THE BIG BOOK OF LIBRARY GRANT MONEY

2004 2005

Profiles of Private and Corporate Foundations and Direct Corporate Givers Receptive to Library Grant Proposals

PREPARED BY

Taft®

FOR THE

American Library Association

AMERICAN LIBRARY ASSOCIATION

Chicago   2004

THOMSON

GALE

The Big Book of Library Grant Money, 2004–2005

ISBN 0-8389-0874-8
ISSN 1086-0568

Printed in the United States of America
10 9 8 7 6 5 4 3 2 1

Contents

The Big Book of Library Grant Money 2004–2005 provides detailed descriptive profiles of more than 2,400 philanthropic programs in the United States—programs associated with private foundations, corporate foundations, and corporate direct givers. All of the funders in this directory have either made grants to libraries within the last few reporting periods or have listed libraries as a typical recipient category on their questionnaires returned to the Taft Group. *The Big Book* provides fund raisers and researchers with quick and convenient access to important information on the major U.S. funding organizations supporting libraries.

The Big Book of Library Grant Money includes current data on over 1,780 of the top private foundations, those with assets or grant distributions of at least $100,000. Interfiled with these major private foundations are over 535 corporate foundations and over 120 hard-to-find direct corporate givers. Collectively, the funders profiled in this edition awarded nearly $13.8 billion during their most recent reporting period to support libraries and other nonprofit organizations.

The directory excludes funders that do not accept unsolicited requests for funds and those funders that give to only preselected recipients. All of the funders included will consider unsolicited proposals.

Content and Arrangement

The funders are arranged alphabetically by the name of the foundation or by the name of the corporation sponsoring the foundation or direct giving program. Foundations named after family members are listed alphabetically by family name. For instance, the Theodore H. Barth Foundation appears alphabetically under "Barth". For corporation names and corporate foundations that are personal names, the user is advised to locate a company first by surname, and if unsuccessful, to try the first element in the name.

Giving profiles are as detailed as permitted by the information available. Contents of a profile can include:

- Foundation name or sponsoring company name and corporate foundation name, if applicable
- Corporate contact information
- Corporate profile information—financial figures, number of employees, parent company, former name(s), SIC(s), Fortune rank, EIN, operating locations, and subsidiary companies
- Giving contact information
- Foundation profile information—year founded, organization type, giving location(s), and grant types
- Financial summary
- Typical recipients
- Application procedures
- Foundation/corporate officials
- Grants lists and analysis

Method of Compilation

The Big Book of Library Grant Money 2004–2005 consists of giving profiles that are compiled for the Taft Group's *Corporate Giving Directory, Foundation Reporter,* and *Prospector's Choice.* Profiles are selected that support libraries and library services. Foundation profiles are updated annually and are based on the most recent Form 990-PF available from the IRS, as well as the foundation's annual reports, grants lists, guidelines, questionnaire responses, and telephone interviews. Profiles of corporate direct-giving programs are based on information provided directly by the companies, press releases, telephone interviews, standard business publications, and data uncovered in extensive surveys of publication in the field.

Indexes

Five indexes allow users to quickly locate information presented in the profiles.

Funders by Headquarters State—Lists foundations and corporations alphabetically by the state of their primary location. Within each state, foundation and corporation names are listed in alphabetical order.

Funders by Operating Locations—Arranges corporations by the states of their major operating locations. Within each state, company names are listed in alphabetical order.

Library Recipients by State—Organizes grants given to libraries and other library-related projects by the state in which the library and/or project is located. Within each state, grants are listed in alphabetical order. When more than one grant has been given to the same organization, such as the New York Public Library, individual grants are listed in descending order by the grant amount.

Officers and Directors by Name—Lists officers, trustees, managers, staff, and contact people in alphabetical order with the name of the funder.

Master Index—Lists in alphabetical order the private foundations, corporate foundations, and corporate direct-giving programs profiled in this directory and includes the page number on which the profile appears. Also listed are former names of funders, as well as parent company names for corporate foundation/direct-giving programs. These citations also include the page number of the profile in which this information is located.

Comments and Suggestions Welcome

We encourage your comments and suggestions on how future editions of *The Big Book of Library Grant Money* may be enhanced to meet your prospecting needs. Please submit comments to:

The Taft Group
27500 Drake Rd.
Farmington Hills, MI 48331-3535
Phone: (248) 699-4253
Toll-free: (800) 347-4253
Fax: (248) 699-8069
URL: www.gale.com
E-mail: BusinessProducts@gale.com

or

Editorial Director
ALA Editions
50 E. Huron St.
Chicago, IL 60611
www.alastore.ala.org

Still one of the most frequently asked questions by members, trustees, and other library professionals who contact the Development Office at the American Library Association (ALA) is "where do I find funders for library initiatives?" *The Big Book of Library Grant Money 2004-2005* goes a long way in helping answer this question. It's a unique resource for anyone contemplating financial support for library-related initiatives, programs, and services.

Now more than ever it is essential for fund-raisers in libraries to be strategic in seeking funds. This has come about mainly because of the economic downturn across the country in the past few years. With less money available, competition for scarce resources by nonprofits is fierce. *The Big Book of Library Grant Money* lists those granting agencies that have or are likely to fund libraries. It will help to focus you on the most probable sources for success.

The Big Book of Library Grant Money may be distinguished from other sources in two important ways. First, it provides depth of information about a breadth of sources not found in a single directory devoted to the content area of libraries. Second, it includes private foundations, corporate foundations, and corporate direct givers that have either indicated interest in funding libraries or have already funded libraries. Therefore, the directory reveals untapped resources about funders who have the potential to fund libraries as well as those who have already done so. Directories typically do one or the other.

Getting Started

Before consulting *The Big Book*, you should have a clear understanding of the program or service that you are trying to fund. Boil the essentials about the program down to no more than one or two pages that include the goals of the program. *The Big Book* will then become a wonderful source as you match the goals of the program to the goals of the funding agencies.

Once you select a list of potential funders, you should check with library staff and trustees to determine if anyone has a contact at the funding agency. It's always better to have a contact within the agency than to go in on a cold call.

However, you can certainly move ahead if you do not know anyone at the foundation by contacting the program officers or other appropriate people. A program officer will be able to communicate a level of interest from the organization based on your brief one- to two-page synopsis about your proposed program.

After a potential funding source is identified, your relationship with the program officer becomes critical. The program officer is responsible for seeking excellent initiatives and programs to fund on behalf of the foundation. Foundations want to make a good investment when they fund programs. Therefore, your program officer and you must work together as you proceed to find funding for your program. The successful development of rapport with the foundation program officer cannot be underestimated. It must turn into a positive experience for both your library and the foundation.

You must be able to give program officers all of the information and statistics that will help them present your project to the foundation board. Some statistics that should help the program officer in preparing a case are found in the following list. Look for statistics or other documentation specific to your library or the community you serve to reinforce your case.

- Americans go to school, public, and academic libraries more than twice as often as they go to the movies.
- Reference librarians in the nation's public and academic libraries answer more than seven million questions weekly. Standing single file, the line of questioners would stretch from Boston to San Francisco.
- Federal spending on libraries annually is only 54¢ per person.
- A 2002 poll conducted by the American Library Association found that 91 percent of respondents expect libraries to be needed in the future, despite the increased availability of information via the Internet.

Public Libraries

- There are more public libraries than McDonald's—a total of 16,220, including branches.

- Americans spend more than three times as much on salty snacks as they do on public libraries.

- Americans check out an average of more than six books a year. They spend $25.25 a year for the public library—much less than the average cost of one hardcover book.

- Public libraries are the number-one point of online access for people without Internet connections at home, school, or work.

- 95 percent of public libraries provide public access to the Internet.

School Libraries

- Research shows the highest achieving students attend schools with good library media centers.

- Americans spend seven times as much money on home video games ($7 billion) as they do on school library materials for their children ($1 billion).

- School library media centers spend an average of $7 per child for books—less than half the average cost of one hardcover school library book.

- Students visit school library media centers almost 1.5 billion times during the school year—about one-and-a-half times the number of visits to state and national parks.

Academic Libraries

- Academic librarians answer 97 million reference questions each year, almost three times the attendance at college football games.

- College libraries receive less than 3¢ of every dollar spent on higher education.

- If the cost of gas had risen as fast as the cost of academic library periodicals since 1990, it would cost $3 to put a gallon of gas in your car.

SOURCES: ALA Office for Research and Statistics, ALA Washington Office, and the Library Research Service, Colorado State Library.

Once you receive your grant, review your agreement with the funder carefully. This is a legally binding document that outlines the expectations of each party in the relationship. If changes are necessary during the implementation phase, these must be communicated to and negotiated with the funder both in person and in writing.

Be sure to utilize as many publicity avenues as you have available. Remember public service announcements and the new opportunities that the Web provides. Recognizing the support of your donors is a wonderful tool in building long-term relationships. There are many ways to acknowledge your donors as well as to get the most out of public relations opportunities for your library and library initiatives. Check with your funder for specific guidelines on press releases.

Using ALA Initiatives to Leverage Local Support

In 2000 ALA adopted ALAction 2005, a five-year initiative to position libraries and librarians for the twenty-first century. Be sure to put the weight of the national organization goals behind your initiatives. For instance, ALA has identified five key action areas: diversity, education and continuous learning, equity of access, intellectual freedom, and twenty-first-century literacy. In order to achieve these goals, ALA leaders have adopted the following targets:

- By 2005 ALA will have increased support for libraries and librarians by communicating clearly and strongly why libraries and librarians are both unique and valuable.

- By 2005 ALA will be recognized as the leading voice for equitable access to information resources in all formats for all people.

- By 2005 ALA will be a leader in the use of technology for communication with, democratic participation by, and shared learning among its members.

- By 2005 ALA will be a leader in continuing education for librarians and library personnel.

Among the initial steps in achieving these goals is the launch of the national Campaign for America's Libraries. For up-to-date information on the campaign and other useful data for your proprosals, you can log on to www.ala.org/@your library.

Additional resources on fund-raising for libraries from ALA Editions can be found online at www.alastore.ala.org.

We wish you luck as you pursue funding for your program. As always, we welcome input for future editions of this book.

Susan Roman
Director, Development Office
American Library Association

Arrangement of Giving Profiles

Giving profiles are arranged alphabetically by the name of the foundation or by the sponsoring company name in the case of corporate foundations and corporate direct-giving programs.

If a giving profile is for a corporate foundation, such as Boeing Corporation/The Boeing Corporation Charitable Trust, the profile has two headings—one for information on the corporation and another for information on the foundation. Giving profiles for private foundations and corporate direct-giving programs have only one profile heading.

Data Elements

Data elements for each type of profile vary. The abbreviated entry shown below illustrates the standard data elements that a giving profile can contain, depending on the nature of the profile—private foundation, corporate foundation, or corporate direct-giving program. Numbered items in the sample are explained in the corresponding numbered paragraphs below.

❚1❚ XYZ Stores
❚2❚ *Company Headquarters*
700 Haywood Rd.
Greenville, SC 29607
Phone: (555) 392-2000
Fax: (508) 392-3000
E-mail: info@xyz.com
URL: http://www.xyz.com
❚3❚ *Company Description*
Founded: 1902
Ticker: XYZ
Exchange: NYSE
Former Name: Archer Inc.
Revenue: US$4 billion (2002)
Profit: US$2 billion (2002)
Employees: 5,000 (2002)
Fortune Rank: 200, per FORTUNE Magazine's list of 500 Largest U.S. Corporations (2003)
SIC(s): 5555 Department stores
❚4❚ *Operating Locations*
CA: XYZ Limited, Los Angeles, San Diego; CT: XYZ Limited, New Haven; ME: XYZ Limited, Bangor; Australia: XYZ Limited, Sydney
❚5❚ *Nonmonetary Support*
Value: $9,000,000 (2002); $4,000,000 (2001)
Type: Donated Products
Note: Product donations are directed primarily to organizations that support overseas educational programs.
❚6❚ XYZ Foundation
❚7❚ *Giving Contact*

Emmit Roman, Executive Director
555 Haywood Rd., Ste. 200
Greenville, SC 29607
Phone: (555) 297-3203
Email: eroman@xyz.com
❚8❚ *Foundation Description*
Founded: 1944
EIN: 551127710
Organization Type: Corporate Foundation
Giving Locations: headquarters and operating communities
Grant Types: General Support, Project, and Research
Note: Employee matching gift ratio: 2 to 1 for contributions over $25 to colleges and universities, up to $2,000 annually; 1 to 1 for gifts to hospitals and cultural institutions, up to $500 annually.
❚9❚ *Donor Information*
Founder: Margaret Burns
❚10❚ *Financial Summary*
Total Giving: $1,800,000 (2003 approx.); $1,752,934 (2002); $1,493,082 (2001); $1,271,427 (2000)
Giving Analysis: Giving for 2002 includes: foundation ($1,715,434); foundation grants to United Way ($37,500).
Assets: $13,974,021 (2002); $12,675,142 (2001); $13,058,376 (2000)
Gifts Received: $242,355 (2002); $224,794 (2001); $99,749 (2000).
Note: Contributions are received from various XYZ Stores.
❚11❚ *Typical Recipients*
Arts & Humanities: Arts Centers, Arts Institutes, Ballet, Community Arts, Historic Preservation, Libraries, Museums/Galleries, Music, Opera, Performing Arts, Public Broadcasting, Theater
Education: Afterschool/Enrichment Programs, Agricultural Education, Arts/Humanities Education, Colleges and Universities
Environment: Resource Conservation, Wildlife Protection
Health: Cancer, Hospitals, Medical Research, Nursing Services
Social Services: YMCA/YMHA/YWCA/YWHA
❚12❚ *Application Procedures*
Initial Contact: Initial contact should be made by letter.
Application Requirements: Proposals should include a summary statement and background information, names of board members, a copy of annual budget and most recent Form 990, the specific monetary amount requested, a budget listing how the funds will be spent, and a copy of the organization's IRS tax-exempt letter.
Deadlines: None.
Review Process: Proposals must be received at least four weeks prior to the month in which the request is to be reviewed.
Evaluative Criteria: Priority is given to organizations serving XYZ employees.
Decision Notification: Final decisions are usually made within eight to ten weeks of receipt.
❚13❚ *Restrictions*
Does not support individuals, political or lobbying groups, or religious organizations for sectarian purposes.
❚14❚ *Additional Information*
XYZ Stores acquired ACME Products in 1999.
Publications: Annual Report; Guidelines
❚15❚ *Corporate Officials*
John C. Belk: chairman B Charlotte, NC 1920. ED Davidson College (1943). PRIM CORP EMPL chairman: Belk Stores Services Inc.

CORP AFFIL director: Lowes Home Centers Inc.; chairman: Parks-Belk Co. Northern Virginia; vice president: Leggett Realty South Boston Virginia; director: Lowes Companies; chairman: Charlotte Belk Inc.; director: Coca-Cola Bottling Co. Consolidated; director: Brothers Investment Co.; director: Chaparral Steel Co.

Montgomery Burns: pres B Springfield, IL 1900. ED Henderson Univ (1922). PRIM CORP EMPL pres: XYZ Stores Services Inc. CORP AFFIL director: Lowes Home Centers Inc.; vice president: Parks-Belk Co. Northern Virginia

Foundation Officials
John A. Kuhne: director
Emmit Roman: executive director
Kate M. Simpson: director

∎16∎ *Grants Analysis*
Disclosure Period: 2002
Total Grants: $1,715,434
Number of Grants: 158
Average Grant: $7,742*
Highest Grant: $500,000
Typical Range: $5,000-$100,000
* Average grant figure excludes highest grant.

∎17∎ *Recent Grants*
Note: Grants derived from 2002 Form 990.
Library-Related

75,000	New York Public Library, New York, NY—Utopia Exhibition
50,000	Columbia University Avery Library

General

500,000	QRS Communications, Boston, MA—toward capital campaign
200,000	Southern Maine Museum of Art, Freeport, ME—toward a new satellite building
175,000	Vermont Artist Visions, Burlington, VT—to support annual programs
50,000	Historical MA—toward capital campaign
25,000	Converse College, Spartanburg, SC—toward capital campaign
15,000	University of South Carolina Lancaster, Lancaster, SC
10,000	Highlands Land Trust—for wetlands preservation projects
10,000	Greenville Free Medical Clinic, Greenville, SC
10,000	Presbyterian Hospital, Charlotte, NC
5,000	Pickens County YMCA, Easley, SC

Description of Numbered Elements

∎1∎ *Company Name.*

∎2∎ *Company Headquarters:* The address, phone, fax, e-mail, and URL for the sponsoring corporation's headquarters locations, when available.

∎3∎ *Company Description:* Includes financial and other statistical information as reported in the April 14, 2003 issue of Fortune magazine (Time, Inc., New York, N.Y.), and several corporate databases available on-line. If the sponsoring company is a subsidiary of or affiliated with another company, this information is listed under **Parent Company. Revenue/sales, profits, number of employees, Fortune rank,** and **SIC(s)** as reported by the company or major business publications, give a capsule look at the financial health and business interests of the profiled company. The entry may also include number of employees, ticker symbol, and stock exchange information for the company. Corporate giving levels are closely tied to a company's sales and profits: the more profitable a company, the greater its philanthropic potential. Many companies base their giving on a percentage of pretax profits,

typically 0.5 percent to 2.5 percent, but occasionally as high as 5 percent. Fortune rank is a classic indicator of how a company compares to its peers. The number of employees also provides a quick measure of a company's size, and corporate programs are usually interested in seeing charitable contributions affect the largest number of corporate employees. Fortune rank, as well as company sales, profits, and number of employees are given where available. SIC information helps identify corporations with a special interest in a particular activity due to the nature of their business.

∎4∎ *Operating Locations:* Company business typically revolves around corporate headquarters and operating locations, and charitable giving information reflects this orientation. Headquarters information is indexed in the index to *Funders by Headquarters State.* Operating locations are indexed in the *Funders by Operating Locations* index. The names and locations of the company's U.S. subsidiaries are also included when available. A company's field of business or marketing orientation often influences its charitable objectives.

∎5∎ *Nonmonetary Support:* Notes the types and amounts of nonmonetary support offered, such as cause-related marketing and promotion, donated equipment, donated products, in-kind services, loaned employees, loaned executives, and workplace solicitation. Also includes the value of such support and whom to contact, if available.

∎6∎ *Foundation Name.*

∎7∎ *Giving Contact:* The name of the person responsible for answering inquiries and receiving grant applications for the foundation, as well as the individual's title, organization name, mailing address, telephone number, fax number, e-mail, and URL, when available.

∎8∎ *Foundation Description:* Listed here is general information about the foundation, such as year **Founded,** its **Employer Identification Number (EIN)**—the unique nine-digit number assigned to a philanthropic institution by the Internal Revenue Service—**Organization Type, Giving Locations, Former Names** and **Grant Types.** Foundations are grouped into four general categories (or **Organization Type**): **Family, General Purpose, Institutional,** or **Special Purpose. Grant Types** lists the financial support typically offered by the foundation using nineteen standard categories ranging from award to seed money. **Giving Locations** indicates the geographic preference for disbursing funds as reported by the foundation or based on analysis of grants lists. Users should review the index to *Funders by Headquarters State* and the *Library Recipients by State* index to gain a greater understanding of a foundation's geographic giving interests. The **Note** section offers any other relevant information pertaining to Grant Types or employee matching gift programs.

∎9∎ *Donor Information:* Contains background information on the donor, his or her family members or spouses, the sources of their wealth or businesses, or their other philanthropies. The specific interests of foundations are frequently oriented toward the philanthropic, business, educational, vocational, religious, political, or social interests of their donors.

❚10❚ *Financial Summary:* For corporate foundations and direct-giving programs, lists giving figures for the three most recent years available, as reported by the company. Also includes information on the scope of the program, including whether the company gives directly, through a foundation, or both. If the company has a foundation, this section lists foundation assets and any gifts the foundation received for the three most recent years available. Use this information to qualify a corporation according to its giving potential and to spot trends in its overall corporate giving. For private foundations, lists the three most current figures of market value of a foundation's assets, along with figures for overall giving (both actual and projected) for at least the three most recent years available. The gifts received category reports, by year, the dollar amount of donations given to a foundation. The source of a gift is explained in the **Financial Note**, when the information is available. Use the information in the Financial Summary to rate foundations according to their financial potential and giving trends.

❚11❚ *Typical Recipients:* Presents an inventory of the types of nonprofit causes that a foundation or direct-giving program most frequently supports, using 215 standard recipient categories under nine broad categories: Arts & Humanities, Civic & Public Affairs, Education, Environment, Health, International, Religion, Science, and Social Services. This section is designed to catalog the kinds of activities supported, rather than indicate priority. A complete list of the 215 recipient organization types, arranged under the 9 major categories, is available starting on page xv.

❚12❚ *Application Procedures:* **Initial Contact, Application Requirements,** and **Deadlines** outline the preferred methods of contacting the company, meeting requirements for proposals, and sending requests within specific time frames, respectively. **Review Process, Evaluative Criteria,** and **Decision Notification** describe the decision-making process foundations or companies follow when reviewing requests, including procedures, the criteria upon which requests are evaluated, and when decisions are made.

❚13❚ *Restrictions:* A brief description of restrictions on eligibility, or types of programs, campaigns, or organizations that are not funded.

❚14❚ *Additional Information:* Reports additional procedures, significant changes in the status of the foundation or company, or policies that could influence solicitation efforts. The **Publications** section lists any printed material provided by the foundation or giving program.

❚15❚ *Corporate Officials:* Provides biographical information on principal corporate officers and contributions program officers, directors, or trustees. When available, includes year and place of birth, education (school, program, degree, and year of graduation), current employment, corporate affiliations, nonprofit affiliations, and club affiliations. This background biographical information helps nonprofits discover connections to development teams and boards of directors, as well as uncover opportunities to cultivate relationships with these decision makers.

Foundation Officials: Provides biographical information on principal foundation officers (usually the chairman, vice chairman, president, vice president, and chief executive officer). When available, includes year and place of birth, education (school, program, degree, and year of graduation), current employment, corporate affiliations, nonprofit affiliations, and club affiliations. This background biographical information helps nonprofits discover connections to development teams and boards of directors, as well as uncover opportunities to cultivate relationships with these decision makers.

❚16❚ *Grants Analysis:* An analytical section which calculates **Total Grants, Number of Grants, Average Grant, Highest Grant,** and **Typical Range.** The **Disclosure Period** indicates the year (actual or fiscal) from which the analytical information was derived. The **Note** contains information on large grants that may skew the average, or any other relevant information pertaining to the grants analysis.

❚17❚ *Recent Grants:* When available, provides a listing of top library-related grants and a general listing of the top 10 recently awarded grants from the following categories: Arts & Humanities, Civic & Public Affairs, Education, Environment, Health, International, Religion, Science, and Social Services. Grants are listed in descending order based on dollar amount. The **Note** at the top of this section indicates the year of the Recent Grants listings.

Abbreviations

A

&	And
AA	Associate of Arts
AB	Arts, Bachelor of
acct	accountant
admin	administration, administrative, administrator
adv	advisor, advisory
AFB	Air Force Base
Aff	Affairs
affil	affiliation
AG	Aktiengesellschaft
Am	America, American
AM	Arts, Master of
Apt	Apartment
APO	Army Post Office
archt	architect
Assn	Association
Assoc(s)	Associate(s), Associated
asst	assistant
atty	attorney
Ave	Avenue

B

b	born
BA	Bachelor of Arts
BBA	Bachelor of Business Administration
bd	board
BD	Bachelor of Divinity
BE	Bachelor of Engineering
BFT	Bachelor of Foreign Trade
Bldg	Building
Blvd	Boulevard
Bros	Brothers
BS	Bachelor of Science
BSChE	Bachelor of Science in Chemical Engineering
BSME	Bachelor of Science in Mechanical Engineering
Bur	Bureau
Bus	Business

C

c/o	care of
CC	Country Club
ceo	chief executive officer
cfo	chief financial officer
Chap	Chapter
Chem	Chemical, Chemist, Chemistry
chmn	chairman
chp	chairperson
chwm	chairwoman
Co	Company
Coll	College
comm	committee
commn	commission
commnr	commissioner
Commun	Communication(s), Community
comptr	comptroller
Conf	Conference
Confed	Confederation
Cong	Congress
Consult	Consultant, Consulting
contr	controller
coo	chief operating officer
Coop	Cooperating, Cooperative, Cooperation
Corp	Corporate, Corporation
Counc	Council
couns	counsel, counseling, counselor
CPA	Certified Public Accountant
Ct	Court
Ctr	Center, Centre
curr	current
cust	customer

D

DB	Divinity, Bachelor of
del	delegate
Dem	Democrat
dep	deputy
Dept	Department
Devel	Development
dir	director
Distr	Distributor, Distribution, Distributing

Div	Division
don	donor
Dr	Doctor
Dr	Drive

E

E	East
Econ	Economic, Economics
Ed	Education, Educational, Educated
EIN	Employer Identification Number
empl	employment
Engg	Engineering
engr	engineer
exec	executive
Expy	Expressway

F

f/b/o	for the benefit of
Fdn	Foundation
fdr	founder
Fed	Federal, Federation, Federated
Fin	Finance, Financial
Fl	Floor
FPO	Fleet Post Office
Ft	Fort
Fwy	Freeway

G

GC	Golf Club
gen	general
gov	governing, governor
govt	government
grad	graduate

H

hon	honorable, honorary
Hosp	Hospital
Hwy	Highway

I

Inc	Incorporated
Indus	Industrial, Industries, Industry
Ins	Insurance
Inst	Institute, Institution
Intl	International

J

JD	Juris Doctor
Jr	Junior

L

Legis	Legislation, Legislative, Legislator
LLB	Laws, Bachelor of
LLD	Laws, Doctor of
Ln	Lane
LP	Limited Partnership
Ltd	Limited

M

MA	Master of Arts
MBA	Master of Business Administration
Med	Medical
mem	member
Meml	Memorial
Metro	Metropolitan
Mfg	Manufacturing
Mfr	Manufacturer
Mgmt	Management
mgr	manager
misc	miscellaneous
Mktg	Marketing
Mng	Managing
MS	Master of Science
Mt	Mount
Mus	Museum

N

N	North
NAACP	National Association for the Advancement of Colored People
N. Ap.	Not Applicable
N. Av	Not Available
Natl	National
NE	North East
No	Number
nonpr	nonprofit
NW	North West

O

off	office, officer
oper	operating, operations
Org	Organization

P

pers	personnel
PhB	Philosophy, Bachelor of
PhD	Philosophy, Doctor of
phil	philanthropic
Pk	Park
Pke	Pike
Pkwy	Parkway
Pl	Place
Plz	Plaza
PO	Post Office
Polytech	Polytechnic, Polytechnical
pres	president
prin	principal
prof	professor
Prov	Province, Provincial
Pt	Point
Pte	Pointe
Ptnr	Partner
pub(s)	publication(s)
pub	public
publ(s)	published, publisher, publishing
Pvt	Private

R

Rd	Road
RD	Rural Delivery
rehab	rehabilitation
rel	religious, religion
rels	relations
rep	representative
Repbl	Republican
Res	Research, Researcher
ret	retired
RFD	Rural Free Delivery
Rm	Room
RR	railroad
RR	Rural Route
Rte	Route
RY	Railway

S

S	South
SB	Science, Bachelor of
Sch	School

SE and following

SE	South East
secy	secretary
sen	senator
SM	Science, Master of
Soc	Society
Sq	Square
Sr	Senior
SR	Star/State Route
St	Saint, State, Street
Sta	Station
Ste	Sainte, Suite
Sub(s)	Subsidiary(ies)
supt	superintendent
supvr	supervisor
Svc(s)	Service(s)
SW	South West
Sys	System(s)

T

Tech	Technological, Technical, Technology
Tel & Tel	Telephone and Telegraph
Terr	Terrace
Tpke	Turnpike
treas	treasurer
trust	trustee

U

Un	United
Univ	University
US	United States
u/w/o	under the will of

V

vchmn	vice chairman
vp	vice president

W

W	West

Y

YC	Yacht Club
YMCA	Young Men's Christian Association
YMHA	Young Men's Hebrew Association
YWCA	Young Women's Christian Association
YWHA	Young Women's Hebrew Association

Nonprofit Recipient Categories and Organization Types

Arts & Humanities ∎ Art History, Arts Appreciation, Arts Associations & Councils, Arts Centers, Arts Festivals, Arts Funds, Arts Institutes, Arts Outreach, Ballet, Community Arts, Dance, Ethnic & Folk Art, Film & Video, Historic Preservation, History & Archeology, Libraries, Literary Arts, Museums/Galleries, Music, Opera, Performing Arts, Public Broadcasting, Theater, Visual Arts

Civic & Public Affairs ∎ African American Affairs, Asian American Affairs, Botanical Gardens/Parks, Business/Free Enterprise, Chambers of Commerce, Civil Rights, Clubs, Community Foundations, Economic Development, Economic Policy, Employment/Job Training, Ethnic Organizations, First Amendment Issues, Gay/Lesbian Issues, Hispanic Affairs, Housing, Inner-City Development, Law & Justice, Legal Aid, Minority Business, Municipalities/Towns, Native American Affairs, Nonprofit Management, Parades/Festivals, Philanthropic Organizations, Professional/Trade Associations, Public Policy, Rural Affairs, Safety, Urban/Community Affairs, Women's Affairs, Zoos/Aquariums

Education ∎ Afterschool Enrichment Programs, Agricultural Education, Arts/Humanities Education, Business Education, Business-School Partnerships, Colleges & Universities, Community/Junior Colleges, Continuing Education, Economic Education, Education Associations, Education Funds, Education Reform, Elementary Education (private), Elementary Education (public), Engineering Education, Environmental Education, Faculty Development, Gifted & Talented Programs, Health & Physical Education, International Exchange, International Studies, Journalism/Media Education, Leadership Training, Legal Education, Literacy, Medical Education, Minority Education, Preschool Education, Private Education (precollege), Public Education (precollege), Religious Education, School Volunteerism, Science/Mathematics Education, Secondary Education (private), Secondary Education (public), Social Sciences Education, Special Education, Student Aid, Vocational/Technical Education

Environment ∎ Air/Water Quality, Energy, Forestry, Protection, Research, Resource Conservation, Sanitary Systems, Watershed, Wildlife Protection

Health ∎ Adolescent Health Issues, AIDS/HIV, Alzheimer's Disease, Arthritis, Cancer, Children's Health/Hospitals, Clinics/Medical Centers, Diabetes, Emergency/Ambulance Services, Eyes/Blindness, Geriatric Health, Health Funds, Health Organizations, Health Policy/Cost Containment, Heart, Home-Care Services, Hospices, Hospitals, Hospitals (university affiliated), Kidney, Long-Term Care, Medical Rehabilitation, Medical Research, Medical Training, Mental Health, Multiple Sclerosis, Nursing Services, Nutrition, Outpatient Health Care, Prenatal Health Issues, Preventive Medicine/Wellness Organizations, Public Health, Research/Studies Institutes, Respiratory, Single-Disease Health Associations, Speech & Hearing, Transplant Networks/Donor Banks, Trauma Treatment

International ∎ Foreign Arts Organizations, Foreign Education Institutions, Health Care/Hospitals, Human Rights, International Affairs, International Development, International Environmental Issues, International Law, International Organizations, International Peace & Security Issues, International Relations, International Relief Efforts, Missionary/Religious Activities, Trade

Religion ∎ Bible Study/Translation, Churches, Dioceses, Jewish Causes, Ministries, Missionary Activities (domestic), Religious Organizations, Religious Welfare, Seminaries, Social/Policy Issues, Synagogues/Temples

Science ∎ Observatories/Planetariums, Science Exhibits/Fairs, Scientific Institutes, Scientific Organizations

Social Services ∎ Animal Protection, At-Risk Youth, Big Brother/Big Sister, Camps, Child Abuse, Child Welfare, Community Centers, Community Service Organizations, Counseling, Crime Prevention, Day Care, Delinquency/Criminal Rehabilitation, Domestic Violence, Emergency Relief, Family Planning, Family Services, Food & Clothing Distribution, Homes, People With Disabilities, Recreation & Athletics, Refugee Assistance, Scouts, Senior Services, Sexual Abuse, Shelters/Homeless, Special Olympics, Substance Abuse, United Funds/United Way, Veterans, Volunteer Services, YMCA/YMHA/YWCA/YWHA, Youth Organizations

PROFILES

1ST SOURCE CORP.

Company Headquarters
100 N. Michigan Street
South Bend, IN 46601
Phone: (219)235-2000
Fax: (219)235-2882
Web: http://www.1stsource.com

Company Description
Founded: 1971
Ticker: SRCE
Exchange: NASDAQ
Assets: US$3.409 billion (2002)
Employees: 1260 (2002)
SIC(s): 6022 State Commercial Banks.

Operating Locations
First Source Corp. (IN--South Bend)

First Source Foundation

Giving Contact
Mary Sonneborn, Trust Officer
Care of First Source Bank
PO Box 1602
South Bend, IN 46601
Phone: (219)235-2790
Fax: (219)235-2771

Description
Founded: 1952
EIN: 356034211
Organization Type: Corporate Foundation
Giving Locations: IN
Grant Types: General Support.

Donor Information
Founder: First Source Bank Charitable Trust

Financial Summary
Total Giving: $325,528 (2000); $229,781 (1999); $1,055,066 (1998)
Giving Analysis: Giving for 2000 includes: foundation grants to United Way ($109,168); foundation ($216,360); 1999: foundation grants to United Way ($55,023); foundation ($174,758); 1998: foundation ($1,055,066);
Assets: $13,025,607 (2000); $12,851,261 (1999); $12,184,556 (1998)
Gifts Received: $700,000 (1999); $951,907 (1998); $2,338,732 (1994). Note: In 1999, contributions were received from First Source Bank.

Typical Recipients
Arts & Humanities: Arts Centers, Arts & Humanities-General, Historic Preservation, History & Archaeology, Libraries, Museums/Galleries, Music, Performing Arts, Public Broadcasting
Civic & Public Affairs: Botanical Gardens/Parks, Business/Free Enterprise, Community Foundations, Economic Development, Economic Policy, Civic & Public Affairs-General, Housing, Minority Business, Municipalities/Towns, Parades/Festivals, Safety, Urban & Community Affairs
Education: Arts/Humanities Education, Business Education, Colleges & Universities, Economic Education, Education Associations, Education Funds, Elementary Education (Private), Engineering/ Technological Education, Education-General, International Exchange, Medical Education, Private Education (Precollege), Public Education (Precollege), Public Education (Precollege), Science/Mathematics

Education, Secondary Education (Private), Secondary Education (Public), Student Aid
Environment: Environment-General
Health: Alzheimers Disease, Children's Health/Hospitals, Diabetes, Health Funds, Health Organizations, Hospices, Hospitals, Kidney, Mental Health, Preventive Medicine/Wellness Organizations, Public Health
Religion: Bible Study/Translation, Churches, Jewish Causes, Religious Organizations, Religious Welfare
Social Services: Animal Protection, Big Brother/Big Sister, Camps, Child Abuse, Community Service Organizations, Crime Prevention, Delinquency & Criminal Rehabilitation, Family Services, Food/Clothing Distribution, Homes, People with Disabilities, Recreation & Athletics, Shelters/Homelessness, Substance Abuse, United Funds/United Ways, Volunteer Services, YMCA/YWCA/YMHA/YWHA, Youth Organizations

Application Procedures
Initial Contact: Submit a written request.
Application Requirements: Requests should include a written statement of purpose concerning grant request.
Deadlines: None.

Corporate Officials
Christopher J. Murphy, III: president, chief executive officer, director B Washington, DC 1946. ED University of Notre Dame BA (1968); University of Virginia JD (1971); Harvard University Graduate School of Business Administration MBA (1973). PRIM CORP EMPL president, chief executive officer, director: First Source Corp. CORP AFFIL director: Trust Corp. Mortgage Inc.; director: Quality Dining Inc.; director: Titan Holding; director: Comair Inc.; director: Omega Health System; chairman: 1st Source Industry Inc.; chairman, chief executive officer: 1st Source Bank; chairman: 1st Source Capital Corp. NONPR AFFIL member: Virginia Bar Association; international board director, member: Young President Organization; member: Saint Joseph County Bar Association; advisory council: Notre Dame College Arts and Letters; member: Robert Morris Associates; director, chairman: National Association Publically Traded Companies; member: National Association Securities Dealers; member: National Association Business Economists; member: Indiana Bar Association; chairman: Medical Education Foundation; member: American Bankers Association; member: American Bar Association.

Foundation Officials
Harry Gerber: director
Christopher J. Murphy, III: director (see above)

Grants Analysis
Disclosure Period: calendar year ending 2000
Total Grants: $216,360*
Number of Grants: 56
Average Grant: $1,970*
Highest Grant: $75,000
Lowest Grant: $250
Typical Range: $1,000 to $5,000
***Note:** Giving excludes United Way. Average grant figure excludes two highest grants.

Recent Grants
Note: Grants derived from 2000 Form 990.

General

92,000	United Way St. Joseph County, South Bend, IN
75,000	Morris Performing Arts Center (MPAC), South Bend, IN
35,000	Morris Performing Arts Center (MPAC), South Bend, IN
10,000	Indiana University South Bend, South Bend, IN -- Toradze Piano Festival
8,500	YMCA, South Bend, IN
7,000	St. Joseph High School, South Bend, IN -- capital campaign
6,000	Jewish Federation of St. Joseph County, South Bend, IN
5,500	Ancilla College, Donaldson, IN
5,000	Community Foundation, South Bend, IN
5,000	Crossing Campaign, South Bend, IN

ABBOTT LABORATORIES

Company Headquarters
100 Abbott Park Road
Abbott Park, IL 60064-2500
Phone: (847)936-1000
Fax: (847)937-1511
Web: http://www.abbott.com

Company Description
Founded: 1900
Ticker: ABT
Exchange: NYSE
Revenue: US$17.684 billion (2002)
Profit: US$2.793 billion (2002)
Employees: 71819 (2002)
Fortune Rank: 100, per FORTUNE Magazine's list of 500 Largest U.S. Corporations (2002).
SIC(s): 2833 Medicinals & Botanicals, 2834 Pharmaceutical Preparations, 2844 Toilet Preparations, 3841 Surgical & Medical Instruments.

Operating Locations
Abbott Ambulatory Infusion Systems (CA--San Diego); Abbott Critical Care Systems (CA--Morgan Hill; UT--Salt Lake City); Abbott Diagnostics (CA--Santa Clara); Abbott Laboratories (KS--McPherson; NJ--Fairfield; NY--Buffalo; NC--Laurinburg, Rocky Mount; OH--Ashland; TX--Austin, Irving); MediSense, Inc. (MA--Bedford); Ross Products (AZ--Casa Grande; MI--Sturgis; OH--Columbus; VA--Altavista); Tap Pharmaceuticals (IL--Deerfield)

Nonmonetary Support
Value: $100,000,000 (2001 approx); $1,850,000 (2000)
Type: Donated Products
Note: Product donations are directed primarily to organizations that support overseas health care programs and disaster relief efforts.

Abbott Laboratories Fund

Giving Contact
Cindy Schwab, Vice President
Abbott Laboratories Fund
Dept. 379, Building AP6D-2
100 Abbott Park Road
Abbott Park, IL 60064-6048
Phone: (847)937-7075
Fax: (847)935-5051
Web: http://abbott.com/community/lab_fund.html

Description
Founded: 1951
EIN: 366069793
Organization Type: Corporate Foundation

Giving Locations: headquarters and operating communities; United Kingdom; Puerto Rico

Grant Types: Employee Matching Gifts, General Support, Research.

Note: Employee matching gift ratio: 1 to 1 for elementary and secondary schools and higher education; public broadcasting; foundations (meeting criteria); and hospitals. Contact Rhonda Rudolph, Matching Grant Coordinator.

Donor Information

Founder: Abbott Laboratories

Financial Summary

Total Giving: $15,547,595 (2001); $11,162,538 (2000); $10,346,876 (1999)

Giving Analysis: Giving for 2000 includes: foundation grants to United Way ($1,627,289); foundation matching gifts ($1,849,993); foundation ($7,685,256); 1999: foundation scholarships ($99,887); foundation grants to United Way ($681,201); foundation matching gifts ($1,499,997); foundation ($8,065,791); 1998: foundation grants to United Way ($1,292,322); foundation matching gifts ($1,606,063); foundation ($7,631,749);

Assets: $130,249,818 (2001); $117,763,266 (2000); $95,027,756 (1999)

Gifts Received: $12,015,796 (2001); $9,300,000 (1998); $2,700,000 (1997). Note: In 2001, contributions were received from Miles White ($5,268), Phil and Sandra Tobin ($5,341), and Abbott Laboratories ($12,000,000).

Typical Recipients

Arts & Humanities: Arts Institutes, Community Arts, Dance, Arts & Humanities-General, Historic Preservation, History & Archaeology, Libraries, Museums/Galleries, Music, Opera, Performing Arts, Public Broadcasting, Theater

Civic & Public Affairs: Botanical Gardens/Parks, Clubs, Community Foundations, Economic Development, Economic Policy, Civic & Public Affairs-General, Hispanic Affairs, Housing, Law & Justice, Professional & Trade Associations, Public Policy, Safety, Urban & Community Affairs, Women's Affairs, Zoos/Aquariums

Education: Business Education, Colleges & Universities, Community & Junior Colleges, Continuing Education, Education Associations, Engineering/Technological Education, Health & Physical Education, Legal Education, Medical Education, Minority Education, Private Education (Precollege), Public Education (Precollege), Religious Education, Science/Mathematics Education, Student Aid

Environment: Forestry, Environment-General

Health: AIDS/HIV, Cancer, Children's Health/Hospitals, Clinics/Medical Centers, Emergency/Ambulance Services, Health-General, Geriatric Health, Health Organizations, Heart, Hospices, Hospitals, Hospitals (University Affiliated), Kidney, Medical Rehabilitation, Medical Research, Medical Training, Nursing Services, Nutrition, Public Health, Research/Studies Institutes, Single-Disease Health Associations

International: Health Care/Hospitals, International Development

Religion: Religious Welfare, Seminaries

Science: Observatories & Planetariums, Science Museums, Scientific Centers & Institutes, Scientific Research

Social Services: Child Welfare, Community Centers, Community Service Organizations, Day Care, Delinquency & Criminal Rehabilitation, Emergency Relief, Family Services, People with Disabilities, Scouts, Sexual Abuse, Shelters/Homelessness, Substance Abuse, United Funds/United Ways, Volunteer Services, YMCA/YWCA/YMHA/YWHA, Youth Organizations

Application Procedures

Initial Contact: Send a written request.

Application Requirements: Include a description of organization's mission; geographic area served; description of project, outlining needs and goals; amount requested; budget information; copy of 501(c)(3) tax-exempt letter; most recent audited financial statement; annual report and other supporting materials; and list of current supporters and donors.

Deadlines: None; contributions committee meets continuously throughout the year.

Evaluative Criteria: Priority is given to organizations serving communities in which Abbott has significant operations or employees; organizations whose activities support professions in health care fields related to Abbott's primary areas of operation; institutions of higher learning which benefit the health care industry and its employees. The fund's primary areas of interest are human health and welfare and higher education. Also of interest are secondary education, elementary education, culture, the arts, and civic activities.

Decision Notification: Final decisions are usually made within eight weeks of receipt.

Restrictions

Does not award grants to individuals, political or lobbying groups, or religious organizations for sectarian purposes; purely social organizations; symposia or conferences; memberships; or business-related purposes. Does not support dinners, special events, ticket purchases, meetings, marketing sponsorships, or goodwill advertising.

Additional Information

The fund gives preference to requests for one-time contributions and for programmatic and operating purposes; multiyear and capital requests are considered as exceptions.

Abbott Laboratories Fund is supported by contributions from Abbott Laboratories employees, retirees, and the corporation.

Publications: Abbott Laboratories Fund Contributions Policy; Annual Report

Corporate Officials

Gary Patrick Coughlan: chief financial officer, senior vice president finance B Fresno, CA 1944. ED Saint Mary's College BA (1966); University of California, Los Angeles MA (1967); Wayne State University MBA (1971). PRIM CORP EMPL chief financial officer, senior vice president finance: Abbott Laboratories ADD CORP EMPL chief financial officer: Abbott Health Products Inc. CORP AFFIL director: Fort James Corp. NONPR AFFIL member: Financial Executives Institute; member advisory council: University Illinois Chicago; member advisory council: De Paul University College Commerce; member: Council Financial Executives; member advisory council: Council Foreign Relations; director: Chicago Horticultural Society; member: Conference Board Inc. CLUB AFFIL Economic Club Chicago.

Miles D. White: chairman, chief executive officer B March 10, 1955. ED Stanford University BS (1978); Stanford University MBA (1980). PRIM CORP EMPL chairman, chief executive officer: Abbott Laboratories.

Foundation Officials

Catherine V. Babington: president, director

Gary Patrick Coughlan: director (see above)

Cindy A. Schwab: vice president

Carol A. Sebesta: treasurer

Brian J. Smith: secretary

Thomas M. Wascoe: director

Grants Analysis

Disclosure Period: calendar year ending 2001

Total Grants: $10,700,286*

Number of Grants: 909

Average Grant: $9,636*

Highest Grant: $1,020,000

Lowest Grant: $100

Typical Range: $500 to $50,000 and $100,000 to $300,000

*Note: Giving excludes matching gifts, scholarship and United Way. Average grant figure excludes two highest grants ($1,960,298).

Recent Grants

Note: Grants derived from 2001 Form 990.

General

1,020,000	American Red Cross National Headquarters, Washington, DC
1,000,000	United Way of America - The September 11th Fund, New York, NY
940,298	Axios Foundation, Cleveland, OH
688,000	Baylor College of Medicine, Houston, TX
525,000	Joffrey Ballet of Chicago, Chicago, IL
424,300	International HIV and AIDS Alliance, London United Kingdom
300,000	Stanford University, Stanford, CA
220,000	Pharmaceutical Manufacturers Association, Washington, DC
205,000	Lyric Opera of Chicago, Chicago, IL
200,000	Milburn School, Wadsworth, IL

ABC, INC.

Company Headquarters

77 W. 66th St.
New York, NY 10023-6298
Web: http://www.abc.go.com

Company Description

Former Name: Capital Cities/ABC.

Employees: 20,200

SIC(s): 2711 Newspapers, 2731 Book Publishing, 4832 Radio Broadcasting Stations, 4833 Television Broadcasting Stations.

Operating Locations

ABC (CA--Los Angeles, San Francisco; CO--Englewood; CT--Bristol, Groton, Guilford, Mystic, North Haven, West Hartford; IL--Belleville, Cahokia, Carol Stream, Chicago, Highland, Lombard, O Fallon; MA--Marshfield; MI--Pontiac; MN--Minneapolis; MO--Clayton, St. Louis; NY--Astoria; NC--Durham, Greensboro; OH--Cleveland; OR--Albany, Ashland, Cottage Grove, Newport, Portland, Sandy, Springfield; PA--Radnor, Wilkes-Barre; RI--Providence, Wakefield; TX--Dallas, Houston; WA--Spokane)

Amon G. Carter Star Telegram Employees Fund

Giving Contact

Nenetta Carter Tatum, President
PO Box 17480
Ft. Worth, TX 76102
Phone: (817)332-3535

Description

Founded: 1945

EIN: 756014850

Organization Type: Corporate Foundation

Giving Locations: TX: Tarrant County

Grant Types: Capital, General Support, Scholarship.

Financial Summary

Total Giving: $1,491,669 (fiscal year ending April 30, 2001); $1,587,067 (fiscal 1999); $1,306,253 (fiscal 1997). Note: Contributes through foundation only.

Giving Analysis: Giving for fiscal 2001 includes: foundation grants to United Way ($25,000); foundation scholarships ($94,000); foundation gifts to individuals ($195,419); foundation ($1,177,500); fiscal 1999: foundation grants to United Way ($25,000); foundation gifts to individuals ($306,328); foundation ($1,255,739); fiscal 1997: foundation scholarships ($103,000); foundation gifts to individuals ($189,403) foundation ($1,013,850)

Assets: $31,392,491 (fiscal 2001); $32,916,443 (fiscal 1999); $30,567,261 (fiscal 1997)

Gifts Received: $10,000 (fiscal 1997); $12,000 (fiscal 1996); $14,000 (fiscal 1995)

Typical Recipients

Arts & Humanities: Arts Associations & Councils, Arts Festivals, Ballet, Historic Preservation, History & Archaeology, Libraries, Museums/Galleries, Music, Opera, Performing Arts, Theater

Civic & Public Affairs: Business/Free Enterprise, Clubs, Civic & Public Affairs-General, Housing, Law & Justice, Municipalities/Towns, Nonprofit Management, Parades/Festivals, Safety, Urban & Community Affairs, Women's Affairs, Zoos/Aquariums

Education: Afterschool/Enrichment Programs, Colleges & Universities, Education Reform, Elementary Education (Private), Education-General, Minority Education, Private Education (Precollege), Public Education (Precollege), School Volunteerism, Special Education

Environment: Environment-General

Health: AIDS/HIV, Cancer, Children's Health/Hospitals, Eyes/Blindness, Health Organizations, Heart, Hospitals, Hospitals (University Affiliated), Medical Research, Mental Health, Nursing Services, Public Health, Research/Studies Institutes, Single-Disease Health Associations, Transplant Networks/Donor Banks

International: Foreign Arts Organizations, Missionary/Religious Activities

Religion: Jewish Causes, Religious Organizations, Religious Welfare

Science: Science Museums, Scientific Research

Social Services: Big Brother/Big Sister, Child Welfare, Community Service Organizations, Counseling, Crime Prevention, Day Care, Domestic Violence, Family Planning, Family Services, Food/Clothing Distribution, People with Disabilities, Recreation & Athletics, Recreation & Athletics, Scouts, Senior Services, Shelters/Homelessness, Social Services-General, Substance Abuse, United Funds/United Ways, YMCA/YWCA/YMHA/YWHA, Youth Organizations

Application Procedures

Initial Contact: Send a brief letter of inquiry.
Application Requirements: One copy of proposal.
Deadlines: None.
Notes: The foundation may request additional information after reviewing initial letter.

Restrictions

Foundation limits its giving to Texas. No grants are given to individuals, except for employee-related scholarships and grants.

Additional Information

Giving is primarily for medical or hardship assistance and pension supplements for Carter Publications, Inc. employees. Scholarships are awarded to children of Star Telegram employees.

Corporate Officials

Richard L. Connor: president, publisher B Bangor, ME 1947. ED Hillsdale College BA (1970). PRIM CORP EMPL president, publisher: Fort Worth Star-Telegram Inc. NONPR AFFIL trustee: Tilton School; director: Wilkes-Barre Chamber of Commerce; trustee: Ft. Worth Academy; trustee: Misericordia College; member: American Society Newspaper Editors; director: Capital Cities Community Minorities Intern

Program; member: American Newspaper Publishers Association.

Grants Analysis

Disclosure Period: fiscal year ending April 30, 1999
Total Grants: $1,177,250*
Number of Grants: 60
Average Grant: $15,716*
Highest Grant: $250,000
Lowest Grant: $1,000
Typical Range: $1,000 to $25,000
*Note: Giving excludes gifts to individuals; scholarships; United Way. Average grant figure excludes highest grant.

Recent Grants

Note: Grants derived from fiscal 2001 Form 990.

General

250,000	Fort Worth Museum of Science and History, Ft. Worth, TX
100,000	Boys and Girls Club of Greater Fort Worth, Ft. Worth, TX
100,000	City of Fort Worth, Ft. Worth, TX
100,000	YMCA of Metropolitan Tarrant County, Ft. Worth, TX
50,000	Gladney Fund, Ft. Worth, TX
50,000	Tarrant County Samaritan Housing, Ft. Worth, TX
50,000	Warm Place, Ft. Worth, TX
35,000	First Texas Council of Camp Fire, Inc., Ft. Worth, TX
25,000	Hope Farm, Ft. Worth, TX
25,000	Learning Center, Ft. Worth, TX

ABELL FOUNDATION

Giving Contact

Robert C. Embry, Jr., President
111 South Calvert Street, Suite 2300
Baltimore, MD 21202
Phone: (410)547-1300
Fax: (410)539-6579
E-mail: abell@abell.org
Web: http://www.abell.org

Description

Founded: 1953
EIN: 526036106
Organization Type: General Purpose Foundation
Giving Locations: MD: Baltimore
Grant Types: Challenge, Employee Matching Gifts, Endowment, Loan, Matching, Project, Research, Scholarship, Seed Money.

Donor Information

Founder: Established in 1953 by the late Harry C. Black , then chairman of A. S. Abell Company, publisher of the Baltimore Sun papers. Formerly known as the A. S. Abell Company Foundation, the Abell Foundation is dedicated to improving the quality of life for the citizens of Maryland. Mr. Black believed it was important "to give something back to the community in such a way that was deemed to be wise and helpful."

Financial Summary

Total Giving: $8,000,000 (2003 approx); $9,000,000 (2002 approx); $11,800,000 (2001)
Giving Analysis: Giving for 2000 includes: foundation matching gifts ($181,035) foundation grants to United Way ($333,333)
Assets: $1,600,000 (2003 approx); $177,560,000 (2002 approx); $264,695,355 (2000)

Typical Recipients

Arts & Humanities: Arts Centers, Arts Festivals, Arts Funds, Arts Institutes, Arts Outreach, Dance, Ethnic & Folk Arts, Arts & Humanities-General, Historic Preservation, Libraries, Literary Arts, Music, Opera, Performing Arts, Theater, Visual Arts

Civic & Public Affairs: African American Affairs, Botanical Gardens/Parks, Business/Free Enterprise, Civil Rights, Community Foundations, Economic Development, Employment/Job Training, Civic & Public Affairs-General, Housing, Legal Aid, Public Policy, Safety, Urban & Community Affairs, Women's Affairs, Zoos/Aquariums

Education: Arts/Humanities Education, Business-School Partnerships, Colleges & Universities, Education Funds, Education Reform, Elementary Education (Private), Elementary Education (Public), Environmental Education, Faculty Development, Education-General, International Studies, Leadership Training, Legal Education, Literacy, Medical Education, Minority Education, Private Education (Precollege), Public Education (Precollege), Science/Mathematics Education, Secondary Education (Public), Social Sciences Education, Special Education, Student Aid

Environment: Air/Water Quality, Environment-General, Resource Conservation

Health: Clinics/Medical Centers, Eyes/Blindness, Health Organizations, Mental Health, Nutrition, Preventive Medicine/Wellness Organizations

International: International Affairs, International Organizations

Religion: Churches, Dioceses, Ministries, Religious Welfare

Science: Science-General, Scientific Centers & Institutes

Social Services: Child Welfare, Community Centers, Community Service Organizations, Crime Prevention, Delinquency & Criminal Rehabilitation, Domestic Violence, Family Planning, Family Services, Food/Clothing Distribution, People with Disabilities, Recreation & Athletics, Scouts, Senior Services, Shelters/Homelessness, Substance Abuse, United Funds/United Ways, Youth Organizations

Application Procedures

Initial Contact: Requests for grants should be initiated by a one-page letter, describing the mission, scope of the activities, a summary of the project with its goals and objectives, and amount requested. Applicants will be asked to submit a formal and detailed application if the board is interested in the preliminary proposal.

Application Requirements: Along with the formal application form, each applicant should include one copy of the following information: a copy of latest IRS determination letter of tax-exempt status; most recent audited financial statement and current operating budget; projected operating budget for each year funding is requested; list of names and professional affiliations of current board; and any other pertinent supporting materials.

Deadlines: January 1 for consideration by the board in February, March 1 for consideration in April, May 1 for consideration in June, August 1 for consideration in September, September 1 for consideration in October, and November 1 for consideration in December.

Review Process: The board usually makes a determination on proposals within a week of the bi-monthly meetings. In essence, the foundation encourages applications that show promise of having a substantial impact on the beneficiaries and the organizations' growth and stability. It also seeks applications for grants that provide creative responses to pressing community needs, demonstrate potential for stimulating new sources of financial support, and strengthen the operational base to ensure more effective and efficient delivery of services for those in need.

Notes: Unless initiated by a trustee, communications with individual trustees regarding proposals are discouraged and will not be helpful. However, the staff welcomes inquiries regarding the grant-making process and specific questions about individual proposals.

A site visit may be requested after the full proposal has been received and acknowledged.

Restrictions

The foundation does not provide funds for individuals, sponsorships, deficit financing, annual sustaining funds, plans, or travel. The foundation does not fund housing projects, hospitals or medical research. It prefers to award grants on a one-time basis, but may make multi-year grants in exceptional cases. If a request is declined, the applicant should wait one year before submitting another proposal.

Grantees must submit post-grant report.

Additional Information

The foundation reports that it also sponsors conferences, seminars, and workshops. On occasion, the foundation requests applications from organizations and initiates its own programs; the foundation also commissions studies to determine community needs.

Publications: Annual Report; Policies and Guidelines; Application Form; Newsletters

Foundation Officials

William Shepherdson Abell, Jr.: trustee B Washington, DC 1943. ED Boston College AB (1963); University of Fribourg (1964); Harvard University MPA (1965); Georgetown University JD (1970). PRIM CORP EMPL partner: Furey, Doolan & Abell.

Gary Black, Jr.: chairman, trustee B 1942. PRIM CORP EMPL co-owner, publisher: Ski Racing Magazine. CORP AFFIL publ: Ski Show Daily.

George Lloyd Bunting, Jr.: trustee B Baltimore, MD 1940. PRIM CORP EMPL president, chief executive officer: Bunting Management Group. CORP AFFIL director: Mercantile Safe Deposit Trust Co.; director: USF&G Corp.; director: Crown Central Petroleum Corp.

Robert C. Embry, Jr.: president, trustee

Robert Garrett: trustee B Morristown, NJ 1937. ED Princeton University AB (1959); Harvard University MBA (1965). PRIM CORP EMPL president: Robert Garrett & Sons Inc. CORP AFFIL president: AdMedia Corp.; director: Mickelberry Communication Inc. CLUB AFFIL River New York Club; University New York Club; Nantucket Yacht Club; Piping Rock Club; Knickerbocker New York Club.

Jaqueline Hrabowski: trustee

Frances Murray Keenan: vice president finance

Sally J. Michel: trustee PRIM NONPR EMPL secretary, director: Maryland Zoological Society. CORP AFFIL trustee: Michel Real Estate. NONPR AFFIL secretary, director: Baltimore Zoo.

Eileen O'Rourke: treasurer

Walter Sondheim, Jr.: trustee

Esthel Summerfield: secretary

Grants Analysis

Disclosure Period: calendar year ending 2000
Total Grants: $11,769,383*
Number of Grants: 314
Average Grant: $37,482
Highest Grant: $807,955
Typical Range: $15,000 to $75,000
*Note: Giving excludes United Way and matching gifts.

Recent Grants

Note: Grants derived from 2000 Form 990.

General

807,955	Baltimore Curriculum Project, Baltimore, MD -- programming
731,243	Ingenuity Project, Baltimore, MD -- programming
534,825	Baltimore City Healthy Start, Baltimore, MD -- programming
440,000	Carson Scholars Fund, Towson, MD -- scholarships
400,500	Center for Fathers, Families and Workforce Development, Baltimore, MD -- programming
333,333	United Way of Central Maryland, Baltimore, MD
250,000	Baltimore Center for Performing Arts, Baltimore, MD
250,000	New Song Community Learning Center, Baltimore, MD -- capital
200,000	Greater Baltimore Committee, Baltimore, MD -- planning
200,000	Men's Centers, Baltimore, MD -- programming

ABELL-HANGER FOUNDATION

Giving Contact

David L. Smith, Executive Director
PO Box 430
Midland, TX 79702
Phone: (915)684-6655
Fax: (915)684-4474
E-mail: ahf@abell-hanger.org
Web: http://www.abell-hanger.org

Description

Founded: 1954
EIN: 756020781
Organization Type: General Purpose Foundation
Giving Locations: TX
Grant Types: Capital, Challenge, Conference/Seminar, Employee Matching Gifts, General Support, Matching, Multiyear/Continuing Support, Operating Expenses, Project.

Donor Information

Founder: Established in Texas in 1954 by George Thomas Abell and his wife, Gladys Hanger Abell .

"Mr. Abell was born in Wakeeney, KS. While attending Colorado A&M (now Colorado State University), he was a member of Gamma Omega, an honorary fraternity, and Sigma Alpha Epsilon, a social fraternity. He graduated with degrees in civil and irrigation engineering and mechanical engineering. In 1927, he moved to Midland, TX, where he trained himself as a geologist and entered the petroleum business as an independent oil operator.

"In addition to his professional endeavors, Mr. Abell was active in many civic, community, cultural, social, educational, and historical activities. He devoted much time to the Boy Scouts of America, serving in various capacities in the Buffalo Trail Council. He led the capital fund campaign which secured the 6,000-acre camp in the Davis mountains. For his service to the Boy Scouts, he was awarded the highest recognition of the Boy Scouts, the Silver Beaver Award.

"While serving as a director of the Midland Chamber of Commerce, Mr. Abell originated the idea for the Permian Basin Petroleum Museum, Library and Hall of Fame. He spent much time and effort collecting antique oil field equipment now displayed on the museum's grounds. Many of the oil paintings of historical events which are on display in the museum were researched by Mr. Abell and commissioned by the Abell-Hanger Foundation.

"In 1939, he married Gladys Hanger of Ft. Worth, TX, the daughter of a pioneer Tarrant County family. She graduated from Paschal High School and attended Texas Christian University and the University of Texas at Austin. Throughout her life, Mrs. Abell was an active champion of civic and cultural causes, contributing her time, talents, energy, and financial resources. An avid American patriot, she was a member of the National Society of Colonial Dames of America, and the Daughters of the American Revolution." 1995 Annual Report

Financial Summary

Total Giving: $7,200,000 (fiscal year ending June 30, 2003 approx); $7,200,000 (fiscal 2002 approx); $8,607,351 (fiscal 2001)

Giving Analysis: Giving for fiscal 2001 includes: foundation matching gifts ($90,187); fiscal 1999: foundation scholarships ($102,500); foundation grants to United Way ($404,338); foundation matching gifts ($781,604); fiscal 1998: foundation grants to United Way ($375,000); foundation scholarships ($529,500) foundation matching gifts ($657,387)

Assets: $130,000,000 (fiscal 2003 approx); $130,000,000 (fiscal 2002 approx); $150,810,640 (fiscal 2001)

Typical Recipients

Arts & Humanities: Arts Associations & Councils, Dance, Historic Preservation, History & Archaeology, Libraries, Literary Arts, Museums/Galleries, Music, Theater

Civic & Public Affairs: Botanical Gardens/Parks, Business/Free Enterprise, Community Foundations, Employment/Job Training, Hispanic Affairs, Housing, Law & Justice, Municipalities/Towns, Philanthropic Organizations, Professional & Trade Associations, Public Policy, Safety, Urban & Community Affairs

Education: Afterschool/Enrichment Programs, Agricultural Education, Colleges & Universities, Community & Junior Colleges, Education Associations, Elementary Education (Public), Engineering/Technological Education, Faculty Development, Education-General, Legal Education, Literacy, Medical Education, Minority Education, Private Education (Precollege), Public Education (Precollege), Science/Mathematics Education, Social Sciences Education, Special Education, Student Aid, Vocational & Technical Education

Environment: Environment-General, Research, Resource Conservation

Health: AIDS/HIV, Alzheimers Disease, Cancer, Children's Health/Hospitals, Emergency/Ambulance Services, Eyes/Blindness, Health Funds, Health Organizations, Hospices, Hospitals, Medical Rehabilitation, Medical Research, Medical Training, Multiple Sclerosis, Nursing Services, Public Health, Single-Disease Health Associations

International: Health Care/Hospitals, Missionary/Religious Activities

Religion: Ministries, Religious Organizations, Religious Welfare, Seminaries

Science: Observatories & Planetariums, Scientific Organizations

Social Services: At-Risk Youth, Camps, Child Abuse, Child Welfare, Community Centers, Community Service Organizations, Counseling, Crime Prevention, Day Care, Delinquency & Criminal Rehabilitation, Domestic Violence, Family Planning, Family Services, Food/Clothing Distribution, Homes, People with Disabilities, Recreation & Athletics, Scouts, Senior Services, Shelters/Homelessness, Substance Abuse, United Funds/United Ways, Veterans, YMCA/YWCA/YMHA/YWHA, Youth Organizations

Application Procedures

Initial Contact: If applicant has never received funding from the Abell-Hanger Foundation, initial contact should be by letter requesting a pre-proposal questionnaire. Upon return of the questionnaire, the trustees will review the request to determine whether it warrants a complete proposal. A full application form will then be sent to the applicant.

Application Requirements: Application should be submitted on the original forms supplied by the foundation. These forms should include the grant affidavit, institutional profile, grant request summary, current year operating budget and current fiscal year budget comparison, staff salaries and benefits, and contributions analysis. The applicant will also be asked to supply the organization's latest audited financial statement. The grant request summary is comprised of five components and serves as a condensation of the detailed proposal: summary statement of request, statement of need, methodology statement, evaluation of project statement, and future funding needs.

Deadlines: Applications will be accepted during the month prior to the trustee meetings in August, November, February, and May. Applicants are strongly encouraged to submit the application as early as possible.

Review Process: Trustee meetings are held in September, December, March, and June. Applicants will be notified within a week after the trustee meeting.

Notes: Please do not make attachments to or bind application forms for presentation; presentations to the trustees are not permitted. Applicants may, at their option, submit any additional proposal information, which will be summarized by foundation staff for the trustees and included with the required application forms.

Restrictions

Specific criteria for awarding a grant include: the organization seeking a grant should be located in Texas or have significant operations in, or provide material benefits to the citizens of, Texas; the applicant must have IRS 501(c)(3) status; and the foundation generally will not contribute to private foundations as defined in Internal Revenue Code 509.

The foundation does not fund loans, grants, scholarships, or fellowships for individual students. Block scholarship grants are made only to institutions of higher education located within Texas. The foundation generally limits its educational grants to institutions of higher education, including religious institutions. Applicants must seek funding for the same proposal from various sources, as sole sponsorship of programs is rarely undertaken. Grants are made without any commitment for future support of operations or specific projects. Unsuccessful proposals may not be resubmitted for at least 12 months.

Additional Information

Publications: Annual Report; Guidelines; Application Form; Pre-Proposal Questionnaire

Foundation Officials

Herbert L. Cartwright, III: comptroller
Arlen L. Edgar: trustee
Jerome M. Fullinwider: trustee PRIM CORP EMPL president: VF - Russia Inc.
Tevis Herd: trustee
Robert C. Leibrock: president CORP AFFIL director: Elcor Corp.
Clarence Scharbauer, III: trustee
David L. Smith: executive director, trustee
Lester Van Pelt, Jr.: secretary-treasurer, trustee
Charles M. Younger, MD: trustee

Grants Analysis

Disclosure Period: fiscal year ending June 30, 2001
Total Grants: $8,517,164*
Number of Grants: 241
Average Grant: $35,340
Highest Grant: $1,000,000
Typical Range: $10,000 to $50,000
*Note: Giving excludes matching program for foundation staff and trustees.

Recent Grants

Note: Grants derived from fiscal 2000 Form 990.

General

1,000,000	Midland College, Midland, TX -- Advanced Technology Center
325,000	Midland College, Midland, TX -- scholarship fund
300,000	Midland College, Midland, TX -- construction of a new building for the Texas Tech Physicians Assistant Program
250,000	United Way Midland, Midland, TX
200,000	Tarleton State University Foundation, Stephenville, TX -- establish Daniel Parker Herd Endowed Scholarship Fund
190,000	City of Midland Aquatics, Midland, TX -- capital campaign
175,000	Midland College, Midland, TX -- for Chaparral Circle Fund
160,960	Permian Basin Petroleum Museum, Library, and Hall of Fame, Midland, TX -- five-year matching grant for the permanent endowment
142,000	University of Texas at Austin, Austin, TX -- Thermal Bioengineering Research Program
125,000	Permian Basin Petroleum Museum, Library, and Hall of Fame, Midland, TX -- operating support

ABERCROMBIE FOUNDATION

Giving Contact

John Backer, General Manager
PO Box 68
Versailles, KY 40383
Phone: (859)873-4477

Alternate Contact

Josephine E. Abercrombie, President

Description

Founded: 1950
EIN: 760229183
Organization Type: Family Foundation
Giving Locations: KY
Grant Types: Department, General Support, Operating Expenses, Project.

Donor Information

Founder: Established in Texas in 1950 with funds donated by James S. Abercrombie , an independent oil man from the Houston area who died in 1975. Mr. Abercrombie founded J. S. Abercrombie Minerals, which discovered oil in Texas and Louisiana. The company is still privately owned. He also founded the Cameron Iron Works, a manufacturer of aerospace products and oil production equipment. Abercrombie's only daughter, Josephine Abercrombie, is the president of the foundation.

In May of 1988, the J. S. Abercrombie Foundation distributed all of its assets and liabilities to the Abercrombie Foundation and the Robinson Foundation, 70% and 30% respectively.

Financial Summary

Total Giving: $1,290,600 (2001); $1,373,910 (2000); $755,950 (1999)
Assets: $5,989,804 (2001); $9,349,552 (2000); $11,347,358 (1999)

Typical Recipients

Arts & Humanities: Arts & Humanities-General, History & Archaeology, Libraries, Museums/Galleries, Music, Visual Arts
Civic & Public Affairs: Botanical Gardens/Parks, Clubs, Civic & Public Affairs-General, Housing, Urban & Community Affairs, Women's Affairs
Education: Colleges & Universities, Education Funds, Elementary Education (Private), Elementary Education (Public), Engineering/Technological Education, Education-General, International Exchange, Leadership Training, Literacy, Medical Education, Private Education (Precollege), Public Education (Precollege), Student Aid
Environment: Environment-General, Resource Conservation, Wildlife Protection
Health: Cancer, Children's Health/Hospitals, Clinics/Medical Centers, Diabetes, Geriatric Health, Medical Research, Mental Health, Prenatal Health Issues, Research/Studies Institutes, Speech & Hearing

Social Services: Animal Protection, At-Risk Youth, Big Brother/Big Sister, Child Welfare, Crime Prevention, Domestic Violence, Emergency Relief, Family Planning, Food/Clothing Distribution, People with Disabilities, Recreation & Athletics, Senior Services, Social Services-General, Special Olympics, Substance Abuse

Application Procedures

Initial Contact: 501(c)(3) organizations are invited to send one copy of a proposal.
Deadlines: May15 and November15.

Additional Information

Publications: Guidelines

Foundation Officials

Josephine E. Abercrombie: donor, president, trustee B Kingston, Jamaica 1926. PRIM CORP EMPL president: Josephine E. Abercrombie Interests. CORP AFFIL president: Pine Oak Stud Inc.

Grants Analysis

Disclosure Period: calendar year ending 2001
Total Grants: $1,290,600
Number of Grants: 30
Average Grant: $19,624*
Highest Grant: $250,000
Lowest Grant: $500
Typical Range: $5,000 to $40,000 and $100,000 to $150,000
*Note: Average grant figure excludes two highest grants totaling $521,310.

Recent Grants

Note: Grants derived from 2001 Form 990.

General

250,000	Sanders Brown Center on Aging, Lexington, KY
200,000	University of Kentucky College of Fine Arts, Lexington, KY
100,000	Cornell University Medical College, New York, NY
100,000	Lexington School, Lexington, KY
100,000	National Center on Addiction and Substance Abuse at Columbia University, New York, NY
100,000	Texas A & M Foundation, College Station, TX
100,000	Texas Children's Hospital, Houston, TX
100,000	University of Kentucky, Lexington, KY -- Equine Research
75,000	University of Kentucky College of Medicine, Lexington, KY
50,000	Weill Medical College of Cornell University, New York, NY

TALBERT AND LEOTA ABRAMS FOUNDATION

Giving Contact

Joe C. Foster, Jr., Secretary & Director
PO Box 27337
Lansing, MI 48909
Phone: (517)706-0000

Description

Founded: 1960
EIN: 386082194
Organization Type: Private Foundation
Giving Locations: MI: Lansing central
Grant Types: Endowment, General Support.

Donor Information

Founder: the late Leota Abrams, Talbert Abrams

Financial Summary

Total Giving: $403,165 (2001); $431,500 (2000); $475,500 (1999)

Giving Analysis: Giving for 2001 includes: foundation grants to United Way ($5,000); 2000: foundation grants to United Way ($5,000); 1999: foundation grants to United Way ($5,000)

Assets: $9,757,838 (2001); $10,482,585 (2000); $10,871,351 (1999)

Gifts Received: $2,358,812 (1992). Note: In fiscal 1992, contributions were received from Talbert Abrams Trust.

Typical Recipients

Arts & Humanities: History & Archaeology, Libraries, Museums/Galleries

Civic & Public Affairs: Clubs, Civic & Public Affairs-General, Philanthropic Organizations

Education: Colleges & Universities, Community & Junior Colleges, Engineering/Technological Education, Literacy, Public Education (Precollege), Special Education

International: Foreign Educational Institutions

Social Services: Counseling, Substance Abuse, United Funds/United Ways, Youth Organizations

Application Procedures

Initial Contact: Send a brief letter of inquiry, not more than two pages. Include proof of tax-exempt status.

Application Requirements: Include description of organization, amount requested, purpose of funds sought, and proof of tax-exempt status.

Deadlines: June 30.

Restrictions

Limited to scientific and educational purposes in central MI.

Additional Information

Publications: Annual Report

Foundation Officials

Kyle C. Abbott: director

Barbara J. Brown: president, director

Craig C. Brown: treasurer, director

Joe C. Foster, Jr.: secretary, director B Lansing, MI 1925. ED Wabash College (1943-1944); University of Michigan JD (1949). PRIM CORP EMPL partner: Fraser, Trebilcock, Davis & Foster. NONPR AFFIL member: Phi Gamma Delta; member: Rotary; member: Phi Beta Kappa; member: International Academy Estate & Trust Law; fellow: Michigan Bar Foundation; fellow: American College Trust & Estate Counsel; member: Florida Bar Association; fellow: American College Tax Counsel; member: American Bar Association; fellow: American Bar Foundation.

Shane A. Patzer: director

Tiffany L. Patzer: director

Thomas M. Schafer: vice president, director

Grants Analysis

Disclosure Period: calendar year ending 2001

Total Grants: $398,165*

Number of Grants: 13

Average Grant: $8,560*

Highest Grant: $174,000

Lowest Grant: $2,500

Typical Range: $5,000 to $20,000

*****Note:** Giving excludes United Way. Average grant figure excludes two highest grants($304,000).

Recent Grants

Note: Grants derived from 2000 Form 990.

Library-Related

195,000	Library of Michigan Foundation, Lansing, MI

General

100,500	Michigan State University, East Lansing, MI
60,000	Utica Community Schools Foundation, Utica, MI
20,000	Charles A Ransom Counseling Center, Lansing, MI
12,500	Council of Michigan Foundations, Lansing, MI
11,000	Lansing Community College Foundation, Lansing, MI
10,000	Junior Achievement, Lansing, MI
6,500	Friends of Historic Meridian
5,000	Capital Area United Way, Lansing, MI
5,000	Rotary Club of Lansing Foundation, Lansing, MI
3,000	Michigan Technological University, Hoaten, MI

ACF INDUSTRIES

Company Headquarters

620 N 2nd St.
St. Charles, MO 63301-5418
Web: http://www.acfindustries.com

Company Description

Employees: 1,548

SIC(s): 3700 Transportation Equipment, 4700 Transportation Services, 6700 Holding & Other Investment Offices.

ACF Foundation

Giving Contact

Nancy Collins, Manager, Treasure Operations
620 North Second Street
St. Charles, MO 63301-2081
Phone: (636)940-5101
Fax: (314)940-5109

Description

EIN: 136085065

Organization Type: Corporate Foundation

Giving Locations: MO

Grant Types: General Support, Matching.

Financial Summary

Total Giving: $43,223 (fiscal year ending April 30, 2001); $41,168 (fiscal 2000); $42,656 (fiscal 1999)

Giving Analysis: Giving for fiscal 2001 includes: foundation matching gifts ($4,010); fiscal 2000: foundation matching gifts ($2,900); foundation ($38,918) fiscal 1999: foundation matching gifts ($2,700)

Assets: $676,908 (fiscal 2001); $654,433 (fiscal 2000); $695,163 (fiscal 1999)

Typical Recipients

Arts & Humanities: Libraries, Museums/Galleries, Music, Public Broadcasting

Civic & Public Affairs: Clubs, Economic Development, Employment/Job Training, Civic & Public Affairs-General, Municipalities/Towns

Education: Business Education, Colleges & Universities, Community & Junior Colleges, Engineering/Technological Education, Education-General, Private Education (Precollege), Religious Education, Special Education, Student Aid, Vocational & Technical Education

Health: Alzheimers Disease, Children's Health/Hospitals, Emergency/Ambulance Services, Health Funds, Hospitals, Mental Health

Religion: Jewish Causes, Religious Organizations, Religious Welfare

Social Services: At-Risk Youth, Child Welfare, Community Centers, Community Service Organizations, Day Care, Food/Clothing Distribution, Homes, People with Disabilities, Scouts, Shelters/Homelessness, Substance Abuse, YMCA/YWCA/YMHA/YWHA, Youth Organizations

Application Procedures

Initial Contact: The foundation has no formal grant application procedure or application form.

Deadlines: None.

Restrictions

Grants are not made to individuals.

Additional Information

Publications: Contributions Guidelines Sheet

Corporate Officials

James C. Bates: vice president, chief financial officer B Saint Louis, MO 1951. ED University of Missouri (1973). PRIM CORP EMPL vice president, chief financial officer: ACF Industries. CORP AFFIL director: Campbell Chemicals; director: Trail Ltd.; vice president: ACF Industries Subs.

Carl Celian Icahn: owner, chairman, director B Queens, NY 1936. ED New York University School of Medicine; Princeton University BA (1957). PRIM CORP EMPL owner, chairman, director: Icahn & Co. CORP AFFIL chairman, president, chief executive officer: Trans World Airlines; chairman, chief executive officer: Starfire Holding Corp.; president: Riverdale Investors Corp., Inc.; Samsonite Corp.; chairman, president: Icahn Holding Corp.; director: Fairchild Corp.; president: Foxfield Thoroughbreds Inc.; chairman: Bayswater Realty & Capital; chairman, chief executive officer, director: ACF Industries Inc.; chairman: American RE Holdings LP. NONPR AFFIL Jewish Guild for the Blind Inc.

Robert J. Mitchell: treasurer PRIM CORP EMPL treasurer: ACF Industries.

James J. Unger: vice chairman, chief executive officer PRIM CORP EMPL vice chairman, chief executive officer: ACF Industries.

Roger D. Wynkoop: president B Oakland, CA 1948. ED Western Maryland College (1970). PRIM CORP EMPL president: ACF Industries. NONPR AFFIL member: National Freight Traffic Association.

Foundation Officials

Gail Golden: secretary, assistant treasurer

Carl Celian Icahn: president, treasurer (see above)

Alfred D. Kingsley: vice president, assistant secretary

Grants Analysis

Disclosure Period: fiscal year ending April 30, 2001

Total Grants: $39,213*

Number of Grants: 42

Average Grant: $934

Highest Grant: $3,000

Lowest Grant: $25

Typical Range: $500 to $2,000

*****Note:** Giving excludes matching grants.

Recent Grants

Note: Grants derived from fiscal 2000 Form 990.

General

3,000	Ranken Technical Institute, St. Louis, MO
2,500	Arkansas Economic Development Foundation, Little Rock, AR
2,000	Junior Achievement - Mississippi Valley, St. Louis, MO
2,000	St. Louis Transitional Hope House, Inc., St. Louis, MO
1,500	Mosaics, St. Charles, MO
1,500	Second Chance Emergency Shelter
1,250	St. Louis Association for Retarded Citizens, St. Louis, MO
1,100	YMCA, St. Charles, MO
1,005	St. Louis University, St. Louis, MO
1,000	American Red Cross, St. Louis, MO

ACHELIS FOUNDATION

Giving Contact

Joseph S. Dolan, Secretary & Executive Director
Morris & McVeigh
767 3rd Avenue, 4th Floor
New York, NY 10017-2023
Phone: (212)644-0322
Fax: (212)759-6510
E-mail: main@achelis-bodman-fnds.org
Web: http://www.fdcenter.org/grantmaker/achelis-bodman

Description

Founded: 1940
EIN: 136022018
Organization Type: General Purpose Foundation
Giving Locations: NY: New York
Grant Types: Capital, Conference/Seminar, Emergency, Employee Matching Gifts, General Support, Matching.

Donor Information

Founder: Established in 1940 with funds donated by the late Elisabeth Achelis , who was born in 1880 in Brooklyn Heights and was active in many social and charitable causes until her death in 1974. The Achelis Foundation is affiliated with the Bodman Foundation, and it reports that they share some officers.

Financial Summary

Total Giving: $2,130,500 (2000); $2,314,300 (1999); $1,540,000 (1998)
Giving Analysis: Giving for 2000 includes: foundation matching gifts ($139,300) 1999: foundation scholarships ($20,000)
Assets: $41,434,574 (2001); $41,487,311 (2000); $43,673,940 (1999)
Gifts Received: $26,000 (1999); $3,080,005 (1998); $1,500 (1993). Note: In 1999, contributions were received from the residuary beneficiary of the Elizabeth Achelis Trust. Gifts represent remainder trusts in 1998.

Typical Recipients

Arts & Humanities: Arts Outreach, Ballet, Dance, Ethnic & Folk Arts, Arts & Humanities-General, Historic Preservation, History & Archaeology, Libraries, Museums/Galleries, Music, Opera, Performing Arts, Public Broadcasting, Theater
Civic & Public Affairs: African American Affairs, Asian American Affairs, Botanical Gardens/Parks, Business/Free Enterprise, Clubs, Community Foundations, Economic Development, Employment/Job Training, Ethnic Organizations, Civic & Public Affairs-General, Housing, Nonprofit Management, Philanthropic Organizations, Public Policy, Urban & Community Affairs, Women's Affairs, Zoos/Aquariums
Education: Afterschool/Enrichment Programs, Arts/Humanities Education, Business Education, Business-School Partnerships, Colleges & Universities, Education Associations, Education Funds, Education Reform, Elementary Education (Private), Environmental Education, Education-General, Legal Education, Literacy, Medical Education, Minority Education, Preschool Education, Private Education (Precollege), Public Education (Precollege), Social Sciences Education, Special Education, Student Aid
Environment: Air/Water Quality, Environment-General, Resource Conservation, Wildlife Protection
Health: AIDS/HIV, Alzheimers Disease, Cancer, Children's Health/Hospitals, Clinics/Medical Centers, Emergency/Ambulance Services, Eyes/Blindness, Health-General, Health Funds, Health Organizations, Hospitals, Hospitals (University Affiliated), Medical Rehabilitation, Medical Research, Medical Training, Mental Health, Nursing Services, Outpatient Health Care, Public Health, Speech & Hearing, Transplant Networks/Donor Banks

International: Foreign Arts Organizations, Health Care/Hospitals, International Development, International Relations, International Relief Efforts
Religion: Churches, Religion-General, Jewish Causes, Ministries, Religious Organizations, Religious Welfare, Social/Policy Issues
Science: Science Museums, Scientific Centers & Institutes, Scientific Labs, Scientific Research
Social Services: Animal Protection, At-Risk Youth, Big Brother/Big Sister, Child Welfare, Community Centers, Community Service Organizations, Counseling, Day Care, Domestic Violence, Emergency Relief, Family Services, Food/Clothing Distribution, People with Disabilities, Recreation & Athletics, Scouts, Senior Services, Shelters/Homelessness, Social Services-General, Substance Abuse, Volunteer Services, YMCA/YWCA/YMHA/YWHA, Youth Organizations

Application Procedures

Initial Contact: Grant requests should be forwarded by letter, one copy only, with the signature of an appropriate officer. Organizations with which the foundation may not be familiar should include a statement of history and purpose for which funds are sought and financial data for both the organization and the proposal itself, along with proof of tax-exempt status.
Deadlines: None.
Review Process: The foundation's board meets in May, September, and December, and holds special meetings whenever warranted. The trustees review all requests for funds from staff recommendations and make all decisions on grant applications. Organizations requesting support must be aware that the foundation can respond affirmatively to only a small number of the many applications received each year.

Restrictions

The foundation's activities are primarily centered in greater NY under the current program. Grants are usually not authorized for travel, publications, films, or conferences. The foundation does not directly engage in research or experimental projects. The foundation does not make loans nor does it make grants to individuals.

Additional Information

Publications: Biennial Report; Guidelines

Foundation Officials

Walter Joseph Patrick Curley, Jr.: trustee B Pittsburgh, PA 1922. ED Yale University BA (1944); Harvard University MBA (1948); University of Oslo (1948). PRIM CORP EMPL president: Curley Land Co. OCCUPATION diplomat, investment banker. CORP AFFIL director: Sotheby Holdings Inc.; director: France Growth Fund. NONPR AFFIL honorary chairman: French-American Foundation; trustee: Frick Collection; member: Counsel Foreign Relations. CLUB AFFIL Yale Club; Saint Stephen's Green Club; Travelers Club; New York Racquet & Tennis Club; Rolling Rock Club; Knickerbocker Club; The Links Club; Golf Morfontaine Club; Kildare Street Club; Bedford Golf Club.
Joseph S. Dolan: executive director, secretary
Anthony Drexel Duke, Sr.: trustee B New York, NY July 28, 1918. ED Princeton University (1941). NONPR AFFIL chairman, president, founder: Boys Harbor.
Peter Frelinghuysen: vice president, trustee ED Princeton University (1963); Yale University (1968). PRIM CORP EMPL attorney: Morris & McVeigh. CORP AFFIL secretary: K O A Holdings Inc.
John N. Irwin, III: chairman, chief executive officer, treasurer, trustee B 1954. ED Princeton University (1976). PRIM CORP EMPL vice president, managing director: Hillside Industries Inc. CORP AFFIL vice president, managing director, director: Hillside Capital Inc. De Corp.

Leslie Lenkowsky, PhD: trustee PRIM NONPR EMPL president, chief executive officer: Hudson Institute Inc. CORP AFFIL director: ITT Educational Services Inc.
Russell Parsons Pennoyer: president, trustee B New York, NY 1951. ED Harvard University BA (1974); Columbia University School of Law JD (1982). PRIM CORP EMPL partner: Benedetto, Gartland & Company Inc.
Mary Stone Phipps: vice president, trustee NONPR AFFIL member-at-large, director: Girl Scout Council Greater New York. CLUB AFFIL Somerset Club; Pilgrims Club; Piping Rock Club; The Links Club; Meadow Brook Club; Colony Club.
Guy G. Rutherfurd: honorary chairman, assistant treasurer, trustee B New York, NY 1913. ED Princeton University BA (1938); University of Virginia LLB (1942). PRIM CORP EMPL partner: Morris & McVeigh.

Grants Analysis

Disclosure Period: calendar year ending 2001
Total Grants: $2,130,500*
Number of Grants: 48
Average Grant: $44,385*
Highest Grant: $100,000
Lowest Grant: $10,000*
Typical Range: $10,000 to $150,000
*Note: Giving excludes matching gifts.

Recent Grants

Note: Grants derived from 2000 Form 990.

Library-Related

100,000	Metropolitan Museum of Art, New York, NY -- Thomas J. Watson, Jr. Memorial Library

General

100,000	Bronx Preparatory Charter School, New York, NY
100,000	Columbia University, New York, NY -- medical scientist training program
100,000	Faith Center for Community Development, New York, NY -- faith-based home ownership program
100,000	Fresh Air Fund, New York, NY -- capital campaigns
100,000	Girl Scout Council of Greater New York, Inc., New York, NY -- school breaks program
100,000	Harvard University, Program on Education Policy and Governance, Cambridge, MA -- "Education Matter" magazine
100,000	Mount Sinai School of Medicine, New York, NY -- medical scientist training program
100,000	New York Blood Center, New York, NY -- minority donor recruitment program
100,000	Rockefeller University, New York, NY -- fellowship for tuberculosis research
75,000	Manhattan Institute for Policy Research, New York, NY

ANNA KEESLING ACKERMAN TRUST

Giving Contact

c/o U.S. Bank National Association
PO Box 3168
Portland, OR 97208
Phone: (503)275-4327

Description

Founded: 1963
EIN: 846032046
Organization Type: Private Foundation

Giving Locations: CO
Grant Types: Endowment, General Support.

Financial Summary

Total Giving: $454,977 (2001); $542,344 (2000); $442,114 (1999)
Giving Analysis: Giving for 2001 includes: foundation scholarships ($3,477)
Assets: $9,197,260 (2001); $10,309,769 (2000); $11,048,567 (1999)

Typical Recipients

Arts & Humanities: Arts Outreach, Libraries, Museums/Galleries, Performing Arts, Theater
Civic & Public Affairs: Community Foundations, Civic & Public Affairs-General, Housing, Urban & Community Affairs, Zoos/Aquariums
Education: Business Education, Colleges & Universities, Education Associations, Education Funds, Education-General, Public Education (Precollege), Social Sciences Education, Student Aid
Environment: Resource Conservation
Health: Children's Health/Hospitals, Diabetes, Emergency/Ambulance Services, Heart, Home-Care Services, Hospices, Mental Health, Multiple Sclerosis, Prenatal Health Issues, Single-Disease Health Associations
Religion: Churches, Ministries, Religious Welfare, Synagogues/Temples
Social Services: Animal Protection, Community Centers, Community Service Organizations, Day Care, Domestic Violence, Family Services, Food/Clothing Distribution, People with Disabilities, Recreation & Athletics, Scouts, Senior Services, Social Services-General, YMCA/YWCA/YMHA/YWHA, Youth Organizations

Application Procedures

Initial Contact: Send a brief letter of inquiry.
Application Requirements: Include purpose of funds sought and proof of tax-exempt status.
Deadlines: None.

Restrictions

Does not provide grants to individuals.

Additional Information

Trust(s): U.S. Bank

Foundation Officials

Harold U. Littrell: co-trustee
Jack H. Webb: co-trustee B Monroe, LA 1936. ED Centenary College BS (1957); Tulane University JD (1960). PRIM CORP EMPL president: Jack M. Webb & Associates. CORP AFFIL director: Scotia Pacific Holdings Co. NONPR AFFIL member: LA Bar Association; member: Texas Bar Association; member: Houston Bar Association; member: American Bar Association.

Grants Analysis

Disclosure Period: calendar year ending 2001
Total Grants: $451,500*
Number of Grants: 33
Average Grant: $10,922*
Highest Grant: $102,000
Typical Range: $3,000 to $15,000
*Note: Giving excludes scholarships. Average grant figure excludes highest grant.

Recent Grants

Note: Grants derived from 2001 Form 990.

General

102,000	Pro Rodeo Hall of Fame, Colorado Springs, CO
50,000	Bust Rodeo Foundation, Colorado Springs, CO
35,000	Cheyenne Mountain Zoo, Colorado Springs, CO
30,000	US Olympic Committee, Colorado Springs, CO
25,000	American Heart Association Pikes Peak Chapter, Colorado Springs, CO
25,000	YMCA of Pikes Peak Region, Colorado Springs, CO
15,000	Boys and Girls Club of Larimer County, Ft. Collins, CO
15,000	Salvation Army, Colorado Springs, CO
12,500	Nature Conservancy, Boulder, CO
10,000	Al Kaly Temple, Pueblo, CO

ACME-MCCRARY CORP./ SAPONA MANUFACTURING CO.

Company Headquarters

PO Box 1287
Asheboro, NC 27204
Web: http://www.saponamfg.com

Company Description

Employees: 900
SIC(s): 2200 Textile Mill Products.

Acme-McCrary and Sapona Foundation

Giving Contact

Fred M. Kearns, Jr., President
PO Box 1287
Asheboro, NC 27204
Phone: (336)625-2161

Description

EIN: 566047739
Organization Type: Corporate Foundation
Giving Locations: NC: Randolph County
Grant Types: Capital, General Support, Scholarship.

Financial Summary

Total Giving: $39,525 (2000); $40,200 (1999); $47,000 (1998). Note: 1997 and 2000 Giving includes United Way ($16,000).
Giving Analysis: Giving for 2000 includes: foundation grants to United Way ($16,000); 1999: foundation grants to United Way ($16,000); foundation ($24,200) 1998: foundation grants to United Way ($16,000)
Assets: $1,383,036 (2000); $1,499,172 (1999); $1,209,498 (1998)
Gifts Received: $39,525 (2000); $50,000 (1998); $50,000 (1997). Note: In 1998, contributions were received from Sapona Manufacturing Co. ($50,000).

Typical Recipients

Arts & Humanities: Arts Associations & Councils, Arts & Humanities-General, Libraries, Museums/Galleries, Music
Civic & Public Affairs: Chambers of Commerce, Clubs, Employment/Job Training, Civic & Public Affairs-General, Housing, Inner-City Development, Professional & Trade Associations, Safety, Zoos/Aquariums
Education: Colleges & Universities, Community & Junior Colleges, Education-General, Health & Physical Education, Medical Education, Minority Education, Preschool Education, Private Education (Precollege), Public Education (Precollege)
Health: Alzheimers Disease, Cancer, Children's Health/Hospitals, Clinics/Medical Centers, Diabetes, Emergency/Ambulance Services, Health-General, Health Organizations, Hospices, Hospitals, Hospitals (University Affiliated), Medical Rehabilitation, Nursing Services, Public Health
Religion: Churches, Religion-General, Religious Organizations

Social Services: Community Centers, Community Service Organizations, Recreation & Athletics, Scouts, Senior Services, Social Services-General, United Funds/United Ways, YMCA/YWCA/YMHA/YWHA, Youth Organizations

Application Procedures

Initial Contact: Send a letter.
Application Requirements: Include purpose of funds sought and the scope of the organization's activities. If the funds are requested for a regular purpose or activity, a description of the purpose or activity should be included.
Deadlines: December 1.

Restrictions

Does not support individuals or political or lobbying groups.

Corporate Officials

Charles W. McCrary, Jr.: chairman, chief executive officer, director PRIM CORP EMPL chairman, chief executive officer, director: Acme-McCrary Corp.
Bruce T. Patram: chief financial officer PRIM CORP EMPL chief financial officer: Acme-McCrary Corp.
William H. Redding, Jr.: president, director PRIM CORP EMPL president, director: Acme-McCrary Corp.
John O. H. Toledano: vice chairman, secretary, director PRIM CORP EMPL vice chairman, secretary, director: Acme-McCrary Corp.

Foundation Officials

Fred M. Kearns, Jr.: president
C.W. McCrary, III: director
Charles W. McCrary, Jr.: vice president (see above)
Bruce T. Patram: secretary, treasurer (see above)
S. Steele Redding: vice president
William H. Redding, Jr.: vice president (see above)
John O. H. Toledano: vice president (see above)
John O.H. Toledano, Jr.: director
Harold J. Weiler: president

Grants Analysis

Disclosure Period: calendar year ending 2000
Total Grants: $23,525*
Number of Grants: 18
Average Grant: $1,310
Highest Grant: $6,250
Lowest Grant: $100
Typical Range: $300 to $4,000
*Note: Giving excludes United Way.

Recent Grants

Note: Grants derived from 2001 Form 990.

General

16,000	United Way of Randolph County, Elkins, WV -- annual fund
6,250	Boy Scouts of America Old North State Council, Greensboro, NC -- park renovation
2,500	Regional Consolidated Services -- annual fund
1,500	North Carolina Zoological Society, NC -- annual fund
1,250	Randolph-Asheboro YMCA, Asheboro, NC -- annual fund
1,000	American Cancer Society, Wallingford, CT -- annual fund
1,000	Asheboro City School Systems, Asheboro, NC -- scholarship
1,000	East Side Improvement Association, Asheboro, NC -- School Renovation Project
1,000	George Washington Carver Community Enrichment Center, Asheboro, NC -- building fund
1,000	Greensboro Symphony Orchestra, Greensboro, NC -- annual fund

Acushnet Foundation

Giving Contact
R. William Blasdale, Foundation Manager
Acushnet Foundation
PO Box 1498
Mattapoisett, MA 02739
Phone: (508)758-6159
Fax: (508)758-8960
E-mail: seamark@ma.ultranet.com

Description
EIN: 046032197
Organization Type: Private Foundation
Giving Locations: MA: New Bedford
Grant Types: Capital, Emergency, General Support, Multiyear/Continuing Support, Scholarship, Seed Money.

Donor Information
Founder: Established by Acushnet Co.

Financial Summary
Total Giving: $510,500 (fiscal year ending June 30, 2001); $521,000 (fiscal 2000); $309,500 (fiscal 1997)
Giving Analysis: Giving for fiscal 2001 includes: foundation grants to United Way ($107,000)
Assets: $9,733,868 (fiscal 2001); $10,786,975 (fiscal 2000); $9,038,211 (fiscal 1997)

Typical Recipients
Arts & Humanities: Arts Associations & Councils, Community Arts, Historic Preservation, History & Archaeology, Libraries, Museums/Galleries, Music, Public Broadcasting, Theater
Civic & Public Affairs: Civil Rights, Community Foundations, Economic Policy, Civic & Public Affairs-General, Law & Justice, Legal Aid, Philanthropic Organizations, Public Policy, Urban & Community Affairs
Education: Business Education, Colleges & Universities, Economic Education, Education Funds, Engineering/Technological Education, Education-General, International Exchange, Minority Education, Public Education (Precollege), Science/Mathematics Education, Secondary Education (Private), Secondary Education (Public), Special Education, Student Aid
Environment: Environment-General
Health: Children's Health/Hospitals, Children's Health/Hospitals, Health Funds, Health Organizations, Hospitals, Medical Rehabilitation, Public Health
Religion: Churches, Religious Organizations, Religious Welfare
Science: Science Exhibits & Fairs
Social Services: Animal Protection, Child Welfare, Community Centers, Community Service Organizations, Day Care, Family Services, Scouts, Substance Abuse, United Funds/United Ways, YMCA/YWCA/YMHA/YWHA, Youth Organizations

Application Procedures
Initial Contact: Send a brief letter of inquiry.
Application Requirements: amount desired, purpose of funds sought, and other pertinent information
Deadlines: None.
Review Process: The board meets when required and notifies applicants within four to six weeks after receipt of letter.

Restrictions
The foundation does not support endowments, operating expenses, or matching gifts. Grants are made in the New Bedford area unless a project receives specific board approval.

Additional Information
The foundation favors organizations with no other means of support. Grant seekers currently receiving government aid are not encouraged to apply.

The Acushnet Co. was the original donor to the Acushnet Foundation. It is currently not involved with administering the foundation.

Foundation Officials
William Blasdale: trustee
Bill Blazedale: trustee
Robert S. Dubiel: trustee PRIM CORP EMPL executive vice president: Acushnet Co. CORP AFFIL president, chief executive officer: Cobra Golf Inc.; president: Titleist Foot-Joy Worldwide.
Grame L. Flanders: trustee
Glenn Johnson: trustee PRIM CORP EMPL vice president: Woburn National Bank Corp.
Edward Powers: foundation managing, trustee
Carl Ribeiro: trustee
Robert Vanz: trustee
Thomas C. Weaver: trustee
Richard B. Young: trustee
William Young: trustee B New Bedford, MA 1943. ED University of Massachusetts, Amherst (1969); Boston University JD (1981). PRIM CORP EMPL vice president, fiduciary tax counsel: Boston Safe Deposit & Trust Co. NONPR AFFIL member: American Bar Association.

Grants Analysis
Disclosure Period: fiscal year ending June 30, 2001
Total Grants: $403,500*
Number of Grants: 59
Average Grant: $6,839
Highest Grant: $50,000
Typical Range: $1,000 to $20,000
*Note: Giving excludes United Way.

Recent Grants
Note: Grants derived from fiscal 1999 Form 990.

General

50,000	Boys and Girls Club of New Bedford, New Bedford, MA
20,000	Old Dartmouth Historical Society, New Bedford, MA
20,000	United Way of New Bedford, Inc., New Bedford, MA
15,000	Boys and Girls Club of New Bedford, New Bedford, MA
15,000	Community Foundation, New Bedford, MA
15,000	Dennison Memorial Community Center, New Bedford, MA
15,000	New Bedford Child and Family Service, New Bedford, MA
15,000	St. Luke's Hospital, New Bedford, MA
15,000	YMCA New Bedford, New Bedford, MA
10,000	Animal Rescue League, New Bedford, MA

Charles E. and Caroline J. Adams Trust

Giving Contact
Sharon M. Driscoll, Executive Account Manager
Charles E. and Caroline J. Adams Trust
Care of Bank Boston
PO Box Box 6767
Providence, RI 02940
Phone: (617)434-5669
Fax: (617)434-7567

Description
Founded: 1955
EIN: 046011995
Organization Type: Private Foundation
Giving Locations: MA: Boston
Grant Types: Capital, General Support.

Donor Information
Founder: the late Charles E. and Caroline J. Adams

Financial Summary
Total Giving: $148,911 (fiscal year ending May 31, 2001); $858,869 (fiscal 1999); $825,723 (fiscal 1997)
Assets: $15,683,700 (fiscal 2001); $15,704,907 (fiscal 1999); $12,873,046 (fiscal 1998)

Typical Recipients
Arts & Humanities: Libraries, Museums/Galleries, Music
Civic & Public Affairs: African American Affairs, Business/Free Enterprise, Economic Development, Employment/Job Training, Civic & Public Affairs-General, Hispanic Affairs, Nonprofit Management, Philanthropic Organizations, Urban & Community Affairs
Education: Colleges & Universities, Education Reform, Engineering/Technological Education, Education-General, Medical Education, Public Education (Precollege), School Volunteerism, Science/Mathematics Education
Science: Science Museums
Social Services: At-Risk Youth, Camps, Child Abuse, Child Welfare, Community Centers, Community Service Organizations, Day Care, Family Services, Youth Organizations

Application Procedures
Initial Contact: Send full proposal.
Application Requirements: Include a description of organization, amount requested, purpose of funds sought, recently audited financial statement, and proof of tax-exempt status.
Deadlines: None.
Review Process: Board meets in March, June, September, and December.

Additional Information
Trust(s): First Natl Bank Boston

Grants Analysis
Disclosure Period: fiscal year ending May 31, 2001
Total Grants: $550,511
Number of Grants: 10
Average Grant: $27,500*
Highest Grant: $165,258
Typical Range: $15,000 to $75,000
*Note: Average grant figure excludes two highest grants ($330,519).

Recent Grants
Note: Grants derived from 2001 Form 990.

General

165,258	Massachusetts Institute of Technology, Cambridge, MA
165,257	Harvard Medical School, Cambridge, MA
75,000	Center for Women and Enterprise, Boston, MA
30,000	Boston Plan for Excellence, Boston, MA
30,000	Career Connections Collaborative, Boston, MA
29,996	Mt. Auburn Associates
20,000	Tri-City Community Action Program, Malden, MA
15,000	Dorchester Bay Economic Development Corp, Dorchester, MA
10,000	Latino Parents Association, Boston, MA
10,000	Suited for Success, Miami, FL

ADC Telecommunications

Company Headquarters
13625 Technology Drive
Eden Prairie, MN 55344-2252
Web: http://www.adc.com

Company Description

Employees: 2,900
SIC(s): 3600 Electronic & Other Electrical Equipment.

Operating Locations

ADC Telecommunications (MN--Minneapolis)

Nonmonetary Support

Type: Donated Equipment; Donated Products; In-kind Services

Giving Contact

Sandra Larson, Manager, Contributions & Community Relations
PO Box 1101
Minneapolis, MN 55440-1101
Phone: (952)946-3113
Fax: (952)946-3292

Description

Organization Type: Corporate Giving Program
Giving Locations: principally near operating locations and to national organizations.
Grant Types: Capital, Emergency, General Support, Operating Expenses, Seed Money.

Financial Summary

Total Giving: Company does not disclose contributions figures.

Typical Recipients

Arts & Humanities: Arts Appreciation, Arts Associations & Councils, Arts Centers, Arts Institutes, Ballet, Community Arts, Dance, Ethnic & Folk Arts, Arts & Humanities-General, Libraries, Museums/Galleries, Music, Opera, Performing Arts, Public Broadcasting, Theater, Visual Arts

Civic & Public Affairs: African American Affairs, Asian American Affairs, Botanical Gardens/Parks, Business/Free Enterprise, Civil Rights, Economic Development, Economic Policy, Employment/Job Training, Ethnic Organizations, Civic & Public Affairs-General, Housing, Inner-City Development, Minority Business, Native American Affairs, Nonprofit Management, Philanthropic Organizations, Public Policy, Urban & Community Affairs, Women's Affairs, Zoos/Aquariums

Education: Afterschool/Enrichment Programs, Arts/Humanities Education, Business Education, Business-School Partnerships, Colleges & Universities, Community & Junior Colleges, Continuing Education, Economic Education, Education Funds, Elementary Education (Public), Engineering/Technological Education, Education-General, Legal Education, Literacy, Minority Education, Preschool Education, Public Education (Precollege), Science/Mathematics Education, Secondary Education (Public), Special Education, Vocational & Technical Education

Environment: Environment-General

Health: Adolescent Health Issues, Clinics/Medical Centers, Health-General, Medical Rehabilitation, Medical Research, Mental Health, Public Health

International: Human Rights, International Affairs, International Relations

Science: Science-General, Science Exhibits & Fairs, Science Museums, Scientific Centers & Institutes, Scientific Labs, Scientific Organizations, Scientific Research

Social Services: At-Risk Youth, Camps, Child Welfare, Community Centers, Community Service Organizations, Counseling, Day Care, Delinquency & Criminal Rehabilitation, Domestic Violence, Emergency Relief, Family Services, Food/Clothing Distribution, Homes, People with Disabilities, Recreation & Athletics, Refugee Assistance, Senior Services, Sexual Abuse, Shelters/Homelessness, Social Services-General, Substance Abuse, United Funds/United Ways, Volunteer Services, Youth Organizations

Application Procedures

Initial Contact: Send a brief letter of inquiry and a full proposal.
Application Requirements: Include a description of organization, amount requested, purpose of funds sought, recently audited financial statement, and proof of tax-exempt status. Also include a list of the board of directors.

Restrictions

Does not support political or lobbying groups or religious organizations for sectarian purposes.

Corporate Officials

Richard R. Roscitt: chairman, chief executive officer PRIM CORP EMPL chairman, chief executive officer: ADC Telecommunications.
Robert E. Switz: senior vice president, chief financial officer PRIM CORP EMPL senior vice president, chief financial officer: ADC Telecommunications ADD CORP EMPL treasurer: ADC Systems Integration Inc.

Grants Analysis

Typical Range: $1,000 to $2,500

DIANA S. ADELSON TRUST

Giving Contact

Edward B. Corcoran
31 America's Cup Ave.
Newport, RI 02840
Phone: (401)847-0872

Description

Founded: 1993
EIN: 050466295
Organization Type: Private Foundation
Giving Locations: RI
Grant Types: General Support.

Financial Summary

Total Giving: $49,000 (2001); $48,400 (2000); $57,900 (1999)
Assets: $700,375 (2001); $756,897 (2000); $780,207 (1999)
Gifts Received: $9,246 (1994); $83,178 (1993); $686,188 (1992). Note: In 1994, contributions were received from the estate of Diana Adelson.

Typical Recipients

Arts & Humanities: Libraries, Music, Public Broadcasting
Civic & Public Affairs: African American Affairs, Civic & Public Affairs-General, Legal Aid, Safety, Urban & Community Affairs
Education: Public Education (Precollege)
Health: Emergency/Ambulance Services, Hospitals, Nursing Services
Religion: Religion-General, Jewish Causes, Religious Organizations, Religious Welfare, Synagogues/Temples
Social Services: Camps, Community Service Organizations, Crime Prevention, Domestic Violence, Family Services, Food/Clothing Distribution, People with Disabilities, Social Services-General, Youth Organizations

Application Procedures

Initial Contact: Send a brief letter of inquiry.
Application Requirements: Include a description of organization and constituents served, general organizational materials, proof of tax-exempt status, and purpose of funds sought.
Deadlines: None.

Restrictions

Supports only 501(c)(3) organizations. No grants are made to individuals.

Foundation Officials

Edwin S. Gozonsky: trustee
Matilda Saver: trustee
Jeffrey J. Teitz: trustee

Grants Analysis

Disclosure Period: calendar year ending 2001
Total Grants: $49,000
Number of Grants: 14
Average Grant: $3,500
Highest Grant: $10,000
Lowest Grant: $1,500
Typical Range: $1,000 to $5,000

Recent Grants

Note: Grants derived from 2001 Form 990.

Library-Related

1,500	Ruth Woolf Adelson Medical Library Fund, Newport, RI

General

10,000	New Visions of Newport County, Newport, RI
10,000	Newport Hospital Foundation, Newport, RI
5,000	Boys and Girls Club of Newport County, Inc, Newport, RI
3,000	Martin Luther King Center, Newport, RI
2,500	Camp Ruggles Rhode Island, Newport, RI
2,500	Child and Family Services, Newport, RI
2,500	Congregation Jesuat Israel, Newport, RI
2,500	Justice Assistance, Providence, RI
2,500	Rhode Island Legal Services, Providence, RI
2,000	Thompson Middle School, Newport, RI

LEO ADLER TRUST

Giving Contact

Marlyn Norquist, Trust Officer
c/o U.S. National Association Bank
PO Box 3168
Portland, OR 97208-3168
Phone: (503)275-4327
E-mail: teresa.ingram@usbank.com
Web: http://www.leoadler.com

Description

Founded: 1995
EIN: 936289087
Organization Type: Private Foundation
Giving Locations: OR: Baker County
Grant Types: General Support, Scholarship.

Financial Summary

Total Giving: $1,072,296 (2002); $1,315,801 (2001); $1,550,093 (2000)
Giving Analysis: Giving for 2002 includes: foundation scholarships ($719,264); 2000: foundation matching gifts ($6,000); foundation scholarships ($782,267); 1999: foundation scholarships ($803,747)
Assets: $21,881,719 (2002); $25,592,850 (2001); $30,896,914 (2000)
Gifts Received: $50 (2002); $150 (2001); $29,300 (2000). Note: Contributions were received from the estate of Leo Adler.

Typical Recipients

Arts & Humanities: History & Archaeology, Libraries, Museums/Galleries, Performing Arts
Civic & Public Affairs: Botanical Gardens/Parks, Employment/Job Training, Civic & Public Affairs-General, Municipalities/Towns, Urban & Community Affairs
Education: Colleges & Universities, Public Education (Precollege), Student Aid
Environment: Environment-General
Health: Clinics/Medical Centers, Emergency/Ambulance Services, Health Organizations, Hospitals
Religion: Religious Welfare
Social Services: Community Centers, Domestic Violence, Family Services, Recreation & Athletics, YMCA/YWCA/YMHA/YWHA

Application Procedures

Initial Contact: Request application form.
Deadlines: October 1 for Community Fund applications, April 1 for first time scholarship applications, March 1 for scholarship renewals.

Restrictions

Grants are not made to support individuals, religious organizations for sectarian purposes, political or lobbying groups, or organizations outside operating areas.

Additional Information

The foundation gives through two funds: a Community Grants fund, with a grant range of $300 to $75,000 and a scholarship fund, with a range of $600 to $5,000. The foundation awards scholarships to students who are graduates of high schools in Baker County, OR, or North Powder High School in Union County, OR. In addition, the Leo Adler Community Fund was created for the purpose of awarding grants to tax-exempt organizations in the Baker County, OR, area.
Trust(s): US Natl Bank OR

Grants Analysis

Disclosure Period: calendar year ending 2002
Total Grants: $353,032*
Number of Grants: 52
Average Grant: $5,942*
Highest Grant: $50,000
Lowest Grant: $300
Typical Range: $1,000 to $10,000
*Note: Giving excludes scholarships. Average grant figure excludes highest grant.

Recent Grants

Note: Grants derived from 2001 Form 990.

General
127,180	Eastern Oregon University, La Grande, OR -- scholarship/education
100,000	Partnership II, Baker City, OR
100,000	St. Elizabeth Health Care Foundation, Baker City, OR
71,783	Oregon State University, Corvallis, OR -- scholarship/education
50,000	Baker Sports Complex, Baker, OR -- to build phase III
47,390	Blue MT Community College, Pendleton, OR -- scholarship/education
38,500	University of Oregon, Eugene, OR -- scholarship/education
34,950	University of Idaho, Moscow, ID -- scholarship and education
34,650	Boise State University, Boise, ID -- scholarship/education
30,000	City of Baker City, Baker City, OR

ADOBE SYSTEMS

Company Headquarters

345 Park Avenue
San Jose, CA 95110-2704
Web: http://www.adobe.com

Company Description

Founded: 1982
Ticker: ADBE
Exchange: NASDAQ
Former Name: Aldus Corp.
Revenue: US$1.164 billion (2002)
Employees: 3341 (2002)
SIC(s): 7300 Business Services.

Operating Locations

Adobe Systems (WA--Seattle)

Nonmonetary Support

Type: Donated Products; In-kind Services

Giving Contact

345 Park Avenue
San Jose, CA 95110
Phone: (408)536-6528
Fax: (408)537-6313
Web: http://www.adobe.com/aboutadobe/philanthropy/main.html

Alternate Contact

Phone: (401)536-3993

Description

Organization Type: Corporate Giving Program
Giving Locations: CA: Seattle/King County, San Francisco Bay area, San Jose, Silicon Valley
Grant Types: Award, Capital, Emergency, General Support, Operating Expenses, Project.

Financial Summary

Total Giving: Company does not disclose contributions figures.

Typical Recipients

Arts & Humanities: Arts Appreciation, Arts Centers, Arts Funds, Arts Outreach, Ballet, Community Arts, Dance, Arts & Humanities-General, Libraries, Literary Arts, Museums/Galleries, Music, Performing Arts, Public Broadcasting, Theater, Visual Arts
Civic & Public Affairs: Botanical Gardens/Parks, Community Foundations, Employment/Job Training, Ethnic Organizations, Civic & Public Affairs-General, Housing, Inner-City Development, Native American Affairs, Nonprofit Management, Women's Affairs, Zoos/Aquariums
Education: Afterschool/Enrichment Programs, Arts/Humanities Education, Business Education, Business-School Partnerships, Faculty Development, Education-General, Literacy, Minority Education, Preschool Education
Environment: Air/Water Quality, Resource Conservation, Wildlife Protection
Health: Adolescent Health Issues, AIDS/HIV, Alzheimers Disease, Arthritis, Cancer, Children's Health/Hospitals, Diabetes, Eyes/Blindness, Health-General, Heart, Hospices
Science: Science-General, Science Exhibits & Fairs, Science Museums, Scientific Research
Social Services: Animal Protection, At-Risk Youth, Child Welfare, Community Centers, Counseling, Delinquency & Criminal Rehabilitation, Domestic Violence, Family Services, Food/Clothing Distribution, People with Disabilities, Recreation & Athletics, Sexual Abuse, Shelters/Homelessness, Social Services-General, United Funds/United Ways, Volunteer Services, Youth Organizations

Application Procedures

Initial Contact: Send postcard with address, call 408/536-3993, or consult the Web site.

Restrictions

Does not support individuals, religious organizations for sectarian purposes, political or lobbying groups, organizations outside operating areas, or organizations which unlawfully discrimate against any kind of person.

Corporate Officials

Bruce Chizen: president, chief executive officer, director B 1955. ED Brooklyn College BS. PRIM CORP EMPL president, chief executive officer, director: Adobe Systems Inc.
Charles Matthew Geschke: co-chairman B Cleveland, OH 1939. ED Carnegie Mellon University PhD; Xavier University AB (1962); Xavier University MS (1963). PRIM CORP EMPL co-chairman: Adobe Systems. NONPR AFFIL member: Math Association America; member: National Academy Engineers; member: Association Computer Math.
Dr. John E. Warnock: co-chairman, chief technology officer B Salt Lake City, UT 1940. ED University of Utah BS (1961); University of Utah MS (1964); University of Utah PhD (1969). PRIM CORP EMPL co-chairman, chief technology officer: Adobe Systems Inc. CORP AFFIL director: Netscape Communications Corp.; director: Red Brick Systems; Evans Sutherland Computer Corp.:. NONPR AFFIL member: NAE; chairman: Tech Museum Innovation; member entrepreneurial board advisory committee: American Film Institute.

Grants Analysis

Typical Range: $3,000 to $30,000

AHMANSON FOUNDATION

Giving Contact

Lee E. Walcott, Jr., Vice President & Managing Director
9215 Wilshire Boulevard
Beverly Hills, CA 90210
Phone: (310)278-0770
Fax: (310)278-4581

Description

Founded: 1952
EIN: 956089998
Organization Type: Family Foundation
Grant Types: Capital, Challenge, Emergency, Endowment, General Support, Matching, Operating Expenses, Project, Scholarship, Seed Money.

Donor Information

Founder: Established in 1952 in California as an independent foundation with funds donated by the late Howard F. Ahmanson and his wife, the late Dorothy G. Sullivan . Other donors include William H. Ahmanson and Robert H. Ahmanson, both nephews.
A graduate of the University of Southern California, Howard Ahmanson built an extensive financial empire consisting primarily of savings and loan associations and insurance companies. A noted philanthropist, yachtsman, and art collector, Howard Ahmanson served on the boards of the Los Angeles County Museum of Art, University of Southern California, Kennedy Center for the Performing Arts, and California Museum of Science and Industry.

Financial Summary

Total Giving: $35,000,000 (fiscal year ending October 31, 2003 approx); $38,000,000 (fiscal 2002 approx); $29,443,705 (fiscal 2001)
Giving Analysis: Giving for fiscal 2000 includes: foundation grants to United Way ($5,000)

Assets: $785,613,165 (fiscal 2001); $964,421,859 (fiscal 2000); $940,763,817 (fiscal 1999)
Gifts Received: $61,330,500 (fiscal 1999); $69,863 (fiscal 1997)

Typical Recipients

Arts & Humanities: Arts Appreciation, Arts Centers, Arts Funds, Arts Institutes, Arts Outreach, Ballet, Dance, Ethnic & Folk Arts, Film & Video, Arts & Humanities-General, Historic Preservation, History & Archaeology, Libraries, Literary Arts, Museums/Galleries, Music, Opera, Performing Arts, Public Broadcasting, Theater, Visual Arts

Civic & Public Affairs: African American Affairs, Botanical Gardens/Parks, Civil Rights, Clubs, Economic Development, Economic Policy, Employment/Job Training, Civic & Public Affairs-General, Hispanic Affairs, Housing, Law & Justice, Legal Aid, Nonprofit Management, Parades/Festivals, Philanthropic Organizations, Public Policy, Safety, Urban & Community Affairs, Zoos/Aquariums

Education: Arts/Humanities Education, Business Education, Colleges & Universities, Education Associations, Education Funds, Education Reform, Elementary Education (Private), Elementary Education (Public), Engineering/Technological Education, Faculty Development, Education-General, Health & Physical Education, International Studies, Journalism/Media Education, Leadership Training, Legal Education, Literacy, Medical Education, Minority Education, Preschool Education, Private Education (Precollege), Public Education (Precollege), School Volunteerism, Science/Mathematics Education, Secondary Education (Private), Social Sciences Education, Special Education, Student Aid, Student Aid, Vocational & Technical Education

Environment: Air/Water Quality, Environment-General, Resource Conservation, Wildlife Protection

Health: Adolescent Health Issues, AIDS/HIV, Alzheimers Disease, Cancer, Children's Health/Hospitals, Clinics/Medical Centers, Emergency/Ambulance Services, Eyes/Blindness, Health Funds, Health Organizations, Heart, Hospitals, Long-Term Care, Medical Research, Mental Health, Multiple Sclerosis, Nursing Services, Outpatient Health Care, Prenatal Health Issues, Public Health, Research/Studies Institutes, Single-Disease Health Associations, Speech & Hearing, Trauma Treatment

International: Foreign Arts Organizations, Foreign Educational Institutions, Health Care/Hospitals, International Development, International Environmental Issues, International Peace & Security Issues, Missionary/Religious Activities

Religion: Churches, Dioceses, Jewish Causes, Religious Organizations, Religious Welfare, Social/Policy Issues, Synagogues/Temples

Science: Science-General, Science Museums, Scientific Centers & Institutes, Scientific Research

Social Services: Animal Protection, At-Risk Youth, Child Welfare, Community Centers, Community Service Organizations, Counseling, Crime Prevention, Day Care, Delinquency & Criminal Rehabilitation, Domestic Violence, Emergency Relief, Family Planning, Family Services, Food/Clothing Distribution, Homes, People with Disabilities, Recreation & Athletics, Senior Services, Shelters/Homelessness, Substance Abuse, Volunteer Services, YMCA/YWCA/YMHA/YWHA, Youth Organizations

Application Procedures

Initial Contact: Applicants should review a copy of the foundation's annual report and guidelines before sending in a proposal. After determining that a proposal matches the foundation's interests, a brief proposal or letter of inquiry should be sent to the managing director.

Application Requirements: Applicants should describe the purpose of the organization, its background, project, and overall funding plan. Also include current annual budget, project budget, amount requested, list of other available sources of support,

audited financial statement, a copy of 501(c)(3) tax-exempt status letter, and a list of the organization's governing board and officers.

Deadlines: None.

Review Process: After reviewing proposals, the foundation may request additional information or an interview. Notification generally occurs within 30 to 60 days; written responses will be sent promptly to those not likely to qualify, to that they may proceed in their search for funding. Others who may qualify will be notified so that a full proposal can be submitted for further consideration.

The foundation evaluates the quality of the program and the organization. Organizations must be well-managed, fiscally sound, have a developed history, and maintain a record of program integrity. Requests for capital support are considered most often after there is clear and assured evidence that the goal of the campaign is going to be achieved and that such will be accomplished within a reasonable time period.

Restrictions

Generally, no grants are made to individuals, or for endowed chairs, annual campaigns, fellowships or exchange programs, continuing support, deficit financing, professorships, internships, individual scholarships, conferences, exhibits, films or video production, or loans.

The foundation generally does not fund organizations which make grants to others, religious organizations for sectarian or propagation of faith purposes, traveling exhibits, performance underwriting, seminars, workshops, studies, surveys, general research and development, operational support of regional and national charities, or political advocacy.

Additional Information

Publications: Annual Report; Guidelines

Foundation Officials

Howard Fieldstead Ahmanson, Jr.: chairman
Robert H. Ahmanson: president, trustee B 1927. PRIM CORP EMPL vice president, director: H.F. Ahmanson & Co.
William H. Ahmanson: vice president, trustee B Omaha, NE 1925. ED University of California, Los Angeles BS (1950). PRIM CORP EMPL H.F. Ahmanson & Co. CORP AFFIL director: Pachmayr Ltd. NONPR AFFIL director: International Shooting Sport Park.
Daniel N. Belin: trustee B 1938. PRIM CORP EMPL partner: Belin Rawling & Badal.
Lloyd Edward Cotsen: trustee B Boston, MA 1929. ED Princeton University BA (1950); Harvard University MBA (1957). PRIM CORP EMPL chairman, chief executive officer, director: Neutrogena Corp.
Robert M. DeKruif: trustee B 1919. PRIM CORP EMPL vice chairman, director: H.F. Ahmanson & Co. CORP AFFIL director vice chairman: Home Savings of America FSB.
Karen A. Hoffman: secretary
Kristen K. O'Connor: treasurer
Stephen D. Rountree: trustee
Leonard E. Walcott, Jr.: vice president, managing director

Grants Analysis

Disclosure Period: fiscal year ending October 31, 2001
Total Grants: $29,443,705
Number of Grants: 501
Average Grant: $44,867*
Highest Grant: $2,600,000
Lowest Grant: $1,000
Typical Range: $10,000 to $100,000
***Note:** Average grant figure excludes three highest grants ($7,100,000).

Recent Grants

Note: Grants derived from 2001 Form 990.

Library-Related

500,000   Henry E. Huntington Library and Art Gallery, San Marino, CA -- book acquisitions

200,000   Library Foundation of Los Angeles, Los Angeles, CA -- reading enrichment programs

General

2,600,000   Museum Associates, Los Angeles, CA -- acquisition of forty-six French oil sketches

2,500,000   University of Southern California, Los Angeles, CA -- construction of Neurogenic Institute of the Keck School of Medicine

2,000,000   HUC Skirball Cultural Center, Los Angeles, CA -- construction of Heritage Hall Amphitheater

800,000   Hathaway Children and Family Services, Sylmar, CA -- infrastructure improvements

750,000   California Lutheran University, Thousand Oaks, CA -- construction of education and technology center

750,000   Pueblo Nuevo Development, Los Angeles, CA -- construction of middle school

500,000   Exposition Park Intergenerational Community Center, Los Angeles, CA -- toward creation of the Exposition Park activities complex

500,000   Goodwill Industries of Southern Georgia, Inc., Albany, GA -- additional support toward the Widening Doors capital campaign

500,000   Museum Associates, Los Angeles, CA -- toward acquisition painting "Persephone Giving Psyche the Water of Beauty"

475,000   Los Angeles Educational Partnership, Los Angeles, CA -- toward establishment of the Excellence in Education Awards Program

CLAUDE W. AND DOLLY AHRENS FOUNDATION

Giving Contact

Claude W. Ahrens, Trustee
Claude W. and Dolly Ahrens Foundation
PO Box 686
Grinnell, IA 50112
Web: http://www.ahrensfoundation.org

Description

Founded: 1994
EIN: 421413842
Organization Type: Private Foundation
Giving Locations: CA; IA

Donor Information

Founder: Established in 1994 by Claude W. Ahrens.

Financial Summary

Total Giving: $582,581 (fiscal year ending October 31, 2000); $928,158 (fiscal 1999); $285,833 (fiscal 1996)
Assets: $14,779,835 (fiscal 2000); $15,408,290 (fiscal 1999); $9,980,452 (fiscal 1996)
Gifts Received: $12,805 (fiscal 1996); $6,630,782 (fiscal 1994). Note: In fiscal 1996, contributions were received from Claude W. Ahrens.

Typical Recipients

Arts & Humanities: Arts Associations & Councils, Libraries
Civic & Public Affairs: Philanthropic Organizations, Safety
Education: Agricultural Education
Health: Clinics/Medical Centers
Social Services: Family Services, Recreation & Athletics

Application Procedures

Initial Contact: Send a brief letter of inquiry.
Deadlines: None.

Foundation Officials

Chad Ahrens: trustee
Claude W. Ahrens: trustee
John Ahrens: trustee
Richard Ahrens: trustee
David Clay: trustee
Randy Juhl: trustee
Dick Muckler: trustee

Grants Analysis

Disclosure Period: fiscal year ending October 31, 2000
Total Grants: $582,581
Number of Grants: 17
Average Grant: $16,474*
Highest Grant: $319,000
Typical Range: $1,000 to $50,000
*Note: Average grant figure excludes highest grant. A more recent grants list was unavailable.

Recent Grants

Note: Grants derived from 1996 Form 990.

Library-Related

25,000	Stewart Library, Grinnell, IA -- automation of library equipment

General

150,000	Ahrens Family Center, Grinnell, IA -- facility addition
100,000	Grinnell Regional Medical Center, Grinnell, IA -- for plaza construction
5,000	Grinnell Area Arts Council, Grinnell, IA -- fundraising for the arts
3,333	Grinnell Volunteer Fire Department, Grinnell, IA -- for rescue truck
2,500	Iowa 4-H Foundation, Ames, IA -- renovation of 4-H Center

AIR FRANCE

Company Headquarters

142 W. 55th St., Fl. 2
New York, NY 10019
Web: http://www.airfrance.com/us

Company Description

Employees: 850
SIC(s): 4500 Transportation by Air.
Parent Company: Groupe Air France, 45 Rue de Paris, Roissy, Charles de Gaulle, France

Operating Locations

Air France (Southwestern Region) (FL--Miami; TX--Houston); Air France (U.S. Pacific Region) (CA--Los Angeles)

Nonmonetary Support

Type: Donated Products

Giving Contact

125 W. 55th St.
New York, NY 10019-3300
Phone: (212)830-4000

Description

Organization Type: Corporate Giving Program
Giving Locations: CA: Los Angeles, San Francisco; DC; FL: Miami; MA: Boston; NY: New York; PA: Philadelphia; TX: Houston generally near "gateway" cities from which Air France flies to Europe.

Typical Recipients

Arts & Humanities: Dance, Historic Preservation, Libraries, Museums/Galleries, Music, Performing Arts, Public Broadcasting, Theater
Civic & Public Affairs: Professional & Trade Associations
Education: International Studies
Health: Hospitals, Medical Research, Single-Disease Health Associations
International: International Relations
Religion: Religious Organizations
Science: Scientific Organizations
Social Services: Child Welfare

Application Procedures

Initial Contact: Initial letter may be submitted at any time to the nearest Air France local sales office. While applications are accepted throughout the year, fall is generally best for funding during the following year. Include a description of organization, number of tickets requested, purpose for which tickets are sought, and the type and level of exposure (advertisements, press releases, etc.) which Air France will gain from making the contribution.

Restrictions

While Air France has no set restrictions on its giving, the company generally prefers to support those organizations whose image is compatible with its own.

Additional Information

Compagnie Nationale Air France in Paris has its own contributions program.

Corporate Officials

Robert C. Iversen: chief operating officer PRIM CORP EMPL chief operating officer: Air France U.S.A.

Grants Analysis

Typical Range: $1,000 to $2,500

AIR PRODUCTS AND CHEMICALS, INC.

Company Headquarters

Allentown, PA
Web: http://www.airproducts.com/maxx

Company Description

Founded: 1940
Ticker: APD
Exchange: NYSE
Revenue: US$5.401 billion (2002)
Profit: US$525.4 million (2002)
Employees: 17200 (2002)
Fortune Rank: 311, per FORTUNE Magazine's list of 500 Largest U.S. Corporations (2002).
SIC(s): 2813 Industrial Gases, 2819 Industrial Inorganic Chemicals Nec, 2873 Nitrogenous Fertilizers, 3443 Fabricated Plate Work--Boiler Shops.

Operating Locations

Air Products & Chemicals, Inc. (AL--Aliceville, Burkville, Decatur, Flomaton, Theodore; AZ--Chandler, Phoenix, Tempe; AR--Fayetteville, Fort Smith, Little Rock, Magnolia; CA--City of Industry, Concord, Fountain Valley, Huntington Beach, Mountain View, Newport Beach, Pleasanton, Sacramento, San Marcos, Santa Clara, Stockton; CO--Denver, Fort Collins; CT--West Hartford; DC--Washington; FL--Fort Walton Beach, Longwood, Miami, Orlando, Pace, Pensacola, Tallahassee; GA--Albany, Atlanta, Conyers, Dalton; IL--Chicago, Granite City, Hennepin, Lisle, Marion, Springfield, Tuscola; IN--Chesterton, Terre Haute; IA--Davenport, Des Moines, Sioux City; KS--Fort Scott, Liberal; KY--Ashland, Louisville, Paducah; LA--Baton Rouge, Convent, Geismar, Monroe, St. Gabriel; MD--Baltimore, Calverton, Elkton, Hyattsville, Salisbury; MA--Hopkinton, Hudson, Marlborough; MI--Saginaw; MS--Greenwood, Southaven; MO--Earth City, Kingsville, Palmyra; NE--Grand Island, Lincoln, Omaha; NJ--Camden, Dayton, Edison, Paulsboro; NM--Rio Rancho; NY--East Fishkill, Glenmont, Latham, New Windsor; NC--Asheville, Durham, Greensboro, Laurinburg, Reidsville; OH--Cincinnati, Cleveland, Columbus, Middletown, North Baltimore; OK--Oklahoma City, Pryor; OR--Eugene, Gresham, Salem, Tualatin; PA--Creighton, Leetsdale, Lyndora, Tamaqua, Wilkes-Barre; SC--Columbia, Florence, Greenville, Taylors; TN--Dyersburg, Kingsport, Knoxville, Memphis; TX--Austin, Dallas, Deer Park, Gruven, Iraan, Irving, La Porte, Midlothian; UT--Centerville; VA--Chester, Hampton, Lynchburg, Roanoke; WA--Puyallup, Renton; WV--Apple Grove, Proctor, Weirton; WI--Green Bay, Oak Creek, Waukesha)

Nonmonetary Support

Type: Donated Equipment; Donated Products; In-kind Services; Loaned Employees; Loaned Executives; Workplace Solicitation
Volunteer Programs: Seventy percent of employees volunteer in community activities. Volunteerism is encouraged and recognized by the company, but it does not have a formal volunteer program.
Contact: Marta Boulos Gabriel, Manager, Community Relations & Philanthropy
Air Products & Chemicals, Inc.
7201 Hamilton Blvd.
Allentown, PA 18195-1501
E-mail: gabrielmb@apci.com

Air Products Foundation

Giving Contact

M.B. Gabriel
7201 Hamilton Boulevard
Allentown, PA 18195-1501
Phone: (610)481-9627
Fax: (610)481-6642
Web: http://www.airproducts.com/social_responsibilities/

Alternate Contact

Phone: (610)481-8814

Description

EIN: 232130928
Organization Type: Corporate Foundation
Giving Locations: headquarters and select operating communities.
Grant Types: Award, Capital, Emergency, Employee Matching Gifts, Matching, Multiyear/Continuing Support, Operating Expenses, Project.
Note: Matching gifts are for higher education, arts and cultural organizations. Employee matching gift ratio: 1 to 1 for gifts to accredited colleges and universities, up to $5,000. Employee matching gift ratio: 2 to 1 for gifts to arts groups, up to $2,000.

Financial Summary

Total Giving: $3,220,117 (fiscal year ending September 30, 2001); $5,000,000 (fiscal 2000 approx); $3,562,613 (fiscal 1999)
Giving Analysis: Giving for fiscal 2001 includes: foundation scholarships ($21,500); foundation grants to United Way ($87,345); foundation matching gifts ($1,435,336); foundation ($1,675,936); fiscal 2000: foundation matching gifts ($597,204); foundation grants to United Way ($1,023,861); corporate direct giving (approx $1,269,467); foundation ($2,109,468);

fiscal 1998: foundation grants to United Way ($153,526); foundation ($597,775) foundation matching gifts ($1,809,626)

Assets: $2,800,289 (fiscal 2001); $6,249,601 (fiscal 2000); $9,401,376 (fiscal 1999)

Gifts Received: $13,237,500 (fiscal 1994). Note: In 1994, the Foundation received contributions from the Prodair Corporation.

Typical Recipients

Arts & Humanities: Arts Festivals, Arts Funds, Community Arts, Dance, Historic Preservation, Libraries, Museums/Galleries, Music, Opera, Performing Arts, Public Broadcasting, Theater

Civic & Public Affairs: Business/Free Enterprise, Civil Rights, Economic Development, Economic Policy, Civic & Public Affairs-General, Housing, Municipalities/Towns, Nonprofit Management, Public Policy, Safety, Urban & Community Affairs, Women's Affairs

Education: Arts/Humanities Education, Business Education, Colleges & Universities, Continuing Education, Economic Education, Education Associations, Education Funds, Education Reform, Engineering/Technological Education, Environmental Education, Environmental Education, Education-General, Legal Education, Literacy, Minority Education, Science/Mathematics Education, Vocational & Technical Education

Environment: Air/Water Quality, Environment-General, Resource Conservation

Health: Cancer, Children's Health/Hospitals, Emergency/Ambulance Services, Health Organizations, Heart, Multiple Sclerosis, Nutrition, Single-Disease Health Associations

International: International Peace & Security Issues

Religion: Religious Welfare

Science: Science Exhibits & Fairs

Social Services: Child Welfare, Community Service Organizations, Counseling, Day Care, Delinquency & Criminal Rehabilitation, Domestic Violence, Emergency Relief, Family Services, Food/Clothing Distribution, Homes, People with Disabilities, Recreation & Athletics, Scouts, Senior Services, Shelters/Homelessness, Substance Abuse, United Funds/United Ways, Volunteer Services, Youth Organizations

Application Procedures

Initial Contact: Submit a written request on organization's letterhead.

Application Requirements: Include information on the purpose and background of the organization, including a list of its board of directors; amount requested; planned use of the contribution, including short- and long-term goals and when and how results will be evaluated; statement of community needs that the organization is addressing; time frame for the project; copy of the organizations Articles of Incorporation and By-Laws; current operating budget; list of current contributions or commitments and follow-up evaluation of contribution impact. Applicants must include a copy of the organization's IRS tax-exempt determination letter. Requests for funding for greater Lehigh Valley/Allentown, PA organizations should be submitted to Marta Boulos Gabriel, Manager of Community Relations and Philanthropy, at the company's Allentown address. For requests outside of this area, submit requests to the nearest Air Products location.

Deadlines: None.

Review Process: Requests are screened by contributions officer, then the committee reviews for approval or denial.

Evaluative Criteria: Committee examines benefit to Air Products community, need, population served, and funding sources.

Decision Notification: Requests are generally processed within 60 days.

Restrictions

Does not support fraternal organizations, labor groups, service clubs, individuals, operating funds for member agencies of the United Way, political or lobbying groups, religious organizations, or veterans organizations.

Additional Information

Company has participated in public/private ventures to rehabilitate abandoned and condemned properties in Allentown, PA.

Corporate Officials

John P. Jones, III: chairman, president, chief executive officer B November 09, 1950. ED Villanova University BSChE (1972). PRIM CORP EMPL chairman, president, chief executive officer: Air Products and Chemicals, Inc.

John R. Owings: vice president, chief financial officer ED Northern Illinois University BS (1971); Northern Illinois University MBA (1976). PRIM CORP EMPL vice president, chief financial officer: Air Products and Chemicals, Inc.

Foundation Officials

Timothy J. Holt: president

Grants Analysis

Disclosure Period: fiscal year ending September 30, 2001

Total Grants: $1,675,936*

Number of Grants: 437

Average Grant: $3,835

Highest Grant: $50,000

Typical Range: $500 to $5,000

*Note: Giving excludes matching gifts, scholarship, and United Way.

Recent Grants

Note: Grants derived from fiscal 2001 Form 990.

General

95,089	United Way of the Greater Lehigh Valley, Bethlehem, PA -- for health and welfare
95,089	United Way of the Greater Lehigh Valley, Bethlehem, PA -- operations support
71,864	United Way of the Greater Lehigh Valley, Bethlehem, PA -- operations support
71,864	United Way of the Greater Lehigh Valley, Bethlehem, PA -- operations support
71,816	United Way of the Greater Lehigh Valley, Bethlehem, PA -- operations support
71,816	United Way of the Greater Lehigh Valley, Bethlehem, PA -- operations support
50,000	Bucknell University, Lewisburg, PA
50,000	United Way of the Greater Lehigh Valley, Bethlehem, PA -- operations support
49,905	United Way of the Greater Lehigh Valley, Bethlehem, PA -- operations support
49,905	United Way of the Greater Lehigh Valley, Bethlehem, PA -- operations support

AK STEEL HOLDING CORP.

Company Headquarters

703 Curtis St.
Middletown, OH 45043
Phone: (513)425-5000

Fax: (513)425-2676
Web: http://www.aksteel.com

Company Description

Founded: 1994
Ticker: AKS
Exchange: NYSE
Acquired: ARMCO (1999).
Revenue: US$4.34 billion (2002)
Employees: 10700 (2001)
Fortune Rank: 376, per FORTUNE Magazine's list of 500 Largest U.S. Corporations (2002).

Nonmonetary Support

Type: Workplace Solicitation
Volunteer Programs: The foundation gives volunteer support donations to community organizations where employees volunteer their time and services.

AK Steel Foundation

Giving Contact

Brian T. Coughlin, Government Affairs Manager; Executive Director
703 Curtis Street
Middletown, OH 45043
Phone: (513)425-2991
Fax: (513)425-5683

Description

Founded: 1990
EIN: 311284344
Organization Type: Corporate Foundation
Formed by Merger of: Armco Inc. (1999).
Giving Locations: operating locations.
Grant Types: Award, Employee Matching Gifts, General Support, Matching, Scholarship.
Note: Employee matching gift ratio: 1 to 1 for educational and cultural institutions.

Donor Information

Founder: Established in 1990 by Armco, Inc., and Kawasaki Steel Investments.

Financial Summary

Total Giving: $1,145,300 (2001); $1,383,333 (2000); $685,299 (1999). Note: Contributes through foundation only.

Giving Analysis: Giving for 2000 includes: foundation scholarships ($7,500); foundation matching gifts ($35,293); foundation grants to United Way ($428,665); 1999: foundation matching gifts ($22,714); foundation scholarships ($119,000); foundation grants to United Way ($210,500); foundation ($333,075); 1998: foundation matching gifts ($10,485); foundation scholarships ($117,500); foundation grants to United Way ($210,500);

Assets: $17,374,380 (2001); $20,930,361 (2000); $9,485,962 (1999)

Gifts Received: $1,000,000 (1995). Note: Gifts are received from Armco, Inc., Kawasaki Steel Investments, Inc, Armco Steel Co., L.P. and Breed, Abbott & Morgan.

Typical Recipients

Arts & Humanities: Arts Associations & Councils, Arts Centers, Arts Festivals, Arts Institutes, Community Arts, Dance, Film & Video, Historic Preservation, History & Archaeology, Libraries, Museums/Galleries, Music, Opera, Performing Arts, Public Broadcasting, Theater

Civic & Public Affairs: Business/Free Enterprise, Chambers of Commerce, Clubs, Community Foundations, Civic & Public Affairs-General, Housing, Law & Justice, Parades/Festivals, Public Policy, Rural Affairs, Safety, Urban & Community Affairs

Education: Afterschool/Enrichment Programs, Business Education, Colleges & Universities, Economic

Education, Education Funds, Engineering/Technological Education, Education-General, International Studies, Public Education (Precollege), Student Aid
Environment: Air/Water Quality, Wildlife Protection
Health: Cancer, Clinics/Medical Centers, Emergency/Ambulance Services, Health Organizations, Heart, Hospices, Hospitals, Public Health, Single-Disease Health Associations
International: Foreign Arts Organizations
Religion: Religious Welfare
Social Services: Child Abuse, Child Welfare, Community Service Organizations, Crime Prevention, Family Services, Homes, People with Disabilities, Recreation & Athletics, Scouts, Senior Services, Shelters/Homelessness, Social Services-General, Substance Abuse, United Funds/United Ways, Veterans, YMCA/YWCA/YMHA/YWHA, Youth Organizations

Application Procedures

Initial Contact: Send a brief letter of inquiry.
Application Requirements: Include a description of organization, amount requested, project description, and proof of tax-exempt status.
Deadlines: None for matching grants; November 30 for scholarship.
Notes: For scholarship or matching grant programs, applicants can request application forms, which include specific criteria for each program.

Additional Information

In 1995, the company reported it changed its name from Armco Steel Company to AK Steel Corporation. The foundation has also undergone a name change; it is now called the AK Steel Foundation. Kawasaki owns approximately 15-16% of AK Steel Corp.'s stock.
AK Steel announced, its merger with Armco Inc. would take effect September 30, 1999. As a result of the merger, the business and operations of Armco will be conducted by and in the name of AK Steel. Armco shares will cease to trade on the New York Stock Exchange as of close of business on September 30, 1999.
Publications: Application Forms; Sons and Daughters of Alaska Steel Corporate Employees Scholarship Program; Employee Matching Gift Program Informational Brochure

Corporate Officials

Richard E. Newsted: executive vice presidento, director PRIM CORP EMPL executive vice president: AK Steel Corp.
Richard M. Wardrop, Jr.: chairman, chief executive officer, director B McKeesport, PA 1945. ED Pennsylvania State University (1968). PRIM CORP EMPL chairman, chief executive officer, director: Alaska Steel Corp. ADD CORP EMPL chairman: AK Steel Holding Corp.

Foundation Officials

Michael T. Adams: secretary
Brian T. Coughlin: executive director, assistant secretary
Brenda S. Harmon: treasurer
John G. Hirtz: president
Alan McCoy: trustee
James L. Wainscott: treasurer

Grants Analysis

Disclosure Period: calendar year ending 2001
Total Grants: $490,900*
Number of Grants: 20
Average Grant: $13,383*
Highest Grant: $125,000
Lowest Grant: $400
Typical Range: $1,000 to $20,000
*Note: Giving excludes matching gifts; scholarship; United Way. Average grant figure excludes two highest grants ($250,000).

Recent Grants

Note: Grants derived from 2001 Form 990.

Library-Related
500	Cameron County Public Library, Emporium, PA

General
288,000	Middletown Community Foundation, Middletown, OH
125,000	Middletown Miami Healthcare Foundation, Middletown, OH
125,000	Middletown Youth Soccer Association, Middletown, OH
89,225	United Way, Middletown, OH
85,000	Butler County United Way, Butler, PA
55,000	United Way of Richland County, Mansfield, OH
50,000	American Red Cross, Davenport, IA
44,613	Middletown United Way, Middletown, OH
44,613	United Way, Middletown, OH
40,000	South Spencer Schools, Evansville, IN

AKC FUND

Giving Contact

Ann Brownell-Sloane, Administrator
67A E. 77th St.
New York, NY 10021
Phone: (212)737-1011

Description

Founded: 1955
EIN: 136091321
Organization Type: Private Foundation
Giving Locations: CT; DC; NY: nationally.
Grant Types: Capital, General Support, Multiyear/Continuing Support, Professorship.

Donor Information

Founder: members of the Childs and Lawrence families

Financial Summary

Total Giving: $225,500 (2001); $209,500 (2000); $271,200 (1999)
Giving Analysis: Giving for 2001 includes: foundation grants to United Way ($6,000); 2000: foundation grants to United Way ($1,000); 1999: foundation grants to United Way ($1,000)
Assets: $5,927,377 (2001); $6,618,492 (2000); $6,660,458 (1999)
Gifts Received: $92,768 (1994). Note: In 1994, contributions were received from the Vannie Hamblet Trust.

Typical Recipients

Arts & Humanities: Arts Festivals, Ballet, Historic Preservation, History & Archaeology, Libraries, Literary Arts, Museums/Galleries, Music, Performing Arts, Public Broadcasting, Theater
Civic & Public Affairs: Community Foundations, Economic Development, Civic & Public Affairs-General, Professional & Trade Associations, Rural Affairs, Urban & Community Affairs, Women's Affairs
Education: Arts/Humanities Education, Colleges & Universities, Education-General, International Studies, Minority Education, Preschool Education, Private Education (Precollege), Public Education (Precollege), Religious Education, Social Sciences Education
Environment: Forestry, Environment-General, Resource Conservation, Wildlife Protection
Health: AIDS/HIV, Clinics/Medical Centers, Health-General, Health Organizations, Hospitals, Medical Research, Mental Health, Prenatal Health Issues, Single-Disease Health Associations

International: Foreign Educational Institutions, International Affairs, International Development, International Environmental Issues, International Organizations
Religion: Churches, Religion-General
Science: Science Museums, Scientific Research
Social Services: Camps, Child Welfare, Community Service Organizations, Family Planning, Recreation & Athletics, Refugee Assistance, Senior Services, Social Services-General, United Funds/United Ways, YMCA/YWCA/YMHA/YWHA, Youth Organizations

Application Procedures

Initial Contact: Send a brief letter of inquiry. Foundation will decide if a full proposal should be submitted.
Deadlines: None.

Restrictions

Emphasis is on education, conservation and preservation, and health and welfare in the Northeast.

Additional Information

Publications: Annual Report

Foundation Officials

Alice Childs Anderson: vice president
Carolyn Schenck Childs: director
Edward Calder Childs: director
Hope S. Childs: secretary
John D. Childs: director
John W. Childs: treasurer
Anne Childs Collins: director
Elizabeth Ransome Garside: director
Elisabeth Childs Gill: president
Starling Anderson Keene: secretary
Barbara Childs Lawrence: president
J. Vinton Lawrence: vice president
Adair Price Mali: director
Jenny Childs Preston: secretary
Susannah C. L. Wood: director

Grants Analysis

Disclosure Period: calendar year ending 2001
Total Grants: $219,500*
Number of Grants: 52
Average Grant: $4,221
Highest Grant: $25,000
Lowest Grant: $1,000
Typical Range: $1,000 to $10,000
*Note: Giving excludes United Way.

Recent Grants

Note: Grants derived from 2001 Form 990.

Library-Related
5,000	Norfolk Library, Norfolk, CT

General
25,000	Geer Foundation, North Canaan, CT
15,000	Phillips Exeter Academy, Exeter, NH
15,000	Student Conservation Association, Charlestown, NJ
15,000	Watertown Cooperative Nursery School, Watertown, MA
14,000	Bard College, East Brunswick, NJ -- Clemenete course in the humanities
10,000	American Farmland Trust, Washington, DC
10,000	Committee to Protect Journalists, New York, NY
10,000	Emory University, Atlanta, GA
10,000	Farm School, Athol, MA
5,000	American Near East Refugee Aid, Washington, DC

AKZO NOBEL CHEMICALS

Company Headquarters

300 S. Riverside Plaza
Chicago, IL 60606
Web: http://www.akzonobelusa.com

Company Description

Former Name: Akzo America.
Employees: 9,000
SIC(s): 2833 Medicinals & Botanicals, 2834 Pharmaceutical Preparations, 2899 Chemical Preparations Nec, 6719 Holding Companies Nec.
Parent Company: Akzo Nobel NV, Velperweg 76, PO Box 9300, Arnhem, Netherlands

Operating Locations

Akzo Chemicals Inc. (NJ--New Brunswick; NY--Burt; TX--Pasadena; WI--Janesville); Akzo Coatings (GA--Atlanta, Baxley; IL--Zion; KY--Louisville; MI--Troy; MS--Clinton; OH--Columbus, Springfield); Akzo Dreeland (CO--Denver); Akzo Electronics Materials Co. (CO--Colorado Springs); Akzo Engineering Plastics (NJ--Neshanic Station); Akzo LanChem Corp. (IL--East St. Louis); Akzo Nobel Chemicals (AL--Birmingham; CA--Los Angeles; CO--Colorado Springs, Denver; GA--Baxley, Norcross; IL--Addison, Chicago, Morton Grove; KY--Louisville; MI--Manistee; NJ--Neshanic Station, New Brunswick, West Orange; NY--New York; NC--Asheville, High Point; OH--Akron, Columbus; OK--Oklahoma City; TN--Rockwood; TX--Pasadena; WI--Janesville); Akzo Nobel Fibers Inc. (NC--Asheville); Akzo Nobel Fortafil Fibers Inc. (TN--Rockwood); Akzo Resins & Vehicles (IL--Addison); Diosynth, Inc. (IL--Chicago); Eka Chemicals North America (GA--Marietta); Fostafil Fibers (TN--Rockwood); Harshaw Filtrol (OH--Solon); Intervet America, Inc. (DE--Millsboro); Organon Inc. (NJ--West Orange); Organon Teknika Corp. (NC--Durham); Pharmaceutical Basics Inc. (CO--Denver; IL--Chicago); Sikkens Aerospace Finishers (CA--Torrance); Sikkens Car Refinishes (CA--Torrance)

Giving Contact

Robin Hall, Gen. Counsel
300 S. Riverside Plz.
Chicago, IL 60606
Phone: (312)906-7500
Fax: (312)906-7680

Description

Organization Type: Corporate Giving Program
Giving Locations: headquarters and operating communities.
Grant Types: Capital, Employee Matching Gifts, Fellowship, Matching, Scholarship.

Donor Information

Founder: Akzo America

Typical Recipients

Arts & Humanities: Community Arts, Arts & Humanities-General, Libraries, Music, Opera, Public Broadcasting
Civic & Public Affairs: Chambers of Commerce, Economic Development, Law & Justice, Philanthropic Organizations, Public Policy, Safety, Urban & Community Affairs
Education: Colleges & Universities, Community & Junior Colleges, Economic Education, Education Associations, Education-General, International Exchange, Minority Education, Science/Mathematics Education, Special Education, Vocational & Technical Education
Environment: Environment-General
Health: AIDS/HIV, Clinics/Medical Centers, Emergency/Ambulance Services, Health Organizations, Heart, Hospitals, Single-Disease Health Associations
Social Services: Child Welfare, Community Service Organizations, United Funds/United Ways, Youth Organizations

Application Procedures

Initial Contact: The foundation has no formal grant application procedure or application form.
Deadlines: None.

Restrictions

Program does not support fraternal, political, or religious organizations. Goodwill advertising is handled by the advertising department.

Additional Information

Akzo Nobel handles contributions for other U.S. subsidiaries of Akzo NV, including Akzo Nobel Chemicals.

Grants Analysis

Typical Range: $500 to $1,000

ALABAMA POWER CO.

Company Headquarters

2046 Patton Chapel Rd.
Birmingham, AL 35216
Web: http://www.alapower.com

Company Description

Employees: 6,865
SIC(s): 4911 Electric Services.
Parent Company: Southern Co., Atlanta, GA, United States

Operating Locations

Alabama Power Co. (AL--Abbeville, Alexander City, Aliceville, Asheville, Ashford, Ashland, Atmore, Auburn, Bankhead Dam, Bay Minette, Bayou La Batre, Blountsville, Bouldin Dam, Brewton, Butler, Carbon Hill, Centerville, Childersburg, Citronelle, Clayton, Columbia, Dadeville, Daleville, Dora, East Jefferson, Enterprise, Eufaula, Flomaton, Florala, Fort Deposit, Gadsden, Gardendale, Georgiana, Goodwater, Greensboro, Greenville, Haleyville, Hamilton, Harris Dam, Headland, Henry Dam, Holt Dam, Jackson, Jacksonville, Jordan Dam, Lay Dam, Leeds, Lineville, Logan Martin Dam, Marion, Martin Dam, Miller, Mobile, Monroeville, Montevallo, Montgomery, Ozark, Parrish, Pell City, Phenix City, Plant Chickasaw, Plant Farley, Plant Gadsden, Plant Gaston, Plant Greene County, Prattville, Prichard, Reform, Saraland, Selma, Smith Dam, Sylacauga, Theodore, Thomasville, Thurlow Dam, Tuscaloosa, Valley, Wedwee, Weiss Dam, West Jefferson, Winfield, Yates Dam)

Nonmonetary Support

Type: In-kind Services; Loaned Employees; Workplace Solicitation
Note: Co. reports that nonmonetary support is limited.

Alabama Power Foundation

Giving Contact

William B. Johnson, President
Alabama Power Foundation
600 N. 18th Street
Birmingham, AL 35291-0011
Phone: (205)257-2508
Fax: (205)257-1860
Note: Proposals should be sent to the manager of the nearest Alabama Power Business Office.

Description

Founded: 1990
EIN: 570901832
Organization Type: Corporate Foundation
Giving Locations: headquarters and operating communities.
Grant Types: Capital, Employee Matching Gifts, Endowment, General Support, Matching, Multiyear/Continuing Support, Project, Scholarship, Seed Money.

Financial Summary

Total Giving: $8,224,218 (2001); $7,937,391 (2000); $6,835,294 (1997). Note: Contributes through corporate direct giving program and foundation. 1997 Giving includes foundation. 1996 Giving includes scholarship ($246,850); matching gifts ($85,782).
Giving Analysis: Giving for 2000 includes: foundation scholarships ($488,553); foundation grants to United Way ($1,012,638) foundation ($6,436,200)
Assets: $136,510,166 (2001); $149,170,931 (2000); $156,135 (1998)
Gifts Received: $513,760 (2001); $687,194 (2000); $2,418,851 (1997). Note: In 2001, contributions were received from Alabama Power Service Organization-State ($75,000), Alabama Power Service Organization-Eastern ($5,000), Alabama Power Service Organization-Southeast ($5,000), Alabama Power Service Organization-Western ($5,000), Camp ASCCA ($75,000), Robert O. Finley, III Foundation ($6,000), Michael D. Garrett ($5,000), Hoover City Schools Foundation, Inc. ($35,000), William B. Hutchins ($50,000), Charles D. McCrary ($100,000), Alan Martin ($5,000), Mike Scott ($10,000), Steve R. Spencer ($50,00), and J.J. Thomley ($50,000). The foundation receives funds from Alabama Power Co., APSO, Birmingham Urban, E.B. Harris, and Robert O'Finley Foundation.

Typical Recipients

Arts & Humanities: Arts Associations & Councils, Arts Centers, Arts Festivals, Community Arts, Dance, Arts & Humanities-General, Historic Preservation, History & Archaeology, Libraries, Museums/Galleries, Music, Performing Arts, Theater, Visual Arts
Civic & Public Affairs: African American Affairs, Botanical Gardens/Parks, Business/Free Enterprise, Chambers of Commerce, Civil Rights, Community Foundations, Economic Development, Civic & Public Affairs-General, Municipalities/Towns, Urban & Community Affairs, Zoos/Aquariums
Education: Business Education, Colleges & Universities, Community & Junior Colleges, Education Funds, Education Reform, Elementary Education (Private), Engineering/Technological Education, Education-General, Literacy, Minority Education, Private Education (Precollege), Public Education (Precollege), Science/Mathematics Education, Student Aid
Environment: Environment-General, Resource Conservation
Health: Cancer, Children's Health/Hospitals, Diabetes, Eyes/Blindness, Health Organizations, Heart, Mental Health, Single-Disease Health Associations
International: International Relief Efforts
Religion: Jewish Causes, Ministries, Missionary Activities (Domestic), Religious Welfare
Science: Science Exhibits & Fairs, Science Museums, Scientific Labs
Social Services: Child Welfare, Community Centers, Community Service Organizations, Delinquency & Criminal Rehabilitation, Family Services, Food/Clothing Distribution, People with Disabilities, Scouts, Senior Services, Shelters/Homelessness, Substance Abuse, United Funds/United Ways, Veterans, Volunteer Services, YMCA/YWCA/YMHA/YWHA, Youth Organizations

Application Procedures

Initial Contact: Send a letter no longer than four pages.
Application Requirements: Include a description of organization, and its mission; previous support from foundation; projects goals and objectives; need project is trying to meet; expected results of project; key staff members, including those directly involved in project; list of board of directors; amount requested; description of use and evidence of need; how results will be measured; how project may be used by others; how project will be sustained once foundation's funding is gone; recently audited financial statements; and proof of tax-exempt status.
Deadlines: None.

Review Process: Manager at local plant will review request and decide whether or not to refer it to the foundation with a recommendation. Foundation will review forwarded proposals and make the final decision.

Evaluative Criteria: Preference is given to programs that have a long-term effect, can be replicated, and respond to issues that concern the customers, employees, and shareholders of Alabama Power Co.; provide opportunities for achievement and leadership to youth, minorities, and elderly; support community development; promote understanding of public issues; identify new programs which can adapt to other communities; or stimulate giving by other organizations.

Decision Notification: Six to eight weeks after application is received.

Restrictions

Does not support individuals, religious organizations for sectarian purposes, political or lobbying groups, or organizations which lack 501(c)(3) status.

Also does not fund organizations which discriminate on the basis of race, color, creed, gender, or national origin or operating expenses which duplicate United Way funding (capital or special project funding will be considered).

Additional Information

Publications: Charitable Giving Pamphlet; Foundation Annual Report

Corporate Officials

Art P. Beattie: vice president, secretary, treasurer B Pittsburgh, PA 1954. ED University of Tennessee BS (1975); University of Alabama MBA (1979). PRIM CORP EMPL vice president, secretary, treasurer: Alabama Power Co. ADD CORP EMPL secretary: Southern Electric Generating Co.

James H. Miller, III: senior vice president

Foundation Officials

Art P. Beattie: treasurer, director (see above)
Thomas E. Chappell: executive vice president, director
Michael D. Garrett: director PRIM CORP EMPL executive vice president: Alabama Power Co.
Stuart L. Griffin: assistant secretary
Elmer Beseler Harris: chairman B Chilton County, AL 1939. ED Auburn University BS (1962); Auburn University MS (1968); Auburn University MBA (1970). CORP AFFIL director: Southern Energy Resources Inc.; director: Southern Co. Services Inc.; president, director: Southern Electric Generating Co.; executive vice president, director: Southern Co. Inc.; director: AmSouth Bank NA; director: SCI Holdings Inc.; director: Alabama Property Co.; director: AmSouth Bancorp. NONPR AFFIL trustee: Southern Research Institute; director: United Way America; member: Southeast Electric Exchange; trustee: Samford University; member: Society American Military Engineers; member advisory board: Saint Vincent Hospital; member: Edison Electric Institute; director: Public Affairs Research Council Alabama; director: Boy Scouts America Birmingham Area Council; director: Alabama Council Economic Education. CLUB AFFIL Summit Club; Montgomery Club; Rotary Club.
Robert Holmes, Jr.: chairman
William Bruce Hutchins, III: president, director B Tuscaloosa, AL 1943. PRIM CORP EMPL executive vice president, chief financial officer: Alabama Power Co. CORP AFFIL director: Southern Electric Generating Co. NONPR AFFIL member: National Association Accountants; member: National Management Association; member: Financial Executives Institute; member: Micron Delta Epsilon; member: Beta Alpha Psi; member: Beta Gamma Sigma.
William B. Johnson: president
William B. Keller: director
Richard S. King: assistant treasurer
C. Alan Martin: director

Charles D. McCrary: director
James H. Miller, III: director (see above)
Rodney O. Mundy: director
William F. Smith: assistant treasurer
Steve R. Spencer: director
Jerry L. Stewart: director
William E. Zales, Jr.: secretary

Grants Analysis

Disclosure Period: calendar year ending 2001
Total Grants: $6,649,914*
Number of Grants: 1,400 (approx)
Average Grant: $4,750 (approx)
Highest Grant: $398,466
Lowest Grant: $20
Typical Range: $500 to $7,500
*Note: Giving excludes United Way and scholarships.

Recent Grants

Note: Grants derived from 2001 Form 990.

General

398,466	Birmingham Urban Revitalization Partnership, Birmingham, AL -- for operating support
314,742	United Way of Central Alabama, Birmingham, AL
174,595	United Way of Central Alabama, Birmingham, AL -- for operating support
160,000	McWane Center, Birmingham, AL -- capital support
150,000	Board of Trustees for the University of Alabama, Tuscaloosa, AL -- for operating
150,000	USS Alabama Battleship Foundation, Inc., Mobile, AL -- for capital support
103,005	Alabama Power Service Organization, Birmingham, AL
100,955	Alabama Power Service Organization, Birmingham, AL
100,000	Alabama Children's Hospital Foundation, Birmingham, AL -- for capital support
100,000	Alabama Institute for Deaf and Blind Foundation, Talladega, AL -- endowment

ALAVI FOUNDATION

Giving Contact

Dr. Mohammad Geramian, President
500 Fifth Avenue, Suite 3900
New York, NY 10110
Phone: (212)944-8333
Fax: (212)921-0325
Web: http://www.alavifoundation.org

Description

Founded: 1973
EIN: 237345978
Organization Type: General Purpose Foundation
Giving Locations: internationally; nationally.
Grant Types: Endowment, Multiyear/Continuing Support, Project.

Donor Information

Founder: Incorporated in 1973 by Bank Melli of Iran.

Financial Summary

Total Giving: $1,765,799 (fiscal year ending March 31, 2002); $994,868 (fiscal 2001); $1,181,765 (fiscal 2000). Note: The figure for 1999 includes $60,838 in nonmonetary support in the form of publicaton and book distributions to educational institutions.
Assets: $85,045,636 (fiscal 2002); $82,555,915 (fiscal 2001); $60,966,919 (fiscal 2000)
Gifts Received: $14,573 (fiscal 2001); $14,850 (fiscal 2000); $11,381 (fiscal 1999)

Typical Recipients

Arts & Humanities: Libraries, Public Broadcasting
Civic & Public Affairs: African American Affairs, Ethnic Organizations, Civic & Public Affairs-General, Safety
Education: Agricultural Education, Colleges & Universities, Community & Junior Colleges, Elementary Education (Private), Education-General, International Studies, Medical Education, Private Education (Precollege), Religious Education, Science/Mathematics Education
Environment: Air/Water Quality
Health: Arthritis, Cancer, Children's Health/Hospitals, Eyes/Blindness, Health Organizations, Heart, Hospitals, Multiple Sclerosis, Single-Disease Health Associations, Transplant Networks/Donor Banks
International: Foreign Educational Institutions, International-General, Health Care/Hospitals, International Organizations, International Peace & Security Issues, International Relief Efforts, Missionary/Religious Activities
Religion: Religion-General, Religious Organizations, Religious Welfare, Seminaries
Social Services: Community Centers, Community Service Organizations, People with Disabilities, Shelters/Homelessness

Application Procedures

Initial Contact: The foundation has no formal application form. Send a letter of inquiry.
Deadlines: None.

Additional Information

The foundation owns four centers in New York, Maryland, Texas, and California that are utilized as educational/religious centers and are open free of charge to all interested parties.

As part of its educational purpose, the foundation operates Saturday Schools in New York and New Jersey for teaching Islamic religion and Middle Eastern languages and cultures. The programs can be utilized by all interested parties.

Foundation Officials

Hoshang Ahmadi: director
Alireza Ebrahimi: secretary
Mohammad Geramian: president
Mehdi Hodjat: director
Abbas Mirakhor: treasurer
Mohammad Pirayandeh: director

Grants Analysis

Disclosure Period: fiscal year ending March 31, 2001
Total Grants: $994,868
Number of Grants: 38
Average Grant: $24,620
Highest Grant: $178,100
Typical Range: $5,000 to $50,000

Recent Grants

Note: Grants derived from 2000 Form 990.

General

127,220	Islamic Institute of New York, Woodside, NY
110,500	Islamic Seminary of New Jersey, NJ
100,000	Islamic Education Center, Tampa, FL
92,000	Razi School, Woodside, NY
90,000	Islamic Education Center, Potomac, MD
68,500	Brooklyn Mosque, Brooklyn, NY
50,000	Al Zahra Islamic Center, Antioch, TN
50,000	American Moslem Foundation, Covington, WA
50,000	Muslim Community School, Potomac, MD
40,000	Islamic Ahlulbelt Association

ALBERTSON'S INC.

Company Headquarters
250 E. Parkcenter Blvd.
Boise, ID 83726
Web: http://www.albertsons.com

Company Description
Founded: 1939
Ticker: ABS
Exchange: NYSE
Acquired: American Stores (1999).
Revenue: US$35.626 billion (2002)
Profit: US$485 million (2002)
Employees: 22000 (2002)
Fortune Rank: 35, per FORTUNE Magazine's list of 500 Largest U.S. Corporations (2002).
SIC(s): 5411 Grocery Stores, 5912 Drug Stores & Proprietary Stores.

Operating Locations
Acme Markets Inc. (PA--Malvern); Albertson's Drug Stores (AZ--Scottsdale); Albertson's Inc. (AR--Hot Springs, Texarkana; CA--Brea, Rocklin; CO--Aurora; OK--Tulsa; OR--Portland; TN--Memphis; TX--Katy, San Antonio; WA--Bellevue); Jewel Food Store (IL--Melrose Park); Max Food & Drug Division (ID--Boise); Osco Drug (AR--Fort Smith); Rx America (UT--Salt Lake City); Sav-on Drugs (CA--Buena Park); Yarnell Ice Cream Co. (AR--Searcy)
Note: Operates in 37 states.

Nonmonetary Support
Type: Cause-related Marketing & Promotion; Donated Products; In-kind Services
Volunteer Programs: The company sponsors the Warren E. McCain Community Volunteer Award. The program annually recognizes employees for volunteer efforts, donating $500 in the name of ten grand award winners to the charity of his/her choice. The company also selects an award winner from each of its operating divisions and donates $250 to each winner's charity of choice.

Giving Contact
Judy McLaughlin, Community Relations Coordinator
PO Box 20
Boise, ID 83726
Phone: (208)395-6200
Fax: (208)395-4382
Web: http://www.albertsons.com/corporate/

Description
Organization Type: Corporate Giving Program
Giving Locations: headquarters and operating communities.
Grant Types: Award, Capital, Conference/Seminar, Emergency, Employee Matching Gifts, Endowment, General Support, Matching, Multiyear/Continuing Support.
Note: Employee matching gift ratio: 1 to 1 for higher education only, up to $1000.

Financial Summary
Total Giving: $63,000,000 (2003 approx); $65,000,000 (2002); $48,000,000 (2001 approx)
Giving Analysis: Giving for 1998 includes: corporate direct giving (approx $3,000,000)
Assets: $115,211,000 (2002); $15,701,000 (2000); $6,233,968 (1999)

Typical Recipients
Arts & Humanities: Arts Appreciation, Arts Centers, Community Arts, Historic Preservation, Libraries, Music, Opera, Performing Arts, Public Broadcasting
Education: Business Education, Colleges & Universities, Community & Junior Colleges, Economic Education, Elementary Education (Private), Minority Education

Health: Emergency/Ambulance Services, Geriatric Health, Hospitals, Medical Rehabilitation, Mental Health, Public Health
Social Services: Child Welfare, Community Centers, Community Service Organizations, Emergency Relief, Food/Clothing Distribution, Senior Services, Shelters/Homelessness, Substance Abuse, United Funds/United Ways, Youth Organizations

Application Procedures
Initial Contact: Submit a full written proposal on the applicant organization's letterhead.
Application Requirements: Proposals should include a cover letter, narrative, and attachments. The cover letter should include a proposal summary and amount requested, and must be signed by the organization's executive director or president. The narrative section should be no longer than five pages, and must include agency information, including a brief a description of organization (history, mission, goals, and objectives), overview of current programs/activities and accomplishments, a description of organization of organizational structure, board/staff responsibilities and level of volunteer involvement, and description of agency affiliation with public agencies; information on the purpose of the grant, including a statement of need, description of constituency served and benefits to constituents, program goals, measurable objectives, program activities planned to accomplish goals (specify whether activities are new or ongoing), timetable for implementation, list of any other organizations participating in the program, list of names and qualifications of key staff members and volunteers responsible for the project, and project budget; and answers to the following questions relating to project evaluation: What results are expected during the funding period? How will success be defined and measured? How will the project's results be used and disseminated? The following attachments must be included with the proposal: board of directors list including occupations, community affiliations, committee assignments, and criteria for board selection; finances including current annual operating budget with summary of itemized revenues and expenses, funding sources for the organization with listing of past major contributions and amounts, anticipated future funding sources, and recently audited financial statement; annual report; and proof of tax-exempt status.
Deadlines: None.
Evaluative Criteria: Present an identifiable community need, tax-exempt status, efficient and effective administration, plentiful volunteer support, serves large population, programs have long-term effects, employee participation, participants encouraged to be self-sufficient, wide community support.
Decision Notification: Company responds to proposals in writing within six to eight weeks.

Restrictions
Does not support religious organizations for sectarian purposes, or political or lobbying groups.

Additional Information
In community fund drives, company generally contributes on a pro rata basis, figuring the number of Albertson's employees as a percentage of private employment in the area.
Publications: Contributions Policy and Procedures

Corporate Officials
Lawrence R. Johnston: chairman, chief executive officer, director B August 29, 1948. ED Stetson University BBA (1972). PRIM CORP EMPL chairman, chief executive officer, director: Albertson's Inc.
Peter L. Lynch: president, chief operating officer PRIM CORP EMPL president, chief operating officer: Albertson's Inc.

Giving Program Officials
Renee Bergquist: director investor relations
John G. Danielson: vice president, treasurer PRIM CORP EMPL vice president, treasurer: Albertson's Inc.

Grants Analysis
Disclosure Period: calendar year ending 2001
Total Grants: $34,000,000 (approx)*
*****Note:** Giving excludes money donated through the Albertson's Community Partners Card program.

ALCOA INC.

Company Headquarters
Pittsburgh, PA
Web: http://www.alcoa.com

Company Description
Founded: 1888
Ticker: AA
Exchange: NYSE
Former Name: Aluminum Co. of America;
Acquired: Reynolds Metals (2000); Cordant Technologies (2000).
Revenue: US$20.263 billion (2002)
Profit: US$420 million (2002)
Employees: 127000 (2002)
Fortune Rank: 82, per FORTUNE Magazine's list of 500 Largest U.S. Corporations (2002).
SIC(s): 2819 Industrial Inorganic Chemicals Nec, 3334 Primary Aluminum, 3353 Aluminum Sheet, Plate & Foil, 3354 Aluminum Extruded Products.

Operating Locations
Alcoa Automotive (OH--Northwood; PA); Alcoa Closure Systems International, Inc. (IN--Crawfordsville); Alcoa Extrusions, Inc. (AR--Magnolia; GA--Fairburn; MS--Hernando); Alcoa Inc. (AL--Cullman; AR--Russellville; CA--Irvine, Visalia; CO--Englewood; FL--Fort Meade; GA--Norcross; IL--Danville, Princeville; IN--Evansville, Lafayette, Richmond; IA--Davenport; KY--Hawesville; LA--Baton Rouge, Vidalia; MI--Southfield; MS--Houston, Olive Branch; MO--St. Louis; NY--Massena; OH--Barberton, Chillicothe, Cleveland, Lima, Sidney, Warren; PA--Lebanon, Leetsdale, Pittsburgh; SC--Gaffney; TN--Elizabethton, Nashville; TX--Dennison, Denton, Rockdale, San Antonio; VA--Stuarts Draft; WA--Auburn)

Alcoa Foundation

Giving Contact
Kathleen W. Buechel, President
Alcoa Foundation
201 Isabella Street
Pittsburgh, PA 15212-5858
Phone: (412)553-2348
Fax: (412)553-4532
Web: http://www.alcoa.com/site/community/homepage/community.asp

Alternate Contact
PO Box 185
Pittsburgh, PA 15230-9897
Phone: (412)553-4731

Description
Founded: 1952
EIN: 251128857
Organization Type: Corporate Foundation
Giving Locations: principally near operating locations and to national organizations.
Grant Types: Award, Capital, Challenge, Conference/Seminar, Emergency, Employee Matching

Gifts, Fellowship, General Support, Matching, Multiyear/Continuing Support, Research, Scholarship, Seed Money.

Note: Employee matching gift ratio: 2 to 1 for higher education.

Financial Summary

Total Giving: $21,326,190 (2001); $20,129,527 (2000); $17,945,924 (1999). Note: Contributes through foundation only.

Giving Analysis: Giving for 1999 includes: foundation grants to United Way ($903,053); foundation matching gifts ($981,000); foundation ($16,061,871); 1996: foundation scholarships ($540,000); foundation matching gifts ($1,605,320) foundation ($10,729,330)

Assets: $409,678,168 (2001); $441,062,746 (2000); $496,340,874 (1999)

Gifts Received: $500,000 (2001); $500,000 (2000); $500,000 (1999). Note: Contributions are received from Alcoa World Alumina.

Typical Recipients

Arts & Humanities: Arts Associations & Councils, Arts Centers, Arts Festivals, Arts Funds, Arts Institutes, Ballet, Community Arts, Dance, Arts & Humanities-General, Historic Preservation, History & Archaeology, Libraries, Literary Arts, Museums/Galleries, Music, Opera, Performing Arts, Public Broadcasting, Theater, Visual Arts

Civic & Public Affairs: African American Affairs, Botanical Gardens/Parks, Business/Free Enterprise, Chambers of Commerce, Civil Rights, Community Foundations, Economic Development, Economic Policy, Employment/Job Training, Civic & Public Affairs-General, Hispanic Affairs, Housing, Law & Justice, Legal Aid, Municipalities/Towns, Parades/Festivals, Philanthropic Organizations, Professional & Trade Associations, Public Policy, Safety, Urban & Community Affairs, Women's Affairs, Zoos/Aquariums

Education: Agricultural Education, Arts/Humanities Education, Business Education, Colleges & Universities, Community & Junior Colleges, Economic Education, Education Associations, Education Funds, Education Reform, Elementary Education (Private), Engineering/Technological Education, Faculty Development, Education-General, Gifted & Talented Programs, International Exchange, International Studies, Journalism/Media Education, Legal Education, Literacy, Medical Education, Minority Education, Preschool Education, Private Education (Precollege), Public Education (Precollege), Science/Mathematics Education, Student Aid

Environment: Environment-General, Protection, Resource Conservation

Health: AIDS/HIV, Cancer, Children's Health/Hospitals, Clinics/Medical Centers, Emergency/Ambulance Services, Health-General, Geriatric Health, Health Policy/Cost Containment, Health Funds, Health Organizations, Heart, Hospices, Hospitals, Medical Rehabilitation, Medical Research, Medical Training, Mental Health, Prenatal Health Issues, Public Health, Single-Disease Health Associations, Speech & Hearing

International: Foreign Arts Organizations, Foreign Educational Institutions, International-General, Health Care/Hospitals, International Development, International Environmental Issues, International Organizations, International Peace & Security Issues, International Relations, International Relief Efforts, Missionary/Religious Activities

Religion: Churches, Jewish Causes, Religious Organizations, Religious Welfare, Seminaries

Science: Science Exhibits & Fairs, Science Museums, Scientific Organizations

Social Services: At-Risk Youth, Big Brother/Big Sister, Child Welfare, Community Centers, Community Service Organizations, Counseling, Day Care, Delinquency & Criminal Rehabilitation, Domestic Violence, Emergency Relief, Family Planning, Family Services, Food/Clothing Distribution, Homes, People with Disabilities, Recreation & Athletics, Senior Services, Shelters/Homelessness, Social Services-General, Special Olympics, Substance Abuse, United Funds/

United Ways, Volunteer Services, YMCA/YWCA/YMHA/YWHA, Youth Organizations

Application Procedures

Initial Contact: Organizations should contact the Alcoa facility nearest them, and the facility will make a recommendation to the foundation for grant awards. Though not encouraged, unsolicited requests may be sent directly to the foundation in the form of a two-page letter.

Application Requirements: Include description of specific project, purpose and objective, procedure to be followed (for research requests), amount requested, budget information, list of other corporate and foundation donors; recently audited financial statement; and proof of tax-exempt status.

Deadlines: None; requests acknowledged upon receipt.

Evaluative Criteria: Compatibility with foundation's five Areas of Excellence, serves area where company operates and has employees.

Decision Notification: Foundation directors usually meet bi-monthly.

Notes: Applicants are encouraged to contact the management of the local Alcoa facility. Management at the local facility will then make recommendations for grant awards to the foundation. National and international organizations should contact Alcoa Foundation in Pittsburgh directly.

Restrictions

In general, foundation does not fund the following: projects outside the area of operation of Alcoa plant or office locations; endowment funds, deficit reduction, or operating reserves; hospital capital campaigns (unless the hospital can present a comprehensive area analysis which justifies, regionally rather than on an individual institutional basis, the need for the capital improvement); individuals (except for the scholarship program for relatives of Alcoa employees); organizations and programs designed to influences legislation or promote political candidates; religious organizations for sectarian purposes; tickets, tables, souvenir programs, advertising, fundraising dinners, golf outings, and the like for benefit purposes, trips, tours or student exchange programs, documentaries, or videos. The foundation only funds organizations classified as public charities and tax-exempt per Section 501(c)(3) of the Internal Revenue Code.

Additional Information

Alcoa merged with Alumax Inc. in 1998.
Recommendations from local Alcoa personnel are important in determining awards.
The foundation reports a growing interest in international giving; international grants tripled between 1993 and 1996.
The Reynolds Metals Company Foundation merged into the Alcoa Foundation February 1, 2001.
The Cordant Technologies Foundation merged into the Alcoa Foundation May 1, 2002.

Publications: Foundation Annual Report
Trust(s): Mellon Bank, N.A.

Corporate Officials

Alain J. P. Belda: chairman, chief executive officer, director B Morocco June 23, 1943. ED MacKenzie University BA (1969). PRIM CORP EMPL chairman, chief executive officer, director: Alcoa Inc. CORP AFFIL director: Cooper Industries Inc.; director: E.I. du Pont de Nemours & Co.; director: Citicorp.

Richard Lawrence Fischer: executive vice president, chairman counsel B Pittsburgh, PA 1936. ED University of Pittsburgh AB (1958); University of Pittsburgh JD (1961); Georgetown University LLM (1965). PRIM CORP EMPL executive vice president, chairman counsel: Alcoa Inc. ADD CORP EMPL president: Alcoa International Holdings Co.

Foundation Officials

Ricardo E. Belda: director
Kathleen W. Buechel: president, treasurer B 1955. ED Harvard University MPA (1988).
Richard Lawrence Fischer: director (see above)
Barbara S. Jeremiah: director B Pittsburgh, PA 1952. PRIM CORP EMPL vice president corporate development: Alcoa Inc. NONPR AFFIL member: American Corp. Counsel Association; member: Federal Energy Bar Association.
Richard B. Kelson: director B Pittsburgh, PA 1946. ED University of Pennsylvania BA (1968); University of Pittsburgh JD (1972). PRIM CORP EMPL executive vice president, chief financial officer: Aluminum Co. of America ADD CORP EMPL executive vice president, chief financial officer: Alcoa Inc. NONPR AFFIL member: Private Sector Councils; director: University Pittsburgh Law School Board Visitors; member: Pennsylvania Economic League; member: Financial Executives Institute Officers Conference Group; director: Pennsylvania Business Roundtable; director: Conference Board Council Financial Executives; member: Financial Executives Institute; member: American Bar Association; member: American Corp. Counsel Association.
William E. Leahey, Jr.: director
G. John Pizzey: director

Grants Analysis

Disclosure Period: calendar year ending 2001
Total Grants: $20,408,090*
Number of Grants: 2,800 (approx)
Average Grant: $7,289 (approx)
Highest Grant: $250,000 (approx)
Lowest Grant: $50
Typical Range: $500 to $25,000
*Note: Giving excludes scholarships.

Recent Grants

Note: Grants derived from 2001 Form 990.

General

250,000	Sao Paulo Education Foundation, Tuscaloosa, AL
166,667	Conservation Student Association, Charlestown, NH
166,667	Nature Conservancy, Arlington, VA
125,000	Great Smoky Mountains Institute, Townsend, TN
100,000	Community Fund of United Blount County, Maryville, TN
100,000	Hill House Association, Pittsburgh, PA
100,000	Muskegon County Community Foundation, Muskegon, MI
100,000	Southwestern United Way, Evansville, IN
83,700	Quad City Area United Way, Davenport, IA
80,000	Carnegie Mellon University, Pittsburgh, PA

ALCON LABORATORIES, INC.

Company Headquarters

Fort Worth, TX
Web: http://www.alconlabs.com

Company Description

Employees: 5,037 (1999)
SIC(s): 2834 Pharmaceutical Preparations, 3841 Surgical & Medical Instruments, 3851 Ophthalmic Goods.

Operating Locations

Alcon Laboratories, Inc. (MD--Elkridge; PA--Sinking Spring; TX--Fort Worth); Alcon Pharma (TX--Fort Worth); Alcon Surgical (TX--Fort Worth); Alcon Systems (TX--Fort Worth)

Nonmonetary Support

Value: $15,000,000 (2000); $10,000,000 (1998)
Type: Donated Equipment; Donated Products
Contact: Winona Edwards, Manager Humanitarian Services
Note: Co. provides nonmonetary support. Products are donated to vision care specialists participating in medical mission trips.

Alcon Foundation

Giving Contact

Mary K. Dulle, Director, Corporate Communications
Alcon Laboratories, Inc.
6201 South Freeway
Ft. Worth, TX 76134-2099
Phone: (817)293-0450
Fax: (817)568-7000
E-mail: Mary.Dulle@alconlabs.com
Web: http://www.alconlabs.com

Description

Founded: 1962
EIN: 756034736
Organization Type: Corporate Foundation
Giving Locations: TX: Ft. Worth nationally.
Grant Types: General Support.

Donor Information

Founder: Alcon Laboratories, Inc.

Financial Summary

Total Giving: $1,177,981 (2001); $625,820 (2000); $983,550 (1999). Note: Contributes through corporate direct giving program and foundation.
Giving Analysis: Giving for 2000 includes: foundation ($625,820); 1998: foundation ($277,194); 1997: foundation ($550,695)
Assets: $8,903 (2001); $1,315 (2000); $1,293 (1998)
Gifts Received: $1,184,750 (2001); $622,000 (2000); $277,000 (1998). Note: The foundation receives donations from Alcon Laboratories, Inc.

Typical Recipients

Arts & Humanities: Arts Associations & Councils, Arts Outreach, Ballet, Libraries, Museums/Galleries, Music, Opera, Performing Arts, Public Broadcasting, Theater
Civic & Public Affairs: African American Affairs, Business/Free Enterprise, Clubs, Civic & Public Affairs-General, Hispanic Affairs, Philanthropic Organizations, Urban & Community Affairs, Women's Affairs, Zoos/Aquariums
Education: Business Education, Colleges & Universities, Community & Junior Colleges, Education Associations, Education-General, Health & Physical Education, Medical Education, Minority Education, Private Education (Precollege), Public Education (Precollege), Science/Mathematics Education, Secondary Education (Private), Secondary Education (Public), Student Aid
Health: Cancer, Cancer, Children's Health/Hospitals, Clinics/Medical Centers, Emergency/Ambulance Services, Eyes/Blindness, Health Funds, Health Organizations, Hospitals, Medical Research, Mental Health, Prenatal Health Issues, Public Health, Single-Disease Health Associations
International: Foreign Educational Institutions, Health Care/Hospitals, International Affairs, International Peace & Security Issues
Religion: Ministries, Religious Welfare, Seminaries
Science: Science-General, Science Museums
Social Services: Camps, Child Welfare, Community Centers, Community Service Organizations, Counseling, Emergency Relief, Family Services, Food/Clothing Distribution, Homes, People with Disabilities, Shelters/Homelessness, Social Services-General, YMCA/YWCA/YMHA/YWHA, Youth Organizations

Application Procedures

Initial Contact: Submit a letter or proposal.
Application Requirements: Include a description of organization; amount requested; purpose of funds sought; a copy of budget or annual financial report indicating sources of funding and how funds are distributed; and proof of tax-exempt status.
Deadlines: None; decisions are announced bi-monthly.

Restrictions

Alcon limits contributions to education and research institutions within Alcon's areas of specialization: ophthalmology, optometry, and vision care. Funding is available for support of community-based activities in areas where Alcon has a facility.

Corporate Officials

C. Allen Baker: executive vice presidento B 1942. PRIM CORP EMPL executive vice president: Alcon Laboratories, Inc.
Timothy R. G. Sear: president, chief executive officer B 1937. ED Manchester University (1962). PRIM CORP EMPL president, chief executive officer: Alcon Laboratories, Inc. CORP AFFIL president: Alcon Puerto Rico Inc.

Foundation Officials

C. Allen Baker: trustee (see above)
Barry Caldwell: trustee
Mary Dulle: chairman PRIM CORP EMPL director professional relations: Alcon Laboratories, Inc.
J. Hiddeman: trustee
Fred Pettinato: trustee
Timothy R. G. Sear: trustee (see above)
John Alexander Walters: trustee B Philadelphia, PA 1938. ED Wagner College BA (1960). PRIM CORP EMPL corporate vice president human resources: Alcon Laboratories, Inc.

Grants Analysis

Disclosure Period: calendar year ending 2001
Total Grants: $1,177,981
Number of Grants: 261
Average Grant: $3,583*
Highest Grant: $150,000
Lowest Grant: $150
Typical Range: $150 to $10,000
***Note:** Average grant figure excludes two highest grants ($250,000).

Recent Grants

Note: Grants derived from 2001 Form 990.

General

150,000	Los Angeles Eye Institute, Los Angeles, CA
100,000	American Red Cross Tarrant County Chapter, Ft. Worth, TX
50,000	Bascom Palmer Eye Institute, Miami, FL
50,000	Cook-Fort Worth Children's Medical Center, Ft. Worth, TX
50,000	University of Colorado, Denver, CO -- Department of Ophthalmology
25,000	Fort Worth Symphony, Ft. Worth, TX
25,000	Fort Worth Zoo, Ft. Worth, TX
25,000	Jules Stein Eye Institute, Los Angeles, CA
25,000	Performing Arts Fort Worth, Ft. Worth, TX
25,000	Southwestern Medical Center Utah, Dallas, TX

GEORGE I. ALDEN TRUST

Giving Contact

Susan Woodbury, III, Chairman
370 Main St., 12th Fl.
Worcester, MA 01608
Phone: (508)798-8621
Fax: (508)791-6454
E-mail: trustees@aldentrust.org
Web: http://www.aldentrust.org

Description

Founded: 1912
EIN: 046023784
Organization Type: General Purpose Foundation
Giving Locations: MA: Worcester New England area.
Grant Types: Capital, Endowment, Project, Scholarship.
Note: Foundation makes restricted endowments primarily for scholarships and not for operating support.

Donor Information

Founder: Established in 1912 in Massachusetts by Mr. George I. Alden , a creative academic innovator who taught mechanical engineering at Worcester Polytechnic Institute for 28 years, served as a trustee of the institute and the Worcester Boys' Trade School, and was a leading member of the Worcester School Committee. Mr. Alden was an inventor; co-founder, president, and chairman of the Norton Company; and the founder and director of America's second hydraulic laboratory. When he died in 1926 at the age of 83, his shares of the Norton Company were bequeathed to the trust.

Financial Summary

Total Giving: $7,250,000 (2003 approx); $8,167,500 (2001); $8,462,500 (2000)
Giving Analysis: Giving for 1998 includes: foundation grants to United Way ($25,000) foundation ($6,922,000)
Assets: $145,000,000 (2003 approx); $159,683,000 (2001); $177,431,000 (2000)

Typical Recipients

Arts & Humanities: Historic Preservation, History & Archaeology, Libraries, Museums/Galleries, Public Broadcasting
Civic & Public Affairs: Botanical Gardens/Parks, Clubs, Community Foundations, Employment/Job Training, Civic & Public Affairs-General, Professional & Trade Associations
Education: Arts/Humanities Education, Colleges & Universities, Community & Junior Colleges, Continuing Education, Education Associations, Engineering/Technological Education, Faculty Development, Education-General, Legal Education, Medical Education, Minority Education, Private Education (Precollege), Religious Education, Science/Mathematics Education, Secondary Education (Private), Student Aid, Vocational & Technical Education
Environment: Environment-General
Health: Clinics/Medical Centers, Emergency/Ambulance Services, Health Organizations, Medical Research
Science: Science Museums, Scientific Centers & Institutes, Scientific Research
Social Services: Child Welfare, Community Service Organizations, Family Planning, YMCA/YWCA/YMHA/YWHA, Youth Organizations

Application Procedures

Initial Contact: Send a request in letter form.
Application Requirements: Requests for funding should include a budget, list goals to be achieved, reasons the applicant is well suited to receive funding, explanation of how applicant's goals fit within existing activities of the foundation, evidence of 501(c)(3) tax-exempt status, an annual report, list of trustees and their other affiliations, and an audited financial statement. Applications must be signed by the organization's chief executive officer. See website for additional details.
Deadlines: None.
Review Process: The trustees meet bimonthly to review applications.

Notes: Proposals should be made in a reasonably brief narrative form with an appropriate budget with enrollment and financial trends in recent years.

Restrictions

No grants are made to individuals or tax-supported institutions. A three year gap applies between grants to any one recipient. The foundation primarily supports preselected organizations.

Additional Information

If grants are given outside the Worcester area, they are only to independent colleges and universities in the United States.
Publications: Annual Report; Guidelines

Foundation Officials

Harry G. Bayliss: treasurer, trustee
Warner S. Fletcher: secretary, trustee B Worcester, MA 1945. ED Williams College BA (1967); Boston University JD (1973). PRIM CORP EMPL treasurer: Fletcher, Tilton & Whipple PC. CORP AFFIL director: Wyman-Gordon Co.
Susan B. Woodbury: trustee

Grants Analysis

Disclosure Period: calendar year ending 2001
Total Grants: $8,167,500
Number of Grants: 178
Average Grant: $79,808*
Highest Grant: $650,000
Lowest Grant: $5,000
Typical Range: $5,000 to $100,000
*Note: Average grant figure excludes highest grant.

Recent Grants

Note: Grants derived from 2000 Form 990.

Library-Related
250,000	Worcester Public Library, Worcester, MA

General
1,200,000	Worcester Polytechnic Institute, Worcester, MA
500,000	YMCA Greater Worcester, Worcester, MA
350,000	American Antiquarian Society, Worcester, MA
300,000	Greater Worcester Community Foundation, Inc., Worcester, MA
250,000	YMCA Greater Worcester, Worcester, MA
200,000	College of the Holy Cross, Worcester, MA
150,000	Becker College, Boston, MA
150,000	Colby College, Waterville, ME
150,000	Worcester Academy, Worcester, MA
100,000	Babson College, Babson Park, MA

JOHN W. ALDEN TRUST

Giving Contact

Olive Kelly, Trust Officer
c/o State Street Bank & Trust Co.
225 Franklin Street
Boston, MA 02110
Phone: (617)664-3358

Description

Founded: 1986
EIN: 222719727
Organization Type: Private Foundation
Giving Locations: MA
Grant Types: Project, Research, Seed Money.

Donor Information

Founder: the late Priscilla Alden

Financial Summary

Total Giving: $699,107 (fiscal year ending September 30, 2001); $579,022 (fiscal 2000); $477,242 (fiscal 1999)
Assets: $10,919,461 (fiscal 2001); $15,813,023 (fiscal 2000); $13,763,072 (fiscal 1999)
Gifts Received: $10,957 (fiscal 1996); $2,584 (fiscal 1992)

Typical Recipients

Arts & Humanities: Arts Associations & Councils, Arts Funds, Arts Institutes, Museums/Galleries, Music
Civic & Public Affairs: Civic & Public Affairs-General, Philanthropic Organizations
Education: Afterschool/Enrichment Programs, Arts/Humanities Education, Colleges & Universities, Leadership Training, Literacy, Medical Education, Private Education (Precollege), Public Education (Precollege), Religious Education, Science/Mathematics Education, Special Education, Vocational & Technical Education
Health: Adolescent Health Issues, Cancer, Children's Health/Hospitals, Clinics/Medical Centers, Eyes/Blindness, Health Organizations, Hospices, Hospitals, Medical Rehabilitation, Medical Research, Mental Health, Prenatal Health Issues, Single-Disease Health Associations
Religion: Religious Welfare
Social Services: At-Risk Youth, Camps, Child Abuse, Child Welfare, Community Service Organizations, Day Care, Delinquency & Criminal Rehabilitation, Family Services, Homes, People with Disabilities, Recreation & Athletics, Youth Organizations

Application Procedures

Initial Contact: Send a brief letter of inquiry.
Application Requirements: Include a description of organization and purpose of funds sought.
Deadlines: None.

Additional Information

Publications: Application Guidelines
Trust(s): State Street Bank & Trust Co

Foundation Officials

William B. Tyler: trustee

Grants Analysis

Disclosure Period: fiscal year ending September 30, 2001
Total Grants: $699,107
Number of Grants: 45
Average Grant: $15,536
Highest Grant: $70,000
Typical Range: $10,000 to $20,000

Recent Grants

Note: Grants derived from fiscal 2000 Form 990.

General
40,000	Associated Day Care Services, Boston, MA -- Building Block Campaign
35,000	McLean Hospital, Belmont, MA -- risk and residency longitudinal study
35,000	Perkins School for the Blind, Watertown, MA -- Toy Lending Library
29,880	Salem State College, Salem, MA -- Computer Literacy Program
25,741	Massachusetts General Hospital, Boston, MA -- support project to prevent ongoing prenatal alcohol damage
25,582	Franciscan Children's Hospital, Boston, MA -- Library Resource Center
25,000	American Academy of Arts and Sciences, Cambridge, MA -- support active girls initiative project
25,000	CAST, Boston, MA -- consortium on universal design for learning
25,000	Margaret Gifford School, Inc. -- building renovations
25,000	Massachusetts General Hospital, Boston, MA -- pediatric study

TOM S. AND MARYE KATE ALDRIDGE CHARITABLE AND EDUCATIONAL TRUST

Giving Contact

Robert S. Aldridge, Director
3035 Northwest 63rd, Suite 207N
Oklahoma City, OK 73116-3606
Phone: (405)840-9916

Description

Founded: 1996
EIN: 731484075
Organization Type: Private Foundation
Giving Locations: headquarters and operating communities.
Grant Types: General Support.

Financial Summary

Total Giving: $174,364 (fiscal year ending June 30, 2001); $135,141 (fiscal 1999); $100,385 (fiscal 1998)
Assets: $3,695,722 (fiscal 2001); $4,110,136 (fiscal 1999); $2,342,030 (fiscal 1997)
Gifts Received: $26,197 (fiscal 1999); $1,901,693 (fiscal 1997). Note: In fiscal 1997, contributions were received from the Tom S. Aldridge Trust.

Typical Recipients

Arts & Humanities: Libraries
Civic & Public Affairs: Law & Justice
Education: Colleges & Universities, Education-General, International Exchange, Public Education (Precollege), Secondary Education (Public)
International: International-General
Religion: Bible Study/Translation, Churches, Ministries
Social Services: Crime Prevention, Food/Clothing Distribution, People with Disabilities, Recreation & Athletics, Social Services-General

Application Procedures

Initial Contact: Send a brief letter of inquiry.
Application Requirements: Include a description of organization proof of tax-exempt status, name and qualifications of the person responsible for the funds, statement of goals and purpose of the program and number of people who will benefit, staff required and their qualifications, itemized budget, amount requested, purpose of funds sought, and other sources of funding.
Deadlines: None.

Restrictions

Requests are not accepted for facility construction or repair, retirement of debt, funding of day to day operations, utilities or other overhead, or fund raising activities.

Foundation Officials

Kimberly F. Aldridge: director
Laverne R. Aldridge: director
M. L. Aldridge: director
Robert S. Aldridge: director
Tom S. Aldridge: director
Parris R. Ferguson: director
Barbara Foerster: director
Nickie Beth Smith: director

Grants Analysis

Disclosure Period: fiscal year ending June 30, 2001
Total Grants: $174,364
Number of Grants: 32
Average Grant: $5,449
Highest Grant: $20,000
Typical Range: $4,500 to $10,000 and $100 to $400

Recent Grants

Note: Grants derived from fiscal 2001 Form 990.

Library-Related

10,000	Lone Oak Area Public Library, Lone Oak, TX
10,000	Navarre Public Library, Navarre, FL

General

20,000	National Institute on Development Delays, Shawnee, OK
17,000	Regional Food Bank of Oklahoma, Oklahoma City, OK
10,000	Crown Center Church, Moore, OK
10,000	Donna Nigh Foundation, Oklahoma City, OK
10,000	Hand Up Ministries, Oklahoma City, OK
10,000	International Student Outreach, Arlington, TX
8,400	University of Central Oklahoma, Edmond, OK
8,000	University of Oklahoma, Norman, OK
7,500	Oklahoma State University, Stillwater, OK
7,275	First Baptist Church of Newalla, Newalla, OK

MARGARET ALEXANDER EDWARDS TRUST

Giving Contact

Julian L. Lapides
807 Cathedral Street
Baltimore, MD 21201-5281
Phone: (410)752-4518

Description

Founded: 1989
EIN: 526389629
Organization Type: Private Foundation
Giving Locations: IL: Chicago; MD: Baltimore
Grant Types: General Support.

Financial Summary

Total Giving: $29,941 (2001); $36,065 (2000); $26,475 (1999)
Assets: $1,017,562 (2001); $1,036,844 (2000); $1,008,257 (1999)
Gifts Received: $4,974 (2001); $650 (2000); $500 (1998). Note: In 1998, contributions were received from C. M. Clapp.

Typical Recipients

Arts & Humanities: Arts Festivals, Libraries, Literary Arts, Theater
Education: Colleges & Universities, Elementary Education (Private), Literacy, Private Education (Precollege), Religious Education, Secondary Education (Private), Secondary Education (Public)

Application Procedures

Initial Contact: The foundation has no formal grant application procedure or application form.
Deadlines: None.

Restrictions

Emphasis is on programs that promote reading among young adults.

Foundation Officials

Anna A. Curry: trustee
Ray M. Fay: trustee
Sara Siebert: trustee

Grants Analysis

Disclosure Period: calendar year ending 2001
Total Grants: $29,941
Number of Grants: 5
Highest Grant: $15,000
Lowest Grant: $2,941
Typical Range: $3,000 to $5,000

Recent Grants

Note: Grants derived from 2000 Form 990.

Library-Related

12,000	American Library Association, Chicago, IL -- Young Adult Reading Project
10,000	American Library Association, Chicago, IL -- Young Adult Reading Project
7,625	American Library Association, Chicago, IL -- Young Adult Reading Project

General

2,500	Baltimore Shakespeare Festival, Baltimore, MD
2,500	Village Learning Place, Inc., Baltimore, MD -- Young Adult Reading Project
1,440	Hannah More School, Reisterstown, MD -- Young Adult Reading Project

JOSEPH ALEXANDER FOUNDATION

Giving Contact

Robert M. Weintraub, President & Director
400 Madison Avenue, Suite 906
New York, NY 10017
Phone: (212)355-3688

Description

Founded: 1960
EIN: 510175951
Organization Type: General Purpose Foundation
Giving Locations: NY: New York nationally.
Grant Types: Capital, Conference/Seminar, Endowment, General Support, Project, Research, Scholarship.

Donor Information

Founder: Established in 1960 by the late Joseph Alexander .

Financial Summary

Total Giving: $613,500 (fiscal year ending October 31, 2001); $639,000 (fiscal 2000); $727,500 (fiscal 1998)
Giving Analysis: Giving for fiscal 2000 includes: foundation scholarships ($12,500); fiscal 1997: foundation fellowships ($7,500) foundation scholarships ($62,500)
Assets: $17,399,960 (fiscal 2001); $19,311,021 (fiscal 2000); $17,948,849 (fiscal 1998)

Typical Recipients

Arts & Humanities: Arts Centers, Arts Festivals, Arts Institutes, Dance, Historic Preservation, History & Archaeology, Libraries, Museums/Galleries, Music, Performing Arts, Public Broadcasting, Visual Arts
Civic & Public Affairs: Clubs, Civic & Public Affairs-General, Philanthropic Organizations, Urban & Community Affairs, Women's Affairs
Education: Arts/Humanities Education, Business Education, Colleges & Universities, Education Funds, Faculty Development, Education-General, Gifted & Talented Programs, Legal Education, Literacy, Medical Education, Private Education (Precollege), Religious Education, Science/Mathematics Education, Special Education, Student Aid
Environment: Environment-General
Health: AIDS/HIV, Alzheimers Disease, Cancer, Children's Health/Hospitals, Clinics/Medical Centers, Diabetes, Emergency/Ambulance Services, Eyes/Blindness, Geriatric Health, Health Funds, Health Organizations, Hospices, Hospitals, Kidney, Long-Term Care, Medical Rehabilitation, Medical Research, Mental Health, Multiple Sclerosis, Nursing Services, Single-Disease Health Associations, Transplant Networks/Donor Banks, Trauma Treatment
International: Foreign Arts Organizations, Foreign Educational Institutions, Health Care/Hospitals, International Organizations, International Peace & Security Issues, International Relations, Missionary/Religious Activities
Religion: Religion-General, Jewish Causes, Religious Organizations, Religious Welfare, Seminaries, Synagogues/Temples
Science: Science Museums
Social Services: Child Welfare, Community Service Organizations, Day Care, Family Planning, Family Services, Homes, People with Disabilities, Senior Services, Social Services-General, Substance Abuse, United Funds/United Ways, Youth Organizations

Application Procedures

Initial Contact: The foundation requests applications be made in writing.
Deadlines: None.
Review Process: The board meets on a regular basis.

Restrictions

Grants are not made to individuals.

Additional Information

Publications: Financial Statement
Trust(s): John Alexander Foundation

Foundation Officials

Arthur S. Alfert: vice president, director
Harvey A. Mackler: director PRIM CORP EMPL executive vice president: Gibraltar Corp. America.
Helen Mackler: secretary, director
Robert M. Weintraub: president, director

Grants Analysis

Disclosure Period: fiscal year ending October 31, 2001
Total Grants: $613,500*
Number of Grants: 52
Average Grant: $11,480*
Highest Grant: $50,000
Lowest Grant: $1,000
Typical Range: $5,000 to $20,000
*Note: Giving excludes scholarships.

Recent Grants

Note: Grants derived from 2001 Form 990.

General

50,000	Bar Ilan University, New York, NY -- program for legal aid advocacy in family law
50,000	Yeshiva University, New York, NY -- Joseph Alexander Science Education Enhancement Program/Stern Yeshiva College
30,000	Genesis Foundation, Staten Island, NY -- auditorium in Beit Shemesh
30,000	University of Pennsylvania, Philadelphia, PA -- Computer Science Program
30,000	Western Wall Heritage Foundation, New York, NY -- unrestricted contribution
25,000	ALS Association Greater Philadelphia,

25,000	Philadelphia, PA -- Scott A. Mackler MD, PhD Assistive Technology Fund
25,000	American Israel Friendship League, New York, NY -- US Israel citizenship through sports youth exchange
25,000	Salk Institute, San Diego, CA -- Alzheimer's disease research
25,000	Union of American Hebrew Congregations, Philadelphia, PA -- health center in Camp Harlem
18,000	Ohr Totah Institution of Israel, New York, NY -- Women's Advocate Program

ROBERT D. AND CATHERINE R. ALEXANDER FOUNDATION

Giving Contact

R. Denny Alexander, Investment Counselor & Trustee
4200 S. Hulen St., Suite 617
Ft. Worth, TX 76109-4913
Phone: (817)731-1317

Description

Founded: 1962
EIN: 756012124
Organization Type: Private Foundation
Giving Locations: TX: Tarrant County, Fort Worth
Grant Types: General Support.

Donor Information

Founder: R. D. Alexander Trust

Financial Summary

Total Giving: $274,425 (2000); $246,900 (1999); $246,900 (1998)
Giving Analysis: Giving for 2000 includes: foundation grants to United Way ($10,000)
Assets: $6,348,911 (2000); $6,250,808 (1999); $5,635,502 (1998)
Gifts Received: $144,063 (1999); $75,000 (1995); $27,604 (1994). Note: In 1996 and 1999, contributions were received from Catherine R. Alexander.

Typical Recipients

Arts & Humanities: Arts Associations & Councils, Ballet, Community Arts, Dance, Libraries, Museums/Galleries, Music, Opera, Performing Arts, Public Broadcasting
Civic & Public Affairs: Clubs, Civic & Public Affairs-General, Housing, Philanthropic Organizations
Education: Business Education, Colleges & Universities, Education-General, Private Education (Precollege), Student Aid
Health: AIDS/HIV, Children's Health/Hospitals, Clinics/Medical Centers, Eyes/Blindness, Health Organizations, Hospitals, Medical Research, Research/Studies Institutes, Single-Disease Health Associations
Religion: Churches, Jewish Causes, Missionary Activities (Domestic), Religious Organizations, Religious Welfare, Social/Policy Issues
Science: Science Museums
Social Services: Camps, Child Welfare, Community Service Organizations, Day Care, Food/Clothing Distribution, People with Disabilities, Shelters/Homelessness, Substance Abuse, United Funds/United Ways, YMCA/YWCA/YMHA/YWHA, Youth Organizations

Application Procedures

Initial Contact: Send a brief letter of inquiry.
Deadlines: None.

Restrictions

Does not support individuals.

Foundation Officials

Catherine R. Alexander: trustee
R. Denny Alexander: investment counsel, trustee PRIM CORP EMPL owner: R. Denny Alexander & Co. CORP AFFIL director: TNP Enterprises Inc.; director: Texas-New Mexico Power Co. NONPR AFFIL director: Cook Childrens Medical Center.

Grants Analysis

Disclosure Period: calendar year ending 2000
Total Grants: $264,425*
Number of Grants: 22
Average Grant: $12,019
Highest Grant: $75,000
Lowest Grant: $1225
Typical Range: $1,000 to $25,000
*Note: Giving excludes United Way.

Recent Grants

Note: Grants derived from 2001 Form 990.

General

77,000	Cook Children's Medical Center, Ft. Worth, TX
52,100	University Christian Church, Ft. Worth, TX
50,000	Camp Carter YMCA, Ft. Worth, TX
42,000	Fort Worth Dallas Ballet, Ft. Worth, TX
25,000	Union Gospel Mission, Ft. Worth, TX
10,000	Texas Christian University, Ft. Worth, TX
10,000	United Way of Metro Tarrant County, Ft. Worth, TX
7,500	Prevent Blindness Texas, Ft. Worth, TX
5,000	Fort Worth Opera, Ft. Worth, TX
2,500	American Fund Raising Professionals, Ft. Worth, TX

WALTER ALEXANDER FOUNDATION

Giving Contact

Stanley F. Staples, Jr., Secretary
PO Box 2137
Wausau, WI 54402-2137
Phone: (715)845-4556

Description

Founded: 1952
EIN: 396044635
Organization Type: Private Foundation
Giving Locations: WI
Grant Types: Capital, Emergency.

Donor Information

Founder: the late Ruth Alexander, the late Anne M. Alexander

Financial Summary

Total Giving: $198,472 (fiscal year ending November 30, 2000); $183,391 (fiscal 1999); $166,504 (fiscal 1998)
Assets: $3,857,363 (fiscal 2000); $3,622,514 (fiscal 1999); $3,804,116 (fiscal 1998)

Typical Recipients

Arts & Humanities: Arts Associations & Councils, Arts Centers, Community Arts, Historic Preservation, History & Archaeology, Libraries, Museums/Galleries, Opera, Performing Arts, Public Broadcasting, Theater

Civic & Public Affairs: Botanical Gardens/Parks, Chambers of Commerce, Community Foundations, Economic Development, Civic & Public Affairs-General, Legal Aid, Municipalities/Towns
Education: Business Education, Colleges & Universities, Education Funds, Education-General, Medical Education, Preschool Education, Private Education (Precollege), Secondary Education (Private), Secondary Education (Public), Student Aid, Vocational & Technical Education
Environment: Air/Water Quality, Environment-General, Resource Conservation, Wildlife Protection
Health: Eyes/Blindness
International: International Development, International Environmental Issues
Religion: Religious Welfare
Social Services: Animal Protection, Camps, Community Service Organizations, Counseling, People with Disabilities, Scouts, Special Olympics, United Funds/United Ways, YMCA/YWCA/YMHA/YWHA, Youth Organizations

Application Procedures

Initial Contact: applications should spell out the activity or capital need for which support is requested.
Application Requirements: Include other sources of funding, proof of tax-exempt status, evaluation procedures, and a commitment to provide any contemplated future sources of income.
Deadlines: None.

Restrictions

Does not support individuals.

Foundation Officials

Nancy Anne Cordaro: director
Jean A. Koskinen: director
Walter Koskinen: vice president, director
John F. Michler: treasurer, director B 1939. ED University of Wisconsin BBA (1962); University of Wisconsin JD (1964). PRIM CORP EMPL vice president: Ruder, Ware & Michler SC. CORP AFFIL secretary: Helke Furniture Co.; secretary: Merrill Manufacturing Corp.
Alexander Reichl: president, director
Stanley F. Staples, Jr.: secretary, director PRIM CORP EMPL president: Alexander Properties Inc. CORP AFFIL director: M & I First American Bank.

Grants Analysis

Disclosure Period: fiscal year ending November 30, 2000
Total Grants: $198,472
Number of Grants: 30
Average Grant: $6,282
Highest Grant: $60,000
Typical Range: $1,000 to $10,000

Recent Grants

Note: Grants derived from fiscal 1999 Form 990.

General

30,000	Wausau Area Community Foundation, Wausau, WI
25,000	Friends of Mosquito Hill, Inc., New London, WI
20,000	University of Wisconsin Madison School of Veterinary Medicine, Madison, WI
15,150	Wisconsin Public Broadcasting Foundation, Milwaukee, WI
15,000	City of Wausau, Wausau, WI
10,000	Boys & Girls Club Fox Valley, Inc., Appleton, WI
10,000	Mount Senario College, Ladysmith, WI
9,777	Lincoln County Humane Society, Inc., Merrill, WI
5,250	Camp Manito-Wish YMCA, Boulder Junction, WI
5,000	Fox Valley Human Association, LTD, Appleton, WI

ALEXANDER STEWART MD FOUNDATION TRUST

Giving Contact
Adelina Martorelli, Trust Officer
c/o Mellon Bank NA
PO Box 7236
Philadelphia, PA 19101-7236
Phone: (215)553-8636

Description
Founded: 1981
EIN: 236732616
Organization Type: Private Foundation
Former Name: Stewart Alexander Foundation (2002).
Giving Locations: PA: Cumberland County, Franklin County, Fulton County, Perry County, Shippensburg County
Grant Types: General Support, Scholarship.

Financial Summary
Total Giving: $374,788 (fiscal year ending June 30, 2001); $371,774 (fiscal 2000); $199,729 (fiscal 1998)
Giving Analysis: Giving for fiscal 2001 includes: foundation grants to United Way ($2,543)
Assets: $8,039,095 (fiscal 2001); $8,343,280 (fiscal 2000); $8,190,980 (fiscal 1998)
Gifts Received: $41,224 (fiscal 1997); $188 (fiscal 1993). Note: In fiscal 1997, contributions were received from Jane Stewart.

Typical Recipients
Arts & Humanities: Arts Associations & Councils, History & Archaeology, Libraries, Music
Civic & Public Affairs: Civic & Public Affairs-General, Housing, Law & Justice, Legal Aid, Rural Affairs, Safety, Women's Affairs
Education: Agricultural Education, Education-General
Environment: Resource Conservation
Health: Cancer, Emergency/Ambulance Services, Home-Care Services, Mental Health, Public Health
Religion: Religious Welfare
Social Services: Animal Protection, Domestic Violence, Family Services, People with Disabilities, Recreation & Athletics, Scouts, Senior Services, Shelters/Homelessness, YMCA/YWCA/YMHA/YWHA

Application Procedures
Initial Contact: Send a brief letter of inquiry.
Application Requirements: Include a description of organization, amount requested, purpose of funds sought, recently audited financial statement, and proof of tax-exempt status.
Deadlines: April 1.

Additional Information
Trust(s): Mellon Bank NA

Grants Analysis
Disclosure Period: fiscal year ending June 30, 2001
Total Grants: $374,788
Number of Grants: 48
Average Grant: $7,755
Highest Grant: $20,000
Typical Range: $1,000 to $12,000

Recent Grants
Note: Grants derived from fiscal 2001 Form 990.

Library-Related
10,000   Franklin County Library System, PA

General
20,000   Lutheran Home Care Services, Chambersburg, PA
20,000   Salvation Army, Chambersburg, PA
20,000   Shippensburg Area Recreation and Parks Department, Shippensburg, PA
16,152   Shook Home for the Aged, Chambersburg, PA
15,000   Agape Residential Ministries & Services, PA
14,000   Buchanan Valley Volunteer Fire Department, Philadelphia, PA
13,500   Quincy United Methodist Home, Quincy, PA
12,000   Cumberland Valley Mental Health Center, PA
12,000   Manito Inc., PA
10,000   Bendersville Community Fire Department, Philadelphia, PA

ALLEGHENY FOUNDATION

Giving Contact
Joanne B. Beyer, President
One Oxford Center
301 Grant Street, Suite 3900
Pittsburgh, PA 15219-6401
Phone: (412)392-2900
Web: http://www.scaife.com

Description
Founded: 1953
EIN: 256012303
Organization Type: General Purpose Foundation
Giving Locations: PA: including western Pennsylvania
Grant Types: General Support, Project.

Donor Information
Founder: Established in 1953 by Richard Mellon Scaife, the Allegheny Foundation makes grants mainly for the benefit of Pittsburgh and western Pennsylvania. Richard Scaife is the son of Sarah Mellon Scaife, and great grandson of Judge Thomas Mellon, founder of Mellon Bank.

Financial Summary
Total Giving: $1,582,500 (2000); $1,209,340 (1999); $1,266,125 (1998)
Giving Analysis: Giving for 2000 includes: foundation scholarships ($50,000)
Assets: $40,398,096 (2001); $42,098,138 (2000); $37,504,049 (1999)
Gifts Received: $681,250 (1999); $130,375 (1993); $1,156,250 (1992). Note: The foundation received contributions in the form of stock from Richard M. Scaife.

Typical Recipients
Arts & Humanities: Arts Associations & Councils, Historic Preservation, History & Archaeology, Libraries, Museums/Galleries, Music, Opera, Theater
Civic & Public Affairs: Botanical Gardens/Parks, Business/Free Enterprise, Clubs, Economic Development, Economic Policy, Employment/Job Training, Civic & Public Affairs-General, Housing, Legal Aid, Municipalities/Towns, Nonprofit Management, Professional & Trade Associations, Public Policy, Urban & Community Affairs
Education: Colleges & Universities, Economic Education, Education Associations, Education Funds, Education Reform, Elementary Education (Private), Environmental Education, Education-General, Leadership Training, Literacy, Medical Education, Private Education (Precollege), Public Education (Precollege), Science/Mathematics Education, Special Education, Student Aid
Environment: Air/Water Quality, Environment-General, Resource Conservation
Health: Cancer
International: Health Care/Hospitals
Religion: Churches, Dioceses, Ministries, Religious Welfare
Science: Scientific Centers & Institutes, Scientific Organizations
Social Services: Animal Protection, Camps, Child Welfare, Community Centers, Community Service Organizations, Counseling, Emergency Relief, Food/Clothing Distribution, People with Disabilities, Recreation & Athletics, Senior Services, Social Services-General, Youth Organizations

Application Procedures
Initial Contact: Letter, signed by the organization's president or authorized representative. The letter should be approved by the organization's board of directors.
Application Requirements: Concise description of the specific project for which funds are sought, annual budget for the project and the organization, latest audited financial statement and annual report, list of board of directors, and proof of tax-exempt status. The foundation may request additional information.
Deadlines: None.
Review Process: The annual meeting is held in December. Proposals are accepted throughout the year, and will be acted upon as soon as possible.

Restrictions
The foundation does not make grants to individuals, or for endowments, scholarships, or fellowships.

Additional Information
Publications: Annual Report; Guidelines

Foundation Officials
Joanne B. Beyer: president
Ralph H. Goettler: trustee B 1929. ED University of Pittsburgh (1957). PRIM CORP EMPL president: Goettler Associates Inc.
Doris O'Donnell: trustee
Margaret R. Scaife: trustee
Richard Mellon Scaife: chairman B Pittsburgh, PA 1932. ED Yale University (1950-1951); University of Pittsburgh BA (1957). PRIM CORP EMPL owner, chairman, publisher: Tribune Review Publishing Co. CORP AFFIL chairman, director: T-R Printing & Publishing Co.; chairman, publisher, director: Tribune Review; partner: 301 Capital Mall Associates; chairman, director: Standard Observer Newspaper.
Nathan Julius Stark: trustee B Minneapolis, MN November 09, 1920. ED Scholl College DHL; Woodrow Wilson Junior College AA (1940); United States Merchant Marine Academy BS (1943); Illinois Institute of Technology JD (1948). CORP AFFIL member advisory board: Health Care Enterprise International. NONPR AFFIL senior vice chancellor emeritus: University Pittsburgh School Health Professions; member: Virginia Scholars Board Governance; president: Pittsburgh University Health Center; member: Southwest Pennsylvania Health Systems Agency; trustee: Pittsburgh Chamber Opera Theatre; vice president: Pittsburgh Opera; member executive board: National Board Medicine Examiners; member: National Academy Sciences Institute Medicine; member: National Academy Social Insurance; member: American Hospital Association; secretary: Eddie Jacobson Memorial Foundation; honorary fellow: American Academy Pediatrics; member: American College Hospital Administration.
George A. Weymouth: trustee PRIM NONPR EMPL chairman, director: Brandywine Conservancy Inc. NONPR AFFIL chairman, director: Brandywine River Museum; chairman, director: Environment Management Center.
Arthur P. Ziegler, Jr.: trustee B Pittsburgh, PA 1937. ED University of Pittsburgh BA (1958); University of Pittsburgh MA (1959); Union Theological Seminary (1960); Case Western Reserve University (1961). PRIM NONPR EMPL president, director: Pittsburgh History & Landmarks. CORP AFFIL director: Steel Heritage Corp. NONPR AFFIL trustee emeritus: Washington National Trust; member, board advisors: Waterfront Center; director: Pittsburgh Partnership Neighborhood Development; trustee: Walden Trust; director: Allegheny County Chamber of Commerce;

trustee: Historic Houses America. CLUB AFFIL City Club.

Grants Analysis

Disclosure Period: calendar year ending 2001
Total Grants: $1,449,000*
Number of Grants: 37
Average Grant: $22,091
Highest Grant: $500,000
Lowest Grant: $1,000
Typical Range: $25,000 to $50,000
*Note: Giving excludes highest grant.

Recent Grants

Note: Grants derived from 2001 Form 990.

Library-Related
40,000	Braddock's Field Historical Society, Braddock, PA -- Braddock Carnegie Library restoration
25,000	Nantucket Athenaeum, Nantucket, MA

General
500,000	Pittsburgh Parks Conservancy, Pittsburgh, PA -- Schenley Park Visitors Center
120,000	Frick Art and Historical Center, Pittsburgh, PA -- Thomas Moran Exhibit
100,000	Intercollegiate Studies Institute, Inc., Wilmington, DE -- Preparatory School Lecture Program
50,000	Boys and Girls Club of Western Pennsylvania, Pittsburgh, PA -- Summer Program
50,000	Brownsville Area Revitalization Corp, Brownsville, PA -- newspaper and education and capital support
50,000	Epiphany Catholic Church, Pittsburgh, PA -- capital support
50,000	Extra-Mile Education Foundation, Inc., Pittsburgh, PA -- Crossroads Scholarship Fund
50,000	Lincoln Institute of Public Opinion Research, Inc., Harrisburg, PA
50,000	Pittsburgh Board of Education, Pittsburgh, PA -- Best Friend Project
50,000	Railroader's Memorial Museum, Altoona, PA

ALLEN BROTHERS FOUNDATION

Giving Contact

Howard Felson
711 5th Ave.
New York, NY 10022
Phone: (212)832-8000
Fax: (212)832-8023
Web: http://www.allenco.com

Description

Founded: 1983
EIN: 133202281
Organization Type: Private Foundation
Giving Locations: NY
Grant Types: General Support.

Financial Summary

Total Giving: $3,200,000 (2001); $1,595,000 (2000); $123,000 (1997)
Assets: $40,258 (2001); $3,198,740 (2000); $3,024,110 (1999)

Typical Recipients

Arts & Humanities: Ethnic & Folk Arts, Film & Video, History & Archaeology, Libraries, Museums/Galleries
Civic & Public Affairs: Civic & Public Affairs-General

Education: Colleges & Universities, Medical Education, Minority Education, Private Education (Precollege), Student Aid
Environment: Resource Conservation, Wildlife Protection
Health: AIDS/HIV, Cancer, Medical Research
International: Foreign Educational Institutions, Health Care/Hospitals, International Environmental Issues, International Relief Efforts
Religion: Jewish Causes, Religious Organizations, Social/Policy Issues
Social Services: Child Welfare, Community Service Organizations, Recreation & Athletics, Substance Abuse

Application Procedures

Initial Contact: Send a brief letter of inquiry.
Application Requirements: Include proof of tax-exempt status.
Deadlines: None.

Foundation Officials

Robert H. Cosgriff: vice president
Richard M. Crooks: director
Paul A. Gould: vice president, director
Irwin H. Kramer: vice president
James W. Quinn: assistant secretary B Bronxville, NY 1945. ED University of Notre Dame AB (1967); Fordham University JD (1971). PRIM CORP EMPL vice president: Allen & Co. NONPR AFFIL member: Am Bar Association; member: Association Bar New York City.
Phillip David Scaturro: director B Newark, NJ 1938. ED Williams College BA (1960); Columbia University JD (1963); Columbia University MBA (1963). PRIM CORP EMPL managing director, executive vice president: Allen & Co. CORP AFFIL director: United Asset Management Co; director: Intrenet; director: Opal Concepts; director: Hi-Tech Manufacturing; director: Asquith Court. NONPR AFFIL director, executive committee finance committee: New York City Opera; member committee alternate investments: Williams College; trustee, member executive committee, chairman audit committee: New School Social Research; member: Century Association. CLUB AFFIL University Club.
Enrique Francisco Senior: director B Havana, Cuba 1943. ED Yale University BA (1964); Yale University BS (1967); Harvard University MBA (1969). CORP AFFIL director: Allen & Co.; director: Dick Clark Productions. NONPR AFFIL member: Phi Beta Kappa; member: Tau Beta Pi. CLUB AFFIL Farmington Country Club; Piping Rock Club; Brook Club.
Stanley S. Shuman: director B Cambridge, MA 1935. ED Harvard University BA (1956); Harvard University JD (1959); Harvard University MBA (1961). PRIM CORP EMPL executive vice president, managing director: Allen & Co. ADD CORP EMPL director: Allen Holdings Inc. CORP AFFIL director: Hudson General Corp.; director: News America Holdings Inc.; director: Bayou Steel Corp.; stockholder, director: GHS Inc.
John Simon: director
Robert H. Werbel: secretary, director
Harold Maurice Wit: director B Boston, MA 1928. ED Harvard University AB (1949); Yale University JD (1954). PRIM CORP EMPL associate, executive vice president: Allen & Co. CORP AFFIL managing director, member executive committee: Toys R Us; director: Allen Investments. NONPR AFFIL member national advisory board: Project Being Dying Upaya Foundation; member: Veterans Foreign Wars; member: Phi Beta Kappa; member: Phi Delta Phi; member: Korean War Veterans Association; trustee: Nature Conservancy S Fork - Shelter Island Chapter; member visitors committee: Harvard University Divinity School; member: American Legion; co-founder: Group South Fork; member. CLUB AFFIL University Club; Harvard Club.

Grants Analysis

Disclosure Period: calendar year ending 2001
Total Grants: $3,200,000
Number of Grants: 2
Highest Grant: $1,600,000

Recent Grants

Note: Grants derived from 2001 Form 990.

General
1,600,000	Hackley School, Tarrytown, NY
1,600,000	Weill Medical College of Cornell University, New York, NY -- professorship of cardiothoracic surgery

NIBS AND EDNA ALLEN FOUNDATION

Giving Contact

Robert C. Lucas, Trustee
Nibs and Edna Allen Foundation
PO Box 250
Miles City, MT 59301
Phone: (406)232-3620

Description

Founded: 1993
EIN: 810480143
Organization Type: Private Foundation
Grant Types: General Support.

Financial Summary

Total Giving: $128,232 (fiscal year ending June 30, 2001); $49,600 (fiscal 1997); $52,018 (fiscal 1996)
Giving Analysis: Giving for fiscal 2001 includes: foundation scholarships ($22,312)
Assets: $2,719,633 (fiscal 2001); $1,149,546 (fiscal 1997); $1,044,104 (fiscal 1996)
Gifts Received: $1,500,000 (fiscal 2001); $750,000 (fiscal 1993). Note: In fiscal 2001, contributions were received from the late Edna Allen. In fiscal 1993, contributions were received from Edna R. Allen.

Typical Recipients

Arts & Humanities: Arts Centers, History & Archaeology, Libraries, Music
Civic & Public Affairs: Community Foundations, Civic & Public Affairs-General, Housing, Parades/Festivals, Safety
Education: Community & Junior Colleges, Education-General, Public Education (Precollege), Secondary Education (Public), Student Aid
Health: Clinics/Medical Centers, Emergency/Ambulance Services, Mental Health
Religion: Religious Organizations
Social Services: At-Risk Youth, Recreation & Athletics, Senior Services, Youth Organizations

Application Procedures

Initial Contact: Send a brief letter of inquiry.
Application Requirements: Inlcude a description of organization, purpose of funds sought, and proof of tax-exempt status.
Deadlines: None. Requests should be made at least two weeks in advance of need.

Restrictions

Contributions are limited to southeastern MT.

Foundation Officials

Edna R. Allen: president
Nancy D. Larsen: secretary, treasurer
Robert C. Lucas: vice president

Grants Analysis

Disclosure Period: fiscal year ending June 30, 2001
Total Grants: $105,920*
Number of Grants: 29

Average Grant: $3,652
Highest Grant: $20,000
Typical Range: $1,000 to $15,000
***Note:** Giving excludes scholarships.

Recent Grants

Note: Grants derived from fiscal 2001 Form 990.

Library-Related

10,000	Miles City Public Library, Miles City, NY

General

20,000	Miles City School District 1, Miles City, MT -- playground equipment
15,000	Parenting Education in East Montana, Miles City, MT
10,000	Miles City Hockey Association, Miles City, MT -- sprinkler system for building
7,500	Miles City School District 1, Miles City, MT -- school bleachers
6,000	Custer County Education Foundation, Miles City, MT -- scholarship fund
5,942	Miles Community College, Miles City, MT -- basketball team
5,000	Custer County High School, Miles City, MT
5,000	Fairgrounds Improvements, Miles City, MT
5,000	Kent Ewalt Fund, Miles City, MT
5,000	Veterans Administration Medical Center Redevelopment Project, Miles City, MT

ALLIANT ENERGY CORP.

Company Headquarters

4902 N. Biltmore Ln.
Madison, WI 53718-2132
Web: http://www.alliant-energy.com

Company Description

Ticker: LNT
Exchange: NYSE
Assets: US$2.777 billion (2001)
Employees: 8000 (2001)
SIC(s): 4911 Electric Services, 4924 Natural Gas Distribution, 4941 Water Supply.

Operating Locations

Wisconsin Power & Light Co. (WI, Madison)

Alliant Energy Foundation, Inc.

Giving Contact

JoAnn Healy, Foundation Administrator
4902 North Biltmore Ln.
PO Box 77007
Madison, WI 53701-1007
Phone: (608)458-3311
Fax: (608)283-6991
Web: http://alliantenergy.com/community/charity.htm
Note: Contact for Wisconsin applications.

Alternate Contact

Jean Bjorseth
Alliant Energy Foundation
200 First Street SE
Cedar Rapids, IA 52401
Note: Contact for Iowa, Minnesota, and Illinois applications.

Description

EIN: 391444065
Organization Type: Corporate Foundation
Former Name: Wisconsin Power & Light Foundation, Inc..

Giving Locations: IL; IA; MN; WI: near headquarters and service areas (central and south central Wisconsin)
Grant Types: Capital, Employee Matching Gifts, General Support.
Note: Employee matching gift ratio: 1 to 1.

Financial Summary

Total Giving: $2,660,932 (2001); $2,328,483 (2000); $2,037,118 (1999)
Giving Analysis: Giving for 2000 includes: foundation scholarships ($79,380); foundation matching gifts ($245,855); foundation grants to United Way ($417,160); foundation ($1,586,088); 1999: foundation matching gifts ($153,534); foundation scholarships ($166,470); foundation grants to United Way ($395,737); foundation ($1,321,377); 1996: foundation scholarships ($2,800); foundation matching gifts ($19,609); foundation grants to United Way ($110,323) foundation ($687,239)
Assets: $27,912,636 (2001); $33,612,218 (2000); $37,744,934 (1999)
Gifts Received: $2,948,250 (1999); $1,200,000 (1997); $1,300,000 (1996). Note: Contributions received from Wisconsin Power & Light Company.

Typical Recipients

Arts & Humanities: Arts Associations & Councils, Arts Centers, Arts Festivals, Community Arts, Historic Preservation, History & Archaeology, Libraries, Museums/Galleries, Music, Performing Arts, Public Broadcasting, Theater
Civic & Public Affairs: African American Affairs, Botanical Gardens/Parks, Business/Free Enterprise, Clubs, Community Foundations, Economic Development, Economic Policy, Employment/Job Training, Civic & Public Affairs-General, Housing, Municipalities/Towns, Parades/Festivals, Professional & Trade Associations, Safety, Urban & Community Affairs
Education: Arts/Humanities Education, Business Education, Colleges & Universities, Community & Junior Colleges, Education Funds, Engineering/Technological Education, Education-General, Education-General, Preschool Education, Private Education (Precollege), Student Aid, Vocational & Technical Education
Environment: Environment-General
Health: Cancer, Children's Health/Hospitals, Clinics/Medical Centers, Emergency/Ambulance Services, Health Organizations, Hospitals, Nursing Services, Public Health, Single-Disease Health Associations
Religion: Religious Welfare
Science: Science-General, Science Museums
Social Services: Child Welfare, Community Centers, Community Service Organizations, Emergency Relief, Family Services, Food/Clothing Distribution, People with Disabilities, Scouts, Senior Services, Shelters/Homelessness, Social Services-General, United Funds/United Ways, YMCA/YWCA/YMHA/YWHA, Youth Organizations

Application Procedures

Initial Contact: Contact the foundation to obtain an Application for Funding form.
Application Requirements: A completed application form must be submitted with a narrative relating to specific topics listed on the application form.
Deadlines: October 1 for funding in the following year.
Review Process: During the review process, the foundation may request additional information or conduct a site visit.
Decision Notification: Grant notification letters are sent in February of each year.

Restrictions

The foundation does not provide grants for individuals; ads in programs, door prizes, raffle tickets, dinner tables, golf outings, or sponsorships of organized sports teams or activities; religious, fraternal or social clubs; endowments; registration fees for fundraising events such as walk-a-thons, runs, or travel funds for tours or tournaments; or books, magazines, or

professional journal articles. Applicants must be classified as 501(c)(3) tax-exempt.

Additional Information

In 1998, WPL Holdings, the parent company of Wisconsin Power and Light Co., was involved in a three-way merger along with IES Industries and Interstate Power Co. The three companies formed Alliant Energy Corporation. Wisconsin Power and Light Co. is now a subsidiary of Alliant Energy Corporation.

Corporate Officials

Erroll Brown Davis, Jr.: chairman, president, chief executive officer B Pittsburgh, PA August 05, 1944. ED Carnegie Mellon University BSEE (1965); University of Chicago MBA (1967). PRIM CORP EMPL chairman, president, chief executive officer: Alliant Energy Corp.; president, chief executive officer, director: Interstate Energy Corp. ADD CORP EMPL chief executive officer: Wisconsin Power & Light Co. CORP AFFIL chief executive officer: Wisconsin Power & Light Co.; director: Sentry Insurance Co.; chief executive officer: Interstate Power Co.; director: PP&G Industries Inc.; chairman: Heartland Development Corp.; chief executive officer: IES Utilities; chief executive officer: Alliant Industries Inc.; director: BP Amoco Corp. NONPR AFFIL director: WI Manufacturing & Commerce; director: WI Utilities Association; member: Selective Service Board; director: Edison Electric Institute; director: Electric Power Research Institute; trustee: Carnegie Mellon University; director: Competitive Wisconsin Inc.; member: Association of Edison Illuminating Companies; member: American Gas Association; member: American Society Corporate Executives; member: American Association Blacks Energy.

Foundation Officials

Edward M. Gleason: secretary-treasurer
Jo Ann Healy: administrator
James E. Hoffman: director
John O. Larsen: director
Steven F. Price: assistant treasurer
Eliot G. Protsch: director
Diane H. Ramsey: vice president
Barbara J. Swan: director
Carol Toussaint: Interim executive director

Grants Analysis

Disclosure Period: calendar year ending 2001
Total Grants: $2,660,932

Recent Grants

Note: Grants derived from 2000 Form 990.

Library-Related

40,000	Greater Cedar Rapids Foundation, Cedar Rapids, IA -- for Skate, Inc., campaign
10,000	Greater Cedar Rapids Foundation, Cedar Rapids, IA -- for Skate, Inc., campaign
8,000	Marion Public Library, Marion, IA -- construction of new facility

General

125,000	East Central United Way, Cedar Rapids, IA
105,197	United Way Dane County, Madison, WI -- 1999 contribution
100,000	Iowa State University Foundation, Ames, IA -- construction of Howe Hall
50,000	Dubuque County Historical Society, Dubuque, IA
50,000	Iowa Great Lakes Maritime Museum, Arnolds Park, IA
50,000	Science Station, Cedar Rapids, IA
50,000	University of Iowa Foundation, Iowa City, IA -- for Arts Share Program
50,000	University of Northern Iowa Foundation, Cedar Falls, IA

42,990   Citizens Scholarship Foundation of America, St. Peter, MN

37,500   American Players Theater, Spring Green, WI -- general support, educational programs

ALLIANZ LIFE INSURANCE COMPANY OF NORTH AMERICA

Company Headquarters

5701 Golden Hill Dr.
Minneapolis, MN 55416
Web: http://www.allianzlife.com

Company Description

Founded: 1896
Assets: US$25.498 billion (2001)
Employees: 0 (2001)
SIC(s): 6311 Life Insurance.
Parent Company: Allianz AG, Koniginstrasse 28, Munich, Germany

Operating Locations

Allianz Life Insurance Company of North America (TX--Dallas); Allianz Underwriters Insurance Co. (CA--Burbank)

Nonmonetary Support

Type: Loaned Employees; Workplace Solicitation

Giving Contact

Julie Letner, Vice President, Human Resources
5701 Golden Hills Drive
Minneapolis, MN 55416
Phone: (763)765-6500
Fax: (763)765-6299
Web: http://www.allianzlife.com

Description

Organization Type: Corporate Giving Program
Giving Locations: near headquarters only.
Grant Types: Capital, General Support, Matching.

Financial Summary

Total Giving: $200,000 (2000 approx); $230,000 (1994)

Typical Recipients

Arts & Humanities: Libraries, Museums/Galleries, Music
Civic & Public Affairs: Economic Development, Housing, Urban & Community Affairs
Education: Colleges & Universities, Economic Education, Education Funds
Health: Health Organizations, Heart, Hospitals
Religion: Churches, Religious Organizations
Social Services: People with Disabilities, Scouts, United Funds/United Ways, YMCA/YWCA/YMHA/YWHA, Youth Organizations

Application Procedures

Initial Contact: Send a brief letter of inquiry and a full proposal. Include a description of organization, amount requested, and purpose of funds sought. It is best to apply by the end of the third quarter, as the review board meets in the fall.

Restrictions

Company does not support individuals, political or lobbying groups, or religious organizations for sectarian purposes.

Additional Information

According to Allianz of America, Inc., each local office administers independent contributions programs, with Allianz Life's being the largest. Local offices decide on recipients and support levels, with nonmonetary support such as loaned employees included in programs.

Corporate Officials

Edward J. Bonachi: senior vice president, treasurer, chief financial officer PRIM CORP EMPL senior vice president, treasurer, chief financial officer: Allianz Life Insurance Co. North America.

Grants Analysis

Typical Range: $1,000 to $2,500

ALLMERICA FINANCIAL CORP.

Company Headquarters

Worcester, MA
Web: http://www.allmerica.com

Company Description

Founded: 1995
Ticker: AFC
Exchange: NYSE
Former Name: State Mutual Life Assurance Co.; Hanover Insurance Co.
Revenue: US$3.419 billion (2002)
Employees: 5600 (2001)
Fortune Rank: 456, per FORTUNE Magazine's list of 500 Largest U.S. Corporations (2002).
SIC(s): 6726 Investment Offices Nec.

Operating Locations

Allmerica Financial Corp. (MA--Worcester)
Note: Operates offices in 22 states and the District of Columbia.

Nonmonetary Support

Type: Donated Equipment; In-kind Services; Loaned Executives; Workplace Solicitation
Volunteer Programs: The company sponsors a Volunteer Incentive Program.

Allmerica Financial Charitable Foundation, Inc.

Giving Contact

Michael Buckley, President
Allmerica Financial Charitable Foundation
440 Lincoln Street
Worcester, MA 01653
Phone: (508)855-1000
Fax: (508)855-6332

Description

Founded: 1991
EIN: 043105650
Organization Type: Corporate Foundation
Giving Locations: MA: Boston, Worcester; MI: Howell
Grant Types: Employee Matching Gifts, General Support.

Financial Summary

Total Giving: $1,093,249 (2001); $962,684 (2000); $955,797 (1999). Note: Contributes through corporate direct giving program and foundation.
Giving Analysis: Giving for 2001 includes: foundation matching gifts ($121,760); foundation grants to United Way ($296,454); foundation ($675,035); 2000: foundation matching gifts ($118,486); foundation grants to United Way ($283,200); foundation ($560,998); 1999: foundation matching gifts ($128,373); foundation ($535,124);

Assets: $4,623,615 (2001); $6,402,814 (2000); $7,191,085 (1999)
Gifts Received: $104,198 (2000); $125,100 (1999); $1,326,661 (1998). Note: Foundation receives contributions from the First Allmerica Financial Life Insurance Company, the Hanover Insurance Company, and Citizens Insurance Company of America.

Typical Recipients

Arts & Humanities: Arts Associations & Councils, Arts Festivals, Arts Outreach, Arts & Humanities-General, History & Archaeology, Libraries, Museums/Galleries, Music, Performing Arts, Theater
Civic & Public Affairs: Business/Free Enterprise, Clubs, Community Foundations, Economic Development, Employment/Job Training, Civic & Public Affairs-General, Hispanic Affairs, Housing, Municipalities/Towns, Parades/Festivals, Philanthropic Organizations, Public Policy, Safety, Urban & Community Affairs, Women's Affairs
Education: Arts/Humanities Education, Business Education, Business-School Partnerships, Colleges & Universities, Community & Junior Colleges, Education Funds, Education Reform, Engineering/Technological Education, Faculty Development, Education-General, Medical Education, Preschool Education, Private Education (Precollege), Public Education (Precollege), Religious Education, School Volunteerism, Student Aid
Environment: Environment-General, Resource Conservation
Health: AIDS/HIV, Cancer, Children's Health/Hospitals, Clinics/Medical Centers, Emergency/Ambulance Services, Eyes/Blindness, Health-General, Health Organizations, Heart, Hospitals, Hospitals (University Affiliated), Medical Research, Nursing Services, Public Health, Single-Disease Health Associations
Religion: Religious Welfare
Science: Scientific Centers & Institutes
Social Services: Big Brother/Big Sister, Child Welfare, Community Centers, Community Service Organizations, Day Care, Domestic Violence, Family Services, Food/Clothing Distribution, Recreation & Athletics, Scouts, Sexual Abuse, Shelters/Homelessness, Social Services-General, Special Olympics, Substance Abuse, United Funds/United Ways, Volunteer Services, YMCA/YWCA/YMHA/YWHA, Youth Organizations

Application Procedures

Initial Contact: Send a brief letter of inquiry.
Application Requirements: The foundation has no formal application policy. Include a description of organization, amount requested, purpose of funds sought, audited financial statement, and proof of tax-exempt status.
Deadlines: None.

Restrictions

The foundation's efforts focus primarily on giving in Worcester, MA.

Corporate Officials

John Francis O'Brien, Jr.: president, chief executive officer B Brockton, MA 1943. ED Harvard College (1965); Harvard University MBA (1968). PRIM CORP EMPL president, chief executive officer: Allmerica Financial Corp. CORP AFFIL director: State Mutual Life Assurance Co.; director: TJX Co. Inc.; chairman: Hanover Insurance Co. Inc.; member, executive committee: Massachusetts Capital Resource Co.; director: First Allmerica Life Insurance Co.; president,ceo: First Allmerica Financial Life Insurance Co.; chairman: Citizens Insurance Co. of America; director: Cabot Corp.; chief executive officer, director, president: Citizens Corp.; president, chief executive officer: Allmerica Financial Corp.; president, chief executive officer, director: Allmerica Property & Casualty Companies Inc.; director: Abiomed Inc.; president: Allmerica Financial Life Insurance and Annuity Co. NONPR AFFIL director: Life Insurance Association of

Massachusetts; trustee: Worcester Polytech Institute; visitors committee board overseers: Harvard College; director: American Council Life Insurance; executive committee: Harvard Alumni Association.

Grants Analysis

Disclosure Period: calendar year ending 2001
Total Grants: $675,035*
Number of Grants: 105
Average Grant: $6,429
Highest Grant: $25,000
Typical Range: $1,000 to $25,000
***Note:** Giving excludes matching gifts and United Way.

Recent Grants

Note: Grants derived from 2001 Form 990.

General

230,000	United Way Central Massachusetts, Worcester, MA
56,984	American Red Cross Disaster Relief Fund, Worcester, MA
50,000	Livingston County United Way, Howell, MI
25,000	LACASA, Howell, MI
25,000	Student Leadership Services, Waterford, MI
22,170	New York Police and Fire Widows and Children's Benefit, Uniondale, NY
20,386	America's Survivor Relief Fund, Farmington, CT
20,000	InVEST, Alexandria, VA
20,000	Volunteer Incentive Program, Wichita, KS
17,500	Alliance for Education, Worcester, MA

ALLYN FOUNDATION

Giving Contact

Meg O'Connell, Executive Director
PO Box 22
Skaneateles, NY 13152
Phone: (315)685-9427

Description

Founded: 1958
EIN: 156017723
Organization Type: Private Foundation
Giving Locations: NY: Cayuga County, Onondaga County
Grant Types: Capital, Fellowship, General Support, Research, Scholarship.

Donor Information

Founder: the late William N. Allyn, William G. Allyn, Welch Allyn, Inc.

Financial Summary

Total Giving: $522,444 (2001); $576,885 (2000); $513,597 (1999)
Giving Analysis: Giving for 2001 includes: foundation scholarships ($23,000); 2000: foundation grants to United Way ($10,435); foundation scholarships ($27,000); 1999: foundation scholarships ($7,000)
Assets: $11,157,063 (2001); $12,474,527 (2000); $12,103,359 (1999)
Gifts Received: $100,000 (2000); $200,000 (1999); $398,121 (1998). Note: In 1995, 1999, and 2000, contributions were received from Welch Allyn.

Typical Recipients

Arts & Humanities: Historic Preservation, Libraries, Museums/Galleries, Music, Performing Arts, Public Broadcasting, Theater
Civic & Public Affairs: African American Affairs, Botanical Gardens/Parks, Chambers of Commerce, Community Foundations, Economic Development, Employment/Job Training, Ethnic Organizations,

Civic & Public Affairs-General, Housing, Native American Affairs, Public Policy, Safety, Urban & Community Affairs, Zoos/Aquariums
Education: Colleges & Universities, Community & Junior Colleges, Education Funds, Literacy, Minority Education, Preschool Education, Private Education (Precollege), Public Education (Precollege), Special Education, Student Aid
Health: Alzheimers Disease, Cancer, Children's Health/Hospitals, Clinics/Medical Centers, Emergency/Ambulance Services, Health Organizations, Hospices, Hospitals, Hospitals (University Affiliated), Long-Term Care, Medical Research, Research/Studies Institutes, Single-Disease Health Associations
International: Missionary/Religious Activities
Religion: Churches, Religious Welfare
Science: Science Museums, Scientific Centers & Institutes
Social Services: Big Brother/Big Sister, Camps, Child Welfare, Community Service Organizations, Counseling, Day Care, Family Planning, Family Services, Food/Clothing Distribution, People with Disabilities, Recreation & Athletics, Scouts, Sexual Abuse, Shelters/Homelessness, Social Services-General, Substance Abuse, YMCA/YWCA/YMHA/YWHA, Youth Organizations

Application Procedures

Initial Contact: Return completed application with proof of tax-exempt status, a list of board members, and recently audited financial statement.
Deadlines: None.

Additional Information

Publications: Application Guidelines

Foundation Officials

Amy Allyn: director
David Allyn: director
Dawn N. Allyn: secretary
Eric R. Allyn: director
Janet J. Allyn: director
Laura Austin Allyn: director
Lew F. Allyn: president B 1941.
Scott Allyn: director
William Finch Allyn: treasurer B Auburn, NY 1935. ED Dartmouth College BA (1958); Syracuse University (1960). PRIM CORP EMPL president: Welch Allyn Inc. CORP AFFIL director: Perfex Corp.; director: Syracuse Research Corp.; director: Oneida Tableware Group; director: Oneida Silver; director: Oneida Silversmiths Division; director: Oneida Ltd.; director: Niagara Mohawk Holdings Inc.; president, chief executive officer: Niagara Mohawk Power Corp.; director: M T Bank; president, director: Grason-Stadler Inc.; president: GSI; president director: C E L Instruments, Ltd.
William G. Allyn: hon officer
Dr. William Scott Allyn: director
Tanya Dillon: director
Tasha A. Falcone: director
Tasha Given: hon director
Marie W. Infanger: hon officer
Donald Nelson: director
Margaret Mary O'Connell: executive director
Elsa A. Soderberg: vice president
Jon Soderberg: director
Libby Soderberg: director
Peer Soderberg: director
Peter Soderberg: director
Robert C. Soderberg: director
Wilbur L. Townsend: director
Charles S. Tracy: director
Sonya Weinfeld: director

Grants Analysis

Disclosure Period: calendar year ending 2001
Total Grants: $499,444*
Number of Grants: 66
Average Grant: $6,898*
Highest Grant: $29,000

Lowest Grant: $500
Typical Range: $2,000 to $15,000
***Note:** Giving excludes scholarship. Average grant excludes two highest grants ($58,000).

Recent Grants

Note: Grants derived from 2001 Form 990.

Library-Related

28,500	Skaneateles Library Association, Skaneateles, NY -- for operating support

General

29,000	Matthew House, Chicago, IL -- for capital improvements
29,000	New York Police and Fire Widows and Orphans Fund, New York, NY -- for 9/11 support
25,000	Native American Service Agency, Syracuse, NY -- for operating support
24,750	East Hill Family Medicine, Auburn, NY -- for school based dental programs
20,000	Hospice of the Finger Lakes, Finger Lakes, NY -- for capital improvements
19,000	Skaneateles Recreational Charitable Trust, Skaneateles, NY -- for capital project
18,900	Cuyaga Boy Scouts, Auburn, NY -- for operating support
15,000	Alzheimer's Disease of Central New York, Syracuse, NY -- for Respite Program
15,000	Auburn YMCA, Auburn, NY -- for capital improvements
15,000	Crouse Health Foundation, Syracuse, NY -- for capital improvements

ELEANORA ALMS TRUST

Giving Contact

Lawra Baumann, Trust Officer
c/o Fifth Third Bank, Department 00864
38 Fountain Square Plaza
Cincinnati, OH 45263
Phone: (513)579-6034

Description

Founded: 1939
EIN: 316019723
Organization Type: Private Foundation
Giving Locations: OH: Cincinnati
Grant Types: Capital, General Support, Seed Money.

Donor Information

Founder: the late Eleanora Alms

Financial Summary

Total Giving: $231,500 (fiscal year ending September 30, 2000); $256,260 (fiscal 1998); $276,260 (fiscal 1997). Note: Fiscal 1997 Giving includes United Way ($6,760).
Giving Analysis: Giving for fiscal 2000 includes: foundation grants to United Way ($25,000); fiscal 1998: foundation grants to United Way ($6,760) foundation ($249,500)
Assets: $6,648,110 (fiscal 2000); $4,462,880 (fiscal 1998); $4,805,912 (fiscal 1997)

Typical Recipients

Arts & Humanities: Arts Associations & Councils, Arts Centers, Arts Funds, Arts Institutes, Ballet, Dance, Arts & Humanities-General, Historic Preservation, Museums/Galleries, Music, Performing Arts, Public Broadcasting
Civic & Public Affairs: Botanical Gardens/Parks, Parades/Festivals, Urban & Community Affairs
Education: Public Education (Precollege)
Environment: Environment-General
Health: Alzheimers Disease
Religion: Churches

Social Services: Community Centers, Family Planning, Family Services, United Funds/United Ways, Youth Organizations

Application Procedures

Initial Contact: Request application.
Deadlines: February 10, May 10, August 10, and November 10.

Restrictions

Does not support individuals, religious organizations for sectarian purposes, or political or lobbying groups.

Additional Information

Publications: Annual Report; Application Form
Trust(s): Fifth Third Bank

Grants Analysis

Disclosure Period: fiscal year ending September 30, 2000
Total Grants: $206,500*
Number of Grants: 7
Average Grant: $17,750*
Highest Grant: $100,000
Typical Range: $10,000 to $25,000
*Note: Giving excludes United Way. Average grant figure excludes highest grant.

Recent Grants

Note: Grants derived from fiscal 2000 Form 990.

General

100,000	Cincinnati Arts Association, Cincinnati, OH -- capital campaign
25,000	Alzheimer's Association, Cincinnati, OH -- in support of the "Family Connections" program
25,000	Professional Flair, Cleveland, OH -- for a fully accessible center for the performing arts for the disabled
25,000	United Way and Community Chest of Greater Cincinnati, Cincinnati, OH -- contribution
16,500	Lorain Public Library, Lorain, OH -- funding for artwork
15,000	Fine Arts Fund, Cincinnati, OH -- contribution
15,000	Louisville Olmsted Parks Conservancy, Louisville, KY -- matching funds for challenge grant
10,000	Fine Arts Fund, Cincinnati, OH -- contribution

BEN J. ALTHEIMER CHARITABLE FOUNDATION

Giving Contact

John S. Selig, President, Secretary & Treasurer
425 W. Capitol Ave., Ste. 1800
Little Rock, AR 72201
Phone: (318)797-2163

Description

Founded: 1995
EIN: 710769229
Organization Type: Private Foundation
Grant Types: General Support.

Financial Summary

Total Giving: $617,286 (2001); $245,774 (2000); $83,376 (1999)
Assets: $4,399,952 (2001); $4,945,432 (2000); $4,743,641 (1999)
Gifts Received: $93 (1998); $2,023,065 (1996).
Note: In 1996, contributions were received from the

Ben J. Altheimer Foundation ($2,018,367); miscellaneous contributions of lessa tha $5,000 each also were received.

Typical Recipients

Civic & Public Affairs: Municipalities/Towns
Education: Colleges & Universities, Legal Education, Medical Education, Private Education (Precollege)
Health: Cancer, Children's Health/Hospitals
Religion: Religion-General
Social Services: Scouts

Application Procedures

Initial Contact: Send a brief letter of inquiry.

Foundation Officials

William H. Bowen: vice president, assistant secretary
John S. Selig: president, secretary, treasurer
Michael J. Selig: vice president
John N. Stern: chairman

Grants Analysis

Disclosure Period: calendar year ending 2001
Total Grants: $617,286
Number of Grants: 11
Highest Grant: $300,000
Lowest Grant: $1,735

Recent Grants

Note: Grants derived from 2000 Form 990.

General

100,000	Arkansas Children's Hospital, Little Rock, AR -- allergy research
50,000	Philander Smith College, Little Rock, AR -- library capital campaign
47,500	University of Arkansas Medical School Foundation, Little Rock, AR -- community medical
41,539	City of Altheimer, Altheimer, AR -- safety
5,000	St. Peters St. Joseph Cemetery
1,735	Quapaw Area Boy Scouts

ALTMAN FOUNDATION

Giving Contact

Karen L. Rosa, Vice President & Executive Director
521 Fifth Ave., 35th Fl.
New York, NY 10175-3599
Phone: (212)682-0970
Web: http://fdncenter.org/grantmaker/altman/

Description

Founded: 1913
EIN: 131623879
Organization Type: General Purpose Foundation
Giving Locations: NY: focusing on the five boroughs of New York City
Grant Types: Project.

Donor Information

Founder: Established in 1913 in New York under the will of Benjamin Altman , the founder of the B. Altman & Company department store, who bequeathed his ownership of the company to the foundation to support charitable and educational institutions in New York.
Since its earliest days, the foundation has reflected Mr. Altman's own philanthropic concern for social service, healthcare, educational and cultural institutions and organizations.

Financial Summary

Total Giving: $10,500,000 (2003 approx); $10,500,000 (2002 approx) $11,248,326 (2000)
Giving Analysis: Giving for 2000 includes: foundation grants to United Way ($100,000) foundation scholarships ($110,000)

Assets: $240,000,000 (2003 approx); $240,000,000 (2002 approx); $251,717,583 (2000)

Typical Recipients

Arts & Humanities: Arts Associations & Councils, Arts Outreach, Historic Preservation, History & Archaeology, Libraries, Museums/Galleries, Music, Performing Arts, Theater
Civic & Public Affairs: Asian American Affairs, Botanical Gardens/Parks, Business/Free Enterprise, Community Foundations, Economic Development, Employment/Job Training, Civic & Public Affairs-General, Housing, Legal Aid, Safety, Urban & Community Affairs, Women's Affairs, Zoos/Aquariums
Education: Afterschool/Enrichment Programs, Arts/Humanities Education, Colleges & Universities, Continuing Education, Education Funds, Elementary Education (Private), Environmental Education, Faculty Development, Education-General, Literacy, Medical Education, Minority Education, Private Education (Precollege), Science/Mathematics Education, Special Education, Student Aid
Environment: Air/Water Quality, Environment-General, Resource Conservation, Wildlife Protection
Health: AIDS/HIV, Cancer, Children's Health/Hospitals, Clinics/Medical Centers, Emergency/Ambulance Services, Eyes/Blindness, Geriatric Health, Health Policy/Cost Containment, Health Funds, Health Organizations, Home-Care Services, Hospitals, Mental Health, Outpatient Health Care, Prenatal Health Issues, Preventive Medicine/Wellness Organizations, Public Health
Religion: Dioceses, Jewish Causes, Religious Organizations, Religious Welfare, Seminaries
Science: Science Museums, Scientific Centers & Institutes
Social Services: Big Brother/Big Sister, Child Abuse, Child Welfare, Community Centers, Community Service Organizations, Day Care, Delinquency & Criminal Rehabilitation, Domestic Violence, Emergency Relief, Family Services, People with Disabilities, Recreation & Athletics, Refugee Assistance, Senior Services, Shelters/Homelessness, Social Services-General, United Funds/United Ways, YMCA/YWCA/YMHA/YWHA, Youth Organizations

Application Procedures

Initial Contact: Submit grant requests in letter form, not exceeding five pages.
Application Requirements: Applicants must describe the project for which funds are being solicited, include a copy of 501(c)(3) most recent audited financial statement, project and organization budgets, a list of major corporate and foundation supporters with amounts, and a list of officers or trustees and their affiliations.
Deadlines: None.
Notes: The Altman Foundation accepts, but does not require, the New York area common grant application form.

Restrictions

No grants are made to individuals. As a general rule, the foundation does not fund bricks and mortar or the purchase of capital equipment. Grant requests from outside the State of New York are generally not considered for funding.

Additional Information

The foundation occasionally initiates discretionary grants and offers ongoing support to organizations that have received previous funding.
Publications: General Guidelines; Application Procedure Brochure; Application Form; Annual Report

Foundation Officials

James M. Burke: trustee
Thomas C. Burke: trustee emeritus
John P. Casey: treasurer B NY 1945. ED City University of New York Bernard M. Baruch College (1971). CORP AFFIL director: Energy Tech International

Corp. NONPR AFFIL vice chairman, director: Saint Agnes Hospital; treasurer: Union League; trustee: Franciscan Services.

Bernard Finkelstein: trustee B New York, NY 1930. ED New York University BA (1951); Yale University LLB (1954). PRIM CORP EMPL partner: Paul, Weiss, Rifkind, Wharton & Garrison. NONPR AFFIL member wills trusts advisory committee: Practicing Law Institute; member: Yale Law School Association; member: Phi Beta Kappa; member: Order Coif; member: Phi Alpha Delta; member: New York State Bar Association; member: Association Bar New York City; member: New York Bar Foundation; fellow: American College Trust & Estate Counsel; member: American Bar Association. CLUB AFFIL Elmwood Country Club.

Anna M. Johnson: administrative assistant

Sharon B. King: trustee, assistant secretary

Justine Koch: accountant

Kate Liebman: program officer

Nina B. Mogilnik: senior program officer

Jane B. O'Connell: president, trustee B New York, NY 1941. ED Manhattanville College BA (1963); New York University MA (1968). PRIM NONPR EMPL school administrator: Convent of Sacred Heart. NONPR AFFIL chairwoman devel committee: Network of Sacred Heart Schools; director: Saint Aloysius Educational Clinic; member: Case Commission Committees; director: City Harvest.

Karen L. Rosa: vice president, executive director

Doriann Sama: administrative assistant

Maurice A. Selinger, Jr.: trustee

Julia V. Shea: secretary, trustee

John W. Townsend, IV: vice president, trustee NONPR AFFIL assistant executive director, assistant secretary: Boettcher Foundation.

Patricia J. Volland: trustee ED Ottawa University; San Diego State University MSW; Loyola College MBA (1981). PRIM NONPR EMPL senior vice president administration finance: New York Academy Medicine. NONPR AFFIL member: National Association Social Workers; director: Planned Parenthood New York; Council Social Work Education; member: Health Care Executive Forum.

Grants Analysis

Disclosure Period: calendar year ending 2000
Total Grants: $10,675,326*
Number of Grants: 232
Average Grant: $46,920
Highest Grant: $564,000
Lowest Grant: $3,500
Typical Range: $25,000 to $100,000
***Note:** Giving excludes scholarships and United Way. Grants analysis provided by foundation.

Recent Grants

Note: Grants derived from 2001 Form 990.

General

1,250,000	New York Botanical Garden, New York, NY -- to provide both operating and endowment support
1,000,000	Graduate School and University Center of City University of New York, New York, NY -- to establish the B. Altman Endowment Fund
250,000	September 11th Fund, New York, NY -- for the benefits of the September 11th fund
225,000	Saint Nicholas Neighborhood Preservation Corporation, Brooklyn, NY -- to support the Model After School Program and Technical Assistance and Training Center
182,000	NPower NY, Inc., New York, NY -- for this new nonprofit designed to aid other New York City Nonprofits
160,000	Bank Street College of Education, New York, NY -- to support the Center for Universal Pre-Kindergarten
150,000	Henry Street Settlement, New York,

	NY -- to renew support for the Community Outreach Initiative
150,000	United Way of New York City, New York, NY -- to renew support for the Child Care and Early Education Fund
140,000	Teak Fellowship, New York, NY -- to help launch an endowment
137,500	New York Academy of Medicine, New York, NY -- for research project and Roundtable Series

MAURICE AMADO FOUNDATION

Giving Contact

Pam Kaizer, Executive Director
3940 Laurel Canyon Boulevard, Suite 809
Studio City, CA 91604
Phone: (818)980-9190
Fax: (818)980-9190
Web: http://www.mauriceamadofdn.org

Description

Founded: 1961
EIN: 956041700
Organization Type: Family Foundation
Giving Locations: CA: Los Angeles; NY: New York
Grant Types: General Support, Project.
Note: Grants also include program and publishing awards.

Donor Information

Founder: Incorporated in 1961 by the late Maurice Amado .

Financial Summary

Total Giving: $1,500,000 (fiscal year ending November 30, 2003 approx); $1,500,000 (fiscal 2002); $1,840,235 (fiscal 2001)
Assets: $30,000,000 (fiscal 2003 approx); $30,000,000 (fiscal 2002); $36,360,759 (fiscal 2001)

Typical Recipients

Arts & Humanities: Arts Centers, Arts Outreach, Ballet, Dance, Ethnic & Folk Arts, Arts & Humanities-General, Libraries, Literary Arts, Museums/Galleries, Music, Opera, Public Broadcasting
Civic & Public Affairs: Ethnic Organizations, Civic & Public Affairs-General, Philanthropic Organizations, Safety, Women's Affairs
Education: Arts/Humanities Education, Colleges & Universities, Education Funds, Education-General, International Exchange, International Studies, Legal Education, Medical Education, Private Education (Precollege), Public Education (Precollege), Religious Education
Health: Cancer, Children's Health/Hospitals, Clinics/Medical Centers, Emergency/Ambulance Services, Geriatric Health, Health Organizations, Hospitals, Hospitals (University Affiliated), Long-Term Care
International: Foreign Arts Organizations, Foreign Educational Institutions, Health Care/Hospitals, International Relief Efforts, Missionary/Religious Activities
Religion: Jewish Causes, Religious Organizations, Synagogues/Temples
Social Services: Camps, Community Centers, Community Service Organizations, Domestic Violence, Family Services, Recreation & Athletics, Senior Services, Social Services-General, United Funds/United Ways, YMCA/YWCA/YMHA/YWHA

Application Procedures

Initial Contact: Initial inquiry should be by letter. Application and procedures will be made available if the foundation would like a full proposal.

Application Requirements: Letters of request should include an overview of the request; a project

description, including activities, timeline, staff, intended audience, and desired outcomes; a budget with projected costs, amount requested from the foundation, and additional funding sources; background information including the applicant's history, mission, goals and objectives, as well as financial statements; proof of non-profit status, including proof of tax exempt 501(c)(3) status; and an evaluation statement of how the progress and success of the program will be measured.

Deadlines: February 15 and August 15.

Review Process: The board meets twice a year, in the fall and the spring, at which time funding decisions are made.

Restrictions

Grants are not made to individuals.

Additional Information

Publications: Guidelines

Foundation Officials

Bernice Amado: vice president, secretary, director

Ralph A. Amado: director

Ralph D. Amado: director ED Stanford University BA (1954); Oxford University PhD (1957). PRIM NONPR EMPL professor: University of Pennsylvania. CORP AFFIL consultant: Los Alamos Science Lab. NONPR AFFIL member: American Association Advancement Science; fellow: American Physics Society.

Renee T. Kaplan: director

Stella Amado Lavis: director

Elaine L. Lindheim: president

Joyce G. Miller: executive director

Regina Amado Tarica: vice president, cfo, director

Samuel R. Tarica: vice president, director

Grants Analysis

Disclosure Period: fiscal year ending November 30, 2001
Total Grants: $1,836,767
Number of Grants: 108
Average Grant: $14,175*
Highest Grant: $100,000
Typical Range: $500 to $100,000
***Note:** Average grant figure excludes highest grant.

Recent Grants

Note: Grants derived from fiscal 2001 Form 990.

Library-Related

15,000	Jewish Community Library of Los Angeles, Los Angeles, CA
9,000	Bala Cynwyd Library, Bala Cynwyd, PA

General

320,000	Jewish Community Foundation, Los Angeles, CA
110,000	University of Pennsylvania, Philadelphia, PA
65,000	Regents University of California, Berkeley, CA
62,700	CUNY Graduate Center, New York, NY
50,000	92nd Street Y, New York, NY
50,000	Foundation for Jewish Camping, New York, NY
50,000	Martha's Vineyard Hospital, Oak Bluff, MA
50,000	Martha's Vineyard Hospital, Oak Bluff, MA
50,000	Saint Louis Symphony Orchestra, St. Louis, MO
50,000	University of Southern California Casden Institute, Los Angeles, CA

AMBASE CORP.

Company Headquarters

51 Weaver St., Bldg. 2
Greenwich, CT 06831

Company Description

Founded: 1975
Ticker: ABCP
Exchange: OTC
Operating Revenue: US$62.1 million (2001)
Employees: 5 (2001)
SIC(s): 6799 Investors Nec.

AmBase Foundation

Giving Contact

Lester J. Mantell, Vice President, Treasurer, Controller & Director
AmBase Foundation
99 University Place, 7th Floor
New York, NY 10003-4528
Phone: (212)473-0028

Description

EIN: 133246657
Organization Type: Corporate Foundation
Giving Locations: NY
Grant Types: General Support.

Financial Summary

Total Giving: $132,750 (2001); $36,800 (2000); $303,000 (1999)
Assets: $132,071 (2001); $252,317 (2000); $253,903 (1999)
Gifts Received: $20,000 (2000). Note: In 2000, contributions were received from Lester J. Mantell.

Typical Recipients

Arts & Humanities: History & Archaeology, Libraries, Museums/Galleries, Public Broadcasting
Civic & Public Affairs: Botanical Gardens/Parks, Legal Aid, Safety, Zoos/Aquariums
Education: Arts/Humanities Education, Colleges & Universities, Private Education (Precollege)
Health: Cancer, Geriatric Health, Hospitals, Medical Research, Mental Health, Public Health
Social Services: Crime Prevention, YMCA/YWCA/YMHA/YWHA

Application Procedures

Initial Contact: Send a brief letter of inquiry.
Deadlines: None.

Corporate Officials

Richard A. Bianco: president, chief executive officer, director PRIM CORP EMPL president, chief executive officer, director: AmBase Corp.

Foundation Officials

Lester J. Mantell: vice president, treasurer, contr, director
David G. Ormsby: president, director
Eben Wright Pyne: director B New York, NY June 14, 1917. ED Princeton University AB (1939). PRIM CORP EMPL director: W.R. Grace & Co. CORP AFFIL director: US International Reins; director: USLIFE Corp.; director: Long Island Lighting Co.; director: Slattery Group; director: Home Insurance Co.; director: General Devel Corp.; vice chairman, director: Home Group. NONPR AFFIL trustee: Saint Lukes Hospital; director: Winthrop University Hospital; member executive committee: Press Prelate Sector Cost Control; trustee, director: New York Zoological Society; member executive committee: Pilgrims U.S.; trustee: Brooklyn Institute Arts & Science; trustee: Juilliard School; advisory board: Boy Scouts America Nassau County. CLUB AFFIL Piping Rock Club; River Club; Bond Racquet & Tennis Club; Ivy Club.
George T. Scharffenberger: president, director

Grants Analysis

Disclosure Period: calendar year ending 2001
Total Grants: $132,750
Number of Grants: 13
Average Grant: $2,729*
Highest Grant: $100,000
Lowest Grant: $500
Typical Range: $1,000 to $5,000
*Note: Average grant figure excludes highest grant.

Recent Grants

Note: Grants derived from 2000 Form 990.

Library-Related
1,000	Greenwich Library, The, Greenwich, CT

General
10,000	Metropolitan Museum of Art, New York, NY
5,000	Brooklyn Museum of Art, Brooklyn, NY
5,000	Greenwich Hospital, Greenwich, CT
5,000	Montefiore Geriatric Training Program
5,000	WNYC Radio, New York, NY
2,500	Welfare Law Center, New York, NY
2,000	Greenwich Country Day School, Greenwich, CT
1,000	Amherst College, Amherst, MA
300	American Museum of Natural History, New York, NY

THE AMBROSE MONELL FOUNDATION

Giving Contact

George Rowe, Jr., President
1 Rockefeller Plaza, Suite 301
New York, NY 10020
Phone: (212)586-0700
Fax: (212)245-1863
E-mail: info@monellvetlesen.org
Web: http://www.monellvetlesen.org/monell/default.htm

Description

Founded: 1952
EIN: 131982683
Organization Type: General Purpose Foundation
Giving Locations: NY: New York metropolitan area nationally.
Grant Types: Capital, Endowment, General Support, Multiyear/Continuing Support, Research.

Donor Information

Founder: The Ambrose Monell Foundation was established in 1952. Funds for its incorporation were donated by Mrs. Maude Monell Vetlesen. Ambrose Monell, who died in 1921, served as president of International Nickel Company.

Financial Summary

Total Giving: $11,177,500 (2001); $11,822,500 (2000); $11,275,000 (1998)
Assets: $217,722,530 (2001); $228,536,489 (2000); $249,855,688 (1998)

Typical Recipients

Arts & Humanities: Arts Funds, Ballet, Dance, Libraries, Museums/Galleries, Music, Opera, Performing Arts, Public Broadcasting, Theater
Civic & Public Affairs: Botanical Gardens/Parks, Economic Development, Employment/Job Training, Civic & Public Affairs-General, Legal Aid, Public Policy
Education: Arts/Humanities Education, Colleges & Universities, Education Associations, Education-General, Health & Physical Education, Literacy, Medical Education, Minority Education, Private Education (Precollege), Public Education (Precollege), Religious Education, Secondary Education (Private)

Environment: Resource Conservation
Health: AIDS/HIV, Alzheimers Disease, Arthritis, Cancer, Clinics/Medical Centers, Clinics/Medical Centers, Emergency/Ambulance Services, Eyes/Blindness, Health-General, Geriatric Health, Hospitals, Hospitals (University Affiliated), Medical Rehabilitation, Medical Research, Mental Health, Public Health, Research/Studies Institutes, Respiratory, Speech & Hearing
International: Health Care/Hospitals, International Peace & Security Issues, International Relief Efforts
Religion: Jewish Causes
Science: Science Museums, Scientific Centers & Institutes, Scientific Research
Social Services: Animal Protection, Delinquency & Criminal Rehabilitation, Homes, Scouts, YMCA/YWCA/YMHA/YWHA, Youth Organizations

Application Procedures

Initial Contact: Send a brief letter to the foundation.
Application Requirements: Letters should include an outline of the proposed project, explain the reason funding is needed and be addressed to the president of the foundation.
Deadlines: December.
Review Process: The board meets on December 1.

Foundation Officials

Eugene P. Grisanti: director B Buffalo, NY 1929. ED College of the Holy Cross AB (1951); Boston University LLB (1953); Harvard University LLM (1954).
Joseph T. C. Hart: treasurer
Ambrose K. Monell: director
Laura Naus: secretary
George Rowe, Jr.: president B Ossining, NY 1922. ED Yale University AB (1943); Columbia University LLB (1948). PRIM CORP EMPL partner: Fulton, Duncombe & Rowe. CORP AFFIL director: International Flavors & Fragrances Inc.

Grants Analysis

Disclosure Period: calendar year ending 2001
Total Grants: $11,177,500
Number of Grants: 127
Average Grant: $88,012
Highest Grant: $600,000
Lowest Grant: $2,500
Typical Range: $25,000 to $200,000

Recent Grants

Note: Grants derived from 2001 Form 990.

Library-Related
100,000	New York Public Library, New York, NY
100,000	Pierpont Morgan Library, New York, NY

General
600,000	Monell Chemical Senses Center, Philadelphia, PA
500,000	Brookdale University Hospital and Medical Center, Brooklyn, NY -- to expand clinic hours at Family Care Center
500,000	Harvard School of Public Health, Boston, MA
500,000	Monell Chemical Senses Center, Philadelphia, PA -- new faculty
500,000	New York Botanical Garden, Bronx, NY
400,000	Educational Broadcasting Corporation, New York, NY
350,000	Institute for Advanced Study, Princeton, NJ -- for Schools of Natural Sciences and Mathematics
350,000	Massachusetts General Hospital, MGH Cancer Center, Quincy, MA
300,000	St. Vincent's Hospital and Medical Center, New York, NY -- for its hospitals
250,000	Jazz at Lincoln Center, New York, NY -- for building campaign

AMCAST INDUSTRIAL CORP.

Company Headquarters

PO Box 98
Dayton, OH 45401
Web: http://www.amcast.com

Company Description

Founded: 1869
Ticker: AIZ
Exchange: NYSE
Revenue: US$576.2 million (2002)
Employees: 4040 (2002)
SIC(s): 3354 Aluminum Extruded Products, 3363 Aluminum Die-Castings, 3366 Copper Foundries, 3400 Fabricated Metal Products.

Operating Locations

Amcast Industrial Corp. (AL--Anniston; AR--Fayetteville; IN--Elkhart, Franklin, Gas City, Geneva, Richmond; MI--Southfield; OH--Wapakoneta; PA--Washington; WI--Cedarburg)
Note: Includes division and plant locations.

Amcast Industrial Foundation

Giving Contact

Samuel Rees, Secretary
Amcast Industrial Foundation
7887 Washington Village Dr.
Dayton, OH 45459
Phone: (937)291-7023

Description

EIN: 316016458
Organization Type: Corporate Foundation
Giving Locations: OH: Dayton
Grant Types: Capital, Challenge, Emergency, Employee Matching Gifts, Multiyear/Continuing Support, Project, Research, Scholarship.

Financial Summary

Total Giving: $85,610 (fiscal year ending August 31, 2001); $161,270 (fiscal 2000); $170,955 (fiscal 1998)
Giving Analysis: Giving for fiscal 2001 includes: foundation grants to United Way ($16,500); foundation scholarships ($19,500); fiscal 2000: foundation scholarships ($13,995); foundation grants to United Way ($54,000); foundation ($107,271) fiscal 1998: foundation grants to United Way ($65,900)
Assets: $346,045 (fiscal 2001); $490,041 (fiscal 2000); $589,109 (fiscal 1998)
Gifts Received: $150,000 (fiscal 1998); $150,000 (fiscal 1996); $100,000 (fiscal 1995). Note: In 1998, contributions were received from Amcast Industrial Corp.

Typical Recipients

Arts & Humanities: Arts Associations & Councils, Arts Centers, Arts Funds, Arts Institutes, Ballet, Arts & Humanities-General, Historic Preservation, History & Archaeology, Libraries, Performing Arts, Theater
Civic & Public Affairs: African American Affairs, Botanical Gardens/Parks, Chambers of Commerce, Community Foundations, Economic Development, Civic & Public Affairs-General, Housing, Inner-City Development, Parades/Festivals, Professional & Trade Associations, Public Policy, Safety, Urban & Community Affairs, Women's Affairs
Education: Business Education, Colleges & Universities, Community & Junior Colleges, Education Funds, Education Reform, Engineering/Technological Education, Education-General, Minority Education, Public Education (Precollege), Science/Mathematics Education, Secondary Education (Public), Student Aid
Environment: Resource Conservation
Health: AIDS/HIV, Alzheimers Disease, Cancer, Children's Health/Hospitals, Health-General, Health Organizations, Heart, Hospices, Hospitals, Medical Research, Prenatal Health Issues
Social Services: Community Centers, Community Service Organizations, Crime Prevention, Emergency Relief, Family Planning, Family Services, Recreation & Athletics, Scouts, Senior Services, Shelters/Homelessness, Social Services-General, United Funds/United Ways, YMCA/YWCA/YMHA/YWHA, Youth Organizations

Application Procedures

Initial Contact: Send a brief letter of inquiry and a full proposal.
Application Requirements: Include a description of organization, amount requested, purpose of funds sought, and proof of tax-exempt status.
Deadlines: None. Requests are processed quarterly in November, February, May, and August.

Restrictions

Does not support individuals, religious organizations for sectarian purposes, political or lobbying groups, organizations outside operating areas, hospitals, organizations receiving support from the United Way, or schools, except in certain situations.

Additional Information

The company sponsors Amcast Engineering Scholarships through the Ohio Foundation of Independent Colleges.
Publications: Operating Guidelines; Matching Gift Program Guidelines

Corporate Officials

Denis G. Daly: secretary financial, chief financial officer PRIM CORP EMPL secretary: Amcast Industrial Corp. ADD CORP EMPL secretary: Elkhart Products Corp.; secretary: Wheeltek Inc.
John Henry Shuey: chairman, president, chief executive officer, director B Monroe, MI 1946. ED University of Michigan BS (1968); University of Michigan MBA (1970). PRIM CORP EMPL chairman, president, chief executive officer, director: Amcast Industrial Corp. ADD CORP EMPL president: Amcast & Elkhart Industries Products; president: Speedline North America Inc.; president: Wheeltek Inc. CORP AFFIL director: Cooper Tire & Rubber Co. NONPR AFFIL trustee: Ohio Foundation of Industries College; director: Wright State University Indiana; member: Financial Executives Institute; trustee: Dayton Ballet.
Douglas D. Watts: vice president financial, chief financial officer PRIM CORP EMPL vice president financial, chief financial officer: Amcast Industrial Corp.

Foundation Officials

Denis G. Daly: secretary (see above)
Francis J. Drew: vice president
Michael R. Higgins: treasurer
Byron O. Pond, Jr.: president
Samuel Rees: secretary
John Henry Shuey: president (see above)
E. Sue Smith: assistant secretary
Douglas D. Watts: vice president (see above)

Grants Analysis

Disclosure Period: fiscal year ending August 31, 2001
Total Grants: $49,610*
Number of Grants: 26
Average Grant: $1,908
Highest Grant: $12,500
Lowest Grant: $50
Typical Range: $1,000 to $3,000
*Note: Giving excludes scholarships, United Way.

Recent Grants

Note: Grants derived from 2000 Form 990.

General

16,000	United Way of Elkhart County, Elkhart, IN
13,995	National Merit Scholarship Corporation, Evanston, IL
12,500	2003 Committee, Dayton, OH
11,500	United Way
11,500	United Way of Steuben County, IN
10,000	Alliance Community Schools, Dayton, OH
7,500	Ohio Foundation of Independent Colleges, Columbus, OH
5,250	University of Iowa Foundation, Iowa City, IA
5,000	Breeden YMCA Learning Center, OH
5,000	St. Joseph Children's Treatment Center, Dayton, OH

AMCORE FINANCIAL, INC.

Company Headquarters

501 7th Street
Rockford, IL 61104
Web: http://www.amcore.com

Company Description

Founded: 1982
Ticker: AMFI
Exchange: NASDAQ
Assets: US$4.522 billion (2002)
Employees: 1333 (2002)

AMCORE Foundation

Giving Contact

James Waddell, Chairman
AMCORE Bank Foundation
501 7th St., PO Box 1537
Rockford, IL 61110
Phone: (815)968-2241
Fax: (815)961-7530
Web: http://www.amcore.com

Description

EIN: 366042947
Organization Type: Corporate Foundation
Giving Locations: IL: Rockford including surrounding communities
Grant Types: Capital, General Support.

Financial Summary

Total Giving: $289,775 (2001); $214,202 (1999); $290,000 (1998 approx)
Giving Analysis: Giving for 2001 includes: foundation grants to United Way ($80,000); foundation ($209,775); 1999: foundation grants to United Way ($72,000) foundation ($142,202)
Assets: $151,284 (2001); $104,783 (1999); $4,147,833 (1998)
Gifts Received: $319,700 (2001); $275,000 (1999); $238,156 (1996). Note: In 2001, 1999 and 1996, contributions were received from Amcore Investment Group NA.

Typical Recipients

Arts & Humanities: Arts Associations & Councils, Arts Festivals, Dance, Arts & Humanities-General, Historic Preservation, Libraries, Literary Arts, Museums/Galleries, Music, Performing Arts, Public Broadcasting, Theater
Civic & Public Affairs: African American Affairs, Botanical Gardens/Parks, Business/Free Enterprise,

Chambers of Commerce, Clubs, Economic Development, Employment/Job Training, Civic & Public Affairs-General, Hispanic Affairs, Housing, Minority Business, Parades/Festivals, Philanthropic Organizations, Public Policy, Safety, Urban & Community Affairs, Women's Affairs

Education: Afterschool/Enrichment Programs, Business Education, Colleges & Universities, Community & Junior Colleges, Economic Education, Education-General, Health & Physical Education, Literacy, Medical Education, Minority Education, Preschool Education, Private Education (Precollege), Public Education (Precollege), Science/Mathematics Education, Secondary Education (Private), Secondary Education (Public), Special Education

Environment: Environment-General

Health: AIDS/HIV, Alzheimers Disease, Cancer, Clinics/Medical Centers, Emergency/Ambulance Services, Health-General, Health Organizations, Hospices, Hospitals, Long-Term Care, Medical Rehabilitation, Mental Health, Nursing Services, Nutrition, Public Health, Single-Disease Health Associations

Religion: Jewish Causes, Religious Welfare

Science: Science Museums

Social Services: Child Welfare, Community Centers, Community Centers, Community Service Organizations, Counseling, Crime Prevention, Day Care, Delinquency & Criminal Rehabilitation, Domestic Violence, Emergency Relief, Family Services, Food/Clothing Distribution, Homes, People with Disabilities, Recreation & Athletics, Scouts, Senior Services, Shelters/Homelessness, Social Services-General, Substance Abuse, United Funds/United Ways, Veterans, Volunteer Services, YMCA/YWCA/YMHA/YWHA, Youth Organizations

Application Procedures

Initial Contact: Submit a written request for funding.
Application Requirements: Include name and a description of organization, number of members, amount requested, purpose of funds sought, federal tax status, a list of officers and board members, most recent annual report, operating budget for last two years, a statement as to how the organization benefits the community, and a list of general sources of funds.
Deadlines: None.
Evaluative Criteria: Perceived effectiveness of the organization within the community and the benefit that the community will derive from AMCORE Bank Foundation support.

Restrictions

Does not support individuals, religious organizations for sectarian purposes, political or lobbying groups, organizations outside operating areas, or loans of any kind.

Corporate Officials

Charles E. Gagnier: chairman, chief executive officer, director PRIM CORP EMPL chairman: AMCORE Bank Rockford.
John Hecht: chief financial officer PRIM CORP EMPL chief financial officer: AMCORE Bank Rockford.
James Warsaw: president, chief executive officer, director PRIM CORP EMPL president, chief executive officer, director: AMCORE Bank Rockford.

Foundation Officials

E. Taylor Carlin: director
Carl J. Dargene: director B Rockford, IL 1930. ED University of Illinois; University of South Carolina (1951). PRIM CORP EMPL chairman: AMCORE Financial Inc. ADD CORP EMPL director: AMCORE Bank NA Rockford; chairman: Amcore Financial Inc. CORP AFFIL director: Woodward Governor Co.
Robert A. Doyle: director
Charles E. Gagnier: president, director (see above)
Mary E. Gerber: secretary
Robert A. Henry, MD: director

Robert Joseph Meuleman: director B South Bend, IN 1939. ED University of Notre Dame BA (1961); Michigan State University MBA (1962). PRIM CORP EMPL president, chief executive officer: Amcore Bank North America. CORP AFFIL director: AMCORE Financial Inc.; director: Rockford Pro - America. NONPR AFFIL mem: Rockford Chamber of Commerce; director: Swedish America Hosp Foundation; mem: Chartered Financial Analysts; mem: Milwaukee Financial Analysts. CLUB AFFIL Rockford Country Club.
William O. Nelson: director

Grants Analysis

Disclosure Period: calendar year ending 1999
Total Grants: $209,775*
Number of Grants: 35
Average Grant: $4,699*
Highest Grant: $50,000
Typical Range: $500 to $5,000 and $12,000 to $30,000
*Note: Giving excludes United Way. Average grant figure excludes highest grant.

Recent Grants

Note: Grants derived from 2001 Form 990.

Library-Related
3,000   Rockford Public Library, Rockford, IL

General
80,000   United Way Rock River Valley, Rockford, IL
50,000   Zion Community Center Corporation, Rockford, IL
30,000   Coronado Theatre, Rockford, IL
15,000   Northwest Community Center, Rockford, IL -- recreational activities for youth
15,000   Sterling Rock Falls Day Care Agency, Inc., Sterling, IL
12,000   Sandler O'Neill Foundation, Rockford, IL
5,200   YMCA Partners with Youth, Rockford, IL
5,000   Crusader Clinic, Rockford, IL
5,000   Epilepsy Foundation, Rockford, IL
5,000   Rock Valley College Foundation, Rockford, IL

AMEREN CORP.

Company Headquarters

St. Louis, MO
Web: http://www.ameren.com

Company Description

Ticker: AEE
Exchange: OTC
Former Name: Union Electric Co.
Assets: US$11.499 billion (2002)
Profit: US$382 million (2002)
Employees: 7447 (2002)
Fortune Rank: 418, per FORTUNE Magazine's list of 500 Largest U.S. Corporations (2002).
SIC(s): 4931 Electric & Other Services Combined.

Operating Locations

Ameren Corp. (MO--Cape Girardeau, Jefferson City); Ameren Corp. (MO--St. Louis)

Nonmonetary Support

Value: $96,312 (1998)
Type: Cause-related Marketing & Promotion; Donated Equipment; Donated Products
Volunteer Programs: Ameren Helping Hands where employees and their families volunteer. VIP/TEAMS Program in which small grants ($50-$500) are given to nonprofits for which Ameren employees volunteer. The company also supports the "Ameren Helping Hands" program which involves group volunteer projects at local nonprofit organizations.

Ameren Corp. Charitable Trust

Giving Contact

Otis Cowan, Manager, Community Relations
Ameren Corporate
PO Box 66149, Mail Code 100
St. Louis, MO 63166-6149
Phone: (314)554-4740
Fax: (314)554-2888
E-mail: ocowan@ameren.com
Web: http://www.ameren.com/community/adc_com_homepage.asp
Note: for nonprofits in the St. Louis, MO area

Alternate Contact

Public Affairs
AmerenCIPS
607 East Adams Street, C1301
Springfield, IL 62739
Note: for nonprofits in the Springfield, IL area

Description

EIN: 436022693
Organization Type: Corporate Foundation
Giving Locations: IL: Peoria, Springfield; MO: St. Louis the company's local district offices.
Grant Types: Award, Capital, Conference/Seminar, Emergency, Employee Matching Gifts, General Support, Multiyear/Continuing Support, Project, Scholarship.
Note: Employee matching gift ratio: 1 to 1 between $10 and $500 annually per employee, for accredited colleges and universities only.

Financial Summary

Total Giving: $2,442,972 (2002); $2,548,344 (2001); $2,652,280 (2000)
Giving Analysis: Giving for 2000 includes: foundation grants to United Way ($965,500); foundation ($1,686,780); 1999: nonmonetary support ($28,881); foundation matching gifts ($54,631); foundation scholarships ($270,000); corporate direct giving ($631,000); foundation grants to United Way ($1,040,500); foundation ($2,054,241); 1998: nonmonetary support ($96,312); corporate direct giving ($582,257); foundation ($2,168,830);
Assets: $8,150,143 (2002); $10,281,558 (2001); $12,010,665 (2000)
Gifts Received: $5,000,000 (2000). Note: Contributions are received from Ameren Corp.

Typical Recipients

Arts & Humanities: Arts Associations & Councils, Arts Centers, Arts Festivals, Arts Funds, Arts Institutes, Community Arts, Dance, Arts & Humanities-General, Historic Preservation, History & Archaeology, Libraries, Museums/Galleries, Music, Opera, Performing Arts, Public Broadcasting, Theater, Visual Arts

Civic & Public Affairs: African American Affairs, Botanical Gardens/Parks, Chambers of Commerce, Economic Development, Civic & Public Affairs-General, Housing, Safety, Urban & Community Affairs, Zoos/Aquariums

Education: Arts/Humanities Education, Business Education, Colleges & Universities, Community & Junior Colleges, Economic Education, Education Funds, Education Reform, Elementary Education (Private), Engineering/Technological Education, Education-General, Minority Education, Private Education (Precollege), Public Education (Precollege), Science/Mathematics Education, Secondary Education (Private), Student Aid, Vocational & Technical Education

Environment: Forestry, Environment-General

Health: AIDS/HIV, Children's Health/Hospitals, Clinics/Medical Centers, Emergency/Ambulance Services, Health Funds, Health Organizations, Multiple Sclerosis

Religion: Dioceses, Jewish Causes, Ministries, Religious Organizations, Religious Welfare
Science: Scientific Centers & Institutes
Social Services: Child Welfare, Community Centers, Community Service Organizations, Counseling, Delinquency & Criminal Rehabilitation, Domestic Violence, Emergency Relief, Family Services, Food/Clothing Distribution, Homes, People with Disabilities, Recreation & Athletics, Scouts, Senior Services, Shelters/Homelessness, United Funds/United Ways, Volunteer Services, YMCA/YWCA/YMHA/YWHA, Youth Organizations

Application Procedures

Initial Contact: Send a letter or proposal on organization's letterhead.
Application Requirements: Include an explanation of project for which funds are requested, along with projected outcomes, statement of organization's mission and how project fits organization's purpose; current status of fundraising for project and end goal; organization's current board-approved operating budget, and audited financial statements; specific amount requested; proof of tax-exempt status; and roster of organization's governing board and staff.
Deadlines: None.
Review Process: Proposals reviewed by contributions committee. Requests for contributions exceeding $10,000 are reviewed and approved by the contributions committee of the Ameren board of directors; contributions of less than $10,000 are awarded directly by the AmerenUE or AmerenCIPS.
Evaluative Criteria: Determining factors include the location of organization in area in which company operates; conformity to company's priorities; overall benefit to community; qualifications, including management experience, of individuals who administer program; total level of support sought by organization throughout community and prospects for obtaining that support; Ameren's current operating situation and priorities relative to overall amount available for contributions.
Decision Notification: Two to three months after biannual meeting.
Notes: Outside the Saint Louis, MO; Springfield, IL; and Peoria, IL areas, request should be sent to AmerenUE, AmerenCIPS, or AmerenCILCO local district offices.

Restrictions

Does not support individuals; political, fraternal, veterans', religious organizations; or social or similar groups.
The company never contributes electric or natural gas service.

Additional Information

Ameren was formed at the end of 1997 as the result of the merger of Union Electric Co. and Central Illinois Public Service Co.
Grantees must submit reports indicating project results.
Items of salvage from company stock are sometimes donated to nonprofit organizations, including utility poles, office furnishings, and other surplus items. Organizations receiving such material must arrange pickup. Same general policies and procedures prevail as with monetary contributions. monetary contributions. monetary contributions. monetary contributions.
Publications: Community Report; Giving Guidelines; Annual Report
Trust(s): Bank of America, NA

Corporate Officials

Susan M. Bell: senior supervisor-corporate communicationslic Policy PRIM CORP EMPL senior supervisor-corporate communications: Ameren Corp.
J. Kay Smith: vice president, Corp. Communications/Public Policy

Foundation Officials

Susan M. Bell: senior supervisor-corporate communications (see above)

Grants Analysis

Disclosure Period: calendar year ending 2001
Total Grants: $1,447,362*
Number of Grants: 96
Average Grant: $15,077
Highest Grant: $135,000
Typical Range: $5,000 to $25,000
*Note: Giving excludes matching gifts; scholarships; United Way.

Recent Grants

Note: Grants derived from 2001 Form 990.

General
845,000	United Way, St. Louis, MO
136,000	Scholarship Foundation of St. Louis, St. Louis, MO
135,000	Scholarship Foundation of St. Louis, St. Louis, MO
125,000	Abraham Lincoln Presidential Library and Museum Foundation, Springfield, IL
114,300	Downtown Now
100,000	University of Illinois, Springfield, IL
100,000	Washington University, St. Louis, MO
100,000	Webster University, St. Louis, MO
85,000	St. Louis Symphony Fund, St. Louis, MO
72,000	Arts and Education Fund of St. Louis, St. Louis, MO

AMERICAN FIDELITY ASSURANCE CO.

Company Headquarters
2000 N. Classen Blvd., Ste 226A
Oklahoma City, OK 73106
Web: http://www.afadvantage.com

Company Description
Employees: 1,100

American Fidelity Corp. Founders Fund

Giving Contact
Joella Ramsey, Secretary
2000 Classen Center
PO Box 25523
Oklahoma City, OK 73125
Phone: (405)523-5008
Fax: (405)523-5421

Description
EIN: 731236059
Organization Type: Corporate Foundation
Giving Locations: OK
Grant Types: General Support.

Financial Summary
Total Giving: $233,977 (2001); $223,385 (2000); $254,080 (1999). Note: Contributes through corporate direct giving program and foundation.
Giving Analysis: Giving for 2000 includes: foundation grants to United Way ($70,000); foundation ($153,385); 1999: foundation grants to United Way ($70,000); foundation ($184,080) 1998: foundation (approx $250,000)
Assets: $4,171,933 (2001); $4,540,413 (2000); $4,783,704 (1999)
Gifts Received: $5,722 (1994); $200,000 (1993); $85,607 (1992). Note: In fiscal 1994, contributions were received from Lenice B. Cameron 1980 Trust

for William M. Cameron; Lenice B. Cameron 1980 Trust for Lynda L. Cameron; C. W. Cameron 1980 Trust for William M. Cameron; C. W. Cameron 1980 Trust for Lynda L. Cameron ($907 each); and Jo Carol Cameron 1980 Trust for William M. Cameron and Jo Carol Cameron 1980 Trust for Lynda L. Cameron ($1,047 each).

Typical Recipients

Arts & Humanities: Arts Associations & Councils, Arts Festivals, Arts Funds, Arts Institutes, Arts Outreach, Ballet, Historic Preservation, History & Archaeology, Libraries, Museums/Galleries, Music, Performing Arts, Public Broadcasting, Theater
Civic & Public Affairs: Botanical Gardens/Parks, Clubs, Community Foundations, Economic Development, Civic & Public Affairs-General, Housing, Municipalities/Towns, Native American Affairs, Nonprofit Management, Public Policy, Urban & Community Affairs, Women's Affairs, Zoos/Aquariums
Education: Business Education, Colleges & Universities, Community & Junior Colleges, Economic Education, Education Funds, Faculty Development, Education-General, Education-General, Literacy, Private Education (Precollege), Public Education (Precollege), Science/Mathematics Education, Social Sciences Education
Environment: Environment-General, Resource Conservation
Health: AIDS/HIV, Arthritis, Cancer, Children's Health/Hospitals, Clinics/Medical Centers, Emergency/Ambulance Services, Health Organizations, Heart, Hospitals, Hospitals (University Affiliated), Medical Rehabilitation, Prenatal Health Issues, Single-Disease Health Associations
International: International Development, International Relief Efforts
Religion: Churches, Ministries, Religious Organizations, Religious Welfare
Science: Science Museums, Scientific Centers & Institutes
Social Services: Big Brother/Big Sister, Child Abuse, Child Welfare, Community Service Organizations, Emergency Relief, Family Services, Food/Clothing Distribution, People with Disabilities, Recreation & Athletics, Scouts, Social Services-General, Substance Abuse, United Funds/United Ways, YMCA/YWCA/YMHA/YWHA, Youth Organizations

Application Procedures
Initial Contact: Submit a letter requesting application form.

Restrictions
The foundation does not support organizations that are not classified as 501(c)(3) tax-exempt by the IRS. No donations are made for propaganda or political purposes, or to any organization that discriminates on the basis of race, color, national origin, sex, or physical disability.

Corporate Officials
Brett Browman: assistant vice president PRIM CORP EMPL assistant vice president: American Fidelity Corp.
William E. Durrett: senior chairman B 1930. ED University of Oklahoma. PRIM CORP EMPL senior chairman: American Fidelity Corp. CORP AFFIL director: OGE Energy Corp.
John Rex: president B 1933. PRIM CORP EMPL president: American Fidelity Corp. CORP AFFIL president, chief operating officer: American Fidelity Assurance Co.; president: American Fidelity Securities.

Foundation Officials
Brett Browman: member (see above)
Joe Carroll Cambrom: member
Laura Cambrom: member
William M. Cambrom: chairman
William E. Durrett: president (see above)

JoElla Ramsey: secretary
John Rex: treasurer (see above)

Grants Analysis

Disclosure Period: calendar year ending 2001
Total Grants: $163,977*
Number of Grants: 123
Average Grant: $1,333
Highest Grant: $70,000
Lowest Grant: $25
Typical Range: $250 to $5,000
***Note:** Giving excludes United Way.

Recent Grants

Note: Grants derived from 2001 Form 990.

General

70,000	United Way, Oklahoma City, OK
18,100	Westminister Presbyterian Church, Oklahoma City, OK
14,400	Allied Arts Foundation, Oklahoma City, OK
10,100	Oklahoma City Public School Foundation, Oklahoma City, OK
8,000	Casady School, Oklahoma City, OK
7,350	Oklahoma City Art Museum, Oklahoma City, OK
7,300	Ballet Oklahoma, Oklahoma City, OK
7,100	Ballet Oklahoma, Oklahoma City, OK
5,555	Last Frontier Council - Boy Scouts of America, Oklahoma City, OK
5,250	Possibilities, Oklahoma City, OK

AMERICAN GENERAL FINANCE

Company Headquarters

Evansville, IN
Web: http://www.agfinance.com

Company Description

Former Name: Credithrift Financial.
Employees: 6,500
SIC(s): 6141 Personal Credit Institutions, 6411 Insurance Agents, Brokers & Service.

Operating Locations

American General Finance (AZ--Tucson; CA--Van Nuys; KY--Dawson Springs, Providence; MT--Bozeman; NJ--Brick, Millville, Pleasantville; PA--Thorndale; TN--Dickson, Tullahoma; WY--Casper)
Note: Operates offices in 42 states.

Nonmonetary Support

Volunteer Programs: The company's Community Spirit Awards program recognizes employees who demonstrate outstanding volunteer service. Award recipients designate $2,500 grants to the organizations they serve.

American General Finance Foundation

Giving Contact

Michelle Dixon, Community Relations Coordinator
American General Finance Corp.
601 NW Second St.
Evansville, IN 47708
Phone: (812)468-5854
Fax: (812)468-5682
Web: http://www.agc.com/agfg2000/agfgweb.nsf

Alternate Contact

PO Box 59
Evansville, IN 47701-0059

Note: Inquiries regarding scholarships should be directed to the University of Southern Indiana, Vice President for Student Affairs.

Description

Founded: 1958
EIN: 356042566
Organization Type: Corporate Foundation
Giving Locations: IN: Evansville including tri-state area
Grant Types: General Support, Matching, Scholarship.
Note: Employee matching gift ratio: 2:1 for employee gifts to institutions of higher education and public broadcasting under the auspices of a university or college; 1:1 for employee gifts to United Way.

Donor Information

Founder: American General Finance, Inc., and subsidiaries

Financial Summary

Total Giving: $370,605 (2000); $356,999 (1999); $317,909 (1998). Note: Contributes through foundation only.
Giving Analysis: Giving for 2000 includes: foundation scholarships ($42,000); 1999: foundation matching gifts ($34,673); foundation scholarships ($47,000); foundation ($122,866); foundation grants to United Way ($152,460); 1998: foundation matching gifts ($15,283); foundation scholarships ($46,000); foundation ($117,524); foundation grants to United Way ($139,102);
Assets: $93,062 (2000); $63,120 (1999); $119,080 (1998)
Gifts Received: $400,000 (2000); $300,000 (1999); $239,000 (1998). Note: In 2000, 1999 and 1998, contributions were received from American General Finance, Inc. and its subsidiaries.

Typical Recipients

Arts & Humanities: Arts Associations & Councils, Dance, Historic Preservation, Libraries, Museums/ Galleries, Music, Public Broadcasting, Theater
Civic & Public Affairs: Botanical Gardens/Parks, Business/Free Enterprise, Clubs, Community Foundations, Economic Development, Civic & Public Affairs-General, Housing, Municipalities/Towns, Parades/Festivals, Safety, Urban & Community Affairs
Education: Agricultural Education, Business Education, Colleges & Universities, Education Funds, Education-General, Literacy, Private Education (Precollege), Public Education (Precollege), Secondary Education (Public), Student Aid
Health: AIDS/HIV, Alzheimers Disease, Arthritis, Cancer, Children's Health/Hospitals, Children's Health/Hospitals, Diabetes, Emergency/Ambulance Services, Heart, Hospices, Hospitals, Medical Rehabilitation, Medical Research, Mental Health, Prenatal Health Issues, Single-Disease Health Associations
Religion: Religious Organizations, Religious Welfare
Science: Science-General, Science Museums
Social Services: Big Brother/Big Sister, Community Service Organizations, Day Care, Domestic Violence, Emergency Relief, Family Services, Food/Clothing Distribution, People with Disabilities, Recreation & Athletics, Scouts, Senior Services, Shelters/Homelessness, Special Olympics, Substance Abuse, United Funds/United Ways, Volunteer Services, YMCA/YWCA/YMHA/YWHA, Youth Organizations

Application Procedures

Initial Contact: Proposals for grants should be made in writing; request application form for scholarships.
Application Requirements: Grant proposals should include the name of the person making the request; a description of organization, including objectives, activities, accomplishments, and geographic scope; purpose of funds sought; amount requested; current budget; list of the names and business or professional affiliations of the organization's officers and board of

directors or trustees; proof of tax-exempt status; and contact name, address, and telephone number for the organization. support continue to be consistent with its exempt status as established in the determination letter; current audited financial statement; other community organizations providing similar service/project/ activity; amount of funds requested; and the name(s) and qualifications of person(s) administering funds support continue to be consistent with its exempt status as established in the determination letter; current audited financial statement; other community organizations providing similar service/project/activity; amount of funds requested; and the name(s) and qualifications of person(s) administering funds
Deadlines: March 1 for scholarships; None for grant proposals.
Review Process: Committee of senior management personnel reviews proposals each quarter, and notifies potential grantees of their decision.

Restrictions

Grants are not made to organizations without 501(c)(3) status; United Way agencies; veterans, labor, religious, political, fraternal, or external athletic groups, except when such groups provided needed benefits or services to the community at large; national organizations; private foundations; individuals; hospitals, unless it is a teaching institution; and international organizations.

Corporate Officials

Frederick Wallace Geissinger: president, vice chairman, chief executive officer B Huntington, PA 1945. ED Dartmouth College AB (1967); University of Chicago MBA (1969). PRIM CORP EMPL president, chief executive officer: American General Finance Inc. ADD CORP EMPL president, chief executive officer: American General Consumer Lending. NONPR AFFIL member: Real Estate Board New York; member: Urban Land Institute. CLUB AFFIL member: Pelham Country Club.

Foundation Officials

Frederick Wallace Geissinger: president (see above)

Grants Analysis

Disclosure Period: calendar year ending 2000
Total Grants: $134,229*
Number of Grants: 23
Average Grant: $5,836
Highest Grant: $21,500
Lowest Grant: $100
Typical Range: $1,000 to $15,500
***Note:** Giving excludes matching gifts; scholarship; and United Way.

Recent Grants

Note: Grants derived from 2000 Form 990.

General

21,500	Evansville Museum of Arts and Science, Evansville, IN
15,500	Evansville Vanderburgh Schools, Evansville, IN
15,000	WNIN Southwest Indiana Public Broadcasting, Evansville, IN
11,000	Evansville Philharmonic Orchestra, Evansville, IN
10,000	American Red Cross, Evansville, IN
5,000	Boys and Girls Club of Evansville, Evansville, IN
5,000	Center City Corp, Evansville, IN
3,250	WNIN Southwest Indiana Public Broadcasting, Evansville, IN
2,500	Arts Council of Southwest Indiana, Evansville, IN
2,500	Big Brothers and Big Sisters, Evansville, IN

AMERICAN HONDA MOTOR COMPANY, INC.

Company Headquarters

1919 Torrance Boulevard
Torrance, CA 90501-2746
Phone: (310)783-2000
Fax: (310)783-2110
Web: http://www.honda.com

Company Description

Employees: 13,774
SIC(s): 3711 Motor Vehicles & Car Bodies, 3714 Motor Vehicle Parts & Accessories, 3751 Motorcycles, Bicycles & Parts, 5012 Automobiles & Other Motor Vehicles.
Parent Company: Honda Motor Co. Ltd., 1-1, 2-chome, Minami-Aoyama, Minato-ku, Tokyo, Japan

Operating Locations

American Honda Finance Corp. (CA--San Ramon, Torrance; GA--Roswell; MA--Longmeadow); American Honda Mid-Atlantic (VA--Richmond); American Honda Motor Co. (CA--Stockton, Torrance; GA--Alpharetta; IA--Davenport; MI--Ann Arbor; OH--Troy; OR--Portland); American Honda Motor Co., Inc. (CA--Richmond); Calhac, Inc. (CA--Anaheim); Celina Aluminum Precision Tech (OH--Celina); Honda of America Manufacturing (OH--Marysville); Honda of America Manufacturing Inc. (OH--East Liberty); Honda Lock (OH--Marysville); Honda Lock American (AL--Selma); Honda North America (CA--Torrance); Honda North America Inc. (CA--Torrance; DC--Washington; MI--Detroit); Honda Power Equipment Manufacturing (NC--Swepsonville); Honda Power Products (ID--Idaho Falls); Honda R&D North America (CA--Torrance); Honda Trading America Corp. (CA--Torrance); Honda Transmissions of America (OH--Russells Point); Indiana Precision Technology (IN--Greenfield); KTH Parts Industries Inc. (OH--St. Paris).

Nonmonetary Support

Volunteer Programs: The company has a commitment to participate actively in community service and encourages employees to play an active role in the community.

American Honda Foundation

Giving Contact

Kathryn Carey, Foundation Manager
American Honda Foundation
1919 Torrance Boulevard
Torrance, CA 90501
Phone: (310)781-4090
Fax: (310)781-4270
Web: http://hondacorporate.com/community/index.html?subsection=foundation

Alternate Contact

Corporate Community Relations Division
American Honda Motor Co.
1919 Torrance Boulevard
Torrance, CA 90501
Phone: (310)783-2000

Description

EIN: 953924667
Organization Type: Corporate Foundation
Giving Locations: nationally.
Grant Types: Challenge, Fellowship, General Support, Matching, Multiyear/Continuing Support, Operating Expenses, Project, Scholarship, Seed Money.

Financial Summary

Total Giving: $1,486,436 (fiscal year ending March 31, 2001); $938,418 (fiscal 2000); $748,905 (fiscal 1999). Note: Contributes through corporate direct giving program and foundation.
Giving Analysis: Giving for fiscal 2001 includes: foundation scholarships ($20,000); foundation ($1,466,436); fiscal 2000: foundation ($938,418); fiscal 1999: foundation ($748,905)
Assets: $28,942,715 (fiscal 2001); $33,082,381 (fiscal 2000); $28,906,994 (fiscal 1999)
Gifts Received: $1,000,000 (fiscal 2001); $1,366,293 (fiscal 2000); $1,000,000 (fiscal 1999). Note: Foundation receives contributions from American Honda Motor Co., Inc.

Typical Recipients

Arts & Humanities: Libraries, Museums/Galleries, Public Broadcasting
Civic & Public Affairs: Employment/Job Training, Public Policy, Zoos/Aquariums
Education: Colleges & Universities, Economic Education, Education Reform, Elementary Education (Private), Elementary Education (Public), Engineering/Technological Education, Environmental Education, Education-General, Gifted & Talented Programs, Health & Physical Education, Leadership Training, Literacy, Minority Education, Preschool Education, Private Education (Precollege), Public Education (Precollege), Science/Mathematics Education, Secondary Education (Public), Student Aid
Environment: Environment-General, Resource Conservation, Wildlife Protection
International: International Organizations
Science: Science Museums, Scientific Centers & Institutes
Social Services: Community Service Organizations, Delinquency & Criminal Rehabilitation, Food/Clothing Distribution

Application Procedures

Initial Contact: Request application form, then send full proposal.
Application Requirements: Include statement of organization's purpose; description of program for which grant is requested; proof of tax-exempt status; copy of most recent Form 990; list of board of directors and a resolution from the board that authorizes request; copy of organization's current budget with comparisons to previous budget and with significant changes reconciled; two most recently audited financial statements; list of current contributions with amounts for each; three- to five-year plan for organization; proposed budget utilizing the grant funds requested with line item detail; and supporting materials.
Deadlines: Applications must be received by November 1 for grants awarded February 1, February 1 for grants awarded May 1, May 1 for grants awarded August 1, and August 1 for grants awarded November 1.
Review Process: In the first month of the quarter, grants are evaluated and approximately 10% of proposals continue in the review process; in the second month, a site visit is conducted; board of directors meets at the end of each quarter to make final decisions on proposals.
Evaluative Criteria: Board looks for proposals that are imaginative, creative, youthful, scientific, humanistic, innovative, and forward thinking; also considered in funding are programs that are: national in scope, broad, soundly managed, financially sound and have a high potential for success, a low degree of duplication of effort, an urgency of need (not merely financial), and a minimal risk for venture capital investment.
Decision Notification: Those applications that do not pass the first review will be notified immediately of the disposition of their proposals. Proposals that go through a full board review will receive notification of the board's decision after the appropriate board meeting in January, April, July, or October.

Notes: Grant applications can be requested in writing at above address. Mark the request Attn: Grant Application Request, and include a self-addressed, stamped envelope. For direct corporate contributions, send a letter of inquiry to Community Relations Department at American Honda Motor Co. No application form is required.

Restrictions

The foundation does not support individuals; for-profit organizations; small, local, community and/or regional projects; scholarships; loans for small businesses; advocacy; foreign exchange programs; sponsorships, conferences, or seminars; veterans or fraternal organizations; labor groups; service club activities; propaganda statements; arts and culture; health, social, or welfare issues; research papers; medical and/or educational research; disaster relief; annual fund drives; corporate memberships; trips or tours; direct support of churches, religious groups, or sectarian organizations; attempts to influence legislation; advertising in charitable publications; hospital operating funds; private foundations; beauty or talent contests; groups serving special interests of their constituencies; marathon-type fundraising; political organizations, programs, campaigns, or candidates; dinners or special events; or organizations outside the United States. Also does not make grants considered to be in the company's self-interest. Organizations should not submit an application more than once in a 12-month period; repeat requests are not considered in the same year. In addition, the foundation does not make gifts or donations of any Honda products for any purpose.

Additional Information

In 1993, company announced a ten-year, $40 million commitment to establish a special alternative secondary school and teacher development center--Eagle Rock School and Professional Development Center, in Estes Park, CO. This school operates independently of the foundation.
Also, Honda of America Manufacturing Co., a subsidiary of American Honda Motor Co., gives through the Honda of America Foundation.
Publications: Policy Statement; Grant Application Form; Guidelines; Newsletter

Corporate Officials

Koichi Amemiya: president, chief executive officer, director B 1941. PRIM CORP EMPL president, chief executive officer, director: American Honda Motor Co., Inc. ADD CORP EMPL president: Honda North America Inc.; president: Honda Trading America Corp. CORP AFFIL president: Honda North America.

Foundation Officials

Kathryn Ann Carey: foundation manager B Los Angeles, CA 1949. ED California State University BA (1971). NONPR AFFIL member: Public Relations Society America; member: Southern California Association Philanthropy; member: Ninety-Nines; member: Ocicats International; member: Humane Society U.S.; member: Los Angeles Society Prevention Cruelty Animals; member: Elsa Wild Animal Appeal; member: Greenpeace; member: American Quarter Horse Association; member: Council Foundations; member: Aircraft Owners & Pilots Association; member: American Humane Association; director: Advocates Nursing Home Reform; president: Affinity Group Japanese Philanthropy. CLUB AFFIL mem: Advertising Los Angeles Club.
Donna Hammond: senior program officer
John Petas: vice president, director
Tom Ross: secretary, treasurer

Grants Analysis

Disclosure Period: fiscal year ending March 31, 2001
Total Grants: $1,466,436*
Number of Grants: 33

Average Grant: $44,437
Highest Grant: $73,339
Lowest Grant: $11,250
Typical Range: $20,000 to $50,000
*Note: Giving excludes scholarships.

Recent Grants

Note: Grants derived from 2001 Form 990.

Library-Related

50,000	Los Angeles County Public Library Foundation, Los Angeles, CA -- Homework Help Center

General

75,000	University of Alabama at Birmingham, Birmingham, AL -- Alabama Hands-on Activity Science Program
73,339	Lee County School District, Opelika, AL -- Extended Day Program
70,065	McWane Center, Birmingham, AL -- science4 adventure road show
65,000	College of Santa Fe, Santa Fe, NM -- mobile science project
63,778	Santa Barbara Museum of Natural History, Santa Barbara, CA -- Los Marineros Program
57,900	Clemson University, Clemson, SC -- series II science and math the go kits
54,370	Show-Me Science Center, Columbia, MO -- funding to purchase new existing kits
52,530	Mercer University, Macon, GA -- Mercer Message
50,000	Chad School, Newark, NJ -- Chad Science Academy
50,000	Children's Museum, Denver, CO -- Earth Balloon Program

AMERICAN OPTICAL CORP.

Company Headquarters
Greenwich, CT

Company Description
Employees: 2,000
SIC(s): 2200 Textile Mill Products, 3000 Rubber & Miscellaneous Plastics Products, 3800 Instruments & Related Products, 5000 Wholesale Trade--Durable Goods.

Operating Locations
American Optical Corp. (MA--Southbridge)

American Optical Foundation

Giving Contact
Gary Bridgeman, Director
PO Box 1, Tax Dept.
Southbridge, MA 01550
Phone: (508)765-9711

Description
EIN: 046028058
Organization Type: Corporate Foundation
Giving Locations: MA
Grant Types: Employee Matching Gifts, General Support, Scholarship.

Financial Summary
Total Giving: $58,782 (2001); $129,121 (2000); $75,525 (1999)
Giving Analysis: Giving for 2001 includes: foundation grants to United Way ($2,000); foundation scholarships ($52,441); 2000: foundation scholarships ($44,681); 1998: foundation scholarships ($36,427) foundation ($57,925)
Assets: $1,607,142 (2001); $1,802,722 (2000); $1,909,900 (1999)
Gifts Received: $18,316 (1995); $25,000 (1994); $26,895 (1993). Note: In 1995, contributions were received from the G. B. Wells Foundation.

Typical Recipients
Arts & Humanities: Arts Centers, Historic Preservation, History & Archaeology, Libraries, Music, Theater
Civic & Public Affairs: Employment/Job Training, Civic & Public Affairs-General, Municipalities/Towns
Education: Colleges & Universities, Community & Junior Colleges, Economic Education, Education Funds, Engineering/Technological Education, Faculty Development, Education-General, International Exchange, Legal Education, Preschool Education, Private Education (Precollege), Public Education (Precollege), Science/Mathematics Education, Secondary Education (Public), Student Aid
Health: Children's Health/Hospitals, Health Organizations, Prenatal Health Issues
International: Health Care/Hospitals
Religion: Religious Welfare
Social Services: Camps, Scouts, Youth Organizations

Application Procedures
Initial Contact: Send a formal letter of application, two letters of recommendation, transcripts, SAT scores, and an essay on career objective.
Deadlines: April 25.

Restrictions
Loans and scholarships are for children of American Optical employees only.

Corporate Officials
Maurice Cunnisse: chairman, president chief financial officer, director PRIM CORP EMPL chairman, president: Am Optical Corp.
John W. Van Dyke: senior vice president, chief financial officer, director B New York, NY 1942. ED Drexel University; Princeton University (1965). PRIM CORP EMPL senior vice president, chief financial officer, director: American Optical Corp. CORP AFFIL senior vice president, chief financial officer, director: Radiac Abrasives; senior vice president, chief financial officer, director: M & R Industries. NONPR AFFIL member: Financial Executives Institute.

Foundation Officials
Steven J. Beckett: trustee B 1946. PRIM CORP EMPL treasurer: American Optical Corp.
Gary Bridgeman: director
Ernest A. Duquette: trustee
Allen Skott: director

Grants Analysis
Disclosure Period: calendar year ending 2001
Total Grants: $4,341*
Number of Grants: 9
Highest Grant: $2,666
Lowest Grant: $10
*Note: Giving excludes scholarships and United Way.

Recent Grants
Note: Grants derived from 2000 Form 990.

Library-Related

34,000	Jacob Edwards Library -- educational

General

27,500	Old Sturbridge Village, Sturbridge, MA -- educational
15,000	Fordham University, New York, NY -- educational
4,500	Heidelberg College, Tiffin, OH -- educational
3,000	Boston College, New York, NY -- educational
3,000	Catholic University of America, Washington, DC -- educational
3,000	Clarkson University, Potsdam, NY -- educational
3,000	Murray State College, Tishomingo, OK -- educational
3,000	Suny College of Fredonia -- educational
2,000	Round Hill Nursery School, Greenwich, CT -- educational
1,500	Clarkson University, Potsdam, NY -- educational

AMERICAN STANDARD INC.

Company Headquarters
1 Centennial Ave.
Piscataway, NJ 08855-6820
Web: http://www.americanstandard.com

Company Description
Ticker: ASD
Exchange: OTC
Revenue: US$7.795 billion (2002)
Profit: US$371 million (2002)
Employees: 38,000
Fortune Rank: 238, per FORTUNE Magazine's list of 500 Largest U.S. Corporations (2002).
SIC(s): 3261 Vitreous Plumbing Fixtures, 3431 Metal Sanitary Ware, 3432 Plumbing Fixtures Fittings & Trim, 3585 Refrigeration & Heating Equipment.

Operating Locations
American Standard Inc. (IL--Skokie; KY--Paintsville; NV--Las Vegas; NJ--Piscataway, Trenton; NC--Greensboro; OH--Tiffin; VA--Arlington); American Standard Medical Systems (NY--New York); Societe Trane (WI--Golbey Cedex); Trane Co. (TX--Tyler; WI--La Crosse); Worldwide Applied Systems (WI--La Crosse)

American Standard Foundation

Giving Contact
G. Peter D'Aloia, President
American Standard Foundation
One Centennial Avenue
Piscataway, NJ 08855-6820
Phone: (732)980-6000
Fax: (732)980-6121

Description
EIN: 256018911
Organization Type: Corporate Foundation
Giving Locations: headquarters and operating communities.
Grant Types: Employee Matching Gifts, General Support, Scholarship.

Financial Summary
Total Giving: $2,297,132 (2001); $1,728,220 (2000); $1,926,011 (1999). Note: Contributes through foundation only.
Giving Analysis: Giving for 2001 includes: foundation scholarships ($51,420); foundation matching gifts ($506,415); foundation ($657,504); foundation grants to United Way ($1,081,793); 2000: foundation ($283,861); foundation matching gifts ($481,696); foundation grants to United Way ($962,663); 1999: foundation matching gifts ($483,060);
Assets: $5,786,941 (2001); $9,249,462 (2000); $11,889,937 (1999)
Gifts Received: $22,999 (1999). Note: In 1999, contributions were received from American Standard Inc.

Typical Recipients

Arts & Humanities: Arts Associations & Councils, Dance, Libraries, Museums/Galleries
Civic & Public Affairs: Business/Free Enterprise, Clubs, Community Foundations, Economic Policy, Employment/Job Training, Civic & Public Affairs-General, Housing, Law & Justice, Legal Aid, Professional & Trade Associations
Education: Agricultural Education, Business Education, Colleges & Universities, Education Funds, Education Reform, Environmental Education, Education-General, International Exchange, Private Education (Precollege), Public Education (Precollege), Religious Education, Secondary Education (Private), Secondary Education (Public), Student Aid, Vocational & Technical Education
Health: Emergency/Ambulance Services, Heart, Single-Disease Health Associations
International: Foreign Educational Institutions, International Affairs, International Development, International Relations
Religion: Religious Organizations, Religious Welfare
Science: Scientific Centers & Institutes
Social Services: Community Service Organizations, Social Services-General, United Funds/United Ways, YMCA/YWCA/YMHA/YWHA

Application Procedures

Initial Contact: Send a brief letter.
Application Requirements: Include purpose, history, and scope of organization; amount requested; purpose for which funds are sought; recently audited financial statement; and proof of tax-exempt status.
Deadlines: None.

Corporate Officials

Fred A. Allardyce: senior vice president chairman, chief financial officerl B Rahway, NJ 1941. ED Yale University BA (1963); University of Chicago Graduate School of Business Administration MBA (1965). PRIM CORP EMPL senior vice president, chairman, chief financial officer: American Standard Inc. ADD CORP EMPL senior vice president: Diasorin Inc.
Adrian B. Deshotel: vice president human resources PRIM CORP EMPL vice president human resources: American Standard Companies Inc.
Horst Hinrichs: vice chairman, director B 1933. ED University of Stuttgart (1958). PRIM CORP EMPL vice chairman, director: American Standard Inc.
Richard A. Kalaher: vice president, secretary, general counsel B Milwaukee, WI 1940. ED Union College AB (1962); Northwestern University JD (1965). PRIM CORP EMPL vice president, secretary, general counsel: American Standard Inc. NONPR AFFIL chairman, legal officer: Conference Board; member: International Bar Association; member: American Bar Association; member: Association Bar City NYK.

Foundation Officials

Fred A. Allardyce: director (see above)
Adrian B. Deshotel: secretary, treasurer (see above)
Richard A. Kalaher: president (see above)

Grants Analysis

Disclosure Period: calendar year ending 2001
Total Grants: $657,504*
Number of Grants: 24
Average Grant: $27,396
Highest Grant: $100,000
Lowest Grant: $1,000
Typical Range: $5,000 to $50,000
*Note: Giving excludes matching gifts, scholarships, and United Way.

Recent Grants

Note: Grants derived from 2001 Form 990.

General
730,311	United Way, Ft. Smith, AR
247,500	United Way, Ft. Smith, AR
100,000	ASA Education Foundation, Inc., Chicago, IL
100,000	Best Friends Foundation, Washington, DC
83,333	American Red Cross
83,333	Salvation Army
83,333	United Way 911 Fund, New York, NY
71,468	American Red Cross
51,420	National Merit Scholarship Corporation, Evanston, IL
39,071	American Standard, Inc., Piscataway, NJ

AMERICAN UNITED LIFE INSURANCE CO.

Company Headquarters
Indianapolis, IN
Web: http://www.aul.com

Company Description
Employees: 880
SIC(s): 6311 Life Insurance.

Operating Locations
American United Life Insurance Co. (CA--Concord, Fresno, Irvine; CO--Denver; FL--St. Petersburg, Tampa; GA--Athens, Atlanta, Decatur; IL--Champaign, Libertyville; IN--Bloomington, Evansville, Lafayette, Muncie, Richmond, Valparaiso; KS--Lawrence, Overland Park, Shawnee Mission, Topeka; KY--Covington; MD--Joppa Heights; MI--Bingham Farms, Grand Blanc, Tawas City, Warren; MN--Mountain Lake; MO--Malden, St. Louis; NJ--Mine Hill, Princeton; NC--Charlotte; OH--Columbus, Dayton; PA--Middletown; SD--Kadoka; TX--Dallas, Houston, New Braunfels; VA--Vinton; WA--Bellevue; WI--Brookfield)

Nonmonetary Support
Value: $5,000 (1998)
Note: Co. currently sponsors a United Way Day of Caring for employees that volunteer.

AUL Foundation Inc.

Giving Contact
James W. Freeman, Chairman, Committee
One American Square
PO Box 368
Indianapolis, IN 46206-0368
Phone: (317)285-1609
Fax: (317)285-1979

Alternate Contact
Phone: (317)285-1489

Description
EIN: 311146437
Organization Type: Corporate Foundation
Giving Locations: IN: headquarters and operating communities.
Grant Types: Capital, Employee Matching Gifts, Endowment, General Support, Operating Expenses.
Note: Matching gifts for higher education only.

Financial Summary
Total Giving: $1,944,000 (2000); $1,936,000 (1999); $2,077,000 (1998). Note: Contributes through corporate direct giving program and foundation.
Giving Analysis: Giving for 2000 includes: foundation ($793,180); corporate direct giving ($1,150,800); 1999: foundation ($810,666); corporate direct giving ($1,125,334); 1998: nonmonetary support ($5,000); foundation ($758,000); corporate direct giving ($1,314,000);
Assets: $5,939,710 (2000); $5,890,321 (1999); $6,222,000 (1998)

Gifts Received: $444,500 (2000); $497,000 (1999); $370,500 (1997). Note: The foundation receives contributions from American United Life Insurance Company.

Typical Recipients
Arts & Humanities: Arts Associations & Councils, Arts Centers, Ethnic & Folk Arts, Historic Preservation, Libraries, Museums/Galleries, Music, Opera, Performing Arts, Public Broadcasting, Theater, Visual Arts
Civic & Public Affairs: Business/Free Enterprise, Economic Development, Employment/Job Training, Civic & Public Affairs-General, Legal Aid, Professional & Trade Associations, Public Policy, Urban & Community Affairs, Zoos/Aquariums
Education: Business Education, Colleges & Universities, Economic Education, Education Funds, Education Reform, Faculty Development, Education-General, Leadership Training, Legal Education, Medical Education, Minority Education, Private Education (Precollege), Student Aid
Health: AIDS/HIV, Cancer, Health Organizations, Hospitals, Medical Rehabilitation, Medical Research, Medical Training, Mental Health, Nursing Services, Public Health, Single-Disease Health Associations
International: Health Care/Hospitals
Religion: Jewish Causes, Seminaries
Social Services: Animal Protection, Child Welfare, Community Centers, Community Service Organizations, Counseling, Day Care, Delinquency & Criminal Rehabilitation, Domestic Violence, Emergency Relief, Family Services, Food/Clothing Distribution, People with Disabilities, Recreation & Athletics, Scouts, Senior Services, Shelters/Homelessness, Special Olympics, Substance Abuse, United Funds/United Ways, Veterans, Volunteer Services, YMCA/YWCA/YMHA/YWHA, Youth Organizations

Application Procedures
Initial Contact: Submit a written request.
Application Requirements: Include description and purpose of the organization, amount requested, purpose of funds sought, recently audited financial statement, other sources of funding, and proof of tax-exempt status.
Deadlines: By the first of each month.
Evaluative Criteria: Based on how request impacts Indianapolis area; requesting organization is generally accepted and respected and provides a needed service to a wide segment of population.

Restrictions
Does not support individuals, religious organizations for sectarian purposes, service clubs, youth groups, organizations with many similar counterparts, or political or lobbying groups. With the exception of college matching gifts, most contributionss limited to indiana. Generally does not support tax-supported organizations.

Additional Information
Company donates at least 2% of its pre-tax income to support charitable organizations.
Publications: Guidelines

Corporate Officials
Jim Freeman: vice president, chairman corporate contributions committee PRIM CORP EMPL vice president, chairman corporate contributions committee: American United Life Insurance Co.
R. Stephen Radcliffe: executive vice president B Winamac, IN 1945. ED Michigan State University BSc (1967); University of Michigan MA (1968). PRIM CORP EMPL executive vice president: American United Life Insurance Co.
Jerry D. Semler: chairman, president, chief executive officer, director B Indianapolis, IN 1937. ED Purdue University BS (1958). PRIM CORP EMPL chairman, president, chief executive officer, director: American United Life Insurance Co. CORP AFFIL chairman,

chief executive officer: State Life Insurance Co.; director: IWC Resources Corp.; director: LIMRA International. NONPR AFFIL director: American Council Life Insurance.

Foundation Officials

Judy Boyle: secretary

James Thomas Morris: director B Terre Haute, IN 1943. ED Indiana University AB (1965); Butler University MBA (1970). CORP AFFIL director: Paul Harris Stores Inc.; director: NiSource Inc.

William R. Riggs: director B Evansville, IN. CORP AFFIL director: American United Life Insurance Co.

Jerry D. Semler: chairman, director (see above)

Grants Analysis

Disclosure Period: calendar year ending 2000
Total Grants: $1,944,000*
Number of Grants: 210*
Average Grant: $9,257
Highest Grant: $150,000
Lowest Grant: $3,000
Typical Range: $1,000 to $50,000
*Note: Grants analysis provided by foundation. Number of grants exclude matching grants.

Recent Grants

Note: Grants derived from 2000 Form 990.

General

150,000	Indiana Sports Corporation, Indianapolis, IN -- NCAA project
150,000	Purdue Foundation, West Lafayette, IN -- endowment
100,000	Educational Choice Charitable Trust, Indianapolis, IN -- support Building Community of Hope Campaign
50,000	Indiana University Foundation, Indianapolis, IN -- school of medicine
25,000	Educational Choice Charitable Trust, Indianapolis, IN -- operating
25,000	Marin College, Indianapolis, IN -- capital campaign
25,000	Young Women's Christian Association, Indianapolis, IN -- for Child and Youth Development Program
21,000	Independent Colleges of Indiana Foundation, Indianapolis, IN -- operating fund
20,000	Christel House, Inc, Indianapolis, IN -- operating fund
20,000	Pleasant Run Children's Home, Indianapolis, IN -- capital campaign

AMERITAS LIFE INSURANCE CORP.

Company Headquarters

Lincoln, NE
Phone: 800-745-6665
Web: http://www.ameritas.com

Company Description

Employees: 800
SIC(s): 6311 Life Insurance, 6321 Accident & Health Insurance, 6324 Hospital & Medical Service Plans.

Ameritas Charitable Foundation

Giving Contact

Scott Stuckey, Assistant Vice President of Corporate Communications
PO Box 81889
Lincoln, NE 68501
Phone: (402)467-1122
Fax: (402)467-7939

Alternate Contact

Lawrence J. Arth
Ameritas Charitable Foundation
5900 "O" Street
Lincoln, NE 68510
Phone: (402)467-7706

Description

Founded: 1985
EIN: 363428705
Organization Type: Corporate Foundation
Giving Locations: NE: Lincoln
Grant Types: Capital, General Support, Multiyear/Continuing Support, Professorship, Project, Research.

Donor Information

Founder: Ameritas Life Insurance Corp.

Financial Summary

Total Giving: $427,425 (2001); $426,975 (2000); $319,125 (1999)
Giving Analysis: Giving for 2001 includes: foundation grants to United Way ($225); foundation scholarships ($10,000); foundation ($417,200); 2000: foundation grants to United Way ($225); foundation ($426,750); 1999: foundation grants to United Way ($225); foundation ($318,900);
Assets: $7,179,188 (2001); $7,692,662 (2000); $7,186,975 (1999)
Gifts Received: $101,167 (2001); $405,966 (2000); $212,534 (1999). Note: Contributions are received from Ameritas Life Insurance Corp.

Typical Recipients

Arts & Humanities: Arts Associations & Councils, Ballet, Dance, Ethnic & Folk Arts, History & Archaeology, Libraries, Museums/Galleries, Music, Performing Arts, Public Broadcasting, Theater
Civic & Public Affairs: Clubs, Community Foundations, Economic Development, Economic Policy, Employment/Job Training, Civic & Public Affairs-General, Housing, Parades/Festivals, Philanthropic Organizations, Professional & Trade Associations, Urban & Community Affairs, Women's Affairs
Education: Business Education, Colleges & Universities, Continuing Education, Economic Education, Education Funds, Faculty Development, Education-General, Health & Physical Education, Leadership Training, Medical Education, Minority Education, Private Education (Precollege), Public Education (Precollege), Religious Education, Science/Mathematics Education, Secondary Education (Private), Special Education, Student Aid
Environment: Environment-General, Resource Conservation
Health: AIDS/HIV, Children's Health/Hospitals, Clinics/Medical Centers, Emergency/Ambulance Services, Health Organizations, Hospitals, Medical Research, Multiple Sclerosis, Public Health, Research/Studies Institutes, Single-Disease Health Associations, Transplant Networks/Donor Banks
Religion: Religious Organizations, Religious Welfare
Science: Scientific Centers & Institutes
Social Services: Animal Protection, At-Risk Youth, Big Brother/Big Sister, Child Welfare, Community Service Organizations, Family Services, Food/Clothing Distribution, Homes, People with Disabilities, Recreation & Athletics, Recreation & Athletics, Scouts, Senior Services, Social Services-General, Special Olympics, Substance Abuse, United Funds/United Ways, YMCA/YWCA/YMHA/YWHA, Youth Organizations

Application Procedures

Initial Contact: Send a written application.
Application Requirements: Include agency name, principal address, phone number, and names of the board of directors and officers; agency purpose; current financial statement, including an analysis of support, revenue, and expenses; balance sheet and statement of changes in retained earnings/fund balances; proposed budget, including sources of funds and analysis of expenses; the organization's tax status; and amount requested and intended use.
Deadlines: None.
Evaluative Criteria: Preference is given to local charitable organizations. Funding requests for the support of hospitals, athletic activities, religious associations, and public activities will be closely reviewed.
Notes: Additional information may be requested as necessary.

Restrictions

Does not support individuals, religious organizations for sectarian purposes, political or lobbying groups, or organizations that require a major portion of budget for administration and solicitation.

Corporate Officials

Kenneth C. Louis: president, chief operating officer, director chief financial officer B Pittsburgh, PA 1938. ED Pennsylvania State University (1961). PRIM CORP EMPL president, chief operating officer, director: Ameritas Life Insurance Corp. CORP AFFIL director: Pathmark Assurance Co.; director: Veritas Corp.; director: Lincoln Gateway Shopping Center Inc.; executive vice president, director: Ameritas Variable Life Insurance Co.; director: First Ameritas Life Insurance Corp. New York; senior vice president, director: Ameritas Investment Corp.; director: Ameritas Managed Dental Plan Inc.; vice president, director: AMAI Corp.; director: Ameritas Investment Advisors Inc.

JoAnn M. Martin: senior vice president, partner, chief financial officer B Plainview, NE 1954. ED University of Nebraska (1975); Colorado State University (1982). PRIM CORP EMPL senior vice president, partner, chief financial officer: Ameritas Life Insurance Corp. ADD CORP EMPL senior vice president, chief financial officer, corporate treasurer: Ameritas Acacia Mutual Holding Co.; chief financial officer, director: Ameritas Managed Dental Plan. CORP AFFIL director, controller: Lincoln Gateway Shopping Center Inc.; compt, director: Pathmark Assurance Co.; comptroller, director: Ameritas Variable Life Insurance Co.; vice president, controller: First Ameritas Life Insurance Corp.; director: Acacia National Life; comptroller: Ameritas Marketing Group. NONPR AFFIL member: American Institute CPAs; fellow, member: Life Management Institute.

Foundation Officials

JoAnn M. Martin: controller (see above)

Grants Analysis

Disclosure Period: calendar year ending 2001
Total Grants: $417,200*
Number of Grants: 65
Average Grant: $4,956*
Highest Grant: $100,000
Lowest Grant: $250
Typical Range: $1,000 to $25,000
*Note: Giving excludes United Way and scholarships. Average grant figure excludes highest grant.

Recent Grants

Note: Grants derived from 2001 Form 990.

General

100,000	University of Nebraska Foundation, Lincoln, NE
30,000	Lincoln Children's Museum, Lincoln, NE
25,000	Boy Scouts of America, Lincoln, NE
22,000	Nebraska Wesleyan University, Lincoln, NE
20,000	Madonna Foundation, Lincoln, NE
20,000	YMCA Lincoln, Lincoln, NE
13,400	Lincoln Public Schools Foundation, Lincoln, NE
10,000	Aksarben Scholarship Fund, Omaha, NE
10,000	American Red Cross Disaster Relief Fund, Washington, DC

10,000   Friendship Home, Lincoln, NE

AMERUS GROUP CO.

Company Headquarters

611 5th Ave.
Des Moines, IA 50309
Web: http://www.amerus.com

Company Description

Founded: 1996
Ticker: AMH
Exchange: NYSE
Former Name: American Mutual Life Insurance Co., Central Companies.
Assets: US$20.293 billion (2002)
Employees: 1415 (2002)
SIC(s): 6311 Life Insurance.

Nonmonetary Support

Type: Donated Equipment; In-kind Services; Loaned Employees; Loaned Executives
Note: Co. provides nonmonetary support.

AmerUs Group Charitable Foundation

Giving Contact

Jonna LaToure, Assistant Director
AmerUs Group Charitable Foundation
699 Walnut Street, 20th Fl.
Des Moines, IA 50309
Phone: (515)557-3910
Fax: (515)283-3269
Web: http://www.amerus.com/about/community.html

Description

EIN: 421431745
Organization Type: Corporate Foundation
Giving Locations: IA
Grant Types: Employee Matching Gifts, General Support.
Note: Employee matching gifts have a $500 maximum.

Financial Summary

Total Giving: $629,181 (2002); $577,895 (2001); $467,760 (2000). Note: Contributes through corporate direct giving program only.
Giving Analysis: Giving for 2001 includes: foundation grants to United Way ($225,956)
Assets: $6,571,849 (2001)

Typical Recipients

Arts & Humanities: Arts Associations & Councils, Arts Centers, Arts Festivals, Arts Funds, Community Arts, Arts & Humanities-General, Libraries, Music, Opera, Performing Arts
Civic & Public Affairs: Business/Free Enterprise, Economic Development, Civic & Public Affairs-General, Housing, Urban & Community Affairs, Women's Affairs
Education: Business-School Partnerships, Colleges & Universities, Community & Junior Colleges, Education-General, Public Education (Precollege), Science/Mathematics Education
Environment: Air/Water Quality, Environment-General
Health: Health-General, Hospices
Science: Scientific Centers & Institutes
Social Services: Animal Protection, Child Welfare, Community Centers, Community Service Organizations, Counseling, Day Care, Emergency Relief, Family Services, Food/Clothing Distribution, Homes, Shelters/Homelessness, Social Services-General,

Substance Abuse, United Funds/United Ways, Volunteer Services, YMCA/YWCA/YMHA/YWHA, Youth Organizations

Application Procedures

Initial Contact: See website for guidelines and application form.
Application Requirements: Include itemized budget reflecting current and anticipated funds (this should include sources of income, contributions received to date, any fundraising expenses, and other expected expenses; recently audited financial statement; proof of tax-exempt status; list of other funding sources approached for support; background information on the sponsoring organization, goals, geographic scope, number of paid employees, total salary expense, and size of volunteer involvement); names and affiliations of officers and board of directors; and amount requested.
Deadlines: March 31 and June 30.
Review Process: Board meetings are generally held three or four times annually.
Notes: Grantees are required to submit annual reports.

Restrictions

Does not support athletes or athletic groups; conference or seminar attendance; courtesy advertising; endowments; fellowships; festival participation; fraternal organizations; hospitals or health care facilities; individuals; individual K-8 schools; organizations, projects, or programs outside the U.S. or whose activities are mainly international; organizations redistributing funds to separate, independent tax-exempt groups (except United Way and independent college funds); political parties, campaigns or candidates, partisan political organizations; private foundations; sectarian, religious, and denominational organizations; social organizations; trade, industry, and professional associations; United Way organizations seeking funds for operating expenses of United Way-funded programs; veterans groups.

Additional Information

Program areas and priorities are United Way, Education, Health and Human Services, Arts and Culture, Civic and Community Programs, and Children At Risk. Company reports that it underwent a merger and a name change in January 1995. Formerly Central Companies, it was known as the American Mutual Life Insurance Company, now known as the AmerUS Group.
Publications: Annual Report

Corporate Officials

Roger Kay Brooks: chairman, director B Clarion, IA 1937. ED University of Iowa BA (1959). PRIM CORP EMPL chairman: AmerUS Group. CORP AFFIL chairman: Amer US Savings Bank; chairman: Central Life Assurance Co. NONPR AFFIL member: Phi Beta Kappa; fellow: Society Actuaries; member: Greater Des Moines Chamber of Commerce; member: Iowa Insurance Hall Fame. CLUB AFFIL Actuaries Des Moines Club; Des Moines Club.
Tom Godlasky: executive vice president, chief investment officer B Tyrone, PA 1955. ED Indiana University of Pennsylvania (1977); University of Pittsburgh (1979). PRIM CORP EMPL executive vice president, chief investment officer: AmerUS Life Holdings Inc.
Sam Charles Kalainov: chairman, president, chief executive officer B Steele, ND 1930. ED North Dakota State University BS (1956); American College Life Underwriters (1966). PRIM CORP EMPL chairman, president, chief executive officer: AmerUS Group. CORP AFFIL director: Bankers Trust Co.; director: Des Moines International Airport; director: AmerUS Life Insurance Co.; chairman: American Mutual Holding Corp.; officer: AmerUS Life Holdings Inc. NONPR AFFIL member: Greater Des Moines Chamber of

Commerce; member: National Association Life Underwriters; trustee: Drake University; member: American Legion; chairman: Corporate International Trade; director: American Council Life Insurance. CLUB AFFIL Rotary Club.
Gary McPhail: president emeritus PRIM CORP EMPL president emeritus: AmerUS Group.
Michael E. Sproule: chief financial officer, director PRIM CORP EMPL chief financial officer, director: Central Life Assurance Co.

Giving Program Officials

Ted W. Wheat: PRIM CORP EMPL director committee relations: AmerUS Group.

Grants Analysis

Disclosure Period: calendar year ending 2001
Total Grants: $351,939*
Number of Grants: 73
Average Grant: $4,821
Highest Grant: $35,000
Lowest Grant: $26
Typical Range: $1,000 to $10,000
***Note:** Giving excludes United Way.

Recent Grants

Note: Grants derived from 2001 Form 990.

Library-Related
1,500   Public Library of Des Moines Foundation, Des Moines, IA

General
215,541   United Way of Central Iowa, Des Moines, IA
35,000   Des Moines Business Education Alliance, Des Moines, IA
25,000   Des Moines Art Center, Des Moines, IA
22,500   Civic Center of Greater Des Moines, Des Moines, IA
21,000   Des Moines Art Festival, Des Moines, IA
20,448   Gifted and Talented Education, Des Moines, IA
15,000   Des Moines Symphony Association, Des Moines, IA
15,000   Iowa College Foundation, Des Moines, IA
15,000   YMCA, Des Moines, IA
13,000   Center for Gifted and Talented Development, Iowa City, IA

AMETEK, INC.

Company Headquarters

Paoli, PA
Web: http://www.ametek.com

Company Description

Founded: 1930
Ticker: AME
Exchange: NYSE
Revenue: US$1.04 billion (2002)
Employees: 7700 (2002)
SIC(s): 3316 Cold-Finishing of Steel Shapes, 3621 Motors & Generators, 3823 Process Control Instruments, 3829 Measuring & Controlling Devices Nec.

Operating Locations

AMETEK Dixson (CO--Grand Junction); AMETEK, Inc. (CA--Costa Mesa; CT--Wallingford; DE--Wilmington; FL--Largo; IL--West Chicago; OH--Kent; PA--Eighty-Four, Feasterville, Horsham, Nesquehoning, Pittsburgh, Sellersville; WA--Redmond); AMETEK Process & Analytical Instruments (DE--Newarkship); AMETEK Rotron Industrial Products (NY--Saugerties); AMETEK Rotron Mil-Aero Products (NY--Woodstock); AMETEK Sensor Technology (MI--Clawson); AMETEK Test & Calibration Instruments (NY--Kew Gardens)

AMETEK Foundation

Giving Contact
Kathryn E. Londra, Secretary, Treasurer
AMETEK Foundation
37 North Valley Road, Bldg. 4
PO Box 1764
Paoli, PA 19301-0801
Phone: (610)647-2121

Description
Founded: 1960
EIN: 136095939
Organization Type: Corporate Foundation
Giving Locations: headquarters and operating communities; nationally.
Grant Types: General Support, Research.

Financial Summary
Total Giving: $1,087,655 (2001); $984,155 (2000); $659,793 (1999). Note: Contributes through foundation only.
Giving Analysis: Giving for 2001 includes: foundation scholarships ($34,750); foundation grants to United Way ($161,103); foundation ($891,802); 2000: foundation grants to United Way ($148,962); foundation ($835,193); 1999: foundation grants to United Way ($167,849); foundation ($491,944);
Assets: $7,623,478 (2001); $7,801,846 (2000); $7,154,137 (1999)
Gifts Received: $650,100 (1996); $650,000 (1995); $650,000 (1994). Note: The foundation receives contributions from AMETEK, Inc.

Typical Recipients
Arts & Humanities: Arts Centers, Arts Funds, Ballet, Dance, Ethnic & Folk Arts, Arts & Humanities-General, Historic Preservation, History & Archaeology, Libraries, Museums/Galleries, Music
Civic & Public Affairs: Botanical Gardens/Parks, Civic & Public Affairs-General, Housing, Municipalities/Towns, Professional & Trade Associations, Safety, Urban & Community Affairs, Women's Affairs, Zoos/Aquariums
Education: Business Education, Colleges & Universities, Community & Junior Colleges, Education Associations, Education Funds, Elementary Education (Private), Engineering/Technological Education, Education-General, International Exchange, Legal Education, Literacy, Medical Education, Private Education (Precollege), Public Education (Precollege), Science/Mathematics Education, Secondary Education (Public), Student Aid, Vocational & Technical Education
Environment: Environment-General, Resource Conservation
Health: Cancer, Clinics/Medical Centers, Diabetes, Emergency/Ambulance Services, Health Funds, Health Organizations, Hospitals, Medical Rehabilitation, Medical Research, Mental Health, Preventive Medicine/Wellness Organizations, Public Health, Single-Disease Health Associations
International: International Affairs
Religion: Jewish Causes, Ministries
Science: Science Museums, Scientific Centers & Institutes
Social Services: At-Risk Youth, Child Welfare, Community Service Organizations, Family Services, Food/Clothing Distribution, Homes, People with Disabilities, Scouts, Senior Services, Shelters/Homelessness, Social Services-General, United Funds/United Ways, YMCA/YWCA/YMHA/YWHA, Youth Organizations

Application Procedures
Initial Contact: Submit brief letter or proposal.
Application Requirements: Submit a description of organization, amount requested, purpose of funds sought, recently audited financial statement, and proof of tax-exempt status.
Deadlines: None.

Restrictions
The foundation does not support political or lobbying groups.

Corporate Officials
Frank S. Hermance: chairman, chief executive officer, director B December 29, 1948. ED Rochester Institute Technology BSEE (1971); Rochester Institute Technology MSEE (1973). PRIM CORP EMPL president, chief executive officer, director: AMETEK, Inc.

Foundation Officials
Helmut N. Friedlaender: director CORP AFFIL director: Ametek Inc.
Frank S. Hermance: president, director (see above)

Grants Analysis
Disclosure Period: calendar year ending 2001
Total Grants: $891,802*
Number of Grants: 71
Average Grant: $10,984*
Highest Grant: $122,941
Lowest Grant: $1,000
Typical Range: $5,000 to $25,000
*Note: Giving excludes United Way and scholarships. Average grant figure excludes highest grant.

Recent Grants
Note: Grants derived from 2001 Form 990.

Library-Related

50,000	Free Library of Philadelphia, Philadelphia, PA
15,000	Alamance Public Library, Burlington, NC
15,000	Gibsonville Public Library, Gibsonville, NC
10,000	Free Library of Philadelphia, Philadelphia, PA
7,500	Alamance County Public Library, Burlington, NC
5,000	Free Library of Philadelphia, Philadelphia, PA -- Summer Reading Program

General

122,941	Binghamton School District, Binghamton, NY
74,635	United Way Southeastern Pennsylvania, Philadelphia, PA
50,000	New Visions for Public Schools, New York, NY -- Neighborhood Literacy Program
30,000	Binghamton Community Resource Center, Binghamton, NY
29,750	National Merit Scholarship Corporation, Evanston, IL
27,500	Paoli Memorial Hospital Foundation, Paoli, PA
25,891	United Way Portage County, Stevens Point, WI
25,000	Central Park Conservancy, New York, NY
25,000	Cornell Cooperative Extension, Binghamton, NY
25,000	Eagles Youth Partnership, Philadelphia, PA

AMGEN, INC.

Company Headquarters
Houston, TX
Web: http://www.amgen.com

Company Description
Ticker: AMGN
Exchange: AMEX
Revenue: US$5.523 billion (2002)
Employees: 4,594 (1999)

Fortune Rank: 305, per FORTUNE Magazine's list of 500 Largest U.S. Corporations (2002).
SIC(s): 5122 Drugs, Proprietaries & Sundries.

Operating Locations
Amgen, Inc. (CA--Newbury Park; CO--Boulder, Longmont; DC--Washington; KY--Louisville; PR--Juncos)

Nonmonetary Support
Type: Donated Equipment; Donated Products
Volunteer Programs: The Amgen Staff Community Involvement Program (SCIP) makes the services of Amgen staff available to nonprofit organizations or needy individuals for community improvement.

Amgen Foundation

Giving Contact
Elizabeth Malkerson, President and Chief Executive Officer
The Amgen Foundation
One Amgen Center Drive
Thousand Oaks, CA 91320-1799
Phone: (805)447-1000
Web: http://www.amgen.com/community/

Description
EIN: 770252898
Organization Type: Corporate Foundation
Giving Locations: headquarters; nationally.
Grant Types: Employee Matching Gifts, General Support.
Note: Employee matching gift ratio: 1 to 1 from $50 to $20,000.

Financial Summary
Total Giving: $2,487,697 (2000); $3,878,374 (1999); $1,532,237 (1998). Note: Contributes through corporate direct giving program and foundation.
Giving Analysis: Giving for 2000 includes: foundation gifts to individuals ($100,000); foundation matching gifts ($1,101,435); foundation ($1,286,262); 1999: foundation matching gifts ($832,911); foundation ($3,045,463) 1998: foundation ($1,532,237)
Assets: $28,808,710 (2000); $5,572,676 (1999); $4,878,296 (1998)
Gifts Received: $25,500,000 (2000); $4,400,000 (1999); $6,303,500 (1998). Note: Contributions are received from Amgen, Inc.

Typical Recipients
Arts & Humanities: Arts Associations & Councils, Arts & Humanities-General, Historic Preservation, History & Archaeology, Libraries, Museums/Galleries, Music
Civic & Public Affairs: Asian American Affairs, Botanical Gardens/Parks, Community Foundations, Gay/Lesbian Issues, Civic & Public Affairs-General, Hispanic Affairs, Housing, Parades/Festivals, Public Policy, Zoos/Aquariums
Education: Business Education, Colleges & Universities, Economic Education, Education Funds, Education Reform, Elementary Education (Private), Engineering/Technological Education, Education-General, Literacy, Medical Education, Private Education (Precollege), Public Education (Precollege), Science/Mathematics Education, Secondary Education (Public), Student Aid, Vocational & Technical Education
Environment: Air/Water Quality, Air/Water Quality, Environment-General, Resource Conservation
Health: AIDS/HIV, Alzheimers Disease, Cancer, Children's Health/Hospitals, Clinics/Medical Centers, Emergency/Ambulance Services, Health Organizations, Heart, Hospices, Hospitals, Medical Research, Preventive Medicine/Wellness Organizations, Public Health, Single-Disease Health Associations
International: Health Care/Hospitals, International Environmental Issues, International Relief Efforts
Religion: Jewish Causes, Religious Welfare

Science: Science Museums, Scientific Centers & Institutes

Social Services: At-Risk Youth, Child Abuse, Child Welfare, Community Service Organizations, Day Care, Family Services, Homes, People with Disabilities, Recreation & Athletics, Scouts, Scouts, Senior Services, Shelters/Homelessness, Social Services-General, United Funds/United Ways, YMCA/YWCA/YMHA/YWHA, Youth Organizations

Application Procedures

Initial Contact: Send a one- to two-page written request.

Application Requirements: The foundation recommends that applicants provide organizational information, a description of the grant request, and documentation. Organization information should include name and address or organization; contact person's name, title, and telephone number; background of the organization; and the target population and geographic area served by the organization. Grant information should include purpose of funds sought and amount requested; project description, including objectives, target population, needs to be addressed, planned activities, staff qualifications and timetable; and allocation of funds requested and percentage of funds spent on administrative expenses. Documentation should include proof of tax-exempt status; current list of corporate funders and amounts of grants; organization's brochure (if available); and current financial statement and budget report.

Deadlines: None; requests for grants must be received at least 90 days prior to desired distribution date.

Review Process: Both the foundation committee and the corporate contribution committee meet quarterly to evaluate proposals.

Notes: All requests should be submitted to the Foundation. If the request is not appropriate for the Foundation, the request will be forwarded to the appropriate corporate contribution committee.

Restrictions

Does not support alumni drives or teacher organizations; construction or building improvements; capital campaigns; city/municipal/federal government departments; endowments and foundations; individuals or scholarships; charitable dinners or sporting events; labor unions; municipal or for-profit hospitals; religious, political, fraternal, service or veterans organizations; professional sports events or athletes; civic organizations that do not serve the areas in which Amgen is located.

Additional Information

Company has established a series of programs that provide its products, including Epogen and Neupogen, to medically needy patients with no insurance or with limited financial resources.

Company's commitment to education extends beyond basic science and the local community to include users of its products. Company also provides educational programs and tools to assist the medical community to better understand its products.

Company also sponsors an annual Teacher Excellence Award.

Company also sponsors an annual Teacher Excellence Award.

Corporate Officials

Kathryn E. Falberg: senior vice president finance, chief financial officer ED University of California, Los Angeles MBA (1981). PRIM CORP EMPL senior vice president finance, chief financial officer: Amgen, Inc.

Kevin W. Sharer: president, chief executive officer ED United States Naval Academy BS (1970); University of Pittsburgh MBA (1982). PRIM CORP EMPL president, chief executive officer: Amgen Inc.

Grants Analysis

Disclosure Period: calendar year ending 2000
Total Grants: $1,286,262*
Number of Grants: 253
Average Grant: $3,517*
Highest Grant: $400,000
Typical Range: $100 to $3,000
*Note: Giving excludes matching gifts and grants to individuals. Average grant figure excludes highest grant.

Recent Grants

Note: Grants derived from 2000 Form 990.

General

400,000	University of Washington, Seattle, WA
50,000	National History Museum of Los Angeles County Foundation, Los Angeles, CA
42,272	National Merit Scholarship Corporation, Evanston, IL
32,294	Fondos Unidos de Puerto Rico, San Juan, PR
25,000	Alliance for Arts, New York, NY
25,000	American Medical Association Foundation
25,000	Chabad of the Conejo Jewish Academy
25,000	Los Angeles Philharmonic Association, Los Angeles, CA
25,000	Mary Health of the Sick, Newbury Park, CA
25,000	Music Center of Los Angeles, Los Angeles, CA

AMP, INC.

Company Headquarters

Harrisburg, PA
Web: http://www.amp.com

Company Description

Employees: 40,000
SIC(s): 3423 Hand & Edge Tools Nec, 3629 Electrical Industrial Apparatus Nec, 3643 Current-Carrying Wiring Devices, 3678 Electronic Connectors.
Parent Company: Tyco International Ltd., 1 Tyco Park, Exeter, NH, United States

Operating Locations

AMP Inc. (CA--Palo Alto; IL--Itasca; IN--Carmel; MI--Comstock Park, Troy; NC--Charlotte, Greensboro, Lowell, Winston-Salem; OR--Sherwood; PA--East Berlin, Jacobus, Loganville, Manheim, Selinsgrove, Seven Valleys, Shrewsbury, Tower City, Williamstown; VA--Harrisonburg, Mount Sidney; AMP Packaging & Carroll Touch Systems Division (TX--Round Rock); M/A-Com Division (MA--Lowell); Madison Cable Corp. (MA--Worcester); Precision Interconnect Division (OR--Portland)

Nonmonetary Support

Type: Donated Equipment; Donated Products
Volunteer Programs: After employees complete 100 hours of volunteer services in a calendar year with a nonprofit organization, the Dollars for Doers program will authorize a $250 contribution from the Foundation to that organization. This is a yearly maximum of $2,000 to one eligible organization.
Note: Nonmonetary support is provided by the company.

Tyco Electronics Foundation

Giving Contact

Mary Rakoczy, Jr., Administrator
Tyco Electronics Corp.
MS 140-10
PO Box 3608, M/S 176-42
Harrisburg, PA 17105-3608

Phone: (717)592-4869
Fax: (717)592-3043
E-mail: mjrakocz@tycoelectronics.com
Web: http://www.tycoelectronics.com/about/foundation

Description

EIN: 232022928
Organization Type: Corporate Foundation
Former Name: AMP Foundation (2002).
Giving Locations: NC: Triad; PA: central Pennsylvania; VA headquarters and operating communities.
Grant Types: Employee Matching Gifts, Multiyear/Continuing Support.
Note: Employee matching gift ratio: 2 to 1 for education, for the first $100 of employee gift, then 1 to 1 up to maximum of $5,000. Employee education matching gift program contributes to accredited secondary schools, colleges and universities.

Financial Summary

Total Giving: $1,200,000 (2002 approx); $1,150,937 (2001); $1,182,596 (2000)
Giving Analysis: Giving for 2000 includes: foundation grants to United Way ($258,922); foundation ($923,674); 1999: foundation grants to United Way ($476,264); foundation ($1,132,808); 1998: foundation grants to United Way ($373,515); foundation ($1,284,842);
Assets: $17,120,000 (2002); $18,490,755 (2001); $20,143,787 (2000)

Typical Recipients

Arts & Humanities: Arts Associations & Councils, Arts Centers, Arts Funds, Ballet, Arts & Humanities-General, Libraries, Museums/Galleries, Music, Opera, Performing Arts, Public Broadcasting, Theater
Civic & Public Affairs: African American Affairs, Business/Free Enterprise, Civil Rights, Clubs, Economic Development, Employment/Job Training, Civic & Public Affairs-General, Hispanic Affairs, Housing, Minority Business, Municipalities/Towns, Professional & Trade Associations, Safety, Urban & Community Affairs
Education: Business Education, Colleges & Universities, Community & Junior Colleges, Education Associations, Education Reform, Elementary Education (Public), Engineering/Technological Education, Environmental Education, Education-General, Literacy, Minority Education, Private Education (Precollege), Public Education (Precollege), School Volunteerism, Science/Mathematics Education, Secondary Education (Private), Vocational & Technical Education
Environment: Environment-General
Health: Cancer, Children's Health/Hospitals, Clinics/Medical Centers, Emergency/Ambulance Services, Health-General, Health Organizations, Hospices, Hospitals, Mental Health, Single-Disease Health Associations
International: International Relations
Religion: Ministries
Science: Science-General, Science Museums, Scientific Centers & Institutes
Social Services: Big Brother/Big Sister, Child Abuse, Child Welfare, Community Centers, Community Service Organizations, Crime Prevention, Family Services, Food/Clothing Distribution, People with Disabilities, Recreation & Athletics, Scouts, Shelters/Homelessness, Social Services-General, Substance Abuse, United Funds/United Ways, YMCA/YWCA/YMHA/YWHA, Youth Organizations

Application Procedures

Initial Contact: Send a brief letter or proposal.
Application Requirements: Provide a description of organization and its purposes; description of the project, including costs, proposed budget, and source of funding; list of board members; proof of IRS section 501(c)(3) status; most recent IRS Form 990.
Deadlines: None. Applications are accepted throughout the year and decisions are made on a quarterly

basis; the majority of grants are budgeted in the first quarter of the year.

Evaluative Criteria: Preference is given to organizations where Tyco Electronics employees volunteer; organizations must be 501(c)(3) non-profit, and operate within geographic areas where Tyco Electronics has employees; organizations should support Tyco's corporate objectives in education, community development, and arts and culture.

Notes: Requests for over $2,500 must answer specific questions on the foundation's application for corporate contributions.

Restrictions

Foundation does not support organizations in geographic areas where Tyco Electronics has few or no employees; individuals; private foundations; national organizations; general operating needs of United Way agencies; service clubs; social, labor, or veterans organizations; political campaigns; organizations or programs that pose a potential conflict of interest for Tyco Electronics; organizations that discriminate based on race, religion, color, nationality, age, sex, physical or mental conditions, veteran status or marital status; programs of churches or religious organizations with the exception of nondenominational programs such as food banks, youth centers or non-sectarian education programs.

Foundation may not support courtesy advertising; testimonial or fund-raising dinners, loans or investments; capital campaigns or other fund-raising of national organizations.

Additional Information

Grant recipients must submit a final report which evaluates the results of the funded program.

Grants Analysis

Disclosure Period: calendar year ending 2001
Total Grants: $668,405*
Number of Grants: 83
Average Grant: $6,283*
Highest Grant: $63,800
Lowest Grant: $250
Typical Range: $250 to $10,000
*Note: Giving excludes educational gifts in individuals and United Way. Average grant figure excludes three highest grants ($165,800).

Recent Grants

Note: Grants derived from 2001 Form 990.

General
75,000	Bay Area, San Francisco, CA
63,800	American Red Cross, Harrisburg, PA
63,800	New York Police and Fire Widows and Children's Fund, New York, NY
56,800	Capital Region, Harrisburg, PA
54,000	Council of the Great City Schools, Washington, DC
48,000	York Technical College, Rock Hill, SC
35,460	York College-York Country Day, York, PA
35,000	Allied Arts Fund, Harrisburg, PA
32,900	Surry Community College, Dobson, NC
32,300	Berks County Arts Council, Reading, PA

AMR CORP.

Company Headquarters

4333 Amon Carter Blvd.
Fort Worth, TX 76155
Web: http://www.amrcorp.com

Company Description

Ticker: AMR
Exchange: OTC
Revenue: US$17.299 billion (2002)
Employees: 92,000

Fortune Rank: 104, per FORTUNE Magazine's list of 500 Largest U.S. Corporations (2002).
SIC(s): 4512 Air Transportation--Scheduled, 6719 Holding Companies Nec.

Operating Locations

American Eagle Airlines Inc. (TX--Fort Worth); AMR Corp. (TX--Fort Worth); AMR Investment Service Inc. (TX--Fort Worth)

Nonmonetary Support

Type: Donated Products; In-kind Services
Volunteer Programs: Company reports that no formal volunteer program exists, other than a volunteer recycling program aboard flights and in offices.
Note: Sales Department provides in-kind services for nonprofits. Company also donates travel vouchers to organizations.

AMR/American Airlines Foundation

Giving Contact

Timothy J. Doke, Secretary
PO Box 619616
Mail Drop 5656
Dallas, TX 75261-9616
Phone: (817)967-3540
Web: http://www.amrcorp.com/corpinfo.htm

Description

EIN: 762086656
Organization Type: Corporate Foundation
Giving Locations: nationally and internationally.
Grant Types: General Support, Matching, Multiyear/Continuing Support, Project, Scholarship.

Financial Summary

Total Giving: $780,169 (2001); $1,265,434 (2000); $1,219,424 (1999)
Giving Analysis: Giving for 2000 includes: foundation ($1,265,434); 1999: foundation grants to United Way ($493,950); foundation ($725,474); 1998: foundation grants to United Way ($365,850); corporate grants to United Way ($481,050); corporate direct giving ($686,379); foundation ($801,579);
Assets: $1,213,126 (2001); $1,843,169 (2000); $2,940,070 (1999)
Gifts Received: $276,565 (2001); $292,098 (2000); $277,173 (1999). Note: In 2001, contributions were received from Flagship Charities. In 1999, contributions were received from Flagship Charities ($274,948) and Chicago Charities ($2,225).

Typical Recipients

Arts & Humanities: Arts Associations & Councils, Arts Centers, Community Arts, Historic Preservation, History & Archaeology, Libraries, Museums/Galleries, Music, Opera, Performing Arts, Public Broadcasting, Theater
Civic & Public Affairs: African American Affairs, Botanical Gardens/Parks, Business/Free Enterprise, Civil Rights, Clubs, Community Foundations, Employment/Job Training, Civic & Public Affairs-General, Hispanic Affairs, Law & Justice, Legal Aid, Minority Business, Municipalities/Towns, Nonprofit Management, Parades/Festivals, Philanthropic Organizations, Professional & Trade Associations, Public Policy, Safety, Urban & Community Affairs, Women's Affairs, Zoos/Aquariums
Education: Arts/Humanities Education, Business Education, Colleges & Universities, Education Reform, Education-General, Leadership Training, Medical Education, Minority Education, Private Education (Precollege), Public Education (Precollege), Religious Education, School Volunteerism, Science/Mathematics Education, Secondary Education (Public), Special Education, Student Aid
Environment: Resource Conservation

Health: AIDS/HIV, Cancer, Children's Health/Hospitals, Clinics/Medical Centers, Diabetes, Emergency/Ambulance Services, Eyes/Blindness, Health Funds, Health Organizations, Heart, Hospitals, Hospitals (University Affiliated), Kidney, Medical Research, Multiple Sclerosis, Public Health, Single-Disease Health Associations, Single-Disease Health Associations, Transplant Networks/Donor Banks
International: Foreign Educational Institutions, Human Rights, International Relations, International Relief Efforts
Religion: Churches, Jewish Causes, Religious Organizations, Religious Welfare
Science: Science Museums
Social Services: At-Risk Youth, Big Brother/Big Sister, Child Welfare, Community Service Organizations, Counseling, Crime Prevention, Emergency Relief, Family Planning, Family Services, Food/Clothing Distribution, People with Disabilities, Recreation & Athletics, Scouts, Senior Services, Shelters/Homelessness, Social Services-General, Substance Abuse, United Funds/United Ways, Volunteer Services, YMCA/YWCA/YMHA/YWHA, Youth Organizations

Application Procedures

Initial Contact: Send a brief letter or proposal.
Application Requirements: Proposals should include contact name, mailing address, phone number, and e-mail address; a description of organization, including overall structure, purpose, and objectives; a list of officers and key staff members; a list of board members and their professional affiliations; amount requested; purpose of funds sought, including objectives, project purpose, and population served; specific reasons why AMR/American Airlines would be an appropriate donor; project budget, including break-out of costs and sources of funding (both committed and expected); size and demographic information about the population to be served; project timetable; methods of evaluating project success; proof of tax-exempt status and a copy of the organization's certification as a 501(c)(3) charitable organization, or preferably the organization's 509(a)(1), (2), or (3); recently audited financial statement; primariy funding sources, including United Way; detailed description of how the Foundation's grant will be acknowledged; and any additional support materials.
Deadlines: None.
Decision Notification: Notice of a decision or request for more information is usually sent within two months of receipt of proposal.
Notes: Foundation requests that organizations contact foundation administrator only.

Restrictions

Does not contribute to the support of organizations lacking proof of 501(c)(3) tax-exempt status; endowments; annual operating support fund drives; organizations that discriminate on the basis of race, religion, sex or national origin; religious, fraternal, social or veterans' organizations; political or partisan organizations established to influence legislation or specific elections; individuals; organizations receiving support from United Way drives; basic academic or scientific research; athletic events or sponsorships; or social functions or advertising in commemorative journals, yearbooks or special event publications.

Additional Information

In 2003, the AMR/American Airlines Foundation announced that it had suspended all cash grants due to the financial crisis in the airline industry. Currently, only requests for air transportation will be considered, albeit on a limited basis. The Foundation intends to resume giving when the industry outlook improves. The American Airlines AAdvantage frequent traveler program sponsors the Miles for Kids in Need program, which provides travel assistance for children facing medical emergencies or requesting special wishes and up to two parents or guardians.

Corporate Officials

Gerard J. Arpey: president, chief executive officer ED University of Texas BBA (1980); University of Texas MBA (1982). PRIM CORP EMPL president, chief executive officer: AMR Corp.

Foundation Officials

Kathy Andersen: administrator

Grants Analysis

Disclosure Period: calendar year ending 2001
Total Grants: $600,169*
Number of Grants: 56
Average Grant: $9,094*
Highest Grant: $100,000
Lowest Grant: $100
Typical Range: $100 to $5,000 and $10,000 to $30,000
*Note: Giving excludes United Way. Average grant excludes highest grant.

Recent Grants

Note: Grants derived from 2001 Form 990.

Library-Related

20,000	Fort Worth Public Library Foundation, Ft. Worth, TX

General

130,000	United Way of Dade County, Miami, FL
100,000	Amon Carter Museum, Ft. Worth, TX
83,334	University of Oklahoma, Norman, OK
50,000	United Way Crusade of Mercy, Chicago, IL
46,250	Marrow Foundation, Washington, DC
30,000	Big Sisters of Los Angeles, Los Angeles, CA
30,000	Community Trust Fund of the VL/SLV, Van Nuys, CA
30,000	Dallas Foundation, Dallas, TX
30,000	Friends of Child Advocates, Monterey Park, CA
30,000	Pediatric and Family Medical Center, Los Angeles, CA

ANDERSEN CORP.

Company Headquarters

100 4th Ave., N
Bayport, MN 55003
Web: http://www.andersencorp.com

Company Description

Revenue: US$1.8 billion (2001)
Employees: 7000 (2001)
SIC(s): 2431 Millwork.

Operating Locations

Andersen Corp. (WI--St. Croix)

Bayport Foundation

Giving Contact

Chloette Haley, Grants Consultant
Bayport Foundation
White Pine Building
342 Fifth Avenue, North
Bayport, MN 55003-0204
Phone: (651)439-1557
Fax: (651)439-9480
E-mail: chloettehaley@scenicriver.org
Web: http://www.scenicriver.org

Alternate Contact

Phone: 888-439-9508

Description

EIN: 416020912
Organization Type: Corporate Foundation
Giving Locations: MN: East Metro area, Washington County; WI: Barron County, Burnett County, Dunn County, Pierce County, Polk County, St. Croix County
Grant Types: Capital, Emergency, General Support, Project.

Financial Summary

Total Giving: $1,900,000 (fiscal year ending November 30, 2003 approx); $2,043,050 (fiscal 2002); $2,069,535 (fiscal 2001). Note: Contributes through corporate direct giving program and foundation.
Giving Analysis: Giving for fiscal 2000 includes: foundation grants to United Way ($79,000) foundation ($2,101,175)
Assets: $38,000,000 (fiscal 2002); $42,837,830 (fiscal 2001); $44,433,993 (fiscal 2000)
Gifts Received: $250,000 (fiscal 2001); $500,000 (fiscal 2000); $70,063 (fiscal 1999). Note: Contributions were received from the Andersen Corporation.

Typical Recipients

Arts & Humanities: Arts Centers, Arts Institutes, Arts & Humanities-General, Historic Preservation, History & Archaeology, Libraries, Museums/Galleries, Music, Public Broadcasting, Theater
Civic & Public Affairs: African American Affairs, Business/Free Enterprise, Civil Rights, Clubs, Community Foundations, Economic Development, Economic Policy, Civic & Public Affairs-General, Housing, Legal Aid, Municipalities/Towns, Philanthropic Organizations, Public Policy, Safety, Urban & Community Affairs, Zoos/Aquariums
Education: Arts/Humanities Education, Colleges & Universities, Economic Education, Education Associations, Education Funds, Elementary Education (Private), Elementary Education (Public), Engineering/Technological Education, Education-General, Minority Education, Preschool Education, Private Education (Precollege), Public Education (Precollege), Religious Education, Science/Mathematics Education, Special Education, Student Aid, Vocational & Technical Education
Environment: Environment-General, Resource Conservation, Wildlife Protection
Health: Cancer, Children's Health/Hospitals, Clinics/Medical Centers, Emergency/Ambulance Services, Eyes/Blindness, Health Funds, Health Organizations, Hospitals, Kidney, Medical Rehabilitation, Medical Research, Public Health, Single-Disease Health Associations, Speech & Hearing
International: International Peace & Security Issues
Religion: Churches, Jewish Causes, Religious Organizations, Religious Welfare
Science: Science Museums
Social Services: Animal Protection, Animal Protection, At-Risk Youth, Camps, Child Welfare, Community Centers, Community Service Organizations, Emergency Relief, Family Planning, Family Services, Food/Clothing Distribution, Homes, People with Disabilities, Recreation & Athletics, Refugee Assistance, Scouts, Substance Abuse, United Funds/United Ways, Volunteer Services, YMCA/YWCA/YMHA/YWHA, Youth Organizations

Application Procedures

Initial Contact: Call the foundation to request guidelines.
Application Requirements: Submit a full written proposal.
Deadlines: None.

Foundation Officials

M. A. Carter: director
J. D. Piepel: director

Grants Analysis

Disclosure Period: fiscal year ending November 30, 2002
Total Grants: $2,043,050
Number of Grants: 151
Average Grant: $17,835
Highest Grant: $500,000
Lowest Grant: $250

Recent Grants

Note: Grants derived from fiscal 2001 Form 990.

General

250,000	Cathedral of St. Paul, St. Paul, MN -- restoration and preservation of Cathedral
125,000	Hudson Medical Center -- health campus capital campaign
100,000	Family Means, Stillwater, MN -- imagine capital campaign
75,000	National Right to Work Legal Defense Foundation, Springfield, VA -- operating support
65,000	Boy Scouts of America Indianhead Council, St. Paul, MN -- operating support
65,000	City of Bayport, Bayport, MN -- remodeling the Bayort Fire Station
65,000	Girl Scout Council of St. Croix Valley, St. Croix, MN -- operating support
65,000	St. Croix United Way, Stillwater, MN -- 2001-2002 campaign
55,000	Independent School District 834, Bayport, MN -- Partnership Plan Programs
55,000	American Red Cross St. Croix Valley Chapter, St. Croix, MN -- operating support

ANDERSEN FOUNDATION

Giving Contact

Mary Gillstrom, Assistant Secretary
Andersen Corp.
100 4th Avenue, North
Bayport, MN 55003-1096
Phone: (651)642-5150
Fax: (651)430-5537

Alternate Contact

Gregory L. Benson, Treasurer, Director
Phone: (651)439-5195
Fax: (651)439-4027

Description

Founded: 1959
EIN: 416020920
Organization Type: General Purpose Foundation
Giving Locations: MN: nationally.
Grant Types: General Support.

Donor Information

Founder: Incorporated in Minnesota in 1959 by the late Fred C. Andersen, who was a director and former president of Andersen Corporation, a producer of wood and vinyl-clad windows and door units. His wife, Katherine B. Andersen, has made several contributions to the foundation.

Financial Summary

Total Giving: $22,175,600 (2001); $21,861,450 (2000); $18,518,198 (1998)
Assets: $440,540,979 (2001); $433,740,871 (2000); $420,488,818 (1998)

Typical Recipients

Arts & Humanities: Arts Centers, Arts Funds, Arts Institutes, Historic Preservation, Libraries, Museums/Galleries, Music, Opera, Performing Arts, Public Broadcasting, Theater

Civic & Public Affairs: Botanical Gardens/Parks, Economic Development, Civic & Public Affairs-General, Minority Business, Municipalities/Towns, Professional & Trade Associations, Public Policy, Safety, Urban & Community Affairs, Zoos/Aquariums

Education: Colleges & Universities, Community & Junior Colleges, Education Funds, Elementary Education (Private), Faculty Development, Education-General, Minority Education, Private Education (Precollege), Public Education (Precollege), Religious Education, Science/Mathematics Education, Secondary Education (Public), Special Education, Student Aid

Environment: Air/Water Quality

Health: Cancer, Children's Health/Hospitals, Clinics/Medical Centers, Emergency/Ambulance Services, Eyes/Blindness, Health Funds, Health Organizations, Heart, Hospices, Hospitals, Kidney, Medical Research, Mental Health, Research/Studies Institutes, Single-Disease Health Associations

International: Foreign Educational Institutions, Health Care/Hospitals

Religion: Churches, Ministries, Religious Organizations, Religious Welfare, Seminaries

Science: Science Museums

Social Services: Animal Protection, Child Welfare, Community Centers, Community Service Organizations, Domestic Violence, Family Services, Food/Clothing Distribution, Homes, People with Disabilities, Recreation & Athletics, Scouts, Senior Services, Social Services-General, Substance Abuse, United Funds/United Ways, Volunteer Services, YWCA/YMHA/YWHA, Youth Organizations

Application Procedures

Initial Contact: The foundation has no formal application requirements or procedures. Prospective applicants should send a letter to the foundation.

Application Requirements: The letter should describe the organization and the project for which funds are sought.

Deadlines: None.

Restrictions

Grants are not given to colleges that receive federal aid.

Foundation Officials

Gregory L. Benson: director, treasurer PRIM CORP EMPL president: First State Bank of Bayport.

Keith R. Clements: president, director

Mary Gillstrom: assistant secretary

George O. Hoel: director

Alan H. Johnson: director B 1932. PRIM CORP EMPL secretary: Andersen Corp.

W. Arvid Wellman: director B 1918.

Jerold W. Wulf: director

Grants Analysis

Disclosure Period: calendar year ending 2001

Total Grants: $22,100,600*

Number of Grants: 153

Average Grant: $138,158*

Highest Grant: $1,100,000

Lowest Grant: $1,500

Typical Range: $10,000 to $200,000

*Note: Giving excludes United Way. Average grant figure excludes highest grant.

Recent Grants

Note: Grants derived from 2001 Form 990.

General

1,100,000	Hudson Medical Center
875,000	Mayo Foundation, Rochester, MN
770,000	Gillette Children's Hospital, St. Paul, MN
750,000	Courage Center, Minneapolis, MN
569,250	Girls Scout Council of St. Croix Valley, St. Paul, MN
560,000	Family Means, Stillwater, MN
450,000	Salvation Army, Bowling Green, KY
413,400	American Red Cross, Concord, NH
300,000	Hope International Family Service
260,000	Children's Home Society of Minnesota, Minneapolis, MN

HUGH J. ANDERSEN FOUNDATION

Giving Contact

Katie Wood, Grants Consultant
PO Box 204
Bayport, MN 55003-0204
Phone: (651)439-1557
Fax: (651)439-9480
E-mail: hjafdn@srinc.biz
Web: http://www.scenicriver.org
Note: Toll Free: (888)439-9508

Description

Founded: 1962

EIN: 416020914

Organization Type: Family Foundation

Giving Locations: MN: St. Paul (secondary focus), St. Croix Valley St. Croix Valley also covers WI; WI: Pierce County, Polk County, St. Croix County

Grant Types: Capital, General Support, Operating Expenses, Project.

Donor Information

Founder: The foundation was established in 1962. Although the foundation began as "a general charitable fund, its resources are now focused primarily on the geographic area surrounding Bayport, Minnesota and western Wisconsin."

Financial Summary

Total Giving: $2,076,024 (fiscal year ending February 28, 2002); $2,050,889 (fiscal 2001); $2,064,423 (fiscal 2000)

Giving Analysis: Giving for fiscal 2001 includes: foundation grants to United Way ($68,300) fiscal 2000: foundation scholarships ($108,500)

Assets: $47,771,866 (fiscal 2002); $49,467,715 (fiscal 2001); $46,731,004 (fiscal 2000)

Gifts Received: $805,566 (fiscal 1995)

Typical Recipients

Arts & Humanities: Arts Centers, Arts Institutes, Arts Outreach, Film & Video, Arts & Humanities-General, History & Archaeology, Libraries, Museums/Galleries, Performing Arts, Public Broadcasting, Theater

Civic & Public Affairs: Business/Free Enterprise, Community Foundations, Economic Development, Employment/Job Training, Hispanic Affairs, Housing, Municipalities/Towns, Native American Affairs, Nonprofit Management, Public Policy, Safety, Urban & Community Affairs, Women's Affairs

Education: Arts/Humanities Education, Colleges & Universities, Elementary Education (Private), Elementary Education (Public), Environmental Education, Faculty Development, Education-General, Health & Physical Education, Literacy, Private Education (Precollege), Public Education (Precollege), Religious Education, Science/Mathematics Education, Social Sciences Education, Special Education, Student Aid, Vocational & Technical Education

Environment: Environment-General, Wildlife Protection

Health: AIDS/HIV, Cancer, Children's Health/Hospitals, Clinics/Medical Centers, Diabetes, Emergency/Ambulance Services, Health Organizations, Hospitals, Medical Rehabilitation, Medical Research, Single-Disease Health Associations

International: International Relief Efforts, Missionary/Religious Activities

Religion: Churches, Ministries, Religious Organizations, Religious Welfare, Seminaries

Science: Science Museums

Social Services: Child Welfare, Community Service Organizations, Counseling, Day Care, Domestic Violence, Emergency Relief, Emergency Relief, Family Planning, Family Services, Food/Clothing Distribution, Homes, People with Disabilities, Recreation & Athletics, Scouts, Senior Services, Sexual Abuse, Social Services-General, Substance Abuse, United Funds/United Ways, Volunteer Services, YMCA/YWCA/YMHA/YWHA, Youth Organizations

Application Procedures

Initial Contact: Prospective applicants should contact the foundation to request guidelines, questionnaire, and a grant proposal checklist. Letters of inquiry are also welcomed by the foundation.

Application Requirements: Applicants must supply the following material: a completed questionnaire; copy of a recent Section 501(c)(3) tax determination letter; copy of the most recent IRS Form 990 or audit; copy of the organization's current budget and project budget; listing of past, current, and pending support; brief history of the organization; description of mission and programs; description of results achieved by organization; detailed project description if special funding is sought; summary of qualifications of key staff; and a list of board members and their affiliations. The materials should be unbound. Proposals should be limited to 10 pages excluding attachments.

Deadlines: The foundation reports that deadlines are March 15, June 15, September 15, and November 15.

Review Process: Grant requests are administered by Scenic River, Inc., Stillwater, MN, and all grant decisions are made by the foundation's board of directors.

Decision Notification: Applicants will be notified within four week of the deadline. Final decisions will be mailed within 2-3 weeks of board meeting.

Notes: Applications faxed will not be considered. The foundation requests that grant applicants do not send videos.

Restrictions

The foundation only responds to personalized requests, not to mass appeals or generic solicitations. The foundation stresses that it is conscious of the environment and does not want proposals to be bound or placed in folders or other casings.

The foundation reports that it does not make loans and does not provide grants or scholarships to individuals. It does not provide grants for lobbying activities, fund-raising dinners and events, or travel. The foundation does not generally consider the following types of organizations and programs for funding: agencies/divisions/councils/programs that have counterparts in St. Paul or the St. Croix Valley; athletic teams; business/economics education; child care centers; civic action groups; immigration/refugee issues and programs; independent media productions; political/voter education; private schools; and religious institutions. The foundation will not generally fund the entire budget for a project, but prefers to be part of an effort that is supported by a number of sources. Major endowment and capital requests are given a low priority.

Additional Information

The foundation accepts the Minnesota Common Grant Application Form.

Publications: Annual Report; Application Guidelines; Application Form; Grant Proposal Checklist

Foundation Officials

Christine E. Andersen: vice president CORP AFFIL director: Andersen Corp.

Sarah J. Andersen: president PRIM CORP EMPL chairman board: Andersen Corp. CORP AFFIL director: Andersen Corp.

William H. Rubenstein: secretary, treasurer

Grants Analysis

Disclosure Period: fiscal year ending February 28, 2002
Total Grants: $2,016,024*
Number of Grants: 213
Average Grant: $8,121*
Highest Grant: $100,000
Lowest Grant: $300
Typical Range: $1,000 to $20,000
***Note:** Giving excludes United Way. Average grant figure excludes four highest grants ($400,000).

Recent Grants

Note: Grants derived from fiscal 2002 Form 990.

General

100,000	Cathedral of Saint Paul, St. Paul, MN -- capital campaign for Remember Restore Rejoice
100,000	Girl Scout Council of St. Croix Valley, St. Croix, MN -- for special program expansion campaign
100,000	Minnesota Children's Museum, St. Paul, MN -- for 3 to Get Ready 4 to Grow campaign
100,000	Twin Cities Habit for Humanity, St. Paul, MN -- for Double the Homes, Double the Hope Campaign
75,000	Family Means, Stillwater, MN -- for capital campaign
65,530	Community Volunteer Service, Stillwater, MN -- for Bayport Senior Center
50,000	Girl Scout Council of St. Croix Valley, St. Croix, MN -- for Warren Township land acquisition
44,745	A Chance to Grow, Minneapolis, MN -- Boost-Up Program
40,000	West Central Wisconsin Community Action, Glenwood City, WI -- for operating support
35,000	Family Means, Stillwater, MN -- operating support

JOHN W. ANDERSON FOUNDATION

Giving Contact

William N. Vinovich, Vice Chairman
402 Wall Street
Valparaiso, IN 46383
Phone: (219)462-4611

Description

Founded: 1967
EIN: 356070695
Organization Type: General Purpose Foundation
Giving Locations: IL: funds some organizations in Northeastern Illinois; IN
Grant Types: Capital, General Support, Operating Expenses, Research.

Donor Information

Founder: Established in Indiana in 1967 with funds donated by the late John W. Anderson , an inventor and president of Anderson Company, a manufacturer of automobile accessories.

Financial Summary

Total Giving: $9,500,000 (2003 approx); $9,400,000 (2002 approx); $10,100,000 (2001 approx)
Assets: $210,000,000 (2003 approx); $210,000,000 (2002); $205,494,000 (2001 approx)

Typical Recipients

Arts & Humanities: History & Archaeology, Libraries, Opera, Public Broadcasting
Civic & Public Affairs: Community Foundations, Economic Development, Employment/Job Training, Civic & Public Affairs-General, Housing, Law & Justice, Legal Aid, Municipalities/Towns, Philanthropic Organizations, Public Policy, Urban & Community Affairs
Education: Business-School Partnerships, Colleges & Universities, Continuing Education, Economic Education, Education Associations, Education Funds, Engineering/Technological Education, Education-General, Legal Education, Medical Education, Minority Education, Preschool Education, Private Education (Precollege), Religious Education, Special Education, Student Aid, Vocational & Technical Education
Health: Cancer, Children's Health/Hospitals, Clinics/Medical Centers, Emergency/Ambulance Services, Health Organizations, Heart, Hospices, Medical Rehabilitation, Mental Health, Nursing Services, Public Health, Research/Studies Institutes, Single-Disease Health Associations
Religion: Churches, Dioceses, Religion-General, Jewish Causes, Religious Welfare
Science: Science Museums
Social Services: At-Risk Youth, Child Welfare, Community Service Organizations, Counseling, Delinquency & Criminal Rehabilitation, Emergency Relief, Family Planning, Family Services, Food/Clothing Distribution, Homes, People with Disabilities, Scouts, United Funds/United Ways, YMCA/YWCA/YMHA/YWHA, Youth Organizations

Application Procedures

Initial Contact: Submit an application.
Application Requirements: Proposals should include the organization's purpose; amount requested; planned use for the grant; list of officers and board of directors; current financial statement and budget (audit and annual report, if available); and proof of tax-exempt status.
Deadlines: None.
Review Process: Grants are awarded in February, April, June, August, October, and December. To be considered at a specific meeting, an application must be received by the 20th day of the month preceding the meeting.
Decision Notification: Applicants will be advised of the status of their requests in writing approximately two to four weeks after the meeting of the Trustees.
Notes: Applications will not be accepted by fax. Applicants should not call regarding the status of their application.

Restrictions

No grants are made to individuals, businesses, for fund raising events advertising, start-up costs, endowment funds, deficit financing, or loans. Applicants must be public charities classified as 501 (c)(3) nonprofits.

Additional Information

Recipients of grants must acknowledge receipt of grants within 30 days.
Organizations may submit an application once in a twelve-month period.
Grants are generally limited to organizations which have been in existence for at least two years, demonstrated service to their community, and received public support. Requests from outside northwest Indiana must state how program or services will benefit northwest Indiana and its residents. Indiana and its residents. Indiana and its residents. Indiana and its residents.
Publications: Brochure; Guidelines

Foundation Officials

Charles W. Conover: trustee
William L. Staehle: trustee
William N. Vinovich: vice chairman, trustee
Bruce W. Wargo: secretary, treasurer B East Chicago, IN 1938. PRIM CORP EMPL chief financial officer: Nyloncraft.
Wilfred G. Wilkins: chairman, trustee

Grants Analysis

Disclosure Period: calendar year ending 2000
Total Grants: $9,400,408*
Number of Grants: 282
Average Grant: $5,000*
Highest Grant: $1,277,112
Lowest Grant: $200
Typical Range: $2,000 to $10,000
***Note:** Grants analysis provided by foundation. Average grant figure excludes highest grants.

Recent Grants

Note: Grants derived from 2000 Form 990.

General

1,500,461	Boys and Girls Clubs of Northwest Indiana, Inc., Gary, IN
1,022,240	Boys and Girls Club of Porter County, Inc., Valparaiso, IN
500,000	Independent Colleges of Indiana Foundation, Indianapolis, IN
500,000	Lake Area United Way, Inc., Griffith, IN
175,000	Cerebral Palsy of Northwest Indiana, Inc., Hobart, IN
175,000	Purdue University Calumet, Hammond, IN
150,000	Indiana University Foundation, Bloomington, IN
150,000	Indiana University School of Medicine, Indianapolis, IN
150,000	Visiting Nurse Association Porter of County, Valparaiso, IN
125,000	Indiana University Northwest, Gary, IN

L. P. AND TERESA ANDERSON FOUNDATION

Giving Contact

Sandra K. Anderson, President
L. P. and Teresa Anderson Foundation
PO Box 190
Miles City, MT 59301-0190
Phone: (406)232-3920

Description

Founded: 1993
EIN: 810479060
Organization Type: Private Foundation
Grant Types: General Support, Scholarship.

Financial Summary

Total Giving: $52,950 (fiscal year ending June 30, 2001); $54,730 (fiscal 2000); $51,650 (fiscal 1999)
Giving Analysis: Giving for fiscal 2001 includes: foundation scholarships ($2,000) fiscal 2000: foundation scholarships ($11,000)
Assets: $1,239,268 (fiscal 2001); $1,230,511 (fiscal 2000); $1,207,491 (fiscal 1999)
Gifts Received: $500,000 (fiscal 1994); $500,000 (fiscal 1993). Note: In fiscal 1994, contributions were received from L. P. Anderson.

Typical Recipients

Arts & Humanities: Arts Centers, History & Archaeology, Libraries
Civic & Public Affairs: Civic & Public Affairs-General, Housing, Parades/Festivals
Education: Agricultural Education, Community & Junior Colleges, Education-General, Private Education (Precollege), Science/Mathematics Education
Health: Cancer, Children's Health/Hospitals
Religion: Religious Organizations, Religious Welfare
Social Services: At-Risk Youth, Big Brother/Big Sister, Community Service Organizations, Domestic Violence, Food/Clothing Distribution, Recreation & Athletics, Scouts, Senior Services, Social Services-General, Substance Abuse, Volunteer Services

Application Procedures

Initial Contact: Send a brief letter of inquiry.
Application Requirements: Include a description of organization, amount requested, purpose of funds sought, recently audited financial statement, and proof of tax-exempt status.
Deadlines: March 1 and September 1.

Restrictions

Preference is given to Miles City and Custer County, MT.

Foundation Officials

Sandra K. Anderson: president
Marilyn Sue Jubb: vice president
Roger Muggli: vice president
Samuel J. Ohnstad: secretary, treasurer

Grants Analysis

Disclosure Period: fiscal year ending June 30, 2001
Total Grants: $50,950*
Number of Grants: 26
Average Grant: $1,960
Highest Grant: $7,500
Lowest Grant: $250
Typical Range: $500 to $3,000
*Note: Giving excludes scholarship.

Recent Grants

Note: Grants derived from fiscal 2000 Form 990.

Library-Related
3,000   Miles City Public Library Foundation, Miles City, MT

General
6,500   Custer County Food Bank, Miles City, MT
5,000   Miles Community College, Miles City, MT -- "enough is enough" Milton Creagh, motivational speaker
2,880   Range Riders, Inc., Miles City, MT -- endowment fund, retirement annuity
2,750   Custer County Art & Heritage Center, Miles City, MT -- education scholarship fund
2,500   Custer County Empty Stocking, Miles City, MT
2,000   Custer County, Miles City, MT -- rural address post
2,000   For One Another, Cancer Family Network, Bozeman, MT -- Camp Southeastern Montana
2,000   Miles City Area Habitat for Humanity, Miles City, MT
1,000   Custer County Council on Aging, Miles City, MT -- to support transportation for the needy
1,000   Miles City Fire Department, Miles City, MT -- substance abuse prevention

M. D. ANDERSON FOUNDATION

Giving Contact

Toloria Allen, Grants Administrator
PO Box 2558
Houston, TX 77252-8037
Phone: (713)216-5348
Fax: (713)216-2119

Description

Founded: 1936
EIN: 746035669

Organization Type: General Purpose Foundation
Giving Locations: TX: Harris County, Houston and metropolitan area
Grant Types: Capital, General Support, Project, Research.

Donor Information

Founder: Established in 1936 to institutionalize the philanthropy of Monroe D. Anderson , a founder of Anderson, Clayton & Co., Houston cotton merchants. Mr. Anderson, who died in 1939, intended the foundation to continue to reflect his interests after his death, although he gave the trustees wide latitude in the choice of funding recipients.

Financial Summary

Total Giving: $5,859,516 (2000); $4,428,424 (1998); $6,146,000 (1997 approx)
Giving Analysis: Giving for 1998 includes: foundation scholarships ($27,500)
Assets: $164,982,332 (2000); $169,532,105 (1999 approx); $154,986,474 (1998)
Gifts Received: $18,050 (1992)

Typical Recipients

Arts & Humanities: Ballet, History & Archaeology, Libraries, Museums/Galleries, Music, Opera, Performing Arts, Theater
Civic & Public Affairs: Botanical Gardens/Parks, Community Foundations, Economic Development, Economic Policy, Employment/Job Training, Civic & Public Affairs-General, Hispanic Affairs, Housing, Law & Justice, Legal Aid, Minority Business, Urban & Community Affairs, Women's Affairs, Zoos/Aquariums
Education: Business Education, Colleges & Universities, Education Associations, Education Reform, Faculty Development, Education-General, International Exchange, Legal Education, Literacy, Medical Education, Minority Education, Private Education (Precollege), Private Education (Precollege), Public Education (Precollege), Science/Mathematics Education, Secondary Education (Private), Social Sciences Education, Special Education
Health: Adolescent Health Issues, Cancer, Children's Health/Hospitals, Clinics/Medical Centers, Emergency/Ambulance Services, Eyes/Blindness, Geriatric Health, Health Policy/Cost Containment, Health Organizations, Heart, Hospices, Hospitals, Medical Rehabilitation, Medical Research, Mental Health, Nursing Services, Prenatal Health Issues, Public Health, Research/Studies Institutes, Single-Disease Health Associations, Transplant Networks/Donor Banks
International: Foreign Educational Institutions
Religion: Churches, Dioceses, Jewish Causes, Religious Welfare, Social/Policy Issues
Science: Science Museums, Science Museums, Scientific Centers & Institutes
Social Services: Animal Protection, At-Risk Youth, Camps, Child Abuse, Child Welfare, Community Centers, Community Service Organizations, Family Planning, People with Disabilities, Recreation & Athletics, Scouts, Senior Services, Shelters/Homelessness, Substance Abuse, YMCA/YWCA/YMHA/YWHA, Youth Organizations

Application Procedures

Initial Contact: Applicants should send a brief letter describing the proposed project, along with an original and four copies of the full proposal. If applying for a matching grant, indicate other sources of funding.
Application Requirements: With the cover letter, include the amount needed and proof of tax-exempt status. If the project falls within the foundation's scope of interest, further information may be requested.

Deadlines: None. Board meetings are held on the third Tuesday of each month. Applications should be received a month prior to the meeting to be considered.
Review Process: The foundation reports that it responds to all proposals by letter detailing whether the application has been approved or denied.

Foundation Officials

Uriel E. Dutton: trustee B Hamilton, TX 1930. ED Howard Payne University (1946-1948); Baylor University LLB (1951). PRIM CORP EMPL partner: Fulbright & Jaworski. CORP AFFIL director: Energy Ventures; director: Grey Wolf Drilling. NONPR AFFIL member: Texas Bar Association; member: Texas Bar Foundation; member: Houston Bar Association; member: Phi Delta Phi; member: American Bar Association; member: American Bar Foundation.
Gibson Gayle, Jr.: president, trustee B Waco, TX 1926. ED Baylor University LLB (1950); Baylor University AB (1950). CORP AFFIL director: Daniel Industries Inc. NONPR AFFIL fellow: Texas Bar Foundation; adj professor: University Texas Law School; member: Texas Bar Association; member: Houston Chamber of Commerce; board governors: Leon Jaworski Foundation; trustee: Baylor College Medicine; member: Houston Bar Association; fellow: American Bar Foundation; member: American Bar Association.
Charles W. Hall: trustee B Dallas, TX 1930. ED University of the South BA (1951); Southern Methodist University JD (1954). PRIM CORP EMPL senior partner, attorney: Fulbright & Jaworski. CORP AFFIL assistant vice chairman: Friedman Industries Inc. NONPR AFFIL member: State Bar Texas; director: Texas Medical Center; trustee: Institute Religion; member: International Bar Association; member: Dallas Bar Association; member: Houston Bar Association; member: American College Tax Counsel; member: American Law Institute; member, chairman national conf lawyers & CPAs: American Bar Association; fellow: American Bar Foundation. CLUB AFFIL River Oaks Country Club; Metro Club; member: Petroleum Club; Coronado Club; Houston City Club.
Ann Trotter: secretary-treasurer
Jack T. Trotter: vice president, trustee CORP AFFIL director: First Interstate Bank Texas.

Grants Analysis

Disclosure Period: calendar year ending 2000
Total Grants: $5,859,516
Number of Grants: 154
Average Grant: $38,049
Highest Grant: $200,000
Typical Range: $5,000 to $50,000

Recent Grants

Note: Grants derived from 2000 Form 990.

General
200,000   Pyramid Community Development Corporation, Houston, TX
200,000   Rice University, Houston, TX
200,000   Southwestern Legal Foundation, Richardson, TX -- for programs
200,000   University of Houston, Houston, TX
200,000   University of Texas Health Science Center, Houston, TX -- to establish the Institute of Molecular Medicine
135,000   Houston Symphony, Houston, TX -- for artistic goals
100,000   Annunciation Orthodox School, Houston, TX
100,000   Baylor College of Medicine, Houston, TX -- to establish an academic chair endowment at the College
100,000   Boys & Girls Clubs of America - Sam Houston Area Council, Houston, TX
100,000   Boys and Girls Clubs of Greater Houston, Houston, TX -- Urban Scouting Program

ANDERSON FOUNDATION (NY)

Giving Contact

E. William Whittaker, Treasurer & Trustee
Chemung Canal Trust Co.
c/o Chemung Canal Trust Co.
PO Box 1522
Elmira, NY 14902
Phone: (607)737-3711

Description

Founded: 1960
EIN: 166024689
Organization Type: Private Foundation
Giving Locations: NY: Elmira
Grant Types: General Support, Operating Expenses, Scholarship.

Donor Information

Founder: Jane G. Anderson, the late Douglas G. Anderson

Financial Summary

Total Giving: $206,240 (fiscal year ending April 30, 2001); $224,402 (fiscal 2000); $144,159 (fiscal 1997)
Giving Analysis: Giving for fiscal 2001 includes: foundation grants to United Way ($13,650); fiscal 2000: foundation grants to United Way ($13,650) fiscal 1997: foundation grants to United Way ($13,000)
Assets: $3,884,217 (fiscal 2001); $4,048,492 (fiscal 2000); $3,679,864 (fiscal 1997)

Typical Recipients

Arts & Humanities: Community Arts, Historic Preservation, History & Archaeology, Libraries, Museums/Galleries, Music, Opera, Performing Arts, Public Broadcasting
Civic & Public Affairs: Community Foundations, Employment/Job Training, Housing, Urban & Community Affairs
Education: Arts/Humanities Education, Business Education, Colleges & Universities, Economic Education, Gifted & Talented Programs, Literacy, Preschool Education
Environment: Environment-General, Resource Conservation
Health: Clinics/Medical Centers, Heart, Hospitals, Long-Term Care, Multiple Sclerosis, Nursing Services
Religion: Religious Welfare
Social Services: Animal Protection, Camps, Child Welfare, Community Centers, Community Service Organizations, Community Service Organizations, Food/Clothing Distribution, People with Disabilities, Recreation & Athletics, Senior Services, Substance Abuse, United Funds/United Ways, Volunteer Services, YMCA/YWCA/YMHA/YWHA, Youth Organizations

Foundation Officials

Elizabeth T. Dalrymple: trust
Clover M. Drinkwater: assistant secretary
Paul Greenlee, Jr.: trustee
J. Philip Hunter: secretary
Robert T. Jones: vice president, trustee
Jane G. Joralemon: president, trustee
Edwin P. Marosek: trustee
Margaret B. Streeter: trust
Kenneth A. Tifft: assistant secretary, trustee
E. William Whittaker: treasurer, trustee
Ethel A. Whittaker: vice president, trustee
Joanne Whittaker Word: trustee

Grants Analysis

Disclosure Period: fiscal year ending April 30, 2001
Total Grants: $192,590*
Number of Grants: 26
Average Grant: $7,407
Highest Grant: $20,000

Lowest Grant: $1,500
Typical Range: $3,000 to $13,000
*Note: Giving excludes United Way.

Recent Grants

Note: Grants derived from fiscal 2001 Form 990.

Library-Related
20,000   Steele Memorial Library, Elmira, NY -- A. Marshall Lowman and Charles A. Winding Material Fund

General
20,000   Community Foundation of the Elmira-Corning Area, Elmira, NY -- S. Roberts Rose Youth Fund Endowment
15,000   Arnot Ogden Medical Center Foundation, Elmira, NY -- CT simulation and planning system package
15,000   Glove House, Elmira, NY -- renovation and consolidation of administrative offices
15,000   St. Joseph's Hospital, Elmira, NY -- bed and mattresses
13,650   United Way of the Southern Tier, Elmira, NY
13,000   Clemens Center for Performing Arts, Elmira, NY -- operating expenses
12,000   Peace by Piece, Inc., Elmira, NY -- operating expense
10,000   Community Foundation of the Elmira-Corning Area, Elmira, NY -- Kenneth A. Tifft/Robert T. Jones Field Experience Fund
10,000   Spencer Van Etten Community Services Corporation, Van Etten, NY -- medical center
10,000   Tanglewood Community Nature Center, Elmira, NY -- capital campaign

ANDERSONS, INC.

Company Headquarters

480 W. Dussel Dr.
Maumee, OH 43537
Web: http://www.andersonsinc.com

Company Description

Founded: 1947
Ticker: ANDE
Exchange: NASDAQ
Former Name: The Andersons.
Revenue: US$984.6 million (2001)
Employees: 3035 (2001)
SIC(s): 0119 Cash Grains Nec, 5153 Grain & Field Beans, 5191 Farm Supplies, 7389 Business Services Nec.

Operating Locations

Andersons Inc. (IN--Poneto; MI--Albion; OH--Bryan, Maumee, Toledo)

Anderson Foundation

Giving Contact

Fredi Heywood, Foundation Services Administrator
608 Madison Avenue, Suite 1540
Toledo, OH 43604
Phone: (419)243-1706

Description

EIN: 346528868
Organization Type: Corporate Foundation
Giving Locations: headquarters and operating communities, including plant locations.
Grant Types: Capital, Employee Matching Gifts, General Support, Project, Scholarship, Seed Money.
Note: Employee matching gift ratio: 1 to 1.

Financial Summary

Total Giving: $286,737 (2001); $520,103 (2000); $614,092 (1999). Note: Contributes through corporate direct giving program and foundation.
Giving Analysis: Giving for 2001 includes: foundation ($128,685); foundation grants to United Way ($158,052); 2000: foundation scholarships ($5,000); foundation grants to United Way ($252,435); foundation ($262,668); 1999: foundation grants to United Way ($303,655); foundation ($310,437);
Assets: $4,559,996 (2001); $5,121,168 (2000); $5,638,249 (1999)
Gifts Received: $25,000 (2001); $50 (2000); $50,000 (1999). Note: Foundation receives contributions from The Andersons, Inc.

Typical Recipients

Arts & Humanities: Arts Associations & Councils, Arts Centers, Arts & Humanities-General, Historic Preservation, History & Archaeology, Libraries, Museums/Galleries, Music, Opera, Performing Arts, Public Broadcasting, Theater
Civic & Public Affairs: African American Affairs, Botanical Gardens/Parks, Clubs, Community Foundations, Economic Development, Economic Policy, Civic & Public Affairs-General, Housing, Municipalities/Towns, Parades/Festivals, Philanthropic Organizations, Public Policy, Rural Affairs, Safety, Urban & Community Affairs, Zoos/Aquariums
Education: Agricultural Education, Business Education, Colleges & Universities, Community & Junior Colleges, Education Associations, Education Funds, Education Reform, Education-General, Literacy, Minority Education, Private Education (Precollege), Public Education (Precollege), Science/Mathematics Education, Secondary Education (Private), Secondary Education (Public), Student Aid, Vocational & Technical Education
Environment: Environment-General, Resource Conservation, Wildlife Protection
Health: Clinics/Medical Centers, Diabetes, Emergency/Ambulance Services, Eyes/Blindness, Health Organizations, Hospices, Hospitals, Medical Research, Mental Health, Nursing Services, Preventive Medicine/Wellness Organizations, Single-Disease Health Associations
Religion: Churches, Dioceses, Jewish Causes, Ministries, Religious Organizations, Religious Welfare
Science: Scientific Centers & Institutes, Scientific Organizations, Scientific Research
Social Services: Animal Protection, Camps, Child Welfare, Community Centers, Community Service Organizations, Day Care, Family Services, Food/Clothing Distribution, People with Disabilities, Recreation & Athletics, Refugee Assistance, Scouts, Senior Services, Social Services-General, United Funds/United Ways, YMCA/YWCA/YMHA/YWHA, Youth Organizations

Application Procedures

Initial Contact: Send written application, of not more than five pages.
Application Requirements: Include amount requested; purpose of funds sought; description of the organization, with organization's purpose and objectives; need the project intends to address; the need the project will address, and geographical area and population to be served; timetable for the project; name(s) and qualifications of the person who will administer the grant; telephone number of an appropriate contact person; how the success of the project will be evaluated; recently audited financial statements; proof of tax-exempt status; organizational budget for the current year showing anticipated expenses and income by sources (if the request is for a capital drive or specific project, also include a budget showing expenses and income for the drive/project); list of officers and directors; and list of major donors within the past 12 months.

Deadlines: At least three weeks before quarterly board meetings, which are in March, June, September, and December.

Restrictions

Does not support individuals, endowment funds, church building or operating funds, or building or operating funds for elementary schools.
The foundation generally does not serve as major or sole funder of projects.

Additional Information

The foundation's major donor is The Andersons, Inc., but the foundation reports that its activities are separate. The company does offer a very limited amount of direct giving in its headquarters area.

Corporate Officials

Thomas Harold Anderson: chairman, director B Toledo, OH 1924. ED Michigan State University BS (1966). PRIM CORP EMPL chairman, director: The Andersons Inc. ADD NONPR EMPL president, director: International Center Preservation Wild Animals. CLUB AFFIL Rotary Club.

Foundation Officials

Charles D. Anderson: trustee B Detroit, MI 1931. ED Michigan School of Mines (1953). PRIM CORP EMPL chairman, president: Anderson Tool Sales Inc. CORP AFFIL chairman: ATD Tools Corp. NONPR AFFIL member: Fraternal Order Eagles.
Jeffrey W. Anderson: trustee
Kevin Anderson: trustee
Mary Anderson: trustee
Thomas Harold Anderson: chairman, trustee (see above)
Martha Corcoran: trustee
John P. Kraus: trustee
Beverly J. Lange: secretary PRIM CORP EMPL secretary: Andersons Management Corp.

Grants Analysis

Disclosure Period: calendar year ending 2001
Total Grants: $128,685*
Number of Grants: 76
Average Grant: $1,693
Highest Grant: $20,000
Lowest Grant: $50
Typical Range: $250 to $5,000
*Note: Giving excludes United Way.

Recent Grants

Note: Grants derived from 2002 Form 990.

Library-Related
5,000	West Jay Community Center, Inc., Dunkirk, IN

General
50,000	United Way of Greater Toledo, Toledo, OH
25,000	United Way of Greater Toledo, Toledo, OH
25,000	United Way of Greater Toledo, Toledo, OH
20,000	Parkland College, Champaign, IL
15,000	Toledo Symphony Orchestra, Toledo, OH
10,000	American Red Cross, Toledo, OH
7,200	United Way Franklin County, Columbus, OH
5,000	ASSETS, Toledo, OH
5,000	Central City Ministries, Toledo, OH
5,000	Crisis Nursery, Urbana, IL

FRANK G. ANDRES CHARITABLE TRUST

Giving Contact

David Myer, Trustee
Frank G. Andres Charitable Trust
c/o First Bank of Tomah
PO Box 753
Tomah, WI 54660
Phone: (608)372-2131

Description

EIN: 510172405
Organization Type: Private Foundation
Giving Locations: WI: Tomah
Grant Types: General Support.

Financial Summary

Total Giving: $113,846 (fiscal year ending June 30, 2001); $108,374 (fiscal 1999); $102,559 (fiscal 1997)
Assets: $2,973,381 (fiscal 2001); $3,348,926 (fiscal 1999); $2,627,055 (fiscal 1997)

Typical Recipients

Arts & Humanities: History & Archaeology, Libraries, Music
Civic & Public Affairs: Botanical Gardens/Parks, Clubs, Employment/Job Training, Civic & Public Affairs-General, Municipalities/Towns, Rural Affairs, Safety, Urban & Community Affairs
Education: Education Funds, Education-General, Public Education (Precollege), Science/Mathematics Education, Vocational & Technical Education
Environment: Environment-General
Health: Emergency/Ambulance Services, Hospices, Hospitals
Social Services: Child Welfare, Community Service Organizations, Recreation & Athletics, Senior Services, Shelters/Homelessness, Substance Abuse, Youth Organizations

Application Procedures

Initial Contact: Application form required.
Deadlines: May15.

Foundation Officials

R. W. Ahlstrom: trustee
Jay Charmichael: trustee
Donald Kortbein: trustee
David Myer: trustee
Roxana O'Connor: trustee, secretary
Raymond Paulis: trustee

Grants Analysis

Disclosure Period: fiscal year ending June 30, 2001
Total Grants: $113,846
Number of Grants: 22
Average Grant: $5,175
Highest Grant: $22,000
Lowest Grant: $1,000
Typical Range: $1,000 to $8,000

Recent Grants

Note: Grants derived from fiscal 2001 Form 990.

Library-Related
3,660	Tomah Public Library, Tomah, WI -- air conditioning for computer room

General
22,000	Tomah Area School District, Tomah, WI -- portable platforms and staging and defibrillator
15,000	Tomah Memorial Hospital, Tomah, WI -- ultrasound for obstetrics and cart for surgical patients
10,000	Boys and Girls Club
10,000	Tomah Memorial Hospital, Tomah, WI -- hospice touch
9,000	Western Wisconsin Technical College,

	La Crosse, WI -- for laptop computers for Tomah
5,584	City of Tomah Fire Department, Tomah, WI -- skid unit for brush truck
5,000	City of Tomah Senior Board, Tomah, WI -- to establish center
5,000	Monroe County Agriculture Society -- toward parking lot project
4,000	Tomah Concert Association, Tomah, WI -- to sponsor a concert
3,750	City of Tomah Ambulance Service, Tomah, WI -- purchase portable suction units

ANDREWS FOUNDATION

Giving Contact

Laura Baxter-Heuer, President & Trustee
925 Euclid Ave., Suite 1525
Cleveland, OH 44115-1407
Phone: (216)621-3215

Description

Founded: 1951
EIN: 346515110
Organization Type: Private Foundation
Giving Locations: OH: including northeastern Ohio
Grant Types: Capital, Endowment, General Support.

Donor Information

Founder: the late Mrs. Matthew Andrews

Financial Summary

Total Giving: $385,700 (2000); $886,394 (1999); $547,167 (1998)
Assets: $11,648,729 (2000); $10,686,660 (1999); $11,984,237 (1998)

Typical Recipients

Arts & Humanities: Arts Centers, Arts Outreach, Ballet, Community Arts, Arts & Humanities-General, Libraries, Museums/Galleries, Music, Performing Arts, Theater
Civic & Public Affairs: Economic Development, Employment/Job Training, Civic & Public Affairs-General, Law & Justice, Municipalities/Towns, Nonprofit Management, Parades/Festivals, Urban & Community Affairs, Women's Affairs
Education: Arts/Humanities Education, Colleges & Universities, Education Funds, Environmental Education, Faculty Development, Education-General, Medical Education, Minority Education, Private Education (Precollege), Public Education (Precollege), Religious Education, Secondary Education (Private), Secondary Education (Public), Special Education, Student Aid
Health: AIDS/HIV, Cancer, Children's Health/Hospitals, Clinics/Medical Centers, Diabetes, Emergency/Ambulance Services, Health Organizations, Heart, Hospitals (University Affiliated), Medical Rehabilitation, Mental Health, Nursing Services, Research/Studies Institutes, Transplant Networks/Donor Banks
Religion: Ministries, Religious Organizations, Religious Welfare, Seminaries
Science: Science Museums
Social Services: At-Risk Youth, Camps, Child Welfare, Community Service Organizations, Day Care, Delinquency & Criminal Rehabilitation, Domestic Violence, People with Disabilities, Substance Abuse, Veterans, Youth Organizations

Application Procedures

Initial Contact: Send a brief letter of inquiry.
Application Requirements: Include a description of organization, purpose of funds sought, and proof of tax-exempt status.
Deadlines: None.

Foundation Officials

Barbara J. Baxter: vice president, trustee
James Howard Dempsey, Jr.: secretary, trustee B Cleveland, OH October 18, 1916. ED Yale University BA (1938); Yale University LLB (1941). PRIM CORP EMPL general partner: Squire, Sanders & Dempsey. NONPR AFFIL member: Ohio Bar Association; trustee: University Hospitals; member: Cleveland Bar Association; member: American Bar Association. CLUB AFFIL Union Club; Pepper Pike Club; Tavern Club; Chagrin Valley Hunt Club; Kirtland Country Club.
Laura Baxter Heuer: assistant secretary, treasurer, trustee
Richard S. Tomer: president, trustee
Richard S. Tomer: vice president, trustee

Grants Analysis

Disclosure Period: calendar year ending 2000
Total Grants: $385,700
Number of Grants: 20
Average Grant: $19,285
Highest Grant: $50,000
Lowest Grant: $2,500
Typical Range: $10,000 to $30,000

Recent Grants

Note: Grants derived from 2001 Form 990.

General

50,000	University Hospitals, Cleveland, OH
40,000	Ratner School, Lyndhurst, OH
35,000	Desert Rehabilitation Services, Inc., Desert Hot Springs, CA
35,000	Hanna Perkins Center, Cleveland, OH
35,000	Hathaway Brown School, Shaker Heights, OH
35,000	Minority Organ Tissue Transplant Education Program (MOTTEP), Washington, DC
34,000	Julie Billiart School, Cleveland, OH
30,000	Great Lakes Theater Festival, Cleveland, OH
25,000	Free Clinic of Greater Cleveland, Cleveland, OH
25,000	Horizon Activities Center, North Olmsted, OH

ANDREWS MCMEEL UNIVERSAL

Company Headquarters

4520 Main St., Ste. 700
Kansas City, MO 64111
Phone: (816)932-6606
Web: http://www.amuniversal.com

Company Description

Revenue: US$130 million (2001)
Employees: 200 (2001)

Andrews McMeel Universal Foundation

Giving Contact

Kathleen W. Andrews, Vice President & Secretary
4520 Main St., Suite 700
Kansas City, MO 64111
Phone: (816)932-6700
Fax: (816)531-5323
E-mail: kandrews@amuniversal.com

Description

Founded: 1991
EIN: 431570308
Organization Type: Private Foundation

Giving Locations: KS; MO, Kansas City metropolitan area: nationally.
Grant Types: General Support.

Donor Information

Founder: Established in 1991 by the United Press Syndicate.

Financial Summary

Total Giving: $309,786 (2001); $362,297 (2000); $419,378 (1999)
Giving Analysis: Giving for 1999 includes: foundation scholarships ($100); foundation grants to United Way ($3,000); 1998: foundation grants to United Way ($2,500); foundation matching gifts ($11,515); foundation ($430,223); 1997: foundation scholarships ($2,000); foundation grants to United Way ($2,500); foundation ($506,142);
Assets: $4,916,268 (2001); $5,118,662 (2000); $5,219,412 (1999)
Gifts Received: $12,937 (2001); $23,357 (2000); $28,717 (1999). Note: In 2001, contributions were received from Starbucks ($11,437) and Kathleen Andrews ($1,500). In 1999, contributions were received from Starbucks.

Typical Recipients

Arts & Humanities: Arts Associations & Councils, Arts Festivals, Arts & Humanities-General, Libraries, Literary Arts, Museums/Galleries, Music, Opera, Theater
Civic & Public Affairs: Clubs, Civic & Public Affairs-General, Housing, Public Policy, Urban & Community Affairs, Women's Affairs, Zoos/Aquariums
Education: Colleges & Universities, Education-General, Gifted & Talented Programs, Journalism/Media Education, Private Education (Precollege), Public Education (Precollege), Secondary Education (Private), Secondary Education (Public), Student Aid, Vocational & Technical Education
Health: Clinics/Medical Centers, Health Organizations, Kidney, Medical Research, Prenatal Health Issues, Single-Disease Health Associations
International: Foreign Arts Organizations, Human Rights
Religion: Jewish Causes, Religious Organizations, Religious Welfare, Seminaries
Science: Science Museums
Social Services: Child Welfare, Community Service Organizations, Domestic Violence, Emergency Relief, People with Disabilities, United Funds/United Ways, Youth Organizations

Application Procedures

Initial Contact: The foundation has no formal grant application procedure or application form.
Application Requirements: Include information that would support the request.
Deadlines: None.

Foundation Officials

Hugh T. Andrews: director
James C. Andrews: director
Kathleen W. Andrews: vice president, secretary ED College of Notre Dame BS (1959); University of Notre Dame MS (1962). PRIM CORP EMPL chief executive officer: Andrews McMeel Publishing ADD CORP EMPL vice chairman: Andrews McMeel Universal. NONPR AFFIL trustee: Notre Dame Colleges; trustee: University Notre Dame; member: Newspaper Features Council; director: NCCJ; member: Newspaper Cartoonists Society; member: Catholic Charities; member: Malta Federation Association; trustee: Avila College; member: American Booksellers Association; trustee: Association Governing Boards Universitys Colleges.
Elena Fallon: director
Thomas I. Gill: assistant secretary
John T. Howard: director
Ole C. Jenson: director
Bridget J. McMeel: director

John Paul McMeel: president, treasurer B South Bend, IN 1936. ED University of Notre Dame BS (1957). PRIM CORP EMPL chairman: Andrews McMeel Publishing. CORP AFFIL director: Universal/ Belo Productions; president: Universal Press Syndicate. NONPR AFFIL member: Sovereign Military Order Malta; member advisory council: University Notre Dame Institute Church Life; director: Newspaper Features Council; member: Intl Press Institute; chairman, director: National Catholic Reporter; co-founder: Christmas October Kansas City; member: Fed Association USA; director: Christmas April USA.
Susan S. McMeel: director
Suzanne E. McMeel: director
Maureen McMeel Jackoboice: director
Dr. Jeffrey F. Rayport: director
Eugene Leslie Roberts, Jr.: director B Goldsboro, NC 1932. ED Mars Hill Junior College AA (1950-1952); University of North Carolina BA (1952-1954); Colby College LLD (1989). PRIM CORP EMPL managing editor: New York Times Co. NONPR AFFIL member: North Carolina Society; member: Society Professional Journalists; member: Cosmos Club; board advisors: Center Foreign Journalists; vice chairman: Commission to Protect Journalists; member: American Society Newspaper Editors; director: Arthur Burns Fellowship; member: American Antiquarian Society; international board: American Commission International Press Institute.
Thomas N. Thornton: director

Grants Analysis

Disclosure Period: calendar year ending 2001
Total Grants: $309,786
Number of Grants: 177
Average Grant: $1,750
Highest Grant: $71,428
Lowest Grant: $50
Typical Range: $50 to $10,000

Recent Grants

Note: Grants derived from 2001 Form 990.

Library-Related

5,000	Harry S. Truman Library Institute, Independence, MO

General

71,428	University of Notre Dame, Notre Dame, IN
50,050	Nelson Atkins Museum of Art, Kansas City, MO
10,000	Christmas in October, Kansas City, MO
10,000	Donnelly College, Kansas City, MO
10,000	International Press Institute, Allentown, PA
10,000	Upper Room, Inc., Kansas City, MO
6,750	Catholic Charities, Kansas City, MO
5,050	Rockhurst College, Kansas City, MO
5,000	ArtsGenesis, Jersey City, NJ
5,000	Catholic Charities, Kansas City, MO

ANHEUSER-BUSCH COMPANIES, INC.

Company Headquarters

St. Louis, MO
Web: http://www.anheuser-busch.com

Company Description

Founded: 1852
Ticker: BUD
Exchange: NYSE
Revenue: US$15.687 billion (2002)
Profit: US$1.933 billion (2002)
Employees: 23432 (2002)
Fortune Rank: 142, per FORTUNE Magazine's list of 500 Largest U.S. Corporations (2002).

SIC(s): 2046 Wet Corn Milling, 2051 Bread, Cake & Related Products, 2082 Malt Beverages, 6719 Holding Companies Nec.

Operating Locations

Anheuser-Busch Companies, Inc. (AR--Jonesboro; CA--Carson, Fairfield, Los Angeles, San Diego, Sylmar, Stockton, Visalia; CO--Denver, Fort Collins, Windsor; FL--Gainesville, Orlando, Tampa, Winter Haven; GA--Cartersville, ID--Idaho Falls; IL--Chicago; LA--New Orleans; MA--Boston; MN--Clearbrook, Moorhead; MO--Arnold, St. Louis; NH--Merrimack; NJ--Newark; NY--Baldwinsville, Newburgh; OH--Aurora, Columbus; OK--Oklahoma City; PA--Langhorne, York; TN--Fayetteville; TX--Houston; VA--Williamsburg; WI--Fort Atkinson, Manitowoc)

Nonmonetary Support

Type: Donated Products
Volunteer Programs: Through the Anheuser-Busch Employee Volunteer Grant Program, the company supports and recognizes its employees who actively volunteer their time and talents to nonprofit organizations by making grants to these organizations for unusual or special projects. An Employee Matching Gifts Program for educational institutions is also offered through the company's charitable foundation.
Note: The company has donated cans of fresh drinking water to victims of natural disasters.

Anheuser-Busch Foundation

Giving Contact

Jayne Nicholson, Specialist, Charitable Contributions
Anheuser-Busch Companies
USBank
PO Box 387, FL-TW-16IT
St. Louis, MO 63166-0587
Phone: (314)418-2168
Fax: (314)577-3251

Description

Founded: 1975
EIN: 510168084
Organization Type: Corporate Foundation
Giving Locations: principally near operating locations and to national organizations.
Grant Types: Capital, Employee Matching Gifts, General Support.

Donor Information

Founder: Anheuser-Busch Co.

Financial Summary

Total Giving: $19,140,827 (2001); $12,648,330 (2000); $6,270,907 (1997). Note: Contributes through corporate direct giving program and foundation.
Giving Analysis: Giving for 2000 includes: foundation grants to United Way ($2,213,907); foundation ($10,434,423); 1997: foundation ($6,270,907); 1996: foundation grants to United Way ($2,025,440) foundation ($7,620,879)
Assets: $40,062,047 (2001); $60,345,116 (2000); $49,286,482 (1997)
Gifts Received: $543,000 (2001); $15,000,000 (2000); $1,024,131 (1997)

Typical Recipients

Arts & Humanities: Arts Associations & Councils, Arts Centers, Arts Funds, Community Arts, Historic Preservation, History & Archaeology, Libraries, Museums/Galleries, Music, Performing Arts, Public Broadcasting, Theater
Civic & Public Affairs: African American Affairs, Botanical Gardens/Parks, Civil Rights, Clubs, Community Foundations, Economic Development, Economic Policy, Employment/Job Training, Civic & Public Affairs-General, Hispanic Affairs, Housing, Law & Justice, Public Policy, Rural Affairs, Urban & Community Affairs, Women's Affairs, Zoos/Aquariums
Education: Agricultural Education, Arts/Humanities Education, Business Education, Colleges & Universities, Community & Junior Colleges, Community & Junior Colleges, Continuing Education, Education Funds, Education Reform, Engineering/Technological Education, Education-General, Health & Physical Education, International Exchange, Legal Education, Literacy, Medical Education, Minority Education, Private Education (Precollege), Public Education (Precollege), Science/Mathematics Education, Secondary Education (Private), Secondary Education (Public), Special Education, Student Aid, Vocational & Technical Education
Environment: Air/Water Quality, Environment-General, Resource Conservation, Wildlife Protection
Health: AIDS/HIV, Alzheimers Disease, Cancer, Children's Health/Hospitals, Emergency/Ambulance Services, Health Policy/Cost Containment, Health Organizations, Heart, Hospitals, Medical Research, Public Health, Single-Disease Health Associations
Religion: Dioceses, Religion-General, Jewish Causes, Religious Organizations, Religious Welfare, Seminaries
Science: Scientific Centers & Institutes, Scientific Organizations, Scientific Research
Social Services: At-Risk Youth, Child Welfare, Community Service Organizations, Counseling, Delinquency & Criminal Rehabilitation, Emergency Relief, Food/Clothing Distribution, People with Disabilities, Recreation & Athletics, Scouts, Senior Services, Shelters/Homelessness, Social Services-General, Substance Abuse, United Funds/United Ways, Volunteer Services, YMCA/YWCA/YMHA/YWHA, Youth Organizations

Application Procedures

Initial Contact: Write or call to request guidelines form.
Application Requirements: The guidelines request the official name of your organization, complete mailing address, phone number, brief general a description of organization of organization's purpose and major activities; purpose of funds sought, including the amount requested and total project budget; dates and amounts of any previous grants received from Anheuser-Busch; whether the applicant is a United Way member agency; and whether the organization has a permanent liquor license. The following items should be attached to the proposal: most recent audited financial statement, current operating budget, apartment (or other materials summarizing programs), list of current board of directors and their affiliations, list of current corporate contributors, IRS letter of tax-exempt certification, do not include videos with proposal.
Deadlines: None.
Evaluative Criteria: Program areas focus on education, health care and human services, minorities and youth, cultural enrichment, and environmental protection in communities where Anheuser-Busch and its subsidiaries operate major facilities and where its employees and their families live and work.
Decision Notification: Review takes approximately six to eight weeks.
Notes: The foundation does not accept videos submitted with proposals.

Restrictions

Does not support organizations that are not designated tax-exempt by the IRS, aid to individualss, political candidates or organizations, religious organizations, organizations with limited constituency such as fraternal or social groups, athletic organizations, or operating funds for hospitals.

Additional Information

As the world's largest brewer, Anheuser-Busch works to encourage responsible drinking among adults who choose to drink and to fight alcohol abuse, drunk driving, and underage drinking. Anheuser-Busch is a major supporter of alcohol education efforts on college campuses, including the BACHUS (Boost Alcohol Consciousness Concerning the Health of University Students) peer-education network, the National Collegiate Athletic Association Foundation's "Choices" grant program, "TIPS for the University" program, and National Collegiate Alcohol Awareness Week.

The company's Busch Gardens and Sea World parks care for endangered and threatened species, such as manatees. The Sea World Parks are known for their rescue and rehabilitation programs. The Anheuser-Busch Theme Parks also support "A Pledge and a Promise" environmental awards program. Established in 1993, the program is held in cooperation with national conservation organizations to honor outstanding efforts of school groups that have made positive contributions to the environment. It offers 13 awards totaling $100,000. The company sponsors an innovative urban beautification program, Operation Brightside, in 12 communities where its breweries are located. The program is based on a public/private partnership designed to involve citizens in cleaning up their cities and, more importantly, in keeping them clean.
Publications: Guidelines; Application Form

Corporate Officials

August Adolphus Busch, III: chairman, chief executive officer B Saint Louis, MO 1937. ED University of Arizona (1957-1958); Siebel Institute of Technology (1960-1961). PRIM CORP EMPL chairman, president, director: Anheuser-Busch Companies, Inc. ADD CORP EMPL chairman, chief executive officer, director: Anheuser-Busch Inc. CORP AFFIL director: Manufacturers Railway Co.; director: General America Life Insurance Co.; director: Emerson Electric Co. NONPR AFFIL director: SBC Community Inc. CLUB AFFIL Saint Louis Country Club; Log Cabin Club.
Patrick T. Stokes: president, chief executive officer PRIM CORP EMPL vice president, group executive: Anheuser-Busch Companies, Inc. ADD CORP EMPL president: Anheuser-Busch Inc.

Giving Program Officials

August Adolphus Busch, III: trustee (see above)

Grants Analysis

Disclosure Period: calendar year ending 2001
Total Grants: $16,926,189*
Number of Grants: 551
Average Grant: $30,000
Highest Grant: $1,000,000
Lowest Grant: $25
Typical Range: $5,000 to $50,000
*Note: Giving excludes United Way.

Recent Grants

Note: Grants derived from 2001 Form 990.

Library-Related
100,000	New York Public Library Astor Lenox and Tilden Foundation, New York, NY

General
1,465,465	United Way Greater St. Louis, St. Louis, MO
1,000,000	Community Foundation for the National Capital Region, Washington, DC
1,000,000	Greater New York Chapter, New York, NY
1,000,000	New York World Trade Center, New York, NY
1,000,000	United Way September 11th Fund, New York, NY

800,000	Washington University, St. Louis, MO
600,000	Cornell University, Ithaca, NY
543,000	Anheuser-Busch Companies, Inc., St. Louis, MO
500,000	Howard University, Washington, DC
500,000	St. Louis University, St. Louis, MO

ANNENBERG FOUNDATION

Giving Contact

Dr. Gail C. Levin, Executive Director
St. Davids Center, Suite A-200
150 Radnor-Chester Road
St. Davids, PA 19087
Phone: (610)341-9066
Fax: (610)964-8688
E-mail: info@annenbergfoundation.org
Web: http://www.annenbergfoundation.org

Description

Founded: 1989
EIN: 236257083
Organization Type: General Purpose Foundation
Giving Locations: nationally.
Grant Types: Project, Seed Money.
Note: The foundation also provides program grants.

Donor Information

Founder: Founder Walter H. Annenberg is the son of Moses Annenberg, who owned the Philadelphia Inquirer and the Daily Racing Form. Walter Annenberg took over the family business in 1940 and launched the very successful TV Guide in 1953. In 1970, he sold the Philadelphia Inquirer to Knight Ridder. Mr. Annenberg sold his other publications to Rupert Murdoch in 1988 for $3 billion. He is an avid art collector, and owns one of the most coveted art collections in the country. The Annenberg Foundation is the successor corporation to the Annenberg School at Radnor, PA, established in 1958. Mr. Annenberg is also the sole trustee of several Annenberg family trusts, including the J.A. Hooker Charitable Trust, the Evelyn A.J. Hall Charitable Trust, the Lita Hazen Charitable Trust, the Esther Simon Charitable Trust, the Polly Annenberg Levee Charitable Trusts, and the Harriett Ames Charitable Trust. He also served as president of the corporate-sponsored M.L. Annenberg Foundation, which has ceased operations. Mr. Annenberg has also been involved in several private philanthropic pursuits. In 1958, he founded and endowed the Annenberg School for Communication, a graduate school at the University of Pennsylvania. He also endowed the Annenberg School for Communication at the University of Southern California; and the Washington Program in Communications Policy Studies of Northwestern University. The Annenberg Foundation provides ongoing support to each of these institutions. Mr. Annenberg has also donated a library and a residence to his alma mater, the Peddie School; in 1983, the school received $12 million. He has given $3 million to the University of Pennsylvania for a performing arts center, $8 million to the University of California, and $10 million to the Annenberg Center for Health Sciences, part of a subsidiary of the Eisenhower Medical Center. Mr. Annenberg has also given major gifts to the Episcopal Academy in Philadelphia, the State of Israel, the Metropolitan Museum of Art, and the Desert Museum in Palm Springs, which he built. In 1993, Mr. Annenberg made several major gifts from his foundation, including a gift to the University of Pennsylvania to endow the Annenberg School for Communication and to establish a Center for Public Policy; a gift to the University of Southern California to establish the Annenberg Center for Communication; a contribution to the Peddie School for an endowment and scholarships; and a gift to Colonial Williamsburg Foundation for an education center, museum, and library. In 1989, he told a Washington Post reporter that "Richard Nixon gave me the greatest honor of my life." In 1968, Nixon appointed Annenberg as Ambassador to the Court of St. James and he served in Great Britain until 1974. The former ambassador remains close to many prominent Republicans, as well as the Royal Family.

Financial Summary

Total Giving: $155,000,000 (fiscal year ending June 30, 2003 approx); $150,000,000 (fiscal 2002 approx); $136,895,959 (fiscal 2001)
Assets: $2,600,000,000 (fiscal 2003 approx); $2,900,000,000 (fiscal 2002 approx); $2,932,205,767 (fiscal 2001)
Gifts Received: $548,509 (fiscal 1992)

Typical Recipients

Arts & Humanities: Arts Appreciation, Arts Associations & Councils, Arts Centers, Arts Funds, Film & Video, Historic Preservation, History & Archaeology, Libraries, Museums/Galleries, Music, Opera, Performing Arts, Public Broadcasting, Theater
Civic & Public Affairs: Business/Free Enterprise, Community Foundations, Civic & Public Affairs-General, Inner-City Development, Legal Aid, Municipalities/Towns, Nonprofit Management, Philanthropic Organizations, Professional & Trade Associations, Public Policy, Rural Affairs, Urban & Community Affairs
Education: Afterschool/Enrichment Programs, Arts/Humanities Education, Colleges & Universities, Community & Junior Colleges, Continuing Education, Education Associations, Education Funds, Education Reform, Education Reform, Elementary Education (Public), Environmental Education, Faculty Development, Education-General, International Studies, Journalism/Media Education, Legal Education, Literacy, Medical Education, Minority Education, Preschool Education, Private Education (Precollege), Public Education (Precollege), Religious Education, Science/Mathematics Education, Vocational & Technical Education
Environment: Environment-General, Resource Conservation, Wildlife Protection
Health: Cancer, Children's Health/Hospitals, Clinics/Medical Centers, Emergency/Ambulance Services, Health Funds, Health Organizations, Hospitals, Medical Research, Mental Health, Nursing Services, Preventive Medicine/Wellness Organizations, Research/Studies Institutes
International: Foreign Arts Organizations, Foreign Educational Institutions, International Affairs, International Development, International Environmental Issues, International Organizations, International Relations, Missionary/Religious Activities
Religion: Churches, Dioceses, Jewish Causes, Ministries, Missionary Activities (Domestic), Religious Organizations, Religious Welfare, Social/Policy Issues, Synagogues/Temples
Science: Science Museums, Scientific Centers & Institutes, Scientific Organizations
Social Services: Animal Protection, Child Welfare, Crime Prevention, Family Planning, Family Services, People with Disabilities, Recreation & Athletics, Scouts, Substance Abuse, United Funds/United Ways, Volunteer Services, Youth Organizations

Application Procedures

Initial Contact: Applicants should submit a brief letter of inquiry.
Application Requirements: Letters should include a brief statement of the need for funds and sufficient factual information to enable the foundation's staff to determine whether or not the application falls within the foundations areas of preferred interest or warrants consideration. If a formal proposal is then requested, it should contain a cover letter providing a brief description of organization, the proposed project, and the amount requested. This proposal should also include background information on the organization, a full description of the proposed project with evidence of its need, an outline for carrying out the project, an evaluation plan, biographical information about the person implementing the program, and principal affiliations of any directors or trustees. In the proposal, a detailed program budget showing sources of funding, a statement concerning plans for continuing support following the foundation's grant, a financial statement, the organization's operating budget during the years of the project, documentation that the organization's board of directors supports the project, and a copy of the organization's exemption letter. Also, advised to consult the Internet site.
Deadlines: None.
Review Process: Following submission of both the letter of inquiry and the full proposal, the review process is generally prompt, but may take up to six months. All grants are approved by the foundation's advisory committee.
A project's contribution to long-term K-12 school reform carries weight, as do fiscal soundness, realistic prospects for future support, and a detailed project budget.
Notes: Applicants should not send a full proposal without preliminary inquiry.

Restrictions

The foundation reports that it does not support individuals, basic research, capital campaigns, construction projects, or operating expenses and is unwilling to offer long-term support of an organization or activity. The foundation does not directly or indirectly support candidates for political office or influence legislation.

Additional Information

The Annenberg Fund, which was established by Walter Annenberg in 1951, has merged with the Annenberg Foundation.
New requests from previously funded organizations will normally be reviewed only after the expiration of the foundation's first grant.
Award recipients are expected to comply with conditions set forth in grant award letters. Challenge grant recipients, working with an independent evaluator, are also responsible for undertaking their own evaluation and documentation. A national assessment of the Annenberg Challenge's impact will be conducted separately. Challenge grants generally cover a period of five years and are tied to progress.
Publications: Guidelines

Foundation Officials

Leonore A. Annenberg: president, director ED Stanford University BA. NONPR AFFIL board: Philadelphia Orchestra; trustee: University Pennsylvania; director: Philadelphia Museum Art; member trustee council: National Gallery Art; honorary trustee: Palm Springs Desert Museum; managing director: Metropolitan Opera Association; honorary trustee: Louisiana Music Center; director: Metropolitan Museum Art; member: Distinguished Daughters Pennsylvania; member: Academy of Music Committee; member: Committee Preservation White House.
Wallis Annenberg: vice president ED Pine Manor College (1959). NONPR AFFIL honorary member: USC Annenberg School for Communication; director: Young Musicians Foundation; trustee emeritus: Pine Manor College; trustee: Entertainment Industries Council Inc.; director: Los Angeles Philharmonic Association.
Lauren Bon: trustee
William J. Henrich, Jr.: secretary, general counsel B Philadelphia, PA 1929. ED LaSalle University BA (1950); Temple University JD (1956). PRIM CORP EMPL senior partner: Dilworth, Paxson, Kalish & Kauffman. CORP AFFIL member board managers: Beneficial Savings Bank; trustee: Philadelphia Consolidated Holding Corp. NONPR AFFIL trustee: University Pennsylvania Annenberg School Communications; trustee: University Southern California Annenberg School Communications; director: LaSalle University; member: Union League Philadelphia; member: American Bar Association; executive vice president: Executive Sounding Board.

Dr. Gail C. Levin: executive director
Dr. Gillian Norris-Szanto: program officer
Meridyth M. Senes: program officer
Charles Weingarten: trustee
Gregory Weingarten: trustee

Grants Analysis

Disclosure Period: fiscal year ending June 30, 2001
Total Grants: $132,384,109*
Number of Grants: 443
Average Grant: $5,000*
Highest Grant: $10,000,000
Lowest Grant: $100
Typical Range: $25,000 to $300,000
*Note: Grants analysis provided by foundation. Average grant reflects median grant amount.

Recent Grants

Note: Grants derived from fiscal 2001 Form 990.

Library-Related

2,000,000	Rancho Mirage Public Library, Rancho Mirage, CA
1,000,000	George Bush Presidential Library Foundation, College Station, TX

General

10,181,700	South Florida Annenberg Challenge, Ft. Lauderdale, FL
6,701,501	Schools of the 21st Century Corporation, Detroit, MI
6,685,200	Chicago Annenberg Challenge, Chicago, IL
5,950,736	California Community Foundation, Los Angeles, CA
5,480,000	Rural School and Community Trust, Washington, DC
5,002,000	Eisenhower Medical Center, Rancho Mirage, CA
4,956,868	Houston Annenberg Challenge, Houston, TX
4,500,000	Corporation for Public Broadcasting, Washington, DC
3,978,000	Center for Arts Education, New York, NY
3,765,000	Trustees of the University of Pennsylvania, Philadelphia, PA

ANSCHUTZ FAMILY FOUNDATION

Giving Contact

Sue Anschutz-Rodgers, President & Executive Director
555 17th Street, Suite 2400
Denver, CO 80202
Phone: (303)293-2338
Fax: (303)299-1235
Web: http://www.anschutzfamilyfoundation.org

Description

Founded: 1982
EIN: 742132676
Organization Type: Family Foundation
Giving Locations: CO
Grant Types: General Support, Project.

Donor Information

Founder: Established in 1982. The donors are Fred B. Anschutz, Marian Pfister Anschutz, Sue Anschutz-Rodgers, and Philip F. Anschutz. Sue Anschutz-Rodgers is primarily responsible for the overall governance of the foundation's philanthropic giving.
Fred and Marian Pfister Anschutz endowed the foundation as a result of their many years of gas and oil, real estate, and livestock ventures. The foundation continues to receive contributions from family members to supplement the annual grant making capacity.

Financial Summary

Total Giving: $2,000,000 (fiscal year ending November 30, 2002 approx); $1,680,430 (fiscal 2001); $1,501,278 (fiscal 2000)
Giving Analysis: Giving for fiscal 1998 includes: foundation scholarships ($21,000)
Assets: $42,524,820 (fiscal 2001); $38,290,237 (fiscal 2000); $38,380,536 (fiscal 1999)
Gifts Received: $12,007,339 (fiscal 1997); $2,214,750 (fiscal 1996); $390,000 (fiscal 1995). Note: In fiscal 1997 contributions were received from Fred B. Anschutz Trust and other contributors.

Typical Recipients

Arts & Humanities: Arts Outreach, Ethnic & Folk Arts, History & Archaeology, Libraries, Museums/Galleries, Opera, Public Broadcasting
Civic & Public Affairs: Asian American Affairs, Botanical Gardens/Parks, Community Foundations, Economic Development, Employment/Job Training, Civic & Public Affairs-General, Hispanic Affairs, Housing, Legal Aid, Municipalities/Towns, Native American Affairs, Nonprofit Management, Professional & Trade Associations, Rural Affairs, Urban & Community Affairs, Women's Affairs, Zoos/Aquariums
Education: Afterschool/Enrichment Programs, Arts/Humanities Education, Business Education, Colleges & Universities, Continuing Education, Education Reform, Elementary Education (Public), Leadership Training, Literacy, Minority Education, Private Education (Precollege), Public Education (Precollege), Science/Mathematics Education, Social Sciences Education, Special Education, Student Aid
Environment: Environment-General
Health: AIDS/HIV, Alzheimers Disease, Cancer, Children's Health/Hospitals, Clinics/Medical Centers, Emergency/Ambulance Services, Geriatric Health, Health Organizations, Heart, Home-Care Services, Hospices, Hospitals, Medical Rehabilitation, Medical Research, Mental Health, Multiple Sclerosis, Nursing Services, Preventive Medicine/Wellness Organizations, Public Health, Research/Studies Institutes, Single-Disease Health Associations, Trauma Treatment
International: Health Care/Hospitals, International Relief Efforts
Religion: Religion-General, Ministries, Religious Organizations, Religious Welfare, Social/Policy Issues
Science: Science Museums
Social Services: At-Risk Youth, Big Brother/Big Sister, Camps, Child Welfare, Community Centers, Community Service Organizations, Counseling, Crime Prevention, Domestic Violence, Family Planning, Family Services, Food/Clothing Distribution, Homes, People with Disabilities, Recreation & Athletics, Scouts, Senior Services, Shelters/Homelessness, Social Services-General, Substance Abuse, Volunteer Services, Youth Organizations

Application Procedures

Initial Contact: Request application guidelines or submit a proposal using the Colorado Common Grant Application.
Application Requirements: Proposals should include a summary of the applicant organization, including the organization's name, address, telephone and fax numbers, email and Web addresses, name of executive director, contact person, amount requested, brief description of request, and signature of chief administrator; organizational information, including mission, purpose, and brief statement of goals, a brief history of organization, summary of the organization's activities, including community/client engagement efforts, and description of the role of volunteers; purpose of grant, including expanded description of goals and measurable objectives, plans for cooperation with other organizations, funding strategies, statement of need and project scope, planned activities and administration, and timetable; evaluation efforts, including anticipated outcomes, how they

will be measured, and organization's evaluation capacity. Attachments should include proof of tax-exempt status, list of key personnel and qualifications, current and future organizational budget, project budget, audited financial statements, list of major contributors, roster of board of directors with affiliations, anti-discrimination statement, and any other material that might be helpful.
Deadlines: Proposals are due February 1 and August 1.
Review Process: Foundation acknowledges the receipt of all proposals; only one proposal per year per organization will be reviewed. Proposals are reviewed semi-annually. Upon review of the application letter, a foundation staff member may request further information. All applicants will be notified whether their requests were denied or granted in writing soon after the May 1 and December 1 semi-annual meetings.
Evaluative Criteria: Alignment with the mission and interests of the Foundation; clearly presented proposal; solid financial sustainability plan; committed board of directors who make financial contributions to the organization; strong volunteer participation; community buy-in; solid effort to engage in the community and/or participants in program development; effective and inspired leadership; an eye on the future that reflects recognition of potential impacts on and opportunities for the organization; geographic location and focus.
Notes: Faxes and emails are not acceptable for transmitting a proposal.

Restrictions

The foundation generally does not support individuals, programs outside of Colorado, graduate or post-graduate research, religious organizations for religious purposes, special events or promotions, candidates for political office, endowments, debt reduction, multi-year grants, or capital campaigns.

Additional Information

The Anschutz Family Foundation receives many requests from very qualified and capable non-profit organizations. Although they provide grants to over 200 Colorado non-profit organizations each year, they cannot be counted on as a sustained giver. In order to be fair in distributing grants, they instituted the "two year rule" in 1990, asking that an organization which receives funding from the Anschutz Family Foundation for two successive years to take one year off before reapplying.
Publications: Annual Report; Guidelines

Foundation Officials

Elizabeth S. Anschutz: trustee
Sue Anschutz-Rodgers: donor, president, executive director, trustee B 1933. NONPR AFFIL director: Up with People.
Hugh C. Braly: secretary, trustee
Melinda A. Rodgers Couzens: trustee
Sarah Anschutz Hunt: trustee
Melissa A. Rodgers Padgett: trustee
Jeff W. Pryor: assistant executive director
Robert S. Rich, Esq.: trustee B New York, NY 1938. ED Harvard University (1961); Yale University (1965). PRIM CORP EMPL partner: Davis, Graham & Stubbs. NONPR AFFIL member: International Bar Association; adjunct faculty: University Denver; Denver World Affairs Council; member: Colorado Bar Association; member: Colorado International Trade Advisory Council; sponsor: American Tax Policy Institute; member: American Bar Association. CLUB AFFIL Yale Club; Mile High Club; Cactus Club; Denver Club.
Susan E. Rodgers Drumm: program ofr, trustee
Brenda Weissman: administrative assistant

Grants Analysis

Disclosure Period: fiscal year ending November 30, 2001
Total Grants: $1,680,430
Number of Grants: 299

Average Grant: $5,620
Highest Grant: $40,000
Lowest Grant: $2,000
Typical Range: $2,500 to $10,000

Recent Grants

Note: Grants derived from fiscal 2001 Form 990.

Library-Related

10,000	Lake County Public Library, Leadville, CO -- support remodel and re-roofing of the library

General

40,000	Greater Denver Neighborhood Partnership, Denver, CO -- support the opportunity for neighborhood representatives to make funding decisions for local projects
20,000	Rocky Mountain Public Broadcasting Network, Denver, CO -- support "Life Wise" programming
15,000	Community Resource Center, Denver, CO -- scholarships
15,000	Habitat for Humanity, Denver, CO -- help provide affordable housing to low-income families
10,000	Colorado Boys Ranch Foundation, La Junta, CO -- provide support for Vocational Education Program
10,000	Colorado Housing, Inc., Pagosa Springs, CO -- support the youth program
10,000	COMPA Food Ministries, Denver, CO -- operating support
10,000	Mount St. Vincent Home, Denver, CO -- provide education and therapy to children
10,000	St. Anne's Episcopal School, Denver, CO -- operating support
10,000	Senior Answers and Services, Denver, CO -- support development of a non-profit entrepreneurial plan

RONALD M. ANSIN FOUNDATION

Giving Contact

Ronald M. Ansin, Trustee
1 Main St.
Leominster, MA 01453
Phone: (978)543-0463

Description

Founded: 1984
EIN: 042786469
Organization Type: Private Foundation
Giving Locations: DC; MA; NY
Grant Types: Emergency, General Support, Project.

Donor Information

Founder: Ronald M. Ansin

Financial Summary

Total Giving: $985,112 (fiscal year ending November 30, 2001); $935,114 (fiscal 2000); $789,782 (fiscal 1999). Note: Contributes through foundation only.
Giving Analysis: Giving for fiscal 2001 includes: foundation grants to United Way ($10,500); fiscal 2000: foundation grants to United Way ($5,400); fiscal 1999: foundation grants to United Way ($10,000);
Assets: $13,454,122 (fiscal 2001); $14,405,724 (fiscal 2000); $11,205,831 (fiscal 1999)
Gifts Received: $271,632 (fiscal 2000); $1,400,000 (fiscal 1993); $3,941,484 (fiscal 1992). Note: In fiscal 1993 and 2000, contributions were received from Ronald M. Ansin.

Typical Recipients

Arts & Humanities: Arts Funds, Community Arts, Arts & Humanities-General, History & Archaeology, Libraries, Museums/Galleries, Music, Performing Arts, Theater
Civic & Public Affairs: Chambers of Commerce, Civil Rights, Clubs, Community Foundations, Gay/Lesbian Issues, Civic & Public Affairs-General, Legal Aid, Municipalities/Towns, Parades/Festivals, Public Policy, Urban & Community Affairs
Education: Colleges & Universities, Community & Junior Colleges, Education Reform, Faculty Development, International Exchange, Legal Education, Private Education (Precollege), Vocational & Technical Education
Environment: Air/Water Quality, Environment-General, Resource Conservation, Watershed
Health: AIDS/HIV, Children's Health/Hospitals, Clinics/Medical Centers, Emergency/Ambulance Services, Hospitals, Mental Health, Single-Disease Health Associations
International: International-General, International Environmental Issues, International Organizations, International Peace & Security Issues, International Relations, International Relief Efforts, Missionary/Religious Activities
Religion: Churches, Jewish Causes, Religious Organizations, Religious Welfare, Synagogues/Temples
Science: Scientific Labs
Social Services: At-Risk Youth, Child Welfare, Community Service Organizations, Domestic Violence, Family Planning, Family Services, People with Disabilities, Recreation & Athletics, Scouts, Senior Services, Social Services-General, Special Olympics, Substance Abuse, United Funds/United Ways, Veterans, Youth Organizations, Youth Organizations

Application Procedures

Initial Contact: Send brief letter describing program.
Application Requirements: Include purpose of funds sought, recently audited financial statement, and proof of 501 (c) (3) status.
Deadlines: None.

Foundation Officials

Ronald M. Ansin: trustee B Worcester, MA 1934. ED Harvard University BA (1955); Yale University JD (1958). PRIM CORP EMPL chairman, treasurer, director: L.B. Evans & Son Co. CORP AFFIL chairman: Merchants National Bank; director, president: Cleghorn Shoe Corp.; director: Cole-Haan; chairman: Anwelt Corp.; chairman: America Footwear Corp.; chairman: Ansewn Shoe Corp. NONPR AFFIL trustee: Fitchburg Saint College; trustee: Leominster Hospital; trustee: Fitchburg Art Museum; trustee: Applewild School.

Grants Analysis

Disclosure Period: fiscal year ending November 30, 2000
Total Grants: $974,612*
Number of Grants: 94
Average Grant: $9,304*
Highest Grant: $100,000
Lowest Grant: $100
Typical Range: $1,000 to $25,000
*Note: Giving excludes United Way. Average grant excludes highest grant.

Recent Grants

Note: Grants derived from fiscal 2001 Form 990.

General

100,000	GLSEN, New York, NY
50,000	American Civil Liberties Union Foundation, Boston, MA
50,000	Fenway Community Health Center, Boston, MA
50,000	Spanish American Center, Leominster, MA
50,000	Victory Foundation, Washington, DC
30,000	ARC Foundation, Washington, DC
30,000	New Israel Fund, Chestnut Hill, MA
25,000	AIDS Action Committee, Boston, MA
25,000	Fitchburg Art Museum, Fitchburg, MA
25,000	Yeshiva Achei Tmimin, Worcester, MA

DANTZLER BOND ANSLEY FOUNDATION

Giving Contact

Kim Williams, Trust Officer, 4th FL
c/o Sun Trust Bank
PO Box 305110
Nashville, TN 37230-5110
Phone: (615)748-4879

Description

Founded: 1980
EIN: 592111990
Organization Type: Private Foundation
Giving Locations: TN: Nashville
Grant Types: Capital, General Support.

Donor Information

Founder: the late Mildred B. Ansley

Financial Summary

Total Giving: $499,890 (fiscal year ending April 30, 1997); $238,500 (fiscal 1995); $272,500 (fiscal 1994). Note: Fiscal 1997 Giving includes United Way ($60,000).
Assets: $10,034,314 (fiscal 1997); $7,693,575 (fiscal 1995); $7,307,800 (fiscal 1994)

Typical Recipients

Arts & Humanities: Historic Preservation, Libraries, Museums/Galleries, Music
Civic & Public Affairs: Civic & Public Affairs-General, Law & Justice, Legal Aid, Municipalities/Towns, Zoos/Aquariums
Education: Colleges & Universities, Continuing Education, Legal Education, Medical Education, Private Education (Precollege), Student Aid
Health: Cancer, Children's Health/Hospitals, Health Organizations, Medical Research, Mental Health, Respiratory, Single-Disease Health Associations, Speech & Hearing
International: International Relief Efforts
Religion: Churches, Ministries, Missionary Activities (Domestic), Religious Organizations, Religious Welfare
Social Services: Child Welfare, Community Centers, Community Service Organizations, Counseling, Family Planning, Family Services, Homes, People with Disabilities, Recreation & Athletics, Scouts, Senior Services, Social Services-General, Special Olympics, Substance Abuse, United Funds/United Ways, YMCA/YWCA/YMHA/YWHA, Youth Organizations

Application Procedures

Initial Contact: The foundation has no formal grant application procedure or application form.
Deadlines: None.

Additional Information

Trust(s): Suntrust Bank
Trust(s): Third Natl Bank

Foundation Officials

Hon. Frank F. Drowota, III: trustee B Williamsburg, KY 1938. ED Vanderbilt University BA (1960); Vanderbilt University JD (1965). PRIM NONPR EMPL associate justice: Tennessee Supreme Court.
Dr. Thomas Fearn Frist, Sr.: trustee B Meridian, MS December 15, 1910. ED University of Mississippi BS (1929); Vanderbilt University MD (1933). PRIM CORP EMPL vice chairman, chief medicine service: Hospital

Corp. of America. CORP AFFIL founder: Park Manor Presbyterian Apartments Elderly; director: Dominion Bank Middle Tennessee; senior member: Frist-Scoville Med Group; vice chairman, founder: America Retirement Corp. NONPR AFFIL member: Sigma Alpha Epsilon; member: TN Heart Association; honorary trustee: Rhodes College; member: Royal Society Internal Medicine; director: Montgomery Bell Academy; member: Nashville Society Internal Medicine; founder: Cumberland Heights Foundation Rehabilitation Alcoholics; director: Medical Benevolence Foundation; fellow: American College Physicians. CLUB AFFIL Lago Mar Golf & Country Club; Belle Meade Country Club.

Fred McFerrin Russell: trustee B Nashville, TN August 27, 1906. ED Vanderbilt University (1927). PRIM CORP EMPL vice president: Nashville Banner. NONPR AFFIL member: Football Writers Association America; chairman honorary court: National Football Foundation & Hall Fame.

Grants Analysis
Disclosure Period: fiscal year ending April 30, 1997
Total Grants: $439,890*
Number of Grants: 63
Average Grant: $6,982
Highest Grant: $30,000
Typical Range: $1,000 to $10,000
***Note:** Giving excludes United Way. A more recent grants list was unavailable.

Recent Grants
Note: Grants derived from fiscal 1997 Form 990.

General

60,000	United Way, Nashville, TN
30,000	Sarah Cannon Cancer Foundation, Nashville, TN
25,000	YMCA, Nashville, TN
20,000	Battle Ground Academy
20,000	Ensworth School, Nashville, TN
20,000	YCAP, Nashville, TN
17,000	Senior Citizens, Nashville, TN
16,000	Jamaican Friends International, Knoxville, TN
15,000	Boy Scouts of America, Nashville, TN
15,000	Girl Scouts of America Cumberland Valley, Nashville, TN

ANTHEM INC.

Company Headquarters
120 Monument Circle
Indianapolis, IN 46204
Web: http://www.anthem.com

Company Description
Ticker: ATH
Exchange: NYSE
Former Name: Anthem Insurance Co. (2001);
Acquired: Southeastern Mutual Insurance (1993); Community Mutual Insurance Co. (1995).
Assets: US$12.293 billion (2002)
Profit: US$549.1 million (2002)
Employees: 19500 (2002)
Fortune Rank: 146, per FORTUNE Magazine's list of 500 Largest U.S. Corporations (2002).
SIC(s): 6311 Life Insurance, 6321 Accident & Health Insurance.

Anthem Foundation, Inc.

Giving Contact
Connie Molland
Anthem Foundation
120 Monument Circle
Indianapolis, IN 46204

Phone: 800-563-5465
Note: Contact and mailing address for applications.

Alternate Contact
Anthem Foundation
9901 Linn Station Road
Louisville, KY 40223
Phone: (502)423-2331
Note: Foundation's official address

Description
Founded: 1990
EIN: 611191499
Organization Type: Corporate Foundation
Giving Locations: KY
Grant Types: Employee Matching Gifts, Project.

Donor Information
Founder: Blue Cross and Blue Shield of Kentucky, Southeastern Mutual Insurance Co.

Financial Summary
Total Giving: $221,447 (2001); $348,000 (2000); $372,498 (1999). Note: Contributes through foundation only.
Giving Analysis: Giving for 2000 includes: foundation grants to United Way ($92,500); foundation ($255,500); 1999: foundation grants to United Way ($43,000); foundation ($329,498); 1998: corporate matching gifts ($6,200); foundation matching gifts ($6,200); corporate grants to United Way ($31,000); foundation grants to United Way ($31,000); corporate direct giving ($255,500);
Assets: $6,578,320 (2001); $6,214,674 (2000); $6,081,416 (1999)
Gifts Received: $12,000 (2001); $12,000 (2000); $12,000 (1998). Note: Contributions are received from SpectraCare.

Typical Recipients
Arts & Humanities: Arts Festivals, Arts Funds, Ballet, History & Archaeology, Libraries, Museums/Galleries, Music, Opera, Public Broadcasting, Theater
Civic & Public Affairs: African American Affairs, Botanical Gardens/Parks, Business/Free Enterprise, Economic Development, Civic & Public Affairs-General, Municipalities/Towns, Professional & Trade Associations, Public Policy, Urban & Community Affairs, Women's Affairs
Education: Arts/Humanities Education, Business Education, Colleges & Universities, Community & Junior Colleges, Economic Education, Education Funds, Education Reform, Education-General, Leadership Training, Medical Education, Minority Education, Private Education (Precollege), Public Education (Precollege), Religious Education, Secondary Education (Private), Secondary Education (Public), Special Education, Student Aid
Environment: Environment-General, Resource Conservation
Health: AIDS/HIV, Cancer, Children's Health/Hospitals, Clinics/Medical Centers, Diabetes, Emergency/Ambulance Services, Health-General, Health Organizations, Heart, Hospitals, Medical Rehabilitation, Multiple Sclerosis, Nursing Services, Prenatal Health Issues, Preventive Medicine/Wellness Organizations, Public Health, Respiratory, Single-Disease Health Associations, Trauma Treatment
Religion: Dioceses, Religious Organizations, Religious Welfare
Science: Scientific Centers & Institutes
Social Services: At-Risk Youth, Camps, Child Abuse, Child Welfare, Community Service Organizations, Food/Clothing Distribution, Scouts, Senior Services, Special Olympics, Substance Abuse, United Funds/United Ways, YMCA/YWCA/YMHA/YWHA

Application Procedures
Initial Contact: Request application form.
Deadlines: None.

Corporate Officials
Larry G. Glasscock: chairman, chief executive officer chief medical officer
Samuel R. Nussbaum, MD: executive vice president, chief medical officer
Michael L. Smith: executive vice president, chief financial officer

Foundation Officials
David R. Frick: chairman PRIM CORP EMPL executive vice president, chief administrative officer: Anthem Insurance Companies. CORP AFFIL officer: Anthem Companies Inc.; officer: Anthem Life Insurance Co.
Larry G. Glasscock: director (see above)
James Lemaster: president B 1938. ADD CORP EMPL president: Truck Maintenance Corp.
George Martin: treasurer
Nancy L. Purcell: secretary PRIM CORP EMPL secretary: Anthem Companies Inc. CORP AFFIL secretary: Anthem Health Indiana; secretary: Anthem Insurance Companies.
M. Ellen Rooze: assistant secretary
Michael L. Smith: director (see above)

Grants Analysis
Disclosure Period: calendar year ending 2001
Total Grants: $117,901*
Number of Grants: 14
Average Grant: $8,422
Highest Grant: $45,000
Lowest Grant: $25
Typical Range: $25 to $20,000
***Note:** Giving excludes United Way.

Recent Grants
Note: Grants derived from 2001 Form 990.

General

103,546	United Way Community Chest, Cincinnati, OH
45,000	Greater Louisville Foundation, Louisville, KY
25,000	BCBS Foundation on Health Care
20,000	Louisville Deaf Oral School, Louisville, KY
15,000	Partners for a Healthy Louisville, Louisville, KY
10,000	Greater Louisville Foundation, Louisville, KY
600	University of Louisville, Louisville, KY
500	Christian Academy, Bowling Green, KY
500	Highview Baptist School
500	St. Xavier High School, Louisville, KY

AOL TIME WARNER

Company Headquarters
75 Rockefeller Plaza
New York, NY 10019
Phone: (212)484-8000
Fax: (212)489-6183
Web: http://www.aoltimewarner.com

Company Description
Founded: 1985
Ticker: AOL
Exchange: NYSE
Acquired: Time Warner (2001);
Former Name: America Online (AOL) (2001);
Acquired: Time Warner Entertainment Co..
Operating Revenue: US$40.961 billion (2002)
Employees: 91250 (2002)
Fortune Rank: 29, per FORTUNE Magazine's list of 500 Largest U.S. Corporations (2002).

Parent Company: AOL Time Warner, 75 Rockefeller Plaza, New York, NY, United States

AOL Time Warner Foundation

Giving Contact
22000 AOL Way
Dulles, VA 20166-9323
Phone: (703)265-2282
E-mail: aoltwfoundation@aol.com
Web: http://aoltwfoundation.org

Alternate Contact
Phone: 800-818-1066

Description
EIN: 541886827
Organization Type: Corporate Foundation
Also Known As: AOL Foundation.
Former Name: Time Warner Foundation.
Giving Locations: nationally.
Grant Types: Capital, Employee Matching Gifts, General Support.

Financial Summary
Total Giving: $6,366,757 (2002 approx); $4,223,324 (2001); $2,311,026 (2000)
Giving Analysis: Giving for 2000 includes: foundation grants to United Way ($500); foundation gifts to individuals ($47,500) foundation ($2,263,026)
Assets: $2,660,422 (2001); $2,849,076 (2000); $2,430,302 (1999)
Gifts Received: $4,551,645 (2001); $5,728,971 (2000); $4,026,465 (1999). Note: In 2001, contributions were received from AOL Time Warner ($4,551,645). In 2000, contributions were received from AOL, Inc. ($5,718,971) and Ikon Office Solutions ($10,000). In 1999, contributions were received from AOL.

Typical Recipients
Arts & Humanities: Arts Associations & Councils, Film & Video, Arts & Humanities-General, History & Archaeology, Libraries, Museums/Galleries, Music
Civic & Public Affairs: African American Affairs, Asian American Affairs, Business/Free Enterprise, Community Foundations, Economic Development, Ethnic Organizations, Civic & Public Affairs-General, Minority Business, Municipalities/Towns, Native American Affairs, Nonprofit Management, Philanthropic Organizations, Urban & Community Affairs
Education: Colleges & Universities, Education Associations, Education Funds, Elementary Education (Public), Education-General, Journalism/Media Education, Literacy, Medical Education, Private Education (Precollege), Public Education (Precollege), Science/Mathematics Education, Secondary Education (Private), Secondary Education (Public), Special Education, Vocational & Technical Education
Health: Cancer, Children's Health/Hospitals, Health-General, Health Organizations, Public Health, Transplant Networks/Donor Banks
International: Foreign Educational Institutions, International Peace & Security Issues
Religion: Ministries, Religious Welfare
Science: Science Museums
Social Services: Community Service Organizations, Counseling, People with Disabilities, Senior Services, Social Services-General, United Funds/United Ways, Youth Organizations

Application Procedures
Initial Contact: An application form is required and may be obtained from the foundation's web site. Telephone requests are not accepted.
Application Requirements: Include organization name and address; brief history; mission statement; contact's name, title, phone number, and e-mail address; amount requested; project start and end dates; project description and evaluation process; other partners working on the project; any additional project funding from other sources; description of how the project fits into one of the four priority areas; project audience; and project budget.
Deadlines: None.
Review Process: Proposals are reviewed throughout the year. Allow 8 to 12 weeks for a response.
Evaluative Criteria: Organizations must have a well-defined purpose which is within the foundation's scope of giving, namely the four key priorities: Equipping Kids for the 21st Century; Extending Internet Benefits to All; Engaging Communities in the Arts; and Empowering Citizens and Civic Participation. They should have a national focus and should be a good strategic partner.

Restrictions
As a general rule, the foundation does not fund unsolicited proposals except under very special circumstances. However, organizations who believe they have an exceptional proposal that falls within the foundation's priorities may submit a request.
AOL Time Warner does not consider funding the following: organizations that do not have 501(c)(3) tax-exempt status; individuals; political, labor, religious or fraternal organizations; amateur or professional sports groups; publications of books or the production of films and music; capital fund drives; or organizations whose missions fall outside the four focus areas.

Additional Information
Time Warner, Inc. and America Online, Inc. merged to form AOL Time Warner, Inc. TW Foundation will dispose of all assets to AOL Time Warner Foundation, Inc. pursuant to the merger.

Corporate Officials
Stephen M. Case: chairman B August 21, 1958. ED Williams College BA (1980). PRIM CORP EMPL chairman: AOL Time Warner Inc.

Grants Analysis
Disclosure Period: calendar year ending 2001
Total Grants: $4,223,324
Number of Grants: 856
Average Grant: $4,934
Highest Grant: $300,000
Lowest Grant: $10
Typical Range: $500 to $2,000 and $1,503 to $93,321

Recent Grants
Note: Grants derived from 2001 Form 990.

Library-Related
25,000	Library of Congress, Washington, DC

General
300,000	Peace Corps, New York, NY
300,000	Virginia Health Care Foundation, Richmond, VA
200,000	Peace Corps, New York, NY
187,500	AOL Time Warner, Dulles, VA
160,500	Pipe Vine
146,882	ePlus Technology, Inc.
100,000	Charities Aid Foundation, Alexandria, VA
100,000	Community Foundation for the National Capital Region, Washington, DC
100,000	CompuMentor, San Francisco, CA
85,308	AOL Time Warner, Dulles, VA

AON CORP.

Company Headquarters
200 E. Randolph
Chicago, IL 60601
Web: http://www.aon.com

Company Description
Founded: 1979
Ticker: AOC
Exchange: NYSE
Revenue: US$8.822 billion (2002)
Profit: US$466 million (2002)
Employees: 53000 (2001)
Fortune Rank: 212, per FORTUNE Magazine's list of 500 Largest U.S. Corporations (2002).
SIC(s): 6411 Insurance Agents, Brokers & Service, 6719 Holding Companies Nec.

Operating Locations
Aon Corp. (MD--Owings Mills; NJ--Lyndhurst; TN--Nashville; TX--Dallas)

Aon Foundation

Giving Contact
Carolyn E. Labutka, Executive Director
AON Foundation
200 East Randolph Street
Chicago, IL 60601
Phone: (312)381-3549
Fax: (312)701-4533

Description
EIN: 363337340
Organization Type: Corporate Foundation
Giving Locations: internationally; operating locations.
Grant Types: Award, Capital, Challenge, Department, Employee Matching Gifts, Endowment, General Support, Operating Expenses, Research.
Note: Employee matching gift ratio: 1 to 1.

Financial Summary
Total Giving: $5,704,663 (2001); $5,567,230 (2000); $5,000,000 (1999 approx). Note: Contributes through foundation only.
Giving Analysis: Giving for 2000 includes: foundation grants to United Way ($468,000); foundation matching gifts ($762,240); foundation ($4,336,990); 1998: foundation fellowships ($21,000); foundation grants to United Way ($45,900); foundation scholarships ($48,313); foundation matching gifts ($500,603); foundation ($3,905,207); 1996: foundation matching gifts ($366,342); foundation grants to United Way ($377,700) foundation ($3,464,129)
Assets: $654,966 (2001); $850,821 (2000); $39,637 (1998)
Gifts Received: $4,748,729 (2001); $6,420,000 (2000); $4,554,000 (1998). Note: In 1998, 2000, and 2001, contributions were received from AON Corporation and its subsidiaries.

Typical Recipients
Arts & Humanities: Arts Associations & Councils, Arts Centers, Arts Festivals, Arts Funds, Arts Institutes, Dance, Historic Preservation, History & Archaeology, Libraries, Museums/Galleries, Music, Opera, Performing Arts, Public Broadcasting, Theater
Civic & Public Affairs: Business/Free Enterprise, Civil Rights, Clubs, Economic Development, Economic Policy, Employment/Job Training, Civic & Public Affairs-General, Law & Justice, Municipalities/Towns, Parades/Festivals, Philanthropic Organizations, Public Policy, Safety, Urban & Community Affairs, Women's Affairs, Zoos/Aquariums
Education: Arts/Humanities Education, Business Education, Business-School Partnerships, Colleges & Universities, Education Associations, Education Funds, Elementary Education (Private), Elementary Education (Public), Faculty Development, Education-General, Health & Physical Education, Legal Education, Preschool Education, Private Education (Precollege), Public Education (Precollege), Religious Education, Science/Mathematics Education, Student Aid
Environment: Environment-General, Resource Conservation

Health: AIDS/HIV, Alzheimers Disease, Cancer, Children's Health/Hospitals, Clinics/Medical Centers, Diabetes, Emergency/Ambulance Services, Health Funds, Hospitals, Hospitals (University Affiliated), Medical Rehabilitation, Medical Research, Multiple Sclerosis, Single-Disease Health Associations
International: Foreign Educational Institutions, International Affairs, International Organizations, International Relations, International Relief Efforts
Religion: Churches, Dioceses, Jewish Causes, Religious Organizations, Religious Welfare
Science: Science Museums, Scientific Centers & Institutes
Social Services: At-Risk Youth, Child Welfare, Community Centers, Community Service Organizations, Counseling, Food/Clothing Distribution, Homes, People with Disabilities, Recreation & Athletics, Refugee Assistance, Scouts, Senior Services, United Funds/United Ways, Volunteer Services, YMCA/YWCA/YMHA/YWHA, Youth Organizations

Application Procedures

Initial Contact: Send a letter or proposal.
Application Requirements: Provide name, address, phone number of organization, and name of executive director; one paragraph description of organization; description of project, including specific objectives, evidence of need, proof that program would not duplicate existing services, and history of organization with such projects; amount requested and purpose of request; list of other potential funding sources and amounts; description of the greatest challenges facing organization in the next two or three years, and evaluation of organization's strengths and weaknesses; list of current contributors and amounts; proof of 501(c)(3) status, and annual report.
Deadlines: None.

Restrictions

Grants are not made to individuals or political organizations. Awards are restricted to charitable, educational (excluding the operation of a secondary educational institution or vocational school, and scientific organizations that qualify as: a) exempt organizations under the 1954 Internal Revenue Code Section 501 (c)(3) (or the corresponding provisions of any future United States revenue law), or (b) organizations described in the 1954 Internal Revenue Code Section 509 (a)(1),(2), or (3) (or the corresponding provisions of any United States revenue law).

Additional Information

AON Corporation was formerly Combined International Corporation. The AON Foundation was formerly the Combined International Foundation.
Publications: Foundation Annual Report

Corporate Officials

Daniel T. Cox: chairman vice president, chief counsel, director B 1946. ED University of North Carolina (1968); Vanderbilt University MA (1971). PRIM CORP EMPL chairman: Aon Corp.
Harvey Norman Medvin: executive vice president, treasurer, chief financial officer B Chicago, IL 1936. ED University of Illinois BS (1958). PRIM CORP EMPL executive vice president, treasurer, chief financial officer: Aon Corp. CORP AFFIL director: Ryan Insurance Group DE; president, treasurer, director: Ryan Warranty Services; director: Combined Insurance Co.
Patrick G. Ryan: chairman, president, chief executive officer B Milwaukee, WI 1937. ED Northwestern University BS (1959). PRIM CORP EMPL chairman, president, chief executive officer: Aon Corp. CORP AFFIL director: Tribune Co.; president: Ryan Properties Inc.; director: Sears, Roebuck & Co.; president: Ryan Companies United States Inc.; chairman, director: Pat Ryan & Associates; president: Ryan Builders Inc.; director: Combined Insurance Co.; director: AON Risk Services Companies; officer: AON Warranty Group; chairman: AON Group Inc. NONPR AFFIL

trustee: Northwestern University; trustee: Rush-Presbyterian-Saint Lukes Medical Center; trustee: Field Museum Natural History.
Raymond Inwood Skilling: executive vice president, chief counsel, director B Enniskillen, United Kingdom 1939. ED Queens University LLB (1961); University of Chicago JD (1962). PRIM CORP EMPL executive vice president, chief counsel, director: Aon Corp. CORP AFFIL executive vice president, chief couns, director: Combined Insurance Co. NONPR AFFIL member: Chicago Bar Association; member: Illinois Bar Association; member: American Bar Association. CLUB AFFIL Racquet Club Chicago; City London Club; Economic Club; Chicago Club; Carlton Club London; Casino Club.

Foundation Officials

Franklin Alan Cole: chairman, director B Park Falls, WI 1926. ED University of Illinois BA (1947); Northwestern University JD (1950). PRIM CORP EMPL chairman: Croesus Corp. CORP AFFIL vice president, director: AON Corp.; director: GATX Corp.; director: America National Bank & Trust Co. Chicago.
Carolyn E. Labutka: vice president, executive director
Andrew James McKenna: director B Chicago, IL 1929. ED University of Notre Dame BS (1951); DePaul University JD (1954). PRIM CORP EMPL chairman, president, chief executive officer: Schwarz Paper Co. CORP AFFIL director: Skyline Corp.; director: Tribune Co.; director: McDonald's Corp.; director: First Chicago NBD Corp.; director: First National Bank Chicago; director: Children's Memorial Hospital; director: Dean Foods Co.; director: Chicago Bears Football Club; director: Chicago National League Baseball Club; director: AON Corp. NONPR AFFIL chairman board trustees: Museum Science & Industry; chairman board trustees: University Notre Dame; director: Catholic Charities Chicago; director: Childrens Memorial Medical Center.
Harvey Norman Medvin: treasurer (see above)
Patrick G. Ryan: president, director (see above)
Raymond Inwood Skilling: director (see above)

Grants Analysis

Disclosure Period: calendar year ending 2000
Total Grants: $4,336,990*
Number of Grants: 325
Average Grant: $13,446
Highest Grant: $500,000
Lowest Grant: $100
Typical Range: $1,000 to $30,000 and $50,000 to $150,000
*Note: Giving excludes matching gifts and United Way.

Recent Grants

Note: Grants derived from 2001 Form 990.

General
500,000	Chicago Symphony Orchestra, Chicago, IL
150,000	St. John's University, New York, NY -- support for 2001
125,000	Northwestern University, Evanston, IL -- professorship in school of education
100,000	Archdiocese of Chicago, Chicago, IL -- annual program support
100,000	Homan Square Community Center Foundation, Chicago, IL -- community center
100,000	Providence-St. Mel School, Chicago, IL -- capital campaign
95,000	Boys and Girls Club, Chicago, IL -- annual support
66,000	Local Initiative Support Corporation, Chicago, IL -- program
65,000	Lyric Opera of Chicago, Chicago, IL -- Opening Night Gala 2001
50,000	Chicago Academy of Sciences, Chicago, IL -- Campaign for 21st Century sponsorship

APPELBAUM-KAHN FOUNDATION

Giving Contact

Carol G. Emerling
201 Ocean Avenue, Apt. 1510B
Santa Monica, CA 90402

Description

Founded: 1999
EIN: 957043271
Organization Type: Private Foundation
Grant Types: General Support.

Financial Summary

Total Giving: $37,250 (fiscal year ending October 31, 2001); $45,250 (fiscal 2000); $35,050 (fiscal 1999)
Assets: $1,055,998 (fiscal 2001); $1,319,310 (fiscal 2000); $1,279,151 (fiscal 1999)
Gifts Received: $460 (fiscal 1999); $1,234,410 (fiscal 1998). Note: In 1998, contributions were received from the Estate of Beatrice A. Kahn.

Typical Recipients

Arts & Humanities: Arts & Humanities-General, Performing Arts
Civic & Public Affairs: Civic & Public Affairs-General
Health: Health Policy/Cost Containment, Hospices
International: Human Rights
Religion: Synagogues/Temples

Application Procedures

Initial Contact: Send a brief letter of inquiry.
Application Requirements: Include a description of organization.
Deadlines: None.

Foundation Officials

Carol G. Emerling: co trustee
Keith S. Emerling: co trustee
Susan C. Emerling: co trustee

Grants Analysis

Disclosure Period: fiscal year ending October 31, 2001
Total Grants: $37,250
Number of Grants: 7
Highest Grant: $20,000
Lowest Grant: $250

Recent Grants

Note: Grants derived from 2000 Form 990.

General
20,000	Montefiore Foundation, Beachwood, OH
5,000	Freedom House Foundation, Glen Gardner, NJ
5,000	Inner City Arts, Los Angeles, CA -- adopt a teacher program
3,000	Austin Riggs Center, Stockbridge, MA -- patient aid director's fund
3,000	Hospice Care in the Berkshire Inc., Pittsfield, MA -- small gift fund, palliative care and community bereavement programs, caring choices library creative passages
2,500	Global Health Council, White River Junction, VT -- Jonathan Mann health and human rights award
2,500	Site Santa Fe, Santa Fe, NM
2,500	Yoga Inside Foundation, Venice, CA
1,500	Harvest Works, New York, NY -- a mechanical medium program
250	Anshe Chesed Fairmont Temple, Beachwood, OH

SCOTT B. AND ANNIE P. APPLEBY TRUST

Giving Contact
Christine A. Butler
c/o Suntrust Bank
PO Box 2018
Sarasota, FL 34230
Phone: (941)951-3324

Description
Founded: 1948
EIN: 526334302
Organization Type: Private Foundation
Giving Locations: DC; FL; GA
Grant Types: General Support.

Financial Summary
Total Giving: $283,298 (2002); $322,000 (2001); $297,500 (2000)
Assets: $4,367,610 (2002); $5,476,631 (2001); $6,339,084 (2000)

Typical Recipients
Arts & Humanities: Arts Institutes, Ballet, Community Arts, Libraries, Museums/Galleries, Music, Performing Arts, Theater
Civic & Public Affairs: Community Foundations, Civic & Public Affairs-General, Housing
Education: Arts/Humanities Education, Colleges & Universities, Environmental Education, Education-General, Minority Education, Private Education (Precollege), Secondary Education (Private), Secondary Education (Public), Special Education
Environment: Environment-General
Health: Cancer, Children's Health/Hospitals, Emergency/Ambulance Services, Health Organizations, Hospices, Hospitals, Mental Health, Multiple Sclerosis, Prenatal Health Issues
Social Services: Child Abuse, Child Welfare, Community Service Organizations, Day Care, Family Services, Food/Clothing Distribution, People with Disabilities, Senior Services, Shelters/Homelessness, Volunteer Services, Youth Organizations

Application Procedures
Initial Contact: Send a brief letter of inquiry.
Application Requirements: Include a description of organization, amount requested, proof of tax-exempt status.
Deadlines: None.

Restrictions
The foundation does not support individuals.

Foundation Officials
Benjamin N. Colby: trustee
F. Jordan Colby: trustee
Sarah Rob Colby Pierce: trustee
Sarah P. Williams: trustee

Grants Analysis
Disclosure Period: calendar year ending 2002
Total Grants: $283,298
Number of Grants: 23
Average Grant: $12,317
Highest Grant: $35,000
Lowest Grant: $1,298
Typical Range: $5,000 to $25,000

Recent Grants
Note: Grants derived from 2001 Form 990.

Library-Related
20,000	Augusta Richmond Public Library
20,000	Augusta Richmond Public Library
5,000	Rye Free Reading Room, Rye, NY

General
40,000	Anthropologist 's Fund Legacy
35,000	Gallaudet University, Washington, DC
35,000	New College Endowment Fund, Sarasota, FL
30,000	Girls, Inc.
20,000	Anthropologist 's Fund Legacy
20,000	Putney School, Putney, VT
15,000	Northern Wings, Portland, ME
15,000	Planned Parenthood of Asheville, Asheville, NC
11,000	Center for Preventive Psychology
10,000	Black Student Fund, Washington, DC

APPLETON PAPERS, INC.

Company Headquarters
825 E. Wisconsin Ave.
Appleton, WI 54912-0359
Web: http://www.appletonideas.com

Company Description
Founded: 1907
SIC(s): 2672 Coated & Laminated Paper Nec, 2679 Converted Paper Products Nec.
Parent Company: Arjo Wiggins Appleton Ltd., St. Clement House, Alencon Link, Basingstoke, HM, England
Parent Revenue: US$4,927,700,000 (2001)

Operating Locations
Appleton Papers Inc. (GA--Atlanta; IA--Daven Port; KS--Kansas City; KY--Florence; NY--Albany, Newton Falls; OH--West Carrollton; OR--Portland; PA--Harrisburg; WI--Combined Locks); Appleton Papers International (PA--Roaring Spring); Appleton Papers-Locks Mills (WI--Combined Locks); Appleton Papers-Portage Plant (WI--Portage); Appleton Papers-Spring Mill (PA--Roaring Spring)

Nonmonetary Support
Type: Donated Equipment; Donated Products
Contact: Billy Van Den Brandt, Staff Public Relations Representative

Giving Contact
Donna Kolb, Contribution Committee
825 East Wisconsin Avenue
PO Box 359
Appleton, WI 54912
Phone: (920)991-7448
Fax: (920)991-8407
E-mail: dkolb@appletonideas.com
Web: http://www.appletonideas.com

Description
Organization Type: Corporate Giving Program
Giving Locations: OH: Dayton; PA: Roaring Spring; WI: Appleton headquarters and operating communities.
Grant Types: Award, Capital, Employee Matching Gifts, General Support, Multiyear/Continuing Support, Project, Scholarship.
Note: Employee matching gift ratio: 1 to 1 for education only.

Financial Summary
Total Giving: $800,000 (2002 approx); $800,000 (2001); $700,000 (2000 approx). Note: Contributes through corporate direct giving program only. Giving includes nonmonetary support.

Typical Recipients
Arts & Humanities: Arts Associations & Councils, Libraries, Museums/Galleries, Music, Performing Arts, Visual Arts
Civic & Public Affairs: Business/Free Enterprise
Education: Colleges & Universities, Economic Education, Engineering/Technological Education, Faculty Development, Minority Education, Science/Mathematics Education, Student Aid
Environment: Environment-General
Health: Single-Disease Health Associations
Social Services: Child Welfare, Community Service Organizations, Counseling, Domestic Violence, Emergency Relief, Food/Clothing Distribution, People with Disabilities, Recreation & Athletics, Senior Services, Shelters/Homelessness, Substance Abuse, United Funds/United Ways, Youth Organizations

Application Procedures
Initial Contact: Send a brief letter of inquiry and proposal.
Application Requirements: Include a description of organization, amount requested, purpose of funds sought, recently audited financial statement, proof of tax-exempt status, number of people benefiting from the project, and extent of Appleton employees' involvement.
Deadlines: None.

Restrictions
The company does not consider funding for the following: dinners or special events, goodwill advertising, member agencies of united funds, individuals, hospitals, fraternal organizations, political or lobbying groups, religious organizations for sectarian purposes, or groups whose agendas differ from the goals of the company.

Giving Program Officials
Dennis N. Hultgren: director B Milwaukee, WI 1946. ED University of Wisconsin (1969); University of Wisconsin (1973). PRIM CORP EMPL director environmental & public affairs: Appleton Papers Inc. CORP AFFIL director: Norwest Bank. NONPR AFFIL member: Rotary International.

Grants Analysis
Typical Range: $5,000 to $10,000

MARIAN MEAKER APTECKAR FOUNDATION

Giving Contact
Care of Chase Bank of TX, NA
PO Box 140
El Paso, TX 79980-0001
Phone: (915)546-6515

Description
Founded: 1997
EIN: 742060589
Organization Type: Private Foundation
Grant Types: General Support.

Financial Summary
Total Giving: $129,446 (fiscal year ending May 31, 2001); $90,000 (fiscal 2000); $72,000 (fiscal 1999)
Assets: $2,336,513 (fiscal 2001); $2,588,912 (fiscal 2000); $2,474,822 (fiscal 1999)

Typical Recipients
Arts & Humanities: Libraries, Museums/Galleries, Music
Education: Colleges & Universities, Education-General
Religion: Jewish Causes

Additional Information
Trust(s): Chase Bank of TX NA

Grants Analysis
Disclosure Period: fiscal year ending May 31, 2001
Total Grants: $129,446
Number of Grants: 6

Highest Grant: $45,489
Lowest Grant: $7,767

Recent Grants

Note: Grants derived from 2001 Form 990.

Library-Related
7,767   El Paso Public Library, El Paso, TX

General
45,489   El Paso Symphony, El Paso, TX
35,889   National Jewish Medical and Research Center
24,767   El Paso Museum of Art, El Paso, TX
7,767   American Association University, New York, NY
7,767   Delta Kappa Gamma Educational

MARY ALICE ARAKELIAN FOUNDATION

Giving Contact

John H. Pramberg, Jr., Trustee
PO Box 510
Newburyport, MA 01950
Phone: (617)346-4000

Description

Founded: 1966
EIN: 046155695
Organization Type: Private Foundation
Grant Types: General Support.

Financial Summary

Total Giving: $345,000 (2001); $356,000 (2000); $335,000 (1999)
Giving Analysis: Giving for 2001 includes: foundation grants to United Way ($25,000); 2000: foundation grants to United Way ($25,000); 1999: foundation grants to United Way ($25,000).
Assets: $7,439,569 (2001); $8,364,314 (2000); $8,323,386 (1999)

Typical Recipients

Arts & Humanities: Arts Associations & Councils, Arts Funds, Community Arts, Historic Preservation, History & Archaeology, Libraries, Museums/Galleries, Public Broadcasting, Theater
Civic & Public Affairs: Botanical Gardens/Parks, Civic & Public Affairs-General, Municipalities/Towns, Safety, Urban & Community Affairs
Education: Colleges & Universities, Special Education
Environment: Environment-General
Health: Health Organizations, Hospitals, Prenatal Health Issues
Religion: Churches, Religious Organizations, Religious Welfare, Synagogues/Temples
Social Services: Community Service Organizations, Recreation & Athletics, United Funds/United Ways, YMCA/YWCA/YMHA/YWHA

Application Procedures

Deadlines: September 15.

Additional Information

Trust(s): Fleet Bank MA NA

Foundation Officials

Rose M. Marshall: co-trustee
Donald D. Mitchell: co-trustee
John H. Pramberg, Jr.: co-trustee
Charles P. Richmond: co-trustee
Mark Welch: co-trustee

Grants Analysis

Disclosure Period: calendar year ending 2001
Total Grants: $320,000*
Number of Grants: 9

Average Grant: $35,556
Highest Grant: $50,000
Lowest Grant: $10,000
Typical Range: $25,000 to $50,000
*****Note:** Giving excludes United Way.

Recent Grants

Note: Grants derived from 2000 Form 990.

Library-Related
20,000   Friends of Newburyport Library, Newburyport, MA

General
120,000   Belleville Improvement Society
100,000   Opportunity Works, Newburyport, MA
30,000   New Hampshire Public Television, Durham, NH
25,000   Anna Jacques Community Health, Newburyport, MA
25,000   United Way of Merrick Valley, Inc.
16,000   Cashman Park Playground
10,000   First Parish Church, Congregational, MA
5,000   Theatre In The Open at Maudsley
5,000   YMCA of Newburyport, Newburyport, MA

ARATA BROTHERS TRUST

Giving Contact

4061 Marsalla Court
Sacramento, CA 95820
Phone: (916)451-5358

Description

Founded: 1976
EIN: 237204615
Organization Type: Private Foundation
Giving Locations: CA
Grant Types: General Support.

Financial Summary

Total Giving: $500,639 (2001); $514,954 (2000); $524,148 (1998)
Assets: $7,517,924 (2001); $8,351,034 (2000); $8,750,302 (1998)
Gifts Received: $4,193,959 (1996)

Typical Recipients

Arts & Humanities: Ballet, Historic Preservation, History & Archaeology, Libraries, Museums/Galleries, Music, Opera, Performing Arts, Public Broadcasting, Theater
Civic & Public Affairs: Clubs, Community Foundations, Employment/Job Training, Civic & Public Affairs-General, Housing, Inner-City Development, Municipalities/Towns, Public Policy, Safety
Education: Business Education, Colleges & Universities, Elementary Education (Private), Elementary Education (Public), Legal Education, Literacy, Private Education (Precollege), Public Education (Precollege), Religious Education, Science/Mathematics Education, Secondary Education (Private)
Health: AIDS/HIV, Arthritis, Cancer, Children's Health/Hospitals, Diabetes, Emergency/Ambulance Services, Health Funds, Health Organizations, Hospitals, Medical Research, Research/Studies Institutes, Respiratory, Single-Disease Health Associations, Speech & Hearing
International: Foreign Educational Institutions
Religion: Churches, Religion-General, Jewish Causes, Ministries, Religious Organizations, Religious Welfare
Social Services: At-Risk Youth, Child Abuse, Child Welfare, Community Service Organizations, Domestic Violence, Family Services, Food/Clothing Distribution, Homes, People with Disabilities, Scouts, Senior Services, Special Olympics, Volunteer Services, YMCA/YWCA/YMHA/YWHA, Youth Organizations

Application Procedures

Initial Contact: Send a brief letter of inquiry.
Application Requirements: Include proof of tax-exempt status and description of program or project.
Deadlines: None.

Foundation Officials

Francis B. Dillon: trustee
Janette Lavezzo: trustee
Renato R. Parenti: trustee
Mark Sewell: trustee

Grants Analysis

Disclosure Period: calendar year ending 2001
Total Grants: $500,639
Number of Grants: 66
Average Grant: $6,932*
Highest Grant: $50,074
Lowest Grant: $750
Typical Range: $2,500 to $15,000
*****Note:** Average grant figure excludes highest grant.

Recent Grants

Note: Grants derived from 2000 Form 990.

General
25,000   Boy Scouts of America, Sacramento, CA -- tax exempt purpose
25,000   Boys and Girls Club, Sacramento, CA -- tax exempt purpose
25,000   Mercy Hospital Foundation, Rancho Cordova, CA -- tax exempt purpose
21,400   St. Patrick's Home for Children, Sacramento, CA -- tax exempt purpose
20,000   St. Hope Academy, Sacramento, CA -- tax exempt purpose
17,000   McGeorge School of Law, Sacramento, CA -- tax exempt purpose
16,000   Sacramento Children's Home and Family Unit, Sacramento, CA -- tax exempt purpose
15,850   YMCA Sacramento, Sacramento, CA -- tax exempt purpose
15,000   Salk Institute, San Diego, CA -- tax exempt purpose
13,000   Passionist Fathers, Citrus Heights, CA -- tax exempt purpose

ARCA FOUNDATION

Giving Contact

Donna F. Edwards, Executive Director
1308 19th St., NW
Washington, DC 20036
Phone: (202)822-9193
Fax: (202)785-1446
E-mail: grants@arcafoundation.org
Web: http://www.arcafoundation.org

Alternate Contact

Jeanne Mathison

Description

Founded: 1952
EIN: 132751798
Organization Type: General Purpose Foundation
Giving Locations: nationally.
Grant Types: Conference/Seminar, General Support, Matching, Multiyear/Continuing Support, Project.

Donor Information

Founder: Nancy Susan Reynolds founded the Arca Foundation, formerly known as the Nancy Reynolds Bagley Foundation, in 1952. By this time she had been active in philanthropy for over two decades. Her main concern was population control, because she felt overpopulation would hinder the standard of living worldwide. Until her death in 1985, she focused on hunger, human and civil rights, peace, a safe and healthy environment, and solar energy. This reflected her belief that ecological soundness is necessary to provide a place where people can create the opportunities to raise their own standard of living.

Nancy Susan Reynolds was the daughter of the late R. J. Reynolds, founder of the R. J. Reynolds Tobacco Company. She was the honorary chairman of the Z. Smith Reynolds Foundation and the vice president of the Sapelo Island Research Foundation.

Financial Summary

Total Giving: $2,900,000 (2003 approx); $2,900,000 (2002 approx); $2,900,000 (2001)
Assets: $73,000,000 (2003 approx); $73,000,000 (2002); $73,300,835 (2000)

Typical Recipients

Arts & Humanities: Ethnic & Folk Arts, Film & Video, Museums/Galleries, Performing Arts, Theater
Civic & Public Affairs: African American Affairs, Civil Rights, Community Foundations, Economic Development, Economic Policy, Employment/Job Training, Ethnic Organizations, First Amendment Issues, Civic & Public Affairs-General, Hispanic Affairs, Law & Justice, Philanthropic Organizations, Public Policy, Rural Affairs, Urban & Community Affairs, Women's Affairs
Education: Colleges & Universities, Education Funds, Education-General, International Exchange, International Studies, Journalism/Media Education, Leadership Training, Legal Education, Literacy
Environment: Environment-General, Resource Conservation
Health: Health Policy/Cost Containment
International: Foreign Arts Organizations, Foreign Educational Institutions, Health Care/Hospitals, Human Rights, International Affairs, International Development, International Environmental Issues, International Organizations, International Peace & Security Issues, International Relations, International Relief Efforts, Missionary/Religious Activities, Trade
Religion: Churches, Ministries, Religious Organizations, Religious Welfare
Social Services: Child Welfare, Community Service Organizations, Food/Clothing Distribution, Refugee Assistance, Substance Abuse

Application Procedures

Initial Contact: The foundation has no formal grant application procedure or application form. Send a clear, concise proposal (one copy).
Application Requirements: The proposal should include a cover letter that describes the project in a brief paragraph, states its total cost, and requests a specific grant amount. It should be signed by the Executive Director and/or Project Director. The proposal should also contain a one page summary, separate from the body of the proposal, highlighting the project's purposes and goals. Include a proposal narrative, of no more than ten pages, that summarizes the policy issue addressed; presents the organization's approach to the problem and specific goals, and provides background on the organization 's history, current range of activities and qualifications for carrying out the project. Organizational information should include short bios or resumes of the project staff and a list of the Board of Directors including affiliations. Also submit financial information including a list of all past Arca grants (year, amount, and project); a list of all grants received for the current year (amount, source, and project), the total organizational budget for the current and previous fiscal year; a list of project grants received in the current year (amount and source), a line-item project budget of income and expense;, and a list of potential funding sources for the project (amounts and contact persons). In addition, submit current IRS documents confirming the organization's status as both tax-exempt (501(c)(3)) and publicly supported (509(a)).

Deadlines: April 1 for the June board meeting; October 1 for the December board meeting.
Review Process: Applicants will receive a postcard acknowledging receipt of their proposal, and the foundation will request further information as needed. Applicants will be informed of the board's decision shortly after the board meets. If an applicant's proposal falls outside guidelines, it will be notified in writing within a month of submission.
Notes: Proposals received via fax will not be considered.

Restrictions

The foundation does not fund direct social services, scholarship funds, scholarly research, individuals, government programs, capital projects/endowments, or groups outside the U.S.

Additional Information

All grantees must submit a narrative and financial progress report prior to submitting additional funding requests. Deadlines for such a report are stipulated in the Grant Agreement that every grantee must sign.
Publications: Annual Report; Grantmaking Guidelines

Foundation Officials

Nancy R. Bagley: vice president
Nicole Bagley: director
Smith Bagley: president PRIM CORP EMPL president: Smith Bagley Inc. CORP AFFIL president, director: Cellular One.
Ellsworth Culver: vice president B Seattle, WA 1927. ED Asbury College BA (1949). PRIM CORP EMPL senior vice president: Mercy Corp.s International. CORP AFFIL president: Culver Stowell Inc. NONPR AFFIL chairman: ProTem Foundation; co-founder: Sports Ambs International People-to-People Program; founder: Oregon Inter-Religious Committee Peace in Middle East; board member: Global Action; director: Mercy Corps Europe.
Donna F. Edwards: executive director
Carolyn Gamerman: administrator
Mary E. King: secretary B Crump, TN 1937. PRIM CORP EMPL vice president benefits development & training, secretary: Cummings.
Walter Russell Mead: director
Bernadette Roberts: program associate
Janet Shenk: director
Eric Sklar: treasurer B 1962. ED University of California at Berkeley (1984); London School of Economics (1985-1986). PRIM CORP EMPL president: Burrito Brothers Inc.
Margery Tabankin: director

Grants Analysis

Disclosure Period: calendar year ending 2000
Total Grants: $2,892,140
Number of Grants: 65
Average Grant: $44,944
Highest Grant: $100,000
Typical Range: $10,000 to $50,000

Recent Grants

Note: Grants derived from 2000 Form 990.

General

350,000	Cuba Policy Foundation, Washington, DC -- to educate the public about US policy toward Cuba through research analysis and dissemination of materials
274,000	Fund for Constitutional Government, Washington, DC -- for the Cuba Policy Foundation project to support educational activities and research on US Cuba policy
80,000	National Interfaith Committee for Worker Justice, Chicago, IL
75,000	Brennan Center for Justice, New York, NY -- support the litigation and pre-litigation
75,000	John F. Kennedy Center for Performing

	Arts, New York, NY -- support the presentation of Ballet National de Cuba on the Kennedy Center stage
75,000	Medical Education Cooperation with Cuba, Atlanta, GA -- support of the organizations work
75,000	National Voting Rights Institute, Boston, MA -- to continue litigation and public education efforts on campaign reform in North Carolina and Vermont
50,000	Center for Voting and Democracy, Takoma Park, MD
50,000	Institute for Southern Studies, Durham, NC -- support the Southern Voting Rights Project building a pro democracy movement in the South through investigative research
50,000	Jobs with Justice Education Fund, Washington, DC

ARCADIA FOUNDATION

Giving Contact

Marilyn L. Steinbright, President
105 East Logan Street
Norristown, PA 19401-3060
Phone: (610)275-8460
Fax: (610)275-8460

Description

Founded: 1964
EIN: 236399772
Organization Type: Family Foundation
Giving Locations: PA: zip codes 18000 to 19800
Grant Types: Capital, Endowment, General Support.
Note: Scholarships are for higher education only-not personally, only to the School.

Donor Information

Founder: Established in 1964 by the late Edith C. Steinbright , and Marilyn Lee Steinbright.

Financial Summary

Total Giving: $6,500,000 (fiscal year ending September 30, 2003 approx); $8,000,000 (fiscal 2002 approx); $7,955,744 (fiscal 2001 approx)
Giving Analysis: Giving for fiscal 1999 includes: foundation scholarships ($25,000)
Assets: $46,000,000 (fiscal 2003 approx); $50,000,000 (fiscal 2002 approx); $49,733,968 (fiscal 2001)
Gifts Received: $22,958 (fiscal 1999); $1,000 (fiscal 1996); $4,389,124 (fiscal 1995). Note: The foundation received gifts from the estate of Edith C. Steinbright.

Typical Recipients

Arts & Humanities: Arts Associations & Councils, Arts Centers, Arts Festivals, Arts Institutes, Arts Outreach, Ballet, Community Arts, Ethnic & Folk Arts, Arts & Humanities-General, Historic Preservation, History & Archaeology, Libraries, Museums/Galleries, Music, Performing Arts, Public Broadcasting, Theater
Civic & Public Affairs: Botanical Gardens/Parks, Clubs, Community Foundations, Economic Development, Ethnic Organizations, Civic & Public Affairs-General, Hispanic Affairs, Housing, Legal Aid, Philanthropic Organizations, Safety, Urban & Community Affairs, Women's Affairs, Zoos/Aquariums
Education: Arts/Humanities Education, Colleges & Universities, Community & Junior Colleges, Education Funds, Engineering/Technological Education, Education-General, Literacy, Medical Education, Private Education (Precollege), Religious Education, Secondary Education (Private), Special Education, Student Aid
Environment: Air/Water Quality, Environment-General, Protection, Resource Conservation, Wildlife Protection

Health: Arthritis, Children's Health/Hospitals, Clinics/ Medical Centers, Diabetes, Emergency/Ambulance Services, Health Organizations, Hospices, Hospitals, Hospitals (University Affiliated), Long-Term Care, Mental Health, Nursing Services, Single-Disease Health Associations

International: International Organizations, International Relations

Religion: Churches, Jewish Causes, Ministries, Religious Organizations, Religious Welfare, Seminaries

Science: Science Museums, Scientific Centers & Institutes, Scientific Organizations

Social Services: Animal Protection, Camps, Child Welfare, Community Centers, Community Service Organizations, Crime Prevention, Day Care, Emergency Relief, Food/Clothing Distribution, People with Disabilities, Recreation & Athletics, Senior Services, Volunteer Services, Youth Organizations

Application Procedures

Initial Contact: Applicants should submit a succinct letter of proposal, no longer than two pages, to the foundation.

Application Requirements: The letter should include a brief hisotry and purpose of organization, the amount of funding requested, how funds will be spent, and proof of the organization's tax-exempt status.

Deadlines: Proposals are accepted only between September 1 and November 1 for the following calendar year.

Review Process: The board meets in December. Notification is usually given within one month.

Notes: The foundation will discard applications that include any extra material, such as brochures, a board of directors list, or treasurer's report.

Restrictions

Grants are not made for, fellowships, conferences, publications, demonstration projects, deficit financing, dinners, special events, fraternal organizations, multiyear grants, political or lobbying groups, or goodwill advertising. New proposals are limited to organizations residing in Pennsylvania within zip codes 18-19800. Grants are not made to individuals.

Additional Information

When requesting a grant for the first time, don't ask for a large amount ($20,000 or more), it will be thrown out immediately.

Publications: Guidelines

Foundation Officials

Harvey S. Shipley Miller: treasurer B Philadelphia, PA 1948. ED Swarthmore College MBA (1970); Harvard University JD (1973). NONPR AFFIL trustee: University Pennsylvania; board overseers: University Pennsylvania School Nursing; trustee: Philadelphia Museum Art; member: Union League; member: Phi Sigma Kappa; member: Philadelphia Art Alliance; member: Metropolitan Museum Art; member: National Gallery Art; member: Collections Comm Historical Society; member: Library College; member: Association Bar New York City; member: Athenaeum Association; member: American Bar Association; member: American Philosophical Society. CLUB AFFIL Harvard Club; Swarthmore Club.

David P. Sandler: secretary B 1935. PRIM CORP EMPL president: Dreslin Co. Inc. CORP AFFIL certified public accountant: Norristown Brick Inc.

Kathleen H. Shellington: vice president

Marilyn L. Steinbright: president

Grants Analysis

Disclosure Period: fiscal year ending September 30, 2001

Total Grants: $7,955,744

Number of Grants: 258

Average Grant: $27,171*

Highest Grant: $500,000

Lowest Grant: $500

Typical Range: $10,000 to $50,000

*Note: Average grant figure excludes two highest grants ($1,000,000).

Recent Grants

Note: Grants derived from fiscal 2002 Form 990.

General

500,000	American Red Cross Southeast Pennsylvania, Philadelphia, PA
500,000	Arcadia University, Glenside, PA
500,000	Cedar Crest College, Allentown, PA
500,000	Lancaster Theological Seminary, Lancaster, PA
500,000	Montgomery Hospital Foundation, Norristown, PA
500,000	Ursinus College, Collegeville, PA
300,000	Philadelphia Museum of Art, Philadelphia, PA
250,000	American Music Theater Festival, Philadelphia, PA
250,000	Franklin Institute, Philadelphia, PA
250,000	National Constitution Center, Philadelphia, PA

ARCANA FOUNDATION

Giving Contact

Joan Kennan, Executive Director
1156 15th Street Northwest, No. 605
Washington, DC 20005
Phone: (202)789-7280
Fax: (202)842-2297
E-mail: arcanajk@aol.com

Description

Founded: 1986
EIN: 521515952
Organization Type: General Purpose Foundation
Giving Locations: DC
Grant Types: General Support.

Donor Information

Founder: Established in 1986 by Ladislaus von Hoffman and his wife, Beatrix von Hoffman.

Financial Summary

Total Giving: $2,429,405 (fiscal year ending September 30, 2001); $2,605,000 (fiscal 1999); $3,143,783 (fiscal 1998)

Giving Analysis: Giving for fiscal 2001 includes: foundation matching gifts ($75,000) foundation scholarships ($181,305)

Assets: $3,341,401 (fiscal 2001); $8,452,267 (fiscal 1999); $12,621,783 (fiscal 1998)

Typical Recipients

Arts & Humanities: Arts Appreciation, Arts Associations & Councils, Arts Outreach, Dance, Libraries, Literary Arts, Museums/Galleries, Music, Performing Arts, Public Broadcasting, Theater

Civic & Public Affairs: Asian American Affairs, Botanical Gardens/Parks, Community Foundations, Employment/Job Training, Civic & Public Affairs-General, Hispanic Affairs, Housing, Urban & Community Affairs, Zoos/Aquariums

Education: Afterschool/Enrichment Programs, Arts/ Humanities Education, Environmental Education, Education-General, International Studies, Literacy, Minority Education, Private Education (Precollege), Public Education (Precollege), Science/Mathematics Education, Secondary Education (Private), Secondary Education (Public), Special Education, Student Aid, Student Aid

Health: Children's Health/Hospitals, Clinics/Medical Centers, Diabetes, Geriatric Health, Health Organizations, Hospices, Long-Term Care, Medical Research, Mental Health, Prenatal Health Issues, Public Health

International: Foreign Arts Organizations, Foreign Educational Institutions, International Organizations, International Peace & Security Issues, International Relations, Trade

Religion: Churches, Ministries, Religious Organizations, Religious Welfare

Social Services: At-Risk Youth, Camps, Child Welfare, Community Centers, Community Service Organizations, Counseling, Day Care, Domestic Violence, Family Planning, Family Services, Food/Clothing Distribution, Homes, People with Disabilities, Refugee Assistance, Senior Services, Shelters/Homelessness, Social Services-General, Substance Abuse, Volunteer Services, YMCA/YWCA/YMHA/ YWHA, Youth Organizations

Application Procedures

Initial Contact: All applications must be submitted in writing.

Restrictions

The foundation does not support sectarian causes, animal rights, individuals, capital campaigns, research, publications, advocacy, media, public policy organizations, legal services, coalitions, or land acquisitions. Applications submitted in writing.

Foundation Officials

George A. Didden, III: director B Washington, DC 1945. ED Boston College (1967); Catholic University America (1973). PRIM CORP EMPL chairman, chief executive officer: National Capital Bank Washington. CORP AFFIL director: Kane Transfer Co. NONPR AFFIL director: Federal Reserve Bank Richmond; trustee: United States Supreme Court Historical Society.

Joan Elisabeth Kennan: executive director B Highland Park, IL 1936. ED University of Paris (1954-1955); Connecticut College BA (1959); University of Washington AM (1984-1985).

Holly Kennedy: secretary

Beatrix von Hoffmann: vice president

Ladislaus von Hoffmann: president, treasurer

Grants Analysis

Disclosure Period: fiscal year ending September 30, 2001

Total Grants: $2,173,100*

Number of Grants: 78

Average Grant: $27,860

Highest Grant: $138,000

Typical Range: $15,000 to $50,000

*Note: Giving excludes scholarships and matching gifts.

Recent Grants

Note: Grants derived from fiscal 2000 Form 990.

Library-Related

100,000	Folger Shakespeare Library, Washington, DC -- for renovation
71,000	Pierpont Morgan Library, New York, NY -- for challenge grant

General

250,000	Our House, Brookeville, MD
155,000	Martha's Table, Washington, DC -- capital expansion
150,000	Institute for Advanced Study, Princeton, NJ
100,000	Camphill Foundation, Kimberton, PA -- endowment
100,000	Camphill Foundation, Kimberton, PA -- endowment
100,000	Camphill Foundation, Kimberton, PA -- endowment
100,000	Institute for Advanced Study, Princeton, NJ
100,000	Studio Theatre, Washington, DC
75,000	Bishop Monamara High School -- scholarship
75,000	Providence Hospital, Washington, DC -- for Perry Family

ADRIAN AND JESSIE ARCHBOLD CHARITABLE TRUST

Giving Contact

Myra Mahon, Director
401 East 60th Street, Suite 36B
New York, NY 10022
Phone: (212)371-1152
Fax: (212)753-9327

Description

Founded: 1976
EIN: 510179829
Organization Type: General Purpose Foundation
Giving Locations: NY: eastern United States
Grant Types: Conference/Seminar, General Support, Multiyear/Continuing Support.

Donor Information

Founder: Established in 1976 by the late Mrs. Adrian Archbold .

Financial Summary

Total Giving: $1,457,000 (fiscal year ending November 30, 2000); $1,500,000 (fiscal 1999 approx); $865,700 (fiscal 1998)
Giving Analysis: Giving for fiscal 2000 includes: foundation scholarships ($50,000)
Assets: $37,723,325 (fiscal 2000); $34,964,281 (fiscal 1998); $30,661,902 (fiscal 1997)

Typical Recipients

Arts & Humanities: Arts Associations & Councils, Ballet, Dance, Historic Preservation, Libraries, Museums/Galleries, Music, Opera, Performing Arts, Theater
Civic & Public Affairs: African American Affairs, Botanical Gardens/Parks, Employment/Job Training, Civic & Public Affairs-General, Legal Aid, Philanthropic Organizations, Public Policy, Safety, Urban & Community Affairs, Women's Affairs
Education: Arts/Humanities Education, Colleges & Universities, Education Reform, Environmental Education, Education-General, Health & Physical Education, Legal Education, Medical Education, Private Education (Precollege), Public Education (Precollege), Secondary Education (Public), Student Aid
Environment: Environment-General, Resource Conservation, Wildlife Protection
Health: AIDS/HIV, Cancer, Children's Health/Hospitals, Clinics/Medical Centers, Emergency/Ambulance Services, Health-General, Health Funds, Health Organizations, Hospitals, Hospitals (University Affiliated), Medical Rehabilitation, Medical Research, Mental Health, Prenatal Health Issues, Public Health, Single-Disease Health Associations
International: Health Care/Hospitals, International Environmental Issues, International Peace & Security Issues, International Relations
Religion: Churches, Dioceses, Religion-General, Religious Organizations, Religious Welfare
Science: Scientific Centers & Institutes, Scientific Labs, Scientific Research
Social Services: At-Risk Youth, Camps, Child Welfare, Community Service Organizations, Day Care, Family Planning, Family Services, Homes, People with Disabilities, Recreation & Athletics, Scouts, Social Services-General, Substance Abuse, United Funds/United Ways, YMCA/YWCA/YMHA/YWHA, Youth Organizations

Application Procedures

Initial Contact: The trust has no formal grant procedure or grant application form.
Deadlines: None.
Review Process: Grants are made throughout the tax year.

Restrictions

The trust makes grants only to organizations that are tax-exempt under IRS tax laws. Grants are made for general charitable purposes with emphasis on medical programs and research. No grants are made to individuals, or for endowment funds, scholarships, fellowships, building funds, or loans.

Additional Information

The trust reports that Chase Manhattan Bank acts as a corporate trustee.
Particular consideration may be given to programs associated with the Archbold Memorial Hospital at the trustee's discretion.
Publications: Program Policy Statement

Foundation Officials

Arthur Joseph Mahon: trustee B New York, NY 1934. ED Manhattan College BA (1955); New York University JD (1958). PRIM CORP EMPL counsel: McDermott, Will & Emery. NONPR AFFIL member: New York State Bar Association; member committee trustee & estate gift plans: Rockefeller University; trustee: Manhattan College; member: Florida Bar Association; trustee: Inner City Scholarship Fund; member: District of Columbia Bar Association; chairman board overseers: Cornell University Medicine College; counselor: Ira W De Camp Foundation; vice president, director: Catholic Communal Fund; chairman planned giving committee: Archdiocese New York; member: Association Bar New York City; director: American Skin Association.
Myra Mahon: director NONPR AFFIL director: Deafness Research Foundation.

Grants Analysis

Disclosure Period: fiscal year ending November 30, 2000
Total Grants: $1,407,000*
Number of Grants: 125*
Average Grant: $8,927*
Highest Grant: $300,000
Lowest Grant: $500
Typical Range: $1,000 to $25,000
*Note: Giving excludes United Way. Average grant figure excludes highest grant.

Recent Grants

Note: Grants derived from fiscal 2000 Form 990.

Library-Related

15,000	Museum of Modern Art, New York, NY	
8,000	Millbrook Free Library, Millbrook, NY	

General

300,000	Weill Medical College of Cornell University, New York, NY
150,000	Weill Medical College of Cornell University, New York, NY
50,000	Inner-city Scholarship Fund, New York, NY
30,000	Overview Foundation, Canaan, CT
25,000	Alfred E. Smith Memorial Foundation, New York, NY
25,000	Archdiocese of New York, New York, NY
25,000	Calvary Hospital Fund, Bronx, NY
25,000	Jordanian Hashemile Development Fund
25,000	New York Weill Cornell Hospital, New York, NY
25,000	Rockefeller University, New York, NY

ARCHER-DANIELS-MIDLAND CO.

Company Headquarters

Decatur, IL
Web: http://www.admworld.com

Company Description

Founded: 1923
Ticker: ADM
Exchange: NYSE
Revenue: US$23.454 billion (2002)
Profit: US$511.1 million (2002)
Employees: 22834 (2002)
Fortune Rank: 71, per FORTUNE Magazine's list of 500 Largest U.S. Corporations (2002).
SIC(s): 2041 Flour & Other Grain Mill Products, 2045 Prepared Flour Mixes & Doughs, 2046 Wet Corn Milling, 2074 Cottonseed Oil Mills.

Operating Locations

ADM Animal Health & Nutrition (NC--Dunn); ADM Arkady Products (IN--Olathe); ADM Bio Products Division (IL--Decatur); ADM Cocoa Division (IL--Decatur); ADM Corn Processing Division (IL--Decatur); ADM/Country Mark (IL--Decatur); ADM Export Co. (IL--Decatur); ADM Growmark (IA--Cedar Rapids); ADM Investor Service Inc. (IL--Chicago); ADM Milling Co. (KS--Overland Park); Agri-Sales Inc. (MI--Saginaw); Agrinational Insurance Co. (IL--Decatur); American River Transportation (IL--Decatur); Archer-Daniels-Midland Shipping (IL--Decatur); Benson-Quinn Co. (MN--Minneapolis); Collingwood Grain Inc. (KS--Hutchinson); Gooch Foods Inc. (NE--Lincoln); Hickory Point Bank & Trust Co. (IL--Decatur); Iowa Interstate Railroad (IA--Iowa City); Moorman's Inc. (IL--Quincy); Southern Cellulose Products (TN--Chattanooga); Southern Cotton Oil Co. (IL--Decatur); Tabor Grain Co. (IL--Macon)

Nonmonetary Support

Value: $3,000,000 (2000)
Type: Donated Equipment; Donated Products
Contact: Larry, senior vice president
Note: Cunningham

Archer-Daniels-Midland Foundation

Giving Contact

Lori Magnussen
Archer-Daniels-Midland Foundation
4666 Faries Parkway
PO Box 1470
Decatur, IL 62525
Phone: (217)424-5957
Fax: (217)424-5581
Web: http://www.admworld.com
Note: Telephone inquiries are strongly discouraged. A contact person is not listed.

Description

Founded: 1953
EIN: 416023126
Organization Type: Corporate Foundation
Giving Locations: nationally, principally near operating locations and to national organizations.
Grant Types: Capital, Employee Matching Gifts, General Support, Matching, Multiyear/Continuing Support.
Note: Employee matching gift ratio: 1 to 1, up to $2,000 annually per recipient per employee.

Financial Summary

Total Giving: $2,600,000 (fiscal year ending June 31, 2002 approx); $2,381,394 (fiscal 2001); $3,866,314 (fiscal 2000). Note: Contributes through foundation only.
Giving Analysis: Giving for fiscal 2002 includes: foundation (approx $2,600,000); fiscal 2001: foundation matching gifts ($806,188); foundation ($1,575,206); fiscal 2000: foundation matching gifts ($616,499); foundation ($3,249,815);
Assets: $112,150 (fiscal 2001); $152,788 (fiscal 2000); $901,439 (fiscal 1999)

Gifts Received: $2,600,000 (fiscal 2002 approx); $2,400,000 (fiscal 2001); $3,600,000 (fiscal 2000). Note: Contributions were received from Archer-Daniels-Midland Company.

Typical Recipients

Arts & Humanities: Arts Associations & Councils, Arts Centers, Arts Festivals, Arts Funds, Arts Institutes, Ethnic & Folk Arts, Historic Preservation, History & Archaeology, Libraries, Museums/Galleries, Music, Opera, Performing Arts, Public Broadcasting, Theater

Civic & Public Affairs: African American Affairs, Business/Free Enterprise, Civil Rights, Clubs, Community Foundations, Economic Development, Economic Policy, Civic & Public Affairs-General, Hispanic Affairs, Law & Justice, Legal Aid, Native American Affairs, Philanthropic Organizations, Professional & Trade Associations, Public Policy, Rural Affairs, Safety, Urban & Community Affairs, Women's Affairs, Zoos/Aquariums

Education: Agricultural Education, Arts/Humanities Education, Business Education, Colleges & Universities, Community & Junior Colleges, Economic Education, Education Associations, Education Funds, Engineering/Technological Education, Faculty Development, Education-General, Health & Physical Education, International Exchange, International Studies, Legal Education, Medical Education, Minority Education, Private Education (Precollege), Religious Education, Science/Mathematics Education, Secondary Education (Private), Student Aid

Environment: Forestry, Environment-General, Resource Conservation

Health: Cancer, Children's Health/Hospitals, Emergency/Ambulance Services, Health Organizations, Hospices, Hospitals, Mental Health, Prenatal Health Issues

International: Foreign Educational Institutions, Health Care/Hospitals, Human Rights, International Affairs, International Development, International Environmental Issues, International Organizations, International Peace & Security Issues, International Relations, International Relief Efforts, Missionary/Religious Activities, Trade

Religion: Churches, Religion-General, Jewish Causes, Missionary Activities (Domestic), Religious Organizations, Religious Welfare

Science: Science-General, Science Museums, Scientific Centers & Institutes

Social Services: Camps, Child Welfare, Community Service Organizations, Day Care, Delinquency & Criminal Rehabilitation, Emergency Relief, Family Planning, Food/Clothing Distribution, People with Disabilities, Recreation & Athletics, Scouts, Senior Services, Shelters/Homelessness, Social Services-General, Substance Abuse, United Funds/United Ways, Volunteer Services, YMCA/YWCA/YMHA/YWHA, Youth Organizations

Application Procedures

Initial Contact: Send a brief letter or proposal.

Application Requirements: Include a description of organization, amount requested, purpose of funds sought, recently audited financial statement, and proof of tax-exempt status.

Deadlines: April 30 for consideration in planned giving for following fiscal year, July 1 to June 30.

Notes: The foundation does not accept phone inquiries.

Restrictions

Grants are not made to individuals.
Generally does not give to united funds except in the form of matching gifts.

Corporate Officials

G. Allen Andreas: chairman, chief executive officer B June 22, 1943. ED Valparaiso University BA (1965); Valparaiso University JD (1968). PRIM CORP EMPL chairman, chief executive officer: Archer Daniels Midland Co.

Richard P. Reising: senior vice president, general counsel, secretary B 1944. ED Stanford University BA; University of Missouri JD (1969). PRIM CORP EMPL senior vice president, general counsel, secretary: Archer-Daniels-Midland Co. ADD CORP EMPL president: Agrinational Insurance Co.; secretary: Coeval Inc. CORP AFFIL director: Hickory Point Bank & Trust.

Foundation Officials

Claudia Madding: president
Richard P. Reising: vice president (see above)

Grants Analysis

Disclosure Period: fiscal year ending June 31, 2001
Total Grants: $1,575,206*
Number of Grants: 113
Average Grant: $13,940*
Highest Grant: $180,000
Lowest Grant: $25
Typical Range: $1,000 to $25,000
*Note: Giving excludes matching gifts. Average grant figure excludes highest grant.

Recent Grants

Note: Grants derived from 2001 Form 990.

Library-Related

60,000	Decatur Public Library, Decatur, IL
50,000	Bush Presidential Library Foundation

General

180,000	Museum of Science and Industry, Chicago, IL
180,000	Museum of Science and Industry, Chicago, IL
180,000	Museum of Science and Industry, Chicago, IL
175,000	Burger King/McLamore Youth Opportunities Foundation
175,000	Clinton County Boys and Girls Club
90,000	Greater Y Capital Campaign
54,597	United Way of Decatur/Macon County, Decatur, IL
50,000	Appeal of Conscience Foundation, New York, NY
50,000	Arthur F Burns Fellowship Programs Inc.
50,000	Woodrow Wilson International Center for Scholars, Washington, DC

NORMAN ARCHIBALD CHARITABLE FOUNDATION

Giving Contact

Chuck Viele, Vice President, Trust Officer
Archibald Charitable Foundation
c/o Wells Fargo Bank
PO Box 21927
Seattle, WA 98111
Phone: (206)292-3533

Description

Founded: 1976
EIN: 911098014
Organization Type: Private Foundation
Giving Locations: WA: Puget Sound region
Grant Types: Capital, General Support, Project, Research

Donor Information

Founder: the late Norman Archibald

Financial Summary

Total Giving: $582,100 (fiscal year ending September 30, 2001); $526,000 (fiscal 2000); $543,500 (fiscal 1999). Note: Giving includes scholarship, United Way.

Giving Analysis: Giving for fiscal 2001 includes: foundation grants to United Way ($75,000); fiscal 2000: foundation grants to United Way ($55,000); fiscal 1998: foundation scholarships ($5,000); foundation grants to United Way ($10,000) foundation ($486,250).

Assets: $9,638,406 (fiscal 2001); $11,587,528 (fiscal 2000); $10,565,927 (fiscal 1998)

Gifts Received: $2,730 (fiscal 1997)

Typical Recipients

Arts & Humanities: Arts Associations & Councils, Arts Centers, Ballet, Dance, Historic Preservation, History & Archaeology, Libraries, Museums/Galleries, Music, Opera, Performing Arts, Theater

Civic & Public Affairs: Botanical Gardens/Parks, Chambers of Commerce, Clubs, Economic Development, Employment/Job Training, Civic & Public Affairs-General, Housing, Municipalities/Towns, Safety, Urban & Community Affairs, Women's Affairs, Zoos/Aquariums

Education: Arts/Humanities Education, Business Education, Colleges & Universities, Community & Junior Colleges, Education Funds, Education Reform, Education-General, Leadership Training, Legal Education, Literacy, Private Education (Precollege), Public Education (Precollege), Religious Education, Secondary Education (Private), Secondary Education (Public), Special Education, Vocational & Technical Education

Environment: Air/Water Quality, Environment-General, Resource Conservation

Health: AIDS/HIV, Alzheimers Disease, Arthritis, Cancer, Children's Health/Hospitals, Clinics/Medical Centers, Emergency/Ambulance Services, Health Organizations, Hospitals, Medical Rehabilitation, Medical Research, Mental Health, Nursing Services, Research/Studies Institutes, Single-Disease Health Associations, Transplant Networks/Donor Banks

International: International Environmental Issues, International Organizations

Religion: Churches, Dioceses, Jewish Causes, Religious Welfare

Science: Science Museums, Scientific Centers & Institutes

Social Services: Animal Protection, At-Risk Youth, Child Welfare, Community Centers, Community Service Organizations, Counseling, Day Care, Domestic Violence, Food/Clothing Distribution, Homes, People with Disabilities, Scouts, Senior Services, Substance Abuse, United Funds/United Ways, Volunteer Services, YMCA/YWCA/YMHA/YWHA, Youth Organizations

Application Procedures

Initial Contact: Applications should be submitted in the form of a letter signed by the chairman of the board, president, or chief operating officer of the organization.

Application Requirements: Include name and address of organization, list of board of directors with principal affiliations, a description of organization, amount requested, list of other funding sources, description of project and what it is designed to achieve, detailed budget for project, location of project and people expected to benefit from it, name of person in charge of the project, financial statements for the past two years, and proof of tax-exempt status.

Deadlines: None.

Restrictions

Does not support individuals, religious organizations, or governmental organizations.

Additional Information

Foundation emphasizes one-time, tangible needs rather than operational or programmatic proposals.
Publications: Annual Report; Application Guidelines
Trust(s): Wells Fargo Bank

Foundation Officials

Durwood Alkire: adv
Robert L. Gerth: adv
Jack Shan Mullin: adv B Bellingham, WA 1934. ED University of Washington BS (1956); University of Washington JD (1958). PRIM CORP EMPL partner: Perkins Cole. NONPR AFFIL trustee: University Washington Law School Foundation; member: Washington State Bar Association; chairman: United Way King County Endowment Fund; member: Seattle International Tax Roundtable; member: Seattle-King County Bar Association; Rotary; co-founder, vice chairman: Seattle Alliance Education; Phi Delta Phi; Phi Gamma Delta; member, director: Fred Hutchinson Cancer Research Center; member: Intl Bar Association; member: Greater Seattle Chamber of Commerce; member, director: American Red Cross; Beta Gamma Sigma; member: American Bar Association. CLUB AFFIL Seattle Tennis Club; Broadmoor Golf Club; Rainier Club.
Stuart H. Prestrud: adv ED University of Washington (1946); Pacific Coast Banking School (1955). CORP AFFIL vice president, director: Aldarra Management Co.; consult: First Interstate Bank Washington.

Grants Analysis

Disclosure Period: fiscal year ending September 30, 2001
Total Grants: $507,100*
Number of Grants: 108
Average Grant: $4,695
Highest Grant: $25,000
Lowest Grant: $1,000
Typical Range: $1,000 to $10,000
***Note:** Giving excludes United Way.

Recent Grants

Note: Grants derived from fiscal 2000 Form 990.

General

40,000	Seattle Art Museum, Seattle, WA
30,000	Puget Sound Blood Center, Seattle, WA
30,000	Seattle Foundation for United Way Gates Foundation, Seattle, WA
25,000	United Way of King County, Seattle, WA
20,000	Museum of Flight, Seattle, WA
20,000	Seattle Opera Association, Seattle, WA
15,000	Pacific Northwest Ballet, Seattle, WA
10,000	Corporate Council for the Arts, Seattle, WA
10,000	Henry Gallery Association, Seattle, WA
10,000	Independent Colleges of Washington, Seattle, WA

ARGUILD FOUNDATION

Giving Contact

Arthur G. Connolly, Jr., Secretary
1220 Market Street
Wilmington, DE 19801
Phone: (302)658-9141

Description

Founded: 1959
EIN: 516016487
Organization Type: Private Foundation
Giving Locations: DE: Wilmington Northeastern United States.
Grant Types: Capital.

Donor Information

Founder: Arthur G. Connolly, Sr.

Financial Summary

Total Giving: $695,206 (2001); $677,071 (2000); $336,104 (1999)
Assets: $7,352,679 (2001); $9,055,587 (2000); $15,801,123 (1999)
Gifts Received: $146,850 (1995); $123,188 (1994); $37,009 (1993). Note: In 1995, contributions were received from Arthur G. Connolly, Sr.

Typical Recipients

Arts & Humanities: Libraries, Music, Public Broadcasting
Civic & Public Affairs: Community Foundations, Employment/Job Training, Civic & Public Affairs-General, Public Policy
Education: Colleges & Universities, Engineering/Technological Education, Education-General, Health & Physical Education, Legal Education, Minority Education, Private Education (Precollege), Secondary Education (Private)
Environment: Environment-General, Resource Conservation
Health: Cancer, Children's Health/Hospitals, Clinics/Medical Centers, Hospices
International: International Relief Efforts
Religion: Dioceses, Jewish Causes, Ministries, Religious Organizations, Religious Welfare
Social Services: Child Welfare, Community Service Organizations, Family Planning, Family Services, Substance Abuse, United Funds/United Ways

Application Procedures

Initial Contact: Send a brief letter of inquiry. Additional materials may be sent at the requesting organization's discretion.
Deadlines: None.

Restrictions

Contributions are made to IRC 501(c)(3) organizations which have demonstrated through past performance a proven excellence and successful accomplishment of objectives. Grants are not made to individuals.

Foundation Officials

Mary Connolly Braun: president
Arthur G. Connolly, Jr. Es: secretary
Arthur Guild Connolly, Sr.: president B Boston, MA November 08, 1905. ED Massachusetts Institute of Technology BS (1927); Harvard University LLB (1930). PRIM CORP EMPL partner emeritus: Connolly, Bove, Lodge & Hutz. NONPR AFFIL fellow: American College Trial Lawyers; member: Delaware Bar Association; member: American Bar Association. CLUB AFFIL Lago Mar Golf & Country Club; Wilmington Country Club; Harvard Club Delaware.
Thomas A. Connolly, Esq.: treasurer

Grants Analysis

Disclosure Period: calendar year ending 2001
Total Grants: $695,206
Number of Grants: 125
Average Grant: $4,346*
Highest Grant: $83,300
Lowest Grant: $1,000
Typical Range: $1,000 to $10,000
***Note:** Average grant figure excludes two highest grants ($160,600).

Recent Grants

Note: Grants derived from 2000 Form 990.

General

50,000	Massachusetts Institute of Technology Alumni Fund, Cambridge, MA
41,000	Arguild Foundation, Boston, MA
25,000	Children's Hospital, Philadelphia, PA
25,000	Children's Hospital, Philadelphia, PA
20,000	Catholic Relief Services, Washington, DC
20,000	Johns Hopkins Prostate Cancer Department, Baltimore, MD
17,000	Aspen Valley Community Foundation, Aspen, CO
15,000	Salvation Army, Wilmington, DE
14,000	Eternal Word Television Network, Birmingham, AL
14,000	Loon Echo Land Trust, Naples, ME

ARGYLE FOUNDATION

Giving Contact

Margo Marbut, President
200 Concord Plaza, Suite 700
San Antonio, TX 78216-6941
Phone: (210)822-3100
Fax: (210)828-7300

Description

Founded: 1997
EIN: 742815647
Organization Type: Private Foundation
Giving Locations: GA; NY; TX
Grant Types: General Support.

Financial Summary

Total Giving: $146,900 (2001); $76,315 (2000); $154,237 (1999)
Giving Analysis: Giving for 2001 includes: foundation grants to United Way ($20,000); 2000: foundation grants to United Way ($10,000) 1998: foundation grants to United Way ($10,000)
Assets: $1,664,726 (2001); $1,851,990 (2000); $2,299,151 (1999)
Gifts Received: $11,000 (2001); $102,900 (1998); $1,000,000 (1997). Note: In 2001, contributions were received from Robert and Margo Marbut.

Typical Recipients

Arts & Humanities: Dance, Libraries, Museums/Galleries, Music, Public Broadcasting
Civic & Public Affairs: Community Foundations, Public Policy
Education: Business Education, Colleges & Universities, International Studies, Preschool Education, Private Education (Precollege), Religious Education, Science/Mathematics Education
Environment: Environment-General
Health: Emergency/Ambulance Services, Health Organizations
International: Foreign Educational Institutions, International Organizations
Religion: Jewish Causes, Synagogues/Temples
Science: Scientific Centers & Institutes
Social Services: Family Planning, Substance Abuse, United Funds/United Ways, YMCA/YWCA/YMHA/YWHA, Youth Organizations

Application Procedures

Initial Contact: The foundation has no formal grant application procedure or application form.
Application Requirements: Provide proof of tax-exempt status.
Deadlines: December 31 for contributions made the following year.

Foundation Officials

Joann Bennett: treasurer
Margo Marbut: trustee
Mike Marbut: director
Robert Marbut: trustee
Patricia Meyer: secretary

Grants Analysis

Disclosure Period: calendar year ending 2001
Total Grants: $126,900*
Number of Grants: 27
Average Grant: $4,700
Highest Grant: $15,000
Lowest Grant: $100
Typical Range: $1,000 to $10,000
*Note: Giving excludes United Way.

Recent Grants

Note: Grants derived from 2000 Form 990.

Library-Related
500	Junior Achievement of South Texas, San Antonio, TX

General
15,000	Harvard Business School, Boston, MA
10,250	Hewitt School, The, New York, NY
10,000	United Way of San Antonio and Bexar County, San Antonio, TX
7,500	Conference of Presidents of Major American Jewish Organizations, New York, NY
7,500	Jewish Community Center, San Antonio, TX
5,000	American Red Cross, San Antonio, TX
5,000	Baylor College of Medicine, Houston, TX
2,000	San Antonio Council on Alcohol and Drug Abuse, San Antonio, TX
1,750	Up with People, Broomfield, CO
1,340	San Antonio Children's Museum, San Antonio, TX

ARGYROS FOUNDATION

Giving Contact

Daniel Russo, Trustee
949 S. Coast Dr., Suite 600
Costa Mesa, CA 92626
Phone: (714)481-5000
Fax: (714)481-5000

Description

Founded: 1979
EIN: 953421867
Organization Type: Private Foundation
Giving Locations: CA
Grant Types: Capital, Project.

Donor Information

Founder: the Argyros Charitable Trusts

Financial Summary

Total Giving: $3,019,323 (fiscal year ending July 31, 2000); $2,565,807 (fiscal 1999); $1,769,336 (fiscal 1998)
Assets: $63,175,655 (fiscal 2000); $53,539,837 (fiscal 1999); $54,658,298 (fiscal 1998)
Gifts Received: $535,870 (fiscal 2000); $1,525,715 (fiscal 1999); $274,075 (fiscal 1998). Note: In fiscal 2000, contributions were received from Argyros Charitable Trust 4 ($309,000) and George L. Argyros ($226,870). In fiscal 1999, contributions were received from Argyros Charitable Trust No. 4. ($315,000), Georgeh Argyros ($1,294,983) and GLA Foundation ($5,732).

Typical Recipients

Arts & Humanities: Arts Associations & Councils, Arts Centers, Arts Funds, Ballet, Arts & Humanities-General, Historic Preservation, History & Archaeology, Libraries, Museums/Galleries, Music, Opera, Performing Arts, Public Broadcasting, Theater
Civic & Public Affairs: Clubs, Economic Development, Economic Policy, Civic & Public Affairs-General, Hispanic Affairs, Philanthropic Organizations, Professional & Trade Associations, Public Policy, Safety, Urban & Community Affairs, Women's Affairs, Zoos/Aquariums
Education: Business Education, Colleges & Universities, Education Funds, Education-General, Student Aid, Vocational & Technical Education
Environment: Air/Water Quality, Resource Conservation, Resource Conservation, Wildlife Protection
Health: AIDS/HIV, Cancer, Children's Health/Hospitals, Clinics/Medical Centers, Diabetes, Eyes/Blindness, Health Organizations, Hospitals, Medical Research, Preventive Medicine/Wellness Organizations, Public Health, Single-Disease Health Associations, Trauma Treatment
International: International Affairs, International Peace & Security Issues, International Relief Efforts
Religion: Churches, Dioceses, Jewish Causes, Religious Organizations, Religious Welfare, Social/Policy Issues
Science: Science Museums, Scientific Centers & Institutes, Scientific Labs, Scientific Organizations
Social Services: Big Brother/Big Sister, Child Abuse, Child Welfare, Community Service Organizations, Domestic Violence, Food/Clothing Distribution, Homes, People with Disabilities, Recreation & Athletics, Scouts, Senior Services, Substance Abuse, United Funds/United Ways, Volunteer Services, YMCA/YWCA/YMHA/YWHA, Youth Organizations

Application Procedures

Initial Contact: Send a brief letter of inquiry.
Application Requirements: a description of organization, purpose of funds sought, proof of tax-exempt status, and federal identification number.
Deadlines: June 1.

Restrictions

Grants are typically awarded for special projects and situations.

Foundation Officials

George L. Argyros: secretary, trustee B Detroit, MI 1937. ED Michigan State University; Chapman College BS (1959). PRIM CORP EMPL chairman, chief executive officer: Arnel & Affiliates. CORP AFFIL director: USC South International, Inc.; director: Rockwell International Corp.; director: Tecstar Inc.; director: First America Finance Corp.; director: First America Title Insurance Co.; director: Applied Solar Energy Corp.; chairman: Arnel Development Co. NONPR AFFIL director: Beckman Laser Institute.
Julie A. Argyros: president, trustee
Carol Campbell: director
Warren Finley: trustee
Charles E. Packard: trustee

Grants Analysis

Disclosure Period: fiscal year ending July 31, 2000
Total Grants: $3,019,323
Number of Grants: 77
Average Grant: $19,673*
Highest Grant: $1,524,200
Lowest Grant: $250
Typical Range: $5,000 to $50,000
*Note: Average grant excludes highest grant.

Recent Grants

Note: Grants derived from 1999 Form 990.

Library-Related
59,200	Richard Nixon Library and Birthplace Foundation, Yorba Linda, CA

General
1,073,890	Chapman University, Orange, CA
267,266	Horatio Alger Association of Distinguished Americans, Alexandria, VA
200,000	California Institute of Technology, Pasadena, CA
150,000	St. Luke's Regional Medical Center, Sun Valley, ID
108,750	Orange County Council, Boy Scouts of America, Costa Mesa, CA
100,000	American Enterprise Institute, Washington, DC
100,000	Crystal Cathedral, Garden Grove, CA
50,000	Center for Strategic and International Studies, Washington, DC
44,926	Orange County Performing Arts Center, Costa Mesa, CA
37,466	Nature Conservancy of Idaho, Sun Valley, ID

BEN H. AND GLADYS ARKELIAN FOUNDATION

Giving Contact

Richard G. McBurnie, Jr., President
PO Box 1825
Bakersfield, CA 93303
Phone: (661)873-0360
Fax: (661)873-0362

Description

Founded: 1959
EIN: 956103223
Organization Type: Private Foundation
Giving Locations: CA
Grant Types: Capital, General Support.

Financial Summary

Total Giving: $153,407 (2001); $149,359 (2000); $103,560 (1999)
Assets: $3,703,026 (2001); $3,617,299 (2000); $3,300,513 (1999)

Typical Recipients

Arts & Humanities: Historic Preservation, History & Archaeology, Libraries, Museums/Galleries, Music, Opera, Public Broadcasting, Theater
Civic & Public Affairs: Clubs, Civic & Public Affairs-General, Legal Aid, Native American Affairs, Rural Affairs
Education: Colleges & Universities, Community & Junior Colleges, Education-General, Legal Education, Preschool Education, Private Education (Precollege), Public Education (Precollege), Secondary Education (Private), Secondary Education (Public)
Environment: Environment-General
Health: Arthritis, Cancer, Children's Health/Hospitals, Clinics/Medical Centers, Emergency/Ambulance Services, Health Funds, Health Organizations, Hospices, Hospitals, Multiple Sclerosis, Single-Disease Health Associations, Transplant Networks/Donor Banks
International: Health Care/Hospitals
Religion: Churches, Religion-General, Religious Organizations, Religious Welfare
Social Services: At-Risk Youth, Child Welfare, Community Service Organizations, Counseling, Crime Prevention, Domestic Violence, Family Services, Homes, People with Disabilities, Recreation & Athletics, Shelters/Homelessness, Social Services-General, Substance Abuse, United Funds/United Ways, Youth Organizations

Application Procedures

Initial Contact: Send a brief letter of inquiry.
Application Requirements: Include a description of program.
Deadlines: None.

Restrictions

Generally, grants are limited to Kern County, CA.

Foundation Officials

Frank I. Ford, Jr.: cfo, secretary, treasurer, director
Richard G. McBurnie: president, director
Mary C. Means: vice president, assistant secretary, director

Grants Analysis

Disclosure Period: calendar year ending 2001
Total Grants: $153,407
Number of Grants: 37
Average Grant: $3,606*
Highest Grant: $20,000
Lowest Grant: $100
Typical Range: $500 to $7,500
*Note: Average grant figure excludes highest grant.

Recent Grants

Note: Grants derived from 2001 Form 990.

General

20,000	Hoffman Hospice, Bakersfield, CA -- capital improvements
20,000	Houchin Blood Bank, Bakersfield, CA -- capital improvements
10,000	California State University, Bakersfield, CA -- capital improvements
10,000	Friends of Mercy Foundation, Bakersfield, CA -- capital improvements
9,800	Emanuel Medical Center, Turlock, CA -- capital improvements
8,300	Bright Beginnings, Bakersfield, CA -- capital improvements
8,000	Bakersfield Homeless Center, Bakersfield, CA -- capital improvements
8,000	Garces Memorial High School, San Francisco, CA -- capital improvements
7,500	Boys and Girls Club, Bakersfield, CA -- capital improvements
6,000	South Fork School and Community, Weldon, CA -- capital improvements

ARKELL HALL FOUNDATION

Giving Contact

Joseph A. Santangelo, Vice President, Treasurer, Administrator
68 Front Street
PO Box 240
Canajoharie, NY 13317-0240
Phone: (518)673-5417
Fax: (518)673-5493

Description

Founded: 1948
EIN: 141343077
Organization Type: General Purpose Foundation
Giving Locations: NY: Western Montgomery County
Grant Types: Award, Capital, Challenge, Endowment, General Support, Matching, Seed Money.

Donor Information

Founder: Established in 1948 by the late Mrs. F. E. Barbour .

Financial Summary

Total Giving: $600,000 (fiscal year ending November 30, 2002 approx); $1,212,395 (fiscal 2001); $600,000 (fiscal 1999). Note: Fiscal 1997 Giving includes scholarship ($33,000).
Giving Analysis: Giving for fiscal 2001 includes: foundation scholarships ($27,000); foundation grants to United Way ($30,000); fiscal 2000: foundation grants to United Way ($40,500) fiscal 1997: foundation scholarships ($33,000).
Assets: $57,181,711 (fiscal 2001); $56,695,842 (fiscal 1997); $51,386,360 (fiscal 1996).
Gifts Received: $950 (fiscal 1997)

Typical Recipients

Arts & Humanities: Arts Centers, History & Archaeology, Libraries, Museums/Galleries, Music, Theater
Civic & Public Affairs: Botanical Gardens/Parks, Clubs, Community Foundations, Economic Development, Civic & Public Affairs-General, Housing, Legal Aid, Municipalities/Towns, Philanthropic Organizations, Urban & Community Affairs
Education: Colleges & Universities, Community & Junior Colleges, Engineering/Technological Education, Environmental Education, Education-General, Health & Physical Education, International Exchange, Legal Education, Literacy, Medical Education, Minority Education, Private Education (Precollege), Public Education (Precollege), Religious Education, Science/Mathematics Education, Secondary Education (Public), Student Aid
Health: Alzheimers Disease, Cancer, Children's Health/Hospitals, Clinics/Medical Centers, Diabetes, Emergency/Ambulance Services, Health-General, Health Funds, Health Organizations, Heart, Hospices, Hospitals, Long-Term Care, Medical Research, Nursing Services, Outpatient Health Care, Prenatal Health Issues, Single-Disease Health Associations
International: International Development, International Relief Efforts
Religion: Churches, Religious Organizations, Religious Welfare
Social Services: Animal Protection, Big Brother/Big Sister, Community Centers, Community Service Organizations, Counseling, Crime Prevention, Domestic Violence, Emergency Relief, Family Services, Food/Clothing Distribution, People with Disabilities, Recreation & Athletics, Scouts, Senior Services, Substance Abuse, United Funds/United Ways, Youth Organizations

Application Procedures

Initial Contact: Applications should be sent in full proposal form. The foundation has no specific application form.
Application Requirements: Grant proposals should include a one- to three-page statement describing, in order: how the project will significantly impact the target community; a description of organization, its staff, its goals, the problem to be addressed, how the proposal addresses the problem; and the funding amount requested. Also include documentation providing financial background on the organization and the proposal, including overall expense and revenue budgets and other funding sources; and an official IRS determination letter documenting the organization's tax-exempt status.
Deadlines: Applications are accepted between August 15 and October 1. Request received between November and May will be denied or returned for later re-submission.
Review Process: Preliminary review of requests is performed upon receipt. Results are forwarded to the applicant within one month. Qualifying requests are then reviewed and acted upon by the foundation's trustees around November 1, with notification and distribution (if awarded) by November 30.
Notes: Visits to the foundation are scheduled only when requested by foundation personnel.

Restrictions

Grants or loans are not made to individuals or to organizations for the express use or benefit of any individual. Grant are made on a single year basis only. No pledges, multiple year commitments, or loans are made. The foundation does not fund operating expenses or wages. Grants limited to Western Montgomery County, NY only.

Additional Information

The foundation is not currently seeking new funding opportunities.
Preferred projects will demonstrate significant volunteer support and have well-defined time periods or will become self-funding after a start-up period.
Publications: Grant Program Guidelines

Foundation Officials

Joyce G. Dresser: trustee
Frances L. Howard: assistant secretary, trustee
Ferdinand C. Kaiser: vice president, secretary, trustee
Joseph A. Santangelo: vice president, treasurer B Norristown, PA 1954. ED Drexel University (1977). PRIM CORP EMPL chief financial officer, secretary, treasurer: FPA Corp. CORP AFFIL vice president: Orleans Construction Corp.; treasurer: Orleans Corp.
Edward W. Shineman, Jr.: president, trustee B Canajoharie, NY April 09, 1915. ED Cornell University AB (1937). CORP AFFIL board director: Fenimore Asset Management; director: Taconic Farms Inc. NONPR AFFIL member: Financial Executives Institute; member: Institute of Management Accountants; member emeritus council: Cornell University.
Charles J. Tallent: trustee
Robert H. Wille: vice president, trustee
Charles E. Wright: trustee B 1942. PRIM CORP EMPL president: W W Custom Clad Inc.

Grants Analysis

Disclosure Period: fiscal year ending November 30, 2001
Total Grants: $1,144,895*
Number of Grants: 56
Average Grant: $6,811*
Highest Grant: $477,051
Typical Range: $1,000 to $15,000
*Note: Giving excludes scholarships and United Way. Average grants excludes two highest grants ($777,051).

Recent Grants

Note: Grants derived from fiscal 2001 Form 990.

Library-Related

10,000	Canajoharie Library and Art Gallery, Canajoharie, NY -- operating support
1,500	Fort Plain Free Library, Ft. Plain, NY -- program support

General

477,051	Arkell Center, Canajoharie, NY -- debt service
300,000	Canajoharie Central School, Canajoharie, NY -- scholarships
60,000	St. Mary's Hospital Foundation, Evansville, IL -- blood administration system
50,000	Village of Canajoharie, Canajoharie, NY
30,000	Amsterdam Memorial Hospital Foundation, Amsterdam, NY -- emergency generators
30,000	United Way of Montgomery County, Amsterdam, NY -- illumination celebration
25,000	Canjoharie Community Services, Canajoharie, NY -- renovation project
20,000	Community Youth Center, Canajoharie, NY -- operating support
20,000	Cornell University College of Human Ecology, Ithaca, NY -- program support
16,000	Twin Rivers Council, Inc. Boy Scouts of America, Albany, NY -- for Woodworth Lake operations

ARNOLD FUND

Giving Contact

John C. Sawyer, Executive Director
1201 W. Peachtree St., Suite 4200
Atlanta, GA 30309
Phone: (404)881-7886

Description

Founded: 1952
EIN: 586032079
Organization Type: Private Foundation
Giving Locations: GA
Grant Types: General Support.

Donor Information

Founder: Florence Arnold

Financial Summary

Total Giving: $1,266,673 (2001); $1,256,760 (2000); $1,171,991 (1999)
Assets: $23,946,331 (2001); $25,461,612 (2000); $27,081,521 (1999)
Gifts Received: $5,029,894 (1992)

Typical Recipients

Arts & Humanities: Ballet, Community Arts, Libraries, Museums/Galleries, Music
Civic & Public Affairs: Clubs, Community Foundations, Civic & Public Affairs-General, Municipalities/Towns, Public Policy, Urban & Community Affairs
Education: Colleges & Universities, Engineering/Technological Education, Literacy, Private Education (Precollege), Public Education (Precollege), Secondary Education (Public), Special Education, Student Aid
Environment: Wildlife Protection
Health: Hospices, Hospitals
Religion: Churches, Religious Welfare
Social Services: Community Service Organizations, People with Disabilities, Recreation & Athletics, Scouts, Special Olympics, United Funds/United Ways, YMCA/YWCA/YMHA/YWHA, Youth Organizations

Application Procedures

Initial Contact: Send a brief letter of inquiry.
Application Requirements: Describe program or project, include purpose of funds sought, area to be served, budget, and other pertinent information.
Deadlines: None.

Foundation Officials

Robert F. Fowler, III: trustee
David Newman: trustee
John C. Sawyer: executive director
Frank B. Turner: trustee

Grants Analysis

Disclosure Period: calendar year ending 2001
Total Grants: $1,266,673
Number of Grants: 46
Average Grant: $17,901*
Highest Grant: $279,043
Lowest Grant: $500
Typical Range: $5,000 to $25,000
*Note: Average grant excludes two highest grants ($479,043).

Recent Grants

Note: Grants derived from 2000 Form 990.

General

200,000	YMCA
165,000	First United Methodist Church, Williamsport, PA
155,150	City of Covington
150,000	Georgia Wildlife Federation, Conyers, GA
120,000	Newton County Public Facilities
70,560	Oxford College, Oxford, GA
70,000	Project Adventure
50,000	Oxford College, Oxford, GA
45,000	Covington Kiwanis Charitable Trust
42,000	Concert Association of Florida, Miami Beach, FL

JOHN ARRILLAGA FOUNDATION

Giving Contact

John Arrillaga, Director
2560 Mission College Blvd., Suite 101
Santa Clara, CA 95054

Phone: (408)980-0130
Fax: (408)988-4893

Description

Founded: 1978
EIN: 942460896
Organization Type: Private Foundation
Giving Locations: CA
Grant Types: Capital, General Support, Scholarship.

Donor Information

Founder: John Arrillaga

Financial Summary

Total Giving: $331,224 (fiscal year ending September 30, 2001); $302,696 (fiscal 2000); $326,720 (fiscal 1999)
Assets: $17,685,488 (fiscal 2001); $15,802,956 (fiscal 2000); $13,265,410 (fiscal 1999)
Gifts Received: $827,853 (fiscal 2000); $3,965,000 (fiscal 1994); $1,000,000 (fiscal 1993). Note: In fiscal 2000, contributions were received from Arrillaga Family Trust. In fiscal 1994, contributions were received from John Arrillaga.

Typical Recipients

Arts & Humanities: Arts Associations & Councils, Arts Centers, Arts Institutes, Dance, Arts & Humanities-General, Historic Preservation, Libraries, Museums/Galleries, Music, Public Broadcasting, Theater, Visual Arts
Civic & Public Affairs: Botanical Gardens/Parks, Clubs, Community Foundations, Employment/Job Training, Law & Justice, Legal Aid, Municipalities/Towns, Parades/Festivals, Philanthropic Organizations, Safety, Urban & Community Affairs
Education: Arts/Humanities Education, Colleges & Universities, Continuing Education, Education Associations, Education Funds, Education Reform, Education-General, Private Education (Precollege), Public Education (Precollege), Secondary Education (Public), Student Aid
Environment: Environment-General
Health: Arthritis, Children's Health/Hospitals, Eyes/Blindness, Health Funds, Heart, Hospices, Hospitals (University Affiliated), Medical Research
International: Health Care/Hospitals
Religion: Bible Study/Translation, Churches, Ministries, Religious Welfare
Social Services: At-Risk Youth, Child Welfare, Community Service Organizations, Counseling, Crime Prevention, Family Services, Food/Clothing Distribution, People with Disabilities, Recreation & Athletics, Scouts, Senior Services, Volunteer Services, YMCA/YWCA/YMHA/YWHA, Youth Organizations

Application Procedures

Application Requirements: Send a brief letter of inquiry. with any applicable brochures.
Deadlines: INone.

Foundation Officials

Frances C. Arrillaga: vice president, director
John Arrillaga, Jr.: treasurer, director
John Arrillaga: president, secretary, director B 1938. ED Stanford University. CORP AFFIL director: Morrison Knudsen Delaware Corp.; director: Morrison Knudsen Ohio Corp.
Laura Arrillaga: secretary, director
Richard Taylor Peery: director B 1940. ED Stanford University. PRIM CORP EMPL co-owner: Peery-Arrillaga.

Grants Analysis

Disclosure Period: fiscal year ending September 30, 2001
Total Grants: $331,224
Number of Grants: 36
Average Grant: $6,485*
Highest Grant: $104,264
Lowest Grant: $150

Typical Range: $1,000 to $10,000
*Note: Average grants excludes highest grant.

Recent Grants

Note: Grants derived from fiscal 2000 Form 990.

General

53,084	Stanford University, Stanford, CA
34,000	Hoover Institution, Stanford, CA
32,540	San Francisco Art Institute, San Francisco, CA
25,000	Palo Alto Endowment Fund, Palo Alto, CA
25,000	St. Mary's Rectory, Greenwich, CT
15,000	Community Foundation Silicon Valley, San Jose, CA
15,000	St. Helena Catholic Church, St. Helena, CA
11,540	Castilleja School, Palo Alto, CA
11,346	Menlo School, Atherton, CA
10,187	Children's Health Council of the Mid-Peninsula, Palo Alto, CA

ARRONSON FOUNDATION

Giving Contact

Joseph C. Kohn, President & Treasurer
One South Broad Street, Suite 2100
Philadelphia, PA 19107-3389
Phone: (215)238-1700

Description

Founded: 1957
EIN: 236259604
Organization Type: Private Foundation
Giving Locations: PA: Philadelphia
Grant Types: Endowment, General Support, Research, Scholarship, Seed Money.

Donor Information

Founder: the late Gertrude Arronson

Financial Summary

Total Giving: $554,585 (fiscal year ending October 31, 2001); $847,140 (fiscal 2000); $662,445 (fiscal 1999)
Giving Analysis: Giving for fiscal 2001 includes: foundation grants to United Way ($8,000); fiscal 2000: foundation grants to United Way ($10,500); fiscal 1999: foundation grants to United Way ($5,000);
Assets: $5,694,064 (fiscal 2001); $7,408,291 (fiscal 2000); $7,660,531 (fiscal 1999)
Gifts Received: $1,500 (fiscal 1998)

Typical Recipients

Arts & Humanities: Arts Associations & Councils, Arts Outreach, Arts & Humanities-General, Historic Preservation, History & Archaeology, Libraries, Museums/Galleries, Music, Opera, Performing Arts, Theater
Civic & Public Affairs: Botanical Gardens/Parks, Employment/Job Training, Civic & Public Affairs-General, Legal Aid, Municipalities/Towns, Philanthropic Organizations, Public Policy, Urban & Community Affairs, Women's Affairs, Zoos/Aquariums
Education: Arts/Humanities Education, Colleges & Universities, Continuing Education, Faculty Development, Education-General, Legal Education, Medical Education, Private Education (Precollege), Religious Education, Secondary Education (Private), Special Education, Student Aid, Vocational & Technical Education
Environment: Air/Water Quality, Resource Conservation
Health: Alzheimers Disease, Cancer, Geriatric Health, Health Organizations, Home-Care Services, Hospices, Hospitals, Medical Rehabilitation, Medical Research, Nursing Services, Single-Disease Health Associations, Trauma Treatment

International: Foreign Arts Organizations, International Relief Efforts, Missionary/Religious Activities
Religion: Churches, Dioceses, Jewish Causes, Religious Organizations, Religious Welfare
Science: Scientific Centers & Institutes
Social Services: Child Welfare, Community Centers, Community Service Organizations, Day Care, Family Planning, Family Services, Homes, People with Disabilities, Recreation & Athletics, Shelters/Homelessness, United Funds/United Ways, YMCA/YWCA/YMHA/YWHA, Youth Organizations

Application Procedures

Initial Contact: Send a brief letter of inquiry.
Application Requirements: Include information on the nature of the organization and its work.
Deadlines: None.

Foundation Officials

Amy Goldberg: vice president
Edith Kohn: vice president, secretary
Ellen Kohn: vice president
Joseph C. Kohn: vice president

Grants Analysis

Disclosure Period: fiscal year ending October 31, 2001
Total Grants: $546,585*
Number of Grants: 34
Average Grant: $16,076
Highest Grant: $100,000
Lowest Grant: $210
Typical Range: $10,000 to $25,000
*Note: Giving excludes United Way.

Recent Grants

Note: Grants derived from 2000 Form 990.

Library-Related

50,000	Easttown Library Foundation, Berwyn, PA

General

100,000	Cumberland College, Williamsburg, KY
100,000	Federation Allied Jewish Appeal, Philadelphia, PA
50,000	Moss Rehabilitation Hospital, Philadelphia, PA
50,000	Regional Performing Arts Center, Philadelphia, PA
30,000	Wilma Theater, Philadelphia, PA
25,000	Academy of Vocal Arts, Philadelphia, PA
25,000	Israel Children's Centers, Deerfield Beach, FL
25,000	Jewish Community Centers of Greater Philadelphia, Philadelphia, PA
25,000	Planned Parenthood of Southeastern Pennsylvania, Philadelphia, PA
25,000	Planned Parenthood of Southeastern Pennsylvania, Philadelphia, PA

ASH CHARITABLE CORP.

Giving Contact

John T. Pollano, Treasurer & Trustee
Ash Charitable Corp.
861 Turnpike St.
North Andover, MA 01845-6105
Phone: (978)683-6700

Description

Founded: 1990
EIN: 222994115
Organization Type: Private Foundation
Giving Locations: MA: North Andover
Grant Types: General Support.

Financial Summary

Total Giving: $55,500 (2000); $53,700 (1999); $50,000 (1997)
Assets: $1,158,421 (2000); $1,156,625 (1999); $1,054,855 (1996)

Typical Recipients

Arts & Humanities: Libraries
Civic & Public Affairs: Community Foundations, Civic & Public Affairs-General, Parades/Festivals, Urban & Community Affairs, Women's Affairs
Education: Colleges & Universities, Education-General, Legal Education, Private Education (Precollege), Secondary Education (Private)
Health: Cancer, Children's Health/Hospitals, Hospitals
International: International Relief Efforts
Religion: Churches, Religion-General, Jewish Causes, Religious Welfare, Synagogues/Temples
Social Services: Child Welfare, Community Centers, Community Service Organizations, Family Services, Recreation & Athletics, Scouts, Social Services-General, Substance Abuse, YMCA/YWCA/YMHA/YWHA, Youth Organizations

Application Procedures

Initial Contact: Send a brief letter of inquiry.
Deadlines: None.

Restrictions

Does not support individuals, religious organizations for sectarian purposes, political or lobbying groups, or organizations outside operating areas.

Foundation Officials

Donald A. George: clerk, trustee
Robert H. Goldstein: president, trustee
John T. Pollano, Esq.: treasurer, trustee

Grants Analysis

Disclosure Period: calendar year ending 2000
Total Grants: $55,500
Number of Grants: 13
Average Grant: $4,269
Highest Grant: $13,500
Lowest Grant: $1,000
Typical Range: $1,000 to $5,000

Recent Grants

Note: Grants derived from 1999 Form 990.

General

5,600	Town of North Andover Public School
5,000	Adelante Inc./Lawrence Youth Center
5,000	Holy Family Hospital
5,000	Merrimack Valley Community Foundation
5,000	St. Michael's Church
5,000	Temple Emanuel
3,000	Suffolk University Law School, Boston, MA
2,500	Gr. Lawrence Council of Churches
2,500	Lawrence Academy
2,500	Pingree School

STANLEY P. AND BLANCHE E. ASH FOUNDATION

Giving Contact

Stanley P. Ash, President
PO Box 310
Greenville, MI 48838-0310
Phone: (616)754-5693

Description

Founded: 1992
EIN: 382966745
Organization Type: Private Foundation
Giving Locations: MI
Grant Types: General Support, Scholarship.

Financial Summary

Total Giving: $213,799 (2001); $185,195 (2000); $136,525 (1999)
Giving Analysis: Giving for 2001 includes: foundation scholarships ($65,978); 2000: foundation scholarships ($55,845) 1999: foundation scholarships ($25,260)
Assets: $3,398,795 (2001); $3,784,654 (2000); $3,623,827 (1998)
Gifts Received: $265,000 (2000); $800,000 (1999); $356,000 (1995). Note: In 1995, 1999 and 2000, donors were Stanley and Blanche Ash ($306,000).

Typical Recipients

Arts & Humanities: Libraries, Literary Arts
Civic & Public Affairs: Botanical Gardens/Parks, Clubs, Community Foundations
Education: Colleges & Universities, Community & Junior Colleges, Engineering/Technological Education, Education-General, Private Education (Precollege), Special Education, Student Aid
Health: Cancer, Single-Disease Health Associations
Religion: Churches, Religion-General
Social Services: Camps, Community Centers, Special Olympics

Application Procedures

Initial Contact: Request application form for scholarship program.
Deadlines: None.

Additional Information

Provides scholarships to students in the Montcalm County, MI, area who show financial need and have satisfactory grades.

Foundation Officials

Blanche E. Ash: vice president
Jennifer K. Ash: director
Stanley P. Ash: president

Grants Analysis

Disclosure Period: calendar year ending 2001
Total Grants: $147,821*
Number of Grants: 63
Average Grant: $771*
Highest Grant: $100,000
Lowest Grant: $15
Typical Range: $100 to $1,000
*Note: Giving excludes scholarships. Average grant figure excludes highest grant.

Recent Grants

Note: Grants derived from 2001 Form 990.

Library-Related

8,000	White Pine Library

General

100,000	Montcalm Community College Foundation, Montcalm, WV
20,000	Greenville Area Community Center
9,000	St. Paul's Lutheran Church
3,500	Faith Lutheran
1,500	Central Michigan University, Mt. Pleasant, MI -- scholarship
1,500	Grand Valley State University, Allendale, MI -- scholarship
1,500	Kalamazoo College, Kalamazoo, MI -- scholarship
1,500	Michigan State University, East Lansing, MI -- scholarship
1,400	Central Michigan University, Mt. Pleasant, MI -- scholarship

1,301 Montcalm Community College Foundation, Montcalm, WV -- scholarship

ASHTABULA FOUNDATION

Giving Contact
Gary Ensign
Ashtabula Foundation
Ashtabula Campus, Kent State University
3325 West 13th Street
Ashtabula, OH 44004
Phone: (440)964-3322

Description
Founded: 1922
EIN: 346538130
Organization Type: Private Foundation
Giving Locations: OH: Ashtabula
Grant Types: General Support, Scholarship.

Financial Summary
Total Giving: $898,845 (2000); $796,233 (1999); $526,847 (1998)
Giving Analysis: Giving for 2000 includes: foundation scholarships ($12,500); foundation grants to United Way ($50,000); 1999: foundation matching gifts ($10,000); foundation scholarships ($15,164); foundation grants to United Way ($50,000); 1998: foundation gifts to individuals ($12,830) foundation grants to United Way ($60,000)
Assets: $17,674,664 (2000); $17,737,370 (1999); $17,499,125 (1998)
Gifts Received: $397,320 (2000); $8,396 (1998); $9,384 (1996). Note: In 1998, contributions were received from Jefferson United Methodist Church ($5,000), Thurgood Marshall Family Resource Center ($2,946) and two others. In 1996, contributions were received from the Jefferson United Methodist Church.

Typical Recipients
Arts & Humanities: Arts Centers, Ballet, History & Archaeology, Libraries, Music
Civic & Public Affairs: Chambers of Commerce, Economic Development, Housing, Urban & Community Affairs
Education: Agricultural Education, Colleges & Universities, Education Reform, Elementary Education (Public), Faculty Development, Education-General, Leadership Training, Private Education (Precollege), Public Education (Precollege), School Volunteerism, Science/Mathematics Education, Secondary Education (Private), Secondary Education (Public), Special Education, Student Aid
Environment: Environment-General, Resource Conservation
Health: Alzheimers Disease, Cancer, Clinics/Medical Centers, Emergency/Ambulance Services, Heart, Prenatal Health Issues, Speech & Hearing
Religion: Bible Study/Translation, Churches, Ministries, Religious Organizations, Religious Welfare
Social Services: Big Brother/Big Sister, Camps, Child Welfare, Community Centers, Community Service Organizations, Family Planning, People with Disabilities, Recreation & Athletics, United Funds/United Ways, Volunteer Services, YMCA/YWCA/YMHA/YWHA

Application Procedures
Initial Contact: Request application form for either grant or scholarship award.
Deadlines: February 1, May 1, August 1, and November 1. Scholarship deadline is May 1.

Additional Information
Provides scholarships to Ashtabula, OH, residents and to Ashtabula County High School football letter winners.
Publications: Application Form

Foundation Officials
Wilbur L. Anderson: trustee
Roy H. Bean: trustee
Dr. Jerome Bockway: trustee
Thad Hague: vice president, trustee
Douglas A. Hedberg: trustee
Eleanor A. Jammal: president, trustee
Robert E. Martin, Jr.: treasurer
Glen W. Warner: treasurer, trust
Barbara P. Wiese: trustee

Grants Analysis
Disclosure Period: calendar year ending 2000
Total Grants: $836,345*
Number of Grants: 41
Average Grant: $15,909*
Highest Grant: $200,000
Lowest Grant: $600
Typical Range: $5,000 to $30,000*
*Note: Giving excludes United Way and scholarships. Average grant excludes highest grant.

Recent Grants
Note: Grants derived from 1999 Form 990.

General
123,151	Jefferson United Methodist Church
78,247	Civic Development Corp of Ashtabula County, Ashtabula, OH -- 1998 foundation pledge
78,247	Civic Development Corp of Ashtabula County, Ashtabula, OH
50,000	United Way of Ashtabula, Ashtabula, OH -- 1999 campaign
35,000	Civic Development Corp of Ashtabula County, Ashtabula, OH -- rails to trails project
32,500	Kent State University, Kent, OH -- construct restroom facilities
20,000	Peoples Missionary Baptist
19,000	Ashtabula County Community, Ashtabula, OH -- new hope housing transitional program
16,182	Conneaut Community Center
15,000	Ashtabula Area City Schools, Ashtabula, OH -- consultant services for continuous improvements

ASPLUNDH FOUNDATION

Giving Contact
Edward K. Asplundh, President
708 Blair Mill Rd.
Willow Grove, PA 19090
Phone: (215)784-4200

Description
Founded: 1953
EIN: 236297246
Organization Type: Private Foundation
Giving Locations: OR; PA; WV
Grant Types: Emergency, Endowment, General Support, Multiyear/Continuing Support, Project.

Donor Information
Founder: the late Carl H. Asplundh, Lester Asplundh

Financial Summary
Total Giving: $636,000 (2001); $610,025 (2000); $673,750 (1999)
Assets: $14,005,679 (2001); $12,428,746 (2000); $12,432,864 (1999)
Gifts Received: $100,000 (2001); $100,500 (2000); $25,500 (1999). Note: In 1993, 1999, 2000, and 2001 contributions were received from the Asplundh Tree Expert Co.

Typical Recipients
Arts & Humanities: Arts Centers, Historic Preservation, History & Archaeology, Libraries, Museums/Galleries, Music, Performing Arts, Visual Arts
Civic & Public Affairs: Botanical Gardens/Parks, Clubs, Employment/Job Training, Civic & Public Affairs-General, Rural Affairs, Safety, Zoos/Aquariums
Education: Colleges & Universities, Elementary Education (Public), Environmental Education, Education-General, Private Education (Precollege), Religious Education, Student Aid
Environment: Environment-General, Resource Conservation
Health: AIDS/HIV, Cancer, Clinics/Medical Centers, Emergency/Ambulance Services, Health Organizations, Hospitals
International: Foreign Educational Institutions, Health Care/Hospitals, International Environmental Issues
Religion: Churches, Churches, Religious Organizations
Science: Science Museums, Scientific Organizations
Social Services: At-Risk Youth, Child Welfare, Community Service Organizations, People with Disabilities, Recreation & Athletics, United Funds/United Ways, Youth Organizations

Application Procedures
Initial Contact: Send a brief letter of inquiry.
Application Requirements: Include a description of organization, amount requested, and purpose of funds sought.
Deadlines: None.

Foundation Officials
Barr E. Asplundh: vice president, director B Bryn Athyn, PA 1925. ED Pennsylvania State University (1952). PRIM CORP EMPL chairman: Asplundh Tree Expert Co. CORP AFFIL director: Tree Preservation Co. Inc.; director: Wilson Tree Co. Inc.; director: Blume Tree Services Inc.; director: Farrens Tree Surgeons Inc.; director: Asplundh Construction Corp.; director: Asplundh Motor Co. Inc.; director: American Lighting Signalization; director: Asplundh Brush Control Co.
Brent D. Asplundh: director B 1961. ED Ohio Wesleyan University (1984). PRIM CORP EMPL president: American Lighting Signalization ADD CORP EMPL vice president: Asplundh Tree Expert Co.; vice president: Blume Tree Services Inc.; vice president: Farrens Tree Surgeons Inc.; vice president: Tree Preservation Co. Inc.; president: Utility Pole Technologies Inc.; vice president: Wilson Tree Co. Inc. CORP AFFIL director: Aslundh Brush Control Co.; director: Asplundh Motor Co. Inc.
Carl H. J. Asplundh, Jr.: director B 1935. PRIM CORP EMPL president: Asplundh Motor Co. Inc. ADD CORP EMPL director: Asplundh Brush Control Co.; vice president: Asplundh Tree Expert Co. Inc.; vice president: Wilson Tree Co. Inc.
Christopher B. Asplundh: president, director B 1939. CORP AFFIL Asplundh Motor Co. Inc.; director: Utility Pole Technologies Inc.; director: Asplundh Construction Corp.; American Lighting Signalization; director: Asplundh Buick GMC Trucks.
E. Boyd Asplundh: secretary, treasurer, director B 1927. CORP AFFIL director: Tree Preservation Co. Inc.; director: Wilson Tree Co. Inc.; director: Farrens Tree Surgeons Inc.; director: Asplundh Tree Expert Co.; director: Blume Tree Services Inc.; director: Asplundh Construction Corp.; director: Asplundh Motor Co. Inc.; director: American Lighting Signalization; director: Asplundh Brush Control Co.
Edward K. Asplundh: president
Gregg G. Asplundh: director PRIM CORP EMPL vice president: Asplundh Tree Expert Co. ADD CORP EMPL vice president: Blume Tree Services Inc.; vice president: Farrens Tree Surgeons Inc.; vice president: Tree Preservation Co. Inc. CORP AFFIL director: American Lighting Signalization; director: Asplundh Construction Corp.

Ian L. Asplundh: director
Paul S. Asplundh: director
Robert H. Asplundh: director B 1929. PRIM CORP EMPL chairman: Asplundh Tree Expert Co. CORP AFFIL director: Tree Preservation Co. Inc.; director: Wilson Tree Co. Inc.; director: Blume Tree Services Inc.; director: Farrens Tree Surgeons Inc.; director: Asplundh Construction Corp.; director: Asplundh Motor Co. Inc.; director: American Lighting Signalization; director: Asplundh Brush Control Co.
Scott M. Asplundh: director
Steven G. Asplundh: director B 1960. ED Stetson University BA (1983); Georgia State University (1986). PRIM CORP EMPL vice president: Asplundh Tree Expert Co. ADD CORP EMPL vice president: Blume Tree Services Inc.; vice president: Farrens Tree Surgeons Inc.; vice president: Tree Preservation Co. Inc.; vice president: Wilson Tree Co. Inc. CORP AFFIL director: Asplundh Construction Co.; director: Asplundh Motor Co. Inc.; director: American Lighting Signalization; director: Asplundh Brush Control Co.
Stewart L. Asplundh: director PRIM CORP EMPL president: American Lighting Signalization ADD CORP EMPL vice president: Asplundh Tree Expert Co.; vice president: Blume Tree Services Inc.; vice president: Farrens Tree Surgeons Inc.; vice president: Tree Preservation Co. Inc. CORP AFFIL director: Asplundh Construction Corp.
George E. Graham, Jr.: director
James E. Graham: director
Emily Jane Lemole: secretary, treasurer

Grants Analysis

Disclosure Period: calendar year ending 2001
Total Grants: $636,000
Number of Grants: 82
Average Grant: $4,707*
Highest Grant: $150,000
Lowest Grant: $100
Typical Range: $500 to $5,000
***Note:** Average grant excludes two highest grants ($250,000).

Recent Grants

Note: Grants derived from 2001 Form 990.

General

150,000	Bryn Athyn Church School, Bryn Athyn, PA -- for church school
100,000	Academy of the New Church Campaign 2000, Bryn Athyn, PA -- for building fund
100,000	Swedenborg Foundation, Chester, PA -- for publishing new edition of Swedenborg writings
50,000	Abington Memorial Hospital Foundation, Abington, PA -- for endowed nursing scholarship
25,000	Carmel Church School, Waterloo, ON Canada -- for expansion
25,000	Doylestown Hospital, Doylestown, PA -- pledge for cardiac unit
25,000	Holy Redeemer Hospital, Meadowbrook, PA -- pledge
25,000	Pittsburgh New Church School, Pittsburgh, PA
10,000	Abington Art Center, Jenkintown, PA
10,000	Academy of the New Church, Bryn Athyn, PA -- for campaign 2000

AT&T CORP.

Company Headquarters

New York, NY
Web: http://www.att.com

Company Description

Founded: 1885
Ticker: T
Exchange: NYSE

Acquired: MediaOne (2000).
Revenue: US$37.827 billion (2002)
Employees: 71000 (2002)
Fortune Rank: 22, per FORTUNE Magazine's list of 500 Largest U.S. Corporations (2002).
SIC(s): 4812 Radiotelephone Communications, 4813 Telephone Communications Except Radiotelephone, 4899 Communications Services Nec.

Operating Locations

ACC Corp. (NY--Rochester); Associated Group (PA--Pittsburgh); At Home Corp. (CA--Redwood City); AT&T Alascam Inc. (AK--Anchorage); AT&T Broadband, LLC (CO--Englewood); AT&T CampusWide Access Solutions Inc. (AZ--Phoenix); AT&T Communication Inc. (NJ--Basking Ridge); AT&T Global Network Services (NJ--Florham Park); AT&T Internet Services (NJ--Bridgewater); AT&T Latin America Corp. (FL--Coral Gables); AT&T Local Service (NJ--Dayton); AT&T Solutions Inc. (NJ--Florham Park); Concert (VA--Reston); Four Media Computer (CA--Burbank); GRC International Inc. (VA--Vienna); Kearns-Tribune Corp. (UT--Salt Lake City); Liberty Digital (NY--New York); Liberty Media Group (CO--Englewood); Management Consulting & Research (VA--McLean); MediaOne Group Inc. (CO--Englewood); Net 2 Phone, Inc. (NJ--Hackensack); Wireless Group (WA--Redmond)

Nonmonetary Support

Type: Cause-related Marketing & Promotion; Donated Products; In-kind Services; Loaned Employees; Loaned Executives
Volunteer Programs: Supports the AT&T CARES program, which makes grants to organizations where employees volunteer, and the Telephone Pioneers of America, a volunteer service organization.
Contact: Jo-Ann Greene, Director, AT&T University Equipment Donation Program
Note: Co. does not accept unsolicited requests for nonmonetary support.

AT&T Foundation

Giving Contact

Vivian Nero, Operations & Local Grants
32 Avenue of the Americas
New York, NY 10013
Phone: (212)387-6557
Fax: (212)387-5098
Web: http://www.att.com/foundation

Description

EIN: 133166495
Organization Type: Corporate Foundation
Giving Locations: headquarters and operating communities; nationally and internationally.
Grant Types: Award, Conference/Seminar, Emergency, Employee Matching Gifts, Fellowship, Matching, Multiyear/Continuing Support, Operating Expenses, Project.
Note: Employee matching gift ratio: 1 to 1 for tax-deductible gifts to higher education and cultural institutions with grants from $25 to $10,000 and a maximum of $50,000 per organization. Foundation also sponsors the AT&T Cares program to provide grants to organisation where employees volunteer at least 50 hours of time.

Financial Summary

Total Giving: $44,196,080 (2001); $45,675,281 (2000); $43,010,493 (1999). Note: Contributes through corporate direct giving program and foundation. 1998 Giving includes foundation.
Giving Analysis: Giving for 2000 includes: foundation matching gifts ($3,634,136); foundation grants to United Way ($3,883,950); 1999: foundation matching gifts ($3,546,921); foundation ($39,463,572); foundation ($45,678,097); 1998: foundation scholarships ($70,243); foundation fellowships ($475,143); foundation matching gifts ($3,059,804); foundation grants to United Way ($4,010,300); foundation ($38,062,607);
Assets: $48,824,236 (2001); $60,219,943 (2000); $75,327,433 (1999)
Gifts Received: $25,199,987 (2001); $36,326,104 (2000); $36,621,716 (1998)

Typical Recipients

Arts & Humanities: Arts Associations & Councils, Arts Centers, Arts Festivals, Arts Funds, Arts Institutes, Ballet, Dance, Historic Preservation, Libraries, Museums/Galleries, Music, Opera, Performing Arts, Theater, Visual Arts
Civic & Public Affairs: African American Affairs, Civil Rights, Community Foundations, Economic Development, Economic Policy, Employment/Job Training, Civic & Public Affairs-General, Hispanic Affairs, Housing, Minority Business, Nonprofit Management, Professional & Trade Associations, Public Policy, Urban & Community Affairs, Women's Affairs
Education: Arts/Humanities Education, Business Education, Colleges & Universities, Education Associations, Education Funds, Education Reform, Elementary Education (Public), Engineering/Technological Education, Faculty Development, Education-General, International Exchange, International Studies, Leadership Training, Legal Education, Literacy, Medical Education, Minority Education, Preschool Education, Public Education (Precollege), Science/Mathematics Education, Secondary Education (Public), Social Sciences Education, Special Education, Student Aid
Environment: Environment-General
Health: Children's Health/Hospitals, Emergency/Ambulance Services, Health Policy/Cost Containment, Hospitals, Speech & Hearing
International: Foreign Arts Organizations, Foreign Educational Institutions, International Affairs, International Relations
Science: Science Museums
Social Services: Child Welfare, Community Service Organizations, Day Care, Emergency Relief, Family Services, People with Disabilities, Recreation & Athletics, Substance Abuse, United Funds/United Ways, Youth Organizations

Application Procedures

Initial Contact: Write for guidelines and application form, then send brief letter with completed application.
Application Requirements: Include brief history of the organization and description of mission; statement relating purpose to interests and priorities of foundation; detailed description of purpose for which grant is sought and amount requested; operating and/or project budget for current year showing anticipated sources of revenue and expenses (if project support sought, include a detailed budget for the project); and proof of 501(c)(3) status.
Deadlines: None.
Review Process: Staff members make recommendations to board of trustees.
Evaluative Criteria: Grants focus on cities and regions with large concentrations of AT&T employees and business operations, with the majority of funds supporting U.S.-based institutions. Organizations must be nonsectarian and nondenominational to receive support; organizations must seek to advance AT&T's goals of promoting diversity and equal opportunity, and that programs will be open and accessible to all segments of society. Grants are awarded in the following program areas: education, civic & community service, and arts and culture through such programs as: AT&T Learning Network grants, direct grants, employee-directed grants, AT&T Cares program, AT&T Employee Matching Gifts Program; arts and cultures programs include AT&T: On Stage, AT&T:NEAT. enhance the quality of life in communities where AT&T employees live and work; utilize technology in inventive ways; or involve employee volunteers.
Decision Notification: Trustees meet monthly.

Notes: For U.S.-based national organizations, apply to foundation. For local projects, apply to Regional Contributions Manager in area; contact information is included in guidelines.

Restrictions

Foundation does not make grants to individuals; organizations whose chief purpose is to influence legislation or to participate or intervene in political campaigns on behalf of or against any candidate for public office, endowments or memorials, construction or renovation projects, sports teams or any sports-related activity or competition even if it addresses our program interests, and fund-raising events or advertising. The Civic & Community Service Program does not support organizations that channel the funds received to third parties, organizations formed to combat specific diseases, medical research, programs to reduce deficits, alcohol-abuse and substance-abuse treatment programs, and programs to alleviate homelessness. The Arts & Culture Program generally does not support student or amateur groups; arts education programs; individual artists; artistic training or scholarships; film and media productions; competitions; arts programs designed primarily for rehabilitation or therapy; public radio and television stations for unrestricted purposes, equipment acquisition or program underwriting; science museums or science/technology exhibitions, except through the AT&T NEAT initiative, and the purchase of equipment.

Additional Information

Guidelines may be obtained by either calling (212) 387-4868, or sending a fax message to (212) 387-4906.

Guidelines include extensive restrictions by program area, and should be carefully reviewed before submitting a request.

The company's nonmonetary support program provides AT&T computer laboratories to selected colleges and universities. This is an invitational program not open to unsolicited requests.

Regional contributions offices for organizations outside the U.S. are as follows:

For organizations in Australia, China, India, Indonesia, Japan, Philippines, South Korea, Taiwan, and Thailand, contact AT&T Asia/Pacific Inc., Shell Tower, Times Sq., 1 Matheson St., 30th Fl., Causeway Bay, Hong Kong, 011-852-2-506-5051.

For organizations in France, contact AT&T France SA, Tour Horizon, 52 quai de Dion-Bouton, 92806 Puteaux, Cedex, France, 011-33-1-4767-4709.

For organizations in Germany, contact AT&T Deutschland, Eschersheimer Landstrasse 14, D-60322, Frankfurt, Germany, 011-49-69-153-06-431.

For organizations in Italy, The Netherlands, Poland, South Africa, and Spain, contact AT&T Communications Service SA, Chaussee de Wavre 1943, B-1160 Brussels, Belgium.

For organizations in Russia, contact AT&T CIS Ltd., Toko Tower,11th Fl., 6, Krasnopresnenskaya, 123242 Moscow, Russia, 011-7-095-974-1462.

For organizations in the United Kingdom, contact AT&T England, Norfolk House, 31 St. James' Sq., London, SW1 4JR, United Kingdom, 011-44-171-925-8116.

For organizations in Canada, c/o AT&T Canada, 320 Front St. West, 17th Fl., Toronto, Ontario, Canada M5V 3B6, 416-204-2908.

For organizations in Argentina, Brazil, Chile, Colombia, Mexico, Puerto Rico, and Venezuela, contact AT&T, 233 Ponce de Leon Blvd., Rm. 941-10, Coral Gables, FL 33134, 305-569-3753.

Publications: Foundation Report; Guidelines

Corporate Officials

C. Michael Armstrong: chairman, chief executive officer, director B Detroit, MI October 1938. ED Miami University BS (1961); Dartmouth College (1976). PRIM CORP EMPL chairman, chief executive officer, director: AT&T Corp. CORP AFFIL director: Times Mirror Co.; chairman, chief executive officer: Hughes Electronics Corp.; director: LA CitiCorp.; chairman board: AT&T Broadband Internet Services; director: Citigroup Inc. NONPR AFFIL vice chairman: World Affairs Council; member advisory board: Yale School Management; member board advisors: University Southern California Business School; vice chairman: Sabriyas Castle Fun Foundation; member supervisory board: Thyssen-Bornemisza Group; member: National Security Telecommunications Advisory Committee; chairman: President's Export Council; member business advisory council: Miami University Ohio; chairman advisory board: Johns Hopkins School Medicine; trustee: Johns Hopkins University; member: Defense Policy Advisory Committee Trade; member: General Motors President Council; member: Council Foreign Relations; trustee: Carnegie Hall.

Harold W. Burlingame: executive vice president wireless group B Zanesville, OH. PRIM CORP EMPL executive vice president wireless group: AT&T Corp.

David W. Dorman: president, director PRIM CORP EMPL president, director: AT&T Corp.

Richard J. Martin: executive vice president public relations employee communications ED Ohio State University BS. PRIM CORP EMPL executive vice president public relations employee communications: AT&T Corp.

Charles H. Noski: vice chairman, chief financial officer, director PRIM CORP EMPL vice chairman, chief financial officer, director: AT&T Corp.

Daniel E. Somers: president, chief executive officer broadband ED Stonehill College BS (1969). PRIM CORP EMPL president, chief executive officer broadband: AT&T Corp.

John D. Zeglis: chairman and chief executive officer wireless group PRIM CORP EMPL chairman and chief executive officer wireless group: AT&T Corp.

Foundation Officials

Robert Angelica: treasurer
Harold W. Burlingame: trustee (see above)
Richard J. Martin: chairman, trustee (see above)
Timothy J. McClimon: executive director B Clinton, IA 1953. ED Luther College BA (1975); Saint Cloud State College MS (1976); Georgetown University JD (1986). NONPR AFFIL director: Theatre Committees Group; member: Volunteer Lawyers Arts; director: Second Stage Theatre; adjunct professor: New York University; director: Performance Space 122; member: New York State Bar Association; consult: National Endowment Arts; member: New York City Bar Association; director: Merce Cunningham Dance Foundation; member: American Bar Association; director: Field Papers.
Vivian Nero: secretary
Marilyn Reznick: vice president education program
Suzanne M. Sato: vice president arts & culture program
Esther Silver-Parker: president, trustee
Mitzi Vaimberg: vice president civic community services

Grants Analysis

Disclosure Period: calendar year ending 2001
Total Grants: $39,753,664*
Number of Grants: 1,536
Average Grant: $26,000
Highest Grant: $500,000
Lowest Grant: $50
Typical Range: $1,000 to $50,000
*Note: Giving excludes matching gifts, United Way, and foundation related expenses.

Recent Grants

Note: Grants derived from 2001 Form 990.

General

850,000	United Way Tri-State, New York, NY -- for operations
500,000	Cambridge University Development Office, New York, NY -- alliance for education
370,000	Mile High United Way, Denver, CO -- for operations
300,000	Children's Partnership, Santa Monica, CA -- for American families in the digital age leadership development for policymakers
275,000	Foundation for Independent High Education, Washington, DC -- for AT&T Learning Network
274,400	United Way of Metropolitan Atlanta, Atlanta, GA -- for operations
250,000	American Red Cross, Washington, DC -- for annual disaster giving program
250,000	American Red Cross, Washington, DC -- for disaster relief efforts
250,000	Exploris, Raleigh, NC -- for Exploris Global Learning Center and School
250,000	Foundation for the National Archives/National Archives and Records Administration, College Park, MD -- preservation and reencasement of the Charters of Freedom

AT&T NATIONAL PRO-AM YOUTH FUND

Giving Contact

Carmel C. Martin, Jr., Secretary & Treasurer
490 Calle Principal
PO Box 112
Monterey, CA 93940
Phone: (831)375-3151

Description

Founded: 1963
EIN: 946050251
Organization Type: Private Foundation
Giving Locations: CA: Monterey County, Santa Cruz County
Grant Types: Capital, General Support, Scholarship.

Donor Information

Founder: The late Bing Crosby.

Financial Summary

Total Giving: $489,625 (fiscal year ending June 30, 2002); $358,650 (fiscal 2001); $470,630 (fiscal 1999) **Giving Analysis:** Giving for fiscal 2001 includes: foundation scholarships ($15,000); fiscal 2000: foundation scholarships ($46,500) fiscal 1999: foundation scholarships ($51,200)
Assets: $195,289 (fiscal 2002); $286,789 (fiscal 2001); $567,174 (fiscal 1999)
Gifts Received: $414,614 (fiscal 2002); $502,165 (fiscal 2001); $512,000 (fiscal 1999). Note: Contributions were received from AT&T Pro-Am Golf Tournament.

Typical Recipients

Arts & Humanities: Arts Associations & Councils, Arts Centers, Arts Outreach, Community Arts, History & Archaeology, Museums/Galleries, Music, Theater
Civic & Public Affairs: Ethnic Organizations, Civic & Public Affairs-General, Housing, Safety, Urban & Community Affairs, Women's Affairs, Zoos/Aquariums
Education: Arts/Humanities Education, Colleges & Universities, Environmental Education, Education-General, International Studies, Journalism/Media Education, Leadership Training, Legal Education, Private Education (Precollege), Public Education (Precollege), Science/Mathematics Education, Secondary Education (Private), Secondary Education (Public), Student Aid
Environment: Environment-General
Health: Health Organizations, Hospitals
International: International Peace & Security Issues, International Relations

Religion: Churches, Religious Organizations, Religious Welfare

Social Services: Big Brother/Big Sister, Camps, Child Welfare, Community Service Organizations, Counseling, Domestic Violence, Family Planning, People with Disabilities, Recreation & Athletics, Scouts, Special Olympics, United Funds/United Ways, Youth Organizations

Application Procedures

Initial Contact: full proposal
Application Requirements: Include a description of organization, amount requested, purpose of funds sought, recently audited financial statement, proof of tax-exempt status, and other sources of funding.
Deadlines: None.

Restrictions

Does not support individuals.

Foundation Officials

Daniel Albert: director
John Burns: trustee
Peter J. Coniglio: trustee
Peter Cutino: director
Nancy Durein: trustee
Jack Holt: trustee
Warner Keeley: trustee
Carmel C. Martin, Jr.: secretary, treasurer
Frank Thacker: chairman
Daniel Tibitts: director
Murray C. Vout: trustee

Grants Analysis

Disclosure Period: fiscal year ending June 30, 2002
Total Grants: $474,625*
Number of Grants: 155
Average Grant: $3,062
Highest Grant: $21,500
Typical Range: $1,000 to $5,000
*Note: Giving excludes scholarship.

Recent Grants

Note: Grants derived from fiscal 2000 Form 990.

General

21,000	Monterey Peninsula College, Monterey, CA
7,500	Lyceum of Monterey County, Monterey, CA
6,000	Carmel Bach Festival, Carmel, CA
5,000	Barracuda Aquatics, Monterey, CA
5,000	Big Brothers Big Sisters of Monterey, Monterey, CA
5,000	California State University Monterey Bay, Seaside, CA
5,000	California Women's Amateur Championship Association, Pebble Beach, CA
5,000	Carmel Unified School District, Carmel, CA
5,000	Carmel Valley Little League, Carmel Valley, CA
5,000	Carmel Valley Village Improvement, Carmel Valley, CA

ATHERTON FAMILY FOUNDATION

Giving Contact

Lissa Schiff, Private Foundation Services Officer
Care of Hawaii Community Foundation
900 Fort Street Mall, Suite 1300
Honolulu, HI 96813
Phone: (808)537-6333
Fax: (808)521-6286
E-mail: lschiff@hcf-hawaii.org

Description

Founded: 1976
EIN: 510175971
Organization Type: General Purpose Foundation
Giving Locations: HI
Grant Types: Capital, Matching, Multiyear/Continuing Support, Project, Scholarship.
Note: The foundation also makes program grants.

Donor Information

Founder: Established in 1975 to continue the charitable work of the original donor and trustees of the Juliette M. Atherton Trust, established in 1915. Juliette M. Atherton was the daughter of pioneer American missionaries in Hawaii. Her husband, Joseph Ballard Atherton, was the son-in-law of Samuel Northrup Castle, the president of Castle and Cooke. Mrs. Atherton entrusted her estate to three of her children, Charles H. Atherton, Mary A. Richards, and Frank C. Atherton, to continue the charitable work in which she was interested. In 1976, the assets of her trust, as well as the assets of the Frank C. Atherton Trust, which had provided support for charitable organizations since 1935, were transferred to the Atherton Family Foundation. The charitable giving patterns of both original trusts were similar through the years. Consolidation of the two trusts was carried out to provide more efficient administration, greater flexibility in foundation policies, and greater protection and growth of the investment assets. It also permitted an increase in the number of members and directors for a broader representation of charitable interests.

Financial Summary

Total Giving: $4,550,075 (2001); $5,056,350 (2000); $3,865,550 (1999)
Giving Analysis: Giving for 2000 includes: foundation scholarships ($128,750); foundation grants to United Way ($277,000); 1999: foundation scholarships ($112,450); foundation grants to United Way ($263,500); 1998: foundation scholarships ($106,650) foundation grants to United Way ($236,500)
Assets: $112,054,947 (2000); $113,520,496 (1999); $96,517,130 (1998)

Typical Recipients

Arts & Humanities: Arts Centers, Arts Funds, Arts Outreach, Ballet, Community Arts, Dance, Arts & Humanities-General, Historic Preservation, History & Archaeology, Libraries, Museums/Galleries, Music, Opera, Performing Arts, Public Broadcasting, Theater, Visual Arts
Civic & Public Affairs: Asian American Affairs, Botanical Gardens/Parks, Business/Free Enterprise, Community Foundations, Economic Development, Employment/Job Training, Civic & Public Affairs-General, Hispanic Affairs, Housing, Legal Aid, Public Policy, Safety, Urban & Community Affairs
Education: Afterschool/Enrichment Programs, Arts/Humanities Education, Business Education, Colleges & Universities, Colleges & Universities, Education Associations, Education Funds, Elementary Education (Private), Faculty Development, Education-General, Gifted & Talented Programs, International Exchange, International Studies, Literacy, Medical Education, Preschool Education, Private Education (Precollege), Public Education (Precollege), Religious Education, Science/Mathematics Education, Secondary Education (Private), Secondary Education (Public), Social Sciences Education, Special Education, Student Aid
Environment: Environment-General, Resource Conservation
Health: Cancer, Children's Health/Hospitals, Clinics/Medical Centers, Emergency/Ambulance Services, Geriatric Health, Health Funds, Health Organizations, Hospices, Hospitals, Long-Term Care, Medical Rehabilitation, Medical Research, Medical Training, Mental Health, Nursing Services, Prenatal Health Issues

International: International Affairs, International Environmental Issues, International Organizations
Religion: Churches, Dioceses, Ministries, Religious Organizations, Religious Welfare
Science: Science Museums, Scientific Centers & Institutes, Scientific Organizations
Social Services: Animal Protection, At-Risk Youth, Big Brother/Big Sister, Camps, Child Welfare, Community Centers, Community Service Organizations, Counseling, Crime Prevention, Delinquency & Criminal Rehabilitation, Domestic Violence, Emergency Relief, Family Planning, Family Services, Food/Clothing Distribution, Homes, People with Disabilities, Recreation & Athletics, Scouts, Senior Services, Shelters/Homelessness, Substance Abuse, United Funds/United Ways, Volunteer Services, YMCA/YWCA/YMHA/YWHA, Youth Organizations

Application Procedures

Initial Contact: Applicants should send a written proposal to the foundation. Guidelines are different for requests for automation equipment and scholarships; contact the foundation for more information.
Application Requirements: The initial proposal should include one, unbound copy, of the following: a description of organization including its history, mission and leadership; brief description of the population to be served or benefited by the project and the approximate size; the need or opportunity for which the proposed activity is a response or solution; project objectives and summary of the activities to be funded; amount requested, duration of time funds will be needed, and anticipated sources of support when foundation funding ceases; method used to determine effectivenss of funded project; information about the organization's staff, including those responsible for the program/project; name and phone number of contact persons; expense budget and revenue plan for the total project budget indicating categories of sources and amounts; a one- or two-page summary of the proposal; and a list of the board of directors, including occupations and affiliation and a statement of board involvement and functions within the organization. Additional materials that must be included are signatures of the presiding officer of the board and the executive director indicating that the board and chief staff person approve of the proposal; IRS determination letter; and the organization's Charter and Bylaws, current annual operating budget, and most recently completed financial statements.
Deadlines: December 1, February 1, April 1, August 1, October 1.
Review Process: If an organization wishes to have its request considered at a particular meeting, its proposal must be received by the first of the month two months prior to the month in which there is a meeting. Meetings are scheduled on the third Wednesday of February, April, June, August, October, and December.

Restrictions

Grants are made only to tax-exempt organizations whose projects or programs will benefit the people of Hawaii. The foundation does not usually support requests for annual operating support, organizations which have already received a grant in the same calendar year, including a grant for automation equipment (exceptions, see "collaborative project"), individuals, with the exception of the Juliette M. Atherton Scholarship Funds, loans, grants for endowment funds, private foundations. The foundation does not award grants for political or lobbying groups. Requests from individual Departments of Education school and organizations intending to redistribute the grant to other beneficiaries (regranting) are not accepted. The University of Hawaii is awarded a grant each year to be expended at the president's discretion, therefore, no other proposals will be accepted from the university for that year, as this considered the universities annual grant.

Additional Information

Any organization receiving a grant from the foundation will be required to submit a brief report summarizing the outcome of the project and a fiscal accounting of the grant expenditures as soon as the operating period for which the funds were used is completed.
Publications: Annual Report; Grant Guidelines; Scholarship Guidelines
Trust(s): Hawaiian Trust Co.

Foundation Officials

Frank C. Atherton: vice president, treasurer, director
Judith Dawson: vice president, secretary, director B Honolulu, HI 1939. ED Wellesley College (1957-1959); University of California BA (1962); University of Hawaii MA (1977). PRIM NONPR EMPL vice president, treasurer: Punahou School. NONPR AFFIL trustee: Oriental Art Society; director: University California Alumni Association; trustee: Hawaiian Mission Childrens Society; member: Hawaii Society Fund-Raising Executive. CLUB AFFIL Oahu Country Club.
Patricia K.R. Henrickson: vice president
Steven Kaneshiro: grant administrator
Robert Richards Midkiff: president, director B Honolulu, HI September 24, 1920. ED Yale University BA (1942); Harvard University AMP (1962). PRIM CORP EMPL chairman, director: American Trust Co. Hawaii PRIM NONPR EMPL chief executive officer, president: American Financial Services. CORP AFFIL director: Persis Corp. NONPR AFFIL member: Profit Sharing Research Foundation; director: Small Business Council America; member: Phi Beta Kappa; member, director: Profit Sharing Council America; director: Hawaii Visitors Bureau; member, board directors: Lahaina Restoration Foundation; treasurer, director: Hawaii Community Foundation; director: Hawaii Theatre Center; director: Downtown Improvement Association; director: Good Beginnings Alliance; member: Council Foundations. CLUB AFFIL Pacific Club; Waialae Country Club; Oahu Country Club.
James F. Morgan, Jr.: vice president, director
Paul F. Morgan: vice president, director
Joan H. Rohlfing: vice president, director
Chris Sunada: grant manager

Grants Analysis

Disclosure Period: calendar year ending 2000
Total Grants: $4,927,600*
Number of Grants: 265
Average Grant: $17,549
Highest Grant: $360,000
Lowest Grant: $1,000
Typical Range: $3,000 to $50,000 and $100,000 to $250,000
*Note: Giving excludes United Way and scholarships.

Recent Grants

Note: Grants derived from 2000 Form 990.

General

360,000	Punahou School, Honolulu, HI -- construction of Science Center
288,000	Mid-Pacific Institute, Honolulu, HI -- capital campaign
240,000	Aloha United Way, Honolulu, HI -- annual campaign
216,000	Hawaii Theater Center, Honolulu, HI -- capital campaign
180,000	Contemporary Museum, Honolulu, HI -- campaign to perpetuate the Spalding House
150,000	Hawaii Preparatory Academy, Honolulu, HI -- constructing and equipping the HPA Technology Center
150,000	Honolulu Academy of Arts, Honolulu, HI -- capital campaign
150,000	YMCA of Oahu, Honolulu, HI -- capital campaign
144,000	Bishop Museum, Honolulu, HI -- Science Learning Center
144,000	Boy Scouts of America Aloha Council, Honolulu, HI -- capital campaign

LEBURTA ATHERTON FOUNDATION

Giving Contact

c/o Pacific Century Trust
PO Box 3170
Honolulu, HI 96802-3170
Phone: (808)538-4472

Description

Founded: 1998
EIN: 943260209
Organization Type: Private Foundation
Giving Locations: CA; CO; HI
Grant Types: General Support.

Financial Summary

Total Giving: $291,000 (2001); $356,500 (2000); $245,000 (1999)
Assets: $6,024,320 (2001); $5,063,112 (2000); $7,016,813 (1999)

Typical Recipients

Arts & Humanities: Arts Centers, Libraries, Theater
Civic & Public Affairs: Clubs, Civic & Public Affairs-General
Education: Preschool Education, Private Education (Precollege)
Health: Hospitals
Religion: Religious Welfare

Additional Information

Trust(s): Bank of Hawaii

Foundation Officials

Frank C. Atherton: director
Leburta G. Atherton: president, director
Balbi A. Brooks: treasurer, director
Marjory A. Newell: vice president, director

Grants Analysis

Disclosure Period: calendar year ending 2001
Total Grants: $291,000
Number of Grants: 12
Average Grant: $24,250
Highest Grant: $100,000
Lowest Grant: $1,000
Typical Range: $5,000 to $50,000

Recent Grants

Note: Grants derived from 2000 Form 990.

Library-Related

25,000	Long Beach Public Library Foundation, Long Beach, CA

General

100,000	La Pietra Hawaii School for Girls, Honolulu, HI
50,000	Hawaii Preparatory Academy, Kamuela, HI
50,000	North Hawaii Community Hospital, Kamuela, HI
50,000	River of Life Mission, Honolulu, HI
25,000	Honolulu Theater for Youth, Honolulu, HI
25,000	Rancho Los Cerritos Foundation, Long Beach, CA
25,000	Volcano Art Center, Hawaii National Park, HI
5,000	Long Beach Rotary Charitable Foundation, Long Beach, CA
1,500	KCAA Pre-School of Hawaii, Honolulu, HI

ATKINSON FOUNDATION

Giving Contact

Elizabeth H. Curtis, Administrator & Director
1720 South Amphlett Blvd.
Suite 100
San Mateo, CA 94402
Phone: (650)357-1101
Fax: (650)357-1101
E-mail: atkinfdn@aol.com

Description

Founded: 1939
EIN: 946075613
Organization Type: General Purpose Foundation
Giving Locations: CA: San Mateo County United States-based international organizations serving Latin America; United States-based international organizations serving the Caribbean.
Grant Types: Capital, General Support, Project, Seed Money.

Donor Information

Founder: Established in 1939 by George H. Atkinson (1905-1978) and his wife Mildred M. Atkinson (1904-1967). George Atkinson, along with his father, co-founded the international construction firm, Guy F. Atkinson Company. He made numerous trips, often accompanied by his wife, to under-developed and developing countries throughout the world. The Atkinsons' "first-hand awareness of the problems of third-world countries and their wish to help the people of these countries created in the foundation a pattern for giving that serves human needs and contributes to the self-esteem and independence of individuals, families, and communities in the developing areas of the world."

George and Mildred made significant contributions to their community in San Mateo County and the San Francisco Bay area. They were leaders in many social service organizations and were actively involved in the Methodist Church, locally, regionally, and nationally.

The value of education, learned while the Atkinsons were both undergraduates at Willamette University in Salem, OR, guides present grants to secondary education, community colleges, and selected universities and black colleges.

Financial Summary

Total Giving: $740,000 (2003); $733,907 (2002); $634,290 (2001)
Giving Analysis: Giving for 1999 includes: foundation program-related investments ($88,350)
Assets: $14,437,183 (2002); $15,761,391 (2001); $15,711,379 (2000)

Typical Recipients

Arts & Humanities: History & Archaeology, Libraries, Museums/Galleries, Public Broadcasting
Civic & Public Affairs: Asian American Affairs, Botanical Gardens/Parks, Business/Free Enterprise, Civil Rights, Community Foundations, Economic Development, Economic Policy, Employment/Job Training, Gay/Lesbian Issues, Civic & Public Affairs-General, Hispanic Affairs, Legal Aid, Municipalities/Towns, Nonprofit Management, Urban & Community Affairs, Women's Affairs
Education: Colleges & Universities, Community & Junior Colleges, Education Associations, Education Reform, Education-General, International Studies, Literacy, Minority Education, Preschool Education, Private Education (Precollege), Public Education (Precollege), Religious Education, Secondary Education (Public), Student Aid, Student Aid
Environment: Environment-General
Health: AIDS/HIV, Alzheimers Disease, Children's Health/Hospitals, Clinics/Medical Centers, Eyes/Blindness, Health-General, Heart, Hospitals, Medical

Rehabilitation, Medical Research, Mental Health, Public Health

International: Foreign Educational Institutions, International-General, Health Care/Hospitals, International Development, International Environmental Issues, International Organizations, International Peace & Security Issues, International Relief Efforts, Missionary/Religious Activities

Religion: Bible Study/Translation, Churches, Ministries, Missionary Activities (Domestic), Religious Welfare

Science: Scientific Centers & Institutes

Social Services: At-Risk Youth, Big Brother/Big Sister, Child Welfare, Community Centers, Community Service Organizations, Community Service Organizations, Counseling, Crime Prevention, Day Care, Delinquency & Criminal Rehabilitation, Domestic Violence, Emergency Relief, Family Planning, Family Services, Food/Clothing Distribution, Homes, People with Disabilities, Recreation & Athletics, Refugee Assistance, Senior Services, Shelters/Homelessness, Social Services-General, Substance Abuse, Volunteer Services, YMCA/YWCA/YMHA/YWHA, Youth Organizations

Application Procedures

Initial Contact: Phone to ascertain whether the proposal is within foundation guidelines and to request application materials. Applications should be submitted in writing.

Application Requirements: Completed foundation coversheet, the organization's name, address, and telephone number, along with the names of the organization's president, executive director, and person to be contacted in connection with the proposal; names and affiliations of officers and directors; brief history and statement of current activities and goals of the organization; description of the proposed program demonstrating the need to be met, population to be served, specific objectives, resources to be applied, description of staff and its qualifications, anticipated outcome, and method of evaluation; program budget with projected income and expenses over a specific period of time, as well as a financial statement for the organization; other sources of funding; copy of IRS letter of tax exemption; and any supplementary information which may significantly strengthen the application.

Deadlines: February 1, May 1, August 1, and November 1.

Review Process: The directors meet quarterly, usually in March, June, September, and December, with distribution committees meeting more frequently. Applicants can expect prompt notification once a decision has been reached. The foundation typically does not meet with grantseekers, and communication with individual foundation directors is discouraged; however, the staff does try to respond to telephone inquiries, and the staff will make occasional site visits and/or meet with grantseekers as necessary to complete or clarify information contained in a grant request.

Evaluative Criteria: Requests are generally viewed more favorably if they are for specific, innovative, and/or non-repetitive purposes. If the project is to continue for an indeterminate period, it is important that the organization indicate future funding plans. Additional positive factors include needs which are not likely to be fully satisfied from other sources, demonstration of cooperation with other donors or agencies, and indication of community support.

Notes: Normally, an applicant will not receive more than one grant per year.

Restrictions

The foundation does not fund grants, scholarships, or loans to individuals; organizations which do not have proof of current tax-exempt status; doctoral study or research; organizations chartered outside the U.S.; fundraising events; media presentations; annual campaigns; sports groups; national or statewide umbrella organizations; grants designed to influence legislation; or travel to conferences or events.

Additional Information

Publications: Annual Report; Guidelines; Proposal Cover Sheet

Foundation Officials

Duane E. Atkinson: president, director B 1927. ED Stanford University BSEE (1951). PRIM CORP EMPL director: Guy F. Atkinson Co. California. CORP AFFIL vice president: Guy F. Atkinson Co. NV; president, general manager: Atkinson Dynamics Co.

Ray N. Atkinson: vice president, director B Portland, OR 1929. ED Stanford University BA (1950). PRIM CORP EMPL director, vice chairman: Guy F. Atkinson Co. California.

James R. Avedisian: director

Elizabeth H. Curtis: director, admin

Thomas J. Henderson: vice president, director B 1931. ED Massachusetts Institute of Technology BS; Massachusetts Institute of Technology MS (1954). PRIM CORP EMPL chairman, president, chief executive officer: Guy F. Atkinson Co. California.

John E. Herrell: treasurer, assistant secretary

James C. Ingwersen: secretary, assistant treasurer, director

Linda L. Lanier: director

Lawrence A. Wright: director

Grants Analysis

Disclosure Period: calendar year ending 2002
Total Grants: $733,907*
Number of Grants: 110
Average Grant: $6,672
Highest Grant: $40,000
Lowest Grant: $2,000
Typical Range: $4,000 to $10,000
*Note: Grants analysis provided by foundation.

Recent Grants

Note: Grants derived from 2001 Form 990.

Library-Related

10,000	South San Francisco Public Library, South San Francisco, CA -- for Homework Assistance Program

General

30,000	San Mateo County Historical Association, San Mateo, CA -- for courthouse campaign
15,000	Samaritan House, San Mateo, CA -- for holiday assistance and Homeless Shelter Programs
12,500	Palcare, Burlingame, CA -- for building expansion capital campaign
12,500	Palcare, Burlingame, CA -- for building expansion capital campaign
10,000	Boys and Girls Club, Half Moon Bay, CA -- for program support
10,000	Catholic Charities of San Francisco, San Francisco, CA -- for San Carlos Adult Day Support Program
10,000	Coastside Adult Day Health Center, Half Moon Bay, CA -- for Alzheimer's Program
10,000	Coastside Opportunity Center, San Francisco, CA -- purchase of replacement paratransit vehicle
10,000	Families On Track Project, San Francisco, CA -- for family and educational services
10,000	International Development Exchange/ IDEX, San Francisco, CA -- for economic development

ATRAN FOUNDATION, INC.

Giving Contact

Diane Fischer, Secretary
23-25 East 21st Street, 3rd Floor
New York, NY 10010
Phone: (212)505-9677

Description

Founded: 1945
EIN: 135566548
Organization Type: General Purpose Foundation
Giving Locations: NY
Grant Types: Conference/Seminar, Emergency, Endowment, Fellowship, General Support, Loan, Multiyear/Continuing Support, Operating Expenses, Project, Research, Scholarship, Seed Money.

Donor Information

Founder: Incorporated in 1945 by the late Frank Z. Atran .

Financial Summary

Total Giving: $591,083 (fiscal year ending November 30, 2001); $540,083 (fiscal 1999); $499,883 (fiscal 1998)
Assets: $17,078,090 (fiscal 2001); $18,273,698 (fiscal 1999); $17,988,177 (fiscal 1998)
Gifts Received: $500 (fiscal 1999); $5,000 (fiscal 1996)

Typical Recipients

Arts & Humanities: Arts Associations & Councils, Arts Centers, Arts Funds, Historic Preservation, Libraries, Museums/Galleries, Performing Arts, Public Broadcasting, Theater

Civic & Public Affairs: African American Affairs, Botanical Gardens/Parks, Economic Policy, Employment/Job Training, Civic & Public Affairs-General, Law & Justice, Philanthropic Organizations, Professional & Trade Associations, Public Policy, Women's Affairs, Zoos/Aquariums

Education: Colleges & Universities, Education Funds, Education Reform, International Studies, Medical Education, Minority Education, Religious Education, Social Sciences Education

Environment: Environment-General

Health: Clinics/Medical Centers, Emergency/Ambulance Services, Geriatric Health, Hospitals, Hospitals (University Affiliated), Long-Term Care, Medical Research, Research/Studies Institutes

International: Foreign Educational Institutions, Human Rights, International Peace & Security Issues, International Relations, International Relief Efforts, Missionary/Religious Activities

Religion: Jewish Causes, Religious Organizations, Religious Welfare, Synagogues/Temples

Social Services: Child Welfare, Community Service Organizations, Homes, People with Disabilities, Senior Services, Special Olympics, United Funds/United Ways, Youth Organizations

Application Procedures

Initial Contact: Send proposals in the form of an informal letter.

Application Requirements: Proposals should include the nature of the project; its objectives including its significance and usefulness; a program or plan for achieving the objectives; estimate time to carry out the program; itemized budget showing the total cost of the project, any contributions by the applicant or others, and the amount requested from the foundation; is the project expected to continue following the achievement of its objectives and what kind of continued financial support will be required; a list of expected sources. Applicants should include whether the results of the project will be disseminated and how, and a copy of the ruling granting federal tax exemption pursuant to section 501 (c)(3).

Deadlines: September 30.

Decision Notification: Only grant recipients will be notified of decisions.

Restrictions

No grants are made to individuals. Only proposals from tax-exempt public organizations will be considered.

Additional Information

Recipients are expected to forward periodic progress reports, and upon termination of the project, to submit a final report detailing the statements of disbursements. Funds not expended are required to be returned to the foundation.
Publications: Application Guidelines

Foundation Officials

Diane Fischer: corporate secretary
Dr. George Kessler Fraenkel: treasurer B Deal, NJ 1921. ED Harvard University BA (1942); Cornell University PhD (1949). NONPR AFFIL member: Phi Kappa Phi; member: Sigma Xi; member: Phi Beta Kappa; dean emeritus: Columbia University; fellow: International Electron Spin Resonance Society; fellow: American Physics Society; member: Association Graduate Schools; fellow: American Association Advancement Science; fellow: American Chemical Society.
William Stern: vice president, director NONPR AFFIL director: Forward Association.

Grants Analysis

Disclosure Period: fiscal year ending November 30, 2001
Total Grants: $591,083
Number of Grants: 33
Average Grant: $17,912
Highest Grant: $107,408
Lowest Grant: $250
Typical Range: $5,000 to $25,000

Recent Grants

Note: Grants derived from fiscal 2001 Form 990.

Library-Related

5,000	New York Public Library, New York, NY

General

107,408	Jewish Labor Committee, New York, NY
90,000	Yivo Institute for Jewish Research, New York, NY
52,000	Columbia University in the City of New York, New York, NY
45,798	Congress for Jewish Culture, New York, NY
45,000	Albert Einstein College of Medicine of Yeshiva University, Bronx, NY
35,000	Foundation of UMDNJ, Newark, NJ
32,500	American Gathering of Jewish Holocaust Survivors, New York, NY
28,000	Brandeis University, Waltham, MA
15,000	Folksbiene Yiddish Theatre, New York, NY
15,000	United Jewish Appeal Federation, New York, NY

AUBURN FOUNDRY

Company Headquarters

1537 W. Auburn Dr.
Auburn, IN 46706

Company Description

Employees: 615
SIC(s): 3300 Primary Metal Industries.

Operating Locations

Auburn Foundry (IN--Auburn)

Auburn Foundry Foundation

Giving Contact

James Westerfield
National City Bank of Indiana
PO Box 110
Ft. Wayne, IN 46801
Phone: (219)461-7126

Description

EIN: 356019220
Organization Type: Corporate Foundation
Giving Locations: headquarters area only.
Grant Types: General Support, Scholarship.

Donor Information

Founder: Auburn Foundry

Financial Summary

Total Giving: $65,000 (fiscal year ending February 28, 2000); $211,532 (fiscal 1999); $223,834 (fiscal 1997)
Giving Analysis: Giving for fiscal 2000 includes: foundation grants to United Way ($9,000); foundation scholarships ($19,000); fiscal 1999: foundation grants to United Way ($8,500); foundation scholarships ($12,000); foundation ($191,032); fiscal 1997: foundation grants to United Way ($8,500); foundation scholarships ($12,000) foundation ($203,334)
Assets: $1,346,850 (fiscal 2000); $1,412,842 (fiscal 1999); $1,431,079 (fiscal 1997)
Gifts Received: $250,000 (fiscal 1997); $50,000 (fiscal 1995); $550,000 (fiscal 1994). Note: In 1997, contributions were received from Auburn Foundry.

Typical Recipients

Arts & Humanities: Arts Associations & Councils, Arts & Humanities-General, Libraries, Music
Civic & Public Affairs: Economic Development, Housing
Education: Business Education, Colleges & Universities, Education Funds, Literacy, Private Education (Precollege), Public Education (Precollege), Science/Mathematics Education
Health: Prenatal Health Issues
Religion: Religious Welfare
Social Services: Food/Clothing Distribution, People with Disabilities, Scouts, Social Services-General, United Funds/United Ways, YMCA/YWCA/YMHA/YWHA

Application Procedures

Initial Contact: The foundation requests applications be made in writing.
Application Requirements: Include purpose of funds sought and proof of tax-exempt status.
Deadlines: None.

Restrictions

Scholarships are limited to Dekalb High School graduates enrolled in a four year accredited school.

Additional Information

Publications: Scholarship application form.
Trust(s): Fort Wayne Natl Bank

Corporate Officials

David Fink: president financial PRIM CORP EMPL president: Auburn Foundry.
William E. Fink: chairman PRIM CORP EMPL chairman: Auburn Foundry.
John Neiger: vice president financial PRIM CORP EMPL vice president financial: Auburn Foundry.

Foundation Officials

Walt Bienz: trustee
William E. Fink: trustee (see above)

Grants Analysis

Disclosure Period: fiscal year ending February 28, 2000
Total Grants: $37,000*
Number of Grants: 13
Average Grant: $1,500*
Highest Grant: $19,000
Lowest Grant: $500
Typical Range: $500 to $5,000
*Note: Giving excludes scholarships; United Way. Average grant figure excludes highest grant.

Recent Grants

Note: Grants derived from fiscal 1999 Form 990.

General

83,332	YMCA DeKalb County, Auburn, IN
55,000	Youth for Christ, Auburn, IN
18,000	Independent Colleges of Indiana, Indianapolis, IN
10,000	Hillsdale College, Hillsdale, MI
8,500	United Way DeKalb County, Auburn, IN
5,000	Science Central, Ft. Wayne, IN
4,000	Tri-State University, Angola, IN
3,000	DeKalb County Habitat for Humanity, Auburn, IN
3,000	Hanover College, Hanover, IN -- scholarship
3,000	Notre Dame University, Notre Dame, IN -- scholarship

AUDUBON STATE BANK

Company Headquarters

315 Broadway St.
Audubon, IA 50025

Audubon State Bank Charitable Foundation

Giving Contact

Gene Karstens, President, Director
315 Broadway, Box 149
Audubon, IA 50025
Phone: (712)563-2644
Fax: (712)563-3654

Description

EIN: 421366431
Organization Type: Corporate Foundation
Giving Locations: IA
Grant Types: General Support.

Financial Summary

Total Giving: $29,455 (2000); $35,007 (1999); $19,370 (1998)
Giving Analysis: Giving for 1999 includes: foundation ($35,007)
Assets: $33,054 (2000); $44,402 (1999); $103,325 (1998)
Gifts Received: $22,000 (2000); $22,000 (1999); $66,150 (1997). Note: In 1996 and 2000, contributions were received from Audubon State Bank.

Typical Recipients

Arts & Humanities: Arts Centers, History & Archaeology, Libraries, Museums/Galleries, Music, Performing Arts, Public Broadcasting
Civic & Public Affairs: Botanical Gardens/Parks, Business/Free Enterprise, Civil Rights, Clubs, Economic Development, Civic & Public Affairs-General, Legal Aid, Municipalities/Towns, Parades/Festivals, Rural Affairs, Safety, Urban & Community Affairs, Women's Affairs
Education: Agricultural Education, Colleges & Universities, Education Funds, Education-General, International Exchange, Public Education (Precollege), Secondary Education (Private), Secondary Education (Public), Student Aid
Environment: Environment-General
Health: Cancer, Diabetes, Emergency/Ambulance Services, Heart, Hospitals, Single-Disease Health Associations, Transplant Networks/Donor Banks
Religion: Churches, Religious Organizations, Religious Welfare
Science: Scientific Centers & Institutes

Social Services: Community Service Organizations, Crime Prevention, Emergency Relief, Family Planning, Family Services, Homes, People with Disabilities, Recreation & Athletics, Scouts, Senior Services, Special Olympics, Substance Abuse, Veterans

Application Procedures

Initial Contact: Send a brief letter of inquiry with an explanation of the purpose of funds sought.
Deadlines: None.

Corporate Officials

Louis Venteicher: chairman, president, chief executive officer PRIM CORP EMPL chairman, president, chief executive officer: Audubon State Bank.

Foundation Officials

M. P. Barron: director
F. J. Boyd: president, director
John Chrystal: director PRIM CORP EMPL chairman: Iowa Savings Bank.
Mary Garst: director
Stephen Garst: director
Richard Harms: secretary, treasurer, director
William C. Hess: vice president, director PRIM CORP EMPL chief executive officer: Iowa Savings Bank.
John C. Parrott, Jr.: director

Grants Analysis

Disclosure Period: calendar year ending 2000
Total Grants: $29,455
Number of Grants: 35
Average Grant: $609*
Highest Grant: $8,750
Lowest Grant: $25
Typical Range: $100 to $2,000
*Note: Average grant excludes highest grant.

Recent Grants

Note: Grants derived from 2001 Form 990.

Library-Related
1,375	Audubon Public Library, Audubon, IA

General
2,231	United Methodist Church, Audubon, IA
2,000	Audubon County Hospital Foundation, Audubon, IA
1,035	Friends of Iowa Public Television, Johnston, IA
1,000	Audubon Community School, Audubon, IA
1,000	Audubon Sports Boosters, Audubon, IA
1,000	Friendship Home, Audubon, IA
1,000	WOI, Ames, IA
970	Our Saviour's Lutheran Church, Audubon, IA
850	Hamlin Lutheran Church, Hamlin, IA
600	Cystic Fibrosis Foundation, Urbandale, IA

CHARLES J. AND BURTON S. AUGUST FAMILY FOUNDATION

Giving Contact

Burton August, Sr., Trustee
Charles J. and Burton S. August Family Foundation
200 Holleder Parkway
Rochester, NY 14615
Phone: (716)647-6400
Note: Ext. 315

Description

Founded: 1989
EIN: 161355601
Organization Type: Private Foundation
Giving Locations: Monroe County.

Grant Types: Capital, Emergency, Project, Scholarship.

Donor Information

Founder: Charles J. August, Burton S. August

Financial Summary

Total Giving: $157,296 (fiscal year ending June 30, 1999); $162,000 (fiscal 1998 approx); $139,335 (fiscal 1997)
Giving Analysis: Giving for fiscal 1999 includes: foundation grants to United Way ($8,000) foundation grants to United Way ($8,000)
Assets: $2,853,544 (fiscal 1999); $2,723,587 (fiscal 1997); $2,526,800 (fiscal 1996)
Gifts Received: $6,170 (fiscal 1997); $81,187 (fiscal 1995); $331,271 (fiscal 1994). Note: In fiscal 1995, contributions were received from Charles J. August ($79,175) and Burton S. August ($2,012).

Typical Recipients

Arts & Humanities: Libraries, Museums/Galleries, Public Broadcasting, Theater
Civic & Public Affairs: Community Foundations, Employment/Job Training, Civic & Public Affairs-General, Housing, Public Policy, Urban & Community Affairs, Zoos/Aquariums
Education: Afterschool/Enrichment Programs, Colleges & Universities, Continuing Education, Engineering/Technological Education, Legal Education, Medical Education, Private Education (Precollege), Special Education
Health: Adolescent Health Issues, Alzheimers Disease, Clinics/Medical Centers, Diabetes, Emergency/Ambulance Services, Health-General, Heart, Medical Rehabilitation, Mental Health, Nursing Services
Religion: Religion-General, Jewish Causes, Religious Welfare, Synagogues/Temples
Science: Science Museums
Social Services: Camps, Child Welfare, Community Centers, Community Service Organizations, Crime Prevention, Domestic Violence, Emergency Relief, Family Planning, Family Services, People with Disabilities, Recreation & Athletics, Scouts, Senior Services, Shelters/Homelessness, United Funds/United Ways, YMCA/YWCA/YMHA/YWHA

Application Procedures

Initial Contact: Send a full proposal.
Application Requirements: Include a description of organization, amount requested, purpose of funds sought, recently audited financial statement, and proof of tax-exempt status.
Deadlines: None. The board meets semi-annually.

Restrictions

Grants are not made to individuals. or for ongoing support.

Foundation Officials

Andrew August: trustee B 1966. PRIM CORP EMPL president: Alternative Sports Inc.
Burton S. August, Sr.: trustee
Charles J. August: trustee
Jan Lise August: trustee
Jean B. August: trustee
John W. August: trustee
Robert W. August: trustee
Cortland L. Brovitz: trustee
Susan Eastwood: trustee
Andrew M. Greenstein: trustee
August Mafreci: trustee
David Mitchell: trustee

Grants Analysis

Disclosure Period: fiscal year ending June 30, 1999
Total Grants: $149,296*
Number of Grants: 47
Average Grant: $2,267*
Highest Grant: $45,000
Typical Range: $200 to $5,000

*Note: Giving excludes United Way. Average grant excludes highest grant.

Recent Grants

Note: Grants derived from fiscal 2000 Form 990.

General
48,000	Park Ridge Foundation, Rochester, NY
16,000	Boy Scouts of America, Rochester, NY
12,500	Boy Scouts of America, Rochester, NY
11,000	Al Sigle Center Partner Agencies
6,000	United Way of Greater Rochester, Rochester, NY
5,000	United Neighborhood Centers, Rochester, NY
5000	Unity Health System, Chesterfield, MO
4,000	Al Sigl Center, Rochester, NY
3,500	Brockport College Foundation
3,000	Norman Howard School Foundation, Rochester, NY

AUTRY FOUNDATION

Giving Contact

Jacqueline Autry, President
4383 Colfax Avenue
Studio City, CA 91604
Phone: (818)752-7770
Fax: (818)752-7779

Description

Founded: 1974
EIN: 237433359
Organization Type: General Purpose Foundation
Giving Locations: CA: including southern California
Grant Types: General Support.

Donor Information

Founder: Established in 1974 by former actor and radio entertainer Gene Autry , who starred in more than 80 western movies and wrote more than 200 songs.

Financial Summary

Total Giving: $1,000,000 (2003 approx); $1,000,000 (2002 approx); $1,080,494 (2000)
Giving Analysis: Giving for 1998 includes: foundation grants to United Way ($1,000,000) 1997: foundation grants to United Way ($1,000,000)
Assets: $18,000,000 (2003 approx); $18,000,000 (2002 approx); $18,687,687 (2000)

Typical Recipients

Arts & Humanities: Arts Associations & Councils, Arts Centers, Arts Funds, Arts Institutes, Ethnic & Folk Arts, Film & Video, Arts & Humanities-General, Historic Preservation, History & Archaeology, Libraries, Museums/Galleries, Music, Opera, Public Broadcasting, Theater
Civic & Public Affairs: African American Affairs, Botanical Gardens/Parks, Business/Free Enterprise, Clubs, Employment/Job Training, Civic & Public Affairs-General, Hispanic Affairs, Professional & Trade Associations, Public Policy, Urban & Community Affairs, Women's Affairs, Zoos/Aquariums
Education: Arts/Humanities Education, Business Education, Colleges & Universities, Education Reform, School Volunteerism, Student Aid
Environment: Energy, Forestry, Environment-General
Health: Alzheimers Disease, Cancer, Children's Health/Hospitals, Clinics/Medical Centers, Diabetes, Eyes/Blindness, Health-General, Health Organizations, Heart, Hospices, Hospitals, Medical Research, Prenatal Health Issues, Public Health, Research/Studies Institutes, Respiratory, Single-Disease Health Associations, Speech & Hearing
International: Human Rights, International Affairs, International Organizations, International Relations, International Relief Efforts

Religion: Jewish Causes, Religious Organizations, Religious Welfare, Social/Policy Issues
Science: Science Museums
Social Services: At-Risk Youth, Child Abuse, Child Welfare, Community Service Organizations, Community Service Organizations, Counseling, Crime Prevention, Delinquency & Criminal Rehabilitation, Domestic Violence, Family Services, Food/Clothing Distribution, People with Disabilities, Recreation & Athletics, Scouts, Shelters/Homelessness, Substance Abuse, United Funds/United Ways, Volunteer Services, YMCA/YWCA/YMHA/YWHA, Youth Organizations

Application Procedures

Initial Contact: Prospective applicants should send a brief letter of inquiry on organization letterhead.
Application Requirements: Applicants should include IRS 501 (c)(3) confirmation.
Deadlines: None.

Foundation Officials

Jacqueline Autry: vice president, director NONPR AFFIL president: Gene Autry Museum of Western Heritage.
Karla Buhlman: vice president music and film
Maxine Hansen: director
Stanley Schneider: treasurer, director NONPR AFFIL vice president, treasurer: Gene Autry Museum of Western Heritage.

Grants Analysis

Disclosure Period: calendar year ending 2000
Total Grants: $1,080,494
Number of Grants: 36
Average Grant: $10,510*
Highest Grant: $712,654
Lowest Grant: $250
Typical Range: $2,500 to $25,000
*Note: Average grant figure excludes highest grant.

Recent Grants

Note: Grants derived from 2000 Form 990.

General
712,654	Autry Museum of Western Heritage, Los Angeles, CA
100,000	P.A.T.H., Los Angeles, CA
100,000	University of Southern California, Los Angeles, CA
25,000	Farm Aid, Champaign, IL
25,000	Project Grad Los Angeles, Inc., Los Angeles, CA
25,000	Ueberroth Family Foundation, Laguna Beach, CA
11,000	Doheny Eye Institute, Los Angeles, CA
10,000	June Ebensteiner Hospice Foundation, Los Angeles, CA
10,000	KCET, Los Angeles, CA
10,000	Los Angeles 2012 Bid Committee, Los Angeles, CA

MILTON AND SALLY AVERY ARTS FOUNDATION

Giving Contact

Sally M. Avery
Milton and Sally Avery Arts Foundation
300 Central Park W.
New York, NY 10024
Phone: (212)595-7338
Fax: (212)595-2840

Description

EIN: 133093638
Organization Type: Private Foundation
Giving Locations: NY: New England states.
Grant Types: General Support.

Donor Information

Founder: Sally M. Avery

Financial Summary

Total Giving: $301,550 (2000); $329,010 (1999); $226,500 (1997)
Assets: $5,404,372 (2000); $5,800,000 (1999); $4,248,888 (1995)
Gifts Received: $636,005 (2000). Note: In 2000, contributions were received from Sally Avery.

Typical Recipients

Arts & Humanities: Arts Associations & Councils, Arts Centers, Arts Festivals, Arts Funds, Arts Institutes, Community Arts, Dance, Arts & Humanities-General, Historic Preservation, Libraries, Literary Arts, Museums/Galleries, Music, Opera, Public Broadcasting, Theater, Visual Arts
Civic & Public Affairs: Women's Affairs
Education: Arts/Humanities Education, Colleges & Universities, Education Reform, Engineering/Technological Education, Private Education (Precollege), Special Education
Environment: Environment-General
International: Foreign Educational Institutions
Religion: Seminaries
Social Services: At-Risk Youth, Community Service Organizations, People with Disabilities

Application Procedures

Initial Contact: Send a brief letter of inquiry and a full proposal.
Application Requirements: Include a description of organization of organization, amount requested, recently audited financial statement, proof of tax-exempt status, and purpose of funds sought.
Deadlines: None.

Restrictions

Awards are restricted to art education and the further development of artists.

Foundation Officials

March A. Cavanaugh: president
Philip Cavanaugh: officer
Sean Avery Cavanaugh: vice president
Harvey Shipley Miller: officer

Grants Analysis

Disclosure Period: calendar year ending 2000
Total Grants: $301,550
Number of Grants: 94
Average Grant: $3,208
Highest Grant: $25,000
Typical Range: $1,000 to $20,000

Recent Grants

Note: Grants derived from 2000 Form 990.

General
25,000	Pitzer College, Claremont, CA
20,000	Moore College of Art, Philadelphia, PA
20,000	New York Studio School, New York, NY
17,000	Purchase College, Purchase, NY
10,000	Bard College, Annandale-on-Hudson, NY
10,000	Bard College, Annandale-on-Hudson, NY
10,000	Bard College, Annandale-on-Hudson, NY
6,000	Greenwich Village Society for Historic Preservation, New York, NY
5,000	Art OMI, New York, NY
5,000	Brooklyn Bureau of Community Service, Brooklyn, NY

AVISTA CORP.

Company Headquarters

Spokane, WA
Web: http://www.avistacorp.com

Company Description

Founded: 1889
Ticker: AVA
Exchange: NYSE
Former Name: Washington Water Power Co. (WWP).
Assets: US$4.037 billion (2001)
Employees: 2175 (2001)
SIC(s): 4931 Electric & Other Services Combined.

Operating Locations

Washington Water Power Co. (ID--Bonners Ferry, Coeur D Alene, Kellogg, Lewiston, Orofino, Post Falls, Sandpoint; OR--Ashland, Klamath Falls, LaGrande, Medford, Roseburg; WA--Colfax, Colville, Othello, Pullman)

Nonmonetary Support

Type: Donated Equipment; In-kind Services; Loaned Employees

Giving Contact

Debbie Simock, Community Relations Coordinator
PO Box 3727
Spokane, WA 99220
Phone: (509)495-8031
Fax: (509)495-4000
E-mail: debbie.simock@avistacorp.com
Web: http://www.avistafoundation.org

Description

Organization Type: Corporate Giving Program
Giving Locations: ID: Northern Idaho service area; WA: Eastern Washington service area, northern Idaho, as well as Sanders County, Montana and South Lake Tahoe, California
Grant Types: General Support, Matching, Multiyear/Continuing Support, Project.

Financial Summary

Total Giving: $745,000 (2003 approx); $735,000 (2002); $550,000 (2001). Note: Contributes through corporate direct giving program only.
Giving Analysis: Giving for 1998 includes: corporate direct giving ($511,146)
Assets: $2,500,000 (2003 approx); $2,000,000 (2002)

Typical Recipients

Arts & Humanities: Arts & Humanities-General, Libraries, Museums/Galleries, Performing Arts, Public Broadcasting, Theater
Civic & Public Affairs: Civic & Public Affairs-General, Safety, Women's Affairs
Education: Colleges & Universities, Community & Junior Colleges, Economic Education, Elementary Education (Private), Engineering/Technological Education, Faculty Development, Minority Education, Public Education (Precollege)
Environment: Environment-General
Social Services: Community Service Organizations, Senior Services, United Funds/United Ways, Youth Organizations

Application Procedures

Initial Contact: Requests must be submitted in writing.
Application Requirements: Include a brief summary of the organization including date of establishment, history, mission statement, and objectives; copy of IRS letter designating the organization's 501(c)(3) status; current financial statement; list of board of

directors and key staff; a brief overview of the program/project for which funding is requested including purpose, targeted population, evaluation strategies, anticipated results, budget, other organizations providing support, and timeline; and current or past corporate involvement, if any, in the organization or program, including employee volunteers, board members, etc.

Deadlines: None.

Review Process: Proposals reviewed by corporate contributions committee.

Evaluative Criteria: Organizations must be tax-exempt and must provide documentation confirming 501(c)(3) status; be located within areas where company operates; show evidence of sound fiscal policies and responsible financial management; have a competent, knowledgeable, and broad-based board of directors with policy-making authority that represents the organization and its members; show a method to evaluate the results of the proposed project; describe collaborative efforts, if applicable, with similar programs/providers and show the project does not represent an unnecessary duplication of effort; and be relevant to company's business interests.

Decision Notification: Requests in excess of $5,000 are reviewed quarterly in February, May, August, and November; requests under $5,000 are usually processed within 30 days.

Notes: Applicants outside Spokane are encouraged to submit requests to regional offices. Contact headquarters for further information. Special attention is given to organizations and programs that serve a large number of people, have long-term benefits, include the company's employees, have broad community support, and are consistent with Avista Corp.'s business interests.

Restrictions

Generally does not contribute to individuals, team or extra-curricular school events, tournament fund raisers, trips or tours, churches or other religious organizations, organizations that discriminate for any reason, endowments or foundations, or hospital or patient care institution operating funds.

Restricts giving to eastern Washington and northern Idaho.

Additional Information

Priority is given to requests that demonstrate partnerships and cooperative efforts between organizations and agencies and which directly benefit people within areas where company conducts business.

Publications: Contributions Guidelines

Corporate Officials

Gary G. Ely: chairman, president, chief executive officer B October 08, 1947. ED Brigham Young University BS (1983). PRIM CORP EMPL chairman, president, chief executive officer: Avista Corp.

Malyn K. Malquist: senior vice president, chief financial officer B Artesia, CA 1952. ED Brigham Young University (1976); Brigham Young University (1978). PRIM CORP EMPL senior vice president, chief financial officer: Avista Corp. CORP AFFIL director: Headwaters Inc.

Giving Program Officials

Debbie Simock: manager community relations

Grants Analysis

Disclosure Period: calendar year ending 2002
Total Grants: $735,000
Number of Grants: 450
Average Grant: $1,000
Highest Grant: $15,000
Lowest Grant: $100
Typical Range: $500 to $1,000

AVON PRODUCTS, INC.

Company Headquarters

New York, NY
Web: http://www.avon.com

Company Description

Founded: 1886
Ticker: AVP
Exchange: NYSE
Revenue: US$6.228 billion (2002)
Profit: US$534.6 million (2002)
Employees: 43800 (2002)
Fortune Rank: 280, per FORTUNE Magazine's list of 500 Largest U.S. Corporations (2002).
SIC(s): 2844 Toilet Preparations, 3961 Costume Jewelry, 5122 Drugs, Proprietaries & Sundries.

Operating Locations

Avon Products, Inc. (CA--Pasadena, Santa Monica; DE--Newark; IL--Glenview, Morton Grove; NY--New York, Rye; OH--Springdale)

Nonmonetary Support

Type: Donated Equipment; Donated Products; In-kind Services
Note: Products are distributed through a partnership with Gifts In Kind.

Avon Products Foundation, Inc.

Giving Contact

Mary P. Quinn, Assistant Secretary & Director
Avon Products Foundation, Inc.
1345 Avenue of the Americas
New York, NY 10105-0196
Phone: (212)282-5517
Fax: (212)282-6049
Web: http://www.avoncompany.com/women/

Description

Founded: 1955
EIN: 136128447
Organization Type: Corporate Foundation
Giving Locations: headquarters and operating communities.
Grant Types: Capital, Challenge, Employee Matching Gifts, Matching, Multiyear/Continuing Support, Scholarship.
Note: The foundation matches Avon associate donations to charitable arts, health, educational, and community and social service organizations through its Matching Gifts Program. Employee matching gift ratio: 1:1 up to $5,000 annually per associate.

Donor Information

Founder: Avon Products

Financial Summary

Total Giving: $39,602,732 (2001); $31,629,489 (2000); $3,332,413 (1999). Note: Contributes through foundation only.
Giving Analysis: Giving for 2001 includes: foundation matching gifts ($238,100); foundation scholarships ($466,335); foundation ($38,898,297); 2000: foundation grants to United Way ($129,250); foundation matching gifts ($181,889); foundation scholarships ($312,600); foundation ($31,005,750); 1999: foundation grants to United Way ($52,500); foundation scholarships ($139,000); foundation matching gifts ($152,199); foundation ($2,988,714);
Assets: $59,103,671 (2001); $38,437,478 (2000); $18,803,317 (1999)
Gifts Received: $101,146,340 (2001); $50,667,895 (2000); $22,145,924 (1999). Note: In 1999, contributions were received from Avon Breast Cancer 3-Day ($16,431,436) and Avon Products, Inc. ($5,714,488).

Typical Recipients

Arts & Humanities: Arts Associations & Councils, Arts Centers, Arts Festivals, Arts Funds, Arts Institutes, Arts Outreach, Community Arts, Dance, Ethnic & Folk Arts, Libraries, Museums/Galleries, Music, Opera, Performing Arts, Public Broadcasting, Theater

Civic & Public Affairs: African American Affairs, Asian American Affairs, Business/Free Enterprise, Chambers of Commerce, Civil Rights, Clubs, Economic Development, Economic Policy, Employment/Job Training, Civic & Public Affairs-General, Hispanic Affairs, Law & Justice, Legal Aid, Native American Affairs, Nonprofit Management, Philanthropic Organizations, Professional & Trade Associations, Public Policy, Public Policy, Rural Affairs, Safety, Urban & Community Affairs, Women's Affairs, Zoos/Aquariums

Education: Afterschool/Enrichment Programs, Arts/Humanities Education, Business Education, Colleges & Universities, Community & Junior Colleges, Economic Education, Education Associations, Education Funds, Environmental Education, Education-General, International Exchange, Leadership Training, Literacy, Medical Education, Minority Education, Science/Mathematics Education, Special Education, Student Aid

Environment: Environment-General, Wildlife Protection

Health: Cancer, Children's Health/Hospitals, Clinics/Medical Centers, Emergency/Ambulance Services, Health-General, Health Funds, Health Organizations, Hospices, Hospitals, Medical Rehabilitation, Medical Research, Mental Health, Outpatient Health Care, Prenatal Health Issues, Single-Disease Health Associations

International: Foreign Educational Institutions, Health Care/Hospitals, International Development, International Organizations, International Relief Efforts

Religion: Religious Welfare

Science: Science Museums, Scientific Centers & Institutes

Social Services: Animal Protection, At-Risk Youth, Big Brother/Big Sister, Child Abuse, Child Welfare, Community Centers, Community Service Organizations, Delinquency & Criminal Rehabilitation, Domestic Violence, Family Services, Food/Clothing Distribution, People with Disabilities, Recreation & Athletics, Refugee Assistance, Scouts, Senior Services, Shelters/Homelessness, Social Services-General, Special Olympics, Substance Abuse, United Funds/United Ways, Volunteer Services, YMCA/YWCA/YMHA/YWHA, Youth Organizations

Application Procedures

Initial Contact: Applicants for Economic Opportunity for Women and Girls funding are encouraged to submit a one-page preliminary application letter. Applicants for scholarships should contact foundation for an application packet. Non-profit, community-based breast health programs wishing to request funding from the Avon Breast Care Fund should contact The Avon Breast Care Fund, 505 Eighth Ave. Suite 2001, New York, NY 10018-6505; telephone: (212) 244-5368; fax: (212) 695-3081; web site: www.avonbreastcare.org.

Application Requirements: Preliminary application letters should include the name, address, telephone number and IRS tax-exempt classification of the organization; a description of organization, including objectives and programs; amount requested, and its proposed use.

Deadlines: None.

Review Process: Preliminary requests for funding are reviewed as they are received.

Evaluative Criteria: Requests asking the foundation to fund a portion of the project will generally receive greater priority than one asking the foundation to be the sole monetary source.

Decision Notification: Responses to preliminary requests generally occurs within 60 days. The foundation will notify the applicant if a formal proposal is needed.

Notes: Preliminary inquiries by telephone or letter are accepted if the applicant has questions regarding funding priorities.

Restrictions

The Foundation does not support individuals; political or lobbying groups; religious, fraternal, or veteran organizations; fundraising events; memberships; journal advertisements; or organizations that discriminate in any way inconsistent with national equal opportunity policies.

Additional Information

Avon sponsors worldwide programs that focus on women's concerns, primarily through cause-related marketing programs. Since 1992, Avon and its sales representatives in the U.S., U.K., Canada, Mexico, Venezuela, the Philippines, and other countries have spearheaded a grass-roots breast cancer awareness campaign to educate women about the importance of early detection and to improve access to mammography exams and breast cancer education. Money raised through the sale of products supports community-based programs worldwide. The company has established a Worldwide Fund for Women's Health, which addresses breast cancer efforts, as well as such other health-related issues as AIDS in Thailand and elder care in Japan, and emotional and financial support for mothers in need in Germany. The company also has awards programs that recognize women's achievements in many fields in Avon countries around the world. The foundation, which has traditionally limited support to U.S. organizations, is expanding its support of women worldwide. Working in partnership with Avon Russia, the foundation agreed to underwrite a series of events in Russia on behalf of Magee Womancare International. Affiliated with the Magee-Women's Hospital of Pittsburgh, PA, this organization seeks to improve the quality of healthcare for women around the world. The first event was a wellness festival held in Moscow in March 1997.

Avon also supports research into alternatives to the use of animal testing in new product development. To strengthen its Global Supplier Code of Conduct, Avon in 1997 implemented a certification and monitoring program to ensure that all suppliers meet and conform to the code. According to the 1996 annual report, "Together with other major corporations and with the guidance of the Council on Economic Priorities, Avon is working to create cooperative certification and monitoring programs that will aid in endorsing those suppliers who meet the agreed-upon criteria." The Avon Women of Enterprise Awards program is a partnership between Avon Products, Inc. and the U.S. Small Business administration. The program recognizes and honors women entrepreneurs who have overcome personal and professional challenges or have exhibited exceptional entrepreneurial skills.

Publications: Information and Guidelines Brochure

Corporate Officials

Andrea Jung: president, chief executive officer ED Princeton University BA (1979). PRIM CORP EMPL president, chief executive officer: Avon Products Inc.

Foundation Officials

Judith Barker: president B Burlington, NC 1941. ED Franklin University; Ohio State University.
Gail Ann Blanke: vice president B Cleveland, OH 1941. ED Sweet Briar College AB. PRIM CORP EMPL senior vice president: Avon Products Inc. NONPR AFFIL member: Society Mayflower Descendants; member: Women's Forum New York; member: National Advertisers; member: American Women in Radio & Television; member: International Association

of Business Communications. CLUB AFFIL Metropolitan Club; Rockaway Hunt Club; Doubles Club; Lawrence Beach Club.
Maria Montoya: director
Mary Quinn: program officer

Grants Analysis

Disclosure Period: calendar year ending 2000
Total Grants: $31,005,750*
Number of Grants: 154
Average Grant: $103,327*
Highest Grant: $10,000,000
Lowest Grant: $1,000
Typical Range: $1,000 to $20,000 and $2,000,000 to $10,000,000
*Note: Giving excludes matching gifts; scholarships; United Way. Average grant figure excludes two highest grants ($15,300,000).

Recent Grants

Note: Grants derived from 2001 Form 990.

General

16,956,340	National Cancer Institute, Bethesda, MD
11,805,701	USCF Comprehensive Cancer Center and San Francisco General Hospital, San Francisco, CA
11,609,910	Massachusetts General Hospital, Boston, MA
11,340,360	Robert H. Lurie Cancer Center of Northwestern University, Chicago, IL
6,111,447	Cicatelli Associates, Inc.
3,120,000	Cancer Care, Inc., New York, NY
2,985,000	Families Referred by Associates
2,500,000	Fred Hutchinson Cancer Research Center, Los Angeles, CA
2,500,000	University of Colorado Comprehensive Cancer Center, Denver, CO
2,200,000	Johns Hopkins University School of Medicine, Baltimore, MD

AYLWARD FAMILY FOUNDATION

Giving Contact

E. W. Aylward, President
PO Box 409
Neenah, WI 54957-0409
Phone: (920)722-0901

Description

Founded: 1953
EIN: 396042143
Organization Type: Private Foundation
Former Name: Neenah Foundry Foundation (1998).
Giving Locations: FL: Palm Beach, West Palm Beach; WI
Grant Types: Capital, General Support, Multiyear/Continuing Support, Operating Expenses.

Donor Information

Founder: Neenah Foundry Co.

Financial Summary

Total Giving: $349,500 (2001); $655,600 (2000); $372,200 (1999)
Giving Analysis: Giving for 2001 includes: foundation grants to United Way ($25,000); 2000: foundation grants to United Way ($25,000); 1999: foundation grants to United Way ($25,000)
Assets: $4,147,412 (2001); $4,408,354 (2000); $4,792,402 (1999)
Gifts Received: $250,000 (1996). Note: In 1996, contributions were received from the Neenah Foundry Co.

Typical Recipients

Arts & Humanities: Arts Associations & Councils, Arts Centers, Ballet, Arts & Humanities-General, History & Archaeology, Libraries, Museums/Galleries, Public Broadcasting, Visual Arts
Civic & Public Affairs: Business/Free Enterprise, Clubs, Economic Development, Civic & Public Affairs-General, Philanthropic Organizations, Safety, Urban & Community Affairs
Education: Business Education, Colleges & Universities, Education Funds, Engineering/Technological Education, Education-General, Private Education (Precollege), Secondary Education (Private), Student Aid, Vocational & Technical Education
Health: Cancer, Children's Health/Hospitals, Health-General, Nursing Services, Single-Disease Health Associations
International: International Environmental Issues
Religion: Churches, Religion-General, Religious Welfare, Religious Welfare
Social Services: Community Service Organizations, Domestic Violence, People with Disabilities, Social Services-General, Substance Abuse, United Funds/United Ways, YMCA/YWCA/YMHA/YWHA, Youth Organizations

Application Procedures

Initial Contact: Send a letter of request detailing need.
Deadlines: October 31.
Notes: Most of the foundation's grants are made to preselected organizations.

Restrictions

Does not make grants to individuals.

Foundation Officials

A. A. Aylward: vice president PRIM CORP EMPL director: Neenah Transport Inc.
E. W. Aylward: president
R.J. Aylward: director

Grants Analysis

Disclosure Period: calendar year ending 2001
Total Grants: $324,500*
Number of Grants: 20
Average Grant: $11,026*
Highest Grant: $115,000
Lowest Grant: $1,000
Typical Range: $2,000 to $15,000
*Note: Giving excludes United Way. Average grant figure excludes highest grant.

Recent Grants

Note: Grants derived from 2001 Form 990.

Library-Related
25,000	Neenah Public Library, Neenah, WI

General
450,000	Rawhide Boys Ranch, New London, WI
25,000	United Way Fox Cities, Menasha, WI
20,000	Goodwill Industries, WI
20,000	United Community Services, Neenah, WI
15,000	Lawrence University, Appleton, WI
15,000	Rawhide Boys Ranch, New London, WI
15,000	Ripon College, Ripon, WI
10,000	ALS Association, Woodland Hills, CA
10,000	Norton Museum of Art, West Palm Beach, FL
10,000	Wayland Academy, Beaver Dam, WI

AYRES FOUNDATION

Giving Contact

John E. D. Peacock, President & Director
5610 West 82nd Street
Indianapolis, IN 46278
Phone: (317)872-5400

Description

Founded: 1944
EIN: 356018437
Organization Type: Private Foundation
Giving Locations: IN: Indianapolis
Grant Types: Capital, General Support, Operating Expenses, Project.

Donor Information

Founder: L.S. Ayres & Co., the late Theodore B. Griffith, Mrs. Theodore B. Griffith

Financial Summary

Total Giving: $232,510 (2000); $146,910 (1999); $175,000 (1998)
Giving Analysis: Giving for 2000 includes: foundation grants to United Way ($2,500) 1999: foundation grants to United Way ($2,250)
Assets: $3,921,134 (2000); $4,116,137 (1999); $2,923,196 (1996)

Typical Recipients

Arts & Humanities: Art History, Arts Institutes, Historic Preservation, History & Archaeology, Libraries, Museums/Galleries, Music, Theater
Civic & Public Affairs: Botanical Gardens/Parks, Community Foundations, Employment/Job Training, Civic & Public Affairs-General, Municipalities/Towns, Zoos/Aquariums
Education: Colleges & Universities, Education Associations, Education Funds, Engineering/Technological Education, Education-General, Medical Education, Private Education (Precollege), Public Education (Precollege)
Environment: Resource Conservation
Health: Cancer, Health Organizations, Home-Care Services, Hospitals, Long-Term Care, Nursing Services, Public Health, Single-Disease Health Associations
International: Foreign Arts Organizations
Religion: Churches, Religious Welfare
Social Services: Animal Protection, Big Brother/Big Sister, Child Welfare, Community Service Organizations, Day Care, Family Planning, Family Services, Food/Clothing Distribution, Homes, People with Disabilities, Scouts, Senior Services, Shelters/Homelessness, Social Services-General, Special Olympics, Substance Abuse, United Funds/United Ways, Volunteer Services, YMCA/YWCA/YMHA/YWHA, Youth Organizations

Application Procedures

Initial Contact: Send brief proposal including name, address, telephone number, financial data, and information on current sources of funding.
Application Requirements: Include a description of organization, amount requested, purpose of funds sought, recently audited financial statement, and proof of tax-exempt status.
Deadlines: None.

Restrictions

Does not support individuals, religious organizations for sectarian purposes, political or lobbying groups, or organizations outside operating areas.

Foundation Officials

David S. Evans: director
Alvin C. Fernandes, Jr.: secretary, director
John E. D. Peacock: president, director
John E. D. Peacock, Jr.: vice president, treasurer, director
William J. Stout: assistant secretary, treasurer B Bloomington, IN December 14, 1914. ED Indiana University AB (1937). CORP AFFIL president, director: Citizens Gas & Coke Utility. NONPR AFFIL director: Saint Richards Day School; director: Saint Vincent Hospital; member: Indianapolis Personnel Association; member: National Retail Merchants Association;

member: Indianapolis Chamber of Commerce; member: Indianapolis Merchants Association; president, director: Flanner House.
Bert M. Wilboith: director

Grants Analysis

Disclosure Period: calendar year ending 2000
Total Grants: $230,010*
Number of Grants: 49
Average Grant: $3,294*
Highest Grant: $42,000
Lowest Grant: $200
Typical Range: $500 to $10,000
*Note: Giving excludes United Way. Average grant figure excludes two highest grants ($75,200).

Recent Grants

Note: Grants derived from 1999 Form 990.

General

32,300	Bosma Industries, Indianapolis, IN
12,500	Indianapolis Day Nursery, Indianapolis, IN
10,000	St. Richard's School, Indianapolis, IN
6,000	Eiteljorg Museum, Indianapolis, IN
5,700	Indiana University Foundation, Indianapolis, IN
5,000	ALS Society, Indianapolis, IN
5,000	Gleaners Food Bank, Indianapolis, IN
5,000	Little Red Door, Indianapolis, IN
5,000	Meals on Wheels, Indianapolis, IN
5,000	Second Helping, Indianapolis, IN

AZADOUTIOUN FOUNDATION

Giving Contact

Carolyn G. Mugar, Trustee
c/o Gravestar
1 Broadway
Cambridge, MA 02142
Phone: (617)492-4118
Fax: (617)492-4118

Description

Founded: 1985
EIN: 042876245
Organization Type: Private Foundation
Giving Locations: MA
Grant Types: General Support, Project.

Donor Information

Founder: Carolyn G. Mugar

Financial Summary

Total Giving: $142,000 (2000); $221,000 (1999); $138,680 (1998)
Assets: $5,431,446 (2000); $4,708,946 (1999); $4,652,866 (1998)
Gifts Received: $151,233 (1999); $45,000 (1996); $153,000 (1995). Note: In 1999 and 1996, contributions were received from Carolyn G. Mugar.

Typical Recipients

Arts & Humanities: Arts Associations & Councils, Historic Preservation
Civic & Public Affairs: Employment/Job Training, Ethnic Organizations, Civic & Public Affairs-General, Public Policy, Urban & Community Affairs, Women's Affairs
Education: Arts/Humanities Education, Business Education, Colleges & Universities, Continuing Education, Education Funds, Elementary Education (Private), Education-General, International Studies, Private Education (Precollege), Social Sciences Education
Environment: Air/Water Quality, Environment-General

Health: Children's Health/Hospitals, Health Policy/Cost Containment, Health Funds
International: Health Care/Hospitals, Human Rights, International Relief Efforts
Religion: Churches, Religious Organizations, Religious Welfare
Social Services: Child Welfare, Community Service Organizations, Day Care, Recreation & Athletics, Youth Organizations

Application Procedures

Initial Contact: Send a brief letter of inquiry describing program or project.
Deadlines: None.

Foundation Officials

Janet Corpus: trustee
Carolyn G. Mugar: trustee
Sidney Peck: trustee
Sharryn Ross: trustee

Grants Analysis

Disclosure Period: calendar year ending 2000
Total Grants: $142,000
Number of Grants: 9
Average Grant: $15,778
Highest Grant: $30,000
Lowest Grant: $5,000
Typical Range: $5,000 to $30,000

Recent Grants

Note: Grants derived from 1999 Form 990.

General

50,000	ANI, Washington, DC
44,000	Armenian Tree Project, Cambridge, MA
40,000	Texans United Education Fund, Houston, TX
30,000	Country Road, Inc., Arlington, VA
22,000	Armenian Assembly of America, Washington, DC
10,000	Human Rights Alliance, Fairfax, VA
10,000	Project Save, Watertown, MA
10,000	Southwest Writers Collection, San Marcos, TX
5,000	Armenian Library and Museum of America, Watertown, MA

MARY REYNOLDS BABCOCK FOUNDATION

Giving Contact

Gayle Williams, Executive Director
2920 Reynolda Road
Winston-Salem, NC 27106-5123
Phone: (336)748-9222
Fax: (336)777-0095
E-mail: info@mrbf.org
Web: http://www.mrbf.org

Description

Founded: 1953
EIN: 560690140
Organization Type: Family Foundation
Giving Locations: Southeastern United States.
Grant Types: Award, Loan, Multiyear/Continuing Support, Seed Money.
Note: Awards organizational development grants.

Donor Information

Founder: Incorporated in North Carolina in 1953 with funds donated by the late Mrs. Mary Reynolds Babcock and Charles H. Babcock. Mary Reynolds was one of four children of R.J. Reynolds, of R.J. Reynolds Tobacco Company.

Financial Summary

Total Giving: $4,777,611 (2000); $4,777,166 (1999); $3,956,230 (1998)
Assets: $118,549,310 (2000); $117,939,218 (1999); $115,618,778 (1998)

Typical Recipients

Arts & Humanities: Arts Centers, Arts Funds, Community Arts, Film & Video, History & Archaeology, Museums/Galleries, Performing Arts, Public Broadcasting

Civic & Public Affairs: African American Affairs, Business/Free Enterprise, Civil Rights, Clubs, Community Foundations, Economic Development, Economic Policy, Employment/Job Training, First Amendment Issues, Civic & Public Affairs-General, Hispanic Affairs, Housing, Law & Justice, Legal Aid, Nonprofit Management, Philanthropic Organizations, Public Policy, Rural Affairs, Safety, Urban & Community Affairs, Women's Affairs

Education: Colleges & Universities, Continuing Education, Economic Education, Education Funds, Education Reform, Education Reform, Elementary Education (Private), Faculty Development, Education-General, Literacy, Preschool Education, Public Education (Precollege), Student Aid

Environment: Air/Water Quality, Environment-General, Resource Conservation, Sanitary Systems, Wildlife Protection

Health: Emergency/Ambulance Services, Health Organizations, Hospitals, Nutrition

International: Human Rights, International Peace & Security Issues, International Relations

Religion: Religion-General, Ministries, Religious Organizations, Religious Welfare

Social Services: Child Welfare, Community Centers, Community Service Organizations, Day Care, Delinquency & Criminal Rehabilitation, Family Planning, Family Services, Food/Clothing Distribution, Volunteer Services, Youth Organizations

Application Procedures

Initial Contact: Call or write foundation for grant application for the Organizational Development program.
Application Requirements: Information needed for two-page Organizational Development Grant Application includes the following: organization's name, contact name, address, phone, and e-mail; description of organization; list of board members including race and gender of each member; list of staff with title, including volunteers if half-time or greater; proof of tax-exempt status; and financial information. Additional information needed for the second part of application form includes the following: description of organization's mission and how it ties to the foundation's goals; description of current activities; definition of organization's current constituency; report on evaluation methods; account of organization's greatest accomplishments and difficult challenges; summary of organization's five-year vision; a description of organization's development work plan; amount of grant request; a cover letter signed by board chair or executive director, and a one page budget.
Deadlines: February 15 for organizational grants; others, none. Applicants can see guidelines and updated information on the foundation's website. Prospective applicants should call the foundation before submitting a letter of request.

Restrictions

Grants are not made to individuals. No grants for international programs, nor for construction.

Additional Information

The foundation reports that it is affiliated with the Z. Smith Reynolds Foundation, Winston-Salem, NC. The foundations share some directors.
Program-related investments are made on a selective basis when a loan is a more appropriate use of the foundation's funds than a grant.

Publications: Annual Report; Guidelines; Application Form

Foundation Officials

Bruce M. Babcock: director
Akosua Barthwell Evans: director
Sybil Jordan Hampton: director
Nathaniel Irvin, II: director
Otis S. Johnson: vice president
Reynolds Lassiter: director
Sandra H. Mikush: assistant director
Barbara B. Millhouse: vice president, director
Katharine Babcock Mountcastle: director B Philadelphia, PA 1931. ED Sweet Briar College BA (1952). NONPR AFFIL director: Fairfield Country Community Foundation.
Katharine Reynolds Mountcastle: director B Greenwich, CT 1963. ED Williams College BA (1985). PRIM CORP EMPL associate producer: CBS News. NONPR AFFIL volunteer: Greater District of Columbia Cares.
Kenneth F. Mountcastle, III: director
Laura Lewis Mountcastle: vice president, director ED Trinity College BA (1978); Yale University MBA (1984). PRIM CORP EMPL vice president planning & investor relations: CMS Energy Corp.
Mary Mountcastle: director NONPR AFFIL assistant director: Center Community Self-Help; director: Tides Indiana Inc.; director: Boggs Rural Life Center; director: Center Community Change.
Zachary Taylor Smith, II: director, secretary B Mount Airy, NC 1923. ED University of North Carolina AB (1947). NONPR AFFIL vice chairman, director: University North Carolina Friends Greensboro Library; life trustee: Wake Forest University; member national development council: University North Carolina; director: University North Carolina Arts Sciences Foundation; member advisory council hospital: Duke University. CLUB AFFIL Rotary Club; Old Town Club.
Gayle Williams: executive director
Carol Prejean Zippert: director

Grants Analysis

Disclosure Period: calendar year ending 2000
Total Grants: $4,777,611
Number of Grants: 138
Average Grant: $34,617
Highest Grant: $577,517
Typical Range: $10,000 to $50,000

Recent Grants

Note: Grants derived from 2001 Form 990.

General

583,334	Reynolda House Museum of American Art, Winston-Salem, NC -- expansion project
421,306	MDC, Inc., Chapel Hill, NC -- grassroots leadership development strategy
386,569	Center for Community Change, Washington, DC -- enterprise and asset development grant
89,500	Reynolda House Museum of American Art, Winston-Salem, NC
87,500	Southern Financial Partners, Arkadelphia, AR -- enterprise and asset development grant
75,000	ALT Consulting, Memphis, TN -- enterprise and asset development grant
75,000	Center for Economic Options, Charleston, WV -- enterprise and asset development grant
75,000	Enterprise Corporation of the Delta, Jackson, MS -- enterprise and asset development grant
75,000	Five Rivers Community Development Corporation, Georgetown, SC -- enterprise and asset development grant
75,000	Good Work, Durham, NC -- enterprise and asset development grant

PAUL AND EDITH BABSON FOUNDATION

Giving Contact

Elizabeth D. Nichols, Grant Administrator
c/o Nichols and Pratt
50 Congress St., Suite 832
Boston, MA 02109
Phone: (617)523-8368
Fax: (617)523-8949
E-mail: pebabsonfdn@babsonfoundations.org
Web: http://www.babsonfoundations.org

Description

Founded: 1957
EIN: 046037891
Organization Type: Private Foundation
Giving Locations: MA: Greater Boston
Grant Types: Capital, General Support, Project.

Donor Information

Founder: the late Paul T. Babson

Financial Summary

Total Giving: $648,543 (2001); $667,340 (2000); $728,160 (1999)
Giving Analysis: Giving for 2001 includes: foundation grants to United Way ($20,000); 2000: foundation grants to United Way ($20,500); 1999: foundation grants to United Way ($25,000);
Assets: $13,166,051 (2001); $14,486,600 (2000); $14,947,823 (1999)

Typical Recipients

Arts & Humanities: History & Archaeology, Libraries, Museums/Galleries, Music, Opera, Performing Arts, Public Broadcasting, Theater

Civic & Public Affairs: African American Affairs, Business/Free Enterprise, Community Foundations, Economic Development, Employment/Job Training, Gay/Lesbian Issues, Civic & Public Affairs-General, Hispanic Affairs, Municipalities/Towns, Native American Affairs, Nonprofit Management, Philanthropic Organizations, Public Policy, Urban & Community Affairs, Women's Affairs

Education: Arts/Humanities Education, Business Education, Colleges & Universities, Education Associations, Engineering/Technological Education, Faculty Development, Education-General, Leadership Training, Medical Education, Minority Education, Private Education (Precollege), Private Education (Precollege), Public Education (Precollege), Science/Mathematics Education, Secondary Education (Private), Student Aid

Environment: Air/Water Quality, Environment-General, Resource Conservation

Health: AIDS/HIV, Hospitals, Medical Research, Mental Health, Public Health

International: Foreign Arts Organizations, Human Rights, International Relief Efforts

Religion: Churches, Religious Organizations, Religious Welfare

Science: Science Museums

Social Services: At-Risk Youth, Child Welfare, Community Centers, Community Service Organizations, Crime Prevention, Family Planning, Family Services, Food/Clothing Distribution, Homes, People with Disabilities, Sexual Abuse, Shelters/Homelessness, United Funds/United Ways, YMCA/YWCA/YMHA/YWHA, YMCA/YWCA/YMHA/YWHA, Youth Organizations

Application Procedures

Initial Contact: Submit two copies of a two-page concept letter and a completed Concept Letter Summary Sheet. The Summary Sheet may be downloaded from the foundation's web site.
Deadlines: February 6 and September 9 for concept letters.

Review Process: The board of trustees review concept letters and invite a limited number of applicants to submit full proposals.
Decision Notification: The board of trustees meets in late May and early December to consider proposals. Decisions are generally communicated to applicants within six weeks of each meeting.

Restrictions

The foundation does not support individuals, films, videos, conferences, fundraising, or donor cultivation events.

Additional Information

Foundation accepts the Common Grant Application of the National Network of Grantmakers for full proposals.
Publications: Guidelines

Foundation Officials

Donald Paul Babson: trustee B Newton, MA 1924. ED Cornell University (1948); Harvard University Graduate School of Business Administration (1950). PRIM CORP EMPL chairman: Babson-United Investment Advs. CORP AFFIL director: South Shore Bank; chairman, president: United Business Service; director: Multibank Financial Corp.
James A. Babson: trustee
Katherine L. Babson: trustee
James R. Nichols: trustee

Grants Analysis

Disclosure Period: calendar year ending 2001
Total Grants: $628,543*
Number of Grants: 96
Average Grant: $6,547
Highest Grant: $25,000
Typical Range: $1,000 to $15,000
*Note: Giving excludes United Way.

Recent Grants

Note: Grants derived from 2001 Form 990.

General

25,000	MACDC Community Business Network
25,000	Trustees of Phillips Academy, Andover, MA
20,000	Associated Grantmakers, Boston, MA
20,000	Newton Wellesley Hospital, Wellesley, MA
20,000	United Way of Massachusetts Bay, Boston, MA
20,000	YMCA of Greater Boston, Boston, MA
15,000	AIDS Action Committee, Boston, MA
15,000	Boston Partners in Education, Boston, MA
15,000	Center for Women and Enterprise, Boston, MA
15,000	Island Alliance, Boston, MA

BEATRICE AND ROY BACKUS FOUNDATION

Giving Contact

Inge T. Stephens, President
378A Heritage Hills
Somers, NY 10589
Phone: (914)277-3024

Description

Founded: 1988
EIN: 133442922
Organization Type: Private Foundation
Giving Locations: CA; MA
Grant Types: Department, General Support, Multiyear/Continuing Support, Research.

Financial Summary

Total Giving: $87,500 (2002 approx); $145,290 (2001); $197,133 (2000)
Assets: $1,691,893 (2001); $1,900,647 (2000); $1,931,611 (1999)

Typical Recipients

Arts & Humanities: Libraries
Education: Afterschool/Enrichment Programs, Education-General, Health & Physical Education, Medical Education, Preschool Education, Science/Mathematics Education
Health: AIDS/HIV, Children's Health/Hospitals, Health Organizations, Hospitals, Medical Rehabilitation, Medical Research, Research/Studies Institutes, Single-Disease Health Associations, Transplant Networks/Donor Banks
Social Services: Child Welfare, Community Service Organizations, Counseling, Day Care, Scouts, Shelters/Homelessness

Application Procedures

Initial Contact: The foundation reports that applications should be submitted in written form detailing the purpose for which the funds will be used.
Deadlines: None.

Restrictions

Grants are limited to programs in the areas of medical research, education, and science.

Foundation Officials

Adolf Haasen: director
Christopher H. Stephens: vice president, director
Inge T. Stephens: treasurer, director
Thomas J. Stephens: president, director

Grants Analysis

Disclosure Period: calendar year ending 2001
Total Grants: $145,290
Number of Grants: 4
Highest Grant: $85,290
Lowest Grant: $20,000

Recent Grants

Note: Grants derived from 2001 Form 990.

General

85,290	Massachusetts General Hospital - Harvard Medical School, Charlestown, MA -- research into pain causation and treatment arising from post-herpetic neuralgia pain
20,000	Massachusetts General Hospital - Harvard Medical School, Charlestown, MA -- funding for the establishment of The Center for Shingles and Post Herpetic Neuralgia
20,000	Parkinson's Institute, Sunnyvale, CA -- for three-year study of the role of Alfa-Synuclein in Parkinson's Disease
20,000	Salk Institute, San Diego, CA -- for Gene Chip Workstation to determine gene function in Parkinson's disease

E. L. AND OMA BACON FOUNDATION

Giving Contact

Staci Adelman
c/o Wells Fargo Bank
PO Box 4010
Grand Junction, CO 81502
Phone: (970)243-1611
Fax: (970)242-1066

Description

Founded: 1978
EIN: 840772667
Organization Type: Private Foundation
Giving Locations: CO
Grant Types: General Support.

Donor Information

Founder: the late E. L. Bacon, the late Oma Bacon

Financial Summary

Total Giving: $184,693 (fiscal year ending August 31, 1996); $184,726 (fiscal 1995); $166,350 (fiscal 1994)
Assets: $3,017,331 (fiscal 1996); $4,218,686 (fiscal 1995); $3,911,550 (fiscal 1994)

Typical Recipients

Arts & Humanities: Arts Associations & Councils, History & Archaeology, Libraries, Museums/Galleries, Music, Public Broadcasting, Theater
Civic & Public Affairs: Civil Rights, Economic Development, Civic & Public Affairs-General, Housing, Municipalities/Towns, Nonprofit Management, Safety, Urban & Community Affairs, Women's Affairs, Zoos/Aquariums
Education: Colleges & Universities, Journalism/Media Education, Preschool Education, Religious Education, Student Aid
Environment: Environment-General
Health: AIDS/HIV, Clinics/Medical Centers, Eyes/Blindness, Hospitals, Medical Rehabilitation, Mental Health, Public Health
Religion: Churches, Religious Organizations, Religious Welfare
Social Services: Child Welfare, Community Service Organizations, Domestic Violence, Food/Clothing Distribution, People with Disabilities, Senior Services, Substance Abuse, United Funds/United Ways, Volunteer Services, Youth Organizations

Application Procedures

Initial Contact: Send a brief letter of inquiry describing program.
Deadlines: None.

Restrictions

Does not support individuals.

Additional Information

Publications: Application Guidelines

Foundation Officials

Herbert L. Bacon: president
Laura May Bacon: treasurer
Patrick A. Gormley: vice president

Grants Analysis

Disclosure Period: fiscal year ending August 31, 1996
Total Grants: $184,693
Number of Grants: 23
Average Grant: $8,030
Highest Grant: $25,000
Typical Range: $500 to $20,000
Note: A more recent grants list was unavailable.

Recent Grants

Note: Grants derived from 1996 Form 990.

Library-Related

1,565	Mesa County Public Library, Grand Junction, CO -- lift for van

General

25,000	Iliff School of Theology, Denver, CO
25,000	Museum of Western Colorado, Grand Junction, CO -- new museum campaign
25,000	Resource Center, Grand Junction, CO
15,000	Marillac Clinic, Grand Junction, CO
15,000	St. Mary's Hospital, Grand Junction, CO -- expansion campaign

13,000	United Way Mesa County, Grand Junction, CO
7,000	Delta Gamma Anchor Center for Blind Children
6,113	Center for Independence, Grand Junction, CO
5,300	Volunteer Central of Mesa County Retired Senior Volunteers, Grand Junction, CO -- salary, computer
5,000	Calvary Episcopal Church, Grand Junction, CO

ROSE M. BADGELEY RESIDUARY CHARITABLE TRUST

Giving Contact

Roberta Grossman, Vice President
Care of HSBC Bank, USA
140 Broadway, 11th Fl.
New York, NY 10005
Phone: 800-975-4722
Fax: (212)658-7790

Description

Founded: 1977
EIN: 136744781
Organization Type: General Purpose Foundation
Former Name: Rose M. Badgeley Charitable Trust.
Giving Locations: NY
Grant Types: General Support, Research.

Donor Information

Founder: Established in 1977 through the will of the late Rose M. Badgeley .

Financial Summary

Total Giving: $1,300,000 (fiscal year ending October 1, 2000 approx); $1,128,648 (fiscal 1999); $682,500 (fiscal 1997)
Assets: $33,025,402 (fiscal 1999); $23,429,692 (fiscal 1997); $15,539,185 (fiscal 1995)
Gifts Received: $111,388 (fiscal 1999); $109,984 (fiscal 1997); $250,379 (fiscal 1995). Note: In 1999, contributions were received from the Rose M. Badgeley Annuity Trust.

Typical Recipients

Arts & Humanities: Film & Video, Libraries, Museums/Galleries, Music, Opera, Performing Arts, Theater
Civic & Public Affairs: Botanical Gardens/Parks, Clubs, Employment/Job Training, Civic & Public Affairs-General, Hispanic Affairs, Housing, Women's Affairs
Education: Arts/Humanities Education, Colleges & Universities, Education-General, Literacy, Minority Education, Preschool Education, Private Education (Precollege), Public Education (Precollege), School Volunteerism, Science/Mathematics Education, Student Aid, Vocational & Technical Education
Environment: Air/Water Quality, Resource Conservation
Health: AIDS/HIV, Alzheimers Disease, Cancer, Children's Health/Hospitals, Clinics/Medical Centers, Emergency/Ambulance Services, Eyes/Blindness, Geriatric Health, Health Organizations, Heart, Hospitals, Hospitals (University Affiliated), Medical Rehabilitation, Medical Research, Mental Health, Nursing Services, Prenatal Health Issues, Single-Disease Health Associations, Transplant Networks/Donor Banks
International: Health Care/Hospitals
Religion: Churches, Dioceses, Jewish Causes, Ministries, Religious Welfare

Social Services: At-Risk Youth, Camps, Child Welfare, Community Centers, Community Service Organizations, Counseling, Family Services, Food/Clothing Distribution, Homes, People with Disabilities, Scouts, Senior Services, Shelters/Homelessness, Substance Abuse, Veterans, Volunteer Services, YMCA/YWCA/YMHA/YWHA, Youth Organizations

Application Procedures

Initial Contact: Letters of inquiry should be directed to the chairman of the trust's grants committee at HSBC.
Application Requirements: Requests should include current financial statements, list of board members and patrons, operating budget, and proof of tax-exempt status.
Deadlines: Applications must be postmarked no earlier than December 1 and no later than March 15.

Additional Information

Publications: Guidelines; Application Form
Trust(s): HSBC Bank USA

Foundation Officials

Roberta Grossman: vice president

Grants Analysis

Disclosure Period: fiscal year ending October 1, 1999
Total Grants: $1,128,648
Number of Grants: 46
Average Grant: $24,536
Highest Grant: $65,000
Lowest Grant: $2,500
Typical Range: $5,000 to $30,000

Recent Grants

Note: Grants derived from fiscal 2000 Form 990.

General

75,000	New York Presbyterian Hospital, New York, NY -- to support programs in research and teaching in Pediatric Cardiology
50,000	Alzheimer's Association, New York, NY -- to help extend and expand the efforts of the New York City Chapter
50,000	Make-A-Wish Foundation, New York, NY -- to support the cost of funding one wish for a critically ill child
50,000	Mount Sinai Medical Center, New York, NY -- support for the clinical development of combination cytotoxic differentiation therapy of colon cancer and prostate cancer
46,000	Carnegie Hall Society, New York, NY -- for the Family Concert Series
46,000	Metropolitan Opera Guild, New York, NY -- to help provide some New York area schools with an affordable and effective opera education program
45,000	New York City Opera, New York, NY
45,000	Skin Cancer Foundation, New York, NY -- to prepare the vaccine needed for the trial and to cover part of the cost of the assays
42,000	AMFAR, Los Angeles, CA -- to research various possible vaccines for treatment of HIV
35,000	Lincoln Center Theater, New York, NY -- to support the audience development and education project

BADGER METER, INC.

Company Headquarters

Milwaukee, WI
Web: http://www.badgermeter.com

Company Description

Founded: 1905
Ticker: BMI
Exchange: AMEX
Revenue: US$138.5 million (2001)
Employees: 936 (2001)
SIC(s): 3823 Process Control Instruments, 3824 Fluid Meters & Counting Devices.

Operating Locations

Badger Meter, Inc. (AZ--Rio Rico; OK--Tulsa)

Badger Meter Foundation

Giving Contact

Beth McCallister, Secretary
4545 West Brown Deer Road
Milwaukee, WI 53223
Phone: (414)371-5704
Fax: (414)371-5956

Description

EIN: 396043635
Organization Type: Corporate Foundation
Giving Locations: WI: Milwaukee
Grant Types: General Support.

Financial Summary

Total Giving: $410,108 (2001); $406,933 (2000 approx); $346,000 (1999 approx)
Giving Analysis: Giving for 2001 includes: foundation scholarships ($6,000); foundation grants to United Way ($92,250); foundation ($311,858); 2000: foundation grants to United Way ($52,000); foundation ($354,933); 1998: corporate matching gifts ($350); foundation matching gifts ($350); corporate scholarships ($1,500); corporate grants to United Way ($46,750); foundation grants to United Way ($55,158); corporate direct giving ($227,558).
Assets: $1,763,808 (2001); $2,099,581 (2000); $2,081,354 (1998)
Gifts Received: $106,000 (2001); $215,000 (2000); $265,271 (1998). Note: Contributions are received from Badger Meter, Inc.

Typical Recipients

Arts & Humanities: Ballet, Arts & Humanities-General, Libraries, Museums/Galleries, Music, Opera, Performing Arts, Theater
Civic & Public Affairs: Botanical Gardens/Parks, Clubs, Economic Development, Employment/Job Training, Civic & Public Affairs-General, Hispanic Affairs, Housing, Law & Justice, Municipalities/Towns, Parades/Festivals, Public Policy, Urban & Community Affairs, Zoos/Aquariums
Education: Arts/Humanities Education, Business Education, Business-School Partnerships, Colleges & Universities, Education Funds, Engineering/Technological Education, Faculty Development, Education-General, Health & Physical Education, Literacy, Medical Education, Minority Education, Private Education (Precollege), Private Education (Precollege), Public Education (Precollege), Religious Education, Science/Mathematics Education, Secondary Education (Private), Secondary Education (Public), Student Aid
Environment: Environment-General, Resource Conservation
Health: Arthritis, Cancer, Health Organizations, Heart, Hospitals, Medical Research, Mental Health, Preventive Medicine/Wellness Organizations, Single-Disease Health Associations, Speech & Hearing, Transplant Networks/Donor Banks
Religion: Religious Welfare
Science: Science Museums
Social Services: Animal Protection, Child Welfare, Community Centers, Community Service Organizations, Day Care, Domestic Violence, Food/Clothing

Distribution, Homes, People with Disabilities, Recreation & Athletics, Scouts, Shelters/Homelessness, Social Services-General, Substance Abuse, United Funds/United Ways, YMCA/YWCA/YMHA/YWHA, Youth Organizations

Application Procedures

Initial Contact: Send a brief letter of inquiry on organization's letterhead.

Application Requirements: Information should include purpose of funds sought; amount requested; and an attached copy of an IRS 501(c)(3) determination letter.

Deadlines: None.

Decision Notification: Board meets in April, August, and December.

Additional Information

RES Grants are awarded solely to charitable, scientific, literary, or educational organizations.

Corporate Officials

Ronald H. Dix: vice president administration & human resources B 1944. ED University of Wisconsin BS (1969). PRIM CORP EMPL vice president administration & human resources: Badger Meter, Inc.

Richard A. Meeusen: vice president, chief financial officer, treasurer B 1954. ED University of Wisconsin, Whitewater BS (1976). PRIM CORP EMPL vice president, chief financial officer, treasurer: Badger Meter, Inc.

James O. Wright: chairman, director B Milwaukee, WI 1921. ED Yale University BS (1944). PRIM CORP EMPL chairman, director: Badger Meter, Inc. CORP AFFIL director: Northwestern Mutual Life Insurance Co.; director: Wisconsin Natural Gas Co.; director: Marshall & Ilsley Corp.; director: Grede Foundries Inc.; director: Marshall & Ilsley Bank; director: Becor Western Inc.

Foundation Officials

Ronald H. Dix: director (see above)
Beth McCallister: secretary
James O. Wright: president, director (see above)

Grants Analysis

Disclosure Period: calendar year ending 2001
Total Grants: $311,858*
Number of Grants: 94
Average Grant: $3,318
Highest Grant: $50,000
Lowest Grant: $25
Typical Range: $500 to $5,000
*Note: Giving excludes United Way and scholarships.

Recent Grants

Note: Grants derived from 2001 Form 990.

General

50,000	Milwaukee Kickers, Milwaukee, WI
50,000	United Way Milwaukee, Milwaukee, WI
40,250	University School Milwaukee, Milwaukee, WI
25,000	Goodwill Industries, Milwaukee, WI
16,000	Friends of Schlitz Audubon Center, Milwaukee, WI
12,500	American Black Holocaust Museum, Milwaukee, WI
10,000	Marcus Center for Performing Arts, Milwaukee, WI
10,000	Urban Day School, Milwaukee, WI -- 12th Street
10,000	Villa Terrace Museum, Milwaukee, WI
7,500	United Performing Arts Fund, Milwaukee, WI

LOUIS W. AND DOLPHA BAEHR FOUNDATION

Giving Contact

Carl F. Gump
c/o Team Bank
PO Box 369
Paola, KS 66071
Phone: (913)294-4311

Description

Founded: 1967
EIN: 486129741
Organization Type: Private Foundation
Giving Locations: MO: Kansas City
Grant Types: Capital, Endowment, Project, Research, Seed Money.

Donor Information

Founder: the late L. W. Baehr, the late Dolpha Baehr

Financial Summary

Total Giving: $362,808 (fiscal year ending April 30, 2001); $363,284 (fiscal 2000); $213,900 (fiscal 1999)
Giving Analysis: Giving for fiscal 2001 includes: foundation grants to United Way ($3,000) fiscal 2000: foundation grants to United Way ($3,000)
Assets: $5,740,131 (fiscal 2001); $6,226,220 (fiscal 2000); $6,569,033 (fiscal 1999)

Typical Recipients

Arts & Humanities: Arts Centers, Historic Preservation, History & Archaeology, Libraries

Civic & Public Affairs: Botanical Gardens/Parks, Civic & Public Affairs-General, Municipalities/Towns, Parades/Festivals, Urban & Community Affairs

Education: Arts/Humanities Education, Colleges & Universities, Community & Junior Colleges, Continuing Education, Education-General, Minority Education, Private Education (Precollege), Public Education (Precollege), Secondary Education (Public)

Health: Children's Health/Hospitals, Health Organizations, Hospitals, Mental Health, Nutrition

International: International Relations

Social Services: Child Welfare, Community Service Organizations, People with Disabilities, Recreation & Athletics, Scouts, United Funds/United Ways, Youth Organizations

Application Procedures

Initial Contact: Send a brief letter of inquiry.

Application Requirements: Include a description of organization, amount requested, purpose of funds sought, recently audited financial statement, and proof of tax-exempt status.

Deadlines: Meetings are scheduled for January, April, August, and October.

Review Process: Proposals must be received at least four weeks prior to the month in which the request is to be reviewed.

Restrictions

Does not support individuals or provide funds for advertising.

Additional Information

Publications: Application Guidelines
Trust(s): Team Bank

Grants Analysis

Disclosure Period: fiscal year ending April 30, 2001
Total Grants: $359,808*
Number of Grants: 17
Average Grant: $12,216*
Highest Grant: $51,000
Lowest Grant: $650
Typical Range: $5,000 to $25,000
*Note: Giving excludes United Way. Average grant figure excludes four highest grants ($201,000).

Recent Grants

Note: Grants derived from fiscal 2000 Form 990.

Library-Related

10,000	Pittsburgh State University, Pittsburg, KS

General

50,000	U.S.D. 368, Paola, KS -- endowment
50,000	Kansas State University Foundation, Manhattan, KS
40,000	Kansas State Historical Society, Topeka, KS
40,000	Lakemary Endowment, Paola, KS
37,500	Children's Mercy Hospital, Kansas City, MO
25,000	Miami County Historical Society, Paola, KS
22,744	U.S.D. 368 Adult Education Center, Paola, KS
11,480	Kansas University Audio Reader, Lawrence, KS
10,000	Lakemary Center, Paola, KS
8,532	Paola Heartland USA, Paola, KS

WILLIAM O. AND CAROLE P. BAILEY FAMILY FOUNDATION

Giving Contact

William O. Bailey, President
c/o US Trust Co.
114 W. 47th St., Tax Svcs.
New York, NY 10036
Phone: (212)852-3834

Description

Founded: 1997
EIN: 541860572
Organization Type: Private Foundation
Grant Types: General Support.

Financial Summary

Total Giving: $101,000 (2001); $98,950 (2000); $62,250 (1999)
Assets: $1,018,569 (2001); $1,363,394 (2000); $1,480,166 (1999)
Gifts Received: $486,887 (2000); $15,276 (1999); $30,888 (1998). Note: In 1999 and 2000, contributions were received from William D. Bailey. In 1998, contributions were received from William O. and Carole P. Bailey.

Typical Recipients

Arts & Humanities: Arts & Humanities-General, History & Archaeology, Libraries

Civic & Public Affairs: Civil Rights, Civic & Public Affairs-General

Education: Business Education, Colleges & Universities, Education-General, Leadership Training, Private Education (Precollege)

Environment: Environment-General, Resource Conservation

Health: Cancer, Hospitals

International: Foreign Arts Organizations

Social Services: Camps

Foundation Officials

Carolyn Bailey Akers: secretary, second vice president

George P. Bailey: secretary, second vice president

William O. Bailey: president

Janet Bailey Faude: assistant treasurer, second vice president

Carole P. Bailey First: vice president, treasurer

Grants Analysis

Disclosure Period: calendar year ending 2001
Total Grants: $101,000
Number of Grants: 26
Average Grant: $3,885
Highest Grant: $17,500
Lowest Grant: $500
Typical Range: $1,000 to $5,000

Recent Grants

Note: Grants derived from 2000 Form 990.

Library-Related
6,000	Wadsworth Atheneum, Hartford, CT

General
21,000	Friends of the Riverfront, Pittsburgh, PA
15,000	Connecticut Valley Hospital, Middletown, CT
10,000	Campaign for the Mar
10,000	Cooley Dickinson Hospital, Inc, Northampton, MA
5,000	Bermuda Fine Arts Foundation, Wilmington, DE
5,000	Bermuda Maritime Museum, Mangrove Bay Bermuda
5,000	Bryn Mawr College, Bryn Mawr, PA
5,000	Dartmouth Alumni Fund, Hanover, NH
2,500	Loomis Chaffee School, Windsor, CT
1,500	Squam Lake Conservation Society, Meredith, NH

CHARLES M. BAIR FAMILY TRUST

Giving Contact

c/o U.S. Bank Trust MT
303 N. Broadway
PO Box 20678
Billings, MT 59115-0678
Phone: (406)657-8083

Description

Founded: 1994
EIN: 816075761
Organization Type: Private Foundation
Giving Locations: MT
Grant Types: General Support.

Donor Information

Founder: Established in 1994 by Alberta M. Bair.

Financial Summary

Total Giving: $476,133 (fiscal year ending April 30, 2001); $900,850 (fiscal 2000); $724,865 (fiscal 1999)
Assets: $51,905,874 (fiscal 2001); $54,049,211 (fiscal 2000); $52,341,421 (fiscal 1999)
Gifts Received: $1,100,097 (fiscal 2001); $250,022 (fiscal 2000); $4,464 (fiscal 1997). Note: In 2000 and 2001, contributions were received from Bair Ranch Foundation. In fiscal 1996 and 1997, contributions were received from the estate of Alberta M. Bair.

Typical Recipients

Arts & Humanities: Arts Centers, Arts Outreach, Arts & Humanities-General, Historic Preservation, History & Archaeology, Libraries, Literary Arts, Museums/Galleries, Music, Public Broadcasting, Theater
Civic & Public Affairs: Botanical Gardens/Parks, Business/Free Enterprise, Civic & Public Affairs-General, Safety, Zoos/Aquariums
Education: Colleges & Universities, Private Education (Precollege), Public Education (Precollege)
Environment: Environment-General
Health: AIDS/HIV, Clinics/Medical Centers, Emergency/Ambulance Services, Mental Health
Religion: Ministries, Religious Welfare
Social Services: Community Service Organizations, Day Care, Domestic Violence, Family Services, Food/Clothing Distribution, Recreation & Athletics, Scouts, Senior Services, YMCA/YWCA/YMHA/YWHA, Youth Organizations

Application Procedures

Initial Contact: Send a brief letter requesting application form.
Deadlines: January 15 and August 1.

Additional Information

Trust(s): U.S. Bank Trust NA

Foundation Officials

Anne M. Hafer: director
Douglas A. Jenkins: director
Gerald B. Murphy: chairman
Lee B. Rostad: vchairman
Roger L. Sullivan: secretary

Grants Analysis

Disclosure Period: fiscal year ending April 30, 2001
Total Grants: $476,133
Number of Grants: 26
Average Grant: $16,845*
Highest Grant: $55,000
Lowest Grant: $3,000
Typical Range: $5,000 to $30,000
*Note: Average grant figure excludes highest grant.

Recent Grants

Note: Grants derived from fiscal 2000 Form 990.

General
225,000	Rocky Mountain College, Billings, MT
50,000	Alberta Bair Theater, Billings, MT
50,000	Upper Musselshell Historical Society, Harlowton, MT
50,000	Yellowstone Art Museum, Billings, MT
40,000	Billings Symphony Society, Billings, MT
40,000	Boys & Girls Club of Billings and Yellowstone County, Billings, MT
35,000	Treasure Trails Girl Scout Council, Billings, MT
30,000	Museum of the Rockies, Bozeman, MT
27,500	St. John's Lutheran Ministries, Billings, MT
25,000	Billings Depot, Inc., Billings, MT

BAIRD BROTHERS CO. FOUNDATION

Giving Contact

Donna Auten
c/o Huntington Trust Co. NA
41 S. High St.
Columbus, OH 43216
Phone: (614)480-3633

Description

EIN: 316194844
Organization Type: Private Foundation
Giving Locations: OH: Nelsonville
Grant Types: General Support.

Financial Summary

Total Giving: $169,561 (fiscal year ending June 30, 2001); $456,242 (fiscal 2000); $187,756 (fiscal 1998)
Assets: $3,988,811 (fiscal 2001); $4,181,726 (fiscal 2000); $5,734,717 (fiscal 1998)

Typical Recipients

Arts & Humanities: Arts Centers, Arts Festivals, Ballet, Arts & Humanities-General, Historic Preservation, History & Archaeology, Libraries, Museums/Galleries, Music, Opera, Performing Arts, Theater
Civic & Public Affairs: Botanical Gardens/Parks, Economic Development, Civic & Public Affairs-General, Municipalities/Towns, Urban & Community Affairs

Education: Colleges & Universities, Economic Education, Engineering/Technological Education, Education-General, Preschool Education, Public Education (Precollege), Science/Mathematics Education
Environment: Environment-General
Health: Children's Health/Hospitals, Diabetes, Eyes/Blindness, Hospitals, Long-Term Care, Transplant Networks/Donor Banks
Religion: Churches, Religious Welfare
Social Services: Animal Protection, Camps, Community Service Organizations, Emergency Relief, Family Services, Food/Clothing Distribution, Recreation & Athletics, Scouts, United Funds/United Ways, YMCA/YWCA/YMHA/YWHA, Youth Organizations

Application Procedures

Initial Contact: The foundation has no formal grant application procedure or application form.
Deadlines: None.

Additional Information

The foundation is no longer associated with the Baird Brothers Co.
Trust(s): Huntington National Bank

Foundation Officials

David S. Fraedrich: director
Jane E. Harmony: director
Wilbert W. Warren, Jr.: director

Grants Analysis

Disclosure Period: fiscal year ending June 30, 2001
Total Grants: $169,561
Number of Grants: 37
Average Grant: $4,582
Highest Grant: $26,400
Lowest Grant: $20
Typical Range: $1,000 to $10,000

Recent Grants

Note: Grants derived from fiscal 2001 Form 990.

Library-Related
5,000	Milwaukee Public Library, Milwaukee, WI

General
80,000	United Way, Milwaukee, WI
47,500	United Performing Arts Fund, Milwaukee, WI
20,182	Wisconsin Council on Economic Education, Milwaukee, WI
18,600	Boys and Girls Clubs of Greater Milwaukee, Milwaukee, WI
17,500	Florida Council on Economic Education, Tampa, FL
15,000	Florida Orchestra, Tampa, FL
15,000	Marquette Center for Family Business, Marquette, WI
15,000	Miller Park Gala
15,000	Outward Bound Inc., Garrison, NY
15,000	Wisconsin Technical College Foundation, Waunakee, WI

BAIRD FOUNDATION

Giving Contact

Catherine F. Schweitzer, Manager
Ellicott Station
PO Box 1210
Buffalo, NY 14205
Phone: (716)883-2429

Description

Founded: 1947
EIN: 166023080
Organization Type: Private Foundation
Giving Locations: NY: Western New York
Grant Types: General Support.

Donor Information

Founder: the late Flora M. Baird, the late Frank B. Baird, Jr., the late Cameron Baird, the late William C. Baird

Financial Summary

Total Giving: $659,461 (2001); $652,770 (2000); $791,222 (1999)
Giving Analysis: Giving for 2000 includes: foundation grants to United Way ($4,000)
Assets: $11,127,368 (2001); $11,703,037 (2000); $12,321,785 (1999)

Typical Recipients

Arts & Humanities: Arts Funds, Arts Institutes, Arts & Humanities-General, Historic Preservation, History & Archaeology, Libraries, Museums/Galleries, Music, Opera, Performing Arts, Public Broadcasting, Theater
Civic & Public Affairs: Botanical Gardens/Parks, Community Foundations, Economic Development, Ethnic Organizations, Civic & Public Affairs-General, Housing, Municipalities/Towns, Parades/Festivals, Professional & Trade Associations, Urban & Community Affairs, Zoos/Aquariums
Education: Arts/Humanities Education, Colleges & Universities, Engineering/Technological Education, Environmental Education, Literacy, Private Education (Precollege), Secondary Education (Private), Special Education
Environment: Air/Water Quality, Environment-General, Resource Conservation, Resource Conservation, Wildlife Protection
Health: Arthritis, Children's Health/Hospitals, Clinics/Medical Centers, Eyes/Blindness, Health Funds, Health Organizations, Hospices, Hospitals, Medical Research, Multiple Sclerosis, Public Health, Speech & Hearing
International: Foreign Educational Institutions, International Organizations
Religion: Churches
Science: Science Museums
Social Services: Animal Protection, Camps, Community Service Organizations, Food/Clothing Distribution, Homes, People with Disabilities, Recreation & Athletics, Senior Services, Social Services-General, Substance Abuse, United Funds/United Ways, Youth Organizations

Application Procedures

Initial Contact: The foundation requests applications be made in writing and include amount requested, purpose of funds sought, proof of tax-exempt status, recently audited financial statement, and a list of board members. The application must be signed by a person receiving no compensation from the organization.
Deadlines: None.

Restrictions

Prefers to award grants in the western New York area.

Foundation Officials

Arthur W. Cryer: trustee
Robert James Armstrong Irwin: trustee B Buffalo, NY 1927. ED Colgate University BA (1949); University of Buffalo (1949-1950); Babson College Institute of Finance (1952-1953). CORP AFFIL member advisory board: Manufacturers & Traders; director: Niagara Share Corp.; director, deputy chairman: ASA Ltd.; member advisory board: First Empire State Corp. NONPR AFFIL trustee: Saint Barnabas College Fund Inc.; director: University Cape Town Fund Inc.; trustee: Old Ft Niagara Association; trustee: Ridley College Scholarship Fund Inc.; director: Hauptman Woodward Medical Research Institute; trustee: Library Foundation Buffalo Erie County. CLUB AFFIL Saturn Club; University Club; Mid-Day Club; Royal Canadian Yacht Club; Buffalo Canoe Club.
William Baird Irwin: trustee
Catherine F. Schweitzer: foundation manager

Grants Analysis

Disclosure Period: calendar year ending 2001
Total Grants: $659,461
Number of Grants: 128
Average Grant: $5,152
Highest Grant: $25,000
Typical Range: $500 to $10,000

Recent Grants

Note: Grants derived from 2001 Form 990.

General

25,000	Old Fort Niagara Association, Youngstown, NY
22,000	Boys and Girls Club of Buffalo, Buffalo, NY
20,000	Boys and Girls Club of Buffalo, Buffalo, NY
20,000	Hauptman-Woodward Medical Research Institute, Buffalo, NY
16,500	Theodore Roosevelt Inaugural Historic Site, Buffalo, NY
15,000	Buffalo Green Fund, Buffalo, NY
12,500	Irish Classical Theater, Buffalo, NY
11,370	Tapestry Charter School, Buffalo, NY
10,000	Buffalo State College Foundation, Buffalo, NY
10,000	Canisius College, Buffalo, NY

GLADYS BAIRD TRUST

Giving Contact

c/o PNC Advisors
PO Box 8480
Erie, PA 16553-8480
Phone: (814)871-9229

Description

Founded: 1998
EIN: 251792867
Organization Type: Private Foundation
Giving Locations: PA
Grant Types: General Support.

Financial Summary

Total Giving: $100,929 (2001); $94,721 (2000); $71,392 (1999)
Assets: $1,413,665 (2001); $1,769,418 (2000); $2,005,885 (1999)

Typical Recipients

Arts & Humanities: Libraries
Education: Colleges & Universities
Health: Hospitals
Social Services: Emergency Relief, Homes, Volunteer Services

Additional Information

Trust(s): PNC Bank

Grants Analysis

Disclosure Period: calendar year ending 2001
Total Grants: $100,929
Number of Grants: 7
Average Grant: $11,590*
Highest Grant: $31,387
Lowest Grant: $3,320
Typical Range: $3,500 to $15,000
*Note: Average grant figure excludes highest grant.

Recent Grants

Note: Grants derived from 2001 Form 990.

Library-Related

14,586	Warren Library Association, Warren, PA

General

31,387	Warren General Hospital, Warren, PA
14,586	North Warren United Presbyterian Church, Warren, PA
14,586	Pennsylvania State University, University Park, PA
14,586	Pennsylvania State University, University Park, PA
7,878	North Warren Volunteer, North Warren, PA
3,320	NWVFD Ambulance Service, North Warren, PA

DEXTER F. AND DOROTHY H. BAKER FOUNDATION

Giving Contact

Dexter F. Baker, Trustee, Chairman
c/o Air Products & Chemicals Inc.
7201 Hamilton Blvd.
Allentown, PA 18195-1501
Phone: (610)481-7357

Description

Founded: 1988
EIN: 232453230
Organization Type: Private Foundation
Giving Locations: FL: Collier; PA: Lehigh Valley
Grant Types: General Support.

Donor Information

Founder: Dexter F. and Dorothy H. Baker

Financial Summary

Total Giving: $661,185 (2000); $407,100 (1999); $404,668 (1996)
Giving Analysis: Giving for 2000 includes: foundation grants to United Way ($10,000); foundation scholarships ($14,500) 1999: foundation scholarships ($63,000)
Assets: $13,831,310 (2000); $13,329,384 (1999); $13,861,923 (1998)
Gifts Received: $452,577 (2000); $601,780 (1998); $389,358 (1996). Note: In 1998 and 2000, contributions were received from Dexter F. Baker.

Typical Recipients

Arts & Humanities: Arts Associations & Councils, Arts Festivals, Ballet, Community Arts, Dance, Historic Preservation, History & Archaeology, Libraries, Museums/Galleries, Music, Opera, Performing Arts, Public Broadcasting, Theater
Civic & Public Affairs: Public Policy, Safety, Urban & Community Affairs, Women's Affairs
Education: Arts/Humanities Education, Colleges & Universities, Engineering/Technological Education, Education-General, Private Education (Precollege), Student Aid
Environment: Resource Conservation
Health: Health Funds, Medical Rehabilitation
Religion: Churches, Religious Welfare
Science: Science Museums
Social Services: Child Welfare, Food/Clothing Distribution, People with Disabilities, Recreation & Athletics, Scouts, Senior Services, Shelters/Homelessness, United Funds/United Ways, Volunteer Services, YMCA/YWCA/YMHA/YWHA, Youth Organizations

Application Procedures

Initial Contact: Request application form.
Deadlines: Deadline for letter of intent is March 15. Application deadline is July 15.

Additional Information

Trust(s): Mellon Bank NA

Foundation Officials

Dexter Farrington Baker: trustee B Worcester, MA 1927. ED Lehigh University BS (1950); Lehigh University MBA (1957). CORP AFFIL director: AMP Inc.

NONPR AFFIL member: National Association Manufacturers; member: Theta Chi; trustee: Harry C. and Mary M. Trexler Foundation; board associates: Muhlenberg College; member: AICHE; member: American Management Association.
Dorothy H. Baker: trustee
Ellen L. Baltz: director, trustee
Richard Shaffer, Esq.: trustee

Grants Analysis

Disclosure Period: calendar year ending 2000
Total Grants: $636,685*
Number of Grants: 31
Average Grant: $6,953*
Highest Grant: $180,000
Lowest Grant: $800
Typical Range: $1,000 to $10,000
*Note: Average grant excludes three highest grants ($442,000). Giving excludes scholarships and United Way.

Recent Grants

Note: Grants derived from 1999 Form 990.

Library-Related
4,000	Allentown Public Library, Allentown, PA

General
105,000	Muhlenberg College, Allentown, PA
102,500	Lehigh University, Bethlehem, PA
58,000	First Presbyterian Church of Allentown, Allentown, PA
40,000	Lehigh University, Bethlehem, PA -- arts scholarships
20,000	Muhlenberg College, Allentown, PA -- arts scholarships
10,000	Lehigh Valley Chamber Orchestra, Allentown, PA
10,000	Minsi Trails Boy Scouts of America, Allentown, PA
7,500	Lehigh Valley Public Broadcasting System, Bethlehem, PA
5,000	Community Music School, Allentown, PA
5,000	Koresh Dance Company, Philadelphia, PA

R. C. Baker Foundation

Giving Contact
Frank L. Scott, Chairman
PO Box 6150
Orange, CA 92863-6150
Phone: (714)750-8987

Description
Founded: 1952
EIN: 951742283
Organization Type: General Purpose Foundation
Giving Locations: western US.
Grant Types: Capital, General Support, Operating Expenses, Research, Scholarship.

Donor Information
Founder: Established in 1952 by the late R. C. Baker Sr. , the foundation takes a broad-based approach to philanthropy. Mr. Baker founded Baker International Corp. (now known as Baker Hughes), a supplier of oilfield tools and services. Because his work was centered in California and in oil-producing and mining areas, many of the foundation's grants are awarded to organizations in those locations.

Financial Summary
Total Giving: $1,200,000 (2003 approx); $1,275,000 (2002); $1,432,050 (2000)
Assets: $33,000,000 (2003 approx); $33,000,000 (2002); $37,178,830 (2000)
Gifts Received: $600,000 (1994); $590,000 (1993); $565,000 (1992)

Typical Recipients

Arts & Humanities: Ballet, History & Archaeology, Libraries, Literary Arts, Museums/Galleries, Music, Performing Arts, Public Broadcasting, Theater
Civic & Public Affairs: Botanical Gardens/Parks, Business/Free Enterprise, Chambers of Commerce, Clubs, Community Foundations, Economic Policy, Employment/Job Training, Civic & Public Affairs-General, Hispanic Affairs, Law & Justice, Legal Aid, Parades/Festivals, Public Policy, Rural Affairs, Safety, Urban & Community Affairs
Education: Arts/Humanities Education, Business Education, Business-School Partnerships, Colleges & Universities, Engineering/Technological Education, Education-General, Private Education (Precollege), Public Education (Precollege), Secondary Education (Private), Secondary Education (Public), Special Education, Student Aid
Environment: Resource Conservation
Health: Cancer, Children's Health/Hospitals, Clinics/Medical Centers, Emergency/Ambulance Services, Eyes/Blindness, Health Organizations, Hospitals, Medical Rehabilitation, Medical Research, Mental Health, Multiple Sclerosis, Nursing Services, Preventive Medicine/Wellness Organizations, Research/Studies Institutes, Single-Disease Health Associations, Speech & Hearing
International: International Peace & Security Issues
Religion: Churches, Jewish Causes, Missionary Activities (Domestic), Religious Organizations, Religious Welfare
Science: Scientific Centers & Institutes
Social Services: Big Brother/Big Sister, Camps, Child Welfare, Community Centers, Community Service Organizations, Day Care, Delinquency & Criminal Rehabilitation, Domestic Violence, Family Services, Food/Clothing Distribution, People with Disabilities, Recreation & Athletics, Senior Services, Shelters/Homelessness, Social Services-General, Substance Abuse, United Funds/United Ways, Volunteer Services, YMCA/YWCA/YMHA/YWHA, Youth Organizations

Application Procedures

Initial Contact: There are no formal application procedures. Applicants should mail a letter to the foundation.
Application Requirements: Include a description of the proposed project and anticipated results, a recently audited financial statement, amount requested, and a listing of other sources of support. Applicants should also include proof of tax-exempt status (if not listed in the IRS Cumulative List of Tax Exempt Organizations).
Deadlines: Applications should be received by May 1 and October 1.
Review Process: No interviews are conducted.

Restrictions

The foundation does not make grants to individuals or to political or lobbying groups. It also does not grant funds for endowments, loans, or capital projects of tax-supported institutions. No grants are made to organizations in the Eastern U.S.

Foundation Officials

Kenneth Dale: trustee
James H. Hickey: trustee
Frank L. Scott: chairman board trustees B Houston, TX 1915. ED University of Houston (1934).
James J. Shelton: trustee B Mayfield, KY 1916. PRIM CORP EMPL senior vice president, director: Baker International Corp. CORP AFFIL director: Epic Microwave Inc.; director: Tetra Tech Inc.
Ronald G. Turner: vice chairman board trustees B Houston, TX 1936. ED University of Houston (1958); University of Houston (1967). PRIM CORP EMPL vice president: Baker Hughes Inc.

Grants Analysis

Disclosure Period: calendar year ending 2000
Total Grants: $1,432,050
Number of Grants: 103
Average Grant: $13,903
Highest Grant: $280,000
Lowest Grant: $250
Typical Range: $500 to $10,000

Recent Grants

Note: Grants derived from 2000 Form 990.

General
280,000	Presbyterian Intercommunity Hospital Foundation, Whittier, CA
112,500	College of the Desert, Palm Desert, CA
105,700	Los Ayudantes de Naranja
100,000	Harvey Mudd College, Claremont, CA
75,000	Speech and Language Development Center, Buena Park, CA
67,000	R.C. Baker Memorial Museum, Coalinga, CA
50,000	St. Anne School, Laguna Niguel, CA
35,000	Marlborough School Foundation, Los Angeles, CA
30,000	Help for Brain Injured Children, La Habra, CA
25,350	Doheny Eye Institute, Los Angeles, CA

William G. Baker, Jr. Memorial Fund

Giving Contact
Melissa Warlon
Latrobe Building, 9th Floor
2 East Read Street
Baltimore, MD 21202
Phone: (410)332-4171
Fax: (410)837-4701

Description
Founded: 1964
EIN: 526057178
Organization Type: General Purpose Foundation
Giving Locations: MD: Baltimore
Grant Types: Capital, Endowment, General Support, Matching, Multiyear/Continuing Support, Project.

Donor Information
Founder: The fund was established in Maryland in 1964.

Financial Summary
Total Giving: $1,963,800 (2001); $1,470,770 (2000); $1,601,133 (1999)
Giving Analysis: Giving for 1998 includes: foundation grants to United Way ($55,000)
Assets: $29,026,715 (2002); $30,840,690 (2001); $43,220,680 (2000)

Typical Recipients

Arts & Humanities: Arts Associations & Councils, Arts Centers, Arts Funds, Arts Institutes, Arts Outreach, Dance, Arts & Humanities-General, Historic Preservation, History & Archaeology, Libraries, Museums/Galleries, Music, Opera, Performing Arts, Public Broadcasting, Theater
Civic & Public Affairs: African American Affairs, Botanical Gardens/Parks, Community Foundations, Economic Development, Employment/Job Training, Civic & Public Affairs-General, Housing, Legal Aid, Nonprofit Management, Parades/Festivals, Philanthropic Organizations, Urban & Community Affairs, Women's Affairs, Zoos/Aquariums
Education: Arts/Humanities Education, Business Education, Colleges & Universities, Community & Junior

Colleges, Education Funds, Education Reform, Education-General, Health & Physical Education, Literacy, Minority Education, Private Education (Precollege), Public Education (Precollege), Secondary Education (Private), Special Education, Student Aid
Environment: Resource Conservation
Health: Children's Health/Hospitals, Clinics/Medical Centers, Emergency/Ambulance Services, Eyes/Blindness, Health-General, Health Funds, Health Organizations, Heart, Hospices, Hospitals, Medical Research, Mental Health, Public Health, Speech & Hearing
Religion: Churches, Religion-General, Jewish Causes, Ministries, Religious Organizations, Religious Welfare, Synagogues/Temples
Science: Science-General, Science-General, Scientific Centers & Institutes, Scientific Research
Social Services: Child Abuse, Child Welfare, Community Centers, Community Service Organizations, Counseling, Crime Prevention, Day Care, Delinquency & Criminal Rehabilitation, Family Services, Food/Clothing Distribution, Homes, People with Disabilities, Recreation & Athletics, Scouts, Senior Services, Shelters/Homelessness, Social Services-General, Special Olympics, Substance Abuse, United Funds/United Ways, YMCA/YWCA/YMHA/YWHA, Youth Organizations

Application Procedures

Initial Contact: The foundation requests applications be made in writing.
Application Requirements: Applicants should submit five copies of a written proposal that includes a cover letter with proposal summary and amount requested; proposal narrative should include agency information including history, mission, goals, programs, future plans, organizational structure, and affiliations; detailed information concerning the purpose of the grant, including goals and objectives; need to be addressed, and activities planned to accomplish goals; and how progress will be evaluated. Attachments should include a list of the board of directors and officers, project budget, list of current donors to the proposed project, financial reports, and the copy of organization's tax-exempt letter.
Deadlines: Please call for deadlines.
Review Process: The review board usually meets four times a year and its decisions are made within three months.
Notes: The fund accepts The Association of Baltimore Area Grantmakers' Grant Application Format. The foundation requests that only organizations described in IRS sections 509(a)(1)(2) and 170(b)(1)(vii) apply.

Restrictions

No grants are made to individuals, or for loans, deficit financing, or annual campaigns. The Fund does not normally make grants for continuing operating support.

Additional Information

Grants for unique and socially significant purposes are encouraged by the Fund; educational concerns are given priority over general welfare projects.
Publications: Application Guidelines

Foundation Officials

Timothy D. Armbruster: governor PRIM NONPR EMPL president, director: Baltimore Community Foundation.
Connie Imboden: governor
J. Marshall Reid: governor, chair PRIM CORP EMPL president: Mercantile Bankshares Corp.
Walter Sondheim, Jr.: governor
Semmes Guest Walsh: governor B Annapolis, MD 1926. ED Yale University BE (1946); Harvard University MBA (1950). NONPR AFFIL director: J. L. Kernan Hospital Foundation.

Grants Analysis

Disclosure Period: calendar year ending 2001
Total Grants: $1,903,800*
Number of Grants: 135*
Average Grant: $13,088*
Highest Grant: $150,000
Lowest Grant: $500
Typical Range: $5,000 to $25,000
*Note: Giving excludes United Way. Average grant figure excludes highest grant.

Recent Grants

Note: Grants derived from 2001 Form 990.

Library-Related
25,000	Enoch Pratt Free Library, Baltimore, MD
25,000	Village Learning Place, Inc, Baltimore, MD

General
150,000	Baltimore Opera Company, Baltimore, MD
85,000	Baltimore Community Foundation, Baltimore, MD
60,000	United Way of Central Maryland, Baltimore, MD
35,000	Baltimore Symphony Orchestra, Baltimore, MD
28,500	Baltimore Community Foundation, Baltimore, MD
25,000	Baltimore Medical System, Baltimore, MD
25,000	Baltimore Museum of Art, Baltimore, MD
25,000	Baltimore Museum of Art, Baltimore, MD
25,000	Catholic Community Elementary/Middle School
25,000	Chesapeake Center for the Creative Arts, Baltimore, MD

BAKER STREET FOUNDATION

Giving Contact

Roy Bukstein, Chief Financial Officer & Director
135 Main St., No. 1140
San Francisco, CA 94105-1815
Phone: (415)904-1992

Description

Founded: 1995
EIN: 943192365
Organization Type: Private Foundation
Giving Locations: CA
Grant Types: General Support.

Donor Information

Founder: Established in 1995 by Robert N. and Mary M. Miner.

Financial Summary

Total Giving: $2,421,500 (1999); $1,822,500 (1998); $1,040,000 (1996). Note: Fiscal 1996 Giving includes scholarship ($50,000).
Giving Analysis: Giving for 1998 includes: foundation scholarships ($50,000)
Assets: $82,130,640 (1999); $39,815,186 (1998); $34,890,929 (1996)
Gifts Received: $11,087,500 (1999); $15,103,100 (1996); $1,785,000 (1994). Note: In 1999, contributions were received from Robert N. and Mary M. Miner. In 1994, contributions were received from Robert N. and Mary M. Miner.

Typical Recipients

Arts & Humanities: Arts Associations & Councils, Ballet, Ethnic & Folk Arts, Libraries, Museums/Galleries, Music, Performing Arts, Public Broadcasting, Theater

Civic & Public Affairs: Botanical Gardens/Parks, Ethnic Organizations, Civic & Public Affairs-General, Women's Affairs
Education: Afterschool/Enrichment Programs, Arts/Humanities Education, Colleges & Universities, Education-General, International Studies, Private Education (Precollege), Public Education (Precollege), Secondary Education (Private), Secondary Education (Public), Student Aid
Health: AIDS/HIV, Alzheimers Disease, Cancer, Clinics/Medical Centers
Science: Scientific Centers & Institutes
Social Services: Community Service Organizations, Family Planning, Food/Clothing Distribution, Recreation & Athletics, Youth Organizations

Application Procedures

Deadlines: June 15.

Foundation Officials

Roy Bukstein: cfo, director
Andrew Dudnick: secretary, director
Justine Miner: director
Mary Miner: president, director
Nicola Miner: director
Helen Sedwick: secretary, director

Grants Analysis

Disclosure Period: calendar year ending 1999
Total Grants: $2,421,500
Number of Grants: 42
Average Grant: $41,988*
Highest Grant: $700,000
Typical Range: $25,000 to $100,000
*Note: Average grant excludes highest grant.

Recent Grants

Note: Grants derived from 1999 Form 990.

Library-Related
200,000	San Francisco Library Foundation, San Francisco, CA

General
700,000	San Francisco Ballet, San Francisco, CA
150,000	Friends of Recreation and Parks, San Francisco, CA
150,000	San Francisco Jazz Festival, San Francisco, CA
150,000	Woodhull Institute
100,000	Memorial Sloan-Kettering Cancer Center, New York, NY
100,000	San Francisco Museum of Modern Art, San Francisco, CA
100,000	University of California San Francisco Foundation, San Francisco, CA -- cancer research
80,000	New Langton Arts, New Langton, CA
75,000	American Conservatory Theater, San Francisco, CA
50,000	French American International School, San Francisco, CA

CLAYTON BAKER TRUST

Giving Contact

John B. Powell, Jr., Trustee
2 East Read Street, Suite 100
Baltimore, MD 21202
Phone: (410)837-3555

Description

Founded: 1960
EIN: 526054237
Organization Type: Private Foundation
Giving Locations: MD: Baltimore
Grant Types: General Support, Operating Expenses, Project, Seed Money.

Donor Information

Founder: Julia C. Baker

Financial Summary

Total Giving: $668,750 (2001); $516,125 (2000); $474,500 (1999)

Giving Analysis: Giving for 2001 includes: foundation grants to United Way ($5,000); 2000: foundation grants to United Way ($10,000); 1999: foundation grants to United Way ($10,000)

Assets: $36,161,552 (2001); $11,437,547 (2000); $11,745,761 (1999)

Gifts Received: $24,243,984 (2001); $502,425 (1998); $202,675 (1994). Note: In 2001, contributions were received from the estate of Julia C. Baker. In 1998, contributions were received from Julia C. Baker.

Typical Recipients

Arts & Humanities: Libraries, Museums/Galleries, Opera, Public Broadcasting

Civic & Public Affairs: Botanical Gardens/Parks, Civil Rights, Clubs, Community Foundations, Economic Development, Employment/Job Training, Civic & Public Affairs-General, Housing, Law & Justice, Legal Aid, Parades/Festivals, Philanthropic Organizations, Public Policy, Urban & Community Affairs

Education: Colleges & Universities, Education Funds, Education Reform, Environmental Education, Education-General, Literacy, Private Education (Precollege), Science/Mathematics Education, Student Aid

Environment: Air/Water Quality, Environment-General, Protection, Resource Conservation, Wildlife Protection

Health: AIDS/HIV, Clinics/Medical Centers, Diabetes, Emergency/Ambulance Services, Health Organizations, Medical Research, Medical Training, Mental Health

International: International Peace & Security Issues

Religion: Churches, Jewish Causes, Ministries, Religious Organizations, Religious Welfare

Science: Scientific Centers & Institutes

Social Services: At-Risk Youth, Big Brother/Big Sister, Child Abuse, Child Welfare, Community Centers, Community Service Organizations, Family Planning, Family Services, Food/Clothing Distribution, Homes, People with Disabilities, Recreation & Athletics, Scouts, Senior Services, Shelters/Homelessness, Substance Abuse, United Funds/United Ways, Youth Organizations

Application Procedures

Initial Contact: Send letter requesting application form and guidelines.

Application Requirements: Applications should include a cover letter and narrative as described in the foundation's guidelines. The following attachments are required: a list of the organization's board of directors, including occupations and/or community affiliations, board committee assignments, and criteria for board selection; financial information, including the organization's current annual operating budget, funding sources for the organization (major past contributors and anticipated funding sources), recently audited financial statement, and list of other foundations to which the proposal has been submitted; an annual report (if available); examples of current relevant newpaper/magazine articles or reviews about the organization's program (if available); and proof of tax-exempt status.

Deadlines: April 5, August 5, and December 5.

Restrictions

The majority of the grants are made within the Baltimore area and seek to aid the disadvantaged through results-oriented projects with an emphasis on children's needs. Grants made outside the Baltimore area are usually limited to organizations concerned with environmental protection, population control, arms control, and nuclear disarmament.

Additional Information

Publications: Application Guidelines

Foundation Officials

Julia Clayton Baker: trustee
William C. Baker: trustee
John B. Powell, Jr.: trustee

Grants Analysis

Disclosure Period: calendar year ending 2001

Total Grants: $663,750*

Number of Grants: 42

Average Grant: $15,804

Highest Grant: $60,000

Lowest Grant: $2,000

Typical Range: $5,000 to $25,000

***Note:** Giving excludes United Way.

Recent Grants

Note: Grants derived from 2001 Form 990.

Library-Related

50,000	Village Learning Place, Inc., Baltimore, MD -- for community development and capital campaign
20,000	Enoch Pratt Free Library, Baltimore, MD -- for youth development, After-School Program at Roland Park Public School

General

60,000	Bryn Mawr School, Baltimore, MD -- for education, Julia C. Baker chair in Environmental Studies
40,000	Baltimore Community Foundation, Baltimore, MD -- for community development, Baltimore Police Foundation
35,000	Chesapeake Bay Foundation, Annapolis, MD -- for environment and Baltimore City Education Program
30,000	Fund for Educational Excellence, Baltimore, MD -- for education "Achievement First" in Baltimore public schools
25,000	Baltimore Community Foundation, Baltimore, MD -- for youth programs and A-teams
25,000	Baltimore Community Foundation, Baltimore, MD -- for youth program, PAL centers and Summer Programs
25,000	Catholic Relief Services, Baltimore, MD
25,000	Kennedy Krieger Institute, Baltimore, MD -- for health care
25,000	Shepherd's Clinic, Baltimore, MD -- for health care, endowment and relocation
20,000	American Civil Liberties Union Foundation of Maryland, Baltimore, MD -- for education and state funding for Baltimore Public Schools

GEORGE F. BAKER TRUST

Giving Contact

Ms. Rocio Suarez, Executive Director
477 Madison Avenue, Suite 1650
New York, NY 10022
Phone: (212)755-1890
Fax: (212)319-6316

Description

Founded: 1937

EIN: 136056818

Organization Type: Family Foundation

Giving Locations: NY: New York Nationally.

Grant Types: General Support, Professorship.

Donor Information

Founder: Established in 1937 by the late George F. Baker , chairman of the First National Bank of New York.

Financial Summary

Total Giving: $2,761,000 (2000); $3,337,316 (1999); $5,095,640 (1998)

Giving Analysis: Giving for 1998 includes: foundation scholarships ($80,000)

Assets: $23,999,200 (2000); $26,000,000 (1999 approx); $27,200,479 (1998)

Typical Recipients

Arts & Humanities: Arts Appreciation, Arts Centers, Ballet, Historic Preservation, History & Archaeology, Libraries, Museums/Galleries, Music, Opera, Performing Arts

Civic & Public Affairs: Clubs, Economic Development, Employment/Job Training, Civic & Public Affairs-General, Legal Aid, Philanthropic Organizations, Public Policy, Safety, Urban & Community Affairs, Women's Affairs, Zoos/Aquariums

Education: Arts/Humanities Education, Business Education, Colleges & Universities, Community & Junior Colleges, Elementary Education (Private), Engineering/Technological Education, Environmental Education, Faculty Development, Education-General, Health & Physical Education, International Studies, Medical Education, Minority Education, Private Education (Precollege), Public Education (Precollege), Religious Education, Science/Mathematics Education, Secondary Education (Private), Social Sciences Education, Special Education, Student Aid

Environment: Air/Water Quality, Environment-General, Resource Conservation, Wildlife Protection

Health: AIDS/HIV, Cancer, Children's Health/Hospitals, Clinics/Medical Centers, Diabetes, Emergency/Ambulance Services, Health-General, Heart, Hospitals, Hospitals (University Affiliated), Medical Rehabilitation, Medical Research, Prenatal Health Issues, Public Health

International: Health Care/Hospitals, Human Rights, International Environmental Issues, International Relations, International Relief Efforts, Missionary/Religious Activities

Religion: Churches, Ministries, Religious Organizations, Religious Welfare

Science: Scientific Labs, Scientific Research

Social Services: Animal Protection, At-Risk Youth, Camps, Child Welfare, Community Centers, Community Service Organizations, Crime Prevention, Family Planning, People with Disabilities, Recreation & Athletics, Social Services-General, Substance Abuse, YMCA/YWCA/YMHA/YWHA, Youth Organizations

Application Procedures

Initial Contact: Applicants should send a brief description of the proposed project. There is no formal application form.

Application Requirements: The initial letter should outline the proposed project, include the amount requested, list other sources of funding, and be signed by an authorized officer. Only the original copy of the application needs to be submitted.

Deadlines: None.

Review Process: Board meetings are held in June and November. Notification of grant approval occurs within six months following proposal receipt. No notice is sent to those applicants who do not receive funding.

Restrictions

No grants are made to individuals, or for scholarships, capital or endowment funds, fellowships, loans, or special projects.

Additional Information

Citibank, N.A. is listed as a corporate trustee of the foundation.

Publications: Annual Report

Trust(s): Citibank N.A.

Foundation Officials

Anthony K. Baker: trustee

George F. Baker, III: trustee B 1939. ED Harvard University AB (1961); Harvard University MBA (1964).

PRIM CORP EMPL general partner: Baker New York Securities ADD CORP EMPL managing partner: Cambridge Capital Fund; chief executive officer, chairman: Whitehall Corp.
Kane K. Baker: trustee
Rocio Suarez: executive director

Grants Analysis

Disclosure Period: calendar year ending 2000
Total Grants: $2,761,000*
Number of Grants: 73
Average Grant: $37,822*
Highest Grant: $250,000
Lowest Grant: $2,000
Typical Range: $1,000 to $25,000 and $50,000 to $250,000
*Note: Giving excludes scholarships.

Recent Grants

Note: Grants derived from 2001 Form 990.

General

450,000	Harvard University, Cambridge, MA
270,000	New York Hospital Cornell Medical Center, New York, NY
100,000	Drexel University, Philadelphia, PA
100,000	Nantucket Historical Association, Nantucket, MA
100,000	Sea Education Association, Inc., Woods Hole, MA
100,000	Wildlife Conservation Society, New York, NY
77,500	YMCA Palm Beaches, West Palm Beach, FL
65,000	Palm Beach Zoo, West Palm Beach, FL
62,500	Baker Boys and Girls
60,000	Brooks School, North Andover, MA

BAKEWELL CORP.

Company Headquarters

7800 Forsyth Blvd.
St. Louis, MO 63105

Company Description

Employees: 25

Operating Locations

Bakewell Corp. (MO--St. Louis)

Edward L. Bakewell, Jr. Family Foundation

Giving Contact

Richard W. Meier, Director & Secretary
7800 Forsyth Boulevard, 8th Floor
St. Louis, MO 63105
Phone: (314)862-5555
Fax: (314)862-5076

Description

Founded: 1987
EIN: 431434313
Organization Type: Corporate Foundation
Giving Locations: AR; CA; CO; IL; MD; MO; NM; VA
Grant Types: Emergency, General Support, Operating Expenses, Research.

Donor Information

Founder: Edward L. Bakewell, Jr., Edward L. Bakewell III, Bakewell Corp.

Financial Summary

Total Giving: $23,835 (2001); $24,100 (2000); $24,158 (1999)
Giving Analysis: Giving for 2000 includes: foundation grants to United Way ($750); 1999: foundation

grants to United Way ($750); foundation ($23,408) 1998: foundation grants to United Way ($750)
Assets: $467,311 (2001); $513,826 (2000); $505,673 (1999)

Typical Recipients

Arts & Humanities: Arts Outreach, Historic Preservation, History & Archaeology, Libraries, Museums/Galleries, Public Broadcasting
Civic & Public Affairs: Botanical Gardens/Parks, Economic Policy, Civic & Public Affairs-General, Public Policy, Zoos/Aquariums
Education: Arts/Humanities Education, Colleges & Universities, Continuing Education, Education-General, International Studies, Private Education (Precollege)
Environment: Research, Resource Conservation
Health: Cancer, Children's Health/Hospitals, Emergency/Ambulance Services, Geriatric Health, Long-Term Care, Medical Research, Multiple Sclerosis, Public Health, Speech & Hearing
International: Health Care/Hospitals, International Relief Efforts, Missionary/Religious Activities
Religion: Churches, Religion-General, Religious Organizations, Religious Organizations, Religious Welfare
Science: Science Museums, Scientific Centers & Institutes
Social Services: Child Welfare, Counseling, Day Care, People with Disabilities, Scouts, Substance Abuse, United Funds/United Ways

Application Procedures

Initial Contact: Send written application.
Application Requirements: Applications should include explanation of the merits of the specific request complete with supporting literature.
Deadlines: Applications are accepted between September 1 and November 30.

Additional Information

Publications: Application Guidelines

Corporate Officials

Edward L. Bakewell, III: chairman, chief executive officer PRIM CORP EMPL chairman, chief executive officer: Bakewell Corp.
Thomas J. Bannister, Jr.: president PRIM CORP EMPL president: Bakewell Corp. ADD CORP EMPL president: Bakewell Investment Co.
Ron Horak: controller PRIM CORP EMPL controller: Bakewell Corp.

Foundation Officials

Edward L. Bakewell, III: president, director (see above)
Richard W. Meier: director, secretary

Grants Analysis

Disclosure Period: calendar year ending 2001
Total Grants: $23,835
Number of Grants: 40
Average Grant: $533*
Highest Grant: $2,500
Typical Range: $100 to $1,000
*Note: Average grant figure excludes highest grant.

Recent Grants

Note: Grants derived from 2001 Form 990.

Library-Related

1,000	Friends of the Saint Louis Public Library, St. Louis, MO -- operating funds

General

2,500	Ashoka, Arlington, VA -- for operating funds
1,500	American Red Cross Armed Forces Emergency Services, Falls Church, VA -- public education, emergency relief and blood services

1,500	St. Louis Children's Hospital, St. Louis, MO -- research/general operating funds
1,375	St. Louis Zoo, St. Louis, MO -- operating funds
1,360	St. Louis Science Center Foundation, St. Louis, MO -- operating funds
1,000	Cardinal Glennon Children's Hospital, St. Louis, MO -- operating funds
1,000	Central Institute for the Deaf, St. Louis, MO -- education/services for the deaf
1,000	Enterprise Mentors International, St. Louis, MO -- for operating funds
1,000	Environic Foundation International, Inc., Chevy Chase, MD -- for operating funds
1,000	Heifer International, Little Rock, AR -- for operating funds

FRED BALDWIN MEMORIAL FOUNDATION

Giving Contact

Janis Reischmann, Grants Administrator
c/o Hawaii Community Foundation
900 Fort Street Mall, Suite 1300
Honolulu, HI 96813
Phone: (808)566-5570
Fax: (808)521-6286

Description

Founded: 1910
EIN: 990075264
Organization Type: Private Foundation
Giving Locations: HI: Maui County
Grant Types: Capital, General Support, Project.

Donor Information

Founder: the late Fred Baldwin, members of the Baldwin family

Financial Summary

Total Giving: $327,500 (2001); $329,082 (2000); $240,384 (1999). Note: 1997 Giving includes United Way ($5,016).
Giving Analysis: Giving for 1999 includes: foundation grants to United Way ($2,000) 1997: foundation grants to United Way ($5,016)
Assets: $6,162,045 (2001); $7,269,533 (2000); $7,764,413 (1999)

Typical Recipients

Arts & Humanities: Arts Associations & Councils, Arts Centers, Community Arts, Dance, Arts & Humanities-General, History & Archaeology, Libraries, Museums/Galleries, Music, Opera, Performing Arts, Public Broadcasting, Theater, Visual Arts
Civic & Public Affairs: Botanical Gardens/Parks, Clubs, Community Foundations, Economic Development, Economic Policy, Employment/Job Training, Civic & Public Affairs-General, Law & Justice, Legal Aid, Parades/Festivals, Professional & Trade Associations, Urban & Community Affairs, Women's Affairs
Education: Arts/Humanities Education, Environmental Education, Education-General, Literacy, Private Education (Precollege), Secondary Education (Public), Special Education
Environment: Environment-General, Resource Conservation
Health: AIDS/HIV, Cancer, Children's Health/Hospitals, Clinics/Medical Centers, Diabetes, Health Organizations, Hospices, Hospitals, Medical Rehabilitation, Nutrition, Single-Disease Health Associations
International: International Affairs, International Relations
Religion: Churches, Dioceses, Ministries, Religious Organizations, Religious Welfare
Social Services: Animal Protection, At-Risk Youth, Big Brother/Big Sister, Child Welfare, Community Service Organizations, Crime Prevention, Emergency

Relief, Family Planning, Family Services, Food/Clothing Distribution, People with Disabilities, Scouts, United Funds/United Ways, Volunteer Services, YMCA/YWCA/YMHA/YWHA, Youth Organizations

Application Procedures

Initial Contact: Send cover letter and full proposal.
Application Requirements: Include a description of organization, amount requested, purpose of funds sought, recently audited financial statement, and proof of tax-exempt status. Also evaluation methods.
Deadlines: January 2 and May 1.

Restrictions

Does not support individuals, political or lobbying groups, or organizations outside operating areas.

Foundation Officials

Bennet M. Baldwin: assistant treasurer, trustee
John C. Baldwin: secretary, trustee B 1937. PRIM CORP EMPL treasurer: HNJ2 Inc. CORP AFFIL officer: Walker Industries Ltd.
Kristina E. Lyons: trustee
Michael H. Lyons, II: president, trustee
Shaun L. Lyons: vice president, assistant secretary, trustee
Elizabeth Norcross: trustee
Wendy Rice Peterson: trustee
Janis A. Reischmann: giving contact B 1955.
Henry F. Rice: treasurer, trustee
Claire C. Sanford: trustee
Mary Cameron Sanford: trustee B 1930. PRIM CORP EMPL chairman: Maui Land & Pineapple Co. CORP AFFIL pub: Maui News; chairman: Maui Publishing Co. Ltd.; director: Haleakala Ranch Co.; director: Kapalua Land Co. Ltd.
Emily B. Young: trustee

Grants Analysis

Disclosure Period: calendar year ending 2001
Total Grants: $327,500
Number of Grants: 49
Average Grant: $6,683
Highest Grant: $15,000
Lowest Grant: $500
Typical Range: $2,000 to $10,000

Recent Grants

Note: Grants derived from 2000 Form 990.

General
22,000	Makawao Union Church
12,500	Maui Arts and Cultural Center, Maui, HI
11,000	Hui No'Eau Visual Arts Center, Makawao, HI
10,000	Community Work Day Program, Puunene, HI
10,000	Friends of Maui Drug Court, Maui, HI
10,000	Hale Makua Foundation, Kahului, HI
10,000	Hospice Hawaii, Honolulu, HI
10,000	Hospice Maui Inc, Maui, HI
10,000	Maui Food Bank Inc, Maui, HI
10,000	Na Leo Pulama O Maui Inc, Maui, HI

L. G. BALFOUR FOUNDATION

Giving Contact

Kerry H. Sullivan, Director, Grants
Care of Fleet National Bank
75 State Street, 7th Floor
Mail Code: MABOFO7B
Boston, MA 02109
Phone: (781)346-2484
Fax: (781)346-2495

Alternate Contact

Christine Feeney
Phone: (617)346-2479

Description

Founded: 1973
EIN: 046397138
Organization Type: General Purpose Foundation
Giving Locations: MA: New England area.
Grant Types: Capital, General Support, Scholarship.

Donor Information

Founder: Lloyd G. Balfour (d.1978) founded and was the sole owner of the L. G. Balfour Company, producer of class rings and fraternity pins. After Mr. Balfour's death in 1973, the company was managed for a number of years by the Bank of New England, first as executor of L. G. Balfour's estate, and then as trustee of the L. G. Balfour Foundation, which was established in 1973. The company was sold in 1983, but the foundation retains a significant financial interest.

Financial Summary

Total Giving: $2,327,400 (1999); $3,088,000 (1998); $3,275,000 (1995 approx)
Giving Analysis: Giving for 1999 includes: foundation scholarships ($275,000)
Assets: $115,006,613 (1999); $102,120,739 (1998); $56,000,000 (1995 approx)

Typical Recipients

Arts & Humanities: Libraries
Education: Colleges & Universities, Education Associations, Education Funds, Minority Education, Public Education (Precollege), Student Aid
Health: Hospitals
Social Services: Day Care

Application Procedures

Initial Contact: Applicants should submit a letter of intent to the trustee for review and response before a formal grant proposal is prepared.
Application Requirements: The letter should describe the nature and objective of the program to be funded and include a list of the organization's board members or trustees along with the names and qualifications of officers and staff; evidence of tax-exempt status; detailed budget for the projects; Form 990 and audited financial statement for the most recent fiscal year; statement of other sources of funding, both private and public; and a statement of agreement to report on the results of the project and on the expenditure of grant funds.
Deadlines: Proposals should be submitted by January 31 for consideration in the spring, or by July 31 for consideration in the fall.
Review Process: The foundation's distribution committee usually meets twice each year, in the spring and fall.

Restrictions

No grants are made to individuals or private foundations. Grant proposals for capital projects such as construction, renovation, or equipment purchase will be considered, but will be given less priority.

Additional Information

Fleet Investment Management is listed as corporate trustee for the foundation.
Publications: Grant Application Procedures

Foundation Officials

Kerry H. Sullivan: trustee officer, director grant making PRIM CORP EMPL vice president: Fleet Investment Services.

Grants Analysis

Disclosure Period: calendar year ending 1999
Total Grants: $2,052,400*
Number of Grants: 25
Average Grant: $82,096
Highest Grant: $250,000
Typical Range: $25,000 to $250,000
***Note:** Giving excludes scholarships.

BALL BROTHERS FOUNDATION

Giving Contact

Douglas A. Bakken, Executive Director
222 South Mulberry
PO Box 1408
Muncie, IN 47308
Phone: (765)741-5500
Fax: (765)741-5518
E-mail: ballfoundation@yahoo.com

Description

Founded: 1926
EIN: 350882856
Organization Type: Family Foundation
Giving Locations: IN: East Central Indiana, Muncie
Grant Types: Capital, General Support, Operating Expenses, Project.

Donor Information

Founder: Established in 1926 by Edmund B. Ball , Frank C. Ball , Lucius L. Ball , and William A. Ball , all of whom are deceased. The estate of Edmund B. Ball provided the foundation's initial endowment, with securities valued at about $3.5 million. His brothers subsequently donated additional money and securities to augment the foundation's assets. The foundation is affiliated with the George and Frances Ball Foundation. Edmund Burke Ball was one of the founders of the Ball Brothers Company, which grew over the years to become the Ball Corporation, a large and diversified manufacturer whose best-known product is the Ball glass preserving jar.

Financial Summary

Total Giving: $4,650,000 (2002 approx); $4,400,000 (2001); $4,656,695 (2000)
Giving Analysis: Giving for 2000 includes: foundation grants to United Way ($85,000)
Assets: $113,767,460 (2000); $100,000,000 (1999); $111,247,784 (1998)
Gifts Received: $1,100,000 (2000); $5,000 (1992). Note: In 2000, contributions were received from the estate of Edmund F. Ball.

Typical Recipients

Arts & Humanities: Arts Associations & Councils, Arts Centers, Arts Funds, Arts Outreach, Arts & Humanities-General, Historic Preservation, History & Archaeology, Libraries, Museums/Galleries, Music, Public Broadcasting, Theater, Visual Arts
Civic & Public Affairs: Botanical Gardens/Parks, Clubs, Community Foundations, Economic Development, Civic & Public Affairs-General, Housing, Municipalities/Towns, Nonprofit Management, Parades/Festivals, Philanthropic Organizations, Public Policy, Rural Affairs, Urban & Community Affairs
Education: Arts/Humanities Education, Business Education, Business-School Partnerships, Colleges & Universities, Economic Education, Education Funds, Elementary Education (Public), Engineering/Technological Education, Education-General, International Exchange, International Studies, Journalism/Media Education, Literacy, Private Education (Precollege), Public Education (Precollege), Science/Mathematics Education, Secondary Education (Public), Student Aid
Environment: Environment-General, Resource Conservation
Health: AIDS/HIV, Children's Health/Hospitals, Diabetes, Health Organizations, Heart, Hospitals, Medical Rehabilitation, Preventive Medicine/Wellness Organizations, Public Health
Religion: Churches, Ministries, Religious Organizations, Religious Welfare

Social Services: Animal Protection, Community Service Organizations, Family Services, People with Disabilities, Recreation & Athletics, Scouts, Social Services-General, Special Olympics, United Funds/United Ways, United Funds/United Ways, YMCA/YWCA/YMHA/YWHA, Youth Organizations

Application Procedures

Initial Contact: Grant seekers can approach the foundation in one of three ways: send a preliminary proposal, and ask for an initial reaction in thirty days; send a complete proposal; or ask for a personal visit to discuss a potential grant request with the Executive Director.

Application Requirements: A preliminary proposal should be one to two pages (not including the cover letter) and include a description of idea; need; who will do the work; and what the project will cost. A complete proposal should be two to five pages (not including cover letter) and include a succinct description of request; an outline; reason for need; when it will be accomplished; who will undertake work; a program budget; an organization budget; evaluation procedures including who will be responsible for evaluation; and an IRS not-for-profit determination letter.

Deadlines: None, but foundation prefers that proposals be submitted between February and May.

Review Process: The grants committee and board of directors review grant applications at committee and board meetings during the year. Grant making takes place April through December each year.

Restrictions

The foundation does not fund individuals, booster organizations, direct scholarships to individuals, or services which the community-at-large should underwrite (e.g. roads, buses, etc.).

Additional Information

The foundation reports that, in addition to grant making, it also offers proposal writing assistance and conducts seminars and workshops.

Publications: Application Guidelines; General Information

Foundation Officials

Douglas Adair Bakken: executive director B Breckenridge, MN 1939. ED North Dakota State University BS (1961); University of Nebraska MA (1967). NONPR AFFIL fellow: Society American Archivists; member: Sports and Hobby Development Group Inc.; member: Minnesota Cultural Foundation; member: Muncie Rotary Club; president: Indiana Donors Alliance Foundation; president: Indiana Dunes Alliance Foundation; member: Independent Colleges Indiana.

Frank E. Ball: vice president, director B 1938. PRIM CORP EMPL president: Minnetrista Corp. CORP AFFIL president: B B & S Properties Inc.

William M. Bracken: director B 1942. ED Carleton College BA (1963); University of Michigan MBA (1965). PRIM CORP EMPL chairman: Northco Corp. CORP AFFIL Northco Investment Group Inc.; Northco Minerals Inc.; Northco Financial Corp.

John Wesley Fisher: president, director B Walland, TN July 15, 1915. ED University of Tennessee BS (1938); Harvard University MBA (1942). PRIM CORP EMPL chairman emeritus: Ball Corp. CORP AFFIL director: Minnetrista Corp.; president: Nature's Catch Inc.; president: Fisher Properties Indiana; director: Kindel Furniture Co.; chairman: CID Partners LP; president: Cardinal Health Systems; chairman: CID Equity Partners; director: America National Trust & Investment Co.; partner: Blackwood & Nichols Corp. NONPR AFFIL member: Muncie Chamber of Commerce; member, director: National Association Manufacturers; member: Indiana Academy; member: Indiana Chamber of Commerce; member: Glass Packaging Institute; member: Grocery Manufacturer Association; member: Delta Tau Delta; chairman board directors: Ball Memorial Hospital; member: Conference Board. CLUB AFFIL Royal Poinciana

Country Club; Skyline Club; Rotary Club; Naples National Golf Club; Naples Yacht Club; Muncie Club; Delaware Country Club; Indianapolis Athletic Club; Columbia Club.

Douglas J. Foy: treasurer, assistant secretary, director PRIM CORP EMPL secretary, director: Pri Pak Inc.

Lucina B. Moxley: director

William L. Peterson: secretary, director

John J. Pruis: director B Borculo, MI 1923. ED Western Michigan University BS (1947); Northwestern University MA (1949); Northwestern University PhD (1951). NONPR AFFIL member: Speech Community Association; director: United Way Delaware County; member: Omicron Delta Kappa; member: Phi Delta Kappa; director: Muncie Symphony Association; director: North Central Association; member: Muncie Chamber of Commerce; director: Big Brothers/Big Sisters; director: Indiana Legal Foundation; chairman, director: Ball Memorial Hospital; member: Beta Gamma Sigma; member: American Association Higher Education. CLUB AFFIL Rotary Club; Blue Key Club.

William L. Skinner: director

Grants Analysis

Disclosure Period: calendar year ending 2000
Total Grants: $4,571,695*
Number of Grants: 47
Average Grant: $29,404*
Highest Grant: $1,890,964
Typical Range: $3,000 to $100,000
*Note: Giving excludes United Way. Average grant figure excludes two highest grants ($3,248,495).

Recent Grants

Note: Grants derived from 2000 Form 990.

Library-Related

50,000	Muncie Public Library, Muncie, IN

General

1,890,964	Minnetrista Cultural Foundation, Muncie, IN
1,357,531	Ball State University Art Museum, Muncie, IN -- gift of Art collection
127,000	Masonic Community Building Foundation, Muncie, IN -- transition funding grant
100,000	Ball State University Foundation, Muncie, IN -- Muncie Center for the Arts Fund
100,000	Ball State University Foundation, Muncie, IN -- Above and Beyond General Campaign
100,000	Ball State University Foundation, Muncie, IN -- Community Wellness/Fisher Initiative
85,000	United Way Delaware County, Muncie, IN
80,000	Sports and Hobby Development Group, Muncie, IN
70,000	Community Foundation of Muncie-Delaware County, Muncie, IN -- Litly Cape initiative
70,000	YMCA Camp Crosley

GEORGE AND FRANCES BALL FOUNDATION

Giving Contact

Joyce M. Beck, Administrative Assistant
PO Box 1408
Muncie, IN 47308
Phone: (765)741-5500
Fax: (317)741-5518
E-mail: jjpcuis@iquest.net

Description

Founded: 1937
EIN: 356033917
Organization Type: General Purpose Foundation
Giving Locations: IN: Delaware County, East Central Indiana, Muncie
Grant Types: Capital, Challenge, Conference/Seminar, General Support, Loan, Multiyear/Continuing Support, Operating Expenses, Project.

Donor Information

Founder: Established in 1937 by the late George A. Ball .

Financial Summary

Total Giving: $4,500,000 (2003); $4,400,000 (2002); $4,548,500 (2001)
Giving Analysis: Giving for 2000 includes: foundation scholarships ($7,000); foundation matching gifts ($15,000) foundation grants to United Way ($115,000)
Assets: $88,000,000 (2003 approx); $88,000,000 (2002); $97,422,000 (2000)

Typical Recipients

Arts & Humanities: Arts Associations & Councils, Arts Centers, Arts Festivals, Arts Funds, Arts Outreach, Film & Video, Historic Preservation, History & Archaeology, Libraries, Museums/Galleries, Music, Public Broadcasting, Visual Arts

Civic & Public Affairs: Botanical Gardens/Parks, Clubs, Community Foundations, Economic Development, Civic & Public Affairs-General, Housing, Municipalities/Towns, Parades/Festivals, Philanthropic Organizations, Safety, Urban & Community Affairs

Education: Arts/Humanities Education, Business Education, Colleges & Universities, Economic Education, Education Funds, Education Reform, Environmental Education, Faculty Development, Education-General, Leadership Training, Medical Education, Minority Education, Public Education (Precollege), Science/Mathematics Education, Secondary Education (Public), Vocational & Technical Education

Environment: Air/Water Quality, Environment-General, Resource Conservation

Health: Children's Health/Hospitals, Emergency/Ambulance Services, Health Organizations, Hospitals, Medical Rehabilitation, Medical Research

Religion: Ministries, Religious Welfare

Social Services: Big Brother/Big Sister, Community Centers, Community Service Organizations, Crime Prevention, Day Care, Emergency Relief, Family Planning, Family Services, Food/Clothing Distribution, People with Disabilities, Recreation & Athletics, Scouts, Special Olympics, Substance Abuse, United Funds/United Ways, YMCA/YWCA/YMHA/YWHA, Youth Organizations, Youth Organizations

Application Procedures

Initial Contact: Applications should be addressed to the administrative assistant of the foundation.

Application Requirements: Applications should include a complete description of the project, budget, time frame, amount requested and brief rationale, and a copy of the organization's IRS tax exemption letter.

Deadlines: None.

Notes: Grants for operational expenses and budget emergencies are seldom made.

Restrictions

The foundation does not make grants to individuals.

Foundation Officials

Stefan Stolen Anderson: director B Madison, WI 1934. ED Harvard University AB (1956); University of

Chicago MBA (1960). PRIM CORP EMPL chairman, chief executive officer: First Merchants Corp. CORP AFFIL director: DE Advancement Corp.; director: Maxon Corp. CLUB AFFIL Rotary Club.

Joyce M. Beck: administrative assistant

Frank A. Bracken: president, director B 1934. PRIM CORP EMPL attorney: Bingham, Summers, Welsh & Spilman ADD CORP EMPL under secretary: Department Interior. CORP AFFIL director: Ball Corp.; chairman: Ball InCon Glass Packaging Corp.

Douglas J. Foy: treasurer, assistant secretary PRIM CORP EMPL secretary, director: Pri Pak Inc.

John J. Pruis: executive vice president, director B Borculo, MI 1923. ED Western Michigan University BS (1947); Northwestern University MA (1949); Northwestern University PhD (1951). NONPR AFFIL member: Speech Community Association; director: United Way Delaware County; member: Omicron Delta Kappa; member: Phi Delta Kappa; director: Muncie Symphony Association; director: North Central Association; member: Muncie Chamber of Commerce; director: Big Brothers/Big Sisters; director: Indiana Legal Foundation; chairman, director: Ball Memorial Hospital; member: Beta Gamma Sigma; member: American Association Higher Education. CLUB AFFIL Rotary Club; Blue Key Club.

Samuel L. Reed: director PRIM CORP EMPL partner: DeFur, Voran, Hanley, Radcliff, Reed.

Robert M. Smitson: director B 1936. ED Purdue University BSME (1958). PRIM CORP EMPL chief executive officer: Maxon Corp. CORP AFFIL director: Dalton Foundries Inc.; vice chairman: First Merchants Bank NA.

Grants Analysis

Disclosure Period: calendar year ending 2001
Total Grants: $4,548,552*
Number of Grants: 46
Average Grant: $30,000*
Highest Grant: $1,000,000
Lowest Grant: $1,500
Typical Range: $5,000 to $50,000
***Note:** Grants analysis provided by foundation.

Recent Grants

Note: Grants derived from 2000 Form 990.

Library-Related

100,000	Muncie Public Library, Muncie, IN -- capital campaign
15,000	Red Trail Conservancy, Inc., Muncie, IN -- for operations
5,000	West Jay Community Center, Inc., Dunkirk, IN -- capital campaign
3,000	Junior Achievement of Central Indiana, Muncie, IN -- for operations

General

1,000,000	Ball State University Foundation, Muncie, IN -- capital campaign
856,255	Minnetrista Cultural Foundation, Muncie, IN -- Oakhurst Gardens
500,000	Keuka College, Keuka Park, NY -- capital campaign
115,000	United Way Delaware County, Muncie, IN -- unrestricted
100,000	Indiana University Foundation, Bloomington, IN -- Muncie Center for Medical Education
60,000	Indiana Nature Conservancy, Indianapolis, IN -- Geography of Hope Capital Campaign
50,000	Berea College, Berea, KY -- unrestricted
50,000	BMH Foundation, Muncie, IN -- for community legacy campaign
50,000	Delaware Advancement Corporation, Muncie, IN -- for Chamber of Commerce incubator
50,000	Delaware County Historical Alliance, Muncie, IN -- for Chamber of Commerce incubator

BALLET MAKERS

Company Headquarters

20-10 Maple Avenue
Fair Lawn, NJ 07410
Web: http://www.balletmakers.com

Company Description

Employees: 600
SIC(s): 2200 Textile Mill Products, 3100 Leather & Leather Products.

Operating Locations

Ballet Makers (NJ--Totowa)

Capezio/Ballet Makers Dance Foundation

Giving Contact

Jane Remer, Grants & Program Director
Capezio/Ballet Makers Dance Foundation
1 Campus Road
Totowa, NJ 07512
Phone: (973)595-9000
Fax: (973)595-0341

Description

Founded: 1953
EIN: 136161198
Organization Type: Corporate Foundation
Giving Locations: nationally.
Grant Types: Award, General Support, Project.

Financial Summary

Total Giving: $103,067 (1999); $95,500 (1998); $85,751 (1995)
Giving Analysis: Giving for 1999 includes: foundation ($103,067)
Assets: $33,147 (1999); $36,687 (1998); $1,407 (1995)
Gifts Received: $100,000 (1999); $100,000 (1998); $84,000 (1995). Note: In 1999, contributions were received from were received from Ballet Makers.

Typical Recipients

Arts & Humanities: Arts Associations & Councils, Arts Funds, Arts Outreach, Dance, Film & Video, Arts & Humanities-General, Libraries, Music, Performing Arts, Public Broadcasting, Theater
Civic & Public Affairs: Employment/Job Training, Civic & Public Affairs-General
Education: Arts/Humanities Education, Colleges & Universities, Education-General
Religion: Churches

Application Procedures

Initial Contact: Send letter requesting application and cover sheet/form.
Application Requirements: In addition to cover sheet/form and application, applicants must provide an audited financial statement, proof of tax-exempt status, a list of the board of directors, and other sources of support.
Deadlines: April 1.

Restrictions

Does not support individuals, religious organizations for sectarian purposes, political or lobbying groups, or organizations outside operating areas.

Additional Information

Grants are limited to service organizations engaged in the promotion of dance in America. Cover sheet/form must accompany application. Company also sponsors the Capezio Dance Award, which is given at the discretion of the trustees and not open for application.

Corporate Officials

Anthony Giacoio: chief executive officer, director PRIM CORP EMPL chief executive officer, director: Ballet Makers.
Nick Terlizzi, Jr.: chairman, director PRIM CORP EMPL chairman, director: Ballet Makers.

Foundation Officials

Robert O. Carr: director
Anthony Giacoio: secretary (see above)
Donald Terlizzi: director PRIM CORP EMPL vice chairman: Ballet Makers.
Nick Terlizzi, Jr.: vice president (see above)

Grants Analysis

Disclosure Period: calendar year ending 1999
Total Grants: $103,067
Number of Grants: 73
Average Grant: $1,250*
Highest Grant: $13,000
Typical Range: $500 to $3,500
***Note:** Average grant excludes highest grant

Recent Grants

Note: Grants derived from 1999 Form 990.

Library-Related

1,000	New York Public Library, New York, NY

General

13,000	Dance USA, Washington, DC
4,750	American College, Bryn Mawr, PA
3,750	American Dance Festival, New York, NY
3,250	Jacob's Pillow Dance Festival, Lee, MA
2,500	Joyce Theater, New York, NY
2,000	Dance Theater Workshop, New York, NY
1,500	New York Foundation for Arts, New York, NY
1,500	Pentacle, New York, NY
1,250	Brooklyn Academy of Music, Brooklyn, NY
1,000	Dance Alliance, Columbus, OH

BALTIMORE EQUITY SOCIETY

Company Headquarters

Baltimore, MD

Company Description

Employees: 10

Baltimore Equitable Insurance Foundation

Giving Contact

Sharon Woodward, President, Chief Executive Officer
21 N. Eutaw Street
Baltimore, MD 21201
Phone: (410)727-1794
Fax: (410)539-1073

Description

EIN: 521645633
Organization Type: Corporate Foundation
Giving Locations: MD
Grant Types: General Support.

Financial Summary

Total Giving: $207,500 (2001); $200,730 (2000); $210,200 (1999)
Giving Analysis: Giving for 2001 includes: foundation grants to United Way ($50,000); 2000: foundation grants to United Way ($50,000); foundation

($150,730); 1999: foundation grants to United Way ($50,000); foundation ($160,200);
Assets: $4,396,453 (2001); $4,324,556 (2000); $4,492,145 (1999)
Gifts Received: $305,920 (2001); $611,919 (1999); $294,316 (1998). Note: In 1998, 1999 and 2001, contributions were received from Baltimore Equitable Society.

Typical Recipients

Arts & Humanities: Libraries, Museums/Galleries, Public Broadcasting
Civic & Public Affairs: Community Foundations, Housing, Safety, Urban & Community Affairs
Education: Religious Education, Student Aid
Religion: Jewish Causes, Religious Welfare
Social Services: Crime Prevention, Recreation & Athletics, United Funds/United Ways

Application Procedures

Initial Contact: The foundation has no formal grant application procedure or application form.
Deadlines: Jan. 1, April 1, July 1, and October 1.

Restrictions

Foundation supports Maryland area organizations only.

Corporate Officials

Stephen J. Bernhardt: chairman, president, chief executive officer, chief financial officer PRIM CORP EMPL chairman, president, chief executive officer, chief financial officer: Balt Equity Soc.

Foundation Officials

Richard O. Berndt: director
Stephen J. Bernhardt: president, treasurer (see above)
Anthony L. Brennan: director
George L. Bunting: director
M. Jenkins Cromwell, Jr.: director CORP AFFIL director: Provident Bank of Maryland; director: Provident Bankshares Corp.
Edward A. Crooke: director B 1938. ED University of Maryland BS (1968); Loyola College MBA (1971). CORP AFFIL director: First Maryland Bancorp; director: First National Bank Maryland Inc.; director: Constellation Energy Group Inc.; chairman: BGE Energy Projects & Services; chairman: BGE Home Products & Services Inc.
Edward K. Dunn, Jr.: director
Edward K. Dunn, Jr.: director
George B. Hess, Jr.: director
Howard D. Jones, III: secretary
Judy J. Mohraz: director
Betsy Nelson: director
Philip J. Raub: director
James S. Riepe: director
Sharon V. Woodward: president, treasurer

Grants Analysis

Disclosure Period: calendar year ending 2001
Total Grants: $157,500*
Number of Grants: 18
Average Grant: $8,750
Highest Grant: $20,000
Lowest Grant: $2,500
Typical Range: $5,000 to $10,000
***Note:** Giving excludes United Way.

Recent Grants

Note: Grants derived from 2000 Form 990.

Library-Related
10,000	Enoch Pratt Free Library, Baltimore, MD -- family place program

General
50,000	United Way of Central Maryland, Baltimore, MD -- for charitable and educational programs
30,000	Baltimore Police Department, Baltimore,

	MD -- police athletic league for Baltimore City youth
10,000	Baltimore Neighborhood Collaborative, Baltimore, MD -- technical support for community, building initiatives and neighborhood associations
10,000	Fire Museum of Maryland, Lutherville, MD -- education outreach on fire safety and prevention program
10,000	Institute for Christian and Jewish Studies, Baltimore, MD -- ICJS high school general project
10,000	St. Ambrose Housing Aid Center, Baltimore, MD -- homeownership counseling program
10,000	St. Ambrose Housing Aid Center, Baltimore, MD -- homesharing program
10,000	South East Community Organization, Baltimore, MD -- crime prevention and public safety program
7,500	The Baltimore Mentoring Partnership, Baltimore, MD -- workplace recruitment campaign 2000
7,500	Fire Museum of Maryland, Lutherville, MD -- educational program including Junior Fire Warden Program II

JOHN ERNEST BAMBERGER AND RUTH ELEANOR BAMBERGER MEMORIAL FOUNDATION

Giving Contact

Eleanor Roser, Chairman
136 South Main Street, Suite 418
Salt Lake City, UT 84101-1690
Phone: (801)364-2045
Fax: (801)322-5284

Description

Founded: 1947
EIN: 876116540
Organization Type: Private Foundation
Giving Locations: UT: Salt Lake City
Grant Types: Loan, Multiyear/Continuing Support, Operating Expenses, Scholarship.

Donor Information

Founder: Established in 1947 by Ernest Bamberger, the late Eleanor F. Bamberger .

Financial Summary

Total Giving: $995,857 (2001); $1,109,661 (2000); $1,150,312 (1998)
Giving Analysis: Giving for 2000 includes: foundation scholarships ($105,736); 1998: foundation grants to United Way ($2,000) foundation scholarships ($99,027)
Assets: $25,892,584 (2001); $30,093,433 (2000); $27,966,977 (1998)

Typical Recipients

Arts & Humanities: Community Arts, History & Archaeology, Libraries, Museums/Galleries, Performing Arts
Civic & Public Affairs: Botanical Gardens/Parks, Clubs, Economic Development, Civic & Public Affairs-General, Housing, Legal Aid, Municipalities/Towns, Native American Affairs, Public Policy, Safety, Urban & Community Affairs
Education: Business Education, Colleges & Universities, Community & Junior Colleges, Elementary Education (Public), Education-General, International Exchange, Legal Education, Literacy, Medical

Education, Private Education (Precollege), Public Education (Precollege), Science/Mathematics Education, Secondary Education (Private), Secondary Education (Public), Social Sciences Education, Special Education
Environment: Environment-General, Resource Conservation, Resource Conservation
Health: Alzheimers Disease, Cancer, Children's Health/Hospitals, Clinics/Medical Centers, Emergency/Ambulance Services, Eyes/Blindness, Health-General, Health Organizations, Hospices, Hospitals, Long-Term Care, Mental Health, Multiple Sclerosis, Nursing Services, Public Health, Respiratory, Single-Disease Health Associations
Religion: Churches, Jewish Causes, Religious Organizations, Religious Welfare
Science: Science Museums
Social Services: Child Welfare, Community Service Organizations, Counseling, Crime Prevention, Domestic Violence, Family Planning, Family Services, Food/Clothing Distribution, Homes, People with Disabilities, Sexual Abuse, Shelters/Homelessness, Social Services-General, Special Olympics, Substance Abuse, United Funds/United Ways, YMCA/YWCA/YMHA/YWHA, Youth Organizations

Application Procedures

Initial Contact: Send a brief letter of inquiry., 6 copies, with copies of 501c3 and 3 copies of last audit.
Deadlines: Each year in January.

Additional Information

Provides undergraduate scholarships for student nurses.

Foundation Officials

Clifford L. Ashton: mem
Clarence Bamberger, Jr.: mem
Margaret D. Olwell: chairperson
William H. Olwell: secretary, treasurer
Roy William Simmons: mem B Portland, OR January 24, 1916. ED University of Utah. PRIM CORP EMPL chairman, director: Zions First National Bank. CORP AFFIL director: O C Tanner Co.; chairman: Zion Bancorp; director: Mountain Fuel Supply Co.; director: Questar Corp.; director: Beneficial Life Insurance Co.; director: Ellison Ranching Co. NONPR AFFIL member: Salt Lake City Chamber of Commerce; member: Sigma Pi.

Grants Analysis

Disclosure Period: calendar year ending 2001
Total Grants: $880,280*
Number of Grants: 87
Average Grant: $10,118
Highest Grant: $25,000
Lowest Grant: $1,000
Typical Range: $5,000 to $20,000
***Note:** Giving excludes scholarships.

Recent Grants

Note: Grants derived from 2001 Form 990.

General
25,000	Nature Conservancy, Arlington, VA
20,000	Junior League of Salt Lake City, Inc., Salt Lake City, UT
15,000	American Indian Services, Salt Lake City, UT
15,000	Davis Applied Technology
15,000	Neighborhood House, Salt Lake City, UT
15,000	YWCA, Salt Lake City, UT
11,000	Homeless Children's Foundation, Salt Lake City, UT
10,000	Artspace, Salt Lake City, UT
10,000	Children's Service Society of Utah, Salt Lake City, UT
10,000	Community Health Center, Burlington, VT

BANDAI AMERICA, INC.

Company Headquarters

5551 Katella Ave.
Cypress, CA 90630
Web: http://www.bandai.com

Company Description

Employees: 22
SIC(s): 5000 Wholesale Trade--Durable Goods.
Parent Company: Bandai Company, Ltd., 5-4 Komagata 2-chome, Taito-ku, Tokyo, Japan

Bandai Foundation

Giving Contact

Alison Miller, Contributions Advisor
Bandai Foundation
c/o The Carmen Group
1299 Pennsylvania Ave. NW, Eighth Fl.
Washington, DC 20004
Web: http://www.bandai.com/about/
bandai_foundation.cfm

Alternate Contact

5551 Katella Avenue
Cypress, CA 90630
Phone: (714)816-9500

Description

Founded: 1994
EIN: 330655933
Organization Type: Corporate Foundation
Giving Locations: CA: nationally.
Grant Types: General Support.

Financial Summary

Total Giving: $352,995 (2001); $443,995 (2000);
$467,645 (1999)
Giving Analysis: Giving for 1999 includes: foundation ($467,645)
Assets: $10,024,855 (2001); $9,519,931 (2000);
$9,526,758 (1999)

Typical Recipients

Arts & Humanities: Film & Video, Libraries, Museums/Galleries, Performing Arts, Public Broadcasting
Civic & Public Affairs: Civil Rights, Civic & Public Affairs-General, Professional & Trade Associations
Education: Afterschool/Enrichment Programs, Arts/Humanities Education, Colleges & Universities, Education-General, Medical Education, Private Education (Precollege)
Health: AIDS/HIV, Arthritis, Cancer, Children's Health/Hospitals, Clinics/Medical Centers, Hospitals (University Affiliated), Medical Research, Single-Disease Health Associations
International: Human Rights, International Organizations, International Relief Efforts
Science: Scientific Centers & Institutes
Social Services: Big Brother/Big Sister, Child Welfare, Community Service Organizations, Family Services, Food/Clothing Distribution, Substance Abuse

Application Procedures

Initial Contact: Send a brief letter of inquiry.
Application Requirements: Include a description of organization, amount requested, purpose of funds sought, and proof of tax-exempt status.
Deadlines: None.

Restrictions

Grants are not made to individuals, religious organizations for sectarian purposes, or political or lobbying groups.

Corporate Officials

Steve Grimes: chief financial officer, president, chief executive officer PRIM CORP EMPL chief financial officer: Bandai America.
Paul Nojima: chairman, president, chief executive officer PRIM CORP EMPL chairman, president, chief executive officer: Bandai America.

Foundation Officials

Seiichi Takeuchi: secretary, treasurer
Masaaki Tsuji: chairman, president

Grants Analysis

Disclosure Period: calendar year ending 2001
Total Grants: $352,995
Number of Grants: 10
Average Grant: $22,555*
Highest Grant: $150,000
Lowest Grant: $1,000
Typical Range: $1,000 to $75,000
*Note: Average grant excludes highest grant.

Recent Grants

Note: Grants derived from 2001 Form 990.

General
10,000   Arthritis Foundation, Fountain Valley, CA -- medical research

BANK OF AMERICA CORP.

Company Headquarters

Bank of America Corporation Center
100 N. Tryon St.
Charlotte, NC 28255
Phone: 888-279-3457
Fax: (704)386-6699
Web: http://www.bankofamerica.com

Company Description

Founded: 1998
Ticker: BAC
Exchange: NYSE
Former Name: BankAmerica Corp. (1999);
Acquired: NationsBank (1998).
Assets: US$662.401 billion (2002)
Profit: US$9.249 billion (2002)
Employees: 133944 (2002)
Fortune Rank: 23, per FORTUNE Magazine's list of 500 Largest U.S. Corporations (2002).
SIC(s): 6021 National Commercial Banks, 6712 Bank Holding Companies.

Nonmonetary Support

Type: Cause-related Marketing & Promotion; Donated Equipment; Loaned Employees
Volunteer Programs: The company sponsors the Volunteer Time for Schools program, which allows each full-time associate to volunteer at a public or private school for up to two hours of paid time per week. The company also sponsors a Volunteer Grants Program. If an associate volunteers 50 or more hours at a nonprofit organization in a calendar year, Bank of America donates $250 to that organization in the associates name; the donation is increased to $500 for those who volunteer 100 or more hours. In addition, the company maintains the Team Bank of America Volunteer Network, which provides volunteer opportunities for Bank of America associates wishing to get involved in any of the approximately 3,000 volunteer events the company sponsors each year.

Bank of America Foundation

Giving Contact

Paula J. Fraher, Corporate Initiatives Executive
100 North Tryon Street
NC1-007-18-01
Charlotte, NC 28255-0001
Phone: (704)388-3183
Web: http://www.bankofamerica.com/foundation

Alternate Contact

401 North Tryon Street
NC1-021-02-20
Charlotte, NC 28255
Phone: (704)386-5659

Description

EIN: 582429625
Organization Type: Corporate Foundation
Giving Locations: headquarters and operating communities, except in Washington State.
Grant Types: Capital, General Support, Project, Seed Money.
Note: Foundation matches gifts. Employee matching gift ratio: 1 to 1, for gifts from $25 to $5,000.

Financial Summary

Total Giving: $86,034,537 (2001); $87,400,000 (2000); $94,700,000 (1999 approx). Note: Contributes through corporate direct giving program and foundation.
Giving Analysis: Giving for 2000 includes: foundation matching gifts (approx $8,000,000); foundation grants to United Way (approx $13,000,000); foundation (approx $66,400,000); 1998: foundation matching gifts ($2,616,875); foundation grants to United Way ($6,117,000); 1996: domestic subsidiaries ($2,350,000) foundation ($18,633,872)
Assets: $2,933,072 (2001); $7,595,703 (1998); $5,048,445 (1996)
Gifts Received: $86,323,627 (2001); $8,850,952 (1998); $20,174,021 (1996). Note: In 2001, contributions were received from Bank of America, N.A. ($84,553,481) and Cassella Trust ($1,770,146). In 1994, gifts were received from BankAmerica Corp. and Seafirst Bank Matching Gifts Program.

Typical Recipients

Arts & Humanities: Arts Appreciation, Arts Associations & Councils, Arts Centers, Arts Festivals, Arts Funds, Arts Institutes, Ballet, Community Arts, Ethnic & Folk Arts, Historic Preservation, Libraries, Museums/Galleries, Music, Opera, Performing Arts, Public Broadcasting, Theater
Civic & Public Affairs: Asian American Affairs, Botanical Gardens/Parks, Business/Free Enterprise, Civil Rights, Community Foundations, Economic Development, Employment/Job Training, Civic & Public Affairs-General, Hispanic Affairs, Housing, Legal Aid, Native American Affairs, Nonprofit Management, Professional & Trade Associations, Public Policy, Rural Affairs, Urban & Community Affairs, Urban & Community Affairs, Women's Affairs, Zoos/Aquariums
Education: Afterschool/Enrichment Programs, Agricultural Education, Business Education, Colleges & Universities, Community & Junior Colleges, Economic Education, Education Funds, Education Reform, Elementary Education (Private), Engineering/Technological Education, Environmental Education, Faculty Development, Education-General, Health & Physical Education, International Exchange, International Studies, Leadership Training, Medical Education, Minority Education, Preschool Education, Public Education (Precollege), Science/Mathematics Education, Student Aid
Environment: Environment-General, Research, Resource Conservation

Health: Children's Health/Hospitals, Clinics/Medical Centers, Emergency/Ambulance Services, Health Organizations, Hospitals, Medical Research, Prenatal Health Issues
International: International Environmental Issues, International Relations
Religion: Dioceses
Science: Science Museums, Scientific Centers & Institutes
Social Services: Child Abuse, Child Welfare, Community Service Organizations, Family Services, Food/Clothing Distribution, People with Disabilities, Shelters/Homelessness, Substance Abuse, United Funds/United Ways, YMCA/YWCA/YMHA/YWHA, Youth Organizations

Application Procedures

Initial Contact: Send a brief letter of inquiry or obtain application form from the foundation's web site.
Application Requirements: Information should include: purpose of funds sought; correct mailing address, name and phone number of contact person; amount requested; brief statement of mission; copy of IRS letter of designation; current list of board members with affiliations; operating budget and project budget if applicable; population and geographic area served; list of sources and amounts of other funding obtained, pledged or requested for this purpose; and financial information for the previous two years, with an audited financial statement, if available.
Deadlines: None.
Evaluative Criteria: Organizations must demonstrate fiscal and administrative stability, good management policies and practices, and the ability to produce a budget and organizational financial statement.
Decision Notification: Decisions regarding funding requests are ongoing. All requests will be reviewed in a competitive process.

Restrictions

Generally not receptive to individuals, organizations without 501(c)(3) public charity status, memorial campaigns, fund-raising events, political activities, religious organizations for sectarian purposes, research, athletic events and programs, endowment campaigns, advertising, member agencies of united funds, book or film or video projects, public or private education (K-12), disease advocacy organizations, or organizations that discriminate on the basis of age, culture, race, gender, or sexual orientation.

Additional Information

In 1992, BankAmerica Corp. and BankAmerica Foundation acquired, respectively, Security Pacific Corp. and Security Pacific Foundation and related entities, Security Pacific Foundation Northwest and Security Pacific Bank Arizona Foundation. The foundations associated with Security Pacific completely dissolved; the giving program for BankAmerica Corp. and its subsidiaries continues to be contained completely within BankAmerica Foundation.
BankAmerica Corp. and NationsBank have merged to create Bank of America.

Corporate Officials

Kenneth D. Lewis: chairman, president, chief executive officer ED Georgia State University BS (1969). PRIM CORP EMPL chairman, president, chief executive officer: Bank of America Corp.

Foundation Officials

J. S. (Steele) Alphin: trustee
Catherine P. Bessant: trustee
Caroline O. Boitano: executive director
Kathleen J. Burke: trustee B 1952. PRIM CORP EMPL vice chairman, personnel relations officer: BankAmerica Corp.
Sandra Cohen: secretary
Barbara J. Desoer: trustee

Lynn E. Drury: president PRIM CORP EMPL executive vice president & corporate affairs: Bank of America Corp.
Paula J. Fraher: corporate initiatives executive
William M. Goodyear: trustee B 1948. ED University of Notre Dame BA (1970); Dartmouth College MBA (1972). PRIM CORP EMPL chairman, chief executive officer: Navigant Consulting, Inc. CORP AFFIL director: Continental Illinois Venture Del.
Judy Granucci-Tufo: charitable contributions analyst
Raymond M. McKee: trustee
R. E. (Gene) Taylor: trustee
James Wagele: senior vice president
Gary S. Williams: treasurer

Grants Analysis

Disclosure Period: calendar year ending 2001
Total Grants: $84,889,537*
Number of Grants: 4,410 (approx)
Average Grant: $19,249
Highest Grant: $1,475,750
Lowest Grant: $100
Typical Range: $1,000 to $25,000
*Note: Giving excludes matching gifts and United Way.

Recent Grants

Note: Grants derived from 2001 Form 990.

General
4,500,000 United Way of America, Alexandria, VA -- for Success by Six Initiatives
3,000,000 United Way of America, Alexandria, VA -- for Success by Six Initiatives
2,500,000 United Way of America, Alexandria, VA -- for Success by Six Initiatives
1,475,750 Joe Martin Scholarship Fund, St. Peter, MN -- for scholarships
1,400,000 United Way Bay Area, San Francisco, CA -- for 2000 campaign
1,100,000 National Council on Economic Education, New York, NY -- for Teacher's Institute
1,000,000 Music Center of Los Angeles County, Los Angeles, CA
1,000,000 National Urban League, Charlotte, NC
1,000,000 University of California, San Francisco, CA -- for transition budget
750,000 United Way of Greater Los Angeles, Los Angeles, CA -- for annual corporate gift

THE BANK OF GREENE COUNTY

Company Headquarters
302 Main St.
Catskill, NY 12414
Web: http://www.thebankofgreenecounty.com

Company Description
Founded: 1889
Parent Company: Greene County Bancorp, Inc., PO Box 470, Catskill, NY, United States

Bank of Greene County Charitable Foundation

Giving Contact
Michelle M. Plummer, Chief Financial Officer
425 Main Street
Catskill, NY 12414-1300
Phone: (518)943-3700
Web: http://www.thebankofgreenecounty.com/Charitable.htm

Description
Founded: 1999
EIN: 141810419
Organization Type: Corporate Foundation
Giving Locations: , NY

Donor Information
Founder: The Bank of Greene County established the Bank of Greene County Charitable Foundation in 1998 in connection with the bank's conversion from a mutual to stock organization.

Financial Summary
Total Giving: $26,500 (fiscal year ending 0, 2002); $20,100 (fiscal 2001); $25,600 (fiscal 2000)
Assets: $752,094 (fiscal 2002); $516,217 (fiscal 2001); $391,623 (fiscal 2000)

Typical Recipients
Arts & Humanities: Museums/Galleries
Civic & Public Affairs: Housing
Science: Scientific Centers & Institutes
Social Services: Animal Protection, Food/Clothing Distribution, Social Services-General, YMCA/YWCA/YMHA/YWHA

Application Procedures
Initial Contact: Requests for grants of $1,000 or less should be submitted in writing to a Bank of Greene County retail branch. Requests for grants of more than $1,000 should be submitted to the Bank's operations office using the New York/New Jersey Area Common Grant Application form.
Application Requirements: Requests for $1,000 or less should include a cover letter on the applicant organization's letterhead detailing the amount requested; purpose of funds sought; and the name, address and telephone number of the contact person. Include a brief description of the organization's purpose, history and forward outlook. Attachments must include a copy of the organization's operating budget for the current and preceding years; a list of the organization's officers and directors; proof of tax-exempt status; and a list of other current sources of financial support, including the purpose and amount received from each. If the organization has previously applied for funding from Bank of Greene County Charitable Foundation, list the dates and amounts of any previous grants received and any applications to the foundation that were not granted.
Requests for more than $1,000 may obtain a copy of the New York/New Jersey Area Common Grant Application form at http://www.nyrag.org.
Deadlines: Requests for funding should be submitted between December 1 and January 15.
Decision Notification: The foundation typically processes applications within 90 days of the close of the application period.
Notes: Generally, the maximum amount that may be requested is $2,500. An organization may submit only one application per foundation fiscal year.

Restrictions
The foundation does not ordinarily support individuals; candidates for political office; religious organizations; sectarian activities; seminars, conferences, or endowments; or activities that would benefit The Bank of Greene County.

Foundation Officials
Bruce P. Egger: secretary
Walter H. Ingalls: director
David H. Jenkins, DVM: director
Raphael Klein: director
Dennis R. O'Grady: director
John M. Olivett: treasurer
Michelle M. Plummer: chief financial officer
Paul Slutzky: director
Martin C. Smith: director
J. Bruce Whittaker: president

Grants Analysis

Total Grants: $26,500
Number of Grants: 18
Average Grant: $1,472
Highest Grant: $2,500
Lowest Grant: $500
Typical Range: $1,000 to $2,500

Recent Grants

Note: Grants derived from fiscal 2002 Form 990.

General

2,500	Community Action of Green County, Inc, Catskill, NY -- senior companion volunteers program
2,500	Mountain Top Arboretum, Tannersville, NY -- computer and software
2,000	Catskill Mountain Foundation, Hunter, NY -- 2002 programming plan
2,000	Catskill Mountain Housing Development Corp, Catskill, NY -- 1st time homebuyer workshops for low/moderate income
2,000	Hunter Foundation, Inc., Hunter, NY -- signage
1,500	Capital District YMCA, Troy, NY -- youth campaign
1,500	Michael J Quill Irish Cultural & Sports Center, East Durham, NY -- support Irish arts week
1,500	St. Patrick's Academy, Catskill, NY -- strategic plan for future viability in community
1,000	Albany County Rural Housing Alliance, Inc., Voorheesville, NY -- 0% loans to low income homeowners
1,000	All Arts Matter, Greenville, NY -- improve and expand programs

BANK OF NEW YORK COMPANY, INC.

Company Headquarters

New York, NY
Web: http://www.bankofny.com

Company Description

Founded: 1968
Ticker: BK
Exchange: NYSE
Assets: US$77.564 billion (2002)
Profit: US$902 million (2002)
Employees: 19435 (2002)
Fortune Rank: 299, per FORTUNE Magazine's list of 500 Largest U.S. Corporations (2002).
SIC(s): 6022 State Commercial Banks, 6712 Bank Holding Companies.

Operating Locations

Bank of New York Co., Inc. (MO--St. Louis; NY--Harrison; TX--Irving; WI--Milwaukee); BNY Financial (Holdings) Ltd. (IL--London); BNY International Financial Corp. (NY--New York); CTC Illinois Trust Co. (IL--Chicago)

Giving Contact

Pat Bicket, Vice President and Assistant Secretary
1 Wall St.
31st Floor
New York, NY 10286
Phone: (212)635-1787
Fax: (212)635-1799

E-mail: gschneider@bankofny.com
Web: http://bankofny.com/pages/acdb_bnyinthecomm.htm

Description

Organization Type: Corporate Giving Program
Giving Locations: DE; NJ; NY
Grant Types: Award, Capital, Conference/Seminar, Emergency, Employee Matching Gifts, Endowment, Fellowship, General Support, Multiyear/Continuing Support.
Note: Employee matching gift ratio: 1 to 1.

Financial Summary

Total Giving: $4,700,000 (1997 approx); $4,680,000 (1996 approx); $4,680,000 (1995 approx). Note: Contributes through corporate direct giving program only.

Typical Recipients

Arts & Humanities: Arts Appreciation, Arts Associations & Councils, Arts Centers, Historic Preservation, Libraries, Literary Arts, Museums/Galleries, Music, Opera, Performing Arts, Public Broadcasting
Civic & Public Affairs: Business/Free Enterprise, Civil Rights, Economic Development, Housing, Zoos/Aquariums
Education: Education Associations, Elementary Education (Private), Minority Education, Private Education (Precollege)
Environment: Environment-General
Health: Health Organizations, Hospitals, Nursing Services, Single-Disease Health Associations
Social Services: Child Welfare, Community Service Organizations, Family Services, Shelters/Homelessness, Substance Abuse, United Funds/United Ways, Volunteer Services, Youth Organizations

Application Procedures

Initial Contact: letter with proposal attached
Application Requirements: goals and financial statement for organization and project; tax identification number
Deadlines: None, but prefers to receive proposals in the fall
Notes: Regional branches have discretionary budgets for contributions to local nonprofits. The headquarters office handles requests from statewide groups.

Restrictions

*Company does not support religious or political organizations or individuals.

Additional Information

Majority of recipients are organizations the company traditionally supports, though policy does not restrict first-time requests.

Corporate Officials

Alan Richard Griffith: vice chairman, chief executive officer, director B Mineola, NY 1941. ED Lafayette College BA (1964); City University of New York MBA (1971). PRIM CORP EMPL vice chairman: Bank of New York Co., Inc. CORP AFFIL vice chairman: Bank New York Co. Inc. NONPR AFFIL trustee: Chesapeake Bay Foundation; trustee: Lafayette College; trustee: Amyotrophic Lateral Sclerosis Association. CLUB AFFIL University Club New York; Marco Polo Club.
Thomas A. Renyi: chairman, chief executive officer, director B Passaic, NJ 1946. ED Rutgers University BA (1967); Rutgers University MBA (1968). PRIM CORP EMPL president, chief executive officer, director: Bank of New York Co., Inc. CORP AFFIL president, director: Bank New York Co. Inc.; chairman: BNY Mortgage Co. Inc.

Grants Analysis

Typical Range: $1,000 to $10,000

BANK ONE CORP.

Company Headquarters

1 Bank One Plaza
Chicago, IL 60670
Web: http://www.bankone.com

Company Description

Ticker: ONE
Exchange: NYSE
Acquired: Polaroid Corp. (2002); First Chicago NBD Corp..
Assets: US$263.023 billion (2002)
Profit: US$3.295 billion (2002)
Employees: 73685 (2002)
Fortune Rank: 79, per FORTUNE Magazine's list of 500 Largest U.S. Corporations (2002).

Nonmonetary Support

Type: Donated Equipment; In-kind Services; Loaned Executives

Bank One Foundation

Giving Contact

James E. Donovan, Treasurer
1 Bank One Plaza, Suite 0308
Chicago, IL 60670
Phone: (312)407-8052
Fax: (312)732-2437

Description

EIN: 366033828
Organization Type: Corporate Foundation
Giving Locations: nationally.
Grant Types: Capital, Employee Matching Gifts, Endowment, Fellowship, General Support, Operating Expenses, Project.

Financial Summary

Total Giving: $30,170,306 (2001); $12,937,895 (2000); $9,708,684 (1999). Note: Contributes through foundation only.
Giving Analysis: Giving for 2000 includes: foundation scholarships ($1,500); foundation matching gifts ($1,939,441); foundation grants to United Way ($4,671,643); foundation ($6,325,311); 1998: foundation matching gifts ($20,350); foundation program-related investments ($537,500); foundation grants to United Way ($1,835,642); 1997: foundation matching gifts ($167,999);
Assets: $55,693,035 (2001); $29,108,221 (2000); $6,637,456 (1999)
Gifts Received: $57,988,173 (2001); $35,333,189 (2000); $7,099,993 (1998). Note: The foundation received contributions in 2001 from First Chicago Investment Corp.; Bank One, NA (Chicago); ANB & Trust Co - Chicago; Bank One, NA (Ohio); Disaster Relief Fund; and others.

Typical Recipients

Arts & Humanities: Arts Associations & Councils, Arts Centers, Arts Festivals, Arts Funds, Arts Institutes, Arts Outreach, Ballet, Community Arts, Dance, Ethnic & Folk Arts, Arts & Humanities-General, Historic Preservation, History & Archaeology, Libraries, Museums/Galleries, Music, Opera, Performing Arts, Public Broadcasting, Theater
Civic & Public Affairs: African American Affairs, Asian American Affairs, Botanical Gardens/Parks, Business/Free Enterprise, Civil Rights, Clubs, Community Foundations, Economic Development, Economic Policy, Civic & Public Affairs-General, Hispanic Affairs, Housing, Law & Justice, Municipalities/

Towns, Municipalities/Towns, Philanthropic Organizations, Public Policy, Urban & Community Affairs, Zoos/Aquariums

Education: Agricultural Education, Arts/Humanities Education, Business Education, Colleges & Universities, Economic Education, Education Associations, Education Funds, Engineering/Technological Education, International Studies, Leadership Training, Minority Education, Private Education (Precollege), Science/Mathematics Education

Environment: Environment-General

Health: Children's Health/Hospitals, Clinics/Medical Centers, Hospitals

Religion: Religious Organizations

Science: Observatories & Planetariums, Science Museums, Scientific Centers & Institutes

Social Services: At-Risk Youth, Big Brother/Big Sister, Child Welfare, Community Service Organizations, Emergency Relief, Family Services, People with Disabilities, Recreation & Athletics, United Funds/United Ways, YMCA/YWCA/YMHA/YWHA, Youth Organizations

Application Procedures

Initial Contact: Send cover letter and proposal.
Application Requirements: Cover letter should briefly describe the specific purpose for which funds are being sought and state the level of funding requested. Include goals and objectives of requesting organization, list of recent achievements, description of programs, list of board members and key personnel and management structure, current budget and principal funding sources and levels, recently audited financial statement or annual report, proof of tax-exempt status. Community/neighborhood organizations should also provide goals and budget for specific program/project to be funded.
Deadlines: None.
Evaluative Criteria: Clear definition of goals and responsibilities; demonstration of effective organizational, programmatic, and financial objective setting and management; evidence of broad-based support; evidence that the service is a response to a valid need and is superior to existing competitors; documentation of past success or sound reasons to expect success in the future.

Restrictions

In general, the foundation does not support individuals; religious or fraternal organizations; preschool, elementary, or secondary schools; public agencies; consecutive multiyear capital pledges; multiyear operating pledges; or agencies receiving United Way/Crusade of Mercy funds.

Additional Information

Foundation Officials

Gerald E. Buldak: vice president
Stanley J. Calderon: vice president
Dennis P. Carroll: assistant treasurer
Michael J. Cavanagh: director, vice president
Daniel P. Cooney: assistant secretary
Mary L. Decker: vice president
David E. Donovan: director, vice president
James E. Donovan: treasurer
Christine A. Edwards: director, vice president
William M. Farrow: vice president
Harry H. Hallowell: assistant treasurer
Jacqueline A. Hurlbutt: vice president
Patricia Hurston: vice president
Marie I. Jordan: secretary
Norma J. Lauder: vice president
Michael Lipsitz: assistant secretary
John Q. McKinnon: vice president
Melinda McMullen: president
Timothy P. Moen: vice president
Margaret E. O'Hara: assistant secretary
Charles A. Peruski: assistant treasurer
Sharon A. Renchof: assistant secretary

Sharon A. Renchof: assistant treasurer
Lesley D. Slavitt: vice president
Diane M. Smith: president, director
Mary K. Walter: assistant secretary
Clark J. Wulf: assistant treasurer

Grants Analysis

Disclosure Period: calendar year ending 2001
Total Grants: $23,693,236*
Number of Grants: 470
Average Grant: $50,000
Highest Grant: $500,000
Lowest Grant: $1,000
Typical Range: $5,000 to $50,000
*Note: Giving excludes United Way, matching gifts and scholarships.

Recent Grants

Note: Grants derived from 2001 Form 990.

General

1,683,500	United Way Crusade of Mercy, Chicago, IL
850,000	United Way of Central Indiana, Indianapolis, IN
710,000	Local Initiatives Support Corporation, Detroit, MI
690,000	United Way Community Services, Detroit, MI
577,100	United Way of Central Ohio, Columbus, OH
506,750	Valley of the Sun United Way, Phoenix, AZ
500,000	Millennium Park, Inc., Chicago, IL
375,000	Greater Columbus Arts Council, Columbus, OH
315,000	United Way of Delaware, Wilmington, DE
300,000	Detroit Institute for Arts, Detroit, MI

BANKATLANTIC BANCORP

Company Headquarters

Fort Lauderdale, FL
Web: http://www.bankatlantic.com

Company Description

Founded: 1952
Ticker: BBX
Exchange: NYSE
Assets: US$4.015 billion (2001)
Employees: 1457 (2001)
SIC(s): 6035 Federal Savings Institutions, 6712 Bank Holding Companies

BankAtlantic Foundation

Giving Contact

Shelley Levan-Margolis, Executive Director
PO Box 8608
Ft. Lauderdale, FL 33310-8608
Phone: (954)760-5458
Web: http://www.bankatlantic.com/communityinvestment/bafoundation.asp

Alternate Contact

1750 East Sunrise Boulevard
Ft. Lauderdale, FL 33304-3013

Description

Founded: 1994
EIN: 650499150
Organization Type: Corporate Foundation
Giving Locations: FL: Southern Florida
Grant Types: Emergency, General Support, Operating Expenses, Project.

Financial Summary

Total Giving: $330,725 (2001); $310,800 (2000); $311,400 (1999)
Giving Analysis: Giving for 2001 includes: foundation ($330,725) 1998: foundation grants to United Way ($10,000)
Assets: $1,071,246 (2001); $1,388,009 (2000); $1,007,791 (1998)
Gifts Received: $950 (2001); $900,000 (2000); $768,000 (1998). Note: In 1998, contributions were received from BankAtlantic.

Typical Recipients

Arts & Humanities: Arts Associations & Councils, Arts Centers, Arts Outreach, Ballet, Dance, Film & Video, Arts & Humanities-General, History & Archaeology, Libraries, Museums/Galleries, Music, Opera, Performing Arts, Public Broadcasting, Theater

Civic & Public Affairs: African American Affairs, Business/Free Enterprise, Civil Rights, Community Foundations, Economic Development, Civic & Public Affairs-General, Housing, Law & Justice, Municipalities/Towns, Nonprofit Management, Professional & Trade Associations, Public Policy, Safety, Urban & Community Affairs, Women's Affairs

Education: Arts/Humanities Education, Business Education, Business-School Partnerships, Colleges & Universities, Colleges & Universities, Community & Junior Colleges, Economic Education, Education Reform, Education-General, Legal Education, Minority Education, Public Education (Precollege), Science/Mathematics Education, Student Aid

Health: AIDS/HIV, Emergency/Ambulance Services, Prenatal Health Issues

International: Human Rights

Religion: Jewish Causes

Science: Science Museums

Social Services: At-Risk Youth, Child Welfare, Community Service Organizations, Day Care, Domestic Violence, Family Services, Food/Clothing Distribution, Homes, People with Disabilities, Scouts, Senior Services, Shelters/Homelessness, Social Services-General, United Funds/United Ways, Volunteer Services, YMCA/YWCA/YMHA/YWHA, Youth Organizations

Application Procedures

Initial Contact: Submit typewritten proposal on organization's letterhead.
Application Requirements: Include the name, address, telephone number of organization; name of the director; brief history of organization; project description, including problem, need, or issue to be addressed; anticipated benefits; total amount requested; dates of proposed project; operating and project budgets; actual and prospective sources of income for the project, including amounts; project director's name, address, and telephone number (if different); project location; proof of tax-exempt status; copy of charitable solicitation license; list of board members and their affiliations; list of any funding received from BankAtlantic during the same calendar year; and the signature of the executive director acknowledging application.
Deadlines: Applications must be received between February 1 and October 1.
Review Process: Applications are generally reviewed within 60 to 90 days.

Restrictions

Does not support social functions or sporting events; religious organizations; capital, building, or endowment campaigns; individuals; purchase of ad space; fundraising events; funds for travel expenses; hospitals, medical research, or national health organizations; K-12 schools; organizations without 501(c)3 status; political or lobbying organizations; programs or organizations operating outside of Florida; or school athletic teams, cheerleading squads, bands, choirs, etc. The foundation will not fund an organization twice in one calendar year or for more than three consecutive years.

Additional Information

Support goes to education, human services, arts, civic organizations, public policy, economic development, and affordable housing.

Corporate Officials

Alan Levan: chairman, president, chief executive officer PRIM CORP EMPL chairman, president, chief executive officer: BankAtlantic Bancorp.

Foundation Officials

Alan Levan: president, trustee (see above)
Shelley Levan: treasurer, trustee

Grants Analysis

Disclosure Period: calendar year ending 2001
Total Grants: $330,725
Number of Grants: 82
Average Grant: $4,033
Highest Grant: $20,000
Typical Range: $1,000 to $5,000

Recent Grants

Note: Grants derived from 2001 Form 990.

General

25,000	South Florida Annenberg Challenge, Ft. Lauderdale, FL
20,000	Community Foundation of Broward, Ft. Lauderdale, FL -- Broward Partnership for the Homeless
20,000	Indian River Community College Foundation, Inc., Ft. Pierce, FL
15,000	Florida Grand Opera, Miami, FL
10,000	Broward Community College Foundation, Ft. Lauderdale, FL
10,000	Collins Center for Public Policy, Miami, FL
10,000	Florida Philharmonic Orchestra, Ft. Lauderdale, FL
10,000	Junior Achievement of the Palm Beaches, Inc., West Palm Beach, FL
5,000	Museum of Discovery and Science, Ft. Lauderdale, FL
5,000	University of Miami, Miami, FL -- Children and Law Clinic

BANTA CORP.

Company Headquarters

Menasha, WI
Web: http://www.banta.com

Company Description

Founded: 1901
Ticker: BN
Exchange: NYSE
Revenue: US$1.366 billion (2002)
Employees: 8300 (2002)
SIC(s): 2732 Book Printing, 2752 Commercial Printing--Lithographic, 2759 Commercial Printing Nec, 7336 Commercial Art & Graphic Design.

Operating Locations

Banta Book Group (TN--Johnson City; UT--Spanish Fork; VA--Harrisonburg; WA--Kent; WI--Appleton, Green Bay, Kaukauna, Menasha); Banta Catalog Group (MN--Maple Grove, St. Paul); Banta Corp. (CA--Rialto; MN--Long Prairie; MO--Liberty; OH--Greenfield; WI--Milwaukee, Neenah, Plover); Banta Ventures, Inc. (WI--Plover)

Banta Corp. Foundation

Giving Contact

Donald D. Belcher, Vice President
Banta Corp. Foundation
PO Box 8003
Menasha, WI 54952-8003
Phone: (920)751-7777
Fax: (920)751-7790

Description

Founded: 1953
EIN: 396050779
Organization Type: Corporate Foundation
Giving Locations: WI: operating locations.
Grant Types: Award, Capital, Employee Matching Gifts, General Support, Multiyear/Continuing Support.
Note: The foundation matches Banta Corp. employee gifts to institutions of higher learning; alumni funds, foundations, or associations; hospitals; and cultural organizations.

Donor Information

Founder: Banta Corp.

Financial Summary

Total Giving: $569,237 (2001); $325,057 (2000); $313,072 (1999). Note: Contributes through corporate direct giving program and foundation.
Giving Analysis: Giving for 2001 includes: foundation matching gifts ($12,579); foundation scholarships ($77,500); foundation ($479,158); 2000: foundation matching gifts ($15,702); foundation scholarships ($130,000); foundation ($179,355); 1999: foundation matching gifts ($19,372); foundation scholarships ($82,450); foundation ($218,531);
Assets: $29,821 (2001); $1,014 (2000); $8,011 (1999)
Gifts Received: $600,000 (2001); $325,000 (2000); $325,000 (1999). Note: Contributions are received from the Banta Corp.

Typical Recipients

Arts & Humanities: Arts Centers, Arts & Humanities-General, History & Archaeology, Libraries, Museums/Galleries, Music, Performing Arts, Public Broadcasting, Theater, Visual Arts
Civic & Public Affairs: Botanical Gardens/Parks, Business/Free Enterprise, Chambers of Commerce, Community Foundations, Economic Development, Civic & Public Affairs-General, Housing, Municipalities/Towns, Parades/Festivals, Urban & Community Affairs
Education: Arts/Humanities Education, Business Education, Colleges & Universities, Education Funds, Engineering/Technological Education, Education-General, Gifted & Talented Programs, International Studies, Medical Education, Minority Education, Preschool Education, Private Education (Precollege), Science/Mathematics Education, Secondary Education (Private), Secondary Education (Private), Student Aid, Vocational & Technical Education
Environment: Environment-General, Resource Conservation
Health: AIDS/HIV, Cancer, Children's Health/Hospitals, Clinics/Medical Centers, Emergency/Ambulance Services, Heart, Hospitals, Mental Health, Nursing Services
Religion: Religious Organizations, Religious Welfare
Social Services: Child Welfare, Community Service Organizations, Counseling, Domestic Violence, Family Services, Food/Clothing Distribution, People with Disabilities, Recreation & Athletics, Scouts, Social Services-General, Substance Abuse, United Funds/United Ways, YMCA/YWCA/YMHA/YWHA, Youth Organizations

Application Procedures

Initial Contact: Send a brief letter of inquiry.
Application Requirements: Include a description of organization, amount requested, purpose of funds sought, recently audited financial statement, and proof of tax exempt status.
Deadlines: November 1.
Decision Notification: The board meets twice annually, in the spring and fall.

Corporate Officials

Donald David Belcher: chairman, president, chief executive officer, director B Kansas City, MO 1938. ED Dartmouth College BA (1960); Stanford University MBA (1964). PRIM CORP EMPL chairman, president, chief executive officer, director: Banta Corp. CORP AFFIL chairman: Packaging Fulfillment Specialists; director: Fellowes Manufacturing Co.; director: Hunt Manufacturing Co. NONPR AFFIL trustee: Lawrence University.
Gerald A. Henseler: executive vice president, chief financial officer, director B Marshfield, WI 1940. ED University of Wisconsin, Madison BS (1962). PRIM CORP EMPL executive vice president, chief financial officer, director: Banta Corp. CORP AFFIL director: First National Bancshares Corp.; vice president: Tidi Products Inc.; director: Banta Healthcare Products Inc.

Foundation Officials

Rosalie N. Barbera: vice president, director PRIM CORP EMPL director employee benefits & compensation: Bonta Corp.
Donald David Belcher: vice president, director (see above)
Gerald A. Henseler: president (see above)
Margaret Banta Humleker: vice president, director
Henry G. Wells: vice president, director

Grants Analysis

Disclosure Period: calendar year ending 2001
Total Grants: $479,158*
Number of Grants: 83
Average Grant: $4,319*
Highest Grant: $125,000
Lowest Grant: $125
Typical Range: $1,000 to $15,000
***Note:** Giving excludes matching gifts; scholarships. Average grant figure excludes highest grant.

Recent Grants

Note: Grants derived from 2001 Form 990.

Library-Related

125,000	Elisha D. Smith Public Library
2,500	Wisconsin Library Association Foundation, Inc., Madison, WI

General

77,500	Banta Scholarship Program, Menasha, WI
30,000	Habitat for Humanity
30,000	Habitat for Humanity
25,000	City of Menasha, Menasha, WI
25,000	Fox Cities Performing Arts Center, Appleton, WI
15,000	Bay-Lakes Council, Boy Scouts of America, Menasha, WI
15,000	Menasha Educational Endowment Fund, Menasha, WI
15,000	Neenah-Menasha YMCA, Neenah, WI
13,000	Wisconsin Foundation of Independent Colleges, Milwaukee, WI
12,900	Wisconsin Public Broadcasting Foundation, Milwaukee, WI

ROBERT BARD FOUNDATION

Giving Contact
Pat Kling, Trust Officer
Robert Bard Foundation
Care of Mellon Bank NA
PO Box 7236, AIM 193 0224
Philadelphia, PA 19101-7236
Phone: (215)553-3208

Description
Founded: 1988
EIN: 236806099
Organization Type: Private Foundation
Giving Locations: PA: Royersford
Grant Types: General Support.

Donor Information
Founder: the late Agnes Cook Bard

Financial Summary
Total Giving: $25,000 (fiscal year ending June 30, 2001); $15,182 (fiscal 1999); $122,350 (fiscal 1998)
Assets: $4,313,448 (fiscal 2001); $4,808,423 (fiscal 1999); $4,476,530 (fiscal 1998)

Typical Recipients
Arts & Humanities: History & Archaeology, Libraries, Music
Civic & Public Affairs: Clubs, Community Foundations, Economic Development, Civic & Public Affairs-General, Urban & Community Affairs, Zoos/Aquariums
Education: Arts/Humanities Education, Colleges & Universities, Private Education (Precollege), Public Education (Precollege)
Environment: Environment-General
Health: Children's Health/Hospitals, Emergency/Ambulance Services, Nursing Services
Social Services: Child Welfare, Community Centers, Community Service Organizations, Counseling, Family Services, Food/Clothing Distribution, People with Disabilities, Senior Services, United Funds/United Ways, Volunteer Services, YMCA/YWCA/YMHA/YWHA, Youth Organizations

Application Procedures
Initial Contact: Send a brief letter of inquiry.
Application Requirements: Include a description of organization, total cost, name of contact person, and IRS determination letter.
Deadlines: April 1.

Restrictions
Preference is first given to charities in Royersford, PA, after which any worthy charities will be considered.

Additional Information
Trust(s): Mellon Bank NA

Foundation Officials
Norman E. Donoghue, II: trustee B Coatesville, PA 1944. ED Williams College BA (1966); Duke University JD (1969). PRIM CORP EMPL partner: Dechert Price & Rhoads. NONPR AFFIL legal counselor, director: International Visitors Council Philadelphia; trustee, legal counselor, corporate secretary: Princess Grace Foundation; member: American Bar Association; fellow: International Academy Trust & Estate Lawyers.

Grants Analysis
Disclosure Period: fiscal year ending June 30, 2001
Total Grants: $25,000
Number of Grants: 1

Recent Grants
Note: Grants derived from fiscal 2001 Form 990.

General
25,000	Spring-Ford Area Historical Society, Spring-Ford, PA

BARDEN PRECISION BEARINGS

Company Headquarters
200 Park Ave.
Danbury, CT 06813
Web: http://www.bardenbearings.com

Company Description
Employees: 850
SIC(s): 3469 Metal Stampings Nec, 3562 Ball & Roller Bearings, 3568 Power Transmission Equipment Nec.

Operating Locations
Barden Corp. (CT--Winsted); Winsted Precision Ball Co. (CT--Winsted)

Barden Foundation, Inc.

Giving Contact
Thomas F. Loughman, Treasurer & Trustee
1146 Barnum Avenue
Bridgeport, CT 06610
Phone: (203)336-7531
Fax: (203)336-6440

Alternate Contact
Scholarship Committee
Barden Foundation, Inc.
200 Park Avenue
Danbury, CT 06810
Phone: (203)744-2211
Note: Application address for scholarships.

Description
Founded: 1959
EIN: 066054855
Organization Type: Corporate Foundation
Giving Locations: CT: Bridgeport, Danbury, Winsted
Grant Types: General Support, Scholarship.

Donor Information
Founder: The Barden Corp.

Financial Summary
Total Giving: $361,500 (fiscal year ending October 31, 2001); $562,500 (fiscal 2000); $364,970 (fiscal 1999). Note: Contributes through foundation only.
Giving Analysis: Giving for fiscal 2001 includes: foundation scholarships ($54,500); foundation grants to United Way ($90,000); foundation ($217,000); fiscal 2000: foundation scholarships ($55,000); foundation grants to United Way ($157,000); foundation ($350,500); fiscal 1999: foundation scholarships ($39,000); foundation grants to United Way ($95,000) foundation ($230,970)
Assets: $6,209,743 (fiscal 2001); $7,511,625 (fiscal 2000); $7,474,662 (fiscal 1999)
Gifts Received: $8,000 (fiscal 1992). Note: Contributions are received from the Barden Corp.

Typical Recipients
Arts & Humanities: Arts Centers, Libraries, Museums/Galleries, Music, Theater
Civic & Public Affairs: African American Affairs, Civil Rights, Clubs, Civic & Public Affairs-General, Municipalities/Towns, Parades/Festivals, Safety, Urban & Community Affairs, Zoos/Aquariums
Education: Business Education, Colleges & Universities, Community & Junior Colleges, Education Funds, Engineering/Technological Education, Education-General, Private Education (Precollege), Public Education (Precollege), Science/Mathematics Education, Student Aid, Vocational & Technical Education
Health: Cancer, Children's Health/Hospitals, Clinics/Medical Centers, Emergency/Ambulance Services, Health Organizations, Hospices, Hospitals, Medical Rehabilitation, Nursing Services, Nursing Services, Single-Disease Health Associations
Religion: Religious Organizations, Religious Welfare
Science: Science Exhibits & Fairs, Science Museums, Scientific Organizations
Social Services: Child Welfare, Community Centers, Community Service Organizations, Day Care, Emergency Relief, Family Services, Homes, People with Disabilities, Recreation & Athletics, Scouts, Social Services-General, Special Olympics, United Funds/United Ways, Volunteer Services, YMCA/YWCA/YMHA/YWHA, Youth Organizations

Application Procedures
Initial Contact: Send a letter of request for grants; request an application for scholarships.
Application Requirements: Requests should include a description of organization, goals and requirements, amount requested, purpose of grant, recent financial statement, and copy of IRS determination letter.
Deadlines: By December for grant award in following year; April 1 for scholarships.
Decision Notification: Trustees meet in February.

Restrictions
Most scholarships are restricted to children of employees of the Barden Corp.
Organizations must be tax-exempt charities.

Additional Information
Publications: Informational Brochure

Corporate Officials
John Emling: vice president B 1956. ED Saint Bonaventure University BBA Marketing. PRIM CORP EMPL vice president: Barden Corp.

Foundation Officials
Robert M. Davis: trustee PRIM CORP EMPL vice president: Barden Corp.
John Emling: trustee (see above)
Thomas F. Loughman: secretary, treasurer, trustee
Robert P. Moore: trustee B 1924. CORP AFFIL president: Lacey Manufacturing Co. Division.
Stanley Noss: trustee

Grants Analysis
Disclosure Period: fiscal year ending October 31, 2001
Total Grants: $217,000*
Number of Grants: 47
Average Grant: $4,617
Highest Grant: $40,000
Lowest Grant: $500
Typical Range: $1,000 to $15,000
*Note: Giving excludes scholarships, and United Way.

Recent Grants
Note: Grants derived from 2001 Form 990.

General
50,000	United Way Northern Fairfield County, Danbury, CT
40,000	Bridgeport Hospital Foundation, Bridgeport, CT
40,000	Danbury Hospital Development Fund, Danbury, CT
20,000	United Way Eastern Fairfield County, Bridgeport, CT
20,000	United Way Northwest Connecticut, Winsted, CT

15,000	DATAHR, Brookfield, CT
10,000	Winsted Area Child Care Center, Winsted, CT
9,000	American Cancer Society, Wilton, CT
8,000	New Milford Hospital, New Milford, CT
5,000	American Red Cross, Bridgeport, CT

BARDES CORP.

Company Headquarters
Cincinnati, OH

Company Description
Employees: 700
SIC(s): 3451 Screw Machine Products, 3643 Current-Carrying Wiring Devices.

Bardes Fund

Giving Contact
Rebecca Autry
Bardes Fund
4730 Madison Road
Cincinnati, OH 45227-1426
Phone: (513)533-6228
Fax: (513)871-4084
E-mail: rautry@ilsco.com

Description
Founded: 1955
EIN: 316036206
Organization Type: Corporate Foundation
Giving Locations: OH: Cincinnati
Grant Types: General Support.

Financial Summary
Total Giving: $292,559 (2000); $180,000 (1999 approx); $180,000 (1998 approx). Note: Contributes through corporate direct giving program and foundation. Giving includes foundation. 1996 Giving includes foundation ($144,545); United Way ($28,000).
Giving Analysis: Giving for 2000 includes: foundation scholarships ($28,200) foundation grants to United Way ($65,500)
Assets: $4,915,820 (2000); $5,000,000 (1999 approx); $3,007,786 (1996)
Gifts Received: $600,000 (1999 approx); $150,000 (1996); $215,000 (1995). Note: Contributions are received from Bardes Corp.

Typical Recipients
Arts & Humanities: Arts Associations & Councils, Arts Centers, Arts Funds, Community Arts, Historic Preservation, History & Archaeology, Libraries, Museums/Galleries, Music, Opera, Performing Arts, Public Broadcasting, Theater
Civic & Public Affairs: Botanical Gardens/Parks, Clubs, Employment/Job Training, Civic & Public Affairs-General, Philanthropic Organizations, Public Policy, Urban & Community Affairs, Zoos/Aquariums
Education: Business Education, Colleges & Universities, Education Associations, Education Funds, Elementary Education (Public), Education-General, Private Education (Precollege), Student Aid, Vocational & Technical Education
Environment: Environment-General, Resource Conservation
Health: AIDS/HIV, Alzheimers Disease, Cancer, Children's Health/Hospitals, Emergency/Ambulance Services, Eyes/Blindness, Heart, Hospices, Hospitals, Medical Rehabilitation, Medical Research, Preventive Medicine/Wellness Organizations, Public Health, Single-Disease Health Associations
International: Foreign Arts Organizations, International Affairs
Religion: Churches, Religious Organizations, Religious Welfare

Social Services: Animal Protection, Camps, Child Welfare, Community Service Organizations, Family Planning, Family Services, Recreation & Athletics, Social Services-General, United Funds/United Ways, Youth Organizations

Application Procedures
Initial Contact: Written request
Deadlines: None.

Corporate Officials
Merrilyn B. Bardes: president B 1945. PRIM CORP EMPL president: Bardes Corp.
Brittain B. Cudlip: chairman B 1948. PRIM CORP EMPL chairman: Bardes Corp. CORP AFFIL president: WRB Inc.; chairman: Walnut Hill Properties Inc.; vice president: Kentucky Connector Corp.; president: New Horizons Madonna Hall; vice president: Ilsco Corp. NONPR AFFIL trustee: Tufts University.
David J. FitzGibbon: president, chief executive officer B 1944. ED Thomas More College (1965). PRIM CORP EMPL president, chief executive officer: Bardes Corp. CORP AFFIL chief operating officer: Ilsco Corp.; president: Kentucky Connector Corp.
J. E. Valentine: chief financial officer PRIM CORP EMPL chief financial officer: Bardes Corp.

Foundation Officials
Rebecca Autry: secretary

Grants Analysis
Disclosure Period: calendar year ending 2000
Total Grants: $198,859*
Number of Grants: 71
Average Grant: $2,801
Highest Grant: $25,000
Lowest Grant: $100
Typical Range: $200 to $10,000
*Note: Giving excludes scholarships and United Way.

Recent Grants
Note: Grants derived from 2001 Form 990.

General
21,000	Lawrenceville School, Lawrenceville, NJ
15,000	National Gallery of Art, Washington, DC
10,000	Boston College, Chestnut Hill, MA
10,000	Jefferson Scholars Program, Charlottesville, VA
9,226	Riverbend Music Center, Riverbend, NJ
7,500	Fine Arts Fund, Cincinnati, OH
6,500	Cincinnati Symphony Orchestra, Cincinnati, OH
5,850	Society of Four Arts, Palm Beach, FL
5,000	NESF, Rosslyn, VA
4,200	Preservation Foundation, Palm Beach, FL

HOLLIS AND HELEN BARIGHT FOUNDATION

Giving Contact
Thomas V. Van Robays, Contact
6015 Northwest Radial Highway
Omaha, NE 68104
Phone: (402)554-4792

Description
Founded: 1995
EIN: 470789577
Organization Type: Private Foundation
Giving Locations: NE: Omaha
Grant Types: General Support, Scholarship.

Donor Information
Founder: Established in 1995 by the late Hollis Baright.

Financial Summary
Total Giving: $401,000 (2001); $429,350 (2000); $427,601 (1999)
Giving Analysis: Giving for 2001 includes: foundation scholarships ($1,000); 2000: foundation scholarships ($1,000); 1999: foundation scholarships ($1,000)
Assets: $5,264,638 (2001); $6,172,107 (2000); $6,762,941 (1999)
Gifts Received: $4,556,340 (1995)

Typical Recipients
Arts & Humanities: Museums/Galleries
Civic & Public Affairs: Botanical Gardens/Parks, Zoos/Aquariums
Education: Colleges & Universities, Student Aid
Social Services: Crime Prevention

Application Procedures
Initial Contact: Send a brief letter of inquiry.
Application Requirements: Include a description of organization, amount requested, and purpose of funds sought.
Deadlines: None.

Restrictions
Donations are not usually made for current operating expenses.

Additional Information
Trust(s): Great Western Bank

Foundation Officials
Ralph W. Palmer: co-trustee
Nick R. Taylor: co-trustee

Grants Analysis
Disclosure Period: calendar year ending 2001
Total Grants: $400,000*
Number of Grants: 3
Highest Grant: $275,000
Lowest Grant: $25,000
*Note: Giving excludes scholarships.

Recent Grants
Note: Grants derived from 2000 Form 990.

Library-Related
103,350	Ralston Public Library Foundation, Ralston, NE

General
275,000	Durham Western Heritage Museum, Omaha, NE
50,000	Omaha Zoo Foundation, Omaha, NE -- for construction of new visitor's center
1,000	University of Nebraska Omaha, Omaha, NE -- scholarships

BARKER FOUNDATION INC.

Giving Contact
Allan M. Barker, Treasurer & Trustee
Barker Foundation Inc
PO Box 328
Nashua, NH 03061-0328
Phone: (603)889-1763

Description
Founded: 1954
EIN: 026005885
Organization Type: Private Foundation
Giving Locations: DC; ME; MA; NH
Grant Types: Emergency, General Support.

Donor Information
Founder: the late Walter Barker, Irene L. Barker

Financial Summary
Total Giving: $292,786 (2001); $296,480 (2000); $281,029 (1999)
Giving Analysis: Giving for 2000 includes: foundation scholarships ($17,000); 1998: foundation grants to United Way ($1,500) foundation scholarships ($33,114)
Assets: $6,097,009 (2001); $6,785,025 (2000); $6,984,334 (1999)

Typical Recipients
Arts & Humanities: Historic Preservation, History & Archaeology, Libraries, Public Broadcasting
Civic & Public Affairs: Community Foundations, Employment/Job Training, Civic & Public Affairs-General, Municipalities/Towns, Safety, Urban & Community Affairs
Education: Colleges & Universities, Elementary Education (Private), Education-General, Private Education (Precollege)
Environment: Environment-General
Health: Arthritis, Cancer, Children's Health/Hospitals, Clinics/Medical Centers, Diabetes, Emergency/Ambulance Services, Eyes/Blindness, Heart, Hospices, Hospitals, Medical Research, Multiple Sclerosis, Nursing Services, Respiratory, Single-Disease Health Associations, Trauma Treatment
Religion: Churches
Social Services: Animal Protection, Big Brother/Big Sister, Child Welfare, Community Service Organizations, Crime Prevention, Day Care, Domestic Violence, Family Services, Food/Clothing Distribution, People with Disabilities, Scouts, Senior Services, Shelters/Homelessness, Special Olympics, United Funds/United Ways, YMCA/YWCA/YMHA/YWHA, Youth Organizations

Application Procedures
Initial Contact: Submit a one-page concept paper.
Application Requirements: Include a description of organization, amount requested, purpose of funds sought, proof of tax-exempt status.
Deadlines: None.
Notes: Due to the volume of applications, individual replies to requests are not possible. Phone inquiries are not accepted.

Restrictions
Does not support individuals, political or lobbying groups, or non tax-exempt organizations. No restrictions by geographical areas, but the majority of requests are from New Hampshire organizations.

Additional Information
Provides scholarships to students demonstrating financial need.

Foundation Officials
Anne M. April: trustee
Allan M. Barker: treasurer, trustee
Dorothy A. Barker: trustee
Douglas M. Barker: secretary
Elizabeth M. Bucknam: president, trustee
Carol A. Larouche: assistant secretary
Edward P. Moran, Jr.: trustee
Susan B. Moran: vice president, trustee
Sidney F. Thaxter: clerk

Grants Analysis
Disclosure Period: calendar year ending 2001
Total Grants: $292,786
Number of Grants: 55
Average Grant: $4,377*
Highest Grant: $52,052
Lowest Grant: $500
Typical Range: $500 to $10,000
*Note: Average grant figure excludes highest grant.

Recent Grants
Note: Grants derived from 2001 Form 990.

General
52,053	Lahey Clinic, Burlington, MA
25,000	American Red Cross Disaster Relief Fund, Washington, DC
15,000	Community Hospice House, Merrimack, NH
12,250	Boy and Girls Club of Greater Nashua, Nashua, NH
12,000	New Hampton School, New Hampton, NH
10,000	Dexter Historical Society, Dexter, ME
10,000	Nashua Soup Kitchen & Shelter, Inc., Nashua, NH
10,000	St. Joseph Community Services, Merrimack, NH
8,000	Colby College, Waterville, ME
6,000	New Hampshire Association for the Blind, Concord, NH

J.M.R. BARKER FOUNDATION

Giving Contact
Robert R. Barker, President, Director & Member
530 5th Ave.
2nd Floor
New York, NY 10036-5101
Phone: (212)371-6777

Description
Founded: 1968
EIN: 136268289
Organization Type: Private Foundation
Giving Locations: MA: Boston; NY: New York
Grant Types: Capital, Endowment, General Support, Multiyear/Continuing Support, Operating Expenses, Project, Research.

Donor Information
Founder: the late James M. Barker, the late Margaret R. Barker, Robert R. Barker

Financial Summary
Total Giving: $1,594,250 (1999); $1,064,500 (1998); $1,297,700 (1996)
Giving Analysis: Giving for 1998 includes: foundation ($1,064,000)
Assets: $26,443,085 (1998); $22,969,192 (1996); $21,248,268 (1995)

Typical Recipients
Arts & Humanities: Community Arts, Libraries, Literary Arts, Museums/Galleries, Music, Performing Arts, Public Broadcasting
Civic & Public Affairs: Civic & Public Affairs-General, Nonprofit Management, Philanthropic Organizations, Public Policy, Urban & Community Affairs
Education: Colleges & Universities, Continuing Education, Engineering/Technological Education, Education-General, Gifted & Talented Programs, International Studies, Legal Education, Minority Education, Private Education (Precollege), Public Education (Precollege), School Volunteerism
Environment: Environment-General, Resource Conservation, Wildlife Protection
Health: Clinics/Medical Centers, Health Funds, Health Organizations, Home-Care Services, Hospitals
International: International Environmental Issues, International Relations, International Relief Efforts, International Relief Efforts
Religion: Churches, Jewish Causes, Religious Organizations
Science: Science Museums, Scientific Centers & Institutes, Scientific Labs

Social Services: Child Welfare, Community Service Organizations, Crime Prevention, Family Planning, Family Services, People with Disabilities, Refugee Assistance, Senior Services, Social Services-General, United Funds/United Ways, Volunteer Services, Youth Organizations

Application Procedures
Initial Contact: Before sending a formal grant proposal, submit a preliminary letter of inquiry.
Application Requirements: Briefly describe the programs of the sponsoring organizations. Indicate amount requested and what will be accomplished as a result of the grant.
Deadlines: November 1.
Notes: Primarily supports preslected organizations.

Foundation Officials
Ann S. Barker: director
Elizabeth S. Barker: vice president, director, mem
James R. Barker: mem B Cleveland, OH 1935. ED Columbia University BA (1957); Harvard University MBA (1963). PRIM CORP EMPL founder, vice chairman, co-owner: Mormac Marine Group. CORP AFFIL director: Pittston Co.; chairman: Lakes Shipping Co.; vice chairman: Moran Towing Co.; chairman: Interlake Holding Co.; chairman, director, president: Interlake Steamship Co.; trustee: Eastern Enterprises; director: GTE Corp. NONPR AFFIL vice chairman, trustee: Stamford Hospital.
Robert R. Barker: president, director, mem
Dr. William Benjamin Barker: director, mem B Stamford, CT 1947. ED Harvard University (1969-1975). PRIM CORP EMPL president, chief executive officer: Data Race Inc. CORP AFFIL general partner: Robert R Barker & Co.
Margaret Barker Clark: director, mem
Robert P. Conner: treasurer, director B New Bedford, MA 1948. ED Boston College BS (1970); Pace University MS (1977). PRIM CORP EMPL senior vice president: J&W Seligman & Co. CORP AFFIL director: CRB Broadcasting Corp. NONPR AFFIL member: Beta Gamma Sigma; member: New York Saint Society CPA's; member: American Institute of CPA's; member: Alpha Sigma Nu.
John W. Holman, Jr.: director PRIM CORP EMPL managing director: Triak Services Corp.
Maureen A. Hopkins: secretary, admin
Richard D. Kahn: assistant secretary, director B New York, NY 1931. ED Harvard University AB (1952); Harvard University JD (1955). PRIM CORP EMPL counsel: Debevoise & Plimpton. NONPR AFFIL member: New York City Bar Association; member: Phi Beta Kappa; director: JMR Barker Foundation; member: Montauk Citizens Advisory Committee; director: Concerned Citizens Montauk; director: Group South Fork. CLUB AFFIL Harvard Club.
Dwight E. Lee: vice president, director
William L. Musser: director
Donna Rosario: assistant treasurer

Grants Analysis
Disclosure Period: calendar year ending 1999
Total Grants: $1,594,250
Number of Grants: 35
Average Grant: $17,402*
Highest Grant: $510,000
Typical Range: $1,000 to $20,000
*Note: Average grant figure excludes two highest grants ($1,020,000).

Recent Grants
Note: Grants derived from 1999 Form 990.

General
510,000	American Museum of Natural History, New York, NY
510,000	Harvard University, Cambridge, MA
100,000	Nursing and Home Care, Wilton, CT
100,000	Waveny Care Center, New Canaan, CT
50,000	San Antonio Symphony, San Antonio, TX

28,750	Amazon Conservation Team, Arlington, VA
25,000	Connecticut Friends School, Wilton, CT
23,500	Grafton Museum of Natural History, Grafton, VT
20,000	Bridge Fund of New York, New York, NY
20,000	Karme-Choling

BARKER WELFARE FOUNDATION

Giving Contact

Sarane H. Ross, President & Director
1007 Glen Cove Ave.
Glen Head, NY 11545
Phone: (516)759-5592
Fax: (516)759-5497
E-mail: barkersmd@aol.com
Web: http://www.barkerwelfare.org

Description

Founded: 1934
EIN: 366018526
Organization Type: General Purpose Foundation
Giving Locations: IL: Chicago; IN: Michigan City; NY: New York
Grant Types: Capital, General Support, Loan, Operating Expenses, Project, Research.

Donor Information

Founder: Established in 1934 by the late Catherine B. Hickox , whose daughter, Mrs. Walter L. Ross II, is the current president. In addition, five relatives are also active in the foundation's activities.

Financial Summary

Total Giving: $2,627,607 (fiscal year ending September 30, 2001); $3,105,000 (fiscal 1999); $2,958,500 (fiscal 1998)
Assets: $60,278,364 (fiscal 2001); $66,538,388 (fiscal 1999); $59,092,655 (fiscal 1998)

Typical Recipients

Arts & Humanities: Arts Centers, Arts Institutes, Arts Outreach, Ballet, Ethnic & Folk Arts, Arts & Humanities-General, Historic Preservation, History & Archaeology, Libraries, Museums/Galleries, Music, Opera, Performing Arts, Public Broadcasting, Theater
Civic & Public Affairs: Botanical Gardens/Parks, Economic Development, Employment/Job Training, Gay/Lesbian Issues, Civic & Public Affairs-General, Hispanic Affairs, Inner-City Development, Legal Aid, Nonprofit Management, Philanthropic Organizations, Urban & Community Affairs, Zoos/Aquariums
Education: Afterschool/Enrichment Programs, Arts/Humanities Education, Colleges & Universities, Education Reform, Elementary Education (Public), Environmental Education, Health & Physical Education, Literacy, Minority Education, Preschool Education, Private Education (Precollege)
Environment: Forestry, Environment-General, Resource Conservation, Wildlife Protection
Health: Adolescent Health Issues, AIDS/HIV, Cancer, Children's Health/Hospitals, Clinics/Medical Centers, Emergency/Ambulance Services, Heart, Home-Care Services, Hospitals, Long-Term Care, Medical Rehabilitation, Medical Training, Mental Health, Nursing Services, Nutrition, Outpatient Health Care, Prenatal Health Issues, Public Health
International: International Environmental Issues
Religion: Dioceses, Religious Organizations, Religious Welfare
Science: Science Museums, Scientific Labs, Scientific Research
Social Services: At-Risk Youth, Big Brother/Big Sister, Camps, Child Abuse, Child Welfare, Community Centers, Community Service Organizations, Crime Prevention, Day Care, Delinquency & Criminal Rehabilitation, Family Planning, Family Services, Food/Clothing Distribution, People with Disabilities, Recreation & Athletics, Scouts, Senior Services, Shelters/Homelessness, Substance Abuse, United Funds/United Ways, Volunteer Services, YMCA/YWCA/YMHA/YWHA, Youth Organizations

Application Procedures

Initial Contact: To apply, a brief two- to three-page letter or telephone call is suggested, describing the organization and the request for which funds are being sought.
Application Requirements: A budget and evidence of tax-exempt status should be included with the letter of inquiry. If the request falls within the current scope of the foundation's interests, the applicant will be asked to submit an application and supply additional information as required.
Deadlines: The foundation requires that completed applications be submitted by February 1 for May board meeting, and by August 1 for November board meeting.
Review Process: Applicants may be notified during the process that funds are not available. Organizations who receive approval for a grant will receive the funds approximately six weeks after the directors meet.
Notes: Organizations in the Michigan City, IN, area must also send an additional copy of complete proposal to Thomas P. McCormick, First Citizens Bank, PO Box 800, Michigan City, IN 46360.

Restrictions

As a general rule, the foundation will not consider support for individual scholarships or fellowships; costs of fund-raising campaigns; endowments; conferences; seminars; conduit organizations; medical research; scientific research; national education, health, or welfare funds; grants to operating foundations; institutions of higher education, private elementary or secondary schools; professional schools or trade organizations; or films.
No grants are made for lobbying or legislative activities, or for start-up organizations, emergency funds, or deficit financing. The foundation also does not accept unsolicited applications for grants in the Chicago, IL, area. the Chicago, IL, area.

Additional Information

The foundation will not accept more than one proposal within a 12-month period.
The foundation suggests submitting completed proposals at least a month before the official deadline so that site visits can be made in a timely matter.
Publications: Application Form; Checklist; Annual Report (including Guidelines)

Foundation Officials

Katrina H. Becker: vice president, secretary, director
Diane Curtis: director
Susan M. DeMaio: assistant secretary
Charles C. Hickox: director ED Columbia University (1961).
John B. Hickox: director
Linda J. Hickox: director
Mary Lou Linnen: director
Alline Matheson: director
Thomas P. McCormick: treasurer
Sarane R. O'Connor: director
Alexander B. Ross: director
Sarane H. Ross: president

Grants Analysis

Disclosure Period: fiscal year ending September 30, 2001
Total Grants: $2,627,607
Number of Grants: 232
Average Grant: $11,326*
Highest Grant: $60,000
Typical Range: $5,000 to $20,000
***Note:** Average grant figure excludes highest grant.

Recent Grants

Note: Grants derived from fiscal 2001 Form 990.

Library-Related
50,000	Chicago Public Library Foundation, Chicago, IL -- for the Family Computer Center
20,000	New York Public Library, New York, NY -- for Page Program

General
60,000	Chicago Youth Centers, Chicago, IL -- for capital improvements
60,000	Wildlife Conservation Society, Bronx, NY -- for the Tiger Kingdom
52,000	Friends of Barker Civic Center, Michigan City, IN -- for repairs and to purchase new furnishings
50,000	Carnegie Hall Society, New York, NY -- for the state-of-the-art venue for music performance and music education
50,000	Chicago Commons Association, Chicago, IL -- for the West Humbolt Settlement House Construction Project
50,000	Metropolitan Opera Association, Inc., New York, NY -- for the Met in the Parks
50,000	Rehabilitation Institute Foundation, Chicago, IL -- for Patient and Family Enrichment Center
50,000	Salvation Army of Michigan City, Michigan City, IN -- for Help Hope Find a Brand New Home Capital Campaign
50,000	YMCA Metropolitan Chicago, Chicago, IL -- for construction of the Mini Field House
27,000	Happiness is Camping, Bronx, NY -- for furnishings, equipment and supplies for the camp

BARNES FOUNDATION

Giving Contact

Sally A. O'Connor, Vice President & Executive Director
PO Box 315
East Hartland, CT 06027-0315
Phone: (860)653-0462
E-mail: barnesfd@erols.com

Description

Founded: 1945
EIN: 066037160
Organization Type: Private Foundation
Giving Locations: CT
Grant Types: Conference/Seminar, Project, Scholarship, Seed Money.

Donor Information

Founder: Carlyle F. Barnes, Aurelia B. Bristow, Louise B. Adams, the late Myrtle I. Barnes, the late Fuller F. Barnes

Financial Summary

Total Giving: $244,000 (2002); $349,250 (2000); $223,000 (1999)
Assets: $7,223,809 (2002); $8,779,385 (2000); $8,066,076 (1999)
Gifts Received: $200 (1998); $300 (1993); $36,000 (1992)

Typical Recipients

Arts & Humanities: Arts Centers, Arts Outreach, Dance, Libraries, Literary Arts, Museums/Galleries, Music, Performing Arts, Public Broadcasting, Theater
Civic & Public Affairs: Botanical Gardens/Parks, Community Foundations, Zoos/Aquariums

Education: Afterschool/Enrichment Programs, Arts/Humanities Education, Colleges & Universities, Education Associations, Education Funds, Elementary Education (Public), Engineering/Technological Education, Environmental Education, Faculty Development, Education-General, Gifted & Talented Programs, International Exchange, International Studies, Leadership Training, Minority Education, Private Education (Precollege), Public Education (Precollege), Science/Mathematics Education, Special Education, Student Aid

Environment: Environment-General, Environment-General

Religion: Churches

Science: Science Museums, Scientific Centers & Institutes

Social Services: Camps, Child Welfare, Community Service Organizations, Family Services, People with Disabilities, Scouts, YMCA/YWCA/YMHA/YWHA, Youth Organizations

Application Procedures

Initial Contact: Send a letter of inquiry requesting application guidelines.

Application Requirements: Include a description of organization, amount requested, purpose of funds sought, recently audited financial statement, and proof of tax-exempt status.

Deadlines: Apply 6 to 12 months in advance.

Notes: Foundation accepts the Common Application Form of the Connecticut Council on Philanthropy.

Restrictions

Limited to federally tax-exempt nonprofit organizations relating to precollegiate education in Connecticut.

Additional Information

Publications: Annual Report (including Application Guidelines)

Foundation Officials

Louise B. Adams: trustee

Carlyle Fuller Barnes: president B Bristol, CT 1924. ED Wesleyan University AB (1948). CORP AFFIL director: Travelers Life & Annuity Co.; director: United Bank & Trust Co.; director: Travelers Insurance Companies; director: Travelers Insurance Co.; director: Travelers Corp.; director: Travelers Indemnity Co. North America. NONPR AFFIL director: Institute Living; trustee: New England Colleges Fund; president: Bristol Hospital Development Foundation.

Elliott B. Bristow: treasurer

Joan B. Flynn: secretary

Sally A. O'Connor: vice president, executive director

Grants Analysis

Disclosure Period: calendar year ending 2002

Total Grants: $244,000

Number of Grants: 31

Average Grant: $7,871

Highest Grant: $20,000

Lowest Grant: $2,500

Typical Range: $2,000 to $10,000

Recent Grants

Note: Grants derived from 2002 Form 990.

General

20,000	MacDuffie School, Springfield, MA -- for improving the technology resources at the school
20,000	Walks Foundation, Simsbury, CT -- for Scholarship Program
15,000	Lake Champlain Maritime Museum, Vergennes, VT -- for Champlain Discovery Program
15,000	Main Street Community Foundation, Bristol, CT -- for a special fund in honor of Hap Barnes
15,000	Walnut Hill School, Natick, MA -- to establish a special fund in honor of Louise B. Adams
10,000	Maritime Aquarium, Norwalk, CT -- for Harbor Seal Census Study
10,000	Science Center of Connecticut, West Hartford, CT -- for collaborative environmental education program
10,000	Teachers College Columbia University, New York, NY -- for the Private School Leadership Program
10,000	University of Hartford, Hartford, CT -- for educational main street - a tutoring program
9,000	New Haven Ecology Project, New Haven, CT -- support for the agricultural, science and environmental education programs

BARNES GROUP, INC.

Company Headquarters

123 Main Street
PO Box 489
Bristol, CT 06011-0489
Phone: (860)583-7070
Fax: (860)589-7466
Web: http://www.barnesgroupinc.com

Company Description

Founded: 1857
Ticker: B
Exchange: NYSE
Revenue: US$784 million (2002)
Employees: 5150 (2002)
SIC(s): 3465 Automotive Stampings, 3493 Steel Springs Except Wire, 3495 Wire Springs, 3496 Miscellaneous Fabricated Wire Products.

Operating Locations

Barnes Group Inc. (CA--Gardena; CT--East Windsor, Windsor; GA--Norcross; IL--Rockford; MI--Lansing, Saline, Ypsilanti; MS--Meridian; NJ--Edison; NY--Syracuse; OH--Cleveland, Dayton; PA--Corry; TN--Memphis; TX--Arlington, Dallas; UT--Ogden; WA--Auburn; WI--Milwaukee, New Berlin)

Barnes Group Foundation Inc.

Giving Contact

Thomas Barnes, Secretary
123 Main Street
PO Box 489
Bristol, CT 06011-0489
Phone: (860)583-7070
Fax: (860)589-7466

Alternate Contact

Scholarship Application Contact
Citizen Scholarship Foundation of America
1505 Riverview Road
PO Box 297
St. Peter, MN 56082
Phone: (603)627-3870

Description

EIN: 237339727
Organization Type: Corporate Foundation
Giving Locations: operating communities.
Grant Types: General Support.

Financial Summary

Total Giving: $670,933 (2001); $674,680 (2000); $450,000 (1999 approx). Note: Contributes through foundation only.

Giving Analysis: Giving for 2001 includes: foundation grants to United Way ($60,699); foundation scholarships ($151,050); foundation scholarship ($459,184); 2000: foundation grants to United Way ($21,050); foundation ($653,630); 1997: foundation grants to United Way ($30,140)

Assets: $1,748,961 (2001); $2,598,194 (2000); $3,587,835 (1998)

Gifts Received: $500,000 (1998); $750,000 (1997); $500,000 (1996). Note: In 1998, contributions were received from Barnes Group Inc.

Typical Recipients

Arts & Humanities: Arts Associations & Councils, Arts Centers, Arts Festivals, Community Arts, Dance, Historic Preservation, Libraries, Museums/Galleries, Music, Opera, Public Broadcasting, Theater

Civic & Public Affairs: African American Affairs, Clubs, Community Foundations, Economic Development, Civic & Public Affairs-General, Housing, Legal Aid, Minority Business, Municipalities/Towns, Public Policy, Safety, Urban & Community Affairs, Zoos/Aquariums

Education: Afterschool/Enrichment Programs, Business Education, Colleges & Universities, Community & Junior Colleges, Education Funds, Engineering/Technological Education, Education-General, Minority Education, Private Education (Precollege), Private Education (Precollege), Public Education (Precollege), Religious Education, Science/Mathematics Education, Secondary Education (Private), Special Education, Student Aid, Vocational & Technical Education

Environment: Air/Water Quality, Environment-General

Health: Cancer, Children's Health/Hospitals, Clinics/Medical Centers, Emergency/Ambulance Services, Hospitals, Medical Research, Single-Disease Health Associations, Trauma Treatment

International: International Relief Efforts

Religion: Religious Organizations

Science: Science Museums

Social Services: Big Brother/Big Sister, Child Welfare, Community Service Organizations, Crime Prevention, Family Services, Homes, People with Disabilities, Recreation & Athletics, Scouts, Senior Services, Special Olympics, Substance Abuse, United Funds/United Ways, United Funds/United Ways, YMCA/YWCA/YMHA/YWHA, Youth Organizations

Application Procedures

Initial Contact: Write or call an operating division of the company requesting application form.

Application Requirements: State purpose, history of organization, describe project, annual itemized budget, project budget, foundation and corporate donors, and 501(c)(3) exemption letter.

Deadlines: March 1.

Decision Notification: Board meets four times per year.

Restrictions

To be an eligible candidate for the scholarship grant, applicants must be a child of either a current Barnes Group employee in the US or Canada who has worked for the company at least one year by the application deadline, or a retired employee.

The foundation does not support political or lobbying efforts.

Additional Information

Publications: Contributions Policy; Guidelines

Corporate Officials

Thomas O. Barnes: board chairmans B 1949. PRIM CORP EMPL board chairman: Barnes Group Inc. CORP AFFIL chairman: Chapman Machine Co. Inc.

John Edward Besser: senior vice president finance & law B Iowa City, IA 1942. ED University of Rochester AB (1964); Northwestern University JD

(1967). PRIM CORP EMPL senior vice president finance & law: Barnes Group Inc. NONPR AFFIL member: Missouri Bar Association; board electors: Wadsworth Atheneum; member: American Bar Association; director: Greater Hartford Arts Council.

Edmund Mogford Carpenter: president, chief executive officer B Lodi, CA December 28, 1941. ED University of Michigan BS (1963); University of Michigan MBA (1964). PRIM CORP EMPL president, chief executive officer: Barnes Group Inc. CORP AFFIL director: Electroglas Inc.; director: ChevronTexaco Inc.; director: Dana Corp.; director: Campbell Soup Co. NONPR AFFIL director: Junior Achievement; member: Machinery & Allied Products Institute.

John J. Locher: vice president, treasurer B 1944. ED Fordham University BA (1966); New York University Leonard N. Stern School of Business MBA (1971). PRIM CORP EMPL vice president, treasurer: Barnes Group Inc.

Foundation Officials

Thomas O. Barnes: secretary (see above)
Wallace W. Barnes: director B Bristol, CT 1926. ED Williams College BA (1949); Yale University LLB (1952); Harvard University Advanced Management Program (1973); Harvard University LLD (1988). CORP AFFIL chairman, director: Tradewind Turbines Corp.; director: Loctite Corp.; director: Rogers Corp.; director: Connecticut Innovations Inc.; director: De-Maria Electro Optics Inc.; director executive committee: Aetna Life & Casualty Co. Inc. NONPR AFFIL director: Great Hartford Chamber of Commerce; member: Newcomen Society; member: Connecticut Business & Industry Association; member: Bristol Historical Society; member: Connecticut Bar Association; member: American Judicature Society; member: American Arbitration Association; member: American Bar Association. CLUB AFFIL Williams Club; Yale Club; Elks Club; Farmington Country Club; Economic Club; American Legion Club; Chippance Golf Club.
John Edward Besser: director (see above)
John J. Locher: treasurer (see above)

Grants Analysis

Disclosure Period: calendar year ending 2001
Total Grants: $459,184*
Number of Grants: 241
Average Grant: $1,905
Highest Grant: $41,986
Lowest Grant: $40
Typical Range: $50 to $4,000
*Note: Giving excludes United Way and scholarships.

Recent Grants

Note: Grants derived from 2001 Form 990.

General

75,525	Citizen's Scholarship Foundation of America, St. Peter, MN
75,525	Citizen's Scholarship Foundation of America, St. Peter, MN
41,985	NYCCPI Twin Towers Fund, New York, NY
20,000	Metropolitan Opera Association, Inc., New York, NY
15,000	Bristol Regional Environmental Center, Bristol, CT
15,000	Bushnell, Hartford, CT
12,500	Connecticut Children's Hospital Center, Hartford, CT
12,000	Greater Hartford Arts Center, Hartford, CT
10,000	Sloan-Kettering Society
10,000	Urban League, Hartford, CT

BARRA FOUNDATION

Giving Contact

William Harral, III, President
8200 Flourtown Avenue, Suite 12
Wyndmoor, DE 19038-7976

Phone: (215)233-5115
Fax: (215)836-1033

Description

Founded: 1963
EIN: 236277885
Organization Type: General Purpose Foundation
Giving Locations: PA: Philadelphia
Grant Types: Conference/Seminar, Matching, Project, Research, Seed Money.

Donor Information

Founder: Established in Delaware in 1963 by Robert L. McNeil Jr., who currently serves as president, treasurer, and director of the foundation.

Financial Summary

Total Giving: $2,294,000 (2001); $3,966,213 (2000); $3,624,416 (1998)
Giving Analysis: Giving for 2000 includes: foundation grants to United Way ($13,500)
Assets: $50,692,059 (2001); $54,500,983 (2000); $49,044,311 (1998)
Gifts Received: $1,003 (2000); $5,034,000 (1997). Note: In 1997, contributions were received from Robert L. McNeil, Jr.

Typical Recipients

Arts & Humanities: Arts Associations & Councils, Arts Centers, Arts Funds, Arts Institutes, Ballet, Community Arts, Dance, Ethnic & Folk Arts, Historic Preservation, History & Archaeology, Libraries, Literary Arts, Museums/Galleries, Opera, Performing Arts, Public Broadcasting, Theater
Civic & Public Affairs: Botanical Gardens/Parks, Business/Free Enterprise, Chambers of Commerce, Civil Rights, Clubs, Community Foundations, Economic Development, Employment/Job Training, First Amendment Issues, Civic & Public Affairs-General, Hispanic Affairs, Housing, Philanthropic Organizations, Professional & Trade Associations, Public Policy, Urban & Community Affairs, Women's Affairs, Zoos/Aquariums
Education: Afterschool/Enrichment Programs, Arts/Humanities Education, Colleges & Universities, Community & Junior Colleges, Economic Education, Education Associations, Education Reform, Education-General, Health & Physical Education, Leadership Training, Literacy, Medical Education, Minority Education, Private Education (Precollege), Religious Education, Science/Mathematics Education, Social Sciences Education
Environment: Air/Water Quality, Environment-General, Resource Conservation, Watershed
Health: Alzheimers Disease, Cancer, Children's Health/Hospitals, Clinics/Medical Centers, Emergency/Ambulance Services, Health-General, Health Organizations, Home-Care Services, Hospices, Hospitals, Hospitals (University Affiliated), Long-Term Care, Medical Rehabilitation, Medical Research, Preventive Medicine/Wellness Organizations, Public Health, Single-Disease Health Associations
International: Foreign Arts Organizations, Foreign Educational Institutions, International Relations, International Relief Efforts
Religion: Churches, Religion-General, Jewish Causes, Religious Organizations, Religious Welfare
Science: Scientific Centers & Institutes, Scientific Research
Social Services: Animal Protection, Child Welfare, Community Service Organizations, Emergency Relief, Family Planning, Family Services, Food/Clothing Distribution, Homes, People with Disabilities, Scouts, Senior Services, Shelters/Homelessness, United Funds/United Ways, Volunteer Services, Youth Organizations

Application Procedures

Initial Contact: Send in a preliminary letter not exceeding two pages.
Application Requirements: The preliminary letter should serve as request for funding, summarizing the

objectives and significance of the project; the methodology; qualifications of the investigator; estimated timetable; project budget and other sources of support; the organization's history and goals; listing of officers and directors; and a copy of the IRS tax-exemption ruling. If the letter indicates that the project may fall within the foundation's interest, a formal application will be sent.
Deadlines: None.
Review Process: Upon receipt, the project will be submitted to the foundation's advisors for evaluation and recommendation to the board of directors. The board meets in November, and as appropriate. The evaluation process may take three to six months. Applicants will be notified of a final decision.

Restrictions

The foundation does not give grants to individuals; for annual or capital campaigns; deficit drives; building renovation or repairs; endowment funds; publications not related to the project; international programs and institutions; operating budgets; scholarships; fellowships; or programs in process. In addition, the foundation will not make loans. Giving restricted to greater Philadelphia.

Additional Information

Publications: Guidelines; Application Form; Program Policy Statement

Foundation Officials

Harry E. Cerino: director
Frank R. Donahue, Jr.: secretary, director
Robert Paul Hauptfuhrer: director B Philadelphia, PA 1931. ED Princeton University BA (1953); Harvard University Graduate School of Business Administration MBA (1957). PRIM CORP EMPL chairman, chief executive officer, director: Oryx Energy Co. CORP AFFIL director: Quaker Chemical Corp. NONPR AFFIL trustee: Princeton University; chairman board advisors: University Pennsylvania Cancer Center; member: National Petroleum Council; member: Natural Gas Supply Association; member, board governors: Dallas Symphony Association; member: National Association Manufacturers; member: Conference Board; member: American Petroleum Institute; director: American Productivity & Quality Control Center. CLUB AFFIL Union League Club; Philadelphia Country Club; Pine Valley Golf Club; Merion Cricket Club.
Herman R. Hutchinson: vice president, director
Victoria M. Levine: director
Joanna M. Lewis: director
Collin F. McNeil: director
Robert L. McNeil, III: director
Robert L. McNeil, Jr.: president, treasurer, director CORP AFFIL director: Arrow International Inc.
Seymour S. Preston, III: director
Lowell S. Thomas, Jr.: director

Grants Analysis

Disclosure Period: calendar year ending 2001
Total Grants: $3,950,003*
Number of Grants: 284
Average Grant: $13,908
Highest Grant: $1,000,000
Lowest Grant: $1,000
Typical Range: $1,000 to $12,500
*Note: Giving excludes United Way.

Recent Grants

Note: Grants derived from 2000 Form 990.

Library-Related

500,000	Library Company of Philadelphia, Philadelphia, PA -- International Fellow Program
50,000	Athenaeum of Philadelphia, Philadelphia, PA -- conference seating
50,000	Library Company of Philadelphia, Philadelphia, PA -- retrospective conversion
7,500	Athenaeum of Philadelphia, Philadelphia, PA -- conference seating

General

1,000,000	Woodmere Art Museum, Philadelphia, PA
500,000	Philadelphia Museum of Art, Philadelphia, PA
250,000	National Constitution Center, Philadelphia, PA
200,000	Chestnut Hill HealthCare, Philadelphia, PA -- Public Emergency Room
74,233	College of Physicians, Philadelphia, PA -- Hippocrates Symposium
50,000	American Philosophical Society
50,000	Metropolitan Career Center, Philadelphia, PA -- Project Future
49,500	Society of Architectural Historians, Philadelphia, PA
47,500	University of Pennsylvania Press, Philadelphia, PA -- Fort Mifflin
45,000	American Revolution Patriots Fund, Conshohocken, PA

BARRINGTON FOUNDATION

Giving Contact
David Strassler, President
Barrington Foundation
PO Box 750
7-11 South Broadway, Suite 200
Great Barrington, MA 01230
Phone: (914)285-9393

Description
Founded: 1978
EIN: 132930849
Organization Type: Private Foundation
Giving Locations: MA
Grant Types: General Support, Multiyear/Continuing Support, Project.

Financial Summary
Total Giving: $897,750 (2002); $1,163,000 (2000); $1,336,580 (1999)
Giving Analysis: Giving for 2002 includes: foundation grants to United Way ($3,000); 2000: foundation grants to United Way ($2,000) 1999: foundation grants to United Way ($3,000)
Assets: $1,056,475 (2002); $1,645,029 (2000); $2,090,390 (1999)
Gifts Received: $763,814 (2002); $425,130 (2000); $5,850 (1999). Note: In 2002, contributions were received from Berkshire Hathaway ($5,814), David Strassler ($203,000), Abbie Strassler ($50,000), Alan Strassler ($30,000), and Robert Strassler ($475,000). In 2000, contributions were received from Berkshire Hathaway ($6,930), David Strassler ($388,200), Abbie Strassler ($20,000), and Kathleen Ward ($10,000). In 1999, contributions were received from Berkshire Hathaway. In 1998, contributions were received from David H. Strassler. In 1994, contributions were received from Alan Strassler ($20,000), Karen Strassler ($20,000), Matthew Strassler ($30,000), Abbie Strassler ($20,000), Gary and Monica Strassler ($6,000), and Berkshire Hathaway ($15,719).

Typical Recipients
Arts & Humanities: Arts Associations & Councils, Arts Funds, Dance, Arts & Humanities-General, Historic Preservation, History & Archaeology, Libraries, Museums/Galleries, Music, Theater
Civic & Public Affairs: Community Foundations, Civic & Public Affairs-General, Hispanic Affairs, Public Policy, Urban & Community Affairs, Women's Affairs
Education: Arts/Humanities Education, Colleges & Universities, Continuing Education, Education-General, International Studies, Private Education (Precollege), Science/Mathematics Education, Student Aid
Environment: Environment-General, Resource Conservation, Wildlife Protection

Health: AIDS/HIV, Cancer, Children's Health/Hospitals, Clinics/Medical Centers, Emergency/Ambulance Services, Hospices, Hospitals, Long-Term Care, Mental Health, Single-Disease Health Associations
International: Foreign Educational Institutions, Human Rights, International Affairs, International Development, Missionary/Religious Activities
Religion: Jewish Causes, Religious Organizations
Social Services: Community Service Organizations, Crime Prevention, Family Planning, Family Services, Food/Clothing Distribution, People with Disabilities, United Funds/United Ways

Application Procedures
Application Requirements: No specific application deadlines.
Deadlines: None.

Foundation Officials
David H. Strassler: president
Robert B. Strassler: secretary, treasurer

Grants Analysis
Disclosure Period: calendar year ending 2002
Total Grants: $894,750*
Number of Grants: 112
Average Grant: $6,739*
Highest Grant: $75,000
Typical Range: $1,000 to $10,000
***Note:** Giving excludes United Way. Average grant excludes two highest grants ($140,000).

Recent Grants
Note: Grants derived from 2001 Form 990.

General

75,000	Princeton University, Princeton, NJ
65,800	Recording for the Blind, Lenox, MA
65,000	Medici Archive Project, New York, NY
54,000	Aston Magna Foundation for Music, Danbury, CT
51,000	Simons Rock College of Bard, Great Barrington, MA
45,000	Ackerman Institute for Family Therapy, New York, NY
33,000	Anti-Defamation League of B'nai B'rith, New York, NY
26,000	Clark University, Worcester, MA
25,000	ACCION International, Boston, MA
25,000	American Academy in Rome, New York, NY

GERALDINE AND R. A. BARROWS FOUNDATION

Giving Contact
Stephen J. Campbell, Trust Officer
c/o UMB Bank
1010 Grand
Kansas City, MO 64106
Phone: (816)860-7711

Description
Founded: 1979
EIN: 431184875
Organization Type: Private Foundation
Giving Locations: MO: Kansas City
Grant Types: Endowment, General Support, Research.

Donor Information
Founder: the late G. M. Barrows

Financial Summary
Total Giving: $365,636 (2001); $462,007 (2000); $494,416 (1999)
Giving Analysis: Giving for 1999 includes: foundation grants to United Way ($2,917) 1998: foundation grants to United Way ($414,700)

Assets: $8,024,702 (2001); $8,546,562 (2000); $8,803,999 (1999)
Gifts Received: In 1991, contributions were received from a trust under the will of G.M. Barrows for benefit of Helen Bueker.

Typical Recipients
Arts & Humanities: Arts Institutes, Ballet, Museums/Galleries, Music, Opera, Performing Arts, Theater
Civic & Public Affairs: Botanical Gardens/Parks, Community Foundations, Civic & Public Affairs-General, Housing, Rural Affairs, Women's Affairs, Zoos/Aquariums
Education: Colleges & Universities, Education-General, Private Education (Precollege)
Health: Cancer, Children's Health/Hospitals, Clinics/Medical Centers, Health Organizations, Hospices, Hospitals, Medical Rehabilitation, Medical Research, Single-Disease Health Associations
Religion: Churches, Religious Welfare, Seminaries
Social Services: At-Risk Youth, Child Welfare, Domestic Violence, People with Disabilities, Recreation & Athletics, Scouts, YMCA/YWCA/YMHA/YWHA, Youth Organizations

Application Procedures
Initial Contact: The foundation requests applications be made in writing.
Deadlines: None.

Restrictions
Limited to underprivileged children and cancer research in the Kansas City, MO area.

Additional Information
Trust(s): UMB Bank

Grants Analysis
Disclosure Period: calendar year ending 2001
Total Grants: $365,636
Number of Grants: 20
Average Grant: $12,665*
Highest Grant: $125,000
Lowest Grant: $1,000
Typical Range: $5,000 to $30,000
***Note:** Average grant figure excludes highest grant.

Recent Grants
Note: Grants derived from 2000 Form 990.

General

50,000	Kansas City Symphony, Kansas City, MO
50,000	Teel Institute, Kansas City, MO
25,000	Wayside WAIFS, Kansas City, MO
25,000	Wyandotte County Parks Foundation Board, Kansas City, KS -- Schlagle Library and Environmental Learning Center
16,573	Kingswood Manor, Kansas City, MO
13,334	Boys and Girls Club, Kansas City, MO
10,000	Central United Methodist Church, Kansas City, MO
10,000	Kansas City Rescue Mission, Kansas City, MO
6,000	St. Paul's Episcopal Day School, Kansas City, MO
5,000	American Humanics, Inc., Kansas City, MO

BARSTOW FOUNDATION

Giving Contact
Bruce M. Groom, Senior Vice President & Senior Trust Officer
c/o Chemical Bank and Trust Co.
333 E. Main St.
Midland, MI 48640
Phone: (517)839-5305

Description

Founded: 1967
EIN: 386151026
Organization Type: Private Foundation
Giving Locations: MI: Midland County
Grant Types: Operating Expenses, Project.

Donor Information

Founder: the late Florence K. Barstow

Financial Summary

Total Giving: $517,100 (2001); $708,773 (2000); $308,242 (1999)
Assets: $6,557,896 (2001); $6,862,453 (2000); $8,702,713 (1999)
Gifts Received: $469,188 (2001); $16,000 (2000); $100,057 (1993). Note: In 2001, contributions were received from Ruth Dixon. In 2000, contributions were received from Sedona Community Food Bank, Seconda, AZ. In 1993, contributions were received from the final distribution of the F. K. Barstow Charitable Annuity Trust.

Typical Recipients

Arts & Humanities: Arts Centers, Dance, Ethnic & Folk Arts, Arts & Humanities-General, History & Archaeology, Libraries, Museums/Galleries, Music, Theater
Civic & Public Affairs: Community Foundations, Civic & Public Affairs-General, Housing, Urban & Community Affairs
Education: Afterschool/Enrichment Programs, Arts/Humanities Education, Colleges & Universities, Environmental Education, Faculty Development, Education-General, Literacy, Minority Education, Science/Mathematics Education, Student Aid
Environment: Air/Water Quality, Forestry, Environment-General, Resource Conservation, Watershed
Health: AIDS/HIV, Mental Health, Prenatal Health Issues, Single-Disease Health Associations
International: Health Care/Hospitals, International Relief Efforts
Religion: Churches, Religious Welfare
Science: Science Museums, Scientific Centers & Institutes
Social Services: Animal Protection, Camps, Community Centers, Community Service Organizations, Domestic Violence, Family Services, Food/Clothing Distribution, Homes, Recreation & Athletics, Shelters/Homelessness, Social Services-General, Youth Organizations

Application Procedures

Initial Contact: Send cover letter and full proposal. Include organization's pamphlet or brochure, if available.
Deadlines: July 31.

Restrictions

Does not support individuals or research programs, or provide loans, scholarships, or fellowships.

Foundation Officials

David O. Barstow: trustee
Frederick E. Barstow: president
John C. Barstow: trustee
Richard G. Barstow: trustee
Robert G. Barstow: trustee
Dr. Robert O. Barstow: trustee
Ruth B. Dixon: chairman
William R. Dixon: trustee
Bruce M. Groom: secretary, trustee

Grants Analysis

Disclosure Period: calendar year ending 2001
Total Grants: $517,100
Number of Grants: 1

Recent Grants

Note: Grants derived from 2000 Form 990.

General

380,000	Midland Community Center, Midland, MI -- for facility improvements
50,591	Friends of Garland Park, Sedona, AZ -- for construction of Teen Center
50,000	Friends of the Colorado River Foundation, Bastrop County, TX -- construction of Amphitheater for recreation and education
50,000	Lutheran Church Missouri Synod, Rimrock, AZ -- construction of youth and family center
25,591	Midland Area Community Foundation, Midland, MI -- for Barstow Family Fund
25,000	CARE, Chicago, IL -- for emergency assistance services
25,000	UNICEF, New York, NY -- eradication of abduction of women and children in Sudan
20,000	Fuller Museum of Art, Brockton, MA -- Children's Discovery Gallery
10,000	AIDS Services of Austin, Austin, TX -- unrestricted grant
10,000	Creative Spirit Center, Midland, MI -- Safety First Project for John Pratt Mosaic House

THE THEODORE H. BARTH FOUNDATION, INC.

Giving Contact

Ellen S. Berelson, Vice President & Director
45 Rockefeller Plaza, Suite 2037
New York, NY 10111
Phone: (212)332-3466

Description

Founded: 1953
EIN: 136103401
Organization Type: General Purpose Foundation
Giving Locations: MA; NY
Grant Types: General Support.

Donor Information

Founder: Incorporated in 1953 by the late Theodore H. Barth .

Financial Summary

Total Giving: $1,692,313 (2000); $1,541,888 (1999); $1,431,385 (1998)
Giving Analysis: Giving for 2000 includes: foundation scholarships ($262,028) 1998: foundation scholarships ($1,100)
Assets: $33,187,196 (2000); $31,464,534 (1998); $27,979,508 (1997)

Typical Recipients

Arts & Humanities: Ballet, Dance, History & Archaeology, Libraries, Literary Arts, Museums/Galleries, Music, Opera, Performing Arts, Public Broadcasting, Theater, Visual Arts
Civic & Public Affairs: Botanical Gardens/Parks, Clubs, Community Foundations, Economic Development, Legal Aid, Urban & Community Affairs, Zoos/Aquariums
Education: Arts/Humanities Education, Colleges & Universities, Education Reform, Education-General, Legal Education, Literacy, Private Education (Precollege), Science/Mathematics Education, Special Education
Environment: Air/Water Quality, Environment-General, Resource Conservation, Wildlife Protection
Health: Children's Health/Hospitals, Clinics/Medical Centers, Health Funds, Health Organizations, Hospices, Hospitals, Kidney, Medical Research, Mental Health, Nursing Services, Public Health, Research/

Studies Institutes, Single-Disease Health Associations, Speech & Hearing, Transplant Networks/Donor Banks
International: Foreign Arts Organizations
Religion: Churches, Jewish Causes, Religious Welfare
Science: Science Museums
Social Services: At-Risk Youth, Big Brother/Big Sister, Child Welfare, Community Centers, Community Service Organizations, Counseling, Day Care, Family Planning, Family Services, Food/Clothing Distribution, People with Disabilities, Scouts, Shelters/Homelessness, United Funds/United Ways, Youth Organizations

Application Procedures

Initial Contact: The foundation requests a general letter of interest.
Deadlines: None.

Restrictions

Grants are not made to individuals.

Foundation Officials

Ellen S. Berelson: vice president, director
Thelma D. Berelson: secretary, director

Grants Analysis

Disclosure Period: calendar year ending 2000
Total Grants: $1,430,285*
Number of Grants: 113
Average Grant: $11,654*
Highest Grant: $125,000
Lowest Grant: $185
Typical Range: $1,000 to $25,000
*Note: Giving excludes scholarships. Average grant figure excludes highest grant.

Recent Grants

Note: Grants derived from 2000 Form 990.

Library-Related

25,000	New York Public Library, New York, NY

General

290,000	League for the Hard of Hearing, New York, NY
100,000	Metropolitan Opera Association, Inc., New York, NY
100,000	Southcoast Health Systems, Inc., New Bedford, MA
75,000	Harvard Law School Fund, Cambridge, MA
75,000	New York and Presbyterian Hospital, New York, NY
30,000	National Book Foundation, New York, NY
25,000	Educational Broadcasting Corporation, New York, NY
25,000	Metropolitan Museum of Art, New York, NY
25,000	New York Botanical Garden, Bronx, NY
25,000	New York City Ballet, Inc., New York, NY

BARTLETT & CO.

Company Headquarters

4800 Main Street, Suite 600
Kansas City, MO 64112
Web: http://www.bartlettandco.com

Company Description

Employees: 525
SIC(s): 0211 Beef Cattle Feedlots, 2041 Flour & Other Grain Mill Products, 5153 Grain & Field Beans.
Parent Company: Legg Mason, Inc., PO Box 1476, Baltimore, MD, United States

Bartlett & Co. Grain Charitable Foundation

Giving Contact

Arnold Wheeler, Chief Financial Officer
4800 Main Street, Suite 600
Kansas City, MO 64112-2510
Phone: (816)753-6300
Fax: (816)753-0062

Description

Founded: 1986
EIN: 436323269
Organization Type: Corporate Foundation
Giving Locations: MO
Grant Types: General Support.

Financial Summary

Total Giving: $96,500 (fiscal year ending April 30, 2001); $105,870 (fiscal 2000); $113,200 (fiscal 1999)
Giving Analysis: Giving for fiscal 2000 includes: foundation ($105,870).
Assets: $1,990,016 (fiscal 2001); $1,715,570 (fiscal 2000); $2,122,138 (fiscal 1999)

Typical Recipients

Arts & Humanities: Arts & Humanities-General, History & Archaeology, Libraries, Museums/Galleries, Opera, Public Broadcasting, Theater
Civic & Public Affairs: Botanical Gardens/Parks, Business/Free Enterprise, Community Foundations, Civic & Public Affairs-General, Law & Justice, Legal Aid, Professional & Trade Associations, Public Policy, Rural Affairs, Urban & Community Affairs
Education: Agricultural Education, Business Education, Colleges & Universities, Education Funds, Faculty Development, Education-General, Private Education (Precollege), Public Education (Precollege)
Environment: Resource Conservation
Health: AIDS/HIV, Children's Health/Hospitals, Health-General, Preventive Medicine/Wellness Organizations, Public Health, Single-Disease Health Associations, Trauma Treatment
International: International-General
Religion: Religion-General, Jewish Causes, Ministries, Religious Welfare
Science: Science-General, Science Museums, Scientific Centers & Institutes
Social Services: At-Risk Youth, Child Welfare, Community Service Organizations, Crime Prevention, People with Disabilities, Recreation & Athletics, Scouts, Social Services-General

Application Procedures

Initial Contact: Send a brief letter of inquiry.
Application Requirements: Include a description of organization, amount requested, and purpose of funds sought.
Deadlines: None.

Restrictions

Does not support individuals, religious organizations for sectarian purposes, or organizations outside operating areas.

Corporate Officials

Paul Dana Bartlett, Jr.: chairman, director B Kansas City, MO September 16, 1919. ED Yale University BA (1941). PRIM CORP EMPL chairman, director: Bartlett & Co. CORP AFFIL director: United Missouri Bancshares; director: United Missouri Bank Financial Corp.
James B. Hebenstreit: president PRIM CORP EMPL president: Bartlett & Co.
Arnold Wheeler: chief financial officer PRIM CORP EMPL chief financial officer: Bartlett & Co.

Foundation Officials

Paul Dana Bartlett, Jr.: trustee (see above)
James B. Hebenstreit: trustee (see above)

Grants Analysis

Disclosure Period: fiscal year ending April 30, 2001
Total Grants: $96,500
Number of Grants: 41
Average Grant: $1,663*
Highest Grant: $30,000
Lowest Grant: $100
Typical Range: $500 to $2,500
*Note: Average grant excludes highest grant.

Recent Grants

Note: Grants derived from fiscal 2000 Form 990.

Library-Related
10,000	Linda Hall Library, Kansas City, MO

General
31,000	Nelson-Atkins Museum of Art, Kansas City, MO -- capital campaign
10,000	Kemper Museum of Contemporary Art and Design, Kansas City, MO
8,000	Pembroke Hill School, Kansas City, MO
5,000	Harry S. Truman Library Institute, Independence, MO
5,000	Kemper Museum of Contemporary Art and Design, Kansas City, MO
3,000	Nelson-Atkins Museum of Art, Kansas City, MO
3,000	Powell Gardens, Kingsville, MO
2,500	Agriculture Future of America, Kansas City, MO
2,500	Heart of America Council of Boy Scouts of America
2,500	Lyric Opera of Kansas City, Kansas City, MO

BAT HANADIV FOUNDATION No. 3

Giving Contact

Jerome Caufield, Attorney
Care of Carter Leoyard & Milburn
2 Wall Street, 13th Floor
New York, NY 10005
Phone: (212)732-3200
Fax: (212)732-3232

Description

Founded: 1981
EIN: 133091620
Organization Type: Specialized/Single Purpose Foundation
Giving Locations: Israel
Grant Types: Fellowship, General Support, Operating Expenses, Project.

Donor Information

Founder: Established in 1981. All support received since its inception has come from non-U.S. organizations, including Bat Hanadiv Foundation and Bat Hanadiv Foundation No. 2.

Financial Summary

Total Giving: $5,000,000 (2000); $4,996,005 (1999); $3,789,848 (1998)
Giving Analysis: Giving for 2000 includes: foundation fellowships ($126,900); 1997: foundation gifts to individuals ($64,544) foundation fellowships ($174,490)
Assets: $230,798,621 (2000); $215,975,141 (1999); $188,397,880 (1998)

Typical Recipients

Arts & Humanities: Film & Video, Arts & Humanities-General, Museums/Galleries, Music
Civic & Public Affairs: Botanical Gardens/Parks, Business/Free Enterprise, Community Foundations, Employment/Job Training, Gay/Lesbian Issues, Civic & Public Affairs-General, Law & Justice
Education: Colleges & Universities, Continuing Education, Economic Education, Education Associations, Education Reform, Education-General, Private Education (Precollege), Religious Education, Science/Mathematics Education
Environment: Environment-General, Resource Conservation
Health: Hospices, Hospitals
International: Foreign Arts Organizations, Foreign Educational Institutions, International-General, Health Care/Hospitals, International Development, International Environmental Issues, Missionary/Religious Activities
Religion: Jewish Causes
Science: Science-General, Scientific Centers & Institutes, Scientific Organizations
Social Services: Child Welfare, Substance Abuse

Application Procedures

Initial Contact: The foundation has no formal grant application procedure or application form.
Deadlines: None.

Additional Information

The foundation lists the Doder Trust, Ltd., Hamilton, Bermuda, as a corporate trustee.
The foundation reports that it is a foreign foundation and that the majority of funds go to international organizations.

Foundation Officials

Jerome Caufield: attorney

Grants Analysis

Disclosure Period: calendar year ending 2000
Total Grants: $5,000,000
Number of Grants: 30
Average Grant: $166,667*
Highest Grant: $750,000
Typical Range: $2,000 to $200,000
*Note: Average grant excludes highest grant.

Recent Grants

Note: Grants derived from 2000 Form 990.

General
750,000	Water Research Insitute
530,000	Jerusalem Music Center -- operations 2000
520,000	C.E.T. -- research and developments
432,825	Institute for Advanced Studies, New York, NY
399,528	Institute for Advanced Studies, New York, NY
320,000	C.E.T. -- English on line
245,339	O.U.I. -- Jewish studies
243,487	O.U.I. -- new campus at Ra'Anana
200,000	O.U.I. Fully Integrated Learning Environments
194,982	Cet-Noor Information & Research Centre, Ramallah

BATTS FOUNDATION

Giving Contact

3777 Sparks Drive SE, Suite 100
Grand Rapids, MI 49546
Phone: (616)956-3053

Description

EIN: 382782168
Organization Type: Private Foundation
Giving Locations: MI: Grand Rapids, Holland
Grant Types: General Support.

Financial Summary

Total Giving: $224,350 (2001); $221,308 (2000); $204,617 (1999)
Giving Analysis: Giving for 1998 includes: foundation grants to United Way ($10,000) 1997: foundation grants to United Way ($10,000)
Assets: $2,555,399 (2001); $3,069,299 (2000); $3,372,838 (1999)
Gifts Received: $250,000 (1994); $250,000 (1992). Note: In 1994, contributions were received from the Batts Group, Ltd.

Typical Recipients

Arts & Humanities: Arts Associations & Councils, Arts Centers, Arts Festivals, Arts & Humanities-General, History & Archaeology, Libraries, Museums/Galleries, Music, Opera, Performing Arts, Public Broadcasting
Civic & Public Affairs: Botanical Gardens/Parks, Chambers of Commerce, Clubs, Community Foundations, Economic Development, Employment/Job Training, Civic & Public Affairs-General, Housing, Municipalities/Towns, Nonprofit Management, Parades/Festivals, Urban & Community Affairs, Women's Affairs, Zoos/Aquariums
Education: Business Education, Colleges & Universities, Community & Junior Colleges, Education Funds, Elementary Education (Private), Education-General, Private Education (Precollege), Public Education (Precollege), Science/Mathematics Education, Student Aid
Environment: Environment-General, Resource Conservation
Health: Cancer, Children's Health/Hospitals, Emergency/Ambulance Services, Health Funds, Health Organizations, Hospices, Hospitals, Long-Term Care, Medical Rehabilitation, Public Health, Research/Studies Institutes, Trauma Treatment
International: Health Care/Hospitals, International Relief Efforts
Religion: Churches, Religious Organizations, Religious Welfare
Social Services: Community Service Organizations, Family Planning, Family Services, Food/Clothing Distribution, Homes, Scouts, Senior Services, Substance Abuse, United Funds/United Ways, Youth Organizations

Application Procedures

Initial Contact: The foundation has no formal grant application procedure or application form.
Deadlines: None.

Foundation Officials

James L. Batts: director
John H. Batts: president, director
John T. Batts: director
Michael A. Batts: director
Robert H. Batts: director
Maurice R. Wertenberger: vice president

Grants Analysis

Disclosure Period: calendar year ending 2001
Total Grants: $224,350
Number of Grants: 44
Average Grant: $5,099
Highest Grant: $25,000
Lowest Grant: $250
Typical Range: $1,000 to $10,000

Recent Grants

Note: Grants derived from 2000 Form 990.

General

20,400	Devos Children's Hospital, Grand Rapids, MI
20,000	Community Foundation, Holland, MI
20,000	Grand Valley State University, Grand Rapids, MI
16,667	Boys and Girls Club, Holland, MI
12,000	Hope College, Holland, MI
10,000	Center for Women in Transition, Grand Rapids, MI
10,000	Grand Valley State University, Grand Rapids, MI
10,000	Heart of West Michigan, Grand Rapids, MI
10,000	St. Johns School Gift Campaign, Grand Rapids, MI
7,000	Holland Community Hospital, Holland, MI

BAUER FAMILY FOUNDATION

Giving Contact

Paul D. Bauer, Trustee
60 Waterfront Cir.
Buffalo, NY 14202
Phone: (716)856-7020

Description

Founded: 1991
EIN: 161390793
Organization Type: Private Foundation
Grant Types: General Support.

Financial Summary

Total Giving: $86,650 (2001); $120,000 (2000); $117,100 (1998)
Giving Analysis: Giving for 2001 includes: foundation scholarships ($21,000) 2000: foundation scholarships ($41,000)
Assets: $1,092,458 (2001); $1,126,806 (2000); $1,126,806 (1999)
Gifts Received: $42,000 (2000); $33,000 (1993). Note: In 1993 and 2000, contributions were received from Paul D. Bauer.

Typical Recipients

Arts & Humanities: Libraries
Civic & Public Affairs: Civic & Public Affairs-General, Women's Affairs
Education: Colleges & Universities, Special Education, Student Aid
Health: AIDS/HIV, Cancer, Children's Health/Hospitals, Hospices, Hospitals
International: Foreign Educational Institutions, Missionary/Religious Activities
Religion: Churches, Dioceses, Religion-General, Ministries, Religious Organizations, Religious Welfare, Seminaries
Social Services: At-Risk Youth, Child Welfare, Emergency Relief, Family Services, Food/Clothing Distribution, People with Disabilities, Shelters/Homelessness, Substance Abuse

Application Procedures

Initial Contact: Send a one-page brief letter.
Application Requirements: Include a a description of organization, amount requested, and proof of tax-exempt status.
Deadlines: None.

Foundation Officials

David P. Bauer: trustee
Lisa M. Bauer: trustee
Mary Grace Bauer: trustee
Paul D. Bauer: trustee

Grants Analysis

Disclosure Period: calendar year ending 2001
Total Grants: $65,650*
Number of Grants: 16

Average Grant: $4,103
Highest Grant: $20,000
Lowest Grant: $500
Typical Range: $1,000 to $5,000
***Note:** Giving excludes scholarships.

Recent Grants

Note: Grants derived from 2000 Form 990.

General

20,000	Bison Fund, Buffalo, NY -- scholarship fund
20,000	Canisius High School, Buffalo, NY -- scholarship fund
20,000	St. Gregory the Great Church, Williamsville, NY -- capital campaign
10,000	Women at the Service of Life, Buffalo, NY -- for program support
8,700	Catholic Charities, Buffalo, NY
6,000	Covenant House, Inc., New York, NY
5,000	Niagara University, Niagara Falls, NY -- for program support
5,000	St. Joseph's Orphanage India
5,000	Sisters of Mercy, Buffalo, NY
2,750	Children's Hospital of Buffalo, Buffalo, NY

CHARLES M. BAUERVIC FOUNDATION

Giving Contact

Executive Director
10260 East Hilltop Road
Suttons Bay, MI 49682
Phone: (248)643-4545

Description

Founded: 1967
EIN: 386146352
Organization Type: Private Foundation
Giving Locations: MI
Grant Types: General Support, Operating Expenses, Project.

Donor Information

Founder: the late Charles M. Bauervic

Financial Summary

Total Giving: $156,500 (2000); $178,000 (1999); $173,000 (1998)
Assets: $4,093,436 (2000); $4,337,640 (1999); $4,198,871 (1998)

Typical Recipients

Arts & Humanities: Arts Centers, Arts Outreach, History & Archaeology, Libraries, Museums/Galleries, Music, Opera, Performing Arts
Civic & Public Affairs: Civil Rights, Employment/Job Training, Civic & Public Affairs-General, Housing, Legal Aid, Public Policy, Safety, Urban & Community Affairs
Education: Arts/Humanities Education, Colleges & Universities, Continuing Education, Elementary Education (Private), Education-General, Leadership Training, Medical Education, Minority Education, Private Education (Precollege), Religious Education, Science/Mathematics Education, Secondary Education (Private), Student Aid
Health: Alzheimers Disease, Clinics/Medical Centers, Emergency/Ambulance Services, Health-General, Health Organizations, Hospices, Long-Term Care, Medical Research, Public Health
International: Foreign Educational Institutions, Health Care/Hospitals
Religion: Dioceses, Religious Organizations, Religious Welfare, Social/Policy Issues
Science: Science Exhibits & Fairs

Social Services: At-Risk Youth, Camps, People with Disabilities, Social Services-General, Special Olympics, Youth Organizations

Application Procedures

Initial Contact: Return completed application form. Include title and description of project, itemized budget, proof of tax-exempt status, any material that will supplement the project proposal, two copies of the past five year's financial reports, and a report of all funds received to date.
Deadlines: April 30.

Restrictions

Grants are awarded primarily for educational purposes.

Additional Information

Publications: Application Form

Foundation Officials

Rose Bauervic-Wright: vice president
Kathryn Leonard: treasurer
Patricia A. Leonard: president, secretary
Theodore J. Leonard: director
Timothy J. Leonard: director

Grants Analysis

Disclosure Period: calendar year ending 2000
Total Grants: $156,500
Number of Grants: 39
Average Grant: $4,013
Highest Grant: $15,000
Lowest Grant: $1,000
Typical Range: $1,000 to $10,000

Recent Grants

Note: Grants derived from 2001 Form 990.

General

15,000	Institute in Basic life Principles, Oak Brook, IL -- for character first program
10,000	Educational Center for Life, Troy, MI -- for educational materials for radio and internet publicity
10,000	Everest Academy, Clarkston, MI -- for library books and the music program
10,000	Franciscan University of Steubenville, Steubenville, OH -- for computer lab equipment update
10,000	Hillsdale College, Hillsdale, MI -- for the Center for Teacher Training
10,000	Madonna University, Livonia, MI -- for dietetics equipment to access therapeutic nutrition
10,000	Seton Home Study School, Front Royal, VA -- for printing of new 5th grade books
10,000	Southwest College of Naturopathic Medicine, Tempe, AZ -- for three document cameras and for visiting instructors education and promotion costs
10,000	Walsh College, Troy, MI -- for Online Learning Program
8,000	Right to Life of Michigan, Grand Rapids, MI -- for Direct Connect Program

BAUERVIC-PAISLEY FOUNDATION

Giving Contact

Beverly Paisley, President & Director
501 E. Mullet Lake Rd.
Indian River, MI 49749
Phone: (231)238-7817

Description

Founded: 1984
EIN: 382494390
Organization Type: Private Foundation
Giving Locations: MI
Grant Types: Capital, Operating Expenses.

Financial Summary

Total Giving: $73,500 (2001); $139,000 (2000); $107,000 (1999)
Giving Analysis: Giving for 1998 includes: foundation scholarships ($5,000)
Assets: $1,725,357 (2001); $2,600,336 (2000); $4,282,891 (1999)

Typical Recipients

Arts & Humanities: Arts Associations & Councils, Libraries, Museums/Galleries, Music, Opera
Civic & Public Affairs: Clubs, Community Foundations, Civic & Public Affairs-General, Municipalities/Towns, Urban & Community Affairs
Education: Afterschool/Enrichment Programs, Business-School Partnerships, Colleges & Universities, Education Funds, Elementary Education (Private), Education-General, International Exchange, Private Education (Precollege), Public Education (Precollege), Science/Mathematics Education, Secondary Education (Private), Student Aid
Health: Alzheimers Disease, Children's Health/Hospitals, Heart, Hospices, Hospitals, Long-Term Care, Mental Health, Prenatal Health Issues, Public Health
Religion: Religious Organizations, Religious Welfare
Science: Scientific Centers & Institutes, Scientific Labs
Social Services: At-Risk Youth, Camps, Community Centers, Community Service Organizations, Delinquency & Criminal Rehabilitation, Family Services, People with Disabilities, Recreation & Athletics, Social Services-General, Substance Abuse, Volunteer Services, Youth Organizations

Application Procedures

Initial Contact: Contact the foundation to obtain an application form.
Application Requirements: Include title and description of project, itemized budget, approval from the institution where the project will be done, year-end financial statement, proof of tax-exempt status, and the way in which project completion will be visually confirmed.
Deadlines: October 1.

Restrictions

No grants are awarded to individuals.

Foundation Officials

Beverly Paisley: president, director
Bonnie Paisley: director
Charles Paisley: director
Martha Paisley: vice president, director
Peter Paisley, Jr.: director
Peter W. Paisley: director

Grants Analysis

Disclosure Period: calendar year ending 2001
Total Grants: $73,500
Number of Grants: 18
Average Grant: $4,083
Highest Grant: $10,000
Lowest Grant: $500
Typical Range: $2,500 to $10,000

Recent Grants

Note: Grants derived from 2001 Form 990.

Library-Related

2,500	St. Mary Catholic Central High -- for Alumni Program

General

10,000	Hospice of the Straits -- for building addition
10,000	Skidmore College, Saratoga Springs, NY -- for Athletic Program
5,000	Academy of Sacred Heart, New Orleans, LA -- for After School Learning Center
5,000	Cheboygan Youth Center, Cheboygan, MI -- enhancement of children's programming
5,000	Friends of the Broadway, Mt. Pleasant, MI -- to organize Broadway Children's Group
5,000	Henry Ford Museum and Greenfield Village, Dearborn, MI -- School Partnership and Scholarship Program
5,000	Hospice of Little Traverse Bay, Petoskey, MI -- counselor for Bereavement Program
5,000	Tuscarora Township, Indian River, MI -- for Project Playland
3,500	Wellspring, Fairfax, VA -- for Academic and Job Development Program
3,400	Novi Community That Cares, Novi, MI -- for building addition

BAUGHMAN FOUNDATION

Giving Contact

Eugene W. Slaymaker, President
PO Box 1356
Liberal, KS 67905-1356
Phone: (620)624-1371
Fax: (620)624-4177
E-mail: baughman@swko.net

Description

Founded: 1958
EIN: 486108797
Organization Type: General Purpose Foundation
Giving Locations: KS: Liberal
Grant Types: Capital, Endowment, Operating Expenses, Project, Scholarship.

Donor Information

Founder: Incorporated in 1958 by the late Robert W. Baughman and John W. Baughman Farms Co.

Financial Summary

Total Giving: $1,290,771 (2001); $1,200,000 (1999 approx); $991,937 (1998)
Giving Analysis: Giving for 2001 includes: foundation grants to United Way ($2,000); 1998: foundation matching gifts ($3,500) foundation scholarships ($213,000)
Assets: $22,000,000 (1999 approx); $27,105,134 (1998); $24,114,193 (1997)

Typical Recipients

Arts & Humanities: Arts Associations & Councils, Arts Funds, Arts Outreach, Ethnic & Folk Arts, Historic Preservation, History & Archaeology, Libraries, Museums/Galleries, Music, Public Broadcasting
Civic & Public Affairs: Chambers of Commerce, Community Foundations, Economic Development, Employment/Job Training, Civic & Public Affairs-General, Housing, Law & Justice, Municipalities/Towns, Parades/Festivals, Philanthropic Organizations, Public Policy, Safety, Urban & Community Affairs
Education: Agricultural Education, Colleges & Universities, Community & Junior Colleges, Economic Education, Education Funds, Faculty Development, Education-General, Leadership Training, Legal Education, Preschool Education, Private Education (Precollege), Public Education (Precollege), Religious Education, Science/Mathematics Education, Student Aid, Vocational & Technical Education
Environment: Environment-General
Health: Alzheimers Disease, Clinics/Medical Centers, Diabetes, Emergency/Ambulance Services,

Health Organizations, Hospitals, Single-Disease Health Associations

Religion: Ministries, Missionary Activities (Domestic), Religious Organizations, Religious Welfare

Science: Science Museums

Social Services: Animal Protection, Big Brother/Big Sister, Child Welfare, Community Centers, Community Service Organizations, Counseling, Crime Prevention, Day Care, Domestic Violence, Emergency Relief, Family Services, Homes, People with Disabilities, Recreation & Athletics, Scouts, Senior Services, Senior Services, Sexual Abuse, Shelters/Homelessness, Social Services-General, Substance Abuse, United Funds/United Ways, Youth Organizations

Application Procedures

Initial Contact: The foundation requests applications be made in writing.

Application Requirements: Applicants should submit proposal stating need, availability of other funding, and amount requested.

Deadlines: None. Applicants must submit proposals prior to 10 a.m. Central Time on the second Wednesday of each month to be reviewed at that month's meeting.

Review Process: The foundation reviews proposals on a monthly basis.

Restrictions

Grants are made only to organizations with tax-exempt status under IRS section 501(c)(3) and which are not private foundations. No grants are given to individuals.

Foundation Officials

Carol Feather-Francis: vice president, trustee
Eugene W. Slaymaker: president, trustee
James R. Yoxall: secretary, treasurer, trustee PRIM CORP EMPL treasurer: Hitch Land & Cattle Co. Inc. CORP AFFIL secretary: Keating Tractor & Equipment.

Grants Analysis

Disclosure Period: calendar year ending 2001
Total Grants: $1,288,771*
Number of Grants: 93
Average Grant: $13,858
Highest Grant: $160,000
Lowest Grant: $500
Typical Range: $1,000 to $20,000
*****Note:** Giving includes United Way.

Recent Grants

Note: Grants derived from 2000 Form 990.

Library-Related
17,320	Liberal Memorial Library, Liberal, KS -- internet access equipment and augment book budget
11,505	Dodge City Public Library, Dodge City, KS -- Literacy Training Program

General
160,000	Seward County Community College Development Foundation, Liberal, KS -- scholarships, student liability premiums, PR, and Epworth Health Center enhancement
85,000	Depot Heritage, Liberal, KS -- to assist restoration of Grier House Hotel Restaurant
70,000	SWKTS Foundation, Liberal, KS -- scholarships and student housing
50,000	City of Liberal, Liberal, KS -- for police department equipment
32,500	Seward County Historical Society, Liberal, KS -- staff development, equipment purchases and brochures
30,000	City of Liberal, Liberal, KS -- for parks and recreation department operations
30,000	Original Town of Liberal Revitalization,

	Liberal, KS -- rehabilitate 509 N. Sherman
30,000	USD 480, Liberal, KS -- Smart Start Program
27,500	Stepping Stone Shelter, Liberal, KS -- operations
27,000	Baker Arts Foundation, Liberal, KS -- year 2000 operations, maintenance, and USD 480 cooperation

BAUSCH & LOMB, INC.

Company Headquarters
Rochester, NY
Web: http://www.bausch.com

Company Description
Founded: 1853
Ticker: BOL
Exchange: NYSE
Revenue: US$1.816 billion (2002)
Employees: 11500 (2002)
SIC(s): 3479 Metal Coating & Allied Services, 3634 Electric Housewares & Fans, 3827 Optical Instruments & Lenses, 3851 Ophthalmic Goods.

Operating Locations
Bausch & Lomb Inc. (CA--Yorba Linda; CT--Lebanon, Storrs; FL--Miami, Sarasota, Summerland Key; GA--Atlanta, Colbert, Tucker; IL--Roanoke; ME--Windham; MA--Norwood, Southbridge, West Brookfield, Wilmington; MI--Portage; MN--Golden Valley; MO--O'Fallen; NE--Omaha; NH--Pittsfield; NJ--Newfield; NY--Williamston; NC--Williamston; PA--Reinholds, Williamsport; SC--Greenville; TX--Houston, San Antonio; VA--Lynchburg)
Note: Operates in Canada, the Caribbean, Latin America, Europe, Australia, and Asia.

Nonmonetary Support
Type: In-kind Services

Bausch & Lomb Foundation, Inc.

Giving Contact
Barbara M. Kelley, Vice President
One Bausch & Lomb Place
Rochester, NY 14604-2701
Phone: (585)338-6000
Fax: (585)338-6007

Description
EIN: 166039442
Organization Type: Corporate Foundation
Giving Locations: NY: Rochester
Grant Types: General Support.

Financial Summary
Total Giving: $1,075,784 (fiscal year ending December 29, 2001); $377,500 (fiscal 2000); $780,000 (fiscal 1999). Note: Contributes through corporate direct giving program and foundation.
Giving Analysis: Giving for fiscal 2000 includes: foundation ($377,500) fiscal 1999: foundation ($780,000)
Assets: $1,987,200 (fiscal 2001); $3,115,801 (fiscal 2000); $3,386,244 (fiscal 1999)
Gifts Received: $386,736 (fiscal 2000); $789,103 (fiscal 1999); $815,000 (fiscal 1998). Note: Contributions are received from Bausch & Lomb Inc.

Typical Recipients
Arts & Humanities: Dance, History & Archaeology, Libraries, Museums/Galleries, Music, Performing Arts, Public Broadcasting, Theater

Civic & Public Affairs: Botanical Gardens/Parks, Business/Free Enterprise, Economic Development, Employment/Job Training, Civic & Public Affairs-General, Housing, Public Policy, Urban & Community Affairs, Women's Affairs, Zoos/Aquariums

Education: Arts/Humanities Education, Business Education, Colleges & Universities, Community & Junior Colleges, Minority Education, Private Education (Precollege), Science/Mathematics Education

Environment: Environment-General

Health: Clinics/Medical Centers, Geriatric Health, Medical Rehabilitation, Nursing Services

Science: Science Museums, Scientific Centers & Institutes

Social Services: Child Welfare, Community Centers, Community Service Organizations, Emergency Relief, Homes, People with Disabilities, Recreation & Athletics, Special Olympics, United Funds/United Ways, Veterans, Youth Organizations

Application Procedures
Initial Contact: Send a written letter proposal.
Application Requirements: Include a full proposal, a brief description, a budget showing revenue and expenses, a list of the organization's board of directors, and proof of tax-exempt status.
Deadlines: None.
Evaluative Criteria: Preference is given to Rochester, NY based projects and organizations.

Additional Information
Company is currently reviewing its policy on international giving.

Corporate Officials
Alan H. Resnick: vice president, treasurer B Boston, MA 1943. ED Tufts University BS (1965); Columbia University MBA (1967). PRIM CORP EMPL vice president, treasurer: Bausch & Lomb Inc. NONPR AFFIL treasurer: Visiting Nurse Foundation Inc.
William H. Waltrip: chairman, director B 1937. PRIM CORP EMPL chairman, director: Bausch & Lomb Inc. CORP AFFIL chairman: Technology Solutions Co.; director: Thomas & Betts Corp.

Foundation Officials
Jean F. Geisel: secretary
Barbara M. Kelley: vice president PRIM CORP EMPL vice president corporate communications: Bausch & Lomb Inc.
Stephen C. McCluski: president, director
Alan H. Resnick: treasurer (see above)
Robert Stiles: director

Grants Analysis
Disclosure Period: fiscal year ending December 29, 2001
Total Grants: $768,284*
Number of Grants: 25
Average Grant: $19,512*
Highest Grant: $300,000
Lowest Grant: $700
Typical Range: $1,800 to $40,000
*****Note:** Giving excludes United Way. Average grant figure excludes highest grant.

Recent Grants
Note: Grants derived from 2001 Form 990.

General
307,500	United Way, Rochester, NY
300,000	University of Rochester, Rochester, NY
75,000	UNCGR Foundation, Rochester, NY
65,584	American Red Cross, Rochester, NY
57,500	Seneca Park Zoo Society, Rochester, NY
40,000	University of Rochester, Rochester, NY -- Science Award Program

37,500	Rochester Philharmonic, Rochester, NY
30,000	Al Sigl Center, Rochester, NY
28,700	George Eastman House, Rochester, NY
22,500	Junior Achievement of Rochester, Rochester, NY

BAY FOUNDATION

Giving Contact

Robert W. Ashton, Executive Director & Secretary
17 W. 94th St.
New York, NY 10025
Phone: (212)663-1115
Fax: (212)932-0316

Description

Founded: 1950
EIN: 135646283
Organization Type: General Purpose Foundation
Giving Locations: nationally, with some preference for the East Coast.
Grant Types: General Support, Project, Research.

Donor Information

Founder: Charles Ulrick Bay, Josephine Bay

Financial Summary

Total Giving: $250,000 (2002 approx); $826,221 (2001); $1,724,220 (2000)
Giving Analysis: Giving for 2001 includes: foundation gifts to individuals ($150,000); 2000: foundation gifts to individuals ($150,000) 1999: foundation gifts to individuals ($168,000)
Assets: $20,252,858 (2001); $22,776,336 (2000); $22,497,939 (1999)

Typical Recipients

Arts & Humanities: Arts Associations & Councils, Arts Centers, Arts Institutes, Arts Outreach, Dance, Film & Video, Arts & Humanities-General, Historic Preservation, History & Archaeology, Libraries, Literary Arts, Museums/Galleries, Music, Opera, Public Broadcasting, Theater
Civic & Public Affairs: Botanical Gardens/Parks, Employment/Job Training, Civic & Public Affairs-General, Hispanic Affairs, Municipalities/Towns, Native American Affairs, Zoos/Aquariums
Education: Arts/Humanities Education, Colleges & Universities, Education Reform, Elementary Education (Public), Engineering/Technological Education, Environmental Education, Education-General, Medical Education, Private Education (Precollege), Public Education (Precollege), Science/Mathematics Education, Special Education
Environment: Air/Water Quality, Environment-General, Protection, Resource Conservation, Wildlife Protection
Health: Medical Rehabilitation, Research/Studies Institutes, Single-Disease Health Associations
International: Foreign Arts Organizations, Foreign Educational Institutions, International Environmental Issues, International Peace & Security Issues, International Relief Efforts
Religion: Religious Organizations, Religious Welfare
Science: Science Museums, Scientific Centers & Institutes, Scientific Labs, Scientific Research
Social Services: At-Risk Youth, Child Welfare, Community Centers, Community Service Organizations, Family Services, Social Services-General, Youth Organizations

Application Procedures

Initial Contact: Send a brief letter and proposal. Include proof of tax-exempt status.
Deadlines: March 1, September 1, and December 1.

Restrictions

Grants restricted to conservation sciences, early education, and the care of cultural collections. Funding is not available for individuals, building campaigns, or non-publicly supported charities.

Additional Information

The foundation reports that first time grants generally fall within the $2,000 to $6,000 range.
Publications: Annual Report

Foundation Officials

Robert W. Ashton: secretary B Memphis, TN 1937. ED University of Michigan BA (1960); Vanderbilt University LLB (1964). OCCUPATION pvt practice. NONPR AFFIL director: Saint Lukes Orchestra; board directors: Saint Matthews & Saint Timothys Neighborhood Center; member: New York City Bar Association; member: New York State Bar Association; member: Century Association; director: Millay Colony Arts; member: American Bar Association. CLUB AFFIL Estate Lawyers Club.
Frederick Bay: chairman
Daniel Anthony Demarest: treasurer B Plainfield, NJ 1924. ED Harvard University BA (1948); Harvard University LLB (1951). NONPR AFFIL member: City Bar Association; member: Phi Beta Kappa. CLUB AFFIL Knickerbocker New York Club.
Hans A. Ege: vice president
Synnova Bay Hayes: president
Corrine Steel: director

Grants Analysis

Disclosure Period: calendar year ending 2001
Total Grants: $826,221
Number of Grants: 133
Average Grant: $5,084
Highest Grant: $125,000
Lowest Grant: $100
Typical Range: $5,000 to $20,000

Recent Grants

Note: Grants derived from 2001 Form 990.

General

125,000	Center for Marine Conservation, Washington, DC
35,000	Heritage Preservation, Inc., Washington, DC
30,000	First Nations Development Institute, Fredericksburg, VA
20,000	Greenwich Village Youth Council, New York, NY
20,000	Mary McDowell Center for Learning, Brooklyn, NY
20,000	Native American Rights Fund, Boulder, CO
18,000	Alliance for Arts, New York, NY
15,000	Environmental Defense Fund
15,000	Goddard Riverside Community Center, New York, NY
15,000	International Biodiversity Observation Year

BAY STATE BANCORP, INC.

Company Headquarters

1299 Beacon St.
Brookline, MA 02446
Web: http://www.baystatefederal.com

Company Description

Founded: 1997
Ticker: BYS
Exchange: AMEX
Assets: US$491.9 million (2001)
Employees: 109 (2001)
SIC(s): 6035 Federal Savings Institutions, 6712 Bank Holding Companies.

Bay State Federal Savings Charitable Foundation

Giving Contact

Susan Kelliher
Bay State Federal Savings Charitable Foundation
1299 Beacon Street
Brookline, MA 02446-5242
Phone: (617)739-9577

Description

Founded: 1999
EIN: 043415547
Organization Type: Corporate Foundation
Giving Locations: Bank's market area, or subject to approval.

Financial Summary

Total Giving: $474,566 (fiscal year ending March 31, 2002); $211,523 (fiscal 2001)
Assets: $6,746,634 (fiscal 2002); $4,638,726 (fiscal 2001)

Typical Recipients

Arts & Humanities: History & Archaeology, Music, Public Broadcasting, Theater
Civic & Public Affairs: Chambers of Commerce, Community Foundations, Civic & Public Affairs-General, Municipalities/Towns, Public Policy
Education: Elementary Education (Public), Public Education (Precollege), Student Aid
Health: Cancer, Children's Health/Hospitals, Emergency/Ambulance Services, Geriatric Health, Health Organizations, Heart, Hospitals, Medical Research, Prenatal Health Issues, Single-Disease Health Associations
Religion: Jewish Causes, Religious Organizations, Religious Welfare
Social Services: Community Centers, Community Service Organizations, Recreation & Athletics, Senior Services, United Funds/United Ways, YMCA/YWCA/YMHA/YWHA, Youth Organizations

Application Procedures

Initial Contact: Send a grant application package or a written letter.
Application Requirements: Include proof of tax-exempt status.
Deadlines: None.

Foundation Officials

Anthony Caruso: director
Michael O. Gilles: senior vice president, treasurer
Jill Lacy: corporate secretary
John E. Murphy: chairman, president, chief executive officer
Phyllis Penta: director
Denise M. Renaghan: executive vice president, director

Grants Analysis

Disclosure Period: fiscal year ending March 31, 2002
Total Grants: $456,191*
Number of Grants: 125
Average Grant: $2,833*
Highest Grant: $55,000
Lowest Grant: $100
Typical Range: $500 to $5,000
*Note: Giving excludes United Way and scholarship. Average grant figure excludes two highest grants totaling $107,753.

Recent Grants

Note: Grants derived from 2002 Form 990.

General

55,000	American Red Cross, Ann Arbor, MI
52,753	Brookline Senior Center, Brookline, MA
27,500	Twin Towers Fund, New York, NY
25,000	Caritas Norwood Hospital
25,000	Friends of Norwood Senior Center
15,000	Coolidge Corner Theater Foundation
15,000	Newton Boys and Girls Club, Newton, MA
11,000	American Lung Association
10,000	Sandler O'Neil Assistance, Rockford, IL
10,000	Westwood Elementary School Coalition, Portland, OR

BAY VIEW BANK

Company Headquarters

1840 Gateway Drive, Suite 300
San Mateo, CA 94404
Web: http://www.bayviewbank.com

Company Description

Employees: 374
SIC(s): 6000 Depository Institutions, 6035 Federal Savings Institutions.
Parent Company: Bay View Capital Corp., 1840 Gateway Dr., Ste. 300, San Mateo, CA, United States

Operating Locations

Bay View Federal Bank (CA--San Mateo)

Nonmonetary Support

Type: Donated Equipment

Giving Contact

Suzanne Vaughan, Marketing Coordinator
1840 Gateway Drive
San Mateo, CA 94404
Phone: (650)312-7200

Description

Organization Type: Corporate Giving Program
Giving Locations: CA: Bay area, San Francisco
Grant Types: General Support, Project, Scholarship.

Financial Summary

Total Giving: $75,000 (1996); $50,000 (1995); $50,000 (1994)

Typical Recipients

Arts & Humanities: Arts Outreach, Community Arts, Ethnic & Folk Arts, Arts & Humanities-General, Libraries, Performing Arts
Civic & Public Affairs: African American Affairs, Asian American Affairs, Community Foundations, Economic Development, Employment/Job Training, Ethnic Organizations, Gay/Lesbian Issues, Civic & Public Affairs-General, Hispanic Affairs, Housing, Inner-City Development, Parades/Festivals, Philanthropic Organizations, Urban & Community Affairs
Education: Afterschool/Enrichment Programs, Education-General, Minority Education, Preschool Education, Public Education (Precollege), Special Education
Health: Adolescent Health Issues, AIDS/HIV, Children's Health/Hospitals, Clinics/Medical Centers, Health-General, Geriatric Health, Medical Research, Single-Disease Health Associations
Social Services: At-Risk Youth, Camps, Community Centers, Community Service Organizations, Counseling, Domestic Violence, Family Services, People with Disabilities, Senior Services, Shelters/Homelessness, Social Services-General, Substance Abuse, United Funds/United Ways, Volunteer Services, Youth Organizations

Application Procedures

Initial Contact: Send a brief letter of inquiry and a full proposal. Include a description of organization, amount requested, purpose of funds sought, and proof of tax-exempt status.
Deadlines: None.

Restrictions

Does not support religous organizations for sectarian purposes or political or lobbying groups. United Way agencies are supported separately.

Corporate Officials

John R. McKean: chairman, director B Evanston, IL 1930. ED University of San Francisco (1951); Golden Gate University (1976). PRIM CORP EMPL chairman, director: Bay View Fed Bank. CORP AFFIL chairman: Bay View Capital Corp.; president: John R McKean Accountants.

Grants Analysis

Typical Range: $50 to $1,000

BCR FOUNDATION

Giving Contact

Betty Gregg-Rainwater, President, Treasurer & Trustee
PO Box 13307
Pensacola, FL 32591-3307
Phone: (850)438-2509

Description

Founded: 1986
EIN: 592728836
Organization Type: Private Foundation
Giving Locations: FL
Grant Types: General Support.

Financial Summary

Total Giving: $56,900 (fiscal year ending August 31, 2000); $51,600 (fiscal 1999); $983,512 (fiscal 1998)
Giving Analysis: Giving for fiscal 1998 includes: foundation grants to United Way ($2,000)
Assets: $8,167,222 (fiscal 2000); $6,843,413 (fiscal 1999); $5,494,766 (fiscal 1998)
Gifts Received: $1,798,824 (fiscal 1998). Note: Contributions were received from the Crawford Rainwater Estate.

Typical Recipients

Arts & Humanities: Arts Associations & Councils, Community Arts, Dance, History & Archaeology, Libraries, Music, Theater
Civic & Public Affairs: Civic & Public Affairs-General, Housing, Urban & Community Affairs
Education: Business Education, Colleges & Universities, Community & Junior Colleges, Education-General, Journalism/Media Education, Literacy, Private Education (Precollege)
Environment: Environment-General, Resource Conservation, Wildlife Protection
Health: AIDS/HIV, Geriatric Health, Medical Rehabilitation, Medical Research, Public Health, Single-Disease Health Associations
International: Health Care/Hospitals, International Environmental Issues
Religion: Churches, Ministries, Religious Welfare
Science: Scientific Centers & Institutes
Social Services: Big Brother/Big Sister, Child Welfare, Community Service Organizations, Crime Prevention, Day Care, Family Planning, Food/Clothing Distribution, People with Disabilities, Scouts, Senior Services, Sexual Abuse, United Funds/United Ways, Youth Organizations

Application Procedures

Initial Contact: The foundation has no formal grant application procedure or application form.
Deadlines: None.

Restrictions

Does not support individuals.

Foundation Officials

Betty Nickenson: secretary, trustee
Betty Gregg Rainwater: president, treasurer, trustee

Grants Analysis

Disclosure Period: fiscal year ending August 31, 2000
Total Grants: $56,900
Number of Grants: 19
Average Grant: $2,688*
Highest Grant: $11,200
Lowest Grant: $200
Typical Range: $500 to $5,000
*Note: Average grant excludes 2 highest grants ($21,200).

Recent Grants

Note: Grants derived from 1999 Form 990.

Library-Related

4,000	Friends of the Pensacola Library, Pensacola, FL

General

10,000	Council On Aging
4,800	United Ministries
3,600	Favor House
3,000	Crime Stoppers
3,000	Junior Achievement, Pensacola, FL
3,000	West Florida Child Care, FL
2,400	Habitat for Humanity, Westminster, CA
2,400	Learn to Read
2,400	Manna Food Bank, Pensacola, FL
1,500	Arts Council

BEAL FOUNDATION

Giving Contact

Spencer E. Beal, Trustee
104 S. Pecos
Midland, TX 79701
Phone: (915)682-3753

Alternate Contact

Bill J. Hill
c/o Nationsbank of Texas
PO Box 270
Midland, TX 79702-0270
Phone: (915)685-2063

Description

Founded: 1962
EIN: 756034480
Organization Type: Private Foundation
Giving Locations: TX: Midland
Grant Types: General Support.

Donor Information

Founder: Carlton Beal, W. R. Davis

Financial Summary

Total Giving: $660,000 (2000); $511,000 (1998); $684,000 (1996). Note: 1996 Giving includes United Way ($140,000).
Giving Analysis: Giving for 2000 includes: foundation grants to United Way ($60,000); 1998: foundation grants to United Way ($100,000) foundation ($411,000)
Assets: $7,736,898 (1999); $4,913,528 (1998); $4,253,598 (1996)

Typical Recipients

Arts & Humanities: Arts Associations & Councils, Ballet, History & Archaeology, Libraries, Museums/Galleries, Music
Civic & Public Affairs: Civic & Public Affairs-General, Hispanic Affairs, Housing, Public Policy, Safety, Urban & Community Affairs
Education: Business Education, Colleges & Universities, Community & Junior Colleges, Continuing Education, Education-General, Private Education (Precollege), Special Education, Student Aid
Health: Cancer, Children's Health/Hospitals, Hospices, Hospitals, Medical Rehabilitation, Medical Research, Public Health, Single-Disease Health Associations
International: Health Care/Hospitals
Religion: Ministries, Religious Organizations, Religious Welfare
Social Services: At-Risk Youth, Big Brother/Big Sister, Child Welfare, Community Service Organizations, Crime Prevention, Day Care, Domestic Violence, Family Planning, Family Services, Food/Clothing Distribution, People with Disabilities, Scouts, Sexual Abuse, Social Services-General, Substance Abuse, United Funds/United Ways, YMCA/YWCA/YMHA/YWHA, Youth Organizations

Application Procedures

Initial Contact: Request application and guidelines.
Deadlines: one month before meetings for first-time applicants; two weeks before meetings for repeat applicants. Board meets on April 1 and November 1.

Additional Information

Publications: Application; Guidelines

Foundation Officials

Barry A. Beal: trustee
Carlton E. Beal, Jr.: trustee
Keleen H. Beal: chairman
Kelly S. Beal: trustee
Spencer E. Beal: trustee
Larry Bell: trustee
Robert J. Cowen: trustee
Karlene Beal Garber: trustee
Bill J. Hill: secretary, treasurer
Jane B. Ramsland: trustee
Smith K. Ray: trustee
Paul Rea: trustee

Grants Analysis

Disclosure Period: calendar year ending 2000
Total Grants: $600,000*
Number of Grants: 61
Average Grant: $7,881*
Highest Grant: $75,000
Lowest Grant: $1,000
Typical Range: $2,000 to $15,000
*Note: Giving excludes United Way. Average grant figure excludes highest two grants (135,000).

Recent Grants

Note: Grants derived from 1999 Form 990.

General

50,000	Trinity School of Midland, Midland, TX -- operating costs
45,000	United Way of Midland, Midland, TX -- operating costs
40,000	Midland College Foundation, Midland, TX -- operating costs
35,000	United Way of Midland, Midland, TX -- operating costs
25,000	Trinity School of Midland, Midland, TX -- operating costs
20,000	Midland Soup Kitchen Ministry, Midland, TX -- operating costs
10,000	Casa de Amigos, Midland, TX -- operating costs
10,000	High Sky Children's Ranch, Midland, TX -- operating costs
10,000	Midland Memorial Foundation, Midland, TX -- operating costs
10,000	Midland Odessa Symphony and Chorale, Midland, TX -- operating costs

NORWIN S. AND ELIZABETH N. BEAN FOUNDATION

Giving Contact

PO Box 326
Manchester, NH 03105-0326
Phone: (603)625-6464
Fax: (603)225-1700
E-mail: ns@nsa.org

Description

Founded: 1957
EIN: 026013381
Organization Type: Private Foundation
Giving Locations: NH: Amherst, Manchester
Grant Types: Conference/Seminar, Emergency, General Support, Loan, Project, Scholarship, Seed Money.

Donor Information

Founder: the late Norwin S. Bean, the late Elizabeth N. Bean

Financial Summary

Total Giving: $1,112,330 (2000); $712,523 (1999); $649,817 (1998)
Giving Analysis: Giving for 1999 includes: foundation grants to United Way ($25,000); 1998: foundation grants to United Way ($6,995) foundation ($642,822)
Assets: $18,207,135 (2000); $19,952,306 (1999); $16,555,179 (1998)

Typical Recipients

Arts & Humanities: Arts Associations & Councils, Arts Centers, Arts Festivals, Arts Institutes, Arts Outreach, Community Arts, Historic Preservation, History & Archaeology, Libraries, Museums/Galleries, Music, Performing Arts, Theater
Civic & Public Affairs: Chambers of Commerce, Community Foundations, Employment/Job Training, Civic & Public Affairs-General, Hispanic Affairs, Housing, Municipalities/Towns, Native American Affairs, Nonprofit Management, Parades/Festivals, Philanthropic Organizations, Safety, Urban & Community Affairs, Women's Affairs
Education: Afterschool/Enrichment Programs, Arts/Humanities Education, Colleges & Universities, Education Reform, Environmental Education, Faculty Development, Education-General, Literacy, Preschool Education, Private Education (Precollege), Public Education (Precollege), School Volunteerism, Science/Mathematics Education, Secondary Education (Private), Secondary Education (Public)
Environment: Forestry, Environment-General, Resource Conservation, Watershed
Health: AIDS/HIV, Alzheimers Disease, Cancer, Children's Health/Hospitals, Clinics/Medical Centers, Emergency/Ambulance Services, Health Organizations, Heart, Mental Health, Nursing Services, Prenatal Health Issues, Respiratory
Religion: Churches, Ministries, Religious Welfare
Social Services: At-Risk Youth, Big Brother/Big Sister, Child Welfare, Community Service Organizations, Counseling, Delinquency & Criminal Rehabilitation, Family Services, Family Services, Food/Clothing Distribution, People with Disabilities, Recreation & Athletics, Scouts, Senior Services, Shelters/Homelessness, Substance Abuse, United Funds/United Ways, YMCA/YWCA/YMHA/YWHA, Youth Organizations

Application Procedures

Initial Contact: Send a cover sheet and a proposal with appropriate enclosures.
Application Requirements: Explain the purpose of the project and describe how that purpose will be accomplished.
Deadlines: December 1, April 1, and September 1 for meetings in February, June, and November.

Restrictions

Does not support individuals or provide funds for scholarships.

Additional Information

Publications: Annual Report; Informational Brochure (including Application Guidelines)

Foundation Officials

Maybelle L. Balsama: trustee
Thomas J. Donovan: trustee
Susan G. Lafond: trustee
James A. Shanahan, Jr.: trustee
Arthur F. Starr: trustee
William G. Steele, Jr.: chairman

Grants Analysis

Disclosure Period: calendar year ending 2000
Total Grants: $1,112,330
Number of Grants: 55
Average Grant: $20,224
Highest Grant: $125,000
Lowest Grant: $1,000
Typical Range: $10,000 to $50,000

Recent Grants

Note: Grants derived from 1999 Form 990.

General

60,000	Summerbridge At Manchester, Manchester, NH -- for the program endowment campaign
50,000	University of New Hampshire at Manchester, Manchester, NH -- to construct a new microbiology laboratory
40,000	Manchester Police Athletic League, Manchester, NH -- capital campaign to purchase and renovate St. Cecilia's Hall
40,000	Webster House, Manchester, NH -- capital campaign
35,000	Audubon Society of New Hampshire, Concord, NH -- capital campaign
35,000	Way Home, Inc., The, Manchester, NH -- to implement a housing advocacy program for low income tenants
31,500	New Hampshire Charitable Foundation, Concord, NH -- annual grant support and services to the field
25,000	Manchester Neighborhood Housing Services, Manchester, NH -- to establish an economic development program in the Center City
25,000	United Way of Greater New Hampshire, Manchester, NH -- new computer system
20,000	Child Health Services, Manchester, NH -- program of health education and clinical services to adolescents

LUCY AND EMILY BEASLEY CHARITABLE TRUST

Giving Contact

Thomas D. Barsody, Trust Officer
c/o Bank One Akron NA
50 S. Main St.
Akron, OH 44308
Phone: (330)972-1732

Description

Founded: 1981
EIN: 341350747
Organization Type: Private Foundation
Giving Locations: OH

Donor Information

Founder: Robert P. Beasley Trust

Financial Summary

Total Giving: $407,741 (fiscal year ending September 30, 1999); $432,999 (fiscal 1998); $309,000 (fiscal 1997)
Assets: $7,880,723 (fiscal 1999); $7,451,539 (fiscal 1998); $7,301,213 (fiscal 1997)
Gifts Received: $224 (fiscal 1999); $35,251 (fiscal 1998); $227,211 (fiscal 1997). Note: In 1999, contributions were received from Robert P. Beasley Trust. In fiscal 1996, contributions were received from the Robert P. Beasley Trust ($1,888) and the estate of Robert P. Beasley ($31,052).

Typical Recipients

Arts & Humanities: Libraries
Civic & Public Affairs: Clubs, Employment/Job Training, Civic & Public Affairs-General, Zoos/Aquariums
Education: Colleges & Universities, Education-General, Private Education (Precollege), Public Education (Precollege)
Environment: Environment-General
Health: Health Organizations
Religion: Churches, Ministries, Religious Welfare
Social Services: Animal Protection, Community Service Organizations, Domestic Violence, Family Services, People with Disabilities, Scouts

Application Procedures

Initial Contact: Send a brief letter of inquiry.
Application Requirements: Include a description of organization and purpose of funds sought.
Deadlines: None.

Additional Information

Trust(s): Bank One Akron NA

Foundation Officials

Howard Cable: adv
L. W. Moore: adv
Francis B. Young: adv

Grants Analysis

Disclosure Period: fiscal year ending September 30, 1999
Total Grants: $407,741
Number of Grants: 36
Average Grant: $8,793*
Highest Grant: $100,000
Typical Range: $1,000 to $20,000
*Note: Average grant figure excludes highest grant. A more recent grants list was unavailable.

Recent Grants

Note: Grants derived from fiscal 2001 Form 990.

General

100,000	Akron Zoological Park, Akron, OH
75,000	H.M. Life Opportunity Services, Akron, OH
75,000	Interval Brotherhood Home, Akron, OH
50,000	Access, Akron, OH
25,000	Project Learn to Summit County, Akron, OH
20,000	University of Akron Foundation, Akron, OH
10,000	Cumberland College, Williamsburg, KY
5,000	Gennesaret, Akron, OH
5,000	Goodwill Industries, Akron, OH
5,000	Great Trail Council, Akron, OH

CORDELIA LEE BEATTIE FOUNDATION

Giving Contact

Debra M. Jacobs, Administrator
1800 2nd St., Suite 750
Sarasota, FL 34236
Phone: (941)957-0442
Fax: (941)957-3135
E-mail: djacobs@selbyfdn.org
Web: http://www.selbyfdn.org/cordeliaLee.html

Description

Founded: 1975
EIN: 596540711
Organization Type: Private Foundation
Giving Locations: FL: Sarasota County
Grant Types: General Support.

Donor Information

Founder: the late Cordelia Lee Beattie

Financial Summary

Total Giving: $104,550 (fiscal year ending October 31, 2002); $150,792 (fiscal 2001); $137,430 (fiscal 2000)
Assets: $2,168,005 (fiscal 2002); $2,487,788 (fiscal 2001); $3,111,250 (fiscal 2000)

Typical Recipients

Arts & Humanities: Arts Associations & Councils, Arts Centers, Arts Festivals, Ballet, Community Arts, Dance, Film & Video, Libraries, Literary Arts, Museums/Galleries, Music, Opera, Performing Arts, Theater, Visual Arts
Civic & Public Affairs: Botanical Gardens/Parks
Education: Arts/Humanities Education, Private Education (Precollege)
Environment: Environment-General
Health: Children's Health/Hospitals
Social Services: Animal Protection

Application Procedures

Initial Contact: Contact the foundation or visit the foundation's web site to obtain guidelines and application format.
Deadlines: November 15.
Notes: The Selby Foundation manages the Cordelia Lee Beattie Foundation's grantmaking.

Restrictions

Does not support endowments, deficit financing, debt reduction, or ordinary operating expenses; conferences, seminars, workshops, travel, surveys, advertising, fundraising costs, or research; annual giving campaigns; projects that have already been completed; or individuals.

Additional Information

Publications: Application Guidelines

Foundation Officials

Debra M. Jacobs: administration agent NONPR AFFIL vice president: Ringling School Art & Design.
Dr. Robert E. Perkins: admin agent

Grants Analysis

Disclosure Period: fiscal year ending October 31, 2002
Total Grants: $104,550
Number of Grants: 9
Average Grant: $11,617*
Highest Grant: $30,000
Lowest Grant: $4,800
Typical Range: $2,500 to $15,000
*Note: Average grant excludes highest grant.

Recent Grants

Note: Grants derived from 2002 Form 990.

General

30,000	Florida West Coast Symphony, Sarasota, FL -- Youth Orchestra Program
20,000	Asolo Performing Arts Center, Sarasota, FL -- for Kaleidoscope Touring Company
13,000	Marie Selby Botanical Gardens, Sarasota, FL -- for Sunday Garden Music series
10,750	Florida Studio Theater, Sarasota, FL -- for VIP Program
10,000	Sarasota Ballet, Sarasota, FL -- for the Nutcracker children's costumes
6,000	Gloria Musicae, Sarasota, FL -- for Venice High School Project
5,000	Theater Works, Sarasota, FL -- for mainstage season
4,800	Pines of Sarasota Inc., Sarasota, FL -- for Continuation of Arts Program

CORDELIA LUNCEFORD BEATTY TRUST

Giving Contact

James R. Rodgers, Trustee
105 North Main
PO Box 514
Blackwell, OK 74631-0514
Phone: (580)363-3684

Description

Founded: 1943
EIN: 736094952
Organization Type: Private Foundation
Giving Locations: OK: Blackwell
Grant Types: Scholarship.

Financial Summary

Total Giving: $166,525 (2000); $135,655 (1999); $112,385 (1998)
Giving Analysis: Giving for 2000 includes: foundation scholarships ($26,674); 1999: foundation scholarships ($16,875) 1998: foundation gifts to individuals ($12,250)
Assets: $3,431,122 (2000); $3,786,418 (1999); $3,555,697 (1998)

Typical Recipients

Arts & Humanities: Libraries, Music
Civic & Public Affairs: Clubs, Civic & Public Affairs-General, Municipalities/Towns, Safety
Education: Afterschool/Enrichment Programs, Agricultural Education, Colleges & Universities, Literacy, Private Education (Precollege), Public Education (Precollege), Religious Education, School Volunteerism, Secondary Education (Public), Special Education, Student Aid
Health: Emergency/Ambulance Services
Religion: Religious Welfare
Social Services: Community Service Organizations, Food/Clothing Distribution, People with Disabilities, Recreation & Athletics, Scouts, Substance Abuse, United Funds/United Ways, YMCA/YWCA/YMHA/YWHA, Youth Organizations

Application Procedures

Initial Contact: The foundation has no formal grant application procedure or application form.
Deadlines: None.

Foundation Officials

James R. Rodgers: trustee
William W. Rodgers: trustee

Grants Analysis

Disclosure Period: calendar year ending 2000
Total Grants: $139,851*
Number of Grants: 33
Average Grant: $2,069*
Highest Grant: $73,646
Lowest Grant: $100
Typical Range: $500 to $5,000*
*Note: Giving excludes scholarships. Average grant excludes highest grant.

Recent Grants

Note: Grants derived from 1999 Form 990.

Library-Related

9,220	Blackwell High School, Blackwell, OK -- computerized library book
1,000	Blackwell Public Library, Blackwell, OK -- children's books

General

7,500	Northern Oklahoma Youth Services, Ponca City, OK -- capital improvement fund
6,500	Blackwell Youth Center, Blackwell, OK
5,825	Northern Oklahoma College, Tonkawa, OK -- fall 1999 scholarships
5,000	Blackwell Baseball Board, Blackwell, OK -- baseball program
5,000	YMCA of Ponca City
4,200	Blackwell High School, Blackwell, OK -- maps
4,000	Blackwell Oklahoma Community Foundation, Blackwell, OK -- repair and maintenance to pool
3,725	Northern Oklahoma College, Tonkawa, OK -- spring 2000 scholarships
2,639	Wal-Mart, Blackwell, OK -- school supplies
2,233	Wal-Mart, Blackwell, OK -- rotary Christmas

BEAUCOURT FOUNDATION

Giving Contact

Peter A. Wilson, Trust Officer
c/o Testa, Hurwitz & Thibeault
125 High St.
Boston, MA 02110
Phone: (617)248-7426
Fax: (617)248-7100

Description

Founded: 1988
EIN: 042979426
Organization Type: Private Foundation
Giving Locations: MA: Boston; NY
Grant Types: General Support.

Financial Summary

Total Giving: $235,000 (2001); $245,000 (2000); $205,000 (1999)
Assets: $3,934,666 (2001); $4,097,085 (2000); $3,987,620 (1999)

Typical Recipients

Arts & Humanities: Libraries
Education: Business Education, Colleges & Universities, Education-General, International Studies
International: Foreign Educational Institutions

Application Procedures

Initial Contact: The foundation has no formal grant application procedure or application form.
Deadlines: None.

Restrictions

Must be an IRS approved charity.

Foundation Officials

Henry W. Comstock, Jr.: clerk, director
Richard J. Testa: president, treasurer, director B Marlboro, MA 1939. ED Assumption College AB (1959); Harvard University LLB (1962). PRIM CORP EMPL managing partner: Testa Hurwitz & Thibeault ADD CORP EMPL vice president: Granite State Phoenix Co. NONPR AFFIL member: American Bar Association.

Grants Analysis

Disclosure Period: calendar year ending 2001
Total Grants: $235,000
Number of Grants: 3
Highest Grant: $80,000
Lowest Grant: $70,000

Recent Grants

Note: Grants derived from 2001 Form 990.

Library-Related

85,000	French Library and Cultural Center, Boston, MA
70,000	French Library and Cultural Center, Boston, MA

General

80,000	Insead Management Education Foundation, New York, NY

BEAZLEY FOUNDATION

Giving Contact

Richard S. Bray, Jr., President
3720 Brighton Street
Portsmouth, VA 23707
Phone: (757)393-1605
Fax: (757)393-4708
Web: http://www.beazleyfoundation.org

Description

Founded: 1948
EIN: 540550100
Organization Type: General Purpose Foundation
Giving Locations: VA: Portsmouth Hampton Roads, VA area.
Grant Types: Capital, General Support, Operating Expenses, Project, Scholarship, Seed Money.

Donor Information

Founder: Established in December 1948 with funds provided by the late Fred W. Beazley , his wife Marie C. Beazley, and son Fred W. Beazley Jr., all of Portsmouth, VA. A sister foundation, Foundation Boys Academy was founded by Mr. Beazley in 1956. In 1986, the charter of Foundation Boys Academy was amended, the name changed to Frederick Foundation and its purpose changed to fund charitable and religious, in addition to educational endeavors. However, in 1993, the Frederick Foundation merged into the Beazley Foundation and now follows its program interests.
The main goal of the chief benefactor of the foundations, Mr. Beazley, was to provide what was not otherwise available to the citizens of Portsmouth, primarily to the youth. He was interested in a quality secondary education for deserving youngsters, as well as recreational facilities for the children of the city. He established the City Dental Clinic in cooperation with the city of Portsmouth to provide dental care to those who could not afford it. Affordable rental housing was also one of his most satisfying accomplishments.

Financial Summary

Total Giving: $1,800,000 (2003 approx); $2,700,179 (2002); $2,947,056 (2001)
Giving Analysis: Giving for 2000 includes: foundation grants to United Way ($28,000) 1998: foundation grants to United Way ($24,750)
Assets: $45,000,000 (2003 approx); $50,943,145 (2002); $73,903,006 (2000)

Typical Recipients

Arts & Humanities: Historic Preservation, History & Archaeology, Libraries, Museums/Galleries, Music
Civic & Public Affairs: African American Affairs, Botanical Gardens/Parks, Business/Free Enterprise, Economic Development, Employment/Job Training, Civic & Public Affairs-General, Housing, Municipalities/Towns, Nonprofit Management, Philanthropic Organizations, Professional & Trade Associations, Safety, Urban & Community Affairs, Zoos/Aquariums
Education: Afterschool/Enrichment Programs, Agricultural Education, Arts/Humanities Education, Business Education, Colleges & Universities, Community & Junior Colleges, Education Funds, Elementary Education (Public), Engineering/Technological Education, Environmental Education, Faculty Development, Education-General, Gifted & Talented Programs, Leadership Training, Legal Education, Literacy, Medical Education, Minority Education, Preschool Education, Private Education (Precollege), Public Education (Precollege), School Volunteerism, Science/Mathematics Education, Secondary Education (Private), Student Aid
Environment: Forestry
Health: AIDS/HIV, Cancer, Children's Health/Hospitals, Clinics/Medical Centers, Emergency/Ambulance Services, Health-General, Geriatric Health, Health Organizations, Hospitals, Hospitals (University Affiliated), Medical Rehabilitation, Public Health, Single-Disease Health Associations
International: Foreign Arts Organizations, International Organizations
Religion: Churches, Ministries, Religious Organizations, Religious Welfare, Seminaries
Science: Observatories & Planetariums, Science Museums
Social Services: At-Risk Youth, Camps, Child Abuse, Child Welfare, Community Centers, Community Service Organizations, Crime Prevention, Day Care, Delinquency & Criminal Rehabilitation, Domestic Violence, Emergency Relief, Family Services, Food/Clothing Distribution, Homes, People with Disabilities, Recreation & Athletics, Scouts, Senior Services, Shelters/Homelessness, Social Services-General, Substance Abuse, United Funds/United Ways, Volunteer Services, YMCA/YWCA/YMHA/YWHA, Youth Organizations

Application Procedures

Initial Contact: Applicants are encouraged to call the foundation to request grant application guidelines.
Deadlines: Quarterly.

Restrictions

The foundation does not fund individuals, conferences, symposia, publications or media projects, international or national programs and institutions, and environmental protection projects. Generally, limited grants are given to the arts and only to programs providing art education directly to elementary and secondary school students.

Additional Information

Publications: Application Guidelines; Foundation Policy; Annual Report

Foundation Officials

Jeannette C. Bridgeman: treasurer, assistant secretary
Leroy T. Canoles, Jr.: trustee B 1925. ED University of Virginia Law School (1951). PRIM CORP EMPL president, director: Kaufman and Canoles PC.

Diane P. Griffin: trustee
Lawrence W. l'Anson, Jr.: president, executive director
W. Ashton Lewis: secretary, trustee
P. Ward Robinett, Jr.: trustee PRIM CORP EMPL president: Branch Banking Trust Co. of Virginia.

Grants Analysis

Disclosure Period: calendar year ending 2001
Total Grants: $2,947,056*
Number of Grants: 90
Average Grant: $23,745
Highest Grant: $357,235
Lowest Grant: $70
Typical Range: $1,000 to $50,000
***Note:** Grants analysis provided by foundation.

Recent Grants

Note: Grants derived from 2000 Form 990.

General

315,000	Portsmouth Health Department, Portsmouth, VA -- City Dental Clinic
91,000	Portsmouth Public Schools, Portsmouth, VA -- Beazley scholarships
90,000	Virginia Foundation for Independent Colleges, Richmond, VA -- support Beazley Scholarships
80,000	Tidewater Scholarship Foundation, Norfolk, VA -- ACCESS program endowment
75,000	Portsmouth School Foundation, Portsmouth, VA -- for ACCESS Program
64,451	Portsmouth Museums, Portsmouth, VA -- Children's Museum
60,000	College Fund/UNCF, Fairfax, VA -- endowed scholarship
54,000	Help and Emergency Response, Portsmouth, VA -- operating expense
50,300	Virginia Air and Space Museum, Hampton, VA -- for Science Program for Portsmouth Students
50,000	Battleship Wisconsin Foundation, Norfolk, VA -- capital endowment

HILDEGARDE D. BECHER FOUNDATION

Giving Contact

Lawrence Dix, Treasurer
PO Box 11
Hartsdale, NY 10530-0011
Phone: (914)997-9888

Description

Founded: 1995
EIN: 133744010
Organization Type: Private Foundation
Grant Types: General Support, Scholarship.

Financial Summary

Total Giving: $272,300 (2001); $258,205 (2000); $234,250 (1999)
Giving Analysis: Giving for 2001 includes: foundation scholarships ($19,800)
Assets: $4,928,876 (2001); $5,630,539 (2000); $5,848,421 (1999)

Typical Recipients

Arts & Humanities: Libraries, Museums/Galleries, Music, Opera
Education: Arts/Humanities Education, Colleges & Universities, Medical Education, Student Aid
Health: Cancer, Hospices, Hospitals, Medical Research, Respiratory
International: Foreign Arts Organizations
Social Services: Animal Protection, Camps, Child Welfare, Substance Abuse, YMCA/YWCA/YMHA/YWHA

Application Procedures

Initial Contact: Send a brief letter of inquiry.
Deadlines: None.

Foundation Officials

Alan Berg: vice president
Lawrence Dix: treasurer
Jack Geogheghan: secretary
Herbert Kroner: president

Grants Analysis

Disclosure Period: calendar year ending 2001
Total Grants: $252,500*
Number of Grants: 21
Average Grant: $7,395*
Highest Grant: $62,000
Lowest Grant: $500
Typical Range: $2,500 to $10,000
***Note:** Giving excludes scholarship. Average grant figure excludes two highest grants ($112,000).

Recent Grants

Note: Grants derived from 2000 Form 990.

General

52,500	Leukemia and Lymphoma Society -- medical research
30,000	New York University - Medical Center, New York, NY -- medical research
25,000	Happiness is Camping, Bronx, NY
22,500	Rye YMCA
18,000	Mannes College of Music, New York, NY -- scholarship
10,000	American Lung Association
10,000	Barnard College, New York, NY
9,125	New York Medical College, Valhalla, NY -- medical research
9,080	Calvary Hospital, Bronx, NY
8,000	Children's Dream Foundation, New York, NY

MARIE H. BECHTEL CHARITABLE REMAINDER UNI-TRUST

Giving Contact

R. Richard Bittner, Trustee
201 West 2nd Street, Ste. 1000
Davenport, IA 52801
Phone: (563)328-3333
Fax: (563)328-3352

Description

Founded: 1978
EIN: 426288500
Organization Type: General Purpose Foundation
Giving Locations: IA: Scott County
Grant Types: Capital, Challenge, Emergency, Endowment, General Support, Matching, Operating Expenses, Scholarship.
Note: A limited number of emergency grants, endowments, operating grants are given.

Donor Information

Founder: The Marie H. Bechtel Charitable Remainder Uni-Trust, established in 1978, is the largest of four trusts and a corporate foundation which were created either by Harold R. Bechtel or by Marie H. Bechtel during their lifetimes. The other charitable organizations are the following: the Bechtel Foundation, the H. Reimers Bechtel Uni-Trust, the H. R. Bechtel Testamentary Charitable Trust, and the Harold R. Bechtel Charitable Remainder Uni-Trust.
The Bechtels were lifetime residents of Scott County, IA. Harold R. Bechtel was one of Iowa's foremost bankers until his death in 1987. Marie H. Bechtel was highly regarded for her cultural activities and interests in Scott County, as well as her devotion to the health care needs of the community.
Both Harold and Marie were born in Davenport, IA. Harold served in both World War I and World War II, rising to the rank of lieutenant colonel. He became engaged in the banking industry in 1935 when the Bechtel Trust Company received its state banking charter.

Financial Summary

Total Giving: $1,008,100 (2001); $1,082,500 (2000); $1,401,000 (1999)
Giving Analysis: Giving for 2000 includes: foundation scholarships ($50,000); 1999: foundation scholarships ($125,000) foundation matching gifts ($127,500)
Assets: $30,861,450 (2001); $32,871,278 (2000); $31,077,354 (1999)

Typical Recipients

Arts & Humanities: Arts Institutes, Community Arts, Libraries, Museums/Galleries
Civic & Public Affairs: Economic Development, Employment/Job Training, Civic & Public Affairs-General, Housing, Legal Aid, Municipalities/Towns, Philanthropic Organizations
Education: Business Education, Colleges & Universities, Community & Junior Colleges, Education-General, Medical Education, Private Education (Precollege), Science/Mathematics Education, Secondary Education (Private)
Environment: Environment-General
Health: Cancer, Public Health
Religion: Churches, Religion-General, Religious Organizations, Religious Welfare
Science: Science Museums
Social Services: At-Risk Youth, Big Brother/Big Sister, Child Welfare, Community Centers, Community Service Organizations, Food/Clothing Distribution, Recreation & Athletics, Senior Services, Social Services-General, YMCA/YWCA/YMHA/YWHA

Application Procedures

Initial Contact: Contact the trust to request a copy of the grant application. Such contact should be written and should provide a brief description of the requested use for funds.
Application Requirements: Grant applications will require the following: a brief a description of organization, including its legal name, history, activities, purpose, and governing body; a clear description of the purpose for which the grant is requested and the goals to be achieved; the amount requested and a list of other current and potential sources of financial support; a copy of the organization's most recent audited financial statement; a copy of the IRS tax-exempt determination letter; and a copy of the organization's last 990-income tax return.
Deadlines: None.
Review Process: The trust will send a written notice to applicants within a reasonable time, whether the request for a grant has been approved or declined.

Restrictions

The foundation generally does not support endowment funds; past operating deficits or debt retirement; general and continuing operating support; or basic scholarly research within established academic disciplines.
Grants are currently confined to nonprofit, public tax-exempt organizations to be used for their charitable purposes. Grants may be made to individuals in the future, but are not currently available.
Grants are generally made to Scott County, IA, with the noted exceptions.

Additional Information

Publications: Guidelines; Application Form; Brochure Explaining Uni-Trust's Philosophy

Foundation Officials
R. Richard Bittner: trustee, director
Lucy Boedeker: office manager

Grants Analysis
Disclosure Period: calendar year ending 2000
Total Grants: $1,008,100*
Number of Grants: 14
Average Grant: $50,578*
Highest Grant: $150,000
Typical Range: $25,000 to $100,000
*Note: Giving excludes scholarship. Average grant figure excludes two highest grants ($300,000).

Recent Grants
Note: Grants derived from 2001 Form 990.

General
150,000	City of Davenport, Davenport, IA -- public charity
150,000	St. Ambrose University, Davenport, IA -- renovation of McMullen Hall
100,000	Junior Achievement of the Quad Cities Area, Inc., Moline, IL -- funding for Exchange City facility
100,000	Museum of Art Foundation, Davenport, IA -- capital funding for construction
100,000	Putnam Museum of History and Natural Science, Davenport, IA -- capital funding for construction of I-Max Theater
100,000	Scott Community College Foundation, Bettendorf, IA -- capital funds for the renovation of the Kahl Educational Center
100,000	Scott County Family YMCA, Davenport, IA -- for Program Development Fund
75,000	City of Davenport, Davenport, IA -- capital funding
50,000	Davenport One Foundation, Davenport, IA -- for community charity
50,000	Friends of Brady Street Stadium, Davenport, IA -- capital funding for renovation

BECHTEL GROUP, INC.

Company Headquarters
San Francisco, CA
Web: http://www.bechtel.com

Company Description
Operating Revenue: US$11.6 billion (2002)
Employees: 47000 (2002)
SIC(s): 1522 Residential Construction Nec, 1541 Industrial Buildings & Warehouses, 1542 Nonresidential Construction Nec, 1611 Highway & Street Construction.

Operating Locations
Bechtel Group, Inc. (CA--Concord, Englewood, Los Angeles; DC--Washington; NV--North Las Vegas; NJ--Florence, Hainesport; NC--Charlotte; PA--Pittsburgh; SC--Cayce; TN--Kingsport)

Nonmonetary Support
Type: In-kind Services
Note: Co. provides limited nonmonetary support.

Bechtel Foundation

Giving Contact
LeeAnne M. Lang, Assistant Secretary
Bechtel Foundation
50 Beale Street
San Francisco, CA 94105
Phone: (415)768-7158
Fax: (415)768-0263
E-mail: lmlang@bechtel.com
Web: http://www.bechtel.com/bechfoun.html

Alternate Contact
E-mail: foundtn@bechtel.com

Description
EIN: 946078120
Organization Type: Corporate Foundation
Giving Locations: internationally, in major operating locations.
Grant Types: Employee Matching Gifts, General Support.
Note: Foundation matches employee gifts to colleges and universities in the United States.

Financial Summary
Total Giving: $3,120,277 (2001); $3,672,966 (2000); $2,842,313 (1999). Note: Contributes through foundation only.
Giving Analysis: Giving for 2001 includes: foundation scholarships ($69,611); foundation grants to United Way ($220,500); foundation ($2,830,166); 2000: foundation grants to United Way ($259,650); foundation ($3,413,316); 1999: foundation grants to United Way (approx $259,820); foundation ($2,582,493);
Assets: $15,653,616 (2001); $17,678,607 (2000); $20,973,216 (1999)

Typical Recipients
Arts & Humanities: Arts Outreach, Community Arts, Ethnic & Folk Arts, Libraries, Museums/Galleries, Performing Arts
Civic & Public Affairs: African American Affairs, Botanical Gardens/Parks, Business/Free Enterprise, Chambers of Commerce, Clubs, Economic Development, Economic Policy, Ethnic Organizations, Civic & Public Affairs-General, Hispanic Affairs, Housing, Legal Aid, Minority Business, Municipalities/Towns, Nonprofit Management, Philanthropic Organizations, Professional & Trade Associations, Public Policy, Urban & Community Affairs, Zoos/Aquariums
Education: Business Education, Business-School Partnerships, Colleges & Universities, Education Funds, Education Reform, Elementary Education (Public), Engineering/Technological Education, Environmental Education, Education-General, International Exchange, International Studies, Legal Education, Literacy, Medical Education, Minority Education, Private Education (Precollege), Public Education (Precollege), Science/Mathematics Education, Secondary Education (Public), Social Sciences Education, Student Aid, Vocational & Technical Education
Environment: Air/Water Quality, Environment-General, Resource Conservation
Health: Adolescent Health Issues, AIDS/HIV, Cancer, Children's Health/Hospitals, Emergency/Ambulance Services, Hospitals, Prenatal Health Issues, Research/Studies Institutes
International: Foreign Educational Institutions, Health Care/Hospitals, International Affairs, International Development, International Organizations, International Peace & Security Issues, International Relations, Missionary/Religious Activities
Religion: Jewish Causes, Religious Welfare
Science: Science Exhibits & Fairs, Science Museums, Scientific Centers & Institutes, Scientific Organizations, Scientific Research
Social Services: Child Welfare, Community Service Organizations, Emergency Relief, Food/Clothing Distribution, Recreation & Athletics, Scouts, Social Services-General, Special Olympics, Substance Abuse, United Funds/United Ways, YMCA/YWCA/YMHA/YWHA, Youth Organizations

Application Procedures
Initial Contact: Send a one- or two-page letter of request.
Application Requirements: Include a description of organization; amount requested; purpose of funds sought; recently audited financial statement; proof of tax-exempt status; and a few pages of backup material.

Deadlines: None.
Notes: Most grants are under $5,000.

Restrictions
The foundation does not support individuals; fraternal, social, or religious organizations; entertainment; limited interest organizations; fellowships, internships, or residencies; endowed or named chairs at educational or research institutions; catalogs and publications; conferences and events.

Corporate Officials
Donald J. Gunther: director, president, director B 1938. ED University of Missouri BScE (1960). PRIM CORP EMPL director: Bechtel Group, Inc. CORP AFFIL president: Bechtel Americas; executive vice president: Bechtel Corp.
Adrian Zaccaria: vice chairman, president, director B 1944. ED United States Merchant Marine Academy BS (1966). PRIM CORP EMPL vice chairman, president, director: Bechtel Group, Inc. CORP AFFIL officer: Bechtel Systems Infrastructure; administration: International Bechtel S De RL; president: Bechtel Overseas Corp.; president: Bechtel Leasing Services Inc.; president: Bechtel North America Power Corp.; executive vice president, director: Bechtel Corp.; president: Bechtel International Inc.; president: America Bechtel Inc.; vice chairman: Bechtel Construction Operations Inc.

Grants Analysis
Disclosure Period: calendar year ending 2001
Total Grants: $2,830,166*
Number of Grants: 480
Average Grant: $4,449*
Highest Grant: $698,913
Lowest Grant: $25
Typical Range: $50 to $5,000 and $10,000 to $50,000
*Note: Giving excludes United Way and scholarships. Average grant figure excludes highest grant.

Recent Grants
Note: Grants derived from 2001 Form 990.

General
698,913	Twin Towers Fund, New York, NY
383,333	Institute for International Studies, Washington, DC
175,000	United Way Bay Area, San Francisco, CA
152,694	Jason Foundation for Education, Needham Hts, MA
60,000	Charities Aid Foundation, Alexandria, VA
60,000	Houston Golf Association, Houston, TX
60,000	National Action Council for Minorities in Engineering, New York, NY
50,000	American School in London Foundation, Princeton, NJ
50,000	Chronicle Season of Sharing Fund, San Francisco, CA
46,000	ActionAIDS, Philadelphia, PA

ARNOLD AND MABEL BECKMAN FOUNDATION

Giving Contact
Jacqueline Dorrance, Executive Director
100 Academy Drive
Irvine, CA 92612
Phone: (949)721-2222
Fax: (949)721-2225
E-mail: jdorrance@beckman-foundation.com
Web: http://www.beckman-foundation.com

Description

Founded: 1977
EIN: 953169713
Organization Type: Specialized/Single Purpose Foundation
Giving Locations: nationally.
Grant Types: Award, Research.

Donor Information

Founder: Established in 1977 by Arnold Orville Beckman and his wife, the late Mabel Meinzer Beckman (d. 1989). In 1934, while a professor of chemistry at the California Institute of Technology, Dr. Beckman invented the glass electrode pH meter. In 1941, he invented the quartz spectrophotometer. He went on to found Beckman Instruments, a company which develops and manufactures analytical and electronic instruments, precision components, and chemical products for medical, industrial, environmental, and scientific applications.

Financial Summary

Total Giving: $20,719,938 (fiscal year ending August 31, 2002); $20,000,000 (fiscal 2001 approx); $5,473,313 (fiscal 1999)
Giving Analysis: Giving for fiscal 1999 includes: foundation scholarships ($953,603)
Assets: $334,260,791 (fiscal 2002); $452,940,223 (fiscal 1999); $358,773,092 (fiscal 1998)
Gifts Received: $95 (fiscal 2002); $55,150 (fiscal 1999); $19,908,399 (fiscal 1997). Note: In fiscal 1999, contributions were received from Dr. Arnold Beckman.

Typical Recipients

Civic & Public Affairs: Civic & Public Affairs-General, Urban & Community Affairs, Zoos/Aquariums
Education: Colleges & Universities, Engineering/Technological Education, Education-General, Science/Mathematics Education, Student Aid
Health: Clinics/Medical Centers, Eyes/Blindness, Medical Research, Research/Studies Institutes, Speech & Hearing
Science: Science-General, Science Museums, Scientific Centers & Institutes, Scientific Organizations, Scientific Research
Social Services: Community Service Organizations

Application Procedures

Initial Contact: The foundation encourages all applicants to go to website for guidelines and application.
Application Requirements: The proposal should consist of a brief four-page description of proposed work, including the rationale for the work, its potential importance, methods of implementation, progress to date, and any significant outcomes; curriculum vitae for the principal investigator; three letters of reference; the completed two-page application. References, diagrams, and drawings should be incorporated with the four page limitations. One copy of all of the proposal materials must be submitted.
Deadlines: October 1 for consideration in the following fiscal year.
Review Process: Recommendations of the foundation's Grants Advisory Council are forwarded to the foundation's board, whose decisions on awards are final. Notifications of awards are made in the spring. Approved grants will normally be paid quarterly over three years.
Notes: Projects will be supported for periods of one to four years. While the foundation has no fixed limits on the size of grants, grants will normally be about $240,000 over the term of the project.

Restrictions

Funding will not be considered for the following: general institutional expenses; general fundraising campaign expenses, such as dinners and mass mailings; unified funds or organizations that grant funds to other organizations; and social science, religious, political,

or other research that does not fall within the foundation's areas of interest.

Additional Information

Funding is limited to principal investigators who have completed no more than three years of their initial appointment as independent researcher (tenure-track assistant professor or equivalent) by the application deadline.
Publications: Statement of Research Grant Policy and Procedures

Foundation Officials

George L. Argyros: chairman, director B Detroit, MI 1937. ED Michigan State University; Chapman College BS (1959). PRIM CORP EMPL chairman, chief executive officer: Arnel & Affiliates. CORP AFFIL director: USC South International, Inc.; director: Rockwell International Corp.; director: Tecstar Inc.; director: First America Finance Corp.; director: First America Title Insurance Co.; director: Applied Solar Energy Corp.; chairman: Arnel Development Co. NONPR AFFIL director: Beckman Laser Institute.
Arnold W. Beckman: director NONPR AFFIL director: Beckman Laser Institute.
G. Patricia Beckman: director
Theodore Lawrence Brown: secretary, director B Green Bay, WI 1928. ED Illinois Institute of Technology BS (1950); Michigan State University PhD (1956). NONPR AFFIL member: Sigma Xi; professor chemical emeritus: University Illinois; member: American Chemical Society; member: American Academy of Arts & Sciences; fellow: American Association Advancement Science; member: Alpha Chi Sigma.
Gerald E. Gallwas: director
Harry Barkus Gray: director B Woodburn, KY 1935. ED Western Kentucky University BS (1957); Northwestern University PhD (1960). NONPR AFFIL vis professor: University Witwatersrand; visitors professor: University Yeshiva; visitors professor: University Copenhagen; visitors professor: University Iowa; member: Royal Danish Academy Science & Letters; visitors professor: University Canterbury; visitors professor: Rockefeller University; visitors professor: Pennsylvania State University; member: Phi Lambda Upsilon; professor chem: California Institute Technology; visitors professor: Harvard University; fellow: American Association Advancement Science; member: American Chemical Society; member: Alpha Chi Sigma.
Gavin Shearer Herbert, Jr.: director B Los Angeles, CA 1932. ED University of Southern California BS (1954). PRIM CORP EMPL co-founder, chairman emeritus: Allergan. CORP AFFIL director: Beckman Instruments; director: Cytel Corp. NONPR AFFIL member: Research Prevent Blindness; trustee: University Southern California; member: Pharmaceutical Manufacturer Association; director: Estelle Doheny Eye Foundation; director: Richard Nixon Presidential Foundation; member: Beta Theta Pi. CLUB AFFIL Pacific Club; Big Canyon Country Club; Newport Harbor Yacht Club; Balboa Bay Yacht Club.
Gary H. Hunt: director B 1948. ED Long Island University BA (1970). CORP AFFIL vice president: Hunt Jaffe; vice president: Milk & Cookie Inc.; vice president: ETV Network.
Gary Wescombe: treasurer

Grants Analysis

Disclosure Period: fiscal year ending August 31, 1999
Total Grants: $3,840,000*
Average Grant: $240,000
Typical Range: $10,000 to $50,000 and $200,000 to $1,000,000
***Note:** Giving excludes scholarships and miscellaneous grants ($15,400).

Recent Grants

Note: Grants derived from 2000 Form 990.

General

3,298,614	Beckman Young Investigators -- scientific research
3,238,675	California Institute of Technology, Pasadena, CA -- scientific research
2,500,000	Discovery Science Center, Santa Ana, CA -- scientific research
2,238,675	University of Illinois, Bloomington, IL -- scientific research
2,000,000	Beckman Research Technology, Austin, TX -- scientific research
1,572,450	Stanford University, Stanford, CA -- scientific research
1,239,337	City of Hope National Medical Center, Duarte, CA -- scientific research
1,187,594	Beckman Scholars Program, Irvine, CA -- scientific research
1,000,000	Chapman University, Orange, CA -- scientific research
500,000	Boys Scouts of America, Costa Mesa, CA -- community support

J. L. Bedsole Foundation

Giving Contact

Mabel B. Ward, Executive Director
PO Box 1137
Mobile, AL 36633
Phone: (251)432-3369
Fax: (251)432-1134
E-mail: bedsole2@bellsouth.net

Alternate Contact

Ken Niemeyer, Vice President and Trust Officer
AmSouth Bank, N.A.
Drawer 1628
Mobile, AL 36633
Phone: (334)438-8260

Description

Founded: 1949
EIN: 237225708
Organization Type: General Purpose Foundation
Giving Locations: AL: Southwest part of the state, Mobile
Grant Types: Award, Capital, Conference/Seminar, Endowment, Operating Expenses, Professorship, Scholarship.

Donor Information

Founder: Established in 1949 by a small donation from J. L. Bedsole to help young people achieve a college education, the foundation was fully funded in 1988 after Mr. Bedsole's death in 1975.
Joseph Linyer Bedsole was born August 7, 1881 in Clarke County, AL. In 1919, he moved to Mobile where he organized the Bedsole-Colvin Drug Company. He was a director of the First National Bank of Mobile for over fifty years and also served as a director of the Alabama Power Company for twenty years.
Mr. Bedsole was active in many charitable enterprises. In 1947, as chairman of the Mobile Infirmary Campaign, he organized the fundraising campaign to build the new hospital, which was dedicated in 1952. In 1951, he was named "Mobilian of the Year" and was selected "Man of the Year" by Howard College (now Samford University), where he served on the board of trustees from 1939-62. Mr. Bedsole also received the first honorary degree awarded by the University of Mobile, where he served as chairman of the board of trustees from 1962-67.
He was married in 1910 to Phala Bradford. Their only child, Lt. Joseph Linyer Bedsole, Jr., a B-17 Bomber pilot with the U.S. Army Air Corps and holder of the

Distinguished Flying Cross, was killed in a bomber raid over Germany in April 1944.

Financial Summary

Total Giving: $4,202,749 (2000); $4,200,000 (1999); $3,155,520 (1998)

Giving Analysis: Giving for 2000 includes: foundation gifts to individuals ($27,000); foundation scholarships ($533,400); foundation ($3,642,349); 1998: foundation gifts to individuals ($28,300); foundation scholarships ($31,700) foundation scholarships ($505,581)

Assets: $77,305,707 (2000); $95,000,000 (1999); $96,915,286 (1998)

Typical Recipients

Arts & Humanities: Arts Associations & Councils, Arts Centers, Arts Festivals, Ballet, Arts & Humanities-General, Historic Preservation, History & Archaeology, Libraries, Museums/Galleries, Music, Opera, Performing Arts, Public Broadcasting, Theater, Visual Arts

Civic & Public Affairs: Botanical Gardens/Parks, Business/Free Enterprise, Chambers of Commerce, Clubs, Community Foundations, Economic Development, Civic & Public Affairs-General, Municipalities/Towns, Parades/Festivals, Philanthropic Organizations, Public Policy, Rural Affairs, Safety, Urban & Community Affairs

Education: Business Education, Colleges & Universities, Community & Junior Colleges, Economic Education, Education Associations, Education Funds, Elementary Education (Private), Elementary Education (Public), Education-General, Leadership Training, Legal Education, Literacy, Medical Education, Private Education (Precollege), Public Education (Precollege), Science/Mathematics Education, Secondary Education (Public), Social Sciences Education, Special Education

Environment: Forestry, Environment-General, Research

Health: Children's Health/Hospitals, Clinics/Medical Centers, Eyes/Blindness, Health-General, Health Organizations, Hospitals, Mental Health, Outpatient Health Care, Public Health, Single-Disease Health Associations

International: International Relief Efforts

Religion: Churches, Religion-General, Religious Organizations, Religious Welfare

Science: Observatories & Planetariums, Science Museums, Scientific Centers & Institutes, Scientific Research

Social Services: Animal Protection, Camps, Child Welfare, Community Centers, Community Service Organizations, Day Care, Emergency Relief, Family Services, Food/Clothing Distribution, People with Disabilities, Recreation & Athletics, Scouts, Shelters/Homelessness, Social Services-General, Substance Abuse, United Funds/United Ways, Veterans, Volunteer Services, YMCA/YWCA/YMHA/YWHA, Youth Organizations

Application Procedures

Initial Contact: Applicants should submit a written request to the foundation. Application forms and descriptive brochures for the Bedsole Scholarship Program are sent to high school counselors in southwest Alabama. Application forms are also sent to individuals upon request.

Application Requirements: The preliminary letter should be short and include the organization name, proof of tax-exempt status, a brief description of the project and the name, address, and telephone number of the contact person.

Deadlines: None for grant requests. Application forms for the Bedsole Scholars Program are due November 30.

Review Process: The board meets every other month. If the foundation has an interest in the proposal

then the applicant will be requested to furnish additional information about the project and the organization.

Restrictions

Grants are limited to Southwest Alabama. Bedsole Scholarships are awarded only to graduates of southwest Alabama high schools who achieve a minimum high school GPA of 2.50. Preference is given to high school seniors attending public or private schools in Mobile, Baldwin, Clarke, Monroe, or Washington Counties and Sweet Water High School in Marengo County.

Additional Information

Publications: Application Form
Trust(s): AmSouth Bank, NA

Foundation Officials

M. Palmer Bedsole: member distribution committee B 1928. PRIM CORP EMPL president, chief executive officer, director: Bedsole Medical Companies Inc.

T. Massey Bedsole: chairman distribution committee, trustee ADD CORP EMPL member: Hand Arendall LLC. CORP AFFIL vice president: Mobile Fixture & Equipment Co.

Travis M. Bedsole, Jr.: member distribution committee

Ken Niemeyer: trustee PRIM CORP EMPL trustee officer: AmSouth Bank.

Mabel B. Ward: executive director

T. Bestor Ward, III: mem distribution comm

Robert Williams: member distribution committee

Grants Analysis

Disclosure Period: calendar year ending 2000
Total Grants: $3,642,349*
Number of Grants: 72
Average Grant: $37,194*
Highest Grant: $538,750
Typical Range: $2,000 to $50,000
*Note: Giving excludes gifts to individuals and scholarships. Average grant figure excludes two highest grants ($1,038,750).

Recent Grants

Note: Grants derived from 2000 Form 990.

Library-Related

100,000	Mobile County Public Library, Mobile, AL
10,000	Grove Hill Public Library, Grove Hill, AL
10,000	Mobile County Public Library, Mobile, AL

General

538,750	J. L. Bedsole Scholars Program, Mobile, AL
500,000	Center for the Living Arts
434,873	Gulf Coast Exploreum Museum of Science, Mobile, AL
317,000	MLK Redevelopment Corporation, Inc. -- for Lincoln Square Shopping Center Phase II
200,000	Mobile Area Chamber of Commerce Foundation, Mobile, AL
200,000	Mobile Symphony Opera Complex, Mobile, AL
200,000	St. Paul's Episcopal School, New Orleans, LA
100,000	Alabama Gulf Coast Chapter of American Red Cross, Mobile, AL
100,000	Community Foundation of South Alabama, Mobile, AL
100,000	Monroeville Area Young Men's Christian Association, Monroeville, AL

FLORENCE SIMON BEECHER FOUNDATION

Giving Contact

c/o Sky Trust, Trust Dept.
PO Box 479
Youngstown, OH 44501-0479
Phone: (330)742-7035

Description

Founded: 1969
EIN: 346613413
Organization Type: Private Foundation
Giving Locations: OH: Youngstown
Grant Types: Capital, General Support, Scholarship.

Donor Information

Founder: Florence Simon Beecher

Financial Summary

Total Giving: $475,233 (2002); $186,766 (2001); $396,917 (2000)

Giving Analysis: Giving for 2002 includes: foundation scholarships ($10,000); foundation grants to United Way ($37,500); 2000: foundation grants to United Way ($25,000) 1999: foundation grants to United Way ($25,000)

Assets: $8,123,933 (2002); $9,028,198 (2001); $9,591,569 (2000)

Gifts Received: $2,150,729 (1992). Note: In 1992, contributions were received from the Florence Simon Beecher Trust.

Typical Recipients

Arts & Humanities: Arts Centers, Arts Institutes, Historic Preservation, History & Archaeology, Libraries, Music, Performing Arts, Theater

Civic & Public Affairs: Botanical Gardens/Parks, Business/Free Enterprise, Urban & Community Affairs

Education: Colleges & Universities, Education-General, Private Education (Precollege), Student Aid

Health: Health Organizations, Hospitals, Long-Term Care, Nursing Services, Public Health, Speech & Hearing

Religion: Churches, Religion-General, Religious Welfare

Social Services: Camps, Community Service Organizations, Domestic Violence, Family Planning, Homes, People with Disabilities, Senior Services, United Funds/United Ways, YMCA/YWCA/YMHA/YWHA, Youth Organizations

Application Procedures

Initial Contact: Send a brief letter of inquiry.

Application Requirements: Include a description of organization, amount requested, purpose of funds sought, recently audited financial statement, and proof of tax-exempt status.

Deadlines: None.

Restrictions

Does not support individuals, religious organizations for sectarian purposes, political or lobbying groups, or organizations outside operating areas.

Additional Information

Trust(s): Sky Trust.

Foundation Officials

Eleanor Beecher Flad: chairman
Erle L. Flad: director
Ward Beecher Flad: director
Gregory L. Ridler: director
Patrick A. Sebastiano: director

Grants Analysis

Disclosure Period: calendar year ending 2002
Total Grants: $427,733*
Number of Grants: 16
Average Grant: $12,695*
Highest Grant: $125,000
Lowest Grant: $500
Typical Range: $5,000 to $20,000
*Note: Giving excludes United Way; scholarship. Average grant figure excludes two highest grants ($250,000).

Recent Grants

Note: Grants derived from 2001 Form 990.

General

25,000	Friends of Fellows Gardens, Youngstown, OH -- for Sheridan Memorial Gardens
18,920	Shrine of Our Lady Comforter, Youngstown, OH -- for painting and repair of windows
18,700	Shrine of Our Lady Comforter, Youngstown, OH -- for roof repair
13,000	Butler Institute of American Art, Youngstown, OH -- for installation of Viola Exhibit
12,500	St. Patrick's Church, Youngstown, OH -- for restoration of stained glass windows
11,000	Youngstown and Mahoning Valley United Way, Youngstown, OH -- for leadership
10,000	Mahoning Valley Historical Society, Youngstown, OH -- endowment fund
10,000	Park Vista Retirement Community, Youngstown, OH -- for Life Care Fund
10,000	St. Elizabeth Development Foundation, Youngstown, OH -- for mobile clinic
10,000	Youngstown Playhouse, Youngstown, OH -- for playhouse presentations

BELK STORES SERVICES, INC.

Company Headquarters

Charlotte, NC
Web: http://www.belk.com

Company Description

Employees: 2,300
SIC(s): 7389 Business Services Nec, 8721 Accounting, Auditing & Bookkeeping.

Operating Locations

Belk Stores Services Inc. (AL; AR; FL; GA; MD; MS; NC; SC; TX; VA; WV)

Nonmonetary Support

Note: In 1998, 10,681 shares of North Carolina Railroad (NCRR) were contributed to 12 different charities at fair market value.

Belk Foundation

Giving Contact

Paul B. Wyche, Jr., Trustee
2801 West Tyvola Road
Charlotte, NC 28217-4500
Phone: (704)357-1000
Fax: (704)357-1883
Web: http://belk.com/main/
about_philanthropic.jsp?bmUID=1029805668286

Alternate Contact

Susan Blount, Administrative Assistant
E-mail: susan_blount@belk.com

Description

Founded: 1988
EIN: 566046450
Organization Type: Corporate Foundation
Giving Locations: GA; NC; SC
Grant Types: Capital, Multiyear/Continuing Support, Project.

Financial Summary

Total Giving: $2,915,731 (fiscal year ending May 31, 2002); $2,900,000 (fiscal 2001 approx); $2,818,404 (fiscal 2000)
Giving Analysis: Giving for fiscal 2001 includes: foundation grants to United Way ($87,725); foundation ($2,730,679); fiscal 1999: foundation grants to United Way ($7,000); foundation ($2,497,914); fiscal 1998: foundation grants to United Way ($5,600) foundation ($1,944,556)
Assets: $50,253,778 (fiscal 2002); $57,019,809 (fiscal 2000); $57,945,928 (fiscal 1999)
Gifts Received: $511,170 (fiscal 2002); $595,651 (fiscal 2000); $1,000,000 (fiscal 1999). Note: In fiscal 2002, contributions were received from Belk Inc. In 1994, contributions were received from Belk stores throughout Georgia and North and South Carolina.

Typical Recipients

Arts & Humanities: Arts Associations & Councils, Ethnic & Folk Arts, History & Archaeology, Libraries, Museums/Galleries, Music, Opera, Public Broadcasting
Civic & Public Affairs: African American Affairs, Botanical Gardens/Parks, Business/Free Enterprise, Clubs, Community Foundations, Employment/Job Training, Civic & Public Affairs-General, Housing, Parades/Festivals, Urban & Community Affairs, Women's Affairs
Education: Afterschool/Enrichment Programs, Arts/Humanities Education, Business Education, Business-School Partnerships, Colleges & Universities, Community & Junior Colleges, Economic Education, Education Associations, Education Funds, Education Reform, Elementary Education (Public), Literacy, Medical Education, Minority Education, Preschool Education, Private Education (Precollege), Public Education (Precollege), Religious Education, Science/Mathematics Education, Vocational & Technical Education
Environment: Environment-General, Resource Conservation
Health: Arthritis, Cancer, Children's Health/Hospitals, Emergency/Ambulance Services, Health Funds, Health Organizations, Heart, Hospitals, Hospitals (University Affiliated), Medical Rehabilitation
Religion: Churches, Ministries, Religious Organizations, Religious Welfare, Seminaries
Social Services: Child Welfare, Community Service Organizations, Emergency Relief, Family Planning, Family Services, Homes, Recreation & Athletics, Scouts, Senior Services, Shelters/Homelessness, Social Services-General, Substance Abuse, United Funds/United Ways, YMCA/YWCA/YMHA/YWHA, Youth Organizations

Application Procedures

Initial Contact: Send a request for grant summary form. Unsolicited grant proposals are not accepted.
Application Requirements: Include with completed form: a description of organization; amount requested; purpose of funds sought; recently audited financial statement; proof of tax-exempt status; and whether single-year or multi-year grant is requested.
Deadlines: None.
Decision Notification: Foundation will review grant request and contact organization if interested in funding proposal.

Additional Information

Each of the Belk stores operate as an individual corp., but contributes through the foundation, including the Belk-Tyler Foundation in Rocky Mountain, NC and Belk-Simpson Foundation in Greenville, SC.
Publications: Grant Summary Form

Corporate Officials

John Montgomery Belk: chairman, chief executive officer B Charlotte, NC 1920. ED Davidson College (1943). PRIM CORP EMPL chairman, chief executive officer: Belk Inc. ADD CORP EMPL chief executive officer, chairman: Belk Stores Services Inc. CORP AFFIL director: Texas Industries Inc.; director: Coca-Cola Bottling Co. Consolidated; director: Brothers Investment Co.; director: Chaparral Steel Co.; chairman: Belk-Hudson Inc. Spartanburg SC. NONPR AFFIL member: National Retail Federation.

Foundation Officials

John Montgomery Belk: member board advisors (see above)
James K. Glenn, Jr.: member board advisors
Katherine B. Morns: member board advisors
Leroy Robinson: member board advisors CORP AFFIL director: Belk-Gallant, La Grange Georgia; director: Charlotte Belk Inc.; director: Belk Department Store, Rock Hill.

Grants Analysis

Disclosure Period: fiscal year ending May 31, 2002
Total Grants: $2,676,531*
Number of Grants: 89
Average Grant: $30,073
Highest Grant: $247,013
Lowest Grant: $1,000
Typical Range: $5,000 to $100,000
*Note: Giving excludes scholarship and United Way.

Recent Grants

Note: Grants derived from 2002 Form 990.

General

247,013	Queens College, Charlotte, NC -- Queens International Experience Program
200,000	Union Theological Seminary, Charlotte, NC -- Satellite Program at Queens College
125,000	High Point University, High Point, NC -- renovation and restoration of MIB Hall
105,175	Queens College, Charlotte, NC -- Queens International Experience Program
100,000	Queens College, Charlotte, NC -- Queens International Experience Program
100,000	Queens College, Charlotte, NC -- Queens International Experience Program
100,000	Wake Forest University, Winston-Salem, NC
98,730	Charlotte Country Day School, Charlotte, NC -- Believe and Achieve Campaign for Tomorrow
98,415	CPCC -- Criminal Justice Program
73,739	High Point University, High Point, NC

JAMES FORD BELL FOUNDATION

Giving Contact

Diane B. Neimann, Executive Director
1818 Oliver Avenue South
Minneapolis, MN 55405
Phone: (612)377-8400

Description

Founded: 1955
EIN: 416023099
Organization Type: Private Foundation
Giving Locations: MN
Grant Types: General Support.

Donor Information

Founder: the late James Ford Bell

Financial Summary

Total Giving: $1,403,884 (2000); $1,096,496 (1998); $1,092,339 (1996). Note: In 1996 Giving includes matching gifts ($3,000).
Giving Analysis: Giving for 2000 includes: foundation matching gifts ($18,698)
Assets: $19,648,976 (2000); $20,750,869 (1998); $19,107,523 (1996)
Gifts Received: $1,000 (1998); $163,426 (1996); $7,000 (1995). Note: In 1995, contributions were received from Penelope B. Hatten.

Typical Recipients

Arts & Humanities: Arts Centers, Arts Institutes, Dance, Historic Preservation, History & Archaeology, Libraries, Museums/Galleries, Music, Opera, Performing Arts, Public Broadcasting, Theater, Visual Arts
Civic & Public Affairs: Botanical Gardens/Parks, Employment/Job Training, Civic & Public Affairs-General, Housing, Public Policy, Urban & Community Affairs, Women's Affairs
Education: Arts/Humanities Education, Colleges & Universities, Environmental Education, Education-General, Legal Education, Private Education (Precollege), Social Sciences Education, Special Education, Student Aid
Environment: Environment-General, Resource Conservation, Wildlife Protection
Health: AIDS/HIV, Children's Health/Hospitals, Diabetes, Health Organizations, Heart
International: Foreign Arts Organizations, Human Rights, International Environmental Issues, International Relief Efforts
Religion: Churches
Science: Scientific Research
Social Services: Big Brother/Big Sister, Child Welfare, Community Centers, Community Service Organizations, Family Planning, Family Services, Food/Clothing Distribution, Recreation & Athletics, Scouts, Shelters/Homelessness, Youth Organizations

Application Procedures

Initial Contact: Applicants are encouraged to submit a letter of inquiry or to discuss request with staff before submitting an application. Trustees usually meet in February, June, and October. Proposals should be received 45 working days before the first day of the month of a board meeting.

Restrictions

No grants are made directly to individuals or for scholarships, fellowships, political campaigns, or to units of local government. High priority is given to projects with historical connections to the Bell family.

Foundation Officials

Ford W. Bell: trustee
Samuel H. Bell, Jr.: trustee B Rochester, NY 1925. ED College of Wooster BA (1947); University of Akron JD (1952). PRIM CORP EMPL judge: United States District Court, Akron Ohio ADD CORP EMPL adj professor: College Wooster; adj professor: University Akron School Law. NONPR AFFIL member: Ohio Historical Society; member: Supreme Court Historical Society; director: Joseph R. Miller Foundation; member: Ohio Bar Association; member: Fed Bar Association; member: Federal Judges Association; member: Charles F. Scanlon Akron Inn Ct.; fellow: Akron Bar Foundation; member: Akron University School Law Alumni Association; member: Akron Bar Association.

CLUB AFFIL Masons Club; Phi Alpha Delta; Akron City Club.
David B. Hartwell: trustee
Diane B. Neimann: executive director

Grants Analysis

Disclosure Period: calendar year ending 2000
Total Grants: $1,385,185*
Number of Grants: 45
Average Grant: $27,795*
Highest Grant: $100,000
Lowest Grant: $50
Typical Range: $5,000 to $50,000
*Note: Giving excludes matching grants. Average grant excludes 2 highest grants ($190,000).

Recent Grants

Note: Grants derived from 1999 Form 990.

General

150,000	Redeemer Restoration Project
148,644	Summit Academy, Minneapolis, MN
125,500	Minneapolis Institute of Arts, Minneapolis, MN
100,000	University of Minnesota Foundation, St. Paul, MN
58,200	Southside Neighborhood Housing Services
51,000	Central Neighborhood, Minneapolis, MN
45,000	Southside Neighborhood Housing Services
30,000	Belwin Foundation, Minneapolis, MN
26,500	Minnesota Humanities Commission, St. Paul, MN
26,000	Greater Minneapolis Council of Churches, Minneapolis, MN

S. Lewis And Lucia B. Bell Foundation

Giving Contact

Joseph M. McElwee
PO Box 832
Chester, SC 29706-0832
Phone: (803)581-9198

Description

Founded: 1991
EIN: 570932788
Organization Type: Private Foundation
Giving Locations: gives nationally.
Grant Types: General Support.

Financial Summary

Total Giving: $74,235 (2001); $62,000 (2000); $49,900 (1999)
Giving Analysis: Giving for 2000 includes: foundation grants to United Way ($1,000); 1999: foundation grants to United Way ($1,000); 1998: foundation grants to United Way ($1,000) foundation ($44,600)
Assets: $1,541,531 (2001); $1,399,765 (2000); $1,283,097 (1999)
Gifts Received: $130,000 (2001); $130,000 (2000); $130,000 (1999). Note: In 1994, contributions were received from the Lucia Beason Bell Trust.

Typical Recipients

Arts & Humanities: Art History
Civic & Public Affairs: Municipalities/Towns
Education: Afterschool/Enrichment Programs, Education-General, Public Education (Precollege), Vocational & Technical Education
Health: Emergency/Ambulance Services, Health-General
Religion: Churches
Social Services: Community Service Organizations, Emergency Relief, People with Disabilities, Scouts, United Funds/United Ways, YMCA/YWCA/YMHA/YWHA, Youth Organizations

Application Procedures

Initial Contact: Send a brief letter of inquiry.
Application Requirements: a description of organization and purpose of funds sought.
Deadlines: None.

Restrictions

Restricted to Chester County, SC.

Foundation Officials

Ladson Stringfellow: trustee
D. C. Wylie, Jr.: trustee

Grants Analysis

Disclosure Period: calendar year ending 2001
Total Grants: $73,235*
Number of Grants: 11
Average Grant: $2,582*
Highest Grant: $30,000
Lowest Grant: $400
Typical Range: $1,000 to $5,000
*Note: Giving excludes United Way. Average grant figure excludes two highest grants ($50,000).

Recent Grants

Note: Grants derived from 2000 Form 990.

General

30,000	York Technical College Foundation
10,900	Chester ARP Church
7,500	Chester Branch YMCA
3,000	Great Falls Rescue Squad
2,500	Chester County DSS Medicine Fund
2,200	Great Falls Home Town Association, Great Falls, MT
1,000	Chester Area United Way, Chester, SC
1,000	Chester County Citizens in Schools
1,000	Chester County Warm Hearth Fund
1,000	Great Falls High School, Great Falls, MT

Bellsouth Corp.

Company Headquarters

1155 Peachtree Street NE
Atlanta, GA 30309-3610
Phone: (404)249-2000
Fax: (404)249-5599
Web: http://www.bellsouthcorp.com

Company Description

Ticker: BLS
Exchange: NYSE
Revenue: US$22.44 billion (2002)
Profit: US$1.423 billion (2002)
Employees: 77000 (2002)
Fortune Rank: 77, per FORTUNE Magazine's list of 500 Largest U.S. Corporations (2002).
SIC(s): 4813 Telephone Communications Except Radiotelephone, 6719 Holding Companies Nec.

Nonmonetary Support

Type: Loaned Executives
Note: Co. also offers corporate leadership and management training conferences.

BellSouth Foundation

Giving Contact

Greg Norton, Grants Administrator
1155 Peachtree Street, NE, Room 7H08
Atlanta, GA 30309-3610
Phone: (404)249-2396
Fax: (404)249-5696
E-mail: grants.manager@bellsouth.com
Web: http://www.bellsouthfoundation.org

Description

Founded: 1986
EIN: 581708046
Organization Type: Corporate Foundation
Giving Locations: principally near operating locations and to national organizations.
Grant Types: Capital, Conference/Seminar, Emergency, Employee Matching Gifts, Endowment, Fellowship, General Support, Matching, Multiyear/Continuing Support.
Note: Employee matching gift ratio: 2 to 1 for education gifts; 1 to 1 for cultural gifts. Corporate contributions fund operating expenses, employee matching gifts, and conference/seminar gifts. Foundation funds policy studies.

Financial Summary

Total Giving: $3,006,850 (2001); $6,431,385 (2000); $3,850,957 (1999). Note: Contributes through corporate direct giving program and foundation.
Giving Analysis: Giving for 2000 includes: foundation ($6,431,385); 1999: foundation ($3,850,957); 1998: foundation ($2,517,386);
Assets: $55,726,884 (2001); $63,347,878 (2000); $66,840,903 (1999)
Gifts Received: $14,000,000 (1996). Note: In 1996, contributions were received from BellSouth Corp.

Typical Recipients

Arts & Humanities: Libraries, Museums/Galleries, Visual Arts
Civic & Public Affairs: Chambers of Commerce, Employment/Job Training, Civic & Public Affairs-General, Public Policy, Urban & Community Affairs
Education: Arts/Humanities Education, Business Education, Business-School Partnerships, Colleges & Universities, Community & Junior Colleges, Education Associations, Education Reform, Elementary Education (Private), Elementary Education (Public), Engineering/Technological Education, Faculty Development, Education-General, Health & Physical Education, International Exchange, Leadership Training, Legal Education, Literacy, Medical Education, Minority Education, Preschool Education, Private Education (Precollege), Public Education (Precollege), School Volunteerism, Science/Mathematics Education, Secondary Education (Public), Special Education, Vocational & Technical Education
Environment: Resource Conservation
Health: Health-General
International: International-General
Science: Science Museums, Scientific Centers & Institutes
Social Services: Child Welfare, Day Care, Family Services, Social Services-General, Youth Organizations

Application Procedures

Initial Contact: Visit website for information on requests for proposals and to apply for an opportunity grant. All applications must be submitted through the website.
Application Requirements: Opportunity grant requests must be submitted as a two-page concept paper using the template available on the website.
Deadlines: Late winter or early spring for foundation Opportunity Grants; the corporation reviews requests on a continuous basis.
Evaluative Criteria: Opportunity Grants will be awarded to programs or projects that: mesh tightly with one of the foundation's strategies; appear to be interesting and valuable endeavors; offer a complementary strategy for the foundation's other work; offer a new and innovative approach to a priority issue; provide a supportive policy-level effort to supplement a foundation priority; or serve as a collaborative practice for a foundation initiative. learned and in replication of successful practices; and are most likely to produce measurable results. learned and in replication of successful practices; and are most likely to

produce measurable results. learned and in replication of successful practices; and are most likely to produce measurable results.
Decision Notification: Applicants will receive an email response to an online request. Foundation will invite suitable applicants to submit a full proposal. Board meets in late spring to make final decisions.

Restrictions

The foundation does not support capital or building campaigns; endowments; general operating expenses; education product development; individuals; individual study, research, or travel grants; for-profit entities or start-up businesses; fundraising events or dinners; scholarships; single K-12 schools that are not part of a larger district reform effort; single discipline curricula unrelated to comprehensive school reform; equipment acquisition; programs that are primarily recreational or community-based and not connected to the educational system; any organization that discriminates on the basis of race, creed, ethnicity, gender, sexual orientation, national origin, or disability; programs outside of operating locations, except when invited; or non-tax-exempt organizations.

Additional Information

Publications: Bellsouth Foundation Grant Guidelines 1996-2000; New Strategies for the Bellsouth Foundation; Annual Report on Grantmaking Activity of the Bellsouth Foundation

Corporate Officials

F. Duane Ackerman: chief executive officer corporate development B Plant City, FL 1942. ED Massachusetts Institute of Technology MS; Rollins College BS (1964); Rollins College MS (1970). PRIM CORP EMPL president, chief executive officer: BellSouth Corp. CORP AFFIL director: Wachovia Bank of Georgia, NA; director: American Business Products Inc.; director: American Heritage Life Insurance Corp.; director: Allstate Corp. NONPR AFFIL director: Ctrl Atlanta Progress; trustee: Rollins College.
Keith O. Cowan: vice president corporate development B Hartford, CT 1956. ED University of North Carolina BS (1978); University of Virginia School of Law JD (1982). PRIM CORP EMPL vice president corporate development: BellSouth Corp. CORP AFFIL director: Medirisk Inc.

Foundation Officials

Alicia Adams: secretary
Bonnie Bush: assistant trustee
Suzanne H. Detlefs: trustee, vice president PRIM CORP EMPL president: BellSouth Advertising & Publishing Corp.
Fran Dramis: trustee
Mark E. Droege: trustee
Margaret H Green: trustee, chairman PRIM CORP EMPL group president: Bell South Telecommunications Inc.
Tom Harvey: assistant treasurer
Nan Johnson: assistant trustee
Donna Lee: trustee
Donna Malone: assistant trustee
Eva Mayhew: assistant trustee
Linda McCann: assistant trustee
Charlotte Mitchell: assistant trustee
Kim Mulkey: director, Technology program
William C. Pate: chairman PRIM CORP EMPL vice president advertising and Public Relations: BellSouth Corp.
Ramon L. Rodriguez: associate director grantmaking
Jacquelyn Tatum: assistant trustee

Grants Analysis

Disclosure Period: calendar year ending 1999
Total Grants: $3,850,957*
Number of Grants: 149
Average Grant: $50,000
Highest Grant: $500,000

Typical Range: $15,000 to $60,000
***Note:** Grants analysis provided by Foundation.

Recent Grants

Note: Grants derived from 2001 Form 990.

General

200,000	Key Largo School -- Power to Learn
193,000	Harrison Central High School
167,500	Mary Scroggs Elementary School, Chapel Hill, NC
144,250	Miami Dade School, Miami, FL
100,000	Board of Regents of the University System of Georgia, Athens, GA
100,000	Center for Leadership in School Reform, Louisville, KY
100,000	Center for Leadership in School Reform, Louisville, KY
100,000	Murray State University, Murray, KY -- Power to Teach
100,000	Murray State University, Murray, KY
100,000	Murray State University, Murray, KY

BELO CORP.

Company Headquarters

400 S. Record Street
Dallas, TX 75202
Phone: (214)977-6606
Fax: (214)977-7655
Web: http://www.belo.com

Company Description

Founded: 1842
Ticker: BLC
Exchange: NYSE
Former Name: A.H. Belo Corp. (2000).
Revenue: US$1.427 billion (2002)
Employees: 7800 (2002)
SIC(s): 2711 Newspapers, 4833 Television Broadcasting Stations.

Operating Locations

A.H. Belo Corp. (CA--Sacramento; LA--Gretna, New Orleans; OK--Tulsa; TX--Cedar Hill, Dallas, Houston, Plano; VA--Hampton, Norfolk; WA--Seattle)

Belo Foundation

Giving Contact

Becky Odlozil, Executive Director
The Belo Foundation
PO Box 655237
Dallas, TX 75265-5237
Phone: (214)977-6661
Fax: (214)977-6620
Web: http://www.belo.com/aboutbelo/philanthropy.html

Description

Founded: 1952
EIN: 752564365
Organization Type: Corporate Foundation
Former Name: Dallas Morning News-WFAA Foundation.
Former Name: A. H. Belo Corp. FND (2001).
Giving Locations: CA: Claremont, Oakland, Pasadena; DC: Washington; GA: Atlanta; ID: Boise; IL: Chicago; KY: Louisville; NY: New York; TX: Austin, Dallas, Ft. Worth; VA: Arlington, Reston
Grant Types: Capital, Endowment, General Support, Matching.

Financial Summary

Total Giving: $3,191,428 (2001); $1,501,928 (2000); $2,345,800 (1999). Note: Contributes through corporate direct giving program and foundation.

Giving Analysis: Giving for 1999 includes: foundation grants to United Way ($250,000); foundation ($2,095,800) 1996: foundation (approx $900,000)
Assets: $45,491,589 (2001); $53,257,593 (2000); $52,043,283 (1999)
Gifts Received: $4,050,000 (2001); $250,000 (1993). Note: Contributions are received from Belo Corp.

Typical Recipients

Arts & Humanities: Arts Associations & Councils, Arts Centers, Ethnic & Folk Arts, Arts & Humanities-General, Historic Preservation, History & Archaeology, Libraries, Museums/Galleries, Music, Public Broadcasting, Theater, Visual Arts
Civic & Public Affairs: African American Affairs, Botanical Gardens/Parks, Community Foundations, Economic Development, Employment/Job Training, First Amendment Issues, Civic & Public Affairs-General, Hispanic Affairs, Law & Justice, Municipalities/ Towns, Nonprofit Management, Professional & Trade Associations, Public Policy, Safety, Urban & Community Affairs
Education: Afterschool/Enrichment Programs, Arts/ Humanities Education, Colleges & Universities, Economic Education, Education Funds, Education-General, Journalism/Media Education, Journalism/Media Education, Legal Education, Literacy, Secondary Education (Private)
Health: AIDS/HIV, Diabetes, Health Organizations, Hospitals
International: International-General, Human Rights
Religion: Dioceses
Social Services: Child Welfare, Community Service Organizations, Family Planning, Shelters/Homelessness, Social Services-General, United Funds/ United Ways, Youth Organizations

Application Procedures

Initial Contact: Send a brief letter of inquiry. Phone calls in advance of the application are encouraged.
Application Requirements: Include a minimum of background material, a list of officers and directors, proof of tax-exempt status.
Deadlines: None.
Review Process: The foundation is governed by a board of trustees; smaller requests are reviewed year-round for community service support; however, capital and endowment grants in the foundation's focus areas are considered three times a year.
Notes: The foundation encourages calls and letters of inquiry before the submission of a full proposal.

Additional Information

A.H. Belo Corp.'s companion philanthropic foundation was established in 1952, named in honor of G.P. Dealey, founder of *The Dallas Morning News* and majority owner of Belo from 1926 until his death in 1946. Its name changed to the Dallas Morning News-WFAA Foundation in 1983, and in 1995, it was renamed the A.H. Belo Corp. Foundation. In 2000, the foundation was one again renamed the Belo Foundation. The above profile reflects contributions by Belo Corp., *The Dallas Morning News,* and WFAA-TV. Wholly-owned operating companies handle local requests for support and public service announcements independently. Contact the appropriate company directly.

Corporate Officials

Robert William Decherd: chairman, president, chief executive officer, director B Dallas, TX 1951. ED Harvard University BA (1973). PRIM CORP EMPL chairman, president, chief executive officer, director: A.H. Belo Corp. CORP AFFIL chairman: Owensboro Messenger Inquirer; chairman: Henderson Gleaner; director: Kimberly-Clark Corp.; chairman, chief executive officer: Audubon Printers Ink Ltd. NONPR AFFIL member: Newspaper Association America; trustee: Tomas Rivera Policy Institute.

Ward L. Huey, Jr.: president broadcast division, vice chairman, director B Dallas, TX 1938. ED Southern Methodist University BA (1960). PRIM CORP EMPL president broadcast division, vice chairman, director: A.H. Belo Corp. CORP AFFIL president: WWL TV Inc.; vice chairman: Maxium Service Television; president: 3rd Avenue Television Inc. NONPR AFFIL member executive committee: State Fair Texas; member: TV Bureau Advertising; trustee: Southern Methodist University; member executive committee: Southern Methodist University Meadows School Arts; director: Dallas Foundation; member: Maxium Service TV Association; Member: Dallas Advertising League; member: Association Broadcast Executives Texas. CLUB AFFIL Salesmanship Club Dallas; Dallas Country Club.
Burl Osborne: president publishing division, director B Jenkins, KY 1937. ED University of Kentucky (1955-1957); Marshall University BA (1960); Harvard University Graduate School of Business Administration AMP (1984); Long Island University MBA (1984). PRIM CORP EMPL president publishing division, director: A.H. Belo Corp. CORP AFFIL director, publisher, editor: Dallas Morning News. NONPR AFFIL member: Organization Professional Journalists; member: Southern Newspaper Publishers Association; director: Newspaper Association America; board member: Nieman Foundation; board member: Harvard University; member journalism advisory committee: Knight Foundation; member: American Society Newspaper Editors.

Foundation Officials

Robert William Decherd: trustee (see above)
Judith M. Garrett: president, executive director
Ward L. Huey, Jr.: vice president, trustee (see above)
James McQueen Moroney, Jr.: trustee B Dallas, TX 1921. ED University of Texas BBA (1943). CORP AFFIL director: A.H. Belo Corp. NONPR AFFIL chairman: University Dallas.
Becky W. Odlozil: executive director
Burl Osborne: chairman, trustee (see above)

Grants Analysis

Disclosure Period: calendar year ending 2001
Total Grants: $3,191,082*
Number of Grants: 45
Average Grant: $27,070*
Highest Grant: $2,000,000
Lowest Grant: $1,000
Typical Range: $2,000 to $100,000
*Note: Grants analysis provided by the foundation. Average grant figure excludes highest grant.

Recent Grants

Note: Grants derived from 2001 Form 990.

General

2,000,000	Southern Methodist University, Dallas, TX -- endowed distinguished chair in journalism
300,000	Texas State History Museum Foundation, Austin, TX -- capital campaign
252,000	United Way of Metropolitan Dallas, Dallas, TX
150,000	Southern Newspaper Publishers Association Foundation, Atlanta, GA -- endowed campaign
125,000	American Red Cross, Washington, DC -- for September 11th fund
50,000	University of North Texas System Center at Dallas, Denton, TX -- capital campaign
30,000	Dallas Theater Center, Dallas, TX -- for site development plan Dean Park
27,313	Dallas Police Memorial, Dallas, TX -- for construction management services
26,000	United Way of Metropolitan Tarrant County, Ft. Worth, TX
25,000	Boys and Girls Club of America, Atlanta, GA -- for annual chairman's dinner

BEMIS COMPANY, INC.

Company Headquarters

222 S. Ninth Street
Suite 2300
Minneapolis, MN 55402-4099
Phone: (612)376-3000
Web: http://www.bemis.com

Company Description

Founded: 1858
Ticker: BMS
Exchange: NYSE
Revenue: US$2.369 billion (2002)
Employees: 11800 (2002)
SIC(s): 2672 Coated & Laminated Paper Nec, 3565 Packaging Machinery.

Operating Locations

Bemis Co., Inc. (CO--Highlands Ranch; FL--Altamonte Springs; IL--Peoria; KS--Shawnee Mission; MI--De Witt; NE--Omaha; NJ--Flemington; NY--Huntington; OH--Cuyahoga Falls; PA--Doylestown, Hazleton; TX--Magnolia, Richardson; WI--Middleton, Neenah)

Bemis Co. Foundation

Giving Contact

Gene H. Seashore, Trustee
Bemis Co. Foundation
222 South 9th Street, Suite 2300
Minneapolis, MN 55402
Phone: (612)376-3093
E-mail: ajkirchner@bemis.com

Description

EIN: 416038616
Organization Type: Corporate Foundation
Giving Locations: MN: Minneapolis principally near operating locations and to national organizations.
Grant Types: Capital, General Support.
Note: Employee matching gift ratio: 2 to 1 for education and Food Shelves. Annual budget is committed to multi-year grants and no more than 20% of annual budget is committed to capital programs.

Financial Summary

Total Giving: $2,452,847 (2002); $2,558,438 (2001); $3,305,748 (2000). Note: Contributes through corporate direct giving program and foundation.
Giving Analysis: Giving for 2001 includes: foundation matching gifts ($288,222); foundation grants to United Way ($310,553); foundation scholarships ($442,046); foundation ($1,517,617); 2000: foundation grants to United Way ($296,355); foundation matching gifts ($298,980); foundation scholarships ($373,308); foundation ($2,337,105); 1999: foundation matching gifts ($170,285); foundation grants to United Way ($282,131); foundation scholarships ($318,700) foundation ($1,403,307)
Assets: $958,191 (2001); $961,616 (1999); $1,113,879 (1998)
Gifts Received: $2,615,000 (2001); $2,055,000 (2000); $2,562,000 (1998). Note: Foundation receives contributions from Bemis Company, Inc.

Typical Recipients

Arts & Humanities: Arts Appreciation, Arts Associations & Councils, Arts Centers, Arts Institutes, History & Archaeology, Libraries, Museums/Galleries, Music, Opera, Performing Arts, Public Broadcasting, Theater, Visual Arts
Civic & Public Affairs: African American Affairs, Botanical Gardens/Parks, Business/Free Enterprise, Community Foundations, Economic Development, Employment/Job Training, Civic & Public Affairs-General, Housing, Public Policy, Safety, Urban & Community Affairs, Women's Affairs, Zoos/Aquariums

Education: Business Education, Colleges & Universities, Community & Junior Colleges, Education Associations, Education Funds, Education Reform, Elementary Education (Private), Engineering/Technological Education, Education-General, Health & Physical Education, International Studies, Legal Education, Medical Education, Minority Education, Preschool Education, Private Education (Precollege), Public Education (Precollege), Religious Education, Student Aid, Vocational & Technical Education

Environment: Environment-General

Health: Clinics/Medical Centers, Diabetes, Emergency/Ambulance Services, Health-General, Health Policy/Cost Containment, Health Funds, Health Organizations, Hospitals, Mental Health, Nursing Services, Prenatal Health Issues, Public Health, Single-Disease Health Associations, Speech & Hearing

International: International Environmental Issues, International Peace & Security Issues

Religion: Bible Study/Translation, Religious Welfare

Science: Science Museums

Social Services: Child Welfare, Community Centers, Community Service Organizations, Counseling, Day Care, Domestic Violence, Emergency Relief, Family Planning, Family Services, Food/Clothing Distribution, Homes, People with Disabilities, Recreation & Athletics, Scouts, Senior Services, Shelters/Homelessness, Substance Abuse, United Funds/United Ways, Volunteer Services, YMCA/YWCA/YMHA/YWHA, Youth Organizations

Application Procedures

Initial Contact: Send a brief letter or proposal by mail.

Application Requirements: Include organization's name and certificate; outline of proposed project; proposed budget; brief description of objectives and how they are to be attained; list of officers and board members; and proof of tax-exempt status.

Deadlines: None.

Evaluative Criteria: Project is within giving categories and proposal displays an innovative approach to effectively serving people. Preference is given to institutions which are supported by Bemis employees through contributions of time or money.

Restrictions

Grants do not support non tax-exempt organizations, individuals, organizations for religious or political purposes, or lobbying efforts or campaigns. Company prefers not to give to educational capital funds, endowments, or trips or tours.

Grants will not exceed 5% of total requirements of any organization or campaign. No grants are approved for more than three years.

Additional Information

The basis for charitable contributions is 2% of company's domestic pretax profits.

Publications: Annual Community Relations Report

Corporate Officials

Jeffrey H. Curler: president, chief executive officer ED University of Wisconsin BS. PRIM CORP EMPL president, chief executive officer: Bemis Co. Inc.

Benjamin R. Field, III: senior vice president, chief financial officer, treasurer B Hartford, CT 1938. ED Williams College BA (1961); Harvard University Graduate School of Business Administration MBA (1963). PRIM CORP EMPL senior vice president, chief financial officer, treasurer: Bemis Co., Inc.

Scott W. Johnson: senior vice president, secretary, general counsel B Saint Paul, MN 1940. ED Harvard University AB (1962); University of Minnesota JD (1966). PRIM CORP EMPL senior vice president, secretary, general counsel: Bemis Co., Inc. NONPR AFFIL chairman: Minneapolis Coalition Educational Reform & Accountability; member: Minnesota State Bar Association. CLUB AFFIL Interlochen Country Club; Minneapolis Club.

Foundation Officials

Audrey Kirchner: secretary PRIM CORP EMPL administrative assistant: Bemis Co. Inc.

Lawrence E. Schwanke: trustee PRIM CORP EMPL vice president human resources: Bemis Co., Inc.

Gene C. Wulf: vice president, controller B 1950. PRIM CORP EMPL vice president, chief financial officer, treasurer: Bemis Co. Inc. CORP AFFIL vice president: Curwood Inc.; treasurer: Perfecseal Inc.

Grants Analysis

Disclosure Period: calendar year ending 2002

Total Grants: $2,452,847

Recent Grants

Note: Grants derived from 2000 Form 990.

General

427,660	Citizens Scholarship Foundation of America, St. Peter, MN -- educational
150,000	Fox Valley Technical College Foundation, Appleton, WI
100,000	Appleton Family YMCA, Appleton, WI
100,000	Ivy Tech State College, Indianapolis, IN
75,000	United Way, Minneapolis, MN
50,000	American Red Cross, Minneapolis, MN
46,500	United Way of Wabash Valley, Terre Haute, IN
30,000	Purdue University Foundation, West Lafayette, IN
25,000	Apple Tree Dental, Minneapolis, MN
25,000	ARC Hennepin-Carver, Minneapolis, MN

BEMIS MANUFACTURING CO.

Company Headquarters

300 Mill Street
PO Box 901
Sheboygan Falls, WI 53085
Phone: 800-558-7651
Fax: (920)467-8573
E-mail: corp@BemisMfg.com
Web: http://www.bemismfg.com

Company Description

Employees: 1,200

SIC(s): 2499 Wood Products Nec, 2511 Wood Household Furniture, 3084 Plastics Pipe, 3089 Plastics Products Nec, 3944 Games, Toys & Children's Vehicles, 3991 Brooms & Brushes.

F.K. Bemis Family Foundation

Giving Contact

Richard A. Bemis, President
PO Box 901
Sheboygan Falls, WI 53085-0901
Phone: (920)467-4621
Fax: (920)467-8573
E-mail: corp@BemisMfg.com

Description

Founded: 1953

EIN: 396067930

Organization Type: Corporate Foundation

Giving Locations: MA; WI: Sheboygan County

Grant Types: Capital, General Support, Scholarship.

Donor Information

Founder: Bemis Manufacturing

Financial Summary

Total Giving: $409,100 (2001); $352,200 (2000); $353,400 (1999). Note: Contributes through foundation only.

Giving Analysis: Giving for 2001 includes: foundation ($2,000); foundation scholarships ($9,000); foundation ($398,100); 2000: foundation grants to United Way ($2,000); foundation scholarships ($11,500); foundation ($338,700); 1999: foundation grants to United Way ($2,000); foundation scholarships ($11,500); foundation ($339,900);

Assets: $17 (2001); $17 (2000); $17 (1999)

Gifts Received: $409,100 (2001); $352,200 (2000); $353,400 (1999). Note: Contributions received from Bemis Manufacturing Co.

Typical Recipients

Arts & Humanities: Arts Associations & Councils, Arts Centers, Arts Festivals, History & Archaeology, Libraries, Museums/Galleries, Music, Performing Arts, Public Broadcasting, Theater

Civic & Public Affairs: Botanical Gardens/Parks, Business/Free Enterprise, Clubs, Employment/Job Training, Civic & Public Affairs-General, Urban & Community Affairs

Education: Business Education, Colleges & Universities, Engineering/Technological Education, Education-General, Private Education (Precollege), Public Education (Precollege), Student Aid, Vocational & Technical Education

Environment: Environment-General

Health: Cancer, Children's Health/Hospitals, Clinics/Medical Centers, Emergency/Ambulance Services, Hospitals, Medical Research

International: Foreign Educational Institutions

Religion: Churches, Religious Welfare

Social Services: Camps, Child Welfare, Community Service Organizations, Day Care, Recreation & Athletics, Scouts, Special Olympics, United Funds/United Ways, YMCA/YWCA/YMHA/YWHA

Application Procedures

Initial Contact: Send a brief letter of inquiry.

Application Requirements: Include purpose of funds sought and proof of tax-exempt status.

Deadlines: None.

Corporate Officials

Richard A. Bemis: president, chief executive officer, director B 1941. ED Denison College BA (1963). PRIM CORP EMPL president, chief executive officer, director: Bemis Manufacturing Co. CORP AFFIL director: WPS Resources Corp.

Peter Lukaszewicz: treasurer, director PRIM CORP EMPL treasurer, director: Bemis Manufacturing Co.

Foundation Officials

Richard A. Bemis: president (see above)

Peter Lukaszewicz: treasurer (see above)

Grants Analysis

Disclosure Period: calendar year ending 2001

Total Grants: $398,100*

Number of Grants: 29

Average Grant: $10,646*

Highest Grant: $100,000

Lowest Grant: $250

Typical Range: $500 to $50,000

***Note:** Giving excludes scholarship; United Way. Average grant figure excludes highest grant.

Recent Grants

Note: Grants derived from 2001 Form 990.

General

100,000	Settler's Park Fund, Sheboygan Falls, WI -- community

50,000	Lakeland College Building Fund, Sheboygan, WI -- education/building
50,000	St. Norbert College, De Pere, WI -- education/building
37,500	John Michael Kohler Arts Center, Sheboygan, WI -- community
25,000	Manitou Girl Scout Council, Sheboygan, WI -- community/youth
25,000	National Plastics Museum, Leominster, MA -- education/youth
20,000	Boy Scouts of America, Sheboygan, WI -- community/youth
15,000	School District of Sheboygan Falls, Sheboygan Falls, WI -- community
12,500	ASA Education Foundation, Inc., Chicago, IL -- education
10,000	Lakeland College Annual Fund, Sheboygan, WI -- education/capital

BEN & JERRY'S HOMEMADE, INC.

Company Headquarters
Waterbury, VT
Web: http://www.benjerry.com

Company Description
Employees: 751 (1999)
SIC(s): 2024 Ice Cream & Frozen Desserts, 5143 Dairy Products Except Dried or Canned, 5812 Eating Places.

Operating Locations
Ben & Jerry's Homemade Inc. (AZ--Scottsdale, Tempe, Tucson; CA--Agoura Hills, Glendale, Los Angeles, Malibu, Manhattan Beach, Roseville, Sacramento, San Diego, San Francisco, San Ramon, Santa Monica, Sherman Oaks, Torrance; CO--Boulder, Denver; CT--Groton, Norwalk; DC--Washington; FL--Key West, Palm Harbor, Sarasota; IL--Vernon Hills, Villa Park; IN--Bloomington, Nashville, West Lafayette; KY--Saratoga Springs; MA--Arlington, Hingham, North Eastham, Pittsfield, Provincetown; NY--Spring Valley; RI--Cranston, Narragansett, Newport, Providence; VT--Rutland; VA--Alexandria, Norfolk, Virginia Beach, Williamsburg)

Nonmonetary Support
Type: Cause-related Marketing & Promotion; Donated Products
Contact: Laura Cunningham-Firkey, Donations Coordinator
Note: Company provides nonmonetary support.

Ben & Jerry's Foundation

Giving Contact
Lisa Pendolino, Executive Director
Ben & Jerry's Foundation
30 Community Drive
South Burlington, VT 05403-6828
Phone: (802)651-9600
Fax: (802)846-1610
Web: http://www.benjerry.com/foundation

Alternate Contact
Debbie Kessler
Phone: (802)846-1500
Note: Phone extension is 7567.

Description
Founded: 1977
EIN: 030300865
Organization Type: Corporate Foundation

Giving Locations: VT: focusing on Community Action Teams U.S.-based organizations.
Grant Types: Award, General Support, Project.

Donor Information
Founder: Ben & Jerry's Homemade

Financial Summary
Total Giving: $1,824,994 (2001); $940,899 (2000); $532,521 (1999). Note: Contributes through corporate direct giving program and foundation.
Giving Analysis: Giving for 2000 includes: foundation ($940,899); 1997: foundation ($456,350); 1996: corporate direct giving ($70,711); domestic subsidiaries ($115,415) foundation ($323,143)
Assets: $5,864,790 (2001); $6,088,111 (2000); $1,130,649 (1999)
Gifts Received: $1,429,857 (2001); $5,812,000 (2000); $86,883 (1997). Note: Contributions are received from Ben & Jerry's, Inc., Ben Cohen, and Jerry Greenfield.

Typical Recipients
Arts & Humanities: Arts Associations & Councils, Arts Outreach, Ethnic & Folk Arts, Film & Video, Arts & Humanities-General, Historic Preservation, Libraries, Music, Public Broadcasting
Civic & Public Affairs: African American Affairs, Asian American Affairs, Business/Free Enterprise, Civil Rights, Clubs, Community Foundations, Economic Development, Economic Policy, Employment/ Job Training, Ethnic Organizations, Gay/Lesbian Issues, Civic & Public Affairs-General, Hispanic Affairs, Housing, Law & Justice, Municipalities/Towns, Native American Affairs, Philanthropic Organizations, Professional & Trade Associations, Public Policy, Rural Affairs, Safety, Urban & Community Affairs, Women's Affairs
Education: Colleges & Universities, Elementary Education (Public), Faculty Development, Education-General, Literacy, Private Education (Precollege), Secondary Education (Public)
Environment: Air/Water Quality, Forestry, Environment-General, Protection, Resource Conservation, Wildlife Protection
Health: AIDS/HIV, Cancer, Medical Rehabilitation, Mental Health
International: Human Rights, International Development, International Environmental Issues, International Peace & Security Issues, International Relief Efforts
Religion: Churches, Religion-General, Religious Welfare
Science: Scientific Organizations
Social Services: Animal Protection, Camps, Child Welfare, Community Centers, Community Service Organizations, Counseling, Crime Prevention, Emergency Relief, Family Services, Food/Clothing Distribution, People with Disabilities, Recreation & Athletics, Refugee Assistance, Senior Services, Shelters/Homelessness, Social Services-General, YMCA/YWCA/YMHA/YWHA, Youth Organizations

Application Procedures
Initial Contact: Call, write, or see website for guidelines, then send two copies of a one-page initial letter of interest attached to foundation cover page.
Application Requirements: Include: a description of organization and indication of competence in the area of proposal; outline of the project, including who will benefit, design of project, and outcomes expected; brief overview of budget, income sources, and expenses for the project.
Deadlines: None for initial inquiries; applications should be submitted by the first of March, July, or November for invited full proposals.
Review Process: Foundation reviews initial requests within eight weeks of receipt, and then invites full proposals for large grants (using the National Network of Grantmakers Common Grant Application); full proposals and small requests (less than $1,000) are reviewed 3 times a year.
Evaluative Criteria: Funds projects that will: lead to societal, institutional, and/or environmental change; address the root causes of social or environmental problems; lead to new ways of thinking and acting. Projects must: help ameliorate an unjust or destructive situation by empowering constituents; facilitate leadership development and strengthen the self-empowerment efforts of those who have traditionally been disenfranchised in our society; support movement building and social action. Applicants should: develop a plan for long-term viability; articulate a clear analysis of the underlying causes of the problem; outline specific goals and strategies of their organizing campaign or program.
Decision Notification: Initial letters are reviewed within six weeks of receipt; final decisions are announced within ten weeks after review meetings.
Notes: Express delivery of packages is strongly discouraged; faxed proposals and inquiries are not accepted. Letters of interest must be readable (with at least a 10 point font, and one-inch margins). The Foundation encourages the use of recycled paper and double-sided copying; avoid using plastic covers, sheet protectors, and glossy photos. Do not send additional backup materials, videos, or cassettes.

Restrictions
Grants are not made to support basic or direct service programs.
Foundation does not fund: discretionary or emergency requests, colleges or universities, individuals, scholarship programs, research projects, capital campaigns, state agencies, religious programs, international or foreign-based programs, or social services programs.

Additional Information
The Foundation generally supports organizations with budgets under $250,000.
Ben and Jerry's Foundation was established in 1985 through a donation of stock in Ben and Jerry's Homemade, Inc.
Approximately 7.5% of pre-tax profits is set aside annually for philanthropy; the foundation, the Community Action Team, and corporate philanthropy each receive a portion of this total.
In April 2000, an agreement was made to sell Ben & Jerry's Homemade, Inc. to Unilever. As part of the terms of agreement, Ben & Jerry's will operate separately from Unilever's existing U.S. ice cream business. In addition, Ben & Jerry's will have an independent board of directors which will concentrate on maintaining Ben & Jerry's social mission and brand integrity.
Publications: Application Packet; Annual Report

Corporate Officials
Jerry Greenfield: co-founder, vice chairman B New York, NY 1950. ED Oberlin College BA (1973). PRIM CORP EMPL co-founder, vice chairman: Ben & Jerry's Homemade Inc.

Foundation Officials
Elizabeth Bankowski: secretary B Boston, MA 1947. ED Boston College (1970). PRIM CORP EMPL director: Ben & Jerry's Homemade, Inc.
Jeffrey Furman: treasurer, trustee PRIM CORP EMPL director: Ben & Jerry's Homemade Inc.
Rebecca Golden: director

Grants Analysis
Disclosure Period: calendar year ending 2000
Total Grants: $1,793,712*
Number of Grants: 446
Average Grant: $4,021
Highest Grant: $150,000
Lowest Grant: $10
Typical Range: $1,000 to $15,000

*Note: Giving excludes matching gifts and United Way.

Recent Grants

Note: Grants derived from 2001 Form 990.

General

160,000	Global Exchange, San Francisco, CA
150,000	United for a Fair Economy, Boston, MA
100,000	Ruckus Society, Berkeley, CA
100,000	Social Venture Fund, Dover, NH
30,000	Ice Center
25,000	Counseling Service of Addison County
25,000	Twenty First Century Foundation
15,000	Citizens Environmental Coalition, Albany, NY
15,000	Gwich'in Steering Committee, Anchorage, AK
15,000	Jacob Riis Neighbor, Long Island City, NY

LEGLER BENBOUGH FOUNDATION

Giving Contact

Peter K. Ellsworth, President
2550 5th Ave., Suite 132
San Diego, CA 92103
Phone: (619)235-8099

Description

Founded: 1985
EIN: 330105049
Organization Type: Private Foundation
Giving Locations: CA: San Diego
Grant Types: General Support, Research.

Donor Information

Founder: Legler Benbough

Financial Summary

Total Giving: $1,661,900 (2001); $1,847,000 (2000); $1,131,960 (1999)
Assets: $40,595,501 (2001); $39,585,481 (2000); $33,647,108 (1999)
Gifts Received: $2,247,335 (2001); $9,412,674 (2000); $23,013,030 (1999). Note: In 2001, contributions were received from Legler Benbough Trust. In 2000, contributions were received from Legler Benbough Trust ($5,144,551) and La Jolla Camino Trust ($4,262,123). In 1998 and 1999, contributions were received from the Legler Benbough Trust.

Typical Recipients

Arts & Humanities: Community Arts, Ethnic & Folk Arts, Historic Preservation, History & Archaeology, Libraries, Museums/Galleries, Music, Performing Arts, Theater, Visual Arts
Civic & Public Affairs: African American Affairs, Civic & Public Affairs-General, Housing, Public Policy, Safety, Urban & Community Affairs, Zoos/Aquariums
Education: Colleges & Universities, Education Funds, Literacy, Private Education (Precollege), Science/Mathematics Education, Secondary Education (Public)
Health: Alzheimers Disease, Arthritis, Cancer, Children's Health/Hospitals, Clinics/Medical Centers, Eyes/Blindness, Health Funds, Health Organizations, Hospices, Medical Research, Prenatal Health Issues, Public Health, Research/Studies Institutes, Single-Disease Health Associations
International: Health Care/Hospitals
Religion: Churches, Religious Organizations, Religious Welfare, Social/Policy Issues
Science: Science Museums, Scientific Centers & Institutes
Social Services: Animal Protection, Big Brother/Big Sister, Camps, Child Welfare, Community Service Organizations, Crime Prevention, Domestic Violence,

Family Services, Food/Clothing Distribution, People with Disabilities, Recreation & Athletics, Scouts, Senior Services, Social Services-General, Special Olympics, Volunteer Services, Youth Organizations

Application Procedures

Initial Contact: Send a brief letter of inquiry.
Application Requirements: Include pertinent information.
Deadlines: March 15 for April 15 grants and September 15 for October 15 grants.

Foundation Officials

Legler Benbough: president
Thomas E. Cisco: treasurer
Winifred Deming: vice president
Peter Kennedy Ellsworth: secretary B Los Angeles, CA 1931. ED Stanford University BA (1953); Stanford University JD (1956). PRIM CORP EMPL president, chief executive officer: Sharp Healthcare. NONPR AFFIL member: California Bar Association; member: Rotary; fellow: American Bar Association.

Grants Analysis

Disclosure Period: calendar year ending 2001
Total Grants: $1,661,900
Number of Grants: 47
Average Grant: $22,998*
Highest Grant: $400,000
Lowest Grant: $1,000
Typical Range: $10,000 to $50,000
*Note: Average grant figure excludes three highest grants ($650,000).

Recent Grants

Note: Grants derived from 2000 Form 990.

General

400,000	Zoological Society of San Diego, San Diego, CA -- Heart of the Zoo Project
250,000	San Diego Natural History Museum, San Diego, CA -- for Legler Benbough Exhibit Hall
200,000	Reuben H. Fleet Science Center, San Diego, CA -- for exploratorium
125,000	San Diego Historical Society, San Diego, CA -- unrestricted
108,000	Boy Scouts of America Desert Pacific Council, San Diego, CA -- for pool at Camp Mataguay
70,000	Salk Institute, San Diego, CA -- for 5 graduate students
50,000	Elderhelp, San Diego, CA -- for case management services
50,000	San Diego Humane Society, San Diego, CA -- for Partners for Life Campaign
50,000	Sharp Health Care Foundation, San Diego, CA -- for mobile clinic in Chula Vista
50,000	Timken Museum of Art, San Diego, CA -- charity for "In the Library" by John Peto

BENDER FOUNDATION

Giving Contact

Julie Bender-Silver, President
1120 Connecticut Ave. NW, Suite 1200
Washington, DC 20036
Phone: (202)828-9000
Fax: (202)785-9347

Description

Founded: 1958
EIN: 526054193
Organization Type: Private Foundation
Giving Locations: DC: Washington
Grant Types: General Support.

Donor Information

Founder: the late Jack I. Bender

Financial Summary

Total Giving: $1,046,675 (2000); $590,871 (1999); $429,105 (1998)
Giving Analysis: Giving for 1999 includes: foundation scholarships ($10,800)
Assets: $13,580,363 (2000); $13,046,290 (1999); $11,854,798 (1998)
Gifts Received: $1,563,688 (2000); $890,000 (1999). Note: In 1999, contributions were received from the Estate of D.G. Bender, and Howard M. Bender.

Typical Recipients

Arts & Humanities: Arts Centers, Arts Festivals, Arts Institutes, Ballet, Dance, Historic Preservation, History & Archaeology, Libraries, Museums/Galleries, Music, Performing Arts, Theater
Civic & Public Affairs: Botanical Gardens/Parks, Civic & Public Affairs-General, Urban & Community Affairs
Education: Colleges & Universities, Education Funds, Elementary Education (Public), Education-General, International Exchange, International Studies, Private Education (Precollege), School Volunteerism, Secondary Education (Private), Secondary Education (Public), Special Education, Student Aid
Health: Cancer, Children's Health/Hospitals, Clinics/Medical Centers, Health-General, Heart, Hospitals, Medical Rehabilitation, Multiple Sclerosis, Prenatal Health Issues, Public Health, Respiratory, Single-Disease Health Associations
International: Foreign Arts Organizations, Foreign Educational Institutions, Health Care/Hospitals, International Organizations, International Peace & Security Issues, International Relief Efforts, Missionary/Religious Activities
Religion: Jewish Causes, Religious Organizations, Religious Welfare
Science: Science Museums
Social Services: Child Welfare, Community Centers, Community Service Organizations, Day Care, Delinquency & Criminal Rehabilitation, Domestic Violence, Family Planning, Family Services, Food/Clothing Distribution, People with Disabilities, Recreation & Athletics, Senior Services, Substance Abuse, United Funds/United Ways, YMCA/YWCA/YMHA/YWHA, Youth Organizations

Application Procedures

Initial Contact: Send a brief letter of inquiry.
Application Requirements: Include brochures describing the program or project, amount requested, proof of charitable status, and purpose of funds sought.
Deadlines: November 30.

Restrictions

Does not support individuals, or political or lobbying groups.

Foundation Officials

Julie Bender Belinkie: president
David S. Bender: vice president
Howard Marvin Bender: executive vice president B Paterson, NJ 1930. ED University of Maryland (1948-1950). PRIM CORP EMPL chairman, director: Blake Construction Co. CORP AFFIL president: Best Mechanical. NONPR AFFIL director: Jewish Community Center Greater Washington; member: Tau Epsilon Phi.
Sondra D. Bender: chairwoman
Stanley Seymour Bender: secretary B Paterson, NJ 1929. ED University of Maryland. PRIM CORP EMPL executive vice president, director: Blake Construction Co. NONPR AFFIL member: Washington Board Realtors.
Barbara Bender-Laskow: vice president
Eileen Bender Greenberg: vice president

Grants Analysis

Disclosure Period: calendar year ending 2000
Total Grants: $1,046,675
Number of Grants: 136
Average Grant: $6,318*
Highest Grant: $100,000
Lowest Grant: $250
Typical Range: $1,000 to $15,000
***Note:** Average grant figure excludes two highest grants ($200,000).

Recent Grants

Note: Grants derived from 1999 Form 990.

Library-Related

50,000	Genesis Foundation, New York, NY -- library

General

100,000	Congregation Beth El, Bethesda, MD -- campaign 2000
50,000	Discovery Creek Children's Museum, Washington, DC
50,000	UJA Federation of Greater Washington, Rockville, MD -- donation
30,000	Jewish Community Center of Greater Washington, Washington, DC -- parenting center
25,000	American University, Washington, DC -- library renovation
25,000	Anti-Defamation League, Washington, DC -- concert
21,100	Discovery Creek Children's Museum, Washington, DC -- fashion show
10,000	American Heart Association
10,000	Children's National Medical Center, Washington, DC -- project champ
10,000	Colorado Academy, Denver, CO -- campaign 2000

LEO H. BENDIT CHARITABLE FOUNDATION

Giving Contact

Dr. Kurt J. Bloch, Trustee
81 Arlington Rd.
Chestnut Hill, MA 02467
Phone: (617)734-3284

Description

Founded: 1963
EIN: 136143764
Organization Type: Private Foundation
Grant Types: General Support.

Financial Summary

Total Giving: $144,166 (2002); $158,503 (2001); $162,000 (2000)
Giving Analysis: Giving for 2002 includes: foundation grants to United Way ($5,000); 2000: foundation grants to United Way ($5,000); 1999: foundation grants to United Way ($5,000)
Assets: $2,667,438 (2002); $3,003,839 (2001); $3,304,856 (2000)
Gifts Received: $42,490 (2002); $48,032 (2001); $83,550 (2000). Note: In 1999, 2000, 2001, and 2002, contributions were received from Margot Bloch. In 1998, contributions were received from Kurt J. Bloch.

Typical Recipients

Arts & Humanities: Historic Preservation, Libraries, Museums/Galleries, Music, Public Broadcasting
Civic & Public Affairs: Civic & Public Affairs-General, Urban & Community Affairs

Education: Colleges & Universities, Education-General, Medical Education, Private Education (Precollege), Secondary Education (Private), Special Education, Student Aid
Environment: Environment-General, Wildlife Protection
Health: AIDS/HIV, Arthritis, Cancer, Emergency/Ambulance Services, Health-General, Health Organizations, Heart, Hospitals, Long-Term Care, Nursing Services, Respiratory, Single-Disease Health Associations
International: Human Rights, International Affairs, International Peace & Security Issues
Religion: Jewish Causes, Religious Welfare
Social Services: Community Service Organizations, Community Service Organizations, Emergency Relief, Family Planning, Food/Clothing Distribution, People with Disabilities, Shelters/Homelessness, United Funds/United Ways

Application Procedures

Initial Contact: Send a brief letter of inquiry.
Deadlines: None.

Restrictions

Grants are not made to individuals.

Foundation Officials

Donald B. Bloch: trustee
Kenneth D. Bloch: trustee
Dr. Kurt Julius Bloch: trustee B Germany 1929. ED City College of New York BS (1951); New York University MD (1955). PRIM CORP EMPL physician, chief clinical immunology: Massachusetts General Hospital. CORP AFFIL professor: Harvard Medical School. NONPR AFFIL member: American Society Clinical Investigation; diplomate: Diagnostic Laboratory Immunology; diplomate: American Board Internal Medicine; member: American Association Physicians; diplomate: American Board Allergy & Immunology.

Grants Analysis

Disclosure Period: calendar year ending 2002
Total Grants: $139,166*
Number of Grants: 49
Average Grant: $2,066*
Highest Grant: $40,000
Lowest Grant: $100
Typical Range: $1,000 to $5,000
***Note:** Giving excludes United Way. Average grant figure excludes highest grant.

Recent Grants

Note: Grants derived from 2001 Form 990.

General

40,000	Massachusetts General Hospital, Boston, MA
23,203	United Jewish Communities, New York, NY
10,000	American Red Cross of Massachusetts Bay, Boston, MA
10,000	Beth Israel Hospital, Boston, MA
10,000	New York Foundation for Nursing Homes, Jamaica, NY
10,000	Planned Parenthood League of Massachusetts, Cambridge, MA
10,000	Self Help Community Services, New York, NY
5,000	Jewish Family and Children's Service, Boston, MA
5,000	United Way of Massachusetts, Boston, MA
4,000	Pine Street Inn, Boston, MA

BENEFICIA FOUNDATION

Giving Contact

Alisha King, Contact
1 Pitcairn Place, Suite 3000
Jenkintown, PA 19046-3593
Phone: (215)887-6700
Fax: (215)881-6092
E-mail: ak3371@pitcairn.com

Description

Founded: 1953
EIN: 246015630
Organization Type: Family Foundation
Giving Locations: no restrictions.
Grant Types: General Support, Project.

Donor Information

Founder: Established in 1953 by members of the Theodore Pitcairn family.

Financial Summary

Total Giving: $1,600,000 (fiscal year ending April 30, 2002 approx); $1,625,000 (fiscal 2001); $1,600,000 (fiscal 2000). Note: The foundation did not give grants in fiscal 1996.
Assets: $15,993,427 (fiscal 2001); $18,491,820 (fiscal 1999); $20,582,849 (fiscal 1998)

Typical Recipients

Arts & Humanities: Arts Centers, Arts Outreach, Historic Preservation, Libraries, Museums/Galleries, Music, Opera, Performing Arts, Public Broadcasting, Theater
Civic & Public Affairs: Botanical Gardens/Parks, Clubs, Economic Development, Civic & Public Affairs-General, Law & Justice, Legal Aid, Public Policy, Urban & Community Affairs, Zoos/Aquariums
Education: Arts/Humanities Education, Colleges & Universities, Education Funds, Education Reform, Education-General, Medical Education, Private Education (Precollege), Science/Mathematics Education, Special Education, Student Aid
Environment: Air/Water Quality, Forestry, Environment-General, Protection, Resource Conservation, Resource Conservation, Watershed, Wildlife Protection
Health: Cancer, Children's Health/Hospitals, Health-General, Nursing Services, Nutrition
International: International Environmental Issues
Religion: Churches, Religious Organizations, Religious Welfare
Science: Scientific Organizations, Scientific Research
Social Services: Community Centers, Community Service Organizations, Crime Prevention, People with Disabilities, United Funds/United Ways, Youth Organizations

Application Procedures

Initial Contact: All applications should be made in writing and addressed to either the Environmental Committee or Arts Committee.
Application Requirements: Applications should include the organization's name and address, proof of U.S. tax-exempt status or affiliation with U.S. based nonprofit, annual report, and a one page project summary. A brief proposal, 10 pages or less, which includes project objectives, project description, expected outcomes, a timetable, a complete budget, and the qualifications of key personnel involved should also be included.
Deadlines: January 31.
Review Process: Committee chairs select proposals for preliminary review at committee meetings in February or March. The full board of directors meets in May to conduct final proposal reviews and make recommendations for funding. Applicants whose proposals are approved will be notified by May 31.

Notes: A final report is required from all grant recipients at the end of the grant year.

Additional Information

Foundation favors programs which are innovative, catalytic, address unmet needs, and strive toward self-sustainability.
Publications: Brochure; Grant List

Foundation Officials

Janet Fishman: contact
John Daniel Mitchell: director B New York, NY 1957. NONPR AFFIL fellow: Linnean Society London; honorary curator: New York Botanical Garden; member: International Association Plant Taxonomists; vice chairman: BAT Conservation International; member: Ecological Society America; member: American Association Advancement Science. CLUB AFFIL Philadelphia Botanical Club; Organization for Flora Neotropica; Explorers Club; New England Botanical Club.
Miriam Pitcairn Mitchell: vice president, director
Eshowe P. Pennink: director
Mark J. Pennink: treasurer, director B 1957. PRIM CORP EMPL partner: Pitcairn Group LP. CORP AFFIL president: Pennink & Arrimour; partner: Pitcairn Finance Management Corp.
Feodor Urban Pitcairn: executive secretary, director B Bergen, Netherlands 1934. ED University of Pennsylvania AB (1959). PRIM CORP EMPL chairman: Pitcairn Financial Management Group. CORP AFFIL director: Infotron System. NONPR AFFIL vice chairman, member: Montgomery County Planning Committee; president: Pennypack Watershed Association; member: Bryn Athyn Planning Committee; director: Center Marine Conservation; trustee: Academy Natural Science; member: Bryn Athyn Borough Authority. CLUB AFFIL Racquet Club.
Kirstin Odhner Pitcairn: director
Laren Pitcairn: president, director PRIM CORP EMPL president: Chief Logan Associates Ltd. CORP AFFIL director: Old York Road Bancorp; director: Pitcairn Co.; director: Bank & Trust Old York Road.
Mary Eleanor Pitcairn: director
Heather C. Reynolds: director

Grants Analysis

Disclosure Period: fiscal year ending April 30, 2001
Total Grants: $1,625,000
Number of Grants: 46
Average Grant: $22,282*
Highest Grant: $600,000
Typical Range: $10,000 to $50,000
*Note: Average grant figure excludes highest grant.

Recent Grants

Note: Grants derived from fiscal 2001 Form 990.

General

600,000	Philadelphia Society of the Lord's New Church, Huntington Valley, PA
160,000	Academy of the New Church, Bryn Athyn, PA -- for the Performing Arts Center
60,000	Center to Prevent Handgun Violence, Washington, DC -- Legal Action Project
60,000	Oxfam America, Boston, MA -- for Central America, Equal Ground and South America and South East Asia
40,000	Philadelphia Museum of Art, Philadelphia, PA
37,000	Southern Poverty Law Center, Montgomery, AL -- for Performing Arts Center
35,000	Academy of the Vocal Arts, Philadelphia, PA -- for Ava Opera Theater
30,000	Center for Marine Conservation, Washington, DC -- Alaska Seas Campaign
30,000	Conservation International, Washington, DC -- for Bilsa Reserve Land Acquisition
30,000	Institute of Systematic Boteny, Bronx, NY -- for Serra Do Teimoso Reserve and Bahia Stewardship

FRANCES AND BENJAMIN BENENSON FOUNDATION

Giving Contact

Charles B. Benenson, President
708 3rd Avenue, 28th Floor
New York, NY 10017
Phone: (212)867-0990
Fax: (212)983-1952

Description

Founded: 1983
EIN: 133267113
Organization Type: Family Foundation
Giving Locations: NY: New York
Grant Types: General Support, Scholarship.

Donor Information

Founder: Established in 1983 by Charles B. Benenson.

Financial Summary

Total Giving: $1,800,000 (fiscal year ending November 30, 2003 approx); $1,900,000 (fiscal 2002 approx); $1,900,000 (fiscal 2001)
Giving Analysis: Giving for fiscal 2000 includes: foundation grants to United Way ($5,250) fiscal 1998: foundation grants to United Way ($5,000)
Assets: $30,000,000 (fiscal 2003 approx); $30,000,000 (fiscal 2002); $38,116,077 (fiscal 2000)
Gifts Received: $2,050,000 (fiscal 2000); $1,400,000 (fiscal 1998); $1,262,500 (fiscal 1996).
Note: In fiscal 2000, contributions were received from Marx Realty and Improvement Co., Inc. ($250,000) and Charles B. Benenson ($1,800,000). In fiscal 1998, contributions were received from Benenson Capital Company and Marx Realty and Improvement Co., Inc. In fiscal 1996, contributions were received from Benenson Capital Co. ($1,075,000) and Marx Realty & Improvement Co., Inc. ($187,500).

Typical Recipients

Arts & Humanities: Arts Associations & Councils, Arts Centers, Arts Institutes, Ethnic & Folk Arts, Film & Video, Arts & Humanities-General, Libraries, Museums/Galleries, Music, Opera, Performing Arts, Public Broadcasting, Theater
Civic & Public Affairs: Botanical Gardens/Parks, Clubs, Economic Development, Civic & Public Affairs-General, Housing, Municipalities/Towns, Philanthropic Organizations, Professional & Trade Associations, Urban & Community Affairs
Education: Arts/Humanities Education, Business Education, Colleges & Universities, Community & Junior Colleges, Education Funds, Elementary Education (Private), Elementary Education (Public), Education-General, Gifted & Talented Programs, International Studies, Literacy, Minority Education, Minority Education, Private Education (Precollege), Secondary Education (Public), Social Sciences Education, Student Aid
Environment: Air/Water Quality, Environment-General, Wildlife Protection
Health: AIDS/HIV, Cancer, Children's Health/Hospitals, Clinics/Medical Centers, Diabetes, Emergency/Ambulance Services, Health Organizations, Hospitals, Single-Disease Health Associations
International: Foreign Arts Organizations, Foreign Educational Institutions, Human Rights, International Relations, International Relief Efforts, Missionary/Religious Activities
Religion: Jewish Causes, Religious Organizations, Religious Welfare, Synagogues/Temples
Science: Scientific Organizations
Social Services: Animal Protection, Child Welfare, Community Centers, Community Service Organizations, Crime Prevention, Family Planning, Family Services, People with Disabilities, Recreation & Athletics, Shelters/Homelessness, Social Services-General,

Substance Abuse, United Funds/United Ways, Youth Organizations

Application Procedures

Initial Contact: The foundation requests applications be made in writing.
Application Requirements: Include a description of organization and amount requested.
Deadlines: None.
Notes: The foundation considers all proposals.

Restrictions

Grants are not made to individuals.

Foundation Officials

Charles B. Benenson: president B New York, NY 1913. ED Yale University BA (1930). PRIM CORP EMPL president: Benenson Realty Co. CORP AFFIL director: Southbury Hilton; director: Southbury Oper Partners LLC; director: Loews Corp.
Anthony J. DiNome: secretary, treasurer
Emanuel Lubin: vice president PRIM CORP EMPL partner: Goldfarb & Fleece.

Grants Analysis

Disclosure Period: fiscal year ending November 30, 2000
Total Grants: $2,185,906*
Number of Grants: 181
Average Grant: $9,366*
Highest Grant: $500,000
Typical Range: $5,000 to $20,000
*Note: Giving excludes United Way. Average grant excludes highest grant.

Recent Grants

Note: Grants derived from fiscal 1999 Form 990.

Library-Related

49,585	New York Public Library, New York, NY

General

375,000	Metropolitan Museum of Art, New York, NY
250,000	Yale University, New Haven, CT
100,000	AJC Kosovo Relief Fund
100,000	American Jewish Committee
100,000	Inner-city Scholarship Fund, New York, NY
100,000	Mosholu Montefiore Community Center, Bronx, NY
100,000	Trust for Public Land
100,000	UJA - Federation of Jewish Philanthropies of New York, New York, NY
75,000	Klein Family Health
50,000	Anti - Defamation League

BENETTON U.S.A. CORP.

Company Headquarters

New York, NY
Web: http://www.benetton.com

Company Description

Employees: 20
SIC(s): 2300 Apparel & Other Textile Products.
Parent Company: Bennetton Group SpA, Via Villa Minelli 1, Ponzano, Treviso, Italy

Operating Locations

Benetton U.S.A. Corp. (NC--New York)

Nonmonetary Support

Type: Donated Products

Giving Contact

Mark Major, Communications Director
597 5th Avenue, 11th Floor
New York, NY 10017-1020

Phone: (212)593-0290
Fax: (212)371-1438

Description

Organization Type: Corporate Giving Program
Giving Locations: no restrictions.
Grant Types: General Support.

Typical Recipients

Arts & Humanities: Dance, Historic Preservation, Libraries, Museums/Galleries, Performing Arts
Education: Colleges & Universities, Private Education (Precollege), Public Education (Precollege)
Health: Hospitals, Medical Research, Single-Disease Health Associations
Science: Scientific Organizations
Social Services: Community Service Organizations, Domestic Violence, People with Disabilities, Refugee Assistance, Substance Abuse, United Funds/United Ways, Youth Organizations

Application Procedures

Initial Contact: Send a brief letter.
Application Requirements: Applications should include a description of organization, amount requested, and purpose of funds sought.
Deadlines: Setember.

Restrictions

Benetton does not support political or lobbying groups.

Corporate Officials

Luciano Benetton: chairman, president, chief executive officer, director B Treviso, Italy 1935. PRIM CORP EMPL chairman, president, chief executive officer, director: Benetton Corp. ADD CORP EMPL co-fdr: Colors Publications; chairman: Fratelli Benetton. CORP AFFIL director: Eliodona Publs.
Carlo Tunioli: vice president, general manager PRIM CORP EMPL vice president, general manager: Benetton U.S.A. Corp.

Grants Analysis

Typical Range: $10,000 to $25,000

CLAUDE BENNETT FAMILY FOUNDATION

Giving Contact

Harold I. Apolinsky, Trustee
2311 Highland Avenue South
Birmingham, AL 35205
Phone: (205)945-4687

Description

Founded: 1993
EIN: 582052917
Organization Type: Private Foundation
Grant Types: General Support.

Financial Summary

Total Giving: $86,450 (2001); $92,730 (2000); $82,225 (1999)
Giving Analysis: Giving for 2001 includes: foundation grants to United Way ($2,500); 2000: foundation scholarships ($1,000); foundation grants to United Way ($2,500); 1999: foundation grants to United Way ($2,500)
Assets: $1,712,454 (2001); $1,977,541 (2000); $2,225,317 (1999)

Typical Recipients

Arts & Humanities: Arts & Humanities-General, Libraries, Museums/Galleries, Music, Opera
Civic & Public Affairs: Botanical Gardens/Parks, Clubs, Civic & Public Affairs-General, Urban & Community Affairs, Zoos/Aquariums

Education: Colleges & Universities, Elementary Education (Private), Education-General, Medical Education, Private Education (Precollege), Student Aid
Health: AIDS/HIV, Alzheimers Disease, Clinics/Medical Centers, Health-General, Health Organizations, Heart, Hospices, Medical Rehabilitation, Medical Research, Prenatal Health Issues, Public Health, Trauma Treatment
International: Health Care/Hospitals
Religion: Churches, Religion-General, Ministries
Science: Science Museums
Social Services: At-Risk Youth, Camps, Child Welfare, Community Centers, Community Service Organizations, Family Planning, Family Services, Food/Clothing Distribution, Senior Services, Shelters/Homelessness, United Funds/United Ways

Application Procedures

Initial Contact: Applications should be submitted in writing.
Application Requirements: Identify the organization, give the organization's tax exempt number and proof of tax-exempt status, state the purpose of funds sought, state the prior experience of the applicant in carrying out such purpose, provide the applicant's plan for carrying out the purpose, list the personnel to be involved in the project, and attach financial statements for the current and the two preceding years.
Deadlines: None.

Foundation Officials

Harold I. Apolinsky: trustee
Clark Bennett: trustee
Nancy Bennett: trustee
Katherine Bennett O'Leary: trustee
J. Miller Piggott: trustee

Grants Analysis

Disclosure Period: calendar year ending 2001
Total Grants: $83,950*
Number of Grants: 32
Average Grant: $2,623
Highest Grant: $15,000
Lowest Grant: $50
Typical Range: $500 to $5,000
*Note: Giving excludes United Way.

Recent Grants

Note: Grants derived from 2001 Form 990.

General

15,000	Birmingham Episcopal Camp, Birmingham, AL
14,200	St. Luke's Episcopal Church
10,650	Alzheimer's of Central Alabama, AL
10,000	Samford University, Birmingham, AL
5,000	Alabama Symphony Orchestra, Birmingham, AL
4,750	South Highland Presbyterian Church, Birmingham, AL
3,000	Food Bank of Larimar County
2,500	United Way, Dubuque, IA
2,000	Botanical Gardens
2,000	Crossroads Safe House, Ft. Collins, CO

BENTON FOUNDATION

Giving Contact

Harry Kirkman, Executive Director
950 18th St., NW
Washington, DC 20006
Phone: (202)638-5770
Fax: (202)638-5771
E-mail: harryk@benton.org
Web: http://www.benton.org

Alternate Contact

E-mail: benton@benton.org

Description

Founded: 1981
EIN: 136075750
Organization Type: Specialized/Single Purpose Foundation
Giving Locations: nationally.
Grant Types: Award, Conference/Seminar, Fellowship, Multiyear/Continuing Support, Project, Research.

Donor Information

Founder: Established in 1981 in Washington, DC, by Charles Benton with the legacy of his father, the late Senator William Benton . The foundation is the successor to a foundation established in 1948 by Senator Benton, who was an advocate of the communications media and involved in advertising, education, government, and publishing.

Financial Summary

Total Giving: $1,061,422 (2000); $669,522 (1999); $468,572 (1998)
Giving Analysis: Giving for 2000 includes: foundation fellowships ($16,000) 1999: foundation fellowships ($5,000)
Assets: $18,023,630 (2000); $19,726,858 (1999); $17,620,317 (1998)
Gifts Received: $5,177,366 (2000); $4,354,062 (1999); $2,799,354 (1998). Note: In 2000, contributions were received from Annie E. Casey Foundation ($100,000), AOL Foundation ($200,500), Aspen Institute ($80,557), AT&T Foundation ($40,000), Bill & Melinda Gates Foundation ($40,000), Casey Family Program ($35,000), David & Lucile Packard Foundation ($209,600), James Irvine Foundation ($50,000), Joyce Foundation ($642,215), Albert A. List Foundation ($30,000), Lucent Technologies Foundation ($40,000), John D. & Catherine T. Macarthur Foundation ($150,000), National Education Association ($300,000), Pew Charitable Trusts ($50,000), Robert Wood Johnson Foundation ($2,016,781), Rockefeller Brothers Foundation ($25,000), Rockefeller Foundation ($100,000), Streaming Media.com ($20,000), Tides Foundation ($10,300), Ford Foundation ($615,000), W.K. Kellogg ($65,000), Markle Foundation ($25,000), Charles Stewart Mott Foundation ($50,000), Philadelphia Foundation ($50,000), and miscellaneous contributions ($232,413). In 1999, contributions were received from The Robert Wood Johnson Foundation, AOL Foundation, the Ford Foundation, the National Endowment for the Arts, The Pew Charitable Trusts, The Aspen Institute, and various others. In 1998 contributions were received from W. K. Kellogg Foundation ($150,000), Robert Wood Johnson Foundation ($866,587), The Joyce Foundation ($251,110), and various other contributors totaling ($2,728,425) in monetary gifts and ($70,929) in computer equipment and software.

Typical Recipients

Arts & Humanities: Arts Associations & Councils, Arts Centers, Arts Festivals, Arts Institutes, Film & Video, Arts & Humanities-General, Libraries, Museums/Galleries, Music, Public Broadcasting, Theater, Visual Arts
Civic & Public Affairs: Botanical Gardens/Parks, Civic & Public Affairs-General, Legal Aid, Nonprofit Management, Philanthropic Organizations, Professional & Trade Associations, Public Policy, Urban & Community Affairs, Women's Affairs
Education: Colleges & Universities, Community & Junior Colleges, International Exchange, Journalism/Media Education, Science/Mathematics Education
Environment: Environment-General
International: International Organizations
Social Services: Child Welfare, People with Disabilities

Application Procedures

Initial Contact: Send a brief letter of inquiry.
Application Requirements: Include a description of the project, budget, and resumes of principal personnel.
Deadlines: NONE

Restrictions

Provides grants to nonprofit organizations for other than general operating support in the communications field of regional/national significance.

Additional Information

The Benton Foundation also provides media technical assistance. The Benton Foundation produces several publications regarding communications and the nonprofit community. Benton bulletins include: Talk Radio, Using Video, Cable Access, and Independent Features.

The foundation's decision to fund only operating projects "has dramatically reduced the foundation's grants budget while increasing the foundation's ability to demonstrate innovative uses of the media for issue advocacy and to help nonprofits advance their strategic use of communications and information technologies and services."
Publications: Mission Statement; Publication Flyers

Foundation Officials

Charles Benton: chairman B 1930.
Craig Benton: director
Marjorie Craig Benton: trustee ED National College of Education LHD (1981); Lincoln College (1982); Columbia College LHD (1983); Northwestern University LHD (1983). CORP AFFIL vice chairman: Pub Media Inc.; director: Royal Packaging Industries. NONPR AFFIL member: Van Leer Group Foundation; cofounder: Womens Issues Network; president: University Chicago Chapin Hall Center Children; honorary chairman: Save Children Federation; co chairman: United States Commr International Year Child; member: Middle East Policy Council; co-founder: Peace Museum; member: Intl Human Rights Law Institute DePaul College Law; member committee university resources: Harvard University; member: Harvard University Institute Social & Economic Policy Middle East; honorary member: Chicago Pediatric Society; chairman, director: Council Foundations; member: Chicago Foundation Women Womens Issues Network; member: American Orthopsychiatric Association; member: Bernard Van Leer Foundation. CLUB AFFIL River New York Club; Arts Chicago Club; Economic Chicago Club.
Adrianne Furness: secretary
Harry Kirkman: secretary, director
Richard Mahoney: director
Richard M. Neustadt: director
Michael Pertschuck: director
Gene Pokorny: director B 1946. PRIM CORP EMPL chairman, director: Cambridge Reports.
Dorothy Sattes Ridings: director B Charleston, WV 1939. ED Randolph-Macon Woman's College (1957-1959); Northwestern University BSJ (1961); University of North Carolina MA (1968). PRIM CORP EMPL president, publisher: Bradenton Herald. NONPR AFFIL president, chief executive officer: Coun on Foundations; trustee: Manatee Community College.
Carolyn Sachs: director

Grants Analysis

Disclosure Period: calendar year ending 2000
Total Grants: $1,045,422*
Number of Grants: 40
Average Grant: $26,136
Highest Grant: $35,000
Lowest Grant: $3,000
Typical Range: $15,000 to $35,000
*****Note:** Giving excludes fellowships.

Recent Grants

Note: Grants derived from 1999 Form 990.

General

50,000	Leeward Community College, Pear City, HI
40,000	Community Media Center, Grand Rapids, MI
40,000	Information Technology Resource Center and Mexican Fine Arts Museum, Chicago, IL
40,000	Ink People Center for The Arts, Eureka, CA
40,000	La Plaza Telecommunity, Taos, NM
40,000	Lewis and Clark State College, Lewiston, ID
40,000	Media Alliance, San Francisco, CA
40,000	Nebraska Arts Council, Omaha, NE
40,000	Squeaky Wheel, Buffalo, NY
40,000	Visual Communications, Los Angeles, CA

BENWOOD FOUNDATION

Giving Contact

Corinne A. Allen, Executive Director
Suntrust Bank Building
736 Market Street, Suite 1600
Chattanooga, TN 37402
Phone: (423)267-4311
Fax: (615)267-9049
E-mail: benwoodfnd@benwood.org

Description

Founded: 1950
EIN: 620476283
Organization Type: General Purpose Foundation
Giving Locations: TN: Chattanooga
Grant Types: Challenge, Matching, Project.

Donor Information

Founder: Established by George T. Hunter , who was chairman of the board of the Coca-Cola Bottling Company (Thomas, Inc.) at the time of his death in 1950. Mr. Hunter's uncle, Benjamin F. Thomas, was one of the founders of the Coca-Cola bottling industry. Most of Mr. Hunter's holdings in the bottling company were bequeathed to the foundation.

Financial Summary

Total Giving: $4,000,000 (2003 approx); $4,209,591 (2002); $6,880,277 (2000)
Giving Analysis: Giving for 2000 includes: foundation grants to United Way ($432,000) 1998: foundation grants to United Way ($75,000)
Assets: $93,000,000 (2003 approx); $93,894,413 (2002); $128,545,288 (2000)

Typical Recipients

Arts & Humanities: Arts Associations & Councils, Arts Funds, Arts Institutes, Ballet, Arts & Humanities-General, History & Archaeology, Libraries, Museums/Galleries, Music, Opera, Performing Arts, Public Broadcasting, Theater
Civic & Public Affairs: African American Affairs, Botanical Gardens/Parks, Business/Free Enterprise, Chambers of Commerce, Clubs, Community Foundations, Economic Development, Civic & Public Affairs-General, Housing, Municipalities/Towns, Parades/Festivals, Professional & Trade Associations, Safety, Urban & Community Affairs, Zoos/Aquariums
Education: Arts/Humanities Education, Business Education, Colleges & Universities, Continuing Education, Education Associations, Education Funds, Education Funds, Education Reform, Elementary Education (Private), Elementary Education (Public), Education-General, Legal Education, Literacy, Medical Education, Private Education (Precollege), Public

Education (Precollege), School Volunteerism, Secondary Education (Private), Secondary Education (Public)
Environment: Air/Water Quality, Environment-General, Resource Conservation, Wildlife Protection
Health: Alzheimers Disease, Clinics/Medical Centers, Emergency/Ambulance Services, Health Organizations, Hospitals, Medical Research, Mental Health, Public Health, Research/Studies Institutes
International: Health Care/Hospitals
Religion: Bible Study/Translation, Churches, Ministries, Religious Organizations, Religious Welfare, Social/Policy Issues
Social Services: Big Brother/Big Sister, Camps, Child Welfare, Community Centers, Community Service Organizations, Family Services, Food/Clothing Distribution, Homes, People with Disabilities, Recreation & Athletics, Scouts, Senior Services, Substance Abuse, United Funds/United Ways, YMCA/YWCA/YMHA/YWHA, Youth Organizations

Application Procedures

Initial Contact: A two-page letter of inquiry should be sent to the foundation.
Application Requirements: The letter should include the need that will be met by the proposed project, how the need will be met, and who will be served; why the applicant is qualified to implement the project and what staff will carry out the project; other sources of possible support; how the project will be measured, how the project will be supported after the requested grant expires, and the timetable for the project; and the amount requested by the foundation to fund the project. In addition to the application letter, a brief background of the organization, a list of board members, a copy of the most recent audited financial statement, a copy of the organization's current operating budget, and an IRS letter of determination indicating tax-exempt status should also be submitted. Applicants should submit six copies of the application.
Deadlines: The board of trustees meets annually in January to consider applications.
Review Process: The board looks favorably on proposals for projects dealing with education, health, the humanities, religion, and social welfare, particularly in and around Chattanooga. The trustees reserve the right to delay final decision on grant requests for a two-month period.

Restrictions

The foundation does not award grants for general operating expenses, endowments, financing deficits, political organizations, fund raising, multi-year grants, agencies outside the United States, or requests that are submitted by an organization that has received funding within the same year. Further, the foundation does not give funds for scholarship, fellowships, or grants directly to individuals.

Additional Information

Publications: Appliation Form; Guidelines

Foundation Officials

Corinne A. Allen: executive director
Sebert Brewer, Jr.: secretary-treasurer
E. Y. Chapin, III: chairman CORP AFFIL director: SunTrust Bank Chattanooga NA.
Susan R. Randolph: vice president
Robert J. Sudderth, Jr.: president B Chattanooga, TN 1942. ED Vanderbilt University (1964). PRIM CORP EMPL chairman, chief executive officer: American National Bank & Trust Co. CORP AFFIL director: Dixie Group Inc.; chairman, chief executive officer, director: SunTrust Bank Chattanooga NA.

Grants Analysis

Disclosure Period: calendar year ending 2000
Total Grants: $6,773,527*
Number of Grants: 129
Average Grant: $52,508
Highest Grant: $675,000

Lowest Grant: $250
Typical Range: $1,000 to $10,000 and $25,000 to $100,000
*Note: Giving excludes United Way.

Recent Grants

Note: Grants derived from 2000 Form 990.

Library-Related

100,000	Chattanooga-Hamilton County Bicentennial Library, Chattanooga, TN

General

675,000	Siskin Foundation, Chattanooga, TN
585,000	University of Tennessee at Chattanooga, Chattanooga, TN
336,000	WTCI-TV 45
320,000	McCallie School, Chattanooga, TN
275,000	Chattanooga Neighborhood Enterprise, Chattanooga, TN
275,000	Lula Lake Land Trust, Chattanooga, TN
252,000	Allied Arts, Oklahoma City, OK
250,000	Chattanooga State Technical Community College, Chattanooga, TN
250,000	Children's Educational Opportunity Foundation, Bentonville, AR
250,000	Friends of the Zoo

DORIS L. BENZ TRUST

Giving Contact

Judith Burrows
One South Street
PO Box 1335
Concord, NH 03302
Phone: (603)225-6641

Description

Founded: 1984
EIN: 046504871
Organization Type: Private Foundation
Giving Locations: MA; NH
Grant Types: General Support, Scholarship.

Donor Information

Founder: the late Doris L. Benz

Financial Summary

Total Giving: $397,677 (fiscal year ending June 30, 2001); $302,514 (fiscal 1999); $338,826 (fiscal 1996)
Assets: $9,786,155 (fiscal 2001); $9,672,973 (fiscal 1999); $7,313,714 (fiscal 1996)

Typical Recipients

Arts & Humanities: Community Arts, History & Archaeology, Libraries, Music, Public Broadcasting, Theater
Civic & Public Affairs: Community Foundations, Economic Development, Civic & Public Affairs-General, Philanthropic Organizations, Safety, Urban & Community Affairs, Zoos/Aquariums
Education: Arts/Humanities Education, Business Education, Colleges & Universities, Community & Junior Colleges, Education Funds, Private Education (Precollege), Public Education (Precollege), Secondary Education (Public), Student Aid
Environment: Environment-General
Health: AIDS/HIV, Cancer, Children's Health/Hospitals, Clinics/Medical Centers, Heart, Home-Care Services, Hospices, Hospitals, Mental Health, Nursing Services, Single-Disease Health Associations
Social Services: Child Welfare, Community Centers, Community Service Organizations, Day Care, Food/Clothing Distribution, People with Disabilities, Recreation & Athletics, Senior Services, Special Olympics, United Funds/United Ways, YMCA/YWCA/YMHA/YWHA, Youth Organizations

Application Procedures

Initial Contact: Return completed application form along with most recent high school or college transcripts, applicant appraisal, and application fee.
Deadlines: None.

Restrictions

No support for religious purposes.

Additional Information

Provides scholarships to residents of Sandwich or Carroll County, NH, who have graduated from high schools in these areas.

Foundation Officials

Wendell P. Weyland: trustee

Grants Analysis

Disclosure Period: fiscal year ending June 30, 2001
Total Grants: $397,677
Number of Grants: 23
Average Grant: $8,191*
Highest Grant: $217,477
Lowest Grant: $500
Typical Range: $1,000 to $10,000
*Note: Average grant figure excludes highest grant.

Recent Grants

Note: Grants derived from fiscal 2001 Form 990.

Library-Related

25,000	Gilmanton Year Round Library, Gilmanton, NH
10,000	Cook Memorial Library, Tamworth, NH

General

217,477	N.H. Charitable Fund, Concord, NH
40,000	Community School, South Tamworth, NH
15,000	Lynn YMCA, Lynn, MA
14,000	Poore Family Foundation, The, Colebrook, NH
12,500	Endicott College, Beverly, MA
10,000	Helen Fava Scholarship Fund, The, Boxford, MA
10,000	North Shore Association for Retarded Citizens, Salem, MA
10,000	North Shore Medical Center, Lynn, MA
5,000	Bear Camp Valley School, Tamworth, NH
5,000	Boys and Girls Club of Lynn, Lynn, MA

BERE FOUNDATION

Giving Contact

Barbara Van Dellen-Bere, President & Director
641 S. Elm Street
Hinsdale, IL 60521-4623
Phone: (312)322-8511

Description

Founded: 1983
EIN: 363272779
Organization Type: Private Foundation
Giving Locations: IL
Grant Types: General Support.

Donor Information

Founder: James F. Bere

Financial Summary

Total Giving: $819,750 (2001); $776,000 (2000); $330,000 (1999)
Giving Analysis: Giving for 2001 includes: foundation grants to United Way ($500); 2000: foundation grants to United Way ($500); 1999: foundation grants to United Way ($500)
Assets: $8,335,833 (2001); $9,594,681 (2000); $10,605,311 (1999)

Gifts Received: In 1991, contributions were received from James F. and Barbara L. Bere.

Typical Recipients

Arts & Humanities: Arts Institutes, History & Archaeology, Libraries, Museums/Galleries, Music, Opera, Public Broadcasting
Civic & Public Affairs: African American Affairs, Economic Development, Employment/Job Training, Civic & Public Affairs-General, Urban & Community Affairs, Zoos/Aquariums
Education: Business Education, Colleges & Universities, Education Reform, Education-General, Legal Education, Private Education (Precollege), Public Education (Precollege), Religious Education, Secondary Education (Private), Student Aid
Health: Children's Health/Hospitals, Health Organizations, Hospitals, Kidney, Medical Rehabilitation, Preventive Medicine/Wellness Organizations, Public Health
International: International Organizations, International Relief Efforts, Missionary/Religious Activities
Religion: Bible Study/Translation, Churches, Religion-General, Ministries, Missionary Activities (Domestic), Religious Organizations, Religious Welfare, Seminaries
Science: Science Museums
Social Services: Child Welfare, Community Service Organizations, Day Care, Family Services, Recreation & Athletics, United Funds/United Ways, YMCA/YWCA/YMHA/YWHA, Youth Organizations

Application Procedures

Initial Contact: The foundation has no formal grant application procedure or application form.
Deadlines: None.

Foundation Officials

Barbara Van Dellen Bere: president, director
David L. Bere: secretary, treasurer
James Frederick Bere, Jr.: vice president, director B Chicago, IL 1922. ED Northwestern University (1946); Northwestern University (1950). CORP AFFIL director: Temple-Inland Tribune Co.; director: York International Corp.; director: K-Mart Corp.; director: Abbott Laboratories; director: Ameritech Corp.
Robert P. Bere: vice president, director
Becky B. Sigfusson: vice president, director
Lynn B. Stine: vice president, director

Grants Analysis

Disclosure Period: calendar year ending 2001
Total Grants: $819,250*
Number of Grants: 54
Average Grant: $8,171*
Highest Grant: $386,200
Lowest Grant: $200
Typical Range: $1,000 to $10,000
*Note: Giving excludes United Way. Average grant figure excludes highest grant.

Recent Grants

Note: Grants derived from 2000 Form 990.

General

387,000	Christ Church of Oak Brook, Oak Brook, IL -- religious
100,500	World Vision
50,200	Community House -- social service
50,000	Fuller Seminary -- education
25,000	Institute for Global Engagement, St. Davids, PA -- social services
25,000	St. Petersburg Theological Seminary Foundation, Oak Brook, IL -- religious
20,000	Metro Chicago Youth For Christ, Chicago, IL -- youth ministry
16,000	Lawndale Community Church, Chicago, IL -- religious
10,000	Intervarsity Christian Fellowship, Madison, WI -- Christian ministry
7,000	Art Institute of Chicago, Chicago, IL -- culture

FRANK AND LYDIA BERGEN FOUNDATION

Giving Contact

Thomas Chiolo
First Union National Bank
401 S. Tyron Street, 4th Floor
Charlotte, NC 28288-1159
Phone: (704)383-5589

Alternate Contact

First Union National Bank
190 Riverpond
Summit, NJ 07901
Note: Address for application submissions.

Description

Founded: 1983
EIN: 226359304
Organization Type: Private Foundation
Giving Locations: NJ: Young American Conductor Projects run throughout the US.
Grant Types: Conference/Seminar, General Support, Multiyear/Continuing Support, Project, Scholarship.

Donor Information

Founder: the late Charlotte V. Bergen

Financial Summary

Total Giving: $597,195 (2001); $715,836 (2000); $944,483 (1999)
Giving Analysis: Giving for 2001 includes: foundation scholarships ($130,850); 2000: foundation scholarships ($94,500) 1999: foundation scholarships ($104,200)
Assets: $9,870,592 (2001); $10,961,662 (2000); $11,285,627 (1999)

Typical Recipients

Arts & Humanities: Arts Associations & Councils, Arts Centers, Arts Festivals, Arts Funds, Arts Institutes, Arts Outreach, Ballet, Dance, Libraries, Music, Opera, Performing Arts, Public Broadcasting
Civic & Public Affairs: Native American Affairs
Education: Arts/Humanities Education, Colleges & Universities, Faculty Development, Private Education (Precollege), Student Aid
Religion: Jewish Causes, Religious Welfare
Social Services: Youth Organizations

Application Procedures

Initial Contact: Send cover letter and a full proposal.
Application Requirements: Include a description of organization, amount requested, purpose of funds sought, recently audited financial statement, and proof of tax-exempt status.
Deadlines: March 15 through September 15.

Restrictions

Grants not made to individuals, endowments, political or lobbying groups, loans, fundraising events, or operating expenses.

Additional Information

Publications: Annual Report; Informational Brochure (including Application Guidelines)
Trust(s): First Union National Bank

Grants Analysis

Disclosure Period: calendar year ending 2001
Total Grants: $466,345*
Number of Grants: 54
Average Grant: $8,636
Highest Grant: $45,000
Lowest Grant: $750
Typical Range: $5,000 to $10,000
*Note: Giving excludes scholarships.

Recent Grants

Note: Grants derived from 2001 Form 990.

General

45,000	New Jersey Symphony Orchestra, Newark, NJ
31,500	Community School of the Arts
25,000	Montclair State University, Upper Montclair, NJ
24,000	New Jersey Chamber Music Society, Montclair, NJ
21,000	Colonial Symphony, Basking Ridge, NJ
19,600	Community Center on the Palisades Music Development, Pacific Palisades, CA
18,000	Bay Atlantic Symphony, Bridgeton, NJ
17,500	Westfield Symphony Orchestra, Westfield, CT
15,000	Mason Gross School of the Arts, New Brunswick, NJ
12,500	New Jersey City University Foundation, New Jersey City, NJ

H. N. AND FRANCES C. BERGER FOUNDATION

Giving Contact

Christopher M. McGuire, Vice President, Assistant Secretary & Director
PO Box 13390
Palm Desert, CA 92255-3390
Phone: (760)341-5293
Web: http://www.hnberger.org

Description

Founded: 1994
EIN: 521757452
Organization Type: Private Foundation
Giving Locations: CA; KY
Grant Types: General Support.

Financial Summary

Total Giving: $10,378,587 (2000); $4,694,000 (1999); $12,043,449 (1998)
Giving Analysis: Giving for 1999 includes: foundation matching gifts ($344,580) foundation scholarships ($405,000)
Assets: $403,833,632 (2000); $370,124,315 (1999); $357,644,178 (1998)
Gifts Received: $1,435,750 (1995); $2,317,000 (1994). Note: In 1995, contributions were received from Berger Family Trust A ($105,750) and the H. N. and Frances C. Berger Trust 1 ($1,330,000).

Typical Recipients

Arts & Humanities: Arts Centers, Libraries
Civic & Public Affairs: Legal Aid, Nonprofit Management, Professional & Trade Associations, Women's Affairs
Education: Business Education, Colleges & Universities, Continuing Education, Education Associations, Faculty Development, Legal Education, Minority Education, Public Education (Precollege), Science/Mathematics Education, Student Aid
Health: AIDS/HIV, Alzheimers Disease, Cancer, Clinics/Medical Centers, Health-General, Hospices, Hospitals, Medical Rehabilitation, Medical Research, Research/Studies Institutes
Religion: Bible Study/Translation, Churches, Missionary Activities (Domestic), Religious Welfare
Social Services: Big Brother/Big Sister, Child Welfare, Community Centers, Domestic Violence, People with Disabilities, Recreation & Athletics, Scouts, Youth Organizations

Application Procedures

Initial Contact: Send a written request by mail only.
Deadlines: None.

Additional Information

The foundation owns real estate which is leased to public charities and also owns and operates senior citizen housing.

Foundation Officials

Shirley Allen: vice president
Joan C. Auen: secretary-treasurer, director
Ronald M. Auen: president, director B 1932.
John N. Berger: vice president, director
Darrell Burrage: vice president
Christopher M. McGuire: vice president, assistant secretary, director
Douglass Vance: vice president, director
Lewis M. Webb, Jr.: vice president, director

Grants Analysis

Disclosure Period: calendar year ending 2000
Total Grants: $10,378,587*
Number of Grants: 85
Average Grant: $69,983*
Highest Grant: $4,500,000
Typical Range: $30,000 to $150,000
*Note: Average grant figure excludes highest grant.

Recent Grants

Note: Grants derived from 1999 Form 990.

General

665,000	College of the Ozarks, Pt. Lookout, MO -- support citizens abroad program
500,000	I Have A Dream Foundation Los Angeles, Los Angeles, CA
375,000	Salk Institute for Biological Studies, San Diego, CA -- support Center for Cellular and Molecular Imaging
250,000	Salk Institute for Biological Studies, San Diego, CA -- help support salaries, help purchase supplies and small equipment
250,000	Southwest Community Church, Palm Desert, CA -- media production expenses
194,580	Desert Rehabilitation Services, Inc., Desert Hot Springs, CA -- support "Can Do It" program
150,000	Henry E. Huntington Library and Art Gallery, San Marino, CA -- construction of Botanical Teaching Center
150,000	University of Arizona Foundation, Tucson, AZ -- support Berger Entrepreneurship program
129,000	Caney Creek Community Center, Whittier, CA -- scholarship program
129,000	Cumberland College, Williamsburg, KY -- support graduate scholarship program

LOUIS AND SANDRA BERKMAN FOUNDATION

Giving Contact

Linda L. Pinkle, Secretary
PO Box 576
Steubenville, OH 43952
Phone: (740)283-3722
Fax: (740)283-1224

Description

Founded: 1952
EIN: 346526694
Organization Type: Private Foundation
Giving Locations: MA; OH; PA
Grant Types: General Support.

Donor Information

Founder: Established in 1952 by the late Louis Berkman Sr. , Mrs. Louis Berkman, the Louis Berkman Co., Follansbee Steel Corp., and others.

Financial Summary

Total Giving: $328,928 (2001); $456,532 (2000); $1,152,488 (1998)

Giving Analysis: Giving for 2000 includes: foundation scholarships ($3,670); 1997: foundation grants to United Way ($1,500) foundation scholarships ($500,000)

Assets: $14,004,765 (2001); $14,269,197 (2000); $14,635,593 (1998)

Gifts Received: $100,000 (2000); $240,773 (1996); $100 (1995). Note: In 1996 and 2000, contributions were received from the Louis Berkman Co.

Typical Recipients

Arts & Humanities: Arts Festivals, History & Archaeology, Music

Civic & Public Affairs: Clubs, Community Foundations, Civic & Public Affairs-General, Housing, Municipalities/Towns, Parades/Festivals, Safety, Zoos/Aquariums

Education: Arts/Humanities Education, Colleges & Universities, Community & Junior Colleges, Minority Education, Private Education (Precollege), Religious Education, Secondary Education (Public), Student Aid

Health: Cancer, Children's Health/Hospitals, Clinics/Medical Centers, Emergency/Ambulance Services, Eyes/Blindness, Health Organizations, Heart, Hospices, Hospitals, Medical Research, Prenatal Health Issues, Public Health, Single-Disease Health Associations, Transplant Networks/Donor Banks

Religion: Churches, Churches, Religion-General, Jewish Causes, Ministries, Missionary Activities (Domestic), Religious Organizations, Religious Welfare, Synagogues/Temples

Science: Scientific Centers & Institutes

Social Services: Community Service Organizations, Crime Prevention, Day Care, Emergency Relief, Family Planning, Food/Clothing Distribution, Recreation & Athletics, Scouts, United Funds/United Ways, Youth Organizations

Application Procedures

Initial Contact: Send a brief letter of inquiry with a complete explanation of purpose of funds sought and a full description of the applicant.

Deadlines: July 1.

Foundation Officials

Louis Berkman: president, trustee B Canton, OH 1909. PRIM CORP EMPL chairman, president, chief executive officer, treasurer, director: Louis Berkman Co. CORP AFFIL president: Scott Lumber; president: Swenson Spreader; president: Meyer Products; president: Orrville Products; president, director: Follansbee Steel Corp.; president: IDL Supplies; chairman: Ampco-Pittsburgh Corp.; president: Dover Parkersburg.

John Koren: secretary, trustee

Robert Arthur Paul: vice president, assistant secretary, assistant treasurer, trustee B New York, NY 1937. ED Cornell University AB (1959); Harvard University JD (1962); Harvard University MBA (1964). PRIM CORP EMPL president, chief executive officer, director: Ampco-Pittsburgh Corp. CORP AFFIL partner: Romar Trading Co.; partner: National City Corp.; executive vice president, assistant secretary, director, trustee: Louis Berkman Co. NONPR AFFIL member: Massachusetts Bar Association; trustee: Presbyterian University Hospital; trustee: Cornell University; member: American Bar Association. CLUB AFFIL Pittsburgh Athletic Association; Harvard Club; Concordia Club; Duquesne Club.

Linda Pirkle: assistant secretary

Grants Analysis

Disclosure Period: calendar year ending 2001

Total Grants: $328,928*

Number of Grants: 43

Average Grant: $2,754*

Highest Grant: $100,000

Lowest Grant: $25

Typical Range: $1,000 to $5,000

*Note: Giving excludes scholarships. Average grant figure excludes three highest grants ($210,498).

Recent Grants

Note: Grants derived from 2001 Form 990.

General

100,000	Cornell University, Akron, OH
60,498	Franciscan University, Steubenville, OH
50,000	Old Fort Steuben Project, Old Fort, OH -- amphitheater project
25,000	West Liberty State College, Wheeling, WV -- advancement fund
20,000	Rodef Shalom Congregation Capital Campaign, Pittsburgh, PA
12,500	American Friends of Union of Progressive Jews in Germany, Austria and Switzerland, Pittsburgh, PA
10,000	Steubenville Jewish Community Council, Steubenville, OH
5,000	Oglebay Park Good Zoo -- education program
5,000	Rodef Shalom Congregation Capital Campaign, Pittsburgh, PA -- Jane Berkman Library Fund
5,000	Rodef Shalom Congregation Capital Campaign, Pittsburgh, PA -- support Sandra W. Berkman Library Fund

ARNOLD BERNHARD FOUNDATION

Giving Contact

Jean B. Buttner, President
220 East 42nd Street, 6th Floor
New York, NY 10017-5806
Phone: (212)907-1620
Fax: (212)226-3935

Description

Founded: 1976
EIN: 136100457
Organization Type: Private Foundation
Giving Locations: CT; NY: nationally.
Grant Types: General Support, Scholarship.

Donor Information

Founder: The foundation was founded by the Arnold Bernhard Charitable Annuity Trust I and the Arnold Bernhard Charitable Annuity Trust II.

Financial Summary

Total Giving: $461,470 (2001); $815,300 (2000); $825,000 (1999)

Giving Analysis: Giving for 2001 includes: foundation gifts to individuals ($10,000) 2000: foundation fellowships ($400,000)

Assets: $8,437,378 (2001); $9,918,475 (2000); $11,237,527 (1999)

Gifts Received: $75,000 (2001); $86,124 (2000); $447,739 (1999). Note: In 2001, contributions were received from Stanford Business School. In 2000, contributions were received from Janet K. Bernhard Charitable Annuity Trusts I and II. In 1999, contributions were received from Arnold Bernhard Charitable Annuity Trust II.

Typical Recipients

Arts & Humanities: Libraries, Opera, Public Broadcasting

Civic & Public Affairs: Economic Development, Employment/Job Training, Civic & Public Affairs-General, Safety

Education: Business Education, Colleges & Universities, Student Aid

Environment: Air/Water Quality, Environment-General

Health: Clinics/Medical Centers, Emergency/Ambulance Services, Hospitals, Medical Research, Single-Disease Health Associations

Religion: Churches, Religious Welfare

Social Services: Domestic Violence, Food/Clothing Distribution, Recreation & Athletics, Youth Organizations

Application Procedures

Initial Contact: Send a brief letter of inquiry.

Deadlines: None.

Foundation Officials

Howard A. Brecher: vice president, director

Jean Bernhard Buttner: president, director B New Rochelle, NY 1934. ED Vassar College BA (1957); Harvard University (1958). PRIM CORP EMPL chairman, chief executive officer, president, director: Value Line. CORP AFFIL chairman, president, chief executive officer, chief operating officer, director: Arnold Bernhard & Co.; chairman, director: Value Line Fund. NONPR AFFIL member visitation committee: Harvard University Business School; trustee: Williams College.

Grants Analysis

Disclosure Period: calendar year ending 2001

Total Grants: $451,470*

Number of Grants: 15

Average Grant: $25,105*

Highest Grant: $100,000

Lowest Grant: $250

Typical Range: $1,000 to $50,000

*Note: Giving excludes gifts to individuals. Average grant excludes highest grant.

Recent Grants

Note: Grants derived from 2000 Form 990.

Library-Related

100,000	Westport Public Library, Westport, CT

General

400,000	Williams College, Williamstown, MA
100,000	New York Presbyterian Hospital, New York, NY
60,000	Quinnipiac College, Hamden, CT
50,000	Colby College, Waterville, MA
40,000	Unitarian Church, Westport, CT
25,000	Skidmore College, Saratoga Springs, NY
15,000	Westport Police Athletic League, Westport, CT
10,000	Girls Incorporated, New York, NY
5,000	Salvation Army of Greater New York, New York, NY
5,000	Vassar College, Poughkeepsie, NY

GRACE AND FRANKLIN BERNSEN FOUNDATION

Giving Contact

Sandra L. Griffin, Administrator
15 West 6th St., Suite 1308
Tulsa, OK 74119-5407
Phone: (918)584-4711
Fax: (918)584-4713
E-mail: info@bernsen.org
Web: http://www.bernsen.org

Alternate Contact
E-mail: Gfbernsen@aol.com

Description
Founded: 1985
EIN: 237009414
Organization Type: Family Foundation
Giving Locations: OK: Tulsa
Grant Types: Capital, Emergency, Matching, Multiyear/Continuing Support, Operating Expenses, Project, Seed Money.

Donor Information
Founder: Established in 1968 by the late Grace Bernsen and the late Franklin Bernsen .

Financial Summary
Total Giving: $1,517,604 (fiscal year ending 0, 2001); $1,747,849 (fiscal 2000); $1,563,375 (fiscal 1999)
Giving Analysis: Giving for fiscal 2000 includes: foundation grants to United Way ($10,000); fiscal 1999: foundation grants to United Way ($10,000) fiscal 1998: foundation grants to United Way ($10,000).
Assets: $30,863,180 (fiscal 2001); $39,505,882 (fiscal 2000); $36,991,640 (fiscal 1999)

Typical Recipients
Arts & Humanities: Arts Associations & Councils, Arts Centers, Ballet, Community Arts, Dance, Historic Preservation, History & Archaeology, Literary Arts, Museums/Galleries, Music, Opera, Performing Arts, Theater
Civic & Public Affairs: Botanical Gardens/Parks, Business/Free Enterprise, Clubs, Community Foundations, Civic & Public Affairs-General, Nonprofit Management, Philanthropic Organizations, Professional & Trade Associations, Public Policy, Urban & Community Affairs, Women's Affairs, Zoos/Aquariums
Education: Business Education, Colleges & Universities, Community & Junior Colleges, Education Funds, Education-General, International Studies, Literacy, Medical Education, Preschool Education, Preschool Education, Private Education (Precollege), Public Education (Precollege), Science/Mathematics Education, Special Education
Environment: Energy, Resource Conservation
Health: Children's Health/Hospitals, Clinics/Medical Centers, Emergency/Ambulance Services, Health Organizations, Heart, Hospices, Hospitals, Medical Rehabilitation, Medical Research, Mental Health, Multiple Sclerosis, Nursing Services, Prenatal Health Issues, Public Health, Respiratory, Single-Disease Health Associations, Speech & Hearing
International: International Affairs, International Relations
Religion: Churches, Ministries, Religious Organizations, Religious Welfare, Seminaries, Social/Policy Issues
Science: Scientific Research
Social Services: Animal Protection, At-Risk Youth, Big Brother/Big Sister, Camps, Child Abuse, Child Welfare, Community Service Organizations, Crime Prevention, Day Care, Delinquency & Criminal Rehabilitation, Domestic Violence, Family Services, Food/Clothing Distribution, People with Disabilities, Scouts, Senior Services, Sexual Abuse, Shelters/Homelessness, Special Olympics, Substance Abuse, United Funds/United Ways, Volunteer Services, YMCA/YWCA/YMHA/YWHA, Youth Organizations

Application Procedures
Initial Contact: Submit a brief letter of inquiry.
Application Requirements: Applications should be submitted in writing by the chief executive officer of the applicant organization. In a summary letter, provide a brief description of the program in need of funding, including an explanation of its importance and clear statement of its goal. Cite the financial need, including the other sources of funds, if any. Attachments should include a list of current officers and board of trustees, documentation of tax-exempt status, most recent audited financial statement, current year-to-date financial statements and budget, project budget and plans to support the project after grant period.
Deadlines: None.
Review Process: Applications are considered at monthly or bi-monthly board meetings. Site visits are often scheduled by the board; proposals are typically processed within two months.
Decision Notification: Decisions on applications are reported in writing or by personal visit.
Notes: There are no set deadlines, but the foundation does request that applications be received by the 12th of each month before the next scheduled board meeting.

Restrictions
The foundation's trustees generally consider funding requests from Tulsa area charitable organizations for projects that will provide a defined benefit, such as capital projects, building programs, or specific program needs of the organizations. The trustees generally only make gifts that will be meaningful in amount and benefit to the recipient. The foundation discourages applications for general support, debt, or continuing support for the same program, although a single grant may extend over a period of several years. No grants are made to elementary or secondary schools, unless the programs are for at-risk, handicapped, or learning disabled children, or if they are innovative and apply to all schools in the system; to individuals; or for the benefit of specific individuals.

Additional Information
Publications: Annual Report; An Introduction to the Grace and Franklin Bernsen Foundation (Brochure); Guidelines

Foundation Officials
Sandra L. Griffin: admin
J. Warren Jackman: trustee
Donald F. Marlar: trustee PRIM CORP EMPL president: Jackman, Pray, Walker.
Donald E. Pray: trustee B Tulsa, OK 1932. ED University of Tulsa BS (1955); University of Oklahoma LLB (1963). PRIM CORP EMPL counsel: Jackman, Pray, Walker. NONPR AFFIL president: Tulsa Estate Planning Forum; president: Tulsa Mineral Lawyers Sect; director: Saint Johns Medical Center; director: Tulsa Ballet Theater; fellow: American Bar Foundation; director: Philbrook Art Museum; member: American Bar Association. CLUB AFFIL president: Summit Club.
John D. Strong, Jr.: trustee
W. Bland Williamson: secretary, trustee PRIM CORP EMPL secretary, director: Lasmo America Ltd.

Grants Analysis
Total Grants: $1,517,604
Number of Grants: 42
Average Grant: $30,917*
Highest Grant: $250,000
Typical Range: $5,000 to $50,000
*Note: Average grant figure excludes highest grant.

Recent Grants
Note: Grants derived from fiscal 2001 Form 990.

General
260,000	University of Tulsa, Tulsa, OK -- provide funds for a student health facility and programs
250,000	Camp Loughridge, Tulsa, OK -- provide funds for capital campaign
100,000	Family and Children Services, Tulsa, OK -- provide funds for capital campaign
100,000	Oklahoma Centennial Commemoration Fund Inc., Oklahoma City, OK -- provide funds for capital dome project
100,000	Tulsa Zoo Friends, Tulsa, OK -- provide funds for capital campaign
90,000	Gilbert and Sullivan Society, Tulsa, OK -- provide funds for programs
80,000	First Presbyterian Church, Tulsa, OK -- provide funds for Children Program and equipment
53,322	Brush Creek Ranch, Jenks, OK -- provide funds for renovations
50,000	Phillips Theological Seminary, Tulsa, OK -- provide funds for capital needs
45,000	Oklahoma State University College of Osteopathic Medicine, Oklahoma City, OK -- provide funds to purchase medical equipment

LOREN M. BERRY FOUNDATION

Giving Contact
William T. Lincoln, Treasurer & Trustee
3055 Kettering Boulevard, Suite 418
Dayton, OH 45439
Phone: (937)293-0398

Description
Founded: 1960
EIN: 316026144
Organization Type: Family Foundation
Giving Locations: OH: Dayton
Grant Types: General Support.

Donor Information
Founder: Established in 1960 by the late Loren M. Berry , who developed a predecessor to today's telephone yellow pages. Berry, who was one of the largest telephone directory publishers in the country, died in 1980.

Financial Summary
Total Giving: $900,000 (2002 approx); $848,100 (2001); $858,304 (2000)
Giving Analysis: Giving for 2001 includes: foundation scholarships ($25,000); 2000: foundation scholarships ($38,070) 1997: foundation scholarships ($14,211)
Assets: $16,163,977 (2001); $16,608,991 (2000); $17,844,127 (1998)

Typical Recipients
Arts & Humanities: Arts Associations & Councils, Arts Centers, Arts Institutes, Community Arts, History & Archaeology, Libraries, Museums/Galleries, Music, Public Broadcasting, Theater
Civic & Public Affairs: Botanical Gardens/Parks, Business/Free Enterprise, Ethnic Organizations, Civic & Public Affairs-General, Philanthropic Organizations, Public Policy, Urban & Community Affairs, Women's Affairs
Education: Business Education, Colleges & Universities, Community & Junior Colleges, Education Funds, Environmental Education, Education-General, Literacy, Private Education (Precollege), Public Education (Precollege), Social Sciences Education, Student Aid
Environment: Air/Water Quality, Environment-General, Wildlife Protection
Health: Alzheimers Disease, Cancer, Children's Health/Hospitals, Clinics/Medical Centers, Emergency/Ambulance Services, Eyes/Blindness, Geriatric Health, Health Organizations, Heart, Hospices, Hospitals, Medical Rehabilitation, Single-Disease Health Associations, Transplant Networks/Donor Banks
International: Human Rights, International Affairs
Religion: Churches, Religious Welfare
Science: Science Museums

Social Services: Animal Protection, At-Risk Youth, Big Brother/Big Sister, Camps, Child Welfare, Community Centers, Community Service Organizations, Crime Prevention, Domestic Violence, Family Planning, Family Services, Food/Clothing Distribution, Homes, People with Disabilities, Recreation & Athletics, Scouts, United Funds/United Ways, YMCA/YWCA/YMHA/YWHA, Youth Organizations

Application Procedures
Initial Contact: Applicants should send a proposal in letter form.
Application Requirements: The letter should include the organization's charitable activities, its history, needs, and goals.
Deadlines: None. Requests may be submitted at any time.
Review Process: Letters are reviewed by the board of trustees.

Restrictions
The foundation does not support individuals.

Foundation Officials
Charles D. Berry: trustee
David L. Berry: trustee B 1927. PRIM CORP EMPL president: Berry & Berry Inc. CORP AFFIL president: Madera Valley Inn Inc.; president: Westgate Building Materials; president: Berry Construction; president: Best Western.
George W. Berry: trustee
John William Berry, Jr.: president, trustee B 1947. PRIM CORP EMPL president, chief executive officer, director: L.M. Berry & Co. CORP AFFIL chief executive officer: Berry Investments Inc.; chairman, director: AcuSport Corp.; chairman: Berry Braiding Inc. NONPR AFFIL director: Air Force Museum Foundation.
Martha B. Fraim: trustee
William L. Fraim: trustee B Santa Monica, CA 1951. ED Occidental College (1974). PRIM CORP EMPL president, director: AcuSport Corp. CORP AFFIL member: National Association Sporting Goods Wholesalers; president, director: Go Sportsmens Supply Inc.; president, director: Midwest Warehouse. NONPR AFFIL member: Benevolent Protectorate Elks.
Elizabeth B. Gray: trustee
Leland W. Henry: trustee
William T. Lincoln: treasurer, trustee B 1943. PRIM CORP EMPL president, director: Berry Investments Inc. ADD CORP EMPL secretary, director: AcuSport Corp.; treasurer: Berry Braiding Inc.; director: Go Sportsmens Supply Inc.
James O. Payne: trustee B 1937. ED University of Dayton; Xavier University MBA. PRIM CORP EMPL executive vice president financial & administration: L.M. Berry & Co. CORP AFFIL treasurer, director: Microwave Sensors Inc.; secretary: Berry Investments Inc. NONPR AFFIL director: Design Forum Inc.

Grants Analysis
Disclosure Period: calendar year ending 2001
Total Grants: $823,100*
Number of Grants: 69
Average Grant: $11,929
Highest Grant: $60,000
Lowest Grant: $150
Typical Range: $5,000 to $20,000
*Note: Giving excludes scholarships.

Recent Grants
Note: Grants derived from 2001 Form 990.

General
60,000	Boonshoft Museum of Discovery, Dayton, OH
60,000	Boonshoft Museum of Discovery, Dayton, OH
50,000	Second & Main Ltd., Dayton, OH
40,000	Cedarville College, Cedarville, OH
40,000	Cox Arboretum, Dayton, OH
37,000	Jefferson Township Local Schools, Dayton, OH
35,000	St. Joseph's Children's Center, Torrington, WY
35,000	United Rehabilitation Services, Dayton, OH
30,000	Franciscan at St. Leonard's, Dayton, OH
25,000	2003 Fund Committee, Dayton, OH

BERTHA FOUNDATION

Giving Contact
Douglas A. Stroud, Vice President & Director
PO Box 1110
Graham, TX 76450
Phone: (940)549-1400

Description
Founded: 1967
EIN: 756050023
Organization Type: Private Foundation
Giving Locations: TX: Young County
Grant Types: General Support, Operating Expenses, Scholarship.

Donor Information
Founder: E. Bruce Street, M. Boyd Street Foundation

Financial Summary
Total Giving: $160,474 (2000); $432,192 (1999); $627,844 (1998)
Giving Analysis: Giving for 2000 includes: foundation scholarships ($35,560)
Assets: $10,395,372 (2000); $10,226,191 (1999); $9,619,360 (1998)
Gifts Received: $8,855 (1999); $41,600 (1998); $1,787,085 (1996). Note: In 1998, contributions were received from E. Bruce Street Charitable Trust ($20,800) and M. Boyd Street Charitable Trust ($20,800). In 1996, contributions were received from E. Bruce Street ($814,305), M. Boyd Street ($931,100), E. Bruce Street Charitable Trust ($20,800), and M. Boyd Street Charitable Trust ($20,800).

Typical Recipients
Arts & Humanities: Arts Associations & Councils, Arts Festivals, Libraries, Literary Arts, Museums/Galleries, Music
Civic & Public Affairs: Botanical Gardens/Parks, Chambers of Commerce, Clubs, Civic & Public Affairs-General, Municipalities/Towns, Rural Affairs, Safety
Education: Business-School Partnerships, Colleges & Universities, Education Funds, Faculty Development, Literacy, Medical Education, Public Education (Precollege), Science/Mathematics Education, Student Aid
Health: Health Organizations, Hospices, Hospitals, Mental Health, Preventive Medicine/Wellness Organizations, Public Health
Religion: Jewish Causes, Religious Organizations
Science: Science Exhibits & Fairs
Social Services: Community Service Organizations, Counseling, Family Services, Scouts, Senior Services, Social Services-General, Substance Abuse, Youth Organizations

Application Procedures
Initial Contact: Send a brief letter of inquiry.
Application Requirements: Include name, address, telephone number, and purpose of funds sought.
Deadlines: None.

Foundation Officials
S. Estess: director
J. R. Montgomery: secretary, director
Alice Ann Street: president, director
E. Bruce Street: director
M. Boyd Street, Jr.: director
M. Boyd Street: director
Douglas A. Stroud: vice president, director

Grants Analysis
Disclosure Period: calendar year ending 2000
Total Grants: $124,914*
Number of Grants: 19
Average Grant: $5,273*
Highest Grant: $30,000
Lowest Grant: $120
Typical Range: $1,000 to $10,000
*Note: Giving excludes scholarships. Average grant excludes highest grant.

Recent Grants
Note: Grants derived from 1999 Form 990.

General
100,000	Old Post Office Museum, Graham, TX -- for construction project
86,651	Graham Civic Services, Graham, TX -- for renovation of American Legion Building
60,970	Ranger Nursing School, Graham, TX -- for nursing school
29,486	Graham ISD, Graham, TX -- for the purchase of Waterford Reading program
25,000	City of Graham, Graham, TX -- for downtown revitalization project
20,975	Graham ISD, Graham, TX -- for SAT/ACT, parents as teachers, accelerator math pilot program and computer lab
10,221	Graham General Hospital, Graham, TX -- for rural scholar recognition program
10,000	Graham Hospital Foundation, Graham, TX -- for construction project
7,658	City of Graham, Graham, TX -- for maintenance and landscaping at library
5,300	Graham Area Crisis Center, Graham, TX -- to replace air conditioning units

BERWIND GROUP

Company Headquarters
3000 Centre Square West
1500 Market Street
Philadelphia, PA 19102
Phone: (215)563-2800
Fax: (215)563-8347
Web: http://www.berwind.com

Company Description
Founded: 1874
Employees: 4,800 (1998)
SIC(s): 2834 Pharmaceutical Preparations, 2865 Cyclic Crudes & Intermediates, 3441 Fabricated Structural Metal, 6519 Real Property Lessors Nec.

Operating Locations
Berwind Corp. (KY--Kimper, Pikeville; MA--Ashland, Sharon; MI--Port Huron; NJ--Neptune; NY--Amherst; OR--Portland; PA--King of Prussia, Philadelphia, Warminster, West Point; TN--LaVergne; WV--Charleston)

Nonmonetary Support
Type: Donated Equipment

Giving Contact
Mary LaRue, Chairperson, Contributions Committee
3000 Centre Square West
1500 Market Street
Philadelphia, PA 19102

Phone: (215)563-2800
Fax: (215)563-1493
E-mail: mlarue@berwind.com
Web: http://www.berwind.com

Description

Organization Type: Corporate Giving Program
Giving Locations: headquarters area only.
Grant Types: Emergency, Employee Matching Gifts, General Support, Matching, Project.
Note: Employee matching gift ratio: 1 to 1 up to $1,000, for education only. $5,000 maximum per employee per year.

Financial Summary

Total Giving: $500,000 (2003 approx); $500,000 (2002); $1,000,000 (2001). Note: Contributes through corporate direct giving program only.

Typical Recipients

Arts & Humanities: Arts Institutes, Arts & Humanities-General, Libraries, Museums/Galleries, Music, Performing Arts, Public Broadcasting, Theater
Civic & Public Affairs: Civic & Public Affairs-General, Women's Affairs, Zoos/Aquariums
Education: Business Education, Colleges & Universities, Education-General, Legal Education, Minority Education
Environment: Environment-General
Health: Health-General, Hospitals
Science: Scientific Centers & Institutes
Social Services: Child Welfare, Community Centers, Delinquency & Criminal Rehabilitation, Family Planning, Food/Clothing Distribution, Senior Services, United Funds/United Ways

Application Procedures

Initial Contact: Send a letter of inquiry.
Application Requirements: Include a description of organization, amount requested, purpose of funds sought, list of organizations which support the work done by your organization, list of board of directors, and IRS 501(c)(3) tax-determination letter.
Deadlines: By November for proceeding year.

Restrictions

Does not support political or lobbying groups.

Grants Analysis

Typical Range: $1,000 to $2,500

BESSER FOUNDATION

Giving Contact

J. Richard Wilson, President
123 N. 2nd Ave.
Alpena, MI 49707-2801
Phone: (989)354-4722
Fax: (989)354-8099
E-mail: bessfdtn@freeway.net

Description

Founded: 1944
EIN: 386071938
Organization Type: Private Foundation
Giving Locations: MI: Alpena
Grant Types: Challenge, General Support, Multiyear/Continuing Support, Operating Expenses.

Donor Information

Founder: the late J. H. Besser, Besser Co.

Financial Summary

Total Giving: $819,649 (2001); $1,768,496 (2000); $802,665 (1999)
Giving Analysis: Giving for 2001 includes: foundation grants to United Way ($42,000); 2000: foundation grants to United Way ($41,000); foundation matching

gifts ($94,000) 1999: foundation grants to United Way ($40,000)
Assets: $16,883,920 (2001); $18,254,098 (2000); $20,024,714 (1999)

Typical Recipients

Arts & Humanities: Arts Associations & Councils, Arts Institutes, Libraries, Museums/Galleries, Theater
Civic & Public Affairs: Community Foundations, Civic & Public Affairs-General, Housing, Legal Aid, Nonprofit Management, Philanthropic Organizations, Professional & Trade Associations, Safety
Education: Business Education, Colleges & Universities, Community & Junior Colleges, Engineering/Technological Education, Education-General, Public Education (Precollege), School Volunteerism, Science/Mathematics Education, Secondary Education (Public), Student Aid, Vocational & Technical Education
Environment: Environment-General
Health: Clinics/Medical Centers, Health-General, Health Organizations, Hospices, Hospitals, Medical Rehabilitation, Mental Health
International: Health Care/Hospitals, International Relief Efforts, Missionary/Religious Activities
Religion: Churches, Religious Organizations, Religious Welfare
Science: Scientific Centers & Institutes
Social Services: At-Risk Youth, Big Brother/Big Sister, Camps, Child Welfare, Community Service Organizations, Domestic Violence, Family Services, Food/Clothing Distribution, Recreation & Athletics, Shelters/Homelessness, Substance Abuse, United Funds/United Ways, Volunteer Services, Youth Organizations

Application Procedures

Initial Contact: Submit a written request.
Application Requirements: Provide a detailed prospectus of the project, including the project name, purpose and historical background of the problem to be addressed; proposal objective, plan of development, expected results, and method of evaluation; how and by whom the expected results will be used, and how results might lead to new methods, changes in practice, service, etc.; detailed information concerning personnel involved with the project; complete financial budget; projected calendar, including stages and the points and which partial results and progress reports will be available; whether similar projects have been undertaken previously; whether support has been or is being requested of other foundations; and the name of the organization sponsoring or proposing the project and a copy of its letter of tax-exempt status.
Deadlines: The end of the first month of each calendar quarter.

Restrictions

Does not support individuals, endowment funds, meeting or conference expenses, or travel expenses. The foundation does not generally consider grant requests from organizations located outside of Alpena, MI.

Additional Information

Publications: Annual Report (including Application Guidelines)

Foundation Officials

Gary Dawley: trustee
Patricia Gardner: trustee
James Charles Park: trustee B Alpena MI 1937. ED University of Michigan (1959); University of Michigan (1961). PRIM CORP EMPL chairman, president, chief executive officer, director: Besser Co. CORP AFFIL chairman: Lithibar Corp.; chairman: Proneq Industries Montreal; chairman: Besser Canada Ltd.; director: Besser Appco. CLUB AFFIL Rotary Club.
Carl F. Reitz: secretary
Harold A. Ruemenapp: trustee
J. Richard Wilson: president

Grants Analysis

Disclosure Period: calendar year ending 2001
Total Grants: $777,649*
Number of Grants: 48
Average Grant: $9,949*
Highest Grant: $220,000
Typical Range: $1,000 to $25,000
*Note: Giving excludes United Way. Average grant excludes two highest grants ($320,000).

Recent Grants

Note: Grants derived from 2001 Form 990.

General

220,000	Jesse Besser Museum, Alpena, MI -- for operating expenses
100,000	Alpena Community College, Alpena, MI -- World Center for Concrete Technology
50,000	Jesse Besser Museum, Alpena, MI -- operating support
42,000	United Way of Alpena County, Alpena, MI -- for administrative expenses
40,000	Child and Family Services, Alpena, MI -- operating expenses
35,000	Sunrise Mission, Alpena, MI -- shelter renovation
26,500	Africare, Washington, DC -- Baroueli School Project
25,000	Boys and Girls Club of Alpena, Alpena, MI -- operating expenses
25,000	Salvation Army, Alpena, MI -- relocation of thrift store
25,000	Thunder Bay Soccer Association, Alpena, MI -- new soccer fields

BURTON G. BETTINGEN CORP.

Giving Contact

Patricia A. Brown, Executive Director
9777 Wilshire Boulevard, Suite 615
Beverly Hills, CA 90212
Phone: (310)276-4115
Fax: (310)276-4693
E-mail: burtonbet@aol.com

Description

Founded: 1984
EIN: 953942826
Organization Type: General Purpose Foundation
Giving Locations: CA: Los Angeles
Grant Types: Capital, Endowment, General Support, Project, Research.

Donor Information

Founder: Established in 1984 by the late Burton G. Bettingen .

Financial Summary

Total Giving: $1,867,620 (fiscal year ending September 30, 2001); $2,760,300 (fiscal 2000 approx); $3,594,495 (fiscal 1999)
Giving Analysis: Giving for fiscal 1999 includes: foundation scholarships ($120,000)
Assets: $15,718,032 (fiscal 2001); $13,995,773 (fiscal 2000 approx); $15,646,490 (fiscal 1999)
Gifts Received: $1,482,145 (fiscal 1999); $1,482,144 (fiscal 1998); $1,482,145 (fiscal 1997). Note: In Fiscal 1998, contributions were received from the Burton G. Bettingen Charitable Lead Annuity Trust.

Typical Recipients

Arts & Humanities: Libraries, Museums/Galleries, Music, Public Broadcasting
Civic & Public Affairs: Botanical Gardens/Parks, Business/Free Enterprise, Community Foundations,

Economic Policy, Hispanic Affairs, Law & Justice, Legal Aid, Native American Affairs, Nonprofit Management, Philanthropic Organizations, Public Policy, Urban & Community Affairs

Education: Afterschool/Enrichment Programs, Arts/Humanities Education, Colleges & Universities, Community & Junior Colleges, Environmental Education, Faculty Development, Education-General, Medical Education, Minority Education, Private Education (Precollege), Public Education (Precollege), Religious Education, Science/Mathematics Education, Secondary Education (Private), Secondary Education (Public), Special Education, Student Aid

Environment: Environment-General, Resource Conservation

Health: AIDS/HIV, Alzheimers Disease, Cancer, Children's Health/Hospitals, Emergency/Ambulance Services, Health Policy/Cost Containment, Health Organizations, Home-Care Services, Hospitals, Hospitals (University Affiliated), Long-Term Care, Medical Research, Mental Health, Preventive Medicine/Wellness Organizations, Research/Studies Institutes, Respiratory, Single-Disease Health Associations

International: Health Care/Hospitals, International Environmental Issues, International Relief Efforts

Religion: Dioceses, Religious Organizations, Religious Welfare

Social Services: At-Risk Youth, Camps, Child Abuse, Child Welfare, Community Service Organizations, Counseling, Crime Prevention, Day Care, Family Planning, Family Services, Homes, People with Disabilities, Sexual Abuse, Shelters/Homelessness, Substance Abuse, YMCA/YWCA/YMHA/YWHA, Youth Organizations

Application Procedures

Initial Contact: Letters of inquiry stating the applicant's background, goals, and objectives and its specific need for funding are welcome; however, the corporation does not generally award unsolicited grant requests.

Deadlines: None.

Notes: Consult the corporation's Grant Policy and Application Guidelines for further information.

Restrictions

The corporation does not award grants to individuals, or to organizations that are themselves grantmaking bodies. In addition, the corporation does not support general fundraising events, dinners, or mass mailings.

Additional Information

Publications: Application Guidelines

Foundation Officials

Patricia A. Brown: secretary, treasurer, executive director, director PRIM CORP EMPL administration director, director: Burton G. Bettingen Corp.

Regina Covitt: assistant treasurer

Sandra G. Nowicki: president, director PRIM CORP EMPL president, director: Burton G. Bettingen Corp.

Stuart Paul Tobisman: vice president, director, counsel B Detroit, MI 1942. ED University of California, Los Angeles BA (1966); University of California, Los Angeles JD (1969). PRIM CORP EMPL partner: O'Melveny & Myers. CORP AFFIL director: Burton G. Bettingen Corp. NONPR AFFIL Order Coif; member: Phi Beta Kappa; fellow: American College Trust & Estate Counsel.

Gyte Van Zyl: vice president, director

Jane Van Zyl: director

Grants Analysis

Disclosure Period: fiscal year ending September 30, 1999

Total Grants: $3,474,495*

Number of Grants: 38

Average Grant: $91,434

Highest Grant: $250,000

Typical Range: $10,000 to $100,000

*Note: Giving excludes scholarships.

Recent Grants

Note: Grants derived from fiscal 2000 Form 990.

General

700,000	Children's Hospital of Los Angeles, Los Angeles, CA
500,000	Hamburger Home (AVIVA), Los Angeles, CA
200,000	Catholic Charities, Los Angeles, CA
200,000	St. John's Hospital and Health Care Center, Santa Monica, CA
120,000	United Negro College Fund, Fairfax, VA
110,000	Public Counsel Center, Los Angeles, CA
100,000	Catholic Charities, Los Angeles, CA
100,000	Children's Bureau, Los Angeles, CA
100,000	Children's Defense Fund, Oakland, CA
100,000	Children's Defense Fund, Washington, DC

BETTS INDUSTRIES

Company Headquarters

1800 Pennsylvania Ave. W.
Warren, PA 16365

Company Description

Employees: 220

SIC(s): 3300 Primary Metal Industries, 3400 Fabricated Metal Products, 3600 Electronic & Other Electrical Equipment, 3700 Transportation Equipment.

Betts Foundation

Giving Contact

Richard T. Betts, Trustee
Betts Foundation
1800 Pennsylvania Avenue W.
Box 88
Warren, PA 16365
Phone: (814)723-1250

Description

EIN: 256035169

Organization Type: Corporate Foundation

Giving Locations: PA: Warren County

Grant Types: General Support.

Financial Summary

Total Giving: $181,281 (2001); $206,616 (2000); $141,344 (1999). Note: 1996 Giving includes scholarship (21,800).

Giving Analysis: Giving for 2001 includes: foundation scholarships ($30,738); 2000: foundation scholarships ($23,500); foundation ($183,116); 1999: foundation grants to United Way ($13,290); foundation scholarships ($25,000); foundation ($103,054);

Assets: $3,120,062 (2001); $3,537,328 (2000); $3,955,098 (1999)

Gifts Received: $25,000 (2001); $75,000 (2000); $225,000 (1999). Note: Contributions were received from Betts Industries.

Typical Recipients

Arts & Humanities: Arts Associations & Councils, Libraries, Music, Performing Arts

Civic & Public Affairs: Botanical Gardens/Parks, Business/Free Enterprise, Economic Development, Economic Policy, Civic & Public Affairs-General, Municipalities/Towns, Parades/Festivals, Public Policy, Safety, Urban & Community Affairs, Women's Affairs

Education: Business Education, Colleges & Universities, Community & Junior Colleges, Economic Education, Education Funds, Engineering/Technological Education, Public Education (Precollege), Secondary Education (Private), Secondary Education (Public), Student Aid, Vocational & Technical Education

Health: Emergency/Ambulance Services, Health Organizations, Hospices

Religion: Churches, Religious Welfare

Social Services: Animal Protection, Camps, Child Welfare, Community Service Organizations, Day Care, Delinquency & Criminal Rehabilitation, Family Services, Homes, Recreation & Athletics, Scouts, Senior Services, Social Services-General, Substance Abuse, United Funds/United Ways, YMCA/YWCA/YMHA/YWHA, Youth Organizations

Application Procedures

Initial Contact: Telephone the foundation or send a brief letter describing program.

Deadlines: None.

Restrictions

Preference is given to educational studies for residents of Warren County, Pennsylvania.

Additional Information

Provides scholarships for higher education.

Corporate Officials

Richard T. Betts: chairman, president, director PRIM CORP EMPL chairman, president, director: Betts Industries.

Foundation Officials

C. R. Betts: trustee

I. R. Betts: trustee

R. E. Betts: trustee

Richard T. Betts: trustee (see above)

M. D. Hedges: trustee

Grants Analysis

Disclosure Period: calendar year ending 2001

Total Grants: $150,543*

Number of Grants: 20

Average Grant: $6,318*

Highest Grant: $30,500

Lowest Grant: $40

Typical Range: $1,500 to $10,000

*Note: Giving excludes scholarships. Average grant figure excludes highest grant.

Recent Grants

Note: Grants derived from 2000 Form 990.

General

50,000	Warren Sports Boosters Inc, Warren, PA
34,574	City of Warren, Warren, PA
25,500	Salvation Army, Warren, PA
20,000	Warren County YMCA, Warren, PA
13,825	United Fund of Warren County, Warren, PA
12,500	Rouse Home, Youngsville, PA
5,000	Warren Senior Center, Warren, PA
3,500	Jamestown Business College, Jamestown, NY -- scholarship
3,500	Warren County Commissioners, Warren, PA
3,116	Warren County School District, North Warren, PA

FRANK STANLEY BEVERIDGE FOUNDATION, INC.

Giving Contact

Philip Caswell, President
301 Northeast 51st Street, Suite 1130
Boca Raton, FL 33431-4929
Phone: (561)241-8388
Fax: (561)241-8332
E-mail: administrator@beveridge.org
Web: http://www.beveridge.org

Description

Founded: 1947
EIN: 046032164
Organization Type: Family Foundation
Giving Locations: CA: Orange County; FL: Boca Raton; HI: Kauai County; MA: Hampden County, Hampshire County; NH; RI
Grant Types: Award, Capital, Emergency, Project, Research, Seed Money.

Donor Information

Founder: Established in 1947 in Massachusetts by the late Frank Stanley Beveridge , who was born in Canada on April 17, 1879. In March 1900, having traveled from Pembrooke Shores, near Yarmouth, Nova Scotia, he arrived at Mount Hermon School in Northfield, MA, with only a quarter. Following Mount Hermon School, Frank moved to upstate New York, married, and he and his wife, Theresa, had two daughters -- Evelyn and Ruth. Later, Mr. Beveridge joined the Fuller Brush Company in Hartford, CT, where he became director of sales.
In 1933, Beveridge founded Stanley Home Products, Inc. in Westfield, MA (Stanhome, Inc.), which now boasts annual sales of nearly $800 million.
In 1947, he founded the Stanley Park of Westfield, Inc., and the Frank Stanley Beveridge Foundation, a trust originally organized to provide funds for the park. Today, Stanley Park consists of over 200 acres of formal gardens, a carillon tower, trails, sports fields, and a substantial nature area. The park continues as the principal recipient of funds from the foundation.

Financial Summary

Total Giving: $1,833,809 (2001); $2,560,800 (2000); $1,634,812 (1998)
Giving Analysis: Giving for 1998 includes: foundation grants to United Way ($5,000)
Assets: $38,879,821 (2001); $56,724,973 (2000); $57,145,524 (1998)

Typical Recipients

Arts & Humanities: Arts Associations & Councils, Arts Centers, Arts Funds, Dance, Historic Preservation, Libraries, Literary Arts, Museums/Galleries, Music, Performing Arts, Public Broadcasting, Theater, Visual Arts
Civic & Public Affairs: African American Affairs, Botanical Gardens/Parks, Community Foundations, Economic Development, Civic & Public Affairs-General, Housing, Nonprofit Management, Philanthropic Organizations, Urban & Community Affairs, Women's Affairs, Zoos/Aquariums
Education: Arts/Humanities Education, Colleges & Universities, Education Associations, Education Funds, Education Reform, Faculty Development, Education-General, Medical Education, Preschool Education, Private Education (Precollege), Private Education (Precollege), Science/Mathematics Education, Secondary Education (Public), Special Education
Environment: Forestry, Environment-General, Resource Conservation, Watershed, Wildlife Protection
Health: Cancer, Clinics/Medical Centers, Diabetes, Emergency/Ambulance Services, Eyes/Blindness, Geriatric Health, Health Organizations, Hospices, Hospitals, Mental Health, Nursing Services, Public Health, Research/Studies Institutes, Single-Disease Health Associations
Religion: Churches, Dioceses, Ministries, Religious Organizations, Religious Welfare, Seminaries
Science: Science Museums
Social Services: Animal Protection, At-Risk Youth, Camps, Child Welfare, Community Centers, Community Service Organizations, Day Care, Emergency Relief, Family Services, Food/Clothing Distribution, People with Disabilities, Recreation & Athletics, Scouts, Senior Services, United Funds/United Ways, Volunteer Services, YMCA/YWCA/YMHA/YWHA, Youth Organizations

Application Procedures

Initial Contact: According to foundation, applications must be made through web site only.
Deadlines: February and August. Applications must be submitted no later than 5:00 p.m. on the first day of the month, two months prior to the next regularly scheduled meeting.
Review Process: Board of directors meets each April and October. Applicants are notified in writing of the action taken by the board relative to grant proposals usually within one month after board meetings.

Restrictions

The foundation usually does not support international affairs programs or foreign organizations or expenditures; member benefit organizations; collection management and preservation; endowments; organizations outside the approved geographic area; individuals, scholarships, professorships, and fellowships; employee matching gifts; operating expenses, except for research or start-up programs; faculty or staff development; budget deficits; program-related investment loans; income and management development; conferences and seminars; units of government; private educational institutions not attended by members of the Beveridge family; other private foundations excluding private operating foundations; federated drives and their foundations, including Catholic Charities, United Jewish Appeal, and United Way; chiefly tax-supported institutions and their foundations; or organizations that receive more than 50% of their operating revenues from taxes.
Any requests outside Hampden or Hampshire County, MA, require the support of one or more directors. Applicants should not solicit such support. The foundation will contact these applicants if interested, after initial proposals are received.

Additional Information

Publications: Annual Report; Guidelines; Application Form

Foundation Officials

Sarah Caswell Bartelt: director
John Beveridge Caswell: director B Hartford, CT 1938. ED Brown University BA (1960); Columbia University MBA (1961). PRIM CORP EMPL president: Omnia Group. CORP AFFIL director, trustee: Berkshire Life Insurance Co. NONPR AFFIL director, trustee: University Tampa.
Philip Caswell: president, director
Ward S. Caswell: director
Latimer B. Eddy: director
Alfred L. Griggs: director B 1940. PRIM CORP EMPL chief executive officer: A.L. Griggs Industries Inc. CORP AFFIL chief executive officer: Classic Foods Coffee Service; chief executive officer: Classic Foods Spring Water; chief executive officer: Classic Foods.
Carole S. Lenhart: treasurer
Ian Campbell Palmer: director
Joseph Beveridge Palmer: director
Richard A. Stebbins: director
Patsy Palmer Stecher: director
J. Thomas Touchton: director PRIM CORP EMPL managing partner: The Witt-Touchton Co. CORP AFFIL officer: Tampa Electric Co.; director: TECO Energy Inc.
David F. Woods: clerk, director B Baltimore, MA 1936. ED Loyola College BS (1964). PRIM CORP EMPL partner: Woods & Livingston Financial Group. CORP AFFIL chairman, director: Baystate Health System; agent: Massachusetts Mutual Life Insurance Co. NONPR AFFIL member: Massachusetts Association Life Underwriters; member: National Association Life Underwriters; member: Association Advanced Life Underwriting.

Grants Analysis

Disclosure Period: calendar year ending 2001
Total Grants: $1,833,809
Number of Grants: 63
Average Grant: $27,520*
Highest Grant: $100,000
Lowest Grant: $1,000
Typical Range: $10,000 to $50,000
*****Note:** Average grant figure excludes highest grant.

Recent Grants

Note: Grants derived from 2001 Form 990.

Library-Related
35,000   Company of the Redwood Library and Athenaeum, Newport, RI -- implementation consultant and sponsor exhibits

General
100,000   Babson College, Wellesley, MA -- class of 1961 fifty reunion gifts program
75,000   Charles River Association for Retarded Citizens, Needham, MA -- Paul D. Merritt Center capital campaign
75,000   Clark School for the Deaf, Northampton, MA -- Rogers Hall exterior renovation
75,000   Western New England College, Springfield, MA -- educational technology initiative
75,000   Young Men's Christian Association Metro Springfield, Springfield, MA -- overhaul boiler system
58,334   Stanley Park, Westfield, MA -- operating support
50,000   American National Red Cross, Washington, DC -- special contribution
50,000   Church of the Atonement (Episcopal), Westfield, CT -- capital campaign
50,000   Community Music School of Springfield, Springfield, MA -- Early Childhood Music and Teacher Training Program
50,000   Foundation for Excellent Schools, Cornwall, VT -- western Massachusetts Excellent Schools Program

KATHRYNE BEYNON FOUNDATION

Giving Contact

Robert D. Bannon, Trustee
199 S. Los Robles Ave., Suite 711
Pasadena, CA 91101
Phone: (626)584-8800
Fax: (626)584-8807

Description

Founded: 1967
EIN: 956197328
Organization Type: Private Foundation
Giving Locations: CA
Grant Types: Capital, Endowment, General Support.

Donor Information

Founder: the late Kathryne Beynon

Financial Summary

Total Giving: $332,210 (fiscal year ending October 31, 2001); $361,600 (fiscal 2000); $228,350 (fiscal 1998)
Giving Analysis: Giving for fiscal 2001 includes: foundation scholarships ($30,000); fiscal 2000: foundation scholarships ($48,200); fiscal 1998: foundation scholarships ($7,750)
Assets: $9,184,681 (fiscal 2001); $10,559,335 (fiscal 2000); $9,362,766 (fiscal 1998)

Typical Recipients

Arts & Humanities: Arts Associations & Councils, Arts Centers, Ethnic & Folk Arts, Historic Preservation, History & Archaeology, Libraries
Civic & Public Affairs: Clubs, Employment/Job Training, Civic & Public Affairs-General, Hispanic Affairs, Philanthropic Organizations, Public Policy, Safety
Education: Colleges & Universities, Legal Education, Preschool Education, Private Education (Precollege), Secondary Education (Public), Student Aid
Health: AIDS/HIV, Cancer, Children's Health/Hospitals, Clinics/Medical Centers, Home-Care Services, Hospitals, Medical Rehabilitation, Prenatal Health Issues, Respiratory
Religion: Churches, Religious Welfare
Social Services: At-Risk Youth, Child Welfare, Community Service Organizations, Day Care, Family Planning, Family Services, Homes, People with Disabilities, Scouts, Social Services-General, Substance Abuse, Youth Organizations

Application Procedures

Initial Contact: Send a brief letter of inquiry.
Application Requirements: Include amount requested, purpose of funds sought, financial statements, and proof of tax-exempt status.
Deadlines: None.

Restrictions

Limited to publicly supported charities in child welfare, education, hospital respiratory units, and alcohol treatment in Southern CA.

Foundation Officials

Mel B. Bannon: trustee
Robert D. Bannon: trustee
Alexandra Laboutin Bannon: trustee
Mary Ellen Lubow: trustee

Grants Analysis

Disclosure Period: fiscal year ending October 31, 2001
Total Grants: $302,210*
Number of Grants: 22
Average Grant: $11,534*
Highest Grant: $60,000
Lowest Grant: $2,500
Typical Range: $5,000 to $20,000
*Note: Giving excludes scholarships. Average grant excludes highest grant.

Recent Grants

Note: Grants derived from 2000 Form 990.

Library-Related
5,000	United Friends of Children, Culver City, CA

General
58,000	Hillside Home for Children, Pasadena, CA -- for permanent endowment
50,000	Huntington Memorial Hospital, Pasadena, CA -- for education and therapy for children
25,000	Westmont College, Santa Barbara, CA -- scholarship
22,200	Friends of Foster Children, Arcadia, CA -- for scholarships and the Christmas program
21,000	Orthopedic Hospital Foundation, Los Angeles, CA
17,000	Assistance League of Southern California, Los Angeles, CA -- for day nursery and children club
17,000	Blind Children's Center, Glendale, CA -- for Anchorland therapeutic playground project
17,000	Young and Healthy, Pasadena, CA
16,000	Boys and Girls Club of Hollywood, Hollywood, CA
15,000	Boys and Girls Club of Pasadena, Pasadena, CA

BICKNELL FUND

Giving Contact

Robert G. Acklin, Secretary & Treasurer
c/o Advisory Services Inc.
1422 Euclid Ave., Rm. 1010
Cleveland, OH 44115-2078
Phone: (216)363-6482
Web: http://fdncenter.org/grantmaker/bicknellfund/

Description

Founded: 1949
EIN: 346513799
Organization Type: Private Foundation
Giving Locations: OH: Cleveland
Grant Types: Capital, General Support, Project, Seed Money.

Donor Information

Founder: Kate H. Bicknell, the late Warren Bicknell, Jr., Warren Bicknell III, Kate B. Kirkham

Financial Summary

Total Giving: $384,765 (2002); $750,000 (2001); $686,000 (2000). Note: 1997 Giving includes United Way ($35,000).
Giving Analysis: Giving for 2002 includes: foundation grants to United Way ($40,000); 2000: foundation scholarships ($32,500); foundation grants to United Way ($38,000); 1999: foundation scholarships ($26,000) foundation grants to United Way ($38,000)
Assets: $6,354,388 (2002); $8,853,247 (2001); $12,747,375 (2000)
Gifts Received: $913,436 (1995); $10,683 (1994); $183,600 (1993). Note: In 1995, contributions were received from Kate H. Bicknell.

Typical Recipients

Arts & Humanities: Arts Associations & Councils, Museums/Galleries, Music, Performing Arts, Theater
Civic & Public Affairs: Botanical Gardens/Parks, Economic Development, Employment/Job Training, Civic & Public Affairs-General, Housing, Urban & Community Affairs, Women's Affairs, Zoos/Aquariums
Education: Colleges & Universities, Community & Junior Colleges, Education-General, Medical Education, Private Education (Precollege), Public Education (Precollege), Special Education, Student Aid
Environment: Protection
Health: Children's Health/Hospitals, Clinics/Medical Centers, Emergency/Ambulance Services, Eyes/Blindness, Health-General, Health Funds, Medical Rehabilitation, Medical Research, Mental Health, Nursing Services, Public Health, Single-Disease Health Associations
Religion: Ministries, Religious Welfare
Social Services: Animal Protection, At-Risk Youth, Camps, Child Abuse, Child Welfare, Community Service Organizations, Counseling, Domestic Violence, Family Planning, Family Services, Food/Clothing Distribution, People with Disabilities, Scouts, Senior Services, Shelters/Homelessness, Substance Abuse, United Funds/United Ways, YMCA/YWCA/YMHA/YWHA, Youth Organizations

Application Procedures

Initial Contact: Send cover letter and full proposal.
Application Requirements: Include current income and expense statement of operation, projected budget showing how the requested funds will be utilized, a description of organization, amount requested, and proof of tax-exempt status.
Deadlines: May 1 and October 1.

Restrictions

Does not support individuals or provide loans.

Additional Information

Majority of grants are for community, medical, and educational purposes.
Publications: Application Guidelines

Foundation Officials

Robert G. Acklin: secretary, treasurer
Warren Bicknell, III: vice president, trustee
Wendy H. Bicknell: trustee
Samantha K. Crowley: trustee
Donald J. Hofman: trustee
Kate B. Kirkham: president, trustee
Henry L. Meyer, III: trustee B Cleveland, OH 1949. ED Colgate University BA (1972); Harvard University MBA (1978). PRIM CORP EMPL chairman, president, chief operating officer: KeyBank of Cleveland. CORP AFFIL director: Society Mortgage Co.; director: National Finance Services Corp.; director: Society Investor Services Corp. NONPR AFFIL trustee: Cleveland Museum Natural History; trustee: Federation for Neighborhood Progress; trustee: American Cancer Society Cuyahoga County Unit; trustee: A. M. McGregor Home. CLUB AFFIL Kirtland Country Club; Union Club.
Alexander S. Taylor, II: trustee PRIM CORP EMPL senior vice president: McDonald & Co.
Lyman H. Treadway, III: trustee

Grants Analysis

Disclosure Period: calendar year ending 2002
Total Grants: $344,765*
Number of Grants: 52
Average Grant: $4,895*
Highest Grant: $50,000
Lowest Grant: $765
Typical Range: $1,000 to $10,000
*Note: Giving excludes United Way. Average grant figure excludes two highest grants ($100,000).

Recent Grants

Note: Grants derived from 2001 Form 990.

General
150,000	South Kent School, South Kent, CT -- for capital campaign
77,000	Salvation Army of Greater Cleveland, Cleveland, OH -- for program funding and operational support
50,000	Cleveland Botanical Garden, Cleveland, OH -- for program funding
38,000	United Way Services, Cleveland, OH -- for operational support
35,000	American Red Cross, Cleveland, OH -- for operational support
25,000	Cleveland Museum of Natural History, Cleveland, OH -- capital campaign
20,000	Hattie Larlham Foundation, Mantua, OH -- for research institute
20,000	Hiram House, Chagrin Falls, OH -- for capital campaign
12,000	Preterm, Cleveland, OH -- for operational support
10,000	Achievement Center for Children, Cleveland, OH -- for operational support

MARY DUKE BIDDLE FOUNDATION

Giving Contact

Dr. James H. Semans, Chairman
1044 West Forest Hills Boulevard
Durham, NC 27707
Phone: (919)493-5591
Fax: (919)489-0118

Alternate Contact
Douglas C. Zinn, Executive Director

Description
Founded: 1956
EIN: 136068883
Organization Type: General Purpose Foundation
Giving Locations: NY; NC
Grant Types: Award, Project, Seed Money.

Donor Information
Founder: Established by a trust agreement signed by Mary Lillian Duke Biddle on September 14, 1956. The first board of trustees included her children, Nicholas Duke Biddle and Mary Duke Biddle Trent Semans, and her son-in-law, Dr. James H. Semans.

Mary Lillian Duke Biddle, the daughter of Sarah Pearson Angier and Benjamin Newton Duke, was born on November 16, 1887, in Durham, NC. In 1907, she graduated from Trinity College (later Duke University) with an English degree. Mrs. Biddle was an accomplished singer and musician. She was active in the civic and cultural life of Durham until she married and moved to New York in 1915. Mrs. Biddle and her husband, A.J. Drexel Biddle, Jr., lived in Irvington-on-Hudson and New York City. They had two children, Mary and Nicholas.

Mrs. Biddle was a niece of James Buchanan Duke, the electric power and tobacco magnate who was a founder of Duke University, and the daughter of Benjamin N. Duke, also one of the University's founders. The personal and business interests of the Duke family have always been centered in North Carolina and New York, the two areas of concern to the Biddle Foundation.

Until her death in 1960, Mrs. Biddle supported the arts, civic organizations, education, religion, and social concerns. She emphasized support of Duke University and other efforts that would "strengthen communities, educate minds, heal bodies, and further the sustaining enrichment of the arts."

The Mary Duke Biddle Foundation is one of three foundations established by members of the Duke family. The others are the Duke Endowment and the Doris Duke Foundation. When Mrs. Biddle died, her will provided for the bulk of her $40 million estate to go to the foundation, which had been established four years earlier. The will also stipulated that half of the annual income of the foundation should go to Duke University for various programs and activities.

Financial Summary
Total Giving: $1,151,724 (2001); $1,158,654 (2000); $1,240,145 (1999)
Giving Analysis: Giving for 2000 includes: foundation scholarships ($22,500); foundation fellowships ($75,594); 1999: foundation scholarships ($45,000); foundation fellowships ($65,543); 1998: foundation scholarships ($36,610)
Assets: $28,094,557 (2001); $30,931,906 (2000); $26,119,546 (1999)

Typical Recipients
Arts & Humanities: Arts Associations & Councils, Arts Centers, Arts Festivals, Arts Funds, Arts Institutes, Arts Outreach, Ballet, Dance, Ethnic & Folk Arts, Film & Video, Historic Preservation, History & Archaeology, Literary Arts, Museums/Galleries, Music, Opera, Performing Arts, Public Broadcasting, Theater
Civic & Public Affairs: Botanical Gardens/Parks, Community Foundations, Economic Development, Civic & Public Affairs-General, Nonprofit Management, Public Policy
Education: Agricultural Education, Arts/Humanities Education, Business Education, Colleges & Universities, Community & Junior Colleges, Environmental Education, Faculty Development, Education-General, International Exchange, International Studies, Medical Education, Minority Education, Public Education

(Precollege), Science/Mathematics Education, Student Aid
Environment: Environment-General
Health: AIDS/HIV, Cancer, Clinics/Medical Centers, Health-General, Geriatric Health, Health Organizations, Hospices, Hospitals (University Affiliated), Medical Rehabilitation, Mental Health
International: Foreign Arts Organizations, International Relations
Religion: Churches, Ministries, Religious Welfare
Social Services: At-Risk Youth, Community Centers, Community Service Organizations, Emergency Relief, People with Disabilities, Senior Services

Application Procedures
Initial Contact: The foundation suggests that applicants call for application guidelines and procedures.
Application Requirements: Letters should include a description of the organization, project description, amount needed, estimated project budget, list of board of directors and staff, and other sources of support. A copy of the applying organization's 501(c)(3) form should also be submitted.
Deadlines: For specific deadlines, please call the foundation.
Review Process: Applicants are notified of the board's decision, usually within one month after the board meeting. A detailed description of the project may be requested at that time. Grant decisions are made at board meetings which are generally held in March, June, September, and December.

Restrictions
Support is not given to individuals or for general operating support, public education, bricks-and-mortar projects, or endowments. Giving is restricted to New York and North Carolina.

Additional Information
Thompson, Siegel & Walmsley of Richmond, VA, gives the foundation investment advice.
Publications: Annual Report

Foundation Officials
Mary Duke Trent Jones: second vchairman, assistant secretary, assistant treasurer, trustee
Thomas Stephen Kenan, III: secretary, treasurer, trustee, secretary investments committee B Durham, NC 1937. ED University of North Carolina BA (1959). CORP AFFIL director: Kenan Transport Co.; member executive committee: Flagler System Inc. NONPR AFFIL trustee: Council National Trust Historic Preservation; trustee: National Tropical Botanical Garden. CLUB AFFIL University Club; Landfall Golf & Tennis Club; Treyburn Country Club; Breakers Beach & Golf Club; Hope Valley Country Club.
John G. Mebane, Jr.: trustee, mem investments comm
James Duke Biddle Trent Semans: trustee
James H. Semans: chairman, trustee, secretary grants comm
Mary Duke Biddle Trent Semans: vchairman, chairman grants comm, donor daughter B New York, NY February 4, 1920. NONPR AFFIL member: League Women Voters; director: North Carolina School Arts; director: Goodwill Industries Research Triangle Area; director: Durham Public Library; director: Executive Mansion Fine Arts Committee; member: Business Professional Womens Club; chairman: Angier B. Duke Memorial. CLUB AFFIL Rotary Club; Altrusa Club; Half Century Club.
Douglas C. Zinn: executive director

Grants Analysis
Disclosure Period: calendar year ending 2000
Total Grants: $1,060,560*
Number of Grants: 236
Average Grant: $4,494
Highest Grant: $37,576
Typical Range: $1,000 to $10,000
*Note: Giving excludes scholarships and fellowships.

Recent Grants
Note: Grants derived from 2001 Form 990.

General

25,000	North Carolina School of the Arts, NC -- support of scholarships
25,000	Reynolda House, Inc., Winston-Salem, NC -- support of the expansion project
12,500	Reynolda House, Inc., Winston-Salem, NC -- support of the expansion project
10,000	Concert Artists Guild, Inc. -- support of programs
8,000	Durham Arts Council, Inc., Durham, NC -- support of the Emerging Artist Program
6,500	Triangle Opera Theater, Durham, NC -- support of Young Artist Sponsorship and North Carolina Artists Sponsorships
6,000	Durham Arts Council, Inc., Durham, NC -- support of the development of North Carolina Arts for Health Network
5,000	Carolina Ballet, Inc., Raleigh, NC -- support to establish an Arts Education Coordinator
5,000	Carolina Chamber Symphony -- support of two performances of Bach's Saint John Possion
5,000	Christ Church United Methodist -- annual support

F. R. BIGELOW FOUNDATION

Giving Contact
Paul A. Verret, President
55 5th Street E, Suite 600
St. Paul, MN 55101-1797
Phone: (651)224-5463
Fax: (651)224-8123
E-mail: inbox@saintpaulfoundation.org
Web: http://www.saintpaulfoundation.org

Description
Founded: 1934
EIN: 510232651
Organization Type: General Purpose Foundation
Giving Locations: MN: St. Paul
Grant Types: Capital, Endowment, Matching, Multiyear/Continuing Support, Operating Expenses, Project, Research, Seed Money.

Donor Information
Founder: Established in 1934 by the late Frederic Russell Bigelow , who served for many years as president and chairman of the board of directors of the St. Paul Fire and Marine Insurance Company, a subsidiary of the St. Paul Companies.

Financial Summary
Total Giving: $6,533,099 (2000); $4,963,223 (1998); $6,092,424 (1997)
Giving Analysis: Giving for 2000 includes: foundation grants to United Way ($412,057); 1998: foundation grants to United Way ($485,312); 1997: foundation grants to United Way ($277,131)
Assets: $140,931,742 (2000); $126,841,954 (1998); $131,992,708 (1997)
Gifts Received: $270,034 (2000). Note: In 2000, contributions were received from Estate of V.J. & I.C. Knutson ($242,966) and Estate of Ida C. Knutson ($4,068).

Typical Recipients
Arts & Humanities: Arts Associations & Councils, Community Arts, History & Archaeology, Libraries, Literary Arts, Museums/Galleries, Music, Opera, Performing Arts, Public Broadcasting, Theater
Civic & Public Affairs: African American Affairs, Asian American Affairs, Botanical Gardens/Parks,

Community Foundations, Economic Development, Economic Policy, Employment/Job Training, Ethnic Organizations, Civic & Public Affairs-General, Hispanic Affairs, Housing, Law & Justice, Legal Aid, Minority Business, Municipalities/Towns, Native American Affairs, Nonprofit Management, Urban & Community Affairs, Women's Affairs, Zoos/Aquariums

Education: Business Education, Colleges & Universities, Continuing Education, Economic Education, Education Associations, Education Funds, Education Reform, Faculty Development, Education-General, Literacy, Minority Education, Private Education (Precollege), Public Education (Precollege), School Volunteerism, Science/Mathematics Education, Special Education, Student Aid, Vocational & Technical Education

Environment: Environment-General

Health: Alzheimers Disease, Cancer, Children's Health/Hospitals, Emergency/Ambulance Services, Health-General, Health Organizations, Hospices, Hospitals, Medical Rehabilitation, Mental Health, Preventive Medicine/Wellness Organizations, Public Health, Research/Studies Institutes, Single-Disease Health Associations

International: Human Rights, International Environmental Issues

Religion: Churches, Religion-General, Jewish Causes, Religious Welfare, Seminaries, Social/Policy Issues

Science: Science Museums

Social Services: At-Risk Youth, Child Welfare, Community Centers, Community Service Organizations, Counseling, Emergency Relief, Family Planning, Family Services, Food/Clothing Distribution, Homes, People with Disabilities, Recreation & Athletics, Scouts, Senior Services, Shelters/Homelessness, Social Services-General, Substance Abuse, United Funds/United Ways, Volunteer Services, YMCA/YWCA/YMHA/YWHA, Youth Organizations

Application Procedures

Initial Contact: The foundation has a set of application requirements available upon request. The applicant may wish to submit a preliminary proposal to ascertain whether the project falls within foundation interests and guidelines. Full proposals may be submitted without preliminary reports.

Application Requirements: Preliminary summary proposals must address the questions in the application concisely, in no more than two or three pages. In the past, the foundation has stipulated that full proposals must include the applicant's name and address; a description of organization's general purpose and objectives; indication of the scope of its operations; copy of the IRS determination letter of tax-exempt status; amount requested; statement of project purpose and objectives; significance of project to society; and an estimate of the number of Minnesota citizens that will benefit from the project. Applicants should also include a project evaluation plan; the applicant's relationship to the organization; detailed budget; indication of other sources of support; statement of need; verification that donated funds will be used solely for the purposes requested and that the applicant will submit progress reports to the foundation; proposed length of time for support (including schedule of support commencement and termination); names and affiliations of board members; qualifications of principal staff members for project implementation; staff availability throughout duration of the project and replaceability should they not be available; recent balance sheet and audited income sheet; acknowledgement that payment of funds will be at the convenience of the foundation and that modifications of original payment agreements may occur; and indication that application has been received and endorsed by the governing body of applicant organization. If possible, a formal board resolution confirming this should be included. Two copies of the proposal must be submitted.

Deadlines: None. The board of trustees meets three times a year, usually in April, August, and November. Generally, full proposals must be received approximately three and a half months prior to a meeting date.

Review Process: Applicants must allow time for ample review prior to formal trustee consideration. Applications that are not adequately reviewed in time for one Trustee meeting are carried forward to the next one. The foundation encourages interviews with applicants when possible. Grant decisions are relayed three to six months after applications are received.

Restrictions

Normally, the foundation will not act as the only source of financial support for a project; make annual or annual operating grants; support sectarian religious groups; make grants to individuals; fund medical research; or make ongoing, open-ended grants.

Additional Information

Publications: Annual Report; List of Application Requirements

Foundation Officials

Carolyn J. Brusseau: trustee
Robert L. Bullard: chairman, trustee
Judi Dutcher: president Minnesota community
Eugene U. Frey: trustee
Joan L. Gardner: trustee CORP AFFIL director: Lifecore Biomedical Inc.
Elizabeth M. Kiernat: trustee NONPR AFFIL director: Amherst H. Wilder Foundation.
Constance Kunin: trustee
Galen T. Pate: trustee PRIM CORP EMPL chairman, chief executive officer, director: Park Financial Corp. ADD CORP EMPL president, director: United Community Bancshares. CORP AFFIL director: Park National Bank; chairman, director: Signal Bank Inc.; director: Goodhue County National Bank; director: Park Financial Bank.
Edward G. Pendergast: trustee B Springfield, MA 1938. ED University of Hartford BA (1973); University of Hartford MBA (1977). PRIM CORP EMPL vice president: Saint Paul Companies. CORP AFFIL vice president: Saint Paul Fire Marine Insurance Co.; director: Seabord Surety Co.
Wendy H. Rubin: vice chairman, trustee
John M. Scanlan: trustee
Jon A. Theobald: trustee B Saint Paul, MN 1945. ED Saint John's University (1967); Saint John's University (1970). PRIM CORP EMPL executive vice president: Resource Trust Co.
Paul A. Verret: secretary, treasurer B 1941. PRIM NONPR EMPL president: Saint Paul Foundation.

Grants Analysis

Disclosure Period: calendar year ending 2000
Total Grants: $6,121,042*
Number of Grants: 145
Average Grant: $37,646*
Highest Grant: $700,000
Typical Range: $15,000 to $50,000
*Note: Giving excludes United Way. Average grant figure excludes highest grant.

Recent Grants

Note: Grants derived from 2001 Form 990.

General

364,903	Greater Twin Cities United Way, Minneapolis, MN -- for the annual campaign
250,000	Minnesota Public Radio, St. Paul, MN -- to help finance construction of new facilities in St. Paul Minnesota
250,000	St. Paul Foundation, St. Paul, MN -- to help finance the Children, Families and Community Initiative
225,000	Saint Paul Foundation, St. Paul, MN -- to help finance Children's Literacy Initiative
200,000	Cathedral of St. Paul, St. Paul, MN --

	for the Remember, Restore, Rejoice Campaign
105,000	Saint Paul Foundation, St. Paul, MN -- to help finance Children's Literacy Initiative
100,000	Children's Home Society of Minnesota, St. Paul, MN -- for the Compassion Under Construction capital campaign
100,000	Friends of the St. Paul Farmers' Market, Shoreview, MN -- for capital campaign
100,000	Girl Scout Council of St. Croix Valley, St. Paul, MN -- for the All the Girls capital campaign
100,000	Goodwill Industries, St. Paul, MN -- for the Creating Solutions Campaign

WILLIAM BINGHAM FOUNDATION

Giving Contact

Laura H. Gilbertson, Director
20325 Center Ridge Rd., Suite 629
Rocky River, OH 44116-3554
Phone: (440)331-6350
E-mail: www.info@wbinghamfoundation.org
Web: http://www.fdncenter.org/grantmaker/bingham/

Description

Founded: 1955
EIN: 346513791
Organization Type: Family Foundation
Giving Locations: CA; DC; NY; OH; RI: United States only.
Grant Types: Award, Capital, Conference/Seminar, Endowment, General Support, Matching, Operating Expenses, Project.

Donor Information

Founder: Incorporated in 1955 by Elizabeth Bingham Blossom in memory of her brother, William Bingham, II.

Initially, the foundation contributed to a wide variety of organizations in education, the arts, health, and human services in the Cleveland area. After the death of Mrs. Blossom in 1970, the foundation continued under the leadership of her daughter, Mary Blossom Lee (d. 1976) and her daughter-in-law, Emily E. Blossom. Over the years, many of the current trustees, all descendants of the founder, have relocated to regions away from Cleveland, and as a result the foundation's objectives have broadened to reflect the needs of the communities in which the Trustees reside.

Financial Summary

Total Giving: $200,000 (2003 approx); $693,175 (2001); $1,396,034 (2000)
Assets: $20,000,000 (2003 approx); $20,830,856 (2001); $25,869,309 (2000)
Gifts Received: $667,693 (1994); $1,000 (1993); $1,000 (1992). Note: In 1994, contributions were received from Society National Bank, trustee for Elizabeth B. Blossom Pension Fund Trust.

Typical Recipients

Arts & Humanities: Arts Appreciation, Arts Associations & Councils, Arts Centers, Arts Funds, Arts Outreach, Ballet, Dance, Film & Video, Historic Preservation, Libraries, Literary Arts, Museums/Galleries, Music, Performing Arts, Public Broadcasting, Theater, Visual Arts

Civic & Public Affairs: Botanical Gardens/Parks, Economic Development, Civic & Public Affairs-General, Housing, Nonprofit Management, Professional & Trade Associations, Women's Affairs, Zoos/Aquariums

Education: Afterschool/Enrichment Programs, Arts/Humanities Education, Business Education, Colleges & Universities, Community & Junior Colleges,

Continuing Education, Economic Education, Education Associations, Elementary Education (Public), Engineering/Technological Education, Environmental Education, Faculty Development, Education-General, Gifted & Talented Programs, International Exchange, International Studies, Legal Education, Preschool Education, Private Education (Precollege), Public Education (Precollege), Science/Mathematics Education, Secondary Education (Private), Special Education, Student Aid

Environment: Air/Water Quality, Environment-General, Resource Conservation, Sanitary Systems, Watershed, Wildlife Protection

Health: Cancer, Clinics/Medical Centers, Diabetes, Hospices, Hospitals, Medical Rehabilitation, Multiple Sclerosis, Nursing Services, Public Health

International: International Environmental Issues, International Relief Efforts, Missionary/Religious Activities

Religion: Religion-General, Ministries

Science: Science Museums, Scientific Centers & Institutes, Scientific Labs, Scientific Organizations

Social Services: Animal Protection, Camps, Child Welfare, Community Service Organizations, Domestic Violence, People with Disabilities, Recreation & Athletics, Senior Services, Sexual Abuse, Shelters/Homelessness, Substance Abuse, YMCA/YWCA/YMHA/YWHA, Youth Organizations

Application Procedures

Initial Contact: Submit a one- to two-page letter; no other attachments or documentation should be included.

Application Requirements: Include the nature of the project, budget requirements, and the amount requested.

Deadlines: None.

Review Process: If the project corresponds with the foundation's interests, the executive director or a trustee may request a meeting or a full proposal. If the foundation requests a full grant proposal, the proposal must be submitted two months before the next meeting of the board of trustees. The trustees act on full grant applications, when requested, at these semi-annual meetings, which occur in the spring and fall.

Notes: The foundation encourages applicants to seek additional funding sources and asks applicants to inform the foundation of other grants received. The foundation expects a grantee to report at least annually on the progress of its program, and to account for funds at the completion of the grant period.

Restrictions

The foundation does not make grants to individuals or to organizations outside the United States.

Additional Information

Publications: Guidelines

Foundation Officials

Thomas F. Allen: secretary

C. Bingham Blossom: trustee, president, chairman investment committee

C. Perry Blossom: trustee, treasurer

Laurel Blossom: trustee, chairman grant eval committee

Robin Dunn Blossom: trustee, chairman education committee

Laura H. Gilbertson: director

Elizabeth Blossom Heffernan: vice president, trustee, chairman public information committee

Grants Analysis

Disclosure Period: calendar year ending 2001

Total Grants: $693,175

Number of Grants: 22

Average Grant: $31,508

Highest Grant: $99,000

Lowest Grant: $5,000

Typical Range: $5,000 to $50,000

Recent Grants

Note: Grants derived from 2001 Form 990.

General

99,000	YMCA of the USA, Chicago, IL -- writers community
50,075	University of Florida Foundation, Gainesville, FL -- environmental education program
50,000	Achievement Center For Children, Cleveland, OH -- building construction
50,000	Hawken School, Cleveland, OH -- athletic facility construction
50,000	Pacific Symphony Association, Santa Ana, CA -- commissioning of symphony
50,000	Yale University, New Haven, CT -- Fox Fellowship Program
45,000	Playhouse Square Foundation, Cleveland, OH -- building renovation
35,000	Partners in Parks, Paonia, CO -- capacity building
30,000	Cuyahoga Valley Environmental Education Center, Peninsula, OH -- environmental education program
25,000	Amos House, Providence, RI -- employment program

WILLIAM BINGHAM SECOND BETTERMENT FUND

Giving Contact

Anna Mosquera, Administrator
c/o Davidson, Dawson & Clark
330 Madison Ave. Rm. 3500
New York, NY 10017
Phone: (212)557-7700
Fax: (212)286-8513

Description

Founded: 1955

EIN: 136072625

Organization Type: General Purpose Foundation

Giving Locations: ME: Western Mountain region.

Grant Types: Capital, Endowment, General Support.

Financial Summary

Total Giving: $1,989,775 (2000); $1,682,469 (1998); $2,865,522 (1996)

Giving Analysis: Giving for 2000 includes: foundation scholarships ($93,000); foundation matching gifts ($245,865); 1998: foundation scholarships ($314,500); foundation matching gifts ($507,319); 1996: foundation scholarships ($15,000) foundation matching gifts ($232,152)

Assets: $43,615,890 (2000); $39,087,387 (1998); $32,998,302 (1996)

Typical Recipients

Arts & Humanities: Arts Associations & Councils, Arts Festivals, Film & Video, Arts & Humanities-General, History & Archaeology, Libraries, Museums/Galleries, Music, Public Broadcasting

Civic & Public Affairs: Chambers of Commerce, Civil Rights, Community Foundations, Economic Development, Economic Policy, Employment/Job Training, Gay/Lesbian Issues, Civic & Public Affairs-General, Housing, Law & Justice, Municipalities/Towns, Nonprofit Management, Philanthropic Organizations, Public Policy, Rural Affairs, Urban & Community Affairs, Women's Affairs

Education: Agricultural Education, Arts/Humanities Education, Colleges & Universities, Education Funds, Education Reform, Environmental Education, Faculty Development, Education-General, Education-General, Health & Physical Education, International Studies, Leadership Training, Literacy, Medical Education, Private Education (Precollege), Public Education

(Precollege), Science/Mathematics Education, Student Aid, Vocational & Technical Education

Environment: Air/Water Quality, Forestry, Environment-General, Resource Conservation, Wildlife Protection

Health: Cancer, Children's Health/Hospitals, Clinics/Medical Centers, Diabetes, Health Funds, Health Organizations, Home-Care Services, Hospitals, Long-Term Care, Medical Research, Nursing Services, Preventive Medicine/Wellness Organizations, Public Health, Respiratory

Religion: Ministries

Science: Science-General, Scientific Labs

Social Services: Camps, Child Welfare, Community Centers, Community Service Organizations, Counseling, Crime Prevention, Family Planning, Family Services, Food/Clothing Distribution, Homes, Recreation & Athletics, Substance Abuse, YMCA/YWCA/YMHA/YWHA, Youth Organizations

Application Procedures

Initial Contact: Applicants should submit, in duplicate, a grant application cover sheet with an accompanying letter. The cover sheet is available from the foundation.

Application Requirements: A more detailed letter may accompany the application form, but applicants are urged to be succinct. After studying the proposal the trustees will request any additional information needed.

Deadlines: Proposals should be submitted by the last day of January, April, July, and October.

Review Process: The fund tries to answer each inquiry it receives, except general mailings and applicants that lie outside the geographical area or fields of interest of the fund. The trustees normally meet in March, June, September and December.

Notes: Each organization receiving a grant is expected to submit an evaluation of the project within six months after the payment of the grant.

Restrictions

The foundation does not make grants or loans to individuals, or for the support of religious activities or programs.

Additional Information

The United States Trust Company of New York is the fund's corporate trustee.

The fund uses the following criteria for grant selection: whether the program is innovative; evidence of substantial support from constituency; ability to demonstrate sufficient fiscal responsibility and management skills; whether organization can demonstrate a realistic plan for the continuance of program or organization after the grant is completed; and collaborative proposals which involve several organizations or groups in the community are given priority.

Publications: Annual Report; Guidelines; Application Form

Foundation Officials

William P. Clough, III: trustee

Carol Berg Geist: trustee

William M. Throop, Jr.: trustee PRIM CORP EMPL partner, chief executive officer: Davidson, Dawson & Clark.

William B. Winship: trustee

Carolyn S. Wollen: trustee NONPR AFFIL vice president, director: Gould Academy.

Grants Analysis

Disclosure Period: calendar year ending 2000

Total Grants: $1,650,910*

Number of Grants: 88

Average Grant: $16,290*

Highest Grant: $150,000

Typical Range: $10,000 to $50,000

*****Note:** Giving excludes scholarships; matching gifts. Average grant figure excludes two highest grants ($250,000).

Recent Grants

Note: Grants derived from 2001 Form 990.

Library-Related

50,000	Maine Community Foundation, Ellsworth, ME
25,000	Brown Memorial Library, East Baldwin, ME
25,000	Ludden Memorial Library, Dixfield, ME
25,000	Maine Community Foundation, Ellsworth, ME
25,000	Norway Medical Library, Norway, ME
25,000	Norway Memorial Library, Norway, ME

General

150,000	Gould Academy, Bethel, ME
100,000	Gould Academy, Bethel, ME
100,000	Maine Public Broadcasting Corporation, Portland, ME
100,000	University of New England, Biddeford, ME
75,000	Appalachian Trail Conference, Harpers Ferry, WV
50,000	Maine Humanities Council, Portland, ME
50,000	New England Forestry Foundation, Cambridge, MA
50,000	New England Medical Center, Boston, MA
50,000	Portland Museum of Art, Portland, ME
35,000	Eastern Maine Technical College, Bangor, ME

BINNEY & SMITH, INC.

Company Headquarters

1100 Church Lane
Easton, PA 18042
Phone: (610)559-6610
Fax: (610)559-6691
Web: http://www.crayola.com

Company Description

Employees: 1,600
SIC(s): 2891 Adhesives & Sealants, 3944 Games, Toys & Children's Vehicles, 3952 Lead Pencils & Art Goods.
Parent Company: Hallmark Cards, Inc., 2501 McGee Street, Kansas City, MO, United States

Nonmonetary Support

Type: Donated Products
Note: Company provides nonmonetary support.
Volunteer Programs: The company provides volunteers for special events.
Contact: Margaret Heckman, Philanthropy Administrator

Giving Contact

Mary Ellyn Volden, Director, Global Philanthropy
PO Box 431
1100 Church Ln.
Easton, PA 18044-0431
Phone: (610)559-6607
Fax: (610)559-6691
E-mail: mvoden@binney-smith.com
Web: http://www.binney-smith.com

Description

Organization Type: Corporate Giving Program
Giving Locations: PA: Easton
Grant Types: Capital, Employee Matching Gifts.

Financial Summary

Total Giving: $300,000 (2000 approx); $305,000 (1999 approx); $305,000 (1998 approx). Note: Contributes through corporate direct giving program only.

Typical Recipients

Arts & Humanities: Arts Appreciation, Arts Associations & Councils, Arts Centers, Arts Festivals, Arts Funds, Arts Institutes, Community Arts, Dance, Film & Video, Historic Preservation, Libraries, Literary Arts, Museums/Galleries, Music, Opera, Performing Arts, Public Broadcasting, Theater, Visual Arts
Civic & Public Affairs: Business/Free Enterprise, Civil Rights, Community Foundations, Economic Development, Economic Policy, First Amendment Issues, Civic & Public Affairs-General, Hispanic Affairs, Philanthropic Organizations
Education: Afterschool/Enrichment Programs, Arts/Humanities Education, Business Education, Colleges & Universities, Community & Junior Colleges, Continuing Education, Economic Education, Education Associations, Education Funds, Elementary Education (Private), Education-General, Literacy, Preschool Education, Private Education (Precollege), Public Education (Precollege), Secondary Education (Private), Secondary Education (Public), Social Sciences Education, Special Education, Student Aid
Environment: Environment-General, Wildlife Protection
Health: Children's Health/Hospitals, Emergency/Ambulance Services, Health-General, Speech & Hearing
International: International Relations
Social Services: At-Risk Youth, Child Welfare, Community Centers, Domestic Violence, Family Services, Sexual Abuse, Shelters/Homelessness, Social Services-General, United Funds/United Ways, Volunteer Services, Youth Organizations

Application Procedures

Initial Contact: Submit a letter of request on organization letterhead.
Application Requirements: Include purpose and background information of the organization, amount requested, purpose of funds sought, recently audited financial statements, copy of IRS 501 (c)(3) tax determination letter, population served, time frame in which contribution is needed, planned use of contributions, and follow-up evaluation of contributions impact.
Deadlines: September 1 prior to the year for which funding is sought.
Review Process: Major contributions are reviewed annually by corporate contributions committee.

Restrictions

The company does not support individuals, individual schools, religious organizations for sectarian purposes, athletic groups, fraternal organizations, national or international organizations, individual child care centers, nursing and convalescent homes, prisoners, conventions, hospitals, endowment funds, labor groups, social clubs, or veteran's organizations. Generally, funding is not given for past operating deficits, travel, conferences, events, non-product goodwill advertising, or undefined operational support. Gives to local organizations only. Does not have out of state beneficiaries.

Additional Information

Publications: Informational Brochure (including Guidelines)

Corporate Officials

Mary Ellen Volden: director global philanthropy

Grants Analysis

Total Grants: $0
Average Grant: $0
Typical Range: $1,000 to $2,500

BINSWANGER COMPANIES

Company Headquarters

Philadelphia, PA
Web: http://www.cbbi.com

Company Description

Employees: 150
SIC(s): 6531 Real Estate Agents & Managers, 6799 Investors Nec.

Binswanger Foundation

Giving Contact

John K. Binswanger, President
2 Logan Square, 4th Floor
Philadelphia, PA 19103
Phone: (215)448-6000
Fax: (215)448-6238
E-mail: info@cbbi.com

Description

EIN: 236296506
Organization Type: Corporate Foundation
Giving Locations: PA
Grant Types: General Support.

Donor Information

Founder: Binswanger Corp.

Financial Summary

Total Giving: $418,592 (2001); $468,263 (2000); $394,784 (1999). Note: Contributes through foundation only.
Giving Analysis: Giving for 2001 includes: foundation grants to United Way ($29,000); foundation ($389,592); 2000: foundation grants to United Way ($34,000); foundation ($434,263); 1999: foundation grants to United Way ($70,000); foundation ($324,784);
Assets: $635,716 (2001); $1,230,006 (2000); $1,644,831 (1999)
Gifts Received: $175,000 (2000); $25,000 (1998); $50,000 (1996). Note: In 2000, contributions were received from John K Binswanger ($25,000) and the Estate of Elizabeth Binswanger ($150,000). In 1998, contributions were received from John K. Binswanger.

Typical Recipients

Arts & Humanities: Arts Associations & Councils, Arts Festivals, Ballet, Community Arts, Arts & Humanities-General, Historic Preservation, History & Archaeology, Libraries, Museums/Galleries, Music, Performing Arts, Public Broadcasting, Theater
Civic & Public Affairs: African American Affairs, Botanical Gardens/Parks, Business/Free Enterprise, Chambers of Commerce, Clubs, Economic Development, Employment/Job Training, Civic & Public Affairs-General, Housing, Law & Justice, Municipalities/Towns, Professional & Trade Associations, Public Policy, Urban & Community Affairs, Zoos/Aquariums
Education: Arts/Humanities Education, Business Education, Business-School Partnerships, Colleges & Universities, Education-General, Minority Education, Minority Education, Private Education (Precollege), Public Education (Precollege)
Health: Cancer, Children's Health/Hospitals, Emergency/Ambulance Services, Eyes/Blindness, Health Organizations, Hospitals, Hospitals (University Affiliated), Medical Research, Mental Health, Public Health, Single-Disease Health Associations
International: Foreign Educational Institutions, International Affairs, International Organizations, International Relations, Missionary/Religious Activities
Religion: Jewish Causes, Religious Organizations, Religious Welfare, Social/Policy Issues
Science: Science Museums, Scientific Centers & Institutes
Social Services: Child Welfare, Community Service Organizations, Crime Prevention, Day Care, Delinquency & Criminal Rehabilitation, Family Planning, Family Services, People with Disabilities, Recreation & Athletics, Recreation & Athletics, Scouts, Shelters/Homelessness, Substance Abuse, United Funds/United Ways, Youth Organizations

Application Procedures

Initial Contact: Send a brief letter of inquiry.
Application Requirements: Include all information pertinent to a decision.
Deadlines: None.
Notes: The foundation has no formal grant application procedure or application form.

Additional Information

Foundation reports their grant making is suspended, but they are still in operation.

Corporate Officials

David R. Binswanger: president, chief executive officer B Abington, PA 1956. ED Bowdoin College (1978); Harvard University MBA (1982). PRIM CORP EMPL president, chief executive officer: Binswanger Companies. CORP AFFIL president: Binswanger International; president: Binswanger Management Corp.
Frank G. Binswanger, Jr.: co-chairman, director B Philadelphia, PA 1928. ED Wesleyan University (1950). PRIM CORP EMPL co-chairman, director: Binswanger Companies. CORP AFFIL cochairman: Binswanger International; chairman: Binswanger Management Corp.
John K. Binswanger: co-chairman, director B Philadelphia, PA 1932. ED Wesleyan University (1954). PRIM CORP EMPL co-chairman, director: Binswanger Companies. CORP AFFIL chairman: Binswanger Management Corp.; co-chairman: Chesterton Blumenauer Binswanger.
Michael J. Brennan: chief financial officer, executive vice president B Philadelphia, PA 1958. ED LaSalle University (1979); Villanova University (1989). PRIM CORP EMPL chief financial officer, executive vice president: Binswanger Companies. CORP AFFIL executive vice president, chief financial officer: Binswanger Management Corp.

Foundation Officials

David R. Binswanger: treasurer (see above)
Frank G. Binswanger, III: secretary CORP AFFIL chief executive officer: Binswanger International; president: Binswanger Management Corp.
John K. Binswanger: chairman (see above)
Robert B. Binswanger: vice chairman

Grants Analysis

Disclosure Period: calendar year ending 2001
Total Grants: $389,592*
Number of Grants: 87
Average Grant: $4,478
Highest Grant: $80,000
Lowest Grant: $250
Typical Range: $250 to $10,000
*Note: Giving excludes United Way.

Recent Grants

Note: Grants derived from 2001 Form 990.

Library-Related

1,000	Rosenbach Museum and Library, Philadelphia, PA

General

80,000	Jewish Federation of Greater Philadelphia, Philadelphia, PA
63,500	Wesleyan University, Wesleyan, MA
44,250	Children's Hospital of Philadelphia, Philadelphia, PA
29,000	United Way Southeastern Pennsylvania, Philadelphia, PA
27,500	Fox Chase Cancer Center, Philadelphia, PA
18,037	Falmount Park Commission, Philadelphia, PA
13,000	Germantown Friends School, Philadelphia, PA
11,050	Academy of Music of Philadelphia, Philadelphia, PA
10,000	Regional Performing Arts Center, Philadelphia, PA

9,500	Police Athletic League of Philadelphia, Philadelphia, PA

BIRDS EYE FOODS, INC.

Company Headquarters

90 Linden Oaks
Rochester, NY 14602-0670
Web: http://www.birdseyefoods.com

Company Description

Former Name: (Parent) Agway, Inc.; Agrilink Foods (2002).
Revenue: US$1 billion (2001)
Employees: 5500 (2001)
SIC(s): 2032 Canned Specialties, 2033 Canned Fruits & Vegetables, 2037 Frozen Fruits & Vegetables, 2038 Frozen Specialties Nec.
Parent Company: Pro-Fac Cooperative, Inc., 90 Linden Oaks, Rochester, NY, United States

Operating Locations

Agrilink Foods, Inc. (GA--Montezuma; IL--Collinsville, Ridgeway; IA--Wall Lake; MI--Benton Harbor, Coloma, Fennville, Sodus; NJ--Vineland; NY--Alton, Barker, Bergen, Gorham, LeRoy, Leicester, Lyons, Red Creek, Shortsville, Waterport; OH--Lodi; PA--Berlin; TX--Alamo; WA--Tacoma)

Nonmonetary Support

Range: $500 - $1,000
Type: Donated Products; Workplace Solicitation
Contact: Bea Slizewski, vice president, corporate communications
Note: Nonmonetary support requests are handled individually by each division.

Agrilink Foods/Pro-Fac Foundation

Giving Contact

Susan C. Riker, Secretary
PO Box 20670
Rochester, NY 14602-0670
Phone: (585)264-3155
Fax: (585)383-1606
Web: http://www.agrilinkfoods.com/corp/about/community/index.html

Description

EIN: 166071142
Organization Type: Corporate Foundation
Giving Locations: headquarters and operating communities.
Grant Types: Capital, Emergency, Endowment, General Support, Matching, Operating Expenses, Scholarship.

Financial Summary

Total Giving: $298,000 (fiscal year ending June 31, 2002 approx); $315,725 (fiscal 2001); $238,209 (fiscal 1999). Note: Contributes through foundation only.
Giving Analysis: Giving for fiscal 2002 includes: foundation ($17,600); corporate direct giving ($280,000); fiscal 2001: foundation scholarships ($17,700); corporate direct giving ($23,850); foundation grants to United Way ($85,225); foundation ($188,950); fiscal 1999: foundation scholarships ($4,000); foundation grants to United Way ($73,379); foundation ($160,830);
Assets: $146,000 (fiscal 2002 approx); $38,583 (fiscal 2001); $111,000 (fiscal 2000 approx)
Gifts Received: $300,000 (fiscal 2002); $300,000 (fiscal 2001); $300,000 (fiscal 2000). Note: In 2001 and 2002, contributions were received from Pro-Fac. Contributions are received from Curtice-Burns Foods Inc.

Typical Recipients

Arts & Humanities: Arts Associations & Councils, Arts Centers, Community Arts, History & Archaeology, Libraries, Museums/Galleries, Music, Performing Arts, Public Broadcasting, Theater
Civic & Public Affairs: African American Affairs, Botanical Gardens/Parks, Business/Free Enterprise, Civil Rights, Clubs, Community Foundations, Economic Development, Employment/Job Training, Civic & Public Affairs-General, Housing, Nonprofit Management, Rural Affairs, Safety, Urban & Community Affairs, Women's Affairs
Education: Agricultural Education, Business Education, Colleges & Universities, Community & Junior Colleges, Education Funds, Education-General, Legal Education, Literacy, Minority Education, Minority Education, Private Education (Precollege), Special Education, Student Aid
Environment: Environment-General, Resource Conservation
Health: Cancer, Children's Health/Hospitals, Clinics/Medical Centers, Emergency/Ambulance Services, Geriatric Health, Health Organizations, Heart, Hospices, Hospitals, Medical Rehabilitation, Mental Health, Nursing Services, Public Health, Single-Disease Health Associations
Religion: Religious Welfare
Science: Science Museums, Scientific Research
Social Services: Animal Protection, Big Brother/Big Sister, Child Welfare, Community Centers, Community Service Organizations, Day Care, Delinquency & Criminal Rehabilitation, Domestic Violence, Emergency Relief, Family Planning, Family Services, Family Services, Food/Clothing Distribution, Homes, People with Disabilities, Recreation & Athletics, Scouts, Senior Services, Shelters/Homelessness, Social Services-General, Substance Abuse, United Funds/United Ways, Veterans, Volunteer Services, YMCA/YWCA/YMHA/YWHA, Youth Organizations

Application Procedures

Initial Contact: Brief letter or proposal.
Application Requirements: a description of organization, amount requested, purpose of funds sought, recently audited financial statement, and copy of IRS 501(c)(3) letter
Deadlines: None.

Restrictions

Contributions are not made to individuals, political groups, dinners or special events, international projects, fraternal organizations, goodwill advertising, or religious activities for sectarian purposes. No awards given outside the United States.

Corporate Officials

Dennis M. Mullen: president, chief executive officer, director B Newark, NJ December 09, 1953. ED Saint Leo College BA. PRIM CORP EMPL president, chief executive officer, director: Agrilink Foods, Inc.
Beatrice B. Slizewski: vice president corporate communications B Rochester, NY 1943. ED State University of New York (1986). PRIM CORP EMPL vice president corporate communications: Agrilink Foods, Inc.

Foundation Officials

Robert V. Call, Jr.: chairman, trustee B Batavia, NY 1926. ED Cornell University (1950); Harvard University (1981). PRIM CORP EMPL chairman, director: Agrilink Foods, Inc. ADD CORP EMPL vice president, director: Call Farms Inc.; vice president: Genesee Farms Inc.; president, director: My-T Acres Inc.
Virginia Ford: trustee CORP AFFIL director: Agrilink Foods, Inc.

Grants Analysis

Disclosure Period: fiscal year ending June 31, 2002
Total Grants: $298,000*
Number of Grants: 148
Average Grant: $2,000

Highest Grant: $20,000
Lowest Grant: $100
Typical Range: $100 to $5,000
*Note: Grants analysis provided by foundation.

Recent Grants

Note: Grants derived from 2001 Form 990.

General

20,000	On Broadway, Green Bay, WI -- for Urban renewal in Green Bay
19,785	United Way Greater Rochester, Rochester, NY -- for corporate matching gift
15,000	United Way Pierce County, Tacoma, WA -- annual campaign
13,530	United Way Greater Rochester, Rochester, NY -- for Employee Matching Gift Program
10,000	Al Sigl Center, Rochester, NY -- for gathering of hearts
10,000	Encompass Child Care, Green Bay, WI -- for capital building campaign
10,000	University of Rochester, Rochester, NY -- for emergency department
9,085	United Way Brown County, Green Bay, WI -- for employee campaign
5,350	United Way Genesee County, Rochester, NY -- annual campaign
5,000	Faces of Hope, Inc., Rochester, NY -- for operating fund

A. G. BISHOP CHARITABLE TRUST

Giving Contact

Pamela W. Taeckens, Vice President
c/o Bank One
111 E. Court Street, Suite 100
Flint, MI 48502
Phone: (810)237-3765
Fax: (810)237-3809
Note: Application address.

Alternate Contact

c/o Bank One Trust Co.
PO Box 1308
Milwaukee, WI 53201
Phone: (414)765-2769

Description

Founded: 1944
EIN: 386040693
Organization Type: Private Foundation
Giving Locations: MI: Flint-Genesee County
Grant Types: Capital, Emergency, Multiyear/Continuing Support, Operating Expenses.

Donor Information

Founder: the late Arthur Giles Bishop

Financial Summary

Total Giving: $671,016 (2001); $686,921 (2000); $591,986 (1999)
Giving Analysis: Giving for 2001 includes: foundation grants to United Way ($100,000); 2000: foundation grants to United Way ($150,000); 1999: foundation grants to United Way ($100,000)
Assets: $12,794,893 (2001); $13,943,274 (2000); $14,045,905 (1999)

Typical Recipients

Arts & Humanities: Arts Associations & Councils, Arts Centers, Arts Institutes, Community Arts, Dance, Ethnic & Folk Arts, History & Archaeology, Libraries, Museums/Galleries, Music, Public Broadcasting, Theater, Visual Arts
Civic & Public Affairs: Botanical Gardens/Parks, Community Foundations, Economic Development,

---

Civic & Public Affairs-General, Hispanic Affairs, Housing, Law & Justice, Urban & Community Affairs
Education: Arts/Humanities Education, Business Education, Colleges & Universities, Community & Junior Colleges, Engineering/Technological Education, Education-General, Private Education (Precollege), Public Education (Precollege)
Environment: Environment-General
Health: Children's Health/Hospitals, Clinics/Medical Centers, Emergency/Ambulance Services, Eyes/Blindness, Geriatric Health, Health Organizations, Medical Research, Public Health, Single-Disease Health Associations
International: International Organizations
Religion: Churches, Ministries, Religious Welfare
Science: Science Museums
Social Services: Animal Protection, Big Brother/Big Sister, Child Abuse, Child Welfare, Community Service Organizations, Crime Prevention, Domestic Violence, Family Planning, People with Disabilities, Recreation & Athletics, Scouts, Shelters/Homelessness, Special Olympics, Substance Abuse, United Funds/United Ways, Volunteer Services, YMCA/YWCA/YMHA/YWHA, Youth Organizations

Application Procedures

Initial Contact: The foundation requests applications be made in writing.
Deadlines: None.

Restrictions

Grants are restricted to qualified tax-exempt organizations.

Additional Information

Trust(s): Bank One

Foundation Officials

Robert J. Bellairs: co-trustee
Elizabeth B. Wentworth: co-trustee

Grants Analysis

Disclosure Period: calendar year ending 2001
Total Grants: $571,016*
Number of Grants: 46
Average Grant: $9,791*
Highest Grant: $50,000
Lowest Grant: $1,500
Typical Range: $1,000 to $20,000
*Note: Giving excludes United Way. Average grant figure excludes three highest grants ($150,000).

Recent Grants

Note: Grants derived from 2000 Form 990.

General

150,000	United Way Genesee and Lapeer Counties, Flint, MI -- operating support
50,000	Flint Cultural Center Corporation, Flint, MI -- operating support
50,000	Goodwill Industries of Mid-Michigan, Inc., Flint, MI
25,000	Flint Cultural Center Corporation, Flint, MI -- operating support
25,000	Shelter of Flint, Flint, MI
20,000	Flint Institute of Music & Arts, Flint, MI -- operating support
20,000	Kettering University, Flint, MI
20,000	Mott Community College, Flint, MI
20,000	Mott Community College, Flint, MI
20,000	YMCA - Flint, Flint, MI

E. K. AND LILLIAN F. BISHOP FOUNDATION

Giving Contact

Tom Nevers, Grants Manager
Care of Bank of America, Trustee
701 5th Avenue, Floor 47
Seattle, WA 98104

Phone: (520)749-2004
Fax: (520)749-2990
E-mail: thomas.nevers@azbar.org

Description

Founded: 1971
EIN: 916116724
Organization Type: General Purpose Foundation
Giving Locations: WA, Grays Harbor County
Grant Types: Award, Capital, Matching, Project, Seed Money.

Donor Information

Founder: Established in 1971 by the late E. K. Bishop and the late Lillian F. Bishop .

Financial Summary

Total Giving: $1,954,647 (fiscal year ending April 30, 2000); $4,132,034 (fiscal 1999); $1,372,814 (fiscal 1998)
Assets: $29,745,740 (fiscal 2000); $28,471,704 (fiscal 1999); $26,000,000 (fiscal 1998 approx)

Typical Recipients

Arts & Humanities: Arts Associations & Councils, Arts Centers, Ballet, Community Arts, Dance, History & Archaeology, Libraries, Museums/Galleries, Music, Opera, Performing Arts, Theater
Civic & Public Affairs: Asian American Affairs, Botanical Gardens/Parks, Business/Free Enterprise, Clubs, Community Foundations, Economic Development, Employment/Job Training, Civic & Public Affairs-General, Housing, Inner-City Development, Municipalities/Towns, Native American Affairs, Parades/Festivals, Philanthropic Organizations, Safety, Urban & Community Affairs, Women's Affairs, Zoos/Aquariums
Education: Afterschool/Enrichment Programs, Agricultural Education, Arts/Humanities Education, Business Education, Colleges & Universities, Community & Junior Colleges, Education Associations, Education Funds, Elementary Education (Private), Elementary Education (Public), Education-General, Private Education (Precollege), Public Education (Precollege), Science/Mathematics Education, Secondary Education (Public), Special Education, Student Aid
Health: Children's Health/Hospitals, Clinics/Medical Centers, Emergency/Ambulance Services, Eyes/Blindness, Health Funds, Heart, Hospitals, Medical Research, Nursing Services, Research/Studies Institutes, Single-Disease Health Associations, Trauma Treatment
International: Human Rights
Religion: Churches, Dioceses, Religious Welfare
Science: Science-General, Science Museums, Scientific Centers & Institutes
Social Services: Big Brother/Big Sister, Camps, Child Welfare, Community Centers, Community Service Organizations, Domestic Violence, Family Planning, Family Services, Food/Clothing Distribution, Recreation & Athletics, Scouts, Shelters/Homelessness, Special Olympics, Substance Abuse, United Funds/United Ways, Volunteer Services, YMCA/YWCA/YMHA/YWHA, Youth Organizations

Application Procedures

Initial Contact: Applicants seeking grants should write to the foundation for a brochure and an application form.
Application Requirements: An original and four copies of the application should be submitted with the following: certificate of tax-exemption from the IRS; list of the applicant's senior officers and directors; most recent financial statements (preferably audited); and proposed budget for use of requested funds.
Deadlines: Applications must be received by the first business day of January, April, July, or October.
Review Process: The awards committee meets quarterly.

Notes: Foundation requests no videotapes be sent. Trustees may request an interview with the applicant or conduct a visit at the applicant's organization.

Restrictions

Grants only made to non-profits for programs that benefit youth (0-23) in the State of Washington.

Additional Information

Priority is accorded to grants that encourage community involvement and are joined with matching funds, public, private, or both. Seafirst Bank is the foundation's corporate trustee.
Publications: Application Guidelines; Application Form

Foundation Officials

Isabelle Smith Lamb: director B Quebec, QC Canada 1922. ED Carleton University (1947). PRIM CORP EMPL president, treasurer, director: Enterprises International Inc. ADD CORP EMPL treasurer, director: EII Ltd./Limitee; vice president, director: Lamb-Grays Harbor Co.; vice president, director: Meridian Machine Works Inc.; treasurer, director: Ovalstrapping Inc. NONPR AFFIL director: Independent College Washington.
James C. Mason: director B 1955. CORP AFFIL president: Mason Timber Inc.
Tom Nevers: grant mgr
Janet T. Skadon: director

Grants Analysis

Disclosure Period: fiscal year ending April 30, 2000
Total Grants: $1,954,647
Number of Grants: 156
Average Grant: $6,159*
Highest Grant: $1,000,000
Lowest Grant: $1,000
Typical Range: $1,000 to $10,000 and $15,000 to $50,000
***Note:** Average grant figure excludes highest grant.

Recent Grants

Note: Grants derived from fiscal 2000 Form 990.

Library-Related
50,000	Seattle Public Library Foundation, Seattle, WA

General
1,000,000	YMCA of Grays Harbor, Aberdeen, WA
71,856	Grays Harbor Children's Center
56,712	Gray Harbor Community Foundation
50,000	YMCA of Greater Seattle, Seattle, WA
43,695	Grays Harbor Community Hospital, Grays Harbor, WA
40,700	Grays Harbor College, Aberdeen, WA
40,000	People Organized to Operate
30,756	Gray Harbor Community Foundation
25,845	Saron Evangelical Lutheran
25,000	Central Puget Sound Council of Camp Fire, Seattle, WA

VERNON AND DORIS BISHOP FOUNDATION

Giving Contact

Vernon Bishop, Trustee
1616 Fieldcrest Road
Lebanon, PA 17042-6413
Phone: (717)273-1462

Description

Founded: 1957
EIN: 236255835
Organization Type: Private Foundation
Giving Locations: PA
Grant Types: General Support.

Financial Summary

Total Giving: $359,840 (2001); $308,219 (2000); $515,052 (1999)
Giving Analysis: Giving for 2001 includes: foundation grants to United Way ($36,140); 2000: foundation grants to United Way ($10,500); 1999: foundation grants to United Way ($10,000)
Assets: $4,420,648 (2001); $5,062,858 (2000); $4,709,934 (1999)
Gifts Received: $351 (1998); $200,000 (1996); $100,000 (1995). Note: In 1996, contributions were received from the Lebanon Chemical Corp.

Typical Recipients

Arts & Humanities: Arts Associations & Councils, Historic Preservation, History & Archaeology, Libraries, Museums/Galleries, Music, Public Broadcasting, Theater
Civic & Public Affairs: Clubs, Employment/Job Training, Civic & Public Affairs-General, Philanthropic Organizations, Professional & Trade Associations, Public Policy
Education: Business Education, Colleges & Universities, Engineering/Technological Education, Education-General, Private Education (Precollege), Religious Education, Secondary Education (Private)
Health: Clinics/Medical Centers, Emergency/Ambulance Services, Health Organizations, Hospitals, Medical Research, Mental Health, Prenatal Health Issues, Public Health
International: Missionary/Religious Activities
Religion: Churches, Ministries, Religious Organizations, Religious Welfare
Science: Scientific Centers & Institutes
Social Services: At-Risk Youth, Camps, Community Service Organizations, People with Disabilities, Scouts, United Funds/United Ways, YMCA/YWCA/YMHA/YWHA, Youth Organizations

Application Procedures

Initial Contact: The foundation requests applications be made in writing.
Deadlines: None.

Foundation Officials

Vernon Bishop: trustee

Grants Analysis

Disclosure Period: calendar year ending 2001
Total Grants: $323,700*
Number of Grants: 39
Average Grant: $3,255*
Highest Grant: $200,000
Lowest Grant: $100
Typical Range: $1,000 to $5,000
***Note:** Giving excludes United Way. Average grant figure excludes highest grant.

Recent Grants

Note: Grants derived from 2000 Form 990.

Library-Related
3,000	Lebanon Community Library, Lebanon, PA

General
100,000	Penn Laurel Girl Scout Council, York, PA
85,768	Good Samaritan Health Services Foundation, Lebanon, PA -- hospital television project
30,000	Lebanon Valley Rails-to-Trails, Cleona, PA
14,169	Lebanon Valley College, Annville, PA
11,232	Good Samaritan Health Services Foundation, Lebanon, PA -- hospital television project
10,500	United Way Lebanon County, Lebanon, PA
10,000	Pennsylvania Historic Dramas, Mt. Gretna, PA
4,000	St. Andrew's Presbyterian Church, Lebanon, PA
3,500	Heritage Foundation, Washington, DC
3,000	Gretna Theater, Mt. Gretna, PA

MONA BISMARCK CHARITABLE TRUST

Giving Contact

Russell M. Porter, Trustee
1133 Avenue of the Americas
New York, NY 10036-6710
Phone: (212)336-2960

Description

Founded: 1986
EIN: 133244269
Organization Type: Private Foundation
Grant Types: General Support.

Donor Information

Founder: Russell M. Porter

Financial Summary

Total Giving: $627,500 (2000); $643,400 (1998); $617,000 (1997)
Assets: $17,904,919 (2000); $16,386,079 (1998); $14,083,557 (1997)

Typical Recipients

Arts & Humanities: History & Archaeology, Libraries
Education: Colleges & Universities
Health: Research/Studies Institutes
International: Foreign Arts Organizations, Foreign Educational Institutions, International-General, International Organizations, International Peace & Security Issues, International Relations, International Relief Efforts

Application Procedures

Initial Contact: Send a brief letter of inquiry describing program or project.
Deadlines: None.

Restrictions

Does not support individuals.

Foundation Officials

Russell M. Porter: trustee

Grants Analysis

Disclosure Period: calendar year ending 2000
Total Grants: $627,500
Number of Grants: 3
Highest Grant: $600,000
Lowest Grant: $7,500

Recent Grants

Note: Grants derived from 1999 Form 990.

General
700,000	Mona Bismaeck Foundation Inc, Paris France -- meet expense on cultural events
20,000	Lafayette Escadrille Memorial Day Association, New York, NY -- upkeep of monument
3,000	American Library in Paris, Paris France -- purchase books

BLANDIN FOUNDATION

Giving Contact

Linda Gibeau, Grants Manager
100 North Pokegama Avenue
Grand Rapids, MN 55744

Phone: (218)326-0523
Fax: (218)327-1949
E-mail: bfinfo@blandinfoundation.org
Web: http://www.blandinfoundation.org

Alternate Contact

Paul M. Olson, President

Description

Founded: 1941
EIN: 416038619
Organization Type: General Purpose Foundation
Giving Locations: MN
Grant Types: Multiyear/Continuing Support, Project, Scholarship, Seed Money.

Donor Information

Founder: Established in 1941 by the late Charles K. Blandin . As owner of a paper mill, Mr. Blandin began his career with the *St. Paul Pioneer Press and Dispatch*, and by the late 1920s, rose to the position of owner and publisher. Eventually he sold the newspaper but retained ownership of the Blandin Paper Company and various other companies. After his death, most of Mr. Blandin's estate was placed in trust for the foundation. Although the trustees sold the trust's stock in Blandin Paper Company in 1977, the foundation remains committed to serving the community where its income was earned. Most of the foundation's income is derived from the Blandin Residuary Trust. Mr. Blandin set no specific funding restrictions on the foundation's areas of interest.

Financial Summary

Total Giving: $15,418,132 (2001); $13,601,341 (2000); $11,853,548 (1999)
Giving Analysis: Giving for 2000 includes: foundation grants to United Way ($10,000); foundation scholarships ($643,203); 1999: foundation grants to United Way ($12,500); foundation scholarships ($612,547); 1998: foundation grants to United Way ($46,500) foundation matching gifts ($381,000)
Assets: $389,600,831 (2001); $457,940,059 (2000); $407,930,875 (1999)
Gifts Received: $18,097,047 (2001); $16,392,372 (2000). Note: Contributions were received from C.K. Blandin Residuary Trust.

Typical Recipients

Arts & Humanities: Arts Appreciation, Arts Associations & Councils, Arts Centers, Arts Institutes, Arts Outreach, Historic Preservation, History & Archaeology, Libraries, Literary Arts, Museums/Galleries, Music, Opera, Performing Arts, Public Broadcasting, Theater
Civic & Public Affairs: Botanical Gardens/Parks, Chambers of Commerce, Clubs, Community Foundations, Economic Development, Employment/Job Training, Civic & Public Affairs-General, Housing, Legal Aid, Municipalities/Towns, Native American Affairs, Nonprofit Management, Philanthropic Organizations, Professional & Trade Associations, Rural Affairs, Safety, Urban & Community Affairs
Education: Agricultural Education, Arts/Humanities Education, Colleges & Universities, Community & Junior Colleges, Education Reform, Elementary Education (Public), Engineering/Technological Education, Environmental Education, Faculty Development, Education-General, Leadership Training, Medical Education, Minority Education, Public Education (Precollege), Science/Mathematics Education, Secondary Education (Public), Social Sciences Education, Special Education, Student Aid
Environment: Air/Water Quality, Forestry, Environment-General, Resource Conservation
Health: Children's Health/Hospitals, Clinics/Medical Centers, Emergency/Ambulance Services, Health Policy/Cost Containment, Health Organizations, Hospices, Long-Term Care, Medical Research, Mental Health, Nursing Services, Outpatient Health Care, Public Health

Religion: Religious Welfare, Religious Welfare
Science: Scientific Research
Social Services: At-Risk Youth, Camps, Child Welfare, Community Centers, Crime Prevention, Domestic Violence, Emergency Relief, Family Services, People with Disabilities, Recreation & Athletics, Substance Abuse, United Funds/United Ways, YMCA/YWCA/YMHA/YWHA, Youth Organizations

Application Procedures

Initial Contact: Submit a short preliminary letter of inquiry, by conventional mail or through the foundation's online inquiry form on the foundation's web site, concerning the nature of request.
Deadlines: The board meets three times a year; January 2, for the April meeting; May 1 for the August meeting; and September 1, for the January meeting.
Review Process: Each proposal is assigned to a member of the program staff when it is received. The staff member presents the proposal, along with the results of any related investigation, and the program staff's composite recommendation to the Board of Trustees. The board commits all grant funds.
Notes: Guidelines differ for organizations located in the foundation's home community of Grand Rapids and Itasca County, MN. Applicants from Grand Rapids/Itasca County should contact the foundation to obtain local grantmaking guidelines and a local grant application form.
The foundation will also accept the Minnesota Common Grant Form.

Restrictions

The foundation does not funds organizations outside the state of Minnesota; capital campaigns for construction, renovation, or purchase of equipment or endowments outside of the greater Grand Rapids/Itasca County area; religious activities; medical research; publications; films or videos; travel grants for individuals or groups; camping programs; ordinary governments services; grants to individuals, except the Blandin Educational Awards Program; grants intended to influence legislation; or general operating funds outside of the greater Grand Rapids/Itasca County area.

Additional Information

In addition to making grants, the foundation provides services for conferences and community leadership training for rural Minnesota.
Publications: Annual Report; Application Guidelines; Program Policy Statement

Foundation Officials

Kenneth Albrecht: trustee emeritus
Dr. Kathleen Annette: vice chairman, trustee
Dr. M. James Bensen: trustee
Vernae Hasbargen: trustee emeritus
John Hawkinson: trustee
Peter A. Heegaard: chairman, member executive committee PRIM CORP EMPL executive vice president: Norwest Bank Minnesota.
James Hoolihan: chairman, trustee B 1952. ED University of Minnesota (1973-1977); William Mitchell College of Law JD (1979). PRIM CORP EMPL president, director: Industrial Lubricant Co.
Kathryn L. Jensen: senior vice president
Sandy Layman: secretary, trustee
Kenneth Lundgren: trustee, director
Marcie Mclaughlin: trustee
Paul M. Olson: president B 1944.
Bruce W. Stender: chairman, member executive committee B 1942. ED Florida State University PhD (1969). PRIM CORP EMPL president, chief operating officer, director: Lyric Block Development Corp. ADD CORP EMPL president, chief operating officer: Holiday Inn; president, chief operating officer: Labovitz Enterprises Inc. CORP AFFIL director: Minnesota Power Inc.; director: Minnesota Power & Light Co.
George Thompson: trustee

Brian Vergin: trustee B 1943. ED Babson College. PRIM CORP EMPL senior vice president marketing, director: Blandin Paper Co.

Grants Analysis

Disclosure Period: calendar year ending 2001
Total Grants: $14,711,651*
Number of Grants: 132*
Average Grant: $79,059*
Highest Grant: $3,400,000
Lowest Grant: $975
Typical Range: $15,000 to $25,000
*Note: Giving excludes United Way and scholarship. Number of grants and average grant exclude $34,015 in miscellaneous grants. Average grant figure excludes two highest grants ($4,400,000).

Recent Grants

Note: Grants derived from 2001 Form 990.

Library-Related

124,000	City of Lavergne, Lavergne, TN -- for the Promise Project

General

3,400,000	Greater Minnesota Housing Fund, St. Paul, MN -- for Minnesota communities
1,000,000	Itasca Community College, Grand Rapids, MN -- for capital and programming support
750,000	Minnesota Public Radio, St. Paul, MN -- for Mainstreet Radio
646,236	Sota Tec Fund, Arden Hills, MN -- administration support for Research and Technology Transfer Program
456,000	Sota Tec Fund, Arden Hills, MN -- administration support for Research and Technology Transfer Program
400,000	Minnesota High Technology Foundation, Bloomington, MN -- for computers for schools
400,000	Sibley County, Gaylord, MN -- for capital campaign
346,000	Minnesota Department of Children, Families and Learning, Minneapolis, MN -- for Educational Leadership Program
336,600	City of Coleraine, Coleraine, MN -- for the Ski Complex Project
330,000	Judy Garland Children's Museum, Grand Rapids, MN -- for three year pilot

RENE BLOCH FOUNDATION

Giving Contact

Care of U.S. Bank Trust Group
PO Box 3168
Portland, OR 97208-3168
Phone: (503)275-4327

Description

Founded: 1997
EIN: 916448421
Organization Type: Private Foundation
Giving Locations: nationally.
Grant Types: General Support.

Financial Summary

Total Giving: $60,000 (2001); $73,500 (2000); $63,000 (1999)
Giving Analysis: Giving for 2001 includes: foundation scholarships ($1,000)
Assets: $1,058,698 (2001); $1,268,038 (2000); $1,439,255 (1999)
Gifts Received: $13,842 (1998); $1,036,518 (1997). Note: In 1998, contributions were received from Rene Bloch estate.

Typical Recipients

Arts & Humanities: Libraries, Opera, Theater
Civic & Public Affairs: Civic & Public Affairs-General, Hispanic Affairs
Education: Colleges & Universities, Education-General, Health & Physical Education
Health: Geriatric Health, Health Organizations, Hospitals, Multiple Sclerosis, Public Health
Religion: Jewish Causes, Ministries
Social Services: Community Service Organizations, People with Disabilities, Youth Organizations

Application Procedures

Deadlines: September 30.

Additional Information

Trusts: US Bank NA OR.
Trust(s): US Bank NA OR

Grants Analysis

Disclosure Period: calendar year ending 2001
Total Grants: $59,000*
Number of Grants: 28
Average Grant: $2,107
Highest Grant: $6,000
Lowest Grant: $1,000
Typical Range: $1,000 to $5,000
***Note:** Giving excludes scholarships.

Recent Grants

Note: Grants derived from 2001 Form 990.

Library-Related

3,000	Library Foundation, Los Angeles, CA
2,500	Gunn Memorial Library, Washington, CT

General

6,000	Seeds of Peace, New York, NY
4,000	New Milford Hospital, New Milford, MA
3,000	Greater Washington Coalition for Jewish Life, Washington, CT
3,000	National Multiple Sclerosis Society, Portland, OR
3,000	Oregon Health Sciences Foundation, Portland, OR
3,000	Scripps College, Claremont, CA
2,500	Lewis & Clark College, Portland, OR
2,500	Oregon Council for Hispanic Advancement, Portland, OR
2,000	Brookdale Center on Aging, Brookdale, NY
2,000	Music Theater Works, New York, NY

WALTER A. BLOEDORN FOUNDATION

Giving Contact

F. Elwood Davis, Chairman
888 17th St. NW, Suite 1075
Washington, DC 20006
Phone: (202)452-8553
Fax: (202)293-8973

Description

Founded: 1966
EIN: 520846147
Organization Type: Private Foundation
Giving Locations: DC: Washington metropolitan area
Grant Types: Capital, General Support, Professorship, Scholarship.

Donor Information

Founder: the late Walter A. Bloedorn

Financial Summary

Total Giving: $185,000 (2002); $292,000 (2001); $392,000 (2000). Note: Contributes through foundation only.

Giving Analysis

Giving Analysis: Giving for 2002 includes: foundation scholarships ($6,000); 2000: foundation scholarships ($20,000); 1999: foundation scholarships ($10,000);
Assets: $6,715,349 (2002); $8,060,156 (2001); $9,354,384 (2000)

Typical Recipients

Arts & Humanities: Dance, Historic Preservation, History & Archaeology, Libraries, Museums/Galleries, Music, Public Broadcasting
Civic & Public Affairs: Business/Free Enterprise, Employment/Job Training, Municipalities/Towns, Philanthropic Organizations, Urban & Community Affairs
Education: Colleges & Universities, Legal Education, Medical Education, Private Education (Precollege), Religious Education, Secondary Education (Private), Social Sciences Education, Special Education, Student Aid
Health: AIDS/HIV, Alzheimers Disease, Children's Health/Hospitals, Emergency/Ambulance Services, Heart, Home-Care Services, Hospices, Hospitals, Hospitals (University Affiliated), Long-Term Care, Outpatient Health Care, Public Health
International: International Relief Efforts
Religion: Churches, Missionary Activities (Domestic), Religious Welfare
Science: Scientific Centers & Institutes, Scientific Organizations
Social Services: Child Welfare, Community Service Organizations, Counseling, Family Services, Food/Clothing Distribution, Homes, People with Disabilities, Recreation & Athletics, Senior Services, Social Services-General, United Funds/United Ways, Youth Organizations

Application Procedures

Initial Contact: Send letter describing program or project.
Application Requirements: Include proof of tax-exempt status.
Deadlines: December 31.
Review Process: Board meets in April.

Foundation Officials

John H. Bloedorn, Jr.: trustee
F. Elwood Davis: trustee
Robert Edwin Davis: trust B Madison, IL 1931. ED University of Missouri BS (1953); Washington University (1953). PRIM CORP EMPL managing director: Axcess Corp. CORP AFFIL director: USF&G Corp.; director: HIMONT; director: Rheometric Science; director: H&R Block. NONPR AFFIL member: American Management Association. CLUB AFFIL Saint Andrews Club; Marriott Seaview Club.
Jack Kleh: trustee
John A. Sargent: trustee
Anne D. Spratt: trustee
John Sumter: trustee
John Winkel: director

Grants Analysis

Disclosure Period: calendar year ending 2002
Total Grants: $179,000*
Number of Grants: 25
Average Grant: $7,160
Highest Grant: $25,000
Lowest Grant: $1,000
Typical Range: $5,000 to $10,000
***Note:** Giving excludes scholarships.

Recent Grants

Note: Grants derived from 2001 Form 990.

General

30,000	George Washington University, Washington, DC -- for WAB Multimedia Center in the Medical School Library
30,000	National Geographic Society Education Foundation, Washington, DC -- for endowment fund for State of Maryland
30,000	Salvation Army, Washington, DC -- for Turning Point Program
25,000	Boys and Girls Club of Greater Washington, Silver Spring, MD
15,000	Easter Seal Society for Disabled Children and Adults, Washington, DC
15,000	Ingleside Presbyterian Retirement Community, Washington, DC
15,000	Ivymount School, Rockville, MD -- for School to Work Program
10,000	Boys and Girls Club of America, Atlanta, GA
10,000	Decatur House, Washington, DC
10,000	Heights School, Potomac, MD -- for scholarships

BLOOD-HORSE CHARITABLE FOUNDATION

Giving Contact

Mr. Stacy V. Bearse, Treasurer
1736 Alexandria Dr.
Lexington, KY 40504
Phone: (606)278-2361

Description

Founded: 1989
EIN: 611142154
Organization Type: Private Foundation
Grant Types: General Support.

Financial Summary

Total Giving: $63,031 (fiscal year ending May 31, 2001); $38,625 (fiscal 1999); $19,195 (fiscal 1997)
Assets: $112,932 (fiscal 2001); $116,377 (fiscal 1999); $84,726 (fiscal 1997)
Gifts Received: $53,900 (fiscal 2001); $42,000 (fiscal 1999); $1,400 (fiscal 1995). Note: In fiscal 1995 and 1999, contributions were received from Morven Stud, Ltd. ($6,000) and Blood-Horse ($36,000).

Typical Recipients

Arts & Humanities: Libraries, Museums/Galleries, Public Broadcasting
Civic & Public Affairs: Philanthropic Organizations
Education: Arts/Humanities Education, Business Education, Colleges & Universities, Medical Education, Science/Mathematics Education, Student Aid
Health: Cancer, Children's Health/Hospitals, Health Organizations, Medical Research
Religion: Ministries
Social Services: Animal Protection, Community Service Organizations, People with Disabilities, Recreation & Athletics, Social Services-General, YMCA/YWCA/YMHA/YWHA

Application Procedures

Initial Contact: Requests should be made in writing.
Application Requirements: Include the purpose of the organization, amount requested, purpose of funds sought, proof of tax-exempt status, and any other pertinent information.
Deadlines: April1.

Foundation Officials

Stacy V. Bearse: treasurer
Robert N. Clay: vice president
G. Watts Humphrey, Jr.: president PRIM CORP EMPL chairman, chief executive officer, chief operating officer: Conair Group.
Raymond S. Paulick: secretary

Grants Analysis

Disclosure Period: fiscal year ending May 31, 2001
Total Grants: $63,031

Number of Grants: 39
Average Grant: $869*
Highest Grant: $30,000
Lowest Grant: $100
Typical Range: $100 to $5,000
*Note: Average grant figure excludes highest grant.

Recent Grants

Note: Grants derived from 2001 Form 990.

Library-Related
1,000   Stonington Free Library, Stonington, CT -- contribution to support organization

General
30,000   University of Kentucky Equine Research Foundation, Lexington, KY -- to support research into the Fetal Loss Syndrome
5,000   Cornell University, Ithaca, NY -- to sponsor the "Cornell at Saratoga Symposium on Equine Health Care"
5,000   High Hope Steeplechase, Lexington, KY -- sponsorship of the Blood Horse Sportsman's Challenge
3,560   University of Illinois Foundation, Urbana, IL -- to sponsor student participation in AAEP national conference
2,500   United States Equestrian Team, Foxboro, MA -- contribution to support organization
1,546   Thoroughbred Retirement Foundation, Shrewsbury, NJ -- contribution to support organization
1,400   WUKY, Lexington, KY -- to sponsor luncheon at Keeneland and to support organization
1,147   American Association of Equine Practitioners, Lexington, KY -- to fund purchase of item for annual fundraising auction
1,000   American Academy of Equine Art, Lexington, KY -- contribution to support organization
1,000   American Cancer Society, Florence, KY -- contribution to support organization

MILDRED WEEDON BLOUNT EDUCATIONAL AND CHARITABLE FOUNDATION

Giving Contact
Arnold B. Dopson, Chairman
Mildred Weedon Blount Educational and Charitable Foundation
PO Box 706
Tallassee, AL 36078
Phone: (334)283-6581
Fax: (334)283-2310

Description
Founded: 1981
EIN: 630817472
Organization Type: Private Foundation
Giving Locations: AL: Elmore County
Grant Types: General Support, Scholarship.

Donor Information
Founder: the late Mildred W. Blount

Financial Summary
Total Giving: $196,000 (fiscal year ending June 30, 2001); $203,500 (fiscal 2000); $146,500 (fiscal 1996)

Giving Analysis: Giving for fiscal 2001 includes: foundation scholarships ($51,500) fiscal 2000: foundation scholarships ($203,500)
Assets: $3,667,748 (fiscal 2001); $3,543,117 (fiscal 2000); $3,465,080 (fiscal 1996)

Typical Recipients
Arts & Humanities: Arts Associations & Councils, Arts Centers, Community Arts, Libraries, Museums/Galleries, Music, Theater
Civic & Public Affairs: Civic & Public Affairs-General, Municipalities/Towns, Urban & Community Affairs, Women's Affairs
Education: Business Education, Colleges & Universities, Medical Education, Public Education (Precollege), Secondary Education (Public)
Health: Emergency/Ambulance Services, Hospitals
Religion: Churches
Social Services: Community Service Organizations, Scouts, Substance Abuse, United Funds/United Ways, Youth Organizations

Application Procedures
Initial Contact: For grants, send a brief letter of inquiry. Students should submit general information to scholarship committees of Elmore County high schools.
Deadlines: Early May.

Additional Information
Provides scholarships for higher education to students from Elmore County, AL.
Publications: Application Procedures

Foundation Officials
J. Herbert Boddie: trustee emeritus
John I. Cottle, III: secretary
Arnold B. Dopson: chairman
Lloyd F. Emfinger, Jr.: trustee
Carl W. Fuller: trustee
Charles B. Funderburk: trustee
John C. Granger: trustee
O. C. Harden, Jr.: trustee
Virgil F. Redden: trustee
Teddy O. Taylor: trustee
Daniel P. Wilbanks: vchairman

Grants Analysis
Disclosure Period: fiscal year ending June 30, 2001
Total Grants: $144,500*
Number of Grants: 23
Average Grant: $6,283
Highest Grant: $15,000
Typical Range: $500 to $10,000
*Note: Giving excludes scholarships.

Recent Grants
Note: Grants derived from fiscal 2001 Form 990.

Library-Related
10,000   Community Library

General
15,000   Tallassee High School, Tallassee, AL -- support Women's Show Choir
10,000   Community Hospital Foundation, Grand Junction, CO
10,000   Elmore County High School
10,000   Reeltown High School, Tallassee, AL
10,000   Reeltown High School, Tallassee, AL -- support athletic department
10,000   St. Vincent de Paul Catholic Church
10,000   Tallassee Historical Preservation Society, Tallassee, AL
10,000   Tallassee Mt. Vernon Theatre, Inc., Tallassee, AL
7,500   Tallassee City Schools, Tallassee, AL -- basketball
5,000   ACTS

BLOWITZ-RIDGEWAY FOUNDATION

Giving Contact
Tina M. Erickson, Administrator
One Northfield Plaza, Suite 528
570 Frontage Road
Northfield, IL 60093-1213
Phone: (847)446-1010
E-mail: brf_mcw@sbcglobal.net
Web: http://fdncenter.org/grantmaker/blowitz/

Description
Founded: 1984
EIN: 362488355
Organization Type: General Purpose Foundation
Giving Locations: IL
Grant Types: Capital, General Support, Operating Expenses, Project, Research.
Note: Foundation also makes program-related investments through the Illinois Facilities Fund.

Donor Information
Founder: The Blowitz-Ridgeway Foundation was founded in 1984 using the proceeds of the sale of Chicago's Ridgeway Hospital, a non-profit, psychiatric facility focusing on low-income adolescents.

Financial Summary
Total Giving: $1,295,678 (fiscal year ending September 30, 2001); $1,333,160 (fiscal 2000); $1,560,082 (fiscal 1999)
Assets: $23,616,527 (fiscal 2001); $23,616,527 (fiscal 2000); $25,461,212 (fiscal 1999)

Typical Recipients
Arts & Humanities: Arts Institutes, Arts Outreach, Libraries, Theater
Civic & Public Affairs: Economic Development, Employment/Job Training, Ethnic Organizations, Civic & Public Affairs-General, Housing, Municipalities/Towns, Nonprofit Management
Education: Afterschool/Enrichment Programs, Business Education, Colleges & Universities, Faculty Development, Education-General, Literacy, Minority Education, Preschool Education, Private Education (Precollege), Science/Mathematics Education, Secondary Education (Private), Special Education, Student Aid
Environment: Resource Conservation
Health: AIDS/HIV, Alzheimers Disease, Arthritis, Cancer, Children's Health/Hospitals, Clinics/Medical Centers, Emergency/Ambulance Services, Eyes/Blindness, Health-General, Health-General, Health Organizations, Home-Care Services, Hospices, Hospitals, Hospitals (University Affiliated), Long-Term Care, Medical Rehabilitation, Medical Research, Mental Health, Nursing Services, Outpatient Health Care, Prenatal Health Issues, Public Health, Respiratory, Single-Disease Health Associations, Speech & Hearing
Religion: Religion-General, Ministries, Religious Organizations, Religious Welfare
Social Services: At-Risk Youth, Big Brother/Big Sister, Child Abuse, Child Welfare, Community Centers, Community Service Organizations, Counseling, Domestic Violence, Emergency Relief, Family Planning, Family Services, Food/Clothing Distribution, Homes, People with Disabilities, Scouts, Senior Services, Sexual Abuse, Shelters/Homelessness, Social Services-General, Special Olympics, Youth Organizations

Application Procedures
Initial Contact: Write the foundation for a formal application form.
Deadlines: None.
Review Process: The board meets monthly.

Evaluative Criteria: Foundation prefers to fund organizations whose programs or services benefit persons who have not yet reached their majority and/or are for the care of individuals who lack sufficient resources to provide for themselves.

Decision Notification: Applications are reviewed in the order they are received. Committee may decline, recommend board approval, request additional information, schedule a site visit, or invite applicant for an interview by the board.

Notes: The foundation reports that the only funding done outside of the state of Illinois is for medical research, unless an out-of-state applicant has been specifically invited to apply.

Restrictions

The foundation does not support government agencies or organizations which subsist mainly on third party funding. Grants are not made to individuals. Grants will not be made for religious or political purposes, nor for the production of audio-visual materials. Fundraising and administrative costs must be within reasonable limits; grants are only made to the organization providing the service to the end user or is conducting the program for which funding is sought. Applicants must be equal opportunity employers and provide equal access to programs or services.

Additional Information

Applicants, if declined, may not reapply for at least one year from the date of the application. Although the foundation does support operating budgets, applicants should not consider the foundation a source of continuing annual funding.

Publications: Annual Report; Guidelines; Application Form

Foundation Officials

Arthur R Collision: trustee
Anthony M. Dean: treasurer, trustee
Rev. James W. Jackson: secretary, trustee
Daniel L. Kline: vice president, trustee
Pierre R. LeBreton, PhD: trustee
Patricia A. MacAlister: trustee
Max Pastin: president, trustee
Marvin J. Pitluk, PhD: trustee
Samuel G. Winston: trustee

Grants Analysis

Disclosure Period: fiscal year ending September 30, 2001
Total Grants: $1,333,160*
Number of Grants: 106
Average Grant: $11,976*
Highest Grant: $63,700
Typical Range: $1,000 to $50,000
*Note: Average grant figure excludes highest grant.

Recent Grants

Note: Grants derived from fiscal 2001 Form 990.

General

63,700	Northwestern University, Chicago, IL -- research project
51,000	Arkansas Children's Hospital, Little Rock, AR -- for 2nd year funding of a research project entitled, How do Neonatal Experiences Alter Brain Development and Subsequent Behavior?
50,000	Northwestern University Medical School, Chicago, IL -- for a childhood cancer research project entitled
30,000	Cradle, Evanston, IL -- for continued support of its Nursery and Special Needs Program, a 24-hour, on-site nursery for infants awaiting adoption
30,000	Deicke Center for Visual Rehabilitation, Wheaton, IL -- to support its capital campaign for Seeing is Believing Program
26,250	Texas Children's Cancer Center, Houston, TX -- research project

25,000	Northwestern University, Chicago, IL -- for a juvenile arthritis research project
25,000	Rush Presbyterian - St. Luke's Medical Center, Chicago, IL -- research for project titled "Gene Therapy for subthalamic delivery of GAD in a non human primate model of Parkinson's Disease"
25,000	Rush Presbyterian - St. Luke's Medical Center, Chicago, IL -- for project titled "In utero exposure to bacterial toxins a possible etiologic factor in Parkinson's Disease"
25,000	Rush University, Chicago, IL -- funding of an asthma research project

BLUE BELL, INC.

Company Headquarters

Greensboro, NC
Web: http://www.bluebell.com

Company Description

SIC(s): 2253 Knit Outerwear Mills, 2311 Men's/Boys' Suits & Coats, 2321 Men's/Boys' Shirts, 2325 Men's/Boys' Trousers & Slacks.
Parent Company: VF Corp., Greensboro, NC, United States

Operating Locations

Blue Bell, Inc. (AL--Birmingham, Mobile, Montgomery, Mooresville; FL--Panama City; KS--Kansas City; LA--Baton Rouge, Ruston; MS--Jackson; OK--Broken Arrow, Oklahoma City; TX--Alvin, Beaumont, Big Spring, Fort Worth, Harlingen, Humble, Lancaster, Lewisville, Longview, New Braunfels, San Antonio, Waco)

Blue Bell Foundation

Giving Contact

Charles Conkin, Vice President Human Resources & Foundation Contact
Blue Bell Foundation
PO Box 21488
Greensboro, NC 27420
Phone: (910)373-3412

Description

EIN: 566041057
Organization Type: Corporate Foundation
Giving Locations: principally near operating locations and to national organizations.
Grant Types: Employee Matching Gifts, General Support.

Financial Summary

Total Giving: $198,587 (2001); $231,575 (2000); $198,169 (1998). Note: Contributes through corporate direct giving program and foundation.
Giving Analysis: Giving for 2000 includes: foundation matching gifts ($35,515); foundation grants to United Way ($50,000); foundation ($146,060); 1998: corporate scholarships ($23,015); foundation matching gifts ($29,275); corporate matching gifts ($29,275); corporate direct giving ($145,879); foundation ($168,894); 1997: foundation matching gifts ($29,934); foundation grants to United Way ($45,000); foundation ($191,318);
Assets: $6,274,401 (2001); $6,858,035 (2000); $6,375,166 (1998)

Typical Recipients

Arts & Humanities: Arts Associations & Councils, Arts Centers, Arts Festivals, Arts Funds, Community Arts, Historic Preservation, Libraries, Museums/Galleries, Music, Theater

Civic & Public Affairs: Botanical Gardens/Parks, Chambers of Commerce, Clubs, Community Foundations, Employment/Job Training, Civic & Public Affairs-General, Housing, Law & Justice, Municipalities/Towns, Public Policy, Safety, Urban & Community Affairs, Zoos/Aquariums

Education: Agricultural Education, Arts/Humanities Education, Business Education, Colleges & Universities, Community & Junior Colleges, Economic Education, Education Associations, Education Funds, Elementary Education (Public), Engineering/Technological Education, Education-General, Education-General, Literacy, Minority Education, Private Education (Precollege), Public Education (Precollege), Science/Mathematics Education, Secondary Education (Private), Secondary Education (Public), Student Aid, Vocational & Technical Education

Environment: Resource Conservation, Wildlife Protection

Health: Cancer, Children's Health/Hospitals, Clinics/Medical Centers, Diabetes, Emergency/Ambulance Services, Heart, Hospices, Hospitals, Medical Rehabilitation, Medical Research, Prenatal Health Issues, Public Health, Respiratory, Single-Disease Health Associations

International: Foreign Arts Organizations, Health Care/Hospitals, International Development

Religion: Churches, Jewish Causes, Ministries, Religious Organizations, Religious Welfare, Social/Policy Issues

Science: Scientific Centers & Institutes

Social Services: At-Risk Youth, Camps, Child Abuse, Child Welfare, Community Centers, Community Service Organizations, Counseling, Day Care, Domestic Violence, Emergency Relief, Family Services, Food/Clothing Distribution, Homes, People with Disabilities, Recreation & Athletics, Scouts, Senior Services, Social Services-General, Special Olympics, Substance Abuse, United Funds/United Ways, YMCA/YWCA/YMHA/YWHA, Youth Organizations

Application Procedures

Initial Contact: Send a letter of request.
Application Requirements: Include a description of organization; IRS tax determination letter; and amount requested.
Deadlines: None.
Decision Notification: Board meets two times per year.

Restrictions

Foundation does not support individuals; grants are made to organizations that directly benefit company's employees.

Additional Information

Trust(s): Wachovia Bank NA

Corporate Officials

John P. Schamberger: president, chairman jeanswear coalition B 1948. ED Saint John's University BS (1969); Saint John's University MBA (1974). PRIM CORP EMPL president, chairman jeanswear coalition: VF Corp.

Foundation Officials

Ed Heim: secretary advisory committee
Donald P. Laws: member advisory committee PRIM CORP EMPL president, Wrangler Westernwear: VF Jeanswear Inc. CORP AFFIL president: VF Corp.
Robert Matthews: member advisory committee
John P. Schamberger: member advisory board (see above)
T. L. Weatherford: member advisory committee

Grants Analysis

Disclosure Period: calendar year ending 2001
Total Grants: $122,485*
Number of Grants: 62
Average Grant: $1,976
Highest Grant: $50,000

Typical Range: $100 to $5,000
*Note: Giving excludes matching gifts; United Way.

Recent Grants

Note: Grants derived from 2001 Form 990.

General

50,000	United Way Greater Greensboro, Greensboro, NC
18,965	Citizens Scholarship Foundation of America, St. Peter, MN
12,500	Page County Habitat for Humanity, Luray, VA
10,000	Greensboro Symphony Orchestra, Greensboro, NC
5,025	David Lipscomb University, Nashville, TN
5,000	Guilford College, Greensboro, NC
5,000	Habitat for Humanity (Donelson/Hermitage Project), Nashville, TN
5,000	Matt Greene Golf Classic, Greensboro, NC
5,000	Old North State Boy Scouts of America, Greensboro, NC
5,000	West Texas Rehabilitation Center, Ozona, TX

HARRY AND MARIBEL G. BLUM FOUNDATION

Giving Contact

H. Jonathan Kovler, Vice President
919 North Michigan Avenue, Suite 2800
Chicago, IL 60611
Phone: (312)664-5050
Fax: (312)664-8983

Description

Founded: 1967
EIN: 366152744
Organization Type: Family Foundation
Giving Locations: IL: nationally.
Grant Types: General Support.

Donor Information

Founder: Established in 1967 by the late Harry Blum .

Financial Summary

Total Giving: $2,306,275 (2001); $2,308,000 (2000); $1,709,000 (1998)
Assets: $38,587,445 (2001); $45,906,192 (2000); $46,218,008 (1998)

Typical Recipients

Arts & Humanities: Arts Centers, Arts Funds, Arts Institutes, Film & Video, Historic Preservation, History & Archaeology, Libraries, Museums/Galleries
Civic & Public Affairs: Employment/Job Training, Civic & Public Affairs-General, Urban & Community Affairs, Women's Affairs, Zoos/Aquariums
Education: Business-School Partnerships, Colleges & Universities, Education-General, Medical Education, Private Education (Precollege), Religious Education
Health: Cancer, Children's Health/Hospitals, Clinics/Medical Centers, Diabetes, Health Organizations, Hospitals, Medical Rehabilitation, Medical Research, Prenatal Health Issues, Single-Disease Health Associations, Transplant Networks/Donor Banks
Religion: Churches, Jewish Causes, Religious Organizations, Synagogues/Temples
Social Services: Animal Protection, At-Risk Youth, Child Welfare, Community Centers, Community Service Organizations, Day Care, Family Services, Food/Clothing Distribution, People with Disabilities, Recreation & Athletics, Scouts, United Funds/United Ways, Youth Organizations

Application Procedures

Initial Contact: The foundation reports that no specific application form is required.
Deadlines: None.

Foundation Officials

H. H. Bregar: secretary, director
Everett Kovler: president
H. Jonathan Kovler: vice president, treasurer
Peter Kovler: assistant secretary

Grants Analysis

Disclosure Period: calendar year ending 2001
Total Grants: $2,306,325*
Number of Grants: 29
Average Grant: $39,873*
Highest Grant: $750,000
Lowest Grant: $100
Typical Range: $2,000 to $10,000
*Note: Average grant figure excludes two highest grants ($1,150,000).

Recent Grants

Note: Grants derived from 2001 Form 990.

General

750,000	American Diabetes Association, Alexandria, VA
510,000	US Holocaust Memorial Museum, Washington, DC
400,000	Lincoln Park Zoological Society, Chicago, IL
200,000	Washington University School of Medicine, St. Louis, MO
147,375	Museum of Contemporary Art, Chicago, IL
100,000	Jewish United Fund of Metropolitan Chicago, Chicago, IL
60,000	Rehabilitation Institute, Chicago, IL
50,100	Northwestern Memorial Hospital, Chicago, IL
33,000	Children's Diabetes Foundation at Denver, Denver, CO
10,000	American Fund for the Tate Gallery, New York, NY

BLUM-KOVLER FOUNDATION

Giving Contact

919 North Michigan Avenue, Suite 2800
Chicago, IL 60611
Phone: (312)664-5050
Fax: (312)664-8983

Description

Founded: 1957
EIN: 362476143
Organization Type: General Purpose Foundation
Giving Locations: DC: Washington; IL: Chicago metropolitan area; NY: New York
Grant Types: General Support.

Donor Information

Founder: Established in 1953 by the late Harry Blum and Everette Kovler, both of whom served as chairman of the James B. Distilling Company, a subsidiary of American Brands, Inc. The Blum-Kovler Foundation is administered primarily by family members. Maribel Blum, widow of Harry Blum, served as the foundation's chairperson until her death in 1985.

Financial Summary

Total Giving: $4,327,172 (2000); $2,739,425 (1998); $2,764,943 (1997)
Assets: $92,081,283 (2000); $88,265,381 (1998); $71,520,369 (1997)

Typical Recipients

Arts & Humanities: Arts Associations & Councils, Arts Centers, Arts Festivals, Arts Funds, Arts Institutes, Dance, Film & Video, Arts & Humanities-General, Historic Preservation, History & Archaeology, Libraries, Museums/Galleries, Music, Opera, Performing Arts, Public Broadcasting, Theater
Civic & Public Affairs: African American Affairs, Botanical Gardens/Parks, Business/Free Enterprise, Civil Rights, Civic & Public Affairs-General, Legal Aid, Philanthropic Organizations, Public Policy, Urban & Community Affairs, Women's Affairs, Zoos/Aquariums
Education: Arts/Humanities Education, Business Education, Business-School Partnerships, Colleges & Universities, Economic Education, Education Associations, Education Funds, Education Reform, Education-General, International Studies, Leadership Training, Legal Education, Medical Education, Minority Education, Preschool Education, Private Education (Precollege), Public Education (Precollege), Science/Mathematics Education, Secondary Education (Private), Social Sciences Education, Student Aid
Environment: Environment-General, Protection
Health: Cancer, Children's Health/Hospitals, Clinics/Medical Centers, Diabetes, Health Funds, Health Organizations, Hospices, Hospitals, Hospitals (University Affiliated), Medical Rehabilitation, Medical Research, Mental Health, Public Health, Research/Studies Institutes, Single-Disease Health Associations, Transplant Networks/Donor Banks
International: Foreign Educational Institutions, International-General, Health Care/Hospitals, International Affairs, International Peace & Security Issues, International Relations, International Relief Efforts, Missionary/Religious Activities
Religion: Churches, Jewish Causes, Religious Organizations, Synagogues/Temples
Science: Science-General, Science Museums
Social Services: Animal Protection, Child Welfare, Community Centers, Community Service Organizations, Family Services, Food/Clothing Distribution, Homes, People with Disabilities, Recreation & Athletics, Refugee Assistance, Shelters/Homelessness, Substance Abuse, United Funds/United Ways, YMCA/YWCA/YMHA/YWHA, Youth Organizations

Application Procedures

Initial Contact: Interested parties may submit proposals, as well as proof of tax exemption under IRS Code 501(c)(3), to the foundation office.
Deadlines: None.

Foundation Officials

H. H. Bregar: secretary
Everett Kovler: president
H. Jonathan Kovler: vice president, treasurer
Peter Kovler: treasurer, assistant secretary

Grants Analysis

Disclosure Period: calendar year ending 2001
Total Grants: $4,327,172
Number of Grants: 267
Average Grant: $14,333*
Highest Grant: $500,000
Typical Range: $5,000 to $30,000
*Note: Average grant figure excludes highest grant.

Recent Grants

Note: Grants derived from 2000 Form 990.

General

500,000	National Organization on Disability, Washington, DC
300,000	John G. Shedd Aquarium, Chicago, IL
293,021	Millennium Park, Chicago, IL
250,000	American Diabetes Association, Alexandria, VA
235,900	Museum of Contemporary Art, Chicago, IL

206,000	Travelers and Immigrants Aid, Chicago, IL
200,000	Washington University School of Medicine, St. Louis, MO
100,000	Barbara Davis Center for Childhood Diabetes, Denver, CO
100,000	Chicago Historical Society, Chicago, IL
100,000	Family Institute, Evanston, IL

BLUMENTHAL FOUNDATION

Giving Contact

Philip Blumenthal, Director
PO Box 34689
Charlotte, NC 28234-4689
Phone: (704)377-6555
Fax: (704)377-9237
Web: http://www.blumenthalfoundation.org
Note: Mr. Blumenthal's phone extention is 2477.

Alternate Contact

Peggy Gartner, Administrator
Radiator Specialty Co.
1900 Wilkinson Boulevard
Charlotte, NC 28208
E-mail: foundation@gunk.com
Note: Foundation office location.

Description

Founded: 1953
EIN: 560793667
Organization Type: Family Foundation
Former Name: Blumenthal Foundation for Charity, Religion and Education.
Giving Locations: NC: Charlote headquarters.
Grant Types: Capital, Challenge, Endowment, General Support, Operating Expenses, Professorship, Project, Research, Scholarship.

Donor Information

Founder: Established in 1953 by members of the Blumenthal family including the late I. D. Blumenthal . Two trustees of the foundation sit on the board of the Radiator Specialty Company. Herman Blumenthal and Alan Blumenthal serve as the chairman and president, respectively.

Financial Summary

Total Giving: $790,000 (fiscal year ending April 30, 2003 approx); $898,000 (fiscal 2002 approx); $1,771,607 (fiscal 2001)
Giving Analysis: Giving for fiscal 2001 includes: foundation grants to United Way ($13,206); fiscal 2000: foundation grants to United Way ($12,500) fiscal 1997: foundation grants to United Way ($10,000)
Assets: $20,746,923 (fiscal 2001); $22,513,319 (fiscal 1999); $20,922,156 (fiscal 1997)
Gifts Received: $1,722,230 (fiscal 1999); $65,000 (fiscal 1995); $75,600 (fiscal 1994). Note: Contributions were received from various contributors.

Typical Recipients

Arts & Humanities: Arts Associations & Councils, Arts Centers, Arts Festivals, Dance, Libraries, Museums/Galleries, Music, Opera, Performing Arts, Public Broadcasting, Theater
Civic & Public Affairs: Civil Rights, Economic Policy, Civic & Public Affairs-General, Nonprofit Management, Philanthropic Organizations, Zoos/Aquariums
Education: Arts/Humanities Education, Business Education, Colleges & Universities, Community & Junior Colleges, Education Funds, Education Reform, Education-General, Preschool Education, Private Education (Precollege), Religious Education, Science/Mathematics Education
Environment: Environment-General, Resource Conservation

Health: Adolescent Health Issues, AIDS/HIV, Clinics/Medical Centers, Health Organizations, Hospitals, Mental Health, Single-Disease Health Associations
International: Foreign Arts Organizations, International Affairs, Missionary/Religious Activities
Religion: Churches, Jewish Causes, Ministries, Religious Organizations, Religious Welfare, Synagogues/Temples
Science: Science Museums
Social Services: Child Welfare, Community Service Organizations, Family Planning, Family Services, Food/Clothing Distribution, Scouts, Senior Services, Social Services-General, Substance Abuse, United Funds/United Ways, YMCA/YWCA/YMHA/YWHA, Youth Organizations

Application Procedures

Initial Contact: Applicants should send one copy of a brief letter proposal.
Application Requirements: The proposal should be signed by an authorized official of the petitioning organization and the first paragraph should contain the amount and purpose of the request. The proposal should also include the following: a concise description of the project; what the project hopes to accomplish; total project cost and its duration; funds currently committed or pledged to the project and from what sources; other prospective funding sources; an evaluation plan and, if needed, how future funding will be obtained. Also include a phone number where a contact person for the project may be reached during normal business hours and the name to whom the check is to be made payable. In addition, materials should be attached to the proposal including the following: a line-item budget for the proposed project, if applicable, and a budget for the organization's total operations including expected income and expenditure; a list of the governing board of the petitioning organization; and a copy of the IRS tax-exempt determination letter, except in the cases of governmental agencies and churches.
Deadlines: None.
Review Process: The foundation's board of trustees meets quarterly to consider grant applications.

Restrictions

No grants are made to individuals for any purpose; does not provide scholarships, fellowships, or loans.

Additional Information

The Blumenthal Foundation addresses additional community needs through the Foundation for the Carolinas, including: The Neighborhood Grants Program, to offer support to low-income neighborhoods through leadership development initiatives; Underwriting for the Peirce Report, an in-depth analysis of the Charlotte region offering recommendations on how to deal with growth and development issues; Underwriting for Central Carolina Choices, to develop a regional network of citizens to solve problems by building consensus; The Summer Freedom School, a Children's Defense Fund Program directed at getting "at-risk" children off the street and into summer enrichment programs. enrichment programs.
Publications: Procedures; Requirements for Submitting Grant Proposals; American Jewish Times Outlook (monthly)

Foundation Officials

Alan Blumenthal: trustee B 1947. ED University of North Carolina (1969). PRIM CORP EMPL president: Radiator Specialty Co.
Anita Blumenthal: trustee
Philip Blumenthal: trustee B 1950. ED University of North Carolina (1972). NONPR AFFIL president, director: Wildacres Retreat.
Samuel Blumenthal, PhD: trustee
Peggy Gartner: admin

Grants Analysis

Disclosure Period: fiscal year ending April 30, 2001
Total Grants: $1,753,401*
Number of Grants: 191
Average Grant: $9,180*
Highest Grant: $100,000
Typical Range: $1,000 to $15,000
*Note: Giving excludes United Way. Average grant figure excludes two highest grants ($200,000).

Recent Grants

Note: Grants derived from fiscal 2001 Form 990.

General

100,000	Jewish Community Center, Charlotte, NC
100,000	Wildacres Retreat, Little Switzerland, NC
60,000	Jewish Federation of Greater Charlotte, Charlotte, NC
60,000	Jewish Federation of Greater Charlotte, Charlotte, NC
60,000	Jewish Federation of Greater Charlotte, Charlotte, NC
60,000	Jewish Federation of Greater Charlotte, Charlotte, NC
60,000	Jewish Federation of Greater Charlotte, Charlotte, NC
58,649	Wildacres Retreat, Little Switzerland, NC
50,000	Queens College, Charlotte, NC
50,000	Wildacres Retreat, Little Switzerland, NC

BODMAN FOUNDATION

Giving Contact

Joseph S. Dolan, Secretary & Executive Director
767 Third Avenue, 4th Floor
New York, NY 10017
Phone: (212)644-0322
Fax: (212)759-6510
E-mail: main@archelis-bodman-fnds.org
Web: http://fdncenter.org/grantmaker/achelis-bodman/

Description

Founded: 1945
EIN: 136022016
Organization Type: General Purpose Foundation
Giving Locations: NJ: Northern New Jersey; NY: New York metropolitan area
Grant Types: Capital, Conference/Seminar, Emergency, Employee Matching Gifts, General Support, Matching.

Donor Information

Founder: Established in 1945 by the late George M. Bodman (d. 1950), a senior partner in the New York City brokerage firm of Cyrus J. Lawrence and Sons. Both Mr. Bodman and his wife, the late Louise C. Bodman (d. 1955), were active in civic and charitable causes in New York City and Monmouth County, NJ, during their lifetimes.

Financial Summary

Total Giving: $2,620,000 (2002); $3,505,000 (2001); $3,916,200 (2000)
Giving Analysis: Giving for 2000 includes: foundation matching gifts ($146,200)
Assets: $2,500,000 (2003 approx); $65,761,931 (2001); $76,686,891 (2000)

Typical Recipients

Arts & Humanities: Ballet, Dance, Historic Preservation, Libraries, Museums/Galleries, Music, Opera, Performing Arts, Public Broadcasting, Theater
Civic & Public Affairs: African American Affairs, Asian American Affairs, Botanical Gardens/Parks,

Business/Free Enterprise, Civil Rights, Economic Development, Employment/Job Training, Civic & Public Affairs-General, Hispanic Affairs, Housing, Nonprofit Management, Philanthropic Organizations, Public Policy, Urban & Community Affairs, Zoos/Aquariums
Education: Afterschool/Enrichment Programs, Arts/ Humanities Education, Business Education, Colleges & Universities, Economic Education, Education Associations, Education Funds, Education Reform, Elementary Education (Private), Elementary Education (Public), Education-General, Legal Education, Literacy, Medical Education, Minority Education, Preschool Education, Private Education (Precollege), Public Education (Precollege), School Volunteerism, Science/Mathematics Education, Social Sciences Education, Special Education, Student Aid
Environment: Air/Water Quality, Environment-General, Resource Conservation, Wildlife Protection
Health: Cancer, Children's Health/Hospitals, Clinics/ Medical Centers, Emergency/Ambulance Services, Eyes/Blindness, Health Funds, Health Organizations, Hospices, Hospitals, Medical Rehabilitation, Medical Research, Outpatient Health Care, Single-Disease Health Associations, Speech & Hearing, Transplant Networks/Donor Banks, Trauma Treatment
International: Human Rights, International Affairs, International Development, Missionary/Religious Activities
Religion: Churches, Dioceses, Religion-General, Jewish Causes, Religious Organizations, Religious Welfare, Seminaries
Science: Science Museums, Scientific Centers & Institutes, Scientific Labs, Scientific Organizations, Scientific Research
Social Services: Animal Protection, At-Risk Youth, Big Brother/Big Sister, Child Abuse, Child Welfare, Community Centers, Community Service Organizations, Counseling, Domestic Violence, Family Services, Food/Clothing Distribution, Homes, People with Disabilities, Recreation & Athletics, Scouts, Senior Services, Shelters/Homelessness, Social Services-General, Substance Abuse, Veterans, Volunteer Services, YMCA/YWCA/YMHA/YWHA, Youth Organizations

Application Procedures

Initial Contact: The foundation has no standard application form. One short, but comprehensive proposal should be made in writing and sent to the foundation. Introductory letters should be no longer than two pages.
Application Requirements: All requests should briefly include the history, purpose, and financial statement of the applying organization, as well as descriptions of current activities and programs. In addition, grant requests should contain names of board members, personnel involved in the project, a vita of author or researcher, purpose of the request, amount needed, research basis, expected client or participant outcomes and measurable program results, and financial data or IRS information supporting the organization's tax-exempt status. Proposals should not exceed five pages.
Deadlines: None.
Review Process: The foundation's trustees meet in May, September, and December to decide on grant requests. When the board makes final decisions on grants, it takes into account the recommendations of its professional staff. Applicants typically receive a written response within six weeks. Personal interviews and site visits are arranged when necessary.
Evaluative Criteria: Special consideration given to self-help, leadership and character development, parental involvement, consumer choice, economic empowerment, independent research, prevention and early intervention, advancing the state of the art, faith-based program, strengthening the two-percent intact family, and client/participant outcomes and measurable program results.

Restrictions

No grants are made to individuals. Foundation does not make loans. Generally, grant requests for conferences, travel, films, housing, and publications are discouraged. The foundation generally will not fund national health and mental health organizations, small performing arts groups, annual appeals, dinner functions, fund raising events, international projects, deficits, endowments, annual capital campaigns, housing, or government-affiliated organizations and agencies. The Foundation funds primarily in New York City, occasionally in New Jersey.

Additional Information

Publications: Biennial Report; Guidelines

Foundation Officials

Walter Joseph Patrick Curley, Jr.: trustee B Pittsburgh, PA 1922. ED Yale University BA (1944); Harvard University MBA (1948); University of Oslo (1948). PRIM CORP EMPL president: Curley Land Co. OCCUPATION diplomat, investment banker. CORP AFFIL director: Sotheby Holdings Inc.; director: France Growth Fund. NONPR AFFIL honorary chairman: French-American Foundation; trustee: Frick Collection; member: Counsel Foreign Relations. CLUB AFFIL Yale Club; Saint Stephen's Green Club; Travelers Club; New York Racquet & Tennis Club; Rolling Rock Club; Knickerbocker Club; The Links Club; Golf Morfontaine Club; Kildare Street Club; Bedford Golf Club.
Joseph S. Dolan: executive director, secretary
Anthony Drexel Duke, Sr.: trustee B New York, NY July 28, 1918. ED Princeton University (1941). NONPR AFFIL chairman, president, founder: Boys Harbor.
Peter Frelinghuysen: vice president, trustee ED Princeton University (1963); Yale University (1968). PRIM CORP EMPL attorney: Morris & McVeigh. CORP AFFIL secretary: K O A Holdings Inc.
John N. Irwin, III: chairman, chief executive officer, treasurer, trustee B 1954. ED Princeton University (1976). PRIM CORP EMPL vice president, managing director: Hillside Industries Inc. CORP AFFIL vice president, managing director, director: Hillside Capital Inc. De Corp.
Leslie Lenkowsky, PhD: trustee PRIM NONPR EMPL president, chief executive officer: Hudson Institute Inc. CORP AFFIL director: ITT Educational Services Inc.
Russell Parsons Pennoyer: president, trustee B New York, NY 1951. ED Harvard University BA (1974); Columbia University School of Law JD (1982). PRIM CORP EMPL partner: Benedetto, Gartland & Company Inc.
Mary Stone Phipps: vice president, trustee NONPR AFFIL member-at-large, director: Girl Scout Council Greater New York. CLUB AFFIL Somerset Club; Pilgrims Club; Piping Rock Club; The Links Club; Meadow Brook Club; Colony Club.
Guy G. Rutherfurd: honorary chairman, assistant treasurer, trustee B New York, NY 1913. ED Princeton University BA (1938); University of Virginia LLB (1942). PRIM CORP EMPL partner: Morris & McVeigh.

Grants Analysis

Disclosure Period: calendar year ending 2000
Total Grants: $3,770,000*
Number of Grants: 76
Average Grant: $49,605
Highest Grant: $250,000
Lowest Grant: $15,000
Typical Range: $25,000 to $75,000
*****Note:** Giving excludes matching grants.

Recent Grants

Note: Grants derived from 2000 Form 990.

General

250,000	Urban League of Hudson County, Jersey City, NJ -- for Schomburg Charter School
250,000	Wildlife Conservation Society, Brooklyn, NY -- for Tiger Kingdom
150,000	New York University School of Medicine, New York, NY -- for Nationwide Medical Program
100,000	Boy Scouts of America, Greater New York Councils, New York, NY -- for Volunteer Leader Training and Scoutreach Programs
100,000	Bronx Preparatory Charter School, New York, NY -- for start-up costs
100,000	Children's Scholarship Fund, New York, NY -- for assistance to disadvantaged Newark families
100,000	Metropolitan Museum of Art, New York, NY -- for Thomas J. Watson Jr. Memorial Library
100,000	National Association of Scholars, Princeton, NJ -- for operations and annual national meeting in NYC
100,000	New York Foundling Hospital, New York, NY -- for Vincent J. Fontana Center for Child Protection
100,000	New York Hospital Cornell Medical Center, New York, NY -- for Tri-Institutional MD - Ph.D. Program

BOE BROTHERS FOUNDATION

Giving Contact

PO Box 1396
Great Falls, MT 59403-1396
Phone: (406)727-4200

Description

Founded: 1997
EIN: 841378691
Organization Type: Private Foundation
Giving Locations: MT: North Central portion of MT known as the Golden Triangle Area
Grant Types: General Support.

Financial Summary

Total Giving: $479,288 (2001); $148,600 (2000); $327,500 (1999)
Giving Analysis: Giving for 2000 includes: foundation scholarships ($35,800)
Assets: $5,093,611 (2001); $5,120,803 (2000); $4,821,634 (1999)

Typical Recipients

Arts & Humanities: Libraries, Museums/Galleries
Civic & Public Affairs: Clubs, Economic Development, Civic & Public Affairs-General, Municipalities/ Towns
Education: Agricultural Education, Colleges & Universities, Public Education (Precollege), Special Education, Student Aid
Health: Health Organizations, Hospitals
Religion: Churches

Application Procedures

Initial Contact: Send a brief letter of inquiry.
Deadlines: None.

Restrictions

The trust generally supports organizations located in the north central portion of Montana.

Foundation Officials

Allen D. Faechner: trustee

Grants Analysis
Disclosure Period: calendar year ending 2001
Total Grants: $479,288*
Typical Range: $1,000 to $10,000
*Note: No grants list available for 2001

Recent Grants
Note: Grants derived from 2000 Form 990.

General
20,000	Concordia College, Moorhead, MN
20,000	Fairfield High School, Fairfield, MT
20,000	Saint Paul Lutheran Church, Fairfield, MT
10,000	Montana State University Foundation, Bozeman, MT -- for scholarship
5,000	Fairfield High Special Education, Fairfield, MT
5,000	Montana State University Foundation, Bozeman, MT -- for scholarship
4,000	Greenfield School District 75 -- for scholarships
4,000	Power High School -- for scholarships
4,000	Teton Medical Center Foundation, Choteau, MT
3,000	Choteau High School, Choteau, MT

BOEHM FOUNDATION

Giving Contact
Robert Boehm, Trustee
500 5th Ave.
New York, NY 10110
Phone: (212)354-9292
E-mail: boehmfdn@aol.com
Web: http://www.members.aol.com/boehmfdn/

Description
Founded: 1963
EIN: 136145943
Organization Type: Private Foundation
Giving Locations: NY
Grant Types: Emergency, General Support, Operating Expenses, Project, Seed Money.

Donor Information
Founder: Robert L. Boehm, Frances Boehm

Financial Summary
Total Giving: $418,250 (2002); $464,750 (2001); $413,700 (2000)
Assets: $40,347 (2002); $376,360 (2001); $988,331 (2000)
Gifts Received: $188,000 (2002); $120,000 (2001); $260,000 (2000). Note: In 2002, contributions were received from Frances Boehm ($94,000) and Robert Boehm ($94,000). In 2001, contributions were received from Frances Boehm ($60,000) and Robert Boehm ($60,000). In 2000, contributions were received from Frances Boehm ($130,000) and Robert Boehm ($130,000). In 1999, contributions were received from Robert Boehm ($156,650), and Frances Boehm ($125,000). In 1996, contributions were received from Robert Boehm ($66,770), Lucille Banta ($150,500), and Frances Boehm ($69,500).

Typical Recipients
Arts & Humanities: Film & Video, Libraries, Public Broadcasting, Theater
Civic & Public Affairs: African American Affairs, Asian American Affairs, Civil Rights, Economic Development, Economic Policy, Employment/Job Training, First Amendment Issues, Gay/Lesbian Issues, Civic & Public Affairs-General, Law & Justice, Legal Aid, Nonprofit Management, Philanthropic Organizations, Public Policy, Rural Affairs, Urban & Community Affairs, Women's Affairs

Education: Colleges & Universities, Economic Education, Education Funds, Education Reform, Education-General, International Exchange, Legal Education, Public Education (Precollege)
Environment: Air/Water Quality, Environment-General, Resource Conservation
Health: AIDS/HIV, Hospitals, Mental Health, Prenatal Health Issues
International: Foreign Arts Organizations, Human Rights, International Affairs, International Development, International Organizations, International Peace & Security Issues, International Relations, International Relief Efforts, Missionary/Religious Activities, Trade
Religion: Religious Organizations, Religious Welfare
Social Services: Child Welfare, Community Centers, Community Service Organizations, Crime Prevention, Refugee Assistance, Sexual Abuse, Youth Organizations

Application Procedures
Initial Contact: The foundation has no formal grant application procedure or application form.
Deadlines: None.

Restrictions
Does not support individuals, individual research, publications, or film and video projects.

Additional Information
Publications: Application Guidelines; Annual Report

Foundation Officials
Judy Austermiller: trustee
Diane Boehm: trustee
Frances Boehm: trustee
Robert L. Boehm: trustee
Ron Daniels: trustee
Reynaldo R. Guerrero: trustee
Glenn Magpantay: trustee
June Markela: trustee
Beth Richie: trustee
Sara Rios: trustee
Edith Tiger: trustee

Grants Analysis
Disclosure Period: calendar year ending 2002
Total Grants: $418,250
Number of Grants: 35
Average Grant: $11,950
Highest Grant: $50,000
Lowest Grant: $1,250
Typical Range: $5,000 to $15,000

Recent Grants
Note: Grants derived from 2001 Form 990.

General
100,000	Center for Constitutional Rights, New York, NY
50,000	National Coalition to Abolish the Death Penalty, Washington, DC -- to establish a Communications Department and expand its Development Department
40,000	United for a Fair Economy, Boston, MA -- to develop and install an interactive Web site
37,000	Institute for Policy Studies, Washington, DC -- for Independent Progressive Politics Network
35,000	National Coalition of Education Activists, Rhinebeck, NY -- to expand its outreach to parent, teacher and community activist and develop its fundraising capabilities
30,000	Africa Fund, New York, NY -- for restructure and merger with American Committee on Africa and the Africa Information Policy Center
30,000	Highlander Research and Education Center, New Market, TN -- to develop the organization's bi-lingual, bi-cultural

capacity to meet the needs of Latino communities in Appalachia and the South
25,000	Lawyers Committee on Nuclear Policy, New York, NY
25,000	Lawyers Committee on Nuclear Policy, New York, NY
10,000	ACLU Foundation, MA -- for Project Hip-Hop

BOETTCHER FOUNDATION

Giving Contact
Timothy W. Schultz, President & Executive Director
600 Seventeenth Street, Suite 2210 South
Denver, CO 80202
Phone: (303)534-1937
E-mail: grants@boettcherfoundation.org
Web: http://www.boettcherfoundation.org

Description
Founded: 1937
EIN: 840404274
Organization Type: General Purpose Foundation
Giving Locations: CO: Denver
Grant Types: Capital, Challenge, Scholarship.

Donor Information
Founder: Established in 1937 in Colorado by the Boettcher family, with substantial gifts from Charles and Fanny Augusta Boettcher, their son Claude K. Boettcher, his wife Edna Boettcher, and other family members. Charles Boettcher (1852-1948), a German immigrant, helped organize the Great Western Sugar Company and the Ideal Cement Company.

Financial Summary
Total Giving: $9,800,000 (2003 approx); $9,887,000 (2002 approx); $9,421,254 (2000)
Giving Analysis: Giving for 2000 includes: foundation grants to United Way ($125,000); foundation scholarships ($2,711,926); 1999: foundation scholarships ($1,969,455); 1998: foundation scholarships ($1,463,554)
Assets: $190,000,000 (2003 approx); $195,000,000 (2002 approx); $200,324,017 (2000)

Typical Recipients
Arts & Humanities: Arts Associations & Councils, Arts Centers, Ballet, Dance, Historic Preservation, History & Archaeology, Libraries, Museums/Galleries, Music, Opera, Performing Arts, Public Broadcasting, Theater
Civic & Public Affairs: African American Affairs, Botanical Gardens/Parks, Business/Free Enterprise, Clubs, Community Foundations, Economic Development, Employment/Job Training, Civic & Public Affairs-General, Hispanic Affairs, Housing, Legal Aid, Municipalities/Towns, Parades/Festivals, Public Policy, Rural Affairs, Urban & Community Affairs, Women's Affairs, Zoos/Aquariums
Education: Arts/Humanities Education, Business Education, Colleges & Universities, Colleges & Universities, Community & Junior Colleges, Economic Education, Education Reform, Elementary Education (Private), Elementary Education (Public), Engineering/Technological Education, Education-General, Literacy, Medical Education, Preschool Education, Private Education (Precollege), Public Education (Precollege), Religious Education, Science/Mathematics Education, Secondary Education (Public), Student Aid
Environment: Forestry, Environment-General, Resource Conservation
Health: AIDS/HIV, Alzheimers Disease, Children's Health/Hospitals, Clinics/Medical Centers, Emergency/Ambulance Services, Eyes/Blindness, Health-General, Hospices, Hospitals, Long-Term Care, Medical Rehabilitation, Mental Health, Multiple Sclerosis,

Preventive Medicine/Wellness Organizations, Public Health, Single-Disease Health Associations
Religion: Churches, Jewish Causes, Ministries, Religious Welfare
Science: Science Museums, Scientific Centers & Institutes
Social Services: At-Risk Youth, Child Welfare, Community Centers, Community Service Organizations, Day Care, Domestic Violence, Family Planning, Family Services, Food/Clothing Distribution, Homes, People with Disabilities, Recreation & Athletics, Scouts, Senior Services, Sexual Abuse, Shelters/Homelessness, Substance Abuse, United Funds/United Ways, Volunteer Services, YMCA/YWCA/YMHA/YWHA, Youth Organizations

Application Procedures

Initial Contact: A preliminary letter should be sent, signed by the head of organization and describing the project for which funding is requested. The letter should include a statement related to the priority of the project within the organization. The Foundation will ask the organization to submit a full proposal if interested.
Application Requirements: Send a full proposal with a copy of recent IRS statement of tax-exempt status; list of officers and directors, including occupations and places of employment; a brief description of organization, including historical background, services provided, population served and measurements of success; a recent audited financial statement; a current operating budget; description of project for which funding is being requested, including amount requested; budget for project showing expenses and anticipated sources of revenue; and statement of the funds currently committed to the project and other requests pending.
Deadlines: None.
Review Process: A preliminary response is made as soon as possible. Applicants should allow two or three months before a final decision.

Restrictions

No new grants are awarded for endowments, scholarships, operations, purchase of tables or tickets for events, out of state projects, conferences, seminars, workshops, travel, media presentations, or to individuals.

Additional Information

Grantees are required to submit reports on the use of grants and project results.
The foundation also makes program-related investments. Applicants should already have between 50% and 75% of the funding goal committed before foundation will consider proposal.
Publications: Annual Report; Biennial Scholarship Report

Foundation Officials

Pamela Beardsley: trustee
E. Atwill Gilman: trustee
A. Barry Hirschfeld: trustee, vice chairman B Denver, CO 1942. ED California State Polytechnic University, Pomona BS (1964); University of Denver MBA (1966). PRIM CORP EMPL president: AB Hirschfeld Press Inc. CORP AFFIL director: New Century Energies Inc.; director: Public Service Co. Colorado; vice president: Colorado Carphone Corp. NONPR AFFIL prefabricated: Rocky Mountain Multiple Sclerosis Center; director: Up with People; member: National Jewish Medical Research Center; member: Mountain Studies Employers Council; prefabricated: National Conference Christians & Jews; member: Harvard Divinity Center Values Public life; member: Mayor's Advisory Committee; member: Cherry Creek Arts Festival; member: Colorado Concern; member: Allied Jewish Federation; member: Boy Scouts America; life trustee: 9 Who Care. CLUB AFFIL One Hundred Club; Metropolitan Denver Executives Club; Mile Hi Stadium Club.

Katie S. Kramer: vice president grants/scholarships
Claudia Boettcher Merthan: chairman, trustee
Frederick K. Trask, III: vice president, assistant secretary ED Harvard University (1960).
Edward D. White, III: trustee

Grants Analysis

Disclosure Period: calendar year ending 2000
Total Grants: $6,584,328*
Number of Grants: 158
Average Grant: $41,673
Highest Grant: $500,000
Typical Range: $3,000 to $50,000 and $80,000 to $500,000
*Note: Giving excludes scholarships; United Way.

Recent Grants

Note: Grants derived from 2000 Form 990.

General

500,000	Children's Hospital, Denver, CO -- toward construction of and equipment for Mae Boettcher Center for Pediatric Imaging
500,000	University of Denver, Denver, CO -- Toward renovation of Arts & Sciences Building
250,000	Boys and Girls Club of Metro Denver, Boulder, CO -- creation of George M. Wilfley branch
250,000	Longmont YMCA, Longmont, CO -- toward capital improvements
250,000	University of Colorado Health Sciences Center, Denver, CO -- toward Charles Boettcher II endowed chair
250,000	University of Denver - College of Law, Denver, CO -- Toward Hover T. Lentz Scholarship Fund
235,000	Long Peak Council - Boy Scouts of America, Greeley, CO -- toward capital improvements at Ben Delatour Scout Ranch
200,000	Denver Botanical Gardens, Denver, CO -- toward renovation of Boettcher Conservatory
200,000	Mount Saint Vincent Home, Denver, CO -- toward construction and remodeling project
175,000	YMCA of Metropolitan Denver, Denver, CO -- toward construction of Susan Duncan Branch

BOISE CASCADE CORP.

Company Headquarters

Boise, ID
Web: http://www.bc.com

Company Description

Founded: 1957
Ticker: BCC
Exchange: NYSE
Revenue: US$7.412 billion (2002)
Profit: US$11.3 million (2002)
Employees: 24111 (2002)
Fortune Rank: 254, per FORTUNE Magazine's list of 500 Largest U.S. Corporations (2002).
SIC(s): 2421 Sawmills & Planing Mills--General, 2436 Softwood Veneer & Plywood, 2439 Structural Wood Members Nec, 2493 Reconstituted Wood Products.

Operating Locations

Boise Cascade Corp. (AL--Jackson; AZ--Phoenix; CA--City of Commerce; CO--Denver; ID--Burley, Emmett, Idaho Falls, Nampa; LA--Florien, Oakdale; MN--International Falls; MT--Billings; OR--Medford, Monmouth, Portland, St. Helens; UT--Lake City; WA--Kettle Falls, Spokane, Wallula, Yakima)

Nonmonetary Support

Range: $50,000 - $400,000
Type: Donated Equipment; Donated Products

Giving Contact

Connie E. Weaver, Manager,Community Relations
1111 West Jefferson Street
PO Box 50
Boise, ID 83728-0001
Phone: (208)384-7673
Fax: (208)384-7224

Description

Organization Type: Corporate Giving Program
Giving Locations: headquarters and operating communities.
Grant Types: Capital, Employee Matching Gifts, Project.
Note: Matching gifts for education only.

Financial Summary

Total Giving: $1,500,000 (2000 approx); $1,500,000 (1997 approx); $500,000 (1993 approx). Note: Contributes through corporate direct giving program only.

Typical Recipients

Arts & Humanities: Community Arts, Dance, Libraries, Museums/Galleries, Music, Opera, Performing Arts, Theater
Civic & Public Affairs: Business/Free Enterprise, Civil Rights, Economic Development, Economic Policy, Public Policy, Women's Affairs, Zoos/Aquariums
Education: Business Education, Colleges & Universities, Community & Junior Colleges, Economic Education, Engineering/Technological Education, Literacy, Minority Education, Special Education
Environment: Environment-General
Health: Emergency/Ambulance Services, Hospitals
Social Services: Community Centers, Homes, Recreation & Athletics, Senior Services, Substance Abuse, United Funds/United Ways, Youth Organizations

Application Procedures

Initial Contact: Write to nearest Boise Cascade facility.
Application Requirements: Include a description of the organization and its purpose; proof of tax-exempt status; list of officers a directors; current operating budget and sources of funding; recently audited financial statement or most recent Form 990; purpose of grant; project budget and estimated fund-raising costs; and sources of funding, both committed and proposed.
Deadlines: None.
Decision Notification: Proposals are reviewed on an ongoing basis.

Restrictions

Company does not support organizations located in areas where the company has few or no operations; individuals; private foundations; international organizations; fraternal, social, labor, or veterans' organizations; requests of a political nature and organizations or programs that are sensitive, controversial, harmful, or which pose a potential conflict of interest for the company; operating expenses of United Way member agencies; school trips or tours; athletic teams, scholarships, or sport vehicles; courtesy advertising; testimonial dinners; loans or investments; or churches or religious organizations.

Company generally will not arrange loans, or support memorials, grants to cover operating deficits, or projects that are primarily fund-raising events; organizations that channel funds to donee agencies, except for United Way; or endowments at educational institutions or funds or associations whose sole purpose is to raise funds for educational institutions or other organizations.

Additional Information

Priority is given to organizations and programs in communities where the company operates and to those in which company employees are involved.
Operating locations manage and distribute their own funds. Grant seekers should contact the location nearest them.
Publications: Guidelines

Grants Analysis

Typical Range: $1,000 to $10,000

BONFILS-STANTON FOUNDATION

Giving Contact

Dorothy Harrell, Executive Director
1601 Arapahoe St., Suite 5
Denver, CO 80202
Phone: (303)825-3774
Web: http://www.bonfils-stantonfoundation.org

Description

Founded: 1962
EIN: 846029014
Organization Type: Private Foundation
Giving Locations: CO
Grant Types: Capital, General Support, Research.

Donor Information

Founder: the late Charles E. Stanton

Financial Summary

Total Giving: $3,872,749 (fiscal year ending June 30, 2001); $3,213,615 (fiscal 2000); $2,500,000 (fiscal 1999 approx)
Giving Analysis: Giving for fiscal 2001 includes: foundation matching gifts ($21,500); foundation scholarships ($25,310); foundation gifts to individuals ($50,000); fiscal 2000: foundation matching gifts ($10,000); foundation scholarships ($13,500) foundation gifts to individuals ($37,500)
Assets: $71,286,373 (fiscal 2001); $71,726,091 (fiscal 2000); $55,832,329 (fiscal 1998)
Gifts Received: $640,787 (fiscal 2001); $403,466 (fiscal 2000); $1,875,045 (fiscal 1997). Note: In fiscal 1996, substantial contributions were received from the estate of Charles Stanton.

Typical Recipients

Arts & Humanities: Arts Associations & Councils, Arts Centers, Ballet, Dance, Historic Preservation, History & Archaeology, Libraries, Museums/Galleries, Music, Opera, Public Broadcasting, Theater
Civic & Public Affairs: Asian American Affairs, Botanical Gardens/Parks, Economic Development, Employment/Job Training, Civic & Public Affairs-General, Public Policy, Urban & Community Affairs, Women's Affairs, Zoos/Aquariums
Education: Arts/Humanities Education, Colleges & Universities, Community & Junior Colleges, Continuing Education, Elementary Education (Private), Education-General, Literacy, Minority Education, Private Education (Precollege), Science/Mathematics Education
Environment: Environment-General, Resource Conservation
Health: Cancer, Cancer, Children's Health/Hospitals, Clinics/Medical Centers, Emergency/Ambulance Services, Eyes/Blindness, Home-Care Services, Hospices, Hospitals, Long-Term Care, Medical Rehabilitation, Medical Research, Single-Disease Health Associations
Religion: Jewish Causes, Seminaries
Science: Science Museums, Scientific Centers & Institutes

Social Services: At-Risk Youth, Child Abuse, Child Welfare, Community Centers, Community Service Organizations, Domestic Violence, Family Planning, Family Services, Food/Clothing Distribution, Homes, People with Disabilities, Senior Services, Substance Abuse, YMCA/YWCA/YMHA/YWHA, Youth Organizations

Application Procedures

Initial Contact: Send a brief letter of inquiry, signed by president or chairman, requesting guidelines.
Deadlines: January 1, April 1, July 1, October 1.

Restrictions

Foundation generally does not support individuals, religious organizations for sectarian purposes, political or lobbying groups, or organizations outside operating areas of Colorado.

Additional Information

Publications: Annual Report (including Application Guidelines)

Foundation Officials

James P. Craig: trustee
Ann Dillon: trustee
Louis J. Duman, MD: trustee
W. Eileen Greenawalt: secretary, trustee
Dorothy Harrell: executive director
Flaminia Odescalchi Kelly: trustee
Johnston R. Livingston: vice president, trustee B Foochow, People's Republic of China 1923. ED Yale University BS (1947); Harvard University MBA (1949). CORP AFFIL director: Construction Tech. NONPR AFFIL member: Sigma Xi; member: Tau Beta Ti; director: Rocky Mountain World Trade Association; director: National Repertory Orchestra; chairman: Rocky Mountain Regional Institute International Education; trustee: Bonfils Stanton Foundation; director: National Home Improvement Council. CLUB AFFIL Denver Country Club.
J. Landis Martin: trustee
John E. Repine, MD: trustee
Robert E. Stanton: president, treasurer, trustee

Grants Analysis

Disclosure Period: fiscal year ending June 30, 2001
Total Grants: $3,775,939*
Number of Grants: 137
Average Grant: $12,451*
Highest Grant: $620,000
Typical Range: $5,000 to $50,000
*Note: Giving excludes matching gifts, scholarships, and gifts to individuals. Average grant figure excludes four highest grants ($2,120,000). ($1,500,000).

Recent Grants

Note: Grants derived from fiscal 2000 Form 990.

General

500,000	Central City Opera House Association, Denver, CO -- for the Bonfils-Stanton Foundation Artist Training Program
500,000	Colorado Seminary, Denver, CO -- capital campaign
500,000	University of Colorado Foundation, Boulder, CO -- to help relocate the May Bonfils Stanton Outpatient Clinics
250,000	National Jewish Center for Immunological and Respiratory Medicine, Denver, CO -- toward funding the furnishings for the renovation of the historic Southside Building
100,000	Colorado Symphony Association, Denver, CO
100,000	Stanley British Primary School, Denver, CO -- to help renovate the Lowry facilities to accommodate the K-1 classes
75,000	Denver Art Museum, Denver, CO -- in support of the sculpture commission
50,000	Bonfils Blood Center Foundation, Denver, CO -- for additional equipment
35,000	Opera Colorado, Denver, CO -- to help with season 2000 opening production of Puccini's Madam Butterfly
30,000	Central City Opera House Association, Denver, CO -- for the Bonfils-Stanton Foundation Artist Training Program

BOOTH FERRIS FOUNDATION

Giving Contact

Hildy Simmons, Co-Trustee
Care of J.P. Morgan Chase
1211 Avenue of Americas
New York, NY 10036
Phone: (212)483-2323
Fax: (212)596-3712

Description

Founded: 1957
EIN: 136170340
Organization Type: General Purpose Foundation
Giving Locations: NY: New York metropolitan area nationally.
Grant Types: Capital, Challenge, General Support, Matching, Multiyear/Continuing Support, Operating Expenses, Project, Seed Money.

Donor Information

Founder: Founded in 1957 through trusts established by Mrs. Chancie Ferris Booth (d. 1957) and from the estate of Willis H. Booth (d. 1958). The combined trusts created the Booth Ferris Foundation in 1964. For many years, Willis Booth served as vice president of Guaranty Trust Company (now Morgan Guaranty Trust Company), and acted as trustee for many different corporations.

Financial Summary

Total Giving: $9,000,000 (2003 approx); $10,000,000 (2002 approx); $12,207,000 (2000)
Assets: $263,445,335 (2000); $278,785,912 (1999); $259,303,863 (1998)
Gifts Received: $64,831 (1998)

Typical Recipients

Arts & Humanities: Arts Associations & Councils, Arts Centers, Arts Funds, Arts Institutes, Arts Outreach, Ballet, Community Arts, Dance, Ethnic & Folk Arts, Film & Video, Historic Preservation, History & Archaeology, Libraries, Literary Arts, Museums/Galleries, Music, Opera, Performing Arts, Public Broadcasting, Theater
Civic & Public Affairs: African American Affairs, Asian American Affairs, Botanical Gardens/Parks, Business/Free Enterprise, Economic Development, Employment/Job Training, Civic & Public Affairs-General, Hispanic Affairs, Housing, Legal Aid, Municipalities/Towns, Nonprofit Management, Philanthropic Organizations, Professional & Trade Associations, Urban & Community Affairs, Women's Affairs
Education: Afterschool/Enrichment Programs, Arts/Humanities Education, Business Education, Colleges & Universities, Education Funds, Education Reform, Engineering/Technological Education, Faculty Development, Education-General, International Studies, Literacy, Minority Education, Private Education (Precollege), Public Education (Precollege), Science/Mathematics Education, Social Sciences Education, Vocational & Technical Education
Environment: Air/Water Quality, Environment-General, Wildlife Protection

Health: Children's Health/Hospitals, Emergency/Ambulance Services, Eyes/Blindness, Health Organizations, Hospitals, Nutrition, Research/Studies Institutes

International: Foreign Arts Organizations, International Peace & Security Issues

Religion: Churches, Jewish Causes, Ministries, Religious Organizations, Religious Welfare, Seminaries, Synagogues/Temples

Science: Science Museums, Scientific Labs

Social Services: At-Risk Youth, Child Welfare, Community Centers, Community Service Organizations, Day Care, Family Planning, Family Services, Food/Clothing Distribution, People with Disabilities, Recreation & Athletics, Shelters/Homelessness, Social Services-General, Substance Abuse, YMCA/YWCA/YMHA/YWHA, Youth Organizations

Application Procedures

Initial Contact: Send a formal proposal.
Application Requirements: Include annual report and financial data, including current budget and latest audited financial report.
Deadlines: None.

Restrictions

The foundation does not give support to organizations operating outside the United States, to individuals, for federated campaigns, to educational institutions for scholarships and fellowships, for restricted endowments, to social service and cultural programs outside the New York City metropolitan area, for specific diseases and disabilities, or for individual research.

Additional Information

Morgan Guaranty Trust Company of New York serves as corporate trustee for the foundation.
Publications: Annual Report
Trust(s): J.P. Morgan Chase Bank

Foundation Officials

Robert J. Murtagh: co-trustee

Grants Analysis

Disclosure Period: calendar year ending 2000
Total Grants: $12,207,000
Number of Grants: 127
Average Grant: $96,118
Highest Grant: $250,000
Lowest Grant: $7,000

Recent Grants

Note: Grants derived from 2001 Form 990.

General

250,000	Abyssinian Development Corp, New York, NY -- capital support
200,000	Cooper Union, New York, NY -- capital support
200,000	Gallaudet University, Washington, DC -- capital support
200,000	New York City Outward Bound Center, New York, NY -- capital support
150,000	Bard College, Annandale-on-Hudson, NY -- capital support
150,000	Big Apple Circus Children's Clown Unit, New York, NY -- capital support
150,000	Brooklyn Philharmonic Orchestra, Brooklyn, NY -- capacity building
150,000	Classroom, Inc., New York, NY -- to strengthen its technological capacity and increase its web-based teacher training
150,000	Cold Spring Harbor Laboratory, Cold Spring, NY -- capital support
150,000	East Harlem Employment Service, New York, NY -- capital support

CHARLES H. AND BERTHA L. BOOTHROYD FOUNDATION

Giving Contact

Donald C. Gancer, President
120 W. Madison Street, Suite 14-L
Chicago, IL 60602
Phone: (312)346-8333

Description

Founded: 1958
EIN: 366047045
Organization Type: Private Foundation
Giving Locations: IL
Grant Types: Research, Scholarship.

Donor Information

Founder: the late Mary T. Palzkill, Agnes K. McAvoy Trust

Financial Summary

Total Giving: $268,500 (fiscal year ending June 30, 2002); $294,000 (fiscal 2001); $255,000 (fiscal 2000)
Giving Analysis: Giving for fiscal 2002 includes: foundation scholarships ($35,000)
Assets: $5,792,306 (fiscal 2002); $6,213,814 (fiscal 2001); $5,687,305 (fiscal 2000)
Gifts Received: $67,166 (fiscal 2002); $260,000 (fiscal 2001); $3 (fiscal 1992). Note: In fiscal 2001 and 2002, contributions were received from Gudrun Alcock Trust. In 1992, contributions were received from Agness K. McAvoy.

Typical Recipients

Arts & Humanities: Arts Institutes, Libraries, Music, Opera, Theater
Civic & Public Affairs: Economic Development, Civic & Public Affairs-General, Law & Justice, Legal Aid, Municipalities/Towns, Women's Affairs
Education: Arts/Humanities Education, Colleges & Universities, Medical Education, Private Education (Precollege), Student Aid
Environment: Resource Conservation
Health: Alzheimers Disease, Clinics/Medical Centers, Health Funds, Health Organizations, Hospitals, Medical Research, Mental Health, Nursing Services, Single-Disease Health Associations
Religion: Religious Welfare
Social Services: Community Service Organizations, Senior Services

Application Procedures

Initial Contact: Send brief letter.
Application Requirements: Individual and organizational applicants must submit a brief resume of academic qualifications, purpose of funds sought, and proof of tax-exempt status. Research grants must include an outline of the proposed investigation and proposed budget.
Deadlines: None.

Foundation Officials

Gudrun Alcock: vice president
Bruce E. Brown: vice president
Donald Charles Gancer: president B Chicago, IL 1933. ED Marquette University LLB (1957). PRIM CORP EMPL principal: Querrey & Harrow Ltd. NONPR AFFIL member: Illinois State Bar Association; member: WI Bar Association; member: Chicago Bar Association; member: Chicago Council Lawyers; member: American Bar Association. CLUB AFFIL Union League Club; Oak Park Tennis Club.
Thomas C. Kaufmann: vice president
Lorraine Marcus: secretary
Dennis A. Marks: vice president

Grants Analysis

Disclosure Period: fiscal year ending June 30, 2002
Total Grants: $268,500
Number of Grants: 17
Average Grant: $19,029
Highest Grant: $35,000
Lowest Grant: $2,500
Typical Range: $8,500 to $20,000

Recent Grants

Note: Grants derived from fiscal 2002 Form 990.

Library-Related

2,500	Newberry Library, Chicago, IL

General

35,000	N. W. University Arts & Sciences, Evanston, IL
26,000	University of Chicago Department of Psychiatry, Chicago, IL
20,000	Bethel New Life, Chicago, IL
20,000	Evans Scholars Foundation, Golf, IL
20,000	H.O.M.E., Chicago, IL
20,000	St. Ignatius College Prep, Chicago, IL
15,000	Alzheimer's Association, Skokie, IL
15,000	Chicago Volunteer Legal Services, Chicago, IL
15,000	Daniel Murphy Scholarship Fund, Chicago, IL
15,000	Golden Apple, Chicago, IL

ALBERT AND ELAINE BORCHARD FOUNDATION

Giving Contact

Willard A. Beling, Chairman & Director
22055 Clarendon St., Suite 210
Woodland Hills, CA 91367
Phone: (818)888-2871

Description

Founded: 1978
EIN: 953294377
Organization Type: Private Foundation
Grant Types: General Support, Scholarship.

Financial Summary

Total Giving: $609,290 (fiscal year ending July 31, 2001); $631,607 (fiscal 2000); $515,898 (fiscal 1998)
Giving Analysis: Giving for fiscal 2001 includes: foundation matching gifts ($5,000); foundation fellowships ($25,000); fiscal 2000: foundation matching gifts ($12,000) foundation fellowships ($15,000)
Assets: $14,952,424 (fiscal 2001); $14,678,216 (fiscal 2000); $13,261,578 (fiscal 1998)
Gifts Received: $5,000 (fiscal 2001); $25,027 (fiscal 2000). Note: In fiscal 2001, contributions were received from Alzheimer's Association. In fiscal 2000, contributions were received from B. Lawrence Brennan ($5,027), Richard E. Kipper ($5,000), O.W. Moyle III ($5,000), Robert K. Johnson ($5,000), and the Alzheimer's Association ($5,000).

Typical Recipients

Arts & Humanities: History & Archaeology, Libraries, Museums/Galleries, Public Broadcasting, Theater
Civic & Public Affairs: Clubs, Employment/Job Training, Housing, Law & Justice, Legal Aid
Education: Afterschool/Enrichment Programs, Arts/Humanities Education, Colleges & Universities, Economic Education, Education Associations, Education Funds, Education Reform, International Exchange, International Studies, Legal Education, Medical Education, Science/Mathematics Education, Social Sciences Education, Special Education
Environment: Protection
Health: Adolescent Health Issues, Alzheimers Disease, Cancer, Children's Health/Hospitals, Emergency/Ambulance Services, Geriatric Health, Health

Policy/Cost Containment, Health Organizations, Medical Research, Prenatal Health Issues, Single-Disease Health Associations
International: Foreign Arts Organizations, Health Care/Hospitals
Religion: Religious Welfare
Social Services: Child Abuse, Child Welfare, Community Centers, Community Service Organizations, Crime Prevention, Delinquency & Criminal Rehabilitation, Family Planning, Family Services, People with Disabilities, Senior Services, United Funds/United Ways, Youth Organizations

Application Procedures

Initial Contact: Submit a written grant request, in triplicate.
Application Requirements: Include full proposal and proof of tax-exempt status.
Deadlines: None.

Restrictions

Does not support individuals.

Foundation Officials

Betty Beling: assoc director
Willard A. Beling: chairman, director B Great Bend, ND 1919. ED University of California, Los Angeles BA (1943); Princeton University PhD (1947). NONPR AFFIL professor: University Southern California.
Carol Spurgeon: assoc director
Edward Dutcher Spurgeon: president, director B Newton, NJ 1939. ED Princeton University AB (1961); Stanford University LLB (1964); New York University LLM (1968). NONPR AFFIL president, director: Sibert & Elaine Borchard Foundation; professor, dean sch law: University GA; member: American Bar Association; member: American Bar Foundation.

Grants Analysis

Disclosure Period: fiscal year ending July 31, 2001
Total Grants: $579,290*
Number of Grants: 62
Average Grant: $9,343
Highest Grant: $33,333
Lowest Grant: $250
Typical Range: $1,000 to $20,000
*Note: Giving excludes fellowships and matching gifts.

Recent Grants

Note: Grants derived from 2000 Form 990.

General

33,333	University of Southern California School of Medicine, Los Angeles, CA -- Borchard Foundation laboratory in Institute of Genetic Medicine
25,000	ABA Fund for Justice Education, Washington, DC -- conference on dementia
25,000	Regents of the University of California, Los Angeles, CA -- grants for Paris Programs in Critical Theory
25,000	University of Southern California, Los Angeles, CA -- reconstructing Russian History
20,000	Princeton University, Princeton, NJ -- council of humanities programs
20,000	University of California Los Angeles Foundation, Los Angeles, CA -- grant to underwrite artist's fee and residency activity of cappella choir
20,000	University of Southern California School of Medicine, Los Angeles, CA -- study on postoperative irradiation
20,000	Utah Legal Services, Salt Lake City, UT -- senior lawyer volunteer project
18,000	Regents of the University of California, Santa Barbara, CA -- conference on "Women and Books in Late Medieval and Renaissance Europe"
18,000	University of Southern California, Los

Angeles, CA -- conference on "Pharmacokinetic Imaging"

BORDEN, INC.

Company Headquarters

180 E. Broad St.
Columbus, OH 43215
Web: http://www.bordenfamily.com

Company Description

Employees: 4,200
SIC(s): 2022 Cheese--Natural & Processed, 2023 Dry, Condensed & Evaporated Dairy Products, 2024 Ice Cream & Frozen Desserts, 2026 Fluid Milk.

Operating Locations

Borden, Inc. (IL--Aurora; KY--Shively; LA--Lafayette, Lake Charles; MD--Ellicott City; MS--Jackson, McComb, Meridian, Petal; NJ--Fair Lawn; NM--Albuquerque, Gallup, Silver City; OH--Cincinnati, Reynoldsburg; OR--LaGrande; PA--Wellsboro; RI--Providence; TX--Abilene, Fort Worth, Houston, Mercedes, Pharr, San Antonio, Texarkana, Tyler, Waco; WA--Kent)

Nonmonetary Support

Type: Donated Products; In-kind Services

Borden Foundation, Inc.

Giving Contact

Colleen Nissl, President
Borden Foundation
180 East Broad Street
24th Floor
Columbus, OH 43215-3799
Phone: (614)225-4580
Fax: (614)225-4066

Description

Founded: 1944
EIN: 136089941
Organization Type: Corporate Foundation
Giving Locations: principally near operating locations and to national organizations.
Grant Types: Challenge, Department, Employee Matching Gifts, General Support, Multiyear/Continuing Support.
Note: Matches gifts for higher education, health care, and youth and arts organisation.

Financial Summary

Total Giving: $835,441 (2001); $1,582,764 (2000); $1,000,000 (1999 approx)
Giving Analysis: Giving for 2000 includes: foundation matching gifts ($103,742); foundation grants to United Way ($215,477); foundation ($1,263,545); 1999: foundation (approx $1,000,000); 1998: foundation scholarships ($37,500); foundation grants to United Way ($241,436) foundation ($1,211,669)
Assets: $1,541,186 (1998); $1,706,045 (1996); $93,925 (1995)
Gifts Received: $835,441 (2001); $1,665,590 (1998); $677,076 (1996)

Typical Recipients

Arts & Humanities: Arts Associations & Councils, Arts Centers, Arts Institutes, Ballet, Community Arts, Dance, Historic Preservation, Libraries, Museums/Galleries, Music, Opera, Performing Arts, Public Broadcasting, Theater
Civic & Public Affairs: African American Affairs, Botanical Gardens/Parks, Business/Free Enterprise, Chambers of Commerce, Civil Rights, Clubs, Community Foundations, Economic Development, Economic Policy, Ethnic Organizations, Civic & Public

Affairs-General, Hispanic Affairs, Law & Justice, Legal Aid, Municipalities/Towns, Nonprofit Management, Parades/Festivals, Philanthropic Organizations, Professional & Trade Associations, Public Policy, Public Policy, Urban & Community Affairs, Women's Affairs, Zoos/Aquariums
Education: Business Education, Colleges & Universities, Continuing Education, Education Associations, Education Funds, Education Reform, Elementary Education (Public), Engineering/Technological Education, Education-General, Literacy, Medical Education, Minority Education, Private Education (Precollege), Public Education (Precollege), Science/Mathematics Education, Special Education, Student Aid
Environment: Environment-General
Health: AIDS/HIV, Arthritis, Cancer, Children's Health/Hospitals, Diabetes, Emergency/Ambulance Services, Eyes/Blindness, Hospitals, Medical Research, Mental Health, Prenatal Health Issues, Public Health, Single-Disease Health Associations, Speech & Hearing
International: Health Care/Hospitals, International Relations, International Relief Efforts, Missionary/Religious Activities
Religion: Churches, Dioceses, Religion-General, Religious Organizations, Religious Welfare
Science: Science Museums, Scientific Centers & Institutes, Scientific Organizations
Social Services: At-Risk Youth, Big Brother/Big Sister, Child Welfare, Community Service Organizations, Domestic Violence, Emergency Relief, Family Services, Food/Clothing Distribution, Homes, People with Disabilities, Recreation & Athletics, Scouts, Shelters/Homelessness, Social Services-General, United Funds/United Ways, Volunteer Services, YMCA/YWCA/YMHA/YWHA, Youth Organizations

Application Procedures

Initial Contact: Send a brief letter or resume.
Application Requirements: Include a description of organization, amount requested, purpose of funds sought, recently audited financial statement, and proof of tax-exempt status. Also provide an outline of a proposed budget with percentages, for the past three years; (7) amount and percentage of total income expended for fund raising, program, administrative, and general operations for the past two years; (8) copy of IRS tax-exemption letter, current financial statement, and most recent financial audit; (9) information on Philanthropic Advisory Service rating; (10) a description of organization's affiliations; (11) purpose of project or request, including whether problem area to be addressed is a special project or part of general operating support; (12) why organization should be the vehicle of support for project and how this project will benefit recipients and total community; (13) how project will be carried out; and (14) principal.
Deadlines: None.
Review Process: Initial screening, research, and evaluation conducted by foundation staff to ensure compliance with grant criteria.
Decision Notification: Notice of approval, rejection, or request for additional information will be sent within three to six months of application.
Notes: Preliminary letters are reviewed within 60 days of receipt. The foundation will notify organization if a formal proposal is needed.

Restrictions

Foundation does not support individuals; endowments; memberships; lobbying organizations; conferences, workshops, or seminars; building or renovation; journal advertisements; political activities or organizations; organizations deriving major support from government funding; or organizations that discriminate in any way consistent with national equal opportunity policies.

Requests to consider a portion of the support for a project will generally receive greater priority. Applicants must be 501(c)(3) or 501(a) organizations.

Additional Information

Foundation requires status reports on the success of project.

Corporate Officials

C. Robert Kidder: chairman, president, chief executive officer, director B Freeport, NY 1943. ED University of Michigan BS (1966); Iowa State University MS (1968). PRIM CORP EMPL chairman, president, chief executive officer, director: Borden, Inc. CORP AFFIL director: Morgan Stanley Dean Witter Co.; director: Resource Partners Inc.; director: Electronic Data Systems Corp.; chairman: Corning Consumer Products Co.; director: Dean Witter Reynolds Inc.; chairman: Borden Foods Corp.; chairman: Borden Holdings Inc.; chairman: Borden Chemicals; director: AEP Industries Inc.; director: B.F. Processing Corp.

Foundation Officials

Frankie Nowland: president, director social responsibilities

Grants Analysis

Disclosure Period: calendar year ending 2001
Total Grants: $722,278*
Number of Grants: 37
Average Grant: $3,397*
Highest Grant: $600,000
Lowest Grant: $200
Typical Range: $500 to $5,000 and $25,000 to $70,000
*****Note:** Giving excludes matching gifts and United Way. Average grant figure excludes highest grant.

Recent Grants

Note: Grants derived from 2001 Form 990.

General

600,000	Columbus Foundation, Columbus, OH -- Grant
91,443	United Way Franklin County, Columbus, OH
21,720	Matching Gift Projection
12,500	Columbus Speech and Hearing, Columbus, OH
10,500	Greater Columbus Chamber of Commerce, Columbus, OH
10,000	Catalyst, New York, NY
8,000	YMCA, Columbus, OH
7,500	Columbus Literacy Council, Columbus, OH
5,000	Center for New Directions, Columbus, OH
5,000	Directions for Youth, Columbus, OH

BORKEE-HAGLEY FOUNDATION

Giving Contact

Henry H. Silliman, Jr., President
PO Box 4590
Greenville, DE 19807
Phone: (302)652-8616

Description

Founded: 1955
EIN: 516011644
Organization Type: Private Foundation
Giving Locations: DE
Grant Types: Capital, General Support.

Financial Summary

Total Giving: $630,500 (2000); $534,000 (1999); $516,000 (1998)
Assets: $10,345,530 (2000); $13,304,791 (1999); $11,268,686 (1998)

Typical Recipients

Arts & Humanities: History & Archaeology, Libraries, Museums/Galleries
Civic & Public Affairs: Clubs, Employment/Job Training, Civic & Public Affairs-General, Housing, Professional & Trade Associations, Public Policy, Urban & Community Affairs, Women's Affairs
Education: Arts/Humanities Education, Business Education, Colleges & Universities, Environmental Education, Education-General, Private Education (Precollege), Public Education (Precollege), Vocational & Technical Education
Environment: Environment-General, Resource Conservation
Health: Emergency/Ambulance Services, Geriatric Health, Health Organizations, Hospices, Hospitals, Long-Term Care, Preventive Medicine/Wellness Organizations, Public Health
Religion: Jewish Causes, Ministries, Religious Organizations, Religious Welfare
Social Services: Big Brother/Big Sister, Big Brother/Big Sister, Child Welfare, Community Centers, Community Service Organizations, Day Care, Family Planning, Family Services, Food/Clothing Distribution, Homes, People with Disabilities, Recreation & Athletics, Senior Services, Social Services-General, Special Olympics, YMCA/YWCA/YMHA/YWHA, Youth Organizations

Application Procedures

Initial Contact: Send a brief letter of inquiry on organization's stationery.
Application Requirements: Includes organization's purpose, proof of tax-exempt status, and details about the area of need for funds requested.
Deadlines: November 1.

Restrictions

Preference is given to organizations engaged in activities benefiting the elderly.

Foundation Officials

Thomas F. Husbands: assistant treasurer
Eleanor Silliman Maroney: secretary
George A. Sandbach: director
Henry Harper Silliman, Jr.: president
John E. Silliman: vice president B Scarsdale, NY 1934. ED Yale University BA (1956); Columbia University LLB (1959). PRIM CORP EMPL partner: Murtha, Cullina, Richter & Pinney.
Robert M. Silliman: vice president, treasurer ED Yale University.
Doris Silliman Stockly: director

Grants Analysis

Disclosure Period: calendar year ending 2000
Total Grants: $630,500
Number of Grants: 62
Average Grant: $10,169
Highest Grant: $50,000
Lowest Grant: $1,000
Typical Range: $3,000 to $20,000

Recent Grants

Note: Grants derived from 2001 Form 990.

General

25,000	Delaware Nature Society, Hockessin, DE -- capital
25,000	St. Anne's Episcopal School, Middletown, DE -- capital
25,000	Tower Hill School, Wilmington, DE -- capital
25,000	Wilmington Youth Rowing Association, Wilmington, DE -- capital
20,000	Christiana Care Foundation, Wilmington, DE -- capital
20,000	Delaware Elwyn, Inc., Wilmington, DE -- capital
20,000	Habitat for Humanity, Wilmington, DE -- capital
20,000	Pilot School, Wilmington, DE -- capital
20,000	Wellness Community, Wilmington, DE -- capital
16,000	Sanford School, Hockessin, DE -- capital

THE BOSTON GLOBE

Company Headquarters

Boston, MA
Web: http://www.boston.com

Company Description

Revenue: US$201 million (2002)
Employees: 2175 (2002)
SIC(s): 2711 Newspapers.
Parent Company: New York Times Co., 229 W. 43rd Street, New York, NY, United States

Operating Locations

The Boston Globe (MA--Billerica, Waltham)

Nonmonetary Support

Type: Cause-related Marketing & Promotion; In-kind Services
Note: Co. provides nonmonetary support. Supports the Globe Santa Program, which raises funds from readers to provide Christmas donations to needy families.

Boston Globe Foundation

Giving Contact

Mrs. Bailey
135 Morrissey Boulevard, 2nd Floor
Boston, MA 02107
Phone: (617)929-3467
Fax: (617)929-2041
E-mail: foundation@globe.com
Web: http://bostonglobe.com/community/index.stm

Description

EIN: 222821421
Organization Type: Corporate Foundation
Giving Locations: MA: Boston, Cambridge, Chelsea, Somerville
Grant Types: Capital, Employee Matching Gifts, General Support, Multiyear/Continuing Support.
Note: Employee matching gift ratio: 1 to 1 to education.

Financial Summary

Total Giving: $345,566 (2001); $2,765,364 (2000); $1,866,436 (1999). Note: Contributes through foundation only. In 2000, the foundation changed from a fiscal year to a calendar year; giving figure for 2000 includes contributions made from July 31, 1999 to December 31, 2000.
Giving Analysis: Giving for 2000 includes: foundation grants to United Way ($41,789); foundation scholarships ($96,231); foundation ($2,627,344); 1999: foundation matching gifts ($32,275); foundation grants to United Way ($295,000) foundation ($1,539,161)
Assets: $108,774 (2001); $4,623,923 (2000); $637,776 (1999)
Gifts Received: $1,241,638 (2001); $1,573,249 (2000); $1,999,315 (1999). Note: Contributions received from Globe Newspaper Company.

Typical Recipients

Arts & Humanities: Arts Associations & Councils, Arts Festivals, Arts Funds, Arts Outreach, Ballet, Dance, Ethnic & Folk Arts, Arts & Humanities-General, Libraries, Museums/Galleries, Music, Performing Arts, Public Broadcasting, Theater, Visual Arts

Civic & Public Affairs: Botanical Gardens/Parks, Business/Free Enterprise, Economic Development, Employment/Job Training, Hispanic Affairs, Housing, Nonprofit Management, Philanthropic Organizations, Professional & Trade Associations, Safety, Urban & Community Affairs, Women's Affairs, Zoos/Aquariums

Education: Afterschool/Enrichment Programs, Business-School Partnerships, Colleges & Universities, Education Reform, Elementary Education (Private), Environmental Education, Faculty Development, Education-General, Journalism/Media Education, Literacy, Medical Education, Minority Education, Preschool Education, Private Education (Precollege), Public Education (Precollege), Science/Mathematics Education, Special Education, Student Aid

Environment: Environment-General, Protection

Health: AIDS/HIV, Children's Health/Hospitals, Clinics/Medical Centers, Health Organizations, Hospitals, Medical Research, Mental Health, Nutrition

International: Foreign Arts Organizations, Human Rights

Religion: Religious Welfare

Science: Science Museums

Social Services: Camps, Child Welfare, Community Centers, Community Service Organizations, Counseling, Crime Prevention, Day Care, Domestic Violence, Family Services, Food/Clothing Distribution, Homes, People with Disabilities, Recreation & Athletics, Shelters/Homelessness, Substance Abuse, United Funds/United Ways, Youth Organizations

Application Procedures

Initial Contact: Apply using the Associated Grantmakers of Massachusetts (AGM) Common Proposal Format and a Boston Globe Foundation Addendum. Contact the AGM and Boston Globe Foundation for forms.

Application Requirements: Completed proposal following the AGM Common Proposal Format and answers to all questions asked on the Boston Globe Foundation's Addendum.

Deadlines: None.

Review Process: Proposals reviewed by foundation staff, agencies investigated, budgetary requirements evaluated, and recommendation made to foundation board which meets February, June and in the fall.

Evaluative Criteria: The foundation's primary funding criteria is to support programs and operations of well-managed, financially viable charitable organizations based in Boston, Cambridge, Somerville and Chelsea, MA that serve youth ages 0-22 who live primarily in low-income neighborhoods. Secondary funding criteria include a preference for programs that foster inclusion of youth not participating fully in society; build bridges for youth across divides (neighborhood borders, varied backgrounds); link youth programs with other neighborhood initiatives, as participants in an integrated community effort; and demonstrate effective and consistent constituency involvement in creation and implementation of programs. The foundation also evaluates whether an agency values inclusion and diversity among staff, clientele and decision-makers; has active governing bodies knowledgeable about the organization's mission and constituents; addresses systemic causes of a problem, or educates the public on important issues.

Decision Notification: Allow four to six months for processing.

Notes: Foundation sponsors meetings on how to shape proposals. Call the foundation for more information regarding community information meetings.

Restrictions

The foundation does not make grants to individuals or for the purchase of tables, tickets, or advertising. The foundation does not make more than one grant per fiscal year to any one organization.

Additional Information

The Globe Santa Fund solicits through advertising and publicity contributions to purchase Christmas gifts for needy children. The company also administers several scholarship programs, including the L.L. Winship Scholarship Fund (for children of full-time company employees), the I. Arthur Seigel Scholarship Fund (athletic), the Marjorie L. Adams Scholarship Fund (for children of employees), and the Louis Shriber Scholarship Fund (for Globe newsboys). The company also sponsors scholastic art awards and the Globe Interscholastic Festival.

The foundation holds bi-weekly informational meetings for grantseekers to help shape proposals. Staff explains funding priorities and application procedures. The contact for these meetings is Sylvia Payton, at (617)929-2895.

The New York Times Company acquired the Globe Newspaper Co.'s parent corporation, Affiliated Publications, in 1993.

Publications: Application; Guidelines; Report to the Community

Foundation Officials

Richard H. Gilman: director
Leslie Griffin: director
Richard Gula: president, director
Al Larkin: president
Suzanne W. Maas: executive director
Mary Marty: assistant treasurer B 1942. ED Marycrest College (1964). PRIM CORP EMPL treasurer: Affiliated Publications Inc. ADD CORP EMPL treasurer: Globe SPLty Products Inc.
Loretta McLaughlin: director
Mary Jane Patrone: director, clerk
Sylvia Payton: program officer
Mariella Puerto: project director
Randall K. Short: assistant treasurer
Benjamin B. Taylor: director B 1947. ED Harvard University. PRIM CORP EMPL president, publisher chairman: Globe Newspaper Co. NONPR AFFIL trustee: Park School; trustee: Radcliffe College.

Grants Analysis

Disclosure Period: calendar year ending 2001
Total Grants: $345,566
Number of Grants: 28 (approx)
Average Grant: $10,129*
Highest Grant: $72,090 (approx)
Lowest Grant: $2,500 (approx)
Typical Range: $10,000 to $50,000
*Note: Average grant figure excludes highest grant.

Recent Grants

Note: Grants derived from 1996 Form 990.

General

70,000	University of Massachusetts Boston, Boston, MA -- support 1996 Taylor Scholars Program
50,000	Boston Globe Foundation, Boston, MA -- for Lead Action Plan
39,000	Project Bread, Boston, MA -- for Emergency Feeding Network
20,000	New England Aquarium, Boston, MA -- program support, capital campaign
15,000	Black Church Capacity Building Project -- support of Black Church Capacity Building Project
15,000	Boston Children's Services, Boston, MA -- for Project Excel
15,000	HSPC Diversity Initiative -- support arts and humanities organizations
15,000	Roca, Inc., Chelsea, MA -- renovations
15,000	WGBH Educational Foundation, Springfield, MA -- for National Center for Accessible Media
13,400	Associated Grantmakers of Massachusetts, Boston, MA -- support services

THE BOTHIN FOUNDATION

Giving Contact

Lyman H. Casey, Executive Director & Treasurer
Presidio Blvd., Suite 1016
PO Box 29906
San Francisco, CA 94129-0906
Phone: (415)561-6540
Fax: (415)561-6477
Web: http://www.pacificfoundationservices.com

Description

Founded: 1926
EIN: 941196182
Organization Type: General Purpose Foundation
Giving Locations: CA: San Francisco metropolitan area
Grant Types: Capital.

Donor Information

Founder: Established as a private foundation in the State of California on September 28, 1917 by Henry E. Bothin, his wife, Ellen Chabot Bothin, and his daughter, Genevieve Bothin de Limur. The foundation is administered by a board of directors, several of whom are members of the Bothin family and was formerly known as the Bothin Helping Fund.

Financial Summary

Total Giving: $1,500,000 (2002 approx); $1,557,117 (2001); $1,751,031 (2000)
Assets: $38,027,684 (2001); $41,462,760 (2000); $33,765,137 (1998)

Typical Recipients

Arts & Humanities: Arts Associations & Councils, Arts Centers, Arts Festivals, Arts Outreach, Ethnic & Folk Arts, Film & Video, Libraries, Museums/Galleries, Music, Public Broadcasting, Theater

Civic & Public Affairs: Asian American Affairs, Botanical Gardens/Parks, Business/Free Enterprise, Community Foundations, Economic Development, Employment/Job Training, Civic & Public Affairs-General, Hispanic Affairs, Housing, Legal Aid, Urban & Community Affairs, Women's Affairs, Zoos/Aquariums

Education: Afterschool/Enrichment Programs, Business Education, Colleges & Universities, Education Funds, Elementary Education (Private), Education-General, Gifted & Talented Programs, Leadership Training, Private Education (Precollege), School Volunteerism, Science/Mathematics Education, Secondary Education (Private), Secondary Education (Public), Special Education, Student Aid

Environment: Environment-General, Resource Conservation, Wildlife Protection

Health: AIDS/HIV, Cancer, Clinics/Medical Centers, Emergency/Ambulance Services, Eyes/Blindness, Health Organizations, Home-Care Services, Hospices, Hospitals, Hospitals (University Affiliated), Kidney, Medical Rehabilitation, Mental Health, Prenatal Health Issues, Speech & Hearing

International: Human Rights, International Environmental Issues, International Relations

Religion: Churches, Ministries, Religious Welfare

Science: Scientific Centers & Institutes, Scientific Research

Social Services: Animal Protection, At-Risk Youth, Camps, Child Welfare, Community Centers, Community Service Organizations, Counseling, Day Care, Domestic Violence, Family Planning, Family Services, Food/Clothing Distribution, People with Disabilities, Recreation & Athletics, Senior Services, Sexual Abuse, Shelters/Homelessness, Social Services-General, Substance Abuse, Volunteer Services, YMCA/YWCA/YMHA/YWHA, Youth Organizations

Application Procedures

Initial Contact: Applicants should submit a brief preliminary letter of request.

Application Requirements: Requests for support should include a description of the goals and objectives of the proposed project; purpose and history of the applying organization; names and qualifications of the project's staff; total operating budget, estimated or proposed budget for the project; amount requested; other sources of income; and proof of tax exemption. If additional information is needed, the foundation will contact the applicant.

Deadlines: Applications should be submitted 12 weeks prior to board meetings.

Review Process: All requests satisfying the guidelines are submitted to the advisory committee for preliminary review before being presented to the board of directors. The board meets three times per year, in February, May, and October. Applicants should expect a waiting period of up to three months before funding decisions are made. All requests are answered with a written response within a reasonable period of time.

Restrictions

Grants are not made to individuals, for endowment drives, general operating expenses, films or other media presentations, religious groups for sectarian purposes, medical research, conferences, program support, or educational institutions other than those directly serving the developmentally or learning disabled. Grants are not made for events, annual appeals, or scholarships.

Additional Information

The foundation prefers that a full three years elapse between grants.

Publications: Biennial Report

Foundation Officials

A. Michael Casey: vice president, treasurer ED University of California at Berkeley (1964); University of California Hastings School Law JD (1967).

Lyman H. Casey: executive director

Genevieve Bothin Lyman di San Faustino: president, director, donor granddaughter

Stephanie MacColl: director NONPR AFFIL director: San Francisco Foundation.

Edmona Lyman Mansell: vice president, director

Gordon E. Miller: director

Rhoda Schultz: director

Grants Analysis

Disclosure Period: calendar year ending 2001
Total Grants: $1,557,117
Number of Grants: 95
Average Grant: $16,390
Highest Grant: $185,000
Lowest Grant: $1,000
Typical Range: $5,000 to $30,000

Recent Grants

Note: Grants derived from 2001 Form 990.

General

185,000	Families On Track Project, San Francisco, CA -- support for academic programs and social services for at-risk students and their families at Parkway Heights Middle School
100,000	California Academy of Science, San Francisco, CA -- toward the California Academy of science capital campaign
50,000	San Francisco Conservatory of Music, San Francisco, CA -- toward the campaign for construction of the new San Francisco Conservatory of Music facility at civic center
25,000	Golden Gate Community Incorporated, San Francisco, CA -- replace roof at

	Oak Street House, a transitional shelter for homeless women and their children
25,000	Kids Street Learning Center -- toward renovation of the Lincoln Arts Center that houses the Kid Street Charter School for the homeless and at-risk children
25,000	Marin General Hospital Foundation, Greenbrae, CA -- purchase IMRT computer software for the Radiation Oncology Department
25,000	Marine Mammal Center, Sausalito, CA -- purchase computer equipment to develop new medical database for the veterinary science program
25,000	Okizu Foundation, Novato, CA -- toward construction of new playground and renovation of existing playground for the childcare programs
25,000	Raphael House, San Francisco, CA -- toward capital campaign to renovate the shelter for homeless families and children
25,000	RCH, Inc., San Francisco, CA -- toward renovation of the therapeutic swimming pool

BOURNS, INC.

Company Headquarters

1200 Columbia Avenue
Riverside, CA 92507
Phone: (909)781-5500
Fax: (909)781-5006
Web: http://www.bourns.com

Company Description

Revenue: US$9 million (2001)
Employees: 150 (2001)
SIC(s): 3676 Electronic Resistors, 3679 Electronic Components Nec, 3699 Electrical Equipment & Supplies Nec.

Operating Locations

Recon-Optical, Inc. (CA--Riverside)

Nonmonetary Support

Type: Donated Equipment

Bourns Foundation

Giving Contact

Gordon L. Bourns, President
1200 Columbia Ave.
Riverside, CA 92507
Phone: (909)781-5084
Fax: (909)781-5203

Description

EIN: 956044472
Organization Type: Corporate Foundation
Giving Locations: CA: focusing on Inland Empire area of Southern California; UT
Grant Types: Capital, Endowment, Multiyear/Continuing Support, Scholarship.

Financial Summary

Total Giving: $31,000 (fiscal year ending November 30, 2001); $1,063,950 (fiscal 2000); $1,425,105 (fiscal 1999). Note: Contributes through foundation only.

Giving Analysis: Giving for fiscal 2000 includes: foundation scholarships ($8,000); foundation ($1,055,950); fiscal 1999: foundation grants to United Way ($4,000); foundation ($1,421,105); fiscal 1998: foundation ($1,696,539);

Assets: $449,648 (fiscal 2001); $452,919 (fiscal 2000); $309,501 (fiscal 1999)

Gifts Received: $1,188,234 (fiscal 2000); $1,328,313 (fiscal 1999); $1,800,000 (fiscal 1998). Note: Contributions were received from Bourns, Inc.

Typical Recipients

Arts & Humanities: Arts & Humanities-General, Museums/Galleries

Civic & Public Affairs: Clubs, Economic Development, Civic & Public Affairs-General

Education: Arts/Humanities Education, Business Education, Colleges & Universities, Education Funds, Engineering/Technological Education, Education-General, Private Education (Precollege), Public Education (Precollege), Religious Education, Science/Mathematics Education, Student Aid

Health: Cancer, Children's Health/Hospitals, Diabetes, Health-General, Hospices, Hospitals, Mental Health

Religion: Religious Welfare

Social Services: Community Service Organizations, Recreation & Athletics, Scouts, Shelters/Homelessness, Social Services-General, United Funds/United Ways, YMCA/YWCA/YMHA/YWHA, Youth Organizations

Application Procedures

Initial Contact: Send a brief letter of inquiry.
Application Requirements: Include description of program, including benefits, and purpose of funds sought.
Deadlines: None.

Corporate Officials

Gordon L. Bourns: chairman finance, chief financial officer, treasurer B 1949. ED University of California, Los Angeles BSEE (1971); University of California, Los Angeles MBA (1973). PRIM CORP EMPL chairman: Bourns, Inc.

William P. McKenna: vice president finance, chief financial officer, treasurer B 1947. ED College of the Holy Cross MA (1968); University of Southern California MBA (1976). PRIM CORP EMPL vice president finance, chief financial officer, treasurer: Bourns, Inc.

Foundation Officials

Gordon L. Bourns: president, trustee (see above)
Linda Bourns Hill: vice president, trustee
Anita L. MacBeth: trustee CORP AFFIL director: Bourns Inc.
Denise L. Moyles: trustee
Gerald T. Young: secretary, treasurer, trustee

Grants Analysis

Disclosure Period: fiscal year ending November 30, 2002
Total Grants: $16,450*
Number of Grants: 5
Average Grant: $2,800*
Highest Grant: $5,200
Lowest Grant: $2,000
Typical Range: $2,000 to $10,000
***Note:** Grants analysis provided by foundation. Giving excludes scholarships. Average grant figure excludes highest grant.

Recent Grants

Note: Grants derived from fiscal 2001 Form 990.

General

10,000	Orange Coast College Foundation, Costa Mesa, CA -- Educational Programs
5,000	Utah State University, Logan, UT -- engineering scholarships
3,750	Valle Monte League, San Jose, CA -- Christmas tree elegance
3,000	University of California Riverside, Riverside, CA -- engineering scholarships
2,500	Newport Harbor High School, Costa Mesa, CA -- Educational Programs
2,500	Regents of the University of California, Riverside, CA -- College of Engineering

2,000	Junior League, Riverside, CA -- Charity Ball campaign
2,000	University of California Riverside, Riverside, CA -- Alumni and Visitor Center
250	Assistance League, Riverside, CA -- underprivileged children

BOUTELL MEMORIAL FUND

Giving Contact
Helen James, Trust Officer
c/o CB Wealth Management
101 N. Washington
Saginaw, MI 48607
Phone: (989)776-7368

Description
Founded: 1961
EIN: 386040492
Organization Type: Private Foundation
Giving Locations: MI: Saginaw County
Grant Types: General Support.

Donor Information
Founder: the late Arnold and Gertrude Boutell

Financial Summary
Total Giving: $470,236 (fiscal year ending March 31, 2002); $344,697 (fiscal 2001); $726,803 (fiscal 2000)
Giving Analysis: Giving for fiscal 2001 includes: foundation grants to United Way ($23,000); fiscal 2000: foundation grants to United Way ($23,000) fiscal 1999: foundation grants to United Way ($105,000)
Assets: $11,829,470 (fiscal 2002); $12,169,683 (fiscal 2001); $14,303,417 (fiscal 2000)

Typical Recipients
Arts & Humanities: Community Arts, Dance, Libraries, Music, Public Broadcasting
Civic & Public Affairs: Community Foundations, Economic Development, Employment/Job Training, Civic & Public Affairs-General, Housing, Municipalities/Towns, Parades/Festivals, Rural Affairs, Safety, Urban & Community Affairs, Zoos/Aquariums
Education: Business-School Partnerships, Colleges & Universities, Public Education (Precollege)
Health: Emergency/Ambulance Services, Health Funds, Hospitals, Prenatal Health Issues
Religion: Religious Welfare
Social Services: At-Risk Youth, Child Abuse, Child Welfare, Community Service Organizations, Crime Prevention, Family Services, Recreation & Athletics, Shelters/Homelessness, United Funds/United Ways, YMCA/YWCA/YMHA/YWHA, Youth Organizations

Application Procedures
Initial Contact: Send letter requesting application guidelines. There are no deadlines.

Restrictions
Does not support individuals.

Additional Information
Trust(s): CB Wealth Management
Publications: Application Guidelines

Grants Analysis
Disclosure Period: fiscal year ending March 31, 2002
Total Grants: $470,236
Number of Grants: 34
Average Grant: $12,128*
Highest Grant: $70,000
Lowest Grant: $1,000
Typical Range: $5,000 to $25,000
*Note: Average grant excludes highest grant.

Recent Grants
Note: Grants derived from 2000 Form 990.

General
100,000	Saginaw County Parks and Recreation Commission, Saginaw, MI
95,100	City of Saginaw School District, Saginaw, MI
75,000	Boys & Girls Club, Saginaw, MI
50,000	City Rescue Mission, Saginaw, MI
50,000	Saginaw Community Foundation, Saginaw, MI
40,000	Opportunities Industrialization, Saginaw, MI
30,000	Healthy Delivery Inc., Saginaw, MI
25,000	Neighborhood Renewal Services, Saginaw, MI
25,000	Neighborhood Renewal Services of Saginaw, Saginaw, MI
25,000	Saginaw Valley State University, University Center, MI

MERVIN BOVAIRD FOUNDATION

Giving Contact
R. Casey Cooper, President & Trustee
401 S. Boston, Suite 3300
Tulsa, OK 74103-4070
Phone: (918)592-3300

Description
Founded: 1955
EIN: 736102163
Organization Type: General Purpose Foundation
Giving Locations: OK: Tulsa metropolitan area
Grant Types: Capital, Challenge, Conference/Seminar, General Support, Matching, Multiyear/Continuing Support, Operating Expenses, Project, Research, Scholarship.

Donor Information
Founder: Established in 1955 by the late Mabel W. Bovaird (1893-1979) to honor her deceased husband, Mervin Bovaird (1890-1949). The Bovairds were longtime residents of Tulsa, OK.

Financial Summary
Total Giving: $1,787,776 (2001); $2,138,776 (2000); $2,346,123 (1999). Note: 1996 Giving includes scholarship ($402,000) and pledges ($915,000).
Giving Analysis: Giving for 2001 includes: foundation grants to United Way ($15,000) 2000: foundation scholarships ($351,000)
Assets: $42,664,096 (2001); $44,952,905 (2000); $40,817,294 (1999)

Typical Recipients
Arts & Humanities: Art History, Arts Associations & Councils, Arts Institutes, Ballet, Dance, Libraries, Literary Arts, Museums/Galleries, Music, Opera, Public Broadcasting, Theater
Civic & Public Affairs: African American Affairs, Botanical Gardens/Parks, Community Foundations, Civic & Public Affairs-General, Legal Aid, Municipalities/Towns, Safety, Urban & Community Affairs, Women's Affairs, Zoos/Aquariums
Education: Colleges & Universities, Community & Junior Colleges, Education Associations, Education Reform, Elementary Education (Private), Elementary Education (Public), Engineering/Technological Education, Gifted & Talented Programs, Legal Education, Preschool Education, Private Education (Precollege), Social Sciences Education, Special Education, Student Aid
Environment: Environment-General, Resource Conservation

Health: Arthritis, Cancer, Children's Health/Hospitals, Clinics/Medical Centers, Emergency/Ambulance Services, Health Policy/Cost Containment, Health Organizations, Heart, Hospices, Hospitals, Kidney, Long-Term Care, Medical Rehabilitation, Medical Research, Mental Health, Multiple Sclerosis, Prenatal Health Issues, Single-Disease Health Associations, Speech & Hearing
Religion: Churches, Religion-General, Religious Welfare
Social Services: At-Risk Youth, Big Brother/Big Sister, Camps, Child Welfare, Community Service Organizations, Day Care, Domestic Violence, Family Planning, Family Planning, Family Services, Food/Clothing Distribution, Homes, People with Disabilities, Scouts, Senior Services, Sexual Abuse, Shelters/Homelessness, Substance Abuse, United Funds/United Ways, Volunteer Services, YMCA/YWCA/YMHA/YWHA, Youth Organizations

Application Procedures
Initial Contact: General grant applicants should send a brief letter to the foundation.
Application Requirements: General grant proposals should include legal name and address of organization; name, title, address, and phone number of primary contact; a description of organization, including summary of its background and qualifications in funding area sought; description of project, its expected achievements, and its importance; descriptions of people, organizations, or groups expected to benefit from project and ways they would benefit; detailed expenditure budget for project, indicating how major elements of expense were estimated, how requested funds are to be spent, and during what periods; description of other possible sources of support, including funds received or pledged; and grant amount sought.
In an appendix, also include photocopies of most recent IRS Section 501(c)(3) and 509(a) rulings; statement signed by CEO that organization's purpose, character, or operations have not changed since IRS's determination; most recently audited completed fiscal year, or most recent IRS Form 990; interim financial statement for current fiscal period; and list of names and primary professional affiliations of governing body, and names and titles of officers.
Deadlines: The general application deadline is November 15, and the scholarship application deadline is in May.
Review Process: Scholarship recipients are chosen by the schools, based on need and ability. The foundation is governed by trustees, presently five, who meet periodically to consider requests for gifts. The bulk of applications will be acted on by the trustees on or about December 1 each year. When an application has been acted on by the trustees, it will be accepted or rejected in writing with a determination being sent to the applicant's mailing address.

Restrictions
Grants are restricted to the metropolitan Tulsa, OK, area. The foundation does not make loans. The foundation makes grants only to nonprofit, tax-exempt organizations in existence at least three years, and occasionally to local government. As a general rule, the foundation does not contribute to any organization whose administrative expense, including fund-raising expense, exceeds 25% of its annual budget.
Scholarship support for Tulsa, OK, high school and Tulsa Community College graduates attending University of Tulsa is based on a student's ability to maintain proper scholastic standing. Scholarships are for undergraduate study only and are limited to $6,000 each per academic year.

Additional Information
Publications: Policies and Procedures

Foundation Officials

Wanda W. Brown: secretary
Richard Casey Cooper: president, trustee B Tulsa, OK 1942. ED University of Tulsa BSBA (1965); University of Tulsa JD (1967). PRIM CORP EMPL managing partner: Boesche McDermott & Eskridge. NONPR AFFIL member: Tulsa County Bar Association; trustee: Tulsa Philharmonic Orchestra; trustee: Philbrook Art Museum; member: American Bar Association; member: Oklahoma Bar Association. CLUB AFFIL Southern Hills Country Club.
T. Hillis Eskridge: trustee, assistant to president
David B. McKinney: vice president, treasurer, trustee B Tulsa, OK 1951. ED Rice University BA (1974); Columbia University JD (1975). PRIM CORP EMPL partner: Boesche McDermott & Eskridge. NONPR AFFIL member, founder: Tulsa Health Care Attorneys; member: Tulsa Pension Attorneys; member: National Health Lawyers Association; trustee: Metropolitan Christian Academy; member: National Association College & University Attorneys.
Lance Stockwell: trustee
Thomas H. Trower: trustee

Grants Analysis

Disclosure Period: calendar year ending 2001
Total Grants: $1,787,776*
Number of Grants: 103
Average Grant: $15,076*
Highest Grant: $250,000
Typical Range: $5,000 to $30,000
*Note: Giving excludes scholarships. Average grant figure excludes highest grant.

Recent Grants

Note: Grants derived from 2001 Form 990.

General

100,000	Tulsa Philharmonic, Tulsa, OK -- Tulsa performances
62,000	Tulsa Boys Home Foundation, Tulsa, OK
57,600	Bacone College, Muskogee, OK
50,000	Life Light, Jenks, OK -- pregnancy crisis centers
50,000	Oklahoma Medical Research Foundation, Oklahoma City, OK
50,000	St. Gregory's University, Shawnee, OK
35,000	Community Action Project of Tulsa County, Tulsa, OK
35,000	Street School, Tulsa, OK -- scholarship fund
30,000	Gilcrease Museum, Tulsa, OK -- Rave Review Exhibition
30,000	Margaret Hudson Program, Tulsa, OK -- girls home and school

BOWATER, INC.

Company Headquarters

55 East Camperdown Way
Greenville, SC 29601
Phone: (864)271-7733
Fax: (864)282-9482
Web: http://www.bowater.com

Company Description

Ticker: BOW
Exchange: NYSE
Revenue: US$2.449 billion (2001)
Employees: 400 (2001)
SIC(s): 2421 Sawmills & Planing Mills--General, 2611 Pulp Mills, 2621 Paper Mills, 2672 Coated & Laminated Paper Nec.

Operating Locations

Bowater Inc. (AL--Albertville; IL--Moline; ME--Millinocket; SC--Catawba; TN--Calhoun)
Note: Also operates in Halifax, Nova Scotia, Canada.

Nonmonetary Support

Type: Donated Products

Giving Contact

Gordon Manuel, Director, Government Affairs
55 East Camperdown Way
Greenville, SC 29601-3597
Phone: (864)271-7733
Fax: (864)282-9594

Description

Organization Type: Corporate Giving Program
Giving Locations: headquarters and operating communities.
Grant Types: Capital, Employee Matching Gifts, General Support.
Note: Employee matching gift ratio: 1 to 1.

Financial Summary

Total Giving: $1,000,000 (2003 approx); $1,000,000 (2002); $1,000,000 (2000 approx). Note: Contributes through corporate direct giving program only.
Assets: $5,000,000,000 (2002)

Typical Recipients

Arts & Humanities: Arts Associations & Councils, Arts Centers, Community Arts, Libraries, Music, Performing Arts, Public Broadcasting
Civic & Public Affairs: Economic Development, Urban & Community Affairs
Education: Business Education, Colleges & Universities, Community & Junior Colleges, Continuing Education, Economic Education, Engineering/Technological Education, Minority Education
Environment: Environment-General
Health: Health Organizations, Hospitals
Social Services: United Funds/United Ways, Youth Organizations

Application Procedures

Initial Contact: letter of inquiry
Application Requirements: a description of organization, amount requested, purpose of funds sought, recently audited financial statement, and IRS tax-determination letter
Deadlines: for small grants, None; for larger grants, July 31.
Evaluative Criteria: requires that the organization requesting funds truly needs the money; that the donation ultimately benefits the company, a significant number of employees, or the operating community; that the contribution must meet the standards of the community and be an appropriate amount; and, whenever possible, donations should be backed by appropriate community participation

Restrictions

Does not support individuals, religious organizations for sectarian purposes, or political or lobbying groups. If the organization requesting a donation is supported by a united fund or if an agency which the contributions committee believes should be a member of a united fund, company will not make a donation.

Additional Information

Each company division has its own contributions budget, with varying application procedures.
Publications: Bowater Incorporated Criteria for Corporate Giving

Corporate Officials

David G. Maffucci: executive vice president, chief financial officero B Stamford, CT 1950. ED Sacred Heart University BA (1972). PRIM CORP EMPL executive vice president, chief financial officer: Bowater Inc. NONPR AFFIL member: Financial Executives Institute; member: National Association Accountants; member: American Institute CPAs.
Arnold M. Nemirow: chairman, president, chief executive officer B March 25, 1943. ED Harvard University

AB (1966); University of Michigan JD (1969). PRIM CORP EMPL chairman, president, chief executive officer: Bowater Inc.

Giving Program Officials

Deborah L. Humphrey: director PRIM CORP EMPL director corporate relations: Bowater Inc.

Grants Analysis

Typical Range: $250 to $1,000

ETHEL N. BOWEN FOUNDATION

Giving Contact

R. W. Wilkinson, President
c/o First Century Bank
500 Federal St.
Bluefield, WV 24701
Phone: (304)325-8181

Description

Founded: 1968
EIN: 237010740
Organization Type: Private Foundation
Giving Locations: VA: Southwestern Virginia; WV: Southern West Virginia
Grant Types: General Support, Scholarship.

Donor Information

Founder: the late Ethel N. Bowen

Financial Summary

Total Giving: $376,189 (2000); $381,806 (1999); $398,443 (1998)
Giving Analysis: Giving for 2000 includes: foundation grants to United Way ($220); foundation scholarships ($10,000); 1999: foundation scholarships ($150); foundation grants to United Way ($1,000); 1998: foundation grants to United Way ($5,000); foundation ($133,682) foundation scholarships ($259,761)
Assets: $10,934,904 (2000); $11,453,910 (1999); $12,149,729 (1998)
Gifts Received: $20,000 (2000)

Typical Recipients

Arts & Humanities: Arts Associations & Councils, Arts Centers, Film & Video, Historic Preservation, History & Archaeology, Libraries, Music
Civic & Public Affairs: Business/Free Enterprise, Clubs, Community Foundations, Economic Policy, Civic & Public Affairs-General, Law & Justice, Municipalities/Towns, Parades/Festivals, Public Policy, Urban & Community Affairs
Education: Business Education, Colleges & Universities, Community & Junior Colleges, Education Funds, Elementary Education (Private), Elementary Education (Public), Education-General, International Studies, Legal Education, Literacy, Medical Education, Private Education (Precollege), Public Education (Precollege), Religious Education, Science/Mathematics Education, Secondary Education (Private), Secondary Education (Public), Social Sciences Education, Student Aid
Health: Cancer, Children's Health/Hospitals, Emergency/Ambulance Services, Home-Care Services, Prenatal Health Issues, Public Health
Religion: Bible Study/Translation, Churches, Religious Organizations, Religious Welfare
Science: Science-General, Scientific Centers & Institutes
Social Services: Animal Protection, Camps, Child Welfare, Community Centers, Counseling, Crime Prevention, Homes, Recreation & Athletics, Scouts, Shelters/Homelessness, Social Services-General, United Funds/United Ways, YMCA/YWCA/YMHA/YWHA, Youth Organizations

Application Procedures

Initial Contact: The foundation has no formal grant application procedure or application form. Students must submit transcripts.

Deadlines: prior to beginning of academic year.

Additional Information

Provides scholarships for higher education to residents of southern WV and southwestern VA.

Trust(s): First Century Bank

Foundation Officials

Henry Bowen: director

Basil L. Jackson: vice president B Portsmouth, VA 1924. ED Virginia Polytechnic Institute & State University (1950); University of Wisconsin (1961). PRIM CORP EMPL chairman: First National Bank of Bluefield. CORP AFFIL director: Flat Top Insurance Agency; chairman: Pocahontas Bankshares Corp.; director: Bluefield Area Development Corp.

Byron K. Satterfield: treasurer PRIM CORP EMPL executive vice president, trust officer, director: First Century Bank NA.

Frank W. Wilkinson: secretary

Richard W. Wilkinson: president B Welch, WV 1932. ED University of Virginia (1955-1962); University of Virginia JD (1962). PRIM CORP EMPL president, chief executive officer, director: First Century Bank NA. CORP AFFIL president, director: Pocahontas Bankshares.

Grants Analysis

Disclosure Period: calendar year ending 2000

Total Grants: $365,969*

Number of Grants: 61

Average Grant: $5,999

Highest Grant: $25,000

Lowest Grant: $100

Typical Range: $1,000 to $10,000

***Note:** Giving excludes scholarships, United Way.

Recent Grants

Note: Grants derived from 1999 Form 990.

General

10,000	University of Virginia Law School, Charlottesville, VA
10,000	Virginia Student Aid Foundation, Richmond, VA
8,750	Alliance for the Arts Limited
7,000	Governor Gaston Caperton Science Fund
5,000	Bluefield Community Center, Bluefield, WV
5,000	Bluefield High School, Bluefield, WV
5,000	Bluefield Middle School, Bluefield, WV
5,000	Eastern Regional Coal Archives, Bluefield, WV
5,000	Elizabeth Bowen Jones Memorial United Methodist
5,000	First Baptist Church

WAYNE AND IDA BOWMAN FOUNDATION

Giving Contact

Donald W. Bowman, President & Director
7 W. Lake Drive
St. Simons Island, GA 31522
Phone: (912)638-8670

Description

Founded: 1995

EIN: 621600157

Organization Type: Private Foundation

Grant Types: General Support, Scholarship.

Financial Summary

Total Giving: $146,518 (fiscal year ending September 30, 2001); $176,468 (fiscal 2000); $80,000 (fiscal 1998)

Giving Analysis: Giving for fiscal 2001 includes: foundation scholarships ($74,000)

Assets: $902,827 (fiscal 2001); $1,076,243 (fiscal 2000); $1,208,706 (fiscal 1998)

Gifts Received: $1,014,391 (fiscal 1996). Note: In fiscal 1996, contributions were received from the Wayne L. Bowman Residuary Trust ($534,634) and the estate of Ida S. Bowman ($479,757).

Typical Recipients

Arts & Humanities: Arts Associations & Councils, Libraries

Education: Arts/Humanities Education, Colleges & Universities, Student Aid

Health: AIDS/HIV

International: Missionary/Religious Activities

Religion: Bible Study/Translation, Churches, Religious Welfare

Application Procedures

Initial Contact: Contact foundation for application instructions.

Deadlines: None.

Foundation Officials

David S. Bowman: director

Donald W. Bowman: president, director

Mayne J. Bowman: vice president

William H. Bowman: secretary, director

Grants Analysis

Disclosure Period: fiscal year ending September 30, 2001

Total Grants: $72,518*

Number of Grants: 9

Average Grant: $6,217*

Highest Grant: $22,783

Lowest Grant: $735

Typical Range: $3,000 to $10,000

***Note:** Giving excludes scholarships. Average grant figure excludes highest grant.

Recent Grants

Note: Grants derived from fiscal 2000 Form 990.

Library-Related

13,468	Georgia, Florida, Oregon and Oklahoma Department of Corrections -- government prison libraries

General

18,000	Montgomery AIDS Outreach, Montgomery, AL
16,000	Berea College, Berea, KY
13,000	Brushy Fork Institution, Berea College, Berea, KY
10,000	Bethel Bible Village, Chattanooga, TN
10,000	Covenant College, Lookout Mountain, GA
5,500	Alabama Art Education Association, Montgomery, AL
5,500	Alabama Institute for Education in the Arts, Montgomery, AL
5,000	Bob Jones University, Greenville, SC
5,000	Pikeville College, Pikeville, KY
5,000	Tennessee Baptist Children's Home, Chattanooga, TN

J. BOWMAN PROPER CHARITABLE TRUST

Giving Contact

Stephen P. Kosak, Consultant
PO Box 374
Oil City, PA 16301
Phone: (412)677-5085

Description

Founded: 1993

EIN: 251670828

Organization Type: Private Foundation

Giving Locations: PA

Grant Types: General Support, Scholarship.

Financial Summary

Total Giving: $141,523 (fiscal year ending September 30, 2001); $147,697 (fiscal 2000); $87,948 (fiscal 1998)

Giving Analysis: Giving for fiscal 2001 includes: foundation scholarships ($15,000); fiscal 2000: foundation scholarships ($14,000); fiscal 1998: foundation scholarships ($6,100) foundation ($81,848)

Assets: $2,347,471 (fiscal 2001); $2,871,108 (fiscal 2000); $2,331,463 (fiscal 1998)

Typical Recipients

Arts & Humanities: History & Archaeology, Libraries

Civic & Public Affairs: Civic & Public Affairs-General, Municipalities/Towns, Safety, Urban & Community Affairs

Education: Agricultural Education, Public Education (Precollege), Student Aid

Health: Emergency/Ambulance Services, Public Health

Religion: Churches, Ministries, Religious Welfare

Social Services: Child Welfare, Community Centers, Community Service Organizations, Recreation & Athletics, Substance Abuse, Veterans, YMCA/YWCA/YMHA/YWHA, Youth Organizations

Application Procedures

Initial Contact: Request application guidelines with a letter explaining purpose of funds sought, amount requested, and when the funds are needed.

Deadlines: April 30.

Additional Information

Publications: Application Guidelines

Trust(s): National City Bank PA

Foundation Officials

Frank Blum: admin comm mem

Paul Blum: admin comm mem

Steve Gilford, Esq.: admin comm mem

Donald Hall, Jr.: administration committee member

Bruce Johnson: admin comm mem

Stephen P. Kosak: consultant

Grants Analysis

Disclosure Period: fiscal year ending September 30, 2001

Total Grants: $126,523*

Number of Grants: 13

Average Grant: $6,811*

Highest Grant: $44,801

Lowest Grant: $1,300

Typical Range: $2,000 to $10,000

***Note:** Giving excludes scholarships. Average grant figure excludes highest grant.

Recent Grants

Note: Grants derived from fiscal 2000 Form 990.

General

61,059	Tionesta Borough Volunteer Fire Department, Tionesta, PA -- exterior improvements
15,572	Tionesta Recreation Board, Tionesta, PA
14,000	Venango Area Community Foundation, Oil City, PA -- scholarships
12,500	Tionesta Ambulance Service, Tionesta, PA -- new equipment
10,000	United Methodist Church of Tionesta, Tionesta, PA -- building project
8,210	Tionesta Borough, Tionesta, PA -- public projects

6,000	Forest-Warren Department of Human Service, Tionesta, PA
5,000	Focus On Forest's Future, Tionesta, PA
4,265	Forest County Historical Society, Tionesta, PA -- property improvement
3,000	Daffy-Forest County Drug and Alcohol Free, Tionesta, PA

ROBERT BOWNE FOUNDATION

Giving Contact

Lena Townsend
345 Hudson St.
New York, NY 10014
Phone: (212)924-5500
Fax: (212)229-3400
Web: http://www.fdncenter.org/grantmaker/bowne/index.html

Description

Founded: 1968
EIN: 132620393
Organization Type: Private Foundation
Giving Locations: NY: Manhattan Boroughs outside of Manhattan, New York
Grant Types: General Support, Multiyear/Continuing Support, Operating Expenses, Project, Seed Money.

Donor Information

Founder: Edmund A. Stanley, Jr., members of the Stanley family

Financial Summary

Total Giving: $1,300,850 (2001); $1,300,000 (2000); $1,200,000 (1999)
Assets: $18,608,408 (2001); $19,614,904 (2000); $20,484,303 (1999)
Gifts Received: $100,000 (2001); $100,000 (2000); $105,000 (1999). Note: Contributions are received from Thomas O. Stanley and Bowne of New York City, Inc.

Typical Recipients

Arts & Humanities: Art History, Arts Centers, Arts & Humanities-General, History & Archaeology, Libraries, Museums/Galleries
Civic & Public Affairs: Economic Development, Employment/Job Training, Civic & Public Affairs-General, Hispanic Affairs, Housing, Nonprofit Management, Urban & Community Affairs, Women's Affairs
Education: Afterschool/Enrichment Programs, Arts/Humanities Education, Education Reform, Leadership Training, Literacy, Science/Mathematics Education, Special Education, Vocational & Technical Education
Health: Clinics/Medical Centers
Religion: Churches, Religious Welfare
Social Services: At-Risk Youth, Child Welfare, Community Centers, Community Service Organizations, Family Services, Recreation & Athletics, Refugee Assistance, Shelters/Homelessness, YMCA/YWCA/YMHA/YWHA, Youth Organizations

Application Procedures

Initial Contact: Initial request should be a letter outlining the project.
Deadlines: None.
Decision Notification: The foundation usually responds to requests within four weeks.

Restrictions

Focus is specifically on innovation in both new and existing youth programs that are willing to take risks and that aspire to make literacy education an integral part of their work. Does not support religious organizations, primary or secondary schools, colleges or universities, except when some aspect of their work is an integral part of a program supported by the foundation. Also does not support individuals, capital campaigns, or endowments.

Additional Information

Publications: Informational Brochure

Foundation Officials

Douglas F. Bauer: secretary, treasurer, trustee B Lackawanna, NY 1942. ED Princeton University AB (1964); Harvard University JD (1967). PRIM CORP EMPL secretary, general counsel: Bowne & Co. Inc. NONPR AFFIL member: New York City Bar Association; member: New York State Bar Association; member: National Association Corp. Directors; member: Fellows Pierpont Morgan Library; counselor: Friends of Princeton University Library; vice president, trustee: Bowne (Robert) House Historical Society; chairman, trustee: American Printing Historical Association; member: American Society of Corporate Secretaries; member: American Bar Association. CLUB AFFIL Grolier Club; Princeton Club.
Suzanne Carothers: trustee
Robert M. Johnson: trustee
Dianne Kangisser: vice president, executive director, trustee
Richard Harvey Koontz: trustee B Bedford, PA 1940. ED Pennsylvania State University BS (1962). PRIM CORP EMPL president, chief executive officer, director: Bowne & Co. Inc.
Hali Hae Kyung Lee: trustee
Edmund Allport Stanley, Jr.: president, chairman, trustee B New York, NY 1924. ED Princeton University AB (1949). PRIM CORP EMPL chairman executive committee: Bowne & Co. Inc. CLUB AFFIL Bond New York Club; Pilgrims Club.
Jennifer Stanley: vice president, trustee
Franz von Ziegesar: vice president, trustee B Sao Paulo, SP Brazil 1924. ED Yale University BA (1948). PRIM CORP EMPL chairman, chief executive officer, director: Bowne & Co. Inc. CORP AFFIL director: Southeastern Industries; director: Zarn Inc.

Grants Analysis

Disclosure Period: calendar year ending 2001
Total Grants: $1,300,850
Number of Grants: 56
Average Grant: $23,229
Highest Grant: $70,000
Lowest Grant: $1,000
Typical Range: $10,000 to $50,000

Recent Grants

Note: Grants derived from 2001 Form 990.

General

70,000	Innovation Network, Inc, Washington, DC
70,000	St. Nicholas Neighborhood Preservation Corporation, Brooklyn, NY
50,000	Interfaith Neighbors, New York, NY
35,000	Concourse House Housing Development Fund Company, Inc., Bronx, NY
35,000	Jamaica Center For Art's & Learning, Inc., Jamaica, NY
34,000	Hartley House, New York, NY
33,500	Mary Mitchell Family and Youth Center, Bronx, NY
30,000	Brooklyn Bureau of Community Service, Brooklyn, NY
30,000	Catholic Charities
30,000	Crenulated Company, LTD, Bronx, NY

BOWSHER-BOOHER FOUNDATION

Giving Contact

Tom Lower, Trust Officer
c/o Wells Fargo Bank of Indiana NA
112 W. Jefferson Blvd.
South Bend, IN 46601
Phone: (219)237-3340
Fax: (219)237-3317

Description

Founded: 1980
EIN: 310979401
Organization Type: Private Foundation
Giving Locations: IN: St. Joseph County, South Bend
Grant Types: General Support.

Financial Summary

Total Giving: $70,600 (fiscal year ending May 31, 2002); $87,900 (fiscal 2001); $82,488 (fiscal 2000)
Assets: $2,043,627 (fiscal 2002); $2,332,061 (fiscal 2001); $2,469,286 (fiscal 2000)

Typical Recipients

Arts & Humanities: Dance, Historic Preservation, History & Archaeology, Libraries
Civic & Public Affairs: African American Affairs, Chambers of Commerce, Clubs, Civic & Public Affairs-General, Hispanic Affairs, Housing, Legal Aid, Minority Business, Urban & Community Affairs, Women's Affairs
Education: Afterschool/Enrichment Programs, Colleges & Universities, Education Funds, Literacy, Science/Mathematics Education, Student Aid
Environment: Environment-General
Health: AIDS/HIV, Health Organizations, Prenatal Health Issues
Religion: Ministries, Religious Organizations, Religious Welfare
Social Services: Big Brother/Big Sister, Camps, Child Welfare, Community Centers, Community Service Organizations, Family Services, People with Disabilities, People with Disabilities, Scouts, Shelters/Homelessness, United Funds/United Ways, YMCA/YWCA/YMHA/YWHA, Youth Organizations

Application Procedures

Initial Contact: The foundation requests applications be made in writing.
Application Requirements: Include a description of organization, amount requested, purpose of funds sought, recently audited financial statement, and proof of tax-exempt status.
Deadlines: April 1 and October 1.

Additional Information

Trust(s): Wells Fargo Bank IN NA

Grants Analysis

Disclosure Period: fiscal year ending May 31, 2002
Total Grants: $70,600
Number of Grants: 4
Highest Grant: $30,000
Lowest Grant: $5,000
Typical Range: $5,000 to $20,000

Recent Grants

Note: Grants derived from 2000 Form 990.

General

19,000	University of Notre Dame, Notre Dame, IN -- NYSP in summer
16,500	Institute for Neighborhoods
10,000	Literacy Council of St. Joe County
9,200	Minority and Women's Business Development -- youth exchange program
9,000	University of Notre Dame, Notre Dame, IN -- lead program 2000
6,500	South Bend Community School Corp, South Bend, IN -- mentoring program
5,600	Goodwill Industries of Michiana, Inc., Michiana, IN
5,000	St. Margaret's House
1,688	Southbend Community School Corp, South Bend, IN -- computer school

BP AMOCO CORP.

Company Headquarters

Chicago, IL
Web: http://www.bpamoco.com

Company Description

Ticker: BP
Exchange: OTC
Former Name: Amoco Corp.;
Acquired: Atlantic Richfield Company (ARCO) (1999).
Employees: 56,450
SIC(s): 1311 Crude Petroleum & Natural Gas, 1321 Natural Gas Liquids, 2221 Broadwoven Fabric Mills--Manmade, 6719 Holding Companies Nec.
Parent Company: BP Plc, Britannic House, 1 Finsbury Circus, London, United Kingdom

Operating Locations

ARCO Metals (KY--Louisville); BP America Inc. (OH--Cleveland); BP Amoco Corp. (NY--New York); BP Corp. (DC--Washington); BP Global Power (TX--Houston); BP Solar Inc. (CA--Fairfield); BP Solarex (MD--Baltimore); Burmah Castrol Chemicals (KS--Kansas City); Castrol North America (NJ--Wayne); Chem-Trend Inc. (MI--Howell); Dussek Campbell Inc. (IL--Skokie); Fosbel Inc. (OH--Berea); Foseco Inc. (OH--Cleveland); Fosroc Inc. (KY--Georgetown); Remet Corp. (NY--Utica); Sericol Inc.P (KS--Kansas City)

Nonmonetary Support

Type: Donated Equipment; In-kind Services; Loaned Employees; Loaned Executives
Volunteer Programs: Through company's Employee Volunteer Grants Program, employees may request grants of up to $500 for nonprofit organizations to which they give at least 12 hours per month of their own time.
Note: Requests for nonmonetary support are handled by each local company's public affairs office.

ARCO Foundation

Giving Contact

Russell G. Sakaguchi, President
333 South Hope Street
Los Angeles, CA 90071
Phone: (213)486-3342
Fax: (213)486-0113
Web: http://ntlf.com/html/grants/5977.htm

Alternate Contact

200 East Randolph Drive
Mail Code
Chicago, IL 60601
Phone: (312)856-3147

Description

EIN: 953222292
Organization Type: Corporate Foundation
Giving Locations: AK: Southwestern United States; Western United States.
Grant Types: Employee Matching Gifts, General Support.
Note: Employee matching gift ratio: 1 to 1.

Financial Summary

Total Giving: $0 (2001); $5,471,025 (2000 approx); $8,919,313 (1999). Note: Contributes through corporate direct giving program and foundation. In 2001, no grants were distributed.
Giving Analysis: Giving for 2000 includes: foundation grants to United Way ($80,988); foundation scholarships ($86,028); foundation ($5,304,009); 1999:

foundation grants to United Way ($1,973,329); foundation ($6,945,985); 1998: foundation grants to United Way ($1,898,685); foundation ($7,950,473);
Assets: $2,000,000 (2001); $2,000,000 (2000); $2,100,000 (1999)
Gifts Received: $5,471,025 (2000); $8,888,335 (1999); $8,355,492 (1998). Note: Contributions are received from Atlantic Richfield Co.

Typical Recipients

Arts & Humanities: Arts Centers, Community Arts, Dance, Ethnic & Folk Arts, Arts & Humanities-General, Historic Preservation, Libraries, Museums/Galleries, Music, Opera, Performing Arts, Public Broadcasting, Theater
Civic & Public Affairs: Asian American Affairs, Civil Rights, Community Foundations, Economic Development, Employment/Job Training, Ethnic Organizations, Civic & Public Affairs-General, Hispanic Affairs, Housing, Minority Business, Municipalities/Towns, Nonprofit Management, Public Policy, Urban & Community Affairs, Women's Affairs, Zoos/Aquariums
Education: Agricultural Education, Arts/Humanities Education, Business Education, Colleges & Universities, Continuing Education, Economic Education, Education Funds, Education Reform, Elementary Education (Public), Engineering/Technological Education, Faculty Development, Education-General, Leadership Training, Literacy, Minority Education, Preschool Education, Private Education (Precollege), Public Education (Precollege), Science/Mathematics Education, Social Sciences Education, Student Aid, Vocational & Technical Education
Environment: Environment-General, Resource Conservation, Wildlife Protection
Health: Children's Health/Hospitals, Research/Studies Institutes
Religion: Religious Welfare
Science: Science Museums
Social Services: At-Risk Youth, Child Welfare, Community Service Organizations, Day Care, Domestic Violence, Family Services, Food/Clothing Distribution, Recreation & Athletics, Scouts, Senior Services, Social Services-General, United Funds/United Ways, Volunteer Services, YMCA/YWCA/YMHA/YWHA, Youth Organizations

Application Procedures

Initial Contact: Submit a full proposal.
Application Requirements: One-page proposal summary, including mission statement, grant amount requested and purpose of grant, legal name of organization, and any past Arco support (with dates and amounts); proposal of not more than five pages, including: proposal summary, mission and history of organization, need for project in view of related work by others, project description, goals, objectives, action plan, expected outcomes or results, method of evaluation, and plan for continuing activity. Required attachments include financial information, including financial statement, income and expense budget, list of other current and projected sources of funding; most recent Form 990; and list of board members, with affiliations.
Deadlines: None.
Evaluative Criteria: Priority of project within Foundation's goals, anticipated results, resources requested and available funds.
Decision Notification: Bimonthly meetings are held for most requests; directors review major education requests in December, and all other major requests periodically.
Notes: Faxed applications and videos are not accepted. Local and regional applicants should apply directly to nearest company field office.

Restrictions

Only nonprofit, tax-exempt public charities as defined in Section 501(c)(3) of the IRS Code are eligible. Does not support individuals; organizations whose services are not provided in a geographic area of

interest to ARCO; film or video projects; religious activities or organizations; specialized single-issue health organizations, except under Foundation's Matching Grants or Volunteer Grants programs; fraternal, professional, or veterans' organizations or similar membership groups; endowments; annual, automatically renewable, or multiyear grants; organizations that discriminate on the basis of race, color, sex, or national origin; or benefit dinners, advertisements, or tables at fund-raising events.

Additional Information

Details regarding the Matching Grants, Volunteer Grants, and United Way programs can be obtained by contacting the ARCO Foundation offices in California, Arkansas, or Texas.
Vastar Resources is a separate corporate entity in Texas that administers grants to qualified nonprofit organizations in the Gulf Coast area.
Publications: Annual Report

Corporate Officials

Michael Ray Bowlin: chairman, chief executive officer, director B Amarillo, TX 1943. ED North Texas State University BBA (1965); North Texas State University MBA (1967). PRIM CORP EMPL chairman, chief executive officer, director: Atlantic Richfield Co. CORP AFFIL chairman, chief executive officer: ARCO International Oil & Gas Co.; officer: Wells Fargo & Co.
Marie L. Knowles: executive vice president, chief financial officer PRIM CORP EMPL executive vice president, chief financial officer: Atlantic Richfield Co. CORP AFFIL director: Phelps Dodge Corp.

Foundation Officials

Michael Ray Bowlin: chairman, director (see above)
M. P. Hoffman: director
James D. McNamara: treasurer
C. Noble: director
Glenn M. Pastrana: research assistant, matching gifts coordinator
Russell G. Sakaguchi: president
B. L. Thelander: director
J. K. Thompson: director
D. R. Voelte: director

Grants Analysis

Disclosure Period: calendar year ending 2000
Total Grants: $5,304,009*
Number of Grants: 313 (approx)
Average Grant: $10,590*
Highest Grant: $2,000,000
Lowest Grant: $25
Typical Range: $1,000 to $25,000
*Note: GEX United Way. Average grant figure excludes highest grant.

Recent Grants

Note: Grants derived from 2000 Form 990.

Library-Related
25,000	Long Beach Public Library Foundation, Long Beach, CA

General
2,000,000	Music Center of Los Angeles, Los Angeles, CA
250,000	Genesis Long Beach Aquarium Foundation, Long Beach, CA
250,000	Stanford University, Stanford, CA
175,000	Genesis - Los Angeles Economic Growth, Los Angeles, CA
100,000	Concerned Citizens of South Central Los Angeles, Los Angeles, CA
50,000	Access Books, Inglewood, CA
48,000	United Way, Anchorage, AK
42,500	Puente Learning Center, Los Angeles, CA
40,000	Achievement Council, Los Angeles, CA
40,000	Collegiate Search Youth Organization, Gardena, CA

DONALD C. BRACE FOUNDATION

Giving Contact

Robert A. Beer, Trustee
c/o Cummings & Lockwood
PO Box 120
Stamford, CT 06904-0120
Phone: (203)351-4294

Description

Founded: 1987
EIN: 133442680
Organization Type: Private Foundation
Giving Locations: Northeast region of US.
Grant Types: General Support.

Donor Information

Founder: Donna Brace Ogilvie

Financial Summary

Total Giving: $542,500 (2002); $728,500 (2001); $635,000 (2000)
Assets: $6,451,278 (2002); $8,938,347 (2001); $11,113,953 (2000)
Gifts Received: $218,997 (2000); $512,000 (1993). Note: In 1993 and 2000, contributions were received from Donna Brace Ogilvie.

Typical Recipients

Arts & Humanities: Arts Associations & Councils, Arts Centers, Arts Institutes, History & Archaeology, Libraries, Literary Arts, Museums/Galleries, Music, Theater
Civic & Public Affairs: Employment/Job Training, Civic & Public Affairs-General
Education: Arts/Humanities Education, Colleges & Universities, Literacy, Private Education (Precollege)
Environment: Environment-General, Protection
Health: Geriatric Health, Health Organizations, Hospices, Hospitals, Medical Research, Multiple Sclerosis
Social Services: Community Centers, Community Service Organizations, Food/Clothing Distribution, People with Disabilities, Senior Services, YMCA/YWCA/YMHA/YWHA, Youth Organizations

Application Procedures

Initial Contact: Send brief letter describing program.
Deadlines: None.

Foundation Officials

Robert A. Beer: trustee
Katharine Butler: trustee B Chicago Heights, IL 1925. ED Western Michigan University BA (1950); Western Michigan University MA (1953); Western Michigan University EdS (1961); Michigan State University PhD (1967). PRIM CORP EMPL professor research, director speech & hearing center: San Jose State University PRIM NONPR EMPL professor research, director: Western Michigan University. CORP AFFIL consult: Virginia Hosp. NONPR AFFIL member: New York Saint Speech Language Hearing Association; researchprofessor, director: Syracuse University Center Language Research; member, treasurer: International Association Applied Psycholinguistics; member: International Association Logopedics & Phonetics; member: Higher Education Consortium Special Education; fellow: International Academy Research Learning Disabilities; director: HEW Office Education; member: California Speech & Hearing Association; member: Council Exceptional Children; director: Bur Education Handicapped; member: California Association Prof Special Education; member: American Psychological Association; fellow, trustee: American Speech Language Hearing Association.
Paul Gitlin, Esq.: trustee
John Brace Latham: trustee

Donna Brace Ogilvie: trustee
Karen Scheid: trustee

Grants Analysis

Disclosure Period: calendar year ending 2002
Total Grants: $542,500
Number of Grants: 12
Average Grant: $10,278*
Highest Grant: $150,000
Lowest Grant: $2,500
Typical Range: $5,000 to $20,000
*Note: Average grant figure excludes three highest grants ($450,000).

Recent Grants

Note: Grants derived from 2001 Form 990.

General

150,000	Girls, Inc., Bloomington, IN -- endowment
150,000	Phillips Academy, Andover, MA -- Richard L. Gelb Science Center
150,000	Phillips Academy, Andover, MA -- Richard L. Gelb Science Center
150,000	Stamford Health Foundation, Inc, Stamford, CT -- Brace Community Conference Center
75,000	Stamford Health Foundation, Inc, Stamford, CT -- Brace Community Conference Center
25,000	Friends of the Teton River -- projects to improve the condition of Teton River
15,000	Westhampton Cultural Consortium, Inc., Westhampton Beach, NY -- concerts on the Village Green in Westhampton Beach
10,000	Stamford Land Conservation Trust, Stamford, CT -- purchase of "Treetops"
2,500	Stamford Center for the Arts, Stamford, CT -- Reach Out and Arts in Education Program
1,000	Meals on Wheels, Stamford, CT -- meals for the homebound

HELEN BRACH FOUNDATION

Giving Contact

Toni Peville, Associate Director
55 W Wacker Dr., Suite 701
Chicago, IL 60601
Phone: (312)372-4417
Fax: (312)372-0290
Note: Foundation accepts faxed requests.

Description

Founded: 1974
EIN: 237376427
Organization Type: General Purpose Foundation
Giving Locations: IL: nationally.
Grant Types: Conference/Seminar, Department, General Support, Operating Expenses, Project, Scholarship.

Donor Information

Founder: Incorporated in 1974 in Chicago, IL. Helen V. Brach was the wife of Frank Brach, owner of the E.J. Brach and Sons Candy Company in Chicago. Frank Brach's father founded the company, which in 1966 was sold upon Frank's retirement. After his death in 1970, Helen Brach became heir to the family fortune.
In February 1977, Helen Brach disappeared without a trace. Seven years later, she was declared legally dead, with her death presumed to have occurred in 1977. As the foundation was the primary beneficiary

under her will, it received a significant bequest from her estate when she was declared deceased. Charles M. Vorhees (Helen Brach's brother) was an original member and director of the foundation, and remains on the board of directors.

Financial Summary

Total Giving: $5,461,000 (fiscal year ending March 31, 2002); $3,473,675 (fiscal 1999); $3,537,235 (fiscal 1997)
Giving Analysis: Giving for fiscal 1999 includes: foundation grants to United Way ($10,000) fiscal 1998: foundation grants to United Way ($10,000)
Assets: $115,983,215 (fiscal 1999); $84,054,260 (fiscal 1997); $69,152,658 (fiscal 1995)
Gifts Received: $95,636 (fiscal 1999). Note: In fiscal 1999, contributions were received from the estate of Helen V. Brach.

Typical Recipients

Arts & Humanities: Arts Centers, Arts Institutes, Community Arts, Dance, Historic Preservation, Libraries, Museums/Galleries, Music, Theater
Civic & Public Affairs: Community Foundations, Economic Development, Employment/Job Training, Civic & Public Affairs-General, Hispanic Affairs, Housing, Inner-City Development, Philanthropic Organizations, Public Policy, Urban & Community Affairs, Women's Affairs, Zoos/Aquariums
Education: Afterschool/Enrichment Programs, Arts/Humanities Education, Colleges & Universities, Community & Junior Colleges, Continuing Education, Education Associations, Education Funds, Education-General, Legal Education, Minority Education, Preschool Education, Private Education (Precollege), Public Education (Precollege), Religious Education, Science/Mathematics Education, Secondary Education (Private), Special Education, Student Aid, Vocational & Technical Education
Environment: Environment-General, Wildlife Protection
Health: AIDS/HIV, Children's Health/Hospitals, Clinics/Medical Centers, Geriatric Health, Health Funds, Health Organizations, Hospices, Hospitals, Long-Term Care, Medical Rehabilitation, Medical Research, Mental Health, Nursing Services, Nutrition, Preventive Medicine/Wellness Organizations, Public Health, Trauma Treatment
International: International Environmental Issues, Missionary/Religious Activities, Trade
Religion: Churches, Dioceses, Ministries, Missionary Activities (Domestic), Religious Organizations, Religious Welfare, Religious Welfare
Science: Science Museums
Social Services: Animal Protection, Child Welfare, Community Centers, Community Service Organizations, Counseling, Family Services, Food/Clothing Distribution, People with Disabilities, Senior Services, Shelters/Homelessness, Volunteer Services, Youth Organizations

Application Procedures

Initial Contact: Applicants should contact the foundation by letter for application form and a report on the foundation.
Application Requirements: The foundation requires seven copies of the completed application form, together with one copy of the following: a cover letter containing a brief summary of the background and purposes of the prospective grantee and the particular project or activity for which funds are requested; a list of the members of the governing board of the requesting organization; evidence of the approval for the submission of the request from the chief executive officer or other authorized individual; a copy of the organization's most recent audited financial statement; and IRS determination of tax exempt status under 501(c)(3) of the Internal Revenue Code.

Deadlines: December 31 for consideration by March 31. To receive optimum consideration, proposals should be received by the foundation in completed form several months before the end of the year and precede a December board meeting.

Review Process: The board follows a schedule of regular quarterly meetings to consider grant applications and to review the progress of currently funded projects. Final consideration is given to all applications received in any year at the board's first meeting the following year, which is usually in March. At the foundation's discretion, a site visit or interview may be scheduled as part of the review process. All eligible requests will be acknowledged.

Restrictions

Except for well-established organizations which the foundation has supported in the past, the board prefers to consider relatively smaller grants and to distribute them among a number of applicants.

The foundation does not make grants to individuals, political campaigns or lobbying groups, or governmental bodies or tax-supported institutions. Grants are not made in excess of 10% of a group's operating budget.

The foundation usually does not make multiyear grants or commitments. Except where the foundation has made an express commitment for successive years' funding, a grant made in one year in no way implies the recipient will receive priority for funding in future years. The foundation does not give internationally.

Additional Information

Publications: Biennial Report; Guidelines; Application Form

Foundation Officials

James John O'Connor: vice president, director B Chicago, IL 1937. ED College of the Holy Cross BS (1958); Harvard University MBA (1960); Georgetown University JD (1963). PRIM CORP EMPL chairman, chief executive officer, director: Unicom Corp. CORP AFFIL director: Tribune Co.; director: UAL Corp.; director: Smurfit-Stone Container Corp.; director: Corning Inc.; director: First National Bank Chicago; director: America National Canada Co.; chairman: Advanced Reactor Corp. NONPR AFFIL trustee: Museum Science & Industry; trustee: Northwestern University; director: Lyric Opera Chicago; member: Illinois Bar Association; member: Illinois Business Roundtable; member: Hundred Club Cook County; director: Chicago Urban League; member: Chicagoland Chamber of Commerce; member: Chicago Symphony Orchestra; director: Chicago Board Trade; member: Chicago Convention & Tourism Bureau; member: Chicago Bar Association; member executive board: Boy Scouts America Chicago Area Council; member: Business Council; trustee: Adler Planetarium. CLUB AFFIL member: Hundred Cook County Club.
Toni Perille: associate director
John J. Sheridan: secretary, treasurer, director
R. Matthew Simon: director
Raymond F. Simon: president, executive director
Charles A. Vorhees: director
Charles M. Vorhees: chairman, director

Grants Analysis

Disclosure Period: fiscal year ending March 31, 1999
Total Grants: $3,463,675*
Number of Grants: 379
Average Grant: $9,139
Highest Grant: $100,000
Lowest Grant: $100
Typical Range: $5,000 to $25,000
*Note: Giving excludes United Way.

Recent Grants

Note: Grants derived from 2000 Form 990.

General

100,000	Big Shoulders Fund, Chicago, IL
100,000	Misericordia Home, Chicago, IL -- to complete major redecoration of a group home, including new floor, wall coverings, and windows
75,000	Loyola University of Chicago, Chicago, IL
60,000	Primarily Primates, San Antonio, TX
60,000	St. Rita High School, Chicago, IL
50,000	Brother Rice High School, Bloomfield, MI
50,000	Catholic Charities, Chicago, IL
50,000	Colombiere Health Care Project -- to assist in providing for increasing healthcare needs of elderly and inform community members
50,000	Cristo Rey Jesuit High School, Chicago, IL
50,000	De LaSalle Institute, Chicago, IL

GEORGE W. BRACKENRIDGE FOUNDATION

Giving Contact

Gilbert M. Denman, Jr., Trustee
711 Navarro Street, Suite 535
San Antonio, TX 78205
Phone: (210)224-1011
Fax: (210)223-3657

Description

Founded: 1920
EIN: 746034977
Organization Type: General Purpose Foundation
Giving Locations: TX
Grant Types: Endowment, Project, Research, Scholarship.

Donor Information

Founder: Established in 1920 by the late George W. Brackenridge .

Financial Summary

Total Giving: $1,184,882 (2001); $1,549,525 (1999); $887,941 (1998)
Giving Analysis: Giving for 2001 includes: foundation grants to United Way ($154,000); 1999: foundation scholarships ($1,270,140); 1997: foundation scholarships ($125,000);
Assets: $27,603,708 (2001); $28,727,722 (1999); $29,514,575 (1998)

Typical Recipients

Arts & Humanities: Arts Associations & Councils, Arts Institutes, Arts Outreach, Ballet, Ethnic & Folk Arts, Libraries, Museums/Galleries, Music, Public Broadcasting
Civic & Public Affairs: Community Foundations, Nonprofit Management, Parades/Festivals, Philanthropic Organizations, Zoos/Aquariums
Education: Arts/Humanities Education, Colleges & Universities, Elementary Education (Private), Engineering/Technological Education, Faculty Development, Education-General, Gifted & Talented Programs, Health & Physical Education, Leadership Training, Medical Education, Minority Education, Private Education (Precollege), Public Education (Precollege), Science/Mathematics Education, Social Sciences Education, Student Aid
Health: Clinics/Medical Centers, Medical Training
Science: Scientific Research
Social Services: YMCA/YWCA/YMHA/YWHA, YMCA/YWCA/YMHA/YWHA, Youth Organizations

Application Procedures

Initial Contact: The foundation requests that the application be made in writing on the organization's letterhead and signed by a member of its board of directors or an officer of the organization.
Application Requirements: The application should contain specific information related to the desired use of the grant, a copy of the organization's charter and by-laws, and a copy of the organization's exemption letter from the IRS, including the most recent financial statement.
Deadlines: None.
Review Process: The board meets in March, June, September, and December.

Restrictions

The organization must be located in Texas and must be an accredited education organization, or the grant must support one or more accredited educational organizations. The foundation does not support individuals; provide general support, continuing support, seed money, or matching gifts; or fund emergency funds, operating budgets, annual campaigns, deficit financing, or land acquisition.

Foundation Officials

Gilbert M. Denman, Jr.: trustee B San Antonio, TX 1921. ED University of Texas BA (1940); University of Texas LLB (1942). PRIM CORP EMPL attorney: Denman, Franklin & Denman.
Leroy G. Denman, Jr.: trustee B San Antonio, TX 1918. ED University of Texas LLB (1939); University of Texas BA (1939). PRIM CORP EMPL attorney: Denman, Franklin & Denman. CORP AFFIL vice president, director: King Ranch Saddle Shop Inc.; vice president, director: Running W Saddle Shop; director: King Ranch Holdings Inc.
John H. Moore: trustee

Grants Analysis

Disclosure Period: calendar year ending 2001
Total Grants: $1,030,882*
Number of Grants: 16
Average Grant: $17,555*
Highest Grant: $750,000
Typical Range: $5,000 to $25,000
*Note: Giving excludes scholarships. Giving excludes United Way. Average grant figure excludes highest grant.

Recent Grants

Note: Grants derived from 2001 Form 990.

General

750,000	University of Texas at San Antonio, San Antonio, TX -- educational purposes, Visiting Professor Program
45,000	San Antonio Museum of Art, San Antonio, TX -- educational programs, art, field trips
37,500	Trinity University, San Antonio, TX -- scholarship program and educational program
36,000	St. Mary's University, San Antonio, TX -- scholarship program
30,000	San Antonio Arts, San Antonio, TX -- educational programs
25,000	Alamo Public Telecommunications, San Antonio, TX -- educational purposes
25,000	Healy Murphy Center, San Antonio, TX -- educational programs
25,000	University of Texas Health Science Center, San Antonio, TX -- for educational programs, nursing program
20,000	Poth Independent School District, Poth, TX -- educational - technology advancements
17,500	San Antonio Zoological Society, San Antonio, TX -- educational programs

GEORGE AND RUTH BRADFORD FOUNDATION

Giving Contact

Robert L. Bradford, Director
PO Box E
San Mateo, CA 94402
Phone: (650)344-0422

Description

Founded: 1985
EIN: 943015722
Organization Type: Private Foundation
Giving Locations: CA: San Francisco Peninsula
Grant Types: General Support, Scholarship.

Donor Information

Founder: Ruth Bradford

Financial Summary

Total Giving: $169,600 (fiscal year ending June 30, 2001); $157,500 (fiscal 2000); $128,700 (fiscal 1999)
Giving Analysis: Giving for fiscal 1999 includes: foundation scholarships ($3,000)
Assets: $2,515,972 (fiscal 2001); $2,402,692 (fiscal 2000); $2,491,423 (fiscal 1999)
Gifts Received: $500 (fiscal 2001); $250 (fiscal 2000); $250 (fiscal 1999)

Typical Recipients

Arts & Humanities: Libraries, Museums/Galleries, Music, Performing Arts, Public Broadcasting, Theater
Civic & Public Affairs: Botanical Gardens/Parks, Business/Free Enterprise, Community Foundations, Employment/Job Training, Civic & Public Affairs-General, Rural Affairs, Zoos/Aquariums
Education: Afterschool/Enrichment Programs, Agricultural Education, Business Education, Colleges & Universities, Education Associations, Education Reform, Elementary Education (Public), Environmental Education, Education-General, Literacy, Religious Education, Secondary Education (Private), Secondary Education (Public), Special Education
Environment: Environment-General, Resource Conservation, Wildlife Protection
Health: Cancer, Children's Health/Hospitals, Clinics/Medical Centers, Diabetes, Hospitals, Long-Term Care, Mental Health, Public Health
Religion: Religious Welfare
Science: Science Museums, Scientific Centers & Institutes
Social Services: Big Brother/Big Sister, Child Welfare, Community Centers, Community Service Organizations, Counseling, Family Services, Food/Clothing Distribution, People with Disabilities, Scouts, Senior Services, Shelters/Homelessness, Volunteer Services, YMCA/YWCA/YMHA/YWHA, Youth Organizations

Application Procedures

Initial Contact: Send a brief letter of inquiry.
Deadlines: None.

Restrictions

Does not support individuals.

Foundation Officials

Robert Bradford: director
Lloyd Haefner: director
Joan Richardson: director

Grants Analysis

Disclosure Period: fiscal year ending June 30, 2001
Total Grants: $169,600
Number of Grants: 50
Average Grant: $2,441*
Highest Grant: $50,000
Typical Range: $1,000 to $5,000
*Note: Average grant figure excludes highest grant.

Recent Grants

Note: Grants derived from fiscal 2000 Form 990.

Library-Related
5,000	Mendocino County Library Foundation, Ukiah, CA -- education

General
10,000	Hidden Villa, Palo Alto, CA -- education
5,000	California Foundation for Agriculture in the Classroom, Sacramento, CA -- education
5,000	Environmental Traveling Companions, San Francisco, CA -- handicapped assistance
5,000	Mary Elizabeth Inn, San Francisco, CA -- social services
5,000	Mendocino Cancer Resource Center, Mendocino, CA -- education
5,000	Point Reyes Bird Observatory, Stinson Beach, CA -- environmental education
5,000	Point Reyes Bird Observatory, Stinson Beach, CA
5,000	Santa Rosa High School, Santa Rosa, CA -- music education
5,000	Second Harvest Food Bank, San Jose, CA -- homeless assistance
4,000	Ronald McDonald House, Palo Alto, CA -- support services

LYNDE AND HARRY BRADLEY FOUNDATION

Giving Contact

Grants Program
Lynde and Harry Bradley Foundation
Attn: Michael W. Grebe
PO Box 510860
Milwaukee, WI 53203-0153
Phone: (414)291-9915
Fax: (414)291-9991
Web: http://www.bradleyfdn.org

Description

Founded: 1942
EIN: 396037928
Organization Type: General Purpose Foundation
Giving Locations: WI: nationally.
Grant Types: Capital, Conference/Seminar, Fellowship, General Support, Matching, Operating Expenses, Project, Research, Scholarship.

Donor Information

Founder: Incorporated as the Allen-Bradley Foundation in Wisconsin in 1942 and funded by contributions from Harry L. Bradley, Caroline D. Bradley, Margaret B. Bradley, the Margaret Loock Trust, and the Allen-Bradley Company. The Allen-Bradley Company, an electronics manufacturing firm, was sold to Rockwell International in 1985, after which the foundation acquired proceeds from that sale. The foundation adopted its present name in April 1985.

Financial Summary

Total Giving: $26,000,000 (2003 approx); $25,146,793 (2002 approx); $35,304,281 (2001)
Giving Analysis: Giving for 1995 includes: foundation scholarships ($4,214,250)
Assets: $532,048,000 (2002 approx); $579,739,000 (2001); $626,124,000 (2000)

Typical Recipients

Arts & Humanities: Arts Associations & Councils, Ballet, Dance, Film & Video, History & Archaeology, Museums/Galleries, Music, Opera, Performing Arts, Public Broadcasting, Theater, Visual Arts
Civic & Public Affairs: African American Affairs, Business/Free Enterprise, Civil Rights, Community Foundations, Economic Development, Economic Policy, Employment/Job Training, Ethnic Organizations, Civic & Public Affairs-General, Hispanic Affairs, Law & Justice, Legal Aid, Nonprofit Management, Parades/Festivals, Philanthropic Organizations, Professional & Trade Associations, Public Policy, Safety
Education: Arts/Humanities Education, Colleges & Universities, Continuing Education, Economic Education, Education Associations, Education Funds, Education Reform, Engineering/Technological Education, Faculty Development, Education-General, Gifted & Talented Programs, International Exchange, International Studies, Journalism/Media Education, Public Education (Precollege), School Volunteerism, Science/Mathematics Education, Secondary Education (Public), Social Sciences Education, Student Aid
Environment: Environment-General
Health: Children's Health/Hospitals, Clinics/Medical Centers, Health Policy/Cost Containment, Hospitals, Transplant Networks/Donor Banks
International: Foreign Educational Institutions, Human Rights, International Affairs, International Development, International Peace & Security Issues, International Relations
Religion: Jewish Causes, Religious Organizations, Religious Welfare, Social/Policy Issues
Science: Scientific Centers & Institutes
Social Services: Community Centers, Community Service Organizations, Crime Prevention, Family Services, Veterans, YMCA/YWCA/YMHA/YWHA, Youth Organizations

Application Procedures

Initial Contact: Applicants should write a brief letter of inquiry to the foundation describing the applicant's organization and intended project. If the foundation determines the project to be within its current program interests, the applicant will be invited to submit a formal proposal.
Application Requirements: The proposal should include a letter presenting a concise description of the project, its objectives and significance, and the qualifications of the organizations and individuals involved. Included with the letter should be a project budget, amount requested, other sources of support, a copy of the IRS determination letter 501(c)(3), and a completed Grantee Tax Exempt Status Information form included with the program guidelines.
Deadlines: Deadlines for full proposals are December 1, March 1, July 1, and September 1.
Review Process: The board meets in February, May or June, September, and November. If the foundation is interested in funding the project, the applicant will receive information regarding the foundation and its guidelines for proposals. Final notification arrives within three to five months.

Restrictions

No grants are made to individuals, organizations that do not have 501(c)(3) tax-exempt status, or strictly denominational organizations. Foundation favors projects not normally financed by public tax funds. Capital requests are considered, but foundation limits grants to a fraction of the total project cost.

Additional Information

The foundation conducts an annual evaluation of grants, and recipients are requested to provide periodic reports on the progress of their work.
Publications: Annual Report; Application Guidelines; Proposal Checklist

Foundation Officials

Robert N. Berkopec: treasurer, assistant secretary
Reed Coleman: director CORP AFFIL director: Fidelity Life Association; director: Lunar Corp.
Terry Considine: director
Pete du Pont, IV: director
Michael W. Grebe: president B Peoria, IL 1940. ED United States Military Academy BS (1962); University of Michigan JD (1970). PRIM CORP EMPL partner:

Foley & Lardner. NONPR AFFIL Order Coif; member: State Bar Wisconsin; member: Milwaukee Bar Association.

James Clayburn La Force: director B San Diego, CA 1928. ED San Diego State University BA (1951); University of California, Los Angeles MA (1958); University of California, Los Angeles PhD (1962). PRIM NONPR EMPL professor emeritus: University of California, Los Angeles Graduate School. CORP AFFIL director: Timken Co.; director: Rockwell International Corp.; director: Payden & Rygel Investment Trust; director: Providence Investment Council Mutual Funds; director: Jacobs Engineering Group Inc.; director: Motor Cargo Industries; director: Blackrock Income Trust Inc.; director: Imperial Credit Industries; director: Black Rock Funds. NONPR AFFIL member: Mont Pelerin Society; member: Phi Beta Kappa; member: Economic History Association; chairman, trustee: Foundation Research Economic Education; chairman advisory committee: California Workmens Compensation.

I. Andrew Rader: director CORP AFFIL director: Clayton Industries.

Thomas L. Rhodes: director, vice chairman

Wayne J. Roper: secretary, director B 1924. ED University of Wisconsin (1946); Harvard University MA, LLB (1949). PRIM CORP EMPL attorney: Von Briesen Purtell & Roper. CORP AFFIL secretary, director: Green Bay Packaging; secretary, director: Runzheimer International Ltd.

Daniel P. Schmidt: executive vice president, chief operating officer

Thomas L. Smallwood: secretary, director

Brother Bob Smith: director

Allen M. Taylor: chairman, director B Cedar Rapids, IA 1923. ED Princeton University AB (1946); Yale University LLB (1949). NONPR AFFIL director: Stark Hospital Foundation; member: Wisconsin Bar Association; chairman capital fund drive: Milwaukee Symphony Orchestra; member steering comm: Pabst Theatre Reconstruction Campaign; ad bd director: Medical College Wisconsin; director: Medical College Wisconsin Health Policy Institute; member: Greater Milwaukee Foundation; member: American Bar Association; member: Association Bank Holding Companies. CLUB AFFIL Princeton Club; Milwaukee Club; Milwaukee Country Club; Cap & Gown Club.

David V. Uihlein, Jr.: director PRIM CORP EMPL president: Uihlein Archts.

Grants Analysis

Disclosure Period: calendar year ending 2001
Total Grants: $35,304,281
Number of Grants: 400 (approx)
Average Grant: $88,261
Highest Grant: $4,000,000
Typical Range: $20,000 to $200,000

Recent Grants

Note: Grants derived from 2001 Form 990.

General

2,700,000	Partners Advancing Values in Education, Milwaukee, WI -- support development of a loan program
1,205,000	Encounter for Culture and Education, Milwaukee, WI -- support Educational Book Program
1,000,000	Milwaukee Art Museum, Inc., Milwaukee, WI -- support capital campaign
831,200	American Enterprise Institute for Public Policy Research, Washington, DC -- support of the Foreign and Defense Policy Studies, Bradley Lecture Series
700,000	American Civil Rights Institute, Sacramento, CA -- support operations and public education campaign
568,750	Heritage Foundation, Washington, DC -- support operations
550,000	American Education Reform Council, Milwaukee, WI -- support operations
500,000	Black Alliance for Educational Options, Washington, DC -- support operations
475,000	Center for the Study of Popular Culture, Los Angeles, CA -- support of operations
400,000	Wisconsin Policy Research Institute, Washington, DC -- operating support

BRADY FOUNDATION

Giving Contact

James C. Brady, President, Treasurer & Trustee
Brady Foundation
PO Box 351
Gladstone, NJ 07934
Phone: (908)719-6658

Description

Founded: 1953
EIN: 136167209
Organization Type: Private Foundation
Giving Locations: NJ
Grant Types: General Support.

Donor Information

Founder: the late Helen M. Cutting, Nicholas Brady

Financial Summary

Total Giving: $348,600 (2000); $211,250 (1999); $274,300 (1998)
Giving Analysis: Giving for 2000 includes: foundation grants to United Way ($2,000); 1999: foundation grants to United Way ($2,000) 1998: foundation grants to United Way ($2,000)
Assets: $9,270,268 (2000); $9,442,465 (1999); $8,630,642 (1998)
Gifts Received: $700 (2000); $500 (1999); $300 (1995)

Typical Recipients

Arts & Humanities: Arts Associations & Councils, Arts Funds, Ballet, Dance, Libraries, Literary Arts, Museums/Galleries, Music, Public Broadcasting
Civic & Public Affairs: Civic & Public Affairs-General, Municipalities/Towns, Philanthropic Organizations, Safety, Urban & Community Affairs
Education: Arts/Humanities Education, Gifted & Talented Programs, Private Education (Precollege)
Environment: Air/Water Quality, Environment-General, Resource Conservation, Watershed, Wildlife Protection
Health: Alzheimers Disease, Cancer, Clinics/Medical Centers, Emergency/Ambulance Services, Health Funds, Health Organizations, Hospitals, Medical Research, Mental Health, Prenatal Health Issues, Public Health, Research/Studies Institutes, Single-Disease Health Associations
Religion: Churches
Science: Scientific Centers & Institutes
Social Services: Big Brother/Big Sister, Camps, Child Welfare, Community Service Organizations, People with Disabilities, Recreation & Athletics, Scouts, United Funds/United Ways, YMCA/YWCA/YMHA/YWHA, Youth Organizations

Application Procedures

Initial Contact: The foundation requests applications be made in writing. and should include a description of organization and amount requested.
Deadlines: None.

Restrictions

The foundation does not fund individuals or political or lobbying groups.

Foundation Officials

James C. Brady, Jr.: president, treasurer, trustee
Nicholas Frederick Brady: trustee B New York, NY 1930. ED Yale University BA (1952); Harvard University MBA (1954). CORP AFFIL director: Amerada

Hess Corp. NONPR AFFIL trustee: Boys Club Newark. CLUB AFFIL Lunch Club; Bond New York Club; The Links Club.
Karen Wisnosky: secretary

Grants Analysis

Disclosure Period: calendar year ending 2000
Total Grants: $346,600*
Number of Grants: 49
Average Grant: $4,183*
Highest Grant: $100,000
Lowest Grant: $100
Typical Range: $500 to $10,000
***Note:** Giving excludes United Way. Average grant excludes two highest grants ($150,000).

Recent Grants

Note: Grants derived from 1999 Form 990.

General

50,000	New Jersey Performing Arts Center Corporation, Newark, NJ
28,000	Boys and Girls Club of Newark, Newark, NJ
20,000	Metropolitan Museum of Art, New York, NY
15,000	Morristown Memorial Health Foundation, Inc., Morristown, NJ
10,000	Nature Conservancy Inc., Pottersville, NJ
10,000	New Jersey Seeds Inc., Peddie School, Hightstown, NJ
10,000	Newark Museum Association, Newark, NJ
5,000	Alzheimer Disease & Related Disorders, St. Louis, MO
5,000	Gladstone Equestrian Association, Gladstone, NJ
5,000	National Museum of Racing, Saratoga Springs, NY

BRAEMAR CHARITABLE TRUST

Giving Contact

Martha B. Cox, Trustee
c/o Trust Management Services
PO Box 1990
Waldport, OR 97394
Phone: (541)563-7279

Description

Founded: 1994
EIN: 936272124
Organization Type: Private Foundation
Giving Locations: OR
Grant Types: General Support.

Donor Information

Founder: Established in 1994 by Hobart and Marian A. Bird.

Financial Summary

Total Giving: $860,444 (fiscal year ending September 30, 2001); $652,854 (fiscal 2000); $356,542 (fiscal 1998)
Giving Analysis: Giving for fiscal 2000 includes: foundation scholarships ($5,000)
Assets: $15,462,143 (fiscal 2001); $20,344,412 (fiscal 2000); $10,585,278 (fiscal 1998)
Gifts Received: $1,276,728 (fiscal 2001); $1,500,000 (fiscal 1998); $1,500,000 (fiscal 1996). Note: Contributions were received from Hobart M. and Marian A. Bird.

Typical Recipients

Arts & Humanities: Arts Associations & Councils, Ballet, History & Archaeology, Libraries, Museums/Galleries, Opera, Public Broadcasting

Civic & Public Affairs: Economic Development, Employment/Job Training, Housing, Nonprofit Management, Women's Affairs
Education: Afterschool/Enrichment Programs, Agricultural Education, Community & Junior Colleges, Literacy, Public Education (Precollege), Science/Mathematics Education, Vocational & Technical Education
Environment: Environment-General, Resource Conservation
Health: Children's Health/Hospitals, Geriatric Health, Heart, Home-Care Services, Nursing Services, Nutrition
Religion: Religious Welfare
Science: Science Museums
Social Services: At-Risk Youth, Child Abuse, Child Welfare, Community Service Organizations, Counseling, Crime Prevention, Domestic Violence, Family Services, Food/Clothing Distribution, People with Disabilities, Scouts, Senior Services, Shelters/Homelessness, Substance Abuse, Volunteer Services, Youth Organizations

Application Procedures

Initial Contact: The foundation requests applications be made in writing.
Application Requirements: Include proof of tax-exempt status, a copy of by-laws and constitution, recently audited financial statement, statement of specific endeavor, record of prior results of similar efforts, and any other pertinent information.
Deadlines: Vary by region in Oregon; contact foundation.

Restrictions

Grants are not made to individuals.

Additional Information

Grants are limited to tax-exempt organizations within Oregon. Maximum grant is $8,000.

Foundation Officials

Gail Atkinson: program manager
Hobart M. Bird: trustee
Marian A. Bird: trustee
Martha B. Cox: trustee
Molly Sue Snyder: trustee

Grants Analysis

Disclosure Period: fiscal year ending September 30, 2001
Total Grants: $860,444
Number of Grants: 143
Average Grant: $6,017
Highest Grant: $11,714
Lowest Grant: $780
Typical Range: $3,000 to $8,000

Recent Grants

Note: Grants derived from fiscal 2000 Form 990.

Library-Related
8,000   Friends of The Coos Bay Public Library, Coos Bay, OR -- education

General
10,175   Southwest Oregon Community Action, OR -- assistance
9,800   Dallas School District 12 Foundation, Dallas, TX -- education
8,000   Albany Free From Drug Abuse, Albany, NY -- for alcohol and drug abuse
8,000   Bay Area Rehabilitation Center, Baytown, TX -- disabled and handicapped
8,000   Boys and Girls Club of Albany, Albany, NY -- for youth activities
8,000   Chemeketa Community College, Salem, OR -- education
8,000   Columbia Gorge Discovery Center -- education
8,000   Deschutes County Historical Society, Bend, OR -- historical preservation

8,000   Eugene Symphonic Association, Inc., Eugene, OR -- cultural
8,000   Gilbert House Children's Museum, Salem, OR -- education

R. B. O. Bragg
Charitable Trust

Giving Contact

Care of Bank of America
PO Box 831041
Dallas, TX 75283-1041
Phone: (214)508-2005

Description

Founded: 1999
EIN: 756521856
Organization Type: Private Foundation
Grant Types: General Support.

Financial Summary

Total Giving: $53,000 (fiscal year ending February 28, 2001); $36,880 (fiscal 1998)
Assets: $1,419,600 (fiscal 2001); $1,108,482 (fiscal 1999); $1,304,083 (fiscal 1998)
Gifts Received: $1,078,114 (fiscal 1998). Note: In fiscal 1998, contributions were received from Dorothy Watson Bragg.

Typical Recipients

Arts & Humanities: Libraries
Education: Colleges & Universities
Health: Children's Health/Hospitals, Health Organizations

Additional Information

Trust(s): Bank of America NA TX

Grants Analysis

Disclosure Period: fiscal year ending February 28, 2001
Total Grants: $53,000
Number of Grants: 4
Highest Grant: $17,666
Lowest Grant: $5,889

Recent Grants

Note: Grants derived from fiscal 2001 Form 990.

Library-Related
5,889   Fairfield Library Association, Fairfield, TX -- for charitable purposes

General
17,666   Shriners Hospital for Children, Galveston, TX -- for charitable purpose
14,723   East Texas Medical Center Foundation, Fairfield, TX -- for equipment, real estate, construction or purchase of hospital facilities
14,722   College of the Ozarks, Pt. Lookout, MO -- for charitable purposes

Braitmayer
Foundation

Giving Contact

Robert L. Kirkpatrick, Jr., Advisory
Middlesex Corp. Center
213 Court St., Suite 1101
Middletown, CT 06457
Phone: (860)638-5026
Fax: (860)638-5069
Web: http://www.braitmayerfoundation.org

Description

Founded: 1964
EIN: 046112131
Organization Type: Private Foundation
Giving Locations: National.
Grant Types: General Support, Project, Seed Money.

Donor Information

Founder: Marian S. Braitmayer

Financial Summary

Total Giving: $227,700 (2001); $230,052 (2000); $193,200 (1999)
Giving Analysis: Giving for 1999 includes: foundation scholarships ($1,500)
Assets: $4,970,454 (2001); $5,462,233 (2000); $5,253,769 (1999)

Typical Recipients

Arts & Humanities: Libraries, Museums/Galleries, Music, Public Broadcasting, Theater
Civic & Public Affairs: Botanical Gardens/Parks, Community Foundations, Civic & Public Affairs-General, Housing, Municipalities/Towns, Urban & Community Affairs
Education: Colleges & Universities, Faculty Development, Education-General, Leadership Training, Private Education (Precollege), Religious Education, Science/Mathematics Education, Secondary Education (Private), Special Education, Student Aid
Environment: Environment-General, Resource Conservation
Science: Scientific Centers & Institutes
Social Services: Child Welfare, Community Service Organizations, Day Care, Family Services, People with Disabilities, Recreation & Athletics, YMCA/YWCA/YMHA/YWHA, Youth Organizations

Application Procedures

Initial Contact: Contact the foundation for their detailed Objectives and Guidelines sheet.
Application Requirements: Include a brief history of the organization, a description of the project (not more than three pages), a budget and time frame, proof of tax-exempt status, list of board members, and recently audited financial statement.
Deadlines: Dates vary depending on the size of the grant. Obtain foundation guideline, as they will include the schedule.

Restrictions

No grants to individuals, no multi-year grants, grants for endowment purposes or building programs, nor to childcare or pre-kindergarten programs.

Foundation Officials

Eric A. Braitmayer: trustee
John W. Braitmayer: trustee
Karen L. Braitmayer: trustee
Nancy W. Corkery: trustee
Kristina B. Hewey: trustee
Anne B. Webb: trustee
R. Davis Webb, Jr.: trustee

Grants Analysis

Disclosure Period: calendar year ending 2001
Total Grants: $227,700
Number of Grants: 19
Average Grant: $12,000
Highest Grant: $35,000
Lowest Grant: $400
Typical Range: $1,000 to $35,000

Recent Grants

Note: Grants derived from 2000 Form 990.

Library-Related
1,000   Elizabeth Tabor Library

General

35,000	Francis W. Parker Charter Essential School
34,900	The Girl's Middle School
34,662	Northwestern University, Chicago, IL
30,160	Vermont Center for the Book, Chester, VT
30,000	Lab School of Washington, Washington, DC
25,000	CAST, Boston, MA
20,130	Mount Holyoke College, Holyoke, MA
10,000	Wesleyan University, Middletown, CT -- Ascend Program
3,200	V.A.S.E.
1,000	Coalition for Buzzards Bay, Buzzards Bay, MA

OTTO BREMER FOUNDATION

Giving Contact

John Kostishack, Executive Director
445 Minnesota Street, Suite 2000
St. Paul, MN 55101-2107
Phone: (651)227-7621
Fax: (651)312-3665
E-mail: obf@bremer.com
Web: http://www.ottobremer.org
Note: Proposals may be submitted through local Bremer First American Bank affiliates. Toll Free: (888)291-1123

Description

Founded: 1944
EIN: 416019050
Organization Type: General Purpose Foundation
Giving Locations: MN; MT; ND; WI
Grant Types: Capital, Challenge, Loan, Matching, Multiyear/Continuing Support, Operating Expenses, Project, Seed Money.

Donor Information

Founder: Otto Bremer , a German immigrant of humble origins, has become an established symbol of philanthropy in the Minnesota, North Dakota, and Wisconsin regions. He began his career as a bookkeeper in the National German American Bank in St. Paul, initiating what proved to be an enduring attachment to that area. Mr. Bremer was an active participant in a wide variety of community affairs throughout his lifetime. In 1921, he became chairman of the American National Bank, and in 1939, he assumed the presidency of the Schmidt Brewing Company.

In addition to these corporate activities, Mr. Bremer was treasurer of the City of St. Paul, aided in the formation of the Minnesota Democratic Farmer-Labor Party, counseled Presidents Woodrow Wilson and Franklin D. Roosevelt, and administered the Federal Home Owners' Loan Corporation in Minnesota. Yet, it was his participation in banking that was most important to Otto Bremer. His holdings were vast, yet his association with "countryside banks" proved to be most satisfying. One of his creeds was that "banks should be home banks, independently operated by people of their communities."

In a biography of Otto Bremer, he is described as firmly believing that individuals do not live or grow in isolation; they fulfill themselves only by helping one another. It was his commitment to this belief that led Mr. Bremer to act with concern for the rural communities in his area that were threatened by poverty. During the Depression, Mr. Bremer liquidated personal assets and placed them in banks serving these rural communities. His support sustained these struggling banks and communities. Later, Mr. Bremer became concerned with maintaining support to these communities after his death. In 1943, he established the Bremer Financial Corporation which received assets from the banks of which Mr. Bremer was principal shareholder. The assets from the Bremer Financial Corporation were then transferred to the Otto Bremer Foundation, which was formed in 1944 due to his deep concern for his holdings in Minnesota, North Dakota, and Wisconsin. Through the foundation, he sought to insure the perpetuation of the Bremer banks and the ultimate return of his wealth to the trade territories of the banks and the city of St. Paul. Money placed in Otto Bremer's banks was funneled into the corporation, and finally to the foundation, which dispensed it to needy causes in the community. In this way, Mr. Bremer formulated an enduring system which would continue to use his wealth to "serve the community in which it was invested first, last and always."

Financial Summary

Total Giving: $20,000,000 (2003 approx); $20,000,000 (2002 approx); $16,080,448 (2001)
Giving Analysis: Giving for 1999 includes: foundation program-related investments ($1,832,000); foundation program-related investments ($3,397,375) foundation program-related investments ($3,538,500)
Assets: $393,777,842 (2001); $308,530,245 (1999); $294,888,232 (1998)

Typical Recipients

Arts & Humanities: Ethnic & Folk Arts, Libraries, Music, Public Broadcasting
Civic & Public Affairs: African American Affairs, Asian American Affairs, Botanical Gardens/Parks, Civil Rights, Community Foundations, Economic Development, Employment/Job Training, Civic & Public Affairs-General, Hispanic Affairs, Housing, Legal Aid, Native American Affairs, Nonprofit Management, Public Policy, Rural Affairs, Urban & Community Affairs, Women's Affairs
Education: Agricultural Education, Colleges & Universities, Community & Junior Colleges, Continuing Education, Education Funds, Environmental Education, Faculty Development, Education-General, Gifted & Talented Programs, International Exchange, Leadership Training, Legal Education, Literacy, Medical Education, Minority Education, Preschool Education, Private Education (Precollege), Public Education (Precollege), Religious Education, Science/Mathematics Education, Social Sciences Education, Vocational & Technical Education
Environment: Resource Conservation
Health: AIDS/HIV, Clinics/Medical Centers, Diabetes, Emergency/Ambulance Services, Geriatric Health, Health Organizations, Hospices, Hospitals, Mental Health, Nursing Services, Outpatient Health Care, Public Health
International: Human Rights, International Development
Religion: Churches, Jewish Causes, Religious Welfare
Science: Scientific Centers & Institutes
Social Services: At-Risk Youth, Camps, Child Welfare, Community Centers, Community Service Organizations, Counseling, Crime Prevention, Day Care, Domestic Violence, Emergency Relief, Family Services, Food/Clothing Distribution, Homes, People with Disabilities, Recreation & Athletics, Refugee Assistance, Senior Services, Shelters/Homelessness, Social Services-General, Substance Abuse, United Funds/United Ways, YMCA/YWCA/YMHA/YWHA, Youth Organizations

Application Procedures

Initial Contact: Applicants should write or call the foundation for an application and for assistance in the development of a proposal. A video on how to apply for a grant is available through the foundation and through First National Bank affiliates.
Application Requirements: A proposal includes the following: legal name, address, and phone number of organization, and name and phone number of contact person; brief a description of organization, including goals, purposes, and short history, if appropriate; description of project for which funds are being sought, what it is designed to achieve, how this will be accomplished; the specific amount requested; documentation of organization's nonprofit and tax-exempt status; names and qualifications of individuals responsible for implementing project; evidence that request is endorsed by board of directors of applicant organization an d list of members; complete budget for project, with projected revenues and expenses; audited financial statement, if available, for organization's previous fiscal year, current operational budget, and copy of most recent IRS Form 990; indication of other funding sources to be used to support project; description of project's future funding plans, where appropriate; description of procedure for reporting expenditures of grant funds and progress of project.
Deadlines: The board of trustees meets monthly; however, proposals should be submitted for review three months prior to the date the funding decision is required. Most applicants are reviewed in a two-step process over two consecutive monthly meetings, about 6-8 weeks on average timetable.
Review Process: All complete proposals will be reviewed first by the staff and then submitted to the trustees, with whom final responsibility for grant approval resides. Applicants receive written notification of board action within a week of the board meeting.
Notes: Grant guidelines are available on the internet.

Restrictions

Grants are given only to projects within the service areas of Bremer-affiliated organizations in Wisconsin, North Dakota, Minnesota, Montana, and within the city of St. Paul. Grants are rarely made to organizations in other communities unless they affect these specified geographic areas. Grants are not made to individuals, K-12 education, sporting activities, or to endowment funds, or to organizations which are not tax exempt as defined under section 501 (c)(3) of the Internal Revenue Service code. Requests for annual fund drives, benefit events, camps, economic development, or medical research are discouraged. The Foundation does not support theatrical productions, books, motion pictures, or other media projects.

Additional Information

Grants are evaluated at the conclusion of the first year of funding. Grants made for more than one year may be reconsidered at the end of each year.
Publications: Annual Report; Guidelines; And Video

Foundation Officials

Charlotte S. Johnson: trustee PRIM CORP EMPL vice president: Bremer Financial Corp.
John Kostishack: executive director B 1941.
Mark Lindberg: senior program officer
William H. Lipschultz: trustee B Saint Paul, MN 1930. ED University of Minnesota (1956). PRIM CORP EMPL vice president, treasurer, director, chairman: Bremer Financial Corp. CORP AFFIL vice president, director: Otto Bremer Co.; vice president: Stone Container Corp. Halper Box Division.
Lynda Marrone: grants mgr
Elsa Vega Perez: program officer
Daniel C. Reardon: trustee
Karen Starr: senior program officer
Kari Suzuki: program associate
Anthony A. Vasquez: computer specialist

Grants Analysis

Disclosure Period: calendar year ending 1999
Total Grants: $15,739,721*
Number of Grants: 586
Average Grant: $20,213
Highest Grant: $243,700
Typical Range: $900 to $150,000
*Note: Giving excludes program related investments, which are eventually repaid to the foundation.

Recent Grants

Note: Grants derived from 2001 Form 990.

General

300,000	Tri-College University, Fargo, ND -- establish Red River Basin Institute
202,150	Prairie Public Broadcasting, Inc, Fargo, ND -- Public Education Program
200,000	American Red Cross Minn-Kota Chapter, Moorhead, MN -- implement community-based flood mitigation project
200,000	St. Paul Foundation, St. Paul, MN -- emergency relief fund
200,000	Tri-College University, Fargo, ND -- establish Red River Basin Institute
194,770	Prairie Public Broadcasting, Inc, Fargo, ND -- Public Education Program
160,000	Higher Education Consortium for Urban Affairs, Inc., St. Paul, MN -- operating expenses
150,000	Fond du Lac Tribal and Community College, Cloquet, MN -- academic building expansion project
140,000	Prairie Public Broadcasting, Inc, Fargo, ND -- River Watch Community Education Program
135,000	Peoples Institute for Survival and Beyond, New Orleans, LA -- establish regional office

BRETZLAFF FOUNDATION

Giving Contact

Michael J. Malarkey, Secretary
Bretzlaff Foundation, Inc.
Weigand Center
165 Liberty Street
Reno, NV 89501
Phone: (775)333-0330

Description

Founded: 1989
EIN: 880241424
Organization Type: Private Foundation
Giving Locations: DC; HI; MI; NV: Northern part of state
Grant Types: Research.

Donor Information

Founder: Established in 1989 by Hazel C. Van Allen.

Financial Summary

Total Giving: $1,210,500 (fiscal year ending June 30, 2001); $1,274,300 (fiscal 2000); $1,000,095 (fiscal 1999 approx)
Giving Analysis: Giving for fiscal 2001 includes: foundation scholarships ($20,000); fiscal 2000: foundation scholarships ($205,000); fiscal 1998: foundation scholarships ($220,000) foundation ($705,000).
Assets: $19,084,601 (fiscal 2001); $22,504,036 (fiscal 2000); $18,317,091 (fiscal 1998)
Gifts Received: $322,121 (fiscal 2001); $1,848,262 (fiscal 2000); $1,200,000 (fiscal 1998). Note: In 2001, contributions were received from the estate of Hazel Van Allen ($156,095), Ruthmary S. Cobb ($7,729), Beverly K. McClendon ($76,222), and Stephen C. Baker ($76,222). Contributions were received from the estate of Hazel C. Van Allen.

Typical Recipients

Arts & Humanities: Arts Associations & Councils, Arts Centers, Ethnic & Folk Arts, Historic Preservation, History & Archaeology, Libraries, Museums/Galleries, Music, Public Broadcasting, Theater
Civic & Public Affairs: Employment/Job Training, Legal Aid, Public Policy
Education: Arts/Humanities Education, Colleges & Universities, Legal Education, Science/Mathematics Education, Student Aid

Environment: Research, Resource Conservation
Health: Health Organizations, Hospices, Hospitals, Medical Rehabilitation, Medical Research, Public Health, Research/Studies Institutes
Religion: Religious Welfare
Social Services: At-Risk Youth, Big Brother/Big Sister, Child Welfare, Community Service Organizations, Delinquency & Criminal Rehabilitation, Family Services, Recreation & Athletics, Youth Organizations

Application Procedures

Initial Contact: Send a brief letter of inquiry.
Application Requirements: Include type of organization, its purpose and nature, and purpose of funds sought.
Deadlines: December 31.

Restrictions

Does not support individuals, religious organizations for sectarian purposes, political or lobbying groups, or organizations outside operating areas.

Foundation Officials

Richard Gilbert: vice president
Michael J. Melarkey: treasurer
Hazel C. (Bretzlaff) Van Allen: president
William G. Van Allen: secretary

Grants Analysis

Disclosure Period: fiscal year ending June 30, 2001
Total Grants: $1,190,500*
Number of Grants: 59
Average Grant: $17,078*
Highest Grant: $200,000
Lowest Grant: $500
Typical Range: $5,000 to $30,000
*Note: Giving excludes scholarships. Average grant excludes highest grant.

Recent Grants

Note: Grants derived from fiscal 2000 Form 990.

General

180,000	Hawaii Justice Foundation, Honolulu, HI
80,000	Truckee Meadows Community College, Reno, NV -- scholarships
60,000	Bishop Museum, Honolulu, HI
60,000	Honolulu Academy of Arts, Honolulu, HI -- cultural education
50,000	Historic Hawaii Foundation, Honolulu, HI -- endowment for preserving Hawaiians
50,000	KNPB Public TV, Reno, NV -- endowment for public TV
50,000	Nature Conservancy -- historic preservation
50,000	Nevada State Museum, NV -- cultural education
50,000	University of Hawaii College of Education, Honolulu, HI -- scholarship
34,000	University of Nevada Reno Foundation, Reno, NV -- scholarships

BRIDGESTONE AMERICAS HOLDING, INC.

Company Headquarters

50 Century Blvd.
Nashville, TN 37214
Web: http://www.bridgestone-firestone.com

Company Description

Founded: 1990
Also Known As: Bridgestone/Firestone.
Revenue: US$389 million (2002)
Employees: 45000 (2002)
SIC(s): 2296 Tire Cord & Fabrics, 3011 Tires & Inner Tubes, 3069 Fabricated Rubber Products Nec, 5014 Tires & Tubes.

Parent Company: Bridgestone Corp., 10-1 Kyobashi 1-chome, Chuo-ku, Tokyo, Japan

Operating Locations

Bridgestone/Firestone Credit Services Co. (OH--Brook Park); Bridgestone/Firestone, Inc. (AR--Russellville; CA--Irvine; FL--Mary Esther, West Palm Beach; GA--Marietta, Norcross, Tucker; IL--Bloomington, Decatur, Rolling Meadows; IN--Indianapolis; IA--Des Moines; MA--Quincy; MI--Southfield; MN--Minneapolis; NY--Clifton Park; NC--Wilson; OH--Akron; OK--Oklahoma City; TN--LaVergne; TX--Corpus Christi, Grand Prairie, Houston); Bridgestone/Firestone Information Services Co. (OH--Akron); Bridgestone/Firestone Off-Road Tire Co. (TN--Nashville); Bridgestone/Firestone Original Equipment Tire Sales Co. (MI--Southfield); Bridgestone/Firestone Research Laboratories (OH--Akron); Bridgestone/Firestone Retail Operations (IL--Rolling Meadows); Bridgestone/Firestone Technology Co. (OH--Akron); Bridgestone/Firestone Tire Manufacturing Operations (TN--Nashville); Bridgestone/Firestone Tire Sales Co. (TN--Nashville); Dayton Tire (OK--Oklahoma City); Firestone Agricultural Tire Co. (IA--Des Moines); Firestone Building Products Co. (IN--Carmel); Firestone Fibers & Textiles Co. (NC--Kings Mountain); Firestone Industrial Products Co. (IN--Carmel); Firestone Synthetic Rubber & Latex Co. (OH--Akron); Firestone Tube Co. (AR--Russellville).
Note: Also operate in Canada, Mexico, Europe, South and Central America, Liberia, and Singapore.

The Bridgestone/ Firestone Trust Fund

Giving Contact

Bernice Csaszar, Administrator
The Bridgestone/Firestone Trust Fund
50 Century Boulevard
Nashville, TN 37214
Phone: (615)872-1415
Fax: (615)872-1414
E-mail: bfstrustfund@bfsusa.com

Description

Founded: 1952
EIN: 346505181
Organization Type: Corporate Foundation
Former Name: Bridgestone/Firestone, Inc. (2003).
Giving Locations: headquarters and operating communities.
Grant Types: Capital, Challenge, Employee Matching Gifts, General Support, Operating Expenses, Project, Scholarship, Seed Money.

Donor Information

Founder: Bridgestone/Firestone, Inc.

Financial Summary

Total Giving: $6,131,633 (2001); $4,664,329 (2000); $3,500,000 (1999 approx). Note: Contributes through foundation only.
Giving Analysis: Giving for 2000 includes: foundation grants to United Way ($585,471); foundation ($4,078,858); 1998: foundation grants to United Way ($471,788); foundation ($2,139,548); 1997: foundation grants to United Way ($409,837) foundation ($1,538,677)
Assets: $38,681,621 (2001); $87,819,753 (2000); $67,994,672 (1998)

Typical Recipients

Arts & Humanities: Arts Associations & Councils, Arts Institutes, Arts Outreach, Ballet, Community Arts, Dance, Arts & Humanities-General, Historic Preservation, Libraries, Museums/Galleries, Music, Opera, Public Broadcasting, Theater

Civic & Public Affairs: African American Affairs, Business/Free Enterprise, Civil Rights, Clubs, Community Foundations, Economic Development, Employment/Job Training, Civic & Public Affairs-General, Housing, Law & Justice, Municipalities/Towns, Professional & Trade Associations, Public Policy, Rural Affairs, Urban & Community Affairs, Zoos/Aquariums
Education: Agricultural Education, Arts/Humanities Education, Business Education, Colleges & Universities, Colleges & Universities, Community & Junior Colleges, Economic Education, Education Funds, Engineering/Technological Education, Education-General, International Studies, Medical Education, Minority Education, Public Education (Precollege), Religious Education, Science/Mathematics Education, Special Education, Student Aid, Vocational & Technical Education
Environment: Environment-General, Resource Conservation
Health: Children's Health/Hospitals, Emergency/Ambulance Services, Health Policy/Cost Containment, Health Organizations, Hospices, Hospitals, Medical Research, Nursing Services, Single-Disease Health Associations
Religion: Ministries
Science: Scientific Centers & Institutes, Scientific Organizations
Social Services: At-Risk Youth, Camps, Child Welfare, Community Centers, Community Service Organizations, Community Service Organizations, Emergency Relief, Family Planning, Family Services, People with Disabilities, Recreation & Athletics, Scouts, Senior Services, Social Services-General, Substance Abuse, United Funds/United Ways, Volunteer Services, YMCA/YWCA/YMHA/YWHA, Youth Organizations

Application Procedures

Initial Contact: Send a brief letter or proposal; organizations in communities where Bridgestone/Firestone operates should write to local major facility.
Application Requirements: Include a description of organization, amount requested, purpose of funds sought, recently audited financial statement, proof of tax-exempt status, 501(C)(3) Federation IRS Form 990 or letter, board of directors, current operating budget, and list of major donors, including each of their contributions.
Deadlines: None.
Review Process: Proposals are reviewed upon receipt; those proposals meeting basic criteria are held for review by the committee that meets several times a year; applicants are notified of committee's decision.

Restrictions

Recipients must have 501(c)(3) status and must operate in accordance with the principle of equal opportunity.
Grants do not support groups that discriminate, partisan political organizations, or groups limited to a single religious organization.

Additional Information

In 1992, the company relocated its corporate headquarters from Akron, OH, to Nashville, TN.
In 1989, Bridgestone U.S.A., Inc., merged with Firestone Tire & Rubber Co. to become Bridgestone/Firestone, Inc., a wholly-owned subsidiary of Bridgestone Corp. of Japan.
Publications: Guidelines

Corporate Officials

Masatoshi Ono: chairman, chief executive officer B 1937. ED Kumamoto University (Japan) BS (1959). PRIM CORP EMPL chairman, chief executive officer: Bridgestone/Firestone, Inc.

Foundation Officials

Bernice Csaszar: administrator
Hal Horton: member
Christine Karbowiak: chairman

Gene Stephens: member
Ronald Tepner: member

Grants Analysis

Disclosure Period: calendar year ending 2001
Total Grants: $6,101,651*
Number of Grants: 1,1228
Average Grant: $4,969
Highest Grant: $800,000
Lowest Grant: $50
Typical Range: $50 to $50,000
*Note: Giving excludes United Way.

Recent Grants

Note: Grants derived from 2001 Form 990.

Library-Related

250,000	Nashville Public Library Foundation, Nashville, TN

General

250,000	Coming Together Project, Akron, OH
184,600	National Merit Scholarship Corporation, Evanston, IL
138,000	Akron Golf Charities Foundation, Akron, OH
100,000	American Red Cross, Concord, NH
100,000	Barton College, Wilson, NC
100,000	Nature Conservancy of Texas, Houston, TX
99,500	Nashville Predators Foundation, Nashville, TN
82,500	Championship Racing Auxiliary
65,000	United Way Summit County, Akron, OH
64,000	National Future Farmers of America Foundation, Madison, WI

ALEXANDER H. BRIGHT CHARITABLE TRUST

Giving Contact

Solange Bell, Operations manager
c/o Boston Family Office
33 Broad Street
Boston, MA 02109
Phone: (617)227-2676
Fax: (617)227-6063

Description

Founded: 1952
EIN: 046013967
Organization Type: Private Foundation
Giving Locations: MA
Grant Types: General Support, Operating Expenses.

Donor Information

Founder: the late Alexander H. Bright

Financial Summary

Total Giving: $110,700 (2000); $121,775 (1999); $106,450 (1996)
Assets: $4,780,142 (2000); $4,328,590 (1999); $2,794,030 (1996)

Typical Recipients

Arts & Humanities: Arts Associations & Councils, Arts Funds, Museums/Galleries, Music, Public Broadcasting, Theater
Civic & Public Affairs: Botanical Gardens/Parks, Clubs, Civic & Public Affairs-General, Municipalities/Towns, Native American Affairs, Rural Affairs, Women's Affairs
Education: Colleges & Universities, Education Funds, Environmental Education, Education-General, Leadership Training, Literacy, Medical Education, Private Education (Precollege)
Environment: Air/Water Quality, Forestry, Environment-General, Protection, Research, Resource Conservation, Wildlife Protection

Health: Emergency/Ambulance Services, Nursing Services
International: Health Care/Hospitals, International Environmental Issues
Religion: Churches, Religious Organizations
Science: Science Museums, Scientific Research
Social Services: Animal Protection, Child Welfare, Family Planning, Recreation & Athletics, United Funds/United Ways, Youth Organizations

Application Procedures

Initial Contact: Send a brief letter of inquiry.
Application Requirements: Include a concise statement of purpose of funds sought, the staff and budget for the project, the current operating budget, recently audited financial statement, a list of board members, resumes of all key staff people, proof of tax-exempt status, and a copy of the most recent Form 990.
Deadlines: February, May, August, and November.

Foundation Officials

Edward W. Weld: trustee

Grants Analysis

Disclosure Period: calendar year ending 2000
Total Grants: $110,700
Number of Grants: 97
Average Grant: $1,141
Highest Grant: $2,500
Lowest Grant: $100
Typical Range: $500 to $2,000

Recent Grants

Note: Grants derived from 1999 Form 990.

General

10,000	Brookline Library Foundation
2,500	Animal Rescue League, Boston, MA
2,500	Boston Symphony Orchestra, Boston, MA
2,500	Earth Island Institute
2,000	Alaska Conservation Foundation, Anchorage, AK
2,000	Arnold Arboretum, Boston, MA
2,000	Bosler Humane Society
2,000	Conservation Law Foundation, Boston, MA
2,000	Museum of Science, Boston, MA
2,000	National Conservancy of California

BRIGHT FAMILY FOUNDATION

Giving Contact

Calvin E. Bright, President
1620 N. Carpenter Rd., Bldg. B
Modesto, CA 95351
Phone: (209)526-8242
Fax: (209)526-8886
Web: http://www.bright-homes.com

Description

Founded: 1986
EIN: 770126942
Organization Type: Private Foundation
Giving Locations: CA
Grant Types: Operating Expenses.

Donor Information

Founder: Calvin Bright, Marjorie Bright

Financial Summary

Total Giving: $548,900 (2000); $465,523 (1999); $371,567 (1998)
Giving Analysis: Giving for 2000 includes: foundation scholarships ($95,500); 1999: foundation scholarships ($96,000) 1998: foundation scholarships ($120,500)

Assets: $11,177,950 (2000); $12,112,860 (1999); $10,451,476 (1998)
Gifts Received: $700,000 (1999); $700,000 (1998); $700,000 (1996). Note: In 1998 and 1999, contributions were received from Calvin and Marjorie Bright.

Typical Recipients

Arts & Humanities: Arts & Humanities-General, Libraries, Museums/Galleries, Music, Performing Arts, Public Broadcasting, Theater
Civic & Public Affairs: Clubs, Economic Development, Civic & Public Affairs-General, Housing, Native American Affairs, Philanthropic Organizations, Safety, Women's Affairs
Education: Arts/Humanities Education, Colleges & Universities, Community & Junior Colleges, Medical Education, Private Education (Precollege), Public Education (Precollege), Secondary Education (Public), Student Aid
Health: Cancer, Clinics/Medical Centers, Health Organizations, Hospices, Hospitals, Research/Studies Institutes, Single-Disease Health Associations
International: Health Care/Hospitals, International Environmental Issues, International Organizations
Religion: Churches, Churches, Jewish Causes, Missionary Activities (Domestic), Religious Organizations, Religious Welfare
Science: Science Museums
Social Services: Child Welfare, Community Service Organizations, Crime Prevention, Domestic Violence, People with Disabilities, Recreation & Athletics, Scouts, Shelters/Homelessness, United Funds/United Ways, Youth Organizations

Application Procedures

Initial Contact: Send a brief letter of inquiry.
Application Requirements: Include a statement of charitable purpose on organization letterhead, including tax I.D. number, or submit information on Bright Family foundations grant application form.
Deadlines: December 1.

Additional Information

Publications: Application Form

Foundation Officials

Calvin E. Bright: president
Lyn Bright: secretary, treasurer
Marjorie Bright: vice president

Grants Analysis

Disclosure Period: calendar year ending 2000
Total Grants: $453,400*
Number of Grants: 48
Average Grant: $9,446
Highest Grant: $40,000
Lowest Grant: $200
Typical Range: $1,000 to $20,000
*Note: Giving excludes scholarships.

Recent Grants

Note: Grants derived from 2001 Form 990.

General

50,000	Central Valley Performing Arts Committee, Modesto, CA
40,000	Children's Crisis Center, Modesto, CA
30,000	California State University Stanislaus, Turlock, CA
30,000	Campus Crusade for Christ, Orlando, FL
30,000	Modesto Gospel Mission, Modesto, CA
30,000	University of California San Francisco School of Medicine, San Francisco, CA
26,000	Modesto Junior College Foundation, Modesto, CA
25,000	Community Hospice, Modesto, CA
25,000	Modesto Junior College Foundation, Modesto, CA
20,000	Shelter Cove Community Church, Modesto, CA

BRILLION IRON WORKS

Company Headquarters

200 Park Avenue
Brillion, WI 54110
Web: http://www.brillionironworks.com

Company Description

Founded: 1934
Revenue: US$126 million (2002)
Employees: 800 (2002)
SIC(s): 3321 Gray & Ductile Iron Foundries, 3523 Farm Machinery & Equipment, 3624 Carbon & Graphite Products.
Parent Company: Transportation Technologies Industries, Inc., 980 N. Michigan Ave., Chicago, IL, United States

Brillion Foundation

Giving Contact

Harold J. Wolf, Secretary & Treasurer
Brillion Foundation
200 Park Ave., Box 127
Brillion, WI 54110-0127
Phone: (920)756-2121

Description

EIN: 396043916
Organization Type: Corporate Foundation
Giving Locations: WI: Brillion
Grant Types: Capital, Challenge, General Support, Operating Expenses, Scholarship.

Financial Summary

Total Giving: $61,810 (fiscal year ending June 30, 2001); $62,000 (fiscal 1998); $134,155 (fiscal 1997). Note: Fiscal 1997 Giving includes scholarship ($7,350).
Giving Analysis: Giving for fiscal 2001 includes: foundation scholarships ($5,700) fiscal 1999: foundation scholarships ($7,550)
Assets: $327,692 (fiscal 2001); $317,206 (fiscal 1999); $342,258 (fiscal 1997)
Gifts Received: $50,000 (fiscal 2001); $50,000 (fiscal 1999); $50,000 (fiscal 1997). Note: In fiscal 1999 and fiscal 2001, contributions were received from Brillion Iron Works Inc.

Typical Recipients

Arts & Humanities: Historic Preservation, History & Archaeology, Libraries, Music, Public Broadcasting
Civic & Public Affairs: Botanical Gardens/Parks, Clubs, Civic & Public Affairs-General, Municipalities/Towns, Urban & Community Affairs
Education: Agricultural Education, Business Education, Colleges & Universities, Economic Education, Education-General, Journalism/Media Education, Public Education (Precollege)
Environment: Environment-General
Health: Cancer, Children's Health/Hospitals, Health Organizations, Public Health, Single-Disease Health Associations
International: International Peace & Security Issues
Religion: Churches, Religion-General, Religious Organizations, Religious Welfare
Science: Observatories & Planetariums
Social Services: Animal Protection, Community Service Organizations, People with Disabilities, Recreation & Athletics, Scouts, Scouts, Special Olympics, Substance Abuse, Youth Organizations

Application Procedures

Initial Contact: Send brief letter.
Deadlines: None.

Additional Information

Include a description of organization, amount requested, purpose of funds sought, audited financial statement, and proof of tax-exempt status. Provides support for churches, public broadcasting, community services, and restricted scholarships.

Corporate Officials

Dennis L. Graven: chief financial officer, vice president finance PRIM CORP EMPL chief financial officer, vice president finance: Brillion Iron Works.
John David McClain: president, chief executive officer B Camp Lajune, NC 1944. ED North Carolina State University (1967). PRIM CORP EMPL president, chief executive officer: Brillion Iron Works.

Foundation Officials

Gary Austin: director
Richard Larson: director
John David McClain: president (see above)
Carl Miller: director
Lowell O. Reese: vice president, director
Lin Wittmann: director
Harold J. Wolf: secretary, treasurer, director

Grants Analysis

Disclosure Period: fiscal year ending June 30, 2001
Total Grants: $56,110*
Number of Grants: 27
Average Grant: $2,078
Highest Grant: $6,000
Typical Range: $500 to $5,000
*Note: Giving excludes scholarships.

Recent Grants

Note: Grants derived from fiscal 2000 Form 990.

General

6,000	Faith United Methodist Church, Brillion, WI
6,000	Peace United Church of Christ, Brillion, WI
6,000	St. Bartholomew's Lutheran Church, Brillion, WI
6,000	St. Mary's Catholic Church, Brillion, WI
6,000	Trinity Evangelical Lutheran Church, Brillion, WI
3,250	Brillion City Community Drive, Brillion, WI
3,000	Community Assembly of God, Brillion, WI
2,500	Brillion Nature Center, Brillion, WI
1,000	"Beat the Heat" Program
1,000	Lakeland College, Shadeygan, WI

BRISTOL-MYERS SQUIBB CO.

Company Headquarters

345 Park Ave.
New York, NY 10154-0037
Web: http://www.bms.com

Company Description

Ticker: BMY
Exchange: NYSE
Operating Revenue: US$18.119 billion (2002)
Profit: US$1.895 billion (2002)
Employees: 44000 (2002)
Fortune Rank: 98, per FORTUNE Magazine's list of 500 Largest U.S. Corporations (2002).

Nonmonetary Support

Value: $35,000,000 (2000 approx)
Type: Donated Products
Note: Contact local operating facilities for local non-monetary giving. Contact Frank Cifuni at the Edition, NJ, facility for international product requests.

Bristol-Myers Squibb Foundation Inc.

Giving Contact

John L. Damonti, Foundation Coordinator
Bristol-Myers Squibb Foundation Inc.
345 Park Avenue
New York, NY 10154
Phone: (212)546-4000
Web: http://www.bms.com/aboutbms/founda/data/index.html

Alternate Contact

David Fritzsche
Bristol-Myers Squibb Company-Wallingford
PO Box 5100
Wallingford, CT 06492-5100
Note: Contact for nonprofit organizations in the Wallingford, Connecticut community

Description

Founded: 1990
EIN: 133127947
Organization Type: Corporate Foundation
Giving Locations: headquarters and operating communities; internationally; nationally.
Grant Types: Employee Matching Gifts, General Support, Project, Research.
Note: Employee matching gift ratio: 1 to 1.

Donor Information

Founder: Bristol-Myers Squibb Co., divisions, and subsidiaries

Financial Summary

Total Giving: $21,716,953 (2001); $15,862,375 (2000); $29,122,295 (1999). Note: Contributes through corporate direct giving program and foundation. Giving includes corporate direct giving, foundation, domestic subsidiaries, international subsidiaries, nonmonetary support.
Giving Analysis: Giving for 2000 includes: foundation scholarships ($396,755); foundation grants to United Way ($1,833,900); foundation matching gifts ($2,383,889); foundation ($11,247,831); 1999: foundation grants to United Way ($1,420,521); foundation matching gifts ($2,161,566); foundation ($6,346,425); corporate direct giving ($19,348,498); 1998: foundation grants to United Way ($1,420,521); foundation matching gifts ($2,161,566); foundation ($6,191,710) corporate direct giving ($12,790,571)
Assets: $40,005,806 (2001); $26,867,580 (2000); $3,756,669 (1998)
Gifts Received: $32,500,000 (2001); $39,091,700 (2000); $14,450,000 (1998). Note: Contributions were received from Bristol-Myers Squibb Co.

Typical Recipients

Arts & Humanities: Arts Associations & Councils, Arts Centers, Arts Funds, Arts Institutes, Arts Outreach, Historic Preservation, Libraries, Museums/Galleries, Music, Opera, Performing Arts, Public Broadcasting, Theater
Civic & Public Affairs: African American Affairs, Botanical Gardens/Parks, Business/Free Enterprise, Community Foundations, Economic Development, Employment/Job Training, Civic & Public Affairs-General, Housing, Law & Justice, Municipalities/Towns, Professional & Trade Associations, Public Policy, Rural Affairs, Safety, Urban & Community Affairs, Women's Affairs, Zoos/Aquariums

Education: Arts/Humanities Education, Business Education, Colleges & Universities, Education Funds, Education Reform, Education-General, Leadership Training, Legal Education, Medical Education, Minority Education, Private Education (Precollege), Religious Education, Social Sciences Education, Special Education, Student Aid
Environment: Air/Water Quality, Environment-General, Resource Conservation
Health: AIDS/HIV, Cancer, Children's Health/Hospitals, Clinics/Medical Centers, Diabetes, Emergency/Ambulance Services, Health-General, Geriatric Health, Health Organizations, Heart, Hospitals, Medical Rehabilitation, Medical Research, Medical Training, Mental Health, Nutrition, Public Health, Research/Studies Institutes, Transplant Networks/Donor Banks
International: Foreign Educational Institutions, Foreign Educational Institutions, International-General, Health Care/Hospitals, International Affairs, International Organizations, International Relations, Missionary/Religious Activities
Religion: Religion-General, Jewish Causes, Missionary Activities (Domestic), Religious Welfare
Science: Science-General, Science Museums, Scientific Centers & Institutes, Scientific Organizations, Scientific Research
Social Services: Community Service Organizations, Crime Prevention, Emergency Relief, Family Services, Food/Clothing Distribution, People with Disabilities, Recreation & Athletics, Shelters/Homelessness, Substance Abuse, United Funds/United Ways, Volunteer Services, Youth Organizations

Application Procedures

Initial Contact: Send a brief letter or proposal no more than five pages.
Application Requirements: Include brief statement of history, goals, and accomplishments to date; amount requested; purpose of funds sought; list of current funding sources; recently audited financial statement; current year's operating budget; current annual report; list of board members; proof of tax-exempt status; most recent IRS Form 990.
Deadlines: October 1; organizations should not submit more than one grant application in a 12-month period.

Restrictions

The foundation does not support organizations receiving support through the United Way or other federated campaigns; conferences, special events, or videos; political, fraternal, social, or veterans organizations; religious or sectarian activities, unless they benefit entire community; endowments; courtesy advertising; or individuals

Additional Information

Organizations located in communities where the company maintains facilities may apply directly to the local office.
Publications: Report of Charitable Contributions

Corporate Officials

Harrison MacKellar Bains, Jr.: vice president, treasurer B Pasadena, CA 1943. ED University of Redlands BA (1964); University of California MBA (1966); Harvard University Graduate School of Business Administration (1983). PRIM CORP EMPL vice president, treasurer: Bristol-Myers Squibb Co. ADD CORP EMPL treasurer: Boclaro Inc.; treasurer: Bristol Caribbean Inc.; treasurer: Bristol-Myers Squibb Laboratories; treasurer: Squibb Manufacturing Inc. NONPR AFFIL treasurer: Food Safety Council; member: National Association of Corporate Treasurers; member: Financial Executives Institute.
Peter R. Dolan: chairman, chief executive officer PRIM CORP EMPL president, chief executive officer, director: Bristol-Myers Squibb Co.
Charles Andreas Heimbold, Jr.: president, chief executive officer B Newark, NJ May 27, 1933. ED Villanova University BA (1954); The Hague Academy of

International Law (1959); University of Pennsylvania LLB (1960); New York University LLM (1966). PRIM CORP EMPL chairman, director: Bristol-Myers Squibb Co. CORP AFFIL director: ExxonMobil Corp. NONPR AFFIL member, board: University Pennsylvania; chairman board overseers: University Pennsylvania Law School; chairman: Phoenix House Foundation Inc.; member: Commonwealth Fund Commission on Womens Health; trustee: International House; member: Association Bar New York City; trustee: American Museum Natural History. CLUB AFFIL Riverside Yacht Club; member: Causeway Club; River Club.
John L. Skule, III: senior vice president public affairs PRIM CORP EMPL senior vice president public affairs: Bristol-Myers Squibb Co.

Foundation Officials

Harrison MacKellar Bains, Jr.: treasurer (see above)
Stephen E. Bear: director
AnnaMaria DeSalva: director
Jeffrey Galik: assistant treasurer
Patricia Georgiadis: director
S. Anders Hedberg, Ph.D.: director
Cindy G. Johnson: director
Kathie L. Karr: director
Sandra Leung: secretary
John McGoldrick: director
Phangisile Mtshali: director
Frederick S. Schiff: director
John L. Skule, III: director (see above)
Laurie Smaldone: director
Richard L. Thompson: director
Sonia Vora: assistant secretary
Lilibeth D. Zandueta: director

Grants Analysis

Disclosure Period: calendar year ending 2001
Total Grants: $18,516,852*
Number of Grants: 288 (approx)
Average Grant: $61,034*
Highest Grant: $1,000,000
Lowest Grant: $1,500
Typical Range: $3,000 to $100,000
*Note: Giving excludes matching gifts, scholarship, United Way. Average grant figure excludes highest grant.

Recent Grants

Note: Grants derived from 2001 Form 990.

General

1,500,000	United Way of Tri-state, New York, NY -- New York City
1,000,000	American Red Cross Disaster Relief Fund, New York, NY -- New York City disaster relief
1,000,000	New York City Police Foundation, New York, NY -- New York City disaster relief
1,000,000	United Way September 11th Fund, New York, NY -- New York City disaster relief fund
750,000	New York Firefighters 9-11 Disaster Relief Fund, New York, NY
750,000	UFA Widow's and Children's Fund, New York, NY -- New York City disaster relief
516,000	Secure the Future, Washington, DC
500,000	John Jay College of Criminal Justice Foundation, New York, NY
406,160	National Merit Scholarship Corporation, Evanston, IL
400,000	Yale University, New Haven, CT -- School of Nursing

BRITTON FUND

Giving Contact

Nick Valentino, Treasurer
1422 Euclid Avenue, Suite 1010
Cleveland, OH 44115-2078
Phone: (216)363-6489

Description

Founded: 1952
EIN: 346513616
Organization Type: Private Foundation
Giving Locations: OH: Greater Cleveland including Cayahoga, Geauga, and lake counties
Grant Types: Capital, Department, Endowment, General Support, Multiyear/Continuing Support.

Donor Information

Founder: Established in 1952 by Gertrude H. Britton, Charles S. Britton, and Brigham Britton.

Financial Summary

Total Giving: $1,818,600 (2001); $1,808,800 (2000); $2,352,200 (1999)
Giving Analysis: Giving for 1998 includes: foundation grants to United Way ($10,000)
Assets: $25,610,926 (2001); $28,376,111 (2000); $33,956,428 (1999)
Gifts Received: $75 (1998); $1,250 (1997); $419,697 (1995). Note: In 1995, contributions were received from the estate of Gertrude H. Britton.

Typical Recipients

Arts & Humanities: Arts Centers, Arts Festivals, Historic Preservation, History & Archaeology, Libraries, Museums/Galleries, Music, Performing Arts, Public Broadcasting, Theater
Civic & Public Affairs: Botanical Gardens/Parks, Economic Development, Employment/Job Training, Civic & Public Affairs-General, Philanthropic Organizations, Urban & Community Affairs, Women's Affairs
Education: Arts/Humanities Education, Colleges & Universities, Continuing Education, Education Associations, Education Funds, Education-General, Medical Education, Minority Education, Private Education (Precollege), Special Education, Student Aid
Health: Alzheimers Disease, Cancer, Children's Health/Hospitals, Clinics/Medical Centers, Emergency/Ambulance Services, Eyes/Blindness, Eyes/Blindness, Geriatric Health, Health Organizations, Hospitals, Hospitals (University Affiliated), Long-Term Care, Medical Rehabilitation, Medical Research, Mental Health, Multiple Sclerosis, Nursing Services, Single-Disease Health Associations, Speech & Hearing
Religion: Religious Welfare
Science: Science Museums
Social Services: Animal Protection, Camps, Child Welfare, Community Centers, Community Service Organizations, Counseling, Day Care, Domestic Violence, Emergency Relief, Family Planning, Family Services, Food/Clothing Distribution, Homes, People with Disabilities, Senior Services, Sexual Abuse, Shelters/Homelessness, United Funds/United Ways, YMCA/YWCA/YMHA/YWHA, YMCA/YWCA/YMHA/YWHA, Youth Organizations

Application Procedures

Initial Contact: Send a brief letter of inquiry and a full proposal.
Application Requirements: Include a description of organization, amount requested, purpose of funds sought, and proof of tax-exempt status.
Deadlines: April 30 and Oct. 31.

Restrictions

Does not support individuals.

Additional Information

Publications: Annual Report

Foundation Officials

Lynda R. Britton: president, trustee
Terence B. Britton: vice president, trustee
Timothy C. Britton: vice president, trustee
Gloria Kirkwood: secretary
Nick Valentino: treasurer

Grants Analysis

Disclosure Period: calendar year ending 2001
Total Grants: $1,818,600
Number of Grants: 50
Average Grant: $30,372*
Highest Grant: $300,000
Lowest Grant: $1,000
Typical Range: $10,000 to $50,000
*Note: Average grant figure excludes highest grant.

Recent Grants

Note: Grants derived from 2001 Form 990.

Library-Related

25,000	Blue Hill Library, Blue Hill, ME -- pledge payment for capital campaign

General

300,000	Cleveland Museum of Natural History, Cleveland, OH
265,200	Institute of Pathology, Cleveland, OH -- Alzheimer research
200,000	Hathaway Brown School, Cleveland, OH
200,000	New York Firefighters 9-11 Disaster Relief Fund, New York, NY
50,000	American Red Cross, Cleveland, OH -- September 11th Tragedy
50,000	Center for Families and Children, Cleveland, OH -- capital campaign
50,000	Cleveland Center for Contemporary Art, Cleveland, OH
50,000	Hiram House, Hiram, OH -- pledge payment
50,000	NYS FOB-Foundation WTC Police Disaster Relief Fund, New York, NY -- aid to families
40,000	Salvation Army, Cleveland, OH

BROADHURST FOUNDATION

Giving Contact

Ann Cassidy Baker, Chairman
Broadhurst Foundation
401 S. Boston, Suite 100
Tulsa, OK 74103
Phone: (918)584-0661

Description

Founded: 1951
EIN: 736061115
Organization Type: Private Foundation
Giving Locations: OK: Midwest region of US.
Grant Types: Capital, Fellowship, Loan, Multiyear/Continuing Support, Research, Scholarship, Seed Money.

Donor Information

Founder: William Broadhurst

Financial Summary

Total Giving: $273,737 (2001); $253,967 (2000); $255,860 (1999)
Giving Analysis: Giving for 2001 includes: foundation scholarships ($131,000); 2000: foundation grants to United Way ($5,000); foundation scholarships ($136,000); 1999: foundation grants to United Way ($10,000); foundation scholarships ($131,000);
Assets: $7,380,696 (2001); $7,073,410 (2000); $6,617,170 (1999)

Typical Recipients

Arts & Humanities: Arts Centers, Ballet, Libraries, Museums/Galleries, Music, Opera
Civic & Public Affairs: Urban & Community Affairs, Zoos/Aquariums
Education: Colleges & Universities, Education-General, Legal Education, Literacy, Medical Education,
Minority Education, Preschool Education, Private Education (Precollege), Religious Education, Student Aid
Health: Cancer, Children's Health/Hospitals, Diabetes, Emergency/Ambulance Services, Eyes/Blindness, Health Organizations, Heart, Medical Research, Mental Health, Multiple Sclerosis, Respiratory, Single-Disease Health Associations
Religion: Churches, Jewish Causes, Religious Organizations, Religious Welfare, Religious Welfare, Seminaries
Social Services: Animal Protection, Child Welfare, Community Service Organizations, Crime Prevention, Food/Clothing Distribution, People with Disabilities, Scouts, Senior Services, Shelters/Homelessness, United Funds/United Ways, Youth Organizations

Application Procedures

Initial Contact: Send a brief letter of inquiry outlining needs.
Application Requirements: Include a description of organization.
Deadlines: None.

Restrictions

Generally limited to educational, religious, and medical research institutions in the Midwest.

Additional Information

Publications: Annual Report

Foundation Officials

Ann Cassidy Baker: chairman
John Cassidy, Jr.: trustee
Clint V. Cox: trustee
Ernestine Broadhurst Howard: vchairman
Wishard Lemons: trustee

Grants Analysis

Disclosure Period: calendar year ending 2001
Total Grants: $142,737*
Number of Grants: 38
Average Grant: $3,756
Highest Grant: $15,000
Lowest Grant: $200
Typical Range: $1,000 to $5,000
*Note: Giving excludes scholarships.

Recent Grants

Note: Grants derived from 2000 Form 990.

General

18,000	Asbury Theological Seminary, Wilmore, KY
18,000	First United Methodist Church, Tulsa, OK
15,000	Schepens Eye Research Institute, Boston, MA
10,000	Goodwill Industries of Tulsa, Tulsa, OK
10,000	Library Books for Children Fund, Tulsa, OK
10,000	National Jewish Center for Immunology and Respiratory Medicine, Denver, CO
10,000	Oklahoma City University, Oklahoma City, OK
9,000	Native American Scholarship Fund, Albuquerque, NM
8,000	Holland Hall School, Tulsa, OK
8,000	John Brown University, Siloam Springs, AR

BRODBECK ENTERPRISES

Company Headquarters

1035 E US Hwy. 151
Platteville, WI 53818

Company Description
Employees: 900
SIC(s): 5400 Food Stores.

Brodbeck Foundation

Giving Contact
Robert J. Brodbeck, President & Chief Executive Officer
PO Box 656
Platteville, WI 53818
Phone: (608)348-2343

Description
Founded: 1987
EIN: 391605932
Organization Type: Corporate Foundation
Giving Locations: WI: Southwestern part of the state
Grant Types: General Support.

Donor Information
Founder: Brodbeck Enterprises

Financial Summary
Total Giving: $53,380 (fiscal year ending August 31, 2001); $90,087 (fiscal 2000); $61,264 (fiscal 1998)
Giving Analysis: Giving for fiscal 2001 includes: foundation grants to United Way ($4,500); fiscal 2000: foundation grants to United Way ($5,000); foundation scholarships ($7,500); foundation ($77,587); fiscal 1998: foundation grants to United Way ($6,000) foundation ($55,264)
Assets: $240,374 (fiscal 2001); $306,312 (fiscal 2000); $166,145 (fiscal 1998)
Gifts Received: $88,516 (fiscal 2001); $118,909 (fiscal 2000); $98,965 (fiscal 1998). Note: In fiscal 1994, 2000, and 2001 contributions were received from Brodbeck Enterprises.

Typical Recipients
Arts & Humanities: Arts Centers, History & Archaeology, Libraries, Performing Arts, Theater
Civic & Public Affairs: Chambers of Commerce, Civic & Public Affairs-General, Public Policy, Urban & Community Affairs
Education: Colleges & Universities, Education-General, Student Aid
Health: Geriatric Health, Health Organizations, Hospitals, Nutrition, Prenatal Health Issues
Science: Science-General
Social Services: Camps, Community Centers, Community Service Organizations, Food/Clothing Distribution, Recreation & Athletics, Scouts, Senior Services, United Funds/United Ways, YMCA/YWCA/YMHA/YWHA

Application Procedures
Initial Contact: Send a brief letter of inquiry.
Application Requirements: Include background information.
Deadlines: None.

Corporate Officials
Robert J. Brodbeck: president, chief executive officer, director PRIM CORP EMPL president, chief executive officer, director: Brodbeck Enterprises.
Richard Taggart: vice president financial, chief financial officer B 1949. ED Adrian College BA (1971); University of Detroit MBA (1976). PRIM CORP EMPL vice president financial, chief financial officer: Brodbeck Enterprises ADD CORP EMPL east secretary: Brodbeck Realty Corp.

Foundation Officials
Barry J. Brodbeck: vice president, treasurer PRIM CORP EMPL vice president human resources, director: Brodbeck Enterprises.
Helen S. Brodbeck: director
Robert J. Brodbeck: secretary (see above)

Grants Analysis
Disclosure Period: fiscal year ending August 31, 2001
Total Grants: $48,880*
Number of Grants: 72
Average Grant: $679
Highest Grant: $6,166
Lowest Grant: $10
Typical Range: $100 to $2,000
***Note:** Giving excludes United Way.

Recent Grants
Note: Grants derived from 2000 Form 990.

General
7,500	Memorial Hospital of Iowa County, Dodgeville, WI
7,500	University of Wisconsin Platteville, Platteville, WI
6,624	BEI Thanksgiving Program
5,914	BEI Donation Program for Schools, Platteville, WI
2,681	Grant County Center on Aging, Lancaster, WI
2,681	Grant County Center on Aging, Lancaster, WI
2,681	Grant County Center on Aging, Lancaster, WI
2,681	Grant County Center on Aging, Lancaster, WI
2,500	Boscobel Area Health Care Foundation, Boscobel, WI
2,500	Hillsdale College, Hillsdale, MI

BRODERBUND LLC

Company Headquarters
500 Redwood Blvd.
Novato, CA 94947
Web: http://www.broderbund.com

Company Description
Former Name: Broderbund Corp.
Revenue: US$68 million (2001)
Employees: 1,129
SIC(s): 3944 Games, Toys & Children's Vehicles, 7372 Prepackaged Software.
Parent Company: Riverdeep Group Plc, Styne House, 3rd Fl., Upper Hatch St., Dublin, Ireland

Operating Locations
Broderbund Software, Inc. (OH--Avon Lake; TX--Dallas)

Carlston Family Foundation

Giving Contact
Nancy Klussman
PO Box 10162
San Rafael, CA 94912
Phone: (415)381-8557
Fax: (415)382-4500

Description
Founded: 1988
EIN: 680154752
Organization Type: Corporate Foundation
Giving Locations: CA: San Francisco Bay area
Grant Types: General Support.

Donor Information
Founder: Broderbund Corp.

Financial Summary
Total Giving: $36,667 (2000); $101,200 (1999); $153,926 (1998). Note: Contributes through foundation only.

Giving Analysis: Giving for 1998 includes: foundation grants to United Way ($78); foundation matching gifts ($14,432); foundation ($139,416); 1997: foundation matching gifts ($10,425); foundation grants to United Way ($31,750); foundation ($216,012); 1996: foundation grants to United Way ($26,550) foundation ($341,957)
Assets: $3,957,058 (2000); $3,832,352 (1999); $3,737,711 (1998)
Gifts Received: $15,062 (1999); $220,216 (1997); $918,000 (1996). Note: Contributions were received from Alice Carlston.

Typical Recipients
Arts & Humanities: Ethnic & Folk Arts, History & Archaeology, Libraries, Literary Arts, Museums/Galleries, Music, Theater
Civic & Public Affairs: Business/Free Enterprise, Employment/Job Training, Civic & Public Affairs-General, Hispanic Affairs, Housing, Native American Affairs, Parades/Festivals, Rural Affairs, Zoos/Aquariums
Education: Afterschool/Enrichment Programs, Agricultural Education, Arts/Humanities Education, Colleges & Universities, Leadership Training, Literacy, Medical Education, Minority Education, Preschool Education, Public Education (Precollege), Religious Education, Science/Mathematics Education, Secondary Education (Private), Secondary Education (Public), Student Aid
Environment: Forestry, Environment-General, Resource Conservation, Wildlife Protection
Health: AIDS/HIV, Alzheimers Disease, Cancer, Children's Health/Hospitals, Emergency/Ambulance Services, Heart, Hospices, Hospitals, Mental Health, Nursing Services, Preventive Medicine/Wellness Organizations, Public Health, Respiratory, Single-Disease Health Associations
International: Health Care/Hospitals, International Environmental Issues, International Peace & Security Issues
Religion: Religion-General, Ministries, Religious Welfare
Science: Science Museums, Scientific Centers & Institutes
Social Services: Animal Protection, At-Risk Youth, Big Brother/Big Sister, Child Abuse, Child Welfare, Community Service Organizations, Counseling, Day Care, Domestic Violence, Family Services, Food/Clothing Distribution, Food/Clothing Distribution, People with Disabilities, Scouts, Senior Services, Sexual Abuse, Shelters/Homelessness, Special Olympics, Substance Abuse, United Funds/United Ways, Volunteer Services, Youth Organizations

Application Procedures
Initial Contact: Send a brief letter of inquiry.
Application Requirements: Include the organization's statement of purpose, amount requested, proposed use of grant and proof of tax-exempt status.
Deadlines: None.
Evaluative Criteria: Employee involvement is a consideration. Preference is given to health, educational social welfare, and environmental organizations in the San Francisco Bay area.

Corporate Officials
Douglas G. Carlston: chairman, chief operating officer PRIM CORP EMPL chairman: Broderbund Software Inc.
Joseph P. Durrett: chief executive officer B 1945. ED Duke University BA; University of Pennsylvania MBA. PRIM CORP EMPL chief executive officer: Broderbund Software Inc.
William M. McDonagh: president, chief operating officer PRIM CORP EMPL president, chief operating officer: Broderbund Software Inc.

Foundation Officials
Douglas G. Carlston: president, director (see above)
Erin G. Carlston: director

William M. McDonagh: director (see above)
Patsy Murphy: secretary, director

Grants Analysis

Disclosure Period: calendar year ending 2000
Total Grants: $36,667
Number of Grants: 3
Highest Grant: $16,667
Lowest Grant: $5,000

Recent Grants

Note: Grants derived from 1999 Form 990.

General

15,000	Community Nursing Care of Marin, Novato, CA
10,000	Global Fund for Women, Palo Alto, CA
10,000	Meals of Marin, San Rafael, CA
7,500	Marin Concerned Citizens, San Anselmo, CA -- support Adopt-A-Family program
5,000	Alliance for Technology Access, San Rafael, CA
5,000	Apple Family Works, San Rafael, CA
5,000	MARC, San Rafael, CA
5,000	Marin Child Care Council, San Rafael, CA
5,000	Marin Humane Society, Novato, CA
5,000	Marine Mammal Center, Sausalito, CA

GUY I. BROMLEY RESIDUARY TRUST

Giving Contact

David P. Ross, Senior Vice President & Trust Officer
Bank of America, NA
1200 Main St., 14th Fl.
PO Box 419119
Kansas City, MO 64141-6119
Phone: (816)979-7481

Description

Founded: 1964
EIN: 436157236
Organization Type: Private Foundation
Giving Locations: KS; MO: Kansas City
Grant Types: General Support, Project.

Donor Information

Founder: Guy I. Bromley

Financial Summary

Total Giving: $254,747 (2001); $496,788 (2000); $201,522 (1999)
Giving Analysis: Giving for 2001 includes: foundation grants to United Way ($500); 2000: foundation grants to United Way ($500); 1999: foundation grants to United Way ($500)
Assets: $6,984,073 (2001); $7,969,279 (2000); $8,798,019 (1999)

Typical Recipients

Arts & Humanities: Arts Associations & Councils, Arts Centers, Arts Festivals, Arts Outreach, Ballet, History & Archaeology, Museums/Galleries, Music, Opera, Theater, Visual Arts
Civic & Public Affairs: Civil Rights, Community Foundations, Economic Development, Employment/Job Training, Civic & Public Affairs-General, Housing, Nonprofit Management, Urban & Community Affairs, Zoos/Aquariums
Education: Agricultural Education, Colleges & Universities, Continuing Education, Education-General, Private Education (Precollege), Public Education (Precollege), Religious Education, Science/Mathematics Education, Secondary Education (Private), Student Aid

Environment: Environment-General, Resource Conservation
Health: Emergency/Ambulance Services, Medical Rehabilitation, Mental Health
Religion: Churches, Dioceses, Religion-General, Religious Organizations, Religious Welfare
Social Services: Child Welfare, Community Centers, Community Service Organizations, Counseling, Crime Prevention, Emergency Relief, Family Services, United Funds/United Ways, YMCA/YWCA/YMHA/YWHA, Youth Organizations

Application Procedures

Initial Contact: Send brief letter of no more than three pages with appropriate attachments.
Deadlines: None.

Additional Information

Trust(s): Bank of America NA MO

Grants Analysis

Disclosure Period: calendar year ending 2001
Total Grants: $254,247*
Number of Grants: 19
Average Grant: $13,381
Highest Grant: $52,947
Lowest Grant: $100
Typical Range: $5,000 to $25,000
*Note: Giving excludes United Way.

Recent Grants

Note: Grants derived from 2001 Form 990.

General

52,947	Catholic Charities Archdiocese of Kansas City, Kansas City, KS
30,000	St. Lawrence Catholic Campus Center, Lawrence, KS -- technology improvements
30,000	Visitation Church, Kansas City, MO -- computer science lab
25,000	Baker University, Baldwin City, KS -- library capital campaign
25,000	Kansas City Church Community Organization, Kansas City, MO -- challenge
25,000	RLDS for Community of Christ, Independence, MO -- 2001 Peace Prize
17,000	Surplus Exchange, Kansas City, MO
12,000	Foundation for Inclusive Religious Education (FIRE), Kansas City, MO -- operating budget
10,000	Bishop Seabury Academy, Lawrence, KS
10,000	Junction City Family YMCA, Junction City, KS -- Water Safety Program

BROOK FAMILY FOUNDATION

Giving Contact

Paul Brook, Secretary/Treasurer
9 Korhonen Road
Norway, ME 04268
Phone: (207)743-5690

Description

Founded: 1997
EIN: 010499178
Organization Type: Private Foundation
Giving Locations: ME; RI; VT
Grant Types: General Support.

Financial Summary

Total Giving: $180,795 (fiscal year ending March 31, 2001); $183,800 (fiscal 2000); $155,996 (fiscal 1999)
Assets: $2,860,645 (fiscal 2001); $3,426,981 (fiscal 2000); $3,450,265 (fiscal 1999)

Typical Recipients

Arts & Humanities: Libraries, Museums/Galleries
Civic & Public Affairs: Civic & Public Affairs-General
Education: Arts/Humanities Education, Environmental Education, Private Education (Precollege), Public Education (Precollege), Secondary Education (Public), Student Aid, Vocational & Technical Education
Health: Emergency/Ambulance Services, Health-General, Hospices
Social Services: Community Service Organizations, Crime Prevention, Recreation & Athletics

Foundation Officials

Jacqueline C. Brook: director
Paul F. Brook: secretary, treasurer
Robert L. Brook: director
Shirley W. Brook: director

Grants Analysis

Disclosure Period: fiscal year ending March 31, 2001
Total Grants: $180,795
Number of Grants: 20
Average Grant: $6,989*
Highest Grant: $48,000
Lowest Grant: $1,500
Typical Range: $1,000 to $10,000
*Note: Average grant figure excludes highest grant.

Recent Grants

Note: Grants derived from 2001 Form 990.

Library-Related

30,000	Oakland Public Library, Oakland, ME -- educational

General

48,000	Uxbridge Public Schools, Uxbridge, MA -- educational
15,000	Brattleboro Union High School, Brattleboro, VT -- educational
10,000	American Red Cross, Auburn, ME -- for disaster relief
10,000	HOPE, South Paris, ME -- for social tolerance
10,000	Inside Out Playground, Waterville, ME -- for youth programs
10,000	Whitingham School, Wilmington, VT -- educational
8,355	Western Maine Health, Norway, ME -- medical
7,000	Rockingham Arts and Museum, Bellow Falls, VT -- for Arts Programs
5,000	Cranston Public Schools, Cranston, RI -- educational
5,000	Grammar School, Putney, VT -- educational

BROOKDALE FOUNDATION

Giving Contact

Stephen L. Schwartz, President
126 E. 56th St., 10th Fl.
New York, NY 10022
Phone: (212)644-0774
Fax: (212)750-0132
Web: http://www.ewol.com/brookdale

Description

Founded: 1950
EIN: 136076863
Organization Type: Private Foundation
Giving Locations: nationally.
Grant Types: Fellowship, Project, Research, Seed Money.

Donor Information
Founder: the late Henry L. Schwartz and his brothers

Financial Summary
Total Giving: $819,515 (fiscal year ending June 30, 2000); $819,515 (fiscal 1999); $953,847 (fiscal 1998)
Assets: $4,912,994 (fiscal 2000); $4,912,994 (fiscal 1999); $7,359,865 (fiscal 1997)

Typical Recipients
Arts & Humanities: Libraries, Visual Arts
Civic & Public Affairs: Civic & Public Affairs-General, Legal Aid, Municipalities/Towns, Public Policy, Urban & Community Affairs
Education: Colleges & Universities, Education-General, Health & Physical Education, Legal Education, Medical Education
Environment: Environment-General
Health: Alzheimers Disease, Cancer, Clinics/Medical Centers, Geriatric Health, Hospitals, Hospitals (University Affiliated), Long-Term Care, Nursing Services, Research/Studies Institutes
Religion: Dioceses, Jewish Causes, Religious Organizations, Religious Welfare
Social Services: Child Welfare, Community Centers, Community Service Organizations, Family Services, Recreation & Athletics, Scouts, Senior Services, Sexual Abuse, YMCA/YWCA/YMHA/YWHA, Youth Organizations

Application Procedures
Initial Contact: Send a brief letter of inquiry.
Application Requirements: Include a description of organization, amount requested, purpose of funds sought, and proof of tax-exempt status.

Restrictions
The foundation does not support individuals.

Additional Information
Publications: Program Policy Statement; Descriptions of Initiatives

Foundation Officials
Victor Biggs: assistant vice president
Stanley Epstein: director
Arthur Norman Field: director B New York, NY 1935. ED City College of New York BBA (1955); Harvard University LLB (1958). PRIM CORP EMPL partner: Shearman & Sterling. CORP AFFIL director: Sunset Realty Corp. NONPR AFFIL member: New York State Bar Association; fellow: New York State Bar Foundation; member: Association Bar New York City; member: New York County Lawyers Association; fellow: American Bar Foundation; member: American Law Institute; member: American Bar Association.
Jeanette Pereira: secretary, treasurer
Stephen L. Schwartz: president
Mary Ann Van Clief: vice president, director PRIM CORP EMPL vice president: Brookdale Management Co.
Roy J. Zuckerberg: director B New York, NY 1936. ED Lowell Technological Institute BS (1958). PRIM CORP EMPL head division: Goldman Sachs & Co. NONPR AFFIL trustee: Jewish Communal Fund; vice chairman: Long Island Jewish Medical Center; American Jewish Joint Distr Comm; trustee: American Red Cross Greater New York; member, board overseers: Albert Einstein College of Medicine. CLUB AFFIL Woodmere Club; Harmonie Club; Mashomack Club.

Grants Analysis
Disclosure Period: fiscal year ending June 30, 2000
Total Grants: $819,515
Number of Grants: 17
Average Grant: $48,207
Highest Grant: $75,000
Lowest Grant: $15,000
Typical Range: $15,000 to $60,000

Recent Grants
Note: Grants derived from fiscal 1999 Form 990.

General
75,000	Research Foundation of the City of New York, New York, NY
70,000	National Institute on Aging, Bethesda, MD
67,500	Fishberg Research Center for Neurobiology, New York, NY
67,500	Regents of the University of California, La Jolla, CA
61,568	Johns Hopkins University, Baltimore, MD
60,000	Baylor College of Medicine, Houston, TX
60,000	Johns Hopkins University School of Medicine, Baltimore, MD
60,000	Trustees of University of PA, Philadelphia, PA
59,814	Trustees of Tufts College, Boston, MA
59,151	Boston University, Boston, MA

GLADYS BROOKS FOUNDATION

Giving Contact
Jessica L. Rutledge, Administrative Assistant
1055 Franklin Avenue, Suite 102
Garden City, NY 11530
Phone: (516)746-6103
Fax: (516)877-1758
Web: http://www.gladysbrooksfoundation.org

Alternate Contact
90 Broad Street
New York, NY 10005

Description
Founded: 1981
EIN: 132955337
Organization Type: General Purpose Foundation
Giving Locations: CT; DE; DC; IN; ME; MD; MA; NH; NJ; NY; NC; OH; PA; RI; SC; VT; VA; WA; WV
Grant Types: Capital, Endowment, Scholarship.

Donor Information
Founder: Established in 1981 by the late Gladys Brooks Thayer .

Financial Summary
Total Giving: $1,285,000 (2001); $1,830,080 (2000); $1,247,000 (1998)
Assets: $36,000,000 (2001); $39,459,852 (2000); $36,709,197 (1998)

Typical Recipients
Arts & Humanities: Arts & Humanities-General, Historic Preservation, History & Archaeology, Libraries, Museums/Galleries
Civic & Public Affairs: Civic & Public Affairs-General, Urban & Community Affairs
Education: Arts/Humanities Education, Business Education, Colleges & Universities, Education-General, Medical Education, Preschool Education, Private Education (Precollege), Public Education (Precollege), Secondary Education (Private), Special Education, Student Aid
Health: Cancer, Children's Health/Hospitals, Clinics/Medical Centers, Emergency/Ambulance Services, Hospitals, Medical Research, Nursing Services, Research/Studies Institutes, Single-Disease Health Associations
International: Foreign Educational Institutions, Missionary/Religious Activities
Religion: Churches, Religious Organizations, Religious Welfare
Science: Observatories & Planetariums, Scientific Labs, Scientific Labs

Social Services: Child Welfare, Family Services, People with Disabilities, Youth Organizations

Application Procedures
Initial Contact: The foundation requests applicants obtain a formal application form from the foundation.
Application Requirements: When submitting application form. the Foundation also requests: a specific budget for the grant, financial statements for the latest fiscal year; an annual report or a brief description of organization; and a specific budget for the project. Applications must be submitted in duplicate.
Deadlines: Within 45 days from the date of the letter from the foundation furnishing the application to the applicant.
Notes: It is the policy of the Foundation not to acknowledge receipt of grant application or indicate reason for non-approval of the same.

Restrictions
As a matter of policy, the foundation will make grants only to private, publicly supported, nonprofit, tax-exempt organizations. Grant applications will only be considered if outside funding (including governmental) is not available; or, if the project will be largely funded by the grant and will not be part of a larger project; or, if the funds will be used for capital projects, including equipment or endowments. In addition, grant applications will only be considered for major expenditures, generally between $50,000 and $100,000. The board follows the practice of determining, at the beginning of each calendar year, a limited scope of activities for which it will consider grant applications for that year. The foundation does not make grants to individuals or to support research projects.

Additional Information
Publications: Program Policy Statement; Annual Report (including Application Guidelines)
Trust(s): US Trust Company of NY

Foundation Officials
James J. Daly: member board governors
Thomas Q. Morris: member board govs B Yonkers, NY 1933. ED University of Notre Dame BS (1954); Columbia University MD (1958). PRIM NONPR EMPL senior associate vice president health sciences: Columbia University College Physicians Surgeons. NONPR AFFIL vice dean faculty medicine: Columbia University College Physicians & Surgeons; senior advisor: New York Academy Medicine. CLUB AFFIL Century Club; Harvey Society.
Jessica L. Rutledge: administrative assistant

Grants Analysis
Disclosure Period: calendar year ending 2000
Total Grants: $1,830,080
Number of Grants: 30
Average Grant: $61,003
Highest Grant: $110,000
Typical Range: $100,000 to $110,000 and $10,000 to $15,000

Recent Grants
Note: Grants derived from 2000 Form 990.

Library-Related
10,000	Friends of the Shelter Island Public Library Society, Shelter Island, NY

General
110,000	University of Notre Dame, Notre Dame, IN
100,000	American University in Beirut, New York, NY
100,000	Bucknell University, Lewisburg, PA
100,000	Cathedral Community Cares
100,000	Churchill School and Center, New York, NY
100,000	Eastern Long Island Hospital, Greenport, NY

100,000	Family and Children's Association
100,000	Mary Imogene Bassett Hospital, Cooperstown, NY
100,000	New Alternatives for Children, New York, NY
100,000	New York Academy of Medicine, New York, NY

BROOMFIELD CHARITABLE FOUNDATION

Giving Contact
William S. Broomfield, President
9910 E. Bexhill Dr.
Kensington, MD 20895
Phone: (301)942-4882

Description
Founded: 1993
EIN: 383083449
Organization Type: Private Foundation
Grant Types: General Support.

Financial Summary
Total Giving: $33,850 (fiscal year ending November 30, 2001); $35,175 (fiscal 2000); $34,400 (fiscal 1999)
Assets: $859,754 (fiscal 2001); $660,736 (fiscal 2000); $679,583 (fiscal 1999)
Gifts Received: $517,688 (fiscal 1993). Note: In fiscal 1993, contributions were received from the Broomfield Campaign Committee.

Typical Recipients
Arts & Humanities: History & Archaeology, Libraries, Museums/Galleries
Civic & Public Affairs: Community Foundations, Civic & Public Affairs-General, Municipalities/Towns
Education: Education Funds, Elementary Education (Public), Private Education (Precollege), Secondary Education (Private), Student Aid
Health: Alzheimers Disease, Arthritis, Cancer, Children's Health/Hospitals, Clinics/Medical Centers, Hospitals, Medical Research, Mental Health, Multiple Sclerosis, Single-Disease Health Associations
Religion: Religious Welfare
Science: Scientific Centers & Institutes
Social Services: Camps, Child Welfare, Community Service Organizations, Delinquency & Criminal Rehabilitation, Domestic Violence, People with Disabilities, Scouts, Substance Abuse, Youth Organizations

Application Procedures
Initial Contact: Applications should include an outline of the proposed project and its objectives, a proposed budget, and proof of tax-exempt status.
Deadlines: None.

Restrictions
Foundation does not support individuals or political or lobbying groups.

Additional Information
Trust(s): Bank One

Foundation Officials
Jane Broomfield: vice president, secretary, treasurer
William S. Broomfield: president
Nancy Broomfield Aiken: director
Barbara Broomfield Shaffer: director

Grants Analysis
Disclosure Period: fiscal year ending November 30, 2001
Total Grants: $33,850
Number of Grants: 21
Average Grant: $1,612*
Highest Grant: $5,000

Lowest Grant: $100
Typical Range: $500 to $2,500
***Note:** Average grant figure excludes highest grant.

Recent Grants
Note: Grants derived from fiscal 2000 Form 990.

General

10,000	Suburban Hospital Foundation, Bethesda, MD
5,000	Children's Hospital of Michigan, Detroit, MI
5,000	Dondero High School Scholarship Fund, Royal Oak, MI
4,000	Children's National Medical Center, Washington, DC
2,500	GRACF - Rochester Hills Museum, Rochester, MI
2,000	VZV Research Foundation, New York, NY
1,650	Connelly School of the Holy Child, Potomac, MD
1,200	Georgetown Preparatory Annual Fund, Rockville, MD
1,000	Boy Scouts of America, Bethesda, MD
1,000	North Bethesda Middle School, Bethesda, MD

WILLIAM AND JEMIMA BROSSMAN CHARITABLE FOUNDATION

Giving Contact
Carl Brubaker, Trust Officer
William and Jemima Brossman Charitable Foundation
c/o Ephrata National Bank
31 E. Main St., PO Box 457
Ephrata, PA 17522
Phone: (717)733-6576

Description
Founded: 1986
EIN: 236087844
Organization Type: Private Foundation
Giving Locations: PA: South Central area of state
Grant Types: General Support.

Donor Information
Founder: the late Bertha Brossman Blair

Financial Summary
Total Giving: $1,048,820 (fiscal year ending October 31, 2001); $1,002,720 (fiscal 2000); $1,000,000 (fiscal 1999 approx)
Giving Analysis: Giving for fiscal 2001 includes: foundation grants to United Way ($11,000); foundation scholarships ($408,000); fiscal 2000: foundation grants to United Way ($10,000); foundation scholarships ($404,000); fiscal 1998: foundation grants to United Way ($10,000); foundation scholarships ($370,625) foundation ($812,960)
Assets: $20,852,111 (fiscal 2001); $22,725,979 (fiscal 2000); $14,763,460 (fiscal 1998)
Gifts Received: $1,346 (fiscal 1993). Note: In fiscal 1993, contributions were received from the estate of Bertha B. Blair.

Typical Recipients
Arts & Humanities: Arts Associations & Councils, Arts Centers, Arts & Humanities-General, Historic Preservation, History & Archaeology, Libraries, Museums/Galleries, Music, Opera, Performing Arts, Public Broadcasting, Theater, Visual Arts
Civic & Public Affairs: Civic & Public Affairs-General, Housing, Zoos/Aquariums

Education: Arts/Humanities Education, Business Education, Colleges & Universities, Engineering/Technological Education, Leadership Training, Private Education (Precollege), Science/Mathematics Education, Student Aid
Health: Alzheimers Disease, Cancer, Emergency/Ambulance Services, Eyes/Blindness, Geriatric Health, Heart, Hospices, Hospitals, Public Health
International: Foreign Educational Institutions, Missionary/Religious Activities
Religion: Churches, Jewish Causes, Ministries, Religious Welfare, Seminaries
Science: Scientific Centers & Institutes
Social Services: Big Brother/Big Sister, Community Service Organizations, Family Planning, Recreation & Athletics, Scouts, United Funds/United Ways, YMCA/YWCA/YMHA/YWHA

Application Procedures
Initial Contact: The foundation has no formal grant application procedure or application form. Send a full proposal.
Application Requirements: Include a description of organization, amount requested, purpose of funds sought, and proof of tax-exempt status.
Deadlines: None.

Restrictions
The foundation does not support individuals or political or lobbying groups. Recipients must be 501(c)(3) organizations.

Additional Information
Trust(s): Ephrata Natl Bank

Grants Analysis
Disclosure Period: fiscal year ending October 31, 2001
Total Grants: $629,820*
Number of Grants: 114
Average Grant: $5,525*
Highest Grant: $50,000
Lowest Grant: $25
Typical Range: $1,000 to $10,000
***Note:** Giving excludes scholarships; United Way.

Recent Grants
Note: Grants derived from 2000 Form 990.

General

356,000	Brossman Scholarship Fund, Ephrata, PA
50,000	Lutheran Theological Seminary, Gettysburg, PA
50,000	Rider University, Lawrenceville, NJ -- annual leadership gift
40,000	Ephrata Public Library, Ephrata, PA -- contribution
38,000	American Red Cross of the Susquehanna Valley, Lancaster, PA
30,000	Franklin and Marshall College, Lancaster, PA
30,000	Thaddeus Stevens Foundation, Lancaster, PA -- grant
25,000	Linden Hall, Lititz, PA -- grant
25,000	Pennsylvania Academy of Music, Lancaster, PA
25,000	Whitaker Center for Science, Harrisburg, PA -- grant

BROWN FOUNDATION

Giving Contact
Nancy Pittman, Executive Director
PO Box 130646
Houston, TX 77219-0646
Phone: (713)523-6867
Fax: (713)523-2917
E-mail: bfi@brownfoundation.org
Web: http://www.brownfoundation.org

Description

Founded: 1951
EIN: 746036466
Organization Type: General Purpose Foundation
Giving Locations: TX: particularly Houston
Grant Types: Capital, Challenge, Employee Matching Gifts, Endowment, Fellowship, General Support, Matching, Operating Expenses, Project.

Donor Information

Founder: Established in July 1951 by Margrett Root Brown , Herman Brown , Alice Pratt Brown , and George R. Brown . Herman and George were founders of Brown & Root, Inc., a construction company whose subsidiaries included oil and gas companies, hotels, real estate companies, paper mills, and mines. Until 1958, all funding was restricted to organizations in Texas. The charter was amended to allow a small amount of funding to be distributed elsewhere in the United States. All of the original donors are now deceased.

Financial Summary

Total Giving: $69,463,862 (fiscal year ending June 30, 2002); $62,456,909 (fiscal 2001); $60,964,045 (fiscal 2000)
Giving Analysis: Giving for fiscal 2001 includes: foundation scholarships ($100,000); foundation grants to United Way ($125,000); fiscal 2000: foundation grants to United Way ($125,000); foundation scholarships ($472,000); fiscal 1999: foundation program-related investments ($14,281); foundation grants to United Way ($125,000); foundation scholarships ($467,500); foundation matching gifts ($4,243,148); foundation matching gifts ($5,694,349)
Assets: $1,040,221,987 (fiscal 2002); $1,323,011,734 (fiscal 2001); $1,434,297,259 (fiscal 2000)
Gifts Received: $1,096 (fiscal 1996)

Typical Recipients

Arts & Humanities: Arts Associations & Councils, Arts Centers, Arts Funds, Arts Institutes, Arts Outreach, Ballet, Dance, Ethnic & Folk Arts, Arts & Humanities-General, Historic Preservation, History & Archaeology, Libraries, Literary Arts, Museums/Galleries, Music, Opera, Performing Arts, Public Broadcasting, Theater, Visual Arts
Civic & Public Affairs: African American Affairs, Botanical Gardens/Parks, Community Foundations, Economic Development, Civic & Public Affairs-General, Hispanic Affairs, Housing, Inner-City Development, Public Policy, Urban & Community Affairs, Women's Affairs, Zoos/Aquariums
Education: Arts/Humanities Education, Business Education, Colleges & Universities, Education Funds, Elementary Education (Private), Elementary Education (Public), Engineering/Technological Education, Environmental Education, Faculty Development, Education-General, International Exchange, International Studies, Leadership Training, Literacy, Medical Education, Preschool Education, Private Education (Precollege), Public Education (Precollege), Religious Education, Science/Mathematics Education, Secondary Education (Private), Social Sciences Education, Special Education, Student Aid, Vocational & Technical Education
Environment: Environment-General, Resource Conservation, Wildlife Protection
Health: Adolescent Health Issues, Alzheimers Disease, Cancer, Children's Health/Hospitals, Clinics/Medical Centers, Health Organizations, Heart, Hospices, Hospitals, Medical Research, Mental Health, Research/Studies Institutes, Single-Disease Health Associations
International: Foreign Arts Organizations, Foreign Educational Institutions, International Environmental Issues, International Organizations, International Relief Efforts
Religion: Religious Welfare

Science: Science Museums, Scientific Centers & Institutes
Social Services: Animal Protection, At-Risk Youth, Camps, Child Abuse, Child Welfare, Community Centers, Community Service Organizations, Counseling, Crime Prevention, Day Care, Delinquency & Criminal Rehabilitation, Domestic Violence, Family Planning, Family Services, People with Disabilities, Recreation & Athletics, Shelters/Homelessness, United Funds/United Ways, YMCA/YWCA/YMHA/YWHA, Youth Organizations

Application Procedures

Initial Contact: Applicants should submit a written proposal. Contact the foundation or visit the foundation's web site to obtain guidelines and a Proposal Summary Form.
Application Requirements: Completed Proposal Summary Forms must be accompanied by the following supporting information: list of board members/officers/advisory board, including the percentage of directors who have contributed financially to the endeavor and the total amount of their contributions; the organization's current operating budget and a budget for the specific program to be funded; a list of other sources of funding for the project, including amounts committed and pending; recently audited financial statement; financial statement of income and expenses from time of last audit to present; and proof of tax-exempt status. The foundation requests that applications be signed by both the chief administrator/executive officer and by the board president or chair, if applicable.
Deadlines: Proposals should be submitted at least four months before funding will be needed but are accepted at any time.
Review Process: Applicants should not inquire about proposal status. Applicants will be informed, in writing, that their proposal has been received at the foundation's office and of the decision of the trustees within 90 days.
Evaluative Criteria: The foundation prefers to fund projects which address root causes of a concern rather than treating symptoms; serve as a catalyst for collaborative efforts by several sectors of the community; result in a growing, long-term impact on the situation beyond the value of the grant itself; and reflect and encourage sound financial planning and management practices in project administration.
Notes: If the foundation requests additional information, failure to submit such within 30 days will result in removal of the proposal from the review process. Video and audio tapes are not accepted.

Restrictions

The foundation does not support individuals; religious organizations for sectarian purposes; testimonial dinners, fundraising events, or marketing efforts; political candidates or causes; private foundations; or grants to cover past operating deficits or debt retirements.

Additional Information

Only one grant request from an organization will be considered in a twelve month period. No proposal from an organization previously funded by the foundation will be reviewed until a full report of the expenditure of the previous grant has been submitted.
Publications: Application Guidelines; Application Form; Annual Report; Proposal Summary Form

Foundation Officials

Nancy I. Abendshein: trustee
John F. Fort, III: secretary, trustee
Isabel S. Lummis: trustee
William Nelson Mathis: trustee
Edgar W. Monteith: secretary, trustee
Leslie N. Negley: trustee
Nancy B. Negley: vice president, trustee
W. Walter Negley: trustee
George R. O'Connor: trustee

Maconda Brown O'Connor: president, trustee B 1930. PRIM CORP EMPL partner: George R. Brown Partnership.
Nancy Pittman: executive director
Ann Prescott: treasurer
Christopher B. Sarofim: trustee
Louisa Stude Sarofim: vice president, trustee ED Smith College. PRIM CORP EMPL partner: George R. Brown Partnership.
Elisa J. Stude: trustee
Herman L. Stude: assistant secretary
Mike S. Stude: chairman, trustee B 1939. PRIM CORP EMPL partner: George R. Brown Partnership.
Nancy Brown Wellin: vice president, trustee PRIM CORP EMPL partner: George R. Brown Partnership.
Isabel Brown Wilson: first vice president, trustee PRIM CORP EMPL partner: George R. Brown Partnership.

Grants Analysis

Disclosure Period: fiscal year ending June 30, 2002
Total Grants: $67,525,862*
Number of Grants: 340
Average Grant: $169,684*
Highest Grant: $5,172,593
Lowest Grant: $500
Typical Range: $50,000 to $300,000 and $500,000 to $1,000,000
***Note:** Giving excludes scholarships and United Way. Average grant excludes two highest grants ($10,172,593).

Recent Grants

Note: Grants derived from fiscal 2001 Form 990.

Library-Related
250,000   San Antonio Public Library Foundation, San Antonio, TX -- Latino Leadership for the Library

General
5,000,000   Museum of Fine Arts of Houston, Houston, TX -- Acquisition of Jasper John's 1984 encaustic painting
5,000,000   Texas State Aquarium, Corpus Christi, TX -- Campaign for Aquarium 2000 (matching grant)
3,893,000   Baylor College of Medicine, Houston, TX -- For the Brain and Behavior Clinical Institute
3,872,048   Smithsonian Institute, Washington, DC -- Acquisition of the Victor Building and
2,000,000   Child Centered School Initiative of the Greater Houston Area, Houston, TX -- Houston Annenberg Challenge for School Reform
2,000,000   Davidson College, Davidson, NC -- Toward construction of a campus center
2,000,000   Rural School and Community Trust, Washington, DC -- General operating fund
1,985,130   Rural School and Community Trust, Washington, DC -- General operating fund
1,455,880   Episcopal High School, Houston, TX -- Financial Aid Endowment
1,200,000   Project YES, Houston, TX -- Capital Campaign - From Experiment to Institution

JAMES GRAHAM BROWN FOUNDATION, INC.

Giving Contact

Mason B. Rummel, Executive Director
4350 Brownsboro Road
Suite 200
Louisville, KY 40207
Phone: (502)896-2440

Fax: (502)896-1774
E-mail: mason@jgbf.org
Web: http://www.jgbf.org

Description

Founded: 1943
EIN: 610724060
Organization Type: General Purpose Foundation
Giving Locations: KY
Grant Types: Capital, Challenge, Endowment, Scholarship.

Donor Information

Founder: Established in 1943 and funded by the late James Graham Brown and his sister, the late Agnes B. Duggan . Mr. Brown's business pursuits included timberland, lumber, mineral holdings, and hotels. His philanthropic interests included the Louisville Zoo and a new Red Cross Blood Bank in Louisville. Each organization received $1.5 million in grants. When Mr. Brown died in March 1969, his will specified twelve bequests to religious and educational institutions totaling $3.05 million. The remainder of his estate, one of the largest ever probated in Kentucky, was left to the foundation.

Financial Summary

Total Giving: $17,000,000 (2003 approx); $21,000,000 (2002 approx); $21,843,310 (2001)
Giving Analysis: Giving for 2000 includes: foundation grants to United Way ($700,000); 1999: foundation grants to United Way ($650,000) 1998: foundation grants to United Way ($575,000)
Assets: $426,367,510 (2001); $445,710,284 (2000); $431,061,882 (1999)

Typical Recipients

Arts & Humanities: Arts Centers, Arts Institutes, Ballet, Ethnic & Folk Arts, Historic Preservation, History & Archaeology, Libraries, Museums/Galleries, Music, Opera, Public Broadcasting, Visual Arts
Civic & Public Affairs: African American Affairs, Botanical Gardens/Parks, Business/Free Enterprise, Chambers of Commerce, Clubs, Economic Development, Employment/Job Training, Civic & Public Affairs-General, Housing, Inner-City Development, Municipalities/Towns, Nonprofit Management, Parades/Festivals, Public Policy, Urban & Community Affairs, Women's Affairs, Zoos/Aquariums
Education: Arts/Humanities Education, Business Education, Colleges & Universities, Economic Education, Education Reform, Education Reform, Education-General, Literacy, Preschool Education, Private Education (Precollege), Public Education (Precollege), Secondary Education (Private), Special Education
Environment: Environment-General, Resource Conservation
Health: Arthritis, Cancer, Children's Health/Hospitals, Clinics/Medical Centers, Emergency/Ambulance Services, Eyes/Blindness, Geriatric Health, Health Organizations, Hospices, Hospitals, Medical Rehabilitation, Mental Health, Multiple Sclerosis, Prenatal Health Issues, Respiratory, Single-Disease Health Associations
Religion: Jewish Causes, Religious Organizations, Religious Welfare, Social/Policy Issues
Science: Science Museums, Scientific Centers & Institutes
Social Services: Animal Protection, Camps, Child Welfare, Community Centers, Community Service Organizations, Counseling, Family Planning, Family Services, Food/Clothing Distribution, Homes, People with Disabilities, Recreation & Athletics, Scouts, Senior Services, Shelters/Homelessness, Special Olympics, Substance Abuse, United Funds/United Ways, Veterans, Volunteer Services, YMCA/YWCA/YMHA/YWHA, Youth Organizations

Application Procedures

Initial Contact: Contact the foundation or visit the foundation web site to obtain a pre-grant application form.
Application Requirements: The Pre-Grant Application must include the name and phone number of contact person; name of the organization's board chair and president or CEO; percentage of board members contributing to the project or campaign; a description of organization; project description; total project cost; amount requested; evidence of community support; board of directors list; and project budget.
Deadlines: None. Funds are dispersed annually at the end of each calendar year; applications received after October 1 will be considered in the following calendar year.
Review Process: The board reviews inquiries and applications monthly. Applicants will receive written notification of the next step, if any, in the application process.

Restrictions

The foundation does not fund grant requests related either directly or indirectly to the performing arts, requests from individuals, primary or secondary schools, national organizations, political entities, religious organizations for religious purposes, annual operating support, or debt reduction.

Additional Information

Publications: Grant application

Foundation Officials

H. Curtis Craig: trustee
Stanley Dickson: trustee
Joan R. Dudley: assistant treasurer
Frank B. Hower, Jr.: trustee
Stanley Hugenberg, Jr.: trustee PRIM CORP EMPL president: Jack Antom Sales Co. CORP AFFIL director: Churchill Downs Inc. NONPR AFFIL director: Kentucky Derby Museum Corp.
Graham B. Loper: vice president, trustee
Ray Loper: trustee
Dorma J. McKenzie: trustee
Barrett Nichols: trustee B 1950. PRIM CORP EMPL secretary: Micropak Inc.
Alex Rankin: trustee
Joe M. Rodes: president, trustee CORP AFFIL director: PNC Bank.
Robert Rounsavall, III: trustee B 1943. PRIM CORP EMPL chief executive officer: Dixie Warehouse Cartage Inc. CORP AFFIL director: PNC Bank Kentucky; chairman: Prolift Industrial Equipment Co.
Robert Lewis Royer: trustee B Louisville, KY 1928. ED Rose-Hulman Institute Technology BS (1949). PRIM CORP EMPL chairman emeritus: Louisville Gas & Electric Co. NONPR AFFIL member: Louisville Chamber of Commerce; member, board managers: Rose-Hulman Institute Technology; member: Executives Club Louisville; member: Institute Electrical & Electronics Engineers. CLUB AFFIL Pendennis Club; Rotary Club; Hurstbourne Country Club.
Mrs. Mason Rummel: executive director, secretary
Sylvia Watson: trustee

Grants Analysis

Disclosure Period: calendar year ending 2001
Total Grants: $21,843,310
Number of Grants: 58
Average Grant: $229,345*
Highest Grant: $4,000,000
Lowest Grant: $500
Typical Range: $100,000 to $500,000
*Note: Average grant figure excludes two highest grants ($9,000,000).

Recent Grants

Note: Grants derived from 2001 Form 990.

Library-Related
250,000 San Antonio Public Library Foundation, San Antonio, TX -- Latino Leadership for the Library Initiative

General
5,409,367 Museum of Fine Arts - Houston, Houston, TX -- acquisition of Jasper John's painting
5,000,000 Baylor College of Medicine, Houston, TX -- brain and behavior clinical institute
5,000,000 Texas State Aquarium, Corpus Christi, TX -- campaign for aquarium
4,000,000 Rural School and Community Trust, Washington, DC -- operating fund
4,000,000 Smithsonian Institute, Washington, DC -- acquisition of the Victor Building
2,000,000 Child Centered School Initiative of the Greater Houston Area, Houston, TX -- Houston Anneberg Challenge
2,000,000 Davidson College, Davidson, NC -- construction of a campus center
1,540,000 Episcopal High School, Houston, TX -- financial aid endowment
1,202,500 Project YES, Houston, TX -- capital campaign
1,025,000 Houston Music Hall Foundation, Houston, TX -- construction of the Hobby Center for Performing Arts

M. K. BROWN FOUNDATION

Giving Contact

Bill W. Waters, Chairman
PO Box 662
Pampa, TX 79066-0662
Phone: (806)669-6851

Description

Founded: 1960
EIN: 756034058
Organization Type: Private Foundation
Giving Locations: TX: Gray County, Pampa County, Panhandle area of Texas
Grant Types: General Support.

Donor Information

Founder: the late M. K. Brown

Financial Summary

Total Giving: $57,500 (2000); $92,500 (1999); $787,086 (1998)
Giving Analysis: Giving for 2000 includes: foundation grants to United Way ($15,000); 1999: foundation grants to United Way ($15,000) 1998: foundation grants to United Way ($14,000)
Assets: $3,401,962 (2000); $3,186,972 (1999); $3,104,658 (1998)

Typical Recipients

Arts & Humanities: Arts Associations & Councils, Ballet, Dance, Historic Preservation, History & Archaeology, Libraries, Museums/Galleries, Music
Civic & Public Affairs: Economic Development, Civic & Public Affairs-General, Municipalities/Towns, Safety, Urban & Community Affairs
Education: Colleges & Universities, Engineering/Technological Education, Medical Education, Public Education (Precollege)
Environment: Environment-General
Health: Alzheimers Disease, Cancer, Hospices, Prenatal Health Issues, Single-Disease Health Associations
Religion: Churches, Religious Welfare
Science: Scientific Centers & Institutes
Social Services: At-Risk Youth, Camps, Child Welfare, Community Service Organizations, Day Care, Family Planning, Food/Clothing Distribution, People

with Disabilities, Recreation & Athletics, Scouts, Senior Services, Substance Abuse, United Funds/ United Ways, Veterans, Youth Organizations

Application Procedures

Initial Contact: The foundation requests applications be made in writing.
Application Requirements: Include a description of organization, purpose of funds sought, affiliation with any other organization, and proof of tax-exempt status.
Deadlines: July 1 and December 1.

Foundation Officials

David Earl Holt: secretary B Magna, UT 1928. ED University of Utah (1946-1947); University of Utah (1952-1954); Brigham Young University BA (1957); Brigham Young University MA (1958); University of Utah (1958-1959); Emory University MLS (1963). PRIM CORP EMPL director: Austin Public Library. NONPR AFFIL member: Texas Library Association; member: Urban Library Council; member: Rotary; member: American Library Association; staff member: Library USA.
Alice T. Smith: vchairman
Bill W. Waters: chairman

Grants Analysis

Disclosure Period: calendar year ending 2000
Total Grants: $42,500*
Number of Grants: 14
Average Grant: $3,035*
Highest Grant: $6,000
Lowest Grant: $500
Typical Range: $1,000 to $5,000
*Note: Giving excludes United Way.

Recent Grants

Note: Grants derived from 1999 Form 990.

General

21,000	Golden Spread Council, Boy Scouts of America, Pampa, TX
15,000	Pampa United Way, Pampa, TX
14,000	St. Matthews Episcopal Church, Pampa, TX
10,000	Panhandle-Plains Museum, Canyon, TX
10,000	Texas Plains Girl Scouts, Pampa, TX
5,000	City of Pampa, Pampa, TX -- public building project
5,000	Good Samaritan Christian Service, Pampa, TX
5,000	Gray County, Texas, Pampa, TX
2,500	Roberts County, Texas, Miami, TX
2,000	Pampa Civic Ballet, Pampa, TX

W. L. Lyons Brown Foundation

Giving Contact

Ina Hamilton-Bond, President
850 Dixie Hwy.
Louisville, KY 40210
Phone: (502)895-6363
E-mail: Brown-Forman@b-f.com
Web: http://www.brown-forman.com

Description

Founded: 1962
EIN: 610598511
Organization Type: Private Foundation
Giving Locations: KY: Louisville
Grant Types: Capital, General Support.

Donor Information

Founder: the late W. L. Lyons Brown

Financial Summary

Total Giving: $935,891 (2001); $1,094,250 (2000); $1,065,615 (1999). Note: 1997 Giving includes United Way ($23,000).
Giving Analysis: Giving for 2001 includes: foundation grants to United Way ($28,000); 2000: foundation grants to United Way ($26,000); 1999: foundation ($1,065,615);
Assets: $20,424,812 (2001); $22,132,417 (2000); $19,554,918 (1999)

Typical Recipients

Arts & Humanities: Arts Festivals, Arts Funds, Community Arts, Ethnic & Folk Arts, Arts & Humanities-General, Historic Preservation, History & Archaeology, Libraries, Museums/Galleries, Music, Public Broadcasting, Theater
Civic & Public Affairs: Botanical Gardens/Parks, Clubs, Community Foundations, Economic Development, Civic & Public Affairs-General, Housing, Public Policy, Urban & Community Affairs, Zoos/Aquariums
Education: Business Education, Colleges & Universities, Education Reform, Environmental Education, Faculty Development, Legal Education, Private Education (Precollege), Public Education (Precollege), Science/Mathematics Education, Secondary Education (Private)
Environment: Air/Water Quality, Forestry, Environment-General, Resource Conservation, Wildlife Protection
Health: Cancer, Clinics/Medical Centers, Hospitals, Nursing Services, Prenatal Health Issues
International: International Environmental Issues
Religion: Churches, Religious Welfare
Science: Scientific Centers & Institutes
Social Services: Community Service Organizations, Family Planning, Family Services, Homes, People with Disabilities, United Funds/United Ways

Application Procedures

Initial Contact: The foundation requests applications be made in writing.
Application Requirements: Include pertinent information that will enable the board to determine if the request satisfies foundation's guidelines.
Deadlines: None.

Restrictions

Priority is given to organizations that seek to improve the quality of life in Louisville, KY, such as zoos, museums, parks, educational institutions, and organizations that support the arts. Support will not be given to organizations operating in fields where there is substantial governmental financial assistance.

Foundation Officials

Ina B. Hamilton Bond: president, trustee
Martin S. Brown: trustee PRIM CORP EMPL chairman, chief executive officer: Jack Daniels Distillery. CORP AFFIL director: Blue Grass Cooperage Co.; director: Brown-Forman Corp.
Owsley Brown, II: treasurer, trustee B Louisville, KY September 10, 1942. ED Yale University BA (1964); Stanford University MBA (1966). PRIM CORP EMPL president, chief executive officer: Brown-Forman Corp. NONPR AFFIL treasurer, trustee: W L Lyons Brown Foundation; director: Greater Louisville Fund Arts. CLUB AFFIL Wynn Stay Club; Louisville Country Club; Pendennis Club; Filson Club.
Mrs. W. L. Lyons Brown: secretary, trustee
William Lee Lyons Brown, Jr.: trustee B Louisville, KY 1936. ED University of Virginia BA (1958); American Graduate School of International Management BS (1960). PRIM CORP EMPL chairman: Brown-Forman Corp. CORP AFFIL director: Stone & Webster; director: National City Corp. Cleveland; director: Standex International Corp.; director: Carter Hawley

Hale Stores Inc.; director: National City Corp.; director: Bank Boston Corp.; director: Bradley Real Estate Trust. NONPR AFFIL member: Presidents Advisory Committee Trade Policy & Negotiations; member: University Virginia Alumni Association; member business committee: Metropolitan Museum Art; chairman: American Business Conference. CLUB AFFIL Travelers Club; University Club; Pendennis Club; River Valley Club; Fishers Club; Louisville Country Club.
Benjamin H. Morris: trustee

Grants Analysis

Disclosure Period: calendar year ending 2001
Total Grants: $907,891*
Number of Grants: 22
Average Grant: $30,395*
Highest Grant: $200,000
Lowest Grant: $4,000
Typical Range: $10,000 to $50,000
*Note: Giving excludes United Way. Average grant figure excludes two highest grants ($300,000).

Recent Grants

Note: Grants derived from 2000 Form 990.

General

200,000	River Fields, Inc, Louisville, KY -- land conservation grant for environmental impact
100,000	Brown Theatre, Columbia, SC -- art grant for building renovation
75,000	Downtown Development Corporation, Louisville, KY -- to underwrite cost of visioning and design process
62,500	University of Virginia, Charlottesville, VA -- for educational grant and capital campaign
50,000	Bernheim Arboretum and Research Forest, Clermont, KY -- to create critically need infrastructure
50,000	Harrods Creek Baptist Church -- capital campaign - construction of community center
50,000	Muhammad Ali Center, Louisville, KY -- grant to promote peace and non-violence
50,000	Transylvania University, Lexington, NY -- educational grant for excellence in teaching
50,000	Waterfront Development Corporation -- grant for conservation and beautification of banks of Ohio
40,000	Christ Church Cathedral, Houston, TX -- for capital campaign and renovation grant

Brown & Williamson Tobacco Corp.

Company Headquarters

401 South 4th Avenue, Suite 200
PO Box 35090
Louisville, KY 40232-5090
Phone: (502)568-7000
Fax: (502)568-7494
Web: http://www.bw.com

Company Description

Employees: 6,600
SIC(s): 2111 Cigarettes, 2131 Chewing & Smoking Tobacco.
Parent Company: British American Tobacco Plc, Globe House, 4 Temple Pl., London, United Kingdom

Operating Locations
Brown & Williamson Tobacco Corp. (NC--Wilson, Winston-Salem)

Nonmonetary Support
Type: Donated Equipment; Workplace Solicitation

Giving Contact
Gail Strange, Senior Manager, Corp. and Community Relations
Brown & Williamson Tower 200
401 S. Fourth St.
PO Box 35090
Louisville, KY 40202
Phone: (502)568-7451
Fax: (502)568-8262
Web: http://www.bw.com

Alternate Contact
Brennan Dawson, Vice President

Description
Organization Type: Corporate Giving Program
Giving Locations: headquarters and operating communities.
Grant Types: Award, Capital, Employee Matching Gifts, General Support, Operating Expenses, Research, Scholarship.

Financial Summary
Total Giving: $1,800,000 (2003 approx); $1,800,000 (2002); $3,000,000 (2001 approx). Note: Contributes through corporate direct giving program only.

Typical Recipients
Arts & Humanities: Arts Associations & Councils, Dance, Ethnic & Folk Arts, Historic Preservation, Libraries, Museums/Galleries, Public Broadcasting
Civic & Public Affairs: Business/Free Enterprise, Economic Development, Employment/Job Training, Law & Justice, Public Policy, Urban & Community Affairs, Women's Affairs, Zoos/Aquariums
Education: Colleges & Universities, Education Associations, Minority Education, Science/Mathematics Education
Environment: Environment-General
Science: Scientific Organizations
Social Services: Child Welfare, Community Centers, Community Service Organizations, Family Services, Senior Services, Substance Abuse, United Funds/United Ways

Application Procedures
Initial Contact: letter requesting formal application form
Application Requirements: description of the organization, amount requested, purpose of funds sought, recently audited financial statement, and proof of tax-exempt status
Deadlines: August.

Restrictions
The company does not support individuals, dinners or special events, fraternal organizations, goodwill advertising, member agencies of united funds, political or lobbying groups, or religious organizations for sectarian purposes.

Corporate Officials
Brennan Dawson: vice president external affairs PRIM CORP EMPL vice president external affairs: Brown & Williamson Tobacco Co.
Susan Ivey: president, chief executive officer PRIM CORP EMPL president, chief executive officer: Brown & Williamson Tobacco Corp.
Michael J. McGraw: senior vice president law & human resources PRIM CORP EMPL senior vice president law & human resources: Brown & Williamson Tobacco Corp.

Grants Analysis
Typical Range: $2,500 to $5,000

BROYHILL FAMILY FOUNDATION

Giving Contact
Paul H. Broyhill, Chairman & Manager
PO Box 500
Golfview Park
Lenoir, NC 28645
Phone: (828)758-6100

Description
Founded: 1945
EIN: 566054119
Organization Type: Family Foundation
Giving Locations: NC: preference to Cardwell County and surrounding areas
Grant Types: General Support, Scholarship.

Donor Information
Founder: Established in 1945. Broyhill Furniture Industries and the Broyhill family members are donors.

Financial Summary
Total Giving: $1,920,508 (2001); $1,881,133 (2000); $1,851,495 (1999)
Giving Analysis: Giving for 2001 includes: foundation grants to United Way ($24,000); 2000: foundation grants to United Way ($28,725); 1998: foundation grants to United Way ($12,000)
Assets: $41,848,607 (2001); $45,785,412 (2000); $45,195,546 (1999)

Typical Recipients
Arts & Humanities: Arts Associations & Councils, Arts Centers, Community Arts, Arts & Humanities-General, History & Archaeology, Libraries, Museums/Galleries, Music
Civic & Public Affairs: Botanical Gardens/Parks, Business/Free Enterprise, Community Foundations, Economic Development, Economic Policy, Employment/Job Training, Civic & Public Affairs-General, Philanthropic Organizations, Professional & Trade Associations, Public Policy, Safety
Education: Arts/Humanities Education, Business Education, Colleges & Universities, Community & Junior Colleges, Continuing Education, Education Funds, Education Reform, Education-General, International Studies, Medical Education, Minority Education, Private Education (Precollege), Public Education (Precollege), Religious Education, School Volunteerism, Science/Mathematics Education, Student Aid
Health: Children's Health/Hospitals, Clinics/Medical Centers, Emergency/Ambulance Services, Eyes/Blindness, Health-General, Health Organizations, Hospices, Hospitals, Medical Research, Mental Health, Preventive Medicine/Wellness Organizations, Public Health, Research/Studies Institutes
Religion: Bible Study/Translation, Churches, Ministries, Missionary Activities (Domestic), Religious Organizations, Religious Welfare, Seminaries
Social Services: At-Risk Youth, Camps, Child Welfare, Community Centers, Community Service Organizations, Counseling, Homes, People with Disabilities, Senior Services, Special Olympics, Substance Abuse, United Funds/United Ways, United Funds/United Ways, Volunteer Services, YMCA/YWCA/YMHA/YWHA, Youth Organizations

Application Procedures
Initial Contact: Potential applicants should submit a brief letter to the foundation.
Deadlines: None.
Review Process: The foundation's board meets quarterly to review proposals.

Restrictions
The foundation does not give loans or scholarships directly to students.

Foundation Officials
Clarence E. Beach: director
E. D. Beach: secretary, treasurer, director PRIM CORP EMPL secretary, treasurer, director: Broyhill Investments Inc.
Faye A. Broyhill: director
M. Hunt Broyhill: president, director B 1964. ED Wake Forest University (1984). PRIM CORP EMPL president, director: Broyhill Investments Inc.
Paul Hunt Broyhill: chairman, director B Lincolnton, NC 1924. ED University of North Carolina (1948). PRIM CORP EMPL chairman, chief operating officer: Broyhill Investments Inc. CORP AFFIL chairman: Broyhill Realty. NONPR AFFIL chairman: BMC Fund, Inc.
Lee E. Pritchard: assistant secretary, assistant treasurer

Grants Analysis
Disclosure Period: calendar year ending 2001
Total Grants: $1,896,500*
Number of Grants: 223
Average Grant: $8,504
Highest Grant: $101,000
Typical Range: $5,000 to $20,000
*Note: Giving excludes United Way.

Recent Grants
Note: Grants derived from 2001 Form 990.

Library-Related
10,000	Jesse Helms Center Foundation, Wingate, NC

General
101,000	Gardner Webb University, Boiling Springs, NC
100,000	Eckerd Youth Camps, NC
100,000	Ridge YMCA
100,000	Tomorrow's America Foundation, Charlotte, NC
90,000	T.H. Broyhill Park Authority, NC
87,500	Caldwell Community College, Caldwell, ID
80,000	Medical Foundation of North Carolina, Chapel Hill, NC
80,000	Wake Forest University, Winston-Salem, NC
75,000	Mars Hill College, Mars Hill, NC -- EDB Endowment
55,000	Caldwell Memorial Hospital Foundation, Lenoir, NC

EVA L. AND JOSEPH M. BRUENING FOUNDATION

Giving Contact
Janet E. Narten, Executive Director
1422 Euclid Avenue, Suite 627
Cleveland, OH 44115-1901
Phone: (216)621-2632
Fax: (216)621-8198
Web: http://www.fmscleveland.com/bruening

Description
Founded: 1988
EIN: 341584378
Organization Type: General Purpose Foundation
Giving Locations: OH: Cuyahoga County
Grant Types: Capital, General Support, Multiyear/Continuing Support, Project, Seed Money.

Donor Information

Founder: Established in 1988 from the estate of the late Eva L. Bruening (d. 1987) and the late Joseph M. Bruening (d. 1987). Although natives of Cincinnati, OH, the Bruenings were residents of Cleveland, OH, for more than 65 years. Mr. Bruening owned the Ohio Ball Bearing Company, which later became Bearings, Inc.

Mr. Bruening was a founding member of Bluecoats, Inc., the organization that helps families of police officers and firefighters killed in the line of duty. Mr. Bruening served many nonprofit organizations during his lifetime including the Cleveland Rotary Club, American Cancer Society, Notre Dame College of Ohio, Society for Crippled Children, Cleveland Zoological Society, and St. Vincent Charity Hospital.

Financial Summary

Total Giving: $4,028,578 (2001); $4,254,319 (2000); $4,025,305 (1999)
Assets: $66,694,994 (2001); $72,189,263 (2000); $73,304,880 (1999)
Gifts Received: $8,695 (1994); $45 (1993); $1,350 (1992)

Typical Recipients

Arts & Humanities: Ballet, Dance, Historic Preservation, Libraries, Museums/Galleries, Music, Performing Arts, Public Broadcasting, Theater
Civic & Public Affairs: Business/Free Enterprise, Clubs, Community Foundations, Economic Development, Employment/Job Training, Civic & Public Affairs-General, Hispanic Affairs, Housing, Municipalities/Towns, Nonprofit Management, Parades/Festivals, Urban & Community Affairs, Women's Affairs, Zoos/Aquariums
Education: Afterschool/Enrichment Programs, Arts/Humanities Education, Business Education, Colleges & Universities, Community & Junior Colleges, Education Funds, Education Reform, Elementary Education (Private), Faculty Development, Education-General, International Studies, Literacy, Minority Education, Private Education (Precollege), Public Education (Precollege), Religious Education, Science/Mathematics Education, Secondary Education (Private), Secondary Education (Public), Special Education, Student Aid
Health: Adolescent Health Issues, AIDS/HIV, Alzheimers Disease, Cancer, Children's Health/Hospitals, Clinics/Medical Centers, Emergency/Ambulance Services, Eyes/Blindness, Geriatric Health, Health Organizations, Hospices, Hospitals, Long-Term Care, Nursing Services, Prenatal Health Issues, Preventive Medicine/Wellness Organizations, Public Health, Research/Studies Institutes, Single-Disease Health Associations, Speech & Hearing
Religion: Churches, Dioceses, Jewish Causes, Ministries, Ministries, Religious Organizations, Religious Welfare, Seminaries
Science: Science Museums, Scientific Centers & Institutes
Social Services: At-Risk Youth, Child Welfare, Community Centers, Community Service Organizations, Counseling, Day Care, Domestic Violence, Family Planning, Family Services, Food/Clothing Distribution, People with Disabilities, Recreation & Athletics, Senior Services, Sexual Abuse, Shelters/Homelessness, Social Services-General, Substance Abuse, United Funds/United Ways, Volunteer Services, YMCA/YWCA/YMHA/YWHA, Youth Organizations

Application Procedures

Initial Contact: Applicants are encouraged to contact the foundation for further clarification of its grant-making policies before submitting a proposal.
Application Requirements: Applications must include two copies of the following: a one-page summary signed by the organization's chief operating officer and chief volunteer officer; a proposal including a description of organization's mission and programs, the problem or issue to be addressed, the clients to be served, the program objectives and methods, the project budget, and an evaluation plan; list of the board of trustees; and a copy of the organization's current operating budget. In addition, applicants should submit organization's IRS letter designating its nonprofit status and a copy of the most recent audited financial statement and/or annual report.
Deadlines: March 1, July 1, and October 1.
Review Process: The distribution committee reviews grant requests three times a year in May, August, and December. Qualifying applicants will receive written notification of the foundation's decision within several weeks of each meeting.
Notes: Proposal pages should be attached with a paper clip and the use of binders or notebooks is discouraged.

Restrictions

The foundation will not make a permanent commitment of support to any type of project. In most cases, the foundation will not consider requests for endowments, general operations, research, publications, symposiums, or seminars. No grants will be awarded to individuals, or in response to mass mailings or annual campaign appeals. Grants are limited to the Greater Cleveland area.

Additional Information

Publications: Annual Report
Trust(s): KeyBank NA

Foundation Officials

Anne B. Blaine: member distribution committee
Kim Cowan: program officer
Marilyn Cunin: chairman distribution committee
John A. Favret: member distribution committee
CORP AFFIL director: Gorman-Lavelle Corp.
Janet E. Narten: executive director
E. Lorrie Robertson: member distribution committee
Cristin Slesh: program officer
Cathy A. Starkey: administration assistant
Margaret S. Wheeler: senior program officer

Grants Analysis

Disclosure Period: calendar year ending 2001
Total Grants: $5,120,669*
Number of Grants: 138
Average Grant: $25,000
Highest Grant: $400,000
Lowest Grant: $300
Typical Range: $5,000 to $50,000
*Note: Grants analysis was provided by the foundation and reflects grants approved.

Recent Grants

Note: Grants derived from 2000 Form 990.

Library-Related
150,000   East Cleveland Public Library, Cleveland, OH -- to renovate and expand the main library

General
300,000   Boys and Girls Clubs of Greater Cleveland, Cleveland, OH -- for costs associated with the construction of the new Broadway Club
250,000   Applewood Centers, Cleveland, OH -- for start-up support of the Independent Living Program
250,000   Metrohealth Foundation, Cleveland, OH -- for a new Center for Skilled Nursing Care
100,000   Center for Families and Children, Cleveland, OH -- for implementation of the technology component of the strategic plan
100,000   City Mission, Cleveland, OH -- to establish a new long term transitional housing program

100,000   Cuyahoga County Board of Commissioners, Cleveland, OH -- for the Early Childhood Initiative
100,000   Eliza Jennings Group, Lakewood, OH -- for renovations
100,000   North Coast Community Homes, Inc., Cleveland, OH -- for the development of two homes
100,000   Saint Vitus Development Corporation, Cleveland, OH -- for capital expenses
100,000   Shorebank Enterprise Group Cleveland, Cleveland, OH -- for capital improvements

CHARLES E. AND EDNA T. BRUNDAGE CHARITABLE, SCIENTIFIC, AND WILDLIFE CONSERVATION FOUNDATION

Giving Contact

Francis X. O'Brien, Secretary & Trustee
c/o Carpenter, Bennett & Morrissey
3 Gateway Ctr.
100 Mulberry St.
Newark, NJ 07102-4079
Phone: (973)622-7711

Description

Founded: 1955
EIN: 226050185
Organization Type: Private Foundation
Giving Locations: NJ
Grant Types: General Support.

Donor Information

Founder: Edna T. Brundage

Financial Summary

Total Giving: $200,500 (2002); $167,500 (2001); $159,000 (2000)
Assets: $3,471,866 (2002); $4,170,392 (2001); $4,678,618 (2000)
Gifts Received: $5,481 (1999); $510,000 (1996); $25,000 (1994). Note: In 1999, contributions were received from William B. Cater, Jr. In 1996, contributions were received from the estate of Edna T. Brundage.

Typical Recipients

Arts & Humanities: Arts Associations & Councils, Community Arts, History & Archaeology, Libraries, Museums/Galleries, Music, Opera, Performing Arts, Public Broadcasting, Theater
Civic & Public Affairs: African American Affairs, Clubs, Community Foundations, Civic & Public Affairs-General, Safety, Urban & Community Affairs
Education: Arts/Humanities Education, Business Education, Colleges & Universities, Education Funds, Education-General, Leadership Training, Literacy, Preschool Education, Private Education (Precollege), Science/Mathematics Education, Student Aid
Environment: Environment-General, Resource Conservation, Wildlife Protection
Health: Children's Health/Hospitals, Clinics/Medical Centers, Emergency/Ambulance Services, Health Funds, Health Organizations, Home-Care Services, Hospices, Prenatal Health Issues, Research/Studies Institutes
International: Health Care/Hospitals, International Organizations
Religion: Churches, Religious Welfare
Science: Science Museums, Scientific Centers & Institutes

Social Services: Camps, Community Centers, Community Service Organizations, Crime Prevention, Delinquency & Criminal Rehabilitation, Family Planning, Family Services, Food/Clothing Distribution, Recreation & Athletics, United Funds/United Ways

Application Procedures

Initial Contact: Send a brief letter of inquiry.
Deadlines: None.

Foundation Officials

Charles B. Cater: trustee
June B. Cater: trustee
Kerry Cater: trustee
William B. Cater: vice president, treasurer, trustee
William B. Cater, Jr.: president, trustee
James A. Jukosky: vice president, trustee
Susan Jukosky: trustee
Thomas L. Morrissey: vice president, secretary, trustee
Francis X. O'Brien: secretary, trustee
Laurence Reich: assistant secretary

Grants Analysis

Disclosure Period: calendar year ending 2002
Total Grants: $200,500
Number of Grants: 51
Average Grant: $3,931
Highest Grant: $22,500
Lowest Grant: $1,000
Typical Range: $1,000 to $5,000

Recent Grants

Note: Grants derived from 2001 Form 990.

General

12,000	New Jersey Symphony Orchestra, Newark, NJ -- operating fund
10,000	Dartmouth College, Hanover, NH
10,000	Newark Museum, Newark, NJ -- operating fund
10,000	Newark Museum, Newark, NJ -- Science Center
8,000	Electronic Information and Education Service, South Orange, NJ -- operating fund
6,000	Vermont Studio Center, Johnson, VT
5,500	Kiwanis Foundation of New Jersey, Clinton, NJ
5,000	Greater Newark Christmas Fund, Newark, NJ
5,000	Lebanon Opera House, Lebanon, NH -- capital campaign
5,000	WNYC Radio Foundation, New York, NY

JOSEPH S. BRUNO CHARITABLE FOUNDATION

Giving Contact

Jera Stribling, Executive Director
PO Box 530727
Birmingham, AL 35253
Phone: (205)879-0799

Description

Founded: 1985
EIN: 630936234
Organization Type: Private Foundation
Giving Locations: AL
Grant Types: General Support, Research.

Donor Information

Founder: Joseph S. Bruno

Financial Summary

Total Giving: $441,000 (fiscal year ending November 30, 2001); $438,700 (fiscal 2000); $377,650 (fiscal 1998)
Giving Analysis: Giving for fiscal 2000 includes: foundation scholarships ($10,000)
Assets: $9,980,597 (fiscal 2001); $10,316,380 (fiscal 2000); $10,208,747 (fiscal 1998)
Gifts Received: $1,722,282 (fiscal 1996); $108,063 (fiscal 1994); $545,313 (fiscal 1993). Note: In fiscal 1996, contributions were received from the estate of Joseph S. Bruno.

Typical Recipients

Arts & Humanities: Arts Festivals, Ballet, Dance, Arts & Humanities-General, Libraries, Museums/Galleries, Performing Arts
Civic & Public Affairs: Civic & Public Affairs-General
Education: Arts/Humanities Education, Business Education, Colleges & Universities, Education Reform, Education-General, Preschool Education, Private Education (Precollege), Secondary Education (Private), Student Aid
Environment: Environment-General
Health: Cancer, Children's Health/Hospitals, Health-General, Heart, Hospitals, Medical Research, Mental Health, Single-Disease Health Associations
Religion: Churches, Dioceses, Jewish Causes, Religious Organizations, Religious Welfare
Social Services: Camps, Child Welfare, Community Service Organizations, Community Service Organizations, Scouts, Social Services-General, United Funds/United Ways, Youth Organizations

Application Procedures

Initial Contact: Contact the executive director for application and deadline information.

Restrictions

Does not support idd.

Foundation Officials

Richard Cohn: director
Anne LaRussa: director
Benny M. LaRussa, Jr.: vice president, treasurer
Robert H. Sprain, Jr.: vice president, secretary
Theresa Sprain: director
Jera G. Stribling: executive director

Grants Analysis

Disclosure Period: fiscal year ending November 30, 2001
Total Grants: $441,000
Number of Grants: 35
Average Grant: $11,500*
Highest Grant: $50,000
Lowest Grant: $2,000
Typical Range: $5,000 to $20,000
*Note: Average grant figure excludes highest grant.

Recent Grants

Note: Grants derived from fiscal 2000 Form 990.

Library-Related

10,000	Emmet O'Neal Library, Mountain Brook, AL -- education

General

50,000	Service Guild, Birmingham, AL -- for civic and community
44,200	Birmingham Southern College, Birmingham, AL -- for education
30,000	John Carroll Catholic High School Education Foundation, Birmingham, AL -- for education
25,000	Carraway Hospitals Foundation, Birmingham, AL -- for health and human services
25,000	First Look, Birmingham, AL -- for civic and community
25,000	St. Vincent's, Birmingham, AL -- for health and human services
20,000	United Cerebral Palsy, Birmingham, AL -- for health and human services
15,000	Birmingham International Festival, Birmingham, AL -- for arts and culture
12,000	Preschool Partners, Birmingham, AL -- for education
10,000	Al Theater for the Performing Arts, Birmingham, AL -- for arts and culture

BRUNSWICK CORP.

Company Headquarters

1 North Field Court
Lake Forest, IL 60045
Phone: (847)735-4469
Fax: (847)735-4481
Web: http://www.brunswickcorp.com

Company Description

Founded: 1845
Ticker: BC
Exchange: NYSE
Revenue: US$3.711 billion (2002)
Profit: US$78.4 million (2002)
Employees: 22700 (2001)
Fortune Rank: 430, per FORTUNE Magazine's list of 500 Largest U.S. Corporations (2002).
SIC(s): 3519 Internal Combustion Engines Nec, 3732 Boat Building & Repairing, 3949 Sporting & Athletic Goods Nec.

Operating Locations

Brunswick Corp. (CA--Orange; GA--Norcross; IL--Glendale Heights, Lombard; PA--Philadelphia)

Brunswick Foundation

Giving Contact

Carol Stame, President
One North Field Court
Lake Forest, IL 60045
Phone: (847)735-4667

Description

EIN: 366033576
Organization Type: Corporate Foundation
Giving Locations: principally near operating locations and to national organizations.
Grant Types: Fellowship, Project, Research, Scholarship.

Financial Summary

Total Giving: $675,850 (2001); $675,850 (2000); $607,950 (1999). Note: Contributes through foundation only.
Giving Analysis: Giving for 2000 includes: foundation ($258,850); foundation scholarships ($417,000); 1999: foundation grants to United Way ($550); foundation ($196,400); foundation scholarships ($411,000) 1998: foundation ($733,047)
Assets: $6,921,257 (2001); $6,921,257 (2000); $7,253,649 (1999)
Gifts Received: $100,000 (1998); $3,895,243 (1996); $1,984,000 (1995). Note: In 1998, contributions were received from Brunswick Corp.

Typical Recipients

Arts & Humanities: Arts Festivals, Arts Funds, Arts Institutes, Community Arts, Dance, Historic Preservation, Libraries, Museums/Galleries, Music, Performing Arts, Theater

Civic & Public Affairs: Asian American Affairs, Botanical Gardens/Parks, Civil Rights, Clubs, Community Foundations, Economic Development, Ethnic Organizations, Civic & Public Affairs-General, Legal Aid, Professional & Trade Associations, Public Policy, Rural Affairs, Urban & Community Affairs, Women's Affairs, Zoos/Aquariums

Education: Business Education, Colleges & Universities, Community & Junior Colleges, Economic Education, Education Associations, Engineering/Technological Education, Environmental Education, Education-General, Gifted & Talented Programs, International Exchange, International Studies, Leadership Training, Literacy, Minority Education, Private Education (Precollege), Public Education (Precollege), Science/Mathematics Education, Secondary Education (Private), Student Aid, Vocational & Technical Education

Environment: Environment-General, Wildlife Protection

Health: Cancer, Children's Health/Hospitals, Clinics/Medical Centers, Diabetes, Emergency/Ambulance Services, Health Organizations, Heart, Hospices, Hospitals, Mental Health, Nursing Services, Prenatal Health Issues, Single-Disease Health Associations

International: International Affairs, International Relations

Religion: Ministries, Religious Welfare

Social Services: At-Risk Youth, Big Brother/Big Sister, Child Welfare, Child Welfare, Community Centers, Community Service Organizations, Day Care, Delinquency & Criminal Rehabilitation, Emergency Relief, Family Planning, Family Services, Food/Clothing Distribution, People with Disabilities, Recreation & Athletics, Scouts, Senior Services, Shelters/Homelessness, Social Services-General, Special Olympics, Substance Abuse, United Funds/United Ways, Volunteer Services, YMCA/YWCA/YMHA/YWHA, Youth Organizations

Application Procedures

Initial Contact: Send a brief letter requesting application form.

Application Requirements: Completed applications will include objectives and purpose for which grant is sought; plans for implementation and evaluation of project; benefits expected; evidence of need for project; budget; list of board of directors, IRS 501(c)(3) verification; and most recently audited financial statement.

Deadlines: None.

Decision Notification: Committee meets as needed.

Notes: Foundation does not accept telephone solicitations.

Restrictions

Foundation does not make grants to individuals or provide loans. Does not support organizations that are not tax-exempt; religious or political organizations, veterans' groups, fraternal orders or labor groups; preschool, or trips, tours, tickets, dinners, special events or advertising. Does not donate company equipment or products.

Additional Information

Foundation is in the process of reorganization.

Publications: Annual Report; Application Forms

Corporate Officials

Peter N. Larson: chairman, chief executive officer, director B Los Angeles, CA 1939. ED Oregon State University BS (1960); Seton Hall University JD (1972). PRIM CORP EMPL chairman, chief executive officer, director: Brunswick Corp. CORP AFFIL director: Coty Corp.; Kimberly-Clark Corp.; director: CIGNA Corp.; director: Compaq Computer Corp.

Foundation Officials

Mary Kay Bottorff: president

Peter Bannerman Hamilton: director B Philadelphia, PA 1946. ED Princeton University AB (1968); Yale University JD (1971). PRIM CORP EMPL vice president, president: Brunswick Corp. CORP AFFIL director: Fidelity Life Association; director: Kemper National Insurance Companies; director: American Motorists Insurance Co.

Michael D. Schmitz: secretary PRIM CORP EMPL assistant secretary: Brunswick Corp.

Geoffrey Smith: treasurer

Kenneth B. Zeigler: director PRIM CORP EMPL vice president, chief human resources officer: Brunswick Corp.

Grants Analysis

Disclosure Period: calendar year ending 2000

Total Grants: $258,850*

Number of Grants: 91*

Average Grant: $1,765*

Highest Grant: $100,000

Typical Range: $100 to $5,000

*Note: Giving excludes scholarships. Average grant figure excludes highest grant.

Recent Grants

Note: Grants derived from 2001 Form 990.

General

100,000	Citizens For A Sound Economy Education, Washington, DC -- Unrestricted
36,000	U.S. China Foundation for International Exchanges, San Francisco, CA -- Unrestricted
36,000	U.S. China Foundation for International Exchanges, San Francisco, CA -- Unrestricted
7,500	Junior Achievement of Chicago, Chicago, IL -- Unrestricted
5,000	Children's Memorial Foundation, Chicago, IL -- Unrestricted
5,000	Committee for Economic Development, New York, NY -- Unrestricted
5,000	Evans Scholars Foundation, Golf, IL -- Unrestricted
5,000	Executive Service Corps of Chicago, Chicago, IL -- Unrestricted
5,000	Family Service of South Lake County, Highland Park, IL -- Unrestricted
5,000	YMCA of Metropolitan Chicago, Chicago, IL -- Unrestricted

BRUSH FOUNDATION

Giving Contact

3135 Euclid Avenue, Suite 102
Cleveland, OH 44115

Phone: (216)881-5121

Fax: (216)881-1834

Description

Founded: 1928

EIN: 346000445

Organization Type: Private Foundation

Giving Locations: Third World countries, nationally, and locally.

Grant Types: Conference/Seminar, Emergency, General Support, Multiyear/Continuing Support, Operating Expenses, Project, Research, Seed Money.

Donor Information

Founder: the late Charles F. Brush, Maurice Perkins

Financial Summary

Total Giving: $383,537 (2000); $299,750 (1999); $350,000 (1998)

Assets: $7,449,849 (2000); $7,560,233 (1999); $5,289,077 (1996)

Typical Recipients

Arts & Humanities: History & Archaeology, Libraries

Civic & Public Affairs: Civil Rights, Civic & Public Affairs-General, Legal Aid, Nonprofit Management, Public Policy, Women's Affairs

Education: Business Education, Colleges & Universities, Education-General, Legal Education, Medical Education, Public Education (Precollege), Student Aid

Health: Clinics/Medical Centers, Health-General, Health Organizations, Prenatal Health Issues, Public Health

International: Health Care/Hospitals, International Environmental Issues, International Organizations, International Peace & Security Issues

Religion: Ministries, Religious Organizations, Social/Policy Issues

Social Services: Big Brother/Big Sister, Child Welfare, Family Planning, Family Services, Food/Clothing Distribution, Scouts, Youth Organizations

Application Procedures

Initial Contact: Send a brief letter of inquiry. Include grant request and purpose of funds sought.

Application Requirements: Include a description of organization, grant request and purpose of funds sought.

Deadlines: None.

Decision Notification: Decisions are made by the Managers at their November and May board meetings.

Restrictions

Grants will be awarded to finance efforts contributing toward betterment of the human stock through research in the field of eugenics and toward regulation of the population. Does not support individuals or provide loans.

Additional Information

Trust(s): Key Trust Co OH NA

Foundation Officials

John J. Beeston, MD: board mem

Barbara Brush Wright: president

Sally F. Burton: vice president

Cindie Carroll: board mem

Michael C. Carter: board mem

Virginia P. Carter: board mem

Doris B. Dingle: board member

Richard Miesse Donaldson: treasurer B Columbus, OH 1929. ED Northwestern University BS (1950); University of Michigan JD (1953); Harvard University LLM (1957); Stanford University Graduate School of Business Administration (1982). NONPR AFFIL member: Ohio Bar Association; member: Ohio Chamber of Commerce; member: Highway Users Federation; advisory committee: A New Day; chairman: Fast Track Task Force; private sector member: Greater Cleveland Infrastructure Task Force; trustee: Childrens Aid Society Cleveland; member visitors committee: Case Western Reserve University Frances P Bolton School Nursing; chairman public committee: Case Western Reserve University Regional Environmental Priorities Project; member: American Petroleum Institute. CLUB AFFIL Cleveland Yacht Club; River Oaks Racquet Club; City Club.

Meacham Hitchcock: secretary

Daniel Earl Pellegrom: board mem B Three Rivers, MI 1944. ED Western Michigan University BA (1966); Union Theological Seminary MDiv (1969). PRIM CORP EMPL president: Pathfinder Intl. NONPR AFFIL director: Interaction; bd overseers: Planned Parenthood League; director: Alan Guttmacher Institute; treasurer, director: Advocates for Youth; member: Am Public Health Association.

Jane Perkins Moffett: board mem

Grants Analysis

Disclosure Period: calendar year ending 2000
Total Grants: $383,537
Number of Grants: 26
Average Grant: $14,751
Highest Grant: $25,000
Typical Range: $5,000 to $25,000

Recent Grants

Note: Grants derived from 1999 Form 990.

General

37,500	Alan Guttmacher Institute, New York, NY
37,500	Catholics for a Free Choice, Washington, DC
25,000	Center for Reproduction Law & Policy, New York, NY
25,000	Free Clinic of Greater Cleveland, Cleveland, OH
25,000	Pathfinder, Watertown, MA
25,000	Planned Parenthood of San Diego, San Diego, CA
21,000	University of Michigan, Ann Arbor, MI
20,000	Minnesota International Health Volunteers, Minneapolis, MN
17,500	Planned Parenthood, Cleveland, OH
15,000	National Abortion Federation, Washington, DC

BRYAN FOODS

Company Headquarters

PO Box 1177
West Point, MS 39773
Web: http://www.bryanfoods.com

Company Description

Employees: 2,200
SIC(s): 2000 Food & Kindred Products, 2011 Meat Packing Plants.
Parent Company: Sara Lee Corp., Chicago, IL, United States

Nonmonetary Support

Type: Donated Products
Volunteer Programs: Company is a partner in education with local public schools.

Giving Contact

Jadas Blissard, Human Resources Assistant
PO Box 1177
West Point, MS 39773
Phone: (662)495-4000
Fax: (662)495-4439
E-mail: hakola@bryanfoods.com

Description

Organization Type: Corporate Giving Program
Giving Locations: headquarters and operating communities.

Financial Summary

Total Giving: $87,560 (1998); $86,146 (1997); $140,000 (1996)

Typical Recipients

Arts & Humanities: Arts Festivals, Arts Outreach, Community Arts, Arts & Humanities-General, Libraries, Performing Arts
Civic & Public Affairs: African American Affairs, Civil Rights, Community Foundations, Economic Development, Civic & Public Affairs-General
Education: Afterschool/Enrichment Programs, Arts/Humanities Education, Business Education, Business-School Partnerships, Elementary Education (Public), Faculty Development, Education-General, Minority Education, Preschool Education, Public Education (Precollege), Special Education

Environment: Resource Conservation, Wildlife Protection
Health: Cancer, Diabetes, Multiple Sclerosis
Social Services: At-Risk Youth, Child Welfare, Domestic Violence, Food/Clothing Distribution, People with Disabilities, Shelters/Homelessness, United Funds/United Ways, Volunteer Services, Youth Organizations

Application Procedures

Initial Contact: Send a brief letter of inquiry and a full proposal.
Application Requirements: Include a description of organization, amount requested, recently audited financial statement, proof of tax-exempt status, and purpose of funds sought.
Notes: Most contributions are made to preselected organizations.

Restrictions

Does not support individuals, religious organizations for sectarian purposes, political or lobbying groups, or organizations outside operating areas.

Corporate Officials

John Bryan, III: chairman, president, chief executive officer PRIM CORP EMPL chairman, president, chief executive officer: Bryan Foods.
Brad Egbert: chief financial officer PRIM CORP EMPL chief financial officer: Bryan Foods.

Grants Analysis

Typical Range: $10 to $1,000
Note: A more recent grants list was unavailable.

Recent Grants

Note: Grants derived from 1996 grants list.

General

Clay County Public Schools, Pheba, MS
Gardner Simmons Home for Girls, Tupelo, MS
Kidtown Committee, West Point, MS
Mississippi Troopers, Jackson, MS
Safe Haven, Columbus, MS
Sally Kate Winters Home for Children, West Point, MS
Sheriff's Boys and Girls Club, Columbus, MS
Special Olympics, Jackson, MS
West Point Public Schools, West Point, MS
NAACP, West Point, MS

THE BRYANT FOUNDATION

Giving Contact

Arthur H. Bryant, Jr., President & Treasurer
PO Box 1239
Stephens City, VA 22655-1239
Phone: (540)868-2183

Description

Founded: 1949
EIN: 546032840
Organization Type: Family Foundation
Giving Locations: VA
Grant Types: General Support.

Donor Information

Founder: Established in 1949 by the late J. C. Herbert Bryant .

Financial Summary

Total Giving: $1,903,680 (2000); $2,509,697 (1999); $3,718,221 (1998)
Assets: $15,391,043 (2000); $16,426,220 (1999); $15,692,821 (1998)

Typical Recipients

Arts & Humanities: Art History, Arts Associations & Councils, Arts Centers, Historic Preservation, History & Archaeology, Libraries, Museums/Galleries
Civic & Public Affairs: Clubs, Civic & Public Affairs-General, Housing, Municipalities/Towns, Nonprofit Management, Safety, Urban & Community Affairs, Women's Affairs, Zoos/Aquariums
Education: Colleges & Universities, Education Funds, Education-General, Legal Education, Private Education (Precollege), Public Education (Precollege), Religious Education, Secondary Education (Private), Social Sciences Education, Student Aid
Environment: Forestry, Environment-General, Wildlife Protection
Health: Cancer, Clinics/Medical Centers, Emergency/Ambulance Services, Health-General, Health Organizations, Health Organizations, Hospitals, Long-Term Care, Medical Rehabilitation, Medical Research, Prenatal Health Issues, Public Health, Respiratory, Single-Disease Health Associations
International: International Peace & Security Issues
Religion: Churches, Religious Organizations, Religious Welfare, Seminaries
Science: Science Museums, Scientific Centers & Institutes
Social Services: Animal Protection, Child Welfare, Community Centers, Community Service Organizations, Day Care, Food/Clothing Distribution, Homes, Recreation & Athletics, Social Services-General, Youth Organizations

Application Procedures

Initial Contact: The foundation has no formal grant application procedure or application form.
Deadlines: None.

Restrictions

The foundation reports that grants are made only to nonprofit, charitable organizations. Grants are not made to individuals.

Foundation Officials

Arthur Herbert Bryant, II: president, treasurer B Washington, DC 1942. ED University of Miami (1963). PRIM CORP EMPL chairman, chief executive officer: O'Sullivan Corp. CORP AFFIL chairman: O'Sullivan Plastics Corp.; chairman: Regalite Plastics Corp. CLUB AFFIL treasurer: Birdwood Golf Course.
Howard W. Smith, Jr.: secretary ED National University (1938). NONPR AFFIL Sons American Revolution. CLUB AFFIL Sulgrave Country Club; Chevy Chase Country Club.

Grants Analysis

Disclosure Period: calendar year ending 2000
Total Grants: $1,903,680
Number of Grants: 63
Average Grant: $30,217
Highest Grant: $300,000
Lowest Grant: $250
Typical Range: $500 to $25,000

Recent Grants

Note: Grants derived from 2000 Form 990.

Library-Related

5,000	Alexandria Library, Alexandria, VA

General

300,000	Virginia Sports Hall of Fame, Portsmouth, VA
200,000	Athletic Educational Foundation of the College of William & Mary, Williamsburg, VA
200,000	Blue Ridge School, Dyke, VA
200,000	Hill School, Middleburg, VA
200,000	Shenandoah University Athletic, Winchester, VA

125,000	Chesapeake Academy, Irvington, VA
100,000	Christchurch School, Christchurch, VA
100,000	LFCC Educational Foundation, Middletown, VA
100,000	Loudon Health Care Foundation, Leesburg, VA
100,000	Virginia Institute of Autism, Gloucester Point, VA

BLANCHE BRYDEN FOUNDATION

Giving Contact
Judy K. Wilson, Manager
800 SW Jackson St., Suite 910
Topeka, KS 66612-1216
Phone: (785)357-1316

Description
Founded: 1992
EIN: 481117045
Organization Type: Private Foundation
Giving Locations: KS: Topeka
Grant Types: General Support.

Donor Information
Founder: the late Blanche Bryden

Financial Summary
Total Giving: $117,671 (fiscal year ending June 30, 2001); $135,120 (fiscal 1999); $115,930 (fiscal 1998)
Giving Analysis: Giving for fiscal 2001 includes: foundation scholarships ($48,800) fiscal 1999: foundation scholarships ($48,940)
Assets: $2,898,130 (fiscal 2001); $3,301,874 (fiscal 1999); $2,433,643 (fiscal 1997)

Typical Recipients
Arts & Humanities: Libraries, Music, Public Broadcasting
Civic & Public Affairs: Employment/Job Training, Safety
Education: Afterschool/Enrichment Programs, Colleges & Universities, Health & Physical Education, International Studies, Medical Education, Public Education (Precollege), Student Aid, Vocational & Technical Education
Health: Arthritis, Clinics/Medical Centers, Hospices, Mental Health
Religion: Religious Welfare, Synagogues/Temples
Social Services: Animal Protection, Child Welfare, Scouts, Senior Services, Substance Abuse, YMCA/YWCA/YMHA/YWHA, Youth Organizations

Application Procedures
Initial Contact: Send a full proposal.
Application Requirements: Include a description of organization, amount requested, purpose of funds sought, recently audited financial statement, and proof of tax-exempt status. Send a brief letter of inquiry.
Deadlines: None.
Evaluative Criteria: Include purpose of funds sought and proof of tax-exempt status.

Restrictions
Grants are not made to individuals.

Additional Information
Trust(s): Mercantile Bank

Foundation Officials
Oscar F. Belin: president, trustee B El Reno, OK. ED University of Kansas LLB; University of Kansas BS. PRIM CORP EMPL partner: Bever Dye Mustard Belin Attorneys. NONPR AFFIL member: Kansas Bar Association; member: Wichita Bar Association.

Shelli Crow-Johnson: secretary, treasurer
Katherine G. Kent: trustee

Grants Analysis
Disclosure Period: fiscal year ending June 30, 2001
Total Grants: $68,871*
Number of Grants: 14
Average Grant: $4,919
Highest Grant: $12,000
Lowest Grant: $400
Typical Range: $1,000 to $10,000
*Note: Giving excludes scholarship.

Recent Grants
Note: Grants derived from fiscal 2001 Form 990.

Library-Related
| 500 | Topeka and Shawnee County Public Library, Topeka, KS |

General
26,800	Washburn Endowment Association, Topeka, KS -- scholarship fund
12,000	Villages, Topeka, KS -- summer education and recreation programs
10,000	Marian Clinic, Topeka, KS -- nurses' salaries
10,000	Stormont-Vail Foundation, Topeka, KS -- for nurses' scholarships
10,000	Topeka High School Stars Program, Topeka, KS
8,500	Washburn University, Topeka, KS -- for Blanche Bryden Sunflower Music Festival Institute
5,000	Stormont-Vail Foundation, Topeka, KS -- for Allied Health Professional scholarships
5,000	Topeka Youth Project, Topeka, KS
5,000	Washburn Endowment Association, Topeka, KS -- for KTWU Channel 11
5,000	Washburn Endowment Association, Topeka, KS -- for Women's Alliance Scholarship Fund

BRYN MAWR BANK CORP.

Company Headquarters
801 Lancaster Avenue
Bryn Mawr, PA 19010-3396
Web: http://www.bmtc.com

Company Description
Founded: 1986
Ticker: BMTC
Exchange: NASDAQ
Assets: US$577.4 million (2002)
Employees: 242 (2002)
SIC(s): 6000 Depository Institutions.

Operating Locations
Bryn Mawr Trust Co. (PA--Havertown, Poole, Wayne)

Nonmonetary Support
Note: Meeting Rooms

Giving Contact
Joe Smith, Vice President
801 Lancaster Ave.
Bryn Mawr, PA 19010
Phone: (610)525-1700
Fax: (610)520-7278
E-mail: joesmith@bmtc.com

Description
Organization Type: Corporate Giving Program
Giving Locations: headquarters area only.
Grant Types: Operating Expenses, Scholarship.

Financial Summary
Total Giving: $72,000 (1999); $43,000 (1998); $43,000 (1997)

Typical Recipients
Arts & Humanities: Arts Associations & Councils, Arts Centers, Arts Festivals, Arts Funds, Arts Institutes, Community Arts, Arts & Humanities-General, Historic Preservation, Libraries, Museums/Galleries, Music, Opera, Performing Arts, Theater
Civic & Public Affairs: African American Affairs, Botanical Gardens/Parks, Business/Free Enterprise, Chambers of Commerce, Civil Rights, Community Foundations, Economic Development, Civic & Public Affairs-General, Housing, Inner-City Development, Municipalities/Towns, Parades/Festivals, Professional & Trade Associations, Zoos/Aquariums
Education: Arts/Humanities Education, Colleges & Universities, Education-General
Environment: Air/Water Quality, Environment-General, Resource Conservation
Health: Arthritis, Cancer, Children's Health/Hospitals, Clinics/Medical Centers, Emergency/Ambulance Services, Health-General, Geriatric Health, Heart, Home-Care Services, Hospices, Hospitals, Long-Term Care, Nursing Services, Prenatal Health Issues, Preventive Medicine/Wellness Organizations
Social Services: Community Centers, Community Service Organizations, Counseling, Day Care, Food/Clothing Distribution, Recreation & Athletics, Senior Services, Shelters/Homelessness, Social Services-General, United Funds/United Ways, Volunteer Services, YMCA/YWCA/YMHA/YWHA

Application Procedures
Initial Contact: Send a brief letter of inquiry.
Application Requirements: Include a description of organization, amount requested, purpose of funds sought, recently audited financial statement, and proof of tax-exempt status.
Deadlines: None.

Restrictions
Does not support individuals, religious organizations for sectarian purposes, political or lobbying groups, or organizations outside operating areas.

Corporate Officials
Joseph W. Rebl: senior vice president financeeo PRIM CORP EMPL senior vice president finance: Bryn Mawr Trust Co.
Robert L. Stevens: chairman, president, chief executive officer B 1937. PRIM CORP EMPL chairman, president, chief executive officer: Bryn Mawr Trust Co. ADD CORP EMPL president: Bryn Mawr Bank Corp.

Grants Analysis
Typical Range: $100 to $1,000

CAROL FRANC BUCK FOUNDATION

Giving Contact
Marya A. Beam, Administrative Assistant
PO Box 6085
Incline Village, NV 89450
Phone: (775)831-6366
Fax: (775)831-8655

Description
Founded: 1979
EIN: 880163505
Organization Type: Private Foundation
Giving Locations: Western US.
Grant Types: Endowment, General Support, Multiyear/Continuing Support, Project.

Donor Information
Founder: Carol S. Sells, John E. Sells

Financial Summary
Total Giving: $805,700 (fiscal year ending November 30, 2001); $735,450 (fiscal 2000); $735,450 (fiscal 1999)
Assets: $15,230,142 (fiscal 2001); $16,147,726 (fiscal 2000); $16,147,726 (fiscal 1999)
Gifts Received: $1,016,287 (fiscal 1994). Note: In fiscal 1994, contributions were received from Carol Plummer.

Typical Recipients
Arts & Humanities: Arts Associations & Councils, Arts Centers, Arts Funds, Arts Institutes, Arts Outreach, Ballet, Dance, Arts & Humanities-General, History & Archaeology, Museums/Galleries, Music, Opera, Performing Arts, Public Broadcasting, Theater, Visual Arts
Civic & Public Affairs: Civic & Public Affairs-General, Urban & Community Affairs
Education: Arts/Humanities Education, Colleges & Universities, Public Education (Precollege), Secondary Education (Public)

Application Procedures
Initial Contact: Telephone foundation or send brief letter of inquiry.
Deadlines: June 1 and December 1.
Review Process: Board meets in January, April, July, and October. Decisions are made within three months.
Evaluative Criteria: Prefer applications from visual and performing arts organizations or for education in the arts.

Restrictions
Does not support individuals or provide funds for deficit financing, land acquisition, renovations, scholarships, fellowships, or loans.

Foundation Officials
Carol F. Buck: trustee
Christian P. Erdman: trustee
Helen J. O'Hanlon: trustee

Grants Analysis
Disclosure Period: fiscal year ending November 30, 2001
Total Grants: $805,700
Number of Grants: 30
Average Grant: $16,878*
Highest Grant: $125,000
Lowest Grant: $1,000
Typical Range: $10,000 to $25,000
***Note:** Average grant excludes three highest grants ($350,000).

Recent Grants
Note: Grants derived from fiscal 2000 Form 990.

General
200,000	San Francisco Opera, San Francisco, CA -- streetcar named desire
125,000	Seattle Opera, Seattle, WA
100,000	Houston Grand Opera, Houston, TX -- flying Dutchman
50,000	San Francisco Symphony, San Francisco, CA -- concert season
39,500	Nevada Festival Ballet, Reno, NV -- underwrite live orchestra nutcracker ballet
25,000	Santa Fe Opera, Santa Fe, NM
25,000	Utah Opera, Salt Lake City, UT -- merry widow
21,000	Music in the Mountains, Nevada City, CA -- concert season
20,000	Reno Chamber Orchestra, Reno, NV
15,000	Children's Museum of Northern Nevada, Carson City, NV -- youth education program

FRANK H. AND EVA B. BUCK FOUNDATION

Giving Contact
Kathy Hazen, Executive Director
PO Box 5610
Vacaville, CA 95696-5610
Phone: (760)446-7700

Description
Founded: 1989
EIN: 770233870
Organization Type: Private Foundation
Giving Locations: CA: Contra Cos County, Napa County, Sacramento County, San Joaquin County, Solano County, Yolo County
Grant Types: Scholarship.

Donor Information
Founder: Robert B. Buck

Financial Summary
Total Giving: $2,051,200 (fiscal year ending March 31, 2000); $1,818,627 (fiscal 1999); $1,932,730 (fiscal 1998)
Giving Analysis: Giving for fiscal 2000 includes: foundation grants to United Way ($1,010); foundation gifts to individuals ($1,892,050) fiscal 1999: foundation scholarships ($1,814,337)
Assets: $72,066,817 (fiscal 2000); $60,674,488 (fiscal 1999); $48,696,853 (fiscal 1997)
Gifts Received: $12,432 (fiscal 1996); $3,616,157 (fiscal 1995); $2,095,900 (fiscal 1994)

Typical Recipients
Arts & Humanities: Libraries, Museums/Galleries
Civic & Public Affairs: Chambers of Commerce, Parades/Festivals
Education: Colleges & Universities, Elementary Education (Public), Education-General, Public Education (Precollege), Secondary Education (Public)
Health: Health Organizations
Social Services: Child Welfare, Community Service Organizations, Social Services-General, Special Olympics, United Funds/United Ways

Application Procedures
Initial Contact: Submit application, teacher's assessment, and parental authorization for release of school records.
Deadlines: December 15.

Restrictions

Additional Information
Provides scholarships to students in the third congressional district of CA.
Publications: Application Form

Foundation Officials
Carol Buck: president
Paul Buck: director
Walter Buck: secretary
Christian P. Erdman: treasurer
Kathy Hazen: executive director
Stacey Morris: director

Grants Analysis
Disclosure Period: fiscal year ending March 31, 2000
Total Grants: $158,140*
Number of Grants: 21
Average Grant: $1,352*
Highest Grant: $131,000
Typical Range: $1,000 to $3,000
***Note:** Giving excludes scholarships to individuals totaling $1,892,051 and United Way. Average grant excludes highest grant.

Recent Grants
Note: Grants derived from 2000 Form 990.

General
131,100	Vacaville Unified School District, Vacaville, CA
16,450	Solano Community Foundation, Vacaville, CA
2,000	Vacaville Century Committee, Vacaville, CA
1,265	Northbay Health Care Foundation, Fairfield, CA
1,010	United Way of the Bay Area, San Francisco, CA
1,000	Festival of Trees, Vacaville, CA
1,000	Vaca High School, Vacaville, CA
1,000	Vacaville Museum, Vacaville, CA
1,000	Vanden Sober Grad Nite, Fairfield, CA
1,000	Will C. Wood Grad Nite, Vacaville, CA

BUCKLEY & SPERLING, INC.

Company Headquarters
347 25th St.
Santa Monica, CA 90402

Company Description
SIC(s): 8100 Legal Services.

Buckley & Sperling Law Firm Foundation

Giving Contact
George E. Sperling, Jr., Senior Partner
347 25th St.
Santa Monica, CA 90402
Phone: (310)393-6905

Description
Founded: 1983
EIN: 770010122
Organization Type: Corporate Foundation
Giving Locations: headquarters area only.
Grant Types: General Support.

Donor Information
Founder: Dennis L. Buckley, Buckley & Sperling, George E. Sperling, Jr., Elizabeth Sperling.

Financial Summary
Total Giving: $6,371 (2000); $4,445 (1999); $4,930 (1998). Note: 1997 Giving includes United Way ($100).
Giving Analysis: Giving for 2000 includes: foundation grants to United Way ($100); 1999: foundation grants to United Way ($100) foundation ($4,345)
Assets: $409 (2000); $205 (1999); $4,126 (1998)
Gifts Received: $7,000 (2000); $5,136 (1999); $5,450 (1998). Note: In 1995, contributions were received from Buckley & Sperling ($2,000) and George E. Sperling, Jr. ($4,000).

Typical Recipients
Arts & Humanities: Libraries, Museums/Galleries, Public Broadcasting, Theater
Civic & Public Affairs: Clubs, Civic & Public Affairs-General, Hispanic Affairs, Housing, Legal Aid, Zoos/Aquariums
Education: Colleges & Universities, Education Funds, Elementary Education (Public), Private Education (Precollege), Secondary Education (Private), Special Education, Student Aid
Health: Alzheimers Disease, Arthritis, Cancer, Clinics/Medical Centers, Emergency/Ambulance Services, Heart, Hospices, Hospitals, Kidney, Medical

Research, Multiple Sclerosis, Single-Disease Health Associations
International: Health Care/Hospitals, Human Rights, International Environmental Issues, International Relief Efforts
Religion: Bible Study/Translation, Churches, Ministries, Religious Welfare
Social Services: Community Service Organizations, Day Care, Homes, People with Disabilities, Senior Services, Shelters/Homelessness, United Funds/United Ways, Veterans, YMCA/YWCA/YMHA/YWHA

Application Procedures

Initial Contact: Send letter of inquiry to foundation president.
Application Requirements: Include a description of organization, amount requested, purpose of funds sought, and proof of tax-exempt status.
Deadlines: None.

Restrictions

Grants are not made to individuals.

Corporate Officials

George E. Sperling, Jr.: senior, partner, president B Philadelphia, PA February 05, 1915. ED Pennsylvania State College AB (1936); Pennsylvania State College MA (1937); University of Michigan JD (1940). PRIM CORP EMPL senior, partner, president: Buckley & Sperling. NONPR AFFIL chairman: Wilshire YMCA; member: Wisconsin Bar Association; member president council: San Francisco Theological Seminary; president: Clara Schmidt Foundation; member: Ohio Bar Association; member: Pennsylvania State College Alumni Association Southern California; member: Navy League; member: Kiwanis; member: Michigan Bar Association; trustee: Bel Air Town & Country School; member: California Bar Association. CLUB AFFIL Riviera Country Club; Toastmasters Club; Presidents Club.

Foundation Officials

Mary E. Phelps: secretary
George E. Sperling, Jr.: president (see above)

Grants Analysis

Disclosure Period: calendar year ending 2000
Total Grants: $6,271*
Number of Grants: 47
Average Grant: $133
Highest Grant: $825
Lowest Grant: $25
Typical Range: $50 to $300
*Note: Giving excludes United Way.

Recent Grants

Note: Grants derived from 1999 Form 990.

General

320	American Heart Institute, Los Angeles, CA
300	Alzheimer's Association, Los Angeles, CA
300	Habitat for Humanity, Los Angeles, CA
300	Los Angeles Mission, Los Angeles, CA
250	Terra Rosa Charter School, Los Angeles, CA
200	American Red Cross, Los Angeles, CA
200	CARE, Los Angeles, CA
200	Greenpeace, Los Angeles, CA
100	Amnesty International, Los Angeles, CA
100	Covenant House, Los Angeles, CA

BUCYRUS INTERNATIONAL, INC.

Company Headquarters

1100 Milwaukee Avenue
South Milwaukee, WI 53172
Web: http://www.bucyrus.com

Company Description

Employees: 1,166
SIC(s): 3532 Mining Machinery, 3533 Oil & Gas Field Machinery.

Operating Locations

Bucyrus-Erie Co. (CA--City of Industry; ND--Jamestown; WI--Milwaukee)

Bucyrus-Erie Foundation

Giving Contact

Carol Wilson, Scholarship Administrator
1020 N. Broadway
Milwaukee, WI 53202
Phone: (414)272-5805
Fax: (414)290-7344
E-mail: cwilson@greatermkefdn.org

Description

EIN: 396075537
Organization Type: Corporate Foundation
Giving Locations: WI: Milwaukee County, Milwaukee South Milwaukee
Grant Types: Capital, Employee Matching Gifts, General Support, Project.
Note: Matching gifts are for education, health and social services, and the arts.

Financial Summary

Total Giving: $889,765 (2001); $870,846 (2000); $914,631 (1999). Note: Contributes through foundation only.
Giving Analysis: Giving for 2000 includes: foundation scholarships ($66,375); foundation grants to United Way ($98,387); foundation ($706,084); 1997: foundation scholarships ($55,743); foundation matching gifts ($65,196); foundation grants to United Way ($109,840) foundation ($547,943)
Assets: $15,977,418 (2001); $17,039,924 (2000); $18,291,386 (1999)

Typical Recipients

Arts & Humanities: Arts Associations & Councils, Arts Funds, Ballet, Dance, Historic Preservation, Libraries, Museums/Galleries, Music, Opera, Performing Arts, Public Broadcasting, Theater
Civic & Public Affairs: African American Affairs, Asian American Affairs, Business/Free Enterprise, Economic Development, Economic Policy, Employment/Job Training, Hispanic Affairs, Housing, Municipalities/Towns, Native American Affairs, Parades/Festivals, Professional & Trade Associations, Public Policy, Safety, Urban & Community Affairs, Zoos/Aquariums
Education: Business Education, Colleges & Universities, Community & Junior Colleges, Economic Education, Education Funds, Elementary Education (Private), Engineering/Technological Education, Education-General, Gifted & Talented Programs, Literacy, Medical Education, Minority Education, Private Education (Precollege), Public Education (Precollege), Religious Education, Science/Mathematics Education, Student Aid
Environment: Energy, Resource Conservation
Health: Children's Health/Hospitals, Clinics/Medical Centers, Health Organizations, Hospitals, Long-Term Care, Medical Rehabilitation, Medical Research, Single-Disease Health Associations
International: Foreign Arts Organizations
Religion: Religious Welfare
Social Services: Big Brother/Big Sister, Child Welfare, Community Centers, Community Service Organizations, Day Care, Domestic Violence, Family Services, Food/Clothing Distribution, Homes, People with Disabilities, Recreation & Athletics, Scouts, Senior Services, Shelters/Homelessness, Substance Abuse, United Funds/United Ways, YMCA/YWCA/YMHA/YWHA, Youth Organizations

Application Procedures

Initial Contact: Send a brief outline on organization's letterhead.
Application Requirements: Include a description of organization; amount requested; purpose of funds sought; size and characteristics of target population; recently audited financial statement; most recent IRS Form 990; and proof of tax-exempt status under IRS code 501(c)(3).
Deadlines: None.
Review Process: Staff reviews proposal, investigates agencies (sometimes involving site visits), evaluates budgetary requirements, and makes recommendations to the board of directors; directors make all final funding decisions.
Decision Notification: Decisions generally are made within three months from the time a proposal is received.
Notes: Contact foundation for complete guidelines before submitting a full proposal.

Restrictions

Does not give to individuals, purchase tickets or tables at dinners or other functions, or purchase goodwill advertising.
Generally does not make more than one grant per fiscal year to any one organization.
Company does not make contributions of equipment or supplies.

Additional Information

Scholarship eligibility requirements are as follows: Applicants must be children or legal wards of active full-time employees of Bucyrus-Erie Co. and any of its divisions or domestic subsidiaries; scholarship recipients must be enrolled in an accredited university or college; children and legal wards of officers and directors of Bucyrus-Erie Co. and any of its divisions or domestic subsidiaries are ineligible. Contact the foundation for more information and for application forms. The Milwaukee Foundation manages the Bucyrus Foundation for the company.
Grants are focused in Milwaukee County only; plant locations of the Bucyrus International companies may also contribute to organizations.
Specific guidelines determine eligibility under matching programs.
Grant inquiries should be directed to the grants manager at (414)272-5805.
Publications: Application Guidelines

Corporate Officials

Norbert J. Verville: vice president, chief financial officer, treasurer, director PRIM CORP EMPL vice president, chief financial officer, treasurer, director: Bucyrus-Erie Co.
William Bergford Winter: president B LaCrosse, WI 1928. ED University of Wisconsin (1951). PRIM CORP EMPL president: Bucyrus-Erie Co. CORP AFFIL director: Wisconsin Gas Co.; director: WICOR Inc. NONPR AFFIL member executive board: YMCA Metropolitan Milwaukee. CLUB AFFIL University Club; Western Racquet Club; Milwaukee Country Club.

Foundation Officials

Sigfredo Guiterrez: secretary, manager, trustee
Mary Ann W. LaBahn: director
Vincent L. Martin: director
Donald E. Porter: director
Brenton H. Rupple: director B Waukesha, WI 1924. ED University of Wisconsin (1948). CORP AFFIL director: Roundy's Inc.
Norbert J. Verville: treasurer (see above)
William Bergford Winter: chairman, president, director (see above)

Grants Analysis

Disclosure Period: calendar year ending 2001
Total Grants: $690,768*
Number of Grants: 361

Average Grant: $1,913
Highest Grant: $19,500
Lowest Grant: $50
Typical Range: $100 to $10,000
***Note:** Giving excludes United Way and scholarships.

Recent Grants

Note: Grants derived from 2000 Form 990.

General

27,250	United Way, Milwaukee, WI -- operating
27,250	United Way, Milwaukee, WI -- operating
27,250	United Way, Milwaukee, WI -- operating
27,250	United Way, Milwaukee, WI -- operating
25,000	YMCA South Shore Branch, Cudahy, WI
19,500	United Performing Arts Fund, Milwaukee, WI
19,500	United Performing Arts Fund, Milwaukee, WI
19,500	United Performing Arts Fund, Milwaukee, WI
19,500	United Performing Arts Fund, Milwaukee, WI
14,921	United Way, Milwaukee, WI -- operating

TEMPLE HOYNE BUELL FOUNDATION

Giving Contact

Susan J. Steele, Executive Director
1666 South University Boulevard, Suite B
Denver, CO 80210
Phone: (303)744-1688
Fax: (303)744-1601
E-mail: ssteele@buellfoundation.org
Web: http://www.buellfoundation.org

Description

Founded: 1962
EIN: 846037604
Organization Type: Family Foundation
Giving Locations: CO
Grant Types: Capital, General Support, Operating Expenses, Project.
Note: The foundation provides technical assistance.

Donor Information

Founder: Incorporated in 1962 by the late Temple Hoyne Buell .

Financial Summary

Total Giving: $4,500,000 (fiscal year ending June 30, 2003 approx); $4,793,350 (fiscal 2002); $4,418,993 (fiscal 2001)
Giving Analysis: Giving for fiscal 2000 includes: foundation grants to United Way ($75,000); foundation scholarships ($152,860) fiscal 1999: foundation scholarships ($70,000)
Assets: $111,000,000 (fiscal 2003 approx); $111,463,748 (fiscal 2002); $110,266,805 (fiscal 2000)
Gifts Received: $358,000 (fiscal 1996); $1,478 (fiscal 1995); $94,505 (fiscal 1994)

Typical Recipients

Arts & Humanities: Arts Centers, Arts Funds, Arts Outreach, Historic Preservation, Libraries, Museums/ Galleries, Music, Performing Arts, Theater
Civic & Public Affairs: African American Affairs, Botanical Gardens/Parks, Business/Free Enterprise, Chambers of Commerce, Clubs, Economic Development, Civic & Public Affairs-General, Hispanic Affairs, Housing, Municipalities/Towns, Native American Affairs, Nonprofit Management, Urban & Community Affairs, Women's Affairs, Zoos/Aquariums
Education: Afterschool/Enrichment Programs, Arts/ Humanities Education, Business Education, Colleges & Universities, Education Funds, Elementary

Education (Public), Engineering/Technological Education, Education-General, Gifted & Talented Programs, Leadership Training, Literacy, Minority Education, Preschool Education, Private Education (Precollege), Public Education (Precollege), Science/ Mathematics Education, Special Education, Student Aid
Health: Cancer, Children's Health/Hospitals, Diabetes, Health Organizations, Heart, Hospitals, Kidney, Mental Health, Prenatal Health Issues, Preventive Medicine/Wellness Organizations, Public Health, Research/Studies Institutes, Single-Disease Health Associations, Speech & Hearing
International: Foreign Educational Institutions
Religion: Churches, Ministries, Religious Organizations, Religious Welfare
Social Services: Camps, Child Welfare, Community Service Organizations, Counseling, Crime Prevention, Day Care, Domestic Violence, Family Planning, Family Services, Food/Clothing Distribution, People with Disabilities, Shelters/Homelessness, United Funds/United Ways, Veterans, YMCA/YWCA/YMHA/ YWHA, Youth Organizations

Application Procedures

Initial Contact: The Foundation request that applicants call the office to receive the appropriate forms. The Foundation uses the Common Grant Application form and asks the applicants to make sure the "Purpose of Grant" fits the foundation's guidelines and that the applicants indicate their "focus area".
Application Requirements: For requests of $5,000 and under, include: a limited version of the Common Grant Application; a letter of intent describing the organization and purpose of request; Summary of Applicant Organization (attached form); balance sheet and income and expense statement for previous fiscal year; program budget or organization's budget (if requesting general support); 501(c)(3) determination letter; anti-discrimination statement; and list of board of directors.
For request over $5,000 submit a Full Common Grant Application with described attachments.
Deadlines: The first business day of January, May and September by 5:00 p.m.
Notes: Do not use bulky notebooks, binders, or include videotapes.

Restrictions

Grants are not made to or for the following: individuals; to cover past operating expenses; the retirement of debt; testimonial dinners; events, annual campaigns, membership drives or conferences; loans; litigation; sectarian programs promoting religion; legislative lobbying or support of political candidates; international organizations; medical programs; multi-year awards; or endowments. No grant request will be considered from an organization unless that organization is determined to be tax-exempt under 501(c)(3) of the Internal Revenue Code and "not a private foundation" under section 509(a) of the Code.

Additional Information

Publications: Application Form; Guidelines; Annual Report

Foundation Officials

Arthur H. Bosworth, II: trustee
Merle Catherine Chambers: trustee B Chicago, IL 1946. ED University of California at Berkeley BA (1968); University of California, San Francisco JD (1977); University of Denver LLM (1984). PRIM CORP EMPL president, chief executive officer: Axem Resources Inc. CORP AFFIL chairman executive committee: Clipper Express Co. NONPR AFFIL member: Colorado Women's Bar Association; director: Women Foundations; member: California Bar Association; member: Colorado Bar Association; director: 1066 Foundation; member: American Bar Association.
Thomas J. Curnes: treasurer, trustee

Jerome L. Lindberg: vice president, trustee
Daniel Lee Ritchie: president, trustee B Springfield, IL 1931. ED Harvard University BA (1954); Harvard University MBA (1956). PRIM NONPR EMPL chancellor: University of Denver. CORP AFFIL owner: Rancho Cielo; owner: Grand River Ranch. NONPR AFFIL chancellor: Colorado Seminary.
Hon. Luis Dario Rovira: trustee, sociology B San Juan, PR 1923. ED University of Colorado BA (1948); University of Colorado LLB (1950). NONPR AFFIL trustee: Denver Foundation; member: Phi Alpha Delta; member: Denver Bar Association; member: Colorado Association Retarded Children; member: Colorado Bar Association; member: American Bar Association; director: Childrens Hospital; member: Alpha Tau Omega. CLUB AFFIL Athletic Club; Denver Country Club.
Susan J. Steele: acting executive director

Grants Analysis

Disclosure Period: fiscal year ending June 30, 2001
Total Grants: $4,418,993*
Number of Grants: 224
Average Grant: $19,728
Highest Grant: $250,000
Lowest Grant: $65
Typical Range: $10,000 to $50,000
***Note:** Grants analysis provided by foundation.

Recent Grants

Note: Grants derived from fiscal 2000 Form 990.

General

500,000	Kidstart Inc., Denver, CO -- expansion into Mesa County
145,000	City and County of Denver, Denver, CO -- head start program
130,000	Durango 4-C Council, Inc., Durango, CO -- early childhood human resource and professional training project
106,758	Rocky Mountain S.E.R/Jobs for Progress, Inc, Denver, CO -- Denver Head Start Career and Professional Development
100,000	Cherokee Ranch and Castle Foundation, Sedalia, CO
75,000	Mile High United Way, Denver, CO -- Ready to Succeed Initiative
74,000	Family Visitor Program, Glenwood Springs, CO -- Family Empowerment Team
70,000	Baca County School District Region 4, Springfield, CO -- capital campaign
65,000	Colorado Children's Campaign, Denver, CO
59,440	Clayton Foundation, Denver, CO -- Clayton-Buell Professional Development Project

BUHL FOUNDATION (PA)

Giving Contact

Doreen E. Boyce, President
650 Smithfield St., Suite 2300
Pittsburgh, PA 15222
Phone: (412)566-2711
Fax: (412)566-2714
E-mail: buhl@buhlfoundation.org

Description

Founded: 1927
EIN: 250378910
Organization Type: General Purpose Foundation
Giving Locations: PA: Pittsburgh metropolitan area
Grant Types: Award, Seed Money.

Donor Information

Founder: The Buhls, a German merchant family for nine generations, immigrated to Zelienople, PA, around 1800. The Buhls established a legacy of concerned citizenship in Pennsylvania, as evidenced by their last heir, Henry Buhl Jr. Trained as a merchant, he and his friend, Russell H. Boggs, established a profitable dry goods store in 1869. As he neared the end of his life, Mr. Buhl considered the future of his fortune. Because he had no children or other direct heirs, he established the Buhl Foundation as a memorial to his wife, Louise C. Buhl, and dedicated it to "charitable, educational, and public uses and purposes," to benefit "the citizens of the City of Pittsburgh and the County of Allegheny, Pennsylvania" first and foremost where he lived and "engaged in business activities and formed friendships." Henry Buhl, Jr., died in 1927.

Financial Summary

Total Giving: $2,648,106 (fiscal year ending June 30, 2002); $4,396,118 (fiscal 2001); $2,579,150 (fiscal 1999 approx)

Giving Analysis: Giving for fiscal 2001 includes: foundation matching gifts ($23,336); fiscal 1999: foundation grants to United Way ($1,000); fiscal 1998: foundation grants to United Way ($221,000)

Assets: $72,319,732 (fiscal 2002 approx); $80,664,699 (fiscal 2001); $4,269,428 (fiscal 2000)

Typical Recipients

Arts & Humanities: Arts Funds, Arts Outreach, Ballet, Film & Video, Arts & Humanities-General, Historic Preservation, History & Archaeology, Libraries, Literary Arts, Museums/Galleries, Music, Opera, Performing Arts, Public Broadcasting, Theater

Civic & Public Affairs: African American Affairs, Business/Free Enterprise, Economic Development, Economic Policy, Employment/Job Training, Civic & Public Affairs-General, Housing, Minority Business, Nonprofit Management, Philanthropic Organizations, Public Policy, Urban & Community Affairs, Women's Affairs

Education: Arts/Humanities Education, Business Education, Colleges & Universities, Community & Junior Colleges, Education Associations, Education Funds, Education Reform, Elementary Education (Private), Environmental Education, Faculty Development, Education-General, Gifted & Talented Programs, Leadership Training, Literacy, Minority Education, Preschool Education, Private Education (Precollege), Public Education (Precollege), School Volunteerism, Science/Mathematics Education, Secondary Education (Private), Secondary Education (Public), Social Sciences Education, Special Education, Vocational & Technical Education

Environment: Environment-General, Wildlife Protection

Health: Cancer, Children's Health/Hospitals, Emergency/Ambulance Services, Health Organizations, Heart, Hospitals, Mental Health, Nursing Services

Religion: Ministries, Religious Organizations, Religious Welfare

Science: Observatories & Planetariums, Scientific Centers & Institutes

Social Services: At-Risk Youth, Child Abuse, Child Welfare, Community Service Organizations, Crime Prevention, Day Care, Delinquency & Criminal Rehabilitation, Food/Clothing Distribution, People with Disabilities, Recreation & Athletics, Scouts, Sexual Abuse, Social Services-General, Substance Abuse, YMCA/YWCA/YMHA/YWHA, Youth Organizations

Application Procedures

Initial Contact: Send a letter of inquiry to the president. A formal proposal will be requested if the foundation is interested.

Application Requirements: Statement of objectives for the project and the means by which they will be achieved, including staff qualifications and a timetable; proof of need for the project, its uniqueness in comparison to other work being done in a similar area, and the result anticipated; documentation of procedures for evaluation of anticipated results; itemized budget indicating resources required for the project, other possible funding sources, and the amount requested of them; general information about the applying agency including its name, address, telephone numb er, contact person, executive director, members of the board, brief history, mission, tax-exempt status, and ability to initiate and sustain project; and a statement that the proposal has been approved for submission to the foundation by the executive director of the applying organization.

Deadlines: None. Organizations should submit proposals at least two months before consideration may be given by the board.

Review Process: If the foundation is interested in the proposed project, an interview will be scheduled. Grant decisions are made at monthly board meetings.

Restrictions

Grants generally are not made for building funds, overhead costs, accumulated deficits, ordinary operating budgets, fundraising campaigns, loans, scholarships, fellowships, nationally funded organized groups, conferences, seminars (unless grant-related), propaganda, sectarian religious activities, or lobbying. Grants are not made to other foundations or to individuals.

Additional Information

Grant recipients will be expected to confer with the foundation on schedules of grant payments, progress reports on program achievements, and an evaluation upon completion of the program.

Publications: Annual Report; Program Guidelines

Foundation Officials

Dr. Doreen Elizabeth Boyce: president B Antofagasta, Chile 1934. ED Oxford University BA (1956); Oxford University MA (1960); University of Pittsburgh PhD (1983); Westminster College B Humane Lit (1986); Washington & Jefferson College DHL (1993). PRIM NONPR EMPL president: Buhl Foundation. CORP AFFIL director: Orbeco Analytical Services, Inc.; director: Duquesne Light Co.; director: Microbac Laboratories Inc.; director: Dollar Bank, FSB; director: DQE Inc. NONPR AFFIL director: Research for Better School; member appeals committee: Somerville College (Oxford, England); member: Grantmakers of Western Pennsylvania; member: International Womens Forum; director: Council Independent Colleges; trustee: Franklin & Marshall College; member: American Economic Association; trustee: Carnegie Science Center; member: American Association Higher Education. CLUB AFFIL member: Duquesne Club.

Francis B. Nimick, Jr.: chairman board directors ED Princeton University (1939); Harvard University (1941). NONPR AFFIL chairman: Allegheny General Hospital; vice president, director: W Pennsylvania School Deaf.

William H. Rea: vchairman B Pittsburgh, PA 1912. PRIM CORP EMPL director: Colt Industries Inc.

Jean A. Robinson: vice chairman

Katharina E. Schumacher: secretary, treasurer ED New York University (1986).

Albert Clarence Van Dusen: vchairman B Tampa, FL August 30, 1915. ED University of Florida BS (1937); University of Florida AM (1938); Northwestern University PhD (1942). CORP AFFIL director: Dollar Bank, FSB. NONPR AFFIL member: W Pennsylvania Council Economic Education; director: YMCA Pittsburgh; member: Sigma Xi; vice chancellor emeritus: University Pittsburgh; member: Pittsburgh Psychological Association; member: Professional School World Affairs Comm; vice chairman board trustees: Pittsburgh History & Landmarks Foundation; member: Pennsylvania Public Television Network Committee; member: Phi Beta Kappa; vice chancellor emeritus, professor emeritus: Northwestern University; fellow: Pennsylvania Psychological Association; fellow: International Foundation Social Economic Development; member: Midwest Psychological Association; member: International Association School Institute Administration; member: Friends Art Pittsburgh Schools; member: International Association Applied Psychology; member: Beta Theta Pi; member: Eastern Psychological Association; member: Association Deans Dir Summer Sessions; member: Beta Gamma Sigma; fellow: American Psychological Society; member: American Personal Guidance Association; fellow: American Psychological Association; member: American College Public Relations Association; director: American Japan Society Pittsburgh. CLUB AFFIL University Pittsburgh Club; Duquesne Club.

Grants Analysis

Disclosure Period: fiscal year ending June 30, 2001

Total Grants: $4,372,782*

Number of Grants: 87

Average Grant: $45,032*

Highest Grant: $500,000

Lowest Grant: $1,000

Typical Range: $20,000 to $100,000

*Note: Giving excludes matching gifts. Average grant figure excludes highest grant.

Recent Grants

Note: Grants derived from fiscal 2000 Form 990.

Library-Related

250,000   Carnegie Library of Pittsburgh, Pittsburgh, PA -- for support of customer research component of "Agenda for Change: Planning for the Future"

131,050   La Roche College, Pittsburgh, PA -- for support of integrated online library system for the college library

General

500,000   National Aviary in Pittsburgh, Washington, DC -- support of Phase II Expansion: The Ends of the Earth

200,000   Carnegie Institute Science Center, Pittsburgh, PA -- for support of Mr. Rogers' Neighborhood Planetarium Show

200,000   Historical Society of Western Pennsylvania, Pittsburgh, PA -- for support of Visitor Center and Pedestrian Wayfinder

200,000   Pittsburgh Foundation, Pittsburgh, PA -- for support of Allegheny County Department of Human Services Data Warehouse

178,000   WQED Pittsburgh, Pittsburgh, PA -- for support of "Something About Oakland"

173,375   Mount Aloysius College, Cresson, PA -- for support in development of interactive classroom

160,000   Robert Morris College, Coraopolis, PA -- for support of computer integrated engineering enterprise

150,000   Board of Education School District of Pittsburgh, Pittsburgh, PA -- support of PRIME Initiative, over three years - payable from the Frick Educational Fund

150,000   Manchester Youth Development, Pittsburgh, PA -- for support of expansion of the center

150,000   Western Pennsylvania School for the Deaf, Pittsburgh, PA -- for support of curricular integration through technology

BUILDING 19 FOUNDATION

Giving Contact

Les MacDonald, Director
319 Lincoln St.
Hingham, MA 02043-1600
Phone: (781)749-6900

Description

Founded: 1990
EIN: 043064072
Organization Type: Private Foundation
Grant Types: Capital, Scholarship.

Donor Information

Founder: Established in 1990 by Building 19, Inc.; S & S Domestic, Inc.; IFC, Inc.; and Paperworks 19, Inc.

Financial Summary

Total Giving: $121,118 (2001); $109,376 (1999); $114,131 (1998)
Assets: $1,027,944 (2001); $1,167,608 (1999); $1,199,434 (1998)
Gifts Received: $170,182 (1994); $187,000 (1993); $213,800 (1992). Note: In 1994, contributions were received from Building 19 Inc. ($83,182), International Floorcrafts ($26,400), Paperworks 19 Inc. ($19,200), and Furniture 19 ($10,800); seven other donors made contributions of $8,400 or less each.

Typical Recipients

Arts & Humanities: Arts Centers, Libraries, Museums/Galleries, Opera
Civic & Public Affairs: Clubs, Economic Development, Civic & Public Affairs-General, Urban & Community Affairs, Zoos/Aquariums
Education: Colleges & Universities, Public Education (Precollege), Secondary Education (Public), Student Aid
Environment: Wildlife Protection
Health: AIDS/HIV, Cancer, Clinics/Medical Centers, Health Organizations, Hospices, Hospitals, Medical Rehabilitation, Mental Health, Multiple Sclerosis, Outpatient Health Care, Single-Disease Health Associations, Trauma Treatment
International: Foreign Educational Institutions, Missionary/Religious Activities
Religion: Churches, Jewish Causes
Science: Science Museums
Social Services: Animal Protection, At-Risk Youth, Community Centers, Community Service Organizations, Domestic Violence, Emergency Relief, Food/Clothing Distribution, Homes, People with Disabilities, Recreation & Athletics, Senior Services, Shelters/Homelessness, Special Olympics

Application Procedures

Initial Contact: Send a brief letter of inquiry.
Deadlines: None.

Foundation Officials

Brian Callum: director
Phyllis Devaney: director
Debra Elovitz: director
Elaine Elovitz: director
Gerald Elovitz: director

Grants Analysis

Disclosure Period: calendar year ending 2001
Total Grants: $121,118
Number of Grants: 332
Average Grant: $365
Highest Grant: $10,000
Lowest Grant: $25
Typical Range: $50 to $500

Recent Grants

Note: Grants derived from 2000 Form 990.

Library-Related

1,000	Hingham Public Library, Hingham, MA

General

26,827	Weymouth United Methodist
5,000	Dana Farber Cancer Institute, Boston, MA
2,500	Germaine Lawrence, Arlington, MA
2,000	Project Bread, Boston, MA
1,500	Anti-Defamation League
1,000	American Association Ben Gurion University
1,000	Friends of Beth Israel Deaconess Medical Center
1,000	Hebrew Rehabilitation Center, MA
1,000	Hingham High Baseball, Hingham, MA
1,000	Interbarth

BUNBURY CO., INC.

Giving Contact

Samuel W. Lambert III, Treasurer
2 Railroad Place
Hopewell, NJ 08525
Phone: (609)333-8800
Fax: (609)333-8900
E-mail: BunburyCo@aol.com
Web: http://www.bunburycompany.org

Description

Founded: 1952
EIN: 136066172
Organization Type: General Purpose Foundation
Giving Locations: , Burlington County, NJ , Camden County , Hunterdon County , Middlesex County , Monmouth County , Ocean County , Somerset County, Mercer County
Grant Types: Capital, Challenge, Endowment, General Support, Matching, Project, Seed Money.
Note: Also funds special initiatives.

Donor Information

Founder: Incorporated in New York in 1952 by the late Dean Mathey .

Financial Summary

Total Giving: $1,084,167 (2001); $1,044,333 (2000); $1,030,501 (1999)
Giving Analysis: Giving for 2001 includes: foundation grants to United Way ($1,000); 2000: foundation grants to United Way ($1,000); 1999: foundation grants to United Way ($1,000)
Assets: $24,045,158 (2001); $24,416,797 (2000); $25,422,308 (1999)

Typical Recipients

Arts & Humanities: Arts Associations & Councils, Arts Centers, Arts Outreach, Ballet, Dance, Historic Preservation, History & Archaeology, Libraries, Museums/Galleries, Music, Performing Arts, Public Broadcasting, Theater
Civic & Public Affairs: Botanical Gardens/Parks, Clubs, Community Foundations, Economic Development, Civic & Public Affairs-General, Hispanic Affairs, Housing, Law & Justice, Municipalities/Towns, Nonprofit Management, Philanthropic Organizations, Professional & Trade Associations, Public Policy, Rural Affairs, Safety, Urban & Community Affairs, Women's Affairs, Zoos/Aquariums
Education: Arts/Humanities Education, Colleges & Universities, Education Funds, Education Reform, Elementary Education (Public), Environmental Education, Education-General, Health & Physical Education, International Exchange, Literacy, Minority Education, Private Education (Precollege), Secondary Education (Public), Special Education, Student Aid, Vocational & Technical Education
Environment: Air/Water Quality, Forestry, Environment-General, Resource Conservation, Watershed
Health: AIDS/HIV, Cancer, Children's Health/Hospitals, Clinics/Medical Centers, Emergency/Ambulance Services, Hospitals, Medical Research, Mental Health, Nursing Services, Public Health
International: Foreign Educational Institutions, Health Care/Hospitals

Religion: Churches, Ministries, Religious Organizations, Religious Welfare
Science: Observatories & Planetariums, Science Museums
Social Services: Animal Protection, At-Risk Youth, Child Welfare, Community Centers, Community Service Organizations, Domestic Violence, Family Planning, Family Services, Food/Clothing Distribution, Homes, People with Disabilities, Recreation & Athletics, Senior Services, Shelters/Homelessness, Substance Abuse, YMCA/YWCA/YMHA/YWHA, Youth Organizations

Application Procedures

Initial Contact: Request guidelines from the foundation via a letter of inquiry or from the foundation's web site.
Application Requirements: Application packages must include seven copies of the following information in this order: complete standard Bunbury application form; cover letter signed by the applicant organization's executive director or project director; a one-page executive summary of the project (separate from the body of the proposal), including purpose of funds sought, goal, collaborative partners, total project cost, and amount requested; proposal narrative (three pages or less) that includes a brief history of the organization and its range of programs and activities, project description, goals, objectives, and timeline, collaborative partners and community support for the project, methods of measuring outcomes, and a plan to complete or sustain project funding, if applicable; profiles or resumes of project staff; lists of board of directors and institutional funding sources over $1,000; IRS 501(c)(3) determination letter or proof of public supported 509(a) status; and financial information including organization budget for current year, year-end figures for previous year, most recent audit, and detailed project budget for its complete duration.
Deadlines: Exact dates vary, but fall within the months of April, June, September, and December. Contact the foundation for this year's deadlines.
Review Process: Grants are reviewed by a joint committee of Bunbury and its sister foundation, the Windham Foundation.
Evaluative Criteria: Although several New Jersey counties are eligible to apply for grants, preference is given to applicants in Mercer County. The foundation reports that it is, "...particularly interested in innovative ideas that can be sustained over time or that can be replicated elsewhere. Collaborative efforts, demonstrating broad community support and the ability to impact positively the quality of life within the community, are highly encouraged."
"In making decisions, the Foundation will look to the accomplishments of the applicant organization, the stability of its financial base, the strength of its leadership, and the long-term viability of the program in question."
The Foundation uses the following four criteria to evaluate applications:
"Ability to impact positively the target area and audience; Significance and depth of project; Feasibility - ability to complete the project successfully, within a realistic time frame, and according to budgeted goals; Ability to measure and evaluate proposed outcomes."
Decision Notification: Applicants are notified of the foundation's decision by mail within 8-10 weeks of the submission deadline.

Restrictions

The foundation does not make grants to individuals, out-of-state organizations, or for building funds, fellowships, or loans.

Additional Information

The foundation is affiliated with the Windham Foundation in Grafton, VT.
Publications: Annual Report; Application Guidelines

Foundation Officials

Charles B. Atwater: director

James Richard Cogan: treasurer, director B Jersey City, NJ 1928. ED Yale University BA (1950); Columbia University LLB (1953). PRIM CORP EMPL partner: Walter Conston Alexander & Green PC. CORP AFFIL chairman board: Grafton Village Cheese Co. NONPR AFFIL trustee: Charlotte Palmer Phillips Foundation; chairman board trustees: Windham Foundation; member: New York County Lawyers Association; member: Association Bar New York City; director: Corporate Relief Widows & Children Clergymen; director: American Friends Plantin-Moretus Museum; member: American Bar Association; member: American College Trust & Estate Counsel. CLUB AFFIL Salmagundi Artists Club; Yale Club.

Samuel Waldron Lambert, III: president, trustee B New York, NY 1938. ED Yale University BA (1960); Harvard University LLB (1963). PRIM CORP EMPL partner: Drinker, Biddle & Reath. NONPR AFFIL member: New Jersey Bar Association; member: Princeton Bar Association; member: American Bar Association.

William McGuigan: assistant treasurer

Stephan A. Morse: director B 1947. PRIM CORP EMPL president, director: Old Tavern at Grafton Inc. ADD CORP EMPL president, administration, director: Grafton Village Cheese Co. CORP AFFIL director: United Bank; director: Vermont Finance Services.

Robert M. Olmsted: director

Barbara L. Ruppert: assistant secretary

Edward Joseph Toohey: president, director B Jersey City, NJ 1930. ED Yale University BA (1953). CORP AFFIL vice president: Old Tavern Grafton Inc. NONPR AFFIL director emeritus: New York City Ballet; vice chairman: Peddie School. CLUB AFFIL Yale Club; Sky Club; University Club; Canoe Brook Country Club; Georgetown Club.

Charles C. Townsend, Jr.: secretary, director PRIM CORP EMPL secretary: The Bunbury Co. CORP AFFIL director: HTI Voice Solutions Inc.; director: Project Orbis International; director: Cary Institutional PRPTS Inc.

William Bigelow Wright: director B Rutland, VT 1924. ED Princeton University AB (1950). NONPR AFFIL president: Princeton Alumni Association Vermont; member, vice president executive committee Class '47: Princeton University Alumni Council; trustee: Calvin Coolidge Memorial Foundation. CLUB AFFIL Ivy Club; Princeton Club.

Edward R. Zuccaro: director B New York, NY 1943. PRIM CORP EMPL partner: Zuccaro, Willis & Bent. CORP AFFIL clerk, director: Phelps Enterprises; clerk, director: Phelps Real Estate; clerk, director: Music Shop; vice president, secretary, director: Old Tavern Grafton Inc.; treasurer: Grafton Village Cheese Co.; clerk, director: Movie World; clerk, director: Dana Jewelry.

Grants Analysis

Disclosure Period: calendar year ending 2001
Total Grants: $1,084,167*
Number of Grants: 124
Average Grant: $8,743
Highest Grant: $60,000
Lowest Grant: $500
Typical Range: $1,000 to $5,000
*****Note:** Giving excludes United Way.

Recent Grants

Note: Grants derived from 2001 Form 990.

Library-Related

15,000	Lanpher Memorial Library
5,000	Huntington Public Library

General

60,000	Windham Foundation, Grafton, VT
50,000	Princeton Day School, Princeton, NJ
40,000	McCarter Theater for Performing Arts, Princeton, NJ
33,333	Princeton Scholarship Foundation, Princeton, NJ
33,333	Young Scholars Institute, Trenton, NJ
30,000	Princeton Academy of the Sacred Heart, Princeton, NJ
25,000	Home Front, Lawrenceville, NJ
25,000	Housing and Community Development Network, Washington, DC
25,000	Institute for Children with Cancer and Blood Disorders, New Brunswick, NJ
25,000	St. Johnsbury Academy, St. Johnsbury, VT

CHARLES E. BURCHFIELD FOUNDATION

Giving Contact

John P. Dee, Attorney
Blair & Roach LLP
2645 Sheridan Dr.
Tonawanda, NY 14150
Phone: (716)834-9181

Description

Founded: 1966
EIN: 166073522
Organization Type: Private Foundation
Giving Locations: CA; DE; NY
Grant Types: Capital, General Support, Multiyear/Continuing Support, Operating Expenses, Scholarship.

Donor Information

Founder: the late Charles E. Burchfield

Financial Summary

Total Giving: $540,600 (2001); $107,000 (2000); $56,700 (1999)
Assets: $2,498,042 (2001); $2,183,390 (2000); $2,248,974 (1999)
Gifts Received: $235,000 (1993). Note: In 1993, contributions were received in the form of paintings.

Typical Recipients

Arts & Humanities: Arts Centers, Arts Institutes, Arts & Humanities-General, History & Archaeology, Libraries, Museums/Galleries
Civic & Public Affairs: Civic & Public Affairs-General, Municipalities/Towns
Education: Arts/Humanities Education

Application Procedures

Initial Contact: Send a brief letter of inquiry; full proposal.
Application Requirements: Include a description of organization.
Deadlines: None.

Additional Information

Publications: Annual Report

Foundation Officials

C. Arthur Burchfield: president, director
Violet P. Burchfield: director
Sally R. Hill: vice president, director
Phyllis S. Mustain: director
Robert D. Mustain: secretary, director

Grants Analysis

Disclosure Period: calendar year ending 2001
Total Grants: $540,600
Number of Grants: 5
Highest Grant: $51,000
Lowest Grant: $1,000

Recent Grants

Note: Grants derived from 2001 Form 990.

General

51,000	Town of West Seneca, West Seneca, NY -- exhibition, recreation and education
20,000	Burchfield Homestead Society, Salem, OH -- exhibition
17,500	Burchfield Penney Art Center, Buffalo, NY -- for endowment, exhibition and restoration
1,100	Friends of Art Valparaiso University, Valparaiso, IN -- for memorial
1,000	Taconic Resources for Independence, Poughkeepsie, NY -- for exhibition

BURLINGTON INDUSTRIES, INC.

Company Headquarters

Greensboro, NC
Web: http://www.burlington.com

Company Description

Founded: 1923
Ticker: BRLG
Exchange: OTC
Revenue: US$933.3 million (2002)
Employees: 7600 (2002)
SIC(s): 2211 Broadwoven Fabric Mills--Cotton, 2221 Broadwoven Fabric Mills--Manmade, 2231 Broadwoven Fabric Mills--Wool, 2273 Carpets & Rugs.

Operating Locations

Burlington Industries, Inc. (CA--San Francisco; DC--Washington; GA--Calhoun, Dahlonega; IL--Chicago; KS--Overland Park; NY--New York; NC--Belmont, Burlington, Denton, Forest City, Gastonia, Mooresville, Mount Olive, Oxford, Rocky Mount, Smithfield, St. Pauls; SC--Bishopville, Greenville; TN--Johnson City; VA--Halifax, Hillsville; WA--Seattle)
Note: Operates in 10 states and 42 communities and maintains plants in Mexico.

Nonmonetary Support

Type: Donated Products; Loaned Executives
Volunteer Programs: Company does not have a formal employee volunteer program, but it provides meeting space on the premises or time off to individual employees who volunteer for Junior Achievement. Company also sponsors two Red Cross Blood Drives annually.
Note: Co. provides nonmonetary support

Burlington Industries Foundation

Giving Contact

Dolores C. Sides, Executive Director
PO Box 21207
Greensboro, NC 27420-1207
Phone: (336)379-2303
Fax: (336)379-4504

Description

EIN: 566043142
Organization Type: Corporate Foundation
Giving Locations: NC; SC; VA: principally near operating locations and to national organizations.
Grant Types: Award, Capital, Conference/Seminar, Employee Matching Gifts, General Support.
Note: Employee matching gift ratio: 1 to 1 up to $5,000 for current employees; up to $1,000 for retired employees.

Financial Summary

Total Giving: $691,212 (fiscal year ending September 30, 2001); $833,546 (fiscal 2000 approx); $1,095,920 (fiscal 1999). Note: Contributes through foundation only.
Giving Analysis: Giving for fiscal 2000 includes: foundation gifts to individuals ($18,588); foundation matching gifts ($181,725); foundation grants to United Way ($194,600); foundation ($438,633); fiscal 1999: foundation gifts to individuals ($56,650); foundation grants to United Way ($165,050); foundation matching gifts ($178,503) foundation ($695,717)
Assets: $2,810,901 (fiscal 2001); $3,656,552 (fiscal 2000); $3,691,096 (fiscal 1999)
Gifts Received: $400,005 (fiscal 2000); $1,000,000 (fiscal 1999); $100 (fiscal 1998)

Typical Recipients

Arts & Humanities: Arts Associations & Councils, Arts Funds, Historic Preservation, Libraries, Museums/Galleries, Music
Civic & Public Affairs: Botanical Gardens/Parks, Business/Free Enterprise, Clubs, Community Foundations, Employment/Job Training, Civic & Public Affairs-General, Housing, Law & Justice, Minority Business, Municipalities/Towns, Nonprofit Management, Philanthropic Organizations, Public Policy, Safety, Urban & Community Affairs
Education: Agricultural Education, Business Education, Colleges & Universities, Community & Junior Colleges, Education Associations, Education Funds, Education Reform, Elementary Education (Public), Engineering/Technological Education, Faculty Development, Education-General, Literacy, Minority Education, Private Education (Precollege), Public Education (Precollege), Science/Mathematics Education, Student Aid, Vocational & Technical Education
Environment: Environment-General, Resource Conservation
Health: AIDS/HIV, Children's Health/Hospitals, Clinics/Medical Centers, Emergency/Ambulance Services, Health Organizations, Hospices, Hospitals, Multiple Sclerosis, Outpatient Health Care, Preventive Medicine/Wellness Organizations, Respiratory, Single-Disease Health Associations
International: International Affairs, International Relations
Religion: Jewish Causes, Ministries, Religious Welfare
Science: Science Museums, Scientific Centers & Institutes
Social Services: Child Welfare, Community Centers, Community Service Organizations, Delinquency & Criminal Rehabilitation, Family Services, People with Disabilities, Recreation & Athletics, Scouts, Scouts, Shelters/Homelessness, Special Olympics, Substance Abuse, United Funds/United Ways, YMCA/YWCA/YMHA/YWHA, Youth Organizations

Application Procedures

Initial Contact: Send a brief letter or proposal.
Application Requirements: Include a description of organization, including its aims and purpose; need and justification for program; evidence that organization and its programs are developed and have direction; information on organization's reputation, efficiency, management ability, financial status, and other income sources; proof that organization is tax-exempt and is not a private foundation.
Deadlines: None.
Notes: Foundation may request additional information.

Restrictions

Contributions generally are not made to national organizations; organizations that are not tax-exempt; fraternal, labor, or veterans' organizations; churches; endowment funds; organizations supported through federated campaigns; private secondary schools; historic preservation projects; outdoor dramas; individuals; workshops, conferences, or seminars; production of films, documentaries, or other similar projects; operating expenses; political organizations, parties, or candidates; or medical research.

Corporate Officials

James M. Guin: vice president human resources & public relations B 1943. ED North Carolina State University BS (1966). PRIM CORP EMPL vice president human resources & public relations: Burlington Industries, Inc.
George W. Henderson, III: chief executive officer, chairman B Roanoke, VA 1948. ED University of North Carolina BA (1970); Emory University MBA (1974). PRIM CORP EMPL president, chief executive officer, director: Burlington Industries, Inc. CORP AFFIL director: Wachovia Bank NA; director: Wachovia Corp.; director: Jefferson Pilot Corp.; director: Jefferson Pilot Life Insurance Co.

Foundation Officials

George W. Henderson, III: director (see above)

Grants Analysis

Disclosure Period: fiscal year ending September 30, 2001
Total Grants: $386,450*
Number of Grants: 46
Average Grant: $8,401
Highest Grant: $37,500
Lowest Grant: $250
Typical Range: $500 to $15,000
*Note: Giving excludes United Way; matching gifts; and gifts to individuals.

Recent Grants

Note: Grants derived from fiscal 2001 Form 990.

General

121,500	Hospice of Greensboro, Greensboro, NC
37,500	Boy Scouts of America Old North State Council, Greensboro, NC
33,333	University of North Carolina Chapel Hill, Chapel Hill, NC
30,000	United Way Greater Greensboro, Greensboro, NC
30,000	United Way Greater Greensboro, Greensboro, NC
25,000	Community Foundation of Greater Greensboro, Greensboro, NC
25,000	New York Police and Fire Widows and Children's Benefit Fund, New York, NY
17,000	Independent College Fund of North Carolina, Winston-Salem, NC
15,871	University of North Carolina Chapel Hill, Chapel Hill, NC
13,000	Appalachian State University, Boone, NC

BURLINGTON NORTHERN SANTA FE CORP.

Company Headquarters

2650 Lou Menk Drive, 2nd Floor
PO Box 961057
Fort Worth, TX 76161-0057
Phone: (817)333-2000
Web: http://www.bnsf.com

Company Description

Founded: 1995
Ticker: BNI
Exchange: NYSE
Operating Revenue: US$8.979 billion (2002)
Profit: US$760 million (2002)
Employees: 36000 (2002)
Fortune Rank: 205, per FORTUNE Magazine's list of 500 Largest U.S. Corporations (2002).

SIC(s): 4011 Railroads--Line-Haul Operating, 4613 Refined Petroleum Pipelines.

Nonmonetary Support

Type: Donated Equipment
Note: Company provides nonmonetary support.

Burlington Northern Santa Fe Foundation

Giving Contact

Richard A. Russack, President
2500 Lou Menk Drive
Ft. Worth, TX 76161
Phone: (708)924-5615
E-mail: sharon.heft@bnsf.com

Description

EIN: 366051896
Organization Type: Corporate Foundation
Giving Locations: principally near operating locations and to national organizations.
Grant Types: Capital, Emergency, Employee Matching Gifts, General Support, Matching, Multiyear/Continuing Support, Project, Scholarship.

Financial Summary

Total Giving: $3,235,146 (2002); $3,378,438 (2001); $3,434,847 (2000). Note: Contributes through corporate direct giving program and foundation.
Giving Analysis: Giving for 2001 includes: foundation matching gifts ($248,777); foundation scholarships ($315,934); foundation grants to United Way ($763,688); 2000: foundation matching gifts ($250,630); foundation scholarships ($430,810); foundation grants to United Way ($816,594); foundation ($1,936,813); 1999: foundation gifts to individuals ($93,155); foundation matching gifts ($280,068); foundation scholarships ($372,708); foundation grants to United Way ($749,843) foundation ($1,956,710)
Assets: $1,888,257 (2002); $1,901,074 (2001); $510,252 (2000)
Gifts Received: $4,675,000 (2001); $3,502,000 (2000). Note: Contributions were received from Burlington Northern Santa Fe Corp.

Typical Recipients

Arts & Humanities: Ballet, Dance, History & Archaeology, Libraries, Museums/Galleries, Music, Opera, Performing Arts
Civic & Public Affairs: Chambers of Commerce, Civic & Public Affairs-General, Zoos/Aquariums
Education: Colleges & Universities, Education-General, Literacy, Minority Education, Private Education (Precollege), Student Aid
Science: Science Museums
Social Services: Child Welfare, Emergency Relief, United Funds/United Ways, YMCA/YWCA/YMHA/YWHA

Application Procedures

Initial Contact: Send a brief letter requesting application form; application packet will be sent pending determination of eligibility.
Application Requirements: Include with completed application: description of the organization, amount requested, copy of IRS tax-exempt ruling, current budget, principal sources and amounts of ongoing annual support, copy of most recently filed Form 990, information on the purpose, need for and relevance of the project, the approach to implementing the project, description of local support and coordination; method of project evaluation; how grant funds will be used; the competence of the organization and its personnel, and outside contractors in a direct or indirect supervisory position over the project; outline of future funding of on-going projects, list of other sources of support.
Deadlines: None.

Review Process: Consideration is given to each proposal to determine eligibility; declined organizations receive notification by mail; approved organizations receive funds shortly after approval.

Evaluative Criteria: Relevance to community needs, management capability, ability to achieve program's objectives, impact on community, level of volunteer participation, current and future sources of financial support

Decision Notification: As long as six months after application.

Restrictions

In general, the foundation does not support capital campaigns; individuals; political, religious, fraternal, or veterans organizations; national health organizations or their local chapters; goodwill advertising; tours, conferences, dinners, seminars, workshops, or testimonials; endowment funds; tax-supported educational institutions or governmental agencies; preschool, primary and secondary educational institutions; organizations already receiving United Way support; community and other foundations that also provide grants; or programs beyond stated geographic areas of interest.

Additional Information

Burlington Northern Santa Fe Corporation was formed by the merger of Burlington Northern Inc. and Santa Fe Pacific Corporation

Corporate Officials

Thomas N. Hund: executive vice president, chief financial officer ED Loyola University Chicago BBA; University of Chicago MBA. PRIM CORP EMPL executive vice president, chief financial officer: Burlington Northern Santa Fe Corp.

Carl R. Ice: executive vice president, chief operating officer PRIM CORP EMPL executive vice president, chief operating officer: Burlington Northern Santa Fe Corp.

Matthew K. Rose: president, chief executive officer, director B April 1959. ED University of Missouri BS (1980). PRIM CORP EMPL president, chief executive officer, director: Burlington Northern Santa Fe Corp.

Foundation Officials

Douglas Babs: director
Jeffrey Moreland: director
Richard A. Russack: president ED Union College BS (1959); New York University BA (1960). PRIM CORP EMPL vice president corporate relations: Burlington Northern Santa Fe Corp.

Grants Analysis

Disclosure Period: calendar year ending 2001
Total Grants: $3,235,146*
Number of Grants: 554
Highest Grant: $100,000
Lowest Grant: $50
*Note: Giving excludes scholarships, matching gifts, United Way. Grants analysis provided by foundation.

Recent Grants

Note: Grants derived from 2001 Form 990.

Library-Related
25,000	Fort Worth Public Library Foundation, Ft. Worth, TX

General
298,750	Scholarship Program Administrators, Nashville, TN
141,000	United Way of Metro Tarrant County, Ft. Worth, TX
100,000	Museum of Science and Industry, Chicago, IL
100,000	Performing Arts Fort Worth, Ft. Worth, TX
100,000	September 11 Fund, New York, NY
92,738	United Way of Greater Topeka, Topeka, KS

60,000	Fort Worth Museum of Science and History, Ft. Worth, TX
50,875	American Indian Science and Engineering Society, Boulder, CO
50,000	American Red Cross Chisholm Trail Chapter, Ft. Worth, TX
50,000	Amon Carter Museum, Ft. Worth, TX

BURLINGTON RESOURCES INC.

Company Headquarters

5051 Westheimer, Ste. 1400
Houston, TX 77056
Web: http://www.br-inc.com

Company Description

Ticker: BR
Exchange: NYSE
Revenue: US$2.964 billion (2002)
Profit: US$45.4 million (2002)
Employees: 2167 (2001)
Fortune Rank: 497, per FORTUNE Magazine's list of 500 Largest U.S. Corporations (2002).

Burlington Resources Foundation

Giving Contact

Gavin H. Smith, President
5051 Westheimer, Suite 1400
Houston, TX 77056-5604
Phone: (817)347-2000

Description

EIN: 760453686
Organization Type: Corporate Foundation
Grant Types: Capital, Employee Matching Gifts, General Support.

Financial Summary

Total Giving: $4,553,336 (2001); $2,804,803 (2000). Note: Contributes through corporate direct giving program and foundation.

Giving Analysis: Giving for 2001 includes: foundation grants to United Way ($168,900); foundation matching gifts ($306,896); foundation ($4,077,540) 2000: foundation ($2,804,803)

Assets: $22,272,848 (2001); $10,905,678 (2000)

Gifts Received: $14,726,291 (2001); $6,280,087 (2000); $1,698,000 (1994). Note: In 2000 and 2001, contributions were received from Burlington Resources Inc. In 1993 and 1994, contributions were received from Meridian Oil Inc.

Typical Recipients

Arts & Humanities: Arts Associations & Councils, Arts Festivals, Arts Funds, Community Arts, Dance, Libraries, Museums/Galleries, Music, Opera, Public Broadcasting, Theater

Civic & Public Affairs: Clubs, Economic Policy, Hispanic Affairs, Housing, Native American Affairs, Philanthropic Organizations, Urban & Community Affairs, Zoos/Aquariums

Education: Arts/Humanities Education, Business Education, Colleges & Universities, Education Associations, Education Funds, Education Reform, Elementary Education (Public), Engineering/Technological Education, Faculty Development, International Studies, Literacy, Medical Education, Minority Education, Private Education (Precollege), Public Education (Precollege), Science/Mathematics Education, Student Aid

Environment: Environment-General, Resource Conservation, Wildlife Protection

Health: Alzheimers Disease, Children's Health/Hospitals, Emergency/Ambulance Services, Heart, Hospices, Medical Research, Nursing Services, Prenatal Health Issues, Preventive Medicine/Wellness Organizations, Public Health, Single-Disease Health Associations

International: International Organizations
Religion: Religious Welfare, Seminaries
Science: Science Museums
Social Services: At-Risk Youth, Child Abuse, Child Welfare, Family Services, Food/Clothing Distribution, Homes, People with Disabilities, Recreation & Athletics, Scouts, United Funds/United Ways, Volunteer Services, YMCA/YWCA/YMHA/YWHA, Youth Organizations

Application Procedures

Initial Contact: Request application form.
Application Requirements: Include the completed application form; financial information, including your total current budget and the principal sources and amounts of ongoing annual support; proof of tax-exempt status; and copy of the organization's most recent Form 990.
Deadlines: None.
Decision Notification: Allow four months for a decision.
Notes: Foundation discourages telephone calls or personal visits. Copies of application forms are not accepted. Forms should not be placed in binders or other types of covers.

Restrictions

Does not support religious organizations for religious purposes; veteran or fraternal organizations; general endowment funds; national health organizations or programs; individuals; fund-raising events; corporate memberships, chambers of commerce, taxpayer associations, and other bodies whose activities are not expected to directly benefit the company; political organizations, campaigns, or candidates; and computers or related computer related projects.

Additional Information

Burlington Resources was separated from Burlington Northern Inc. in 1988. It operates its own foundation out of Ft. Worth, TX.

Burlington Resources Foundation gives on behalf of El Paso Natural Gas Co., El Paso, TX; Glacier Park Co., Seattle, WA; Meridian Oil Inc., Houston, TX; and Meridian Minerals Co., Englewood, CO.

Corporate Officials

Jeffery P. Monte: secretary

Foundation Officials

Ernesto Gomez: tax officer
Ann P. Graves: assistant treasurer
L. David Hanower: senior vice president, director B New York, NY 1959. ED Harvard University (1981); University of Chicago Law School (1985). PRIM CORP EMPL senior vice president law: Burlington Resources Inc.
Daniel D. Hawk: vice president, treasurer
Joseph P. McCoy: vice president, controller
Jeffery P. Monte: secretary (see above)
Frederick J. Plaeger, II: senior vice president, assistant secretary, general counsel
Bobby S. Shackouls: chairman, director
Steven J. Shapiro: senior vice president, chief financial officer
Gavin H. Smith: president, director
Anne V. Vaughan: assistant secretary
Dane E. Whitehead: vice president

Grants Analysis

Disclosure Period: calendar year ending 2001
Total Grants: $4,077,540*
Number of Grants: 222
Average Grant: $14,509*
Highest Grant: $300,000

Lowest Grant: $200
Typical Range: $1,000 to $50,000 and $100,000 to $300,000
***Note:** Giving excludes United Way and matching grants. Average grant figure excludes three highest grants ($900,000).

Recent Grants

Note: Grants derived from 2001 Form 990.

Library-Related

100,000	Morgan Library, New York, NY

General

300,000	Mississippi State University Foundation, Mississippi State, MS
300,000	Mississippi State University Foundation, Mississippi State, MS
300,000	Texas Children's Hospital, Houston, TX
200,000	Baylor College of Medicine, Houston, TX
200,000	University of Texas M.D. Anderson Cancer Center, Houston, TX
200,000	University of Texas M.D. Anderson Cancer Center, Houston, TX
200,000	University of Texas M.D. Anderson Cancer Center, Houston, TX
100,000	Texas Heart Institute, Houston, TX
100,000	University of Notre Dame, Notre Dame, IN
75,000	American Red Cross, Central Panhandle Chapter

ALPHONSE A. BURNAND MEDICAL AND EDUCATIONAL FOUNDATION

Giving Contact

Alphonse A. Burnand, III, President
PO Box 59
Borrego Springs, CA 92004
Phone: (760)767-5314
Fax: (760)767-5912

Description

Founded: 1957
EIN: 956083677
Organization Type: Private Foundation
Giving Locations: CA: San Diego County, Borrego Springs
Grant Types: General Support.

Financial Summary

Total Giving: $300,000 (2000); $207,500 (1999); $243,820 (1998)
Assets: $4,801,401 (2000); $5,982,171 (1999); $2,734,926 (1998)

Typical Recipients

Arts & Humanities: Libraries, Music, Performing Arts, Public Broadcasting
Civic & Public Affairs: Botanical Gardens/Parks, Chambers of Commerce, Clubs, Civic & Public Affairs-General, Legal Aid, Safety, Urban & Community Affairs, Women's Affairs, Zoos/Aquariums
Education: Colleges & Universities, Education Funds, Education-General, Public Education (Precollege), Special Education, Student Aid
Environment: Resource Conservation
Health: Cancer, Children's Health/Hospitals, Emergency/Ambulance Services, Health Organizations, Hospitals, Medical Research, Public Health, Single-Disease Health Associations, Transplant Networks/Donor Banks
International: Health Care/Hospitals, International Organizations
Religion: Churches

Social Services: Animal Protection, Camps, Child Welfare, Community Centers, Community Service Organizations, Day Care, Domestic Violence, People with Disabilities, Recreation & Athletics, Scouts, United Funds/United Ways, YMCA/YWCA/YMHA/YWHA, Youth Organizations

Application Procedures

Initial Contact: Send a brief letter of inquiry.
Application Requirements: Include a full explanation of request and proof of tax-exempt status.
Deadlines: None.

Restrictions

Does not support individuals.

Foundation Officials

Alphonse A. Burnand, III: president
Audrey Steele Burnand: treasurer
Alice G. Hansen: secretary

Grants Analysis

Disclosure Period: calendar year ending 2000
Total Grants: $300,000
Number of Grants: 26
Average Grant: $5,435*
Highest Grant: $75,000
Lowest Grant: $1,000
Typical Range: $1,000 to $10,000
***Note:** Average grant figure excludes three highest grants ($175,000).

Recent Grants

Note: Grants derived from 2001 Form 990.

Library-Related

5,000	San Diego County Library, San Diego, CA -- charitable

General

50,000	Borrego Community Health Foundation, Borrego Springs, CA -- charitable
50,000	Boys and Girls Club of Borrego Springs, Ramona, CA -- charitable
25,000	Borrego Springs Fire Protection District, Borrego Springs, CA -- charitable
15,000	Borrego Springs Little League, Borrego Springs, CA -- charitable
15,000	Borrego Springs Performing Arts Center, Borrego Springs, CA -- charitable
10,000	Borrego Springs Educational Foundation, Borrego Springs, CA -- charitable
10,000	Borrego Springs Youth Center, Borrego Springs, CA -- charitable
10,000	Christmas Circle Community Park, Borrego Springs, CA -- charitable
5,500	Braille Institute, Los Angeles, CA -- charitable
5,000	Borrego Springs Children's Center, Borrego Springs, CA -- charitable

LEO BURNETT CO.

Company Headquarters

Chicago, IL
Web: http://www.leoburnett.com

Company Description

Employees: 9,029
SIC(s): 7311 Advertising Agencies.

Operating Locations

Leo Burnett Co. (CA--Los Angeles; FL--Coral Gables; NY--New York)

Nonmonetary Support

Type: Cause-related Marketing & Promotion
Volunteer Programs: Company sponsors "Give Back Day," a day when about 500 employees volunteer in local schools.

Leo Burnett Co. Charitable Foundation

Giving Contact

Christian Kimball, Vice President
35 West Wacker Drive
Chicago, IL 60601
Phone: (312)220-5959
Fax: (312)220-6523

Description

EIN: 363379336
Organization Type: Corporate Foundation
Giving Locations: IL: Chicago
Grant Types: Employee Matching Gifts, General Support, Operating Expenses, Project.

Financial Summary

Total Giving: $1,149,773 (2001); $961,292 (2000); $793,807 (1999). Note: Contributes through corporate direct giving program and foundation.
Giving Analysis: Giving for 2000 includes: foundation grants to United Way ($165,000); foundation matching gifts ($291,742); foundation ($504,549) 1998: foundation grants to United Way ($160,500)
Assets: $1,016,301 (2001); $1,836,560 (2000); $2,665,680 (1999)
Gifts Received: $250,000 (2001); $149,231 (1998); $106 (1996). Note: Contributions are received from the Leo Burnett Co.

Typical Recipients

Arts & Humanities: Arts Centers, Arts Funds, Arts Institutes, Ballet, Film & Video, Arts & Humanities-General, Historic Preservation, History & Archaeology, Libraries, Museums/Galleries, Music, Opera, Performing Arts, Public Broadcasting, Theater
Civic & Public Affairs: African American Affairs, Business/Free Enterprise, Chambers of Commerce, Civil Rights, Economic Development, Civic & Public Affairs-General, Hispanic Affairs, Housing, Law & Justice, Municipalities/Towns, Professional & Trade Associations, Public Policy, Rural Affairs, Urban & Community Affairs, Women's Affairs, Zoos/Aquariums
Education: Agricultural Education, Arts/Humanities Education, Business Education, Business Education, Colleges & Universities, Community & Junior Colleges, Education Funds, Education Reform, Engineering/Technological Education, Education-General, International Studies, Medical Education, Minority Education, Preschool Education, Private Education (Precollege), Public Education (Precollege), Science/Mathematics Education, Secondary Education (Private), Student Aid
Environment: Environment-General, Resource Conservation, Wildlife Protection
Health: AIDS/HIV, Arthritis, Cancer, Children's Health/Hospitals, Clinics/Medical Centers, Emergency/Ambulance Services, Health Organizations, Heart, Hospices, Hospitals, Medical Research, Mental Health, Multiple Sclerosis, Single-Disease Health Associations
International: Foreign Arts Organizations, Health Care/Hospitals, Human Rights, International Affairs, International Environmental Issues, International Organizations, International Peace & Security Issues, International Relations, International Relief Efforts, Missionary/Religious Activities
Religion: Jewish Causes, Religious Organizations, Religious Welfare
Science: Science-General, Observatories & Planetariums, Science Museums
Social Services: Animal Protection, At-Risk Youth, Child Welfare, Community Centers, Community Service Organizations, Family Planning, Family Services, Food/Clothing Distribution, People with Disabilities,

Recreation & Athletics, Scouts, Senior Services, Shelters/Homelessness, United Funds/United Ways, YMCA/YWCA/YMHA/YWHA, Youth Organizations

Application Procedures

Initial Contact: Send a brief letter of inquiry.
Application Requirements: Include a description of organization, financial statement, listing of board of directors and IRS statement.
Deadlines: None.
Evaluative Criteria: Supports disadvantaged groups in the Chicago area; supports social and economic structure of Chicago; supports education in the creative fields.
Decision Notification: After bi-annual meetings.

Restrictions

The foundation does not provide grants to individuals or religious groups.

Corporate Officials

Kristin Anderson: vice president, director community affairs PRIM CORP EMPL vice president, director community affairs: Leo Burnett Co.
Richard B. Fizdale: chairman, chief executive officer, director B 1938. PRIM CORP EMPL chairman, chief executive officer, director: Leo Burnett Co. Inc. CORP AFFIL chairman: Leo Burnett Worldwide Inc.

Foundation Officials

Kristin Anderson: secretary, contact (see above)

Grants Analysis

Disclosure Period: calendar year ending 2001
Total Grants: $626,959*
Number of Grants: 116
Average Grant: $5,405
Highest Grant: $50,000
Lowest Grant: $25
Typical Range: $5,000 to $15,000
***Note:** Giving excludes matching gifts and United Way.

Recent Grants

Note: Grants derived from 2001 Form 990.

General

165,000	United Way, Chicago, IL
50,000	Off the Street Club, Chicago, IL
50,000	United States of America for United Nations High Commission, Washington, DC
42,473	Off the Street Club, Chicago, IL
41,000	Creative Development Fund
35,101	United Way, Chicago, IL
25,000	Advertising Council, New York, NY
25,000	Mental Health Association
20,000	Chicago Coalition for the Homeless, Chicago, IL
20,000	Greater Chicago Food Depository, Chicago, IL

THE BURNETT FOUNDATION

Giving Contact

Thomas F. Beech, Executive Vice President
801 Cherry Street, Suite 1585
Unit 16
Ft. Worth, TX 76102-6881
Phone: (817)877-3344
Fax: (817)338-0448

Description

Founded: 1978
EIN: 751638517
Organization Type: General Purpose Foundation

Giving Locations: NM: Santa Fe; TX: Ft. Worth occasionally grants are provided nationally, at the trustee's discretion.
Grant Types: Capital, Challenge, Endowment, General Support, Matching, Operating Expenses.

Donor Information

Founder: Established in 1978 by Anne Burnett Tandy in memory of her husband, Charles D. Tandy (d. 1978). Mr. Tandy bought Radio Shack in 1963 and built it from a debt-ridden chain of nine electronics stores to a national chain with over 7,000 outlets.

Financial Summary

Total Giving: $11,625,000 (2003 approx); $11,625,000 (2002 approx); $13,880,745 (2001)
Giving Analysis: Giving for 1998 includes: foundation scholarships ($5,000); foundation matching gifts ($25,000); foundation grants to United Way ($87,000) 1997: foundation grants to United Way ($50,000)
Assets: $205,000,000 (2003 approx); $205,000,000 (2002 approx); $263,614,624 (2001)

Typical Recipients

Arts & Humanities: Arts Associations & Councils, Arts Centers, Arts Festivals, Arts Institutes, Arts Outreach, Ballet, Dance, Historic Preservation, Libraries, Museums/Galleries, Music, Opera, Performing Arts, Theater, Visual Arts
Civic & Public Affairs: African American Affairs, Botanical Gardens/Parks, Community Foundations, Economic Development, Employment/Job Training, Civic & Public Affairs-General, Hispanic Affairs, Housing, Municipalities/Towns, Nonprofit Management, Parades/Festivals, Public Policy, Rural Affairs, Urban & Community Affairs, Women's Affairs, Zoos/Aquariums
Education: Afterschool/Enrichment Programs, Arts/Humanities Education, Colleges & Universities, Colleges & Universities, Education Funds, Education Reform, Elementary Education (Private), Engineering/Technological Education, Environmental Education, Faculty Development, Education-General, Leadership Training, Medical Education, Minority Education, Preschool Education, Private Education (Precollege), Public Education (Precollege), Special Education, Student Aid
Environment: Research
Health: AIDS/HIV, Alzheimers Disease, Cancer, Children's Health/Hospitals, Clinics/Medical Centers, Emergency/Ambulance Services, Health Policy/Cost Containment, Hospitals, Medical Research, Mental Health, Prenatal Health Issues, Research/Studies Institutes, Single-Disease Health Associations
International: Health Care/Hospitals, International Affairs, International Development
Religion: Ministries, Religious Organizations, Religious Welfare, Social/Policy Issues
Science: Science Museums
Social Services: At-Risk Youth, Big Brother/Big Sister, Child Abuse, Child Welfare, Community Centers, Community Service Organizations, Crime Prevention, Day Care, Domestic Violence, Emergency Relief, Family Planning, Family Services, Food/Clothing Distribution, People with Disabilities, Recreation & Athletics, Scouts, Senior Services, Sexual Abuse, Shelters/Homelessness, Substance Abuse, United Funds/United Ways, YMCA/YWCA/YMHA/YWHA, Youth Organizations

Application Procedures

Initial Contact: Applicants are encouraged to write a letter of inquiry.
Application Requirements: Include a description of organization, the specific program to be considered, the amount requested, and a budget summary.

Deadlines: None.
Review Process: If the program fits within the foundation's guidelines and priorities, a more detailed application will be requested. Formal grant review meetings are held three times a year, usually in March, June, and November.

Restrictions

Funding is limited to organizations with 501(c)(3) status. The foundation will not fund individuals.

Additional Information

Publications: Annual Report; Guidelines

Foundation Officials

Thomas Foster Beech: executive vice president B Saint Paul, MN 1939. ED Carleton College BA (1961).
Benjamin J. Fortson: trustee
Anne Windfohr Grimes: trustee
Edward R. Hudson, Jr.: vice president, trustee, secretary, treasurer
Anne W. Marion: president, trustee B 1939. ED Briarcliffe Junior College; University of Geneva; University of Texas. NONPR AFFIL trustee: Modern Art Museum Fort Worth; honorary trustee: Texas Technology University; member: Memorial Sloan-Kettering Cancer Center; member executive committee: Fort Worth Stock Show; director: Fort Worth Zoological Association.
John Louis Marion: trustee B New York, NY 1933. ED Fordham University BS (1956); Columbia University (1960-1961). PRIM CORP EMPL honorary chairman: Sotheby's Inc. CORP AFFIL director: Sotheby Holdings Inc. NONPR AFFIL member: Appraisers Association America; director: International Foundation Art Research; chairman finance arts committee: American Cancer Society New York City. CLUB AFFIL Shady Oaks Country Club; Vintage Club; Eldorado Country Club; Lotos Club.

Grants Analysis

Disclosure Period: calendar year ending 2001
Total Grants: $13,880,745
Number of Grants: 69
Average Grant: $186,677*
Highest Grant: $1,000,000
Lowest Grant: $3,000
Typical Range: $5,000 to $50,000 and $100,000 to $800,000
***Note:** Provided by foundation. Average grant figure excludes highest grant.

Recent Grants

Note: Grants derived from 2000 Form 990.

General

4,000,000	MPA Foundation, Ft. Worth, TX -- new facility for Modern Art Museum of Fort Worth
2,900,000	Georgia O'Keeffe Museum, Santa Fe, NM -- construction and equipment expenses at research center
2,200,000	Georgia O'Keeffe Museum, Santa Fe, NM -- operating expenses
1,066,459	Downtown Fort Worth Initiatives, Ft. Worth, TX -- maintenance of Burnett Park
1,000,000	Amon Carter Museum, Ft. Worth, TX -- museum expansion campaign
1,000,000	National Cowgirl Museum and Hall of Fame, Ft. Worth, TX -- capital campaign
1,000,000	Texas Christian University, Ft. Worth, TX -- William E and Jean Jones Tucker Technology Center
750,000	Lensic Performing Arts Center, Santa Fe, NM -- capital campaign
650,000	Site Santa Fe, Santa Fe, NM -- operating expenses
610,000	Georgia O'Keeffe Museum, Santa Fe, NM -- restoration expenses at Ghost Ranch property

MARGARET E. BURNHAM CHARITABLE TRUST

Giving Contact

Thomas M. Pierce, Trustee
Care of H.M. Payson & Co.
PO Box 31
Portland, ME 04112-0031
Phone: (207)772-3761
Fax: (207)871-7508
Web: http://www.megrants.org/Burnham.htm

Description

Founded: 1995
EIN: 010496879
Organization Type: Private Foundation
Giving Locations: ME
Grant Types: General Support.

Financial Summary

Total Giving: $359,200 (2000); $353,800 (1999); $340,500 (1998)
Giving Analysis: Giving for 2000 includes: foundation grants to United Way ($18,000); 1999: foundation grants to United Way ($15,000); 1998: foundation grants to United Way ($15,000) foundation ($325,500)
Assets: $7,886,400 (2000); $7,829,550 (1999); $8,113,489 (1998)

Typical Recipients

Arts & Humanities: Ethnic & Folk Arts, Historic Preservation, History & Archaeology, Libraries, Museums/Galleries, Music
Civic & Public Affairs: Civic & Public Affairs-General, Safety, Urban & Community Affairs, Zoos/Aquariums
Education: Arts/Humanities Education, Colleges & Universities, Education Funds, Education-General, Leadership Training, Public Education (Precollege), Student Aid, Vocational & Technical Education
Environment: Environment-General, Resource Conservation
Health: AIDS/HIV, Clinics/Medical Centers, Emergency/Ambulance Services, Health Organizations, Home-Care Services, Hospitals, Single-Disease Health Associations
Religion: Religious Welfare
Social Services: Camps, Child Welfare, Community Centers, Community Service Organizations, Counseling, Domestic Violence, Emergency Relief, Scouts, Social Services-General, Substance Abuse, United Funds/United Ways, Volunteer Services, YMCA/YWCA/YMHA/YWHA, Youth Organizations

Application Procedures

Initial Contact: Send completed application form supplied by the foundation.
Application Requirements: Include proof of tax-exempt status, recently audited financial statement, and a list of officers or directors.
Deadlines: October 15.

Foundation Officials

Thomas M. Pierce: trustee
Clifford H. Sinnett: trustee

Grants Analysis

Disclosure Period: calendar year ending 2000
Total Grants: $341,200*
Number of Grants: 86
Average Grant: $3,967
Highest Grant: $15,000
Typical Range: $1,000 to $5,000
***Note:** Giving excludes United Way.

Recent Grants

Note: Grants derived from 2001 Form 990.

Library-Related

5,000	Brown Memorial Library, East Baldwin, ME
5,000	Falmouth Memorial Library, Falmouth, ME

General

20,000	United Way of Greater Portland, Portland, ME
10,000	Falmouth Education Foundation, Falmouth, MA
10,000	Maine Medical Center, Portland, ME
10,000	Portland Museum of Art, Portland, ME
10,000	Rippleffect, Portland, OR
7,500	Catholic Charities, ME
7,500	Gulf of Maine Aquarium, Portland, ME
7,500	Miles Memorial Hospital, Damariscotta, ME
7,500	St. Lawrence Arts and Community Center, Portland, ME
7,500	University of New England, Biddeford, ME

BURNS & MCDONNELL

Company Headquarters

9400 Ward Parkway
Kansas City, MO 64114
Web: http://www.burnsmcd.com

Company Description

Former Name: Burns & McDonnell Engineering Co.
Operating Revenue: US$186 million (2002)
Employees: 1500 (2002)
SIC(s): 8700 Engineering & Management Services, 8711 Engineering Services, 8712 Architectural Services, 8748 Business Consulting Services Nec.

Burns & McDonnell Foundation

Giving Contact

David E. Christianson, Vice President
Burns & McDonnell Foundation
PO Box 419173
Kansas City, MO 64141-6173
Phone: (816)333-9400
Fax: (816)333-3690

Description

Founded: 1988
EIN: 431448871
Organization Type: Corporate Foundation
Giving Locations: MO: Kansas City metropolitan area
Grant Types: General Support.

Donor Information

Founder: the Burns & McDonnell Corporation

Financial Summary

Total Giving: $155,598 (2001); $200,743 (2000); $118,928 (1999)
Giving Analysis: Giving for 2001 includes: foundation ($58,000); 2000: foundation ($97,743); foundation grants to United Way ($103,000); 1999: foundation grants to United Way ($300); foundation ($118,628)
Assets: $4,097,914 (2001); $4,097,930 (2000); $3,919,444 (1999)
Gifts Received: $18,000 (1993); $36,000 (1992).
Note: In 1993, contributions were received from Burns & McDonnell Engineering Co.

Typical Recipients

Arts & Humanities: Ballet, History & Archaeology, Libraries, Museums/Galleries, Music, Opera, Public Broadcasting, Theater
Civic & Public Affairs: Civic & Public Affairs-General, Housing, Professional & Trade Associations, Urban & Community Affairs, Women's Affairs, Zoos/Aquariums
Education: Colleges & Universities, Engineering/Technological Education, Education-General, International Exchange, Minority Education, Science/Mathematics Education
Environment: Environment-General
Health: Cancer, Diabetes, Medical Research, Multiple Sclerosis, Single-Disease Health Associations
Science: Scientific Organizations
Social Services: Child Welfare, Community Service Organizations, Crime Prevention, Recreation & Athletics, Scouts, United Funds/United Ways, Youth Organizations

Application Procedures

Initial Contact: The foundation has no formal grant application procedure or application form.
Deadlines: None.

Restrictions

The foundation does not make contributions to political or religious causes.

Additional Information

Company reports 60% of contributions support education; 30% civic and public affairs; and 5% each to arts and health/human services programs.

Corporate Officials

Dave G. Ruf, Jr.: chairman, president, chief executive officer, director B Kansas City, MO 1938. ED Kansas City Junior College (1958); University of Kansas (1960). PRIM CORP EMPL chairman, president, chief executive officer, director: Burns & McDonnell.
Mark Taylor: vice president PRIM CORP EMPL vice president: Burns & McDonnell ADD CORP EMPL vice president: Burns McDonnell Engineering Co.

Foundation Officials

Gerard T. Bukowski, Jr.: secretary PRIM CORP EMPL vice president, counsel: Burns & McDonnell.
Joel A. Cerwick: director
David E. Christianson: vice president
Barbara L. Graham: assistant secretary
Darrell M. Hosler: vice president, director B Beloit, KS 1936. ED Kansas State University (1959). PRIM CORP EMPL executive vice president, secretary, director: Burns & McDonnell. CORP AFFIL president, managing director: Burns & McDonnell International; director: Nofsinger Co.
Paul A. Hustad: director
Dave G. Ruf, Jr.: chairman, president, director (see above)
James Schorgl: assistant treasurer
Howard E. Wolfrom, Jr.: treasurer, assistant secretary PRIM CORP EMPL controller: Burns & McDonnell.

Grants Analysis

Disclosure Period: calendar year ending 2001
Total Grants: $97,598*
Number of Grants: 43
Average Grant: $2,269
Highest Grant: $11,000
Lowest Grant: $75
Typical Range: $500 to $5,000
***Note:** Giving excludes United Way.

Recent Grants

Note: Grants derived from 2000 Form 990.

General

103,000	United Way, New York, NY
11,000	KCP-TV, Kansas City, MO
6,000	Iowa State University, Ames, IA
6,000	Kansas State University, Manhattan, KS
6,000	University of Kansas, Lawrence, KS
6,000	University of Missouri - Rolla, St. Louis, MO
5,500	University of Missouri - Columbia, St. Louis, MO
4,500	University of Nebraska, Lincoln, NE
4,250	Kansas City Symphony Ball, Kansas City, MO
4,000	South Dakota State University, Brookings, SD

ROBERT HAROLD BURTON PRIVATE FOUNDATION

Giving Contact

Richard G. Horne, executive Director
c/o First Security Bank of UT NA
PO Box 58477
Salt Lake City, UT 84158
Phone: (801)715-7140

Description

Founded: 1985
EIN: 742425567
Organization Type: Private Foundation
Giving Locations: UT: Salt Lake County
Grant Types: General Support.

Donor Information

Founder: the late Robert H. Burton

Financial Summary

Total Giving: $2,151,102 (1999); $1,708,951 (1998); $995,224 (1996)
Assets: $59,470,635 (1999); $50,536,901 (1998); $13,507,696 (1997)
Gifts Received: $5,996 (1995); $2,613 (1993)

Typical Recipients

Arts & Humanities: Arts Centers, Dance, Ethnic & Folk Arts, Libraries, Literary Arts, Museums/Galleries, Music, Opera, Performing Arts, Public Broadcasting, Theater
Civic & Public Affairs: Botanical Gardens/Parks, Civic & Public Affairs-General, Law & Justice, Legal Aid, Public Policy, Safety, Urban & Community Affairs
Education: Arts/Humanities Education, Colleges & Universities, Elementary Education (Public), Engineering/Technological Education, Faculty Development, Education-General, Legal Education, Literacy, Medical Education, Preschool Education, Private Education (Precollege), Public Education (Precollege), Secondary Education (Private), Student Aid, Vocational & Technical Education
Environment: Resource Conservation, Wildlife Protection
Health: Children's Health/Hospitals, Emergency/Ambulance Services, Health-General, Health Organizations, Long-Term Care, Nursing Services
Religion: Churches, Religious Welfare, Social/Policy Issues
Science: Science Museums
Social Services: Child Welfare, Community Centers, Community Service Organizations, Crime Prevention, Family Services, Social Services-General, Substance Abuse, United Funds/United Ways, YMCA/YWCA/YMHA/YWHA, Youth Organizations

Application Procedures

Initial Contact: The foundation has no formal grant application procedure or application form.
Deadlines: None.

Additional Information

Trust(s): First Security Bank NA

Foundation Officials

Richard R. Burton: chairman
Fred A. Moreton, Jr.: member
Judith Burton Moyle: mem

Grants Analysis

Disclosure Period: calendar year ending 1999
Total Grants: $2,151,102
Number of Grants: 47
Average Grant: $45,768
Highest Grant: $231,285
Typical Range: $10,000 to $100,000

Recent Grants

Note: Grants derived from 2001 Form 990.

General

414,776	University of Utah, Salt Lake City, UT
264,000	Red Butt Gardens and Arboretum, Salt Lake City, UT
200,000	Western Folklife, Elko, NV
150,000	Life Care, Salt Lake City, UT
100,000	And Justice For All, Salt Lake City, UT
100,000	Westminster College, Salt Lake City, UT
77,068	KUED, Salt Lake City, UT
50,000	Guadalupe Schools, Salt Lake City, UT
50,000	National Conference For Community and Justice, Salt Lake City, UT
50,000	Ronald McDonald House Charities, Salt Lake City, UT

EDYTH BUSH CHARITABLE FOUNDATION, INC.

Giving Contact

David A. Odahowski, President
199 East Welbourne Avenue
PO Box 1967
Winter Park, FL 32790-1967
Phone: 888-647-4322
Fax: (407)647-7716
E-mail: dhessler@edythbush.org
Web: http://www.edythbush.org

Description

Founded: 1966
EIN: 237318041
Organization Type: General Purpose Foundation
Giving Locations: FL: Lake County, Orange County, Osceola County, Seminole County
Grant Types: Award, Capital, Challenge, Matching, Multiyear/Continuing Support, Project.

Donor Information

Founder: Incorporated in 1966 in Minnesota by the late Edyth Bush and reincorporated in 1973 in Florida.

Financial Summary

Total Giving: $2,868,800 (fiscal year ending August 31, 2002 approx); $3,230,791 (fiscal 2001); $2,647,607 (fiscal 1999)
Giving Analysis: Giving for fiscal 2001 includes: foundation matching gifts ($98,764) fiscal 1999: foundation grants to United Way ($10,000)
Assets: $75,176,198 (fiscal 2001); $82,605,768 (fiscal 1999); $68,468,724 (fiscal 1998)

Typical Recipients

Arts & Humanities: Arts Appreciation, Arts Outreach, Arts & Humanities-General, Music, Public Broadcasting
Civic & Public Affairs: Business/Free Enterprise, Community Foundations, Civic & Public Affairs-General, Housing, Municipalities/Towns, Nonprofit Management, Professional & Trade Associations
Education: Business Education, Colleges & Universities, Education-General, Literacy, Public Education (Precollege), Science/Mathematics Education
Health: Alzheimers Disease, Cancer, Clinics/Medical Centers, Eyes/Blindness, Health Organizations, Hospitals, Mental Health, Nursing Services, Single-Disease Health Associations
Religion: Churches, Dioceses, Ministries, Religious Organizations, Religious Welfare
Science: Scientific Centers & Institutes
Social Services: Animal Protection, Animal Protection, At-Risk Youth, Big Brother/Big Sister, Child Welfare, Community Centers, Community Service Organizations, Counseling, Emergency Relief, Family Services, Food/Clothing Distribution, People with Disabilities, Senior Services, Shelters/Homelessness, Social Services-General, Volunteer Services, YMCA/YWCA/YMHA/YWHA, Youth Organizations

Application Procedures

Initial Contact: Applicants are encouraged to contact the foundation first by telephone. The foundation requests applications be made in writing.
Application Requirements: The foundation specifies that it needs two sets of a proposal. Requests for support should include contact information, amount requested with statement of why the grant is needed, position or relationship to the applicant organization of the individual signing the grant request, list of contributions received during each of the preceding three years and current year, and a list of potential funding sources. Applications should include a description of goals the grant is expected to accomplish, the method of financing the project after funds from the foundation are expended, and the criteria judging the effectiveness of the grant. Also required are a detailed project budget, statement that applicant will furnish a report detailing fund expenditures, timetable for project, and the names, occupations, and business affiliations of each of the board members, trustees, and key personnel. Applicants also must furnish copies of most recent 501(c)(3) letter of exemption and 509(a) status letter; statement that 501(c)(3) and 509(a) status has not been revoked or modified; government relationship, if applicable; latest annual balance sheet and detailed income statement; and the most recent quarterly or monthly management financial statement, if the annual statement is more than three months old.
Applicants submitting construction or renovation requests should provide a current contractor's estimate of costs broken down by subcontracts. Requests for loans require a list of collateral to be tendered and a schedule of principal and interest payments. The foundation suggests talking with its officers before filing a loan request.
Deadlines: None.
Review Process: The foundation conducts a site visit after a complete grant request has been received. A representative of the foundation will meet with both the organization's staff and board members or trustees, and review the organization's operations. After the site visit, completed requests are presented to the grants committee and then to the board of directors. The board generally meets in February, May, August, and November.

Restrictions

The foundation ordinarily will not fund tax-supported institutions, individual scholarships or individual research; alcohol or drug abuse programs; foreign organizations or foreign use of funds; travel projects; fellowships; organizations for sacramental, denominational, or interdenominational purposes; advocacy organizations; cultural or arts organizations, unless their work is of a demonstrated, nationally recognized quality, or for the demonstrated educational value of children, K-12th grade; or organizations having revenues from memberships or contributions of less than $25,000 in the previous year. The foundation discourages requests for routine operating expenses, to pay off deficits, or for endowment funds. The foundation will not accept proposals by facsimile.

Additional Information

Approximately 50% of foundation grants are made on a challenge or match basis. Large grants are typically paid in installments over two or three years. The foundation also provides program-related investment loans to nonprofit organizations

Publications: Outline of Grant Request Requirements; Grants Policies and Procedures; Guidelines

Foundation Officials

Frederick Belloff: director
Mary Gretchen Belloff: vice chairman, director
Michael R. Cross: vice president finance, treasurer
Deborah Hessler: secretary
Gerald F. Hilbrich: director
Herbert W. Holm: director
H. Clifford Lee: chairman, director
John S. Lord: director
David A. Odahowski: president, director
Robert E. Waggoner: director

Grants Analysis

Disclosure Period: fiscal year ending August 31, 2001
Total Grants: $3,230,791*
Number of Grants: 94*
Average Grant: $31,710*
Highest Grant: $250,000
Typical Range: $2,000 to $100,000
*Note: Grants analysis provided by the foundation. Average grant figure excludes highest grant.

Recent Grants

Note: Grants derived from 2001 Form 990.

General

250,000	Seniors First, Orlando, FL -- to purchase five ambulatory passenger vehicles equipped with wheelchair lifts
233,453	Community Foundation of Central Florida, Inc., Orlando, FL -- for new philanthropy for the Millennium Program
200,000	National Center for Social Entrepreneurs, Golden Valley, MN -- for the Orlando Project for Social Entrepreneurs
183,852	United Arts of Central Florida, Orlando, FL -- for new philanthropy for the millennium
150,000	Children's Home Society of Florida, Winter Park, FL -- to relocate corporate headquarter offices to Orlando, Florida
133,209	Habitat for Humanity of Greater Orlando, Orlando, FL -- to create a regional warehouse to reduce costs and to increase housing production
129,317	American Cancer Society Orange County Region, Orlando, FL -- for additional staff for the Patient Service Center
126,825	Central Florida YMCA, Orlando, FL -- lead gift to kick off the New Horizon Campaign
115,000	Consumer Credit Counseling Service, Orlando, FL -- to purchase a management information system
114,000	Healthy Initiative of Greater Orlando, Orlando, FL -- for Community Capacity Building Project

BUSH FOUNDATION

Giving Contact

Anita M. Pampusch, President
332 Minnesota Street, E-900
St. Paul, MN 55101
Phone: (651)227-0891
Fax: (651)297-6485
E-mail: info@bushfoundation.org
Web: http://www.bushfoundation.org

Description

Founded: 1953
EIN: 416017815
Organization Type: General Purpose Foundation
Giving Locations: MN; ND; SD: nationally.
Grant Types: Capital, Fellowship, Multiyear/Continuing Support, Project.

Donor Information

Founder: Established in 1953 by Archibald Granville Bush and his wife, Edyth Bassler Bush . Mr. Bush was born in 1887 on his family farm near Granite Falls, MN, the third of five children. He grew up on the farm, attended the Granite Falls public schools, and intended to be a farmer. However, hay fever allergy in 1908 forced him to seek a more pollen-free climate. He moved to Duluth, MN, enrolled in the six-month business course at Duluth Business University, and in 1909 went to work for the 3M Company as assistant bookkeeper. His 57-year career at 3M was mainly in sales and general management. He was chairman of the corporation's executive committee at his death in 1966. Bush also was active in St. Paul civic affairs, and was a trustee of Hamline University. In 1919, Bush married Edyth Bassler of Chicago, a professional actress and dancer. Although Mrs. Bush ceased her stage career, she maintained a strong interest in theater and the arts. In St. Paul, she founded the Edyth Bush Theatre and served there as playwright, producer, and occasional actress. She was chairman of the board of The Bush Foundation from 1966 until her death in 1972. Ill health, however, prevented her active participation in that role for most of those years.

Financial Summary

Total Giving: $36,360,000 (fiscal year ending November 30, 2002 approx); $37,181,023 (fiscal 2001); $44,852,609 (fiscal 2000)
Giving Analysis: Giving for fiscal 2001 includes: foundation grants to United Way ($500,000); foundation fellowships ($2,664,414); fiscal 2000: foundation grants to United Way ($300,000) foundation fellowships ($2,515,685)
Assets: $608,650,000 (fiscal 2002 approx); $726,484,372 (fiscal 2001); $836,335,488 (fiscal 2000)
Gifts Received: $900,000 (fiscal 2001). Note: In fiscal 2001, contributions were received from the Hewlett Foundation.

Typical Recipients

Arts & Humanities: Arts Associations & Councils, Arts Centers, Arts Outreach, Ethnic & Folk Arts, Arts & Humanities-General, Historic Preservation, History & Archaeology, Libraries, Museums/Galleries, Music, Opera, Performing Arts, Public Broadcasting, Theater, Visual Arts
Civic & Public Affairs: Asian American Affairs, Civil Rights, Community Foundations, Economic Development, Employment/Job Training, Civic & Public Affairs-General, Housing, Legal Aid, Native American Affairs, Nonprofit Management, Public Policy, Urban & Community Affairs, Women's Affairs, Zoos/Aquariums
Education: Business Education, Colleges & Universities, Community & Junior Colleges, Education Associations, Education Funds, Engineering/Technological Education, Environmental Education, Faculty

Development, Education-General, International Exchange, Education-General, Leadership Training, Legal Education, Literacy, Medical Education, Minority Education, Public Education (Precollege), School Volunteerism, Science/Mathematics Education, Secondary Education (Private), Social Sciences Education, Special Education, Vocational & Technical Education
Environment: Air/Water Quality, Environment-General, Resource Conservation, Wildlife Protection
Health: AIDS/HIV, Children's Health/Hospitals, Clinics/Medical Centers, Health-General, Geriatric Health, Health Organizations, Medical Rehabilitation, Medical Training, Mental Health, Nursing Services, Public Health, Research/Studies Institutes
Religion: Churches, Religion-General, Jewish Causes, Religious Organizations, Religious Welfare, Seminaries
Science: Science Museums
Social Services: At-Risk Youth, Big Brother/Big Sister, Child Welfare, Community Centers, Community Service Organizations, Day Care, Domestic Violence, Emergency Relief, Family Planning, Family Services, Food/Clothing Distribution, People with Disabilities, Recreation & Athletics, Refugee Assistance, Senior Services, Sexual Abuse, Shelters/Homelessness, Social Services-General, Substance Abuse, United Funds/United Ways, Youth Organizations

Application Procedures

Initial Contact: The foundation encourages potential applicants to submit a brief letter of inquiry.
Application Requirements: Letters of inquiry should include a project description, amount requested, and the length of time for the expenditure of grant funds. A full proposal should be submitted in duplicate and should include a cover sheet form (available from the foundation); proof of tax-exempt status and the organization's IRS status as a private foundation, private operating foundation, or not a private foundation; the names and primary professional affiliations of the organization's directors and trustees; a description of organization, including its background, purpose, and experience in the area for which funds are requested (limit to one page); the organization's financial information, including operating income and expense projections in a multi-year format for the organization's immediate past year, current year, and for one or more future fiscal years (include line items for major expense categories and sources of support and the main assumptions upon which the projetions are based such as inflation rates and program growth); a copy of the organization's latest complete audit; a proposal narrative, and a proposal budget.
Deadlines: March 1, for consideration at the July board meeting; July 1, for consideration at the November meeting; and November 1, for consideration at the March meeting.
Review Process: Foundation staff reviews letters of inquiry to help applicants gauge the likelihood of Foundation support for a particular proposal. Replies generaly range from "possible" to "unlikely." Applicants may then take this assessment into account when determining whether or not to submit a full proposal.
The board meets to consider proposals in March, July, and November. Ordinarily, one member of the program staff is assigned to work on a specific proposal. As necessary, this individual will contact the applicant, seek outside opinions, obtain consultant review assistance, and undertake background research. The results will be presented to the grants committee and the board. The grants committee reviews proposals and makes recommendations to the board. All commitments of grant funds are made by the board. Written notice of grant decisions is usually sent within ten days of a board meeting.

Restrictions

The foundation only contributes to nonprofit, tax-exempt organizations. The foundation does not make grants to individuals except through its fellowship programs. The foundation is unlikely to approve grants for general and continuing operating support; past operating deficits, cash reserve funds, or debt reduction; endowment of health and human service agencies, and of public colleges and universities; small remodeling projects or the purchase of office furnishings, computers, vehicles, and other equipment that are not part of a comprehensive capital campaign; individual concerts or concert series, individual exhibitions, festivals, conferences, performances, or one-time cultural events; media projects such as manuscripts, films, television shows, documentaries, or video projects; capital projects to preserve individual, historic structures; capital or program grants for county historical societies; building purchase, construction, or remodeling projects for charter schools, church sanctuaries, community centers, nursing homes, day care centers for children or adults, municipal and other government agencies, nature centers, public colleges, and universities; research in the biomedical and health sciences and in established academic disciplines; projects outside the United States; efforts to increase public awareness of a social problem without suggesting an approach to prevent, solve, or reduce it; general grants to individual day care centers for children or adults, nature centers, nursing homes, senior citizen centers, and youth recreation and camping programs; newly established arts and humanities organizations; arts organizations that do not pay artistic personnel; or government agencies.

Additional Information

The foundation requires progress reports from grant recipients. The reports should include a list of expenditures. Uncommitted funds must be returned at the end of the grant period.

Fellowship grants limited to Minnesota, North Dakota, South Dakota, and western Wisconsin.

Publications: Annual Report; Application Form; Guidelines

Foundation Officials

Esperanza Guerro Anderson: director
Sharon Sayles Belton: director B Saint Paul, MN 1951. ED Macalester College. PRIM NONPR EMPL mayor: City of Minneapolis. NONPR AFFIL director: Search Institute; director: United States Conference Mayors; director: One to One Mentoring Program; director: President Committee Critical Infrastructure Protection; assistant director: Minneapolis Program for Victims of Sexual Assault; director: National League Cities; member: American Bar Association.
Lee-Hoon Benson: program officer
Ivy S. Bernhardson: treasurer B Fargo, ND 1951. ED Gustavus Adolphus College (1973); University of Minnesota (1978). PRIM CORP EMPL vice president, associate general counsel, corporate secretary: General Mills, Inc. NONPR AFFIL member: Hennepin County Bar Association; member: Minneapolis Bar Association; director: Fairview Southdale Hospital; member: American Society Corporate Secretary; director: Fairview Hospital & Healthcare Services; member: American Bar Association.
Wilson Bradshaw: director
Shirley M. Clark: second vice chairman PRIM CORP EMPL vice chancellor academic affairs: Oregon State System Higher Education. NONPR AFFIL adj professor education policy & management: University Oregon.
Dudley Cocke: director
Merlin E. Dewing: director B Portal, ND 1934. ED University of North Dakota BS (1956); University of North Dakota MS (1958). PRIM CORP EMPL founder, chief executive officer: Dewing Financial Services. NONPR AFFIL director: Lutheran Health System; member: Minnesota Society CPA's; member: Greater Minneapolis Chamber of Commerce; member: American Institute of Certified Public Accountants. CLUB AFFIL Downtown Kiwanis Club.
Jose Gonzalez: program director health
Diana E. Murphy: director B Faribault, MN 1934. ED University of Minnesota BA (1954); Johannes Gutenberg University (1954-1955); University of Minnesota

(1955-1958); University of Minnesota JD (1974). PRIM NONPR EMPL judge: U.S. Court Appeals. NONPR AFFIL treasurer, trustee: University Minnesota Foundation; trustee: University Saint Thomas; member: University Minnesota Alumni Association; board overseers school theology: Saint Johns University; director: United Way Minneapolis; member: Order Coif; member: Phi Beta Kappa; member: National Association Governing Boards Universitys Colleges; treasurer: National Association Women Judges; director: Minnesota Opera; member: Minnesota Women Lawyers; member: Minnesota Bar Association; member: Federal Judicial Center; member: Hennepin County Bar Association; member: American Judicature Society; member: American Law Institute; member: American Bar Association; fellow: American Bar Foundation.
Anita Marie Pampusch, PhD: president B Saint Paul, MN 1938. ED College of Saint Catherine BA (1962); University of Notre Dame MA (1970); University of Notre Dame PhD (1972). CORP AFFIL director: Saint Paul Companies Inc. NONPR AFFIL trustee: University Notre Dame; member executive committee: Women's College Coalition; member: Saint Paul Chamber of Commerce; member: Phi Beta Kappa; district chairman: Rhodes Scholarship Selection Committee; member, chairman: Council Independent Colleges; member: American Philosophical Association; member advisory committee: Columbia University Institutional Leadership Project. CLUB AFFIL Minneapolis Club; Saint Paul Athletic Club.
William Peter Pierskalla: director B Saint Cloud, MN 1934. ED Harvard University AB Economics (1956); Harvard University MBA (1958); University of Pittsburgh MS Math (1962); Stanford University PhD (1965); University of Pennsylvania MA (1978). PRIM NONPR EMPL dean, professor: John E. Anderson Graduate School of Management, UCLA. CORP AFFIL director: North Trust Corp. California. NONPR AFFIL member: Operations Research Society America; consult: Project Hope; member: Omega Rho; member: Institute for Management Sciences; member: International Federation Operational Research Society.
Catherine V. Piersol: director
Gordon M. Sprenger: director B Albert Lea, MN 1937. ED Saint Olaf College BA (1959); University of Minnesota MA (1961). PRIM CORP EMPL chief executive officer, director principal: Allina Health System ADD CORP EMPL principal: Abbott-Northwestern Hospital. CORP AFFIL director: Medtronic Inc.; director: Saint Paul Companies Inc.
Kathryn H. Tunheim: director
W. Richard West, Jr.: secretary B San Bernardino, CA 1943. ED University of Redlands BA (1965); Harvard University AM (1968); Stanford University JD (1971). NONPR AFFIL honorary counselor: Wings America; member advisory committee: Winslow Foundation; trustee: University Redlands; national support committee: Native American Rights Fund; founding director: Smithsonian Institute National Museum American Indian; trustee: Education Foundation America; member, board trustees: Environmental Defense Fund; member: American Indian Bar Association; treasurer: American Indian Lawyer Training Program.
Frank B. Wilderson, Jr.: first vice chair B Lutcher, LA.
C. Angus Wurtele: director B Minneapolis, MN 1934. ED Yale University BA (1956); Stanford University MBA (1961). CORP AFFIL director: IDS Mutual Fund Group; director: Spectro Alloys Corp.; secretary, director: FFS Inc.; director: General Mills Inc.; director: Bemis Co. Inc. NONPR AFFIL member, director: National Paint & Coatings Association; member advisory council: Stanford University Graduate School Business; member: American Business Conference. CLUB AFFIL Minneapolis Club.
Ann Wynia: chair B Fort Worth, TX 1943. ED University of Texas BA (1965); University of Wisconsin MA

(1968). NONPR AFFIL commissioner: Minnesota Department Human Services; instructor: North Hennepin Community College.

Grants Analysis

Disclosure Period: fiscal year ending November 30, 2002
Total Grants: $35,060,000*
Number of Grants: 193
Average Grant: $181,658
Highest Grant: $3,000,000
Typical Range: $25,000 to $300,000
*Note: Giving excludes fellowship.

Recent Grants

Note: Grants derived from fiscal 2001 Form 990.

General

3,000,000	American Indian College Fund, New York, NY -- Toward a capital campaign for building projects at 30 tribal colleges in the American Indian College Fund's consortium
1,000,000	Family Housing Fund of Minneapolis and St. Paul, Minneapolis, MN -- To develop new models to support and deliver services to homeless families
1,000,000	Family Housing Fund for Minneapolis and St. Paul, Minneapolis, MN -- to develop new models to support and deliver services to homeless families
1,000,000	Hampton University, Hampton, VA -- Toward the capital and endowment goals of the Campaign for Hampton
1,000,000	People Serving People, Inc., Minneapolis, MN -- For a capital campaign to renovate a building to house and serve homeless people
1,000,000	People Serving People, Inc., Minneapolis, MN -- for capital campaign
1,000,000	United Negro College Fund, Fairfax, VA -- To support the Technology Enhancement Capital Campaign
920,000	Amherst H. Wilder Foundation, St. Paul, MN -- Toward development and evaluation of a comprehensive school reform project that integrates educational and social services
817,569	Bush Leadership Fellows Programs, St. Paul, MN -- 2000 Program
750,000	Goodwill Industries, St. Paul, MN -- for a new building for employment and training programs

PATRICK AND AIMEE BUTLER FAMILY FOUNDATION

Giving Contact

Kerrie Blevins, Program Director
Patrick and Aimee Butler Family Foundation
332 Minnesota Street, Suite E-1420
St. Paul, MN 55101-1369
Phone: (651)222-2565
E-mail: info@butlerfamilyfoundation.org
Web: http://www.butlerfamilyfoundation.org

Description

Founded: 1951
EIN: 416009902
Organization Type: Private Foundation
Giving Locations: MN: Minneapolis, St. Paul
Grant Types: General Support, Multiyear/Continuing Support, Project.

Donor Information

Founder: the late Patrick Butler and family

Financial Summary

Total Giving: $3,558,470 (2001); $2,878,058 (2000); $1,800,000 (1999 approx)

Giving Analysis: Giving for 2001 includes: foundation scholarships ($10,000); foundation grants to United Way ($40,000); 2000: foundation scholarships ($10,000); foundation grants to United Way ($1,284,598); 1999: foundation grants to United Way ($816,000).

Assets: $53,238,857 (2001); $54,394,211 (2000); $50,795,364 (1999)

Gifts Received: $350,000 (2001); $424,048 (2000); $350,000 (1999). Note: In 2001, 2000 and 1999, contributions were received from Aimee Mott Butler Irrevocable Trust. In 1996, contributions were received from the estate of Aimee Mott Butler ($834,630), the Aimee Mott Butler Irrevocable Trust ($350,000), and Sandra K. Butler ($4,032).

Typical Recipients

Arts & Humanities: Arts Centers, Arts Institutes, Community Arts, Historic Preservation, Libraries, Literary Arts, Museums/Galleries, Public Broadcasting, Theater

Civic & Public Affairs: Botanical Gardens/Parks, Employment/Job Training, Civic & Public Affairs-General, Housing, Native American Affairs, Rural Affairs, Urban & Community Affairs, Women's Affairs, Zoos/Aquariums

Education: Arts/Humanities Education, Education-General, Leadership Training, Literacy, Minority Education

Environment: Air/Water Quality, Environment-General, Resource Conservation

Religion: Jewish Causes, Religious Welfare

Science: Science Museums

Social Services: Child Welfare, Community Centers, Community Service Organizations, Counseling, Domestic Violence, Family Services, Senior Services, Shelters/Homelessness, Social Services-General, Substance Abuse, United Funds/United Ways, Youth Organizations

Application Procedures

Initial Contact: Contact foundation for application form, then send a full proposal.

Application Requirements: Include a description of organization, amount requested, purpose of funds sought, recently audited financial statement, proof of tax-exempt status, and Butler Family Foundation application form.

Deadlines: Call for deadlines.

Restrictions

Does not support criminal justice, economic education, employment and vocational programs, films, health, hospitals, loans, or grants to individuals, medicine research secondary and elementary education, music, or dance.

Additional Information

Faxed applications not accepted.

Publications: Financial Statement; Annual Report; Informational Brochure (including Application Guidelines)

Foundation Officials

Kerrie Blevins: program officer
Brigid M. Butler: trustee
Catherine Butler: trustee
Cecelia M. Butler: trustee
John K. Butler: treasurer, trustee
Patricia M. Butler: trustee
Patrick Butler: vice president, trustee
Paul S. Butler: trustee
Peter M. Butler: president, trustee
Sandra K. Butler: trustee

Terence N. Doyle: secretary B Minneapolis, MN 1936. ED Saint Thomas College BA (1958); University of Minnesota JD (1961). NONPR AFFIL member: Minnesota Law Alumni Association; member: Order Coif; fellow: American College Trust & Estate Counsel; member: Minnesota Bar Association; director: AH South Foundation; member: American Bar Association. CLUB AFFIL Minnesota Club.

Suzanne A. Lefevour: trustee
Jude M. Peterson: trustee
Kate B. Peterson: trustee

Grants Analysis

Disclosure Period: calendar year ending 2001
Total Grants: $3,508,470*
Number of Grants: 126
Average Grant: $12,336*
Highest Grant: $1,966,470
Lowest Grant: $500
Typical Range: $1,000 to $20,000
*Note: Giving excludes United Way and scholarships. Average grant figure excludes highest grant.

Recent Grants

Note: Grants derived from 2000 Form 990.

Library-Related
75,000	The Friends of the St. Paul Public Library, St. Paul, MN -- support for the renewal campaign

General
1,249,598	United Way of the St. Paul Area, St. Paul, MN -- endowment support
100,000	HEARTH Connection, Minneapolis, MN -- support for the supportive housing and managed care pilot program
100,000	Minnesota Book and Literary Arts Building, Inc., Minneapolis, MN -- support for the open book
100,000	The Trust for Public Lands, St. Paul, MN -- capital support for the lower Phalen Creek project
75,000	Project for Pride in Living, Inc., Minneapolis, MN -- support for the Joe Selvaggio initiative
45,000	Minnesota Children's Museum, St. Paul, MN -- contribution for the endowment support
35,000	United Way of the St. Paul Area, St. Paul, MN -- operating support
30,000	Catholic Charities, Minneapolis, MN -- contribution for the visitation transitional housing for single women
30,000	Twin Cities Habit for Humanity, St. Paul, MN -- operating support
25,000	Conservation Fund, Chicago, IL -- support for technical assistance and capacity building with man based environmental groups working on the upper Mississippi River corridor

BUTZ FOUNDATION

Giving Contact

Thomas N. Boyden, Trust Officer
c/o Northern Trust Co.
50 S. LaSalle St., L-5
Chicago, IL 60675
Phone: (312)630-6000
Fax: (312)444-4122

Description

Founded: 1951
EIN: 366008818
Organization Type: Private Foundation
Giving Locations: IL
Grant Types: General Support, Multiyear/Continuing Support, Operating Expenses, Research.

Donor Information

Founder: the late Theodore C. Butz, Jean Butz James

Financial Summary

Total Giving: $247,000 (2002); $274,000 (2001); $173,000 (2000)

Giving Analysis: Giving for 2000 includes: foundation scholarships ($19,500) 1999: foundation scholarships ($16,500)

Assets: $3,867,616 (2002); $4,814,652 (2001); $5,464,792 (2000)

Gifts Received: $21,150 (1998); $550 (1995). Note: In 1998, contributions were received from Robert T. Butz ($6,000), Thompsom H. Butz ($5,000), Theodore H. Butz ($5,000), Gregory and Karen Hall ($50), and Vera Dover ($100). In 1995, contributions were received from Jean Butz James.

Typical Recipients

Arts & Humanities: Arts Associations & Councils, Arts Festivals, Community Arts, Libraries, Music, Performing Arts, Visual Arts

Civic & Public Affairs: Botanical Gardens/Parks, Hispanic Affairs, Law & Justice, Zoos/Aquariums

Education: Colleges & Universities, Education Funds, Education-General, Literacy, Private Education (Precollege), Special Education, Student Aid

Environment: Wildlife Protection

Health: AIDS/HIV, Cancer, Clinics/Medical Centers, Diabetes, Emergency/Ambulance Services, Eyes/Blindness, Hospitals, Medical Research, Multiple Sclerosis, Prenatal Health Issues, Single-Disease Health Associations, Speech & Hearing

Religion: Religion-General

Science: Science-General, Science Museums, Science Associations, Scientific Centers & Institutes

Social Services: Community Service Organizations, Counseling, Family Services, People with Disabilities, Recreation & Athletics, Shelters/Homelessness

Application Procedures

Initial Contact: The foundation has no formal grant application procedure or application form.
Deadlines: None.

Restrictions

Does not support individuals.

Foundation Officials

Barbara T. Butz: director
Elvira M. Butz: vice president
Theodore H. Butz: president
Thompson H. Butz: treasurer
Vera M. Dover: secretary
Jean Butz James: director
Ronald E. James: director

Grants Analysis

Disclosure Period: calendar year ending 2002
Total Grants: $247,000
Number of Grants: 23
Average Grant: $8,400*
Highest Grant: $30,000
Lowest Grant: $1,000
Typical Range: $5,000 to $10,000
*Note: Average grant figure excludes three highest grants ($79,000).

Recent Grants

Note: Grants derived from 2001 Form 990.

General
60,000	St. Dominic School, Post Falls, ID -- for gutter system and engineering bridge for handicapped entrance
30,000	St. Peter's Parish, Poolesville, MD
30,000	St. Peter's Parish, Poolesville, MD
30,000	St. Peter's Parish, Poolesville, MD
30,000	University of Richmond, Richmond, VA -- for scholarship fund

25,000	International Rett Syndrome Association, Clinton, MD -- for research fund
20,000	St. Olaf College, Northfield, MN -- for scholarship fund
15,000	Evanston Northwestern Healthcare Corporation, Evanston, IL -- research
10,000	Field Museum of Natural History, Chicago, IL -- for exhibit expenses
10,000	Kennedy Center for the Performing Arts, Washington, DC -- education and public service

BYDALE FOUNDATION

Giving Contact

Milton D. Solomon, Vice President, Secretary & Trustee
11 Martine Ave., Ste. 775
White Plains, NY 10606-1934
Phone: (914)683-3519

Description

Founded: 1965
EIN: 136195286
Organization Type: Private Foundation
Giving Locations: NY: New York
Grant Types: Conference/Seminar, General Support, Multiyear/Continuing Support, Operating Expenses, Project, Research, Seed Money.

Donor Information

Founder: the late James P. Warburg

Financial Summary

Total Giving: $748,250 (2001); $753,000 (2000); $712,000 (1999)
Assets: $13,591,815 (2001); $14,498,103 (2000); $14,683,530 (1999)

Typical Recipients

Arts & Humanities: Arts Centers, Arts Outreach, Film & Video, Libraries, Literary Arts, Music, Opera, Performing Arts, Public Broadcasting
Civic & Public Affairs: Botanical Gardens/Parks, Civil Rights, Economic Policy, Civic & Public Affairs-General, Nonprofit Management, Parades/Festivals, Professional & Trade Associations, Public Policy, Rural Affairs, Urban & Community Affairs, Women's Affairs
Education: Arts/Humanities Education, Colleges & Universities, Engineering/Technological Education, Education-General, International Studies, Literacy, Private Education (Precollege), Vocational & Technical Education
Environment: Air/Water Quality, Environment-General
International: Foreign Arts Organizations, Human Rights, International Affairs, International Environmental Issues, International Peace & Security Issues, International Relations, Missionary/Religious Activities
Religion: Jewish Causes, Religious Organizations, Religious Welfare, Synagogues/Temples
Social Services: Community Service Organizations, Day Care, Family Planning, Family Services, Food/Clothing Distribution, Social Services-General, YMCA/YWCA/YMHA/YWHA

Application Procedures

Initial Contact: Send a brief letter of inquiry describing program or project.
Deadlines: November 1.

Restrictions

Does not support individuals or provide funds for loans, deficit financing, demonstration projects, capital funds, scholarships, or fellowships.

Foundation Officials

Sarah W. Bliumis: trustee
Frank J. Kick: treasurer
Milton D. Solomon: vice president, secretary, trustee
James P. Warburg, Jr.: trustee
Jennifer J. Warburg: trustee
Joan M. Warburg: president, trustee
Philip N. Warburg: trustee

Grants Analysis

Disclosure Period: calendar year ending 2001
Total Grants: $748,250
Number of Grants: 68
Average Grant: $9,825*
Highest Grant: $90,000
Lowest Grant: $1,000
Typical Range: $2,000 to $15,000
*Note: Average grant excludes highest grant.

Recent Grants

Note: Grants derived from 2001 Form 990.

General

90,000	American for Peace Now, Washington, DC
50,000	Foundation on Economic Trends, Washington, DC
50,000	Grassroots Policy Project, Washington, DC
30,000	New Israel Fund, Washington, DC
25,000	Poets House, New York, NY
25,000	WNYC Radio Foundation, New York, NY
20,000	Equality Now, New York, NY
20,000	Public Media, Inc., New York, NY
15,000	Channel 13, New York, NY
15,000	Feminist Majority Foundation

BYRNE FOUNDATION

Giving Contact

Dorothy M. Byrne, President
35 Rope Ferry Road
Hanover, NH 03755
Phone: (603)643-4555

Description

Founded: 1993
EIN: 020462931
Organization Type: Private Foundation
Giving Locations: NH: Upper Valley Region; VT: Upper Valley Region

Donor Information

Founder: Established in 1993 by John J. Byrne.

Financial Summary

Total Giving: $3,917,550 (2000); $3,164,200 (1998); $2,495,483 (1997)
Giving Analysis: Giving for 1998 includes: foundation grants to United Way ($5,000)
Assets: $31,225,657 (2000); $30,403,555 (1998); $26,179,670 (1997)
Gifts Received: $1,206 (2000); $2,436 (1998); $14,355 (1997). Note: In 1996, contributions were received from John J. Byrne ($13,000) and Berkshire Hathaway ($14,400).

Typical Recipients

Arts & Humanities: Community Arts, History & Archaeology, Libraries, Performing Arts, Public Broadcasting
Civic & Public Affairs: Business/Free Enterprise, Civil Rights, Clubs, Community Foundations, Gay/Lesbian Issues, Civic & Public Affairs-General, Housing, Parades/Festivals, Philanthropic Organizations, Public Policy, Urban & Community Affairs

Education: Colleges & Universities, Environmental Education, Education-General, Literacy, Minority Education, Private Education (Precollege), Public Education (Precollege), Science/Mathematics Education, Student Aid
Environment: Air/Water Quality, Environment-General, Resource Conservation
Health: Cancer, Children's Health/Hospitals, Clinics/Medical Centers, Emergency/Ambulance Services, Health Organizations, Hospices, Hospitals, Medical Rehabilitation, Medical Research, Multiple Sclerosis, Public Health, Respiratory
International: Foreign Educational Institutions, International-General, Human Rights, International Relations, International Relief Efforts, Missionary/Religious Activities
Religion: Churches, Dioceses, Religion-General, Jewish Causes, Religious Welfare
Science: Scientific Centers & Institutes
Social Services: Child Abuse, Child Welfare, Community Service Organizations, Family Services, Food/Clothing Distribution, People with Disabilities, Recreation & Athletics, Senior Services, Special Olympics, Substance Abuse, United Funds/United Ways, Youth Organizations

Application Procedures

Initial Contact: Send a brief letter of inquiry.
Deadlines: None.

Restrictions

Primary interests are cancer research, Dartmouth Community College, and general philanthropy.

Foundation Officials

Dorothy M. Byrne: president
John J. Byrne, III: director
Mark J. Byrne: director
Patrick M. Byrne: director
Robert E. Snyder: vice president, secretary, treasurer

Grants Analysis

Disclosure Period: calendar year ending 2000
Total Grants: $3,917,550*
Number of Grants: 189
Average Grant: $18,585*
Highest Grant: $405,000
Lowest Grant: $500
Typical Range: $100 to $20,000
*Note: Average grant excludes highest grant. Grants analysis provided by foundation.

Recent Grants

Note: Grants derived from 2000 Form 990.

General

405,000	Memorial Sloan-Kettering Cancer Center, New York, NY
389,900	Norris Cotton Cancer Center, Hanover, NH
310,000	Tuck School, Hanover, NH
300,000	St. Mary's Church, Park City, UT
208,000	Kingswood Oxford School, West Hartford, CT
196,000	Upper Valley Haven, White River Junction, VT
110,000	Friends of Grafton County Seniors, Lebanon, NH
110,000	Lebanon College, Lebanon, NH
100,000	Dana Farber Cancer Institute Jimmy Fund, Boston, MA
75,000	Diocese of Manchester, Manchester, NY

C. E. AND S. FOUNDATION

Giving Contact

Bruce A. Maza, Executive Director
1650 National City Tower
Louisville, KY 40202

Phone: (502)583-0546
Fax: (502)583-7648
E-mail: bruce@cesfoundation.com
Web: http://www.cesfoundation.com/

Description

Founded: 1984
EIN: 592466943
Organization Type: Private Foundation
Giving Locations: KY: Louisville Louisville, KY
Grant Types: Capital, Endowment, General Support, Scholarship.

Donor Information

Founder: David A. Jones

Financial Summary

Total Giving: $2,418,776 (2002); $2,904,055 (2001); $3,029,751 (2000)
Giving Analysis: Giving for 2002 includes: foundation scholarships ($120,500); foundation matching gifts ($167,900); foundation grants to United Way ($200,000); 2001: foundation matching gifts ($48,550); foundation grants to United Way ($200,000); 2000: foundation grants to United Way ($59,799); foundation matching gifts ($117,500);
Assets: $40,000,000 (2002 approx); $37,033,833 (2001); $56,986,546 (2000)
Gifts Received: $616 (2001); $1,000,000 (2000); $1,945,575 (1999). Note: In 2001, contributions were received from David A. Jones. In 2000, contributions were received from W. T. Young Foundation. In 1999, contributions were received from David A. Jones ($1,807,272) and J.G. Funding ($138,303). In 1996 and 1998, contributions were received from David A. Jones.

Typical Recipients

Arts & Humanities: Arts Centers, Community Arts, History & Archaeology, Libraries, Music, Performing Arts, Public Broadcasting
Civic & Public Affairs: African American Affairs, Botanical Gardens/Parks, Community Foundations, Housing
Education: Afterschool/Enrichment Programs, Arts/Humanities Education, Business Education, Colleges & Universities, Faculty Development, Education-General, International Studies, Legal Education, Literacy, Private Education (Precollege), Religious Education, Science/Mathematics Education, Social Sciences Education, Student Aid, Vocational & Technical Education
Environment: Resource Conservation
International: Foreign Educational Institutions, Health Care/Hospitals, International Development, International Relations, International Relief Efforts, Missionary/Religious Activities
Religion: Churches, Churches, Ministries, Religious Welfare, Seminaries
Social Services: Community Centers, Community Service Organizations, Food/Clothing Distribution, Homes, People with Disabilities, United Funds/United Ways, Youth Organizations

Application Procedures

Initial Contact: Request executive director to request an application form.
Deadlines: None.

Foundation Officials

A. Robert Doll: president PRIM CORP EMPL senior partner: Greenebaum, Doll & McDonald.
Bruce A. Maza: executive director

Grants Analysis

Disclosure Period: calendar year ending 2002
Total Grants: $1,930,376*
Number of Grants: 107
Average Grant: $14,574*
Highest Grant: $385,500
Lowest Grant: $250

Typical Range: $5,000 to $25,000
***Note:** Giving excludes matching gifts, scholarship, and United Way. Average grant figure excludes highest grant.

Recent Grants

Note: Grants derived from 2001 Form 990.

General

1,000,000	Transylvania University, Lexington, KY -- Clive M. Beck Athletic Recreation Center
478,500	University of Louisville Foundation, Louisville, KY -- higher education initiative
200,000	Metro United Way, Inc., Louisville, KY -- participate in business challenge
100,000	Yale China Association, New Haven, CT -- centennial campaign
85,000	Louisville Presbyterian Theological Seminary, Louisville, KY -- support of foreign and domestic seminary students
81,440	Bellarmine College, Louisville, KY -- support teacher formation
75,000	Yale University, New Haven, CT -- Yale Law School China Institute
69,500	Cathedral Heritage Foundation, Louisville, KY -- community dining room
57,535	Yale University, New Haven, CT -- Global Constitutionalism Symposium of Yale Law School
50,000	Bellarmine College, Louisville, KY -- to fund international student travel, internships and foreign language, faculty development

C. LOUIS AND MARY C. CABE FOUNDATION

Giving Contact

Anita Cabe, Secretary & Treasurer
108 Front St.
Gurdon, AR 71743
Phone: (870)353-2063

Description

Founded: 1990
EIN: 710685612
Organization Type: Private Foundation
Giving Locations: AR; TX
Grant Types: Capital, General Support.

Donor Information

Founder: Established in 1990 by Mary C. Cabe and C. Louis Cabe.

Financial Summary

Total Giving: $84,306 (2001); $86,050 (2000); $88,619 (1999)
Giving Analysis: Giving for 2001 includes: foundation grants to United Way ($1,000) 1998: foundation grants to United Way ($1,000)
Assets: $2,321,758 (2001); $2,322,624 (2000); $2,365,893 (1999)
Gifts Received: $750,000 (1996). Note: In 1989, contributions were received from from C. Louis Cabe ($250,000) and Mary C. Cabe ($250,000).

Typical Recipients

Arts & Humanities: Libraries, Museums/Galleries
Civic & Public Affairs: African American Affairs, Civic & Public Affairs-General, Municipalities/Towns
Education: Arts/Humanities Education, Colleges & Universities, Education Funds, Literacy, Public Education (Precollege), Secondary Education (Public), Student Aid
Environment: Environment-General
Health: Children's Health/Hospitals, Hospitals, Preventive Medicine/Wellness Organizations
Religion: Churches, Religious Welfare

Social Services: Camps, Child Welfare, Recreation & Athletics, Senior Services, Social Services-General, Youth Organizations

Application Procedures

Initial Contact: Applicants should contact the foundation for an application form.
Deadlines: None.

Restrictions

Grants are usually restricted to charitable and educational organizations operating in AR and TX.

Foundation Officials

Anita B. Cabe: secretary, treasurer, director
Charles L. Cabe, Jr.: president, director
Mary C. Cabe: vice president, director
Marianne Cabe Long: vice president, director

Grants Analysis

Disclosure Period: calendar year ending 2001
Total Grants: $84,306*
Number of Grants: 51
Average Grant: $1,653*
Highest Grant: $5,000
Lowest Grant: $50
Typical Range: $50 to $5,000
***Note:** Average grant figure excludes highest grant.

Recent Grants

Note: Grants derived from 2001 Form 990.

General

5,000	Arkansas Sheriff Boys and Girls Ranches, Batesville, AR
5,000	Children's Village, New York, NY
5,000	Fishing Hall of Fame Inc.
5,000	Gurdon Schools, Gurdon, AR -- football
4,500	Arkansas Children's Hospital, Little Rock, AR
3,000	Clark County T.E.A Coalition
3,000	Gurdon Schools, Gurdon, AR -- scholarships
3,000	Gurdon Schools, Gurdon, AR -- football
3,000	Gurdon Schools, Gurdon, AR -- auditorium fund
3,000	Hot Springs Documentary Film Institute, Hot Springs, AR

ROBERT G. CABELL III AND MAUDE MORGAN CABELL FOUNDATION

Giving Contact

John B. Werner, Executive Director
PO Box 85678
Richmond, VA 23285-5678
Phone: (804)780-2000
Fax: (804)697-2989

Description

Founded: 1957
EIN: 546039157
Organization Type: Family Foundation
Giving Locations: VA: Richmond
Grant Types: Capital, Matching.

Donor Information

Founder: Incorporated in 1957 by the late Robert G. Cabell II and the late Maude Morgan Cabell .

Financial Summary

Total Giving: $4,000,000 (2003 approx); $4,000,000 (2002 approx); $4,400,000 (2001)
Assets: $84,000,000 (2002 approx); $93,029,169 (2000); $92,693,397 (1999)

Gifts Received: $38,502,636 (1997). Note: In 1997, contributions were received from Morgan A. Reynolds.

Typical Recipients

Arts & Humanities: Arts Associations & Councils, Arts Centers, Arts & Humanities-General, Historic Preservation, History & Archaeology, Libraries, Museums/Galleries, Music, Performing Arts, Theater

Civic & Public Affairs: Botanical Gardens/Parks, Clubs, Community Foundations, Economic Development, Civic & Public Affairs-General, Housing, Municipalities/Towns, Philanthropic Organizations, Urban & Community Affairs, Women's Affairs, Zoos/Aquariums

Education: Agricultural Education, Arts/Humanities Education, Colleges & Universities, Education Funds, Faculty Development, Education-General, Gifted & Talented Programs, Legal Education, Literacy, Science/Mathematics Education, Social Sciences Education

Environment: Air/Water Quality, Forestry, Environment-General, Resource Conservation

Health: Alzheimers Disease, Arthritis, Children's Health/Hospitals, Clinics/Medical Centers, Diabetes, Emergency/Ambulance Services, Geriatric Health, Health Organizations, Heart, Hospitals, Public Health, Research/Studies Institutes, Single-Disease Health Associations, Transplant Networks/Donor Banks

Religion: Churches, Religion-General, Ministries, Religious Organizations, Religious Welfare, Seminaries

Science: Science Museums

Social Services: Animal Protection, Child Abuse, Child Welfare, Community Service Organizations, Domestic Violence, Family Planning, Family Services, Food/Clothing Distribution, Homes, People with Disabilities, Recreation & Athletics, Senior Services, Shelters/Homelessness, United Funds/United Ways, YMCA/YWCA/YMHA/YWHA, Youth Organizations

Application Procedures

Initial Contact: The foundation has no formal grant procedure or grant application form. Submit proposals in writing.

Application Requirements: Include a brief description of the mission; how the specific project supports the mission; planned budget; additional sources of support; current operating budget and recent financial statement; a list of officer's and Board of Directors; support for non-exempt status; a cover letter from the CEO, stating support for proposal.

Deadlines: April 1 and October 1.

Restrictions

Grants are restricted to the state of Virginia. The foundation does not support individuals, endowment funds, operating budgets, special interest groups, or research programs.

Additional Information

Publications: Application Guidelines

Foundation Officials

Joseph L. Antrim, III: director PRIM CORP EMPL executive vice president, director: Davenport & Co. LLC.

J. Read Branch, Jr.: director

J. Read Branch: president, treasurer

Patteson Branch, Jr.: director

Charles L. Cabell: secretary PRIM CORP EMPL attorney: Williams Mullen Christian & Dobbins. CORP AFFIL director: Pleasants Hardware Inc.; director: CF Sauer Co. Inc.; director: High's Ice Cream Corp.; director: Metrolina Plastics Inc.; director: C & T Refinery Quincy Inc.; director: Dean Foods Co.; director: C & T Quincy Inc.

John Branch Cabell: director

Elizabeth Cabell Jennings: director

Edmund A. Rennolds, Jr.: director

John B. Werner: executive director B Saint Marys, PA 1931. ED Randolph-Macon College BA (1953); University of Virginia postgrad (1953-1955); Rutgers University postgrad (1965). PRIM CORP EMPL senior executive vice president: Sovran Fin Corp. NONPR AFFIL member: Robert Morris Associates; member: Virginia Chamber of Commerce; trustee, member finance committee: Randolph-Macon College; member: Comptroller Currencys National Advisory Comm; member: Poplar Forest Foundation. CLUB AFFIL Commonwealth Club.

Mary Z. (Rennolds) Zeugner: director

Grants Analysis

Disclosure Period: calendar year ending 2000

Total Grants: $4,677,500

Number of Grants: 37

Average Grant: $93,456*

Highest Grant: $500,000

Typical Range: $50,000 to $250,000

*Note: Average grant figure excludes three top grants.

Recent Grants

Note: Grants derived from 2000 Form 990.

Library-Related

500,000	Thomas Jefferson Memorial Foundation, Charlottesville, VA -- Jefferson Research Library
50,000	Friends of the Mathews Memorial Library, Mathews, VA -- renovation and expansion

General

500,000	Mount Vernon Ladies Association, Mt. Vernon, VA -- auditorium and gift shop
500,000	Richmond Riverfront Development Corp, Richmond, VA -- Canal Walk Project
300,000	Valentine Museum, Richmond, VA -- capital improvements
250,000	Boys and Girls Club of Metro Richmond, Richmond, VA -- Robinson Street Club
200,000	Science Museum of Virginia Foundation, Richmond, VA -- interactive granite sculpture
150,000	Nature Conservancy Virginia Chapter, Charlottesville, VA -- land acquisition
150,000	Randolph-Macon Women's College, Lynchburg, VA -- renovation of auditorium
122,000	Jamestown-Yorktown Foundation, Williamsburg, VA -- new facility at pier
100,000	Better Housing Coalition, Richmond, VA -- childcare center equipment
100,000	Emory and Henry College, Emory, VA -- Academic Center

CABOT CORP.

Company Headquarters

Boston, MA

Web: http://www.cabot-corp.com

Company Description

Founded: 1882

Ticker: CBT

Exchange: NYSE

Revenue: US$1.557 billion (2002)

Employees: 4500 (2002)

SIC(s): 2819 Industrial Inorganic Chemicals Nec, 2821 Plastics Materials & Resins, 2895 Carbon Black, 3061 Mechanical Rubber Goods.

Operating Locations

Cabot Corp. (MA--Billerica)

Nonmonetary Support

Type: Donated Equipment; Donated Products; In-kind Services; Loaned Employees; Loaned Executives

Note: Nonmonetary support is provided by the co. and the foundation. For information on nonmonetary support, contact local Cabot facilities manager.

Cabot Corp. Foundation

Giving Contact

Dorothy L. Forbes, Executive Director, Vice President

Two Seaport Ln., Ste. 1300

Boston, MA 02210

Phone: (617)342-6004

Fax: (617)342-6312

E-mail: dorothy_forbes@cabot-corp.com

Alternate Contact

Phone: (617)342-6002

Note: The alternate phone number is to answer preliminary inquiries. Organizations can also contact local Cabot facilities.

Description

EIN: 046035227

Organization Type: Corporate Foundation

Giving Locations: principally near operating locations and to national organizations.

Grant Types: Capital, Challenge, Employee Matching Gifts, Fellowship, General Support, Professorship, Project, Research, Scholarship, Seed Money.

Note: Employee matching gift ratio: 1 to 1 for schools and united funds only.

Financial Summary

Total Giving: $1,035,082 (fiscal year ending September 30, 2001); $1,036,883 (fiscal 2000); $1,098,690 (fiscal 1999). Note: Contributes through corporate direct giving program and foundation. Giving includes foundation.

Giving Analysis: Giving for fiscal 1999 includes: foundation scholarships ($17,400); foundation gifts to individuals ($19,000); foundation matching gifts ($311,030); foundation ($751,260); fiscal 1998: foundation gifts to individuals ($17,700) foundation matching gifts ($327,809)

Assets: $1,627,896 (fiscal 2001); $2,300,000 (fiscal 2000); $2,855,709 (fiscal 1999)

Gifts Received: $500,000 (fiscal 2001); $1,571,760 (fiscal 1999); $1,059,655 (fiscal 1997)

Typical Recipients

Arts & Humanities: Arts Appreciation, Arts Associations & Councils, Arts Centers, Arts Funds, Arts Institutes, Arts Outreach, Community Arts, Dance, Ethnic & Folk Arts, Arts & Humanities-General, Historic Preservation, Libraries, Literary Arts, Museums/Galleries, Music, Opera, Performing Arts, Theater

Civic & Public Affairs: African American Affairs, Botanical Gardens/Parks, Business/Free Enterprise, Community Foundations, Economic Development, Economic Policy, Employment/Job Training, Civic & Public Affairs-General, Law & Justice, Legal Aid, Municipalities/Towns, Public Policy, Safety, Urban & Community Affairs, Women's Affairs, Zoos/Aquariums, Zoos/Aquariums

Education: Business Education, Colleges & Universities, Community & Junior Colleges, Economic Education, Education Funds, Education Reform, Elementary Education (Private), Engineering/Technological Education, Faculty Development, Education-General, Health & Physical Education, International Exchange, International Studies, Literacy, Medical Education,

Minority Education, Preschool Education, Private Education (Precollege), Public Education (Precollege), Science/Mathematics Education, Social Sciences Education, Special Education, Student Aid

Environment: Air/Water Quality, Environment-General, Wildlife Protection

Health: Cancer, Children's Health/Hospitals, Clinics/Medical Centers, Diabetes, Health-General, Health Organizations, Heart, Hospitals, Prenatal Health Issues, Public Health

International: Foreign Arts Organizations, Foreign Educational Institutions, International-General, Health Care/Hospitals, International Development, International Organizations, International Relations, International Relief Efforts

Religion: Ministries

Science: Science Exhibits & Fairs, Science Museums, Scientific Organizations

Social Services: At-Risk Youth, Camps, Child Abuse, Child Welfare, Community Centers, Community Service Organizations, Counseling, Day Care, Domestic Violence, Emergency Relief, Food/Clothing Distribution, Homes, People with Disabilities, Recreation & Athletics, Scouts, Senior Services, Shelters/Homelessness, Social Services-General, Substance Abuse, United Funds/United Ways, Volunteer Services, YMCA/YWCA/YMHA/YWHA, Youth Organizations

Application Procedures

Initial Contact: Send a written proposal.

Application Requirements: Include statement of proposed project (no more than two pages), including its purpose, uniqueness, long-term goals, specific short-term objectives, estimated time required for completion, and manner by which results are measured; brief background information on organization, board of directors, and those leading proposed effort; proof of tax-exempt status; total project cost, present and potential funding sources, and amount requested of Cabot; include latest audited financial statement if organization's budget exceeds $100,000.

Deadlines: Proposals must be received at least one month before board meetings held in March, June, September, and December.

Review Process: Grant requests for/from communities where Cabot has operations are reviewed at the local level by community relations teams; if appropriate for foundation funding, they are forwarded to the executive director; further information and site visits may be necessary; approval is made by the directors of the foundation.

Evaluative Criteria: Year-end reports, audits, community relations team recommendation, employee involvement.

Decision Notification: Quarterly.

Restrictions

Cabot Corporation Foundation does not make contributions to individuals, political or fraternal organizations, religious institutions for sectarian purposes, advertising, or dinner-table sponsorship.

Additional Information

Cabot strongly encourages requests from projects under way in plant locations. The contributions program has expanded its involvement in plant communities, tying contributions more closely to the nature of business, encouraging greater employee participation in community volunteer activities, and addressing significant societal concerns. Foundation particularly considers recommendations from teams formed by local employees, which initiate community projects and consider local requests for support.

Company prefers to support specific projects or programs rather than general operating expenses.

Strong consideration is given to projects that combine financial support with company manpower, technical assistance, or in-kind support to achieve objectives.

Company often conducts "needs assessments" surveys to determine if projects will have a long-term effect on the community they serve.

Cabot is especially interested in projects involved with science and technology.

Organizations receiving grants are expected to provide periodic progress reports.

Publications: Guidelines

Corporate Officials

Kennett F. Burnes: chairman, chief executive officer, president PRIM CORP EMPL chairman, chief executive officer, president: Cabot Corp.

Foundation Officials

Susan H. Alexander: director
Robert L. Culver: director
Dorothy L. Forbes: executive director
Paul J. Gormisky: director
Margaret J. Hanratty: treasurer
John J. Lawler: director
John P. McGann: clerk
Sarah W. Saunders: clerk

Grants Analysis

Disclosure Period: fiscal year ending September 30, 1999

Total Grants: $751,260*
Number of Grants: 59
Average Grant: $12,733
Highest Grant: $168,894
Lowest Grant: $500
Typical Range: $1,000 to $10,000
*Note: Giving excludes matching gifts; scholarships; volunteer grants.

Recent Grants

Note: Grants derived from fiscal 2001 Form 990.

General

75,000	Museum of Science, Boston, MA -- for the current Science and Technology Center
55,814	Boyertown Area United Way, Boyertown, PA -- matching grant
50,000	Massachusetts General Hospital - Harvard Medical School, Charlestown, MA -- for MGS Clinical Facility Fund
50,000	New England Aquarium, Boston, MA -- for capital campaign
50,000	Northeastern University, Boston, MA -- for the Godfrey Lowell Cabot Physical Education Center
50,000	Twin Towers Fund, New York, NY -- for the workers in New York disaster
45,000	WGBH Education Foundation, Boston, MA -- to sponsorship of the Science Tuesday series
35,780	United Way of Massachusetts Bay, Boston, MA -- matching grant
34,000	Citizens Scholarship Foundation of America -- for Cabot's College Scholarship Program
30,000	Courageous Sailing Center, Boston, MA -- for Summer Programs

CABOT FAMILY CHARITABLE TRUST

Giving Contact

Ruth C. Scheer, Executive Director
70 Federal St.
Boston, MA 02110
Phone: (617)451-1744

Description

Founded: 1942
EIN: 046036446
Organization Type: Private Foundation

Giving Locations: CA; MA
Grant Types: Capital, Endowment, General Support, Multiyear/Continuing Support, Project.

Donor Information

Founder: Established in 1942 by the late Godfrey L. Cabot.

Financial Summary

Total Giving: $3,034,500 (2001); $1,167,663 (2000); $1,603,417 (1998)

Giving Analysis: Giving for 2001 includes: foundation grants to United Way ($25,000)

Assets: $53,100,042 (2001); $37,931,079 (2000); $27,766,493 (1998)

Gifts Received: $750,000 (1996). Note: In 1996, contributions were received from the estate of Thomas D. Cabot.

Typical Recipients

Arts & Humanities: Arts Associations & Councils, Arts Funds, Arts Institutes, Arts Outreach, Ballet, Dance, Film & Video, Arts & Humanities-General, Historic Preservation, History & Archaeology, Libraries, Literary Arts, Museums/Galleries, Music, Opera, Public Broadcasting, Theater

Civic & Public Affairs: Civil Rights, Clubs, Economic Development, Employment/Job Training, Civic & Public Affairs-General, Municipalities/Towns, Native American Affairs, Philanthropic Organizations, Public Policy, Urban & Community Affairs, Women's Affairs, Zoos/Aquariums

Education: Afterschool/Enrichment Programs, Colleges & Universities, Education Associations, Education-General, Health & Physical Education, International Studies, Journalism/Media Education, Leadership Training, Legal Education, Medical Education, Private Education (Precollege), Public Education (Precollege), Science/Mathematics Education, Secondary Education (Private)

Environment: Environment-General, Protection, Resource Conservation

Health: Children's Health/Hospitals, Clinics/Medical Centers, Health Organizations, Hospitals, Mental Health, Public Health

International: Foreign Educational Institutions, Health Care/Hospitals, Human Rights, International Development, International Environmental Issues, International Peace & Security Issues, International Relief Efforts

Religion: Churches, Jewish Causes, Social/Policy Issues

Science: Science Museums, Scientific Centers & Institutes, Scientific Labs, Scientific Organizations

Social Services: Camps, Child Welfare, Child Welfare, Community Service Organizations, Day Care, Family Planning, Family Services, People with Disabilities, Recreation & Athletics, Refugee Assistance, United Funds/United Ways, YMCA/YWCA/YMHA/YWHA, Youth Organizations

Application Procedures

Initial Contact: Send a brief letter of inquiry.
Deadlines: April 1 and October 1.

Restrictions

Limited to organizations that deal with population control, environmental quality, and educational awards.

Additional Information

Publications: Annual Report

Foundation Officials

Jane C. Bradley: trustee
John Godfrey Lowell Cabot: trustee B Rio de Janeiro, RJ Brazil 1934. ED Harvard University AB (1956); Harvard University MBA (1960). PRIM CORP EMPL vice chairman, director: Cabot Corp. CORP AFFIL director: Eaton Vance Corp.; director: Hollingsworth & Vose Co.; director: Distrigas Massachusetts Corp.; director: America Oil & Gas Corp.; director:

Cabot Oil & Gas Corp. NONPR AFFIL trustee: Tufts University; overseer: WGBH Education Foundation; overseer, government: New England Medical Center; member corporate: Massachusetts General Hospital; chairman, director: New England Legal Foundation. **Louis Wellington Cabot:** trustee B Boston, MA 1921. ED Harvard University AB (1943); Harvard University MBA (1948). CORP AFFIL director: Kendall Sq Research. NONPR AFFIL member: Sigma Xi; member: U.S. Chamber of Commerce; member: Phi Beta Kappa; trustee: National Humanities Center; trustee: Northeastern University; member: National Council US-China Trade; member corporate: Massachusetts Institute Technology; trustee: Museum Science Boston; member: Massachusetts Business Roundtable; member: Conference Board; member: Council Foreign Relations; trustee: Brookings Institution; member: Business Council; fellow: American Academy of Arts & Sciences. CLUB AFFIL Wianno Club; Somerset Club; New York Yacht Club; River Club; Metropolitan Club; Commercial Club; Harvard Club. **Ruth C. Scheer:** executive director

Grants Analysis

Disclosure Period: calendar year ending 2001
Total Grants: $3,034,500*
Number of Grants: 85
Average Grant: $30,700*
Highest Grant: $400,000
Lowest Grant: $5,000
Typical Range: $10,000 to $50,000
*Note: GEX United Way. Average grant figure excludes highest grants.

Recent Grants

Note: Grants derived from 2001 Form 990.

Library-Related

50,000	Library of the Boston Athenaeum, Boston, MA

General

400,000	School of the Museum of Fine Arts, Boston, MA
200,000	Harvard School of Public Health, Boston, MA
100,000	Museum of Science, Boston, MA
100,000	New England Conservatory, Boston, MA
100,000	Smithsonian Tropical Research Institute, Washington, DC
100,000	Trustees of Reservations, Beverly, MA
60,000	Island Alliance, Boston, MA
50,000	Academy of Pacific Rim Charter School
50,000	American Academy of Arts and Sciences, Cambridge, MA
50,000	Boston Ballet, Boston, MA

CHARLES AND MARIE CAESTECKER FOUNDATION

Giving Contact

Thomas E. Caestecker, Trustee
Charles and Marie Caestecker Foundation
20 S. Clark, Suite 2310
Chicago, IL 60603-1802
Phone: (312)726-2468
Fax: (312)726-2741

Alternate Contact

Guidance Counselor
Green Lake Public High School
Green Lake, WI 54941
Note: Alternate address is for scholarship applications.

Description

Founded: 1967
EIN: 363154453
Organization Type: Private Foundation
Giving Locations: AZ; WI
Grant Types: Operating Expenses, Scholarship.

Donor Information

Founder: the late Charles E. Caestecker

Financial Summary

Total Giving: $110,583 (fiscal year ending April 30, 2002); $164,707 (fiscal 2001); $1,132,716 (fiscal 1999)
Giving Analysis: Giving for fiscal 2002 includes: foundation scholarships ($39,583); fiscal 2001: foundation scholarships ($37,707) fiscal 1999: foundation scholarships ($50,256)
Assets: $1,715,124 (fiscal 2002); $1,906,838 (fiscal 2001); $2,144,453 (fiscal 1999)
Gifts Received: $3,000 (fiscal 2002)

Typical Recipients

Arts & Humanities: Historic Preservation, History & Archaeology, Libraries
Education: Colleges & Universities, Engineering/Technological Education, Religious Education, Science/Mathematics Education, Student Aid
Health: Clinics/Medical Centers, Hospitals
Religion: Churches, Religious Welfare
Social Services: Community Service Organizations

Application Procedures

Initial Contact: Request application form for scholarships.
Deadlines: February 1 of graduation year.

Additional Information

Provides scholarships to graduates of Green Lake, WI, public high schools for attendance at a four-year college or university.

Foundation Officials

Thomas E. Caestecker: trustee
Frank Andrew Karaba: trustee B Chicago, IL 1927. ED Northwestern University BS (1949); Northwestern University JD (1951). PRIM CORP EMPL senior counsel: Crowley, Barrett & Karaba. CORP AFFIL director: A&R Printers; director: Lyrick Corp. NONPR AFFIL member: Illinois Bar Association; member: Order Coif; member: American Bar Association; assistant counselor: Emergency Commission Crime. CLUB AFFIL Law Club; Legal Club.

Grants Analysis

Disclosure Period: fiscal year ending April 30, 2002
Total Grants: $71,000*
Number of Grants: 5
Average Grant: $14,200
Highest Grant: $25,000
Lowest Grant: $1,000
Typical Range: $10,000 to $25,000
*Note: Giving excludes scholarships.

Recent Grants

Note: Grants derived from fiscal 2002 Form 990.

Library-Related

25,000	Caestecker Public Library Foundation, Green Lake, WI

General

25,000	Ripon College, Ripon, WI
14,583	University of Wisconsin Eau Claire, Eau Claire, WI
12,500	Arizona State University, Tempe, AZ
12,500	Lawrence University, Appleton, WI -- scholarship
10,000	Berlin Memorial Hospital, Berlin, WI
10,000	Ripon Medical Center Foundation, Ripon, WI
1,000	Ripon College, Ripon, WI -- Education Foundation

MORRIS AND GWENDOLYN CAFRITZ FOUNDATION

Giving Contact

Anne Allen, Executive Director
1825 K Street Northwest, Suite 1400
Washington, DC 20006
Phone: (202)223-3100
Fax: (202)296-7567
E-mail: grantscoord@cafritzfoundation.org
Web: http://www.cafritzfoundation.org

Description

Founded: 1948
EIN: 526036989
Organization Type: General Purpose Foundation
Giving Locations: DC: Washington including metropolitan area
Grant Types: Award, Challenge, General Support, Matching, Operating Expenses, Project, Scholarship, Seed Money.

Donor Information

Founder: Established in 1948 by the late Morris Cafritz (d. 1964), a major real estate developer and prominent philanthropist in the Washington, DC, area, and his wife, the late Gwendolyn Cafritz (d. 1988).

Financial Summary

Total Giving: $17,000,000 (fiscal year ending April 30, 2003 approx); $16,706,820 (fiscal 2002); $16,648,176 (fiscal 2001)
Giving Analysis: Giving for fiscal 1999 includes: foundation matching gifts ($227,819) foundation scholarships ($549,564)
Assets: $340,000,000 (fiscal 2003 approx); $346,922,783 (fiscal 2002); $336,242,000 (fiscal 2001)
Gifts Received: $7,188,739 (fiscal 1999); $1,575,477 (fiscal 1997); $19,041,036 (fiscal 1995). Note: Fiscal 1999 contribution from the Gwendolyn D. Cafritz Estate.

Typical Recipients

Arts & Humanities: Arts Associations & Councils, Arts Centers, Arts Festivals, Arts Institutes, Arts Outreach, Ballet, Community Arts, Dance, Historic Preservation, History & Archaeology, Libraries, Literary Arts, Museums/Galleries, Music, Opera, Performing Arts, Public Broadcasting, Theater
Civic & Public Affairs: Botanical Gardens/Parks, Civil Rights, Community Foundations, Economic Development, Employment/Job Training, Hispanic Affairs, Housing, Legal Aid, Nonprofit Management, Professional & Trade Associations, Urban & Community Affairs
Education: Afterschool/Enrichment Programs, Arts/Humanities Education, Business Education, Colleges & Universities, Education Associations, Education Funds, Education Reform, Environmental Education, Faculty Development, Education-General, International Studies, Medical Education, Minority Education, Preschool Education, Private Education (Precollege), Public Education (Precollege), Science/Mathematics Education, Secondary Education (Public), Special Education, Student Aid, Vocational & Technical Education
Environment: Air/Water Quality, Environment-General, Resource Conservation, Watershed
Health: Adolescent Health Issues, AIDS/HIV, Children's Health/Hospitals, Diabetes, Emergency/Ambulance Services, Geriatric Health, Health Organizations, Hospices, Hospitals, Long-Term Care, Medical

Rehabilitation, Mental Health, Nursing Services, Prenatal Health Issues, Single-Disease Health Associations

Religion: Jewish Causes, Religious Welfare

Science: Scientific Centers & Institutes, Scientific Organizations, Scientific Research

Social Services: At-Risk Youth, Child Welfare, Community Centers, Community Service Organizations, Counseling, Crime Prevention, Day Care, Delinquency & Criminal Rehabilitation, Domestic Violence, Emergency Relief, Family Planning, Family Services, Food/Clothing Distribution, People with Disabilities, Recreation & Athletics, Refugee Assistance, Scouts, Senior Services, Shelters/Homelessness, Social Services-General, Substance Abuse, United Funds/United Ways, Volunteer Services, Youth Organizations

Application Procedures

Initial Contact: The foundation requests that all grantseekers use the Washington Regional Association of Grantmakers Common Grant Application Format. Send one unbound copy of the properly formatted proposal.

Application Requirements: The application should include a maximum two page cover letter; a ten-page maximum narrative, including organization information, purpose of grant and evaluation; financial information, including project budget, previous and current operating budget, most recent annual financial statement, other sources of funding, and agency affiliation with federation funds or public agencies. Include the following attachments: a copy of IRS determination letter, list of Board of Directors, letters of support, annual report and relevant articles or reviews about organizations pro grams.

Deadlines: Submit proposals by March 1, July 1, and November 1 by 4:00 p.m. Applications received between deadlines will be held until the next deadline.

Review Process: Applicants are notified as soon as possible after proposals are reviewed by the foundation's advisory board or board of directors. It takes six-to-nine months from the deadline date to process a proposal before submitting it to the board of directors.

Restrictions

Grants generally are made on a project basis. Support is not given to individuals, or for capital purposes, special events or endowments. It is not a general policy to commit funds for a project for more than one year at a time. Grants are only awarded to organizations that are tax-exempt under the IRS code.

Additional Information

Publications: Annual Report; Application Procedures; Grant Guidelines

Foundation Officials

John H. C. Barron: secretary

Daniel Joseph Boorstin: director B Atlanta, GA October 01, 1914. ED Harvard University AB (1934); Oxford University Balliol College BA (1936); Inner Temple, London (1934-1937); Oxford University Balliol College BCL (1937); Yale University JSD (1940). CORP AFFIL member board editors: Encyclopaedia Britannica Inc. NONPR AFFIL trustee: Thomas Gilcrease Museum; trustee: Woodrow Wilson Center International Scholars; member: Phi Beta Kappa; librarian emeritus: Library of Congress; member: Organization American Historians; member: International House Japan; trustee: John F. Kennedy Center Performing Arts; member: Colonial Society Massachusetts; trustee: Colonial Williamsburg Foundation; member: American Philosophical Society; member: American Studies Association; honorary fellow: American Geographical Society; member: American Academy of Arts & Sciences; member: American Antiquarian Society. CLUB AFFIL National Press Club; Cosmos Club; Elizabethan Club.

John Carter Brown: director B Providence, RI 1934. ED Harvard University AB (1956); Harvard University

MBA (1958); University of Munich postgrad (1958). PRIM NONPR EMPL director emeritus: National Gallery Art. CORP AFFIL chairman: Ovation Inc.; director: Nordstern Insurance Co. America. NONPR AFFIL treasurer: White House Historical Association; trustee: World Monuments Fund; member, honorary trustee: Touro Synagogue National Heritage Trust; chairman: U.S. Commission of Fine Arts; member: State Hermitage Museum Advisory Board; trustee: Storm King Art Center; chairman: Pritzker Architecture Prize Jury; honorary fellow: Royal Academy Arts; trustee: National Geographic Society; member: Phi Beta Kappa; member: National Advisory Council Leonard Bernstein Center Education Arts; chairman: National Cultural Alliance; chairman: Leadership Council; fellow: National Academy Design; trustee: John F. Kennedy Center Performing Arts; trustee: Federal City Council; treasurer, member: Federal Council Arts & Humanities; board governors, trustee: Brown University; director, member: Committee Preservation White House; trustee: John Nicolas Brown Center Study American Civilization; board governors: John Carter Brown Library Association; chairman: Arts Network; member, honorary life trustee: Association Art Museum Directors; honorary member: American Institute Architects; member: American Philosophical Society; trustee: American Academy Rome; trustee: American Federation Arts; fellow: American Academy of Arts & Sciences.

Calvin Cafritz: chairman, president, chief executive officer B Washington, DC 1931. PRIM CORP EMPL founder, president: Calvin Cafritz Enterprises. CORP AFFIL director: Cafritz Co.

Daniel J. Callahan, III: director vice chairman treasurer PRIM CORP EMPL chairman, chief executive officer, director: USLICO Corp.

Terence C. Golden: director B Honesdale, PA 1944. ED University of Notre Dame BS (1966); Massachusetts Institute of Technology MS (1967); Harvard University MBA (1970). PRIM CORP EMPL chairman: Bailey Management Corp. ADD CORP EMPL director: Host Mariott Corp. CORP AFFIL president, chief executive officer: Host Marriott Corp.; director: Prime Retail; director: D.R. Horton; chairman: Bailey Realty Corp.; director: Cousins Properties Inc.

Guy T. Steuart, II: director B 1934. PRIM CORP EMPL president, director: Steuart Investment Co. CORP AFFIL president, director: Steuart Kret Development Co.; director: Steuart Petroleum; chairman: Half Moon Bay Ltd.; vice president: Steuart Holding Co.

Grants Analysis

Disclosure Period: fiscal year ending April 30, 2001
Total Grants: $16,648,176
Number of Grants: 273
Average Grant: $60,982
Highest Grant: $1,000,000
Lowest Grant: $2,000
Typical Range: $10,000 to $100,000

Recent Grants

Note: Grants derived from fiscal 2001 Form 990.

General

1,000,000	Seed Foundation, Inc., Washington, DC -- to acquire the Weatherless School
1,000,000	Seed Foundation, Inc., Washington, DC -- to acquire the Weatherless School
400,000	Planned Parenthood, Portland, OR
400,000	Planned Parenthood, Portland, OR
225,000	Washington Regional Association of Grantmakers, Washington, DC -- for HIV/AIDS epidemic in the Washington Metropolitan area
225,000	Washington Regional Association of Grantmakers, Washington, DC -- for HIV/AIDS epidemic in the Washington Metropolitan area

200,000	Chesapeake Bay Foundation, Annapolis, MD -- for the Covenant to Save the Chesapeake Bay
200,000	Chesapeake Bay Foundation, Annapolis, MD -- for the Convenant to Save the Chesapeake Bay
200,000	Corcoran Gallery and School of Art, Washington, DC -- support for the museum and school
200,000	Field School, Washington, DC -- for scholarship assistance

EFFIE AND WOFFORD CAIN FOUNDATION

Giving Contact

Lynn Fowler, Executive Director, Secretary & Treasurer
4131 Spicewood Springs Road, Suite A-1
Austin, TX 78759
Phone: (512)346-7490
Fax: (512)346-7491
E-mail: mbratz@cainfoundation.org

Description

Founded: 1952
EIN: 756030774
Organization Type: Family Foundation
Giving Locations: TX
Grant Types: Endowment, Operating Expenses, Project, Research, Scholarship.

Donor Information

Founder: Incorporated in Texas in 1952 by Effie Marie Cain and the late Wofford R. Cain .

Financial Summary

Total Giving: $4,500,000 (fiscal year ending October 31, 2003 approx); $4,500,000 (fiscal 2002 approx); $4,468,033 (fiscal 2001)

Giving Analysis: Giving for fiscal 2000 includes: foundation grants to United Way ($5,000); foundation scholarships ($561,070); fiscal 1999: foundation grants to United Way ($17,000); foundation scholarships ($249,450) fiscal 1998: foundation grants to United Way ($24,500)

Assets: $90,000,000 (fiscal 2003 approx); $90,000,000 (fiscal 2002 approx); $95,664,554 (fiscal 2001)

Gifts Received: $22,155 (fiscal 2000); $500,000 (fiscal 1999); $1,503,200 (fiscal 1998). Note: In fiscal 2000, contributions were received from the Estate of Effie Marie Cain. Previous contributions were received from Effie Marie Cain in the form of cash and securities.

Typical Recipients

Arts & Humanities: Arts Centers, Arts Outreach, Film & Video, Historic Preservation, Libraries, Museums/Galleries, Music, Public Broadcasting, Theater

Civic & Public Affairs: Botanical Gardens/Parks, Clubs, Employment/Job Training, Civic & Public Affairs-General, Housing, Municipalities/Towns, Nonprofit Management, Parades/Festivals, Philanthropic Organizations

Education: Arts/Humanities Education, Colleges & Universities, Education Reform, Elementary Education (Public), Engineering/Technological Education, Education-General, International Exchange, International Studies, Legal Education, Medical Education, Minority Education, Private Education (Precollege), Public Education (Precollege), Religious Education, Science/Mathematics Education, Student Aid, Student Aid

Environment: Forestry, Wildlife Protection

Health: Alzheimers Disease, Arthritis, Cancer, Children's Health/Hospitals, Clinics/Medical Centers, Diabetes, Emergency/Ambulance Services, Health Organizations, Heart, Hospitals, Hospitals (University

Affiliated), Medical Research, Medical Training, Mental Health, Public Health, Respiratory, Single-Disease Health Associations

Religion: Churches, Jewish Causes, Ministries, Missionary Activities (Domestic), Religious Organizations, Religious Welfare, Seminaries

Social Services: At-Risk Youth, Camps, Child Abuse, Child Welfare, Community Centers, Community Service Organizations, Domestic Violence, Emergency Relief, Food/Clothing Distribution, Homes, People with Disabilities, Recreation & Athletics, Scouts, Substance Abuse, United Funds/United Ways, YMCA/YWCA/YMHA/YWHA, Youth Organizations

Application Procedures

Initial Contact: Prospective grantees should call the foundation to request application guidelines.

Application Requirements: Include a description of organization, what it does, and magnitude of its activities; amount requested with explanation of purpose of grant and magnitude of total project or program; and what other efforts are being pursued to raise balance of total cost of project or program; a copy of IRS determination letter; a signed letter from an authorized representative of organization, stating there is no knowledge that the IRS has given notice of change in status to such organization. Additional information may be requested after receipt of the first letter.

Deadlines: None.

Review Process: Application letters are processed for consideration as they arrive. Status reports will be made when appropriate.

Restrictions

The Cain Foundation provides grants and contributions, on a highly selective basis, primarily to scientific, medical, and educational institutions. Substantially all of the grants and contributions are made to organizations with which the Cain Foundation has an existing relationship. Grants are not made to, or for the benefit of, individuals. The foundation does not accept unsolicited grant applications from organizations outside of Texas. Qualified organizations may re-apply for funding every other fiscal year.

Additional Information

In addition to its grant making activities, the foundation also provides direct technical assistance to charitable organizations.

Foundation Officials

Effie Marie Cain: honorary president, director
James B. Cain: vice president, director ED University of Texas LLB; University of Texas BBA.
John C. Cain: director, vice president
F. Wofford Denius: vice president, director B Athens, TX 1945. ED University of Texas LLB; University of Texas BBA. PRIM CORP EMPL attorney: Franklin Wofford Denius Law Offices. CORP AFFIL chairman emeritus, director: Southern Union Co. CLUB AFFIL member: Masons Club.
Frank W. Denius: executive vice president, director B Athens, TX 1925. ED University of Texas LLB (1949); University of Texas BBA (1949). PRIM CORP EMPL attorney: Franklin Wofford Denius Law Offices. CORP AFFIL chairman emeritus, director: Southern Union Co.; director: Chase Bank Texas. NONPR AFFIL member: American Bar Association. CLUB AFFIL Masons Club.
Charmaine D. McGill: director, vice president
Joyce Reynolds: assistant secretary
Harvey L. Walker: executive director, secretary, treasurer

Grants Analysis

Disclosure Period: fiscal year ending October 31, 2001
Total Grants: $4,468,033*
Number of Grants: 110

Average Grant: $40,618*
Highest Grant: $455,000
Lowest Grant: $200
Typical Range: $1,000 to $50,000
*Note: Grant analysis excludes United Way; scholarships. Grants analysis provided by foundation.

Recent Grants

Note: Grants derived from 2000 Form 990.

Library-Related

28,000   Texas College, Tyler, TX -- choral scholarship fund

General

350,000   Texas A&M University Development Foundation, College Station, TX -- endowed college scholarships

300,000   Baylor College of Medicine, Houston, TX -- endowed research scholar in cardiology

291,692   University of Texas Southwestern Medical Center, Dallas, TX -- endowed research scholar in angiogenesis

272,500   University of Texas at Austin, Austin, TX -- endowment for internship program

250,000   Texas A and M University Development Foundation, College Station, TX -- pathology chair

250,000   University of Texas at Austin, Austin, TX -- acquisition and conservation of painting

212,407   Baylor College of Medicine, Houston, TX -- Alzheimer's Professorship

150,000   University of Texas Southwestern Medical Center, Dallas, TX -- endowed chair in clinical research

125,000   University of Texas Health Center at Tyler, Tyler, TX -- endowed chair for tuberculosis research

101,000   University of Austin at Austin, Austin, TX -- capital campaign

GORDON AND MARY CAIN FOUNDATION

Giving Contact

James D. Weaver, President
8 Greenway Plaza, Suite 702
Houston, TX 77046
Phone: (713)960-9283
Fax: (713)877-8107

Description

Founded: 1988
EIN: 760251558
Organization Type: Family Foundation
Giving Locations: FL: Lake Wales; NC: Linville Houston, TX.
Grant Types: Capital, General Support, Multiyear/Continuing Support, Operating Expenses, Project, Research.

Donor Information

Founder: Established in 1988 by Gordon A. Cain and Mary H. Cain.

Financial Summary

Total Giving: $9,114,338 (2000); $4,120,600 (1999); $6,228,350 (1998)
Giving Analysis: Giving for 2000 includes: foundation matching gifts ($20,000); foundation scholarships ($899,000); 1999: foundation matching gifts ($20,000); foundation matching gifts ($170,000); foundation scholarships ($272,500) 1998: foundation grants to United Way ($10,000)
Assets: $169,586,932 (2000); $149,392,515 (1999); $128,800,598 (1998)
Gifts Received: $54,197,348 (2000); $6,087,500 (1998); $29,684,991 (1997). Note: In 1998 and 2000,

contributions were received from Gordon and Mary Cain.

Typical Recipients

Arts & Humanities: Arts Associations & Councils, Arts Centers, Arts Outreach, Ballet, Dance, History & Archaeology, Libraries, Museums/Galleries, Music, Opera, Public Broadcasting, Theater

Civic & Public Affairs: African American Affairs, Botanical Gardens/Parks, Business/Free Enterprise, Clubs, Community Foundations, Economic Development, Economic Policy, Housing, Law & Justice, Legal Aid, Parades/Festivals, Philanthropic Organizations, Professional & Trade Associations, Public Policy, Urban & Community Affairs, Women's Affairs, Zoos/Aquariums

Education: Arts/Humanities Education, Business Education, Business-School Partnerships, Colleges & Universities, Community & Junior Colleges, Economic Education, Education Associations, Education Funds, Education Reform, Engineering/Technological Education, Environmental Education, Education-General, Literacy, Medical Education, Minority Education, Private Education (Precollege), Religious Education, Science/Mathematics Education, Special Education, Student Aid

Environment: Environment-General, Resource Conservation, Wildlife Protection

Health: AIDS/HIV, Cancer, Children's Health/Hospitals, Clinics/Medical Centers, Diabetes, Emergency/Ambulance Services, Eyes/Blindness, Health Policy/Cost Containment, Heart, Hospices, Hospitals, Medical Rehabilitation, Medical Research, Public Health, Single-Disease Health Associations

International: International-General, Health Care/Hospitals, International Organizations

Religion: Churches, Jewish Causes, Religious Welfare

Science: Science Museums, Scientific Centers & Institutes

Social Services: At-Risk Youth, Camps, Child Welfare, Community Centers, Community Service Organizations, Day Care, Family Planning, Homes, Recreation & Athletics, Scouts, Shelters/Homelessness, Social Services-General, Substance Abuse, United Funds/United Ways, YMCA/YWCA/YMHA/YWHA, Youth Organizations

Application Procedures

Initial Contact: The foundation has no application form. Written requests should be mailed directly to the foundation.

Application Requirements: Written proposals should include a statement of purpose of the organization; project description, including objectives and community need; brief history of the organization and those whom it serves; most recent audited financial statement, budget with balance sheet, fund balance, and number of employees; current and itemized annual budget and project budget if applicable; amount of grant being requested; list of major sources of support, staff description, breakdown of proposed expenses, and list of Board of Trustees; the latest copy of the organization's IRS 501(c)(3) tax-exempt status letter; a description of an evaluation plan; and specifics of why organization will make a difference and how program will be stable enough to survive.

Deadlines: Proposals should be received on the last day of the month prior to a board meeting, generally April 30, August 31, and November 30.

Review Process: The board meets three times a year, usually in May, September, and December. Applicants should contact the foundation to determine the date of the next board meeting.

Restrictions

Grants are not made to individuals.

Additional Information

Publications: Guidelines

Foundation Officials

Mary H. Cain: vice president
William A. McMinn: vice president B 1931. PRIM CORP EMPL director, chairman: Texas Petrochemical Holdings ADD CORP EMPL chairman: Texas Petrochemicals Corp. CORP AFFIL director: Sterling Chemicals; director: Purina Mills Inc.; director: Lexicon Genetics Inc.; director: P M Holdings Corp. NONPR AFFIL trustee: Vanderbilt University.
Margaret W. Oehmig: vice president
William C. Oehmig: secretary, treasurer PRIM CORP EMPL principal: Sterling Group. CORP AFFIL director: PM Holdings Corp.; director: Purina Mills Inc.
John M. Sullivan: assistant secretary, treasurer
James D. Weaver: president B 1918. PRIM CORP EMPL chairman board, director: Weaver Trucking Inc.
Sharyn A. Weaver: vice president

Grants Analysis

Disclosure Period: calendar year ending 2000
Total Grants: $8,195,338*
Number of Grants: 129
Average Grant: $56,214*
Highest Grant: $1,000,000
Lowest Grant: $500
Typical Range: $1,000 to $50,000 and $100,000 to $500,000
*Note: Giving excludes matching gifts, scholarships.

Recent Grants

Note: Grants derived from 2000 Form 990.

General

1,000,000	Appalachian State University, Boone, NC -- Science Teacher's Program
500,000	Rice University, Houston, TX
500,000	Texas Children's Hospital, Houston, TX -- capital campaign
500,000	University of Texas M.D. Anderson Cancer Center, Houston, TX -- research
400,000	Nature Conservancy, Durham, NC
390,000	National Center for Excellence in Urban Teaching, Houston, TX -- scholarships
375,000	Louisiana State University Foundation, Baton Rouge, LA -- fellowship fund
300,000	Louisiana State University Foundation, Baton Rouge, LA -- research center
250,000	Houston Music Hall Foundation, Houston, TX
250,000	Spring Branch Center Building Foundation, Houston, TX -- capital campaign

LOUIS CALDER FOUNDATION

Giving Contact

Allison Sargent, Grant Program Manager
230 Park Avenue, Room 1525
New York, NY 10169
Web: http://www.lcfnyc.org

Description

Founded: 1951
EIN: 136015562
Organization Type: General Purpose Foundation
Giving Locations: New York City.
Grant Types: Capital, Endowment, Multiyear/Continuing Support, Project, Scholarship.

Donor Information

Founder: Established in 1951 by the late Louis Calder (d. 1963), who was chairman of the board of Perkins-Goodwin Co. The foundation was funded by gifts from Mr. Calder during his lifetime and later by a residuary bequest in his will.

Financial Summary

Total Giving: $8,569,232 (fiscal year ending October 31, 2000); $7,363,092 (fiscal 1999); $5,982,164 (fiscal 1998)
Giving Analysis: Giving for fiscal 2000 includes: foundation scholarships ($233,000); fiscal 1999: foundation matching gifts ($37,500) foundation scholarships ($225,000)
Assets: $180,168,264 (fiscal 2000); $179,279,261 (fiscal 1999); $164,419,538 (fiscal 1998)

Typical Recipients

Arts & Humanities: Arts Outreach, Ballet, Libraries, Museums/Galleries, Music, Public Broadcasting, Theater
Civic & Public Affairs: Botanical Gardens/Parks, Business/Free Enterprise, Community Foundations, Economic Development, Employment/Job Training, Civic & Public Affairs-General, Housing, Legal Aid, Urban & Community Affairs
Education: Afterschool/Enrichment Programs, Arts/Humanities Education, Business-School Partnerships, Colleges & Universities, Elementary Education (Private), Faculty Development, Education-General, Health & Physical Education, Leadership Training, Literacy, Minority Education, Private Education (Precollege), Public Education (Precollege), Religious Education, School Volunteerism, Science/Mathematics Education, Secondary Education (Private), Special Education, Special Education, Student Aid
Health: Adolescent Health Issues, AIDS/HIV, Cancer, Children's Health/Hospitals, Health Organizations, Heart, Hospitals, Research/Studies Institutes
Religion: Churches, Religious Organizations, Religious Welfare
Science: Science Museums
Social Services: At-Risk Youth, Big Brother/Big Sister, Child Welfare, Community Centers, Community Service Organizations, Crime Prevention, Day Care, Family Services, People with Disabilities, Recreation & Athletics, Scouts, United Funds/United Ways, YMCA/YWCA/YMHA/YWHA, Youth Organizations

Application Procedures

Initial Contact: The foundation has no formal application form, but requests organizations use the New York Regional Association of Grantmakers Common Application Form. The foundation does not accept unsolicited formal proposals from organizations unfamiliar to the foundation, but such organizations may submit a letter of inquiry. If the request falls within the parameters of the foundation's current grantmaking interests, the foundation will request a full proposal.
Application Requirements: Proposals should consist of a one- to three-page letter with a concise statement of the purpose of the grant and the amount. The letter should be accompanied by a copy of IRS 501(c)(3) determination letter; brief a description of organization's history and activities; current list of organization members, trustees, directors, and officers; latest audited financial report; detailed project or organization budget; and an accounting of other foundation support.
Deadlines: None.
Review Process: The trustees have no set schedule of meetings.
Decision Notification: Decisions are base upon the nature of the proposal, availability of funding, and the applicant's fiscal year. It is contemplated that all decisions upon pending proposals will be determined by September 30.

Restrictions

Grants are not made to individuals, private foundations, government organizations, or publicly operated educational and medical institutions. Grants for endowments, building funds, capital development, and grants payable over several years are made occasionally. Grants to performing arts institutions or to private colleges and universities are made only at the invitation of the Foundation.

Additional Information

Chase Manhattan Bank is listed as a trustee of the foundation.
Publications: Annual Report; Guidelines

Foundation Officials

Paul R. Brenner: trustee B Yonkers, NY 1942. ED Fordham University AB (1964); Fordham University JD (1967); New York University LLM (1968). PRIM CORP EMPL partner, attorney: Kelley, Drye & Warren.
Peter D. Calder: trustee ED University of Rhode Island BA (1974); University of Rhode Island MA (1977).
Allison Sargent: grant program manager

Grants Analysis

Disclosure Period: fiscal year ending October 31, 2000
Total Grants: $8,336,232*
Number of Grants: 236
Average Grant: $35,323
Highest Grant: $500,000
Typical Range: $10,000 to $50,000
*Note: Giving excludes scholarships.

Recent Grants

Note: Grants derived from 2001 Form 990.

Library-Related

100,000	Patrons Program, New York, NY -- Library Connections Program
50,000	Brooklyn Public Library, Brooklyn, NY -- for an initiative aimed at promoting reading readiness and making life longer readers for children

General

250,000	American Museum of Natural History, New York, NY -- education web site
250,000	American Museum of Natural History, New York, NY -- for an education web site
200,000	Boys Club of New York, New York, NY -- to create a Technology Initiative
200,000	New Visions for Public Schools, New York, NY -- to revitalize 4 public elementary or middle school libraries in Queens and Brooklyn
175,000	St. John's University, New York, NY -- for financial aid endowment for low-income New York City students
175,000	St. Joseph High School, Brooklyn, NY -- for renovation of the science and computer labs
150,000	Fordham Preparatory High School, Bronx, NY -- for the renovation of their 30 year-old library
125,000	Boys Club of New York, New York, NY -- for Summer School Program
125,000	Boys and Girls Harbor, New York, NY -- funding to support the creation of the Engineering Track Science Lab
125,000	YMCA of Greater New York, New York, NY -- for capital campaign for kids

KENNETH L. CALHOUN CHARITABLE TRUST

Giving Contact

Karen Krino, Trust Administrator
c/o Key Trust Co. of Ohio NA
157 S. Main St.
Akron, OH 44308
Phone: (330)379-1647

Description
Founded: 1982
EIN: 341370330
Organization Type: Private Foundation
Giving Locations: OH: Akron including surrounding area
Grant Types: General Support.

Donor Information
Founder: the late Kenneth Calhoun

Financial Summary
Total Giving: $481,033 (fiscal year ending July 31, 2001); $302,023 (fiscal 1999); $342,898 (fiscal 1998)
Giving Analysis: Giving for fiscal 2001 includes: foundation fellowships ($4,000)
Assets: $6,355,413 (fiscal 2001); $7,392,289 (fiscal 1999); $6,586,007 (fiscal 1998)

Typical Recipients
Arts & Humanities: Arts Associations & Councils, Ballet, Film & Video, Historic Preservation, History & Archaeology, Libraries, Museums/Galleries, Music, Performing Arts, Public Broadcasting, Theater
Civic & Public Affairs: Botanical Gardens/Parks, Community Foundations, Economic Development, Civic & Public Affairs-General, Law & Justice, Parades/Festivals, Urban & Community Affairs, Zoos/Aquariums
Education: Arts/Humanities Education, Colleges & Universities, Education Funds, Education Reform, Education-General, Medical Education, Minority Education, Private Education (Precollege), Public Education (Precollege), Secondary Education (Private), Special Education
Health: Children's Health/Hospitals, Emergency/Ambulance Services, Health Organizations, Heart, Heart, Hospices, Hospitals, Medical Research, Mental Health, Nursing Services, Public Health
International: International Environmental Issues
Religion: Churches, Ministries, Religious Organizations, Religious Welfare
Science: Science Museums, Scientific Centers & Institutes
Social Services: Big Brother/Big Sister, Child Welfare, Community Service Organizations, Crime Prevention, Delinquency & Criminal Rehabilitation, Domestic Violence, Family Services, Food/Clothing Distribution, People with Disabilities, Scouts, Senior Services, Shelters/Homelessness, United Funds/United Ways, Volunteer Services, YMCA/YWCA/YMHA/YWHA, Youth Organizations

Application Procedures
Initial Contact: Send a brief letter of inquiry describing program or project.
Application Requirements: Include a description of organization, date and amount requested, purpose of funds sought, and proof of tax-exempt status.
Deadlines: June 30.

Additional Information
Trust(s): Key Bank Co OH NA.
Trust(s): Key Trust Co OH NA

Grants Analysis
Disclosure Period: fiscal year ending July 31, 2001
Total Grants: $477,033*
Number of Grants: 119
Average Grant: $4,009
Highest Grant: $25,000
Lowest Grant: $500
Typical Range: $1,000 to $25,000
*Note: No grants list available for fiscal 1999.

Recent Grants
Note: Grants derived from 2001 Form 990.

General
25,000	Akron General Development Foundation, Akron, OH
15,000	University of Akron Foundation, Akron, OH
13,000	Ohio Chamber Ballet, Akron, OH
10,000	Daybreak Productions, Aurora, OH
10,000	Hanna Perkins School, Akron, OH
10,000	In His Steps Foundation
10,000	Kevin Coleman Foundation, Kent, OH
10,000	University of Akron Foundation, Akron, OH
10,000	YMCA, Akron, OH
8,000	American Heart Association, Akron, OH

CALIFORNIA BANK & TRUST

Company Headquarters
San Francisco, CA
Web: http://www.calbanktrust.com

Company Description
Acquired: Sumitomo Bank of California (1998).
Employees: 1,500
SIC(s): 6082 Foreign Trade & International Banks.
Parent Company: Zions Bancorp, Salt Lake City, UT, United States

Operating Locations
California Bank & Trust (CA--Albany, Alhambra, Anaheim, Brea, Claremont, Costa Mesa, Cupertino, Fresno, Gardena, Hacienda Heights, Hayward Millbrae, La Palma, Long Beach, Los Angeles, Monterey, Mountain View, Oxnard, Pleasant Hill, Pomona, Sacramento, San Francisco, San Jose, San Mateo, Santa Monica, Stockton, Torrance, Watsonville, West Hollywood); Sumitomo Bank of California (CA--San Francisco); Sumitomo Bank Capital Markets (NY--New York); Sumitomo Bank Financial Services (NY--New York); Sumitomo Bank Investment Management (NY--New York); Sumitomo Bank Leasing & Finance (NY--New York); Sumitomo Bank, Ltd.-Atlanta Agency (GA--Atlanta); Sumitomo Bank, Ltd., Chicago Branch (IL--Chicago); Sumitomo Bank, Ltd.-Houston Agency (TX--Houston); Sumitomo Bank, Ltd., Los Angeles Branch (CA--Los Angeles); Sumitomo Bank, Ltd., New York Branch (NY--New York); Sumitomo Bank, Ltd., San Francisco Branch (CA--San Francisco); Sumitomo Bank, Ltd.-Seattle Representative Office (WA--Seattle); Sumitomo Bank of New York Trust Co. (NY--New York); Sumitomo Bank Securities (NY--New York)

Nonmonetary Support
Type: Donated Equipment; In-kind Services; Loaned Employees
Volunteer Programs: Employees are encouraged to become involved in their communities through participation in local civic and government groups and whose primary focus is to improve economic development in the community.
Contact: Steve Nelson

Giving Contact
Lynda Buckner, Vice President and Manager
Community Development Department
11622 El Camino Real, Suite 200
San Diego, CA 92130
Phone: (858)793-7470
Fax: (858)793-7438
Web: http://www.calbanktrust.com/

Description
Organization Type: Corporate Giving Program
Giving Locations: CA: Supports organizations within the state of California with priority given to those with whom we have a banking relationship headquarters area only.

Grant Types: General Support, Loan, Operating Expenses.
Note: Employee matching gift ratio: 1 to 1.

Financial Summary
Total Giving: $750,000 (2001 approx); $1,000,000 (2000 approx); $827,500 (1999)
Assets: $6,900,000,000 (2000); $6,566,985,000 (1999)

Typical Recipients
Arts & Humanities: Community Arts, Libraries, Museums/Galleries, Music
Civic & Public Affairs: Economic Development, Employment/Job Training, Housing, Urban & Community Affairs
Education: Colleges & Universities, Public Education (Precollege)
Health: Health Organizations
Social Services: Community Service Organizations, Family Services, People with Disabilities, United Funds/United Ways, Youth Organizations

Application Procedures
Initial Contact: Send a written proposal.
Application Requirements: Send a a description of organization and name of contact person, a statement of purpose, a request for a specific amount of funding, an explanation of why funds are needed and how they will be used, a list of contributors, list of board of directors and their business affiliations, a recently audited financial statement including income and expenses, proof of tax-exempt status.
Deadlines: None.
Notes: Individual branches administer small budgets; large grants are referred to the Community Development Department or the Regional Headquarters in San Francisco, Los Angeles, or San Diego.

Restrictions
Does not support individuals, religious organizations for sectarian purposes, or organizations outside operating areas.

Additional Information
In March 1997, Sumitomo Bank announced its 1997 Community Outreach Plan, which contains the bank's CRA (Community Reinvestment Act) goals. The bank has doubled a commitment made in 1993 and will target $1 billion in CRA loans by the year 2003. In addition, the company expanded its Community Advisory Board from five to ten members, and expects to aim for greater diversity in its use of vendors and in its philanthropic support of community organizations. In 1997, the company's goal was to donate 2% of net income, with a greater emphasis given to educational, business, and job development needs in the communities it serves.
Publications: Guidelines Sheet; Annual Report

Grants Analysis
Disclosure Period: calendar year ending 1999
Total Grants: $827,500*
Number of Grants: 293
Average Grant: $2,800
Highest Grant: $40,000
Typical Range: $2,500 to $5,000
*Note: Grants analysis provided by company.

CALLAWAY FOUNDATION, INC.

Giving Contact
H. Speer Burdette, President
209 Broome Street
PO Box 790
LaGrange, GA 30241

Phone: (706)884-7348
Fax: (706)884-0201

Description

Founded: 1943
EIN: 580566147
Organization Type: General Purpose Foundation
Giving Locations: GA: LaGrange including Troup County
Grant Types: Capital, Challenge, Matching.

Financial Summary

Total Giving: $8,900,000 (fiscal year ending September 30, 2003 approx); $8,864,000 (fiscal 2002 approx); $10,414,462 (fiscal 2001)
Giving Analysis: Giving for fiscal 1998 includes: foundation grants to United Way ($36,625)
Assets: $188,000,000 (fiscal 2003 approx); $187,400,000 (fiscal 2002 approx); $196,549,371 (fiscal 2001)

Typical Recipients

Arts & Humanities: Arts Associations & Councils, Arts Centers, Ballet, Community Arts, Historic Preservation, History & Archaeology, Libraries, Museums/Galleries, Music, Performing Arts
Civic & Public Affairs: African American Affairs, Botanical Gardens/Parks, Business/Free Enterprise, Clubs, Economic Development, Employment/Job Training, Civic & Public Affairs-General, Housing, Municipalities/Towns, Philanthropic Organizations, Urban & Community Affairs, Women's Affairs, Zoos/Aquariums
Education: Arts/Humanities Education, Business Education, Colleges & Universities, Economic Education, Education Associations, Education Funds, Education Reform, Engineering/Technological Education, Education-General, International Exchange, Literacy, Literacy, Medical Education, Preschool Education, Private Education (Precollege), Public Education (Precollege), Special Education, Student Aid, Vocational & Technical Education
Environment: Environment-General, Resource Conservation
Health: AIDS/HIV, Alzheimers Disease, Cancer, Clinics/Medical Centers, Emergency/Ambulance Services, Eyes/Blindness, Health Policy/Cost Containment, Health Organizations, Heart, Hospitals, Long-Term Care, Medical Rehabilitation, Public Health, Single-Disease Health Associations, Transplant Networks/Donor Banks
International: Foreign Educational Institutions
Religion: Churches, Jewish Causes, Ministries, Religious Organizations, Religious Welfare, Synagogues/Temples
Science: Science Museums, Scientific Centers & Institutes, Scientific Labs
Social Services: Animal Protection, Camps, Community Centers, Community Service Organizations, Emergency Relief, Family Planning, People with Disabilities, Recreation & Athletics, Scouts, Social Services-General, Special Olympics, Substance Abuse, United Funds/United Ways, Youth Organizations

Application Procedures

Initial Contact: Applicants should send a letter containing pertinent information about the organization to the foundation office.
Application Requirements: Initial letters should contain an outline of the purpose of the request, a proposed budget, amount raised, the needs of the applicant, other material information substantiating the validity of the project, and proof of tax-exempt status. Notification will be given if additional information or interviews are considered necessary.

Deadlines: None. The board of trustees meets in January, April, July, and October; optimum time for application is four to six weeks before the quarterly meetings.

Restrictions

Grants are not made for endowment, debt retirement, loans, or repetitive year-to-year funds for a program. No grants are made to individuals.

Additional Information

The foundation prefers to support organizations on a one-time basis rather than on a long-term basis.
Publications: Annual Report

Foundation Officials

Mark Clayton Callaway: trustee B 1956. ED La-Grange College BA (1981); New York University (1981-1982). CLUB AFFIL Piedmont Driving Club; Rotary Club; Highland Country Club.
Jane Alice Craig: trustee
James Thomas Gresham: president, general manager B Griffin, GA 1937. ED Georgia Technology University BS (1960). PRIM CORP EMPL director: Atlantic Realty Co. NONPR AFFIL member: Sigma Chi; honorary member: Tau Beta Pi; honorary member: Phi Kappa Phi; trustee: Georgia Technology Research Corp.; trustee: Medical Park Foundation; trustee: Georgia Heart Clinic Inc.; trustee: Georgia Technology Foundation; deacon: First Baptist Church, LaGrange; president, trustee: Enoch Callaway Cancer Clinic. CLUB AFFIL member: Highland Country Club.
Ellen H. Harris: trustee
Charles D. Hudson, Jr.: trustee
D. Ray McKenzie, Jr.: vice president
C. L. Pitts: secretary
Esther Rainey: treasurer

Grants Analysis

Disclosure Period: fiscal year ending September 30, 2001
Total Grants: $10,414,462
Number of Grants: 91
Average Grant: $76,163*
Highest Grant: $2,250,000
Lowest Grant: $59
Typical Range: $1,000 to $100,000
*Note: Average grant figure excludes two highest grants.

Recent Grants

Note: Grants derived from fiscal 2000 Form 990.

Library-Related

93,176	Troup Harris Coweta Regional Library, La Grange, GA -- integrated library computer system

General

1,000,000	Georgia Tech Athletic Association, Atlanta, GA -- renovation and expansion project
1,000,000	Trust for Public Land, Atlanta, GA -- Chattahoochee River Greenway land purchase
641,681	City of LaGrange, La Grange, GA -- Softball Complex Project
500,000	University of Georgia Foundation, Athens, GA -- funds for expansion projects
336,000	First United Methodist Church, La Grange, GA -- permanent improvements
326,262	LaGrange College, La Grange, GA -- operating and maintaining property
312,500	West Georgia Health System, Inc., La Grange, GA -- project to purchase land and building
250,000	Woodward Academy, Inc., College Park, GA -- construction project
221,444	LaGrange College, La Grange, GA -- operating and maintaining property
220,000	Lafayette Society of Performing Arts, Inc., La Grange, GA

CAMBRIDGE MUSTARD SEED FOUNDATION

Giving Contact

Vauntina Franklin, Client Contact Representative
Cambridge Mustard Seed Foundation
c/o Fleet National Bank
100 Federal Street
Boston, MA 02109-1810
Phone: (617)346-2472
Fax: (617)346-2495

Description

Founded: 1985
EIN: 046527529
Organization Type: Private Foundation
Giving Locations: MA
Grant Types: General Support.

Donor Information

Founder: Sarah C. Doering, R & T Liquidating Trust

Financial Summary

Total Giving: $205,000 (fiscal year ending July 31, 2001); $178,000 (fiscal 2000); $1,790,191 (fiscal 1997)
Assets: $6,497,061 (fiscal 2001); $6,763,587 (fiscal 2000); $4,846,688 (fiscal 1997)
Gifts Received: $32,575 (fiscal 1992). Note: In fiscal 1992, contributions were received from R&T Liquidating Trust ($31,575) and Elizabeth Bullitt, M.D. ($1,000).

Typical Recipients

Arts & Humanities: History & Archaeology, Libraries, Music, Public Broadcasting
Civic & Public Affairs: African American Affairs, Civic & Public Affairs-General, Housing, Municipalities/Towns, Urban & Community Affairs, Women's Affairs
Education: Afterschool/Enrichment Programs, Arts/Humanities Education, Colleges & Universities, Community & Junior Colleges, Elementary Education (Private), Education-General, International Studies, Leadership Training, Private Education (Precollege), Public Education (Precollege), Religious Education, Science/Mathematics Education, Secondary Education (Private), Secondary Education (Public), Student Aid
Environment: Environment-General
Health: Heart, Hospices, Hospitals, Medical Research, Public Health
International: International Affairs, International Peace & Security Issues, International Relations
Religion: Ministries
Social Services: Child Welfare, Community Service Organizations, Day Care, Family Planning, Family Services, Food/Clothing Distribution, Recreation & Athletics, Shelters/Homelessness, United Funds/United Ways, Volunteer Services, Youth Organizations

Application Procedures

Initial Contact: Send a brief letter of inquiry stating proposal.
Deadlines: None.

Additional Information
Trust(s): Fleet Natl Bank

Grants Analysis
Disclosure Period: fiscal year ending July 31, 2001
Total Grants: $205,000
Number of Grants: 15
Average Grant: $13,667
Highest Grant: $30,000
Typical Range: $5,000 to $25,000

Recent Grants
Note: Grants derived from 2000 Form 990.

General
34,000	Harvard School of Public Health, Boston, MA
30,000	Odwin Learning Center, Dorchester, MA
20,000	Planned Parenthood League of Massachusetts, Boston, MA
15,000	KCTS Television, Seattle, WA
10,000	Community Day Charter School, Lawrence, MA
10,000	Community Education Center, East Boston, MA
10,000	Jane Doe, Inc., Boston, MA
10,000	Medical Foundation, Boston, MA
10,000	Peace Games, Somerville, MA
10,000	Presentation of Mary Academy, Methuen, MA

APOLLOS CAMP AND BENNET HUMISTON TRUST

Giving Contact
Neil C. Bach, Chairman
300 W. Washington St.
Pontiac, IL 61764
Phone: (815)844-6155
Fax: (815)842-2977

Description
Founded: 1925
EIN: 370701044
Organization Type: Private Foundation
Giving Locations: IL: Pontiac
Grant Types: Capital, Operating Expenses.

Financial Summary
Total Giving: $334,226 (fiscal year ending April 30, 2002); $312,470 (fiscal 2001); $277,403 (fiscal 2000)
Assets: $7,895,757 (fiscal 2002); $7,844,591 (fiscal 2001); $7,566,349 (fiscal 2000)
Gifts Received: $50 (fiscal 1997); $5,451 (fiscal 1996). Note: In fiscal 1996, contributions were received from Humiston Haven.

Typical Recipients
Arts & Humanities: Historic Preservation, Libraries, Music, Performing Arts
Civic & Public Affairs: Botanical Gardens/Parks, Chambers of Commerce, Clubs, Economic Development, Civic & Public Affairs-General, Housing, Municipalities/Towns, Parades/Festivals, Safety, Urban & Community Affairs, Zoos/Aquariums
Education: Arts/Humanities Education, Education-General, Public Education (Precollege), Secondary Education (Public)
Environment: Environment-General
Health: Clinics/Medical Centers, Long-Term Care, Public Health
Religion: Religious Welfare
Social Services: Child Welfare, Community Service Organizations, Family Services, Recreation & Athletics, Social Services-General, Substance Abuse, Youth Organizations

Application Procedures
Initial Contact: The foundation requests applications be made in writing. Include amount requested and purpose of funds sought.
Deadlines: None.

Foundation Officials
Neil C. Bach: chairman, trustee
David R. Harding: trustee
William C. Harris: trustee
Louis Lyons: trustee

Grants Analysis
Disclosure Period: fiscal year ending April 30, 2002
Total Grants: $334,226
Number of Grants: 21
Average Grant: $10,785*
Highest Grant: $69,000
Lowest Grant: $708
Typical Range: $5,000 to $25,000
*****Note:** Average grant excludes two highest grants ($129,320).

Recent Grants
Note: Grants derived from fiscal 2000 Form 990.

General
60,000	Boys & Girls Club, Pontiac, IL
53,320	Humiston Woods Nature Center, Pontiac, IL
38,000	City of Pontiac, Pontiac, IL -- riverside park
25,000	Livingston County Alternative School, Pontiac, IL
20,000	Livingston County Special Services, Pontiac, IL
20,000	Pontiac High School Health, Pontiac, IL
16,433	Humiston Woods Nature Center, Pontiac, IL
14,000	Pontiac Township High School, Pontiac, IL -- band instruments
10,000	Habitat for Humanity, Pontiac, IL
8,000	Needy Kids Foundation, Pontiac, IL

CAMP YOUNTS FOUNDATION

Giving Contact
Bobby B. Worrell, Executive Director
PO Box 813
Franklin, VA 23851
Phone: (757)562-3439
Fax: (757)569-7839

Description
Founded: 1955
EIN: 586026001
Organization Type: Family Foundation
Giving Locations: VA: southeastern states.
Grant Types: General Support.

Donor Information
Founder: Established in 1955 by the late Charles Younts and the late Willie Camp Younts .

Financial Summary
Total Giving: $2,817,157 (2001); $2,919,657 (1998); $2,150,157 (1997)
Giving Analysis: Giving for 1998 includes: foundation grants to United Way ($8,000)
Assets: $46,276,243 (2001); $51,025,542 (1998); $46,036,573 (1997)
Gifts Received: $97,384 (1993)

Typical Recipients
Arts & Humanities: Arts Centers, Community Arts, Historic Preservation, History & Archaeology, Libraries, Museums/Galleries, Music, Performing Arts, Theater

Civic & Public Affairs: Botanical Gardens/Parks, Community Foundations, Civic & Public Affairs-General, Municipalities/Towns, Philanthropic Organizations, Public Policy, Urban & Community Affairs
Education: Agricultural Education, Business Education, Colleges & Universities, Community & Junior Colleges, Education Reform, Engineering/Technological Education, Environmental Education, Medical Education, Private Education (Precollege), Public Education (Precollege), Science/Mathematics Education, Special Education, Student Aid
Environment: Environment-General
Health: Cancer, Geriatric Health, Hospitals, Nursing Services, Single-Disease Health Associations
Religion: Churches, Ministries, Religious Organizations, Religious Welfare
Science: Science Museums
Social Services: Animal Protection, Child Welfare, Community Centers, Community Service Organizations, Food/Clothing Distribution, Homes, People with Disabilities, Recreation & Athletics, Shelters/Homelessness, United Funds/United Ways, YMCA/YWCA/YMHA/YWHA, Youth Organizations

Application Procedures
Initial Contact: Applications must be made in writing.
Application Requirements: Application must include an IRS tax-exempt letter.
Deadlines: September 1.

Restrictions
Grants are not made to individuals.

Foundation Officials
Harold S. Atkinson, Jr.: trustee
John M. Camp, Jr.: director, trustee
Robert R. Long: trustee
Paul C. Marks: director, trustee
Robert Mays: vice president
Harry Webster Walker, II: director, trustee B Bridgeport, CT 1921. PRIM CORP EMPL president, chief executive officer, director: Sunsweet Fruit Inc. CORP AFFIL president: Indian River Elite Citrus Inc.; director: Walker Group Inc.; director: Carpenter Technology Corp. NONPR AFFIL director: Vero Beach YMCA; devel board: Yale University; member: United States Yacht Racing Union; chairman: Piedmont College; member: Rotary Club; chairman: Olympic International Star Class Yacht Racing Association; director: Blue Ridge Assemblies, Inc.; member: National Boating Safety; member: Association Yale University Alumni.

Grants Analysis
Disclosure Period: calendar year ending 2001
Total Grants: $2,817,157*
Number of Grants: 407
Average Grant: $6,123*
Highest Grant: $200,000
Typical Range: $1,000 to $10,000
*****Note:** Giving excludes United Way. Average grant figure excludes two highest grants ($325,000).

Recent Grants
Note: Grants derived from 2001 Form 990.

General
200,000	Southampton Academy, Courtland, VA -- operating support
125,000	Piedmont College, Demorest, GA -- operating support
72,357	Elms, Franklin, VA -- operating support
50,000	Southampton Academy, Courtland, VA -- operating support
40,900	Virginia Military Institute, Lexington, VA -- operating support
39,500	Virginia Polytechnic Institute, Blacksburg, VA -- operating support
37,500	Taft School, Watertown, CT -- operating support
35,000	Chowan College, Murfreesboro, NC -- operating support

35,000	Virginia Military Institute, Lexington, VA -- operating support
30,000	Bay Leaf Baptist Church, Raleigh, NC -- operating support

BUSHROD H. CAMPBELL AND ADAH E. HALL CHARITY FUND

Giving Contact

Kathryn Frost, Foundation Administrator
c/o Palmer & Dodge
1 Beacon St., Rm. 2200
Boston, MA 02108
Phone: (617)573-0100

Description

Founded: 1956
EIN: 046013598
Organization Type: Private Foundation
Giving Locations: MA: Boston including metropolitan area
Grant Types: Capital, Conference/Seminar, Fellowship, Multiyear/Continuing Support, Operating Expenses, Project, Seed Money.

Donor Information

Founder: the late Bushrod H. Campbell, the late Adah F. Hall

Financial Summary

Total Giving: $1,074,085 (fiscal year ending May 31, 2001); $618,640 (fiscal 1998); $566,625 (fiscal 1997)
Assets: $22,184,381 (fiscal 2001); $19,541,611 (fiscal 1998); $17,803,730 (fiscal 1997)

Typical Recipients

Arts & Humanities: Historic Preservation, Libraries, Opera, Public Broadcasting
Civic & Public Affairs: Asian American Affairs, Civil Rights, Economic Development, Employment/Job Training, Civic & Public Affairs-General, Hispanic Affairs, Housing, Urban & Community Affairs, Women's Affairs
Education: Afterschool/Enrichment Programs, Colleges & Universities, Engineering/Technological Education, Education-General, Literacy, Medical Education, Minority Education, School Volunteerism, Special Education
Health: AIDS/HIV, Alzheimers Disease, Clinics/Medical Centers, Geriatric Health, Health Funds, Health Organizations, Home-Care Services, Hospices, Hospitals, Long-Term Care, Medical Research, Nursing Services, Public Health
International: Health Care/Hospitals
Religion: Churches, Religious Organizations, Social/Policy Issues
Social Services: Community Service Organizations, Day Care, Domestic Violence, Family Planning, Family Services, Food/Clothing Distribution, People with Disabilities, Senior Services, Shelters/Homelessness, Social Services-General, United Funds/United Ways, YMCA/YWCA/YMHA/YWHA, Youth Organizations

Application Procedures

Initial Contact: Send cover letter and formal proposal.
Application Requirements: Include a description of organization, amount requested, purpose of funds sought, recently audited financial statement, and proof of tax-exempt status.
Deadlines: January 1, April 1, August 1, and October 1.

Restrictions

Preference is given to teaching hospitals, organizations providing services to the elderly, and population control efforts.

Additional Information

Publications: Application Guidelines

Foundation Officials

Casimir de Rham, Jr.: trustee B New York, NY 1924. ED Yale University (1943-1944); Harvard University AB (1946); Harvard University JD (1949). PRIM CORP EMPL officer counsel: Palmer & Dodge. NONPR AFFIL treasurer, trustee: Mt Auburn Hospital; director: Womens Education & Industry Union; member: Massachusetts Bar Association; trustee: Mt Auburn Foundation; treasurer: Little Harbor Chapel; member: Masons; honorary trustee: Sterling & Francine Clark Art Institute; trustee: Commonwealth School; member: Cambridge-Arlington-Belmont Bar Association; honorary trustee: Center Blood Research Boston; member: Boston Bar Association; sr advisory board: Boys & Girls Clubs Boston; member: American Bar Foundation; member: American Legion; member: American Bar Association. CLUB AFFIL Saint Botolph Club.
Arthur B. Page: trustee
Curtis Prout, MD: trustee B Swampscott, MA October 13, 1915. ED Harvard University AB (1937); Harvard University MD (1941). OCCUPATION physician. NONPR AFFIL director, treasurer: Medical Foundation; director: National Comm Correctional Health Care; fellow: Massachusetts Medicine Society; fellow: American College Physicians; member: American Medical Association; member: American Clinical & Climatological Association.

Grants Analysis

Disclosure Period: fiscal year ending May 31, 2001
Total Grants: $1,074,085
Number of Grants: 124
Average Grant: $8,662
Highest Grant: $37,500
Typical Range: $2,000 to $20,000

Recent Grants

Note: Grants derived from 2000 Form 990.

General

162,557	Harvard Medical School, Cambridge, MA
162,557	Massachusetts Institute of Technology, Cambridge, MA
75,000	YMCA of Greater Boston, Boston, MA
50,000	Boston Workforce Development Coalition, Boston, MA
30,000	Suffolk University, Boston, MA
25,000	Dorchester Bay Economic Development Corp, Dorchester, MA
25,000	United Way Special Fund for Emergency Assistance
20,000	Chelsea Community YMCA, Chelsea, MA
20,000	La Alianza Hispana, Boston, MA
20,000	Peace at Home, Boston, MA

J. BULOW CAMPBELL FOUNDATION

Giving Contact

Betsy Hamilton, Associate Director
50 Hurt Plaza, Suite 850
Atlanta, GA 30303-2917
Phone: (404)658-9066
Fax: (404)659-4802

Description

Founded: 1940
EIN: 580566149
Organization Type: General Purpose Foundation
Giving Locations: AL; FL; GA: Atlanta including surrounding area; NC; SC; TN
Grant Types: Capital, Challenge.

Donor Information

Founder: Established in 1940 in accordance with the will of J. Bulow Campbell (1870-1946), who was chairman of the Campbell Coal Company. He was also chairman of the Berry Schools and Rabun Gap-Nacoochee School, chairman of the executive committee of Columbia Theological Seminary, and a trustee of Agnes Scott College and the YMCA. Mr. Campbell's philanthropic interests were strongly influenced by his Christian faith and close ties to the Southern Presbyterian Church.

Financial Summary

Total Giving: $32,000,000 (2003 approx); $32,000,000 (2002 approx); $35,983,616 (2001)
Giving Analysis: Giving for 1999 includes: foundation grants to United Way ($1,000,000)
Assets: $600,000,000 (2003 approx); $600,000,000 (2002 approx); $641,312,031 (2001)
Gifts Received: $60,000 (2000); $145,970,246 (1999); $2,587,459 (1998). Note: In 1999 and 2000, contributions were received from The estate of Virginia C. Courts. In 1998, contributions were received from the J. Bulow Campbell Trust.

Typical Recipients

Arts & Humanities: Arts Centers, Arts Festivals, History & Archaeology, Libraries, Museums/Galleries, Music
Civic & Public Affairs: Botanical Gardens/Parks, Chambers of Commerce, Community Foundations, Civic & Public Affairs-General, Hispanic Affairs, Housing, Law & Justice, Legal Aid, Municipalities/Towns, Nonprofit Management, Urban & Community Affairs, Zoos/Aquariums
Education: Arts/Humanities Education, Business Education, Colleges & Universities, Economic Education, Education Reform, Education-General, Health & Physical Education, International Studies, Literacy, Medical Education, Private Education (Precollege), Religious Education, Science/Mathematics Education, Special Education, Student Aid
Environment: Environment-General, Resource Conservation
Health: Cancer, Children's Health/Hospitals, Clinics/Medical Centers, Emergency/Ambulance Services, Health Organizations, Hospices, Hospitals, Long-Term Care, Medical Research, Mental Health, Nursing Services, Single-Disease Health Associations
International: Missionary/Religious Activities
Religion: Bible Study/Translation, Churches, Religion-General, Jewish Causes, Ministries, Religious Organizations, Religious Welfare, Seminaries
Science: Science Museums
Social Services: Animal Protection, At-Risk Youth, Big Brother/Big Sister, Camps, Child Welfare, Community Service Organizations, Counseling, Emergency Relief, Family Services, Homes, People with Disabilities, Scouts, Senior Services, Shelters/Homelessness, Social Services-General, United Funds/United Ways, YMCA/YWCA/YMHA/YWHA, Youth Organizations

Application Procedures

Initial Contact: The foundation does not provide an application form. Initial contact should be made through a letter of request.
Application Requirements: The letter of request must be limited to one page. It should include the full legal name and a concise a description of organization, its purpose, and its program; specific amount requested; brief description of the purpose for which the grant would be used; definite plan and timetable

for successful completion of the project; and the signature of the principal officer of the governing board and the chief administrative officer of the institution. A copy of the organization's IRS determination letter of tax-exempt status should be enclosed.

Deadlines: Applications submitted by January 1, April 1, July 1, and October 1 will be given preliminary consideration at the board meeting held in each of those months. However, organizations are encouraged to submit applications well in advance of the deadlines.

Review Process: All grants must be approved by the seven-member board of trustees. During preliminary consideration, the board will decide whether or not to consider an application. The applicant will be notified in writing either that the board has declined the proposal or that it has decided to pursue the matter. If further consideration is undertaken, foundation staff will conduct a more detailed study of the proposal. The staff will usually conduct at least one site visit at this stage and submit a report to the board for consideration at the next quarterly board meeting. executive director are often helpful, as are consultations with him prior to submitting a formal letter of application. executive director are often helpful, as are consultations with him prior to submitting a formal letter of application.

Restrictions

The foundation makes no grants or loans of any kind to individuals. It discourages requests from local church congregations. Grants are generally limited exclusively to Georgia, but will occasionally consider grants in South Carolina, North Carolina, Tennessee, Alabama, and Florida.

Additional Information

The Trust Company of Georgia serves as corporate trustee for the foundation.

Applicants are asked to wait at least one year from the date of any previous application before submitting another request.

Publications: General Information Pamphlet; Application Guidelines

Trust(s): SunTrust Bank, Atlanta

Foundation Officials

David E. Boyd: member
Peter M. Candler: member
R. W. Courts, II: chairman
Betsy Hamilton: grants director
Larry L. Prince: trustee B Dyersburg, TN 1937. PRIM CORP EMPL chairman, chief executive officer, director: Genuine Parts Co. CORP AFFIL director: Trust Co. Georgia; director: UAP Inc.(Canadian Corp.); director: SunTrust Banks Inc.; director: So Mills; director: SP Richards Co.; chairman, chief executive officer, director: NAPA Distribution Center; director: Lesker Office Furniture; chairman, chief executive officer, director: NAPA Auto Parts; director: John H. Harland Co.; director: Crawford & Co.; director: Equifax Inc.
Yvonne Quick: secretary
Joseph T. Spence: member
John W. Stephenson: executive director
Barry L. Teague: member
Lawrence Barry Teague: trustee
Robert Ray Woodson: trustee B Thomaston, GA 1932. ED University of Georgia BS (1958). PRIM CORP EMPL director, president, chief executive officer: John H. Harland Co. ADD CORP EMPL chairman: Hartland Dataprint. CORP AFFIL director: Haverty Furniture Companies Inc.; director: Allied Holdings. NONPR AFFIL member: American Institute of Certified Public Accountants.

Grants Analysis

Disclosure Period: calendar year ending 2001
Total Grants: $35,983,616
Number of Grants: 51
Average Grant: $619,672*

Highest Grant: $5,000,000
Lowest Grant: $8,275
Typical Range: $100,000 to $500,000 and $1,000,000 to $5,000,000
***Note:** Average grant figure excludes highest grant.

Recent Grants

Note: Grants derived from 2001 Form 990.

General

5,000,000	Lovett School, Atlanta, GA
3,500,000	Georgia Institute of Technology, Atlanta, GA
2,000,000	Georgia State University Foundation, Atlanta, GA
1,981,180	Agnes Scott College, Decatur, GA
1,928,779	Corporation of Mercer University, Macon, GA
1,928,779	Morehouse College, Atlanta, GA
1,300,000	Trust for Public Land, Atlanta, GA
1,200,000	Trust for Public Land, Atlanta, GA
1,000,000	Brenau University, Gainesville, GA
1,000,000	Latin American Association, Atlanta, GA

CAMPBELL FOUNDATION (MD)

Giving Contact

William B. Campbell, President
100 W. Pennsylvania Avenue
Baltimore, MD 21204
Phone: (410)825-0545

Description

EIN: 520794348
Organization Type: Private Foundation
Giving Locations: MD: Baltimore including metropolitan area
Grant Types: Capital, Endowment, Operating Expenses, Project.

Donor Information

Founder: R. McLean Campbell

Financial Summary

Total Giving: $147,000 (2000); $144,900 (1999); $144,700 (1998)
Assets: $2,962,867 (2000); $2,771,235 (1999); $2,850,223 (1998)
Gifts Received: $10,000 (1996). Note: In 1996, contributions were received from the estate of Bruce S. Campbell, Jr.

Typical Recipients

Arts & Humanities: Arts Centers, Arts Institutes, Arts Outreach, Community Arts, Arts & Humanities-General, Historic Preservation, History & Archaeology, Libraries, Museums/Galleries, Music, Opera, Performing Arts, Theater
Civic & Public Affairs: Botanical Gardens/Parks, Clubs, Economic Development, Employment/Job Training, Civic & Public Affairs-General, Housing, Parades/Festivals, Professional & Trade Associations, Urban & Community Affairs, Zoos/Aquariums
Education: Arts/Humanities Education, Colleges & Universities, Education Funds, Environmental Education, Education-General, Literacy, Medical Education, Minority Education, Private Education (Precollege), Science/Mathematics Education, Special Education, Special Education, Student Aid
Environment: Environment-General, Resource Conservation
Health: AIDS/HIV, Children's Health/Hospitals, Clinics/Medical Centers, Eyes/Blindness, Hospices, Hospitals, Research/Studies Institutes
Science: Scientific Centers & Institutes

Social Services: Animal Protection, Camps, Child Welfare, Community Service Organizations, Counseling, Crime Prevention, Family Planning, Food/Clothing Distribution, People with Disabilities, Recreation & Athletics, Shelters/Homelessness, Special Olympics, Substance Abuse, United Funds/United Ways, YMCA/YWCA/YMHA/YWHA, Youth Organizations

Application Procedures

Initial Contact: Send a full proposal.
Application Requirements: Include a description of organization, amount requested, purpose of funds sought, recently audited financial statement, and proof of tax-exempt status, and description of project.
Deadlines: October 15.

Restrictions

Grants are primarily in support of education, civic, cultural, and health programs. Does not support individuals.

Foundation Officials

Carolyn C. Beall: assistant treasurer
Bruce S. Campbell, III: treasurer
J. Tyler Campbell: director
Mary Jo Campbell: assistant treasurer
William B. Campbell: president
Margaret C. W. Davis: treasurer

Grants Analysis

Disclosure Period: calendar year ending 2000
Total Grants: $147,000
Number of Grants: 74
Average Grant: $1,986
Highest Grant: $10,000
Lowest Grant: $500
Typical Range: $500 to $5,000

Recent Grants

Note: Grants derived from 2001 Form 990.

Library-Related

5,000	Baltimore County Public Library, Towson, MD -- capital campaign

General

15,000	Roland Park Country School, Baltimore, MD -- capital campaign
15,000	St. Paul's School for Girls, Brooklandville, MD -- capital campaign
10,000	Odyssey School, Baltimore, MD -- capital campaign
10,000	Walters Art Gallery, Baltimore, MD -- for capital campaign
5,000	Independent College Fund of Maryland, Baltimore, MD
5,000	Jubilee Baltimore, Inc., Baltimore, MD -- capital campaign
5,000	St. James Academy, Baltimore, MD -- capital campaign
3,000	Baltimore Educational Scholarship Trust, Baltimore, MD
2,500	Women's Industrial Exchange, Baltimore, MD -- capital campaign
2,000	Center for Poverty Solutions, Baltimore, MD -- capital campaign

RUTH AND HENRY CAMPBELL FOUNDATION

Giving Contact

Donald D. Koonce, Trust Officer
c/o Bank of America
PO Box 26903
Richmond, VA 23261
Phone: (804)788-2573

Description

Founded: 1957
EIN: 546031023
Organization Type: Private Foundation
Giving Locations: VA
Grant Types: General Support.

Financial Summary

Total Giving: $1,025,365 (2000); $1,012,500 (1999); $835,955 (1998)
Assets: $18,667,844 (2000); $21,118,480 (1999); $18,751,788 (1998)
Gifts Received: $30,500 (2000); $4,000 (1999); $35,500 (1998)

Typical Recipients

Arts & Humanities: Arts Associations & Councils, Arts Funds, Ethnic & Folk Arts, Historic Preservation, History & Archaeology, Libraries, Museums/Galleries, Opera, Theater
Civic & Public Affairs: Clubs, Community Foundations, Civic & Public Affairs-General, Municipalities/Towns, Parades/Festivals, Philanthropic Organizations, Public Policy, Safety, Urban & Community Affairs
Education: Agricultural Education, Business Education, Colleges & Universities, Community & Junior Colleges, Education Funds, Faculty Development, Minority Education, Private Education (Precollege), Public Education (Precollege), Religious Education, Student Aid
Environment: Environment-General, Resource Conservation, Wildlife Protection
Health: Children's Health/Hospitals, Clinics/Medical Centers, Health Organizations, Heart, Home-Care Services, Hospices, Hospitals, Nursing Services
Religion: Churches, Dioceses, Religious Welfare, Seminaries
Science: Science Museums, Scientific Centers & Institutes
Social Services: Child Welfare, Community Centers, Community Service Organizations, Emergency Relief, Family Services, Homes, People with Disabilities, Recreation & Athletics, Scouts, Volunteer Services, YMCA/YWCA/YMHA/YWHA, Youth Organizations

Application Procedures

Initial Contact: The foundation requests applications be made in writing.
Application Requirements: Include information about individual or organization.
Deadlines: None.

Additional Information

Trust(s): Bank of America

Foundation Officials

John M. Camp, Jr.: director
Paul D. Camp, III: director
Paul Camp Marks: director
Harry W. Walker, III: director

Grants Analysis

Disclosure Period: calendar year ending 2000
Total Grants: $1,025,365
Number of Grants: 110
Average Grant: $7,416*
Highest Grant: $124,415
Lowest Grant: $1,000
Typical Range: $2,000 to $20,000
*Note: Average grant excludes two highest grants ($224,415).

Recent Grants

Note: Grants derived from 1999 Form 990.

General

500,000	Franklin Area Flood Fund, Franklin, VA
76,000	Southampton Academy, Courtland, VA
56,500	Southampton County, Virginia, Courtland, VA
30,000	Southampton County Historical Society, Newsoms, VA
27,000	Virginia Foundation for Independent Colleges, Richmond, VA
25,000	The Elms Foundation, Franklin, VA
20,000	St. John's Museum of Art, Wilmington, NC
19,500	Southeast 4-H Educational Center, Wakefield, VA
17,000	Science Museum of Virginia, Richmond, VA
15,000	Salvation Army/Franklin Division, Alexandria, VA

CAMPBELL SOUP CO.

Company Headquarters

Camden, NJ
Web: http://www.campbellsoup.com

Company Description

Founded: 1922
Ticker: CPB
Exchange: NYSE
Revenue: US$6.133 billion (2002)
Profit: US$525 million (2002)
Employees: 25000 (2002)
Fortune Rank: 286, per FORTUNE Magazine's list of 500 Largest U.S. Corporations (2002).
SIC(s): 2032 Canned Specialties, 2037 Frozen Fruits & Vegetables, 2051 Bread, Cake & Related Products, 2052 Cookies & Crackers.

Operating Locations

Campbell Soup Co. (CA--Dixon, Modesto, Sacramento, Stockton; CT--Norwalk; GA--Douglas; IL--Downers Grove, West Chicago; IN--Brighton; MI--Bridgeport, Glenn, Memphis, West Bloomfield; NE--Omaha, Tecumseh; NY--New York; NC--Maxton; OH--Jackson, Napoleon, Wauseon; PA--Denver, Downingtown, Evansville, Reading; TX--Paris); Campbell Soup Co. (WI); Campbell Soup Co. (WI--Paris)
Note: Operates in Europe and South America.

Nonmonetary Support

Range: $1,000,000 - $4,000,000
Type: Donated Equipment; Donated Products; In-kind Services; Workplace Solicitation
Volunteer Programs: Foundation operates a Dollars for Doers fund to support and reward company employees who volunteer in their communities; also supports a program in which employees tutor disadvantaged youth. Giving to the United Way is determined by employee involvement.
Contact: Joan Berger, Grant Administrator

Campbell Soup Foundation

Giving Contact

J. S. Buckley, Chairman
Campbell Place
Camden, NJ 08103-1799
Phone: (856)342-4800
Web: http://www.campbellsoupcompany.com/community_center.asp

Description

EIN: 216019196
Organization Type: Corporate Foundation
Giving Locations: headquarters and operating communities.
Grant Types: Challenge, Employee Matching Gifts, General Support, Project.
Note: Employee matching gift ratio: 1 to 1 for education and the United Way.

Financial Summary

Total Giving: $1,930,413 (fiscal year ending June 31, 2001); $1,707,839 (fiscal 1999); $1,875,000 (fiscal 1998 approx). Note: Contributes through corporate direct giving program and giving.
Giving Analysis: Giving for fiscal 2001 includes: foundation matching gifts ($228,287); foundation program-related investments ($398,595); foundation grants to United Way ($647,125); foundation ($656,406); fiscal 1999: foundation matching gifts ($110,298); foundation grants to United Way ($583,086); foundation ($1,014,455); fiscal 1997: foundation matching gifts ($280,345); foundation grants to United Way ($420,000) foundation ($1,269,841)
Assets: $23,747,296 (fiscal 2001); $26,485,431 (fiscal 1999); $24,000,000 (fiscal 1998 approx)
Gifts Received: $1,000,000 (fiscal 1995); $2,000,000 (fiscal 1994). Note: Foundation receives contributions from the Campbell Soup Company.

Typical Recipients

Arts & Humanities: Arts Centers, Community Arts, Arts & Humanities-General, Historic Preservation, Libraries, Museums/Galleries, Music, Performing Arts, Public Broadcasting, Visual Arts
Civic & Public Affairs: African American Affairs, Botanical Gardens/Parks, Business/Free Enterprise, Chambers of Commerce, Economic Development, Economic Policy, Employment/Job Training, Civic & Public Affairs-General, Hispanic Affairs, Housing, Law & Justice, Minority Business, Professional & Trade Associations, Urban & Community Affairs, Zoos/Aquariums
Education: Afterschool/Enrichment Programs, Business Education, Colleges & Universities, Community & Junior Colleges, Education Funds, Education Reform, Elementary Education (Public), Faculty Development, Education-General, Education-General, Gifted & Talented Programs, Legal Education, Literacy, Medical Education, Minority Education, Private Education (Precollege), Public Education (Precollege), Science/Mathematics Education, Vocational & Technical Education
Health: Cancer, Children's Health/Hospitals, Clinics/Medical Centers, Diabetes, Emergency/Ambulance Services, Eyes/Blindness, Health-General, Heart, Hospitals, Kidney, Medical Research, Nutrition, Single-Disease Health Associations
International: International Development, International Relief Efforts
Religion: Churches, Religious Welfare
Science: Science Museums
Social Services: Animal Protection, Big Brother/Big Sister, Community Centers, Community Service Organizations, Counseling, Crime Prevention, Day Care, Family Services, Food/Clothing Distribution, Recreation & Athletics, Scouts, Shelters/Homelessness, Social Services-General, Special Olympics, United Funds/United Ways, YMCA/YWCA/YMHA/YWHA, Youth Organizations

Application Procedures

Initial Contact: Submit a succinct proposal in letter form.
Application Requirements: Summary grant proposal and full narrative proposal, including: description of the organization, including name, address, and telephone number of contact; project objective; target population; major activities planned; timetable; project staff; means of measuring goals; historical sketch of agency and statement of current goals; statement of primary interest; project budget; other sources of funding; and proof of tax-exempt status.
Deadlines: None.
Review Process: An initial review is conducted by foundation staff; qualifying proposals are forwarded to board of trustees for a final decision. The review process may take up to three months.

Cargill Foundation

Giving Contact
Toni Green, Senior Program Officer
Cargill Foundation
PO Box 5650
Minneapolis, MN 55440-5650
Phone: (952)742-6290
E-mail: toni_green@cargill.com
Web: http://www.cargill.com/commun/found.htm

Alternate Contact
Stacey Smida, Grants Administrator
Cargill Foundation
Phone: (952)742-4311
E-mail: stacey_smida@cargill.com

Description
EIN: 416020221
Organization Type: Corporate Foundation
Giving Locations: MN: Minneapolis including western and northern suburbs headquarters and operating locations; internationally; nationally.
Grant Types: Capital, Emergency, Employee Matching Gifts, General Support, Multiyear/Continuing Support, Project.

Financial Summary
Total Giving: $6,122,457 (2001); $8,568,521 (1999); $14,153,000 (1998). Note: Contributes through corporate direct giving program and foundation.
Giving Analysis: Giving for 2001 includes: foundation grants to United Way ($1,109,268); foundation ($5,013,189); 1999: foundation grants to United Way ($1,242,365); foundation ($7,326,156); 1998: foundation ($4,500,000); corporate direct giving ($9,650,000);
Assets: $66,814,267 (2001); $95,051,167 (1999); $68,401,382 (1997)
Gifts Received: $250,000 (2001); $2,600,000 (1999); $2,600,000 (1997). Note: Contributions were received from Cargill, Inc., Cargill Financial Services Corp., and North Star Steel Co.

Typical Recipients
Arts & Humanities: Arts Associations & Councils, Arts Centers, Arts Institutes, Arts Outreach, Ethnic & Folk Arts, Arts & Humanities-General, History & Archaeology, Libraries, Museums/Galleries, Music, Opera, Public Broadcasting, Theater
Civic & Public Affairs: African American Affairs, Botanical Gardens/Parks, Chambers of Commerce, Economic Development, Employment/Job Training, Ethnic Organizations, Civic & Public Affairs-General, Housing, Law & Justice, Legal Aid, Minority Business, Native American Affairs, Nonprofit Management, Public Policy, Rural Affairs, Safety, Urban & Community Affairs, Women's Affairs, Zoos/Aquariums
Education: Agricultural Education, Arts/Humanities Education, Business Education, Colleges & Universities, Community & Junior Colleges, Economic Education, Education Funds, Education Reform, Elementary Education (Private), Engineering/Technological Education, Faculty Development, Education-General, Leadership Training, Literacy, Medical Education, Minority Education, Preschool Education, Private Education (Precollege), Public Education (Precollege), Religious Education, Science/Mathematics Education, Social Sciences Education, Special Education, Student Aid, Vocational & Technical Education
Environment: Environment-General, Resource Conservation
Health: AIDS/HIV, Cancer, Children's Health/Hospitals, Clinics/Medical Centers, Emergency/Ambulance Services, Eyes/Blindness, Health Organizations, Hospitals
International: International Environmental Issues, International Relief Efforts
Religion: Churches, Religious Welfare
Science: Science Museums, Scientific Centers & Institutes
Social Services: At-Risk Youth, Big Brother/Big Sister, Child Welfare, Community Centers, Community Service Organizations, Crime Prevention, Day Care, Domestic Violence, Family Planning, Family Services, Food/Clothing Distribution, People with Disabilities, Recreation & Athletics, Scouts, Senior Services, Substance Abuse, United Funds/United Ways, YMCA/YWCA/YMHA/YWHA, Youth Organizations

Application Procedures
Initial Contact: Contact the foundation or visit the foundation's web site to obtain guidelines and an application cover sheet.
Application Requirements: Initial applications should be no more than two typed pages plus a completed application cover sheet. All applications should include proof of tax-exempt status; a description of organization, its mission, and a brief organization history; and a statement of what type of funding is being requested (General Operating, Project, Program, Innovation, or Capital). The foundation requests that all applications (except Capital Grant requests) address the following questions in this order: (1) How does your organization, project, program or concept "Prepare the next generation for success in school, work and life?" (2) How does your organization and/or program demonstrate leadership and effectiveness? (3) Describe the project, program or proposed concept for which you are requesting funds, and explain the need. If a project or program, is it existing or new? If existing, how old is it? (4) Which Cargill Foundation priority or priorities does your organization, project, program, or proposed concept serve? (6) Is there a specific gender or ethnic group that your organization, project, program, or proposed concept serves?
For a Capital Grant, the following questions should be answered: Why is capital support needed? Are you currently in a capital campaign? If so, how much have you raised to date? How will capital dollars strengthen your organization?
Deadlines: None.
Review Process: The initial application is reviewed by foundation staff to ensure that the applicant's activities and programs coincide with the foundation's mission. If the foundation approves of the initial application, the applicant will be asked to schedule a site visit. The site visit will allow the foundation staff to observe the organization and its programs, and discuss the applicant's proposal. Upon a successful site visit, the foundation will send a letter confirming its interest in the applicant's proposal, and will request additional information to generate a formal proposal. Formal proposals are considered by foundation staff prior to being presented to the foundation's board of directors.
Evaluative Criteria: The foundation prefers to fund organizations with a well-articulated mission; a clear strategic plan; programs that are considered models in their field; a strong executive director and motivated staff; solid financial reporting and performance; a board the governs responsibly; an entrepreneurial approach; carefully-determined program goals and objectives with documented results; and a demonstrated willingness and ability to take calculated risks.
Decision Notification: Initial applications are responded to by mail within four weeks.
Notes: The Cargill Citizenship Committee addresses regional and national organizations seeking support for community service initiatives or projects in the company's operating communities outside the Twin Cities area. The Committee's corporate grantmaking guidelines were under review at press time. The company reported that revised guidelines should be available on Cargill's web site in late 2003.

Restrictions
The foundation does not support individuals; athletic scholarships; religious organizations for sectarian purposes; membership in civic organizations or trade associations; benefit fundraising events or tickets; endowments or endowment campaigns; recognition or testimonial events; fundraising campaigns for disease-specific organizations or for medical research; fraternal, veterans', or professional associations; public service or political campaigns/lobbying; conferences; or travel expenses.
Due to funding limitations, no funding is provided for youth facing physical or mental challenges; programs that primarily serve adults; summer programs; juvenile offender programs; faith-based organizations; programs that serve children whose parents are incarcerated or have serious medical problems; homes or shelters for children; or organizations that serve the medical or dental needs of children.

Additional Information
Cargill is taking steps toward achieving a target of two percent of domestic pre-tax earnings for its U.S.-based contributions.
Publications: Guidelines Sheet

Corporate Officials
Robbin S. Johnson: corporate vice president public affairs PRIM CORP EMPL senior vice president, corporate affairs: Cargill Inc.
James D. Moe: corporate vice president, general counsel, secretary ED Stanford University AB (1962); University of Minnesota LLB (1965). PRIM CORP EMPL corporate vice president, general counsel, secretary: Cargill Inc.
Warren R. Staley: chairman, chief executive officer B May 14, 1942. ED Kansas State University BA (1965); Cornell University MBA (1967). PRIM CORP EMPL chairman, chief executive officer: Cargill Inc.
Tyrone K. Thayer: corp. vice president PRIM CORP EMPL corp. vice president: Cargill Inc. CORP AFFIL director: North Star Steel Co.

Giving Program Officials
James D. Moe: member contributions committee ED Stanford University AB (1962); University of Minnesota LLB (1965). PRIM CORP EMPL corporate vice president, general counsel, secretary: Cargill Inc.
Nancy P. Siska: member contributions committee
Warren R. Staley: member contributions committee B May 14, 1942. ED Kansas State University BA (1965); Cornell University MBA (1967). PRIM CORP EMPL chairman, chief executive officer: Cargill Inc.
Tyrone K. Thayer: member contributions committee (see above)

Foundation Officials
Robbin S. Johnson: vice president (see above)
Katherine Kersten: director, vice president PRIM NONPR EMPL chairman: Center for the American Experiment.
Frank Sims: director, vice president

Grants Analysis
Disclosure Period: calendar year ending 2001
Total Grants: $5,013,189*
Number of Grants: 175
Average Grant: $17,317*
Highest Grant: $2,000,000
Typical Range: $5,000 to $50,000 and $50,000 to $150,000
*Note: Giving excludes United Way. Average grant figure excludes highest grant.

Recent Grants
Note: Grants derived from 2001 Form 990.

General

2,000,000	University of Minnesota Foundation, Minneapolis, MN
725,000	United Way of Minneapolis Area, Minneapolis, MN
246,000	Neighborhood Involvement Program, Minneapolis, MN

Evaluative Criteria: Proposal must apply to one of the foundation's giving areas; organization must demonstrate it has a positive history and strong leadership; proposal must be clear and compelling as well as produce measurable results; project must be visible enough to solicit additional support from other funding sources.
Decision Notification: Applicant will be notified of any delays. Decision is received in writing.

Restrictions
The foundation does not make multiyear grants.
The foundation only accepts proposals submitted in writing. An organization can only submit similar proposals once in a 12-month period. Grants do not exceed $100,000.
The foundation does not support individuals; organizations outside the United States; discriminatory organizations; organizations not defined as tax-exempt under Section 501(c)(3) of the Internal Revenue Code; fraternal, political, or lobbying organizations; or goodwill advertising, dinners, or special events. tax-exempt under Section 501(c)(3) of the Internal Revenue Code; fraternal, political, or lobbying organizations; or goodwill advertising, dinners, or special events.

Additional Information
The foundation is increasing emphasis on reinforcing employee charitable activities. Because of this increased emphasis, the foundation is no longer funding initiatives in the area of diet and health.
Publications: Foundation Annual Report

Corporate Officials
Jerry S. Buckley: senior vice president public affairs B 1954. PRIM CORP EMPL vice president public affairs: Campbell Soup Co.
Douglas R. Conant: president, chief executive officer, director B 1951. PRIM CORP EMPL president, chief executive officer, director: Campbell Soup Co.
Donald R. Lanning: vice president grocery operations CORP AFFIL president: Campbell's Fresh Inc.

Foundation Officials
Jerry S. Buckley: trustee (see above)
Carlos del Sol: vice president, trustee
A. Fred George: trustee PRIM CORP EMPL branch manager: Campbell Soup Co.
Steve M. Jander: trustee
Ellen O. Kaden: senior vice president B New York, NY 1951. ED Cornell University BA (1972); Chicago State University MA (1973); Columbia University JD (1977). PRIM CORP EMPL senior vice president Law & government: Campbell Soup Co. NONPR AFFIL trustee: Institute Judicial Administration; member: National Legal Aid & Defender Association; trustee: Columbia University; member: Committee Civil Rights.

Grants Analysis
Disclosure Period: fiscal year ending June 31, 2001
Total Grants: $656,406*
Number of Grants: 80
Average Grant: $6,600*
Highest Grant: $135,000
Typical Range: $500 to $25,000
*Note: Giving excludes matching gifts; United Way; and program-related investments. Average grant figure excludes highest grant.

Recent Grants
Note: Grants derived from 2001 Form 990.

General

450,000	United Way of Camden County, Camden, NJ
135,000	St. Joseph's Carpenter Society, Camden, NJ
42,958	United Way of Henry County, Napoleon, OH
35,000	Cooper's Ferry Development Association, Camden, NJ
35,000	Hopeworks' N Camden, Camden, NJ
35,000	Scotia Village Foundation
34,153	United Way of Lamar County, Paris, TX
32,600	Dooley House, NJ
31,058	United Way of Lancaster County, Lancaster, PA
30,000	Camden City Garden Club, Inc, Camden, NJ

Frank A. Campini Foundation

Giving Contact
Paul J. Ruby, Director
220 Sansome St., Suite 700
San Francisco, CA 94104
Phone: (415)421-4171
Fax: (415)391-9997

Description
Founded: 1960
EIN: 946107956
Organization Type: Private Foundation
Giving Locations: CA: San Francisco Bay Area
Grant Types: General Support.

Donor Information
Founder: the late Frank A. Campini

Financial Summary
Total Giving: $1,156,000 (2001); $1,080,200 (2000); $1,000,400 (1999)
Giving Analysis: Giving for 2001 includes: foundation scholarships ($34,000) 2000: foundation scholarships ($10,000)
Assets: $23,176,214 (2001); $22,722,799 (2000); $23,404,400 (1999)

Typical Recipients
Arts & Humanities: Libraries, Museums/Galleries, Music, Opera, Public Broadcasting, Theater
Civic & Public Affairs: Botanical Gardens/Parks, Civic & Public Affairs-General, Urban & Community Affairs, Zoos/Aquariums
Education: Colleges & Universities, Economic Education, Environmental Education, Health & Physical Education, International Studies, Private Education (Precollege), Secondary Education (Public), Student Aid
Environment: Forestry, Environment-General, Resource Conservation
Health: AIDS/HIV, Cancer, Children's Health/Hospitals, Clinics/Medical Centers, Hospices, Medical Research, Preventive Medicine/Wellness Organizations, Single-Disease Health Associations
International: Foreign Educational Institutions, Missionary/Religious Activities
Religion: Jewish Causes, Religious Welfare
Science: Scientific Centers & Institutes, Scientific Centers & Institutes
Social Services: Child Welfare, Community Service Organizations, Crime Prevention, Domestic Violence, Family Services, Food/Clothing Distribution, Homes, Youth Organizations

Application Procedures
Initial Contact: Send a brief letter of inquiry.
Application Requirements: Include a description of organization, proof of tax-exempt status, amount requested, recently audited financial statement, and purpose of funds sought.
Deadlines: October 1.

Restrictions
Does not support individuals, religious organizations for sectarian purposes, political or lobbying groups, or organizations outside operating areas.

Foundation Officials
Alan Neys: director
Hendrika C. Neys: director
Patricia Neys: secretary, treasurer
Paul J. Ruby: director

Grants Analysis
Disclosure Period: calendar year ending 2001
Total Grants: $1,122,000*
Number of Grants: 89
Average Grant: $11,614*
Highest Grant: $100,000
Lowest Grant: $1,000
Typical Range: $5,000 to $20,000
*Note: Giving excludes scholarships. Average grant figure excludes highest grant.

Recent Grants
Note: Grants derived from 2001 Form 990.

General

104,000	Boys and Girls Club of San Francisco, San Francisco, CA
60,000	Audubon Canyon Ranch, Stinson Beach, CA
50,000	Alan Neys Memorial Fund
50,000	Family House, San Francisco, CA -- capital campaign
50,000	Fine Arts Museums of San Francisco, San Francisco, CA -- Rebuild de Young Fund
50,000	Friends of Recreation and Parks, San Francisco, CA -- Windmill Project
50,000	Jewish Federation of the Greater East Bay, San Francisco, CA
47,000	University of California San Francisco, San Francisco, CA -- Scientist Fellow Program
35,000	University of California San Francisco, San Francisco, CA -- Pediatric Oncology Clinical Research
25,000	California Academy of Sciences, San Francisco, CA

Candlesticks, Inc.

Company Headquarters
New York, NY

Company Description
Employees: 5
SIC(s): 2300 Apparel & Other Textile Products, 5100 Wholesale Trade--Nondurable Goods.

Lawrence Foundation

Giving Contact
Leonard Bernstein, Trustee
Lawrence Foundation
112 West 34th Street
Room 911
New York, NY 10120-0101
Phone: (212)947-8900
Fax: (212)643-9653

Description
EIN: 132880731
Organization Type: Corporate Foundation
Grant Types: General Support.

Financial Summary
Total Giving: $62,300 (fiscal year ending September 30, 2001); $61,100 (fiscal 2000); $58,000 (fiscal 1999)
Giving Analysis: Giving for fiscal 2001 includes: foundation scholarships ($4,000); fiscal 2000: foundation scholarships ($4,000); fiscal 1999: foundation scholarships ($4,000) foundation ($54,000)

Assets: $1,284,378 (fiscal 2001); $1,271,626 (fiscal 2000); $1,214,520 (fiscal 1999)
Gifts Received: $5,000 (fiscal 2001); $43,000 (fiscal 2000); $43,000 (fiscal 1998). Note: Contributions were received from Candlesticks, Inc. and Lancaster Industries.

Typical Recipients

Arts & Humanities: History & Archaeology, Libraries, Literary Arts, Public Broadcasting
Civic & Public Affairs: African American Affairs, Civil Rights, Economic Development, Gay/Lesbian Issues, Civic & Public Affairs-General, Safety, Urban & Community Affairs
Education: School Volunteerism
Environment: Air/Water Quality
Health: Cancer, Hospitals
International: Human Rights, International Peace & Security Issues, International Relations
Religion: Churches, Jewish Causes, Religious Organizations, Religious Welfare
Social Services: Animal Protection, Community Centers, Community Service Organizations, Crime Prevention, Delinquency & Criminal Rehabilitation, Domestic Violence, Senior Services, Shelters/Homelessness, Substance Abuse

Application Procedures

Initial Contact: Send a brief letter of inquiry.
Application Requirements: Include a description of organization, purpose of funds sought, and proof of tax-exempt status.
Deadlines: None.

Restrictions

Foundation does not support individuals or religious organizations.

Additional Information

Provides scholarships to students of Donegal High School, Mount Joy, PA.

Corporate Officials

Leonard S. Bernstein: chairman, president, chief executive officer B 1931. PRIM CORP EMPL chairman, president, chief executive officer: Candlesticks ADD CORP EMPL president: Donegal Industries Inc.; president: Lawrence Childrens Underwear Co.

Foundation Officials

Jay S. Bernstein: trustee B 1934. PRIM CORP EMPL vice president: Candlesticks Inc. ADD CORP EMPL vice president: Donnegal Industries Inc.; secretary: Lawrence Children's Underwear Co.
Lawrence Bernstein: trustee PRIM CORP EMPL vice president: Candlesticks Inc.
Leonard S. Bernstein: trustee (see above)

Grants Analysis

Disclosure Period: fiscal year ending September 30, 2001
Total Grants: $58,300*
Number of Grants: 19
Average Grant: $3,068
Highest Grant: $7,000
Lowest Grant: $500
Typical Range: $1,000 to $5,000
***Note:** Giving excludes scholarship.

Recent Grants

Note: Grants derived from fiscal 2000 Form 990.

General

7,000	American Civil Liberties Union
7,000	Fresh Air Fund, New York, NY
6,500	Phoenix House, New York, NY
6,000	Center to Prevent Handgun Violence, Washington, DC
6,000	Coalition for Homeless
4,000	Memorial Sloan Kettering Cancer Center, New York, NY
3,500	Coalition Against Domestic Violence
3,000	Gay Men's Health Crisis, New York, NY
2,500	God's Love We Deliver, New York, NY
2,000	Concord Coalition, Concord, MA

The Cannon Foundation, Inc.

Giving Contact

Frank Davis, Executive Director
57 Union Street South
PO Box 548
Concord, NC 28026-0548
Phone: (704)786-8216
Fax: (704)785-2052
E-mail: fdavis@cannonfoundationinc.org
Web: http://www.thecannonfoundationinc.org

Description

Founded: 1943
EIN: 566042532
Organization Type: General Purpose Foundation
Giving Locations: NC
Grant Types: Capital, Challenge, Project.

Donor Information

Founder: Established in 1943 by the late Charles A. Cannon , who was president and chairman of Cannon Mills for more than 50 years.

Financial Summary

Total Giving: $9,800,000 (fiscal year ending September 30, 2003 approx); $9,800,000 (fiscal 2002 approx); $9,822,749 (fiscal 2001)
Assets: $205,000,000 (fiscal 2003 approx); $205,000,000 (fiscal 2002 approx); $182,160,484 (fiscal 2001)

Typical Recipients

Arts & Humanities: Historic Preservation, History & Archaeology, Libraries, Museums/Galleries, Music, Performing Arts
Civic & Public Affairs: Employment/Job Training, Civic & Public Affairs-General, Legal Aid, Nonprofit Management, Philanthropic Organizations, Public Policy, Safety, Urban & Community Affairs, Women's Affairs
Education: Agricultural Education, Arts/Humanities Education, Business-School Partnerships, Colleges & Universities, Community & Junior Colleges, Environmental Education, Faculty Development, Education-General, Health & Physical Education, Literacy, Minority Education, Private Education (Precollege), Public Education (Precollege), Religious Education, Science/Mathematics Education, Social Sciences Education
Environment: Air/Water Quality, Energy, Forestry, Resource Conservation
Health: Adolescent Health Issues, AIDS/HIV, Children's Health/Hospitals, Clinics/Medical Centers, Emergency/Ambulance Services, Health-General, Geriatric Health, Health Organizations, Home-Care Services, Hospices, Hospitals, Nutrition, Prenatal Health Issues, Public Health, Research/Studies Institutes, Transplant Networks/Donor Banks
Religion: Churches, Ministries, Religious Organizations, Religious Welfare, Seminaries
Science: Science Museums, Scientific Centers & Institutes
Social Services: Camps, Child Welfare, Community Centers, Community Service Organizations, Domestic Violence, Family Planning, Family Services, Food/Clothing Distribution, Homes, People with Disabilities, People with Disabilities, Recreation & Athletics, Scouts, Senior Services, Social Services-General, Special Olympics, Substance Abuse, YMCA/YWCA/YMHA/YWHA, Youth Organizations

Application Procedures

Initial Contact: Applicants should send a proposal of no more than five pages to the foundation. The foundation provides an application form.
Application Requirements: Proposals should include an explanation of the need for the project; objectives and purposes, and how they will be met; description of applying organization; qualifications of persons responsible for project or program; form 990; location and duration of program; evaluative criteria; most recent audit report and one-page line item budget; list of the organization's governing board; and proof of tax-exempt status.
Deadlines: The foundation receives and considers applications on a quarterly basis. Applications are due by January 15, April 15, July 15, or October 15.

Restrictions

The foundation does not make loans or grants to individuals or for endowments. Scholarship grants and recurring grants are not funded.

Additional Information

Applicants must show evidence that the project can be sustained on a continuing basis.
Publications: Guidelines; Application Form

Foundation Officials

G. A. Batte, Jr.: director, member
W. C. Cannon, Jr.: director, member
W. S. Fisher: vice president, director, member
Thomas M. Grady: member, director
D. L. Gray: assistant secretary, treasurer, director, member
Mariam C. Hayes: president, director, member B 1918. PRIM CORP EMPL president: Central Distributing Co.
R. C. Hayes: director, member
T. C. Haywood: director
Elizabeth L. Quick: director, member B Izmir, Turkey 1948. ED Duke University AB (1970); University of North Carolina JD (1974). PRIM CORP EMPL attorney: Womble Carlyle Sandridge & Rice. NONPR AFFIL member: Forsyth County Bar Association; member: North Carolina Bar Association; member: American Bar Association; member: Fellow American College Trust & Estate Counsel.

Grants Analysis

Disclosure Period: fiscal year ending September 30, 2000
Total Grants: $9,250,163*
Number of Grants: 150
Average Grant: $61,668
Highest Grant: $2,000,000
Lowest Grant: $300
Typical Range: $5,000 to $50,000
***Note:** Grants analysis provided by foundation.

Recent Grants

Note: Grants derived from fiscal 2000 Form 990.

Library-Related

25,000	Friends of Madison County Library, Marshall, NC -- construction of a new library

General

2,000,000	Cabarrus Memorial Hospital, Concord, NC -- for health service delivery enhancement
1,000,000	Cabarrus County Boys and Girls Club, Concord, NC -- capital campaign
1,000,000	Cannon Memorial YMCA and Community Center, Kannapolis, NC -- renovations and expansions
500,000	Avery Health Care System, Inc., Linville, NC -- for Charles A. Cannon, Jr. Memorial Hospital
430,000	Cabarrus Memorial Hospital, Concord, NC -- Northeast Medical Center Professional Education Program
250,000	American National Red Cross Cabarrus County Chapter, Concord, NC -- Hurricane Floyd Relief in North Carolina
250,000	Athletic Foundation of the University of North Carolina at Charlotte, Charlotte, NC -- Barnhardt Student Activity Center
150,000	Lead-McRae College, Banner Elk, NC -- facility upgrades
150,000	Pfeiffer University, Misenheimer, NC -- technology plan
150,000	Wingate University, Wingate, NC -- technology improvements

Canon U.S.A., Inc.

Company Headquarters

1 Canon Plaza
Great Neck, NY 11024-1198
Web: http://www.usa.canon.com

Company Description

Employees: 8,700
SIC(s): 3577 Computer Peripheral Equipment Nec.
Parent Company: Canon, Inc., 30-2, Shimomaruko 3-chome, Ohta-ku, Tokyo, Japan

Operating Locations

Ambassador Office Equipment (IL--Schaumburg); Astro Business Solutions (CA--Gardena); Canon Computer Systems (CA--Costa Mesa); Canon Financial Services (NJ--Burlington); Canon Latin America (FL--Miami); Canon U.S.A. (NY--Lake Success); Dupli-fax (NJ--Burlington); MCS Business Solutions (NY--New York)

Nonmonetary Support

Type: Donated Equipment; Donated Products

Giving Contact

John Lese, Asst. Dir. Corp. Programs
One Canon Plz.
Lake Success, NY 11042
Phone: (516)328-4928
Fax: (516)328-5149

Description

Organization Type: Corporate Giving Program

Typical Recipients

Arts & Humanities: Arts Centers, Historic Preservation, Libraries, Museums/Galleries, Performing Arts, Public Broadcasting
Civic & Public Affairs: Municipalities/Towns, Urban & Community Affairs, Women's Affairs
Education: Colleges & Universities, Elementary Education (Private)
Environment: Resource Conservation
Health: Health Organizations, Medical Research
Religion: Religious Organizations
Social Services: Community Service Organizations, People with Disabilities, United Funds/United Ways, Youth Organizations

Application Procedures

Initial Contact: Send a brief introductory letter on organizational letterhead.

Additional Information

Canon U.S.A. sponsors a "Clean Earth Campaign" in conjunction with the National Wildlife Federation and the Nature Conservancy. The program has several purposes: it helps to keep the environment clean by encouraging customers to return used toner cartridges to the company, free of charge, instead of disposing of them in the trash; it conserves industrial resources by utilizing the recyclable portion of the cartridge to create new ones; and it helps to protect wildlife and the environment because the National Wildlife Federation and the Nature Conservancy share equally a $1-per-cartridge contribution from Canon. For more information, contact Canon U.S.A., Inc., at 1-800-962-2708. Canon also has manufacturing subsidiaries operating in California and Virginia and research and development operations in California.

Corporate Officials

Seymour Liebman: executive vice president finance, chief financial officer PRIM CORP EMPL executive vice president finance, chief financial officer: Canon U.S.A.
Haruo Murase: chairman, president, chief executive officer PRIM CORP EMPL chairman, president, chief executive officer: Canon U.S.A.

Cape Branch Foundation

Giving Contact

Scarlet S. Johnson, Trustee
PO Box 86
Oldwick, NJ 08858
Phone: (908)439-2357
Fax: (609)452-1025

Description

Founded: 1964
EIN: 226054886
Organization Type: Private Foundation
Giving Locations: NJ
Grant Types: Capital, General Support, Research.

Financial Summary

Total Giving: $1,536,060 (2001); $986,336 (2000); $810,500 (1998)
Giving Analysis: Giving for 1998 includes: foundation ($810,500)
Assets: $23,068,840 (2001); $23,944,789 (2000); $21,582,255 (1998)

Typical Recipients

Arts & Humanities: Arts Associations & Councils, Arts Centers, Arts Outreach, Dance, Arts & Humanities-General, Libraries, Museums/Galleries, Music, Performing Arts
Civic & Public Affairs: Civic & Public Affairs-General, Law & Justice, Municipalities/Towns, Urban & Community Affairs, Women's Affairs
Education: Arts/Humanities Education, Colleges & Universities, Education Funds, Education-General, Literacy, Medical Education, Private Education (Precollege), Public Education (Precollege), Secondary Education (Private), Student Aid
Environment: Air/Water Quality, Environment-General, Protection, Resource Conservation, Watershed
Health: AIDS/HIV, Health-General, Hospitals, Medical Rehabilitation, Medical Research, Research/Studies Institutes, Single-Disease Health Associations
International: Health Care/Hospitals
Religion: Churches, Jewish Causes, Religious Welfare
Science: Scientific Research
Social Services: Camps, Community Service Organizations, Day Care, Family Planning, Family Services, People with Disabilities, Recreation & Athletics, Youth Organizations

Application Procedures

Initial Contact: Send a brief letter of inquiry.
Application Requirements: Outline purpose of funds sought and include amount requested.
Deadlines: None.

Restrictions

The foundation does not support individuals, religious organizations for sectarian purposes, or political or lobbying groups.

Foundation Officials

Gordon O. Danser: trustee
Frank Joseph Hoenemeyer: truste
director: American International Grou
Gretchen W. Johnson: trustee, dire
James Lawrence Johnson: directo
1927. ED Texas Technology Univers
PRIM CORP EMPL chairman emeri
CORP AFFIL director: Walter Industri
First Federal Savings & Loan Assoc
Mutual Life Insurance Co.; director:
director: BC Telecommunications
Bloomington Unlimited. NONPR A
Wesleyan Associates; member: Wesle
member: National Association Accour
McLean County Association Comme
trustee, member advisory council: Me
tal; member advisory council: Illinois S
College Business; director: Illinois Tele
ation; member: Financial Executives I
AFFIL Rotary Club; Woodway C
Bloomington Country Club; Crestwicke

Grants Analysis

Disclosure Period: calendar year end
Total Grants: $1,536,059
Number of Grants: 21
Average Grant: $43,903*
Highest Grant: $500,000
Typical Range: $5,000 to $100,000
***Note:** Average grant figure excludes grants. .

Recent Grants

Note: Grants derived from 2001 Form 9

General

500,000	Willow School, Gladstone, N
201,889	Edison Wetlands Associatior NJ
150,000	Matheny School and Hospita NJ -- arts auditorium campai
125,000	Institute for Democracy Studi York, NY
100,000	Town of Jupiter Island, Hobe FL -- for land conservation
100,000	United States Equestrian Tea stone, NJ
75,000	Artistic Realization Technolog Belle Mead, NJ
52,171	Blairsden Association, New Y
50,000	Center for Law and Reproduct icy, New York, NY
50,000	Girls, Inc., New York, NY

Cargill, Inc.

Company Headquarters

Minneapolis, MN
Web: http://www.cargill.com

Company Description

Revenue: US$50.826 billion (2002)
Employees: 97000 (2002)
SIC(s): 2041 Flour & Other Grain Mill Produc Deep Sea Domestic Transportation of Freigl Grain & Field Beans, 6221 Commodity Contra kers & Dealers.

Operating Locations

Cargill Inc. (CA--Newark; FL--Riverview; ID Falls; IL--Chicago; MA--Beverly; MN--Minne Monticello, Wayzata; TN--Cordova; WI--Jef Sheboygan)

Nonmonetary Support

Type: Donated Equipment; Donated Pro Loaned Executives
Contact: Mark Murphy
Note: Co. provides nonmonetary support.

218,549	University of Minnesota Foundation, Minneapolis, MN
128,184	Minnesota Humanities Commission, St. Paul, MN -- capital support
125,000	Indian Hills Community College Foundation, Ottumwa, IA
118,963	Pillsbury United Communities, Minneapolis, MN
100,000	St. Paul Chamber Orchestra, St. Paul, MN
100,000	YMCA Metropolitan Minneapolis, Minneapolis, MN
85,000	Minnesota Historical Society, St. Paul, MN -- Hi-Jinx programs

CARILLON IMPORTERS, LTD.

Company Headquarters

Teaneck, NJ

Company Description

Employees: 54
SIC(s): 2084 Wines, Brandy & Brandy Spirits, 2085 Distilled & Blended Liquors.
Parent Company: Diageo Plc, 8 Henrietta Place, London, United Kingdom

Grand Marnier Foundation

Giving Contact

Jerry Ciraulo, Treasurer
80 Route 4 East, 1st Floor
Paramus, NJ 07652
Phone: (201)368-9500

Description

EIN: 133258414
Organization Type: Corporate Foundation
Giving Locations: CA; MD; NY: nationally.
Grant Types: General Support.

Financial Summary

Total Giving: $485,900 (2001); $428,507 (2000); $408,380 (1999). Note: Contributes through foundation only.
Giving Analysis: Giving for 1999 includes: foundation ($408,380)
Assets: $5,665,145 (2001); $6,355,906 (2000); $6,699,487 (1999)

Typical Recipients

Arts & Humanities: Arts Associations & Councils, Arts Centers, Arts Institutes, Arts Outreach, Ballet, Dance, Ethnic & Folk Arts, Film & Video, Arts & Humanities-General, History & Archaeology, Libraries, Museums/Galleries, Music, Opera, Performing Arts, Public Broadcasting, Theater
Civic & Public Affairs: Botanical Gardens/Parks, Clubs, Employment/Job Training, Civic & Public Affairs-General, Hispanic Affairs, Housing, Native American Affairs, Parades/Festivals, Professional & Trade Associations, Women's Affairs
Education: Arts/Humanities Education, Business Education, Colleges & Universities, Continuing Education, Engineering/Technological Education, Education-General, International Studies, International Studies, Leadership Training, Literacy, Medical Education, Minority Education, Private Education (Precollege), Public Education (Precollege), Science/Mathematics Education, Student Aid
Environment: Air/Water Quality
Health: AIDS/HIV, Alzheimers Disease, Cancer, Children's Health/Hospitals, Clinics/Medical Centers,

Emergency/Ambulance Services, Health Organizations, Heart, Hospitals, Medical Research, Nutrition, Single-Disease Health Associations
International: Foreign Arts Organizations, Foreign Educational Institutions, International Development, International Organizations, International Peace & Security Issues, International Relations, International Relief Efforts, Missionary/Religious Activities
Religion: Churches, Jewish Causes, Religious Welfare, Synagogues/Temples
Social Services: Child Abuse, Child Welfare, Community Service Organizations, Crime Prevention, Emergency Relief, Family Services, Food/Clothing Distribution, Recreation & Athletics, Shelters/Homelessness, Social Services-General, Youth Organizations

Application Procedures

Initial Contact: Submit a brief letter.
Application Requirements: Include a description of organization, amount requested, purpose of funds sought, recently audited financial statement, and proof of tax-exempt status.
Deadlines: None.

Corporate Officials

Michel Roux: president, chief executive officer, director B 1941. PRIM CORP EMPL president, chief executive officer, director: Carillon Importers, Ltd.

Foundation Officials

Jerry Ciraulo: treasurer, director PRIM CORP EMPL chief executive officer: Carillon Importers Ltd.
Maxime Coury: director B Alexandria, Egypt 1925.
Michel Roux: president, director (see above)

Grants Analysis

Disclosure Period: calendar year ending 2001
Total Grants: $485,900
Number of Grants: 100
Average Grant: $4,290*
Highest Grant: $61,200
Lowest Grant: $150
Typical Range: $200 to $10,000
*Note: Average grant figure excludes highest grant.

Recent Grants

Note: Grants derived from 2001 Form 990.

General

61,200	City Meals on Wheels, New York, NY
50,000	French Institute Alliance Francaise, New York, NY
39,000	Friends of the Israel Defense Forces, Hauppauge, NY
35,000	Maryland Public Television, Owings Mills, MD
25,000	Bergen County 200 Club, Hackensack, NJ
25,000	Culinary Institute of America, Hyde Park, NY -- scholarship funds
25,000	Windows of Hope Family Relief Fund, New York, NY
16,000	Columbia University in the City of New York, New York, NY -- for Maison Francaise
15,750	American Heart Association, Chicago, IL
13,000	New York University Center for French Civilization and Culture, New York, NY

CARLS FOUNDATION

Giving Contact

Elizabeth A. Stieg, Executive Director
333 W. Fort Street, Suite 1940
Detroit, MI 48226
Phone: (313)965-0990
Fax: (313)965-0547
Web: http://www.carlsfdn.org/

Description

Founded: 1961
EIN: 386099935
Organization Type: Private Foundation
Giving Locations: MI: Huron Valley
Grant Types: General Support, Scholarship.

Donor Information

Founder: William Carls

Financial Summary

Total Giving: $6,245,242 (2001); $8,010,008 (2000); $3,607,322 (1999)
Assets: $109,738,312 (2001); $120,599,915 (2000); $120,708,912 (1999)
Gifts Received: $36,446,672 (1998); $6,915,833 (1996); $110,000 (1995). Note: In 1998, contributions were received from William Carls Estate Trust.

Typical Recipients

Arts & Humanities: Libraries, Music
Civic & Public Affairs: Community Foundations, Employment/Job Training, Civic & Public Affairs-General
Education: Colleges & Universities, Engineering/Technological Education, Environmental Education, Education-General, Minority Education, Private Education (Precollege), Public Education (Precollege), Special Education, Student Aid, Vocational & Technical Education
Environment: Resource Conservation
Health: Alzheimers Disease, Cancer, Children's Health/Hospitals, Clinics/Medical Centers, Diabetes, Eyes/Blindness, Geriatric Health, Health Organizations, Home-Care Services, Hospitals, Mental Health, Prenatal Health Issues, Public Health, Speech & Hearing, Transplant Networks/Donor Banks
International: Health Care/Hospitals, International Relief Efforts
Religion: Ministries, Ministries, Religious Welfare
Science: Scientific Centers & Institutes
Social Services: Big Brother/Big Sister, Camps, Child Welfare, Community Service Organizations, Day Care, Family Services, Homes, People with Disabilities, Senior Services, Substance Abuse, YMCA/YWCA/YMHA/YWHA, Youth Organizations

Application Procedures

Initial Contact: The foundation has no formal grant application procedure or application form. Send a brief letter of inquiry.
Deadlines: November 1, March 1, and July 1. Board meets in January, May, and September.

Restrictions

Grants are awarded for the purpose of providing for children's welfare, with special emphasis on the prevention and treatment of hearing impairment and recreational, educational, and welfare programs, especially for children who are disadvantaged for economic and/or health reasons. Grants also awarded for preservation of natural areas, open space and historic buildings and areas having special beauty or significance in maintaining America's heritage and historic ideals, through assistance to land trusts and conservancies and directly related to environmental educational programs.

Additional Information

Provides scholarships to students of the Huron Valley public school system.

Foundation Officials

Arthur Derisley: president, treasurer, trustee
Henry Fleischer: trustee
Theresa Krieger: trustee
Elizabeth A. Stieg: assistant secretary, trustee
Harold E. Stieg: vice president, secretary, trustee

Grants Analysis
Disclosure Period: calendar year ending 2001
Total Grants: $6,245,242
Number of Grants: 66
Average Grant: $39,142*
Highest Grant: $750,000
Lowest Grant: $2,725
Typical Range: $10,000 to $50,000
*Note: Average grant excludes eight highest grant ($3,975,000).

Recent Grants
Note: Grants derived from 2001 Form 990.

General
750,000	Detroit Institute for Children, Detroit, MI -- for the renovation of the facility
500,000	Central Michigan University, Mt. Pleasant, MI -- capital support for clinical wing
500,000	Community Foundation for Southeast Michigan, Detroit, MI -- for GreenWays Initiative
500,000	Detroit 300, Inc., Detroit, MI -- for conservancy endowment
500,000	Detroit Science Center, Detroit, MI -- for Science Stage Air Show, Power of Air, and the Williams Carls Exhibit
500,000	North Oakland Medical Center, Pontiac, MI -- support renovation of Neonatal Intensive Care Unit
375,000	Grand Traverse Regional Land Conservancy, Traverse City, MI -- for Lasting Landscapes Project
300,000	Lion's Visually Impaired Youth Camp, Lake Orion, MI -- for construction of Main Lodge for a camp for children with physical disabilities
250,000	Alternatives for Girls, Detroit, MI -- for capital funds
250,000	Mel Trotter Ministries, Grand Rapids, MI -- for the purchase of a new camp serving the homeless inner city youth

CARLSON COMPANIES, INC.

Company Headquarters
1405 Xenium Lane N.
Plymouth, MN 55441
Web: http://www.carlson.com

Company Description
Founded: 1938
Revenue: US$6.5 billion (2002)
Employees: 180,000 (2002)
SIC(s): 4729 Passenger Transportation Arrangement Nec, 5812 Eating Places, 5961 Catalog & Mail-Order Houses, 7359 Equipment Rental & Leasing Nec.

Curtis L. Carlson Family Foundation

Giving Contact
Donna Snyder, Secretary
301 Carlson Parkway, Suite 102
Minnetonka, MN 55305
Phone: (952)404-5600
Fax: (952)404-5601

Description
Founded: 1959
EIN: 416028973
Organization Type: Corporate Foundation
Giving Locations: MN
Grant Types: General Support.

Donor Information
Founder: Curtis L. Carlson, Arleen M. Carlson, Glen D. Nelson, Marylyn C. Nelson

Financial Summary
Total Giving: $2,518,248 (2001); $2,098,132 (2000); $194,318 (1999 approx). Note: Contributes through corporate direct giving program and foundation.
Giving Analysis: Giving for 2000 includes: foundation matching gifts ($27,600); foundation grants to United Way ($170,000); foundation ($1,900,532); 1998: foundation grants to United Way ($83,000); foundation ($383,040); 1997: foundation grants to United Way ($2,600) foundation ($1,724,200)
Assets: $54,571,233 (2001); $56,062,053 (2000); $34,204,474 (1998)
Gifts Received: $7,432,483 (2001); $7,488,060 (2000); $204,384 (1997). Note: In 2000 and 2001, contributions were received from Arleen M. Carlson. In 1997, contributions were received from Edwin C. Gage and Barbara C. Gage.

Typical Recipients
Arts & Humanities: Arts Centers, Arts Funds, Arts Institutes, Community Arts, Libraries, Museums/Galleries, Music, Opera, Public Broadcasting, Theater
Civic & Public Affairs: Business/Free Enterprise, Clubs, Ethnic Organizations, Civic & Public Affairs-General, Professional & Trade Associations, Urban & Community Affairs, Women's Affairs, Zoos/Aquariums
Education: Business Education, Colleges & Universities, Education Funds, Education-General, Gifted & Talented Programs, International Studies, Leadership Training, Minority Education, Private Education (Precollege), Student Aid
Environment: Forestry, Wildlife Protection
Health: AIDS/HIV, Cancer, Children's Health/Hospitals, Clinics/Medical Centers, Diabetes, Emergency/Ambulance Services, Eyes/Blindness, Health Organizations, Heart, Hospitals, Medical Research, Multiple Sclerosis, Public Health, Research/Studies Institutes, Single-Disease Health Associations
International: Health Care/Hospitals, International Organizations, International Relations
Religion: Churches, Jewish Causes, Ministries, Religious Organizations, Religious Welfare, Seminaries
Science: Science Museums
Social Services: Animal Protection, Big Brother/Big Sister, Camps, Child Welfare, Community Service Organizations, Family Services, Food/Clothing Distribution, People with Disabilities, Recreation & Athletics, Scouts, Shelters/Homelessness, Substance Abuse, United Funds/United Ways, United Funds/United Ways, YMCA/YWCA/YMHA/YWHA, Youth Organizations

Application Procedures
Initial Contact: Write to request application guidelines, then send a written proposal.
Application Requirements: Include name of organization, address, and contact information; history and general purpose of the organization; three-year budget history and projected budget of organization; copy of IRS tax-exempt ruling; copy of most recent Form 990; list of board of directors and their affiliations; purpose of request; amount requested; program budget; evidence of cooperation with other similar agencies; evidence of evaluation system for program; and description of how program will be funded on an ongoing basis.
Deadlines: September 1 for organizations seeking grants before the end of the calendar year.
Review Process: Contributions committee reviews requests.
Evaluative Criteria: Purpose of grant, other sources of support, practicality of proposed plan, plans for future support. Supported programs meet one or more of the following guidelines: self-sufficiency, self-sustaining, performance, potential benefit, and cooperation and coordination.
Decision Notification: Quarterly.

Restrictions
Foundation generally does not fund dinners, benefits, or conferences; travel costs; individuals; political activities or causes; athletic events; endowments; and organizations that are not tax-exempt.

Additional Information
Company has operating locations in nearly all 50 states.
Publications: Guidelines and Policy

Corporate Officials
Barbara C Gage: director vice president, chief financial officer PRIM CORP EMPL director: Carlson Companies Inc. ADD CORP EMPL director: Carlson Holdings Inc. CORP AFFIL director: Gage Marketing Group LLC.
Marilyn Carlson Nelson: chairman, chief executive officer B Minneapolis, MN August 19, 1939. ED Smith College BA (1961). PRIM CORP EMPL chairman, chief executive officer: Carlson Companies Inc. CORP AFFIL director: ExxonMobil Corp.; director: US West Inc.; chairman, director: Citizens State Bank Waterville; director, president: Carlson Holdings Inc.; chairman: Citizens State Bank Montgomery; president: Adams Martin & Nelson Inc.
Martyn R. Redgrave: executive vice president, chief financial officer B 1952. ED New York University MBA; Princeton University BA. PRIM CORP EMPL executive vice president, chief financial officer: Carlson Companies Inc. CORP AFFIL chief financial officer: Carlson Holdings Inc.

Foundation Officials
Arleen M. Carlson: emeritus director
Barbara C Gage: president (see above)

Grants Analysis
Disclosure Period: calendar year ending 2001
Total Grants: $2,071,100*
Number of Grants: 74
Average Grant: $3,300*
Highest Grant: $500,000
Lowest Grant: $250
Typical Range: $50 to $100,000
*Note: Giving excludes United Way, scholarship, and matching gifts. Average grant figure excludes seven highest grants totaling $1,850,000.

Recent Grants
Note: Grants derived from 2001 Form 990.

General
500,000	University of Minnesota Foundation, Minneapolis, MN -- Gateway Pledge
500,000	University of Minnesota Foundation, Minneapolis, MN -- Gateway Pledge
250,000	American Swedish Institute, Minneapolis, MN -- Selma Garden
200,000	Penn State University, Pittsburgh, PA -- scholarship fund
200,000	United Way, Minneapolis, MN -- operating support
100,000	World Childhood Foundation, New York, NY -- operating support
100,000	World Childhood Foundation, New York, NY -- operating support
86,500	Bakken, Minneapolis, MN -- operating support
64,000	World Childhood Foundation, New York, NY -- operating support
27,000	Hennepin Avenue United Methodist Church, Minneapolis, MN -- annual pledge

CARNAHAN-JACKSON FOUNDATION

Giving Contact

Carnahan-Jackson Foundation
c/o Fleet Trust Co.
PO Box 3326
Jamestown, NY 14702
Phone: (716)726-8050

Description

Founded: 1972
EIN: 166151608
Organization Type: Private Foundation
Giving Locations: NY: Jamestown
Grant Types: Capital, General Support, Project, Scholarship, Seed Money.

Donor Information

Founder: the late Katharine J. Carnahan

Financial Summary

Total Giving: $564,700 (fiscal year ending July 31, 2001); $625,913 (fiscal 2000); $733,533 (fiscal 1998). Note: Fiscal 1997 Giving includes United Way ($10,000).
Giving Analysis: Giving for fiscal 2001 includes: foundation grants to United Way ($10,000); fiscal 1998: foundation grants to United Way ($10,000) foundation ($723,533)
Assets: $13,469,505 (fiscal 2001); $14,335,943 (fiscal 2000); $14,069,737 (fiscal 1998).

Typical Recipients

Arts & Humanities: Ballet, Dance, Arts & Humanities-General, History & Archaeology, Libraries, Music, Performing Arts, Public Broadcasting
Civic & Public Affairs: Clubs, Economic Development, Municipalities/Towns
Education: Business Education, Colleges & Universities, Education Funds, Medical Education, Minority Education, Preschool Education, Public Education (Precollege), Student Aid
Environment: Environment-General, Resource Conservation, Wildlife Protection
Health: Hospitals
International: International Organizations
Religion: Churches, Religious Welfare
Social Services: Animal Protection, Child Welfare, Community Centers, Community Service Organizations, Crime Prevention, Day Care, People with Disabilities, Recreation & Athletics, Scouts, Substance Abuse, United Funds/United Ways, YMCA/YWCA/YMHA/YWHA, Youth Organizations

Application Procedures

Initial Contact: Send a brief letter of inquiry.
Application Requirements: Include purpose of funds sought and proof of tax-exempt status.
Deadlines: Applications are considered in June and September.

Restrictions

Preference is given to educational institutions and charitable organizations in the Jamestown, NY, area.

Additional Information

Trust(s): Fleet Trust Co

Grants Analysis

Disclosure Period: fiscal year ending July 31, 2001
Total Grants: $554,700*
Number of Grants: 23
Average Grant: $14,986*
Highest Grant: $140,000
Typical Range: $5,000 to $30,000
*Note: Giving excludes United Way. Average grant figure excludes two highest grants ($240,000).

Recent Grants

Note: Grants derived from 1999 Form 990.

Library-Related
100,000	James Prendergast Library, Jamestown, NY
25,000	Patterson Library, Westfield, NY
25,000	Sinclairville Free Library, Sinclairville, NY
5,000	Cuba Circulating Library, Cuba, NY

General
237,300	Chautauqua Institution, Jamestown, NY
65,000	Denison University, Granville, OH
50,000	YMCA Camp Onyahsa
25,000	WNEO Public Broadcasting Association, Youngstown, OH
15,000	Chautauqua Regional Youth Ballet, Jamestown, NY
15,000	Davis & Elkins College, Elkins, WV
15,000	Nature Conservancy
13,900	Jamestown Audubon Society, Jamestown, NY
13,000	Junior Achievement, Providence, RI
10,000	Independent College Fund

CARNEGIE CORP. OF NEW YORK

Giving Contact

Adam Liebling, Grants Associate
437 Madison Avenue
New York, NY 10022
Phone: (212)371-3200
Fax: (212)754-4073
Web: http://www.carnegie.org

Description

Founded: 1938
EIN: 131628151
Organization Type: General Purpose Foundation
Giving Locations: internationally, especially to countries that are or have been members of the British commonwealth.
Grant Types: General Support, Project, Research, Seed Money.

Donor Information

Founder: Andrew Carnegie was born in Scotland in 1835. He moved to the United States 13 years later, beginning work as a boobin boy in the cotton mill. After holding various joubs with Western Union and the Pennsylvania Railroad, Carnegie resigned in 1865 to establish his own business enterprises and eventually organized the Carnegie Steel Company. At the turn of the century, he sold his major Pittsburgh steel company to J.P. Morgan for $400 million. Carnegie was one of the first wealthy Americans to believe that the well-to-do had a moral responsibility to assist the less fortuante. Carnegie's personal philanthropy began in his thrities with a large gift to his hometown of Dunfermline, Scotland. One of his earliest interests was the establishment of free public libraries throughout the United States, a cause to which he donated over $56 million. Other interests included adult education and education in the fine arts. Over the years, Carnegie established seven philanthropic and educational organizations in the United States, and several more in Europe to carry out theses and other programs. In the United States, he established the Carnegie Foundation for the Advancement of Teaching, the Carnegie Institute (Pittsburgh), the Carnegie Mellon University (formed by the 7 merger of the Mellon Institute and the Carnegie Institute of Technology), the Carnegie Endowment for International Peace, and the Carnegie Institution of Washington. Overseas, Mr. Carnegie established the Carnegie Trust for the Universities of Scotland to assis students and fund expansion and research, and the Carnegie Dunfermline and United Kingdom Trusts to improve social conditions in his native town, and the well-being of the people of Great Britain and Ireland through aid to community service, arts and crafts, and leadership training. Mr. Carnegie also established hero funds in the United States, the United Kingdom, and Europe to recognize heroic acts performed in peaceful nations. In all, Mr. Carnegie's gifts and bequests totaled over $350 million.

Financial Summary

Total Giving: $80,000,000 (fiscal year ending September 30, 2003 approx); $76,301,020 (fiscal 2002); $84,353,909 (fiscal 2001)
Assets: $1,627,733,524 (fiscal 2002); $1,711,510,640 (fiscal 2001); $1,705,527,531 (fiscal 1999)
Gifts Received: $50,015 (fiscal 1999). Note: In fiscal 1999, contributions were received from the estate of Peter Economos.

Typical Recipients

Arts & Humanities: Libraries, Public Broadcasting
Civic & Public Affairs: African American Affairs, Asian American Affairs, Civil Rights, Economic Development, Economic Policy, Civic & Public Affairs-General, Hispanic Affairs, Law & Justice, Legal Aid, Native American Affairs, Nonprofit Management, Philanthropic Organizations, Professional & Trade Associations, Public Policy, Urban & Community Affairs, Women's Affairs
Education: Afterschool/Enrichment Programs, Arts/Humanities Education, Colleges & Universities, Education Associations, Education Reform, Elementary Education (Public), Faculty Development, Education-General, Health & Physical Education, International Exchange, International Studies, Journalism/Media Education, Legal Education, Literacy, Medical Education, Minority Education, Preschool Education, Public Education (Precollege), Science/Mathematics Education, Secondary Education (Public), Social Sciences Education, Special Education, Vocational & Technical Education
Health: Adolescent Health Issues, Children's Health/Hospitals, Clinics/Medical Centers, Health Policy/Cost Containment, Health Organizations, Medical Research, Mental Health, Prenatal Health Issues, Public Health
International: Foreign Arts Organizations, Foreign Educational Institutions, International-General, Health Care/Hospitals, Human Rights, International Affairs, International Development, International Organizations, International Peace & Security Issues, International Relations, Missionary/Religious Activities, Trade
Science: Scientific Centers & Institutes, Scientific Organizations
Social Services: At-Risk Youth, Child Abuse, Child Welfare, Community Service Organizations, Crime Prevention, Day Care, Family Planning, Family Services, Refugee Assistance, Substance Abuse, Volunteer Services, Youth Organizations

Application Procedures

Initial Contact: The corporation does not have application forms. Initial contact should be by letter.
Application Requirements: The initial proposal should be a brief written statement describing the project's aims, duration, methods, personnel, and the amount of financial support required.
The following points may be helpful in preparing a proposal or preproposal. Although the questions need not be answered individually, they indicate the types of concerns program staff members have in mind when reviewing requests: What problem does your project address? Why is this issue significant? What is the relationship of the problem/issue to the corporation's program? How will your project or activity deal with the stated problem? What do you intend to demonstrate or prove? What means will you use, and

what methodology will you apply? If the project is already under way, what have you accomplished so far? What outcomes do you expect for the project, both immediate and long term? How will you assess the success or effectiveness of your work? What strengths and skills do the organization and personnel bring to this project? In short, what makes this organization the right one to conduct this project? If the organization has not received a grant from the corporation before, please include background information such as an annual report, audited financial statement, or mission statement. Finally, what is the overall cost of the project? How much are you requesting and over how long a period? What other sources of support are you pursuing for this project?

Corporation officers will request supplementary information or a personal discussion when necessary. The endorsement of the administrative head of the requesting institution need not be sent with the initial proposal, but it will be required before a favorable recommendation is made to the corporation's trustees.

Deadlines: None.

Review Process: Corporation officers consider each project. If they decide to evaluate a project for funding, a more developed project proposal will be requested. Specific criteria will be given in the descriptions of each program area. The corporation's board meets in October, February, April, and June.

Notes: The corporation does not, as a matter of policy, provide to prospective grantseekers copies of successful proposals.

Restrictions

The corporation does not operate scholarship, fellowship, or travel grant programs; it does not make grants for basic operating expenses, endowments, or facilities of educational or human services institutions; nor does it make program-related investments.

The corporation does not generally make grants to individuals. On occasion, it will make a grant to a highly qualified individual for a project that is central to its stated program interests.

Additional Information

The corporation also does not fund individual schools, or curriculum projects within individual schools.

Publications: Annual Report; General Information Pamphlet; Carnegie Quarterly; Carnegie Special Report; Carnegie Meeting Papers; Carnegie Occasional Papers; Andrew Carnegie Pamphlet; Carnegie Newslines

Foundation Officials

Bruce Michael Alberts, PhD: trustee B Chicago, IL 1938. ED Harvard College AB (1960); Harvard University PhD (1965). PRIM NONPR EMPL president: National Academy of Sciences. CORP AFFIL member advisory board: Bethesda Research Laboratories; member advisory board: Life Techs Inc. NONPR AFFIL chairman: NRC; member: Phi Beta Kappa; member advisory board: National Science Resource Center Smithsonian Institute; member, president: NAS; committee member: National Board Professional Teaching Standards; committee member department biology: Massachusetts Institute Technology; member science advisory committee: Marine Biology Laboratory; member: Markey Foundation; member science advisory board: Fred Hutchinson Cancer Research Center; director: Federal American Society Experimental Biology; member: Genetics Society America; member department embryology: Carnegie Institute; member: European Molecular Biology Organization; member: American Society Microbiology; member: American Society Biochemistry & Molecular Biology; member: American Society Cell Biology; member: American Chemical Society; member: American Philosophical Society; member: American Association Advancement Science.

Deana Arsenian: senior program officer international peace

Geoffrey T. Boisi: trustee PRIM CORP EMPL vice chairman investment banking: J.P. Morgan Chase.

Gloria Primm Brown: senior program officer international development

Matthew Day, Jr.: member

Karin P. Egan: program officer education

Neil R. Grabois: vice president/director for strategic planning

Vartan Gregorian: president B Tabriz, Iran 1934. ED College of Armenia (1955); Stanford University BA (1958); Stanford University PhD (1964). CORP AFFIL director: McGraw-Hill Inc. NONPR AFFIL trustee: Museum Modern Art; member: Phi Beta Kappa; member: Mid-East Studies Association; director: Institute International Education; member: International Federation Library Association; member: Institute Advanced Studies; chairman board visitors: City University New York Graduate School & University Center; member: Council Foreign Relations; president: Carnegie Corp. New York; director: Brookings Institution; president: Brown University; member: American Historical Association; member: American Philosophical Society; member: American Association Advancement Slavic Studies; fellow: American Academy of Arts & Sciences; member: American Antiquarian Society. CLUB AFFIL Round Table Club; Grolier Club; Century Club; Economic Club.

David A. Hamburg: president emeritus B Evansville, IN 1925. ED Indiana University MD (1947). NONPR AFFIL trustee: President Committee Advisory Science & Technology; director: Rockefeller University; member: Phi Beta Kappa; deputy chairman: Federal Reserve Bank New York; member: National Academy Sciences; member: Association Research Nervous & Mental Diseases; member: American Philosophical Society; member: American Psychiatric Association; trustee: American Museum Natural History; member: American Academy of Arts & Sciences; member: American Association Advancement Science; member: Alpha Omega Alpha.

Idalia Holder: director human resources

James B. Hunt: trustee

Helene L. Kaplan: chairman, trustee B New York, NY 1933. ED Barnard College AB (1953); New York University JD (1967). PRIM CORP EMPL of counsel: Skadden, Arps, Slate, Meagher & Flom. CORP AFFIL director: Metro Life Insurance Co.; director: Verizon Communications Inc.; director: ExxonMobil Corp.; director: May Department Stores Co.; director: Chase Manhattan Corp. NONPR AFFIL trustee: Olive Free Library; member: Women's Forum; member: New York State Bar Association; vice chairman, trustee: Mount Sinai Medical Center; vice chairman, trustee: Mount Sinai School of Medicine; member: Century Association; trustee: Institute Advanced Studies; trustee: Barnard College; member: American Philosophical Society; member: Association Bar New York City; member: American Bar Association; trustee, vice chairman: American Museum Natural History; member: American Academy of Arts & Sciences. CLUB AFFIL Cosmopolitan Club.

Susan Robinson King: vice president public affairs

Martin L. Leibowitz: vice chairman ED New York University PhD; University of Chicago MA; University of Chicago BA. PRIM CORP EMPL vice chairman, chief investment officer: TIAA-CREF.

Geraldine P. Mannion: program chair U.S. democracy

William McDonough: trustee

Sam Nunn: trustee PRIM CORP EMPL senior partner: King & Spalding.

Olara A. Otunnu: trustee PRIM NONPR EMPL special representative: United Nations.

William A. Owens: trustee

Thomas R. Pickering: trustee

Patricia L. Rosenfield: chair Carnegie Scholars program

Robert J. Seman: finance director

Edward Sermier: vice president, chief administrative officer NONPR AFFIL chief financial officer, director: Philharmonic Symphony Society New York.

D. Ellen Shuman: vice president, chief investment officer

Ruth J. Simmons: trustee PRIM NONPR EMPL president: Brown University.

Raymond W. Smith: trustee B Pittsburgh, PA 1937. ED Carnegie Mellon University BS (1959); University of Pittsburgh MBA (1967). CORP AFFIL director: USAirways Group Inc.; director: Westinghouse Electric Corp.; chairman: Bell Atlantic Maryland. NONPR AFFIL member: Library Congress James Madison National Council; member national advisory board: Private Sector Councils; member board advisors: Arden Theatre Co.; member: Business Roundtable.

David C. Speedie, III: program chairman international peace and security

Marta Tienda, PhD: trustee B TX. ED University of Texas PhD (1977). PRIM NONPR EMPL director: Princeton University, Office Population Research. NONPR AFFIL member: Population Association America; associate director: Population Research Center; research assistant: Ogburn Stouffer Center; fellow: Center Advanced Study Behavioral Science; member: International Union Science Study Population; member: American Sociological Association; trustee: Carnegie Corp. New York; fellow: American Academy of Arts & Sciences; member: American Economic Association.

Judy Woodruff: trustee B Tulsa, OK 1946. ED Meredith College (1964-1966); Duke University BA (1968). PRIM CORP EMPL anchor & senior correspondent: Cable News Network. NONPR AFFIL member: National Academy Television Arts & Sciences; member: White House Correspondents Association; director: International Womens Media Foundation; member, board advisors: Knight Fellowship in Journalism; member: Commonwealth Fund; trustee: Duke University; member: Commission on Womens Health.

Grants Analysis

Disclosure Period: fiscal year ending September 30, 2001

Total Grants: $84,353,909*

Number of Grants: 241

Average Grant: $350,016*

Highest Grant: $2,671,100

Typical Range: $25,000 to $350,000

*Note: Grants analysis provided by foundation.

Recent Grants

Note: Grants derived from fiscal 2001 Form 990.

General

1,764,417	University of Dar es Salaam United Republic of Tanzania -- Scholarship Program for undergraduate women
500,000	United Nations Office of the High Commissioner for Human Rights, Geneva Switzerland -- world conference against racism, racial discrimination
402,350	Nelson Mandela Metropolitan Municipal Library Services- -- activities to increase services for children, expand services in under served areas
307,484	Durban Metropolitan Library Services Republic of South Africa -- increase literacy and information service development
304,367	University of Natal, Durban Republic of South Africa -- establish the KwaZulu Natal Centre for HIV/AIDS Network
289,600	University of South Africa, Pretoria Republic of South Africa -- establishment of the Centre for the Improvement of Mathematics, Science, and Technology Education
275,912	Free State Provincial Library and Information Services -- activities to expand services
275,000	African Women's Development Fund, London United Kingdom

266,838 Northern Cape Provincial Library and Information Services Republic of South Africa -- activities to increase literacy, preserve indigenous languages, enhance technology and train staff

248,910 University of Dar es Salaam United Republic of Tanzania -- Scholarship Program for undergraduate women

CARNIVAL CORP.

Company Headquarters

3655 Northwest 87th Avenue
Miami, FL 33178-2428
Phone: (305)599-2600
Fax: (305)406-4758
Web: http://www.carnivalcorp.com

Company Description

Founded: 1974
Ticker: CCL
Exchange: NYSE
Revenue: US$4.535 billion (2001)
Employees: 33200 (2001)
SIC(s): 7999 Amusement & Recreation Nec.

Operating Locations

Carnival Cruise Lines Inc. (FL--Miami); Gray Line (AK--Anchorage, Fairbanks, Healy); Holland America Line (WA--Seattle)

Arison Foundation

Giving Contact

Madelon Rosenberg, Assistant to the President
3655 NW 87th Avenue
Miami, FL 33178-2428
Phone: (305)599-2600

Description

Founded: 1981
EIN: 592128429
Organization Type: Corporate Foundation
Former Name: Arison Foundation.
Giving Locations: FL: Miami including surrounding area
Grant Types: General Support.

Financial Summary

Total Giving: $10,151,522 (2001); $11,997,688 (2000); $11,060,017 (1999). Note: Contributes through corporate direct giving program and foundation.
Giving Analysis: Giving for 2001 includes: foundation grants to United Way ($1,400,000); foundation ($8,751,522); 2000: foundation scholarships ($62,500); foundation grants to United Way ($1,800,000); foundation ($10,135,188); 1999: foundation grants to United Way ($1,478,817); foundation ($9,581,200);
Assets: $250,771,018 (2001); $286,985,260 (2000); $239,249,044 (1999)
Gifts Received: $630,000 (2001); $5,705,396 (2000); $1,753 (1999). Note: In 2001, contributions were received from the Ted Arison Charitable Trust. In 1999, contributions were received from Shari Arison.

Typical Recipients

Arts & Humanities: Arts Associations & Councils, Arts Festivals, Arts Funds, Dance, Film & Video, Arts & Humanities-General, History & Archaeology, Museums/Galleries, Music, Performing Arts, Theater, Visual Arts
Civic & Public Affairs: Civil Rights, Clubs, Community Foundations, Economic Policy, Civic & Public Affairs-General, Municipalities/Towns, Public Policy, Urban & Community Affairs

Education: Arts/Humanities Education, Business Education, Colleges & Universities, Education Associations, Education Funds, Engineering/Technological Education, Education-General, International Studies, Medical Education, Minority Education, Public Education (Precollege), Religious Education, Science/Mathematics Education, Student Aid
Health: Cancer, Children's Health/Hospitals, Clinics/Medical Centers, Eyes/Blindness, Health-General, Geriatric Health, Health Organizations, Hospices, Hospitals, Medical Research, Public Health, Single-Disease Health Associations
International: Foreign Arts Organizations, Foreign Educational Institutions, International-General, Health Care/Hospitals, International Environmental Issues, International Organizations, International Peace & Security Issues, International Relations, International Relief Efforts, Missionary/Religious Activities
Religion: Religion-General, Jewish Causes, Religious Welfare, Social/Policy Issues, Synagogues/Temples
Science: Science-General
Social Services: At-Risk Youth, Child Welfare, Community Service Organizations, People with Disabilities, Recreation & Athletics, Shelters/Homelessness, Social Services-General, United Funds/United Ways, Youth Organizations

Application Procedures

Initial Contact: Send brief letter or proposal.
Application Requirements: Include a description of organization, amount requested, purpose of funds sought, recently audited financial statement, and proof of tax-exempt status.
Deadlines: None.

Additional Information

Foundation's giving is very limited in scope and frequently committed well in advance.

Corporate Officials

M. Micky Arison: chairman, chief executive officer, director secretary B Tel Aviv, Israel 1949. ED University of Miami. PRIM CORP EMPL chairman, chief executive officer, director: Carnival Corp. CORP AFFIL director: CHC International Inc.; managing general partner: Miami Heat; chairman: Air Holding Co.; chairman, chief executive officer, managing partner: Carnival Cruise Lines.
Shari Arison: director PRIM CORP EMPL director: Carnival Corp.
Arnaldo Perez: vice president, general counsel, secretary ED Miami University BBA (1982); Columbia University JD (1985). PRIM CORP EMPL vice president, general counsel, secretary: Carnival Corp.

Foundation Officials

M. Micky Arison: trustee (see above)
Madeleine Arison: trustee
Marilyn Arison: trustee
Shari Arison: president (see above)
Jean Collier: comptroller
William J. Conaty: director
Michael J. Cosgrove: treasurer
Pamela Daley: director
Shalom C. Elcott: president
Benjamin W. Heineman, Jr.: director
Joyce Hergenhan: director
Gisele N. Hill: secretary
Henry A. Hubschman: director
Arnaldo Perez: assistant vice president, secretary (see above)
Keith S. Sherin: director
Robert Sturges: vice president
Lloyd G. Trotter: director

Grants Analysis

Disclosure Period: calendar year ending 2001
Total Grants: $8,751,522*
Number of Grants: 100

Average Grant: $87,515
Highest Grant: $3,333,333
Lowest Grant: $1,000
Typical Range: $5,000 to $50,000 and $100,000 to $1,000,000
***Note:** Giving excludes United Way.

Recent Grants

Note: Grants derived from 2001 Form 990.

General

3,333,333 Performing Arts Center Foundation of Greater Miami, Miami, FL -- for operations

1,000,000 Duke University, Durham, NC -- for Duke University Basketball Legacy Fund and the campaign for Duke

1,000,000 Trust for Jewish Philanthropy, New York, NY -- for Matan endowment

554,688 PEF Israel Endowment Funds Inc, New York, NY -- for charitable programs

544,600 Trust for Jewish Philanthropy, New York, NY -- for Mifgash Program

530,000 United Way International, Alexandria, VA -- for operating budget

500,000 United Way International, Alexandria, VA -- for operations

362,425 Friends of Tel Aviv Sourasky Medical Center, New York, NY -- for electrical configuration beds for the Arison Tower

300,000 Greater Miami Jewish Federation, Miami, FL -- for charitable programs

200,000 United Way International, Alexandria, VA -- for allocations 2001

CAROLYN FOUNDATION

Giving Contact

Rebecca L. Erdahl, Executive Director
901 Marquette Ave., Suite 2630
Minneapolis, MN 55402-3230
Phone: (612)596-3279
Fax: (612)338-2084
E-mail: berdahl.carolyn@winternet.com
Web: http://www.carolynfoundation.org

Description

Founded: 1964
EIN: 416044416
Organization Type: General Purpose Foundation
Giving Locations: CT: New Haven; MN: Minneapolis-St. Paul
Grant Types: Capital, Endowment, General Support, Operating Expenses, Project, Seed Money.

Donor Information

Founder: Established in Minnesota in 1964 under the terms of the will of Carolyn McKnight Christian (d. 1964), who was the daughter of real estate entrepreneur and lumberman, Sumner T. McKnight.

Financial Summary

Total Giving: $1,900,000 (2002 approx); $2,300,000 (2001); $2,917,050 (2000)
Assets: $30,000,000 (2001); $48,073,470 (2000); $54,620,400 (1999)

Typical Recipients

Arts & Humanities: Arts Associations & Councils, Arts Centers, Arts Festivals, Arts Funds, Arts Outreach, Ballet, Community Arts, Dance, Ethnic & Folk Arts, Arts & Humanities-General, Historic Preservation, History & Archaeology, Libraries, Museums/Galleries, Music, Opera, Performing Arts, Public Broadcasting, Theater
Civic & Public Affairs: Asian American Affairs, Botanical Gardens/Parks, Chambers of Commerce, Clubs, Community Foundations, Economic Development, Economic Policy, Employment/Job Training,

Civic & Public Affairs-General, Hispanic Affairs, Housing, Native American Affairs, Nonprofit Management, Parades/Festivals, Public Policy, Public Policy, Rural Affairs, Safety, Urban & Community Affairs, Women's Affairs, Zoos/Aquariums

Education: Afterschool/Enrichment Programs, Arts/Humanities Education, Colleges & Universities, Education Associations, Education Reform, Elementary Education (Private), Education-General, Literacy, Private Education (Precollege), Public Education (Precollege), School Volunteerism, Science/Mathematics Education, Special Education, Vocational & Technical Education

Environment: Air/Water Quality, Energy, Forestry, Environment-General, Resource Conservation, Watershed, Wildlife Protection

Health: Children's Health/Hospitals, Clinics/Medical Centers, Emergency/Ambulance Services, Health Organizations, Hospitals, Medical Rehabilitation, Mental Health, Nursing Services, Research/Studies Institutes

International: Foreign Arts Organizations, Health Care/Hospitals, Human Rights, International Environmental Issues

Religion: Churches, Religious Welfare

Science: Science Museums, Scientific Organizations

Social Services: Animal Protection, At-Risk Youth, Child Abuse, Child Welfare, Community Centers, Community Service Organizations, Counseling, Crime Prevention, Day Care, Domestic Violence, Emergency Relief, Family Planning, Family Services, Food/Clothing Distribution, Homes, People with Disabilities, Recreation & Athletics, Senior Services, Shelters/Homelessness, Social Services-General, Substance Abuse, United Funds/United Ways, YMCA/YWCA/YMHA/YWHA, Youth Organizations, Youth Organizations

Application Procedures

Initial Contact: Minnesota common application form; written proposals should be sent to the foundation.

Application Requirements: Applicants must provide the name and address of the contact person; a description of organization; a list of officers, directors, and executive staff; their IRS number and a copy of their determination letter; state registration certificate; the amount requested; timetable; and purpose, objective, and goals of the project. Applicants also should include a history of the project; an operational plan; future plans; licensing requirements; evaluation methods; the reason the foundation is being approached for funding; a detailed budget; income from prior three years; provisions for financial support of project in future; audited financial report; and an annual report.

Deadlines: Applications are to be submitted by January 31 to considered at the June meeting of the trustees, and by July 31 to considered at the December meeting.

Restrictions

The foundation does not fund individuals, religious organizations for religious purposes, political or veterans organizations, annual fund drives, debts, or legal costs. The foundation generally will not sponsor conferences, seminars, or projects in foreign countries.

Additional Information

Publications: Annual Report; Guidelines

Foundation Officials

Anne T. Calabresi: trustee
Guido Calabresi: trustee emeritus B Milan, Italy 1932. ED Yale University BS (1953); Oxford University BA (1955); Yale University LLB (1958); Oxford University MA (1959). PRIM NONPR EMPL judge: U.S. Court Appeals Second Circuit. NONPR AFFIL Sterling professor emeritus: Yale University Law School; trustee: Yale University Saint Thomas More Chapel; professor emeritus: Yale University; fellow: Royal Swedish Academy Sciences; fellow: Timothy

Dwight College; member: Connecticut Bar Association; member: Association American Law Schools; fellow: Associazione Italiana Di Diritto Comparato; member: American Philosophical Society; fellow: Accademia Delle Scienze Di Torino; fellow: American Academy of Arts & Sciences; fellow: Academia Nazionale dei Lincei.

Eugenie T. Copp: trustee
Edwin L. Crosby: chairman, trustee
Franklin M. Crosby, III: trustee
G. Christian Crosby: trustee
Harriett Crosby: trustee
Sumner McKnight Crosby, Jr.: vice chairman, trustee
Thomas Manville Crosby, Jr.: trustee B Minneapolis, MN 1938. ED Yale University BA (1960); Yale University JD (1965). PRIM CORP EMPL attorney: Faegre & Benson. NONPR AFFIL member: American Bar Association.
Charles C. Dobson: trustee
Carol J. Fetzer: fdn admin, secretary, trustee
Sumner McKnight-Crosby, III: trustee
Lucy C. Mitchell: trustee

Grants Analysis

Disclosure Period: calendar year ending 2000
Total Grants: $2,672,880*
Number of Grants: 107
Average Grant: $24,979
Highest Grant: $75,000
Typical Range: $5,000 to $30,000
*Note: Giving excludes United Way and matching gifts.

Recent Grants

Note: Grants derived from 2000 Form 990.

General

200,000	United Way of Clallam County, Port Angeles, WA -- for support of Prevention Works! Coalition	
150,000	Minnetonka Center for the Arts, Minneapolis, MN -- capital campaign	
75,000	Blake School, Hopkins, MN -- support of Learning Works at Blake	
75,000	Community Foundation for Greater New Haven, New Haven, CT -- to establish the Greater New Haven area as a National Arts Stabilization Project Site	
75,000	Graves Academy, St. Louis Park, MN -- for "Think of the Possibilities" capital campaign	
75,000	Neighborhood Music School, New Haven, CT -- capital campaign	
75,000	New Haven Festival of Arts and Ideas, New Haven, CT -- support of its Youth Program agenda	
50,000	Chrysalis Center for Women, Minneapolis, MN -- to construct a new facility	
50,000	Leadership, Education, and Athletics in Partnership for New Haven Youth, New Haven, CT	
50,000	Minnesota Diversified Industries, St. Paul, MN -- for capital campaign	

CARPENTER FOUNDATION

Giving Contact

Jane Carpenter, President, Trustee
711 E. Main St., Suite 10
Medford, OR 97504
Phone: (541)772-5851

Description

Founded: 1957
EIN: 930491360
Organization Type: Private Foundation
Giving Locations: OR: Jackson and Josephine counties

Grant Types: General Support, Operating Expenses, Seed Money.

Donor Information

Founder: the late Helen Bundy Carpenter, the late Alfred S.V. Carpenter, Harlow Carpenter

Financial Summary

Total Giving: $935,725 (fiscal year ending June 30, 2001); $792,828 (fiscal 1999); $811,412 (fiscal 1998). Note: Fiscal 1997 Giving includes United Way ($16,500).

Giving Analysis: Giving for fiscal 2001 includes: foundation grants to United Way ($35,000); foundation scholarships ($127,130); fiscal 1999: foundation grants to United Way ($29,000) foundation scholarships ($101,230)

Assets: $18,538,935 (fiscal 2001); $19,548,514 (fiscal 1999); $16,940,092 (fiscal 1997)

Gifts Received: $212,266 (fiscal 2001); $1,000 (fiscal 1997); $1,000 (fiscal 1996)

Typical Recipients

Arts & Humanities: Arts Associations & Councils, Arts Festivals, Arts Outreach, Arts & Humanities-General, History & Archaeology, Libraries, Literary Arts, Museums/Galleries, Music, Opera, Performing Arts, Public Broadcasting, Theater, Visual Arts

Civic & Public Affairs: Economic Development, Employment/Job Training, Civic & Public Affairs-General, Hispanic Affairs, Housing, Legal Aid, Municipalities/Towns, Native American Affairs, Parades/Festivals

Education: Afterschool/Enrichment Programs, Colleges & Universities, Community & Junior Colleges, Education Funds, Elementary Education (Public), Faculty Development, International Studies, Preschool Education, Public Education (Precollege), Secondary Education (Public), Student Aid, Student Aid

Environment: Air/Water Quality, Forestry, Environment-General, Resource Conservation

Health: Children's Health/Hospitals, Clinics/Medical Centers, Long-Term Care, Mental Health, Nursing Services, Public Health

Social Services: At-Risk Youth, Child Abuse, Child Welfare, Community Centers, Community Service Organizations, Counseling, Crime Prevention, Day Care, Delinquency & Criminal Rehabilitation, Domestic Violence, Emergency Relief, Family Services, Food/Clothing Distribution, People with Disabilities, Recreation & Athletics, Scouts, Senior Services, Shelters/Homelessness, Substance Abuse, United Funds/United Ways, YMCA/YWCA/YMHA/YWHA, Youth Organizations

Application Procedures

Initial Contact: Send a brief letter of inquiry.
Application Requirements: Include a description of organization, proof of tax-exempt status, purpose of funds sought, organization budget, project budget, plan employed to accomplish the project, evidence of other financial support for the project, and a list of the board of directors.
Deadlines: None.

Restrictions

Grants are not made outside Jackson or Josephine counties, or to individuals. Grants are not made to individuals.

Additional Information

Publications: Application Guidelines; Annual Report

Foundation Officials

Karen C. Allan: secretary, trustee
Pat Blair: pub trustee
Kathy Burkey: pub trustee
Dunbar Carpenter: treasurer, trustee
Jane H. Carpenter: president, trustee
William E. Duhaime: pub trustee
William R. Moffat: trustee

Grants Analysis

Disclosure Period: fiscal year ending June 30, 2001
Total Grants: $773,595*
Number of Grants: 67
Average Grant: $11,546
Highest Grant: $40,000
Typical Range: $5,000 to $20,000
*****Note:** Giving excludes United Way and scholarship.

Recent Grants

Note: Grants derived from fiscal 2000 Form 990.

Library-Related

25,000	Jackson County Library Foundation, Medford, OR

General

40,000	Oregon Shakespeare Festival, Ashland, OR -- second of three payments for a new theater
32,402	Rogue Valley Art Association - Rouge Gallery, Medford, OR
25,000	Craterian Performances Company, Medford, OR
25,000	Oregon Shakespeare Festival, Ashland, OR -- to underwrite student and senior half-price matinees for Rogue Valley residents
25,000	Southern Oregon University, Ashland, OR -- final payment for the Southern Oregon Center for the Visual Arts
25,000	Southern Oregon University, Ashland, OR
20,000	Bear Creek Greenway Foundation, Medford, OR -- towards completion of the Bear Creek Greenway trail and bridges. First of three payments
20,000	Boys & Girls Club/ Jackson Co., Medford, OR
20,000	Britt Festivals, Medford, OR
20,000	United Way of Jackson County, Jackson, MI

E. Rhodes And Leona B. Carpenter Foundation

Giving Contact

Joseph A. O'Connor, Jr., Contact
PO Box 58880
Philadelphia, PA 19102-8880
Phone: (215)963-5212
Web: http://www.ats.edu/faculty/external/spons/C0000259.HTML

Description

Founded: 1975
EIN: 510155772
Organization Type: General Purpose Foundation
Giving Locations: VA: east of the Mississippi River.
Grant Types: Capital, Challenge, Emergency, General Support, Project, Scholarship.

Donor Information

Founder: Established in 1975 by the late E. Rhodes Carpenter and Leona B. Carpenter.

Financial Summary

Total Giving: $10,626,225 (2000); $10,563,917 (1999); $9,281,126 (1998)
Giving Analysis: Giving for 1998 includes: foundation scholarships ($472,000)
Assets: $237,865,221 (2000); $254,533,775 (1999); $221,888,302 (1998)

Gifts Received: $7,158 (1996); $2,492,586 (1995); $2,000,000 (1993). Note: In 1995, the foundation received a gift of $2,492,586 form the estate of Leona B. Carpenter.

Typical Recipients

Arts & Humanities: Arts Associations & Councils, Arts Centers, Arts Funds, Arts Institutes, Arts Outreach, Ballet, Community Arts, Dance, Ethnic & Folk Arts, Historic Preservation, History & Archaeology, Libraries, Museums/Galleries, Music, Opera, Performing Arts, Public Broadcasting, Theater
Civic & Public Affairs: Asian American Affairs, Botanical Gardens/Parks, Economic Development, Civic & Public Affairs-General, Housing, Municipalities/Towns, Philanthropic Organizations, Women's Affairs
Education: Arts/Humanities Education, Colleges & Universities, Education Funds, Elementary Education (Private), Elementary Education (Public), Education-General, Health & Physical Education, International Studies, International Studies, Medical Education, Public Education (Precollege), Religious Education, Science/Mathematics Education, Secondary Education (Public), Student Aid
Environment: Environment-General
Health: AIDS/HIV, Cancer, Children's Health/Hospitals, Clinics/Medical Centers, Emergency/Ambulance Services, Health Policy/Cost Containment, Health Organizations, Hospices, Hospitals, Medical Rehabilitation, Nursing Services, Public Health, Research/Studies Institutes, Single-Disease Health Associations
International: Foreign Arts Organizations, International Environmental Issues, International Peace & Security Issues, International Relations, Missionary/Religious Activities
Religion: Churches, Jewish Causes, Ministries, Religious Organizations, Religious Welfare, Seminaries
Science: Science Museums, Science Museums, Scientific Centers & Institutes
Social Services: Child Welfare, Community Centers, Community Service Organizations, Day Care, Delinquency & Criminal Rehabilitation, Domestic Violence, Family Planning, Family Services, Food/Clothing Distribution, Homes, People with Disabilities, Recreation & Athletics, Sexual Abuse, Shelters/Homelessness, Substance Abuse, Youth Organizations

Application Procedures

Initial Contact: Informal letter applications are sufficient.
Application Requirements: The letter application should include a brief history of the purpose of the organization, the dollar amount requested, a description of the specific project or program for which the amount is being requested, and a copy of the organization's ruling that it is a 509(a)(1) or (2) institution.
Deadlines: Applications should be postmarked or fax dated on or before March 15 to be considered at the spring meeting and on or before September 15 for the autumn meeting.

Restrictions

Generally, the foundation will not consider grant requests to support private secondary education, nor will it as a general rule consider grant requests from large public charities such as the Red Cross, American Cancer Society, or United Fund. Also the foundation generally will not transfer funds from its endowment to the endowment of another organization. Grants are made for specific projects or programs. The foundation does not support individuals.

Additional Information

Publications: Application Guidelines

Foundation Officials

Ann B. Day: president, director
Paul B. Day, Jr.: vice president, secretary, treasurer
M. H. Reinhart: director PRIM CORP EMPL president: E.R. Carpenter Co.

Grants Analysis

Disclosure Period: calendar year ending 2000
Total Grants: $10,626,224
Number of Grants: 161
Average Grant: $54,253*
Highest Grant: $1,000,000
Typical Range: $100,000 to $250,000 and $10,000 to $50,000
*****Note:** Average grant excludes two highest grants ($2,000,000).

Recent Grants

Note: Grants derived from 2000 Form 990.

General

1,000,000	Johns Hopkins University School of Nursing, Baltimore, MD -- endowment
1,000,000	Virginia Museum of Fine Arts, Richmond, VA -- underwrite part of the cost of expansion of Asian art galleries and care of Asian art collections
537,570	Art Institute of Chicago, Chicago, IL -- support exhibition "Taoism and the Arts of China"
303,490	Science Museum of Virginia, Richmond, VA -- support creative productions for 2001-2002
229,325	Nelson-Atkins Museum of Art, Kansas City, MO -- help underwrite publication cost of exhibition catalogue
200,000	Richmond Ballet, Richmond, VA -- underwrite new building
200,000	Virginia Opera, Richmond, VA -- underwrite costs of a new Friday opening night series
180,000	Pacific School of Religion, Berkeley, CA -- underwrite costs for a Center for Lesbian and Gay Studies in Religion and Ministries
180,000	Pacific School of Religion, Berkeley, CA -- support for Center for Lesbian and Gay Studies in Religion
170,000	Princeton University, Princeton, NJ -- cover costs of six seminary-trained theologians as visiting scholars

CARRIS REELS

Company Headquarters

439 W. St.
Rutland, VT 05701
Web: http://www.carris.com

Company Description

Revenue: US$107 million (2002)
Employees: 900 (2002)
SIC(s): 2499 Wood Products Nec, 3089 Plastics Products Nec, 3499 Fabricated Metal Products Nec.

Operating Locations

Carris Reels (MI--Galien; NC--Statesville; VT--Brandon)

Carris Corp. Foundation

Giving Contact

Karen O'Brien, Foundation Bookkeeper
PO Box 696
Rutland, VT 05702-0696
Phone: (802)773-9111

Description

Founded: 1990
EIN: 030326934
Organization Type: Corporate Foundation
Giving Locations: headquarters and operating communities.
Grant Types: General Support.

Donor Information
Founder: Carris Reels, Bridge Mfg., Vermont Tubbs

Financial Summary
Total Giving: $216,952 (2001); $414,843 (2000); $277,067 (1999)
Giving Analysis: Giving for 2001 includes: foundation grants to United Way ($39,105); foundation ($177,847); 2000: foundation grants to United Way ($10,422); foundation ($404,421); 1999: foundation grants to United Way ($38,394) foundation ($238,673)
Assets: $149,814 (2001); $227,069 (2000); $561,881 (1999)
Gifts Received: $130,034 (2001); $60,000 (2000); $153,500 (1999). Note: In 2001, contributions were received from Carris Reels, Inc. In 2000, contributions were received from Carris Reels, Inc. ($60,000). In 1999, contributions were received from Carris Reels, Inc. ($143,500) and Carris Reels of Connecticut ($10,000).In 1996, contributions were received from Carris Reels ($209,679), Carris Reels of Connecticut ($92,351), Vermont Tubbs ($53,630), and Carris Reels of California ($1,502).

Typical Recipients
Arts & Humanities: Arts Associations & Councils, Arts Centers, History & Archaeology, Libraries, Museums/Galleries, Music, Public Broadcasting, Theater, Visual Arts
Civic & Public Affairs: Civil Rights, Clubs, Community Foundations, Employment/Job Training, Civic & Public Affairs-General, Housing, Native American Affairs, Parades/Festivals
Education: Afterschool/Enrichment Programs, Colleges & Universities, Elementary Education (Public), Education-General, Literacy, Private Education (Precollege), Public Education (Precollege), Science/Mathematics Education, Secondary Education (Public)
Environment: Environment-General
Health: AIDS/HIV, Cancer, Children's Health/Hospitals, Diabetes, Emergency/Ambulance Services, Health-General, Health Organizations, Health Organizations, Heart, Hospitals, Nursing Services, Prenatal Health Issues, Public Health, Single-Disease Health Associations
International: Missionary/Religious Activities
Religion: Churches, Religion-General, Jewish Causes, Religious Welfare
Science: Scientific Centers & Institutes
Social Services: Animal Protection, Big Brother/Big Sister, Camps, Child Abuse, Child Welfare, Community Centers, Community Service Organizations, Delinquency & Criminal Rehabilitation, Domestic Violence, Emergency Relief, Family Services, Food/Clothing Distribution, Homes, People with Disabilities, Recreation & Athletics, Scouts, Senior Services, Social Services-General, Special Olympics, Substance Abuse, United Funds/United Ways, United Funds/United Ways, Veterans, Volunteer Services, YMCA/YWCA/YMHA/YWHA

Application Procedures
Initial Contact: The foundation supports organizations nominated by committees of employee owners.

Corporate Officials
William H. Carris: chairman, president, chief executive officer PRIM CORP EMPL chairman, president, chief executive officer: Carris Reels.
David Fitz-Gerald: chief financial officer PRIM CORP EMPL chief financial officer: Carris Reels.

Foundation Officials
Barbara T. Carris: vice president PRIM CORP EMPL vice president, director: Carris Reels.
William H. Carris: president (see above)
Thomas Dowling: secretary
David Fitz-Gerald: treasurer (see above)

Grants Analysis
Disclosure Period: calendar year ending 2001
Total Grants: $177,847*
Number of Grants: 61
Average Grant: $2,916
Highest Grant: $50,000
Lowest Grant: $100
Typical Range: $1,000 to $10,000
*Note: Giving excludes United Way.

Recent Grants
Note: Grants derived from 2001 Form 990.

General
80,103	Carving Studio, West Rutland, VT
20,691	United Way Rutland County, Rutland, VT
15,000	College of St. Joseph, VT
13,500	American Red Cross, Rutland, VT
9,500	United Way of Madera County
8,995	New York State World Trade Center Relief Fund, New York, NY
7,500	Rutland Dismas House, Rutland, VT
5,416	United Way of Iredell County, Statesville, NC
5,000	Meals on Wheels, Somerset, PA
5,000	Rutland Area Visiting Nurse Association, Rutland, VT

CARTER FAMILY FOUNDATION

Giving Contact
Debbie Lester
Carter Family Foundation
c/o United National Bank, Trust Department
129 Main Street
Beckley, WV 25801
Phone: (304)256-7262

Description
Founded: 1981
EIN: 550606479
Organization Type: Private Foundation
Giving Locations: WV: Raleigh County
Grant Types: Project, Scholarship.

Donor Information
Founder: Bernard E. Carter, the late Georgia Carter

Financial Summary
Total Giving: $74,400 (fiscal year ending June 30, 2001); $241,374 (fiscal 1999); $769,538 (fiscal 1998). Note: Fiscal 1997 Giving includes scholarship ($10,000); United Way ($2,000).
Giving Analysis: Giving for fiscal 1998 includes: foundation grants to United Way ($71,000) foundation ($698,538).
Assets: $13,316,260 (fiscal 2001); $13,045,261 (fiscal 1999); $12,098,204 (fiscal 1998)
Gifts Received: $258,009 (fiscal 1998); $1,500 (fiscal 1995); $50,000 (fiscal 1994). Note: In 1998, contributions were received from Bernard E. Carter. In fiscal 1994, contributions were received from the estate of Bernard E. and Georgia Carter.

Typical Recipients
Arts & Humanities: Libraries, Museums/Galleries, Public Broadcasting, Theater
Civic & Public Affairs: Community Foundations, Employment/Job Training, Housing, Women's Affairs
Education: Colleges & Universities, Engineering/Technological Education, Medical Education, Minority Education, Private Education (Precollege), Religious Education, Secondary Education (Public), Student Aid, Vocational & Technical Education
Environment: Protection

Health: Alzheimers Disease, Arthritis, Cancer, Children's Health/Hospitals, Emergency/Ambulance Services, Eyes/Blindness, Health Organizations, Heart, Hospices, Hospitals, Kidney, Medical Research, Multiple Sclerosis, Prenatal Health Issues, Single-Disease Health Associations
International: Health Care/Hospitals, International Peace & Security Issues, International Relief Efforts, Missionary/Religious Activities
Religion: Bible Study/Translation, Churches, Religious Organizations, Religious Welfare, Synagogues/Temples
Social Services: Animal Protection, Camps, Child Welfare, Community Service Organizations, Homes, Scouts, Shelters/Homelessness, United Funds/United Ways, YMCA/YWCA/YMHA/YWHA, Youth Organizations

Application Procedures
Initial Contact: Send letter and resume.
Deadlines: None.
Notes: The foundation provides scholarships and student loans to individuals willing to continue their education and teaching profession within the state of West Virginia.

Additional Information
Trust(s): United National Bank

Grants Analysis
Disclosure Period: fiscal year ending June 30, 2001
Total Grants: $74,400*
Number of Grants: 4
Average Grant: $7,008*
Highest Grant: $50,000
Lowest Grant: $4,400
Typical Range: $500 to $20,000
*Note: Giving excludes United Way. Average grant figure excludes highest grant.

Recent Grants
Note: Grants derived from fiscal 2001 Form 990.

Library-Related
10,000	Friends of Shady Spring Library

General
50,000	YMCA Youth Soccer Complex
10,000	Theater West Virginia, Beckley, WV
4,400	Ohio West Virginia YMCA Youth Opportunity Camp

AMON G. CARTER FOUNDATION

Giving Contact
John H. Robinson, Grant Administrator-Executive Vice President
PO Box 1036
Ft. Worth, TX 76101-1036
Phone: (817)332-2783
Fax: (817)332-2787
E-mail: jrobinson@agcf.org
Web: http://www.agcf.org

Description
Founded: 1945
EIN: 756000331
Organization Type: General Purpose Foundation
Giving Locations: TX: Fort Worth including Tarrant County
Grant Types: Capital, Challenge, Endowment, General Support, Matching, Operating Expenses, Project, Seed Money.

Donor Information
Founder: Established in 1945 by Amon G. Carter, publisher of the *Fort Worth Star Telegram* and founder of Carter Publications. Ruth Carter Stevenson, the

donor's daughter and the only living member of the Carter family, is president of the foundation. The Carter family's interests in art are reflected in the Amon Carter Museum, which specializes in western and early American art.

Financial Summary

Total Giving: $14,640,000 (2003 approx); $14,640,000 (2002 approx); $17,167,151 (2000). **Giving Analysis:** Giving for 2000 includes: foundation grants to United Way ($1,000) 1997: foundation grants to United Way ($100,000) **Assets:** $284,000,000 (2003 approx); $284,000,000 (2002 approx); $335,901,614 (2000)

Typical Recipients

Arts & Humanities: Arts Associations & Councils, Arts Centers, Arts Festivals, Ballet, Community Arts, Ethnic & Folk Arts, Film & Video, Arts & Humanities-General, Historic Preservation, History & Archaeology, Libraries, Museums/Galleries, Music, Opera, Performing Arts, Public Broadcasting, Theater **Civic & Public Affairs:** Botanical Gardens/Parks, Community Foundations, Economic Development, Civic & Public Affairs-General, Housing, Law & Justice, Municipalities/Towns, Philanthropic Organizations, Safety, Urban & Community Affairs, Women's Affairs, Zoos/Aquariums **Education:** Afterschool/Enrichment Programs, Arts/Humanities Education, Colleges & Universities, Community & Junior Colleges, Economic Education, Education Associations, Education Reform, Elementary Education (Private), Engineering/Technological Education, Education-General, Medical Education, Minority Education, Private Education (Precollege), Public Education (Precollege), School Volunteerism, Science/Mathematics Education, Special Education, Student Aid **Environment:** Air/Water Quality, Environment-General, Wildlife Protection **Health:** AIDS/HIV, Alzheimers Disease, Cancer, Children's Health/Hospitals, Clinics/Medical Centers, Diabetes, Emergency/Ambulance Services, Health Policy/Cost Containment, Health Organizations, Hospices, Hospitals, Hospitals (University Affiliated), Medical Rehabilitation, Medical Research, Mental Health, Nursing Services, Prenatal Health Issues, Public Health, Research/Studies Institutes, Respiratory, Single-Disease Health Associations, Transplant Networks/Donor Banks **International:** International Affairs, International Relief Efforts **Religion:** Churches, Dioceses, Religious Organizations, Religious Welfare **Science:** Science Exhibits & Fairs, Science Museums, Scientific Research **Social Services:** At-Risk Youth, Big Brother/Big Sister, Camps, Child Welfare, Community Centers, Community Service Organizations, Counseling, Crime Prevention, Day Care, Delinquency & Criminal Rehabilitation, Family Planning, Family Services, Food/Clothing Distribution, Homes, People with Disabilities, Recreation & Athletics, Scouts, Senior Services, Shelters/Homelessness, Social Services-General, Substance Abuse, United Funds/United Ways, Volunteer Services, YMCA/YWCA/YMHA/YWHA, Youth Organizations

Application Procedures

Initial Contact: Applicants should contact the foundation by letter. **Application Requirements:** Letters of request should include proof of the organization's tax-exempt status and the purpose of the requested grant. The foundation may require additional information at a later date. **Deadlines:** None. **Review Process:** All grants must be approved by the five-member board of directors, which meets three times a year.

Restrictions

No grants are made to individuals or for loans. Applying organizations usually must qualify for exemption under Section 501(c)(3) of the Internal Revenue Code. Special consideration is required if an applying organization is not exempt as a private foundation under Section 509(a) of the Code. Grants outside the Fort Worth area are initiated only by the staff and board of directors.

Additional Information

Publications: Annual Report; Policy and Guidelines Statement

Foundation Officials

Robert William Brown, MD: vice president, director B Seattle, WA 1924. ED Tulane University MD (1950). PRIM CORP EMPL president: American Baseball League. **W. Patrick Harris:** executive vice president investments ED Louisiana State University. NONPR AFFIL treasurer: Amon Carter Museum Western Art. **Kate L. Johnson:** director **Mark L. Johnson:** treasurer, director **Sheila B. Johnson:** secretary, director **John H. Robinson:** executive vice president **Ruth Carter Stevenson:** president, director, donor daughter B Fort Worth, TX 1925. ED Sarah Lawrence College BA (1945). NONPR AFFIL president: Amon Carter Museum Western Art.

Grants Analysis

Disclosure Period: calendar year ending 2000 **Total Grants:** $17,166,151* **Number of Grants:** 150 **Average Grant:** $34,446* **Highest Grant:** $7,000,000 **Typical Range:** $10,000 to $100,000 *Note: Giving excludes United Way. Average grant excludes two highest grants ($12,068,191).

Recent Grants

Note: Grants derived from 2000 Form 990.

General

7,000,000	Amon Carter Museum, Ft. Worth, TX -- for expansion support
5,068,191	Amon Carter Museum, Ft. Worth, TX
1,000,000	Modern Art Museum of Fort Worth, Ft. Worth, TX -- for capital campaign
500,000	Fort Worth Zoological Society, Ft. Worth, TX -- capital campaign
500,000	Trinity Valley School, Ft. Worth, TX -- capital campaign
250,000	Huguley Memorial Medical Center, Ft. Worth, TX -- construction support
250,000	Texas Christian University, Ft. Worth, TX -- for capital campaign
150,000	Carter Blood Center, Ft. Worth, TX -- for special program
150,000	Performing Arts Fort Worth, Ft. Worth, TX -- for capital campaign
140,000	All Saints Episcopal School -- capital campaign

BEIRNE CARTER FOUNDATION

Giving Contact

Lucille A. Lindamood, Grant Administrator
1802 Bayberry Ct., No. 301
Richmond, VA 23226
Phone: (804)521-0272
Fax: (804)521-0274
E-mail: bcarterfn@aol.com
Web: http://www.bcarterfdn.org

Alternate Contact

Phone: (804)788-2288

Description

Founded: 1986
EIN: 541397827
Organization Type: General Purpose Foundation
Giving Locations: VA
Grant Types: Capital, Conference/Seminar, Project, Research, Scholarship, Seed Money.

Donor Information

Founder: Established in 1986 by the late Beirne B. Carter .

Financial Summary

Total Giving: $1,293,000 (2001); $1,638,135 (2000); $1,560,080 (1999) **Assets:** $28,373,630 (2001); $35,345,841 (2000); $37,709,992 (1999) **Gifts Received:** $3,243 (1995). Note: In 1995, contributions were received from the refund of 1994 990-PF excise tax.

Typical Recipients

Arts & Humanities: Arts Associations & Councils, Arts Centers, Arts Festivals, Ballet, Ethnic & Folk Arts, Film & Video, Arts & Humanities-General, Historic Preservation, History & Archaeology, Libraries, Museums/Galleries, Music, Opera, Performing Arts, Public Broadcasting, Theater **Civic & Public Affairs:** Botanical Gardens/Parks, Clubs, Community Foundations, Economic Development, Civic & Public Affairs-General, Hispanic Affairs, Housing, Legal Aid, Nonprofit Management, Philanthropic Organizations, Professional & Trade Associations, Public Policy, Urban & Community Affairs, Women's Affairs, Zoos/Aquariums **Education:** Afterschool/Enrichment Programs, Agricultural Education, Arts/Humanities Education, Business Education, Colleges & Universities, Community & Junior Colleges, Education Funds, Engineering/Technological Education, Environmental Education, Education-General, Medical Education, Private Education (Precollege), Public Education (Precollege), Science/Mathematics Education, Social Sciences Education, Special Education, Student Aid **Environment:** Air/Water Quality, Forestry, Environment-General, Resource Conservation, Watershed, Wildlife Protection **Health:** AIDS/HIV, Arthritis, Cancer, Children's Health/Hospitals, Clinics/Medical Centers, Emergency/Ambulance Services, Hospices, Hospitals, Hospitals (University Affiliated), Medical Research, Mental Health, Nursing Services, Preventive Medicine/Wellness Organizations, Public Health, Research/Studies Institutes, Respiratory, Single-Disease Health Associations, Transplant Networks/Donor Banks **International:** Human Rights **Religion:** Churches, Ministries, Religious Welfare, Seminaries **Science:** Science Museums **Social Services:** Animal Protection, At-Risk Youth, Big Brother/Big Sister, Camps, Child Abuse, Child Welfare, Community Service Organizations, Day Care, Domestic Violence, Emergency Relief, Family Planning, Family Services, Food/Clothing Distribution, Homes, People with Disabilities, Recreation & Athletics, Scouts, Senior Services, Shelters/Homelessness, Social Services-General, YMCA/YWCA/YMHA/YWHA, Youth Organizations

Application Procedures

Initial Contact: The foundation requests applications be made in writing and be submitted in quadruplicate. Applications should be accompanied by an Application Summary Form, which can be obtained from the foundation's web site or directly from the foundation. **Application Requirements:** Brief description of the organization, its history, and its purpose; a concise

description of the project or activity proposed, including the specific purpose for which the grant is requested, the benefits to be provided, and the needs to be met; a detailed financial plan that includes the total cost, amount requested, amount raised to date, plans for procuring the remainder, other funding sources, and provision for contingencies and ongoing support; brief biographical information on the person who will conduct or supervise the proposed project; plans for evaluating the project's results and for sustaining the project after grant funds expire; the names and affiliations of the organization's trustees, directors, administrators, and principal staff; and a cover letter from an official of the organization stating that the organization has formally approved the proposed project. One copy of the following attachments should be included with a proposal: proof of tax-exempt status and financial statements for the current and two prior years. A new organization should submit prospective pro forma financial statements to assure statements covering at least two years are provided.
Deadlines: February 1 and August 1.
Review Process: The board meets in the spring and fall to review applications.

Restrictions

The foundation does not make grants to individuals. In general, grants are not made to endowment funds, for ongoing general operating expenses, existing deficits, debt reduction, organizations supported primarily by government funds, or to churches and related organizations.

Additional Information

Funding requests that are not of a recurring nature are given preference.
Publications: Informational Brochure (including Application Guidelines)

Foundation Officials

Mary Ross Carter Hutcheson: president
Talfourd H. Kemper: secretary, treasurer PRIM CORP EMPL principal: Woods Rogers & Hazlegrove PLC.
Kenneth C. Laughon: director
Mary T. Bryan Perkins: vice president

Grants Analysis

Disclosure Period: calendar year ending 2001
Total Grants: $1,293,000
Number of Grants: 55
Average Grant: $14,962*
Highest Grant: $250,000
Typical Range: $5,000 to $30,000
*Note: Average grant excludes two highest grants ($500,000).

Recent Grants

Note: Grants derived from 2001 Form 990.

Library-Related
10,000	Charles P. Jones Memorial Library, Covington, VA -- expansion and renovation of the library

General
250,000	St. Catherine's School, Richmond, VA -- construction of an athletic, wellness and fitness center
250,000	St. Christopher's School, Richmond, VA -- capital campaign
50,000	Chip of Roanoke, Roanoke, VA -- renovation of new building
50,000	Richmond Hill, Richmond, VA -- renovation of facility
50,000	University of Virginia Beirne B. Carter Center for Immunology Research, Charlottesville, VA -- for the grant-in-aid program and upgrade of flow cytometer
25,000	Children's Home Society, Richmond, VA -- renovate and furnish the Richmond office

25,000	Goodwill Industries of the Valleys, Inc., Roanoke, VA -- purchase and install new computer equipment
25,000	Instructive Visiting Nurse Association, Richmond, VA -- acquire a new facility
25,000	Jackson-Field Episcopal Home, Jarrah, VA -- renovate gymnasium
25,000	Richmond Goodwill Industries, Richmond, VA -- construct an addition

EVELYN C. CARTER TRUST

Giving Contact

Care of Bank One Trust Co.
PO Box 1308
Milwaukee, WI 53201
Phone: (414)765-2017

Description

Founded: 1997
EIN: 556129783
Organization Type: Private Foundation
Giving Locations: WV: Bridgeport
Grant Types: General Support.

Financial Summary

Total Giving: $72,800 (2001); $55,494 (2000); $60,941 (1999)
Giving Analysis: Giving for 2001 includes: foundation scholarships ($18,203); 2000: foundation scholarships ($13,872); 1999: foundation scholarships ($15,236);
Assets: $1,793,617 (2001); $1,904,747 (2000); $1,902,231 (1999)

Typical Recipients

Arts & Humanities: Libraries
Civic & Public Affairs: Safety
Religion: Churches

Application Procedures

Initial Contact: No specific format is required.
Deadlines: April 30.

Restrictions

Scholarships are restricted to graduates of Bridgeport High School who are attending West Virginia University and demonstrate financial need.

Additional Information

Trust(s): Bank One Trust Company

Grants Analysis

Disclosure Period: calendar year ending 2001
Total Grants: $54,597*
Number of Grants: 3
Average Grant: $18,199
Typical Range: $10,000 to $20,000
*Note: Giving excludes scholarships.

Recent Grants

Note: Grants derived from 2001 Form 990.

Library-Related
18,199	Bridgeport Public Library, Bridgeport, WV

General
18,199	Bridgeport United Methodist Church, Bridgeport, WV
18,199	Bridgeport Volunteer Fire Department, Bridgeport, WV

THOMAS AND AGNES CARVEL FOUNDATION

Giving Contact

Ann McHugh
35 East Grassy Sprain Road
Yonkers, NY 10710
Phone: (914)793-7300
Fax: (914)793-7381

Description

Founded: 1976
EIN: 132879673
Organization Type: General Purpose Foundation
Giving Locations: NY: Westchester County
Grant Types: Capital, General Support.

Donor Information

Founder: Established in 1976 by the late Agnes Carvel and the late Thomas Carvel . The foundation is also affiliated with the International Institute of Health Foods, Inc.

Financial Summary

Total Giving: $2,000,000 (fiscal year ending November 30, 2003 approx); $2,000,000 (fiscal 2002 approx); $2,043,590 (fiscal 2000)
Giving Analysis: Giving for fiscal 2000 includes: foundation scholarships ($3,500)
Assets: $32,000,000 (fiscal 2003 approx); $30,000,000 (fiscal 2002 approx); $39,641,646 (fiscal 2000)
Gifts Received: $22,304,500 (fiscal 1999)

Typical Recipients

Arts & Humanities: Ballet, History & Archaeology, Libraries, Museums/Galleries, Music, Performing Arts, Public Broadcasting, Theater
Civic & Public Affairs: Civil Rights, Economic Development, Civic & Public Affairs-General
Education: Arts/Humanities Education, Colleges & Universities, Education Funds, Elementary Education (Public), Education-General, Private Education (Precollege), Social Sciences Education, Special Education
Environment: Environment-General, Wildlife Protection
Health: Cancer, Children's Health/Hospitals, Clinics/Medical Centers, Emergency/Ambulance Services, Health-General, Hospices, Hospitals, Medical Rehabilitation, Medical Research, Nursing Services, Nutrition, Outpatient Health Care, Prenatal Health Issues, Single-Disease Health Associations, Transplant Networks/Donor Banks
International: International Organizations
Religion: Churches, Dioceses, Religion-General, Religious Organizations, Religious Welfare, Seminaries
Social Services: At-Risk Youth, Camps, Community Centers, Community Service Organizations, Domestic Violence, Recreation & Athletics, Social Services-General, Substance Abuse, United Funds/United Ways, Youth Organizations

Application Procedures

Initial Contact: Applications must be made in writing.
Application Requirements: Applications must be supported by a budget and any additional information that may seem necessary.
Deadlines: October 1.

Foundation Officials

Robert H. Abplanalp: director B 1922. ED Villanova University. PRIM CORP EMPL chief executive officer, president: Precision Valve Corp. CORP AFFIL president: Adirondack Fisheries Inc. CLUB AFFIL president: Walker's Cay Club Ltd.
Brendan T. Byrne: director PRIM CORP EMPL partner, vice president: Carella, Byrne, Bain, Gilfilla.

CORP AFFIL director: Elizabethtown Corp.; director: Elizabethtown Water Co.; director: Chelsea GCA Realty Inc.

Lawrence Fay: director

William E. Griffin: president, director B 1932. PRIM CORP EMPL president: Griffin Coogan & Venaruso PC. CORP AFFIL chairman, director: Hudson Valley Bank; chairman, director: Hudson Valley Holding Corp.; secretary: Adirondack Fisheries Inc.

Ann McHugh: vice president, treasurer, director

Salvador Molella: vice president, treasurer

Grants Analysis

Disclosure Period: fiscal year ending November 30, 2000
Total Grants: $2,042,090*
Number of Grants: 60
Average Grant: $35,208
Highest Grant: $200,000
Lowest Grant: $390
Typical Range: $5,000 to $50,000
*Note: Giving excludes scholarships.

Recent Grants

Note: Grants derived from fiscal 2000 Form 990.

Library-Related
200,000   Children's Hospital

General
200,000   Helping Hands, Dallas, TX -- endowment fund
200,000   New York Foundling Hospital, New York, NY
165,000   Blythdale Children's Hospital, White Plains, NY
120,000   Richmond Children's Center, Richmond, VA
100,000   Archdiocese of Newark, Newark, NJ -- scholarship fund
75,000   St. Agnes Children's Hospital, Fond du Lac, WI
50,000   Carmelite Communion
50,000   Fordham University, Bronx, NY
50,000   Garden State Cancer Center -- biologics production facility
50,000   Learning Project, New York, NY

ROY J. CARVER CHARITABLE TRUST

Giving Contact

Troy K. Ross, Executive Administrator
202 Iowa Avenue
Muscatine, IA 52761-3733
Phone: (563)263-4010
Fax: (563)263-1547
E-mail: info@carvertrust.org
Web: http://www.carvertrust.org

Description

Founded: 1982
EIN: 421186589
Organization Type: General Purpose Foundation
Giving Locations: IA: organizations with which the founder had significant involvement.
Grant Types: Award, Capital, Challenge, Project, Research, Scholarship, Seed Money.

Donor Information

Founder: Established in 1982 under the will of Roy J. Carver , an Iowa industrialist and philanthropist whose interests and activities were worldwide. Mr. Carver founded Bandag, Inc., the Carver Pump Company, and Carver Foundry Products, and remained active in the management of each firm until his death in 1981.

Financial Summary

Total Giving: $14,473,871 (fiscal year ending April 30, 2001); $12,819,754 (fiscal 1999); $11,443,410 (fiscal 1998)
Assets: $273,351,348 (fiscal 2001); $285,341,419 (fiscal 1999); $265,845,844 (fiscal 1998)

Typical Recipients

Arts & Humanities: Arts Outreach, Community Arts, Ethnic & Folk Arts, History & Archaeology, Libraries, Museums/Galleries, Music, Visual Arts
Civic & Public Affairs: Asian American Affairs, Employment/Job Training, Civic & Public Affairs-General, Hispanic Affairs, Municipalities/Towns, Philanthropic Organizations, Urban & Community Affairs, Zoos/Aquariums
Education: Arts/Humanities Education, Colleges & Universities, Community & Junior Colleges, Education Funds, Education Reform, Elementary Education (Private), Engineering/Technological Education, Education-General, Leadership Training, Legal Education, Literacy, Medical Education, Private Education (Precollege), Public Education (Precollege), School Volunteerism, Science/Mathematics Education, Secondary Education (Private), Student Aid, Vocational & Technical Education
Environment: Environment-General, Research, Resource Conservation, Wildlife Protection
Health: AIDS/HIV, Alzheimers Disease, Cancer, Children's Health/Hospitals, Emergency/Ambulance Services, Eyes/Blindness, Hospitals (University Affiliated), Medical Research, Nursing Services
Religion: Religious Welfare
Science: Observatories & Planetariums, Science Museums, Scientific Centers & Institutes, Scientific Research
Social Services: Child Abuse, Child Welfare, Community Service Organizations, Day Care, Domestic Violence, Family Services, People with Disabilities, Recreation & Athletics, Scouts, YMCA/YWCA/YMHA/YWHA, Youth Organizations

Application Procedures

Initial Contact: The Trust encourages initial telephone or written inquires.
Application Requirements: The proposal should contain a complete standardized application cover sheet, which is provided by the foundation; a description of organization, including its purpose, activities, and governing board; clear description of the desired purpose and goals; amount of the request and potential sources of funding; a statement of why support from the trust is vital to the success of the project; a plan for evaluating the project; and information on possible sources of funding after the grant period. Applicants should also include a copy of the IRS determination letter indicating 501(c)(3) tax-exempt status, copy of the organization's most recent audited financial statement, name of the contact person, and telephone number. contact person, and telephone number.
Deadlines: None.
Review Process: The board of trustees meets in January, April, July, and October and makes decisions on the third Friday of each of these months. Staff will consider meeting with applicants after reading their proposals. All grants are acted upon by the board of trustees after thorough screening and evaluation by the staff. The trust will send written notices to applicants within a reasonable time period.

Restrictions

The trust does not provide annual operating support or award endowments except under unusual circumstances, direct grants to individuals, or fund religious activities. It does not support political parties, offices, or candidates; fund-raising benefits; program advertising, or organizations without 501(c)(3) status.

Additional Information

Once a grant is approved, the grantee must accept the terms and conditions of an Agreement of Donee, which includes financial reporting and summary results. This practice enables the trust to review and evaluate grant performance periodically.
Publications: Biennial Report; Guidelines for Youth Recreation and Iowa Public Library; Application Form

Foundation Officials

Willard Lee Boyd: trustee B Saint Paul, MN 1927. ED University of Minnesota BS (1949); University of Minnesota LLB (1951); University of Michigan LLM (1952); University of Michigan SJD (1962). NONPR AFFIL president: National Committee Accrediting; president emeritus: University Iowa Law School; board member: Metropolitan Opera Association; director: National Arts Stabilization Fund; president emeritus: Field Museum Natural History; director: Harry S Truman Library Institute; chairman: American Association of Universities; member: American Bar Association.
Lucille Avis Carver: secretary, trustee B 1912. PRIM CORP EMPL treasurer: Bandag, Inc. CORP AFFIL treasurer: Carver Pump Co.
Roy James Carver, Jr.: vice chairman, trustee B Davenport, IA 1943. ED University of Iowa MA (1968); University of California at Berkeley (1970). PRIM CORP EMPL chairman, chief executive officer: Carver Pump Co. CORP AFFIL director: Met-Coil System Corp.; chief executive officer, director: RM Acquisitions Inc.; director: Iowa First Bancshares Inc.; director: GlobalKey; chief executive officer, chairman: Harrington Signal Inc.; president: Downtown Drug & Hardware; president: Carver Hotel Enterprises Inc.; director: Catalyst International Inc.; president: Carver Hardware Inc.; director: Bandag Inc.; president: Carver Aero Inc.
William F. Cory: trustee
J. Larry Griffith: trustee B 1937. PRIM CORP EMPL president, director: Mosebach Griffith.
Clay Le Grand: trustee B Saint Louis, MO February 26, 1911. ED Saint Ambrose College (1931); Catholic University America LLB (1934). NONPR AFFIL member: Iowa Bar Association; member: Scott County Bar Association; member: Institute Judicial Administration; member: American Bar Association; member: American Judicature Society.

Grants Analysis

Disclosure Period: fiscal year ending April 30, 2001
Total Grants: $14,473,871
Number of Grants: 108
Average Grant: $100,710*
Highest Grant: $2,000,000
Typical Range: $50,000 to $200,000
*Note: Average grant excludes four highest grants ($4,000,000).

Recent Grants

Note: Grants derived from fiscal 2000 Form 990.

Library-Related
55,000   Bettendorf Public Library, Bettendorf, IA
50,000   Carver Youth Recreation Program, Muscatine, IA
50,000   Carver Youth Recreation Program, Muscatine, IA

General
2,000,000   University of Illinois Urbana-Champaign, Urbana, IL
1,600,000   Iowa State University Foundation, Ames, IA -- plant sciences initiative
1,050,000   University of Iowa Foundation, Iowa City, IA -- construct new medical education and biomedical research facility
1,000,000   Iowa College Foundation, Des Moines, IA -- funding to continue the Communications Technology Challenge program
1,000,000   Iowa State University Foundation, Ames, IA -- C. Scholars

530,000   Iowa State University Foundation, Ames, IA -- establish a magnetoelectronic research foundations
305,000   City of Muscatine, Muscatine, IA
300,000   Iowa School for the Deaf, Council Bluffs, IA
300,000   Iowa State University Foundation, Ames, IA -- support image guided surgery research
275,200   University of Iowa Foundation, Iowa City, IA

MARY FLAGLER CARY CHARITABLE TRUST

Giving Contact
Edward A. Ames, Trustee
122 E 42nd St., Rm. 3505
New York, NY 10168
Phone: (212)953-7700
Fax: (212)953-7720
E-mail: info@carytrust.org
Web: http://www.carytrust.org

Description
Founded: 1968
EIN: 136266964
Organization Type: General Purpose Foundation
Giving Locations: NY: New York City including metropolitan area; for music and urban environment grants eastern coastal states for conservation grants.
Grant Types: General Support, Matching, Operating Expenses, Project.

Donor Information
Founder: Established in 1968 under the will of the late Mary Flagler Cary , the daughter of Harry Harkness and Anne Lamont Flagler and the wife of Melbert B. Cary, Jr., a graphic design expert. Her family was involved in the original Standard Oil Company. Mrs. Cary was interested in music, particularly the problems of young musicians trying to develop professional careers. She was also interested in the beauty of the countryside and natural landscape. Mrs. Cary owned over 1,800 acres of farmland near Millbrook, NY. Other interests are evident in the Carys' collections of fine prints, music manuscripts, and playing cards.

Financial Summary
Total Giving: $7,000,000 (fiscal year ending June 30, 2003 approx); $8,140,089 (fiscal 2002); $8,016,583 (fiscal 2001)
Assets: $100,000,000 (fiscal 2003 approx); $100,000,000 (fiscal 2002); $122,106,442 (fiscal 2001)

Typical Recipients
Arts & Humanities: Arts Associations & Councils, Arts Centers, Arts Funds, Arts Outreach, Community Arts, Dance, Arts & Humanities-General, Historic Preservation, Libraries, Museums/Galleries, Music, Opera, Performing Arts, Theater
Civic & Public Affairs: Botanical Gardens/Parks, Economic Development, Employment/Job Training, Civic & Public Affairs-General, Inner-City Development, Philanthropic Organizations, Urban & Community Affairs
Education: Arts/Humanities Education, Colleges & Universities, Engineering/Technological Education, Environmental Education
Environment: Air/Water Quality, Environment-General, Protection, Research, Resource Conservation, Watershed, Wildlife Protection
International: International Environmental Issues
Science: Scientific Research
Social Services: Community Service Organizations

Application Procedures
Initial Contact: The trust does not use an application form; send a written request.
Application Requirements: After studying a letter of request, if the trustees decide that there is a possibility of support, additional information will be requested. Trustees will want to see complete tax information, including a concise statement of the program or project; amount requested and how it fits within the applicant's overall budget; a description of organization; proof of tax-exempt status; a copy of the applicant's most recent audited financial statement; its legal name; an official letter of request on the organization's letterhead, signed by its chief executive officer on behalf of its governing body; and current list of officers, directors or trustees.
Deadlines: None. Guidelines, including application deadlines, are available for music commissioning and recording grants.
Review Process: The trustees meet at least once every month.

Restrictions
Grants are not made to individuals, international organizations, or primary or secondary schools. With certain exceptions, grants are not made to colleges, universities, or private foundations, or for building or endowment funds. Grants under the trust's music and urban environment programs are restricted to New York City.

Additional Information
Publications: Annual Report; Program Guidelines; General Information Pamphlet

Foundation Officials
Edward A. Ames: trustee
Paul Bernard Guenther: trustee B New York, NY 1940. ED Fordham University BS (1962); Columbia University MBA (1964). CORP AFFIL director: Consolidated Freightways; member advisory committee: Walden Capital Partners LP. NONPR AFFIL chairman: Philharmonic Symphony Society New York; trustee governing committee: Scholastic Achievement, Mary Flagler Cary Charitable Trust; chairman: Frost Valley YMCA; member: Institute Chartered Financial Analysts; member board overseers: Columbia University; trustee: Fordham University.
Phyllis J. Mills: trustee NONPR AFFIL vice chairman, director: Philharmonic Symphony Society New York.
Gayle Morgan: program director music
Lois M. Regan: admin, program officer urban environment

Grants Analysis
Disclosure Period: fiscal year ending June 30, 2001
Total Grants: $8,016,583*
Number of Grants: 127
Average Grant: $35,805*
Highest Grant: $3,505,152
Typical Range: $15,000 to $75,000
*Note: Average grant figure excludes highest grants.

Recent Grants
Note: Grants derived from fiscal 2000 Form 990.

Library-Related
36,500   Yale University, New Haven, CT -- support for the revision of Redesigning the American Lawn

General
3,162,050   Institute of Ecosystem Studies, Millbrook, NY -- for stewardship of Mary Flagler Cary Arboretum
1,185,000   Institute of Ecosystem Studies, Millbrook, NY -- capital campaign
500,000   Nature Conservancy, Arlington, VA -- for the Broadwater Project of the Virginia Coast Reserve
450,000   Nature Conservancy, Arlington, VA --

for TNC's Atlantic Coast Ecosystem Project
367,500   American Music Center, New York, NY -- for the live Music for Dance Program
355,000   Southern Environmental Law Center, Charlottesville, VA -- capital campaign
303,500   Concert Artists Guild, New York, NY -- support for a Recording Program
225,000   Citizens Committee for New York City, New York, NY -- support of the Neighborhood Leadership Institute
125,500   Concert Artists Guild, New York, NY -- for Commissioning Program
116,500   Trust for Public Land, New York, NY -- for Neighborhood Open Space Management Program

EUGENE B. CASEY FOUNDATION

Giving Contact
Betty Brown-Casey, Chairman, President & Treasurer
800 South Frederick Avenue
Suite 100
Gaithersburg, MD 20877
Phone: (301)948-4595
Fax: (301)948-9159

Description
Founded: 1981
EIN: 526220316
Organization Type: General Purpose Foundation
Giving Locations: DC: Washington including metropolitan area
Grant Types: Capital, General Support.

Donor Information
Founder: The foundation was established in 1981 by Eugene B. Casey.

Financial Summary
Total Giving: $9,570,000 (fiscal year ending August 31, 2000); $6,729,900 (fiscal 1999); $1,379,260 (fiscal 1997)
Assets: $188,222,802 (fiscal 2000); $193,315,458 (fiscal 1999); $174,157,102 (fiscal 1997)
Gifts Received: $4,900 (fiscal 1999); $68,000 (fiscal 1997); $74,528,657 (fiscal 1996). Note: In fiscal 1999, contributions were received from Heartland Development. In fiscal 1997, contributions were received from Blandford Casey, Rockville Development, and Nancy Corp.

Typical Recipients
Arts & Humanities: Arts Associations & Councils, Ballet, Historic Preservation, History & Archaeology, Libraries, Museums/Galleries, Opera, Performing Arts, Public Broadcasting, Theater, Visual Arts
Civic & Public Affairs: Business/Free Enterprise, Civil Rights, Clubs, Economic Development, Economic Policy, Employment/Job Training, Housing, Law & Justice, Native American Affairs, Parades/Festivals, Philanthropic Organizations, Public Policy, Rural Affairs, Women's Affairs
Education: Arts/Humanities Education, Colleges & Universities, Education Reform, Environmental Education, Faculty Development, Education-General, Journalism/Media Education, Literacy, Medical Education, Minority Education, Private Education (Precollege), Secondary Education (Private), Social Sciences Education, Special Education, Student Aid
Environment: Environment-General
Health: Cancer, Children's Health/Hospitals, Clinics/Medical Centers, Emergency/Ambulance Services, Eyes/Blindness, Health Funds, Health Organizations, Heart, Hospices, Hospitals, Hospitals (University Affiliated), Medical Research, Mental Health, Nutrition

Religion: Churches, Religion-General, Religious Organizations, Religious Welfare, Social/Policy Issues
Science: Scientific Centers & Institutes
Social Services: Child Abuse, Child Welfare, Community Centers, Community Service Organizations, Domestic Violence, Family Planning, Food/Clothing Distribution, People with Disabilities, Recreation & Athletics, Senior Services, Shelters/Homelessness, Substance Abuse, Veterans, YMCA/YWCA/YMHA/ YWHA, Youth Organizations

Application Procedures

Initial Contact: The foundation has no formal grant application procedure or grant application form.
Application Requirements: Applicants should submit written proposals that include an annual report, the purpose for which the funds are requested, form of project control, and the amount and proportions of funds requested compared with the total sought from other organizations.
Deadlines: None.

Foundation Officials

Betty Brown Casey: chairman, president, treasurer, trustee B 1928. ED Washington College. PRIM CORP EMPL president: Casey Engineering.
Douglas R. Casey: trustee
Stephen N. Jones: vice president, secretary, trustee
William James Price, IV: trustee B Baltimore, MD 1924. ED Yale University BS (1949). CORP AFFIL board director: Alex Brown Cash Reserve Fund. NONPR AFFIL trustee: Saint Pauls School; trustee: Washington College; member: National Association Securities Dealers.

Grants Analysis

Disclosure Period: fiscal year ending August 31, 2000
Total Grants: $9,570,000
Number of Grants: 28
Average Grant: $187,308*
Highest Grant: $2,700,000
Lowest Grant: $5,000
Typical Range: $5,000 to $25,000 and $100,000 to $300,000
*Note: Average grant figure excludes two highest grants.

Recent Grants

Note: Grants derived from 2000 Form 990.

General

2,700,000	Suburban Hospital, Bethesda, MD -- for the Eugene B. Casey Center for Diagnostic Cardiology
2,000,000	Garden Club of America, New York, NY
1,100,000	WETA, Washington, DC -- for program underwriting
1,000,000	Georgetown University, Washington, DC -- renovation of St. Mary's Hall at Georgetown's School of Nursing
1,000,000	National Gallery of Art, Washington, DC
1,000,000	Washington Opera, Washington, DC
100,000	Duke Ellington School of Arts, Washington, DC -- for Denyce Graves Endowment Fund
100,000	Georgetown University Medical Center, Washington, DC -- for planning for and establishment of Georgetown University Spine Center
100,000	Georgetown Visitation Preparatory School, Washington, DC -- for Performing Arts Center
100,000	Montgomery Hospice Foundation, Rockville, MD -- for Eugene B. Casey Endowment Fund

O. W. Caspersen Foundation For Aid To Health And Education

Giving Contact

Lucille Keegan, Secretary
PO Box 617
Gladstone, NJ 07934-0617
Phone: (908)719-8876

Description

Founded: 1964
EIN: 510101350
Organization Type: Private Foundation
Giving Locations: East coast.
Grant Types: Capital, Emergency, Multiyear/Continuing Support, Operating Expenses, Research.

Donor Information

Founder: the late O. W. Caspersen

Financial Summary

Total Giving: $1,626,141 (2000); $1,883,356 (1999); $448,088 (1998)
Assets: $17,143,172 (2000); $15,063,767 (1999); $16,387,961 (1998)
Gifts Received: $743,028 (2000); $961,358 (1999); $574,504 (1998). Note: In 1998 and 1999, contributions were received from the Freda R. Caspersen Charitable Lead Unitrust.

Typical Recipients

Arts & Humanities: Arts Associations & Councils, Arts Funds, Historic Preservation, Libraries
Education: Colleges & Universities, Education-General, Legal Education, Private Education (Precollege), Science/Mathematics Education
Environment: Environment-General, Resource Conservation, Watershed, Wildlife Protection
Health: Emergency/Ambulance Services, Health Funds, Health Organizations, Hospitals, Single-Disease Health Associations
Religion: Churches
Social Services: Recreation & Athletics, Scouts, YMCA/YWCA/YMHA/YWHA

Application Procedures

Initial Contact: The foundation has no formal grant application procedure or application form.
Deadlines: None.

Restrictions

Support is given for health and education grants only.

Foundation Officials

Barbara M. Caspersen: vice president, treasurer
Erik Michael Westby Caspersen: vice president, director
Finn M. W. Caspersen, Jr.: vice president, director
Finn M. W. Caspersen, Sr.: president B New York, NY 1941. ED Brown University BA (1963); Harvard University LLB (1966). CORP AFFIL vice president: Westby Corp.; director: Beneficial Bank PLC; member executive committee, director: Beneficial National Bank. NONPR AFFIL director: Shelter Harbor Fire District; chairman: U.S. Equestrian Team; chairman: Prosperty New Jersey; member: Partnership for New Jersey; trustee, chairman: Peddie School; member: New York State Bar Association; chairman dean advisory board: Harvard University Law School; advisory board: Institute for Law & Economic; member: Harvard Resources Comm; member: Florida Bar Association; chairman: Gladstone Equestrian Association Inc.; director: Drumthwacket Foundation; chairman: Coalition Better Transportation; chairman: Coalition Service Industry; emeritus trustee: Brown University; member: American Finance Services Association;

trustee: BGCN Life Camp Inc. CLUB AFFIL Wilmington Country Club; Knickerbocker Club; University Club; Harvard Club.
Samuel Michael Westby Caspersen: vice president, director
Lois E. Hansen: secretary, assistant treasurer
John O. Williams: assistant secretary, treasurer

Grants Analysis

Disclosure Period: calendar year ending 2000
Total Grants: $1,626,141
Number of Grants: 33
Average Grant: $49,277
Highest Grant: $278,438
Lowest Grant: $500
Typical Range: $10,000 to $100,000

Recent Grants

Note: Grants derived from 1999 Form 990.

General

1,000,000	Drew University, Madison, NJ
525,000	Matheny School, Peapack, NJ
250,000	Morristown Memorial Health Foundation, Inc., Morristown, NJ
48,356	Statue of Liberty Ellis Island Foundation, New York, NY
15,000	Groton School, Groton, MA
9,000	Epiphany Prep School, Dorchester, MA
7,500	Pomfret School, Pomfret, CT
5,000	Fund for Johns Hopkins, Baltimore, MD
5,000	Peck School, Morristown, NJ
5,000	Peddie School, Hightstown, NJ

Louis N. Cassett Foundation

Giving Contact

Malcolm B. Jacobson, Trustee
1 Penn Center, Suite 335
Philadelphia, PA 19103
Phone: (215)563-8886

Description

Founded: 1946
EIN: 236274038
Organization Type: Private Foundation
Giving Locations: Northeast.
Grant Types: Capital, General Support.

Donor Information

Founder: the late Louis N. Cassett

Financial Summary

Total Giving: $636,350 (2000); $626,905 (1999); $497,500 (1998). Note: 1996 Giving includes United Way ($15,000).
Giving Analysis: Giving for 2000 includes: foundation grants to United Way ($15,000); 1999: foundation grants to United Way ($17,000) 1998: foundation grants to United Way ($15,000)
Assets: $12,255,521 (2000); $13,250,629 (1999); $12,205,904 (1998)

Typical Recipients

Arts & Humanities: Arts Centers, Arts Institutes, Arts Outreach, Ballet, Community Arts, Historic Preservation, Libraries, Museums/Galleries, Music, Performing Arts, Public Broadcasting, Theater
Civic & Public Affairs: Civil Rights, Civic & Public Affairs-General, Law & Justice, Public Policy, Zoos/ Aquariums
Education: Arts/Humanities Education, Colleges & Universities, Education-General, Legal Education, Minority Education, Special Education
Environment: Environment-General, Resource Conservation
Health: Alzheimers Disease, Cancer, Children's Health/Hospitals, Clinics/Medical Centers, Diabetes,

Hospitals, Medical Research, Nursing Services, Nutrition, Public Health, Single-Disease Health Associations

International: International Relief Efforts, Missionary/Religious Activities

Religion: Churches, Jewish Causes, Religious Organizations, Religious Welfare

Social Services: Big Brother/Big Sister, Community Service Organizations, Day Care, Family Planning, People with Disabilities, Senior Services, Substance Abuse, United Funds/United Ways, Volunteer Services

Application Procedures

Initial Contact: Send a brief letter of inquiry.

Application Requirements: Include a description of organization, amount requested, purpose of funds sought, recently audited financial statement, and proof of tax-exempt status.

Deadlines: None.

Restrictions

Does not support individuals.

Foundation Officials

Albert J. Elias: trustee

Carol Gerstley-Hofheimer: trustee

Malcolm B. Jacobson: trustee

Grants Analysis

Disclosure Period: calendar year ending 2000

Total Grants: $621,350*

Number of Grants: 220 (approx)

Average Grant: $2,824

Highest Grant: $25,000

Typical Range: $500 to $5,000

***Note:** Giving excludes United Way.

Recent Grants

Note: Grants derived from 1999 Form 990.

General

25,000	Fairfield University, Fairfield, CT
25,000	United Cerebral Palsy, New York, NY
25,000	United Cerebral Palsy of New York, New York, NY
15,000	Philadelphia Orchestra, Philadelphia, PA
10,000	First Unitarian Church, West Palm Beach, FL
10,000	Friends of the Unitarian Universalist Union, Boston, MA
10,000	New Bolton Center Tees of University of Pennsylvania, Philadelphia, PA
10,000	Raymond F. Kravis Center, West Palm Beach, FL
10,000	Tiferet Israel Congregation, Blue Bell, PA
7,500	Tiferet Bet Israel, Blue Bell, PA

HAROLD K. L. CASTLE FOUNDATION

Giving Contact

Katherine F. Braden, Vice President & Treasurer
146 Hekili Street, Suite 203A
Kailua, HI 96734
Phone: (808)262-9413
Fax: (808)261-6918
E-mail: bradenkf@aloha.com
Web: http://www.castlefoundation.org

Description

Founded: 1962

EIN: 996005445

Organization Type: General Purpose Foundation

Giving Locations: HI: focusing on Windward Oahu

Grant Types: Capital, Challenge, Matching, Multiyear/Continuing Support, Seed Money.

Note: Grants are awarded for program start-up or expansion through matching, challenge, and multiyear grants. Capital grants are awarded up to five years and project/program grants up to three years.

Donor Information

Founder: The foundation was established in 1962, with the late Harold K. L. Castle and his wife, the late Alice Hedemann Castle , as donors. Mr. Castle, a prominent landowner and community leader, owned the Kaneohe Ranch. The ranch company was dissolved upon Mr. Castle's death; some of the land and commercial properties from the original ranch provide the base for the foundation's assets. The foundation is the largest private foundation based in Hawaii.

Financial Summary

Total Giving: $9,000,000 (2003 approx); $9,000,000 (2002 approx); $8,334,203 (2000)

Giving Analysis: Giving for 2000 includes: foundation grants to United Way ($110,000); 1998: foundation grants to United Way ($110,000); 1997: foundation grants to United Way ($100,000) foundation matching gifts ($175,450)

Assets: $180,000,000 (2003 approx); $180,000,000 (2002); $178,786,279 (2000)

Typical Recipients

Arts & Humanities: Arts Associations & Councils, Arts Centers, Community Arts, Ethnic & Folk Arts, Arts & Humanities-General, Historic Preservation, History & Archaeology, Libraries, Museums/Galleries, Music, Opera, Performing Arts, Public Broadcasting, Theater, Visual Arts

Civic & Public Affairs: Botanical Gardens/Parks, Business/Free Enterprise, Community Foundations, Economic Development, Employment/Job Training, Civic & Public Affairs-General, Housing, Legal Aid, Philanthropic Organizations, Public Policy, Urban & Community Affairs, Zoos/Aquariums

Education: Afterschool/Enrichment Programs, Arts/Humanities Education, Colleges & Universities, Economic Education, Elementary Education (Private), Elementary Education (Public), Environmental Education, Education-General, Gifted & Talented Programs, International Studies, Literacy, Preschool Education, Private Education (Precollege), Public Education (Precollege), Science/Mathematics Education, Secondary Education (Private), Secondary Education (Public), Student Aid

Environment: Air/Water Quality, Environment-General, Resource Conservation, Wildlife Protection

Health: AIDS/HIV, Cancer, Children's Health/Hospitals, Clinics/Medical Centers, Emergency/Ambulance Services, Health Organizations, Heart, Hospices, Hospitals, Medical Rehabilitation, Mental Health, Prenatal Health Issues, Single-Disease Health Associations

International: International Affairs, International Development, International Environmental Issues

Religion: Churches, Ministries, Religious Organizations, Religious Welfare

Science: Science-General, Science Museums, Scientific Centers & Institutes

Social Services: Animal Protection, At-Risk Youth, Big Brother/Big Sister, Camps, Child Abuse, Community Centers, Community Service Organizations, Day Care, Delinquency & Criminal Rehabilitation, Domestic Violence, Family Services, Food/Clothing Distribution, People with Disabilities, Scouts, Senior Services, Shelters/Homelessness, Substance Abuse, United Funds/United Ways, YMCA/YWCA/YMHA/YWHA, Youth Organizations

Application Procedures

Initial Contact: Applicants should send a preliminary letter to the foundation requesting guidelines. Prior to submitting a proposal, consult with the foundation to determine whether a pre-submittal meeting with the staff is desirable, to clarify what the proposal should

include, and to clarify whether the proposal is within the foundation's interests.

Application Requirements: Submit one original and six copies of a written proposal with a cover letter or executive summary signed by the organization's board chairman and president as well as a contact person's name and daytime telephone number. The proposal should include the purpose of the requested grant, the budget for the organization and the specific project for which funds are being requested, together with an indication of other funding sources. A list of the organization's current officers and directors should also be included as well as a description of what will be done to determine the effectiveness of the project. Also include the organization's most recent annual report or audited financial statements, and a copy of the IRS Section 501(c)(3) determination letter, together with a letter signed by an officer stating the IRS letter has not been modified.

Deadlines: None. Submit proposals by the first of the month prior to the month of the meeting date (i.e., January 1, March 1, May 1, etc.). The board generally meets every other month.

Review Process: The foundation directors will generally notify recipients within one week of the meeting. Larger grants (more than $100,000) are usually paid in December.

Restrictions

Eligible grantees include nonprofit organizations in Hawaii with IRS code Section 501(c)(3) "public" charity status, and government in areas not primarily tax-supported. The foundation does not give grants to individuals. Presentations cannot be made at a meeting of the foundation's directors.

Additional Information

All funded organizations are required to sign a written grant agreement detailing the use of the grant funds, reporting requirements, and other specifics of the grant.

The foundation approves about 30-35% of all proposals it receives.

Organizations should not resubmit a proposal until the next fiscal year.

As stated in the guidelines, applicants are welcome to contact staff prior to submittal to discuss proposals.

Publications: Annual Report; Guidelines

Foundation Officials

William C. Aull: director B 1922. PRIM NONPR EMPL treasurer, director: Mid Pacific Institute. CORP AFFIL director: Victoria Ward Ltd. NONPR AFFIL director: Hawaii Pacific University; treasurer: Mid-Pacific Institute.

John C. Baldwin: secretary, director B 1937. PRIM CORP EMPL treasurer: HNJ2 Inc. CORP AFFIL officer: Walker Industries Ltd.

Katherine F. Braden: vice president, treasurer B 1948. ED University of Hawaii (1989).

Henry Mitchell D'Olier: president, director B Chicago, IL 1946. ED University of Iowa BA (1968); University of Iowa JD (1972). PRIM CORP EMPL partner tax & health management committee: Goodsil, Anderson, Quinn & Stifel. CORP AFFIL president: Victoria Ward Ltd.; director: Reyns Mens Wear. NONPR AFFIL vice president: Central Union Church.

James C. McIntosh: director

Randolph G. Moore: director B Honolulu, HI 1939. ED Swarthmore College (1961); Stanford University (1963). PRIM CORP EMPL chief executive officer: Kaneohe Ranch. CORP AFFIL director: Hawaii Stevedores; director: Maui Land & Pineapple Co.; director: Grove Farm Co. Ltd.

Grants Analysis

Disclosure Period: calendar year ending 2000

Total Grants: $8,224,203*

Number of Grants: 74

Average Grant: $68,277*

Highest Grant: $3,240,000

Lowest Grant: $170
Typical Range: $5,000 to $25,000 and $50,000 to $100,000
*Note: Giving excludes United Way. Average grant figure excludes highest grant.

Recent Grants

Note: Grants derived from 2000 Form 990.

General

3,240,000	La Jardin Academy, Kailua, HI -- towards first phase of campus relocation capital campaign
600,000	Honolulu Academy of Arts, Honolulu, HI -- for the "Renaissance Campaign" to fund renovation and construction projects
333,333	Castle Medical Center, Honolulu, HI -- capital campaign
333,333	Contemporary Museum, Honolulu, HI -- construction budget
333,333	Reproductive and Biology Research Department, Honolulu, HI
250,000	All Kinds of Minds, Carrboro, NC
250,000	La Pietra Hawaii School for Girls, Honolulu, HI -- towards construction of science facility
250,000	Oceanic Institute, Honolulu, HI -- for expansion of the Center for Applied Aquaculture and Marine Biotechnology
200,000	Mid-Pacific Institute, Honolulu, HI
200,000	St. Mark Lutheran Church and School, Kaneohe, HI -- capital campaign to build new multipurpose building and classrooms

SAMUEL N. AND MARY CASTLE FOUNDATION

Giving Contact

Alfred L. Castle, Executive Director
The Pacific Garden Center, Makai Tower
733 Bishop Street, Suite 1275
Honolulu, HI 96813
Phone: (808)522-1101
Fax: (808)522-1103
E-mail: acastle@aloha.net
Web: http://fdncenter.org/grantmaker/castle/

Description

Founded: 1925
EIN: 996003321
Organization Type: General Purpose Foundation
Giving Locations: HI
Grant Types: Award, Capital, Challenge, Multiyear/Continuing Support, Project, Seed Money.

Donor Information

Founder: In 1898, Mary Tenney Castle (d. 1907), the widow of Samuel Northrop Castle (1809-1894), set aside one quarter of her estate to establish the Mary Castle Fund. Her husband had been a congregational missionary and a businessman who co-founded Castle & Cooke, one of Hawaii's largest corporations. In 1925, the Samuel N. and Mary Castle Foundation was incorporated with the transfer of assets from the Mary Castle Fund.

Financial Summary

Total Giving: $2,400,000 (2002 approx); $2,352,000 (2001); $2,100,000 (2000 approx)
Assets: $45,000,000 (2002 approx); $50,200,263 (2001); $60,000,000 (2000 approx)
Gifts Received: $1,350 (2001)

Typical Recipients

Arts & Humanities: Arts Centers, Arts Festivals, Arts Outreach, Arts & Humanities-General, History & Archaeology, Libraries, Literary Arts, Museums/Galleries, Music, Opera, Public Broadcasting, Theater, Visual Arts
Civic & Public Affairs: Asian American Affairs, Botanical Gardens/Parks, Community Foundations, Economic Development, Employment/Job Training, Civic & Public Affairs-General, Nonprofit Management, Parades/Festivals, Public Policy, Urban & Community Affairs, Women's Affairs
Education: Afterschool/Enrichment Programs, Arts/Humanities Education, Business Education, Colleges & Universities, Education Associations, Education Reform, Elementary Education (Private), Elementary Education (Public), Environmental Education, Faculty Development, Education-General, Gifted & Talented Programs, International Studies, Literacy, Preschool Education, Private Education (Precollege), Public Education (Precollege), Religious Education, Science/Mathematics Education, Secondary Education (Private), Secondary Education (Public), Special Education, Student Aid, Vocational & Technical Education
Environment: Environment-General, Research, Resource Conservation
Health: AIDS/HIV, Cancer, Children's Health/Hospitals, Emergency/Ambulance Services, Health Organizations, Hospices, Hospitals, Mental Health, Prenatal Health Issues, Respiratory, Speech & Hearing
International: Foreign Educational Institutions, International Affairs, International Organizations, International Relations
Religion: Churches, Religion-General, Ministries, Missionary Activities (Domestic), Religious Organizations, Religious Welfare
Science: Scientific Centers & Institutes
Social Services: Animal Protection, At-Risk Youth, Camps, Child Welfare, Community Centers, Community Service Organizations, Day Care, Family Services, Food/Clothing Distribution, People with Disabilities, Recreation & Athletics, Scouts, Special Olympics, Substance Abuse, United Funds/United Ways, YMCA/YWCA/YMHA/YWHA, Youth Organizations

Application Procedures

Initial Contact: Applicants should write or call the foundation for priorities and grantmaking policies. Grant seekers are encouraged to call, visit, or e-mail the foundation to determine the appropriateness of an application before submitting a complete proposal.
Application Requirements: Written proposals must contain a brief summary describing the organization, with history, mission, goals and major achievements; population to be served and any relevant characteristics; community opportunity or need which proposal addresses; program or project objectives, a summary of activities to be funded, and any other programmatic details that help clarify the request; amount requested, the duration of time over which foundation funds will be needed, and anticipated sources of support when foundation funding ceases; proposed methods of program/project evaluation; and information about the applicant organization's staff, including those responsible for the program/project.
One copy of each of the following attachments should be included with a proposal: IRS determination letter; the organization's charter and bylaws; most recently completed financial statements for the organization's operation for a full year, preferably audited, showing the year's income and expenses, fund balances at year's end and an explanation for anything unusual in the statements; a copy of the organization's current operating budget; a cover letter signed by the presiding officer of the board and the executive director of the organization, indicating that both the board and the chief staff person have approved the proposal; and the name and phone number of the contact person.

Proposals should also be accompanied by two copies of the following: a oneor two-page executive summary; an expense budget for the proposed activity and the revenue plan for the budget with two categories of sources and amounts; and a list of the board of directors, with occupations or positions and a statement of board involvement and functions within the organization.
Deadlines: February 1 for the April meeting, June 1 for the August meeting, and October 1 for the December meeting. Organizations seeking $25,000 or more for major capital must submit proposals by October 1, for review at the December meeting.

Restrictions

Grants are not made to organizations that cannot confirm their 501(c)(3) status. The foundation does not generally award grants to organizations located outside of the state of Hawaii; for programs or projects for which funds are based solely on an organizational need rather than in response to a documented community need; where foundation support would exceed 50% of the program or project budget; to endowment funds; or to third party regranting organizations. Program and project support does not generally exceed three years, and all funding myst be applied for on a yearly basis.

Additional Information

Organizations requesting funds from the Henry and Dorothy Castle Memorial Fund should submit requests directly to the Samuel N. and Mary Castle Foundation.
Organizations receiving support from the foundation must submit a brief report summarizing the outcome of the project and a financial accounting of the grant expenditures.
Publications: Annual Report; Requests for Proposals for the Henry and Dorothy Castle Memorial Fund
Trust(s): Bank of Hawaii

Foundation Officials

John C. Baldwin: president B 1937. PRIM CORP EMPL treasurer: HNJ2 Inc. CORP AFFIL officer: Walker Industries Ltd.
Alfred L. Castle: executive director, treasurer, trustee B Washington, DC 1948. ED University of New Mexico; Colorado State University BA (1971); Colorado State University MA (1972); Columbia University (1980). PRIM NONPR EMPL vice president development: Hawaii Pacific University. NONPR AFFIL member: San Diego Council Grantmakers; trustee: Trimble Charitable Trust; trustee: Robert Black Memorial Trust; trustee: Hawaiian Historical Society; executive director: NMMI Federation; trustee: Hawaii School Girls; member: Governors Council Children Youth; trustee: Hawaii Food Bank; member: Council Foundations; member: Association Grantmakers Hawaii; trustee: Henry & Dorothy Castle Fund; trustee: Academy Pacific.
William Donald Castle: secretary, trustee
James C. McIntosh: trustee
Cynthia Quisenberry: trustee

Grants Analysis

Disclosure Period: calendar year ending 2001
Total Grants: $2,352,000
Number of Grants: 101
Average Grant: $23,287
Highest Grant: $200,000
Lowest Grant: $2,000
Typical Range: $5,000 to $50,000

Recent Grants

Note: Grants derived from 2001 Form 990.

General

200,000	Hanahau'oli School, Honolulu, HI -- capital campaign to repair & renovate facilities

200,000	Hanahau'oli School, Honolulu, HI -- capital campaign to repair & renovate facilities
200,000	Maui Arts and Cultural Center, Kahului, HI -- educational complex improvement
200,000	Montessori School of Maui, Makawao, HI -- purchase of land
100,000	Hanalani Schools, Mililani, HI -- construction of a student activity center
100,000	Hanalani Schools, Mililani, HI -- construction of a student activity center
100,000	Hawaii Public Television Foundation, Honolulu, HI -- capital campaign to convert to digital broadcasting
100,000	Hawaiian Mission Children's Society, Honolulu, HI -- preservation of Historic Chamberlain House
84,000	Chaminade University of Honolulu, Honolulu, HI -- Castle Colleagues Program Funding
50,000	J. Walter Cameron Center, Wailuku, HI -- construction of infant and children facility

CASTLE ROCK FOUNDATION

Giving Contact
Sally Rippey, Secretary
4100 East Mississippi Avenue, 1850
Denver, CO 80246
Phone: (303)388-1636
Fax: (303)388-1684
E-mail: generalinfo@castlerockfdn.org
Web: http://www.castlerockfoundation.org

Alternate Contact
John W. Jackson, National Program Advisor

Description
Founded: 1993
EIN: 841243301
Organization Type: Private Foundation
Giving Locations: nationally.
Grant Types: General Support, Project, Scholarship.

Financial Summary
Total Giving: $2,900,000 (fiscal year ending November 30, 2003 approx); $2,900,000 (fiscal 2002 approx); $3,397,000 (fiscal 2001)
Giving Analysis: Giving for fiscal 1999 includes: foundation scholarships ($100,000)
Assets: $50,000,000 (fiscal 2003 approx); $50,000,000 (fiscal 2002 approx); $50,862,306 (fiscal 2001)
Gifts Received: $36,596,253 (fiscal 1994). Note: Contributions were received from Adolph Coors Foundation.

Typical Recipients
Arts & Humanities: Ethnic & Folk Arts, Historic Preservation, History & Archaeology, Libraries, Museums/Galleries
Civic & Public Affairs: African American Affairs, Botanical Gardens/Parks, Civil Rights, Community Foundations, Economic Development, Economic Policy, Civic & Public Affairs-General, Law & Justice, Legal Aid, Native American Affairs, Philanthropic Organizations, Professional & Trade Associations, Public Policy, Urban & Community Affairs, Women's Affairs
Education: Arts/Humanities Education, Colleges & Universities, Economic Education, Education Associations, Education Reform, Faculty Development, Education-General, Journalism/Media Education, Leadership Training, Legal Education, Minority Education, Private Education (Precollege), Social Sciences Education, Student Aid, Student Aid
Environment: Environment-General

Health: Cancer, Clinics/Medical Centers, Health Policy/Cost Containment, Medical Research, Preventive Medicine/Wellness Organizations
International: Health Care/Hospitals
Religion: Dioceses, Ministries, Religious Organizations, Religious Welfare, Social/Policy Issues
Social Services: Community Centers, Family Services, Scouts, Youth Organizations

Application Procedures
Initial Contact: One copy of a proposal.
Application Requirements: Legal name and address of organization; most recent copy of IRS letter of exemption; date of establishment, brief history and mission statement; purpose and amount of grant, as well as a description of the project and a project budget; current and/or proposed income and expense budget for the organization; anticipated results; financial statements for most recent fiscal year (preferably copy of audit); funding sources and amounts; names and occupations of board of directors and officers; names and addresses of those who have benefited from the organization's work.
Deadlines: April 30.
Review Process: The board of trustees meets once a year in the late fall to consider requests. An on-site visit may be conducted.

Restrictions
The foundation will generally not consider support of the following: human service agencies; museums or museum projects; organizations primarily supported by tax-derived funding; individuals; endowments; scientific or medical research projects; publications or production of films or other media-related projects; churches or church projects; funding of deficits or retirement of debt; special events; out of country projects; or purchase of computer equipment.

Additional Information
Publications: Annual Report

Foundation Officials
Holland H. Coors: ambassador
Jeffrey H. Coors: treasurer B Denver, CO 1944. ED Cornell University BSChE (1967); Cornell University MSChE (1968). PRIM CORP EMPL co-president, chief executive officer: ACX Technologies Inc. CORP AFFIL officer: Golden Photon Inc.; president, chief executive officer: Graphic Packaging Corp.; officer: Golden Genesis Co. Inc.
William K. Coors: trustee B Golden, CO August 11, 1916. ED Princeton University BSChE (1938); Princeton University MSChE (1939). PRIM CORP EMPL chairman, president, chief executive officer, director: Adolph Coors Co.
Linda S. Tafoya: secretary
Rev. Robert G. Windsor: trustee

Grants Analysis
Disclosure Period: fiscal year ending November 30, 2001
Total Grants: $3,397,000
Number of Grants: 43
Average Grant: $68,976*
Highest Grant: $500,000
Typical Range: $30,000 to $100,000
*Note: Average grant figure excludes highest grant.

Recent Grants
Note: Grants derived from fiscal 2001 Form 990.

General
500,000	Episcopal Diocese of Massachusetts, Boston, MA -- capital support for religious camp and conference center
250,000	Boy Scouts of America Denver Area Council, Denver, CO -- Inner City Scouting Program
250,000	Mount Vernon Ladies Association of the Union, Mt. Vernon, VA -- support George Washington Education Center

200,000	American Battle Monuments Commission, Arlington, VA -- operating support
200,000	Heritage Foundation, Washington, DC
200,000	John Wayne Cancer Institute, Santa Monica, CA -- support of cancer research and treatment agency
190,000	Hillsdale College, Hillsdale, MI -- Center for Constructive Alternatives
150,000	Marshall Area Community Center, Inc., Marshall, MN -- capital support for Community Center
100,000	Denver Foundation, Denver, CO -- support for educational options for children
75,000	Institute for Justice, Washington, DC -- support of public interest law firm

CATERPILLAR INC.

Company Headquarters
100 NE Adams St.
Peoria, IL 61629
Web: http://www.cat.com

Company Description
Founded: 1925
Ticker: CAT
Exchange: NYSE
Revenue: US$20.152 billion (2002)
Profit: US$798 million (2002)
Employees: 68990 (2002)
Fortune Rank: 85, per FORTUNE Magazine's list of 500 Largest U.S. Corporations (2002).
SIC(s): 3272 Concrete Products Nec, 3511 Turbines & Turbine Generator Sets, 3519 Internal Combustion Engines Nec, 3531 Construction Machinery.

Operating Locations
Caterpillar Inc. (AL--Opelika; AZ--Green Valley; CO--Denver; DC--Washington; FL--Jacksonville; GA--Atlanta; IL--Aurora, Decatur, Joliet, Lisle, Morton Grove, Mossville, Pontiac, Springfield; IN--Indianapolis, Lafayette; MS--Corinth; NC--Clayton; PA--Camp Hill, York; TX--Houston, Irving; WA--Spokane; WI--Edgerton)

Nonmonetary Support
Value: $700,000 (1999)
Type: Donated Equipment; In-kind Services; Loaned Executives
Contact: Henry Holling

Caterpillar Foundation

Giving Contact
Henry Holling, Vice President
Caterpillar Foundation
100 NE Adams Street
Peoria, IL 61629-1480
Phone: (309)675-4464
Fax: (309)675-5815
Web: http://www.cat.com/foundation

Description
Founded: 1952
EIN: 376022314
Organization Type: Corporate Foundation
Giving Locations: operating locations; educational matching gifts program is international.
Grant Types: Capital, Employee Matching Gifts, General Support, Scholarship.
Note: Employee matching gift ratio: 1 to 1 for higher education only.

Donor Information
Founder: Caterpillar

Financial Summary
Total Giving: $11,900,000 (2002 approx); $11,753,614 (2001); $14,008,424 (2000)
Giving Analysis: Giving for 2001 includes: foundation grants to United Way ($1,053,750); foundation ($10,699,864); 2000: nonmonetary support ($650,000); foundation grants to United Way ($930,150); foundation matching gifts ($1,129,822); corporate direct giving ($1,478,424); foundation ($9,820,028); 1999: foundation matching gifts ($1,039,079); foundation grants to United Way ($1,602,641); corporate direct giving ($1,894,328) foundation ($12,261,654)
Assets: $54,805,299 (2001); $54,700,692 (2000); $33,500,000 (1999)
Gifts Received: $11,900,000 (2002); $14,100,000 (2001); $12,000,000 (2000). Note: Contributions are received from Caterpillar, Inc.

Typical Recipients
Arts & Humanities: Arts Centers, Community Arts, Arts & Humanities-General, Historic Preservation, History & Archaeology, Museums/Galleries, Music, Performing Arts, Public Broadcasting, Theater
Civic & Public Affairs: African American Affairs, Botanical Gardens/Parks, Business/Free Enterprise, Civil Rights, Community Foundations, Economic Development, Economic Policy, Employment/Job Training, Ethnic Organizations, Civic & Public Affairs-General, Hispanic Affairs, Housing, Law & Justice, Municipalities/Towns, Nonprofit Management, Public Policy, Safety, Urban & Community Affairs
Education: Business Education, Colleges & Universities, Community & Junior Colleges, Economic Education, Education Funds, Education Reform, Engineering/Technological Education, Faculty Development, Education-General, International Studies, Medical Education, Minority Education, Private Education (Precollege), Public Education (Precollege), Science/Mathematics Education, Student Aid, Vocational & Technical Education
Environment: Environment-General, Resource Conservation
Health: Cancer, Emergency/Ambulance Services, Health Organizations, Hospices, Hospitals, Medical Rehabilitation, Mental Health, Single-Disease Health Associations
International: International Environmental Issues, International Peace & Security Issues, Trade
Religion: Religion-General, Ministries, Missionary Activities (Domestic), Religious Welfare
Science: Science Museums
Social Services: Camps, Child Welfare, Community Centers, Community Service Organizations, Domestic Violence, Emergency Relief, Family Services, Homes, People with Disabilities, Scouts, Sexual Abuse, Social Services-General, Special Olympics, Substance Abuse, United Funds/United Ways, YMCA/YWCA/YMHA/YWHA, Youth Organizations

Application Procedures
Initial Contact: Submit a brief proposal to the nearest Caterpillar facility.
Application Requirements: Include the date; organization's name, address, phone and fax; name, address, phone and position of contact person; a description of organization; proof of tax-exempt status; purpose of the project or campaign, total goal, portion of the total already on hand, and if the funds will be used for operating or capital items; reason that Caterpillar should contribute to the cause, and the benefit to Caterpillar; list of other organizations providing similar support and how they provide it; amount requested and why; number of Caterpillar employees or family members are members of the applicant organization; number of Caterpillar employees or family members that might benefit from this project and how; whether the proposal is for an annual request for funds; whether funds are also being sought or obtained from others such as governmental bodies, United Way, etc., and to what degree; and, where appropriate, information on the details of the proposal, copy of current budget, copy of the most recent audited financial report, list of major donors/pledges, and list of board members and their affiliations.
Deadlines: None.
Decision Notification: Notice of approval or rejection is usually sent within one month of proposal receipt.

Restrictions
In general, company does not support individuals, fraternal organizations, religious organizations whose services are limited to any one sectarian group, political activity, tickets or advertising for fund-raising benefits, or general operations or ongoing programs of agencies funded by the United Way.

Foundation Officials
Glen A. Barton: chairman, chief executive officer
Henry W. Holling: vice president
Alan J. Rassi: vice president PRIM CORP EMPL vice president: Caterpillar Inc.
T. Thorstenson: vice president

Grants Analysis
Disclosure Period: calendar year ending 2001
Total Grants: $10,699,864*
Number of Grants: 571
Average Grant: $18,739
Highest Grant: $630,000
Typical Range: $1,000 to $25,000
*Note: Giving excludes United Way; corporate direct giving.

Recent Grants
Note: Grants derived from 2001 Form 990.

General
900,000	United Way HOIUW Excellence Fund
630,000	Bradley University, Peoria, IL
548,623	Educational Grants
500,000	Valparaiso University, Valparaiso, IN
320,466	Cultural
300,000	American Red Cross, Washington, DC
250,000	Eureka College, Eureka, IL
200,000	Abraham Lincoln Presidential Library and Museum Foundation, Springfield, IL
200,000	Youth Farm, Peoria, IL
165,000	Illinois Central College Foundation, Chicago, IL

JOHN AND MILDRED CAUTHORN CHARITABLE TRUST

Giving Contact
Jessie Kerbow, Secretary
PO Box 678
Sonora, TX 76950
Phone: (915)387-2711

Description
Founded: 1985
EIN: 751977779
Organization Type: Private Foundation
Giving Locations: TX: including the Sutton County area
Grant Types: General Support, Operating Expenses, Scholarship.

Financial Summary
Total Giving: $725,117 (2001); $640,618 (2000); $419,926 (1999)
Giving Analysis: Giving for 2001 includes: foundation scholarships ($61,000); 2000: foundation scholarships ($54,000) 1999: foundation scholarships ($60,000)
Assets: $5,779,105 (2001); $4,983,121 (2000); $4,671,962 (1999)

Typical Recipients
Arts & Humanities: Historic Preservation, History & Archaeology, Libraries, Music
Civic & Public Affairs: Clubs, Community Foundations, Housing, Municipalities/Towns, Urban & Community Affairs
Education: Agricultural Education, Education Reform, Education-General, Leadership Training, Public Education (Precollege), Special Education, Student Aid
Health: Cancer, Emergency/Ambulance Services, Health Funds, Hospitals
Religion: Churches, Religious Organizations, Religious Welfare
Social Services: Child Welfare, Community Service Organizations, Homes, Scouts, Senior Services, Youth Organizations

Application Procedures
Initial Contact: The foundation has no formal grant application procedure or application form.
Deadlines: None.

Restrictions
Giving is restricted to entities and individuals in Sutton County, Texas.

Foundation Officials
Michael V. Hale: trustee
JoAnn Jones: trustee
Nelda Mayfield: trustee
Nelson Stubblefield: trustee
Bob Teaff: trustee

Grants Analysis
Disclosure Period: calendar year ending 2001
Total Grants: $664,117*
Number of Grants: 12
Average Grant: $3,767*
Highest Grant: $293,890
Lowest Grant: $500
Typical Range: $500 to $5,000
*Note: Giving excludes scholarships. Average grant figure excludes three highest grants ($630,217).

Recent Grants
Note: Grants derived from 2001 Form 990.

General
293,890	Presbyterian Children Services, Austin, TX -- operating funds
195,927	Church of the Good Shephard, Sonora, TX -- operating funds
140,000	Sutton County, Sonora, TX -- building repair
61,000	Sonora Independent School District, Sonora, TX -- scholarship
16,400	Bronco Booster Club, Sonora, TX -- school athletic
9,500	Sonora Ministerial Alliance, Sonora, TX -- operating funds
3,000	Community Action Team, Sonora, TX -- Project Graduation
1,500	American Cancer Society, Sonora, TX -- operating fund
1,000	Helping Hand Fund, Sonora, TX -- operating funds
1,000	Sutton County Child Protection, Sonora, TX -- operating funds

CAYUGA FOUNDATION

Giving Contact
Edwin Diener, Trust Officer
c/o Key Trust Co. of Ohio
PO Box 10099
Toledo, OH 43699-0099
Phone: (419)259-8372

Description

Founded: 1960
EIN: 346504822
Organization Type: Private Foundation
Giving Locations: NY; OH, Toledo
Grant Types: Capital, General Support, Scholarship.

Financial Summary

Total Giving: $200,000 (2001); $212,000 (2000); $200,000 (1999)
Giving Analysis: Giving for 2001 includes: foundation grants to United Way ($4,000); 2000: foundation grants to United Way ($4,200) 1999: foundation grants to United Way ($2,000)
Assets: $3,290,939 (2001); $3,960,001 (2000); $4,475,478 (1999)

Typical Recipients

Arts & Humanities: Community Arts, Libraries, Museums/Galleries, Public Broadcasting
Civic & Public Affairs: Botanical Gardens/Parks, Economic Development, Civic & Public Affairs-General, Housing, Municipalities/Towns, Public Policy, Safety, Urban & Community Affairs
Education: Colleges & Universities, Elementary Education (Public), Environmental Education, International Exchange, Leadership Training, Minority Education, Preschool Education, Private Education (Precollege), Public Education (Precollege)
Environment: Environment-General, Research, Resource Conservation, Wildlife Protection
Health: Cancer, Clinics/Medical Centers, Health-General, Health Organizations, Hospices, Hospitals, Long-Term Care, Medical Rehabilitation, Single-Disease Health Associations
International: Foreign Educational Institutions, Human Rights, International Environmental Issues, International Organizations, International Relations
Religion: Churches, Ministries, Religious Organizations, Religious Welfare
Social Services: Child Welfare, Community Service Organizations, Family Planning, Family Services, Recreation & Athletics, Scouts, United Funds/United Ways, Volunteer Services, Youth Organizations

Application Procedures

Initial Contact: Send brief letter and a full proposal. Include a description of organization, recently audited financial statement, proof of tax-exempt status, and purpose of funds sought.
Deadlines: None.

Restrictions

The foundation does not support individuals, religious organizations for sectarian purposes, political or lobbying groups, or organizations outside operating areas.

Additional Information

Trust(s): Key Trust Co OH NA

Foundation Officials

Sandra Fritch: adv
Donald J. Keune: adv
Elizabeth M. Pfenninger: adv

Grants Analysis

Disclosure Period: calendar year ending 2001
Total Grants: $196,000*
Number of Grants: 32
Average Grant: $5,290*
Highest Grant: $32,000
Lowest Grant: $2,000
Typical Range: $2,000 to $10,000
***Note:** Giving excludes United Way. Average grant figure excludes highest grant.

Recent Grants

Note: Grants derived from 2001 Form 990.

Library-Related
6,000   Aurora Free Library Association, Aurora, NY

General
32,000   New York City Outward Bound, New York, NY
12,000   Comfortcare of Cayuga County, Inc, Auburn, NY -- for operations
12,000   United Ministry, Aurora, NY -- for operations
12,000   Village of Cayuga, Cayuga, NY -- for operations
10,000   Peachtown Elementary School, Aurora, NY -- educational
10,000   Wells College, Aurora, NY -- for operations
8,000   Cayuga County Habitat for Humanity, Inc, Auburn, NY -- for operations
8,000   Faatz Crofut Home for the Elderly, Auburn, NY -- for operations
8,000   Ocean Reef Volunteer Fire Department, Inc, Key Largo, FL -- for operations
8,000   Sloan-Kettering Institute for Cancer Research, New York, NY -- for operations and medical research

CBS CORP.

Company Headquarters

51 West 52nd Street
New York, NY 10019
Phone: (212)975-4321
Fax: (212)975-4516
Web: http://www.cbs.com

Company Description

Employees: 28,900 (1999)
Parent Company: Viacom, Inc., 1515 Broadway, New York, NY, United States

Nonmonetary Support

Type: In-kind Services

CBS Foundation

Giving Contact

Ken Silverman, Foundation Contact
Viacom, Inc.
51 West 52nd Street
New York, NY 10019
Phone: (212)975-3773

Description

EIN: 136099759
Organization Type: Corporate Foundation
Giving Locations: markets where CBS has major ownership presence.
Grant Types: Employee Matching Gifts, General Support, Multiyear/Continuing Support, Operating Expenses, Project, Scholarship.

Financial Summary

Total Giving: $770,651 (2000); $1,196,924 (1999); $2,385,428 (1998)
Giving Analysis: Giving for 2000 includes: foundation matching gifts ($78,151); foundation ($692,500); 1999: foundation grants to United Way ($30,000); foundation matching gifts ($222,480); foundation ($944,444); 1998: foundation grants to United Way ($123,000); foundation matching gifts ($215,183); foundation ($2,047,245);
Assets: $3,155,957 (2000); $3,294,050 (1999); $4,771,159 (1998)

Gifts Received: $802,555 (2000). Note: In 2000, contributions were received from Westinghouse Foundation.

Typical Recipients

Arts & Humanities: Arts Associations & Councils, Arts Centers, Dance, Film & Video, Arts & Humanities-General, Libraries, Literary Arts, Museums/Galleries, Music, Performing Arts, Public Broadcasting, Theater
Civic & Public Affairs: African American Affairs, Chambers of Commerce, Clubs, Community Foundations, Civic & Public Affairs-General, Hispanic Affairs, Law & Justice, Municipalities/Towns, Nonprofit Management, Professional & Trade Associations, Public Policy, Urban & Community Affairs, Women's Affairs
Education: Afterschool/Enrichment Programs, Arts/Humanities Education, Business-School Partnerships, Colleges & Universities, Education Funds, Education Reform, Education-General, Journalism/Media Education, Minority Education, Minority Education, Science/Mathematics Education, Social Sciences Education, Special Education, Student Aid
Environment: Air/Water Quality, Environment-General
Religion: Religious Welfare
Science: Scientific Centers & Institutes
Social Services: Child Welfare, Community Service Organizations, People with Disabilities, Social Services-General, United Funds/United Ways, YMCA/YWCA/YMHA/YWHA, Youth Organizations

Application Procedures

Initial Contact: Submit a full proposal.
Application Requirements: Include an outline of project and expected benefits; a copy of 501(c)(3) determination letter; financial plan; list of board of directors and officers; and a copy of organization's latest audited financial statements.
Deadlines: None.

Restrictions

Company only supports charitable organizations with IRS 501(c)(3) tax-exempt status.

Does not support projects that are directly associated with the internal operations of divisions of CBS; organizations via advertisements in journals; endowment or capital costs, including construction, renovation, and/or equipment; internal programs and institutions; or individuals.

Additional Information

In December 1997, the corporation changed its name from Westinghouse Electric Corp. to CBS Corp., recognizing it was nearing completion of its transformation to a pure media company.

Corporate Officials

Preston Robert Tisch: co-chairman, co-chief executive officer, director B Brooklyn, NY 1926. ED Bucknell University (1943-1944); University of Michigan BA (1948). PRIM CORP EMPL co-chairman, director: Loews Corp. ADD CORP EMPL owner, chief executive officer, chairman: New York Football Giants Inc. CORP AFFIL director: Transcontinental Insurance Co. New York; director: Hasbro Inc.; director: Rite Aid Corp.; director: CNA Financial Corp.; director: Bulova Corp. NONPR AFFIL trustee: New York University; member: Sigma Alpha Mu; chairman emeritus: New York Convention & Visitor Bureau; president: City-meals Wheels; member: Governments Business Advisory Council New York. CLUB AFFIL Rye Racquet Club; Century Country Club.

Foundation Officials

David Zemelman: trustee

Grants Analysis

Disclosure Period: calendar year ending 2000
Total Grants: $692,500*
Number of Grants: 124
Average Grant: $5,585

Highest Grant: $50,000
Lowest Grant: $500
Typical Range: $1,500 to $10,000
***Note:** Giving excludes matching gifts.

Recent Grants

Note: Grants derived from 2000 Form 990.

Library-Related
25,000	New York Public Library, New York, NY

General
78,151	CBS Gift Match Program, New York, NY
50,000	New York Restoration Project, New York, NY
50,000	Sam Houston State University, Huntsville, TX
50,000	Take the Field, New York, NY
40,000	Advertising Council, New York, NY
40,000	National Corporate Theatre Fund, New York, NY
35,000	American Film Institute, New York, NY
32,500	Barnard College, New York, NY
30,000	Hispanic Association of Colleges, Novato, CA
30,000	League of Women Voters NYS Education, New York, NY

CCB FINANCIAL CORP.

Company Headquarters
Durham, NC
Web: http://www.ccbonline.com

Company Description
Employees: 2,891
SIC(s): 6022 State Commercial Banks, 6712 Bank Holding Companies.

Operating Locations
CCB Financial Corp. (SC--Durham)

CCB Foundation

Giving Contact
John D. Ramsey, President
CCB Foundation
PO Box 931
Durham, NC 27702-0931
Phone: (919)683-7251
Fax: (919)682-3870

Description
Founded: 1985
EIN: 581611223
Organization Type: Corporate Foundation
Giving Locations: headquarters area only.
Grant Types: General Support.

Financial Summary
Total Giving: $1,414,563 (2000); $955,657 (1998); $768,196 (1997)
Giving Analysis: Giving for 2000 includes: foundation matching gifts ($62,504); foundation grants to United Way ($371,144); foundation ($980,915); 1998: foundation matching gifts ($47,692); foundation grants to United Way ($194,506); 1997: foundation matching gifts ($37,694) foundation grants to United Way ($172,835).
Assets: $1,420,847 (2000); $1,616,995 (1998); $1,378,459 (1997)
Gifts Received: $1,661,125 (2000); $1,123,300 (1998); $984,000 (1997). Note: In 2000, contributions were received from Central Carolina Bank ($1,660,000); Durham Crime Stoppers, Inc. ($1,000); and North Carolina State University ($125). In 1998, contributions were received from Central Carolina Bank.

Typical Recipients
Arts & Humanities: Arts Associations & Councils, Dance, Arts & Humanities-General, History & Archaeology, Libraries, Museums/Galleries, Music, Performing Arts, Public Broadcasting, Theater
Civic & Public Affairs: Business/Free Enterprise, Chambers of Commerce, Economic Development, Civic & Public Affairs-General, Housing, Urban & Community Affairs
Education: Arts/Humanities Education, Business Education, Colleges & Universities, Community & Junior Colleges, Education Reform, Faculty Development, Education-General, Health & Physical Education, Public Education (Precollege)
Health: Cancer, Emergency/Ambulance Services, Health-General, Health Organizations, Hospitals
Religion: Religious Welfare
Science: Science Museums
Social Services: Child Welfare, Community Service Organizations, Community Service Organizations, Crime Prevention, Emergency Relief, Recreation & Athletics, Shelters/Homelessness, Social Services-General, United Funds/United Ways, YMCA/YWCA/YMHA/YWHA

Application Procedures
Initial Contact: Send a full proposal.
Application Requirements: Include a description of organization, amount requested, purpose of funds sought, and proof of tax-exempt status.
Deadlines: None.
Review Process: Requests are considered on a monthly basis.

Restrictions
Does not support individuals, religious organizations for sectarian purposes, political or lobbying groups, or organizations outside operating areas.

Grants Analysis
Disclosure Period: calendar year ending 2000
Total Grants: $980,915*
Number of Grants: 189
Average Grant: $5,190
Highest Grant: $54,500
Typical Range: $2,500 to $5,000
***Note:** Giving excludes matching gifts; United Way.

Recent Grants
Note: Grants derived from 2000 Form 990.

General
122,000	United Way Triangle Area, Raleigh, NC
115,000	United Way Triangle Area, Raleigh, NC
54,500	Carolina Business Review on UNC-TV, Durham, NC
28,000	North Carolina Museum of Life and Science, Durham, NC
25,000	North Carolina State University College of Management, Raleigh, NC
25,000	North Carolina Transportation Museum Foundation, Spencer, NC
25,000	North Carolinians for Educational Opportunity, Durham, NC
25,000	St. Joseph's Historic Foundation, Durham, NC
24,000	United Way of Greenville County, Greenville, SC
20,000	Durham Technical Community College, Durham, NC

CEMALA FOUNDATION

Giving Contact
Priscilla P. Taylor, Executive Director
Cemala Foundation
122 N. Elm Street, Suite 816
Greensboro, NC 27401-2842
Phone: (336)274-3541

E-mail: Cemala@cemala.org
Web: http://www.cemala.org

Description
Founded: 1986
EIN: 561528982
Organization Type: Private Foundation
Giving Locations: NC: Guilford County
Grant Types: Capital, General Support.

Donor Information
Founder: the late Martha A. Cone, the late Ceasar Cone II

Financial Summary
Total Giving: $2,889,540 (2002); $1,512,210 (2001); $1,649,799 (2000)
Giving Analysis: Giving for 2002 includes: foundation grants to United Way ($181,000); 2000: foundation grants to United Way ($40,000); 1999: foundation grants to United Way ($38,500)
Assets: $38,486,684 (2002); $43,476,576 (2001); $45,356,558 (2000)
Gifts Received: $12,409,058 (1998); $420,000 (1997); $412,277 (1996). Note: Contributions were received from the Martha A. Cone Trust.

Typical Recipients
Arts & Humanities: Historic Preservation, History & Archaeology, Libraries, Museums/Galleries, Music, Public Broadcasting, Visual Arts
Civic & Public Affairs: Community Foundations, Economic Development, Civic & Public Affairs-General, Law & Justice, Nonprofit Management, Public Policy, Rural Affairs, Urban & Community Affairs, Women's Affairs
Education: Business Education, Colleges & Universities, Elementary Education (Private), Private Education (Precollege), Public Education (Precollege)
Environment: Environment-General
Health: AIDS/HIV, Cancer, Clinics/Medical Centers, Emergency/Ambulance Services, Health Organizations, Hospices
Religion: Religion-General, Ministries, Religious Welfare
Science: Science Museums, Scientific Centers & Institutes
Social Services: Child Welfare, Community Centers, Community Service Organizations, Emergency Relief, Family Planning, Family Services, People with Disabilities, Scouts, Shelters/Homelessness, Social Services-General, United Funds/United Ways, YMCA/YWCA/YMHA/YWHA

Application Procedures
Initial Contact: Submit a completed application form signed and dated by the chief executive officer or chairman of the organization. A proposal of not more than two pages should also be sent, and should include (in this order): a short introductory paragraph with a concise statement of the purpose of funds sought and amount requested; a detailed project description covering the issue being addressed, what will be different and why it is important, the outcomes to be achieved, plans for accomplishing the outcomes and project timetable, capacity of the organization to carry out the plan; if this is a collaborative effort, the role of each partner, and how the success and effectiveness of the program will be evaluated; a description of organization, its history, mission, and activities; project budget; organization operating budget; list of board members and their affiliations; recently audited financial statement; and proof of tax-exempt status.
Deadlines: March 1 and September 1.

Restrictions
Does not provide endowment or operating funds.

Additional Information
Publications: Application Form; Guidelines

Foundation Officials

Carole W. Bruce: director
Ashley E. Cone: secretary
Ceasar Cone, III: president, director
Janet G. Cone: director
Walter C. Cone: director
Betty T. Day: assistant secretary, assistant treasurer
William L. Hemphill: director
John Richmond: treasurer
Katherine K. Richmond: director
Matthew D. Richmond: director
Merritt Richmond: treasurer
William R. Rogers: director
Priscilla P. Taylor: executive director
Robert B. White: secretary, treasurer
Martha C. Wright: vice president, director

Grants Analysis

Disclosure Period: calendar year ending 2002
Total Grants: $2,708,540*
Number of Grants: 46
Average Grant: $17,984*
Highest Grant: $1,899,257
Lowest Grant: $2,500
Typical Range: $10,000 to $40,000
*Note: Giving excludes United Way. Average grant figure excludes highest grant.

Recent Grants

Note: Grants derived from 2001 Form 990.

Library-Related
25,000	Conservation Trust for North Carolina, Raleigh, NC -- for operations

General
150,000	Greensboro Urban Ministry, Greensboro, NC -- for operations
125,000	Hospice at Greensboro, Inc., Greensboro, NC -- for operations
100,000	Triad Stage, Greensboro, NC -- for operations
70,000	Community Foundation of Greater Greensboro, Greensboro, NC -- for operations
60,000	United Way of Greater High Point, Inc., High Point, NC -- for operations
50,000	North Carolina Institute of Government Foundation, Chapel Hill, NC -- for operations
50,000	September 11th Fund, New York, NY -- for operations
50,000	Women's Resource Center, Greensboro, NC -- for operations
44,000	United Way of Greater Greensboro, Greensboro, NC -- for operations
40,000	Junior Achievement of Central North Carolina, Greensboro, NC -- for operations

CENTERPOINT ENERGY, INC.

Company Headquarters

1111 Louisiana St.
Houston, TX 77002
Web: http://www.centerpointenergy.com

Company Description

Founded: 1976
Ticker: CNP
Exchange: NYSE
Former Name: Houston Industries, Inc. (1999); Reliant Energy, Inc. (2002).
Assets: US$30.18 billion (2002)
Employees: 11000 (2002)
Fortune Rank: 236, per FORTUNE Magazine's list of 500 Largest U.S. Corporations (2002).

SIC(s): 4841 Cable & Other Pay Television Services, 4911 Electric Services, 5063 Electrical Apparatus & Equipment, 6719 Holding Companies Nec.

Operating Locations

Reliant Energy HL&P (TX--Houston); Reliant Energy Minnegasco (MN--Minneapolis); Reliant Enrergy Arkla (AR--Little Rock); Reliant Entex (TX--Houston)

Nonmonetary Support

Type: Donated Equipment; In-kind Services; Loaned Employees; Loaned Executives

Reliant Resources Foundation

Giving Contact

Robert Gibbs, Director, Corporate Community Relations
PO Box 4567
Houston, TX 77210
Phone: (713)207-5155
Fax: (713)207-0207
Web: http://www.reliantenergy.com/company/community/

Description

Founded: 1997
EIN: 760537222
Organization Type: Corporate Foundation
Former Name: Houston Industries, Inc. (1999).
Former Name: Reliant Energy Foundation.
Giving Locations: headquarters and operating communities, mainly TX.
Grant Types: Capital, General Support, Research, Seed Money.

Financial Summary

Total Giving: $5,818,098 (fiscal year ending , 2001); $6,554,892 (fiscal 2000); $3,655,039 (fiscal 1998). Note: Contributes through corporate direct giving program and foundation. Company does not disclose contributions figures.
Giving Analysis: Giving for fiscal 2000 includes: foundation scholarships ($56,800); foundation grants to United Way ($1,173,921); foundation ($5,324,171); fiscal 1998: corporate scholarships ($327,650); corporate grants to United Way ($699,150) corporate direct giving ($2,628,239)
Assets: $14,960,363 (fiscal 2001); $21,971,181 (fiscal 2000); $20,143,422 (fiscal 1998)
Gifts Received: $363,736 (fiscal 2000). Note: In 2000, contributions were received from Reliant Energy Ventures.

Typical Recipients

Arts & Humanities: Arts Associations & Councils, Arts Centers, Arts Funds, Community Arts, Dance, Ethnic & Folk Arts, Historic Preservation, Libraries, Museums/Galleries, Music, Performing Arts, Public Broadcasting, Theater
Civic & Public Affairs: African American Affairs, Botanical Gardens/Parks, Business/Free Enterprise, Economic Development, Employment/Job Training, Civic & Public Affairs-General, Housing, Law & Justice, Municipalities/Towns, Parades/Festivals, Professional & Trade Associations, Public Policy, Rural Affairs, Safety, Urban & Community Affairs, Women's Affairs, Zoos/Aquariums
Education: Business Education, Colleges & Universities, Community & Junior Colleges, Economic Education, Economic Education, Education Funds, Engineering/Technological Education, Education-General, Literacy, Medical Education, Minority Education, Public Education (Precollege), Science/Mathematics Education, Student Aid, Vocational & Technical Education
Environment: Environment-General, Resource Conservation, Wildlife Protection

Health: Cancer, Children's Health/Hospitals, Diabetes, Emergency/Ambulance Services, Health Organizations, Heart, Hospitals, Medical Research, Mental Health, Single-Disease Health Associations
Religion: Religious Welfare
Science: Science Museums, Scientific Organizations
Social Services: Child Welfare, Community Centers, Community Service Organizations, Delinquency & Criminal Rehabilitation, Family Services, Food/Clothing Distribution, People with Disabilities, Recreation & Athletics, Refugee Assistance, Scouts, Senior Services, Substance Abuse, United Funds/United Ways, Volunteer Services, YMCA/YWCA/YMHA/YWHA, Youth Organizations

Application Procedures

Initial Contact: The foundation requests applications be made in writing.
Application Requirements: Send written request to Robert W. Gibbs, Jr., PO Box 4567, Houston, Texas, 77710-4567, telephone (713)207-5155, include the name of the organization, contact person, address, phone and fax numbers setting out specifically the amount and purpose of the request. A copy of the IRS tax status letter, Form 990, financial statements and list of board of directors should accompany the request.
Deadlines: None.

Restrictions

Does not support dinners or special events, fraternal organizations, individuals, political or lobbying groups, or religious organizations for sectarian purposes.

Additional Information

In 1999, Houston Industries, Inc. reported that information related to changes in its giving program was not yet available.

Corporate Officials

Robert W. Harvey: vice chairman, executive vice president, chief financial officer PRIM CORP EMPL vice chairman: Reliant Energy Inc.
Lee W. Hogan: vice chairman, executive vice president PRIM CORP EMPL vice chairman, executive vice president: Reliant Energy Inc.
R. Steve Letbetter: chairman, president, chief executive officer PRIM CORP EMPL chairman, president, chief executive officer: Reliant Energy Inc.
Stephen W. Naeve: vice chairman, executive vice president, chief financial officer PRIM CORP EMPL vice chairman, executive vice president, chief financial officer: Reliant Energy Inc.

Giving Program Officials

Robert Gibbs: PRIM CORP EMPL director corporate & community relations: Reliant Energy Inc.

Foundation Officials

Richard B. Dauphin: assistant secretary
Linda Geiger: assistant secretary
Hugh Rice Kelly: secretary
Marc Kilbride: treasurer
David M. McClanahan: director
William S. Waller: assistant treasurer

Grants Analysis

Total Grants: $4,489,922*
Number of Grants: 189
Average Grant: $24,000*
Highest Grant: $1,000,000
Typical Range: $2,000 to $50,000
*Note: Giving excludes scholarships and United Way. Average grant figure excludes highest grantss.

Recent Grants

Note: Grants derived from 2001 Form 990.

General
1,000,000	Texas A&M Foundation, College Station, TX

650,000	Houston Livestock Show and Rodeo, Houston, TX
250,000	American Red Cross, Houston, TX
225,000	United Way of the Texas Gulf Coast, Houston, TX
225,000	United Way of the Texas Gulf Coast, Houston, TX
225,000	United Way of the Texas Gulf Coast, Houston, TX
225,000	United Way of the Texas Gulf Coast, Houston, TX
186,666	McCombs School of Business, Austin, TX
183,333	Texas Heart Institute, Houston, TX
167,000	Baylor University - School of Engineering, Waco, TX

CENTRAL HUDSON GAS & ELECTRIC CORP.

Company Headquarters

Poughkeepsie, NY
Web: http://www.cenhud.com

Company Description

Employees: 1,260
SIC(s): 4900 Electric, Gas & Sanitary Services.

Nonmonetary Support

Type: Donated Equipment; Loaned Employees; Loaned Executives

Giving Contact

Joseph J. DeVirgilio, Jr., Vice President, Human Resources & Administration
284 South Ave.
Poughkeepsie, NY 12601
Phone: (845)452-2000
Fax: (845)486-5894
E-mail: jdvirgilio@cenhud.com

Description

Organization Type: Corporate Giving Program
Giving Locations: corporate operating locations.
Grant Types: Capital, Matching.

Typical Recipients

Arts & Humanities: Arts Associations & Councils, Arts Funds, Historic Preservation, Libraries, Performing Arts
Civic & Public Affairs: Economic Development, Housing, Philanthropic Organizations, Professional & Trade Associations
Education: Colleges & Universities, Science/Mathematics Education
Health: Hospices, Hospitals, Mental Health
Science: Science Exhibits & Fairs
Social Services: Child Welfare, Community Centers, Community Service Organizations, Domestic Violence, Food/Clothing Distribution, Homes, Senior Services, Shelters/Homelessness, United Funds/United Ways, Volunteer Services, Youth Organizations

Application Procedures

Initial Contact: Send brief letter of inquiry.
Application Requirements: Include a description of organization, amount requested, purpose of funds sought, recently audited financial statments, and proof of tax-exempt status.
Deadlines: None.

Restrictions

Does not support individuals, religious organizations for sectarian purposes, organizations outside the company's service territory, or political or lobbying groups.

Corporate Officials

Paul J. Ganci: president, chief operating officer B New York, NY 1938. ED Rensselaer Polytechnic Institute (1960); Union College (1969). PRIM CORP EMPL president, chief operating officer: Central Hudson Gas & Electric Corp. CORP AFFIL director: Fleet Bank Southeast New York; director: Mid Hudson Pattern Progress. NONPR AFFIL trustee: Mt Saint Marys College; vice chairman: Vassar Brothers Hospital.
Steven V. Lant: chief financial officer B Albany, NY 1957. ED State University of New York Albany (1979); State University of New York Albany (1984). PRIM CORP EMPL chief financial officer: Central Hudson Gas & Electric Corp.
John E. Mack, III: chairman, chief executive officer B Poughkeepsie, NY 1934. ED Siena College BS (1956); Siena College MBA (1966); Mount Saint Mary's College LHD (1994). PRIM CORP EMPL chairman, chief executive officer: Central Hudson Gas & Electric Corp. CORP AFFIL president: Empire State Electric Energy Research Corp.; director: New York Business Development Corp. NONPR AFFIL chairman executive committee: New York Power Pool; chairman: New York Saint Energy Association; director: Mid Hudson Medical Center; director: Edison Electric Institute; director: Marist College; director: Astor Home for Children; president: Boy Scouts America Hudson Valley Council; member: American Gas Association.

CENTRAL MAINE POWER CO.

Company Headquarters

83 Edison Dr.
Augusta, ME 04336
Web: http://www.cmpco.com

Company Description

Employees: 1,607 (1999)
SIC(s): 4931 Electric & Other Services Combined.
Parent Company: Energy East Corp., PO Box 12904, Albany, NY, United States

Operating Locations

Central Maine Power Co. (ME--West Buxton); Yankee Atomic Electric Co. (ME--West Buxton)
Note: Operates 14 district offices throughout Maine.

Nonmonetary Support

Range: $25,000 - $50,000
Type: Donated Equipment; Donated Products; In-kind Services
Note: Provides mentoring-engineering help with science program. Portland employees employees donate time in elementary schools.

Giving Contact

John H. Carroll, Community Relations Specialist
83 Edison Dr.
Augusta, ME 04336
Phone: (207)623-3521
Fax: (207)623-5908
Note: Mr. Carroll's extension is 2493.

Description

Organization Type: Corporate Giving Program
Giving Locations: ME: primarily central and southern Maine
Grant Types: Award, Capital, Challenge, Conference/Seminar, Emergency, Employee Matching Gifts, General Support, Matching, Multiyear/Continuing Support, Project, Research, Scholarship, Seed Money.
Note: Employee matching gift ratio: 1 to 1.

Financial Summary

Total Giving: $100,000 (2002 approx); $100,000 (2001 approx); $100,000 (2000 approx). Note: Contributes through corporate direct giving program only.
Giving Analysis: Giving for 2000 includes: nonmonetary support (approx $25,000) foundation (approx $75,000)

Typical Recipients

Arts & Humanities: Arts Associations & Councils, Arts Festivals, Arts Institutes, Community Arts, Dance, Ethnic & Folk Arts, Arts & Humanities-General, Historic Preservation, Libraries, Literary Arts, Museums/Galleries, Music, Performing Arts, Public Broadcasting, Theater, Visual Arts
Civic & Public Affairs: Civil Rights, Economic Development, Economic Policy, Employment/Job Training, Housing, Professional & Trade Associations, Public Policy, Rural Affairs, Safety, Urban & Community Affairs, Women's Affairs
Education: Arts/Humanities Education, Business Education, Colleges & Universities, Community & Junior Colleges, Continuing Education, Economic Education, Education Associations, Education Funds, Elementary Education (Private), Engineering/Technological Education, Faculty Development, Literacy, Minority Education, Preschool Education, Public Education (Precollege), Science/Mathematics Education, Social Sciences Education, Student Aid
Environment: Environment-General
Health: Emergency/Ambulance Services, Health-General, Geriatric Health, Health Organizations, Hospices, Hospitals, Medical Rehabilitation, Mental Health, Nutrition, Public Health, Single-Disease Health Associations
Science: Science Exhibits & Fairs, Scientific Centers & Institutes
Social Services: Child Welfare, Community Centers, Community Service Organizations, Counseling, Day Care, Delinquency & Criminal Rehabilitation, Domestic Violence, Emergency Relief, Family Planning, Family Services, Food/Clothing Distribution, People with Disabilities, Recreation & Athletics, Senior Services, Shelters/Homelessness, Social Services-General, Substance Abuse, United Funds/United Ways, Volunteer Services, Youth Organizations

Application Procedures

Initial Contact: Send a brief letter of inquiry.
Application Requirements: Include a description of organization, amount requested, purpose of funds sought, recently audited financial statement, and proof of tax-exempt status.
Deadlines: None.
Decision Notification: Proposals are reviewed monthly.

Restrictions

Company does not support individuals, religious organizations for sectarian purposes, political or lobbying groups, or organizations outside operating areas.

Additional Information

In December 1999, the company's future merge with Energy East was approved.

Corporate Officials

Sara J. Burns: president, director PRIM CORP EMPL president, director: Central Maine Power Co.
Curtis Call: treasurer

Grants Analysis

Disclosure Period: calendar year ending 2000
Total Grants: $100,000 (approx)
Typical Range: $250 to $5,000

CENTRAL NATIONAL BANK

Company Headquarters

8th & Washington
Junction City, KS 66441

Company Description

Employees: 150
SIC(s): 6000 Depository Institutions.

Central Charities Foundation

Giving Contact

Edward C. Rolfs, Chairman, President & Chief Executive Officer
PO Box 700
Junction City, KS 66441-0700
Phone: (785)238-4114
Fax: (785)238-6299

Description

EIN: 486143983
Organization Type: Corporate Foundation
Giving Locations: KS: including surrounding areas
Grant Types: General Support.

Financial Summary

Total Giving: $108,500 (2001); $104,595 (2000); $116,860 (1999). Note: 1996 Giving includes United Way ($7,512).
Giving Analysis: Giving for 2001 includes: foundation grants to United Way ($15,957); 2000: foundation grants to United Way ($13,723); 1999: foundation grants to United Way ($12,367); foundation ($104,493);
Assets: $1,576,239 (2001); $1,641,044 (2000); $1,623,615 (1999)
Gifts Received: $21,170 (2001); $66,293 (2000); $16,784 (1999). Note: In 1998, contributions were received from Genevieve M. Beerhalter Trust ($58,966), and miscellaneous donations of less than $5,000 each ($12,207).

Typical Recipients

Arts & Humanities: Arts Associations & Councils, Historic Preservation, Libraries, Literary Arts, Museums/Galleries, Opera, Theater
Civic & Public Affairs: Business/Free Enterprise, Economic Policy, Civic & Public Affairs-General, Safety
Education: Agricultural Education, Colleges & Universities, Economic Education, Private Education (Precollege), Secondary Education (Public)
Environment: Wildlife Protection
Health: Cancer, Children's Health/Hospitals, Clinics/Medical Centers, Emergency/Ambulance Services, Health-General, Geriatric Health, Hospices, Hospitals
Religion: Churches, Religious Welfare
Social Services: At-Risk Youth, Community Centers, Community Service Organizations, Crime Prevention, Emergency Relief, Recreation & Athletics, Scouts, Scouts, United Funds/United Ways, YMCA/YWCA/YMHA/YWHA

Additional Information

Publications: Application Form

Corporate Officials

Edward C. Rolfs: chairman, president, chief executive officer, director PRIM CORP EMPL chairman, president, chief executive officer, director: Central National Bank.

Foundation Officials

DeCourcy Eyre McIntosh: mem B Baltimore, MD 1942. ED Harvard University BA (1965). NONPR AFFIL director: Pittsburgh Parks & Playgrounds Fund; member: Walpole Society; executive director: Frick Art & History Center; trustee: Pittsburgh History & Landmarks Foundation; trustee: Art Services International; member: Century Association; member: American Association Museums. CLUB AFFIL Pittsburgh Golf Club.
Edward C. Rolfs: mem (see above)
Edward J. Rolfs: mem PRIM CORP EMPL chairman: Central National Bank.
James R. Waters: member
Robert K. Weary: mem
Bruce J. Woner: member

Grants Analysis

Disclosure Period: calendar year ending 2001
Total Grants: $92,543*
Number of Grants: 27
Average Grant: $3,428
Highest Grant: $11,000
Lowest Grant: $59
Typical Range: $1,000 to $5,000
*Note: Giving excludes United Way.

Recent Grants

Note: Grants derived from 2001 Form 990.

Library-Related
1,752	Frank Carlson Library

General
11,000	Junction City Family YMCA, Junction City, KS
10,250	Coronado Area Council, BSA, Salina, KS
10,000	Geary County Extension, Junction City, KS
10,000	Geary County Red Cross, ARC, Junction City, KS
10,000	Geary County Salvation Army, Junction City, KS
10,000	Junction City Good Samaritan Center, Junction City, KS
10,000	Kaw Valley Girl Scout, Topeka, KS
9,611	United Way Junction City/ Geary County, Junction City, KS
5,000	Art of the Ages
3,094	United Way of Greater Topeka, Topeka, KS

CENTRAL SOYA CO.

Company Headquarters

1946 W. Cook Rd
Fort Wayne, IN 46818
Web: http://www.centralsoya.com

Company Description

Employees: 1,200
SIC(s): 2075 Soybean Oil Mills, 5153 Grain & Field Beans.
Parent Company: Beghin-Say S.A., 14 Blvd. Du General Leclerc, Neuilly-sur-Seine, France
Parent Revenue: US$13,987,000,000 (2001)

Operating Locations

Cerestar U.S.A. (IN--Hammond); Intermarine U.S.A. (GA--Savannah)

Central Soya Foundation

Giving Contact

Theresa J. Tracey, President
National City Bank of Indiana
PO Box 110
Ft. Wayne, IN 46801
Phone: (219)461-6218
E-mail: carl.hausman@centralsoya.com

Description

Founded: 1954
EIN: 356020624
Organization Type: Corporate Foundation
Giving Locations: operating locations.
Grant Types: Capital, General Support, Matching, Operating Expenses, Research, Scholarship.

Donor Information

Founder: Central Soya Co., Inc.

Financial Summary

Total Giving: $175,682 (2000); $351,946 (1999); $46,110 (1998). Note: Contributes through foundation only.
Giving Analysis: Giving for 2000 includes: foundation grants to United Way ($50,166); 1999: foundation matching gifts ($2,735); foundation scholarships ($14,838); foundation grants to United Way ($100,746) foundation ($233,627)
Assets: $241,060 (2000); $197,450 (1999); $320,885 (1998)
Gifts Received: $200,000 (2000); $200,000 (1998); $200,000 (1997). Note: Contributions are received from Central Soya Company.

Typical Recipients

Arts & Humanities: Arts Appreciation, Arts Associations & Councils, Arts Funds, History & Archaeology, Museums/Galleries, Music, Opera, Public Broadcasting, Theater, Visual Arts
Civic & Public Affairs: African American Affairs, Chambers of Commerce, Clubs, Community Foundations, Economic Development, Municipalities/Towns, Parades/Festivals, Philanthropic Organizations, Professional & Trade Associations, Rural Affairs, Safety, Urban & Community Affairs, Women's Affairs, Zoos/Aquariums
Education: Agricultural Education, Business Education, Colleges & Universities, Education Associations, Education Funds, Education-General, Health & Physical Education, Minority Education, Public Education (Precollege), Religious Education, Science/Mathematics Education, Special Education, Student Aid
Environment: Environment-General
Health: Children's Health/Hospitals, Emergency/Ambulance Services, Health Funds, Health Organizations, Hospitals, Medical Rehabilitation, Prenatal Health Issues, Public Health, Single-Disease Health Associations
Religion: Churches, Ministries, Religious Organizations, Religious Welfare
Science: Scientific Centers & Institutes
Social Services: Child Welfare, Community Service Organizations, Day Care, Food/Clothing Distribution, People with Disabilities, Recreation & Athletics, Scouts, United Funds/United Ways, YMCA/YWCA/YMHA/YWHA, Youth Organizations

Application Procedures

Initial Contact: Send a letter that includes a description of organization and its goals, outline of proposed project, and proof of tax-exempt status.
Deadlines: None.

Restrictions

Does not support individuals.

Additional Information

Trust(s): Ft. Wayne National Bank

Corporate Officials

Carl L. Hausmann: chairman, president, chief executive officer B 1946. ED Boston College BS (1968). PRIM CORP EMPL chairman, president, chief executive officer: Central Soya Co. CORP AFFIL president, chief executive officer: Cerestar USA.

Grants Analysis

Disclosure Period: calendar year ending 2000
Total Grants: $125,516*
Number of Grants: 25
Average Grant: $5,021
Highest Grant: $16,035
Lowest Grant: $660
Typical Range: $1,000 to $10,000
*Note: Giving excludes United Way.

Recent Grants

Note: Grants derived from 1999 Form 990.

General

35,000	United Way Allen County, Inc., Ft. Wayne, IN
35,000	United Way Allen County, Inc., Ft. Wayne, IN
15,000	Fort Wayne Philharmonic, Ft. Wayne, IN
14,687	United Way Adams County, Monroe, IN
14,530	National Merit Scholarship Corp, Evanston, IL
14,500	Arts United, Ft. Wayne, IN
14,000	Arts United, Ft. Wayne, IN
13,620	United Way Adams County, Monroe, IN
12,000	Independent Colleges of Indiana, Indianapolis, IN
8,000	Embassy Theater Foundation, Inc., Ft. Wayne, IN -- Hotel/Stage Renovation

CENTRAL VERMONT PUBLIC SERVICE CORP.

Company Headquarters

Rutland, VT
Web: http://www.cvps.com

Company Description

Founded: 1929
Ticker: CV
Exchange: NYSE
Assets: US$521.7 million (2001)
Employees: 572 (2001)
SIC(s): 4911 Electric Services.

Operating Locations

Central Vermont Public Service Corp. (VT--Middleburg, Montpelier, Randolph, St. Albans, St. Johnsbury, Woodstock); Vermont Yankee Nuclear Power Corp. (VT--Woodstock)

Giving Contact

Andrea Bove, Exec. Asst.
77 Grove Street
Rutland, VT 05701
Phone: (802)747-5672
Fax: (802)747-2188
E-mail: above@cvps.com
Web: http://www.cvps.com

Description

Organization Type: Corporate Giving Program
Giving Locations: VT
Grant Types: Emergency, Endowment, General Support, Multiyear/Continuing Support.

Financial Summary

Total Giving: $127,000 (2003 approx); $200,000 (2002); $202,332 (1994)

Typical Recipients

Arts & Humanities: Community Arts, Libraries, Museums/Galleries, Music, Public Broadcasting
Civic & Public Affairs: Economic Development, Nonprofit Management
Education: Colleges & Universities
Environment: Environment-General
Health: Mental Health
Science: Science Exhibits & Fairs
Social Services: Community Service Organizations

Application Procedures

Initial Contact: Send brief letter of inquiry, including a description of organization, amount requested, and purpose of funds sought. Deadline for January 1 Fiscal year is August 15th.

Restrictions

Does not support individuals, religious organizations for sectarian purposes, political or lobbying groups, or organizations outside operating areas.

Corporate Officials

Frederic Howard Bertrand: chairman, chief executive officer B Montpelier, VT 1936. ED Norwich University BScE (1958); Georgetown University Law Center (1961-1963); College of William & Mary JD (1967); Carnegie Mellon University (1967-1968). PRIM CORP EMPL chairman: Central Vermont Public Service Corp. CORP AFFIL director: Union Mutual Fire Insurance Co.; director: New England Guaranty Insurance Co.; director: Chittenden Trust Co.; chairman, chief executive officer: National Life Insurance Co.; director: Central Vermont Public Services Corp. NONPR AFFIL director: Vermont Business Roundtable; member: Washington County Bar Association; member: Vermont Bar Association; member: Epsilon Tau Sigma; member: Theta Chi; director: Central Vermont Economic Development Corp.; member: American Council Life Insurance.
F. Ray Keyser, Jr.: chairman, director B Chelsea, VT 1927. ED Boston University Law School LLB (1952); Tufts University LLD (1961); Norwich University LLD (1962). PRIM CORP EMPL chairman, director: Central Vermont Public Service Corp. CORP AFFIL director: Vermont Yankee Nuclear Power Co.; director: Vermont Electric Power Corp.; director: Lakey Hitchcock Clinic; director: Union Mutual Fire Insurance Co.; director: Keystone Custodian Funds; director: ICI Mutual Insurance Co.; of counsel: Keyser Crowley Meub Zayden Kulig & Sullivan PC; director: Grand Trunk Corp. NONPR AFFIL member: Masons; member: Vermont Bar Association; member: American Legion; member: American Bar Association.
Robert Harris Young: president, chief executive officer B New York, NY 1947. ED Beloit College (1970); Stanford University (1975). PRIM CORP EMPL president, chief executive officer: Central Vermont Public Service Corp. CORP AFFIL president, chief executive officer, director: SmartEnergy Services; president, chief executive officer, director: Summersville Hydro Corp.; director: Rutland Regional Medical Center; president, chief executive officer, director: Gauley River Management Corp.; director: Green Mountain Bank; president, chief executive officer, director: East Barnet Hydroelectric; president, chief executive officer, director: Equinox Vermont Corp.; president, chief executive officer, director: CV Energy Resources; president, chief executive officer, director: CV Realty; president, chief executive officer, director: Catamount Williams Lake Ltd.; president, chief executive officer, director: Connecticut Valley Electric Co.; president, chief executive officer, director: Catamount Thetford Corp.; president, chief executive officer, director: Catamount Rumford; president, chief executive officer, director: Catamount Rupert Corp.; president, chief executive officer, director: Catamount Energy Corp.;

president, chief executive officer, director: Catamount Glenns Ferry Corp.; president, chief executive officer, director: Appomattox Vermont Corp.; director: Associated Industries Vermont.

Grants Analysis

Typical Range: $1,000 to $2,500

CERTAINTEED CORP.

Company Headquarters

750 E. Swedesford Rd.
Valley Forge, PA 19482
Web: http://www.certainteed.com

Company Description

Revenue: US$2.607 billion (2002)
Employees: 8,231 (2002)
SIC(s): 2421 Sawmills & Planing Mills--General, 2426 Hardwood Dimension & Flooring Mills, 3087 Custom Compound of Purchased Resins, 3271 Concrete Block & Brick.
Parent Company: Compagnie de Saint-Gobain, Les Miroirs, 18 Ave. d'Alsace, La Defense, Paris, France

Operating Locations

Bay Mills (Delaware) (DE--Wilmington); Bayex (NY--Albion); Bird Inc. (MA--Norwood); Bird Roofing Products (MA--Norwood); Cerbay Co. (TX--Wichita Falls); CertainTeed Corp. (CA--Chowchilla, Placentia; FL--Gainesville; GA--Social Circle; KS--Kansas City, McPherson; LA--Westlake; MN--Alberta Lea; PA--Mountain Top, Nesquehoning; SC--Spartanburg; TX--Waco); CertainTeed Foreign Sales Corp. (PA--Valley Forge); CertainTeed International (PA--Valley Forge); CertainTeed Ventures (PA--Valley Forge); CertainTeed Weaving Corp. (PA--Valley Forge); Diamond Film Divison (MA--Northborough); Ecophon CertainTeed (PA--Valley Forge); Insulate LLC (WA--Auburn); Lake Keowee Country Club, Inc. (PA--Valley Forge); Ludowici Celedon (OH--New Lexington); Ludowici Roof Tile (OH--New Lexington); Maxitile (CA--Carson); Perma Glas-Mesh (OH--Dover); Pro-Cut Products, Inc (TX--Dallas); Vetrotex CertainTeed Corp. (TX--Wichita Falls); Wolverine Technologies (IA--Grinnell; MI--Jackson); Wolverine Vinyl Siding (PA--Valley Forge)

Nonmonetary Support

Type: Cause-related Marketing & Promotion; Donated Equipment; Donated Products; In-kind Services; Loaned Employees; Workplace Solicitation
Note: Volunteer recognition award program is designed to acknowledge the volunteer activities of these groups for the benefit of their communities.

Saint-Gobain Corporation Foundation

Giving Contact

Dorothy Wackerman, Vice President
PO Box 860
Valley Forge, PA 19482-0101
Phone: (610)341-7000
Fax: (610)341-7777

Description

Founded: 1955
EIN: 236242991
Organization Type: Corporate Foundation
Former Name: CertainTeed Corp. Foundation (2002).
Formed by Merger of: CertainTeed and Norton Company Foundation merged to become Saint-Gobain Corporation Foundation (2003).
Giving Locations: principally near operating locations and to national organizations.

Grant Types: Employee Matching Gifts, General Support.

Donor Information

Founder: CertainTeed Products Corp.

Financial Summary

Total Giving: $532,380 (2001); $412,152 (2000); $500,000 (1999 approx). Note: Contributes through foundation only.

Giving Analysis: Giving for 2000 includes: foundation scholarships ($210); foundation grants to United Way ($23,000); foundation matching gifts ($114,883); foundation ($274,059); 1998: foundation grants to United Way ($24,450); foundation matching gifts ($126,795); 1996: foundation grants to United Way ($21,600) foundation matching gifts ($96,500)

Assets: $32,875 (2001); $160,397 (2000); $261,448 (1998)

Gifts Received: $426,300 (2001); $346,807 (2000); $465,702 (1998)

Typical Recipients

Arts & Humanities: Arts Associations & Councils, Arts Institutes, Ballet, Community Arts, Film & Video, Arts & Humanities-General, Historic Preservation, History & Archaeology, Libraries, Museums/Galleries, Music, Performing Arts, Public Broadcasting, Theater

Civic & Public Affairs: African American Affairs, Business/Free Enterprise, Clubs, Community Foundations, Economic Development, Economic Policy, Employment/Job Training, Ethnic Organizations, Civic & Public Affairs-General, Hispanic Affairs, Housing, Law & Justice, Legal Aid, Municipalities/Towns, Professional & Trade Associations, Public Policy, Safety, Urban & Community Affairs, Women's Affairs, Zoos/Aquariums

Education: Arts/Humanities Education, Business Education, Colleges & Universities, Community & Junior Colleges, Education Funds, Education Reform, Elementary Education (Private), Elementary Education (Public), Engineering/Technological Education, Education-General, International Exchange, International Studies, Legal Education, Literacy, Medical Education, Minority Education, Private Education (Precollege), Public Education (Precollege), Religious Education, Secondary Education (Private), Secondary Education (Public), Student Aid

Environment: Environment-General, Resource Conservation, Wildlife Protection

Health: Alzheimers Disease, Cancer, Children's Health/Hospitals, Clinics/Medical Centers, Emergency/Ambulance Services, Health Organizations, Heart, Hospices, Hospitals, Medical Research, Multiple Sclerosis, Prenatal Health Issues, Public Health, Single-Disease Health Associations

International: Foreign Arts Organizations, Foreign Educational Institutions, Health Care/Hospitals, International Development, International Organizations, International Relations, International Relief Efforts, Trade

Religion: Churches, Religion-General, Jewish Causes, Religious Organizations, Religious Welfare, Seminaries

Science: Science Museums

Social Services: At-Risk Youth, Big Brother/Big Sister, Child Abuse, Child Welfare, Community Centers, Community Service Organizations, Domestic Violence, Food/Clothing Distribution, Homes, People with Disabilities, Recreation & Athletics, Scouts, Shelters/Homelessness, Substance Abuse, United Funds/United Ways, Volunteer Services, YMCA/YWCA/YMHA/YWHA, Youth Organizations

Application Procedures

Initial Contact: Send a brief letter requesting application form, specifying whether request is for direct or in-kind/product support.

Application Requirements: Include proof of tax-exempt status, a description of organization, amount requested, purpose for which funds are sought, and a recently audited financial statement.

Deadlines: None.

Notes: Matching gifts are for the homeless, education, and charitable programs and require formal applications. Organizations must have IRS determination as a 501(c)(3) organization.

Restrictions

Foundation does not make grants to individuals, religious organizations for sectarian purposes, or organizations receiving more than 20% of support from United Way or government agencies.

Additional Information

As noted above, Caccini is president of Saint-Gobain NA and, therefore, oversees the company's U.S. holdings, which include CertainTeed Corp.

Corporate Officials

Dennis J. Baker: vice president, director, director PRIM CORP EMPL vice president, director: CertainTeed Corp.

Bruce H. Cowgill: president PRIM CORP EMPL president: CertainTeed Corp.

Bradford C. Mattson: executive vice president exterior building products B Duluth, MN 1952. ED University of Nebraska (1974); Stanford University (1976). PRIM CORP EMPL executive vice president exterior building products: CertainTeed Corp. CORP AFFIL executive vice president: Saint-Gobain Corp.; president: Vetrotex CertainTeed Corp.; chairman: Bird Inc.

Jean-Francois Phelizon: chairman, chief executive officer, director PRIM CORP EMPL chief executive officer, senior vice president: Compagnie de Saint-Gobain ADD CORP EMPL chairman, chief executive officer, director: CertainTeed Corp.

Michael J. Walsh: vice president B Portland, OR 1932. ED University of Portland BA (1954); Georgetown University JD (1959-1959). PRIM CORP EMPL vice president: CertainTeed Corp. NONPR AFFIL member: Oregon Bar Association; member: Portland Chamber of Commerce; member: National Association College & University Attorneys; chairman: Employees Compensation Appeals Board; member: Multnomah County Bar Association; member: American Trial Lawyers Association; member: DC Bar Association; member: American Judicature Society; member: American Arbitration Association. CLUB AFFIL Georgetown University Club.

Foundation Officials

Dennis J. Baker: director (see above)

David Boivin: director, vice president

James F. Harkins, Jr.: treasurer B 1953. ED Villanova University BA. PRIM CORP EMPL vice president, treasurer: CertainTeed Corp. CORP AFFIL treasurer: Saint-Gobain Corp.; treasurer: Vetrotex CertainTeed Corp.; treasurer: Norton Performance Plastics; treasurer: Carborundum Specialty Products; treasurer: Norton Co.; treasurer: Ball-Foster Glass Container Co. LLC.

James E. Hilyard: vice president, director B New Castle, PA 1941. ED Carnegie Mellon University BS (1963); Case Western Reserve University MBA (1970). CORP AFFIL vice chairman, president, director: Ludowici Roof Tile Inc.; president: Celadon; president: Bird Inc. NONPR AFFIL member: National Tile Roofing Manufacturer Association; member: Philadelphia Council on World Affairs; member: National Roofing Contractors Association; member: Asphalt Roofing Manufacturing Association; admissions counselor: Carnegie Mellon University; member: America Production Control Society; member: America AICE. CLUB AFFIL Chesapeake Bay Yacht Club Association; Castle Harbor Yacht Club.

Mark E. Mathisen: director, vice president

John R. Mesher: assistant secretary B 1952. ED Duquesne University; Indiana University of Pennsylvania BA. PRIM CORP EMPL vice president, secretary, deputy general counsel: CertainTeed Corp. CORP AFFIL officer: Saint-Gobain Corp.

Jean-Francois Phelizon: president, director (see above)

Mark J. Scott: director, vice president

Dorothy C. Wackerman: director, vice president, secretary

Grants Analysis

Disclosure Period: calendar year ending 2001

Total Grants: $256,155*

Number of Grants: 569 (approx)

Average Grant: $450

Highest Grant: $60,000

Lowest Grant: $100

Typical Range: $100 to $5,000

*Note: Giving excludes matching gifts, United Way, and scholarships.

Recent Grants

Note: Grants derived from 2001 Form 990.

General

60,000	Regional Performing Arts Center, Philadelphia, PA
28,000	Assumption of Mary Catholic Church, Wichita Falls, TX
22,500	Assumption of Mary Catholic Church, Wichita Falls, TX
10,500	United Way, Wichita Falls, TX
10,000	United Way Chester County, Exton, PA
6,000	Berlin-Milan Local Schools, Milan, OH
5,375	Make-A-Wish Foundation, Wichita, KS
5,375	United Way of Wyandotte County, Kansas City, MO
5,000	Baker Industries, Pauli, PA
5,000	Committee for Economic Development, New York, NY -- Strategy 21

CESSNA AIRCRAFT CO.

Company Headquarters

5211 E. Pawnee St.
Wichita, KS 67218
Web: http://www.cessna.com

Company Description

Employees: 6,900
SIC(s): 3721 Aircraft, 3728 Aircraft Parts & Equipment Nec.

Operating Locations

Cessna Aircraft Co. (OH--Vandalia)

Cessna Foundation, Inc.

Giving Contact

Marilyn Richwine, Secretary & Treasurer
Cessna Foundation
PO Box 7706
Wichita, KS 67277-7706
Phone: (316)517-7810
Fax: (316)517-7812

Description

Founded: 1952
EIN: 486108801
Organization Type: Corporate Foundation
Giving Locations: KS: Wichita including surrounding area principally near operating locations and to national organizations.
Grant Types: Capital, Emergency, Employee Matching Gifts, Multiyear/Continuing Support.
Note: Employee matching gift ratio: 2 to 1.

Donor Information

Founder: Cessna Aircraft Co.

Financial Summary

Total Giving: $1,744,180 (2001); $783,457 (2000); $1,610,959 (1999)

Giving Analysis: Giving for 2000 includes: foundation scholarships ($30,227); foundation matching gifts ($182,630); foundation grants to United Way ($256,150); foundation ($314,450); 1997: foundation scholarships ($71,300); foundation matching gifts ($120,077); foundation grants to United Way ($277,350) foundation ($665,634)

Assets: $15,561,756 (2001); $15,690,434 (2000); $14,122,860 (1999)

Gifts Received: $1,500,000 (2001); $2,250,000 (2000); $750,000 (1999). Note: Contributions are received from Cessna Aircraft Co.

Typical Recipients

Arts & Humanities: Arts Associations & Councils, Arts Centers, Arts Outreach, Libraries, Museums/Galleries, Music, Performing Arts, Theater

Civic & Public Affairs: African American Affairs, Clubs, Community Foundations, Employment/Job Training, Civic & Public Affairs-General, Housing, Professional & Trade Associations, Safety, Urban & Community Affairs, Zoos/Aquariums

Education: Agricultural Education, Business Education, Colleges & Universities, Community & Junior Colleges, Economic Education, Education Funds, Education Reform, Engineering/Technological Education, Medical Education, Private Education (Precollege), Public Education (Precollege), Science/Mathematics Education, Special Education, Student Aid, Vocational & Technical Education

Health: AIDS/HIV, Cancer, Children's Health/Hospitals, Clinics/Medical Centers, Emergency/Ambulance Services, Health Funds, Health Organizations, Heart, Hospices, Hospitals, Multiple Sclerosis, Preventive Medicine/Wellness Organizations, Single-Disease Health Associations

International: Missionary/Religious Activities

Religion: Churches, Ministries, Missionary Activities (Domestic), Religious Organizations, Religious Welfare, Social/Policy Issues

Science: Science Museums, Scientific Centers & Institutes

Social Services: Big Brother/Big Sister, Child Welfare, Community Centers, Community Service Organizations, Family Services, Food/Clothing Distribution, People with Disabilities, Recreation & Athletics, Scouts, Special Olympics, Substance Abuse, United Funds/United Ways, YMCA/YWCA/YMHA/YWHA, Youth Organizations

Application Procedures

Initial Contact: Send a brief letter or proposal.

Application Requirements: Include a description of organization, amount requested, purpose of funds sought, recently audited financial statement, and proof of tax-exempt status.

Deadlines: None for grants; board meets quarterly. Scholarship applications are due May 15.

Corporate Officials

Charles B. Johnson: president vice president human resources B 1949. ED Simpson College. PRIM CORP EMPL executive vice president operation: Cessna Aircraft Co.

John E. Moore: executive vice president human resources B Charleston, WV 1943. ED Washington & Lee University BS (1965); University of Kentucky JD (1968). PRIM CORP EMPL executive vice president human resources: Cessna Aircraft Co.

Foundation Officials

Jordan L. Haines: trustee CORP AFFIL director: KN Energy Inc.; director: Q'west Communication International Inc.

Charles B. Johnson: trustee (see above)

John E. Moore: vice president (see above)

Marilyn Richwine: secretary, treasurer

Grants Analysis

Disclosure Period: calendar year ending 2001

Total Grants: $636,350*

Number of Grants: 44

Average Grant: $14,462

Highest Grant: $100,000

Lowest Grant: $500

Typical Range: $500 to $15,000

*Note: Grants analysis provided by foundation. Giving excludes matching gifts, scholarships, and United Way.

Recent Grants

Note: Grants derived from 2000 Form 990.

General

81,250	United Way of the Plains, Wichita, KS
81,250	United Way Plains, Wichita, KS
81,250	United Way of the Plains, Wichita, KS
50,000	Kansas State University Foundation, Manhattan, KS
50,000	Kansas University Endowment Association, Lawrence, KS
50,000	Wichita State University, Wichita, KS
26,000	Wichita Symphony Society, Wichita, KS
20,000	Center for Health and Wellness, Wichita, KS
20,000	Newman University, Wichita, KS
20,000	Rainbows United, Wichita, KS

CH FOUNDATION

Giving Contact

Nelda Thompson, Secretary & Trustee
PO Box 16458
Lubbock, TX 79490
Phone: (806)799-3250

Description

Founded: 1976

EIN: 751534816

Organization Type: Private Foundation

Giving Locations: TX: South Plains including surrounding area

Grant Types: Capital, General Support, Matching, Research, Scholarship.

Donor Information

Founder: the late Christine DeVitt

Financial Summary

Total Giving: $3,816,160 (2000); $3,000,592 (1999); $2,290,097 (1998)

Giving Analysis: Giving for 2000 includes: foundation grants to United Way ($60,000) 1999: foundation grants to United Way ($55,000)

Assets: $90,511,407 (2000); $91,396,968 (1999); $72,184,318 (1998)

Typical Recipients

Arts & Humanities: Ballet, Ethnic & Folk Arts, Historic Preservation, History & Archaeology, Libraries, Literary Arts, Museums/Galleries, Music, Public Broadcasting, Theater

Civic & Public Affairs: Community Foundations, Civic & Public Affairs-General, Hispanic Affairs, Urban & Community Affairs

Education: Agricultural Education, Arts/Humanities Education, Colleges & Universities, Education Reform, Elementary Education (Private), Elementary Education (Public), Engineering/Technological Education, Faculty Development, Literacy, Medical Education, Preschool Education, Private Education (Precollege), Public Education (Precollege), Science/Mathematics Education, Secondary Education (Public), Student Aid

Environment: Environment-General

Health: Alzheimers Disease, Cancer, Children's Health/Hospitals, Eyes/Blindness, Hospices, Hospitals, Medical Research

Science: Science Museums, Scientific Centers & Institutes, Scientific Organizations

Social Services: At-Risk Youth, Child Welfare, Community Centers, Family Services, Food/Clothing Distribution, People with Disabilities, Scouts, Senior Services, United Funds/United Ways, Volunteer Services, YMCA/YWCA/YMHA/YWHA, Youth Organizations

Application Procedures

Initial Contact: Send a brief letter of inquiry and a full proposal.

Application Requirements: Include background of the organization, a description of the project and its objectives and goals, purpose of funds sought, a detailed budget, other sources of funding, a specific amount requested, proof of tax-exempt status, recently audited financial statement, a statement of approval of the request signed by the chief administrator and the chairman of the board and the name of the primary contact person, and the plan for sustaining the project after grant funds expire.

Deadlines: May 1.

Foundation Officials

Helen DeVitt Jones: hon chairman, trustee

Don Graf: president, trustee

Kevin McMahon: trustee

Kay Sanford: trustee

Nelda Thompson: secretary, trustee

Louise Wilson Arnold: treasurer, trustee

Grants Analysis

Disclosure Period: calendar year ending 2000

Total Grants: $3,756,160*

Number of Grants: 67

Average Grant: $37,972*

Highest Grant: $1,250,000

Typical Range: $10,000 to $50,000

*Note: Average grant excludes highest grant. Giving excludes United Way.

Recent Grants

Note: Grants derived from 1999 Form 990.

Library-Related

45,000	Texas Tech University, Lubbock, TX -- for library
31,500	Texas Tech Museum, Lubbock, TX -- for Southwest Collection Library

General

1,250,000	Texas Tech University, Lubbock, TX -- for the museum auditorium
100,000	American Wind Power Center, Lubbock, TX
100,000	Joe Arrington Cancer Research and Treatment Center, Lubbock, TX
75,000	YWCA, Lubbock, TX -- for capital campaign
67,000	Bean Elementary School, Lubbock, TX -- for CORE curriculum
60,000	Early Learning Center, Lubbock, TX
57,000	Texas Tech University Museum, Lubbock, TX
55,000	United Way Lubbock, Lubbock, TX
50,000	Lubbock Area Foundation, Texas Aviation, Lubbock, TX
49,960	Volunteer Center, Lubbock, TX

DOROTHY JORDAN CHADWICK FUND

Giving Contact

c/o US Trust Co. of NY
114 West 47th Street
New York, NY 10036
Phone: (212)852-1000

Description

Founded: 1957
EIN: 136069950
Organization Type: Private Foundation
Giving Locations: DC: Washington; NY: New York
Grant Types: General Support.

Donor Information

Founder: the late Dorothy J. Chadwick, Dorothy R. Kidder

Financial Summary

Total Giving: $1,443,600 (fiscal year ending May 31, 2001); $953,825 (fiscal 1999); $590,900 (fiscal 1997)
Assets: $27,077,858 (fiscal 2001); $27,427,365 (fiscal 1999); $19,673,118 (fiscal 1997)
Gifts Received: $3,046,464 (fiscal 1996)

Typical Recipients

Arts & Humanities: Arts Associations & Councils, Arts Centers, Arts Outreach, Arts & Humanities-General, Libraries, Literary Arts, Museums/Galleries, Music, Performing Arts, Public Broadcasting, Theater
Civic & Public Affairs: Botanical Gardens/Parks, Community Foundations, Civic & Public Affairs-General, Municipalities/Towns, Urban & Community Affairs, Zoos/Aquariums
Education: Arts/Humanities Education, Colleges & Universities, Education Reform, Environmental Education, Education-General, Private Education (Precollege), Science/Mathematics Education, Student Aid
Environment: Environment-General, Resource Conservation, Wildlife Protection
Health: Alzheimers Disease, Clinics/Medical Centers
International: International Environmental Issues, International Peace & Security Issues
Religion: Churches, Religion-General
Social Services: At-Risk Youth, Camps, Child Welfare, Food/Clothing Distribution, Senior Services, Youth Organizations

Application Procedures

Initial Contact: Send a brief letter of inquiry.
Application Requirements: Describe program or project.
Deadlines: None.

Additional Information

Trust(s): US Trust Co NY

Foundation Officials

Berkley D. Johnson, Jr.: trustee

Grants Analysis

Disclosure Period: fiscal year ending May 31, 2001
Total Grants: $1,443,600
Number of Grants: 43
Average Grant: $31,381*
Highest Grant: $125,600
Typical Range: $10,000 to $50,000
*Note: Average grant figure excludes highest grant.

Recent Grants

Note: Grants derived from 2000 Form 990.

General

125,600	Proctor Academy, Andover, NH -- operational
99,521	Friends of the Natural Arboretum -- operational
90,000	Warner Christian Academy -- religious
80,000	African Wildlife Foundation, Washington, DC -- operational
70,000	African Wildlife Foundation, Washington, DC -- operational
50,000	Unity Health Care, Washington, DC -- operational
41,079	Camp Dudley YMCA, Westport, NY -- operational
40,000	Washington College, Chestertown, MD -- educational
38,600	Proctor Academy, Andover, NH -- operational
38,600	Voyage of The Spray, Inc, Salem, MA -- operational

CHAMBERLAIN FOUNDATION

Giving Contact

Calvin M. Chamberlain, President, Director
37000 N. Woodward Ave., Suite 101
Bloomfield Hills, MI 48304
Phone: (248)540-7200

Description

Founded: 1989
EIN: 382837915
Organization Type: Private Foundation
Grant Types: Department, General Support.

Financial Summary

Total Giving: $18,975 (fiscal year ending May 31, 2001); $17,900 (fiscal 2000); $20,300 (fiscal 1999)
Giving Analysis: Giving for fiscal 2000 includes: foundation scholarships ($2,000)
Assets: $155,878 (fiscal 2001); $203,703 (fiscal 2000); $226,441 (fiscal 1999)
Gifts Received: $1,500 (fiscal 1996). Note: In fiscal 1996, contributions were received from Calvin M. Chamberlain.

Typical Recipients

Arts & Humanities: Arts Outreach, Libraries
Civic & Public Affairs: Civic & Public Affairs-General, Hispanic Affairs, Municipalities/Towns, Public Policy, Safety, Urban & Community Affairs
Education: Colleges & Universities, Education Funds, International Exchange, Medical Education, Private Education (Precollege), Secondary Education (Private), Student Aid
Environment: Resource Conservation
Health: Alzheimers Disease, Cancer, Children's Health/Hospitals, Clinics/Medical Centers, Diabetes, Hospices, Medical Research, Multiple Sclerosis, Prenatal Health Issues, Public Health, Single-Disease Health Associations
International: Health Care/Hospitals, International Relief Efforts
Religion: Churches, Religious Welfare
Social Services: At-Risk Youth, Child Welfare, Community Service Organizations, Community Service Organizations, People with Disabilities, Recreation & Athletics, Special Olympics, United Funds/United Ways, Youth Organizations

Application Procedures

Initial Contact: Send a brief letter of inquiry.
Application Requirements: Include a description of organization and purpose of funds sought.
Deadlines: None.

Foundation Officials

Calvin M. Chamberlain: director

Grants Analysis

Disclosure Period: fiscal year ending May 31, 2001
Total Grants: $18,975
Number of Grants: 16
Average Grant: $1,186
Highest Grant: $5,000
Lowest Grant: $100
Typical Range: $200 to $2,000

Recent Grants

Note: Grants derived from 2000 Form 990.

Library-Related

250	Crooked Tree District Library, Walloon Lake, MI

General

3,700	Crossroads for Youth, Oxford, MI
2,500	Spanish Language Institute, Miami, FL
2,000	Community Living Centers, Farmington, MI
2,000	Rotary Club of Petoskey, Petoskey, MI -- Strive Scholarship
1,500	First Presbyterian Church, Royal Oak, MI
1,500	North Central Michigan College, Petoskey, MI
1,500	University of Michigan, Ann Arbor, MI
750	Salvation Army, Pontiac, MI
300	Karmanos Cancer Institute, Detroit, MI
300	Michigan Special Olympics, Mt. Pleasant, MI

CHAMIZA FOUNDATION

Giving Contact

Sandra Edelman, Executive Director
1301 Luisa St.
Santa Fe, NM 87505
Phone: (505)986-5044

Description

Founded: 1989
EIN: 850373197
Organization Type: Private Foundation
Giving Locations: NM
Grant Types: Project.

Donor Information

Founder: Established in 1989 by Gifford Phillips.

Financial Summary

Total Giving: $162,070 (2000); $121,742 (1999); $93,698 (1998)
Assets: $2,764,569 (2000); $2,791,118 (1999); $2,811,405 (1998)
Gifts Received: $100 (2000); $55,000 (1999); $87,866 (1998). Note: In 1999, contributions were received from Gifford Phillips.

Typical Recipients

Arts & Humanities: Arts Associations & Councils, Arts Centers, Community Arts, Ethnic & Folk Arts, Arts & Humanities-General, Historic Preservation, History & Archaeology, Libraries, Museums/Galleries, Music
Civic & Public Affairs: Community Foundations, Civic & Public Affairs-General, Native American Affairs, Women's Affairs
Education: Arts/Humanities Education, Education-General, Literacy, Minority Education, Private Education (Precollege), Public Education (Precollege), Social Sciences Education
Environment: Environment-General, Resource Conservation
Health: Preventive Medicine/Wellness Organizations
Social Services: Child Welfare, Family Services

Application Procedures

Initial Contact: Submit applications in letter format.
Application Requirements: Include description of the project, amount requested, personnel to implement the project, expected impact on the Pueblo Indian community.
Deadlines: January 20, April 15, August 15.

Restrictions

Grants are made only for cultural preservation and education projects among the Pueblo Indian population of NM.

Additional Information

Trust(s): Charles Schwab & Co.

Foundation Officials

Jonathan Batkin: director
Agnes M. Dill: director
Sandra A. Edelman: executive director
George H. Ewing: director
Mrs. Paul C. Frank: vice president, director
Julia Herrera: director
Robert Montoya: treasurer
Gifford Phillips: president, director
James L. Phillips: director
Joann K. Phillips: secretary, assistant treasurer, director
Diane Reyna: director
Joe Sando: director

Grants Analysis

Disclosure Period: calendar year ending 2000
Total Grants: $162,070
Number of Grants: 23
Average Grant: $5,170*
Highest Grant: $48,320
Lowest Grant: $500
Typical Range: $1,000 to $10,000
*Note: Average grant figure excludes highest grant.

Recent Grants

Note: Grants derived from 1999 Form 990.

General

17,919	Lina, Pueblo, NM -- language training program
7,883	Shiwi Wan Museum, Zuni Pueblo, NM -- youth cultural education program
7,425	Pueblo of Jemez, Jemez Pueblo, NM -- traditional arts program
6,700	Pueblo of Tesuque, Tesuque, NM -- youth cultural education program
6,000	Pueblo of Nambe, Santa Fe, NM -- youth cultural education program
5,177	Tesuque Pueblo, Tesuque, NM -- youth cultural education program
5,000	Cornerstones, Santa Fe, NM -- Gasper Internship
5,000	Santo Domingo Pueblo, Santo Domingo, NM -- youth cultural education program
4,000	Pueblo of Zuni -- ceremonial life preservation program
3,900	Santa Fe Forum, Santa Fe, NM -- healing spaces grant

CHAMPLIN FOUNDATION

Giving Contact

Keith Lang, Executive Director
300 Centerville Road, Suite 300S
Warwick, RI 02886-0226
Phone: (401)736-0370
Fax: (401)736-7248
E-mail: champlinfdns@worldnet.att.net
Web: http://www.fndcenter.org/grantmaker/champlin

Description

Founded: 1932
EIN: 516010168
Organization Type: General Purpose Foundation
Giving Locations: RI: Providence
Grant Types: Capital.
Note: Capital grants generally take the form of direct grants for the purchase of equipment or real property, the reduction of mortgages, and construction or renovation.

Donor Information

Founder: The Champlin Foundation Trust was established in 1932 in Delaware by George S. Champlin (d. 1980), Hope C. Neaves (d. 1987), and Florence C. Hamilton (d. 1970). They founded the Second Champlin Foundation Trust in 1947. In 1975, George S. Champlin founded the Third Champlin Foundation.

Financial Summary

Total Giving: $18,700,000 (2003 approx); $18,700,000 (2002 approx); $20,742,979 (2001)
Assets: $400,000,000 (2003 approx); $400,000,000 (2002 approx); $432,332,498 (2001)

Typical Recipients

Arts & Humanities: Arts Centers, Historic Preservation, History & Archaeology, Libraries, Museums/Galleries, Music, Performing Arts
Civic & Public Affairs: African American Affairs, Botanical Gardens/Parks, Economic Development, Employment/Job Training, Civic & Public Affairs-General, Hispanic Affairs, Legal Aid, Municipalities/Towns, Nonprofit Management, Philanthropic Organizations, Safety, Urban & Community Affairs, Zoos/Aquariums
Education: Agricultural Education, Arts/Humanities Education, Business Education, Colleges & Universities, Community & Junior Colleges, Education-General, International Studies, Private Education (Precollege), Public Education (Precollege), Science/Mathematics Education, Secondary Education (Private), Secondary Education (Public), Special Education, Vocational & Technical Education
Environment: Environment-General, Resource Conservation
Health: Clinics/Medical Centers, Emergency/Ambulance Services, Health-General, Geriatric Health, Health Funds, Health Organizations, Heart, Hospices, Hospitals, Long-Term Care, Medical Rehabilitation, Nursing Services, Prenatal Health Issues, Public Health, Transplant Networks/Donor Banks
Religion: Churches, Religion-General, Jewish Causes, Religious Welfare
Science: Science Museums
Social Services: Animal Protection, Camps, Child Welfare, Community Centers, Community Service Organizations, Crime Prevention, Family Planning, Family Services, Food/Clothing Distribution, Homes, People with Disabilities, Recreation & Athletics, Recreation & Athletics, Refugee Assistance, Scouts, Senior Services, Shelters/Homelessness, Social Services-General, United Funds/United Ways, Volunteer Services, YMCA/YWCA/YMHA/YWHA, Youth Organizations

Application Procedures

Initial Contact: Applicants should send a one-page letter.
Application Requirements: The letter should include a description of the project and its intended purpose, costs, amount requested, an accounting of other fund-raising efforts, and a listing of other sources of available funds. An applicant should also submit copies of its IRS 501(c)(3) exemption and 509(a) letters.
Deadlines: Requests should be submitted between March 1 and June 30. The distribution committees meet annually in November to accept or reject grant recommendations. Funds are distributed in December. The foundations report that funds are seldom available for applications filed at the last minute.
Review Process: After acknowledging a request, the foundations may request additional information concerning fund-raising efforts. The foundations like to see fund-raising plans with some favorable results. If fund-raising is not totally successful, the foundations are interested in what parts of the project will proceed and the costs. Mortgage status and evidence of ability to pay for increased operating costs may also be requested.

Site visits by members of the investigating committee are scheduled between May 1 and September 30. Committee members prefer to meet with the chief of operations, selected staff members, and the treasurer in a very informal manner. Prepared speeches and slide shows should be omitted.

Restrictions

Grants are not awarded on a continuing basis, but applicants may qualify annually. Grants are not made for program or operating expenses. No grants are awarded to individuals. Public school requests are considered only if they are solicited by the foundation.

Additional Information

Publications: Annual Report; Guidelines
Trust(s): PNC Bank-Delaware

Foundation Officials

John Gorham: chairman distribution comm, mem investigating comm
Louis R. Hampton: mem distribution comm B Hartford, CT 1920. ED University of Rhode Island BSME (1942). PRIM CORP EMPL chairman executive committee, director: Providence Energy Corp. CORP AFFIL director: Providence Gas Co.
Earl W. Harrington, Jr.: mem distribution comm
Robert W. Kenyon: mem distribution comm
David A. King: executive director, mem distribution & investigating comm
Norma B. LaFreniere: member distribution comm
Keith H. Lang: member dist committee, member investigating committee
John W. Linnell: mem distribution comm
Carol B. Wilmot: secretary

Grants Analysis

Disclosure Period: calendar year ending 2000
Total Grants: $23,726,939*
Number of Grants: 221
Average Grant: $89,667
Highest Grant: $4,000,000
Lowest Grant: $429
Typical Range: $15,000 to $25,000 and $100,000 to $500,000
*Note: Grants analysis provided by foundation.

Recent Grants

Note: Grants derived from 2001 Form 990.

General

1,045,000	YMCA Greater Providence, Providence, RI -- North Kingston building
350,000	Rhode Island Hospital, Providence, RI -- purchase new radiographic and fluoroscopic system
300,000	Providence Community Health Foundation, Providence, RI -- building
267,717	Rhode Island College, Providence, RI -- renovations
250,000	Children's Friend and Service, Providence, RI -- construction of Family Support Center
250,000	Saint Elizabeth Community, Providence, RI -- capital campaign
200,000	Burrillville Glocester Youth Soccer, Pascoag, RI -- completion of soccer field construction
200,000	Dorcas Place, Providence, RI -- purchase and renovate building
148,200	Independence Square Foundation, Pawtucket, RI -- heating upgrade
117,037	Corliss Institute, Inc., Warren, RI -- rehabilitation of building

CHAPIN FOUNDATION OF MYRTLE BEACH, SOUTH CAROLINA

Giving Contact

Harold D. Clardy, Chairman Emeritus
PO Box 2568
Myrtle Beach, SC 29577
Phone: (803)255-7411

Description

Founded: 1943
EIN: 566039453
Organization Type: Private Foundation
Grant Types: Operating Expenses.

Donor Information

Founder: S. B. Chapin

Financial Summary

Total Giving: $492,400 (fiscal year ending July 31, 2001); $511,237 (fiscal 2000); $886,626 (fiscal 1998)
Assets: $26,414,566 (fiscal 2001); $23,532,284 (fiscal 2000); $18,661,131 (fiscal 1998)

Typical Recipients

Arts & Humanities: Libraries
Education: Elementary Education (Public), Private Education (Precollege)
Religion: Churches, Dioceses, Jewish Causes, Ministries, Religious Organizations, Religious Welfare, Synagogues/Temples
Social Services: Community Service Organizations, YMCA/YWCA/YMHA/YWHA, Youth Organizations

Application Procedures

Initial Contact: Send a brief letter of inquiry.
Application Requirements: Include proof of tax-exempt status and statement of purpose.
Deadlines: None.

Restrictions

Generally grants are restricted to Myrtle Beach, SC, area.

Foundation Officials

Harold D. Clardy: chairman
Claude M. Epps, Jr.: secretary
Ruth T. Gore: director
Harold Hartshorne, Jr.: director

Grants Analysis

Disclosure Period: fiscal year ending July 31, 2001
Total Grants: $492,400
Number of Grants: 14
Average Grant: $30,138*
Highest Grant: $100,600
Lowest Grant: $12,000
Typical Range: $20,000 to $50,000
***Note:** Average grant figure excludes highest grant.

Recent Grants

Note: Grants derived from 2000 Form 990.

Library-Related

135,600	Chapin Memorial Library, Myrtle Beach, SC
6,000	St. Andrews School Library, Myrtle Beach, SC

General

59,000	First Presbyterian Church, Myrtle Beach, SC
45,000	First United Methodist Church, Myrtle Beach, SC
37,500	Grand Stand Family YMCA, Myrtle Beach, SC
30,000	St. Andrews Catholic Church, Myrtle Beach, SC
25,000	Ocean View Baptist Church, Myrtle Beach, SC
25,000	Socastee Pentecostal Holiness Church, Myrtle Beach, SC
16,000	Agape Christian Fellowship, Myrtle Beach, SC
15,000	Light Sound of Praise Church, The, Myrtle Beach, SC
15,000	Miracle Tabernacle of Prayer, Myrtle Beach, SC
14,937	First Church of God, Myrtle Beach, SC

HOWARD AND BESS CHAPMAN CHARITABLE CORP.

Giving Contact

Peter M. Dunn, Secretary & General Counsel
Care of Alliance Bank, Trust Dept.
160 Main Street
Oneida, NY 13421-1675
Phone: (315)363-1409

Description

Founded: 1991
EIN: 161373396
Organization Type: Private Foundation
Giving Locations: NY: Oneida including surrounding area
Grant Types: Capital, General Support.

Donor Information

Founder: Established in 1991 from the estate of Howard Chapman.

Financial Summary

Total Giving: $187,552 (fiscal year ending October 31, 2001); $179,999 (fiscal 2000); $183,075 (fiscal 1999)
Giving Analysis: Giving for fiscal 2001 includes: foundation grants to United Way ($2,000).
Assets: $3,419,453 (fiscal 2001); $3,684,815 (fiscal 2000); $3,765,854 (fiscal 1999)
Gifts Received: In fiscal 1991, contributions were received from the estate of Howard Chapman.

Typical Recipients

Arts & Humanities: Arts Associations & Councils, Arts Centers, Arts & Humanities-General, History & Archaeology, Libraries
Civic & Public Affairs: Clubs, Civic & Public Affairs-General, Philanthropic Organizations, Urban & Community Affairs
Education: Colleges & Universities, Education Funds, Education-General, Literacy, School Volunteerism, Student Aid
Health: Emergency/Ambulance Services, Health Organizations, Hospitals
Religion: Churches, Religious Welfare
Social Services: Camps, Child Welfare, Community Centers, Community Service Organizations, Food/Clothing Distribution, People with Disabilities, Recreation & Athletics, Senior Services, Social Services-General, United Funds/United Ways, YMCA/YWCA/YMHA/YWHA, Youth Organizations

Application Procedures

Initial Contact: Send a brief letter of inquiry and a full proposal.
Application Requirements: Include a description of organization, amount requested, purpose of funds sought, recently audited financial statement, and proof of tax-exempt status.
Deadlines: None.

Restrictions

Does not support individuals, religious organizations for sectarian purposes, political or lobbying groups, or organizations outside operating areas.

Foundation Officials

Peter M. Dunn, Esq.: secretary, general counsel
Robert H. Fearon, Jr.: vice president
John G. Haskell: president
Dr. Steven Schneeweiss: treasurer
Rowland Stevens: trustee

Grants Analysis

Disclosure Period: fiscal year ending October 31, 2001
Total Grants: $185,552*
Number of Grants: 17
Average Grant: $4,910*
Highest Grant: $107,000
Lowest Grant: $1,000
Typical Range: $1,000 to $10,000
***Note:** Giving excludes United Way. Average grant excludes highest grant.

Recent Grants

Note: Grants derived from 2000 Form 990.

Library-Related

12,000	Hamilton Public Library, Hamilton, NY

General

44,000	Madison County ARC, Oneida, NY -- for building fund
44,000	Oneida Health Care Facility, Oneida, NY
5,000	Community Memorial Hospital, Hamilton, NY
3,000	Orchard Hill Club, Oneida, NY
2,500	Oneida Area Arts, Oneida, NY
2,000	Community Action, Morrisville, NY
2,000	Madison Oneida Red Cross, Oneida, NY
2,000	Salvation Army, Oneida, NY
2,000	Tri-Valley YMCA, Oneida, NY
2,000	United Way of Oneida, Oneida, NY

H. A. AND MARY K. CHAPMAN CHARITABLE TRUST

Giving Contact

Donne Pitman, Trustee
One Warren Place, Suite 1816
6100 South Yale Avenue
Tulsa, OK 74136
Phone: (918)496-7882
Fax: (918)496-7887

Alternate Contact

J. Jerry Dickman, Trustee

Description

Founded: 1976
EIN: 736177739
Organization Type: General Purpose Foundation
Giving Locations: OK: Tulsa
Grant Types: Award, Capital, Conference/Seminar, Emergency, General Support, Matching, Multiyear/Continuing Support.

Donor Information

Founder: The H. A. and Mary K. Chapman Charitable Trust was established in 1976 by the late H. A. Chapman.

Financial Summary

Total Giving: $3,880,000 (2001 approx); $3,644,000 (2000); $3,129,475 (1999)
Giving Analysis: Giving for 1999 includes: foundation grants to United Way ($6,000) 1997: foundation grants to United Way ($50,000)
Assets: $75,000,000 (2001 approx); $82,236,870 (1999); $73,627,473 (1998)

Typical Recipients

Arts & Humanities: Arts Associations & Councils, Arts Centers, Ballet, Dance, History & Archaeology, Libraries, Literary Arts, Museums/Galleries, Music, Opera, Performing Arts
Civic & Public Affairs: Botanical Gardens/Parks, Business/Free Enterprise, Clubs, Civic & Public Affairs-General, Law & Justice, Municipalities/Towns, Nonprofit Management, Philanthropic Organizations, Urban & Community Affairs, Zoos/Aquariums
Education: Business Education, Colleges & Universities, Continuing Education, Education Associations, Education Funds, Education Reform, Education-General, International Studies, Legal Education, Literacy, Medical Education, Preschool Education, Private Education (Precollege), Private Education (Precollege), Public Education (Precollege), Religious Education, Science/Mathematics Education, Secondary Education (Private), Student Aid
Environment: Research, Resource Conservation, Wildlife Protection
Health: Cancer, Children's Health/Hospitals, Clinics/Medical Centers, Health-General, Geriatric Health, Health Organizations, Hospices, Hospitals, Medical Research, Mental Health, Nursing Services, Prenatal Health Issues, Public Health, Research/Studies Institutes, Respiratory, Single-Disease Health Associations, Speech & Hearing
Religion: Churches, Religion-General, Ministries, Religious Organizations, Religious Welfare, Seminaries
Science: Science Museums
Social Services: Animal Protection, At-Risk Youth, Camps, Child Abuse, Child Welfare, Community Service Organizations, Day Care, Domestic Violence, Family Services, Food/Clothing Distribution, Homes, People with Disabilities, Scouts, Senior Services, Shelters/Homelessness, Special Olympics, Substance Abuse, United Funds/United Ways, Volunteer Services, YMCA/YWCA/YMHA/YWHA, Youth Organizations

Application Procedures

Initial Contact: Applications will be mailed upon request.
Application Requirements: Organizations must submit proof of IRS 501(c)(3) status, and public charity classification. Applications and required information are to be presented in triplicate and hole-punched for insertion into a 3-ring binder.
Deadlines: February 20, May 20, August 20, and November 20.

Foundation Officials

J. Jerry Dickman: trustee
Donne W. Pitman: trustee B 1940. PRIM CORP EMPL president, director: Chapman Exploration Inc. CORP AFFIL director: F & M Bank Trust Co.

Grants Analysis

Disclosure Period: calendar year ending 2001
Total Grants: $3,129,475*
Number of Grants: 69*
Average Grant: $45,354*
Highest Grant: $505,000
Typical Range: $2,000 to $50,000
*Note: Total analysis excludes United Way.

Recent Grants

Note: Grants derived from 2000 Form 990.

General

500,000	University of Tulsa, Tulsa, OK
250,000	Oklahoma Medical Research Foundation, Oklahoma City, OK
250,000	Philbrook Museum of Art, Tulsa, OK
250,000	University of Oklahoma Foundation, Oklahoma City, OK
150,000	M.D. Anderson Cancer Center, Houston, TX
100,000	12 and 12 Transition House, Tulsa, OK
100,000	Family and Children Services, Tulsa, OK
100,000	Holland Hall School, Tulsa, OK
100,000	Junior Achievement of Greater Tulsa, Tulsa, OK
100,000	McCall's Chapel School, Ada, OK

CHARITABLE VENTURE FOUNDATION

Giving Contact

William D. Dessingue, Executive Director
747 Pierce Road
Clifton Park, NY 12065
Phone: (518)877-8454
Fax: (518)877-6260

Alternate Contact

c/o Conway, Lavelle & Finn
450 New Karner Road
Albany, NY 12205

Description

Founded: 1992
EIN: 141751211
Organization Type: Private Foundation
Giving Locations: NY
Grant Types: General Support, Loan, Multiyear/Continuing Support, Scholarship.

Donor Information

Founder: Established in 1992 by Herbert K. Liebich and Isabel C. Liebich.

Financial Summary

Total Giving: $1,320,244 (2001); $1,658,248 (2000); $1,464,914 (1999)
Giving Analysis: Giving for 2001 includes: foundation scholarships ($111,000); 2000: foundation scholarships ($34,000); foundation matching gifts ($355,000) 1999: foundation matching gifts ($20,000)
Assets: $6,223,011 (2001); $8,738,898 (2000); $8,647,591 (1999)
Gifts Received: $117,605 (1999); $14,494 (1996); $5,018,750 (1992). Note: In 1999, contributions were received from New York State. In 1996, contributions were received from Herbert K. Leibich.

Typical Recipients

Arts & Humanities: Arts & Humanities-General
Civic & Public Affairs: African American Affairs, Botanical Gardens/Parks, Community Foundations, Employment/Job Training, Civic & Public Affairs-General, Hispanic Affairs, Housing, Urban & Community Affairs
Education: Business Education, Colleges & Universities, Education Reform, Engineering/Technological Education, Faculty Development, Education-General, Literacy, Medical Education, Public Education (Precollege), Science/Mathematics Education, Secondary Education (Public), Student Aid, Vocational & Technical Education
Environment: Resource Conservation
Health: Alzheimers Disease, Hospitals, Medical Rehabilitation
Religion: Religious Welfare

Social Services: At-Risk Youth, Community Service Organizations, Crime Prevention, Family Services, People with Disabilities, Recreation & Athletics, Social Services-General, Youth Organizations

Application Procedures

Initial Contact: Send a brief letter of inquiry (maximum of 2 pages).
Application Requirements: Include a description of organization, amount requested, and purpose of funds sought.
Deadlines: None.

Restrictions

The foundation does not award grants to arts organizations. Applicants should have limited resources.

Foundation Officials

Arthur Bates: trustee
Jennifer Cornell: giving contact
William Dessingue: executive director
Donald H. Liebich: trustee
Herbert K. Liebich: trustee
Kurt Liebich: trustee
Richard C. Liebich: trustee
Daniel P. Nolan: trustee
Jennifer Patterson: office administrator

Grants Analysis

Disclosure Period: calendar year ending 2001
Total Grants: $1,209,244*
Number of Grants: 29
Average Grant: $30,687*
Highest Grant: $350,000
Lowest Grant: $1,000
Typical Range: $15,000 to $50,000
*Note: Giving excludes scholarships. Average grant figure excludes highest grant.

Recent Grants

Note: Grants derived from 2001 Form 990.

General

350,000	Project Lead The Way Inc. -- PLTW Programs
176,000	Foundation for Excellent Schools, Cornwall, VT -- Adirondack Excellent Schools Program
114,723	Council of Community Services, Albany, NY -- Community Voice Mail Program
111,000	College of Saint Rose, Albany, NY -- future applied technology educators scholarship fund
105,000	University of Albany Foundation, Albany, NY -- science research
53,709	Junior Achievement Capital District New York, Schenectady, NY -- Rural Outreach Program
40,540	Career Links, Albany, NY -- Opportunities that Last Program
38,023	Interfaith Partnership for the Homeless, Albany, NY -- Homeless Intervention Program
35,000	Parsons Child and Family Center, Albany, NY -- work appreciation for youth
34,544	Merrimack Valley CSD, Penacook, NH -- school equipment

CHARITY RANDALL FOUNDATION

Giving Contact

Robert P. Randall, President
71 Progress Avenue
Cranberry Township, PA 16066-3511
Phone: (724)776-7000

Description

EIN: 251329778
Organization Type: Private Foundation
Giving Locations: headquarters and operating communities.
Grant Types: General Support, Scholarship.

Donor Information

Founder: Earl R. Randall

Financial Summary

Total Giving: $220,040 (fiscal year ending June 30, 2002); $205,750 (fiscal 2001); $160,000 (fiscal 2000 approx)
Giving Analysis: Giving for fiscal 2002 includes: foundation scholarships ($20,000); fiscal 2000: foundation scholarships ($30,000); fiscal 1999: foundation scholarships ($40,000)
Assets: $4,163,963 (fiscal 2002); $4,643,698 (fiscal 2001); $4,100,325 (fiscal 1999)
Gifts Received: $50,000 (fiscal 2002); $201,100 (fiscal 2001); $200,025 (fiscal 1999). Note: In fiscal 1998, 2000, and 2002, contributions were received from Three Rivers Aluminum Co.; and miscellaneous contributions of $50 also was received. In fiscal 1999 contributions were received from Three Rivers Aluminum Co. ($200,000) and miscellaneous contributions of $25 also was received.

Typical Recipients

Arts & Humanities: Arts Associations & Councils, Arts Centers, Ballet, Dance, History & Archaeology, Libraries, Literary Arts, Museums/Galleries, Music, Opera, Performing Arts, Public Broadcasting, Theater
Civic & Public Affairs: Botanical Gardens/Parks, Employment/Job Training, Civic & Public Affairs-General, Public Policy, Zoos/Aquariums
Education: Colleges & Universities, Economic Education, Education Funds, Private Education (Precollege), Student Aid
Environment: Environment-General, Protection, Resource Conservation, Wildlife Protection
Health: Cancer, Children's Health/Hospitals, Hospitals
International: Foreign Arts Organizations, International Environmental Issues
Science: Scientific Centers & Institutes
Social Services: Animal Protection, Animal Protection, Big Brother/Big Sister, Community Service Organizations, Youth Organizations

Application Procedures

Initial Contact: Send a brief letter of inquiry.
Application Requirements: Individuals should include a brief resume of academics. Research grants should include outline of proposed investigation and proposed budget. Organizations should request the Foundation's grant application.
Deadlines: None.
Decision Notification: Applicants are usually notified within one month of application.

Restrictions

Does not support individuals, religious organizations for sectarian purposes, political or lobbying groups, or organizations outside operating areas.

Additional Information

Grants to individuals are limited to people attending educational institutions beyond the secondary level. Recipients are selected on the basis of need, prior scholastic achievements, and area of study, with preference given to literary and environmental conservation endeavors.
Publications: Application Form

Foundation Officials

Robert G. Panagulias: assistant treasurer
Brett R. Randall: treasurer
Rita M. Randall: secretary

Robert P. Randall: treasurer
Robin S. Randall: secretary

Grants Analysis

Disclosure Period: fiscal year ending June 30, 2002
Total Grants: $200,040*
Number of Grants: 21
Average Grant: $2,502*
Highest Grant: $150,000
Lowest Grant: $40
Typical Range: $1,000 to $5,000
*Note: Giving excludes scholarships. Average grant figure excludes highest grant.

Recent Grants

Note: Grants derived from fiscal 2000 Form 990.

Library-Related

5,000	Cranberry Public Library, Cranberry Township, PA -- for education purposes

General

40,000	Carnegie Mellon University, Pittsburgh, PA
15,000	Phipps Conservatory and Botanical Garden, Pittsburgh, PA
10,000	Western Pennsylvania Conservancy, Pittsburgh, PA -- for land conservation
10,000	Zoological Society of Pittsburgh, Pittsburgh, PA -- for maintenance of zoological garden
5,000	Civic Light Opera Association of Greater Pittsburgh, Pittsburgh, PA -- for fine arts
5,000	International Poetry Forum, Pittsburgh, PA -- for fine arts
5,000	La Roche College, Pittsburgh, PA -- for presidential scholarship fund
5,000	Make A Wish Foundation, Pittsburgh, PA
5,000	Pennsylvania Partnership for Economic Education, Pittsburgh, PA -- for educational purposes
5,000	Pittsburgh Public Theater, Pittsburgh, PA -- for fine arts

CHARLES SCHWAB CORP.

Company Headquarters

101 Montgomery St.
San Francisco, CA 94104
Web: http://www.schwab.com

Company Description

Ticker: SCH
Exchange: OTC
Acquired: U.S. Trust Corp. (2000).
Revenue: US$4.48 billion (2002)
Profit: US$109 million (2002)
Employees: 13,192
Fortune Rank: 364, per FORTUNE Magazine's list of 500 Largest U.S. Corporations (2002).

Nonmonetary Support

Type: Donated Equipment
Volunteer Programs: The company has a formal employee volunteer program and sponsors various volunteer programs during the year throughout the U.S., including Habitat for Humanity and Christmas in April.
Note: Foundation provides nonmonetary support. Application procedure is the same as for printing. In-kind services are for printing only.

Charles Schwab Corp. Foundation

Giving Contact

Elinore Robey, Senior Manager, Community Investor Services
Charles Schwab Corp. Foundation
101 Montgomery St., 28th Floor
MS-SF120KNY-28-353
San Francisco, CA 94104
Phone: 877-408-5438
Fax: (415)636-3262
E-mail: CIS@schwab.com
Web: http://www.aboutschwab.com/sstory/communityservices.html

Description

EIN: 943192615
Organization Type: Corporate Foundation
Giving Locations: CA: San Francisco communities where there are Schwab branch offices.
Grant Types: Capital, Conference/Seminar, Emergency, Employee Matching Gifts, General Support, Multiyear/Continuing Support, Project.
Note: Employee matching gift ratio: 2 to 1 up to $5,000.

Financial Summary

Total Giving: $3,700,000 (fiscal year ending June 31, 2004 approx); $3,700,000 (fiscal 2003 approx); $4,699,859 (fiscal 2000). Note: Contributes through corporate direct giving program and foundation.
Giving Analysis: Giving for fiscal 2000 includes: foundation grants to United Way ($74,401); foundation ($4,625,458); fiscal 1999: foundation grants to United Way ($126,291); foundation ($2,738,297) foundation matching gifts ($2,844,009)
Assets: $6,066,079 (fiscal 2000); $7,970,625 (fiscal 1999); $5,650,600 (fiscal 1998)
Gifts Received: $2,611,365 (fiscal 2000); $6,244,048 (fiscal 1999); $2,050,775 (fiscal 1998). Note: Contributions are received from Charles Schwab & Co.

Typical Recipients

Arts & Humanities: Arts Associations & Councils, Arts Centers, Arts Festivals, Arts Outreach, Ballet, Community Arts, Ethnic & Folk Arts, Historic Preservation, Libraries, Museums/Galleries, Music, Opera, Performing Arts, Public Broadcasting
Civic & Public Affairs: African American Affairs, Asian American Affairs, Botanical Gardens/Parks, Business/Free Enterprise, Civil Rights, Clubs, Community Foundations, Economic Development, Employment/Job Training, Gay/Lesbian Issues, Civic & Public Affairs-General, Hispanic Affairs, Housing, Law & Justice, Nonprofit Management, Philanthropic Organizations, Professional & Trade Associations, Public Policy, Urban & Community Affairs, Women's Affairs, Zoos/Aquariums
Education: Afterschool/Enrichment Programs, Arts/Humanities Education, Business Education, Colleges & Universities, Economic Education, Education Reform, Elementary Education (Public), Faculty Development, Leadership Training, Minority Education, Private Education (Precollege), Public Education (Precollege), School Volunteerism, Science/Mathematics Education, Secondary Education (Private), Secondary Education (Public), Special Education, Student Aid, Vocational & Technical Education
Environment: Environment-General, Protection, Resource Conservation, Wildlife Protection
Health: AIDS/HIV, Cancer, Children's Health/Hospitals, Clinics/Medical Centers, Diabetes, Emergency/Ambulance Services, Health Organizations, Heart, Home-Care Services, Hospices, Kidney, Medical Research, Mental Health, Multiple Sclerosis, Nursing

Services, Prenatal Health Issues, Single-Disease Health Associations, Transplant Networks/Donor Banks

International: Health Care/Hospitals, International Environmental Issues, International Organizations, International Relief Efforts

Religion: Religion-General, Jewish Causes, Ministries, Religious Welfare

Science: Science Museums, Scientific Centers & Institutes

Social Services: Animal Protection, Big Brother/Big Sister, Child Welfare, Community Service Organizations, Day Care, Domestic Violence, Emergency Relief, Family Planning, Family Services, Food/Clothing Distribution, People with Disabilities, Recreation & Athletics, Senior Services, Shelters/Homelessness, United Funds/United Ways, Volunteer Services, Volunteer Services, YMCA/YWCA/YMHA/YWHA, Youth Organizations

Application Procedures

Initial Contact: Call or write for guidelines, then submit a formal proposal.

Application Requirements: Include mission statement, program objectives, amount requested and how funds will be used, population served, plan for evaluation, names of any Schwab employee volunteers, and name of nearest Schwab branch. Attachments should include list of board of director; list of foundation and corporate funders, most recent annual report or Form 990, proof of tax-exempt status, current operating and program budgets, and list of board of directors or trustees.

Deadlines: None.

Decision Notification: Applicants will receive a written response within 60 days of receipt.

Notes: Schwab employees personally involved with a nonprofit organization applying for funding are encouraged to attach a letter of endorsement to the organization's grant proposal.

Restrictions

Foundation does not fund: advertising; athletic or sporting activities, teams or students associations; business development activities; cause-related marketing projects; conferences or seminars; fraternal or exclusive membership organizations; fundraising events; individuals; organizations that engage in discriminatory practices; organizations without current nonprofit 501(c)(3) status; political or lobbying organizations; private foundations; publications, films, videos, or television programs; religious or sectarian organizations; sponsorships or promotional events; or group travel. The foundation does not provide capital, challenge, or seed funding and rarely funds institutions of higher learning, hospitals, or single-disease associations (although such organizations may be funded through employee matching gifts).

Additional Information

The Charles Schwab Corporation Foundation was created in December 1993.

Publications: Program Guidelines

Corporate Officials

David Steven Pottruck: president, co-chief executive officer, director B 1948. ED University of Pennsylvania BA (1970); University of Pennsylvania MBA (1972). PRIM CORP EMPL president, co-chief executive officer, director: Charles Schwab & Co., Inc. CORP AFFIL president, chief operating officer: Charles Schwab Corp.; director: Preview Travel Inc.; director: Intel Corp.; director: McKesson Corp.; director: Decibel Instruments Inc. NONPR AFFIL trustee: University Pennsylvania.

Charles R. Schwab: chairman, co-chief executive officer, director B Sacramento, CA 1937. ED Stanford

University MBA (1959); Stanford University MBA (1961). PRIM CORP EMPL chairman, co-chief executive officer, director: Charles Schwab & Co., Inc. CORP AFFIL director: Siebel Systems, Inc.; director: TransAmerica Corp.; director: The Gap Inc.; chairman: Schwab Holding Inc.

Foundation Officials

Charles R. Schwab: chairman (see above)

Grants Analysis

Disclosure Period: fiscal year ending June 31, 2000
Total Grants: $4,625,458*
Number of Grants: 1,986
Average Grant: $2,329
Highest Grant: $210,766
Typical Range: $1,000 to $5,000
*Note: Giving excludes United Way. Giving includes matching gifts.

Recent Grants

Note: Grants derived from 2000 Form 990.

General

210,766	PGA Tour Charities, Inc, Ponte Vedra Beach, FL
177,753	San Francisco AIDS Foundation, San Francisco, CA
121,671	American National Red Cross, Columbus, OH
81,119	Phoenix Children's Hospital, Phoenix, AZ
67,808	Los Angeles Gay and Lesbian Center, Los Angeles, CA
57,792	Susan G. Komen Breast Cancer Foundation, San Francisco, CA
52,804	United Way Bay Area, San Francisco, CA
46,771	Leukemia Society of America, Cincinnati, OH -- Team in Training
45,304	San Francisco Zoological Society, San Francisco, CA
42,828	YMCA, San Francisco, CA

CHARTWELL FOUNDATION

Giving Contact

Margaret Perenchio, President
1999 Avenue of the Stars, Suite 3050
Los Angeles, CA 90067
Phone: (310)556-7600
Fax: (310)556-3568

Description

Founded: 1986
EIN: 954080111
Organization Type: Private Foundation
Giving Locations: CA
Grant Types: General Support.

Donor Information

Founder: A. Jerrold Perenchio

Financial Summary

Total Giving: $4,478,500 (fiscal year ending November 30, 1999); $169,000 (fiscal 1998); $4,511,114 (fiscal 1997)
Assets: $55,568 (fiscal 2000); $10,028 (fiscal 1999); $2,296,336 (fiscal 1998)
Gifts Received: $634,509 (fiscal 1999); $11,090,763 (fiscal 1996); $1,199,629 (fiscal 1995). Note: In fiscal 1996 and 1999, contributions were received from A. Jerrold Perenchio.

Typical Recipients

Arts & Humanities: Arts Centers, Arts Funds, Arts Institutes, Film & Video, Historic Preservation, History & Archaeology, Libraries, Museums/Galleries, Music, Opera, Performing Arts, Public Broadcasting

Civic & Public Affairs: African American Affairs, Civic & Public Affairs-General, Hispanic Affairs, Public Policy, Women's Affairs

Education: Arts/Humanities Education, Business Education, Colleges & Universities, Continuing Education, Education Reform, Engineering/Technological Education, Literacy, Medical Education, Private Education (Precollege), Public Education (Precollege), Religious Education, Student Aid

Environment: Air/Water Quality, Environment-General, Resource Conservation

Health: AIDS/HIV, Alzheimers Disease, Cancer, Children's Health/Hospitals, Clinics/Medical Centers, Diabetes, Emergency/Ambulance Services, Eyes/Blindness, Hospitals, Medical Research, Mental Health, Multiple Sclerosis, Prenatal Health Issues, Research/Studies Institutes, Single-Disease Health Associations, Transplant Networks/Donor Banks

International: Foreign Arts Organizations, Foreign Educational Institutions, Human Rights, International Organizations, International Relief Efforts, Missionary/Religious Activities

Religion: Jewish Causes, Missionary Activities (Domestic), Religious Welfare, Social/Policy Issues

Social Services: Child Welfare, Community Centers, Community Service Organizations, Domestic Violence, Family Planning, Family Services, Food/Clothing Distribution, People with Disabilities, Recreation & Athletics, Scouts, Senior Services, Sexual Abuse, Shelters/Homelessness, Substance Abuse, Veterans, Volunteer Services, Youth Organizations

Application Procedures

Initial Contact: The foundation requests applications be made in writing.

Application Requirements: Includes proof of tax-exempt status.

Deadlines: None.

Restrictions

Does not support individuals.

Foundation Officials

Robert V. Cahill: vice president
Andrew Jerrold Perenchio: president B Fresno, CA 1930. ED University of California, Los Angeles BS (1954). PRIM CORP EMPL president: Chartwell Partnerships Group. CLUB AFFIL Friars Club; Westchester Country Club; Bel-Air Country Club.
John Perenchio: vice president

Grants Analysis

Disclosure Period: fiscal year ending November 30, 2000
Total Grants: $0
Note: Average grant excludes 3 highest grants ($1,200,000).

Recent Grants

Note: Grants derived from fiscal 1999 Form 990.

General

400,000	American Jazz Philharmonic, Los Angeles, CA
400,000	Children's Scholarship Fund, New York, NY
400,000	Geffen Playhouse, Los Angeles, CA
334,000	Los Angeles County Museum of Art, Los Angeles, CA
250,000	Motion Picture and Television Fund Foundation, Woodland Hills, CA
250,000	Muhammad Ali Center, Louisville, KY
150,000	Metropolitan Opera Association, New York, NY
100,000	American Red Cross - Los Angeles Chapter, Los Angeles, CA
81,600	American Friends of the National Gallery London, New York, NY
50,000	AMFAR, New York, NY

RICHARD ALLEN CHASE CHARITABLE FOUNDATION

Giving Contact
Richard Allen Chase, President
27 Hooks Ln.
Baltimore, MD 21208
Phone: (410)653-8200

Description
Founded: 1989
EIN: 521601909
Organization Type: Private Foundation
Grant Types: General Support.

Donor Information
Founder: Established in 1989 by Richard Allen Chase.

Financial Summary
Total Giving: $43,500 (2001); $55,000 (2000); $52,950 (1998)
Assets: $475,472 (2001); $703,996 (2000); $786,271 (1998)
Gifts Received: $50,000 (1996); $44,595 (1995); $65,000 (1994). Note: In 1996, contributions were received from Richard Allen Chase.

Typical Recipients
Arts & Humanities: History & Archaeology, Libraries, Museums/Galleries, Music, Performing Arts, Public Broadcasting
Civic & Public Affairs: Botanical Gardens/Parks, Clubs, Civic & Public Affairs-General
Education: Colleges & Universities, Continuing Education, Medical Education, Minority Education
Environment: Environment-General
Health: AIDS/HIV, Hospitals, Mental Health, Research/Studies Institutes, Single-Disease Health Associations
International: International Environmental Issues
Religion: Churches

Application Procedures
Initial Contact: Send a brief letter of inquiry.
Application Requirements: Include a description of organization and purpose of funds sought.
Deadlines: None.

Restrictions
Limited to charities in the areas of health and education.

Foundation Officials
Richard Allen Chase: president
Robert Mathias Hoffman: secretary

Grants Analysis
Disclosure Period: calendar year ending 2001
Total Grants: $43,500
Number of Grants: 6
Highest Grant: $25,000
Lowest Grant: $2,000

Recent Grants
Note: Grants derived from 2000 Form 990.

General
25,000	Harvard University, Cambridge, MA
5,000	Fund for Johns Hopkins, Baltimore, MD
5,000	Yale University Child Study Center, New Haven, CT
3,000	Metropolitan Museum of Art, New York, NY
3,000	University of Chicago, Chicago, IL
2,000	College of Physicians and Surgeons, New York, NY

1,500	Ascension Music, New York, NY
1,000	American Foundation For AIDS Research, New York, NY
1,000	Central Park Conservancy, New York, NY
1,000	Colonial Williamsburg Foundation, Williamsburg, VA

ALFRED E. CHASE CHARITY FOUNDATION

Giving Contact
Kerry Herlihy Sullivan, Directory, Fleet Foundation and Philanthropic Serv.
PO Box 6767
Providence, RI 02940-6767
Phone: (401)276-7316

Description
Founded: 1956
EIN: 046026314
Organization Type: Private Foundation
Giving Locations: MA
Grant Types: Capital, General Support, Operating Expenses, Project.

Donor Information
Founder: the late Alfred E. Chase

Financial Summary
Total Giving: $363,000 (fiscal year ending October 31, 2001); $275,000 (fiscal 2000); $170,000 (fiscal 1998)
Assets: $8,336,654 (fiscal 2001); $8,738,493 (fiscal 2000); $8,081,213 (fiscal 1998)
Gifts Received: $3 (fiscal 1992)

Typical Recipients
Arts & Humanities: Arts Festivals, Ballet, Ethnic & Folk Arts, Libraries, Music, Performing Arts, Public Broadcasting
Civic & Public Affairs: Asian American Affairs, Economic Development, Employment/Job Training, Ethnic Organizations, Civic & Public Affairs-General, Hispanic Affairs, Housing, Philanthropic Organizations, Urban & Community Affairs
Education: Colleges & Universities, Education Reform, Education-General, Preschool Education, Private Education (Precollege), Public Education (Precollege)
Environment: Environment-General
Health: Cancer, Clinics/Medical Centers, Health Funds, Hospices, Hospitals, Mental Health, Prenatal Health Issues, Single-Disease Health Associations
International: International Peace & Security Issues
Religion: Religion-General, Religious Organizations
Science: Science Museums
Social Services: Animal Protection, Child Abuse, Child Welfare, Community Centers, Community Service Organizations, Day Care, Delinquency & Criminal Rehabilitation, Domestic Violence, Family Services, Food/Clothing Distribution, Homes, People with Disabilities, Shelters/Homelessness, United Funds/United Ways, YMCA/YWCA/YMHA/YWHA, Youth Organizations

Application Procedures
Initial Contact: Send a brief letter of inquiry requesting guidelines.
Deadlines: February 15.

Restrictions
Videotapes are not accepted. Grants not made to individuals.

Additional Information
Preference is given to minority education, preventative health care, and family Service.
Publications: Application Guidelines; Application Form
Trust(s): Fleet National Bank MA NA

Foundation Officials
Kerry H. Sullivan: director grant making PRIM CORP EMPL vice president: Fleet Investment Services.

Grants Analysis
Disclosure Period: fiscal year ending October 31, 2001
Total Grants: $363,000
Number of Grants: 20
Average Grant: $18,150
Highest Grant: $50,000
Lowest Grant: $5,000
Typical Range: $10,000 to $25,000

Recent Grants
Note: Grants derived from 2000 Form 990.

General
50,000	St. Mary's Women and Infants Center, Boston, MA
25,000	Boston Renaissance Charter School, Boston, MA
25,000	Colonel Daniel Marr, Dorchester, MA
25,000	Colonel Marr Boys and Girls, Dorchester, MA
20,000	Germaine Lawrence Inc., Arlington, MA
15,000	Boys and Girls Club of Lynn, Lynn, MA
10,000	Community Minority Center, Lynn, MA
10,000	Help for Abused Women, Salem, MA
10,000	Steppingstone Foundation, Boston, MA
5,000	Boston Chinatown Neighborhood Center, Boston, MA

ALICE P. CHASE TRUST

Giving Contact
Emma Greene, Trust Officer
c/o Boston Safe Deposit and Trust Co.
1 Boston Pl., AIM 024-009D
Boston, MA 02108
Phone: (617)722-7341

Description
Founded: 1956
EIN: 046093897
Organization Type: Private Foundation
Giving Locations: MA: Boston including the North Shore area, Lynn
Grant Types: Capital, General Support, Project.

Donor Information
Founder: the late Alice P. and Alfred E. Chase

Financial Summary
Total Giving: $455,000 (fiscal year ending August 31, 1999); $218,000 (fiscal 1996); $226,500 (fiscal 1995)
Assets: $455,000 (fiscal 1999); $5,465,833 (fiscal 1996); $5,028,321 (fiscal 1995)

Typical Recipients
Arts & Humanities: Arts Associations & Councils, Arts Institutes, Ballet, Community Arts, Dance, Ethnic & Folk Arts, History & Archaeology, Libraries, Museums/Galleries, Music
Civic & Public Affairs: Botanical Gardens/Parks, Clubs, Community Foundations, Economic Development, Civic & Public Affairs-General, Hispanic Affairs,

Housing, Municipalities/Towns, Native American Affairs, Philanthropic Organizations, Urban & Community Affairs
Education: Arts/Humanities Education, Colleges & Universities, Education-General, Leadership Training, Medical Education, Private Education (Precollege), Public Education (Precollege), Vocational & Technical Education
Environment: Environment-General
Health: AIDS/HIV, Cancer, Children's Health/Hospitals, Clinics/Medical Centers, Diabetes, Health Organizations, Hospitals, Medical Research, Public Health
International: Health Care/Hospitals
Religion: Churches, Religious Welfare
Science: Science Museums
Social Services: Camps, Child Welfare, Community Centers, Community Service Organizations, Crime Prevention, Family Services, Food/Clothing Distribution, Recreation & Athletics, Shelters/Homelessness, United Funds/United Ways, Veterans, YMCA/YWCA/YMHA/YWHA, Youth Organizations

Application Procedures

Initial Contact: Send a brief letter of inquiry.
Application Requirements: a concise statement of the purpose of funds sought, the current year's operating budget, recently audited financial statement, a list of board members, resumes of all key staff people, and proof of tax-exempt status.
Deadlines: in February, May, August, and November.

Restrictions

Does not support individuals or provide funds for matching gifts.

Additional Information

Publications: Application Guidelines
Trust(s): Boston Safe Deposit & Trust Co

Grants Analysis

Disclosure Period: fiscal year ending August 31, 1999
Total Grants: $455,000
Number of Grants: 10
Highest Grant: $100,000
Typical Range: $10,000 to $50,000

Recent Grants

Note: Grants derived from 1999 Form 990.

General

100,000	Boston Medical Center, Boston, MA -- in support of "reach out and read" program
75,000	Boys and Girls Club of Boston, Boston, MA -- to rehabilitate the building and teen education room
50,000	Allston-Brighton Community Development Corporation, Allston, MA -- for proposed economic literacy and asset building program
50,000	Franklin Institute, Philadelphia, PA -- for the Mellon Computer Center
40,000	Food Project, Lincoln, MA -- for a youth development program
40,000	Massachusetts Eye & Ear Infirmary, Boston, MA -- for research on age related muscular degeneration
25,000	Art Institute of Boston, Boston, MA -- for young artists program
25,000	Community Investment Opportunities Initiative
20,000	Mytown -- to become founding corporate sponsor/support walking tours
20,000	United Way, Dubuque, IA -- for continued investment in the jobs for youth financial services training program

CHATLOS FOUNDATION

Giving Contact

William J. Chatlos, President
PO Box 915048
Longwood, FL 32791-5048
Phone: (407)862-5077
Web: http://www.chatlos.org

Description

Founded: 1953
EIN: 136161425
Organization Type: Family Foundation
Giving Locations: nationally.
Grant Types: General Support, Matching, Operating Expenses, Project.

Donor Information

Founder: William Frederick Chatlos , the foundation's donor, was born in Bridgeport, CT, in 1889. In his youth, he began working for a builder and lumberman while studying the drafting of housing plans in night school at the YMCA. At the age of 17, Mr. Chatlos built his first house. He continued to construct buildings in Connecticut, New York, New Jersey, and Florida until his death in 1977. Mr. Chatlos established the foundation in 1953.

Financial Summary

Total Giving: $4,000,000 (2003 approx); $4,000,000 (2002 approx); $5,951,786 (2000)
Giving Analysis: Giving for 2000 includes: foundation matching gifts ($1,000); foundation scholarships ($366,875); 1998: foundation matching gifts ($12,000) foundation scholarships ($267,000)
Assets: $100,000,000 (2003 approx); $100,000,000 (2002 approx); $121,912,941 (2001)
Gifts Received: $50,000 (1999); $50,000 (1998)

Typical Recipients

Arts & Humanities: Historic Preservation, Libraries
Civic & Public Affairs: Civic & Public Affairs-General, Housing, Professional & Trade Associations, Safety, Women's Affairs
Education: Colleges & Universities, Faculty Development, Leadership Training, Medical Education, Minority Education, Religious Education, Science/Mathematics Education, Special Education, Student Aid
Environment: Protection
Health: AIDS/HIV, Arthritis, Cancer, Children's Health/Hospitals, Clinics/Medical Centers, Emergency/Ambulance Services, Eyes/Blindness, Health Organizations, Heart, Hospitals, Hospitals (University Affiliated), Long-Term Care, Medical Research, Nursing Services, Public Health, Trauma Treatment
International: Foreign Educational Institutions, International-General, Health Care/Hospitals, International Development, International Environmental Issues, International Peace & Security Issues, International Relief Efforts, Missionary/Religious Activities
Religion: Bible Study/Translation, Churches, Ministries, Missionary Activities (Domestic), Religious Organizations, Religious Welfare, Seminaries, Social/Policy Issues
Social Services: Child Welfare, Community Centers, Food/Clothing Distribution, People with Disabilities, Shelters/Homelessness

Application Procedures

Initial Contact: The foundation requests that all inquiries be submitted in writing.
Application Requirements: All requests must include a cover letter with the amount requested and plans for the monies; most recent budget; a one- to two-page proposal summary; and evidence of IRS tax exempt status. Include a completed application form, which may be obtained by writing the foundation or from the foundation's web site. If a proposal is to be brought before the full board, additional information

will be requested to make the file complete, including: a full proposal, not to exceed ten pages; notarized affidavit certifying current tax exempt status and adherence to IRS criteria; copies of the organization's audited financial statement and Form 990's as submitted to the IRS; project budget; a listing of actual commitments toward the projected budget of the project, and any other information which may be necessary in consideration of your request; and a listing of all current officers and directors.
Deadlines: None. Although there are no deadlines, proposals may be forwarded for consideration at a subsequent meeting.
Review Process: The full board meets in February, May, August and November. A preliminary review committee considers all proposals at its monthly meetings. If significant interest is evidenced, a proposal is considered by the full board. Applicants are notified if their proposal is to be considered by the full board and will be asked to provide additional information. Meetings with the foundation are by appointment only, and are not granted initially.
Decision Notification: Requests are responded to in writing. The review process takes approximately 120 days.

Restrictions

The foundation does not support medical research, individual church congregations, individuals, the arts, state universities, primary or secondary schools, or organizations in existence for less than two years. It also does not provide seed money, loans, deficit financing, or endowment funds. Grants requests for bricks and mortar, conference and administrative expenses, multi-year support, and computer implementation are given very low priority. Do not bind proposals.

Additional Information

Organizations are allowed to submit a proposal every six months. However, no more than one project will be funded in a twelve month period.
The Foundation does not make scholarship grants directly to individuals but rather to educational institutions which in turn select recipients.
For first time applicants, the foundation tends to fund requests for amounts less than $10,000.
For first time applicants, the foundation tends to fund requests for amounts less than $10,000.
Publications: Application Guidelines; Application Form

Foundation Officials

Carol J. Chatlos: secretary, trustee
William J. Chatlos: president, treasurer, trustee
CORP AFFIL president: Sun Ray Homes Inc.
Joy E. D'Arata: vice president, trustee
Esther J. Kemsey: trustee
Charles O. Morgan, Jr.: trustee
Kathryn A. Randle: chairman, trustee
Michele C. Roach: assistant secretary, assistant treasurer, trustee

Grants Analysis

Disclosure Period: calendar year ending 2001
Total Grants: $5,403,717*
Number of Grants: 340
Average Grant: $16,442*
Highest Grant: $600,000
Lowest Grant: $100
Typical Range: $1,000 to $50,000 and $100,000 to $400,000
*Note: Giving excludes United Way. Grants analysis provided by foundation.

Recent Grants

Note: Grants derived from 2000 Form 990.

Library-Related

50,000	Florida College, Temple Terrace, FL -- west wing of the William F. Chatlos Library

50,000	Kentucky Mountain Bible College, Oakland City, IN -- construction funds to complete town house apartment complex

General

535,692	National Retinitis Pigmentosa Foundation, Hunt Valley, MD -- medical research
250,000	Haggai Institute for Advanced Leadership Training, Atlanta, GA -- sponsor a training session
250,000	Philadelphia College of Bible, Langhorne, PA -- Biblical Learning Center
181,444	Harvard University, Cambridge, MA
150,000	Adventist Health System/Sunbelt, Inc., Orlando, FL -- implementation of the next phase of the Interactive Simulation Healthcare Education Network project
100,000	Dallas Theological Seminary, Dallas, TX -- emergency aid fund
59,080	University of Miami School of Medicine, Miami, FL -- purchase of a real-time digital imaging and analysis system
55,516	University of Pennsylvania Health System, Philadelphia, PA -- final phase of trial treatment in Retinitis Pigmentosa
54,170	Campus Crusade for Christ International, Orlando, FL -- help fund S.A.Y. Yes Centers
50,000	Atlantic City Rescue Mission, Atlantic City, NJ -- Women's Overcomers Program

CHAZEN FOUNDATION

Giving Contact

Jerome A. Chazen, Trustee
Chazen Foundation
767 5th Avenue, 26th Floor
New York, NY 10153
Phone: (212)269-4141

Description

Founded: 1985
EIN: 133229474
Organization Type: Private Foundation
Giving Locations: NY: New York
Grant Types: Capital.

Donor Information

Founder: Jerome A. Chazen

Financial Summary

Total Giving: $2,194,715 (2001); $2,540,845 (2000); $2,340,406 (1999)
Giving Analysis: Giving for 1999 includes: foundation scholarships ($211,561) 1998: foundation scholarships ($58,750)
Assets: $37,127,964 (2001); $39,000,886 (2000); $36,999,596 (1999)
Gifts Received: $2,145,313 (2000); $1,527,003 (1999); $3,175,000 (1998). Note: In 1999, contributions were received from Jerome Chazen ($1,507,500) and Sean Sovak ($19,503). In 1994 and 1998, contributions were received from Jerome and Simona Chazen.

Typical Recipients

Arts & Humanities: Arts Associations & Councils, Arts Centers, Arts Funds, Arts Institutes, Community Arts, Dance, Ethnic & Folk Arts, Libraries, Museums/Galleries, Music, Opera, Performing Arts, Public Broadcasting, Theater, Visual Arts
Civic & Public Affairs: Civil Rights, Economic Development, Gay/Lesbian Issues, Civic & Public Affairs-General, Hispanic Affairs, Nonprofit Management, Parades/Festivals, Public Policy, Urban & Community Affairs, Women's Affairs

Education: Arts/Humanities Education, Business Education, Colleges & Universities, Education-General, Medical Education, Private Education (Precollege), Secondary Education (Public), Social Sciences Education, Student Aid, Student Aid
Environment: Air/Water Quality, Forestry
Health: AIDS/HIV, Arthritis, Cancer, Emergency/Ambulance Services, Eyes/Blindness, Health Organizations, Heart, Hospitals, Medical Research, Prenatal Health Issues, Single-Disease Health Associations
International: Foreign Arts Organizations, Foreign Educational Institutions, International Relations, Missionary/Religious Activities
Religion: Religion-General, Jewish Causes, Religious Organizations, Religious Welfare, Social/Policy Issues, Synagogues/Temples
Science: Science Museums
Social Services: Animal Protection, Camps, Child Welfare, Community Centers, Community Service Organizations, Counseling, Emergency Relief, Family Planning, Family Services, People with Disabilities, Recreation & Athletics, Scouts, Shelters/Homelessness, United Funds/United Ways, Volunteer Services, YMCA/YWCA/YMHA/YWHA, Youth Organizations

Application Procedures

Initial Contact: Send a letter stating the purpose of funds sought.
Deadlines: None.

Foundation Officials

Jerome A. Chazen: trustee B New York, NY 1927. ED University of Wisconsin BA (1948); Columbia University MBA (1950). ADD CORP EMPL chairman: Liz Claiborne Foreign Holdings Inc.
Simona A. Chazen: trustee

Grants Analysis

Disclosure Period: calendar year ending 1999
Total Grants: $2,128,845*
Number of Grants: 143
Average Grant: $14,887
Highest Grant: $333,333
Typical Range: $200 to $25,000
*Note: Giving excludes scholarships.

Recent Grants

Note: Grants derived from 2001 Form 990.

General

89,930	Playing to Win, New York, NY
60,000	American Craft Museum, New York, NY
39,620	Volunteer Counseling Service, Rockland, NY
33,480	Jazz Aspen, Aspen, CO
31,000	National Jewish Center for Immunological and Respiratory Medicine, Denver, CO
25,000	92nd Street Y, New York, NY
23,000	Helen Hayes Performing Arts Center
18,600	United Jewish Appeal Federation, New York, NY
15,500	NOW Legal Defense and Education Fund, New York, NY
14,900	Temple Beth Torah, New York, NY

CHC FOUNDATION

Giving Contact

Ralph Isom, President
PO Box 1644
Idaho Falls, ID 83403
Phone: (208)522-2368

Description

Founded: 1984
EIN: 820211282
Organization Type: Private Foundation

Giving Locations: ID: especially eastern ID
Grant Types: Capital, General Support, Matching.

Financial Summary

Total Giving: $1,019,736 (2001); $750,083 (2000); $491,301 (1999)
Giving Analysis: Giving for 2001 includes: foundation grants to United Way ($10,000)
Assets: $14,364,307 (2001); $17,004,828 (2000); $14,303,140 (1999)
Gifts Received: $3,878,561 (2000)

Typical Recipients

Arts & Humanities: Arts Associations & Councils, History & Archaeology, Libraries, Museums/Galleries, Music, Performing Arts, Public Broadcasting, Theater
Civic & Public Affairs: Botanical Gardens/Parks, Chambers of Commerce, Clubs, Economic Development, Employment/Job Training, Civic & Public Affairs-General, Housing, Municipalities/Towns, Safety, Urban & Community Affairs, Zoos/Aquariums
Education: Agricultural Education, Arts/Humanities Education, Colleges & Universities, Education Funds, Elementary Education (Public), Education-General, Gifted & Talented Programs, Public Education (Precollege), Secondary Education (Public), Vocational & Technical Education
Environment: Environment-General, Resource Conservation, Wildlife Protection
Health: Emergency/Ambulance Services, Health Organizations, Hospices, Hospitals, Prenatal Health Issues
Religion: Ministries
Science: Science Museums, Scientific Centers & Institutes
Social Services: Animal Protection, At-Risk Youth, Child Welfare, Community Service Organizations, Counseling, Crime Prevention, Domestic Violence, Emergency Relief, Family Planning, Family Services, Homes, People with Disabilities, Recreation & Athletics, Scouts, Senior Services, Social Services-General, Substance Abuse, Volunteer Services, YMCA/YWCA/YMHA/YWHA

Application Procedures

Initial Contact: Send 13 copies of a written proposal detailing the project and budget.
Application Requirements: Include a description of organization, amount requested, purpose of funds sought, recently audited financial statement, and proof of tax-exempt status.
Deadlines: Proposals are due in spring and fall; February 1, and September 1.

Restrictions

Foundation supports only tax-exempt nonprofit organizations. Foundation does not support individuals; religious groups or churches; political or legislative action groups; athletic teams, bands, trips or tours; contests and competitions; scholarships; general operating expenses of organizations; annual fund drives; advertising for benefit purposes; general activities not clearly linked to specific charitable objectives; general planning or work in which achievements cannot be measured; projects that involve the basic delivery of educational services, except for unique or innovative special programs that serve students or enhance teaching skills or otherwise add a desirable educational dimension not provided by or appropriately printed by regular school operating budgets; national or regional organizations except as may be a specific project or activity within the foundation's region. Foundation prefers short-term projects.

Additional Information

The CHC Foundation, an independent philanthropic foundation, was created in 1985. Its immediate antecedent was Community Hospital of Idaho Falls, which owned the hospital until 1984.

Foundation Officials

Milton F. Adam: secretary
Donald R. Bjornson, MD: director
Joan Chesbro: director
Ernest C. Craner: director
Joan C. Hahn-Struhs: president
Ralph Isom: director
Deborah Jenkins: director
Forde Johnson: treasurer
Janice C. Matthews: treasurer
Maureen McFadden: director
Charles M. Rice: vice president
John I. Sackett: director
Peggy Sharp: director
Anne S. Voilleque: director

Grants Analysis

Disclosure Period: calendar year ending 2001
Total Grants: $1,009,736*
Number of Grants: 76
Average Grant: $10,232*
Highest Grant: $242,338
Lowest Grant: $98
Typical Range: $5,000 to $30,000
*Note: Giving excludes United Way. Average grant figure excludes highest grant.

Recent Grants

Note: Grants derived from 2001 Form 990.

General

242,338	City of Idaho Falls Tautphaus Park Zoo, Idaho Falls, ID -- charitable
80,000	Eagle Rock Art Guild, Idaho Falls, ID -- charitable
56,000	Lemhi County Crisis Intervention Center, Salmon, ID -- charitable
39,780	Idaho Falls Symphony, Idaho Falls, ID -- charitable
39,780	Idaho Falls Symphony, Idaho Falls, ID -- charitable
36,000	Family Care Center, Carondelet, MO -- charitable
35,000	Shepeherds Inn, Idaho Falls, ID -- charitable
29,648	Teton Valley Museum, Idaho Falls, ID -- charitable
27,000	Ashton Memorial Hospital, Ashton, ID -- charitable
25,000	American Red Cross, Idaho Falls, ID -- charitable

OWEN CHEATHAM FOUNDATION

Giving Contact

Celeste W. Cheatham, President & Director
11444 Lost Tree Way
North Palm Beach, FL 33408

Description

Founded: 1957
EIN: 136097798
Organization Type: Private Foundation
Giving Locations: NY
Grant Types: General Support, Operating Expenses, Project, Scholarship.

Donor Information

Founder: the late Gwen Robertson Cheatham, the late Celeste W. Cheatham

Financial Summary

Total Giving: $404,830 (2001); $406,280 (2000); $397,865 (1999)
Assets: $6,942,145 (2001); $8,179,336 (2000); $9,354,982 (1999)

Typical Recipients

Arts & Humanities: Arts Associations & Councils, Arts Funds, Arts Institutes, Ballet, Community Arts, Dance, Historic Preservation, Libraries, Museums/Galleries, Music, Opera, Performing Arts, Public Broadcasting, Theater
Civic & Public Affairs: Civic & Public Affairs-General, Philanthropic Organizations, Public Policy
Education: Colleges & Universities, Legal Education, Minority Education, Private Education (Precollege)
Environment: Environment-General
Health: Alzheimers Disease, Cancer, Clinics/Medical Centers, Emergency/Ambulance Services, Eyes/Blindness, Heart, Hospices, Hospitals, Hospitals (University Affiliated), Kidney, Medical Research, Mental Health, Mental Health, Single-Disease Health Associations
International: Foreign Arts Organizations, Foreign Educational Institutions, Human Rights, International Development, International Organizations
Religion: Churches, Jewish Causes, Religious Organizations, Religious Welfare, Synagogues/Temples
Social Services: Animal Protection, At-Risk Youth, Child Welfare, Community Service Organizations, Family Services, People with Disabilities, Recreation & Athletics, Shelters/Homelessness, Social Services-General, Substance Abuse, United Funds/United Ways, Youth Organizations

Application Procedures

Initial Contact: Send a request on organization's stationery giving complete details of the purpose of funds sought.
Deadlines: None.

Foundation Officials

MacDonald Budd: secretary, director
Celeste Wickliffe Cheatham: president, director
Kenneth Kennedy: director
Edward Arthur Reilly: vice president, treasurer B New York, NY 1943. ED Princeton University AB (1965); Duke University JD (1968). PRIM CORP EMPL partner: Morris & McVeigh. NONPR AFFIL member: Florida Bar Association; member: New York State Bar Association; fellow: American College Trust & Estate Counsel; member: Connecticut Bar Association.
Celeste W. Weisglass: president, director
Stephen S. Weisglass: vice president, treasurer, director

Grants Analysis

Disclosure Period: calendar year ending 2001
Total Grants: $404,830
Number of Grants: 69
Average Grant: $5,867
Highest Grant: $50,000
Lowest Grant: $50
Typical Range: $1,000 to $10,000

Recent Grants

Note: Grants derived from 2001 Form 990.

General

50,000	Fore Augusta Foundation, Augusta, GA
39,300	Lenox Hill Hospital, New York, NY
29,000	Choate Rosemary Hall, Wallingford, CT
26,000	Miami City Ballet, Miami, FL
26,000	Spence School, New York, NY
15,200	Hospice of Wake County, Raleigh, NC
15,000	Flushing Town Hall
15,000	New Concord Presbyterian Church, New Concord, OH
10,000	Freedom Institute, New York, NY
10,000	Metropolitan Opera Association, New York, NY

TRUST FOR THE CHEEK FAMILY FOUNDATION

Giving Contact

Ronald Lelen, Vice President & Trust Officer
c/o The Chase Manhattan Bank
1211 6th Avenue, 34th Floor
New York, NY 10036
Phone: (212)789-4076

Description

Founded: 1990
EIN: 136930808
Organization Type: Private Foundation
Grant Types: General Support.

Financial Summary

Total Giving: $88,880 (fiscal year ending 8, 2001); $147,608 (fiscal 2000); $107,200 (fiscal 1999)
Giving Analysis: Giving for fiscal 2000 includes: foundation grants to United Way ($10,000)
Assets: $1,823,524 (fiscal 2001); $2,057,757 (fiscal 2000); $1,856,395 (fiscal 1999)

Typical Recipients

Arts & Humanities: Ballet, History & Archaeology, Libraries, Music, Opera
Civic & Public Affairs: Civic & Public Affairs-General, Housing, Urban & Community Affairs
Education: Colleges & Universities, Student Aid
Health: Cancer
Religion: Churches, Religious Organizations
Social Services: Animal Protection, Child Welfare, United Funds/United Ways, YMCA/YWCA/YMHA/YWHA

Application Procedures

Initial Contact: Send a brief letter of inquiry.
Deadlines: None.

Additional Information

Trust(s): Chase Manhattan Bank

Grants Analysis

Total Grants: $78,880*
Number of Grants: 40
Average Grant: $1,972
Highest Grant: $10,000
Typical Range: $500 to $50,000
*Note: Giving excludes United Way.

Recent Grants

Note: Grants derived from fiscal 2001 Form 990.

Library-Related

5,000	Thomas Jefferson Memorial Foundation, Charlottesville, VA

General

10,000	United Way Services, Richmond, VA
10,000	University of Richmond, Richmond, VA
5,000	Better Housing Coalition, Richmond, VA
5,000	Gore Place Society, Waltham, MA
5,000	Richmond Ballet, Richmond, VA
5,000	Trustees of Reservations
5,000	YWCA
3,000	Richmond Ballet, Richmond, VA
2,500	Richmond Society for Prevention of Cruelty to Animals, Richmond, VA
2,500	Virginia Union University, Richmond, VA

MRS. CHEEVER PORTER FOUNDATION

Giving Contact

Clifford E. Starkins, Director
c/o Adams and Becker CPA's
22 Oakwood Road
Huntington, NY 11743
Phone: (631)423-6634

Description

Founded: 1962
EIN: 136093181
Organization Type: Private Foundation
Giving Locations: NH; NJ; NY
Grant Types: General Support.

Financial Summary

Total Giving: $298,500 (fiscal year ending June 30, 2001); $478,500 (fiscal 2000); $521,500 (fiscal 1999)
Assets: $3,398,278 (fiscal 2001); $4,008,172 (fiscal 2000); $3,739,640 (fiscal 1999)

Typical Recipients

Arts & Humanities: Arts Associations & Councils, Arts Centers, Ballet, Libraries, Literary Arts, Museums/Galleries, Music, Opera, Public Broadcasting, Theater
Civic & Public Affairs: Botanical Gardens/Parks, Chambers of Commerce, Civic & Public Affairs-General, Municipalities/Towns, Public Policy, Safety, Urban & Community Affairs, Zoos/Aquariums
Education: Colleges & Universities, Medical Education, Private Education (Precollege)
Environment: Air/Water Quality, Environment-General, Resource Conservation, Wildlife Protection
Health: Cancer, Children's Health/Hospitals, Clinics/Medical Centers, Health-General, Geriatric Health, Hospitals, Hospitals (University Affiliated), Medical Research, Prenatal Health Issues
International: Foreign Arts Organizations, Foreign Educational Institutions
Religion: Churches, Religious Welfare
Science: Scientific Centers & Institutes
Social Services: Animal Protection, Community Service Organizations, Day Care, Family Planning, Homes, People with Disabilities, Scouts, Social Services-General, Youth Organizations

Application Procedures

Initial Contact: Send brief letter describing program.
Deadlines: None.

Foundation Officials

Alton Emil Peters: director B Albany, NY 1935. ED Harvard University AB (1955); Harvard University LLB (1958). PRIM CORP EMPL partner: Kelley, Drye & Warren. NONPR AFFIL fellow: Pierpont Morgan Library; honorary trustee: Signet Associates; member: New York State Bar Association; chairman executive committee, managing director: Metropolitan Opera Association; president, director: Metropolitan Opera Guild; director: Lincoln Center Performing Arts; fellow: Frick Collection; chairman, director: Goodwill Industries Greater New York; director: English Speaking Union U.S. New York Branch; trustee: Cathedral Saint John Divine; member: Century Association; member: Association Bar New York City; chairman, director: British American Arts Association; member council: American Museum Britain; vice president, director: American Friends Covent Garden & Royal Balet; member: American Judicature Society; member: American College Probate Counsel; treasurer, trustee: Academy American Poets; member: American Bar Association. CLUB AFFIL Pilgrims Club; Church Club; Harvard Club.
Edgar Scott, Jr.: director
Clifford E. Starkins: director

Grants Analysis

Disclosure Period: fiscal year ending June 30, 2001
Total Grants: $298,500
Number of Grants: 61
Average Grant: $4,893
Highest Grant: $30,000
Lowest Grant: $1,000
Typical Range: $1,000 to $15,000

Recent Grants

Note: Grants derived from fiscal 2001 Form 990.

General

30,000	Huntington Townwide Fund, Yorktown Heights, NY
25,000	Nassau Suffolk Autism Society
15,000	AOH
10,000	Pederson-Krag Center, Huntington Station, NY
10,000	Philips Exeter Academy, Exeter, NH
10,000	St. Paul's Center, NY
8,000	Cooley's Anemia Foundation
6,000	Metropolitan Museum of Art, New York, NY
5,000	Babylon Child Care Center, Inc., West Babylon, NY
5,000	Bridgehampton Child Care, Bridgehampton, NY

BEN B. CHENEY FOUNDATION

Giving Contact

William O. Rieke, Executive Director
1201 Pacific Avenue South, Suite 1600
Tacoma, WA 98402
Phone: (253)572-2442
Fax: (253)572-2902
E-mail: info@benbcheneyfoundation.org
Web: http://www.benbcheneyfoundation.org/

Description

Founded: 1955
EIN: 916053760
Organization Type: General Purpose Foundation
Giving Locations: CA: Del Norte, Humboldt, Lassen, Shasta, Siskiyou, and Trinity Counties in northern CA, especially northern CA; OR: especially southwestern OR; WA: especially southwestern WA, Tacoma-Pierce County
Grant Types: Capital, Emergency, Project, Seed Money.

Donor Information

Founder: The foundation was established in 1955 by the late Ben B. Cheney , who died in 1971, and Marian Cheney Olrogg , who died in 1975. Mr. Cheney founded the Cheney Lumber Company in 1936, and remained in the industry until his death. In 1975, the foundation began active grant making and offices were established in Tacoma, WA.

Financial Summary

Total Giving: $3,200,000 (2002 approx); $4,039,700 (2001); $3,976,172 (2000)
Giving Analysis: Giving for 2000 includes: foundation scholarships ($280,000) 1998: foundation scholarships ($82,400)
Assets: $65,000,000 (2002 approx); $78,702,955 (2001); $86,734,337 (2000)

Typical Recipients

Arts & Humanities: Arts Associations & Councils, Arts Centers, Arts Outreach, Ballet, Community Arts, Dance, Arts & Humanities-General, Historic Preservation, History & Archaeology, Libraries, Museums/Galleries, Music, Opera, Performing Arts, Public Broadcasting, Theater, Visual Arts

Civic & Public Affairs: African American Affairs, Botanical Gardens/Parks, Community Foundations, Economic Development, Employment/Job Training, Civic & Public Affairs-General, Housing, Municipalities/Towns, Nonprofit Management, Parades/Festivals, Philanthropic Organizations, Safety, Urban & Community Affairs, Women's Affairs, Zoos/Aquariums
Education: Afterschool/Enrichment Programs, Arts/Humanities Education, Arts/Humanities Education, Business Education, Colleges & Universities, Community & Junior Colleges, Education Reform, Faculty Development, Education-General, Literacy, Private Education (Precollege), Science/Mathematics Education, Secondary Education (Private), Special Education, Student Aid
Environment: Forestry, Environment-General, Resource Conservation, Wildlife Protection
Health: AIDS/HIV, Cancer, Children's Health/Hospitals, Clinics/Medical Centers, Emergency/Ambulance Services, Eyes/Blindness, Health Funds, Health Organizations, Heart, Hospitals, Long-Term Care, Medical Training, Mental Health, Single-Disease Health Associations, Speech & Hearing
Religion: Ministries, Missionary Activities (Domestic), Religious Organizations, Religious Welfare
Science: Science Exhibits & Fairs, Science Museums, Scientific Centers & Institutes
Social Services: Animal Protection, Camps, Child Welfare, Community Centers, Community Service Organizations, Counseling, Day Care, Domestic Violence, Emergency Relief, Family Services, Food/Clothing Distribution, Homes, People with Disabilities, Recreation & Athletics, Scouts, Senior Services, Shelters/Homelessness, Social Services-General, Special Olympics, Substance Abuse, United Funds/United Ways, Volunteer Services, YMCA/YWCA/YMHA/YWHA, Youth Organizations

Application Procedures

Initial Contact: Applicants should mail a one- to two-page query letter to the executive director.
Application Requirements: Query letters should provide a short history and mission of the applicant, the scope of operations, and summarize the proposal to be considered. This summary should include the nature of the need(s) to be addressed, the goal of the project, and the amount and purpose of funds requested of the foundation, the total project budget, and a plan for how other monies will be raised.
Deadlines: None.
Review Process: Agenda items for board meetings are set six to eight weeks in advance of meetings. Board meetings are held in April, June, September, and December.
The foundation considers requests on the basis of priorities and funds available. Queries go to a review committee, and if the committee deems a proposal to be of interest to the foundation, a staff contact and application form will follow. The foundation responds to all serious inquiries.

Restrictions

The foundation does not contribute to programs where government funding is available; for operating budgets, research, loans, or endowments; religious organizations for sectarian purposes; the preparation or publication of books, videos, or films; for seminars; to individuals; or for groups raising money for school-related tours.

Additional Information

The foundation awards grants primarily in southwestern Washington, Tacoma-Pierce County, southern Oregon (particularly around Medford), and the seven northernmost counties of California where the Cheney Lumber Company was active.
CF Investments of Tacoma, WA, provides accounting and investment services.
Publications: Application Guidelines; Application Form; Annual Report

Foundation Officials

Bradbury B. Cheney: president, director
Piper Cheney: treasurer, director
R. Gene Grant: director
John F. Hansler: secretary, director
Elgin E. Olrogg: vice president, director
William Oliver Rieke, MD: executive director B Odessa, WA 1931. ED Pacific Lutheran University BA (1953); University of Washington MD (1958). NONPR AFFIL president emeritus: Pacific Lutheran University.
Kenneth I. Ristine: program officer

Grants Analysis

Disclosure Period: calendar year ending 2001
Total Grants: $3,759,700*
Number of Grants: 129
Average Grant: $29,145
Highest Grant: $100,000
Lowest Grant: $1,500
Typical Range: $5,000 to $50,000
*Note: Giving excludes scholarships.

Recent Grants

Note: Grants derived from 2001 Form 990.

Library-Related

50,000	Pierce County Library Foundation, Tacoma, WA -- purchase and equip a kids bookmobile
43,000	Coos County Library Service District, Coos Bay, OR -- upgrade the computer network serving all Coos County libraries
38,000	Ezra Meeker Historical Society Foundation Center, Puyallup, WA -- install a new heating system

General

100,000	American Red Cross, Olympia, WA -- support disaster relief in the aftermath of terrorist attacks
100,000	Annie Wright School, Tacoma, WA -- support campaign
100,000	Bellarmine Preparatory School, Tacoma, WA -- expand and renovate math/science building
100,000	Museum of Glass, Tacoma, WA -- construction of the new Museum of Glass
100,000	Oregon Shakespeare Festival Association, Ashland, OR -- complete construction and equipping of new theatre
100,000	Tacoma Art Museum, Tacoma, WA -- build new art museum
100,000	Tacoma Rescue Mission, Tacoma, WA -- build and relocate Mission
75,000	Girl Scouts - Pacific Peaks Council, Tumwater, WA -- support the Make a Promise capital campaign
65,000	Ben B. Cheney Scholarship Program, Tacoma, WA -- provide college scholarships to students from Pierce County High Schools
55,000	CRISTA Ministries, Seattle, WA -- renovate and add cabins at Miracle Ranch

ELIZABETH F. CHENEY FOUNDATION

Giving Contact

Elizabeth Geraghty, III, Administrative Director
120 S. LaSalle St., Suite 1740
Chicago, IL 60603
Phone: (312)782-1234
E-mail: egeraghty@cheneyfoundation.org
Web: http://www.cheneyfoundation.org/

Description

Founded: 1985
EIN: 363375377
Organization Type: Private Foundation
Giving Locations: IL: Chicago
Grant Types: General Support.
Note: project.

Donor Information

Founder: Elizabeth F. Cheney Trust

Financial Summary

Total Giving: $862,095 (fiscal year ending May 31, 2001); $794,500 (fiscal 1999); $578,750 (fiscal 1997)
Assets: $15,298,388 (fiscal 2001); $16,433,979 (fiscal 1999); $12,988,809 (fiscal 1997)

Typical Recipients

Arts & Humanities: Arts Associations & Councils, Arts Centers, Arts Festivals, Arts Institutes, Ballet, Community Arts, Dance, Historic Preservation, History & Archaeology, Libraries, Museums/Galleries, Music, Opera, Performing Arts, Public Broadcasting, Theater
Civic & Public Affairs: Employment/Job Training, Civic & Public Affairs-General, Parades/Festivals
Education: Colleges & Universities

Application Procedures

Initial Contact: Application forms available from foundation administration director. ICI a brief letter of inquiry.
Application Requirements: purpose of funds sought, proof of tax-exempt status.
Deadlines: 30 days prior to quarterly meetings of directors.

Restrictions

Most grants awarded to artistic and cultural organizations.

Additional Information

Publications: Application Form

Foundation Officials

Lawrence L. Belles: president, director
Allan I. Drebin: treasurer, director
Howard McDowell McCue, III: secretary, director B Sumter, SC 1946. ED Princeton University AB (1968); Harvard University JD (1971). PRIM CORP EMPL partner: Mayer, Brown & Platt. NONPR AFFIL director: Lawrence Hall Youth Services; director, chairman board governors: Northwestern University Library Council; member: Illinois Bar Association; director: International Academy Estate & Trust Law; adj professor: Chicago Kent College Law; director: Harvard Law Society Illinois; director, member: Chicago Bar Foundation; director: Art Institute of Chicago; member federal tax committee: Chicago Bar Association; member: American College Trust & Estate Counsel; member: American Bar Association; member: American College Tax Counsel. CLUB AFFIL Chicago Club.

Grants Analysis

Disclosure Period: fiscal year ending May 31, 2001
Total Grants: $862,095
Number of Grants: 121
Average Grant: $7,125
Highest Grant: $47,000
Typical Range: $2,000 to $15,000

Recent Grants

Note: Grants derived from 2000 Form 990.

General

69,000	Orchestral Association, Chicago, IL -- for civic orchestra
40,000	Columbia College, Chicago, IL -- for white oak project
38,000	Art Institute of Chicago, Chicago, IL -- for Cleopatra project
35,000	Columbia College, Chicago, IL -- for Skrebneski Exhibit
33,000	Northwestern University, Evanston, IL -- for winter chamber music festival
25,000	Chicago Chamber Musicians, Chicago, IL -- to underwrite two concerts
25,000	Grant Park Music Festival, Chicago, IL -- for summer 2000 performances
25,000	Lyric Opera of Chicago, Chicago, IL -- for rising stars concert
25,000	Ravinia Festival, Highland Park, IL -- for rising stars series
25,000	Window to the World Communications, Chicago, IL -- for "Star Crossed Lovers" production

CHESAPEAKE CORP.

Company Headquarters

Richmond, VA
Web: http://www.cskcorp.com

Company Description

Founded: 1918
Ticker: CSK
Exchange: NYSE
Revenue: US$822.2 million (2002)
Employees: 5801 (2002)
SIC(s): 2435 Hardwood Veneer & Plywood, 2621 Paper Mills, 2631 Paperboard Mills, 2653 Corrugated & Solid Fiber Boxes.

Operating Locations

Chesapeake Corp. (IA--West Des Moines; KY--Louisville; MD--Pocomoke City, Princess Anne; NJ--Pennsauken; NY--Binghamton, Buffalo, North Tonawanda, Scotia; NC--Elizabeth City, Greensboro, Winston-Salem; OH--Madison, Sandusky; VA--Keysville, Milford, Norfolk, West Point, Williamsburg; WI--Appleton, Menasha)

Nonmonetary Support

Contact: Molly Remes, Director, Corporate Communications
Note: Co. provides nonmonetary support to nonprofits.

Chesapeake Corp. Foundation

Giving Contact

PO Box 2350
Richmond, VA 23218
Phone: (804)697-1000
Fax: (804)697-1199

Alternate Contact

Fran Boroughs, Assistant Secretary
Phone: (804)697-1132

Description

EIN: 540605823
Organization Type: Corporate Foundation
Giving Locations: operating locations.
Grant Types: Award, Capital, Employee Matching Gifts, Scholarship.

Financial Summary

Total Giving: $235,171 (2001); $310,504 (2000); $512,890 (1999). Note: Contributes through corporate direct giving program and foundation.
Giving Analysis: Giving for 2001 includes: foundation matching gifts ($54,530); foundation scholarships ($71,371); 1999: foundation matching gifts ($61,829); foundation scholarships ($80,611); foundation ($370,450); 1998: foundation matching gifts

($62,929); foundation scholarships ($73,366); foundation grants to United Way ($101,450); foundation ($345,450);

Assets: $1,617,138 (2001); $1,866,905 (2000); $2,120,030 (1999)

Gifts Received: $605,580 (1999); $540,000 (1998); $512,500 (1996). Note: Contributions are received from the Chesapeake Corporation.

Typical Recipients

Arts & Humanities: Arts Associations & Councils, Arts Centers, Arts Funds, Community Arts, Historic Preservation, History & Archaeology, Libraries, Museums/Galleries, Music, Theater

Civic & Public Affairs: African American Affairs, Asian American Affairs, Botanical Gardens/Parks, Community Foundations, Economic Development, Employment/Job Training, Civic & Public Affairs-General, Housing, Municipalities/Towns, Nonprofit Management, Philanthropic Organizations, Professional & Trade Associations, Public Policy, Safety, Urban & Community Affairs, Women's Affairs

Education: Agricultural Education, Business Education, Colleges & Universities, Community & Junior Colleges, Continuing Education, Education Associations, Education Funds, Engineering/Technological Education, Environmental Education, Education-General, Literacy, Minority Education, Private Education (Precollege), Public Education (Precollege), School Volunteerism, Science/Mathematics Education, Secondary Education (Private), Special Education, Student Aid, Vocational & Technical Education

Environment: Air/Water Quality, Forestry, Environment-General, Resource Conservation

Health: Cancer, Children's Health/Hospitals, Clinics/Medical Centers, Diabetes, Emergency/Ambulance Services, Health Organizations, Hospitals, Medical Rehabilitation, Mental Health, Multiple Sclerosis, Research/Studies Institutes

International: Health Care/Hospitals, International Relief Efforts

Religion: Religious Welfare

Science: Observatories & Planetariums, Science Museums, Scientific Centers & Institutes

Social Services: Community Service Organizations, Domestic Violence, Family Services, Homes, People with Disabilities, Recreation & Athletics, Scouts, Social Services-General, United Funds/United Ways, YMCA/YWCA/YMHA/YWHA, Youth Organizations

Application Procedures

Initial Contact: Send a letter of inquiry with a brief statement of the applicant's need for funds; foundation will respond to all preliminary inquiries.

Application Requirements: If the foundation requests a full proposal, it should include specific purpose of request and results sought; budget for project including the month in which it is requested that the grant be paid; recently audited financial statement; identity and qualifications of personnel involved in project; members of governing body; a list of other primary funding sources, particularly the United Way; evidence of tax-exempt status; statement that application has been reviewed and approved by organization's governing body.

Deadlines: December 1 for full grant applications; foundation trustees meet in January.

Decision Notification: Decisions are made at trustee meetings; secretary attempts to promptly notify organizations that do not fall within the foundation's scope.

Notes: Applications for operating grants should be for amounts not less than $1,000. Applications for capital grants should be for amounts not less than $5,000 and should not be payable over more than five years.

Restrictions

Foundation does not support individuals, organizations which are not tax-exempt under IRS standards, school athletic programs or athletic scholarships, religious or fraternal groups unless activities support the general community, school athletic programs or scholarships, political or lobbying groups organizations or candidates, or activities outside the company's geographical operating areas.

Additional Information

After the organization has received a grant, the Foundation requires an accounting of the distribution of funds and recent financial statements.

The Foundation reviews all specific requests for funds but does not respond to routine fund-raising appeals. A budget for the year is finalized in January and includes grants to education, health, community service, and cultural organizations to which the foundation regularly contributes.

Company gives directly through marketing or public affairs departments within each operating group.

Corporate Officials

Christopher R. Burgess: assistant vice president PRIM CORP EMPL assistant vice president: Chesapeake Corp.

John Paul Causey, Jr.: senior vice president, secretary, general counsel B Takoma Park, MD 1943. ED Davidson College AB (1965); University of Richmond TC Williams School of Law JD (1968). PRIM CORP EMPL senior vice president, secretary, general counsel: Chesapeake Corp. NONPR AFFIL member: American Corporate Counsel Association; member: American Society of Corporate Secretaries.

Joseph Carter Fox: chairman, president, chief executive officer B Petersburg, VA 1939. ED Washington & Lee University BS (1961); University of Virginia MBA (1963). PRIM CORP EMPL chairman, president, chief executive officer: Chesapeake Corp. CORP AFFIL director: Crestar Financial Corp. NONPR AFFIL director: American Forest & Paper Association.

Louis K. Matherne: treasurer B Brownsville, TN 1951. ED University of Virginia (1973); University of Pennsylvania (1978). PRIM CORP EMPL treasurer: Chesapeake Corp.

Foundation Officials

John Paul Causey, Jr.: chairman, trustee (see above)

Charles Sal Cianciola: trustee B Milwaukee, WI 1933. ED Lawrence University BS (1955). CORP AFFIL director: Associate First Bank of Neenah. CLUB AFFIL Viking Beach Club; Elks Club.

T. G. Harris: trustee

Bruce M. Pinover: trustee PRIM CORP EMPL vice president: Chesapeake Display & Packaging Co.

Brenda L. Skidmore: trustee

E. Massey Valentine: trustee ED University of Virginia (1956).

Grants Analysis

Disclosure Period: calendar year ending 2001

Total Grants: $72,000*

Number of Grants: 23

Average Grant: $3,130

Highest Grant: $20,000

Lowest Grant: $1,000

Typical Range: $1,000 to $10,000

*Note: Giving excludes matching gifts; scholarships; United Way. Grants analysis provided by foundation.

Recent Grants

Note: Grants derived from 2001 Form 990.

Library-Related

2,000	Warren County Memorial Library
1,000	Elis Olsson Memorial Library Fund, West Point, VA

General

20,000	Science Museum, Richmond, VA
18,000	United Way Forsyth County, Winston-Salem, NC
10,000	Lexington County Memorial Hospital
10,000	Robinson/Sture Olsson Auditorium and Fine Arts Center
8,700	United Way Broome, Binghamton, NY
5,000	Delran Emergency Squad
5,000	Habitat for Humanity, Gateway, MO
3,500	United Way, Richmond, VA
3,000	United Way Greater Richmond, Richmond, VA
3,000	Virginia Foundation for Independent Colleges, Richmond, VA

CHEVRONTEXACO CORP.

Company Headquarters

6001 Bollinger Canyon Rd.
San Ramon, CA 94583
Web: http://www.chevrontexaco.com

Company Description

Founded: 1926
Ticker: CVX
Exchange: NYSE
Acquired: Texaco (2001);
Former Name: Chevron Corp. (2001).
Revenue: US$98.691 billion (2002)
Profit: US$1.132 billion (2002)
Employees: 53014 (2002)
Fortune Rank: 7, per FORTUNE Magazine's list of 500 Largest U.S. Corporations (2002).
SIC(s): 1311 Crude Petroleum & Natural Gas, 1382 Oil & Gas Exploration Services, 2911 Petroleum Refining, 2992 Lubricating Oils & Greases.

Operating Locations

Chevron Corp. (AK--Delta Junction, Glennallen; CA--Anaheim, Concord, El Segundo, La Habra, Oxnard, Richmond, San Francisco, San Ramon, Ventura; CO--Denver, Englewood, Rangely; FL--Hollywood; GA--Athens, Atlanta; HI--Hilo, Kahului; IN--Elkhart; LA--Winnsboro; MD--Baltimore; MS--Pascagoula; NM--Santa Fe; OR--Portland, St. Helens; PA--Mercer; TX--Bryan, El Paso, Fredericksburg, Houston, Port Arthur, San Antonio, Segno, Silsbee; UT--Park City, Salt Lake City; WA--Spokane; WY--Evanston); ChevronCorp. (WA--Seattle)

Nonmonetary Support

Type: Donated Equipment
Note: Equipment is book value. Chevron has also donated land. Contact Chevron operating locations for local nonmonetary support.

Giving Contact

Manager, Corporate Contributions
ChevronTexaco Corp.
Worldwide Headquarters
575 Market Street
San Francisco, CA 94105
Phone: (925)842-1000
Fax: (415)894-3583
E-mail: comment@chevrontexaco.com
Web: http://www.chevronTEXACO.com/ social_responsibility/community/ annual_contributions.asp

Description

Organization Type: Corporate Giving Program
Giving Locations: corporate operating locations nationally and internationally.
Grant Types: Award, Employee Matching Gifts, General Support.
Note: Employee/director/retiree matching programs are available for educational institutions and arts and cultural organisation. Gifts to higher educational institutions will be matched up to $5,000 for employees, and up to $1,000 for retirees. Arts-related cultural gifts and gifts to precollege educational institutions will be matched up to $500 per individual annually.

Financial Summary

Total Giving: $48,518,964 (2002); $34,520,367 (2000); $20,900,000 (1999 approx). Note: Contributes through corporate direct giving program only. Total giving for 1998 and 1999 reflects Chevron's corporate giving. Total giving for 2000 reflects the combined totals of Chevron corporate contributions program and Texaco Foundation giving.

Giving Analysis: Giving for 2000 includes: foundation ($7,323,718); corporate direct giving ($27,196,649); 1998: corporate grants to United Way ($2,456,438) corporate direct giving ($23,415,476)

Typical Recipients

Arts & Humanities: Arts Associations & Councils, Arts Centers, Arts Festivals, Arts Funds, Ballet, Community Arts, Dance, Film & Video, Historic Preservation, Libraries, Museums/Galleries, Music, Opera, Performing Arts, Public Broadcasting, Theater

Civic & Public Affairs: African American Affairs, Business/Free Enterprise, Economic Development, Economic Policy, Employment/Job Training, Civic & Public Affairs-General, Hispanic Affairs, Housing, Law & Justice, Legal Aid, Municipalities/Towns, Nonprofit Management, Professional & Trade Associations, Public Policy, Rural Affairs, Safety, Urban & Community Affairs, Women's Affairs, Zoos/Aquariums

Education: Agricultural Education, Arts/Humanities Education, Business Education, Colleges & Universities, Economic Education, Education Associations, Education Funds, Education Reform, Elementary Education (Private), Engineering/Technological Education, Faculty Development, Education-General, International Studies, Journalism/Media Education, Literacy, Minority Education, Public Education (Precollege), Science/Mathematics Education, Student Aid

Environment: Environment-General, Resource Conservation, Wildlife Protection

Health: AIDS/HIV, Clinics/Medical Centers, Emergency/Ambulance Services, Health Policy/Cost Containment, Health Funds, Health Organizations, Hospices, Hospitals, Medical Rehabilitation, Mental Health, Public Health, Single-Disease Health Associations

International: Foreign Educational Institutions, International-General, Health Care/Hospitals, International Affairs, International Development, International Environmental Issues, International Peace & Security Issues, International Relations, International Relief Efforts

Science: Observatories & Planetariums, Science Exhibits & Fairs, Scientific Centers & Institutes, Scientific Organizations

Social Services: Child Welfare, Community Centers, Community Service Organizations, Crime Prevention, Day Care, Delinquency & Criminal Rehabilitation, Domestic Violence, Emergency Relief, Family Services, Food/Clothing Distribution, Homes, People with Disabilities, Refugee Assistance, Senior Services, Shelters/Homelessness, Substance Abuse, United Funds/United Ways, Volunteer Services, Youth Organizations

Application Procedures

Initial Contact: ChevronTexaco is currently undergoing a review of its grant programs and guidelines. As of press time, the company was not accepting grant proposals. Once new guidelines become available, they will be posted on the company's web site.

Additional Information

In October 2001, Chevron and Texaco merged to become ChevronTexaco. The company is honoring all existing commitments to community partnership programs and grants made by Chevron, Texaco, and Caltex. At press time for this edition, the company was developing grant guidelines that will reflect the new company's program focus. not been deleted from

this entry. When new information is available, the entry will be re-written.

When grants are approved, Chevron requires recipients to sign grant agreements which state that financial and progress reports will be submitted to Chevron to help it monitor the effectiveness of its program. Chevron also requires completion of a substantiation form for grants totaling $250 or more.

Please do not send video or audio tapes. Submitted materials use as a guide for proposals.

If funding is sought for the environment or education, and it is broad in scope, requests for a Chevron Investment Grant application form should be made. Unsolicited proposals outside these two areas of emphasis are not encouraged by this grant program.

Publications: Philanthropy Report

Corporate Officials

Lydia I. Beebe: corporate secretaryc B McPherson, KS 1952. ED University of Kansas (1974); Golden Gate University (1980). PRIM CORP EMPL corporate secretary: Chevron Corp. NONPR AFFIL member: American Bar Association.

R. Bruce Marsh: general tax counsel B New Orleans, LA 1942. ED University of Texas (1966). PRIM CORP EMPL general tax counsel: Chevron Corp. NONPR AFFIL member: Mid-Continent Oil Gas Association; member: Tax Executives Institute; member: American Petroleum Institute.

David J. O'Reilly: chairman, chief executive officer, director B January 1947. ED University College of Dublin (1968). PRIM CORP EMPL chairman, chief executive officer, director: ChevronTexaco Corp. NONPR AFFIL board governors: San Francisco Symphony; member: Western Studies Petroleum Association; member: JP Morgan International Council; member: National Petroleum Council; member: Business Council; member: Business Roundtable; director: American Petroleum Institute; member: Bay Area Council.

Glenn F. Tilton: vice chairman, director ED University of South Carolina BA (1970). PRIM CORP EMPL vice chairman, director: ChevronTexaco Inc.

Giving Program Officials

Skip Rhodes: manager corporate contributions

Grants Analysis

Disclosure Period: calendar year ending 2000
Total Grants: $34,520,367*
Typical Range: $2,000 to $10,000 and $25,000 to $100,000

*Note: Grants analysis includes Chevron corporate contributions and Texaco Foundation grants made in 2000.

Recent Grants

Note: Grants derived from 1998 Form 990.

General

980,000	Unrestricted Fund, San Francisco, CA
671,077	Stanford University, Stanford, CA
550,000	Contra Costa County Department of Health Services, Martinez, CA
272,376	Ugborodo Town Relocation Project, Ugborodo Nigeria
270,005	University of California, Berkeley, Berkeley, CA
258,039	TB Moblie Clinic Kazakhstan
248,294	Nigerian Conservation Foundation, Lagos Nigeria
232,015	Dolisie Project, Dolisie Republic of the Congo
219,205	Chevron Scholarship Progam for Employees' Children
217,500	Yayasan Sosial Chevron dan Texaco Indonesia, Jakarta Indonesia

Company Description

Revenue: US$2.027 billion (2001)
Employees: 700 (2001)
SIC(s): 6231 Security & Commodity Exchanges.

Chicago Board of Trade Foundation

Giving Contact

Julia Spraggs, Administrator
141 W. Jackson Blvd.
Chicago, IL 60604
Phone: (312)435-3500

Description

Founded: 1984
EIN: 363348469
Organization Type: Corporate Foundation
Giving Locations: IL
Grant Types: General Support.

Donor Information

Founder: Chicago Board of Trade

Financial Summary

Total Giving: $190,280 (fiscal year ending June 30, 2001); $170,000 (fiscal 1999); $155,000 (fiscal 1998)
Assets: $3,924,656 (fiscal 2001); $4,188,683 (fiscal 1999); $3,878,396 (fiscal 1998)
Gifts Received: $764 (fiscal 2001); $203,010 (fiscal 1994); $100,000 (fiscal 1992)

Typical Recipients

Arts & Humanities: Arts Festivals, Arts Institutes, Ballet, Community Arts, History & Archaeology, Libraries, Museums/Galleries, Music, Opera, Public Broadcasting, Theater

Civic & Public Affairs: Employment/Job Training, Civic & Public Affairs-General, Parades/Festivals, Philanthropic Organizations, Urban & Community Affairs, Zoos/Aquariums

Education: Business-School Partnerships, Education Associations, Literacy, Private Education (Precollege), Secondary Education (Private), Special Education, Student Aid

Health: Cancer, Children's Health/Hospitals, Clinics/Medical Centers, Diabetes, Medical Rehabilitation, Multiple Sclerosis, Public Health, Single-Disease Health Associations

Religion: Jewish Causes, Ministries, Religious Organizations, Religious Welfare

Science: Observatories & Planetariums, Science Museums, Scientific Centers & Institutes

Social Services: At-Risk Youth, Child Welfare, Community Service Organizations, Domestic Violence, Emergency Relief, Food/Clothing Distribution, Homes, People with Disabilities, Scouts, Shelters/Homelessness, United Funds/United Ways, Youth Organizations

Application Procedures

Initial Contact: Send brief letter describing program.
Deadlines: None.

Restrictions

Does not support: individuals, religious organizations for sectarian purposes, political or lobbying groups, or hospitals.

Corporate Officials

Patrick H. Arbor: chairman, chief executive officer PRIM CORP EMPL chairman: Chicago Board of Trade.

Thomas Roy Donovan: president, chief executive officer B Chicago, IL 1937. ED Illinois Institute of Technology BA (1972); Illinois Institute of Technology MPA (1975). PRIM CORP EMPL president, chief executive officer: Chicago Board of Trade. CORP AFFIL director: MidAm. NONPR AFFIL director, member: National Futures Association; council: Northwestern University Associates; director: Illinois Leadership Council Agricultural Education; director; member: De La Salle Institute; council: Grad School Business University; director, member executive committee: Chicago Association Commerce Industry; member: Chicago Central Area Comm. CLUB AFFIL Communal Chicago Club; Executive Club Chicago.

Foundation Officials

David P. Brennan: chairman
Thomas P. Cunningham: director
David J. Fisher: director
Glen M. Johnson: treasurer
Francis X. O'Donnell: director

Grants Analysis

Disclosure Period: fiscal year ending June 30, 2001
Total Grants: $190,280
Number of Grants: 32
Average Grant: $5,946
Highest Grant: $20,000
Lowest Grant: $2,000
Typical Range: $2,500 to $10,000

Recent Grants

Note: Grants derived from fiscal 2000 Form 990.

General

20,000	Adler Planetarium, Chicago, IL
20,000	Field Museum, Chicago, IL
10,000	Family Shelter Service, Glen Ellyn, IL
10,000	Infant, Lincolnwood, IL
10,000	J Kyle Braid Foundation, Village Grove, CO
7,500	Gus Foundation, Chicago, IL
5,000	Blessed Sacrament, North Aurora, IL
5,000	Brookfield Zoo, Brookfield, IL
5,000	Children's Heart Foundation, Chicago, IL
5,000	Cristo Rey Jesuit High School, Chicago, IL

CHICAGO RAWHIDE CO.

Company Headquarters

735 Tollgate Road
Elgin, IL 60123-9332
Web: http://www.chicago-rawhide.com

Company Description

Former Name: CR Industries.
Employees: 1,800
SIC(s): 3053 Gaskets, Packing & Sealing Devices, 3714 Motor Vehicle Parts & Accessories.
Parent Company: SKF U.S.A., Inc., Northtown, PA, United States
Parent Revenue: US$5,096,900,000 (2001)

Operating Locations

Chicago Rawhide Manufacturing Co. (IL--Elgin); Chicago Rawhide Manufacturing Co. (IN; KS; MO; OK; SD)

Nonmonetary Support

Type: Donated Equipment; Loaned Executives

Giving Contact

Wally Borduer, Development Manager
900 N. State
Elgin, IL 60123
Phone: (847)742-7840
Fax: (847)742-0970

Description

Organization Type: Corporate Giving Program
Giving Locations: headquarters and operating communities.
Grant Types: Capital, Challenge, Endowment, General Support, Project, Research, Seed Money.

Typical Recipients

Arts & Humanities: Arts Associations & Councils, Arts Centers, Historic Preservation, Libraries, Museums/Galleries, Music, Performing Arts
Civic & Public Affairs: Business/Free Enterprise, Economic Development, Law & Justice, Professional & Trade Associations, Public Policy, Urban & Community Affairs, Zoos/Aquariums
Education: Business Education, Colleges & Universities, Economic Education, Engineering/Technological Education
Health: Hospitals
Social Services: Community Service Organizations, People with Disabilities, Substance Abuse, United Funds/United Ways

Application Procedures

Initial Contact: Submit a brief letter or proposal, including proof of tax-exempt status, a description of organization, and the purpose of funds sought. Applications are accepted any time.

Restrictions

The following are not considered for charitable contributions: fraternal organizations, goodwill advertising, or religious organizations for fraternal purposes.

Corporate Officials

Kent Alcott: chief financial officer, chief executive officer PRIM CORP EMPL chief financial officer: Chicago Rawhide Manufacturing Co.
Gary Butcher: president, chief executive officer PRIM CORP EMPL president, chief executive officer: Chicago Rawhide Manufacturing Co.

Grants Analysis

Typical Range: $1,000 to $2,500

CHICAGO TITLE CORP.

Company Headquarters

171 N. Clark Street
Chicago, IL 60601
Phone: (312)630-2000
Fax: (312)223-5955
Web: http://www.ctt.com

Company Description

Employees: 10,550 (1998)
Parent Company: Fidelity National Financial Inc., 3916 State St., Suite 300, Santa Barbara, CA, United States

Chicago Title and Trust Co. Foundation

Giving Contact

Eileen Hughes, Treasurer
171 N. Clark Street, 9TF
Chicago, IL 60601-3294
Phone: (312)335-9386

Description

Founded: 1951
EIN: 366036809
Organization Type: Corporate Foundation
Giving Locations: IL: Chicago
Grant Types: Award, Employee Matching Gifts, General Support, Matching.

Donor Information

Founder: Chicago Title and Trust Co.

Financial Summary

Total Giving: $285,577 (2001); $512,187 (2000); $678,009 (1998). Note: Contributes through corporate direct giving program and foundation.
Giving Analysis: Giving for 2000 includes: foundation grants to United Way ($163,248); foundation ($348,939); 1998: foundation matching gifts ($90,490); foundation grants to United Way ($147,639) foundation ($439,880)
Assets: $2,399,779 (2001); $2,540,103 (1998); $2,382,819 (1997)
Gifts Received: $650,000 (2000); $360,000 (1998); $180,000 (1997). Note: In 1998, contributions were received from Chicago Title and Trust Co.

Typical Recipients

Arts & Humanities: Arts Appreciation, Arts Centers, Arts Festivals, Arts Institutes, Community Arts, Arts & Humanities-General, Libraries, Museums/Galleries, Music, Opera, Performing Arts, Public Broadcasting, Theater
Civic & Public Affairs: African American Affairs, Asian American Affairs, Botanical Gardens/Parks, Business/Free Enterprise, Chambers of Commerce, Clubs, Economic Development, Employment/Job Training, Civic & Public Affairs-General, Housing, Law & Justice, Legal Aid, Nonprofit Management, Philanthropic Organizations, Public Policy, Urban & Community Affairs, Women's Affairs, Zoos/Aquariums
Education: Business Education, Colleges & Universities, Economic Education, Economic Education, Education Funds, Education-General, Journalism/Media Education, Legal Education, Literacy, Medical Education, Minority Education, Public Education (Precollege), School Volunteerism, Secondary Education (Private), Student Aid
Health: Cancer, Children's Health/Hospitals, Clinics/Medical Centers, Diabetes, Emergency/Ambulance Services, Eyes/Blindness, Health Organizations, Hospitals, Long-Term Care, Multiple Sclerosis, Respiratory, Single-Disease Health Associations, Trauma Treatment
Religion: Jewish Causes, Religious Welfare
Social Services: At-Risk Youth, Big Brother/Big Sister, Child Abuse, Child Welfare, Community Service Organizations, Crime Prevention, Delinquency & Criminal Rehabilitation, Family Planning, Food/Clothing Distribution, Scouts, Senior Services, Shelters/Homelessness, United Funds/United Ways, YMCA/YWCA/YMHA/YWHA, Youth Organizations

Application Procedures

Initial Contact: Send a written proposal.
Application Requirements: Include a description of organization, its purpose, history, programs, and achievements; statement describing the specific purpose of grant request; a plan for evaluating program; current operating budget and budget for proposed project; audited financial statement; copy of certificate of tax exemption; list of officers and board members; and sources of income.
Deadlines: March 1 and September 1.
Evaluative Criteria: Applicant organization contributes to improving the quality of community life, with an emphasis on the urban community; organization is tax-exempt; organization does not show evidence of discrimination; and program qualifies under established priorities of foundation.

Decision Notification: The board meets in April and October.

Notes: Proposals should generally not exceed 10 pages in length. Elaborate, costly proposals are discouraged.

Restrictions

Foundation does not support religious or political activities, funds for reducing or eliminating a budget deficit, or individuals.

Additional Information

Although multi-year grants may be made, grants are not automatically renewed. Requests must be submitted annually, along with a financial statement and an account of accomplishments with the expenditure of funds.

Publications: Application Guidelines

Corporate Officials

Stuart Douglas Bilton: president, chief executive officerhuman resources B Croydon, United Kingdom 1946. ED London School of Economics (1967); University of Wisconsin (1970). PRIM CORP EMPL president, chief executive officer: Chicago Trust Co. CORP AFFIL executive vice president: Chicago Title & Trust Co.; director: Security Trust Co.; president: Alleghany Asset Management Inc.; director: Baldwin & Lyons Inc.

Richard L. Pollay: vice chairman emeritus, director B 1932. ED University of Chicago BS (1952); University of Chicago JD (1955). PRIM CORP EMPL vice chairman emeritus, director: Chicago Title and Trust Co.

Richard Paul Toft: chairman B Saint Louis County, MO 1936. ED University of Missouri (1958). PRIM CORP EMPL chairman: Chicago Title and Trust Co. CORP AFFIL director: Cologne Life Reinsurance Co.; director: Peoples Energy Corp.; chairman, chief executive officer: Alleghany Asset Management Inc.; chairman: Chicago Title Insurance Co.

S. LaNette Zimmerman: senior vice president human resources B Newark, AR 1944. ED University of Wisconsin (1969); University of Wisconsin (1975). PRIM CORP EMPL executive vice president, chief human resources officer: Chicago Title and Trust Co.

Foundation Officials

Stuart Douglas Bilton: trustee (see above)
Norman Bobins: trustee
Edson Burton: trustee
William Foley: vice chairman
Thomas Hodges: secretary
Eileen Hughes: treasurer
Nancy Labik: foundation coord
Marguerite Leanne Lachman: trustee B Vancouver, BC Canada 1943. ED University of Southern California BA (1964); Claremont Graduate School MA (1966). PRIM CORP EMPL managing director: Schroder Real Estate Associates. CORP AFFIL managing director: Schroder Mortgage Associates; director: Liberty Property Trust; director: Lincoln National Corp.; director: Chicago Title Corp. NONPR AFFIL trustee, vice president: Urban Land Foundation; trustee, vice president: Urban Land Institute; member: New York Womens Forum. CLUB AFFIL Commercial Club Chicago.

Peter Leemputte: trustee
Margaret (Pontius) "Mardie" Mac Kimm: trustee B Chicago, IL 1933. ED College of William & Mary BA (1955). PRIM CORP EMPL senior vice president corporate communications: Kraft Foods, Inc. CORP AFFIL director: FW Woolworth Co.; director: E.I. du Pont de Nemours & Co.; director: Venator Group Inc.; director: Chicago Title Insurance Co.; director: Chicago Title & Trust Co. NONPR AFFIL executive committee: Chicago Community Trust. CLUB AFFIL Womens Athletic Club.

Richard L. Pollay: trustee (see above)

John E. Rau: trustee B Milwaukee, WI 1948. ED Boston College BS (1970); Harvard University Graduate School of Business Administration MBA (1972). ADD CORP EMPL president: Chicago Title & Trust Co.; president: Chicago Title Insurance Co. MO; president: Security Union Title Insurance Co.; president, chief executive officer: Ticor Title Insurance Co. CORP AFFIL director: LaSalle National Bank; director: Nicor Inc.; director: Borg-Warner Automotive Inc.; director: First Industrial Realty Corp.

Robert Stuker: trustee
Richard Paul Toft: trustee (see above)
Richard Williamson: trustee
S. LaNette Zimmerman: trustee (see above)

Grants Analysis

Disclosure Period: calendar year ending 2001
Total Grants: $265,577*
Number of Grants: 44
Average Grant: $6,036
Highest Grant: $30,000
Lowest Grant: $500
Typical Range: $1,000 to $10,000
***Note:** Giving excludes United Way.

Recent Grants

Note: Grants derived from 2001 Form 990.

General

30,000	Commercial Club Foundation, Chicago, IL
20,000	Chicago Shakespeare Theater, Chicago, IL
20,000	Neighborhood Housing Services, Chicago, IL
20,000	United Way, Philadelphia, PA
15,000	Chicago Shakespeare Theater, Chicago, IL
10,000	Boys and Girls Club, Chicago, IL
10,000	Chicago Humanities Festival, Chicago, IL
10,000	Chicago Shakespeare Theater, Chicago, IL
10,000	Evanston Northwestern Hospital, Evanston, IL
10,000	Goodman Theater, Chicago, IL

CHICAGO TRIBUNE DIRECT MARKETING

Company Headquarters

505 NW Ave.
Northlake, IL 60164
Web: http://www.tribune.com

Company Description

Employees: 10,700
SIC(s): 2711 Newspapers, 7331 Direct Mail Advertising Services, 8742 Management Consulting Services.
Parent Company: Tribune Co., 435 N. Michigan Avenue, Chicago, IL, United States

Operating Locations

Chicago Tribune Co. (FL--Hollywood; GA--Atlanta; IL--Countryside, Freeport, Homewood, Rosemont, Schaumburg, Vernon Hills, Warrenville; NY--New York; TX--Dallas)

Nonmonetary Support

Type: Cause-related Marketing & Promotion
Volunteer Programs: The company's TribUnity program directs volunteer efforts toward reading and hunger issues.
Note: Nonmonetary support is no longer offered.

Chicago Tribune Foundation

Giving Contact

Frank Gihan, President
Chicago Tribune Foundation
435 N. Michigan Ave., Suite 200
Chicago, IL 60611-4041
Phone: (312)222-4300
Fax: (312)222-3751
E-mail: ctcommunityrelations@tribune.com
Web: http://www.chicagotribune.com/extras/comrel/

Description

EIN: 366050792
Organization Type: Corporate Foundation
Giving Locations: IL: Chicago including metropolitan area
Grant Types: Employee Matching Gifts, General Support, Project.
Note: Employee matching gift ratio: 2 to 1.

Financial Summary

Total Giving: $750,000 (2002); $685,614 (2001); $1,080,142 (2000). Note: Contributes through corporate direct giving program and foundation.
Giving Analysis: Giving for 2000 includes: foundation matching gifts ($196,842); foundation ($883,300); 1999: foundation matching gifts ($114,192); foundation grants to United Way ($475,000); foundation ($598,002); 1998: foundation scholarships ($112,627); foundation grants to United Way ($472,745); foundation ($945,844);
Assets: $5,000,000 (2002 approx); $6,001,961 (2001); $7,163,024 (2000)
Gifts Received: $408,893 (1999); $867,446 (1998); $1,475,000 (1996). Note: The foundation is supported by funds from the Chicago Tribune Company.

Typical Recipients

Arts & Humanities: Arts Associations & Councils, Arts Centers, Arts Funds, Arts Institutes, Arts Outreach, Community Arts, Dance, Ethnic & Folk Arts, Arts & Humanities-General, History & Archaeology, Libraries, Literary Arts, Museums/Galleries, Music, Opera, Performing Arts, Public Broadcasting, Theater
Civic & Public Affairs: African American Affairs, Asian American Affairs, Chambers of Commerce, Civil Rights, Clubs, Economic Development, Employment/Job Training, Civic & Public Affairs-General, Hispanic Affairs, Housing, Minority Business, Municipalities/Towns, Native American Affairs, Nonprofit Management, Philanthropic Organizations, Professional & Trade Associations, Professional & Trade Associations, Public Policy, Urban & Community Affairs, Women's Affairs, Zoos/Aquariums
Education: Arts/Humanities Education, Business Education, Colleges & Universities, Economic Education, Engineering/Technological Education, Education-General, Journalism/Media Education, Legal Education, Literacy, Minority Education, Private Education (Precollege), Public Education (Precollege), Religious Education, Secondary Education (Public), Student Aid, Vocational & Technical Education
Environment: Environment-General
Health: AIDS/HIV, Children's Health/Hospitals, Emergency/Ambulance Services, Health Organizations, Prenatal Health Issues, Transplant Networks/Donor Banks
International: Human Rights
Religion: Jewish Causes, Ministries, Religious Organizations, Religious Welfare
Science: Science Museums
Social Services: Child Abuse, Child Welfare, Community Service Organizations, Delinquency & Criminal Rehabilitation, Domestic Violence, Family Services, Food/Clothing Distribution, People with Disabilities, Senior Services, Shelters/Homelessness, Social Services-General, Substance

Abuse, United Funds/United Ways, Volunteer Services, Youth Organizations

Application Procedures

Initial Contact: Send cover letter and grant proposal, preferably using the Chicago Area Grant Application Form. For application forms and information, call (312) 222-4300.

Application Requirements: The application should be accompanied by a one-sided, one-page list of board of directors; copy of the most recent IRS tax-exempt status form; audited financial statements or Form 990 from the most recent fiscal year; organization budget for year in which funding is being sought; sources of support, listing which funds have been committed; annual report or other literature on the organization's programmatic, financial, and managerial accomplishments.

Deadlines: February 1 for culture proposals, June 1 for journalism proposals. Civic proposals are considered by invitation only.

Decision Notification: Board meeting for culture proposals is held in late May and for journalism proposals in late September. All requests for support will be acknowledged.

Restrictions

Grants are generally not made to capital campaigns, endowments, or individuals. Because grants are a more cost-effective mode of support, the company does not generally purchase tables at fund-raising events benefiting nonprofit organizations. The company does not fund international projects.

Additional Information

The Chicago Tribune Company works in partnership with the Robert R. McCormick Tribune Foundation to assist local philanthropy. Company assists foundation in raising monies for two of its funds: Chicago Tribune Charities and the Chicago Tribune Holiday Fund. The Chicago Tribune uses articles, columns, and other aspects of the newspaper to solicit donations from its readers to finance the Chicago Tribune Holiday Fund, which addresses the needs of children, the homeless, hunger and developmental disability in metropolitan Chicago. These funds are matched by the McCormick Tribune Foundation and used to disburse gifts of toys and books to children during the holiday season. Support also goes to organizations that combat child abuse and developmental delay. Other areas of support include programs or organizations that provide immediate shelter needs for the homeless, and hunger programs that subsidize food banks or alleviate hunger. Chicago Tribune Charities receives funds from the sponsorship endeavors of the Chicago Tribune Company. These monies are used to combat illiteracy and unemployment in the Chicago area. Eligible programs include job preparation and training as well as adult education programs, GED preparation and English as a Second Language programs. The Robert R. McCormick Tribune Foundation also supports programs that enhance the independence of persons with debilitating mental and physical disabilities. All money donated by the public or raised through sponsorship by the Chicago Tribune is matched by the Robert R. McCormick Tribune Foundation. Requests for support in these areas require a completed application form to be sent to the foundation in care of the Chicago Tribune Charities or the Chicago Tribune Holiday Fund at 435 North Michigan Avenue, Chicago, Illinois, 60611. Fund at 435 North Michigan Avenue, Chicago, Illinois, 60611. Fund at 435 North Michigan Avenue, Chicago, Illinois, 60611. Fund at 435 North Michigan Avenue, Chicago, Illinois, 60611. Fund at 435 North Michigan Avenue, Chicago, Illinois, 60611.

Publications: Annual Report; Grantmaking Guidelines

Corporate Officials

Denise Palmer: vice president, strategy & finance B 1957. ED Northwestern University Kellogg Graduate School of Business Administration; University of Dayton BS. PRIM CORP EMPL vice president, strategy & finance: Chicago Tribune Co.

Grants Analysis

Disclosure Period: calendar year ending 2001
Total Grants: $552,850*
Number of Grants: 45
Average Grant: $12,286
Highest Grant: $45,000
Lowest Grant: $1,350
Typical Range: $5,000 to $25,000
*Note: Giving excludes matching gifts.

Recent Grants

Note: Grants derived from 2001 Form 990.

Library-Related

7,500	North Suburban Library Foundation, Wheeling, IL -- operating support

General

45,000	Roosevelt University, Chicago, IL -- support media high-tech newsroom
25,000	American Society of Newspaper Editors Foundation, Reston, VA -- Diversity Projects
25,000	Art Institute of Chicago, Chicago, IL -- for the endowment for the Gene Siskel Film Center
25,000	Community Renewal Society, Chicago, IL -- for internships at the "Chicago Reporter"
25,000	Illinois Conservation Foundation, Chicago, IL -- John Husar Outdoor Education Endowment
25,000	Investigative Reporters and Editors, Columbia, MD -- convention support
25,000	Youth Communication/Chicago Center, Chicago, IL
20,000	United Negro College Fund, Chicago, IL
19,500	Literary Prizes, Chicago, IL -- Nelson Algren and Heartland Literacy Awards
19,000	Chicago Cultural Center Foundation, Chicago, IL -- for Chicago Tribute

CHILDREN'S FOUNDATION OF ERIE COUNTY

Giving Contact

Ann M. Denman, Treasurer
P.O. Box 560
Kenmore, NY 14217
Phone: (716)877-0418

Description

Founded: 1836
EIN: 166000171
Organization Type: Private Foundation
Giving Locations: NY: Erie County
Grant Types: General Support.

Donor Information

Founder: Founded by the late Ida Z. Welt.

Financial Summary

Total Giving: $262,400 (2001); $250,200 (2000); $215,000 (1999)
Assets: $4,818,865 (2001); $5,230,694 (2000); $5,448,477 (1999)
Gifts Received: $25 (1996); $1,540 (1995); $395 (1994). Note: In 1994, contributions were received from the estate of Ida Z. Welt.

Typical Recipients

Arts & Humanities: Arts Outreach, Arts & Humanities-General, Libraries, Music, Theater
Civic & Public Affairs: Civic & Public Affairs-General, Urban & Community Affairs
Education: Arts/Humanities Education, Education Reform, Education-General, Leadership Training, Preschool Education, Private Education (Precollege), Special Education
Environment: Air/Water Quality, Environment-General
Health: Children's Health/Hospitals, Diabetes, Heart, Hospices, Single-Disease Health Associations
International: International Affairs
Religion: Churches, Ministries, Religious Welfare
Social Services: At-Risk Youth, Camps, Child Welfare, Community Centers, Community Service Organizations, Day Care, Family Planning, Family Services, People with Disabilities, Recreation & Athletics, Scouts, Social Services-General, United Funds/United Ways, YMCA/YWCA/YMHA/YWHA, Youth Organizations

Application Procedures

Initial Contact: Send a brief letter of inquiry requesting application guidelines.
Application Requirements: Include a description of program for which funds are requested, amount requested, purpose of funds sought, recently audited financial statement, proof of tax-exempt status, and how the program will benefit at-risk minors.
Deadlines: January 15.

Restrictions

Limited to organizations serving needy children in Erie County, NY.

Foundation Officials

Hilary P. Bradford: trustee
Winthrop Lawrence Buck: trustee
David Edmunds: trustee
Rosa Gonzelez: trustee
Charles J. Hahn: president
Calvin J. Haller: trustee B Buffalo, NY 1925. ED University of Buffalo BS (1949). NONPR AFFIL chairman board trustee: YMCA Greater Buffalo; trustee: YMCA Metropolitan Buffalo & Erie County; member: University Buffalo Alumni Association; director: Niagara Lutheran Nursing Home; member: Savings Banks Association New York State; member: New York Society Security Analysts; member: Newcomen Society North America; member: National Association Mutual Savings Banks; member: Masons; member: National Association Business Economists; director: Cerebral Palsy Association; director: Children's Foundation; director: Buffalo Federation Neighborhood Center; member: Beta Gamma Sigma; member: Buffalo Area Chamber of Commerce; member: American Institute Banking. CLUB AFFIL Equality Club; Buffalo Country Club; Bond Club; Buffalo Club.
Lewis F. Hazel: treasurer
Mary G. Howland: vice president, trustee
Betsy Mitchell: trustee
Susan Russ: trustee
Amelia Sherrets: trustee
Kevin I. Sullivan: trustee
Edward F. Walsh, Jr.: secretary, trustee

Grants Analysis

Disclosure Period: calendar year ending 2001
Total Grants: $262,400
Number of Grants: 71
Average Grant: $3,696
Highest Grant: $20,000
Lowest Grant: $1,200
Typical Range: $1,000 to $5,000

Recent Grants

Note: Grants derived from 2000 Form 990.

Library-Related

20,000	The Library Foundation of Buffalo

General

30,000	Success by 6
10,000	Planned Parenthood
9,000	Gateway-Longview Day Care Center
7,800	Buffalo Audubon Society
7,000	Child & Family Services
7,000	The Salvation Army
5,000	Buffalo Federation of Neighborhood Centers
5,000	Camp Fire Boys & Girls of Buffalo
5,000	Parents Anonymous of Buffalo
5,000	St. Augustine's Center Inc.

ROBERTA M. CHILDS CHARITABLE FOUNDATION

Giving Contact

John R. D. McClintock, Trustee
PO Box 639
North Andover, MA 01845-0639
Phone: (978)685-4113

Description

Founded: 1978
EIN: 042660275
Organization Type: Private Foundation
Giving Locations: MA
Grant Types: General Support, Operating Expenses.

Donor Information

Founder: the late Roberta M. Childs

Financial Summary

Total Giving: $641,500 (fiscal year ending March 31, 2002); $314,000 (fiscal 2000); $278,000 (fiscal 1999)
Assets: $6,837,285 (fiscal 2002); $7,463,583 (fiscal 2000); $6,890,152 (fiscal 1999)

Typical Recipients

Arts & Humanities: Ethnic & Folk Arts, Historic Preservation, Libraries, Public Broadcasting
Civic & Public Affairs: Economic Development, Civic & Public Affairs-General, Housing, Law & Justice, Philanthropic Organizations, Urban & Community Affairs
Education: Colleges & Universities, Education-General, Legal Education, Medical Education, Minority Education, Private Education (Precollege), Public Education (Precollege), Special Education, Student Aid
Environment: Environment-General, Resource Conservation, Wildlife Protection
Health: Children's Health/Hospitals, Clinics/Medical Centers, Home-Care Services, Hospitals, Medical Rehabilitation, Medical Research, Single-Disease Health Associations, Trauma Treatment
Religion: Ministries, Religious Organizations, Religious Welfare
Social Services: Animal Protection, Animal Protection, At-Risk Youth, Child Welfare, Community Service Organizations, Counseling, Delinquency & Criminal Rehabilitation, Emergency Relief, Family Services, Homes, People with Disabilities, Refugee Assistance, Senior Services, Shelters/Homelessness, Substance Abuse, YMCA/YWCA/YMHA/YWHA, Youth Organizations

Application Procedures

Initial Contact: The foundation has no formal grant application procedure or application form.
Deadlines: None.

Foundation Officials

John R. D. McClintock: trustee

Grants Analysis

Disclosure Period: fiscal year ending March 31, 2002
Total Grants: $641,500
Number of Grants: 105
Average Grant: $5,447*
Highest Grant: $75,000
Lowest Grant: $2,000
Typical Range: $3,000 to $10,000
*Note: Average grant figure excludes highest grant.

Recent Grants

Note: Grants derived from 2000 Form 990.

General

5,000	Accelerated School, Los Angeles, CA
5,000	Adolescent Consultation Services, Cambridge, MA
5,000	Alice Lloyd College, Grayson, KY
5,000	Alice Lloyd College, Pippa Passes, KY
5,000	Berea College, Berea, KY
5,000	Boston Biomedical Research Institute, Boston, MA
5,000	Boys and Girls Club of Boston, Boston, MA
5,000	Brighten Your Future, Logan, OH
5,000	David Jon Louison Foundation, Inc., Brockton, MA
5,000	FCD Educational Services, Needham, MA

CHILES FOUNDATION

Giving Contact

Earle M. Chiles, President & Trustee
111 Southwest Fifth Avenue, Suite 4050
Portland, OR 97204
Phone: (503)222-2143
Fax: (503)228-7079
E-mail: cf@qwest.net

Description

Founded: 1941
EIN: 936031125
Organization Type: Family Foundation
Giving Locations: primarily Pacific Northwest.
Grant Types: General Support, Project, Research, Scholarship.

Donor Information

Founder: Incorporated in 1949 in Oregon by the late Eva Chiles Meyer, the late Earle A. Chiles, and Virginia H. Chiles.

Financial Summary

Total Giving: $1,784,150 (2001); $2,251,500 (2000); $2,006,600 (1999)
Giving Analysis: Giving for 2001 includes: foundation ($2,021,100) 1998: foundation scholarships ($194,400)
Assets: $19,325,175 (2001); $22,393,165 (2000); $24,436,913 (1999)

Typical Recipients

Arts & Humanities: Arts Festivals, Dance, Arts & Humanities-General, Historic Preservation, History & Archaeology, Libraries, Museums/Galleries, Music, Opera, Performing Arts, Public Broadcasting, Theater
Civic & Public Affairs: African American Affairs, Botanical Gardens/Parks, Community Foundations, Ethnic Organizations, Civic & Public Affairs-General, Municipalities/Towns, Public Policy, Rural Affairs, Safety, Urban & Community Affairs, Women's Affairs, Zoos/Aquariums

Education: Afterschool/Enrichment Programs, Agricultural Education, Arts/Humanities Education, Business Education, Colleges & Universities, Education-General, International Studies, Leadership Training, Legal Education, Minority Education, Private Education (Precollege), Public Education (Precollege), Religious Education, Science/Mathematics Education, Secondary Education (Public), Student Aid
Environment: Environment-General
Health: Cancer, Clinics/Medical Centers, Emergency/Ambulance Services, Health Funds, Health Organizations, Heart, Hospitals, Medical Research, Multiple Sclerosis, Nursing Services, Prenatal Health Issues, Public Health, Single-Disease Health Associations
International: Foreign Educational Institutions, Health Care/Hospitals, International Affairs, International Organizations, International Peace & Security Issues, International Relations, Missionary/Religious Activities
Religion: Churches, Dioceses, Religion-General, Jewish Causes, Religious Organizations, Religious Welfare
Science: Science Museums
Social Services: Child Welfare, Community Service Organizations, Homes, Recreation & Athletics, Scouts, Youth Organizations

Application Procedures

Initial Contact: Applicants should contact a foundation officer by phone to obtain an application form before submitting a complete proposal.
Deadlines: Proposals are accepted from January 1 to February 15 of each year.
Review Process: The trustees meet periodically to consider proposals.

Restrictions

Grants are not made to individuals. No grants are made for deficit financing, mortgage reduction, litigation projects, loans, or conferences already in progress.

Additional Information

Publications: Informational Brochure

Foundation Officials

Michael Arthur: secretary, trustee
Earle M. Chiles: president, trustee
Pedro Garcia: trustee
Sharron Mathews: director operations

Grants Analysis

Disclosure Period: calendar year ending 2001
Total Grants: $1,784,150
Number of Grants: 53
Average Grant: $18,568*
Highest Grant: $347,100
Typical Range: $5,000 to $30,000
*Note: Average grant figure excludes three highest grants ($800,000).

Recent Grants

Note: Grants derived from 2001 Form 990.

Library-Related

1,000	French Library and Cultural Center, Boston, MA -- operating support

General

347,100	Boston University, Boston, MA -- operating support
252,900	University of Portland, Portland, OR -- academic assistance, building repairs, athletic programs support
200,000	Providence Portland Medical Foundation, Portland, OR -- support research programs
170,500	Stanford University, Palo Alto, CA -- academic assistance, operating support, and building construction

139,000	Ludwig Maximilians University, Munich Germany -- support research programs
90,000	Institute of International Education, San Francisco, CA -- academic assistance
85,000	Boston Symphony Orchestra, Boston, MA -- operating support
83,200	High Desert Museum, Bend, OR -- operating support
46,450	Menlo College, Atherton, CA -- operating support
45,000	Oregon Public Broadcasting, Portland, OR -- operating support

M. A. CHISHOLM FOUNDATION

Giving Contact

c/o US Trust Co. of New York
114 W. 47th St.
New York, NY 10036-1510
Phone: (212)852-1000

Description

Founded: 1995
EIN: 136984354
Organization Type: Private Foundation
Giving Locations: nationally.
Grant Types: General Support.

Donor Information

Founder: Established in 1995 by the late Margaret A. Chisholm.

Financial Summary

Total Giving: $797,500 (fiscal year ending November 30, 2001); $1,021,775 (fiscal 2000); $683,100 (fiscal 1999)
Assets: $13,802,086 (fiscal 2001); $23,040,803 (fiscal 2000); $9,437,972 (fiscal 1999)
Gifts Received: $28,624 (fiscal 1996); $486,998 (fiscal 1994). Note: In fiscal 1994, contributions were received from the estate of Margaret A. Chisholm.

Typical Recipients

Arts & Humanities: Arts Outreach, Historic Preservation, History & Archaeology, Libraries, Museums/Galleries, Music, Opera, Performing Arts, Theater
Civic & Public Affairs: Asian American Affairs, Botanical Gardens/Parks, Community Foundations, Employment/Job Training, Civic & Public Affairs-General, Municipalities/Towns, Women's Affairs
Education: Arts/Humanities Education, Colleges & Universities, Community & Junior Colleges, Faculty Development, International Studies, Leadership Training, Private Education (Precollege), Religious Education, Student Aid
Environment: Resource Conservation, Wildlife Protection
Health: Health-General, Health Policy/Cost Containment, Transplant Networks/Donor Banks
Religion: Churches, Religion-General, Seminaries
Social Services: Child Welfare, Social Services-General, Youth Organizations

Application Procedures

Initial Contact: Send a brief letter of inquiry.
Application Requirements: Include purpose of funds sought.
Deadlines: None.

Additional Information

Trust(s): US Trust Co NY

Foundation Officials

Cynthia C. Saint-Amand: trustee

Grants Analysis

Disclosure Period: fiscal year ending November 30, 2001
Total Grants: $797,500

Number of Grants: 59
Average Grant: $13,517
Highest Grant: $50,000
Lowest Grant: $100
Typical Range: $5,000 to $30,000

Recent Grants

Note: Grants derived from fiscal 2001 Form 990.

Library-Related

25,000	Morgan Library, New York, NY
10,000	Morgan Library, New York, NY

General

50,000	Greenwich Country Day School, Greenwich, CT
50,000	Juilliard School, New York, NY
50,000	Mississippi Center for Non-Profit, MS
50,000	Mount Vernon Association, Mt. Vernon, VA
50,000	St. John's Episcopal Church, Newark, NJ
50,000	Washington State University, Pullman, WA
25,000	Grace Children's Foundation, New York, NY
25,000	Grameen USA Poverty Alleviation Collaborative, Washington, DC
25,000	Lauren Rogers Museum of Art, Laurel, MS
25,000	Metropolitan Opera Guild, New York, NY

L. C. CHRISTENSEN CHARITABLE AND RELIGIOUS FOUNDATION

Giving Contact

Stephen J. Smith, Secretary
L. C. Christensen Charitable and Religious Foundation
c/o Hostak, Henzl and Bichler
PO Box 516
Racine, WI 53401-0516
Phone: (414)632-7541

Alternate Contact

Harold K. Christensen, Jr.
403 Spruce St.
Abbotsford, WI 54405
Phone: (715)223-6345

Description

Founded: 1966
EIN: 396096022
Organization Type: Private Foundation
Giving Locations: WI: Abbotsford, Racine nationally.
Grant Types: General Support.

Donor Information

Founder: the late Harold K. Christensen, Sr.

Financial Summary

Total Giving: $149,150 (2001); $151,800 (2000); $148,920 (1999)
Assets: $3,413,827 (2001); $3,472,587 (2000); $3,299,882 (1999)

Typical Recipients

Arts & Humanities: Arts Associations & Councils, Arts Funds, Arts Outreach, Community Arts, Historic Preservation, Libraries, Museums/Galleries, Music, Performing Arts, Theater
Civic & Public Affairs: Botanical Gardens/Parks, Housing, Municipalities/Towns, Safety, Urban & Community Affairs, Women's Affairs, Zoos/Aquariums
Education: Colleges & Universities, Education Funds, Leadership Training, Literacy, Minority Education, Private Education (Precollege), Public Education

(Precollege), Science/Mathematics Education, Secondary Education (Private), Secondary Education (Public), Student Aid
Environment: Environment-General
Health: Children's Health/Hospitals, Geriatric Health, Health Organizations, Medical Research
Religion: Churches, Churches, Religious Welfare
Social Services: Camps, Child Welfare, Community Service Organizations, Family Services, Homes, People with Disabilities, Recreation & Athletics, Scouts, Senior Services, Social Services-General, Substance Abuse, YMCA/YWCA/YMHA/YWHA, Youth Organizations

Application Procedures

Initial Contact: The foundation requests applications be made in writing. Send cover letter and six copies of proposal.
Application Requirements: Include a description of organization, amount requested, purpose of funds sought, and proof of tax-exempt status.
Deadlines: None.
Notes: Primarily supports preselected organizations.

Foundation Officials

Carol Christensen: director
Harold K. Christensen, Jr.: president
John E. Erskine, Jr.: director
Russel L. Kortendick, Sr.: vice president
Dennis E. Schelling: treasurer
Stephen J. Smith: secretary

Grants Analysis

Disclosure Period: calendar year ending 2001
Total Grants: $149,150
Number of Grants: 44
Average Grant: $2,771*
Highest Grant: $30,000
Lowest Grant: $500
Typical Range: $1,000 to $5,000
*Note: Average grant excludes highest grant.

Recent Grants

Note: Grants derived from 2001 Form 990.

Library-Related

5,000	Abbotsford Library, Abbotsford, WI -- for 10 books on CD format and encyclopedias

General

30,000	Wastum Museum Art Association, Racine, WI -- capital campaign
24,000	Racine Theatre Guild, Inc., Racine, WI -- for final payment on grant
12,000	Racine YMCA, Racine, WI -- for youth programs and capital campaign
8,500	Christ Lutheran Church, Abbotsford, WI -- for church and parking lot
8,500	St. Monica's Senior Citizens Home, Racine, WI -- towards replacing water pipes and computers
6,000	Marshfield Medical Research Foundation, Marshfield, WI -- for Man to Man Prostate Cancer Education and Support Group
6,000	Racine Habitat for Humanity, Racine, WI -- to assist in a building new house
5,500	St. Paul's Lutheran Church, Curtiss, WI -- toward paying for church
5,000	Luther College, Deborah, IA -- towards theater and dance design club
4,800	City of Abbotsford-Abby Athletic Youth Association and Baseball Team, Abbotsford, WI -- for new bases and field screens

CHRISTIAN DIOR PERFUMES, INC.

Company Headquarters

9 W. 57th Street, Suite 39
New York, NY 10019
Web: http://www.dior.com

Company Description

Employees: 50
SIC(s): 6700 Holding & Other Investment Offices.
Parent Company: Christian Dior SA, 30, Avenue Montaigne, Paris, France

Operating Locations

Christian Dior New York (NY--New York)

Nonmonetary Support

Type: Donated Products

Giving Contact

Amy Raiter, Events Planner
712 5th Ave., 37th Fl.
New York, NY 10019
Phone: (212)582-0500
Fax: (212)581-0788
E-mail: araiter@christiandior.fr

Alternate Contact

Danielle McGarr, Special Events

Description

Organization Type: Corporate Giving Program
Giving Locations: NY: New York nationally.

Financial Summary

Total Giving: Company does not disclose contributions figures.

Typical Recipients

Arts & Humanities: Art History, Arts Appreciation, Arts Associations & Councils, Arts Centers, Arts Festivals, Arts Funds, Arts Institutes, Arts Outreach, Ballet, Community Arts, Dance, Ethnic & Folk Arts, Film & Video, Arts & Humanities-General, Historic Preservation, History & Archaeology, Libraries, Literary Arts, Museums/Galleries, Music, Opera, Performing Arts, Public Broadcasting, Theater, Visual Arts
Education: Colleges & Universities, Education Associations, Education-General, International Studies
Health: AIDS/HIV, Cancer, Health-General, Single-Disease Health Associations, Speech & Hearing
Social Services: People with Disabilities, Social Services-General, Youth Organizations

Application Procedures

Initial Contact: Send a brief letter or proposal, including a description of the organization and purpose of funds sought.

Corporate Officials

Jillian Hirsch: chief financial officer, chief executive officer PRIM CORP EMPL chief financial officer: Christian Dior New York.
Thierry Letrillart: president, chief executive officer PRIM CORP EMPL president, chief executive officer: Christian Dior New York.

CHRISTY-HOUSTON FOUNDATION

Giving Contact

Robert B. Mifflin, Executive Director
1296 Dow Street
Murfreesboro, TN 37130
Phone: (615)898-1140

Fax: (615)895-9524
E-mail: christy-houston@mindspring.com

Description

Founded: 1987
EIN: 621280998
Organization Type: General Purpose Foundation
Giving Locations: TN: Rutherford County
Grant Types: Capital, Operating Expenses.

Donor Information

Founder: The foundation was established in 1987 with funding from the sale of a hospital.

Financial Summary

Total Giving: $4,641,636 (2001); $4,200,000 (2000); $4,050,000 (1999 approx)
Giving Analysis: Giving for 1999 includes: foundation scholarships ($76,515)
Assets: $80,075,099 (2001); $91,383,701 (2000); $90,257,860 (1999)

Typical Recipients

Arts & Humanities: History & Archaeology, Libraries, Museums/Galleries, Music
Civic & Public Affairs: Civic & Public Affairs-General, Rural Affairs
Education: Colleges & Universities, Medical Education, Private Education (Precollege), Student Aid, Vocational & Technical Education
Health: Clinics/Medical Centers, Emergency/Ambulance Services, Health Organizations, Heart, Hospices, Hospitals, Kidney, Public Health
Religion: Religious Welfare
Social Services: Community Service Organizations, Domestic Violence, Food/Clothing Distribution, Scouts, YMCA/YWCA/YMHA/YWHA, Youth Organizations

Application Procedures

Initial Contact: Interested organizations should contact the foundation for application information and forms.
Application Requirements: All applicants will be requested to provide the following information: the name and address of the applicant; specific geographic target area; affiliations with any other organization; list of any other organizations doing the same or similar work in that geographic area; and a statement explaining how future funding for the project will be handled. The applicant will also be requested to submit a program description which includes the objectives and purposes of the project, a planned method for evaluation, and the amount of funding requested with an explanation of why funding from the Christy-Houston Foundation is needed. Along with the application, organizations will be required to attach a copy of their most recent determination letter from the IRS, a copy of their most recent Form 990, a list of governing board members and their affiliations, a list of any officers or paid staff, identity of other sources of funding currently solicited, and a copy of their most recent financial statement together with a line-item operating budget incidental to the proposed project.
Deadlines: 28 February to be considered for a grant in March.
Review Process: All applications are evaluated on individual merit, and final approval is determined by the board of directors which meets monthly.

Restrictions

The foundation does not support organizations that do not have tax-exempt status, legislative or lobbying efforts, religious organizations or endeavors, veterans organizations, any program supported with tax funds, or payment to physicians or surgeons except for radical or extraordinary treatment. Public charities located in Rutherford County have priority and in most instances, those charities exhaust the funds.

Additional Information

Publications: Application Form

Foundation Officials

Granville S. R. Bouldin: director
Henry King Butler: director
Ed Delbridge: director
Ed Elam: director
Larry N. Haynes: director
William H. Huddleston: director B 1929. ED Yale University (1950). PRIM CORP EMPL president: Huddleston Steel Engineering.
Roger C. Maples: director
Hubert McCullough: director
Robert B. Mifflan: executive director
Matt B. Murfree, III: director

Grants Analysis

Disclosure Period: calendar year ending 2001
Total Grants: $4,641,636*
Number of Grants: 13
Average Grant: $92,898*
Highest Grant: $2,515,523
Lowest Grant: $3,172
Typical Range: $50,000 to $2,000,000
*Note: Average grant excludes two highest grants ($3,433,961). Giving excludes scholarships.

Recent Grants

Note: Grants derived from 2001 Form 990.

Library-Related

56,000	Linebaugh Public Library, Murfreesboro, TN -- equipment for expansion of genealogy section

General

2,515,523	Community Care Center, Murfreesboro, TN -- nursing home building renovation
918,438	City of Murfreesboro, Murfreesboro, TN -- Rutherford County Health Department
396,239	Domestic Violence, Murfreesboro, TN -- new office and shelter building
182,000	Salvation Army, Murfreesboro, TN -- building repairs and construction of warehouse
150,000	Middle Tennessee State University, Murfreesboro, TN -- nursing scholarships
110,357	Rutherford County Emergency Medical Service, Murfreesboro, TN -- emergency ambulance and van
103,464	Consolidated Water District, Murfreesboro, TN -- extension of Rock Springs water line
60,000	Middle Tennessee State University, Murfreesboro, TN -- dyslexia gene research
55,000	Community Helpers, Murfreesboro, TN -- for prescription drugs for the indigent
47,542	Tennessee Technology Center, Murfreesboro, TN -- equipment for nursing and surgical technician training

CHURCH & DWIGHT COMPANY, INC.

Company Headquarters

469 N. Harriston St.
Princeton, NJ 08540
Web: http://www.churchdwight.com

Company Description

Founded: 1846
Ticker: CHD
Exchange: NYSE
Revenue: US$1.047 billion (2002)
Employees: 2099 (2002)

SIC(s): 2812 Alkalies & Chlorine, 2819 Industrial Inorganic Chemicals Nec, 2841 Soap & Other Detergents, 2842 Polishes & Sanitation Goods.

Operating Locations
Church & Dwight Co., Inc. (CA--Irvine, Petaluma; CO--Evergreen; FL--Altamonte Springs; GA--Norcross; MA--Wakefield; MN--Apple Valley; MO--Nixa; OH--Old Fort; SC--Taylors; TX--Dallas; WA--Federal Way)

Nonmonetary Support
Type: Donated Equipment; Donated Products; In-kind Services; Loaned Employees; Loaned Executives

Giving Contact
Steven Cugini, Vice President, Human Resources
Church & Dwight Co., Inc.
469 North Harrison Street
Princeton, NJ 08543-5297
Phone: (609)683-5900
Fax: (609)497-7177
Web: http://www.churchdwight.com

Description
Organization Type: Corporate Giving Program
Giving Locations: NJ
Grant Types: Employee Matching Gifts, Research.

Financial Summary
Total Giving: $100,000 (2001); $100,000 (2000 approx); $100,000 (1999 approx). Note: Contributes through corporate direct giving program only. Giving includes corporate direct giving; domestic subsidiaries.

Typical Recipients
Arts & Humanities: Community Arts, Historic Preservation, Libraries, Museums/Galleries, Music, Public Broadcasting
Civic & Public Affairs: Urban & Community Affairs
Education: Agricultural Education, Arts/Humanities Education, Business Education, Colleges & Universities
Environment: Environment-General
Health: Emergency/Ambulance Services, Health Funds, Health Organizations, Hospitals, Medical Research, Mental Health
Science: Scientific Organizations
Social Services: Animal Protection, Community Service Organizations, Emergency Relief, Food/Clothing Distribution, United Funds/United Ways, Youth Organizations

Application Procedures
Initial Contact: letter of inquiry
Application Requirements: a description of organization, amount requested, purpose of funds sought, recently audited financial statements, and proof of tax-exempt status
Deadlines: None.

Restrictions
Does not support individuals, religious organizations for sectarian purposes, or political or lobbying groups.

Corporate Officials
Dwight Church Minton: chairman, director B North Hills, NY 1934. ED Yale University BA (1959); Stanford University Graduate School of Business Administration MBA (1961). PRIM CORP EMPL chairman, director: Church & Dwight Co., Inc. CORP AFFIL director: Medusa Corp.; director: Medusa Cement Corp.; director: Crane Co.; director: First Brands Corp. NONPR AFFIL trustee: Morehouse College; trustee: National Environmental Education & Training Foundation; chairman: Greater Yellowstone Coalition; member: Grocery Manufacturer America; member: Chemical Manufacturers Association. CLUB AFFIL

Yale Club; Racquet & Tennis Club; Seawanhaka Corinthian Yacht Club; Lotos Club.

CIBC WORLD MARKETS

Company Headquarters
200 Liberty St.
New York, NY 10281
Web: http://www.cibcwm.com

Company Description
Former Name: Canadian Imperial Bank of Commerce; CIBC Wood Gundy Securities Corp.
Employees: 185
SIC(s): 6211 Security Brokers & Dealers, 6221 Commodity Contracts Brokers & Dealers.
Parent Company: Canadian Imperial Bank of Commerce, Commerce Ct., Toronto, ON, Canada

Operating Locations
Canadian Imperial Holding Co. (DE--Wilmington; NY--New York); Canadian Imperial Service Co. (NY--New York); CIBC (GA--Atlanta; NY--New York); CIBC Aviation (NY--New York); CIBC Oppenheimer (CA--Los Angeles, San Francisco; GA--Atlanta; IL--Chicago; NY--New York; TX--Houston); CIBC Wood Gundy Securities Corp. (NY--New York); Oppenheimer Capital (NY--New York)

Nonmonetary Support
Type: Cause-related Marketing & Promotion; Donated Equipment

Giving Contact
Ashley Johansen, Charitable Contributions Coordinator
425 Lexington Avenue, 9th Floor
New York, NY 10017
Phone: (212)667-7000
Fax: (212)856-3996
Web: http://www.cibcwm.com

Description
Organization Type: Corporate Giving Program
Giving Locations: CA: Los Angeles, Menlo Park, San Francisco; DC; FL: Boca Raton, Fort Lauderdale, Miami; GA: Atlanta; IL: Chicago; MA: Boston; MO: Saint Louis; NY: New York City; TX: Dallas, Houston; WA: Seattle headquarters and operating communities.
Grant Types: General Support, Loan, Operating Expenses, Project, Seed Money.

Financial Summary
Total Giving: $1,216,441 (1997); $450,000 (1995); $250,000 (1994). Note: Contributes through corporate direct giving program only.

Typical Recipients
Arts & Humanities: Libraries
Civic & Public Affairs: Chambers of Commerce, Economic Development, Employment/Job Training, Housing, Inner-City Development, Legal Aid, Municipalities/Towns, Urban & Community Affairs
Education: Business Education
Social Services: United Funds/United Ways, YMCA/YWCA/YMHA/YWHA

Restrictions
Does not support individuals, religious organizations for sectarian purposes, political or lobbying groups, or organizations outside operating areas.

Additional Information
The company is restructuring its giving program.

Corporate Officials
Al Flood: chairman, chief executive officer, director B Monkton, ON Canada 1935. ED Harvard University. PRIM CORP EMPL chairman, chief executive officer: Canadian Imperial Bank of Commerce. CORP AFFIL chairman, chief executive officer: CIBC Subs. NONPR AFFIL director: Council for Canadian Unity; trustee: Hospital for Sick Children; chairman: Business Council National Issues.
John Hunkin: president B Toronto, ON Canada 1945. ED University of Manitoba BS (1967); York University MBA (1969). PRIM CORP EMPL president: CIBC Oppenheimer.
Matt Singleton: vice president, chief executive officer, director PRIM CORP EMPL vice president, chief executive officer, director: CIBC Oppenheimer.

Grants Analysis
Typical Range: $1,000 to $2,500

CIGNA CORP.

Company Headquarters
Philadelphia, PA
Web: http://www.cigna.com

Company Description
Founded: 1982
Ticker: CI
Exchange: NYSE
Assets: US$88.95 billion (2002)
Employees: 41200 (2002)
Fortune Rank: 87, per FORTUNE Magazine's list of 500 Largest U.S. Corporations (2002).
SIC(s): 6282 Investment Advice, 6311 Life Insurance, 6331 Fire, Marine & Casualty Insurance, 6719 Holding Companies Nec.

Operating Locations
CIGNA Corp. (CT--Hartford)

Nonmonetary Support
Value: $6,900,000 (2000 approx); $47,250 (1998)
Type: Cause-related Marketing & Promotion; Donated Equipment
Volunteer Programs: Foundation sponsors three "Employee Recognition Awards," which acknowledge employee volunteer efforts. Through the "Grants for Givers" program, employees and retirees who volunteer a significant amount of their time to qualifying nonprofits can request foundation grants of $100 for their organizations. If three or more employees volunteer for the same project, the organization could receive up to $5,000 through the CIGNA Team Award. The Volunteer of the Month award recognizes superior employee volunteer efforts with a $500 grant to the organization benefiting from the employee's volunteerism.
Contact: Deborah Veney Robinson, Technical Consultant

CIGNA Foundation

Giving Contact
Deborah Veney-Robinson, Director, Civic Affairs
CIGNA Contributions and Civic Affairs
Tax Department
1601 Chestnut Street, TL06B
Philadelphia, PA 19192
Phone: (215)761-1000
Fax: (215)761-5632
E-mail: deborah.veney-robinson@cigna.com
Web: http://www.cigna.com/general/about/community/index.html

Alternate Contact

Arnold W. Wright, Jr., Director of Civic Affairs
900 Cottage Grove Road, W-A
Hartford, CT 06152-5001
Phone: (215)761-1000
Note: Alternate contact is for the Hartford area only.

Description

EIN: 236261726
Organization Type: Corporate Foundation
Giving Locations: CT: Hartford including metropolitan area; PA: Philadelphia including metropolitan area
Grant Types: Conference/Seminar, Department, Employee Matching Gifts, General Support, Operating Expenses, Project.
Note: Employee matching gift ratio: 1 to 1 for culture and art organisation.

Financial Summary

Total Giving: $9,265,851 (2001); $9,167,922 (2000); $10,014,950 (1999). Note: Contributes through corporate direct giving program and foundation.
Giving Analysis: Giving for 2000 includes: foundation grants to United Way ($1,329,000); foundation matching gifts ($1,556,490); corporate direct giving ($2,575,855); foundation ($6,592,067); 1999: foundation scholarships ($63,375); foundation matching gifts ($1,529,383); foundation grants to United Way ($1,633,500); corporate direct giving ($2,759,411); foundation ($4,029,281) 1997: corporate direct giving ($2,608,421)
Assets: $1,209,158 (2001); $1,121,024 (2000); $1,045,998 (1999)
Gifts Received: $8,724,515 (2001); $6,445,287 (2000); $7,669,045 (1999)

Typical Recipients

Arts & Humanities: Arts Associations & Councils, Arts Festivals, Ballet, Ethnic & Folk Arts, Arts & Humanities-General, History & Archaeology, Libraries, Literary Arts, Museums/Galleries, Music, Opera, Performing Arts, Public Broadcasting, Theater
Civic & Public Affairs: African American Affairs, Business/Free Enterprise, Chambers of Commerce, Economic Development, Economic Policy, Employment/Job Training, Civic & Public Affairs-General, Hispanic Affairs, Law & Justice, Municipalities/Towns, Nonprofit Management, Philanthropic Organizations, Professional & Trade Associations, Public Policy, Safety, Urban & Community Affairs, Women's Affairs, Zoos/Aquariums
Education: Arts/Humanities Education, Business Education, Business Education, Business-School Partnerships, Colleges & Universities, Education Reform, Elementary Education (Private), Faculty Development, Education-General, Health & Physical Education, International Exchange, Legal Education, Literacy, Medical Education, Private Education (Precollege), Public Education (Precollege), Secondary Education (Public), Special Education, Student Aid
Environment: Energy, Resource Conservation
Health: Adolescent Health Issues, Cancer, Children's Health/Hospitals, Clinics/Medical Centers, Health-General, Health Organizations, Hospitals, Prenatal Health Issues, Public Health
International: Human Rights
Religion: Religious Welfare
Science: Science Museums, Scientific Centers & Institutes
Social Services: Big Brother/Big Sister, Child Welfare, Child Welfare, Community Service Organizations, Crime Prevention, Family Services, Food/Clothing Distribution, People with Disabilities, Social Services-General, Special Olympics, United Funds/United Ways, Volunteer Services

Application Procedures

Initial Contact: Send one- or two-page letter of inquiry.
Application Requirements: Include a description of organization (including name, history, activities, purpose, and board members); description of program for which grant is requested; objectives and evaluative criteria; most recently audited financial statement; copy of IRS 501(c)(3) letter; copy of the most recent Form 990.
Deadlines: None; however, the foundation recommends that proposals be submitted by September 1 for funding in the next year.
Decision Notification: Ongoing; allow six weeks for initial review.

Restrictions

CIGNA Foundation generally will not provide funds to the following categories: individuals, political organizations, religious activities or organizations that are denominational or sectarian, organizations receiving substantial support through United Way or other CIGNA-supported federated funding agencies, endowment drives or capital campaigns, or hospital capital improvements or expansions.

Additional Information

Publications: Annual Report; Contributions Report

Corporate Officials

H. Edward Hanway: chairman, chief executive officer B West Chester, PA 1952. ED Loyola College BA (1974); Widener University MBA (1984). PRIM CORP EMPL president, chief executive officer: CIGNA Corp. NONPR AFFIL member: PICPA; member: World Affairs Council Philadelphia; member: American Institute CPAs.
Judith Soltz: executive vice president PRIM CORP EMPL chief counsel: CIGNA Corp.

Foundation Officials

Paul Bergsteinsson: vice president PRIM CORP EMPL vice president: Cigna Healthcare of Maine, Inc.. CORP AFFIL vice president: Recovery Services International.
John J. Corcoran: assistant secretary
Michael Fernandez: president
Lee R. Hoffman: assistant secretary
Arnold W. Wright, Jr.: vice president, executive director

Grants Analysis

Disclosure Period: calendar year ending 2001
Total Grants: $5,835,051*
Number of Grants: 134 (approx)*
Average Grant: $26,000*
Highest Grant: $1,400,000
Typical Range: $5,000 to $38,000
*Note: Giving excludes matching gifts, scholarships, and United Way. Number of grants also excludes grants of less than $5,000 each not listed. Average grant amount requested excludes two highest grants ($2,400,000).

Recent Grants

Note: Grants derived from 2002 Form 990.

General

1,400,000	American Enterprise Institute for Public Policy Research, Washington, DC
1,000,000	Regional Performing Arts Center, Philadelphia, PA
515,000	United Way of the Capital Area, Hartford, CT
500,000	New York City Public and Private Initiatives, New York, NY
500,000	United Way of New York City, New York, NY
400,027	United Way Field Agencies, Alexandria, VA
400,000	United Way Southeastern Pennsylvania, Philadelphia, PA
255,000	Morehouse School of Medicine, Atlanta, GA
185,500	Susan G. Komen Breast Cancer Foundation, Aspen, CO
125,000	News for Students Foundation, San Diego, CA

JAMES AND BARBARA CIMINO FOUNDATION

Giving Contact

Christine Bender, Secretary, Treasurer & Director
James and Barbara Cimino Foundation
PO Box 448
Sun Valley, ID 83353-0448
Phone: (208)622-4556

Description

Founded: 1995
EIN: 820474867
Organization Type: Private Foundation

Financial Summary

Total Giving: $81,200 (fiscal year ending June 30, 2001); $19,500 (fiscal 1997); $8,500 (fiscal 1996)
Assets: $1,138,565 (fiscal 2001); $975,994 (fiscal 1997); $926,370 (fiscal 1996)
Gifts Received: $60,000 (fiscal 2001); $954,308 (fiscal 1996). Note: In fiscal 2001, contributions were received from J & B Cimino. In fiscal 1996, contributions were received from James Cimino ($182,929), Barbara Cimino ($71,379), James and Barbara Cimino ($450,000), and Robert Cimino ($250,000).

Typical Recipients

Arts & Humanities: Arts Associations & Councils, Libraries, Public Broadcasting
Civic & Public Affairs: Civic & Public Affairs-General, Hispanic Affairs
Education: Colleges & Universities, Community & Junior Colleges, Education Funds, Elementary Education (Private), Elementary Education (Public), Student Aid
Environment: Environment-General, Resource Conservation, Wildlife Protection
Health: Hospices
International: Foreign Educational Institutions, Health Care/Hospitals
Religion: Churches
Social Services: At-Risk Youth

Application Procedures

Initial Contact: Send a brief letter of inquiry.
Application Requirements: Include a specific explanation of the program for which funds are sought and proof of tax-exempt status.
Deadlines: None.

Additional Information

Trust(s): Bank AM IL

Foundation Officials

Christine Bender: secretary, treasurer, director
Barbara Cimino: vice president, director
David Cimino: director
James A. Cimino: director
James N. Cimino: president, director
Robert Cimino: director

Grants Analysis

Disclosure Period: fiscal year ending June 30, 2001
Total Grants: $81,200
Number of Grants: 21
Average Grant: $2,810*
Highest Grant: $25,000

Typical Range: $1,000 to $5,000
*Note: Average grant figure excludes highest grant.

Recent Grants

Note: Grants derived from fiscal 2001 Form 990.

Library-Related
5,000   Community Library Association, Ketchum, ID

General
25,000   DePaul University, Chicago, IL
5,000   Idaho Public Television, Boise, ID
5,000   Nature Conservancy of Idaho, Sun Valley, ID
5,000   Peregrine Fund, Boise, ID
5,000   Rinaldi Foundation
4,000   Boise State University, Boise, ID
2,500   Mills College Alumnae Foundation, Oakland, CA
2,500   National Foundation for Advancement in the Arts, Miami, FL
2,500   University of Waitako, Hamilton New Zealand
2,000   Hospice of Wood River Valley, Ketchum, ID

CINERGY CORP.

Company Headquarters

139 E. 4th St.
Cincinnati, OH 45202
Web: http://www.cinergy.com

Company Description

Founded: 1994
Ticker: CIN
Exchange: NYSE
Assets: US$13.307 billion (2002)
Employees: 7823 (2002)

Nonmonetary Support

Value: $30,000 (1998 approx)
Type: Cause-related Marketing & Promotion; Donated Equipment; Donated Products; In-kind Services; Loaned Employees; Loaned Executives; Workplace Solicitation
Contact: Karol King, Cinergy Foundation

Cinergy Foundation

Giving Contact

Karol King, Foundation Manager
139 E. 4th St.
Cincinnati, OH 45202
Phone: (513)287-1251
Fax: (513)651-9196
E-mail: kking@cinergy.com
Web: http://www.cinergy.com/Community/default.asp

Alternate Contact

Phone: 800-262-3000

Description

Founded: 1992
EIN: 351755088
Organization Type: Corporate Foundation
Former Name: PSI Energy Foundation.
Giving Locations: IN: company service area; KY: Northern Kentucky (company service area); OH: company service area
Grant Types: Award, Employee Matching Gifts, Matching, Multiyear/Continuing Support, Project, Research, Scholarship.

Financial Summary

Total Giving: $5,200,000 (2000 approx); $5,571,237 (1999); $5,385,337 (1998)
Giving Analysis: Giving for 1997 includes: foundation grants to United Way ($562,019) foundation ($4,458,170)
Assets: $47,452 (1998); $14,426 (1997); $468,821 (1996)
Gifts Received: $5,493,942 (1998); $4,675,368 (1997); $6,209,653 (1996)

Typical Recipients

Arts & Humanities: Arts Associations & Councils, Arts Centers, Arts Festivals, Arts Funds, Ballet, Community Arts, Arts & Humanities-General, Historic Preservation, History & Archaeology, Libraries, Museums/Galleries, Music, Opera, Performing Arts, Public Broadcasting, Theater
Civic & Public Affairs: African American Affairs, Botanical Gardens/Parks, Chambers of Commerce, Community Foundations, Economic Development, Civic & Public Affairs-General, Municipalities/Towns, Nonprofit Management, Public Policy, Urban & Community Affairs, Zoos/Aquariums
Education: Arts/Humanities Education, Business Education, Business-School Partnerships, Colleges & Universities, Education Funds, Education Reform, Elementary Education (Private), Engineering/Technological Education, Faculty Development, Education-General, Leadership Training, Literacy, Private Education (Precollege), Public Education (Precollege), Student Aid
Environment: Environment-General, Resource Conservation
Health: Children's Health/Hospitals, Emergency/Ambulance Services, Health-General, Hospitals, Mental Health, Prenatal Health Issues, Single-Disease Health Associations
International: Health Care/Hospitals
Religion: Religious Welfare
Social Services: Child Welfare, People with Disabilities, Recreation & Athletics, Scouts, Social Services-General, Special Olympics, Substance Abuse, United Funds/United Ways, YMCA/YWCA/YMHA/YWHA, Youth Organizations

Application Procedures

Initial Contact: Telephone to request application guidelines and grant application form, then send full proposal.
Application Requirements: Grant application form requests the following information: organization name, address, phone number, and federal tax identification number; name and title of contact person; a brief a description of organization's mission, goals, and objectives; and project information, including name and dates of project, total project cost, dollar amount requested, number of people project benefits, county within which project is located, additional counties benefiting from project, plan for recognizing contributors, project description, a list of Cinergy employees involved in the project and a description of their roles. Attachments requested include a copy of 501(c)(3) tax exemption letter; a copy of organization's current budget and the project budget, showing all project revenues and expenses; timetable for becoming self-sufficient; plan for project evaluation; the names and addresses of the organization's board of directors; clear, measurable project objectives; and other supplementary material that describes the organization.
Deadlines: The 15th of March, June, and September.
Review Process: Grant requests are reviewed on a quarterly basis; applicants are encouraged to submit grant applications as far in advance of the project dates above as possible.
Evaluative Criteria: How project benefits citizens and communities, especially within company's service area.

Decision Notification: organizations receive notification of grant approximately six weeks after submission deadline. Applications received after the deadline will automatically be considered at the next grant application deadline.
Notes: Applicants are encouraged to call the foundation to discuss their proposals prior to submission. Applicants are requested to submit their grant application to the district office closest to them for review and endorsement by the district manager. Managers and employees are involved in the decision-making process, and the foundation reports it is important for the Cinergy district manager in applicant's service area to be well informed about project.

Restrictions

The foundation does not fund capital campaigns; advertising; membership dues; non-tax exempt organizations; post-prom or post-graduation activities; programs posing a conflict of interest; recognition or academic awards programs (unless part of a staff or workforce development program); technology and audiovisual equipment; travel expenses; uniforms; post-event funding; organizations benefiting an individual or a few persons; capital or endowment campaigns; construction projects; auctions; textbooks purchases, for schools or fundraising events; or veterans, labor, religious, political, or fraternal groups. Generally, gifts for competitions, golf events, and athletic programs and facilities are beyond the scope of foundation's program.

Additional Information

Company is looking for partnerships between the company and organizations that enhance the future of Indiana communities. Grants are for specific projects or designated programs. Grants are made on a one-year basis. Re-application is necessary for consideration of a grant renewal. Special consideration is given to programs with a statewide scope that benefit citizens in company's service area. Some organizations receiving grants from the Cinergy Foundation will be offered the added benefit of an energy audit of their facilities at Cinergy's expense. The audit provides the organization with recommendations to save on energy costs.
Publications: Guidelines; Annual Report

Corporate Officials

William J. Grealis: vice president, president, chief executive officer, director B Olmsted Falls, OH 1945. ED Ohio University (1967); University of Akron (1972). PRIM CORP EMPL vice president: Cinergy Corp. ADD CORP EMPL president, director: Cincergy Investments; president, director: Cinergy Communication Inc.; president: Lawrenceburg Gas Co. CORP AFFIL president corp. development, chief strategic officer: Cincinnati Gas & Electric Co. Inc.
James E. Rogers, Jr.: vice chairman, president, chief executive officer, director B Birmingham, AL 1947. ED University of Kentucky BBA (1970); University of Kentucky JD (1974). PRIM CORP EMPL vice chairman, president, chief executive officer, director: Cinergy Corp. ADD CORP EMPL president: Cinergy Service Inc.; vice chairman: Lawrenceburg Gas Co.; chief executive officer: PSI Energy Inc.; chairman: Power Equipment Supply Co.; vice chairman: Union Light Heat & Power Co. Inc. CORP AFFIL vice president: Roger Petroleum Service Inc.; director: Duke Realty Investments Inc.; director: Fifth Third Bancorp. NONPR AFFIL director: Edison Electric Institute.

Foundation Officials

Phillip R. Cox: director B 1946. ED Xavier University (1967-1969). PRIM CORP EMPL president: Cox Financial Corp. ADD CORP EMPL secretary: Crown Mortgage Services Inc. CORP AFFIL director: Cincinnati Bell Inc.; director: Cinergy Corp.
William J. Grealis: director (see above)

J. Joseph Hale, Jr.: president, director PRIM CORP EMPL vice president corporate communications: Cinergy Corp.

John A. Hillenbrand, II: chairman, president B 1932. PRIM CORP EMPL chairman, president, chief executive officer: Glynnadam, Inc. CORP AFFIL director: Hillenbrand Industries; vice chairman: Pri Pak Inc.; director: Able Body Corp.; director: Cinergy Corp.

George C. Juilfs: president, chief executive officer, director B 1939. PRIM CORP EMPL president, chief executive officer: SENCORP. CORP AFFIL director: Cinergy Corp.; chairman: SENCO Products Inc.

James E. Rogers, Jr.: chairman, director (see above)

Grants Analysis

Disclosure Period: calendar year ending 1999
Total Grants: $5,571,237*
Number of Grants: 1,600*
Average Grant: $3,500
Highest Grant: $550,000*
Typical Range: $200 to $5,000
*Note: Grants analysis provided by Foundation.

Recent Grants

Note: Grants derived from 1999 Form 990.

General

140,000	Fine Arts Fund, Cincinnati, OH -- 1998 campaign corp.
75,000	United Way, Indianapolis, IN -- employee match
70,000	Contemporary Arts Center, New Orleans, LA -- educational component
63,500	Greater Cincinnati Chamber of Commerce, Cincinnati, OH -- models for improving the quality of life and economics vitality
62,500	Cincinnati Arts Association, Cincinnati, OH -- Aronoff Center
60,000	Cincinnati Scholarship Foundation, Cincinnati, OH -- scholarships for dependent employees
55,000	Cincinnati Horticultural Society, Cincinnati, OH -- flower shows
50,000	Boy Scouts of America, Melbourne, FL -- The Right Direction, a camp developing youth campaign
50,000	Children's Museum, Cincinnati, OH -- relocation
50,000	Cincinnati 2012, Cincinnati, OH -- summer Olympics

CISCO SYSTEMS, INC.

Company Headquarters

San Jose, CA
Web: http://www.cisco.com

Company Description

Founded: 1984
Ticker: CSCO
Exchange: NASDAQ
Revenue: US$18.915 billion (2002)
Profit: US$1.893 billion (2002)
Employees: 36000 (2002)
Fortune Rank: 95, per FORTUNE Magazine's list of 500 Largest U.S. Corporations (2002).
SIC(s): 3577 Computer Peripheral Equipment Nec.

Cisco Systems Foundation

Giving Contact

Lynne Elliott
170 West Tasman Drive
San Jose, CA 95134
Phone: (408)526-4000

Web: http://www.cisco.com/warp/public/750/philanthropy/

Description

EIN: 770443347
Organization Type: Corporate Foundation
Giving Locations: CA: San Jose area; MA; NY; NC
Grant Types: General Support.

Financial Summary

Total Giving: $7,187,424 (fiscal year ending July 31, 2001); $14,190,789 (fiscal 2000)
Giving Analysis: Giving for fiscal 2001 includes: foundation matching gifts ($2,494,266); foundation ($4,693,158) fiscal 2000: foundation matching gifts ($1,608,820)
Assets: $125,001,798 (fiscal 2001); $132,211,438 (fiscal 2000)
Gifts Received: $199,559 (fiscal 2001); $91,024,874 (fiscal 2000). Note: In 2001, contributions were received from United Airlines ($184,359) and various contributors donating less than $5,000. In 2000, contributions were received from Cisco Systems Corp.

Typical Recipients

Arts & Humanities: Museums/Galleries, Music, Public Broadcasting
Civic & Public Affairs: Botanical Gardens/Parks, Clubs, Economic Development, Employment/Job Training, Civic & Public Affairs-General, Hispanic Affairs, Housing, Legal Aid, Municipalities/Towns, Public Policy, Urban & Community Affairs, Women's Affairs
Education: Business Education, Education Reform, Elementary Education (Public), Faculty Development, Education-General, Private Education (Precollege)
Health: AIDS/HIV, Cancer, Children's Health/Hospitals, Clinics/Medical Centers, Health Organizations, Hospices, Single-Disease Health Associations
International: International-General
Religion: Religion-General, Ministries, Religious Organizations, Religious Welfare
Science: Science Museums
Social Services: Child Welfare, Community Centers, Community Service Organizations, Crime Prevention, Domestic Violence, Family Services, Food/Clothing Distribution, People with Disabilities, Scouts, Shelters/Homelessness, Social Services-General, Substance Abuse, YMCA/YWCA/YMHA/YWHA, Youth Organizations

Application Procedures

Initial Contact: Call or see website for application guidelines, then send a written request.
Application Requirements: Include proof of tax-exempt status.
Deadlines: April and November.
Review Process: Foundation makes funding decisions twice each year, for funding in August and March.
Evaluative Criteria: Organizations must be nonprofits under Section 501(c)(3) and public charities, and must operate within 50 miles of Cisco's San Jose headquarters. Programs must leverage existing resources within the larger organization and community; serve the community at large; and have overhead expenses that do not exceed 25% of total operating budget.

Restrictions

Does not fund athletic events, competitions, or tournaments; capital building funds; conferences/seminars; fundraising events or sponsorships; general operating expenses; individuals; multi-year grants; religious, political, or sectarian organizations; research programs; scholarships or stipends; schools, school systems, or school foundations; start-up programs; or grantmaking organizations.

Additional Information

In May of 2003, Cisco donated $2.6 million in networking equipment and services to China's Ministry of Health in order to fight the spread of Severe Acute Respiratory Syndrome (SARS).

Foundation Officials

Barbara Beck: vice president, director
Larry R. Carter: trustee
John T. Chambers: trustee
John P. Morgridge: trustee
Jean Taylor: assistant secretary

Grants Analysis

Disclosure Period: fiscal year ending July 31, 2001
Total Grants: $4,693,158*
Number of Grants: 115
Average Grant: $32,396*
Highest Grant: $1,000,000
Typical Range: $10,000 to $100,000
*Note: Giving excludes matching gifts. Average grant figure excludes highest grant.

Recent Grants

Note: Grants derived from 2001 Form 990.

General

1,000,000	Habitat for Humanity -- equipment and volunteer support
706,099	Second Harvest Food Bank of Santa Clara and San Mateo, San Jose, CA
545,000	Southern Poverty Law Center, Montgomery, AL -- Tolerance Program
425,000	Education Broadcasting Corporation, New York, NY -- National Teacher Training Institute
333,333	American Red Cross, Washington, DC -- Disaster Giving Program
330,000	City Year, San Jose, CA -- tech team training
200,000	City Year, San Jose, CA -- national leadership partner
197,500	Brave Kids, San Francisco, CA -- utilizing the power of internet to help seriously ill children
125,000	Education Broadcasting Corporation, New York, NY -- National Teacher Training Institute
115,236	Food Bank, Memphis, TN

CIT GROUP, INC.

Company Headquarters

1 CIT Dr.
Livingston, NJ 07039
Web: http://www.cit.com

Company Description

Founded: 1908
Ticker: CIT
Exchange: NYSE
Assets: US$42.71 billion (2002)
Employees: 5835 (2002)
Fortune Rank: 317, per FORTUNE Magazine's list of 500 Largest U.S. Corporations (2002).
SIC(s): 6141 Personal Credit Institutions, 6153 Short-Term Business Credit, 6159 Miscellaneous Business Credit Institutions, 6719 Holding Companies Nec.
Parent Company: Dai-Ichi Kangyo Bank, Ltd., 1-1-5 Uchi-Saiwaicho, Chiyoda-ku, Tokyo, Japan

Operating Locations

CIT Group/Business Credit (NY--New York); CIT Group/Capital Finance (NY--New York); CIT Group/Commercial Services (NY--New York); CIT Group/Credit Finance (NY--New York); CIT Group/Equipment Financing (NJ--Livingston); CIT Group/Equity Investments (NJ--Livingston); CIT Group Holdings (NY--New York); The CIT Group, Inc. (NJ--Livingston;

NY--New York); CIT Group/Industrial Financing (NJ--Livingston); CIT Group/Sales Financing (NJ--Livingston); Dai-Ichi Kangyo Bank of California (CA--San Jose, Torrance); Dai-Ichi Kangyo Bank of California-Los Angeles (CA--Los Angeles); Dai-Ichi Kangyo Bank, Ltd.-Atlanta (GA--Atlanta); Dai-Ichi Kangyo Bank, Ltd.-Chicago (IL--Chicago); Dai-Ichi Kangyo Bank, Ltd.-Houston (TX--Houston); Dai-Ichi Kangyo Bank, Ltd.-Los Angeles (CA--Los Angeles); Dai-Ichi Kangyo Bank, Ltd.-New York (NY--New York); Dai-Ichi Kangyo Bank, Ltd.-San Francisco (CA--San Francisco); Dai-Ichi Kangyo Trust Co. of New York (NY--New York); DKB Data Services (U.S.A.) (NJ--Jersey City); DKB Financial Futures Corp. (IL--Chicago); DKB Financial Products (NY--New York); DKB Securities Corp. (NY--New York)

CIT Group Foundation

Giving Contact

Kelley Gibson
CIT Group Foundation
1211 Avenue of the Americas
New York, NY 10036
Phone: (973)740-5200
Fax: (973)740-5264
Web: http://www.cit.com/about_us/corp_giving.html

Description

EIN: 136083856
Organization Type: Corporate Foundation
Giving Locations: nationally, with an emphasis on headquarters area only.
Grant Types: General Support, Scholarship.

Financial Summary

Total Giving: $2,485,864 (2001); $2,209,917 (2000); $2,036,015 (1999). Note: Contributes through corporate direct giving program and foundation.
Giving Analysis: Giving for 2001 includes: foundation scholarships ($6,000); foundation grants to United Way ($500,349); foundation ($1,979,515); 2000: foundation matching gifts ($139,319); foundation scholarships ($260,180); foundation grants to United Way ($333,413); foundation ($1,477,005); 1998: foundation matching gifts ($67,704); foundation scholarships ($97,027); foundation grants to United Way ($300,000); foundation ($1,437,633);
Assets: $190,447 (2001); $14,172 (2000); $74,089 (1999)
Gifts Received: $2,663,354 (2001); $2,150,000 (2000); $2,100,000 (1999). Note: Contributions received from CIT Group.

Typical Recipients

Arts & Humanities: Arts Funds, Community Arts, History & Archaeology, Libraries, Museums/Galleries, Music, Performing Arts, Public Broadcasting, Theater
Civic & Public Affairs: African American Affairs, Business/Free Enterprise, Community Foundations, Economic Development, Economic Policy, Civic & Public Affairs-General, Housing, Municipalities/Towns, Philanthropic Organizations, Professional & Trade Associations, Public Policy, Urban & Community Affairs, Women's Affairs
Education: Arts/Humanities Education, Business Education, Colleges & Universities, Continuing Education, Education Funds, Education Reform, Engineering/Technological Education, Education-General, Journalism/Media Education, Legal Education, Minority Education, Private Education (Precollege), Private Education (Precollege), Public Education (Precollege), Secondary Education (Private), Secondary Education (Public), Special Education, Student Aid
Health: AIDS/HIV, Arthritis, Cancer, Children's Health/Hospitals, Clinics/Medical Centers, Diabetes, Emergency/Ambulance Services, Health Organizations, Heart, Hospitals, Medical Research, Mental

Health, Nursing Services, Single-Disease Health Associations, Transplant Networks/Donor Banks, Trauma Treatment
International: International Peace & Security Issues, International Relations, Missionary/Religious Activities
Religion: Dioceses, Religion-General, Jewish Causes, Religious Organizations, Religious Welfare
Science: Scientific Centers & Institutes
Social Services: Child Welfare, Community Centers, Community Service Organizations, Community Service Organizations, Food/Clothing Distribution, Homes, People with Disabilities, Recreation & Athletics, Scouts, Shelters/Homelessness, Social Services-General, Substance Abuse, United Funds/United Ways, Veterans, Volunteer Services, YMCA/YWCA/YMHA/YWHA, Youth Organizations

Application Procedures

Initial Contact: Send a written proposal in letter form.
Application Requirements: Include a description of organization, amount requested, purpose of funds sought, audited financial statement, annual report, and proof of tax-exempt status.
Deadlines: None.

Restrictions

Does not support political or lobbying groups, or grants to individuals.

Corporate Officials

Albert R. Gamper, Jr.: president, chief executive officer, chairman B 1942. ED Harvard University PMD; Rutgers University BA. PRIM CORP EMPL president, chief executive officer, chairman: The CIT Group, Inc.

Foundation Officials

Albert R. Gamper, Jr.: president, chief executive officer, director (see above)

Grants Analysis

Disclosure Period: calendar year ending 2001
Total Grants: $1,979,515*
Number of Grants: 585
Average Grant: $3,384
Highest Grant: $200,000
Lowest Grant: $25
Typical Range: $500 to $10,000
*Note: Giving excludes scholarships and United Way.

Recent Grants

Note: Grants derived from 2001 Form 990.

General

200,349	United Way, Tri-State, NY
200,000	Saint Barnabas Medical Centers, Livingston, NJ
163,250	New Jersey Performing Arts Center, Livingston, NJ
163,250	New Jersey Performing Arts Center, Newark, NJ
100,000	United Way, Tri-State, NY
100,000	United Way, Tri-State, NY
100,000	United Way, Tri-State, NY
66,667	American Red Cross, East Orange, NJ
50,000	Business Executives for National Security, Washington, DC
48,750	New Jersey Institute of Technology, Newark, NJ

CITIGROUP INC.

Company Headquarters

399 Park Ave.
New York, NY 10043
Phone: (212)559-1000
Fax: (212)793-3946
Web: http://www.citigroup.com

Company Description

Founded: 1998
Ticker: C
Exchange: NYSE
Assets: US$10.971 billion (2002)
Profit: US$15.276 billion (2002)
Employees: 255000 (2002)
Fortune Rank: 6, per FORTUNE Magazine's list of 500 Largest U.S. Corporations (2002).

Nonmonetary Support

Type: Donated Equipment
Volunteer Programs: The corporation's volunteer incentive program provides up to $500 for organizations to which employees volunteer.

Citigroup Foundation

Giving Contact

Charles V. Raymond, President
Citigroup Foundation
850 Third Avenue, 13th Floor
New York, NY 10043
Phone: (212)559-9163
Fax: (212)793-5944
E-mail: citigroupfoundation@citigroup.com
Web: http://www.citigroup.com

Description

EIN: 133781879
Organization Type: Corporate Foundation
Giving Locations: NY: New York headquarters and operating communities.
Grant Types: Employee Matching Gifts, Fellowship, General Support, Multiyear/Continuing Support, Project.
Note: Employee matching gift ratio: 1 to 1.

Financial Summary

Total Giving: $56,788,899 (2002); $67,644,961 (2001); $43,068,029 (2000). Note: Contributes through corporate direct giving program and foundation.
Giving Analysis: Giving for 2001 includes: foundation matching gifts ($1,169,217); corporate direct giving ($3,556,500); domestic and international subsidiaries ($13,355,182); foundation ($49,564,061); 2000: foundation ($43,068,029); 1999: corporate direct giving ($1,180,000); foundation grants to United Way ($1,399,450); foundation ($9,015,606);
Assets: $140,404,667 (2002); $179,182,168 (2000); $136,206,912 (1998)
Gifts Received: $2,381,908 (2002); $108,991,700 (2000); $9,015,606 (1999). Note: Foundation receives contributions from Citicorp and Citibank.

Typical Recipients

Arts & Humanities: Arts Appreciation, Arts Associations & Councils, Arts Centers, Arts Festivals, Arts Funds, Arts Institutes, Dance, Ethnic & Folk Arts, Historic Preservation, Libraries, Museums/Galleries, Music, Opera, Performing Arts, Public Broadcasting, Theater
Civic & Public Affairs: Asian American Affairs, Business/Free Enterprise, Civil Rights, Economic Development, Economic Policy, Employment/Job Training, Civic & Public Affairs-General, Housing, Native American Affairs, Nonprofit Management, Philanthropic Organizations, Public Policy, Urban & Community Affairs, Women's Affairs, Zoos/Aquariums
Education: Arts/Humanities Education, Business Education, Colleges & Universities, Colleges & Universities, Community & Junior Colleges, Continuing Education, Economic Education, Education Associations, Education Funds, Education Reform, Elementary Education (Private), Faculty Development, Education-General, International Exchange, International Studies, Literacy, Minority Education, Private Education (Precollege), Public Education (Precollege), Science/

Mathematics Education, Special Education, Student Aid

Environment: Environment-General

Health: Children's Health/Hospitals, Emergency/Ambulance Services, Health Policy/Cost Containment, Health Organizations, Hospices, Hospitals, Hospitals (University Affiliated), Medical Research, Single-Disease Health Associations, Transplant Networks/Donor Banks

International: Foreign Educational Institutions, International-General, Health Care/Hospitals, International Development, International Peace & Security Issues, International Relations, International Relief Efforts

Religion: Missionary Activities (Domestic)

Science: Science Museums

Social Services: Child Welfare, Community Centers, Community Service Organizations, Day Care, Emergency Relief, Family Services, Food/Clothing Distribution, Homes, People with Disabilities, Shelters/Homelessness, Substance Abuse, United Funds/United Ways, Volunteer Services, YMCA/YWCA/YMHA/YWHA, Youth Organizations

Application Procedures

Initial Contact: Call for guidelines.

Application Requirements: Proposals should include amount requested; proposal objective; itemized budget; brief statement of organization's history, goals, and accomplishments to date; current annual report; proof of tax-exempt status; current year's budget showing anticipated expenses and income; list of current corporate and foundation funding sources, public and private, with amounts received within the most recent 12 months or last fiscal year (for both the organization and the specific programs for which funds are requested); recently audited financial statement; board of directors list; and list of accrediting agencies, if applicable. Cultural organizations should submit their most recent 12-month audience statistics.

Deadlines: None.

Review Process: Initial review by contributions staff and committee members, who may deny a request or make a recommendation to the full committee or policy committee.

Evaluative Criteria: Provide evidence of clearly delineated goals and effective, innovative programs that conform to bank's giving priorities; have stable management, and sound financial status; strong leadership to strengthen communities in which bank operates and serve as a model for other nonprofits; and opportunities for employee volunteer involvement.

Decision Notification: Ongoing; contributions committee meets as required; in most cases, applicants learn of a decision in writing within sixty to ninety days.

Notes: Many contributions committees use a proposal application form, available from local contact person.

Restrictions

The company does not support individuals; political causes or candidates; religious, veteran, or fraternal organizations, unless project significantly benefits entire community; fundraising dinners, benefits, or events; or courtesy advertising.

Additional Information

Citicorp Foundation and Travelers Foundation merged to form the Citigroup Foundation in 1999. Company and foundation prefer to initiate grants, but will consider unsolicited proposals.

The company generally prefers to support specific, one-year programs in areas of charitable interest.

Potential for combination with volunteers, in-kind services, or other direct Citibank involvement is frequently a deciding factor in grant decisions. Citibank also makes housing, small business, and student loans; is involved with programs to hire minority youth and to pay summer interns at community nonprofit

organizations; provides technical assistance; and encourages employees to participate in the matching gifts program.

Publications: Public Responsibility at Citibank; Guidelines

Corporate Officials

Paul John Collins: vice chairman, director B West Bend, WI 1936. ED University of Wisconsin BBA (1958); Harvard University MBA (1961). PRIM CORP EMPL vice chairman, director: Citibank. CORP AFFIL director: Kimberly-Clark Corp.; director: Nokia Corp. NONPR AFFIL trustee: Central Park Conservancy; trustee: Glyndeburne Arts Trust; trustee: Carnegie Hall. CLUB AFFIL River Club.

Deryck C. Maughan: vice chairman B Consett, United Kingdom 1947. ED University of London Kings College BA (1969); Stanford University MBA (1978). PRIM CORP EMPL vice chairman: Citigroup Inc. CORP AFFIL officer: New York Stock Exchange Inc.; director: Salomon Brothers Inc.; vice chairman: Citigroup Inc.

Paul Michael Ostergard: vice president, director corporate contributions B Akron, OH 1939. ED University of Madrid (1959-1960); Case Western Reserve University AB (1961); University of Michigan JD (1964); Harvard University MPA (1969). PRIM CORP EMPL vice president, director corporate contributions: Citibank. NONPR AFFIL member: Omicron Delta Kappa; member: Phi Beta Kappa; director: ARC Greater Greater New York; director: Junior Achievement New York; member, board: American Council Arts. CLUB AFFIL Wexford Plantation Club; Harvard Club.

William Reginald Rhodes: vice chairman B New York, NY 1935. ED Brown University BA History (1957). PRIM CORP EMPL vice chairman: Citibank. CORP AFFIL director: Conoco Inc.; vice chairman: Citigroup Inc. NONPR AFFIL member: Venezuela-American Chamber of Commerce; board overseers: Watson Institute International Studies; member executive committee: United States-Russia Business Council; member: United States-Egyptian President Council; founding member: United States National Council International Management Center Budapest; director: Private Export Funding Corp.; government: New York Presbyterian Hospital; chairman: Northfield Mt Hermon School; director: New York City Partnership; member: Lincoln Center Corporate Leadership Committee; vice chairman: Metropolitan Museum Business Committee; vice chairman: Institute International Finance Inc.; director: Foreign Policy Association; director: Institute East-West Studies; member: Council Foreign Relations; trustee: Brown University; trustee: Council Americas; member executive committee: Bretton Woods Committee; member: Bankers Association Foreign Trade; member: Bankers Roundtable; director: Americas Society; director: African-American Institute.

Herman Onno Ruding: vice chairman B Breda, Netherlands 1939. ED Erasmus University (Netherlands) School of Economics MA (1964); Erasmus University (Netherlands) School of Economics PhD (1969). PRIM CORP EMPL vice chairman: Citibank Corp. CORP AFFIL director: Corning Inc.; vice chairman, director: Citicorp. NONPR AFFIL director: Sinai Hospital; member: Trilateral Commission; member: Committee Monetary Union Europe; member: Christian Democratic Alliance.

Sanford I. Weill: chairman B New York, NY 1933. ED Cornell University BA (1955); Cornell University Graduate School Business & Public Administration (1954-1955). PRIM CORP EMPL chairman: Citigroup. CORP AFFIL director: E.I. du Pont de Nemours & Co.; director: IDS Mutual Fund Group; director: AT&T Corp. NONPR AFFIL member business committee: Museum Modern Art; member: New York Society Security Analysts; member, board overseers: Cornell University Medicine College; chairman: Carnegie Hall Society Inc.; vice chairman advisory council: Cornell University Johnson Graduate School Management; founder: Academy Financial. CLUB AFFIL Cornell Club; Harmonie Club; Century Country Club.

Robert B. Willumstad: president, director ED Adelphi University BA. PRIM CORP EMPL president, director: Citigroup Inc. CORP AFFIL director: MasterCard International. NONPR AFFIL board member: Habitat for Humanity.

Giving Program Officials

Alan Okada: PRIM CORP EMPL vice president health programs: Citibank. CORP AFFIL vice president health programs: Citibank NA.

Peter C. Thorp: PRIM CORP EMPL vice president university relations: Citibank.

Foundation Officials

Patricia Byrne: vice president

Paul Michael Ostergard: president (see above)

Charles V. Raymond: president, chief executive officer

Daria Sheehan: secretary

Grants Analysis

Disclosure Period: calendar year ending 2002

Total Grants: $53,063,030*

Number of Grants: 3,066 (approx)

Average Grant: $17,307 (approx)

Highest Grant: $1,150,000

Lowest Grant: $500

Typical Range: $5,000 to $50,000

*****Note:** Giving excludes corporate direct giving, matching gifts, and United Way.

Recent Grants

Note: Grants derived from 2002 Form 990.

Library-Related

150,000	Dade Public Education Fund, Miami, FL -- Citibank Family Tech Program

General

1,150,000	National Academy Foundation, New York, NY -- operating support
1,000,000	Habitat for Humanity, Atlanta, GA
1,000,000	Raza Development Fund, AR -- NCLR Partnership
800,000	Asia Society, New York, NY
600,000	Grameen Foundation USA, Washington, DC -- microcredit in China
500,000	Alvin Ailey American Dance Theater, New York, NY -- Campaign for Ailey
500,000	Local Initiatives Support Corporation, New York, NY -- Community Development Leadership Initiative
500,000	National Community Reinvestment Coalition, Washington, DC -- Citigroup Financial Literacy Leadership Initiative
470,000	Microfinance Opportunities -- financial education for microborrowers
400,000	Women's World Banking, Charleston, WV -- integrated service offerings

CITIZENS FINANCIAL GROUP, INC.

Company Headquarters

1 Citizens Plaza
Providence, RI 02903
Web: http://www.citizensbank.com

Company Description

Employees: 2,167

SIC(s): 6022 State Commercial Banks.

Parent Company: Royal Bank of Scotland Plc, 30 St. Andrew Sq., Edinburgh, United Kingdom

Operating Locations

Citizens Bank of Connecticut (CT--New London); Citizens Bank of Massachusetts (MA--Fairhaven); Citizens Financial Group (RI--Providence); Citizens Financial Services Corp. (RI--Providence); Citizens

Leasing Corp. (RI--Providence); Citizens Mortgage Corp. (GA--Atlanta); Citizens Savings Bank (RI--Providence); Citizens Trust Co. (RI--Providence); Gulf State Mortgage (GA--Atlanta); Royal Bank of Scotland Plc (CA--San Francisco; NY--New York)

Nonmonetary Support

Type: Cause-related Marketing & Promotion; Donated Equipment; Loaned Employees

Citizens Charitable Foundation

Giving Contact

D. Faye Sanders, Senior Vice President
Citizens Charitable Foundation
1 Citizens Plaza
Providence, RI 02903-1339
Phone: (401)456-7285
Fax: (401)456-7644

Description

EIN: 056022653
Organization Type: Corporate Foundation
Giving Locations: RI
Grant Types: General Support.

Financial Summary

Total Giving: $2,749,785 (2001); $1,948,535 (2000); $1,596,117 (1999). Note: Contributes through foundation only.
Giving Analysis: Giving for 2001 includes: foundation scholarships ($40,000); foundation grants to United Way ($476,365); foundation ($2,233,420); 2000: foundation scholarships ($42,500); foundation grants to United Way ($430,170); foundation ($1,475,865); 1999: foundation scholarships ($5,000); foundation grants to United Way ($417,416); foundation ($1,173,701);
Assets: $10,650,030 (2001); $13,470,838 (2000); $4,613,784 (1999)
Gifts Received: $526,139 (2001); $11,153,438 (2000); $26,900 (1999). Note: The foundation receives contributions from Citizens Bank of Rhode Island and Citizens Bank of Connecticut.

Typical Recipients

Arts & Humanities: Arts Associations & Councils, Arts Centers, Arts Funds, Arts Institutes, Arts & Humanities-General, History & Archaeology, Libraries, Literary Arts, Museums/Galleries, Music, Performing Arts, Theater
Civic & Public Affairs: African American Affairs, Botanical Gardens/Parks, Business/Free Enterprise, Community Foundations, Economic Development, Employment/Job Training, Civic & Public Affairs-General, Hispanic Affairs, Housing, Law & Justice, Municipalities/Towns, Philanthropic Organizations, Public Policy, Urban & Community Affairs, Women's Affairs, Zoos/Aquariums
Education: Afterschool/Enrichment Programs, Arts/Humanities Education, Business Education, Colleges & Universities, Community & Junior Colleges, Economic Education, Education Associations, Education Funds, Education-General, Literacy, Medical Education, Private Education (Precollege), Secondary Education (Public), Student Aid
Environment: Environment-General
Health: AIDS/HIV, Children's Health/Hospitals, Clinics/Medical Centers, Emergency/Ambulance Services, Geriatric Health, Health Organizations, Hospices, Hospitals, Medical Rehabilitation, Medical Research, Mental Health, Nursing Services, Prenatal Health Issues, Public Health, Single-Disease Health Associations
International: Foreign Arts Organizations, Health Care/Hospitals

Religion: Churches, Dioceses, Jewish Causes, Ministries, Missionary Activities (Domestic), Religious Organizations, Religious Welfare
Science: Science Museums, Scientific Centers & Institutes
Social Services: Camps, Child Welfare, Community Centers, Community Service Organizations, Day Care, Emergency Relief, Family Services, Food/Clothing Distribution, Homes, People with Disabilities, Recreation & Athletics, Scouts, Senior Services, Sexual Abuse, Shelters/Homelessness, Substance Abuse, United Funds/United Ways, Volunteer Services, YMCA/YWCA/YMHA/YWHA, Youth Organizations

Application Procedures

Initial Contact: Send a letter of proposal.
Application Requirements: Include a description of agency, its purpose, history, and programs; summary of need, amount requested, and description of agencies providing similar services; financial data on organization, such as independent audit, budget with sources of income, breakdown of expenditures by program, administration, and personnel; brief explanation why Citizens Charitable Foundation would be an appropriate donor; list of board of directors; copy of IRS tax-determination letter; and copy of affirmative action/equal opportunity policy.
Deadlines: None.
Decision Notification: Board meets quarterly; allow 60 to 90 days for a reply.

Restrictions

The foundation does not award grants to the following: member agencies of federated organizations, including United Way agencies, except for major capital campaigns; sectarian programs, including capital campaigns for church buildings; public and quasi-governmental agencies and organizations; operating budget deficits of any agencies; annual campaigns; local affiliates of national organizations; endowments and funds for general operating support; individuals; agencies and organizations outside of the geographical area served by Citizens bank; labor and fraternal organizations or programs and projects of a political nature; or advertising and fund-raising activities. or advertising and fund-raising activities.

Additional Information

All organizations requesting funding must agree to evaluation procedures including on-site visits and community interviews. The foundation may request periodic reports from organizations receiving funding. The foundation will not contribute in excess of 1% of the total goal to capital fund campaigns. Generally, payments are made within a three- to five-year period in order to eliminate an accumulation of substantial pledges in future years.
Publications: Annual Report (including Application Guidelines)

Corporate Officials

Lawrence K. Fish: chairman, chief executive officer, president B Chicago, IL 1944. ED Drake University (1966); Harvard University Graduate School of Business Administration MBA (1968). PRIM CORP EMPL chairman, chief executive officer, president: Citizens Financial Group Inc. CORP AFFIL director: MasterCard Inc.; director: Textron Inc.; chairman: Citizens Bank Massachusetts; director: John Hancock Mutual Life Insurance Co.; chairman, chief executive officer: Bank New England. NONPR AFFIL president: Institute Contemporary Art Boston; overseer: New England Conservatory Music. CLUB AFFIL Longwood Club.
Mark J. Formica: vice president, director B 1948. PRIM CORP EMPL president: Citizens Bank Rhode Island.

Foundation Officials

Lawrence K. Fish: trustee (see above)
Mark J. Formica: trustee (see above)
D. Faye Sanders: senior vice president

Grants Analysis

Disclosure Period: calendar year ending 2001
Total Grants: $2,233,420*
Number of Grants: 238
Average Grant: $9,384
Highest Grant: $68,483
Typical Range: $1,000 to $10,000
*Note: Giving excludes scholarships and United Way.

Recent Grants

Note: Grants derived from 2001 Form 990.

General

245,000	United Way of SENE, Providence, RI
125,000	United Way of Massachusetts Bay, Boston, MA
100,000	Johnson and Wales University, Providence, RI
97,000	Providence College, Providence, RI
90,959	American Red Cross, Providence, RI
68,483	American Red Cross of Massachusetts Bay, Boston, MA
66,922	American Red Cross of Massachusetts Bay, Boston, MA
60,000	Acorn Housing Corporation
51,865	United Way, Providence, RI
50,000	Diocese of Providence, Providence, RI

CITIZENS FIRST NATIONAL BANK

Company Headquarters

606 S. Main Street
Princeton, IL 61356
Web: http://www.citizens1st.com

Company Description

Assets: US$420 million (2001)
Employees: 200 (2001)
SIC(s): 6000 Depository Institutions.
Parent Company: First National Corp., 950 John C. Calhoun Dr., SE, Orangeburg, SC, United States

Operating Locations

Citizens First National Bank (IA--Storm Lake)

Citizens First National Bank Foundation

Giving Contact

George H. Schaller, Trustee
Drawer 1227
Storm Lake, IA 50588-1227
Phone: (712)732-5440

Description

EIN: 426073539
Organization Type: Corporate Foundation
Giving Locations: IA: Early, Storm Lake
Grant Types: Capital, General Support.

Financial Summary

Total Giving: $20,600 (2000); $20,445 (1999); $18,973 (1998)
Giving Analysis: Giving for 1999 includes: foundation ($20,445).
Assets: $402,338 (2000); $423,450 (1999); $405,407 (1998)
Gifts Received: $2,935 (2000)

Typical Recipients

Arts & Humanities: Arts Associations & Councils, Historic Preservation, History & Archaeology, Libraries, Museums/Galleries

Civic & Public Affairs: Botanical Gardens/Parks, Business/Free Enterprise, Clubs, Community Foundations, Employment/Job Training, Civic & Public Affairs-General, Housing, Municipalities/Towns, Safety

Education: Colleges & Universities, Education-General, Private Education (Precollege), Public Education (Precollege), Secondary Education (Public), Student Aid

Health: Emergency/Ambulance Services, Health Organizations, Hospitals

Religion: Bible Study/Translation, Churches, Religion-General, Religious Organizations, Religious Welfare

Social Services: Community Service Organizations, Crime Prevention, Delinquency & Criminal Rehabilitation, Domestic Violence, Food/Clothing Distribution, Recreation & Athletics, Recreation & Athletics, Shelters/Homelessness, United Funds/United Ways

Application Procedures

Initial Contact: Send brief letter describing program. Include any information relevant to the request.
Deadlines: November 1.

Corporate Officials

George H. Schaller: president, chief executive officer PRIM CORP EMPL president, chief executive officer: Citizens First National Bank.

Harry W. Schaller: chairman B Storm Lake, IA 1905. ED Columbia University (1926). PRIM CORP EMPL chairman: Citizens First National Bank. CORP AFFIL chairman, director: First National Co.; president, director: Schaller Co.; chairman: Citizens Credit Corp.; chairman: First Leasing Co.

Foundation Officials

Gaylord Sadusky: trust
George H. Schaller: trustee (see above)
Harry W. Schaller: trustee (see above)

Grants Analysis

Disclosure Period: calendar year ending 2000
Total Grants: $20,600
Number of Grants: 55
Average Grant: $374
Highest Grant: $3,500
Typical Range: $100 to $500

Recent Grants

Note: Grants derived from 1999 Form 990.

General

2,650	Methodist Manor, Storm Lake, IA
2,500	Gingerbread House, Storm Lake, IA
2,000	Buena Vista University, Storm Lake, IA
1,500	Church of Christ, Storm Lake, IA
1,250	First Baptist Church, Storm Lake, IA
1,000	Friends of St. Mary's, Storm Lake, IA
750	City of Early, Early, IA
750	Lakeside Presbyterian Church, Storm Lake, IA
500	Buena Vista Work Activity Center, Storm Lake, IA
500	City of Lakeside, Lakeside, IA

CITIZENS UNION BANK

Company Headquarters

200 N. East St.
Greensboro, GA 30642

Company Description

Employees: 43
SIC(s): 6000 Depository Institutions.

Citizens Union Bank Foundation

Giving Contact

Bobby Voyles, Chairman
PO Box 89
Greensboro, GA 30642
Phone: (706)453-2236
Fax: (706)453-9172

Alternate Contact

Dean B. Rizner, Secretary & Treasurer

Description

EIN: 581541701
Organization Type: Corporate Foundation
Giving Locations: GA: Greene County
Grant Types: General Support, Scholarship.

Financial Summary

Total Giving: $15,345 (2001); $4,850 (2000); $7,000 (1999)
Giving Analysis: Giving for 2001 includes: foundation scholarships ($11,000); 2000: foundation ($850); foundation scholarships ($4,000); 1999: foundation scholarships ($7,000);
Assets: $478,978 (2001); $496,803 (2000); $431,597 (1999)
Gifts Received: $50,000 (2000); $150,895 (1998). Note: In 2000, contributions were received from Citizens Union Bank. In 1998, contributions were received from Citizens Union Bank ($150,000) and the Rotary Club of Greene County ($895).

Typical Recipients

Arts & Humanities: Libraries
Education: Continuing Education, Education-General, Vocational & Technical Education
Health: Hospitals
Religion: Churches
Social Services: Animal Protection

Application Procedures

Initial Contact: Recipients are nominated by students and faculty. All information is submitted by the local high school.
Deadlines: None.

Restrictions

Does not support individuals, religious organizations for sectarian purposes, political or lobbying groups, or organizations outside operating areas.

Additional Information

Provides scholarships for higher education to residents of Greene County, GA.

Corporate Officials

Harold Reynolds: chairman, chief executive officer PRIM CORP EMPL chairman, chief executive officer: Citizens Union Bank.
Bobby Voyles: president PRIM CORP EMPL president: Citizens Union Bank.

Foundation Officials

W. Seaborn Ashley, Jr.: director
Neal Dolvin: director
Lanier Rhodes: director
Dean B. Rizner: secretary, treasurer
Frances Strickland: director
Bobby Voyles: chairman (see above)

Grants Analysis

Disclosure Period: calendar year ending 2001
Total Grants: $4,245*
Number of Grants: 5
Highest Grant: $2,000
Lowest Grant: $245
***Note:** Giving excludes scholarships.

Recent Grants

Note: Grants derived from 2000 Form 990.

Library-Related

250	Greene County Library, Greensboro, GA

General

500	Oconee Regional Humane Society, Eatonton, GA
100	Springfield Baptist Church

CITY NATIONAL BANK & TRUST CO.

Company Headquarters

PO Box 873
Gloversville, NY 12078
Web: http://www.citynatlbank.com

Company Description

Employees: 74
SIC(s): 6021 National Commercial Banks.
Parent Company: CNB Bancorp Inc., 10-24 N. Main St., Gloversville, NY, United States.

City National Bank Foundation

Giving Contact

William N. Smith, President
14 N. Main St.
Gloversville, NY 12078
Phone: (518)773-7911
Fax: (518)773-8867

Description

EIN: 222816974
Organization Type: Corporate Foundation
Giving Locations: NY: Gloversville
Grant Types: General Support.

Financial Summary

Total Giving: $60,173 (2001); $52,720 (2000); $52,770 (1999)
Giving Analysis: Giving for 2001 includes: foundation grants to United Way ($16,000); 2000: foundation grants to United Way ($16,000); 1999: foundation grants to United Way ($16,000); foundation ($36,770);
Assets: $76,311 (2001); $82,335 (2000); $59,943 (1999)
Gifts Received: $50,000 (2001); $70,000 (2000); $37,500 (1999). Note: In 1998, 1999, and 2001, contributions were received from City National Bank and Trust Company.

Typical Recipients

Arts & Humanities: History & Archaeology, Libraries, Museums/Galleries, Opera, Performing Arts, Theater

Civic & Public Affairs: Chambers of Commerce, Clubs, Civic & Public Affairs-General, Housing, Municipalities/Towns, Safety, Urban & Community Affairs

Education: Agricultural Education, Community & Junior Colleges, Literacy, School Volunteerism, Science/Mathematics Education, Student Aid

Health: Cancer, Children's Health/Hospitals, Emergency/Ambulance Services, Heart, Hospices, Hospitals, Long-Term Care, Medical Research, Respiratory, Single-Disease Health Associations

Religion: Churches, Jewish Causes, Religious Welfare

Social Services: Animal Protection, Child Welfare, Child Welfare, Community Centers, Community Service Organizations, Family Services, Food/Clothing Distribution, Homes, Recreation & Athletics, Senior

Services, United Funds/United Ways, YMCA/YWCA/YMHA/YWHA

Application Procedures

Initial Contact: Send a brief letter of inquiry.
Application Requirements: Include amount requested and purpose of funds sought.
Deadlines: None.

Restrictions

Grants limited to local organizations and government subdivisions.

Additional Information

Trust(s): City National Bank

Corporate Officials

Michael J. Frank: committee partner, vice president PRIM CORP EMPL committee partner, vice president: City National Bank and Trust Co.
George A. Morgan: executive vice president PRIM CORP EMPL executive vice president: City National Bank and Trust Co.
Bill Smith: chief executive officer PRIM CORP EMPL chief executive officer: City National Bank and Trust Co.
William N. Smith: president, chief executive officer, director PRIM CORP EMPL president, chief executive officer, director: City National Bank and Trust Co.

Foundation Officials

Clark Easterly: trustee B Gloversville, NY 1926. ED North Carolina State University. PRIM CORP EMPL president, director: Johnstown Knitting Mill Co. CORP AFFIL director: First America Bank New York. NONPR AFFIL member: Masons.
Leon Finkle: trustee
Brian Hanaburgh: trustee
Richard E. Hathaway: trustee
Theodore E. Hoye, Jr.: trustee
Robert L. Maider: trustee B Gloversville, NY 1932. ED Hamilton College (1953); Cornell University (1958). PRIM CORP EMPL director: CNB Bancorp.
John C. Miller: trustee
George A. Morgan: trustee (see above)
Frank E. Perrella: trustee
Deborah H. Rose: trustee
William N. Smith: president, trustee (see above)
Clark D. Subik: trustee

Grants Analysis

Disclosure Period: calendar year ending 2001
Total Grants: $44,173*
Number of Grants: 12
Average Grant: $2,198*
Highest Grant: $20,000
Lowest Grant: $200
Typical Range: $500 to $5,000
***Note:** Giving excludes United Way. Average grant excludes highest grant.

Recent Grants

Note: Grants derived from 2001 Form 990.

General

20,000	Nathan Littauer Hospital, Gloversville, NY -- for public support
16,000	United Way of Fulton County, Gloversville, NY -- for public support
10,000	Senior Citizens Center, Gloversville, NY -- for public support
5,000	City of Gloversville, Gloversville, NY -- for public support
3,973	Victims and Families Related, Baltimore, MD -- for public support
1,000	Habitat for Humanity, Johnstown, NY -- for public support
1,000	Jewish Community Center, Gloversville, NY -- for public support
1,000	St. Jude's Children Research, Memphis, TN -- for public support
500	Fulton County YMCA, Gloversville, NY -- for public support
500	James Brennan Humane Society, Gloversville, NY -- for public support

LIZ CLAIBORNE AND ART ORTENBERG FOUNDATION

Giving Contact

James Murtaugh, Program Director
650 5th Avenue, 15th Floor
New York, NY 10019
Phone: (212)333-2536
Fax: (212)956-3531
E-mail: lcaof@fcc.net
Web: http://www.lcaof.org

Description

Founded: 1984
EIN: 133200329
Organization Type: General Purpose Foundation
Giving Locations: internationally especially undeveloped countries; Northern Rockies area and nationally.
Grant Types: Multiyear/Continuing Support, Project.

Donor Information

Founder: The foundation was established in 1984 by Arthur Ortenberg and Elisabeth Claiborne, who founded Liz Claiborne, Inc., the largest seller of women's sportswear in department stores.

The couple started the clothing company in 1976 with an initial investment of $250,000. They contributed $50,000 themselves and borrowed $200,000 from family and friends. Mr. Ortenberg and Ms. Claiborne are no longer on the board of directors of Liz Claiborne, Inc. They no longer hold Liz Claiborne, Inc., stock.

Ms. Claiborne was born in Brussels in 1929 while her father, a banker from New Orleans, was posted overseas. She attended the Art School in Brussels in 1947 and the Academie des Beaux Arts in Paris in 1948, where she studied painting. She decided to remain in the United States when she won a Harper's Bazaar design contest while she was vacationing in New Orleans in 1949. She is a direct descendant of William C. C. Claiborne, Louisiana's governor during the War of 1812.

Ms. Claiborne made a name for herself as a designer in New York at Jonathan Logan, where she spent 16 years designing moderately priced junior dresses. Elisabeth Claiborne and Arthur Ortenberg were married in 1957. They both had children by a previous marriage. He has two children and she has one, Alexander G. Schultz.

Financial Summary

Total Giving: $1,800,000 (fiscal year ending January 31, 2003 approx); $1,800,000 (fiscal 2002 approx); $1,837,149 (fiscal 2001)
Giving Analysis: Giving for fiscal 1999 includes: foundation grants to United Way ($1,000)
Assets: $42,000,000 (fiscal 2003 approx); $42,000,000 (fiscal 2002 approx); $42,315,477 (fiscal 2001)
Gifts Received: $75,000 (fiscal 1999); $75,000 (fiscal 1998); $300,000 (fiscal 1997). Note: The foundation receives contributions from Arthur and Elisabeth C. Ortenberg.

Typical Recipients

Arts & Humanities: Arts Centers, Arts Funds, History & Archaeology, Libraries, Museums/Galleries, Music, Public Broadcasting
Civic & Public Affairs: African American Affairs, Botanical Gardens/Parks, Community Foundations, Economic Development, Economic Policy, Ethnic Organizations, Civic & Public Affairs-General, Municipalities/Towns, Native American Affairs, Philanthropic Organizations, Public Policy, Urban & Community Affairs, Women's Affairs
Education: Arts/Humanities Education, Colleges & Universities, Elementary Education (Private), Elementary Education (Public), Environmental Education, Private Education (Precollege), Public Education (Precollege), Science/Mathematics Education
Environment: Air/Water Quality, Forestry, Environment-General, Research, Resource Conservation, Wildlife Protection, Wildlife Protection
Health: AIDS/HIV, Emergency/Ambulance Services, Health Organizations, Hospitals, Single-Disease Health Associations
International: Health Care/Hospitals, Human Rights, International Environmental Issues, International Peace & Security Issues
Religion: Religious Organizations
Science: Science Museums, Scientific Labs
Social Services: Animal Protection, Counseling, Crime Prevention, Delinquency & Criminal Rehabilitation, Family Planning, People with Disabilities, Recreation & Athletics, United Funds/United Ways, YMCA/YWCA/YMHA/YWHA, Youth Organizations

Application Procedures

Initial Contact: Send a brief letter of inquiry. All requests must be in writing.
Application Requirements: Applicants should include a brief description of the project, the amount requested, and the contact person in charge of the project.
Deadlines: None.

Foundation Officials

Robert Dewar: director
James Murtaugh: program director CORP AFFIL director: Hypres Inc.
Arthur Ortenberg: don, trustee, director B 1926.
Elisabeth Claiborne Ortenberg: donor, director, trustee B Brussels, Belgium 1929. ED Art School Brussels (1948-1949); Academie Nice (France) (1950). NONPR AFFIL director: Fire Island Lighthouse Restoration Comm; guest lecturer: Parsons School Design; guest lecturer: Fashion Institute Technology; director: Council American Fashion Designers; member: Fashion Group.
Mary Corliss Pearl: director B New York, NY 1950. ED Yale University BA (1972); Yale University MPh (1976); Yale University PhD (1982). NONPR AFFIL board governors: Society Conservation Biology; assistant director: Wildlife Conservation Society; member: International Union Conservation Nature; trustee: Gomez Foundation; member: International Primatology Society; member: American Society Primatologists; founder: Council Higher Education Group Rainforest Alliance; member: American Association Advancement Science. CLUB AFFIL Explorers Club.
David Quammen: director
Dr. David Western: director

Grants Analysis

Disclosure Period: fiscal year ending January 31, 2001
Total Grants: $1,837,149*
Number of Grants: 147
Average Grant: $12,498
Highest Grant: $300,000
Lowest Grant: $200
Typical Range: $1,000 to $50,000
***Note:** Grants analysis provided by foundation.

Recent Grants

Note: Grants derived from 2000 Form 990.

Library-Related

227,000	Library of Congress, Washington, DC
6,220	Lincoln Public Schools Library, Lincoln, NE

General

323,360	Missouri Botanical Garden, St. Louis, MO

194,700	Wildlife Conservation Society, Washington, DC
168,080	Wildlife Preservation Trust International, Washington, DC
115,000	Montana Audubon Council, Helena, MT
100,000	Montana Land Reliance, Helena, MT
100,000	Nature Conservancy of Montana, Helena, MT
86,500	African Conservation Center
50,000	African Wildlife Foundation, Washington, DC
50,000	Malpai Borderlands Group, Douglas, AZ
50,000	Peregrine Fund, Boise, ID

CLANEIL FOUNDATION

Giving Contact
Cathy M. Weiss, Executive Director
630 West Germantown Pike, Suite 400
Plymouth Meeting, PA 19462-1074
Phone: (610)828-6331
Fax: (610)828-6405

Description
Founded: 1968
EIN: 236445450
Organization Type: Private Foundation
Giving Locations: MA; PA, Philadelphia metro area
Grant Types: Capital, Conference/Seminar, General Support, Loan, Professorship, Project, Research, Seed Money.

Donor Information
Founder: Established in 1968 the late Henry S. McNeil and Langhorne B. Smith.

Financial Summary
Total Giving: $2,948,246 (2001); $2,237,520 (2000); $2,000,000 (1999 approx)
Assets: $51,265,949 (2001); $48,500,939 (2000); $47,000,000 (1999 approx)
Gifts Received: $13,078,940 (2001); $10,096,939 (2000); $10,000,000 (1999 approx). Note: In 2001 and 2000, contributions were received from Claneil Enterprises Inc.

Typical Recipients
Arts & Humanities: Arts Institutes, Arts Outreach, Arts & Humanities-General, Historic Preservation, History & Archaeology, Museums/Galleries, Public Broadcasting, Theater
Civic & Public Affairs: Community Foundations, Economic Development, Employment/Job Training, Civic & Public Affairs-General, Hispanic Affairs, Housing, Law & Justice, Native American Affairs, Rural Affairs, Safety, Urban & Community Affairs, Women's Affairs, Zoos/Aquariums
Education: Afterschool/Enrichment Programs, Arts/Humanities Education, Colleges & Universities, Community & Junior Colleges, Education Funds, Environmental Education, Faculty Development, Education-General, Medical Education, Minority Education, Preschool Education, Private Education (Precollege), Special Education
Environment: Air/Water Quality, Forestry, Environment-General, Resource Conservation, Watershed
Health: AIDS/HIV, Alzheimers Disease, Cancer, Children's Health/Hospitals, Clinics/Medical Centers, Geriatric Health, Health Funds, Health Organizations, Home-Care Services, Hospitals, Long-Term Care, Medical Research, Mental Health, Prenatal Health Issues, Preventive Medicine/Wellness Organizations, Single-Disease Health Associations, Trauma Treatment
International: Health Care/Hospitals, International Organizations, International Relief Efforts
Religion: Churches, Dioceses, Religious Welfare
Science: Science Museums

Social Services: At-Risk Youth, Child Welfare, Community Centers, Community Service Organizations, Domestic Violence, Family Planning, Family Services, Scouts, Senior Services, Shelters/Homelessness, Substance Abuse, YMCA/YWCA/YMHA/YWHA, Youth Organizations

Application Procedures
Initial Contact: Organizations that have never applied to the Claneil Foundation, those which have applied within the last three years but have not received a grant, and those who are applying for a grant larger than $10,000 must submit a letter of intent prior to submitting a full proposal. All others may submit a full proposal; guidelines may be requested from the foundation.
Application Requirements: Letters of intent should briefly describe the organization and the purpose for which funding is requested.
Deadlines: Letters of intent must be submitted prior to December 15 for the spring cycle and June 30 for the fall cycle. Proposals are accepted up to March 1 for the spring cycle and August 15 for the fall cycle.
Decision Notification: After reviewing the letters of intent, the Claniel Foundation will notify applicants whether or not a full proposal is invited. Grants resulting from full proposals are awarded in June for the spring cycle and in November for the fall cycle.
Notes: The foundation reports that it is in a transitional period and therefore may change its guidelines from time to time over the short term. It is recommended that potential applicants contact the foundation to obtain updated guidelines.

Restrictions
Does not support individuals. Grants for more than $10,000, or those made outside Southeast Pennsylvania are by invitation only.

Foundation Officials
Joanne Bailey: assistant secretary
Marjorie M. Findlay: director
Barbara M. Jordan: director
Henry A. Jordan: secretary, director
Lois F. McNeil: president, director
Robert D. McNeil: director
Langhorne B. Smith: treasurer, director

Grants Analysis
Disclosure Period: calendar year ending 2000
Total Grants: $2,237,520
Number of Grants: 234
Average Grant: $9,562
Highest Grant: $150,000
Typical Range: $5,000 to $20,000

Recent Grants
Note: Grants derived from 2000 Form 990.

General
150,000	St. Luke's Roosevelt Hospital Center, New York, NY -- Richard Eaton Hand Fellowship Endowment
95,000	Chester County Community Foundation, Coatesville, PA -- Community Foundation and affiliated funds
60,000	Pocono Medical Center, East Stroudsburg, PA -- comprehensive capital campaign
56,208	Massachusetts Indian Association, Carlisle, MA -- graduate student scholarship fund
50,000	Farmers' Market Trust, Philadelphia, PA -- School Market Project
50,000	Franklin Institute, Philadelphia, PA -- capital campaign
50,000	Pilot School, Wilmington, DE -- facility renovation
50,000	Please Touch Museum, Philadelphia, PA -- capital campaign
50,000	St. Thomas' Church, Ft. Washington, PA -- rose window

40,000	Eastern National Park and Monument Association, Philadelphia, PA -- Independence Park Institute

GEORGE H. AND ANNE L. CLAPP CHARITABLE AND EDUCATIONAL TRUST

Giving Contact
Annette Calgaro, Assistant Vice President
George H. and Anne L. Clapp Charitable and Educational Trust
c/o Mellon Bank
PO Box 185
Pittsburgh, PA 15230
Phone: (412)234-1634

Description
EIN: 256018976
Organization Type: Private Foundation
Giving Locations: PA: Pittsburgh including metropolitan area
Grant Types: General Support.

Donor Information
Founder: the late George H. Clapp

Financial Summary
Total Giving: $1,025,500 (fiscal year ending September 30, 2001); $1,244,000 (fiscal 2000); $1,064,000 (fiscal 1998)
Assets: $20,036,379 (fiscal 2001); $24,509,682 (fiscal 2000); $21,913,867 (fiscal 1998)

Typical Recipients
Arts & Humanities: Historic Preservation, History & Archaeology, Libraries, Museums/Galleries, Music, Opera, Public Broadcasting
Civic & Public Affairs: Economic Development, Employment/Job Training, Civic & Public Affairs-General, Housing, Public Policy, Safety, Women's Affairs, Zoos/Aquariums
Education: Business Education, Colleges & Universities, Education Funds, Education Reform, Engineering/Technological Education, Education-General, Legal Education, Minority Education, Private Education (Precollege), Public Education (Precollege), Science/Mathematics Education, Special Education, Student Aid
Environment: Environment-General, Resource Conservation
Health: Cancer, Children's Health/Hospitals, Clinics/Medical Centers, Emergency/Ambulance Services, Eyes/Blindness, Health Organizations, Hospices, Hospitals, Long-Term Care, Medical Rehabilitation, Medical Research, Mental Health, Multiple Sclerosis, Nursing Services, Nutrition, Prenatal Health Issues, Single-Disease Health Associations
International: International Environmental Issues
Religion: Religious Organizations, Religious Welfare
Science: Science Museums, Scientific Centers & Institutes
Social Services: Child Welfare, Community Centers, Community Service Organizations, Family Planning, Family Services, Food/Clothing Distribution, People with Disabilities, Sexual Abuse, Shelters/Homelessness, United Funds/United Ways, YMCA/YWCA/YMHA/YWHA, Youth Organizations

Application Procedures
Initial Contact: Phone for application requirements.
Application Requirements: Completed applications will include a description of organization, purpose of funds sought, and proof of tax-exempt status.
Deadlines: Proposals are accepted from January 31 through May 31.

Restrictions

Foundation does not support individuals, religious organizations for sectarian purposes, political or lobbying groups, or organizations outside operating areas.

Additional Information

Trust(s): Mellon Bank NA

Foundation Officials

Annette Calgaro: assistant vice president

Grants Analysis

Disclosure Period: fiscal year ending September 30, 2001
Total Grants: $1,025,500
Number of Grants: 87
Average Grant: $10,762*
Highest Grant: $100,000
Typical Range: $5,000 to $20,000
***Note:** Average grant figure excludes highest grant.

Recent Grants

Note: Grants derived from fiscal 2000 Form 990.

General

50,000	Carnegie, The, Pittsburgh, PA -- arts and music grant
27,500	Morris Museum of Arts and Sciences, Augusta, GA
25,000	Carnegie Institute, Pittsburgh, PA
25,000	Sewickley YMCA, Sewickley, PA
20,000	Children's Hospital of Pittsburgh, Pittsburgh, PA
20,000	Hotchkiss School, Lakeville, CT
20,000	Laughlin Children's Center, Sawickley, PA
20,000	Sewickley Public Library, Sewickley, PA
20,000	Sewickley Valley Hospital, Sewickley, PA
20,000	University of Pittsburgh, Pittsburgh, PA -- for scholarship fund

CLARCOR, INC.

Company Headquarters

Rockford, IL
Web: http://www.clarcor.com

Company Description

Founded: 1904
Ticker: CLC
Exchange: NYSE
Revenue: US$715.6 million (2002)
Employees: 4545 (2002)
SIC(s): 3411 Metal Cans, 3564 Blowers & Fans, 3569 General Industrial Machinery Nec, 3714 Motor Vehicle Parts & Accessories.

Operating Locations

CLARCOR Inc. (AL--Birmingham; CA--Corona; GA--Atlanta; IL--Downers Grove; IN--New Albany; KY--Louisville; NE--Kearney; OH--Cincinnati; TN--Nashville; TX--Dallas, Garland)

Nonmonetary Support

Type: Loaned Executives
Note: Nonmonetary support is for United Way only, and is approximately $20,000 annually.

CLARCOR Foundation

Giving Contact

David J. Lindsay, Chairman
2323 6th Street
P.O. Box 7007
Rockford, IL 61125

Phone: (815)962-8867
Fax: (815)962-0417

Alternate Contact

Sue Berg, Foundation Secretary

Description

EIN: 366032573
Organization Type: Corporate Foundation
Giving Locations: operating locations only.
Grant Types: Capital, Employee Matching Gifts, General Support, Multiyear/Continuing Support.
Note: Employee matching gift ratio: 1 to 1 to educational institutions.

Financial Summary

Total Giving: $512,068 (2001); $588,157 (2000); $479,162 (1999). Note: Contributes through corporate direct giving program and foundation.
Giving Analysis: Giving for 2000 includes: foundation grants to United Way ($138,079); foundation ($450,078); 1999: foundation grants to United Way ($116,833); foundation ($362,329); 1998: foundation grants to United Way ($109,212); foundation ($385,730);
Assets: $8,753,503 (2001); $9,788,761 (2000); $10,436,933 (1999)

Typical Recipients

Arts & Humanities: Arts Associations & Councils, Dance, Ethnic & Folk Arts, Arts & Humanities-General, History & Archaeology, Libraries, Museums/Galleries, Music, Opera, Public Broadcasting, Theater
Civic & Public Affairs: African American Affairs, Botanical Gardens/Parks, Community Foundations, Economic Development, Employment/Job Training, Civic & Public Affairs-General, Hispanic Affairs, Housing, Minority Business, Municipalities/Towns, Parades/Festivals, Women's Affairs
Education: Business Education, Colleges & Universities, Economic Education, Faculty Development, Education-General, Legal Education, Literacy, Private Education (Precollege), Public Education (Precollege)
Health: Cancer, Clinics/Medical Centers, Clinics/Medical Centers, Emergency/Ambulance Services, Health Funds, Health Organizations, Hospices, Hospitals, Long-Term Care, Mental Health, Nursing Services, Public Health, Respiratory, Single-Disease Health Associations
Religion: Churches, Religion-General, Jewish Causes, Religious Welfare
Science: Science-General, Science Museums
Social Services: At-Risk Youth, Big Brother/Big Sister, Child Welfare, Community Centers, Community Service Organizations, Crime Prevention, Day Care, Emergency Relief, Family Services, Food/Clothing Distribution, Homes, People with Disabilities, Recreation & Athletics, Scouts, Social Services-General, Special Olympics, Substance Abuse, United Funds/United Ways, Veterans, YMCA/YWCA/YMHA/YWHA, Youth Organizations

Application Procedures

Initial Contact: Request grant application form.
Application Requirements: Proposals should include completed application form, amount requested, purpose for which funds are sought, a description of organization, recently audited financial statement, and proof of tax-exempt status.
Deadlines: None.
Decision Notification: Quarterly.

Additional Information

In 1988, J.L. Clark Manufacturing Co. was reincorporated as CLARCOR Inc. The foundation name was changed from the Clark Foundation to the CLARCOR Foundation.
Publications: Foundation Guidelines

Corporate Officials

Bruce A. Klein: chief financial officer, vice president B Louisville, KY 1947. ED University of Louisville BA (1973); University of Chicago MBA (1976). PRIM CORP EMPL chief financial officer, vice president: CLARCOR Inc. ADD CORP EMPL treasurer: J.L. Clark Inc. Delaware. CORP AFFIL director: Peoples Insurance Agency; director: Suntec Industries Inc.
William F. Knese: vice president, treasurer B 1948. PRIM CORP EMPL vice president, treasurer: CLARCOR Inc.
David J. Lindsay: vice president B 1955. ED University of Illinois BS (1977). PRIM CORP EMPL vice president: CLARCOR Inc.

Foundation Officials

David Anderson: trustee
Sue M. Berg: secretary
Marcia Blaylock: trustee
Lawrence Eugene Gloyd: trustee B Milan, IN 1932. ED Hanover College BA (1954). ADD CORP EMPL chairman: Airguard industries Inc.; chairman: Baldwin Filters Inc.; chairman, chief executive officer: Clark Filter Inc.; director: J.L. Clark Inc. CORP AFFIL director: United Air Specialists Inc.; director: Woodward Governor Co.; director: Ruppman Marketing Inc.; director: Thomas Industries Inc.; director: AMCORE Financial Inc.; director: GUD Holdings Ltd. NONPR AFFIL member: National Association Manufacturers; member: President Association; director: Illinois Council Economic Education; member: Illinois Manufacturer Association; director: Council 100; member: Hardware Group Association; member: American Hardware Manufacturer Association; national director: Big Brothers/Big Sisters. CLUB AFFIL Masons Club.
Norman E. Johnson: trustee B Lake Mills, IA 1948. ED University of Iowa (1970); Drake University (1972). PRIM CORP EMPL president, chief executive officer: Clarcor Inc. CORP AFFIL president: Baldwin Filters Inc.; chairman: JL Clark Inc.
Bruce A. Klein: trustee (see above)
William F. Knese: chairman, trustee (see above)
David J. Lindsay: trustee (see above)

Grants Analysis

Disclosure Period: calendar year ending 2001
Total Grants: $359,788*
Number of Grants: 51
Average Grant: $4,455*
Highest Grant: $50,000
Lowest Grant: $500
Typical Range: $500 to $25,000
***Note:** Giving excludes United Way and miscellaneous grants of less than $500 each. Average grant figure excludes three highest grants ($145,950).

Recent Grants

Note: Grants derived from 2001 Form 990.

General

50,000	Friends of the Coronado, Rockford, IL
50,000	Zion Gateway Center, Rockford, IL
45,950	United Way of RR Valley, Rockford, IL
33,238	United Way of Kearney, Kearney, NE
30,000	Rockford Pro/Am, Rockford, IL
25,175	Rockford Park District, Rockford, IL
25,000	Illinois Growth Enterprises, Chicago, IL
21,927	United Way of Greensboro, Greensboro, NC
18,109	United Way of Lancaster County, Lancaster, PA
15,500	Blackhawk Area Council, Rockford, IL

CLARK FOUNDATION (NY)

Giving Contact

Charles Hamilton, Executive Director
One Rockefeller Plaza, 31st Floor
New York, NY 10020-2102

Phone: (212)977-6900
Fax: (212)977-3424

Description

Founded: 1931
EIN: 135616528
Organization Type: General Purpose Foundation
Giving Locations: NY: Cooperstown, New York nationally.
Grant Types: Capital, General Support, Scholarship.

Donor Information

Founder: The Clark Foundation was established in 1931 in New York by members of the Clark family, including Edwin Severin Clark, Stephen Carlton Clark, and Frederick Ambrose Clark. The donors were heirs to the Clark family fortune, which originated in the 1800s with Edward Clark, a Cooperstown lawyer who was one of the founders of the Singer Company. The foundation has made major contributions to the residents of Cooperstown through gifts of a museum, a hospital affiliated with Columbia University, a community recreation center, and a college scholarship program for local students. In 1973, the foundation merged with the Scriven Foundation, another Clark endowment. The foundation is governed by a thirteen-member board of directors, including two members of the Clark family.

Financial Summary

Total Giving: $16,000,000 (fiscal year ending June 30, 2003 approx); $16,286,400 (fiscal 2002 approx); $18,533,634 (fiscal 2001)
Giving Analysis: Giving for fiscal 2001 includes: foundation fellowships ($143,429); foundation grants to United Way ($420,000); foundation scholarships ($2,660,775); fiscal 2000: foundation fellowships ($158,097); foundation gifts to individuals ($183,769); foundation grants to United Way ($760,000); foundation scholarships ($2,489,990); fiscal 1999: nonmonetary support ($115,000); foundation gifts to individuals ($132,023); foundation fellowships ($180,991) foundation scholarships ($2,295,383)
Assets: $425,000,000 (fiscal 2003 approx); $480,000,000 (fiscal 2002 approx); $495,890,546 (fiscal 2001)
Gifts Received: $1,214,221 (fiscal 2001); $1,000 (fiscal 2000); $724,856 (fiscal 1999). Note: In fiscal 2001, contributions were received from Trust for Dorthy Dewart. In fiscal 1995, contributions were received from Trust for Frieda Shipley.

Typical Recipients

Arts & Humanities: Ballet, Arts & Humanities-General, History & Archaeology, Libraries, Museums/Galleries, Music, Opera, Performing Arts, Public Broadcasting, Theater
Civic & Public Affairs: Business/Free Enterprise, Civil Rights, Community Foundations, Economic Development, Employment/Job Training, Civic & Public Affairs-General, Housing, Legal Aid, Nonprofit Management, Professional & Trade Associations, Safety, Urban & Community Affairs, Women's Affairs, Zoos/Aquariums
Education: Afterschool/Enrichment Programs, Arts/Humanities Education, Business Education, Colleges & Universities, Education Funds, Education Reform, Elementary Education (Private), Elementary Education (Public), Education-General, Leadership Training, Literacy, Medical Education, Minority Education, Private Education (Precollege), Public Education (Precollege), School Volunteerism, Social Sciences Education, Special Education, Student Aid, Vocational & Technical Education
Environment: Air/Water Quality, Environment-General, Resource Conservation, Wildlife Protection
Health: AIDS/HIV, Cancer, Clinics/Medical Centers, Emergency/Ambulance Services, Health Funds, Health Organizations, Hospitals, Kidney, Medical Training, Mental Health, Outpatient Health Care
International: International Development

Religion: Churches, Religious Organizations, Religious Welfare
Science: Science Museums
Social Services: At-Risk Youth, Big Brother/Big Sister, Child Welfare, Community Centers, Community Service Organizations, Crime Prevention, Day Care, Delinquency & Criminal Rehabilitation, Family Planning, Family Services, Homes, People with Disabilities, Recreation & Athletics, Senior Services, Shelters/Homelessness, Substance Abuse, United Funds/United Ways, Veterans, Volunteer Services, YMCA/YWCA/YMHA/YWHA, Youth Organizations

Application Procedures

Initial Contact: Applicants should send a preliminary letter to the foundation.
Application Requirements: The letter should include a description of the project, amount requested, audited financial report, budget, and proof of tax-exempt status. If the foundation is interested in the project, further information will be requested.
Deadlines: None. The foundation's board of directors meets in October and May and at other times during the year. The grants committee, however, meets more frequently.
Review Process: The grants committee has the authority to approve some grants, but its general function is to make recommendations to the board of directors concerning grant requests. Decisions usually are made by the entire board.

Restrictions

The foundation does not fund deficit financing, matching gifts, gifts to individuals, or loans. Grants are not made outside New York.

Additional Information

Publications: Program Policy Statement; Application Guidelines

Foundation Officials

Kent L. Barwick: director B 1941. NONPR AFFIL president: Municipal Art Society of New York.
Jane Forbes Clark: president, donor daughter, director B New York, NY 1955. ED Bennett College AA (1975); Marymount Manhattan College MS (1979). PRIM CORP EMPL chairman: Clark Estates Inc. CORP AFFIL vice president: Otesaga Hotel; vice president: Cooper Inn; vice president: Leatherstocking Corp. NONPR AFFIL vice chairman: National Baseball Hall & Museum; senior vice president, director: U.S. Equestrian Team. CLUB AFFIL vice president: Leatherstocking Golf Course.
Leonard S. Coleman, Jr.: director B Montclair, NJ 1949. ED Harvard University MPA; Princeton University. PRIM CORP EMPL president: National League, Major League Baseball. CORP AFFIL director: Omnicom Group Inc.; director: Owens Corning; director: H.J. Heinz Co.; director: New Jersey Resources Corp.; director: Beneficial Corp.; director: Cendant Corp.; director: Avis Rent-A-Car Inc.
William Maxwell Evarts, Jr.: director B New York, NY 1925. ED Harvard University AB (1949); Harvard University LLB (1952). PRIM CORP EMPL partner: Winthrop, Stimson, Putnam & Roberts. NONPR AFFIL director: Trust Public Land; director: Union Hospital Fund New York; director: Scenic Hudson; member: Association Bar New York City; member distr committee: New York Community Trust; member: American Bar Association.
Gates Helms Hawn: director PRIM CORP EMPL chief operating officer: Donaldson, Lufkin & Jenrette Inc. CORP AFFIL chief operating officer: Pershing Trust Co. Division.
Archie F. MacAllaster: director
Joan B. S. McMenamin: director B New York, NY 1925. ED Smith College BA (1946). NONPR AFFIL trustee: Robert College Istanbul Turkey; trustee: WICAT Foundations; member: New York State Association Independent Schools; special advisor: Parents

League; trustee: Laurenceville School; member: National Association Principal's Girls School. CLUB AFFIL Bridgehampton Club; Cosmopolitan Club.
Kevin S. Moore: treasurer, director PRIM CORP EMPL chief financial officer, senior vice president, director: Clark Estates Inc. CORP AFFIL director: Leatherstocking Corp.; director: Ducommun Inc. NONPR AFFIL treasurer: National Baseball Hall Fame & Museum.
Anne Labouisse Peretz: director B 1939. PRIM CORP EMPL co-owner: New Report Inc. NONPR AFFIL president: Family Center Inc.
Edward William Stack: vice president, director B Rockville Centre, NY 1935. ED Pace University BBA (1956). PRIM CORP EMPL president, director: Clark Estates Inc. CORP AFFIL secretary, treasurer, director: New Republic Inc.; director: Otesaga Hotel; director: Cooper Inn; director: Leatherstocking Corp.; regional advisory board: Chase Banking Corporate. NONPR AFFIL secretary, trustee: New York Saint Historical Association; advisory council: Salvation Army Nassau County; trustee: Hartwick College; chairman: National Baseball Hall Fame & Museum; member: Downtown Association; vice chairman, director: Farmers Museum; vice president, trustee: Mary Imogene Bassett Hospital. CLUB AFFIL Mohican Club; director: Leatherstocking Golf Course.
John Hoyt Stookey: director B New York, NY 1930. ED Amherst College BA (1952); Columbia University BS (1955). CORP AFFIL director: US Trust Co.; trustee: US Trust Co. New York; chairman: Per Scholas Inc.; chairman, director: Suburban Propane Partners; director: Chesapeake Corp.; director: Cyprus Amax Minerals Co.; director: ACX Technologies Inc.
Richard C. Vanison: assistant treasurer PRIM CORP EMPL treasurer: Clark Estates Inc. CORP AFFIL treasurer: Leatherstocking Corp.

Grants Analysis

Disclosure Period: fiscal year ending June 30, 2001
Total Grants: $15,309,427*
Number of Grants: 155
Average Grant: $91,947*
Highest Grant: $1,149,662
Typical Range: $50,000 to $200,000
***Note:** Giving excludes scholarships, United Way, and fellowship. Average grant figure excludes highest grant.

Recent Grants

Note: Grants derived from fiscal 2000 Form 990.

General
1,000,000	Clara Welch Thanksgiving Home, Cooperstown, NY
760,000	United Way New York City, New York, NY
330,000	Center for Children and Families, New York, NY
300,000	Public/Private Ventures, New York, NY
250,000	Hudson Guild, New York, NY
215,000	Foundation for Excellent Schools, Cornwall, VT
200,000	East Harlem Employment Service, New York, NY
200,000	Episcopal Social Services, New York, NY
200,000	Family Center, Somerville, MA
200,000	Graham-Windham, New York, NY

Lynn And Helen Clark Fund

Giving Contact

Steve Melvin, Trust Officer
c/o First National Bank of Longmont
PO Box 1159
Longmont, CO 80501

Phone: (303)776-5800
Fax: (303)776-8475

Description
Founded: 1993
EIN: 846270492
Organization Type: Private Foundation
Giving Locations: CO: Longmont limited to the St. Vrain School District, including the city of Longmont, CO
Grant Types: General Support.

Financial Summary
Total Giving: $175,192 (fiscal year ending September 30, 2001); $189,788 (fiscal 2000); $172,900 (fiscal 1998)
Giving Analysis: Giving for fiscal 2001 includes: foundation scholarships ($15,000) fiscal 2000: foundation scholarships ($28,500)
Assets: $3,036,166 (fiscal 2001); $3,649,334 (fiscal 2000); $3,339,799 (fiscal 1998)

Typical Recipients
Arts & Humanities: Arts Associations & Councils, Arts Centers, Arts & Humanities-General, History & Archaeology, Museums/Galleries, Music
Civic & Public Affairs: Botanical Gardens/Parks, Community Foundations, Urban & Community Affairs, Women's Affairs
Education: Education Funds, Faculty Development, Education-General, Minority Education, Preschool Education, Public Education (Precollege), Student Aid
Health: Emergency/Ambulance Services, Hospices, Hospitals, Medical Rehabilitation, Public Health
Religion: Churches, Religion-General
Social Services: Animal Protection, Community Centers, Community Service Organizations, Domestic Violence, Family Planning, Family Services, Food/Clothing Distribution, Homes, Senior Services, YMCA/YWCA/YMHA/YWHA, YMCA/YWCA/YMHA/YWHA, Youth Organizations

Application Procedures
Initial Contact: There is no formal application form or guidelines.
Deadlines: May 1.

Restrictions
Grants are limited to St. Vrain Valley School District inhabitants.

Additional Information
The fund is set aside for charitable, religious, literacy, and educational purposes.
Trust(s): First Natl Bank Longmont

Grants Analysis
Disclosure Period: fiscal year ending September 30, 2001
Total Grants: $160,192*
Number of Grants: 23
Average Grant: $6,965
Highest Grant: $12,000
Lowest Grant: $1,000
Typical Range: $3,000 to $10,000
*Note: Giving excludes scholarships.

Recent Grants
Note: Grants derived from fiscal 2000 Form 990.

General

20,000	Longmont United Hospital, Longmont, CO -- building of education resources library
15,288	Special Transit, Boulder, CO -- transportation expenses
15,000	St. Vrain Historical Society, Longmont, CO -- Hoverhome capital campaign
13,500	Longmont YMCA, Longmont, CO --

	membership, youth activities, and childcare
12,000	First Congregational Church, Longmont, CO
10,000	Alternatives for Youth, Inc, Longmont, CO -- Clearview Educational Center academic programs
10,000	Friends First, Longmont, CO
10,000	Longmont Coalition for Women in Crisis, Longmont, CO
10,000	Longmont YMCA, Longmont, CO -- childcare scholarships
10,000	Teen Cafi, Longmont, CO

JOHN CLARKE TRUST

Giving Contact
PO Box 6767
PO Box 1861
Providence, RI 02940-6767
Phone: (617)434-4644

Description
EIN: 056006062
Organization Type: Private Foundation
Giving Locations: RI
Grant Types: General Support.

Financial Summary
Total Giving: $174,675 (2000); $216,550 (1999); $351,874 (1998)
Giving Analysis: Giving for 1998 includes: foundation grants to United Way ($12,500) foundation ($339,374)
Assets: $4,321,026 (2000); $4,410,227 (1999); $4,387,620 (1998)

Typical Recipients
Arts & Humanities: Arts Associations & Councils, Libraries, Music, Theater
Civic & Public Affairs: African American Affairs, Chambers of Commerce, Civic & Public Affairs-General, Legal Aid, Municipalities/Towns, Urban & Community Affairs, Women's Affairs
Education: Afterschool/Enrichment Programs, Arts/Humanities Education, Colleges & Universities, Education Funds, Engineering/Technological Education, Education-General, Medical Education, Private Education (Precollege), Public Education (Precollege), Religious Education, Secondary Education (Private), Secondary Education (Public), Student Aid
Environment: Wildlife Protection
Health: Eyes/Blindness, Health Organizations, Home-Care Services, Hospitals, Medical Research, Mental Health, Nursing Services
International: International Affairs
Religion: Churches, Churches, Ministries, Religious Organizations, Religious Welfare
Science: Science Museums
Social Services: At-Risk Youth, Big Brother/Big Sister, Camps, Child Welfare, Community Centers, Community Service Organizations, Day Care, Domestic Violence, Family Services, Scouts, Shelters/Homelessness, Substance Abuse, United Funds/United Ways, Volunteer Services, YMCA/YWCA/YMHA/YWHA, Youth Organizations

Application Procedures
Initial Contact: The foundation has no formal grant application procedure or application form.
Deadlines: None.

Restrictions
Grants provided for the relief of the poor and education of children.

Additional Information
Trust(s): BankBoston NA

Foundation Officials
William W. Corcoran, Esq.: co-trustee
Wilbur Nelson, Jr.: co-trustee

Grants Analysis
Disclosure Period: calendar year ending 2000
Total Grants: $174,675
Number of Grants: 41
Average Grant: $4,260
Highest Grant: $10,000
Lowest Grant: $1,000
Typical Range: $1,000 to $10,000

Recent Grants
Note: Grants derived from 2000 Form 990.

Library-Related

5,000	Providence Public Library, Providence, RI

General

10,000	Newport Hospital Foundation, Newport, RI
10,000	Rogers High School, Newport, RI -- scholarships
10,000	University of Rhode Island, Providence, RI
7,200	Community Preparatory School, Providence, RI
5,000	East Providence Community Center, Providence, RI
5,000	Middletown High School, Middletown, RI
5,000	New Visions for Newport County, Newport, RI
5,000	Newman Bird Sanctuary, Middletown, RI
5,000	Portsmouth High School, Portsmouth, RI -- scholarships
5,000	Providence In-Town Churches, Providence, RI

EUGENE M. CLARY FOUNDATION, INC.

Giving Contact
Eugene M. Clary, President
4701 Post Oak Tritt Rd.
Marietta, GA 30062
Phone: (770)993-3562

Description
Founded: 1997
EIN: 582310406
Organization Type: Private Foundation
Grant Types: General Support.

Financial Summary
Total Giving: $104,730 (2001); $97,190 (2000); $83,140 (1999)
Assets: $1,351,181 (2001); $1,404,248 (2000); $1,591,899 (1999)
Gifts Received: $50,000 (2000); $10,000 (1999); $1,131,523 (1997). Note: In 1997, 1999 and 2000, contributions were received from Eugene M. Clary.

Typical Recipients
Arts & Humanities: Libraries
Civic & Public Affairs: Civic & Public Affairs-General, Urban & Community Affairs
Education: Education-General
Environment: Wildlife Protection
Health: Alzheimers Disease, Cancer, Children's Health/Hospitals, Diabetes, Emergency/Ambulance Services, Eyes/Blindness, Health-General, Medical Research, Prenatal Health Issues
Social Services: At-Risk Youth, People with Disabilities

Foundation Officials

Eugene M. Clary: president
Kenneth B. Clary: director
William C. Clary, Jr.: chief financial officer

Grants Analysis

Disclosure Period: calendar year ending 2001
Total Grants: $104,730
Number of Grants: 20
Average Grant: $1,160*
Highest Grant: $40,000
Lowest Grant: $10
Typical Range: $100 to $500
***Note:** Average grant figure excludes three highest grant ($85,000).

Recent Grants

Note: Grants derived from 2000 Form 990.

Library-Related

23,000	Harlem Library Fund

General

70,000	Alexander Tharpe Fund, Atlanta, GA
600	Recording for the Blind and Dyslexic
500	Guiding Eyes for the Blind, Yorktown Heights, NY
300	Alzheimer's Disease and Related Disorders
300	American Diabetes Association
250	Georgia Spit Tobacco Education, GA
200	National Stroke Council
100	American Foundation for the Blind, New York, NY
100	American Institute for Cancer Research
100	Aria, Homewood, IL

CLAY FOUNDATION

Giving Contact

Charles M. Avampato, President
1426 Kanawha Boulevard, East
Charleston, WV 25301
Phone: (304)344-8656
Fax: (304)344-3805
E-mail: cfiwv@aol.com

Description

Founded: 1987
EIN: 550670193
Organization Type: General Purpose Foundation
Giving Locations: WV
Grant Types: Award, Challenge, Endowment, Matching, Research, Seed Money.

Donor Information

Founder: The foundation was established in 1987 by Lyell B. Clay, the chairman of the foundation, and Buckner Clay, also chairman of the foundation. Lyell B. Clay is the chairman of the board of Clay Communications, Inc.

Financial Summary

Total Giving: $1,000,000 (fiscal year ending October 31, 2003 approx); $1,000,000 (fiscal 2002 approx); $1,710,141 (fiscal 2001)
Giving Analysis: Giving for fiscal 2001 includes: foundation scholarships ($25,000); foundation grants to United Way ($65,000) fiscal 1998: foundation grants to United Way ($50,000)
Assets: $63,000,000 (fiscal 2003 approx); $63,000,000 (fiscal 2002 approx); $61,881,185 (fiscal 1998)
Gifts Received: $660,489 (fiscal 1992). Note: Contributions were received from Lyell B. and Buckner W. Clay.

Typical Recipients

Arts & Humanities: Arts Centers, Arts Funds, Historic Preservation, History & Archaeology, Libraries, Museums/Galleries, Music, Opera, Public Broadcasting, Theater
Civic & Public Affairs: Botanical Gardens/Parks, Chambers of Commerce, Community Foundations, Economic Development, Civic & Public Affairs-General, Housing, Law & Justice, Legal Aid, Nonprofit Management, Philanthropic Organizations, Professional & Trade Associations, Public Policy, Urban & Community Affairs
Education: Afterschool/Enrichment Programs, Arts/Humanities Education, Business-School Partnerships, Colleges & Universities, Continuing Education, Education-General, Health & Physical Education, Legal Education, Literacy, Medical Education, Private Education (Precollege), Public Education (Precollege), Science/Mathematics Education, Social Sciences Education, Student Aid
Health: Children's Health/Hospitals, Clinics/Medical Centers, Health Policy/Cost Containment, Health Organizations, Hospices, Hospitals, Mental Health, Preventive Medicine/Wellness Organizations, Speech & Hearing
International: International Organizations
Religion: Churches, Religious Organizations, Religious Welfare
Science: Science Museums
Social Services: Animal Protection, At-Risk Youth, Camps, Child Welfare, Community Service Organizations, Counseling, Family Services, Food/Clothing Distribution, Homes, People with Disabilities, Recreation & Athletics, Scouts, Shelters/Homelessness, United Funds/United Ways, Volunteer Services, YMCA/YWCA/YMHA/YWHA, YMCA/YWCA/YMHA/YWHA, Youth Organizations

Application Procedures

Initial Contact: The foundation reports that applicants should submit, in triplicate, a letter of inquiry (two to three pages) that briefly describes the proposed project.
Application Requirements: Letters should include the name, address, and phone number of the organization; contact's name; descriptive title of project; amount of funds requested; timetable for use of funds; outline of objectives, specific goals, and target population; methods which will be used to accomplish these goals; other sources of funding for the project; and plans for evaluation of the project (if applicable). Attachments should include information about the sponsoring organization, names and brief statements of qualification for individuals who will be involved in the project, most recently audited financial statement, and tax-exempt identification.
Deadlines: None.
Review Process: All grant requests are first reviewed to determine if the request falls within the current program interest of the foundation. Only those requests that clearly fall outside the foundation's priorities are declined on the first review.

In reviewing grant applications, the foundation gives careful consideration to: the potential impact of the request and the number of people who will benefit; the degree to which the applicant works with, or complements, the services of other community organizations; the organization's fiscal responsibility and management qualifications; the possibility of the use of its grants as seed money for matching funds from other sources; the ability of the program to obtain necessary additional funding to implement the project; the commitment of the organization's board of directors; the imaginative and experimental quality of the proposed project; the extent of local volunteer involvement and support for the project; and the ability of the organization to provide ongoing funding after the term of the grant.

The foundation may request additional information and, in some cases, may arrange for the applicant to meet with the staff for further discussion. A project site visit may be scheduled, and the advice of outside consultants may be sought.

Final approval of each major grant is the responsibility of the board of directors. Certain other grants that require a smaller amount of support may be authorized by the president of the foundation. All grants are subject to the same review and monitoring criteria. Applicants should allow the foundation 60 working days to review a request. If the foundation's priorities and resources permit consideration of the request, a detailed proposal may be requested. The board of directors meets four times a year, generally in January, April, July, and October.

Restrictions

In general, the foundation does not fund ongoing normal operations, debt retirement or operational deficits, national fundraising campaigns, endowment or scholarship funds, religious organizations for religious purposes, or conduit organizations. The foundation may not award grants to individuals, designate funds for legislation, or support activities that seek to influence the legislative process.

Foundation Officials

Charles M. Avampato: president
James Knight Brown: secretary B Rainelle, WV 1929. ED West Virginia University BS (1951). PRIM CORP EMPL member: Jackson & Kelly. CORP AFFIL director: One Valley Bancorp West Virginia, Inc. NONPR AFFIL member: Phi Beta Kappa; member: West Virginia State Bar; member: Order Coif; member: American Bar Association.
Buckner W. Clay: chairman
Hamilton G. Clay: vice president
Lyell Buffington Clay: chairman B Baltimore, MD 1923. ED Williams College BA (1944); University of Virginia LLB (1948); Marshall University MA (1956); Harvard University (1967); West Virginia University MBA (1975). NONPR AFFIL member: West Virginia Press Association; member: West Virginia State Bar; member: Charleston Area Chamber of Commerce; member: American Newspaper Publishers Association. CLUB AFFIL Charleston Rotary Club.
Whitney Clay Diller: treasurer
Louis Sweetland Southworth, II: assistant secretary-treasurer B Huntington, WV 1943. ED Marshall University AB (1965); West Virginia University JD (1968); New York University LLM (1970). PRIM CORP EMPL attorney: Jackson & Kelly. NONPR AFFIL trustee: Kanawha Valley Foundation; trustee: University Charleston; director: CAMC Foundation; fellow: American College Tax Counsel. CLUB AFFIL Rotary Club; Edgewood Country Club.

Grants Analysis

Disclosure Period: fiscal year ending October 31, 2001
Total Grants: $1,620,141*
Number of Grants: 22
Average Grant: $48,748*
Highest Grant: $596,425
Lowest Grant: $1,711
Typical Range: $5,000 to $60,000
***Note:** Giving excludes United Way and scholarships. Average grant figure excludes highest grant.

Recent Grants

Note: Grants derived from 1999 Form 990.

Library-Related

80,000	Library Foundation of Kanawha County, Charleston, WV -- library automation
7,620	Kanawha County Schools, Charleston, WV -- library automation

General

1,300,000	Center for Arts and Sciences of West Virginia, Charleston, WV -- new arts center
571,425	University of Charleston, Charleston, WV -- information & science center

100,000	University of Virginia, Charlottesville, VA -- Law School Foundation
80,000	BIDCO Foundation, Charleston, WV -- economic development programs
62,500	YWCA of Charleston, Charleston, WV -- renovation of women's & children's shelter
60,000	Fund for the Arts, Charleston, WV -- annual campaign
50,000	United Way Kanawha Valley, Charleston, WV -- annual fund raising
50,000	West Virginia Health Right, Inc., Charleston, WV -- construction of a new health clinic
39,000	Religious Coalition for Community Renewal, Charleston, WV -- Jubilee Housing Project
25,000	Neediest Cases, Charleston, WV -- Christmas help for indigent families

SILAS AND RUTH CLAYPOOL FOUNDATION

Giving Contact

Jimmy Rogers
c/o Old National Trust
PO Box 10
Oblong, IL 62449
Phone: (618)592-5029

Description

Founded: 1991
EIN: 376288069
Organization Type: Private Foundation
Giving Locations: IL: Crawford County
Grant Types: General Support.

Financial Summary

Total Giving: $37,493 (2001); $52,490 (2000); $27,908 (1999)
Assets: $810,515 (2001); $846,811 (2000); $839,250 (1999)
Gifts Received: In 1991, contributions were received from the Ruth Claypool Living Trust.

Typical Recipients

Arts & Humanities: Arts Associations & Councils, Historic Preservation, History & Archaeology, Libraries, Music, Theater
Civic & Public Affairs: Community Foundations, Civic & Public Affairs-General, Housing, Municipalities/Towns, Safety, Urban & Community Affairs
Education: Agricultural Education, Education-General, Literacy, Preschool Education, Public Education (Precollege), Secondary Education (Public)
Health: Emergency/Ambulance Services
International: International-General, International Affairs
Religion: Churches
Social Services: Animal Protection, Community Service Organizations, Domestic Violence, Food/Clothing Distribution, Recreation & Athletics, Social Services-General, Veterans

Application Procedures

Initial Contact: Send a brief letter of inquiry.
Application Requirements: Include name and address of organization, amount requested, description of project, and the name of the contact person.
Deadlines: May 1 and November 1.

Restrictions

Limited to organizations in Crawford County, IL.

Foundation Officials

Barbara Sue Bailey: trustee
Edward Carpenter: trustee
Tom Eden: trustee

David L. Musgrave: trustee
Allen R. Price: trustee

Grants Analysis

Disclosure Period: calendar year ending 2001
Total Grants: $37,493
Number of Grants: 20
Average Grant: $1,875
Highest Grant: $7,000
Lowest Grant: $600
Typical Range: $1,000 to $3,000

Recent Grants

Note: Grants derived from 2000 Form 990.

Library-Related
6,870	Palestine Public Library District -- public welfare

General
7,000	Robinson High School -- education
6,000	Eastern Illinois Assembly -- public welfare
5,200	Oblong Community Unit School District 4
4,130	Palestine Preservation Projects Society -- recreation
3,800	Crawford County Development Association -- public welfare
3,500	Crawford County Habitat for Humanity
2,000	Hutsonville Community Unit School District 1 -- education
2,000	Crawford County Health Deptartment -- public welfare
2,000	Flat Rock Fire Protection Distributors -- public welfare
2,000	Lamotte Township Park District -- recreation

CLAYTON FUND

Giving Contact

William Askey
Chase Bank of Texas
600 Travis, 7th Fl.
Houston, TX 77002
Phone: (713)216-1453

Alternate Contact

Anne Bryant

Description

Founded: 1989
EIN: 760285764
Organization Type: General Purpose Foundation
Giving Locations: nationally.
Grant Types: Fellowship, General Support, Professorship.

Donor Information

Founder: Established in Texas as a trust in 1952 through donations by the late William L. Clayton and his late wife, Susan V. Clayton . William L. Clayton, founder of the insurance and food processing company, Anderson, Clayton and Company, was also active in the federal government, including his service as Assistant Secretary of State. He was also vice president of the Export-Import Bank, and wrote extensively on international trade, economics, and foreign affairs. The William L. Clayton Center for International Economic Affairs at the Fletcher School of Law and Diplomacy of Tufts University is named after him.

Financial Summary

Total Giving: $2,353,350 (fiscal year ending December 01, 2001); $3,012,000 (fiscal 2000); $2,391,485 (fiscal 1998)
Giving Analysis: Giving for fiscal 1998 includes: foundation ($2,391,485)

Assets: $48,832,420 (fiscal 2001); $56,130,249 (fiscal 2000); $53,609,243 (fiscal 1998)
Gifts Received: $2,501,206 (fiscal 1996); $365,395 (fiscal 1995)

Typical Recipients

Arts & Humanities: Arts Associations & Councils, Historic Preservation, Libraries, Museums/Galleries, Music, Opera, Theater
Civic & Public Affairs: African American Affairs, Botanical Gardens/Parks, Clubs, Community Foundations, Economic Development, Civic & Public Affairs-General, Hispanic Affairs, Housing, Nonprofit Management, Public Policy, Rural Affairs, Urban & Community Affairs
Education: Afterschool/Enrichment Programs, Agricultural Education, Arts/Humanities Education, Business Education, Colleges & Universities, Education Reform, Engineering/Technological Education, Education-General, Literacy, Medical Education, Minority Education, Private Education (Precollege), Public Education (Precollege), Religious Education, Special Education, Student Aid
Environment: Environment-General, Resource Conservation, Wildlife Protection
Health: Cancer, Children's Health/Hospitals, Clinics/Medical Centers, Emergency/Ambulance Services, Health Organizations, Heart, Hospitals, Hospitals (University Affiliated), Medical Rehabilitation, Mental Health, Prenatal Health Issues, Public Health, Single-Disease Health Associations, Speech & Hearing, Transplant Networks/Donor Banks
International: Health Care/Hospitals, International Peace & Security Issues, International Relations, International Relief Efforts, Missionary/Religious Activities
Religion: Churches, Ministries, Religious Welfare
Social Services: At-Risk Youth, Camps, Child Welfare, Community Centers, Community Service Organizations, Domestic Violence, Family Planning, Family Planning, Family Services, Food/Clothing Distribution, People with Disabilities, Recreation & Athletics, Scouts, Shelters/Homelessness, Social Services-General, YMCA/YWCA/YMHA/YWHA, Youth Organizations

Application Procedures

Initial Contact: Four copies of a brief proposal
Application Requirements: a summary concerning the applicant, details of the project, amount requested, total amount required for the project, income and expense budget for project, including other sources of funding, a copy of the determination letter issued to the applicant by the I.R.S., and a narrative of three to five pages.
Deadlines: February 1, May 1, August 1, and November 1.
Review Process: Attempts are made to provide applicants with a response within eight weeks of receiving the application.

Restrictions

The foundation generally does not make grants to building or endowment funds. No grants are made to individuals.

Foundation Officials

William Hartman Askey: treasurer, secretary B Williamsburg, PA June 21, 1919. ED Bucknell University BA (1941); University of Pittsburgh JD (1951). PRIM NONPR EMPL magistrate: U.S. District Court. NONPR AFFIL member: Lycoming Law Association; member: Pennsylvania Bar Association; honorary member: Federation Bar Association; member: Federation Magistrate Judges Association; member: American Bar Association. CLUB AFFIL Ross Club; Masons Club.
William C. Baker: trustee
William L. Garwood, Jr.: vice president
Burdine C. Johnson: president

Grants Analysis

Disclosure Period: fiscal year ending December 01, 2001
Total Grants: $2,353,350
Number of Grants: 88
Average Grant: $20,635*
Highest Grant: $200,000
Lowest Grant: $2,000
Typical Range: $10,000 to $40,000
*Note: Average grant figure excludes four highest grants ($620,000).

Recent Grants

Note: Grants derived from 2000 Form 990.

General

300,000	Rice University, Houston, TX -- to help create and endow the William L. Clayton Fellowship
200,000	Chesapeake Bay Foundation, Annapolis, MD -- toward support of the Environment Education Program
140,000	Bryn Mawr College, Bryn Mawr, PA -- to endow the Chair in Environmental Stewardship honoring Julia Clayton Baker
125,000	Houston CEO Foundation, Houston, TX -- toward program support and the Children's Scholarship Fund
100,000	Planned Parenthood of Houston and Southeast Texas, Houston, TX -- toward program support
100,000	Rice University, Houston, TX -- to help create and endow the William L. Clayton Fellowship
75,000	Institute for Rehabilitation and Research Foundation, Houston, TX -- to help fund it scientific research team for "Mission Connect"
75,000	Planned Parenthood Federation of America, Inc., New York, NY -- toward support of its adolescent reproductive health projects in Cameroon, Uganda, Ecuador and Mexico
50,000	Anne Arundel Medical Center, Annapolis, MD -- to help the Medical Center provide state-of-the-art healthcare
50,000	Annunciation Orthodox School, Houston, TX -- for master facilities plan

CLEARY FOUNDATION

Giving Contact

Gail Cleary, President
301 Sky Harbour Dr.
La Crosse, WI 54603
Phone: (608)783-7500

Description

Founded: 1982
EIN: 391426785
Organization Type: Private Foundation
Giving Locations: WI
Grant Types: Endowment, General Support.

Donor Information

Founder: Russell G. Cleary, Gail K. Cleary

Financial Summary

Total Giving: $345,805 (fiscal year ending November 30, 2001); $414,495 (fiscal 2000); $262,451 (fiscal 1999)
Giving Analysis: Giving for fiscal 2001 includes: foundation grants to United Way ($30,800); fiscal 2000: foundation grants to United Way ($31,000); fiscal 1999: foundation grants to United Way ($35,000); **Assets:** $8,667,682 (fiscal 2001); $8,040,694 (fiscal 2000); $5,376,725 (fiscal 1999)
Gifts Received: $604,139 (fiscal 2000); $50,439 (fiscal 1998); $15,062 (fiscal 1996). Note: In fiscal 2000,

contributions were received from Estate of Lillian Hope Kumm. In fiscal 1996, contributions were received from Russell G. and Gail K. Cleary.

Typical Recipients

Arts & Humanities: Arts Associations & Councils, Arts Funds, Community Arts, Ethnic & Folk Arts, Historic Preservation, History & Archaeology, Libraries, Museums/Galleries, Music, Performing Arts, Public Broadcasting, Theater
Civic & Public Affairs: Clubs, Economic Development, Housing, Parades/Festivals, Public Policy, Urban & Community Affairs
Education: Business Education, Colleges & Universities, Legal Education, Minority Education, Public Education (Precollege), Student Aid, Vocational & Technical Education
Environment: Resource Conservation, Wildlife Protection
Health: Emergency/Ambulance Services, Health-General, Geriatric Health, Health Funds, Hospitals, Long-Term Care, Medical Research, Single-Disease Health Associations
International: International Organizations
Religion: Churches, Religious Welfare
Social Services: Animal Protection, Community Centers, Community Service Organizations, Counseling, Crime Prevention, Domestic Violence, Family Services, Food/Clothing Distribution, People with Disabilities, Recreation & Athletics, Scouts, Substance Abuse, United Funds/United Ways, YMCA/YWCA/YMHA/YWHA, Youth Organizations

Application Procedures

Initial Contact: Send a brief letter of inquiry describing program.
Application Requirements: Include proof of tax-exempt status, amount requested, and abbreviated amount of supporting detail.
Deadlines: None.

Restrictions

Does not make contributions to individuals.

Foundation Officials

Gail K. Cleary: vice president, secretary, director
Kristine H. Cleary: director
Russell George Cleary: president, treasurer, director B Chippewa Falls, WI 1933. ED University of Wisconsin LLB (1957). PRIM CORP EMPL chairman, chief executive officer, director: Cleary Management Corp. CORP AFFIL director: AO Smith Corp.; director: Protection Mutual Insurance Co.; chairman: First State Bancorp; director: Kohler Co.; director: Ecolab Inc. NONPR AFFIL trustee: WI Alumni Research Foundation.
Sandra G. Cleary: director
L. Hope Kumm: director

Grants Analysis

Disclosure Period: fiscal year ending November 30, 2001
Total Grants: $315,005*
Number of Grants: 76
Average Grant: $2,800*
Highest Grant: $105,025
Typical Range: $500 to $5,000
*Note: Giving excludes United Way. Average grant figure excludes highest grant.

Recent Grants

Note: Grants derived from fiscal 2000 Form 990.

Library-Related

1,000	La Crosse Public Library, La Crosse, WI -- public library association
1,000	Riverfront, Inc., La Crosse, WI -- employment for developmentally handicapped

General

195,500	First Presbyterian Church, La Crosse, WI -- religious and community activities
47,400	Riverland Girl Scouts, La Crosse, WI -- youth education and training
42,000	Health Science Consortium, La Crosse, WI -- community health education
31,000	La Crosse Area United Way, La Crosse, WI -- community agencies support
30,000	Children's Museum, La Crosse, WI -- children's educational exhibits
15,130	Boys & Girls Club of La Crosse, La Crosse, WI -- youth education and rehabilitation
7,200	Boy Scouts of America, La Crosse, WI -- youth education
6,550	WWTC Foundation, La Crosse, WI -- educational scholarship and building funds
6,100	Salvation Army, La Crosse, WI -- agency support
2,500	Marquette Law School, Milwaukee, WI -- youth education scholarship

CLEMENS MARKETS

Company Headquarters

1555 Bustard Road
Kulpsville, PA 19443
Web: http://www.clemensmarkets.com

Company Description

Employees: 2,000
SIC(s): 5400 Food Stores.

Clemens Foundation

Giving Contact

Jack Clemons, Jr., Treasurer
P.O. Box 1555
Kulpsville, PA 19443
Phone: (215)361-9000
Web: http://www.clemensmarkets.com/Community/Community_Involvement.htm

Description

EIN: 231675035
Organization Type: Corporate Foundation
Giving Locations: PA
Grant Types: Capital, General Support, Scholarship.

Financial Summary

Total Giving: $111,300 (fiscal year ending September 30, 2000); $107,275 (fiscal 1999); $105,975 (fiscal 1998). Note: Fiscal 1997 Giving includes United Way ($13,400); sch ($3,000).
Giving Analysis: Giving for fiscal 2000 includes: foundation scholarships ($10,800); foundation grants to United Way ($37,800); fiscal 1999: foundation scholarships ($500); foundation grants to United Way ($16,200); fiscal 1998: foundation scholarships ($500); foundation grants to United Way ($16,200) foundation ($89,275)
Assets: $821,234 (fiscal 2000); $708,843 (fiscal 1999); $613,019 (fiscal 1998)
Gifts Received: $108,411 (fiscal 2000); $80,000 (fiscal 1999); $80,000 (fiscal 1997). Note: In fiscal 1997 and 1999, contributions were received from Clemens Markets Corp., James S. Clemens Markets, Inc., and Abraham and Lillian Clemens.

Typical Recipients

Arts & Humanities: Historic Preservation, Libraries
Civic & Public Affairs: Civic & Public Affairs-General, Housing, Safety
Education: Colleges & Universities, Private Education (Precollege), Religious Education, Secondary Education (Private), Student Aid
Health: Cancer, Children's Health/Hospitals, Emergency/Ambulance Services, Geriatric Health, Hospitals, Medical Rehabilitation, Medical Research, Mental Health

International: Missionary/Religious Activities
Religion: Bible Study/Translation, Churches, Religion-General, Jewish Causes, Ministries, Missionary Activities (Domestic), Religious Organizations, Religious Welfare, Seminaries
Social Services: Camps, Community Service Organizations, Family Services, Food/Clothing Distribution, Homes, United Funds/United Ways, United Funds/United Ways, YMCA/YWCA/YMHA/YWHA, Youth Organizations

Application Procedures

Initial Contact: Return completed application form.
Application Requirements: Include recently audited financial statement, list of sources of revenue, actual cost of raising funds, and the compensation of officers, directors, trustees, and officials in charge of overall direction of management.
Deadlines: November 1.

Corporate Officials

James S. Clemens, Jr.: chairman, president, chief executive officer, director PRIM CORP EMPL chairman, president, chief executive officer, director: Clemens Markets.
G. Christian Limbert, Jr.: chief financial officer, treasurer PRIM CORP EMPL chief financial officer, treasurer: Clemens Markets.

Foundation Officials

Abram S. Clemens: president
James S. Clemens, Jr.: treasurer (see above)
Lillan H. Clemens: trustee
Matilda S. Clemens: vice president
Suzanne C. Harris: assistant treasurer
Jill Clemens Kulp: trustee PRIM CORP EMPL director human resources: Clemens Markets.
Jules Pearlstine: assistant secretary
R. Carl Rhoads: trustee
Janice C. Tyson: secretary

Grants Analysis

Disclosure Period: fiscal year ending September 30, 2000
Total Grants: $62,700*
Number of Grants: 103
Average Grant: $609
Highest Grant: $5,000
Typical Range: $100 to $2,000
*Note: Giving excludes United Way and scholarships.

Recent Grants

Note: Grants derived from fiscal 1999 Form 990.

General

8,000	North Penn United Way, Lansdale, PA -- corporate
5,000	Gideons International
5,000	St. Joseph's University, Philadelphia, PA
3,750	Eastern College, St. Davids, PA
3,400	North Penn United Way, Lansdale, PA -- executive
3,000	Juniata College
3,000	North Pennsylvania Valley Boys and Girls Club, Lansdale, PA
2,500	Harleysville Community Fire Department
2,200	Bucks County United Way, PA
2,000	Calvary Baptist Theological Seminary

CLEMENTS FOUNDATION

Giving Contact

Shirley Warren
1901 N. Akard St.
Dallas, TX 75201
Phone: (214)720-0377

Description

Founded: 1968
EIN: 756065076
Organization Type: Private Foundation
Giving Locations: TX: Dallas including metropolitan area
Grant Types: General Support, Scholarship.

Financial Summary

Total Giving: $140,275 (2000); $181,360 (1999); $109,591 (1998). Note: Giving includes United Way ($10,000).
Giving Analysis: Giving for 2000 includes: foundation grants to United Way ($200); 1999: foundation grants to United Way ($10,200); 1998: foundation grants to United Way ($10,000) foundation ($99,591)
Assets: $13,305,201 (2000); $12,333,256 (1999); $11,258,959 (1998)
Gifts Received: $255,000 (1993). Note: In 1993, contributions were received from William P. Clements, Jr.

Typical Recipients

Arts & Humanities: Arts Outreach, Historic Preservation, History & Archaeology, Libraries, Museums/Galleries
Civic & Public Affairs: Botanical Gardens/Parks, Clubs, Community Foundations, Civic & Public Affairs-General, Parades/Festivals, Philanthropic Organizations, Safety, Urban & Community Affairs, Zoos/Aquariums
Education: Arts/Humanities Education, Colleges & Universities, Education Funds, Engineering/Technological Education, Faculty Development, Education-General, Medical Education, Private Education (Precollege), Public Education (Precollege), Secondary Education (Private), Secondary Education (Public)
Environment: Wildlife Protection
Health: Arthritis, Cancer, Clinics/Medical Centers, Health Organizations, Hospitals, Nutrition, Public Health
International: Health Care/Hospitals, International Affairs
Religion: Churches, Religious Welfare
Science: Science Museums
Social Services: Child Welfare, Community Service Organizations, Crime Prevention, Family Services, People with Disabilities, Recreation & Athletics, Scouts, Substance Abuse, United Funds/United Ways, YMCA/YWCA/YMHA/YWHA, Youth Organizations

Application Procedures

Initial Contact: Send a detailed, written statement outlining the course of study the applicant wishes to pursue, prior publications (if any), grade reports and/or aptitude scores, and financial need.
Deadlines: None.

Additional Information

Provides scholarships to students pursuing a course of study involving the history of the state of TX, the Greater Southwest, or related matters of historical value.
Publications: Application Guidelines

Foundation Officials

B. Gill Clements: vice president
William P. Clements, Jr.: president B Dallas, TX April 13, 1917. ED Southern Methodist University DHL (1974). CORP AFFIL chairman: SEDCO; director: General Motors Corp.; director: Interfirst Corp. NONPR AFFIL member: Southern Methodist University; member: Southwest Medicine School; member national executive board: Boy Scouts America; member: International Association Drilling Contractors; member: American Association Oil Well Drilling Contractors.
Nancy Clements Seay: vice president

Grants Analysis

Disclosure Period: calendar year ending 2000
Total Grants: $140,075*
Number of Grants: 45
Average Grant: $2,047*
Highest Grant: $50,000
Typical Range: $500 to $5,000
*Note: Giving excludes United Way. Average grant excludes highest grant.

Recent Grants

Note: Grants derived from 1999 Form 990.

Library-Related

2,795	Kaufman County Library, Kaufman, TX

General

50,000	Southern Methodist University in Taos - SMU, Dallas, TX
20,000	The William Booth Society of The Salvation Army, Dallas, TX
15,000	St. Michael and All Angels Church, Dallas, TX
11,100	Southern Methodist University, Dallas, TX
11,000	University of Texas Southwestern Medical Center at Dallas, Dallas, TX
10,000	United Way, Dallas, TX
5,000	All Saints Health Foundation, Ft. Worth, TX
5,000	Dallas Museum of Natural History, Dallas, TX
5,000	Hockaday School, Dallas, TX
5,000	Junior League of Dallas, Dallas, TX

CLEVELAND-CLIFFS, INC.

Company Headquarters

1100 Superior Ave., Fl. 18
Cleveland, OH 44114
Web: http://www.cleveland-cliffs.com

Company Description

Founded: 1847
Ticker: CLF
Exchange: NYSE
Revenue: US$330.4 million (2001)
Employees: 3376 (2001)
SIC(s): 1011 Iron Ores.

Operating Locations

Cleveland-Cliffs, Inc. (MI--Ishpeming; TX--Houston)

Nonmonetary Support

Type: Loaned Executives; Workplace Solicitation

The Cleveland-Cliffs Foundation

Giving Contact

Dana W. Byrne, Vice President, Assistant Treasurer
1100 Superior Avenue East
Cleveland, OH 44114-2589
Phone: (216)694-5700
Fax: (216)694-6741
Web: http://www.cleveland-cliffs.com/GeneralInformation

Description

EIN: 346525124
Organization Type: Corporate Foundation
Giving Locations: DC: Washington; MI; OH; nationally; Canada: nationally.
Grant Types: Capital, Employee Matching Gifts, General Support, Matching, Multiyear/Continuing Support.

Financial Summary

Total Giving: $461,006 (2001); $601,103 (1999); $624,384 (1998). Note: Contributes through foundation only.

Giving Analysis: Giving for 2001 includes: foundation grants to United Way ($57,562); foundation matching gifts ($58,914); 1999: foundation scholarships ($5,000); foundation grants to United Way ($56,955); foundation matching gifts ($61,683); foundation ($477,465); 1998: foundation grants to United Way ($56,109); foundation matching gifts ($84,410); foundation ($483,675);

Assets: $638,000 (2001); $1,154,583 (1999); $1,502,619 (1998)

Gifts Received: $200,000 (2000); $200,000 (1999); $400,000 (1998). Note: The foundation receives contributions from Cleveland-Cliffs, Inc.

Typical Recipients

Arts & Humanities: Arts Associations & Councils, Arts Centers, Ballet, Arts & Humanities-General, Historic Preservation, History & Archaeology, Libraries, Museums/Galleries, Music, Opera, Performing Arts, Public Broadcasting, Theater

Civic & Public Affairs: Botanical Gardens/Parks, Business/Free Enterprise, Chambers of Commerce, Clubs, Community Foundations, Economic Development, Employment/Job Training, Civic & Public Affairs-General, Housing, Legal Aid, Municipalities/Towns, Parades/Festivals, Philanthropic Organizations, Public Policy, Rural Affairs, Urban & Community Affairs, Zoos/Aquariums

Education: Afterschool/Enrichment Programs, Arts/Humanities Education, Business Education, Business-School Partnerships, Colleges & Universities, Community & Junior Colleges, Continuing Education, Economic Education, Education Associations, Education Funds, Education Reform, Engineering/Technological Education, Education-General, Minority Education, Private Education (Precollege), Public Education (Precollege), Science/Mathematics Education, Secondary Education (Private), Secondary Education (Public), Student Aid

Environment: Environment-General, Resource Conservation, Wildlife Protection

Health: Cancer, Children's Health/Hospitals, Clinics/Medical Centers, Emergency/Ambulance Services, Health Organizations, Heart, Hospitals, Preventive Medicine/Wellness Organizations, Public Health

International: Health Care/Hospitals, International Affairs

Religion: Religious Welfare, Seminaries

Science: Science Museums, Scientific Centers & Institutes, Scientific Centers & Institutes

Social Services: Camps, Child Welfare, Community Service Organizations, Counseling, Crime Prevention, Delinquency & Criminal Rehabilitation, Emergency Relief, Family Services, Food/Clothing Distribution, People with Disabilities, Recreation & Athletics, Scouts, Senior Services, United Funds/United Ways, Volunteer Services, YMCA/YWCA/YMHA/YWHA, Youth Organizations

Application Procedures

Initial Contact: Submit a brief letter of inquiry.

Application Requirements: Include a description of organization, amount requested, purpose of funds sought, recently audited financial statements, and proof of tax-exempt status.

Deadlines: None.

Review Process: Vice president evaluates requests and submits them to distribution committee for their approval; a letter is sent regarding final decision.

Restrictions

Foundation does not support individuals or political or lobbying groups.

Additional Information

Publications: Guidelines Sheet

Corporate Officials

Cynthia B. Bezik: senior vice president finance B Youngstown, OH 1953. ED Youngstown State University (1970); Case Western Reserve University (1980). PRIM CORP EMPL senior vice president finance: Cleveland-Cliffs, Inc. CORP AFFIL chief financial officer: Cliffs Resources Inc.; manager financial analysis: Pickands Mather; member: Cleveland Cliffs Iron Co. NONPR AFFIL member: National Association Accountants; member: Planning Forum; member: Financial Executives Institute; member: American Iron & Steel Institute; member: American Society Women Accountants. CLUB AFFIL Womens City Club.

John S. Brinzo: president, chief executive officer B Cleveland, OH 1942. ED Kent State University BSBA (1964); Case Western Reserve University MBA (1968). PRIM CORP EMPL chairman, chief executive officer: Cleveland-Cliffs, Inc. NONPR AFFIL member: American Iron & Steel Institute; director: National Mining Association.

Edward C. Dowling: senior vice president, operations PRIM CORP EMPL senior vice president, operations: Cleveland-Cliffs, Inc.

Robert Emmet: vice president financial planning, treasurer B 1945. ED Yale University BA (1967); Harvard University MBA (1973). PRIM CORP EMPL vice president financial planning, treasurer: Cleveland-Cliffs, Inc. ADD CORP EMPL vice president: Cleveland-Cliffs Iron Co.

Donald J. Gallagher: vice president, sales PRIM CORP EMPL vice president, sales: Cleveland-Cliffs, Inc.

John E. Lenhard: secretary, associate general counsel PRIM CORP EMPL secretary, associate general counsel: Cleveland-Cliffs, Inc.

Robert J. Leroux: vice president, controller PRIM CORP EMPL vice president, controller: Cleveland-Cliffs, Inc.

Richard F. Novak: vice president human resources PRIM CORP EMPL vice president human resources: Cleveland-Cliffs, Inc.

Thomas J. O'Neil: president, chief operating officer PRIM CORP EMPL president, chief operating officer: Cleveland-Cliffs, Inc.

John W. Sanders: senior vice president, international development PRIM CORP EMPL senior vice president, international development: Cleveland-Cliffs, Inc.

James A. Trethewey: senior vice president, operations services PRIM CORP EMPL senior vice president, operations services: Cleveland-Cliffs, Inc.

A. Stanley West: senior vice president, sales & commercial planning PRIM CORP EMPL senior vice president, sales & commercial planning: Cleveland-Cliffs, Inc.

Foundation Officials

John S. Brinzo: trustee (see above)
D. L. Gardner: vice president, assistant treasurer
Thomas J. O'Neil: trustee (see above)
John W. Sanders: trustee (see above)
A. Stanley West: trustee (see above)

Grants Analysis

Disclosure Period: calendar year ending 2001
Total Grants: $344,530*
Number of Grants: 109
Average Grant: $3,161
Highest Grant: $42,437
Typical Range: $250 to $10,000
*Note: Giving excludes matching gifts; United Way.

Recent Grants

Note: Grants derived from 2001 Form 990.

Library-Related

5,000	Peter White Library, Marquette, MI	

General

50,000	Suntrac, Ishpeming, MI	
45,857	United Way Services, Cleveland, OH	
42,437	American Red Cross Disaster Relief Fund, Washington, DC	
25,000	Cleveland Orchestra, Cleveland, OH	
20,000	Michigan Technological University, Houghton, MI	
10,000	Negaunee Performing Arts, Negaunee, MI	
10,000	Northern Michigan University Ice Arena, Marquette, MI	
10,000	Two Harbors Area Fund, Duluth, MN	
9,728	Northern Michigan University Development Fund, Marquette, MI	
8,750	Cleveland Tomorrow, Cleveland, OH	

CLOROX CO.

Company Headquarters

1221 Broadway
Oakland, CA 94612-1888
Phone: (510)271-7000
Fax: (510)832-1463
Web: http://www.clorox.com

Company Description

Founded: 1913
Ticker: CLX
Exchange: NYSE
Acquired: First Brands Corp. (1999).
Revenue: US$4.061 billion (2002)
Profit: US$322 million (2002)
Employees: 9500 (2002)
Fortune Rank: 394, per FORTUNE Magazine's list of 500 Largest U.S. Corporations (2002).
SIC(s): 2033 Canned Fruits & Vegetables, 2034 Dehydrated Fruits, Vegetables & Soups, 2035 Pickles, Sauces & Salad Dressings, 2842 Polishes & Sanitation Goods.

Operating Locations

Clorox Co. (AL--Birmingham; CA--Laguna Hills, Los Angeles; GA--Forest Park; IL--Chicago, Naperville; MD--Aberdeen; MN--Bloomington; MS--Pearl; MO--Kansas City; NH--Nashua; OH--Cleveland; TX--Farmers Branch, Houston)
Note: Operates over 30 plants in the USA and internationally.

Nonmonetary Support

Type: Donated Equipment; Donated Products; In-kind Services; Workplace Solicitation
Volunteer Programs: The company reports that more than one-third of employees in its General Offices and its Technical Center volunteer time at more than 375 agencies. The Clorox Employee Volunteer Program identifies volunteer opportunities, disseminates information about community agencies and programs to employees, and helps match volunteers with organizations. Company awards $200 grants to organizations where employees volunteer.
Note: Support is given to Second Harvest Food Bank and for disaster relief.

Clorox Co. Foundation

Giving Contact

Carmella J. Johnson, Contributions Manager
1221 Broadway, 13th Floor
Oakland, CA 94612-1888
Phone: (510)271-2199
Fax: (510)271-7757
E-mail: community.relations@clorox.com
Web: http://www.clorox.com/company/foundation
Note: This is the application address for organizations located in the Oakland, CA area. Applicants located

outside of Oakland should submit their requests to the n

Alternate Contact

Clorox Co. Foundation
PO Box 24305
Oakland, CA 94623-9981
Phone: (510)271-2965

Description

Founded: 1980
EIN: 942674980
Organization Type: Corporate Foundation
Giving Locations: CA: Oakland, San Francisco including metropolitan area operating locations.
Grant Types: Capital, Employee Matching Gifts, Endowment, General Support, Operating Expenses, Project, Scholarship.
Note: Employee matching gift ratio: 1 to 1 for educational institutions and the United Way.

Donor Information

Founder: Clorox Co.

Financial Summary

Total Giving: $2,403,711 (fiscal year ending June 31, 2001); $2,993,729 (fiscal 2000); $3,258,786 (fiscal 1999)
Giving Analysis: Giving for fiscal 2001 includes: foundation grants to United Way ($69,630); foundation program-related investments ($85,000); foundation scholarships ($137,842); foundation ($947,206); foundation matching gifts ($1,164,034); fiscal 2000: foundation grants to United Way ($105,050); foundation scholarships ($125,080); foundation matching gifts ($1,229,185); foundation ($1,536,414); fiscal 1999: foundation grants to United Way ($331,051); foundation matching gifts ($1,442,000) foundation ($1,485,735)
Assets: $3,114,125 (fiscal 2001); $5,276,748 (fiscal 2000); $8,157,591 (fiscal 1999)
Gifts Received: $345,000 (fiscal 2001); $7,547 (fiscal 2000); $2,355,044 (fiscal 1999). Note: In fiscal 2001, contributions were received from the Clorox Co.

Typical Recipients

Arts & Humanities: Arts Appreciation, Arts Associations & Councils, Arts Centers, Arts Festivals, Arts Outreach, Ballet, Community Arts, Dance, Ethnic & Folk Arts, Film & Video, Arts & Humanities-General, Historic Preservation, Libraries, Literary Arts, Museums/Galleries, Music, Opera, Performing Arts, Public Broadcasting, Theater, Visual Arts
Civic & Public Affairs: African American Affairs, Asian American Affairs, Botanical Gardens/Parks, Chambers of Commerce, Civil Rights, Clubs, Community Foundations, Economic Development, Employment/Job Training, Civic & Public Affairs-General, Hispanic Affairs, Law & Justice, Legal Aid, Municipalities/Towns, Nonprofit Management, Public Policy, Safety, Urban & Community Affairs, Women's Affairs, Zoos/Aquariums
Education: Arts/Humanities Education, Business Education, Business-School Partnerships, Colleges & Universities, Community & Junior Colleges, Continuing Education, Economic Education, Education Associations, Education Funds, Education Reform, Elementary Education (Private), Elementary Education (Public), Environmental Education, Faculty Development, Education-General, Journalism/Media Education, Literacy, Minority Education, Preschool Education, Private Education (Precollege), Public Education (Precollege), Religious Education, School Volunteerism, Science/Mathematics Education, Secondary Education (Public), Special Education, Student Aid, Student Aid
Environment: Environment-General, Resource Conservation, Wildlife Protection
Health: Children's Health/Hospitals, Clinics/Medical Centers, Emergency/Ambulance Services, Geriatric Health, Health Funds, Health Organizations, Hospices, Hospitals, Mental Health, Prenatal Health Issues, Public Health, Research/Studies Institutes, Single-Disease Health Associations
International: International Affairs, International Development
Religion: Religion-General, Jewish Causes, Ministries, Religious Organizations, Religious Welfare
Science: Science Exhibits & Fairs, Scientific Centers & Institutes
Social Services: Animal Protection, At-Risk Youth, Big Brother/Big Sister, Child Welfare, Community Centers, Community Service Organizations, Counseling, Day Care, Delinquency & Criminal Rehabilitation, Domestic Violence, Family Planning, Family Services, Food/Clothing Distribution, People with Disabilities, Recreation & Athletics, Scouts, Senior Services, Shelters/Homelessness, Substance Abuse, United Funds/United Ways, Volunteer Services, YMCA/YWCA/YMHA/YWHA, Youth Organizations

Application Procedures

Initial Contact: Send a brief letter of inquiry or phone call to request application guidelines and proposal cover sheet form. Guidelines and cover sheet form may also be obtained from the company's web site.
Application Requirements: Include the cover sheet and a typewritten, single-spaced proposal of not more than three pages. The proposal should consist of the following questions answered in the order provided (typing the number and question followed by the answer): 1) What are some of your recent accomplishments? Emphasize achievements of the past year, both quantitative and qualitative. 2) Briefly describe the population that you serve with the funds requested, including the number of individuals, geographic location, age, socio-economic status, race, ethnicity, language, gender, etc. For cultural organizations, include this information for your audience and/or participants. Include a breakdown of the population served by racial/ethnic group and gender using percentages. 3) What are the expected outcomes of the project for which you are requesting funds? Describe the program/activities that will lead to these outcomes. Include the methods that will be used to evaluate the project. 4) Do you collaborate with other agencies? If so, which ones?
Attachments should include a copy of the organization's most recent IRS letter indicating tax status; list of current officers and directors, including professional affiliations; staff list including position titles and indication of full- or part-time and number of volunteers, as well as a breakdown of current staff by racial/ethnic group and gender percentages; project budget; agency budget; financial statement; budget narrative explaining any significant changes in revenues or expenses between years, the nature and purpose of any cash reserves or endowment, and a list of in-kind or other non-cash contributions; a list of organization's funders and amounts received during previous fiscal year from all sources; a list of funding sources being solicited for this project indicated committed and pending funds; and a confirmation latter from your fiscal agent (if appropriate).
Deadlines: Applications for foundation grants are accepted August 1 to June 1 of each fiscal year ending June 30; deadlines are July 1, October 1, January 1, and April 1; requests for special events sponsorship should be submitted in writing at least sixty days prior to the event.
Review Process: For grants in excess of $2,500, applications are reviewed by contributions committee, which advises the board of trustees; grants in excess of $10,000 must be reviewed by the board.
Evaluative Criteria: Foundation favors applicants whose programs focus on direct delivery of services; launch programs or services in an innovative manner; promote volunteer participation and citizen involvement; encourage self-reliance and personal growth among individuals served; have a broad base of financial support and a reasonable fund development plan; and include Clorox employee involvement. Other criteria for selection include: clarity of purpose, outcomes related to performance, strategies that will achieve the stated outcomes, sound evaluation procedures, sound fiscal and management practices, involvement of board members, demonstrated collaborative relationships, fundraising capacity, nondiscrimination policies and practices, and diversity of board, staff, clients, etc.
Decision Notification: Contributions committee meets quarterly.
Notes: Endowment/capital campaign requests include building funds, purchase of major equipment, or general operating reserve funds. However, the foundation discourages contributions to endowments. The company's operating facilities each have their own particular funding priorities and independent review processes. A complete list of contributions programs at Clorox locations is contained within the guidelines.

Restrictions

The foundation will not provide grants to political parties, organizations, candidates, or issues; exclusive membership organizations; religious-based activities for the purpose of furthering religious doctrine; individuals; benefit or raffle tickets; conferences, conventions or meetings; media productions; athletic leagues or events; national projects; advertising or promotional sponsorships; association or membership dues; fundraising events; deficits or retroactive funding; field trips, tours, or travel expenses; or organizations which receive more than 15% of funding from United Way or government sources.
Only one grant request per organization will be considered within a fiscal year time period (July 1 through June 30). Applicants must possess an IRS ruling confirming their classification as a 501(c)(3) organization or be sponsored by a qualified fiscal agent.

Additional Information

First-time grants generally range from $1,000 to $5,000 for general operating support and special projects. The foundation considers itself to be a supplemental funding source, seeking points of intervention where modest grants can be leveraged for greater change.
In addition to cash contributions by the company and foundation, Clorox has invested more than $60 million in low-income housing projects nationwide. Such investments are expected to increase to approximately $100 million.
The Clorox Co. is a U.S. affiliate of Henkel KGAA, which has a 28% investment in Clorox. Other U.S. affiliates are Loctite Corp. (29%) and Ecolab (25%).
Publications: Guidelines; Application Form; Foundation Annual Report

Corporate Officials

Peter D. Bewley: senior vice president, general counsel, secretary B Atlantic City, NJ 1946. ED Princeton University BA (1968); Stanford University JD (1971). PRIM CORP EMPL senior vice president, general counsel, secretary: The Clorox Co. CORP AFFIL secretary: Atlantic Health Group Inc.; senior vice president, secretary, general secretary: Nova Care Inc.
Gerald E. Johnston: president, chief executive officer B 1947. ED California State University, Fullerton BS. PRIM CORP EMPL president, chief executive officer: Clorox Co.
Karen M. Rose: group vice president, chief financial officer B Chicago, IL 1949. ED University of Pennsylvania MBA (1978). PRIM CORP EMPL group vice president, chief financial officer: Clorox Co. ADD CORP EMPL treasurer: Brita Products Co.; treasurer: Clorox International Co. Inc.; treasurer: Clorox Products Manufacturing Co.
G. Craig Sullivan: chairman B 1940. ED Boston College BS (1964). PRIM CORP EMPL chairman: Clorox Co.

Giving Program Officials

Karen M. Rose: member contributions committee (see above)

Foundation Officials

Peter D. Bewley: vice president, secretary (see above)
Gerald E. Johnston: trustee (see above)
G. Craig Sullivan: chairman (see above)

Grants Analysis

Disclosure Period: fiscal year ending June 31, 2001
Total Grants: $947,206*
Number of Grants: 174
Average Grant: $5,444
Highest Grant: $100,000
Typical Range: $2,500 to $25,000
*Note: Giving excludes program-related investments, matching gifts, scholarships, United Way.

Recent Grants

Note: Grants derived from 2001 Form 990.

Library-Related

10,000	Oakland Public Library Foundation, Oakland, CA -- PASS Program

General

100,000	University of California Berkeley Incentive Awards Program, Berkeley, CA -- Incentive Awards Program
87,020	Citizens Scholarship Foundation of America, St. Peter, MN -- 2001 Scholarship Program
75,000	East Oakland Youth Development Center, Oakland, CA -- support of three core program
70,000	Oakland Unified School District, Oakland, CA -- Oakland open court reading adoption
30,000	Oakland Ballet Association, Inc., Oakland, CA -- operating support
30,000	Oakland Unified School District, Oakland, CA -- support teacher training
18,000	Marcus A. Foster Educational Institute, Oakland, CA -- Clorox Partners' scholarship match
15,000	Junior Achievement of the Bay Area, San Francisco, CA -- help fund programs in Oakland and Tri-Valley
15,000	Oakland Museum of California Foundation, Oakland, CA -- sponsor 2001 Youth and Education Programs
15,000	United Negro College Fund, San Francisco, CA -- funding for scholarships for disadvantage Bay Area students

CLOVER FOUNDATION

Giving Contact

Luis Tellez, Treasurer
20 Nassau St., Suite 232
Princeton, NJ 08542
Phone: (609)688-1020

Description

Founded: 1986
EIN: 742390003
Organization Type: Private Foundation
Giving Locations: internationally; nationally.
Grant Types: General Support.

Donor Information

Founder: Alberto Pacheco, Educational Aid Fund

Financial Summary

Total Giving: $2,722,500 (2000); $1,003,206 (1998); $501,565 (1996)
Assets: $27,303,839 (2000); $28,239,712 (1998); $19,521,169 (1996)

Gifts Received: $200,465 (2000); $10,859,439 (1998); $1,194,895 (1996). Note: In 2000, contributions were received from the Perochena Estate. In 1998, contributions were received from Gerona Enterprises Ltd. ($10,422,685), Alberto Martinez Fernandez ($250,000) and others. In 1996, contributions were received from Jose Luis Razo, Victor Cano, and others.

Typical Recipients

Arts & Humanities: Libraries
Education: Colleges & Universities, Education Funds, International Exchange, International Studies
International: Foreign Educational Institutions, International-General, Health Care/Hospitals, International Development, International Organizations, International Peace & Security Issues, International Relations

Application Procedures

Initial Contact: Application form required.
Deadlines: None.

Additional Information

Publications: Application Form

Foundation Officials

Ralph Coti: secretary, director
Francisco Gomez Franco: president, director
Begona Laresgoitide Gomez: vice president, director
Luis E. Tellez: treasurer, director

Grants Analysis

Disclosure Period: calendar year ending 2000
Total Grants: $2,722,500
Number of Grants: 8
Highest Grant: $1,000,000
Lowest Grant: $25,000
Typical Range: $25,000 to $100,000

Recent Grants

Note: Grants derived from 1999 Form 990.

Library-Related

158,471	Roman Athenaeum Foundation, New Rochelle, NY

General

500,000	University Pan AM. Cultur De Me, Mexico City, DF Mexico -- to establish medical school education endowment at The Universidad Pan-American
125,000	Global Work Ethic, Inc., Washington, DC -- vocational and job development program development in third world countries
60,000	Princeton University, Princeton, NJ
20,000	Association Cultural International, Mexico City, DF Mexico

CLOWES FUND

Giving Contact

Elizabeth A. Casselman, Exec.Dir.
320 N. Meridian, Suite 316
Indianapolis, IN 46204-1722
Phone: (317)833-0144
Fax: (317)833-0145
E-mail: staff@clowesfund.org
Web: http://www.clowesfund.org

Description

Founded: 1952
EIN: 351079679
Organization Type: General Purpose Foundation
Giving Locations: IN: Indianapolis; MA
Grant Types: Capital, Endowment, General Support, Matching, Operating Expenses, Professorship, Project, Research, Scholarship, Seed Money.

Donor Information

Founder: The Clowes Fund was established in 1952 by the late Edith W. Clowes , George H. A. Clowes, and Allen W. Clowes.

Financial Summary

Total Giving: $3,712,975 (2002); $3,600,000 (2000 approx); $3,200,000 (1999 approx)
Giving Analysis: Giving for 1997 includes: foundation scholarships ($64,000); 1996: foundation scholarships ($58,000) foundation matching gifts ($250,000)
Assets: $75,947,500 (2001); $93,913,813 (1998); $78,020,114 (1997)

Typical Recipients

Arts & Humanities: Arts Associations & Councils, Arts Centers, Arts Outreach, Ballet, Community Arts, Dance, Ethnic & Folk Arts, Film & Video, Arts & Humanities-General, Historic Preservation, History & Archaeology, Libraries, Museums/Galleries, Music, Opera, Performing Arts, Public Broadcasting, Theater, Visual Arts

Civic & Public Affairs: African American Affairs, Botanical Gardens/Parks, Employment/Job Training, Civic & Public Affairs-General, Housing, Law & Justice, Nonprofit Management, Philanthropic Organizations, Public Policy, Urban & Community Affairs, Women's Affairs, Zoos/Aquariums

Education: Arts/Humanities Education, Business-School Partnerships, Colleges & Universities, Colleges & Universities, Education Associations, Elementary Education (Public), Faculty Development, Education-General, Gifted & Talented Programs, Leadership Training, Literacy, Medical Education, Minority Education, Preschool Education, Private Education (Precollege), Public Education (Precollege), Religious Education, Science/Mathematics Education, Secondary Education (Private), Student Aid, Vocational & Technical Education

Environment: Environment-General, Resource Conservation, Wildlife Protection

Health: Children's Health/Hospitals, Clinics/Medical Centers, Diabetes, Health Funds, Health Organizations, Hospices, Hospitals, Hospitals (University Affiliated), Medical Research, Nursing Services, Outpatient Health Care, Respiratory

International: Foreign Arts Organizations, Foreign Educational Institutions, International Development, International Relief Efforts

Religion: Churches, Ministries, Missionary Activities (Domestic), Religious Organizations, Religious Welfare, Seminaries

Science: Scientific Centers & Institutes, Scientific Labs, Scientific Organizations

Social Services: At-Risk Youth, Big Brother/Big Sister, Camps, Child Abuse, Child Welfare, Community Centers, Community Service Organizations, Day Care, Domestic Violence, Family Planning, Family Services, Food/Clothing Distribution, Homes, People with Disabilities, Recreation & Athletics, Scouts, Senior Services, Shelters/Homelessness, Substance Abuse, United Funds/United Ways, YMCA/YWCA/YMHA/YWHA, Youth Organizations, Youth Organizations

Application Procedures

Initial Contact: Applicants should submit a letter or proposal to the fund.
Application Requirements: Proposals should include a description of organization, purpose for which the grant is sought, specific amount requested, budget for the proposal, financial statement, and copy of the IRS ruling of tax-exempt status. Two copies of this information is required. If any of the listed criteria is not included in the proposal, it will be considered unacceptable with no written notice given.
Deadlines: January 31.
Review Process: The fund's board meets once a year between April 1 and June 1 to consider proposals.

Restrictions

The fund does not make grants to individuals, or for publications, conferences, seminars, or religious evangelical doctrine.

Additional Information

The fund does not acknowledge receipt of grant proposals. The fund does not make available any kind of printed material for distribution and does not have a printed application.

Foundation Officials

Margaret C. Bowles: secretary

Elizabeth A. Casselman: assistant secretary, treasurer

Alexander W. Clowes: president B 1946. ED Harvard University AB (1968); Harvard University MD (1972). PRIM NONPR EMPL department vice chairman vascular surgery: University of Washington. NONPR AFFIL member: Society Vascular Surgery; chief division vascular surgery: University Washington; trustee: Seattle Symphony; member: Sigma Xi; trustee: Marine Biology Laboratory (Woods Hole MA); member: Seattle Surgical Society; member: International Society Applied Cardiovascular Biology; member: American Society Cell Biology; member: American Surgical Association; member: American Heart Association; member: American Association Pathologists. CLUB AFFIL Quisset Yacht Club; Cruising Club America Club.

Jonathan J. Clowes: director

Margaret J. Clowes: vice president ED Bryn Mawr College (1937).

Thomas J. Clowes: director

William H. Marshall: treasurer

Donna J. Wiley: director

Grants Analysis

Disclosure Period: calendar year ending 2002
Total Grants: $3,402,975*
Number of Grants: 92
Average Grant: $30,802*
Highest Grant: $600,000
Lowest Grant: $5,000
Typical Range: $10,000 to $50,000
*Note: Giving excludes scholarships. Average grant figure excludes highest grant.

Recent Grants

Note: Grants derived from 2001 Form 990.

General

4,200,000	Indianapolis Museum of Art, Indianapolis, IN -- for Sir Peter Paul Rubens painting
700,000	Harvard University Medical School, Boston, MA -- for operations
166,667	Boy Scouts of America National Council, Indianapolis, IN -- for camp facility
156,937	Oberlin College, Oberlin, OH -- for education
125,000	Orchard School Foundation, Indianapolis, IN -- for Performing Arts Center
100,000	Indiana University Foundation, Bloomington, IN -- for operations
100,000	James Whitcomb Riley Memorial Association, Indianapolis, IN -- for Riley Outpatient Center
100,000	Sea Education Association, Woods Hole, MA -- endowment for scholarships
100,000	Seattle Center Foundation, Seattle, WA -- for operations
90,000	Indianapolis Museum of Art, Indianapolis, IN -- for the Clowes Collection

CNA FINANCIAL CORP.

Company Headquarters

CNA Plaza
Chicago, IL 60685
Web: http://www.cna.com

Company Description

Ticker: CNA
Exchange: OTC
Acquired: Buckeye Union Insurance Co..
Assets: US$65.968 billion (2001)
Employees: 17274 (2001)
SIC(s): 6311 Life Insurance, 6321 Accident & Health Insurance, 6331 Fire, Marine & Casualty Insurance.

Operating Locations

CNA (FL--Orlando; PA--Reading; TN--Nashville)

Nonmonetary Support

Type: Donated Equipment; In-kind Services
Note: Co. provides nonmonetary support.

CNA Foundation

Giving Contact

Andrea Sinisi, Executive Director
CNA Plaza
Chicago, IL 60685

Description

Founded: 1995
EIN: 364029026
Organization Type: Corporate Foundation
Giving Locations: in communities where co. has a presence.
Grant Types: Employee Matching Gifts, General Support, Multiyear/Continuing Support, Operating Expenses, Scholarship.
Note: Employee matching gift ratio: 1 to 1.

Financial Summary

Total Giving: $2,286,319 (2001); $2,538,738 (2000); $2,205,611 (1999). Note: Contributes through corporate direct giving program and foundation.
Giving Analysis: Giving for 2000 includes: foundation grants to United Way ($357,500); foundation matching gifts ($430,734); foundation ($1,750,504); 1999: foundation grants to United Way ($325,500); foundation matching gifts ($567,321); foundation ($1,312,790); 1998: foundation grants to United Way ($360,500); foundation matching gifts ($552,430); foundation ($1,445,501)
Assets: $22,309,578 (2001); $25,188,752 (2000); $27,448,174 (1999)
Gifts Received: $1,000,000 (1998); $481,000 (1997); $284,694 (1995). Note: Contributions were received from CNA.

Typical Recipients

Arts & Humanities: Arts Associations & Councils, Arts Institutes, Arts Outreach, Dance, Historic Preservation, History & Archaeology, Libraries, Literary Arts, Museums/Galleries, Music, Opera, Performing Arts, Theater
Civic & Public Affairs: Botanical Gardens/Parks, Business/Free Enterprise, Chambers of Commerce, Clubs, Community Foundations, Employment/Job Training, Civic & Public Affairs-General, Housing, Law & Justice, Nonprofit Management, Philanthropic Organizations, Professional & Trade Associations, Public Policy, Safety, Urban & Community Affairs, Women's Affairs, Zoos/Aquariums
Education: Arts/Humanities Education, Business Education, Colleges & Universities, Continuing Education, Continuing Education, Economic Education, Education Associations, Education Funds, Faculty Development, Education-General, Literacy, Minority Education, Preschool Education, Private Education (Precollege), Public Education (Precollege), Science/Mathematics Education, Student Aid
Health: AIDS/HIV, Children's Health/Hospitals, Diabetes, Emergency/Ambulance Services, Health-General, Health Organizations, Heart, Hospitals, Medical Research, Mental Health
International: Missionary/Religious Activities

Religion: Jewish Causes, Religious Organizations, Religious Welfare
Social Services: Child Abuse, Child Welfare, Community Service Organizations, Counseling, Delinquency & Criminal Rehabilitation, Family Services, Food/Clothing Distribution, People with Disabilities, Recreation & Athletics, Scouts, Shelters/Homelessness, Social Services-General, United Funds/United Ways, YMCA/YWCA/YMHA/YWHA, Youth Organizations

Application Procedures

Initial Contact: Request guidelines; then submit proposal.
Application Requirements: Include a description of the organization with its mission and project to be supported, a needs statement and objectives (no more than one page); amount requested and rationale; latest audited financial statement; proof of tax-exempt status; and names and amounts of other contributors; description of benefits to be realized and population to be served; plans for evaluating and reporting results; a current budget; and the names and affiliations of trustees or board of directors.
Deadlines: None.

Restrictions

Does not support individuals; religious organizations for sectarian purposes; capital campaigns; political or lobbying groups; veterans, labor, alumni, military, or fraternal organizations; social clubs; professional associations; organizations that discriminate by race, color, creed, gender, national origin or disability; endowed chairs or professorships; general endowments; United Way affiliated agencies; ad books, goodwill advertising, raffles, etc.; tickets for testimonials or benefits; documentaries, films, videos, or media projects; national groups whose local chapters receive CNA support; foundations that make grants; trips or travel by student groups; or organizations, programs or projects that pose a conflict of interest. The foundation does not make grants to organizations that are not classified as 501(c)(3) tax-exempt.

Additional Information

Company publishes a corporate contribution guidelines sheet.
CNA Insurance Companies is affiliated with CNA Financial Corporation, Continental Casualty Company, and Continental Assurance Company. Company. Company. Company.

Corporate Officials

Antoinette Cook Bush: partnerchr, co-chief executive officer, director PRIM CORP EMPL partner: Skadden, Arps, Slate, Meagher & Flom. CORP AFFIL director: CNA Financial Corp.

Peter E. Jokiel: senior vice president, chief financial officer B 1947. ED Northern Illinois University (1972). PRIM CORP EMPL senior vice president, chief financial officer: CNA Financial Corp. CORP AFFIL chief financial officer: Transportation Insurance Co.; vice president: Valley Forge Life Insurance Co.; chief financial officer: Transcontinental Insurance Co. New York; chief financial officer: Continental Loss Adjusting Services; vice president: Firemens Insurance Newark New Jersey; vice president: Continental Insurance Co. New Jersey; chief financial officer: Continental Casualty Co.; vice president: Continental Corp.; senior vice president: Continental Assurance Co.; chief financial officer: CNA Casualty California; chief financial officer: Columbia Casualty Corp.; senior vice president: American Casualty Reading Pennsylvania.

Preston Robert Tisch: co-chairman, co-chief executive officer, director B Brooklyn, NY 1926. ED Bucknell University (1943-1944); University of Michigan BA (1948). PRIM CORP EMPL co-chairman, director: Loews Corp. ADD CORP EMPL owner, chief executive officer, chairman: New York Football Giants Inc. CORP AFFIL director: Transcontinental Insurance

Co. New York; director: Hasbro Inc.; director: Rite Aid Corp.; director: CNA Financial Corp.; director: Bulova Corp. NONPR AFFIL trustee: New York University; member: Sigma Alpha Mu; chairman emeritus: New York Convention & Visitor Bureau; president: City-meals Wheels; member: Governments Business Advisory Council New York. CLUB AFFIL Rye Racquet Club; Century Country Club.

Foundation Officials

Charles Boesel: contributions committee
Joyce Donaly: treasurer
Karen Foley: president, director
Karen Harngan: contributions committee
Dennis Hemme: vice president
Robert M. Mann: vice president, secretary
Michael McGavick: director
Edward J. Noha: chairman B New York, NY 1926. ED Pace University BBA (1951). CORP AFFIL director: Loews Corp.; chairman: National Fire Insurance Co. Hartford; chief executive officer, director: CNA Financial Corp.; chairman: Continental Loss Adjusting Services.
Tom Pontarelli: director
Michael Ragan: contributions committee
Mary Ribikawskis: assistant vice president, assistant secretary
William Seyboth: contributions committee
Andrea Sinisi: executive director, contributions committee
John Sullivan: group vice president
Laurence Alan Tisch: senior vice president, director B New York, NY March 05, 1923. ED New York University BS (1942); University of Pennsylvania MA (1943); Harvard University Law School (1946). PRIM CORP EMPL co-chairman, director: Loews Corp. ADD CORP EMPL chief executive officer: Continental Loss Adjusting Service. CORP AFFIL director: Petrie Stores Corp.; director: Transcontinental Insurance Co. New York; director: CNA Financial Corp.; director: Automatic Data Processing Inc.; director: Bulova Corp. NONPR AFFIL chairman board trustees: New York University; director: United Jewish Appeal Federation; trustee: New York Public Library; member: Council Foreign Relations; trustee: Metropolitan Museum Art.
Preston Robert Tisch: president, donor, director (see above)
Theresa Unkrur: contributions committee
Peter Wilson: director
Gloria Woods: contributions committee

Grants Analysis

Disclosure Period: calendar year ending 2000
Total Grants: $1,750,504*
Number of Grants: 56
Average Grant: $18,924*
Highest Grant: $433,619
Lowest Grant: $500
Typical Range: $1,000 to $25,000
*Note: Giving excludes United Way; matching gifts. Average grant figure excludes two highest grants totaling $728,619.

Recent Grants

Note: Grants derived from 2001 Form 990.

General

420,570	Mathcounts Foundation, St. Paul, MN
200,000	Millenium Park, Inc.
177,185	National Merit Scholarship Corporation, Evanston, IL
160,000	KaBOOMI, Washington, DC
150,000	Chicago Symphony Orchestra, Chicago, IL
147,500	KaBOOMI, Washington, DC
147,500	KaBOOMI, Washington, DC
75,000	University of Chicago Graduate School, Chicago, IL
73,750	KaBOOMI, Washington, DC
50,000	Chicago Manufacturing Center, Chicago, IL

COBB FAMILY FOUNDATION

Giving Contact

Charles E. Cobb, Jr., President
255 Aragon Avenue, Suite 333
Coral Gables, FL 33134
Phone: (305)441-1700
Fax: (305)445-5674

Description

Founded: 1984
EIN: 592477459
Organization Type: Private Foundation
Giving Locations: FL: Dade County
Grant Types: Capital, General Support.

Donor Information

Founder: Charles E. Cobb, Jr.

Financial Summary

Total Giving: $528,345 (fiscal year ending September 30, 2001); $518,559 (fiscal 2000); $516,899 (fiscal 1998)
Giving Analysis: Giving for fiscal 2001 includes: foundation scholarships ($2,000); foundation grants to United Way ($35,000); fiscal 2000: foundation scholarships ($2,500); foundation grants to United Way ($70,000); fiscal 1997: foundation grants to United Way ($25,000) foundation ($416,195)
Assets: $9,194,561 (fiscal 2001); $11,070,578 (fiscal 2000); $9,986,653 (fiscal 1997)
Gifts Received: $144,688 (fiscal 2001); $216,875 (fiscal 2000); $490,250 (fiscal 1997). Note: In fiscal 1994, 2000, and 2001, contributions were received from Charles E. Cobb, Jr.

Typical Recipients

Arts & Humanities: Arts Centers, Arts Funds, Film & Video, Libraries, Music, Public Broadcasting
Civic & Public Affairs: Clubs, Ethnic Organizations, Civic & Public Affairs-General, Municipalities/Towns, Philanthropic Organizations, Urban & Community Affairs, Zoos/Aquariums
Education: Business Education, Colleges & Universities, Elementary Education (Public), International Exchange, Leadership Training, Legal Education, Medical Education, Private Education (Precollege), Science/Mathematics Education, Student Aid
Environment: Environment-General, Resource Conservation
Health: Cancer, Emergency/Ambulance Services, Medical Research, Prenatal Health Issues, Single-Disease Health Associations, Trauma Treatment
International: International Affairs, International Organizations, International Peace & Security Issues, Trade
Religion: Churches, Jewish Causes, Religious Welfare, Social/Policy Issues
Social Services: At-Risk Youth, Camps, Child Welfare, Emergency Relief, Family Services, People with Disabilities, Recreation & Athletics, Shelters/Homelessness, Social Services-General, United Funds/United Ways, Youth Organizations

Application Procedures

Initial Contact: Send a brief letter of inquiry.
Application Requirements: Include a description of organization, list of members of the board of directors and senior executives, current annual budget, percent of management/administration costs to dollars distributed, purpose of funds sought, amount requested, and proof of tax-exempt status.
Deadlines: None.

Restrictions

Contributions are made to institutions of higher education and selected charities that promote the quality of life in communities where the Cobb family has an established interest.

Foundation Officials

Charles E. Cobb, Jr.: president B Fresno, CA 1936. ED Stanford University BA (1958); Stanford University MBA (1962). PRIM CORP EMPL senior partner: Cobb Partners. CORP AFFIL chairman, chief executive officer: Pan America Corp. NONPR AFFIL chairman board trustees: University Miami.
Christian M. Cobb: vice president
Sue M. Cobb: vice president
Tobin T. Cobb: vice president

Grants Analysis

Disclosure Period: fiscal year ending September 30, 2001
Total Grants: $491,345*
Number of Grants: 109
Average Grant: $3,392*
Highest Grant: $125,000
Lowest Grant: $500
Typical Range: $1,000 to $5,000
*Note: Giving excludes scholarships and United Way. Average grant figure excludes highest grant.

Recent Grants

Note: Grants derived from fiscal 2000 Form 990.

General

125,000	University of Miami, Miami, FL -- for Cobb Stadium
70,000	United Way of Dade County, Miami, FL -- pledge
50,000	University of Miami, Miami, FL -- for presidents fund
25,000	Stanford University, Stanford, CA -- for Cobb track and Angell field
20,000	University of Miami, Miami, FL -- for James W. McLamore Distinguished fellows fund
13,000	Dade Schools Athletic Foundation, Miami, FL
12,500	University of Miami, Miami, FL -- for hurricane club
10,217	Department of St. Award for the Career Foreign Service Officer in Trade, Washington, DC -- for the Cobb award
10,000	Annenberg Foundation, Miami, FL
10,000	Goodwill Industries, Miami, FL

COCA-COLA CO.

Company Headquarters

1 Coca-Cola Plaza
Atlanta, GA 30313
Web: http://www.cocacola.com

Company Description

Founded: 1886
Ticker: KO
Exchange: NYSE
Revenue: US$19.564 billion (2002)
Profit: US$3.05 billion (2002)
Employees: 56000 (2002)
Fortune Rank: 92, per FORTUNE Magazine's list of 500 Largest U.S. Corporations (2002).
SIC(s): 2037 Frozen Fruits & Vegetables, 2086 Bottled & Canned Soft Drinks, 2087 Flavoring Extracts & Syrups Nec, 2099 Food Preparations Nec.

Operating Locations

Coca-Cola Co. (FL--Maitland; IL--Downers Grove; OH--Cincinnati; PA--Blandon)

Nonmonetary Support

Type: Donated Equipment; Donated Products
Note: NOT Company donates computers recently removed from service.
Volunteer Programs: Company sponsors an employee volunteer reaching-out program.
Contact: Kirk Glaze

Coca-Cola Foundation

Giving Contact

Ingrid Saunders Jones, Chairman
Coca-Cola Foundation
One Coca-Cola Plaza NW
Atlanta, GA 30313
Phone: (404)676-3525
Fax: (404)676-8804
Web: http://www2.coca-cola.com/citizenship/foundation.html

Alternate Contact

Phone: (404)676-6480

Description

Founded: 1984
EIN: 581574705
Organization Type: Corporate Foundation
Giving Locations: internationally; nationally.
Grant Types: Capital, Challenge, Employee Matching Gifts, Endowment, Fellowship, General Support, Multiyear/Continuing Support, Project, Scholarship.
Note: Employee matching gift ratio: 2 to 1.

Financial Summary

Total Giving: $12,141,774 (2001); $12,182,611 (2000); $11,543,211 (1999). Note: Contributes through corporate direct giving program and foundation.
Giving Analysis: Giving for 2000 includes: foundation fellowships ($719,000); foundation scholarships ($3,292,111); foundation ($8,171,500); foundation ($12,182,611); 1999: foundation scholarships ($2,483,500); foundation ($9,059,711) 1998: foundation ($12,504,811).
Assets: $59,075,032 (2001); $68,176,408 (2000); $27,640,690 (1999)
Gifts Received: $51,302,278 (2000); $200,001 (1998); $4,928,297 (1996). Note: In 1998 and 1999, contributions were received from the Coca-Cola Company.

Typical Recipients

Arts & Humanities: Arts Festivals, Ballet, Arts & Humanities-General, Historic Preservation, History & Archaeology, Libraries, Museums/Galleries, Music, Opera, Theater
Civic & Public Affairs: African American Affairs, Botanical Gardens/Parks, Civic & Public Affairs-General, Hispanic Affairs, Native American Affairs, Public Policy, Urban & Community Affairs
Education: Afterschool/Enrichment Programs, Arts/Humanities Education, Business Education, Colleges & Universities, Continuing Education, Education Associations, Education Funds, Education Reform, Elementary Education (Private), Engineering/Technological Education, Environmental Education, Faculty Development, Education-General, Health & Physical Education, International Exchange, International Studies, Leadership Training, Legal Education, Literacy, Medical Education, Minority Education, Private Education (Precollege), Public Education (Precollege), Science/Mathematics Education, Social Sciences Education, Student Aid, Vocational & Technical Education

International: Foreign Educational Institutions, Health Care/Hospitals, International Affairs, International Development, International Environmental Issues, International Relief Efforts
Science: Science Museums, Scientific Centers & Institutes
Social Services: Recreation & Athletics, YMCA/YWCA/YMHA/YWHA, Youth Organizations

Application Procedures

Initial Contact: Call or check the company's web site to obtain an application form.
Application Requirements: Completed application with program summary of no more than five pages. Information should include organization's mission; general program description, an explanation of why it is appropriate for Coca-Cola Foundation to help fund the project; financial statement; board of directors; proof of tax-exempt status; a statement on letterhead indicating that there is no change in purpose of organization since the issuance of the IRS letters; total project cost and amount requested; and a plan for measuring the success of the project.
Deadlines: None.
Decision Notification: Applications are accepted and reviewed continuously; notification is made within 60 days.
Notes: If proposal is being considered for funding, further communication may be required.

Restrictions

Foundation does not make grants to individuals; religious organizations or endeavors; political, legislative, lobbying or fraternal organizations; fundraising events; advertising, magazines, or articles in professional journals; or organizations that do not have tax-exempt status under IRS Code Section 501(c)(3).

Additional Information

Foundation prefers to support direct service projects and programs rather than making contributions to intermediary funding agencies.

Preference is given to proposals that identify clearly defined need, describe an innovative way to meet that need, demonstrate the applicant's ability to implement the process, and show how the program will benefit the general community.

Special consideration is given to organizations that effectively engage volunteers in reaching their goals.

Corporate Officials

Douglas N. Daft: chairman, chief executive officer B March 20, 1943. ED University of New England (Australia) BS; University of New South Wales Bus Admin. PRIM CORP EMPL chairman, chief executive officer: Coca-Cola Co. CORP AFFIL director: SunTrust Banks Inc. NONPR AFFIL Grocery Manufacturers of America; Woodruff Arts Center; CERGE-EI Foundation; board governors: Boys & Girls Clubs America.

Foundation Officials

John Richard Alm: director B Jamestown, NY 1946. ED State University of New York BS (1972). PRIM CORP EMPL chief operating officer, president: Coca-Cola Enterprises Inc. CORP AFFIL vice president, chief financial officer: Johnston Coca-Cola Bottling Group. NONPR AFFIL member: Financial Executives Institute; member: Minnesota Society CPA's.
Frank P. Bifulco, Jr.: director
James Chestnut: director
Carlton L. Curtis: director
John H. Downs, Jr.: director
Gary P. Fayard: treasurer, director
William Hawkins: general tax council
Carol Hayes: general counsel
Ingrid Saunders Jones: chairman, director B Detroit, MI 1945. ED Michigan State University BA (1968); Eastern Michigan University MA (1972). PRIM CORP EMPL senior vice president: The Coca-Cola Co.

Joseph West Jones: secretary, director B Georgetown, DE 1912. ED Beacom College BA (1932). PRIM CORP EMPL chairman: Ichauway Inc.
Melody Justice: director
Helen Smith Price: executive director, officer
Susan E. Shaw: assistant secretary

Grants Analysis

Disclosure Period: calendar year ending 2001
Total Grants: $7,668,384*
Number of Grants: 110
Average Grant: $69,713
Highest Grant: $250,000
Lowest Grant: $10,000
Typical Range: $25,000 to $150,000
***Note:** Giving excludes scholarship.

Recent Grants

Note: Grants derived from 2001 Form 990.

General

1,149,890	United Negro College Fund, Atlanta, GA -- scholarship program
300,000	University System of Georgia, Atlanta, GA -- for Prep Program
250,000	Intercultural Development Research Association, San Antonio, TX -- Coca-Cola Valued Youth Program Into The Next Millennium
250,000	National Park Foundation, Washington, DC -- National Park Discovery Centers
250,000	Project GRAD Atlanta, Atlanta, GA -- for Project GRAD Programs
225,000	College Fund/UNCF, Atlanta, GA
225,000	College Fund/UNCF, Atlanta, GA -- annual support
200,000	American Indian College Fund, Denver, CO -- for scholarships
200,000	Atlanta International School, Atlanta, GA -- capital campaign
200,000	Atlanta Symphony Orchestra, Atlanta, GA -- for next generation concerts

COCKRELL FOUNDATION

Giving Contact

M. Nancy Williams, Executive Vice President
1600 Smith, Suite 3900
Houston, TX 77002-7348
Phone: (713)209-7500
Fax: (713)209-7599
E-mail: foundation@cockrell.com
Web: http://www.cockrell.com/foundation/default.asp

Description

Founded: 1966
EIN: 746076993
Organization Type: Family Foundation
Giving Locations: TX: Houston
Grant Types: Capital, Endowment, General Support, Matching, Multiyear/Continuing Support, Operating Expenses.

Donor Information

Founder: Established in 1957 by Mrs. Dula Cockrell and Ernest Cockrell Jr. . Incorporated in 1966, the foundation's assets increased substantially, with almost $4 million bequeathed by Mr. Cockrell's estate. Members of the Cockrell family are among the six-member board of directors.

Financial Summary

Total Giving: $8,249,001 (2002); $7,690,000 (2001); $8,375,001 (2000)
Giving Analysis: Giving for 2000 includes: foundation grants to United Way ($3,030); 1999: foundation grants to United Way ($14,450); foundation matching gifts ($139,450) foundation scholarships ($1,050,000)

Assets: $158,707,288 (2000); $169,671,221 (1999); $175,573,945 (1998)

Typical Recipients

Arts & Humanities: Arts Outreach, Arts & Humanities-General, Historic Preservation, Libraries, Museums/Galleries, Music, Theater

Civic & Public Affairs: Botanical Gardens/Parks, Business/Free Enterprise, Clubs, Economic Development, Economic Policy, Civic & Public Affairs-General, Hispanic Affairs, Housing, Law & Justice, Municipalities/Towns, Safety, Urban & Community Affairs, Women's Affairs, Zoos/Aquariums

Education: Business Education, Colleges & Universities, Economic Education, Education Associations, Engineering/Technological Education, Faculty Development, Education-General, Legal Education, Literacy, Medical Education, Public Education (Precollege), Special Education, Student Aid

Environment: Environment-General, Resource Conservation

Health: Adolescent Health Issues, Alzheimers Disease, Cancer, Children's Health/Hospitals, Clinics/Medical Centers, Diabetes, Emergency/Ambulance Services, Eyes/Blindness, Health Organizations, Heart, Hospices, Hospitals, Medical Research, Mental Health, Prenatal Health Issues, Single-Disease Health Associations, Speech & Hearing

International: International Relief Efforts

Religion: Churches, Jewish Causes, Ministries, Religious Organizations, Religious Welfare

Science: Science Museums

Social Services: At-Risk Youth, Camps, Child Abuse, Child Welfare, Community Centers, Community Service Organizations, Day Care, Family Planning, Family Services, Food/Clothing Distribution, Homes, People with Disabilities, Recreation & Athletics, Scouts, Senior Services, Shelters/Homelessness, Social Services-General, United Funds/United Ways, YMCA/YWCA/YMHA/YWHA, Youth Organizations

Application Procedures

Initial Contact: The foundation has no standard application form. Organizations should send a detailed letter of inquiry outlining their grant proposal.

Application Requirements: Applicants should include in the letter: a brief statement of need; statement of goals; a project budget including the total cost; amount raised to date, including other sources of funding (i.e. private, government, individuals, board members, etc.); plans for raising any uncovered balance; statement of project status; amount requested; description of plans for putting project on self-sustaining basis, plus an estimate of cost; and a list of officers and directors of the organization. Also include a copy of the IRS letter of 501(c)(3) tax exemption, a copy of current annual budget and latest Form 990, and latest audited financial statement.

Deadlines: None.

Review Process: The foundation board meets in Spring and Fall. Generally, decisions are made within six weeks of the meetings.

Restrictions

The foundation does not give to individuals or fund political or lobbying groups.

Additional Information

Publications: Annual Report; Guidelines

Foundation Officials

Douglas E. Bryant: secretary, treasurer

Ernest Harris Cockrell: president, director B Houston, TX 1945. ED University of Texas, Austin BS (1967); University of Texas MBA (1970). PRIM CORP EMPL president, chief executive officer, director: Cockrell Oil Corp. CORP AFFIL director: Pennzoil Co.

Janet S. Cockrell: director

Carol Cockrell Curran: director CORP AFFIL officer: Cockrell Oil Corp.; officer: Cockrell Resources Inc.

Richard B. Curran: director CORP AFFIL director: Intellicall Inc.

Milton T. Graves: vice president, director B Okmulgee, OK 1936. ED Sam Houston State University BBA (1958). PRIM CORP EMPL executive vice president, chief financial officer, director: Cockrell Oil Corp. CORP AFFIL vice president, director: Cockrell Resources Inc.; president, director: Texas Production Co.; president, director: Cockrell Interests Inc.

J. Webb Jennings, III: director

Laura Jennings Turner: director

M. Nancy Williams: executive vice president PRIM CORP EMPL secretary, treasurer: Sprint Press.

Grants Analysis

Disclosure Period: calendar year ending 2002

Total Grants: $8,249,001*

Number of Grants: 29

Average Grant: $131,920*

Highest Grant: $4,423,320

Lowest Grant: $1,500

Typical Range: $1,000 to $50,000

*Note: Giving excludes scholarships and United Way. Average grant excludes highest grant.

Recent Grants

Note: Grants derived from 2002 Form 990.

General

3,333,000	Boy Scouts of America, Houston, TX -- constructing Cockrell Memorial Scout Training and Service Center
1,423,320	Baylor College of Medicine, Houston, TX -- funding researchers for clinical research initiative
750,000	Texas Heart Institute, Houston, TX -- capital campaign
550,000	University of Texas Engineering, Austin, TX -- scholarship fund
400,000	TIRR Foundation, Houston, TX -- endowment campaign
300,000	American Red Cross, Houston, TX -- capital campaign "Keeping the Promise"
250,000	Houston CEO Foundation, Houston, TX -- Scholarship program
250,000	University of Texas Health Science Center, Houston, TX -- TexGen Project
200,000	Greater Houston Collaborative for Children, Houston, TX -- program costs and collaborative support
200,000	Houston Museum of Natural Science, Houston, TX -- Technology Improvement Program

GEORGE W. CODRINGTON CHARITABLE FOUNDATION

Giving Contact

c/o Key Trust Co. of OH, N.A.
127 Public Square, 17th Floor
Cleveland, OH 44114
Phone: (216)689-3000

Description

Founded: 1955

EIN: 346507457

Organization Type: Private Foundation

Giving Locations: OH: Cuyahoga County including surrounding area

Grant Types: General Support.

Donor Information

Founder: the late George W. Codrington

Financial Summary

Total Giving: $1,292,000 (2000); $1,372,500 (1999); $1,045,000 (1998)

Giving Analysis: Giving for 2000 includes: foundation grants to United Way ($15,800); foundation scholarships ($115,000); 1999: foundation grants to United Way ($93,050) foundation scholarships ($96,500)

Assets: $22,867,114 (2000); $24,275,429 (1999); $22,527,291 (1998)

Gifts Received: $556,880 (1992). Note: In 1992, contributions were received from William S. McKinstry.

Typical Recipients

Arts & Humanities: Arts Centers, Arts Institutes, Arts Outreach, Ballet, Community Arts, Dance, Historic Preservation, History & Archaeology, Libraries, Museums/Galleries, Music, Opera, Performing Arts, Public Broadcasting, Theater

Civic & Public Affairs: Botanical Gardens/Parks, Business/Free Enterprise, Community Foundations, Employment/Job Training, Civic & Public Affairs-General, Legal Aid, Parades/Festivals, Public Policy, Safety, Urban & Community Affairs

Education: Business Education, Colleges & Universities, Community & Junior Colleges, Economic Education, Education Funds, Education Reform, Faculty Development, Education-General, Minority Education, Minority Education, Private Education (Precollege), Public Education (Precollege), Science/Mathematics Education, Social Sciences Education, Student Aid

Environment: Environment-General

Health: AIDS/HIV, Cancer, Children's Health/Hospitals, Clinics/Medical Centers, Diabetes, Emergency/Ambulance Services, Eyes/Blindness, Health-General, Hospitals, Hospitals (University Affiliated), Medical Research, Nursing Services, Prenatal Health Issues, Public Health, Speech & Hearing

International: Foreign Arts Organizations, International Affairs

Religion: Ministries, Religious Organizations, Religious Welfare

Science: Science Museums, Scientific Centers & Institutes

Social Services: Camps, Child Welfare, Community Centers, Community Service Organizations, Domestic Violence, Family Planning, Family Services, Food/Clothing Distribution, People with Disabilities, Scouts, Senior Services, Substance Abuse, United Funds/United Ways, Volunteer Services, YMCA/YWCA/YMHA/YWHA, Youth Organizations

Application Procedures

Initial Contact: Send a brief letter of inquiry.

Application Requirements: Include amount requested, purpose of funds sought, a brief history of the organization, the area served by the applicant, a description of the applicant's contributions to the area, and a listing of the applicant's officers and trustees.

Review Process: Supervisory board meets in March, June, September, November, and December to review applications.

Restrictions

Provides only annual grants. Does not support individuals or provide loans.

Additional Information

Publications: Annual Report (including Application Guidelines)

Trust(s): Key Bank OH NA

Foundation Officials

Kenneth Allen Ashmus: secretary supervisory board B Cleveland, OH 1949. ED Michigan State University BA (1971); Michigan State University MA (1972); Yale University JD (1974). PRIM CORP EMPL partner: Thompson, Hine & Flory. NONPR AFFIL member: Public Sector Labor Relations Association; trustee: Smaller Enterprises Council; member: Ohio Bar Association; member: Cleveland Bar Association; member: Defense Research Institute; member: California State Bar Association.

John J. Dwyer: mem supervisory board

William E. McDonald: mem supervisory board B Murphy, NC 1942. ED Western Carolina University (1967); East Tennessee State University (1979). PRIM CORP EMPL president, chief operating officer: United Telephone System Southeast. CORP AFFIL president: Sprint Mid-Atlantic Telecom.

Curtis E. Moll: member supervisory board B 1939. ED Ohio Wesleyan University (1961); Southern Methodist University (1963). PRIM CORP EMPL chairman, chief executive officer, director: MTD Products Inc. CORP AFFIL director: Valley City Steel Co.; director: Society National Bank; director: Standard Products Co.; director: KeyCorp; director: Sherwin-Williams Co.; chairman, director: Arnold Distributors Inc.; director: Cub Cadet Corp. NONPR AFFIL trustee: Goodwill Industries.

Raymond Terry Sawyer: chairman B Cleveland, OH 1943. ED Yale University BA (1965); Harvard University LLB (1968). PRIM CORP EMPL partner: Thompson, Hine & Flory. NONPR AFFIL director: Premix; member: Yale University Alumni Association; secretary, member executive committee: Metro Health System; member: Ohio State Bar Association; member: Cleveland Bar Association; trustee: Cleveland Orchestra; member: American Bar Association; trustee: Cleveland Ballet.

William Robert Seelbach: mem supervisory board B Lakewood, OH 1948. ED Yale University BS (1970); Stanford University MBA (1972). PRIM CORP EMPL chairman: Inverness Partners. CORP AFFIL director: Lumitex Inc. NONPR AFFIL trustee: Playhouse Square Foundation; trustee: University School; trustee: Nebraska Ohio Council; trustee: Enterprise Development Council.

Grants Analysis

Disclosure Period: calendar year ending 2000
Total Grants: $1,161,200*
Number of Grants: 131
Average Grant: $8,864
Highest Grant: $100,000
Typical Range: $5,000 to $20,000
*Note: Giving excludes United Way and scholarships.

Recent Grants

Note: Grants derived from 1999 Form 990.

General

200,000	Case Western Reserve University, Cleveland, OH -- development of an expanded academic medical center and biotechnology complex
90,000	Cleveland Summit on Education, Cleveland, OH
50,000	City Mission Women's Ministry, Cleveland, OH -- expansion of mission program
35,000	Case Western Reserve, Cleveland, OH -- support of Homenet
35,000	Cleveland Orchestra, Cleveland, OH
35,000	Ohio Canal Corridor, OH
33,000	Educational Television Association of Metropolitan Cleveland, Cleveland, OH
30,000	Access to the Arts, Cleveland, OH -- support of the Malicky Center for Social Sciences
20,000	Cleveland Botanical Gardens, Cleveland, OH -- capital campaign
20,000	John Carroll University, University Heights, OH -- summer research program

CHARLES S. AND MARY COEN FAMILY FOUNDATION

Giving Contact
Mona L. Thompson, Trustee
PO Box 34
Washington, PA 15301
Phone: (724)223-5503

Description
Founded: 1959
EIN: 256033877
Organization Type: Private Foundation
Giving Locations: PA: Washington; WV: St. Mary's
Grant Types: General Support.

Donor Information
Founder: the late C. S. Coen, the late Mary Coen, Charles R. Coen, C. S. Coen Land Co.

Financial Summary
Total Giving: $705,010 (fiscal year ending February 28, 2002); $598,090 (fiscal 2001); $403,975 (fiscal 2000)
Giving Analysis: Giving for fiscal 2002 includes: foundation grants to United Way ($6,000); fiscal 2001: foundation grants to United Way ($4,500); fiscal 2000: foundation grants to United Way ($4,000)
Assets: $9,050,468 (fiscal 2002); $7,889,299 (fiscal 2001); $7,726,901 (fiscal 2000)
Gifts Received: $227,680 (fiscal 2002); $76,000 (fiscal 2001); $50,000 (fiscal 2000). Note: In fiscal 1999, 2000, 2001, and 2002 contributions were received from the estate of C. S. Coen.

Typical Recipients
Arts & Humanities: History & Archaeology, Libraries, Museums/Galleries, Music
Civic & Public Affairs: Botanical Gardens/Parks, Clubs, Civic & Public Affairs-General, Housing, Safety
Education: Business Education, Colleges & Universities, Education Funds, Literacy, Minority Education, Private Education (Precollege), Public Education (Precollege)
Environment: Resource Conservation
Health: Children's Health/Hospitals, Clinics/Medical Centers, Hospices, Hospitals, Long-Term Care, Medical Research, Single-Disease Health Associations
International: Health Care/Hospitals
Religion: Churches, Religious Welfare
Social Services: Big Brother/Big Sister, Child Welfare, Community Service Organizations, Homes, People with Disabilities, Recreation & Athletics, Scouts, Senior Services, Substance Abuse, United Funds/United Ways, YMCA/YWCA/YMHA/YWHA, Youth Organizations

Application Procedures
Initial Contact: Send a brief letter of inquiry.
Deadlines: None.

Restrictions
Does not support individuals.

Foundation Officials
Charles R. Coen: trustee
Mona Thompson: trustee
Lawrence A. Withum, Jr.: trustee

Grants Analysis
Disclosure Period: fiscal year ending February 28, 2002
Total Grants: $699,010*
Number of Grants: 105
Average Grant: $5,808*
Highest Grant: $95,000
Lowest Grant: $100

Typical Range: $1,000 to $10,000
*Note: Giving excludes United Way. Average grant excludes highest grant.

Recent Grants
Note: Grants derived from fiscal 2000 Form 990.

Library-Related

5,000	Pleasants County Public Library, St. Marys, WV
3,000	Citizens Library, Washington, PA

General

75,000	Wilson College, Chambersburg, PA
70,000	Washington and Jefferson College, Washington, DC
40,000	Washington Hospital Foundation, Washington, PA
36,000	Church of the Covenant, Washington, PA
20,000	Ohio State University Development Account 536315, Columbus, OH
20,000	Presbyterian Senior Care, Washington, PA
20,000	Waynesburg College, Waynesburg, PA
20,000	Youth for Christ, Washington, PA
11,000	Foundation for California University of Pennsylvania, California, PA
10,000	Westminster College, New Wilmington, PA

COGSWELL BENEVOLENT TRUST

Giving Contact
David P. Goodwin, Trustee
1001 Elm St.
Manchester, NH 03101
Phone: (603)622-4013

Description
Founded: 1929
EIN: 020235690
Organization Type: Private Foundation
Giving Locations: NH
Grant Types: Endowment, General Support, Operating Expenses.

Donor Information
Founder: the late Leander A. Cogswell

Financial Summary
Total Giving: $1,151,296 (2002); $917,749 (2001); $1,134,681 (2000)
Giving Analysis: Giving for 2002 includes: foundation grants to United Way ($55,000); 2000: foundation grants to United Way ($50,000); 1999: foundation grants to United Way ($35,000);
Assets: $20,518,169 (2002); $25,230,873 (2001); $23,924,941 (2000)

Typical Recipients
Arts & Humanities: Arts Associations & Councils, Arts Centers, Community Arts, Arts & Humanities-General, Historic Preservation, History & Archaeology, Libraries, Museums/Galleries, Music, Performing Arts, Public Broadcasting, Theater
Civic & Public Affairs: Botanical Gardens/Parks, Chambers of Commerce, Ethnic Organizations, Civic & Public Affairs-General, Housing, Municipalities/Towns, Urban & Community Affairs
Education: Arts/Humanities Education, Colleges & Universities, Faculty Development, Health & Physical Education, Minority Education, Preschool Education, Private Education (Precollege), Science/Mathematics Education, Secondary Education (Private), Special Education, Student Aid
Environment: Forestry, Environment-General, Resource Conservation, Watershed

Health: AIDS/HIV, Children's Health/Hospitals, Clinics/Medical Centers, Emergency/Ambulance Services, Eyes/Blindness, Geriatric Health, Health Policy/Cost Containment, Hospices, Hospitals, Long-Term Care, Medical Rehabilitation, Mental Health, Prenatal Health Issues, Research/Studies Institutes, Respiratory
Religion: Churches, Religious Welfare
Science: Scientific Centers & Institutes
Social Services: Animal Protection, At-Risk Youth, Camps, Child Welfare, Community Centers, Community Service Organizations, Day Care, Family Services, Food/Clothing Distribution, Homes, People with Disabilities, Recreation & Athletics, Scouts, Senior Services, Shelters/Homelessness, Social Services-General, Special Olympics, United Funds/United Ways, YMCA/YWCA/YMHA/YWHA, Youth Organizations

Application Procedures

Initial Contact: Send a brief letter of inquiry describing program or project.
Application Requirements: Include amount requested, purpose of funds sought, and name, address, and telephone number of contact person.
Deadlines: None.

Restrictions

The trust is restricted by will to donate 90 percent of funds within NH.

Foundation Officials

David P. Goodwin: trustee
Mark Northridge: trustee
Theodore Wadleigh: trustee

Grants Analysis

Disclosure Period: calendar year ending 2002
Total Grants: $1,096,296*
Number of Grants: 79
Average Grant: $12,773*
Highest Grant: $100,000
Lowest Grant: $1,000
Typical Range: $5,000 to $25,000
*Note: Giving excludes United Way. Average grant figure excludes highest grants.

Recent Grants

Note: Grants derived from 2001 Form 990.

General
60,000	Child Health Services, Manchester, NH -- for emergency operating expenses
50,000	Girls Incorporated, NH -- for Norwell Home Program support
50,000	Salvation Army of Manchester, Manchester, NH -- for Camp Expansion Program
50,000	United Way of Greater Manchester, Manchester, NH -- annual campaign
40,000	Weeks Medical Center, Lancaster, NH -- for purchase of mobile health care van
30,000	Cedarcrest Foundation, Keene, NH -- for building expansion project
25,000	Girls Incorporated, NH -- for emergency funding to meet immediate needs of children
25,000	Habitat for Humanity of Mount Washington Valley
25,000	New Horizons of New Hampshire, Manchester, NH -- for 8th annual Thanksgiving breakfast
25,000	Odyssey House, Manchester, NH -- for Youthbuild Odyssey Program

NAOMI AND NEHEMIAH COHEN FOUNDATION

Giving Contact

Allison McWilliams, Associate Director
PO Box 73708
Washington, DC 20056
Phone: (202)234-5454
Fax: (202)234-8797
E-mail: nncf@starpower.net

Description

Founded: 1959
EIN: 526054166
Organization Type: Family Foundation
Giving Locations: DC: Washington; Israel
Grant Types: Capital, General Support, Operating Expenses, Project.

Donor Information

Founder: Established in 1959 by the late Israel Cohen and the late Naomi Cohen . Mr. Cohen left the majority of his estimated $101 million estate to the foundation, boosting the foundation's assets to about $75 million.

Financial Summary

Total Giving: $3,300,000 (2002 approx); $3,379,200 (2001); $3,400,000 (2000 approx)
Assets: $81,000,000 (2002 approx); $87,419,263 (2001); $84,200,000 (2000 approx)
Gifts Received: $12,000,000 (2002 approx); $10,208,399 (2001); $35,010,090 (1998)

Typical Recipients

Arts & Humanities: Arts Centers, Arts & Humanities-General, Libraries, Museums/Galleries, Music, Opera, Performing Arts, Public Broadcasting, Theater
Civic & Public Affairs: Community Foundations, Economic Development, Economic Policy, Employment/Job Training, Civic & Public Affairs-General, Housing, Law & Justice, Philanthropic Organizations, Professional & Trade Associations, Public Policy, Safety, Urban & Community Affairs, Women's Affairs
Education: Agricultural Education, Colleges & Universities, Community & Junior Colleges, Education Funds, Education-General, Legal Education, Medical Education, Minority Education, Preschool Education, Private Education (Precollege), Religious Education, Science/Mathematics Education, Secondary Education (Private), Special Education, Student Aid
Environment: Energy, Environment-General, Protection, Resource Conservation, Wildlife Protection
Health: Arthritis, Cancer, Children's Health/Hospitals, Clinics/Medical Centers, Diabetes, Emergency/Ambulance Services, Eyes/Blindness, Health-General, Health Organizations, Heart, Hospices, Hospitals, Hospitals (University Affiliated), Long-Term Care, Mental Health, Prenatal Health Issues, Single-Disease Health Associations
International: Foreign Arts Organizations, Foreign Educational Institutions, Health Care/Hospitals, International Organizations, International Peace & Security Issues, Missionary/Religious Activities
Religion: Churches, Religion-General, Jewish Causes, Jewish Causes, Ministries, Religious Organizations, Religious Welfare, Social/Policy Issues, Synagogues/Temples
Science: Observatories & Planetariums, Scientific Centers & Institutes, Scientific Research
Social Services: Child Welfare, Community Centers, Community Service Organizations, Crime Prevention, Delinquency & Criminal Rehabilitation, Family Planning, Food/Clothing Distribution, Homes, Recreation & Athletics, Senior Services, Shelters/Homelessness, Social Services-General, Substance Abuse, United Funds/United Ways, Youth Organizations

Application Procedures

Initial Contact: The foundation has no formal grant procedure or grant application form. Send a brief letter of inquiry accompanied by a current operating budget, a list of institutional funders and the amounts of their grants, and a copy of your organization's IRS determination letter of 501(c)(3) tax-exempt status. Please do not send letters of inquiry by fax, Federal Express, or messenger.
Deadlines: None.

Restrictions

Grants are not made to individuals.

Foundation Officials

Dr. Diane Solomon Brown: vice president
Lillian Cohen-Solomon: president
Daniel Solomon: secretary
David Solomon: treasurer

Grants Analysis

Disclosure Period: calendar year ending 2001
Total Grants: $3,379,200*
Number of Grants: 122
Average Grant: $27,700
Highest Grant: $150,000
Typical Range: $1,000 to $50,000
*Note: Grants analysis provided by foundation.

Recent Grants

Note: Grants derived from 2000 Form 990.

Library-Related
525,000	Library of Congress, Washington, DC

General
4,250,000	Jewish Federation of Greater Washington, Rockville, MD
200,000	Americans for Peace Now, Washington, DC
200,000	PEF Israel Endowment Fund, New York, NY
100,000	American Friends of Weizmann Institute of Science, Washington, DC
100,000	Israel Policy Forum, New York, NY
100,000	Salvation Army, Washington, DC
85,000	Bread for the City and Zacchaeus Free Clinic, Washington, DC
75,000	Planned Parenthood of Metropolitan Washington, Washington, DC
50,000	American Friends of Israel Union for Environmental Defense, Bethesda, MD
50,000	American Friends of Melitz, Baltimore, MD

COLBURN FUND

Giving Contact

Richard D. Colburn, Director
1120 La Collina Road
Beverly Hills, CA 90210
Phone: (310)273-3607
Fax: (310)273-7904

Description

Founded: 1985
EIN: 954018318
Organization Type: Private Foundation
Giving Locations: CA
Grant Types: General Support.

Donor Information

Founder: Richard D. Colburn, Consolidated Electrical Distributors, U.S. Rentals

Financial Summary

Total Giving: $450,011 (2001); $486,100 (2000); $275,730 (1999)
Assets: $185,395 (2001); $221,223 (2000); $331,562 (1999)

Gifts Received: $400,000 (2001); $375,000 (2000); $350,000 (1999). Note: Contributions are received from Consolidated Electrical Distributors, Inc.

Typical Recipients

Arts & Humanities: Arts Associations & Councils, Arts Centers, Arts Funds, Arts Institutes, Community Arts, Film & Video, Arts & Humanities-General, History & Archaeology, Libraries, Museums/Galleries, Music, Opera, Performing Arts, Public Broadcasting, Theater

Civic & Public Affairs: Community Foundations, Civic & Public Affairs-General, Municipalities/Towns, Parades/Festivals, Philanthropic Organizations, Public Policy, Women's Affairs

Education: Arts/Humanities Education, Colleges & Universities, Continuing Education, Education-General, International Studies, Private Education (Precollege), Social Sciences Education

Environment: Environment-General, Resource Conservation, Wildlife Protection

Health: AIDS/HIV, Cancer, Diabetes, Emergency/Ambulance Services, Heart, Hospitals, Medical Research, Mental Health

International: Foreign Arts Organizations, International Development, International Environmental Issues, International Organizations, International Relations, Missionary/Religious Activities

Religion: Religion-General, Religious Organizations

Social Services: Community Service Organizations, Family Services, Recreation & Athletics

Application Procedures

Initial Contact: The foundation has no formal grant application procedure or application form.
Deadlines: None.

Additional Information

Emphasis is on music, music related endeavors, fine arts, and performing arts, including their sponsoring organizations, such as orchestral and opera societies, galleries, theatre groups, and civic and other charitable organizations with similar purposes. The fund may also support any other tax exempt organization that is operated exclusively for the charitable, scientific, literary, or educational purposes.

Foundation Officials

Richard Dunton Colburn: director B Carpentersville, IL 1911. ED Antioch College (1933). PRIM CORP EMPL chairman: Decco/Edmundson Electric. CORP AFFIL director: Rolled Alloys Inc.; chairman: U South Rentals Inc.; director: Hajoca Corp.; director: Consolidated Electrical Distributors; director: Edmundson International.
Bernard E. Lyons: director

Grants Analysis

Disclosure Period: calendar year ending 2001
Total Grants: $450,011
Number of Grants: 55
Average Grant: $8,182
Highest Grant: $56,200
Lowest Grant: $200
Typical Range: $1,000 to $15,000

Recent Grants

Note: Grants derived from 2001 Form 990.

General

56,200	Colburn School for Performing Arts, CA
50,000	Antioch College, Yellow Springs, OH
33,200	International Festival Society, Los Angeles, CA
31,500	Fraternity of Friends, Los Angeles, CA
25,589	Los Angeles Opera, Los Angeles, CA
25,000	American Friends of the Bayreuth Festival, Los Angeles, CA
25,000	American Friends of the Israel Philharmonic Orchestra, New York, NY
25,000	American Youth Symphony, Los Angeles, CA

25,000	Community Partners FBO Opus Chamber Orchestra
15,000	American Symphony Orchestra, New York, NY

OLIVE B. COLE FOUNDATION

Giving Contact

John E. Hogan, Executive Vice President & Treasurer
6207 Constitution Drive
Ft. Wayne, IN 46804
Phone: (260)436-2182
Fax: (260)432-3146

Description

Founded: 1954
EIN: 356040491
Organization Type: General Purpose Foundation
Giving Locations: IN: North Eastern Indiana, Noble, La Grange, De Kalb, and Steuben counties
Grant Types: Capital, General Support, Loan, Operating Expenses, Project, Scholarship.

Donor Information

Founder: The Olive B. Cole Foundation was established in Indiana in 1954 with funds donated by the late Richard R. Cole and Olive B. Cole . Mr. Cole set up the foundation in honor of his mother. The money for the foundation came from stock in Flint and Walling, a water pump and conditioner manufacturer.

Financial Summary

Total Giving: $1,200,000 (fiscal year ending March 31, 2003 approx); $1,200,000 (fiscal 2002); $1,202,122 (fiscal 2001). Note: Fiscal 1997 Giving includes scholarship ($167,669); 1996 scholarship ($176,217).
Giving Analysis: Giving for fiscal 2001 includes: foundation scholarships ($260,423) fiscal 1999: foundation scholarships ($185,221)
Assets: $29,748,768 (fiscal 2001); $32,259,842 (fiscal 1999); $32,000,000 (fiscal 1998 approx)

Typical Recipients

Arts & Humanities: Arts Appreciation, Arts Institutes, Arts Outreach, Dance, Historic Preservation, Libraries, Literary Arts, Museums/Galleries, Music, Opera, Public Broadcasting, Theater

Civic & Public Affairs: Botanical Gardens/Parks, Chambers of Commerce, Community Foundations, Economic Development, Employment/Job Training, Civic & Public Affairs-General, Municipalities/Towns, Parades/Festivals, Philanthropic Organizations, Safety, Urban & Community Affairs, Zoos/Aquariums

Education: Arts/Humanities Education, Business Education, Colleges & Universities, Education Associations, Education Funds, Engineering/Technological Education, Environmental Education, Education-General, International Studies, Literacy, Private Education (Precollege), Public Education (Precollege), Science/Mathematics Education, Secondary Education (Public), Special Education, Student Aid

Environment: Air/Water Quality, Environment-General, Resource Conservation

Health: AIDS/HIV, Alzheimers Disease, Cancer, Children's Health/Hospitals, Clinics/Medical Centers, Emergency/Ambulance Services, Health Organizations, Home-Care Services, Hospices, Trauma Treatment

Religion: Churches, Religious Welfare

Science: Science Exhibits & Fairs, Science Museums

Social Services: At-Risk Youth, Big Brother/Big Sister, Child Welfare, Community Centers, Community Service Organizations, Crime Prevention, Day Care, Emergency Relief, Family Services, Food/Clothing

Distribution, People with Disabilities, People with Disabilities, Recreation & Athletics, Scouts, Senior Services, Shelters/Homelessness, United Funds/United Ways, Volunteer Services, YMCA/YWCA/YMHA/YWHA, Youth Organizations

Application Procedures

Initial Contact: A letter of inquiry is the preferred method of initial contact.
Application Requirements: Applicants must complete an application form that is supplied upon request.
Deadlines: None.
Review Process: The board meets in February, May, August, and November. Applicants will be notified of the board's decision after four months.

Restrictions

Scholarship eligibility is limited to residents or graduates of secondary schools in North Eastern Indiana, Noble, La Grange, DeKalb, and Steuben counties in Indiana. Grants are not given to individuals, to religious organizations, or for funds for redistribution.

Additional Information

Scholarship applications also are available at high school offices throughout Noble County, IN.
Publications: Application Form; Statement of Program Policy

Foundation Officials

John E. Hogan: executive vice president, treasurer
Maclyn T. Parker, Esq.: president, director B 1929. ED DePauw University AB (1951); University of Michigan JD (1954). PRIM CORP EMPL member: Baker & Daniels.
Emily E. Pichon: secretary
John N. Pichon, Jr.: chairman
Paul Schirmeyer: director
Gwendlyn I. Tipton: scholarship admin, director

Grants Analysis

Disclosure Period: fiscal year ending March 31, 2001
Total Grants: $936,699*
Number of Grants: 33
Average Grant: $19,897*
Highest Grant: $300,000
Lowest Grant: $660
Typical Range: $10,000 to $40,000
*Note: Giving excludes scholarships. Average grant excludes highest grant.

Recent Grants

Note: Grants derived from 2000 Form 990.

Library-Related

2,500	Eckhart Public Library, Auburn, IN -- young adult program

General

500,000	Breeden YMCA Learning Center, OH
150,000	Central Noble School Corporation, Albion, IN -- additional center stage fund
75,000	Kendallville Day Care Center, Kendallville, IN -- addition/expansion
70,000	Four County Area Vocational Cooperative, Garrett, IN -- vocational equipment
5,0000	Junior Achievement of East-Central Noble County, Ft. Wayne, IN -- special K fund
35,000	Nature Conservancy, Indianapolis, IN -- fish creek project
34,000	Kendallville Windmill Museum and Historical Society, Kendallville, IN -- Mid-America Windmill Museum
30,000	Fort Wayne Children's Zoo, Ft. Wayne, IN -- heart of the zoo campaign
25,390	Kendallville Park and Recreation Department, Kendallville, IN -- Sunset Park Improvements
25,000	Anthony Wayne Council Boy Scouts of

America, Ft. Wayne, IN -- capital campaign

QUINCY COLE TRUST

Giving Contact
Rita Smith, Trust Officer
c/o Bank of America
PO Box 26688
Richmond, VA 23261
Phone: (804)788-2143

Description
EIN: 546086247
Organization Type: Private Foundation
Giving Locations: VA: Richmond including metropolitan area
Grant Types: General Support.

Donor Information
Founder: the late Quincy Cole

Financial Summary
Total Giving: $847,849 (fiscal year ending June 30, 2000); $905,872 (fiscal 1999); $552,896 (fiscal 1997)
Assets: $14,340,971 (fiscal 2000); $14,153,141 (fiscal 1999); $10,734,328 (fiscal 1997)

Typical Recipients
Arts & Humanities: Arts Associations & Councils, Arts Centers, Ballet, Community Arts, Dance, Historic Preservation, History & Archaeology, Libraries, Museums/Galleries, Music, Opera
Civic & Public Affairs: Botanical Gardens/Parks, Clubs, Civic & Public Affairs-General, Municipalities/Towns, Public Policy
Education: Afterschool/Enrichment Programs, Arts/Humanities Education, Colleges & Universities, Private Education (Precollege), Public Education (Precollege), Science/Mathematics Education
Environment: Environment-General
Health: Clinics/Medical Centers, Research/Studies Institutes, Single-Disease Health Associations
International: Foreign Arts Organizations
Religion: Churches, Religious Organizations, Seminaries
Science: Science Museums
Social Services: Child Welfare, Community Service Organizations, Family Services, Food/Clothing Distribution, Homes, People with Disabilities, Recreation & Athletics, Scouts, Shelters/Homelessness, YMCA/YWCA/YMHA/YWHA, Youth Organizations

Application Procedures
Initial Contact: Send a brief letter of inquiry.
Application Requirements: Include a description of organization and purpose of funds sought.
Deadlines: April 20.

Additional Information
Trust(s): Bank of America NA

Grants Analysis
Disclosure Period: fiscal year ending June 30, 2000
Total Grants: $847,849
Number of Grants: 34
Average Grant: $23,361*
Highest Grant: $76,949
Typical Range: $10,000 to $50,000
*Note: Average grant excludes highest grant.

Recent Grants
Note: Grants derived from fiscal 2000 Form 990.

Library-Related
25,000   Steward School, Richmond, VA -- grant for construction of a new library

General
76,949   Windsor House, Richmond, VA -- upkeep and maintenance of house
50,000   Foundation for the Preservation of Virginia's Executive Mansion, Richmond, VA
50,000   Maymont Foundation, Richmond, VA
50,000   Richmond Home For Ladies, Richmond, VA -- grant for relocation purposes
50,000   Virginia Home, Richmond, VA -- grant for completing the vision project
50,000   YWCA of Richmond, Richmond, VA -- grant for equipment and furnishings
40,000   Virginia Commonwealth University Foundation, Richmond, VA -- grant for renovation to Franklin St. House
30,000   Science Museum of Virginia Foundation, Richmond, VA -- grant for DNA model display
30,000   YMCA of Richmond, Richmond, VA -- grant for headquarters renovation
25,000   Boys and Girls Club of Richmond, Richmond, VA -- grant for renovation program

GEORGE E. COLEMAN FOUNDATION

Giving Contact
Denis Loncto, Trustee
c/o Neville, Rodie & Shaw
200 Madison Ave.
New York, NY 10016
Phone: (212)725-1440
Fax: (212)689-8746

Description
Founded: 1979
EIN: 133025258
Organization Type: Private Foundation
Giving Locations: DC: Washington; NY; PA
Grant Types: General Support, Research.

Donor Information
Founder: the late George E. Coleman, Jr.

Financial Summary
Total Giving: $654,750 (2000); $679,600 (1999); $464,700 (1998)
Assets: $9,856,686 (2000); $11,245,727 (1999); $10,459,062 (1998)

Typical Recipients
Arts & Humanities: Historic Preservation, History & Archaeology, Libraries, Museums/Galleries, Music, Public Broadcasting
Civic & Public Affairs: Business/Free Enterprise, Economic Policy, Civic & Public Affairs-General, Legal Aid, Municipalities/Towns, Philanthropic Organizations, Public Policy, Urban & Community Affairs, Women's Affairs, Zoos/Aquariums
Education: Arts/Humanities Education, Colleges & Universities, Economic Education, Education Funds, Education Reform, Education-General, International Studies, Journalism/Media Education, Private Education (Precollege), Secondary Education (Private), Social Sciences Education
Environment: Environment-General, Resource Conservation, Wildlife Protection
Health: Health Policy/Cost Containment, Public Health
International: Health Care/Hospitals, International Affairs, International Environmental Issues, International Peace & Security Issues, International Relations, Missionary/Religious Activities
Religion: Churches, Religious Organizations, Religious Welfare, Social/Policy Issues
Social Services: Community Service Organizations, Youth Organizations

Application Procedures
Initial Contact: Send a brief letter of inquiry.
Application Requirements: Indicate type of organization and purpose of funds sought.
Deadlines: None.

Foundation Officials
Denis Loncto: trustee
Daniel Oliver: trustee
Louise Oliver: trustee

Grants Analysis
Disclosure Period: calendar year ending 2000
Total Grants: $654,750
Number of Grants: 42
Average Grant: $13,165*
Highest Grant: $115,000
Typical Range: $5,000 to $25,000
*Note: Average grant figure excludes highest grant.

Recent Grants
Note: Grants derived from 1999 Form 990.

Library-Related
16,100   John Carter Brown Library, Providence, RI

General
125,000   Fidelity Investments Charitable Gift Fund, Boston, MA
100,000   Pacific Research Institute for Public Policy, San Francisco, CA
59,000   Claremont Institute, Claremont, CA
50,000   Intercollegiate Studies Institute, Wilmington, DE
50,000   National Review Institute, New York, NY
37,000   The Heritage Foundation, Washington, DC
26,000   Fund for Living American Government, Washington, DC
25,000   Locke Institute
20,000   American Enterprise Institute, Washington, DC
20,000   American Spectator Educational Foundation, Arlington, VA

COLEMAN FOUNDATION (IL)

Giving Contact
Michael W. Hennessy, President
575 West Madison Street, Suite 4605
Chicago, IL 60661-2549
Phone: (312)902-7120
Fax: (312)902-7124
E-mail: Coleman@colemanfoundation.org
Web: http://www.colemanfoundation.org

Description
Founded: 1953
EIN: 363025967
Organization Type: General Purpose Foundation
Giving Locations: IL: Chicago nationally; especially the midwest.
Grant Types: Capital, Challenge, Conference/Seminar, General Support, Matching, Multiyear/Continuing Support, Project, Research.

Donor Information
Founder: The Foundation was established in 1953 by the late J. D. Stetson Coleman and the late Dorothy W. Coleman. The Colemans owned Fannie May Candies from 1936 through 1977.

Financial Summary
Total Giving: $6,000,000 (2003 approx); $6,000,000 (2002); $7,130,578 (2000)
Giving Analysis: Giving for 2000 includes: foundation scholarships ($73,800); foundation matching gifts

($190,105); 1999: foundation grants to United Way ($4,000); foundation scholarships ($90,000); 1998: foundation scholarships ($39,000) foundation matching gifts ($277,423)
Assets: $150,000,000 (2003 approx); $150,000,000 (2002); $191,309,383 (2000)

Typical Recipients

Arts & Humanities: Arts Centers, Arts & Humanities-General, History & Archaeology, Libraries, Museums/Galleries, Music, Theater

Civic & Public Affairs: Asian American Affairs, Business/Free Enterprise, Clubs, Community Foundations, Economic Development, Employment/Job Training, Civic & Public Affairs-General, Hispanic Affairs, Housing, Municipalities/Towns, Nonprofit Management, Philanthropic Organizations, Public Policy, Safety, Urban & Community Affairs, Women's Affairs

Education: Business Education, Colleges & Universities, Education Associations, Education Funds, Elementary Education (Public), Engineering/Technological Education, Education-General, International Studies, Medical Education, Minority Education, Preschool Education, Private Education (Precollege), Public Education (Precollege), Religious Education, Secondary Education (Private), Secondary Education (Public), Student Aid

Health: AIDS/HIV, Cancer, Clinics/Medical Centers, Eyes/Blindness, Health Organizations, Hospices, Hospitals, Hospitals (University Affiliated), Medical Rehabilitation, Medical Research, Preventive Medicine/Wellness Organizations, Public Health, Research/Studies Institutes, Single-Disease Health Associations

Religion: Churches, Dioceses, Jewish Causes, Missionary Activities (Domestic), Religious Welfare

Science: Scientific Research

Social Services: Child Welfare, Community Centers, Community Service Organizations, Emergency Relief, Food/Clothing Distribution, People with Disabilities, Sexual Abuse, Shelters/Homelessness, Social Services-General, YMCA/YWCA/YMHA/YWHA, Youth Organizations

Application Procedures

Initial Contact: Submit a brief letter of inquiry (2 pages maximum).

Application Requirements: Include history of the organization, explanation of need, explanation of goals and objectives, amount requested, complete proposal along with project budget, names of other donors with amounts, and alternative sources of funding. All grant applicants must qualify under current IRS Laws and Code Sections 509(a)(1), (2), or (3) or 501(c)(3) and/or other applicable sections of the Internal Revenue Code.

Deadlines: None.

Review Process: The board generally meets in February, May, August, and November. Applicants will be notified of a decision about three months after receipt of proposal.

Restrictions

The foundation does not respond to unsolicited grant proposals, form letters, telephone solicitations, mass mailings, or requests for ticket purchases. The foundation does not make grants to individuals, for deficit financing, for loans, or for programs outside the United States. Applicants should not expect ongoing support. Grant agreements are required before funds are disbursed.

Additional Information

Publications: Financial Statement; Guidelines; Application Procedures and History

Foundation Officials

C. Hugh Albers: chairman
Trevor C. Davies: chief financial officer treasurer, assistant secretary
R. Michael Furlong: director

Michael W. Hennessy: president, chief executive officer, director B 1951. ED University of Colorado (1973). PRIM CORP EMPL chairman, president, chief executive officer, director: Lovejoy Inc.

John Edwin Hughes: chairman B Beloit, WI 1927. ED Northwestern University; University of Illinois. PRIM CORP EMPL chairman, president, chief executive officer: J.E. Hughes Enterprises. NONPR AFFIL chairman: Council Entrepreneurship Awareness & Education; member: Institute of Management Accountants; member: American Accounting Association; member: American Institute of Certified Public Accountants.

James H. Jones: section, assistant treasurer, PRIM CORP EMPL treasurer, secretary: Archibald Candy Corp.

Grants Analysis

Disclosure Period: calendar year ending 2000
Total Grants: $7,130,578
Number of Grants: 253
Average Grant: $28,184
Highest Grant: $400,000
Typical Range: $5,000 to $50,000

Recent Grants

Note: Grants derived from 2000 Form 990.

General

400,000	Providence-St. Mel High School, Chicago, IL -- support
364,150	Wellness House, Hinsdale, IL
362,000	Rush Presbyterian St. Luke's Medical Center, Chicago, IL -- program development
200,000	Cristo Rey Jesuit High School, Chicago, IL
200,000	Northwestern University Medical School, Chicago, IL
160,000	United States Association for Small Business and Entrepreneurship, Madison, WI
150,000	North Central College, Naperville, IL -- professorships
145,000	Institute for Entrepreneurship, Greenville, WI -- education
121,000	Rush Presbyterian St. Luke's Medical Center, Chicago, IL -- program development
114,000	St. Louis University, St. Louis, MO

COLLINS FOUNDATION

Giving Contact

Dr. Jerry E. Hudson, Executive Vice President
1618 Southwest 1st Avenue, Suite 505
Portland, OR 97201-5706
Phone: (503)227-7171
Fax: (503)295-3794
E-mail: information@collinsfoundation.org
Web: http://www.collinsfoundation.org

Description

Founded: 1947
EIN: 936021893
Organization Type: Family Foundation
Giving Locations: OR
Grant Types: Award, Capital, Challenge, General Support, Project.

Donor Information

Founder: The Collins Foundation was established in Oregon in 1947 by members of the Collins family. The Collins family is involved in the lumber and wood products industry. Family members serve on the board of directors of the Collins Pine Company.

Financial Summary

Total Giving: $7,986,550 (2001); $7,996,859 (2000); $8,559,848 (1999)
Giving Analysis: Giving for 1999 includes: foundation grants to United Way ($1,000)
Assets: $166,235,818 (2001); $180,072,848 (2000); $171,933,982 (1999)

Typical Recipients

Arts & Humanities: Arts Associations & Councils, Arts Centers, Arts Festivals, Arts Institutes, Arts Outreach, Ballet, Dance, Ethnic & Folk Arts, Arts & Humanities-General, Historic Preservation, History & Archaeology, Libraries, Museums/Galleries, Music, Opera, Performing Arts, Public Broadcasting, Theater

Civic & Public Affairs: Botanical Gardens/Parks, Community Foundations, Economic Development, Employment/Job Training, Civic & Public Affairs-General, Housing, Urban & Community Affairs, Zoos/Aquariums

Education: Afterschool/Enrichment Programs, Arts/Humanities Education, Colleges & Universities, Education Funds, Environmental Education, Education-General, Health & Physical Education, Leadership Training, Legal Education, Literacy, Minority Education, Preschool Education, Private Education (Precollege), Religious Education, Science/Mathematics Education, Special Education, Student Aid

Environment: Air/Water Quality, Environment-General, Resource Conservation

Health: Alzheimers Disease, Cancer, Children's Health/Hospitals, Clinics/Medical Centers, Emergency/Ambulance Services, Health Funds, Health Organizations, Heart, Hospices, Hospitals, Hospitals (University Affiliated), Medical Research, Mental Health, Prenatal Health Issues, Preventive Medicine/Wellness Organizations, Public Health, Research/Studies Institutes, Trauma Treatment

International: Health Care/Hospitals, International Environmental Issues

Religion: Churches, Churches, Ministries, Religious Organizations, Religious Welfare, Seminaries

Science: Science Museums

Social Services: Animal Protection, Child Welfare, Community Centers, Community Service Organizations, Day Care, Family Planning, Family Services, Food/Clothing Distribution, Homes, People with Disabilities, Recreation & Athletics, Scouts, Senior Services, Shelters/Homelessness, Substance Abuse, United Funds/United Ways, Volunteer Services, YMCA/YWCA/YMHA/YWHA, Youth Organizations

Application Procedures

Initial Contact: Interested organizations should submit a written application to the foundation.

Application Requirements: Applications must include the name of the charitable organization; date the grant is needed; budget; copy of IRS determination letter of tax-exempt status; description of project; list of the board of directors; estimated total funds required and amount needed from the foundation; anticipated sources of remaining funds; list of other contributors; and other sources being approached for funding.

Deadlines: None.

Review Process: Processing of applications requires four to eight weeks.

Restrictions

The foundation does not give grants to individuals.

Additional Information

Publications: Annual Report; Guidelines

Foundation Officials

Timothy R. Bishop: treasurer B 1951. ED University of Oregon BS (1974). PRIM CORP EMPL vice president, treasurer: Collins Pine Co. CORP AFFIL treasurer: Collins Resources Int Ltd.; vice president, treasurer: Ostrander Resources Co.

Ralph Bolliger: vice president, trustee
Maribeth Wilson Collins: president, trustee B Portland, OR October 27, 1918. ED University of Oregon BA (1940). CORP AFFIL director: Ostrander Resources Co.; director: CP Specialties Division; director: Kane Hardwood Division; director: Collins Holding Co.; director: Collins Pine Co.; director: Chester Division; director: Builders Supply Division. NONPR AFFIL member: Gamma Phi Beta; member executive committee, secretary board trustees: Willamette University. CLUB AFFIL University Club.
Truman W. Collins, Jr.: vice president, trustee
Jerry E. Hudson: executive vice president B Chattanooga, TN 1938. ED David Lipscomb College BA (1959); Tulane University MA (1961); Tulane University PhD (1965). CORP AFFIL director: Portland General Electric Co. NONPR AFFIL director: National Association Independent Colleges & Universities; member: Phi Alpha Theta; director: EIIA.
Cherida C. Smith: vice president, trustee CORP AFFIL director: CP Specialties Division; director: Kane Hardwood Division; director: Collins Pine Co.; director: Builders Supply Division; director: Chester Division.

Grants Analysis

Disclosure Period: calendar year ending 2000
Total Grants: $7,996,859*
Number of Grants: 268
Average Grant: $33,046
Highest Grant: $650,000
Lowest Grant: $500
Typical Range: $2,500 to $50,000
***Note:** Giving excludes United Way.

Recent Grants

Note: Grants derived from 2000 Form 990.

Library-Related

100,000	Eugene Public Library Foundation, Eugene, OR -- construction of new library

General

300,000	Reed College, Portland, OR -- renovation and expansion of Reed College biology building
300,000	Willamette University, Portland, OR -- construction of new student recreation and activities center
225,000	Ecumenical Ministries of Oregon, Portland, OR -- support of programs and renovation of the Patton Home
200,000	Oregon Public Broadcasting, Portland, OR -- support of the World of Learning Campaign and sponsorship of two OPB programs
200,000	St. Vincent Medical Foundation, Portland, OR -- purchase of a prototype robotic cardiac surgical system
175,000	Oregon Food Bank, Portland, OR -- construction of warehouse and office facility
150,000	Portland Opera Association, Portland, OR -- enhancement of artistic venture fund
150,000	United Methodist Church, Oregon-Idaho Annual Conference, Portland, OR -- continued support of programs
100,000	Caitlin Gabel School, Portland, OR -- construction o upper school library
100,000	George Fox University, Newberg, OR -- construction of Edward Stevens Center

George And Jennie Collins Foundation

Giving Contact

Roger B. Collins, Chairman
2627 E. 21st St., Suite 200
Tulsa, OK 74114-1710
Phone: (918)744-5607

Description

Founded: 1943
EIN: 736093053
Organization Type: Private Foundation
Giving Locations: OK
Grant Types: Capital, General Support, Scholarship.

Donor Information

Founder: George F. Collins, Jr., Liberty Glass Co., and others

Financial Summary

Total Giving: $329,399 (2002); $351,870 (2001); $455,670 (2000)
Assets: $5,151,084 (2002); $5,273,647 (2001); $6,128,622 (2000)
Gifts Received: $100 (1999); $100 (1996); $500 (1995)

Typical Recipients

Arts & Humanities: Community Arts, Arts & Humanities-General, History & Archaeology, Libraries, Museums/Galleries, Music
Civic & Public Affairs: Civic & Public Affairs-General, Housing
Education: Business Education, Colleges & Universities, Education Funds, Faculty Development, Private Education (Precollege)
Health: Alzheimers Disease, Health Organizations, Hospices, Hospitals
Religion: Churches, Missionary Activities (Domestic), Religious Organizations, Religious Welfare
Social Services: Child Welfare, Community Service Organizations, Recreation & Athletics, Sexual Abuse, Shelters/Homelessness, Social Services-General, United Funds/United Ways, YMCA/YWCA/YMHA/YWHA

Application Procedures

Initial Contact: Send a brief letter of inquiry.
Application Requirements: Include a description of organization amount requested, purpose of funds sought, proof of tax-exempt status.
Deadlines: None.

Restrictions

Does not support individuals, religious organizations for sectarian purposes, political or lobbying groups, organizations outside operating areas

Foundation Officials

Frances R. Collins: trustee
Fulton Collins: trustee B 1943. ED Stanford University BA; Stanford University MBA; Stanford University MS. PRIM CORP EMPL chairman, director: Summit Acceptance Corp.
Roger B. Collins: chairman

Grants Analysis

Disclosure Period: calendar year ending 2002
Total Grants: $329,399
Number of Grants: 11
Average Grant: $11,567*
Highest Grant: $125,300
Lowest Grant: $2,500
Typical Range: $5,000 to $25,000
***Note:** Average grant figure excludes two highest grants ($225,300).

Recent Grants

Note: Grants derived from 2001 Form 990.

General

150,000	First Presbyterian Church, Tulsa, OK -- for operations
118,000	Holland Hall, Tulsa, OK -- for operations
40,000	Baker University, Baldwin City, KS -- for operations
20,370	Salvation Army, Tulsa, OK -- for operations
10,000	University of Tulsa, Tulsa, OK -- for operations
5,000	Habitat for Humanity, Tulsa, OK -- for operations
3,000	Tulsa Philharmonic, Tulsa, OK -- for operations
1,500	12 and 12, Inc., Tulsa, OK -- for operations
1,500	University of Tulsa, Tulsa, OK -- for operations
1,200	Junior Achievement of Tulsa, Tulsa, OK -- for operations

George Fulton Collins, Jr. Foundation

Giving Contact

Fulton Collins, Chairman
1924 S. Utica, Suite 800
Tulsa, OK 74104
Phone: (918)748-9860

Description

Founded: 1968
EIN: 237008179
Organization Type: Private Foundation
Giving Locations: OK
Grant Types: Capital, Scholarship.

Financial Summary

Total Giving: $215,000 (2001); $210,000 (2000); $112,000 (1999)
Assets: $3,846,918 (2001); $4,089,195 (2000); $4,446,178 (1999)
Gifts Received: $500 (2000); $500 (1996). Note: In 1996, contributions were received from G. Fulton Collins III.

Typical Recipients

Arts & Humanities: Community Arts, Libraries, Museums/Galleries
Civic & Public Affairs: Women's Affairs, Zoos/Aquariums
Education: Colleges & Universities, Literacy, Private Education (Precollege), Public Education (Precollege), Secondary Education (Private)
Health: Emergency/Ambulance Services, Health Funds, Health Organizations
Religion: Churches, Religious Organizations, Religious Welfare
Social Services: Child Welfare, Community Service Organizations, Counseling, Food/Clothing Distribution, Recreation & Athletics, Sexual Abuse, Shelters/Homelessness, YMCA/YWCA/YMHA/YWHA

Application Procedures

Initial Contact: Send a brief letter of inquiry.
Application Requirements: Include purpose of funds sought, amount requested, and how funds will be utilized.
Deadlines: None.

Foundation Officials

Fulton Collins: chairman B 1943. ED Stanford University BA; Stanford University MBA; Stanford University MS. PRIM CORP EMPL chairman, director: Summit Acceptance Corp.
Roger B. Collins: treasurer
Suzanne M. Collins: secretary

Grants Analysis

Disclosure Period: calendar year ending 2001
Total Grants: $215,000
Number of Grants: 1

Recent Grants

Note: Grants derived from 2001 Form 990.

General

215,000   University of Tulsa, Tulsa, OK

COLLINS MEDICAL TRUST

Giving Contact

Nancy L. Helseth, Administrator
1618 SW 1st Avenue, Suite 500
Portland, OR 97201-5706
Phone: (503)227-1219

Description

Founded: 1956
EIN: 936021895
Organization Type: Private Foundation
Giving Locations: OR: OR
Grant Types: Research, Scholarship.

Donor Information

Founder: the late Truman W. Collins

Financial Summary

Total Giving: $325,600 (fiscal year ending September 30, 2001); $323,291 (fiscal 2000); $348,650 (fiscal 1998). Note: In fiscal 1997, Giving includes scholarship ($25,000).
Giving Analysis: Giving for fiscal 2001 includes: foundation scholarships ($60,000); fiscal 2000: foundation scholarships ($35,000); fiscal 1998: foundation scholarships ($31,500) foundation ($317,150)
Assets: $6,559,797 (fiscal 2001); $6,952,913 (fiscal 2000); $6,589,420 (fiscal 1998)

Typical Recipients

Arts & Humanities: Libraries, Museums/Galleries
Education: Colleges & Universities, Education Funds, Engineering/Technological Education, Health & Physical Education, Medical Education, Science/Mathematics Education, Student Aid
Health: Alzheimers Disease, Clinics/Medical Centers, Eyes/Blindness, Health-General, Health Policy/Cost Containment, Health Organizations, Heart, Hospices, Hospitals, Medical Research, Medical Training, Nursing Services, Public Health, Single-Disease Health Associations, Speech & Hearing
Science: Scientific Research
Social Services: Child Welfare, Community Service Organizations, Family Services, Veterans

Application Procedures

Initial Contact: Send a brief letter of inquiry.
Application Requirements: Include a description of organization of project, amount requested, and proof of tax-exempt status.
Deadlines: None.

Restrictions

Grants restricted to research, education, and work in the medical research field.

Foundation Officials

Timothy R. Bishop: treasurer B 1951. ED University of Oregon BS (1974). PRIM CORP EMPL vice president, treasurer: Collins Pine Co. CORP AFFIL treasurer: Collins Resources Int Ltd.; vice president, treasurer: Ostrander Resources Co.
Maribeth Wilson Collins: trustee B Portland, OR October 27, 1918. ED University of Oregon BA (1940). CORP AFFIL director: Ostrander Resources Co.; director: CP Specialties Division; director: Kane Hardwood Division; director: Collins Holding Co.; director: Collins Pine Co.; director: Chester Division; director: Builders Supply Division. NONPR AFFIL member: Gamma Phi Beta; member executive committee, secretary board trustees: Willamette University. CLUB AFFIL University Club.

Truman W. Collins, Jr.: trustee
Nancy L. Helseth: admin
Joseph F. Paquet, MD: trustee
James Randolph Patterson: trustee B Lancaster, PA 1942. ED University of Pennsylvania AB (1964); Columbia University MD (1968). CORP AFFIL pulmonary & critical care specialist: Oregon Clinic. NONPR AFFIL member: Pacific Interurban Clinic; member: Pacific Society Internal Medicine; member: Oregon Society Critical Care Medicine; member: Oregon Lung Association; member: Oregon Medicine Association; clinical professor medicine: Oregon Health Sciences University; member: Multnomah County Medicine Society; member: North Pacific Society Internal Medicine; member: American Thoracic Society; member: American Board Internal Medicine; member: American College Chest Physicians.

Grants Analysis

Disclosure Period: fiscal year ending September 30, 2001
Total Grants: $256,600*
Number of Grants: 13*
Average Grant: $20,431
Highest Grant: $30,000
Lowest Grant: $5,000
Typical Range: $10,000 to $25,000
*Note: Giving excludes scholarships.

Recent Grants

Note: Grants derived from fiscal 2000 Form 990.

General

35,000	Linfield College School of Nursing, McMinnville, OR -- nursing scholarship
34,975	Oregon Health Sciences Foundation, Portland, OR -- establishing a site for drug intervention in glaucoma
25,040	Oregon Health Sciences Foundation, Portland, OR -- role of bacterial vaginosis in post-cesarean uterine infection
25,000	Oregon Health Sciences Foundation, Portland, OR -- genetic mechanisms of cardia arrhythmia in heart failure
25,000	Oregon Health Sciences Foundation, Portland, OR -- acanthamoeba eye infections
25,000	Oregon Health Sciences Foundation, Portland, OR -- effects of iugur in microswine on renal versus extrarenal vascular function in adult offspring
25,000	Oregon Hospice Association, Portland, OR -- hospice and palliative care
25,000	Portland Veterans Affairs Medical, Portland, OR -- novel antimalarial drug development
23,650	Oregon Health Sciences Foundation, Portland, OR -- connective tissue changes in pelvic organ prolapse in women
20,500	Oregon Health Sciences Foundation, Portland, OR -- dangerous decibels: preventing hearing loss in children

COLLIS FOUNDATION

Giving Contact

Astrid C. Womble, Executive Director
30 Spruce Street
Riverside, CT 06878
Phone: (203)637-8329

Description

Founded: 1997
EIN: 061472006
Organization Type: Private Foundation
Giving Locations: New England area.
Grant Types: General Support.

Financial Summary

Total Giving: $494,500 (fiscal year ending 8, 2002); $388,525 (fiscal 2001); $289,500 (fiscal 2000)
Giving Analysis: Giving for fiscal 2001 includes: foundation scholarships ($18,000) fiscal 2000: foundation scholarships ($108,000)
Assets: $9,073,941 (fiscal 2002); $10,304,135 (fiscal 2001); $10,794,965 (fiscal 2000)
Gifts Received: $5,000,153 (fiscal 1997). Note: In fiscal 1997, contributions were received from Charles A. Collis.

Typical Recipients

Arts & Humanities: History & Archaeology, Libraries, Museums/Galleries, Music
Civic & Public Affairs: Civic & Public Affairs-General, Women's Affairs
Education: Education-General, Private Education (Precollege)
Religion: Religious Welfare
Social Services: Community Service Organizations, Food/Clothing Distribution, YMCA/YWCA/YMHA/YWHA, Youth Organizations

Application Procedures

Initial Contact: Submit a two- to three-page letter of inquiry.
Application Requirements: Include a brief statement of the organization's purpose and goals; a description of the project, the need it addresses, and the target population (if applicable); the capability of the leadership to implement the proposed project; anticipated short- and long-term outcomes; method for evaluating success; amount requested; recently audited financial statement; a statement about the total agency budget and project budget, if different; committed and anticipated funding sources for the agency and/or project; proof of tax-exempt status; and a copy of the organization's budget.
Deadlines: None.
Notes: If the proposal is for $1,000 or less, the foundation may be able to evaluate the request based on the letter of inquiry.
Current grantees should contact the executive director before submitting a new proposal.

Restrictions

The foundation funds only charitable organizations located in New England.

Foundation Officials

Charles A. Collis: director
Elfried A. Collis: director
Astrid C. Womble: executive director, president, director

Grants Analysis

Total Grants: $370,525*
Number of Grants: 25
Average Grant: $10,063*
Highest Grant: $105,025
Lowest Grant: $2,500
Typical Range: $5,000 to $20,000
*Note: Average grant excludes highest grant. Giving excludes scholarship.

Recent Grants

Note: Grants derived from fiscal 2001 Form 990.

Library-Related

10,000	Providence Public Library, Providence, RI -- program for young readers

General

105,025	Community Preparatory School, Providence, RI -- endowment
62,500	Gordon School, Providence, RI -- for capital campaign
40,000	San Miguel Education Center, San Diego, CA -- support of center
25,000	Rhode Island Philharmonic, Providence, RI -- for capital

15,000	Dorcas Place Literacy Center, Providence, RI -- support of center
15,000	Moses Brown School, Providence, RI -- for scholarship
15,000	Moses Brown School, Providence, RI -- for Access Program
15,000	Rhode Island Community Food Bank, Warwick, RI -- for operating budget
10,000	Amos House, Providence, RI -- for operating budget
10,000	Children's Museum of Rhode Island, Providence, RI -- for museum support

COLONIAL LIFE & ACCIDENT INSURANCE CO.

Company Headquarters
1200 Colonial Life Blvd., W.
Columbia, SC 29210
Web: http://www.coloniallife.com

Company Description
Founded: 1939
Parent Company: UnumProvident, 1 Fountain Sq., Chattanooga, TN, United States

Nonmonetary Support
Type: Donated Equipment; In-kind Services; Loaned Employees; Loaned Executives

Giving Contact
Donna Northam, Assistant Vice President
Corporate & External Communication
1200 Colonial Life Blvd.
PO Box 1365
Columbia, SC 29202
Phone: (803)213-5634
Fax: (803)213-7461
E-mail: dcnortham@unum.com
Web: http://www.coloniallife.com/about/ColonialCares.asp

Description
Organization Type: Corporate Giving Program
Giving Locations: SC
Grant Types: General Support.

Financial Summary
Total Giving: $560,000 (1996 approx); $500,000 (1994 approx); $500,000 (1993 approx). Note: Contributes through corporate direct giving program only.

Typical Recipients
Arts & Humanities: Arts Appreciation, Arts Associations & Councils, Arts Centers, Arts Festivals, Arts Institutes, Community Arts, Dance, Ethnic & Folk Arts, Historic Preservation, Libraries, Museums/Galleries, Music, Opera, Performing Arts, Theater, Visual Arts
Civic & Public Affairs: Business/Free Enterprise, Economic Development, Economic Policy, Employment/Job Training, Housing, Law & Justice, Legal Aid, Nonprofit Management, Philanthropic Organizations, Professional & Trade Associations, Safety, Zoos/Aquariums
Education: Agricultural Education, Arts/Humanities Education, Business Education, Colleges & Universities, Community & Junior Colleges, Economic Education, International Exchange, International Studies, Private Education (Precollege), Public Education (Precollege), Student Aid
Environment: Environment-General
Health: Emergency/Ambulance Services, Geriatric Health, Health Policy/Cost Containment, Hospices, Hospitals, Medical Research, Medical Training, Mental Health, Nursing Services, Public Health, Single-Disease Health Associations
Social Services: Animal Protection, Child Welfare, Community Centers, Community Service Organizations, Counseling, Day Care, Delinquency & Criminal Rehabilitation, Domestic Violence, Emergency Relief, Family Planning, Family Services, Food/Clothing Distribution, Homes, People with Disabilities, Recreation & Athletics, Refugee Assistance, Senior Services, Substance Abuse, United Funds/United Ways, Volunteer Services, Youth Organizations

Application Procedures
Initial Contact: Send a brief letter of inquiry.
Application Requirements: Include a description of organization, amount requested, purpose of funds sought, recently audited financial statements, and proof of tax-exempt status.
Deadlines: September 1 for the following year.

Restrictions
The company does not support beauty contests, fashion shows, adversarial groups, individuals, religious organizations for sectarian purposes, or political or lobbying groups.

Giving Program Officials
Edwina Carms: PRIM CORP EMPL community service administration: Colonial Life & Accident Insurance Co.

Grants Analysis
Typical Range: $1,000 to $2,500

COLONIAL OAKS FOUNDATION

Giving Contact
Kristin E. McGlinn, Co-Executive Director
850 N. Wyomissing Boulevard, Suite 200
Wyomissing, PA 19610
Phone: (610)988-2400

Description
Founded: 1992
EIN: 232705277
Organization Type: Private Foundation
Giving Locations: PA: Berks County
Grant Types: General Support.

Donor Information
Founder: Established in 1992 by Terrence J. McGlinn.

Financial Summary
Total Giving: $799,220 (fiscal year ending September 30, 2000); $1,012,100 (fiscal 1999); $584,850 (fiscal 1998)
Giving Analysis: Giving for fiscal 2000 includes: foundation grants to United Way ($10,000); fiscal 1999: foundation grants to United Way ($10,000) fiscal 1998: foundation grants to United Way ($20,000)
Assets: $17,256,590 (fiscal 2000); $17,017,996 (fiscal 1999); $17,500,394 (fiscal 1998)
Gifts Received: $1,627,000 (fiscal 1998); $6,588,450 (fiscal 1997); $4,000 (fiscal 1996). Note: In 1998, contributions were received from James A. Walker ($5,000) and Terrence J. McGlinn ($1,622,000). In fiscal 1995, contributions were received from Terrence J. McGlinn.

Typical Recipients
Arts & Humanities: Arts Institutes, History & Archaeology, Libraries, Museums/Galleries, Music
Civic & Public Affairs: Clubs, Civic & Public Affairs-General, Housing, Philanthropic Organizations
Education: Arts/Humanities Education, Business Education, Colleges & Universities, Community & Junior Colleges, Education Funds, Education-General, Literacy, Private Education (Precollege), Public Education (Precollege), Secondary Education (Private), Special Education, Student Aid
Environment: Resource Conservation
Health: AIDS/HIV, Arthritis, Cancer, Children's Health/Hospitals, Clinics/Medical Centers, Emergency/Ambulance Services, Hospices, Hospitals, Long-Term Care, Medical Research, Prenatal Health Issues, Single-Disease Health Associations
Religion: Churches, Jewish Causes, Ministries, Religious Organizations, Religious Welfare
Social Services: At-Risk Youth, Child Welfare, Community Service Organizations, Domestic Violence, Food/Clothing Distribution, Recreation & Athletics, Scouts, Shelters/Homelessness, Substance Abuse, United Funds/United Ways, Youth Organizations

Application Procedures
Initial Contact: Send a brief letter of inquiry.
Deadlines: None.

Foundation Officials
Barbara T. McGlinn: assistant secretary
John F. McGlinn, II: assistant treasurer
Terrence J. McGlinn, Jr.: director
Terrence J. McGlinn: president
Christine R. McGlinn Auman: executive director, secretary
Margaret M. Shields: treasurer

Grants Analysis
Disclosure Period: fiscal year ending September 30, 2000
Total Grants: $789,220*
Number of Grants: 75
Average Grant: $8,706*
Highest Grant: $145,000
Typical Range: $1,000 to $20,000
*****Note:** Giving excludes United Way. Average grant excludes highest grant.

Recent Grants
Note: Grants derived from fiscal 1999 Form 990.

General
308,000	Holy Name High School, Reading, PA -- expand and improve the school
103,000	St. Ignatius RC Church, Sinking Spring, PA -- church and rectory renovation campaigns
50,500	Caron Foundation, Wernersville, PA
25,000	Alvernia College, Reading, PA -- student center building campaign
25,000	Bethany Children's Home, Womelsdorf, PA -- capital campaign for shelter care housing and program for children in crisis situation
25,000	Easter Seal Society, Reading, PA -- research cause and prevention of birth defects
25,000	Hospice of St. Joseph County, South Bend, IN -- build facility to assist terminally ill patients and their families
25,000	Reading Hospital and Medical Center, Reading, PA
25,000	St. Katherine of Siena Parish, Wayne, PA -- parish campaign to renovate church and school
25,000	Wyomissing Institute of Fine Arts, Wyomissing, PA

JAMES J. COLT FOUNDATION

Giving Contact
Thomas H. Heard, President & Director
PO Box 9130
Lyndhurst, NJ 07071
Phone: (201)804-8322

Description

Founded: 1952
EIN: 136112997
Organization Type: Private Foundation
Giving Locations: CA; FL: Miami including surrounding area; NY
Grant Types: General Support, Scholarship.

Donor Information

Founder: the late James J. Colt

Financial Summary

Total Giving: $88,450 (2001); $69,300 (2000); $145,750 (1999)
Assets: $266,755 (2001); $358,941 (2000); $419,174 (1999)
Gifts Received: $89,740 (1994). Note: In 1994, contributions were received from the estate of Anita Heard.

Typical Recipients

Arts & Humanities: Historic Preservation, History & Archaeology, Libraries, Literary Arts, Museums/Galleries, Public Broadcasting
Civic & Public Affairs: Clubs, Civic & Public Affairs-General, Municipalities/Towns, Parades/Festivals, Safety, Urban & Community Affairs
Education: Colleges & Universities, Education-General, Medical Education, Preschool Education, Private Education (Precollege), Public Education (Precollege), School Volunteerism
Environment: Environment-General, Resource Conservation
Health: AIDS/HIV, Cancer, Children's Health/Hospitals, Clinics/Medical Centers, Diabetes, Emergency/Ambulance Services, Eyes/Blindness, Health Organizations, Heart, Hospitals, Medical Rehabilitation, Medical Research, Prenatal Health Issues, Single-Disease Health Associations
International: Missionary/Religious Activities
Religion: Churches, Jewish Causes, Ministries, Religious Welfare, Synagogues/Temples
Social Services: Animal Protection, At-Risk Youth, Child Welfare, Community Service Organizations, Crime Prevention, Emergency Relief, Homes, People with Disabilities, Recreation & Athletics, Senior Services, YMCA/YWCA/YMHA/YWHA, Youth Organizations

Application Procedures

Initial Contact: Send a brief letter of inquiry on organization's letterhead.
Application Requirements: Describe program and charitable purpose; include proof of tax-exempt status.
Deadlines: None.

Foundation Officials

Vaughn Durbin: secretary
Jane Heard: director
Karen Heard: director
Thomas H. Heard: vice president, director
Donald Oresman: treasurer B New York, NY 1925. ED Oberlin College BA (1946); Columbia University School of Law LLB (1957). CORP AFFIL officer: Movado Group Inc.; managing partner: Wellspring Associatess.

Grants Analysis

Disclosure Period: calendar year ending 2001
Total Grants: $88,450
Number of Grants: 24
Average Grant: $3,685
Highest Grant: $20,000
Lowest Grant: $100
Typical Range: $500 to $5,000

Recent Grants

Note: Grants derived from 2001 Form 990.

Library-Related

10,000	Morgan Library, New York, NY	

General

20,000	Project Newborn, Miami, FL
20,000	Women's Cancer League and Partners, Miami Beach, FL
10,000	Florida Derby Gala, Gainesville, FL
10,000	Grolier Club, New York, NY
5,000	Jackson Memorial Foundation, Miami, FL
5,000	Thoroughbred Retirement Foundation, Shrewsbury, NJ
2,500	Grace Presbyterian Church, Dalton, GA
2,500	Miami Heart Research Institute, Miami, FL
1,000	American Red Cross Disaster Relief Fund, New York, NY
1,000	Bascom Palmer Eye Institute, Miami, FL

COLUMBIA FOUNDATION

Giving Contact

Susan R. Clark, Executive Director
One Lombard Street, Suite 305
San Francisco, CA 94111
Phone: (415)986-5179
Fax: (415)986-1732
E-mail: susan@columbia.org
Web: http://www.columbia.org

Description

Founded: 1940
EIN: 941196186
Organization Type: General Purpose Foundation
Giving Locations: CA: especially northern California, San Francisco including metropolitan area; England : London
Grant Types: Capital, Project, Seed Money.

Donor Information

Founder: The Columbia Foundation was established in 1940 by Madeline Haas Russell, donor and president of the foundation. Mrs. Russell is a member of the Haas family, which owns Levi-Strauss and Company, the nation's largest manufacturer of apparel.
Mrs. Russell has been active in Democratic politics, and served on the boards at the San Francisco Museum of Art and the Asia Foundation, located in San Francisco. She has also been active in public broadcasting, health care, and education.
Christine H. Russell, the foundation's treasurer, is also a donor to the foundation.

Financial Summary

Total Giving: $3,398,521 (fiscal year ending May 31, 2001); $3,266,082 (fiscal 1999); $4,410,650 (fiscal 1998)
Assets: $80,355,102 (fiscal 2001); $86,965,250 (fiscal 1999); $70,694,573 (fiscal 1997)
Gifts Received: $42,080 (fiscal 2001); $39,274 (fiscal 1999); $6,019,085 (fiscal 1997). Note: In fiscal 2001, contributions were received from Madeleine H. Russell 1982 Charitable Lead Trust ($32,660) and SIT Investment ($9,420). In fiscal 2000, contributions were received from $38,624 from Madeleine H. Russell 1982 Charitable Lead Trust.

Typical Recipients

Arts & Humanities: Arts Associations & Councils, Arts Centers, Arts Funds, Arts Institutes, Ballet, Community Arts, Dance, Ethnic & Folk Arts, Film & Video, Arts & Humanities-General, Historic Preservation, History & Archaeology, Libraries, Literary Arts, Museums/Galleries, Music, Opera, Public Broadcasting, Theater, Visual Arts
Civic & Public Affairs: Asian American Affairs, Botanical Gardens/Parks, Civil Rights, Clubs, Community Foundations, Economic Development, Economic Policy, Employment/Job Training, First Amendment Issues, Gay/Lesbian Issues, Hispanic Affairs, Housing, Law & Justice, Legal Aid, Municipalities/Towns, Native American Affairs, Nonprofit Management, Philanthropic Organizations, Professional & Trade Associations, Public Policy, Rural Affairs, Urban & Community Affairs, Women's Affairs
Education: Afterschool/Enrichment Programs, Agricultural Education, Business Education, Colleges & Universities, Education Funds, International Studies, Private Education (Precollege), Public Education (Precollege), Vocational & Technical Education
Environment: Air/Water Quality, Forestry, Environment-General, Protection, Research, Resource Conservation, Wildlife Protection
Health: AIDS/HIV, Emergency/Ambulance Services, Health Policy/Cost Containment, Health Funds, Hospices, Long-Term Care, Medical Research, Nutrition, Preventive Medicine/Wellness Organizations, Public Health
International: Foreign Arts Organizations, Foreign Educational Institutions, Health Care/Hospitals, Human Rights, International Development, International Environmental Issues, International Organizations, International Peace & Security Issues, International Relations, Missionary/Religious Activities
Religion: Jewish Causes, Ministries, Religious Organizations, Religious Welfare, Synagogues/Temples
Science: Science Museums, Scientific Research
Social Services: At-Risk Youth, Community Centers, Community Service Organizations, Crime Prevention, Delinquency & Criminal Rehabilitation, Domestic Violence, Food/Clothing Distribution, Homes, Recreation & Athletics, Refugee Assistance, Shelters/Homelessness, Social Services-General, Volunteer Services, Youth Organizations

Application Procedures

Initial Contact: Send a letter of inquiry with an application cover sheet (available from the foundation). A full proposal will be requested if the foundation selects the application for further consideration.
Application Requirements: The letter of inquiry should be no longer than four pages and include: a description of organization; the purpose for which funds are being requested; amount requested; project budget and other sources of support; plan of action including cooperating agencies, intended results, and measurable objective if applicable. Submission of the cover sheet and letter of inquiry is sufficient for meeting the application deadline.
If the foundation requests a full proposal, it should include: a proposal narrative describing the need for the program or the problem to be addressed; plan of action including a theoretical base or rationale for this approach; the impact and significance of project, including its potential relevance; qualifications of organization and staff to implement project; relationship of program to other similar programs or agencies; how program will be evaluated; and plans for the future of program; including dissemination of results. Financial information should include the following: a line-item budget for fiscal year; statement of actual expenses and revenue for the last two years for the organization and for the project (include an audited statement if available); a list of other contributions and sources of support for project including those currently being considered. Organizational information should include: a history of organization including a description of current activities and an annual report; list of board of directors, including affiliations and occupations; a copy of IRS tax-exempt letter; and copies of articles or other publicity about organization or project.
Deadlines: Deadlines are September 1 for Human Rights; December 15 for Sustainable Communities and Economies; and June 1 for Arts and Culture. February 1. All materials should be postmarked by

the application deadline, or the following business day if the deadline falls on a weekend or holiday.

Review Process: A screening process to select applications to be considered further is completed within approximately 10 weeks after the deadline, after which all applicants are notified. At this time, those to be considered are asked to submit a full proposal. After proposals are reviewed, the staff makes recommendations to the board of directors, which makes a final decision at a meeting held in late spring or late fall. The foundation reports that it only grants funds to about thirty new applicants each year.

Notes: The foundation does not accept faxed proposals. Applicants should submit proposals on two-sided recycled paper. The duration of the project may be up to five years on a single application.

Restrictions

The foundation does not customarily provide support for operating budgets of established agencies, for recurring expenses for direct services or ongoing administrative costs, for individual fellowships or scholarships, or for agencies wholly supported by federated campaigns or heavily subsidized by government funds.

Additional Information

The foundation considers proposals only from organizations certified by the IRS as public charities.

The foundation does not assume an obligation for ongoing support for any activity. It awards a few large multi-year grants of $300,000 to $1,000,000 paid over three to five years, designed to allow an organization to make a major contribution to its field. Grants of $25,000 to $100,000 may be awarded as a single grant or as a multi-year pledge. The foundation focuses its grant making on major arts organizations in San Francisco and London, as well as the Creative Work Fund which, in turn, awards grants to individual artists.

Publications: Application Guidelines; Program Policy Statement; Annual Report; Grants list; Five-year report

Foundation Officials

Susan R. Clark: executive director

Charles P. Russell: vice president, board of director

Christine Haas Russell: secretary, program consult, donor PRIM CORP EMPL chief financial officer: Persistence Software Inc.

Madeleine Haas Russell: president, donor B San Francisco, CA 1915. ED Smith College BA (1937). NONPR AFFIL trustee: Brandeis University; trustee: San Francisco Museum Modern Art.

Alice Russell-Shapiro: treasurer, board directors

Grants Analysis

Disclosure Period: fiscal year ending May 31, 2001
Total Grants: $3,266,082
Number of Grants: 92
Average Grant: $28,890*
Highest Grant: $333,000
Typical Range: $10,000 to $50,000
*Note: Average grant figure excludes two highest grants ($666,000).

Recent Grants

Note: Grants derived from 2000 Form 990.

General

333,000	Congregation Emanu-El, San Francisco, CA -- to establish an endowment
333,000	San Francisco Opera, San Francisco, CA -- to establish an endowment
150,000	Walter and Elise Haas Fund, San Francisco, CA -- for the Creative Work Fund
100,000	Asia Foundation, San Francisco, CA -- to support the Human Rights Program in Asia
100,000	Community Center Project, San Francisco, CA -- for capital campaign
100,000	Compassion in Dying Federation of

America, Portland, OR -- for organizational development and for assistance in starting up local chapters

100,000	Gay, Lesbian and Straight Education Network, San Mateo, Millbrae, CA -- to support its Western Organizing Project
100,000	Materials for the Future Foundation, San Francisco, CA -- to increase financial tools and resources to create jobs in low-income Bay Area neighborhoods
100,000	Save the Redwoods League, San Francisco, CA -- for the Redwoods to The Sea Wildlife Corridor
100,000	Tides Center, The, San Francisco, CA -- for Urban Habitat Program

COLUMBUS DISPATCH PRINTING CO.

Company Headquarters
Columbus, OH

Company Description
Employees: 1,900
SIC(s): 6200 Security & Commodity Brokers.

Operating Locations
Columbus Dispatch Printing Co. (OH--Columbus)

Nonmonetary Support
Type: In-kind Services

Wolfe Associates, Inc.

Giving Contact
Rita Wolfe Hoag, Vice President & Trustee
Wolfe Associates, Inc.
770 Twin Rivers Drive
Columbus, OH 43215
Phone: (614)460-3782
E-mail: comrel@dispatch.com
Web: http://www.dispatch.com

Description
Founded: 1973
EIN: 237303111
Organization Type: Corporate Foundation
Giving Locations: OH: Central Ohio and other areas in which the corporate donors have a substantial presence
Grant Types: Capital, Conference/Seminar, Endowment, General Support, Project, Scholarship.

Financial Summary
Total Giving: $3,329,866 (fiscal year ending June 31, 2001); $2,298,011 (fiscal 2000); $2,353,871 (fiscal 1997). Note: Contributes through foundation only.
Giving Analysis: Giving for fiscal 2001 includes: foundation grants to United Way ($869,219); foundation ($2,460,647); fiscal 2000: foundation scholarships ($31,000); foundation grants to United Way ($471,575); foundation ($1,795,436); fiscal 1997: foundation grants to United Way ($315,866); foundation ($2,038,005);
Assets: $8,582,601 (fiscal 2001); $9,722,053 (fiscal 2000); $6,001,608 (fiscal 1997)
Gifts Received: $1,989,860 (fiscal 2001); $734,313 (fiscal 2000); $1,057,900 (fiscal 1997). In fiscal 2001, contributions were received from Dispatch. In fiscal 2000, contributions were received from Dispatch ($421,363); WTHR ($191,500); WBNS ($107,000); and DCS ($14,450). In fiscal 1997 contributions were received from Dispatch Printing Co., WBNS-TV, Inc., The Ohio Co., and WTHR.

Typical Recipients
Arts & Humanities: Arts Associations & Councils, Arts Centers, Arts Funds, Arts Institutes, Ballet, Dance, Historic Preservation, History & Archaeology, Libraries, Literary Arts, Museums/Galleries, Music, Opera, Performing Arts, Public Broadcasting, Theater
Civic & Public Affairs: African American Affairs, Business/Free Enterprise, Chambers of Commerce, Clubs, Community Foundations, Economic Development, Economic Policy, Employment/Job Training, Ethnic Organizations, Civic & Public Affairs-General, Housing, Law & Justice, Legal Aid, Municipalities/Towns, Philanthropic Organizations, Safety, Urban & Community Affairs, Zoos/Aquariums
Education: Arts/Humanities Education, Business Education, Colleges & Universities, Economic Education, Education Associations, Education Funds, Education-General, International Studies, Leadership Training, Legal Education, Literacy, Minority Education, Private Education (Precollege), Public Education (Precollege), Religious Education, Secondary Education (Private), Social Sciences Education, Student Aid
Environment: Resource Conservation
Health: Cancer, Children's Health/Hospitals, Clinics/Medical Centers, Emergency/Ambulance Services, Health-General, Health Funds, Heart, Hospices, Hospitals, Long-Term Care, Medical Rehabilitation, Medical Research, Single-Disease Health Associations
International: Health Care/Hospitals, International Relations, Trade
Religion: Churches, Dioceses, Jewish Causes, Ministries, Missionary Activities (Domestic), Religious Welfare
Science: Scientific Centers & Institutes
Social Services: Animal Protection, Child Welfare, Community Centers, Community Service Organizations, Crime Prevention, Family Planning, Food/Clothing Distribution, People with Disabilities, Senior Services, Shelters/Homelessness, Social Services-General, United Funds/United Ways, YMCA/YWCA/YMHA/YWHA, Youth Organizations

Application Procedures
Initial Contact: Submit a written request.
Application Requirements: Include a cover letter with a brief summary of purpose of funds sought, amount requested, proof of tax-exempt status, financial statements, and a copy of the organization's most recent Form 990.
Deadlines: None.

Restrictions
Foundation does not support individuals, public school systems, research and demonstration projects, publications, or conferences.

Additional Information
Corporate donors to the foundation are the Dispatch Printing Company, the Ohio Company, WBNS TV Inc., and RadiOhio Inc.

Grants are not automatically renewable and current recipients must reapply annually for continued support.

Foundation may require annual progress reports and notice of any material modification to project during the funding year.

The Columbus Dispatch also provides support directly through their community relations department. They work to develop programs that range from supporting the arts and nurturing Ohio's children, to providing music and excitement for the community through concerts and special events. For more information, contact Community Relations: (614)461-5225.

Corporate Officials
A. Kenneth Pierce, Jr.: vice president, chief financial officer, director B 1930. PRIM CORP EMPL vice president, chief financial officer, director: Dispatch Printing Co. CORP AFFIL vice president, secretary, director: Ohio Magazine Inc.

Foundation Officials

Nancy Wolfe Lane: vice president B 1939. ED Bryn Mawr College (1961). PRIM CORP EMPL vice president: Wolfe Associates, Inc.

A. Kenneth Pierce, Jr.: vice president, secretary, treasurer (see above)

William C. Wolfe, Jr.: vice president B 1951. PRIM CORP EMPL vice president, director: Dispatch Printing Co. CORP AFFIL vice president, director: Wolfe Enterprises Inc.

Grants Analysis

Disclosure Period: fiscal year ending June 31, 2001
Total Grants: $2,460,647*
Number of Grants: 194
Average Grant: $10,677*
Highest Grant: $400,000
Typical Range: $500 to $50,000
*Note: Giving excludes United Way. Average grant figure excludes highest grant.

Recent Grants

Note: Grants derived from 2001 Form 990.

General

400,000	Children's Hospital Foundation, Columbus, OH
274,648	United Way of Franklin County, Columbus, OH -- employee match
268,491	United Way, Columbus, OH
200,000	Center for Science and Industry, Columbus, OH
200,000	Diocese of Columbus, Columbus, OH -- challenge for the changing times campaign
100,000	Case Western Reserve University, Cleveland, OH -- final payment of pledge
100,000	Community Shelter Board, Columbus, OH
100,000	Salvation Army, Columbus, OH
100,000	United Way, Columbus, OH
89,455	United Way of Franklin County, Columbus, OH -- employee match

COMER FOUNDATION (AL)

Giving Contact

R. Larry Edmunds, Secretary & Treasurer
PO Box 302
Sylacauga, AL 35150
Phone: (256)249-2962
Fax: (256)249-2962

Description

Founded: 1945
EIN: 636004424
Organization Type: Private Foundation
Giving Locations: AL: Birmingham
Grant Types: Capital, General Support, Operating Expenses, Research.

Donor Information

Founder: Avondale Mills, Comer-Avondale Mills, Inc., Cowikee Mills

Financial Summary

Total Giving: $1,011,250 (2000); $1,020,361 (1999); $1,018,178 (1998)
Giving Analysis: Giving for 2000 includes: foundation grants to United Way ($4,000); foundation scholarships ($184,000); 1999: foundation grants to United Way ($4,000); foundation scholarships ($182,240); 1998: foundation grants to United Way ($4,000) foundation scholarships ($153,452)
Assets: $14,816,313 (2000); $15,244,077 (1999); $15,021,401 (1998)

Typical Recipients

Arts & Humanities: Arts Associations & Councils, Ballet, Libraries, Museums/Galleries, Music, Theater
Civic & Public Affairs: Botanical Gardens/Parks, Civic & Public Affairs-General, Housing, Municipalities/Towns, Urban & Community Affairs
Education: Afterschool/Enrichment Programs, Colleges & Universities, Economic Education, Education Funds, Education Reform, Engineering/Technological Education, Education-General, Literacy, Medical Education, Public Education (Precollege), Science/Mathematics Education, Special Education, Student Aid, Vocational & Technical Education
Environment: Environment-General
Health: Children's Health/Hospitals, Clinics/Medical Centers, Hospices, Medical Rehabilitation, Medical Research, Medical Training, Nursing Services, Respiratory
Religion: Religious Welfare
Science: Science Exhibits & Fairs, Science Museums
Social Services: Animal Protection, Camps, Child Welfare, Community Service Organizations, Family Services, People with Disabilities, Recreation & Athletics, Scouts, Substance Abuse, United Funds/United Ways, YMCA/YWCA/YMHA/YWHA, Youth Organizations

Application Procedures

Initial Contact: Send a brief letter of inquiry describing program or project.
Deadlines: None.

Foundation Officials

Richard J. Comer, Jr.: chairman
Francis H. Crockard: trustee
Marie M. Edmunds: assistant secretary, assistant treasurer
R. Larry Edmunds: secretary, treasurer
Gillian C. Goodrich: trustee
Dr. Hugh C. Nabers, Jr.: trustee
Jane B. Selfe: trustee

Grants Analysis

Disclosure Period: calendar year ending 2000
Total Grants: $823,250*
Number of Grants: 38
Average Grant: $17,791*
Highest Grant: $165,000
Lowest Grant: $250
Typical Range: $5,000 to $30,000
*Note: Giving excludes scholarships; United Way. Average grant figure excludes highest grant.

Recent Grants

Note: Grants derived from 1999 Form 990.

Library-Related

180,000	B.B. Comer Memorial School, Sylacauga, AL -- library operations and expansion of facility
50,000	Mountain Brook Library Foundation, Mountain Brook, AL -- expansion of facility

General

125,000	Greater Alabama Council Boy Scouts of America, AL -- renovate Camp Comer
61,000	Auburn University, Auburn, AL -- scholarship
50,000	Alabama Symphonic Association, Birmingham, AL -- assistance for operations
50,000	Service Guild of Birmingham, Birmingham, AL -- support program for children with spinal bifida, down syndrome
48,000	University of Alabama Birmingham, Birmingham, AL -- scholarships
33,000	University of Alabama, Tuscaloosa, AL -- scholarships
30,000	Jimmy Hale Mission -- assistance for operations center
30,000	McWane Center, Birmingham, AL -- support operations
30,000	Sylacauga Park and Recreation Board, Sylacauga, AL -- assistance of programs and operation
25,000	A Education Foundation, Montgomery, AL -- to improve reading achievement of Alabama public schools

COMERICA INC.

Company Headquarters

Comerica Tower
500 Woodward Avenue
Detroit, MI 48226
Phone: (313)222-7356
Fax: (313)222-3240
Web: http://www.comerica.com

Company Description

Founded: 1982
Ticker: CMA
Exchange: NYSE
Assets: US$53.301 billion (2002)
Profit: US$601 million (2002)
Employees: 11792 (2002)
Fortune Rank: 433, per FORTUNE Magazine's list of 500 Largest U.S. Corporations (2002).
SIC(s): 6022 State Commercial Banks, 6712 Bank Holding Companies.

Operating Locations

Comerica Inc. (CA--San Jose; FL--Boca Raton; IL--Franklin Park; MI--Battle Creek, Comstock Park, Grand Rapids, Marne; OH--Toledo); Comerica Inc. (TX--Dallas)

Nonmonetary Support

Type: In-kind Services
Volunteer Programs: Company offers Comerica Cares program in which employees participate in volunteer activities of community organizations.
Contact: Charlene Cole, Education/Volunteer Program Manager

Comerica Charitable Foundation

Giving Contact

Caroline Solomon-Chambers, Corporate Contributions Vice President
500 Woodward Avenue
Detroit, MI 48226-3352
Phone: (313)222-3571
Fax: (313)222-8720
E-mail: caroline_chambers@comerica.com
Web: http://Comerica.com/cma/cda/main/0,1555,1_A_1472,00.html

Description

Founded: 1997
EIN: 383373052
Organization Type: Corporate Foundation
Former Name: Comerica Foundation (2000).
Giving Locations: CA; FL; MI: especially southeastern MI; TX
Grant Types: Capital, Employee Matching Gifts, General Support, Operating Expenses, Scholarship.
Note: Employee matching gift ratio: 1 to 1 for gifts to colleges and universities, up to $2,000 per employee annually. Company sponsors a special one-time holiday match program.

Financial Summary

Total Giving: $6,101,689 (2001); $5,206,095 (2000); $4,857,422 (1998). Note: Contributes through foundation and corporate direct giving.

Giving Analysis: Giving for 2000 includes: foundation scholarships ($35,550); foundation grants to United Way ($1,088,850); foundation ($4,077,614); 1998: corporate direct giving ($656,641); foundation grants to United Way ($944,333) foundation ($3,256,448)

Assets: $12,281,827 (2001); $13,740,367 (2000)

Gifts Received: $5,000,000 (2001); $11,000,000 (2000); $2,000,000 (1998). Note: The foundation receives gifts from Comerica, Inc. and subsidiaries.

Typical Recipients

Arts & Humanities: Arts Festivals, Arts Institutes, History & Archaeology, Libraries, Museums/Galleries, Music, Opera, Public Broadcasting

Civic & Public Affairs: Business/Free Enterprise, Clubs, Community Foundations, Economic Development, Employment/Job Training, Civic & Public Affairs-General, Housing, Municipalities/Towns, Parades/Festivals, Public Policy, Urban & Community Affairs, Zoos/Aquariums

Education: Arts/Humanities Education, Business Education, Colleges & Universities, Education Funds, Education-General, Legal Education, Minority Education, Private Education (Precollege), Public Education (Precollege), Student Aid

Health: Cancer, Children's Health/Hospitals, Emergency/Ambulance Services, Health Organizations, Health Organizations, Hospices, Hospitals, Medical Rehabilitation, Mental Health, Single-Disease Health Associations

Religion: Jewish Causes, Religious Welfare

Science: Scientific Centers & Institutes

Social Services: At-Risk Youth, Community Service Organizations, Food/Clothing Distribution, People with Disabilities, Recreation & Athletics, Scouts, Senior Services, Social Services-General, United Funds/United Ways, Volunteer Services, Youth Organizations

Application Procedures

Initial Contact: Send a written proposal.

Application Requirements: Include concise statements about project or agency describing programs, need, budget, management, goals, and accomplishments; amount requested; itemized projection of program costs; organizational operating budgets for past two years (preferably audited statements); list of existing funding sources; current board of directors; documentation on the method in which the contribution will be used in the program; and proof of tax-exempt status.

Deadlines: None.

Review Process: After initial staff review, proposals go to corporate contributions committee which determines specific amounts or terms of contributions; organizations will receive written notification of funding decision within 60 days of receipt of request.

Notes: Organizations in Southeastern Michigan may apply to above address; other organizations should contact nearest bank branch. Comerica Foundation board ratifies final decisions concerning contributions allocations.

Restrictions

The company does not support individuals; religious, fraternal, or political organizations; charitable golf events, recreational and athletic programs; multiyear pledges; endowment funds; non-tax-exempt organizations; or organizations supported by united funds. The company avoids controversial organizations and causes.

Additional Information

The company gives primarily to private and public 501(c)(3) organizations, and prefers innovative organizations which demonstrate the ability to solve problems and provide direct services relating to economic development. Approximately 30% of Comerica's contributions are made through headquarters direct giving and 70% of contributions are made through the Comerica Foundation.

The company reports that three permanent funds have been established with the Community Foundation of Southeastern Michigan to address specific needs of the community in the areas of the arts, youth activities, and economic development. Contact the Community Foundation of Southeastern Michigan at (313) 961-6675, or submit a proposal to Vice President of Programs, 333 W. Fort Street, Suite 2010, Detroit, MI 48226.

Publications: Comerica Contributions Policy

Corporate Officials

John D. Lewis: vice chairman B 1950. PRIM CORP EMPL vice chairman: Comerica Inc. ADD CORP EMPL vice chairman: Comerica Bank; director: Comerica Bank California.

Foundation Officials

Karen Batchelor: director
Richard A. Collister: president
Linda Forte: director
Sharon McMurray: director
Karen Mulvahill: director
Mark Yonkman: director

Grants Analysis

Disclosure Period: calendar year ending 2001
Total Grants: $4,830,239*
Number of Grants: 622
Average Grant: $7,766
Highest Grant: $250,000
Lowest Grant: $25
Typical Range: $100 to $50,000 and $100,000 to $250,000
*Note: Giving excludes scholarship and United Way.

Recent Grants

Note: Grants derived from 2001 Form 990.

General

728,000	United Way, Detroit, MI -- corporate campaign
250,000	American Red Cross, New York, NY -- for New York and Washington relief efforts
217,000	Detroit 300, Inc., Detroit, MI
200,000	Detroit Institute of Arts Founders Society, Detroit, MI -- capital campaign
166,000	United Way, Detroit, MI -- for New Detroit Fund
150,000	Detroit Symphony Orchestra Hall, Detroit, MI
123,200	United Way, Detroit, MI -- for capital funds
115,000	Detroit Educational Television Foundation WTVS, Channel 56 in Detroit, Detroit, MI -- for programs
100,000	Barbara Ann Karmanos Cancer Institute, Detroit, MI
100,000	City Year, NH

COMMERCE BANCSHARES, INC.

Company Headquarters

Kansas City, MO
Web: http://www.commercebank.com

Company Description

Founded: 1966
Ticker: CBSH
Exchange: NASDAQ
Assets: US$13.308 billion (2002)
Employees: 5302 (2002)

SIC(s): 6021 National Commercial Banks, 6712 Bank Holding Companies.

Operating Locations

Commerce Bancshares, Inc. (MO--Springfield); Commerce Bancshares, Inc. (MO--St. Joseph, St. Louis); Commerce Bancshares, Inc. (NE)

Nonmonetary Support

Volunteer Programs: The company actively encourages employee volunteerism. Employees and executives also are active in United Way, Habitat for Humanity, and numerous community organizations.

Commerce Bancshares Foundation

Giving Contact

Michael D. Fields, President
PO Box 13095
Kansas City, MO 64199-3095
Phone: (816)234-2985

Alternate Contact

Sheila Rice
Phone: (816)234-8670

Description

Founded: 1952
EIN: 446012453
Organization Type: Corporate Foundation
Giving Locations: IL: West Central; KS; MO
Grant Types: General Support.

Donor Information

Founder: Commerce Bank of Kansas City, NA, Commerce Bank of Kansas City, NA, Commerce Bank of Springfield, NA

Financial Summary

Total Giving: $1,159,337 (2002); $1,265,561 (2001); $1,205,589 (2000). Note: Contributes through corporate direct giving program and foundation.

Giving Analysis: Giving for 1997 includes: foundation grants to United Way ($285,886) foundation ($739,366)

Assets: $4,688,206 (2002); $2,086,555 (2001); $3,128,751 (2000)

Gifts Received: $997,639 (1996); $16,453 (1993); $657,899 (1992). Note: In 1996, contributions were received from from Commerce Bancshares Inc.

Typical Recipients

Arts & Humanities: Arts Associations & Councils, Arts Centers, Community Arts, Historic Preservation, History & Archaeology, Libraries, Museums/Galleries, Music, Opera, Public Broadcasting, Theater

Civic & Public Affairs: African American Affairs, Botanical Gardens/Parks, Business/Free Enterprise, Community Foundations, Economic Development, Civic & Public Affairs-General, Housing, Legal Aid, Municipalities/Towns, Nonprofit Management, Parades/Festivals, Urban & Community Affairs, Zoos/Aquariums

Education: Afterschool/Enrichment Programs, Agricultural Education, Arts/Humanities Education, Business Education, Business-School Partnerships, Colleges & Universities, Education Funds, Education-General, Literacy, Private Education (Precollege), Private Education (Precollege), Public Education (Precollege), Secondary Education (Private), Secondary Education (Public)

Environment: Environment-General, Resource Conservation, Wildlife Protection

Health: Cancer, Children's Health/Hospitals, Clinics/Medical Centers, Emergency/Ambulance Services, Health-General, Health Organizations, Hospitals, Public Health, Single-Disease Health Associations

International: International Affairs

Religion: Dioceses, Missionary Activities (Domestic), Religious Organizations, Religious Welfare
Science: Science Exhibits & Fairs, Science Museums, Science Museums, Scientific Centers & Institutes
Social Services: Child Welfare, Community Centers, Community Service Organizations, Counseling, Domestic Violence, Family Planning, Family Services, Food/Clothing Distribution, Scouts, Shelters/Homelessness, Substance Abuse, United Funds/United Ways, YMCA/YWCA/YMHA/YWHA, Youth Organizations

Application Procedures

Initial Contact: Address letter of inquiry to local branch president.
Application Requirements: Include a description of organization and its purpose, amount requested, time frame, proof of tax-exempt status, a list of the board of directors, an audited financial statement, specific program budget, a list of other donors, and proof of 501(c)(3) status.
Deadlines: None.
Review Process: All requests for support originate from the communities served; local bank presidents forward requests to the foundation; if additional information is required, the foundation requests it.
Evaluative Criteria: Ability to help target constituency.
Decision Notification: Review process is ongoing; organization should set aside at least six months for a specific request.

Restrictions

The foundation does not support private foundations.

Corporate Officials

David Woods Kemper: chairman, president, chief executive officer, director B Kansas City, MO 1950. ED Harvard University AB (1972); Oxford University Worcester College MA (1974); Stanford University Graduate School of Business Administration MBA (1976). PRIM CORP EMPL chairman, president, chief executive officer, director: Commerce Bancshares, Inc. CORP AFFIL director: SLH Corp.; director: Wave Technologies International Inc.; director: Seafield Capital Corp.; director: Lab Holdings Inc.; director: Ralcorp Holdings Inc.; chairman: City National Bank Pittsburgh; director: Commerce Bank Saint Louis; director: Business Mens Assurance Co. NONPR AFFIL trustee: Saint Louis Symphony Orchestra; trustee: Washington University; trustee: Missouri Botanical Gardens; member: American Academy of Arts & Sciences; member: Bankers Roundtable. CLUB AFFIL Saint Louis Country Club; University Club; River Club; Saint Louis Club; Racquet Club; Kansas City Country Club; Old Warson Country Club.
Jonathan McBride Kemper: vice chairman B Kansas City, MO 1953. ED Harvard University AB (1975); Harvard University MBA (1979). PRIM CORP EMPL vice chairman, chief executive officer, director: Commerce Bank, NA ADD CORP EMPL vice chairman: Commerce Bancshares Inc.; president, chief executive officer, director: Commerce Bank Kansas City. NONPR AFFIL director: Greater Kansas City Community Foundation.

Foundation Officials

Jonathan McBride Kemper: director (see above)
Edward J. Reardon, II: director PRIM CORP EMPL director: Commerce Bank, NA.
J. Daniel Stinnett: director B Great Falls, MT 1945. ED Vanderbilt University (1967); University of Missouri, Kansas City (1972). PRIM CORP EMPL vice president, general counsel, secretary: Commerce Bancshares, Inc. CORP AFFIL secretary: Commerce Bank NA.

Grants Analysis

Disclosure Period: calendar year ending 2002
Total Grants: $1,159,337*
Number of Grants: 695

Highest Grant: $184,360
Lowest Grant: $50
Typical Range: $50 to $184,360
*Note: Grants analysis provided by foundation. Giving includes United Way.

Recent Grants

Note: Grants derived from 2001 Form 990.

General
50,175	United Way Plains, Wichita, KS
44,747	United Way of Greater St. Louis, St. Louis, MO
44,747	United Way of Greater St. Louis, St. Louis, MO
44,747	United Way of Greater St. Louis, St. Louis, MO
44,747	United Way of Greater St. Louis, St. Louis, MO
27,500	Heart of America United Way, Kansas City, MO
27,500	Heart of America United Way, Kansas City, MO
27,500	Heart of America United Way, Kansas City, MO
27,500	Heart of America United Way, Kansas City, MO
25,000	United Way of Greater St. Louis, St. Louis, MO

COMMERCIAL INTERTECH FOUNDATION

Giving Contact

Mary Ann Tanner, Executive Assistant to Chief Executive Officer
PO Box 239
Youngstown, OH 44501
Phone: (330)746-8011
Fax: (330)746-0422

Description

EIN: 346517437
Organization Type: Corporate Foundation
Giving Locations: OH
Grant Types: Award, Conference/Seminar, Employee Matching Gifts, Fellowship, General Support.

Financial Summary

Total Giving: $314,909 (fiscal year ending October 31, 2000); $312,758 (fiscal 1998); $270,849 (fiscal 1997). Note: Contributes through corporate direct giving program and foundation.
Giving Analysis: Giving for fiscal 1998 includes: foundation matching gifts ($1,875); foundation grants to United Way ($132,500); foundation ($178,383); fiscal 1997: foundation grants to United Way ($132,700); foundation ($138,149); fiscal 1996: corporate direct giving ($35,000) foundation ($364,265)
Assets: $550,860 (fiscal 2000); $663,262 (fiscal 1998); $696,678 (fiscal 1997)
Gifts Received: $243,565 (fiscal 2000); $240,000 (fiscal 1998); $240,000 (fiscal 1997). Note: Contributions are received from Commercial Intertech Corp.

Typical Recipients

Arts & Humanities: Arts Associations & Councils, Arts Institutes, Arts & Humanities-General, History & Archaeology, Libraries, Music, Performing Arts, Public Broadcasting
Civic & Public Affairs: Botanical Gardens/Parks, Business/Free Enterprise, Economic Development, Civic & Public Affairs-General, Legal Aid, Municipalities/Towns, Philanthropic Organizations, Professional & Trade Associations, Public Policy, Urban & Community Affairs
Education: Arts/Humanities Education, Business Education, Colleges & Universities, Economic Education, Education Funds, Engineering/Technological

Education, Faculty Development, Education-General, Minority Education, Private Education (Precollege), Public Education (Precollege), Social Sciences Education, Special Education
Environment: Energy
Health: Cancer, Children's Health/Hospitals, Children's Health/Hospitals, Clinics/Medical Centers, Diabetes, Emergency/Ambulance Services, Health-General, Health Organizations, Heart, Home-Care Services, Hospices, Hospitals, Long-Term Care, Multiple Sclerosis, Public Health, Single-Disease Health Associations, Speech & Hearing
International: International Affairs, International Relations
Religion: Ministries, Religious Welfare
Social Services: Camps, Child Welfare, Community Service Organizations, Day Care, Domestic Violence, Emergency Relief, Family Planning, People with Disabilities, Recreation & Athletics, Scouts, Senior Services, Social Services-General, Substance Abuse, United Funds/United Ways, Volunteer Services, YMCA/YWCA/YMHA/YWHA, Youth Organizations

Application Procedures

Initial Contact: Send a brief letter describing program.
Application Requirements: Include a description of organization, amount requested, purpose of funds sought, board of directors, list of management, recently audited financial statement, and proof of tax-exempt status.
Deadlines: None.

Corporate Officials

Steven J. Hewitt: senior vice president, chief financial officer B 1949. PRIM CORP EMPL senior vice president, chief financial officer: Commercial Intertech Corp.

Foundation Officials

Gerald C. McDonough: trustee B Cleveland, OH 1928. ED Case Western Reserve University (1953). CORP AFFIL director: Commercial Intertech Corp.; director: York International Corp.
Shirley M. Shields: secretary PRIM CORP EMPL secretary: Commercial Intertech Corp. CORP AFFIL secretary: Cylinder City Inc.
George M. Smart: trustee B Conneaut, OH 1945. ED Defiance College (1967); University of Pennsylvania Wharton School (1969). PRIM CORP EMPL Strategic Development Inc.. CORP AFFIL director: FirstEnergy Corp.; director: Ohio Edison Co.; director: Commercial Intertech Corp.
Bruce C. Wheatley: vice president B Du Quoin, IL 1942. ED Southern Illinois University (1963); University of Denver (1966). PRIM CORP EMPL senior vice president administration: Commercial Intertech Corp.

Grants Analysis

Disclosure Period: fiscal year ending October 31, 1997
Total Grants: $178,383*
Number of Grants: 56
Average Grant: $3,185
Highest Grant: $50,000
Typical Range: $25 to $5,000
*Note: Giving excludes United Way, matching gifts.

Recent Grants

Note: Grants derived from 2001 Form 990.

General
36,250	United Way, Youngstown, OH
36,250	United Way, Youngstown, OH
36,250	United Way, Youngstown, OH
36,250	United Way - MV
12,000	Ohio Foundation of Independent Colleges, Columbus, OH
10,000	Youngstown Symphony Society, Youngstown, OH
5,500	Youngstown Symphony Society, Youngstown, OH

5,000	Butley Institute
5,000	Friends, Riverside, CA
5,000	Industrial Information Institute, Youngstown, OH

COMMONWEALTH EDISON CO.

Company Headquarters

Chicago, IL
Web: http://www.ceco.com

Company Description

Employees: 16,800
SIC(s): 4911 Electric Services.

Operating Locations

Commonwealth Edison Co. (IL--Bradley, Fox River Grove, Romeoville)

Nonmonetary Support

Type: Donated Equipment; In-kind Services

Giving Contact

Steve Salomon, Corporate Affairs Associate
PO Box 767
Chicago, IL 60690
Phone: (312)394-4361
Fax: (312)394-3552
E-mail: leslie.jackson@exeloncorp.com

Alternate Contact

Phone: 800-344-7661

Description

Organization Type: Corporate Giving Program
Giving Locations: IL: Chicago including surrounding area
Grant Types: Capital, Employee Matching Gifts, General Support, Matching, Multiyear/Continuing Support.
Note: Employee matching gift ratio: 1 to 1 for education only. The company also reports benefits as a typical grant type.

Financial Summary

Total Giving: $3,800,000 (2000 approx); $3,900,000 (1999 approx); $3,394,000 (1998). Note: Contributes through corporate direct giving program only.
Giving Analysis: Giving for 1998 includes: corporate direct giving ($3,394,000); 1997: nonmonetary support ($24,000); corporate matching gifts ($134,800) corporate direct giving ($3,899,800)

Typical Recipients

Arts & Humanities: Arts Institutes, Community Arts, Dance, Ethnic & Folk Arts, Libraries, Museums/Galleries, Opera, Performing Arts, Public Broadcasting, Theater
Civic & Public Affairs: Civil Rights, Economic Development, Housing, Urban & Community Affairs, Zoos/Aquariums
Education: Colleges & Universities
Health: Health Organizations, Hospitals, Single-Disease Health Associations
Social Services: Community Service Organizations, Substance Abuse, United Funds/United Ways, Youth Organizations

Application Procedures

Initial Contact: Send a brief letter of inquiry.
Application Requirements: Include outline of proposal, history and a description of organization, amount requested, purpose of funds sought, proof of tax-exempt status, key staff, list of board of directors, an audited financial statement, budget, and a listing of funding sources.
Deadlines: None.

Review Process: Corporate responsibility committee evaluates most requests.
Evaluative Criteria: Priority is given to organizations and programs which are innovative and utilize their resources most effectively or fill a need in the community that is not already being addressed. Generally supports organizations where employees are actively involved.
Decision Notification: Committee meets in February, May, August, and November.
Notes: Company accepts the Chicago Area Grant Application Form. Requests of $2,000 or less may be reviewed and decided upon by a subcommittee.

Restrictions

The company does not purchase ads for benefit programs or make grants to religious or political organizations, individuals, fraternal or veterans organizations, or municipal, state, or federal agencies, departments, or public schools. Company does not make contributions to United Way supported agencies. Specific elementary or secondary schools are not funded, nor are national or international organizations that do not benefit ComEd or its customers. Capital support typically is limited to one-half of 1% of total campaign. Company indicates that currently applications are accepted only from organizations that have previously received funding.

Corporate Officials

John T. Costello: vice president corporate relations PRIM CORP EMPL vice president corporate relations: Commonwealth Edison Co.
John W. Rowe: chairman, chief executive officer, president, director B Dodgeville, WI 1945. ED University of Wisconsin BS; University of Wisconsin JD. PRIM CORP EMPL chairman, president, chief executive officer: Unicom Corp. ADD CORP EMPL chairman, chief executive officer, president, director: Commonwealth Edison Co. CORP AFFIL director: Unum Corp.; director: Bank of Boston Corp.; director: PepsiCo. NONPR AFFIL trustee: Pioneer Institute; president: Worcester Mcpl. Research Bur; member: Order Coif; member: Phi Beta Kappa; member: Massachusetts Business Roundtable; trustee: Mechanics Hall; director: Field Museum Natural History; director: Dana Farber Cancer Institute; director: Edison Electric Institute. CLUB AFFIL Chicago Club.
Pamela B. Strobel: chief executive officer B Chicago, IL 1952. ED University of Illinois BS (1974); University of Illinois JD (1977). PRIM CORP EMPL senior vice president, general counsel: Commonwealth Edison of Indiana. CORP AFFIL senior vice president, general counsel: Commonwealth Edison Co.; senior vice president, general counsel: Unicom Corp.; director: Badger Meter Inc.

Giving Program Officials

John T. Costello: member corporate responsibility committee (see above)
Edward M. Peterson: Corporate responsibility manager (see above)
Pamela B. Strobel: member corporate responsibility committee (see above)

Foundation Officials

John W. Rowe: membership corporate responsibility committee (see above)

Grants Analysis

Disclosure Period: calendar year ending 1998
Total Grants: $3,394,000*
Number of Grants: 400 (approx)
Average Grant: $8,485
Typical Range: $1,000 to $10,000
*Note: Grants analysis provided by the company.

THE COMMONWEALTH FUND

Giving Contact

Andrea C. Landes, Director, Grants Management
1 East 75th Street
New York, NY 10021-2692
Phone: (212)606-3858
Fax: (212)606-3500
E-mail: cmwf@cmwf.org
Web: http://www.cmwf.org

Description

Founded: 1918
EIN: 131635260
Organization Type: General Purpose Foundation
Giving Locations: nationally; some emphasis on New York City.
Grant Types: Fellowship, Project, Research.

Donor Information

Founder: The Commonwealth Fund was established in 1918 with a gift of about $10 million from Anna M. Harkness . Her husband, Stephen (d. 1888), was a founding investor in Standard Oil Company. Her son, Edward S. Harkness, was the fund's president until his death in 1940 and developed the fund's basic programs. In 1986, the fund was given the assets of the James Picker Foundation.

Financial Summary

Total Giving: $14,000,000 (fiscal year ending June 30, 2002 approx); $15,349,829 (fiscal 2001); $15,912,356 (fiscal 1999)
Giving Analysis: Giving for fiscal 2001 includes: foundation matching gifts ($575,858) foundation fellowships ($1,026,175)
Assets: $550,680,215 (fiscal 2001); $554,246,808 (fiscal 1999); $536,800,000 (fiscal 1998)
Gifts Received: $50,000 (fiscal 1999); $1,663,818 (fiscal 1996). Note: In 1999, contributions were received from Professor Frances Cooke Macgregor.

Typical Recipients

Arts & Humanities: Arts Funds, History & Archaeology, Libraries, Public Broadcasting
Civic & Public Affairs: Botanical Gardens/Parks, Business/Free Enterprise, Employment/Job Training, Civic & Public Affairs-General, Housing, Law & Justice, Municipalities/Towns, Nonprofit Management, Philanthropic Organizations, Professional & Trade Associations, Public Policy, Safety, Urban & Community Affairs, Women's Affairs
Education: Business Education, Colleges & Universities, Education Reform, Faculty Development, Education-General, Health & Physical Education, Leadership Training, Legal Education, Medical Education, Public Education (Precollege), Science/Mathematics Education, Social Sciences Education, Special Education, Student Aid, Vocational & Technical Education
Environment: Energy, Environment-General, Resource Conservation, Wildlife Protection
Health: Adolescent Health Issues, Cancer, Children's Health/Hospitals, Clinics/Medical Centers, Diabetes, Health-General, Geriatric Health, Health Policy/Cost Containment, Health Funds, Health Organizations, Heart, Home-Care Services, Hospitals, Long-Term Care, Medical Research, Medical Training, Mental Health, Nursing Services, Prenatal Health Issues, Preventive Medicine/Wellness Organizations, Public Health, Research/Studies Institutes
International: International-General, Health Care/Hospitals, Human Rights, International Organizations
Science: Scientific Centers & Institutes
Social Services: At-Risk Youth, Child Welfare, Community Service Organizations, Day Care, Domestic Violence, Emergency Relief, Family Planning, Family Services, Homes, Recreation & Athletics, Senior Services, Substance Abuse, Youth Organizations

Application Procedures

Initial Contact: Applicants should submit a letter of inquiry via regular or electronic mail. Letters should be brief and no more than three pages.

Application Requirements: The letter of inquiry should include contact name, legal name of grantee organization, complete mailing address, phone numbers, e-mail address, purpose of grants, description of the project's targeted audience, estimated total project cost, total dollar amount requested from the Fund, project design, including schedule and workplan, description of the project's expected outcomes, and organization staffing and financial resources.

Deadlines: None. Applicants may send requests any time.

Review Process: Applications are reviewed by the staff to judge merit. Applicants will be notified within two months of initial review. Those viewed favorably are reviewed and voted upon by the board of directors, which meets three times a year.

Restrictions

Grants are not provided for general planning, ongoing activities, or work for which achievements cannot be measured. The fund does not make grants to individuals or make contributions used for general support, endowments, buildings, renovations of facilities, or major equipment. The funds does not typically support major media projects or documentaries. Grants rarely provide support for longer than three years.

Additional Information

Preference is given to proposals to clarify the scope of serious and neglected problems, especially those affecting vulnerable groups of Americans; to analyze the impact of policies and trends on well-defined issues; or to develop and test practical solutions.

Publications: Annual Report; Recent Grants Release

Foundation Officials

John Edwin Craig, Jr.: executive vice president, treasurer B Lancaster, SC 1944. ED Davidson College BA (1966); Princeton University MA (1968). NONPR AFFIL chairman investment committee: Social Science Research Council; member, board: US-Australia-New Zealand Council; member government council: Rockefeller Archives Center; chairman investment committee: Investment Fund Foundations; chairman: Nonprofit Coordinating Committee; member: Foundation Administration Group; member: Foundation Financial Officer Group; member, board visitors: Davidson College. CLUB AFFIL mem: University Club.

Karen Padgett Davis: president, director B Blackwell, OK 1942. ED Rice University BA (1965); Rice University PhD (1969). CORP AFFIL director: Somatix Therapy Corp.

Samuel C. Fleming: director PRIM CORP EMPL chairman, chief executive officer: Decision Resources Inc.

Lawrence Smith Huntington: chairman finance committee, director B New York, NY 1935. ED Harvard University BA (1957); New York University LLB (1964). PRIM CORP EMPL chairman, chief executive officer, chairman executive committee, director: Fiduciary Trust Co. International. CORP AFFIL director: Princeton Packet Inc. NONPR AFFIL director: Woods Hole Research Center; director: World Wildlife Fund; vice chairman, treasurer, trustee: South Street Seaport Museum; director: Trinity Church; trustee: Saint Lukes Roosevelt Hospital Center; trustee: Santa Fe Institute; member advisory board: New York State Common Retirement Fund; trustee: Opsail; member advisory board: NASD International Markets; chairman: New York Law School; director: Business Executives National Security; trustee: Citizens Budget Committee. CLUB AFFIL trust: New York Yacht Club; American Alpine Club; Century Association.

Helene L. Kaplan: director, vice chairman B New York, NY 1933. ED Barnard College AB (1953); New York University JD (1967). PRIM CORP EMPL of counsel: Skadden, Arps, Slate, Meagher & Flom. CORP AFFIL director: Metro Life Insurance Co.; director: Verizon Communications Inc.; director: ExxonMobil Corp.; director: May Department Stores Co.; director: Chase Manhattan Corp. NONPR AFFIL trustee: Olive Free Library; member: Women's Forum; member: New York State Bar Association; vice chairman, trustee: Mount Sinai Medical Center; vice chairman, trustee: Mount Sinai School of Medicine; member: Century Association; trustee: Institute Advanced Studies; trustee: Barnard College; member: American Philosophical Society; member: Association Bar New York City; member: American Bar Association; trustee, vice chairman: American Museum Natural History; member: American Academy of Arts & Sciences. CLUB AFFIL Cosmopolitan Club.

Dr. Walter Eugene Massey: director B Hattiesburg, MS 1938. ED Morehouse College BS (1958); Washington University MA (1966); Washington University PhD (1966). PRIM NONPR EMPL president: Morehouse College. CORP AFFIL director: Motorola Inc.; director: BP Amoco Corp.; director: McDonalds Corp.; director: BankAmerica Corp. NONPR AFFIL member: American Physics Society; member: Sigma Xi; member: American Association Advancement Science.

Robert Marchant O'Neil: director B Boston, MA 1934. ED Harvard University AB (1956); Harvard University AM (1957); Harvard University LLB (1961). CORP AFFIL director: James River Corp. Inc.; director: Fort James Corp. NONPR AFFIL trustee: Teachers Insurance & Annuity Association; law professor: University Virginia; director: Public Television Station WVPT; director: American Law Institute.

Roswell Burchard Perkins: honorary director B Boston, MA 1926. ED Harvard University AB (1945); Harvard University LLD (1949). CORP AFFIL director: Fiduciary Trust Co. International; member legal committee board directors: New York Stock Exchange Inc. NONPR AFFIL member national executive committee: New York Lawyers Commission Civil Rights; member: New York State Bar Association; member: Harvard University Alumni Association; member, chairman council: American Law Institute; member: Association Bar New York City; member: American Arbitration Association; member: American Bar Association.

Charles Addison Sanders: chairman board directors B Dallas, TX 1932. ED University of Texas MD (1955). NONPR AFFIL chairman: Project Hope; trustee: University North Carolina; director: National Foundation Biomedical Research; member: President Council Advisor Science Technology; member: American Heart Association; member: Massachusetts Medicine Society; member: American College Physicians.

James J. Tallon, Jr.: director PRIM CORP EMPL chairman: Educational Resources Systems. NONPR AFFIL director: New York Academy Medicine.

Samuel O. Thier, MD: director

Grants Analysis

Disclosure Period: fiscal year ending June 30, 2001
Total Grants: $13,747,796*
Number of Grants: 274
Average Grant: $50,174
Highest Grant: $284,000
Typical Range: $25,000 to $100,000
*Note: Giving excludes fellowship and matching gifts gifts to individuals.

Recent Grants

Note: Grants derived from fiscal 2001 Form 990.

General

360,000	Harvard Medical School, Boston, MA -- university fellowship in minority health policy
354,355	Johns Hopkins University School of Hygiene and Public Health, Baltimore, MD -- support Healthy Steps for Young Children Program
326,320	Princeton Survey Research Associates, Princeton, NJ -- survey on disparities in quality of health care
321,827	ICF Incorporated, Fairfax, VA -- Health Steps for Young Children Program
255,925	Harvard Medical School, Boston, MA -- university fellowship in minority health policy
247,636	George Washington University, Washington, DC -- monitoring the impact of medicarechoice programs on the elderly
237,500	Urban Institute, Washington, DC -- Medicare's future support
231,917	Massachusetts General Hospital, Boston, MA -- task force on academic health care
221,500	Urban Institute, Washington, DC -- Medicare's future support
207,600	Princeton Survey Research Associates, Princeton, NJ -- assessing stability and quality of health insurance

COMMUNITY ENTERPRISES

Giving Contact

William H. Hightower, Jr., President
PO Box 1089
Thomaston, GA 30286
Phone: (706)647-7131
Fax: (706)646-5094

Description

Founded: 1944
EIN: 586043415
Organization Type: Private Foundation
Giving Locations: GA: Thomaston including area within approximately 100 miles of Thomaston
Grant Types: General Support, Multiyear/Continuing Support, Scholarship.

Donor Information

Founder: Julian T. Hightower, Thomaston Cotton Mills

Financial Summary

Total Giving: $568,306 (fiscal year ending June 30, 2001); $629,509 (fiscal 2000); $659,087 (fiscal 1999). Note: Giving includes United Way ($13,500); scholarship ($364,669).
Giving Analysis: Giving for fiscal 2001 includes: foundation grants to United Way ($10,000); fiscal 2000: foundation grants to United Way ($10,000); fiscal 1999: foundation grants to United Way ($13,500) foundation scholarships ($18,500)
Assets: $11,002,025 (fiscal 2001); $10,546,202 (fiscal 2000); $13,163,754 (fiscal 1999)

Typical Recipients

Arts & Humanities: Arts Associations & Councils, Historic Preservation, Libraries
Civic & Public Affairs: Civic & Public Affairs-General, Housing, Municipalities/Towns, Urban & Community Affairs
Education: Business Education, Colleges & Universities, Education Funds, Engineering/Technological Education, Education-General, Private Education (Precollege), Public Education (Precollege), Science/Mathematics Education, Student Aid, Vocational & Technical Education
Environment: Wildlife Protection
Health: Cancer, Heart, Hospitals
Religion: Churches, Missionary Activities (Domestic), Religious Organizations, Religious Welfare
Science: Science Museums
Social Services: Community Service Organizations, Recreation & Athletics, Scouts, Shelters/Homelessness, United Funds/United Ways, Youth Organizations

Application Procedures

Initial Contact: Send a brief letter of inquiry.
Application Requirements: Include a description of organization, amount requested, purpose of funds sought, recently audited financial statement, and proof of tax-exempt status.
Deadlines: December 31.

Additional Information

The foundation is affiliated with Thomaston Mills. See separate entry for financial data on this company.

Foundation Officials

George H. Hightower, Jr.: vice president, trustee PRIM CORP EMPL executive vice president, director: Thomaston Mills.

Neil Hamilton Hightower: secretary, treasurer, trustee B Atlanta, GA 1940. ED Georgia Institute of Technology BS (1963); Harvard University (1974). PRIM CORP EMPL chairman, president, chief executive officer, director: Thomaston Mills. CORP AFFIL director: NationsBank; director: GA NationsBank. NONPR AFFIL director, member: Textile Education Foundation; member: Textile Traffic Association; member: Southern Industry Relations Conf; member: Georgia Textile Manufacturer Association; director, member: National Cotton Council America; member: Georgia Chamber of Commerce; president, member: American Textile Manufacturer Institute; member: American Yarn Spinners Association. CLUB AFFIL Kiwanis Club.

William H. Hightower, Jr.: president, trustee B Atlanta, GA 1936. ED Georgia Institute of Technology (1958). CORP AFFIL director: Thomaston Mills.

Grants Analysis

Disclosure Period: fiscal year ending June 30, 2001
Total Grants: $558,306*
Number of Grants: 37
Average Grant: $9,953*
Highest Grant: $200,000
Typical Range: $1,500 to $20,000
***Note:** Giving excludes United Way. Average grant figure excludes highest grant.

Recent Grants

Note: Grants derived from fiscal 2000 Form 990.

Library-Related

38,000	Pine Mountain Regional Library System
5,000	Yatesville Public Library Fund

General

200,000	First United Methodist Church, Grand Rapids, MI
50,000	City Thomaston -- industrial development
14,964	Hightower Memorial United Methodist Church
12,145	Upson County Hospital Trust Fund
10,275	East Thomaston Baptist Church
10,000	Thomaston-Upson Arts Council
10,000	Upson County United Way
6,000	Flint River Council Boy Scouts of America
5,000	Harbor House
2,000	Pine Valley Girl Scout Council

COMMUNITY TRUST BANCORP, INC.

Company Headquarters

PO Box 2947
Pikeville, KY 41501
Web: http://www.ctbi.com

Company Description

Founded: 1980
Ticker: CTBI
Exchange: NASDAQ
Former Name: Commercial Bank.
Assets: US$2.487 billion (2002)
Employees: 883 (2002)
SIC(s): 6000 Depository Institutions.
Parent Company: Commercial Bank of Grayson, 208 E. Main St., Grayson, KY, United States

Operating Locations

Community Trust Bank (KY--Lexington)

Commercial Bank Foundation

Giving Contact

Jack W. Strother, Trustee
208 E. Main St.
Grayson, KY 41143
Phone: (606)474-7811

Description

EIN: 611087988
Organization Type: Corporate Foundation
Giving Locations: KY: Carter County
Grant Types: Scholarship.

Financial Summary

Total Giving: $33,540 (2001); $28,000 (2000); $23,682 (1999)
Giving Analysis: Giving for 1999 includes: foundation ($11,682); foundation scholarships ($12,000) 1998: foundation scholarships ($6,000)
Assets: $563,434 (2001); $561,770 (2000); $554,769 (1999)
Gifts Received: $25,000 (2001); $25,000 (2000); $100,000 (1999). Note: Contributions were received from The Commercial Bank.

Typical Recipients

Arts & Humanities: Libraries
Civic & Public Affairs: Civic & Public Affairs-General
Education: Business Education, Colleges & Universities, Private Education (Precollege), Public Education (Precollege), Secondary Education (Public), Student Aid
Religion: Ministries, Religious Welfare
Social Services: Substance Abuse

Application Procedures

Initial Contact: Application form required for scholarships. Other applications should be made in writing. Deadline for graduating seniors is April 15.

Additional Information

Provides higher education scholarships to graduates of Carter County, KY, high schools only.
Publications: Application Form

Corporate Officials

Burlin Coleman: chairman, president, chief executive officer PRIM CORP EMPL chairman, president, chief executive officer: Community Trust Bank.
Richard Levy: chief financial officer PRIM CORP EMPL chief financial officer: Community Trust Bank.

Foundation Officials

Jack W. Strother, Jr.: co-trustee
Jack W. Strother, Sr.: co-trustee

Grants Analysis

Disclosure Period: calendar year ending 2001
Total Grants: $19,540*
Number of Grants: 4
Highest Grant: $5,000
***Note:** Giving excludes scholarships to individuals.

Recent Grants

Note: Grants derived from 2001 Form 990.

General

5,000	Community Hospice, Ashland, KY -- Capital Campaign
5,000	Kentucky Christian College, Grayson, KY
5,000	Kentucky Christian College, Grayson, KY
4,540	Morehead State University, Morehead, KY -- Learning Lab Grant

COMSAT INTERNATIONAL

Company Headquarters

6560 Rock Spring Drive
Bethesda, MD 20817
Web: http://www.comsat.com

Company Description

Former Name: Communications Satellite Corp.
Employees: 1,644
SIC(s): 4800 Communications.

Operating Locations

COMSAT Corp. (VA--Sterling); COMSAT Video Enterprises (DC; MD); Lockheed Martin Aeronautics Co. (TX--Fort Worth)

Giving Contact

Charles Manner, V.P. Communications
6560 Rock Springs Dr.
Bethesda, MD 20817
Phone: (301)214-3000
Fax: (301)214-7100

Description

Organization Type: Corporate Giving Program
Giving Locations: nationally.
Grant Types: Employee Matching Gifts.

Financial Summary

Total Giving: Company does not disclose contributions figures.

Typical Recipients

Arts & Humanities: Arts Centers, Community Arts, Arts & Humanities-General, Libraries, Museums/Galleries, Music, Public Broadcasting, Theater
Education: Colleges & Universities, Community & Junior Colleges, Education Funds, Education-General, Vocational & Technical Education

Restrictions

Does not support individuals, religious organizations for sectarian purposes, or political or lobbying groups.

Corporate Officials

Betty L. Alewine: president, chief executive officer PRIM CORP EMPL president, chief executive officer: COMSAT Corp. ADD CORP EMPL president: Comcast International Communication.
Edwin I. Colodny: chairman PRIM CORP EMPL chairman: COMSAT Corp.
Allen E. Flower: chief financial officer, vice president PRIM CORP EMPL chief financial officer, vice president: COMSAT Corp.

Grants Analysis

Typical Range: $10 to $1,000

CONE-BLANCHARD CORP.

Company Headquarters

7 Everett Lane
Windsor, VT 05089

Company Description
Revenue: US$10.8 million (2001)
Employees: 60 (2001)
SIC(s): 3500 Industrial Machinery & Equipment, 7300 Business Services.

Cone Automatic Machine Co. Charitable Foundation

Giving Contact
W. Red McCullough, Treasurer
PO Box 757
Windsor, VT 05089
Phone: (802)674-2161

Description
EIN: 036004866
Organization Type: Corporate Foundation
Giving Locations: VT: Windsor including surrounding area
Grant Types: Scholarship.

Financial Summary
Total Giving: $58,500 (fiscal year ending October 31, 2001); $35,500 (fiscal 2000); $35,500 (fiscal 1999)
Assets: $922,818 (fiscal 2001); $1,061,280 (fiscal 2000); $1,061,280 (fiscal 1999)

Typical Recipients
Arts & Humanities: Arts & Humanities-General, History & Archaeology, Libraries, Museums/Galleries, Public Broadcasting
Civic & Public Affairs: Civic & Public Affairs-General, Urban & Community Affairs
Education: Colleges & Universities, Engineering/Technological Education, Faculty Development, Education-General, Science/Mathematics Education, Student Aid, Vocational & Technical Education
Health: Arthritis, Clinics/Medical Centers, Emergency/Ambulance Services, Health-General, Health Organizations, Home-Care Services, Hospitals, Nursing Services, Public Health
Religion: Religious Welfare
Social Services: Community Service Organizations, Homes, People with Disabilities, Scouts, Senior Services, Social Services-General, Volunteer Services, Youth Organizations

Application Procedures
Initial Contact: Send brief letter of inquiry, including a description of organization, amount requested, purpose of funds sought, and proof of tax-exempt status.
Deadlines: August 31.

Restrictions
Does not support individuals (except for scholarships for children or grandchildren of employees), religious organizations for sectarian purposes, or political or lobbying groups.

Corporate Officials
Hunter Banbury: president, chief executive officer, treasurer PRIM CORP EMPL president, chief executive officer, treasurer: Cone-Blanchard Corp.
Jack Keibaum: general manager PRIM CORP EMPL general manager: Cone-Blanchard Corp.

Foundation Officials
Alden P. Dana: trustee
W. R. McCullough: trustee
Wayne E. Pfenning: trustee

Grants Analysis
Disclosure Period: fiscal year ending October 31, 2001
Total Grants: $58,500
Number of Grants: 36

Average Grant: $1,625
Highest Grant: $3,500
Lowest Grant: $150
Typical Range: $250 to $2,500

Recent Grants
Note: Grants derived from 2000 Form 990.

Library-Related
1,000	Windsor Library Association, Windsor, CT

General
4,000	Mt. Ascutney Hospital, Windsor, VT
3,000	University of Maine, Orono, ME
2,500	Castleton State College
2,500	Visiting Nurse Alliance of Vermont and New Hampshire
2,000	College of St. Joseph, Rutland, VT
2,000	University of Vermont, Burlington, VT
1,500	College of the Ozarks, Pt. Lookout, MO
1,500	Franklin Pierce College, Rindge, NH
1,500	Loyola College in Maryland, Baltimore, MD
1,500	Lyndon State College, Lyndonville, VT

MICHAEL J. CONNELL FOUNDATION

Giving Contact
Michael J. Connell, President & Director
225 S. Lake Avenue, Suite 271
Pasadena, CA 91101
Phone: (323)681-8085

Description
Founded: 1931
EIN: 956000904
Organization Type: Private Foundation
Giving Locations: CA: Los Angeles including metropolitan area
Grant Types: Fellowship, Project.

Donor Information
Founder: the late Michael J. Connell

Financial Summary
Total Giving: $780,615 (fiscal year ending June 30, 2001); $951,826 (fiscal 2000); $821,428 (fiscal 1999)
Giving Analysis: Giving for fiscal 2001 includes: foundation grants to United Way ($10,000); fiscal 2000: foundation grants to United Way ($10,000) fiscal 1999: foundation grants to United Way ($10,000)
Assets: $14,018,791 (fiscal 2001); $15,207,750 (fiscal 2000); $16,251,505 (fiscal 1999)

Typical Recipients
Arts & Humanities: Arts Centers, Arts Outreach, Community Arts, Libraries, Museums/Galleries, Music, Public Broadcasting, Theater
Civic & Public Affairs: Botanical Gardens/Parks, Civic & Public Affairs-General, Nonprofit Management, Safety, Urban & Community Affairs
Education: Arts/Humanities Education, Colleges & Universities, Elementary Education (Public), Gifted & Talented Programs, Minority Education, Private Education (Precollege), Science/Mathematics Education, Vocational & Technical Education
Environment: Environment-General, Resource Conservation
Health: Children's Health/Hospitals, Emergency/Ambulance Services, Eyes/Blindness
Religion: Religious Welfare
Social Services: Child Welfare, Community Service Organizations, Family Services, Homes, United Funds/United Ways

Application Procedures
Initial Contact: Include a cover letter and a full proposal.
Application Requirements: The cover letter should include the name of the applicant organization; appropriate contact person; an outline of the proposed project and its objectives; total project cost and amount requested; and anticipated date of completion. The proposal must include a description of organization, including the organization's history, current programs, key leadership, and major funding sources; a complete project description, including need, target populations, project strategy, staff requirements and qualifications, and implementation timetable; and an evaluation plan explaining methods of project evaluation and a clear statement of project objetives and an outline of evaluation activities. Financial information must be attached, including management letters and notes for the last two fiscal years; the organization's operating budget and organizational budget for the current fiscal year, with actuals to date (if applicant organization has no audited statements, in-house statements verified and signed by two of the organization's officers are acceptable). Required attachments include copes of both the organization's original and federal tax exemption letter under section 501(c)(3) and the subsequent final determination letter on private foundation status; a letter signed by an officer of the board of directors stating that the proposal is submitted with the board's knowledge and endorsement; and a roster of the organization's board of directors, including each member's full name, address, profession, and notation of office held on board (if applicable).
Deadlines: February 15, May 15, August 15, and November 15.
Review Process: Proposals are initially reviewed to determine whether it fits within the foundation's current areas of interest. Proposals that are aligned with the foundation's interest will be reviewed at the upcoming board meeting.
Decision Notification: The foundation notifies applicants of the receipt of their proposals as soon as possible.
Notes: The Connell Foundation generally discourages unsolicited grant requests because it generally initiates and pursues its own programs in the social, cultural, educational, and medical fields. Application guidelines are supplied for those organizations who desire to apply after taking this into consideration.

Restrictions
Does not support individuals.

Foundation Officials
Mary C. Bayless: director
Michael J. Connell: president, director
Ruth E. Dodd: secretary
Richard A. Grant: vice president, director
Richard A. Wilson: treasurer, director

Grants Analysis
Disclosure Period: fiscal year ending June 30, 2001
Total Grants: $770,615*
Number of Grants: 16
Average Grant: $28,258*
Highest Grant: $250,000
Lowest Grant: $1,826
Typical Range: $10,000 to $50,000
*****Note:** Giving excludes United Way. Average grant figure excludes two highest grants ($375,000).

Recent Grants
Note: Grants derived from fiscal 2000 Form 990.

Library-Related
25,000	Library Foundation of Los Angeles, Los Angeles, CA

General
250,000	Community Television, Los Angeles, CA
100,000	University of Southern California, Los

	Angeles, CA -- support Department of Cell and Neurobiology
75,000	Rancho Santa Ana Botanical Garden, Claremont, CA
50,000	Hollygrove, Los Angeles, CA
35,000	Concern Resource, Ojai, CA -- training youths to care for parks and trails
33,000	Armory Center for the Arts, Pasadena, CA -- support individual arts program
25,000	Ganna Walska Lotusland Foundation, Santa Barbara, CA
20,000	Pacific Oaks College, Pasadena, CA
20,000	Shakespeare Festival, Los Angeles, CA -- art enrichment
10,000	Don Bosco Technical Institute, Rosemead, CA

CONNELLY FOUNDATION

Giving Contact

E. Ann Wilcox, Grants Administrator
One Tower Bridge, Suite 1450
West Conshohocken, PA 19428
Phone: (610)834-3222
Fax: (610)834-0866
E-mail: eawilcox@connellyfdn.org
Web: http://www.connellyfdn.org

Description

Founded: 1955
EIN: 236296825
Organization Type: Family Foundation
Giving Locations: PA: Philadelphia Greater Delaware Valley Region.
Grant Types: Capital, General Support, Operating Expenses, Project.

Donor Information

Founder: John F. Connelly and his wife, Josephine Connelly, established the Connelly Foundation in Pennsylvania in 1955. The foundation's assets consist largely of stock in Crown Cork & Seal Company, of which John Connelly was chairman from 1956 until his death in 1990.

Financial Summary

Total Giving: $11,500,803 (2002); $17,000,082 (1999 approx); $20,410,868 (1998)
Giving Analysis: Giving for 1998 includes: foundation grants to United Way ($31,000)
Assets: $201,300,000 (2002); $312,403,154 (1999); $315,682,501 (1998)

Typical Recipients

Arts & Humanities: Arts Centers, Arts Institutes, Arts Outreach, Historic Preservation, History & Archaeology, Libraries, Museums/Galleries, Music, Opera, Performing Arts, Theater
Civic & Public Affairs: Economic Development, Civic & Public Affairs-General, Hispanic Affairs, Housing, Public Policy, Urban & Community Affairs, Zoos/Aquariums
Education: Afterschool/Enrichment Programs, Arts/Humanities Education, Colleges & Universities, Education Associations, Education Funds, Elementary Education (Private), Engineering/Technological Education, Faculty Development, Education-General, Leadership Training, Literacy, Medical Education, Minority Education, Preschool Education, Private Education (Precollege), Public Education (Precollege), Religious Education, School Volunteerism, Science/Mathematics Education, Secondary Education (Private), Secondary Education (Public), Special Education, Student Aid, Vocational & Technical Education
Environment: Environment-General
Health: AIDS/HIV, Alzheimers Disease, Cancer, Children's Health/Hospitals, Clinics/Medical Centers, Emergency/Ambulance Services, Geriatric Health, Health Funds, Health Organizations, Heart, Home-Care Services, Hospices, Hospitals, Hospitals (University Affiliated), Long-Term Care, Medical Rehabilitation, Medical Research, Nursing Services, Outpatient Health Care, Prenatal Health Issues, Preventive Medicine/Wellness Organizations, Public Health, Research/Studies Institutes, Transplant Networks/Donor Banks
International: Foreign Arts Organizations, Foreign Educational Institutions, Health Care/Hospitals, International Relief Efforts, Missionary/Religious Activities
Religion: Churches, Dioceses, Jewish Causes, Ministries, Religious Organizations, Religious Welfare, Seminaries, Social/Policy Issues
Science: Science Museums, Scientific Centers & Institutes
Social Services: Child Abuse, Child Welfare, Community Centers, Community Service Organizations, Day Care, Domestic Violence, Family Planning, Family Services, Food/Clothing Distribution, Homes, People with Disabilities, Recreation & Athletics, Senior Services, Shelters/Homelessness, Social Services-General, Substance Abuse, United Funds/United Ways, YMCA/YWCA/YMHA/YWHA, Youth Organizations

Application Procedures

Initial Contact: The foundation provides application guidelines. Initial contact should be in writing.
Application Requirements: Proposals should include the following: an executive summary of the project, its goals, and financial requirements and status (a specific grant amount must be requested); brief history of the organization, an annual report, financial statements from the two most recent years, and the names and occupations of all directors and trustees; detailed proposal including project objectives, budget, revenue plan, timetable and target population (capital expenses must be documented); prospective and committed funding sources to date; evaluation plan and prospects for continued support of the project; resume of project officer and a list of key staff; and a copy of the IRS determination letter granting tax-exempt status.
Deadlines: None.
Review Process: The board of directors meets five times a year with the annual meeting at the foundation's office on the last Monday in January. Proposals are acknowledged upon receipt. The foundation does not grant interviews. Final notification takes three to six months.
Notes: The foundation also accepts the Delaware Valley Grantmakers Application Form.

Restrictions

The foundation does not make grants to individuals, political organizations, or other foundations, nor does it generally respond to annual appeals or letters of solicitation.

Additional Information

Publications: Biennial Report; Guidelines

Foundation Officials

William Joseph Avery: trustee B Chicago, IL 1940. ED University of Chicago (1965). PRIM CORP EMPL chairman: Crown Cork & Seal Co. Inc. CORP AFFIL director: Rohm and Haas Co. NONPR AFFIL chairman: YMCA Philadelphia.
Dr. Lewis William Bluemle, Jr.: senior vice president, trustee B Williamsport, PA 1921. ED Johns Hopkins University AB (1943); Johns Hopkins University MD (1946). CORP AFFIL consult: National Institute Health; director: Teleflex Inc.; director: Greater Philadelphia First Corp.; director, member executive committee: Mellon Bank East. NONPR AFFIL fellow: Royal College Physicians Edinburgh; president: Thomas Jefferson University; member advisory board Philadelphia chapter: Physicians Social Responsibility; member: Phi Beta Kappa; member: Philadelphia Association Clinic Trails; member: Association Academy Health Centers; fellow: College Physicians Philadelphia; member: American Society Artificial Internal Organs; member: American Society Nephrology; member: American Clinical & Climatological Association; fellow: American College Physicians; member: Alpha Omega Alpha. CLUB AFFIL Philadelphia Club; Union League Club.
Ira Brind: trustee B Philadelphia, PA 1941. ED University of Pennsylvania AB (1963); University of Pennsylvania JD (1967). PRIM CORP EMPL managing director: Brind Lindsay & Co. Inc. CORP AFFIL director: Today's Man Inc.; director: Trala; director: Shooting Star; director: Thomas Jefferson University Hospital; director: Philadelphia School; director: Delta Paper; director: Nationalease System; director: J. E. Berkowitz LP; director: Blue Ribbon; officer: Aydin Corp. NONPR AFFIL officer: University Arts; director: Wistar Institute of Anatomy & Biology; member: Truck Rental Leasing Association; director: Philadelphia College Arts; member: Philadelphoa Bar Association; member: American Bar Association; member: Pennsylvania Bar Association. CLUB AFFIL Locust Club.
Christine C. Connelly: trustee
Daniele Connelly: trustee
Thomas S. Connelly: trustee, donor son B 1945. PRIM CORP EMPL Connelly Containers ADD CORP EMPL manager: Georgia Pacific Corp.
Caroline M. Crowley: trustee
Eleanor L. Davis: trustee
Philippe Delouvrier: trustee B 1950. PRIM CORP EMPL president: Eastern Industrial Minerals. NONPR AFFIL member: Phi Beta Kappa. CLUB AFFIL Knickerbocker Club.
Thomas F. Donovan: trustee B 1934. CORP AFFIL chairman, chief executive officer: Mellon Bank East.
Victoria K. Flaville: vice president, secretary
Chester C. Hilinski: trustee emeritus B Bethlehem, PA March 26, 1917. ED University of Pennsylvania BS (1938); University of Pennsylvania JD (1941). PRIM CORP EMPL senior partner: Dechert Price & Rhoads. CORP AFFIL director: Connelly Containers; director: Crown Cork & Seal Co. Inc. NONPR AFFIL member: Pennsylvania State Bar Association; member: Philadelphia Bar Association; member: American Bar Association.
Josephine C. Mandeville: chairman, chief executive officer, president, trustee, donor daughter CORP AFFIL director: Crown Cork & Seal Co. Inc.
Peter O. Mandeville: trustee
Lawrence T. Mangan: vice president, treasurer
Emily C. Riley: executive vice president, trustee B 1946. CORP AFFIL director: Connelly Containers. NONPR AFFIL trustee: Villanova University.

Grants Analysis

Disclosure Period: calendar year ending 1998
Total Grants: $20,379,868*
Number of Grants: 547*
Average Grant: $37,258
Highest Grant: $2,000,625
Typical Range: $5,000 to $50,000
*Note: Giving excludes United Way.

Recent Grants

Note: Grants derived from 2000 Form 990.

Library-Related

150,000	Rosenbach Museum and Library, Philadelphia, PA -- restoration of two historic buildings that house the museum on Delancey Place

General

1,000,000	Georgetown University, Washington, DC -- capital campaign
813,824	Chestnut Hill College, Philadelphia, PA -- in support of Phase I - The Commons
657,975	Holy Redeemer Health System, Huntington Valley, PA -- support for "Manor Bridge," capital campaign
581,000	Archdiocese of Philadelphia-Josephine

	C. Connelly Achievement Awards, Philadelphia, PA -- tuition scholarship awards
500,000	Country Day School of the Sacred Heart, Bryn Mawr, PA -- for renovations and addition to the Marie Cornelia Dooley Building
500,000	Gateway Visitor Center Corporation, Philadelphia, PA -- in support of the creation of a regional orientation facility in the heart of Philadelphia
500,000	Gwynedd Mercy College, Gwynedd Valley, PA -- for the Josephine C. Connelly Scholarships
491,952	Archdiocese of Philadelphia-Neumann Scholars Program, Philadelphia, PA -- for tuition assistance scholarships
465,965	Holy Ghost Preparatory School, Bensalem, PA -- for capital campaign
405,093	St. Elizabeth High School, Wilmington, DE -- capital campaign

CONNEMARA FUND

Giving Contact

Herrick Jackson, Trustee
c/o Glen Mede Trust Co.
1650 Market Street, Suite 1200
Philadelphia, PA 19103
Phone: (215)419-6000

Description

Founded: 1968
EIN: 566096063
Organization Type: Private Foundation
Giving Locations: New England.
Grant Types: General Support, Multiyear/Continuing Support.

Donor Information

Founder: the late Mary R. Jackson

Financial Summary

Total Giving: $517,000 (fiscal year ending June 30, 2001); $405,000 (fiscal 2000); $346,567 (fiscal 1998)
Assets: $8,789,366 (fiscal 2001); $11,013,752 (fiscal 2000); $9,426,457 (fiscal 1998)

Typical Recipients

Arts & Humanities: Arts Associations & Councils, Arts Centers, Arts & Humanities-General, Libraries, Museums/Galleries, Music, Public Broadcasting
Civic & Public Affairs: Civil Rights, Civic & Public Affairs-General, Legal Aid, Native American Affairs, Philanthropic Organizations, Public Policy, Zoos/Aquariums
Education: Arts/Humanities Education, Colleges & Universities, Elementary Education (Private), Education-General, Leadership Training, Preschool Education, Private Education (Precollege)
Environment: Environment-General, Resource Conservation
Health: Cancer, Emergency/Ambulance Services, Health-General, Hospitals, Medical Research, Mental Health, Prenatal Health Issues, Preventive Medicine/Wellness Organizations, Single-Disease Health Associations
International: International-General, International Affairs, International Development, International Peace & Security Issues, International Relief Efforts, Missionary/Religious Activities
Religion: Churches, Religion-General, Ministries, Missionary Activities (Domestic), Religious Welfare, Social/Policy Issues, Synagogues/Temples
Social Services: Child Welfare, People with Disabilities, Shelters/Homelessness, United Funds/United Ways, Youth Organizations

Application Procedures

Initial Contact: Send a brief letter of inquiry.
Application Requirements: Include proof of tax-exempt status.
Deadlines: None.

Restrictions

Does not support individuals.

Foundation Officials

Herrick Jackson: trustee
Sister Maria Jackson: trustee
Polly B. Jackson: trustee
Alison Jackson Van Dyk: trustee

Grants Analysis

Disclosure Period: fiscal year ending June 30, 2001
Total Grants: $517,000
Number of Grants: 78
Average Grant: $6,628
Highest Grant: $40,000
Lowest Grant: $1,000
Typical Range: $1,000 to $10,000

Recent Grants

Note: Grants derived from fiscal 2000 Form 990.

General

45,000	Trustees of Westminster School, Simsbury, CT
40,000	Orleans Church Building Foundation, Inc., Orleans, MA
40,000	Temple of Understanding, New York, NY
30,000	Children's Hospital Corporation, Boston, MA
30,000	Temple of Understanding, New York, NY
20,000	American Psychoanalytic Association, New York, NY
15,000	St. Luke's Foundation, New Canaan, CT
12,000	Hope Directory, Lindale, TX
10,000	Becket Fund, Washington, DC
10,000	CACLD, East Norwalk, CT

CONSECO, INC.

Company Headquarters

11825 N. Pennsylvania St.
Carmel, IN 46032
Web: http://www.conseco.com

Company Description

Founded: 1979
Ticker: CNCE
Exchange: OTC
Former Name: American Life
Chap. 11 Reorg. Bankruptcy (2002).
Revenue: US$6.147 billion (2002)
Employees: 3,000
Fortune Rank: 284, per FORTUNE Magazine's list of 500 Largest U.S. Corporations (2002).
SIC(s): 6000 Depository Institutions, 6100 Nondepository Institutions, 6300 Insurance Carriers, 6700 Holding & Other Investment Offices.

Operating Locations

Conseco (IN--Carmel)

Nonmonetary Support

Type: Donated Equipment; In-kind Services
Note: Conseco will consider requests for in-kind contributions. Determinations will be based on need and the availability of resources to provide requested items.

Giving Contact

Sheila Taylor, Supervisor
Conseco Services, LLC
11815 N. Pennsylvania Street
PO Box 1911
Carmel, IN 46082-1911
Phone: 800-888-4918
Fax: (317)817-6721
Web: http://

Description

Organization Type: Corporate Giving Program
Giving Locations: IN: Indianapolis metropolitan area, including Marion County and nine surrounding counties
Grant Types: Capital, Operating Expenses, Research, Seed Money.

Typical Recipients

Arts & Humanities: Art History, Arts Appreciation, Arts Institutes, Ballet, Libraries, Museums/Galleries, Performing Arts, Public Broadcasting, Theater
Civic & Public Affairs: African American Affairs, Botanical Gardens/Parks, Chambers of Commerce, Community Foundations, Economic Development, Inner-City Development, Parades/Festivals, Philanthropic Organizations, Safety, Urban & Community Affairs, Women's Affairs, Zoos/Aquariums
Education: Afterschool/Enrichment Programs, Arts/Humanities Education, Business Education, Colleges & Universities, Continuing Education, Economic Education, Education Reform, Elementary Education (Private), Leadership Training, Literacy, Minority Education, Preschool Education, Private Education (Precollege), Public Education (Precollege), Secondary Education (Private), Secondary Education (Public), Special Education
Environment: Environment-General, Wildlife Protection
Health: Adolescent Health Issues, AIDS/HIV, Alzheimers Disease, Arthritis, Cancer, Children's Health/Hospitals, Diabetes, Health Organizations, Heart, Hospitals, Hospitals (University Affiliated), Long-Term Care, Medical Research, Medical Training, Mental Health, Multiple Sclerosis, Nursing Services, Single-Disease Health Associations
Social Services: At-Risk Youth, Big Brother/Big Sister, Camps, Child Abuse, Child Welfare, Community Centers, Community Service Organizations, Crime Prevention, Domestic Violence, Family Planning, Food/Clothing Distribution, Homes, People with Disabilities, Recreation & Athletics, Scouts, Senior Services, Shelters/Homelessness, Social Services-General, Special Olympics, United Funds/United Ways, Volunteer Services, Youth Organizations

Application Procedures

Deadlines: January 1, April 1, July 1, and October 1. Applicants are encouraged to submit their requests well in advance of the deadline, allowing community relations adequate time for additional research, if necessary. Proposals postmarked on the deadline but not received at Conseco until after the deadline will not be considered until the following quarter. Proposals may not be submitted by fax machine. Applications for Pacers/Colts Charity Program grants are accepted year-round; however, please note that applications for both programs must be received by the July 1 deadline to be considered for the upcoming season.

Restrictions

Requests are not considered from organizations without 501(c)(3) tax-exempt status; veterans groups, service clubs, or fraternal organizations; conferences, workshops, or seminars; religiously-affiliated causes, multiple-year gifts; endowments; projects or groups benefiting an individual or just a few people; re-granting organizations (other than the United Way); political or lobbying groups; or post-event funding.

Additional Information

A proposal asking Conseco to consider providing a portion of the support for a project will generally receive greater preference than one seeking Conseco as the exclusive funding source.

The Community Action Committee requires that proposals offer three sponsorship/donation levels.

For organizations and projects new to the company, it is preferred to start funding at a more modest level and work toward building a relationship.

Conseco's grant-making policy places more emphasis on specific project proposals than on general operating fund or capital campaign proposals.

If renewed funding is desired, an organization must submit a formal request. The Community Action Committee supports new and opportune projects each year. Therefore, a grant given in any one year does not ensure future funding.

The Community Action Committee will consider only one grant request per project in each calendar year. Multiple projects may be submitted during the same funding cycle; a separate application must be filled out for each project.

Organizations that receive a grant will be required to send in a completed Conseco Post-Grant Evaluation form within one month after the completion of the project or program. Future grants will not be awarded to organizations that have a Post Grant Evaluation form outstanding after the deadline.

Grant recipients must use the funds, as agreed upon, within six months of the event or of receiving the funds. The company sponsors several special programs, including the Pacers/Colts Charity Programs. Each season, Conseco selects 18 community organizations to participate in the Indiana Pacers/Conseco Three-Point Charity Program. Each organization receives 20 admission tickets to two Indiana Pacers home games, as well as a financial contribution at the end of the season. Conseco contributes $50 to a fund for every three-point shot the Pacers make throughout the season. The overall total is divided equally among the participating organizations. One community organization is selected each year to participate in the Indianapolis Colts/Conseco First Down Charity Program. For every first down the Colts make in the RCA Dome, Conseco contributes $75 to the recipient organization. A check presentation is made at the end of the season.

Corporate Officials

Rollin M. Dick: executive vice president, chief financial officers, chief executive officer PRIM CORP EMPL executive vice president, chief financial officer: Conseco.

Stephen C. Hilbert: founder, chairman, president, chief executive officer B 1946. PRIM CORP EMPL founder, chairman, president, chief executive officer: Conseco. CORP AFFIL director: CCP Insurance; chief executive officer: Colonial Penn Life Insurance Co.; director: Bankers Life Holding Corp.

Grants Analysis

Typical Range: $1,500 to $10,000

CONSTELLATION ENERGY GROUP, INC.

Company Headquarters

39 W. Lexington Street
Baltimore, MD 21201
Phone: (410)234-5678
Fax: (410)234-5220
Web: http://www.constellationenergy.com

Company Description

Founded: 1995
Ticker: CEG
Exchange: NYSE

Former Name: Baltimore Gas & Electric (1999).
Assets: US$4.703 billion (2002)
Profit: US$525.6 million (2002)
Employees: 8700 (2002)
Fortune Rank: 352, per FORTUNE Magazine's list of 500 Largest U.S. Corporations (2002).
SIC(s): 4931 Electric & Other Services Combined, 4932 Gas & Other Services Combined, 5722 Household Appliance Stores.

Operating Locations

Baltimore Gas & Electric Co. (MD--Baltimore, Lusby); Baltimore Gas & Electric Home Products & Services Inc. (MD--Columbia, Elkridge, Glen Burnie); Church Street Stateion Inc. (FL--Orlando); Constellation Energy Source (TX--Houston); Safe Harbor Water Power Corp. (PA--Conestoga)

Nonmonetary Support

Value: $50,000 (2003 approx); $43,250 (2002); $59,260 (2001)
Type: Donated Equipment; Donated Products; In-kind Services
Note: NOT Nonmonetary support is provided by the company.
Volunteer Programs: The company sponsors an employee volunteer program aimed at increasing pride, motivation, and participation by allowing volunteers to direct their own program.

Giving Contact

Malinda B. Small, Director, National-State Affairs & Corporate Contributions
Constellation Energy Group
PO Box 1475
Baltimore, MD 21203-1475
Phone: (410)783-3273
Fax: (410)783-3279
E-mail: Malinda.B.Small@constellation.com
Web: http://www.constellation.com/about/givingfocus.asp

Description

Founded: 1986
Organization Type: Corporate Foundation
Giving Locations: headquarters and operating communities.
Grant Types: Capital, Employee Matching Gifts, General Support, Multiyear/Continuing Support, Operating Expenses, Project, Scholarship.
Note: Employee matching gift ratio: 1 to 1 between $25 and $2,000 annually per employee.

Donor Information

Founder: Baltimore Gas and Electric Co.

Financial Summary

Total Giving: $4,000,000 (2003 approx); $4,000,000 (2002 approx); $5,000,000 (2001 approx). Note: Contributes through corporate direct giving program and foundation.
Giving Analysis: Giving for 2000 includes: foundation grants to United Way ($876,865); foundation ($2,038,140); 1999: foundation grants to United Way ($1,004,993) foundation ($1,759,029)
Assets: $288,895 (2001); $161,214 (2000); $2,477,650 (1999)
Gifts Received: $1,713,000 (2001); $575,000 (2000); $2,024,500 (1999). Note: In 2001, contributions were received from Constellation Energy Group, Inc. and Baltimore Gas and Electric Company. Contributions prior to 2001 were received from Baltimore Gas and Electric Company.

Typical Recipients

Arts & Humanities: Arts Festivals, Dance, Historic Preservation, History & Archaeology, Libraries, Museums/Galleries, Music, Performing Arts, Theater
Civic & Public Affairs: Business/Free Enterprise, Economic Development, Civic & Public Affairs-General, Housing, Law & Justice, Professional & Trade

Associations, Urban & Community Affairs, Zoos/Aquariums
Education: Arts/Humanities Education, Business-School Partnerships, Colleges & Universities, Continuing Education, Education Funds, Faculty Development, Education-General, Health & Physical Education, Literacy, Medical Education, Minority Education, Preschool Education, Religious Education, Science/Mathematics Education, Social Sciences Education, Special Education, Student Aid
Environment: Air/Water Quality, Environment-General, Resource Conservation
Health: Clinics/Medical Centers, Health Organizations, Hospices, Hospitals, Public Health
Religion: Dioceses, Jewish Causes, Ministries, Religious Welfare, Seminaries
Science: Science Museums, Scientific Centers & Institutes, Scientific Research
Social Services: At-Risk Youth, Child Abuse, Child Welfare, Community Service Organizations, Family Services, People with Disabilities, Scouts, Senior Services, Special Olympics, United Funds/United Ways, Veterans, Volunteer Services, YMCA/YWCA/YMHA/YWHA, Youth Organizations

Application Procedures

Initial Contact: Obtain the appropriate guidelines and application forms from the company's web site. Submit two copies of grant requests, or a single copy of sponsorship or in-kind requests.
Deadlines: None for requests of less than $10,000; May 1 and September 1 for requests of $10,000 or more.
Evaluative Criteria: Preference will be given to organizations for which company employees and board members serve as volunteers; organizations whose purposes are aligned with the company's philanthropic focus areas; and organizations that demonstrate a broad base of community support.
Decision Notification: All applicants will receive a response in writing after a funding decision has been made. Allow six to eight weeks for processing grant requests of less than $10,000, sponsorships, and in-kind requests. Grant requests of more than $10,000 are considered at Corporate Contributions Committee meetings in June and October.

Restrictions

Does not normally fund member agencies of the United Way. Company does not support individuals, churches for religious causes, organizations in conflict with company goals, start-up funding, or hospitals' capital campaigns. The company will only consider one contribution request per organization per year. Applicants must be 501(c)(3) tax-exempt nonprofit organizations located in an area where the company has significant business interests.

Additional Information

Publications: Guidelines

Corporate Officials

Mayo A. Shattuck, III: president, chief executive officer, chairman
Malinda B. Small: director national-state affairs & corporate contributions

Foundation Officials

Christian Herndon Poindexter: chairman, president B Evansville, IN 1938. ED United States Naval Academy BS (1960); Loyola College MBA (1976). ADD CORP EMPL director, president, chairman, chief executive officer: Constellation Energy Group Inc. CORP AFFIL director: Mercantile Bankshares Corp.; director: Dome Corp.; director: KMS Group Inc.; chairman, chief executive officer: Constellation Investments Inc.; chairman, chief executive officer: Constellation Properties Inc.; chairman, chief executive officer: Constellation Biogas Inc. NONPR AFFIL trustee: Villa Julie College; secretary, director: YMCA

Anne Arundel County; trustee: Morgan State University; president, director: Scholarships Scholars Inc.; trustee: Johns Hopkins University; trustee: Maryland Academy Science; member: Engineering Society Baltimore; member: Institute Electrical & Electronics Engineers; member executive board: Boy Scouts America Baltimore Area Council.

Thomas E. Ruszin, Jr.: treasurer ADD CORP EMPL treasurer, assistant secretary: Constellation Energy Group Inc.

Malinda B. Small: assistant secretary, assistant treasurer (see above)

Grants Analysis

Disclosure Period: calendar year ending 2002
Total Grants: $4,000,000*
Number of Grants: 878
Average Grant: $4,120
Highest Grant: $100,000
Lowest Grant: $25
Typical Range: $25,000 to $100,000
*Note: Grants analysis provided by foundation.

Recent Grants

Note: Grants derived from 2001 Form 990.

Library-Related

20,000	Kennedy Krieger Institute, Baltimore, MD -- capital campaign

General

725,000	United Way of Central Maryland, Baltimore, MD -- 2000 corporate campaign
200,000	Johns Hopkins University, Baltimore, MD -- School of Continuing Studies
200,000	United States Naval Academy Foundation, Annapolis, MD -- pledge to capital campaign
125,000	Baltimore Center for Performing Arts, Baltimore, MD -- Hippodrome Performing Arts Center
125,000	Baltimore Children's Museum, Baltimore, MD -- capital campaign
125,000	University of Maryland Foundation, Adelphi, MD -- pledge to BGE Teaching Fund
100,000	Archdiocese of Baltimore, Baltimore, MD -- Partners in Excellence Program
100,000	Baltimore Symphony Orchestra, Baltimore, MD -- sustaining greatness campaign
100,000	University of Maryland College Park, College Park, MD -- "Bright Future" campaign
70,000	Maryland Historical Society, Baltimore, MD -- establishment of new education and Public Programs Center

Consumers Energy Co.

Company Headquarters

212 W. Michigan Ave.
Jackson, MI 49201
Web: http://www.consumersenergy.com

Company Description

Revenue: US$4.104 billion (2001)
Employees: 1,475 (2001)
Parent Company: CMS Energy Co., 330 Town Center Dr., Ste. 100, Dearborn, MI, United States

Nonmonetary Support

Type: In-kind Services

Consumers Energy Foundation

Giving Contact

Carolyn A. Bloodworth, Secretary/Treasurer
Consumers Energy Foundation
One Energy Plaza
Jackson, MI 49201
Phone: (517)788-0432
Fax: (517)788-2281
E-mail: foundation@consumersenergy.com
Web: http://www.consumersenergy.com/welcome.htm

Alternate Contact

Phone: 877-501-4952

Description

EIN: 382935534
Organization Type: Corporate Foundation
Giving Locations: MI; nationally.
Grant Types: Capital, Employee Matching Gifts, General Support, Operating Expenses, Project.
Note: Employee matching gift ratio: 1 to 1 for donations to colleges, universities, and Michigan food banks and community foundations, up to $5,000 per employee or retiree annually.

Financial Summary

Total Giving: $600,000 (2004 approx); $600,000 (2003 approx); $1,500,000 (2002)
Giving Analysis: Giving for 2000 includes: foundation grants to United Way ($517,400); foundation matching gifts ($544,469); foundation ($802,922); 1997: foundation matching gifts ($199,635); foundation grants to United Way ($374,892) foundation ($745,986)
Assets: $1,000,000 (2004 approx); $2,000,000 (2003 approx); $3,400,000 (2002)
Gifts Received: $7,000,000 (2001); $2,000,000 (2000); $4,000,000 (1998). Note: Contributions are received from Consumers Energy Company.

Typical Recipients

Arts & Humanities: Arts Associations & Councils, Arts Funds, Arts Institutes, Community Arts, Arts & Humanities-General, Historic Preservation, History & Archaeology, Libraries, Museums/Galleries, Music, Opera, Performing Arts, Public Broadcasting, Theater
Civic & Public Affairs: Botanical Gardens/Parks, Chambers of Commerce, Clubs, Community Foundations, Economic Development, Employment/Job Training, Civic & Public Affairs-General, Housing, Municipalities/Towns, Nonprofit Management, Parades/Festivals, Philanthropic Organizations, Professional & Trade Associations, Public Policy, Urban & Community Affairs, Zoos/Aquariums
Education: Agricultural Education, Arts/Humanities Education, Business Education, Business-School Partnerships, Colleges & Universities, Community & Junior Colleges, Economic Education, Engineering/Technological Education, Legal Education, Minority Education, Public Education (Precollege), Science/Mathematics Education, Secondary Education (Public)
Environment: Energy, Environment-General, Resource Conservation, Watershed, Wildlife Protection
Health: Alzheimers Disease, Cancer, Children's Health/Hospitals, Emergency/Ambulance Services, Hospitals
International: International Relations
Religion: Religious Welfare
Science: Scientific Centers & Institutes
Social Services: Camps, Community Centers, Community Service Organizations, Family Services, Food/Clothing Distribution, People with Disabilities, Recreation & Athletics, Scouts, Senior Services, Shelters/Homelessness, Substance Abuse, United Funds/United Ways, United Funds/United Ways, Volunteer Services, YMCA/YWCA/YMHA/YWHA, Youth Organizations

Application Procedures

Initial Contact: Request or see foundation website for application guidelines, then send a cover letter and the Council of Michigan Foundation's Common Grant Application.
Application Requirements: Cover letter should include a description of a program that is supported by the general public, businesses, and other foundations and governments; and should make a strategic link between proposal and foundation's interests. Attachments to completed application should include plans for evaluating the program, current realistic budget including other sources of funding, most recent audited financial statement, list of board of directors, and proof of tax-exempt status.
Deadlines: None; requests reviewed quarterly.
Review Process: Applications are reviewed locally and at company headquarters, then sent to foundation board for consideration; after preliminary review, applicant may be asked to provide additional information. Small grants of less than $5,000 can be approved at any time; larger grants need prior board approval.
Evaluative Criteria: Indications of effective governing board, realistic budget, clearly defined program that is supported by the public, business, and other foundations (if appropriate); and record of accomplishment.
Decision Notification: The foundation tries to respond within six to eight weeks.
Notes: The foundation will not respond to telephone requests. Facsimile requests are discouraged. Funds primarily given to organizations located in the state of Michigan.

Restrictions

Funds only groups to which donations are tax-deductible.

Does not support individuals, political or lobbying groups, endowments, organizations whose operating status is supported by the United Way, religious organizations for sectarian purposes, or labor, veterans, fraternal and social clubs.

Also does not contribute to organizations which discriminate on the basis of sex, age, height, weight, marital status, race, religion, creed, color, nationality or origin, ancestry, disability, handicap, or veteran status. The Foundation does not buy tickets or make payments to events or celebrations to raise funds or charitable purposes, or sponsor advertising to support these efforts.

Additional Information

Consumers Energy Foundation looks for grant recipients that provide solutions to problems faced by individuals and families who are unable to address their own needs without help; protect and enhance the natural environment; improve the availability and quality of education while stressing cost effectiveness; back the improvement and effectiveness of the public's health care systems, with special emphasis on reducing patient costs; participate in community and civic activities for the betterment of the citizenry and their governments; and increase an awareness of the values of artistic and cultural achievements and encourage their growth.

The foundation considers requests from qualified organizations to support operating budgets and capital fund programs for construction, refurbishment or purchase of buildings, structures, equipment or other physical enhancements.

A contribution from Consumers Energy Foundation is more likely to be approved when grant seekers' programs are focused on high priority needs which they are capable of addressing successfully.

Corporate Officials

Paul A. Elbert: president, chief executive officer natural gas B 1950. ED Ohio State University BA; University of Illinois MA. PRIM CORP EMPL president, chief executive officer natural gas: Consumers Energy Co. CORP AFFIL chairman: Michigan Gas Storage Co.; director: Sugar Monitor Co.

David W. Joos: president, chief executive officer electric, executive vice president B Fargo, ND 1953. ED Iowa State University of Science & Technology (1975); Iowa State University of Science & Technology (1976). PRIM CORP EMPL president, chief executive officer electric, executive vice president: Consumers Energy Co. NONPR AFFIL member: American Society Mechanical Engineers; member: Registered Professional Engineers; member: American Nuclear Society.

William Thomas McCormick, Jr.: chairman, chief executive officer, director B Washington, DC 1944. ED Cornell University BS (1966); Massachusetts Institute of Technology PhD (1969). PRIM CORP EMPL chairman, chief executive officer, director: CMS Energy Corp. ADD CORP EMPL chairman: Consumers Energy Co.; chairman: Consumers Power Co. CORP AFFIL director: First Chicago NBD Corp.; director: Rockwell International Corp.; director: Bank One Corp.; chairman, chief executive officer, director: CMS Enterprises Co. NONPR AFFIL director, member: Greater Detroit Chamber of Commerce; director: Schumberger; director: American Gas Association; director: Edison Electric Institute.

Giving Program Officials
Carolyn A. Bloodworth: secretary-trs PRIM CORP EMPL director community relations: CMS Energy Corp.

Foundation Officials
Carolyn A. Bloodworth: secretary-treasurer (see above)
John W. Clark: president B 1945. ED Indiana University (1968). PRIM CORP EMPL senior vice president communications: CMS Energy Corp. ADD CORP EMPL senior vice president, chief financial officer: Consumers Energy Co.
Carl L. English: director
Victor J. Fryling: director B 1948. ED Wayne State University BS (1970). PRIM CORP EMPL president, chief operating officer: CMS Energy Corp. ADD CORP EMPL chairman: CMS Marketing Service Trading Co.; president: CMS Enterprises Co.; chairman: CMS Gas Transmission & Storage Co.; chairman: CMS Generation Co.; chairman: CMS Generation Operating Co.; chairman: CMS Generation Filer City; president: CMS Generation Filer Cy Operating Co.; principal: CMS Generation Grayling Co.; chairman: CMS Generation Recycling Co.; president: CMS Midland Inc.; chairman: CMS NOMECO Oil & Gas Co.; president: Consumers Energy Co.; chairman: Panhandle Eastern Pipe Line Co.
William Thomas McCormick, Jr.: chairman (see above)
David G. Mengebier: president
John G. Russell: director
Alan M. Wright: director

Grants Analysis
Disclosure Period: calendar year ending 2002
Total Grants: $1,500,000
Number of Grants: 145
Average Grant: $3,200
Highest Grant: $350,000
Lowest Grant: $100

Recent Grants
Note: Grants derived from 2001 Form 990.

General

62,500	United Way Jackson County, Jackson, MI
62,500	United Way Jackson County, Jackson, MI
62,500	United Way Jackson County, Jackson, MI
62,500	United Way Jackson County, Jackson, MI

50,000	Detroit Institute of Arts, Detroit, MI
40,000	Inroads, Grand Rapids, MI
33,010	Michigan State University, East Lansing, MI
28,750	United Way Community Services, Detroit, MI
28,750	United Way Community Services, Detroit, MI
28,750	United Way Community Services, Detroit, MI

CONTEMPO COMMUNICATIONS

Company Headquarters
Sherman, CT

Contempo Communications Foundation for the Arts, Inc.

Giving Contact
Joan F. Marshall, Vice President & Director
Contempo Communications Foundation for the Arts, Inc.
9686 Casa Mar Circle
Ft. Myers, FL 33919
Phone: (941)466-7262

Description
EIN: 136209719
Organization Type: Corporate Foundation
Giving Locations: NY: New York including metropolitan area
Grant Types: General Support.

Financial Summary
Total Giving: $9,079 (fiscal year ending March 31, 2001); $8,669 (fiscal 1999); $7,882 (fiscal 1997)
Giving Analysis: Giving for fiscal 2001 includes: foundation ($9,079) fiscal 1999: foundation ($8,669)
Assets: $179,045 (fiscal 2001); $190,376 (fiscal 1999); $175,076 (fiscal 1997)

Typical Recipients
Arts & Humanities: Arts Centers, Dance, Arts & Humanities-General, Libraries, Museums/Galleries, Music, Performing Arts, Public Broadcasting, Theater, Visual Arts
Civic & Public Affairs: Botanical Gardens/Parks, Clubs, Civic & Public Affairs-General, Legal Aid, Municipalities/Towns, Parades/Festivals, Public Policy, Safety, Urban & Community Affairs, Women's Affairs
Education: Arts/Humanities Education, Colleges & Universities, Education-General, Minority Education
Environment: Environment-General, Resource Conservation, Wildlife Protection
Health: Cancer, Emergency/Ambulance Services, Health-General, Hospices, Hospitals, Mental Health, Single-Disease Health Associations, Single-Disease Health Associations
International: Health Care/Hospitals, International Relief Efforts, Missionary/Religious Activities
Religion: Churches, Religion-General, Jewish Causes, Religious Organizations, Synagogues/Temples
Science: Science Museums, Scientific Organizations
Social Services: Child Welfare, Community Service Organizations, Family Planning, Food/Clothing Distribution, United Funds/United Ways, YMCA/YWCA/YMHA/YWHA, Youth Organizations

Application Procedures
Initial Contact: The foundation has no formal grant application procedure or application form. Send a brief letter of inquiry.
Application Requirements: Include all relevant information, including amount requested and purpose of funds sought.
Deadlines: None.

Corporate Officials
Joan F. Marshall: president PRIM CORP EMPL president: Contempo Communications.

Foundation Officials
David B. Marshall: president, director
David L. Marshall: secretary, treasurer, director B Madison, NJ 1939. ED Princeton University (1961); Pennsylvania State University (1962). CORP AFFIL chairman: Brinks.
Joan F. Marshall: vice president, director (see above)

Grants Analysis
Disclosure Period: fiscal year ending March 31, 2001
Total Grants: $9,079
Number of Grants: 46
Average Grant: $105*
Highest Grant: $4,350
Typical Range: $20 to $200
*****Note:** Average grant figure excludes highest grant.

Recent Grants
Note: Grants derived from 2001 Form 990.

General

4,850	University of Michigan, Ann Arbor, MI
1,650	Temple Beth Am, New York, NY
300	United Jewish Appeal Federation, New York, NY
126	American Parkinson's Disease Association, Staten Island, NY
125	City of Sanibel, Sanibel, FL
100	Doctors Without Borders, New York, NY
100	Hillel Foundation, Washington, DC
100	Muscular Dystrophy Association, Denver, CO
100	YWCA
75	Ding Darling Wildlife Society, Sanibel, FL

CONTIGROUP COMPANIES, INC.

Company Headquarters
277 Park Ave.
New York, NY 10172
Web: http://www.contigroup.com

Company Description
Former Name: Continental Grain Co. (2001).
Revenue: US$3.3 billion (2001)
Employees: 14500 (2001)
SIC(s): 0211 Beef Cattle Feedlots, 0213 Hogs, 0251 Broiler, Fryer & Roaster Chickens, 2041 Flour & Other Grain Mill Products, 2048 Prepared Feeds Nec, 6159 Miscellaneous Business Credit Institutions.

Operating Locations
Continental Grain Co. (NY--New York)

ContiGroup Companies Foundation

Giving Contact
Susan McIntyre, Assistant Secretary
277 Park Avenue
New York, NY 10172-0003

Phone: (212)207-5879
Fax: (212)207-5163

Description
EIN: 136160912
Organization Type: Corporate Foundation
Giving Locations: NY: Midwest.
Grant Types: General Support, Scholarship.

Financial Summary
Total Giving: $371,970 (fiscal year ending January 31, 2002); $274,620 (fiscal 2001); $290,937 (fiscal 2000)
Giving Analysis: Giving for fiscal 2002 includes: foundation scholarships ($17,330); foundation ($354,640); fiscal 2001: foundation ($274,620) fiscal 2000: foundation ($290,937)
Assets: $332 (fiscal 2002); $142 (fiscal 2001); $82 (fiscal 2000)
Gifts Received: $372,185 (fiscal 2002); $283,230 (fiscal 2001); $296,937 (fiscal 2000). Note: In fiscal 2001 and 2002, contributions were received from ContiGroup Companies.

Typical Recipients
Arts & Humanities: Arts Centers, Arts Outreach, Dance, Historic Preservation, Libraries, Museums/Galleries, Music, Opera, Performing Arts, Theater
Civic & Public Affairs: African American Affairs, Business/Free Enterprise, Chambers of Commerce, Civic & Public Affairs-General, Legal Aid, Professional & Trade Associations, Public Policy, Rural Affairs, Urban & Community Affairs, Women's Affairs
Education: Agricultural Education, Business Education, Colleges & Universities, Education Funds, Education Reform, Elementary Education (Public), Education-General, International Studies, Legal Education, Minority Education, Religious Education, Science/Mathematics Education, Secondary Education (Private), Student Aid, Student Aid
Environment: Resource Conservation
Health: Alzheimers Disease, Cancer, Children's Health/Hospitals, Clinics/Medical Centers, Emergency/Ambulance Services, Hospitals, Multiple Sclerosis, Nursing Services, Single-Disease Health Associations
International: Health Care/Hospitals, Human Rights, International Development, International Organizations, International Peace & Security Issues, International Relations, International Relief Efforts
Religion: Churches, Religion-General, Jewish Causes, Religious Welfare, Seminaries
Science: Science Museums
Social Services: Animal Protection, At-Risk Youth, Child Welfare, Community Service Organizations, Family Services, People with Disabilities, Social Services-General, Substance Abuse, United Funds/United Ways, Volunteer Services, YMCA/YWCA/YMHA/YWHA, Youth Organizations

Application Procedures
Initial Contact: Send a brief letter of inquiry detailing purpose for which grant is requested.
Deadlines: None.

Corporate Officials
James John Bigham: executive vice president, chief financial officer, director B Waterbury, CT 1937. ED Fairfield University BS (1959); Columbia University MBA (1961); Harvard University Graduate School of Business Administration (1970). PRIM CORP EMPL executive vice president, chief financial officer, director: Continental Grain Co.
Dwight C. Coffin: vice president human resources PRIM CORP EMPL vice president human resources: Continental Grain Co.
Paul J. Fribourg: chairman, president, chief executive officer ED Amherst College BA; Harvard University MA. PRIM CORP EMPL chairman, president, chief executive officer: ContiGroup Companies Inc.

Donald L. Staheli: chairman, director B Hurricane, UT 1931. ED University of Illinois PhD; University of Illinois MS; Utah State University BS. PRIM CORP EMPL chairman, director: Continental Grain Co.

Foundation Officials
Dwight C. Coffin: vice president, secretary, director (see above)
Gerald Frenchman: vice president
Donald L. Staheli: vice president, director (see above)
Lawrence G. Weppler: assistant secretary
Daniel J. Willet: treasurer

Grants Analysis
Disclosure Period: fiscal year ending January 31, 2002
Total Grants: $354,640*
Number of Grants: 47
Average Grant: $7,545
Highest Grant: $50,525
Lowest Grant: $35
Typical Range: $250 to $15,000
*Note: Giving excludes scholarships.

Recent Grants
Note: Grants derived from 2002 Form 990.

Library-Related
20,000	Library of Congress, Washington, DC

General
50,525	American Red Cross Disaster Relief Fund, New York, NY
45,000	National FFA Foundation, Indianapolis, IN
25,000	Appeal of Conscience Foundation, New York, NY
25,000	Virtual Y, New York, NY
17,330	National Merit Scholarship Corporation, Evanston, IN
12,500	National Committee on US-China Relations, New York, NY
10,000	Amherst College, Amherst, MA
10,000	Animal Agriculture Alliance, Arlington, VA
10,000	Carnegie Hall Society, New York, NY
10,000	Catalyst, New York, NY

CONTRAN CORP.

Company Headquarters
5430 Lyndon B. Johnson Freeway, Ste. 1700
Dallas, TX 75240

Company Description
Revenue: US$1.1 billion (2002)
Employees: 7,300 (2002)
SIC(s): 1311 Crude Petroleum & Natural Gas, 2063 Beet Sugar, 2421 Sawmills & Planing Mills--General, 5812 Eating Places.

Operating Locations
Operates internationally.

Harold Simmons Foundation, Inc.

Giving Contact
Lisa Simmons Epstein, President
Harold Simmons Foundation
5430 LBJ Freeway, Suite 1700
Dallas, TX 75240-2697
Phone: (972)991-2400
Fax: (972)448-1456

Alternate Contact
Keith A. Johnson, Controller
Harold Simmons Foundation
Phone: (972)233-1700

Description
Founded: 1988
EIN: 752222091
Organization Type: Corporate Foundation
Giving Locations: TX: Dallas including metropolitan area
Grant Types: Capital, General Support.

Donor Information
Founder: NL Industries and subsidiaries and Contran Corp.

Financial Summary
Total Giving: $2,497,353 (2001); $6,171,733 (2000); $3,312,399 (1999). Note: Contributes through foundation only.
Giving Analysis: Giving for 2000 includes: foundation grants to United Way ($133,486); foundation ($6,038,247); 1999: foundation grants to United Way ($70,304) foundation ($3,242,095)
Assets: $7,813,555 (2001); $9,119,616 (2000); $11,258,963 (1999)
Gifts Received: $450,000 (2001); $1,750,000 (2000); $2,800,000 (1999). Note: Contributions are received from Contran Corp.

Typical Recipients
Arts & Humanities: Arts Centers, Arts Festivals, Arts Outreach, Dance, Historic Preservation, Libraries, Museums/Galleries, Music, Performing Arts, Public Broadcasting, Theater
Civic & Public Affairs: Botanical Gardens/Parks, Clubs, Community Foundations, Economic Development, Employment/Job Training, Civic & Public Affairs-General, Housing, Nonprofit Management, Philanthropic Organizations, Professional & Trade Associations, Public Policy, Urban & Community Affairs, Women's Affairs, Zoos/Aquariums
Education: Arts/Humanities Education, Business Education, Colleges & Universities, Community & Junior Colleges, Education Funds, Education Reform, Faculty Development, Education-General, Leadership Training, Legal Education, Literacy, Medical Education, Preschool Education, Private Education (Precollege), Public Education (Precollege), Religious Education, Secondary Education (Public)
Environment: Environment-General
Health: AIDS/HIV, Cancer, Children's Health/Hospitals, Clinics/Medical Centers, Health Organizations, Hospitals, Hospitals (University Affiliated), Kidney, Medical Research, Mental Health, Multiple Sclerosis, Nursing Services, Prenatal Health Issues, Public Health, Single-Disease Health Associations, Transplant Networks/Donor Banks
International: Health Care/Hospitals, International Development, International Relief Efforts
Religion: Churches, Religion-General, Jewish Causes, Ministries, Missionary Activities (Domestic), Religious Welfare, Religious Welfare, Social/Policy Issues
Science: Science-General, Science Museums
Social Services: At-Risk Youth, Camps, Child Welfare, Community Service Organizations, Counseling, Crime Prevention, Domestic Violence, Emergency Relief, Family Planning, Family Services, Food/Clothing Distribution, Homes, People with Disabilities, Recreation & Athletics, Scouts, Shelters/Homelessness, Substance Abuse, United Funds/United Ways, Volunteer Services, YMCA/YWCA/YMHA/YWHA, Youth Organizations

Application Procedures
Initial Contact: Send a written proposal. An application form is not required.
Application Requirements: Include a brief history of organization and its purpose; explanation of proposed

project, and amount of funds requested; plans for evaluation of project; list of foundation's directors, including professional affiliations; description of staff; description of use of volunteers; list of major donors; copy of organization's tax determination letter from IRS; financial information; most recent audited statement or Form 990; current year's budget for organization and project; fundraising costs and total fundraising goal.
Deadlines: None.
Review Process: If initial criteria are met, further information may be requested.
Decision Notification: Two to three months after receipt of proposal.

Restrictions

Foundation does not support individuals, endowments, deficit financing, or organizations that discriminate on the basis of race, religion, or sex. Multiyear grants are limited in number. Applicants must be classified as a 501(c)(3) organization.

Corporate Officials

Eugene Karl Anderson: vice president, director B Omaha, NE 1935. ED Wayne State University (1958); University of Nebraska (1962). PRIM CORP EMPL vice president, assistant treasurer: Contran Corp. ADD CORP EMPL vice president: NAT City Lines Inc.; vice president: Valcor Inc.; vice president, assistant treasurer: Valhi Inc.
Glenn Reuben Simmons: vice chairman B Golden, TX 1928. ED Texas Christian University; East Texas State University BS (1950). PRIM CORP EMPL vice chairman: Contran Corp. CORP AFFIL director: Valhi Group Inc.; vice chairman: Valhi Inc.; vice chairman: Valcor Inc.; director: NL Industries Inc.; chairman: Sherman Wire Caldwell Inc.; chairman, chief executive officer, director: Keystone Consolidated Industries; vice chairman: National City Lines Inc.; chief executive officer: Fox Valley Steel Wire Co.; chairman: DeSoto Inc.; president: Flight Proficiency Service Inc.
Steven L. Watson: president, director PRIM CORP EMPL president, director: Contran Corp. CORP AFFIL secretary: Flight Proficiency Service Inc.; secretary: National City Lines Inc.; secretary: Dallas Compressor Co.

Foundation Officials

Eugene Karl Anderson: treasurer (see above)
Lisa K. Simmons Epstein: president
John Mark Hollingsworth: assistant secretary B Dallas, TX 1951. ED Rhodes College BA (1973); Southern Methodist University JD (1977). PRIM CORP EMPL general corporate counsel: Valhi Inc.
Keith A. Johnson: controller
Harold Clark Simmons: chairman, director B Alba, TX 1931. ED University of Texas BA (1951); University of Texas MA (1952). PRIM CORP EMPL chairman, chief executive officer: Valhi Inc. ADD CORP EMPL chairman, chief executive officer: Contran Corp. CORP AFFIL chairman: Valcor Inc.; director: Kronos Inc.; chairman: NL Industries Inc. NONPR AFFIL member: Phi Beta Kappa.
Steven L. Watson: vice president, secretary, director (see above)

Grants Analysis

Disclosure Period: calendar year ending 2001
Total Grants: $2,412,475*
Number of Grants: 199
Average Grant: $12,123
Highest Grant: $300,000
Lowest Grant: $100
Typical Range: $1,000 to $50,000
*Note: Giving excludes United Way.

Recent Grants

Note: Grants derived from 2001 Form 990.

General

300,000	Southern Methodist University, Dallas,

TX -- for President's Scholars endowments
100,000	Crystal Charity Ball, Dallas, TX -- benefiting Baylor Health Care System Foundation
100,000	East Dallas Community School, Dallas, TX -- for capital campaign
100,000	Fellowship of Christian Athletes, Greater Dallas Chapter, Dallas, TX -- for open golf tournament
100,000	Greenhill School, Dallas, TX -- for Tennis Center
100,000	Human Rights Initiative of North Texas, Dallas, TX -- for operating expenses
100,000	University of Texas at Austin, Austin, TX -- for the Longhorn Legacy for renovation and construction of Darrell K. Royal-Texas Memorial Stadium
87,500	Violence Intervention Prevention Coalition, Dallas, TX -- for operating expenses
65,000	Family Place, Dallas, TX -- for capital campaign
40,000	United Way of Santa Barbara County, Santa Barbara, CA -- to sponsor 200 children for 2002 Fun in the Sun

CARLE C. CONWAY SCHOLARSHIP FOUNDATION

Giving Contact

Scholarship and Recognition Program
PO Box 6731
Princeton, NJ 08541

Description

Founded: 1950
EIN: 136088936
Organization Type: Private Foundation
Giving Locations: nationally.
Grant Types: Scholarship.

Donor Information

Founder: Continental Can Co., Inc.

Financial Summary

Total Giving: $676,124 (fiscal year ending June 30, 2001); $433,961 (fiscal 2000); $340,330 (fiscal 1998). Note: Fiscal 1998 Giving includes scholarship ($265,330).
Giving Analysis: Giving for fiscal 2001 includes: foundation scholarships ($676,124) fiscal 2000: foundation scholarships ($433,961)
Assets: $7,605,445 (fiscal 2001); $9,072,752 (fiscal 2000); $9,313,728 (fiscal 1998)
Gifts Received: $5,656,069 (fiscal 1994)

Typical Recipients

Arts & Humanities: Libraries
Education: Arts/Humanities Education, Colleges & Universities, Engineering/Technological Education, Faculty Development, Medical Education, Science/Mathematics Education, Social Sciences Education, Student Aid, Vocational & Technical Education
Social Services: Family Services

Application Procedures

Initial Contact: Send a written application consisting of student and employee information.
Deadlines: November 30.

Restrictions

Maximum grant does not exceed $8,500 a year for four years. Scholarships awarded only to children of employees who have at least six months continuous service up to the Vice President level.

Foundation Officials

R. E. Adams: vice president
Stephen Bermas: president B New York, NY 1925. ED Cornell University BS (1949); Cornell University JD (1950); New York University LLM (1957). PRIM CORP EMPL vice president, general counsel: Continental Plastic Containers. NONPR AFFIL member: American Bar Association.
M. Colten: vice president, secretary, treasurer
J. Hereford: vice president

Grants Analysis

Disclosure Period: fiscal year ending June 30, 2000
Note: Giving excludes scholarship.

Recent Grants

Note: Grants derived from fiscal 2000 Form 990.

Library-Related

10,000	Woodbury University, Burbank, CA

General

40,000	University of Illinois at Urbana-Champaign, Urbana, IL
20,000	Bowling Green State University, Bowling Green, OH
20,000	Marquette University, Milwaukee, WI
20,000	New York University, New York, NY
20,000	University of Scranton, Scranton, PA
17,325	Penn State University, University Park, PA
16,328	SUNY, Binghamton, NY
14,779	Sam Houston State University, Huntsville, TX
10,000	Creighton University, Omaha, NE
10,000	Florida State University, Tallahassee, FL

LOUELLA COOK FOUNDATION

Giving Contact

James Bittel, Vice President & Trust Officer
c/o US Trust Company of New York
114 W. 47th Street
New York, NY 10036
Phone: (212)852-1000

Description

Founded: 1976
EIN: 911098016
Organization Type: Private Foundation
Giving Locations: WA: Seattle
Grant Types: Operating Expenses.

Financial Summary

Total Giving: $261,350 (fiscal year ending July 31, 2000); $197,000 (fiscal 1998); $108,250 (fiscal 1997)
Assets: $5,840,757 (fiscal 2000); $5,527,287 (fiscal 1998); $5,174,091 (fiscal 1997)
Gifts Received: $125,002 (fiscal 1998); $200,023 (fiscal 1997). Note: In 1998 contributions were received from Shelley B. Jansing.

Typical Recipients

Arts & Humanities: Libraries
Civic & Public Affairs: Botanical Gardens/Parks, Clubs, Philanthropic Organizations
Education: Colleges & Universities, Literacy, Private Education (Precollege), Student Aid
Environment: Resource Conservation
Health: Cancer, Children's Health/Hospitals, Clinics/Medical Centers, Emergency/Ambulance Services, Health Funds, Medical Research, Preventive Medicine/Wellness Organizations, Trauma Treatment
International: Human Rights, International Environmental Issues

Religion: Churches, Religion-General, Missionary Activities (Domestic), Religious Organizations, Religious Welfare

Social Services: Community Centers, Community Service Organizations, Crime Prevention, Day Care, Food/Clothing Distribution, Homes, Shelters/Homelessness, United Funds/United Ways, YMCA/YWCA/YMHA/YWHA, Youth Organizations

Application Procedures

Initial Contact: Send a brief letter of inquiry.
Application Requirements: Include purpose of funds sought.
Deadlines: None.

Additional Information

Trust(s): US Trust Co.

Foundation Officials

Caroline C. Jansing: trustee
Christopher C. Jansing: trustee
John Cook Jansing: trustee

Grants Analysis

Disclosure Period: fiscal year ending July 31, 2000
Total Grants: $261,350*
Average Grant: $4,925*
Typical Range: $200 to $5,000
*Note: No grants list was available for 2000. Average grant figure reflects the foundation's typical average.

Recent Grants

Note: Grants derived from 1998 Form 990.

General

100,000	Dartmouth College, New Haven, CT
25,000	Seattle University, Seattle, WA
5,000	Catholic Community Services, Seattle, WA
5,000	Christ Memorial Chapel, Hobe Sound, FL
5,000	Downtown Emergency Services, Seattle, WA
5,000	Jupiter Medical Center Foundation, Jupiter, FL
5,000	Northern Michigan Hospital Burns Clinic Foundation, Petoskey, MI
5,000	The Salvation Army, Seattle, WA
3,000	American Red Cross, Seattle, WA
3,000	Bread of Life Mission, Seattle, WA -- Grant

KELLY GENE COOK, SR. CHARITABLE FOUNDATION

Giving Contact

Peggy C. Pool, President
278 Waterford Way
Montgomery, TX 77356
Phone: (936)449-6272
E-mail: pegpool@aol.com

Description

Founded: 1986
EIN: 760201807
Organization Type: Specialized/Single Purpose Foundation
Giving Locations: MS: internationally; nationally.
Grant Types: Challenge, Endowment, General Support, Scholarship.

Donor Information

Founder: Established in 1986 by the late Kelly G. Cook and Peggy J. Cook.

Financial Summary

Total Giving: $1,622,776 (2001); $1,631,003 (2000); $1,453,617 (1998)
Giving Analysis: Giving for 2001 includes: foundation scholarships ($540,922); 2000: foundation scholarships ($429,617); 1997: foundation gifts to individuals ($8,562) foundation scholarships ($537,972)
Assets: $33,329,720 (2001); $35,975,941 (2000); $35,187,265 (1998)
Gifts Received: $27,977 (1993); $890,296 (1992).
Note: Contributions were received from the estate of Kelly Gene Cook.

Typical Recipients

Arts & Humanities: Libraries
Civic & Public Affairs: Civic & Public Affairs-General, Municipalities/Towns, Parades/Festivals, Philanthropic Organizations
Education: Business Education, Colleges & Universities, Community & Junior Colleges, Education Reform, Elementary Education (Private), Elementary Education (Public), Faculty Development, Education-General, Journalism/Media Education, Legal Education, Medical Education, Preschool Education, Private Education (Precollege), Public Education (Precollege), Religious Education, Secondary Education (Public), Special Education, Student Aid
Health: Medical Training, Mental Health
Religion: Religious Organizations, Seminaries
Social Services: Community Service Organizations, Day Care, Domestic Violence, Family Services, People with Disabilities, Shelters/Homelessness, Substance Abuse, Youth Organizations

Application Procedures

Application Requirements: Prospective applicants for scholarships should contact the director of financial aid at Millsaps College, the University of Mississippi, or Mississippi State University. Other scholarship programs are administered at the foundation's initiation.
Deadlines: April 15.
Review Process: Applications are reviewed by the institutions and forwarded to the foundation. The foundation then selects those to be interviewed and notifies the applicant. Individual interviews are administered by the foundation. Recipients are chosen based on financial need, potential, and motivation.

Restrictions

To be eligible, an applicant must: be a full-time student with a minimum of 15 academic hours per semester; maintain a satisfactory grade point average as determined by the foundation; not be a physical education major; not be married or have a child; and demonstrate need.

Additional Information

Scholarship recipients who maintain an overall GPA of 3.0 or above in their undergraduate studies are eligible to receive $4,000 ($2,000 per semester) for the first year of graduate studies.
For more information from a specific institution contact:
Mr. Jack L. Woodward, Director of Financial Aid, Millsaps College, Jackson, MS 39210;
Mr. Thomas G. Hood, Director of Student Financial Aid, Division of Student Personnel, University of Mississippi, University, MS 38677; or
Ms. Teresa Bost, Assistant Director of Scholarships, Mississippi State University, PO Box AB, Mississippi State, MS 39762.

Foundation Officials

Corbin Barnes: treasurer
Robert B. Kneppler, Jr.: director
Ray S. Mikell: vice president NONPR AFFIL secretary: French Camp Academy.
Peggy Cook Pool: president
Deborah Rochelle: secretary

Grants Analysis

Disclosure Period: calendar year ending 2001
Total Grants: $881,854*
Number of Grants: 32
Average Grant: $27,558*
Highest Grant: $200,000
Lowest Grant: $250
Typical Range: $15,000 to $50,000
*Note: Giving excludes scholarships. Average grant figure excludes highest grant.

Recent Grants

Note: Grants derived from 2001 Form 990.

General

200,000	Mississippi State University, Starkville, MS -- for Civil Engineering Department
110,000	Boys and Girls Country, Hockley, TX -- campaign for new administration and admission building
100,000	Center for Hearing and Speech, Houston, TX -- Tuition Assistance Program
100,000	Magnolia Speech School, Jackson, MS
86,782	Options Inc., Hammond, LA -- community-based education project
75,000	French Camp Academy, French Camp, MS -- matching grant
50,000	Boys and Girls Country, Hockley, TX
50,000	Briarwood School, Houston, TX -- Teacher Intensive Program
50,000	Holy Child Jesus Catholic School, Canton, MS -- Teacher Intensive Program
50,000	Montgomery Walker County Council on Alcohol and Drug Abuse, Huntsville, TX -- After-School tutorial Program

COOKE FOUNDATION

Giving Contact

Lisa Schiff, Grants Administrator
1164 Bishop Street, 8th Floor
Honolulu, HI 96813
Phone: (808)537-6333
Fax: (808)521-6286
E-mail: info@hcf-hawaii.org
Web: http://www.hcf-hawaii.org

Description

Founded: 1920
EIN: 237120804
Organization Type: General Purpose Foundation
Giving Locations: HI: especially Oahu
Grant Types: Capital, Multiyear/Continuing Support, Project.

Donor Information

Founder: The Cooke Foundation was established in 1920 as the Charles M. Cooke and Anna C. Cooke Trust, with funds bequeathed by their estates. The Cooke family was one of the early pioneers in the development of Hawaii. The family was instrumental in the growth of the Honolulu Academy of Arts, and, to this day, in honor of Anna C. Cooke, the first grant authorized by the foundation's trustees each fiscal year goes to the academy. Through the Cooke Foundation, the Cooke family continues to support the interests and needs of Hawaii.

Financial Summary

Total Giving: $1,478,950 (fiscal year ending June 30, 2002); $1,537,970 (fiscal 2001); $1,667,425 (fiscal 2000)

Giving Analysis: Giving for fiscal 1997 includes: foundation grants to United Way ($12,000)
Assets: $24,604,882 (fiscal 2002); $29,390,021 (fiscal 2001); $36,737,372 (fiscal 2000)
Gifts Received: $500 (fiscal 1999)

Typical Recipients

Arts & Humanities: Arts Associations & Councils, Arts Centers, Arts Festivals, Arts Funds, Ethnic & Folk Arts, Film & Video, Arts & Humanities-General, Historic Preservation, History & Archaeology, Libraries, Literary Arts, Museums/Galleries, Music, Opera, Performing Arts, Public Broadcasting, Theater, Visual Arts
Civic & Public Affairs: Asian American Affairs, Botanical Gardens/Parks, Business/Free Enterprise, Clubs, Community Foundations, Economic Development, Employment/Job Training, Civic & Public Affairs-General, Hispanic Affairs, Housing, Legal Aid, Nonprofit Management, Parades/Festivals, Philanthropic Organizations, Public Policy, Urban & Community Affairs, Zoos/Aquariums
Education: Afterschool/Enrichment Programs, Arts/Humanities Education, Colleges & Universities, Economic Education, Education Funds, Elementary Education (Public), Environmental Education, International Exchange, International Studies, Preschool Education, Private Education (Precollege), Public Education (Precollege), Science/Mathematics Education, Secondary Education (Private), Secondary Education (Public), Social Sciences Education, Special Education, Student Aid
Environment: Air/Water Quality, Environment-General, Resource Conservation, Wildlife Protection
Health: AIDS/HIV, Alzheimers Disease, Cancer, Children's Health/Hospitals, Clinics/Medical Centers, Emergency/Ambulance Services, Health-General, Health Policy/Cost Containment, Health Organizations, Heart, Hospices, Hospices, Hospitals, Medical Research, Mental Health, Prenatal Health Issues, Public Health, Single-Disease Health Associations
International: International Environmental Issues, International Organizations
Religion: Churches, Dioceses, Religion-General, Ministries, Missionary Activities (Domestic), Religious Organizations, Religious Welfare, Seminaries
Science: Science-General, Science Museums, Scientific Centers & Institutes, Scientific Research
Social Services: Animal Protection, At-Risk Youth, Big Brother/Big Sister, Child Welfare, Community Centers, Community Service Organizations, Counseling, Crime Prevention, Domestic Violence, Emergency Relief, Family Planning, Family Services, Food/Clothing Distribution, People with Disabilities, Recreation & Athletics, Scouts, Senior Services, Shelters/Homelessness, Social Services-General, Substance Abuse, United Funds/United Ways, Volunteer Services, YMCA/YWCA/YMHA/YWHA, Youth Organizations

Application Procedures

Initial Contact: Funding requests must be made in writing and must include foundation request cover sheet. Contact foundation for application guidelines.
Application Requirements: The following information should be included: one copy of a proposal, including a brief summary of organization, its history, mission, goals, and major achievements; population served by project and any relevant characteristics; community need, problem, or opportunity addressed by project; program objectives, and summary of activities to be funded; amount requested, duration of time funds will be needed, anticipated sources of future support; method to determine effectiveness of project; and information on key staff. Attachments will include one copy of the IRS determination letter, organization charter and bylaws, most recent financial statement, organization's current operating budget, signatures indicating that both the board and executive director have approved submission of proposal, and name and phone number of contact person. Include a one-

totwo page executive summary of proposal; an expense budget for the proposed activity; and list of the board of directors, including occupations, statement of board involvement, and functions within the organization.
Deadlines: Proposals must be postmarked by July 1 for review at the September meeting; November 1 for the January meeting; and March 1 for the May meeting.
Review Process: Requests for major projects (requests of more than $25,000) are considered at the last meeting of the fiscal year, held in May.
Notes: Organizations receiving grants must submit a brief report summarizing the outcome of the project and an expenditure report at the completion of the project or accounting period.

Restrictions

Grants are not made to individuals; to churches not affiliated with foundation trustees or Cooke family forebears; for scholarships; for re-granting or discretionary funds; or for loans to individuals or institutions. Only one grant will be awarded to an organization in any one year.

Additional Information

The Hawaii Community Foundation is the grants administrator for the Cooke Foundation, Ltd.
Publications: Annual Report; Application Procedures

Foundation Officials

Dale Bachman: trustee
Anna Derby Blackwell: trustee B Honolulu, HI 1932. ED Vassar College (1950-1952); University of Hawaii (1952-1953); University of Canterbury (New Zealand) (1985); Hawaii Pacific University BA (1991). PRIM CORP EMPL consultant: ANNAgram. NONPR AFFIL member: Women in Communications Inc.; founder: Women's Fund Hawaii; assistant manager: Cathedral Associates Saint Marks; member: Public Relations Society America.
Richard A. Cooke, Jr.: trustee
Samuel A. Cooke: president, trustee PRIM NONPR EMPL chairman: Honolulu Academy Arts.
Betty P. Dunford: vice president, trustee NONPR AFFIL director: Family Support Services West Hawaii.
Lynne Johnson: secretary
Charles C. Spalding: vice president, trustee

Grants Analysis

Disclosure Period: fiscal year ending June 30, 2002
Total Grants: $1,478,950
Number of Grants: 97
Average Grant: $14,364*
Highest Grant: $100,000
Lowest Grant: $2,000
Typical Range: $5,000 to $25,000
*Note: Average grant figure excludes highest grant.

Recent Grants

Note: Grants derived from fiscal 2002 Form 990.

General

121,000	St. Andrew's Priory School, Honolulu, HI -- landscaping for playground at Queen Emma Preschool
100,000	Honolulu Academy of Arts, Honolulu, HI -- for annual grant
50,000	Daughters of Hawaii, Honolulu, HI -- for Queen Emma Summer Palace
50,000	Hanahauoli School, Honolulu, HI -- capital campaign
50,000	La Pietra, Honolulu, HI -- capital campaign
50,000	Volcano Art Center, Hawaii National Park, HI -- for construction of administration and arts education facilities
30,000	Missionary Church, Inc., Mililani, HI -- for Punawai Ola Center Programs
25,000	Academy of the Pacific, Honolulu, HI -- for technology upgrade project
25,000	Assets School, Honolulu, HI -- for library expansion
25,000	Boy Scouts of America Aloha Council, Honolulu, HI -- for capital campaign

V. V. COOKE FOUNDATION CORP.

Giving Contact

Theodore L. Merhoff, Jr., Executive Director
V. V. Cooke Foundation Corp.
PO Box 202
Pewee Valley, KY 40056-0202
Phone: (502)241-0303

Description

Founded: 1947
EIN: 616033714
Organization Type: Private Foundation
Giving Locations: KY
Grant Types: General Support.

Donor Information

Founder: the late V. V. Cooke, Cooke Chevrolet Co., Cooke Pontiac Co.

Financial Summary

Total Giving: $299,510 (fiscal year ending August 31, 2001); $318,385 (fiscal 2000); $327,750 (fiscal 1998)
Giving Analysis: Giving for fiscal 2001 includes: foundation grants to United Way ($9,000) fiscal 1998: foundation grants to United Way ($7,500)
Assets: $6,143,748 (fiscal 2001); $6,848,934 (fiscal 2000); $6,466,806 (fiscal 1998)
Gifts Received: $2,556 (fiscal 1998); $193,390 (fiscal 1997)

Typical Recipients

Arts & Humanities: Arts Centers, Arts Funds, Libraries, Music
Civic & Public Affairs: Botanical Gardens/Parks, Clubs, Civic & Public Affairs-General, Housing, Women's Affairs, Zoos/Aquariums
Education: Business Education, Colleges & Universities, Economic Education, Education Funds, Legal Education, Private Education (Precollege), Public Education (Precollege), Special Education
Environment: Forestry
Health: AIDS/HIV, Alzheimers Disease, Cancer, Children's Health/Hospitals, Emergency/Ambulance Services, Hospices, Medical Research, Research/Studies Institutes, Single-Disease Health Associations
Religion: Churches, Ministries, Religious Organizations, Religious Welfare, Seminaries
Social Services: At-Risk Youth, Child Welfare, Community Service Organizations, Day Care, Family Services, People with Disabilities, Scouts, Senior Services, United Funds/United Ways, Volunteer Services, YMCA/YWCA/YMHA/YWHA, Youth Organizations

Application Procedures

Initial Contact: Applications may be in letter format.
Application Requirements: Letter should outline the applicant's goals and purposes, the intended use, and the amount of the grant requested. Include proof of tax-exempt status.
Deadlines: Middle of the following months: January, April, July, and October.

Restrictions

Grants are limited to organizations located in the Louisville, KY area. Grant purposes must be religious, educational, civic or humanitarian.

Foundation Officials

Tracy A. Cooke: director
V. V. Cooke, Jr.: president
Jane C. Cross: vice president
Joe D. Cross, Jr.: director
Frank P. Hilliard: director
June C. Hook: director
Robert L. Hook, Jr.: director
Robert L. Hook, Sr.: secretary, treasurer

Grants Analysis

Disclosure Period: fiscal year ending August 31, 2001
Total Grants: $290,510*
Number of Grants: 80
Average Grant: $3,631
Highest Grant: $54,000
Typical Range: $100 to $25,000
*Note: Giving excludes United Way.

Recent Grants

Note: Grants derived from 2001 Form 990.

Library-Related
5,000	Prescott Public Library, Prescott, AZ

General
54,000	Walnut Street Baptist Church, Louisville, KY
32,120	Broadway Baptist Church, Louisville, KY
27,750	Baptist Theological Seminary, Richmond, VA
7,000	Metro United Way, Louisville, KY
7,000	St. Paul's Episcopal Church, Alexandria, VA
6,800	St. Francis in the Fields Episcopal Church
6,000	Cabbage Patch Settlement House, Louisville, KY
6,000	University of Virginia, Charlottesville, VA -- for Jefferson Scholars Program
5,000	First Baptist Church of Boynton Beach, Boynton Beach, FL
5,000	Habitat for Humanity - Prescott

COOPER FOUNDATION

Giving Contact

E. Arthur Thompson, President
211 N. 12th St., No. 304
Lincoln, NE 68508
Phone: (402)476-7571
Fax: (402)476-2356
E-mail: art@cooperfoundation.org
Web: http://www.cooperfoundation.org

Description

Founded: 1934
EIN: 470401230
Organization Type: Private Foundation
Giving Locations: NE: Lincoln including Lancaster County
Grant Types: Emergency, General Support, Research, Scholarship, Seed Money.

Donor Information

Founder: the late Joseph H. Cooper

Financial Summary

Total Giving: $580,000 (2003 approx); $584,612 (2002); $801,288 (1999)
Giving Analysis: Giving for 1999 includes: foundation matching gifts ($5,000); foundation grants to United Way ($10,741) foundation scholarships ($26,000)
Assets: $115,000,000 (2003 approx); $114,958,173 (2002); $22,057,684 (1999)
Gifts Received: $459,376 (1999). Note: In 1999, contributions were received from E.N. Thompson.

Typical Recipients

Arts & Humanities: Arts Associations & Councils, Arts Centers, Arts Festivals, Ballet, Community Arts, Arts & Humanities-General, History & Archaeology, Libraries, Museums/Galleries, Music, Opera, Performing Arts, Public Broadcasting, Theater
Civic & Public Affairs: Asian American Affairs, Business/Free Enterprise, Community Foundations, Economic Policy, Hispanic Affairs, Housing, Municipalities/Towns, Native American Affairs, Public Policy, Zoos/Aquariums
Education: Arts/Humanities Education, Business Education, Colleges & Universities, Community & Junior Colleges, Economic Education, Education Associations, Education Funds, Elementary Education (Private), Faculty Development, Education-General, International Studies, Legal Education, Literacy, Medical Education, Minority Education, Private Education (Precollege), Public Education (Precollege), Religious Education, Science/Mathematics Education, Secondary Education (Private), Secondary Education (Public), Student Aid
Environment: Environment-General, Resource Conservation
Health: Cancer, Children's Health/Hospitals, Emergency/Ambulance Services, Hospitals, Kidney, Prenatal Health Issues, Public Health
International: International Organizations
Religion: Churches, Religious Organizations, Religious Welfare
Social Services: At-Risk Youth, Child Welfare, Community Centers, Community Service Organizations, Crime Prevention, Delinquency & Criminal Rehabilitation, Domestic Violence, Family Services, Food/Clothing Distribution, Homes, People with Disabilities, Recreation & Athletics, Scouts, Shelters/Homelessness, Substance Abuse, United Funds/United Ways, Volunteer Services, YMCA/YWCA/YMHA/YWHA, Youth Organizations

Application Procedures

Initial Contact: Application form required.
Deadlines: None. Applications are reviewed monthly at board meetings.

Restrictions

Supports programs that benefit children and youth in Lincoln and Lancaster counties, or Nebraska statewide.

Additional Information

Publications: Biennial Report (including Application Guidelines); Informational Brochure

Foundation Officials

Jack D. Campbell: trustee
Kathryn Druliner: trustee
Jane Hood: trustee
Margaret Huff: secretary
W. W. Nuernberger: trustee
John E. Olsson: trustee
Susan Renken: trustee
William C. Smith: trustee
E. Arthur Thompson: president
E. N. Thompson: chairman
Jack Edward Thompson: trustee B Central City, NE 1924. ED Northwestern University (1942-1943); Colorado School of Mines DEngg (1945). PRIM CORP EMPL president, chief executive officer: Homestake Mining Co. NONPR AFFIL member: Mining & Metallurgical Society America; member: President Council Co. School Mines; member: Mining Foundation Southwest; member: American Institute Mining Metallurgical Petroleum Engineers; chairman, trustee: Minerals Industry Education Foundation. CLUB AFFIL Tucson Country Club.
Durward B. Varner: trustee
Richard Vierk: trustee
Norton Warner: trustee

Grants Analysis

Disclosure Period: calendar year ending 1999
Total Grants: $759,547*
Number of Grants: 61
Average Grant: $12,451
Highest Grant: $60,000
Typical Range: $1,000 to $25,000
*Note: Giving excludes matching gifts, scholarships, United Way.

Recent Grants

Note: Grants derived from 1999 Form 990.

General
60,000	Nebraska Cultural Endowment, NE -- cultural endowment
50,000	Lincoln Public Schools Foundation, Lincoln, NE -- comprehensive health initiative
41,000	Audubon Nebraska, NE
41,000	Audubon Nebraska, NE
40,000	University of Nebraska Lincoln, E.N. Thompson Forum on World Issues, Lincoln, NE -- Desmond Tutu and a panel presentation
35,000	Doane College, Crete, NE -- equipment for new Lied Science and Mathematics building
26,400	University Place Art Center -- expansion of art education program for children and adults
25,256	Norfolk Arts Center -- creation of computer classroom for graphic arts and technology education
25,000	Doane College, Crete, NE -- Cooper Undergraduate Research Pilot program
25,000	Doane College, Crete, NE -- Cooper Undergraduate Research Pilot program

COOPER INDUSTRIES LTD.

Company Headquarters

600 Travis St., Ste. 5800
Houston, TX 77002-1001
Web: http://www.cooperindustries.com

Company Description

Founded: 1833
Ticker: CBE
Exchange: NYSE
Revenue: US$3.96 billion (2002)
Employees: 30520 (2002)

Nonmonetary Support

Type: Donated Equipment; Donated Products; In-kind Services
Volunteer Programs: The company sponsors a volunteer Spirit Awards program at all of its international locations. In 1996, Cooper recognized 31 volunteers in nine countries, enabling them to direct cash contributions totaling $46,500 to the nonprofit organizations of their choice.
Note: Nonmonetary support is handled through local contacts.

Cooper Industries Foundation

Giving Contact

Jennifer L. Evans, Director, Community Affairs
Cooper Industries Foundation
PO Box 4446
Houston, TX 77210-4446
Phone: (713)209-8607
Fax: (713)209-8982
Web: http://www.cooperindustries.com/about/index.htm

Note: Subsidiaries have separate contact persons; call the foundation office for information.

Description

EIN: 316060698
Organization Type: Corporate Foundation
Giving Locations: operating locations.
Grant Types: Capital, Challenge, Emergency, Employee Matching Gifts, General Support, Matching, Multiyear/Continuing Support.
Note: Employee matching gift ratio: 1 to 1; 2 to 1 for volunteer services.

Financial Summary

Total Giving: $3,032,117 (2001); $2,773,586 (2000); $2,843,956 (1999). Note: Contributes through corporate direct giving program and foundation.
Giving Analysis: Giving for 2001 includes: foundation matching gifts ($401,217); foundation grants to United Way ($941,104); foundation ($1,606,751); 2000: foundation scholarships ($27,197); foundation matching gifts ($423,285); foundation grants to United Way ($890,404); foundation ($1,432,700); 1999: foundation matching gifts ($344,286); foundation grants to United Way ($1,013,994); foundation ($1,485,676);
Assets: $221,782 (2001); $1,762,474 (2000); $4,568,408 (1999)
Gifts Received: $1,500,000 (2001); $1,000 (1998); $9,856,410 (1997). Note: In 2001, contributions were received from Cooper Industries.

Typical Recipients

Arts & Humanities: Arts Associations & Councils, Arts Funds, Ballet, Dance, Historic Preservation, Libraries, Museums/Galleries, Music, Opera, Performing Arts, Public Broadcasting, Theater
Civic & Public Affairs: African American Affairs, Botanical Gardens/Parks, Business/Free Enterprise, Economic Development, Economic Policy, Employment/Job Training, Civic & Public Affairs-General, Housing, Law & Justice, Municipalities/Towns, Professional & Trade Associations, Public Policy, Safety, Urban & Community Affairs, Women's Affairs, Zoos/Aquariums
Education: Arts/Humanities Education, Business Education, Colleges & Universities, Community & Junior Colleges, Economic Education, Education Associations, Education Funds, Engineering/Technological Education, Literacy, Medical Education, Minority Education, Private Education (Precollege), Public Education (Precollege), Science/Mathematics Education, Secondary Education (Public), Student Aid, Vocational & Technical Education
Environment: Environment-General
Health: Cancer, Children's Health/Hospitals, Emergency/Ambulance Services, Health Funds, Health Organizations, Heart, Hospices, Hospitals, Mental Health, Single-Disease Health Associations
International: Health Care/Hospitals, International Affairs
Religion: Religious Welfare
Science: Science Museums, Scientific Centers & Institutes
Social Services: Animal Protection, Child Welfare, Community Centers, Community Service Organizations, Emergency Relief, Food/Clothing Distribution, People with Disabilities, Recreation & Athletics, Senior Services, Substance Abuse, United Funds/United Ways, YMCA/YWCA/YMHA/YWHA, Youth Organizations

Application Procedures

Initial Contact: Send a brief letter or proposal.
Application Requirements: Include concise a description of organization and its mission, purpose of funds sought including fundraising goals, amount requested, budget information and funding sources, list of board members, and proof of tax-exempt status.
Deadlines: None; budget is set in the fall for the following year.

Review Process: Review team evaluates requests on an ongoing basis; response within four to six weeks of receipt.
Evaluative Criteria: Programs must benefit a community where Cooper is a significant employer, must be endorsed by local management (where applicable), must not duplicate efforts of company-created programs, must have objectives that coincide with those of the company, and must fulfill an important community need.
Notes: Organizations in communities where Cooper has a plant facility should direct their requests to local facilities.

Restrictions

The following types of organizations normally are not eligible for grants: religious organizations, national health and welfare organizations (except through a local united fund or community chest, or through and for the use and benefit of local chapters), fraternal or veterans' organizations (except for special philanthropic projects that benefit a wide spectrum of community life), endowment funds, political candidates or organizations, labor organizations, or lobbying organizations. The company does not support individuals.

Corporate Officials

D. Bradley McWilliams: chief financial officer, senior vice president financerc B 1941. ED New York University; University of Texas BBA (1966); University of Texas JD (1971). PRIM CORP EMPL chief financial officer, senior vice president finance: Cooper Industries, Inc. CORP AFFIL director: Kronos Data Systems Inc.; director: Kronos Inc.
H. John Riley, Jr.: chairman, president, chief executive officer, director B Syracuse, NY 1940. ED Syracuse University BS (1961); Harvard University (1985). PRIM CORP EMPL chairman, president, chief executive officer, director: Cooper Industries, Inc. CORP AFFIL director: Wyman-Gordon Co.; director: Baker Hughes Inc.; director: Central Houston Inc. NONPR AFFIL trustee: Manufacturer Alliance Productivity & Innovation.

Giving Program Officials

Jennifer L. Evans: manager, secretary PRIM CORP EMPL manager corporate giving programs: Cooper Industries Inc.

Foundation Officials

D. Bradley McWilliams: vice president (see above)
H. John Riley, Jr.: chairman, president, chief executive officer (see above)

Grants Analysis

Disclosure Period: calendar year ending 2001
Total Grants: $1,606,751*
Number of Grants: 201
Average Grant: $7,994
Highest Grant: $80,000
Typical Range: $5,000 to $15,000
*Note: Giving excludes matching gifts, scholarships, and United Way.

Recent Grants

Note: Grants derived from 2001 Form 990.

General

127,271	United Way of Waukesha County, Waukesha, WI
97,373	United Way of the Texas Gulf Coast, Houston, TX
92,995	United Way Central New York, Syracuse, NY
80,000	Houston Grand Opera, Houston, TX
63,428	United Way Greater St. Louis, St. Louis, MO
61,775	United Way of West Central Mississippi, Vicksburg, MS
60,000	Alley Theater, Houston, TX
58,250	City of Hope, Los Angeles, CA
57,080	United Way of the Texas Gulf Coast, Houston, TX
57,000	Lowe's Home Safety Council, Wilkesboro, NC

COOPER TIRE & RUBBER CO.

Company Headquarters

701 Lima Ave.
Findlay, OH 45840
Web: http://www.coopertire.com

Company Description

Founded: 1914
Ticker: CTB
Exchange: NYSE
Revenue: US$3.154 billion (2001)
Employees: 23268 (2001)

Nonmonetary Support

Type: Donated Equipment; Donated Products

Cooper Tire & Rubber Foundation

Giving Contact

Philip G. Weaver, Trustee
701 Lima Ave.
Findlay, OH 45840
Phone: (419)423-1321
Fax: (419)424-4212
Web: http://www.cooperindustries.com/about/index.htm

Description

EIN: 237025013
Organization Type: Corporate Foundation
Giving Locations: OH: operating locations.
Grant Types: Employee Matching Gifts, General Support.

Financial Summary

Total Giving: $944,743 (2001); $733,339 (2000); $678,000 (1999). Note: Contributes through corporate direct giving program and foundation.
Giving Analysis: Giving for 2001 includes: foundation scholarships ($2,200); foundation grants to United Way ($252,978); foundation ($689,569); 2000: foundation grants to United Way ($170,900) foundation ($562,439);
Assets: $149,608 (2001); $1,064,261 (2000); $783,026 (1997)
Gifts Received: $38,919 (2001); $501,400 (2000); $700,000 (1997)

Typical Recipients

Arts & Humanities: Arts Associations & Councils, Arts & Humanities-General, Libraries, Museums/Galleries, Public Broadcasting
Civic & Public Affairs: Chambers of Commerce, Clubs, Community Foundations, Employment/Job Training, Civic & Public Affairs-General
Education: Arts/Humanities Education, Business Education, Colleges & Universities, Education Funds, Engineering/Technological Education, Faculty Development, Education-General, Literacy, Private Education (Precollege), Science/Mathematics Education, Secondary Education (Private), Student Aid, Vocational & Technical Education
Health: Cancer, Clinics/Medical Centers, Emergency/Ambulance Services, Health-General, Hospitals, Medical Rehabilitation, Public Health
Religion: Religious Welfare, Seminaries

Science: Scientific Centers & Institutes
Social Services: Community Centers, Community Centers, People with Disabilities, Scouts, Senior Services, Social Services-General, United Funds/United Ways, YMCA/YWCA/YMHA/YWHA

Application Procedures

Initial Contact: Send a brief letter.
Application Requirements: Include a description of organization, amount requested, purpose of funds sought, recently audited financial statement, and proof of tax-exempt status.
Deadlines: None.

Restrictions

Company does not award grants to individuals.

Corporate Officials

Thomas A. Dattilo: chairman, president, chief executive officer B June 12, 1951. ED Ohio State University BA (1973); University of Toledo JD (1977). PRIM CORP EMPL chairman, president, chief executive officer: Cooper Tire & Rubber Co.
Philip G. Weaver: executive vice president, chief financial officer, trustee PRIM CORP EMPL vice president, chief financial officer, trustee: Cooper Tire & Rubber Co.

Foundation Officials

Philip G. Weaver: trustee (see above)

Grants Analysis

Disclosure Period: calendar year ending 2001
Total Grants: $689,569*
Number of Grants: 260
Average Grant: $2,276*
Highest Grant: $100,000
Lowest Grant: $50
Typical Range: $100 to $15,000
*Note: Giving excludes United Way and scholarships.

Recent Grants

Note: Grants derived from 2001 Form 990.

General

100,000	American Red Cross -- for operating
95,800	United Way Hancock County, Findlay, OH -- for operating
70,000	Findlay Family YMCA, Findlay, OH -- for operating
26,620	University of Findlay, Findlay, OH -- for operating
25,000	Ohio Foundation of Independent Colleges, Columbus, OH -- for operating
25,000	Scott County Community Foundation -- for operating
20,000	Karmanos Cancer Institute, Detroit, MI -- for operating
20,000	Kettering University, Flint, MI -- for operating
20,000	Montgomery Community College Foundation, Rockville, MD -- for operating
19,000	United Way Greater Texarkana, Texarkana, AR -- for operating

ADOLPH COORS FOUNDATION

Giving Contact

Salley Rippey, Executive Director
4100 East Mississippi Avenue, Suite 1850
Denver, CO 80246
Phone: (303)388-1636
Fax: (303)388-1684
E-mail: generalinfo@acoorsfdn.org
Web: http://www.adolphcoors.org

Description

Founded: 1975
EIN: 510172279
Organization Type: Family Foundation
Giving Locations: CO
Grant Types: Capital, Endowment, General Support, Operating Expenses, Project, Scholarship.

Donor Information

Founder: Adolph Coors, Sr., a native German, came to the United States to escape his country's political and economic oppression. In 1873, he founded the Coors brewery in Golden, CO.
In 1912, Adolph Coors, Jr., became brewery superintendent and continued the profitable operation of the family's brewery and porcelain company. Later, during the prohibition years, he established what has become one of the largest malted milk operations in the country. Adolph Coors Jr., died in 1970. In October 1975, the Adolph Coors Foundation was established with funds from his trust.

Financial Summary

Total Giving: $8,745,315 (fiscal year ending November 30, 2001); $8,029,309 (fiscal 1999); $7,458,005 (fiscal 1998)
Giving Analysis: Giving for fiscal 1999 includes: foundation grants to United Way ($20,000)
Assets: $140,247,354 (fiscal 2001); $183,144,109 (fiscal 1999); $188,000,000 (fiscal 1998 approx)
Gifts Received: $160,795,564 (fiscal 1996); $9,456,288 (fiscal 1995). Note: In fiscal 1995, the foundation received the contribution from the Janet H. Coors Estate.

Typical Recipients

Arts & Humanities: Arts Associations & Councils, Arts Centers, Ethnic & Folk Arts, Film & Video, Historic Preservation, History & Archaeology, Libraries, Museums/Galleries, Music, Performing Arts, Public Broadcasting, Theater
Civic & Public Affairs: Botanical Gardens/Parks, Business/Free Enterprise, Chambers of Commerce, Clubs, Community Foundations, Economic Development, Economic Policy, Employment/Job Training, First Amendment Issues, Civic & Public Affairs-General, Hispanic Affairs, Housing, Law & Justice, Legal Aid, Municipalities/Towns, Native American Affairs, Nonprofit Management, Parades/Festivals, Professional & Trade Associations, Public Policy, Rural Affairs, Urban & Community Affairs, Urban & Community Affairs, Women's Affairs, Zoos/Aquariums
Education: Arts/Humanities Education, Business Education, Colleges & Universities, Continuing Education, Economic Education, Education Associations, Education Funds, Education Reform, Engineering/Technological Education, Education-General, Gifted & Talented Programs, Health & Physical Education, Journalism/Media Education, Leadership Training, Literacy, Minority Education, Private Education (Precollege), Public Education (Precollege), Religious Education, Science/Mathematics Education, Secondary Education (Public), Student Aid
Environment: Environment-General
Health: AIDS/HIV, Children's Health/Hospitals, Clinics/Medical Centers, Emergency/Ambulance Services, Health Organizations, Hospitals, Medical Rehabilitation, Medical Research, Mental Health, Nursing Services, Preventive Medicine/Wellness Organizations, Public Health, Single-Disease Health Associations
International: International Development, International Peace & Security Issues
Religion: Churches, Jewish Causes, Ministries, Religious Organizations, Religious Welfare
Science: Science Museums, Scientific Organizations
Social Services: At-Risk Youth, Camps, Child Welfare, Community Centers, Community Service Organizations, Day Care, Delinquency & Criminal Rehabilitation, Domestic Violence, Emergency Relief, Family Services, Food/Clothing Distribution, Homes, People with Disabilities, Recreation & Athletics, Scouts, Senior Services, Sexual Abuse, Shelters/Homelessness, Substance Abuse, United Funds/United Ways, Volunteer Services, YMCA/YWCA/YMHA/YWHA, Youth Organizations

Application Procedures

Initial Contact: A preliminary letter with a general description of the proposed project is suggested and should be sent to the executive director.
Application Requirements: After the initial letter is sent, the applying organization should send one copy of a complete proposal, including the organization's legal name and address; contact person and phone number; proof of tax exemption; history, description, and goals of the organization; factors which set the proposed project apart from similar programs; amount needed and how it will be spent; project budget, proof of need, and expected goals of project; other sources of funding and amounts; list of board members (indicate occupations); financial statement of most recent year (foundation prefers a copy of audit); and current and/or proposed income and expense budget.
Deadlines: Applications must be received at least eight weeks prior to the meeting at which consideration is desired.
Review Process: The board of trustees generally meets in March, July, and October to select grant recipients.

Restrictions

The foundation does not make grants to individuals, or for endowment funds, research, film production or other media projects, churches, preschools, day-care centers, nursing homes, extended care centers, conduit funding, deficit financing or retirement of debt, special benefit programs, purchase of membership, or purchase of blocks of tickets. Funding is primarily restricted to Colorado programs.

Additional Information

Presentations by applicants are to be made to staff rather than to board members. If possible, an on-site visit will be conducted as a part of the application review process. If a proposal is approved, a grant agreement is required.
Publications: Annual Report

Foundation Officials

Hon. Holland H. Coors: trustee NONPR AFFIL trustee: Heritage Foundation, Washington DC.
Jeffrey H. Coors: treasurer, trustee B Denver, CO 1944. ED Cornell University BSChE (1967); Cornell University MSChE (1968). PRIM CORP EMPL co-president, chief executive officer: ACX Technologies Inc. CORP AFFIL officer: Golden Photon Inc.; president, chief executive officer: Graphic Packaging Corp.; officer: Golden Genesis Co. Inc.
William K. Coors: president B Golden, CO August 11, 1916. ED Princeton University BSChE (1938); Princeton University MSChE (1939). PRIM CORP EMPL chairman, president, chief executive officer, director: Adolph Coors Co.
Linda S. Tafoya: executive director, secretary
Rev. Robert G. Windsor: trustee

Grants Analysis

Disclosure Period: fiscal year ending November 30, 1999
Total Grants: $8,184,380*
Number of Grants: 120
Average Grant: $62,474*
Highest Grant: $750,000
Lowest Grant: $400
Typical Range: $10,000 to $50,000
*Note: Grants analysis excludes United Way. Average grant figure excludes highest grant.

Recent Grants

Note: Grants derived from fiscal 2001 Form 990.

General

2,000,000	Denver Museum of Nature and Science, Denver, CO -- for the Space Science Initiative
1,000,000	Johnson and Wales University, Providence, RI -- to establish the hospitality and culinary arts campus in Denver
500,000	Colorado College, Colorado Springs, CO -- for construction
500,000	Rocky Mountain Public Broadcasting, Denver, CO -- for capital support to aid in digital conversion of equipment
500,000	University of Denver, Denver, CO -- capital support to build a new performing arts center
250,000	Colorado Outward Bound School, Denver, CO -- to assist with costs to renovate space at new headquarters facility
225,000	YMCA Pikes Peak Region, Colorado Springs, CO -- for capital support for construction of new facility
192,000	Colorado School of Mines Foundation, Golden, CO -- for the Herman F. Coors Professional Chair in Ceramics
160,500	Boy Scouts of America Greater Southwest Council, Albuquerque, NM -- development of infrastructure near Delores, Colorado
150,000	Boys and Girls Club of Larimer County, Ft. Collins, CO -- for capital support

COPIC MEDICAL FOUNDATION

Giving Contact

Kathy Brown, Vice President Marketing & COIs
c/o Copic Insurance Co.
7351 Lowry Blvd.
Denver, CO 80230
Phone: (720)858-6066
Web: http://callcopic.com/cmf/index.htm

Description

Founded: 1992
EIN: 841197083
Organization Type: Private Foundation
Giving Locations: CO
Grant Types: General Support, Operating Expenses.

Donor Information

Founder: Established in 1992 by the Copic Insurance Co.

Financial Summary

Total Giving: $228,938 (2002); $323,662 (2001); $387,453 (2000)
Assets: $3,516,105 (2002); $5,283,954 (2001); $5,324,966 (2000)
Gifts Received: $250,000 (2001); $250,000 (2000); $500,200 (1999). Note: In 2000 and 2001, contributions were received from In 1999, contributions were received from the COPIC Trust ($500,000) and Valerie Farnham ($200).

Typical Recipients

Arts & Humanities: Libraries
Civic & Public Affairs: Urban & Community Affairs
Education: Education-General, Literacy, Medical Education, Science/Mathematics Education
Health: Alzheimers Disease, Clinics/Medical Centers, Emergency/Ambulance Services, Health-General, Health Policy/Cost Containment, Health Organizations, Hospitals, Medical Research, Multiple Sclerosis, Nursing Services, Preventive Medicine/Wellness Organizations, Public Health, Research/Studies Institutes, Respiratory, Transplant Networks/Donor Banks
Religion: Religious Welfare
Science: Science Museums
Social Services: Child Welfare, Domestic Violence, Emergency Relief, Family Services, Shelters/Homelessness, Social Services-General, Substance Abuse

Application Procedures

Initial Contact: Send a brief letter of inquiry requesting application form or download application and guidelines from the foundation's web site.
Application Requirements: Proposals should include a completed application, copy of 501(c)(3) letter, total project cost and amount requested, recently audited financial statement, and most recent audit report.
Deadlines: None.

Restrictions

Restricted to purposes related to medicine, medical education, medical research, and other medical charitable purposes. Grants are not made to individuals.

Foundation Officials

A. Lee Anneberg, MD: director
Jerome M. Buckley, MD: director, chairman PRIM CORP EMPL chief executive officer: Copic Insurance Co.
Georgia L. Buford: secretary
George D. Dikeou, Esq.: director
Stuart L. Greisman, D.O.: director
Erroll C. Hossack: treasurer
K. Mason Howard, M.D.: president, director
Alethia Morgan, M.D.: director
Ronald C. Ochsner, M.D.: director
Merlin G. Otteman, M.D.: director
Barbara Reed, M.D.: director
Bruce C. Richards, M.D.: director
Amilu S. Rothhammer, M.D.: director
Steve Rubin: treasurer
Steven J. Thorson, M.D.: director
Larry W. Thrower: vice president, director
David M. West, M.D.: director
Harold Williamson: director

Grants Analysis

Disclosure Period: calendar year ending 2002
Total Grants: $228,938
Number of Grants: 57
Average Grant: $4,016
Highest Grant: $45,000
Lowest Grant: $250
Typical Range: $250 to $10,000

Recent Grants

Note: Grants derived from 2002 Form 990.

General

45,000	Colorado Academy of Family Physicians, Denver, CO -- for program support
30,000	Colorado Medical Society Foundation, Denver, CO -- for program support
25,000	Colorado Prevention Center, Denver, CO -- for program support
15,000	Inner City Health Center, Denver, CO -- for program support
12,000	University of Colorado Health Sciences Center, Denver, CO -- for program support
10,500	Doctors Care, Littleton, CO -- for program support
10,000	Family Pathways of Colorado, Wheat Ridge, CO -- for program support
10,000	Rocky Mountain Multiple Sclerosis Center, Englewood, CO -- for program support
10,000	St. Francis Center, Denver, CO -- for program support
8,250	American Lung Association of Colorado,

Denver, CO -- for Champ Camp Scholarship

COPLEY PRESS, INC.

Company Headquarters

7776 Ivanhoe Ave.
La Jolla, CA 92037
Web: http://www.copleynews.com

Company Description

Revenue: US$534 million (2001)
Employees: 3500 (2001)
SIC(s): 2711 Newspapers.

Operating Locations

Copley Press, Inc. (CA--San Diego, San Pedro, Santa Monica; IL--Aurora, Elgin, Joliet, Lincoln Park, Springfield, Waukegan)

James S. Copley Foundation

Giving Contact

PO Box 1530
La Jolla, CA 92038-1530
Phone: (858)454-0411

Description

EIN: 956051770
Organization Type: Corporate Foundation
Giving Locations: in immediate circulation areas only.
Grant Types: Capital, Employee Matching Gifts, Endowment, Multiyear/Continuing Support, Scholarship.
Note: Employee matching gift ratio: 1 to 1 for gifts to education institutions, up to $1,000 annually.

Financial Summary

Total Giving: $4,975,000 (2002 approx); $2,600,000 (2001); $2,742,298 (2000). Note: Contributes through corporate direct giving program and foundation.
Giving Analysis: Giving for 2002 includes: foundation (approx $2,000,000); 2001: foundation (approx $2,600,000); 2000: foundation grants to United Way ($350,500); foundation ($2,391,798).
Assets: $25,576,325 (2001); $28,428,345 (2000); $30,903,356 (1999)
Gifts Received: $30,531 (2001); $17,160 (2000); $21,182 (1999). Note: Foundation receives contributions from the San Diego Union Shoe Fund.

Typical Recipients

Arts & Humanities: Arts Centers, Dance, Ethnic & Folk Arts, Arts & Humanities-General, History & Archaeology, Libraries, Literary Arts, Museums/Galleries, Music, Opera, Performing Arts, Public Broadcasting, Theater, Visual Arts
Civic & Public Affairs: Botanical Gardens/Parks, Community Foundations, Civic & Public Affairs-General, Housing, Law & Justice, Professional & Trade Associations, Public Policy, Urban & Community Affairs, Zoos/Aquariums
Education: Arts/Humanities Education, Colleges & Universities, Education Funds, Education-General, Leadership Training, Literacy, Medical Education, Minority Education, Private Education (Precollege), Public Education (Precollege), Secondary Education (Private), Student Aid
Environment: Resource Conservation
Health: AIDS/HIV, Alzheimers Disease, Children's Health/Hospitals, Clinics/Medical Centers, Health-General, Hospices, Hospitals, Medical Rehabilitation, Mental Health, Preventive Medicine/Wellness Organizations, Public Health, Research/Studies Institutes, Single-Disease Health Associations, Transplant Networks/Donor Banks

International: Foreign Arts Organizations, Foreign Educational Institutions, International Organizations
Religion: Dioceses, Religious Welfare
Science: Science Museums, Scientific Organizations
Social Services: Animal Protection, Child Abuse, Child Welfare, Community Centers, Community Service Organizations, Food/Clothing Distribution, Homes, People with Disabilities, Recreation & Athletics, Scouts, Senior Services, Senior Services, Shelters/Homelessness, Social Services-General, Substance Abuse, United Funds/United Ways, YMCA/YWCA/YMHA/YWHA, Youth Organizations

Application Procedures

Initial Contact: Submit letter.
Application Requirements: Include an outline of the specific need with a copy of tax exempt certificate, a list of board/trustee members, and financial budgetary information.
Deadlines: January 2 yearly for annual meeting held in February; otherwise accepted throughout the year.
Review Process: The board meets sometime in the spring to review requests; usually responds within 30 days.
Notes: The foundation does not accept faxed applications or videotapes.

Restrictions

Foundation does not make grants to individuals, fundraising events, goodwill advertising, or political or lobbying groups. Grants generally are not made for unrestricted purposes, budgetary support, operating expenses, or seed money.

Grants generally are not made to organizations receiving support from United Way; loans; general fund drives or annual appeals; debt retirement or operational deficits; state universities and colleges; grantmaking organizations; national organizations; public elementary and secondary schools; organizations whose activities are mainly international; research projects; government and public agencies; religious, fraternal, or athletic organizations; conferences or seminars; organizations for distribution to beneficiaries of their own choosing; or for production costs of films, videos, television programs, or books.

Scholarship funds are only contributed to colleges and universities for distribution, not to individuals. Grants are limited primarily to the immediate circulation areas of Copley Newspapers located in California, Illinois, and Ohio.

Additional Information

Foundation does not grant interviews.
Contributions are made for one year and imply no commitment to repeat donations.
Publications: Giving Guidelines

Corporate Officials

David C. Copley: president, chief executive officer, director, senior management board B 1952. ED Menlo College BSBA. PRIM CORP EMPL president, chief executive officer, director, senior management board: Copley Press, Inc. ADD CORP EMPL publisher: Borrego Sun; president: Copley Northwest Inc.; president: Copley News Service; president: Puller Paper Co. CORP AFFIL member editorial Bd: San Diego Union-Tribune; officer: Peoria Journal Star Inc.; chairman, chief executive officer: Fox Valley Press Inc. NONPR AFFIL president: University San Diego President Club; member president associates: Zoological Society San Diego; member: U.S. Humane Society; director: San Diego Museum Art; member president council: Scripps Clinic & Research Foundation; member president council: San Diego Kind Corp.; member: San Diego Hall Science; member: San Diego Historical Society; trustee: San Diego Crew Classic Foundation; member: San Diego Aerospace Museum; member advisory board: San Diego Automotive Museum; member: National Newspaper Association; director:

Saint Vincent de Paul Society; trustee emeritus: Museum Photog Arts; member: FOCAS; trustee emeritus: La Jolla Playhouse; trustee: Canterbury School; trustee emeritus: American Craft Council. CLUB AFFIL Bachelor San Diego Club.
Dean P. Dwyer: vice president finance, treasurer, senior management board PRIM CORP EMPL vice president finance, treasurer, senior management board: Copley Press, Inc. CORP AFFIL treasurer, director: Fox Valley Press Inc.; assistant secretary: Peoria Journal Star Inc.
Charles F. Patrick: executive vice president, chief operating officer, senior management board PRIM CORP EMPL executive vice president, chief operating officer, senior management board: Copley Press, Inc.

Foundation Officials

Anita A. Baumgardner: secretary, trustee
David C. Copley: president, trustee (see above)
Helen K. Copley: chairman B Cedar Rapids, IA 1922. ED Hunter College (1945). ADD CORP EMPL publisher: San Diego Union-Tribune. CORP AFFIL chairman, editorial board: Union Tribune Publishing Co.; officer: Peoria Journal Star Inc.; director: Fox Valley Press Inc. NONPR AFFIL honorary chairman: Washington Crossing Foundation; member: YWCA; life member: Scripps Memorial Hospital Auxiliary; life member: Star of India Auxiliary; member: San Diego Symphony Association; life member: San Diego Zoological Society; member: San Diego Society Natural History; life member: San Diego Hall Science; life member: San Diego Opera Association; honorary chairman: San Diego Council Literacy; life patroness: Makua Auxiliary; member: Newspaper Association America; member: La Jolla Town Council; member: Inter-American Press Association; life member: La Jolla Museum Contemporary Art; life member: Friends of International Center; member: California Press Association; member: California Press Institute; member: California Newspaper Publishers Association; member: American Press Institute. CLUB AFFIL San Francisco Press Club; LA Press Club.
Robert F. Crouch: vice president, trustee CORP AFFIL officer: Fox Valley Press Inc.
Alex De Bakcsy: vice president, trustee CORP AFFIL director: Copley Press Inc.
Terry Gilbert: secretary
Charles F. Patrick: treasurer, trustee (see above)
Karl ZoBell: vice president, trustee B La Jolla, CA 1932. ED Utah State University (1949-1951); Columbia University (1951-1952); Columbia University AB (1953); Stanford University JD (1958). PRIM CORP EMPL partner: Gray, Cary, Ames & Frye. CORP AFFIL director, founder: La Jolla Bank & Trust Co.; vice president, director: Geisel-Seuss Enterprises Inc. NONPR AFFIL trustee: Dr Seuss Foundation; member: Lambda Alpha; director: James C Copley Charitable Foundation; fellow: American College Trust & Estate Counsel; member: California Bar Association; member: American Bar Association. CLUB AFFIL La Jolla Beach & Tennis Club.

Grants Analysis

Disclosure Period: calendar year ending 2001
Total Grants: $2,076,561*
Number of Grants: 290
Average Grant: $7,200
Highest Grant: $500,000
Lowest Grant: $15
Typical Range: $100 to $10,000
*Note: Giving excludes United Way.

Recent Grants

Note: Grants derived from 2001 Form 990.

General

500,000	La Jolla Playhouse, La Jolla, CA
250,000	Old Globe Theatre, San Diego, CA
200,000	Museum of Photographic Arts, San Diego, CA
200,000	San Diego Natural History Museum, San Diego, CA
100,000	Mingei International Museum of World Folk Art, La Jolla, CA
100,000	Museum of Contemporary Art, San Diego, CA
56,250	United Way of San Diego County, San Diego, CA
56,250	United Way of San Diego County, San Diego, CA
56,250	United Way of San Diego County, San Diego, CA
50,000	Children's Museum of San Diego, San Diego, CA -- Museo de los Ninos

CORBETT FOUNDATION

Giving Contact

Karen P. McKim, Executive Director
127 West 9th Street, Suite 3
Cincinnati, OH 45202
Phone: (513)241-3320
Fax: (513)723-4422

Description

Founded: 1958
EIN: 316050360
Organization Type: General Purpose Foundation
Giving Locations: OH: Cincinnati
Grant Types: Capital, Matching, Project.

Donor Information

Founder: Established in 1958 by the late J. Ralph Corbett and Patricia Corbett.

Financial Summary

Total Giving: $1,924,104 (fiscal year ending April 30, 2002); $1,279,936 (fiscal 2001); $2,027,888 (fiscal 1999)
Assets: $19,586,459 (fiscal 2002); $24,103,851 (fiscal 2001); $26,552,389 (fiscal 1999)
Gifts Received: $250 (fiscal 1999); $1,500,025 (fiscal 1992). Note: Contributions were received from Patricia A. Corbett.

Typical Recipients

Arts & Humanities: Arts Associations & Councils, Arts Centers, Arts Festivals, Arts Institutes, Arts Outreach, Ballet, Dance, Ethnic & Folk Arts, Film & Video, Arts & Humanities-General, Historic Preservation, History & Archaeology, Libraries, Museums/Galleries, Music, Opera, Performing Arts, Public Broadcasting, Theater
Civic & Public Affairs: Chambers of Commerce, Civic & Public Affairs-General, Urban & Community Affairs, Women's Affairs
Education: Afterschool/Enrichment Programs, Arts/Humanities Education, Colleges & Universities, Private Education (Precollege), Public Education (Precollege), Religious Education, Secondary Education (Public), Special Education, Student Aid
Environment: Environment-General
Health: Alzheimers Disease, Nutrition, Preventive Medicine/Wellness Organizations
International: Foreign Arts Organizations
Religion: Ministries, Religious Welfare
Science: Science Museums
Social Services: Child Welfare, Community Service Organizations, Senior Services, Substance Abuse, United Funds/United Ways

Application Procedures

Initial Contact: The foundation requests applications be made in writing.
Application Requirements: Applicants should describe the program and need, budget and include a copy of the exempted organization's IRS letter regarding its classification under section 501(c)(3).

Deadlines: None. Proposals are accepted throughout the year.
Review Process: Applicants are usually notified within two months whether the application has been approved, rejected, or if more information is necessary before a decision can be made.

Restrictions

Grants are not made to individuals. The foundation supports projects in the greater Cincinnati area only.

Foundation Officials

Patricia A. Corbett: chairman, president
Thomas R. Corbett: trustee B 1936. ED Williams College (1956). PRIM CORP EMPL president, treasurer: Corbett Lighting Inc. CORP AFFIL president, treasurer: CLI Holdings Inc.
Karen P. McKim: secretary, executive director
Jean S. Reis: vice president, treasurer, trustee
Nancy Walker: trustee

Grants Analysis

Disclosure Period: fiscal year ending April 30, 2001
Total Grants: $1,924,104
Number of Grants: 28
Average Grant: $21,575*
Highest Grant: $600,000
Typical Range: $5,000 to $30,000
***Note:** Average grant figure excludes three highest grants ($1,320,000).

Recent Grants

Note: Grants derived from fiscal 2002 Form 990.

General

600,000	Soc Pres Music Hall
520,000	AAAE -- assist in funding programs
200,000	WCET, Cincinnati, OH
115,000	May Festival
100,000	Cincinnati Art School, Cincinnati, OH
65,000	Cincinnati Opera, Cincinnati, OH
50,000	Cincinnati Institute of Fine Arts, Cincinnati, OH
38,000	WGUC Radio Station, Cincinnati, OH
30,000	School of Creative and Performing Arts, Cincinnati, OH
26,000	American Classical Music Hall of Fame

E. L. CORD FOUNDATION

Giving Contact

William O. Bradley, Trustee
1 East 1st Street, Number 901
Reno, NV 89501
Phone: (775)323-0373
Fax: (775)325-8523

Description

Founded: 1962
EIN: 366072793
Organization Type: General Purpose Foundation
Giving Locations: NV: northern and rural counties
Grant Types: Capital, General Support, Operating Expenses, Project, Scholarship.

Donor Information

Founder: Established in 1962 by the late E. L. Cord , who owned business ventures in automobile manufacturing, airplane and boat engine manufacturing, the airline industry, shipbuilding, electrical appliance manufacturing, real estate, and investments. When Mr. Cord died in 1974, his will provided that the major portion of his estate be given to the foundation after bequests to his family members were paid.

Financial Summary

Total Giving: $4,500,000 (2003 approx); $5,186,125 (2000); $5,224,765 (1999)
Giving Analysis: Giving for 1998 includes: foundation scholarships ($209,680)

Assets: $108,657,900 (2000); $105,848,945 (1999); $101,040,208 (1998)

Typical Recipients

Arts & Humanities: Arts Associations & Councils, Arts Centers, Ballet, Dance, Film & Video, Historic Preservation, History & Archaeology, Libraries, Literary Arts, Museums/Galleries, Music, Opera, Performing Arts, Public Broadcasting, Theater
Civic & Public Affairs: Botanical Gardens/Parks, Chambers of Commerce, Employment/Job Training, Civic & Public Affairs-General, Hispanic Affairs, Housing, Law & Justice, Legal Aid, Safety, Women's Affairs, Zoos/Aquariums
Education: Afterschool/Enrichment Programs, Arts/Humanities Education, Business Education, Colleges & Universities, Community & Junior Colleges, Elementary Education (Private), Elementary Education (Public), Engineering/Technological Education, Faculty Development, Education-General, Legal Education, Medical Education, Minority Education, Private Education (Precollege), Public Education (Precollege), Science/Mathematics Education, Secondary Education (Public), Student Aid
Environment: Research
Health: Cancer, Children's Health/Hospitals, Clinics/Medical Centers, Diabetes, Emergency/Ambulance Services, Health-General, Hospices, Hospitals, Medical Research, Single-Disease Health Associations
Religion: Churches, Religious Organizations, Religious Welfare
Science: Scientific Centers & Institutes, Scientific Labs
Social Services: Camps, Child Welfare, Community Service Organizations, Counseling, Domestic Violence, Family Services, Food/Clothing Distribution, Homes, People with Disabilities, Recreation & Athletics, Scouts, Senior Services, Shelters/Homelessness, Substance Abuse, United Funds/United Ways, YMCA/YWCA/YMHA/YWHA, Youth Organizations

Application Procedures

Initial Contact: Applicants should write the foundation for application procedures before submitting a formal application.
Application Requirements: All applications must include a concise statement of the project; a statement of the organization's background and its purpose and objectives (the most recent annual report containing such information will suffice); financial information, including a copy of the audited financial statement for the prior fiscal year, a copy of the organizational budget for the current year, the most recent unaudited operating and other available financial statements, and a statement of the major sources of financial support; a statement of how the applicant and the foundation will be able to determine the results of the project upon its completion; evidence of tax-exempt status copy of the determination letter from the IRS stating that the organization is exempt from taxation as defined under Section 501(c)(3) of the Internal Revenue Code and further that the organization is not a private foundation as defined in Section 509 (a); and a list of names of the board members, showing their business, professional, or community affiliations. Any trustee of the foundation, serving as a member, director, trustee, officer, or employee of an organization requesting a grant, will abstain from voting on any matter pertaining to the organization with which the common relationship exists.
Deadlines: October 15.
Review Process: After an organization submits a formal application, the foundation may request an interview, a site visit to the project, or have a telephone discussion with the applicant before the formal proposal is submitted to the board.

Restrictions

Funding will not be considered for organizations that do not have a tax-exempt status or do not comply with other terms or provisions of the foundation's application procedures; general fund-raising events, campaigns, memorial campaigns, deficit funding, conferences or seminars, dinners, or mass mailings; direct aid to individuals; grants to organizations who use funds to support other organizations; grants to religious organizations for sectarian purposes; or any request that will require permanent or continuing support by the foundation.

Additional Information

Characteristics that the foundation looks for in submitted proposals include: institutions and organizations with a history of achievement and good management; institutions that demonstrate a current stable financial condition; programs and projects that become self-sufficient, rather than continuing dependence on the foundation; and projects with a measurable impact.
Publications: Guidelines

Foundation Officials

Joseph S. Bradley: trustee
William O. Bradley: trustee
Robert L. Sims: trustee

Grants Analysis

Disclosure Period: calendar year ending 2000
Total Grants: $5,186,125
Number of Grants: 151
Average Grant: $34,345
Highest Grant: $250,000
Lowest Grant: $2,000
Typical Range: $5,000 to $55,000

Recent Grants

Note: Grants derived from 2000 Form 990.

Library-Related

50,000	Washoe Library Foundation, Reno, NV -- to construct Verdi Nature Center

General

250,000	Auburn Cord Duesenberg Museum, Auburn, IN -- for 7000 sq ft expansion project
250,000	Cate School, Carpinteria, CA -- for construction to faculty housing
250,000	KNPB/Channel 5, Reno, NV -- second installment
250,000	KNPB/Channel 5, Reno, NV -- final payment
199,000	University of Nevada Reno Foundation, Reno, NV -- for computers, timing system for aquatic facility and Soviet Medical Library
100,000	Care Chest, Reno, NV -- for partial payment on construction loans for Community Campus Project
100,000	Great Basin College Foundation, Elko, NV -- for endowment of college assistance
100,000	National Automobile Museum, Reno, NV -- to pay construction dept, and endowment
100,000	Nevada Museum of Art, Reno, NV -- to expand museum
100,000	Reno Performing Arts Center, Reno, NV -- to improve Pioneer Center Plaza

PETER C. CORNELL TRUST

Giving Contact

John A. Mitchell, Trustee
c/o Fiduciary Services, Inc.
4476 Main, No. 206
Snyder, NY 14226-2783
Phone: (716)839-3005

Description
Founded: 1949
EIN: 951660344
Organization Type: Private Foundation
Giving Locations: NY: Buffalo including Erie County
Grant Types: Capital, Emergency, General Support, Multiyear/Continuing Support, Operating Expenses, Seed Money.

Donor Information
Founder: the late Peter C. Cornell, M.D.

Financial Summary
Total Giving: $523,746 (fiscal year ending September 30, 2001); $202,000 (fiscal 1999); $280,000 (fiscal 1998)
Assets: $7,144,694 (fiscal 2001); $6,997,687 (fiscal 1999); $5,674,470 (fiscal 1998)

Typical Recipients
Arts & Humanities: Arts Institutes, Arts Outreach, Arts & Humanities-General, History & Archaeology, Libraries, Music, Opera, Public Broadcasting, Theater
Civic & Public Affairs: African American Affairs, Economic Development, Civic & Public Affairs-General, Housing, Municipalities/Towns, Safety, Urban & Community Affairs, Women's Affairs, Zoos/Aquariums
Education: Arts/Humanities Education, Business-School Partnerships, Colleges & Universities, Continuing Education, Education Funds, Education Reform, Faculty Development, Legal Education, Literacy, Medical Education, Minority Education, Preschool Education, Private Education (Precollege), Public Education (Precollege), Science/Mathematics Education, Special Education, Student Aid
Environment: Wildlife Protection
Health: AIDS/HIV, Alzheimers Disease, Children's Health/Hospitals, Clinics/Medical Centers, Emergency/Ambulance Services, Health Organizations, Hospices, Hospitals, Long-Term Care, Nursing Services, Single-Disease Health Associations, Speech & Hearing
International: International-General, International Development
Religion: Churches, Dioceses, Ministries, Religious Organizations, Religious Welfare, Seminaries
Science: Science Museums, Scientific Centers & Institutes, Scientific Organizations
Social Services: Camps, Child Welfare, Community Service Organizations, Counseling, Family Planning, Family Services, Food/Clothing Distribution, People with Disabilities, Scouts, Senior Services, Social Services-General, Substance Abuse, United Funds/United Ways, YMCA/YWCA/YMHA/YWHA, Youth Organizations

Application Procedures
Initial Contact: Request application form and guidelines.
Deadlines: October 15 and April 15.

Restrictions
Does not provide loans or support individuals, demonstration projects, publications, or conferences.

Additional Information
Publications: Application Form; Guidelines

Foundation Officials
John A. Mitchell: trustee
J. Donald Schumacher: trustee
Susan Cornell Wilkes: trustee

Grants Analysis
Disclosure Period: fiscal year ending September 30, 2001
Total Grants: $523,746
Number of Grants: 34
Average Grant: $14,507*

Highest Grant: $45,000
Lowest Grant: $1,000
Typical Range: $5,000 to $25,000
*Note: Average grant figure excludes highest grant.

Recent Grants
Note: Grants derived from fiscal 2000 Form 990.

General
35,000	AIDS Community Services of Western New York, Buffalo, NY
35,000	AIDS Community Services of Western New York, Buffalo, NY -- to hire a fundraiser
25,000	Hospice Buffalo, Buffalo, NY
25,000	Nicholas School, Durham, NC -- for capital campaign
25,000	Nicholas School, Durham, NC -- for capital campaign
25,000	Western New York Public Broadcasting Association, Buffalo, NY -- for friendship program
20,000	Blind Association, Buffalo, NY -- for capital campaign
20,000	International Development Conference, New York, NY -- for challenge grant
20,000	Planned Parenthood -- for askable parent program
18,000	Try Program -- for operating funds

CORNING INC.

Company Headquarters
1 Riverfront Plaza
Corning, NY 14831-0001
Web: http://www.corning.com

Company Description
Founded: 1936
Ticker: GLW
Exchange: NYSE
Acquired: Oak Industries, Inc. (1999).
Revenue: US$2.467 billion (2002)
Employees: 31700 (2002)
Fortune Rank: 455, per FORTUNE Magazine's list of 500 Largest U.S. Corporations (2002).
SIC(s): 3229 Pressed & Blown Glass Nec, 3661 Telephone & Telegraph Apparatus, 3821 Laboratory Apparatus & Furniture, 3826 Analytical Instruments.

Operating Locations
Corning Inc. (ME--Kennebunk, Scarborough; MA--Acton; NY--Oneonta)

Nonmonetary Support
Type: Loaned Executives
Note: Co. provides nonmonetary support.

Corning Inc. Foundation

Giving Contact
Kristin A. Swain, President
MP-LB-02
Corning, NY 14831
Phone: (607)974-8719
Fax: (607)974-4756
E-mail: martinkc@corning.com
Web: http://www.corning.com/inside_corning/foundation.asp

Alternate Contact
Karen C. Martin, Program Officer

Description
EIN: 166051394
Organization Type: Corporate Foundation
Giving Locations: headquarters and operating communities and nationally; internationally to U.S.-based organizations.

Grant Types: Employee Matching Gifts, Fellowship, Project.
Note: Employee matching gift ratio: 1 to 1 up to $5,000 per employee annually; institutions may receive up to $20,000 in matched payments per calendar year.

Financial Summary
Total Giving: $4,718,947 (2001); $5,179,390 (2000); $4,121,681 (1999). Note: Contributes through corporate direct giving program and foundation.
Giving Analysis: Giving for 2001 includes: foundation scholarships ($50,000); foundation matching gifts ($617,686); foundation grants to United Way ($629,570); foundation grants to United Way ($667,075); foundation ($3,421,691); foundation ($5,180,391); 2000: foundation fellowships ($152,200); foundation grants to United Way ($460,010); foundation matching gifts ($1,037,280); foundation ($3,529,900); 1999: foundation grants to United Way ($438,450); foundation matching gifts ($857,134); foundation ($2,826,097);
Assets: $22,686,811 (2001); $24,832,560 (2000); $9,539,807 (1999)
Gifts Received: $405,058 (2001); $9,350,177 (1999); $441,353 (1998). Note: Contributions were received from Corning, Inc.

Typical Recipients
Arts & Humanities: Arts Associations & Councils, Arts Outreach, Community Arts, Arts & Humanities-General, Historic Preservation, Libraries, Museums/Galleries, Music, Opera, Performing Arts, Public Broadcasting, Theater, Visual Arts
Civic & Public Affairs: Community Foundations, Economic Development, Employment/Job Training, Civic & Public Affairs-General, Municipalities/Towns, Nonprofit Management, Professional & Trade Associations, Public Policy, Urban & Community Affairs, Women's Affairs, Zoos/Aquariums
Education: Afterschool/Enrichment Programs, Business Education, Business-School Partnerships, Colleges & Universities, Community & Junior Colleges, Education Associations, Education Funds, Education Reform, Engineering/Technological Education, Environmental Education, Faculty Development, Education-General, International Studies, Minority Education, Public Education (Precollege), Science/Mathematics Education, Student Aid
Environment: Environment-General, Resource Conservation
Health: Clinics/Medical Centers, Emergency/Ambulance Services, Hospices, Hospitals (University Affiliated), Medical Rehabilitation
International: Foreign Educational Institutions
Religion: Jewish Causes
Science: Science Museums, Scientific Centers & Institutes, Scientific Organizations
Social Services: At-Risk Youth, Big Brother/Big Sister, Community Centers, Community Service Organizations, Family Planning, Recreation & Athletics, Scouts, Senior Services, Substance Abuse, United Funds/United Ways, YMCA/YWCA/YMHA/YWHA, Youth Organizations

Application Procedures
Initial Contact: Send a two- to three-page letter of inquiry signed by the senior administrative officer of the organization.
Application Requirements: When submitting a full proposal, provide a project description, including project's purpose, details on how its objectives are to be attained and evaluated, demonstration of how project promotes cooperation among other organizations in the same field, project timetable, amount requested and when funds are needed, itemized project budget, other potential and secured sources of support, and how the project fits Corning Foundation interests. In addition, a proposal must include a description of organization, list of officers and board members, proof of tax-exempt status, and organization's budget and copy of the organization's latest audited financial

statement. Organizations requesting renewed operating support must also include a long-range plan for generating other funding and attaining self-sufficiency.

Deadlines: None.

Decision Notification: Written responses usually follow within four weeks of receipt of inquiries; if interested, foundation will ask for a full proposal. Board meets in March, June, September, and November.

Notes: Eligible organizations located near Corning operations should submit requests for funding directly to local Corning management.

Restrictions

Grants are not made to individuals; political parties, campaigns, or causes; labor or veterans' organizations; religious groups; fraternal orders; for fundraising events; athletic activities; to volunteer emergency squads; or for goodwill advertising.

Additional Information

Publications: Guidelines; Foundation Annual Report

Corporate Officials

James B. Flaws: executive vice president, chief financial officer, director B 1948. ED Tufts University BS (1971); Dartmouth College MBA (1973). PRIM CORP EMPL executive vice president, chief financial officer, director: Corning Inc.

James Richardson Houghton: chairman emeritus B Corning, NY April 06, 1936. ED Harvard University AB (1958); Harvard University MBA (1962). PRIM CORP EMPL chairman emeritus: Corning Inc. CORP AFFIL director: JP Morgan & Co. Inc.; director: Harvard Corp.; director: Metropolitan Life Insurance Co.; director: ExxonMobil Corp. NONPR AFFIL member business council: Trilateral Commission. CLUB AFFIL University Club; Tarratine Club; River Club; Rolling Rock Club; Harvard Club; Laurel Valley Golf Club; Brookline Country Club; Corning Country Club; Augusta National Golf Club.

E. Marie McKee: senior vice president B Columbus, IN 1951. ED Simmons College MBA; Purdue University BA (1973); Purdue University MA (1976). PRIM CORP EMPL senior vice president: Corning Inc. ADD CORP EMPL president: Corning Museum Glass; chairman: Steuben Glass. CORP AFFIL director: Carolina Power Co.

Peter F. Volanakis: president Corning technologies ED Dartmouth College BA; Dartmouth College MA. PRIM CORP EMPL president Corning technologies: Corning Inc.

Wendell P. Weeks: president, chief operating officer, director ED Harvard University MBA; Lehigh University BA. PRIM CORP EMPL president, chief operating officer, director: Corning Inc.

Foundation Officials

Thomas S. Buechner: trustee B New York, NY 1926. ED Princeton University (1945); Arts Students League New York City (1946); Ecole des Beaux Arts (1946); Institut voor Pictologie (1947); University of Paris (1947). PRIM CORP EMPL counsel: Corning Glass Works. NONPR AFFIL trustee: Pilchuck School; trustee: Rockwell Museum; member: National Collection Fine Arts; member: Century Association; trustee: Corning Museum Glass; member: Brooklyn Institute Arts & Science; director: Brooklyn Museum; trustee: Arnot Art Museum Arts Southern Finger Lakes; member faculty art school: Bild-Werk Fravenau Germany.

James Richardson Houghton: trustee (see above)

Karen C. Martin: program officer

E. Marie McKee: chairman, trustee (see above)

Kristin A. Swain: president

William C. Ughetta: trustee B New York, NY 1933. ED Princeton University AB (1954); Harvard University LLB (1959). PRIM CORP EMPL senior vice president, general counsel: Corning Inc. CORP AFFIL director: Siecor Corp.; director: Covance Inc.; director: GlobalLift Technologies; director: Chemung Canal Trust Co.; director: Corning International Corp.

NONPR AFFIL officer: Corning Glass Works Foundation; officer: Corning Museum Glass; member: Association Bar New York City; director: Boy Scouts America; member: American Bar Association; member: American Corporate Counsel Association. CLUB AFFIL Princeton Club; University Club; Corning Country Club.

Grants Analysis

Disclosure Period: calendar year ending 2001

Total Grants: $3,421,691*

Number of Grants: 184

Average Grant: $18,596

Highest Grant: $470,883

Lowest Grant: $200

Typical Range: $5,000 to $25,000

*Note: Giving excludes matching gifts, scholarships, and United Way.

Recent Grants

Note: Grants derived from 2001 Form 990.

Library-Related

50,000	New York Public Library, New York, NY -- for program support

General

470,883	Goddard Riverside Community Center, New York, NY -- for Education and Career Counseling Program
335,000	United Way of Southern Tier, Corning, NY
300,000	Chemung County Performing Arts, Elmira, NY
300,000	One Seventy One Cedar, Corning, NY -- for renovation and expansion project
265,000	YMCA, Corning, NY -- for expansion and renovation
150,000	Regional Science and Discovery Center, Corning, NY -- for Educational Outreach and Expansion Project
125,000	Chemung Valley Arts Council, Corning, NY -- for regional cultural plan
105,750	United Way of New York City, New York, NY -- for disaster relief fund
100,000	Three Rivers Development Foundation, Corning, NY -- for city plan
80,000	Five Rivers Council, Horseheads, NY -- for camp improvements

COUNTRY CURTAINS, INC.

Company Headquarters

705 Pleasant St.
Lee, MA 01238

Company Description

Employees: 137

SIC(s): 2299 Textile Goods Nec.

Operating Locations

Country Curtains, Inc. (CT--Avon, Westport; DE--Greenville; MD--Annapolis; MA--Beverly, Stockbridge, Sturbridge, Sudbury; NJ--Far Hills, Ridgewood, Shrewsbury; NY--Fishkill, Rochester; RI--Cranston; VA--Arlington)

High Meadow Foundation

Giving Contact

John H. Fitzpatrick, President
High Meadow Foundation
PO Box 955
Stockbridge, MA 01262
Phone: (413)243-1474
Fax: (413)243-1067

Description

EIN: 222527419

Organization Type: Corporate Foundation

Giving Locations: MA: Berkshire County, MA

Grant Types: Capital, General Support.

Financial Summary

Total Giving: $1,280,109 (fiscal year ending September 30, 2001); $1,363,877 (fiscal 1999); $1,319,791 (fiscal 1998). Note: Contributes through foundation only.

Giving Analysis: Giving for fiscal 1999 includes: foundation scholarships ($18,533); corporate fellowships ($30,000); foundation grants to United Way ($40,000); foundation ($1,275,344); fiscal 1996: foundation grants to United Way ($37,200); foundation scholarships ($112,500) foundation ($1,567,623)

Assets: $1,953,334 (fiscal 2001); $2,027,799 (fiscal 1999); $1,948,279 (fiscal 1998)

Gifts Received: $1,422,520 (fiscal 2001); $1,216,411 (fiscal 1999); $1,477,125 (fiscal 1998). Note: Contributions were received from Fitzpatrick Companies, Red Lion Inn, Country Curtains Retail, Country Curtains Mail Order, Housatonic Curtain, More Window Ways, Blantyre, John H. and Jane P. Fitzpatrick, JoAnn Brown, Nancy J. Fitzpatrick, and employee donations through the Zoa Fund.

Typical Recipients

Arts & Humanities: Arts Appreciation, Arts Associations & Councils, Arts Centers, Arts Festivals, Dance, Arts & Humanities-General, Historic Preservation, History & Archaeology, Libraries, Museums/Galleries, Music, Opera, Performing Arts, Public Broadcasting, Theater

Civic & Public Affairs: Botanical Gardens/Parks, Business/Free Enterprise, Community Foundations, Economic Development, Civic & Public Affairs-General, Native American Affairs, Parades/Festivals, Professional & Trade Associations, Public Policy, Urban & Community Affairs, Women's Affairs, Zoos/Aquariums

Education: Agricultural Education, Arts/Humanities Education, Business Education, Colleges & Universities, Community & Junior Colleges, Education Associations, Education Funds, Education-General, International Studies, Legal Education, Minority Education, Private Education (Precollege), Public Education (Precollege), Student Aid

Environment: Resource Conservation

Health: AIDS/HIV, Children's Health/Hospitals, Clinics/Medical Centers, Emergency/Ambulance Services, Hospices, Hospitals, Nursing Services, Public Health

International: Foreign Arts Organizations, Human Rights

Religion: Churches, Religious Welfare

Social Services: Child Welfare, Community Centers, Community Service Organizations, Counseling, Family Planning, Family Services, People with Disabilities, Recreation & Athletics, Shelters/Homelessness, United Funds/United Ways, Youth Organizations

Application Procedures

Initial Contact: Send a brief letter.

Application Requirements: Information includes a description of program, brief history, and amount sought.

Deadlines: None.

Restrictions

The foundation limits the majority of gifts to charitable organizations in Berkshire County, MA.

Corporate Officials

Jane P. Fitzpatrick: chairman, chief executive officer, treasurer B 1925. PRIM CORP EMPL chairman, chief executive officer, treasurer: Country Curtains, Inc. CORP AFFIL treasurer: Housatonic Curtain Co.

Inc.; treasurer: Red Lion Inc.; chairman: Country Curtains Mail Order Inc.; chairman: Fitzpatrick Companies Inc.

Robert B. Trask: president, chief operating officer, director B Springfield, MA 1946. ED Western New England College (1971). PRIM CORP EMPL president, chief operating officer, director: The Fitzpatrick Companies Inc. ADD CORP EMPL vice president, clearing houserk, director: Red Lion Inc. CORP AFFIL vice president: Lee Community Development Corp.; director: More Window Ways Inc.; director: Housatonic Curtain Co. Inc.; clerk, director: Country Curtains Retail Inc.; director: Fitzpatrick Retail & Realty Co. Inc.; trustee: City Savings Bank; president, chief operating officer, director: Country Curtains Mail Order Inc.; director: Berkshire Gas Co., Inc.; corporator: Berkshire Health Systems. NONPR AFFIL member: New England Mail Order Association; corporator: North Adams State College Foundation; member: Knights of Columbus; secretary, treasurer: High Meadow Foundation Inc.; member: Institute of Management Accountants; trustee: Berkshire Theatre Festival; member: Direct Marketing Association; member: American Institute CPAs; trustee: Berkshire Community College.

Foundation Officials

Jane P. Fitzpatrick: chairman (see above)
John H. Fitzpatrick: president B 1925. PRIM CORP EMPL president, director: Housatonic Curtain Co. Inc. CORP AFFIL vice chairman: Country Curtains Retail Inc.; director: Fitzpatrick Retail & Realty Co. Inc.
Tamara Stevens: administrator
Robert B. Trask: clerk, trustee (see above)

Grants Analysis

Disclosure Period: fiscal year ending September 30, 2001
Total Grants: $1,237,009*
Number of Grants: 308
Average Grant: $4,016
Highest Grant: $127,480
Typical Range: $100 to $5,000
*Note: Giving excludes United Way.

Recent Grants

Note: Grants derived from fiscal 2001 Form 990.

Library-Related
21,210	New York Public Library, New York, NY
5,000	Lenox Library Association, Lenox, MA

General
127,480	Berkshire Theatre Festival, Stockbridge, MA
100,000	Boston Symphony Orchestra, Boston, MA -- Presidents at Pops
60,000	Norman Rockwell Museum, Stockbridge, MA
57,500	Boston Symphony Orchestra, Boston, MA -- Presidents at Pops
50,000	Lee Visiting Nurse Association Fund Drive, Lee, MA
50,000	Shakespeare and Company, Cambridge, MA
37,000	Berkshire United Way, Pittsfield, MA
30,000	Massachusetts Museum of Contemporary Art Foundation, North Adams, MA
29,611	Berkshire Theatre Festival, Stockbridge, MA
26,000	Green Mountain College, Poultney, VT

COVE CHARITABLE TRUST

Giving Contact

Emma M. Green, Trust Officer
c/o Boston Safe Deposit and Trust Co.
1 Boston Pl. Aim 024-0073
Boston, MA 02108
Phone: (617)722-7341

Description

Founded: 1964
EIN: 046118955
Organization Type: Private Foundation
Giving Locations: MA
Grant Types: Capital, General Support, Multiyear/Continuing Support, Operating Expenses, Project, Seed Money.

Donor Information

Founder: the late Aileen Kelly Pratt, the late Edwin H. B. Pratt

Financial Summary

Total Giving: $283,500 (2001); $280,000 (2000); $295,500 (1999)
Giving Analysis: Giving for 1999 includes: foundation scholarships ($24,000)
Assets: $4,896,375 (2001); $5,463,698 (2000); $5,884,060 (1999)

Typical Recipients

Arts & Humanities: Historic Preservation, History & Archaeology, Libraries, Music, Public Broadcasting
Civic & Public Affairs: Civil Rights, Community Foundations, Civic & Public Affairs-General, Housing, Native American Affairs, Urban & Community Affairs, Women's Affairs
Education: Business Education, Colleges & Universities, Education-General, Health & Physical Education, Leadership Training, Literacy, Student Aid
Environment: Environment-General, Resource Conservation
Health: Emergency/Ambulance Services, Health Funds, Health Organizations, Hospices, Hospitals, Prenatal Health Issues, Preventive Medicine/Wellness Organizations, Public Health
International: International Development
Religion: Churches, Religion-General, Ministries, Religious Organizations, Religious Welfare
Social Services: Animal Protection, Child Welfare, Community Service Organizations, Domestic Violence, Emergency Relief, Family Services, Food/Clothing Distribution, People with Disabilities, Recreation & Athletics, Social Services-General, YMCA/YWCA/YMHA/YWHA, Youth Organizations

Application Procedures

Initial Contact: Call Ms. Emma Green for application information.
Deadlines: None.

Additional Information

Trust(s): Boston Safe Deposit & Trust Co

Grants Analysis

Disclosure Period: calendar year ending 2001
Total Grants: $283,500
Number of Grants: 27
Average Grant: $10,500
Highest Grant: $55,000
Lowest Grant: $1,000
Typical Range: $1,000 to $20,000

Recent Grants

Note: Grants derived from 2001 Form 990.

General
55,000	Emmanuel Gospel Center, Boston, MA -- for operations
55,000	Social Action Ministries
33,500	Coalition of Buzzards Bay -- assist in Watershed Campaign
20,000	Bowling Green State University Foundation, Bowling Green, OH -- support for Ned E. Baker Lecture Series
12,500	Sippican Lands Trust, Marion, MA -- for operations
10,000	American Red Cross -- for disaster relief
10,000	Hartford Foundation for Public Giving, Hartford, CT -- support the Boyd and Wendy Hinds Scholarship Fund
10,000	Old Colony Hospice, Inc., Stoughton, MA -- support for the Hospice Housing Project
8,000	New York City Radio, New York, NY -- support to help replace the destroyed tower
7,500	National Association of County and City Health Officials, Washington, DC -- support for Public Health Partners Coalition

LOUETTA M. COWDEN FOUNDATION

Giving Contact

David P. Ross, Senior Vice President & Trust Officer
c/o Bank of America, N.A.
1200 Main Street, 14th Floor
Kansas City, MO 64105
Phone: (816)979-7481
Fax: (816)979-7916

Description

Founded: 1964
EIN: 436052617
Organization Type: Private Foundation
Giving Locations: MO
Grant Types: Capital, Emergency, Project, Seed Money.

Donor Information

Founder: the late Louetta M. Cowden

Financial Summary

Total Giving: $907,977 (2000); $793,339 (1999); $661,833 (1998)
Giving Analysis: Giving for 2000 includes: foundation grants to United Way ($15,000)
Assets: $16,898,467 (2000); $17,782,175 (1999); $16,863,627 (1998)

Typical Recipients

Arts & Humanities: Ballet, Historic Preservation, Libraries, Literary Arts, Museums/Galleries, Opera, Theater
Civic & Public Affairs: Business/Free Enterprise, Employment/Job Training
Education: Colleges & Universities, Literacy, Private Education (Precollege), Science/Mathematics Education, Special Education, Student Aid
Environment: Resource Conservation
Health: Children's Health/Hospitals, Hospitals, Mental Health, Nursing Services, Research/Studies Institutes
Religion: Jewish Causes, Ministries, Religious Organizations, Religious Welfare
Science: Science Museums
Social Services: Child Welfare, Community Centers, Community Service Organizations, Domestic Violence, Food/Clothing Distribution, Recreation & Athletics, Scouts, Senior Services, United Funds/United Ways, YMCA/YWCA/YMHA/YWHA, Youth Organizations

Application Procedures

Initial Contact: Send a brief letter (no more than three pages) with appropriate attachments. Deadlines vary.

Restrictions

Does not support individuals. Grants are limited to organizations in the state of Missouri.

Additional Information

Publications: Application Guidelines
Trust(s): Bank of America, N.A.

Foundation Officials

Arthur H. Bowen, Jr.: trustee

Grants Analysis

Disclosure Period: calendar year ending 2000
Total Grants: $892,977*
Number of Grants: 19
Average Grant: $44,054*
Highest Grant: $100,000
Typical Range: $25,000 to $75,000
***Note:** Giving excludes United Way. Average grant figure excludes highest grant.

Recent Grants

Note: Grants derived from 1999 Form 990.

General

50,000	American Jazz Museum, Kansas City, MO -- archivist to oversee and implement John Baker collection initiative
50,000	Children's Center Campus, Kansas City, MO -- to support construction of their new campus capital campaign
50,000	St. Luke's Hospital Foundation, Kansas City, MO -- support of their capital campaign
50,000	State Ballet of Missouri, Kansas City, MO -- matching gift program
45,000	Genesis School, Kansas City, MO -- to open a charter school and to provide technology
45,000	Starlight Theater, Kansas City, MO -- final installment of a two-year grant in support of the capital campaign and new stage project
40,000	Big Brothers Big Sisters, Kansas City, MO -- in support of their capital campaign
35,000	Science City at Union Station, Kansas City, MO -- support of the development of their science museum
34,000	Science City at Union Station, Kansas City, MO -- support of the development of their science museum
33,500	Harvesters/Community Food Network, Kansas City, MO -- in support of your capital technology improvement efforts final payment on a 74,500 grant

S. H. COWELL FOUNDATION

Giving Contact

Susan T. Vandiver, Vice President Grants Programs
120 Montgomery St., Suite 2570
San Francisco, CA 94104
Phone: (415)397-0285
Fax: (415)986-6786
Web: http://www.shcowell.org

Description

Founded: 1955
EIN: 941392803
Organization Type: General Purpose Foundation
Giving Locations: CA
Grant Types: Capital, Challenge, Matching, Project.

Donor Information

Founder: The S. H. Cowell Foundation was established in 1955 through the will of Samuel Henry Cowell. S. H. Cowell's father, Henry, was a noted businessman who made his fortune during the famous California Gold Rush of the 1850s. By 1888, Henry Cowell owned the thriving Henry Cowell Lime and Cement Company, various warehouses and storage companies, prime San Francisco financial district properties, and 82,491 acres of land stretching from Texas Island, Canada, to San Louis Obispo, CA. Henry Cowell's net worth was estimated at $3,000,000. S. H. Cowell, although one of four surviving heirs, eventually inherited this estate in its totality. When S. H. Cowell died

in 1955, his will provided for the creation of a foundation that would continue his family's philanthropy. The original assets bequested to the foundation exceeded $12,560,363.

Financial Summary

Total Giving: $7,934,750 (1999); $9,302,765 (1998); $8,900,008 (1997)
Giving Analysis: Giving for 1998 includes: foundation matching gifts ($30,550) foundation grants to United Way ($77,000)
Assets: $195,452,445 (1999); $175,819,032 (1998); $202,372,340 (1997)

Typical Recipients

Arts & Humanities: Ballet, Ethnic & Folk Arts, History & Archaeology, Libraries, Literary Arts, Museums/Galleries, Opera, Performing Arts, Theater, Visual Arts
Civic & Public Affairs: Asian American Affairs, Botanical Gardens/Parks, Clubs, Community Foundations, Economic Development, Employment/Job Training, Civic & Public Affairs-General, Hispanic Affairs, Housing, Parades/Festivals, Public Policy, Urban & Community Affairs, Women's Affairs, Zoos/Aquariums
Education: Afterschool/Enrichment Programs, Colleges & Universities, Education Associations, Education Funds, Education Reform, Elementary Education (Private), Elementary Education (Public), Faculty Development, Education-General, Health & Physical Education, Journalism/Media Education, Leadership Training, Literacy, Minority Education, Preschool Education, Private Education (Precollege), Public Education (Precollege), Religious Education, School Volunteerism, Secondary Education (Public), Special Education
Environment: Environment-General, Protection, Resource Conservation
Health: AIDS/HIV, Cancer, Children's Health/Hospitals, Clinics/Medical Centers, Health Organizations, Medical Research, Nutrition, Public Health, Trauma Treatment
International: Foreign Educational Institutions, Health Care/Hospitals, International Affairs, International Development, International Environmental Issues, International Organizations, International Peace & Security Issues, International Relief Efforts
Religion: Religion-General, Jewish Causes, Religious Welfare, Religious Welfare
Science: Scientific Centers & Institutes
Social Services: Animal Protection, Child Abuse, Child Welfare, Community Centers, Community Service Organizations, Counseling, Day Care, Delinquency & Criminal Rehabilitation, Domestic Violence, Family Planning, Family Services, Food/Clothing Distribution, Homes, People with Disabilities, Recreation & Athletics, Shelters/Homelessness, Social Services-General, Special Olympics, Substance Abuse, United Funds/United Ways, YMCA/YWCA/YMHA/YWHA, Youth Organizations

Application Procedures

Initial Contact: Contact the foundation by telephone to discuss the likelihood of support for a project. Applicants may then be asked to submit a brief letter of inquiry.
Application Requirements: The letter should be two or three pages in length and should include a summary of history, purpose, and goals of the applying agency; scope, budget, and timetable for the project; specific amount requested from the foundation and an explanation of the particular uses to which these funds would be applied; list of other funding sources and amount solicited or received; and a copy of the most recent IRS determination letter of tax-exempt status.
Deadlines: None.
Review Process: The foundation board generally meets monthly to consider requests. The foundation will request further information as needed, and in most

cases a site visit is arranged. Generally, three to six months are required for review from the time of initial inquiry and action by the board.

Restrictions

The foundation normally does not make grants outside northern California or to support individuals. It generally does not fund start-ups of new organizations not included within its affirmative interests; academic or other research unless significantly related to policies or activities of an organization within its affirmative interest fields; general support, routine program administration, and operating expenses; endowments and repayment of indebtedness, except in unusual cases; annual fund-raising and development campaigns; government or governmental agencies; churches or sectarian religious programs; hospitals or programs and projects under hospital sponsorship; medical research or treatment; conferences, seminars, workshops, symposia, or related activities; media projects, including publications and communications projects; or political lobbying.

Additional Information

Grants to organizations outside northern California are made strictly on the Foundation's initiative.
The foundation "prefers to make grants for unusual capital needs or specific projects, rather than for general support, operating expenses, or repayment of indebtedness." Priority is given to applicants who have not received previous grants from the foundation. The foundation is continually increasing its number of matching and challenge grants to provide agencies with leverage in fund raising and to amplify the effect of its support.
A 1997 education guidelines statement from the foundation stated: "The Foundation is in the process of re-evaluating priorities for education grantmaking. In the meantime... limited funds are available to improve student learning; to increase attendance, graduation rates, parent and neighborhood involvement; and to support winning teachers. Qualified applicants must be established public school programs with a solid track record of successful results. We are also interested in funding private schools for outreach/cooperative programs and scholarships serving public school students. The Foundation has been working in several northern California neighborhoods to develop family resource centers. We are interested in linking those community-based efforts with local public schools to meet shared goals for the neighborhood, children, and families."
In 1995, the foundation began to phase out its support for food and clothing programs and for disabled assistance.
Publications: Annual Report

Foundation Officials

Leslie Albrecht: grants assistant
Jack W. Chu: treasurer, director ED Golden Gate University MA; University of California at Berkeley BS. PRIM CORP EMPL certified public accountant, founder, managing partner: Chu and Waters LLP. CORP AFFIL director: Community Bank of the Bay; member: American Institute Certified Public Accountants; member: California Society Certified Public Accountants. NONPR AFFIL director: East Bay Asian Local Development Corp.
Ken Doane: program officer education
Lise Einfeld Maisano: senior program officer
Mary Seawell Metz: president, director B Rockhill, SC 1937. ED Furman University BA (1958); Institute Phonetique (1962-1963); Sorbonne University (1962-1963); Louisiana State University PhD (1966). CORP AFFIL director: Union Bank; director: SBC Communications Inc.; director: Union Bancal Corp.; director: PacTel PacBell; director: PG&E Corp.; director: Longs Drug Stores Corp.; director: Pacific Telesis Group. NONPR AFFIL member: Women's Forum W; member: World Affairs Council Northern California; member: Women's College Coalition; advisory council:

Stanford University Graduate School Business; member: Western College Association; member: Phi Kappa Phi; member: Southern Conference Language Teaching; member: Phi Beta Kappa; associate: Gannett Center Media Studies; member: National Association Independent Colleges & Universities; member: Association Independent Colleges & Universities; member: Business Higher Education Forum.

Fredric C. Nelson: secretary, director

Cora M. Tellez: vice president, director B Manila, Philippines 1949. ED Mills College BA (1972); California State University MA (1979). PRIM NONPR EMPL vice president, regional manager: Kaiser Foundation Health Plan. CORP AFFIL board member: Golden State Bank Board; board member: California Association Health Plans. NONPR AFFIL board member: Institute for the Future; board member: Institute Medical Quality; board member: Holy Names College; board member: Asian Community Mental Health Services.

Susan T. Vandiver: vice president grant programs

Greg Wendt: director ED Harvard University MBA; University of Chicago BS. PRIM CORP EMPL senior vice president: Capital Research Co. NONPR AFFIL director: Larkin Street Youth Services; board member: Teach for America; board member: American Conservatory Theatre San Francisco.

Mary Lee Widener: director PRIM CORP EMPL co-founder, president, chief executive officer: Neighborhood Housing Services America ADD CORP EMPL chairman: Federal Home Loan Bank San Francisco.

Grants Analysis

Disclosure Period: calendar year ending 1998
Total Grants: $9,272,215*
Number of Grants: 156
Average Grant: $59,437
Highest Grant: $334,000
Typical Range: $30,000 to $100,000
*Note: Giving excludes matching gifts.

Recent Grants

Note: Grants derived from 2000 Form 990.

General

500,000	Commonwealth Club of California, San Francisco, CA
400,000	St. Elizabeth Seton School, Palo Alto, CA
350,000	Jewish Family and Children's Services, San Francisco, CA
350,000	Mid-Peninsula Housing Coalition, Redwood City, CA
236,000	Resources for Community Development, Berkeley, CA
200,000	Association for Community Based Education, Washington, DC
175,000	Food and Nutrition Services, Aptos, CA
160,000	Mount Diablo Habitat for Humanity, Concord, CA
150,000	Boys & Girls Club, Bakersfield, CA
150,000	Christian Church Homes of Northern California, Oakland, CA

COWLES CHARITABLE TRUST

Giving Contact

Mary Croft, Secretary & Treasurer
PO Box 219
Rumson, NJ 07760
Phone: (732)936-9826

Description

Founded: 1948
EIN: 136090295
Organization Type: Family Foundation
Giving Locations: FL; NY: New York City nationally.

Grant Types: Capital, Emergency, Endowment, General Support, Operating Expenses, Project, Scholarship.

Donor Information

Founder: Established in 1948 by Gardner Cowles Jr. Mr. Cowles, along with his father, Gardner Cowles, Sr., and brother, John Cowles, built a media empire which included the *Des Moines Register*, the *Evening Tribune*, the *Minneapolis Star*, *Look Magazine*, and radio and television stations. In 1985, the Des Moines Register and Tribune Company, owned primarily by the Cowles, sold its newspapers to Gannett Company for $260 million. Cowles Media of Minneapolis, MN, a private corporation, is owned almost entirely by descendants of John Cowles, Sr.

Financial Summary

Total Giving: $950,500 (2001); $905,740 (2000); $794,500 (1999)
Giving Analysis: Giving for 2000 includes: foundation grants to United Way ($2,500) 1999: foundation grants to United Way ($5,000)
Assets: $22,137,911 (2001); $22,288,235 (2000); $20,509,696 (1999)

Typical Recipients

Arts & Humanities: Arts Appreciation, Arts Associations & Councils, Arts Centers, Arts Festivals, Arts Funds, Arts Institutes, Ballet, Community Arts, Dance, Arts & Humanities-General, Historic Preservation, History & Archaeology, Libraries, Museums/Galleries, Music, Opera, Performing Arts, Public Broadcasting, Theater, Visual Arts

Civic & Public Affairs: African American Affairs, Botanical Gardens/Parks, Civil Rights, Clubs, Employment/Job Training, Civic & Public Affairs-General, Housing, Legal Aid, Municipalities/Towns, Urban & Community Affairs, Women's Affairs, Zoos/Aquariums

Education: Arts/Humanities Education, Colleges & Universities, Colleges & Universities, Faculty Development, Education-General, International Studies, Literacy, Medical Education, Minority Education, Private Education (Precollege), Public Education (Precollege), Social Sciences Education, Special Education

Environment: Environment-General, Wildlife Protection

Health: AIDS/HIV, Cancer, Children's Health/Hospitals, Clinics/Medical Centers, Emergency/Ambulance Services, Health Organizations, Hospitals, Hospitals (University Affiliated), Medical Rehabilitation, Medical Research, Mental Health, Single-Disease Health Associations

International: Foreign Arts Organizations, Foreign Educational Institutions, International Relief Efforts

Religion: Religious Organizations, Religious Welfare

Science: Scientific Centers & Institutes

Social Services: Animal Protection, At-Risk Youth, Child Welfare, Community Centers, Community Service Organizations, Counseling, Crime Prevention, Delinquency & Criminal Rehabilitation, Domestic Violence, Emergency Relief, Family Planning, Family Services, Food/Clothing Distribution, People with Disabilities, Senior Services, Shelters/Homelessness, Substance Abuse, United Funds/United Ways, Volunteer Services, Youth Organizations

Application Procedures

Initial Contact: Send a brief letter requesting a foundation application form.

Application Requirements: The application should include a brief description of organization and scope of current activities; need for project or activity; objectives of project; description of activities to be included and timetable for their accomplishment; and overall cost of project, amount requested from Cowles Charitable Trust, and amounts, sources, and statuses

(committed or pending) of additional support. The application packet should also include Cowles Charitable Trust proposal cover sheet, including signature of CEO; project budget, including projected re venue and expenses; organization's current annual operating budget, including revenues and expenses; governing body and officers, showing business, professional, and community affiliations; and single copies of letter from IRS determining organization's tax-exempt status under sections 501(c)(3) and 509(a), most recent audited financial statement, and other supporting documents.

Deadlines: Any eligible request that arrives too late for one meeting will be placed on the agenda of the following meeting. Proposals must be received at the trust office by 5 p.m. on the following dates to be included on the agendas noted: December 1 for January agenda, March 1 for April agenda; June 1 for July agenda; and September 1 for October agenda. If any of the above dates fall on a weekend or holiday, the deadline is 5 p.m. on the first working day following the published deadline.

Review Process: The board meets in January, April, July, and October to review proposals. The trust will notify, in writing, all grant applicants generally within two weeks of a board meeting.

Notes: Only written applications can be considered. The trust does not accept proposals by fax. Videos and other supplementary material cannot be returned to applicants. Material should not be bound, inserted in protective sleeves, or prepared in other notebook form.

Restrictions

Grants are not made to individuals. The trust will also not consider more than one application from any one organization within a 12 month period. The trust does not consider applications from any nonprofit receiving a multiyear grant until payment of that grant is completed.

Additional Information

Publications: Annual Report; Guidelines; Application Form

Foundation Officials

Charles Cowles: trustee B Santa Monica, CA 1941. ED Stanford University (1963). PRIM CORP EMPL president, director: Charles Cowles Gallery. NONPR AFFIL trustee: New York Studio School; trustee: Wolfsonian; member: Art Dealers Association America; trustee: Lanmeier Sculpture Park.

Gardner Cowles, III: president, trustee B 1936. PRIM CORP EMPL president: Northern Suffolk Publishing Corp.

Jan S. Cowles: trustee B Berkeley, CA 1918.

Mary Croft: secretary, treasurer

Lois Cowles Harrison: trustee B 1934. ED Wellesley College BA (1956). NONPR AFFIL member: Wellesley College Alumnae Association.

Lois Eleanor Harrison: trustee

Kate Cowles Nichols: trustee

Virginia Cowles Schroth: trustee

Grants Analysis

Disclosure Period: calendar year ending 2001
Total Grants: $948,000*
Number of Grants: 144
Average Grant: $6,583
Highest Grant: $37,500
Lowest Grant: $1,000
Typical Range: $1,000 to $10,000
*Note: Giving excludes United Way.

Recent Grants

Note: Grants derived from 2001 Form 990.

Library-Related

10,000	New York Public Library, New York, NY

General

47,240	Miami Art Museum, Miami, FL
37,500	Planned Parenthood of Southwest and Central Florida, Inc
32,500	Polk Museum of Art, Lakeland, FL
30,000	Beth Israel Medical Center North
30,000	Grant Foundation, Pittsburgh, PA
30,000	Museum of Modern Art, New York, NY
30,000	National Council on Crime and Delinquency, San Francisco, CA
27,500	Allen-Stevenson School, New York, NY
25,000	Artists Space, Boston, MA
25,000	East Harlem Tutorial Program, New York, NY

A. G. COX CHARITABLE TRUST

Giving Contact
Sandra M. Wallick
Bank One Trust Co.
70 W. Madison
Chicago, IL 60670
Phone: (312)732-7785

Description
Founded: 1924
EIN: 366011498
Organization Type: Private Foundation
Giving Locations: CA; IL; WA
Grant Types: General Support.

Financial Summary
Total Giving: $602,333 (2001); $636,498 (2000); $628,375 (1999)
Giving Analysis: Giving for 1999 includes: foundation scholarships ($8,000)
Assets: $13,650,810 (2001); $13,578,669 (2000); $12,920,774 (1999)

Typical Recipients
Arts & Humanities: History & Archaeology, Libraries
Civic & Public Affairs: Urban & Community Affairs
Education: Colleges & Universities, Education Funds, Education-General, Health & Physical Education, Medical Education, Preschool Education, Special Education, Student Aid
Environment: Environment-General, Resource Conservation
Health: Arthritis, Cancer, Children's Health/Hospitals, Diabetes, Emergency/Ambulance Services, Health Organizations, Heart, Hospitals, Kidney, Medical Rehabilitation, Medical Research, Nursing Services, Prenatal Health Issues, Respiratory, Single-Disease Health Associations
International: Human Rights
Religion: Churches, Religious Organizations, Religious Welfare
Science: Science Museums
Social Services: At-Risk Youth, Child Welfare, Community Service Organizations, Day Care, Domestic Violence, Emergency Relief, People with Disabilities, Scouts, United Funds/United Ways, Veterans, YMCA/YWCA/YMHA/YWHA, Youth Organizations

Application Procedures
Initial Contact: Send a brief letter of inquiry.
Deadlines: None.

Additional Information
Trust(s): Bank One Trust Co.

Grants Analysis
Disclosure Period: calendar year ending 2001
Total Grants: $602,333
Number of Grants: 31
Average Grant: $19,430
Highest Grant: $100,000

Lowest Grant: $2,000
Typical Range: $5,000 to $30,000

Recent Grants
Note: Grants derived from 2001 Form 990.

General

100,000	American Red Cross, Chicago, IL
100,000	University of Southern California, Los Angeles, CA
90,000	American Cancer Society, Chicago, IL
61,333	Salvation Army of Chicago, Chicago, IL
35,000	Shriners Hospitals for Children, Chicago, IL
30,000	Rehabilitation Institute of Chicago, Chicago, IL
25,000	Mayo Foundation Cancer Research Center, Scottsdale, AZ
15,000	Virginia Mason Foundation, Seattle, WA
12,000	Amyotropic Lateral Sclerosis Association, Chicago, IL
10,000	American Diabetes Association, Chicago, IL

JESSIE B. COX CHARITABLE TRUST

Giving Contact
Susan M. Fish, Grants Administrator
Select Client Services
Hemenway & Barnes
60 State Street
Boston, MA 02109-1899
Phone: (617)227-7940
Fax: (617)227-0781
E-mail: dso@hembar.com
Web: http://www.hembar.com/cox

Description
Founded: 1982
EIN: 046478024
Organization Type: Family Foundation
Giving Locations: New England.
Grant Types: Challenge, Multiyear/Continuing Support, Project, Seed Money.

Donor Information
Founder: The trust was established in 1982 by funds from the estate of Jessie B. Cox . Jessie B. Cox (d. 1982) was a granddaughter of Clarence Barron, who launched the Dow Jones media empire. Her husband, William C. Cox (d. 1970), was a senior director of Dow Jones & Company.

Financial Summary
Total Giving: $3,590,230 (2003 approx); $3,590,230 (2002 approx); $3,059,230 (1999 approx)
Assets: The annual range for assets is between $52,000,000 and $60,000,000.

Typical Recipients
Arts & Humanities: Arts Associations & Councils, Arts Outreach, History & Archaeology, Libraries, Museums/Galleries, Music, Performing Arts, Public Broadcasting
Civic & Public Affairs: African American Affairs, Botanical Gardens/Parks, Community Foundations, Employment/Job Training, Civic & Public Affairs-General, Housing, Law & Justice, Nonprofit Management, Philanthropic Organizations, Public Policy, Women's Affairs, Zoos/Aquariums
Education: Arts/Humanities Education, Colleges & Universities, Education Associations, Education Reform, Elementary Education (Private), Environmental Education, Faculty Development, Education-General, Leadership Training, Literacy, Medical Education, Minority Education, Private Education (Precollege), Public Education (Precollege), School Volunteerism, Science/Mathematics Education, Special Education

Environment: Air/Water Quality, Energy, Forestry, Environment-General, Protection, Research, Resource Conservation, Watershed, Wildlife Protection
Health: Adolescent Health Issues, AIDS/HIV, Children's Health/Hospitals, Diabetes, Health-General, Health Policy/Cost Containment, Health Organizations, Home-Care Services, Hospitals, Hospitals (University Affiliated), Medical Research, Mental Health, Nursing Services, Nutrition, Prenatal Health Issues, Preventive Medicine/Wellness Organizations, Public Health, Respiratory
International: International Environmental Issues
Science: Science Museums, Scientific Centers & Institutes, Scientific Labs, Scientific Research
Social Services: Child Welfare, Community Service Organizations, Family Planning, Family Services, Food/Clothing Distribution, People with Disabilities, Senior Services, Substance Abuse

Application Procedures
Initial Contact: The trust recommends that prospective applicants call to discuss the appropriateness of their request. The trust has a two-step application process. All applicants are asked to first submit a three to four page concept paper signed by the Executive Director or Board President.
Application Requirements: A concept paper should describe the background and purpose of the organization, the project, amount desired, and how the project will enable the applicant organization to reach its goals. A budget and evidence of 501(c)(3) status must accompany the concept paper.
Deadlines: Concept papers may be submitted at any time but must be received by January 15 for the March trustees' meeting, April 15 for the June meeting, July 15 for the September meeting, and October 15 for the December meeting.
Review Process: Concept papers are reviewed by the staff and trustees, following which the trustees will invite full proposals from a limited number. Letters requesting a full proposal are mailed within two weeks of meeting. Trustees tend to favor organizations which have not received prior trust support and which suggest new approaches toward problems. Preference is given to organizations located in New England.
Notes: The trust does not accept facsimile submissions.

Restrictions
The trust will consider multiple-year grants where necessary to accomplish the project.
The trust generally will not support capital projects for buildings, equipment or land purchase; endowments, scholarship funds or fundraising activities; loans; deficits or normal operating budgets or where the trust may become the organization's predominant source of support; programs or projects usually supported by the public sector; any attempt to influence legislation; requests from individuals; sectarian religious activity; organizations or activities outside of New England; or recent grantees, or extension of multiple-year awards.

Additional Information
Publications: Annual Report; Guidelines

Foundation Officials
William Coburn Cox, Jr.: trustee B 1931.
Roy A. Hammer: trustee B New York, NY 1934. ED Yale University BA (1956); Columbia University MA (1957). PRIM CORP EMPL partner: Hemenway & Barnes. CORP AFFIL director: Dow Jones & Co. Inc.
Jane Cox MacElree: trustee B 1929. ED University of Pennsylvania (1949). CORP AFFIL director: Dow Jones & Co. Inc.
Katherine S. McHugh: director
Rachel L. Pohl: program officer
George T. Shaw: trustee ED Trinity College (1962); Harvard University (1965). PRIM CORP EMPL partner: Hemenway & Barnes.
Ann Fowler Wallace: program office

Grants Analysis

Disclosure Period: calendar year ending 1997
Total Grants: $3,059,230
Number of Grants: 81
Average Grant: $37,768
Highest Grant: $125,000
Lowest Grant: $18,500
Typical Range: $25,000 to $75,000
Note: A more recent grants list was unavailable.

Recent Grants

Note: Grants derived from 2001 Form 990.

General

75,000	Center for Public Interest Research, Boston, MA -- New England Climate Action Project
75,000	Essex County Community Foundation, Topsfield, MA -- challenge grant
75,000	University of Pennsylvania, Philadelphia, PA -- The Children's Education Endowment
70,000	Harvard School of Public Health, Boston, MA -- Healthy Public Housing Initiative
65,000	American Cancer Society New England Division, Inc., Framingham, MA -- regional health campaign
60,000	Health Care Without Harm Campaign, Jamaica Plain, MA -- continued support of Boston-New England Organizing Project
55,000	Audubon Society of New Hampshire, Concord, NH -- The New England Science Center
50,000	Alliance for Community Supports, Inc., Concord, NH -- Building Blocks Training Initiative
50,000	American Lung Association of Maine, Augusta, ME -- collaborative of Association and eastern Canada for the International Centre for Action on Air Quality and Human Health
50,000	Cobscook Bay Resource Center, Eastport, ME -- support and strengthen community-based marine conservation and management organizations

COX ENTERPRISES, INC.

Company Headquarters

1400 Lake Hearn Dr., NE
Atlanta, GA 30319
Web: http://www.coxenterprises.com

Company Description

Revenue: US$8.805 billion (2002)
Employees: 77000 (2002)
SIC(s): 2711 Newspapers, 4832 Radio Broadcasting Stations, 4833 Television Broadcasting Stations, 4841 Cable & Other Pay Television Services.

Operating Locations

Cox Enterprises Inc. (AZ--Mesa, Phoenix, Yuma; CA--Anaheim, City of Commerce, Eureka, Fresno, Goleta, Los Angeles, Oakland, Riverside, San Diego; CT--Manchester; FL--Gainesville, Lakeland, Ocala, Ocoee, Orlando, Pensacola, St. Petersburg; GA--Atlanta, Macon, Red Oak; IL--Fairview Heights, Moline; IA--Cedar Rapids; LA--Harahan, New Orleans; MA--Woburn; MI--Saginaw, Southfield; MO--Kansas City; NE--Omaha; NY--Great Neck, New York; NC--Charlotte; OH--Dayton; OK--Oklahoma City; PA--Bala-Cynwyd, Gibsonia, Pittsburgh; RI--Cranston; SC--Myrtle Beach; TX--Austin, Lufkin, Waco; VA--Fredericksburg, Roanoke; WA--Spokane; WI--Caledonia)

Nonmonetary Support

Type: Cause-related Marketing & Promotion; Donated Equipment; In-kind Services
Note: Each company operating location can be contacted for nonmonetary support.

James M. Cox Foundation

Giving Contact

Leigh Ann Launius, Assistant Secretary
PO Box 105357
Atlanta, GA 30348
Phone: (404)843-5000
Fax: (404)843-5599
E-mail: LeighAnn.Launius@cox.com

Alternate Contact

PO Box 105720
Atlanta, GA 30348
Phone: (404)843-5300

Description

EIN: 586032469
Organization Type: Corporate Foundation
Giving Locations: GA: Atlanta headquarters and operating communities.
Grant Types: Capital, Project.

Financial Summary

Total Giving: $3,242,500 (2001); $3,196,123 (2000); $1,857,500 (1998). Note: Contributes through corporate direct giving program and foundation.
Giving Analysis: Giving for 2000 includes: foundation ($3,196,123) 1998: foundation ($1,857,500)
Assets: $5,717,486 (2001); $7,113,129 (2000); $6,732,828 (1998)
Gifts Received: $3,000,000 (2001); $3,000,000 (2000); $1,550,000 (1998). Note: Contributions received from Cox Enterprises.

Typical Recipients

Arts & Humanities: Arts Associations & Councils, Arts Centers, Arts Festivals, Arts Institutes, Historic Preservation, History & Archaeology, Libraries, Museums/Galleries, Music, Opera, Performing Arts, Public Broadcasting, Theater
Civic & Public Affairs: African American Affairs, Botanical Gardens/Parks, Business/Free Enterprise, Community Foundations, Economic Development, Employment/Job Training, Ethnic Organizations, Civic & Public Affairs-General, Hispanic Affairs, Housing, Public Policy, Urban & Community Affairs, Women's Affairs, Zoos/Aquariums
Education: Colleges & Universities, Community & Junior Colleges, Education Associations, Education Reform, Engineering/Technological Education, Education-General, International Studies, Journalism/Media Education, Leadership Training, Literacy, Medical Education, Private Education (Precollege), Public Education (Precollege), School Volunteerism, Special Education, Student Aid
Environment: Air/Water Quality, Environment-General, Resource Conservation, Wildlife Protection
Health: Arthritis, Cancer, Children's Health/Hospitals, Clinics/Medical Centers, Emergency/Ambulance Services, Health-General, Health Policy/Cost Containment, Hospices, Hospitals, Medical Rehabilitation, Multiple Sclerosis, Preventive Medicine/Wellness Organizations, Public Health, Single-Disease Health Associations, Transplant Networks/Donor Banks
International: Health Care/Hospitals, International Relations
Religion: Jewish Causes, Religious Organizations, Religious Welfare
Science: Science Museums, Science Museums, Scientific Centers & Institutes

Social Services: Animal Protection, At-Risk Youth, Camps, Child Abuse, Child Welfare, Community Service Organizations, Counseling, Family Services, Food/Clothing Distribution, Homes, Recreation & Athletics, Shelters/Homelessness, Social Services-General, United Funds/United Ways, Volunteer Services, YMCA/YWCA/YMHA/YWHA, Youth Organizations

Application Procedures

Initial Contact: Send three copies of written request.
Application Requirements: Outline of needs and goals; copy of IRS tax-exemption letter; list of recent donors, including dollar amounts; annual report and other financial information, including audited financial statements (or most recent Form 990); history of organization; list of board members and officers with salaries; copy of current or project budget.
Deadlines: Established one month before quarterly board meetings.
Review Process: Local management recommends grants; foundation trustees make grant decisions.
Decision Notification: The foundation makes its decision at semi-annual meetings.

Restrictions

All potential recipients must be tax-exempt under IRS standards and have support of local management. Grants are generally restricted to operating areas. No grants are made to individuals.

Additional Information

The foundation does not accept personal interviews.

Corporate Officials

David E. Easterly: president, chief operating officer affairs, secretary B Denison, TX 1942. ED University of Texas; Austin College BA (1965). PRIM CORP EMPL president, chief operating officer: Cox Enterprises Inc. CORP AFFIL director: Cox Communications Inc.; vice president: Grand Junction Newspapers. NONPR AFFIL member: Newspaper Association America; member, director: Southern Newspaper Publishers Association; member: Associated Press.
Timothy W. Hughes: senior vice president B 1943. ED Bellarmine College AB (1965); Cleveland State University JD (1973). PRIM CORP EMPL senior vice president: Cox Enterprises Inc.
Richard J. Jacobson: vice president, treasurer B 1956. ED Georgia State University (1980). PRIM CORP EMPL vice president, treasurer: Cox Enterprises Inc.
James Cox Kennedy: chairman, chief executive officer, director B 1947. ED University of Denver BBA (1970). PRIM CORP EMPL chairman, chief executive officer, director: Cox Enterprises Inc. ADD CORP EMPL chairman, president: National Auto Dealers Exchange. CORP AFFIL director: Manheim Auctions Inc.; director: National Service Industries Inc.; Flagler System Inc.; chairman, director: Cox Communications Inc.; director: Cox Radio Inc.; advisory director: Chase Bank Texas.
Andrew Austin Merdek: vice president legal affairs, secretary B Portland, ME 1950. ED Middlebury College AB (1972); University of Virginia JD (1978). PRIM CORP EMPL vice president legal affairs, secretary: Cox Enterprises Inc. ADD CORP EMPL secretary: Cox Texas Pubs Inc.; secretary: Cox Broadcasting Inc.; secretary: Cox Communications Inc.; secretary: Cox Interactive Media Inc.; secretary: Cox NC Pubs Inc.; secretary: Cox Newspapers Inc.; secretary, director: Dayton Newspapers Inc.; secretary: Eagle Research Group Inc.; secretary, director: GA Television Co.; secretary: Hospitality Network Inc.; secretary, director: Manheim Auction Government Service; secretary: Manheim Auctions Inc.; secretary, director: Manheim Metro Detroit Auto Auction; secretary,director: Palm Beach Newspapers Inc.; secretary: WFTV Inc. NONPR AFFIL member: Order Coif; member: Phi Beta Kappa; chairman: Newspaper Association America Legal Affairs Committee; member: American

Corporate Counsel Association; member: American Society of Corporate Secretaries; member: American Bar Association.

Foundation Officials

Barbara Cox Anthony: chairman B Honolulu, HI 1923. PRIM CORP EMPL chairman: Dayton Newspapers Inc. CORP AFFIL director: Cox Enterprises Inc.
John G. Boyette: treasurer B 1944. ED Augusta College BBA (1968). PRIM CORP EMPL senior vice president finance & administration: Cox Broadcasting Inc. ADD CORP EMPL vice president: Cox Enterprises Inc.
Anne Cox Chambers: chairman, trustee B Dayton, OH 1919. ED Finch Junior College. PRIM CORP EMPL chairman: Atlanta Journal-Constitution. CORP AFFIL director: Cox Enterprises Inc. NONPR AFFIL director: New York Botanical Garden; member national committee: Whitney Museum American Art; director: Metropolitan Museum Art; trustee: Museum Modern Art; member: LaCoste School Arts; director: MacDowell Colony; director: High Museum Art; director: Emory Museum Art & Archaeology; director: Forward Arts Foundation; director: Cities Schs; member: Council Foreign Relations; director: American Ambassadors Chmns Council; director: Atlanta Arts Alliance.
Timothy W. Hughes: vice president, trustee (see above)
Leigh Ann (Korns) Launius: assistant secretary PRIM CORP EMPL administration assistant: Cox Enterprises Inc.
Andrew Austin Merdek: secretary (see above)

Grants Analysis

Disclosure Period: calendar year ending 2001
Total Grants: $3,242,500
Number of Grants: 53
Average Grant: $61,179
Highest Grant: $250,000
Lowest Grant: $3,500
Typical Range: $10,000 to $100,000

Recent Grants

Note: Grants derived from 2001 Form 990.

Library-Related
25,000	Mesa County Public Library Foundation, Grand Junction, CO -- capital campaign

General
250,000	High Museum of Art, Atlanta, GA -- capital campaign
250,000	Michael C. Carlos Museum, Atlanta, GA -- capital campaign
250,000	Mighty Eighth Air Force Heritage Museum, Atlanta, GA
250,000	National Cable Television Center and Museum, Denver, CO -- endowment
200,000	Carter Center, Atlanta, GA -- endowment
200,000	Nature Conservancy, TN -- special projects
166,000	Dayton Foundation Performing Arts Fund, Dayton, OH -- capital campaign
125,000	American Red Cross, Atlanta, GA -- September 11th Disaster Relief Fund
125,000	Georgia Department of Natural Resources, Atlanta, GA -- capital campaign
125,000	Piedmont Park Conservancy, Atlanta, GA -- capital campaign

DAVE COY FOUNDATION

Giving Contact

Greg Muenster, Vice President
c/o Bank of America
PO Box 121, Trust Dept.
San Antonio, TX 78291-0121
Phone: (210)270-5371

Description

Founded: 1992
EIN: 746394909
Organization Type: Private Foundation
Giving Locations: TX: Bexar County
Grant Types: General Support.

Financial Summary

Total Giving: $648,456 (fiscal year ending July 31, 2001); $68,000 (fiscal 2000); $450,400 (fiscal 1998)
Giving Analysis: Giving for fiscal 2001 includes: foundation scholarships ($15,000); fiscal 2000: foundation scholarships ($25,000); fiscal 1998: foundation scholarships ($30,000) foundation ($420,400)
Assets: $3,416,101 (fiscal 2001); $4,350,038 (fiscal 2000); $4,935,214 (fiscal 1998)

Typical Recipients

Arts & Humanities: Arts Outreach, Libraries, Museums/Galleries, Music, Public Broadcasting
Civic & Public Affairs: Clubs, Economic Development, Employment/Job Training, Civic & Public Affairs-General, Hispanic Affairs, Housing, Nonprofit Management, Urban & Community Affairs, Women's Affairs
Education: Afterschool/Enrichment Programs, Education Funds, Education-General, Literacy, Private Education (Precollege), Science/Mathematics Education, Secondary Education (Private), Student Aid
Health: AIDS/HIV, Cancer, Children's Health/Hospitals, Clinics/Medical Centers, Emergency/Ambulance Services, Health-General, Health Organizations, Hospitals, Mental Health, Nursing Services, Prenatal Health Issues, Public Health, Single-Disease Health Associations
Religion: Jewish Causes, Ministries, Religious Welfare, Social/Policy Issues
Social Services: At-Risk Youth, Child Welfare, Community Centers, Community Service Organizations, Counseling, Day Care, Domestic Violence, Family Services, Food/Clothing Distribution, People with Disabilities, Scouts, Shelters/Homelessness, YMCA/YWCA/YMHA/YWHA, Youth Organizations

Application Procedures

Initial Contact: Send a full proposal.
Application Requirements: Include description of organization, purpose of funds sought, amount requested, and proof of tax-exempt status.
Deadlines: June 1.

Restrictions

Awards grants to benefit the poor and needy of Bexar County, TX.

Additional Information

Trust(s): Bank of America

Foundation Officials

A. B. Crowther: co-trustee

Grants Analysis

Disclosure Period: fiscal year ending July 31, 2001
Total Grants: $633,456*
Number of Grants: 38
Average Grant: $14,418*
Highest Grant: $100,000
Typical Range: $5,000 to $30,000
*Note: Giving excludes scholarships. Average grant figure excludes two highest grants ($200,000).

Recent Grants

Note: Grants derived from 2000 Form 990.

General
100,000	Catholic Charities, San Antonio, TX -- crisis intervention program
100,000	Salvation Army, San Antonio, TX -- operating support for male substance abusers
40,000	Santa Rosa Children's Hospital, San Antonio, TX -- Miracle 2000 campaign
30,000	Family Services Association, San Antonio, TX -- parenting programs-divorce, child abuse
30,000	Respite Care of San Antonio, Inc., San Antonio, TX -- medical wellness clinic
25,000	Mission Road Developmental Center, San Antonio, TX -- replant Mockingbird property
25,000	San Antonio Metropolitan Ministry Inc, San Antonio, TX -- living and learning center
22,000	San Antonio Lighthouse, San Antonio, TX -- technology upgrades
20,000	Any Baby Can of San Antonio, San Antonio, TX -- assistance for critically ill children
16,000	Christian Assistance Ministry, San Antonio, TX -- food collection and distribution

CRAIL-JOHNSON FOUNDATION

Giving Contact

Carolyn E. Johnson, President
222 W. 6th St., Suite 1010
San Pedro, CA 90731
Phone: (310)519-9500
E-mail: Craig-Johnson@crail-johnson.org
Web: http://www.crail-johnson.org/

Description

Founded: 1987
EIN: 330247161
Organization Type: Private Foundation
Giving Locations: CA: Los Angeles
Grant Types: General Support, Project.

Donor Information

Founder: the late Robert Johnson

Financial Summary

Total Giving: $2,640,140 (2000); $2,001,596 (1999); $2,616,650 (1997)
Assets: $14,204,354 (2000); $14,124,170 (1999); $9,546,158 (1996)
Gifts Received: $2,425,000 (2000); $2,150,000 (1999); $2,253,000 (1996). Note: In 1999, contributions were received from Eric C. Johnson, Craig C. Johnson, Alan C. Johnson, and L. Johnson ($100,000 each), and the Robert Johnson Charitable Lead Trust ($1,750,000). In 1996, contributions were received from the Robert Johnson Charitable Lead Trust ($1,750,000), Eric C. Johnson ($103,000), Craig C. Johnson, Alan C. Johnson, and Ann L. Johnson ($100,000 each), and the Jessie L.Crail Trust ($100,000).

Typical Recipients

Arts & Humanities: Ballet
Civic & Public Affairs: African American Affairs, Clubs, Civic & Public Affairs-General, Legal Aid, Nonprofit Management, Public Policy, Urban & Community Affairs, Women's Affairs, Zoos/Aquariums
Education: Business Education, Education Reform, Elementary Education (Public), Education-General, Literacy, Minority Education, Preschool Education, Private Education (Precollege), Public Education (Precollege), School Volunteerism, Science/Mathematics Education, Secondary Education (Public), Special Education
Environment: Environment-General
Health: AIDS/HIV, Cancer, Children's Health/Hospitals, Clinics/Medical Centers, Emergency/Ambulance Services, Heart, Hospices, Hospitals, Prenatal Health Issues, Public Health
Religion: Religious Welfare
Science: Scientific Centers & Institutes

Social Services: Animal Protection, At-Risk Youth, Big Brother/Big Sister, Camps, Child Welfare, Community Centers, Community Service Organizations, Counseling, Crime Prevention, Day Care, Domestic Violence, Emergency Relief, Family Planning, Family Services, Food/Clothing Distribution, Homes, People with Disabilities, Recreation & Athletics, Shelters/Homelessness, Social Services-General, Special Olympics, Substance Abuse, YMCA/YWCA/YMHA/YWHA, Youth Organizations

Application Procedures

Initial Contact: Send letter of inquiry describing applicant organization.
Application Requirements: Include a description of organization, purpose of funds sought, amount requested, proof of tax-exempt status, methods to be employed, the results expected, a preliminary budget, purpose of project and need it meets and duration.
Deadlines: None.
Decision Notification: Applicants will be notified within one month of receipt of request.

Restrictions

Does not support individuals, religious organizations for sectarian purposes, political or lobbying groups, organizations outside operating areas, University level education, or research.

Additional Information

The foundation provides financial support primarily through grants to public non-profit organizations which are exempt under Section 501(c)(3) of the Internal Revenue Service and are not a private foundation under Section 509(a).
Publications: Brochure; Grant application form.

Foundation Officials

John Berwald: director
Mary Castagne: director
S. L. Hutchison: chief financial officer, director
Alan C. Johnson: vice president, director
Ann L. Johnson: vice president, director
Carolyn E. Johnson: assistant secretary, director
Craig C. Johnson: vice president, director
Eric C. Johnson: chief executive officer, director
Stephon R. Mueller: director
John S. Peterson: secretary, director

Grants Analysis

Disclosure Period: calendar year ending 2000
Total Grants: $2,640,140
Number of Grants: 82
Average Grant: $26,405*
Highest Grant: $501,320
Lowest Grant: $50
Typical Range: $10,000 to $50,000
***Note:** Average grant figure excludes highest grant.

Recent Grants

Note: Grants derived from 1999 Form 990.

General

126,700	Los Angeles Maritime Institute, San Pedro, CA
100,000	Harbor Interfaith Shelter, San Pedro, CA
62,000	Council on Foundations, Washington, DC
52,500	San Pedro Boys and Girls Club, San Pedro, CA
45,000	Holy Family Services, Los Angeles, CA
30,000	Girls, Inc.
30,000	Harbor Area Gang Prevention Program
30,000	Harbor Interfaith Shelter, San Pedro, CA
30,000	Hospice Foundation, Torrance, CA
30,000	National Conference for Community and Justice, Inc., New York, NY

CRALLE FOUNDATION

Giving Contact

James T. Crain, Jr., Executive Director
620 W. Main St., Suite 320
Louisville, KY 40202
Phone: (502)581-1148

Description

Founded: 1990
EIN: 611179672
Organization Type: Private Foundation
Giving Locations: KY
Grant Types: General Support.

Financial Summary

Total Giving: $1,142,508 (2001); $1,205,544 (2000); $1,205,544 (1999)
Assets: $6,444 (2001); $14,789,808 (2000); $14,789,808 (1999)
Gifts Received: $8,066 (2001); $14,650 (2000); $88,573 (1998). Note: In 2001, contributions were received from Joan Day. In 1998, contributions were received from Joan Day and the estate of Lee E. Cralle.

Typical Recipients

Arts & Humanities: Ballet, Dance, Ethnic & Folk Arts, History & Archaeology, Libraries, Museums/Galleries, Public Broadcasting
Civic & Public Affairs: Botanical Gardens/Parks, Community Foundations, Civic & Public Affairs-General, Housing, Philanthropic Organizations, Urban & Community Affairs, Women's Affairs, Zoos/Aquariums
Education: Afterschool/Enrichment Programs, Business Education, Colleges & Universities, Economic Education, Education-General, Medical Education, Preschool Education, Private Education (Precollege), Secondary Education (Private), Special Education
Environment: Environment-General
Health: Emergency/Ambulance Services, Geriatric Health, Preventive Medicine/Wellness Organizations, Single-Disease Health Associations
Religion: Ministries, Religious Organizations, Religious Welfare
Science: Scientific Centers & Institutes
Social Services: At-Risk Youth, Big Brother/Big Sister, Camps, Child Welfare, Community Centers, Community Service Organizations, Day Care, Family Planning, Family Services, Food/Clothing Distribution, Homes, People with Disabilities, Scouts, Shelters/Homelessness, Social Services-General, Substance Abuse, YMCA/YWCA/YMHA/YWHA, Youth Organizations

Application Procedures

Initial Contact: Request application form.
Deadlines: None.

Additional Information

Publications: Application Form

Foundation Officials

James T. Crain, Jr.: executive director
James S. Welch: director

Grants Analysis

Disclosure Period: calendar year ending 2001
Total Grants: $1,142,508
Number of Grants: 65
Average Grant: $14,960*
Highest Grant: $125,000
Lowest Grant: $765
Typical Range: $5,000 to $20,000
***Note:** Average grant figure excludes two highest grants ($200,000).

Recent Grants

Note: Grants derived from 2001 Form 990.

General

125,000	Home of the Innocents, Louisville, KY -- capital campaign
75,000	Centre College, Danville, KY -- endowment
57,500	Spina Bifida Association of Kentucky, Louisville, KY -- Cycle for Life Project
50,000	Spalding University, Louisville, KY -- Cralle Scholars
35,000	Louisville Diversified Services, Louisville, KY -- Schlachter House
30,840	Saint Catherine College, St. Catherine, KY -- computers and workstations
25,000	Cathedral Heritage Foundation, Louisville, KY -- festival
25,000	David School, David, KY -- operating costs
25,000	Spava, Louisville, KY -- scholarships
24,483	YMCA, Louisville, KY -- Camp Piomingo

ARTHUR CRAMES FAMILY FOUNDATION

Giving Contact

Arthur Crames, Director
19 Briarcliff Road
Upper Saddle River, NJ 07458
Phone: (212)372-1520

Description

Founded: 1991
EIN: 133544875
Organization Type: Private Foundation
Giving Locations: NJ; NY
Grant Types: General Support.

Financial Summary

Total Giving: $50,750 (2001); $25,800 (2000); $26,000 (1999)
Assets: $63,067 (2001); $26,127 (2000); $18,130 (1999)
Gifts Received: $81,975 (2001); $37,063 (2000); $39,777 (1999). Note: In 2000 and 2001, contributions were received from Arthur Crames. In 1999, contributions were received from Arthur Crames. In 1996, contributions were received from Arthur Crames ($47,000) and the Monterey Fund ($3,874).

Typical Recipients

Arts & Humanities: History & Archaeology, Libraries
Civic & Public Affairs: Clubs, Community Foundations, Civic & Public Affairs-General, Housing, Municipalities/Towns, Safety, Urban & Community Affairs
Education: Colleges & Universities, Public Education (Precollege)
Health: Cancer, Clinics/Medical Centers, Emergency/Ambulance Services, Eyes/Blindness, Heart, Hospitals
Religion: Religion-General, Religious Organizations, Religious Welfare
Social Services: Child Welfare, Community Service Organizations, Crime Prevention, Delinquency & Criminal Rehabilitation, Recreation & Athletics, Veterans, Volunteer Services

Application Procedures

Initial Contact: The foundation has no formal grant application procedure or application form.
Deadlines: None.

Foundation Officials

Arthur Crames: director
Dale Crames: director
Gail T. Winawer: director

Grants Analysis

Disclosure Period: calendar year ending 2001
Total Grants: $50,750
Number of Grants: 19
Average Grant: $2,671
Highest Grant: $14,000
Lowest Grant: $100
Typical Range: $500 to $5,000

Recent Grants

Note: Grants derived from 2000 Form 990.

Library-Related

2,500	Galway Public Library, Galway, NY

General

4,000	St. Charles, New York, NY
2,500	Boca Raton Community Hospital, Boca Raton, FL
2,500	Campus Crusade, Upper Saddle River, NJ
2,500	Police Pipes and Drums, The, Upper Saddle River, NJ
2,500	Upper Saddle River PBA Local 218, Upper Saddle River, NJ
2,000	Iona College, New Rochelle, NY
1,000	New York City Board of Education, New York, NY
1,000	St. Joseph's Hospital, Paterson, NJ
1,000	Upper Saddle River Fire Department, Upper Saddle River, NJ
1,000	Upper Saddle River Fire Department, Upper Saddle River, NJ

CRAMPTON TRUST

Giving Contact

R. B. Doyle, III, Trust Officer
c/o Regions Bank
PO Box 2527
Mobile, AL 36622-0001
Phone: (334)690-1411
Fax: (334)690-1591

Description

Founded: 1994
EIN: 636181261
Organization Type: Private Foundation
Giving Locations: AL
Grant Types: General Support.

Donor Information

Founder: Established in 1994 by the late Katherine C. Cochrane.

Financial Summary

Total Giving: $1,065,009 (2000); $653,441 (1999); $542,093 (1998)
Assets: $22,241,517 (2000); $22,529,602 (1999); $22,210,935 (1998)
Gifts Received: $1,000 (1993). Note: In 1993, contributions were received from the estate of Katherine C. Cochrane.

Typical Recipients

Arts & Humanities: Ballet, Libraries, Museums/Galleries
Civic & Public Affairs: Civic & Public Affairs-General, Municipalities/Towns, Safety
Education: Business Education, Colleges & Universities, Medical Education, Private Education (Precollege), Public Education (Precollege), Science/Mathematics Education, Secondary Education (Public), Student Aid
Health: Cancer, Children's Health/Hospitals, Clinics/Medical Centers, Emergency/Ambulance Services, Geriatric Health, Heart, Hospitals, Mental Health, Nutrition, Single-Disease Health Associations
Religion: Churches, Religious Organizations, Religious Welfare

Science: Science Museums
Social Services: At-Risk Youth, Food/Clothing Distribution, Homes, People with Disabilities, United Funds/United Ways, YMCA/YWCA/YMHA/YWHA, Youth Organizations

Application Procedures

Initial Contact: Request guidelines.
Deadlines: None.

Additional Information

Trust(s): Regions Bank

Foundation Officials

John C. Johnson: member
Mabel B. Ward: member

Grants Analysis

Disclosure Period: calendar year ending 2000
Total Grants: $1,065,009
Number of Grants: 25
Average Grant: $26,740*
Highest Grant: $300,000
Typical Range: $15,000 to $50,000
*Note: Average grant excludes two highest grants ($450,000).

Recent Grants

Note: Grants derived from 1999 Form 990.

Library-Related

100,000	Mobile Public Library, Mobile, AL -- new equipment

General

150,000	Mobile Museum of Art, Mobile, AL -- capital campaign
50,000	City of Mobile, Mobile, AL -- Nicholas and Alexandra Exhibition
50,000	McGill Toolen High School -- equipment
49,500	Spring Hill College, Mobile, AL -- furniture and equipment
30,225	Bay Area Food Bank, Mobile, AL -- capital fund
30,000	Mercy Medical -- mercy cares project
25,000	America's Junior Miss -- operations
25,000	Mobile Ballet, Mobile, AL -- capital campaign
25,000	Ronald McDonald House, Mobile, AL -- project expenses
24,495	University of South Alabama, Mobile, AL -- medical college professorship

J. FORD CRANDALL MEMORIAL FOUNDATION

Giving Contact

Robert J. Christian, Secretary
26 Market Street, Suite 904
Youngstown, OH 44503
Phone: (330)744-2125

Description

Founded: 1975
EIN: 346513634
Organization Type: Private Foundation
Giving Locations: OH: Mahoning County
Grant Types: Capital, Endowment, General Support, Scholarship.

Donor Information

Founder: the late J. Ford Crandall

Financial Summary

Total Giving: $257,199 (2001); $271,723 (2000); $208,451 (1999)
Giving Analysis: Giving for 2000 includes: foundation scholarships ($22,500) 1999: foundation scholarships ($22,500)

Assets: $5,686,376 (2001); $5,830,274 (2000); $5,519,478 (1999)

Typical Recipients

Arts & Humanities: Arts Associations & Councils, Community Arts, Historic Preservation, Libraries, Music, Public Broadcasting
Civic & Public Affairs: Botanical Gardens/Parks, Economic Development, Civic & Public Affairs-General, Legal Aid, Urban & Community Affairs
Education: Colleges & Universities, Education-General, Preschool Education, Private Education (Precollege), Student Aid
Health: Alzheimers Disease, Children's Health/Hospitals, Clinics/Medical Centers, Emergency/Ambulance Services, Hospices, Hospitals, Research/Studies Institutes
Religion: Churches, Jewish Causes, Missionary Activities (Domestic), Religious Organizations, Religious Welfare
Social Services: Camps, Child Welfare, Community Centers, Community Service Organizations, Counseling, Domestic Violence, Family Services, Food/Clothing Distribution, People with Disabilities, Recreation & Athletics, Senior Services, Shelters/Homelessness, Substance Abuse, United Funds/United Ways, Veterans, Volunteer Services, YMCA/YWCA/YMHA/YWHA, Youth Organizations

Application Procedures

Initial Contact: The foundation has no formal grant application procedure or application form.
Deadlines: December 1.

Foundation Officials

Andrew G. Bresko: trustee
Amy H. Gambrel: trustee
William M. Marshall: trustee

Grants Analysis

Disclosure Period: calendar year ending 2001
Total Grants: $257,199
Number of Grants: 10
Average Grant: $16,525*
Highest Grant: $62,500
Lowest Grant: $1,000
Typical Range: $10,000 to $25,000
*Note: Average grant excludes two highest grants ($125,000).

Recent Grants

Note: Grants derived from 2001 Form 990.

General

62,500	Fellows Riverside Gardens, Youngstown, OH -- for capital improvements
62,500	YMCA, Youngstown, OH -- for capital improvements
35,000	Mill Creek Park Foundation, Canfield, OH -- for operations
25,000	HELP Hotline Crisis Center, Youngstown, OH -- for operations
20,000	Hillsville Charitable Foundation, Lowellville, OH -- for operations
18,570	D & E Counseling Camp Challenge, Youngstown, OH -- for operations
16,580	Volunteer Services Agency, Youngstown, OH -- for operations
15,000	Park Vista Senior Independence, Youngstown, OH -- for operations
1,049	Youngstown Area Arts Council, Youngstown, OH -- for operations
1,000	Rescue Mission, Youngstown, OH -- for operations

CRANE CO.

Company Headquarters

100 1st Stamford Pl., Ste. 300
Stamford, CT 06902
Web: http://www.craneco.com

Company Description

Founded: 1855
Ticker: CR
Exchange: NYSE
Acquired: Stockham Valves & Fittings Inc.
Revenue: US$1.516 billion (2002)
Employees: 9500 (2002)
SIC(s): 3052 Rubber & Plastics Hose & Belting, 3494 Valves & Pipe Fittings Nec, 3594 Fluid Power Pumps & Motors, 3621 Motors & Generators, 5074 Plumbing & Hydronic Heating Supplies.

Operating Locations

Crane Co. (AZ--Goodyear; CA--Burbank; FL--Jacksonville; IL--Joliet; MO--Chesterfield, St. Louis; NY--New Rochelle; NC--Marion; OH--Salem, Washington Court House; PA--King of Prussia, Warrington)

Crane Foundation

Giving Contact

Gil Dickoff, Treasurer
Crane Foundation
100 First Stamford Pl.
Stamford, CT 06902
Phone: (203)363-7268
Fax: (203)363-7295
E-mail: crfdn@craneco.com

Description

Founded: 1951
EIN: 436051752
Organization Type: Corporate Foundation
Giving Locations: headquarters and operating communities.
Grant Types: Emergency, Employee Matching Gifts, General Support.
Note: Employee matching gift ratio: 1 to 1 to educational institutions, to a maximum of $2,500 per employee annually.

Donor Information

Founder: UMC Industries, Inc.

Financial Summary

Total Giving: $355,715 (2001); $359,017 (2000); $214,974 (1998)
Giving Analysis: Giving for 2000 includes: foundation scholarships ($4,000); corporate matching gifts ($36,408); foundation ($318,609); 1998: corporate scholarships ($3,000); corporate matching gifts ($49,230) corporate direct giving ($162,744)
Assets: $7,599,446 (2001); $8,049,038 (2000); $6,538,757 (1998)

Typical Recipients

Arts & Humanities: Arts Associations & Councils, Arts Centers, Ballet, Historic Preservation, History & Archaeology, Libraries, Museums/Galleries, Music, Performing Arts, Public Broadcasting, Theater
Civic & Public Affairs: Botanical Gardens/Parks, Business/Free Enterprise, Community Foundations, Economic Development, Economic Policy, Civic & Public Affairs-General, Hispanic Affairs, Housing, Law & Justice, Legal Aid, Minority Business, Parades/Festivals, Public Policy, Safety, Urban & Community Affairs, Women's Affairs, Zoos/Aquariums
Education: Arts/Humanities Education, Business Education, Colleges & Universities, Community & Junior Colleges, Economic Education, Education Funds, Education Funds, Education Reform, Elementary Education (Public), Faculty Development, Education-General, International Studies, Legal Education, Literacy, Minority Education, Private Education (Precollege), Public Education (Precollege), Science/Mathematics Education, Secondary Education (Private), Secondary Education (Public), Student Aid
Environment: Environment-General, Wildlife Protection

Health: Cancer, Diabetes, Emergency/Ambulance Services, Eyes/Blindness, Health Organizations, Hospitals, Medical Research, Mental Health, Multiple Sclerosis, Public Health, Single-Disease Health Associations, Transplant Networks/Donor Banks
International: International-General, Health Care/Hospitals, International Development, International Environmental Issues, International Organizations, International Peace & Security Issues, International Relief Efforts
Religion: Bible Study/Translation, Religious Welfare
Science: Scientific Centers & Institutes
Social Services: Animal Protection, At-Risk Youth, Child Abuse, Child Welfare, Community Service Organizations, Domestic Violence, Emergency Relief, Food/Clothing Distribution, Homes, People with Disabilities, Recreation & Athletics, Scouts, Shelters/Homelessness, Social Services-General, Special Olympics, Substance Abuse, United Funds/United Ways, Volunteer Services, YMCA/YWCA/YMHA/YWHA, Youth Organizations

Application Procedures

Initial Contact: Send brief letter on organization letterhead.
Application Requirements: Include a description of organization and proof of tax-exempt status.
Deadlines: None.

Restrictions

Grants are not made to individuals.

Corporate Officials

Gil A. Dickoff: treasurer taxes B New York, NY 1961. ED State University of New York (1983); State University of New York (1984). PRIM CORP EMPL treasurer: Crane Co.
Augustus I. DuPont: vice president, general counsel, secretary ED Stanford University BA (1975); University of Chicago JD (1978). PRIM CORP EMPL vice president, general counsel, secretary: Crane Co.
Robert Sheldon Evans: chairman B Pittsburgh, PA 1944. ED University of Pennsylvania BA (1966); Columbia University MBA (1968). PRIM CORP EMPL chairman: Crane Co. CORP AFFIL director: Mid-Ocean Ltd.; director: HBD Industries; chairman: Medusa Corp.; director: Fansteel. NONPR AFFIL member deans advisory council: Columbia University Graduate School Business; trustee: Eaglebrook School; trustee: Allen Stevenson School.
Eric C. Fast: president, chief executive officer PRIM CORP EMPL president, chief executive officer: Crane Co.
Elise M. Kopczick: vice president human resources
T. M. Noonan: vice president taxes

Foundation Officials

Gil A. Dickoff: treasurer (see above)
Augustus I. DuPont: vice president, secretary, director (see above)
Robert Sheldon Evans: chairman, director (see above)
Eric C. Fast: director (see above)
Elise M. Kopczick: vice president (see above)
T. M. Noonan: vice president (see above)
M. L. Raithel: vice president, director

Grants Analysis

Disclosure Period: calendar year ending 2001
Total Grants: $329,225*
Number of Grants: 69
Average Grant: $4,771
Highest Grant: $25,000
Lowest Grant: $100
Typical Range: $500 to $5,000
*Note: Giving excludes matching gifts.

Recent Grants

Note: Grants derived from 2001 Form 990.

Library-Related

10,000	Greenwich Library, Greenwich, CT -- for Peterson Business Award Dinner
5,000	Morgan Library, New York, NY
2,000	New York Public Library, New York, NY

General

25,000	Glendale Community College, Glendale, AZ
25,000	McDowell YMCA, Marion, NC
20,000	Soundwaters, Inc.
20,000	United States Squash Racquets Association
20,000	Washington Legal Foundation, Washington, DC
15,000	Columbia School of Business, New York, NY -- 2001 annual dinner
15,000	McDowell Technical Community College Foundation, Marion, NC
10,000	American Diabetes Association, Pensacola, FL
10,000	Etobicoke Hospital Foundation
10,000	Foundation for Teaching Economics, Davis, CA

CRANSTON PRINT WORKS CO.

Company Headquarters

1381 Cranston St.
Cranston, RI 02920
Web: http://www.cpw.com

Company Description

Employees: 1,175
SIC(s): 2261 Finishing Plants--Cotton, 3552 Textile Machinery, 3554 Paper Industries Machinery.

Operating Locations

Cranston Print Works Co. (LA--Denham Springs; MA--Webster; NY--New York; NC--Fletcher; RI--East Providence, Pawtucket, Providence)

Cranston Foundation

Giving Contact

Carolyn Lake, Administrator
1381 Cranston St.
Cranston, RI 02920
Phone: (401)943-4800
Fax: (401)943-3971
E-mail: cpw@cpw.com

Description

EIN: 056015348
Organization Type: Corporate Foundation
Giving Locations: FL; MA; NY; RI
Grant Types: Employee Matching Gifts, General Support, Scholarship.

Financial Summary

Total Giving: $220,283 (fiscal year ending June 31, 2001); $187,103 (fiscal 2000); $238,928 (fiscal 1999).
Note: Contributes through foundation only.
Giving Analysis: Giving for fiscal 2001 includes: foundation scholarships ($154,935); fiscal 2000: foundation grants to United Way ($15,000); foundation ($22,997); foundation matching gifts ($28,266); foundation scholarships ($120,840); fiscal 1999: foundation ($238,928).
Assets: $13,726 (fiscal 2001); $3,646 (fiscal 2000); $177,450 (fiscal 1998)
Gifts Received: $230,307 (fiscal 2001); $163,499 (fiscal 2000); $24,902 (fiscal 1997)

Typical Recipients

Arts & Humanities: Ethnic & Folk Arts, History & Archaeology, Libraries, Museums/Galleries

Civic & Public Affairs: Civic & Public Affairs-General, Safety

Education: Arts/Humanities Education, Business Education, Colleges & Universities, Community & Junior Colleges, Engineering/Technological Education, Journalism/Media Education, Medical Education, Minority Education, Science/Mathematics Education, Social Sciences Education, Student Aid, Vocational & Technical Education

Environment: Environment-General, Resource Conservation

Health: Emergency/Ambulance Services, Hospitals, Kidney, Prenatal Health Issues

Religion: Jewish Causes, Religious Welfare

Social Services: Big Brother/Big Sister, Community Service Organizations, Scouts, United Funds/United Ways, YMCA/YWCA/YMHA/YWHA, Youth Organizations

Application Procedures

Initial Contact: Send a written request.

Application Requirements: Include details of project; funding requirements; budget information; organization's management structure, purpose, operation, and goals; copy of IRS classification letter; and recent financial statements.

Deadlines: Before May 15 for funding during that fiscal year.

Decision Notification: Trustees normally meet twice per year.

Restrictions

The foundation only makes contributions to domestic organizations which have been ruled by the IRS as tax exempt under Section 501(c)(3) of the Internal Revenue Code.

Additional Information

Publications: Guidelines

Corporate Officials

Bryan Adriance: vice president, finance & administration PRIM CORP EMPL vice president finance & administration: Cranston Print Works Co.

George Whitcomb Shuster: president, chief executive officer, director B Trenton, NJ 1946. ED Yale University (1967); Yale University Law School (1973). PRIM CORP EMPL president, chief executive officer, director: Cranston Print Works Co. CORP AFFIL director: Ashwright Inc. NONPR AFFIL director: Kent County Memorial Hospital.

Foundation Officials

Bryan Adriance: member (see above)
John Menzies: member
George Whitcomb Shuster: trustee (see above)
Shelley Wollseiffen: member

Grants Analysis

Disclosure Period: fiscal year ending June 31, 2001
Total Grants: $21,700*
Number of Grants: 19
Average Grant: $1,142
Highest Grant: $7,500
Typical Range: $250 to $1,500
*Note: Giving excludes matching gifts, scholarship, United Way.

Recent Grants

Note: Grants derived from 2001 Form 990.

General

10,000	United Way of Southeastern New England, Providence, RI -- charitable gift
10,000	United Way Webster-Dudley, Webster, MA -- operating funds
9,815	Eastern Connecticut State University,

9,583	Willimantic, CT -- scholarship to dependent child of employee
	University of Rhode Island, Kingston, RI -- scholarship to dependent child of employee
8,442	Worcester State College, Worcester, MA -- scholarship to dependent child of employee
8,000	Assumption College, Worcester, MA -- scholarship to dependent child of employee
7,500	Hubbard Regional Hospital, Webster, MA -- operating support
7,439	Rhode Island College, Providence, RI -- scholarship to dependent child of employee
7,355	Quinsigamond Community College, Worcester, MA -- scholarship to dependent child of employee
6,099	University of Massachusetts Amherst, Amherst, MA -- scholarship to dependent child of employee

BRUCE L. CRARY FOUNDATION

Giving Contact

Euphemia V. Hall, President
PO Box 396
Elizabethtown, NY 12932
Phone: (518)873-6496

Description

Founded: 1973
EIN: 237366844
Organization Type: Private Foundation
Giving Locations: NY: Essex County
Grant Types: General Support, Scholarship.

Donor Information

Founder: Crary Public Trust, the late Bruce L. Crary

Financial Summary

Total Giving: $397,329 (fiscal year ending June 30, 2001); $358,920 (fiscal 2000); $353,040 (fiscal 1999). Note: Fiscal 1997 Giving includes scholarship ($292,630).

Giving Analysis: Giving for fiscal 2001 includes: foundation scholarships ($370,785) fiscal 1999: foundation scholarships ($327,185)

Assets: $9,907,950 (fiscal 2001); $10,630,163 (fiscal 2000); $10,276,863 (fiscal 1999)

Gifts Received: $5,225 (fiscal 2001)

Typical Recipients

Arts & Humanities: Arts Centers, Historic Preservation, History & Archaeology, Libraries, Theater

Civic & Public Affairs: Municipalities/Towns, Nonprofit Management, Urban & Community Affairs

Education: Community & Junior Colleges, Literacy, Secondary Education (Private), Student Aid

Environment: Air/Water Quality, Environment-General

Health: Emergency/Ambulance Services, Hospices, Hospitals, Mental Health

Social Services: Animal Protection, Child Welfare, Community Service Organizations, Domestic Violence, Family Planning

Application Procedures

Initial Contact: Student aid applications are available at guidance offices in area high schools. For charitable grants, there are no formal requirements.

Deadlines: March 31 for student aid.

Additional Information

Provides scholarships to individuals for higher education.

Foundation Officials

G. Gordon Davis, Esq.: secretary, gov, trustee B Richmond, VA 1941. ED Yale University BE (1964); University of Virginia JD (1967). PRIM CORP EMPL senior up, general counsel: Ecologically Sustainable Development. CORP AFFIL senior partner: Davis & Finucane. NONPR AFFIL member: New York State Bar Association; member: Virginia State Bar Association; member: National Comm US-China Relations; president: Dry Gulch Vineyards.

Janet Decker: gov

Euphemia V. Hall: vice president, gov, trustee

Richard Wesley Lawrence, Jr.: president, gov, trustee B New York, NY January 16, 1909. ED Princeton University BS (1931); Columbia University LLB (1934). PRIM CORP EMPL president, director: Conservation Management. CORP AFFIL vice president, director: Umont Mining. NONPR AFFIL director: New York Parks & Conservation Association; trustee: New York Saint Historical Association; honorary member: New York Library Association; member: Essex County Historical Society; member: Governments Commission Future Adirondacks 21st Century; president: Crary Education Foundation; chairman: Commissioner Eds Comm Reference & Research Library Resources. CLUB AFFIL Union League Club; Explorers Club; Princeton Club; Ausable Club.

Meredith Prime: gov

Gail Rogers-Rice: gov

Arthur V. Savage, Esq.: treasurer, gov, trustee

Grants Analysis

Disclosure Period: fiscal year ending June 30, 2001
Total Grants: $26,544*
Number of Grants: 17
Average Grant: $603*
Highest Grant: $16,894
Typical Range: $100 to $1,000
*Note: Giving excludes scholarships. Average grant excludes highest grant.

Recent Grants

Note: Grants derived from fiscal 2000 Form 990.

General

5,000	Rhode Island School of Design, Providence, RI -- for scholarships
5,000	Union College, Schenectady, NY -- for scholarships
5,000	University of Maine, Orono, ME -- for scholarships
1,500	Cornell University, Ithaca, NY -- for scholarships
1,500	Siena College, Siena, NY -- for scholarships
1,500	SUNY, Plattsburgh, NY -- for scholarships
1,500	SUNY, Potsdam, NY -- for scholarships
1,500	SUNY, Potsdam, NY -- for scholarships
1,500	SUNY, Potsdam, NY -- for scholarships
1,200	Adirondack Community College, Queensbury, NY -- for scholarships

E. R. CRAWFORD ESTATE TRUST FUND A

Giving Contact

George F. Young, Jr., Trustee
PO Box 487
Mc Keesport, PA 15134
Phone: (412)751-2770

Description

Founded: 1936
EIN: 256031554
Organization Type: Private Foundation
Giving Locations: PA
Grant Types: Operating Expenses, Scholarship.

Donor Information

Founder: E. R. Crawford

Financial Summary

Total Giving: $370,674 (2000); $373,225 (1999); $420,176 (1998)
Giving Analysis: Giving for 2000 includes: foundation gifts to individuals ($2,424) 1999: foundation gifts to individuals ($5,475)
Assets: $7,754,069 (2000); $7,501,227 (1999); $8,268,747 (1998)

Typical Recipients

Arts & Humanities: Arts & Humanities-General, Historic Preservation, History & Archaeology, Libraries, Literary Arts, Music, Theater
Civic & Public Affairs: Chambers of Commerce, Clubs, Civic & Public Affairs-General, Municipalities/Towns, Philanthropic Organizations, Professional & Trade Associations, Women's Affairs
Education: Business Education, Colleges & Universities, Community & Junior Colleges, Education-General, Gifted & Talented Programs, Literacy, Preschool Education, Student Aid
Health: Cancer, Children's Health/Hospitals, Diabetes, Emergency/Ambulance Services, Health Organizations, Hospitals, Medical Research, Multiple Sclerosis, Single-Disease Health Associations
Religion: Churches, Religious Organizations, Religious Welfare, Religious Welfare, Synagogues/Temples
Social Services: Child Welfare, Community Service Organizations, Food/Clothing Distribution, Homes, Recreation & Athletics, YMCA/YWCA/YMHA/YWHA, Youth Organizations

Application Procedures

Initial Contact: Individuals should request an application form.
Application Requirements: Public charities should submit a proposal stating general background information, the purposes and nature of the organization, and purpose of funds sought.
Deadlines: None.

Foundation Officials

William O. Hunter: trustee
Francis E. Neish, Jr.: trustee
George F. Young, Jr.: trustee

Grants Analysis

Disclosure Period: calendar year ending 2000
Total Grants: $368,250*
Number of Grants: 103
Average Grant: $3,575
Highest Grant: $45,000
Typical Range: $1,000 to $10,000
***Note:** Giving excludes grants to individuals.

Recent Grants

Note: Grants derived from 1999 Form 990.

Library-Related

30,000	Carnegie Free Library of McKeesport, McKeesport, PA

General

45,000	McKeesport Heritage Center, McKeesport, PA
35,000	YMCA of McKeesport, McKeesport, PA
25,000	South Hills Health System Foundation, Jefferson Boro, PA
20,000	McKeesport Area Meals on Wheels, McKeesport, PA
20,000	McKeesport Hospital Foundation, McKeesport, PA
20,000	Salvation Army, McKeesport, PA
10,000	Community Food Bank, McKeesport, PA
10,000	Kane Foundation, McKeesport, PA
10,000	McKeesport Symphony Society, McKeesport, PA
10,000	Pauline Auberle Foundation, McKeesport, PA

EVAH C. CRAY RESIDUARY CHARITABLE TRUST

Giving Contact

Gay L. Wright, Trust Officer
UMB Bank
626 Commercial
Atchison, KS 66002
Phone: (913)367-3412
Fax: (913)367-7125

Description

Founded: 1995
EIN: 486320070
Organization Type: Private Foundation
Giving Locations: KS: Atchison County
Grant Types: General Support, Matching.

Financial Summary

Total Giving: $393,417 (fiscal year ending June 30, 2001); $416,305 (fiscal 2000); $235,807 (fiscal 1999)
Giving Analysis: Giving for fiscal 2000 includes: foundation grants to United Way ($5,000) fiscal 1999: foundation grants to United Way ($10,000)
Assets: $4,854,205 (fiscal 2001); $5,170,871 (fiscal 2000); $5,641,706 (fiscal 1999)

Typical Recipients

Arts & Humanities: Arts Associations & Councils, History & Archaeology, Libraries, Museums/Galleries, Theater
Civic & Public Affairs: Business/Free Enterprise, Chambers of Commerce, Housing, Municipalities/Towns
Education: Colleges & Universities, Community & Junior Colleges, Elementary Education (Private), Education-General, Private Education (Precollege), Student Aid
Environment: Resource Conservation
Health: Emergency/Ambulance Services, Home-Care Services
International: Health Care/Hospitals
Religion: Churches
Social Services: At-Risk Youth, Community Centers, Community Service Organizations, Family Services, Scouts, United Funds/United Ways, YMCA/YWCA/YMHA/YWHA

Application Procedures

Initial Contact: The foundation has no formal grant application procedure or application form. Send a brief letter of inquiry.
Application Requirements: Include a description of organization, amount requested, purpose of funds sought, proof of tax-exempt status, proof of matched funds.
Deadlines: None.

Restrictions

Does not support organizations outside operating areas. Grants are generally restricted to charitable organizations within Atchison County, KS.

Additional Information

All requests for funds must be matched.
Trust(s): UMB Bank

Foundation Officials

Cloud Cray: co-trustee B Detroit, MI 1922. ED Case Institute of Technology BS (1943). PRIM CORP EMPL president, director: Midwest Solvents Co. of Illinois. CORP AFFIL chairman: Midwest Grain Products Inc. NONPR AFFIL president: Cray Medicine Research Foundation; director: Riverbend Regional Health Systems; chairman: Atchison Hospital Foundation.
Jeri Kurth: co-trustee
June Lynn: co-trustee
Gay Wright: trust officer, trustee

Grants Analysis

Disclosure Period: fiscal year ending June 30, 2001
Total Grants: $388,417*
Number of Grants: 16
Average Grant: $10,000*
Highest Grant: $238,417
Lowest Grant: $1,000
Typical Range: $5,000 to $10,000
***Note:** Giving excludes United Way. Average grant figure excludes highest grant.

Recent Grants

Note: Grants derived from fiscal 2000 Form 990.

General

259,455	Evah C. Cray Home Museum, Atchison, KS -- museum
75,000	Benedictine College, Atchison, KS -- education
25,000	City of Atchison, Atchison, KS -- education
13,000	First Presbyterian Church, Atchison, KS
7,500	Doves Inc., Atchison, KS
6,000	Happy Hearts, Atchison, KS
5,000	Atchison Area United Way, Atchison, KS
5,000	Atchison Child Care Association, Atchison, KS -- education
5,000	Atchison County Historical Society, Atchison, KS -- museum
5,000	Mount Community Center, Atchison, KS

CREDIT SUISSE FIRST BOSTON CORP.

Company Headquarters

11 Madison Ave.
New York, NY 10010-3629
Web: http://www.csfb.com

Company Description

Former Name: First Boston.
Revenue: US$1.366 billion (2001)
Employees: 28,415 (2001)
SIC(s): 6211 Security Brokers & Dealers.
Parent Company: Credit Suisse Group, Paradeplatz 8, PO Box 1, Zurich, Switzerland

Operating Locations

Credit Suisse First Boston (NY--New York; PR--Hato Rey); Swiss American Securities (NY--New York)
Note: Operates throughout the USA.

Nonmonetary Support

Volunteer Programs: The company encourages employee volunteerism in programs such as Publicolor, Habitat for Humanity, Everybody Wins, and Big Brothers/Big Sisters.

Credit Suisse First Boston Foundation Trust

Giving Contact

Ms. Casey Karel, Vice President
Credit Suisse First Boston Foundation Trust
11 Madison Ave.
New York, NY 10010
Phone: (212)325-2389
Fax: (212)538-4633
E-mail: casey.karel@csfb.com
Web: http://www.csfb.com/about_csfb/
company_information/foundation/index.shtml

Description

Founded: 1959
EIN: 046059692
Organization Type: Corporate Foundation
Giving Locations: NY: New York headquarters and operating communities; nationally.
Grant Types: General Support, Project.
Note: The foundation also awards mini-grants to employees.

Donor Information

Founder: The First Boston Corp.

Financial Summary

Total Giving: $5,000,000 (2004 approx); $5,000,000 (2003 approx); $6,000,000 (2002 approx). Note: Contributes through corporate direct giving program and foundation.
Giving Analysis: Giving for 2002 includes: foundation (approx $5,000,000); 2001: foundation (approx $4,422,023); corporate direct giving (approx $10,830,000) 1998: foundation ($1,000,000)
Assets: $24,000,000 (2003 approx); $24,000,000 (2002 approx); $24,677,227 (2001)
Gifts Received: $31,675,934 (2001); $4,708,373 (2000); $557,600 (1996). Note: The foundation received contributions from Credit Suisse First Boston Corporation.

Typical Recipients

Arts & Humanities: Arts Associations & Councils, Arts Centers, Arts Funds, Arts Institutes, Ballet, Dance, Arts & Humanities-General, Libraries, Museums/Galleries, Music, Opera, Performing Arts, Public Broadcasting, Theater
Civic & Public Affairs: African American Affairs, Botanical Gardens/Parks, Business/Free Enterprise, Civil Rights, Clubs, Community Foundations, Economic Development, Economic Policy, Employment/Job Training, Civic & Public Affairs-General, Housing, Law & Justice, Municipalities/Towns, Philanthropic Organizations, Professional & Trade Associations, Public Policy, Urban & Community Affairs, Women's Affairs
Education: Arts/Humanities Education, Business Education, Business Education, Colleges & Universities, Continuing Education, Economic Education, Education Funds, Education Reform, Engineering/Technological Education, Education-General, Leadership Training, Minority Education, Preschool Education, Private Education (Precollege), Public Education (Precollege), School Volunteerism, Science/Mathematics Education, Special Education, Student Aid, Vocational & Technical Education
Environment: Air/Water Quality, Resource Conservation
Health: Cancer, Children's Health/Hospitals, Clinics/Medical Centers, Emergency/Ambulance Services, Hospitals, Medical Research, Mental Health, Prenatal Health Issues, Single-Disease Health Associations, Transplant Networks/Donor Banks
International: Health Care/Hospitals, International Relations
Religion: Religious Welfare

Social Services: At-Risk Youth, At-Risk Youth, Big Brother/Big Sister, Child Welfare, Community Centers, Community Service Organizations, Emergency Relief, Family Services, Food/Clothing Distribution, People with Disabilities, Recreation & Athletics, Scouts, Shelters/Homelessness, Social Services-General, Special Olympics, United Funds/United Ways, Volunteer Services, YMCA/YWCA/YMHA/YWHA, Youth Organizations

Application Procedures

Initial Contact: See website for application guidelines, then submit a letter of inquiry.
Application Requirements: Letters of inquiry should not exceed two pages and must include contact information; a description of organization; purpose of funds sought; population served; estimated overall project budget; and time period for which funds are requested.
Deadlines: None for letters of inquiry. February 15 and August 15 for proposals.
Review Process: If the foundation determines that an inquiry fits the foundation's guidelines and current focus, the applicant will be contacted and invited to submit a full proposal. The foundation's board of trustees holds three grant making meetings from April through September of each year.
Evaluative Criteria: Proposals should be clear and concise. The foundation prefers programs that are consistent with the foundation's mission; provide volunteer opportunities for CSFB employees; for which the foundation's grant money can make a difference; and will be likely to attract the support of other funders in subsequent years. The foundation also strongly prefers organizations with stable financials.
Decision Notification: Letters of inquiry generally receive a response within 90 working days. Review of full proposals may take three to four months.
Notes: Do not send videotapes unless specifically requested.

Restrictions

Foundation does not support capital campaigns; dinners or events; endowments; individuals or scholarship programs; matching gifts; medical research; public or private schools; religious programs; sponsorships; or veteran, fraternal and political programs.

Additional Information

In 1994, the company reported that it changed its name. The company was formerly known as First Boston Inc., but is now known as Credit Suisse First Boston Corp. Additionally, the company's trust has changed its name from First Boston Foundation Trust to Credit Suisse First Boston Foundation Trust.
Publications: Guidelines

Corporate Officials

John J. Mack: chief executive officer
Stephen R. Volk: chairman
Barbara Yastine: chief financial officer

Foundation Officials

Richard E. Thornburgh: chief financial officer, member

Grants Analysis

Disclosure Period: calendar year ending 2002
Total Grants: $6,000,000
Number of Grants: 250
Average Grant: $15,000
Highest Grant: $650,000
Lowest Grant: $500
Typical Range: $5,000 to $15,000
Note: Grants analysis provided by foundation.

Recent Grants

Note: Grants derived from 2001 Form 990.

General

5,000,000	Fire Widows Association
150,000	Robin Hood Foundation, New York, NY
100,000	American Red Cross of Greater New York, New York, NY
100,000	CARE, Inc., New York, NY
100,000	City Parks Foundation, New York, NY
100,000	Pride First Corporation, New York, NY
75,000	City Parks Foundation, New York, NY
75,000	Good Shepherd Services, New York, NY
75,000	Henry Street Settlement, New York, NY
75,000	Junior Achievement, New York, NY

CREMER FOUNDATION

Giving Contact

James A. Berkenstadt, Administrator
PO Box 1
Madison, WI 53701
Phone: (608)837-5166
E-mail: mlpp@globaldialog.com
Note: Mr. Berkenstadt may be reached at extension 330.

Description

Founded: 1965
EIN: 396086822
Organization Type: Private Foundation
Giving Locations: WI: Madison and surrounding metropolitan area
Grant Types: General Support, Seed Money.

Financial Summary

Total Giving: $240,680 (2001); $260,730 (2000); $244,750 (1999)
Giving Analysis: Giving for 1999 includes: foundation grants to United Way ($20,000)
Assets: $3,549,126 (2001); $3,980,812 (2000); $4,060,239 (1999)
Gifts Received: $70,000 (1996). Note: In 1996, contributions were received from Helen and Garvin Cremer.

Typical Recipients

Arts & Humanities: Libraries
Civic & Public Affairs: Employment/Job Training, Hispanic Affairs, Housing
Education: Literacy, Medical Education, Public Education (Precollege), Special Education, Student Aid
Health: Eyes/Blindness, Health-General, Geriatric Health, Medical Research, Mental Health, Nursing Services
Religion: Churches, Religious Welfare
Social Services: At-Risk Youth, Child Welfare, Community Centers, Community Service Organizations, Domestic Violence, Family Planning, Family Services, Food/Clothing Distribution, Homes, People with Disabilities, Scouts, Senior Services, Shelters/Homelessness, Social Services-General, United Funds/United Ways, YMCA/YWCA/YMHA/YWHA, Youth Organizations, Youth Organizations

Application Procedures

Initial Contact: The foundation requests applications be made in writing. Send a full proposal.
Application Requirements: Include a description of organization, amount requested, purpose of funds sought, recently audited financial statement, and proof of tax-exempt status; also list sources of other contributionss received.
Deadlines: None.

Restrictions

The foundation does not support individuals, religious organizations for sectarian purposes, political or lobbying groups, or organizations outside operating areas.

Additional Information

Publications: Application Guidelines

Foundation Officials

James A. Berkenstadt: admin
Frances H. Cremer: president
Holly L. Cremer: treasurer
Helen A. George: secretary
Robert R. Stroud: vice president
James T. Sykes: president

Grants Analysis

Disclosure Period: calendar year ending 2001
Total Grants: $240,680
Number of Grants: 30
Average Grant: $8,023
Highest Grant: $30,500
Lowest Grant: $500
Typical Range: $5,000 to $15,000

Recent Grants

Note: Grants derived from 2000 Form 990.

General

35,000	Madison Mutual Housing Association, Madison, WI
35,000	Traditional Housing, Madison, WI
25,000	Briarpatch, Madison, WI
18,000	Salvation Army, Madison, WI
17,500	Hello Friend, Inc., Madison, WI
13,400	Sun Prairie School District, Sun Prairie, WI
12,680	Madison Literacy Council, Madison, WI
11,555	Colonial Club Adult Day Center, Sun Prairie, WI
10,000	Harambee Dental Clinic, Inc., Madison, WI
7,500	Sun Prairie YMCA, Sun Prairie, WI

CRESTLEA FOUNDATION

Giving Contact

Stephen A. Martinenza, Secretary & Treasurer
100 W. 10th Street, Suite 1109
Wilmington, DE 19801
Phone: (302)654-2477
Fax: (302)654-2323

Description

Founded: 1955
EIN: 516015638
Organization Type: General Purpose Foundation
Giving Locations: DE: Wilmington including surrounding area
Grant Types: Capital, Seed Money.

Donor Information

Founder: Incorporated in 1955 by the late Henry B. duPont .

Financial Summary

Total Giving: $823,285 (2001); $3,037,285 (2000); $2,055,178 (1999)
Giving Analysis: Giving for 2001 includes: foundation grants to United Way ($40,000); 2000: foundation grants to United Way ($40,000); 1998: foundation grants to United Way ($35,000)
Assets: $35,528,984 (2001); $41,069,564 (2000); $44,966,118 (1998)
Gifts Received: $541,101 (2001); $714,442 (2000); $665,062 (1998). Note: In 1998 and 2000, contributions were received from the Wilmington Trust Co.

Typical Recipients

Arts & Humanities: Art History, Arts Centers, Arts Funds, Arts Institutes, Ballet, Arts & Humanities-General, Historic Preservation, History & Archaeology, Libraries, Museums/Galleries, Music, Opera, Performing Arts, Theater, Visual Arts
Civic & Public Affairs: Business/Free Enterprise, Clubs, Community Foundations, Economic Development, Employment/Job Training, Civic & Public Affairs-General, Housing, Law & Justice, Native American Affairs, Nonprofit Management, Professional & Trade Associations, Public Policy, Urban & Community Affairs, Women's Affairs, Zoos/Aquariums
Education: Arts/Humanities Education, Colleges & Universities, Community & Junior Colleges, Education Associations, Education-General, Health & Physical Education, Leadership Training, Literacy, Medical Education, Private Education (Precollege), Science/Mathematics Education, Secondary Education (Private), Secondary Education (Public), Student Aid, Vocational & Technical Education
Environment: Air/Water Quality, Environment-General, Resource Conservation
Health: Alzheimers Disease, Cancer, Children's Health/Hospitals, Clinics/Medical Centers, Geriatric Health, Health Organizations, Hospices, Hospitals, Long-Term Care, Preventive Medicine/Wellness Organizations, Public Health, Single-Disease Health Associations
Religion: Churches, Ministries, Religious Organizations, Religious Welfare
Science: Science-General, Science Museums, Scientific Centers & Institutes
Social Services: Animal Protection, Animal Protection, Camps, Child Welfare, Community Centers, Community Service Organizations, Counseling, Day Care, Family Planning, Family Services, Food/Clothing Distribution, Homes, People with Disabilities, Recreation & Athletics, Scouts, Senior Services, Social Services-General, Special Olympics, United Funds/United Ways, Veterans, YMCA/YWCA/YMHA/YWHA, Youth Organizations

Application Procedures

Initial Contact: The foundation requests applications be made in writing.
Application Requirements: Applicants should include the reason for the grant, any pertinent financial statements, and a copy of the IRS exemption approval letter.
Deadlines: Applications must be received by 3lNovember 1.

Restrictions

Some grants are made at the discretion of the Board of Trustees regardless of geographic location. Solicitation for grantss are only considered from organizations DE and nearby Southern Chester County, PA. Grants are not made to individuals.

Foundation Officials

Otto C. Fad: vice president
Stephen A. Martinenza: treasurer

Grants Analysis

Disclosure Period: calendar year ending 2001
Total Grants: $783,285*
Number of Grants: 67
Average Grant: $11,691*
Highest Grant: $82,785
Typical Range: $5,000 to $20,000
*Note: Giving excludes United Way. Average grant figure excludes highest grant.

Recent Grants

Note: Grants derived from 2001 Form 990.

Library-Related

5,000	Hagley Museum and Library, Wilmington, DE -- operating support
5,000	Library Company, Philadelphia, PA -- operating support
5,000	Northeast Harbor Library, Northeast Harbor, ME -- operating support

General

112,500	Philadelphia Museum of Art, Philadelphia, PA -- operating support
82,785	Pomfret School, Pomfret, CT -- capital improvements
55,000	Delaware Lacrosse Foundation, Wilmington, DE -- program support
40,000	United Way of Delaware, Wilmington, DE -- annual appeal
25,000	Boys & Girls Clubs of DE, Wilmington, DE -- capital campaign for renovations
25,000	Delaware Nature Society, Hockessin, DE -- capital improvements
25,000	Episcopal Academy, Merion, PA -- operating support
25,000	Independence School, Newark, DE -- Caoutak campaign for renovations
25,000	Wilmington Senior Center, Wilmington, DE -- equipment purchases
20,000	Mystic Seaport Museum, Inc., Mystic, CT -- operating support

MARY A. CROCKER TRUST

Giving Contact

Charles Crocker, Trustee
233 Post Street, 2nd Floor
San Francisco, CA 94108
Phone: (415)982-0138
Fax: (415)982-0141
Web: http://www.mactrust.org

Description

Founded: 1889
EIN: 946051917
Organization Type: Private Foundation
Giving Locations: CA: San Francisco including metropolitan area
Grant Types: Capital, Emergency, General Support, Project, Seed Money.

Donor Information

Founder: Established by the late Mary A. Crocker .

Financial Summary

Total Giving: $520,000 (2001); $600,000 (2000); $545,500 (1999)
Assets: $12,264,570 (2001); $12,424,274 (2000); $14,114,033 (1999)

Typical Recipients

Arts & Humanities: Community Arts, Film & Video, Libraries, Museums/Galleries, Public Broadcasting
Civic & Public Affairs: Botanical Gardens/Parks, Business/Free Enterprise, Community Foundations, Employment/Job Training, Ethnic Organizations, Civic & Public Affairs-General, Hispanic Affairs, Housing, Municipalities/Towns, Nonprofit Management, Philanthropic Organizations, Professional & Trade Associations, Public Policy, Rural Affairs, Urban & Community Affairs, Women's Affairs
Education: Colleges & Universities, Education Funds, Education Reform, Environmental Education, Faculty Development, Education-General, Leadership Training, Literacy, Minority Education, Preschool Education, Private Education (Precollege), Public Education (Precollege), School Volunteerism, Science/Mathematics Education, Secondary Education (Private), Secondary Education (Public), Special Education, Student Aid
Environment: Air/Water Quality, Forestry, Environment-General, Research, Resource Conservation, Watershed, Wildlife Protection

Health: Clinics/Medical Centers, Hospitals, Medical Research, Prenatal Health Issues, Research/Studies Institutes
International: Health Care/Hospitals, International Development
Religion: Churches, Religious Welfare
Science: Science Museums, Scientific Centers & Institutes, Scientific Organizations, Scientific Research
Social Services: At-Risk Youth, Child Welfare, Community Centers, Community Service Organizations, Emergency Relief, Family Planning, Family Services, Food/Clothing Distribution, People with Disabilities, Recreation & Athletics, Volunteer Services, Youth Organizations

Application Procedures

Initial Contact: Submit a brief letter of inquiry.
Application Requirements: If the foundation requests a full proposal, it should include amount requested; statement of necessity; description of the project plan, intended outcome, and any innovative features of the proposal; budget and organization budget; information on aid from others; and persons to contact for further information.
Deadlines: None.

Restrictions

Does not support individuals, annual campaigns, continuing support, deficit financing, or sectarian purposes. Building funds, operating budgets, scholarships, and equipment purchases are a low priority. Grants are made primarily to charitable organizations in the San Francisco Bay area.

Additional Information

Publications: Application Guidelines

Foundation Officials

Elizabeth Atcheson: trustee
Lucy Blake: trustee
Charles Crocker: trustee
Tania W. Stepanian: chairperson
Fredrick W. Whitridge: trustee

Grants Analysis

Disclosure Period: calendar year ending 2001
Total Grants: $520,000
Number of Grants: 40
Average Grant: $13,000
Highest Grant: $30,000
Lowest Grant: $1,000
Typical Range: $1,000 to $20,000

Recent Grants

Note: Grants derived from 2001 Form 990.

Library-Related
15,000	San Francisco Public Library, San Francisco, CA -- Wallace Stegner Environmental Center

General
35,000	Kids Turn, San Francisco, CA -- workshops
30,000	Greenbelt Alliance, San Francisco, CA -- protect open space and curb urban sprawl
25,000	Bay Nature, Berekely, CA -- local Bay area magazine launching
25,000	Exploratorium, San Francisco, CA -- training for beginning math and sciences teachers
25,000	First Resort, Oakland, CA -- course teaching consequences of early sexual activity
25,000	Gateway High School, San Francisco, CA -- start up expenses
25,000	Hamilton School, San Francisco, CA -- capital campaign
25,000	Omega Boys Club, San Francisco, CA -- Academic Programs
25,000	Park Day School, Oakland, CA -- Community Outreach Program
25,000	Project HELP, Sunnyvale, CA -- Model Academy safety net

CROMPTON CORP.

Company Headquarters

One American Lane
Greenwich, CT 06831
Phone: (203)552-2000
Fax: (203)552-2870
Web: http://www.cromptoncorp.com

Company Description

Founded: 1999
Ticker: CK
Exchange: NYSE
Former Name: Witco Chemical Corp.;
Formed by Merger of: Crompton & Knowles and Witco Chemical Corp.
Revenue: US$2.546 billion (2002)
Employees: 7340 (2002)
SIC(s): 2869 Industrial Organic Chemicals Nec, 2899 Chemical Preparations Nec, 2951 Asphalt Paving Mixtures & Blocks, 2992 Lubricating Oils & Greases.

Operating Locations

Witco Corp. (AL--Phenix City; CA--City of Commerce, City of Industry, Los Angeles, Rancho Dominguez, Richmond, Santa Fe Springs; CT--Greenwich; IL--Blue Island, Chicago, Mapleton; IN--Indianapolis; IA--Spencer; KS--Olathe; LA--Gretna, Harahan; MI--Highland Park; MS--Philadelphia; NE--Omaha; NV--Las Vegas; NJ--Brainards, Oakland, Perth Amboy; NY--Beacon, New York; OH--Dublin; OK--Ponca City; OR--Klamath Falls; PA--Bradford, Petrolia, Trainer; TN--Memphis; TX--Houston, La Porte, Marshall, Sunray; WI--Janesville)

Subsidiary Companies

CT: Uniroyal Chemical Co., Waterbury; Davis-Standard Corp., Pawcatuck

Robert I. Wishnick Foundation

Giving Contact

William Wishnick, President & Director
1 American Lane
Greenwich, CT 06831
Phone: (212)371-1844

Alternate Contact

c/o Robert I. Wishnick Foundation
PO Box 681869
Park City, UT 84068
Phone: (435)647-0967

Description

EIN: 136068668
Organization Type: Corporate Foundation
Giving Locations: operating communities.
Grant Types: Conference/Seminar, Endowment, Fellowship, General Support, Research, Scholarship.

Donor Information

Founder: Witco Chemical Corp.

Financial Summary

Total Giving: $456,020 (2001); $590,850 (1999); $696,291 (1998). Note: Contributes through foundation only.
Giving Analysis: Giving for 2001 includes: foundation scholarships ($1,100); foundation ($454,920); 1999: foundation ($590,850) 1998: foundation ($696,291)

Assets: $7,716,934 (2001); $8,033,500 (1999); $8,387,248 (1998)
Gifts Received: $100,000 (1998); $200,000 (1994); $31,569 (1992). Note: Contributions are received from William Wishnick.

Typical Recipients

Arts & Humanities: Arts Associations & Councils, Arts Centers, Arts Festivals, Arts Institutes, Ballet, Dance, Arts & Humanities-General, Libraries, Museums/Galleries, Music, Opera, Performing Arts, Theater, Visual Arts
Civic & Public Affairs: Civil Rights, Clubs, Civic & Public Affairs-General, Law & Justice, Native American Affairs, Parades/Festivals, Safety, Urban & Community Affairs, Women's Affairs
Education: Afterschool/Enrichment Programs, Arts/Humanities Education, Business Education, Colleges & Universities, Engineering/Technological Education, Education-General, Legal Education, Medical Education, Minority Education, Preschool Education, Private Education (Precollege), Private Education (Precollege), Public Education (Precollege), School Volunteerism, Student Aid
Environment: Air/Water Quality, Environment-General, Wildlife Protection
Health: AIDS/HIV, Cancer, Children's Health/Hospitals, Clinics/Medical Centers, Emergency/Ambulance Services, Geriatric Health, Home-Care Services, Hospitals, Medical Research, Multiple Sclerosis, Single-Disease Health Associations
International: Foreign Educational Institutions, Health Care/Hospitals, International Peace & Security Issues, International Relations, Missionary/Religious Activities
Religion: Churches, Religion-General, Jewish Causes, Religious Organizations, Religious Welfare, Synagogues/Temples
Science: Scientific Centers & Institutes, Scientific Organizations
Social Services: Animal Protection, Camps, Child Welfare, Child Welfare, Community Service Organizations, Crime Prevention, Family Planning, Family Services, Homes, People with Disabilities, Recreation & Athletics, Scouts, Sexual Abuse, Shelters/Homelessness, Social Services-General, United Funds/United Ways, Veterans, Youth Organizations

Application Procedures

Initial Contact: Send a brief letter.
Application Requirements: Include a description of program, amount of funds requested.
Deadlines: None.
Decision Notification: Board meets quarterly; decisions take six to eight weeks.

Restrictions

Foundation does not support individuals or matching gifts. Loans are not made.

Additional Information

The foundation and corporation operate as separate entities.

Foundation Officials

Lisa Wishnick: director
William Wishnick: president, director B Brooklyn, NY 1924. ED Carnegie Institute of Technology; University of Texas BBA (1949). CORP AFFIL chairman emeritus, director: Witco Corp.

Grants Analysis

Disclosure Period: calendar year ending 2001
Total Grants: $454,920*
Number of Grants: 91
Average Grant: $4,266*
Highest Grant: $71,000
Lowest Grant: $125
Typical Range: $250 to $15,000
*Note: Giving excludes scholarship. Average grant figure excludes highest grant.

Recent Grants

Note: Grants derived from 2001 Form 990.

General

71,000	United Jewish Appeal - Federation of Jewish Philanthropies of New York, New York, NY
35,000	Jerusalem Foundation, Inc., New York, NY
35,000	Thatcher School, Ojai, CA
32,570	Adopt a Native American Elder, Park City, UT
18,000	National Dance Institute, New York, NY
15,400	New York City Ballet, New York, NY
15,000	Brotherhood Synagogue, New York, NY
13,850	National Ability Center of Park City, Park City, UT
10,850	Park City Jewish Center (Temple Har Shalom), Park City, UT
10,000	Appleseed Foundation, Houston, TX

CROSSWICKS FOUNDATION

Giving Contact

Crosswicks Foundation
924 West End Ave., Suite 95
New York, NY 10025
Phone: (860)496-8119

Description

Founded: 1972
EIN: 132732197
Organization Type: Private Foundation
Grant Types: Multiyear/Continuing Support, Scholarship.

Financial Summary

Total Giving: $182,000 (fiscal year ending November 30, 2001); $167,500 (fiscal 2000); $195,000 (fiscal 1998)
Assets: $3,635,375 (fiscal 2001); $3,482,623 (fiscal 2000); $3,573,409 (fiscal 1998)

Typical Recipients

Arts & Humanities: Ballet, Libraries, Literary Arts, Music, Opera, Theater
Civic & Public Affairs: Civic & Public Affairs-General
Education: Arts/Humanities Education, Private Education (Precollege)
Environment: Forestry, Resource Conservation, Wildlife Protection
Health: Cancer, Eyes/Blindness, Hospices, Hospitals, Long-Term Care
International: Foreign Educational Institutions, Health Care/Hospitals
Religion: Churches, Religion-General, Religious Organizations, Religious Welfare
Social Services: At-Risk Youth, Homes, Scouts, Social Services-General, Youth Organizations

Application Procedures

Initial Contact: Send a written request.
Application Requirements: Include a description of organization, amount requested, purpose of funds sought, recently audited financial statement, and proof of tax-exempt status.
Deadlines: November 1.

Restrictions

Grants are not made to individuals.

Foundation Officials

Bion Franklin: treasurer
Laurie Franklin: secretary
Edward A. Jones: director
Josephine Jones: vice president

Madeleine L'Engle Franklin: president B New York, NY 1918. ED Smith College AB (1941); New School for Social Research (1941-1942); Columbia University (1960-1961). CORP AFFIL teacher: Saint Hildas & Saint Hughes Sch; writer-in-residence: Wheaton Coll; writer-in-residence: Cathedral Saint John Divine. NONPR AFFIL member: Colonial Dames; member: Writers Guild America; president, member council & memberbership committee: Authors Guild; member council: Authors League.
Morton L. Price: secretary
Maria R. Rooney: vice president
Madeleine J. Roy: treasurer

Grants Analysis

Disclosure Period: fiscal year ending November 30, 2001
Total Grants: $182,000
Number of Grants: 41
Average Grant: $4,439
Highest Grant: $13,000
Lowest Grant: $500
Typical Range: $1,000 to $10,000

Recent Grants

Note: Grants derived from fiscal 2000 Form 990.

General

16,500	Cathedral of St. John the Divine, New York, NY -- for cathedral library
10,000	Charlotte Hungerford Hospital, Torrington, CT
10,000	Colon Cancer Alliance, New York, NY
10,000	Community of the Holy Spirit, New York, NY
10,000	Connecticut Junior Republic, Litchfield, CT
5,000	Alaskan Raptor Rehabilitation Center, Sitka, AK
5,000	Church of the Holy Apostle Soup Kitchen, New York, NY
5,000	Eye Bank for Sight Restoration, New York, NY
5,000	Holy Apostles Monastery, New York, NY
5,000	Holy Cross Monastery, West Park, NY

HENRY P. AND SUSAN C. CROWELL TRUST

Giving Contact

John T. Bass, President & Secretary
1800 Office Club Pointe, Suite 220
Colorado Springs, CO 80920
Phone: (719)272-8300
Fax: (719)272-8305
E-mail: crowellhp@aol.com
Web: http://www.crowellfoundation.org

Description

Founded: 1927
EIN: 366038028
Organization Type: Specialized/Single Purpose Foundation
Giving Locations: nationally.
Grant Types: Challenge, General Support, Project.

Donor Information

Founder: The trust was established in 1927 and funded by the late Henry P. Crowell , an early leader of the Quaker Oats Company.

Financial Summary

Total Giving: $3,947,000 (2001); $5,000,000 (2000 approx); $5,465,000 (1999)
Assets: $99,932,026 (2001); $115,000,000 (1999 approx); $117,141,308 (1998)

Gifts Received: $1,758,348 (2001). Note: In 2001, contributions were received from Henry P. Crowell for Irene Goodson.

Typical Recipients

Arts & Humanities: Libraries, Public Broadcasting
Civic & Public Affairs: Clubs, Economic Development, Civic & Public Affairs-General, Hispanic Affairs, Public Policy, Urban & Community Affairs
Education: Colleges & Universities, Education-General, International Exchange, International Studies, Private Education (Precollege), Religious Education, Science/Mathematics Education, Secondary Education (Private), Student Aid, Vocational & Technical Education
Health: Clinics/Medical Centers, Hospitals
International: Foreign Arts Organizations, Foreign Educational Institutions, International-General, Health Care/Hospitals, International Affairs, International Development, International Environmental Issues, International Organizations, International Relations, International Relief Efforts, Missionary/Religious Activities
Religion: Bible Study/Translation, Churches, Religion-General, Religion-General, Jewish Causes, Ministries, Missionary Activities (Domestic), Religious Organizations, Religious Welfare, Seminaries, Social/Policy Issues
Social Services: Family Services, Refugee Assistance, Social Services-General

Application Procedures

Initial Contact: Requests should be addressed to the executive director.
Application Requirements: Proposals should clearly set forth the need, purpose, and amount of request. A list of the organization's governing board; history of organization and its mission; problem that project addresses; latest audited financial statement; current year's organizational budget; project budget; and a copy of the organization's IRS letter of tax-exempt and non-private foundation status should be included.
Deadlines: The trust's board meets in May and November. Grant applicants will be advised of meeting date during which the proposal will be considered.

Foundation Officials

John T. Bass: vice chairman, treasurer
Edwin L. Frizen, Jr.: chairman, trustee B Chicago, IL 1925. PRIM NONPR EMPL executive director: Interdenominational Foreign Mission Association ADD NONPR EMPL member missions committee: World Evang Fellowship; treasurer editorial com: Evang Missions Information Service.
Lowell L. Kline: executive director, president
John F. Robinson: trustee

Grants Analysis

Disclosure Period: calendar year ending 2001
Total Grants: $3,947,000
Number of Grants: 101
Average Grant: $34,313*
Highest Grant: $350,000
Lowest Grant: $5,000
Typical Range: $10,000 to $50,000
*Note: Average grant figure excludes two highest grants ($550,000).

Recent Grants

Note: Grants derived from 2001 Form 990.

General

350,000	Pioneers, Orlando, FL -- for operating budget
250,000	Moody Bible Institute, Chicago, IL -- operating budget
200,000	Pioneers, Orlando, FL -- capital fund campaign
130,000	Mexican Mission Ministries, Pharr, TX -- for the WGE Center

130,000	Mission Training International, Colorado Springs, CO -- for van replacement
100,000	Columbia International University, Columbia, SC -- for operating budget
75,000	English Language Institute, San Dimas, CA -- for Teaching Program
75,000	Overseas Council, Indianapolis, IN -- for the Christian Leadership Program
75,000	Partners International, San Jose, CA -- for IT system upgrade
75,000	Peter Deyneka Russian Ministries, Wheaton, IL -- for operating budget

ARIE AND IDA CROWN MEMORIAL

Giving Contact
Susan Crown, President
222 North LaSalle Street, Suite 2000
Chicago, IL 60601
Phone: (312)236-6300
Fax: (312)984-1499
E-mail: aicm@crown-chicago.com

Description
Founded: 1947
EIN: 366076088
Organization Type: General Purpose Foundation
Giving Locations: IL: Chicago including Cook County
Grant Types: Capital, Emergency, Employee Matching Gifts, Endowment, General Support, Multiyear/Continuing Support, Operating Expenses, Project.

Donor Information
Founder: The foundation was established in honor of Arie and Ida Crown by their children in 1947. The Crown family was headed by noted industrialist Henry Crown. Henry and his brother Sol started a building supply company that became the largest in the Chicago area, and the basis for the Crown family fortune. John J. Crown, Lester Crown and Joanne Crown have all donated more than 2% of the total contributions received by the foundation.

Financial Summary
Total Giving: $10,216,560 (2000); $10,092,000 (1999); $8,887,127 (1998)
Giving Analysis: Giving for 2000 includes: foundation grants to United Way ($102,000) 1997: foundation grants to United Way ($26,500)
Assets: $204,471,731 (2000); $208,813,486 (1998); $206,555,116 (1997)
Gifts Received: $42,641 (2000); $23,949,096 (1997). Note: In 2000, contributions were received from Lester Crown.

Typical Recipients
Arts & Humanities: Arts Associations & Councils, Arts Festivals, Arts Institutes, Community Arts, Dance, History & Archaeology, Libraries, Museums/Galleries, Music, Opera, Performing Arts, Public Broadcasting, Theater
Civic & Public Affairs: Asian American Affairs, Botanical Gardens/Parks, Civil Rights, Community Foundations, Employment/Job Training, Civic & Public Affairs-General, Hispanic Affairs, Municipalities/Towns, Public Policy, Urban & Community Affairs, Women's Affairs, Zoos/Aquariums
Education: Arts/Humanities Education, Business Education, Colleges & Universities, Education Funds, Education Reform, Engineering/Technological Education, Education-General, Health & Physical Education, Legal Education, Literacy, Preschool Education, Private Education (Precollege), Religious Education
Environment: Air/Water Quality, Resource Conservation, Wildlife Protection

Health: Alzheimers Disease, Children's Health/Hospitals, Clinics/Medical Centers, Diabetes, Eyes/Blindness, Health-General, Health Organizations, Hospitals, Hospitals (University Affiliated), Medical Rehabilitation, Medical Research, Mental Health, Public Health, Single-Disease Health Associations
International: Foreign Educational Institutions, International Affairs, International Peace & Security Issues, International Relations, Missionary/Religious Activities
Religion: Jewish Causes, Seminaries
Science: Observatories & Planetariums, Science Museums
Social Services: At-Risk Youth, Child Welfare, Community Centers, Community Service Organizations, Community Service Organizations, Delinquency & Criminal Rehabilitation, Domestic Violence, Emergency Relief, Family Planning, Family Services, Food/Clothing Distribution, Homes, People with Disabilities, Refugee Assistance, Scouts, Senior Services, Shelters/Homelessness, Substance Abuse, United Funds/United Ways, Youth Organizations

Application Procedures
Initial Contact: Prospective applicants should submit a letter of inquiry before submitting a proposal. A full proposal and grant application will be requested by the foundation.
Application Requirements: The letter of intent should not be longer than two pages and include the nature of the organization's work, budget size, proposed project, project budget, amount requested, and an attached copy of IRS determination letter.
Deadlines: None.
Review Process: The board meets twice annually, in the spring and fall.

Restrictions
The foundation does not support government sponsored programs, individuals, special events, conferences, or film projects.

Foundation Officials
Arie Steven Crown: vice president, director B Chicago, IL 1952. ED Claremont McKenna College (1974); University of California, Los Angeles MBA (1977). PRIM CORP EMPL general partner: Henry Crown & Co. CORP AFFIL director: Hilton Hotels Corp.; president: Ojai Resort Management Inc.; director: Aspen Ski Co.; director: Farmers Investment Co.
James Schine Crown: vice president, director B Chicago, IL 1953. ED Hampshire College BA (1976); Stanford University JD (1980). PRIM CORP EMPL general partner: Henry Crown & Co. CORP AFFIL director: Sara Lee Corp.; vice president: Woodard Inc.; principal: Pec Israel Economic Corp.; board directors: General Dynamics Corp.; ltd. partner: New York Yankees Partnership; vice president, director: Exchange Building Corp.; vice president, director: CC Industries Inc.; director: Citation Oil & Gas Corp.; director: Bank One Corp. NONPR AFFIL trustee: Orchestral Association; trustee: University Chicago; trustee: Museum Science & Industry.
Lester Crown: treasurer, director B Chicago, IL 1925. ED Northwestern University BScE (1946); Harvard University MBA (1949). PRIM CORP EMPL chairman, director: Material Service Corp. CORP AFFIL ltd. partner: New York Yankees Partnership; director: Santa Cruz Valley Pecan Co.; director: Maytag Appliances; director: Maytag Corp.; director: Marblehead Lime Co.; chairman: Material Service Resources Co.; chairman executive committee, director: General Dynamics Corp.; director: Green Valley Pecan; general partner: Henry Crown Co.; director: Farmers Investment Co.; chairman, director: CC Industries Inc.; director: Country Estates Pecan; director: 360 Communication Co. NONPR AFFIL trustee: Michael Reese Foundation; member: Tau Beta Pi; member: Phi Eta Sigma; member: Pi Mu Epsilon; director: Lyric Opera Corp.; trustee: Northwestern University; director: Childrens

Memorial Medical Center; member: Jewish Theological Seminary; trustee: Aspen Institute Humanistic Studies; member, board advisors: Chicago Zoological Society. CLUB AFFIL Standard Club; Mid-America Club; Northmoor Country Club; Lake Shore Country Club; Marco Polo Club; Economic Club; John Evans Club Northwestern University; Chicago Club; Commercial Club.
Rebecca Crown: vice president, director
Susan Crown: president, director PRIM CORP EMPL vice president: Henry Crown & Co. CORP AFFIL director: Baxter International Inc.; director: Illinois Tool Works Inc.
William Crown: director, vice president
Sara Crown Star: director, vice president
Charles Goodman: vice president, director PRIM CORP EMPL vice president: Henry Crown & Co. CORP AFFIL director: General Dynamics Corp.; vice president, director: Monticello Realty Corp.; vice president, director: Exchange Building Corp.; vice president, director: CC Industries Inc.; director: Citation Oil & Gas Corp.
Jennifer Jacoby: associate director
Barbara Goodman Manilow: vice president, director NONPR AFFIL secretary, director: Chicago Children's Museum.
Arnold R. Weber: director, vice president

Grants Analysis
Disclosure Period: calendar year ending 2001
Total Grants: $10,216,560*
Number of Grants: 678
Average Grant: $15,000*
Highest Grant: $1,700,000
Lowest Grant: $100
*Note: Grants analysis provided by the foundation.

Recent Grants
Note: Grants derived from 2000 Form 990.

General
1,000,000	Jewish United Fund of Metropolitan Chicago, Chicago, IL
500,000	Aspen Institute, Queenstown, MD
400,000	Covenant Foundation, Chicago, IL
290,000	Covenant Foundation, Chicago, IL
280,000	Duke University, Durham, NC
250,000	HA-Am, New York, NY
250,000	Lincoln Park Zoological Society, Chicago, IL
200,000	Children's Memorial Medical Center, Chicago, IL
200,000	Family Institute, Chicago, IL
200,000	Field Museum of Natural History, Chicago, IL

ROY E. CRUMMER FOUNDATION

Giving Contact
Jean Crummer-Coburn, President & Trustee
130 Newport Center Dr., No. 140-B
Newport Beach, CA 92660-6923
Phone: (949)644-4702
Fax: (949)252-8959

Description
Founded: 1964
EIN: 886004422
Organization Type: Private Foundation
Giving Locations: CA
Grant Types: General Support.

Financial Summary
Total Giving: $300,180 (2000); $330,000 (1999); $310,000 (1998)
Giving Analysis: Giving for 1999 includes: foundation grants to United Way ($500)

Assets: $6,909,183 (2000); $6,872,394 (1999); $6,787,397 (1998)

Typical Recipients

Arts & Humanities: Arts Associations & Councils, Film & Video, Historic Preservation, History & Archaeology, Libraries, Museums/Galleries, Public Broadcasting, Theater

Civic & Public Affairs: Clubs, Civic & Public Affairs-General, Hispanic Affairs, Housing, Parades/Festivals

Education: Colleges & Universities, Education-General, Legal Education, Minority Education, Private Education (Precollege), Religious Education

Environment: Air/Water Quality, Environment-General, Resource Conservation, Wildlife Protection

Health: AIDS/HIV, Cancer, Children's Health/Hospitals, Clinics/Medical Centers, Heart, Hospitals, Medical Research, Single-Disease Health Associations

International: International Environmental Issues, International Relief Efforts, Missionary/Religious Activities

Religion: Religious Welfare, Social/Policy Issues

Social Services: Animal Protection, At-Risk Youth, Camps, Child Welfare, Community Centers, Day Care, Domestic Violence, Family Planning, Food/Clothing Distribution, Shelters/Homelessness, United Funds/United Ways, YMCA/YWCA/YMHA/YWHA, Youth Organizations

Application Procedures

Initial Contact: Send a brief letter of inquiry.
Application Requirements: Submit a description of the organization, purpose of funds sought, and IRS exemption number.
Deadlines: October 31.

Foundation Officials

Margarite Brown: secretary, treasurer, trustee
Jean Crummer Coburn: president, trustee
Milton Coburn: vice president, trustee
Ian F. Gow: director, trustee
Lee D. Strom: director

Grants Analysis

Disclosure Period: calendar year ending 2000
Total Grants: $300,180
Number of Grants: 80
Average Grant: $3,752
Highest Grant: $40,000
Typical Range: $1,000 to $10,000

Recent Grants

Note: Grants derived from 1999 Form 990.

Library-Related
5,000	Friends of the Rancho Mirage Library

General
50,000	Cate, Carpinteria, CA
25,000	Palm Springs Desert Museum, Palm Springs, CA
15,550	Living Desert, Oakland, CA
15,000	Shelter for the Storm, Inc., Palm Desert, CA
10,000	Malama Pono Kauai AIDS Project, Lihue, HI
10,000	Nazareth House, Los Angeles, CA -- sister of the poor section
10,000	People Assisting the Homeless (PATH), Los Angeles, CA
10,000	Pepperdine University, Malibu, CA
10,000	Venice Family Clinic, Venice, CA
7,000	Para Los Ninos, Los Angeles, CA

CRYSTAL TRUST

Giving Contact

Stephen C. Doberstein, Director
1088 Du Pont Building
Wilmington, DE 19898
Phone: (302)651-0533

Description

Founded: 1947
EIN: 516015063
Organization Type: Family Foundation
Giving Locations: nationally.
Grant Types: Capital, Emergency, Seed Money.

Donor Information

Founder: The donor of the trust, the late Irenee du Pont, established the trust in 1947. Under the terms of Mr. du Pont's will, the trust received an additional endowment in 1964, and has since operated under its present name. Mr. du Pont served as president of E. I. du Pont de Nemours & Co., a Wilmington-based manufacturing and chemical firm. Currently, the board of advisory trustees includes three descendants of the donor.

Financial Summary

Total Giving: $7,117,600 (2000); $6,417,200 (1998); $9,302,721 (1997)
Giving Analysis: Giving for 2000 includes: foundation grants to United Way ($50,000)
Assets: $161,870,151 (2000); $151,680,772 (1998); $141,502,879 (1997)

Typical Recipients

Arts & Humanities: Arts Institutes, Arts & Humanities-General, Historic Preservation, History & Archaeology, Libraries, Museums/Galleries, Music, Opera, Public Broadcasting, Theater

Civic & Public Affairs: Clubs, Economic Development, Employment/Job Training, Civic & Public Affairs-General, Housing, Nonprofit Management, Public Policy, Urban & Community Affairs, Zoos/Aquariums

Education: Arts/Humanities Education, Business Education, Colleges & Universities, Continuing Education, Economic Education, Education Associations, Elementary Education (Public), Engineering/Technological Education, Education-General, Gifted & Talented Programs, Medical Education, Private Education (Precollege), Science/Mathematics Education, Secondary Education (Private), Student Aid, Vocational & Technical Education

Environment: Environment-General, Protection, Resource Conservation, Wildlife Protection

Health: Cancer, Clinics/Medical Centers, Health-General, Geriatric Health, Health Funds, Health Organizations, Hospices, Hospitals, Long-Term Care, Medical Research, Mental Health, Preventive Medicine/Wellness Organizations, Public Health, Single-Disease Health Associations

Religion: Churches, Ministries, Religious Welfare

Science: Observatories & Planetariums, Science Museums, Scientific Centers & Institutes, Scientific Organizations, Scientific Research

Social Services: Child Abuse, Child Welfare, Community Centers, Community Service Organizations, Counseling, Day Care, Domestic Violence, Family Planning, Family Services, Food/Clothing Distribution, Homes, People with Disabilities, Recreation & Athletics, Scouts, Senior Services, Social Services-General, Special Olympics, United Funds/United Ways, Veterans, YMCA/YWCA/YMHA/YWHA, Youth Organizations

Application Procedures

Initial Contact: The trust does not use standard application forms. Detailed letters of request should be submitted.
Application Requirements: Letters should include a history of the applicant organization, organizational purposes and activities, details about the proposal and its priority within the applicant organization, certification of tax-exempt status, and information on the governing group, staff and finances of the organization.
Deadlines: Requests should be submitted by September 30 of each year. Early application is recommended.

Review Process

Review Process: Grant decisions are made toward the end of the year. Exceptions are considered only when there is a crucial factor of timing.

Restrictions

The trust does not support individuals, endowment funds, research, scholarships, fellowships, matching programs, loans, or continuing expenses of operations or deficits.

Additional Information

In unique cases, requests can be considered at times other than those specified by the trust. One-time support is preferred, usually for capital or for the needs of a program in its early stages.

Requests should be submitted by an appropriate volunteer officer or board member of the organization, or by a member of its executive staff to whom the responsibility is specifically delegated by its governing body.

Foundation Officials

Stephen C. Doberstein: director
Irenee du Pont, Jr.: trustee B 1920. ED Dartmouth College; Massachusetts Institute of Technology. PRIM CORP EMPL vice president: Longwood Gardens.
David Greenewalt: adv trustee
Eleanor Silliman Maroney: trustee, advisory

Grants Analysis

Disclosure Period: calendar year ending 2000
Total Grants: $7,067,600*
Number of Grants: 84
Average Grant: $61,055*
Highest Grant: $2,000,000
Typical Range: $30,000 to $100,000
***Note:** Giving excludes United Way. Average grant figure excludes the highest grant.

Recent Grants

Note: Grants derived from 2000 Form 990.

Library-Related
200,000	Friends of the Concord Pike Library, Wilmington, DE -- capital campaign

General
2,000,000	Wilmington College, New Castle, DE -- capital campaign
350,000	Wilmington Montessori, Wilmington, DE -- capital campaign
300,000	Washington College, Chestertown, MD -- capital campaign
250,000	Academy of Natural Sciences, Philadelphia, PA -- environment
250,000	Academy of Natural Sciences Estuarine Research Center, St. Leonard, MD -- environment
250,000	Delaware Nature Society, Hockessin, DE -- capital campaign
200,000	Claymont Community Center, Claymont, DE -- capital campaign
200,000	Mary Campbell Center, Wilmington, DE -- building renovation
200,000	St. Francis Health Care Services Foundation, Wilmington, DE -- capital campaign
150,000	Baldwin School, Bryn Mawr, PA -- technology needs

CTW FOUNDATION, INC.

Giving Contact

Robert A. Tucker, President
PO Box 911
Wilmington, DE 19899-0911
Phone: (302)429-9425

Description

Founded: 1954
EIN: 516011637
Organization Type: Private Foundation
Giving Locations: nationally.
Grant Types: Capital, Scholarship.

Financial Summary

Total Giving: $741,266 (2001); $624,875 (2000); $2,441,992 (1998)
Giving Analysis: Giving for 2000 includes: foundation scholarships ($144,875); 1998: foundation scholarships ($295,750); 1997: foundation scholarships ($276,895)
Assets: $15,273,811 (2001); $16,247,111 (2000); $17,096,155 (1998)
Gifts Received: $51,156 (2000); $2,628,750 (1998); $800,000 (1997). Note: In 2000, contributions were received from Charles W. Bower. Foundation receives contributions from Beneficial Tax Masters, Inc.

Typical Recipients

Arts & Humanities: Arts Associations & Councils, Arts Festivals, Arts Funds, Libraries, Museums/Galleries, Opera, Theater
Civic & Public Affairs: Botanical Gardens/Parks
Education: Arts/Humanities Education, Colleges & Universities, Economic Education, Education Funds, Engineering/Technological Education, International Studies, Legal Education, Medical Education, Minority Education, Private Education (Precollege), Religious Education, Student Aid
Environment: Environment-General, Resource Conservation
Health: Cancer, Children's Health/Hospitals, Clinics/Medical Centers, Health Funds, Health Organizations, Hospices, Hospitals, Medical Rehabilitation, Medical Research, Medical Training, Preventive Medicine/Wellness Organizations, Public Health
Religion: Churches, Religious Welfare, Seminaries
Social Services: Domestic Violence, Emergency Relief, Homes, People with Disabilities, Scouts, Youth Organizations

Application Procedures

Initial Contact: Send proposal in letter form.
Application Requirements: A description of organization; amount requested; purpose of funds sought; recently audited financial statement; proof of tax-exempt status.
Deadlines: October 1. April 15 for scholarships.
Notes: Application forms are available for scholarships.

Additional Information

Household International acquired Beneficial Corp. in second quarter of 1998. Following the merger, Beneficial Foundation changed its name to CTW Foundation. The foundation is no longer affiliated with either company.

Foundation Officials

Finn M. W. Caspersen, Sr.: vice president, director B New York, NY 1941. ED Brown University BA (1963); Harvard University LLB (1966). CORP AFFIL vice president: Westby Corp.; director: Beneficial Bank PLC; member executive committee, director: Beneficial National Bank. NONPR AFFIL director: Shelter Harbor Fire District; chairman: U.S. Equestrian Team; chairman: Prosperty New Jersey; member: Partnership for New Jersey; trustee, chairman: Peddie School; member: New York State Bar Association; chairman dean advisory board: Harvard University Law School; advisory board: Institute for Law & Economic; member: Harvard Resources Comm; member: Florida Bar Association; chairman: Gladstone Equestrian Association Inc.; director: Drumthwacket Foundation; chairman: Coalition Better Transportation; chairman: Coalition Service Industry; emeritus trustee: Brown University; member: American Finance Association; trustee: BGCN Life

Camp Inc. CLUB AFFIL Wilmington Country Club; Knickerbocker Club; University Club; Harvard Club.
E. D. Dickey: secretary
Wheeler K. Neff: assistant secretary, director B 1948. ED Bucknell University (1970); Temple University (1974). PRIM CORP EMPL secretary, director: Beneficial National Bank ADD CORP EMPL vice president, assistant general counsel: Beneficial Corp.
Robert A. Tucker: president, director B Brooklyn, NY 1926. ED Wesleyan University (1948); Brown University (1951). CORP AFFIL director: Beneficial Corp.
John O. Williams: director

Grants Analysis

Disclosure Period: calendar year ending 2001
Total Grants: $637,500*
Number of Grants: 16
Average Grant: $13,393*
Highest Grant: $250,000
Lowest Grant: $2,500
Typical Range: $5,000 to $25,000
*Note: Giving excludes scholarships. Average grant figure excludes two highest grants ($450,000).

Recent Grants

Note: Grants derived from 2001 Form 990.

Library-Related

250,000	John Carter Brown Library, Providence, RI

General

200,000	Seeing Eye, Inc., Morristown, NJ
25,000	American Red Cross New York City 9/11 Catastrophe Fund, Washington, DC
25,000	Drew University, Madison, NJ
25,000	Peddie School, Hightstown, NJ
25,000	Salvation Army Twin Towers Relief Fund, West Nyack, NY
15,000	New Jersey Shakespeare Festival, Madison, NJ
10,000	Harness Racing Museum and Hall of Fame, Goshen, NY
10,000	Morgan State University Foundation, Baltimore, MD
10,000	Nature Conservancy Inc., Chester, NJ
10,000	New Jersey Museum of Agriculture, New Brunswick, NJ

PATRICK AND ANNA M. CUDAHY FUND

Giving Contact

Judith Borchers, Executive Director
1007 Church St., Suite 414
Evanston, IL 60201
Phone: (847)866-0760
Fax: (847)475-0679
E-mail: secretary@cudahyfund.org
Web: http://www.cudahyfund.org

Description

Founded: 1934
EIN: 390991972
Organization Type: Family Foundation
Giving Locations: IL: Chicago; WI internationally; nationally.
Grant Types: General Support, Multiyear/Continuing Support, Operating Expenses, Project.

Donor Information

Founder: Michael F. Cudahy established the Patrick and Anna M. Cudahy Fund in 1934 in honor of his parents, and incorporated it in Wisconsin in 1949. Patrick Cudahy (1849-1919) was a partner in Armour and Company and organized the Cudahy Brothers Packing Company. Michael Cudahy served as president of the fund and was succeeded by his son, Richard D. Cudahy. The current president is Janet S. Cudahy, M.D., wife of Richard D. Cudahy.

Financial Summary

Total Giving: $1,936,930 (2002 approx); $2,420,433 (2001); $2,033,675 (1998)
Assets: $23,552,805 (2001); $30,279,051 (1998); $28,356,436 (1997)

Typical Recipients

Arts & Humanities: Arts Funds, Arts Institutes, Dance, Historic Preservation, Libraries, Museums/Galleries, Performing Arts, Public Broadcasting
Civic & Public Affairs: African American Affairs, Asian American Affairs, Civil Rights, Economic Development, Employment/Job Training, Hispanic Affairs, Housing, Law & Justice, Municipalities/Towns, Nonprofit Management, Professional & Trade Associations, Public Policy, Rural Affairs, Urban & Community Affairs, Women's Affairs
Education: Afterschool/Enrichment Programs, Business Education, Colleges & Universities, Education Reform, Environmental Education, Education-General, Legal Education, Literacy, Minority Education, Preschool Education, Private Education (Precollege), Private Education (Precollege), Public Education (Precollege), Religious Education, Science/Mathematics Education, Secondary Education (Private), Secondary Education (Public), Vocational & Technical Education
Environment: Environment-General
Health: Clinics/Medical Centers, Geriatric Health, Health Organizations, Long-Term Care, Preventive Medicine/Wellness Organizations, Public Health
International: Foreign Educational Institutions, Health Care/Hospitals, Human Rights, International Development, International Environmental Issues, International Organizations, International Relations, Missionary/Religious Activities
Religion: Churches, Dioceses, Religion-General, Ministries, Missionary Activities (Domestic), Religious Organizations, Religious Welfare
Social Services: At-Risk Youth, Camps, Child Welfare, Community Centers, Community Service Organizations, Community Service Organizations, Day Care, Domestic Violence, Emergency Relief, Family Planning, Family Services, Food/Clothing Distribution, Homes, People with Disabilities, Recreation & Athletics, Scouts, Senior Services, Shelters/Homelessness, Social Services-General, Special Olympics, Substance Abuse, Volunteer Services, YMCA/YWCA/YMHA/YWHA, Youth Organizations

Application Procedures

Initial Contact: Prospective recipients should call or write the fund for guidelines and proposal cover sheet.
Application Requirements: Completed one page Cudahy form entitled "Summary and Request for Funding"; a brief description of the organization and an outline of the proposed project, which should not exceed five pages in length; a projected income and expense breakdown for the organization and the project; a list of the major institutional donors to the organization during the past five years (maximum of ten names with amounts); a complete, current list of the board of directors of the organization; a copy of the Internal Revenue Service ruling that the organization has 501(c)(3) status; a complete copy of the most recent audited financial statement. If the organization is not required to be audited, a detailed balance sheet of actual income and expenses, assets and liabilities for the past fiscal year.
Deadlines: Applicants should submit the proposals eight weeks before a meeting.
Review Process: The board meets quarterly, on January 5, April 5, July 5, and October 5. Notification of decisions will be two weeks after meetings.

Restrictions

No grants are given to individuals or for endowments, and no loans are made. The fund also does not support organizations outside of U.S. who are not represented by a U.S.-based 501(c)(3) organization.

Additional Information

Publications: Guidelines; Application Form; Annual Grants List

Foundation Officials

James D. Bailey: director
Judith Borchers: executive director
Janet S. Cudahy, MD: president, director, donor daughter-in-law
Richard D. Cudahy, Jr.: director, donor grandson
Richard D. Cudahy: chairman, director, donor son B Milwaukee, WI 1926. ED United States Military Academy BS (1948); Yale University JD (1955). PRIM NONPR EMPL federal judge: U.S. Court Appeals. NONPR AFFIL judge: U.S. Court Appeals 7th Federal Circuit; member: Wisconsin Bar Association; member: Milwaukee Bar Association; member board directors: Federal Judges Association; member: Law Club Chicago; trustee: Catholic Theological Union; member: Chicago Bar Association; member: American Law Institute; member: American Bar Association; board selectors: American Institute Public Service.
Annette Stoddard Freeman: director
Dudley J. Godfrey, Jr.: director B 1926. ED University of Wisconsin BBA (1949); University of Michigan LLB (1952). PRIM CORP EMPL senior partner: Godfrey & Kahn SC. CORP AFFIL director: Manpower Inc.; director: Powers Holding Inc.
Jean Holtz: director
Philip Lerman: director
Louise A. McMenamin: secretary, treasurer, director
Wesley L. Scott: director

Grants Analysis

Disclosure Period: calendar year ending 2002
Total Grants: $1,936,930*
Number of Grants: 187
Average Grant: $10,358
Highest Grant: $30,000
Lowest Grant: $500
Typical Range: $5,000 to $20,000
*Note: Grants analysis provided by foundation.

Recent Grants

Note: Grants derived from 2001 Form 990.

Library-Related
200,000   Cudahy Public Library Expansion Committee, Cudahy, WI

General
47,640   Maryknoll Sisters, Maryknoll, NY -- mission projects in four countries
35,000   Little Sisters of the Poor/St. Joseph's Home for the Elderly, Chicago, IL
35,000   St. Ann Center for Intergenerational Care, Milwaukee, WI -- Adopt-A-Life program
31,500   Maryknoll Sisters, Maryknoll, NY -- mission projects in four countries
30,000   Lakefront Single-Room Occupancy Corporation, Chicago, IL
30,000   Oxfam America, Boston, MA
25,000   Alexian Brothers/Bonaventure House, Chicago, IL
25,000   American Youth Hostels, Inc, San Diego, CA
25,000   Center for Deaf-Blind Persons, Milwaukee, WI
25,000   Grand Avenue Club, Milwaukee, WI

THE CULLEN FOUNDATION

Giving Contact

Alan M. Stewart, Executive Director
601 Jefferson, Suite 4000
Houston, TX 77002

Phone: (713)651-8835
Fax: (713)651-2374
Web: http://www.cullenfdn.org

Description

Founded: 1947
EIN: 746048769
Organization Type: Family Foundation
Giving Locations: TX: Houston including surrounding area
Grant Types: Capital, Endowment, Fellowship, General Support, Matching, Multiyear/Continuing Support, Operating Expenses, Professorship, Project, Research, Scholarship.

Donor Information

Founder: The Cullen foundation was established in 1947 by Hugh Roy Cullen, a Houston oilman. The original grant funding the foundation was in the form of oil properties. The donor's daughter and grandsons serve on the board of trustees.

Financial Summary

Total Giving: $10,450 (2003 approx); $12,485,000 (2002); $14,001,667 (2001)
Giving Analysis: Giving for 2000 includes: foundation grants to United Way ($250,000) 1998: foundation grants to United Way ($250,000)
Assets: $180,000,000 (2002); $286,607,589 (2000); $304,000,000 (1999 approx)

Typical Recipients

Arts & Humanities: Arts Associations & Councils, Ballet, Dance, Film & Video, Historic Preservation, History & Archaeology, Libraries, Museums/Galleries, Music, Opera, Public Broadcasting, Theater, Visual Arts
Civic & Public Affairs: African American Affairs, Botanical Gardens/Parks, Employment/Job Training, Civic & Public Affairs-General, Hispanic Affairs, Housing, Legal Aid, Municipalities/Towns, Philanthropic Organizations, Safety, Zoos/Aquariums
Education: Afterschool/Enrichment Programs, Arts/Humanities Education, Colleges & Universities, Education Reform, Education-General, Legal Education, Literacy, Medical Education, Private Education (Precollege), Public Education (Precollege), Science/Mathematics Education, Secondary Education (Private), Special Education, Student Aid
Environment: Environment-General
Health: AIDS/HIV, Alzheimers Disease, Cancer, Children's Health/Hospitals, Clinics/Medical Centers, Emergency/Ambulance Services, Heart, Hospices, Hospitals, Medical Rehabilitation, Medical Research, Speech & Hearing
Religion: Churches, Religious Welfare, Social/Policy Issues
Science: Science Museums, Scientific Centers & Institutes
Social Services: Animal Protection, At-Risk Youth, Camps, Child Abuse, Family Planning, Food/Clothing Distribution, Scouts, Shelters/Homelessness, Substance Abuse, United Funds/United Ways, YMCA/YWCA/YMHA/YWHA, Youth Organizations

Application Procedures

Initial Contact: Send a letter of application on the organization's letterhead signed by the chief executive officer (e.g. president, executive) and including a statement that the chief executive officer has seen and approved the request, and endorses the request as a priority.
Application Requirements: Provide the name, title, and telephone number of the contact person; evidence from the IRS that the applicant organization is a public charity and not a private foundation, and that the donee organization is exempt from federal income taxes under section 501(c)(3) or 170(c) of the Internal Revenue Code. Als include a brief statement of the grant request, including amount requested, total funds

needed for the project, and timing of the grant, including installation payments if required; purpose of funds sought and statement of need; other sources of funds received or anticipated for the project, as well as the existence of a challenge grant, including the name of the grantor; sources of funds available for project apart from grants; how project will be funded after the Foundation's funding ends; and proposed method for evaluating the project. In addition, provide, a description of organization that describes where the organization has previously or is currently operating under a name other than the name on the IRS determination letter; purpose, scope of operations, history, and affiliations (if any); a list of the trustees or directors, officers, and managers; a list of principal contributors during past years and currently, including dollar amounts of major grants; the most recent year's income and expense statement or audited financial report; a complete copy of the organization's most recent IRS Form 990; and balance sheet and budget for the coming year. If the request is for building construction, renovation, or purchase of real property, also attach an architectural rendering or drawing of the facilities to be built or renovated or a photograph of property to be acquired; a description of the property including such items as type of construction, square footage, and special features; and a cost estimate.
Deadlines: None. However, if funding is needed by a specific date, the foundation suggestions that applications be submitted four to six months in advance.
Review Process: The review process may take several months.
Decision Notification: Funding decisions are communicated in writing.

Restrictions

Grants and rewards are restricted to Texas-based organizations, primarily in Houston. The foundation makes grants only to 501(c)(3) or 170(c)(1) organizations, and does not make grants to businesses, individuals, or for loans. The foundation prefers not to fund galas, testimonials, and other fundraising events; organizations that in turn provide grants to others; activities whose sole purpose is the promotion or support of a specific religion, denomination or church; purchase of uniforms, equipment, or trips for school-related organizations or amateur sports teams. Generally, the foundation will not consider applications from an organization more than once every 12 months or an organization that has received a multi-year grant from the foundation until all payments of that grant have been made.

Additional Information

Publications: Guidelines

Foundation Officials

Isaac Arnold, Jr.: vice president, trustee B 1932. CORP AFFIL director: Nuevo Energy Co.; chairman, president, director: Quintana Petroleum Corp.
Bert Louis Campbell: trustee B Tyler, TX 1939. ED University of Texas BA (1961); University of Texas JD (1970). PRIM CORP EMPL partner: Vinson & Elkins. CORP AFFIL secretary: Quintana Minerals Corp. NONPR AFFIL member: Houston Bar Association; member: Texas Bar Association; member: American Health Lawyers Association; member: American Arbitration Association; member: American Bar Association.
Roy Henry Cullen: president, trustee B 1929. CORP AFFIL director: Quintana Petroleum Corp.
William H. Drushel, Jr.: trustee B 1938. ED University of Texas Law School (1960). PRIM CORP EMPL partner: Vinson & Elkins. CORP AFFIL secretary: Quintana Petroleum Corp.
Wilhelmina Cullen Robertson Morian: secretary-treasurer, trustee B 1923. ED Sweet Briar College. CORP AFFIL director: Quintana Petroleum Corp.
Alan M. Stewart: executive director

Grants Analysis

Disclosure Period: calendar year ending 2000
Total Grants: $14,387,749*
Number of Grants: 61
Average Grant: $148,065*
Highest Grant: $3,000,000
Lowest Grant: $17,500
Typical Range: $50,000 to $400,000
*Note: Giving excludes United Way. Average grant figure excludes three highest grants ($5,800,000).

Recent Grants

Note: Grants derived from 2000 Form 990.

General

3,000,000	Baylor College of Medicine, Houston, TX -- The Cullen Endowment
1,800,000	University of Houston System, Houston, TX -- restoration of Robertson Stadium
1,000,000	University of Houston System, Houston, TX -- for expansion and renovations
600,000	Museum of Fine Arts of Houston, Houston, TX -- for new museum building and renovation of existing one
500,000	Neighborhood Center, Houston, TX -- for capital campaign
500,000	Texas Heart Institute, Houston, TX -- for "Raising the Standard: The Texas Heart Institute Campaign"
400,000	Houston Music Hall Foundation, Houston, TX -- toward construction of new Hobby Center for the Performing Arts
400,000	Memorial Hermann Healthcare System, Houston, TX -- the capital campaign
333,333	Episcopal High School, Bellaire, TX -- for construction of a new Field House
333,333	Houston Christian High School, Houston, TX -- construction of the new high school

DAPHNE SEYBOLT CULPEPER MEMORIAL FOUNDATION

Giving Contact

Nicholas J. Nardi, Secretary & Treasurer
PO Box 206
Norwalk, CT 06852-0206
Phone: (203)762-3984

Description

Founded: 1983
EIN: 222478755
Organization Type: Private Foundation
Giving Locations: CT; FL
Grant Types: General Support, Multiyear/Continuing Support.

Donor Information

Founder: the late Daphne Seybolt Culpeper

Financial Summary

Total Giving: $964,350 (2002); $1,019,357 (2000); $837,950 (1999)
Giving Analysis: Giving for 2002 includes: foundation grants to United Way ($10,500); 2000: foundation matching gifts ($1,000); foundation grants to United Way ($10,000); foundation scholarships ($13,500); 1999: foundation scholarships ($8,000); foundation grants to United Way ($10,000);
Assets: $15,537,552 (2002); $19,769,301 (2000); $19,797,618 (1999)

Typical Recipients

Arts & Humanities: Arts Centers, Historic Preservation, History & Archaeology, Libraries, Museums/Galleries, Music, Opera, Theater

Civic & Public Affairs: Botanical Gardens/Parks, Civil Rights, Housing, Zoos/Aquariums
Education: Arts/Humanities Education, Colleges & Universities, Community & Junior Colleges, Education-General, International Studies, Legal Education, Medical Education, Minority Education, Private Education (Precollege), School Volunteerism, Science/Mathematics Education, Secondary Education (Private), Special Education, Student Aid, Vocational & Technical Education
Environment: Environment-General
Health: AIDS/HIV, Cancer, Clinics/Medical Centers, Emergency/Ambulance Services, Health Organizations, Heart, Hospices, Hospitals, Medical Research, Prenatal Health Issues, Single-Disease Health Associations
International: International Relief Efforts
Religion: Churches, Religious Organizations, Religious Welfare
Science: Scientific Centers & Institutes
Social Services: Child Welfare, Community Service Organizations, Counseling, Crime Prevention, Day Care, Domestic Violence, Family Services, Food/Clothing Distribution, People with Disabilities, Recreation & Athletics, Scouts, Senior Services, Shelters/Homelessness, United Funds/United Ways, YMCA/YWCA/YMHA/YWHA, Youth Organizations

Application Procedures

Initial Contact: Send a brief letter of inquiry.
Application Requirements: Provide a description of the proposed program; proof of tax-exempt status; recently audited financial statement; detailed budget, with starting and completing dates; list of names, residences, and business addresses of governing board; and sources of other support.
Deadlines: None.

Restrictions

Does not provide fund individuals; endowments, conferences, forums, seminars, gratuities, honorariums, travel, meals and lodging; or loans.

Additional Information

Publications: Application Guidelines

Foundation Officials

Rodney S. Eielson: president
Nicholas J. Nardi: secretary, treasurer

Grants Analysis

Disclosure Period: calendar year ending 2002
Total Grants: $953,850*
Number of Grants: 283
Average Grant: $3,370
Highest Grant: $75,000
Typical Range: $1,000 to $10,000
*Note: Giving excludes United Way.

Recent Grants

Note: Grants derived from 2002 Form 990.

General

75,000	Bethesda Hospital Foundation Inc., Boynton Beach, FL -- for Critical Care services and Emergency Services Center
65,000	Advent Lutheran Church, Boca Raton, FL -- for Mosaic and additional lighting
50,000	Florida Atlantic University, Boca Raton, FL -- for multiple myeloma cancer research
50,000	Norwalk Hospital Foundation, Norwalk, CT -- for departments of medicine and emergency medicine
35,000	AIDS Project New Haven, Inc., New Haven, CT
25,000	All Saints Catholic School, Madison Lake, MN -- for Technology Program
25,000	Bethany Covenant Church, Berlin, CT -- for Construction Program

25,000	Boca Raton Museum of Art, Boca Raton, FL -- for Educational and Visual Arts Program
25,000	Habitat for South Palm Beach, Boca Raton, FL
25,000	Norwalk Community College Foundation, Norwalk, CT -- for computer security laboratory equipment

JAMES H. CUMMINGS FOUNDATION

Giving Contact

William J. McFarland, Executive Director & Secretary
1807 Elmwood Ave., Rm. 112
Buffalo, NY 14207
Phone: (716)874-0040
Fax: (716)874-0040

Description

Founded: 1962
EIN: 160864200
Organization Type: General Purpose Foundation
Giving Locations: NY: Buffalo; NC: Hendersonville; Canada : Toronto, ON
Grant Types: Capital, Research, Seed Money.

Donor Information

Founder: The James H. Cummings Foundation was established in 1962, under the will of James H. Cummings. Mr. Cummings was a prominent manufacturer of pharmaceuticals with operations in Buffalo, NY, and Toronto, Ontario.

Financial Summary

Total Giving: $1,675,271 (fiscal year ending May 31, 2001); $1,515,660 (fiscal 2000); $1,249,608 (fiscal 1999)
Giving Analysis: Giving for fiscal 1999 includes: foundation grants to United Way ($133,000).
Assets: $34,573,099 (fiscal 2001); $31,581,390 (fiscal 2000); $29,000,000 (fiscal 1999 approx)

Typical Recipients

Arts & Humanities: Arts Institutes, Film & Video, History & Archaeology, Libraries, Music, Public Broadcasting
Civic & Public Affairs: Clubs, Employment/Job Training, Civic & Public Affairs-General, Housing, Municipalities/Towns, Urban & Community Affairs, Zoos/Aquariums
Education: Colleges & Universities, Community & Junior Colleges, Education-General, Minority Education, Preschool Education, Private Education (Precollege), Science/Mathematics Education, Secondary Education (Public), Special Education, Student Aid
Environment: Environment-General
Health: Cancer, Children's Health/Hospitals, Clinics/Medical Centers, Health-General, Geriatric Health, Health Organizations, Heart, Hospices, Hospitals, Medical Rehabilitation, Medical Rehabilitation, Medical Research, Medical Training, Nursing Services, Prenatal Health Issues, Public Health, Respiratory, Speech & Hearing
International: Foreign Educational Institutions, Health Care/Hospitals
Religion: Churches, Jewish Causes, Ministries, Religious Organizations, Religious Welfare
Science: Science Museums, Scientific Centers & Institutes
Social Services: Animal Protection, At-Risk Youth, Camps, Child Welfare, Community Centers, Community Service Organizations, Day Care, Family Planning, Family Services, Food/Clothing Distribution, Homes, People with Disabilities, Recreation & Athletics, Scouts, Social Services-General, Substance Abuse, United Funds/United Ways, United Funds/

United Ways, YMCA/YWCA/YMHA/YWHA, Youth Organizations

Application Procedures

Initial Contact: A preliminary letter or telephone inquiry concerning the foundation's policies is encouraged.

Application Requirements: Eight copies of a formal proposal (limited to two pages) should be submitted. The proposal should include: the name and address of the organization; short history of the agency, with specific purpose, amount requested, and expected goals of the project; project budget; other sources being approached for funding; any other essential facts, including when the grant would be needed. Also include eight copies of the organization's most recently audited financial statement and list of current directors, as well as one copy of the IRS tax-exemption certification letter. Canadian organizations should submit tax-exemption certification from the Department of National Revenue, Ottawa. The application should be signed by the CEO of the organization.

Deadlines: The board of directors meets quarterly. To be considered at the next meeting, a proposal should be received no later than the middle of the month preceding a board meeting. Applications which are not adequately reviewed in time for one meeting are carried forward to the next one.

Restrictions

Grants, including scholarships and fellowships, are not made to individuals. Grants are not made for operating expenses, deficit financing, contingency reserves, or endowments, or to national health organizations.

Additional Information

The foundation strongly encourages applicants to follow the guidelines.

The foundation asks recipient organizations to submit progress reports and, at the termination of the grant, file an accounting of how the funds were disbursed, with an evaluation of the result. Unexpended funds must be returned to the foundation.

Publications: Annual Report; Guidelines

Foundation Officials

William George Gisel: president, director B Jamestown, NY 1916. ED Miami University (1937).

Robert James Armstrong Irwin: treasurer, director B Buffalo, NY 1927. ED Colgate University BA (1949); University of Buffalo (1949-1950); Babson College Institute of Finance (1952-1953). CORP AFFIL member advisory board: Manufacturers & Traders; director: Niagara Share Corp.; director, deputy chairman: ASA Ltd.; member advisory board: First Empire State Corp. NONPR AFFIL trustee: Saint Barnabas College Fund Inc.; director: University Cape Town Fund Inc.; trustee: Old Ft Niagara Association; trustee: Ridley College Scholarship Fund Inc.; director: Hauptman Woodward Medical Research Institute; trustee: Library Foundation Buffalo Erie County. CLUB AFFIL Saturn Club; University Club; Mid-Day Club; Royal Canadian Yacht Club; Buffalo Canoe Club.

Charles F. Kreiner, Jr.: director PRIM CORP EMPL secretary: Kreiner Co. Inc. NONPR AFFIL secretary: Child & Family Services.

William J. McFarland: executive director, secretary

John Patrick Naughton, MD: director B West Nanticoke, PA 1933. ED Cameron State College AA (1952); Saint Louis University BS (1954); University of Oklahoma MD (1958). PRIM NONPR EMPL vice president client affairs: State University of New York. NONPR AFFIL member, president: New York State Heart Association; dean, professor: State University New York Buffalo School Medicine; director: National Exercise Heart Disease Project; member: New York State Department Health Advisory Commission Physician Recredentialing; fellow: American College Physicians; fellow: American College Sports Medicine;

fellow: American College Cardiology; fellow: American College Chest Physicians.

Theodore I. Putnam, MD: director
Robert S. Scheu: director
John N. Walsh, Jr.: vice president

Grants Analysis

Disclosure Period: fiscal year ending May 31, 2001
Total Grants: $1,675,271*
Number of Grants: 29
Average Grant: $40,310
Highest Grant: $281,000
Typical Range: $5,000 to $50,000
*Note: Grants analysis provided by foundation.

Recent Grants

Note: Grants derived from 2000 Form 990.

General

133,933	Roswell Park Cancer Institute, Buffalo, NY -- spectral karyotying system
100,000	Child and Family Services, Buffalo, NY -- repairs
82,992	University of Buffalo Foundation, Buffalo, NY -- pet project
71,107	University Health Network Toronto General Hospital, Toronto, ON Canada -- equipment
53,053	Salvation Army, Buffalo, NY -- heating and ventilation air conditioning
50,000	Blue Ridge Community College, Hendersonville, NC -- learning center
50,000	Boys and Girls Club of Hendersonville, Hendersonville, NC -- build cultural center
50,000	Boys Scouts of America, Buffalo, NY -- construction of shower facility
50,000	Buffalo Association of Western New York, Buffalo, NY -- capital campaign
50,000	Buffalo Audubon Society, Buffalo, NY -- renovations

THE FRANCES L. AND EDWIN L. CUMMINGS MEMORIAL FUND

Giving Contact

Elizabeth H. Costas, Administrative Director
501 Fifth Ave., Suite 708
New York, NY 10017-6103
Phone: (212)286-1778
Fax: (212)682-9458
Note: Faxed proposals are not accepted.

Description

Founded: 1982
EIN: 136814491
Organization Type: General Purpose Foundation
Giving Locations: NY: New York including surrounding area
Grant Types: Challenge, Endowment, Professorship, Project, Seed Money.
Note: The fund also reports that it gives grants for program expansion, staff additions, and technical assistance.

Donor Information

Founder: "The fund was established by Frances L. Cummings and Edwin L. Cummings in 1982. Fran and Ed Cummings were a couple with simple tastes and generally frugal tendencies. They did not "strike it rich" through speculative ventures nor did they amass a fortune through personal business successes. It was not until 1958 that the Cummings received a sizable block of IBM stock from a wealthy, childless aunt. Despite their new-found wealth, the Cummings refrained from significantly enhancing

their "middle class" ways. Indeed, like many Americans who had endured the hard times of the great Depression in the 1930s, they retained a fiscally conservative lifestyle. By their later years, the Cummings, who had no children, saw their IBM stock increase considerably in value, and decided that the bulk of their estates should be distributed for charitable purposes." The Frances L. & Edwin Cummings Memorial Fund Biennial Report 2001-2002

Financial Summary

Total Giving: $1,876,000 (fiscal year ending July 31, 2002); $2,365,700 (fiscal 2001); $2,120,000 (fiscal 2000). Note: Fiscal 2001 giving includes board designated grants ($8,000).
Assets: $41,741,286 (fiscal 2001); $54,117,798 (fiscal 2000); $47,349,623 (fiscal 1999)

Typical Recipients

Arts & Humanities: Libraries

Civic & Public Affairs: African American Affairs, Asian American Affairs, Business/Free Enterprise, Clubs, Community Foundations, Economic Development, Employment/Job Training, Gay/Lesbian Issues, Civic & Public Affairs-General, Hispanic Affairs, Housing, Law & Justice, Municipalities/Towns, Nonprofit Management, Philanthropic Organizations, Public Policy, Safety, Urban & Community Affairs, Women's Affairs

Education: Afterschool/Enrichment Programs, Colleges & Universities, Education Associations, Education Reform, Elementary Education (Public), Environmental Education, Education-General, Journalism/Media Education, Literacy, Minority Education, Preschool Education, Public Education (Precollege), Religious Education, Secondary Education (Private), Secondary Education (Public), Social Sciences Education, Special Education, Student Aid

Health: AIDS/HIV, Cancer, Children's Health/Hospitals, Clinics/Medical Centers, Eyes/Blindness, Health Organizations, Home-Care Services, Hospitals, Medical Rehabilitation, Medical Research, Mental Health, Outpatient Health Care, Public Health

Religion: Churches, Religion-General, Ministries, Religious Organizations, Religious Welfare, Synagogues/Temples

Social Services: At-Risk Youth, Big Brother/Big Sister, Child Abuse, Child Welfare, Community Centers, Community Service Organizations, Crime Prevention, Day Care, Delinquency & Criminal Rehabilitation, Domestic Violence, Emergency Relief, Family Planning, Family Services, People with Disabilities, Senior Services, Shelters/Homelessness, Social Services-General, Substance Abuse, Volunteer Services, YMCA/YWCA/YMHA/YWHA, Youth Organizations

Application Procedures

Initial Contact: The organization should submit one original and three copies of a concise statement, no longer than seven pages in length, which describes the project. Contact foundation for detailed guidelines.

Application Requirements: Attached to the letter should be a specific amount of the request and an itemized project budget including the portion(s) of the budget being requested from the Fund; population to be served, how they are selected, tne number involved, and how they will benefit; specific and measurable goals of the project which the organization hopes to meet at the conclusion of the grant period and how the results will be measured; and an indication of the relevance of this program to both present objectives of the application organization and to future plans. An indication of plans to secure future funding for the program should also be included.

All applicants collate the following attachments with the original and copies of the proposal: audited financial statements; organization's operating budget; names of other foundations, corporations, and/or individuals to whom same grant request is being submitted and the respective amounts solicited; and names of other foundations, corporations, and/or individuals who have already significantly contributed to the project, and their respective amounts. Additionally, an organization must submit one copy of its IRS tax-exempt letter. Proposals should be clipped or stapled together, not permanently bound.

Deadlines: April 1 for review in June and October 1 for review in December. Early submissions are encouraged. Groups submitting early will have a greater chance of having a site visit.

Review Process: The Co-Trustees and Board of Advisors meet twice a year to consider grant requests. Once a full proposal has been received, the Co-Trustees will review the request to determine whether it will be submitted to the Board of Advisors for their consideration. If the Co-Trustees should decide to deny funding for any request without submitting it to the Board of Advisors, organizations will be notified prior to the Board meeting. The Co-Trustees have final responsibility for all grant proposal approvals and rejections.

Site visits are given high priority by the Co-Trustees of the Cummings Fund. They are, however, arranged only at the request of the Co-Trustees. The Co-Trustees will not meet with any organization until a complete grant request together with all supporting documentation has been submitted to the Fund.

Notes: The Cummings Fund will agree to consider up to two different grant requests at any given time from any one organization.

Restrictions

The Cummings Fund is legally restricted from contributing, in any manner, to the cultural arts. Further, as a matter of practice, the Fund does not approve grant requests within the following categories: general operating expenses; building, equipment, and other capital expenses; capital campaigns; legal aid programs; support to private individuals; activities which function primarily outside of the New York metropolitan area; organizations which are not tax-exempt under section 501(c)(3) of the Internal Revenue Code; organizations without audited financial statements; alcoholism and drug addiction treatment programs; camping programs; conferences; day care programs; environmental programs; moving expenses; public opinion polls, surveys, and research studies; public policy and/or advocacy groups; programs for senior citizens; soup kitchens and/or food banks; and well-endowed institutions. Also not funded are documentaries, films, and videos; private elementary and secondary schools; and scholarship programs. The Co-Trustees generally give higher priority to programs which have not received prior support from the fund.

Additional Information

The trust discourages elaborate, expensively prepared proposals. The value of the proposal lies in the quality of its ideas. Grant requests which lack sophistication will never be discarded on that basis alone.

The Board of Advisors may direct $1,000 per member to charities of their choosing annually.

To enable the trust's small professional staff to actively work with grantees, the fund generally prefers to support worthwhile nonprofit groups operating in its region. The fund usually makes one-year grants, and considers up to two requests per organization at any given time.

Publications: Biennial Report; Application Guidelines

Trust(s): Bank of New York

Foundation Officials

Elizabeth Costas: administration director
J. Andrew Lark: co-trustee
Dottye Riley-Chen: secretary

Grants Analysis

Disclosure Period: fiscal year ending July 31, 2002
Total Grants: $1,876,000
Number of Grants: 58

Average Grant: $32,345
Highest Grant: $100,000
Lowest Grant: $500
Typical Range: $10,000 to $50,000

Recent Grants

Note: Grants derived from 2001 Form 990.

General

250,000	Boys and Girls Clubs Union County, Union, NJ
167,000	Foundation Fighting Blindness
100,000	Cancer Research Institute, New York, NY
100,000	New York City Partnership Foundation Inc., New York, NY
90,000	Boys & Girls Clubs of America, New York, NY
75,000	Saint Vincent's Medical Centers of New York, New York, NY
73,500	Community Health Project, New York, NY
52,500	Saint Dominic's Home
50,000	Boys & Girls Clubs of Hudson County
50,000	Center for Alternative Sentencing and Employment Services, New York, NY

CUMMINS, INC.

Company Headquarters

PO Box 3005
Columbus, IN 47202
Web: http://www.cummins.com

Company Description

Founded: 1919
Ticker: CUM
Exchange: NYSE
Former Name: Cummins Engine Co..
Revenue: US$5.853 billion (2002)
Employees: 23,700 (2002)
SIC(s): 3519 Internal Combustion Engines Nec, 3714 Motor Vehicle Parts & Accessories, 7549 Automotive Services Nec.

Operating Locations

Cummins Engine Co. (AL--Huntsville; IN--Columbus, Seymour; IA--Lake Mills; MN--Fridley; NY--Jamestown; NC--Rocky Mount; OH--Findlay; SC--Charleston; TN--Cookeville, Memphis; TX--El Paso)

Nonmonetary Support

Type: Donated Equipment; Donated Products; Loaned Executives

Cummins Foundation

Giving Contact

Tracy H. Souza, President
Cummins Foundation
Box 3005, Mail Code 60909
Columbus, IN 47202-3005
Phone: (812)377-3746
Fax: (812)377-7897
Web: http://www.cummins.com/na/pages/en/whoweare/foundation.cfm

Alternate Contact

Sheri W. Bishop
Cummins Foundation
500 Jackson Street
Columbus, IN 47201
Phone: (812)377-5000
Fax: (812)377-3334

Description

EIN: 356042373
Organization Type: Corporate Foundation
Former Name: Cummins Engine Foundation.
Giving Locations: operating locations.
Grant Types: General Support, Multiyear/Continuing Support.

Financial Summary

Total Giving: $1,677,812 (2003); $1,368,878 (2002); $3,010,805 (2001). Note: Contributes through corporate direct giving program and foundation.
Giving Analysis: Giving for 2002 includes: corporate direct giving ($143,022); 2001: corporate direct giving ($337,319); foundation ($2,665,214) 1999: foundation ($2,774,145)
Assets: $1,724,498 (2001); $4,429,981 (2000); $962,191 (1999)
Gifts Received: $2,000,000 (2003 approx); $1,000,000 (2002 approx); $353,600 (2001). Note: In 2001, contributions were received from Cummins, Inc. In 1999, contributions were received from Fleetguard, Inc.

Typical Recipients

Arts & Humanities: Arts Appreciation, Arts Associations & Councils, Arts Festivals, Arts Funds, Arts Outreach, Community Arts, Dance, Historic Preservation, History & Archaeology, Libraries, Museums/Galleries, Music, Performing Arts, Public Broadcasting

Civic & Public Affairs: African American Affairs, Botanical Gardens/Parks, Chambers of Commerce, Civil Rights, Community Foundations, Economic Development, Economic Policy, Employment/Job Training, Civic & Public Affairs-General, Housing, Legal Aid, Municipalities/Towns, Nonprofit Management, Philanthropic Organizations, Public Policy, Rural Affairs, Safety, Urban & Community Affairs, Women's Affairs, Zoos/Aquariums

Education: Afterschool/Enrichment Programs, Arts/Humanities Education, Business Education, Business-School Partnerships, Colleges & Universities, Community & Junior Colleges, Education Associations, Education Funds, Education Reform, Elementary Education (Private), Elementary Education (Public), Engineering/Technological Education, Education-General, International Exchange, Minority Education, Private Education (Precollege), Public Education (Precollege), Science/Mathematics Education, Student Aid

Environment: Environment-General, Resource Conservation, Wildlife Protection

Health: Children's Health/Hospitals, Eyes/Blindness, Heart, Hospices, Hospitals, Mental Health, Preventive Medicine/Wellness Organizations, Public Health, Research/Studies Institutes

International: Foreign Arts Organizations, Foreign Educational Institutions, Human Rights, International Peace & Security Issues, International Relations

Religion: Religious Welfare, Seminaries

Social Services: Child Welfare, Community Centers, Community Service Organizations, Counseling, Day Care, Domestic Violence, Emergency Relief, Family Planning, Family Services, Food/Clothing Distribution, Recreation & Athletics, Scouts, Senior Services, Shelters/Homelessness, Substance Abuse, United Funds/United Ways, Volunteer Services, YMCA/YWCA/YMHA/YWHA, Youth Organizations

Application Procedures

Initial Contact: Submit a preliminary proposal. Local projects outside Indiana should be sent to local plant manager; proposals from Indiana communities should be directed to the foundation.

Application Requirements: Inquiries should include a brief description of problem being addressed, what the programs aims to achieve, operating plan and cost, description of key leadership, criteria for evaluating program success, and documentation of tax-exempt status.

Deadlines: None.

Review Process: Foundation staff will respond regarding the possibility of funding.

Decision Notification: Directors meet three to four times a year; small grants are made from a discretionary budget between meetings.

Restrictions

Does not support political causes or candidates, sectarian religious activities, or individuals.

Additional Information

Cummins contributes 5% of its domestic pretax profits and 1% of its international profits for charitable activities.

Corporate Officials

Jean Blackwell: vice president, human resources
Jack Kenneth Edwards: executive president, group president power generation B Erie, PA 1944. ED Claremont McKenna College BA (1966); Vanderbilt University MA (1972). PRIM CORP EMPL president: Cummins Engine Co. Inc.
Mark R. Gerstle: vice president, cummins business services
Thomas Linebarger: vice president, chief financial officer ED Stanford University MS (1994); Stanford University MBA (1994). PRIM CORP EMPL vice president, chief financial officer: Cummins Engine Co.
Frank J. McDonald: vice president, quality
Rick J. Mills: president, fleetguard
Theodore Matthew Solso: chairman, chief executive officer, director B Spokane, WA 1947. ED DePauw University (1969); Harvard University MBA (1971). PRIM CORP EMPL chairman, chief executive officer, director: Cummins Engine Co. Inc. CORP AFFIL director: Cyprus Amax Minerals Co.; director: Irwin Financial Corp.; director: BP Amoco Corp.; president: Cummins Americas Inc.
Christina M. Vujovich: vice president environmental policy
John C. Wall: vice president, chief technical office

Foundation Officials

Jack Kenneth Edwards: director (see above)
Mark R. Gerstle: director (see above)
William Irwin Miller: director B Columbus, IN 1956. ED Yale University BA (1978); Stanford University MBA (1981). PRIM CORP EMPL chairman: Irwin Financial Corp. CORP AFFIL chairman: Irwin Management Co. Inc.; chairman: Tipton Lakes Co.; director: Cummins Engine Co. Inc. NONPR AFFIL trustee: Christian Theological Seminary; trustee: Taft School; director: American Public Radio Minneapolis.
Theodore Matthew Solso: chairman (see above)
Tracy H. Souza: president
Christina M. Vujovich: director (see above)

Grants Analysis

Disclosure Period: calendar year ending 2002
Total Grants: $1,368,878
Number of Grants: 152
Highest Grant: $300,000
Lowest Grant: $50
Typical Range: $1,000 to $15,000

Recent Grants

Note: Grants derived from 2001 Form 990.

General

700,000	Bartholomew Consolidated School, Columbus, IN
475,000	United Way Bartholomew County, Columbus, IN
144,500	Ashoka, Arlington, VA -- support for fellowships in Mexico, Brazil and India
100,000	Asociacion Filantropica, New York, NY
97,775	Bartholomew Consolidated School Corporation, Columbus, IN -- for architect fees for new Central Middle School
76,390	United Way Minneapolis, Minneapolis, MN
50,000	Heritage Fund of Bartholomew County, Columbus, IN -- for capital endowment campaign
50,000	kidscommons, Columbus, IN
50,000	National Civil Rights Museum, Memphis, TN -- support for building fund
50,000	New York Firefighters, New York, NY -- support for families of firefighters lost 9/11/01

CUNA MUTUAL GROUP

Company Headquarters

Madison, WI
Web: http://www.cunamutual.com

Company Description

Assets: US$3.921 billion (2001)
Employees: 5000 (2001)
SIC(s): 6311 Life Insurance, 6321 Accident & Health Insurance, 6399 Insurance Carriers Nec.

Operating Locations

CUNA Mutual Group (CA--Pomona; GA--Duluth; IA--Waverly; MI--Bingham Farms; NY--Albany; PA--Harrisburg; TX--Dallas; WA--Federal Way)

Nonmonetary Support

Type: Donated Equipment
Volunteer Programs: The company's Dollars for Doers program provides cash grants to qualifying nonprofit organizations for which employees and company board members volunteer.
Note: Nonmonetary support budget is approximately $5,000 annually.

CUNA Mutual Group Foundation, Inc.

Giving Contact

Terri J. Fiez, Executive Director
CUNA Mutual Group Foundation
5910 Mineral Point Rd.
Madison, WI 53701
Phone: (608)231-7908
Fax: (608)236-7908
Web: http://www.cunamutual.com/cmg/freeFormDetail/0,1248,888,00.html
Note: Toll free: (800)937-2644. Foundation is the point of contact for contributions in Madison or field locations.

Alternate Contact

Corporate Contributions
CUNA Mutual Life Insurance Co.
200 Heritage Way
Waverly, IA 50677
Phone: (319)483-2333
Fax: (319)352-1272
Note: Contact for requests in Waverly.

Description

EIN: 396105418
Organization Type: Corporate Foundation
Former Name: CUNA Mutual Foundation, Inc.
Giving Locations: CA: Rancho Cucamonga primary location; GA: Duluth secondary location; IA: Waverly primary location; MI: Southfield secondary location; MN: Bloomington secondary location; NY: Albany secondary location; TX: Dallas secondary location; WI: Madison primary location generally in communities where CUNA Mutual is located.
Grant Types: Capital, Emergency, Employee Matching Gifts, Matching, Multiyear/Continuing Support.
Note: The company matches employee and retiree gifts to institutions of higher learning, the Filene Research Institute, and the Credit Union Foundation.

Financial Summary

Total Giving: $751,691 (2001); $642,250 (2000); $534,141 (1998). Note: Contributes through corporate direct giving program and foundation.
Giving Analysis: Giving for 2000 includes: foundation grants to United Way ($226,800); foundation ($415,450); 1998: foundation ($534,141); 1997: foundation ($234,794); foundation grants to United Way ($242,555)
Assets: $497,182 (2001); $606,063 (2000); $515,372 (1997)
Gifts Received: $660,000 (2001); $660,000 (2000); $563,000 (1997). Note: The foundation receives contributions from CUNA Mutual Group and its companies.

Typical Recipients

Arts & Humanities: Arts Associations & Councils, Arts Centers, Arts Festivals, Arts Funds, Community Arts, Dance, Arts & Humanities-General, Historic Preservation, History & Archaeology, Libraries, Museums/Galleries, Music, Opera, Performing Arts, Public Broadcasting, Theater
Civic & Public Affairs: African American Affairs, Botanical Gardens/Parks, Business/Free Enterprise, Community Foundations, Economic Development, Employment/Job Training, Civic & Public Affairs-General, Housing, Law & Justice, Minority Business, Municipalities/Towns, Parades/Festivals, Philanthropic Organizations, Public Policy, Safety, Urban & Community Affairs, Zoos/Aquariums
Education: Business Education, Business Education, Business-School Partnerships, Colleges & Universities, Education Associations, Education Funds, Elementary Education (Public), Engineering/Technological Education, Education-General, Gifted & Talented Programs, Legal Education, Minority Education, Public Education (Precollege), Religious Education, Science/Mathematics Education, Secondary Education (Public), Student Aid, Vocational & Technical Education
Environment: Energy, Resource Conservation
Health: AIDS/HIV, Cancer, Children's Health/Hospitals, Clinics/Medical Centers, Diabetes, Emergency/Ambulance Services, Health-General, Geriatric Health, Health Policy/Cost Containment, Health Organizations, Hospitals, Medical Rehabilitation, Medical Research, Mental Health, Nursing Services, Prenatal Health Issues, Public Health, Single-Disease Health Associations
International: International Organizations
Religion: Religious Welfare
Social Services: At-Risk Youth, Big Brother/Big Sister, Camps, Child Welfare, Community Centers, Community Service Organizations, Crime Prevention, Day Care, Emergency Relief, Family Services, Food/Clothing Distribution, Homes, People with Disabilities, Recreation & Athletics, Scouts, Senior Services, Shelters/Homelessness, Social Services-General, Special Olympics, United Funds/United Ways, YMCA/YWCA/YMHA/YWHA, Youth Organizations

Application Procedures

Initial Contact: Call to request guidelines and application.
Application Requirements: Include completed application form, list of current board of directors, most recent audited financial statement, current operating budget (and project budget, if applicable), copy of annual report, copy of IRS tax exemption letter, and any supporting material.
Deadlines: None, for funding under $5,000; requests over $5,000 must be received six weeks before the board meets to be considered for funding at the meeting; contact the foundation executive director for exact dates.
Evaluative Criteria: Program serves communities where company employees live and work or where employees are active volunteers; involves training, management assistance, and involvement by employees and not just monetary assistance; leverages

funds through challenge grants, matching funds or cooperative funding from other sources; reduces duplication and provides cost-effective services; proposal benefits a large section of the community at a low per-capita cost; provides direct services rather than general operations; and demonstrates significant, measurable outcomes.

Decision Notification: Board reviews proposals three times annually, in February, May, and October.

Restrictions

The foundation will not provide grants for organizations without IRS 501(c)(3) nonprofit status; individuals; political parties, candidates, or partisan political campaigns; professional associations; religious purposes; endowment funds; the purchase of tickets or items for fundraising events; or for organizations that conflict with the company's goals, products, or policyowners.

The foundation will generally not consider grants for travel funds, benefit tickets, or courtesy advertising; athletic activities; regional or national programs; organizations that receive a major portion of their funding from government sources; grantmaking bodies; service clubs; general operating support; capital campaigns, unless approved by the Capital Fund Raising Committee in Madison, Wisconsin; or programs that receive United Way funding. Community Cornerstone Funding is not available for secondary locations.

Additional Information

Madison, WI; Pomona, CA; and Waverly, IA are considered "primary locations" for grant consideration. The foundation has four corporate giving and volunteer strategies: Community Cornerstone Grants supporting community organizations; Focused Grants supporting a specific community challenge (the current target population is families of working poor and individuals transitioning from welfare to work); Employee Involvement Grants, which has two major programs, including Dollars for Doers providing cash grants and The Matching Gift Program; and Credit Union Movement Grants supporting charitable causes related to credit unions.

Publications: Application Guidelines; Application Form

Corporate Officials

Loretta M. Burd: chairman
Terri Fiez: manager community relations
Michael B. Kitchen: president, chief executive officer, director B Toronto, ON Canada 1945. ED Ryerson Polytechnic Institute (1968). PRIM CORP EMPL president, chief executive officer, director: CUNA Mutual Insurance Group ADD CORP EMPL president: Members Life Insurance Co.; president: CUNA Mutual Insurance Society; president: CUNA Mutual Insurance Agency; president: CUNA Mutual Investment Corp.; president: CUNA Mutual Life Insurance Co. CORP AFFIL director: CUMIS General Insurance Co.; director: CUMIS Life Insurance Co.; director: Canadian Northern Shield Insurance Co.

Foundation Officials

Larry Blanchard: assistant secretary, treasurer
James L. Bryan: president
Loretta M. Burd: vice president (see above)
Janice C. Doyle: assistant secretary
Terri Fiez: executive director (see above)
Michael B. Kitchen: secretary, treasurer, executive officer (see above)
Tracy K. Lien: assistant secretary
Geoffrey McCloskey: assistant treasurer
Faye A. Patzner: assistant secretary
Neil A. Springer: vice president, director PRIM CORP EMPL treasurer: Cuna Mutual Insurance Agency. CORP AFFIL officer: CUNA Mutual Insurance Group; officer: CUNA Mutual Life Insurance Co.
Helen M. Wagabaza: assistant secretary
Larry Wilson: president, director CORP AFFIL director: CUNA Mutual Insurance Group.

Grants Analysis

Disclosure Period: calendar year ending 2001
Total Grants: $515,641*
Number of Grants: 187
Average Grant: $2,757
Highest Grant: $100,000
Lowest Grant: $25
Typical Range: $100 to $5,000 and $10,000 to $25,000
*Note: Giving excludes United Way.

Recent Grants

Note: Grants derived from 2001 Form 990.

Library-Related
5,000   Waverly Public Library, Waverly, IA

General
230,050   United Way Dane County, Madison, WI
100,000   Worldwide Foundation for Credit Unions, Inc.
62,100   American Red Cross, Concord, NH
50,000   Madison Area Rehabilitation Center, Madison, WI
29,200   Children's Miracle Network, Marshfield, WI
25,000   Center for Prevention and Intervention
20,000   Juvenile Diabetes Foundation, Newport Beach, CA
15,000   Wisconsin Center for Academically Talented Youth, Madison, WI
12,000   New England Credit Union Heritage Foundation
11,350   National Credit Union Foundation

CUNEO FOUNDATION

Giving Contact

John F. Cuneo, Jr., President
9101 Greenwood Avenue, Suite 210
Niles, IL 60714
Phone: (847)296-3351
Fax: (847)296-3310

Description

Founded: 1945
EIN: 362261606
Organization Type: Family Foundation
Giving Locations: IL: Chicago including metropolitan area
Grant Types: Capital, General Support, Matching.

Donor Information

Founder: Incorporated in 1945 by John F. Cuneo and the Milwaukee Golf Development Corporation.

Financial Summary

Total Giving: $659,000 (1999 approx); $623,930 (1998); $659,191 (1996)
Assets: $34,816,261 (1998); $28,189,976 (1996)
Gifts Received: $1,250 (1994)

Typical Recipients

Arts & Humanities: Libraries, Music, Opera
Civic & Public Affairs: Gay/Lesbian Issues, Civic & Public Affairs-General, Law & Justice
Education: Business Education, Colleges & Universities, Medical Education, Private Education (Precollege), Public Education (Precollege), Religious Education, Secondary Education (Private), Secondary Education (Public)
Health: Alzheimers Disease, Cancer, Children's Health/Hospitals, Geriatric Health, Health Funds, Heart, Hospices, Hospitals, Long-Term Care, Medical Research, Public Health, Single-Disease Health Associations
International: International Relief Efforts
Religion: Bible Study/Translation, Churches, Religion-General, Religious Organizations, Religious Welfare, Seminaries

Science: Science Museums, Science Museums
Social Services: Child Welfare, Community Service Organizations, Food/Clothing Distribution, Homes, People with Disabilities, Recreation & Athletics, Scouts, Shelters/Homelessness, Social Services-General, United Funds/United Ways, YMCA/YWCA/YMHA/YWHA, Youth Organizations

Application Procedures

Initial Contact: The foundation requests applications be made in writing.
Application Requirements: Applications should include any supporting materials that might be necessary before a decision can be made.
Deadlines: None.
Review Process: The board of directors meets in May and October of each year. Decisions are usually made within two months.
Notes: The foundation reports that at least 60% of annual contributions are for religious, charitable, educational, or scientific purposes directly or indirectly associated with the Roman Catholic Church.

Restrictions

The foundation has set no fixed limit on the amount of the grants, but its policy has been to confine the amounts to no more than $75,000 in any one year. At present, grants are not being made to individuals, or for scholarships, fellowships, research projects, or loans.

Foundation Officials

Herta Cuneo: director B 1933. PRIM CORP EMPL secretary, director: Hawthorn Corp.
John F. Cuneo, Jr.: president, director B Chicago, IL 1931. ED Georgetown University. CORP AFFIL president: Hawthorn Corp.
Andrea Hasten: director PRIM CORP EMPL director: Jerusalem Foundation. CORP AFFIL director: Northern Trust Corp.
Consuela Cuneo McAlister: director
Tim McAlister: director
Rosemary McEvoy: director
James Nolan: director
Father George Rassas: director
John Tomisek: secretary, treasurer, director

Grants Analysis

Disclosure Period: calendar year ending 1998
Total Grants: $623,930
Number of Grants: 108
Average Grant: $5,777
Highest Grant: $50,000
Typical Range: $1,000 to $15,000

Recent Grants

Note: Grants derived from 1999 Form 990.

General
50,000   St. Mary Fremont Center
25,000   Cenacle, Chicago, IL
25,000   Holy Family Preservation Society, Chicago, IL
25,000   St. Mary of the Angels, Chicago, IL
25,000   St. Mary of the Lake Seminary, Chicago, IL
25,000   Stritch School of Medicine, Chicago, IL
23,500   Boys and Girls Club of Chicago, Chicago, IL
23,250   Children's Home and Aid Society, Chicago, IL
18,000   Loyola University of Chicago, Chicago, IL
17,600   Catholic Charities, Chicago, IL

D&B

Company Headquarters

1 Diamond Hill Rd.
Murray Hill, NJ 07974-1218
Web: http://www.dnb.com

Company Description

Founded: 1841
Ticker: DNB
Exchange: NYSE
Former Name: Dun & Bradstreet Corp. (2001).
Operating Revenue: US$1.275 billion (2002)
Employees: 10100 (2002)
SIC(s): 2731 Book Publishing, 2741 Miscellaneous Publishing, 7319 Advertising Nec, 7323 Credit Reporting Services.

Operating Locations

Dun & Bradstreet Corp. (CA--Campbell, San Diego, San Jose; CO--Aurora; FL--Cape Coral, Hollywood; IL--Carbondale; LA--New Orleans; MD--Rockville; MS--Jackson; NJ--Berkeley Heights, Florham Park, New Providence; NY--Amherst, New York; NC--Greensboro; OR--Eugene; PA--Pittsburgh; TN--Oak Ridge; UT--Salt Lake City; VA--Falls Church, Richmond)

Dun & Bradstreet Corp. Foundation, Inc.

Giving Contact

Rosanne Miller
Dun & Bradstreet Corp. Foundation
1 Diamond Hill Road
Murray Hill, NJ 07974
Phone: (908)665-8052
Fax: (908)665-5022

Alternate Contact

512 Seventh Avenue
11th Floor
New York, NY 10018
Phone: (908)665-5000

Description

EIN: 136148188
Organization Type: Corporate Foundation
Giving Locations: nationally.
Grant Types: Employee Matching Gifts, General Support.

Financial Summary

Total Giving: $946,251 (2001); $1,516,736 (2000); $1,132,364 (1999). Note: Contributes through foundation only.
Giving Analysis: Giving for 2000 includes: foundation ($1,516,736); 1999: foundation ($388,879); foundation ($388,879); foundation matching gifts ($743,485) foundation matching gifts ($743,485)
Assets: $576,771 (2001); $1,078,465 (2000); $5,816,216 (1999)
Gifts Received: $550,000 (2001); $2,250,000 (2000); $1,200,000 (1999)

Typical Recipients

Arts & Humanities: Arts Associations & Councils, Arts Centers, Dance, Arts & Humanities-General, Historic Preservation, Libraries, Museums/Galleries, Performing Arts, Public Broadcasting, Theater
Civic & Public Affairs: African American Affairs, Business/Free Enterprise, Civil Rights, Clubs, Economic Development, Economic Policy, Law & Justice, Municipalities/Towns, Professional & Trade Associations, Public Policy, Urban & Community Affairs
Education: Business Education, Colleges & Universities, Community & Junior Colleges, Education Associations, Education Funds, Education-General, International Studies, Literacy, Minority Education, Student Aid
Health: AIDS/HIV, Cancer, Emergency/Ambulance Services, Health Organizations, Hospitals, Mental Health, Single-Disease Health Associations, Speech & Hearing
Religion: Religious Welfare
Science: Scientific Centers & Institutes

Social Services: At-Risk Youth, Child Welfare, Community Centers, Community Service Organizations, Family Services, Food/Clothing Distribution, People with Disabilities, Recreation & Athletics, Special Olympics, Substance Abuse, United Funds/United Ways, YMCA/YWCA/YMHA/YWHA, Youth Organizations

Application Procedures

Initial Contact: Send brief letter or proposal.
Application Requirements: Include a description of organization, amount requested, purpose of funds sought, recently audited financial statement, and copy of IRS Code Section 501(c)(3) tax-exempt status.
Deadlines: None.

Restrictions

Foundation does not make grants for dinners or special events, fraternal organizations, political or lobbying groups, religious organizations for sectarian purposes, goodwill advertising, or individuals. Foundation will not consider organizations without an IRS 501(c)(3) tax exempt status.

Additional Information

In 1997 the foundation restructured its giving guidelines and priorities.

Corporate Officials

Allan Z. Loren: chairman, chief executive officer, director B May 03, 1938. ED Queens College BS (1960). PRIM CORP EMPL chairman, chief executive officer, director: Dun & Bradstreet Corp.

Foundation Officials

Edwin A. Bescherer, Jr.: trustee B Brooklyn, NY 1933. ED Purdue University BS (1955). NONPR AFFIL member: Financial Executives Institute.
Dennis N. Pidherny: assistant treasurer PRIM CORP EMPL assistant treasurer: Dun & Bradstreet Corp.

Grants Analysis

Disclosure Period: calendar year ending 2001
Total Grants: $604,519*
Number of Grants: 175 (approx)
Average Grant: $3,454 (approx)*
Typical Range: $500 to $5,000
*Note: Giving excludes matching gifts. Number of grants and average grant figures are approximate. A more recent grants list was unavailable.

Recent Grants

Note: Grants derived from 1996 Form 990.

General

250,000	United Way Tri-State Area, New York, NY
200,000	University of Connecticut, Stamford, CT
60,558	National Merit Scholarship Fund, Evanston, IL
60,000	Wilton Family Y, Wilton, CT
55,000	United Way, New York, NY
50,000	Norwalk Community College, Norwalk, CT
41,567	National Merit Scholarship Fund, Evanston, IL
36,000	Jackie Robinson Foundation, New York, NY
30,000	Fairfield County Commission, Norwalk, CT
30,000	Wilton Family Y, Wilton, CT

DAILY NEWS, L.P.

Company Headquarters

450 W. 33rd St.
New York, NY 10001
Web: http://www.nydailynews.com

Company Description

Founded: 1919
Employees: 1,600
SIC(s): 2711 Newspapers.

Operating Locations

Daily News (CA--Woodland Hills)

Tribune New York Foundation

Giving Contact

John Campi, Vice President, Promotions
450 West 33rd Street, 3rd Floor
New York, NY 10001
Phone: (212)210-2100

Alternate Contact

Tribune New York Foundation
220 East 42nd Street, 10th Floor
New York, NY 10017
Phone: (212)210-2686

Description

Founded: 1958
EIN: 136161525
Organization Type: Corporate Foundation
Former Name: Daily News Foundation.
Giving Locations: CT; NJ; NY: New York
Grant Types: General Support.
Note: Employee matching gift ratio: 2 to 1. $25 is the minimum for individual matching grants. A specified fund or particular area of support may by indicated.

Donor Information

Founder: New York News

Financial Summary

Total Giving: $341,260 (2001); $397,096 (2000); $381,544 (1999)
Giving Analysis: Giving for 2000 includes: foundation matching gifts ($10,096); foundation ($387,000); 1999: foundation matching gifts ($14,544); foundation ($367,000) 1996: foundation matching gifts ($9,165)
Assets: $6,413,707 (2001); $6,743,877 (2000); $6,991,480 (1999)

Typical Recipients

Arts & Humanities: Arts Associations & Councils, Arts Centers, Arts Funds, Arts Institutes, Arts Outreach, Ballet, Community Arts, Dance, Ethnic & Folk Arts, Film & Video, Arts & Humanities-General, Historic Preservation, Libraries, Museums/Galleries, Music, Performing Arts, Public Broadcasting, Theater, Visual Arts
Civic & Public Affairs: African American Affairs, Asian American Affairs, Botanical Gardens/Parks, Clubs, Economic Development, Ethnic Organizations, Gay/Lesbian Issues, Civic & Public Affairs-General, Hispanic Affairs, Housing, Municipalities/Towns, Public Policy, Women's Affairs, Zoos/Aquariums
Education: Afterschool/Enrichment Programs, Arts/Humanities Education, Colleges & Universities, Education Funds, Education Reform, Journalism/Media Education, Legal Education, Minority Education, Private Education (Precollege), Religious Education, School Volunteerism, Special Education
Environment: Resource Conservation, Wildlife Protection
Health: Cancer, Hospitals, Long-Term Care, Medical Research, Single-Disease Health Associations
International: Foreign Arts Organizations, Foreign Educational Institutions
Religion: Churches, Dioceses, Religion-General, Jewish Causes, Religious Organizations, Religious Welfare
Science: Science Museums, Scientific Centers & Institutes

Social Services: At-Risk Youth, Child Welfare, Community Service Organizations, Family Planning, Family Services, Food/Clothing Distribution, Food/Clothing Distribution, People with Disabilities, Recreation & Athletics, Substance Abuse, United Funds/United Ways, Volunteer Services, Youth Organizations

Application Procedures

Initial Contact: Contact the foundation for an application form and guidelines.

Application Requirements: Return the application, in the exact form specified by the guidelines, accompanied by a certificate of tax-exempt status signed by an officer of the organization; the organization's most recent tax-exempt determination letter; recently audited financial statement or IRS Form 990; line-item budget for the organization for the year of the request; a line-item program budget, if applicable; a list of board members, with principal business or professional affiliations; a list of the five largest grants received from corporations and/or foundations during the same fiscal year of the audit or Form 990 included with the application, including dollar amounts; and an annual report, if available. If the proposal is for salary support, include a job description and, if available, the resume of the person who will fill the position.

Deadlines: None.

Notes: Handwritten applications are not accepted. Application materials should not be bound, nor should they be submitted on colored paper.

Restrictions

For matching grants, non-eligible parties include, university athletic associations or booster clubs, memberships, subscriptions, fees or tuition, or payment for services.

Corporate Officials

Fred Drasner: co-founder, president, chief executive officer, co-publisher, director PRIM CORP EMPL co-founder, president, chief executive officer, co-publisher, director: U.S. News & World Report.

Les Goodstein: president

Foundation Officials

Carlos Austin: secretary, director
Betty Ellen Berlamino: president, director
Michael Eigner: president, director
Vincent Giannini: treasurer, assistant secretary, director
Steve Mulderrig: director
Bill Shaw: director

Grants Analysis

Disclosure Period: calendar year ending 2001
Total Grants: $332,000*
Number of Grants: 35
Average Grant: $9,486
Highest Grant: $15,000
Lowest Grant: $7,500
Typical Range: $7,500 to $10,000
*Note: Giving excludes matching gifts.

Recent Grants

Note: Grants derived from 2001 Form 990.

Library-Related

10,000	Brooklyn Public Library, Brooklyn, NY
200	New York Public Library, New York, NY -- for Employee Matching Gift Program

General

15,000	Queens Museum of Art, Flushing Meadows, NY
12,000	Emma L. Bowen Foundation for Minority Interests in Media, New York, NY
10,000	Arts Connection, New York, NY
10,000	Association of Hispanic Arts, New York, NY
10,000	Bronx Museum of the Arts, Bronx, NY
10,000	Brooklyn Academy of Music, Brooklyn, NY
10,000	Caribbean Cultural Center, New York, NY
10,000	Children's Express, Washington, DC
10,000	Citymeals-on-Wheels, New York, NY
10,000	Dance Theater of Harlem, New York, NY

DAIMLERCHRYSLER AG

Company Headquarters

Epplestrasese 225
D-70546 Stuttgart, Germany

Fax: GER 711 17-94022
Web: http://www.daimlerchrysler.com/

Company Description

Founded: 1998
Ticker: DCX
Exchange: NYSE
Formed by Merger of: Daimler-Benz AG; Chrysler Corp.
Revenue: US$156.838 billion (2002)
Employees: 365571 (2002)
SIC(s): 3700 Transportation Equipment, 6100 Non-depository Institutions, 6500 Real Estate, 6700 Holding & Other Investment Offices.

Nonmonetary Support

Type: Donated Equipment; Donated Products
Note: Nonmonetary support is principally in the form of vehicles donated to educational institutions for use in training mechanics.

DaimlerChrysler Corp. Fund

Giving Contact

Brian G. Glowiak, Vice President & Secretary
DaimlerChrysler Corp. Fund
CIMS: 485-10-94
1000 Chrysler Dr.
Auburn Hills, MI 48326-2766
Phone: (248)512-2500
Fax: (248)512-2503
Web: http://www.daimlerchrysler.com/company/dccfund/dccfund_e.htm
Note: Contact for national, international, and southeast Michigan organizations. Organizations serving communities where Chrysler Corp. has a facility with a large number of employees should address

Description

Founded: 1953
EIN: 386087371
Organization Type: Corporate Foundation
Giving Locations: headquarters and operating communities and nationally.
Grant Types: Emergency, Employee Matching Gifts, General Support, Project.
Note: Employee matching gift ratio: 2 to 1 up to $5,000 per employee annually.

Donor Information

Founder: Chrysler Corp.

Financial Summary

Total Giving: $21,832,877 (2001); $29,619,272 (2000); $27,487,427 (1999). Note: Contributes through corporate direct giving program and foundation.
Giving Analysis: Giving for 2000 includes: foundation grants to United Way ($3,456,295); foundation grants ($26,162,977); 1999: foundation grants to United Way ($2,637,102); foundation ($24,850,325); 1998: foundation grants to United Way ($3,328,070); foundation ($22,070,414);
Assets: $46,799,509 (2001); $66,738,102 (2000); $89,069,844 (1999)
Gifts Received: $255,928 (2001); $18,940,000 (2000); $33,573,000 (1999). Note: Contributions were received from DaimlerChrysler Corp., formerly Chrysler Corp.

Typical Recipients

Arts & Humanities: Arts Associations & Councils, Arts Centers, Arts Funds, Arts Institutes, Community Arts, Ethnic & Folk Arts, Arts & Humanities-General, Historic Preservation, History & Archaeology, Libraries, Museums/Galleries, Music, Opera, Performing Arts, Public Broadcasting, Theater

Civic & Public Affairs: African American Affairs, Business/Free Enterprise, Chambers of Commerce, Community Foundations, Economic Development, Economic Policy, Employment/Job Training, Ethnic Organizations, Civic & Public Affairs-General, Housing, Minority Business, Municipalities/Towns, Nonprofit Management, Parades/Festivals, Professional & Trade Associations, Public Policy, Rural Affairs, Safety, Safety, Urban & Community Affairs, Women's Affairs, Zoos/Aquariums

Education: Agricultural Education, Arts/Humanities Education, Business Education, Colleges & Universities, Community & Junior Colleges, Continuing Education, Economic Education, Education Associations, Education Funds, Education Reform, Engineering/Technological Education, Faculty Development, Education-General, Health & Physical Education, International Studies, Literacy, Minority Education, Private Education (Precollege), Public Education (Precollege), Science/Mathematics Education, Student Aid

Environment: Environment-General

Health: Cancer, Diabetes, Emergency/Ambulance Services, Eyes/Blindness, Health Organizations, Hospices, Hospitals, Speech & Hearing

International: Foreign Educational Institutions, International Development, International Relief Efforts

Religion: Jewish Causes, Religious Welfare

Science: Scientific Centers & Institutes

Social Services: Animal Protection, Child Welfare, Community Centers, Community Service Organizations, Emergency Relief, Food/Clothing Distribution, People with Disabilities, Recreation & Athletics, Scouts, Senior Services, Substance Abuse, United Funds/United Ways, Volunteer Services, YMCA/YWCA/YMHA/YWHA, Youth Organizations

Application Procedures

Initial Contact: Requests from organizations that are located in Southeastern Michigan or that are national or international in scope must be submitted using the company's on-line application tool (available at http://www.daimlerchrysler.com/company/dccfund/dccfund_e.htm). Local requests (from organizations outside of Michigan) should be submitted in writing to your local DaimlerChrysler facility.

Application Requirements: National, international, or Southeastern Michigan applicants should have the following items available prior to beginning the on-line application process: the organization's IRS determination letter, most recent annual report and a summary description or synopsis outlining the proposal. The synopsis should provide, as briefly as possible, information on the following topics: a. What issue or problem does your program or project address? b. How does this issue relate to DaimlerChrysler Corporation Fund's goals, areas of focus and criteria? c. What are the credentials or special capabilities of your organization to address this issue? d. What is the scope of your program? e. Who are the clients, audience or people served by this program? f. What is the goal or expected outcome of the program for which you seek support? g. What specifically are you requesting of DaimlerChrysler Corporation Fund? h. What is the rationale for this request and the amount requested of the Fund? i. What are the key program or deadline dates? j. How will you measure results or success of this program? k. How will you sustain this program after DaimlerChrysler Corporation Fund support ends? l. What will your organization expect of the Fund in the future?

Local requests should follow the same guidelines, but should be submitted in writing to the local DaimlerChrysler facility.

Deadlines: None.

Evaluative Criteria: Supported programs demonstrate: leadership, innovation, a model of effective change, organizational self-sufficiency, empowered people, involved employees, teamwork, continuous improvement, and results; grants are increasingly made on the initiative of the company or through competitive grants.

Notes: The fund asks that organizations review guidelines prior to submitting a formal letter. Applications are accepted online.

Restrictions

The fund does not support organizations without 501(c)(3) status; individuals; discriminatory organizations; endowment funds; conferences, seminars, trips, tours or similar events; religious organizations for religious purposes; fraternal, athletic, or social clubs; veterans or labor organizations, or similar associations; political organizations or campaigns; requests for loans or debt retirement programs; programs or projects involving the delivery of direct health care; disease-specific organizations; multi-year requests; capital campaigns; operating expenses of United Way local agencies (except through the company's support of annual United Way campaigns in operating communities); fund-raising activities related to individual sponsorship; or the purchase of courtesy advertising.

No support is given to organizations that might in any way pose a conflict with Chrysler's mission, goals, programs, products or employees. Projects and organizations without connection to a major DaimlerChrysler Corp. plant community will not be considered. Neither the DaimlerChrysler Corp. Fund nor DaimlerChrysler Corp. donates vehicles for on-road use.

Additional Information

In May of 1998, Daimler-Benz of Stuttgart, Germany, and Chrysler Corp. of Auburn Hills, MI, merged to create DaimlerChrysler.

Publications: Community Involvement Guidelines

Corporate Officials

Dr. Manfred Bischoff: aerospace and industrial businesses PRIM CORP EMPL aerospace and industrial businesses: DaimlerChrysler Corp.

Thomas Patrick Capo: director B Detroit, MI 1951. ED University of Detroit (1973); University of Detroit (1975). PRIM CORP EMPL director: DaimlerChrysler Corp. CORP AFFIL director: Chrysler Canada Ltd.; director: Chrysler Financial Corp.

W. Frank Fountain, Jr.: vice president government affairs B Brewton, AL 1944. ED Hampton Institute (1966); University of Pennsylvania (1973). PRIM CORP EMPL vice president government affairs: DaimlerChrysler Corp.

Arthur C. Liebler: vice president communications B Pittsburgh, PA 1942. ED Wayne State University; Marquette University AB (1964). PRIM CORP EMPL vice president communications: DaimlerChrysler Corp. NONPR AFFIL director: American Advertising Federation; director: Public Relations Society America. CLUB AFFIL member: Detroit Adcraft Club; member: Detroit Golf Club.

Jurgen E. Schrempp: chairman B Stuttgart, Germany 1944. PRIM CORP EMPL chairman of management board: DaimlerChrysler.

Gary C. Valade: executive vice president, chief financial officer B Detroit, MI 1942. ED Michigan State University BS (1966); Michigan State University MBA (1968). PRIM CORP EMPL executive vice president finance, chief financial officer: Chrysler Corp. ADD

CORP EMPL global procurement: DaimlerChrysler Corp. CORP AFFIL trustee: Henry Ford Health System; chairman: Daimler-Chrysler Aviation Inc. NONPR AFFIL chairman: Michigan Colleges Foundation; member, director: Michigan State University Eli Broad College Business Alumni Association; trustee: Chrysler Corp. Fund; member corp. counsel: Interlochen Center Arts; trustee: Adrian College.

Foundation Officials

W. Frank Fountain, Jr.: president (see above)
Arthur C. Liebler: trustee (see above)
William J. O'Brien, III: trustee B 1943. ED College of the Holy Cross BS (1965); University of Grenoble (1967); Yale University LLB (1969).
E. Thomas Pappert: trustee
Gary C. Valade: trustee (see above)

Grants Analysis

Disclosure Period: calendar year ending 2001
Total Grants: $18,804,882 (approx)*
Number of Grants: 720
Average Grant: $27,372
Highest Grant: $1,100,000
Lowest Grant: $100
Typical Range: $1,000 to $50,000
*Note: Giving excludes United Way.

Recent Grants

Note: Grants derived from 2001 Form 990.

General

2,300,500	United Way Community Services, Detroit, MI
1,100,000	Detroit Symphony Orchestra Hall, Detroit, MI
1,000,000	Detroit 300, Inc., Detroit, MI
701,550	Citizens Scholarship Foundation of America, St. Peter, MN
635,000	Focus HOPE, Detroit, MI
582,000	Michigan Colleges Foundation, Inc., Southfield, MI
500,000	World Childhood Foundation, New York, NY
460,000	New Detroit, Inc., Detroit, MI
400,000	Detroit Zoological Society, Royal Oak, MI
359,610	Michigan State University, East Lansing, MI

HARRY L. DALTON FOUNDATION

Giving Contact

Elizabeth D. Brand, President, Treasurer & Director
736 Wachovia Center
Charlotte, NC 28285
Phone: (704)332-5380
Fax: (704)332-5380

Description

Founded: 1979
EIN: 566061267
Organization Type: Private Foundation
Grant Types: General Support.

Financial Summary

Total Giving: $373,058 (fiscal year ending July 31, 2001); $251,240 (fiscal 2000); $161,020 (fiscal 1998). Note: 1997 Giving includes United Way ($4,000).
Giving Analysis: Giving for fiscal 2001 includes: foundation grants to United Way ($10,000); fiscal 2000: foundation scholarships ($1,000) foundation grants to United Way ($10,000)
Assets: $5,645,734 (fiscal 2001); $5,287,811 (fiscal 2000); $4,819,743 (fiscal 1998)

Typical Recipients

Arts & Humanities: Arts Associations & Councils, Community Arts, Historic Preservation, Libraries, Museums/Galleries, Music, Performing Arts, Theater
Civic & Public Affairs: Clubs, Community Foundations, Civic & Public Affairs-General, Zoos/Aquariums
Education: Colleges & Universities, Private Education (Precollege)
Environment: Environment-General
Health: Cancer, Health Organizations, Hospitals
International: International Affairs, International Relief Efforts
Religion: Churches, Ministries, Religious Welfare
Social Services: Child Abuse, Child Welfare, Community Service Organizations, Day Care, Recreation & Athletics, Shelters/Homelessness, Special Olympics, Substance Abuse, United Funds/United Ways, YMCA/YWCA/YMHA/YWHA, Youth Organizations, Youth Organizations

Application Procedures

Initial Contact: Send brief letter describing program.
Deadlines: None.

Foundation Officials

Elizabeth D. Brand: secretary, vice president
R. Alfred Brand, III: vice president, director
Deeda Coffey: secretary, director
Mary K. Dalton: president, treasurer, director

Grants Analysis

Disclosure Period: fiscal year ending July 31, 2001
Total Grants: $363,058*
Number of Grants: 28
Average Grant: $3,079*
Highest Grant: $206,500
Lowest Grant: $500
Typical Range: $1,000 to $5,000
*Note: Giving excludes United Way. Average excludes two highest grants ($283,000).

Recent Grants

Note: Grants derived from 2000 Form 990.

Library-Related

3,000	Public Library of Charlotte and Mecklenburg, NC

General

77,000	Family Center, Greenwich, CT
76,000	Charlotte Country Day School, Charlotte, NC
10,000	Crisis Assistance Ministry, Charlotte, NC
10,000	United Way of Central Carolinas, Charlotte, NC
6,000	Arts and Science Council, Charlotte, NC
6,000	UNC Lineberger Comprehensive Cancer Center
5,000	Agnes Scott College, Decatur, GA
5,000	Mint Museum of Art, Charlotte, NC
5,000	North Carolina Blumenthal Performing Arts Center, Charlotte, NC
5,000	Sharon Towers

ELEANOR NAYLOR DANA CHARITABLE TRUST

Giving Contact

c/o Trustees
375 Park Avenue, Suite 3807
New York, NY 10152
Phone: (212)754-2890
Fax: (212)754-2892
Note: All correspondence should be addressed to the trustees. A contact person is not listed.

Description

Founded: 1979
EIN: 132992855
Organization Type: General Purpose Foundation
Giving Locations: NY: New York including the East Coast.
Grant Types: General Support, Project, Research.

Donor Information

Founder: Established in 1979 by the late Eleanor Naylor Dana , the wife of Charles A. Dana (also deceased), an attorney and New York State legislator who founded Dana Corporation. The Danas established the Charles A. Dana Foundation in 1950.

Financial Summary

Total Giving: $4,000,000 (fiscal year ending May 31, 2002); $2,888,144 (fiscal 2000); $4,767,527 (fiscal 1999)
Assets: $8,788,752 (fiscal 2000); $7,613,185 (fiscal 1999); $8,267,278 (fiscal 1998)
Gifts Received: $4,197,096 (fiscal 2000); $4,197,096 (fiscal 1999); $4,197,096 (fiscal 1998). Note: Contributions are received from a trust established by Eleanor N. Dana.

Typical Recipients

Arts & Humanities: Arts Associations & Councils, Arts Centers, Arts Festivals, Ballet, Dance, Ethnic & Folk Arts, Arts & Humanities-General, Libraries, Music, Opera, Performing Arts, Public Broadcasting, Theater
Civic & Public Affairs: Community Foundations, Municipalities/Towns
Education: Arts/Humanities Education, Business Education, Colleges & Universities, Elementary Education (Private), Legal Education, Medical Education, Private Education (Precollege), Public Education (Precollege), Secondary Education (Private)
Environment: Wildlife Protection
Health: AIDS/HIV, Cancer, Children's Health/Hospitals, Clinics/Medical Centers, Diabetes, Eyes/Blindness, Heart, Hospitals, Hospitals (University Affiliated), Medical Research, Mental Health, Public Health, Transplant Networks/Donor Banks, Trauma Treatment
International: Health Care/Hospitals, International Affairs, International Development
Religion: Churches, Jewish Causes, Religious Welfare
Science: Scientific Research
Social Services: Family Planning, Senior Services, Youth Organizations

Application Procedures

Initial Contact: Initial inquiries should be submitted as a brief letter of intent, not to exceed one thousand words. Selected applicants will be invited to submit detailed proposals.
Deadlines: February 1, May 1, September 1 and November 1.

Additional Information

In general, biomedical research grants are limited to no more than three years and must not exceed $100,000. Performing arts grants must not exceed $100,000 and must show: anticipated benefit and long-range potential as a result of grant; stature of organization; need for the grant; and financial viability.
Publications: Informational Brochure

Foundation Officials

Robert Alan Good, MD: trustee B Crosby, MN 1922. ED University of Minnesota BA (1944); University of Minnesota MB (1946); University of Minnesota PhD (1947); University of Minnesota MD (1947). NONPR AFFIL professor department pediatrics: University South Florida; member: Western Association Immunologists; member: Transplantion Society; member: Society Experimental Biology & Medicine; member: Society Pediatric Research; member: Sigma Xi; member: Reticuloendothelial Society; fellow: Royal Society Medicine; member: Practitioners Society; honorary fellow: Philippine Pediatric Society; member: Pioneer; member: Phi Beta Kappa; fellow: New York Academy Science; member: Northwest Pediatric Society; member: National Academy Sciences Institute Medicine; member: Minnesota State Medicine Association; member: National Academy Sciences; member: Minneapolis Pediatric Society; member: International Society Nephrology; member: International Society for Transplantation Biology; member: International Society Immunopharmacology; member: International Society Blood Transfusion; member: International Society Experimental Hematology; member advisory committee: International Bone Marrow Transplant Registry; member: Infectious Diseases Society America; member: International Academy Pathology; member: Harvey Society; member: Central Society Clinical Research; member: Detroit Surgical Association; member: Association American Physicians; member: American Society Microbiology; honorary member: American Society Transplant Surgeons; member: American Rheumatism Association; member: American Federation Clinical Research; member: American Pediatric Society; fellow: American College Allergy & Immunology; member: American Association Pathologists; member: American Clinical & Climatological Association; member: American Association Immunologists; member: American Association Anatomists; member: American Association History Medicine; fellow: American Association Advancement Science; fellow: American Academy of Arts & Sciences; fellow: American Academy Pediatrics; member: Alpha Omega Alpha; fellow: Academy Multidisciplinary Research; physician-in-chief: All Childrens Hospital; foreign advisor: Academy Medical Science.
Valerie Harper: admin
A. J. Signorile: treasurer, trustee
Robert Edward Wise, MD: trustee B Pittsburgh, PA May 21, 1918. ED University of Pittsburgh BS (1941); University of Maryland MD (1943). PRIM NONPR EMPL chief executive officer, chairman board governors, radiologist: Lahey Clinic Foundation. CORP AFFIL director: Bay Saint Skills Corp. NONPR AFFIL member: Radiological Society North America; chairman: Robert E. Wise Medicine Research Education Institute; member: New England Roentgen Ray Society; member: North Suburban Chamber of Commerce; member: Massachusetts Radiological Society; corporator: New England Deaconess Hospital; member: Massachusetts Medicine Society; chairman: Lahey Clinic Foundation; trustee: Lahey Clinic Hospital; board governor: Historical Society Palm Beach County; adj staff: Cleveland Clinic Foundation; member: Eastern Radiological Society; clinical professor radiology: Boston University Medicine School; director: Boston Opera Association; director: Boston Public Library Foundation; member: American Medical Association; trustee: Boston Ballet Co.; member: American College Radiology. CLUB AFFIL Webhannet Golf Club; Kennebunk River Club; La Coquille Club; Braeburn Country Club; Atlantis Golf Club; Beach Club; Algonquin Club.

Grants Analysis

Disclosure Period: fiscal year ending May 31, 2000
Total Grants: $2,888,144
Number of Grants: 152
Average Grant: $19,001
Highest Grant: $100,000
Typical Range: $5,000 to $50,000

Recent Grants

Note: Grants derived from 2000 Form 990.

General

100,000	Cleveland Clinic Florida, Ft. Lauderdale, FL -- research support
100,000	Cleveland Clinic Florida, Ft. Lauderdale, FL -- Colorectal Surgery Research and Education Fund
100,000	Jewish Communal Fund, New York, NY
100,000	Lahey Clinic Foundation, Burlington, MA -- continuation of hereditary colo-rectal cancer registry
100,000	Lahey Clinic Foundation, Burlington, MA -- support building expansion initiative
100,000	New York City Opera, New York, NY -- support the new production of Porgy and Bess
100,000	Roundabout Theater Company, New York, NY -- support "The New 42nd St" campaign
80,000	All Children's Hospital, St. Petersburg, FL -- support the stable mixed chimerism
80,000	All Children's Hospital, St. Petersburg, FL -- develop alternative approach for autologous bone marrow transplantation
80,000	All Children's Hospital, St. Petersburg, FL -- cytokines and HIV research

CHARLES A. DANA FOUNDATION

Giving Contact

William Safire, Chairman & Chief Executive Officer
745 Fifth Avenue, Suite 900
New York, NY 10151
Phone: (212)223-4040
Fax: (212)317-8721
E-mail: danainfo@dana.org
Web: http://www.dana.org

Description

Founded: 1950
EIN: 066036761
Organization Type: General Purpose Foundation
Giving Locations: nationally.
Grant Types: Award, Challenge, Conference/Seminar, General Support, Project, Research.

Donor Information

Founder: Established in 1950 by Charles A. Dana .

Financial Summary

Total Giving: $13,023,387 (2002); $12,184,332 (2001); $13,884,221 (2000)
Assets: $288,357,723 (2002); $324,635,937 (2001); $330,431,279 (2000)

Typical Recipients

Arts & Humanities: Arts Associations & Councils, Arts Festivals, History & Archaeology, Libraries, Literary Arts, Museums/Galleries, Music, Performing Arts, Public Broadcasting
Civic & Public Affairs: Municipalities/Towns, Professional & Trade Associations, Public Policy, Zoos/Aquariums
Education: Arts/Humanities Education, Colleges & Universities, Economic Education, Education Reform, Elementary Education (Private), Engineering/Technological Education, Faculty Development, Education-General, Legal Education, Literacy, Medical Education, Minority Education, Private Education (Precollege), Public Education (Precollege), School Volunteerism, Science/Mathematics Education, Social Sciences Education, Special Education, Student Aid
Environment: Environment-General, Wildlife Protection, Wildlife Protection
Health: AIDS/HIV, Cancer, Children's Health/Hospitals, Clinics/Medical Centers, Emergency/Ambulance Services, Health-General, Geriatric Health, Health Policy/Cost Containment, Health Organizations, Heart, Hospitals, Medical Research, Medical Training, Mental Health, Multiple Sclerosis, Public Health,

Single-Disease Health Associations, Speech & Hearing
International: Foreign Educational Institutions
Religion: Religious Welfare
Science: Scientific Centers & Institutes, Scientific Labs, Scientific Research
Social Services: Day Care, People with Disabilities, Recreation & Athletics, Substance Abuse, Volunteer Services

Application Procedures

Initial Contact: Science and health grants are generally provided through a Request for Proposals (RFP) process and invitational programs for research grants. Requests for Proposals are genearlly sent to the deans of U.S. Schools of Medicine and Public Health and other invited institutions. Additional information on these programs can be found on the foundation's web site.

The foundation's Arts Education program is not currently accepting inquiries or proposals. Updates on this program and its guidelines can be obtained from the foundation's web site. The foundation's grant support of innovations in K-12 education is provided through the Dana Center for Educational Innovation (www.utdanacenter.org). All other foundation support of educational projects is generally by invitation only. Charles A. Dana Awards are by nomination only.

Deadlines: The board of directors meets in April, June, and October to consider grant proposals.

Review Process: The foundation acknowledges receipt of proposals and grants interviews with applicants after a proposal letter has passed review. Supporting materials should not be submitted until requested and should include proof of the organization's tax-exempt status.

Notes: Faxed proposals will not be accepted; however, letters of inquiry may be submitted by e-mail at the above address.

Restrictions

Requests from organizations outside the United States or organizations that conduct activities outside the United States are not considered for grants. Aside from the Dana Awards, grants are not made directly to individuals. The foundation generally declines requests to support operating funds of professional organizations. Requests for endowment and support for facilities generally are not accepted, although they are not excluded. The grantees are generally expected to share the cost of the project or raise matching funds. No grants are made for deficit reduction, capital campaigns, or individuals sabbaticals.

Additional Information

The Charles A. Dana Awards for Pioneering Achievements in Health and Education Program is suspended.
Publications: Annual Report; Quarterly Newsletter; Guidelines

Foundation Officials

Dr. Edward C. Andrews, Jr.: honorary director B Rockland, ME 1925. ED Middlebury College AB (1946); Johns Hopkins University MD (1951). PRIM CORP EMPL president: Maine Medical Center. CORP AFFIL director: Ventrex Laboratory; director: Chittenden Trust Co.; director: Medical Mutual Insurance Co. NONPR AFFIL professor pathology: University Vermont; director: Vermont Higher Education Council; member: Portland Chamber of Commerce; member: Association American Medical Colleges; member: Maine Hospital Association; member: American Hospital Association.

Barbara D. Best: director

Wallace Lawrence Cook: director B New York, NY 1939. ED Harvard University AB (1961); University of Virginia LLB (1964). PRIM CORP EMPL investment counselor: Rockefeller & Co. NONPR AFFIL member: Association Bar New York City; member: New York

State Bar Association; member: American Bar Association.

Josephine C. Donahue: director administration
Barbara E. Gill: vice president public affairs CLUB AFFIL Union Club.
Dr. LaSalle D. Leffall, Jr.: director
Donald Baird Marron: director B Goshen, NY 1934. ED City University of New York Bernard M. Baruch College (1949-1951); City University of New York Bernard M. Baruch College (1955-1957). ADD CORP EMPL chairman, chief executive officer: Paine Webber Inc. CORP AFFIL co-founder: Data Resources. NONPR AFFIL director: New York City Partnership; member: President Committee Arts & Humanities; member board overseers: Memorial Sloan-Kettering Cancer Center; vice chairman board trustee: Museum Modern Art; member: Council Foreign Relations; member: Governor School & Business Alliance Task Force; director: Business Committee Arts.
Ann McLaughlin: director
Burton M. Mirsky: vice president finance
Jane Nevins: vice president, Dana Press editor
L. Guy Palmer, II: director B New York, NY.
Edward F. Rover: president B New York, NY 1938. ED Fordham University AB (1961); Harvard University JD (1964). PRIM CORP EMPL partner: White & Case. CORP AFFIL director: Cranshaw Corp. NONPR AFFIL director: Rumsey-Carter Foundation; director: Waterford School; member: New York State Bar Association; director: Norton Simon Art Museum; director: Harvard-Mahoney Neuroscience Institute; member: New York County Bar Association; director: EN Dana Institute; secretary: Guggenheim Museum; director: Brearley School; member: Century Association; member: American Bar Association; member: Association Bar New York City. CLUB AFFIL Scarsdale Golf Club; Harvard Club.
William L. Safire: chairman B New York, NY 1929. ED Syracuse University (1947-1949). PRIM CORP EMPL columnist: New York Times Co. NONPR AFFIL member: Pulitzer Prize Board; trustee: Syracuse University.
Herbert Jay Siegel: director B Philadelphia, PA 1928. ED Lehigh University BA (1950). PRIM CORP EMPL chairman, president: Chris-Craft Industries Inc. CORP AFFIL chairman: United Television.
Clark M. Whittemore, Jr.: secretary, treasurer, director ED Harvard University AB; University of Virginia LLB. PRIM CORP EMPL attorney: Whitman & Ransom.

Grants Analysis

Disclosure Period: calendar year ending 2001
Total Grants: $12,184,332
Number of Grants: 62
Average Grant: $144,950*
Highest Grant: $3,342,377
Lowest Grant: $8,402
Typical Range: $20,000 to $250,000
*Note: Average grant figure excludes highest grant.

Recent Grants

Note: Grants derived from 2000 Form 990.

General

3,534,297	Dana Alliance for Brain Initiatives, Inc., New York, NY -- public education campaign on neuroscience research
1,066,000	University of Texas at Austin, Austin, TX -- Charles A. Dana Center for Educational Innovation
781,208	Harvard Medical School, Cambridge, MA -- Harvard-Mahoney Neuroscience Institute
500,000	Columbia University College of Physicians and Surgeons, New York, NY -- Neuroscience Research Program
500,000	Dana Farber Cancer Institute, Boston, MA -- David Mahoney Center for Neuro-oncology
400,000	American Association for the Advancement of Science, Washington, DC --

	electronic management of scientific information
334,000	Cold Spring Harbor Laboratory Association, Cold Spring Harbor, NY -- train doctoral scholars in biological sciences
229,400	Thirteen/WNET, New York, NY -- Educational Outreach Program
167,714	Parents as Teachers National Center, Inc., St. Louis, MO -- involvement of parents in early childhood education
150,000	Harvard Medical School, Cambridge, MA -- molecular mechanisms of membrane functions

DANIEL FOUNDATION OF ALABAMA

Giving Contact

S. Garry Smith, Executive Director
820 Shades Creek Parkway, Suite 1200
Birmingham, AL 35209
Phone: (205)879-0902
Fax: (205)879-0906

Description

Founded: 1977
EIN: 630736444
Organization Type: General Purpose Foundation
Giving Locations: AL: southeastern states.
Grant Types: General Support.

Donor Information

Founder: The Daniel Foundation of Alabama was founded in 1977, with assets transferred from the Daniel Foundation of South Carolina. The latter was established posthumously in 1947 by Charles E. Daniel and R. Hugh Daniel. Charles E. Daniel (1895-1964) organized, and was chairman of, Daniel Construction Company. He also was a trustee of Clemson University.

Financial Summary

Total Giving: $3,409,000 (2001); $3,898,000 (2000); $1,311,500 (1998)
Giving Analysis: Giving for 2001 includes: foundation grants to United Way ($25,000); 2000: foundation grants to United Way ($20,000) 1997: foundation grants to United Way ($11,000)
Assets: $81,804,260 (2001); $75,694,070 (2000); $78,502,652 (1998). Note: 0.

Typical Recipients

Arts & Humanities: Arts Associations & Councils, Arts Festivals, Arts Funds, Ballet, History & Archaeology, Libraries, Museums/Galleries, Music, Opera, Theater
Civic & Public Affairs: Botanical Gardens/Parks, Clubs, Economic Development, Economic Policy, Civic & Public Affairs-General, Housing, Municipalities/Towns, Nonprofit Management, Safety, Urban & Community Affairs
Education: Arts/Humanities Education, Business Education, Colleges & Universities, Community & Junior Colleges, Education Funds, Education Reform, Elementary Education (Public), Engineering/Technological Education, Education-General, Legal Education, Literacy, Medical Education, Private Education (Precollege), Public Education (Precollege), Religious Education, Science/Mathematics Education, Secondary Education (Private), Special Education
Environment: Environment-General, Resource Conservation, Wildlife Protection
Health: AIDS/HIV, Cancer, Children's Health/Hospitals, Clinics/Medical Centers, Eyes/Blindness, Health Organizations, Hospices, Hospitals, Long-Term Care, Medical Rehabilitation, Medical Research, Mental Health, Multiple Sclerosis, Public Health, Research/Studies Institutes, Single-Disease Health Associations

International: Health Care/Hospitals
Religion: Churches, Jewish Causes, Ministries, Religious Welfare
Science: Science Museums, Scientific Centers & Institutes
Social Services: Animal Protection, At-Risk Youth, Camps, Child Abuse, Child Welfare, Community Service Organizations, Family Services, People with Disabilities, Recreation & Athletics, Scouts, Senior Services, Social Services-General, Substance Abuse, United Funds/United Ways, YMCA/YWCA/YMHA/YWHA, Youth Organizations

Application Procedures

Initial Contact: Preliminary contact should be made in writing.
Application Requirements: The letter should include a description of the proposed program, its purpose, and a breakdown of how the grant will be used. Any applicable brochures regarding the organization, as well.
Deadlines: None. Applications should be received in time for board meetings in April and October.

Restrictions

Limited to organizations located in the southeast region of U.S.

Foundation Officials

Frances Daniel Branum: director
Charles W. Daniel: president CORP AFFIL director: Compass Bancshares; director: Compass Bank.
M. C. Daniel: chairman
S. Garry Smith: secretary, treasurer, foundation manager, executive director

Grants Analysis

Disclosure Period: calendar year ending 2001
Total Grants: $3,384,000*
Number of Grants: 110
Average Grant: $26,218*
Highest Grant: $500,000
Lowest Grant: $1,000
Typical Range: $10,000 to $50,000
*Note: Giving excludes United Way. Average grant figure excludes highest grant.

Recent Grants

Note: Grants derived from 2001 Form 990.

General

500,000	Citadel, Charleston, SC
250,000	Birmingham-Southern College, Birmingham, AL
200,000	City of Vernon
200,000	Piedmont College, Demorest, GA
150,000	Alabama Symphonic Association, Birmingham, AL
150,000	Birmingham Museum of Art, Birmingham, AL
100,000	Big Oak Ranch, Gadsden, AL
100,000	Children's Hospital of Alabama, Birmingham, AL
100,000	Discovery 2000, Birmingham, AL
100,000	Judson College, Marion, AL

EDGAR FOSTER DANIELS FOUNDATION

Giving Contact

Jane Douthitt, Secretary, Treasurer & Director
450 Circle Dr.
Santa Fe, NM 87501-8882
Phone: (505)989-3310

Description

Founded: 1996
EIN: 850435024
Organization Type: Private Foundation

Giving Locations: NM; NY
Grant Types: General Support.

Donor Information

Founder: Established in 1996 by Edgar Foster Daniels.

Financial Summary

Total Giving: $1,410,000 (2000); $1,859,500 (1999); $1,037,910 (1998)
Assets: $309,749 (2000); $303,369 (1999); $561,531 (1998)
Gifts Received: $1,456,291 (2000); $1,623,707 (1999); $776,614 (1998). Note: In 1996, 1998, 1999, and 2000 contributions were received from Edgar Foster Daniels.

Typical Recipients

Arts & Humanities: Arts Associations & Councils, Arts Festivals, Arts & Humanities-General, Libraries, Museums/Galleries, Music, Opera, Performing Arts, Theater
Civic & Public Affairs: Botanical Gardens/Parks, Civic & Public Affairs-General, Parades/Festivals
Education: Arts/Humanities Education, Colleges & Universities, Elementary Education (Private), Preschool Education, Private Education (Precollege)
Health: AIDS/HIV, Diabetes, Health Organizations, Hospitals, Kidney
International: Foreign Arts Organizations, International Environmental Issues, International Organizations
Religion: Religious Welfare
Social Services: Animal Protection, Child Welfare, Community Service Organizations, Family Services

Application Procedures

Initial Contact: Send a written request.
Deadlines: None.

Restrictions

Applicants must qualify as tax-exempt, non-profit organizations.

Foundation Officials

Edgar F. Daniels: president, director
Jane Douthitt: secretary, treasurer, director
Kurt A. Sommer: director

Grants Analysis

Disclosure Period: calendar year ending 2000
Total Grants: $1,410,000
Number of Grants: 16
Average Grant: $54,393*
Highest Grant: $358,500
Typical Range: $25,000 to $100,000
*Note: Average grant figure excludes two highest grants ($648,500).

Recent Grants

Note: Grants derived from 2001 Form 990.

Library-Related

2,000	North Carolina School of Arts Foundation, Winston-Salem, NC

General

518,264	Metropolitan Opera Association, New York, NY
286,754	Dallas Opera, Dallas, TX
251,600	Houston Grand Opera, Houston, TX
185,000	Lyric Opera of Chicago, Chicago, IL
150,000	Santa Fe Opera, Santa Fe, NM
117,380	Covent Garden, New York, NY
100,000	St. Vincent Hospital Foundation, Santa Fe, NM
100,000	San Francisco Opera Association, San Francisco, CA
80,000	Spanish Colonial Arts Society Museum, Santa Fe, NM
27,500	International Festival Society, Los Angeles, CA

FRED HARRIS DANIELS FOUNDATION

Giving Contact

Bruce G. Daniels, Chairman & Director
Fred Harris Daniels Foundation
c/o Fleet National Bank
446 Main Street
Worcester, MA 01608-1438
Phone: (617)434-1670

Description

Founded: 1949
EIN: 046014333
Organization Type: Private Foundation
Giving Locations: MA: Worcester
Grant Types: Capital, Emergency, Endowment, Fellowship, General Support, Multiyear/Continuing Support, Operating Expenses, Professorship, Project.

Donor Information

Founder: the late Fred H. Daniels, Riley Stoker Co.

Financial Summary

Total Giving: $555,000 (fiscal year ending October 31, 2001); $681,832 (fiscal 2000); $623,252 (fiscal 1999)
Giving Analysis: Giving for fiscal 2001 includes: foundation grants to United Way ($5,000); fiscal 2000: foundation grants to United Way ($30,000); fiscal 1998: foundation grants to United Way ($30,000) foundation ($564,606)
Assets: $16,555,562 (fiscal 2001); $18,046,344 (fiscal 2000); $18,384,197 (fiscal 1999)
Gifts Received: $1,725 (fiscal 1995); $2,928 (fiscal 1994)

Typical Recipients

Arts & Humanities: Ethnic & Folk Arts, Historic Preservation, History & Archaeology, Libraries, Museums/Galleries, Music, Public Broadcasting, Theater
Civic & Public Affairs: Botanical Gardens/Parks, Community Foundations, Civic & Public Affairs-General, Safety, Urban & Community Affairs
Education: Colleges & Universities, Community & Junior Colleges, Education-General, Literacy, Preschool Education, Private Education (Precollege), Public Education (Precollege), Student Aid
Environment: Environment-General
Health: Cancer, Clinics/Medical Centers, Health Funds, Health Organizations, Hospitals, Medical Research, Nursing Services, Public Health
Science: Scientific Centers & Institutes, Scientific Labs
Social Services: Big Brother/Big Sister, Child Welfare, Community Service Organizations, Family Planning, Family Services, Social Services-General, United Funds/United Ways, YMCA/YWCA/YMHA/YWHA, Youth Organizations

Application Procedures

Initial Contact: Send a brief letter of inquiry.
Application Requirements: Include a description of organization, proof of tax-exempt status, amount requested and purpose of funds sought.
Deadlines: None.
Review Process: Meetings are held in March, June, September, and December to review applications.

Restrictions

Does not support individuals or provide funds for seed money or deficit financing.

Foundation Officials

Jonathan D. Blake: director
Eleanor D. Bronson: director
Bruce G. Daniels: president
Fred H. Daniels, II: director
Janet B. Daniels: director

Eleanor D. Hodge: director
Amy Bronson Key: director
Carol Lawrence: assistant secretary
Sarah D. Morse: director
David A. Nicholson: director
William S. Nicholson: director
William O. Pettit, Jr.: treasurer, director
Meridith D. Wesby: director

Grants Analysis

Disclosure Period: fiscal year ending October 31, 2001
Total Grants: $550,000*
Number of Grants: 59
Average Grant: $9,322
Highest Grant: $50,000
Lowest Grant: $1,000
Typical Range: $5,000 to $20,000
***Note:** Giving excludes United Way.

Recent Grants

Note: Grants derived from 2000 Form 990.

General

80,000	Worcester Academy Development Office, Worcester, MA
65,000	Worcester Art Museum, Worcester, MA
40,000	Worcester Arts Museum, Worcester, MA
35,000	American Antiquarian Society, Worcester, MA
35,000	EcoTarium, Worcester, MA
33,000	UMASS Memorial Hahnemann and Cardiac Test, Worcester, MA
30,000	Mechanics Hall of Worcester, Worcester, MA
30,000	United Way of Central Massachusetts, Worcester, MA
20,000	Quinsigamond Community College, Worcester, MA
15,000	Preservation Worcester, Worcester, MA

DARBY FOUNDATION

Giving Contact

Katherine Brady, Trustee
PO Box 1410
Easton, MD 21601
Phone: (410)820-4300

Description

Founded: 1966
EIN: 136212178
Organization Type: Private Foundation
Giving Locations: northeastern United States.
Grant Types: General Support.

Donor Information

Founder: Nicholas F. Brady

Financial Summary

Total Giving: $191,000 (2001); $162,700 (2000); $154,000 (1998)
Giving Analysis: Giving for 2001 includes: foundation grants to United Way ($5,000) 1998: foundation grants to United Way ($2,500)
Assets: $2,244,789 (2001); $2,293,328 (2000); $2,012,342 (1998)

Typical Recipients

Arts & Humanities: Arts Associations & Councils, Historic Preservation, History & Archaeology, Libraries, Museums/Galleries, Opera, Performing Arts, Theater
Civic & Public Affairs: Botanical Gardens/Parks, Clubs, Civic & Public Affairs-General, Public Policy, Safety, Zoos/Aquariums
Education: Business Education, Colleges & Universities, Education-General, Medical Education, Private Education (Precollege), Student Aid

Environment: Environment-General, Resource Conservation
Health: Clinics/Medical Centers, Diabetes, Emergency/Ambulance Services, Eyes/Blindness, Hospices, Hospitals, Medical Research, Research/Studies Institutes, Single-Disease Health Associations
International: Foreign Educational Institutions, Health Care/Hospitals, Human Rights, International Development, Missionary/Religious Activities
Religion: Churches
Social Services: Big Brother/Big Sister, Child Abuse, Child Welfare, Community Service Organizations, Day Care, Delinquency & Criminal Rehabilitation, Domestic Violence, Food/Clothing Distribution, Recreation & Athletics, Scouts, Senior Services, Shelters/Homelessness, Social Services-General, United Funds/United Ways, YMCA/YWCA/YMHA/YWHA, Youth Organizations

Application Procedures

Initial Contact: Send a brief letter of inquiry.
Deadlines: None.
Notes: Primarily supports preselected organizations.

Foundation Officials

Katherine D. Brady: trustee
Nicholas Frederick Brady: trustee B New York, NY 1930. ED Yale University BA (1952); Harvard University MBA (1954). CORP AFFIL director: Amerada Hess Corp. NONPR AFFIL trustee: Boys Club Newark. CLUB AFFIL Lunch Club; Bond New York Club; The Links Club.

Grants Analysis

Disclosure Period: calendar year ending 2001
Total Grants: $186,000*
Number of Grants: 22
Average Grant: $8,455
Highest Grant: $25,000
Lowest Grant: $2,000
Typical Range: $5,000 to $10,000
***Note:** Giving excludes United Way.

Recent Grants

Note: Grants derived from 2001 Form 990.

General

25,000	Skillman Association
25,000	Vice President's House
15,000	Lyford Cay Foundation, Nassau Bahamas
10,000	C.S.W.I.
10,000	Friends of the Island Academy, NY
10,000	Iona Senior Services, Washington, DC
10,000	National Gallery of Art, Washington, DC
10,000	National Museum of Racing, Saratoga Springs, NY
10,000	National Museum of Women in the Arts, Washington, DC
10,000	Talbot Hospice Foundation, Easton, MD

HUGH AND HAZEL DARLING FOUNDATION

Giving Contact

Richard L. Stack, Trustee
520 S. Grand Ave. 7th Floor
Los Angeles, CA 90071-2645
Phone: (213)683-5200
Fax: (213)627-7795
E-mail: rstack@dhrlaw.com

Description

Founded: 1988
EIN: 956874901
Organization Type: General Purpose Foundation
Giving Locations: CA
Grant Types: Capital, Endowment, Multiyear/Continuing Support.

Donor Information

Founder: The foundation was established in 1988 from the estate of Hugh Darling and Hazel Darling after Mr. Darling passed away in 1986 and Mrs. Darling passed away in 1987.
Mr. Darling was a prominent lawyer in Southern California for more than 50 years. As an undergraduate, he attended the University of California at Berkeley, and he received his LL.B degree from the University of Southern California School of Law in 1927. He opened a law office with a partner in 1928 that today is known as the law firm of Darling, Hall & Rae in Los Angeles, CA. Mr. Darling developed an expertise in aviation law and served on the board of directors for Western Airlines.
He also belonged to many civic associations, and served as the mayor of Beverly Hills in 1960-61. A former president of the Los Angeles County Bar Association, he visited law schools as a speaker and used his influence to further the support of legal education in California.

Financial Summary

Total Giving: $2,003,500 (2001); $2,100,000 (2000); $2,011,000 (1999)
Giving Analysis: Giving for 2001 includes: foundation scholarships ($130,000) 2000: foundation scholarships ($124,000)
Assets: $32,209,866 (2001); $34,958,662 (2000); $34,773,303 (1999)
Gifts Received: $27,000,000 (1996); $135,664 (1995); $102,000 (1994). Note: The foundation received a one time gift from the will of Thomas C. Case.

Typical Recipients

Arts & Humanities: Libraries, Public Broadcasting
Civic & Public Affairs: Legal Aid, Public Policy
Education: Afterschool/Enrichment Programs, Business Education, Colleges & Universities, Education Funds, Education-General, Legal Education, Private Education (Precollege), Religious Education, Science/Mathematics Education, Special Education, Student Aid
Health: Speech & Hearing
International: Foreign Educational Institutions
Religion: Religious Welfare, Seminaries
Science: Science Museums
Social Services: At-Risk Youth, Community Centers, Crime Prevention, People with Disabilities, Recreation & Athletics, Scouts, Social Services-General, YMCA/YWCA/YMHA/YWHA, Youth Organizations

Application Procedures

Initial Contact: Applicants should submit a detailed one- or two-page letter of proposal.
Application Requirements: Letters should include appropriate contact and mailing information, a description of the project, and the amount requested.
Deadlines: None.

Restrictions

Grants are limited to California educational institutions with a primary emphasis on legal education. The foundation does not make grants to individuals.

Foundation Officials

Richard L. Stack: trustee B Los Angeles, CA 1947. ED University of California, Los Angeles BA (1969); Loyola University JD (1973). PRIM CORP EMPL attorney: Darling Hall & Rae. NONPR AFFIL member: Saint Thomas More Society.

Grants Analysis

Disclosure Period: calendar year ending 2001
Total Grants: $1,873,500*
Number of Grants: 25
Average Grant: $51,500*
Highest Grant: $250,000
Lowest Grant: $2,500
Typical Range: $20,000 to $150,000

*Note: Giving excludes scholarships. Average grant figure excludes highest grant.

Recent Grants

Note: Grants derived from 2001 Form 990.

General

250,000	Chapman University, Orange, CA -- books and publications for library
250,000	Loyola Law School, Los Angeles, CA -- library renovation
200,000	California Lutheran University, Thousand Oaks, CA -- facilities construction
200,000	University of San Francisco of Law School, San Francisco, CA -- facilities renovation
200,000	University of Southern California Law School, Los Angeles, CA -- library renovation
200,000	Westmont College, Santa Barbara, CA -- facilities construction
185,000	Hope International University, Fullerton, CA -- student scholarships
150,000	Deep Springs College, Deep Springs, CA -- construction of facilities
50,000	Pacific Research Institute, San Francisco, CA -- public education
30,000	St. James School, Los Angeles, CA -- facilities construction

CHARLES H. DATER FOUNDATION

Giving Contact

Bruce A. Krone, Secretary & Trustee
602 Main Street, Suite 302
Cincinnati, OH 45202
Phone: (513)241-2734
E-mail: info@DaterFoundation.org
Web: http://www.daterfoundation.org

Description

Founded: 1985
EIN: 311150951
Organization Type: Private Foundation
Giving Locations: OH: Cincinnati including the greater metropolitan area
Grant Types: Capital, General Support, Multiyear/Continuing Support, Project, Scholarship, Seed Money.

Financial Summary

Total Giving: $2,633,500 (fiscal year ending August 31, 2001); $2,510,500 (fiscal 2000); $2,074,000 (fiscal 1998)
Giving Analysis: Giving for fiscal 2001 includes: foundation scholarships ($60,000); fiscal 2000: foundation scholarships ($70,000) fiscal 1998: foundation ($2,074,000)
Assets: $51,474,475 (fiscal 2001); $64,052,100 (fiscal 2000); $50,257,022 (fiscal 1998)
Gifts Received: $17,502,704 (fiscal 1995); $3,646,578 (fiscal 1994); $78,285 (fiscal 1992). Note: In fiscal 1995, contributions were received from the Charles H. Dater Trust.

Typical Recipients

Arts & Humanities: Arts Associations & Councils, Arts Outreach, Arts & Humanities-General, Historic Preservation, History & Archaeology, Libraries, Museums/Galleries, Music, Opera, Performing Arts, Public Broadcasting, Theater
Civic & Public Affairs: Clubs, Community Foundations, Women's Affairs, Zoos/Aquariums
Education: Arts/Humanities Education, Business Education, Colleges & Universities, Education-General, International Studies, Literacy, Private Education

(Precollege), Public Education (Precollege), Secondary Education (Public), Special Education, Student Aid
Environment: Environment-General
Health: Cancer, Children's Health/Hospitals, Hospitals, Multiple Sclerosis, Prenatal Health Issues, Public Health, Single-Disease Health Associations, Speech & Hearing
International: International Peace & Security Issues
Religion: Churches, Dioceses, Ministries, Religious Organizations, Religious Welfare, Social/Policy Issues
Science: Science Museums
Social Services: Child Abuse, Child Welfare, Community Centers, Community Service Organizations, Day Care, Delinquency & Criminal Rehabilitation, Domestic Violence, Family Services, Food/Clothing Distribution, Homes, People with Disabilities, Recreation & Athletics, Shelters/Homelessness, United Funds/United Ways, YMCA/YWCA/YMHA/YWHA, Youth Organizations

Application Procedures

Initial Contact: Return completed application form. along with proof of tax-exempt status.
Deadlines: None.

Restrictions

Focus is on the children in the greater Cincinnati, OH, area. Also does not fund individuals, capital funds, or scholarships directly to individuals.

Additional Information

Publications: Application Form

Foundation Officials

Stanley J. Frank, Jr.: vice president, trustee
Bruce A. Krone: secretary, trustee
Dorothy G. Krone: vice president, trustee
David L. Olberding: vice president, trustee
John Donald Silvati: vice president, trustee B Cincinnati, OH 1937. ED Xavier University BSBA (1959). PRIM CORP EMPL president, manager: Merrill Lynch. NONPR AFFIL member: Institute Certified Financial Planners; member: International Association Financial Planners. CLUB AFFIL member: Kenwood Country Club.

Grants Analysis

Disclosure Period: fiscal year ending August 31, 2001
Total Grants: $2,573,500*
Number of Grants: 117
Average Grant: $20,892*
Highest Grant: $150,000
Lowest Grant: $3,000
Typical Range: $10,000 to $50,000
*Note: Giving excludes scholarships. Average grant figure excludes highest grant.

Recent Grants

Note: Grants derived from 2000 Form 990.

Library-Related

90,000	Public Library of Cincinnati and Hamilton County, Cincinnati, OH -- for Westwood Branch expansion
30,000	Public Library of Cincinnati and Hamilton County, Cincinnati, OH -- for expansion of the Westwood branch

General

100,000	Channel 48, WCET -- for "enriching our lives" campaign
100,000	Children's Hospital Medical Center -- research for the cure of leukemia
100,000	Emmanuel Community Center, Inc., Louisville, KY
100,000	YMCA - Clippard Family Branch -- aquatic center

75,000	WVXU -- for youth programs
65,000	Children's Theater -- 2000-2001 season sponsor
65,000	Cincinnati Museum Center, Cincinnati, OH -- for youth and educational floor programs
65,000	CISE, Cincinnati, OH -- transportation and admissions for field trips
60,000	Perlman Center of CHMC -- for technology program
50,000	Cincinnati Opera, Cincinnati, OH -- for education and outreach program

DAUGHERTY FOUNDATION

Giving Contact

Alex R. Hoffman
15 W. South Temple, Second Floor
Salt Lake City, UT 84101

Description

Founded: 1965
EIN: 826010665
Organization Type: Private Foundation
Giving Locations: ID: including eastern Idaho
Grant Types: General Support.

Donor Information

Founder: US Bank Idaho NA

Financial Summary

Total Giving: $727,356 (2002); $827,201 (2001); $814,893 (2000)
Assets: $582,013 (2002); $1,292,453 (2001); $2,113,113 (2000)

Typical Recipients

Arts & Humanities: Arts Associations & Councils, Arts Centers, Arts Outreach, Libraries, Music
Civic & Public Affairs: Clubs, Community Foundations, Employment/Job Training, Housing, Law & Justice, Legal Aid, Zoos/Aquariums
Education: Arts/Humanities Education, Business Education, Colleges & Universities, Elementary Education (Private), Elementary Education (Public), Education-General, Medical Education, Public Education (Precollege), Secondary Education (Public), Student Aid
Environment: Environment-General
Health: Children's Health/Hospitals, Clinics/Medical Centers, Diabetes, Emergency/Ambulance Services, Health-General, Hospices, Hospitals, Medical Rehabilitation, Public Health, Research/Studies Institutes
Religion: Churches, Religion-General, Ministries, Religious Welfare
Social Services: At-Risk Youth, Big Brother/Big Sister, Child Welfare, Community Service Organizations, Family Services, Food/Clothing Distribution, Homes, People with Disabilities, Recreation & Athletics, Scouts, Shelters/Homelessness, Social Services-General, Special Olympics, United Funds/United Ways, YMCA/YWCA/YMHA/YWHA, Youth Organizations

Application Procedures

Initial Contact: Send a brief letter of inquiry.
Application Requirements: Include amount requested, purpose of funds sought, and proof of tax-exempt status.
Deadlines: July 31.

Restrictions

Limited to eastern ID youth organizations.

Additional Information

Publications: Informational Brochure (including Application Guidelines)
Trust(s): U.S. Bank National Association IN

Grants Analysis

Disclosure Period: calendar year ending 2002
Total Grants: $727,356
Number of Grants: 19
Average Grant: $9,698*
Highest Grant: $145,471
Lowest Grant: $1,000
Typical Range: $5,000 to $15,000
*Note: Average grant figure excludes four highest grants ($581,884).

Recent Grants

Note: Grants derived from 2001 Form 990.

General

165,440	Elks Rehabilitation Hospital, Boise, ID
165,440	Pworth Village, NE
165,440	Shriners Hospital, Salt Lake City, UT
165,440	Shriners Hospital, Salt Lake City, UT
70,000	Idaho Community Foundation, Boise, ID
20,000	Idaho State University, Boise, ID -- for Performing Arts Center
10,000	Harbor House Shelter, Idaho Falls, ID
7,124	Family Service Alliance, Pocatello, ID
5,000	Big Brothers Big Sisters, Idaho Falls, ID
5,000	Development Workshop, Idaho Falls, ID

DAVENPORT-HATCH FOUNDATION

Giving Contact

Bill McKee, Contact
Care of Fleet Trust Co.
1 East Ave.
Rochester, NY 14604
Phone: (716)238-3300

Description

Founded: 1952
EIN: 166027105
Organization Type: General Purpose Foundation
Giving Locations: NY: Rochester including surrounding metropolitan area
Grant Types: Capital, Multiyear/Continuing Support, Project, Scholarship, Seed Money.

Donor Information

Founder: Established in 1952 by the late Augustus Hatch .

Financial Summary

Total Giving: $1,858,620 (fiscal year ending May 31, 2002); $2,105,376 (fiscal 2001); $1,796,171 (fiscal 1999)
Giving Analysis: Giving for fiscal 1999 includes: foundation scholarships ($29,000); foundation grants to United Way ($50,000) foundation grants to United Way ($100,000)
Assets: $37,645,592 (fiscal 2002); $42,178,183 (fiscal 2001); $41,170,672 (fiscal 1999)
Gifts Received: $4,569 (fiscal 1992)

Typical Recipients

Arts & Humanities: Arts Festivals, Arts Outreach, Dance, Film & Video, Historic Preservation, History & Archaeology, Libraries, Museums/Galleries, Music, Opera, Performing Arts, Public Broadcasting, Theater
Civic & Public Affairs: African American Affairs, Business/Free Enterprise, Clubs, Economic Development, Employment/Job Training, Civic & Public Affairs-General, Housing, Urban & Community Affairs, Women's Affairs, Zoos/Aquariums
Education: Arts/Humanities Education, Business Education, Colleges & Universities, Community & Junior Colleges, Elementary Education (Private), Engineering/Technological Education, Education-General, Literacy, Medical Education, Private Education (Precollege), Public Education (Precollege), Science/

Mathematics Education, Secondary Education (Private), Student Aid
Health: AIDS/HIV, Alzheimers Disease, Cancer, Clinics/Medical Centers, Emergency/Ambulance Services, Health-General, Geriatric Health, Health Organizations, Heart, Home-Care Services, Hospices, Hospitals, Kidney, Long-Term Care, Medical Rehabilitation, Medical Research, Medical Training, Mental Health, Multiple Sclerosis, Nursing Services, Prenatal Health Issues, Public Health, Single-Disease Health Associations, Speech & Hearing, Trauma Treatment
International: Foreign Arts Organizations, International Peace & Security Issues
Religion: Churches, Religion-General, Jewish Causes, Religious Organizations, Religious Organizations, Religious Welfare, Synagogues/Temples
Science: Science Museums, Scientific Centers & Institutes, Scientific Research
Social Services: Camps, Child Welfare, Community Centers, Community Service Organizations, Crime Prevention, Day Care, Domestic Violence, Emergency Relief, Family Planning, Family Services, Homes, People with Disabilities, Recreation & Athletics, Scouts, Senior Services, Shelters/Homelessness, Social Services-General, Substance Abuse, United Funds/United Ways, Veterans, Volunteer Services, YMCA/YWCA/YMHA/YWHA, Youth Organizations

Application Procedures

Initial Contact: The foundation has no formal grant procedure or grant application form.
Deadlines: None.

Restrictions

The foundation does not make grants to individuals.

Foundation Officials

Robert J. Brinkman: director B 1944. ED University of Denver BA (1967). PRIM CORP EMPL president: Albert Gates Inc.
William L. Ely: director B 1940. ED Syracuse University BS (1962). PRIM CORP EMPL president, treasurer, secretary: Samuel Sloan & Co. Inc. ADD CORP EMPL president: Heyer Metro Distributors Inc.; president: Metro Associates. CORP AFFIL officer: Saint Augustine Road Corp.
Helen H. Heller: secretary, treasurer, director
A. Thomas Hildebrandt: director
Austin E. Hildebrandt: president, director
Mary Hildebrandt: director
Lindsey Knoble: director
John Ross: director
David H. Taylor: vice president, director B 1944. PRIM CORP EMPL president, treasurer, director: Hart Taylor Lincoln Mercury.
Douglas F. Taylor: director PRIM CORP EMPL vice president, secretary, director: Hart Taylor Lincoln Mercury.
Shirley Warren: director

Grants Analysis

Disclosure Period: fiscal year ending May 31, 2002
Total Grants: $1,803,620*
Number of Grants: 50
Average Grant: $36,072
Highest Grant: $200,000
Lowest Grant: $1,000
Typical Range: $10,000 to $75,000
*Note: Giving excludes United Way.

Recent Grants

Note: Grants derived from 2002 Form 990.

General

200,000	Eastman School of Music, Rochester, NY -- for capital
125,000	Hillside Children's Center, Rochester, NY -- for capital
100,000	Al Sigl Center, Rochester, NY -- for the Respite Home Campaign
100,000	American Red Cross, New York, NY -- for New York City Relief Fund
100,000	Lakeside Health System, Brockport, NY -- building for next generation
100,000	Nazareth College, Rochester, NY -- for capital
100,000	RIT -- for new field house and activities center
100,000	University of Rochester, Rochester, NY -- for Resource Center
75,000	Otetiana Council -- for Camp Pioneer facilities
70,000	Geva Theater, Rochester, NY -- to refurbish main stage area

DAVENPORT TRUST FUND

Giving Contact

Richard E. Jackson, Trustee
55 Front St.
Bath, ME 04530
Phone: (207)443-3431

Description

Founded: 1927
EIN: 016009246
Organization Type: Private Foundation
Giving Locations: ME: Bath
Grant Types: General Support, Loan, Scholarship.

Donor Information

Founder: the late George P. Davenport

Financial Summary

Total Giving: $319,060 (2001); $298,704 (2000); $278,715 (1999). Note: Giving includes scholarships ($125,000).
Giving Analysis: Giving for 2001 includes: foundation scholarships ($140,000); 2000: foundation scholarships ($104,650); 1999: foundation scholarships ($123,975);
Assets: $6,721,170 (2001); $6,874,948 (2000); $6,704,734 (1999)
Gifts Received: $126,185 (2001); $500 (2000); $500 (1999). Note: In 2001, contributions were received from Ruby G. Beggs Charitable Remainder Unitrust. In 1993, contributions were received from the Maine Woman's Christian Temperance Union ($3,000).

Typical Recipients

Arts & Humanities: Libraries, Public Broadcasting
Civic & Public Affairs: Clubs, Civic & Public Affairs-General, Municipalities/Towns, Urban & Community Affairs, Women's Affairs
Education: Arts/Humanities Education, Colleges & Universities, Engineering/Technological Education, Education-General, Literacy, Medical Education, Public Education (Precollege), Special Education, Student Aid, Vocational & Technical Education
Health: Clinics/Medical Centers, Health Organizations, Hospitals, Medical Rehabilitation, Mental Health, Public Health
Religion: Churches, Religion-General, Religious Organizations, Religious Welfare
Social Services: Animal Protection, At-Risk Youth, Big Brother/Big Sister, Child Welfare, Emergency Relief, Food/Clothing Distribution, People with Disabilities, YMCA/YWCA/YMHA/YWHA, Youth Organizations

Application Procedures

Initial Contact: Application form required for scholarships. For non-scholarship grants send a brief letter of inquiry.
Application Requirements: Include amount requested, purpose of funds sought, and a budget and financial statements.
Deadlines: None.

Additional Information

Provides undergraduate scholarships to local students.

Publications: Application Form

Foundation Officials

John Wendell Coombs: trustee B Salt Lake City, UT January 29, 1905. ED University of Utah BA (1926); George Washington University LLB (1934). PRIM CORP EMPL chairman: Transintl Hotel Co. CORP AFFIL consult: Transam Corp.; consult: Transam Mtg Adv.

J. Franklin Howe: trustee

Richard E. Jackson: trustee

Barry M. Sturgeon: trustee

Grants Analysis

Disclosure Period: calendar year ending 2001

Total Grants: $179,060*

Number of Grants: 31

Average Grant: $5,776

Highest Grant: $25,000

Lowest Grant: $330

Typical Range: $1,000 to $10,000

***Note:** Giving excludes scholarships.

Recent Grants

Note: Grants derived from 2001 Form 990.

General

25,000	Merrymeeting Center for Child Development
24,000	Elmhurst, Inc., Bath, ME
18,090	City Bath, Bath, ME
15,000	Small Point Baptist Church, Small Point, ME
10,100	Bath Area Family YMCA, Bath, ME
10,000	American Red Cross
10,000	Midcoast Hospital, Inc., Brunswick, ME
9,000	University of Southern Maine, Portland, ME
7,000	Catholic Charities of Maine, Portland, ME
6,000	Colby-Sawyer College, New London, NY

EDWARD H. DAVIES BENEVOLENT FUND

Giving Contact

John D. Duncan, Trustee
c/o Verrill and Dana
1 Portland Sq.
PO Box 586
Portland, ME 04112-0586
Phone: (207)774-4000

Description

Founded: 1992

EIN: 010473137

Organization Type: Private Foundation

Giving Locations: ME: Portland

Grant Types: General Support.

Financial Summary

Total Giving: $145,410 (2001); $91,350 (2000); $106,000 (1999)

Giving Analysis: Giving for 2001 includes: foundation grants to United Way ($58,000)

Assets: $2,270,042 (2001); $2,479,877 (2000); $2,378,650 (1999)

Typical Recipients

Arts & Humanities: Ballet, Arts & Humanities-General, Historic Preservation, History & Archaeology, Libraries, Museums/Galleries, Music, Performing Arts, Theater

Civic & Public Affairs: African American Affairs, Civic & Public Affairs-General, Housing, Urban & Community Affairs, Women's Affairs, Zoos/Aquariums

Education: Arts/Humanities Education, Business Education, Colleges & Universities, Leadership Training

Environment: Environment-General, Resource Conservation

Health: Cancer, Clinics/Medical Centers, Emergency/Ambulance Services, Hospices

Religion: Churches, Religious Welfare

Social Services: Camps, Child Welfare, Community Centers, Community Service Organizations, Counseling, Family Services, Food/Clothing Distribution, People with Disabilities, Substance Abuse, United Funds/United Ways, YMCA/YWCA/YMHA/YWHA, Youth Organizations

Application Procedures

Initial Contact: Send a written proposal.

Application Requirements: Include general information about the program or project, financial information, and proof of tax-exempt status.

Decision Notification: Decisions are made in early December.

Restrictions

Contributionss are awarded to IRS approved tax-exempt organizations engaged in charitable activities, in the Portland, ME area.

Foundation Officials

John D. Duncan, Esq.: trustee

Alden Sawyer, Jr.: trustee

Frederic Thompson: trustee

Grants Analysis

Disclosure Period: calendar year ending 2001

Total Grants: $87,410*

Number of Grants: 29

Average Grant: $3,014

Highest Grant: $5,000

Lowest Grant: $400

Typical Range: $1,000 to $5,000

***Note:** Giving excludes United Way.

Recent Grants

Note: Grants derived from 2000 Form 990.

General

5,350	University of Southern Maine, Portland, ME -- Lifeline Center for Fitness
5,000	Liberty Ship Memorial Bug Light Enhancement
5,000	Maine Center for the Blind and Visually Impaired, Portland, ME
5,000	Portland Trails, Portland, ME
4,000	Peregrine Corporation
3,500	Community Counseling Center, Portland, ME
3,500	Holy Trinity Greek Orthodox Church
3,000	East End Kids Katering Inc.
3,000	Portland West Neighborhood Planning Council, Portland, ME
3,000	State YMCA Maine, Winthrop, ME

EDWIN W. AND CATHERINE M. DAVIS FOUNDATION

Giving Contact

Bette D. Moorman, President & Director
332 Minnesota St., Suite 2100
St. Paul, MN 55101-1308
Phone: (651)228-0935

Description

Founded: 1956

EIN: 416012064

Organization Type: Family Foundation

Giving Locations: nationally.

Grant Types: Fellowship, General Support, Operating Expenses, Project, Research, Scholarship.

Donor Information

Founder: Edwin Weyerhaeuser Davis, members of the Davis family

Financial Summary

Total Giving: $762,221 (2000); $625,932 (1999); $637,869 (1998)

Giving Analysis: Giving for 2000 includes: foundation scholarships ($97,000) 1999: foundation scholarships ($80,000)

Assets: $13,596,601 (2000); $15,017,667 (1999); $12,145,705 (1998)

Gifts Received: $191,348 (2000); $67,944 (1999); $84,733 (1998). Note: In 2000, contributions were received from 1993 Irrevocable Trust of M. E. Davis ($81,348) and the Estate Trust of Anne O'C Davis ($110,000). In 1998 and 1999, contributions were received from 1993 Irrevocable Trust of M. E. Davis.

Typical Recipients

Arts & Humanities: Arts Associations & Councils, Arts Centers, Arts Outreach, Historic Preservation, History & Archaeology, Libraries, Museums/Galleries, Music, Opera, Public Broadcasting, Theater

Civic & Public Affairs: Asian American Affairs, Botanical Gardens/Parks, Business/Free Enterprise, Civil Rights, Community Foundations, Housing, Nonprofit Management, Philanthropic Organizations, Public Policy, Safety, Zoos/Aquariums

Education: Colleges & Universities, Education Reform, Elementary Education (Public), Education-General, International Studies, Medical Education, Minority Education, Private Education (Precollege), Religious Education, Social Sciences Education, Student Aid

Environment: Environment-General, Resource Conservation, Wildlife Protection

Health: AIDS/HIV, Cancer, Children's Health/Hospitals, Clinics/Medical Centers, Emergency/Ambulance Services, Eyes/Blindness, Health-General, Health Policy/Cost Containment, Health Funds, Health Organizations, Hospitals, Medical Rehabilitation, Medical Research, Mental Health, Nursing Services, Research/Studies Institutes, Single-Disease Health Associations

International: Health Care/Hospitals, Human Rights, International Environmental Issues, International Peace & Security Issues, International Relations, International Relief Efforts

Religion: Churches

Science: Science Museums

Social Services: Animal Protection, Camps, Child Welfare, Community Service Organizations, Day Care, Emergency Relief, Family Planning, Family Services, Recreation & Athletics, Refugee Assistance, United Funds/United Ways, YMCA/YWCA/YMHA/YWHA, Youth Organizations

Application Procedures

Initial Contact: Send a brief letter of inquiry.

Application Requirements: Include proof of tax-exempt status.

Deadlines: None.

Restrictions

The foundation does not make grants to individuals, although it may support scholarships, fellowships, and research programs of established organizations. The foundation generally does not make grants for capital purposes, building and equipment, endowment, or loans. The foundation also prefers not to make long-term commitments in order to preserve flexibility for changing social conditions.

Additional Information

The Davis family is related to the Weyerhaeuser family, who founded the Weyerhaeuser Company.
Publications: Report on Programs; Policies and Procedures

Foundation Officials

Frederick W. Davis, II: secretary, director
Mary E. Davis: vice president, director
Richard T. Holm: assistant treasurer
Joseph S. Micallef: assistant secretary, director B 1933. PRIM CORP EMPL president, chief executive officer, treasurer, director: Fiduciary Counselling Inc. PRIM NONPR EMPL sec-treas: Rock Island Co. CORP AFFIL secretary, treasurer: Rock Island Co.
Bette D. Moorman: president, director CORP AFFIL director: NCR Corp.

Grants Analysis

Disclosure Period: calendar year ending 2000
Total Grants: $665,221*
Number of Grants: 57
Average Grant: $10,804*
Highest Grant: $60,221
Typical Range: $5,000 to $20,000
*Note: Average grant excludes highest grant. Giving excludes scholarship.

Recent Grants

Note: Grants derived from 1999 Form 990.

General

104,831	Fulfillment Fund, Los Angeles, CA -- children's program
50,000	National Tropical Botanical Garden, La-wai, HI
40,000	Regents of the University of California Los Angeles, Los Angeles, CA
30,000	National Medical Fellowships, New York, NY
30,000	University of California Los Angeles Foundation, Los Angeles, CA
28,000	International Rescue Committee, New York, NY
25,000	Teach for America, Oakland, CA
20,000	Camp Nor'wester, Lopez, WA -- memorial
20,000	Children's Health Council, Palo Alto, CA -- scholarship
20,000	International Dyslexia Association, Baltimore, MD

EVELYN Y. DAVIS FOUNDATION

Giving Contact

Evelyn Y. Davis, Trustee
Watergate Office Building
2600 Virginia Ave., NW, Suite 215
Washington, DC 20037-1905
Phone: (202)737-7755

Description

Founded: 1989
EIN: 521632305
Organization Type: Private Foundation
Grant Types: General Support.

Financial Summary

Total Giving: $137,002 (2001); $74,500 (2000); $47,100 (1996)

Assets: $1,772,040 (2001); $1,579,528 (2000); $659,665 (1996)
Gifts Received: $300,000 (2001); $300,000 (2000); $200,000 (1993). Note: In 2000 and 2001, contributions were received from Evelyn Y. Davis. In 1993, contributions were received from Evelyn Y. Davis.

Typical Recipients

Arts & Humanities: Arts Associations & Councils, Arts Centers, Arts Institutes, Libraries, Museums/Galleries, Music, Performing Arts
Civic & Public Affairs: Botanical Gardens/Parks
Education: Colleges & Universities, Journalism/Media Education, Student Aid
Health: Cancer, Hospitals
Social Services: Community Service Organizations, People with Disabilities, Senior Services

Application Procedures

Initial Contact: Application should be in writing describing the organization requesting funds and the purpose of funds sought. The application should be signed by the executive director or president of the organization.
Deadlines: November 15.

Restrictions

Special emphasis is placed on activities in journalism and business.

Foundation Officials

Evelyn Y. Davis: trustee

Grants Analysis

Disclosure Period: calendar year ending 2001
Total Grants: $137,002
Number of Grants: 4
Highest Grant: $70,450
Lowest Grant: $1,962

Recent Grants

Note: Grants derived from 2000 Form 990.

General

25,000	New Jersey Performing Arts Center, Newark, NJ
25,000	Scottsdale Cultural Council, Scottsdale, AZ
14,500	Woodruff Arts Center, Atlanta, GA
10,000	Johns Hopkins Institution, Baltimore, MD

IRENE E. AND GEORGE A. DAVIS FOUNDATION

Giving Contact

Mary Walachy, Executive Director
One Monarch Place, Suite 1450
Springfield, MA 01144
Phone: (413)734-8336
Fax: (413)734-7845
E-mail: info@davisfdn.org
Web: http://www.davisfdn.org

Description

Founded: 1970
EIN: 237102734
Organization Type: General Purpose Foundation
Giving Locations: MA
Grant Types: Award, Challenge, General Support, Matching, Multiyear/Continuing Support, Scholarship.

Donor Information

Founder: Established in 1970 by the late Irene E. Davis and George A. Davis, and was incorporated

under the laws of the Commonwealth of Massachusetts in 1972.

Financial Summary

Total Giving: $4,415,084 (2000); $4,033,144 (1999); $3,390,979 (1998)
Giving Analysis: Giving for 2000 includes: foundation grants to United Way ($135,370); 1997: foundation scholarships ($521,000) 1995: foundation scholarships ($10,000)
Assets: $69,752,912 (2000); $69,572,033 (1999); $64,314,907 (1998)
Gifts Received: $2,002,720 (2000); $4,006,314 (1998); $7,154,196 (1997). Note: In 1998 and 2000, contributions were received from American Saw and Manufacturing Co.

Typical Recipients

Arts & Humanities: Arts Associations & Councils, Arts Festivals, Arts Funds, Historic Preservation, History & Archaeology, Libraries, Museums/Galleries, Public Broadcasting
Civic & Public Affairs: African American Affairs, Clubs, Community Foundations, Economic Development, Employment/Job Training, Civic & Public Affairs-General, Housing, Native American Affairs, Nonprofit Management, Public Policy, Urban & Community Affairs, Women's Affairs, Zoos/Aquariums
Education: Arts/Humanities Education, Business Education, Colleges & Universities, Education Associations, Education Funds, Elementary Education (Public), Education-General, International Exchange, International Studies, Minority Education, Private Education (Precollege), Public Education (Precollege), School Volunteerism, Science/Mathematics Education, Secondary Education (Private), Special Education, Student Aid, Vocational & Technical Education
Environment: Environment-General, Wildlife Protection
Health: AIDS/HIV, Children's Health/Hospitals, Clinics/Medical Centers, Emergency/Ambulance Services, Geriatric Health, Health Organizations, Hospitals, Mental Health, Nursing Services, Prenatal Health Issues, Public Health, Research/Studies Institutes, Single-Disease Health Associations
International: Foreign Arts Organizations, Foreign Educational Institutions, Health Care/Hospitals, International Affairs
Religion: Churches, Dioceses, Religion-General, Jewish Causes, Religious Welfare
Social Services: At-Risk Youth, Big Brother/Big Sister, Child Welfare, Community Centers, Community Service Organizations, Domestic Violence, Food/Clothing Distribution, People with Disabilities, Recreation & Athletics, Scouts, Social Services-General, United Funds/United Ways, Volunteer Services, YMCA/YWCA/YMHA/YWHA, Youth Organizations

Application Procedures

Initial Contact: Send letter of intent or call to request an application.
Application Requirements: Initial letter should outline the purpose, scope, estimated cost, and method of evaluation of specific goals. The organization will be notified if the foundation would like to review a full proposal. If requested, the original proposal (and two copies) should be submitted, unbound, and must include a complete application form; a copy of the most recent letter of exemption under Section 501(c)(3) of the IRS Code; a copy of a form or letter classifying the applicant under Section 509(a) of the IRS Code; an affirmation letter on separate letterhead of the organization, signed by a responsible officer, director, trustee, or chief executive officer, that the IRS determination has not been revoked and that the present operation and sources of support are not inconsistent with the organization's continuing classification as set forth in the determination letter; one copy of the latest audited statement; the project budget; a list of sources of funding; three bids if the funding is for a construction

project; a statement that the grant request is executed by a person authorized to submit on behalf of the organization; the names and affiliation of board members responsible for project management; and the name and qualifications of the proposed grant administrator. All proposals should include a description of the measurable program objectives to be achieved.
Deadlines: Complete proposals must be received no later than February 1, May 1, August 1, or November 1 for review at the next regularly scheduled meeting.
Review Process: The trustees meet quarterly (March, June, September, December) to review proposals. Applicants will be notified in writing of the action taken by the foundation, usually within two weeks of the board meeting.

Restrictions

The foundation's guidelines usually preclude support for individuals, endowments, scholarships, internships, continuing support of current programs, debt reduction, multiple proposals per year from the same organization, other private foundations, and program-related loans. Limited to the Hamden County, Massachusetts area.

Additional Information

The foundation encourages collaborative proposals involving multiple providers.

Foundation Officials

John H. Davis: trustee B 1949. ED Nichols College (1972). PRIM CORP EMPL president, treasurer, director: America Saw & Manufacturing Co.
Mary E. Davis: trustee CORP AFFIL director: American Saw & Manufacturing Co.
Stephen A. Davis: trustee B 1957. PRIM CORP EMPL president: America Saw & Manufacturing Co.
Ann T. Keiser: mgr fin admin
Robert R. Lepak: trustee
Mary E. Walacky: executive director

Grants Analysis

Disclosure Period: calendar year ending 2000
Total Grants: $4,279,714*
Number of Grants: 192
Average Grant: $22,290
Highest Grant: $300,000
Lowest Grant: $100
Typical Range: $5,000 to $50,000
*Note: Giving excludes United Way.

Recent Grants

Note: Grants derived from 2000 Form 990.

Library-Related

250,000	East Longmeadow Public Library, East Longmeadow, MA -- for expansion and renovation of the East Longmeadow Public Library

General

300,000	Roman Catholic Diocese of Springfield, Springfield, MA -- for Future of Hope Campaign
260,000	Bay Path College, Longmeadow, MA -- for development of Technology Education Center
250,000	Nichols College, Dudley, MA
250,000	Nichols College, Dudley, MA
200,000	Roman Catholic Diocese of Springfield, Springfield, MA -- for Future of Hope Campaign
125,000	Children's Study Home, Springfield, MA -- for Mill Pond Campus expansion
106,000	Community United Way of Pioneer Valley, Springfield, MA -- corporate pledge
100,000	Boston College, New York, NY -- to establish scholarship fund for Hampden County students
100,000	Dunbar Community Center, Inc., Springfield, MA -- for capital campaign

75,000	Forest Park Zoological Society, Forest Park, MA

JAMES A. AND JULIET L. DAVIS FOUNDATION

Giving Contact

Merl F. Sellers, President
1 Compound Drive
Hutchinson, KS 67502
Phone: (620)662-8331

Description

Founded: 1954
EIN: 486105748
Organization Type: Private Foundation
Giving Locations: KS: Hutchinson including metropolitan area
Grant Types: General Support, Scholarship.

Financial Summary

Total Giving: $244,965 (2001); $256,915 (2000); $236,514 (1999)
Giving Analysis: Giving for 2001 includes: foundation gifts to individuals ($16,000); foundation scholarships ($71,100); 2000: foundation scholarships ($66,250); 1999: foundation gifts to individuals ($82,750);
Assets: $4,676,348 (2001); $5,371,177 (2000); $5,380,183 (1999)

Typical Recipients

Arts & Humanities: Arts Associations & Councils, Community Arts, History & Archaeology, Libraries, Museums/Galleries, Music, Public Broadcasting, Theater
Civic & Public Affairs: Clubs, Community Foundations, Employment/Job Training, Civic & Public Affairs-General, Housing, Zoos/Aquariums
Education: Afterschool/Enrichment Programs, Colleges & Universities, Community & Junior Colleges, Education Funds, Literacy, Preschool Education, Private Education (Precollege), Public Education (Precollege), Science/Mathematics Education, Student Aid
Environment: Energy, Environment-General
Health: Clinics/Medical Centers, Emergency/Ambulance Services, Health-General, Hospices, Mental Health, Single-Disease Health Associations
Religion: Churches, Dioceses, Ministries, Religious Organizations, Religious Welfare
Social Services: Big Brother/Big Sister, Child Welfare, Community Service Organizations, Day Care, Emergency Relief, Family Planning, Food/Clothing Distribution, People with Disabilities, Scouts, Shelters/Homelessness, United Funds/United Ways, YMCA/YWCA/YMHA/YWHA, Youth Organizations

Application Procedures

Initial Contact: The foundation has no formal grant application procedure or application form.
Deadlines: March 15.

Additional Information

Provides scholarships to students graduating from Hutchinson High School.

Foundation Officials

William Y. Chalfant: secretary, treasurer
Ray E. Dillon, III: trustee
R. A. Edwards: trustee
Allen K. Fee: trustee
Kent Longenecker: trustee
Peter M. McDonald: president
Merl F. Sellers: vice president
V. Carol Winkley: assistant secretary, assistant treasurer

Grants Analysis

Disclosure Period: calendar year ending 2001
Total Grants: $157,865*
Number of Grants: 46
Average Grant: $2,397*
Highest Grant: $50,000
Lowest Grant: $165
Typical Range: $1,000 to $5,000
*Note: Giving excludes gifts to individuals; scholarships. Average grant figure excludes highest grant.

Recent Grants

Note: Grants derived from 2001 Form 990.

General

50,000	Reno County Historical Society, Hutchinson, KS -- for Salt Museum and supplies for children's place
25,000	New Beginnings Homeless Shelter, Hutchinson, KS -- for operations and public building fund
25,000	Salvation Army, Hutchinson, KS -- for public building fund
8,000	Boys and Girls Club of Hutchinson, Hutchinson, KS
8,000	Hutchinson Community College, Hutchinson, KS -- for scholarships
5,500	Training and Evaluation Center of Hutchinson, Inc., Hutchinson, KS -- for public unrestricted
3,000	Hutchinson Community Foundation, Hutchinson, KS -- living land foundation
2,500	Interfaith Housing Services, Hutchinson, KS
2,000	New Beginnings Homeless Shelter, Hutchinson, KS -- for operations and public building fund
2,000	Reno County Historical Society, Hutchinson, KS -- for Salt Museum and supplies for children's place

JOE C. DAVIS FOUNDATION

Giving Contact

Anne Fergerson, Administrative Assistant
908 Audubon Drive
Nashville, TN 37204
Phone: (615)297-1030
Fax: (615)463-2763
E-mail: bartonshan@home.com

Alternate Contact

28 White Bridge Road, Suite 210
Nashville, TN 37205

Description

Founded: 1976
EIN: 626125481
Organization Type: General Purpose Foundation
Giving Locations: TN: Nashville including metropolitan area
Grant Types: Capital, Challenge, Loan, Matching, Project, Research, Scholarship, Seed Money.

Donor Information

Founder: The foundation was established in 1976 by the late Joe C. Davis .

Financial Summary

Total Giving: $4,191,000 (fiscal year ending September 30, 2000); $4,241,000 (fiscal 1999); $2,663,421 (fiscal 1997)
Giving Analysis: Giving for fiscal 2000 includes: foundation grants to United Way ($10,000)
Assets: $92,558,288 (fiscal 2000); $92,558,288 (fiscal 1999); $63,459,454 (fiscal 1997)

Gifts Received: $70,038 (fiscal 1999); $69,999 (fiscal 1997); $103,381 (fiscal 1996). Note: Contributions were received from JCD Lead Trust.

Typical Recipients

Arts & Humanities: Libraries, Performing Arts
Civic & Public Affairs: Botanical Gardens/Parks, Clubs, Community Foundations, Economic Development, Civic & Public Affairs-General, Housing, Municipalities/Towns, Nonprofit Management, Philanthropic Organizations, Public Policy, Urban & Community Affairs
Education: Arts/Humanities Education, Business Education, Colleges & Universities, Continuing Education, Education Reform, Education-General, Legal Education, Medical Education, Preschool Education, Private Education (Precollege), Public Education (Precollege), Student Aid
Health: Alzheimers Disease, Cancer, Children's Health/Hospitals, Clinics/Medical Centers, Diabetes, Health Policy/Cost Containment, Health Organizations, Hospices, Hospitals, Hospitals (University Affiliated), Medical Research, Public Health, Speech & Hearing
Religion: Churches, Ministries, Religious Organizations, Religious Welfare
Social Services: At-Risk Youth, Big Brother/Big Sister, Camps, Child Welfare, Community Centers, Community Service Organizations, Counseling, Crime Prevention, Day Care, Family Services, Food/Clothing Distribution, Homes, Recreation & Athletics, Scouts, Senior Services, Shelters/Homelessness, Social Services-General, Substance Abuse, United Funds/United Ways, YMCA/YWCA/YMHA/YWHA, Youth Organizations

Application Procedures

Initial Contact: Send a two page letter proposal.
Application Requirements: Describe purpose, need, and budget.
Deadlines: July 1.

Restrictions

The foundation seeks to help people help themselves, encouraging individual initiative and responsibility. The foundation prefers one-time grants, rather than funding operating costs on a multi-year basis. The foundation only supports 501(c)(3) organizations.

Additional Information

Publications: Guidelines

Foundation Officials

Shannon Barton: program officer
Bond D. DeLoache: co-trustee
William R. DeLoache, Jr.: co-trustee
Dr. William R. DeLoache: co-trustee B Camden, SC March 27, 1920. ED Furman University (1937-1938); Vanderbilt University BA (1941); Vanderbilt University MD (1943). NONPR AFFIL member: Southern Society Pediatric Research; member advisory board: Vanderbilt University Medical Center; member: Southern Perinatal Association; senior associate: Greenville Memorial Hospital; member: South Carolina Medical Association; member: Greenville County Medical Society; member: American Medical Association; member: Greenville Chamber of Commerce; member: American Academy Pediatrics. CLUB AFFIL Poinsett Club; Rotary Club; Greenville Country Club.
Anne Fergerson: contact

Grants Analysis

Disclosure Period: fiscal year ending September 30, 2001
Total Grants: $4,241,000*
Number of Grants: 40
Average Grant: $106,025*
Highest Grant: $500,000
Typical Range: $5,000 to $50,000 and $200,000 to $500,000
*Note: Giving excludes United Way.

Recent Grants

Note: Grants derived from fiscal 2000 Form 990.

Library-Related
525,000   Nashville Public Library Foundation, Nashville, TN -- capital campaign

General
750,000   YMCA, Nashville, TN -- Outdoor Center
550,000   Montgomery Bell Academy, Nashville, TN -- scholarships and Teacher Programs
500,000   Vanderbilt Ingram Cancer Center, Nashville, TN -- research projects
500,000   Vanderbilt Medical Center, Nashville, TN -- research projects
500,000   Westminster School, Nashville, TN -- capital campaign
200,000   St. Vincent de Paul School, Nashville, TN -- capital campaign
150,000   Dede Wallace Center, Nashville, TN -- for programs
100,000   Senior Citizens, Nashville, TN -- capital campaign
100,000   Tennessee Golf Foundation, Franklin, TN -- First Tee Program
72,000   Vanderbilt University School of Law, Nashville, TN -- law and economics project

ARTHUR VINING DAVIS FOUNDATIONS

Giving Contact

Dr. Jonathan T. Howe, Executive Director
225 Water St., Ste. 1510
Jacksonville, FL 32202-5185
Phone: (904)359-0670
Fax: (904)359-0675
E-mail: arthurvining@bellsouth.net
Web: http://www.jvm.com/davis/

Description

Founded: 1952
EIN: 256018909
Organization Type: General Purpose Foundation
Giving Locations: nationally.
Grant Types: Capital, Challenge, Department, Endowment, Fellowship, General Support, Operating Expenses, Professorship, Project, Research, Scholarship.

Financial Summary

Total Giving: $361,643 (2001); $11,220,072 (2000); $11,226,128 (1999)
Assets: $227,318,646 (2002); $7,377,420 (2001); $244,353,000 (2000)

Typical Recipients

Arts & Humanities: Arts Centers, Film & Video, History & Archaeology, Libraries, Museums/Galleries, Music, Public Broadcasting, Theater
Civic & Public Affairs: Civic & Public Affairs-General, Nonprofit Management
Education: Arts/Humanities Education, Colleges & Universities, Continuing Education, Engineering/Technological Education, Environmental Education, Faculty Development, Education-General, International Studies, Leadership Training, Literacy, Medical Education, Minority Education, Private Education (Precollege), Public Education (Precollege), Religious Education, Science/Mathematics Education, Social Sciences Education, Student Aid
Environment: Resource Conservation
Health: Cancer, Children's Health/Hospitals, Clinics/Medical Centers, Health-General, Health Policy/Cost Containment, Health Organizations, Hospices, Hospitals, Hospitals (University Affiliated), Medical Research, Mental Health, Research/Studies Institutes

International: Foreign Educational Institutions, International Peace & Security Issues, Missionary/Religious Activities
Religion: Religious Organizations, Religious Welfare, Seminaries
Science: Scientific Centers & Institutes, Scientific Labs, Scientific Research
Social Services: Community Service Organizations, United Funds/United Ways

Application Procedures

Initial Contact: Applicants should submit a simple statement describing the proposed project. A budget outline should also be appended.
Application Requirements: All proposals must emanate from the president or other primary executive of an institution.
Deadlines: None.
Review Process: After evaluation of the initial proposal, further detailed information may be requested. Copies of audited financial statements for the past three years are normally requested.
Notes: Additional information is available from the Annual Report, guidelines, and the foundations Website: www.jvm.com/davis/.

Restrictions

The foundations do not support organizations outside of the U.S. and its possessions; individuals, except participants chosen by the grantee institution under an organized scholarship program; voter registration drives; voter education; efforts to influence elections or legislation; expenditures for non-charitable purposes; institutions primarily supported by governmental funds (except in healthcare and secondary education programs); projects incurring obligations extending over several years; private foundations within Sec. 509(A) of the 1969 Tax Reform Act.

Additional Information

The three foundations' assets are invested by corporate trustees and administered as separate legal entities. For the purposes of grantmaking, however, the three foundations function as a single philanthropic organization. The foundations also share a single administrative office in Jacksonville, FL.

Grants generally are made out of annual income, with minimal future commitments. Grantees are expected to prepare a brief written progress report one year after receipt of a grant, or sooner if the project is completed. A more detailed final report also will be required.

The foundations state that a decision not to fund a project is more often the result of funding limitations rather than a judgment of the quality of an applicant or its program. A decision not to fund does not preclude the future submission of a new proposal.

Mellon Bank, N.A., of Pittsburgh, PA, serves as corporate trustee for Foundations No. 1 and No. 2. SunTrust/North Florida, N.A., of Jacksonville, FL, serves as corporate trustee for Foundation No. 3.
Publications: Annual Report; Guidelines

Foundation Officials

Charlene Cook: admin assistant
Holbrook R. Davis: trustee ED Harvard University (1943).
J. H. Dow Davis: chairman
Joel P. Davis: trustee PRIM CORP EMPL senior vice president corporate planning & development: Gillette Co.
Jane M. Estes: chief financial officer
Doreen A. Flippin: grants administrator
Rev. Davis Given: trustee
Dr. Jonathan T. Howe: executive director B San Diego, CA 1935. ED United States Naval Academy BS (1957); Tufts University MA (1968); Tufts University PhD (1969).
William C. Keator: program director
Dr. Max King Morris: trustee B Springfield, MO 1924. ED United States Naval Academy BS (1947); Tufts

University MA Law (1960); Tufts University MA Economics (1961); Tufts University PhD (1967). PRIM CORP EMPL president: Thalassa Res Co. CORP AFFIL director: Jacksonville Electric Authority. NONPR AFFIL member: Middle East Institute; member: U.S. Naval Institute; member: Institute International Strategic Studies; member: Council Foreign Relations. CLUB AFFIL New York Yacht Club; Ponte Vedra Club; Belfry Club; Florida Yacht Club.
Dr. Ann O'Keefe: senior program officer
William R. Wright: trustee

Grants Analysis

Disclosure Period: calendar year ending 2002
Total Grants: $8,740,053*
Number of Grants: 47
Average Grant: $175,313
Highest Grant: $400,000
Lowest Grant: $30,000
***Note:** Grants analysis provided by foundation.

Recent Grants

Note: Grants derived from 2000 Form 990.

General

50,000	Hamilton College, Clinton, NY
50,000	University of Notre Dame, Notre Dame, IN
29,930	Institute for Educational Inquiry, Seattle, WA
25,000	DePauw University, Greencastle, IN
25,000	KCET Hollywood Bowl, Los Angeles, CA -- Woodrow Wilson Series
25,000	Pacific School of Religion, Berkeley, CA
25,000	University of Georgia, Athens, GA
25,000	Wofford College, Spartanburg, SC
24,506	University of Virginia School of Medicine, Charlottesville, VA
20,000	WETA, Washington, DC -- A Force More Powerful

WILLAMETTA K. DAY FOUNDATION

Giving Contact

Jonathan D. Jaffrey, Vice President, Secretary
865 S. Figueroa St., Suite 700
Los Angeles, CA 90017
Phone: (213)891-6300
Fax: (213)891-6300

Description

Founded: 1954
EIN: 956092476
Organization Type: Private Foundation
Giving Locations: CA
Grant Types: General Support.

Donor Information

Founder: the late Willametta K. Day

Financial Summary

Total Giving: $4,607,660 (2000); $1,784,225 (1999); $2,293,500 (1998)
Giving Analysis: Giving for 2000 includes: foundation grants to United Way ($60,000); 1999: foundation scholarships ($15,000); foundation grants to United Way ($37,500); 1998: foundation scholarships ($26,250); foundation grants to United Way ($68,250) foundation ($2,299,000)
Assets: $86,509,422 (2000); $80,154,409 (1999); $58,352,375 (1998)

Typical Recipients

Arts & Humanities: Arts Institutes, Community Arts, Film & Video, Arts & Humanities-General, Historic Preservation, History & Archaeology, Libraries, Museums/Galleries, Music, Opera

Civic & Public Affairs: Clubs, Community Foundations, Civic & Public Affairs-General, Hispanic Affairs, Housing, Legal Aid, Municipalities/Towns, Public Policy, Urban & Community Affairs
Education: Agricultural Education, Business Education, Colleges & Universities, Community & Junior Colleges, Education Reform, Elementary Education (Public), Education-General, Legal Education, Private Education (Precollege), Public Education (Precollege), Secondary Education (Public)
Health: AIDS/HIV, Cancer, Children's Health/Hospitals, Clinics/Medical Centers, Diabetes, Health Organizations, Hospices, Hospitals
International: International Affairs, International Organizations, International Relations, International Relief Efforts
Religion: Dioceses, Religious Organizations, Religious Welfare
Science: Science Museums, Scientific Centers & Institutes
Social Services: Child Welfare, Community Service Organizations, Delinquency & Criminal Rehabilitation, Food/Clothing Distribution, Recreation & Athletics, United Funds/United Ways, YMCA/YWCA/YMHA/YWHA, Youth Organizations

Application Procedures

Initial Contact: The foundation has no formal grant application procedure or application form.

Restrictions

Does not support individuals.

Foundation Officials

Jerry W. Carlton: president, trustee
Dorothy W. Day: trustee
Howard M. Day: vice president, trustee PRIM CORP EMPL general partner: Crescent Investment Co.
Robert A. Day, Jr.: chairman, trustee B 1945. ED Claremont McKenna College (1965). PRIM CORP EMPL founder, chairman, chief executive officer: TCW Asset Management Co. CORP AFFIL chairman, chief executive officer, director: Trust Co. West; chairman, chief executive officer: TCW Capital Investment Corp.; chairman, director: TCW Group Inc.; director: Freeport-McMoRan Copper Gold Inc.; chairman, director: Oakmont Corp.; general partner: Crescent Investment Co.; director: Fisher Scientific International Inc. NONPR AFFIL chairman investments committee, trustee: Claremont McKenna College.
Tammis M. Day: vice president, trustee PRIM CORP EMPL general partner: Crescent Investment Co.
Theodore J. Day: vice president, trustee PRIM CORP EMPL general partner: Crescent Investment Co.
Joseph Deegan-Day: trustee
Lucinda Fournier: trustee
Steven D. Holzman: secretary
Jonathan D. Jaffrey: vice president, secretary
Javier G. Rodriguez: cfo, treasurer

Grants Analysis

Disclosure Period: calendar year ending 2000
Total Grants: $4,547,660*
Number of Grants: 129
Average Grant: $19,904*
Highest Grant: $2,000,000
Lowest Grant: $500
Typical Range: $5,000 to $50,000
***Note:** Giving excludes UNW. Average grant figure excludes highest grant.

Recent Grants

Note: Grants derived from 1999 Form 990.

General

300,000	Stanford University Graduate School of Business, Stanford, CA
100,000	Robert Louis Stevenson School, Pebble Beach, CA
75,000	Claremont McKenna College, Claremont, CA

75,000	Linfield College, McMinnville, OR
75,000	Linfield College, McMinnville, OR
75,000	National Cowboy Hall of Fame, Oklahoma City, OK
75,000	Northeastern Nevada Historical Society, Elko, NV
75,000	University of Nevada Reno Foundation, Reno, NV
67,500	Marylhurst University, Marylhurst, OR
52,500	Dechutes County Fair

DAYTON POWER AND LIGHT CO.

Company Headquarters

1900 Dryden Rd.
Dayton, OH 45439
Web: http://www.waytogo.com/

Company Description

Employees: 2,908
SIC(s): 4911 Electric Services, 4924 Natural Gas Distribution, 4961 Steam & Air-Conditioning Supply.
Parent Company: DPL, Inc., 1065 Woodman Dr., Dayton, OH, United States

Nonmonetary Support

Range: $30,000 - $50,000
Type: Donated Equipment; In-kind Services
Note: Funds goodwill advertising, and dinner/benefit tickets. Requests for nonmonetary support are handled directly by area managers.

Dayton Power and Light Co. Foundation

Giving Contact

Virginia Strausburg, Executive Director
Dayton Power and Light Co. Foundation
PO Box 20331
Dayton, OH 45420
Phone: (937)258-8841
Fax: (937)259-7245
Web: http://www.waytogo.com/support_community.html

Description

EIN: 311138883
Organization Type: Corporate Foundation
Giving Locations: headquarters and operating communities.
Grant Types: Capital, General Support, Multiyear/Continuing Support, Project, Scholarship.

Financial Summary

Total Giving: $1,695,807 (2001); $1,797,879 (2000); $1,483,052 (1999). Note: Contributes through corporate direct giving program and foundation.
Giving Analysis: Giving for 2000 includes: foundation scholarships ($5,000); foundation grants to United Way ($219,010); foundation ($1,573,869); 1999: foundation ($203,122); foundation ($1,279,930); 1998: foundation grants to United Way ($210,051); foundation ($1,263,526)
Assets: $33,287,502 (2001); $45,408,169 (2000); $36,114,271 (1999)
Gifts Received: $12,504,041 (2000)

Typical Recipients

Arts & Humanities: Arts Associations & Councils, Arts Centers, Arts Funds, Arts Institutes, Arts Outreach, Ballet, Dance, Ethnic & Folk Arts, Historic Preservation, History & Archaeology, Libraries, Museums/Galleries, Music, Opera, Performing Arts, Public Broadcasting, Theater, Visual Arts

Civic & Public Affairs: African American Affairs, Botanical Gardens/Parks, Clubs, Community Foundations, Economic Development, Economic Policy, Employment/Job Training, Civic & Public Affairs-General, Housing, Municipalities/Towns, Parades/Festivals, Philanthropic Organizations, Public Policy, Urban & Community Affairs, Women's Affairs

Education: Business Education, Business Education, Colleges & Universities, Community & Junior Colleges, Education Reform, Engineering/Technological Education, Faculty Development, Education-General, Minority Education, Public Education (Precollege), Science/Mathematics Education, Secondary Education (Public), Student Aid

Environment: Energy, Environment-General, Resource Conservation

Health: Alzheimers Disease, Cancer, Children's Health/Hospitals, Heart, Transplant Networks/Donor Banks

Religion: Churches, Religious Welfare, Social/Policy Issues

Science: Science Exhibits & Fairs, Science Museums

Social Services: Big Brother/Big Sister, Child Welfare, Community Service Organizations, Crime Prevention, Domestic Violence, Emergency Relief, Food/Clothing Distribution, People with Disabilities, Recreation & Athletics, Scouts, Senior Services, Substance Abuse, United Funds/United Ways, Veterans, YMCA/YWCA/YMHA/YWHA, Youth Organizations

Application Procedures

Initial Contact: Send a proposal letter with financial attachments.

Application Requirements: Include description of the history, structure, purpose and program of the organization; amount requested, and purpose of funds sought; a specific description of the support needed; status and results of any programs previously supported by DP&L Foundation; and a list of donors and level of support received, committed, or requested. Proposals must be accompanied by detailed organizational financial data, including an independent financial audit, budget, sources of income, and expenditures by programs, administration and fundraising; proof of tax-exempt status; and a copy of the organization's most recent Form 990.

Deadlines: None.

Decision Notification: Distribution committee normally meets quarterly.

Restrictions

Does not support individuals; individual members of federated campaigns; fraternal, labor, or veterans organizations; political or lobbying groups; religious organizations; conduit organizations; college fundraising associations; capital campaigns; endowment or development funds; hospital operating budgets; sports leagues; telephone or mass-mail solicitations; or national organizations outside the DP&L service territory. The foundation rarely makes contributions to tax supported institutions.

Corporate Officials

Allen M. Hill: president, chief executive officer, chief financial officer B Dayton, OH 1945. ED University of Dayton BS (1967); University of Dayton MBA (1972). PRIM CORP EMPL president, chief executive officer: Dayton Power & Light Co. NONPR AFFIL president, chief executive officer, director: DPL Inc.

Caroline E. Muhlenkamp: group vice president, chief financial officer

Foundation Officials

Stephen F. Koziar, Jr.: president, trustee B Webster, MA 1944. ED University of Dayton BSIE (1967); Salmon P. Chase College of Law JD (1971). PRIM CORP EMPL president, chief executive officer: Dayton Power & Light Co. CORP AFFIL president: Miami Valley Development Co.; president: Miami Valley Resources Inc.; secretary: DPL Inc.

Judy W. Lansaw: secretary, trustee B Dayton, OH 1951. ED Wright State University BA (1988). PRIM CORP EMPL group vice president: Dayton Power & Light Co. CORP AFFIL group vice president: DPL Inc.

Caroline E. Muhlenkamp: treasurer, trustee (see above)

Virginia M. Strausburg: executive director

Judy Wyatt: secretary, trustee

Grants Analysis

Disclosure Period: calendar year ending 2001
Total Grants: $1,517,393*
Number of Grants: 86
Average Grant: $6,726
Highest Grant: $350,000
Lowest Grant: $50
Typical Range: $1,000 to $50,000
*Note: Giving excludes United Way.

Recent Grants

Note: Grants derived from 2001 Form 990.

Library-Related
5,000	St. Paris Public Library, St. Paris, OH

General
350,000	Art Center Project Fund, Dayton, OH
200,000	SCOPE, Dayton, OH
170,000	United Way Greater Dayton Area, Dayton, OH
100,000	Dayton Regional Development Alliance, Dayton, OH
100,000	Midwest Energy Research Center, Findlay, OH
75,000	Dayton Art Institute, Dayton, OH
70,000	Boy Scouts of America Miami Valley Council, Dayton, OH
50,000	American Red Cross, Washington, DC
50,000	Buy Com Dayton Open, Centerville, OH
50,000	Riverscape Project, Dayton, OH

DAYWOOD FOUNDATION

Giving Contact

William W. Booker, Secretary & Treasurer
PO Box 2031
1600 Bank One Center
Charleston, WV 25301
Phone: (304)345-8900

Description

Founded: 1958
EIN: 556018107
Organization Type: Private Foundation
Giving Locations: WV: Barbour County, Charleston County, Greenbrier County, Kanawha County, Lewisburg County
Grant Types: Capital, Emergency, General Support, Seed Money.

Donor Information

Founder: the late Ruth Woods Dayton

Financial Summary

Total Giving: $1,227,000 (2000); $1,065,500 (1999); $947,100 (1998)
Giving Analysis: Giving for 2000 includes: foundation matching gifts ($15,000); foundation grants to United Way ($85,000); foundation scholarships ($87,000); 1999: foundation grants to United Way ($60,000); foundation scholarships ($79,500); 1998: foundation grants to United Way ($60,000)
Assets: $24,008,619 (2000); $26,473,985 (1999); $22,753,130 (1998)

Typical Recipients

Arts & Humanities: Arts Centers, Arts Funds, Community Arts, Film & Video, Arts & Humanities-General, History & Archaeology, Libraries, Museums/Galleries, Music, Opera, Theater

Civic & Public Affairs: Economic Development, Civic & Public Affairs-General

Education: Colleges & Universities, Education Funds, Faculty Development, Education-General, Minority Education, Student Aid

Health: Health-General, Health Organizations, Hospices, Mental Health

Social Services: At-Risk Youth, Camps, Child Welfare, Community Service Organizations, Counseling, Domestic Violence, Emergency Relief, Family Services, Food/Clothing Distribution, Recreation & Athletics, Scouts, Scouts, Senior Services, Shelters/Homelessness, Social Services-General, United Funds/United Ways, YMCA/YWCA/YMHA/YWHA, Youth Organizations

Application Procedures

Initial Contact: Submit a brief letter of inquiry.
Application Requirements: Include a description of organization, amount requested, purpose of funds sought, proof of tax-exempt status, and a recently audited financial statement.
Deadlines: September 15.

Restrictions

The foundation does not make grants to individuals, political or lobbying groups, organizations outside operating areas.

Foundation Officials

William W. Booker: secretary, treasurer

Richard Edmond Ford: vice president B Ronceverte, WV 1927. ED University of North Carolina (1950); West Virginia University BS (1951); West Virginia University LLB (1954). PRIM CORP EMPL partner: Hayne Ford & Rowe. CORP AFFIL director: WV Power Co.; director: First National Bank Ronceverte; director: Greenbrier Cable Corp. NONPR AFFIL member: WV University Alumni Association; director: WV University Foundation; member: WV Bar Association; member: WV Law School Association; member: Phi Delta Phi; member: Sigma Chi; member: Phi Beta Kappa; member: National Conference Commrs Uniform Saint Laws; member: Order of Vandalia; member: Greenbrier County Bar Association; director: Faculty Merit Foundation; member advisory board: Greenbrier Community College Center; vice president, director: Daywood Foundation; fellow: American Judicature Society; member executive board: Boy Scouts America; member: American College Real Estate Lawyers; member: American Bar Association; fellow: American Bar Foundation. CLUB AFFIL Shriners Club; Lewisburg Elks Club; Masons Club; Kentucky Club.

John Oscar Kizer: secretary, treasurer B Wheeling, WV March 06, 1913. ED West Virginia University AB (1934); West Virginia University LLB (1936). PRIM CORP EMPL partner: Kay, Casto, Chaney, Love & Wise. NONPR AFFIL member: WV Bar Association; member: WV State Bar; member: Delta Tau Delta; member: American Bar Association; director, past president: Childrens Museum Charleston. CLUB AFFIL Berry Hills Country Club.

L. Newton Thomas, Jr.: president

Grants Analysis

Disclosure Period: calendar year ending 2000
Total Grants: $1,040,000*
Number of Grants: 50
Average Grant: $10,426*
Highest Grant: $300,000
Typical Range: $5,000 to $30,000
*Note: Giving excludes United Way, matching gifts, and scholarship. Average grant figure excludes three highest grants ($550,000). ($400,000).

Recent Grants

Note: Grants derived from 1999 Form 990.

Library-Related
10,000	Greenbrier County Library, Lewisburg, WV -- for program support

General

200,000	Clay Center for The Arts and Sciences, Charleston, WV -- supplemental grant
200,000	Clay Center for The Arts and Sciences, Charleston, WV -- capital campaign
150,000	Carnegie Hall, New York, NY -- for capital debt grant
50,000	Greenbrier Valley Theater, Lewisburg, WV -- for capital campaign
50,000	United Way of Kanawha Valley, Charleston, WV -- for program support
50,000	West Virginia Health Right, Inc., Charleston, WV -- for capital campaign
32,500	Davis & Elkins College, Elkins, WV -- for scholarship program
30,000	West Virginia Wesleyan College, Buckhannon, WV -- for scholarships
17,000	University of Charleston, Charleston, WV -- for nursing scholarships
16,000	Fund for the Arts, Charleston, WV -- for program support

DBH FOUNDATION FOR LAW, LAND, AND THE FELICITOUS ENVIRONMENT

Giving Contact

Dr. Suzanne Keller, Chairman
Princeton University
Department of Sociology
Princeton, NJ 08540
Phone: (201)684-4100

Description

Founded: 1992
EIN: 222953497
Organization Type: Private Foundation
Giving Locations: NY
Grant Types: General Support.

Financial Summary

Total Giving: $28,100 (2000); $36,435 (1998); $24,000 (1996)
Assets: $1,014,803 (2000); $917,504 (1998); $801,241 (1996)
Gifts Received: $19,477 (1998); $3,000 (1992). Note: In 1998, contributions were received from Charles M. Haar.

Typical Recipients

Arts & Humanities: Arts Associations & Councils, Dance, Libraries, Museums/Galleries, Theater
Civic & Public Affairs: Clubs, Civic & Public Affairs-General, Law & Justice, Legal Aid, Urban & Community Affairs
Education: Colleges & Universities, Legal Education, Private Education (Precollege), Social Sciences Education
Environment: Environment-General
Health: Heart
International: Foreign Educational Institutions, International Organizations
Religion: Jewish Causes, Seminaries, Synagogues/Temples
Social Services: Social Services-General

Application Procedures

Initial Contact: Request guidelines. Send a brief letter of inquiry and a full proposal.
Deadlines: None.

Restrictions

Does not support religious organizations for sectarian purposes, or political or lobbying groups.

Additional Information

Publications: Guidelines

Foundation Officials

Charles M. Haar: director
Susan E. Haar: director
Steven G. Horowitz: director
Jerold Kayden: director
Dr. Suzanne Keller: chairman

Grants Analysis

Disclosure Period: calendar year ending 2000
Total Grants: $28,100
Number of Grants: 24
Average Grant: $1,171
Highest Grant: $5,000
Lowest Grant: $100
Typical Range: $100 to $5,000

Recent Grants

Note: Grants derived from 2000 Form 990.

General

5,000	Carlo Mongardini Amalfi Foundation
3,000	World Society of Ekistics, Athens Greece
2,500	Princeton University Department of Sociology, Princeton, NJ
1,800	Stern College for Women, New York, NY
1,000	American Academy of the Arts and Sciences, Cambridge, MA
1,000	Citizens Union Foundation, New York, NY
1,000	Contemporary Dance Theater, New York, NY
1,000	Fogg Art Museum
1,000	Harvard Hillel
1,000	Lawyers Alliance, New York, NY

SARAH K. DE COIZART PERPETUAL CHARITABLE TRUST

Giving Contact

Philip DiMaulo, Vice President
c/o Chase Manhattan Bank
1211 Avenue of the Americas, 34th Floor
New York, NY 10036
Phone: (212)789-4159

Description

Founded: 1995
EIN: 137046581
Organization Type: Private Foundation
Giving Locations: nationally.
Grant Types: General Support.

Donor Information

Founder: Established in 1995 by the late Sarah de Coizart and with funds from the Andre de Coizart Interim Trust.

Financial Summary

Total Giving: $1,150,925 (fiscal year ending January 31, 2001); $2,231,279 (fiscal 2000); $1,000,000 (fiscal 1997)
Giving Analysis: Giving for fiscal 2001 includes: foundation grants to United Way ($25,000); fiscal 2000: foundation scholarships ($35,000) fiscal 1997: foundation scholarships ($15,000)
Assets: $39,276,619 (fiscal 2001); $38,031,709 (fiscal 2000); $24,139,903 (fiscal 1998)

Gifts Received: $10,000 (fiscal 2001); $3,109,301 (fiscal 2000); $10,268,407 (fiscal 1997). Note: In fiscal 1996, contributions were received from the estate of Sarah de Coizart ($3,500,000) and the Andre de Coizart Interim Trust ($10,649,355).

Typical Recipients

Arts & Humanities: Community Arts, Libraries, Museums/Galleries
Civic & Public Affairs: Civic & Public Affairs-General, Philanthropic Organizations, Urban & Community Affairs
Education: Colleges & Universities
Environment: Protection, Resource Conservation
Health: Arthritis, Cancer, Eyes/Blindness, Health-General, Hospitals, Nursing Services, Public Health
Religion: Religious Welfare
Science: Science Museums
Social Services: At-Risk Youth, Child Welfare, Community Centers, Community Service Organizations, Family Services, People with Disabilities, Recreation & Athletics, United Funds/United Ways, YMCA/YWCA/YMHA/YWHA

Application Procedures

Initial Contact: The foundation has no formal grant application procedure or application form.
Deadlines: None.

Additional Information

Trust(s): Chase Manhattan Bank

Foundation Officials

Carl S. Forsythe, III: trustee

Grants Analysis

Disclosure Period: fiscal year ending January 31, 2001
Total Grants: $1,125,925*
Number of Grants: 83
Average Grant: $13,567
Highest Grant: $40,000
Typical Range: $5,000 to $50,000
***Note:** Giving excludes United Way.

Recent Grants

Note: Grants derived from 2001 Form 990.

Library-Related

25,000	Desert Foothills Library, Carefree, AZ
20,000	Museum of Modern Art, New York, NY

General

40,000	VNA of Hudson Valley
35,000	Arthritis Foundation, Reno, NV
35,000	Family Centers, Inc, Greenwich, CT
30,000	Bruce Museum, Greenwich, CT
30,000	Greenwich Land Trust, Greenwich, CT
30,000	Interplast, Inc., Mountain View, CA
25,000	Interfaith Neighbors, Inc., Asbury Park, NJ
25,000	Manchester Health Services, Manchester Center, VT
25,000	Northshire Civic Center, Manchester Center, VT
25,000	Posse Foundation, The, New York, NY

DE QUEEN REGIONAL MEDICAL CENTER

Giving Contact

Charles Long
c/o Cossatot Technical College
De Queen, AR 71832
Phone: (870)584-4471
Fax: (870)584-4100

Description
Founded: 1984
EIN: 710405256
Organization Type: Private Foundation
Grant Types: General Support, Scholarship.

Financial Summary
Total Giving: $2,058,350 (1999); $150,200 (1998); $162,538 (1996)
Giving Analysis: Giving for 1999 includes: foundation scholarships ($350); 1998: foundation gifts to individuals ($700) foundation matching gifts ($92,500)
Assets: $1,639,756 (1999); $3,656,598 (1998); $3,481,170 (1996)

Typical Recipients
Arts & Humanities: Libraries, Museums/Galleries
Civic & Public Affairs: Urban & Community Affairs
Education: Colleges & Universities, Student Aid, Vocational & Technical Education
Health: Emergency/Ambulance Services, Health-General, Hospitals
Social Services: People with Disabilities, Youth Organizations

Application Procedures
Initial Contact: Applications available at Cossatot Technical College.
Deadlines: None.

Additional Information
Provides scholarships to individuals studying for a medical profession.

Foundation Officials
Donn Allison: secretary
Frank Daniel, MD: director
C. E. Hendrix, Jr.: president
Jonathon Hoyt, MD: director
Charles N. Jones, MD: vice president
Ray Kimball: director
Jim Pearce: treasurer
Randell Wright: director

Grants Analysis
Disclosure Period: calendar year ending 1999
Total Grants: $2,058,000*
Number of Grants: 4
Highest Grant: $2,000,000
Typical Range: $100 to $25,000
*Note: Giving excludes scholarships.

Recent Grants
Note: Grants derived from 1999 Form 990.

General
2,000,000	De Queen General Hospital, De Queen, AR
52,500	Christus St. Michael Healthcare, Texarkana, TX
5,500	Community Care Closet, De Queen, AR
350	Arkansas Tech University, Russellville, AR -- scholarship

DEC INTERNATIONAL, INC. SMS/NELLES CHEESE EQUIPMENT

Company Headquarters
PO Box 8662
Madison, WI 53708
Web: http://www.sanimatic.com

Company Description
Employees: 1,030
SIC(s): 2000 Food & Kindred Products, 3500 Industrial Machinery & Equipment, 6700 Holding & Other Investment Offices.

Operating Locations
DEC International, Inc. (WI--Lodi, Stanley)

DEC International-Albrecht Foundation

Giving Contact
Randal A. Albrecht, Secretary
PO Box 8050
Madison, WI 53708-8050
Phone: (608)224-2885

Description
EIN: 396075225
Organization Type: Corporate Foundation
Giving Locations: WI: Dane County
Grant Types: Capital, General Support, Matching, Multiyear/Continuing Support.

Financial Summary
Total Giving: $73,168 (2000); $69,755 (1999); $71,063 (1998)
Giving Analysis: Giving for 2000 includes: foundation grants to United Way ($17,500); 1999: foundation grants to United Way ($16,000); foundation ($53,755) 1998: foundation grants to United Way ($16,000)
Assets: $388 (2000); $306 (1999); $311 (1998)
Gifts Received: $73,250 (2000); $69,750 (1999); $72,650 (1998)

Typical Recipients
Arts & Humanities: Arts Centers, Arts Festivals, Arts Outreach, Community Arts, Arts & Humanities-General, Libraries, Music, Performing Arts, Public Broadcasting, Theater
Civic & Public Affairs: Botanical Gardens/Parks, Business/Free Enterprise, Economic Development, Civic & Public Affairs-General, Housing, Parades/Festivals, Rural Affairs, Safety, Zoos/Aquariums
Education: Afterschool/Enrichment Programs, Agricultural Education, Business Education, Colleges & Universities, Economic Education, Public Education (Precollege)
Health: Cancer, Children's Health/Hospitals, Emergency/Ambulance Services, Heart, Hospices, Multiple Sclerosis, Public Health, Single-Disease Health Associations
Religion: Religious Welfare, Religious Welfare
Social Services: Animal Protection, At-Risk Youth, Big Brother/Big Sister, Camps, Child Welfare, Community Centers, Community Service Organizations, Emergency Relief, Family Planning, Food/Clothing Distribution, Homes, People with Disabilities, Recreation & Athletics, Scouts, Senior Services, Special Olympics, United Funds/United Ways, Volunteer Services, YMCA/YWCA/YMHA/YWHA, Youth Organizations

Application Procedures
Initial Contact: Send a brief letter of inquiry.
Application Requirements: Include a description of organization, amount requested, purpose of funds sought, and proof of tax-exempt status.
Deadlines: September 15. Requests are reviewed quarterly.

Restrictions
Does not support individuals, religious organizations for sectarian purposes, political or lobbying groups, or organizations outside operating areas.

Additional Information
DEC International was in Capter 11 Bankruptcy at the time this entry was updated. They reported that a new company may emerge after fourth quarter 2002, but the information was not available.

Corporate Officials
Henrik Moe: president B Fort Atkinson, WI 1940. ED Northwestern University (1962); Stanford University (1965). PRIM CORP EMPL president: DEC International. CORP AFFIL director: Sub Zero Freezer Co. NONPR AFFIL member: American Institute of CPA's.

Foundation Officials
Randal A. Albrecht: secretary

Grants Analysis
Disclosure Period: calendar year ending 2000
Total Grants: $55,668*
Number of Grants: 83
Average Grant: $386*
Highest Grant: $24,000
Typical Range: $75 to $500
*Note: Giving excludes United Way. Average grant figure excludes highest grant.

Recent Grants
Note: Grants derived from 2001 Form 990.

General
1,000	Edgewood High School, Madison, WI -- Athletic Department
975	Wisconsin Chamber Orchestra, Madison, WI
750	Badger State Games, Madison, WI -- winter games
750	Salvation Army, Madison, WI
692	In Business, Madison, WI
600	Childreach, Warwick, RI
600	Wisconsin Badger Camp, Inc., Platteville, WI
500	Cystic Fibrosis Foundation, Madison, WI
500	Hospice Care, Madison, WI
500	National Multiple Sclerosis Society, Madison, WI

IRA W. DECAMP FOUNDATION

Giving Contact
Lisa L. Philp, Vice President
Care of J.P. Morgan Private Bank
Global FoundationS Group
60 Wall Street, 36th Floor
New York, NY 10260
Phone: (212)483-2323
Fax: (212)648-5082
Web: http://fdncenter.org/grantmaker/decamp/

Description
Founded: 1975
EIN: 510138577
Organization Type: Specialized/Single Purpose Foundation
Giving Locations: NY: New York including the metropolitan area
Grant Types: Capital, General Support, Multiyear/Continuing Support, Research, Scholarship.

Donor Information
Founder: Established in New York in 1975 with funds from the estate of the late Elizabeth DeCamp McInerny .

Financial Summary
Total Giving: $4,915,000 (fiscal year ending October 31, 2001 approx); $3,530,500 (fiscal 2000); $3,494,000 (fiscal 1999)
Giving Analysis: Giving for fiscal 1999 includes: foundation scholarships ($10,000)
Assets: $87,725,298 (fiscal 2001); $111,896,045 (fiscal 2000); $104,898,935 (fiscal 1999)
Gifts Received: $89 (fiscal 1992)

Typical Recipients

Arts & Humanities: Historic Preservation, Libraries, Public Broadcasting

Civic & Public Affairs: Community Foundations, Economic Development, Employment/Job Training, Civic & Public Affairs-General, Hispanic Affairs, Housing, Inner-City Development, Nonprofit Management, Philanthropic Organizations, Urban & Community Affairs, Women's Affairs

Education: Arts/Humanities Education, Business Education, Colleges & Universities, Education Reform, Engineering/Technological Education, Education-General, Health & Physical Education, International Studies, Legal Education, Medical Education, Preschool Education, Private Education (Precollege), Religious Education, Science/Mathematics Education, Special Education, Student Aid, Vocational & Technical Education

Environment: Environment-General

Health: AIDS/HIV, Alzheimers Disease, Cancer, Children's Health/Hospitals, Clinics/Medical Centers, Emergency/Ambulance Services, Eyes/Blindness, Geriatric Health, Health Funds, Health Organizations, Heart, Hospices, Hospitals, Hospitals (University Affiliated), Kidney, Long-Term Care, Medical Rehabilitation, Medical Research, Medical Training, Mental Health, Nursing Services, Outpatient Health Care, Public Health, Research/Studies Institutes, Single-Disease Health Associations, Speech & Hearing, Transplant Networks/Donor Banks

International: Health Care/Hospitals, International Environmental Issues, International Organizations

Religion: Churches, Religion-General, Religious Organizations, Religious Welfare, Seminaries

Science: Scientific Labs, Scientific Organizations, Scientific Research

Social Services: Big Brother/Big Sister, Child Welfare, Community Service Organizations, Counseling, Food/Clothing Distribution, Homes, People with Disabilities, Recreation & Athletics, Scouts, Senior Services, Shelters/Homelessness, Substance Abuse, United Funds/United Ways, Volunteer Services, Youth Organizations

Application Procedures

Initial Contact: Applicants should contact foundation for funding guidelines and application requirements.

Application Requirements: Full proposals will include primary goals of organization, need or problem addressed, and population served; most recent annual report; brief history of the organization; list of directors or trustees with affiliations; brief biography of executive director and key project staff; most recent financial audit; current operating budget; list of foundation and corporate support with amounts for the most recently completed fiscal year; proof of tax-exempt status and Form 990; description of project, including statement of primary purpose and need addressed, population served and how they will benefit, anticipated duration, current budget, and list of funding sources.

Deadlines: March 15 and July 15.

Review Process: Grants are reviewed in the spring and fall. Applicants generally will be notified of the foundation's final decision on their proposal within six weeks of the trustees' meeting.

Restrictions

No grants are made to individuals, private foundations, endowments, scholarships, fellowships, or for matching gifts or loans.

Additional Information

Chase Manhattan Bank serves as a corporate trustee for the foundation.

Foundation Officials

Kari Floren: foundation administrator

Grants Analysis

Disclosure Period: fiscal year ending October 31, 2000

Total Grants: $3,530,500

Number of Grants: 80

Average Grant: $44,125

Highest Grant: $200,000

Typical Range: $50,000 to $150,000

Recent Grants

Note: Grants derived from 2001 Form 990.

Library-Related

75,000	Replications, Inc., New York, NY -- for capacity building
50,000	Pius XII Foundation, New York, NY -- to support the reconfiguration of the library

General

200,000	Rockefeller University Center for Studies in Physics & Biology, New York, NY -- to support new interdisciplinary research in the connection between neurobiology and behavior
165,000	Inner City Scholarship Endowment Fund, New York, NY -- to support the preschool support initiative
150,000	New York University, New York, NY -- for Law School
125,000	Dartmouth Medical School, Hanover, NH -- for the Hanover NH Brain Imaging Analysis
125,000	Hospital for Special Surgery, New York, NY
125,000	New York Foundling Hospital, New York, NY -- for capital campaign
125,000	Weill Cornell Medical School, NY
100,000	Calvary Hospital, Bronx, NY
100,000	DOROT, Inc., New York, NY -- for capital support
100,000	El Puente De Williamsburg, Inc., Brooklyn, NY -- for capital projects

DECHERD FOUNDATION

Giving Contact

Lucy Gonzalez
400 S. Record St., 2nd Fl.
Dallas, TX 75202-4819
Phone: (214)977-8293

Description

Founded: 1993

EIN: 752507229

Organization Type: Private Foundation

Giving Locations: TX: nationally and internationally.

Grant Types: General Support.

Donor Information

Founder: Established in 1993 by Mr. and Mrs. Robert Decherd.

Financial Summary

Total Giving: $437,350 (1999); $540,500 (1998); $96,000 (1996)

Giving Analysis: Giving for 1999 includes: foundation grants to United Way ($22,600); 1998: foundation grants to United Way ($22,000) foundation ($518,500)

Assets: $9,313,341 (1999); $8,331,267 (1998); $3,465,540 (1996)

Gifts Received: $5,313,781 (1998); $1,171,443 (1996); $1,020,000 (1994). Note: In 1998, contributions were received from Mr. and Mrs. Robert Decherd.

Typical Recipients

Arts & Humanities: Libraries

Civic & Public Affairs: Business/Free Enterprise

Education: Colleges & Universities, Education-General, Minority Education, Private Education (Precollege), Student Aid

Health: Eyes/Blindness, Mental Health

Religion: Churches, Religious Welfare

Social Services: Community Centers, Community Service Organizations, Substance Abuse, United Funds/United Ways, YMCA/YWCA/YMHA/YWHA, Youth Organizations

Application Procedures

Initial Contact: Send a brief letter of inquiry.

Application Requirements: Include proof of tax-exempt status, recently audited financial statement, and list of board of directors.

Deadlines: None.

Foundation Officials

William Bennett Cullum: secretary, treasurer

Maureen H. Decherd: president

Robert William Decherd: chairman B Dallas, TX 1951. ED Harvard University BA (1973). PRIM CORP EMPL chairman, president, chief executive officer, director: A.H. Belo Corp. CORP AFFIL chairman: Owensboro Messenger Inquirer; chairman: Henderson Gleaner; director: Kimberly-Clark Corp.; chairman, chief executive officer: Audubon Printers Ink Ltd. NONPR AFFIL member: Newspaper Association America; trustee: Tomas Rivera Policy Institute.

Terri W. Johnson: administrator

Grants Analysis

Disclosure Period: calendar year ending 1999

Total Grants: $414,750*

Number of Grants: 26

Average Grant: $6,990*

Highest Grant: $147,000

Typical Range: $1,000 to $20,000

*****Note:** Giving excludes United Way. Average grant figure excludes 2 highest grants ($247,000).

Recent Grants

Note: Grants derived from 1999 Form 990.

Library-Related

1,000	Friends of the Dallas Public Library, Dallas, TX

General

147,000	St. Mark's School of Texas, Dallas, TX
51,000	Harvard Crimson Trust II, Cambridge, MA
33,000	Betty Ford Center at Eisenhower, Rancho Mirage, CA
25,000	University of Texas at Austin, Austin, TX
22,600	United Way of Metropolitan, Dallas, TX
20,250	St. Michael and All Angels Episcopal Church, Dallas, TX
12,500	Harvard College, Cambridge, MA
5,000	9Ursuline Academy, Dallas, TX
5,000	Hockaday School, Dallas, TX
5,000	Salvation Army, Dallas, TX

ARTHUR J. DECIO FOUNDATION

Giving Contact

Ronald F. Kloska, Trustee
c/o Skyline Corp.
2520 By-Pass Rd.
Elkhart, IN 46515
Phone: (219)294-6521
Fax: (219)293-7574

Description
Founded: 1970
EIN: 237083597
Organization Type: Private Foundation
Giving Locations: IN
Grant Types: General Support.

Donor Information
Founder: Arthur J. Decio

Financial Summary
Total Giving: $85,500 (fiscal year ending September 30, 2001); $66,000 (fiscal 2000); $62,175 (fiscal 1998)
Assets: $2,317,725 (fiscal 2001); $1,894,773 (fiscal 2000); $2,638,752 (fiscal 1998)

Typical Recipients
Arts & Humanities: Arts Festivals, Arts Outreach, Arts & Humanities-General, History & Archaeology, Libraries, Music, Performing Arts, Public Broadcasting
Civic & Public Affairs: Community Foundations, Employment/Job Training, Ethnic Organizations, Civic & Public Affairs-General, Parades/Festivals, Women's Affairs
Education: Business Education, Colleges & Universities, Education Funds, Education-General, Private Education (Precollege), Student Aid
Health: Cancer, Emergency/Ambulance Services, Heart, Hospices, Hospitals, Medical Research, Mental Health, Single-Disease Health Associations
Religion: Religious Organizations, Religious Welfare, Seminaries
Social Services: Community Service Organizations, Domestic Violence, Family Planning, People with Disabilities, Substance Abuse, Youth Organizations

Application Procedures
Initial Contact: Send a brief letter of inquiry.
Deadlines: None.

Foundation Officials
Arthur J. Decio: trustee B Elkhart, IN 1930. ED DePaul University (1949-1950); University of Notre Dame LLD (1975); Indiana State University LLD (1978). PRIM CORP EMPL chairman, chief executive officer, director: Skyline Corp. CORP AFFIL director: Schwarz Paper Co.; director: NIPSCO Industries Inc.; director: Quality Housing. NONPR AFFIL fellow, trustee: University Notre Dame; member: World Business Council; director: Special Olympics International; member: Mobile Home Manufacturer Association; life member, vice chairman advisory board: National Salvation Army; life member, trust: Marmion Military Acad; member: Knights Malta; member: Manufactured Housing Institute; trustee: Holy Cross College; president: Elkhart General Hospital Foundation; member advisory board: Goshen College; member: Chief Executives Organization; counc adv: Center Homeless; member: Chicago Presidents Association. CLUB AFFIL Tavern Club; Ocean Florida Club; Signal Point Country Club; Delray Beach Yacht Club; Chicago Club; Country Club Florida.
Patricia C. Decio: trustee
Terrence M. Decio: trustee
Ronald Frank Kloska: trustee B Grand Rapids, MI 1933. ED University of Montreal MBA (1955); University of Michigan PhB (1957). PRIM CORP EMPL vice chairman, deputy chief executive officer, chief administrative officer, director: Skyline Corp. CORP AFFIL director: NBD Bank. NONPR AFFIL member: Indiana Certified Public Accountant Society; member: Michigan Society CPA's; member: American Institute of CPA's. CLUB AFFIL SouthBend Country Club.
Andrew James McKenna: trustee B Chicago, IL 1929. ED University of Notre Dame BS (1951); DePaul University JD (1954). PRIM CORP EMPL chairman, president, chief executive officer: Schwarz Paper Co. CORP AFFIL director: Skyline Corp.; director: Tribune Co.; director: McDonald's Corp.; director: First Chicago NBD Corp.; director: First National Bank

Chicago; director: Children's Memorial Hospital; director: Dean Foods Co.; director: Chicago Bears Football Club; director: Chicago National League Baseball Club; director: AON Corp. NONPR AFFIL chairman board trustees: Museum Science & Industry; chairman board trustees: University Notre Dame; director: Catholic Charities Chicago; director: Childrens Memorial Medical Center.
Richard M. Treckelo: trustee B Elkhart, IN 1926. ED University of Michigan AB (1951); University of Michigan JD (1953). PRIM NONPR EMPL partner: Barnes & Thornburg. NONPR AFFIL director: Elkhart Park Foundation; member: Indiana Bar Association; director: Elkhart General Hospital Foundation; co-chairman: Elkhart Constitutional Bicentennial Comm; member: Elkhart County Bar Association; member: American Bar Association; member: Elkhart City Bar Association. CLUB AFFIL Rotary Club; Christiana Country Club; Presidents University Michigan Club.

Grants Analysis
Disclosure Period: fiscal year ending September 30, 2001
Total Grants: $85,500
Number of Grants: 13
Average Grant: $4,958*
Highest Grant: $26,000
Lowest Grant: $1,000
Typical Range: $1,000 to $10,000
*Note: Average grant figure excludes highest grant.

Recent Grants
Note: Grants derived from fiscal 2000 Form 990.

General
26,000	Channel 34, Elkhart, IN -- charitable
22,000	University of Notre Dame, Notre Dame, IN -- educational
10,000	American Heart Association -- charitable
2,500	Elkhart General Hospital Foundation, Elkhart, IN -- charitable
2,000	Elkhart County Symphony Association, Elkhart, IN -- charitable
1,000	Junior Achievement of Elkhart County, Elkhart, IN -- educational

DR. G. CLIFFORD AND FLORENCE B. DECKER FOUNDATION

Giving Contact
Gerald E. Putman, Executive Director
8 Hawley St.
Binghamton, NY 13905
Phone: (607)722-0211
Web: http://www.pronetisp.net/~deckerfn/

Description
Founded: 1979
EIN: 161131704
Organization Type: Private Foundation
Giving Locations: NY
Grant Types: General Support, Scholarship.

Donor Information
Founder: the late G. Clifford Decker

Financial Summary
Total Giving: $2,814,034 (2001); $2,002,670 (2000); $1,851,665 (1999)
Giving Analysis: Giving for 2001 includes: foundation grants to United Way ($55,000); foundation scholarships ($200,000); 2000: foundation grants to United Way ($52,000); 1999: foundation scholarships ($21,400); foundation grants to United Way ($50,000); foundation fellowships ($600,000);
Assets: $41,084,733 (2001); $43,634,916 (2000); $49,597,832 (1999)

Gifts Received: $179,854 (1999). Note: In 1999, contributions were received from the Mrs. Korn Trust.

Typical Recipients
Arts & Humanities: Arts Associations & Councils, Arts Outreach, Arts & Humanities-General, History & Archaeology, Libraries, Museums/Galleries, Music, Opera, Performing Arts, Public Broadcasting
Civic & Public Affairs: Economic Development, Civic & Public Affairs-General, Legal Aid, Nonprofit Management, Professional & Trade Associations, Public Policy, Urban & Community Affairs
Education: Arts/Humanities Education, Colleges & Universities, Community & Junior Colleges, Education-General, Health & Physical Education, Literacy, Medical Education, Preschool Education, Science/Mathematics Education, Student Aid
Health: Clinics/Medical Centers, Emergency/Ambulance Services, Health Organizations, Home-Care Services, Hospitals, Mental Health, Public Health
Religion: Churches, Religious Welfare
Science: Science Museums, Scientific Centers & Institutes
Social Services: Child Welfare, Community Service Organizations, Counseling, Day Care, Family Services, Food/Clothing Distribution, People with Disabilities, Recreation & Athletics, United Funds/United Ways, YMCA/YWCA/YMHA/YWHA, Youth Organizations

Application Procedures
Initial Contact: Request application form.
Application Requirements: Include proof of tax-exempt status along with complete summary form, history, and development of organization, needs to be met by project, purpose of program, name, position and qualification of people in charge of project. Include funding list of actual and potential funding sources and how project will be funded in the future and current board members. See application form. for full requirements.
Deadlines: None.

Additional Information
Publications: Grant application form.

Foundation Officials
Ferris G. Akel: chairman PRIM CORP EMPL director: Bsb Bancorp Inc. ADD CORP EMPL director: Bsb Bank & Trust Co.
Donna Bechdel: executive director
James A. Carrigg: trustee B Johnson City, NY 1933. ED Broome Community College AAS; University of Michigan Graduate School of Business Administration; Union College (1951-1953). PRIM CORP EMPL chairman, president, chief executive officer: New York State Electric & Gas Co. CORP AFFIL director: Utilities Mutual Insurance Co.; director: Security Mutual Life Insurance Co.; chairman: UN MedManagement Inc.; director: Security Equity Life Insurance Co.; director: M&T Bank-Endicott Trust Division; director: Partnership 2000; director: First Empire State Corp.; director: Home Mutual Insurance Co.; director: Empire State Electric Energy Research Corp. NONPR AFFIL director: United Health Services Hospitals Inc.; director: United Health Services Inc.; trustee: Public Policy Institute; trustee: Independent College Fund; director: New York Business Development Corp.; director: Broome County Community Charities; director: Foundation SUNY; trustee: Broome Community College. CLUB AFFIL Broome Country Club.
Dr. C. Arnold Decker: chairman emeritus
Mary Lou Faust: trustee
Douglas Johnson: treasurer
Eugene E. Peckham: secretary B Stamford, CT 1940. ED Wesleyan University BA (1962); Harvard University JD (1965). PRIM CORP EMPL partner: Hinman, Howard & Kattell. NONPR AFFIL member: New York State Bar Association; adj professor acctg: State University New York Binghamton; member:

House of Delaware; treasurer: Joint Legislative Advisory Committee Estates Powers & Trusts Law & Surrogates Court Procedure Act; member: Broome County Bar Association; member: Federal Bar Associations 6th Judicial District; fellow: American College Trust & Estate Counsel; trustee: Binghampton Boys Girls Club.
Gerald Putman: executive director
Alice Wales: vchairman

Grants Analysis

Disclosure Period: calendar year ending 2001
Total Grants: $2,559,034*
Number of Grants: 15
Average Grant: $75,753*
Highest Grant: $650,000
Lowest Grant: $4,600
Typical Range: $30,000 to $125,000
*Note: Giving excludes United Way and scholarship. Average grant figure excludes three highest grants ($1,650,000).

Recent Grants

Note: Grants derived from 2001 Form 990.

General

650,000	Roberson Memorial, Inc. -- capital campaign
500,000	Lourdes Hospital Foundation, Binghamton, NY -- 2001 renew campaign
500,000	Phelps Mansion Foundation, Binghamton, NY -- replicate mansard roof
250,000	Discovery Center of Southern Tier, Inc. -- capital project
200,000	Broome Community College Foundation, Binghamton, NY -- endowment for scholarships
150,000	Broome County Council of Churches, Binghamton, NY -- expansion and renovation and relocation
150,000	Imaginarium for Health, Healing and The Arts, Inc. -- development and implementation of After-School Program
125,000	Tri-Cities Opera, Binghamton, NY -- expanding and upgrading
100,000	Foundation of the State University of New York, Binghamton, NY -- equipment for Doctoral Program
55,000	United Way of Broome County, Binghamton, NY -- annual campaign

DEDALUS FOUNDATION

Giving Contact

Richard Rubin, President
555 W. 57th St., Suite 1222
New York, NY 10019
Phone: (212)220-4220

Description

Founded: 1981
EIN: 133091704
Organization Type: Private Foundation
Grant Types: General Support.

Donor Information

Founder: the late Robert Motherwell

Financial Summary

Total Giving: $1,670,100 (2000); $2,076,694 (1999); $2,561,691 (1998)
Giving Analysis: Giving for 2000 includes: foundation gifts to individuals ($62,500); 1998: foundation gifts to individuals ($28,250) foundation ($2,533,441)
Assets: $47,912,940 (2000); $47,119,926 (1999); $47,796,105 (1998)
Gifts Received: $9,915,470 (1996); $19,442,993 (1993). Note: In 1993, contributions were received from the estate of Robert Motherwell.

Typical Recipients

Arts & Humanities: Arts Centers, Arts Institutes, Arts Outreach, Arts & Humanities-General, Libraries, Literary Arts, Museums/Galleries, Visual Arts
Education: Arts/Humanities Education
International: Foreign Arts Organizations
Religion: Jewish Causes

Application Procedures

Initial Contact: Send a brief letter of inquiry followed by a full proposal.
Application Requirements: Include a description of organization, amount requested, purpose of funds sought, and proof of tax-exempt status.
Deadlines: October 1.
Notes: Primarily supports preselected organizations.

Additional Information

Although the foundation gives grants to preselected organizations and does not accept unsolicited requests for funds, it does have three separate grant programs offered to individuals. They are: Senior Fellowship Program, which is open to art historians, critics, and curators pursuing projects related to the study of modern art and modernism. The applicant does not have to be affiliated with an educational institution or a museum and cannot be a candidate for a degree. Applicants must be a U.S. citizen. Awards will be made for a period of up to one year, with a maximum of $25,000 annually. The application must be submitted by October 1st. Decisions made by the end of December; the PhD Dissertation Fellowship, provides support for a graduate student studying any aspect of the modernist tradition. Departments of art history at colleges and universities in the United States are invited to nominate one student each for consideration. Nominees must have completed all course requirements and examinations and must have advanced to candidacy for the PhD. The foundation mails the program information and application to the chairperson of graduate departments a few months in advance of the deadline. The amount of award is $15,000 for award year July 1 to June 30. Nominations and all accompanying materials must be received at the foundation no later than December 1st. Decisions made the following April; and the MFA Fellowship, provides support for graduate students of painting and sculpture who are about to enter their last year of candidacy for the MFA degree at an American college, university, or art school. Graduate departments of art are invited to nominate one student each for consideration. The foundation mails the program information and application to the chairperson of graduate departments a few months in advance of the deadline. Nomination and all accompanying materials must be received at the foundation no later than July 1st. Decisions made in December.

Foundation Officials

Dore Ashton: director B Newark, DE 1925. ED University of Wisconsin BA (1949); Harvard University MA (1950). PRIM CORP EMPL professor: Cooper Union. NONPR AFFIL member advisory board: John Simon Guggenheim Foundation; member: Phi Beta Kappa.
Joan Banach: secretary
John Elderfield: director
Jack Flam: director
Lynn Kearney: director
Renate Pousold Motherwell: chairman
David Rosand: director B Brooklyn, NY 1938. ED Columbia College AB (1959); Columbia University MA (1962); Columbia University PhD (1965). PRIM CORP EMPL professor art history: Meyer Schapiro. NONPR AFFIL member executive board: Renaissance Society America; member general committee: Save Venice; member: Ateneo Veneto; member: College Art Association America.
Richard Rubin: president

Grants Analysis

Disclosure Period: calendar year ending 2000
Total Grants: $1,607,600*
Number of Grants: 15
Average Grant: $40,633*
Highest Grant: $560,000
Typical Range: $20,000 to $65,000
*Note: Giving excludes individuals. Average grant figure excludes two highest grants.

Recent Grants

Note: Grants derived from 1999 Form 990.

General

704,000	Philadelphia Museum of Art, Philadelphia, PA -- to educate the public about the art of Robert Motherwell and modernism
480,000	North Carolina Museum of Art, Raleigh, NC -- to educate the public about the art of Robert Motherwell and modernism
290,000	Massachusetts Institute of Technology, Cambridge, MA -- to educate the public about the art of Robert Motherwell and modernism
240,500	Modern Art Museum of Fort Worth, Ft. Worth, TX -- to educate the public about the art of Robert Motherwell and modernism
180,500	National Gallery of Art, Washington, DC -- to educate the public about the art of Robert Motherwell and modernism
25,000	Art Gallery of Ontario, Toronto, ON Canada -- support for Robert Motherwell Collection
21,750	Museum of Contemporary Art, Los Angeles, CA -- support of exhibition "In Memory of My Feeling"
20,000	Master Drawings, New York, NY -- support of symposium on the art of abstract expressionism and publication of Master Drawings
15,000	New York University Conservation Center of The Institute of Fine Arts, New York, NY -- support of the Dedalus Foundation fellow in conservation
15,000	University of California Press, Berkeley, CA -- support for translation of Ilia Dorontchenkov's Russian and Soviet view of modern western art

LAWRENCE T. AND JANET T. DEE FOUNDATION

Giving Contact

David Buchman, Trust Officer
c/o Wells Fargo Bank Northwest, NA
PO Box 25491
Salt Lake City, UT 84125
Phone: (801)246-1436

Description

Founded: 1971
EIN: 876150803
Organization Type: Private Foundation
Giving Locations: UT
Grant Types: Capital, Emergency, General Support, Research, Scholarship.

Donor Information

Founder: the late L. T. Dee, the late Janet T. Dee

Financial Summary

Total Giving: $725,256 (2000); $681,000 (1999); $614,300 (1998)
Giving Analysis: Giving for 1999 includes: foundation grants to United Way ($1,500)
Assets: $15,658,162 (2000); $16,648,604 (1999); $15,049,399 (1998)

Gifts Received: $100,000 (1996); $404,802 (1995); $350,000 (1994)

Typical Recipients

Arts & Humanities: Arts Centers, Ballet, Community Arts, Dance, Arts & Humanities-General, Historic Preservation, History & Archaeology, Libraries, Museums/Galleries, Music, Opera, Performing Arts, Public Broadcasting, Theater

Civic & Public Affairs: Botanical Gardens/Parks, Civic & Public Affairs-General, Legal Aid, Native American Affairs, Urban & Community Affairs, Women's Affairs

Education: Arts/Humanities Education, Colleges & Universities, Education-General, Literacy, Medical Education, Private Education (Precollege), Public Education (Precollege)

Environment: Environment-General, Resource Conservation

Health: Alzheimers Disease, Arthritis, Cancer, Children's Health/Hospitals, Emergency/Ambulance Services, Eyes/Blindness, Health Organizations, Hospitals, Prenatal Health Issues, Respiratory, Single-Disease Health Associations

Religion: Churches, Religious Welfare

Science: Science Museums, Scientific Research

Social Services: Camps, Child Welfare, Community Centers, Community Service Organizations, Family Planning, People with Disabilities, Senior Services, YMCA/YWCA/YMHA/YWHA, Youth Organizations

Application Procedures

Initial Contact: Send a brief letter of inquiry.
Deadlines: September 30.

Additional Information

Trust(s): First Security Bank UT NA

Foundation Officials

David L. Dee: vice chairman
Thomas D. Dee, III: vchairman
Thomas D. Dee, II: chairman B Ogden, UT 1920. ED Stanford University (1941). PRIM CORP EMPL president: Dee Co. CORP AFFIL director: First Security Corp.

Grants Analysis

Disclosure Period: calendar year ending 2000
Total Grants: $725,256*
Number of Grants: 45
Average Grant: $9,570*
Highest Grant: $162,500
Typical Range: $5,000 to $20,000
*Note: Average grant figure excludes two highest grants ($313,756).

Recent Grants

Note: Grants derived from 2001 Form 990.

General

75,000	Nature Conservancy of Utah, Salt Lake City, UT
60,000	Weber State University, Ogden, UT -- College of Health Professions
57,500	University of Utah, Salt Lake City, UT -- Department of Educational Psychology
50,000	University of Utah, Salt Lake City, UT -- J. Willard Marriott Library
40,000	Ogden Nature Center, Ogden, UT
30,000	Westminster College, Salt Lake City, UT
25,000	Utah Open Lands, Salt Lake City, UT
25,000	Utah State University College of Humanities, Logan, UT
20,000	Utah Symphony, Salt Lake City, UT
15,000	Kolob Foundation, Salt Lake City, UT

DEERE & CO.

Company Headquarters

Moline, IL
Web: http://www.johndeere.com

Company Description

Founded: 1837
Ticker: DE
Exchange: NYSE
Revenue: US$13.947 billion (2002)
Profit: US$319.2 million (2002)
Employees: 45100 (2001)
Fortune Rank: 135, per FORTUNE Magazine's list of 500 Largest U.S. Corporations (2002).
SIC(s): 3519 Internal Combustion Engines Nec, 3523 Farm Machinery & Equipment, 3524 Lawn & Garden Equipment, 3531 Construction Machinery.

Operating Locations

Deere & Co. (GA--Conyers; IA--Ankeny, Davenport, Dubuque; KS--St. Marys; MN--Bloomington; MO--Kansas City; NY--Syracuse; OR--Portland; SC--Clover; TX--Dallas)

Nonmonetary Support

Type: Donated Products; Loaned Executives
Note: Nonmonetary support is provided by the company.

John Deere Foundation

Giving Contact

Judy A. Chistison, Manager Contributions and Community Relations
1515 River Drive
Moline, IL 61265
Phone: (309)765-4137
Fax: (309)765-9855
E-mail: DP51104@deere.com
Web: http://www.deere.com/en_US/compinfo/johndeere_foundations/contributions_index.html ?sidenavstate=00000000001

Alternate Contact

James H. Collins, president

Description

EIN: 366051024
Organization Type: Corporate Foundation
Giving Locations: principally near operating locations and to national organizations.
Grant Types: Award, Capital, Department, Emergency, Fellowship, General Support, Multiyear/Continuing Support, Project, Scholarship.

Financial Summary

Total Giving: $5,883,725 (fiscal year ending October 31, 2001); $5,888,073 (fiscal 2000 approx); $6,512,967 (fiscal 1999). Note: Contributes through corporate direct giving program and foundation.
Giving Analysis: Giving for fiscal 2001 includes: corporate direct giving ($1,700,000); foundation ($5,800,000); fiscal 2000: corporate direct giving ($1,900,000); foundation ($5,800,000); fiscal 1999: foundation grants to United Way ($1,541,400); foundation ($5,067,531);
Assets: $20,552,254 (fiscal 2000); $23,455,558 (fiscal 1999); $23,940,678 (fiscal 1998)
Gifts Received: $1,495,000 (fiscal 2000); $5,987,805 (fiscal 1999); $210,000 (fiscal 1998). Note: Foundation received contributions from Deere & Co., John Deere Insurance Company, Deere & Company - Kansas City Branch, Heritage National Healthplan Services, Inc.

Typical Recipients

Arts & Humanities: Arts Centers, Community Arts, Arts & Humanities-General, Historic Preservation, History & Archaeology, Libraries, Museums/Galleries, Music, Opera, Public Broadcasting, Theater, Visual Arts

Civic & Public Affairs: Botanical Gardens/Parks, Business/Free Enterprise, Chambers of Commerce, Community Foundations, Economic Development,

Civic & Public Affairs-General, Municipalities/Towns, Parades/Festivals, Professional & Trade Associations, Public Policy, Rural Affairs, Urban & Community Affairs, Zoos/Aquariums

Education: Afterschool/Enrichment Programs, Agricultural Education, Arts/Humanities Education, Business Education, Colleges & Universities, Community & Junior Colleges, Economic Education, Engineering/Technological Education, Education-General, Education-General, Minority Education, Private Education (Precollege), Public Education (Precollege), Science/Mathematics Education, Secondary Education (Private), Vocational & Technical Education

Environment: Environment-General, Research, Resource Conservation

Health: Emergency/Ambulance Services, Health-General, Health Policy/Cost Containment, Health Organizations, Hospices, Outpatient Health Care, Public Health, Transplant Networks/Donor Banks

International: Foreign Educational Institutions, International-General, International Relief Efforts

Religion: Religious Welfare

Science: Science Museums

Social Services: Child Welfare, Community Centers, Community Service Organizations, Day Care, Domestic Violence, Family Services, Homes, People with Disabilities, Recreation & Athletics, Scouts, Senior Services, Social Services-General, Substance Abuse, United Funds/United Ways, YMCA/YWCA/YMHA/YWHA, Youth Organizations

Application Procedures

Initial Contact: Request guidelines, then send written proposal. Organizations in the Moline, IL area and organizations of a national scope should send applications to the foundation. OrganizationS serving other operating communities should direct inquiries to the general manager of the local unit.

Application Requirements: Applications should include a description of organization and statement of objectives and goals; recent audited financial statement; annual report; program budget if the request is for a specific project; proof of tax-exempt status; complete explanation of the activity; goals of program and deadlines for results; description of benefits; geographic area to be served.

Deadlines: None.

Review Process: Requests are reviewed in order of receipt; board meets as needed; initial response can be expected in four to six weeks.

Evaluative Criteria: "The John Deere Foundation considers requests only from tax-exempt, nonprofit organizations, located in the U.S. or its possessions.... Supports programs that address specific community needs, solve problems, and develop activities that create opportunities for individuals to gain skills and knowledge that will assist them in accomplishing positive social goals. The Contributions Committee at Deere & Company, a second grant-making group, evaluates requests on their business merits. Priority funding centers upon programs in this order: health and human services; education, including K-12, university, and college efforts that are important to our employee recruiting, research, and training; community revitalization efforts; and cultural organizations." *Deere & Company Corporate Contributions Program 2000 Report of Contributions* **Notes:** Organizations located in Moline, IL area or which are national in scope should direct requests to the foundation; other organizations should send requests to the manager of operating unit in community.

Restrictions

John Deere Foundation will not provide support for individuals; dinners or special events; fraternal organizations; goodwill advertising; or political or lobbying groups.

Additional Information

Publications: Annual Contributions Report

Corporate Officials

John K. Lawson: senior vice president B Moline, IL 1940. ED Iowa State University BA (1962). PRIM CORP EMPL senior vice president: John Deere & Co. ADD CORP EMPL vice president: John Deere Commercial Products. CORP AFFIL director: Deere Marketing Services Inc. NONPR AFFIL director: Iowa State University Foundation; director: Research Board; governor: Iowa College Foundation; director: Arrowhead Ranch.

Giving Program Officials

Donald R. Margenthaler: president, director PRIM CORP EMPL director community relations: Deere Co.

Foundation Officials

Samuel R. Allen: director
James H. Collins: president
Barron W. Curtis: assistant treasurer
Darlene S. Ellis: assistant secretary
James R. Jenkins: director
Nathan J. Jones: director
Robert W. Lane: vice president, director
John K. Lawson: director (see above)
Curtis G. Linke: chairman, director
Donald R. Margenthaler: executive officer, director (see above)
Michael P. Orr: director
Sonja J. Sterling: secretary

Grants Analysis

Disclosure Period: fiscal year ending October 31, 2001
Total Grants: $5,883,725*
Number of Grants: 519
Average Grant: $11,337
Highest Grant: $300,000
Lowest Grant: $500
Typical Range: $1,000 to $25,000
*Note: Grants analysis provided by foundation.

Recent Grants

Note: Grants derived from 2001 Form 990.

General

796,000	United Way of the Quad Cities Area, Davenport, IA
320,000	Cedar Valley United Way, Waterloo, IA
300,000	Dubuque County Historical Society, Dubuque, IA
250,000	Lincoln Park Zoo, Chicago, IL
200,000	Abraham Lincoln Presidential Library and Museum Foundation, Springfield, IL
125,000	Northwestern University, Evanston, IL
125,000	Putnam Museum, Davenport, IA
108,000	United Way Services, Dubuque, IA
100,000	Friends of the Horicon Marsh International Education Center, Horicon, WI
100,000	Loras College, Dubuque, IA

MIGNON SHERWOOD DELANO FOUNDATION

Giving Contact

Dorothy L. Sullivan, Senior Vice President & Senior Trust Officer
c/o NCB
108 E. Michigan Ave., K-B01-2A
Kalamazoo, MI 49007
Phone: (616)376-8029

Description

Founded: 1985
EIN: 382557743
Organization Type: Private Foundation

Giving Locations: MI: Allegan
Grant Types: General Support.

Donor Information

Founder: the late Mignon Sherwood Delano

Financial Summary

Total Giving: $247,317 (2000); $193,461 (1999); $191,106 (1998)
Assets: $5,076,479 (2000); $5,448,822 (1999); $4,862,103 (1998)

Typical Recipients

Arts & Humanities: Arts Associations & Councils, Arts Festivals, Arts Funds, Community Arts, Historic Preservation, History & Archaeology, Libraries, Theater
Civic & Public Affairs: Civic & Public Affairs-General, Housing, Municipalities/Towns, Urban & Community Affairs, Women's Affairs
Education: Agricultural Education, Arts/Humanities Education, Colleges & Universities, Elementary Education (Public), Education-General, Literacy, Preschool Education, Public Education (Precollege), School Volunteerism
Environment: Energy
Health: Cancer, Clinics/Medical Centers, Emergency/Ambulance Services, Eyes/Blindness, Hospices, Hospitals, Mental Health, Preventive Medicine/Wellness Organizations
Religion: Religion-General, Religious Welfare
Social Services: Camps, Child Abuse, Child Welfare, Community Centers, Community Service Organizations, Domestic Violence, Family Planning, Family Services, Food/Clothing Distribution, People with Disabilities, Recreation & Athletics, Social Services-General, Special Olympics, Substance Abuse, United Funds/United Ways, Volunteer Services, Youth Organizations

Application Procedures

Initial Contact: Application form available.
Deadlines: Deadline is September 15.

Additional Information

Publications: Application Form
Trust(s): National City Bank MI NA

Foundation Officials

Ellen Altamore: adv
Rebecca Burnett: adv
G. Phillip Dietrich: adv
Bernard Riker: adv
David Ticknor: adv

Grants Analysis

Disclosure Period: calendar year ending 2000
Total Grants: $247,317
Number of Grants: 26
Average Grant: $9,512
Highest Grant: $30,000
Typical Range: $500 to $20,000

Recent Grants

Note: Grants derived from 1999 Form 990.

General

20,000	Allegan Jaycees, Allegan, MI -- equipment
15,500	Sylvia's Place, Inc, Allegan, MI -- operations, equipment
12,000	Wings of Hope Hospice, Plainwell, MI -- programming
10,000	Allegan Area Arts Council, Allegan, MI -- programming
10,000	Allegan Ministerium Central Food Pantry, Allegan, MI -- operations
10,000	Allegan Public Schools/Allegan Arts Council, Allegan, MI -- programming
10,000	Child and Family Services of Western Michigan, Holland, MI -- programming
10,000	Christian Neighbors, Otsego, MI -- programming
10,000	Family Planning Association of Allegan County, Inc, Allegan, MI -- programming
9,138	Allegan County Intermediate Schools, Allegan, MI -- programming

HAZEL DELL FOUNDATION

Giving Contact

J. Dunlop, Hazel Dell Foundation
1013 Centre Road, No. 350
Wilmington, DE 19809

Description

Founded: 1956
EIN: 136161744
Organization Type: Private Foundation
Giving Locations: CT; MA; NJ
Grant Types: General Support.

Donor Information

Founder: the late Harry C. McClarity

Financial Summary

Total Giving: $114,000 (2000); $114,000 (1999); $188,000 (1998)
Assets: $3,358,863 (2000); $7,824,737 (1999); $6,757,570 (1998)
Gifts Received: $526,019 (1996). Note: In 1996, contributions were received from the June McClarity Powers Trust.

Typical Recipients

Arts & Humanities: Arts Festivals, Ballet, Libraries, Music, Theater
Civic & Public Affairs: Civic & Public Affairs-General, Housing, Municipalities/Towns, Native American Affairs, Parades/Festivals, Safety
Education: Arts/Humanities Education, Colleges & Universities, Engineering/Technological Education, Medical Education, Minority Education, Private Education (Precollege), Public Education (Precollege), Secondary Education (Public)
Environment: Wildlife Protection
Health: Children's Health/Hospitals, Clinics/Medical Centers, Emergency/Ambulance Services, Health Organizations, Hospitals, Medical Rehabilitation, Medical Research
International: Health Care/Hospitals, International Environmental Issues, International Relief Efforts, Missionary/Religious Activities
Religion: Churches, Religion-General, Religious Welfare
Social Services: Animal Protection, Child Welfare, Community Service Organizations, Counseling, Crime Prevention, Family Services, Recreation & Athletics, United Funds/United Ways, Youth Organizations

Application Procedures

Initial Contact: The foundation has no formal grant application procedure or application form.
Deadlines: None.

Restrictions

No support for individuals.

Foundation Officials

Joy S. Dunlop: president, director
Gail A. Fallon: secretary, director
Diane Schroeder: director
William J. Sullivan: treasurer, director PRIM CORP EMPL director advisor: Rolex Watch U.S.A. Inc.

Grants Analysis

Disclosure Period: calendar year ending 2000
Total Grants: $114,000
Number of Grants: 29
Average Grant: $2,357*
Highest Grant: $48,000
Lowest Grant: $300
Typical Range: $1,000 to $5,000
*Note: Average grant figure excludes highest grant.

Recent Grants

Note: Grants derived from 2001 Form 990.

General

24,000	United States Rugby Football Foundation, Boston, MA
2,500	Fairfield Fire Department, Fairfield, CT
2,500	New England Ballet Company, Orange, CT
2,000	Hospital for Special Surgery, New York, NY
2,000	Montana Wildlife Federation, Helena, MT
2,000	Mount Ida College, Newton Center, MA
2,000	New England College, Henniker, NH
2,000	Rocky Mountain Elk Foundation, Missoula, MT
2,000	St. Luke's Catholic Church, Westport, CT
2,000	Sisters of New Skete, Cambridge, NY

GLADYS KRIEBLE DELMAS FOUNDATION

Giving Contact

Joseph C. Mitchell, Trustee
521 5th Avenue, Suite 1612
New York, NY 10175-1699
Phone: (212)687-0011
Web: http://www.delmas.org

Description

Founded: 1976
EIN: 510193884
Organization Type: Private Foundation
Giving Locations: nationally and internationally.
Grant Types: General Support, Research.

Donor Information

Founder: the late Gladys Krieble Delmas, the late Jean Delmas

Financial Summary

Total Giving: $3,119,179 (2000); $2,909,429 (1999); $2,813,181 (1998). Note: 1996 Giving includes scholarship.
Giving Analysis: Giving for 2000 includes: foundation matching gifts ($10,000); foundation fellowships ($60,000); foundation gifts to individuals ($141,334); 1999: foundation scholarships ($10,000); foundation gifts to individuals ($140,570); foundation fellowships ($175,000); foundation matching gifts ($196,750) 1998: foundation gifts to individuals ($128,381)
Assets: $66,326,848 (2000); $70,657,633 (1999); $71,271,167 (1998)
Gifts Received: $701,899 (1995); $818,586 (1993); $30,229,874 (1992). Note: In 1995, contributions were received from the estate of Gladys K. Delmas.

Typical Recipients

Arts & Humanities: Arts Associations & Councils, Arts Festivals, Arts Outreach, Ballet, Dance, Arts & Humanities-General, Historic Preservation, History & Archaeology, Libraries, Literary Arts, Museums/Galleries, Music, Opera, Performing Arts, Theater
Civic & Public Affairs: Civic & Public Affairs-General, Nonprofit Management, Parades/Festivals, Professional & Trade Associations, Public Policy

Education: Arts/Humanities Education, Colleges & Universities, Continuing Education, Education Associations, Education-General, International Studies, Legal Education, Private Education (Precollege), Social Sciences Education, Student Aid
Environment: Environment-General
Health: Hospitals, Research/Studies Institutes
International: Foreign Arts Organizations, Foreign Educational Institutions, International Organizations, International Relations, Missionary/Religious Activities
Science: Scientific Centers & Institutes
Social Services: Community Service Organizations, Social Services-General

Application Procedures

Initial Contact: Application to the humanities, library, and performing arts programs are by invitation only. For other programs and deadline information, contact foundation.

Foundation Officials

Patricia Hochschild Labalme: trustee B New York, NY 1927. ED Bryn Mawr College BA (1948); Harvard University MA (1950); Harvard University PhD (1958). PRIM CORP EMPL assistant director: Princeton University Institute Advanced Study. NONPR AFFIL member: Renaissance Society America; member: Society Renaissance Studies; member: Phi Beta Kappa; honorary trustee: Brearley School; member: Cream Hill Lake Association; trustee: American Rome; member: Ateneo Veneto; member: American Historical Association. CLUB AFFIL Cosmopolitan Club; Harvard Club.
Joseph C. Mitchell: trustee
David Harry Stam: trustee B Paterson, NJ 1935. ED Wheaton College BA (1955); University of Edinburgh New College (1955-1956); Rutgers University MLS (1962); City University of New York (1963-1964); Northwestern University PhD (1978). PRIM CORP EMPL senior scholar: Syracuse University. NONPR AFFIL member: American Antiquarian Society; member: American Historical Association. CLUB AFFIL Princeton New York Club; Caxton Club; Grolier Club.

Grants Analysis

Disclosure Period: calendar year ending 2000
Total Grants: $2,907,845*
Number of Grants: 140
Average Grant: $20,770
Highest Grant: $100,000
Typical Range: $10,000 to $40,000
*Note: Giving excludes fellowships, matching gifts, and grants to individuals.

Recent Grants

Note: Grants derived from 2001 Form 990.

Library-Related

50,000	Library Company of Philadelphia, Philadelphia, PA -- dissertation fellowship
40,000	Frick Collection, New York, NY -- historic archives

General

141,000	Woodrow Wilson National Fellowship Foundation, Princeton, NJ -- Millicent C. McIntosh Fellowships Program
100,000	New York City Ballet, New York, NY -- Archive Project
100,000	New York City Opera, Inc., New York, NY -- support for seasons
100,000	Woodrow Wilson National Fellowship Foundation, Princeton, NJ -- Woodrow Wilson Postdoctoral Fellowships
70,000	People and Stories, Trenton, NJ -- operating support
50,000	Bennington College Corporation, Bennington, VT -- Masters Program
50,000	Brooklyn Academy of Music, Brooklyn, NY -- theater programs
50,000	Brooklyn Academy of Music, Brooklyn, NY -- opera
50,000	University of Toronto, Toronto, ON Canada
50,000	Yale University, New Haven, CT

N. DEMOS FOUNDATION

Giving Contact

Diane Day, Secretary
c/o The Northern Trust Co.
50 S. LaSalle St.
Chicago, IL 60675
Phone: (312)630-6000
Fax: (312)444-4122
E-mail: ddm@ntrs.com

Description

Founded: 1964
EIN: 366165689
Organization Type: Private Foundation
Giving Locations: Greece
Grant Types: General Support, Scholarship.

Donor Information

Founder: the late Nicholas Demos

Financial Summary

Total Giving: $419,000 (fiscal year ending June 30, 2001); $419,000 (fiscal 2000); $332,120 (fiscal 1999)
Assets: $5,178,252 (fiscal 2001); $6,452,776 (fiscal 2000); $5,548,094 (fiscal 1999)

Typical Recipients

Arts & Humanities: Arts Centers, Libraries
Civic & Public Affairs: Civic & Public Affairs-General
Education: Agricultural Education, Arts/Humanities Education, Colleges & Universities, Education-General, Private Education (Precollege)
Health: Children's Health/Hospitals, Clinics/Medical Centers, Medical Research, Mental Health
International: Foreign Educational Institutions, International-General, Health Care/Hospitals, International Organizations, International Peace & Security Issues, International Relief Efforts, Missionary/Religious Activities
Religion: Religious Organizations, Religious Welfare
Social Services: Child Welfare, Community Service Organizations, Family Services, People with Disabilities, Social Services-General, Veterans, Youth Organizations

Application Procedures

Initial Contact: Send a brief letter of inquiry, then a full proposal.
Application Requirements: Include a description of organization, amount requested, purpose of funds sought, recently audited financial statement, and proof of tax-exempt status.
Deadlines: Applications are due by annual meeting.

Restrictions

Limited to charities in Greece involved in various social work activities.

Additional Information

Publications: Application Guidelines

Foundation Officials

Mrs. Desi Bakalis: director
Elizabeth R. Gebhard: director
Charles M. Gray: president
Metropolitan Iakovos: director
Bishop Iakvos: director
Judge Paul C. Lillios: director
Diane Day Miles: secretary
J. Terrance Murray: treasurer
Robert F. Reusche: chairman B New Rochelle, NY 1927. ED Ohio State University BS (1949); University

of Chicago MBA (1955). PRIM CORP EMPL vice chairman, director: Northern Trust Co. CORP AFFIL chairman, director: Northern Trust FloridaCorp.; director: Banque Scandinave Suisse; director: Griffin Group. NONPR AFFIL director: JR Bowman Health Center; trustee: Ravinia Festival Association; member: Financial Analysts Federation; trustee: Chicago Home Incurables; member: Corp. Fiduciary Association; member: American Bankers Association; member advisory board: Catholic Charities.

Mrs. Irving Seaman, Jr.: director

Gordon H. Smith: director B Syracuse, NY 1915. ED Princeton University BA (1932-1936); Yale University LLB (1939). PRIM CORP EMPL counsel, partner: Gardner, Carton & Douglas. NONPR AFFIL member: American Society of Corporate Secretaries; member: Illinois Bar Association; member: American Bar Association. CLUB AFFIL Economic Chicago Club; Law Club Chicago; Commercial Chicago Club.

Mrs. Theodore D. Tieken: director

Alison Winter: treasurer

Grants Analysis

Disclosure Period: fiscal year ending June 30, 2001
Total Grants: $419,000
Number of Grants: 22
Average Grant: $14,200*
Highest Grant: $70,000
Lowest Grant: $5,000
Typical Range: $5,000 to $30,000
***Note:** Average grant figure excludes two highest grants ($135,000).

Recent Grants

Note: Grants derived from fiscal 2000 Form 990.

General

65,000	Spastics Society, Athens
60,000	Trustees of Anatolia College
6,0000	Workshop -- special training and placement "virgin Mary the merciful"
35,000	Social Work Foundation
30,000	Trustees of American Farm School
20,500	Friends of the Deaf of Thessalonikiki
20,000	Margarita
16,000	American School of Classical Studies, New York, NY
15,000	American College of Greece
15,000	Foundation for the Deaf and Public Hard of Hearing

DEMOULAS SUPERMARKETS, INC.

Company Headquarters

875 E. St.
Tewksbury, MA 01876

Company Description

Founded: 1954
Revenue: US$1.9 billion (2001)
Employees: 7,000
SIC(s): 5411 Grocery Stores, 6512 Nonresidential Building Operators.

Operating Locations

Demoulas Supermarkets Inc. (MA--Andover, Bellingham, Burlington, Chelmsford, Chelsea, Danvers, Haverhill, Lawrence, Leominster, Lowell, Middleton, Newburyport, North Andover, North Billerica, Raynham, Rowley, Westford, Wilmington, Woburn; NH--Concord, Hudson, Londonderry, Milford, Plaistow, Portsmouth, Rindge, Rochester, Seabrook, Somersworth, Stratham)

Demoulas Foundation

Giving Contact

Telemachus A. Demoulas, Trustee
Demoulas Foundation
286 Chelmsford Street
Chelmsford, MA 01824
Phone: (978)224-1024
Fax: (978)640-8392

Description

Founded: 1964
EIN: 042723441
Organization Type: Corporate Foundation
Giving Locations: primarily New England.
Grant Types: Endowment, General Support.

Donor Information

Founder: Demoulas Supermarkets, Inc., and members of the Demoulas family

Financial Summary

Total Giving: $1,276,100 (2001); $2,259,443 (2000); $1,755,500 (1999). Note: Contributes through foundation only.
Giving Analysis: Giving for 2000 includes: foundation ($2,259,443) 1999: foundation ($1,755,500)
Assets: $36,142,070 (2001); $35,489,175 (2000); $37,880,279 (1999)

Typical Recipients

Arts & Humanities: Arts Associations & Councils, Arts Centers, Ballet, Dance, Arts & Humanities-General, Historic Preservation, History & Archaeology, Libraries, Literary Arts, Museums/Galleries, Music, Opera
Civic & Public Affairs: Botanical Gardens/Parks, Clubs, Civic & Public Affairs-General, Housing, Municipalities/Towns, Parades/Festivals, Philanthropic Organizations, Safety, Urban & Community Affairs, Women's Affairs
Education: Arts/Humanities Education, Business Education, Colleges & Universities, Education Funds, Education-General, International Studies, Leadership Training, Medical Education, Minority Education, Private Education (Precollege), Religious Education, Secondary Education (Private), Secondary Education (Private), Special Education, Student Aid
Environment: Environment-General
Health: Cancer, Children's Health/Hospitals, Diabetes, Geriatric Health, Health Organizations, Hospices, Hospitals, Long-Term Care, Medical Rehabilitation, Medical Research, Respiratory, Single-Disease Health Associations, Trauma Treatment
Religion: Churches, Dioceses, Religion-General, Religious Organizations, Religious Welfare
Science: Science Museums
Social Services: Camps, Community Centers, Community Service Organizations, Food/Clothing Distribution, Homes, People with Disabilities, Recreation & Athletics, Scouts, Senior Services, Social Services-General, Substance Abuse, Veterans, YMCA/YWCA/YMHA/YWHA, Youth Organizations

Application Procedures

Initial Contact: Send a brief letter of inquiry.
Application Requirements: Include a brief history of organization and description of need.
Deadlines: None.

Corporate Officials

Julien Lacourse: executive vice president

Grants Analysis

Disclosure Period: calendar year ending 2001
Total Grants: $1,276,100
Number of Grants: 169
Average Grant: $7,551
Highest Grant: $110,000

Lowest Grant: $100
Typical Range: $5,000 to $25,000

Recent Grants

Note: Grants derived from 2001 Form 990.

General

110,000	Boys and Girls Club of Lowell, Lowell, MA
100,000	Diocese of Boston Hellenic Orthodox Center, Boston, MA
100,000	Whistler House Museum of Art, Lowell, MA
60,000	Celebrity Series, Boston, MA
40,000	University of Arizona, Tucson, AZ -- scholarship fund
33,000	Boston College, Boston, MA
25,000	Catholic Schools Foundation, Brighton, MA
25,000	Hellenic College, Brookline, MA
25,000	Lowell Plan, Lowell, MA
25,000	Massachusetts General Hospital Roman DeSanctis Scholarship Fund, Boston, MA

DENDROICA FOUNDATION

Giving Contact

Leonard Richards, Vice President
Mellon Bank, NA
Three Mellon Bank Center
Pittsburgh, PA 15259-0001
Phone: (412)234-5892

Description

Founded: 1997
EIN: 237912826
Organization Type: Private Foundation
Giving Locations: Northeastern United States.
Grant Types: General Support, Project.

Financial Summary

Total Giving: $245,000 (2000); $216,100 (1999); $35,000 (1998)
Assets: $12,494,000 (2000); $5,639,972 (1999); $5,313,789 (1998)
Gifts Received: $7,096,000 (2000); $61,659 (1997)

Typical Recipients

Arts & Humanities: Libraries
Civic & Public Affairs: Botanical Gardens/Parks
Education: Environmental Education, Student Aid
Environment: Environment-General, Resource Conservation, Wildlife Protection

Application Procedures

Initial Contact: Contact the foundation for application procedures.
Notes: Most grantees are pre-selected by the distribution committee.

Restrictions

Grants are almost exclusively in the areas of nature conservation, preservation of biological diversity, and environmental education and research.

Additional Information

Trust(s): Mellon Bank NA

Grants Analysis

Disclosure Period: calendar year ending 2000
Total Grants: $245,000
Number of Grants: 13
Average Grant: $18,846
Highest Grant: $40,000
Typical Range: $5,000 to $30,000

Recent Grants

Note: Grants derived from 1999 Form 990.

Library-Related

5,000	New York Botanical Gardens, Bronx, NY

General

30,000	Nature Conservancy, Brunswick, ME
30,000	Nature Conservancy New Jersey Chapter, NJ
20,000	Natural Resources Council of Maine, Augusta, ME
20,000	RARE Center for Tropical Conservation, Philadelphia, PA
20,000	Trust for Public Lands Mid-Atlantic Region, New York, NY
15,000	American Farmland Trust, Washington, DC
15,000	Wildlife Conservation Society, New York, NY
15,000	Yale University School of Forestry and Environmental Studies, New Haven, CT
10,000	Nature Conservancy, Brunswick, ME
10,000	RARE Center for Tropical Conservation, Philadelphia, PA

HELEN PUMPHREY DENIT TRUST FOR CHARITABLE AND EDUCATIONAL PURPOSES

Giving Contact

Richard Adams, Trust Officer
c/o Bank of America
100 South Charles Street, MD4-325-09-03
Baltimore, MD 21201
Phone: (410)547-4333
Fax: (410)837-3096
E-mail: richard.adams@am.bankofamerica.com
Web: http://www.bankofamerica.com

Alternate Contact

Phone: 800-527-5394

Description

Founded: 1989
EIN: 526401248
Organization Type: Private Foundation
Giving Locations: DC
Grant Types: General Support.

Donor Information

Founder: the late Helen P. Denit

Financial Summary

Total Giving: $900,000 (fiscal year ending June 30, 2002 approx); $1,030,000 (fiscal 2001); $650,000 (fiscal 2000)
Assets: $6,500,000 (fiscal 2002 approx); $10,227,077 (fiscal 2001); $6,000 (fiscal 2000)

Typical Recipients

Arts & Humanities: Arts Festivals, History & Archaeology, Libraries, Museums/Galleries, Theater
Civic & Public Affairs: Botanical Gardens/Parks, Community Foundations, Civic & Public Affairs-General, Zoos/Aquariums
Education: Arts/Humanities Education, Colleges & Universities, Private Education (Precollege), Religious Education, Student Aid
Health: Cancer, Heart, Hospitals
Religion: Jewish Causes, Seminaries
Social Services: Child Abuse, Child Welfare, Food/Clothing Distribution, Recreation & Athletics

Application Procedures

Initial Contact: Send a brief letter of inquiry.
Application Requirements: Include amount requested and purpose of funds sought.
Deadlines: None.

Additional Information

Foundation/Giving Program still in operation, but grant making has been suspended. We have preferred charities indicated by Mrs. Denits will, and several multiyear commitments that will effectively limit consideration of additional grants for at least the next five years.
Trust(s): Bank of America

Grants Analysis

Disclosure Period: fiscal year ending June 30, 2001
Total Grants: $1,030,000
Number of Grants: 18
Average Grant: $51,176*
Highest Grant: $160,000
Typical Range: $5,000 to $60,000
*Note: Average grant figure excludes highest grant. Grant analysis provided by foundation.

Recent Grants

Note: Grants derived from fiscal 1999 Form 990.

General

100,000	American Heart Association, Baltimore, MD
60,000	George Washington University, Washington, DC
60,000	Greenebaum Cancer Center, Baltimore, MD
60,000	Montgomery General Hospital, Olney, MD
60,000	Wesley Theological Seminary, Washington, DC
50,000	Western Maryland College, Westminster, MD
20,000	Institute for Christian and Jewish Studies, Baltimore, MD
15,000	Baltimore Child Abuse Center, Inc., Baltimore, MD
15,000	Baltimore's Festival of the Arts, Baltimore, MD
15,000	Center for Poverty Solutions, Baltimore, MD

DENTSPLY INTERNATIONAL, INC.

Company Headquarters

PO Box 872
York, PA 17405-0872
Web: http://www.dentsply.com

Company Description

Founded: 1899
Ticker: XRAY
Exchange: NASDAQ
Revenue: US$1.513 billion (2002)
Employees: 7800 (2002)
SIC(s): 3800 Instruments & Related Products.

Operating Locations

Dentsply International Inc. (DE--Milford; OH--Cincinnati, Maumee)
Note: Includes division locations

Nonmonetary Support

Type: Donated Equipment; Donated Products

Dentsply International Foundation

Giving Contact

Dentsply International Foundation
Tax Dept.
570 W. College Ave.
York, PA 17405
Phone: (717)845-7511

Description

EIN: 236297307
Organization Type: Corporate Foundation
Giving Locations: nationally.
Grant Types: Award, Capital, General Support, Multiyear/Continuing Support, Research.

Financial Summary

Total Giving: $120,710 (2001); $122,500 (2000); $147,540 (1999)
Giving Analysis: Giving for 2001 includes: foundation grants to United Way ($48,000); foundation ($72,710); 2000: foundation grants to United Way ($15,000); 1999: foundation grants to United Way ($30,000); foundation ($117,540).
Assets: $75,616 (2001); $35,864 (2000); $32,534 (1999)
Gifts Received: $160,000 (2001); $125,000 (2000); $150,000 (1999). Note: Contributions were received from Dentsply International.

Typical Recipients

Arts & Humanities: Arts Funds, Arts & Humanities-General, Historic Preservation, History & Archaeology, Libraries, Museums/Galleries, Music, Performing Arts, Theater
Civic & Public Affairs: Botanical Gardens/Parks, Chambers of Commerce, Clubs, Community Foundations, Civic & Public Affairs-General, Hispanic Affairs, Housing, Philanthropic Organizations, Professional & Trade Associations, Public Policy, Safety, Urban & Community Affairs
Education: Arts/Humanities Education, Business Education, Colleges & Universities, Continuing Education, Education-General, Health & Physical Education, Medical Education, Minority Education, Public Education (Precollege), Student Aid
Environment: Resource Conservation
Health: AIDS/HIV, Cancer, Children's Health/Hospitals, Clinics/Medical Centers, Diabetes, Health-General, Geriatric Health, Health Organizations, Heart, Hospices, Hospitals, Medical Research, Nursing Services, Public Health, Single-Disease Health Associations, Transplant Networks/Donor Banks
Religion: Churches, Religion-General, Religious Organizations, Religious Welfare
Social Services: Animal Protection, At-Risk Youth, Big Brother/Big Sister, Child Abuse, Child Welfare, Community Service Organizations, Day Care, Family Services, Food/Clothing Distribution, People with Disabilities, Recreation & Athletics, Senior Services, Shelters/Homelessness, United Funds/United Ways, YMCA/YWCA/YMHA/YWHA, Youth Organizations

Application Procedures

Initial Contact: The foundation has no formal grant application procedure or application form.
Deadlines: None.

Restrictions

Does not support individuals, religious organizations for sectarian purposes, political or lobbying groups, or organizations outside operating areas.

Additional Information

Provides grants for dental health and higher education.

Corporate Officials

Leslie A. Jones: chairman vice president, chief financial officer PRIM CORP EMPL chairman: Dentsply International.

Gary Kunkle: president, chief operating officer PRIM CORP EMPL president, chief operating officer: Dentsply International.

John C. Miles, II: president, chief executive officer, director B Portland, ME 1942. ED Lehigh University (1964); New York University (1971). PRIM CORP EMPL president, chief executive officer, director: Dentsply International. CORP AFFIL director: Dental Manufacturers America.

Edward D. Yates: senior vice president, chief financial officer PRIM CORP EMPL senior vice president, chief financial officer: Dentsply International.

Foundation Officials

Brian M. Addison: trustee

Burton C. Borgelt: trustee B Cincinnati, OH 1933. ED University of Toledo.

J. Patrick Clark: secretary

Marcus K. Dixon: trustee B Baltimore, MD 1945. ED University of Baltimore (1966). PRIM CORP EMPL treasurer: Dentsply International.

William R. Jellison: trustee

John C. Miles, II: trustee (see above)

Edward D. Yates: trustee (see above)

Grants Analysis

Disclosure Period: calendar year ending 2001
Total Grants: $72,710*
Number of Grants: 31
Average Grant: $999*
Highest Grant: $42,750
Lowest Grant: $250
Typical Range: $500 to $3,500
***Note:** Giving excludes United Way. Average grant figure excludes highest grant.

Recent Grants

Note: Grants derived from 2001 Form 990.

Library-Related

500	Intercollegiate Studies Institute, Inc., Wilmington, DE -- community service

General

40,500	United Way of York County, York, PA -- community service
10,000	New York Fire Fighters Fund, New York, NY -- community service
7,000	United Way of Delaware, Wilmington, DE -- community service
2,500	Junior Achievement of Delaware, Wilmington, DE -- community service
1,000	American Heart Association, Georgetown, DE -- community service
1,000	Community Programs Council, Inc., York, PA -- community service
1,000	Friends of the Capitol Theater, Dover, DE -- community service
1,000	Manito, Inc., PA -- community service
1,000	Noah's Place, York, PA -- community service
1,000	Tressler Lutheran Services -- community service

DEROY TESTAMENTARY FOUNDATION

Giving Contact

Julie Rodecker Holly, Vice President
26999 Central Park Boulevard, Suite 160N
Southfield, MI 48076

Phone: (248)827-0920
Fax: (248)827-0922
E-mail: DeRoyFdtn@aol.com

Description

Founded: 1979
EIN: 382208833
Organization Type: General Purpose Foundation
Giving Locations: MI: Metropolitan Detroit
Grant Types: Award, General Support, Multiyear/Continuing Support, Professorship, Project, Scholarship.

Donor Information

Founder: Established in 1979 by the late Helen L. DeRoy .

Financial Summary

Total Giving: $2,060,000 (2002 approx); $1,920,612 (2001); $2,437,339 (2000)
Giving Analysis: Giving for 2001 includes: foundation grants to United Way ($34,000); 1999: foundation grants to United Way ($8,500); 1998: foundation grants to United Way ($8,500)
Assets: $46,724,275 (2001); $45,790,291 (2000); $40,723,787 (1999)

Typical Recipients

Arts & Humanities: Arts Associations & Councils, Arts Centers, Arts Funds, Arts Institutes, Arts Outreach, Arts & Humanities-General, Historic Preservation, History & Archaeology, Libraries, Literary Arts, Museums/Galleries, Music, Opera, Performing Arts, Public Broadcasting, Theater
Civic & Public Affairs: Clubs, Civic & Public Affairs-General, Housing, Municipalities/Towns, Parades/Festivals, Public Policy, Urban & Community Affairs, Women's Affairs, Zoos/Aquariums
Education: Agricultural Education, Arts/Humanities Education, Business Education, Colleges & Universities, Community & Junior Colleges, Education Funds, Engineering/Technological Education, Faculty Development, Education-General, Education-General, International Exchange, Leadership Training, Legal Education, Medical Education, Minority Education, Preschool Education, Private Education (Precollege), Public Education (Precollege), Religious Education, Science/Mathematics Education, Secondary Education (Private), Student Aid
Environment: Air/Water Quality, Environment-General
Health: Cancer, Children's Health/Hospitals, Clinics/Medical Centers, Emergency/Ambulance Services, Eyes/Blindness, Health Organizations, Hospices, Hospitals, Long-Term Care, Medical Rehabilitation, Medical Research, Mental Health, Nursing Services, Prenatal Health Issues, Public Health, Trauma Treatment
Religion: Churches, Jewish Causes, Religious Organizations, Religious Welfare, Synagogues/Temples
Science: Scientific Centers & Institutes
Social Services: Animal Protection, At-Risk Youth, Camps, Child Welfare, Community Centers, Community Service Organizations, Counseling, Day Care, Domestic Violence, Family Planning, Family Services, Homes, People with Disabilities, Recreation & Athletics, Senior Services, United Funds/United Ways, Youth Organizations

Application Procedures

Initial Contact: The foundation reports that applications may vary depending upon the nature of the request.
Deadlines: None.

Restrictions

The foundation reports that it principally makes grants to institutions of established excellence in Michigan. Grants are not made to individuals.

Foundation Officials

Arthur Rodecker: president, trustee B 1926. PRIM CORP EMPL president: Rodecker & Co. Investment Brokers.

Grants Analysis

Disclosure Period: calendar year ending 2002
Total Grants: $2,060,000*
Number of Grants: 152
Average Grant: $11,000
Highest Grant: $250,000
Lowest Grant: $1,000
Typical Range: $5,000 to $25,000
***Note:** Grants analysis was provided by the foundation.

Recent Grants

Note: Grants derived from 2001 Form 990.

General

100,000	Detroit Science Center, Detroit, MI
75,000	Detroit Institute of Arts, Detroit, MI
75,000	Detroit Symphony Orchestra Hall, Detroit, MI
50,000	Brandeis University, Boston, MA
50,000	Community House, Birmingham, MI
50,000	Detroit Zoological Society, Royal Oak, MI
50,000	Jewish Federation of Metropolitan Detroit, Detroit, MI
50,000	Leader Dogs for the Blind, Rochester, MI
50,000	Michigan State University, Lansing, MI
50,000	Oakwood Healthcare System Foundation, Dearborn, MI

LEROY E. DETTMAN FOUNDATION

Giving Contact

Gregory L. Dettman, Secretary & Director
1615 S. Federal Hwy., Ste. 300
Boca Raton, FL 33432-7534
Phone: (561)362-9104

Description

Founded: 1978
EIN: 591784551
Organization Type: Private Foundation
Grant Types: Endowment, Scholarship.

Donor Information

Founder: the late Leroy E. Dettman

Financial Summary

Total Giving: $153,340 (fiscal year ending October 31, 2001); $191,539 (fiscal 2000); $187,815 (fiscal 1999)
Giving Analysis: Giving for fiscal 2001 includes: foundation grants to United Way ($1,500); foundation scholarships ($72,000); fiscal 1999: foundation scholarships ($74,500); fiscal 1998: foundation scholarships ($67,500)
Assets: $1,780,497 (fiscal 2001); $2,804,229 (fiscal 2000); $3,001,778 (fiscal 1999)

Typical Recipients

Arts & Humanities: Arts Associations & Councils, Arts & Humanities-General, Libraries, Museums/Galleries, Music, Public Broadcasting, Theater
Civic & Public Affairs: Clubs, Community Foundations, Civic & Public Affairs-General, Housing, Public Policy, Women's Affairs
Education: Business Education, Colleges & Universities, Community & Junior Colleges, Faculty Development, Private Education (Precollege), Public Education (Precollege), Special Education, Student Aid
Environment: Environment-General

Health: Children's Health/Hospitals, Diabetes, Emergency/Ambulance Services, Heart, Hospices, Hospitals, Medical Research, Single-Disease Health Associations
International: International Relations, International Relief Efforts
Religion: Churches, Religion-General, Religious Organizations, Religious Welfare
Science: Scientific Organizations
Social Services: Community Service Organizations, Food/Clothing Distribution, People with Disabilities, Recreation & Athletics, Social Services-General, United Funds/United Ways, Youth Organizations

Application Procedures

Initial Contact: Return completed application form along with transcripts, SAT or ACT scores, and financial statements.
Deadlines: March 15.
Decision Notification: Grant awards will be announced by June. Funds will be disbursed in August.

Additional Information

Provides scholarships to children of employees of Interim Services.
Publications: Application Guidelines

Foundation Officials

Douglas R. Dettman: president, director
Gregory L. Dettman: secretary, director
Barbara Jane Fleming: vice president, director
Carolyn D. Rubin: treasurer, director

Grants Analysis

Disclosure Period: fiscal year ending October 31, 2001
Total Grants: $81,340*
Number of Grants: 59
Average Grant: $1,379
Highest Grant: $10,000
Lowest Grant: $100
Typical Range: $100 to $5,000
*Note: Giving excludes scholarships and United Way.

Recent Grants

Note: Grants derived from 2000 Form 990.

Library-Related

22,039	Fau Foundation, Boca Raton, FL
19,350	Broward Public Library Foundation, Ft. Lauderdale, FL
19,200	Broward Public Library Foundation, Ft. Lauderdale, FL
15,789	Fau Foundation, Boca Raton, FL

General

31,550	St. Marks School, New York, NY
30,000	Anderson School at UCLA, Los Angeles, CA
22,550	North Carolina Wesleyan College, Rocky Mount, NC
20,000	University of California Los Angeles, Los Angeles, CA
20,000	University of California Los Angeles, Los Angeles, CA
19,850	St. Lawrence Chapel
19,750	Morikami Museum, Delray Beach, FL
19,550	Coral Springs Charter School, Coral Springs, FL
19,300	Easter Seals
19,200	JR Welfare, Manors, FL

GEORGE H. DEUBLE FOUNDATION

Giving Contact

Andrew H. Deuble, Secretary & Trustee
c/o DCC Corp.
5757 Mayfair Rd.
PO Box 2288
North Canton, OH 44720-1546
Phone: (330)828-9770

Description

Founded: 1947
EIN: 341806245
Organization Type: Private Foundation
Grant Types: General Support.

Donor Information

Founder: Established in 1947 by the late George H. Deuble .

Financial Summary

Total Giving: $1,690,061 (2000); $1,745,961 (1999); $1,513,845 (1998)
Giving Analysis: Giving for 2000 includes: foundation grants to United Way ($73,000) 1999: foundation grants to United Way ($625)
Assets: $32,582,412 (2000); $33,918,085 (1999); $32,955,512 (1998)

Typical Recipients

Arts & Humanities: Arts Centers, Arts Festivals, Historic Preservation, Libraries, Museums/Galleries, Music
Civic & Public Affairs: Economic Development, Civic & Public Affairs-General, Housing, Urban & Community Affairs
Education: Business Education, Colleges & Universities, Education Reform, Private Education (Precollege), Public Education (Precollege), Student Aid
Health: Health Funds, Heart, Hospitals, Medical Research
Religion: Religious Welfare
Social Services: Family Services, Recreation & Athletics, United Funds/United Ways, Youth Organizations

Application Procedures

Initial Contact: Send a brief letter of inquiry.
Application Requirements: purpose of funds sought and amount requested.
Deadlines: None.

Foundation Officials

Andrew H. Deuble: secretary, trustee
Steven G. Deuble: president, trustee B Canton, OH 1947. ED Ohio Wesleyan University (1969). PRIM CORP EMPL chief executive officer, director: DCC Corp. CORP AFFIL president, director: Massillon Plaque Co.
Walter C. Deuble: trustee B 1921. PRIM CORP EMPL chairman board, director: DCC Corp.
Walter J. Deuble: trustee

Grants Analysis

Disclosure Period: calendar year ending 2000
Total Grants: $1,617,061*
Number of Grants: 171
Average Grant: $3,242*
Highest Grant: $1,120,000
Typical Range: $1,000 to $10,000
*Note: Giving excludes United Way. Average grant figure excludes highest grant.

Recent Grants

Note: Grants derived from 2000 Form 990.

Library-Related

50,000	National First Ladies Library, Canton, OH

General

125,000	Walsh University, Canton, OH
112,000	Aultman Hospital, Canton, OH
110,000	Stark Community Foundation, Canton, OH
100,000	North Canton Medical Foundation, Canton, OH
75,000	JR Coleman Family Services Corp., Canton, OH
55,000	Community Capital Campaign, Canton, OH
54,333	Education Enhancement Partnership, Canton, OH
50,000	Echoing Hills Village, Warsaw, OH
50,000	United Way Central Stark County, Canton, OH
38,200	Blue Coats Drum and Bugle Corps

DEVORE FOUNDATION

Giving Contact

Richard A. DeVore, President & Secretary
PO Box 782615
Wichita, KS 67278-2615
Phone: (316)634-1275

Description

Founded: 1953
EIN: 486109754
Organization Type: Private Foundation
Giving Locations: KS: Wichita
Grant Types: Capital, Endowment, General Support, Multiyear/Continuing Support, Operating Expenses, Project.

Donor Information

Founder: the late Floyd DeVore, Richard A. DeVore, William O. DeVore

Financial Summary

Total Giving: $237,850 (fiscal year ending November 30, 2001); $275,752 (fiscal 2000); $266,695 (fiscal 1998)
Giving Analysis: Giving for fiscal 2001 includes: foundation grants to United Way ($5,000); fiscal 2000: foundation scholarships ($1,280); foundation grants to United Way ($5,000) fiscal 1998: foundation grants to United Way ($5,000)
Assets: $7,584,791 (fiscal 2001); $8,181,626 (fiscal 2000); $6,164,415 (fiscal 1998)
Gifts Received: $5,000 (fiscal 2000); $5,000 (fiscal 1997); $142,000 (fiscal 1996). Note: In fiscal 1997 and 2000, contributions were received from Devore and Sons. In fiscal 1996, contributions were received from R.A. Devore and William Devore.

Typical Recipients

Arts & Humanities: Arts Associations & Councils, Arts Centers, Arts & Humanities-General, History & Archaeology, Libraries, Museums/Galleries, Music, Performing Arts
Civic & Public Affairs: Business/Free Enterprise, Clubs, Community Foundations, Employment/Job Training, Civic & Public Affairs-General, Municipalities/Towns, Native American Affairs, Public Policy, Urban & Community Affairs, Zoos/Aquariums
Education: Colleges & Universities, Education Funds, Education-General, Literacy, Private Education (Precollege), Student Aid
Environment: Air/Water Quality
Health: AIDS/HIV, Cancer, Children's Health/Hospitals, Geriatric Health, Hospices, Hospitals, Medical Research, Public Health, Single-Disease Health Associations
Religion: Churches, Ministries, Religious Welfare
Social Services: At-Risk Youth, Big Brother/Big Sister, Child Welfare, Community Service Organizations, Crime Prevention, Family Services, Homes, People with Disabilities, Scouts, Senior Services, Social Services-General, Special Olympics, Substance Abuse, United Funds/United Ways, YMCA/YWCA/YMHA/YWHA, Youth Organizations

Application Procedures

Initial Contact: Send a brief letter of inquiry.
Application Requirements: Include a description of organization, amount requested, purpose of funds sought, recently audited financial statement, and proof of tax-exempt status.
Deadlines: None.

Decision Notification: Contributions are planned in advance and donations requiring a rapid decision are rarely made.

Restrictions

The foundation makes contributions to operating and educational organizations only.

Additional Information

Publications: Application Guidelines; Annual Report

Foundation Officials

Richard A. DeVore: president, secretary
William O. DeVore: vice president, treasurer

Grants Analysis

Disclosure Period: fiscal year ending November 30, 2001
Total Grants: $232,850*
Number of Grants: 101
Average Grant: $1,140*
Highest Grant: $90,000
Lowest Grant: $100
Typical Range: $100 to $5,000
*Note: Giving excludes United Way. Average grant figure excludes two highest grants ($120,000).

Recent Grants

Note: Grants derived from fiscal 2000 Form 990.

General

125,000	City of Wichita, Wichita, KS -- sculpture program
30,000	Old Cowtown Museum, Wichita, KS
12,500	First Presbyterian Church, Wichita, KS
10,000	City of Wichita, Wichita, KS
10,000	Stage One, Wichita, KS
5,000	Friends of the Wichita Art Museum, Wichita, KS
5,000	Hospice, Wichita, KS
5,000	United Way of the Plains, Wichita, KS
5,000	Wichita YMCA, Wichita, KS
3,000	Wichita Art Museum, Wichita, KS

RICHARD AND HELEN DEVOS FOUNDATION

Giving Contact

Ginny Vander Hart, Foundation Director
126 Ottowa Northwest, Suite 500
Grand Rapids, MI 49503
Phone: (616)454-4114
Fax: (616)454-0970
E-mail: virginiav@rdvcorp.com

Description

Founded: 1969
EIN: 237066873
Organization Type: Family Foundation
Giving Locations: FL: including central Florida; MI: Grand Rapids nationally.
Grant Types: Capital, Challenge, General Support, Matching, Operating Expenses, Project, Seed Money.

Donor Information

Founder: The foundation was established in Michigan in 1969 by Richard M. DeVos, co-founder and president of the Amway Corporation, and his wife, Helen DeVos. Periodic contributions from the DeVos family increase the foundation's asset level. Executive personnel of the Amway Corporation provide management and administrative aid to the foundation. Mr. Devos purchased the National Basketball Association's Orlando Magic franchise in 1991 for a reported $85 million.

Financial Summary

Total Giving: $26,574,754 (2001); $33,614,934 (2000); $17,544,364 (1998)
Giving Analysis: Giving for 1998 includes: foundation scholarships ($200,000) foundation grants to United Way ($315,000)
Assets: $97,048,407 (2001); $123,862,317 (2000); $148,606,486 (1998)
Gifts Received: $3,596,869 (2001); $18,416,788 (1998); $10,002,230 (1995). Note: In 2001, contributions were received from Richard M. Devos Clat 2. In 1998, contributions were received from Amway Corp. ($4,000,000) and Richard Devos ($14,416,788).

Typical Recipients

Arts & Humanities: Arts Associations & Councils, Arts Centers, Arts Funds, Libraries, Museums/Galleries, Music, Public Broadcasting
Civic & Public Affairs: Botanical Gardens/Parks, Business/Free Enterprise, First Amendment Issues, Civic & Public Affairs-General, Housing, Inner-City Development, Law & Justice, Philanthropic Organizations, Public Policy, Urban & Community Affairs, Zoos/Aquariums
Education: Business Education, Business-School Partnerships, Colleges & Universities, Education Funds, Education Reform, Engineering/Technological Education, Education-General, Private Education (Precollege), Religious Education, Secondary Education (Public), Student Aid
Environment: Air/Water Quality, Environment-General
Health: Clinics/Medical Centers, Emergency/Ambulance Services, Health-General, Health Funds, Health Organizations, Hospitals, Long-Term Care, Medical Research, Prenatal Health Issues, Public Health, Single-Disease Health Associations, Transplant Networks/Donor Banks
International: Health Care/Hospitals, International Affairs, International Development, International Organizations, International Relations, International Relief Efforts, Missionary/Religious Activities
Religion: Bible Study/Translation, Churches, Religion-General, Ministries, Missionary Activities (Domestic), Religious Organizations, Religious Welfare, Seminaries, Social/Policy Issues
Social Services: Camps, Child Welfare, Community Centers, Community Service Organizations, Delinquency & Criminal Rehabilitation, Family Planning, Family Services, Food/Clothing Distribution, Homes, Homes, People with Disabilities, Recreation & Athletics, Scouts, Senior Services, Social Services-General, United Funds/United Ways, YMCA/YWCA/YMHA/YWHA, Youth Organizations

Application Procedures

Initial Contact: Prospective applicants should send a letter of proposal.
Application Requirements: In the preliminary letter, describe the project and organization for which funds are sought. The foundation asks that applicants specify amounts.
Deadlines: None.

Additional Information

Publications: Guidelines

Foundation Officials

William Boer: vice president, assistant secretary
Helen June (Van Wesep) DeVos: president
Robert H. Schierbeek: treasurer
Jerry L. Tubergen: vice president, secretary, chief operating officer CORP AFFIL director: Genmar Holdings Inc.

Grants Analysis

Disclosure Period: calendar year ending 2001
Total Grants: $25,974,754*
Number of Grants: 155
Average Grant: $59,613*
Highest Grant: $3,000,000

Lowest Grant: $199
Typical Range: $10,000 to $100,000
*Note: Giving excludes United Way. Average grant excludes eleven highest grants ($17,390,500).

Recent Grants

Note: Grants derived from 2001 Form 990.

General

3,000,000	Grand Rapids Christian School Association, Grand Rapids, MI
2,590,000	Grand Action Foundation, Grand Rapids, MI
2,015,500	Calvin College, Grand Rapids, MI
2,000,000	Gospel Communications International, Muskegon, MI
1,435,000	Grand Valley State University Foundation, Grand Rapids, MI
1,315,000	Grand Rapids Symphony, Grand Rapids, MI
1,030,000	Holland Home, Grand Rapids, MI
1,005,000	Ada Christian School, Ada, MI
1,000,000	Lee University, Cleveland, TN
1,000,000	National Constitution Center, Philadelphia, PA

DEWAR FOUNDATION

Giving Contact

Frank W. Getman, President & Director
PO Box 613
Oneonta, NY 13820
Phone: (607)432-3530

Description

Founded: 1947
EIN: 166054329
Organization Type: Private Foundation
Giving Locations: NY: including Oneonta and surrounding area
Grant Types: General Support.

Donor Information

Founder: the late Jessie Smith Dewar

Financial Summary

Total Giving: $548,150 (2000); $725,746 (1999); $564,490 (1997)
Giving Analysis: Giving for 2000 includes: foundation grants to United Way ($10,000) 1999: foundation grants to United Way ($10,000)
Assets: $13,522,053 (2000); $15,043,790 (1999); $13,052,070 (1997)
Gifts Received: $7,995 (1994); $2,221,500 (1993). Note: In 1994, contributions were received from the estate of Wendall F. Couse.

Typical Recipients

Arts & Humanities: Arts Centers, History & Archaeology, Libraries, Museums/Galleries, Music, Opera, Public Broadcasting, Theater
Civic & Public Affairs: Employment/Job Training, Civic & Public Affairs-General, Municipalities/Towns, Rural Affairs, Safety, Urban & Community Affairs
Education: Colleges & Universities, Community & Junior Colleges, Education-General, Legal Education, Minority Education, Private Education (Precollege), Public Education (Precollege), Science/Mathematics Education, Student Aid
Environment: Environment-General
Health: Cancer, Emergency/Ambulance Services, Heart, Hospices, Hospitals, Medical Research, Single-Disease Health Associations
Religion: Churches, Jewish Causes, Religious Organizations, Religious Welfare, Synagogues/Temples
Social Services: Animal Protection, Child Welfare, Community Service Organizations, Family Planning, Family Services, Homes, People with Disabilities,

Recreation & Athletics, Scouts, Senior Services, Social Services-General, United Funds/United Ways, YMCA/YWCA/YMHA/YWHA, Youth Organizations

Application Procedures

Initial Contact: Send a brief letter of inquiry describing program or project.
Application Requirements: Include statement of need and purpose of funds sought.
Deadlines: None.

Foundation Officials

Frank W. Getman, Esq.: president, director
Michael F. Getman: treasurer, director
Sidney Levine: director
Nancy Ann Lynch: secretary, director B Brooklyn, NY 1948. ED Brooklyn College BS (1968); Massachusetts Institute of Technology PhD (1972). PRIM CORP EMPL professor: Massachusetts Institute Technology. NONPR AFFIL member: Association Computing Machinery.

Grants Analysis

Disclosure Period: calendar year ending 2000
Total Grants: $538,150*
Number of Grants: 73
Average Grant: $5,720*
Highest Grant: $67,000
Typical Range: $1,000 to $10,000
***Note:** Giving excludes United Way. Average grant figure excludes two highest grants ($132,000).

Recent Grants

Note: Grants derived from 2001 Form 990.

General

150,000	State University College Oneonta, Oneonta, NY
125,000	Fox Memorial Hospital, Oneonta, NY
55,000	Temple Beth El, Oneonta, NY
51,000	Saint Mary's School, Oneonta, NY
35,000	Catskill Area Hospice and Palliative Care, Inc., Oneonta, NY
25,000	College Foundation at Delhi, Inc., Delhi, NY
25,000	College of St. Rose, Albany, NY
25,000	Greater Oneonta Historical Society, Oneonta, NY
25,000	Opportunities for Otsego, Inc., Oneonta, NY
25,000	SUNY Cobleskill, Cobleskill, NY

HENRIETTA DEXTER CHARITABLE TRUST

Giving Contact

Thea Katsounakis, Trust Officer
c/o Fleet PCG
Charitable Trusts
PO Box 6767
Providence, RI 02940-6767

Description

Founded: 1946
EIN: 046018698
Organization Type: Private Foundation
Giving Locations: MA, Sringfield including greater metropolitan are
Grant Types: Capital, Conference/Seminar, Seed Money.

Donor Information

Founder: the late Henrietta F. Dexter

Financial Summary

Total Giving: $740,681 (2001); $554,225 (2000); $562,565 (1999)

Giving Analysis: Giving for 1999 includes: foundation grants to United Way ($18,500)
Assets: $14,427,429 (2001); $15,061,947 (2000); $16,785,454 (1999)

Typical Recipients

Arts & Humanities: Arts Associations & Councils, Arts Centers, Arts Festivals, Community Arts, History & Archaeology, Libraries, Literary Arts, Museums/Galleries, Music, Performing Arts, Theater
Civic & Public Affairs: African American Affairs, Asian American Affairs, Business/Free Enterprise, Community Foundations, Economic Development, Employment/Job Training, Ethnic Organizations, Civic & Public Affairs-General, Hispanic Affairs, Housing, Municipalities/Towns, Philanthropic Organizations, Professional & Trade Associations, Urban & Community Affairs, Zoos/Aquariums
Education: Arts/Humanities Education, Colleges & Universities, Education Reform, Education-General, International Studies, Leadership Training, Literacy, Minority Education, Public Education (Precollege), School Volunteerism, Special Education, Student Aid
Environment: Environment-General
Health: AIDS/HIV, Children's Health/Hospitals, Clinics/Medical Centers, Emergency/Ambulance Services, Health Organizations, Hospitals, Mental Health, Nursing Services, Outpatient Health Care, Prenatal Health Issues, Research/Studies Institutes
International: Foreign Arts Organizations, International Affairs
Religion: Churches, Jewish Causes, Religious Organizations, Religious Welfare
Social Services: At-Risk Youth, Child Welfare, Community Centers, Community Service Organizations, Crime Prevention, Day Care, Family Planning, Family Services, Food/Clothing Distribution, People with Disabilities, Recreation & Athletics, Scouts, Senior Services, Shelters/Homelessness, United Funds/United Ways, YMCA/YWCA/YMHA/YWHA, Youth Organizations

Application Procedures

Initial Contact: Send a brief letter of inquiry.
Deadlines: None.

Restrictions

Does not support individuals. Gives only to charitable organizations in the city of Springfield, Massachusetts.

Additional Information

Publications: Informational Brochure (including Application Guidelines)
Trust(s): Fleet National Bank NA

Grants Analysis

Disclosure Period: calendar year ending 2001
Total Grants: $740,681
Number of Grants: 80
Average Grant: $9,259
Highest Grant: $26,500
Typical Range: $2,000 to $20,000

Recent Grants

Note: Grants derived from 2001 Form 990.

General

26,500	Springfield Southwest Community Health Center, Springfield, MA
26,500	Springfield Southwest Community Health Center, Springfield, MA
25,000	Springfield Home for Friendless Women and Children, Inc., Springfield, MA
23,000	Western New England College, Springfield, MA
21,000	Friends of the Homeless, Springfield, MA
20,000	Springfield Library and Museums Association, Springfield, MA
20,000	Trinity United Methodist Church, Springfield, MA
15,164	Community Foundation of Western Massachusetts, Springfield, MA
15,164	Community Foundation of Western Massachusetts, Springfield, MA
15,164	Community Foundation of Western Massachusetts, Springfield, MA

DIBNER FUND

Giving Contact

Marci B. Sternheim, Executive Director
PO Box 7575
Wilton, CT 06897
Phone: (203)761-9904
Fax: (203)761-9989
E-mail: Dibnerfund@worldnet.att.net

Description

Founded: 1957
EIN: 066038482
Organization Type: Family Foundation
Giving Locations: nationally and internationally.
Grant Types: Conference/Seminar, Scholarship.

Donor Information

Founder: The fund was established in 1957 by David Dibner, the late Bern Dibner , and the late Barbara Dibner . It continues to be supported by the Dibner family.

Financial Summary

Total Giving: $4,879,483 (2000); $6,270,239 (1999); $3,230,300 (1998)
Giving Analysis: Giving for 2000 includes: foundation grants to United Way ($7,500); 1999: foundation grants to United Way ($5,000); 1998: foundation grants to United Way ($5,000);
Assets: $97,036,357 (2000); $104,592,354 (1999); $91,722,037 (1998)
Gifts Received: $250,314 (2000); $725,546 (1999); $319,200 (1997). Note: In 2000, contributions were received from the Barbara Dibner Trust ($125,449) and the Bern Dibner Trust ($124,865). In 1997, contributions were received from the Bern Dibner Trust ($159,600) and the Barbara Dibner Trust ($159,600).

Typical Recipients

Arts & Humanities: Film & Video, Arts & Humanities-General, Historic Preservation, History & Archaeology, Libraries, Literary Arts, Museums/Galleries, Music, Public Broadcasting
Civic & Public Affairs: Botanical Gardens/Parks, Civic & Public Affairs-General, Municipalities/Towns, Native American Affairs, Nonprofit Management, Philanthropic Organizations, Professional & Trade Associations, Zoos/Aquariums
Education: Business Education, Colleges & Universities, Education Funds, Education Reform, Engineering/Technological Education, Education-General, Health & Physical Education, Minority Education, Private Education (Precollege), Public Education (Precollege), Science/Mathematics Education, Student Aid
Environment: Air/Water Quality, Environment-General, Research, Resource Conservation
Health: Cancer, Children's Health/Hospitals, Diabetes, Emergency/Ambulance Services, Hospices, Hospitals, Single-Disease Health Associations
International: Foreign Arts Organizations, Foreign Educational Institutions, International-General, Health Care/Hospitals, International Organizations, International Relief Efforts, Missionary/Religious Activities

Religion: Churches, Jewish Causes
Science: Science Exhibits & Fairs, Science Museums, Scientific Centers & Institutes, Scientific Organizations
Social Services: Community Centers, Family Services, People with Disabilities, Recreation & Athletics, Shelters/Homelessness, United Funds/United Ways, Youth Organizations

Application Procedures

Initial Contact: No special form is required.
Application Requirements: Customary grant request data should be included in proposal.
Deadlines: None.

Restrictions

The Dibner Fund considers grants on a very focused and limited basis in the areas of history of science and technology and science education, and specifically discourages unsolicited applications removed from its fields of interest. It specifically avoids grants for capital programs, general-purpose support, individuals, and religious institutions.

Additional Information

Publications: Guidelines Mission Statement

Foundation Officials

Dr. Paul Busch: trustee
Brent Dibner: trustee
David Dibner: president, treasurer, trustee B New York, NY 1927. PRIM CORP EMPL chairman: Bundy Corp.
Frances K. Dibner: vice president, treasurer, trustee
Stewart Greenfield: trustee B 1931. ED Saint John's College (1949-1953). PRIM CORP EMPL partner: Alternative Investment LP. CORP AFFIL partner: Oak Investment Partners II.
Warren Shine: trustee
Marci B. Sternheim: executive director
George Michael Szabad: secretary, treasurer, trustee B Nizhni Novgorod, Russia February 21, 1917. ED Columbia University BS (1937); Columbia University LLB (1939). PRIM CORP EMPL attorney: Blum Haimoff Gersen Lipson Slavin & Szabad. NONPR AFFIL member: American Federal Bar Association; member: Association Bar New York City; member: American Arbitration Association.

Grants Analysis

Disclosure Period: calendar year ending 2000
Total Grants: $4,871,983*
Number of Grants: 96
Average Grant: $33,670*
Highest Grant: $1,673,350
Lowest Grant: $1,000
Typical Range: $1,000 to $50,000
*Note: Giving excludes United Way. Average grant figure excludes highest grant.

Recent Grants

Note: Grants derived from 2000 Form 990.

Library-Related
2,000   Wilton Public Library, Wilton, CT

General
35,000   Maritime Aquarium, South Norwalk, CT
25,000   Rockefeller University, New York, NY
25,000   Water Environment Research Foundation, Alexandria, VA
25,000   WNYC Radio, New York, NY
20,000   Yivo Institute for Jewish Research, New York, NY
15,000   Worldwise, Dayton, OH
15,000   Yale School of Forestry
10,000   United Jewish Appeal, Westport, CT
10,000   University of Albany Foundation, Albany, NY
10,000   Wilton High School Little Theatre, Wilton, CT

VOLNEY E. DIBRELL CHARITABLE TRUST

Giving Contact

William Clyborne, Vice President & Trust Officer
c/o Frost National Bank
PO Box 2950
San Antonio, TX 78299-2950
Phone: (210)220-4449

Description

Founded: 1993
EIN: 746396825
Organization Type: Private Foundation
Giving Locations: TX
Grant Types: General Support.

Financial Summary

Total Giving: $21,205 (fiscal year ending March 31, 2001); $23,500 (fiscal 2000); $28,500 (fiscal 1998)
Assets: $968,027 (fiscal 2001); $1,019,898 (fiscal 2000); $944,184 (fiscal 1998)
Gifts Received: $692,152 (fiscal 1993)

Typical Recipients

Education: Public Education (Precollege)
Health: Children's Health/Hospitals, Health Organizations, Medical Research
Social Services: Community Service Organizations, Family Planning, Recreation & Athletics

Application Procedures

Initial Contact: Written application should include charter and by-laws, financial statement, and proof of tax-exempt status.
Deadlines: None.

Restrictions

Limited to TX.

Additional Information

Trust(s): Frost National Bank

Grants Analysis

Disclosure Period: fiscal year ending March 31, 2001
Total Grants: $21,205
Number of Grants: 4
Average Grant: $5,301
Highest Grant: $6,000

Recent Grants

Note: Grants derived from 2001 Form 990.

General
6,000   Children's Inn, Boerne, TX
6,000   Little League Baseball, Inc.-Alamo Heights, San Antonio, TX
6,000   National Kidney Foundation of Southeast Texas, Houston, TX
5,205   Planned Parenthood of San Antonio, San Antonio, TX

HARRIET FORD DICKENSON FOUNDATION

Giving Contact

James Largey, Vice President
Care of Morgan Guaranty Trust Trustee
3450 Park Avenue
New York, NY 10154
Phone: (212)464-1937
Fax: (212)464-1919

Description

Founded: 1958
EIN: 136047225
Organization Type: Private Foundation
Giving Locations: NY: Broome County
Grant Types: General Support.

Donor Information

Founder: Harriet Ford Dickenson

Financial Summary

Total Giving: $1,458,000 (2001); $20,123,500 (2000); $2,755,975 (1999)
Giving Analysis: Giving for 2000 includes: foundation grants to United Way ($2,200)
Assets: $43,626,741 (2001); $46,339,506 (2000); $65,831,023 (1999)
Gifts Received: $193,617 (1998)

Typical Recipients

Arts & Humanities: Arts Associations & Councils, Ballet, Historic Preservation, History & Archaeology, Libraries, Museums/Galleries, Music, Opera, Performing Arts, Public Broadcasting
Civic & Public Affairs: Botanical Gardens/Parks, Clubs, Civic & Public Affairs-General, Housing, Law & Justice, Legal Aid, Urban & Community Affairs
Education: Arts/Humanities Education, Colleges & Universities, Community & Junior Colleges, Legal Education, Private Education (Precollege), Student Aid
Environment: Air/Water Quality, Environment-General, Resource Conservation
Health: Hospitals
Religion: Churches, Religious Organizations, Religious Welfare
Science: Science Museums, Scientific Centers & Institutes
Social Services: Camps, Child Welfare, Child Welfare, Community Service Organizations, Counseling, Family Planning, Family Services, Food/Clothing Distribution, Homes, People with Disabilities, Recreation & Athletics, Scouts, United Funds/United Ways, YMCA/YWCA/YMHA/YWHA

Application Procedures

Initial Contact: Send a brief letter of inquiry.
Application Requirements: Describe program and amount requested.
Deadlines: None.

Additional Information

Trust(s): Morgan Guaranty Trust

Foundation Officials

Gillian Attfield: advisory committee member
Ann Hubbard: advisory committee member
David Hubbard: advisory committee member
Tom Hubbard: advisory committee member
John Keeler: advisory committee member
Shirley Keeler: advisory committee member

Grants Analysis

Disclosure Period: calendar year ending 2000
Total Grants: $20,121,300*
Number of Grants: 85
Average Grant: $236,721
Highest Grant: $2,200,000
Lowest Grant: $1,000
Typical Range: $1,000 to $25,000 and $500,000 to $2,200,000
*Note: Does not include grants to United Way.

Recent Grants

Note: Grants derived from 2001 Form 990.

Library-Related
33,750   Cornwall Public Library, Cornwall, CT
5,000   New York Public Library, New York, NY
5,000   Pierpont Morgan Library, New York, NY

General

330,000	New York City Ballet, New York, NY
205,000	New York Botanical Gardens, Bronx, NY
101,000	Smith College, Northampton, MA
100,000	Metropolitan Opera Association, New York, NY
70,000	United Church of Christ, Cornwall, CT
40,000	Binghamton University Foundation, Binghamton, NY
35,000	Discovery Center of the Southern Tier, Binghamton, NY
25,000	Adirondack Council, Elizabethtown, NY
25,000	National Audubon Society of New York State, Albany, NY
25,000	Nature Conservancy of New York, New York, NY

DICKLER FAMILY FOUNDATION

Giving Contact

Lauren Katzowtiz
130 E. 59th St., 12th Fl.
New York, NY 10022
Phone: (212)836-1577

Description

Founded: 1996
EIN: 133864553
Organization Type: Private Foundation
Former Name: Ruth and Gerald Dickler Foundation (2000).
Giving Locations: NY: also areas where trustees reside
Grant Types: General Support.

Financial Summary

Total Giving: $575,000 (2001); $540,000 (2000); $394,500 (1999)
Giving Analysis: Giving for 2000 includes: foundation scholarships ($2,000) 1999: foundation scholarships ($10,000)
Assets: $11,591,357 (2001); $12,889,556 (2000); $12,551,472 (1999)
Gifts Received: $104,089 (1996)

Typical Recipients

Arts & Humanities: Museums/Galleries, Music
Civic & Public Affairs: Economic Policy, Civic & Public Affairs-General, Women's Affairs
Education: Arts/Humanities Education, Education Reform, Literacy, Special Education
Health: Health-General
Social Services: Child Welfare, Community Service Organizations, Family Planning, Family Services

Application Procedures

Initial Contact: Send a brief letter of inquiry.
Application Requirements: Include description of organization, past and present year's budget, and references.
Deadlines: None.

Restrictions

Emphasis is on international population control and New York City early childhood education.

Foundation Officials

Ruth Dickler: president
Susan Dickler: executive vice president
Fred C. Farkouh: treasurer
Lauren Katzowitz: secretary
Jane Lebow: vice president
Abby Pratt: vice president

Grants Analysis

Disclosure Period: calendar year ending 2001
Total Grants: $575,000*
Number of Grants: 67
Average Grant: $8,582
Highest Grant: $25,000
Lowest Grant: $1,000
Typical Range: $1,000 to $20,000
***Note:** Giving excludes scholarships.

Recent Grants

Note: Grants derived from 2001 Form 990.

General

25,000	American Museum of Natural History, New York, NY -- to establish and maintain the museum and library of natural history
25,000	IPAS, New York, NY -- to increase women's abortion access in South Africa
20,000	Campaign for Fiscal Equality, New York, NY -- to reform the system of funding for public education throughout New York State
20,000	Education Through Music, New York, NY -- teaches music to children in public schools to improve academic skills
20,000	New Visions for Public Schools, New York, NY -- aims to improve the quality of education children received in NYC public schools
20,000	Population Media Center, Shelburne, VT -- to promote the use of effective communication strategies for promoting behavior change to encourage family and reproductive health
20,000	Studio In A School Association, New York, NY -- to work with New York City Public Schools and child care center to make art a part of children's daily life
17,500	United Neighborhood Houses, New York, NY -- to initiate a collaboration to replicate the east side house settlement's early childhood transition program
15,000	Abortion Access Project, Inc., Cambridge, MA -- to implement and expand its advocacy organizing education training and policy work
15,000	Henry Street Settlement, New York, NY -- to provide arts instructions and cultural programs to student and staff at PS 20 in New York City

WILLIAM B. DIETRICH FOUNDATION

Giving Contact

William B. Dietrich, President
PO Box 58177
Philadelphia, PA 19102-8177
Phone: (215)979-1919

Description

Founded: 1936
EIN: 231515616
Organization Type: Private Foundation
Giving Locations: PA
Grant Types: Capital, Operating Expenses, Project, Research.

Donor Information

Founder: Daniel W. Dietrich Foundation, the late Henry D. Dietrich, Dietrich American Foundation

Financial Summary

Total Giving: $988,700 (2001); $1,038,135 (2000); $838,635 (1999)

Assets: $17,349,999 (2001); $19,382,601 (2000); $20,745,878 (1999)
Gifts Received: $189 (1998); $500,000 (1993); $375,000 (1992). Note: In 1993, contributions were received from Dietrich American Foundation.

Typical Recipients

Arts & Humanities: Arts Associations & Councils, Community Arts, Ethnic & Folk Arts, Arts & Humanities-General, Historic Preservation, History & Archaeology, Libraries, Museums/Galleries, Music
Civic & Public Affairs: Botanical Gardens/Parks, Civic & Public Affairs-General, Municipalities/Towns, Safety, Urban & Community Affairs, Zoos/Aquariums
Education: Arts/Humanities Education, Colleges & Universities, Medical Education, Private Education (Precollege), Religious Education
Environment: Watershed
Health: AIDS/HIV, Cancer, Children's Health/Hospitals, Emergency/Ambulance Services, Geriatric Health, Health Organizations, Hospices, Hospitals, Medical Research, Single-Disease Health Associations
Religion: Churches
Science: Scientific Centers & Institutes
Social Services: Animal Protection, Community Service Organizations, Crime Prevention, Food/Clothing Distribution, Recreation & Athletics, Senior Services, YMCA/YWCA/YMHA/YWHA

Application Procedures

Initial Contact: Send a brief letter of inquiry.
Application Requirements: Include a description of organization, purpose of funds sought, and proof of tax-exempt status.
Deadlines: None.

Foundation Officials

Frank G. Cooper, Esq.: secretary, assistant treasurer
William B. Dietrich: president, treasurer

Grants Analysis

Disclosure Period: calendar year ending 2001
Total Grants: $988,700
Number of Grants: 39
Average Grant: $13,965*
Highest Grant: $237,000
Lowest Grant: $500
Typical Range: $5,000 to $25,000
***Note:** Average grant figure excludes two highest grants ($472,000).

Recent Grants

Note: Grants derived from 2000 Form 990.

General

350,500	Shipley School, Bryn Mawr, PA -- Beechwood Restoration
237,250	Fairmount Park Historic Preservation Trust, Philadelphia, PA -- Sheep Barn Restoration
229,885	Rosenbach Museum and Library, Philadelphia, PA -- Historic Preservation
100,000	Trustees of the University of Pennsylvania, Philadelphia, PA -- gallery renovations by The University Museum of Archaeology and Anthropology first installment
82,500	Fairmount Park Historic Preservation Trust, Philadelphia, PA -- Exterior Fencing and Landscaping of Sedgley Porter's House
10,000	AIDS Project, Los Angeles, CA
10,000	University of Southern California School of Medicine, Los Angeles, CA -- AIDS Research
6,000	Church Farm School, Paoli, PA
6,000	Options in Aging, Ardmore, PA -- funding for Daily Hot Lunch Program

5,000   Make-A-Wish Foundation of Philadelphia and Southwestern Pennsylvania,
Plymouth Meeting, PA -- benefit a seri-
ously ill child

DILLON FOUNDATION

Giving Contact

Peter W. Dillon, President & Director
PO Box 537
Sterling, IL 61081
Phone: (815)626-9000
Fax: (815)626-4000

Description

Founded: 1953
EIN: 366059349
Organization Type: Family Foundation
Giving Locations: IL: Sterling including metropoli-
tan area
Grant Types: Capital, Emergency, Fellowship, Gen-
eral Support, Matching, Multiyear/Continuing Sup-
port, Research, Scholarship, Seed Money.

Donor Information

Founder: Incorporated in 1953 by members of the
Dillon family.

Financial Summary

Total Giving: $2,810,096 (fiscal year ending October
31, 2003 approx); $3,746,795 (fiscal 2002);
$3,885,286 (fiscal 2001)
Giving Analysis: Giving for fiscal 1998 includes:
foundation grants to United Way ($76,000)
Assets: $53,387,951 (fiscal 2003 approx);
$71,183,935 (fiscal 2002); $75,770,685 (fiscal 2001)

Typical Recipients

Arts & Humanities: History & Archaeology, Libraries,
Museums/Galleries, Music, Opera, Visual Arts
Civic & Public Affairs: Botanical Gardens/Parks,
Community Foundations, Economic Development,
Employment/Job Training, Civic & Public Affairs-Gen-
eral, Housing, Municipalities/Towns, Safety, Urban &
Community Affairs, Zoos/Aquariums
Education: Colleges & Universities, Community &
Junior Colleges, Economic Education, Education As-
sociations, Education Funds, Elementary Education
(Public), Education-General, Private Education (Pre-
college), Public Education (Precollege), Science/
Mathematics Education, Secondary Education
(Public)
Environment: Environment-General, Resource Con-
servation
Health: Cancer, Children's Health/Hospitals, Clinics/
Medical Centers, Emergency/Ambulance Services,
Health Organizations, Hospices, Hospitals, Medical
Rehabilitation, Medical Research, Public Health, Re-
search/Studies Institutes, Single-Disease Health As-
sociations
International: International Organizations
Religion: Churches, Religious Organizations, Reli-
gious Welfare
Social Services: At-Risk Youth, Community Service
Organizations, Family Planning, People with Disabili-
ties, Recreation & Athletics, Scouts, Senior Services,
Social Services-General, United Funds/United Ways,
YMCA/YWCA/YMHA/YWHA, Youth Organizations

Application Procedures

Initial Contact: The foundation requests applications
be made in writing.
Application Requirements: Written proposals
should describe the details of the program or project
for which the applicant is requesting assistance.
Deadlines: None.

Restrictions

No grants are made to individuals. The foundation
does not make loans.

Foundation Officials

James M. Boesen: treasurer, director
John Paul Conway: vice president, secretary, direc-
tor B Summit, NJ 1924. ED Northern Illinois Univer-
sity; Loras College BA (1949). NONPR AFFIL direc-
tor: Catholic Foundation Rockford Diocese.
Margo Dillon: assistant secretary, director
Peter W. Dillon: president, director
Gale Inglee: assistant treasurer, director

Grants Analysis

Disclosure Period: fiscal year ending October 31,
2001
Total Grants: $3,790,687*
Number of Grants: 129
Average Grant: $30,118*
Highest Grant: $940,000
Lowest Grant: $250
Typical Range: $1,000 to $30,000
*Note: Giving excludes United Way. Grants analysis
provided by foundation.

Recent Grants

Note: Grants derived from 2000 Form 990.

Library-Related
429,250   Sterling Rock Falls Day Care Agency,
Inc., Sterling, IL
11,500   Sterling Public Library, Sterling, IL

General
500,200   Sterling Rock Falls YMCA, Sterling, IL
333,726   City of Sterling, Sterling, IL
324,406   Sterling Park District, Sterling, IL
300,000   Sterling Industrial Development Council,
Sterling, IL
250,550   Town of Sterling, Sterling, OK
194,988   Community Unit School District 5, Sterling, IL
85,000   United Way of Sterling Rock Falls, Inc.,
Sterling, IL
57,668   Sauk Valley Community College, Dixon,
IL
50,220   Whiteside Area Vocational Center, Sterling, IL
50,000   Winning Wheels, Inc., Lyndon, IL

DIME BANK OF NORWICH CONNECTICUT

Company Headquarters

290 Salem Turnpike
Norwich, CT 06360
Web: http://www.dimesavingsbank.com

Dime Savings Bank of Norwich Foundation

Giving Contact

Wilma Sullivan, Secretary
Dime Savings Bank Foundation
290 Salem Turnpike
Norwich, CT 06360-0070
Phone: (860)889-2317

Description

Founded: 1998
EIN: 061507800
Organization Type: Corporate Foundation
Giving Locations: CT
Grant Types: General Support.

Financial Summary

Total Giving: $73,309 (2001); $76,244 (2000);
$75,163 (1999)
Assets: $1,367,087 (2001); $1,176,522 (2000);
$1,344,346 (1999)
Gifts Received: $309,978 (2001). Note: In 2001, con-
tributions were received from Dime Savings Bank of
Norwich.

Typical Recipients

Arts & Humanities: Arts & Humanities-General, Li-
braries
Civic & Public Affairs: Civic & Public Affairs-Gen-
eral, Housing
Education: Business Education, Public Education
(Precollege)
Health: Children's Health/Hospitals, Clinics/Medical
Centers, Health-General, Hospices, Hospitals, Medi-
cal Rehabilitation, Nursing Services
Social Services: Community Centers, Community
Service Organizations, Family Services, People with
Disabilities

Application Procedures

Initial Contact: Submit a brief letter of inquiry.
Application Requirements: Include a description of
organization, amount requested, purpose of funds
sought, recently audited financial statement, and
proof of tax-exempt status.
Deadlines: September 30.

Restrictions

Applicants must be located within the company's operating area.

Foundation Officials

Michael G. Betten: director
Francis J. Buckley, Jr.: director
James P. Cronin: president, treasurer
James P. Cronin: director
Roland J. Harris: director
Paul M. Higgins: director
James M. Kirker: director
Richard J. Legare: director
Robert A. Staley: director
Bradley J. Sullivan: assistant treasurer
Wilma J. Sullivan: secretary
Charles O. Treat: vice president

Grants Analysis

Disclosure Period: calendar year ending 2001
Total Grants: $73,309
Number of Grants: 22
Average Grant: $3,332
Highest Grant: $10,000
Lowest Grant: $1,500
Typical Range: $1,500 to $5,000

Recent Grants

Note: Grants derived from 2001 Form 990.

Library-Related
2,800   Otis Library, Los Angeles, CA -- financial assistance for microfilming archived
local newspaper

General
10,000   WW Backus Hospital -- radiation therapy building
5,000   AmeriCares, New Canaan, CT -- funding for walk-in clinic in Norwich
5,000   Ledyard Center School PTO -- purchase library equipment
5,000   Norwich Social Services Safety Net
Team, Norwich, CT -- funding for fuel,
food, children's supplies
5,000   Southeastern Association the Retarded -- recreational and respite services for families with retarded dependents
3,750   High Horses Therapeutic Riding, Etna,

	NH -- scholarships for special needs student
3,500	East Lyme High School -- student fine arts publication
3,000	Madonna Place, Norwich, CT -- staffing for court ordered supervised visits
3,000	Thames River Community Service, Inc. -- funding support for families in transition from public assistance
2,900	Easter Seals, CT -- purchase of therapeutic devices

DIMEO CONSTRUCTION CO.

Company Headquarters

75 Chapman Street
Providence, RI 02905-5496
Web: http://www.dimeo.com

Company Description

Operating Revenue: US$149 million (2002)
Employees: 200 (2002)
SIC(s): 1500 General Building Contractors, 1700 Special Trade Contractors, 8700 Engineering & Management Services.

Nonmonetary Support

Type: In-kind Services; Loaned Executives; Workplace Solicitation

Giving Contact

Kimberly Hall
75 Chapman St.
Providence, RI 02905
Phone: (401)781-9800
Fax: (401)461-4580

Description

Organization Type: Corporate Giving Program
Giving Locations: RI
Grant Types: General Support.

Typical Recipients

Arts & Humanities: Arts Appreciation, Arts Associations & Councils, Arts Centers, Arts Festivals, Community Arts, Historic Preservation, Libraries, Museums/Galleries, Music, Opera, Performing Arts, Theater
Civic & Public Affairs: Economic Development, Housing, Municipalities/Towns, Safety, Women's Affairs, Zoos/Aquariums
Education: Arts/Humanities Education, Business Education, Colleges & Universities, Community & Junior Colleges, Continuing Education, Economic Education
Health: Health Funds, Health Organizations, Hospitals, Mental Health, Nutrition, Single-Disease Health Associations
International: International Peace & Security Issues
Religion: Churches, Religious Organizations, Synagogues/Temples
Social Services: Animal Protection, Child Welfare, Community Centers, Community Service Organizations, Counseling, Family Planning, Senior Services, Substance Abuse

Application Procedures

Initial Contact: Send a brief letter of inquiry.
Application Requirements: Include a description of organization, amount requested, purpose of funds sought, recently audited financial statement, and proof of tax-exempt status.
Deadlines: None.

Restrictions

Does not support individuals.

Corporate Officials

Bradford S. Dimeo: vice president PRIM CORP EMPL vice president: Dimeo Construction Co.
Thomas P. Dimeo: chairman, president, chief executive officer, director B Providence, RI 1930. ED Brown University BA (1952). PRIM CORP EMPL chairman, president, chief executive officer, director: Dimeo Enterprises. CORP AFFIL director: Old Stone Bank; director: Providence Mutual Fire Insurance Co.; chairman: Dimeo Construction Co. NONPR AFFIL member corporate: RI Hospital; director: YMCA Greater Providence; trustee: Cathedral Saint John Divine; trustee: Johnson Wales College.

DIMMER FAMILY FOUNDATION

Giving Contact

Diane C. Dimmer, Executive Director
1019 Pacific Avenue, Suite 916
Tacoma, WA 98402
Phone: (253)759-1318

Description

Founded: 1994
EIN: 911622059
Organization Type: Private Foundation
Giving Locations: WA: Pierce County, Tacoma County
Grant Types: General Support.

Donor Information

Founder: Established in 1994 by John C. Dimmer.

Financial Summary

Total Giving: $769,831 (2000); $419,621 (1999); $361,457 (1998)
Giving Analysis: Giving for 1999 includes: foundation scholarships ($19,211)
Assets: $15,147,517 (2000); $8,294,421 (1999); $8,822,997 (1998)
Gifts Received: $456,994 (2000); $8,509,628 (1999); $51,610 (1998). Note: In 1998, 1999 and 2000, contributions were received from John C. Dimmer and Key Bank. In 1994, contributions were received from John C. Dimmer.

Typical Recipients

Arts & Humanities: Arts Associations & Councils, Arts & Humanities-General, History & Archaeology, Libraries, Museums/Galleries, Music, Opera, Performing Arts, Theater
Civic & Public Affairs: Clubs, Civic & Public Affairs-General, Housing, Parades/Festivals, Zoos/Aquariums
Education: Business Education, Colleges & Universities, Community & Junior Colleges, Elementary Education (Public), Environmental Education, Education-General, Legal Education, Literacy, Private Education (Precollege), Science/Mathematics Education, Special Education, Student Aid
Environment: Wildlife Protection
Health: AIDS/HIV, Arthritis, Cancer, Children's Health/Hospitals, Health Funds, Heart, Hospitals, Mental Health, Prenatal Health Issues, Single-Disease Health Associations
Religion: Churches, Ministries, Religious Welfare
Science: Science Museums, Scientific Centers & Institutes
Social Services: Animal Protection, Camps, Child Welfare, Community Service Organizations, Crime Prevention, Day Care, Food/Clothing Distribution, Homes, People with Disabilities, Recreation & Athletics, Scouts, YMCA/YWCA/YMHA/YWHA, Youth Organizations

Application Procedures

Initial Contact: Send a brief letter of inquiry or complete application.
Application Requirements: Include a description of organization, purpose of funds sought, amount requested, and recently audited financial statement.
Deadlines: None.

Restrictions

Restricted to Tacoma-Pierce county, WA organizations which qualify as 501(c)(3).

Foundation Officials

Carolyn J. Dimmer: vice president
Diane C. Dimmer: secretary
John B. Dimmer: treasurer
John C. Dimmer: president
Marilyn J. Dimmer: vice president

Grants Analysis

Disclosure Period: calendar year ending 2000
Total Grants: $769,831
Number of Grants: 145
Average Grant: $4,444*
Highest Grant: $74,392
Typical Range: $1,000 to $10,000
*Note: Average grant excludes two highest grants ($134,395).

Recent Grants

Note: Grants derived from 1999 Form 990.

General

25,000	Cystic Fibrosis Foundation, Tacoma, WA
25,000	Washington State Historical Society, Tacoma, WA -- donation for historic anchor retrieval
25,000	YMCA, Tacoma, WA -- for new building
20,000	Pacific Harbor Boy Scouts, Seattle, WA
19,151	Mary Bridge Children's Hospital, Tacoma, WA -- festival of trees - tree purchase donated for charity
12,000	Tacoma Actors Guild, Tacoma, WA
10,000	Boys & Girls Club, Tacoma, WA
10,000	Children's Museum of Tacoma, Tacoma, WA
10,000	SMART, Portland, OR
10,000	University of Washington Tacoma, Tacoma, WA -- scholarship donations

MICHAEL D. DINGMAN FOUNDATION

Giving Contact

Lenora Jennings, Assistant Secretary
1 Liberty Ln.
Hampton, NH 03842
Phone: (603)929-2203

Description

Founded: 1986
EIN: 943080164
Organization Type: Private Foundation
Giving Locations: nationally.
Grant Types: Department, General Support.

Donor Information

Founder: Henley Manufacturing Charitable Fdn.

Financial Summary

Total Giving: $1,185,596 (2001); $958,100 (2000); $978,918 (1999)
Giving Analysis: Giving for 1999 includes: foundation grants to United Way ($10,000); 1998: foundation grants to United Way ($10,000) foundation ($2,616,698)

Assets: $707,666 (2001); $1,808,023 (2000); $2,573,626 (1999)
Gifts Received: $32,000 (2001); $32,000 (2000); $32,000 (1999). Note: Contributions are received from Michael D. Dingman, and Winthrop, Inc.

Typical Recipients

Arts & Humanities: Historic Preservation, History & Archaeology, Libraries, Museums/Galleries, Music, Theater
Civic & Public Affairs: Botanical Gardens/Parks, Business/Free Enterprise, Economic Policy, Employment/Job Training, Civic & Public Affairs-General, Housing, Legal Aid, Public Policy, Safety, Urban & Community Affairs, Zoos/Aquariums
Education: Agricultural Education, Business Education, Colleges & Universities, Education Funds, Education-General, Minority Education, Private Education (Precollege), Student Aid
Environment: Environment-General, Resource Conservation, Wildlife Protection
Health: Cancer, Clinics/Medical Centers, Emergency/Ambulance Services, Eyes/Blindness, Health-General, Health Funds, Health Organizations, Hospices, Hospitals, Medical Rehabilitation, Medical Research, Nursing Services, Public Health, Single-Disease Health Associations
International: Foreign Arts Organizations, Foreign Educational Institutions, Health Care/Hospitals, International Development, International Organizations, International Relations, Missionary/Religious Activities
Religion: Churches, Jewish Causes, Ministries, Missionary Activities (Domestic), Religious Organizations, Religious Welfare
Science: Science Museums
Social Services: Animal Protection, Camps, Child Welfare, Community Service Organizations, Crime Prevention, Emergency Relief, People with Disabilities, Recreation & Athletics, Social Services-General, Substance Abuse, United Funds/United Ways, Volunteer Services, Youth Organizations

Application Procedures

Initial Contact: Send a brief letter of inquiry.
Deadlines: None.

Foundation Officials

John Bletzner: vice president, treasurer
Edwin H. Danenhauer: assistant secretary
Elizabeth T. Dingman: vice president
Michael David Dingman: president B New Haven, CT 1931. ED University of Maryland. PRIM CORP EMPL president, chief executive officer: Shipston Group Ltd. CORP AFFIL director: Ford Motor Co.; director: Fisher Scientific International Inc. NONPR AFFIL member: Institute Electrical & Electronics Engineers. CLUB AFFIL San Diego Yacht Club; Union Club; New York Yacht Club; The Links Club; Lyford Cay Club; La Jolla Country Club; Bohemian Club; Cruising Club America Club.
Lenore Jennings: assistant secretary
Edward Kavanaugh: vice president, treasurer, secretary
Daniel Shanahan: secretary

Grants Analysis

Disclosure Period: calendar year ending 2001
Total Grants: $1,185,596
Number of Grants: 47
Average Grant: $17,078*
Highest Grant: $400,000
Lowest Grant: $1,000
Typical Range: $5,000 to $20,000
*Note: Average grant figure excludes highest grant.

Recent Grants

Note: Grants derived from 2001 Form 990.

General

400,000	Business & Management Foundation of MD, Inc., College Park, MD
116,440	Lyford Cay School Development Fund, Nassau Bahamas
100,000	Bahamas Mission of Florida, Inc., Nassau Bahamas
55,000	St. George's School, Newport, RI
50,000	Boston College, Chestnut Hill, MA
50,000	Historic Charleston Foundation, Charleston, SC
50,000	Historic Deerfield, Inc, Deerfield, MA
50,000	Hun School of Princeton, Princeton, NJ
50,000	Medical University of South Carolina, Charleston, SC
20,000	Farnsworth Art Museum, Rockland, ME

H. E. AND KATE DISHMAN CHARITABLE FOUNDATION TRUST

Giving Contact

Trust Officer
c/o Hibernia National Bank
PO Box 3928
Beaumont, TX 77704-3928
Phone: (409)880-1415

Description

Founded: 1985
EIN: 766024806
Organization Type: Private Foundation
Giving Locations: TX: Georgetown
Grant Types: Capital, General Support, Project.

Donor Information

Founder: Dishman Foundation, the late H. E. Dishman, Kate Dishman Foundation

Financial Summary

Total Giving: $195,542 (2001); $190,842 (2000); $233,667 (1999)
Giving Analysis: Giving for 1999 includes: foundation grants to United Way ($20,000)
Assets: $3,523,101 (2001); $3,801,757 (2000); $3,949,823 (1999)

Typical Recipients

Arts & Humanities: Arts Associations & Councils, Arts Outreach, Libraries, Museums/Galleries, Music, Public Broadcasting
Civic & Public Affairs: African American Affairs, Community Foundations, Civic & Public Affairs-General, Nonprofit Management, Philanthropic Organizations
Education: Business Education, Colleges & Universities, Education-General, Public Education (Precollege), Science/Mathematics Education, Secondary Education (Private)
Health: Emergency/Ambulance Services, Hospitals, Medical Research, Nutrition, Single-Disease Health Associations, Transplant Networks/Donor Banks
Religion: Churches, Religious Organizations, Religious Welfare
Science: Science Museums
Social Services: At-Risk Youth, Camps, Child Welfare, Community Service Organizations, Crime Prevention, Family Services, Food/Clothing Distribution, Homes, People with Disabilities, Scouts, Senior Services, Shelters/Homelessness, Substance Abuse, United Funds/United Ways, Volunteer Services

Application Procedures

Initial Contact: Send a brief letter of inquiry and a full proposal.
Application Requirements: Include a description of organization, amount requested, purpose of funds sought, and proof of tax-exempt status.
Deadlines: None.

Restrictions

Does not support individuals, religious organizations for sectarian purposes, political or lobbying groups, or organizations outside operating areas.

Additional Information

Trust(s): Hiberia National Bank

Grants Analysis

Disclosure Period: calendar year ending 2000
Total Grants: $190,842*
Number of Grants: 11
Average Grant: $14,084*
Highest Grant: $50,000
Typical Range: $5,000 to $25,000
*Note: Average grant excludes highest grant.

Recent Grants

Note: Grants derived from 1999 Form 990.

General

66,667	Goodwill Industries of Southeast Texas, Beaumont, TX -- park street property acquisition
50,000	Friends of Spindletop, Beaumont, TX -- marketing, administration and office
20,000	One Church One Child of East Texas, Beaumont, TX -- program expenses and office equipment
20,000	Some Other Place, Beaumont, TX -- funding for back to school program
20,000	United Way of Beaumont, Beaumont, TX -- annual campaign
10,000	Art Museum of Southeast Texas, Beaumont, TX -- educational programming
10,000	Beaumont Police Activities League, Beaumont, TX -- expenses toward juvenile crime prevention
10,000	KVLU, Beaumont, TX -- purchase digital equipment
10,000	Lamar University, Beaumont, TX -- Texas honors leadership program
5,000	Boy Scouts of America, Beaumont, TX -- Scoutnet 2000 Project

CLIFTON C. AND HENRYETTA C. DOAK CHARITABLE TRUST

Giving Contact

Kenneth Loke, Trust Officer
c/o Wells Fargo Bank Texas
PO Drawer 913
Bryan, TX 77805-0913
Phone: (979)776-3267

Description

Founded: 1993
EIN: 746402510
Organization Type: Private Foundation
Giving Locations: TX: Brazos County
Grant Types: General Support.

Donor Information

Founder: Established in 1993 by the late Henryetta C. Doak.

Financial Summary

Total Giving: $258,800 (2001); $140,300 (2000); $142,800 (1999)
Giving Analysis: Giving for 2001 includes: foundation grants to United Way ($10,000); 2000: foundation grants to United Way ($5,000); 1999: foundation grants to United Way ($15,000)
Assets: $4,055,197 (2001); $4,467,112 (2000); $4,707,429 (1999)

Gifts Received: $9,840 (2001); $28,454 (2000); $3,094,886 (1993). Note: In 2000 and 2001, contributions were received from Christopher Lew Trust. In 1993, contributions were received from the estate of Henryetta C. Doak.

Typical Recipients

Arts & Humanities: Arts & Humanities-General, Libraries, Museums/Galleries, Music
Civic & Public Affairs: Clubs, Civic & Public Affairs-General, Housing, Municipalities/Towns, Urban & Community Affairs
Education: Colleges & Universities, Elementary Education (Public), Private Education (Precollege), Student Aid
Health: Clinics/Medical Centers, Emergency/Ambulance Services, Health-General, Health Organizations, Hospices, Medical Rehabilitation, Mental Health
Religion: Religious Welfare
Science: Science Museums
Social Services: Food/Clothing Distribution, Homes, Social Services-General, United Funds/United Ways, Veterans, Youth Organizations

Application Procedures

Initial Contact: submit requests on bank trust department's grant application form
Deadlines: March 15.

Additional Information

Trust(s): Wells Fargo Bank Texas

Grants Analysis

Disclosure Period: calendar year ending 2001
Total Grants: $248,800*
Number of Grants: 21
Average Grant: $11,848
Highest Grant: $31,000
Lowest Grant: $300
Typical Range: $5,000 to $15,000
*Note: Giving excludes United Way.

Recent Grants

Note: Grants derived from 2001 Form 990.

Library-Related
12,500   Bryan City Library, Bryan, TX -- for educational purposes

General
31,000	Hospice Brazos Valley, Bryan, TX -- for charitable purposes
30,000	Brazos Valley Museum, Bryan, TX -- for educational purposes
30,000	Habitat for Humanity, Bryan, TX -- for charitable purposes
20,000	Brazos Valley Rehabilitation Center, Bryan, TX -- for charitable purposes
15,000	Brazos Food Bank, Bryan, TX -- for charitable purposes
15,000	Doak Carter Boys Club, Bryan, TX -- for charitable purposes
15,000	Trinity University, San Antonio, TX -- for educational purposes
14,000	Health for All, Inc., Bryan, TX -- for health care improvements and education
12,500	College Station City Library, College Station, TX -- for educational purposes
10,500	University of North Texas, Denton, TX -- for educational purposes

DR. SEUSS FOUNDATION

Giving Contact

Audrey S. Geisel, President & Assistant Secretary
7301 Encelia Dr.
La Jolla, CA 92037-5279
Phone: (858)454-7384

Description

Founded: 1958
EIN: 956029752
Organization Type: Private Foundation
Giving Locations: CA: national organizations.
Grant Types: General Support.

Donor Information

Founder: the late Theodor S. Geisel

Financial Summary

Total Giving: $207,642 (2001); $255,726 (2000); $209,533 (1999)
Giving Analysis: Giving for 1998 includes: foundation grants to United Way ($2,000)
Assets: $2,192,308 (2001); $2,568,258 (2000); $2,961,238 (1999)

Typical Recipients

Arts & Humanities: Arts Funds, Arts Outreach, Ballet, Dance, Ethnic & Folk Arts, Arts & Humanities-General, Libraries, Literary Arts, Museums/Galleries, Music, Opera, Performing Arts, Public Broadcasting, Theater, Visual Arts
Civic & Public Affairs: Botanical Gardens/Parks, Civil Rights, Community Foundations, Civic & Public Affairs-General, Hispanic Affairs, Parades/Festivals, Philanthropic Organizations, Public Policy, Rural Affairs, Safety, Urban & Community Affairs, Women's Affairs, Zoos/Aquariums
Education: Business Education, Colleges & Universities, Education Funds, Education Reform, Education-General, Literacy, Private Education (Precollege), Public Education (Precollege), Secondary Education (Private), Special Education
Environment: Forestry, Environment-General
Health: AIDS/HIV, Alzheimers Disease, Cancer, Children's Health/Hospitals, Clinics/Medical Centers, Emergency/Ambulance Services, Hospices, Hospitals (University Affiliated), Medical Research, Mental Health, Prenatal Health Issues, Preventive Medicine/Wellness Organizations, Research/Studies Institutes
International: Foreign Arts Organizations, Health Care/Hospitals, Human Rights, International Affairs, International Organizations, International Relief Efforts
Religion: Churches, Religious Welfare
Science: Science Museums, Scientific Organizations
Social Services: Child Welfare, Family Planning, Food/Clothing Distribution, Homes, People with Disabilities, Recreation & Athletics, Scouts, Senior Services, Social Services-General, Substance Abuse, YMCA/YWCA/YMHA/YWHA, Youth Organizations

Application Procedures

Initial Contact: The foundation has no formal grant application procedure or application form.
Deadlines: None.

Restrictions

Grants are not made to individuals.

Foundation Officials

R. L. Bernstein: vice president
Audrey S. Geisel: president, assistant secretary
Edward Lathem: director
Claudia Prescott: chief financial officer
Karl ZoBell: secretary B La Jolla, CA 1932. ED Utah State University (1949-1951); Columbia University (1951-1952); Columbia University AB (1953); Stanford University JD (1958). PRIM CORP EMPL partner: Gray, Cary, Ames & Frye. CORP AFFIL director, founder: La Jolla Bank & Trust Co.; vice president, director: Geisel-Seuss Enterprises Inc. NONPR AFFIL trustee: Dr Seuss Foundation; member: Lambda Alpha; director: James C Copley Charitable Foundation; fellow: American College Trust & Estate Counsel; member: California Bar Association; member: American Bar Association. CLUB AFFIL La Jolla Beach & Tennis Club.

Grants Analysis

Disclosure Period: calendar year ending 2001
Total Grants: $207,642
Number of Grants: 139
Average Grant: $1,494
Highest Grant: $10,000
Lowest Grant: $150
Typical Range: $500 to $5,000

Recent Grants

Note: Grants derived from 2001 Form 990.

General
10,000	San Diego Opera, San Diego, CA
10,000	University of California San Diego Affairs Development, San Diego, CA
8,900	UC Regents, Los Angeles, CA
7,195	San Diego Museum of Art, San Diego, CA
6,750	Vista Hill Foundation, San Diego, CA
5,100	University of California San Diego Foundation, San Diego, CA
3,900	Salvation Army Women's Auxiliary, Dallas, TX
3,500	Episcopal Community Service
3,500	San Diego Symphony, San Diego, CA
3,000	City Ballet, Knoxville, TN

CLEVELAND H. DODGE FOUNDATION

Giving Contact

Phyllis M. Criscuoli, Executive Director & Treasurer
670 West 247th Street
Bronx, NY 10471
Phone: (718)543-1220
Fax: (718)543-0737
E-mail: chdodgefdn@aol.com
Web: http://www.chdodgefoundation.org

Description

Founded: 1917
EIN: 136015087
Organization Type: General Purpose Foundation
Giving Locations: AZ; NM; NY: New York including metropolitan area Northeastern United States.
Grant Types: Capital, Endowment, General Support, Matching, Multiyear/Continuing Support, Operating Expenses, Project.

Donor Information

Founder: The Cleveland H. Dodge Foundation was established in 1917 by Cleveland Hoadley Dodge, whose father headed Phelps Dodge Corporation, a copper company.

Financial Summary

Total Giving: $2,000,000 (2002 approx); $2,300,000 (2001); $2,409,757 (1998). Note: 1996 Giving includes matching gifts ($284,723). 1995 Giving includes matching gifts ($278,304).
Giving Analysis: Giving for 1998 includes: foundation scholarships ($211,500); foundation matching gifts ($572,241) 1997: foundation matching gifts ($316,860)
Assets: $52,000,000 (2001); $50,820,718 (1998); $45,000,000 (1997)

Typical Recipients

Arts & Humanities: Arts Associations & Councils, Arts Outreach, Historic Preservation, History & Archaeology, Libraries, Museums/Galleries, Performing Arts
Civic & Public Affairs: Botanical Gardens/Parks, Clubs, Community Foundations, Employment/Job Training, Civic & Public Affairs-General, Nonprofit Management, Philanthropic Organizations, Public Policy, Urban & Community Affairs, Zoos/Aquariums

Education: Arts/Humanities Education, Colleges & Universities, Education Reform, Elementary Education (Public), Faculty Development, Education-General, International Exchange, International Studies, Leadership Training, Minority Education, Private Education (Precollege), Public Education (Precollege), School Volunteerism, Science/Mathematics Education, Student Aid

Environment: Air/Water Quality, Environment-General, Environment-General, Wildlife Protection

Health: Emergency/Ambulance Services, Health Organizations, Nursing Services, Public Health

International: Foreign Educational Institutions, Health Care/Hospitals, International Affairs, International Environmental Issues, International Organizations, International Peace & Security Issues, International Relations

Religion: Churches, Religious Welfare

Science: Observatories & Planetariums, Science Museums

Social Services: Big Brother/Big Sister, Child Welfare, Community Centers, Community Service Organizations, Emergency Relief, Family Planning, Family Services, People with Disabilities, Recreation & Athletics, Senior Services, Shelters/Homelessness, Volunteer Services, YMCA/YWCA/YMHA/YWHA, Youth Organizations

Application Procedures

Initial Contact: To apply for a grant, organizations may send a brief letter to the foundation's executive director and treasurer. There are no application forms.

Application Requirements: Letters of application should describe the proposed project and include a budget. After a preliminary review, a detailed proposal may be requested.

Deadlines: Applications should be submitted prior to January, April, and October 15. The board of directors meets in June to determine dates for the other board meetings.

Review Process: At the board meetings, the directors review the activities of recipient organizations to ensure that they are "being maintained at a satisfactory level." The remainder of the yearly income is disbursed in the form of one-time grants for capital campaigns and special projects.

Restrictions

The foundation does not make loans or grants to individuals. Low priority is given to cultural organizations, such as museums, libraries, or exhibitions; and to research institutes, preparatory schools, colleges, and universities. The foundation generally does not fund medical research or health care and training, and it is not interested in managing programs or projects of unestablished organizations.

Additional Information

"To encourage the descendants of the Founder to take an interest in philanthropy, the Foundation matches, to a limited extent, their individual grants made to agencies in which they are actively involved."

Publications: Annual Report

Foundation Officials

Phyllis M. Criscuoli: administration director, treasurer

Cleveland Earl Dodge, Jr.: president, chairman executive committee, member finance committee B New York, NY 1922. ED Princeton University BSME (1943). PRIM CORP EMPL president, treasurer, director: International Dodge Inc.

David S. Dodge: mem executive comm, director NONPR AFFIL chairman, director: Near East Foundation.

Gilbert Kerlin: secretary, mem executive & fin comms, director B Camden, NJ October 10, 1909. ED Harvard University (1933); Trinity College (1936). PRIM CORP EMPL counsel: Shearman & Sterling.

CORP AFFIL director: Wave Hill Inc.; president, director: Windward Oil & Gas Corp.; chairman: Silver Resources Corp.; president, director: PI Corp.; director: Silver Jacket Corp.; secretary, director: Malher Mining Co.; chairman board, chairman executive committee: North Central Oil Corp.; chairman: Exmin Corp.; director: Hicks Dome Corp.

William Dodge Rueckert: chairman fin comm, mem executive comm, director ED University of New Hampshire (1977).

Ingrid R. Warren: mem executive comm, director

Mary Rea Weidlein: director

Grants Analysis

Disclosure Period: calendar year ending 1998
Total Grants: $1,875,320*
Number of Grants: 94
Average Grant: $24,197*
Highest Grant: $375,000*
Lowest Grant: $500
Typical Range: $2,000 to $20,000
*Note: Giving excludes matching gifts and scholarships. Average grant figure excludes highest grant.

Recent Grants

Note: Grants derived from 1998 Form 990.

Library-Related
20,000   Carnegie Institute, Pittsburgh, PA

General
375,000   Antique Boat Museum, Clayton, NY -- for Elizabeth Dodge Haxall Building fund
200,000   American University of Beirut, New York, NY
200,000   Teachers College, New York, NY -- Grace Dodge Hall Renovations project
150,000   Princeton University, Princeton, NJ -- environmental program
125,000   Wave Hill, Inc., Bronx, NY -- Ruth Rea Howell Interpretive Gardnership
100,000   American Museum of Natural History, New York, NY
100,000   New York Botanical Garden, Bronx, NY -- children's adventure project
100,000   Springfield College, Springfield, MA -- US Fitness Center for the Disabled
100,000   Wildlife Conservation Society, Bronx, NY -- Congo Gorilla Project
75,000   Planned Parenthood of New York City, Inc., New York, NY -- emergency contraceptives program

GERALDINE R. DODGE FOUNDATION

Giving Contact

David Grant, Executive Director
163 Madison Avenue
PO Box 1239
Morristown, NJ 07962-1239
Phone: (973)540-8442
Fax: (973)540-1211
E-mail: info@grdodge.org
Web: http://www.grdodge.org

Description

Founded: 1974
EIN: 237406010
Organization Type: General Purpose Foundation
Giving Locations: NJ: nationally.
Grant Types: Challenge, Conference/Seminar, Department, Emergency, Employee Matching Gifts, General Support, Matching, Operating Expenses, Project, Seed Money.

Donor Information

Founder: Established in 1974 in accordance with the will of the late Geraldine R. Dodge (d. 1973), the daughter of William Rockefeller (a former president of Standard Oil) and the niece of John D. Rockefeller. Her husband, Marcellus Hartley Dodge, was chairman of the Remington Arms Co. Mrs. Dodge was an avid dog breeder and pet lover and she established an animal shelter at the time of her death.

Financial Summary

Total Giving: $20,689,816 (2001); $24,623,000 (2000); $19,476,286 (1999)
Assets: $306,376,880 (2001); $337,658,000 (2000); $320,000,000 (1999)
Gifts Received: $135,050 (1997); $100,000 (1996); $16,250 (1995)

Typical Recipients

Arts & Humanities: Arts Appreciation, Arts Associations & Councils, Arts Centers, Arts Festivals, Arts Outreach, Ballet, Community Arts, Dance, Ethnic & Folk Arts, History & Archaeology, Libraries, Literary Arts, Museums/Galleries, Music, Opera, Performing Arts, Public Broadcasting, Theater, Visual Arts

Civic & Public Affairs: Botanical Gardens/Parks, Business/Free Enterprise, Employment/Job Training, Civic & Public Affairs-General, Nonprofit Management, Public Policy, Rural Affairs, Urban & Community Affairs, Women's Affairs

Education: Afterschool/Enrichment Programs, Arts/Humanities Education, Colleges & Universities, Education Associations, Education Reform, Elementary Education (Private), Elementary Education (Public), Engineering/Technological Education, Environmental Education, Faculty Development, Education-General, Gifted & Talented Programs, International Exchange, International Studies, Leadership Training, Literacy, Medical Education, Minority Education, Private Education (Precollege), Public Education (Precollege), School Volunteerism, Science/Mathematics Education, Secondary Education (Public), Social Sciences Education, Student Aid

Environment: Air/Water Quality, Energy, Forestry, Environment-General, Protection, Resource Conservation, Watershed, Wildlife Protection

Health: Medical Research

International: Health Care/Hospitals, International Affairs, International Development, International Environmental Issues, International Peace & Security Issues

Science: Science Museums, Scientific Centers & Institutes

Social Services: Animal Protection, Domestic Violence, Family Planning, Family Services, Recreation & Athletics, Shelters/Homelessness, Youth Organizations

Application Procedures

Initial Contact: A one-page letter of inquiry is encouraged, to determine if a project falls within the foundation's guidelines.

Application Requirements: The Foundation accepts the New York Area Common Application Form. Grant proposals should begin with a one-page summary of the project, followed by the main body, which should be a fuller description of no more than six pages. The foundation prefers 12-point type or larger for the text. The proposal should describe the project and the need for it; the qualifications and past accomplishments of the sponsoring organization; how the project is to proceed and who is to carry it out; a time frame and budget; the benefits to be gained and for whom; and the plans for evaluating and funding the project in the future. Also included should be a recent financial statement, together with the names and occupations of the trustees of the organization, as well as IRS confirmation of tax-exempt status. The foundation requests that the proposal be presented in an environmentally sensitive manner. Proposals should

use two-sided copies without binders or plastic packaging. No faxed proposals are accepted, and the foundation prefers that express mail carriers not be used.
Deadlines: Program deadlines are November 1 for education requests, March 1 for arts grants, June 1 for Morris County, June 1 animal welfare requests, and June 1 for critical issue applications.
Review Process: The board of trustees meets four times yearly. It considers pre-collegiate education in March, the arts in June, local projects and the welfare of animals in September, and critical issues in November.

Restrictions

The foundation does not consider grants for higher education, health, or religion. Grants are not usually made for capital programs, equipment purchases, indirect costs, endowment funds, or deficit operations. Grants typically are not made to individuals, scholarship funds, or grants to conduit organizations.

Additional Information

Grant recipients are asked to make periodic progress reports, and at the termination of a grant, to submit a narrative report and an accounting of all disbursements. It is customary for an organization, whether it is funded or not, to wait one year before submitting another proposal.
Publications: Annual Report; Guidelines

Foundation Officials

Robert Hayes Burns Baldwin: chairman, director B East Orange, NJ July 09, 1920.
Alexandra Christy: senior program officer
Ross Danis: program officer
Barbara Knowles Debs: trustee B Eastham, MA 1931. ED Vassar College BA (1953); Harvard University PhD (1967); New York Law School LLD (1979); Manhattanville College LHD (1985). NONPR AFFIL member: Renaissance Society America; member: Young Audiences; president, chief executive officer, director: New York Historical Society; member: Phi Beta Kappa; member advisory board: Greenwich Historical Society; honorary trustee: Manhattanville College; member: Council Foreign Relations; board governors: Foreign Policy Association; trustee: Brooklyn Museum Art; member: College Art Association; member: American Council Education; member executive board: Bard Center Decorative Arts. CLUB AFFIL Cosmopolitan Club; Hundred Club Westchester; Century Association.
Christopher J. Elliman: trustee NONPR AFFIL vice chairman: Environmental Defense Fund.
Lisa Garrison: program officer
David Grant: executive director
Henry U. Harder: trustee emeritus
John Lloyd Huck: trustee B Brooklyn, NY 1922. ED Pennsylvania State University BS (1946). CLUB AFFIL Morris County Golf Club; Pipers Landing Country Club.
Robert LeBuhn: president, trustee B Davenport, IA 1932. ED Northwestern University BS (1954); University of Pennsylvania MBA (1957). PRIM CORP EMPL chairman: Investor International Inc. CORP AFFIL director: USAir Group Inc.; director: USAir Inc.; director: Enzon Inc.; director: Acceptance Insurance Companies Inc.; director: Cambrex Corp.
Nancy D. Lindsay: trustee
Betsy S. Michel: trustee CORP AFFIL director: Seligman Growth Fund Inc.; director: Seligman Income Fund Inc.; director: Seligman Cash Management Fund; director: Seligman Common Stock Fund.
Walter J. Neppl: trustee emeritus
Paul J. O'Donnell: trustee
Robert Perry: program officer
Janet Rodriguez: program officer
James W. Stevens: trustee
John Edward Yingling, Jr.: chief administrative and financial officer B Baltimore, MD 1935. ED Yale University BA (1955); Johns Hopkins University MLA (1967); New York University MBA (1977). CLUB AFFIL Yale Central New Jersey Club.

Grants Analysis

Disclosure Period: calendar year ending 2001
Total Grants: $20,689,816
Number of Grants: 557
Average Grant: $37,145
Highest Grant: $600,000
Lowest Grant: $50
Typical Range: $10,000 to $100,000

Recent Grants

Note: Grants derived from 2002 Form 990.

General
1,000,000 New Jersey Symphony Orchestra, Newark, NJ
375,000 Geraldine R. Dodge Foundation, New Jersey Animal Assistance Program, Morristown, NJ -- to support the efforts of 33 humane organizations in New Jersey
350,000 New Jersey Teaching and Learning Collaborative, NJ -- to establish a new statewide intermediary education organization
300,000 Woodrow Wilson National Fellowship Foundation, Princeton, NJ -- to continue the expansion of "Teachers as Scholars"
250,000 Network for Family Life Education, New Brunswick, NJ -- to continue implementation of the New Jersey Sexuality Education Staff Development Initiative
200,000 Association of New Jersey Environmental Commission, Mendham, NJ -- to support a "Smart Growth Assistance Program"
200,000 Eastern Environmental Law Center, Newark, NJ -- to support two activities at the Center
200,000 Geraldine R. Dodge Foundation Initiative for Veterinary Students, Morristown, NJ -- to again fund the "Frontiers for Veterinary Medicine" Program
200,000 New Jersey Conservation Foundation, Far Hills, NJ -- to support the Garden State Greenways Initiative
200,000 Newark Lighthouse Initiative, Trenton, NJ -- to develop three models of early care and educational excellence in Newark, New Jersey

DODGE JONES FOUNDATION AND SUBSIDIARY

Giving Contact

Lawrence Gill, Grants Administrator
PO Box 176
Abilene, TX 79604
Phone: (915)673-6429
Fax: (915)673-2028

Description

Founded: 1954
EIN: 756006386
Organization Type: General Purpose Foundation
Giving Locations: TX
Grant Types: Capital, Challenge, General Support, Operating Expenses.

Donor Information

Founder: The foundation was established in 1954 by the late Ruth Leggett Jones .

Financial Summary

Total Giving: $7,017,637 (2001); $7,003,182 (2000); $6,293,527 (1998)

Giving Analysis: Giving for 1998 includes: foundation grants to United Way ($13,000)
Assets: $106,756,286 (2001); $110,356,720 (2000); $93,772,401 (1998)
Gifts Received: $580,500 (2001); $250 (1994); $6,900 (1993). Note: In 2001, contributions were received from Julia Jones Matthews.

Typical Recipients

Arts & Humanities: Arts Associations & Councils, Ethnic & Folk Arts, Arts & Humanities-General, Historic Preservation, History & Archaeology, Libraries, Literary Arts, Museums/Galleries, Music, Opera, Performing Arts, Public Broadcasting, Theater, Visual Arts
Civic & Public Affairs: African American Affairs, Botanical Gardens/Parks, Business/Free Enterprise, Chambers of Commerce, Civil Rights, Clubs, Community Foundations, Economic Development, Employment/Job Training, Civic & Public Affairs-General, Housing, Legal Aid, Municipalities/Towns, Nonprofit Management, Professional & Trade Associations, Public Policy, Rural Affairs, Safety, Urban & Community Affairs, Zoos/Aquariums
Education: Agricultural Education, Business Education, Business-School Partnerships, Colleges & Universities, Education Funds, Elementary Education (Private), Engineering/Technological Education, Faculty Development, Education-General, Health & Physical Education, Legal Education, Literacy, Medical Education, Private Education (Precollege), Public Education (Precollege), Science/Mathematics Education, Secondary Education (Public), Social Sciences Education, Special Education, Student Aid, Vocational & Technical Education
Environment: Environment-General
Health: AIDS/HIV, Alzheimers Disease, Cancer, Children's Health/Hospitals, Clinics/Medical Centers, Emergency/Ambulance Services, Geriatric Health, Health Policy/Cost Containment, Health Organizations, Heart, Hospices, Hospitals, Medical Rehabilitation, Medical Research, Mental Health, Public Health, Speech & Hearing
International: Foreign Arts Organizations
Religion: Churches, Ministries, Religious Organizations, Religious Welfare
Science: Scientific Organizations
Social Services: At-Risk Youth, Big Brother/Big Sister, Camps, Child Welfare, Community Centers, Community Service Organizations, Crime Prevention, Day Care, Family Planning, Family Services, Food/Clothing Distribution, People with Disabilities, Recreation & Athletics, Scouts, Senior Services, Shelters/Homelessness, Social Services-General, Substance Abuse, United Funds/United Ways, YMCA/YWCA/YMHA/YWHA, Youth Organizations

Application Procedures

Initial Contact: The foundation reports that applicants should submit a letter of request describing the purpose for the proposed funding.
Deadlines: None.

Restrictions

The foundation does not make grants to individuals, or to organizations on behalf of individuals.

Foundation Officials

Thomas R. Allen: vice president, chief financial officer
Linda Buckner: secretary, treasurer
Joseph E. Canon: executive vice president, executive director CORP AFFIL director: First Financial Bankshares.
Lawrence Gill: vice president
Joseph B. Matthews: director
Julia Jones Matthews: president, director
Kade L. Matthews: director

Grants Analysis

Disclosure Period: calendar year ending 2001
Total Grants: $6,772,637*
Number of Grants: 150
Average Grant: $38,742*
Highest Grant: $1,000,065
Lowest Grant: $500
Typical Range: $5,000 to $100,000
*Note: Giving excludes United Way and scholarship; average grant excludes highest grants.

Recent Grants

Note: Grants derived from 2001 Form 990.

General

1,000,065	Hendrick Medical Center Foundation, Abilene, TX -- Trauma Center
600,000	Grace Museum, Abilene, TX -- endowment fund grant
600,000	Grace Museum, Abilene, TX -- endowment fund grant
500,000	McMurry University, Abilene, TX -- provide funds for purchase of land for future expansion
350,000	12th Armored Division Memorial Museum Foundation, Abilene, TX -- fund equipment needs and future operations
250,000	Harmony Family Services, Abilene, TX -- renovate existing space
225,000	Abilene Hope Haven, Abilene, TX -- assist with renovations
225,000	Grady McWhiney Research Foundation, Abilene, TX -- operational support for the Buffalo Gap Historic Village
225,000	Hardin-Simmons University, Abilene, TX -- to fund construction of Elwin L. Skiles Social Sciences Building
200,000	Pastoral Care and Counseling Center, Abilene, TX -- forgiveness of loan

CARRIE ESTELLE DOHENY FOUNDATION TRUST

Giving Contact

Shirley Bernard, Senior Grants Administrator
707 Wilshire Boulevard, Suite 4960
Los Angeles, CA 90017
Phone: (213)488-1122
Fax: (213)488-1544
E-mail: doheny@dohenyfoundation.org
Web: http://www.dohenyfoundation.org

Description

Founded: 1948
EIN: 952051633
Organization Type: General Purpose Foundation
Giving Locations: nationally.
Grant Types: Award, Capital, Challenge, General Support, Matching, Multiyear/Continuing Support, Research.

Donor Information

Founder: Mrs. Edward Lawrence Doheny established the foundation in 1948, as a result of her lifelong devotion to charitable and public benefactions. Her husband (1856-1935) was chairman of Petroleum Securities Company, and president of Doheny-Stone Drilling Company and Los Nietos Producing and Refining Company. Mrs. Doheny spent years helping the sick, needy, and those suffering from loss and impairment of vision. Her interest in optical problems led her to set up the Estelle Doheny Eye Foundation, which receives annual contributions from the foundation, to support laboratory research and services, and an eye bank. Today, the eye foundation is considered one of the leading opthalmological facilities.

Financial Summary

Total Giving: $6,500,000 (2003 approx); $7,000,000 (2002 approx); $9,661,245 (2000)
Giving Analysis: Giving for 1997 includes: foundation grants to United Way ($160,000)
Assets: $130,000,000 (2003 approx); $135,000,000 (2002 approx); $191,351,663 (2000)

Typical Recipients

Civic & Public Affairs: Employment/Job Training, Civic & Public Affairs-General, Hispanic Affairs, Housing, Nonprofit Management, Urban & Community Affairs, Women's Affairs
Education: Colleges & Universities, Education Funds, Education-General, Preschool Education, Private Education (Precollege), Public Education (Precollege), Religious Education, Secondary Education (Private), Secondary Education (Public), Student Aid, Vocational & Technical Education
Health: Cancer, Children's Health/Hospitals, Clinics/Medical Centers, Emergency/Ambulance Services, Eyes/Blindness, Health Organizations, Heart, Hospitals, Long-Term Care, Medical Research, Medical Training, Nutrition, Prenatal Health Issues, Public Health, Research/Studies Institutes, Single-Disease Health Associations, Speech & Hearing
International: Missionary/Religious Activities
Religion: Churches, Dioceses, Religion-General, Missionary Activities (Domestic), Religious Organizations, Religious Welfare, Seminaries
Social Services: At-Risk Youth, Child Welfare, Community Centers, Community Service Organizations, Domestic Violence, Emergency Relief, Family Planning, Family Services, Food/Clothing Distribution, Homes, People with Disabilities, Recreation & Athletics, Scouts, Senior Services, Shelters/Homelessness, United Funds/United Ways, Youth Organizations

Application Procedures

Initial Contact: The foundation currently has no formal grant application procedure or application form; requests should be made in letter form. Beginning in 2001, and application form will be required. The form will be availabele via mail, fax, or website.
Application Requirements: Requests should be concise and contain a brief description of the project, clearly stating its objectives; preliminary budget; and a description of organization. Copies of an IRS determination letter of tax exemption must be included, along with financial statements.
Deadlines: None.
Review Process: The board of directors meets monthly to review proposals.
Notes: Video tapes cannot be returned.

Restrictions

No grants are made to organizations not certified as nonprofit and tax-exempt by the IRS, individuals, or tax-supported entities; or for scholarships, political purposes, goodwill advertisement, travel funds, radio or television programming, or book publishing.

Additional Information

Publications: Annual Report

Foundation Officials

Robert F. Erburu: director B Ventura, CA 1930. ED University of Southern California BA (1952); Harvard University JD (1955). PRIM CORP EMPL director: The Times Mirror Co. CORP AFFIL director: Marsh & McLennan Companies Inc.; director: Tejon Ranch Co.; director: Cox Communications Inc. NONPR AFFIL chairman board trustee: H.E. Huntington Library Art Gallery; life director: Independent Colleges Southern California; member: American Bar Association.
George Gibbs: director
Joseph Nally: director B 1934. PRIM NONPR EMPL president: Pacific-Western Inc.
Rev. F. David Pansini: director

Mrs. Terry Seidler: director PRIM CORP EMPL tru: Loyola Marymount University.
Robert A. Smith, III: director

Grants Analysis

Disclosure Period: calendar year ending 2000
Total Grants: $9,661,245*
Number of Grants: 389
Average Grant: $19,433*
Highest Grant: $1,101,833
Lowest Grant: $800
Typical Range: $1,500 to $50,000
*Note: Average grant excludes two highest grants ($1,000,000, $1,101,833).

Recent Grants

Note: Grants derived from 2000 Form 990.

General

1,000,000	Doheny Eye Institute, Los Angeles, CA -- Tower campaign
700,000	Archdiocese of Los Angeles, Los Angeles, CA -- construction of the new Our Lady Queen of Angels cathedral
300,000	Archdiocese of Los Angeles, Los Angeles, CA -- upkeep of inner-city schools
260,000	Independent Colleges of Southern California, Los Angeles, CA -- support for the Independent Colleges
250,000	Loyola Marymount University, Los Angeles, CA -- construction of the new Health/Recreation/Athletic Center
250,000	University of San Diego, Los Angeles, CA -- construction of athletics arena
150,000	St. Vincent Medical Center, Los Angeles, CA
139,441	St. Mary's Seminary, Santa Barbara, CA -- capital improvements
133,863	St. Mary's Seminary, Santa Barbara, CA -- capital improvements
125,000	Hospitaler Foundation of California, Los Angeles, CA -- care of sick and elderly

HENRY L. AND GRACE DOHERTY CHARITABLE FOUNDATION

Giving Contact

Walter R. Brown, President
Henry L. and Grace Doherty Charitable Foundation
Care of McGrath, Doyle & Phair
150 Broadway, Suite 1703
New York, NY 10038
Phone: (212)571-2300

Description

Founded: 1947
EIN: 136401292
Organization Type: Private Foundation
Giving Locations: nationally.
Grant Types: General Support, Research.

Donor Information

Founder: the late Mrs. Henry L. Doherty, the late Helen Lee Lassen

Financial Summary

Total Giving: $897,275 (2001); $904,069 (2000); $933,950 (1999)
Giving Analysis: Giving for 2001 includes: foundation grants to United Way ($10,000); 2000: foundation grants to United Way ($10,000); 1999: foundation grants to United Way ($9,000);
Assets: $19,024,391 (2001); $21,062,560 (2000); $18,794,451 (1999)

Typical Recipients

Arts & Humanities: Arts Associations & Councils, Arts Centers, Arts & Humanities-General, History & Archaeology, Libraries, Museums/Galleries, Music, Theater

Civic & Public Affairs: Asian American Affairs, Civic & Public Affairs-General, Parades/Festivals, Urban & Community Affairs

Education: Colleges & Universities, Engineering/Technological Education, Faculty Development, Education-General, Leadership Training, Legal Education, Minority Education, Private Education (Precollege), Public Education (Precollege), Science/Mathematics Education

Environment: Environment-General, Resource Conservation, Wildlife Protection

Health: Alzheimers Disease, Cancer, Clinics/Medical Centers, Diabetes, Emergency/Ambulance Services, Health Organizations, Hospices, Hospitals, Medical Research, Mental Health, Nursing Services, Single-Disease Health Associations

International: Foreign Educational Institutions, Health Care/Hospitals, International Organizations, International Relations, International Relief Efforts

Religion: Churches, Religious Organizations, Religious Welfare

Science: Observatories & Planetariums, Scientific Centers & Institutes, Scientific Labs

Social Services: At-Risk Youth, Camps, Child Welfare, Community Service Organizations, Crime Prevention, People with Disabilities, Scouts, Senior Services, United Funds/United Ways, YMCA/YWCA/YMHA/YWHA, Youth Organizations

Application Procedures

Initial Contact: Send a brief letter of inquiry.

Application Requirements: Include a description of organization, its activities, and its purpose; proof of tax-exempt status; a statement regarding if the applicant is controlled by, related to, connected with, or sponsored by another organization; a list of board members; whether the applicant has applied for a grant from this foundation in the past; purpose of funds sought; amount requested; and the name of contact person who will be administering the proposed program.

Deadlines: None.

Restrictions

Preference is given to marine research and oceanography. Does not support individuals.

Foundation Officials

James R. Billegsly: director
Helen Lee Billingsley: director
James Ray Billingsley: vice president, treasurer B Rome, GA 1927. ED New York University (1945); North Georgia College (1945); University of Mississippi JD (1950). PRIM CORP EMPL managing partner: Tolten LP. CORP AFFIL senior vice president: AT&T. NONPR AFFIL member: New York State Bar Association; member, board advisors: University Mississippi Center Telecommunications; member: Fed Communications Bar Association; member: American Bar Association.
Kiyoko O. Brown: director
Walter R. Brown: president
Jacob C. Hardin, Jr.: director
Dorothy R. McCall: vice president

Grants Analysis

Disclosure Period: calendar year ending 2001
Total Grants: $887,275*
Number of Grants: 48
Average Grant: $4,162*
Highest Grant: $500,000
Lowest Grant: $50
Typical Range: $100 to $15,000
***Note:** Giving excludes United Way. Average grant figure excludes three highest grants ($700,000).

Recent Grants

Note: Grants derived from 2001 Form 990.

Library-Related
15,000   Rye Free Reading Room, Rye, NY

General
500,000   University of Mississippi Foundation, University, OK
100,000   Florida Institute of Technology, Melbourne, FL
100,000   Marine Biological Laboratories, Woods Hole, MA
50,000   Charles Hollister Foundation, Woods Hole, MA
15,000   Hackley School, Tarrytown, NY
15,000   Huntington Museum of Art, Huntington, WV
10,200   National Maritime Historical Society, Peekskill, NY
10,000   Charlottesville Catholic School, Charlottesville, VA
10,000   Maine Coast Heritage Trust, Topsham, ME
10,000   St. Joseph Catholic Church, Huntington, WV

DOMINIC FOUNDATION

Giving Contact

Richard A. Berlanti, President
777 S. Wadsworth Boulevard
Suite 4-280
Lakewood, CO 80226
Phone: (303)985-0041

Description

Founded: 1995
EIN: 521905243
Organization Type: Private Foundation
Giving Locations: nationally and internationally.
Grant Types: General Support.

Donor Information

Founder: Established in 1995 by Richard A. Berlanti, Todd A. Berlanti and Merryl A. Berlanti.

Financial Summary

Total Giving: $92,500 (2001); $231,100 (2000); $198,000 (1999)
Giving Analysis: Giving for 1997 includes: foundation ($129,550)
Assets: $2,564,947 (2001); $1,804,792 (2000); $1,855,411 (1999)
Gifts Received: $1,410,938 (1994). Note: In 1994, contributions were received from Richard A. Berlanti, Todd A. Berlanti, and Merryl A. Berlanti ($470,313) each.

Typical Recipients

Arts & Humanities: Arts Festivals, Ballet, Arts & Humanities-General, History & Archaeology, Libraries, Museums/Galleries

Civic & Public Affairs: Clubs, Civic & Public Affairs-General, Safety

Education: Arts/Humanities Education, Colleges & Universities, Secondary Education (Private), Special Education

Environment: Resource Conservation

Health: Cancer, Children's Health/Hospitals, Hospices

Religion: Churches, Religious Welfare

Science: Science Museums

Social Services: Animal Protection, Child Welfare, Community Service Organizations, Family Services, Food/Clothing Distribution, Homes, People with Disabilities, Recreation & Athletics, Shelters/Homelessness

Application Procedures

Initial Contact: Applicant must submit letter with exemption certificate attached.
Deadlines: None.

Foundation Officials

Merryl A. Berlanti: vice president
Richard A. Berlanti: president
Todd A. Berlanti: secretary, treasurer
John P. Hill, Jr.: administrator

Grants Analysis

Disclosure Period: calendar year ending 2001
Total Grants: $92,500
Number of Grants: 35
Average Grant: $2,643
Highest Grant: $10,000
Lowest Grant: $500
Typical Range: $1,000 to $10,000

Recent Grants

Note: Grants derived from 2001 Form 990.

Library-Related
5,000   Mary S. Biesecker Library, Somerset, PA

General
10,000   Northern New Mexico Animal Protection Society, Espanola, NM
9,000   Laurel Arts, Somerset, PA
5,000   Boca Raton Museum of Art, Boca Raton, FL
5,000   Humanitarian Society, Boca Raton, FL
5,000   Meals on Wheels, Somerset, PA
5,000   Norton Museum of Art, West Palm Beach, FL
4,000   James P. Beckwourth Mountain Club, Denver, CO
3,500   Children's Aid Home and Society of Somerset County, Somerset, PA
3,500   Children's Place at Home Safe, Lake Worth, FL
3,000   Borough of Somerset, Somerset, PA

DOMINION

Company Headquarters

120 Tredegar Street
Richmond, VA 23219
Phone: (804)819-2000
E-mail: dominion_resources@domres.com
Web: http://www.dom.com

Company Description

Founded: 1983
Ticker: D
Exchange: NYSE
Assets: US$37.909 billion (2002)
Profit: US$1.362 billion (2002)
Employees: 17000 (2002)
Fortune Rank: 184, per FORTUNE Magazine's list of 500 Largest U.S. Corporations (2002).

Subsidiary Companies

OH: East Ohio Gas Co., Cleveland

Nonmonetary Support

Type: Donated Equipment; In-kind Services; Loaned Employees; Loaned Executives

Giving Contact

Renee Johnson, Contributions Coordinator
PO Box 26532
Richmond, VA 23261
Phone: (804)819-2580
Fax: (804)819-2217
E-mail: reneejohnson@dom.com
Web: http://www.dom.com/about/community/index.jsp

Description

Organization Type: Corporate Giving Program
Giving Locations: operating locations.
Grant Types: Capital, Employee Matching Gifts, General Support.
Note: Employee matching gift ratio: 0.5 to 1. The company matches gifts from $25 to $1,000 per employee annually.

Financial Summary

Total Giving: $2,150,000 (2002 approx); $2,150,000 (2001 approx); $2,150,000 (2000 approx). Note: Contributes through corporate direct giving program only.

Typical Recipients

Arts & Humanities: Arts Associations & Councils, Arts Centers, Arts Festivals, Community Arts, Dance, Libraries, Literary Arts, Museums/Galleries, Music, Opera, Performing Arts, Public Broadcasting, Theater, Visual Arts
Civic & Public Affairs: Employment/Job Training, Housing, Safety, Urban & Community Affairs, Women's Affairs
Education: Colleges & Universities, Education Funds, Engineering/Technological Education
Environment: Environment-General
Health: Emergency/Ambulance Services, Health Organizations, Hospices, Hospitals, Mental Health
Social Services: Child Welfare, Food/Clothing Distribution, Homes, People with Disabilities, Senior Services, Shelters/Homelessness, Substance Abuse

Application Procedures

Initial Contact: Submit a letter or proposal.
Application Requirements: Include organization's purpose and goals, most recent financial statement, proof of tax-exempt status, amount of grant requested and total goal for contributions from individuals and corp.s, and a description of intended use of requested funds.
Deadlines: None.
Evaluative Criteria: Priority is given to organizations that address issues critical to the company's objectives; organizations that promote research and coalition-building rather than duplicating efforts; organizations that are tax-exempt; and organizations that operate within the northeastern quadrant of the United States.
Decision Notification: Statewide requests are reviewed quarterly and notices are sent in April, July, October, and December; other organizations receive notice within approximately 45 days.

Restrictions

Support is not given to organizations benefiting an individual or family; religious, political, fraternal, veteran, professional or membership organization; operating grants to organizations supported by the United Way; historic restoration; individual Scout troops, except area scouting councils that are not supported by the United Way; organizations that discriminate on the basis of race, creed, color, sex or national origin; or elementary and secondary schools. In the area of human and social services the company does not make grants to national health organizations; for medical equipment or research; tax-supported hospitals or hospitals operated for-profit; or campaigns for sponsorship through program advertising. In the area of education the company does not support private foundations benefiting from tax-supported education institutions; individual research or scholarship; operating support for individual universities; or athletic and extracurricular activities.
In the area of arts and humanities the company does not support film or video projects; endowment programs; or individual high school or college performing arts groups.
In the area of the environment the company does not make grants to groups whose objectives are inconsistent with the company's best interests; political or lobbying groups; or research or issues for which significant information is already available.

Additional Information

In January 2000, Dominion Resources merged with Consolidated Natural Gas Co. Under the terms of the merger agreement, Consolidated Natural Gas Co. became a direct subsidiary of Dominion.
Local community organizations should apply to nearest company offices. Addresses and phone numbers are listed in the Corporate Giving Program brochure, available upon request from the contributions administrator.
Grants for economic development are administered as a separate program by the Economic Development section of the company's Customer Service and Marketing Department.
Organizations that receive a capital grant must wait two years after receiving final payment to apply for another grant.
Publications: Corporate Giving Program Brochure

Giving Program Officials

Eva S. Teig: PRIM CORP EMPL senior vice president: Virginia Electric & Power Co. NONPR AFFIL director: Christian Childrens Fund Inc.

OLIVER S. AND JENNIE R. DONALDSON CHARITABLE TRUST

Giving Contact

Linda Franciscovich, Managing Director
P.O. Box 2004
New York, NY 10109-1910
Phone: (212)852-1000
Fax: (212)852-3377

Description

Founded: 1969
EIN: 046229044
Organization Type: General Purpose Foundation
Giving Locations: northeastern United States.
Grant Types: General Support, Operating Expenses, Project, Research, Seed Money.

Donor Information

Founder: Established in 1969 by the late Oliver S. Donaldson .

Financial Summary

Total Giving: $1,753,750 (2001); $1,477,334 (2000); $839,795 (1998)
Giving Analysis: Giving for 2001 includes: foundation scholarships ($66,600)
Assets: $28,833,712 (2001); $35,738,193 (2000); $34,363,090 (1998)
Gifts Received: $24,397 (1993)

Typical Recipients

Arts & Humanities: Arts Associations & Councils, Arts Festivals, Arts & Humanities-General, Historic Preservation, Libraries, Museums/Galleries, Opera, Public Broadcasting, Theater
Civic & Public Affairs: Clubs, Community Foundations, Employment/Job Training, Civic & Public Affairs-General, Hispanic Affairs, Housing, Urban & Community Affairs, Zoos/Aquariums
Education: Colleges & Universities, Community & Junior Colleges, Education Associations, Legal Education, Private Education (Precollege), Secondary Education (Private), Secondary Education (Public)
Environment: Forestry, Environment-General, Resource Conservation, Wildlife Protection
Health: Cancer, Children's Health/Hospitals, Clinics/Medical Centers, Emergency/Ambulance Services,
Health-General, Health Organizations, Heart, Hospitals, Medical Research, Mental Health, Nursing Services, Preventive Medicine/Wellness Organizations, Research/Studies Institutes, Single-Disease Health Associations
International: Health Care/Hospitals, Human Rights, International Affairs, International Environmental Issues, International Relations
Religion: Churches, Religious Organizations, Religious Welfare, Synagogues/Temples
Science: Scientific Centers & Institutes, Scientific Labs
Social Services: Animal Protection, At-Risk Youth, Big Brother/Big Sister, Child Abuse, Child Welfare, Community Centers, Community Service Organizations, Emergency Relief, Family Services, Homes, People with Disabilities, Recreation & Athletics, Social Services-General, United Funds/United Ways, Volunteer Services, YMCA/YWCA/YMHA/YWHA, Youth Organizations

Application Procedures

Initial Contact: The foundation requests applications be made in writing, using a common application form.
Deadlines: Applicants should fax the foundation to request guidelines and application form.
Review Process: Grants are generally made twice a year.

Restrictions

Funds are restricted to the U.S.; no requests from international organizations will be considered. Grants are not made to individuals.

Additional Information

Publications: Application Guidelines; Application Forms

Foundation Officials

Marjorie Atwood: trustee
Carolyn Lark: vice president
Dr. Elizabeth Atwood Lawrence: trustee
William E. Murray: trustee B 1926. PRIM CORP EMPL chairman board, chief executive officer, director: East Bay Company Ltd.
John F. Sisk: trustee

Grants Analysis

Disclosure Period: calendar year ending 2001
Total Grants: $1,687,150*
Number of Grants: 62*
Average Grant: $16,053*
Highest Grant: $250,000
Lowest Grant: $1,000
Typical Range: $2,000 to $20,000
*Note: Giving excludes scholarships; also excludes three highest paid grants.

Recent Grants

Note: Grants derived from 2001 Form 990.

Library-Related
10,000	Thomas Crane Public Library, Quincy, MA -- for April 2001 grants	
5,000	Redwood Library and Athenaeum, Newport, RI	

General
150,6500	Massachusetts General Hospital, Boston, MA -- grants for palliative care	
250,000	Cold Spring Harbor Laboratory Association, Cold Spring Harbor, NY -- support of stem cell research	
250,000	Spoleto Festival, Charleston, SC -- for April 2001 grants	
140,000	St. Anne's Hospital, Fall River, MA	
100,000	Newport Hospital Foundation, Newport, RI -- to benefit fundraising effort for cancer treatment	
80,000	Charlton Memorial Hospital, New Bedford, MA -- for the repair of the roof of	

	the warren G Atwood medical patient care facility
75,000	Marymount Manhattan College, New York, NY -- per instruction from Pamela Curtis
50,000	Dartmouth College, Hanover, NH -- for April 2001 grants
50,000	Nature Conservancy, Providence, RI -- grants for Tiverton Forest Block Initiative
50,000	St. Anne's Hospital, Fall River, MA -- for April 2001 grants

DONALDSON COMPANY, INC.

Company Headquarters

Minneapolis, MN
Web: http://www.donaldson.com

Company Description

Founded: 1915
Ticker: DCI
Exchange: NYSE
Revenue: US$1.126 billion (2002)
Employees: 8230 (2002)
SIC(s): 3519 Internal Combustion Engines Nec.

Operating Locations

Donaldson Co., Inc. (CA--Covina, San Ramon, Santa Ana; FL--Plantation; IL--Dixon, Galesburg; IN--Frankfort, Indianapolis, South Bend; IA--Grinnell, Oelwein; KS--Shawnee Mission; LA--Jefferson; MI--Brighton; MO--Chillicothe; NY--Skaneateles; NC--Morrisville; OH--Cincinnati, Cleveland, Reynoldsburg; OK--Oklahoma City; PA--Pittsburgh; TX--Houston, Richardson; WA--Bellevue; WI--Baldwin, Brookfield, Stevens Point)
Note: Operates plants in all locations.

Donaldson Foundation

Giving Contact

Norman C. Linnell, President & Trustee
PO Box 1299 MS 100
Minneapolis, MN 55440
Phone: (612)703-4999
Fax: (952)887-3005
E-mail: donaldsonfoundation@mail.donaldson.com
Web: http://www.donaldson.com/en/about/community/foundation.html/html

Description

EIN: 416052950
Organization Type: Corporate Foundation
Giving Locations: headquarters and operating communities.
Grant Types: Award, Capital, General Support, Multiyear/Continuing Support, Scholarship.

Financial Summary

Total Giving: $836,717 (fiscal year ending July 31, 2001); $800,000 (fiscal 1999 approx); $744,949 (fiscal 1998). Note: Contributes through corporate direct giving program and foundation.
Giving Analysis: Giving for fiscal 2001 includes: foundation matching gifts ($14,530); foundation scholarships ($131,860); foundation grants to United Way ($264,052); foundation ($426,275); fiscal 1998: foundation matching gifts ($4,500); foundation scholarships ($114,000); foundation grants to United Way ($241,413) foundation ($384,636).
Assets: $2,979,987 (fiscal 2001 approx); $3,992,732 (fiscal 1998); $1,950,000 (fiscal 1997 approx)
Gifts Received: $900,000 (fiscal 2001); $2,310,000 (fiscal 1998); $1,200,000 (fiscal 1996). Note: Contributions are received from Donaldson Company.

Typical Recipients

Arts & Humanities: Arts Centers, Arts Funds, Arts Institutes, Community Arts, Dance, Historic Preservation, History & Archaeology, Libraries, Museums/Galleries, Music, Opera, Performing Arts, Public Broadcasting, Theater
Civic & Public Affairs: Botanical Gardens/Parks, Business/Free Enterprise, Clubs, Community Foundations, Economic Development, Employment/Job Training, Civic & Public Affairs-General, Housing, Nonprofit Management, Safety, Women's Affairs, Zoos/Aquariums
Education: Agricultural Education, Business Education, Business-School Partnerships, Colleges & Universities, Community & Junior Colleges, Economic Education, Education Funds, Education Reform, Elementary Education (Public), Engineering/Technological Education, Faculty Development, Education-General, Health & Physical Education, Legal Education, Literacy, Minority Education, Private Education (Precollege), Public Education (Precollege), Science/Mathematics Education, Secondary Education (Public), Special Education, Student Aid, Vocational & Technical Education
Environment: Forestry, Environment-General, Resource Conservation, Wildlife Protection
Health: Children's Health/Hospitals, Clinics/Medical Centers, Emergency/Ambulance Services, Health Funds, Health Organizations, Hospices, Hospitals, Medical Rehabilitation, Mental Health, Preventive Medicine/Wellness Organizations, Public Health
Religion: Religious Welfare
Science: Observatories & Planetariums, Science Museums
Social Services: Big Brother/Big Sister, Child Welfare, Community Centers, Community Service Organizations, Counseling, Day Care, Delinquency & Criminal Rehabilitation, Domestic Violence, Emergency Relief, Family Planning, Family Services, Food/Clothing Distribution, Homes, People with Disabilities, Recreation & Athletics, Senior Services, Shelters/Homelessness, Substance Abuse, United Funds/United Ways, Volunteer Services, YMCA/YWCA/YMHA/YWHA, Youth Organizations

Application Procedures

Initial Contact: Send a brief letter of inquiry.
Application Requirements: Provide a description of organization, a list of officers and directors, a description of the program or project needing assistance, explanation of current progress toward goal, a budget and list of contributors, IRS tax exemption letter, and IRS letter stating organization is not a private foundation.
Deadlines: None.
Decision Notification: Trustees review grants in September, January, and May; annual budget set at August meeting.

Restrictions

The foundation limits its support to local or regional drives in communities where Donaldson employees live. The foundation does not support individuals, organizations for religious purposes, groups that influence legislation, political campaigns, or national drives. Applicants must qualify for tax exemption under the IRS Code and cannot be a private foundation.

Additional Information

The foundation considers capital grants, but limits them to 30% of annual giving.

Applicants receiving grants are furnished with a Statement of Donee form, which must be returned to the foundation before payments can be made. The statement may be recalled for any future grant payments.

Publications: Application Guidelines; Annual Report

Corporate Officials

Norman C. Linnell: vice president, general counselo, director B 1959. ED University of Minnesota (1981); University of Minnesota (1984). PRIM CORP EMPL vice president, general counsel: Donaldson Co., Inc.
William Grant Van Dyke: chairman, president, chief executive officer, director B Minneapolis, MN 1945. ED University of Minnesota BA (1967); University of Minnesota MBA (1972). PRIM CORP EMPL chairman, president, chief executive officer, director: Donaldson Co., Inc. ADD CORP EMPL president: Advanced Filtration Systems. CORP AFFIL director: Graco Inc. NONPR AFFIL member: Kappa Sigma Alumni Association.

Foundation Officials

Tim Grafe: trustee
Norman C. Linnell: president, trustee (see above)

Grants Analysis

Disclosure Period: fiscal year ending July 31, 2001
Total Grants: $426,275*
Number of Grants: 57
Average Grant: $5,932*
Highest Grant: $50,000
Typical Range: $1,000 to $5,000
*Note: Giving excludes matching gifts, scholarships, and United Way. Average grant figure excludes two highest grants ($100,000).

Recent Grants

Note: Grants derived from 2001 Form 990.

General

187,000	United Way Minneapolis, Minneapolis, MN
120,660	Citizens Scholarship Foundation of America, St. Peter, MN
50,000	SHAPE, Minneapolis, MN
50,000	University of Minnesota Foundation, Duluth, MN
45,000	Rebuild Resources, Minneapolis, MN
40,000	Community Action Council, Minneapolis, MN
35,000	Women in Transition, Minneapolis, MN
32,000	Tree Trust, St. Louis Park, MN
23,000	Lifeworks Services, Eagan, MN
21,000	United Way Portage County, Stevens Point, WI

DOROT FOUNDATION

Giving Contact

Prof. Ernest S. Frerichs, Executive Director
c/o Marks Paneth ET AL
622 Third Avenue
New York, NY 10017-6701
Phone: (212)503-8800
E-mail: info@dorot.org
Web: http://www.dorot.org

Description

Founded: 1958
EIN: 136116927
Organization Type: General Purpose Foundation
Giving Locations: U.S.-based affiliates of Israeli organizations; northeast United States.
Grant Types: Fellowship.

Donor Information

Founder: The foundation was established in 1958 by Joy G. Ungerleider-Mayerson, D.S., and the R. H. Gottesman Foundation.

Financial Summary

Total Giving: $11,866,252 (fiscal year ending March 31, 2002); $2,877,927 (fiscal 2001); $2,760,520 (fiscal 1999)

Giving Analysis: Giving for fiscal 2001 includes: foundation fellowships ($703,092); fiscal 1999: foundation fellowships ($317,124) fiscal 1995: foundation fellowships ($260,975)
Assets: $49,704,771 (fiscal 2002); $49,662,944 (fiscal 2001); $37,252,803 (fiscal 1999)
Gifts Received: $2,683,031 (fiscal 2002); $2,683,031 (fiscal 2001); $2,683,030 (fiscal 1999). Note: In fiscal 2001, contributions were received from Jeane Ungerleider. In fiscal 1999, contributions were received from the Yesod Fund.

Typical Recipients

Arts & Humanities: Arts Appreciation, Historic Preservation, History & Archaeology, Libraries, Museums/ Galleries, Performing Arts, Public Broadcasting, Theater
Civic & Public Affairs: Civil Rights, Community Foundations, Civic & Public Affairs-General, Law & Justice, Legal Aid, Public Policy, Safety, Urban & Community Affairs, Women's Affairs
Education: Arts/Humanities Education, Colleges & Universities, Economic Education, Education-General, Gifted & Talented Programs, International Exchange, International Studies, Medical Education, Preschool Education, Private Education (Precollege), Religious Education, Secondary Education (Private), Special Education, Student Aid, Vocational & Technical Education
Environment: Environment-General
Health: AIDS/HIV, Clinics/Medical Centers, Hospices, Medical Research, Medical Training, Mental Health, Public Health
International: Foreign Arts Organizations, Foreign Educational Institutions, International-General, Human Rights, International Environmental Issues, International Organizations, International Peace & Security Issues, Missionary/Religious Activities
Religion: Bible Study/Translation, Churches, Religion-General, Jewish Causes, Religious Organizations, Religious Welfare, Synagogues/Temples
Science: Scientific Centers & Institutes
Social Services: Camps, Community Service Organizations, Family Services, People with Disabilities, Social Services-General, Substance Abuse, YMCA/ YWCA/YMHA/YWHA, Youth Organizations

Application Procedures

Initial Contact: Applicants should submit a preliminary letter of proposal. The foundation reports that it does not have any formal proposal guidelines. Fellowship applications and guidelines may be downloaded from the foundation's Web site.

Foundation Officials

Steven Baum: secretary, treasurer
Dina Charan: contact
Eilean Crean: assistant secretary
Ernest S. Frerichs: executive director B Staten Island, NY 1925. ED Brown University AB (1948); Harvard University AM (1949); Boston University STB (1952); Boston University PhD (1957); Hebrew Union College DHL (1992). NONPR AFFIL member: Phi Beta Kappa; member: Society Biblical Literature; professor religious studies; director Judaic stud: Brown University; member: American Academy Religion; vice president, trustee: American Schools Oriental Research; trustee: Albright Institute Archeological Research.
Jeane Ungerleider: president
Steven Ungerleider: vice president

Grants Analysis

Disclosure Period: fiscal year ending March 31, 2002
Total Grants: $9,183,222*
Number of Grants: 30
Average Grant: $306,107*
Highest Grant: $800,000
Typical Range: $30,000 to $100,000

*Note: Giving excludes fellowship. Average grant figure excludes highest grant.

Recent Grants

Note: Grants derived from 2002 Form 990.

Library-Related
800,000   New York Public Library, New York, NY

General
9,000,000   Tides Foundation, New York, NY
250,000   Jewish Board of Family and Children's Services, New York, NY
250,000   Temple Beth Israel, New York, NY
230,000   New Israel Fund, New York, NY
182,099   Albright Institute of Archaeological Research
87,000   Alliance for Justice, Washington, DC
55,000   New York University, New York, NY
50,000   Jewish Braille Institute of America, New York, NY
50,000   Jewish Women's Archive, Brookline, MA
40,000   Bet Tzedek Legal Services, Los Angeles, CA

M. S. DOSS FOUNDATION, INC.

Giving Contact

Joe K. McGill, President
PO Box 1677
Seminole, TX 79360-1677
Phone: (915)758-2770
Fax: (915)758-9591

Description

Founded: 1984
EIN: 751945227
Organization Type: General Purpose Foundation
Giving Locations: NM: eastern New Mexico; TX: western Texas
Grant Types: Capital, General Support, Scholarship.

Donor Information

Founder: Established by the late M. S. Doss and the late Meek Lane Doss .

Financial Summary

Total Giving: $1,375,243 (2002 approx); $2,388,043 (2001); $2,065,727 (1999)
Giving Analysis: Giving for 2001 includes: foundation scholarships ($3,437); 1999: foundation scholarships ($16,960) 1998: foundation scholarships ($4,466)
Assets: $53,439,176 (2001); $44,158,390 (1999); $49,608,627 (1998)
Gifts Received: $8,100 (1993)

Typical Recipients

Arts & Humanities: Historic Preservation, Libraries, Museums/Galleries, Music, Theater
Civic & Public Affairs: Botanical Gardens/Parks, Community Foundations, Economic Development, Civic & Public Affairs-General, Housing, Municipalities/Towns, Nonprofit Management, Parades/Festivals, Professional & Trade Associations, Rural Affairs, Urban & Community Affairs
Education: Afterschool/Enrichment Programs, Agricultural Education, Business Education, Colleges & Universities, Engineering/Technological Education, Education-General, Medical Education, Private Education (Precollege), Public Education (Precollege), Student Aid
Health: Children's Health/Hospitals, Clinics/Medical Centers, Diabetes, Hospices, Hospitals, Medical Rehabilitation, Single-Disease Health Associations
Religion: Churches, Religion-General, Religious Organizations, Religious Welfare

Social Services: Animal Protection, At-Risk Youth, Big Brother/Big Sister, Camps, Child Abuse, Child Welfare, Community Centers, Community Service Organizations, Day Care, Delinquency & Criminal Rehabilitation, Domestic Violence, Family Services, Food/ Clothing Distribution, Homes, People with Disabilities, Recreation & Athletics, Scouts, Senior Services, Shelters/Homelessness, Social Services-General, Substance Abuse, Volunteer Services, YMCA/YWCA/ YMHA/YWHA, Youth Organizations

Application Procedures

Initial Contact: The foundation reports that organizations submitting a proposal for the first time should send a brief letter of inquiry. Organizations applying for grants for a second time should send a grant application packet.
Deadlines: None.

Restrictions

Applications for youth organizations are restricted to West Texas and East New Mexico. Scholarship applications are restricted to Gaines County youth homes to which the foundation has made grants.

Additional Information

The foundation also funds scholarships for certain needy students, and supports the Community Chapel, the Doss Museum, and the Scout Center, all in Seminole, TX. The foundation prefers to support charitable youth organizations.

Foundation Officials

Joe K. McGill: president, chairman, trustee
Julia Narvarte: assistant treasurer, trustee
Stuart Robertson: treasurer, trustee
Richard Spraberry: vice president, trustee
Billie Thompson: secretary, trustee PRIM CORP EMPL vice president: First National Bank Temple.

Grants Analysis

Disclosure Period: calendar year ending 2001
Total Grants: $2,384,606*
Number of Grants: 48
Average Grant: $44,353*
Highest Grant: $300,000
Typical Range: $20,000 to $100,000
*Note: Giving excludes scholarships. Average grant figure excludes highest grant.

Recent Grants

Note: Grants derived from 2001 Form 990.

General
325,000   Boys and Girls Club of Greater Fort Worth, Ft. Worth, TX -- endowment and maintenance
200,000   Permian Basin Area Foundation, Midland, TX -- non binding recommendation for future funding
150,000   Boys and Girls Club of Vernon, Inc., Vernon, TX -- capital campaign
150,000   Ronald McDonald House Charities, El Paso, TX -- building construction
150,000   South Plains Food Bank, Lubbock, TX -- renovations/truck
110,385   M.S. Doss Youth Center, Seminole, TX -- operations, renovations, and air conditioner
100,000   Blue Haven Youth Camp, Inc., Canyon, TX -- waste water treatment system
100,000   Concho Resource Center, San Angelo, TX -- building renovation
100,000   Concho Valley Home for Girls, San Angelo, TX -- building construction
100,000   Young Men's Christian Association, Ft. Worth, TX -- building renovations

JAMES R. DOUGHERTY, JR. FOUNDATION

Giving Contact

Daren R. Wilder, Assistant Secretary & Assistant Treasurer
PO Box 640
Beeville, TX 78104-0640
Phone: (361)358-3560

Description

Founded: 1950
EIN: 746039858
Organization Type: Family Foundation
Giving Locations: TX: nationally and internationally.
Grant Types: Capital, General Support, Operating Expenses, Project, Research, Scholarship, Seed Money.

Donor Information

Founder: the late James R. Dougherty, members of the Dougherty family

Financial Summary

Total Giving: $505,055 (fiscal year ending November 30, 2002); $514,201 (fiscal 2001); $466,875 (fiscal 2000)
Giving Analysis: Giving for fiscal 1999 includes: foundation grants to United Way ($4,000); fiscal 1998: foundation grants to United Way ($5,000) foundation ($675,035)
Assets: $9,349,060 (fiscal 2002); $9,760,250 (fiscal 2001); $9,710,907 (fiscal 2000)
Gifts Received: $2,080 (fiscal 2001)

Typical Recipients

Arts & Humanities: Arts Associations & Councils, Arts Outreach, Dance, Film & Video, Arts & Humanities-General, Historic Preservation, History & Archaeology, Libraries, Museums/Galleries, Opera, Performing Arts, Public Broadcasting
Civic & Public Affairs: Botanical Gardens/Parks, Ethnic Organizations, Civic & Public Affairs-General, Hispanic Affairs, Housing, Legal Aid, Native American Affairs, Philanthropic Organizations, Public Policy, Safety, Urban & Community Affairs, Women's Affairs
Education: Arts/Humanities Education, Colleges & Universities, Education Funds, Education Reform, Elementary Education (Public), Environmental Education, Faculty Development, Education-General, Leadership Training, Private Education (Precollege), Private Education (Precollege), Public Education (Precollege), Religious Education, Science/Mathematics Education, Social Sciences Education, Student Aid
Environment: Environment-General, Resource Conservation, Watershed, Wildlife Protection
Health: AIDS/HIV, Cancer, Children's Health/Hospitals, Clinics/Medical Centers, Emergency/Ambulance Services, Health Organizations, Heart, Hospitals, Medical Rehabilitation, Medical Research, Mental Health, Prenatal Health Issues, Public Health, Single-Disease Health Associations
International: Foreign Arts Organizations, Foreign Educational Institutions, International-General, Health Care/Hospitals, Human Rights, International Development, International Environmental Issues, International Organizations, International Peace & Security Issues, International Relations, International Relief Efforts, Missionary/Religious Activities
Religion: Churches, Dioceses, Jewish Causes, Religious Organizations, Religious Welfare, Synagogues/Temples
Science: Scientific Centers & Institutes
Social Services: At-Risk Youth, Child Welfare, Community Centers, Community Service Organizations, Domestic Violence, Emergency Relief, Family Planning, Family Services, Food/Clothing Distribution, Homes, People with Disabilities, Sexual Abuse, Shelters/Homelessness, Social Services-General, Substance Abuse, United Funds/United Ways, YMCA/YWCA/YMHA/YWHA, Youth Organizations

Application Procedures

Initial Contact: a brief letter of inquiry
Application Requirements: Include a description of organization, purpose of funds sought, amount requested, and proof of tax-exempt status.
Deadlines: None.

Restrictions

No grants are made to individuals. Does not provide multiple-year funding.

Additional Information

The board of directors meets twice a year, usually in the spring and fall.

Foundation Officials

F. William Carr, Jr.: trustee
Rachael Carr: trustee
Kevin Dougherty: trustee
Mary Patricia Dougherty: secretary, treasurer, trustee
May Dougherty King: chairman, trustee
Erin Marcotte: trustee
Beatrice Rossi-Landi: trustee
Frances Carr Tapp: trustee
Ben F. Vaughan, III: trustee
Genevieve Vaughan: trustee
Daren R. Wilder: assistant secretary, assistant treasurer

Grants Analysis

Disclosure Period: fiscal year ending November 30, 2002
Total Grants: $505,055
Number of Grants: 80
Average Grant: $3,255*
Highest Grant: $167,460
Lowest Grant: $50
Typical Range: $500 to $5,000
*Note: Average grant figure excludes two highest grants ($251,190).

Recent Grants

Note: Grants derived from fiscal 2001 Form 990.

General

20,000	Utah State University, Logan, UT -- for Autoimmunity-Cytokines in Autism
15,000	Dougherty Historical Foundation, Beeville, TX -- for operating expenses
15,000	Dougherty Historical Foundation, Beeville, TX -- for operating expenses
14,000	Dougherty Historical Foundation, Beeville, TX -- for operating expenses
14,000	Mount St. Mary's College, Los Angeles, CA -- for Women's Leadership Program
13,200	Seabury School, Tacoma, WA
13,200	Utah State University, Logan, UT -- for research for Autism Research-Viral-Autoimmunity in Older Autistic Subjects
12,000	Sisterhood is Global Institute, Montreal Canada -- for Learning Partnership Project
10,000	American Himalayan Foundation, San Francisco, CA -- to help support the hospital and rehabilitation for disabled children
10,000	Kennedy Krieger Research Institute, Baltimore, MD -- for research with adrenoleukodystrophy

ALFRED AND MARY DOUTY FOUNDATION

Giving Contact

Judith L. Bardes, Executive Director & Trustee
PO Box 540
Plymouth Meeting, PA 19462
Phone: (610)828-8145
Fax: (610)834-8175

Description

Founded: 1968
EIN: 236463709
Organization Type: Private Foundation
Giving Locations: PA: Philadelphia including metropolitan area in Philadelphia and Montgomery counties
Grant Types: General Support, Project, Seed Money.

Donor Information

Founder: the late Alfred Douty, the late Mary M. Douty

Financial Summary

Total Giving: $292,950 (2001); $292,450 (2000); $259,380 (1999)
Assets: $6,585,650 (2001); $7,742,068 (2000); $8,687,190 (1999)
Gifts Received: $180,158 (1995). Note: In 1995, contributions were received from Alfred and Mary Douty Unitrust.

Typical Recipients

Arts & Humanities: Community Arts, Arts & Humanities-General, Libraries, Performing Arts
Civic & Public Affairs: Asian American Affairs, Botanical Gardens/Parks, Community Foundations, Economic Development, Employment/Job Training, Civic & Public Affairs-General, Hispanic Affairs, Housing, Law & Justice, Philanthropic Organizations, Safety, Urban & Community Affairs, Women's Affairs
Education: Afterschool/Enrichment Programs, Arts/Humanities Education, Colleges & Universities, Community & Junior Colleges, Education Funds, Education Reform, Elementary Education (Public), Education-General, Literacy, Minority Education, Preschool Education, Private Education (Precollege), Public Education (Precollege), School Volunteerism, Science/Mathematics Education
Health: Adolescent Health Issues, Children's Health/Hospitals, Children's Health/Hospitals, Prenatal Health Issues, Public Health
Religion: Ministries
Social Services: At-Risk Youth, Camps, Child Welfare, Community Centers, Community Service Organizations, Crime Prevention, Delinquency & Criminal Rehabilitation, Domestic Violence, Family Planning, Family Services, Homes, Social Services-General, YMCA/YWCA/YMHA/YWHA, Youth Organizations

Application Procedures

Initial Contact: Request application guidelines in a brief letter of inquiry, then send full proposal.
Application Requirements: Include name and a description of organization; purpose of funds sought; special nature of the project; leadership involved in the project; evidence that staff involved in the project are able to work with and understand the needs of the population to be served; amount requested and total funds needed; other funds available or anticipated; recently audited financial statement including most recent audited annual report, annual budget, and balance sheet; information on the organization's leadership, including board of directors/trustees; and proof of tax-exempt status.
Deadlines: February 15, April 15, and October 15.
Evaluative Criteria: The foundation favors educational projects and projects that promote positive social change and benefit disadvantaged people.

Restrictions

Foundation does not support individuals, nor religious or political organizations. The following are low funding priorities for the foundation: capital expenditures; endowments; or agency promotion such as marketing, development, publication of annual reports, or fundraising events.

Additional Information

Publications: Annual Report (including Application Guidelines)
Trust(s): PNC Bank NA

Foundation Officials

Richard G. Alexander: trustee
Judith L. Bardes: executive director, trustee
Lynette E. Campbell: trustee
Norma Elias: trustee
Thomas B. Harvey, Esq.: trustee
Nancy J. Kirby: trustee
Carrolle F. Perry: trustee

Grants Analysis

Disclosure Period: calendar year ending 2001
Total Grants: $292,950
Number of Grants: 91
Average Grant: $3,219
Highest Grant: $10,000
Typical Range: $1,000 to $5,000

Recent Grants

Note: Grants derived from 2001 Form 990.

Library-Related
5,000   Free Library of Philadelphia, Philadelphia, PA -- for cultural and educational programming

General
10,000   Children's Hospital of Philadelphia, Philadelphia, PA -- for Bridging the Gaps Consortium
10,000   Delaware Valley Habitat for Humanity, Philadelphia, PA
6,000   Greater Philadelphia Federation of Settlements, Philadelphia, PA -- for 2001 Summer Career Exploration Program
6,000   Korean Community Development Services Center, Philadelphia, PA -- for 2001 Summer Career Exploration Program
6,000   Respond, Camden, NJ -- for 2001 Summer Career Exploration Program
5,000   Asian Arts Initiative, Philadelphia, PA -- for Youth Arts Workshop
5,000   Assets Montco, Norristown, PA
5,000   CHOICE, Philadelphia, PA -- for Teen Pregnancy Prevention Program
5,000   Community Learning Center, Philadelphia, PA
5,000   Family Care Solutions, Inc., Philadelphia, PA

DOVER FOUNDATION

Giving Contact

Hoyt Q. Bailey, President
PO Box 208
Shelby, NC 28151
Phone: (704)487-8890
Fax: (704)482-6818
E-mail: doverfnd@shelby.net

Description

Founded: 1944
EIN: 560769897
Organization Type: General Purpose Foundation
Giving Locations: NC
Grant Types: Challenge, Endowment, General Support, Operating Expenses, Scholarship.

Donor Information

Founder: The Dover foundation was founded in 1944 by John Randolph Dover Jr. and Charles Irvin Dover for the purpose of assisting religious, charitable, scientific, literary, and educational organizations.

Financial Summary

Total Giving: $1,500,000 (fiscal year ending August 31, 2002); $1,317,675 (fiscal 2001); $1,200,000 (fiscal 2000)
Giving Analysis: Giving for fiscal 2001 includes: foundation grants to United Way ($5,000); foundation scholarships ($60,000); fiscal 1999: foundation scholarships ($52,000) fiscal 1998: foundation grants to United Way ($5,000)
Assets: $23,000,000 (fiscal 2002 approx); $25,823,307 (fiscal 2001); $29,229,776 (fiscal 1999)
Gifts Received: In 1991, contributions were received from the estate of Charles I. Dover.

Typical Recipients

Arts & Humanities: Arts Associations & Councils, Dance, Libraries, Museums/Galleries, Theater
Civic & Public Affairs: Botanical Gardens/Parks, Clubs, Community Foundations, Employment/Job Training, Civic & Public Affairs-General, Housing, Law & Justice, Municipalities/Towns, Safety, Urban & Community Affairs
Education: Afterschool/Enrichment Programs, Agricultural Education, Arts/Humanities Education, Colleges & Universities, Community & Junior Colleges, Education-General, Medical Education, Preschool Education, Public Education (Precollege), Science/Mathematics Education, Secondary Education (Public), Student Aid
Environment: Resource Conservation
Health: Cancer, Clinics/Medical Centers, Emergency/Ambulance Services, Geriatric Health, Health Funds, Health Organizations, Heart, Hospices, Hospitals, Kidney, Medical Research, Mental Health, Preventive Medicine/Wellness Organizations, Public Health, Research/Studies Institutes, Respiratory
Religion: Churches, Ministries, Religious Organizations, Religious Welfare
Science: Science Museums
Social Services: Animal Protection, At-Risk Youth, Child Abuse, Child Welfare, Community Centers, Community Service Organizations, Crime Prevention, Domestic Violence, Family Planning, Family Services, Scouts, Senior Services, Shelters/Homelessness, United Funds/United Ways, YMCA/YWCA/YMHA/YWHA, Youth Organizations

Application Procedures

Initial Contact: A formal grant request may be submitted to the foundation by letter.
Application Requirements: The applicant's proposal letter must include the following information: the full legal name of the organization; a brief description of the organization, its purpose, and program; the specific amount of money requested; a brief description of the purpose for which the grant would be used; a definite plan for the successful completion of the project; the signature of the principal officer of the governing board; and the signature of the organization's chief administrative officer. Detailed supporting information about the program or project may be attached to the grant request. The applicant must also attach a copy of the organization's most recent tax exemption letter from the IRS and a list of the organization's board of directors. One copy of the proposal is sufficient.
Deadlines: Deadlines for grant requests to be considered at the next meeting are: December 1, for the January meeting; March 1, for the April meeting; June 1, for the July meeting; and September 1, for the October meeting.
Review Process: The foundation board of directors meets four times a year to consider grant awards. These meetings are in January, April, July, and October.

Restrictions

The foundation does not ordinarily make grants to political entities or for their activities, to individuals or their projects, advertising, newsletters, magazines, books, trips, tours, or to organizations whose principal activities take place outside the United States.

Additional Information

Publications: Application Form; Guidelines

Foundation Officials

Hoyt Q. Bailey: president
W. W. Gainey, Jr.: treasurer
Harvey B. Hamrick: secretary
Kathleen D. Hamrick: vice president

Grants Analysis

Disclosure Period: fiscal year ending August 31, 2001
Total Grants: $1,252,675*
Number of Grants: 156
Average Grant: $6,107*
Highest Grant: $200,000
Lowest Grant: $100
Typical Range: $1,000 to $10,000
*Note: Giving excludes scholarships and United Way. Average grant figure excludes highest grant.

Recent Grants

Note: Grants derived from 2001 Form 990.

Library-Related
10,000   Cleveland County Library System, Shelby, NC

General
200,000   Gardner-Webb University, Boiling Springs, NC
100,000   YMCA, Shelby, NC
75,200   Cleveland County Council on Aging, Shelby, NC
60,000   Dover Scholarships, Shelby, NC
50,000   American Red Cross, Washington, DC
50,000   Heineman Medical Research Center, Charlotte, NC
35,000   Kings Mountain Baptist Association, Shelby, NC
30,000   Duke University Duke Gardens, Durham, NC
30,000   North Carolina State University, Raleigh, NC
25,500   Cleveland County Health Department, Shelby, NC

DOW CORNING CORP.

Company Headquarters

PO Box 994
Midland, MI 48686-0994
Phone: (517)496-4400
Web: http://www.dowcorning.com

Company Description

Employees: 6,000
SIC(s): 2821 Plastics Materials & Resins, 2869 Industrial Organic Chemicals Nec.
Parent Company: Dow Chemical Co., 2030 Dow Center, Midland, MI, United States

Operating Locations

Dow Corning Corp. (CA--Irvine; DC--Washington; GA--Roswell; IA--Davenport; KY--Carrollton, Elizabethtown; MI--Freeland, Hemlock; NJ--Budd Lake; NC--Greensboro; SC--Fort Mill; WA--Silverdale)

Dow Corning Foundation

Giving Contact

Anne M. DeBoer, Executive Director
CO2210
Midland, MI 48686-0994
Phone: (989)496-1863
Fax: (989)496-4393
E-mail: a.m.deboer@dowcorning.com
Web: http://www.dowcorning.com/content/about/
aboutcomm/aboutcomm_guidelines1.asp

Alternate Contact

220 W. Salzburg Road
PO Box 994
Midland, MI 48686-0994

Description

EIN: 382376485
Organization Type: Corporate Foundation
Giving Locations: headquarters and operating communities.
Grant Types: Capital, Multiyear/Continuing Support, Project.

Financial Summary

Total Giving: $774,507 (2000); $665,400 (1999); $654,900 (1998). Note: Contributions through foundation.
Giving Analysis: Giving for 2000 includes: foundation ($774,507); 1999: foundation ($665,400) 1998: foundation ($654,900)
Assets: $15,076,237 (2000); $15,294,604 (1999); $14,313,282 (1998)
Gifts Received: $1,262 (1994); $350 (1993). Note: In 1994, foundation received funds from Dow Corning Corp.

Typical Recipients

Arts & Humanities: Arts Associations & Councils, Arts Centers, Arts Festivals, Arts Institutes, Community Arts, Dance, Arts & Humanities-General, Historic Preservation, Libraries, Museums/Galleries, Music, Performing Arts, Public Broadcasting, Theater, Visual Arts
Civic & Public Affairs: Chambers of Commerce, Community Foundations, Economic Development, Employment/Job Training, Municipalities/Towns, Native American Affairs, Parades/Festivals, Philanthropic Organizations, Professional & Trade Associations, Safety, Urban & Community Affairs, Women's Affairs, Zoos/Aquariums
Education: Arts/Humanities Education, Colleges & Universities, Community & Junior Colleges, Engineering/Technological Education, Faculty Development, Education-General, Education-General, International Exchange, International Studies, Minority Education, Public Education (Precollege), Science/Mathematics Education
Environment: Environment-General
Health: Medical Research
Religion: Religious Welfare
Science: Science Exhibits & Fairs, Scientific Centers & Institutes
Social Services: Child Abuse, Community Centers, Community Service Organizations, Family Services, Recreation & Athletics, Scouts, United Funds/United Ways, YMCA/YWCA/YMHA/YWHA, Youth Organizations

Application Procedures

Initial Contact: Contributions can be made by individual Dow Corning sites, through the US Corporate Contributions Committee, or by the Dow Corning Foundation. Individual sites make small contributions that benefit local communities; US Corporate Contributions funds projects that drive change in operating communities, and grants range from $2,000 to $25,000; the Foundation focuses on education and environmental projects, and grants range from $10,000 to $100,000. Contact appropriate giving program via telephone or letter for detailed application guidelines.
Review Process: Foundation executive director reviews applications and makes a recommendation to the foundation board, which meets quarterly.
Evaluative Criteria: Foundation-supported applicants must meet the following criteria: address a clearly defined need, and describe organization's ability and qualifications to meet the need; outline expected improvements, results, beneficiaries, and how they will be impacted by the program; include plan to secure ongoing funding; contain measurable objectives and plan for reporting progress.
Decision Notification: For foundation grants, decisions are communicated within three weeks following a board meeting.
Notes: Foundation requires a final report from grantees.

Restrictions

Does not support individuals; political or veterans organizations; religious organizations for sectarian purposes; intercollegiate athletics; health-related research or services; public advertisements; conferences, travel costs, dinners or fund-raising events; or ongoing operational support. Foundation does not fund scholarships or provide on-going support.

Additional Information

Contributions of Dow Corning products, material, or equipment are not provided; promotional items and samples are distributed when appropriate.
Dow Corning also sponsors a speakers' bureau.
Publications: Guidelines

Corporate Officials

Gary E. Anderson: chairman, president, chief executive officero PRIM CORP EMPL chairman, president, chief executive officer: Dow Corning Corp.
Gifford E. Brown: global vice president, chief financial officer PRIM CORP EMPL global vice president, chief financial officer: Dow Corning Corp.

Foundation Officials

Barbara S. Carmichael: trustee PRIM CORP EMPL vice president: Dow Corning Corp.
Thomas H. Lane: trustee
Paul A. Marcela: secretary

Grants Analysis

Disclosure Period: calendar year ending 2000
Total Grants: $774,507
Number of Grants: 25
Average Grant: $30,980
Highest Grant: $125,000
Lowest Grant: $8,837
Typical Range: $10,000 to $50,000

Recent Grants

Note: Grants derived from 2001 Form 990.

General

125,000	Midland Community Center, Midland, MI -- heat plant
50,000	City Rescue Mission, Saginaw, MI -- building addition
50,000	Elizabethtown Community College, Elizabethtown, KY -- for Workforce Development Training Center
50,000	Saginaw Valley State University Foundation, University Center, MI -- education professorship
50,000	South Dakota School of Mines and Technology, Rapid City, SD -- chemical engineering laboratory
35,400	Adventure Learning Center at Eagle Village, Hersey, MI -- Violence Prevention Program
35,000	Purdue University School of Chemical Engineering, West Lafayette, IN -- lab equipment
34,000	United Negro College Fund, Fairfax, VA -- fund drive
33,000	Western Michigan University, Kalamazoo, MI -- middle school Math Program
30,000	West Midland Family Center, Midland, MI -- building expansion

HERBERT H. AND GRACE A. DOW FOUNDATION

Giving Contact

Margaret A. Riecker, President
1018 West Main Street
Midland, MI 48640-4292
Phone: (989)631-3699
Fax: (989)631-0675
E-mail: info@hhdowfoundation.org
Web: http://www.hhdowfoundation.org

Description

Founded: 1936
EIN: 381437485
Organization Type: Family Foundation
Giving Locations: MI: statewide, Midland
Grant Types: Capital, Endowment, Matching, Multiyear/Continuing Support, Operating Expenses, Project, Seed Money.

Donor Information

Founder: The foundation was established by Mrs. Grace A. Dow in 1936 in memory of her husband, Dr. Herbert H. Dow, founder of the Dow Chemical Company. Dr. Dow maintained two strong interests during his lifetime: horticulture and an obligation to the workers and families at Dow Chemical Company "to share in the growing physical and cultural benefits which an industrially healthy community could provide." Mrs. Dow was a school teacher in Midland, and avidly studied the town's history. The foundation's trustees hope to perpetuate and expand its donors' interests in these areas.

Financial Summary

Total Giving: $23,722,000 (2001); $19,110,237 (2000); $18,114,256 (1999)
Giving Analysis: Giving for 2001 includes: foundation grants to United Way ($150,000); 1999: foundation grants to United Way ($120,000) foundation grants to United Way matching gifts ($916,000)
Assets: $446,515,000 (2001); $500,159,393 (2000); $571,212,294 (1999)
Gifts Received: $1,889 (2000); $1,855,995 (1998); $56,000 (1997). Note: In 1998, contributions were received from Dorothy D. Arbury. In 1996, donations were received from the Dow Chemical Company, Dept. of Agriculture, Awards Management Division, and other undisclosed sources.

Typical Recipients

Arts & Humanities: Arts Centers, Historic Preservation, History & Archaeology, Libraries, Public Broadcasting
Civic & Public Affairs: Botanical Gardens/Parks, Chambers of Commerce, Community Foundations, Economic Development, Economic Policy, Employment/Job Training, Civic & Public Affairs-General, Municipalities/Towns, Native American Affairs, Nonprofit Management, Parades/Festivals, Philanthropic Organizations, Safety, Urban & Community Affairs, Zoos/Aquariums
Education: Agricultural Education, Colleges & Universities, Continuing Education, Education Associations, Education Funds, Elementary Education (Public), Faculty Development, Education-General, Leadership Training, Preschool Education, Private

Education (Precollege), Public Education (Precollege), Science/Mathematics Education, Secondary Education (Public), Student Aid

Environment: Environment-General, Resource Conservation, Watershed, Wildlife Protection

Health: Children's Health/Hospitals, Clinics/Medical Centers, Emergency/Ambulance Services, Geriatric Health, Health Policy/Cost Containment, Hospitals, Medical Rehabilitation, Public Health

Religion: Churches, Ministries, Religious Organizations, Religious Welfare, Synagogues/Temples

Science: Science-General, Science Museums, Scientific Centers & Institutes

Social Services: Community Centers, Community Service Organizations, Crime Prevention, Family Services, Homes, People with Disabilities, Recreation & Athletics, Senior Services, Social Services-General, Special Olympics, Substance Abuse, United Funds/United Ways, Youth Organizations, Youth Organizations

Application Procedures

Initial Contact: The foundation has no formal application form. Applicants should submit a written proposal.

Application Requirements: Proposals should include a letter setting forth the nature and potential results of the program for which funding is sought; total project cost including any endowment for operations; amount requested, and how and over what period of time the grant may be disbursed; proof of tax-exempt status; a detailed annual budget and audited financial statement for the organization; and the names of the organization's management and trustees/directors.

Deadlines: None.

Review Process: After initial evaluation, proposals are referred to the appropriate program committee for full consideration. Additional information, site visits, or meetings in Midland may be requested. The board meets periodically during the year to make final grant decisions. Grants and installments on grants are usually disbursed late in December.

Evaluative Criteria: The trustees have a preference for funding opportunities where a grant of seed money or a matching grant will stimulate broad public participation in an artistic, recreational or cultural project so that the project can become self-sustaining. Projects that benefit youngsters or senior citizens are of special interest. The foundation also may be interested in a program that needs launching or requires changes. Requests for general support for ongoing programs are unlikely to be funded.

Restrictions

The foundation does not fund individuals, organizations outside of Michigan, or those which are not tax-exempt; political or lobbying groups; organizations that discriminate by race, sex, creed, age, or national origins; and religious organizations for sectarian purposes (except churches in the Midland community).

Additional Information

Publications: Annual Report

Foundation Officials

Julie Carol Arbury: trustee, donor great granddaughter

Herbert Dow Doan: chairman B Midland, MI 1922. ED Cornell University BS (1949). PRIM CORP EMPL chairman: Doan Resources Group. CORP AFFIL director: Elisa Technologies; director: Neogen Corp.; director: Chemical Bank & Trust Co.; director: Applied Intelligent Systems; director: Arch Development Corp. NONPR AFFIL chairman: Michigan Molecular Institute; member: Sigma Xi; member: Commission Physical Sciences Math Applications; member: American Chemical Society; member: American Institute Chemical Engineers.

Michael Lloyd Dow: treasurer B Saginaw, MI 1935. ED Williams College (1953-1956); Michigan State University BS (1961). PRIM CORP EMPL chairman:

Michael L. Dow, Associates. CORP AFFIL director: Dow Howell Gilmore Associates; founder, chairman, chief executive officer: General Aviation; director: Dow Chemical Co.; vice president, director: Central Michigan Inns Inc.; director: Chemical Finance Corp.

Diane D. Hullet: trustee

Bonnie B. Matheson: trustee

Michael D. Parker: trustee

Frank Popott: trustee

Margaret Ann Riecker: president, donor granddaughter

Margaret E. Thompson: trustee

Ruth B. Wheeler: trustee

Macauley Whiting: secretary

Grants Analysis

Disclosure Period: calendar year ending 2001

Total Grants: $23,572,000*

Number of Grants: 102

Average Grant: $231,098

Highest Grant: $2,171,000

Typical Range: $10,000 to $500,000

*Note: Giving excludes United Way.

Recent Grants

Note: Grants derived from 2000 Form 990.

General

2,325,000 Dow Gardens -- annual support for operations, research, education and capital improvements

1,620,000 Midland Center for the Arts, Midland, MI -- operating budget, endowment and historical society

1,500,000 Saginaw Valley State University, Saginaw, MI -- for a visiting scholar program to enrich the intellectual lives of the students

1,138,000 Michigan Molecular Institute, Midland, MI -- endowment pledge and for a grant for the Computer Consortium Project

1,000,000 Homer Township Emergency Services -- for a new facility to house the Fire Department, ambulance and 911 service

1,000,000 Michigan Technological University - Environmental Science Building, Houghton, MI -- part of a $5 million pledge to the Environmental Science and Engineering Building

1,000,000 Western Michigan University, Kalamazoo, MI -- for a project aimed at improving the teaching and learning of math in Michigan

750,000 West Midland Family Center, Midland, MI -- for building expansion

562,000 Meridian Public School District, Meridian, MS -- for a major upgrade and expansion of the school's computerization

500,000 Albion College, Albion, MI -- for the Herbert H. and Grace A. Dow Science Laboratory and the Dow Professorship

DOW JONES & COMPANY, INC.

Company Headquarters

New York, NY

Web: http://www.dowjones.com

Company Description

Ticker: DJ

Exchange: OTC

Employees: 8,300

SIC(s): 2711 Newspapers.

Operating Locations

Dow Jones & Co., Inc. (AZ--Phoenix; AR--Little Rock; CA--Fresno, Los Angeles, Palo Alto, San Diego; CO--Englewood; DC--Washington; FL--Coral Gables, Jacksonville, Tampa; GA--Atlanta; IL--Chicago, Highland, Lisle, Niles, Northbrook; IN--Indianapolis; IA--West Des Moines; MD--Baltimore, Silver Spring; MA--Boston; MI--Detroit; MO--St. Louis; NJ--Monmouth, Union; NY--Albany, Buffalo, Liverpool; NC--Charlotte; OH--Bowling Green; OK--Tulsa; PA--Philadelphia, West Middlesex; RI--East Providence; TX--Dallas, Houston, Irving, Lubbock; UT--Holladay; VA--Richmond; WA--Bellevue; WI--Milwaukee)

Note: Operates internationally.

Dow Jones Foundation

Giving Contact

Leonard E. Doherty, Administrative Officer
Dow Jones Foundation
PO Box 300
Princeton, NJ 08543
Phone: (609)520-5143
Fax: (609)520-5180

Description

EIN: 136070158

Organization Type: Corporate Foundation

Giving Locations: principally near operating locations and to national organizations.

Grant Types: General Support.

Financial Summary

Total Giving: $1,519,446 (2001); $1,488,244 (2000); $1,472,320 (1998). Note: Contributes through corporate direct giving program and foundation.

Giving Analysis: Giving for 2001 includes: foundation grants to United Way ($299,700); foundation scholarships ($317,346); foundation ($902,400); 2000: foundation scholarships ($287,694); foundation grants to United Way ($299,700); foundation ($900,850); 1998: foundation grants to United Way ($301,000); foundation scholarships ($342,770); foundation ($828,550);

Assets: $314,100 (2001); $311,324 (2000); $1,553,750 (1998).

Gifts Received: $1,500,000 (2001); $1,000,000 (1998); $1,125,000 (1997). Note: In 1998 and 2001, contributions were received from Dow Jones and Co.

Typical Recipients

Arts & Humanities: Arts Associations & Councils, History & Archaeology, Libraries, Museums/Galleries, Music, Theater

Civic & Public Affairs: African American Affairs, Asian American Affairs, Botanical Gardens/Parks, Clubs, Economic Development, Economic Policy, First Amendment Issues, Gay/Lesbian Issues, Civic & Public Affairs-General, Hispanic Affairs, Native American Affairs, Professional & Trade Associations, Public Policy, Urban & Community Affairs, Women's Affairs

Education: Arts/Humanities Education, Business Education, Colleges & Universities, Education Associations, Education-General, International Studies, Journalism/Media Education, Minority Education, Private Education (Precollege), Special Education, Student Aid

Health: Clinics/Medical Centers, Hospitals, Hospitals

International: Human Rights, International Organizations, International Relations

Social Services: Child Welfare, Community Service Organizations, Family Services, People with Disabilities, United Funds/United Ways, Volunteer Services

Application Procedures

Initial Contact: Send brief letter or proposal.

Application Requirements: Include outline of proposed purpose of grant and proof of tax-exempt status.

Deadlines: None.
Decision Notification: Annual meeting in November.

Restrictions

Does not currently support medical and scientific research or cultural activities.

Additional Information

Foundation has policy of considering contributions to institutions and causes where there has been a history of active participation and support by company employees.

Foundation reports U.S. Trust Co. of New York as corporate trustee.

The Dow Jones Foundation routinely makes its largest grant to the Dow Jones Newspaper Fund, a program which supports journalism education for minority high school and college students. The fund also provides internships and fellowships. internships and fellowships. internships and fellowships. internships and fellowships.

Corporate Officials

Kenneth L. Burenga: president, chief operating officer, chief executive officer B Somerville, NJ 1944. ED Rider College BS (1970). PRIM CORP EMPL president, chief operating officer, chief executive officer: Dow Jones & Co., Inc. CORP AFFIL general manager: Wall Street Journal; director: Telerate Holdings Inc.; chief executive officer: Dow Jones Telerate Inc.; director: Ottaway Newspapers Inc. NONPR AFFIL chairman: Better Business Bureau New York Inc.

Peter Robert Kann: chairman, chief executive officer, director B New York, NY December 13, 1942. ED Harvard University BA (1964). PRIM CORP EMPL chairman, chief executive officer, director: Dow Jones & Co., Inc. ADD CORP EMPL publisher: Wall Street Journal. NONPR AFFIL trustee: Aspen Institute; trustee: Institute Advanced Study. CLUB AFFIL Spee Club.

James Haller Ottaway, Jr.: senior vice president, director B Binghamton, NY 1938. ED Yale University BA (1960). PRIM CORP EMPL senior vice president, director: Dow Jones & Co., Inc. CORP AFFIL chairman, director, chief executive officer: Ottaway Newspapers Inc.; chairman: Inquirer & Mirror Inc. NONPR AFFIL chairman: World Press Freedom Comm; trustee: World Wildlife Foundation USA; trustee: Storm King Art Center; member: Newspaper Association America; trustee: Phillip Exeter Academy; president: Magazine Group; member: American Society Newspaper Editors; director: Arden Hill Hospital Foundation; trustee: American School Classical Studies Athens; member: American Newspaper Publishers Association.

Foundation Officials

Peter Robert Kann: member advisory committee (see above)
James Haller Ottaway, Jr.: member advisory committee (see above)
Elizabeth R. Steele: member advisory committee

Grants Analysis

Disclosure Period: calendar year ending 2001
Total Grants: $902,400*
Number of Grants: 78
Average Grant: $11,569
Highest Grant: $20,000
Lowest Grant: $800
Typical Range: $1,000 to $20,000
*Note: Giving excludes United Way and scholarships.

Recent Grants

Note: Grants derived from 2001 Form 990.

Library-Related
10,000	Chicopee Public Library, Chicopee, MA
10,000	New York Public Library, New York, NY
10,000	Princeton Public Library, Princeton, NJ
10,000	South Brunswick Public Library Foundation, Monmouth Junction, NJ

General
450,000	Dow Jones Newspaper Fund, New York, NY
302,596	National Merit Scholarship Corporation, Evanston, IL
55,000	United Way of Pioneer Valley, Springfield, MA
55,000	United Way of Tri-State, New York, NY
50,000	Dow Jones Newspaper Fund, New York, NY
43,000	United Way of Mercer County, Lawrenceville, NJ
20,000	Online News Association, Evanston, IL
20,000	United Way of Central New Jersey, Milltown, NJ
20,000	United Way of Hudson County, Jersey City, NJ
15,000	Children's Home Society, Trenton, NJ

DOYLE FOUNDATION

Giving Contact

Frederick E. Fisher, Director
The Doyle Foundation
1901 Ulmerton Rd., Suite 750
Clearwater, FL 33762
Phone: (727)942-7003

Description

Founded: 1995
EIN: 593311469
Organization Type: Private Foundation
Grant Types: General Support.

Donor Information

Founder: Established in 1995 by Dan Doyle.

Financial Summary

Total Giving: $106,500 (2001); $202,925 (2000); $220,000 (1998)
Giving Analysis: Giving for 1998 includes: foundation ($220,000) 1997: foundation matching gifts ($23,357)
Assets: $3,021,847 (2001); $3,321,123 (2000); $3,339,887 (1998)
Gifts Received: $1,105,390 (1996). Note: In 1996, contributions were received from Dan Doyle.

Typical Recipients

Arts & Humanities: Arts Centers, Ballet, Libraries
Civic & Public Affairs: Community Foundations, Civic & Public Affairs-General, Zoos/Aquariums
Education: Colleges & Universities, Private Education (Precollege), Public Education (Precollege)
Health: Clinics/Medical Centers, Public Health
Religion: Churches, Religious Organizations, Religious Welfare
Social Services: Child Abuse, Child Welfare, Food/Clothing Distribution, People with Disabilities, Recreation & Athletics, Shelters/Homelessness, Social Services-General, Youth Organizations

Application Procedures

Initial Contact: Request application form.
Application Requirements: Return completed application form with proof of tax-exempt status, evidence of current accreditation (for educational institutions), recently audited financial statement, and a list of current board members.
Deadlines: Applications are accepted from October 1 to November 30.

Foundation Officials

Daniel M. Doyle, Jr.: director
Daniel M. Doyle: president, director
Rosaleen J. Doyle: vice president, director
Margaret Doyle Carter: director
Frederick E. Fisher: secretary, director

Grants Analysis

Disclosure Period: calendar year ending 2001
Total Grants: $106,500
Number of Grants: 14
Average Grant: $7,607
Highest Grant: $20,000
Lowest Grant: $500
Typical Range: $5,000 to $10,000

Recent Grants

Note: Grants derived from 2000 Form 990.

Library-Related
10,000	Greater Clearwater Public Library Foundation, Clearwater, FL

General
25,000	Long Center Foundation, The, Clearwater, FL
20,000	Morton Plant Mease Foundation, Clearwater, FL
15,000	Clearwater Marine Aquarium, Clearwater, FL
15,000	Lowry Park Zoo, Tampa, FL
12,825	St. Vincent de Paul, St. Petersburg, FL
10,000	Berkeley School, Tampa, FL
10,000	RCS - Food Pantry, Clearwater, FL
10,000	RCS - The Haven, Clearwater, FL
10,000	St. Cecilia's School, Clearwater, FL
10,000	US Ski Team, Park City, UT

DREYFUS CORP.

Company Headquarters

200 Park Avenue, 7th Floor
New York, NY 10166-0039
Web: http://www.dreyfus.com

Company Description

Employees: 1,800
SIC(s): 6200 Security & Commodity Brokers.

Operating Locations

Dreyfus Corp. (NJ--East Orange)

Giving Contact

Patrice M. Kozolowski, Vice President, Corporate Communications
200 Park Ave., 55th Fl.
New York, NY 10166
Phone: (212)922-6000
Fax: (212)922-8620
E-mail: stile.j@dreyfus.com

Description

Organization Type: Corporate Giving Program
Giving Locations: principally near operating locations and to national organizations.
Grant Types: Employee Matching Gifts, General Support, Scholarship.

Financial Summary

Total Giving: Company does not disclose contributions figures.

Typical Recipients

Arts & Humanities: Arts Appreciation, History & Archaeology, Libraries, Museums/Galleries, Opera, Theater
Civic & Public Affairs: Public Policy, Women's Affairs
Education: Afterschool/Enrichment Programs, Business Education, Colleges & Universities, Economic Education, Education Funds, Journalism/Media Education, Literacy
Environment: Protection
Health: Adolescent Health Issues, Children's Health/Hospitals, Clinics/Medical Centers, Diabetes, Health Organizations, Hospitals, Medical Research, Multiple

Sclerosis, Prenatal Health Issues, Research/Studies Institutes, Single-Disease Health Associations
International: International Affairs
Religion: Religious Welfare
Science: Science Museums
Social Services: At-Risk Youth, Community Centers, Recreation & Athletics, Volunteer Services, Youth Organizations

Application Procedures

Initial Contact: Send a brief letter of inquiry and a full proposal. Include a description of organization, amount requested, and purpose of funds sought.

Additional Information

Company reports 40% of contributions support education. Approximately 20% each support the arts and humanities, health and human services, and neighborhood/economic development.

Corporate Officials

Christopher M. Condron: president, chief executive officer PRIM CORP EMPL president, chief executive officer: Dreyfus Corp.
William Thomas Sandalls, Jr.: senior vice president, chief financial officer B Newport, RI 1944. ED Yale University (1966); Harvard University Graduate School of Business Administration (1972). PRIM CORP EMPL senior vice president, chief financial officer: Dreyfus Corp. CORP AFFIL chairman, director: Cirrus System; director: MasterCard International Inc. NONPR AFFIL trustee: Taxpayers Foundation; chairman finance committee: Town Weston MA; member: Tax Executives Institute; member: Financial Executives Institute; member: Massachusetts Society Certified Public Accountants; director-at-large: Bank Administration Institute; corporateorator: Boston Museum Science; member: American Institute of CPA's.
W. Keith Smith: chairman PRIM CORP EMPL chairman: Dreyfus Corp.

Recent Grants

Note: Grants derived from 1998 Form 990.

Library-Related
New York Public Library, New York, NY

General
American Ireland Fund, New York, NY
American Museum of Natural History, New York, NY
Columbia University Business School, New York, NY
Council on Economic Priorities, New York, NY
Cystic Fibrosis Foundation, New York, NY
Financial Women's Association, New York, NY
Franciscan Sisters of the Poor, New York, NY
March of Dimes, Long Island, NY
Reach Out and Read, New York, NY
Metropolitan Museum of Art, New York, NY

Max And Victoria Dreyfus Foundation, Inc.

Giving Contact

Lucy Gioia, Office Administrator
50 Main Street, Suite 1000
White Plains, NY 10606
Phone: (914)682-2008

Description

Founded: 1965
EIN: 131687573
Organization Type: General Purpose Foundation
Giving Locations: nationally.
Grant Types: General Support, Project, Research.

Donor Information

Founder: The foundation was established in New York in 1965 by the late Victoria Dreyfus . When Mrs. Dreyfus died in 1976, her assets were bequeathed to the foundation. Mrs. Dreyfus was the wife of the late Max Dreyfus, a leading figure in the music publishing business and one of the founding members of ASCAP.

Financial Summary

Total Giving: $5,066,900 (2000); $3,989,200 (1998); $2,994,281 (1997)
Giving Analysis: Giving for 1998 includes: foundation grants to United Way ($20,000) foundation scholarships ($70,000)
Assets: $89,129,711 (2000); $91,171,833 (1998); $78,444,446 (1997)

Typical Recipients

Arts & Humanities: Arts Appreciation, Arts Associations & Councils, Arts Centers, Arts Festivals, Arts Outreach, Ballet, Community Arts, Dance, Ethnic & Folk Arts, Arts & Humanities-General, Historic Preservation, Libraries, Literary Arts, Museums/Galleries, Music, Opera, Performing Arts, Public Broadcasting, Theater, Visual Arts
Civic & Public Affairs: Community Foundations, Economic Development, Employment/Job Training, Hispanic Affairs, Housing, Law & Justice, Legal Aid, Municipalities/Towns, Native American Affairs, Nonprofit Management, Parades/Festivals, Philanthropic Organizations, Public Policy, Safety, Safety, Urban & Community Affairs, Zoos/Aquariums
Education: Agricultural Education, Arts/Humanities Education, Business Education, Colleges & Universities, Education Associations, Engineering/Technological Education, Environmental Education, Education-General, Leadership Training, Legal Education, Medical Education, Minority Education, Private Education (Precollege), Public Education (Precollege), Science/Mathematics Education, Secondary Education (Private), Secondary Education (Public), Special Education, Student Aid, Vocational & Technical Education
Environment: Environment-General, Resource Conservation, Wildlife Protection
Health: AIDS/HIV, Cancer, Children's Health/Hospitals, Clinics/Medical Centers, Emergency/Ambulance Services, Eyes/Blindness, Health-General, Health Organizations, Health Organizations, Heart, Home-Care Services, Hospices, Hospitals, Hospitals (University Affiliated), Medical Rehabilitation, Medical Research, Mental Health, Single-Disease Health Associations
Religion: Churches, Dioceses, Religion-General, Jewish Causes, Religious Organizations, Religious Welfare
Science: Science Museums, Scientific Research
Social Services: Animal Protection, At-Risk Youth, Child Welfare, Community Centers, Community Service Organizations, Counseling, Crime Prevention, Day Care, Delinquency & Criminal Rehabilitation, Emergency Relief, Family Planning, Family Services, Food/Clothing Distribution, People with Disabilities, Recreation & Athletics, Scouts, Senior Services, Sexual Abuse, Shelters/Homelessness, Social Services-General, Substance Abuse, United Funds/United Ways, Volunteer Services, YMCA/YWCA/YMHA/YWHA, Youth Organizations

Application Procedures

Initial Contact: Send a letter of request, not exceeding three pages.
Application Requirements: An outline of the project, a copy of an IRS tax-exempt determination letter, budget sheet for project/program and explanation of purpose of grants.
Deadlines: None.
Decision Notification: The board reviews applications every four months.

Restrictions

The foundation does not support individuals or foreign organizations.

Additional Information

Publications: Guidelines

Foundation Officials

Lucy Gioia: office administrator
Nancy E. Oddo: vice president, director
David Jerome Oppenheim: chairman, director B Detroit, MI 1922. OCCUPATION musician. NONPR AFFIL member: Society Fellows; member, board directors: Town Hall Foundation; member: New York State Arts Deans; member: National Society Literature & Arts International; board advisory: New School Concerts; member: Council Fine Arts Deans; member, board directors: Film Society Lincoln Center; member: American Federation Arts; member, board directors: American Stefan Wolpe Society.
Norman S. Portenoy: vice president, director B 1919. PRIM CORP EMPL chairman: PSC Systems Inc. CORP AFFIL officer: EMP Industries Inc.; officer: RJ Simpson Ltd.; officer: Business Link Systems Inc.
Winifred Riggs Portenoy: president, director
Mary P. Surrey: secretary, treasurer, director

Grants Analysis

Disclosure Period: calendar year ending 2000
Total Grants: $5,066,900*
Number of Grants: 554
Average Grant: $9,146
Highest Grant: $62,500
Lowest Grant: $1,000
Typical Range: $5,000 to $10,000
***Note:** Giving excludes scholarships, United Way.

Recent Grants

Note: Grants derived from 2000 Form 990.

General

62,500	Animal Medical Center, New York, NY -- for Cancer Research Programs
60,000	Friends of the National Zoo, Washington, DC -- for Panda Habitat Renovations and operating support
50,000	Gonzaga Preparatory School, Spokane, WA -- for Youth Service Program
50,000	Juilliard School, New York, NY -- for music education
35,000	School District of Oconee County, Walhalla, SC -- for Music and Art Programs
30,000	Federal City Council, Washington, DC -- for National Music Museum and Performance Center
30,000	Olney Theater Corporation, Olney, MD -- for performing arts
30,000	St. Ann's Center for Intergenerational Care, Milwaukee, WI -- for Building Program
30,000	Washington Theater Awards Society, Washington, DC -- for Washington Theatre Legacy Project
25,000	District of Columbia Developing Families Center, Washington, DC -- for The Birth Center

Jean And Louis Dreyfus Foundation

Giving Contact

Edmee de Montmollin Firth, Executive Director
420 Lexington Avenue, Suite 626
New York, NY 10170
Phone: (212)599-1931
Fax: (212)599-2956
E-mail: jldreyfusfdtn@hotmail.com
Web: http://fdncenter.org/grantmaker/dreyfus/

Description

Founded: 1978
EIN: 132947180
Organization Type: Family Foundation
Giving Locations: NY: New York
Grant Types: General Support, Matching.

Donor Information

Founder: Incorporated in 1979 by the late Louis Drey-fus , a music publisher, and his wife, Jean.

Financial Summary

Total Giving: $1,093,000 (2002 approx); $1,352,500 (2001); $1,491,800 (2000)
Assets: $22,000,000 (2001 approx); $25,033,391 (2000); $23,073,212 (1997)

Typical Recipients

Arts & Humanities: Arts Associations & Councils, Arts Centers, Arts Funds, Arts Institutes, Arts Outreach, Ballet, Dance, Ethnic & Folk Arts, Historic Preservation, Libraries, Literary Arts, Museums/Galleries, Music, Opera, Performing Arts, Theater
Civic & Public Affairs: Asian American Affairs, Botanical Gardens/Parks, Business/Free Enterprise, Community Foundations, Economic Development, Employment/Job Training, Gay/Lesbian Issues, Civic & Public Affairs-General, Hispanic Affairs, Housing, Law & Justice, Legal Aid, Municipalities/Towns, Parades/Festivals, Public Policy, Urban & Community Affairs, Women's Affairs
Education: Afterschool/Enrichment Programs, Afterschool/Enrichment Programs, Arts/Humanities Education, Colleges & Universities, Education Reform, Education-General, Literacy, Medical Education, Minority Education, Private Education (Precollege), Public Education (Precollege), Special Education, Student Aid
Environment: Air/Water Quality, Environment-General
Health: Adolescent Health Issues, AIDS/HIV, Alzheimers Disease, Cancer, Children's Health/Hospitals, Clinics/Medical Centers, Geriatric Health, Health Policy/Cost Containment, Health Funds, Health Organizations, Home-Care Services, Hospitals, Long-Term Care, Medical Training, Mental Health, Nursing Services, Nutrition, Prenatal Health Issues, Public Health
International: Foreign Educational Institutions, Health Care/Hospitals, International Organizations
Religion: Churches, Religion-General, Jewish Causes, Religious Welfare
Social Services: At-Risk Youth, Child Welfare, Community Centers, Community Service Organizations, Crime Prevention, Day Care, Delinquency & Criminal Rehabilitation, Family Planning, Family Services, Food/Clothing Distribution, Scouts, Senior Services, Shelters/Homelessness, Social Services-General, Substance Abuse, Volunteer Services, YMCA/YWCA/YMHA/YWHA, Youth Organizations

Application Procedures

Initial Contact: Submit an initial inquiry consisting of a one- to two-page letter.
Application Requirements: Include a description of organization and an outline of the project.
Deadlines: Letters of inquiry are due February 1 and August 1 for spring and fall board meetings, respectively.
Review Process: All inquiries will be acknowledged in writing indicating whether or not an application is justified. If so, the foundation will provide an application form. result in a request for repayment to the foundation or discontinuance of payment by the foundation.

Restrictions

The Foundation has no direct charitable activities. Grants are not made to individuals. Grants are made only to tax-exempt organizations.

Foundation Officials

Edmee de Montmollin Firth: executive director
Katherine V. Firth: vice president
Nicholas L. D. Firth: president NONPR AFFIL director: American Society Composers Authors Publishers.
Thomas J. Hubbard: secretary NONPR AFFIL chairman, director: Metropolitan Opera Guild.
Thomas Joseph Sweeney, Jr.: vice president, treasurer B New York, NY 1923. ED New York University BA (1947); Columbia University JD (1949). PRIM CORP EMPL partner: Decker, Hubbard, Welden & Sweeney. CORP AFFIL chairman inst trustee & investment committee: Morgan Guaranty Trust Co. New York. NONPR AFFIL director: WR Kenan Fund; member: New York State Bar Association.

Grants Analysis

Disclosure Period: calendar year ending 2001
Total Grants: $1,352,500
Number of Grants: 84
Average Grant: $16,101
Highest Grant: $75,000
Lowest Grant: $5,000
Typical Range: $5,000 to $20,000

Recent Grants

Note: Grants derived from 2000 Form 990.

General

75,000	Chancellor's Office for Development, Brooklyn, NY
50,000	Brookdale Center on Aging, New York, NY
50,000	Center for Arts Education, New York, NY
50,000	New York City Opera, New York, NY
30,000	Columbia Presbyterian, New York, NY
25,000	Big Apple Circus, New York, NY
25,000	Burden Center For The Aging, New York, NY
25,000	Center to Prevent Handgun Violence, Washington, DC
25,000	Chamber Music Society of Lincoln Center, New York, NY
25,000	Institute for Democracy Studies, New York, NY

DRISCOLL FOUNDATION

Giving Contact

W. John Driscoll, President & Director
332 Minnesota St., Suite 2100
St. Paul, MN 55101-1308
Phone: (651)228-0935

Description

Founded: 1962
EIN: 416012065
Organization Type: Private Foundation
Giving Locations: CA: San Francisco; MN: Minneapolis, Saint Paul
Grant Types: Capital, General Support, Research.

Donor Information

Founder: members of the Driscoll family

Financial Summary

Total Giving: $730,000 (fiscal year ending February 28, 2001); $640,000 (fiscal 2000); $545,000 (fiscal 1998). Note: Fiscal 1997 Giving includes United Way ($20,000).
Giving Analysis: Giving for fiscal 2000 includes: foundation grants to United Way ($25,000); fiscal 1998: foundation grants to United Way ($25,000) foundation ($520,000)
Assets: $14,482,018 (fiscal 2001); $15,576,506 (fiscal 2000); $13,220,027 (fiscal 1998)

Gifts Received: $421,260 (fiscal 2001); $214,713 (fiscal 2000); $235,988 (fiscal 1998). Note: In fiscal 2001, contributions were received from the Revocable Trust of W. John Driscoll ($410,550) and Berkshire Hathaway ($10,710). In fiscal 2000, contributions were received from the Revocable Trust of W. John Driscoll ($205,209) and Berkshire Hathaway ($9,504).

Typical Recipients

Arts & Humanities: Arts Festivals, Arts Funds, Arts Institutes, Ballet, Community Arts, History & Archaeology, Libraries, Museums/Galleries, Music, Opera, Performing Arts, Public Broadcasting, Theater
Civic & Public Affairs: Botanical Gardens/Parks, Civic & Public Affairs-General, Women's Affairs
Education: Arts/Humanities Education, Colleges & Universities, Literacy, Minority Education, Private Education (Precollege), Religious Education, Special Education
Environment: Environment-General, Wildlife Protection
Health: AIDS/HIV, Children's Health/Hospitals, Hospitals, Medical Research, Speech & Hearing
International: Foreign Educational Institutions, International Environmental Issues
Religion: Seminaries
Science: Science Museums, Science Museums, Scientific Centers & Institutes
Social Services: Child Welfare, Community Service Organizations, Emergency Relief, Family Services, Recreation & Athletics, Substance Abuse, United Funds/United Ways, Volunteer Services, Youth Organizations

Application Procedures

Initial Contact: Send cover letter and full proposal.
Application Requirements: Include a description of organization, amount requested, purpose of funds sought, recently audited financial statement, and proof of tax-exempt status.
Deadlines: None.

Restrictions

Does not support individuals or provide funds for conferences, travel, publications, or films.

Additional Information

Publications: Annual Report; Application Guidelines

Foundation Officials

Elizabeth S. Driscoll: director
Rudolph Weyerhaeuser Driscoll: vice president, director B Saint Paul, MN 1933. ED Yale University BA (1955).
Walter John Driscoll: president, director B Saint Paul, MN 1929. ED Yale University BS (1951). CORP AFFIL director: Northern Studies Power Co.; director: Weyerhaeuser Co.
Michael J. Giefer: treasurer
Joseph S. Micallef: secretary B 1933. PRIM CORP EMPL president, chief executive officer, treasurer, director: Fiduciary Counselling Inc. PRIM NONPR EMPL sec-treas: Rock Island Co. CORP AFFIL secretary, treasurer: Rock Island Co.

Grants Analysis

Disclosure Period: fiscal year ending February 28, 2001
Total Grants: $730,000
Number of Grants: 15
Average Grant: $21,167*
Highest Grant: $250,000
Lowest Grant: $1,000
Typical Range: $10,000 to $30,000
*Note: Average grant figure excludes three highest grant ($476,000).

Recent Grants

Note: Grants derived from fiscal 2000 Form 990.

Library-Related

5,000	James J. Hill Reference Library, St. Paul, MN -- operating support

General

150,000	St. Paul Academy and Summit School, St. Paul, MN -- capital campaign
104,000	Yale University, New Haven, CT -- alumni fund/capital campaign
75,000	Friends of the St. Paul Public Library, St. Paul, MN -- renewal campaign
75,000	Santa Fe Opera, Santa Fe, NM -- opera underwriting
70,100	Minneapolis Institute of Arts, Minneapolis, MN -- endowment fund/annual fund
50,000	Science Museum of Minnesota, St. Paul, MN -- capital campaign
30,000	Minnesota Landscape Arboretum, Chanhassen, MN -- slade perennial gardens
25,000	United Way of St. Paul Area, St. Paul, MN -- operating support
10,000	Single House, Minneapolis, MN -- operating support
10,000	Tacoma Art Museum, Tacoma, WA -- capital campaign

JOSEPH DROWN FOUNDATION

Giving Contact

Wendy Wachtell, Vice President, Program Director
1999 Avenue of the Stars, Suite 1930
Los Angeles, CA 90067
Phone: (310)277-4488
Fax: (310)277-4573
E-mail: staff@jdrown.org
Web: http://www.jdrown.org

Description

Founded: 1953
EIN: 956093178
Organization Type: General Purpose Foundation
Giving Locations: CA
Grant Types: General Support, Matching, Operating Expenses, Project, Research, Scholarship.

Donor Information

Founder: The foundation was established in 1953 in California by Joseph W. Drown (d. 1982). Mr. Drown was a hotel builder and developer in California. His prize hotel, which he personally developed in 1945, was the Hotel Bel-Air in Los Angeles, CA. The foundation still has the original officers chosen by Mr. Drown.

Financial Summary

Total Giving: $4,767,660 (fiscal year ending March 31, 2002); $5,290,671 (fiscal 2001); $5,312,050 (fiscal 2000)
Giving Analysis: Giving for fiscal 2000 includes: foundation matching gifts ($60,000); foundation scholarships ($345,000) fiscal 1999: foundation scholarships ($370,000)
Assets: $90,190,854 (fiscal 2002); $92,370,042 (fiscal 2001); $107,116,104 (fiscal 2000)

Typical Recipients

Arts & Humanities: Arts Centers, Film & Video, Arts & Humanities-General, Libraries, Museums/Galleries, Music, Public Broadcasting, Theater
Civic & Public Affairs: African American Affairs, Botanical Gardens/Parks, Community Foundations, Economic Development, Civic & Public Affairs-General, Hispanic Affairs, Nonprofit Management, Public Policy, Urban & Community Affairs, Women's Affairs

Education: Afterschool/Enrichment Programs, Arts/Humanities Education, Business Education, Colleges & Universities, Education Funds, Education Reform, Faculty Development, Education-General, Gifted & Talented Programs, Health & Physical Education, Leadership Training, Legal Education, Literacy, Medical Education, Minority Education, Preschool Education, Public Education (Precollege), Science/Mathematics Education, Student Aid
Health: Adolescent Health Issues, Alzheimers Disease, Arthritis, Cancer, Children's Health/Hospitals, Clinics/Medical Centers, Diabetes, Emergency/Ambulance Services, Eyes/Blindness, Health-General, Geriatric Health, Health Organizations, Heart, Hospitals (University Affiliated), Long-Term Care, Medical Research, Mental Health, Outpatient Health Care, Preventive Medicine/Wellness Organizations, Research/Studies Institutes, Single-Disease Health Associations, Speech & Hearing
International: Foreign Educational Institutions, Health Care/Hospitals, International Relief Efforts, Missionary/Religious Activities
Religion: Churches, Jewish Causes
Science: Scientific Centers & Institutes, Scientific Research
Social Services: Animal Protection, At-Risk Youth, Child Welfare, Community Service Organizations, Crime Prevention, Day Care, Family Planning, Family Services, Food/Clothing Distribution, People with Disabilities, Senior Services, Substance Abuse, United Funds/United Ways, YMCA/YWCA/YMHA/YWHA, Youth Organizations

Application Procedures

Initial Contact: Prospective applicants should send a proposal and description of their organization.
Application Requirements: Proposals should include: a letter with information about both the organization as a whole and the particular project; an IRS tax-exempt determination letter; the most recent audited financial statement; budget information; a copy of the most recent Form 990 filed with the IRS; and a list of the organization's officers and directors. Any additional materials, such as annual reports and press releases, may also be included.
Deadlines: Applications must be received on or before January 15, April 15, July 15, and October 15.
Review Process: The board meets in the second month following each deadline. All proposals must be received by 5 p.m. on the day of the deadline to be considered.
Notes: Proposals should be addressed to Norman C. Obrow, President of the foundation.

Restrictions

The foundation does not make grants to individuals, endowments, capital campaigns, or building funds. It does not underwrite annual meetings, conferences, or special events. Does not fund religious programs or purchase tickets to events. No unsolicited proposals for medical and scientific research are funded. Funding is limited to California organizations.

Additional Information

Publications: Guidelines

Foundation Officials

Benton C. Coit: director
Milton Franklin Fillius, Jr.: chairman, director B New York, NY 1922. ED Hamilton College BA (1946); University of Michigan JD (1949). NONPR AFFIL member: State Bar California; member: Theta Delta Chi; member: Phi Alpha Delta; member: San Diego Chamber of Commerce.
Philip S. Magaram: secretary, treasurer, director B 1937. ED University of California, Los Angeles Law School. PRIM CORP EMPL president: Rose Valensi & Plc Magaram.
Elaine Mahoney: director
Thomas C. Marshall: vice president, director
Norman C. Obrow: president, director

Wendy Wachtell Schine: vice president, program director B White Plains, NY 1961. ED Wellesley College BA (1983); University of Southern California MA (1987). NONPR AFFIL advisor: Psychological Trauma Center; director: Southern California Association Philanthropy; board directors: Los Angeles Urban Funders; oversight committee: Big Sisters Los Angeles Pathways Project; advisor: Center Talented Youth.

Grants Analysis

Disclosure Period: fiscal year ending March 31, 2002
Total Grants: $4,487,660*
Number of Grants: 120
Average Grant: $37,397
Highest Grant: $381,000
Lowest Grant: $3,000
Typical Range: $10,000 to $50,000
*Note: Giving excludes United Way and scholarship.

Recent Grants

Note: Grants derived from 2002 Form 990.

General

250,000	Accelerated School, Los Angeles, CA -- capital campaign
200,000	Cedars-Sinai Medical Center - Gene Therapeutics Research Institute, Los Angeles, CA -- operating support
100,000	Betty Ford Center, Rancho Mirage, CA -- Children's Program
100,000	Buck Institute for Age Research, Novato, CA -- support research
100,000	California State University Northridge Foundation, Northridge, CA -- operating support
100,000	Families in Schools, Los Angeles, CA -- Mother/Daughter College Preparation Program
100,000	Phoenix Houses of California, Lake View Terrace, CA -- operating support
100,000	Planned Parenthood World Population, Los Angeles, CA -- operating support
100,000	Scripps Clinic, La Jolla, CA -- research in sleep apnea
100,000	United Way of New York, New York, NY -- relief efforts

DTE ENERGY CO.

Company Headquarters

2000 2nd Ave.
Detroit, MI 48226-1279
Web: http://www.dteenergy.com

Company Description

Founded: 1995
Ticker: DTE
Exchange: NYSE
Former Name: Detroit Edison Co.;
Acquired: Michigan Consolidated Gas Co..
Assets: US$19.238 billion (2002)
Employees: 11905 (2002)

Nonmonetary Support

Value: $50,000 (2000)
Type: Donated Equipment; In-kind Services
Note: The company also donates office space.

DTE Energy Foundation

Giving Contact

Karla Hall, Secretary & Director
DTE Energy Foundation
2000 Second Avenue, Rm. 1046 WCB
Detroit, MI 48226-1279
Phone: (313)235-9416
Fax: (313)235-0285

E-mail: hallk@dteenergy.com
Web: http://www.dteenergy.com/community/foundation/index.html
Note: Ms. Hall is also Administrator, Corporate Contributions.

Description

EIN: 382708636
Organization Type: Corporate Foundation
Giving Locations: MI: headquarters and operating communities, Detroit
Grant Types: Capital, Emergency, Employee Matching Gifts, Endowment, General Support, Multiyear/Continuing Support, Operating Expenses, Project.
Note: Foundation matches employee gifts to all educational and Michigan cultural institutions up to a limit of $5,000 per donor annually. Foundation also sponsors "Holiday Season Matching Gifts" program between November 1 and December 31 annually, through which it matches employee gifts to agencies that provide emergency food and shelter services.

Financial Summary

Total Giving: $5,000,000 (2001 approx); $3,807,028 (2000); $3,911,030 (1998). Note: Contributes through corporate direct giving program and foundation.
Giving Analysis: Giving for 2000 includes: foundation matching gifts ($322,066); corporate direct giving (approx $625,000); foundation grants to United Way ($780,250); foundation ($2,704,712); 1998: foundation matching gifts ($256,091); corporate direct giving ($588,447); foundation grants to United Way ($1,053,250); foundation ($2,013,212); 1997: corporate direct giving ($326,000); foundation ($3,300,000);
Assets: $11,150,513 (2000); $14,136,782 (1998); $13,390,127 (1997)
Gifts Received: $3,000,000 (1998); $2,240,000 (1997); $2,250,000 (1996). Note: Gifts are received from the Detroit Edison Co.

Typical Recipients

Arts & Humanities: Arts Associations & Councils, Arts Centers, Arts Institutes, Arts Outreach, Ethnic & Folk Arts, Arts & Humanities-General, Historic Preservation, History & Archaeology, Libraries, Museums/Galleries, Music, Opera, Performing Arts, Public Broadcasting, Theater
Civic & Public Affairs: African American Affairs, Business/Free Enterprise, Chambers of Commerce, Civil Rights, Community Foundations, Economic Development, Economic Policy, Ethnic Organizations, Civic & Public Affairs-General, Housing, Municipalities/Towns, Parades/Festivals, Professional & Trade Associations, Public Policy, Safety, Urban & Community Affairs, Women's Affairs, Zoos/Aquariums
Education: Agricultural Education, Arts/Humanities Education, Business Education, Business-School Partnerships, Colleges & Universities, Community & Junior Colleges, Economic Education, Education Associations, Education Funds, Engineering/Technological Education, Environmental Education, Education-General, Literacy, Medical Education, Minority Education, Private Education (Precollege), Public Education (Precollege), School Volunteerism, Science/Mathematics Education, Student Aid, Vocational & Technical Education
Environment: Environment-General, Wildlife Protection
Health: Children's Health/Hospitals, Emergency/Ambulance Services, Eyes/Blindness, Health Funds, Health Organizations, Hospices, Hospitals, Mental Health, Public Health, Single-Disease Health Associations
Religion: Religious Welfare
Science: Scientific Centers & Institutes, Scientific Centers & Institutes, Scientific Organizations
Social Services: Child Welfare, Community Centers, Community Service Organizations, Delinquency & Criminal Rehabilitation, Family Services, Food/Clothing Distribution, Recreation & Athletics, Substance Abuse, United Funds/United Ways, Youth Organizations

Application Procedures

Initial Contact: Submit a written proposal.
Application Requirements: The foundation uses the Council of Michigan Common Grant Application Procedure. The foundation requests that applicants complete the Common Grant Application Cover Sheet, and include a cover letter signed by the applicant organization's chief executive or senior development officer of the organization or chair of the volunteer board. The foundation has a specific format for applications, which can be referenced on the web at: http://www.dteenergy.com/community/apply.html. Applications should be typed double-space, and must include a Narrative comprised of the Executive Summary, Purpose of Grant, Evaluation, Budget Narrative/Justification, and Organization Information. The Executive Summary should describe why the organization is requesting funds, how the money will be spent, and anticipated outcomes. Purpose of Grant must include a statement of needs to be addressed, description of target population and how they will benefit; project goals, measurable objectives, action plans, and statements as to whether this is a new or ongoing initiative for the organization; a timetable for implementation; a list of any partners in the project and their roles; a description of similar existing projects, how this proposal differs from them, and what effort might be made to work cooperatively; an explanation of the active involvement of constituents in defining the needs/problems to be addressed and in making policy and planning the program; and long-term strategies for funding the project at the end of the grant period. Evaluation should include plans for project evaluation; how evaluation results will be used and/or disseminated; and a description of how constituents will be actively involved in the evaluation process. The Budget Narrative/Justification section should provide a grant budget, an explanation of how each budget item relates to the project and how the budget was calculated; other sources of funding and current funding requests; and an indication of priority items in the budget in the event that the full request cannot be accommodated. Organization Information should include the organization's history and goals; description of current projects, activities, and accomplishments; and an organizational chart, including board, staff and volunteer involvement. Attachments must include proof of tax-exempt status; list of the board of directors and their affiliations; organization's current annual operating budget, including expenses and revenue; and most recent annual financial statement (and Form 990 if financial statement is unaudited). Optional attachments include letters of support, annual report, and donor recognition opportunities, key publicity-related dates, fundraising plan, a list of other corporate and foundation funders with amounts, description of any cooperative actions with similar organizations to advance mutual goals and prevent duplication, and a description of quantity and types of support given by non-volunteer boards.
Deadlines: March 15, June 15, September 15, and December 15.
Review Process: Proposals are reviewed upon receipt and then referred to contributions committee for consideration.
Evaluative Criteria: Evidence of cooperative working arrangements among local organizations addressing same or similar goals.
Decision Notification: Quarterly, usually within 60-90 days after receipt of proposal.
Notes: Faxes and videos are discouraged. Requests must be made in writing.

Restrictions

Support is not provided for individuals (including direct scholarships); political parties, organizations, or activities; religious organizations for sectarian purposes; organizations that cannot demonstrate a commitment to equality and diversity; student group trips; national or international organizations, unless providing benefits directly to DTE Energy service-area residents; projects which may result in undue personal benefit to a member of the DTE Energy Foundation board or any DTE Energy director or employee; or conferences unless they are aligned with DTE Energy's business interests.

Additional Information

Prefers to fund specific projects rather than annual operating budgets or multi-purpose capital campaigns.
Publications: Guidelines; Application Form; Annual Report

Corporate Officials

Susan M. Beale: vice president, secretary chief financial officer B Richmond, IN 1948. ED Michigan State University BS (1970); University of Michigan JD (1976). PRIM CORP EMPL vice president, corporate secretary: DTE Energy Co. ADD CORP EMPL vice president, secretary: Detroit Edison Co. CORP AFFIL director: Edison Illuminating Co. Detroit; director: Saint Clair Energy Corp.
Robert J. Buckler: chief executive officer, president B Flint, MI 1949. ED University of Michigan BSME (1971); University of Michigan MSME (1973). PRIM CORP EMPL president, chief operating officer: DTE Energy Distribution Inc. ADD CORP EMPL chief executive officer, president: Detroit Edison Co.
Anthony Francis Earley, Jr.: chairman, chief executive officer, director B Jamaica, NY July 29, 1949. ED University of Notre Dame BS (1971); University of Notre Dame MS (1979); University of Notre Dame MS (1979). PRIM CORP EMPL chairman, chief executive officer, director: DTE Energy Co. ADD CORP EMPL chairman, chief executive officer, director: Detroit Edison Co. CORP AFFIL director: Mutual America. NONPR AFFIL vice chairman: Michigan Chamber of Commerce; member advisory council: University Notre Dame College Engineering; member: American Bar Association.
David E. Meador: senior vice president, chief financial officer ED Wayne State University BA; Wayne State University MBA. PRIM CORP EMPL senior vice president, chief financial officer: DTE Energy Co.
S. Martin Taylor: senior vice president human resources & corporate affairs ED Western Michigan University BS. PRIM CORP EMPL senior vice president human resources & corporate affairs: DTE Energy Co. ADD CORP EMPL senior vice president human resources: Detroit Edison Co.

Foundation Officials

Susan M. Beale: member (see above)
Robert J. Buckler: director (see above)
Anthony Francis Earley, Jr.: director (see above)
S. Martin Taylor: president, director (see above)

Grants Analysis

Disclosure Period: calendar year ending 2000
Total Grants: $2,704,712*
Number of Grants: 239
Average Grant: $11,317
Highest Grant: $170,000
Typical Range: $500 to $20,000
*Note: Giving excludes matching gifts; United Way.

Recent Grants

Note: Grants derived from 2000 Form 990.

General

170,000	Detroit 300, Inc., Detroit, MI
150,000	Detroit Symphony Orchestra Hall, Detroit, MI
150,000	Founders Society Detroit Institute of Arts, Detroit, MI
133,385	United Way Community Services, Detroit, MI
133,385	United Way Community Services, Detroit, MI

133,385	United Way Community Services, Detroit, MI
133,385	United Way Community Services, Detroit, MI
100,000	Habitat for Humanity of Michigan, Lansing, MI
98,852	United Way Monroe County, Monroe, MI
75,000	Greater Downtown Partnership, Detroit, MI

DUCHOSSOIS FAMILY FOUNDATION

Giving Contact

Kimberly T. Duchossois, President
Duchossois Family Foundation
845 Larch Ave.
Elmhurst, IL 60126-1196
Phone: (847)381-6278
Fax: (847)381-4102

Description

Founded: 1985
EIN: 363327987
Organization Type: Corporate Foundation
Former Name: Duchossois Foundation.
Giving Locations: IL: Chicago
Grant Types: General Support, Multiyear/Continuing Support.

Financial Summary

Total Giving: $501,177 (2001); $3,694,911 (2000); $996,600 (1998). Note: Contributes through foundation only.
Giving Analysis: Giving for 2001 includes: foundation scholarships ($3,500); foundation grants to United Way ($4,000); foundation ($493,677); 2000: foundation grants to United Way ($4,000); 1998: foundation grants to United Way ($3,500);
Assets: $3,905,550 (2001); $4,951,242 (2000); $6,152,703 (1998)
Gifts Received: $3,715,574 (2000); $2,500,000 (1998); $2,000,000 (1997). Note: In 2000, contributions were received from Duchossois Technology Partners, LLC. In 1998 and 1997, contributions were received from Duchossois Industries.

Typical Recipients

Arts & Humanities: Arts Associations & Councils, Arts Festivals, Arts Funds, Arts Institutes, Arts Outreach, Ballet, Community Arts, Dance, Ethnic & Folk Arts, Arts & Humanities-General, History & Archaeology, Libraries, Literary Arts, Museums/Galleries, Music, Opera, Performing Arts, Public Broadcasting, Theater, Visual Arts
Civic & Public Affairs: Botanical Gardens/Parks, Business/Free Enterprise, Chambers of Commerce, Clubs, Community Foundations, Economic Development, Civic & Public Affairs-General, Hispanic Affairs, Housing, Parades/Festivals, Philanthropic Organizations, Public Policy, Safety, Urban & Community Affairs, Urban & Community Affairs, Women's Affairs, Zoos/Aquariums
Education: Afterschool/Enrichment Programs, Arts/Humanities Education, Business Education, Colleges & Universities, Community & Junior Colleges, Education Funds, Education Reform, Elementary Education (Private), Engineering/Technological Education, Faculty Development, Education-General, Medical Education, Minority Education, Private Education (Precollege), Public Education (Precollege), Secondary Education (Public), Special Education, Student Aid
Environment: Forestry, Environment-General, Resource Conservation

Health: AIDS/HIV, Cancer, Children's Health/Hospitals, Clinics/Medical Centers, Diabetes, Health-General, Geriatric Health, Health Funds, Health Organizations, Hospices, Hospices, Hospitals, Hospitals (University Affiliated), Medical Rehabilitation, Medical Research, Mental Health, Prenatal Health Issues, Research/Studies Institutes, Single-Disease Health Associations, Speech & Hearing
International: International-General, Health Care/Hospitals, International Affairs, International Environmental Issues, Missionary/Religious Activities
Religion: Churches, Jewish Causes, Religious Organizations, Religious Welfare, Seminaries
Science: Science Museums, Scientific Organizations
Social Services: Animal Protection, At-Risk Youth, Child Welfare, Community Centers, Community Service Organizations, Family Services, Homes, People with Disabilities, Recreation & Athletics, Scouts, Shelters/Homelessness, Social Services-General, Substance Abuse, United Funds/United Ways, Volunteer Services, Youth Organizations

Application Procedures

Initial Contact: Send a one-page summary-request letter.
Application Requirements: Include a description of organization; its specific needs and purposes; the amount of support requested; list of board of directors and their business or professional affiliations. Attach proof of tax-exempt status and latest annual report.
Deadlines: None.
Review Process: Foundation will either reject initial inquiry or request a full proposal.
Decision Notification: Board meets semi-annually or as needed; major funding commitments are made at the January meeting.

Restrictions

The foundation does not support individuals, including scholarships or fellowships; lobbying groups; religious organizations for sectarian purposes; or organizations that are not tax-exempt.

Additional Information

Publications: Guidelines

Corporate Officials

Craig J. Duchossois: chief executive officer B 1944. ED Southern Methodist University MBA (1968). PRIM CORP EMPL chief executive officer: Duchossois Industries Inc. CORP AFFIL chairman: Saco Defense Inc.; chairman, chief executive officer, director: Thrall Car Manufacturing Co.; chairman: Chamberlain Group Inc.; director: Hill n Dale Farms Inc.
Richard Louis Duchossois: chairman, chief executive officer, director B Chicago, IL 1921. ED Washington & Lee University. PRIM CORP EMPL chairman, chief executive officer, director: Duchossois Industries Inc. CORP AFFIL chairman: Transportation Corp. Am; vice chairman: Thrall Car Manufacturing Co.; chairman: Duchossois Communication Co.; director: Hill n Dale Farms Inc.; director: Chamberlain Manufacturing Corp.; chairman: Arlington Management Services; director: Chamberlain Group Inc.; chairman: Arlington International Racecourse Ltd. NONPR AFFIL member: Chief Executives Organization. CLUB AFFIL Executive Club; Jockey Club; Economic Club.

Foundation Officials

Craig J. Duchossois: director (see above)
Dayle Paige Duchossois: director
Kimberly Duchossois: president
Richard Louis Duchossois: secretary (see above)

Grants Analysis

Disclosure Period: calendar year ending 2001
Total Grants: $493,677*
Number of Grants: 52
Average Grant: $7,719*
Highest Grant: $100,000

Lowest Grant: $500
Typical Range: $1,000 to $20,000
*Note: Giving excludes United Way and scholarships. Average grant figure excludes highest grant.

Recent Grants

Note: Grants derived from 2001 Form 990.

General

100,000	Northwestern University Medical School, Evanston, IL -- for Core Virology Program
50,000	Chicago Public Education Fund, Chicago, IL
25,000	American Cancer Society, Chicago, IL -- for Barrington Relay for Life
25,000	Illinois Institute of Technology, Chicago, IL
25,000	University of Chicago Hospitals, Chicago, IL
20,000	Barrington Youth Dance Ensemble, Barrington, IL
20,000	Beverly Duchossois Cancer Fund, Chicago, IL
20,000	Beverly Duchossois Cancer Fund, Chicago, IL
17,527	Robert Komosa Fund, Rolling Meadows, IL
15,000	Chicago Symphony Orchestra, Chicago, IL

DUCOMMUN AND GROSS FOUNDATION

Giving Contact

Robert Ducommun, President
1155 Park Avenue
New York, NY 10128

Description

Founded: 1968
EIN: 956210834
Organization Type: Private Foundation
Giving Locations: CA; DC: Washington; MA; NY: New York
Grant Types: General Support.

Financial Summary

Total Giving: $247,000 (2001); $245,500 (2000); $271,000 (1999)
Assets: $5,202,645 (2001); $5,082,039 (2000); $4,921,734 (1999)
Gifts Received: $197,087 (2001); $194,640 (2000); $194,640 (1999). Note: Contributions are received from Charles E. and Palmer G. Ducommun Charitable Annuity Trust.

Typical Recipients

Arts & Humanities: Historic Preservation, Libraries, Museums/Galleries, Public Broadcasting
Civic & Public Affairs: Clubs, Community Foundations, Civic & Public Affairs-General, Safety, Zoos/Aquariums
Education: Colleges & Universities, Private Education (Precollege), Public Education (Precollege)
Environment: Environment-General, Resource Conservation
Health: Children's Health/Hospitals, Emergency/Ambulance Services, Medical Research
Science: Science Museums, Scientific Centers & Institutes
Social Services: Child Welfare, Day Care, Emergency Relief, Food/Clothing Distribution, Recreation & Athletics, Scouts, Youth Organizations

Application Procedures

Initial Contact: Send a brief letter of inquiry.
Application Requirements: Include a description of organization, amount requested, purpose of funds sought, and proof of tax-exempt status.
Deadlines: None.

Restrictions

Does not support individuals, religious organizations for sectarian purposes, or political or lobbying groups.

Foundation Officials

Robert E. Ducommun: president
Electra Ducommun Depeyster: vice president, treasurer
Courtlandt D. Gross: adv director
Frederick Alexander Richmand: secretary
Anthony C. Ward: adv director

Grants Analysis

Disclosure Period: calendar year ending 2001
Total Grants: $247,000
Number of Grants: 19
Average Grant: $13,000
Highest Grant: $60,000
Lowest Grant: $2,500
Typical Range: $5,000 to $20,000

Recent Grants

Note: Grants derived from 2001 Form 990.

Library-Related

2,500	David Hale Library, Larkspur, CA

General

60,000	Stanford University, Stanford, CA
25,000	Saint Georges School, Newport, RI
20,000	National Public Radio, Washington, DC
20,000	Woods Hole Oceanographic Institute, Woods Hole, MA
15,000	Harvard College Fund, Cambridge, MA
15,000	Sarah Lawrence College, Bronxville, NY
11,000	National History Museum, Los Angeles, CA
10,000	American Red Cross, Los Angeles, CA
10,000	City of Hope, Los Angeles, CA
10,000	KQED, San Francisco, CA

DUCOMMUN, INC.

Company Headquarters

PO Box 22677
Long Beach, CA 90801-5677
Web: http://www.ducommun.com

Company Description

Founded: 1849
Ticker: DCO
Exchange: NYSE
Revenue: US$212.4 million (2002)
Employees: 1300 (2002)
SIC(s): 3600 Electronic & Other Electrical Equipment, 3700 Transportation Equipment, 5000 Wholesale Trade--Durable Goods.

Operating Locations

Ducommun Inc. (CA--Carson)

Giving Contact

Kenneth R. Pearson, Vice President, Human Resources
111 W. Ocean Bld., Ste. 900
Long Beach, CA 90802
Phone: (562)951-1742
Fax: (562)624-0799

Description

Organization Type: Corporate Giving Program

Typical Recipients

Arts & Humanities: Historic Preservation, Libraries, Museums/Galleries, Public Broadcasting
Civic & Public Affairs: Economic Development, Zoos/Aquariums
Education: Colleges & Universities, Private Education (Precollege), Student Aid
Environment: Environment-General
Health: Emergency/Ambulance Services, Medical Research
International: International Environmental Issues
Science: Science Museums, Scientific Centers & Institutes
Social Services: Youth Organizations

Corporate Officials

Norman A. Barkeley: chairman emeritus B Grand Rapids, MI 1930. ED Michigan State University BS BA (1953). PRIM CORP EMPL chairman emeritus: Ducommun Inc. CORP AFFIL director: Golden Sys Inc.
Joseph C. Berenato: president, chief executive officer B Atlantic City, NJ. ED United States Military Academy (1969); University of Virginia MS (1976); New York University MBA (1979). PRIM CORP EMPL president, chief executive officer: Ducommun.
James S. Heiser: chief financial officer B Evanston, IL 1956. ED University of Virginia (1977); Stanford University (1980). PRIM CORP EMPL chief financial officer: Ducommun. NONPR AFFIL member: American Bar Association.

Grants Analysis

Note: A more recent grants list was unavailable.

Recent Grants

Note: Grants derived from 1997 Form 990.

Library-Related

2,500	David Hale Library, Larkspur, CA

General

30,000	St. George's School, Newport, RI
15,000	National Public Radio, Washington, DC
10,000	American Red Cross, Los Angeles, CA
10,000	Design Industries Foundation, New York, NY
10,000	Harvard College Fund, Cambridge, MA -- for financial aid
10,000	Monterey Bay Aquarium, Monterey, CA
10,000	Stanford University Art Museum for Print, Stanford, CA
10,000	Stanford University School of Education, Stanford, CA
10,000	WGBH, Brighton, MA
10,000	Woods Hole Oceanographic Institute, Woods Hole, MA

DUFFIELD FAMILY FOUNDATION

Giving Contact

Laurie Peek, Secretary
2223 Santa Clara Ave., Ste. B
Alameda, CA 94501
Phone: (510)337-8989
Fax: (510)337-8988
E-mail: info@maddiesfund.org
Web: http://www.maddiesfund.org

Description

Founded: 1995
EIN: 680339626
Organization Type: Private Foundation
Giving Locations: CA
Grant Types: General Support.

Donor Information

Founder: Established in 1995 by David A. Duffield.

Financial Summary

Total Giving: $8,267,988 (fiscal year ending August 31, 2001); $1,305,000 (fiscal 2000 approx); $2,655,971 (fiscal 1999)
Assets: $181,435,997 (fiscal 2001); $148,328,858 (fiscal 1999); $106,225,090 (fiscal 1998)
Gifts Received: $40,314,200 (fiscal 2001); $19,875,000 (fiscal 1995). Note: Contributions were received from David A. Duffield.

Typical Recipients

Arts & Humanities: Museums/Galleries
Civic & Public Affairs: Zoos/Aquariums
Education: Colleges & Universities, Medical Education
Environment: Environment-General, Wildlife Protection
Health: Cancer, Children's Health/Hospitals
International: Health Care/Hospitals
Social Services: Animal Protection, Child Abuse, Community Service Organizations, People with Disabilities, United Funds/United Ways, Youth Organizations

Application Procedures

Initial Contact: Send a brief letter of inquiry.
Application Requirements: Applications should include a description of organization, purpose of funds sought, and proposed follow-up with the foundation.
Deadlines: None.

Restrictions

Support is limited to programs for domestic animal welfare.

Foundation Officials

Cheryl D. Duffield: director
David A. Duffield: director
Laurie E. Duffield: director
Michael D. Duffield: director
Margaret L. Taylor: treasurer, chief financial officer
Amy D. Zeifang: secretary

Grants Analysis

Disclosure Period: fiscal year ending August 31, 2001
Total Grants: $8,267,988
Number of Grants: 13
Average Grant: $201,510*
Highest Grant: $4,798,820
Lowest Grant: $10,000
Typical Range: $50,000 to $400,000
***Note:** Average grant excludes two highest grants ($6,051,373).

Recent Grants

Note: Grants derived from 2001 Form 990.

General

4,798,820	California Veterinary Medical Association, Sacramento, CA -- low income programs for cats and dogs
1,252,553	Best Friends Animal Sanctuary, Salt Lake City, UT -- Utah Project
864,957	Animal Rescue Foundation, Walnut Creek, CA -- capital project
439,513	Humane Society of Austin and Travis County, Austin, TX -- community collaboration
406,563	University of California Davis School of Veterinary Medicine, Davis, CA -- Shelter Medicine Program
305,000	Alabama Veterinary Medical Association, Montgomery, AL -- low income dogs and cats project
77,800	Animal Friends Connection, Lodi, CA -- Lodi Project

62,000	Dane County Veterinary Medical Association, Middleton, WI -- Feral Cat Project
21,000	Dane County Humane Society, Madison, WI -- operating expenses
15,000	Seattle Animal Control, Seattle, WA -- Help the Animals Program

DUKE ENDOWMENT

Giving Contact

David H. Roberson, Director, Communications
100 North Tryon Street, Suite 3500
Charlotte, NC 28202-4012
Phone: (704)376-0291
Fax: (704)376-9336
E-mail: droberson@tde.org
Web: http://www.dukeendowment.org

Description

Founded: 1924
EIN: 560529965
Organization Type: General Purpose Foundation
Giving Locations: NC; SC
Grant Types: Capital, Challenge, Conference/Seminar, Department, Emergency, Endowment, Fellowship, General Support, Loan, Matching, Multiyear/Continuing Support, Operating Expenses, Professorship, Project, Research, Scholarship, Seed Money.

Donor Information

Founder: Established in 1924 by James Buchanan Duke (d. 1925) with a $40 million endowment. The Duke family derived its wealth from tobacco, textiles, and the development of hydroelectric power in North and South Carolina. The family tobacco business began shortly after the Civil War. In 1884, the small firm gambled on an innovation--automation--and the cottage industry grew into the American Tobacco Company with James Duke as president. The company was dissolved in 1911 when the Supreme Court upheld the Sherman Anti-Trust Act; but the Duke family had already turned their attention to hydroelectric power in 1905. This led to the founding of Duke Power Company in 1907. Mr. Duke also had business investments in textiles and blocks of shares of Aluminum Company of America.

During the family's years of prosperity, they generously contributed to orphanages, hospitals, the Methodist Church, and Trinity College, which became Duke University when the Duke Endowment was founded.

The Duke Endowment is also closely affiliated with Angier B. Duke Memorial, NC, and Nanaline Duke Fund for Duke University, NC. Doris Duke , former trustee and late daughter of the donor, established the Doris Duke Charitable Foundation under her will. Ms. Duke died in April 1993.

Financial Summary

Total Giving: $116,554,909 (2002); $105,192,626 (2001); $99,226,727 (2000)
Assets: $2,100,000,000 (2002 approx); $2,489,158,509 (2001); $2,800,000,000 (2000 approx)
Gifts Received: $127,260,880 (1995)

Typical Recipients

Arts & Humanities: Libraries
Civic & Public Affairs: Botanical Gardens/Parks
Education: Arts/Humanities Education, Colleges & Universities, Engineering/Technological Education, Faculty Development, International Studies, Leadership Training, Medical Education, Minority Education, Religious Education, Science/Mathematics Education, Social Sciences Education, Student Aid
Health: Adolescent Health Issues, AIDS/HIV, Alzheimers Disease, Cancer, Children's Health/Hospitals, Clinics/Medical Centers, Diabetes, Emergency/Ambulance Services, Health-General, Geriatric Health,

Health Policy/Cost Containment, Health Organizations, Heart, Home-Care Services, Hospices, Hospitals, Hospitals (University Affiliated), Long-Term Care, Medical Rehabilitation, Medical Research, Medical Training, Nursing Services, Nutrition, Outpatient Health Care, Prenatal Health Issues, Preventive Medicine/Wellness Organizations, Public Health, Respiratory
Religion: Churches, Religious Organizations, Religious Welfare, Seminaries
Social Services: Camps, Child Welfare, Day Care, Family Planning, Family Services, Homes, People with Disabilities, Substance Abuse

Application Procedures

Initial Contact: Applicants should mail a letter of inquiry describing the proposed project. Eligible requests will be referred to the appropriate program officer in education, health care, child care, or the rural Methodist church.
Application Requirements: A program officer may request a full proposal, including project description, budget, funding sources, proof of tax-exempt status, audited financial statements, list of board members, and other pertinent information.
Deadlines: None. The board makes final decisions at its meetings which are held ten times per year.
Review Process: Applications are screened by trustee committees and sent with recommendations to the full board. Letters of inquiry are usually answered within thirty days. If a meeting is desirable, the program officer will arrange it. It may take between two and six months for a final decision on a proposal.

Additional Information

In addition to its grant-making activities, the endowment also sponsors conferences, seminars/workshops, and technical assistance consulting for eligible beneficiaries. The endowment's library is designated a Foundation Center cooperating collection. Their library is open to grantseekers daily, Monday through Friday. Grantsmanship seminars are also held for area nonprofits.
Publications: Annual Report; Guidelines; Brochures Issues Magazine

Foundation Officials

Dr. William George Anlyan: trustee B Alexandria, Egypt 1925. ED Yale University BS (1945); Yale University MD (1949). NONPR AFFIL member: Surgical Biology Club II; member: Allen O. Whipple Surgical Society; member: Southern Medicine Association; member: Southern Surgical Association; member: Society University Surgeons; member: Society Vascular Surgery; member: Society Medical Administrations; member: Sigma Xi; member: Society Clinical Surgery; member: Research America; member: National Academy of Sciences Institute Medicine; member: Phi Beta Kappa; member: International Cardiovascular Society; member: Halsted Society; member: Industrial Research Roundtable - NAS; member: Council Deans; member: Association American Medical Colleges; member: Coordinating Council Medicine Education; member: Association Academy of Health Centers; member: American Medical Association; member: American Surgical Association; member: American Heart Association; member: Alpha Omega Alpha; fellow: American College Surgeons. CLUB AFFIL Rotary Club.

Erskine B. Bowles: trustee
Hugh McMaster Chapman: vice chairman, trustee B Spartanburg, SC 1932. ED University of North Carolina BSBA (1955); Rutgers University Stonier Graduate School of Banking (1966). CORP AFFIL director: West Point Stevens; director: South Carolina Pipeline Corp.; director: Spartan Mills; director: South Carolina Electric & Gas Co.; director: South Carolina Generating Co.; director: Scana Resources Inc.; director: SCANA Corp.; vice president: SCANA Propane Gas, Inc.; director: Primesouth Inc.; director: PrintPak Inc.; director: Inman Mills; director: Palmark Inc.; director:

Inman Holding Co. NONPR AFFIL trustee: East Lake Community Federation.
Eugene W. Cochrane, Jr.: vice president and director health care division
John Hope Franklin: trustee B Rentiesville, OK January 02, 1915. ED Fisk University AB (1935); Harvard University AM (1936); Harvard University PhD (1941). NONPR AFFIL chairman: President Initiative on Race; member: Southern Historical Association; member: Phi Beta Kappa; member: Organization American Historians; member: Phi Alpha Theta; director: DuSable Museum; member: American Studies Association; member: Association Study Afro-American Life & History; member: American Philosophical Society; member: American Association University Professors; member: American Historical Association; fellow: American Academy of Arts & Sciences.
Constance F. Gray: trustee
Richard Hampton Jenrette: trustee B Raleigh, NC 1929. ED University of North Carolina BA (1951); Harvard University MBA (1957). CORP AFFIL director: McGraw-Hill Inc.; director: Standard & Poors Ratings Group; director: AXA Group; senior advisor: Donaldson Lufkin & Jenrette Inc.; director: Alliance Capital Management. NONPR AFFIL member: Phi Beta Kappa; member, board directors, executive committee: Securities Industry Association; member: New York Society Security Analysts; director: Historic Hudson Valley; member: Institute Chartered Financial Analysts; director: Business Foundation North Carolina; director: Business Roundtable. CLUB AFFIL The Links Club; University Club; Harvard Business School Club; Harvard Club; Brook Club; Carolina Yacht Club.
Mary Duke Trent Jones: trustee
Thomas Stephen Kenan, III: trustee B Durham, NC 1937. ED University of North Carolina BA (1959). CORP AFFIL director: Kenan Transport Co.; member executive committee: Flagler System Inc. NONPR AFFIL trustee: Council National Trust Historic Preservation; trustee: National Tropical Botanical Garden. CLUB AFFIL University Club; Landfall Golf & Tennis Club; Treyburn Country Club; Breakers Beach & Golf Club; Hope Valley Country Club.
Juanita Morris Kreps: trustee B Lynch, KY 1921. ED Berea College AB (1942); Duke University MA (1944); Duke University PhD (1948). CORP AFFIL director: Stone Mountain Industrial Park. NONPR AFFIL trustee: University North Carolina Kenan Institute Private Enterprise; trustee: University North Carolina Wilmington; director: Research Triangle Foundation; member: Southern Economic Association; director: National Arts Stabilization Fund; member: National Manpower Policy Task Force; member executive committee: Industrial Relations Research Association; vice chairman: MDistrict of Columbia Inc.; member: American Economic Association; James B Duke professor emerita, vice president emerita: Duke University; member: American Association University Women; director: American Council Germany; fellow: American Academy of Arts & Sciences; member: American Association University Professors.
Elizabeth Hughes Locke: president and director education division B Norfolk, VA 1939. ED Duke University BA (1964); University of North Carolina MA (1966); Duke University PhD (1972). NONPR AFFIL member: Phi Beta Kappa; board visitors: Johnson C. Smith University; member: National Task Force; member: English Speaking Union; member: Independent Sector; board visitors: Davidson College; board visitors: Duke University; board visitors: Charlotte Country Day School; consult communication: Council Foundations.
Rhett N. Mabry: director child care division
John Grimes Medlin, Jr.: trustee B Benson, NC 1933. ED University of North Carolina BS (1956). PRIM CORP EMPL chairman emeritus, director: Wachovia Corp. CORP AFFIL director: National Service Industries Inc.; director: USAir Group Inc.; director: Media Gen Inc.; director: BellSouth Corp.; director:

Burlington Industries Inc. NONPR AFFIL trustee: Research Triangle Fund; trustee: Wake Forest University; member: Phi Delta Theta; director: Kenan Institute Arts; trustee: National Humanities Center.

Russell M. Robinson, II: trustee B Charlotte, NC 1932. ED Princeton University (1950-1952); Duke University School of Law LLB (1956). PRIM CORP EMPL partner: Robinson, Bradshaw & Hinson. CORP AFFIL director: Caraustar Indiana Inc.; director: Duke Energy Corp.; director: Cadmus Communications Corp.

Mary Duke Biddle Trent Semans: chairman, trustee B New York, NY February 21, 1920. NONPR AFFIL member: League Women Voters; director: North Carolina School Arts; director: Goodwill Industries Research Triangle Area; director: Durham Public Library; director: Executive Mansion Fine Arts Committee; member: Business Professional Womens Club; chairman: Angier B. Duke Memorial. CLUB AFFIL Rotary Club; Altrusa Club; Half Century Club.

Minor Mickel Shaw: trustee

Jean G. Spaulding: trustee ED Columbia University; Duke University MD. OCCUPATION psychiatrist. CORP AFFIL director: Wachovia Bank North Carolina.

Louis Cornelius Stephens, Jr.: vchairman, trustee B Dunn, NC 1921. ED University of North Carolina BS (1942); Harvard University MBA (1947). PRIM CORP EMPL vice president, director: Jefferson-Pilot Corp. CORP AFFIL president, director: JP Morgan Investment Management Co.; director: Pilot Life Insurance Co.; treasurer: JP Morgan Growth Fund Inc.; director: Jefferson-Pilot Southern Fire Casuality Companies; director: Jefferson-Pilot Title Insurance Co. NONPR AFFIL director: Salem College Academy; board directors: University North Carolina Greensboro Excellence Fund; director: Research Triangle Institute; director: Ecumenical Institute; director: North Carolina Leadership Institute; director: Belmont Abbey College.

Neil Williams: trustee B Charlotte, NC 1936. ED Duke University AB (1958); Duke University JD (1961). PRIM CORP EMPL partner: Alston & Bird. CORP AFFIL director: National Data Corp.; director: Printpack Inc.; director: Attorney Liability Assurance Society Inc. NONPR AFFIL member: State Bar Georgia; trustee: Vasser Woolley Foundation; member: Omicron Delta Kappa; member: Phi Beta Kappa; member: Atlanta Chamber of Commerce; trustee: Brevard Music Center; member: American Law Institute; director: American Symphony Orchestra; member: American Bar Association; member: American Bar Foundation. CLUB AFFIL member: University Club; member: Commerce Club; member: Piedmont Driving Club.

Grants Analysis

Disclosure Period: calendar year ending 2002
Total Grants: $116,554,909*
Number of Grants: 775 (approx)
Average Grant: $128,624*
Highest Grant: $17,000,000
Lowest Grant: $200
Typical Range: $20,000 to $200,000
*Note: Average grant figure excludes highest grant.

Recent Grants

Note: Grants derived from 2001 Form 990.

General

5,106,623   Duke Endowment, Durham, NC -- to establish the Duke Endowment for Flood Relief
4,000,000   Benjamin N. Duke Leadership Program, Durham, NC
3,500,000   Angier B. Duke Memorial Scholarship Program Endowment, Durham, NC
3,500,000   Benjamin N. Duke Leadership Summer Project, Durham, NC
2,000,000   Davidson College, Davidson, NC
2,000,000   Duke University Divinity School, Durham, NC -- chapel

1,900,000   Furman University, Greenville, SC -- James B. Duke Library
1,693,000   Davidson College, Davidson, NC
1,693,000   Furman University, Greenville, SC -- capital campaign
1,297,000   Johnson C. Smith University, Charlotte, NC

DUKE ENERGY CORP.

Company Headquarters

526 S. Church St.
Charlotte, NC 28202-1803
Web: http://www.duke-energy.com

Company Description

Ticker: DUK
Exchange: OTC
Former Name: Duke Power Co.
Assets: US$60.966 billion (2002)
Profit: US$1.034 billion (2002)
Employees: 22000 (2002)
Fortune Rank: 118, per FORTUNE Magazine's list of 500 Largest U.S. Corporations (2002).
SIC(s): 4911 Electric Services.

Operating Locations

Duke Energy (DE--Wilmington; NC--Burlington, Chapel Hill, Gastonia, Greensboro, Hendersonville, Hickory, Rutherfordton, Salisbury, Winston-Salem; SC--Anderson, Lancaster, Spartanburg)

Subsidiary Companies

MA: Algonquin Gas Transmission Co., Brighton

Nonmonetary Support

Type: Donated Equipment; In-kind Services
Volunteer Programs: Community Volunteer Grants provide $1,000 for materials for employees and retirees who volunteer time to one-time, hands-on projects, and $1,000 grants to organizations where employees help achieve significant strategic objectives.
Note: Co. provides nonmonetary support.

Duke Energy Foundation

Giving Contact

Sabrina Austin, Executive Director, Secretary
422 S. Church Street
Charlotte, NC 28202-1904
Phone: (704)373-6885
Web: http://www.duke-energy.com/company/community/foundation/

Description

EIN: 581586283
Organization Type: Corporate Foundation
Former Name: Duke Power Co. Foundation.
Giving Locations: NC; SC: headquarters and operating communities.
Grant Types: Award, Capital, Challenge, Conference/Seminar, Employee Matching Gifts, General Support, Multiyear/Continuing Support, Project, Scholarship.
Note: Employee matching gift ratio: 1 to 1 for gifts up to $5,000 per employee annually with a $50 minimum, for gifts to education, culture and the arts, and medical organizations.

Financial Summary

Total Giving: $17,531,797 (2001); $10,052,743 (2000); $10,181,149 (1999). Note: Contributes through corporate direct giving program and foundation.
Giving Analysis: Giving for 2001 includes: foundation grants to United Way ($46,674); 2000: foundation

grants to United Way ($26,365); foundation scholarships ($546,690); foundation ($9,479,688); 1999: foundation grants to United Way ($258,319); foundation ($9,922,930);
Assets: $12,457,452 (2001); $5,258,123 (2000); $11,042,799 (1999)
Gifts Received: $24,113,400 (2001); $3,679,890 (2000); $12,220,987 (1999). Note: In 2001, contributions were received from Duke Energy Corp. ($23,330,000) and general public ($783,400). In 2000, contributions were received from Duke Energy Corp. ($3,000,000), and general public ($679,890).

Typical Recipients

Arts & Humanities: Arts Associations & Councils, Arts Centers, Arts Festivals, Arts Funds, Ballet, Community Arts, Dance, Ethnic & Folk Arts, Historic Preservation, History & Archaeology, Libraries, Museums/Galleries, Music, Opera, Performing Arts, Theater
Civic & Public Affairs: African American Affairs, Business/Free Enterprise, Chambers of Commerce, Civil Rights, Community Foundations, Economic Development, Civic & Public Affairs-General, Housing, Legal Aid, Municipalities/Towns, Philanthropic Organizations, Professional & Trade Associations, Public Policy, Rural Affairs, Safety, Urban & Community Affairs, Women's Affairs, Zoos/Aquariums, Zoos/Aquariums
Education: Agricultural Education, Arts/Humanities Education, Business Education, Colleges & Universities, Economic Education, Education Associations, Education Funds, Education Reform, Elementary Education (Private), Engineering/Technological Education, Faculty Development, Education-General, Literacy, Medical Education, Minority Education, Private Education (Precollege), Public Education (Precollege), Religious Education, Science/Mathematics Education, Social Sciences Education, Student Aid
Environment: Environment-General, Resource Conservation
Health: Adolescent Health Issues, Emergency/Ambulance Services, Health-General, Health Policy/Cost Containment, Health Organizations, Hospices, Hospitals, Mental Health, Nutrition, Single-Disease Health Associations
International: International Development, International Peace & Security Issues, International Relations
Religion: Churches, Jewish Causes, Ministries, Religious Welfare
Science: Science Exhibits & Fairs, Science Museums, Scientific Centers & Institutes, Scientific Organizations
Social Services: Animal Protection, Child Abuse, Child Welfare, Community Centers, Community Service Organizations, Counseling, Day Care, Domestic Violence, Emergency Relief, Family Planning, Family Services, Food/Clothing Distribution, People with Disabilities, Recreation & Athletics, Scouts, Senior Services, Substance Abuse, United Funds/United Ways, Volunteer Services, YMCA/YWCA/YMHA/YWHA, Youth Organizations

Application Procedures

Initial Contact: Call or write for application form, then submit written proposal.
Application Requirements: Completed application form; proposal including a description of organization, amount requested, purpose of funds sought; proof of tax-exempt status; list of board members with affiliations; current budget.
Deadlines: None; February 15 for scholarships.
Evaluative Criteria: Broad base of support, affects company service area, annual budget approved by board, board is active and responsible, clear statement of purpose, measurable objectives, nonduplication of services. Each grant must have an internal Duke Energy business "sponsor" and a clear business reason for making the contribution.
Notes: Foundation indicates that most grant money is already dedicated to certain causes or organizations.

Almost no funds are available for unsolicited grant applications.

Restrictions

Foundation does not support organizations that discriminate by race, creed, gender, age or national origin; political activities and organizations; individual agencies of the United Way or the Charlotte Arts and Science Council; health or human service agencies, besides the United Way; capital campaigns and endowments, except in extremely rare and specialized situations that relate directly to company's areas of expertise in business; individuals; athletics, including individual sports teams and all-star teams; underwriting of films, video and television productions; reducing the cost of utility service; sectarian or religious activities; conferences, trips, or tours; fraternal, veteran or labor groups serving only their members; advertising; membership fees or association fees. Dinners or tables at fundraisers are rarely considered.

Additional Information

In June of 1997, Duke Power Company and PanEnergy Corporation merged to create Duke Energy Corporation.

Foundation also matches gifts to the Share the Warmth program, a heating bill assistance program, with a maximum corporate contribution of $500,000 annually.

Publications: Application Form

Corporate Officials

Fred J. Fowler: group president, Energy Transmission PRIM CORP EMPL group president, Energy Transmission: Duke Energy Corp.

Harvey J. Padewer: group president, Energy Services PRIM CORP EMPL group president, Energy Services: Duke Energy Corp.

Richard B. Priory: chairman, president, chief executive officer B May 15, 1946. PRIM CORP EMPL chairman, president, chief executive officer: Duke Energy Corp.

Phyllis T. Simpson: secretary PRIM CORP EMPL secretary: Duke Energy Corp.

Foundation Officials

Sabrina Austin: executive director
Richard W. Blackburn: trustee
Roberta B. Bowman: vice president
Robert P. Brace: trustee
Scott C. Carlberg: assistant vice president
S. Dock Kornegay: director, secretary
Sherwood L. Love: assistant treasurer PRIM CORP EMPL assistant treasurer - cash management: Duke Energy Corp.
Richard J. Osborne: trustee
Ruth G. Shaw: president, trustee
Phyllis T. Simpson: assistant secretary (see above)

Grants Analysis

Disclosure Period: calendar year ending 2001
Total Grants: $17,485,123*
Number of Grants: 1,764 (approx)
Average Grant: $9,912
Highest Grant: $335,000
Lowest Grant: $25
Typical Range: $1,000 to $20,000
*Note: Giving excludes United Way.

Recent Grants

Note: Grants derived from 2001 Form 990.

General

500,000	American Red Cross, Charlotte, NC
348,000	North Carolina State University, Raleigh, NC
335,000	Arts and Science Council, Charlotte, NC
328,612	American Red Cross, Charlotte, NC
250,000	Arts and Science Council, Charlotte, NC
250,000	National Council of Teachers of Mathematics, Reston, VA
250,000	South Carolina First Steps to School, Columbia, SC
217,282	Foundation of the University of North Carolina at Charlotte, Inc., Charlotte, NC
200,000	Arts and Science Council, Charlotte, NC
150,793	Foundation for the Carolinas, Charlotte, NC

DORIS DUKE FOUNDATION

Giving Contact

Director of Operations and Administration
650 Fifth Avenue
New York, NY 10019
Phone: (212)974-7006

Description

Founded: 1934
EIN: 131655241
Organization Type: Private Foundation
Giving Locations: CA; NJ; NY
Grant Types: General Support, Multiyear/Continuing Support.

Donor Information

Founder: the late Doris Duke

Financial Summary

Total Giving: $190,000 (2000); $413,500 (1998); $400,000 (1997)
Giving Analysis: Giving for 2000 includes: foundation matching gifts ($10,000) 1997: foundation grants to United Way ($5,000)
Assets: $190,000 (2000); $6,150,037 (1998); $3,194,304 (1996)
Gifts Received: $3 (1994); $10,726,840 (1993); $755,000 (1992)

Typical Recipients

Arts & Humanities: Arts Associations & Councils, Ballet, Dance, Ethnic & Folk Arts, Historic Preservation, History & Archaeology, Libraries, Museums/Galleries
Civic & Public Affairs: Botanical Gardens/Parks, Clubs, Civic & Public Affairs-General, Safety, Women's Affairs, Zoos/Aquariums
Education: Agricultural Education, Arts/Humanities Education, Colleges & Universities, Medical Education, Secondary Education (Private)
Environment: Wildlife Protection
Health: AIDS/HIV, Cancer, Children's Health/Hospitals, Clinics/Medical Centers, Emergency/Ambulance Services, Eyes/Blindness, Hospitals, Medical Research, Single-Disease Health Associations
International: Foreign Arts Organizations, Health Care/Hospitals, Human Rights, International Relief Efforts
Religion: Churches, Religious Organizations, Religious Welfare
Science: Scientific Organizations
Social Services: Animal Protection, At-Risk Youth, Child Welfare, Community Service Organizations, Crime Prevention, Delinquency & Criminal Rehabilitation, People with Disabilities, Recreation & Athletics, Senior Services, Social Services-General, United Funds/United Ways, YMCA/YWCA/YMHA/YWHA, Youth Organizations

Application Procedures

Initial Contact: Submit a proposal in letter form.
Application Requirements: The foundation has no prescribed proposal format.
Deadlines: None.

Foundation Officials

Bernard Lafferty: president, director
George W. Reed: secretary, treasurer, director

Grants Analysis

Disclosure Period: calendar year ending 2000
Total Grants: $180,000*
Number of Grants: 8
Average Grant: $3,071*
Highest Grant: $158,500
Lowest Grant: $1,000
Typical Range: $1,000 to $5,000
*Note: Giving excludes matching gifts. Average grant figure excludes highest grant.

Recent Grants

Note: Grants derived from 1999 Form 990.

General

572,075	Newport Restoration Foundation, Newport, RI
10,000	Somerset Valley YMCA, Somerset, NJ
8,000	Hillsborough Boys Football Association
5,000	ARC of Somerset County, The
5,000	Greyhound Pets of America
5,000	Potter League for Animals, RI
3,000	St. Hubert's Geralda, Madison, NJ
1,000	Somerset County 4-H Association, Somerset, NJ

CALEB C. AND JULIA W. DULA EDUCATIONAL AND CHARITABLE FOUNDATION

Giving Contact

James F. Mauze, General Counsel
112 South Hanley Road, 2nd Floor
St. Louis, MO 63105-3418
Phone: (314)726-2800
Fax: (314)863-3821

Description

Founded: 1939
EIN: 431716767
Organization Type: General Purpose Foundation
Giving Locations: MO; NY
Grant Types: Operating Expenses.

Donor Information

Founder: Established in 1939 by the late Julia W. Dula .

Financial Summary

Total Giving: $2,289,000 (2000); $2,100,200 (1998); $1,876,000 (1997)
Assets: $46,450,638 (2000); $45,672,064 (1998); $40,007,805 (1997)

Typical Recipients

Arts & Humanities: Arts Associations & Councils, Arts Centers, Arts Funds, Arts Outreach, Dance, Film & Video, Historic Preservation, History & Archaeology, Libraries, Museums/Galleries, Music, Opera, Performing Arts, Public Broadcasting, Theater
Civic & Public Affairs: Botanical Gardens/Parks, Business/Free Enterprise, Clubs, First Amendment Issues, Civic & Public Affairs-General, Parades/Festivals, Public Policy, Urban & Community Affairs, Zoos/Aquariums
Education: Afterschool/Enrichment Programs, Agricultural Education, Arts/Humanities Education, Colleges & Universities, Education-General, Health & Physical Education, Medical Education, Private Education (Precollege), Secondary Education (Public), Special Education, Special Education, Student Aid

Environment: Environment-General, Resource Conservation, Wildlife Protection
Health: Alzheimers Disease, Cancer, Children's Health/Hospitals, Clinics/Medical Centers, Diabetes, Emergency/Ambulance Services, Health Organizations, Hospitals, Nursing Services, Preventive Medicine/Wellness Organizations, Single-Disease Health Associations
Religion: Churches, Missionary Activities (Domestic), Religious Organizations, Religious Welfare
Science: Science Museums, Scientific Centers & Institutes
Social Services: Animal Protection, At-Risk Youth, Camps, Child Welfare, Community Service Organizations, Crime Prevention, Day Care, Family Planning, Family Services, People with Disabilities, Scouts, Senior Services, Shelters/Homelessness, Social Services-General, United Funds/United Ways, Youth Organizations

Application Procedures

Initial Contact: The foundation has no formal grant application procedure or application form.
Deadlines: Proposals must be sent to the trustees by April 1 for the Spring meeting and by October 1 for the Fall meeting.
Review Process: The trustees generally meet four times a year to consider the distribution of funds.

Restrictions

Grants are made only to tax-exempt organizations. The foundation does not support individuals or make loans.

Foundation Officials

Margaret C. Gunter: trustee
Margaret W. Kobusch: trustee
Orrin S. Wightman, III: trustee

Grants Analysis

Disclosure Period: calendar year ending 2000
Total Grants: $2,289,000
Number of Grants: 114
Average Grant: $17,173*
Highest Grant: $100,000
Lowest Grant: $5,000
Typical Range: $5,000 to $35,000
*Note: Average grant excludes four highest grants ($400,000).

Recent Grants

Note: Grants derived from 2000 Form 990.

General

100,000	Eaglebrook School, Deerfield, MA
100,000	Washington University Visual Arts and Design Center
100,000	Whitfield School, St. Louis, MO
100,000	Williams College, Williamstown, MA
75,000	Eaglebrook School, Deerfield, MA
50,000	Center of Contemporary Arts, University City, MO
50,000	Film Arts Foundation, San Francisco, CA
50,000	Missouri Historical Society, St. Louis, MO
50,000	Taproots Association, St. Louis, MO
50,000	Washington University Visual Arts and Design Center

EZEKIEL R. AND EDNA WATTIS DUMKE FOUNDATION

Giving Contact

Claire D. Ryberg, Vice President, Director
PO Box 776
Kaysville, UT 84037-0776
Phone: (801)497-9474

Description

Founded: 1959
EIN: 876119783
Organization Type: Private Foundation
Giving Locations: ID; MT; NM; UT
Grant Types: Research.

Financial Summary

Total Giving: $866,000 (1999); $638,143 (1998); $522,103 (1997)
Giving Analysis: Giving for 1998 includes: foundation grants to United Way ($25,350)
Assets: $22,655,241 (1999); $19,417,200 (1998); $11,876,241 (1996)

Typical Recipients

Arts & Humanities: Arts Associations & Councils, Arts Centers, Arts Outreach, Ballet, Dance, Arts & Humanities-General, Historic Preservation, Libraries, Museums/Galleries, Music, Opera, Performing Arts, Public Broadcasting, Theater, Visual Arts
Civic & Public Affairs: Asian American Affairs, Botanical Gardens/Parks, Community Foundations, Parades/Festivals, Safety, Zoos/Aquariums
Education: Afterschool/Enrichment Programs, Agricultural Education, Arts/Humanities Education, Business Education, Colleges & Universities, Environmental Education, Education-General, Literacy, Medical Education, Minority Education, Preschool Education, Science/Mathematics Education
Environment: Environment-General, Research, Resource Conservation
Health: Alzheimers Disease, Arthritis, Cancer, Children's Health/Hospitals, Clinics/Medical Centers, Diabetes, Emergency/Ambulance Services, Eyes/Blindness, Health Policy/Cost Containment, Health Organizations, Heart, Hospices, Hospitals, Hospitals (University Affiliated), Medical Rehabilitation, Medical Research, Medical Training, Prenatal Health Issues, Public Health, Single-Disease Health Associations
Religion: Religious Welfare
Science: Observatories & Planetariums, Science Museums
Social Services: Camps, Child Abuse, Child Welfare, Community Service Organizations, Counseling, Crime Prevention, Day Care, Domestic Violence, Family Planning, Family Services, Food/Clothing Distribution, People with Disabilities, Senior Services, Sexual Abuse, Shelters/Homelessness, YMCA/YWCA/YMHA/YWHA

Application Procedures

Initial Contact: Send a brief letter of inquiry.
Application Requirements: Include a description of organization, purpose of funds sought, and proof of tax-exempt status.
Deadlines: Approximately January 15 and July 15. Call the foundation to confirm the exact dates.

Restrictions

Grants are not made to individuals. or religious organizations for sectarian purposes.

Additional Information

Publications: Grant Application; Agreement

Foundation Officials

Edmund E. Dumke: treasurer, director, invest adv
Ezekiel R. Dumke, Jr.: president, director
Valerie Dumke: assistant secretary, director
Denise R. Johnsen: foundation manager
Claire Dumke Ryberg: vice president, director
Nancy Healy Schwanfelder: secretary, director

Grants Analysis

Disclosure Period: calendar year ending 1999
Total Grants: $866,000
Number of Grants: 43
Average Grant: $18,238*
Highest Grant: $100,000

Typical Range: $2,000 to $50,000
*Note: Average grant excludes highest grant.

Recent Grants

Note: Grants derived from 1999 Form 990.

General

100,000	Nature Conservancy of Utah, Salt Lake City, UT -- preservation of the Hill, Call Wiser & Duckworth properties on the Great Salt Lake
75,000	Nature Conservancy of Idaho, Sun Valley, ID -- support of Vanishing Rivers campaign and Hemingway House
57,500	Ogden Union Station Foundation, Ogden, UT -- refurbish model railroad exhibit
50,000	Advocates for Survivors of Domestic Abuse, Hailey, ID -- shelter for abused women and their children
50,000	Blaine County Seniors Council, Inc., Hailey, ID -- purchase 2000 Champion bus equipped with wheelchair lift
50,000	Lee David Pesky Center for Learning Enrichment, Boise, ID -- present "Every Child Ready to Read" to day care providers and preschooler teachers
50,000	National Ability Center, Park City, UT -- construction of barn and indoor riding arena
25,000	Diabetes Control Project, Montezuma Creek, UT -- reduce complications of diabetes among the Navajo population
25,000	Foundation for the Santa Fe Community College, Santa Fe, NM -- create ASL videotapes for health care workers
25,000	Health Centers of Northern New Mexico, Espanola, NM -- purchase medical equipment for new clinic

DUNAGAN FOUNDATION

Giving Contact

Kathlyn C. Dunagan, President
PO Box 387
Monahans, TX 79756
Phone: (915)943-2571

Description

Founded: 1976
EIN: 751561848
Organization Type: Private Foundation
Giving Locations: TX
Grant Types: General Support, Professorship, Project, Scholarship.

Donor Information

Founder: J. Conrad Dunagan, Kathlyn C. Dunagan, John C. Dunagan

Financial Summary

Total Giving: $236,775 (2002); $305,429 (2001); $213,211 (2000)
Giving Analysis: Giving for 1998 includes: foundation scholarships ($2,000) foundation ($228,700)
Assets: $4,056,284 (2002); $4,344,820 (2001); $4,356,777 (2000)
Gifts Received: $1,000 (2002); $7,375 (2001); $254,461 (2000). Note: In 1999, 2000, 2001, and 2002, contributions were received from William C. Dunagan. In 1998, contributions were received from Deanna Dunagan ($212,938), John Charles Dunagan ($58,375), William C. Dunagan ($7,882), and Kathleen Dunagan ($115,786). In 1996, contributions were received from Deanna Dunagan ($5,000), John Charles Dunagan ($5,000), Carol Husbands ($500), and Kathleen Dunagan ($500).

Typical Recipients

Arts & Humanities: Arts Centers, Arts & Humanities-General, Historic Preservation, History & Archaeology, Libraries, Literary Arts, Museums/Galleries, Public Broadcasting, Theater

Civic & Public Affairs: Botanical Gardens/Parks, Community Foundations, Employment/Job Training, Civic & Public Affairs-General, Housing

Education: Business Education, Colleges & Universities, Education Funds, Education-General, Legal Education, Medical Education, Private Education (Precollege), Public Education (Precollege), Student Aid

Environment: Air/Water Quality, Environment-General, Resource Conservation, Wildlife Protection

Health: AIDS/HIV, Cancer, Children's Health/Hospitals, Clinics/Medical Centers, Health Funds, Hospices, Hospitals, Hospitals, Hospitals (University Affiliated), Medical Research, Mental Health, Public Health, Research/Studies Institutes, Single-Disease Health Associations

International: Health Care/Hospitals, International Peace & Security Issues

Religion: Churches, Dioceses, Religious Organizations, Religious Welfare

Science: Science Museums, Scientific Centers & Institutes

Social Services: Child Welfare, Community Service Organizations, Counseling, Family Planning, Family Services, Scouts, United Funds/United Ways, Veterans, Youth Organizations

Application Procedures

Initial Contact: Send a brief letter of inquiry.
Application Requirements: Include a description of organization, purpose of funds sought, latest budget information, latest financial statement, and proof of tax-exempt status.
Deadlines: None.

Restrictions

Foundation makes contributions to organizations with exempt certification from the IRS.

Foundation Officials

John C. Dunagan: vice president
Kathleen Dunagan: secretary
Kathlyn C. Dunagan: president
Richard J. Hoyer: assistant secretary, treasurer
Rena Shelton: assistant secretary
Charles N. Wade: treasurer

Grants Analysis

Disclosure Period: calendar year ending 2002
Total Grants: $236,775
Number of Grants: 43
Average Grant: $3,580*
Highest Grant: $50,000
Lowest Grant: $200
Typical Range: $1,000 to $5,000
*Note: Average grant figure excludes two highest grants ($90,000).

Recent Grants

Note: Grants derived from 2001 Form 990.

General

60,000	University of Texas of the Permian Basin, Odessa, TX -- to support educational activities
40,000	Lawrenceville School, Lawrenceville, NJ -- support educational activities
35,000	Boys and Girls Club of Monahans, Monahans, TX -- to support charitable activities
21,000	Mary Institute and St. Louis Country Day School, St. Louis, MO -- to support educational activities
20,000	Dana-Farber Cancer Institute, Boston, MA -- to support medical activities

20,000	Green Farms Academy, Farm, CT -- to support educational activities
11,110	Permian Historical Society, Midland, TX -- to support literary activities
11,000	Parks and Wildlife Foundation, Dallas, TX -- to support parks and wildlife activities
10,000	Buffalo Trail Council of Boy Scouts, Midland, TX -- support charitable activities
10,000	KOCV-TV, Odessa, TX -- to support literacy activities

L. H. AND C. W. DUNCAN FOUNDATION

Giving Contact

Debbie Gibson, Contact
The Chase Bank of Texas
PO Box 2558
Houston, TX 77252-8037
Phone: (713)216-1451
Fax: (713)216-2119

Description

Founded: 1964
EIN: 746064215
Organization Type: Private Foundation
Giving Locations: TX
Grant Types: General Support.

Donor Information

Founder: the late C. W. Duncan

Financial Summary

Total Giving: $500,600 (fiscal year ending September 30, 2001); $360,750 (fiscal 2000); $270,213 (fiscal 1999)
Giving Analysis: Giving for fiscal 2000 includes: foundation grants to United Way ($22,000)
Assets: $7,041,776 (fiscal 2001); $9,075,266 (fiscal 2000); $8,057,144 (fiscal 1999)
Gifts Received: $496,006 (fiscal 2000). Note: In 2000, contributions were received from Lillian H. Duncan CRAT.

Typical Recipients

Arts & Humanities: Ballet, Ethnic & Folk Arts, Film & Video, Arts & Humanities-General, Historic Preservation, Libraries, Museums/Galleries, Music, Performing Arts, Theater

Civic & Public Affairs: Botanical Gardens/Parks, Community Foundations, Civic & Public Affairs-General, Hispanic Affairs, Housing, Municipalities/Towns, Public Policy, Urban & Community Affairs, Zoos/Aquariums

Education: Arts/Humanities Education, Business Education, Colleges & Universities, Education Associations, Education Reform, Medical Education, Preschool Education, Private Education (Precollege), Public Education (Precollege), School Volunteerism, Science/Mathematics Education, Special Education

Environment: Resource Conservation, Wildlife Protection

Health: AIDS/HIV, Cancer, Children's Health/Hospitals, Clinics/Medical Centers, Eyes/Blindness, Health-General, Geriatric Health, Heart, Hospices, Hospitals, Hospitals (University Affiliated), Long-Term Care, Medical Research, Multiple Sclerosis, Prenatal Health Issues, Speech & Hearing

International: International Affairs

Religion: Churches, Dioceses, Jewish Causes, Ministries, Missionary Activities (Domestic), Religious Organizations, Religious Welfare

Science: Science Museums

Social Services: Child Welfare, Community Service Organizations, People with Disabilities, Recreation & Athletics, Substance Abuse, United Funds/United Ways, Volunteer Services, YMCA/YWCA/YMHA/YWHA, Youth Organizations

Application Procedures

Initial Contact: Submit a brief letter of inquiry.
Application Requirements: Include a description of organization, amount requested, purpose of funds sought, proof of tax-exempt status.
Deadlines: None.

Foundation Officials

Mary Anne Duncan Dingus: director
Anne S. Duncan: director
Brenda Duncan: director
C. W. Duncan, III: director
Charles William Duncan, Jr.: chairman, director B Houston, TX 1926. ED Rice University BSChE (1947); University of Texas (1948-1949). CORP AFFIL director: United Technologies Inc.; director: American Express Co.; director: Newfield Exploration Co. NONPR AFFIL member: Sigma Alpha Epsilon; member: Sigma Iota Epsilon; trustee emeritus: Rice University; member: Council Foreign Relations. CLUB AFFIL River Oaks Country Club; Allegro Club; Houston Country Club.
John H. Duncan, Jr.: director
John H. Duncan, Sr.: president, director B Houston, TX 1928. ED University of Texas BBA (1949). CORP AFFIL director: Texas Commerce Bancshares; director: Mosher Inc.; director: Proler International Corp.; director: Group 1 Automotive; director: King Ranch Inc. NONPR AFFIL member: Sigma Alpha Epsilon. CLUB AFFIL Houston Country Club; River Oaks Country Club.
Robert J. Faust: secretary, treasurer, director
Jeaneane Duncan Marsh: vice president, director

Grants Analysis

Disclosure Period: fiscal year ending September 30, 2001
Total Grants: $500,600
Number of Grants: 16
Average Grant: $24,662*
Highest Grant: $60,000
Lowest Grant: $1,000
Typical Range: $10,000 to $60,000
*Note: Average grant figure excludes three highest grants ($180,000).

Recent Grants

Note: Grants derived from fiscal 2000 Form 990.

General

40,000	Depelchin Children Center, Houston, TX -- capital campaign
25,000	Baylor College of Medicine Department of Urology, Houston, TX -- support of learning resource center
25,000	Episcopal High School, Bellaire, TX -- capital campaign
20,000	Greater Houston Community Foundation, Houston, TX -- support of Brenda and John H. Duncan Rise School of Houston
20,000	Kincaid School, Houston, TX -- construction fund
20,000	Texas Heart Institute, Houston, TX -- build new building and education for causes, prevention and treatment of cardiovascular disease
15,000	Brookwood Community Center, Brookshire, TX -- community volunteers benefit luncheon
15,000	Depelchin Children Center, Houston, TX -- support of luncheon
12,500	University of Texas Health Science Center Houston, Houston, TX -- PET center
10,000	Communities in Schools Houston, Inc., Houston, TX -- program support

JOHN G. DUNCAN TRUST

Giving Contact
Yvonne Baca, Trust Officer
c/o Wells Fargo Bank
PO Box 5825
Denver, CO 80217
Phone: (303)392-5324

Description
Founded: 1955
EIN: 846016555
Organization Type: Private Foundation
Giving Locations: CO
Grant Types: General Support.

Donor Information
Founder: the late John G. Duncan

Financial Summary
Total Giving: $445,600 (2002); $399,669 (2001); $414,281 (2000)
Giving Analysis: Giving for 1997 includes: foundation ($198,000)
Assets: $6,420,041 (2002); $7,261,244 (2001); $8,302,265 (2000)

Typical Recipients
Arts & Humanities: Arts Centers, Arts Outreach, History & Archaeology, Libraries, Museums/Galleries, Music, Opera, Performing Arts, Public Broadcasting, Theater
Civic & Public Affairs: African American Affairs, Botanical Gardens/Parks, Clubs, Community Foundations, Employment/Job Training, Civic & Public Affairs-General, Hispanic Affairs, Housing, Legal Aid, Native American Affairs, Urban & Community Affairs, Women's Affairs, Zoos/Aquariums
Education: Afterschool/Enrichment Programs, Colleges & Universities, Continuing Education, Elementary Education (Private), Education-General, Minority Education, Preschool Education, Private Education (Precollege), Science/Mathematics Education
Environment: Forestry
Health: Alzheimers Disease, Cancer, Children's Health/Hospitals, Clinics/Medical Centers, Emergency/Ambulance Services, Geriatric Health, Health Organizations, Heart, Home-Care Services, Hospices, Hospitals, Long-Term Care, Medical Rehabilitation, Medical Research, Public Health, Respiratory, Single-Disease Health Associations, Speech & Hearing, Transplant Networks/Donor Banks
International: Health Care/Hospitals, International Organizations, International Peace & Security Issues, International Relief Efforts
Religion: Jewish Causes, Religious Organizations, Religious Welfare, Synagogues/Temples
Social Services: Animal Protection, At-Risk Youth, Big Brother/Big Sister, Child Welfare, Community Centers, Community Service Organizations, Crime Prevention, Domestic Violence, Emergency Relief, Family Services, Food/Clothing Distribution, Homes, People with Disabilities, Recreation & Athletics, Scouts, Senior Services, Shelters/Homelessness, Special Olympics, Substance Abuse, Volunteer Services, Youth Organizations

Application Procedures
Initial Contact: The foundation requests applications be made in writing.
Deadlines: None.

Additional Information
Publications: Application Guidelines
Trust(s): Wells Fargo Bank

Grants Analysis
Disclosure Period: calendar year ending 2002
Total Grants: $445,600
Number of Grants: 135

Average Grant: $3,301
Highest Grant: $12,000
Lowest Grant: $1,000
Typical Range: $1,000 to $5,000

Recent Grants
Note: Grants derived from 2001 Form 990.

General
24,535	Denver Museum of Nature and Science, Denver, CO
18,000	Youth Biz, Inc., Denver, CO
14,715	Children's Hospital Foundation
10,418	National Center for Children, Families and Communities
10,000	American Red Cross, Atchison, KS
10,000	Boys and Girls Club of Pueblo County, Inc, Pueblo, CO
10,000	Denver Botanical Gardens, Denver, CO
10,000	Denver Summerbridge, Denver, CO
10,000	Kids In Need of Dentistry, Denver, CO
10,000	St. Francis Center, Denver, CO

LOUISE HEAD DUNCAN TRUST

Giving Contact
David Wolfe, Trust Officer
PO Box 248
La Grange, KY 40031
Phone: (606)231-2428
Fax: (606)231-2694

Alternate Contact
Bank One Trust Co.
PO Box 1308
Milwaukee, WI 53201
Phone: (414)765-2017

Description
Founded: 1991
EIN: 616183556
Organization Type: Private Foundation
Giving Locations: KY: Oldham County
Grant Types: General Support.

Donor Information
Founder: Established in 1991 by the late Louise Head Duncan.

Financial Summary
Total Giving: $455,488 (2001); $316,379 (2000); $329,650 (1999)
Assets: $8,465,627 (2001); $9,095,560 (2000); $8,848,562 (1999)
Gifts Received: $683,651 (1992). Note: In 1992, contributions were received from the estate of Louise Duncan.

Typical Recipients
Arts & Humanities: History & Archaeology, Libraries, Performing Arts
Civic & Public Affairs: African American Affairs, Botanical Gardens/Parks, Employment/Job Training, Civic & Public Affairs-General, Housing, Law & Justice, Municipalities/Towns, Safety, Urban & Community Affairs, Women's Affairs
Education: Afterschool/Enrichment Programs, Arts/Humanities Education, Business Education, Elementary Education (Public), Education-General, Private Education (Precollege), Public Education (Precollege)
Environment: Environment-General, Wildlife Protection
Health: Emergency/Ambulance Services, Health Organizations
Religion: Churches, Religion-General, Religious Organizations

Social Services: Big Brother/Big Sister, Child Welfare, Community Centers, Community Service Organizations, Family Services, People with Disabilities, Recreation & Athletics, Recreation & Athletics, Scouts, Shelters/Homelessness, Social Services-General, YMCA/YWCA/YMHA/YWHA, Youth Organizations

Application Procedures
Initial Contact: Send letter to the foundation requesting application form and guidelines.

Restrictions
Grants limited to 501(c)(3) organizations benefiting residents of Oldham County, Kentucky.

Additional Information
Publications: Application Form
Trust(s): Bank One Trust Company NA

Foundation Officials
Thomas W. Gaines, Jr.: adv comm
J. W. Hall, Jr.: adv comm
Rose Ethel Hall: adv comm
John F. Payne: adv comm

Grants Analysis
Disclosure Period: calendar year ending 2001
Total Grants: $455,488
Number of Grants: 22
Average Grant: $12,024*
Highest Grant: $115,000
Lowest Grant: $2,225
Typical Range: $5,000 to $25,000
*Note: Average grant figure excludes two highest grants ($215,000).

Recent Grants
Note: Grants derived from 2001 Form 990.

General
115,000	Oldham County Historical Society, Inc., Prospect, KY
100,000	Oldham County Family YMCA, La-Grange, KY
50,000	Yew Dell, Inc., Crestwood, KY
28,000	Center For Women in Crisis, LaGrange, KY
25,000	City of La Grange, La Grange, GA
25,000	Greenways for Oldham County, Inc., Crestwood, PA
18,000	Applepatch Community, Crestwood, KY
10,000	First Baptist Church of LaGrange, La-Grange, KY
10,000	Oldham Little League, LaGrange, KY
8,100	Ballardsville Fire Protection Dist., Crestwood, KY

DUNKIN' DONUTS, INC.

Company Headquarters
Randolph, MA 02368
Web: http://www.dunkindonuts.com

Company Description
Founded: 1950
Acquired: Mister Donut (1990).
Employees: 1345
SIC(s): 2024 Ice Cream & Frozen Desserts, 5812 Eating Places, 6794 Patent Owners & Lessors.

Operating Locations
Dunkin' Ventures Corp. (MA--Randolph); Mister Donut of America (MA--Randolph); Wine Alliance (CA--Healdsburg)

Nonmonetary Support

Type: Donated Equipment; Donated Products; In-kind Services

Giving Contact

Attn: Dunkin Donuts
15 Pacella Dr.
PO Box 317
Randolph, MA 02368
Phone: (781)961-4020
Fax: (781)986-7490

Description

Organization Type: Corporate Giving Program
Grant Types: General Support.

Financial Summary

Total Giving: Company does not disclose contributions figures.

Typical Recipients

Arts & Humanities: Libraries
Education: Education-General
Health: Alzheimers Disease, Children's Health/Hospitals, Diabetes, Heart
Social Services: At-Risk Youth, Child Welfare, Shelters/Homelessness, Volunteer Services

Application Procedures

Initial Contact: Send a letter of inquiry and brief proposal.

Additional Information

Company reported in June 1998 that Allied Domecq Plc merged three of its U.S. subsidiaries, Baskin-Robbins, Dunkin' Donuts, and Togo's, into one entity, Allied Domecq Retailing U.S.A.

Corporate Officials

Stephen Alexander: chief executive
Tony Hales: chairman
Sir Christopher Anthony Hogg: chairman B London, United Kingdom 1936. ED Oxford University Trinity College BA (1960); Harvard University MBA (1962). PRIM CORP EMPL chairman: Allied Domecq PLC. NONPR AFFIL chairman: Royal National Theatre.
Kim Lopdrup: board member
Jack Shafer: board member
John (Jack) D. Shafer: president PRIM CORP EMPL president: Allied Domecq Retailing U.S.A.

DUNSPAUGH-DALTON FOUNDATION

Giving Contact

William A. Lane, Jr., President
1533 Sunset Drive, Suite 150
Coral Gables, FL 33143
Phone: (305)668-4192
Fax: (305)361-2818

Description

Founded: 1963
EIN: 591055300
Organization Type: General Purpose Foundation
Giving Locations: CA; FL: Dade County; NC nationally.
Grant Types: Capital, Endowment, General Support, Multiyear/Continuing Support, Project, Research.

Donor Information

Founder: The will of Ann V. Dalton created the Dunspaugh-Dalton Foundation in 1963.

Financial Summary

Total Giving: $2,059,700 (2001); $2,059,700 (2000); $1,976,800 (1998)
Giving Analysis: Giving for 1998 includes: foundation grants to United Way ($5,000); 1997: foundation scholarships ($1,000) foundation grants to United Way ($5,000)
Assets: $54,397,309 (2001); $54,397,309 (2000); $56,522,272 (1998)

Typical Recipients

Arts & Humanities: Arts Associations & Councils, Arts Outreach, Community Arts, Historic Preservation, History & Archaeology, Museums/Galleries, Music, Performing Arts, Public Broadcasting, Theater
Civic & Public Affairs: Botanical Gardens/Parks, Clubs, Civic & Public Affairs-General, Housing, Law & Justice, Legal Aid, Parades/Festivals, Urban & Community Affairs, Zoos/Aquariums
Education: Afterschool/Enrichment Programs, Arts/Humanities Education, Colleges & Universities, Education Funds, Engineering/Technological Education, Faculty Development, Education-General, Health & Physical Education, Legal Education, Medical Education, Minority Education, Private Education (Precollege), Public Education (Precollege), Social Sciences Education
Environment: Environment-General
Health: Alzheimers Disease, Cancer, Children's Health/Hospitals, Clinics/Medical Centers, Emergency/Ambulance Services, Geriatric Health, Health Organizations, Hospices, Hospitals, Hospitals (University Affiliated), Long-Term Care, Medical Rehabilitation, Medical Research, Mental Health, Nursing Services, Research/Studies Institutes, Single-Disease Health Associations, Speech & Hearing
International: Foreign Educational Institutions
Religion: Churches, Jewish Causes, Ministries, Missionary Activities (Domestic), Religious Organizations, Religious Welfare
Science: Observatories & Planetariums
Social Services: At-Risk Youth, Big Brother/Big Sister, Camps, Child Welfare, Community Service Organizations, Counseling, Family Planning, Family Services, Food/Clothing Distribution, Homes, People with Disabilities, Recreation & Athletics, Scouts, Senior Services, Shelters/Homelessness, Social Services-General, Substance Abuse, United Funds/United Ways, YMCA/YWCA/YMHA/YWHA, Youth Organizations

Application Procedures

Initial Contact: The foundation has no formal guidelines for application. Prospective grantees should submit a letter of inquiry.
Application Requirements: Letters of inquiry should provide the organization's name and address, project name, and IRS exemption number.
Deadlines: None.

Restrictions

Grants restricted to United States and its territories, for religious, educational, or scientific purposes.

Additional Information

Publications: Annual Report

Foundation Officials

Sarah H. Bonner: vice president, trustee
William A. Lane, Jr.: president B 1954. PRIM CORP EMPL president, director: Lane Winpak Inc.
Thomas Wakefield: secretary, treasurer, trustee

Grants Analysis

Disclosure Period: calendar year ending 2001
Total Grants: $2,059,700
Number of Grants: 101

Average Grant: $14,623*
Highest Grant: $312,000
Lowest Grant: $2,000
Typical Range: $5,000 to $30,000
***Note:** Average grant figure excludes two highest grants ($612,000).

Recent Grants

Note: Grants derived from 2000 Form 990.

General
312,000	Barry University, Miami Shores, FL
300,000	Duke University, Durham, NC -- support of the Hartman Center
105,000	Shake a Leg, Miami, FL
100,000	Carmel by the Sea Sunset Center, Carmel by the Sea, CA
70,000	Monterey Bay Aquarium Foundation, Monterey, CA -- capital campaign for new exhibit wing
60,000	Close Up Foundation of America, Alexandria, VA
60,000	New World Symphony, Miami, FL
55,000	Hearing Research Institute, South Miami, FL
50,000	Kampong of the National Tropical Botanical Garden, Miami, FL -- for the building fund
45,000	Community Hospital Foundation, Monterey, CA

ALFRED I. DUPONT FOUNDATION

Giving Contact

Rosemary C. Wills, Director
4600 Touchton Rd. East, Bldg. 200, Suite 120
Jacksonville, FL 32246
Phone: (904)232-4123

Description

Founded: 1936
EIN: 591297267
Organization Type: General Purpose Foundation
Giving Locations: FL: southeastern United States.
Grant Types: Emergency, General Support.

Donor Information

Founder: The foundation was incorporated in 1936 by the late Jessie Dew Ball duPont .

Financial Summary

Total Giving: $1,376,640 (2001); $1,767,373 (1998); $1,328,149 (1997)
Giving Analysis: Giving for 2001 includes: foundation gifts to individuals ($442,524) 1998: foundation gifts to individuals ($400,650)
Assets: $34,267,614 (2001); $32,538,629 (1998); $35,029,643 (1997)

Typical Recipients

Arts & Humanities: Historic Preservation, History & Archaeology, Libraries, Museums/Galleries, Music, Theater
Civic & Public Affairs: Economic Policy, Employment/Job Training, Civic & Public Affairs-General, Law & Justice, Philanthropic Organizations, Public Policy, Zoos/Aquariums
Education: Afterschool/Enrichment Programs, Agricultural Education, Colleges & Universities, Community & Junior Colleges, Continuing Education, Education Funds, Education-General, Medical Education, Minority Education, Private Education (Precollege), Religious Education, Science/Mathematics Education, Special Education, Student Aid
Environment: Environment-General
Health: Alzheimers Disease, Arthritis, Children's Health/Hospitals, Clinics/Medical Centers, Emergency/Ambulance Services, Health Organizations,

Hospices, Long-Term Care, Medical Rehabilitation, Multiple Sclerosis, Nursing Services, Public Health, Single-Disease Health Associations
International: Foreign Educational Institutions, Health Care/Hospitals
Religion: Churches, Ministries, Religious Organizations, Religious Welfare
Science: Science Museums
Social Services: At-Risk Youth, Child Welfare, Community Service Organizations, Emergency Relief, Food/Clothing Distribution, Homes, People with Disabilities, Senior Services, Shelters/Homelessness, Social Services-General, United Funds/United Ways, YMCA/YWCA/YMHA/YWHA, Youth Organizations

Application Procedures

Initial Contact: The foundation reports that requests should be made for a formal application form.
Application Requirements: Grants are given to individuals and charitable organizations. Individual grants are generally limited to elderly individuals residing in the southeastern U.S. who are in distressed economic situations.
Deadlines: None.
Review Process: After receiving request, forms are mailed to the applicant.

Restrictions

The foundation reports that individual grants are generally limited to elderly individuals residing in the southeastern United States who are in distressed economic situations.

Foundation Officials

Edward Carter Brownlie: assistant secretary, assistant treasurer B Birmingham, AL 1937. ED Samford University (1963). PRIM CORP EMPL vice president administration: St Joe Paper Co. CORP AFFIL vice president, director: Saint Joseph Land & Development Co.; director: Saint Joseph Tel & Tel Co.
Lillie S. Land: secretary, director
Robert E. Nedley: president B 1938. PRIM CORP EMPL president, chief operating officer, director: St Joe Paper Co. CORP AFFIL president: Saint Joe Industries Inc.; vice president, director: Saint Joseph Tel & Tel Co.
Rosemary C. Wills: assistant secretary, assistant treasurer

Grants Analysis

Disclosure Period: calendar year ending 2001
Total Grants: $934,115*
Number of Grants: 119
Average Grant: $7,000
Highest Grant: $75,000
Lowest Grant: $250
Typical Range: $1,000 to $10,000
*Note: Giving excludes gifts to individuals.

Recent Grants

Note: Grants derived from 2001 Form 990.

General

75,000	Maclay School, Tallahassee, FL
50,000	Chipola Junior College, Marianna, FL
50,000	Gulf Coast Community College Foundation, Panama City, FL
35,000	Stetson University, De Land, FL
30,000	Flagler College, St. Augustine, FL
25,000	Cumberland College, Williamsburg, KY
25,000	Florida Legal Foundation, Inc., Tallahassee, FL
25,000	Historic Apalachicola Foundation, Apalachicola, FL
20,000	BETA, Inc.
20,000	Southern Scholarship Foundation, Inc., Tallahassee, FL

CHICHESTER DUPONT FOUNDATION

Giving Contact

Gregory F. Fields, Secretary
3120 Kennett Pike
Wilmington, DE 19807
Phone: (302)658-5244
Fax: (302)658-5091

Description

Founded: 1946
EIN: 516011641
Organization Type: Family Foundation
Giving Locations: mid-Atlantic United States; northeastern United States.
Grant Types: Capital, Endowment, General Support, Operating Expenses.

Donor Information

Founder: The foundation was incorporated in 1946 by A. Felix duPont Jr., Alice duPont Mills, the late Lydia Chichester duPont , and the late Mary Chichester duPont Clark .

Financial Summary

Total Giving: $3,800,000 (2000); $4,600,000 (1999 approx); $3,300,000 (1998 approx)
Assets: $63,699,546 (2000); $80,000,000 (1999 approx); $72,543,713 (1997)

Typical Recipients

Arts & Humanities: Arts Associations & Councils, Arts Centers, Arts Funds, Ballet, Community Arts, Historic Preservation, History & Archaeology, Libraries, Museums/Galleries, Music, Opera, Performing Arts, Theater
Civic & Public Affairs: Botanical Gardens/Parks, Economic Development, Employment/Job Training, Civic & Public Affairs-General, Municipalities/Towns, Rural Affairs, Safety, Urban & Community Affairs, Zoos/Aquariums
Education: Business Education, Colleges & Universities, Community & Junior Colleges, Environmental Education, Education-General, Literacy, Medical Education, Private Education (Precollege), Public Education (Precollege), Science/Mathematics Education, Secondary Education (Private), Special Education, Student Aid
Environment: Air/Water Quality, Forestry, Environment-General, Research, Resource Conservation, Watershed, Wildlife Protection
Health: Arthritis, Cancer, Children's Health/Hospitals, Clinics/Medical Centers, Emergency/Ambulance Services, Health Organizations, Heart, Hospices, Hospitals, Long-Term Care, Medical Rehabilitation, Medical Research, Nursing Services, Preventive Medicine/Wellness Organizations, Public Health, Single-Disease Health Associations
Religion: Churches, Religion-General, Ministries, Religious Welfare
Science: Science Museums
Social Services: Animal Protection, Camps, Child Abuse, Child Welfare, Community Centers, Community Centers, Community Service Organizations, Counseling, Crime Prevention, Day Care, Family Planning, Food/Clothing Distribution, Homes, People with Disabilities, Recreation & Athletics, Senior Services, Social Services-General, Special Olympics, Substance Abuse, United Funds/United Ways, YMCA/YWCA/YMHA/YWHA, Youth Organizations

Application Procedures

Initial Contact: The foundation has no formal grant application procedure or application form. Applicants should provide a complete statement of the grant request.
Deadlines: October 1.

Restrictions

Grants are not made to individuals.

Foundation Officials

Christopher T. du Pont: vice president, trustee
Gregory F. Fields: secretary
Alexis duPont Gahagan: trustee
Katharine G. Gahagan: president
Caroline J. du Pont Prickett: trustee B 1942. PRIM CORP EMPL chairman, director: Summit Aviation Inc.
Mary Mills Abel Smith: trustee
Phyllis Mills Wyeth: trustee NONPR AFFIL trustee: National Trust Historic Preservation.

Grants Analysis

Disclosure Period: calendar year ending 2000
Total Grants: $3,800,000
Number of Grants: 45
Average Grant: $56,818*
Highest Grant: $1,300,000
Lowest Grant: $10,000
Typical Range: $10,000 to $100,000
*Note: Average grant figure excludes highest grant.

Recent Grants

Note: Grants derived from 2000 Form 990.

General

1,300,000	Children's Beach House, Wilmington, DE -- for annual operating and building fund
200,000	Piedmont Environmental Council, Warrenton, VA -- for Land Conservation Program
170,000	University of Pennsylvania, Philadelphia, PA -- for New Bolton Center Building Project
100,000	Brandywine Conservancy, Chadds Ford, PA -- for operating expenses of the Environmental Management Center
100,000	Christ Church, Greenville, DE -- for "Growing in Faith" Campaign
100,000	Farnsworth Art Museum, Rockland, ME -- for "Julia's Gallery for Young Artists" Program
100,000	H. John Heinz III Center for Science, Economics, and the Environment, Washington, DC -- for costs of disseminating the Center's reports pertaining to the Sustainable Oceans, Coasts and Waterways Programs
100,000	Three Bays Preservation, Inc, Osterville, MA -- for Water Quality Monitoring Program
100,000	Union Hospital, Elkton, MD -- for building program
85,000	Cecil County Society for Prevention of Cruelty to Animals, Chesapeake City, MD -- for building project

DURA AUTOMOTIVE SYSTEMS INC.

Company Headquarters

2791 Research Dr.
Rochester Hills, MI 48309
Web: http://www.duraauto.com

Company Description

Ticker: DRRA
Exchange: AMEX
Acquired: Excel Industries (1999).
Revenue: US$2.477 billion (2001)
Employees: 20,000 (2001)

Dura Automotive Systems Inc. Charitable Foundation

Giving Contact
2791 Research Dr.
Rochester Hills, MI 48309
Phone: (248)299-7500

Description
EIN: 311243165
Organization Type: Corporate Foundation
Former Name: Excel Industries Charitable Foundation (1999).
Former Name: Excel Industries Charitable Foundation (2001).
Giving Locations: IN
Grant Types: Award, General Support.

Financial Summary
Total Giving: $216,702 (2000); $55,530 (1998); $46,031 (1997)
Giving Analysis: Giving for 2000 includes: foundation grants to United Way ($35,912); 1998: foundation grants to United Way ($1,000) 1997: foundation grants to United Way ($7,856)
Assets: $441,881 (2000); $545,422 (1998); $429,298 (1997)
Gifts Received: $118,000 (1998); $105,000 (1997); $77,000 (1996). Note: Contributions received from Excel Industries, Inc.

Typical Recipients
Arts & Humanities: Arts Associations & Councils, Arts & Humanities-General, Libraries, Music, Performing Arts, Public Broadcasting, Theater
Civic & Public Affairs: Clubs, Civic & Public Affairs-General, Minority Business, Professional & Trade Associations
Education: Afterschool/Enrichment Programs, Business Education, Colleges & Universities, Economic Education, Education Funds, Engineering/Technological Education, Education-General, Minority Education, Private Education (Precollege), Public Education (Precollege), Science/Mathematics Education, Secondary Education (Public), Student Aid, Vocational & Technical Education
Health: Cancer, Children's Health/Hospitals, Emergency/Ambulance Services, Health Policy/Cost Containment, Hospices, Hospitals, Medical Research, Mental Health
Religion: Religious Welfare
Social Services: At-Risk Youth, Child Abuse, Child Welfare, Community Centers, Community Service Organizations, Crime Prevention, Family Services, Food/Clothing Distribution, People with Disabilities, Scouts, Shelters/Homelessness, United Funds/United Ways, YMCA/YWCA/YMHA/YWHA, Youth Organizations

Application Procedures
Initial Contact: Send a brief letter of inquiry.
Application Requirements: Include a description of organization, amount requested, purpose of funds sought, and proof of tax-exempt status. Requests should be submitted by November for funding the following year.

Restrictions
Does not support individuals, religious organizations for sectarian purposes, political or lobbying groups, or organizations outside operating areas.

Additional Information
In 1999, Excel Industries merged with Dura Automotive Systems, Inc.
Trust(s): Key Trust Co IN NA

Corporate Officials
James O. Futterknecht, Jr.: chairman, president, chief executive officer, chief operating officer, director B Detroit, MI 1947. ED University of Texas (1969). PRIM CORP EMPL chairman, president, chief executive officer, chief operating officer, director: Excel Industries. NONPR AFFIL member: American Society Body Engineers; member: Society Automotive Engineers.
Joseph A. Robinson: chief financial officer, secretary, treasurer, director B Kenton, OH 1938. ED University of Cincinnati BBA (1961). PRIM CORP EMPL chief financial officer, secretary, treasurer, director: Excel Industries. NONPR AFFIL member: Financial Executives Institute; member: Ohio Society CPA's; member: American Institute CPA's. CLUB AFFIL Elcona Country Club; Lakewood Country Club.

Foundation Officials
James O. Futterknecht, Jr.: president (see above)
Joseph A. Robinson: secretary (see above)

Grants Analysis
Disclosure Period: calendar year ending 2000
Total Grants: $180,890*
Number of Grants: 16
Average Grant: $2,059*
Highest Grant: $150,000
Typical Range: $500 to $5,000
*Note: Giving excludes United Way. Average grant figure excludes highest grant.

Recent Grants
Note: Grants derived from 1999 Form 990.

Library-Related
1,000	W. Union Library

General
10,000	University of Notre Dame, Notre Dame, IN
5,000	American Red Cross - Lawrence County, TN
5,000	First The Competition
5,000	Hoffman T.E.C.H. Center Operating Fund
5,000	YMCA/YWCA, Elkhart, IN
4,200	United Way, Detroit, MI
2,860	WNIT, Elkhart, IN
2,000	Dean's Discretionary Fund
1,500	Fulton Rotary Club
1,500	Rockford Symphony Orchestra, Rockford, IL

DURFEE FOUNDATION

Giving Contact
Claire Peeps, Executive Director
1453 3rd Street Promenade, Suite 312
Santa Monica, CA 90401
Phone: (310)890-5120
Fax: (310)899-5121
E-mail: admin@durfee.org
Web: http://www.durfee.org

Description
Founded: 1960
EIN: 952223738
Organization Type: Private Foundation
Giving Locations: CA
Grant Types: Fellowship, General Support, Project.

Donor Information
Founder: Ray Stanton Avery, the late Dorothy Durfee Avery

Financial Summary
Total Giving: $920,122 (2001); $1,057,786 (2000); $1,089,699 (1999)
Giving Analysis: Giving for 2001 includes: foundation gifts to individuals ($75,000); foundation fellowships ($203,856); 2000: foundation gifts to individuals ($75,000); foundation fellowships ($95,000) 1999: foundation gifts to individuals ($170,004)
Assets: $26,759,480 (2001); $28,878,981 (2000); $32,967,928 (1999)
Gifts Received: $35,000 (2001); $500 (1995). Note: In 2001, contributions were received from Judith Avery.

Typical Recipients
Arts & Humanities: Arts Centers, Arts Funds, Arts Institutes, Community Arts, Arts & Humanities-General, History & Archaeology, Libraries, Museums/Galleries, Music, Opera, Public Broadcasting, Theater, Visual Arts
Civic & Public Affairs: Asian American Affairs, Community Foundations, Economic Development, Economic Policy, Civic & Public Affairs-General, Hispanic Affairs, Housing, Nonprofit Management, Philanthropic Organizations, Professional & Trade Associations, Urban & Community Affairs, Women's Affairs
Education: Colleges & Universities, Community & Junior Colleges, Engineering/Technological Education, Education-General, Gifted & Talented Programs, International Exchange, International Studies, Minority Education, Private Education (Precollege), Science/Mathematics Education
Environment: Air/Water Quality, Environment-General, Protection, Resource Conservation
Health: Health Organizations, Mental Health, Public Health, Research/Studies Institutes
International: Foreign Arts Organizations, Foreign Educational Institutions, International Environmental Issues
Religion: Churches
Social Services: Animal Protection, Child Welfare, Community Service Organizations, Social Services-General, Substance Abuse, Youth Organizations

Application Procedures
Initial Contact: Send a brief letter of inquiry.
Application Requirements: Describe the problems, issues, goals, or purposes the proposal intends to address; the proposed solution or activity and its cost and schedule; who would benefit from this endeavor, and in what ways; and who would carry out this endeavor and their current tax status.
Deadlines: None.
Review Process: Selection of grantees is usually initiated by the Trustees.

Restrictions
Majority of grants are in the educational, community, cultural, and historical fields. Does not fund endowments or operating budgets.

Foundation Officials
Caroline Avery: president
Halina Avery: trustee, director
Diana Newkirk: trustee
Jonathan Newkirk: secretary
Judith A. Newkirk: chairman
Michael A. Newkirk: vice president, treasurer
Claire Peeps: executive director

Grants Analysis
Disclosure Period: calendar year ending 2001
Total Grants: $641,266*
Number of Grants: 27
Average Grant: $16,267*
Highest Grant: $218,315
Typical Range: $5,000 to $30,000

*Note: Giving excludes fellowships and gifts to individuals. Average grant figure excludes highest grant.

Recent Grants

Note: Grants derived from 2001 Form 990.

General
49,100	California Institute for the Arts, Valencia, CA
35,000	Odyssey Theater, Los Angeles, CA
35,000	P.F. Breese Foundation, Los Angeles, CA
35,000	Strategic Actions for a Just Economy, Los Angeles, CA
25,000	Community Coalition for Substance Abuse and Prevention and Treatment, Los Angeles, CA
25,000	Los Angeles Conservancy, Los Angeles, CA
25,000	Los Angeles Metropolitan Churches, Los Angeles, CA
25,000	Mental Health Advocacy Services, Los Angeles, IN
25,000	Pueblo Nuevo Enterprises, Inc., Los Angeles, CA -- to hire a manager for the janitorial collective
22,909	Streetlights Production Assistance Program, Los Angeles, CA

DYNAMET, INC.

Company Headquarters

195 Museum Rd.
Washington, PA 15301
Phone: 800-237-9655
Web: http://www.dynamet.com

Company Description

Founded: 1967
Employees: 290
SIC(s): 3356 Nonferrous Rolling & Drawing Nec, 3463 Nonferrous Forgings, 3599 Industrial Machinery Nec.
Parent Company: Carpenter Technology Corp., 1047 North Park Road, Wyomissing, PA, United States

Operating Locations

Dynamet, Inc. (PA--Washington)

Giving Contact

Katharine Marshall, Director of Communications
101 West Burn Street
Reading, PA 19601
Phone: (610)208-2000
Fax: (610)736-6232
Web: http://www.cartech.com

Description

Organization Type: Corporate Giving Program
Giving Locations: PA: Pittsburgh
Grant Types: General Support.

Financial Summary

Total Giving: $785,640 (1998); $767,620 (1997); $503,640 (1996). Note: Contributes through corporate direct giving program only. Foundation dissolved in 1997.
Giving Analysis: Giving for 1998 includes: foundation grants to United Way ($10,000) foundation ($775,640)
Assets: $21,446,952 (1998); $18,455,525 (1997); $10,375,126 (1996)
Gifts Received: $7,304,979 (1997); $1,172,500 (1996); $500,000 (1993). Note: Contributions received from Dynamet, Inc.

Typical Recipients

Arts & Humanities: Arts Centers, Arts Funds, Arts Institutes, Ballet, Film & Video, Historic Preservation, History & Archaeology, Libraries, Museums/Galleries, Music, Opera, Performing Arts, Public Broadcasting, Theater
Civic & Public Affairs: Economic Development, Employment/Job Training, Housing, Parades/Festivals, Philanthropic Organizations, Public Policy, Urban & Community Affairs, Zoos/Aquariums
Education: Colleges & Universities, Economic Education, Education Reform, Engineering/Technological Education, Education-General, Preschool Education, Religious Education, Science/Mathematics Education, Secondary Education (Public), Special Education
Environment: Resource Conservation
Health: Cancer, Children's Health/Hospitals, Clinics/Medical Centers, Diabetes, Emergency/Ambulance Services, Eyes/Blindness, Health Organizations, Hospices, Hospitals, Kidney, Medical Rehabilitation, Medical Research, Mental Health, Single-Disease Health Associations
International: Health Care/Hospitals, International Affairs, International Organizations, International Relations
Religion: Religious Organizations, Religious Welfare, Seminaries
Science: Scientific Centers & Institutes, Scientific Organizations, Scientific Research
Social Services: Camps, Child Welfare, Community Centers, Community Service Organizations, Food/Clothing Distribution, Homes, People with Disabilities, Recreation & Athletics, Scouts, Senior Services, Shelters/Homelessness, Special Olympics, Substance Abuse, United Funds/United Ways, Volunteer Services, YMCA/YWCA/YMHA/YWHA, Youth Organizations

Application Procedures

Initial Contact: Contact co.

Additional Information

Foundation has recently dissolved; contact company for direct giving.

Corporate Officials

Alan Rossin: materials director PRIM CORP EMPL materials director: Dynamet Inc.

Grants Analysis

Disclosure Period: calendar year ending 1998
Total Grants: $775,640*
Number of Grants: 50
Average Grant: $15,513
Highest Grant: $250,000
Typical Range: $1,000 to $50,000
*Note: Giving excludes United Way.

Recent Grants

Note: Grants derived from 1998 Form 990.

Library-Related
10,000	Carnegie Institute, Pittsburgh, PA -- Scientific research
1,000	Carnegie Institute, Pittsburgh, PA -- Powdermill Natural Program

General
250,000	Pittsburgh Theological Seminary, Pittsburgh, PA -- Educational assistance
250,000	Washington and Jefferson College, Washington, PA -- Educational assistance
125,000	Carnegie Mellon University, Pittsburgh, PA -- Educational programs
25,000	South Dakota School of Mines and Technology, Rapid City, SD -- Educational assitance
25,000	Washington Hospital Foundation, Inc., Washington, PA -- Scientific charity
20,000	Coalition for Christian Outreach, Pittsburgh, PA -- Ministry on college campus
10,000	Pittsburgh Trust for Cultural Resources, Pittsburgh, PA -- Recreational cultural organization
10,000	The United Way of Southwest Pennsylvania, Pittsburgh, PA -- United Way
5,000	Childrens Hospital of Pittsburgh, Pittsburgh, PA -- Scientific research
5,000	St. Vincent Archabbey, Latrobe, PA -- Church related renovations

DYSON FOUNDATION

Giving Contact

Diana M. Gurieva, Executive Director
25 Halcyon Road
Millbrook, NY 12545-9611
Phone: (845)677-0644
Fax: (845)677-0650
E-mail: info@dyson.org
Web: http://www.dyson.org

Description

Founded: 1957
EIN: 136084888
Organization Type: General Purpose Foundation
Giving Locations: NY: Mid-Hudson Valley nationally.
Grant Types: Capital, Challenge, Conference/Seminar, Fellowship, General Support, Loan, Matching, Multiyear/Continuing Support, Professorship, Project, Research, Scholarship, Seed Money.

Donor Information

Founder: The Dyson Foundation was established in 1957 by Charles H. Dyson and Margaret M. Dyson as a means of formalizing and furthering their family's charitable giving. Their daughter, Anne E. Dyson, MD, serves as the foundation's president, and their son, Robert R. Dyson is on the foundation's board of directors. Margaret M. Dyson passed away in 1990. Charles H. Dyson died in 1997.

Financial Summary

Total Giving: $14,400,000 (fiscal year ending December 30, 2002); $12,503,211 (fiscal 2001); $14,093,743 (fiscal 2000)
Giving Analysis: Giving for fiscal 2000 includes: foundation scholarships ($616,500) fiscal 1999: foundation grants to United Way ($38,000)
Assets: $296,534,202 (fiscal 2001); $323,869,688 (fiscal 2000); $332,798,464 (fiscal 1999)
Gifts Received: $5,523,289 (fiscal 1999); $150,410,144 (fiscal 1998); $11,578,050 (fiscal 1992)

Typical Recipients

Arts & Humanities: Arts Associations & Councils, Arts Outreach, Ballet, Dance, Historic Preservation, History & Archaeology, Libraries, Museums/Galleries, Music, Opera, Performing Arts, Public Broadcasting
Civic & Public Affairs: Botanical Gardens/Parks, Community Foundations, Economic Development, Civic & Public Affairs-General, Housing, Law & Justice, Legal Aid, Nonprofit Management, Public Policy, Women's Affairs, Zoos/Aquariums
Education: Afterschool/Enrichment Programs, Arts/Humanities Education, Business Education, Colleges & Universities, Environmental Education, Faculty Development, Education-General, Legal Education, Literacy, Medical Education, Preschool Education, Private Education (Precollege), Religious Education, Science/Mathematics Education, Secondary Education (Public), Social Sciences Education, Special Education, Student Aid
Environment: Air/Water Quality, Environment-General, Sanitary Systems, Wildlife Protection
Health: AIDS/HIV, Cancer, Children's Health/Hospitals, Eyes/Blindness, Geriatric Health, Health Funds, Health Organizations, Hospitals, Medical Rehabilitation, Medical Research, Prenatal Health Issues, Public Health, Trauma Treatment
Religion: Churches, Ministries, Religious Organizations, Religious Welfare

Social Services: Child Welfare, Community Centers, Community Service Organizations, Crime Prevention, Day Care, Family Planning, Family Planning, Family Services, Food/Clothing Distribution, Homes, People with Disabilities, Recreation & Athletics, Scouts, Substance Abuse, United Funds/United Ways, Volunteer Services, YMCA/YWCA/YMHA/YWHA, Youth Organizations

Application Procedures

Initial Contact: The foundation welcomes telephone inquiries concerning its interest in charitable projects. The foundation does not accept unsolicited proposals, but applicants may send brief (two- or three-page) letters of inquiry.

Application Requirements: Submit a two- to three-page letter of inquiry addressing the following guidelines: Include a brief statement of the organizations purpose and goals; a description of the project, the need, and its targeted population; information about the capability of the leadership; expected outcomes; grant amount, total project budget, and other funding sources being approached, detailing committed and projected sources of support. Do not include annual reports, brochures, or additional pages of illustrative materials. Please do not send unsolicited videotapes, curricula, reports, etc.

Deadlines: None.

Review Process: All potential applicants will receive a written response to their letter of inquiry. If interested, the foundation will invite applicants to submit a fully developed proposal. During the review, representatives of the foundation will research the proposal through telephone inquiries, site visits, and meetings with staff, board, volunteers, and clients as necessary. Generally, it can take at least six months from time of inquiry to the accrual award of a grant. Directors of the Dyson Foundation meet quarterly.

Evaluative Criteria: The foundation supports organizations that are tax-exempt under Sec. 501(c)(3) of the IRS Code, and are not classified as foundations under Sec. 509(A) of the Code. Occasionally the foundation will consider grants to eligible organizations acting as fiscal sponsors to other non-qualifying organizations. Generally the foundation does not fund projects sponsored by governmental bodies (such as public schools) but will evaluate particularly innovative requests on a case-by-case basis.

Notes: The Foundation prefers to fund special projects rather than general operating expenses. It will consider grants for management or technical assistance, demonstration or pilot projects, start-up costs, evaluation, advocacy, limited equipment purchases, and small-scale publications or conferences. The Foundation will also consider multi-year awards, as well as challenge grants.

Restrictions

The foundation will not make grants to individuals (this includes scholarships, which are only provided though grants to academic institutions) or international projects (to organizations operating outside the U.S.). It will not make grants for debt reduction, direct-mail campaigns, and fund-raising events. Exceptions may occasionally be made for an organization that has an established long-term relationship with the Foundation. The foundation will not award grants support to organizations which, in their constitution, by-laws or practices, discriminate against a person or group on the basis of age, race, national origin, ethnicity, gender, disability, sexual orientation, political affiliation or religious belief. (Grantees may target services to a particular population when the targeted groups require specialized programs to meet specific needs not shared by the general population.)

Additional Information

The foundation is affiliated with the Dyson Charitable Fund, also located in New York.

The foundation prefers to fund special projects rather than general operating expenses.

The Foundation's interests are ever-changing. Potential applicants should review the current year's guidelines for areas of interest and not rely on what or whom the Foundation has funded in the past.

Publications: Annual Report; Guidelines

Foundation Officials

Robert R. Dyson: president, director B 1946. ED Cornell University MBA; Marietta College BA. PRIM CORP EMPL chairman, chief executive officer: Dyson-Kissner-Moran Corp. CORP AFFIL chairman, chief executive officer: D K M Ltd.; chairman: Kearney-National Inc.; director: Centre Foundry & Machine Co.; director: Chrisolm Corp.

John S. FitzSimons: secretary B 1948. ED Princeton University BA (1970); New York University JD (1973). PRIM CORP EMPL secretary, general counsel: Dyson-Kissner-Moran Corp. ADD CORP EMPL secretary, general counsel: DKM Properties Corp. CORP AFFIL secretary, director: Kearney-National Inc.

Diana M. Gurieva: executive vice president

Lynn A. McCluskey: assistant secretary, assistant treasurer PRIM CORP EMPL treasurer, secretary: M.S. Chambers & Sons. CORP AFFIL vice president, secretary, director: Patterson Planning & Services.

David Nathan, MD: director

Grants Analysis

Disclosure Period: fiscal year ending December 30, 2000

Total Grants: $13,477,243*

Number of Grants: 96

Average Grant: $141,065*

Highest Grant: $2,750,000

Lowest Grant: $1,500

Typical Range: $5,000 to $50,000

*Note: Giving excludes scholarships and fellowships. Average grant excludes highest grant.

Recent Grants

Note: Grants derived from 2000 Form 990.

General

2,750,000   Dana Farber Cancer Institute, Boston, MA -- for the Anne E. Dyson Chair in Women's Cancer

1,000,000   Marietta College, Marietta, OH -- for renovation and expansion

1,000,000   Weill Medical College of Cornell University, New York, NY -- for New Horizons for Medicine Campaign

685,000   Dana Farber Cancer Institute, Boston, MA -- support of the David G. Nathan Chair in Pediatric Hematology Oncology

500,000   Columbia University, New York, NY -- for pediatric residency training innovation

500,000   High Mowing School, Wilton, NH -- capital campaign

500,000   University of California San Diego School of Medicine, San Diego, CA -- for pediatric residency training innovation

500,000   University of Hawaii, Honolulu, HI -- for pediatric residency training innovation

497,000   Medical College of Wisconsin, Milwaukee, WI -- for pediatric residency training innovation

487,000   Children's Hospital of Philadelphia, Philadelphia, PA -- for pediatric residency training innovation

E.I. DU PONT DE NEMOURS & CO.

Company Headquarters

Wilmington, DE
Web: http://www.dupont.com

Company Description

Founded: 1802

Ticker: DD

Exchange: NYSE

Acquired: Pioneer Hi-Bred (1999).

Revenue: US$24.006 billion (2002)

Employees: 9300 (2002)

SIC(s): 1222 Bituminous Coal--Underground, 1311 Crude Petroleum & Natural Gas, 1321 Natural Gas Liquids, 2822 Synthetic Rubber.

Operating Locations

E.I. du Pont de Nemours & Co. (AL--Axis; AR--Hazen, Lonoke; CA--Antioch, Santa Clara; CO--Commerce City, Rangely; CT--Danbury; DE--Edge Moor, Glasgow, Newark, Newport, Wilmington; FL--Starke; GA--Athens; IL--El Paso; IN--East Chicago, Kokomo; IA--Fort Madison; KS--Kansas City; KY--Wurtland; LA--Darrow, Egan, Grand Chenier, Lake Charles, Westlake; MA--Boston; MI--Mason, Montague, Mount Clemens, Troy; MS--Pass Christian; NJ--Deepwater, Gibbstown, Linden, Pompton Lakes; NM--Bloomfield, Maljamar; NY--Buffalo, Niagara Falls, Rochester; NC--Brevard, Denton, Fayetteville, Kinston, Wilmington; OH--Circleville, Findlay, Stow, Toledo; OK--Ada, Hennessy, Medford, Ponca City, Tuttle; PA--Boothwyn, Philadelphia, Pittsburgh, Towanda; SC--Camden, Florence; TN--Chattanooga, Memphis, New Johnsonville; TX--Beaumont, El Dorado, Hamlin, Houston, La Porte, McKinney, Mertzon, Mont Belvieu, Orla, Pasadena, Round Rock, San Angelo, Victoria; VA--Front Royal, Martinsville, Mavisdale, Waynesboro; WV--Belle, Martinsburg, Moundsville)

Subsidiary Companies

IA: Pioneer Hi-Bred International, Inc., Des Moines

Nonmonetary Support

Type: Donated Equipment

Note: Company also donates property. For nonmonetary support contact nearest company site.

Giving Contact

Pat Eggert, Contributions Coordinator
DuPont Public Affairs
Corporate Contributions Office
1007 Market Street
Wilmington, DE 19898

Phone: (302)774-2036

Fax: (302)773-2919

Web: http://www1.dupont.com/NASApp/dupontglobal/corp/index.jsp?page=/content/US/en_US/social/outreach/index.html

Alternate Contact

DuPont Office of Education
Barley Mill Plaza 16/2150
PO Box 80016
Wilmington, DE 19880-0016

Note: Contact for DuPont Education programs.

Description

Organization Type: Corporate Giving Program

Giving Locations: headquarters and operating communities.

Grant Types: Capital, Conference/Seminar, Emergency, Fellowship, General Support, Multiyear/Continuing Support.

Financial Summary

Total Giving: $30,000,000 (2000 approx); $28,000,000 (1999 approx); $28,000,000 (1998 approx). Note: Contributes through corporate direct giving program only.

Typical Recipients

Arts & Humanities: Arts Appreciation, Arts Associations & Councils, Arts Centers, Arts Festivals, Arts Funds, Arts Institutes, Community Arts, Dance, Ethnic & Folk Arts, Historic Preservation, Libraries, Literary Arts, Museums/Galleries, Music, Opera, Performing Arts, Public Broadcasting, Theater, Visual Arts

Civic & Public Affairs: Business/Free Enterprise, Civil Rights, Economic Development, Economic Policy, Employment/Job Training, Housing, Law & Justice, Legal Aid, Municipalities/Towns, Nonprofit Management, Philanthropic Organizations, Professional & Trade Associations, Public Policy, Safety, Urban & Community Affairs, Women's Affairs, Zoos/Aquariums

Education: Agricultural Education, Business Education, Colleges & Universities, Community & Junior Colleges, Economic Education, Education Associations, Education Funds, Engineering/Technological Education, Faculty Development, International Exchange, International Studies, Journalism/Media Education, Legal Education, Literacy, Minority Education, Preschool Education, Private Education (Precollege), Public Education (Precollege), Science/Mathematics Education, Social Sciences Education, Student Aid

Environment: Environment-General

Health: Emergency/Ambulance Services, Geriatric Health, Health Policy/Cost Containment, Health Organizations, Hospices, Hospitals, Medical Rehabilitation, Medical Research, Medical Training, Mental Health, Single-Disease Health Associations

International: Foreign Educational Institutions, Health Care/Hospitals, International Peace & Security Issues, International Relations

Science: Science Exhibits & Fairs, Scientific Centers & Institutes, Scientific Organizations

Social Services: Animal Protection, Child Welfare, Community Centers, Community Service Organizations, Counseling, Day Care, Delinquency & Criminal Rehabilitation, Domestic Violence, Emergency Relief, Family Services, Food/Clothing Distribution, Homes, People with Disabilities, Recreation & Athletics, Senior Services, Shelters/Homelessness, Substance Abuse, United Funds/United Ways, Volunteer Services, Youth Organizations

Application Procedures

Initial Contact: Submit a written proposal.

Application Requirements: Provide a one-to two-page a description of organization and program to be funded and an explanation of how it relates to the mission, operating philosophy, and areas of support of the DuPont Community Involvement Program. Requests should be sent to the above address to the attention of the appropriate committee:

The Committee on Contributions and Memberships reviews all requests for non-education financial contributions.

The Committee on Educational Aid reviews requests for financial contributions to educational institutions.

Deadlines: None.

Review Process: The Committee on Contributions and Memberships generally reviews requests in May and September.

Evaluative Criteria: For Community Social Progress and Economic Success requests, DuPont prefers programs that both address a community need and reflect positively on the reputation and image of DuPont; programs that have extensive DuPont employee volunteer involvement; proposals that have well-defined goals and objectives and a method for evaluating results; and programs designed with long-lasting results in mind.

In the area of Environmental Excellence, DuPont has a preference for organizations that can provide evidence of demonstrated, credible environmental performance; proposals that leverage non-cash resources; proposals that involve partnerships and collaboration between industry, governmental, and community-based organizations; programs which involve DuPont employees; and programs that reflect favorably on DuPont's reputation and image.

DuPont focuses its funding in the Education program area on learning readiness, hands-on science, discovery math, work force readiness, and teacher preparation.

Decision Notification: Applicants are notified in writing.

Restrictions

DuPont does not support U.S. nonprofit organizations not eligible for support under the U.S. IRS Code; disease-specific organizations; endowments; fraternal and veterans groups; individuals; political organizations or campaigns; sectarian organizations whose programs are limited to members of one religious group; organizations which discriminate based on age, race, religion, color, sex, disability, national origin, ancestry, marital status, sexual orientation, or veteran status. presence.

Additional Information

The company awards between 5,000 and 6,000 grants annually.

DuPont contributions are focused on three areas of support:

Community Social Progress and Economic Success, particularly those programs that provide access to opportunity to people for whom that access does not currently adequately exist; help children, youth and families; foster understanding and respect between community members; revitalize neighborhoods; and help people achieve self-sufficiency.

Environmental Excellence, through support of initiatives that produce significant, measurable results in four major areas of environmental quality: conservation, public policy, research and education, and environmental management.

Send non-education requests to the DuPont Corporate Contributions Office.

Education, by funding programs that support improvements in pre-school to grade 12 education. At the college/university level, DuPont opens access to leading-edge research and introduces talented students to the company.

Send education-related requests to the DuPont Office of Education.

Publications: Brochure

Corporate Officials

Thomas M. Connelly: senior vice president, chief science & technology officer B Toledo, OH. PRIM CORP EMPL senior vice president, chief science & technology officer: E.I. du Pont de Nemours & Co.

Richard Goodmanson: executive vice president, chief operating officer PRIM CORP EMPL executive vice president, chief operating officer: E.I. du Pont de Nemours & Co.

Charles O. Holliday, Jr.: chairman, chief executive officer, director B March 09, 1948. ED University of Tennessee BS. PRIM CORP EMPL chairman, chief executive officer, director: E.I. du Pont de Nemours & Co.

Stacey J. Mobley: senior vice president, chief administrative officer, general counsel B Chester, PA. PRIM CORP EMPL senior vice president, chief administrative officer, general counsel: E.I. du Pont de Nemours & Co.

Grants Analysis

Disclosure Period: calendar year ending 2000
Total Grants: $30,000,000 (approx)
Typical Range: $5,000 to $10,000

EARHART FOUNDATION

Giving Contact

David B. Kennedy, President
2200 Green Road, Suite H
Ann Arbor, MI 48105

Phone: (734)761-8592
Fax: (734)761-2722

Description

Founded: 1929
EIN: 386008273
Organization Type: Specialized/Single Purpose Foundation
Grant Types: Fellowship, Research, Scholarship.

Donor Information

Founder: The foundation was organized in 1929 by the late Harry Boyd Earhart , the principal donor. Born in Pennsylvania, Mr. Earhart was the son of a village storekeeper. After completing the eighth grade and a brief commercial business course, he became a cargo broker on the Great Lakes, a designer and salesman of logging machinery, and a manufacturer and distributor of lubricating oils and related petroleum products. Mr. Earhart founded the White Star Refining Company, now a part of Mobil Oil Corporation.

Financial Summary

Total Giving: $4,705,024 (2002); $5,053,293 (2000); $4,014,013 (1998)
Giving Analysis: Giving for 2000 includes: foundation fellowships ($1,964,919); 1998: foundation fellowships ($1,759,947) 1997: foundation fellowships ($1,401,891)
Assets: $66,670,425 (2002); $95,889,657 (2000); $98,042,651 (1998)
Gifts Received: $200,000 (1995)

Typical Recipients

Arts & Humanities: History & Archaeology, Libraries, Literary Arts

Civic & Public Affairs: Civil Rights, Economic Policy, Employment/Job Training, Civic & Public Affairs-General, Law & Justice, Philanthropic Organizations, Public Policy, Urban & Community Affairs

Education: Arts/Humanities Education, Business Education, Colleges & Universities, Continuing Education, Economic Education, Education Associations, Education Reform, Engineering/Technological Education, Faculty Development, Education-General, International Exchange, International Studies, Journalism/Media Education, Legal Education, Literacy, Religious Education, Science/Mathematics Education, Secondary Education (Public), Social Sciences Education, Student Aid

Environment: Environment-General, Research

International: Foreign Educational Institutions, Foreign Educational Institutions, International-General, International Affairs, International Development, International Environmental Issues, International Organizations, International Peace & Security Issues, International Relations, Missionary/Religious Activities

Religion: Social/Policy Issues

Social Services: Community Centers, People with Disabilities

Application Procedures

Initial Contact: Organizations or individuals may submit a letter of inquiry or may telephone the foundation for complete application guidelines.

Application Requirements: Institutions seeking grants must complete an application including a general a description of organization, status of eligibility for support from private foundations, current audit or financial statement, list of other institutional supporters, statement of the project with amount requested and budget, and an evaluation with follow-up procedures.

Individuals applying for fellowship research grants must include a personal history statement, full description of proposed research, abstract of approximately 250 words or one page, intended use or publication, budget and time schedule, list of references, and a statement of applications pending elsewhere. elsewhere.

Deadlines: None. The foundation will acknowledge receipt of proposals. In the case of individuals seeking fellowship research grants, applications should be submitted at least 120 days before the commencement of the projected work.

Review Process: If an institutional project is of interest, one copy of a completed proposal will be required. Interviews may be requested.

Restrictions

No grants are made for capital, building, or endowment funds; conferences; operating budgets; continuing support; annual campaigns; seed money; emergency funds; deficit financing; matching gifts; or loans.

Additional Information

H. B. Earhart Fellowships are awarded only to individuals who are nominated by designated faculty sponsors. Direct applications from candidates or from non-invited sponsors are not accepted.

A copy of foundation's annual report is available at the foundation's office for inspection during normal office hours.

Publications: Annual Report

Foundation Officials

Dennis L. Bark: chairman, trustee ED Stanford University (1964).

Thomas Joseph Bray: trustee B New York, NY 1941. ED Princeton University AB (1963). PRIM CORP EMPL editorial page editor: Detroit News. NONPR AFFIL member: American Society Newspaper Editors; member: National Conference Editorial Writers. CLUB AFFIL mem: Birmingham Athletic Club; mem: Detroit Athletic Club.

Kathleen B. Harrington: assistant treasurer

Earl I. Heenan, Jr.: vchairman, trustee

Ann K. Irish: trustee NONPR AFFIL board member, director: North Central Michigan College; secretary, director: Northern Michigan Hospital.

David Boyd Kennedy: president B Ann Arbor, MI 1933. ED McGill University (1951-1952); University of Michigan (1952-1954); Indiana University AB (1958); University of Michigan LLB (1963). NONPR AFFIL director: Philanthropy Roundtable; member: Wyoming Bar Association; member: Mont Pelerin Society; chairman, director: Institute Justice; member: Michigan Bar Association; director: Citizens Research Council Michigan.

Paul Winston McCracken: trustee B Richland, IA December 29, 1915. ED William Penn College (1937); Harvard University MA (1942); Harvard University PhD (1948). NONPR AFFIL member: Royal Economic Society; professor emeritus: University Michigan; trustee: National Bureau Economic Research; fellow: American Statistical Association; member, council: Harvard Graduate Society; member: American Financial Association; member public oversight board: American Institute of Certified Public Accountants; member: American Economic Association. CLUB AFFIL Cosmos Club; Harvard Club.

John H. Moore: trustee

Robert L. Queller: trustee

Edward H. Sichler, III: treasurer B Detroit, MI 1935. ED University of Michigan (1956); University of Michigan (1958). PRIM CORP EMPL executive vice president: Key Bank. NONPR AFFIL member: Chartered Financial Analysts; member: Financial Analysts Society Detroit. CLUB AFFIL Rotary Club.

Antony T. Sullivan: secretary, program officer NONPR AFFIL member: Financial Analysts Society Detroit; member: Institute Chartered Financial Analysts.

Richard Anderson Ware: president emeritus, trustee B New York, NY November 07, 1919. ED Lehigh University BA (1941); Wayne State University MA (1943). NONPR AFFIL member: Phi Beta Kappa; trustee: Smith College Center Study Social & Political Change; trustee: Pequawket Foundation; member: Phi Alpha Theta; director: Liberty Fund Inc.; member: Mont Pelerin Society; trustee: Intercollegiate Studies

Institute; trustee: Institute Foreign Policy Analysis; trustee: Institute Political Economy; member: American Political Science Association; member: Government Research Association. CLUB AFFIL Cosmos Club; North Conway Country Club; Ann Arbor Club.

Grants Analysis

Disclosure Period: calendar year ending 2000
Total Grants: $3,088,374*
Number of Grants: 212
Average Grant: $14,568
Highest Grant: $75,000
Typical Range: $1,000 to $20,000
*Note: Giving excludes fellowships.

Recent Grants

Note: Grants derived from 2000 Form 990.

General

75,000	Jamestown Foundation, Washington, DC -- provide general operating support
50,000	American Enterprise Institute for Public Policy Research, Washington, DC -- support for journal articles and book on regulation, communications, and information technology by Thomas Hazlett
50,000	Association of Literary Scholars and Critics, Berkeley, CA
50,000	Citizens Research Council of Michigan, Detroit, MI
50,000	Intercollegiate Studies Institute, Inc., Wilmington, DE -- for renewal of support for the Richard M. Weaver Fellowship Program
50,000	Social Philosophy and Policy Foundation, Bowling Green, OH -- support for up to six visiting scholars in the fields of history and philosophy
42,600	Intercollegiate Studies Institute, Inc., Wilmington, DE -- for renewal of support for the Richard M. Weaver Fellowship Program
40,000	Institute of World Politics, Washington, DC -- operating support
40,000	Manhattan Institute for Policy Research, New York, NY -- support during 1998 preparation of a book in the growing racial gap in educational performance
35,000	American Friends Fund of the Institute of the US Studies in the University of London, Carlisle, PA -- to provide one graduate fellowship in American Studies

EARLY FOUNDATION

Giving Contact

Jeanette B. Early, President
6319 Mimosa Ln.
Dallas, TX 75230
Phone: (214)373-7114

Description

Founded: 1963
EIN: 756011853
Organization Type: Private Foundation
Giving Locations: TX
Grant Types: General Support.

Donor Information

Founder: Jeannette B. Early

Financial Summary

Total Giving: $247,650 (fiscal year ending May 31, 2000); $220,000 (fiscal 1999); $180,000 (fiscal 1998)
Giving Analysis: Giving for fiscal 1998 includes: foundation grants to United Way ($1,500) foundation ($178,500)
Assets: $3,882,773 (fiscal 2000); $4,612,978 (fiscal 1999); $4,134,046 (fiscal 1998)
Gifts Received: $30,000 (fiscal 1996)

Typical Recipients

Arts & Humanities: Arts Centers, Ballet, Dance, History & Archaeology, Libraries, Museums/Galleries, Music, Opera, Performing Arts, Public Broadcasting, Theater
Civic & Public Affairs: Economic Development, Gay/Lesbian Issues, Civic & Public Affairs-General, Hispanic Affairs, Housing, Parades/Festivals, Public Policy, Urban & Community Affairs, Zoos/Aquariums
Education: Arts/Humanities Education, Business Education, Colleges & Universities, Community & Junior Colleges, Education Reform, Engineering/Technological Education, Education-General, Leadership Training, Literacy, Medical Education, Minority Education, Private Education (Precollege), Public Education (Precollege), Religious Education, Religious Education, Special Education, Student Aid
Environment: Environment-General
Health: Alzheimers Disease, Children's Health/Hospitals, Clinics/Medical Centers, Eyes/Blindness, Health Organizations, Heart, Hospices, Medical Research, Mental Health, Nursing Services, Prenatal Health Issues, Single-Disease Health Associations
International: Foreign Arts Organizations, International Development, International Relations, International Relief Efforts, Missionary/Religious Activities
Religion: Churches, Religion-General, Ministries, Religious Organizations, Religious Welfare, Seminaries
Science: Science Museums
Social Services: Child Welfare, Community Service Organizations, Delinquency & Criminal Rehabilitation, Family Services, Homes, People with Disabilities, Substance Abuse, United Funds/United Ways, Volunteer Services, YMCA/YWCA/YMHA/YWHA, Youth Organizations

Application Procedures

Initial Contact: The foundation has no formal grant application procedure or application form.
Application Requirements: Proof of tax exempt satus is required.
Deadlines: None.

Additional Information

Publications: Annual Report

Foundation Officials

Jeannette B. Early: president

Grants Analysis

Disclosure Period: fiscal year ending May 31, 2000
Total Grants: $247,650
Number of Grants: 34
Average Grant: $7,284
Highest Grant: $25,000
Typical Range: $2,000 to $15,000

Recent Grants

Note: Grants derived from 2002 Form 990.

General

25,000	Dallas Children's Theater, Dallas, TX -- provides drama programs and theater to the children of Dallas
25,000	Grace Presbyterian Village, Dallas, TX -- for retirement home and hospital care for retired citizens
25,000	Total Learning Project, Centennial, CO -- support schools and provides training to those with learning disabilities
20,000	Total Learning Project, Centennial, CO -- support schools and provides training to those with learning disabilities
15,000	Presbyterian Children's Home and Service Agency, Austin, TX -- provides homes and special services to children
15,000	Presbyterian Pan American School, Kingsville, TN -- preparatory school for

students to learn English before going to college

15,000	Science Place, Dallas, TX -- provides hands-on physics gallery and science center to 225,000 school children year round
10,000	Agape Medical Clinic, Dallas, TX -- care of persons in need of health care in East Dallas
10,000	Austin Presbyterian Theological Seminary, Austin, TX -- for graduate school to train church professionals for positions in US and abroad
10,000	Austin Presbyterian Theological Seminary, Austin, TX -- for graduate school to train church professionals for positions in US and abroad

ANDREW H. AND ANNE O. EASLEY TRUST

Giving Contact
Andrew H. and Anne O. Easley Trust
PO Box 27602
Richmond, VA 23261
Phone: (804)697-6901

Description
Founded: 1968
EIN: 546074720
Organization Type: Private Foundation
Giving Locations: VA: Lynchburg
Grant Types: General Support.

Donor Information
Founder: the late Andrew H. Easley

Financial Summary
Total Giving: $508,498 (fiscal year ending June 30, 2001); $530,571 (fiscal 2000); $377,297 (fiscal 1997)
Assets: $407,887,389 (fiscal 2001); $12,062,833 (fiscal 2000); $8,884,803 (fiscal 1997)

Typical Recipients
Arts & Humanities: Arts Associations & Councils, Arts Centers, Community Arts, Historic Preservation, Libraries, Museums/Galleries, Music, Performing Arts, Theater
Civic & Public Affairs: Economic Development, Employment/Job Training, Civic & Public Affairs-General, Housing, Legal Aid, Native American Affairs, Urban & Community Affairs, Women's Affairs
Education: Agricultural Education, Arts/Humanities Education, Colleges & Universities, Community & Junior Colleges, Education Associations, Education-General, Private Education (Precollege), Science/Mathematics Education
Environment: Forestry, Environment-General
Health: Public Health, Single-Disease Health Associations
International: Human Rights
Religion: Religious Welfare
Social Services: Animal Protection, Camps, Child Welfare, Child Welfare, Community Centers, Community Service Organizations, Day Care, Family Planning, Family Services, Food/Clothing Distribution, Homes, Recreation & Athletics, Shelters/Homelessness, United Funds/United Ways, YMCA/YWCA/YMHA/YWHA, Youth Organizations

Application Procedures
Initial Contact: Request application guidelines.
Deadlines: April 1 and October 1.

Additional Information
Publications: Application Guidelines
Trust(s): Wachovia Bank

Grants Analysis
Typical Range: $3,000 to $50,000

Recent Grants
Note: Grants derived from fiscal 2001 Form 990.

General
50,000	Arc of Central Virginia, Richmond, VA
25,000	Lynchburg Sheltered Industries, Inc., Lynchburg, VA
15,345	Virginia School of the Arts, Lynchburg, VA
15,000	Central Virginia Community College, Lynchburg, VA
15,000	Ferrum College, Ferrum, VA
15,000	Hampden-Sydney College, Hampden-Sydney, VA
15,000	Lynchburg College, Lynchburg, VA
15,000	Randolph-Macon Woman's College, Lynchburg, VA
15,000	Sweet Briar College, Sweet Briar, VA
13,550	Adult Care Center

EAST CAMBRIDGE SAVINGS BANK

Company Headquarters
292 Cambridge St.
Cambridge, MA 02141
Web: http://www.ecsb.com

Company Description
Founded: 1854

East Cambridge Savings Charitable Foundation

Giving Contact
East Cambridge Savings Bank
292 Cambridge Street
East Cambridge, MA 02141-1263
Phone: (617)354-7700

Description
Founded: 1997
EIN: 043399319
Organization Type: Corporate Foundation
Giving Locations: , MA
Grant Types: General Support, Scholarship.

Financial Summary
Total Giving: $110,850 (2001); $122,840 (2000); $75,370 (1998)
Giving Analysis: Giving for 2001 includes: foundation grants to United Way ($5,000) foundation scholarships ($6,000)
Assets: $351,951 (2001); $553,619 (2000); $988,885 (1998)

Typical Recipients
Arts & Humanities: Arts Centers, Libraries
Civic & Public Affairs: Community Foundations, Ethnic Organizations, Civic & Public Affairs-General, Municipalities/Towns, Philanthropic Organizations
Education: Arts/Humanities Education, Colleges & Universities, Faculty Development, Public Education (Precollege)
Health: Nursing Services
Religion: Churches
Social Services: Child Welfare, Community Service Organizations, United Funds/United Ways, YMCA/YWCA/YMHA/YWHA

Application Procedures
Initial Contact: Write the foundation to request an application form.

Foundation Officials
Joseph A. Amoroso, Jr.: director
Charles Aufieror: director
Lee C. Craig: director
Tyler H. Foster: director
Susan LaPierre: vice president community relations
Daniel A. Leone: director
Gisela L. Margotta: treasurer
William F. McGilvreay: president, director
Gilda M. Nogueira: clerk
Albert M. Pacheco: director
Arthur C. Spears: executive vice president
Philip A. Trussell: director
George E. Wilson: director

Grants Analysis
Disclosure Period: calendar year ending 2001
Total Grants: $99,850*
Number of Grants: 82
Average Grant: $1,218
Highest Grant: $13,000
Lowest Grant: $25
Typical Range: $100 to $5,000
*Note: Giving excludes scholarships; United Way.

Recent Grants
Note: Grants derived from 2000 Form 990.

Library-Related
| 5,000 | Cambridge Public library, Cambridge, MA -- for 2000 Summer Reading Program |

General
20,000	City of Cambridge, Cambridge, NE -- contribution for the purchase of thermal imaging camera
13,000	DOC Linskey Road Race Scholarship Fund, Cambridge, MA -- for corporate sponsor 18th annual
10,000	Cambridge Family YMCA, Cambridge, MA -- annual campaign
10,000	East End House, Cambridge, MA -- for annual fund campaign
5,000	Cambridge Community Foundation, Cambridge, MA -- for George E. Wilson Campers Fund
5,000	Longy School of Music, Cambridge, MA -- support for scholarship and outreach program
5,000	Sacred Heart of Jesus Church, Cambridge, MA -- to assist in restoring the Sacred Heart Church
5,000	United Way of Massachusetts Bay, Boston, MA -- for annual contribution
3,900	Cambridge Housing Assistance Fund, Somerville, MA -- for celebrating Latin music
2,200	Consumer Credit Counseling Service, Cambridge, MA -- annual appeal

EASTERN BANK

Company Headquarters
Salem, MA
Web: http://www.easternbank.com

Company Description
Employees: 731

Operating Locations
Eastern Bank (MA--Beverly, Boston, Braintree, Hingham, Lynnfield, Malden, Medford, Melrose, Quincy, Salem, Saugus, Shrewsbury, Stoughton, Swampscott, Wakefield, Weymouth)

Eastern Bank Charitable Foundation

Giving Contact

Sumner W. Jones, Executive Vice President
217 Essex Street
Salem, MA 01970
Phone: (978)740-6319
Fax: (978)740-6329
Web: http://www.easternbank.com/
a_charitable_foundation.html

Description

Founded: 1985
EIN: 223317340
Organization Type: Corporate Foundation
Giving Locations: MA: market area
Grant Types: Capital, General Support, Scholarship.

Financial Summary

Total Giving: $1,037,702 (2001); $546,828 (2000); $526,982 (1999). Note: Contributes through foundation only.

Giving Analysis: Giving for 2001 includes: foundation scholarships ($6,340); foundation grants to United Way ($66,000); foundation matching gifts ($206,475); foundation ($758,887); 2000: foundation scholarships ($7,200); foundation grants to United Way ($60,000); foundation ($479,628); 1999: foundation grants to United Way ($65,000); foundation ($461,982);

Assets: $17,571,768 (2001); $17,415,552 (2000); $15,306,660 (1999)

Gifts Received: $202,396 (1995); $105 (1993). Note: Foundation receives contributions from Eastern Bank.

Typical Recipients

Arts & Humanities: Arts Centers, Community Arts, Arts & Humanities-General, Historic Preservation, History & Archaeology, Libraries, Museums/Galleries, Music, Performing Arts, Public Broadcasting

Civic & Public Affairs: African American Affairs, Asian American Affairs, Business/Free Enterprise, Chambers of Commerce, Civil Rights, Clubs, Community Foundations, Economic Development, Employment/Job Training, Ethnic Organizations, Civic & Public Affairs-General, Hispanic Affairs, Housing, Native American Affairs, Nonprofit Management, Parades/Festivals, Philanthropic Organizations, Safety, Urban & Community Affairs, Women's Affairs

Education: Afterschool/Enrichment Programs, Arts/Humanities Education, Business-School Partnerships, Colleges & Universities, Colleges & Universities, Community & Junior Colleges, Education Reform, Education-General, Medical Education, Private Education (Precollege), Science/Mathematics Education, Secondary Education (Private), Student Aid

Health: AIDS/HIV, Cancer, Children's Health/Hospitals, Clinics/Medical Centers, Health-General, Health Organizations, Heart, Hospices, Hospitals, Mental Health, Preventive Medicine/Wellness Organizations, Single-Disease Health Associations

International: International Affairs

Religion: Jewish Causes, Religious Welfare, Synagogues/Temples

Social Services: Camps, Child Welfare, Community Centers, Community Service Organizations, Counseling, Day Care, Delinquency & Criminal Rehabilitation, Domestic Violence, Family Services, Family Services, Food/Clothing Distribution, People with Disabilities, Recreation & Athletics, Shelters/Homelessness, Social Services-General, United Funds/United Ways, YMCA/YWCA/YMHA/YWHA, Youth Organizations

Application Procedures

Initial Contact: Contact foundation for guidelines, then letter or full proposal.

Application Requirements: For grants under $10,000: brief letter describing background of organization, amount requested and purpose of funds sought, and proof of tax-exempt status; grants of $10,000 or more must be requested using Associated Grantmakers of Massachusetts application form and Eastern Bank Donation Request form.

Deadlines: For grants $10,000 to $25,000: the 1st of May or November; for grants of less than $10,000: None.

Decision Notification: Major gifts ($10,000 to $25,000) are considered in June and December.

Restrictions

Recipients of major gifts may not reapply for funding for three years.

Does not support individuals or political or lobbying groups.

Additional Information

Foundation divides its annual giving budget, with half of contributions going to a few major gifts ($10,000 to $25,000), and half distributed broadly with smaller grants.

Publications: Annual Report

Corporate Officials

Sumner Jones: executive vice presidento PRIM CORP EMPL executive vice president: Eastern Bank.

Stanley J. Lukowski: chairman, chief executive officer PRIM CORP EMPL chairman, chief executive officer: Eastern Bank ADD CORP EMPL chairman: Eastern Bank Corp.; chairman: Eastern Bank and Trust Co. Inc.; chairman: Eastern Securities Corp. NONPR AFFIL chairman: Massachusetts Bankers Association.

Foundation Officials

Wendell J. Knox: trustee

Grants Analysis

Disclosure Period: calendar year ending 2000
Total Grants: $479,628*
Number of Grants: 224
Average Grant: $2,035*
Highest Grant: $25,900
Lowest Grant: $50
Typical Range: $100 to $6,000 and $10,000 to $25,000
*Note: Giving excludes United Way and scholarship. Average grant figure excludes highest grant.

Recent Grants

Note: Grants derived from 2000 Form 990.

Library-Related
25,000	Friends of Newburyport Library, Newburyport, MA

General
60,000	United Way of Massachusetts Bay, Boston, MA
25,900	St. Pius V School, Lynn, MA
25,000	United South End Settlements, Boston, MA
22,000	Colonel Daniel Marr Capital Youth Center, Boston, MA
15,360	Salem State College, Salem, MA
15,000	Lynn Shelter Association, Lynn, MA
12,000	South Shore Habitat for Humanity, Whitman, MA
10,000	Boys and Girls Club, Brockton, MA
10,000	Hospice of the South Shore, Braintree, MA
10,000	Melrose Family YMCA, Melrose, MA

EASTERN SAVINGS AND LOAN FOUNDATION

Giving Contact

Carol A. Cieslukowski, Secretary
Eastern Savings & Loan Foundation
257 Main Street
PO Box 709
Norwich, CT 06360-5837
Phone: (860)889-7381
Fax: (860)889-4779
Note: Phone ext. 145.

Description

Founded: 1999
EIN: 061539443
Organization Type: Corporate Foundation
Giving Locations: , CT

Financial Summary

Total Giving: $21,000 (fiscal year ending 0, 2001); $19,000 (fiscal 2000)

Assets: $394,588 (fiscal 2001); $354,729 (fiscal 2000)

Gifts Received: $10,000 (fiscal 2001). Note: In fiscal 2001, contributions were received from Eastern Savings and Loan Association.

Typical Recipients

Arts & Humanities: Libraries

Civic & Public Affairs: Community Foundations, Civic & Public Affairs-General, Women's Affairs

Health: Hospices, Hospitals

Social Services: At-Risk Youth, Community Service Organizations, Family Services, Food/Clothing Distribution

Application Procedures

Initial Contact: Contact the foundation to request a grant application form.

Deadlines: March 31.

Decision Notification: The board's funding decisions are communicated by mail in May.

Notes: Grants are distributed in June.

Restrictions

Grants must be used for a specific program, project or scholarships. Grants are not provided for general operating expenses.

Foundation Officials

Linda M. Adelman: director
Carol A. Cieslukowski: secretary
Donald A. Cipriani: president
Joseph A. Fatone: director
John R. FitzGerald: director
Richard A. Friedrich, Sr.: vice president
D. William Kelleher: director
Anthony G. Madiera: treasurer
Andre J. Messier, Jr.: director
Jerald I. Navick: director
Bernard G. Park: director
Rick L. Rarogiewicz: vice president
Peter H. Shea: director

Grants Analysis

Total Grants: $21,000
Number of Grants: 15
Average Grant: $1,400
Highest Grant: $2,500
Lowest Grant: $1,000
Typical Range: $1,000 to $2,000

Recent Grants

Note: Grants derived from fiscal 2001 Form 990.

Library-Related
2,000	Slater Library -- purchase series of 86 books "Opposing Viewpoints"

1,000	Voluntown Public Library, Voluntown, CT -- expand and re-do youth biography section of library

General

2,500	Natchaug Hospital, Mansfield Center, CT -- renovation project to provide 42,500sq ft to in-patient, out-patient, and education facilities
2,000	Bethesda Community, Inc. -- assisting in creating computer training center to train women for entering workplace
2,000	Madonna Place, Norwich, CT -- family visitation center program
2,000	Martin House, Trenton, NJ -- contributions match for adult education program
1,000	Griswold Volunteer Fire Department -- purchase thermal imaging camera
1,000	Hospice of Southeastern Connecticut, Uncasville, CT -- support of services and equipment provided to patients
1,000	Norwich Arts Council, Norwich, CT -- provide performance at Winter Festival
1,000	Norwich Social Services Safety Net Team, Norwich, CT -- assist people to become self-sufficient through various programs
1,000	Salvation Army, Norwich, CT -- provide 8 scholarships to children for Camp Connri for one week
1,000	Thames River Family Program -- to staff alumni organization

EASTMAN KODAK CO.

Company Headquarters

Rochester, NY
Web: http://www.kodak.com

Company Description

Founded: 1881
Ticker: EK
Exchange: NYSE
Revenue: US$12.835 billion (2002)
Profit: US$770 million (2002)
Employees: 70000 (2002)
Fortune Rank: 150, per FORTUNE Magazine's list of 500 Largest U.S. Corporations (2002).
SIC(s): 2843 Surface Active Agents, 2865 Cyclic Crudes & Intermediates, 3081 Unsupported Plastics Film & Sheet, 3861 Photographic Equipment & Supplies.

Operating Locations

Eastman Kodak Co. (AL--Huntsville, Mobile; AK--Anchorage; AZ--Scottsdale; AR--Little Rock; CA--Fresno, Irvine, Los Angeles, San Diego, San Francisco, San Jose, Ventura, Woodland Hills; CO--Englewood, Windsor; DC--Washington; FL--Fort Lauderdale, Miami, Orlando, Pensacola, Winter Park; GA--Atlanta, Norcross; HI--Mililani; ID--Boise; IL--Chicago, Hinsdale, Springfield; KS--Overland Park, Wichita; KY--Lexington, Louisville; LA--Lafayette, New Orleans; MD--Columbia, Severna Park; MA--Chelmsford, Wellesley Hills; MI--Bingham Farms, Bloomfield Hills, Grand Rapids, Lansing; MN--Minnetonka; MS--Jackson; MO--St. Louis; NV--Las Vegas; NJ--Princeton; NY--Albany, Amherst, Endwell, Fishkill, Latham, New York, Rome, Scottsville, Uniondale; NC--Charlotte, Greensboro, Morrisville; OH--Cincinnati, Dayton, Dublin, Hudson, Toledo; OR--Portland; PA--Camp Hill, Erie, Horsham; SC--Charleston; TN--Knoxville, Nashville; TX--Fort Worth, Houston, Irving, San Antonio; VA--Arlington, Herndon, Norfolk, Reston, Richmond; WA--Spokane; WI--Madison, Middleton, Waukesha)

Nonmonetary Support

Type: Donated Equipment; Donated Products
Volunteer Programs: Company offers "Dollars for Doers" program through which it makes small donations to nonprofit organizations where company employees serve as volunteers; supports Global Service Day; when all employees are encouraged to volunteer in their communities.
Note: Co. donates property. Nonmonetary support budget is separate from the corporate giving budget.

Eastman Kodak Charitable Trust

Giving Contact

Essie B. Calhoun, Director
343 State Street
Rochester, NY 14650-0517
Phone: (716)724-2434
Fax: (716)724-1376
Web: http://www.kodak.com/US/en/corp/community.shtml

Alternate Contact

Care of JP Morgan Chase Bank
PO Box 31412
Rochester, NY 14603
Phone: (716)258-5322

Description

EIN: 166015274
Organization Type: Corporate Foundation
Giving Locations: nationally, especially in operating locations.
Grant Types: Award, Capital, Department, Emergency, Endowment, Fellowship, General Support, Matching, Multiyear/Continuing Support, Research, Scholarship.

Donor Information

Founder: Chase Manhattan Bank, trustee

Financial Summary

Total Giving: $10,905,115 (2001); $9,919,373 (2000); $4,360,327 (1999). Note: Contributes through corporate direct giving program and foundation.
Giving Analysis: Giving for 2000 includes: foundation grants to United Way ($2,497,800); foundation ($7,421,573); 1999: foundation ($2,092,827); foundation grants to United Way ($2,267,500); 1998: foundation grants to United Way ($2,245,300); foundation ($7,713,151);
Assets: $62,916 (2001); $1,086,216 (2000); $528,193 (1999)
Gifts Received: $10,866,809 (2001); $10,146,540 (2000); $21,000,000 (1996)

Typical Recipients

Arts & Humanities: Arts Associations & Councils, Arts Funds, Dance, Arts & Humanities-General, History & Archaeology, Libraries, Museums/Galleries, Music, Performing Arts
Civic & Public Affairs: African American Affairs, Botanical Gardens/Parks, Business/Free Enterprise, Chambers of Commerce, Clubs, Community Foundations, Economic Development, Economic Policy, Employment/Job Training, Ethnic Organizations, Civic & Public Affairs-General, Housing, Minority Business, Parades/Festivals, Professional & Trade Associations, Public Policy, Safety, Urban & Community Affairs, Women's Affairs, Zoos/Aquariums
Education: Arts/Humanities Education, Business Education, Colleges & Universities, Community & Junior Colleges, Education Funds, Education Funds, Education Reform, Elementary Education (Public), Engineering/Technological Education, Education-General, Health & Physical Education, International Studies, Minority Education, Preschool Education, Private Education (Precollege), Public Education (Precollege), Religious Education, School Volunteerism, Science/Mathematics Education, Secondary Education (Private), Secondary Education (Public), Special Education, Student Aid, Vocational & Technical Education
Environment: Environment-General, Resource Conservation
Health: Adolescent Health Issues, Cancer, Clinics/Medical Centers, Emergency/Ambulance Services, Health-General, Health Organizations, Hospitals, Medical Rehabilitation, Mental Health, Nursing Services, Single-Disease Health Associations
International: Foreign Arts Organizations, Foreign Educational Institutions, International-General, Health Care/Hospitals, International Development, International Environmental Issues, International Organizations, International Relations, International Relief Efforts, Missionary/Religious Activities
Religion: Jewish Causes, Religious Welfare
Science: Science Museums, Scientific Centers & Institutes, Scientific Organizations
Social Services: Animal Protection, At-Risk Youth, Child Welfare, Community Centers, Community Service Organizations, Day Care, Emergency Relief, Family Services, Food/Clothing Distribution, Homes, People with Disabilities, Recreation & Athletics, Scouts, United Funds/United Ways, Youth Organizations

Application Procedures

Initial Contact: Send a written proposal.
Application Requirements: Cover letter should include legal name of the organization, mission statement, grant amount requested, and purpose of grant. Proposal (not to exceed five pages) should include proposal summary (one or two pages); mission of the organization; history of the organization; need for the project (in view of related work by others); project description; audience served; goals, objectives, and action plan; expected quantifiable outcomes or results; method of evaluation of proposed outcomes; other sources of support; and, if appropriate, plan for continuing the project beyond company support. Attachments should include most recent organizational financial statement and income and expense budget, list of other current and projected sources of funding, most recent Form 990, proof of tax-exempt status, and list of board members and affiliations.
Deadlines: Applications are accepted between January 1 and April 30.
Review Process: Kodak board of directors approves budget based on recommendation of company's corporate contributions council.
Evaluative Criteria: Funded programs support societal needs in communities where substantial numbers of active and potential employees live and work, and reflect global corporate goals in recruitment, technology strength, market growth, public policy, diversity, and environment.
Decision Notification: Within 45 days of receipt.

Restrictions

Kodak does not support individuals; a commitment beyond three to five years (unless a specific strategic rationale exists and the contribution is reviewed in three years); endowed chairs or university capital campaigns; event sponsorships; operating costs of organizations that receive funds from a Kodak-supported United Way; legislators, political organizations, or campaigns; or sectarian organizations whose programs are limited to members of one religious group.

Additional Information

Charitable trust generally does not solicit funding requests.

Kodak recycles more than a half billion pounds of material a year and supports a World Wildlife Fund program to increase the environmental literacy of students. Copies of Kodak's annual environmental report

are available by writing: Principles and Progress, Coordinator of Environmental Communications, Eastman Kodak Company, Rochester, NY 14650-0518.
Publications: Contributions Program Brochure

Corporate Officials

Michael P. Benard: vice president, director communications & public affairs ED John Carroll University BA; Temple University MEd. PRIM CORP EMPL vice president, director communications & public affairs: Eastman Kodak Co.

Daniel A. Carp: chairman, chief executive officer B 1948. ED Massachusetts Institute of Technology MS; Ohio University BBA; Rochester Institute Technology MBA. PRIM CORP EMPL chairman, chief executive officer, director: Eastman Kodak Co. CORP AFFIL director: Texas Instruments Inc.

Giving Program Officials

Michael P. Benard: member (see above)

Foundation Officials

Essie L. Calhoun: vice president PRIM CORP EMPL director community relations & contributions: Eastman Kodak Co.

Grants Analysis

Disclosure Period: calendar year ending 2001
Total Grants: $8,328,815*
Number of Grants: 382
Average Grant: $21,803
Highest Grant: $445,000
Lowest Grant: $300
Typical Range: $300 to $50,000 and $100,000 to $250,000
***Note:** Giving excludes scholarship, United Way.

Recent Grants

Note: Grants derived from 2001 Form 990.

General

600,000	United Way of Greater Rochester, Rochester, NY
600,000	United Way of Greater Rochester, Rochester, NY
600,000	United Way Greater Rochester, Rochester, NY
600,000	United Way Greater Rochester, Rochester, NY
445,000	World Wildlife Fund, Washington, DC
250,000	University of Rochester, Rochester, NY
200,000	Achieve, San Jose, CA
200,000	United Kingdom Committee for UNICEF United Kingdom
200,000	United Kingdom Committee for UNICEF United Kingdom
160,000	People for the American Way Foundation, Washington, DC

EATON CORP.

Company Headquarters

Eaton Center
Cleveland, OH 44114-2584
Phone: (216)523-5000
Fax: (216)523-4787
Web: http://www.eaton.com

Company Description

Founded: 1916
Ticker: ETN
Exchange: NYSE
Acquired: Aeroquip-Vickers (1999).
Revenue: US$7.209 billion (2002)
Profit: US$281 million (2002)
Employees: 48000 (2002)
Fortune Rank: 258, per FORTUNE Magazine's list of 500 Largest U.S. Corporations (2002).
SIC(s): 3452 Bolts, Nuts, Rivets & Washers, 3559 Special Industry Machinery Nec, 3561 Pumps &

Pumping Equipment, 3714 Motor Vehicle Parts & Accessories.

Operating Locations

Eaton Corp. (AL--Arab; CA--Costa Mesa, El Segundo, San Diego; CT--Bethel, Danbury; FL--Oldsmar, Sarasota; IL--Carol Stream, Rochelle; IN--Auburn, Greenfield, Hamilton, Winamac; IA--Belmond, Shenandoah, Spencer; KS--Hutchinson; MD--Elkridge; MA--Beverly; MI--Galesburg, Marshall, Rochester Hills, Saginaw, Three Rivers; MO--Eden Prairie; NE--Hastings; NY--Horseheads; NC--Asheville, Charlotte, Fayetteville, Fletcher, Kings Mountain, Laurinburg, Roxboro, Sanford, Selma; OH--Brunswick, Cleveland, Eastlake, Westerville; OK--Oklahoma City, Shawnee; PA--Beaver, Pittsburgh; SC--Greenville, Pageland, Sumter; TN--Cleveland, Shelbyville; TX--Austin, Brownsville; WA--Everett; WI--Milwaukee, Watertown, Wauwatosa)

Nonmonetary Support

Value: $19,723 (2002); $31,152 (2001)
Type: Donated Products
Volunteer Programs: Volunteer services of all types are encouraged. Volunteers support many causes including teaching reading to the illiterate, coaching little league softball, organizing school aid programs, serving food at hunger centers, building houses for the needy, and chairing United Way campaigns.
Company sponsors the James R. Stover Awards to recognize employee volunteers, and makes cash grants to organizations where employees contribute their time and talents.

Eaton Charitable Fund

Giving Contact

James L. Mason, Vice President, Public & Community Affairs
1111 Superior Avenue
Cleveland, OH 44114-2584
Phone: (216)523-4944
Fax: (216)479-7013
E-mail: jamesmason@eaton.com
Web: http://www.eaton.com/about/report.html

Description

Founded: 1953
EIN: 346501856
Organization Type: Corporate Foundation
Giving Locations: corporate operating locations.
Grant Types: Capital, Employee Matching Gifts, General Support, Project.
Note: Employee matching gift ratio: 1 to 1 to arts, and cultural institutions; American Red Cross; Salvation Army; and Habitat for Humanity. Employee matching gift ratio: 2 to 1 to accredited colleges, universities, and secondary schools. Also matches employee gifts to United Way organizations that average at least 50 percent of the employee donations in the prior year.

Financial Summary

Total Giving: $4,300,000 (2003 approx); $1,814,290 (2002); $4,937,778 (2001). Note: Contributes through corporate direct giving program and foundation.
Giving Analysis: Giving for 2001 includes: nonmonetary support ($31,152); corporate direct giving ($113,904); foundation matching gifts ($631,914); foundation grants to United Way ($1,724,855); foundation ($2,435,953); 2000: foundation matching gifts ($566,646); foundation grants to United Way ($1,799,805); foundation ($2,879,312); 1998: foundation matching gifts ($471,874); foundation grants to United Way ($1,265,595) foundation ($2,941,624)
Assets: $7,500,000 (2003 approx); $11,979,741 (2002); $5,748,748 (2001)
Gifts Received: $12,475 (2000); $10,000,000 (1998); $400,000 (1995). Note: Contributions are received from Eaton Corporation.

Typical Recipients

Arts & Humanities: Arts Associations & Councils, Arts Centers, Arts Festivals, Arts Funds, Ballet, Community Arts, Dance, Historic Preservation, Libraries, Museums/Galleries, Music, Opera, Performing Arts, Public Broadcasting, Theater, Visual Arts

Civic & Public Affairs: Business/Free Enterprise, Community Foundations, Economic Development, Economic Policy, Employment/Job Training, Civic & Public Affairs-General, Hispanic Affairs, Housing, Law & Justice, Legal Aid, Municipalities/Towns, Parades/Festivals, Professional & Trade Associations, Public Policy, Rural Affairs, Safety, Urban & Community Affairs, Zoos/Aquariums, Zoos/Aquariums

Education: Business Education, Colleges & Universities, Community & Junior Colleges, Economic Education, Education Associations, Education Funds, Education Reform, Engineering/Technological Education, Education-General, Medical Education, Minority Education, Private Education (Precollege), Public Education (Precollege), Religious Education, Science/Mathematics Education, Secondary Education (Public), Student Aid

Environment: Environment-General, Watershed

Health: Cancer, Clinics/Medical Centers, Emergency/Ambulance Services, Health Policy/Cost Containment, Health Funds, Health Organizations, Hospices, Hospitals, Hospitals (University Affiliated), Nursing Services, Public Health, Single-Disease Health Associations

International: International Organizations, International Relations

Religion: Ministries, Religious Welfare, Seminaries

Science: Science Museums, Scientific Centers & Institutes

Social Services: Child Welfare, Community Centers, Community Service Organizations, Counseling, Delinquency & Criminal Rehabilitation, Emergency Relief, Family Services, Food/Clothing Distribution, Homes, People with Disabilities, Recreation & Athletics, Scouts, Senior Services, Shelters/Homelessness, Social Services-General, United Funds/United Ways, Volunteer Services, YMCA/YWCA/YMHA/YWHA, Youth Organizations

Application Procedures

Initial Contact: Contact the company for guidelines; then submit an unbound written proposal.

Application Requirements: Proposals should consist of three components: a cover letter, program detail summary, and attachments. A one-page cover letter (on the organization's letterhead) should summarize the project, its purpose, amount requested, primary program activities, and the population that will benefit from the grant. The program detail component should be three pages or less, and must provide a written summary of the program, including specific project goals and how they relate the applicant organization's mission and to Eaton's grant guidelines; specific population that will benefit; description of what will be accomplished during the grant period; project budget; and an explanation of how the effectiveness of the project will be evaluated and communicated to Eaton and the community. The following attachments are required: the organization's history and purpose; identification of other sources of funding for the program and the amounts committed; names of Eaton employees and a description of their involvement, if applicable; recently audited financial statement and current budget; names and affiliations of officers and directors/trustees; and proof of tax-exempt status.

Deadlines: None.

Review Process: Requests should be made through local Eaton plant or human resources manager. Eaton managers submit requests to the Corporate Contributions Committee, which meets regularly to review requests; written notification of decisions is sent.

Evaluative Criteria: The evaluative process takes into account the importance of the project to Eaton Corporation employees and their families; importance to the community with significant Eaton Corporation employment; contributions from other companies similar to Eaton Corporation; participation of Eaton Corporation employees in direction of the institution; and recommendation by an Eaton manager. Projects supported are aimed at prevention rather than reaction, have clearly defined objectives, measurable results and benchmarks to evaluate progress, efficient administration, ethical fundraising methods, and adequate budgetary controls.

Notes: Grants are typically limited to one year, except in the case of capital grants. Eaton requests that proposals not be submitted in binders or with videotapes, CD-ROMs, and/or in other costly manners.

Restrictions

Grants not awarded to religious, fraternal, or labor organizations; to individuals or individual endeavors; to annual operating budgets of United Way agencies or hospitals; for endowment funds; for fundraising benefits and sponsorships; for medical research; or debt retirement.

Additional Information

Branch facilities may make grants up to $1,000 without headquarters approval.

Eaton limits funding to specific projects or programs which address their priorities or to capital campaigns which meet their criteria. The priorities are education and community improvement.

In April 1999, Eaton Corp. acquired Aeroquip-Vickers, Inc.

Publications: Contributions Guidelines

Giving Program Officials
Kristen Bihary: vice president

Foundation Officials
James L. Mason: vice president, director public affairs B Joliet, IL 1938. ED John Carroll University (1960); Case Western Reserve University (1967).

Grants Analysis
Disclosure Period: calendar year ending 2002
Total Grants: $1,814,290*
Number of Grants: 198
Average Grant: $9,163
Highest Grant: $100,000
Lowest Grant: $500
Typical Range: $1,000 to $100,000
*Note: Grants analysis provided by foundation.

Recent Grants
Note: Grants derived from 2001 Form 990.

Library-Related
25,000	Belmond Public Library, Belmond, IA

General
100,000	Case Western Reserve University, Cleveland, OH
100,000	Cleveland Clinic Foundation, Cleveland, OH
91,751	United Way Services, Cleveland, OH
75,000	Case Western Reserve University, Cleveland, OH
75,000	Cleveland Tomorrow, Cleveland, OH
70,000	Toledo Museum of Art, Toledo, OH
60,000	Toledo Symphony Orchestra, Toledo, OH
50,000	Musical Arts Association, Cleveland, OH
40,000	American Red Cross, Cleveland, OH
40,000	Belmond Community Hospital, Belmond, IA

CYRUS EATON FOUNDATION

Giving Contact
Henry W. Gulick, Treasurer & Trustee
24200 Chagrin Blvd., Suite 233
Beachwood, OH 44122-5531
Phone: (216)360-9550

Description
Founded: 1955
EIN: 237440277
Organization Type: Private Foundation
Giving Locations: OH: Cleveland
Grant Types: Endowment, General Support, Project, Seed Money.

Financial Summary
Total Giving: $178,500 (2000); $211,000 (1999); $114,700 (1995)
Assets: $4,635,846 (2000); $4,170,271 (1999); $2,809,861 (1995)

Typical Recipients
Arts & Humanities: Arts Associations & Councils, Arts Centers, Arts Festivals, Arts Institutes, Arts Outreach, Community Arts, Dance, Arts & Humanities-General, Historic Preservation, History & Archaeology, Libraries, Museums/Galleries, Music, Opera, Performing Arts, Public Broadcasting, Theater
Civic & Public Affairs: African American Affairs, Botanical Gardens/Parks, Clubs, Economic Development, Economic Policy, First Amendment Issues, Gay/Lesbian Issues, Civic & Public Affairs-General, Municipalities/Towns, Public Policy, Urban & Community Affairs
Education: Arts/Humanities Education, Colleges & Universities, Community & Junior Colleges, Education-General, International Studies, Private Education (Precollege), Student Aid
Environment: Resource Conservation
Health: AIDS/HIV, Children's Health/Hospitals, Clinics/Medical Centers, Hospices, Medical Research, Multiple Sclerosis, Single-Disease Health Associations
International: Foreign Educational Institutions, Health Care/Hospitals, International Environmental Issues, International Organizations, International Peace & Security Issues
Science: Science Museums, Scientific Centers & Institutes
Social Services: Camps, Child Welfare, Community Centers, Community Service Organizations, Domestic Violence, Family Planning, Shelters/Homelessness

Application Procedures
Initial Contact: Send a brief letter of inquiry.
Application Requirements: budget for project, financial statements, and proof of tax-exempt status.
Deadlines: October 31.

Foundation Officials
Barring Coughlin: assistant secretary, trustee B Wilkes-Barre, PA December 19, 1913. ED Princeton University BA (1935); Harvard University JD (1938). NONPR AFFIL trustee: Gun Safety Institute; member: Ohio Bar Association; member: American Law Institute; member: American Bar Association. CLUB AFFIL Union Club; Edgewater Yacht Club; Princeton Club; City Club; Adirondack League Club; Chagrin Valley Hunt Club.
Mary Stephens Eaton: vice president, trustee
Alice J. Gulick: trustee
Henry W. Gulick: president, trustee
Ralph P. Higgins: treasurer, trustee
Raymond Szabo: secretary, trustee

Grants Analysis
Disclosure Period: calendar year ending 2000
Total Grants: $178,500
Number of Grants: 39
Average Grant: $4,577
Highest Grant: $15,000
Typical Range: $1,000 to $10,000

Recent Grants
Note: Grants derived from 1999 Form 990.

Library-Related
15,000	Cleveland Public Library, Cleveland, OH

General
25,000	City Club Form Foundation, Cleveland, OH
15,000	American Academy of Arts and Sciences, Cambridge, MA
15,000	Free Medical Clinic of Greater Cleveland, Cleveland, OH
15,000	Hospice of the Western Reserve, Cleveland, OH
10,000	Eco - City Cleveland, Cleveland Heights, OH
10,000	Friends of Cleveland School of the Arts, Cleveland, OH
6,000	McMaster University, Hamilton, ON Canada
6,000	WCPN Cleveland Public Radio, Cleveland, OH
5,000	Camp Ho Mita Koda, Cleveland, OH
5,000	Cleveland Museum of Art, Cleveland, OH

EBERLY FOUNDATION

Giving Contact
Robert E. Eberly, Sr., President
PO Box 2023
Uniontown, PA 15401-1643
Phone: (724)438-3789
Web: http://www.psu.edu/

Description
Founded: 1963
EIN: 237070246
Organization Type: Private Foundation
Giving Locations: PA
Grant Types: General Support.

Financial Summary
Total Giving: $3,494,803 (2001); $18,799,868 (2000); $9,054,128 (1999)
Giving Analysis: Giving for 2000 includes: foundation matching gifts ($770,000); foundation scholarships ($2,025,000); 1999: foundation scholarships ($5,931); foundation matching gifts ($10,000) foundation grants to United Way ($100,000)
Assets: $17,694,731 (2001); $21,167,233 (2000); $34,031,053 (1999)
Gifts Received: $51,198 (1995); $16,918,780 (1994); $1,650,000 (1993). Note: In 1995, contributions were received from Greystone Productions.

Typical Recipients
Arts & Humanities: Arts Outreach, Dance, Ethnic & Folk Arts, Arts & Humanities-General, History & Archaeology, Libraries, Museums/Galleries, Music, Opera, Performing Arts, Public Broadcasting, Theater
Civic & Public Affairs: Botanical Gardens/Parks, Chambers of Commerce, Economic Development, Economic Policy, Civic & Public Affairs-General, Municipalities/Towns, Public Policy, Safety, Urban & Community Affairs
Education: Afterschool/Enrichment Programs, Business Education, Colleges & Universities, Elementary Education (Public), Faculty Development, Medical Education, Public Education (Precollege), Science/Mathematics Education
Environment: Air/Water Quality, Environment-General
Health: Children's Health/Hospitals, Clinics/Medical Centers, Emergency/Ambulance Services, Heart, Hospitals
International: International Organizations
Religion: Religious Welfare
Science: Scientific Centers & Institutes
Social Services: Camps, Community Centers, Community Service Organizations, Family Services, People with Disabilities, Recreation & Athletics, Scouts, Senior Services, United Funds/United Ways, YMCA/YWCA/YMHA/YWHA, Youth Organizations

Application Procedures

Initial Contact: Send a brief letter of inquiry.
Application Requirements: Includes purpose of funds sought, employer identification number, copy of latest Form 990, and proof of tax-exempt status.
Deadlines: August 1.

Foundation Officials

Carolyn E. Blaney: director
Ruth Ann Carter: director
Carolyn Jill Drost: director
Paul O. Eberly: director
Robert E. Eberly, Sr.: director B Greensboro, PA July 14, 1918. ED Pennsylvania State University BA (1939). PRIM CORP EMPL chairman: Eberly & Meade. CORP AFFIL chairman: Greystone Resources; director: Integra Financial Corp.; chairman: Chalk Hill Gas; chairman: Gallatin National Bank. NONPR AFFIL director: WQED/WQEX-TV; member: WV Oil Gas Association; member: Western Pennsylvania Conservancy; trustee emeritus: Uniontown Hospital Association; director: Uniontown Industry Fund; member: Pennsylvania Geological Society; member: Pennsylvania Oil Gas Association; director: Penns Southwest Association; member: OK Independent Petroleum Association; member: OK Oil Gas Association; member: Indepdendent Petroleum Association; member: Ohio Oil Gas Association; member: Greater Uniontown Chamber of Commerce; treasurer: Campaign Penn St; director: Fayette Heritage.
Robert E. Eberly, Jr.: director
Margaret E. George: director
Patricia Hillman Miller: director

Grants Analysis

Disclosure Period: calendar year ending 2000
Total Grants: $16,004,868*
Number of Grants: 140
Average Grant: $59,772*
Highest Grant: $3,000,000
Typical Range: $25,000 to $100,000
*Note: Giving excludes matching gifts, scholarships. Average grant figure excludes five highest grants ($7,931,274). ($4,250,000).

Recent Grants

Note: Grants derived from 1999 Form 990.

General

1,125,000	Pennsylvania State University, University Park, PA -- chair, professorships and scholarship
1,125,000	Pennsylvania State University, University Park, PA -- Fayette Business School
1,000,000	Pennsylvania State University, University Park, PA -- for the Virtual Hospital Hershey Medical Center
1,000,000	Pennsylvania State University, University Park, PA -- for the Virtual Hospital-Hershey Medical Center
540,000	Greater Uniontown Heritage Consortium, Uniontown, PA -- pledge
300,000	Children's Hospital of Pittsburgh, Pittsburgh, PA -- for chair in pediatric otolaryngology
250,000	California University of Pennsylvania Foundation, California, PA -- science and technology building
250,000	California University of Pennsylvania Foundation, California, PA -- science and technology building
250,000	National Park Foundation, Farmington, PA
250,000	Pennsylvania Economy League, Pittsburgh, PA -- for New Interpretive Center

EBSCO INDUSTRIES, INC.

Company Headquarters

Birmingham, AL
Web: http://www.ebsco.com

Company Description

Revenue: US$1.375 billion (2002)
Employees: 4500 (2002)
SIC(s): 2542 Partitions & Fixtures Except Wood, 2721 Periodicals, 2752 Commercial Printing--Lithographic, 2759 Commercial Printing Nec.

Operating Locations

Ebsco Industries, Inc. (IL--Belleville; MD--Bowie; MN--Long Lake; NJ--Shrewsbury; PA--Horsham, Pittsburgh; TX--Plano)

Nonmonetary Support

Type: Donated Products; Workplace Solicitation

Giving Contact

Dell Brooke, Corp. Sec.
PO Box 1943
Birmingham, AL 35201
Phone: (205)991-1197
Fax: (205)995-1517
E-mail: wdimon@ebsco.com
Web: http://www.ebsco.com

Description

Organization Type: Corporate Giving Program
Giving Locations: AL
Grant Types: General Support.

Financial Summary

Total Giving: Contributes through corporate direct giving program only.

Typical Recipients

Arts & Humanities: Arts & Humanities-General, Libraries
Civic & Public Affairs: Civic & Public Affairs-General
Education: Education-General
Health: Health-General
Social Services: Social Services-General

Application Procedures

Initial Contact: Send a breif letter of inquiry. Deadlines: 2/None.
Deadlines: None.
Notes: The company is not currently accepting proposals.

Additional Information

In 1993 the company reported that two substantial long-term commitments have put the giving program over budget for the next four years.
The directors of the giving program report that the office is overwhelmed with requests that they do not have the time to read or the funds to support. Funding to new programs or organizations has ceased.
The company gives approximately 5% of pre-tax earnings.

Corporate Officials

Elton Bryson Stephens: founder, chairman B Clio, AL August 04, 1911. ED Birmingham-Southern College BA (1932); University of Alabama Law School LLB (1936). PRIM CORP EMPL founder, chairman: Ebsco Industries, Inc. CORP AFFIL chairman: Highland Bank; chairman, secretary: Ebsco Investment Services Inc.; chairman, vice president: Franklin Square Agency Overseas Inc.; chairman: CANEBSCO Subscription Services Ltd.; trustee, founder: Ebsco Employee Savings & Profit Sharing Trust; director: RA Brown Agency Ltd.'s; trustee: AlabamaBancorp Savings & Profit Sharing Trust; chairman: Bennett-Ebsco Subscription Services; chairman, founder: AlabamaBancorp. NONPR AFFIL chairman: TN-Tombigbee Waterway Authority Economic Pension Comm; member, don: Un Arts Fund/Metropolitan Arts Council; member: Phi Alpha Delta; chairman: Birmingham-Southern College Executive Comm; member: Omicron Delta Kappa; trustee: Birmingham Metropolitan YMCA; member: Alpha Tau Omega; director: Birmingham Chamber of Commerce. CLUB AFFIL Shades Valley Rotary Club; Summit Club; Mountain Brook Country Club; Birmingham Press Club; The Club.
James T. Stephens: president, director B 1939. ED Yale University BA (1961); Harvard University MBA (1964). PRIM CORP EMPL president, director: Ebsco Industries, Inc. CORP AFFIL president: Plastic Research & Development Corp.

Giving Program Officials

Elton Bryson Stephens: (see above)

WILLARD L. ECCLES CHARITABLE FOUNDATION

Giving Contact

Clark P. Giles
PO Box 628
Salt Lake City, UT 84110
Phone: (801)463-9580

Description

Founded: 1981
EIN: 942759395
Organization Type: Family Foundation
Giving Locations: UT: primarily Salt Lake City and Ogden
Grant Types: Capital, Challenge, Fellowship, General Support, Multiyear/Continuing Support, Project, Research.

Donor Information

Founder: The Willard L. Eccles Charitable Foundation was established in 1981 in Utah.

Financial Summary

Total Giving: $2,460,026 (fiscal year ending March 31, 2000); $2,108,172 (fiscal 1999); $1,919,676 (fiscal 1998)
Giving Analysis: Giving for fiscal 2000 includes: foundation grants to United Way ($5,000) fiscal 1999: foundation grants to United Way ($5,000)
Assets: $60,125,647 (fiscal 2000); $50,508,309 (fiscal 1999); $46,240,631 (fiscal 1998)
Gifts Received: $1,381 (fiscal 1997); $54,854 (fiscal 1995); $8,006 (fiscal 1992)

Typical Recipients

Arts & Humanities: Arts Centers, Arts Funds, Ballet, Libraries, Museums/Galleries, Opera, Performing Arts, Public Broadcasting, Theater
Civic & Public Affairs: Clubs, Community Foundations, Municipalities/Towns, Safety, Zoos/Aquariums
Education: Colleges & Universities, Environmental Education, Education-General, Medical Education, Private Education (Precollege), Public Education (Precollege), School Volunteerism, Science/Mathematics Education, Secondary Education (Public), Special Education
Environment: Environment-General, Resource Conservation, Wildlife Protection
Health: AIDS/HIV, Alzheimers Disease, Cancer, Children's Health/Hospitals, Clinics/Medical Centers, Emergency/Ambulance Services, Eyes/Blindness,

Eyes/Blindness, Health-General, Health Organizations, Hospices, Hospitals, Medical Research, Medical Training, Mental Health, Multiple Sclerosis, Nursing Services, Prenatal Health Issues, Preventive Medicine/Wellness Organizations, Public Health, Respiratory, Single-Disease Health Associations
Religion: Religious Organizations, Religious Welfare
Science: Science Museums, Scientific Research
Social Services: Animal Protection, Big Brother/Big Sister, Camps, Community Centers, Community Service Organizations, Domestic Violence, Family Planning, Food/Clothing Distribution, People with Disabilities, Scouts, Senior Services, Shelters/Homelessness, United Funds/United Ways, YMCA/YWCA/YMHA/YWHA, Youth Organizations

Application Procedures

Initial Contact: Applicants should submit a brief letter or proposal, no specific form is required.
Application Requirements: Requests for grants should specifically describe the purpose of the grant and the proposed use of the funds and the benefits to be derived by the public from the grant. If the requesting organization has not previously submitted a request, background information with respect to the organization and evidence of tax-exempt status should be included. Where practicable, eight copies should be submitted.
Deadlines: Requests may be submitted at any time, but the deadline for consideration at the subsequent meetings of the Advisory Committee are February 1, June 1, and September 1.
Review Process: Proposals are reviewed at the next committee meeting.

Restrictions

The foundation does not support individuals, only exempt charitable organizations; grants for land acquisition, construction or building purposes, or endowments are lim ited to special circumstances.

Foundation Officials

Barbara E. Coit: committee member
Susan E. Coit: committee member
William E. Coit: committee member
Julie Denkers: committee member
Stephen G. Denkers: committee member
Susan E. Denkers: committee member
Clark P. Giles: committee member B 1937. PRIM CORP EMPL president: Ray, Quinney & Nebeker PC.

Grants Analysis

Disclosure Period: fiscal year ending March 31, 2000
Total Grants: $2,455,026*
Number of Grants: 86
Average Grant: $28,547
Highest Grant: $250,000
Typical Range: $1,000 to $100,000
*Note: Giving excludes United Way.

Recent Grants

Note: Grants derived from 2000 Form 990.

Library-Related
200,000	Provo City Library, Provo, UT

General
250,000	Nature Conservancy of Idaho, Sun Valley, ID
200,000	Nature Conservancy of Oregon, Portland, OR
200,000	Nature Conservancy of Utah, Salt Lake City, UT
200,000	University of Utah, Salt Lake City, UT
150,000	Friends of the Bear River Refuge, Logan, UT
100,000	Utah State University, Logan, UT
92,964	Utah State University, Logan, UT
69,274	University of Utah, Salt Lake City, UT
50,200	University of Utah, Salt Lake City, UT
50,000	Nature Conservancy of Oregon, Portland, OR

GEORGE S. AND DOLORES DORE ECCLES FOUNDATION

Giving Contact

Lisa Eccles, Executive Director
Deseret Building
79 South Main Street, 12th Floor
Salt Lake City, UT 84111
Phone: (801)246-5336
Fax: (801)350-3510

Description

Founded: 1958
EIN: 876118245
Organization Type: General Purpose Foundation
Giving Locations: UT: preference for Intermountain area of United States.
Grant Types: Challenge, Department, Fellowship, General Support, Multiyear/Continuing Support, Operating Expenses, Project, Scholarship.

Donor Information

Founder: Established in 1958 by George Stoddard Eccles and Dolores Dore 'Lolie' Eccles. George and Dolores Eccles met as undergraduates at Columbia University in New York City, married in 1925, and "became partners in a lifelong adventure -- a spirited trek through banking, international business and civic reponsibilities."
Throughout his respected business career, George Eccles sat on the boards of many corporations including Texas Gulf Sulfur Co., Amalgamated Sugar, Utah Construction, Union Pacific, and Husky Oil. He was also an original board member for the Salt Lake City-based First Security Corporation. George Eccles died on January 20, 1982, and his estate continues to fund the foundation.
Dolores Dore Eccles is known for her dedication to charities. Besides having served on the boards of several nonprofits including Ballet West and Westminster College, she also founded the Ogden Junior League. Dolores Dore Eccles continues to attend every meeting of the foundation's directors.
In 1981, the foundation absorbed the Lillian Ethel Dufton Charitable Trust.

Financial Summary

Total Giving: $6,796,000 (2003 approx); $9,819,334 (2002); $20,621,709 (2001)
Giving Analysis: Giving for 1998 includes: foundation matching gifts ($15,000) foundation grants to United Way ($100,000)
Assets: $703,246,088 (2000); $644,540,875 (1998); $578,634,739 (1997)
Gifts Received: $50,000,000 (1995 approx); $749,700 (1994). Note: The foundation receives contributions from the estate of George S. Eccles.

Typical Recipients

Arts & Humanities: Arts Associations & Councils, Arts Centers, Arts Festivals, Arts Outreach, Ballet, Community Arts, Dance, Arts & Humanities-General, Historic Preservation, History & Archaeology, Libraries, Literary Arts, Museums/Galleries, Music, Opera, Performing Arts, Public Broadcasting, Theater
Civic & Public Affairs: Botanical Gardens/Parks, Chambers of Commerce, Clubs, Community Foundations, Economic Development, Economic Policy, Civic & Public Affairs-General, Housing, Legal Aid, Municipalities/Towns, Parades/Festivals, Urban & Community Affairs, Zoos/Aquariums
Education: Arts/Humanities Education, Business Education, Colleges & Universities, Colleges & Universities, Community & Junior Colleges, Education Associations, Education Reform, Elementary Education

(Public), Education-General, Health & Physical Education, International Studies, Leadership Training, Legal Education, Medical Education, Minority Education, Preschool Education, Private Education (Precollege), Public Education (Precollege), Science/Mathematics Education, Secondary Education (Public), Student Aid, Vocational & Technical Education
Environment: Air/Water Quality, Environment-General, Resource Conservation
Health: Arthritis, Clinics/Medical Centers, Eyes/Blindness, Health Organizations, Hospices, Hospitals, Medical Research, Mental Health, Nursing Services, Outpatient Health Care, Preventive Medicine/Wellness Organizations, Public Health, Research/Studies Institutes, Single-Disease Health Associations, Speech & Hearing
Religion: Churches, Religious Organizations, Religious Welfare, Synagogues/Temples
Science: Science-General, Science Museums, Scientific Centers & Institutes
Social Services: At-Risk Youth, Camps, Child Welfare, Community Centers, Community Service Organizations, Counseling, Domestic Violence, Family Services, Homes, People with Disabilities, Recreation & Athletics, Scouts, Senior Services, Shelters/Homelessness, United Funds/United Ways, YMCA/YWCA/YMHA/YWHA, Youth Organizations

Application Procedures

Initial Contact: Prospective applicants should request an application form from the foundation.
Application Requirements: Organizations should complete the application form and send one additional copy to the foundation; attachments should include proof of tax-exempt status, financial statement and most recent operating budget, list of board of directors, and any additional information.
Deadlines: None. Proposals should reach the foundation four weeks prior to quarterly meetings.
Review Process: The board meets quarterly to set policies, review proposals, and make final decisions on awarding grants.
Notes: The foundation only accepts requests from organizations exempt by 501(c)(3) status under the Internal Revenue Code.

Restrictions

The foundation does not make grants to individuals, or for loans or endowment funds. Also not funded are operating costs, conduit organizations such as united funds, conferences and seminars, or governmental or quasi-governmental entities other than colleges and universities.
The foundation primarily funds organizations in Utah.

Additional Information

In addition to reviewing proposals submitted by qualified organizations and institutions, the foundation will seek out grant opportunities on its own initiative as funds permit and as the purposes of the foundation are seen as being served by such initiatives.
Publications: Application Form

Foundation Officials

Lisa Eccles: executive assistant to chairman
Spencer Fox Eccles: president, director B Ogden, UT 1934. ED University of Utah BS (1956); Columbia University MA (1959). PRIM CORP EMPL chairman, chief executive officer, director, president: First Security Corp. CORP AFFIL director: Zions Corp. Mercantile; director: Zions Corp.; director: First Security Insurance Inc.; director: Union Pacific Corp.; director: Anderson Lumber Co. NONPR AFFIL director: Merc Institute; member advisory council: University Utah Business College; member: Bankers Roundtable; member: American Bankers Association. CLUB AFFIL mem: Alta Club; mem: Salt Lake Country Club.
David Pierpont Gardner: chairman, director B Berkeley, CA 1933. ED Brigham Young University BS (1955); University of California at Berkeley MA (1959);

University of California at Berkeley PhD (1966). CORP AFFIL director: First Security Corp.; director: Fluor Corp. NONPR AFFIL fellow: American Academy of Arts & Sciences; member: American Philosophical Society.

Robert M. Graham: treasurer

Alonzo Wallace Watson, Jr.: secretary, director B Salt Lake City, UT 1922. ED University of Utah AB (1943); Georgetown University BSFS (1947); University of Utah JD (1951). PRIM CORP EMPL chairman, director: Ray, Quinney & Nebeker.

Grants Analysis

Disclosure Period: calendar year ending 2000
Total Grants: $30,496,586*
Number of Grants: 334
Average Grant: $73,343*
Highest Grant: $5,000,000
Lowest Grant: $1,000
Typical Range: $1,200 to $50,000 and $56,000 to $500,000
*Note: Giving excludes United Way; matching gifts; average grant excludes two highest grants ($1,000,000 and $5,000,000).

Recent Grants

Note: Grants derived from 2000 Form 990.

General

5,000,000	University of Utah, Salt Lake City, UT -- renovate and restore Commander's House and renovate and restore Officer's Club at historic Fort Douglas
1,500,000	Nature Conservancy of Utah, Salt Lake City, UT -- support Utah Second Century campaign
1,350,000	Utah State University, Logan, UT -- to build the Eccles Science Learning Center
1,000,000	University of Utah, Salt Lake City, UT -- construction of a new wing to Museum of Fine Arts
750,000	Alf Engen Ski Museum Foundation, Salt Lake City, UT -- construct the Joe Quinney Winter Sports Center
600,000	Utah Symphony, Salt Lake City, UT -- support for 1999-2000 season
503,214	University of Utah, Salt Lake City, UT -- payment for design and construction of University Penrose Drive property
502,385	This is The Place Foundation, Salt Lake City, UT -- to make improvements to Heritage Park
500,000	Artspace, Salt Lake City, UT -- support the ArtSpace Bridge projects
500,000	Calvary Baptist Church, Salt Lake City, UT -- assist in construction of the education and recreation portion of the new Calvary Baptist Church complex

MARRINER S. ECCLES FOUNDATION

Giving Contact

Shannon K. Toronto, Executive Director
P. O. Box 628
Salt Lake City, UT 84110-0628
Phone: (801)246-1436

Description

Founded: 1973
EIN: 237185855
Organization Type: General Purpose Foundation
Giving Locations: UT
Grant Types: General Support, Matching, Operating Expenses, Professorship, Project, Research, Scholarship.

Donor Information

Founder: The foundation was established in 1979. Marriner Eccles (1890-1977) was the son of banker David Eccles, a co-founder of Utah Construction, which built railroads, bridges, and the Grand Coulee and Hoover Dams. The company, which became Utah International, also had extensive coal and copper mining interests. Marriner S. Eccles was chairman of the company until 1971. Mr. Eccles was Federal Reserve chairman for fourteen years, and proposed many of the New Deal economic reforms, including the minimum wage and federal bank-deposit insurance. His widow, Sara M. Eccles, was the foundation's chairman.

Financial Summary

Total Giving: $2,172,334 (fiscal year ending March 31, 2001); $1,690,467 (fiscal 1999); $1,700,000 (fiscal 1998 approx)
Giving Analysis: Giving for fiscal 2001 includes: foundation grants to United Way ($37,500) fiscal 1999: foundation grants to United Way ($10,000)
Assets: $36,488,522 (fiscal 2001); $38,263,585 (fiscal 1999); $37,000,000 (fiscal 1998 approx)
Gifts Received: $123,635 (fiscal 2001); $7,843 (fiscal 1997); $78,944 (fiscal 1995). Note: Contributions were received from the estate of Marriner Eccles.

Typical Recipients

Arts & Humanities: Arts Associations & Councils, Arts Centers, Arts Festivals, Ballet, Community Arts, Dance, Libraries, Museums/Galleries, Music, Opera, Performing Arts, Public Broadcasting, Theater
Civic & Public Affairs: Botanical Gardens/Parks, Community Foundations, Economic Development, Employment/Job Training, Civic & Public Affairs-General, Housing, Law & Justice, Legal Aid, Native American Affairs, Nonprofit Management, Rural Affairs, Urban & Community Affairs, Zoos/Aquariums
Education: Arts/Humanities Education, Business Education, Colleges & Universities, Community & Junior Colleges, Medical Education, Private Education (Precollege)
Environment: Environment-General
Health: AIDS/HIV, Arthritis, Cancer, Children's Health/Hospitals, Clinics/Medical Centers, Diabetes, Emergency/Ambulance Services, Eyes/Blindness, Health-General, Geriatric Health, Health Organizations, Hospices, Hospitals, Mental Health, Nursing Services, Public Health, Respiratory, Single-Disease Health Associations
International: Foreign Arts Organizations
Religion: Churches, Religious Organizations, Religious Welfare
Social Services: Camps, Child Welfare, Community Centers, Community Service Organizations, Counseling, Day Care, Family Planning, Family Services, Food/Clothing Distribution, Homes, People with Disabilities, Recreation & Athletics, Senior Services, Shelters/Homelessness, Social Services-General, Special Olympics, Substance Abuse, YMCA/YWCA/YMHA/YWHA, Youth Organizations

Application Procedures

Initial Contact: Call or write for application form.
Application Requirements: Application must include an IRS form 501 (c)(3), an outline of the Organization, statement of request, and description of project and determination.
Deadlines: April 15.
Review Process: The foundation's board meets approximately four times a year.

Restrictions

Capital grants are made for equipment acquisition but not for bricks-and-mortar projects. Grants are strictly limited to organizations located within the state of Utah. Grants are not made to individuals.

Additional Information

First Security Bank of Utah, N.A. serves as a corporate trustee for the foundation.
Publications: Application Form; Application Guidelines

Foundation Officials

C. Hope Eccles: committee member
Spencer Fox Eccles: committee member B Ogden, UT 1934. ED University of Utah BS (1956); Columbia University MA (1959). PRIM CORP EMPL chairman, chief executive officer, director, president: First Security Corp. CORP AFFIL director: Zions Corp. Mercantile Institute; director: Zions Corp.; director: First Security Insurance Inc.; director: Union Pacific Corp.; director: Anderson Lumber Co. NONPR AFFIL director: Merc Institute; member advisory council: University Utah Business College; member: Bankers Roundtable; member: American Bankers Association. CLUB AFFIL mem: Alta Club; mem: Salt Lake Country Club.
James M. Steele: committee member
Shannon K. Toronto: executive director
Elmer D. Tucker: comm mem
Alonzo Wallace Watson, Jr.: committee member B Salt Lake City, UT 1922. ED University of Utah AB (1943); Georgetown University BSFS (1947); University of Utah JD (1951). PRIM CORP EMPL chairman, director: Ray, Quinney & Nebeker.

Grants Analysis

Disclosure Period: fiscal year ending March 31, 2001
Total Grants: $2,134,834*
Number of Grants: 123
Average Grant: $17,356*
Highest Grant: $183,000
Lowest Grant: $2,000
Typical Range: $10,000 to $35,000
*Note: Giving excludes United Way.

Recent Grants

Note: Grants derived from 2002 Form 990.

General

183,000	University of Utah Health Science, Salt Lake City, UT
110,000	University of Utah, Salt Lake City, UT
58,500	Boys and Girls Club of Salt Lake, Salt Lake City, UT
50,000	University of Utah, Salt Lake City, UT
50,000	Utah Symphony, Salt Lake City, UT
50,000	Wasatch Homeless Health Care, Salt Lake City, UT
50,000	Westminster College, Salt Lake City, UT
45,000	Planned Parenthood Association, Salt Lake City, UT
45,000	University of Utah, Salt Lake City, UT
45,000	Utah Opera, Salt Lake City, UT

RALPH M. AND ELLA M. ECCLES FOUNDATION

Giving Contact

Emily Eisenman, Trust Officer
c/o National City Bank of Pennsylvania
20 Stanwix St.
Pittsburgh, PA 15222
Phone: (216)222-3668

Description

Founded: 1972
EIN: 237261807
Organization Type: Private Foundation

Giving Locations: PA: limited to Union School District of Clarion County
Grant Types: Capital, Emergency, General Support, Multiyear/Continuing Support, Operating Expenses.

Financial Summary

Total Giving: $272,779 (2000); $137,003 (1999); $184,234 (1998)
Assets: $4,643,329 (2000); $4,925,821 (1999); $4,438,706 (1998)

Typical Recipients

Arts & Humanities: Libraries
Civic & Public Affairs: Economic Development, Municipalities/Towns, Safety
Education: Colleges & Universities, Education Funds, Environmental Education, Public Education (Precollege), School Volunteerism
Health: Clinics/Medical Centers, Hospitals, Prenatal Health Issues
Religion: Churches, Religious Welfare
Social Services: Community Service Organizations, Recreation & Athletics, Youth Organizations

Application Procedures

Initial Contact: Send a brief letter of inquiry.
Application Requirements: Include purpose of funds sought and proof of tax-exempt status.
Deadlines: None.

Restrictions

Foundation contributes to organizations serving Clarion County.

Additional Information

Trust(s): Natl City Bank PA

Grants Analysis

Disclosure Period: calendar year ending 2000
Total Grants: $272,779
Number of Grants: 5
Highest Grant: $192,000

Recent Grants

Note: Grants derived from 1999 Form 990.

Library-Related

117,778	Eccles Lesher Memorial Library, Rimersburg, PA

General

19,070	Rimersburg Medical Center, Rimersburg, PA
155	Union High School, Rimersburg, PA

ECG FOUNDATION

Giving Contact

Amber Carden, Trust Officer
c/o Bank of America
PO Box 908
Austin, TX 78781
Phone: (512)397-2717

Description

Founded: 1986
EIN: 742418070
Organization Type: Private Foundation
Giving Locations: TX: nationally.
Grant Types: General Support.

Donor Information

Founder: Ellen Clayton Garwood

Financial Summary

Total Giving: $185,742 (fiscal year ending April 30, 2001); $160,547 (fiscal 2000); $111,250 (fiscal 1998)
Giving Analysis: Giving for fiscal 2001 includes: foundation grants to United Way ($5,000)
Assets: $3,557,200 (fiscal 2001); $4,249,603 (fiscal 2000); $3,429,356 (fiscal 1998)

Typical Recipients

Arts & Humanities: Arts Associations & Councils, Film & Video, Historic Preservation, Libraries, Literary Arts, Museums/Galleries, Music, Performing Arts, Public Broadcasting, Theater
Civic & Public Affairs: Civil Rights, Civic & Public Affairs-General, Hispanic Affairs, Legal Aid, Public Policy, Urban & Community Affairs, Women's Affairs
Education: Colleges & Universities, Education-General, International Studies, Private Education (Precollege), Secondary Education (Public), Social Sciences Education, Vocational & Technical Education
Health: Cancer, Children's Health/Hospitals, Clinics/Medical Centers, Heart, Hospitals
International: International Peace & Security Issues, International Relations
Religion: Religious Organizations, Religious Welfare
Social Services: Camps, Child Welfare, Community Service Organizations, Counseling, Domestic Violence, Family Services, Recreation & Athletics, United Funds/United Ways, Youth Organizations

Application Procedures

Initial Contact: Request application form.
Deadlines: None.

Restrictions

Limited to organizations with section 501(c)(3) IRS code status.

Additional Information

Publications: Application Form
Trust(s): Bank of America

Foundation Officials

Mary Margaret Farabee: director
William L. Garwood, Jr.: vice president, secretary, director
Lew Little: treasurer, director
Howard Yancy: president, director
Mary Garwood Yancy: president, director

Grants Analysis

Disclosure Period: fiscal year ending April 30, 2001
Total Grants: $180,742*
Number of Grants: 17
Average Grant: $6,449*
Highest Grant: $54,000
Lowest Grant: $2,000
Typical Range: $1,000 to $10,000
*Note: Giving excludes United Way. Average grant figure excludes two highest grants ($84,000).

Recent Grants

Note: Grants derived from fiscal 2000 Form 990.

Library-Related

5,000	Austin Public Library, Austin, TX

General

35,000	Caritas, Austin, TX
34,000	St. Andrew's Episcopal School, Austin, TX
18,000	People's Community Clinic, Austin, TX
12,500	West Austin Youth Association, Austin, TX
10,000	Any Baby Can of Austin, Austin, TX
10,000	St. Edward's University, Austin, TX
5,000	Austin Film Festival, Austin, TX
5,000	LifeWorks, Austin, TX
5,000	Safeplace, Austin, TX
5,000	Seton Fund, Austin, TX

SAMUEL AND RAE ECKMAN CHARITABLE FOUNDATION

Giving Contact

Stephen F. Selig, President & Director
c/o Baer, Marks & Upham
805 3rd Avenue
New York, NY 10022
Phone: (212)702-5700

Description

Founded: 1970
EIN: 237051411
Organization Type: Private Foundation
Giving Locations: NY: primarily New York City
Grant Types: General Support, Research.

Donor Information

Founder: the late Rae Eckman, the late Samuel Eckman

Financial Summary

Total Giving: $251,500 (2000); $219,000 (1999); $232,000 (1998)
Assets: $2,812,960 (2000); $2,964,755 (1999); $2,552,688 (1998)

Typical Recipients

Arts & Humanities: Arts Centers, Ballet, Dance, Arts & Humanities-General, Libraries, Museums/Galleries, Music, Opera, Performing Arts, Theater
Civic & Public Affairs: Botanical Gardens/Parks, Economic Policy, Gay/Lesbian Issues, Civic & Public Affairs-General, Municipalities/Towns, Safety, Urban & Community Affairs
Education: Colleges & Universities, Legal Education
Environment: Air/Water Quality
Health: AIDS/HIV, Cancer, Clinics/Medical Centers, Emergency/Ambulance Services, Hospitals, Medical Research, Public Health, Single-Disease Health Associations
International: Missionary/Religious Activities
Religion: Jewish Causes, Ministries, Religious Organizations, Synagogues/Temples
Social Services: Community Service Organizations, People with Disabilities, Senior Services, YMCA/YWCA/YMHA/YWHA

Application Procedures

Initial Contact: Send a brief letter of inquiry. Include a description of organization, amount requested, purpose of funds sought, recently audited financial statement, and proof of tax-exempt status.
Deadlines: None.

Restrictions

Grants are awarded for medical research, assistance to and support for aged persons, and education of indigent or underprivileged children.

Foundation Officials

Abraham Jacob Briloff: assistant secretary, assistant treasurer B New York, NY July 19, 1917. ED City College of New York BBA (1937); City College of New York MS (1941); New York University PhD (1965). PRIM CORP EMPL partner: AJ & LA Briloff PRIM NONPR EMPL professor emeritus: City University of New York, Baruch College. NONPR AFFIL member: New York Saint Society Certified Public Accountants; member: New York State Society of CPA's; member: American Institute of CPA's.
Arthur Murphy: director
William Benjamin Norden, Esq.: secretary, treasurer, director B Brooklyn, NY 1945. ED Brooklyn College BS (1967); New York University JD (1969). PRIM CORP EMPL partner: Baer Marks & Upham.
Stephen F. Selig, Esq.: president, director

Grants Analysis

Disclosure Period: calendar year ending 2000
Total Grants: $251,500
Number of Grants: 30
Average Grant: $8,383
Highest Grant: $20,000
Lowest Grant: $2,500
Typical Range: $2,500 to $15,000

Recent Grants

Note: Grants derived from 1998 Form 990.

General

20,000	American Foundation for AIDS Research, New York, NY
15,000	Metropolitan Museum, New York, NY
15,000	Metropolitan Opera Association, New York, NY
12,500	Jewish Guild for the Blind, New York, NY
10,000	Calvary Fund, Bronx, NY
10,000	Cancer Care
10,000	Friends New York Fire Department Collection
10,000	Jewish Board of Family and Children's Services, New York, NY
10,000	New York City Ballet, New York, NY
10,000	Philharmonic Society, Hazleton, PA

ECOLAB, INC.

Company Headquarters

370 N. Wabasha St.
St. Paul, MN 55102
Web: http://www.ecolab.com

Company Description

Founded: 1923
Ticker: ECL
Exchange: NYSE
Revenue: US$3.403 billion (2002)
Profit: US$209.8 million (2002)
Employees: 204400 (2002)
Fortune Rank: 457, per FORTUNE Magazine's list of 500 Largest U.S. Corporations (2002).
SIC(s): 2841 Soap & Other Detergents, 2879 Agricultural Chemicals Nec, 2899 Chemical Preparations Nec, 7342 Disinfecting & Pest Control Services.

Operating Locations

Ecolab (MN--St. Paul); Ecolab Inc. (AL--Birmingham, Mobile; CA--Carlsbad, Roseville, San Jose, Simi Valley, Tulare; CO--Denver; CT--Tolland; DC--Washington; FL--Altamonte Springs, Fort Myers, Tampa; GA--McDonough; HI--Honolulu; IL--Glen Ellyn, Joliet, Lombard, Peoria; IN--Granger, Huntington, Indianapolis; IA--West Des Moines; KS--Lenexa; LA--Shreveport, St. Rose; ME--Brewer; MD--Gaithersburg, Ocean City; MA--Norwood, Wilmington; MI--Farmington Hills, Traverse City; MN--Eagan, Mendota Heights, Minnetonka; MO--Kansas City, Springfield; NE--Omaha; NV--North Las Vegas, Reno; NH--Amherst, Lebanon; NM--Albuquerque; NY--East Syracuse, New Hyde Park, New York, Rochester; NC--Burlington, Charlotte, Winston-Salem; OH--Cleveland, Hebron, Pickerington; OK--Oklahoma City, Tulsa; PA--Allentown, Erie, Harrisburg, Lancaster, Plumsteadville; PR--Dorado; SC--Columbia, North Charleston; TN--Brentwood, Knoxville, Memphis, Murfreesboro; TX--Garland, Grand Prairie, Houston; UT--Midvale; VA--Roanoke, Virginia Beach; WA--Gig Harbor, Renton; WI--Janesville, Milwaukee, Sun Prairie)

Nonmonetary Support

Type: In-kind Services
Note: In-kind services are offered in times of disasters.

Volunteer Programs: Employees volunteer as classroom speakers and with Business/Education Partnership. Company also provides technical assistance and coordinates volunteer projects for two weekends of the United Way's Week of Caring, Volunteer Fair, and provides contributions to nonprofit organizations to reward employee volunteers.
Contact: James Dietz, Distribution
Note: Foundation provides nonmonetary support.

Ecolab Foundation

Giving Contact

Lois J. West Duffy, Director, Community & Public Relations
Ecolab Inc.
370 North Wabasha Street N.
St. Paul, MN 55102
Phone: (651)293-2658
Fax: (651)225-3123
Web: http://www.ecolab.com/companyprofile/foundation/default.asp

Alternate Contact

Phone: (651)293-2259

Description

EIN: 411372157
Organization Type: Corporate Foundation
Giving Locations: MN: St. Paul areas where company has a major presence, and large numbers of employees live and work.
Grant Types: General Support.

Financial Summary

Total Giving: $2,723,000 (2002 approx); $3,034,923 (2001); $2,156,822 (2000). Note: Contributes through corporate direct giving program and foundation.
Giving Analysis: Giving for 2000 includes: foundation ($2,600,000); 1998: foundation grants to United Way ($194,008); foundation ($1,624,510); 1997: foundation scholarships ($26,822); foundation grants to United Way ($221,941) foundation ($1,454,870)
Assets: $5,485,860 (2001); $5,236,442 (2000); $4,894,063 (1998).
Gifts Received: $3,402,584 (2001); $2,359,000 (2000); $2,020,000 (1998). Note: In 2000 and 2001, contributions were received from Ecolab Inc. In 1998, contributions were received from the Ida C. Koran Trust.

Typical Recipients

Arts & Humanities: Arts Associations & Councils, Arts Funds, Arts Outreach, Arts & Humanities-General, History & Archaeology, Libraries, Museums/Galleries, Music, Opera, Performing Arts, Public Broadcasting, Theater
Civic & Public Affairs: African American Affairs, Business/Free Enterprise, Economic Development, Employment/Job Training, Ethnic Organizations, Civic & Public Affairs-General, Hispanic Affairs, Housing, Law & Justice, Municipalities/Towns, Nonprofit Management, Parades/Festivals, Professional & Trade Associations, Urban & Community Affairs, Women's Affairs, Zoos/Aquariums
Education: Business Education, Business-School Partnerships, Colleges & Universities, Continuing Education, Economic Education, Education Associations, Education Funds, Education Reform, Elementary Education (Public), Environmental Education, Faculty Development, Education-General, International Exchange, Minority Education, Public Education (Precollege), School Volunteerism, Science/Mathematics Education, Secondary Education (Public), Special Education, Student Aid
Environment: Environment-General, Resource Conservation
Health: AIDS/HIV, Cancer, Children's Health/Hospitals, Clinics/Medical Centers, Emergency/Ambulance

Services, Hospitals, Long-Term Care, Medical Rehabilitation, Nutrition, Public Health, Speech & Hearing
International: Foreign Arts Organizations, International Environmental Issues
Religion: Churches, Religion-General, Jewish Causes, Religious Welfare
Science: Science Museums, Science Museums
Social Services: Animal Protection, At-Risk Youth, Big Brother/Big Sister, Child Welfare, Community Service Organizations, Day Care, Delinquency & Criminal Rehabilitation, Emergency Relief, Family Planning, Family Services, Food/Clothing Distribution, People with Disabilities, Scouts, Senior Services, Shelters/Homelessness, Social Services-General, Substance Abuse, United Funds/United Ways, Volunteer Services, YMCA/YWCA/YMHA/YWHA, Youth Organizations

Application Procedures

Initial Contact: Submit a one-page letter describing the program and how it fits within the foundation's guidelines.
Application Requirements: Full proposals to the foundation should be made using the Minnesota Common Grant Application Form, and must include proof of tax-exempt status.
Deadlines: August 31.
Review Process: The foundation will respond to initial proposals within 2-4 weeks with a postcard indicating whether or not a complete proposal is requested.
Evaluative Criteria: Priority given to programs in company operating areas that leverage corporate dollars with volunteer time and technical expertise; encourage self-sufficiency among disadvantaged groups in the community; encompass creative programs that are not duplicated through existing community organizations and resources; involve a significant number of employees; and have a direct impact on the end user.
Decision Notification: Most funding decisions are made in late fall for the following year, and grantees are notified after January 15.

Restrictions

Grants are made for general operations and specific projects. The company does not award grants for individuals; fundraisers or advertisements; religious organizations for sectarian or denominational programs; disease-specific organizations; sports or athletic programs; industry, trade, political, professional, or business associations; or loans or investments.

Additional Information

Company sponsors an Employee Volunteer Bonus Program (to provide grants to nonprofits in recognition of significant employee volunteer commitments), a Community Involvement Program (to recognize employees who serve on the boards of nonprofits), and a matching gifts program.
The company allocates 1% of pretax U.S. profits to charitable contributions each year.
Ecolab is a U.S. affiliate of Henkel KGAA, which has a 25% investment in the company. Other U.S. affiliates are Loctite Corp. (29%) and Clorox Co. (28%).
Publications: Annual Giving Report; Application Guidelines

Corporate Officials

Douglas Baker, Jr.: president, chief operating officer
Lawrence T. Bell: vice president law, general counsel B 1947. PRIM CORP EMPL vice president law, general counsel: Ecolab Inc.
Bruno Deschamps: president, chief operating officer PRIM CORP EMPL president, chief operating officer: Ecolab Inc.
John G. Forsythe: vice president tax and public affairs B Chicago, IL 1947. ED Loyola University (1969); Northwestern University (1973). PRIM CORP EMPL vice president tax and public affairs: Ecolab Inc. NONPR AFFIL chairman: Chemical Specialties Manufacturing Association.

Steven L. Fritze: vice president, controller B Saint Paul, MN 1954. ED University of Minnesota (1975); University of Minnesota (1977). PRIM CORP EMPL vice president, chief financial officer: Ecolab Inc. NONPR AFFIL member: Financial Executives Institute.

Kenneth A. Iverson: vice president, corporate secretary B 1945. ED College of Saint Thomas BA (1967); University of Notre Dame JD (1970). PRIM CORP EMPL vice president, corporate secretary: Ecolab Inc.

Diana D. Lewis: vice president human resources PRIM CORP EMPL vice president human resources: Ecolab Inc.

Richard L. Marcantonio: vice president, chairman PRIM CORP EMPL vice president, chairman: Ecolab Inc.

Michael J. Monahan: vice president external affairs PRIM CORP EMPL vice president external affairs: Ecolab Inc.

Maurizio Nisita: senior vice president global operations PRIM CORP EMPL senior vice president global operations: Ecolab Inc.

Allan L. Schuman: chairman, chief executive officer, director B Sheridan, WY May 24, 1934. ED New York University BS (1955). PRIM CORP EMPL president, chief executive officer: Ecolab Inc. CORP AFFIL director: Northern Studies Power Co.; director: Northern Studies Power Co. Minnesota; chairman: Industrial Maintenance Corp.

Giving Program Officials

Lawrence T. Bell: member, corporate contributions committee (see above)

John G. Forsythe: member corporate contributions committee (see above)

Diana D. Lewis: member corporate contributions committee (see above)

William A. Mathison: member corporate contributions committee (see above)

Michael J. Monahan: president corporate contributions committee (see above)

Foundation Officials

Dave Duvick: secretary
Thomas Hill: treasurer

Grants Analysis

Disclosure Period: calendar year ending 2001
Total Grants: $2,688,165*
Number of Grants: 1,059
Average Grant: $2,538
Highest Grant: $125,000
Lowest Grant: $500
Typical Range: $1,500 to $10,000
*Note: Giving excludes United Way.

Recent Grants

Note: Grants derived from 2001 Form 990.

General

125,000	Guthrie Theater, Minneapolis, MN
60,000	Minnesota Children's Museum, St. Paul, MN
50,000	St. Paul Chamber Orchestra, St. Paul, MN
50,000	Saint Paul Chamber Orchestra, St. Paul, MN
50,000	YMCA Greater St. Paul, St. Paul, MN
50,000	YMCA Greater St. Paul, St. Paul, MN
45,000	Girl Scout Council St. Croix Valley, St. Paul, MN
45,000	Greater Twin Cities United Way, Minneapolis, MN
45,000	Greater Twin Cities United Way, Minneapolis, MN
45,000	United Way of the St. Paul Area, St. Paul, MN

C. K. Eddy Family Memorial Fund

Giving Contact

Helen James, Trust Administrator
c/o Citizens Bank Saginaw
101 N. Washington Ave., MC 332021
Saginaw, MI 48607
Phone: (517)776-7368
Fax: (517)776-7309

Description

Founded: 1925
EIN: 386040506
Organization Type: Private Foundation
Giving Locations: MI: limited to Saginaw County
Grant Types: Project, Scholarship.

Donor Information

Founder: the late Arthur D. Eddy

Financial Summary

Total Giving: $988,541 (fiscal year ending June 30, 2000); $645,902 (fiscal 1999); $547,101 (fiscal 1997)
Giving Analysis: Giving for fiscal 2000 includes: foundation grants to United Way ($21,000); foundation scholarships ($237,400); fiscal 1999: foundation grants to United Way ($63,000) foundation scholarships ($217,800)
Assets: $16,755,632 (fiscal 2000); $16,633,096 (fiscal 1998); $14,455,448 (fiscal 1997)
Gifts Received: $247,578 (fiscal 1997); $269,788 (fiscal 1996)

Typical Recipients

Arts & Humanities: Dance, Historic Preservation, History & Archaeology, Libraries, Museums/Galleries, Music, Performing Arts, Theater
Civic & Public Affairs: African American Affairs, Business/Free Enterprise, Community Foundations, Employment/Job Training, Civic & Public Affairs-General, Housing, Municipalities/Towns, Safety, Urban & Community Affairs, Zoos/Aquariums
Education: Business Education, Colleges & Universities, Engineering/Technological Education, Public Education (Precollege), Student Aid
Health: Children's Health/Hospitals, Clinics/Medical Centers, Health Funds, Hospitals, Medical Rehabilitation, Nursing Services
Religion: Religion-General, Religious Welfare
Social Services: Big Brother/Big Sister, Child Welfare, Community Centers, Community Centers, Community Service Organizations, Crime Prevention, Food/Clothing Distribution, Recreation & Athletics, United Funds/United Ways, Volunteer Services, YMCA/YWCA/YMHA/YWHA, Youth Organizations

Application Procedures

Initial Contact: For scholarships, return completed application form along with transcripts and financial information; for grants, send a proposal with a one-page cover letter.
Application Requirements: Include explanation of name of program, purpose of funds sought, amount requested, period of program or project, contact person, a description of organization, statement of expected accomplishments, time schedule for completion of project, program budget, and future activities and funding.
Deadlines: None, for scholarships; May 1 for grants

Restrictions

Limited to organizations and residents of Saginaw County or City, MI.

Additional Information

Provides scholarships to residents of Saginaw County for higher education.
Publications: Application Guidelines
Trust(s): Citizens Bank Saginaw

Grants Analysis

Disclosure Period: fiscal year ending June 30, 2000
Total Grants: $730,141*
Number of Grants: 23
Average Grant: $21,083*
Highest Grant: $266,308
Typical Range: $500 to $30,000
*Note: Giving excludes scholarships to individuals totalling $237,400 and United Way. Average grant excludes highest grant.

Recent Grants

Note: Grants derived from fiscal 2000 Form 990.

General

265,308	Saginaw Community Foundation, Saginaw, MI
88,244	Saginaw Eddy Band, Saginaw, MI
80,748	City of Saginaw, Saginaw, MI
63,157	City of Saginaw, Saginaw, MI
30,000	First Ward Community Service, Saginaw, MI
25,000	Saginaw County Community Action Committee, Saginaw, MI
25,000	Saginaw Habitat for Humanity, Saginaw, MI
25,000	Saint Mary's, Saginaw, MI
24,600	Saginaw Valley Zoological Society, Saginaw, MI
21,000	United Way, Saginaw, MI

Eden Hall Foundation

Giving Contact

George C. Greer, Chairman
600 Grant, Suite 3232
Pittsburgh, PA 15219
Phone: (412)642-6697
Fax: (412)642-6698

Alternate Contact

Josephine K. Crane, Administrations Manager

Description

Founded: 1984
EIN: 251384468
Organization Type: General Purpose Foundation
Giving Locations: PA: primarily western area
Grant Types: Capital, Endowment, Project, Research, Scholarship.

Donor Information

Founder: The Eden Hall Foundation was established in 1984 by Eden Hall Farm.

Financial Summary

Total Giving: $9,765,730 (2000); $13,500,951 (1998); $8,651,942 (1997)
Giving Analysis: Giving for 2000 includes: foundation scholarships ($180,500); foundation grants to United Way ($300,000) 1998: foundation grants to United Way ($500,000)
Assets: $194,219,827 (2000); $215,778,020 (1998); $198,304,984 (1997)

Typical Recipients

Arts & Humanities: Arts Associations & Councils, Arts Centers, Arts Outreach, Arts & Humanities-General, Historic Preservation, History & Archaeology, Libraries, Museums/Galleries, Music, Public Broadcasting, Theater
Civic & Public Affairs: African American Affairs, Business/Free Enterprise, Clubs, Community Foundations, Economic Development, Employment/Job Training, Civic & Public Affairs-General, Housing, Parades/Festivals, Philanthropic Organizations, Public Policy, Urban & Community Affairs, Women's Affairs, Zoos/Aquariums

Education: Afterschool/Enrichment Programs, Arts/Humanities Education, Business Education, Colleges & Universities, Education Associations, Education Funds, Environmental Education, Education-General, Gifted & Talented Programs, Health & Physical Education, Literacy, Medical Education, Minority Education, Preschool Education, Private Education (Precollege), Religious Education, Science/Mathematics Education, Special Education, Student Aid
Environment: Wildlife Protection
Health: AIDS/HIV, Arthritis, Cancer, Children's Health/Hospitals, Clinics/Medical Centers, Diabetes, Emergency/Ambulance Services, Health Funds, Health Organizations, Hospices, Hospitals, Kidney, Medical Rehabilitation, Mental Health, Multiple Sclerosis, Nursing Services, Prenatal Health Issues, Research/Studies Institutes, Single-Disease Health Associations
International: International Affairs
Religion: Religion-General, Ministries, Religious Organizations, Religious Welfare
Science: Scientific Centers & Institutes
Social Services: Big Brother/Big Sister, Camps, Child Welfare, Community Centers, Community Service Organizations, Counseling, Day Care, Delinquency & Criminal Rehabilitation, Domestic Violence, Family Planning, Family Services, Food/Clothing Distribution, Homes, People with Disabilities, Scouts, Senior Services, Shelters/Homelessness, Substance Abuse, United Funds/United Ways, YMCA/YWCA/YMHA/YWHA, Youth Organizations

Application Procedures

Initial Contact: Initial requests should be in letter form.
Application Requirements: Requests should include the purpose of the applying organization, current financial statement including the organization's other sources of funding, specific purposes for which the grant is to be used, and proof of IRS tax-exempt status.
Organizations receiving funds must acknowledge receipt in writing, stating that the grant will be used for the purpose for which it was made. When the organization expends the funds, a written report giving details and verification of the expenditures is required by the foundation.
Deadlines: None.
Review Process: The board of directors usually meets quarterly to consider grant proposals. Applicants will receive notification of the board's decision.

Restrictions

Requests to cover operating expenses, accumulated deficits, and general fund-raising campaigns are discouraged. Grants are not made to individuals or private foundations.

Additional Information

Interviews or site visits may be required for additional information and confirmation.
Publications: Application Guidelines

Foundation Officials

D. S. Foster: secretary
George C. Greer: chairman B Sharon, PA 1932. ED Pennsylvania State University (1954); University of Pennsylvania School of Law (1957). PRIM CORP EMPL vice president organization development & administration: H.J. Heinz Co. CORP AFFIL director: Hartwell-Pacific (HK) Ltd.
John Mazur: treasurer
E. H. Shifler: director

Grants Analysis

Disclosure Period: calendar year ending 2000
Total Grants: $9,285,230*
Number of Grants: 72
Average Grant: $128,962
Highest Grant: $800,000

Typical Range: $10,000 to $30,000 and $100,000 to $500,000
*Note: Giving excludes United Way.

Recent Grants

Note: Grants derived from 2000 Form 990.

General

800,000	Holy Family Institute, Pittsburgh, PA -- Family Life Center
670,000	St. Vincent College, Latrobe, PA -- Pathways Program
500,000	Point Park College, Pittsburgh, PA -- purchase property for future construction
500,000	Wilson College, Chambersburg, PA -- fitness and health facility
400,000	Carlow College, Pittsburgh, PA -- equip and furnish labs for chemistry and computer science department
400,000	YWCA of Greater Pittsburgh, Pittsburgh, PA -- renovation of headquarters
359,600	Carnegie Mellon University, Pittsburgh, PA -- science van
300,000	Duquesne University, Pittsburgh, PA -- reading clinic and computer camp
300,000	United Way Allegheny County, Pittsburgh, PA -- annual campaign
300,000	YWCA of Greater Pittsburgh, Pittsburgh, PA -- adolescent girl programming

CHARLES EDISON FUND

Giving Contact

John Keegan, President & Chairman
One Riverfront Plaza, 4th Floor
Newark, NJ 07102-5401
Phone: (973)648-0500
Fax: (973)648-0400
E-mail: alberta@charlesedisonfund.org
Web: http://www.charlesedisonfund.org

Description

Founded: 1948
EIN: 221514861
Organization Type: General Purpose Foundation
Giving Locations: NJ: primarily metropolitan area; NY: primarily metropolitan area
Grant Types: General Support, Multiyear/Continuing Support, Project, Research, Seed Money.

Donor Information

Founder: The Charles Edison Fund was incorporated in 1948 as the Brook Foundation. Charles Edison , who died in 1969, was the founder and principal donor. The son of inventor Thomas A. Edison, he left the bulk of his estate (between $8 and $12 million) to the Brook Foundation, which later became the Charles Edison Fund.
Charles Edison was born in Llewellyn Park, West Orange, NJ, in 1890 and spent most of his life there. He attended the Hotchkiss School, Lakeville, CT, and received a degree in electrical engineering at Massachusetts Institute of Technology in 1913. He went on to become governor of New Jersey and secretary of the Navy. His personal interests were music and literature.

Financial Summary

Total Giving: $160,000 (2002 approx); $1,354,748 (2000); $1,378,500 (1998)
Assets: $41,612,123 (2000); $41,587,257 (1997); $36,855,869 (1996)
Gifts Received: $2,014 (2000); $3,779 (1998); $4,234 (1997)

Typical Recipients

Arts & Humanities: Arts Associations & Councils, Film & Video, Arts & Humanities-General, Historic Preservation, History & Archaeology, Libraries, Museums/Galleries, Music, Performing Arts, Public Broadcasting
Civic & Public Affairs: Botanical Gardens/Parks, Community Foundations, Ethnic Organizations, Civic & Public Affairs-General, Municipalities/Towns, Nonprofit Management, Parades/Festivals, Philanthropic Organizations, Public Policy, Urban & Community Affairs, Women's Affairs
Education: Arts/Humanities Education, Colleges & Universities, Community & Junior Colleges, Education Associations, Engineering/Technological Education, Education-General, Medical Education, Minority Education, Private Education (Precollege), Public Education (Precollege), Science/Mathematics Education, Secondary Education (Private), Secondary Education (Public), Secondary Education (Public), Social Sciences Education, Special Education, Student Aid
Environment: Energy, Wildlife Protection
Health: Arthritis, Cancer, Children's Health/Hospitals, Clinics/Medical Centers, Diabetes, Eyes/Blindness, Hospitals, Hospitals (University Affiliated), Medical Rehabilitation, Medical Research, Medical Training, Mental Health, Prenatal Health Issues, Single-Disease Health Associations, Speech & Hearing, Trauma Treatment
International: Foreign Arts Organizations
Religion: Churches, Religious Organizations, Religious Welfare
Science: Scientific Centers & Institutes, Scientific Organizations
Social Services: Camps, Community Service Organizations, People with Disabilities, Recreation & Athletics, Scouts, Senior Services, Veterans, YMCA/YWHA/YMHA/YWHA, Youth Organizations

Application Procedures

Initial Contact: The fund does not have a formal grant application. Applicants may submit a request on organization's letterhead, signed by an official on behalf of the governing board.
Application Requirements: Proposal should detail the applying organization's history, explain the project, and outline its expected costs. A financial report, current budget, and proof of tax exemption also should be included.
Deadlines: None, but requests must be submitted three weeks prior to meeting to be considered at that meeting.
Review Process: The fund meets in February or March, June, and December. Applicants will be notified of the board's decision within three months.
Notes: Progress reports and a final accounting of the use of grant funds are required and determine eligibility for continuing grants.

Restrictions

No grants are made to individuals, or for endowments or building funds. Continuing grants are made only under special circumstances.

Additional Information

In addition to its grant-making function, the fund provides a variety of services to museums, libraries, and educational institutions. Some of the trustees and staff members pay periodic visits to museums and render assistance in special projects. The fund also provides the services of a professional museum coordinator who visits the more than 80 museums at which it has exhibits, and works closely with producers of educational films and documentaries on Thomas A. Edison. The Charles Edison Fund cooperates with various public television stations throughout the country, providing television of educational science films and videos, and is associated with the Library of Congress Motion Picture Section and the Smithsonian Institute Department of Science and Invention.

Other services of the fund include: providing Edison science-oriented teaching kits; arranging science exhibits; repairing Edison phonographs at museums throughout the country; promoting experimentation in speech therapy through its phonograph collection at Syracuse University, in conjunction with the Voice Foundation of America; loaning rubber molds for the casting of bronze busts of Thomas A. Edison to museums and historical organizations; and working with various state energy educational departments throughout the nation in conjunction with conservation of energy and ecology.

The fund cooperates with the New Jersey Historical Society, New Jersey Historical Commission, Friends of Edison National Historic Site (West Orange, NJ), Edison Birthplace Museum (Milan, OH), Edison Institute (Dearborn, MI), and Edison Winter Home Museum and Laboratory (Ft. Myers, FL). It also assists the Edison Tower of Light (Menlo Park, NJ) and the Thomas A. Edison Papers Project, a twenty year program identifying and organizing millions of historic papers, laboratory notes, photographs, related correspondence and inventions of Thomas Edison.

The fund has recently completed its commitment to the Science of Technology Center in New Jersey, a "hands-on" museum, which will, in part, memorialize Thomas A. Edison and his achievements.

Publications: Brochure (including Guidelines for Application)

Foundation Officials

Edward Lee Allman: trustee B Poplar, MD 1926. ED Georgia Institute of Technology BS (1948). PRIM CORP EMPL chairman: Meggitt-USA Inc. CORP AFFIL director: Canterbury Shaker Village; office: Oneida Tableware Group; director: Amoskeag Industries.
Nancy Miller Arnn: trustee
Alberta Ench: secretary
William M. Henderson: trustee NONPR AFFIL director: Saint Margaret Memorial Hospital Foundation.
James Everett Howe: trustee, chairman investment comm B New York, NY 1930. ED Williams College BA (1952); Columbia University MBA (1954). NONPR AFFIL member: New York Society Security Analysts; member: Princeton Co.; member: Machinery Analysts New York; member: Environmental Control Analysts New York; member: Jamestown Society; member: Alpha Kappa Psi; member: Association Investment Management & Research. CLUB AFFIL Genesee Valley Club; Short Hills Club.
John Phillip Keegan: president, treasurer B 1927.
Robert E. Murray: vice president
John N. Schullinger, MD: trustee
J. Thomas Smoot, Jr.: trustee CORP AFFIL president: Smoot Adams Edwards Green Pennsylvania.
Thomas J. Ungerland: trustee

Grants Analysis

Disclosure Period: calendar year ending 2000
Total Grants: $1,354,748
Number of Grants: 61
Average Grant: $22,209
Highest Grant: $165,000
Lowest Grant: $210
Typical Range: $5,000 to $30,000

Recent Grants

Note: Grants derived from 2000 Form 990.

General

165,000	Edison Preservation, Newark, NJ
100,000	University of Notre Dame, Notre Dame, IN
83,710	Pediatric Research, New York, NY
70,000	Edison Preservation, Newark, NJ
55,000	Edison Preservation, Newark, NJ
50,000	Edison Preservation, Newark, NJ
50,000	Thomas A. Edison Foundation, East Orange, NJ
50,000	Thomas A. Edison Preservation Foundation, East Orange, NJ

50,000	Thomas A. Edison Preservation Foundation, East Orange, NJ
45,000	Edison Preservation, Newark, NJ

EDISON INTERNATIONAL

Company Headquarters

2244 Walnut Grove Avenue
Rosemead, CA 91770
Phone: (626)302-1212
Fax: (626)302-2517
Web: http://www.edison.com

Company Description

Founded: 1987
Ticker: EIX
Exchange: NYSE
Also Known As: Southern California Edison.
Assets: US$33.284 billion (2002)
Profit: US$1.077 billion (2002)
Employees: 15038 (2002)
Fortune Rank: 163, per FORTUNE Magazine's list of 500 Largest U.S. Corporations (2002).
SIC(s): 4911 Electric Services.

Operating Locations

Edison International (AZ--Phoenix; CA--Alhambra, Apple Valley, Arcadia, Barstow, Bell, Bell Gardens, Bellflower, Brea, Buena Park, Burbank, Camarillo, Cathedral City, Cerritos, Chino, Claremont, Corona, Costa Mesa, Covina, Cudahy, Cypress, Delano, Downey, Duarte, Fontana, Fountain Valley, Fullerton, Garden Grove, Glendora, Hanford, Hawthorne, Hemet, Highland, Huntington Beach, Huntington Park, Inglewood, La Canada, La Habra, La Mirada, La Puente, Laguna Beach, Lakewood, Lancaster, Lawndale, Long Beach, Los Angeles, Lynwood, Manhattan Beach, Mission Viejo, Monrovia, Montclair, Montebello, Moorpark, Moreno Valley, Newport Beach, Norco, Ontario, Orange, Oxnard, Palm Springs, Palo Verde, Paramount, Pico Rivera, Placentia, Port Hueneme, Porterville, Rancho Cucamonga, Rancho Palos Verdes, Redondo Beach, Rialto, Ridgecrest, Rosemead, San Bruno, San Dimas, San Fernando, San Gabriel, Santa Barbara, Santa Clarita, Santa Monica, Santa Paula, Simi Valley, South Gate, South Pasadena, Stanton, Thousand Oaks, Torrance, Tulare, Tustin, Victorville, Visalia, Walnut, West Covina, Westminster, Whittier, Yorba Linda)

Nonmonetary Support

Type: Donated Equipment; In-kind Services; Loaned Executives
Contact: Marilyn Kalenda, Corp. Contributions Budget Analyst

Giving Contact

Lucia Galindo, Manager, Corporate Contributions
Southern California Edison Co.
Edison International
2244 Walnut Grove Ave. Room 100 G04
PO Box 800
Rosemead, CA 91770
Phone: (626)302-9853
Fax: (626)302-8114
E-mail: Lucia.Galindo@.sce.com
Web: http://www.edison.com

Description

Organization Type: Corporate Giving Program
Giving Locations: CA: primarily in company's Southern CA service area; strategic giving outside traditional service territory
Grant Types: Employee Matching Gifts, General Support.
Note: Also awards special initative grants.

Financial Summary

Total Giving: $2,700,000 (2003 approx); $2,900,000 (2002); $8,500,000 (2001). Note: Contributes through corporate direct giving program and foundation.
Giving Analysis: Giving for 1999 includes: corporate matching gifts (approx $402,734); corporate scholarships (approx $1,375,000); corporate grants to United Way (approx $2,890,000); corporate direct giving (approx $3,832,266); 1998: foundation ($1,015,000) corporate direct giving ($7,290,000)

Typical Recipients

Arts & Humanities: Arts Associations & Councils, Arts Centers, Arts Institutes, Community Arts, Dance, Ethnic & Folk Arts, Historic Preservation, Libraries, Museums/Galleries, Music, Opera, Performing Arts, Public Broadcasting, Theater
Civic & Public Affairs: Business/Free Enterprise, Civil Rights, Economic Development, Economic Policy, Housing, Law & Justice, Professional & Trade Associations, Public Policy, Safety, Urban & Community Affairs, Women's Affairs, Zoos/Aquariums
Education: Business Education, Colleges & Universities, Economic Education, Engineering/Technological Education, Faculty Development, Education-General, Literacy, Minority Education, Private Education (Precollege), Science/Mathematics Education, Special Education
Environment: Environment-General
Health: Geriatric Health, Health Organizations, Hospices, Hospitals, Nursing Services
Science: Science Exhibits & Fairs, Scientific Centers & Institutes, Scientific Organizations
Social Services: Child Welfare, Community Centers, Community Service Organizations, Counseling, Emergency Relief, Family Services, People with Disabilities, Recreation & Athletics, Senior Services, Substance Abuse, United Funds/United Ways, Volunteer Services, Youth Organizations

Application Procedures

Initial Contact: Send a brief letter or proposal.
Application Requirements: Include organization name and contact information; a description of organization, including objectives, accomplishments, and current programs; amount requested and purpose of funds sought, list of officers and board of directors; list of current contributors and partners; recently audited financial statement, and proof of tax-exempt status.
Deadlines: None.

Restrictions

Company does not support fraternal, political, veterans, religious organizations, labor groups, commercial for-profit agencies, or public agencies.

Additional Information

Edison International is the parent company of Southern California Edison and handles all requests for charitable contributions.
Publications: Guidelines

Corporate Officials

John E. Bryson: chairman, chief executive officer, director B New York, NY 1943. ED Stanford University BA (1965); Freie University Berlin (1965-1966); Yale University JD (1969). PRIM CORP EMPL chairman, chief executive officer: Edison International. CORP AFFIL chairman, chief executive officer: Southern California Edison Co.; director: Times Mirror Co.; director: Mission Group Inc.; director: Pacific America Income Shares Inc.; director: Boeing Co.; chairman: Edison Mission Energy. NONPR AFFIL director: World Resources Institute; member, board editors, associate editor: Yale University Law Journal; member: Phi Beta Kappa; member: Stanford University Alumni Association; member: District of Columbia Bar Association; member: Oregon Bar Association; member: California Water Rights Law Review Committee;

trustee: Claremont University Center; member: California Bar Association; member: California Pollution Control Financing Authority.

Stephen E. Frank: president, chief operating officer, director B 1938. PRIM CORP EMPL president, chief executive officer, director: Southern California Edison Co. CORP AFFIL director: Edison International; director: Arkwright Insurance Co. NONPR AFFIL director: University Virginia.

Grants Analysis
Typical Range: $500 to $10,000

DEAN S. EDMONDS FOUNDATION

Giving Contact
Marjorie Thompson, Vice President
c/o The Bank of New York
1 Wall St., 28th Fl.
New York, NY 10286
Phone: (212)635-1520

Description
Founded: 1959
EIN: 136161381
Organization Type: Private Foundation
Grant Types: General Support.

Financial Summary
Total Giving: $195,000 (2000); $175,000 (1999); $134,700 (1998)
Assets: $3,367,329 (2000); $3,643,903 (1999); $3,396,011 (1998)

Typical Recipients
Arts & Humanities: Arts & Humanities-General, Historic Preservation, History & Archaeology, Libraries, Museums/Galleries, Music, Opera, Performing Arts, Public Broadcasting
Civic & Public Affairs: Clubs, Community Foundations, Civic & Public Affairs-General, Philanthropic Organizations, Professional & Trade Associations, Public Policy, Rural Affairs, Safety, Women's Affairs
Education: Arts/Humanities Education, Business Education, Colleges & Universities, Continuing Education, Engineering/Technological Education, Faculty Development, Medical Education, Private Education (Precollege), Science/Mathematics Education, Student Aid
Health: Cancer, Children's Health/Hospitals, Diabetes, Eyes/Blindness, Hospices, Hospitals
International: Foreign Educational Institutions
Religion: Churches
Science: Science-General, Scientific Organizations
Social Services: Community Service Organizations

Application Procedures
Deadlines: January 31.
Notes: Primarily supports preselected organizations.

Restrictions
Does not fund individuals or political or lobbying groups.

Additional Information
Trust(s): The Bank New York

Foundation Officials
Douglas J. Boyle: vice president
Dean S. Edmonds, III: trustee

Grants Analysis
Disclosure Period: calendar year ending 2000
Total Grants: $195,000
Number of Grants: 59
Average Grant: $3,305

Highest Grant: $20,000
Typical Range: $1,000 to $5,000

Recent Grants
Note: Grants derived from 1999 Form 990.

General
20,000	National Air & Space Musuem- Dulles Center -- Smithsonian Institution
15,000	Metropolitan Opera Association, New York, NY
10,000	Boston University Professor's Program, Boston, MA
10,000	Connecticut Valley Railroad Museum, Hartford, CT
7,000	Schepens Eye Research Institute, Boston, MA
6,000	Boston University, Boston, MA -- distinguished lecture
5,000	Boston University, Boston, MA -- friends of the library
5,000	E.A.A.- National Chapter, Oshkosh, WI
5,000	Immokalee Foundation, Inc., Naples, FL
5,000	Mary Baldwin College, Staunton, VA

EDUCATIONAL FOUNDATION OF AMERICA

Giving Contact
Diane M. Allison, Executive Director
35 Church Lane
Westport, CT 06880-3515
Phone: (203)226-6498
Fax: (203)227-0424
E-mail: efa@efaw.org
Web: http://www.efaw.org

Description
Founded: 1959
EIN: 133424750
Organization Type: Family Foundation
Giving Locations: nationally.
Grant Types: Project, Seed Money.

Donor Information
Founder: Established in 1959 by Richard Prentice Ettinger , who died in 1971. Although he provided the initial funding, other family members have added capital to the asset base over the years.
Mr. Ettinger began his career as a law professor at New York University, and later helped establish the Prentice-Hall publishing company. His career remained closely tied to higher education, as his publishing company concentrated on the development of teaching materials. Mr. Ettinger also was one of the first to grant financial aid scholarships to community and junior college graduates to further their education at four-year institutions.
Afflicted by cancer, he also became interested in cancer research and health care. He inaugurated a cancer fellowship program and the idea of minimum-care floors for ambulatory patients in hospitals.

Financial Summary
Total Giving: $14,503,569 (2000); $11,589,202 (1998); $20,629,359 (1997)
Giving Analysis: Giving for 2000 includes: foundation matching gifts ($5,625) 1998: foundation grants to United Way ($750)
Assets: $252,631,343 (2000); $240,888,907 (1998); $210,326,050 (1997)
Gifts Received: $69,214 (2000); $69,214 (1998); $69,214 (1997). Note: Contributions were received from the Virginia P. Andrews Trust.

Typical Recipients
Arts & Humanities: Arts Institutes, Museums/Galleries, Music, Opera, Performing Arts, Theater
Civic & Public Affairs: Economic Policy, Employment/Job Training, Civic & Public Affairs-General, Legal Aid, Native American Affairs, Public Policy, Rural Affairs, Safety, Women's Affairs
Education: Agricultural Education, Arts/Humanities Education, Business Education, Colleges & Universities, Community & Junior Colleges, Education Associations, Elementary Education (Public), Environmental Education, Faculty Development, Education-General, Leadership Training, Legal Education, Medical Education, Minority Education, Preschool Education, Private Education (Precollege), Public Education (Precollege), Science/Mathematics Education, Social Sciences Education, Special Education, Student Aid
Environment: Air/Water Quality, Energy, Forestry, Environment-General, Protection, Research, Resource Conservation
Health: Cancer, Children's Health/Hospitals, Clinics/Medical Centers, Geriatric Health, Medical Research, Prenatal Health Issues, Public Health
International: Health Care/Hospitals, Human Rights, International Affairs, International Environmental Issues, International Peace & Security Issues
Religion: Religious Organizations, Social/Policy Issues
Science: Scientific Centers & Institutes, Scientific Labs
Social Services: Animal Protection, Child Welfare, Community Service Organizations, Family Planning, Food/Clothing Distribution, Senior Services, Substance Abuse

Application Procedures
Initial Contact: Applicants should submit a letter of inquiry prior to consideration of a proposal. Foundation staff will review the letter and notify applicant if a full proposal is required.
Application Requirements: A letter of inquiry should be no more that two pages printed back to back on one sheet of unbleached recycled paper. The letter should identify the organization, including its mission, date of founding, location, region of focus, past and current projects, name(s) and brief description of the founder(s), and affiliations with other organizations; description of purpose of project, intended results, timeline, amount requested, and funding strategy for project; total amount budgeted for project, total amount budgeted for organization for the current year and a copy of the IRS determination letter.
Proposal should be submitted only after letter of inquiry has been approved. Send a completed EFA Information Request Form along with two copies of proposal. Proposal should be unbound, printed back to back on unbleached paper, single spaced, in 10 to 12 point font and no more than ten pages. Proposals should include the following: an executive summary; statement of problem being addressed; solution to problem, including organization's mission, goals and objectives, brief history and record of achievements; describe other organizations modeled after, influenced by, or building on your organization's work; description of project for which funding is sought, including specifics such as plan of execution, time frame, intended impact, amount requested and an explanation of project budget; describe any other organizations working on similar projects and how the two projects could cooperate; describe methods to evaluate objective, specific and quantifiable criteria, as well as subjective, general, and qualitative criteria; and explanation of funding sources. Also include the following attachments: a line item budget for project; line item annual budget for organization; most current financial statement; brief biographical information and qualification of key staff; list of board members and related qualifications (one page maximum); and a copy of the most recent IRS tax exempt letter and Form 990. and Form 990.
Deadlines: None.

Review Process: When a full proposal is received it will be reviewed by the staff. If all guidelines have been met and review receives a favorable evaluation, staff will then submit it to the Board of EFA for consideration at the next director's meeting. EFA normally meets quarterly. If the Board is interested in the proposal, a letter of invitation and guidelines will be sent describing how to submit a full proposal.

Evaluative Criteria: Characteristics that the foundation focuses on during review of letters of inquiry and proposals include an organization's record of achievement, intended broad impact, sound financial practices, increasing independence, and correspondence with EFA objectives.

Decision Notification: Staff will notify applicants of a decision usually within two weeks after the meeting at which the proposal was considered.

Notes: A final report is required from all grantees.

Restrictions

Foundation does not provide funds for endowments, endowed faculty chairs, building programs, annual fund-raising campaigns, religious purposes, indirect costs, overhead or general support, or to individuals.

Additional Information

Adjunct directors are related to the founder.
Publications: Annual Report; Guidelines

Foundation Officials

Diane M. Allison: executive director B 1953.
Paul R. P. Andrews: adjunct director
Jerry Babicka: director
Laren Babicka: adjunct director
Shelley E. Babicka: adjunct director
Barbara Bohart: director
James Bohart, Jr.: adjunct director
C. Bartley Bragg: adjunct director
Carole P. Bragg: adjunct director
David W. Ehrenfeld: director B New York, NY 1938. ED Harvard University BA (1959); Harvard University Medical School MD (1963); University of Florida PhD (1966). PRIM CORP EMPL professor biology: Cook College, Rutgers University. NONPR AFFIL trustee: E. F. Schumacher Society; member: Sustainable Use of Wild Species; member: International Union Conservation Nature; member: Marine Turtle Specialist Group; trustee: Caribbean Conservation Corp.; member: Ecological Society America; fellow: American Association Advancement Science.
Christian P. Ettinger: adjunct director
Deborah W. P. Ettinger: adjunct director
Heidi P. Ettinger: senior director
James O. Ettinger: adjunct director
Jean Ellen Ettinger: adjunct director
Leland P. Ettinger: adjunct director
Matthew Ettinger: adjunct director
Ronene Ann Ettinger: adjunct director
Sharon W. Ettinger: director
Wendy W. P. Ettinger: director
Elaine P. Hapgood: president
Derek McLane: adjunct director
John P. Powers: senior director
Trevor Renner: adjunct director
Beth Scribner: program officer
Francis Stott: director

Grants Analysis

Disclosure Period: calendar year ending 2000
Total Grants: $14,497,944*
Number of Grants: 202
Average Grant: $71,772
Highest Grant: $280,000
Typical Range: $1,000 to $100,000
*Note: Giving includes matching gifts.

Recent Grants

Note: Grants derived from 2000 Form 990.

General

280,000	Colorado Environmental Coalition, Denver, CO -- Colorado conservation network
230,000	New Jersey Conservation Foundation, Morristown, NJ -- Conservation Assistance and Coordination Program
210,000	San Juan Citizens Alliance, Durango, CO -- western coalbed methane project
203,100	Land and Water Fund of the Rockies, Boulder, CO -- Southern Rockies Forest network
178,650	Oberlin College, Oberlin, OH -- Oberling climate neutral project
166,000	Ambulatory Pediatric Association, McLean, VA -- National Fellowship Training Program
150,000	Foundation on Economic Trends, Washington, DC -- biotech litigation/public education
150,000	League of Conservation Voters Education Fund, Washington, DC -- Southwest Regional Program
125,000	Colorado Public Interest Research Foundation, Denver, CO -- livable communities project
125,000	Mineral Policy Center, Washington, DC -- citizen's campaign for environmental protection

EL PASO CORP.

Company Headquarters

1001 Louisana St.
Houston, TX 77002
Web: http://www.epenergy.com

Company Description

Founded: 1928
Ticker: EP
Exchange: NYSE
Former Name: El Paso Natural Gas Co.;
Acquired: Sonat (1999);
Former Name: El Paso Energy Co. (2001);
Acquired: Coastal Corp. (2001).
Assets: US$46.224 billion (2002)
Profit: US$644 million (2002)
Employees: 11855 (2002)
Fortune Rank: 152, per FORTUNE Magazine's list of 500 Largest U.S. Corporations (2002).
SIC(s): 4923 Gas Transmission & Distribution.

Operating Locations

El Paso Energy Co. (TX--Agua Dulce, El Paso, Freeport, Houston)

El Paso Corporate Foundation

Giving Contact

Gloria Moritz, Community Relations Coordinator
El Paso
1001 Louisiana Street
Houston, TX 77002
Phone: (713)420-5192

Description

Founded: 1992
EIN: 742638185
Organization Type: Corporate Foundation
Former Name: El Paso Energy Foundation.
Giving Locations: AZ; CA; CO; NM; TX: western area nationally.

Grant Types: Award, Challenge, Department, Employee Matching Gifts, General Support, Matching, Multiyear/Continuing Support.

Financial Summary

Total Giving: $9,670,078 (2001); $5,427,182 (2000); $3,017,636 (1999). Note: Contributes through foundation only.
Giving Analysis: Giving for 2000 includes: foundation gifts to individuals ($71,860); foundation grants to United Way ($1,263,771); foundation ($4,091,551); 1999: foundation scholarships ($33,100); foundation grants to United Way ($431,441); foundation ($2,553,095); 1998: corporate scholarships ($28,060); corporate grants to United Way ($397,362); corporate direct giving ($2,858,708);
Assets: $20,852,761 (2001); $11,957,306 (2000); $426,928 (1999)
Gifts Received: $18,000,000 (2001); $4,300,000 (2000); $1,200,000 (1999). Note: In 2001, contributions were received from El Paso Corp.

Typical Recipients

Arts & Humanities: Arts Associations & Councils, Arts Centers, Ballet, History & Archaeology, Libraries, Museums/Galleries, Music, Opera, Performing Arts, Public Broadcasting, Theater
Civic & Public Affairs: Chambers of Commerce, Clubs, Community Foundations, Economic Development, Economic Policy, Civic & Public Affairs-General, Hispanic Affairs, Housing, Native American Affairs, Nonprofit Management, Public Policy, Safety, Urban & Community Affairs, Women's Affairs, Zoos/Aquariums
Education: Afterschool/Enrichment Programs, Agricultural Education, Arts/Humanities Education, Business Education, Colleges & Universities, Community & Junior Colleges, Education Reform, Engineering/Technological Education, Education-General, International Studies, Legal Education, Literacy, Minority Education, Private Education (Precollege), Public Education (Precollege), School Volunteerism, Science/Mathematics Education, Student Aid
Environment: Protection, Resource Conservation
Health: Alzheimers Disease, Cancer, Clinics/Medical Centers, Hospices, Hospitals (University Affiliated), Medical Rehabilitation, Medical Research, Nursing Services, Prenatal Health Issues, Public Health
International: Foreign Arts Organizations, International Development, International Organizations
Religion: Ministries, Religious Welfare
Science: Scientific Centers & Institutes
Social Services: Animal Protection, At-Risk Youth, Child Abuse, Child Welfare, Community Centers, Community Service Organizations, Community Service Organizations, Day Care, Domestic Violence, Family Services, Food/Clothing Distribution, People with Disabilities, Recreation & Athletics, Scouts, Senior Services, Substance Abuse, United Funds/United Ways, YMCA/YWCA/YMHA/YWHA, Youth Organizations

Application Procedures

Initial Contact: Send letter requesting an application form.
Application Requirements: When submitting a completed application form, the following attachments are required: a financial statement, preferably audited; proof of tax-exempt status; and a copy of the organization's most recent Form 990. information on the use of outside consultants.
Deadlines: None.
Review Process: The evaluation process takes four months. The foundation requests that no inquiries be made during this process.
Decision Notification: All applicants receive written notification of a funding decision when it has been reached.

Notes: The foundation emphasizes that incomplete applications or applications incorrectly completed will be returned.

Restrictions

Does not support religious organizations for religious purposes; war veterans and fraternal service organizations; endowment funds; national health organizations and programs; grants or loans to individuals; fundraising events, including tickets, dinners, and telethons; corporate memberships or contributions to chambers of commerce, taxpayer associations, and other bodies whose activities are expected to directly benefit the company; political organizations, campaigns, or candidates; computers or computer-related projects; or operating expenses.

The foundation does not generally does not fund scholarship programs, as the foundation supports its own scholarship program.

Additional Information

Company was formerly known as the El Paso Natural Gas Company.

Publications: application form. and Funding guidelines

Corporate Officials

H. Brent Austin: executive vice president, chief financial officer, director B Dallas, TX 1954. ED University of Texas BA (1975); University of Texas MBA (1978). PRIM CORP EMPL executive vice president, chief financial officer, director: El Paso Corp. CORP AFFIL Leviathon Gas: Pipeline Partner LP.

Norma F. Dunn: vice president investor & public relations PRIM CORP EMPL vice president investor & public relations: El Paso Energy Co.

Douglas L. Foshee: president, chief executive officer

Ronald L. Kuehn, Jr.: chairman, chief executive officer B Brooklyn, NY 1935. ED Fordham University BS (1957); Fordham University LLB (1964). PRIM CORP EMPL chairman, chief executive officer: El Paso Corp. CORP AFFIL director: Transocean Offshore Inc.; director: Union Carbide Corp.; director: Protective Life Corp.; director: Southern Natural Gas Co.; director: Praxair Inc.; director: America South Bancorp; director: Dun & Bradstreet Corp. NONPR AFFIL trustee: Tuskegee University; member president council: University Alabama Birmingham; member: Newcomen Society; director: National Petroleum Council; member: New York Bar Association; director: Gas Research Institute; director: Interstate Natural Gas Association America; member: Fed Energy Bar Association; trustee: Boys Club America; member: Bretton Woods Committee; member: Association Bar New York City; director: Boy Scouts America; member: American Bar Association.

D. Dwight Scott: executive vice president, chief financial officer

Foundation Officials

Robert W. Baker: senior vice president, deputy general counsel

Jeffrey I. Beason: senior vice president, controller

Norma F. Dunn: president (see above)

Ralph Eads: director

Norbert R. Grijalva: tax officer

Peggy A. Heeg: executive vice president, general counsel, director

John J. Hopper: vice president, treasurer

Kelly J. Jameson: assistant secretary

Greg G. Jenkins: director

Robert G. Phillips: director

Joel Richards, III: vice president, director B Salt Lake City, UT 1946. ED Brigham Young University BA (1969); Brigham Young University MA (1971). PRIM CORP EMPL executive vice president human resources administration: El Paso Energy Co. CORP AFFIL executive vice president: El Paso Tennessee Pipeline Co.; executive vice president: El Paso Natural Gas Co. NONPR AFFIL member: Pacific Coast Gas Association; member: Southern Gas Association; member: National Gas Transmission Employee Relations Group; member: Labor Policy Association.

Margaret E. Roark: assistant secretary

D. Dwight Scott: executive vice president (see above)

David L. Siddall: vice president, associate general counsel

John W. Somerhalder, II: director

Judy A. Vandagriff: senior vice president

Gregory W. Watkins: vice president

Basil R. Woller: senior vice president

David E. Zerhusen: senior vice president

Grants Analysis

Disclosure Period: calendar year ending 2001

Total Grants: $8,064,238*

Number of Grants: 696

Average Grant: $8,751*

Highest Grant: $1,000,000

Typical Range: $100 to $10,000 and $25,000 to $100,000

*Note: Giving excludes gifts to individuals; United Way. Average grant figure excludes three highest grants ($2,000,000).

Recent Grants

Note: Grants derived from 2001 Form 990.

General

1,000,000	World Trade Center Port Authority, Jersey City, NJ
779,993	United Way of the Texas Gulf Coast, Houston, TX
500,000	Baylor College of Medicine, Houston, TX
500,000	Baylor College of Medicine, Houston, TX
500,000	Rice University, Houston, TX
317,128	United Way of Central Alabama, Birmingham, AL
200,000	Memorial Hermann Foundation, Houston, TX
200,000	University of Texas at El Paso, El Paso, TX
200,000	University of Texas at El Paso, El Paso, TX
150,000	United Way of San Antonio and Bexar Counties, San Antonio, TX

EL POMAR FOUNDATION

Giving Contact

William J. Hybl, Chairman & Chief Executive Officer
10 Lake Circle
Colorado Springs, CO 80906
Phone: (719)633-7733
Fax: (719)577-5702
E-mail: grants@elpomar.org
Web: http://www.elpomar.org

Alternate Contact

Phone: 800-554-7711
Note: Toll-free telephone number.

Description

Founded: 1937
EIN: 846002373
Organization Type: General Purpose Foundation
Giving Locations: CO
Grant Types: Capital, General Support, Project.

Donor Information

Founder: The El Pomar Foundation was established in 1937 by the late Spencer Penrose . Upon his death in 1939, the foundation received a portion of his estate. Mrs. Spencer Penrose, who died in 1956, also made gifts to the foundation. Mr. Penrose and his associate, Charles L. Tutt, were involved in the gold and copper mining and real estate businesses. He

was founder of the Utah Copper Company, and built the Broadmoor Hotel in Colorado Springs. His private zoo became the Cheyenne Mountain Zoo, which the foundation still supports.

Financial Summary

Total Giving: $15,755,587 (2001); $17,916,087 (2000); $15,358,845 (1999)

Giving Analysis: Giving for 2001 includes: foundation grants to United Way ($176,048).

Assets: $464,243,436 (2001); $489,651,559 (2000); $492,653,986 (1999)

Gifts Received: $29,812 (2000). Note: In 2000, contributions were received from Penrose Trust ($29,762) and other donors.

Typical Recipients

Arts & Humanities: Arts Associations & Councils, Arts Centers, Community Arts, Ethnic & Folk Arts, Historic Preservation, History & Archaeology, Libraries, Museums/Galleries, Music, Opera, Performing Arts, Public Broadcasting, Theater

Civic & Public Affairs: African American Affairs, Botanical Gardens/Parks, Chambers of Commerce, Economic Development, Civic & Public Affairs-General, Hispanic Affairs, Housing, Legal Aid, Municipalities/Towns, Nonprofit Management, Parades/Festivals, Public Policy, Urban & Community Affairs, Zoos/Aquariums

Education: Afterschool/Enrichment Programs, Arts/Humanities Education, Business Education, Colleges & Universities, Community & Junior Colleges, Continuing Education, Economic Education, Education Reform, Elementary Education (Private), Education-General, Leadership Training, Minority Education, Preschool Education, Private Education (Precollege), Public Education (Precollege), Student Aid

Environment: Environment-General, Resource Conservation

Health: Alzheimers Disease, Arthritis, Cancer, Children's Health/Hospitals, Clinics/Medical Centers, Diabetes, Emergency/Ambulance Services, Eyes/Blindness, Health-General, Health Organizations, Hospices, Hospitals, Long-Term Care, Medical Rehabilitation, Medical Research, Mental Health, Nursing Services, Preventive Medicine/Wellness Organizations, Public Health, Transplant Networks/Donor Banks

International: Foreign Educational Institutions

Religion: Jewish Causes, Religious Welfare, Seminaries

Science: Science Museums, Scientific Centers & Institutes

Social Services: At-Risk Youth, Child Welfare, Community Centers, Community Service Organizations, Day Care, Domestic Violence, Emergency Relief, Family Services, Food/Clothing Distribution, Homes, People with Disabilities, Recreation & Athletics, Scouts, Senior Services, Shelters/Homelessness, Substance Abuse, United Funds/United Ways, Volunteer Services, YMCA/YWCA/YMHA/YWHA, Youth Organizations

Application Procedures

Initial Contact: There are no set application forms. A detailed and complete application should be sent to: Board of Trustees, El Pomar Foundation, 10 Lake Circle, Colorado Springs, C0 80906.

Application Requirements: One copy of the application should be sent. Include the name and address of the tax exempt organization applying; a description of organization, including its mission, history, programs, and accomplishments; concise statement of purpose of funds sought and amount requested, including anticipated outcomes and methods for measuring the project's success; organization's budget for the current year and project budget, including total amount to be raised, anticipated funding sources, and long-term funding solutions, if applicable; and a statement indicating whether the applicant has sought aid from other foundations during the previous three years, and a list of the granting foundation(s) and amount received from each, if any. In addition, the applicant should furnish the relationship and capacity of the person signing the application; a list of members of the governing body; a statement that notes that the grant purpose has been approved by the applicant's governing body; endorsement from outside authorities, and copies of regulatory agency approvals, if necessary; copy of current IRS determination letter; the organization's three most recent years of audited financial statements, and the organization's latest IRS Form 990. The foundation also requests that applicants furnish up to three pictures (photographs, architectural renderings, etc.) that portray the specific project, issue, or operations of the organization for use in presenting the application to the board of trustees. Applications for funding of a technology projects must clearly state how the project will benefit the functioning of the nonprofit organization. The foundation considers technology projects under the categories of software applications, computers and peripheral devices, network equipment, and internetworking equipment. Such requests should also include an itemization of equipment and/or software, including a description and purchase price; implementation costs of the technology project, such as installation, consulting or training; and a description of how the project will be implemented including, where applicable, the timeline for installation and training.

Deadlines: None.

Decision Notification: Applications are acted upon within 90 days of receipt.

Restrictions

The foundation does not grant funds for the following: an organization which grants money to recipients of its own selection; discriminatory organizations; deficits, debt elimination, or endowments; making films or other media projects; K-12 education (except for capital requests from non-publicly funded secondary schools); research or studies; organizations which do not have fiscal responsibility for the project; nonprofit organizations that do not have proof of active 501(c)(3) status; travel, conferences, conventions, group meetings, or seminars; camps, camp programs, or other seasonal activities; individuals; religious organizations for support of religious programs; political or lobbying groups; or funding for software development projects. Grant requests of more than $500,000 will rarely be considered. Applicants must be based in Colorado or have a proposed activity that takes place within Colorado. Grantees are precluded from applying for a grant for three years following notification of a grant. Applicants whose proposals are not funded must wait one year before they are eligible to submit another proposal.

Additional Information

The foundation reports that it also sponsors a limited number of seminars, workshops, and conferences. The foundation requires grant recipients to report on expended grant funds and to return any unexpended funds. If a grant is made, grant recipients should not use plaques or memorials relating to El Pomar Foundation without the foundation's approval.

Publications: Annual Report; Guidelines; Program Brochures

Foundation Officials

Judy Bell: trustee

Steve R. Benson: director administration

Cortland S. Dietler: trustee B Denver, CO 1921. ED University of Tulsa (1947); Hillsdale College (1996). PRIM CORP EMPL chairman, chief executive officer: Transmontaigne Oil Co. CORP AFFIL director: PanEnergy Corp.; director: Key Production Co. Inc.; director: Grease Monkey Holding Corp.; director: Hallador Petroleum Co. NONPR AFFIL trustee: University Tulsa.

Theophilus Gregory: director outreach programs

Robert Hilbert: secretary, treasurer, vice president admin, trustee PRIM CORP EMPL secretary, treasurer, director: Garden City Co.

William J. Hybl: chairman, chief executive officer, trustee B Des Moines, IA 1942. ED Colorado College BA (1964); University of Colorado JD (1967). PRIM CORP EMPL vice chairman, director: Broadmoor Hotel, Inc. CORP AFFIL director: Manitou & Pikes Peak RY Co.; director: USAA; director: KN Energy Inc.; director: FirstBank Vail; president, director: Garden City Co.; director: FirstBank Holding Co. Colorado.

Tony Koren: director programs

Kent Oliver Olin: trustee B Chicago, IL 1930. ED Ripon College BS (1955). CORP AFFIL board directors: Bank One Colorado. NONPR AFFIL trustee: Falcon Foundation. CLUB AFFIL Broadmoor Golf Club.

David J. Palenchar: vice president programs, trustee

Brenda J. Smith: trustee

Russell Thayer Tutt, Jr.: president, trustee B 1955. ED Princeton University (1977); Duke University (1979). PRIM CORP EMPL vice president, director: Garden City Co. CORP AFFIL director: Bank One Colorado Springs NA; treasurer, director: Broadmoor Hotel Inc.

William R. Ward: trustee

Grants Analysis

Disclosure Period: calendar year ending 2001

Total Grants: $15,025,837*

Number of Grants: 404

Average Grant: $37,193

Highest Grant: $2,000,000

Typical Range: $2,500 to $25,000 and $50,000 to $125,000

*Note: Giving excludes in-kind support grants totaling $553,702 and United Way.

Recent Grants

Note: Grants derived from 2000 Form 990.

Library-Related

265,000	Pikes Peak Library District, Colorado Springs, CO -- Carnegie Library restoration

General

2,500,000	American Red Cross Pikes Peak Chapter, Colorado Springs, CO -- Montgomery Center for emergency services
2,000,000	Colorado College, Colorado Springs, CO -- new Science Center
2,000,000	University of Colorado at Colorado, CO -- library, communication and technology building
2,000,000	YMCA/USO of the Pikes Peak Region, Colorado Springs, CO -- new facility in southeast Colorado Springs
500,000	St. Paul Catholic Church, Highland, IL -- Julie Penrose Community Center
400,000	Colorado Outward Bound School, Denver, CO -- capital campaign
300,000	Community Health Centers, Colorado Springs, CO -- Direct Services Program
300,000	Conservation Fund A Nonprofit Corporation -- land conservation along I-25 corridor
250,000	Colorado Springs Youth Sports Complex, Colorado Springs, CO -- construction of complex
250,000	Fountain Valley School of Colorado, Colorado Springs, CO -- renovation of Boies Penrose Hall

ELF ATOCHEM NORTH AMERICA, INC.

Company Headquarters

Philadelphia, PA

Company Description

Employees: 3,600

SIC(s): 1479 Chemical & Fertilizer Mining Nec, 2812 Alkalies & Chlorine, 2813 Industrial Gases, 2819 Industrial Inorganic Chemicals Nec.

Operating Locations

Accecones Ricci U.S.A. (NY--New York); Ato-Findley (WI--Wauwatosa); Atochem (MI--Wyandotte; MN--Blooming Prairie; OK--Pryor; SC--Andrews); Atochem Services (PA--Valley Forge); Aviation & Performance Chemicals Division (PA--Philadelphia); Decco Division (CA--Monrovia); Elf Aquitaine (NY--New York); Elf Aquitaine Asphalt (MO--St. Louis); Elf Atochem North America, Agrichemicals Division (PA--Philadelphia); Elf Atochem North America Basic Chemicals Division (PA--Philadelphia); Elf Atochem North America, Fluorochemical Division (PA--Philadelphia); Elf Atochem North America, Inc. (AL--Mobile; CA--Los Angeles, Monrovia; GA; KY--Calvert City, Carrollton; MI--Wyandotte; NY--Buffalo, Homer; OH--Delaware; OK--Pryor, Tulsa; PA--Cornwells Heights, King of Prussia, Philadelphia; TX--Beaumont, Seagraves; WA--Tacoma; Elf Atochem Organic Peroxides Plant (NY--Buffalo); Elf Exploration (TX--Houston); Elf Sanofi (NY--New York); Elf Trading (TX--Houston); Genetic Systems Corp. (WA--Seattle); Parfums Van Cleef & Arpels (NY--New York); Pharmasol Corp. (MA--South Easton); Sanofi (IA--Fort Dodge); Sanofi Beaute (NY--New York); Sanofi Diagnostias Pasteur (MN--Chaska); Sanofi Pharmaceuticals (NY--New York); Sanofi Research (NY--New York); Sanofi Research Division (PA--Malvern); Specialty Chemicals (PA--Philadelphia); Stendhal (NY--New York); Turco Products Division (CA--Long Beach, Westminster; OH--Marion)

Atofina Chemicals Foundation

Giving Contact

George L. Hagar, Executive Secretary
c/o Atofina Chemicals, Inc.
2000 Market Street
Philadelphia, PA 19103-3222
Phone: (215)419-7000
Fax: (215)419-5494

Description

Founded: 1957

EIN: 236256818

Organization Type: Corporate Foundation

Giving Locations: nationally; operating location communities.

Grant Types: Capital, Employee Matching Gifts, General Support.

Note: Employee matching gift ratio: 1 to 1 to colleges and universities, public broadcasting and cultural and performing arts organizations.

Donor Information

Founder: Atochem North America

Financial Summary

Total Giving: $691,059 (2000); $582,333 (1999); $634,070 (1998). Note: Contributes through corporate direct giving program and foundation.

Giving Analysis: Giving for 2000 includes: foundation matching gifts ($38,639); foundation grants to United Way ($64,400); foundation ($588,020); 1999: foundation matching gifts ($51,512); foundation grants to United Way ($88,443); foundation ($442,388); 1998: foundation matching gifts ($28,462); foundation grants to United Way ($86,152); foundation ($519,462);

Assets: $5,129 (2000); $81,073 (1999); $107,982 (1998)

Gifts Received: $600,000 (2000); $557,143 (1999); $527,143 (1998). Note: In 2000, contributions were received from Atofina Chemicals, Inc. In 1998 and 1999, contributions were received from Elf Atochem North American, Inc.

Typical Recipients

Arts & Humanities: Arts Centers, Ballet, Community Arts, Dance, Historic Preservation, History & Archaeology, Libraries, Museums/Galleries, Music, Opera, Performing Arts, Public Broadcasting, Theater
Civic & Public Affairs: Business/Free Enterprise, Chambers of Commerce, Economic Development, Economic Policy, Employment/Job Training, Civic & Public Affairs-General, Law & Justice, Municipalities/Towns, Philanthropic Organizations, Professional & Trade Associations, Public Policy, Safety, Urban & Community Affairs, Zoos/Aquariums
Education: Arts/Humanities Education, Business Education, Colleges & Universities, Community & Junior Colleges, Economic Education, Education Reform, Engineering/Technological Education, Environmental Education, Education-General, Minority Education, Private Education (Precollege), Public Education (Precollege), Science/Mathematics Education, Student Aid
Environment: Environment-General
Health: Clinics/Medical Centers, Emergency/Ambulance Services, Hospitals, Medical Rehabilitation, Medical Research
International: Foreign Educational Institutions
Science: Science Museums, Scientific Centers & Institutes, Scientific Organizations
Social Services: Big Brother/Big Sister, Community Service Organizations, People with Disabilities, United Funds/United Ways, Volunteer Services, YMCA/YWCA/YMHA/YWHA, Youth Organizations

Application Procedures

Initial Contact: Send a brief letter or proposal.
Application Requirements: Include a description of organization, amount requested, purpose of funds sought, recently audited financial statement, proof of tax-exempt status.
Deadlines: None.

Restrictions

The foundation generally does not support political or lobbying groups, member agencies of united funds, or international organizations.

Additional Information

In 1991, the company changed its name from Atochem North America to Elf Atochem North America. The company was also formerly known as Pennwalt Corp.
The Foundation gives preference to qualified charitable organizations whose activities enhance Elf Atochem North America, Inc.'s employees' health and welfare (social, cultural or educational) and/or neighborhoods surrounding the company's plants and offices.

Corporate Officials

Bernard Azoulay: president, chief executive officeraffairs B 1940. ED Ecole Polytechnique (1977). PRIM CORP EMPL president, chief executive officer: Atofina Chemical Inc.
Peter John McCarthy: vice president public affairs B Philadelphia, PA 1943. ED Temple University; LaSalle College (1964). PRIM CORP EMPL vice president public affairs: Elf Atochem North America, Inc.

Foundation Officials

Bernard Azoulay: trustee (see above)
George L. Hagar: executive secretary PRIM CORP EMPL executive secretary: Elf Atochem North America, Inc.
F. H. Lauchert: trustee
Peter John McCarthy: trustee (see above)

Grants Analysis

Disclosure Period: calendar year ending 2000
Total Grants: $588,020*
Number of Grants: 58
Average Grant: $6,807*
Highest Grant: $200,000
Lowest Grant: $15
Typical Range: $50 to $7,500
*Note: Giving excludes matching gifts, and United Way. Average grant figure excludes highest grant.

Recent Grants

Note: Grants derived from 2000 Form 990.

General

200,000	School District of Philadelphia, Philadelphia, PA
135,435	Atofina Chemicals, Philadelphia, PA
100,000	WHYY-TV, Philadelphia, PA
20,000	Chemical Heritage Society, Philadelphia, PA
20,000	Philadelphia Orchestra Association, Philadelphia, PA
20,000	Philadelphia Orchestra Association, Philadelphia, PA
17,000	United Way Calvert Area, Calvert City, KY
15,000	Philadelphia Museum of Art, Philadelphia, PA
12,500	Opera Company of Philadelphia, Philadelphia, PA
12,000	United Way Southwest Alabama, Axis, AL

ELI LILLY & CO.

Company Headquarters

Indianapolis, IN
Web: http://www.lilly.com

Company Description

Founded: 1876
Ticker: LLY
Exchange: NYSE
Revenue: US$11.077 billion (2002)
Profit: US$2.707 billion (2002)
Employees: 43700 (2002)
Fortune Rank: 172, per FORTUNE Magazine's list of 500 Largest U.S. Corporations (2002).
SIC(s): 2833 Medicinals & Botanicals, 2834 Pharmaceutical Preparations.

Operating Locations

Eli Lilly & Co. (AL--Birmingham; AZ--Phoenix; CA--Fresno, Sacramento, Solana Beach, Woodland Hills; CO--Englewood; CT--Enfield; FL--Jacksonville, Tampa; GA--Atlanta; IN--Clinton, Greenfield, Indianapolis, Lafayette; IA--Cedar Rapids; KY--St. Matthews; LA--Metairie; MD--Rockville; MA--Braintree; MN--Bloomington; MS--Brandon; MO--St. Louis; NE--Omaha; NJ--Parsippany; NY--Albany, Melville; NC--Charlotte; OH--Cincinnati, Cleveland; PA--Bala-Cynwyd, Pittsburgh; TN--Knoxville, Memphis, Nashville; TX--Dallas; WA--Kirkland, Spokane; WV--Charleston)

Nonmonetary Support

Value: $176,576,789 (2001); $120,000,000 (2000); $96,000,000 (1999)
Type: Donated Products
Contact: Pat Gibson, Product Contributions Specialist
Note: Donations are in the form of pharmaceuticals (wholesale cost) to nonprofit organizations for disaster assistance.

Eli Lilly Foundation

Giving Contact

Thomas A. King, President
Eli Lilly Co. Foundation
Tax Division
Lilly Corporate Center
Indianapolis, IN 46285
Phone: (317)276-3743
Fax: (317)277-6719
E-mail: tom@lilly.com
Web: http://www.lilly.com/about/community/foundation/cash/index.html

Alternate Contact

Kendy Smith, Senior Contributions Assistant

Description

EIN: 356202479
Organization Type: Corporate Foundation
Giving Locations: headquarters and operating communities; international organizations; national organizations.
Grant Types: Capital, Employee Matching Gifts, General Support, Multiyear/Continuing Support.
Note: Employee matching gift ratio: 1 to 1.

Financial Summary

Total Giving: $233,542,420 (2001); $140,000,000 (2000 approx); $130,425,553 (1999 approx)
Giving Analysis: Giving for 2001 includes: corporate direct giving (approx $12,500); foundation grants to United Way ($4,475,004); foundation matching gifts ($5,689,835); foundation ($9,026,234); international subsidiaries ($9,077,737); domestic subsidiaries ($28,684,321); nonmonetary support ($176,576,789); 2000: foundation ($17,427,525); nonmonetary support (approx $120,000,000); 1999: corporate direct giving (approx $132,850); international subsidiaries (approx $6,276,269); domestic subsidiaries ($11,812,858); foundation ($16,203,582) nonmonetary support (approx $96,000,000)
Assets: $115,325,584 (2001); $137,636,700 (2000); $10,406,705 (1998)
Gifts Received: $23,750,000 (1998); $16,540,606 (1997); $13,722,596 (1996). Note: Gifts are received from Eli Lilly & Co.

Typical Recipients

Arts & Humanities: Arts Associations & Councils, Arts Funds, Arts Outreach, Ballet, Community Arts, Dance, Ethnic & Folk Arts, Historic Preservation, History & Archaeology, Libraries, Museums/Galleries, Music, Opera, Performing Arts, Public Broadcasting, Theater
Civic & Public Affairs: African American Affairs, Botanical Gardens/Parks, Business/Free Enterprise, Chambers of Commerce, Civil Rights, Community Foundations, Economic Development, Economic Policy, Employment/Job Training, Civic & Public Affairs-General, Hispanic Affairs, Housing, Law & Justice, Municipalities/Towns, Parades/Festivals, Professional & Trade Associations, Public Policy, Rural Affairs, Rural Affairs, Urban & Community Affairs, Zoos/Aquariums
Education: Business Education, Business-School Partnerships, Colleges & Universities, Education Associations, Education Funds, Education Reform, Engineering/Technological Education, Faculty Development, Education-General, Health & Physical Education, International Studies, Leadership Training, Medical Education, Minority Education, Private Education (Precollege), Public Education (Precollege), Religious Education, Science/Mathematics Education, Secondary Education (Private), Student Aid
Environment: Environment-General
Health: AIDS/HIV, Cancer, Children's Health/Hospitals, Diabetes, Emergency/Ambulance Services,

Health Policy/Cost Containment, Health Organizations, Heart, Medical Research, Mental Health, Mental Health, Prenatal Health Issues, Public Health, Single-Disease Health Associations, Trauma Treatment
International: Health Care/Hospitals, International Affairs
Religion: Ministries, Religious Welfare
Social Services: Camps, Child Welfare, Community Service Organizations, Homes, People with Disabilities, Recreation & Athletics, Scouts, United Funds/United Ways, YMCA/YWCA/YMHA/YWHA, Youth Organizations

Application Procedures

Initial Contact: Submit a written proposal.
Application Requirements: Include letter from IRS stating 501(c)(3) tax-exempt status, apartment, explanation of amount requested and purpose of request, and purpose of organization (see guidelines at www.lilly.com).
Deadlines: June 30 and December 31.
Review Process: A postcard will be sent upon receipt of proposal which will indicate the quarter in which the proposal will be reviewed. Applicants are notified in writing as soon as possible after the proposal has been reviewed to explain what action has been taken on the request.
Notes: Grants are offered in four areas: health and welfare, education, cultural, and civic.

Restrictions

Does not support individuals; organizations without 501(c)(3) status; endowments; debt reduction; religious or sectarian programs for religious purposes; fraternal, labor, athletic, bands, or veterans organizations; political contributions; beauty or talent contests; fundraising activities related to individual sponsorship; conferences or media productions (though such proposals relating to Lilly products or research may be directed to the company's appropriate product or operating group); non-accredited educational groups; or memorials.

Additional Information

Products, including insulin and anticancer agents, are donated throughout the developing world, to Eastern Europe, summer camp programs for children with diabetes, and emergency relief agencies.
Physician requests for the Lilly Cares--Indigent Patient Program should contact Lilly Cares Program Administrator, PO Box 9105, McLean, VA 22102-0105, (800)545-6962. of victims, families, and relief workers during times of disaster. of victims, families, and relief workers during times of disaster.
Publications: Charitable Contributions Report

Corporate Officials

Mitchell E. Daniels, Jr.: senior vice president, chief financial officer PRIM CORP EMPL director of the office of management and budget: The Office of Management and Budget. CORP AFFIL director: Indianapolis Power & Light Co.; director: Ipalco Enterprises.
Charles E. Golden: executive vice president, chief financial officer PRIM CORP EMPL executive vice president, chief financial officer: Eli Lilly & Co.
Sidney Taurel: chairman, president, chief executive officer B February 09, 1949. ED Columbia University MBA (1971). PRIM CORP EMPL chairman, president, chief executive officer: Eli Lilly & Co.

Foundation Officials

Mitchell E. Daniels, Jr.: chairman, treasurer (see above)
Pedro P. Granadillo: director
Rebecca O. Kendall: director
Thomas A. King: president
John C. Lechleiter: director
Gerhard Mayr: director
August M. Watanabe: director

Grants Analysis

Disclosure Period: calendar year ending 2001
Total Grants: $9,038,738*
Average Grant: $32,586 (approx)*
Typical Range: $10,000 to $50,000
*Note: Number of grants and average grant excludes matching gifts; nonmonetary support; United Way; and cash grants by domestic and international components.

Recent Grants

Note: Grants derived from 2001 Form 990.

General
1,852,363	United Way Central Indiana, Indianapolis, IN -- support programs
1,852,363	United Way Central Indiana, Indianapolis, IN -- support programs
1,000,000	American Red Cross National Headquarters, Washington, DC -- support of New York efforts
525,000	Cathedral High School, Indianapolis, IN -- Project IMPACT
500,000	Indiana University School of Medicine, Indianapolis, IN -- construction of new facility
424,836	Indiana University Foundation, Bloomington, IN
375,000	National Mental Health Association, Alexandria, VA -- assistance to form coalition of organizations
320,000	Purdue University School of Chemical Engineering, West Lafayette, IN
250,000	World Health Organization Switzerland -- Nations for Mental Health Initiative
246,483	United Way Greater Lafayette, Lafayette, IN -- support programs

MARGARET AND JAMES A. ELKINS, JR. FOUNDATION

Giving Contact

James A. Elkins, Jr., President
Margaret and James A. Elkins Jr. Foundation
1001 Fannin St., Suite 1166
Houston, TX 77002
Phone: (713)652-2051

Description

Founded: 1956
EIN: 746051746
Organization Type: Private Foundation
Giving Locations: TX: Houston
Grant Types: General Support.

Financial Summary

Total Giving: $1,680,000 (fiscal year ending October 31, 2000); $1,680,000 (fiscal 1999); $895,000 (fiscal 1998)
Giving Analysis: Giving for fiscal 2000 includes: foundation grants to United Way ($25,000) fiscal 1998: foundation grants to United Way ($25,000)
Assets: $35,756,559 (fiscal 2000); $35,756,559 (fiscal 1999); $33,445,700 (fiscal 1998)
Gifts Received: $10,056,282 (fiscal 1998); $5,815,344 (fiscal 1997); $2,212,568 (fiscal 1995).
Note: In fiscal 1998, contributions were received from James A. Elkins, Jr., and Margaret Elkins.

Typical Recipients

Arts & Humanities: Community Arts, Dance, History & Archaeology, Libraries, Literary Arts, Museums/Galleries, Music, Opera, Performing Arts, Public Broadcasting, Theater
Civic & Public Affairs: Botanical Gardens/Parks, Economic Development, Housing, Municipalities/Towns, Safety, Urban & Community Affairs, Zoos/Aquariums

Education: Arts/Humanities Education, Colleges & Universities, Engineering/Technological Education, Education-General, International Studies, Literacy, Medical Education, Private Education (Precollege), Public Education (Precollege), Secondary Education (Private)
Environment: Environment-General
Health: Cancer, Children's Health/Hospitals, Eyes/Blindness, Geriatric Health, Hospices, Hospitals, Prenatal Health Issues
International: Health Care/Hospitals
Religion: Churches, Dioceses, Religious Organizations, Religious Welfare, Social/Policy Issues
Social Services: Animal Protection, Child Welfare, Community Centers, Community Service Organizations, Day Care, Family Planning, Family Services, Homes, Scouts, Shelters/Homelessness, Substance Abuse, United Funds/United Ways, Youth Organizations

Application Procedures

Initial Contact: Send a brief letter of inquiry.
Application Requirements: Include a description of organization, amount requested, purpose of funds sought, recently audited financial statement, and proof of tax-exempt status. Also include a list of donors.
Deadlines: None.

Restrictions

Does not support individuals or political or lobbying group. Does not make grants for operating support.

Foundation Officials

James Anderson Elkins, Jr.: president B Galveston, TX March 24, 1919. ED Princeton University BA (1941). CORP AFFIL director: Central Houston Inc. NONPR AFFIL member: Christ Cathedral; director: Houston Grand Opera; chairman, trustee: Baylor University College Medicine.
Pete Seale: trust

Grants Analysis

Disclosure Period: fiscal year ending October 31, 2000
Total Grants: $1,655,000*
Number of Grants: 21
Average Grant: $37,105*
Highest Grant: $500,000
Typical Range: $15,000 to $50,000
*Note: Giving excludes United Way. Average grant figure two excludes highest grants ($950,000).

Recent Grants

Note: Grants derived from 2000 Form 990.

Library-Related
20,000	Library of Congress, Houston, TX

General
500,000	M D Anderson Cancer Center, Houston, TX
450,000	Texas Children's Hospital, Houston, TX
100,000	Christ Church Cathedral, Houston, TX
100,000	Junior League of Houston, Houston, TX
100,000	Rice University, Houston, TX
100,000	University of Houston, Houston, TX
50,000	Houston Symphony Society, Houston, TX
25,000	Fort Worth Zoo, Ft. Worth, TX
25,000	Houston Grand Opera, Houston, TX
25,000	Stages Repertory Theater, Houston, TX

ELLIS FOUNDATION

Giving Contact

Michael Ellis, Director
5070 Santa Fe Street
San Diego, CA 92109
Phone: (619)490-5222

Description
Founded: 1997
EIN: 330771069
Organization Type: Private Foundation
Grant Types: General Support.

Financial Summary
Total Giving: $331,821 (2000); $15,620 (1998)
Giving Analysis: Giving for 2000 includes: foundation gifts to individuals ($19,885) 1998: foundation gifts to individuals ($15,620)
Assets: $1,243,820 (2000); $1,124,294 (1998); $250,000 (1997)

Typical Recipients
Arts & Humanities: Libraries
Civic & Public Affairs: Civic & Public Affairs-General, Rural Affairs
Education: Colleges & Universities, Education-General, Public Education (Precollege)
Health: Hospitals
Social Services: Community Service Organizations, Youth Organizations

Foundation Officials
Michael Ellis: director
Monica Ellis: director

Grants Analysis
Disclosure Period: calendar year ending 2000
Total Grants: $311,936*
Number of Grants: 8
Highest Grant: $100,000
Lowest Grant: $2,000
*Note: Giving excludes individuals.

Recent Grants
Note: Grants derived from 2001 Form 990.

Library-Related
10,000	San Diego Public Library, San Diego, CA

General
500,000	Campanile Foundation, San Diego, CA
135,000	Community Education Enhancement, San Diego, CA
25,000	St. Jude Hospital, Memphis, TN
22,500	Sweetwater High School, San Diego, CA
20,000	South Bay Community Services, San Diego, CA
5,000	Country Friends, Santa Fe, CA
5,000	Laurels for Leaders, San Diego, CA
2,000	Children's Experimental Trust, Zeeland, MI
1,000	Boys and Girls Club, San Diego, CA

CHARLES E. ELLIS GRANT AND SCHOLARSHIP FUND

Giving Contact
Patricia Blakely, Program Director
c/o White, Williams Scholars
215 S Broad St.
Philadelphia, PA 19107
Phone: (215)735-4483
Fax: (215)735-4485
E-mail: info@wwscholars.org
Web: http://www.wwscholars.org
Note: All inquiries and grant requets should be submitted to White, Williams Scholars, the foundation's agent.

Description
Founded: 1981
EIN: 236725618
Organization Type: Specialized/Single Purpose Foundation

Giving Locations: PA: Philadelphia County
Grant Types: Scholarship.

Donor Information
Founder: The fund was established in 1981 by the Orphan's Court of Philadelphia under the will of Charles E. Ellis .

Financial Summary
Total Giving: $2,400,000 (fiscal year ending June 30, 2000 approx); $1,491,715 (fiscal 1999); $1,403,344 (fiscal 1998)
Giving Analysis: Giving for fiscal 1999 includes: foundation scholarships ($1,491,715)
Assets: $48,550,448 (fiscal 1999); $45,229,940 (fiscal 1998); $38,394,523 (fiscal 1997)

Typical Recipients
Arts & Humanities: Libraries, Theater
Civic & Public Affairs: Employment/Job Training, Civic & Public Affairs-General, Women's Affairs
Education: Arts/Humanities Education, Colleges & Universities, Education Funds, Education Reform, Education-General, International Studies, Minority Education, Private Education (Precollege), Student Aid, Vocational & Technical Education
Religion: Dioceses, Religious Organizations, Religious Welfare
Science: Scientific Centers & Institutes

Application Procedures
Initial Contact: The fund requests applications be made in writing.
Deadlines: Deadline for diocesan schools is in early April and for independent schools, in early March.

Additional Information
The fund provides high school scholarships to female students in single or no parent families who are residents of Philadelphia County, PA.
White, Williams Scholars handles all application procedures for the fund.
Publications: Guidelines; Application Form

Foundation Officials
Brooke Cheston: vice president

Grants Analysis
Disclosure Period: fiscal year ending June 30, 1999
Total Grants: $1,491,716*
Number of Grants: 1,000 (approx)
Average Grant: $1,492 (approx)
Highest Grant: $4,000 (approx)
Typical Range: $100 to $4,000
*Note: All grants are scholarships for individuals payable through institutional and programmatic entities.

Recent Grants
Note: Grants derived from fiscal 1998 Form 990.

General
1,284,214	White Williams Scholars, Philadelphia, PA -- scholarships
119,130	White-Williams Scholars, Philadelphia, PA -- agent-administrator fees

RUTH H. AND WARREN A. ELLSWORTH FOUNDATION

Giving Contact
Sumner B. Tilton, Jr., Trustee
Ruth H. and Warren A. Ellsworth Foundation
370 Main Street, 12th Floor
Worcester, MA 01608
Phone: (508)798-8621
Fax: (508)791-6454
E-mail: stilton@ftwaw.com

Description
Founded: 1964
EIN: 046113491
Organization Type: Private Foundation
Giving Locations: MA: Worcester
Grant Types: Capital, Emergency, General Support, Multiyear/Continuing Support, Operating Expenses.

Donor Information
Founder: the late Ruth H. Ellsworth

Financial Summary
Total Giving: $976,250 (2001); $990,450 (2000); $829,500 (1999)
Giving Analysis: Giving for 2001 includes: foundation grants to United Way ($4,000); foundation matching gifts ($46,250); 2000: foundation grants to United Way ($12,500); 1999: foundation grants to United Way ($12,850); foundation matching gifts ($40,150);
Assets: $19,465,677 (2001); $21,894,212 (2000); $23,382,592 (1999)

Typical Recipients
Arts & Humanities: Community Arts, Historic Preservation, History & Archaeology, Libraries, Museums/Galleries, Music, Theater
Civic & Public Affairs: Clubs, Community Foundations, Housing, Urban & Community Affairs
Education: Colleges & Universities, Education Reform, Engineering/Technological Education, Education-General, Private Education (Precollege), Science/Mathematics Education, Secondary Education (Private), Student Aid
Environment: Environment-General, Resource Conservation
Health: Cancer, Children's Health/Hospitals, Clinics/Medical Centers, Health Funds, Health Organizations, Hospices, Hospitals, Hospitals (University Affiliated), Medical Rehabilitation, Medical Research, Nursing Services, Public Health, Research/Studies Institutes
International: Foreign Arts Organizations
Religion: Churches, Dioceses, Jewish Causes
Science: Scientific Centers & Institutes, Scientific Organizations, Scientific Research
Social Services: At-Risk Youth, Big Brother/Big Sister, Child Abuse, Child Welfare, Community Centers, Community Service Organizations, Crime Prevention, Family Planning, Family Services, Senior Services, United Funds/United Ways, YMCA/YWCA/YMHA/YWHA, Youth Organizations

Application Procedures
Initial Contact: Send a brief letter of inquiry.
Application Requirements: Include goals and objectives of the request, plan for accomplishing these goals, proof of tax-exempt status, and project budget.
Deadlines: June 1.

Restrictions
Organizations must be recognized by the IRS in the cumulative listing.

Foundation Officials
David H. Ellsworth: trustee
Joy W. Hall: trustee
Sumner B. Tilton, Jr.: trustee PRIM CORP EMPL clerk: New England Newspaper Supply Co. CORP AFFIL clerk: Whitinsville Water Co.; clerk: Whiteater Inc.; clerk: NDI Inc.; clerk: R H White Co. Inc.; officer: Fletcher, Tilton & Whipple PC. NONPR AFFIL president: Greater Worcester Community Foundation.
Joy Wetzel: trustee
Mark R. Wetzel: trustee
Todd H. Wetzel: trustee

Grants Analysis
Disclosure Period: calendar year ending 2001
Total Grants: $926,000*
Number of Grants: 48
Average Grant: $15,239*

Highest Grant: $125,000
Lowest Grant: $1,000
Typical Range: $5,000 to $60,000
*Note: Giving excludes United Way and matching gifts. Average grant figure excludes two highest grants ($225,000).

Recent Grants

Note: Grants derived from 2001 Form 990.

Library-Related

30,000	Friends of the Worcester Public Library, Worcester, MA -- capital project for the expansion and renovation of Salem Square

General

125,000	Bancroft School, Worcester, MA -- for campus programs and needs
100,000	Children's Friend, Inc., Worcester, MA -- for capital campaign Putting Kids First
60,000	New England Science Center, Worcester, MA -- capital campaign support
60,000	New England Science Center, Worcester, MA -- for construction projects
60,000	Worcester Art Museum, Worcester, MA -- centennial campaign
60,000	YOU, Worcester, MA -- for Children's Diagnostic Center
40,000	Massachusetts College of Pharmacy and Health Sciences, Boston, MA -- for the creation of Worcester Campus
30,000	Assumption College, Worcester, MA -- for science building
30,000	Greater Worcester Community Foundation, Worcester, MA -- for December 3rd Fund
30,000	UMASS Memorial Health Care, Worcester, MA -- for Ambulatory Center at Hahnemann Campus

FRED L. EMERSON FOUNDATION, INC.

Giving Contact

Ronald D. West, Executive Director & Secretary
PO Box 276
Auburn, NY 13021
Phone: (315)253-9621
Fax: (315)253-5235
Web: http://www.iath.virginia.edu/readings/emerson.html

Description

Founded: 1943
EIN: 156017650
Organization Type: Family Foundation
Giving Locations: NY: Cayuga County, Upstate, Auburn
Grant Types: Capital, Challenge, Emergency, Endowment, General Support, Matching, Multiyear/Continuing Support, Project, Research, Scholarship.

Donor Information

Founder: Established in 1932 by the late Fred L. Emerson , president of Dunn and McCarthy, Inc., a manufacturer of women's shoes in Auburn, NY.

Financial Summary

Total Giving: $4,319,369 (2000); $3,840,758 (1999); $3,437,196 (1998)
Giving Analysis: Giving for 2000 includes: foundation grants to United Way ($146,269) 1997: foundation grants to United Way ($120,930)
Assets: $90,438,488 (2000); $92,158,304 (1999); $84,608,024 (1998)

Typical Recipients

Arts & Humanities: Arts Associations & Councils, Arts Centers, Arts Festivals, Arts Institutes, Dance, Historic Preservation, History & Archaeology, Libraries, Museums/Galleries, Music, Opera, Performing Arts, Public Broadcasting, Theater
Civic & Public Affairs: African American Affairs, Botanical Gardens/Parks, Chambers of Commerce, Economic Development, Civic & Public Affairs-General, Municipalities/Towns, Nonprofit Management, Parades/Festivals, Public Policy, Safety, Urban & Community Affairs
Education: Arts/Humanities Education, Business Education, Colleges & Universities, Community & Junior Colleges, Education Reform, Elementary Education (Public), Environmental Education, Faculty Development, Leadership Training, Preschool Education, Private Education (Precollege), Science/Mathematics Education, Student Aid, Vocational & Technical Education
Environment: Air/Water Quality
Health: Cancer, Emergency/Ambulance Services, Eyes/Blindness, Health-General, Health Organizations, Heart, Hospices, Hospitals, Long-Term Care, Medical Rehabilitation, Medical Research, Single-Disease Health Associations
International: Missionary/Religious Activities
Religion: Churches, Ministries, Religious Welfare
Science: Science Museums
Social Services: Animal Protection, Child Welfare, Community Service Organizations, Crime Prevention, Family Planning, Homes, People with Disabilities, Recreation & Athletics, Scouts, Senior Services, Shelters/Homelessness, Social Services-General, Substance Abuse, United Funds/United Ways, Volunteer Services, YMCA/YWCA/YMHA/YWHA, Youth Organizations

Application Procedures

Initial Contact: Applicants should send a proposal in letter form to the foundation.
Application Requirements: Proposals should detail the project for which support is sought. Attachments should include copies of current financial statements, a list of other sources of support, and a copy of the IRS determination letter of tax-exempt status.
Deadlines: Proposals should be received no later than May 1 and November 1.
Review Process: Most major grants are made in early December. Meetings may be arranged with the foundation's grants officers if the applicant's program falls within the foundation's areas of interest.

Restrictions

The foundation does not make grants to individuals or for deficit financing or loans. The foundation prefers not to fund operating expenses.

Additional Information

Publications: Application Guidelines

Foundation Officials

William Finch Allyn: director B Auburn, NY 1935. ED Dartmouth College BA (1958); Syracuse University (1960). PRIM CORP EMPL president: Welch Allyn Inc. CORP AFFIL director: Perfex Corp.; director: Syracuse Research Corp.; director: Oneida Tableware Group; director: Oneida Silver; director: Oneida Silversmiths Division; director: Oneida Ltd.; director: Niagara Mohawk Holdings Inc.; president, chief executive officer: Niagara Mohawk Power Corp.; director: M T Bank; president, director: Grason-Stadler Inc.; president: GSI; president director: C E L Instruments, Ltd.
Christopher S. Emerson: director
David L. Emerson: director
Heather A. Emerson: director
Peter J. Emerson: director PRIM NONPR EMPL executive vice president: Dunn & McCarthy Inc.
W. Gary Emerson: president
Anthony D. Franceschelli: vice president

Dr. J. David Hammond: treasurer
Lori E. Robinson: director
Kristen E. Rubacka: director
Sally E. Wagner: director
Ronald D. West: executive director, secretary

Grants Analysis

Disclosure Period: calendar year ending 2000
Total Grants: $4,173,100*
Number of Grants: 57
Average Grant: $73,212
Highest Grant: $506,000
Lowest Grant: $250
Typical Range: $5,000 to $250,000
*Note: Giving excludes United Way.

Recent Grants

Note: Grants derived from 2000 Form 990.

General

506,000	Gunnery, Washington, DC -- annual fund
505,000	Syracuse University, Syracuse, NY -- challenge grant
255,000	Skaneateles Recreational Charitable Trust, Skaneateles, NY -- toward new recreational center
250,000	Al Sigl Center for Rehabilitation Agencies, Rochester, NY -- challenge grant
250,000	Paul Smith's College, Paul Smiths, NY -- Adirondack Information Resource Center Library
250,000	Sage College, Troy, NY -- new fine arts building
250,000	St. John Fisher College, Rochester, NY -- toward student dining facility
250,000	Union College, Schenectady, NY -- challenge grant
225,000	Merry Go Round Playhouse, Auburn, NY -- capital campaign
221,783	Foundation Historical Association, Inc., Auburn, NY -- operating funds

THOMAS J. EMERY MEMORIAL

Giving Contact

Lee A. Carter, President
2120 US Bank
425 Walnut St.
Cincinnati, OH 45202
Phone: (513)621-3124
Fax: (513)651-8403

Description

Founded: 1925
EIN: 310536711
Organization Type: General Purpose Foundation
Giving Locations: OH: Cincinnati
Grant Types: Capital, Matching, Project, Seed Money.

Donor Information

Founder: Incorporated in 1925 by the late Mary Muhlenberg Emery .

Financial Summary

Total Giving: $1,350,633 (2001); $2,306,263 (2000); $2,000,000 (1999 approx)
Giving Analysis: Giving for 2001 includes: foundation grants to United Way ($115,500); 2000: foundation grants to United Way ($87,500) 1998: foundation grants to United Way ($74,000)
Assets: $29,854,500 (2001); $33,046,004 (2000); $34,864,150 (1998)
Gifts Received: $26,000 (1996); $133,000 (1995).
Note: In 1996, contributions were received from C. G. & E.

Typical Recipients

Arts & Humanities: Arts Associations & Councils, Arts Centers, Arts Institutes, Arts Outreach, Ballet, Arts & Humanities-General, Historic Preservation, History & Archaeology, Libraries, Museums/Galleries, Music, Opera, Performing Arts, Public Broadcasting, Theater

Civic & Public Affairs: African American Affairs, Botanical Gardens/Parks, Clubs, Community Foundations, Economic Development, Employment/Job Training, Civic & Public Affairs-General, Housing, Legal Aid, Municipalities/Towns, Nonprofit Management, Parades/Festivals, Public Policy, Urban & Community Affairs, Women's Affairs, Zoos/Aquariums

Education: Arts/Humanities Education, Business Education, Colleges & Universities, Colleges & Universities, Continuing Education, Economic Education, Education Funds, Elementary Education (Private), Education-General, Minority Education, Preschool Education, Private Education (Precollege), Public Education (Precollege), Science/Mathematics Education, Secondary Education (Private), Secondary Education (Public), Special Education, Student Aid, Vocational & Technical Education

Environment: Environment-General

Health: Cancer, Children's Health/Hospitals, Clinics/Medical Centers, Diabetes, Emergency/Ambulance Services, Eyes/Blindness, Health-General, Health Organizations, Hospices, Hospitals, Long-Term Care, Medical Rehabilitation, Mental Health, Prenatal Health Issues, Public Health, Research/Studies Institutes, Single-Disease Health Associations, Speech & Hearing, Transplant Networks/Donor Banks

International: International Development

Religion: Churches, Dioceses, Religion-General, Ministries, Religious Organizations, Religious Welfare, Seminaries

Social Services: Child Welfare, Community Centers, Community Service Organizations, Counseling, Day Care, Domestic Violence, Family Planning, Family Services, Food/Clothing Distribution, Homes, People with Disabilities, Recreation & Athletics, Scouts, Senior Services, Shelters/Homelessness, Social Services-General, Substance Abuse, United Funds/United Ways, YMCA/YWCA/YMHA/YWHA, Youth Organizations

Application Procedures

Initial Contact: The foundation requests that applicants call for application guidelines.
Application Requirements: Send a brief letter of inquiry.
Deadlines: None.
Review Process: The board meets in April, September, and December.

Restrictions

None.

Additional Information

Publications: Guidelines

Foundation Officials

John F. Barrett: treasurer B 1949. ED University of Cincinnati (1971). PRIM CORP EMPL president, chief executive officer, director: Western & Southern Life Insurance Co. ADD CORP EMPL president: Western Southern Life Assurance Co. CORP AFFIL director: Fifth Third Bank; director: Fifth Third Bancorp; director: Cincinnati Bell Inc.; director: Convergys Corp.; director: Andersons Inc. NONPR AFFIL vice chairmanr: Greater Cincinnati Chamber of Commerce.
Lee A. Carter: president, trustee
Frank T. Hamilton: trustee
John T. Lawrence, Jr.: vice president, trustee CORP AFFIL director: America Annuity Group Inc.

Grants Analysis

Disclosure Period: calendar year ending 2001
Total Grants: $1,235,133*
Number of Grants: 56

Average Grant: $22,056
Highest Grant: $121,000
Lowest Grant: $2,500
Typical Range: $15,000 to $50,000
*Note: Giving excludes United Way.

Recent Grants

Note: Grants derived from 2001 Form 990.

General

121,000	Cincinnati Institute of Fine Arts, Cincinnati, OH
115,000	United Way, Cincinnati, OH
100,000	Greater Cincinnati Foundation, Cincinnati, OH
75,000	Local Initiatives Support Corporation, Cincinnati, OH
62,500	YMCA of Greater Cincinnati, Cincinnati, OH
50,000	Children's Hospital Medical Center, Cincinnati, OH
50,000	Cincinnati Country Day School, Cincinnati, OH
50,000	Cincinnati Development Fund, Cincinnati, OH
50,000	National Underground Railroad Museum, Cincinnati, OH
50,000	Seven Hills School, Cincinnati, OH

EMPLOYERS MUTUAL CASUALTY CO.

Company Headquarters

Des Moines, IA
Web: http://www.emcins.com

Company Description

Employees: 1,795
SIC(s): 6311 Life Insurance, 6321 Accident & Health Insurance, 6331 Fire, Marine & Casualty Insurance.
Parent Company: Employers Mutual, Inc., 1000 Riverside Ave., Ste. 400, Jacksonville, FL, United States
Parent Assets: US$758,300,000 (2001)

Operating Locations

Employers Mutual Casualty Co. (AL--Birmingham; IL--Oak Brook; IA--Des Moines; ND--Bismarck)
Note: Operates branch offices in 17 states.

Nonmonetary Support

Type: Donated Equipment; Loaned Executives

Employers Mutual Charitable Foundation

Giving Contact

Joe Smith, Manager, Executive Director
Employers Mutual Charitable Foundation
PO Box 712
Des Moines, IA 50303-0712
Phone: (515)280-2171
Web: http://www.emcins.com/about/communityinvolvement.htm

Description

EIN: 421343474
Organization Type: Corporate Foundation
Giving Locations: IA
Grant Types: General Support.

Financial Summary

Total Giving: $477,360 (2001); $604,451 (2000); $813,042 (1999). Note: Contributes through foundation only.
Giving Analysis: Giving for 2000 includes: foundation grants to United Way ($215,378); foundation ($389,073); 1999: foundation grants to United Way ($238,934); foundation ($574,108); 1998: foundation grants to United Way ($129,402);
Assets: $2,753,559 (2001); $2,998,255 (2000); $3,367,565 (1999)
Gifts Received: $48,350 (2001); $94,756 (1998); $2,050,986 (1997). Note: Contributions are received from Employers Mutual Charitable Trust and Employers Mutual Casualty Company.

Typical Recipients

Arts & Humanities: Arts Associations & Councils, Arts Centers, Arts Festivals, Ballet, Arts & Humanities-General, Historic Preservation, History & Archaeology, Libraries, Literary Arts, Museums/Galleries, Music, Opera, Performing Arts, Public Broadcasting

Civic & Public Affairs: African American Affairs, Botanical Gardens/Parks, Business/Free Enterprise, Civil Rights, Clubs, Community Foundations, Civic & Public Affairs-General, Housing, Municipalities/Towns, Parades/Festivals, Public Policy, Safety, Urban & Community Affairs, Women's Affairs, Zoos/Aquariums

Education: Business Education, Colleges & Universities, Education Funds, Elementary Education (Private), Elementary Education (Public), Education-General, International Studies, Minority Education, Preschool Education, Private Education (Precollege), Public Education (Precollege), Secondary Education (Public), Student Aid

Environment: Environment-General, Resource Conservation

Health: Cancer, Children's Health/Hospitals, Diabetes, Emergency/Ambulance Services, Eyes/Blindness, Health-General, Health Policy/Cost Containment, Hospices, Hospitals, Multiple Sclerosis

International: International Relations

Religion: Jewish Causes, Religious Welfare

Science: Scientific Centers & Institutes

Social Services: Camps, Child Welfare, Community Centers, Community Service Organizations, Family Services, Food/Clothing Distribution, People with Disabilities, Recreation & Athletics, Scouts, Senior Services, Senior Services, Shelters/Homelessness, Social Services-General, Special Olympics, United Funds/United Ways, Volunteer Services, YMCA/YWCA/YMHA/YWHA, Youth Organizations

Application Procedures

Initial Contact: Send a letter of inquiry.
Application Requirements: Include intended use of funds, verification of tax-exempt status, and a list of major donors.
Deadlines: None.

Corporate Officials

Richard W. Hoffmann: general counsel, chief operating officer B Des Moines, IA 1953. ED Dartmouth College (1976); University of Colorado (1979). PRIM CORP EMPL general counsel: Employers Mutual Casualty Co. ADD CORP EMPL general counsel: American Liberty Insurance Co.; general counsel: Illinois EMCASCO Insurance Co.; general counsel: Dakota Fire Insurance Co.; general counsel: EMC Insurance Group Inc.; general counsel: EMC Reinsurance Co.; general counsel: EMCASSCO Insurance Co.; general counsel: Employers Modern Life Co.; general counsel: Farm and City Insurance Co.; general counsel: Union Insurance Co. of Providence ADD NONPR EMPL member legal committee: Alliance of American Insurers. NONPR AFFIL member: American Corp. Counsel Association; member: American Council Life Insurers; member: American Bar Association.

Fredrick A. Schiek: executive vice president, chief operating officer B Readlyn, IA 1934. ED Drake University (1959). PRIM CORP EMPL director: EMC Insurance Group Co. CORP AFFIL director: Mutual Reinsurance Bureau. NONPR AFFIL director: Employers Mutual; vice chairman: Union Insurance Co. of Providence; director: CCIC; director: Alliance American Insurers.

Foundation Officials

Ronald D. Herman: treasurer
Bruce Gunn Kelley: vice president, director B Philadelphia, PA 1954. ED Dartmouth College AB (1976); University of Iowa Law School JD (1979). PRIM CORP EMPL president, chief executive officer, director: Employers Mutual Casualty Co. ADD CORP EMPL president, chief executive officer: EMC Insurance Group Inc.; treasurer: EMC Underwriters Ltd. Inc. CORP AFFIL chairman: Illinois Emcasco Insurance Co.; chief executive officer: Employers Modern Life Co.; chairman: Farm City Insurance Co.; director: Alliance America Insurance Co.; chairman: American Liberty Insurance Co. NONPR AFFIL president: Midlowa Council Boy Scouts America; trustee: National Committee Drunk Drivers; member: Iowa Bar Association; member advisory board: Iowa Public Employees Retirement Systems; director: Des Moines Arts Center; director: Greater Des Moines Sports Authority. CLUB AFFIL Masons Club; Rotary Club; Des Moines Club.
George W. Kochheiser: vice president
Joseph A. Smith: manager, executive director

Grants Analysis

Disclosure Period: calendar year ending 2001
Total Grants: $361,072*
Number of Grants: 75
Average Grant: $4,814
Highest Grant: $100,000
Lowest Grant: $50
Typical Range: $500 to $10,000
*****Note:** Giving excludes United Way.

Recent Grants

Note: Grants derived from 2001 Form 990.

General

116,288	United Way, Washington, DC
100,000	Salisbury House Foundation, Des Moines, IA
25,000	Iowa Dollars for Scholars, Des Moines, IA
25,000	Living History Farms, Des Moines, IA
15,000	Des Moines Symphony, Des Moines, IA
12,500	Iowa Games, Ames, IA
10,000	American Institute of Business, Des Moines, IA
10,000	Blank Children's Hospital Foundation, Des Moines, IA
10,000	Camp Hantessa, Boone, IA
10,000	Civic Center of Greater Des Moines, Des Moines, IA

ENERGEN CORP.

Company Headquarters

605 Richard Arrington Jr. Boulevard, N.
Birmingham, AL 35203-2707
Web: http://www.energen.com

Company Description

Founded: 1978
Ticker: EGN
Exchange: NYSE
Revenue: US$677.2 million (2002)
Employees: 1,533 (2002)
SIC(s): 4900 Electric, Gas & Sanitary Services.
Parent Company: Energen Corp., 605 Richard Arrington Jr. Boulevard, N., Birmingham, AL, United States

Nonmonetary Support

Type: Donated Equipment; In-kind Services; Loaned Employees; Loaned Executives; Workplace Solicitation

Giving Contact

R. William Barber, Director, Corporate Contributions & New Business Administration
605 Richard Arrington, Jr. Blvd N.
Birmingham, AL 35203-2707
Phone: (205)326-8198

Description

Organization Type: Corporate Giving Program
Giving Locations: headquarters area only.
Grant Types: Award, Capital, Emergency, Employee Matching Gifts, General Support, Multiyear/Continuing Support, Operating Expenses, Professorship, Scholarship.

Typical Recipients

Arts & Humanities: Arts Associations & Councils, Arts Festivals, Ballet, Community Arts, Dance, Arts & Humanities-General, Historic Preservation, Libraries, Museums/Galleries, Music, Opera, Performing Arts, Public Broadcasting, Theater
Civic & Public Affairs: Chambers of Commerce, Civil Rights, Community Foundations, Civic & Public Affairs-General, Inner-City Development, Law & Justice, Philanthropic Organizations, Public Policy, Urban & Community Affairs, Zoos/Aquariums
Education: Colleges & Universities, Education Funds, Elementary Education (Public), Faculty Development, Education-General, Literacy, Minority Education, Science/Mathematics Education, Secondary Education (Public)
Health: AIDS/HIV, Arthritis, Cancer, Children's Health/Hospitals, Clinics/Medical Centers, Diabetes, Eyes/Blindness, Health-General, Heart, Hospices, Hospitals, Kidney, Medical Rehabilitation, Mental Health, Multiple Sclerosis, Respiratory, Single-Disease Health Associations
Religion: Religious Welfare
Social Services: At-Risk Youth, Child Welfare, Community Service Organizations, Family Services, People with Disabilities, Recreation & Athletics, Scouts, Senior Services, Shelters/Homelessness, Social Services-General, United Funds/United Ways, Volunteer Services, YMCA/YWCA/YMHA/YWHA

Application Procedures

Initial Contact: Send a brief letter of inquiry and a full proposal. Include a description of organization, amount requested, purpose of funds sought, recently audited financial statement, and proof of tax-exempt status. Also include a listing of salaries and benefits paid to staff members of the organizations requesting a contribution.

Restrictions

Does not support individuals, religious organizations for sectarian purposes, political or lobbying groups, organizations outside operating areas, or fraternal organizations.

Additional Information

Publications: Guidelines

Corporate Officials

Geoff C. Ketcham: executive vice president, treasurer, chief financial officero, director B Birmingham, AL 1951. ED Auburn University. PRIM CORP EMPL executive vice president, treasurer, chief financial officer: Alabama Gas Corp.
William Michael Warren, Jr.: chairman, president, chief executive officer, chief operating officer, director B Bryan, TX 1947. ED Auburn University BA (1968); Duke University JD (1971). PRIM CORP EMPL chairman, president, chief executive officer, chief operating officer, director: Energen Corp. ADD CORP EMPL chief executive officer: Alabama Gas Co.; chief executive officer: Energen Resources Corp. CORP AFFIL director: AmSouth Bank NA.

Recent Grants

Note: Grants derived from 1998 Form 990.

General

Big Oak Ranch, Gadsden, AL
United Negro College Fund, Birmingham, AL
United Way, Birmingham, AL -- operating support
YWCA Capital Camp, Birmingham, AL
Alabama Independent Colleges, Birmingham, AL

MICHAEL S. ENGL FAMILY FOUNDATION

Giving Contact

Michael S. Engl, Director
PO Box 2500
Sun Valley, ID 83353-2500
Phone: (208)726-8151

Description

Founded: 1994
EIN: 820474079
Organization Type: Private Foundation

Financial Summary

Total Giving: $150,500 (2001); $49,500 (1999); $160,869 (1998)
Assets: $2,825,495 (2001); $3,013,454 (1999); $2,197,644 (1998)
Gifts Received: $486,976 (1999); $1,029,910 (1994). Note: In 1994 and 1999, contributions were received from Michael S. Engl.

Typical Recipients

Arts & Humanities: Arts Centers, Museums/Galleries, Performing Arts
Civic & Public Affairs: Civic & Public Affairs-General, Municipalities/Towns
Education: Minority Education, Public Education (Precollege), Special Education
Environment: Environment-General, Resource Conservation
Religion: Religious Organizations

Application Procedures

Initial Contact: The foundation requests applications be made in writing. Include purpose of funds sought and a description of organization.
Deadlines: None.

Foundation Officials

Dana Riley DeGroot: director
Leslie Engl: director
Michael S. Engl: director

Grants Analysis

Disclosure Period: calendar year ending 2001
Total Grants: $150,500
Number of Grants: 18
Average Grant: $8,361
Highest Grant: $30,000
Lowest Grant: $500
Typical Range: $1,000 to $15,000

Recent Grants

Note: Grants derived from 2000 Form 990.

General

60,000	Lensic Performing Arts Center, Santa Fe, NM -- benevolent contribution
20,000	Monastery of Christ in the Desert, Abiquiu, NM -- benevolent contribution
20,000	Wood River Land Trust, Ketchum, ID -- benevolent contribution
15,000	Sun Valley Center for the Arts, Sun Valley, ID -- benevolent charity
10,000	Blaine County Citizens for Smart Growth, Ketchum, ID -- benevolent contribution

10,000	Nature Conservancy, Ketchum, ID -- benevolent contribution
6,023	Community School, Sun Valley, ID -- benevolent contribution
5,000	Ketchum Sun Valley Heritage and Ski Museum, Ketchum, ID -- benevolent contribution
3,000	Idaho Conservation League, Boise, ID -- benevolent contribution
3,000	Snake River Alliance, Ketchum, ID -- benevolent contribution

ENSIGN-BICKFORD INDUSTRIES

Company Headquarters
Simsbury, CT
Web: http://www.ensign-bickford.com

Company Description
Employees: 153
SIC(s): 2672 Coated & Laminated Paper Nec, 2823 Cellulosic Manmade Fibers.

Nonmonetary Support
Type: Donated Equipment

Ensign-Bickford Foundation

Giving Contact
Linda Angelastro, Executive Director, Corporate Communications
10 Grist Mill Road
Simsbury, CT 06070
Phone: (860)658-4411
Fax: (860)843-2805
Web: http://www.e-bind.com/community.html

Description
Founded: 1952
EIN: 066041097
Organization Type: Corporate Foundation
Giving Locations: CT: Avon, Simsbury primarily in areas of company operations.
Grant Types: Capital, Conference/Seminar, Employee Matching Gifts, General Support, Multiyear/ Continuing Support, Project, Research, Scholarship, Seed Money.

Donor Information
Founder: Ensign-Bickford Industries, Inc.

Financial Summary
Total Giving: $95,000 (2002 approx); $223,190 (2001); $229,108 (2000). Note: Contributes through corporate direct giving program and foundation.
Giving Analysis: Giving for 2000 includes: foundation scholarships ($53,000); foundation ($176,108); 1999: foundation grants to United Way ($2,199); foundation scholarships ($5,250); foundation ($212,306); 1997: foundation scholarships ($16,000); foundation ($201,634).
Assets: $147,272 (2001); $112,114 (2000); $89,287 (1999)
Gifts Received: $250,000 (2001); $250,360 (2000); $264,000 (1999). Note: Contributions are received from Ensign-Bickford Industries.

Typical Recipients
Arts & Humanities: Arts Associations & Councils, Arts Centers, Dance, Arts & Humanities-General, Historic Preservation, History & Archaeology, Libraries, Museums/Galleries, Music, Opera, Performing Arts, Theater

Civic & Public Affairs: Botanical Gardens/Parks, Chambers of Commerce, Clubs, Economic Development, Employment/Job Training, Civic & Public Affairs-General, Housing, Legal Aid, Municipalities/ Towns, Parades/Festivals, Professional & Trade Associations, Public Policy, Safety, Urban & Community Affairs, Women's Affairs

Education: Arts/Humanities Education, Business Education, Colleges & Universities, Elementary Education (Public), Engineering/Technological Education, Education-General, Medical Education, Private Education (Precollege), Public Education (Precollege), Secondary Education (Public), Student Aid

Environment: Environment-General, Sanitary Systems, Watershed

Health: Cancer, Children's Health/Hospitals, Diabetes, Health Organizations, Heart, Hospitals, Medical Research, Multiple Sclerosis, Nursing Services, Single-Disease Health Associations

International: Health Care/Hospitals

Religion: Churches, Religious Organizations, Religious Welfare

Science: Science Museums, Scientific Organizations

Social Services: Big Brother/Big Sister, Camps, Child Welfare, Community Centers, Community Service Organizations, Crime Prevention, Emergency Relief, Food/Clothing Distribution, People with Disabilities, Recreation & Athletics, Scouts, Senior Services, Social Services-General, United Funds/United Ways, Volunteer Services, YMCA/YWCA/YMHA/ YWHA, Youth Organizations

Application Procedures
Initial Contact: Send brief letter.
Application Requirements: Include purpose of request, annual budget, other funding, and geographic areas in which proceeds will be distributed.
Deadlines: None.

Restrictions
Grants are generally given to organizations within the local geographic area of the foundation's corporate offices.

Corporate Officials
Linda W. Angelastro: director corporate communications PRIM CORP EMPL director corporate communications: Ensign-Bickford Industries.
Herman J. Fonteyne: president, chief executive officer, director B Ghent, Belgium 1939. ED University of Louvain (1961); University of Ghent (1963). PRIM CORP EMPL president, chief executive officer, director: Ensign-Bickford Industries Inc. CORP AFFIL officer: Ensign-Bickford Haz-Pros Inc.; chairman: Ensign-Bickford Realty Corp.; director: CT Natural Gas Corp.; chairman, chief executive officer, director: Ensign-Bickford Co.
Joseph Ensign Lovejoy: chairman, director B Boston, MA 1940. ED Nichols College (1963). PRIM CORP EMPL chairman, director: Ensign-Bickford Industries Inc. ADD CORP EMPL director: Ensign-Bickford Co.

Foundation Officials
Linda W. Angelastro: executive director (see above)
Robert Edward Darling, Jr.: chairman B Oakland, CA 1937. ED San Francisco State University BA (1959); Yale University School of Drama MFA (1963). PRIM CORP EMPL artistic producer: Acorn Theatre. CORP AFFIL manager: MG Taylor Corp.; manager: Darling Associates Garden Design; director: Ensign-Bickford Industries; vice president: Bushnell Horace Memorial Hall Corp. NONPR AFFIL member: Un Scenic Artists; member: Washington Daffodil Society; member, panelist: Opera America; panelist: National Institute Music Theater; panelist: National Opera Institute; member: Logan Circle Association; member: Actors Equity - Canada; member: American Guild Musical Artists.
Janet DeLissio: treasurer

Michael Thomas Long: director B Hartford, CT 1942. ED University of Notre Dame BA (1964); University of Connecticut JD (1967). PRIM CORP EMPL vice president, general counsel, secretary: Ensign-Bickford Industries Inc. CORP AFFIL director: Windsor Locks; president, director: Ensign-Bickford Haz-Pros Inc.; secretary, director: Ensign-Bickford Realty Corp.; administration, director: Ensign-Bickford Co. NONPR AFFIL member: International Society Explosive Engineers; scholarship chairman: University Notre Dame Alumni Clubs Greater Hartford; member: Hartford County Bar Association; board governors: Institute Makers Explosives; member: Connecticut Bar Association; member: Greater Hartford Chamber of Commerce; director: American Corporate Counsel Association; chairman: Bradley International Airport Committee; member: American Bar Association. CLUB AFFIL Simsbury Farms Men's Club; Hop Meadow Country Club.

Grants Analysis
Disclosure Period: calendar year ending 2001
Total Grants: $223,190
Note: Grants went to qualified charitable organizations.

Recent Grants
Note: Grants derived from 2000 Form 990.

General
50,000	Strive, Inc.
50,000	University of Connecticut, Hartford, CT
25,000	American Heart Association, Wolf Lake, IL
17,450	Science Center of Connecticut, Hartford, CT
16,000	Science Center of Connecticut, Hartford, CT
13,000	Connecticut Engineering Education Association
11,000	CCSU Foundation, New Britain, CT
10,000	Growth Council
7,000	McLean Association Golf Tournament
6,000	St. Ann's, Warsaw, MO

EQUIFAX, INC.

Company Headquarters
Atlanta, GA
Web: http://www.equifax.com

Company Description
Founded: 1899
Ticker: EFX
Exchange: NYSE
Revenue: US$1.139 billion (2001)
Employees: 5200 (2001)
SIC(s): 6411 Insurance Agents, Brokers & Service, 7323 Credit Reporting Services, 7374 Data Processing & Preparation, 7389 Business Services Nec.

Operating Locations
Equifax Inc. (AL--Lillian; AZ--Phoenix; AR--Little Rock; CA--Oroville, San Bruno; DE--New Castle; FL-- Fort Lauderdale, Orlando, St. Petersburg; GA--Atlanta, Doraville, Marietta; ID--Boise; IL--Chicago, Downers Grove, Lisle, Westchester; KS--Shawnee Mission; MD--Pikesville; MA--Woburn; MI--Grand Rapids, Southfield; MN--Brooklyn Center; NJ--Eatontown; NM--Albuquerque; NY--Albany, Amherst, Troy, Yonkers; NC--Charlotte; OK--Oklahoma City; OR-- Portland; PA--Pittsburgh; SC--North Augusta; TX--Arlington, El Paso, San Antonio, Willis; VA--Glen Allen, Richmond; WA--Federal Way; WI--Wisconsin Rapids)
Note: Operates throughout the USA; locations above include affiliate operations.

Nonmonetary Support

Value: $100,000 (2001 approx)
Type: Donated Equipment; Loaned Employees; Loaned Executives; Workplace Solicitation
Volunteer Programs: The Hearts and Hands program recognizes employees for volunteer efforts in their communities. Employees who reach milestones in hours of service are rewarded with Hearts and Hands shirts, event tickets, etc. Volunteers may participate in company-organized activities or may initiate activities on their own.

Equifax Foundation

Giving Contact

Kirby Thompson
Equifax Foundation
1550 Peachtree Street NW, Drop H-46
Atlanta, GA 30309
Phone: (404)885-8000
Fax: (404)885-8215
E-mail: kirby.thompson@equifax.com
Web: http://www.equifax.com

Description

EIN: 581296807
Organization Type: Corporate Foundation
Giving Locations: GA: Atlanta primarily metro area
Grant Types: Capital, Emergency, Employee Matching Gifts, Endowment, General Support, Matching, Multiyear/Continuing Support.

Financial Summary

Total Giving: $1,000,000 (2002 approx); $824,060 (2001); $1,000,000 (2000 approx). Note: Contributes through corporate direct giving program and foundation.
Giving Analysis: Giving for 2001 includes: nonmonetary support ($100,000); foundation ($364,133); 2000: foundation ($623,318); 1999: foundation matching gifts ($82,226); foundation grants to United Way ($328,579) foundation ($491,266);
Assets: $1,687,898 (2001); $2,000,000 (2000 approx); $1,831,518 (1999)
Gifts Received: $300,000 (2001); $475,000 (2000); $1,500,000 (1999). Note: Contributions received from Equifax Inc.

Typical Recipients

Arts & Humanities: Arts Associations & Councils, Arts Centers, Arts Funds, Ballet, Ethnic & Folk Arts, Historic Preservation, Libraries, Music, Performing Arts, Theater
Civic & Public Affairs: Botanical Gardens/Parks, Business/Free Enterprise, Chambers of Commerce, Civil Rights, Community Foundations, Economic Development, Economic Policy, Employment/Job Training, Ethnic Organizations, Civic & Public Affairs-General, Housing, Legal Aid, Municipalities/Towns, Urban & Community Affairs, Women's Affairs, Zoos/Aquariums
Education: Agricultural Education, Arts/Humanities Education, Business Education, Business-School Partnerships, Colleges & Universities, Economic Education, Education Associations, Education Funds, Education Funds, Education Reform, Engineering/Technological Education, Education-General, Literacy, Medical Education, Minority Education, Preschool Education, Private Education (Precollege), Special Education
Environment: Environment-General
Health: Cancer, Children's Health/Hospitals, Emergency/Ambulance Services, Health-General, Health Organizations, Heart, Hospices, Hospitals, Kidney, Medical Rehabilitation, Multiple Sclerosis, Nursing Services, Prenatal Health Issues, Public Health, Research/Studies Institutes, Single-Disease Health Associations

International: Foreign Arts Organizations, Health Care/Hospitals, International Development, International Organizations, International Peace & Security Issues, International Relations, Missionary/Religious Activities
Religion: Jewish Causes, Religious Welfare
Science: Observatories & Planetariums, Science Museums
Social Services: Big Brother/Big Sister, Camps, Child Welfare, Community Centers, Community Service Organizations, Day Care, Delinquency & Criminal Rehabilitation, Emergency Relief, Family Services, Food/Clothing Distribution, People with Disabilities, Senior Services, Shelters/Homelessness, Social Services-General, Special Olympics, Substance Abuse, United Funds/United Ways, Youth Organizations

Application Procedures

Initial Contact: Request application guidelines, then send written proposal.
Application Requirements: Include a description of organization, purpose of funds sought, proof of tax-exempt status, explanation of how funds will be used, annual report, list of officers and directors, and why Equifax would be an appropriate donor.
Review Process: Proposals reviewed by foundation vice president prior to consideration by donations committee, then submitted to foundation committee for approval; committee consists of four executives.

Restrictions

Foundation primarily supports organizations with which it has an established relationship.
Does not support fraternal organizations, goodwill advertising, individuals, political or lobbying groups, member agencies of united funds, or religious organizations for sectarian purposes.
In general, will not give grants for memorials, to cover operating deficits, to projects that are primarily fundraising events, or to local or regional chapters of national organizations. that are primarily fundraising events, or to local or regional chapters of national organizations.

Additional Information

Grants are not renewed automatically. Organizations must re-apply for funding each year unless multi-year campaigns have been approved by the Donations Committee.
The Donations Committee, the panel which directs Equifax's contributions program, is made up of executive officers.
Trust Company Bank, Atlanta, GA, is also listed as the foundation's corporate trustee. corporate trustee. corporate trustee. corporate trustee.

Corporate Officials

John T. Chandler: corporate vice president, chief administrative officer B 1948. PRIM CORP EMPL corporate vice president, chief administrative officer: Equifax Inc. ADD CORP EMPL vice president: Equifax Payment Service Inc.
Karen H. Gaston: chief executive officer PRIM CORP EMPL chief executive officer: Equifax Inc.
David A. Post: corporate vice president, chief financial officer B Canfield, OH 1953. ED Ohio University BBA (1975). PRIM CORP EMPL corporate vice president, chief financial officer: Equifax Inc. ADD CORP EMPL chief financial officer: Equifax Credit Information Service.

Foundation Officials

John T. Chandler: trustee (see above)
Thomas F. Chapman: trustee
Philip J. Mazzilli: trustee
David A. Post: vice president (see above)
Kirby A. Thompson: trustee

Grants Analysis

Disclosure Period: calendar year ending 2001
Total Grants: $372,883*
Number of Grants: 50
Average Grant: $7,500
Highest Grant: $50,000
Lowest Grant: $500
Typical Range: $1,300 to $24,000
*****Note:** Giving excludes matching gifts, scholarships, and United Way.

Recent Grants

Note: Grants derived from 2001 Form 990.

General

100,000	United Way Metro Atlanta, Atlanta, GA
100,000	United Way Metro Atlanta, Atlanta, GA
50,000	Gettysburg College, Gettysburg, PA
50,000	Woodruff Arts Center, Atlanta, GA
40,000	Atlanta Botanical Gardens, Atlanta, GA
36,300	Woodruff Arts Center, Atlanta, GA
33,333	East Lake Community Foundation, Atlanta, GA
32,500	Habitat for Humanity, Atlanta, GA
24,000	United Way of Pinellas County, Clearwater, FL
17,000	Carter Center Atlanta Project, Atlanta, GA

ARMAND G. ERPF FUND

Giving Contact

Sue E. Van de Bovenkamp, President
640 Park Ave.
New York, NY 10021
Phone: (212)535-6678

Description

Founded: 1951
EIN: 136085594
Organization Type: Private Foundation
Giving Locations: NY
Grant Types: General Support.

Donor Information

Founder: the late Armand G. Erpf

Financial Summary

Total Giving: $517,213 (fiscal year ending November 30, 2000); $556,917 (fiscal 1999); $538,762 (fiscal 1998)
Assets: $14,899,265 (fiscal 2000); $14,465,272 (fiscal 1999); $12,958,481 (fiscal 1998)
Gifts Received: $287,493 (fiscal 2000); $251,469 (fiscal 1999); $206,283 (fiscal 1998). Note: In fiscal 1998, 1999 and 2000, contributions were received from from the ERPF Charitable Trust.

Typical Recipients

Arts & Humanities: Arts Associations & Councils, Arts Centers, Arts Institutes, Ballet, Community Arts, Dance, Historic Preservation, Libraries, Museums/Galleries, Music, Opera, Public Broadcasting, Theater
Civic & Public Affairs: Asian American Affairs, Botanical Gardens/Parks, Economic Development, Ethnic Organizations, Civic & Public Affairs-General, Philanthropic Organizations, Zoos/Aquariums
Education: Arts/Humanities Education, Colleges & Universities, Environmental Education, Education-General, International Studies, Private Education (Precollege)
Environment: Environment-General, Resource Conservation, Wildlife Protection
Health: Hospitals, Single-Disease Health Associations

International: Foreign Educational Institutions, Health Care/Hospitals, International Development, International Environmental Issues, International Organizations, International Peace & Security Issues, International Relations, International Relief Efforts
Religion: Churches, Religious Organizations
Science: Science Museums, Scientific Centers & Institutes, Scientific Labs
Social Services: Child Welfare, Crime Prevention, Youth Organizations

Application Procedures

Initial Contact: The foundation has no formal grant application procedure or application form.
Deadlines: None.

Foundation Officials

Gina Caimi: secretary
Douglas Campbell: vice president
Armand B. Erpf: director
Cornelia A. Erpf: director
Henry B. Hyde: director
Carl L. Kempner: treasurer
Robert B. Oxnam: director
Roger David Stone: director B New York, NY 1934. ED Yale University BA (1955). NONPR AFFIL director: Scenic Hudson; president: Sustainable Development Institute; vice chairman: ECO; member: Century Association; member: Council Foreign Relations; member: Center Inter-American Relations; director: Asian Institute Technology Foundation; director: Caribbean Conservation Corp.; member: Arts International; member: ACCION International; member: Ams Foundation.
Sue Erpf Van de Bovenkamp: president, director

Grants Analysis

Disclosure Period: fiscal year ending November 30, 2000
Total Grants: $517,213
Number of Grants: 126
Average Grant: $4,105
Highest Grant: $50,000
Typical Range: $1,000 to $10,000

Recent Grants

Note: Grants derived from fiscal 2002 Form 990.

Library-Related
10,000	New York Public Library, New York, NY

General
50,000	Amazon Conservation Team, Washington, DC
35,000	Wildlife Conservation Society, New York, NY
30,000	World Wildlife Fund, Washington, DC
25,000	Catskill Center for Conservation and Development, Arkville, NY
25,000	Catskill Center for Conservation and Development, Arkville, NY
25,000	Conservation International, Washington, DC
25,000	Wildlife Conservation Society, New York, NY
20,000	World Wildlife Fund, Washington, DC
20,000	World Wildlife Fund, Washington, DC
15,000	Convent of the Sacred Heart, New York, NY

ERVING INDUSTRIES

Company Headquarters

120 E. Main St.
Erving, MA 01344
Web: http://www.fiberclaycouncil.org/erving

Company Description

Former Name: Erving Paper Mills.
Employees: 500
SIC(s): 2621 Paper Mills, 6719 Holding Companies Nec.

Operating Locations

Erving Industries (MA--Erving)

Housen Foundation

Giving Contact

Denis L. Emmett, Treasurer
120 E. Main Street
Erving, MA 01344
Phone: (978)544-3335
Fax: (978)544-2865

Alternate Contact

Personnel Administrator
Erving Paper Mills
97 E. Main Street
Erving, MA 01344
Note: Contact to request application forms.

Description

Founded: 1968
EIN: 046183673
Organization Type: Corporate Foundation
Giving Locations: MA
Grant Types: Award, Capital, Emergency, Employee Matching Gifts, Endowment, Fellowship, General Support, Multiyear/Continuing Support, Operating Expenses, Project, Scholarship.

Donor Information

Founder: Erving Paper Mills, Brattleboro Paper Products, Inc.

Financial Summary

Total Giving: $214,308 (2000); $165,121 (1999); $151,729 (1998)
Giving Analysis: Giving for 2000 includes: foundation scholarships ($1,800); foundation grants to United Way ($2,000); foundation ($210,508); 1999: foundation grants to United Way ($1,500); foundation scholarships ($1,800); foundation ($161,821); 1998: foundation scholarships ($1,800); foundation ($149,929);
Assets: $326,764 (2000); $424,068 (1999); $424,680 (1998)
Gifts Received: $100,000 (2000); $150,000 (1999); $40,000 (1998). Note: Contributions are received from Erving Paper Mills.

Typical Recipients

Arts & Humanities: Arts Associations & Councils, Arts Funds, Arts & Humanities-General, Libraries, Music, Performing Arts
Civic & Public Affairs: Botanical Gardens/Parks, Clubs, Community Foundations, Ethnic Organizations, Civic & Public Affairs-General, Housing, Municipalities/Towns, Philanthropic Organizations
Education: Business-School Partnerships, Colleges & Universities, Community & Junior Colleges, Education Funds, Elementary Education (Public), Engineering/Technological Education, Education-General, Health & Physical Education, Literacy, Medical Education, Private Education (Precollege), Public Education (Precollege), Science/Mathematics Education, Secondary Education (Public), Social Sciences Education, Student Aid, Vocational & Technical Education
Health: Cancer, Children's Health/Hospitals, Clinics/Medical Centers, Emergency/Ambulance Services, Health-General, Heart, Home-Care Services, Hospices, Hospitals, Hospitals (University Affiliated), Preventive Medicine/Wellness Organizations

International: International Peace & Security Issues, Missionary/Religious Activities
Religion: Churches, Religion-General, Jewish Causes, Synagogues/Temples
Science: Science Museums
Social Services: At-Risk Youth, Child Abuse, Child Welfare, Crime Prevention, Domestic Violence, Food/Clothing Distribution, Recreation & Athletics, Scouts, Shelters/Homelessness, Social Services-General, United Funds/United Ways, Veterans, YMCA/YWCA/YMHA/YWHA, Youth Organizations

Application Procedures

Initial Contact: Application forms are available upon request from the personnel administrator.
Deadlines: February 28.

Restrictions

Does not support individuals (except employee-related scholarships).

Additional Information

Provides scholarships to children of employees of Erving Industries and its subsidiaries.

Corporate Officials

Denis L. Emmett: chief financial officer, president, chief executive officer, director B 1954. ED University of Massachusetts BA (1976). PRIM CORP EMPL treasurer: Industries Inc. ADD CORP EMPL treasurer: Erving Paper Products Inc.; treasurer: Erving Paper Mills Inc.
Charles B. Housen: chairman, president, chief executive officer, director B 1932. PRIM CORP EMPL chairman, president, chief executive officer, director: Erving Industries Inc. ADD CORP EMPL chairman: Erving Paper Miles Inc.; president: Erving Paper Products Inc.; president: Flamingo Products Inc. CORP AFFIL director: Massachusetts Electric Co.

Foundation Officials

Charles B. Housen: president, director (see above)
Morris Housen: secretary, director PRIM CORP EMPL treasurer: Erving Industries Inc. ADD CORP EMPL assistant treasurer: Erving Paper Products Inc.
Morton A. Slavin: clerk, director

Grants Analysis

Disclosure Period: calendar year ending 2000
Total Grants: $210,508*
Number of Grants: 23
Average Grant: $5,238*
Highest Grant: $50,000
Lowest Grant: $250
Typical Range: $1,000 to $50,000
*Note: Giving excludes scholarships; United Way. Average grant figure excludes two highest grants totaling $100,000.

Recent Grants

Note: Grants derived from 2001 Form 990.

General
50,000	Brandeis University, Waltham, MA -- GSIEF pioneers fund
50,000	Brandeis University, Waltham, MA -- Annual alumni fund
25,000	Brandeis University, Waltham, MA -- GSIEF Dean's discretionary fund
15,000	Hadassah, Palm Beach, FL
7,702	Erving Elementary School, Erving, MA -- Annual Read-A-Thon
5,000	Anti-Defamation League, New York, NY
5,000	Combined Jewish Philanthropies, Boston, MA
3,000	Greenfield Community College Foundation, Greenfield, MA
2,000	Athol Area United Way, Athol, MA -- 2001 campaign
2,000	Athol Area United Way, Athol, MA -- 2002 campaign

ESSICK FOUNDATION

Giving Contact

Robert Essick, President, Treasurer
1379 La Solana Dr.
Altadena, CA 91001
Phone: (818)449-1120

Description

Founded: 1947
EIN: 956048985
Organization Type: Private Foundation
Giving Locations: CA: primarily in southern area; MA; NY; VA; WA
Grant Types: General Support.

Donor Information

Founder: the late Jeanette Marie Essick, Bryant Essick, Essick Investment Co.

Financial Summary

Total Giving: $136,300 (2001); $137,000 (2000); $147,250 (1999)
Assets: $3,024,853 (2001); $3,104,453 (2000); $3,151,971 (1999)

Typical Recipients

Arts & Humanities: Arts Institutes, Ethnic & Folk Arts, Libraries, Literary Arts, Museums/Galleries, Public Broadcasting
Civic & Public Affairs: Clubs, Philanthropic Organizations, Zoos/Aquariums
Education: Business Education, Colleges & Universities, Education Funds, Engineering/Technological Education, Science/Mathematics Education, Vocational & Technical Education
Health: Alzheimers Disease, Children's Health/Hospitals, Clinics/Medical Centers, Emergency/Ambulance Services, Eyes/Blindness, Health Organizations, Hospitals, Medical Research, Prenatal Health Issues, Preventive Medicine/Wellness Organizations, Research/Studies Institutes, Single-Disease Health Associations, Speech & Hearing
International: Foreign Arts Organizations
Religion: Churches, Religious Welfare
Social Services: Child Welfare, Community Service Organizations, Homes, People with Disabilities, Recreation & Athletics, Scouts, Special Olympics, United Funds/United Ways, Volunteer Services, YMCA/YWHA/YMHA/YWHA, Youth Organizations

Application Procedures

Initial Contact: Send a brief letter of inquiry.
Application Requirements: Include purpose of funds sought and proof of tax-exempt status.
Deadlines: None.

Foundation Officials

Bryant Essick: president
Robert N. Essick: president, vice president B Los Angeles, CA 1942. PRIM NONPR EMPL professor: University of California, Riverside. NONPR AFFIL member, board overseers: Huntington Library; member: Modern Language Association.
Jenijoy LaBelle: secretary
Dr. James Stanger: director

Grants Analysis

Disclosure Period: calendar year ending 2001
Total Grants: $136,300
Number of Grants: 7
Average Grant: $5,571*
Highest Grant: $97,300
Typical Range: $1,000 to $25,000
*Note: Average grant figure excludes highest grant.

Recent Grants

Note: Grants derived from 2001 Form 990.

Library-Related
97,300   Huntington Library, San Marino, CA

General
25,000   University of Virginia, Charlottesville, VA
5,000   University of Rochester, Rochester, NY
4,000   California Institute of Technology, Pasadena, CA
3,000   William College Alumni, Williamstown, MA
1,000   Boy Scouts of America, Redlands, CA
1,000   Boy Scouts of America, Tacoma, WA

ETHYL CORP.

Company Headquarters

Richmond, VA
Web: http://www.ethyl.com

Company Description

Founded: 1942
Ticker: EY
Exchange: NYSE
Revenue: US$656.4 million (2002)
Employees: 1100 (2002)
SIC(s): 2869 Industrial Organic Chemicals Nec, 5169 Chemicals & Allied Products Nec.

Operating Locations

Ethyl Corp. (DC--Washington; MI--Southfield; NY--Clarence Center; TX--Houston)

Nonmonetary Support

Type: Donated Equipment; Loaned Employees

Giving Contact

Diane Hazelwood
330 S. 4th St.
Richmond, VA 23219
Phone: (804)788-5522
Fax: (804)788-5636
E-mail: contributions@ethyl.com
Web: http://www.ethyl.com/contact/contributions.html
Note: Also contact nearest field location.

Description

Organization Type: Corporate Giving Program
Giving Locations: headquarters and operating communities.
Grant Types: Capital, Challenge, Employee Matching Gifts, Endowment, General Support, Professorship, Scholarship.
Note: Employee matching gift ratio: 1 to 1.

Financial Summary

Total Giving: $1,300,000 (1998 approx); $1,400,000 (1997 approx); $1,300,000 (1996 approx). Note: Contributes through corporate direct giving program only.

Typical Recipients

Arts & Humanities: Arts Associations & Councils, Arts Centers, Arts Funds, Community Arts, Historic Preservation, Libraries, Museums/Galleries, Music, Opera, Performing Arts, Public Broadcasting
Civic & Public Affairs: Business/Free Enterprise, Economic Development, Urban & Community Affairs
Education: Colleges & Universities, Economic Education, Science/Mathematics Education
Environment: Environment-General
Health: Emergency/Ambulance Services, Health Organizations, Hospitals
Science: Observatories & Planetariums, Science Exhibits & Fairs, Scientific Centers & Institutes, Scientific Organizations

Social Services: Community Service Organizations, Shelters/Homelessness, United Funds/United Ways, Youth Organizations

Application Procedures

Initial Contact: Send a brief letter of inquiry.
Application Requirements: Include a statement of purpose; brief description of nature and scope of activities; current financial condition (balance sheet); list of board members and staff manager; copy of IRS determination letter; rationale for why company is appropriate donor.
Deadlines: Before September 1.
Review Process: The program is administered from headquarters; community relations committees (plant manager, office manager, department head, deputy) determine involvement on local level, with vice president of external affairs acting as liaison; top management official at each field location responsible for budgeting annual support.
Decision Notification: The annual budget is presented and approved in late fall; contributions on an unbudgeted basis are extremely limited.

Restrictions

Contributions are not made to religious organizations for religious purposes, individuals in support of a personal project for profit, fraternal groups, local organizations in communities where company does not have significant operations, or in response to telephone or mass mail solicitations.
The corporation does not directly support political contributions. However, limited contributions are made through Ethyl Corporation Political Action Committee, which consists of funds contributed by Ethyl employees. Political Action Committee, which consists of funds contributed by Ethyl employees. Foundation primarily funds preselected organizations.

Additional Information

Company annually budgets a limited amount to support charitable organizations with small advertisements in printed programs aimed at raising funds.

Corporate Officials

Thomas E. Gottwald: president, chief executive officer B 1962. ED Virginia Military Institute BS (1983); Harvard University MBA (1984). PRIM CORP EMPL president, chief executive officer: Ethyl Corp. ADD CORP EMPL president, director: Ethyl Petroleum Additives Inc.; president: Ethyl Additives Corp.

Giving Program Officials

Thomas E. Gottwald: B 1962. ED Virginia Military Institute BS (1983); Harvard University MBA (1984). PRIM CORP EMPL president, chief executive officer: Ethyl Corp. ADD CORP EMPL president, director: Ethyl Petroleum Additives Inc.; president: Ethyl Additives Corp.
Henry C. Page, Jr.: PRIM CORP EMPL vice president human resources & external affairs: Ethyl Corp.

Grants Analysis

Typical Range: $1,000 to $5,000

EDWARD P. EVANS FOUNDATION

Giving Contact

Edward P. Evans, Officer
Edward P. Evans Foundation
PO Box 46, Route 602
Casanova, VA 20139
Phone: (212)765-9500

Description

Founded: 1991
EIN: 256232129
Organization Type: Private Foundation
Grant Types: General Support.

Donor Information

Founder: Established in 1991 by Edward P. Evans.

Financial Summary

Total Giving: $287,514 (fiscal year ending November 30, 2001); $549,048 (fiscal 2000); $712,541 (fiscal 1999)
Assets: $4,026,953 (fiscal 2001); $5,798,624 (fiscal 2000); $7,332,352 (fiscal 1999)
Gifts Received: $2,142,538 (fiscal 1999). Note: In fiscal 1999, contributions were received from The Evans Foundation. In fiscal 1989, contributions were received from Edward P. Evans.

Typical Recipients

Arts & Humanities: Arts Associations & Councils, Dance, Historic Preservation, Libraries, Museums/Galleries, Music
Civic & Public Affairs: Botanical Gardens/Parks, Civic & Public Affairs-General, Zoos/Aquariums
Education: Business Education, Colleges & Universities, Education Reform, Elementary Education (Private), Education-General, Private Education (Precollege), Public Education (Precollege), Social Sciences Education, Student Aid
Environment: Environment-General, Resource Conservation, Wildlife Protection
Health: AIDS/HIV, Cancer, Children's Health/Hospitals, Hospices, Hospitals, Medical Research, Single-Disease Health Associations
International: Foreign Arts Organizations, Foreign Educational Institutions, Human Rights, International Affairs
Religion: Churches
Social Services: Animal Protection, Animal Protection, Child Welfare, Community Service Organizations, Recreation & Athletics, United Funds/United Ways

Application Procedures

Initial Contact: The foundation has no formal grant application procedure or application form.
Deadlines: None.

Foundation Officials

Edward Parker Evans: off B Pittsburgh, PA 1942. ED Yale University BA (1964); Harvard University MBA (1967). CORP AFFIL owner: Spring Hill Farm Virginia; director: HBD Industries. NONPR AFFIL member: Andover Development Board. CLUB AFFIL Round Hill Club; Spouting Rock Beach Association; Rolling Rock Club; Lyford Cay Club; River Club; Harvard Business School Club; Blind Brook Country Club; Duquesne Club.
Dorsey Gardner: trustee
Charles J. Queenan, Jr.: trustee

Grants Analysis

Disclosure Period: fiscal year ending November 30, 2001
Total Grants: $287,514
Number of Grants: 20
Average Grant: $3,739*
Highest Grant: $202,210
Lowest Grant: $25
Typical Range: $1,000 to $5,000
*Note: Average grant figure excludes two highest grants ($220,210).

Recent Grants

Note: Grants derived from fiscal 2000 Form 990.

Library-Related

125,000	National Sporting Library, Middleburg, VA

General

300,000	CAP Cure, Santa Monica, CA
25,000	Highland School, Warrenton, VA
25,000	Lawyers Committee for Human Rights, New York, NY
10,000	Eaglebrook Alumni Fund, Deerfield, MA
10,000	Harvard Business School, Cambridge, MA
10,000	Piedmont Environmental Council, Warrenton, VA
10,000	University of Pittsburgh Cancer Institute, Pittsburgh, PA
9,532	Circles of the Kennedy Center, The, Washington, DC -- National Symphony Orchestra
9,530	Society of Memorial Sloan-Kettering Cancer Center, New York, NY
6,936	Central Park Conservatory, New York, NY

LETTIE PATE EVANS FOUNDATION, INC.

Giving Contact

Charles H. McTier, President
50 Hurt Plaza, Suite 1200
Atlanta, GA 30303
Phone: (404)522-6755
Fax: (404)522-7026
E-mail: fdns@woodruff.org
Web: http://www.lpevans.org

Description

Founded: 1945
EIN: 586004644
Organization Type: General Purpose Foundation
Giving Locations: GA: emphasis on Atlanta; VA
Grant Types: Capital, Matching, Project, Seed Money.
Note: The foundation also supports land and equipment acquisition.

Donor Information

Founder: Mrs. Lettie Pate Evans established this foundation in Georgia in 1945. It is one of three related foundations. The other two, the Lettie Pate Whitehead Foundation and the Joseph B. Whitehead Foundation, were set up by Mrs. Evans' children by her first marriage. All three foundations share the same office and staff. The foundation also shares a common administrative arrangement with the Robert W. Woodruff Foundation.

Financial Summary

Total Giving: $2,310,000 (2003 approx); $1,000,000 (2002 approx); $1,750,000 (2001 approx)
Assets: $245,000,000 (2003 approx); $247,967,996 (2002); $325,782,581 (2000). Note: Asset increase from rise in value of foundation's holdings of Coca Cola stock, which doubled after a two-for-one split.

Typical Recipients

Arts & Humanities: Arts Centers, Arts Festivals, Arts Funds, Ballet, Dance, Ethnic & Folk Arts, Film & Video, Historic Preservation, History & Archaeology, Libraries, Museums/Galleries, Music, Opera, Performing Arts, Theater
Civic & Public Affairs: African American Affairs, Botanical Gardens/Parks, Business/Free Enterprise, Community Foundations, Nonprofit Management, Women's Affairs, Zoos/Aquariums
Education: Business Education, Colleges & Universities, Economic Education, Education Associations, Education Funds, Education Reform, Faculty Development, Education-General, International Studies, Leadership Training, Literacy, Minority Education, Private Education (Precollege), Public Education (Precollege), Science/Mathematics Education, Special Education, Student Aid
Environment: Environment-General, Resource Conservation
Health: Cancer, Health Organizations, Hospitals, Nursing Services, Public Health
Religion: Religious Welfare, Seminaries
Science: Science Museums
Social Services: Child Welfare, Community Centers, Homes, YMCA/YWCA/YMHA/YWHA, Youth Organizations

Application Procedures

Initial Contact: There is no standard application form. Organizations are encouraged to make an informal inquiry before sending a proposal. Proposals should be made in letter form.
Application Requirements: Proposal letters should include a brief description of organization, its purposes, programs, staffing and governing board; the organization's latest financial statements, including the most recent audit report; a description of the proposed project and full justification for its funding; an itemized project budget, including other sources of support in hand or anticipated; and evidence from the IRS of the organization's tax-exempt status and that the applicant organization is not a private foundation.
Deadlines: February 1 for the April meeting and September 1 for the November meeting.
Review Process: Requests are reviewed upon receipt. If a proposal clearly is not within the giving interests of the foundation, the applicant will be notified immediately. The foundation grants an interview at the request of an applicant, but only after the proposal is determined to be of interest. Applicants are given final notification of grant decisions within thirty days of board meetings.

Restrictions

Grants are limited to tax-exempt public charities and governmental agencies restricted to the metropolitan Atlanta area. The foundation does not make loans or give grants to individuals. The foundation does not give grants for regular operating expenses. The foundation does not make grants to any institution or agency if a substantial part of its activities consists of carrying on propaganda or otherwise attempting to influence legislation.

Additional Information

Occasionally, the foundation provides support to institutions in Virginia favored by Mrs. Evans. The foundation prefers to make grants for one-time capital projects; awards for basic operating expenses are usually avoided.

The foundation shares offices and administrative staff with the Robert W. Woodruff Foundation, Joseph B. Whitehead Foundation, Lettie Pate Whitehead Foundation, and Ichauway, Inc. Grant and proposals submitted to the Lettie Pate Evans Foundation may also be considered by one or more of the associated foundations. It is not necessary to communicate separately with more than one of these foundations in seeking information or requesting grant support.
Publications: guidelines; brochure

Foundation Officials

P. Russell Hardin: vice president, secretary PRIM NONPR EMPL vice president-secretary: Ichauway Inc. NONPR AFFIL vice president-secretary: Joseph W Jones Ecological Research Center.
Joseph West Jones: chairman emeritus B Georgetown, DE 1912. ED Beacom College BA (1932). PRIM CORP EMPL chairman: Ichauway Inc.
Wilton D. Looney: trustee B 1919. PRIM CORP EMPL honorary chairman, director: Genuine Parts Co. CORP AFFIL director: RPC Inc.; director: Rollins Inc.; director: Coca-Cola Enterprises Inc.; trustee: Ichauway Inc. NONPR AFFIL trustee: Joseph W Jones Ecological Research Center.
Charles Harvey McTier: president B Columbus, GA 1939. ED Emory University BBA (1961). PRIM CORP EMPL president: Ichauway Inc. CORP AFFIL director:

SunTrust Bank Georgia Inc.; director: SunTrust Bank Atlanta. NONPR AFFIL trustee: North Georgia United Methodist Foundation; member: President Cir National Academy Sciences Institute Medicine; president: Joseph W Jones Ecological Research Center; member: Management Executives Society; chairman board trustee: Foundation Center; pub member: Joint Commission Accreditation Health Care Organizations; vice chairman, chairman management committee: Council Foundations; member: Association Emory Alumni. CLUB AFFIL Druid Hills Golf Club; Piedmont Driving Club; director: Commerce Club.

James Malcolm Sibley: trustee B Atlanta, GA August 05, 1919. ED Princeton University AB (1941); Woodrow Wilson School of Law (1942); Harvard University Law School (1945-1946). CORP AFFIL director: Summit Industries; director: Rock-Tenn Co.; director: Ichauway Inc. NONPR AFFIL member: Georgia Bar Association; trustee: AG Rhodes Home; member: Atlanta Bar Association; member: American College Probate Counsel; member: American Law Institute; member: American Bar Foundation; member: American Bar Association. CLUB AFFIL Piedmont Driving Club; Commerce Club.

Hughes Spalding, Jr.: vice chairman, trustee ED Georgetown University; University of Georgia.

J. Lee Tribble: treasurer PRIM CORP EMPL treasurer: Ichauway Inc. NONPR AFFIL treasurer: Joseph W Jones Ecological Research Center.

James Bryan Williams: trustee B Sewanee, TN 1933. ED Emory University AB (1955). PRIM CORP EMPL chairman, chief executive officer, director: SunTrust Banks, Inc. CORP AFFIL director: Sonat Inc.; director: RPC Energy Services Inc.; director: RPC Inc.; director: Georgia-Pacific Corp.; director: Rollins Inc.; director: Coca-Cola Co.; director: Genuine Parts Co.; director: Boral Industries Inc. NONPR AFFIL director: Federal Reserve Bank Atlanta; chairman board trustees: Robert R Woodruff Health Science Center; trustee: Emory University; member: Bankers Roundtable. CLUB AFFIL Piedmont Driving Club; member: Ocean Forest Golf Club; Peachtree Golf Club; Capital City Club; Commerce Club.

Grants Analysis

Disclosure Period: calendar year ending 2000
Total Grants: $5,358,000*
Number of Grants: 9
Average Grant: $256,444*
Highest Grant: $2,050,000
Lowest Grant: $8,000
Typical Range: $250,000 to $500,000
*Note: Grants analysis provided by foundation. Average grant excludes two highest grants ($2,050,000 and $1,000,000).

Recent Grants

Note: Grants derived from 2000 Form 990.

General

2,050,000	Children's Health Care of Atlanta, Atlanta, GA -- for Pediatric Residency Program
1,000,000	Georgia Partnership for Excellence in Education, Atlanta, GA -- establishment of a fund to enable Georgia teachers to pursue certification by the National Board for Professional Teaching Standards
500,000	Atlanta Ballet, Atlanta, GA -- for campaign to purchase, renovate and expand
500,000	Episcopal High School, Alexandria, VA -- for construction of a new Fine Arts Center
500,000	Virginia Museum of Fine Arts Foundation, Richmond, VA -- for Lattie Pate Whitehead Evans Exhibition Fund
500,000	Wesleyan School, Atlanta, GA -- toward purchase of land and classroom trailers
250,000	Washington and Lee University, Lexington, VA -- renovation of Reid Hall
50,000	State YMCA Georgia, Atlanta, GA -- for renovation of headquarters building
8,000	Daughters of the American Revolution, Yorktown, VA -- for architectural and engineering study of renovations

THOMAS J. EVANS FOUNDATION

Giving Contact

J. Gilbert Reese, Chairman & Chief Executive Officer
36 N. 2nd Street
Newark, OH 43055-0764
Phone: (740)345-3431

Description

Founded: 1965
EIN: 316055767
Organization Type: General Purpose Foundation
Giving Locations: OH: Licking County
Grant Types: Capital, General Support, Operating Expenses, Scholarship, Seed Money.

Donor Information

Founder: the late Thomas J. Evans

Financial Summary

Total Giving: $395,292 (fiscal year ending October 31, 2001); $47,093 (fiscal 2000); $635,962 (fiscal 1998)
Assets: $21,886,153 (fiscal 2001); $22,698,591 (fiscal 2000); $21,720,617 (fiscal 1998)
Gifts Received: $700 (fiscal 2000)

Typical Recipients

Arts & Humanities: Arts Associations & Councils, History & Archaeology, Libraries, Museums/Galleries, Theater, Visual Arts
Civic & Public Affairs: Botanical Gardens/Parks, Clubs, Community Foundations, Economic Development, Civic & Public Affairs-General, Housing, Municipalities/Towns, Urban & Community Affairs
Education: Colleges & Universities, Education Reform, Elementary Education (Public), Public Education (Precollege), Student Aid
Environment: Environment-General
Religion: Churches, Ministries, Religious Organizations, Religious Welfare
Social Services: Community Service Organizations, Recreation & Athletics, Senior Services, Social Services-General, YMCA/YWCA/YMHA/YWHA, Youth Organizations

Application Procedures

Initial Contact: The foundation has no formal grant application procedure or application form. Send a brief letter of inquiry.
Deadlines: None.

Restrictions

Grants are not made to individuals. Grants are restricted to organizations in Licking County, Ohio.

Foundation Officials

J. Gilbert Reese: chairman, chief executive officer B 1926. PRIM CORP EMPL chairman board, director: First Federal Saving & Loan Association.
Louella H. Reese: vice president, treasurer
Sarah R. Wallace: president, secretary PRIM CORP EMPL chairman: First Federal Saving & Loan Association.

Grants Analysis

Disclosure Period: fiscal year ending October 31, 2001
Total Grants: $395,292
Number of Grants: 8

Highest Grant: $155,190
Lowest Grant: $50

Recent Grants

Note: Grants derived from 2000 Form 990.

General

15,000	Catholic Social Service, Sacramento, CA -- repairs
7,500	Licking County Housing Authority -- downtown restoration
5,903	Ohio State University, Columbus, OH -- property improvements
5,412	55/61 North 6th Street -- for property held for charitable use
4,515	YMCA, Franklin, PA -- reimburse real estate taxes
2,950	A Frame -- for property held for charitable use
2,500	Licking County Housing Authority -- repairs
1,570	Granville Garden Club, Granville, OH -- daffodil
1,000	Licking County Housing Authority -- playground
376	Central School -- repairs

EVENING POST PUBLISHING CO.

Company Headquarters

134 Columbus St.
Charleston, SC 29403
Web: http://www.esequelsolutions.com

Company Description

Employees: 650
SIC(s): 2711 Newspapers.

Operating Locations

Evening Post Publishing Co. (AZ--Tucson; CO--Pueblo; ID--Nampa; MT--Butte, Missoula; NY--New York; SC--Aiken, Charleston, Kingstree)

Post and Courier Foundation

Giving Contact

J. Douglas Donehue, Administrator
134 Columbus Street
Charleston, SC 29403-4800
Phone: (843)937-5789

Description

EIN: 576020356
Organization Type: Corporate Foundation
Giving Locations: headquarters area only.
Grant Types: Award, Capital, Challenge, General Support.

Financial Summary

Total Giving: $770,614 (2000); $955,944 (1999); $965,040 (1998). Note: Contributes through foundation only.
Giving Analysis: Giving for 2000 includes: foundation scholarships ($1,873); foundation grants to United Way ($60,119); foundation ($708,652); 1999: foundation scholarships ($1,575); foundation grants to United Way ($54,504); foundation ($899,865); 1998: foundation scholarships ($4,850); foundation grants to United Way ($49,765)
Assets: $8,338,992 (2000); $8,045,522 (1999); $8,207,299 (1998)
Gifts Received: $534,825 (2000); $497,505 (1999); $579,133 (1998). Note: Contributions are received from the Evening Post Publishing Company.

Typical Recipients

Arts & Humanities: Arts Associations & Councils, Arts Centers, Arts Festivals, Ballet, Arts & Humanities-General, Historic Preservation, History & Archaeology, Libraries, Museums/Galleries, Music, Performing Arts, Theater

Civic & Public Affairs: Botanical Gardens/Parks, Business/Free Enterprise, Chambers of Commerce, Clubs, Community Foundations, Economic Development, Civic & Public Affairs-General, Parades/Festivals, Professional & Trade Associations, Safety, Urban & Community Affairs, Women's Affairs, Zoos/Aquariums

Education: Arts/Humanities Education, Business Education, Colleges & Universities, Education Funds, Education Reform, Education-General, Health & Physical Education, Literacy, Medical Education, Private Education (Precollege), Public Education (Precollege), Secondary Education (Private), Student Aid

Environment: Environment-General, Resource Conservation, Wildlife Protection

Health: Cancer, Health-General, Hospices, Medical Rehabilitation, Preventive Medicine/Wellness Organizations, Speech & Hearing

International: Trade

Religion: Jewish Causes, Religious Welfare

Social Services: Animal Protection, Community Service Organizations, People with Disabilities, Recreation & Athletics, Scouts, Social Services-General, United Funds/United Ways, YMCA/YWCA/YMHA/YWHA, Youth Organizations

Application Procedures

Initial Contact: Send a brief letter.
Application Requirements: Include program description, amount requested, purpose of grant sought, and any other pertinent information.
Deadlines: None.

Restrictions

Does not support individuals, religious organizations for sectarian purposes, political or lobbying groups, or organizations outside operating areas.

Corporate Officials

Peter Manigault: chairman, director B Charleston, SC 1927. ED Princeton University AB (1950). PRIM CORP EMPL chairman: Evening Post Publishing Co. NONPR AFFIL member: Audubon Society.

Travis O. Rockey: vice president, director B 1950. ED University of Florida BS (1973); Winthrop College MA (1979); Indiana University MA (1987). PRIM CORP EMPL vice president, director: Evening Post Publishing Co. CORP AFFIL secretary: KXLF Communications Inc.; treasurer: Sawtooth Communications Inc.; secretary, director: KTVQ Communications Inc.; secretary, director: Cordillera Communications Inc.; secretary: KETZ Communications Inc.

Giving Program Officials

James W. Martin: B 1943. ED Western Michigan University (1965). PRIM CORP EMPL treasurer, chief financial officer, director: Evening Post Publishing Co.

Foundation Officials

Peter Manigault: president (see above)

Grants Analysis

Disclosure Period: calendar year ending 2000
Total Grants: $708,652*
Number of Grants: 72
Average Grant: $9,842
Highest Grant: $80,000
Typical Range: $1,000 to $12,000
*Note: Giving excludes scholarships; United Way.

Recent Grants

Note: Grants derived from 2000 Form 990.

General

80,000	Nature Conservancy, Charleston, SC -- Winyah Bay Capital Project
76,466	Salvation Army, Charleston, SC -- support homeless shelter for men, women and children meals and financial assistance
66,361	Catholic Charities, Charleston, SC -- provide hot meals, clothing and financial assistance for needy at Christmas
66,361	Star Gospel Mission, Charleston, SC -- for Good Cheer Christmas Fund
60,119	Trident United Way, Charleston, SC -- annual operating fund
50,000	South Carolina Historical Society, Charleston, SC -- capital project
50,000	Spoleto Festival USA, Charleston, SC -- annual operating fund
25,524	Association for the Blind, Charleston, SC -- to provide food and clothing for blind people at Christmas
25,524	Carolina Youth Development Center, N. Charleston, SC -- for operating fund
25,000	Community Foundation, Charleston, SC

EVERETT CHARITABLE TRUST

Giving Contact

c/o Fleet National Bank, Trustee
One East Avenue
Rochester, NY 14604
Phone: (716)546-9289

Description

Founded: 1957
EIN: 156018093
Organization Type: Private Foundation
Giving Locations: NY: Auburn and Cayuga counties, NY
Grant Types: General Support.

Donor Information

Founder: the late Fred M. Everett

Financial Summary

Total Giving: $91,175 (2000); $94,928 (1999); $96,235 (1998). Note: 1996 Giving includes United Way ($49,991).
Giving Analysis: Giving for 2000 includes: foundation grants to United Way ($44,650) 1999: foundation grants to United Way ($42,452)
Assets: $2,788,169 (2000); $2,812,066 (1999); $2,768,155 (1998)
Gifts Received: $1,725 (1992)

Typical Recipients

Arts & Humanities: Arts Associations & Councils, Arts Centers, Historic Preservation, History & Archaeology, Libraries, Museums/Galleries, Music, Performing Arts

Civic & Public Affairs: Civic & Public Affairs-General

Education: Colleges & Universities, Community & Junior Colleges, Student Aid

Health: Emergency/Ambulance Services, Hospitals, Long-Term Care

International: Human Rights

Religion: Churches

Social Services: Animal Protection, Child Welfare, Community Service Organizations, Recreation & Athletics, Scouts, United Funds/United Ways, YMCA/YWCA/YMHA/YWHA, Youth Organizations

Application Procedures

Initial Contact: Send a brief letter of inquiry.
Application Requirements: Include amount requested, and purpose of funds sought.
Deadlines: November 1

Additional Information

Trust(s): Fleet Trust Co

Grants Analysis

Disclosure Period: calendar year ending 2000
Total Grants: $46,525*
Number of Grants: 17
Average Grant: $2,737
Highest Grant: $8,930
Typical Range: $1,000 to $5,000
*Note: Giving excludes United Way.

Recent Grants

Note: Grants derived from 2002 Form 990.

General

48,369	United Way of Cayuga County, Auburn, NY
11,173	Westminster Presbyterian Church, Austin, TX
5,586	Auburn Memorial Hospital, Auburn, NY
5,586	Trinity United Church of Christ, Union Springs, NY
5,586	YMCA of Auburn, Auburn, NY
2,500	United Way of Cayuga County, Auburn, NY
2,500	United Way of Cayuga County, Auburn, NY
2,500	United Way of Cayuga County, Auburn, NY

H. T. EWALD FOUNDATION

Giving Contact

Shelagh Kuprenski, Secretary
15450 E. Jefferson Ave., Suite 180
Grosse Pointe Park, MI 48230
Phone: (313)821-1278

Description

Founded: 1928
EIN: 386007837
Organization Type: Private Foundation
Giving Locations: MI: Detroit including metropolitan area
Grant Types: General Support, Scholarship.

Donor Information

Founder: the late Henry T. Ewald

Financial Summary

Total Giving: $121,448 (2000); $123,155 (1999); $127,378 (1998)
Giving Analysis: Giving for 2000 includes: foundation grants to United Way ($500); foundation scholarships ($113,313); 1999: foundation grants to United Way ($1,000); foundation scholarships ($108,800); 1998: foundation grants to United Way ($1,000); foundation ($13,778); foundation scholarships ($112,600);
Assets: $3,556,546 (2000); $4,095,908 (1999); $4,111,012 (1998)
Gifts Received: $435 (2000); $1,470 (1999); $4,057 (1998). Note: In 1999, contributions were received from James and Dorothy Bashaw ($1,000) and miscellaneous donations of less than $500 each. In 1994, contributions were received from Mr. and Mrs. Henry Ewald ($100,000), and Charles B. Johnson ($500).

Typical Recipients

Arts & Humanities: Arts Institutes, History & Archaeology, Libraries, Public Broadcasting

Civic & Public Affairs: Clubs, Civic & Public Affairs-General, Housing, Law & Justice, Urban & Community Affairs, Women's Affairs, Zoos/Aquariums

Education: Arts/Humanities Education, Business Education, Colleges & Universities, Engineering/Technological Education, Education-General, Legal Education, Minority Education, Private Education (Precollege), Student Aid
Social Services: At-Risk Youth, Camps, Child Welfare, Community Service Organizations, Recreation & Athletics, United Funds/United Ways, Veterans, YMCA/YWCA/YMHA/YWHA, Youth Organizations

Application Procedures

Initial Contact: send complete application
Application Requirements: three letters of recommendation, a photo biography, high school transcripts, and SAT or ACT scores
Deadlines: April 1.

Additional Information

Provides scholarships to residents of the metropolitan Detroit, MI, area all residents must be in their senior year to apply.
Publications: Informational Brochure (including Application Guidelines)

Foundation Officials

Carolyn T. Ewald: vice president
Holly Ewald: vice president
John Clifford Ewald: vice president
Kristi Ewald: vice president
Shelagh Kuprenski: secretary
Shirley E. Pfeifer: vice president

Grants Analysis

Disclosure Period: calendar year ending 2000
Total Grants: $7,635*
Number of Grants: 34
Average Grant: $225*
Highest Grant: $750
Typical Range: $50 to $500
*Note: Giving excludes scholarships; United Way.

Recent Grants

Note: Grants derived from 1999 Form 990.

General

5,000	DAPCEP, Detroit, MI
3,000	Concordia College -- scholarship
3,000	Dartmouth College, Dartmouth, MA -- scholarship
3,000	Hope College, Holland, MI -- scholarship
3,000	Kalamazoo College, Kalamazoo, MI -- scholarship
3,000	University of Notre Dame, Notre Dame, IN -- scholarship
2,500	Alma College, Alma, MI -- scholarship
2,500	Kettering University, Flint, MI -- scholarship
2,500	Michigan State University, Detroit, MI -- scholarship
2,500	University of Michigan Dearborn, Dearborn, MI -- scholarship

EXCEL CORP.

Company Headquarters

3201 W. Hwy. 154
Dodge City, KS 67801

Company Description

Employees: 14,220
SIC(s): 2000 Food & Kindred Products.
Parent Company: Cargill, Inc., Minneapolis, MN, United States

Operating Locations

Excel Corp. (KS--Wichita; MN--Minneapolis)

Nonmonetary Support

Type: Donated Products

Giving Contact

Scott Eilert, Excel Cargill Cares Chairperson
151 North Main Street
Wichita, KS 67202
Phone: (316)291-2500
Fax: (316)291-3499
E-mail: contactexcel@cargill.com

Description

Organization Type: Corporate Giving Program
Giving Locations: headquarters and operating communities.
Grant Types: Employee Matching Gifts, Multiyear/Continuing Support, Scholarship.

Financial Summary

Total Giving: $260,000 (1998 approx); $220,000 (1997 approx); $170,000 (1996 approx). Note: Contributes through corporate direct giving program only.

Typical Recipients

Arts & Humanities: Libraries, Literary Arts, Public Broadcasting
Civic & Public Affairs: Chambers of Commerce, Community Foundations, Civic & Public Affairs-General, Zoos/Aquariums
Education: Agricultural Education, Colleges & Universities, Elementary Education (Public), Education-General, Literacy
Health: Health-General, Medical Rehabilitation
Social Services: At-Risk Youth, Emergency Relief, Social Services-General, United Funds/United Ways

Corporate Officials

Bill Buckner: president, chief executive officer
Derek Kennedy: chief financial officer

Grants Analysis

Typical Range: $10 to $1,000

EXCHANGE BANK

Company Headquarters

PO Box 403
Santa Rosa, CA 95402
Web: http://www.exchangebank.com

Company Description

Founded: 1890
Ticker: EXSR
Exchange: OTC
Assets: US$974.2 million (2001)
Employees: 450 (2001)
SIC(s): 6000 Depository Institutions.

Operating Locations

Exchange Bank (CA--Santa Rosa)

Exchange Bank Foundation

Giving Contact

Sharon E. Stockham, Senior Vice President & Human Resources Administrator
Exchange Bank
PO Box 403
Santa Rosa, CA 95402
Phone: (707)524-3117

Alternate Contact

Shirley Kielty
Exchange Bank
Note: Contact to request application form.

Description

Founded: 1979
EIN: 942576480
Organization Type: Corporate Foundation
Giving Locations: CA: Sonoma County
Grant Types: Capital, General Support, Scholarship.

Financial Summary

Total Giving: $57,430 (2001); $43,250 (2000); $53,050 (1999)
Giving Analysis: Giving for 2001 includes: foundation scholarships ($4,000) 1999: foundation ($53,050)
Assets: $63,090 (2001); $19,899 (2000); $62,460 (1999)
Gifts Received: $100,000 (2001); $50,000 (1999); $60,000 (1998). Note: In 2001, contributions were received from Exchange Bank.

Typical Recipients

Arts & Humanities: Arts Associations & Councils, Arts Centers, Libraries, Museums/Galleries, Music, Opera, Performing Arts, Theater
Civic & Public Affairs: Economic Development, Employment/Job Training, Safety
Education: Business Education, Business-School Partnerships, Colleges & Universities, Preschool Education, Student Aid
Environment: Resource Conservation
Health: AIDS/HIV, Children's Health/Hospitals, Clinics/Medical Centers, Hospices, Hospitals, Medical Rehabilitation, Research/Studies Institutes, Respiratory
Religion: Religious Welfare
Science: Observatories & Planetariums
Social Services: Animal Protection, At-Risk Youth, Community Centers, Community Service Organizations, Counseling, Family Services, People with Disabilities, People with Disabilities, Recreation & Athletics, Scouts, Senior Services, Shelters/Homelessness, Volunteer Services, YMCA/YWCA/YMHA/YWHA, Youth Organizations

Application Procedures

Initial Contact: Call the foundation contact to request an application form.
Application Requirements: Provide a completed application form including description of the benefit to be achieved, number of people that will benefit, names of other contributors and amount requested from each, budget for current fiscal year, copy of most recent annual audit, list of board of directors and their business and/or home addresses, organization's bylaws and articles of incorporation, proof of tax-exempt status, a geographic breakdown of the area served, and organization's membership structure
Deadlines: None.

Restrictions

Preference is given to organizations supporting youth, the disabled, or the indigent. No grants are made for scholarships, seed money, private schools, or for program or operating expenses.

Additional Information

The company's largest shareholder is the Doyle Trust, which recently has contributed more than $3.5 million annually to the Doyle Scholarship Program for students attending Santa Rosa Junior College.
Publications: Application Form; Guidelines

Corporate Officials

Bruce DeCrona: chief financial officer, controller, vice president finance PRIM CORP EMPL chief financial officer, controller, vice president finance: Exchange Bank.

C. William Reinking: president, chief executive officer, director PRIM CORP EMPL president, chief executive officer, director: Exchange Bank.

Andrew J. Shepard: chairman, director B Chicago, IL 1924. ED Stanford University (1949); Pacific Coast Banking School (1954). PRIM CORP EMPL chairman, director: Exchange Bank. NONPR AFFIL chairman: LPGA.

Foundation Officials

Marlene S. Barney: director
Charles R. Bartley, Sr.: vchairman
Jean E. Destruel: director
Samuel L. Jones, III: director
John E. McDonald: director
C. William Reinking: director (see above)
James M. Ryan: director
Andrew J. Shepard: chairman (see above)
Robert G. Stone: director

Grants Analysis

Disclosure Period: calendar year ending 2001
Total Grants: $53,430*
Number of Grants: 20
Average Grant: $2,672
Highest Grant: $5,000
Lowest Grant: $500
Typical Range: $1,000 to $3,000
***Note:** Giving excludes scholarship.

Recent Grants

Note: Grants derived from 2000 Form 990.

Library-Related
5,000	Rohnert Park/Cotati Library Committee, Rohnert Park, CA -- support construction costs for new library

General
5,000	City of Santa Rosa Police Department Mounted Enforcement Unit, Santa Rosa, CA -- equipment
5,000	Cloverdale Senior Center Building Fund, Cloverdale, CA -- assist in building senior center
5,000	Social Advocates for Youth (SAY), Santa Rosa, CA -- assist with purchase of van
4,000	Earle Baum Center of the Blind, Santa Rosa, CA -- purchase of sit-down mower for the Center
4,000	Sonoma State University, Rohnert Park, CA -- scholarship fund
3,000	Junior Achievement of the Redwood Empire, Santa Rosa, CA -- 2000 campaign
2,500	Family Service Agency, Santa Rosa, CA -- computer networking
2,500	Sonoma State University, Rohnert Park, CA -- athletic department
2,000	Old Adobe Development Services, Petaluma, CA -- computer system upgrade
1,500	Private Industry Council, Santa Rosa, CA -- Youth 2000 Program

EXELON

Company Headquarters
10 S. Dearborn Street, 37th Floor
Chicago, IL 60690-3005
Phone: (312)394-7398
Web: http://www.exeloncorp.com

Company Description
Founded: 2000
Ticker: EXC
Exchange: NYSE
Acquired: Unicom Corp. (2000);
Former Name: PECO Energy Co. (2000).
Assets: US$4.118 billion (2002)
Profit: US$1.44 billion (2002)

Employees: 29000 (2002)
Fortune Rank: 126, per FORTUNE Magazine's list of 500 Largest U.S. Corporations (2002).
SIC(s): 4931 Electric & Other Services Combined.

Operating Locations
PECO Energy Co. (NJ--Hancock's Bridge; PA--Bristol, Chester, Eddystone, Limerick Township, New Florence, Peach Bottom, Philadelphia, Shelocta)

Nonmonetary Support
Type: Donated Equipment; In-kind Services; Loaned Employees; Loaned Executives

Giving Contact
Exelon Corp.
10 South Dearborn Street, 37th Floor
P.O. Box 805379
Chicago, IL 60690-3005
Phone: (312)394-7398

Description
Organization Type: Corporate Giving Program
Giving Locations: PA: Bucks County, Chester County, Delaware County, Montgomery County, York County
Grant Types: Capital, General Support, Operating Expenses.

Financial Summary
Total Giving: $3,000,000 (1999 approx); $3,000,000 (1998 approx). Note: Contributes through corporate direct giving program only.

Typical Recipients
Arts & Humanities: Arts Funds, Dance, Ethnic & Folk Arts, Libraries, Music, Opera
Civic & Public Affairs: Housing, Law & Justice, Urban & Community Affairs
Education: Business Education, Colleges & Universities, Community & Junior Colleges, Education Funds, Education-General, Public Education (Precollege)
Environment: Environment-General
Health: Hospitals
Social Services: Child Welfare, United Funds/United Ways

Application Procedures
Initial Contact: brief letter
Application Requirements: a description of organization and its mission; detailed description of project and amount requested; list of organization's board of directors, trustees, officers, and other key people and their affiliations; copy of current year's organizational budget and/or project budget; and copy of 501(c)(3) letter of determination
Deadlines: None.

Corporate Officials
Corbin Asahel McNeill, Jr.: president, chief executive officer, director, chairman B Santa Fe, NM 1939. ED United States Naval Academy BS (1962); Naval Nuclear Power School (1962-1963); University of California at Berkeley (1975-1976); Syracuse University (1983-1984). PRIM CORP EMPL president, chief executive officer, director, chairman: PECO Energy Co. CORP AFFIL president, chief executive officer, chairman: Philadelphia Electric Co.; president: Adwin Equipment Co.; president, director: Adwin Realty Co. NONPR AFFIL director: Drexel University; director: Nuclear Utility Management Resources Council; director: American Nuclear Energy Council; member: American Nuclear Society; director: American Gas Association.

Foundation Officials
Anne Baker: manager corporate contributions

EXXONMOBILE CORP.

Company Headquarters
5959 Las Colinas Blvd.
Irving, TX 75039-2298
Web: http://www2.exxonmobile.com

Company Description
Founded: 1999
Ticker: XOM
Exchange: NYSE
Revenue: US$204.506 billion (2002)
Employees: 123000 (2002)

Exxon Mobil Foundation

Giving Contact
Edward F. Ahnert, Manager, Contributions
Exxon Mobil Corp. Contributions
5959 Las Colinas Boulevard
Irving, TX 75039-2298
Phone: (972)444-1104
Fax: (972)444-1405
E-mail: contributions@exxonmobil.com
Web: http://www2.exxonmobil.com/Corporate/Newsroom/Publications/c_cc_02/index.htm

Alternate Contact
Matching Gifts Program
PO Box 7288
Princeton, NJ 08543-7288
Phone: 877-807-0204
E-mail: exxonmobil@easymatch.com

Description
EIN: 136082357
Organization Type: Corporate Foundation
Former Name: Exxon Education Foundation (1999).
Giving Locations: internationally; nationally.
Grant Types: Employee Matching Gifts, General Support, Matching, Multiyear/Continuing Support.
Note: Employee matching gift ratio: 3 to 1 up to $5,000 per employee per year to colleges and universities, and to the United Negro College Fund, the American Indian College Fund, and the Hispanic Association of Colleges & Universities. Educational matching gifts are handled through the foundation. Employee matching gift ratio: 1 to 1 up to $1,000 per employee annually to the arts and humanities. Cultural matching gifts are handled through the corporation. Matching gift contact information should be used by employees, retirees, surviving spou.

Financial Summary
Total Giving: $98,000,000 (2002 approx); $32,667,911 (2001); $42,188,567 (2000). Note: Contributes through corporate direct giving program and foundation.
Giving Analysis: Giving for 2001 includes: corporate direct giving ($18,152,241); foundation matching gifts (approx $20,000,000); 2000: foundation grants to United Way ($279,200); foundation matching gifts ($16,863,974); foundation ($25,045,393); 1999: foundation grants to United Way ($2,773,501); corporate grants to United Way ($3,327,650) foundation matching gifts ($18,152,241).
Assets: $70,171,738 (2001); $71,180,930 (2000); $84,184,471 (1999)
Gifts Received: $36,749,080 (2001); $26,550,000 (2000); $93,621,000 (1999). Note: In 2001, contributions were received from Exxon Mobil Corp. ($35,400,000) and Enjay Inc. ($1,349,080). In 2000, contributions were received from Exxon Corporation

($21,550,000) and ExxonMobil Biomedical Sciences ($5,000,000). In 1999, contributions were received from ExxonMobil Research Engineering Co. ($58,000,000); Exxon Corporation ($19,636,000); ExxonMobil Biomedical Sciences ($15,000,000) and other ExxonMobil companies. In 1998, contributions were received from Exxon Corporation.

Typical Recipients

Arts & Humanities: Arts Associations & Councils, Arts Centers, Arts Festivals, Arts Institutes, Arts Outreach, Community Arts, Dance, Ethnic & Folk Arts, Historic Preservation, Libraries, Museums/Galleries, Music, Opera, Performing Arts, Public Broadcasting, Theater

Civic & Public Affairs: African American Affairs, Botanical Gardens/Parks, Business/Free Enterprise, Community Foundations, Economic Development, Economic Policy, Employment/Job Training, Civic & Public Affairs-General, Hispanic Affairs, Housing, Law & Justice, Minority Business, Municipalities/Towns, Nonprofit Management, Professional & Trade Associations, Public Policy, Safety, Urban & Community Affairs, Women's Affairs, Zoos/Aquariums

Education: Business Education, Business-School Partnerships, Colleges & Universities, Economic Education, Education Associations, Education Funds, Education Reform, Engineering/Technological Education, Environmental Education, Faculty Development, Education-General, Health & Physical Education, International Studies, Leadership Training, Medical Education, Minority Education, Public Education (Precollege), Science/Mathematics Education, Secondary Education (Public), Special Education, Student Aid

Environment: Air/Water Quality, Energy, Forestry, Environment-General, Resource Conservation, Wildlife Protection

Health: Cancer, Clinics/Medical Centers, Emergency/Ambulance Services, Health Organizations, Hospitals, Hospitals, Medical Rehabilitation, Medical Research, Medical Training, Nursing Services, Public Health

International: Health Care/Hospitals, International Affairs, International Environmental Issues, International Peace & Security Issues, International Relations

Science: Science-General, Science Museums, Scientific Centers & Institutes, Scientific Labs, Scientific Research

Social Services: At-Risk Youth, Child Welfare, Community Service Organizations, Counseling, Day Care, Delinquency & Criminal Rehabilitation, Emergency Relief, Family Services, Scouts, Shelters/Homelessness, Substance Abuse, United Funds/United Ways, Volunteer Services, YMCA/YWCA/YMHA/YWHA, Youth Organizations

Application Procedures

Initial Contact: The foundation has no formal grant application procedure or application form. Submit a brief written request (preferably under five pages).

Application Requirements: Grant requests should include a brief history of the organization, a description of its current work, and an explanation of the significance of that work; the organization's current general operating budget; recently audited financial statement; background information on those responsible for administering and developing the organization's programs; a list of the members of the board of directors; a list of current public and private contributors, including their levels of support; and proof of tax-exempt status. If the request is for a specific project, the request should also include a description of the project and explanation of its significance; background information on the individuals who will be carrying out the project; total project budget; amount requested; and a list of others who are or will be providing project funds.

Deadlines: None.

Decision Notification: Review process is continuous.

Notes: All requests will be considered by both the foundation and the corporation.

Restrictions

Neither the company nor the foundation makes grants to individuals, local organizations or activities (unless they are geographically located in an area where Exxon Mobil has significant facilities or numbers of employees), or for political or religious causes. Generally, support is not provided for endowments or operating support to agencies funded by the United Way. Scholarships are provided only on a preselected basis and are offered by ExxonMobil recruiters to attract selected students to employment with the company.

Additional Information

The Exxon Education Foundation's name was changed to Exxon Mobil Foundation as a result of the merger of Exxon Corp. and Mobil Corp. in 1999. The Exxon Mobil Foundation gives to education only and is separate from the corporate direct giving program and the Mobil Foundation.

The National Fish and Wildlife Foundation and Exxon Corp. established the Save the Tiger Fund in 1995 to help fund tiger conservation projects in Asia and research at universities and zoos. The funds also supports education programs to make the public aware that the tiger is near extinction in the wilderness.

Corporate Officials

Edward F. Ahnert: corporate contribution manager PRIM CORP EMPL corporate contribution manager: Exxon Mobil Corp.

Rene Dahan: senior vice president B Fez, Morocco 1941. ED Ecole Nationale D'Officiers De Marine (1959); Ecole d'Hydrographie (1961). ADD CORP EMPL president: Exxon International Services.

Harry J. Longwell: senior vice president B Bunkie, LA 1941. ED Louisiana State University (1963). PRIM CORP EMPL senior vice president, director: ExxonMobil Corp.

Lee R. Raymond: chairman, president, chief executive officer B Watertown, SD 1938. ED University of Wisconsin BSChE (1960); University of Minnesota PhD (1963). PRIM CORP EMPL chairman, chief executive officer: Exxon Mobil Corp. ADD CORP EMPL senior vice president, director: Esso International-AM Inc. CORP AFFIL director: Morgan Guaranty Trust Co.; director: JP Morgan & Co. Inc. NONPR AFFIL member: University Wisconsin Foundation; trustee: Wisconsin Alumni Research Foundation; director: United Negro College Fund; member, board governors: United Way America; trustee: Southern Methodist University; member: Trilateral Commission; director: Project Shelter Pro-Am; member: Singapore-U.S. Business Council; partner emeritus: New York City Partnership; member: Occupational Physicians Scholarship Fund; member: National Petroleum Council; director: New American Schools Development Corp.; director: Jason Foundation for Education; member, director: National Academy Engineering; member: Emergency Committee American Trade; director: Dallas Citizens Council; member: Dallas Committee Foreign Relations; member: College Board; member: Council Foreign Relations; director: Business Council International Understanding Inc.; member: Business Roundtable; member: Business Council; member: American Society Engineering Educators; member, founder: American Society Royal Botanical Garden; director: American Petroleum Institute; member national advisory council: American Society Engineering; member: American Council Germany.

Foundation Officials

Edward F. Ahnert: president (see above)
D. P. Bailey: trustee
D. L. Bard, Jr.: trustee
F. W. Bass: trustee
J. E. Bayne: treasurer

Ken P. Cohen: chairman, trustee
J. C. Glaubig: trustee
P. A. Hanson: controller
W. N. Huplits: assistant controller
M. K. Ivey: assistant secretary
A. E. Lawson: executive director
A. M. Lopez: trustee
B. G. Macklin: trustee
L. D. Meyer: assistant treasurer
S. A. Millican: assistant secretary
C. T. Olson: vice president
S. B.L. Penrose: treasurer
R. V. Pisarczyk: trustee
F. A. Risch: trustee
D. H. Samson: assistant treasurer
F. B. Sprow: trustee
P. A. Wetz: trustee

Grants Analysis

Disclosure Period: calendar year ending 2002
Total Grants: $42,325,600*
Number of Grants: 2000 (approx)
Average Grant: $21,163
Highest Grant: $6,213,789
Lowest Grant: $250
Typical Range: $1,000 to $50,000
*Note: Grants analysis provided by foundation.

Recent Grants

Note: Grants derived from 2001 Form 990.

General
4,173,500	Volunteer Involvement Fund, Irving, TX -- for program
2,000,000	Educational Alliance Program, Irving, TX
1,315,000	National Science Teachers Association, Arlington, VA
500,000	National Fish and Wildlife Foundation, Washington, DC -- for programs
500,000	National Fish and Wildlife Foundation, Washington, DC -- for Tiger Program
459,000	California Foundation on the Environment and the Economy, San Francisco, CA -- for clean air challenge
448,748	Mobil Retiree Volunteer Program, Irving, TX -- for program
330,000	Harvard University School of Public Health, Boston, MA -- for Harvard Malaria Initiative
300,000	Carnegie Mellon University, Pittsburgh, PA -- for center for the study and improvement of regulations
270,000	National Action Council for Minorities in Engineering, New York, NY

FAB STEEL PRODUCTS CO.

Company Headquarters
Clovis, NM

Fab Steel Products Foundation

Giving Contact
Nanette B. Winton, Secretary, Treasurer & Director
Fab Steel Products Foundation
4600 Mabry Drive
Clovis, NM 88101
Phone: (505)763-4414

Description
EIN: 850339249
Organization Type: Corporate Foundation
Giving Locations: NM; TX
Grant Types: General Support.

Financial Summary

Total Giving: $11,200 (2000); $10,050 (1999); $10,700 (1998)

Giving Analysis: Giving for 1999 includes: foundation ($10,050)

Assets: $161,666 (2000); $165,162 (1999); $154,401 (1998)

Gifts Received: $9,634 (2000); $10,000 (1999); $19,000 (1997)

Typical Recipients

Arts & Humanities: Libraries
Education: Student Aid
Religion: Churches, Religious Welfare
Social Services: Camps, Youth Organizations

Application Procedures

Initial Contact: Send a formal written request.
Deadlines: None.

Corporate Officials

Stanley Glenn: president, chief executive officer PRIM CORP EMPL president, chief executive officer: Fab Steel Product Co.

Foundation Officials

M. Virginia Glenn: director
Ted Van Soelen: president, director
Nanette B. Winton: secretary, treasurer, director PRIM CORP EMPL vice president, controller: Fab Steel Product Co.

Grants Analysis

Disclosure Period: calendar year ending 2000
Total Grants: $11,200
Number of Grants: 3
Highest Grant: $6,000
Lowest Grant: $2,000

Recent Grants

Note: Grants derived from 1999 Form 990.

General

5,000	First Methodist Church, Clovis, NM
4,000	New Mexico Girls and Boys Ranch, Albuquerque, NM
1,050	Lighthouse Mission, Clovis, NM

FAIR OAKS FOUNDATION

Giving Contact

Rose Hoover, Secretary
Fair Oaks Foundation
600 Grant Street, Suite 4600
Pittsburgh, PA 15219
Phone: (412)456-4418

Description

Founded: 1988
EIN: 251576560
Organization Type: Private Foundation
Giving Locations: NY
Grant Types: General Support, Scholarship.

Donor Information

Founder: Pittsburgh Forgings Foundation, Ampco-Pittsburgh Foundation

Financial Summary

Total Giving: $452,675 (2000); $432,115 (1999); $421,370 (1998)

Giving Analysis: Giving for 2000 includes: foundation grants to United Way ($28,600); 1999: foundation grants to United Way ($28,500) 1998: foundation grants to United Way ($28,500)

Assets: $5,539,621 (2000); $5,375,615 (1999); $5,840,437 (1998)

Typical Recipients

Arts & Humanities: Arts Associations & Councils, Arts Centers, Arts Festivals, Ballet, Community Arts, History & Archaeology, Libraries, Museums/Galleries, Music, Opera, Public Broadcasting, Theater

Civic & Public Affairs: African American Affairs, Asian American Affairs, Botanical Gardens/Parks, Civil Rights, Clubs, Economic Development, Civic & Public Affairs-General, Parades/Festivals, Professional & Trade Associations, Public Policy, Safety, Urban & Community Affairs, Women's Affairs, Zoos/Aquariums

Education: Business Education, Colleges & Universities, Community & Junior Colleges, Education Funds, Legal Education, Medical Education, Minority Education, Private Education (Precollege), Student Aid

Environment: Environment-General

Health: Arthritis, Cancer, Children's Health/Hospitals, Emergency/Ambulance Services, Hospitals, Single-Disease Health Associations

International: International Affairs, International Relief Efforts

Religion: Jewish Causes, Religious Organizations, Religious Welfare, Social/Policy Issues

Social Services: Community Centers, Community Service Organizations, Crime Prevention, Family Planning, Food/Clothing Distribution, People with Disabilities, Recreation & Athletics, Scouts, Substance Abuse, United Funds/United Ways, YMCA/YWCA/YMHA/YWHA, Youth Organizations

Application Procedures

Initial Contact: The foundation has no formal grant application procedure or application form.
Deadlines: October 31.

Additional Information

Provides scholarships to individuals for higher education.

Foundation Officials

Louis Berkman: chairman, trustee B Canton, OH 1909. PRIM CORP EMPL chairman, president, chief executive officer, treasurer, director: Louis Berkman Co. CORP AFFIL president: Scott Lumber; president: Swenson Spreader; president: Meyer Products; president: Orrville Products; president, director: Follansbee Steel Corp.; president: IDL Supplies; chairman: Ampco-Pittsburgh Corp.; president: Dover Parkersburg.

Rose Hoover: secretary

Robert Arthur Paul: president, trustee B New York, NY 1937. ED Cornell University AB (1959); Harvard University JD (1962); Harvard University MBA (1964). PRIM CORP EMPL president, chief executive officer, director: Ampco-Pittsburgh Corp. CORP AFFIL partner: Romar Trading Co.; partner: National City Corp.; executive vice president, assistant secretary, director, trustee: Louis Berkman Co. NONPR AFFIL member: Massachusetts Bar Association; trustee: Presbyterian University Hospital; trustee: Cornell University; member: American Bar Association. CLUB AFFIL Pittsburgh Athletic Association; Harvard Club; Concordia Club; Duquesne Club.

Grants Analysis

Disclosure Period: calendar year ending 2000
Total Grants: $424,075*
Number of Grants: 94
Average Grant: $1,349*
Highest Grant: $200,000
Typical Range: $500 to $5,000
*Note: Giving excludes United Way. Average grant figure excludes two highest grants ($300,000).

Recent Grants

Note: Grants derived from 1999 Form 990.

General

200,000	Harvard University, Boston, MA -- for programs
100,000	Cornell University Ornithology, Ithaca, NY -- for programs
50,000	United Jewish Federation, Pittsburgh, PA -- for programs
20,000	United Way of Southwestern Pennsylvania, Pittsburgh, PA -- for programs
5,000	Carnegie Mellon University, Pittsburgh, PA -- for programs
5,000	Engineers Society of Western Pennsylvania, Pittsburgh, PA -- for programs
5,000	Harvard Business School, Boston, MA -- for programs
3,500	Pittsburgh Cultural Trust, Pittsburgh, PA -- for programs
3,000	United Way of Central Virginia, Lynchburg, VA -- for programs
2,500	United Way of Tonawandas, Tonawanda, NY -- for programs

FAIR PLAY FOUNDATION

Giving Contact

Blaine T. Phillips, Executive Director
100 W. 10th Street, Suite 1010
Wilmington, DE 19801
Phone: (302)777-4711
Fax: (302)658-1192
E-mail: bthillips@pac.delware.com

Description

Founded: 1983
EIN: 516017779
Organization Type: Private Foundation
Giving Locations: DE
Grant Types: Capital, General Support.

Financial Summary

Total Giving: $908,750 (2000); $893,082 (1999); $800,000 (1998)

Assets: $17,358,530 (2000); $19,446,547 (1999); $17,745,492 (1998)

Typical Recipients

Arts & Humanities: Arts Centers, Arts Festivals, Arts Institutes, Arts & Humanities-General, Historic Preservation, History & Archaeology, Libraries, Museums/Galleries, Music, Theater

Civic & Public Affairs: Botanical Gardens/Parks, Community Foundations, Civic & Public Affairs-General, Philanthropic Organizations, Public Policy, Urban & Community Affairs, Zoos/Aquariums

Education: Agricultural Education, Arts/Humanities Education, Colleges & Universities, Education Funds, Environmental Education, Legal Education, Private Education (Precollege)

Environment: Air/Water Quality, Environment-General, Protection, Research, Resource Conservation, Watershed, Wildlife Protection

Health: Arthritis, Hospices, Long-Term Care, Medical Research, Single-Disease Health Associations

International: International Environmental Issues, International Relief Efforts

Religion: Churches

Science: Science Museums, Scientific Centers & Institutes

Social Services: Child Welfare, Community Service Organizations, Day Care, Family Planning, Family Services, Recreation & Athletics, YMCA/YWCA/YMHA/YWHA, Youth Organizations

Application Procedures

Initial Contact: Send a brief letter of inquiry describing program or project.
Deadlines: None.

Foundation Officials

James F. Burnett: vice president, trustee
Thomas H. Fooks, V: trustee
L. E. Grimes: treasurer, trustee

Blaine T. Phillips: president, trustee
D. P. Ross, Jr.: trustee

Grants Analysis

Disclosure Period: calendar year ending 2000
Total Grants: $908,750
Number of Grants: 52
Average Grant: $13,475*
Highest Grant: $125,000
Typical Range: $5,000 to $30,000
*Note: Average grant excludes two highest grants ($235,000).

Recent Grants

Note: Grants derived from 1999 Form 990.

Library-Related

25,000	Wilmington Library, Wilmington, DE -- restoration and hanging of North Carolina Wyeth paintings

General

114,402	Winterthur Museum, Greenville, DE -- enchanted woods children's garden improvements
100,000	Chesapeake Bay Foundation, Annapolis, MD -- oyster restoration, crab protection program
75,000	University of Virginia, Charlottesville, VA -- Carr's Hill landscaping improvements, law school professorship search
50,000	African Wildlife Foundation, Washington, DC -- Amboselli Elephant Research Project
50,000	Delaware Wild Lands, Odessa, DE -- restoration project
25,580	Hagley Museum & Library, Wilmington, DE -- relocating manuscript division
25,000	Salisbury State Teachers College, Salisbury, MD -- history/genealogical education projects
25,000	Stroud Water Research Center, Avondale, PA -- increase public services availability of staff
25,000	Vail Valley Foundation, Vail, CO -- community projects
25,000	Winterthur Museum, Greenville, DE -- point-to-point course improvements

SHERMAN FAIRCHILD FOUNDATION, INC.

Giving Contact

Bonnie Himmelman, President
5454 Wisconsin Ave. Suite 1205
Chevy Chase, MD 20815
Phone: (301)913-5990
Fax: (301)913-9444
Web: http://www.990pf.org

Description

Founded: 1955
EIN: 131951698
Organization Type: General Purpose Foundation
Giving Locations: NY: New York including metropolitan area nationally.
Grant Types: Capital, Endowment, Fellowship, General Support, Project, Research, Scholarship.

Donor Information

Founder: The Sherman Fairchild Foundation was incorporated in 1955 by Sherman M. Fairchild , inventor of the Fairchild aerial camera, chairman of Fairchild Camera Instrument Co. and of Fairchild Hiller Corp., owner of Fairchild Recording Equipment Co., and one of the largest single stockholders of IBM. When Mr. Fairchild died in 1971, he left most of his estate to the foundation.

Financial Summary

Total Giving: $18,955,435 (2001); $18,991,027 (2000); $19,229,566 (1998)
Giving Analysis: Giving for 1998 includes: foundation scholarships ($10,000)
Assets: $435,835,204 (2001); $510,359,835 (2000); $361,922,366 (1998)
Gifts Received: $4,475 (1998); $4,346 (1996); $2,608 (1995). Note: The foundation receives contributions from the Sherman M. Fairchild Annuity Trust.

Typical Recipients

Arts & Humanities: Arts Centers, Arts Institutes, Arts & Humanities-General, Historic Preservation, Libraries, Museums/Galleries, Music, Performing Arts, Visual Arts
Civic & Public Affairs: Botanical Gardens/Parks, Civic & Public Affairs-General
Education: Arts/Humanities Education, Colleges & Universities, Engineering/Technological Education, Faculty Development, Education-General, International Studies, Legal Education, Medical Education, Minority Education, Private Education (Precollege), Religious Education, Science/Mathematics Education, Secondary Education (Private), Student Aid
Health: Cancer, Children's Health/Hospitals, Clinics/Medical Centers, Health Funds, Hospitals, Medical Research
International: International Peace & Security Issues
Religion: Dioceses, Religion-General, Jewish Causes, Missionary Activities (Domestic), Religious Welfare, Seminaries
Science: Science Museums, Scientific Research
Social Services: Animal Protection, At-Risk Youth, Child Welfare, Community Service Organizations, Family Services, Recreation & Athletics, Shelters/Homelessness, YMCA/YWCA/YMHA/YWHA, Youth Organizations

Application Procedures

Initial Contact: Send a a brief letter of inquiry.
Application Requirements: Include a description of the proposed project and proof of the organization's tax-exempt status.
Deadlines: None.

Restrictions

No grants are made to individuals.

Foundation Officials

Walter Burke: treasurer, director
Walter F. Burke, III: director, chairman
Robert P. Henderson: director PRIM CORP EMPL managing partner: Greylock Ltd. Partnership. CORP AFFIL director: Cabot Corp.; director: Allmerica Asset Management; director: Allmerica Financial Corp. NONPR AFFIL chairman: Museum Fine Arts Boston.
Bonnie Himmelman: president, director
Michele Tolela Myers: director B Rabat, Morocco 1941. ED University of Paris (1962); University of Denver MA (1966); University of Denver PhD (1967); Trinity University MA (1977). PRIM CORP EMPL president: Sarah Lawrence College. NONPR AFFIL director, member: American Council Education; director: National Association Independent Colleges & Universities. CLUB AFFIL 100 San Antonio Club.
Paul Donnelly Paganucci: director B Waterville, ME 1931. ED Dartmouth College AB (1953); Dartmouth College Amos Tuck Graduate School of Business Administration MBA (1954); Harvard University JD (1957). PRIM CORP EMPL chairman: Ledyard National Bank. CORP AFFIL director: Urstadt Biddle Properties; officer: Vineland Laboratories; director: Hypertherm Inc.; director: IGI Inc.; director: EVSCO Pharmaceuticals; director: Filene's Basement Corp.; trustee: Allmerica Securities Trust Inc. NONPR AFFIL member: Institute Chartered Financial Analysts; member: President Private Sector Survey Cost Control; overseer: Dartmouth Catholic Student Center; director: Grace Institute; trustee: Casque & Gauntlet; trustee: Colby College. CLUB AFFIL Union Club;

president, director: Dartmouth New York Club; member: Knights of Malta.
Dr. Agnar Pytte: director B Kongsberg, Norway 1932. ED Princeton University AB (1953); Harvard University AM (1954); Harvard University PhD (1958). PRIM CORP EMPL president: Case Western Reserve University. CORP AFFIL director: AO Smith Corp.; director: Goodyear Tire & Rubber Co. NONPR AFFIL director: United Way; trustee: University Research Association; director: Sherman Fairchild Foundation Inc.; member: Sigma Xi; member: Ohio Science Technology Council; member: Phi Beta Kappa; trustee: Ohio Aerospace Institute; member: Ohio Council Research & Economic Development; member: Cleveland Roundtable; member: Cleveland Technology Leadership Council; trustee: Cleveland Institute Music; trustee: Cleveland Orchestra; member: American Physical Society; director: Cleveland Growth Association.
James Wright: director

Grants Analysis

Disclosure Period: calendar year ending 2001
Total Grants: $13,588,435*
Number of Grants: 54
Average Grant: $104,254*
Highest Grant: $2,000,000
Lowest Grant: $20,000
Typical Range: $50,000 to $200,000
*Note: Giving excludes a scholarships. Average grant figure excludes five highest grants ($8,480,000).

Recent Grants

Note: Grants derived from 2001 Form 990.

General

5,000,000	California Institute of Technology, Pasadena, CA -- for Postdoctoral Scholars Program
2,000,000	Sara Lawrence College, Bronxville, NY -- President's Discretionary Fund
1,660,000	Metropolitan Museum of Art, New York, NY -- for works on paper and photographs Conservation Center
1,600,000	Metropolitan Museum of Art, New York, NY -- for construction of the Center for Objects Conservation at the Cloisters
1,000,000	Case Western Reserve University, Cleveland, OH -- for Professorship in Physics Program
1,000,000	Salvation Army of New York, New York, NY
1,000,000	University of California San Francisco, San Francisco, CA -- for protein research
500,000	Denison University, Granville, OH -- facility enhancement fund
500,000	Inner-city Scholarship Fund, New York, NY -- endowment
500,000	New York University Institute of Fine Arts, New York, NY -- endowment

FREEMAN E. FAIRCHILD-MEEKER CHARITABLE TRUST

Giving Contact

Judy Dowling, Trust Officer
c/o Wells Fargo Bank
633 17th St.
Denver, CO 80270
Phone: (303)293-5365
Fax: (303)293-5632

Description

Founded: 1969
EIN: 846068906
Organization Type: Private Foundation

Giving Locations: CO: Meeker
Grant Types: General Support, Scholarship.

Donor Information
Founder: the late Freeman E. Fairfield

Financial Summary
Total Giving: $174,790 (fiscal year ending November 30, 2001); $179,961 (fiscal 2000); $103,169 (fiscal 1998). Note: Fiscal 1997 Giving includes scholarship ($173,415).
Giving Analysis: Giving for fiscal 2001 includes: foundation scholarships ($63,400)
Assets: $4,801,106 (fiscal 2001); $5,175,258 (fiscal 2000); $4,939,751 (fiscal 1998)

Typical Recipients
Arts & Humanities: Community Arts, Historic Preservation, History & Archaeology, Libraries, Music
Civic & Public Affairs: Chambers of Commerce, Economic Development, Civic & Public Affairs-General, Municipalities/Towns, Parades/Festivals, Safety, Urban & Community Affairs
Education: Colleges & Universities, Community & Junior Colleges, Education Funds, Engineering/Technological Education, Education-General, Literacy, Private Education (Precollege), Public Education (Precollege), Science/Mathematics Education, Secondary Education (Public), Student Aid
Health: Health-General, Hospitals, Medical Rehabilitation
Religion: Churches, Religious Welfare
Social Services: Community Service Organizations, Family Services, Recreation & Athletics, Scouts, Veterans

Application Procedures
Initial Contact: Send a brief letter of inquiry describing program.
Deadlines: None.

Additional Information
Provides scholarships to graduates of Meeker High School.
Trust(s): Wells Fargo Bank

Foundation Officials
Rev. Paul Brisbane: trustee
Kim Cook: trustee
Dave McGraw: trustee
Larry Shutis: trustee
Glenn Trobster: trustee
Pete Waller: trustee

Grants Analysis
Disclosure Period: fiscal year ending November 30, 2001
Total Grants: $111,390*
Number of Grants: 14
Average Grant: $3,646*
Highest Grant: $37,640
Lowest Grant: $1,000
Typical Range: $1,000 to $5,000
*Note: Giving excludes scholarships. Average grant figure excludes two highest grants ($67,640).

Recent Grants
Note: Grants derived from fiscal 2000 Form 990.

General

50,000	Pioneer Hospital, Meeker, CO -- charitable
33,000	Rio Blanco Fire Protection District, Meeker, CO -- charitable
26,466	Meeker Civic Improvement Corporation, Meeker, CO -- charitable
16,670	Rio Blanco County Historical Society, Meeker, CO -- charitable
8,000	Mesa State College, Grand Junction, CO -- scholarship
6,700	University of Northern Colorado, Greeley, CO -- scholarship
4,800	Colorado State University, Ft. Collins, CO -- scholarship
4,600	Rio Blanco RE-1 School District, Meeker, CO -- charitable
3,200	Fort Lewis College, Durango, CO -- scholarship
3,000	Northwest Colorado Dental Coalition, Craig, CO -- charitable

FAITH FOUNDATION

Giving Contact
Daniel L. Kerr, Secretary & Treasurer
Attn: Grants
2746 Front St. NE
Salem, OR 97303-6554
Phone: (503)364-6777

Description
Founded: 1993
EIN: 931115227
Organization Type: Private Foundation
Giving Locations: OR
Grant Types: Loan.

Donor Information
Founder: Established in 1993 by Richard Faith.

Financial Summary
Total Giving: $298,496 (2000); $148,035 (1999); $44,500 (1998)
Assets: $14,386,034 (2000); $11,858,393 (1999); $9,325,339 (1998)
Gifts Received: $2,000,000 (2000); $2,201,000 (1999); $1,500,000 (1998). Note: In 1998, 1999 and 2000, contributions were received from Richard Faith. In 1996, contributions were received from Richard Faith & Dan Kerr. In 1995, contributions were received from Richard Faith.

Typical Recipients
Arts & Humanities: Libraries
Education: Public Education (Precollege)
International: Foreign Educational Institutions, International Environmental Issues, International Organizations, Missionary/Religious Activities
Religion: Churches, Ministries, Missionary Activities (Domestic), Religious Welfare
Social Services: Recreation & Athletics, Social Services-General, Youth Organizations

Application Procedures
Initial Contact: Send a brief letter of inquiry
Application Requirements: a description of organization, amount requested, purpose of funds sought, proof of tax-exempt status, project description and timeline.
Deadlines: None.

Restrictions
Does not support individuals.

Additional Information
The foundation funds causes through low interest capital improvement loans.

Foundation Officials
Richard G. Faith: president, director
Daniel L. Kerr: secretary, treasurer
Jennifer Rowland: vice president
Jodie Schwanke: vice president

Grants Analysis
Disclosure Period: calendar year ending 2000
Total Grants: $298,496
Number of Grants: 11
Average Grant: $19,850*

Highest Grant: $100,000
Typical Range: $5,000 to $30,000
*Note: Average grant excludes highest grant.

Recent Grants
Note: Grants derived from 1999 Form 990.

General

35,000	Frontier Lodge, St. Hermeneglide, QC Canada -- for sewer line
34,260	Blanchett School, Salem, OR -- for heating systems
16,000	Boys and Girls Club, Salem, MA -- for building fund
10,000	Gospel Missionary Union, Kansas City, MO
10,000	Northgate Wesleyan Church, Salem, OR -- for building fund
6,500	Halbert Baptist, Salem, OR -- for vehicle purchase
5,000	Gospel Ministries/Deaf, Portland, OR
5,000	Lourde School, Scio, OR
1,000	Africa Mission, Jacksonville, FL
275	Auburn Baseball Club, Inc., Auburn, WA

MAURICE FALK MEDICAL FUND

Giving Contact
Sigo Falk, Chairman
3315 Grant Bldg.
Pittsburgh, PA 15219
Phone: (412)261-2485

Description
Founded: 1960
EIN: 251099658
Organization Type: Private Foundation
Giving Locations: PA
Grant Types: Conference/Seminar, Endowment, General Support, Multiyear/Continuing Support, Project, Seed Money.

Donor Information
Founder: Maurice and Laura Falk Foundation

Financial Summary
Total Giving: $520,578 (fiscal year ending August 31, 2001); $827,064 (fiscal 2000); $130,310 (fiscal 1996)
Assets: $17,559,288 (fiscal 2001); $19,103,272 (fiscal 2000); $12,895,316 (fiscal 1996)
Gifts Received: $37,663 (fiscal 2001); $33,294 (fiscal 2000); $16,000 (fiscal 1996). Note: In fiscal 2001, contributions were received from Loti G. Gaffney ($25,389) and Jeannette Falk ($12,274). In fiscal 2000, contributions were received from Loti G. Gaffney ($23,332) and Jeannette Falk ($9,962). In fiscal 1996, contributions were received from Loti G. Gaffney.

Typical Recipients
Arts & Humanities: Arts Centers, Arts Funds, Arts Outreach, Community Arts, Film & Video, Historic Preservation, History & Archaeology, Libraries, Public Broadcasting, Theater, Visual Arts
Civic & Public Affairs: African American Affairs, Civil Rights, Economic Development, Housing, Legal Aid, Nonprofit Management, Philanthropic Organizations, Public Policy, Urban & Community Affairs, Women's Affairs
Education: Colleges & Universities, Education Funds, Health & Physical Education, International Studies, Medical Education, Minority Education, Private Education (Precollege), Social Sciences Education
Health: AIDS/HIV, Health Funds, Health Organizations, Hospitals, Mental Health, Public Health, Research/Studies Institutes, Single-Disease Health Associations

International: Foreign Arts Organizations, Health Care/Hospitals, International Organizations, International Peace & Security Issues, International Relations
Religion: Religious Organizations, Religious Welfare
Science: Scientific Research
Social Services: Child Welfare, Community Centers, Counseling, Crime Prevention, Family Planning, Family Services, People with Disabilities, Youth Organizations

Application Procedures

Initial Contact: Send detailed letter of inquiry describing program or project.
Application Requirements: Include history of organization, goals of project, budget, endorsements, and proof of tax-exempt status.
Deadlines: None.

Restrictions

Grants are made primarily to projects in mental health and health related fields. Does not support individuals or provide loans.

Additional Information

Publications: Application Guidelines; Occasional Report

Foundation Officials

Bertram S. Brown, MD: trustee
Estelle Comay: secretary, treasurer
Sigo Falk: chairman B Pittsburgh, PA 1934. ED Harvard University (1957); Carnegie Mellon University (1960). CORP AFFIL trustee: McKee Income Realty Trust; director: National Intergroup; director: DQE Inc.; director: Duquesne Light Co.
Philip Burgh Hallen: president B Buffalo, NY 1930. ED Syracuse University BA (1952); Syracuse University MA (1954); Yale University MS (1958). NONPR AFFIL director: Pittsburgh Oratorio Society; vice chairman board directors: Urban League Pittsburgh; director: Pittsburgh Opera Theater; director: Pittsburgh Chamber Music Society; director: Pittsburgh Filmakers; chairman: Pennsylvania Humanities Council; member: Pennsylvania Public Health Association; chairman: National Cathedral Association Southwest Pennsylvania; director: National Institute Against Prejudiced Violence; chairman: Local Initiatives Services Corp.; trustee: National Cathedral Association; sr fellow: Council Foundations; director: Dollar Energy Fund; fellow: American Psychiatric Association; fellow: American Public Health Association. CLUB AFFIL Harvard-Yale-Princeton Club; Junta Club.
Kerry J. O'Donnell: president
Julian Ruslander, Esq.: trustee
Eric W. Springer: trustee B New York, NY 1929. ED Rutgers University AB (1950); New York University LLB (1953). CORP AFFIL director: Duquesne Light Co. NONPR AFFIL fellow: American Public Health Association; member: National Bar Association; member: American Bar Association; honorary fellow: American College Healthcare Executives; member: Allegany County Bar Association; member: American Academy Hospital attorneys. CLUB AFFIL Order of Coif.

Grants Analysis

Disclosure Period: fiscal year ending August 31, 2001
Total Grants: $520,578*
Typical Range: $100 to $7,000
*Note: Grants list for fiscal 2001 incomplete.

Recent Grants

Note: Grants derived from 2000 Form 990.

General

2,500	Pittsburgh AIDS Task Force, Pittsburgh, PA -- support for the 14th annual aids benefit at the Pittsburgh Public Theater
2,000	National Video Resources, New York, NY -- support for the activities of grantmakers in film and electronic media
1,750	Urban League of Pittsburgh, Pittsburgh, PA -- support for the fourth annual Ronald H. Brown Leadership Banquet
1,714	Council on Foundations, Washington, DC -- support of program activities
1,000	Foundation Center, New York, NY -- support of program activities
500	University of Pittsburgh School of Medicine Western Psychiatric Institute and Clinic, Pittsburgh, PA -- support for a reception for two community psychiatrist
500	Women and Philanthropy, Washington, DC -- support for membership dues

FANNIE MAE

Company Headquarters

Washington, DC
Web: http://www.fanniemae.com

Company Description

Founded: 1938
Ticker: FNM
Exchange: NYSE
Former Name: Federal National Mortgage Association.
Assets: US$887.515 billion (2002)
Profit: US$4.618 billion (2002)
Employees: 4800 (2002)
Fortune Rank: 16, per FORTUNE Magazine's list of 500 Largest U.S. Corporations (2002).
SIC(s): 6111 Federal & Federally-Sponsored Credit.

Operating Locations

Fannie Mae (AL--Birmingham; AZ--Phoenix; CA--Pasadena; CT--Hartford; FL--Orlando; GA--Atlanta; IL--Chicago; IA--Des Moines; MA--Boston; MI--Detroit; MN--St. Paul; MS--Jackson; MO--St. Louis; NE--Lincoln; NY--New York; NC--Charlotte; OH--Columbus; OR--Portland; PA--Philadelphia; TX--Houston, San Antonio; WA--Seattle)
Note: Operates nationally, through headquarters and 5 regional offices.

Nonmonetary Support

Type: Loaned Employees

Fannie Mae Foundation

Giving Contact

Grants Management
Fannie Mae Foundation
North Tower, Suite One
4000 Wisconsin Avenue, NW
Washington, DC 20016-2804
Phone: (202)274-8062
Fax: (202)274-8111
E-mail: grants@fanniemaefoundation.org
Web: http://www.fanniemaefoundation.org

Description

Founded: 1979
EIN: 521172718
Organization Type: Corporate Foundation
Giving Locations: DC: Washington national organizations; operating locations.
Grant Types: Award, Capital, Conference/Seminar, Emergency, Employee Matching Gifts, Endowment, General Support, Loan, Matching, Multiyear/Continuing Support.
Note: Employee matching gift ratio: 2 to 1 up to $500 annually. Employee matching gift ratio: 1 to 1 for gifts over $500.

Financial Summary

Total Giving: $39,100,000 (2003 approx); $38,058,078 (2002); $34,874,351 (2001). Note: Contributes through foundation only.
Giving Analysis: Giving for 2001 includes: foundation grants to United Way ($200,041); foundation gifts to individuals ($567,500); foundation matching gifts ($1,790,862); foundation ($32,276,944); 2000: foundation ($36,521,087); 1999: foundation grants to United Way ($105,000); foundation ($33,821,500);
Assets: $333,496,929 (2002); $468,969,010 (2001); $272,988,815 (2000);
Gifts Received: $300,000,000 (2001); $30,000,000 (2000); $154,687,624 (1999). Note: Contributions received from Fannie Mae.

Typical Recipients

Arts & Humanities: Arts Outreach, Dance, History & Archaeology, Museums/Galleries, Music, Opera, Performing Arts, Public Broadcasting, Theater
Civic & Public Affairs: African American Affairs, Asian American Affairs, Business/Free Enterprise, Community Foundations, Economic Development, Employment/Job Training, Ethnic Organizations, Civic & Public Affairs-General, Hispanic Affairs, Housing, Municipalities/Towns, Professional & Trade Associations, Public Policy, Rural Affairs, Urban & Community Affairs, Women's Affairs
Education: Afterschool/Enrichment Programs, Business Education, Colleges & Universities, Community & Junior Colleges, Education-General, Legal Education, Minority Education, Religious Education, Student Aid, Vocational & Technical Education
Environment: Environment-General
Health: Nursing Services, Single-Disease Health Associations
International: Health Care/Hospitals, International Relief Efforts
Religion: Jewish Causes, Religious Welfare
Social Services: Camps, Child Abuse, Community Centers, Community Service Organizations, Emergency Relief, Family Services, Homes, Recreation & Athletics, Refugee Assistance, Senior Services, Shelters/Homelessness, United Funds/United Ways, Volunteer Services, Youth Organizations

Application Procedures

Initial Contact: The foundation accepts unsolicited proposals only once per year--and posts deadlines, guidelines, and other grant information at the website by December 31 each year for the subsequent year.
Application Requirements: The foundation awards most of its grants by soliciting proposals from organizations with both the capacity and proven track record to engage in strong partnerships with the Foundation. In order to allow us also to identify potential future partners or respond to unique community needs, the foundation sets aside a limited amount of grant funding each year for which nonprofit organizations may apply through a competitive process. the program's target population; and geographic area (s) to benefit from the request. The narrative should include a description of organization including its history, mission, programs/services offered, and recent accomplishments; a description of the request, including its principal objectives and anticipated outcomes; problems and issues the program or organization will address; qualifications of the organization and its principal personnel to implement the objectives and achieve the expected outcomes; degree to which the program will build on existing services in the community rather than duplicating them; funding received to date for the program (or for the organization, if the request is for general operating support), as well as other sources from which
Deadlines: Deadlines posted on the website.
Evaluative Criteria: The foundation's national work is organized around the following four interconnected initiatives: Increase the affordable housing supply. The foundation seeks to produce and preserve high

quality affordable housing that sustains healthy neighborhoods and offers opportunities to create individual and community wealth. Generally, we seek to enhance the operations of particularly effective and accountable non-profit organizations working on housing production and/or preservation, rather than to direct our grant funds to specific affordable housing development projects. Create wealth through homeownership: The foundation works to increase sustainable homeownership that builds individual and community wealth. This initiative focuses on providing high-quality, comprehensive personal finance and homeownership information and education and strives to help bring mainstream financial services to underserved communities. Bring Wall Street to Main Street: The Foundation strives to attract Wall Street investors-including individuals, corporations, governments, and foundations-to investments in affordable housing and housing-related community development. The foundation also works to improve the capacity of financial intermediaries, including their interconnection with mainstream players in the larger capital markets. Create and Share Knowledge: The Foundation creates and shares relevant and innovative information in order to help advance practice, policy and through in the fields of affordable housing and community development. Primary audiences for this shared knowledge are nonprofit organization staffs, affordable housing practitioners, government officials, academics and private developers. The Foundation's primary vehicle for sharing data is www.knowledgeplex.org, the Foundation's premier portal for housing and community development information.

Decision Notification: The foundation acknowledges receipt of proposal within 15 days.
Notes: The foundation's Innovation, Research, and Technology grant program have a separate set of guidelines. See the foundation's web site.
The foundation frequently makes Requests For Applications; these initiatives may have specific deadlines.

Restrictions

Does not support projects, programs or organizations that do not fit within the foundation's areas of interest or for which the foundation is asked to serve as the sole funder; individuals; organizations without Section 501(c)(3) status; private foundations; organizations that channel funds received to third parties; political campaigns, candidates or lobbying organizations; sectarian purposes; endowment and capital campaigns; in-classroom components of K-12 public or private schools; existing program or organizational deficits; organizations that already have an active grant with the foundation; or local affiliates of larger national organizations, if the foundation has a relationship with the national organization.

Additional Information

Applications should be sent to regional offices; contact information is included in application guidelines.
Publications: Application Form; Foundation Annual Report; Application Guidelines

Corporate Officials

Kenneth J. Bacon: senior vice president B Houston, TX 1954. ED Stanford University (1976); Harvard University (1982). PRIM CORP EMPL senior vice president: Fannie Mae.
Jamie Shona Gorelick: vice chair B New York, NY 1950. PRIM CORP EMPL vice chair: Fannie Mae. CORP AFFIL member: Local Initiatives Support Corp. NONPR AFFIL member: Washington Legal Clinic for Homeless; member: Women's Bar Association; member: National Park Foundation; member: National Women's Law Center; member: National Community Support Law Enforcement; member: National Legal Center Public Interest; member: District of Columbia College Access; member: Carnegie Endowment; member: Council Foreign Relations; member: American Promise - Alliance for Youth; member: Bazelon

Center Mental Health Law; follow: American Bar Foundation; member: American Law Institute.
William R. Maloni: senior vice president policy & public affairs B Pittsburgh, PA 1944. ED Duquesne University (1968). PRIM CORP EMPL senior vice president policy & public affairs: Fannie Mae.
Franklin Delano Raines: chairman, chief executive officer B Seattle, WA 1949. ED Harvard University BA (1971); Oxford University (1971-1973); Harvard University JD (1976). PRIM CORP EMPL chairman, chief executive officer: Fannie Mae. CORP AFFIL director: Pfizer Inc.; director: AOL Time Warner Inc.; director: PepsiCo. NONPR AFFIL member: White House Conference Children Youth.
Barry Zigas: senior vice president B New York, NY 1951. ED Grinnell College (1973). PRIM CORP EMPL senior vice president: Federal National Mortgage Association. NONPR AFFIL director: National Housing Trust; director: Yachad Inc.; director: Mercy Housing; trustee: Enterprise Foundation; secretary, treasurer, director: Hands Net Inc.

Foundation Officials

Kenneth J. Bacon: director (see above)
Peter Beard: vice president national philanthropy
James H. Carr: senior vice president
Rev. Dr. Floyd Harold Flake: director B Los Angeles, CA 1945. ED Northeastern University; Wilberforce University BA (1967); United Theology Seminary D Ministry (1995). PRIM CORP EMPL pastor: Allen AME Church. NONPR AFFIL senior fellow: Manhattan Institute Policy Research.
Stephen Goldsmith: director
Jamie Shona Gorelick: vice chair (see above)
Chuck Greener: director
Colleen Hernandez: director
Glen S. Howard: secretary, director
Louis W. Hoyes: director
Anastasia Kelly: secretary, director
Stewart Kwoh: director
Robert J. Levin: director
William R. Maloni: director (see above)
Ann D. McLaughlin: director
Dan Mudd: director
Tom Nides: treasurer, director
Franklin Delano Raines: chairman (see above)
John Sasso: director
Rebecca Senhauser: director
Stacey Davis Stewart: president, chief executive officer, director
H. Patrick Swygert: director
Ann Marie Wheelock: president, chief executive officer
Karen Hastie Williams: director B Washington, DC 1944. ED University of Neuchatel (Switzerland) (1965); Bates College BA (1966); Tufts University MA (1967); Catholic University America JD (1973). PRIM CORP EMPL partner: Crowell & Moring. CORP AFFIL director: SunAmerica Inc.; director: Washington Gas Light Co.; director: Gannett Co. Inc.; director: Crestar Financial Services Corp.; director: Federal National Mortgage Association; director: Continental Airlines Inc. NONPR AFFIL member: National Contract Management Association; member: Washington Bar Association; member: National Bar Association; chairman, trustee: Greater Washington Research Center; member, director legal defense fund: NAACP; member: American Bar Association.
Barry Zigas: director (see above)

Grants Analysis

Disclosure Period: calendar year ending 2002
Total Grants: $38,058,078*
Number of Grants: 834
Average Grant: $43,140
Highest Grant: $4,000,000
Lowest Grant: $500
Typical Range: $20,000 to $100,000
***Note:** Analysis provided by the foundation.

Recent Grants

Note: Grants derived from 2001 Form 990.

General

2,317,906	Community Foundation for the National Capital Region, Washington, DC -- homeless campaign
750,000	Local Initiatives Support Corporation, New York, NY -- affordable housing and community development
500,000	Enterprise Foundation, Columbia, MD -- programs
500,000	Enterprise Foundation, Columbia, MD -- programs
400,000	National Council of La Raza, Washington, DC -- Partnerships of Hope Program
361,868	President and Fellows of Harvard College, Cambridge, MA -- development of case studies
350,000	National Urban League, New York, NY -- support of a capacity building initiative
300,000	George Washington University School of Business, Washington, DC -- excellence in municipal management
250,000	District of Columbia College Access Program, Washington, DC -- support of a program which provides financial aid and admissions counseling
250,000	Enterprise Foundation, Columbia, MD -- programs

MAX AND MARIAN FARASH CHARITABLE FOUNDATION

Giving Contact

Max M. Farash, Trustee
919 Winton Rd. S.
Rochester, NY 14618-1633
Phone: (716)244-1886

Description

Founded: 1989
EIN: 222948675
Organization Type: Private Foundation
Giving Locations: NY: Rochester including metropolitan area; PA
Grant Types: General Support.

Financial Summary

Total Giving: $431,600 (2001); $213,000 (2000); $214,000 (1999)
Giving Analysis: Giving for 1997 includes: foundation grants to United Way ($6,000)
Assets: $4,115,068 (2001); $4,961,141 (2000); $4,891,138 (1999)

Typical Recipients

Arts & Humanities: Arts Associations & Councils, Arts & Humanities-General, History & Archaeology, Libraries, Museums/Galleries, Music, Theater
Civic & Public Affairs: Employment/Job Training, Civic & Public Affairs-General, Urban & Community Affairs
Education: Arts/Humanities Education, Business Education, Colleges & Universities, Community & Junior Colleges, Medical Education, Student Aid
Health: Cancer, Clinics/Medical Centers, Health Organizations, Hospitals, Medical Rehabilitation, Medical Research, Single-Disease Health Associations
International: Missionary/Religious Activities
Religion: Jewish Causes, Religious Organizations
Science: Science Museums
Social Services: Child Welfare, Community Centers, Community Service Organizations, Homes, Senior

Services, United Funds/United Ways, Volunteer Services, Youth Organizations

Application Procedures

Initial Contact: Send a brief letter of inquiry on organization's letterhead.
Application Requirements: Include statement of purpose, amount requested, and proof of tax-exempt status.
Deadlines: March 1.

Restrictions

Organized charitable organizations qualifying as such under the Internal Revenue code.

Foundation Officials

Marian M. Farash: trustee
Max M. Farash: trustee
Eric R. Fox: trustee

Grants Analysis

Disclosure Period: calendar year ending 2001
Total Grants: $431,600
Number of Grants: 6
Highest Grant: $200,000
Lowest Grant: $2,500

Recent Grants

Note: Grants derived from 2001 Form 990.

General

200,000	Catholic Family Services
100,000	University of Pennsylvania - The Wharton School, Philadelphia, PA
50,000	Jewish Community Center
50,000	Jewish Home Foundation, Rochester, NY
29,100	George Eastman House, Rochester, NY
2,500	Suny College at Alfred

WILLIAM STAMPS FARISH FUND

Giving Contact

Martha L. Gary, President
10000 Memorial Drive, Suite 920
Houston, TX 77024
Phone: (713)686-7373

Description

Founded: 1951
EIN: 746043019
Organization Type: General Purpose Foundation
Giving Locations: KY: Lexington; NY; TX: Houston
Grant Types: Capital, Challenge, Conference/Seminar, Project, Research, Scholarship.

Donor Information

Founder: Mrs. Libbie Rice Farish, wife of William Stamps Farish, established the William Stamps Farish Fund in 1951 in Texas. Mr. Farish was one of the Humble Oil Company organizers. The fund receives contributions from various family trusts.

Financial Summary

Total Giving: $10,300,000 (fiscal year ending June 30, 2000); $8,400,000 (fiscal 1998); $6,300,000 (fiscal 1997)
Giving Analysis: Giving for fiscal 1998 includes: foundation gifts to individuals ($120,000) foundation scholarships ($795,000)
Assets: $198,319,288 (fiscal 2000); $176,678,403 (fiscal 1998); $155,658,310 (fiscal 1997)

Typical Recipients

Arts & Humanities: Arts Associations & Councils, Arts Centers, Arts Outreach, Ballet, Dance, History & Archaeology, Libraries, Museums/Galleries, Music, Opera, Performing Arts, Public Broadcasting, Theater, Visual Arts
Civic & Public Affairs: Botanical Gardens/Parks, Business/Free Enterprise, Urban & Community Affairs, Women's Affairs
Education: Afterschool/Enrichment Programs, Arts/Humanities Education, Business Education, Colleges & Universities, Education Associations, Education Funds, Faculty Development, Education-General, Literacy, Medical Education, Minority Education, Preschool Education, Private Education (Precollege), Public Education (Precollege), Religious Education, Science/Mathematics Education, Secondary Education (Private), Social Sciences Education, Special Education, Student Aid
Environment: Environment-General, Resource Conservation
Health: Cancer, Clinics/Medical Centers, Emergency/Ambulance Services, Eyes/Blindness, Health-General, Health Funds, Health Organizations, Hospices, Hospitals, Hospitals (University Affiliated), Medical Research, Mental Health, Prenatal Health Issues, Public Health, Single-Disease Health Associations, Speech & Hearing
Religion: Churches, Religious Organizations, Religious Welfare
Science: Science Museums, Scientific Centers & Institutes, Scientific Labs, Scientific Research
Social Services: Animal Protection, Camps, Child Abuse, Child Welfare, Community Service Organizations, Community Service Organizations, Day Care, Family Planning, Family Services, Food/Clothing Distribution, People with Disabilities, Recreation & Athletics, Scouts, Sexual Abuse, Substance Abuse, Volunteer Services, Youth Organizations

Application Procedures

Initial Contact: Applicants should send a copy of a full proposal to the fund.
Application Requirements: A complete proposal must include proof of tax-exempt status; brief history of the organization; description of the proposed project and a concise statement of the necessity for such a project; copy of a detailed financial statement; and an explanation of the proposed use of funds, detailed project budget, other potential sources of funding, and specific amount requested.
Deadlines: None.
Review Process: The board meets annually.

Restrictions

The fund does not make contributions for endowments, ongoing operating expenses, or to individuals.

Additional Information

Publications: Application Guidelines

Foundation Officials

Laura Farish Chadwick: trustee
Cornelia Gerry Corbett: trustee
Martha Farish Gerry: president, trustee NONPR AFFIL director: Cold Spring Harbor Laboratory.
Caroline P. Rotan: secretary
Terry W. Ward: vice president, treasurer

Grants Analysis

Disclosure Period: fiscal year ending June 30, 2000
Total Grants: $10,300,000
Number of Grants: 104
Average Grant: $99,038
Highest Grant: $600,000
Lowest Grant: $5,000
Typical Range: $10,000 to $75,000 and $100,000 to $500,000

Recent Grants

Note: Grants derived from fiscal 2000 Form 990.

General

600,000	Independent Day School, Tampa, FL -- for capital campaign
600,000	South Kent School Corporation, South Kent, CT -- annual giving and capital campaign
540,000	Lexington School, Lexington, KY -- annual giving and capital campaign
500,000	Morehouse School of Medicine, Atlanta, GA -- capital campaign
500,000	University of Kentucky Chandler Medical Center, Lexington, KY -- establishment of Chair in Urology Department
400,000	Episcopal High School, Bellaire, TX -- for New Learning Center
320,000	Healthways, Inc., Monticello, FL -- for clinic renovation and supplies
310,000	Ephraim McDowell Cancer Research, Lexington, KY -- annual giving and Leshney research
300,000	Boys' Country of Houston, Inc., Hockley, TX -- capital campaign
300,000	Cold Spring Harbor Laboratory Association, Cold Spring Harbor, NY -- for development of Graduate Program

FARMER FAMILY FOUNDATION

Giving Contact

Amy F. Joseph, Trustee
c/o Summer Hill
PO Box 625737
Cincinnati, OH 45262-5737
Phone: (513)459-1085

Description

Founded: 1988
EIN: 311256614
Organization Type: Private Foundation
Grant Types: General Support.

Donor Information

Founder: Richard T. Farmer

Financial Summary

Total Giving: $950,000 (2000); $552,596 (1999); $538,185 (1998)
Assets: $33,355,183 (2000); $17,740,644 (1999); $23,541,732 (1998)
Gifts Received: $7,673,592 (2000); $4,960,299 (1998); $1,434,375 (1997). Note: In 2000, contributions were received from Richard T. Farmer 2000 Charitable Trust ($4,371,416), Richard T. Farmer ($3,101,954) and Scott D. Farmer ($200,222). In 1998, contributions were received from Richard T. Farmer ($4,360,380), Brynne F. Coletti ($199,973), Scott D. Farmer ($199,973), and Amy F. Joseph ($199,973). In 1994, contributions were received from Joyce E. Farmer ($1,390,000) and Brynne F. Coletti ($36,000).

Typical Recipients

Arts & Humanities: Arts Associations & Councils, Arts Centers, Libraries, Museums/Galleries, Performing Arts
Civic & Public Affairs: Community Foundations, Civic & Public Affairs-General, Urban & Community Affairs, Zoos/Aquariums
Education: Business Education, Colleges & Universities, Education Reform, Education-General, Journalism/Media Education, Private Education (Precollege), Student Aid
Health: Children's Health/Hospitals, Clinics/Medical Centers, Diabetes, Hospices, Hospitals, Single-Disease Health Associations
Religion: Churches
Science: Scientific Organizations
Social Services: At-Risk Youth, Food/Clothing Distribution, People with Disabilities, Scouts, YMCA/YWCA/YMHA/YWHA, Youth Organizations

Application Procedures

Initial Contact: Send a brief letter of inquiry.
Application Requirements: purpose of funds sought, description and background of organization, amount requested, charitable status, and list of board members.
Deadlines: None.

Additional Information

The foundation was established to assist children, the handicapped, and programs that aid people in entering the work force.

Foundation Officials

Brynne F. Coletti: president, treasurer, trustee
Robert E. Coletti: trustee
Amy Joseph: vice president, secretary, trustee

Grants Analysis

Disclosure Period: calendar year ending 2000
Total Grants: $950,000
Number of Grants: 43
Average Grant: $10,590*
Highest Grant: $166,000
Typical Range: $5,000 to $20,000
*Note: Average grant figure excludes four highest grants ($537,000)

Recent Grants

Note: Grants derived from 1999 Form 990.

General

167,000	Good Samaritan Hospital Foundation, Cincinnati, OH
150,000	Tyler Davidson Fund, Cincinnati, OH
67,500	Xavier University, Cincinnati, OH
33,000	Children's Hospital Medical Foundation, Cincinnati, OH
25,000	Jason Foundation for Education, Waltham, MA
20,000	YWCA, Cincinnati, OH
10,000	Children's Museum of Cincinnati, Cincinnati, OH
10,000	National Geographic Society, Washington, DC
7,500	Miami University Foundation, Cincinnati, OH
5,000	Children's Hospital Foundation, Cincinnati, OH

FARMER JACK SUPERMARKETS

Company Headquarters

18718 Borman St.
Detroit, MI 48228
Web: http://www.farmerjack.com

Company Description

Founded: 1928
Former Name: Borman's Inc..
Employees: 8,500
SIC(s): 5411 Grocery Stores, 5912 Drug Stores & Proprietary Stores.
Parent Company: Great Atlantic & Pacific Tea Company, Inc., 2 Paragon Drive, Montvale, NJ, United States

Operating Locations

Borman's Inc. (MI--Southfield)
Note: Operates 2 divisions in Detroit, MI.

Borman's Inc. Fund

Giving Contact

Paul Borman, President
Borman's Inc. Fund
20500 Civic Center Drive, Suite 2750
Southfield, MI 48076

Phone: (248)350-0300
Fax: (248)350-2920

Description

EIN: 386069267
Organization Type: Corporate Foundation
Giving Locations: MI: Southeastern Michigan
Grant Types: Award, General Support, Project.

Donor Information

Founder: Borman's Inc., Paul Borman

Financial Summary

Total Giving: $16,105 (2000); $400,000 (1999 approx); $408,916 (1998). Note: Contributes through corporate direct giving program and foundation.
Giving Analysis: Giving for 2000 includes: foundation ($16,105); 1998: foundation grants to United Way ($1,250); foundation ($407,666); 1995: foundation grants to United Way ($1,250) foundation ($510,322)
Assets: $350,630 (2000); $493,744 (1998); $689,538 (1995)
Gifts Received: $5,210 (2000); $129,960 (1998); $311,984 (1995). Note: In 1995, contributions were received from Great Atlantic & Pacific Tea Company ($300,000), Paul Borman ($5,000), and other sources ($6,984).

Typical Recipients

Arts & Humanities: Art History, Arts Associations & Councils, Arts Centers, Arts Institutes, Community Arts, Dance, Ethnic & Folk Arts, Historic Preservation, Libraries, Literary Arts, Museums/Galleries, Music, Performing Arts, Theater
Civic & Public Affairs: Civil Rights, Civic & Public Affairs-General, Housing, Parades/Festivals, Philanthropic Organizations, Public Policy, Urban & Community Affairs, Zoos/Aquariums
Education: Colleges & Universities, Environmental Education, International Exchange, Minority Education, Private Education (Precollege), Religious Education, Science/Mathematics Education, Secondary Education (Public), Student Aid
Environment: Environment-General
Health: AIDS/HIV, Alzheimers Disease, Alzheimers Disease, Cancer, Children's Health/Hospitals, Diabetes, Emergency/Ambulance Services, Eyes/Blindness, Geriatric Health, Health Organizations, Hospices, Hospitals, Long-Term Care, Mental Health, Multiple Sclerosis, Single-Disease Health Associations
International: Foreign Educational Institutions, Health Care/Hospitals, International Affairs, International Organizations, International Relief Efforts, Missionary/Religious Activities
Religion: Churches, Jewish Causes, Religious Organizations, Religious Welfare, Seminaries, Synagogues/Temples
Science: Scientific Centers & Institutes, Scientific Organizations
Social Services: Animal Protection, Child Welfare, Community Centers, Community Service Organizations, Day Care, Delinquency & Criminal Rehabilitation, Domestic Violence, Emergency Relief, Family Planning, Family Services, Food/Clothing Distribution, People with Disabilities, Recreation & Athletics, Senior Services, Shelters/Homelessness, Substance Abuse, United Funds/United Ways, Youth Organizations

Application Procedures

Initial Contact: Send a written request.
Application Requirements: Include amount needed, purpose of the grant, and organizational and financial information.
Deadlines: None.

Restrictions

The company does not support individuals, political or lobbying groups.

Corporate Officials

Paul Borman: chief executive officer B Detroit, MI 1932. ED Michigan State University (1954). PRIM CORP EMPL chairman: Borman's Inc. CORP AFFIL director: First Federal Michigan.

Foundation Officials

Paul Borman: president, director (see above)

Grants Analysis

Disclosure Period: calendar year ending 2000
Total Grants: $16,105
Number of Grants: 23
Average Grant: $700
Highest Grant: $2,500
Lowest Grant: $25
Typical Range: $100 to $5,000

Recent Grants

Note: Grants derived from 2000 Form 990.

General

2,500	Scheie Eye Institute, Philadelphia, PA
2,312	American ORT Federation, New York, NY
2,000	Karmanos Cancer Institute, Detroit, MI
1,005	Hillel Day School, Farmington Hills, MI
1,000	Michigan Humane Society, Auburn Hills, MI
1,000	Mikveh Israel, Oak Park, MI
1,000	Spaulding for Children, Southfield, MI
750	Women's American ORT Federation, New York, NY
613	Jewish Theological Seminary, New York, NY
500	American Friends of the Israel Museum, New York, NY

FRANK M. AND ALICE M. FARR TRUST

Giving Contact

James E. Koepke, Trustee
1101 12th St.
Aurora, NE 68818
Phone: (402)694-3136
Fax: (402)694-3136

Description

Founded: 1985
EIN: 476144457
Organization Type: Private Foundation
Giving Locations: DC; IA; NE: Hamilton County
Grant Types: Capital, Emergency, Endowment, General Support, Operating Expenses.

Financial Summary

Total Giving: $278,017 (2001); $239,993 (2000); $250,013 (1999)
Assets: $4,862,853 (2001); $5,054,179 (2000); $5,219,126 (1999)

Typical Recipients

Arts & Humanities: Historic Preservation, History & Archaeology, Libraries, Music
Civic & Public Affairs: Botanical Gardens/Parks, Chambers of Commerce, Clubs, Community Foundations, Ethnic Organizations, Civic & Public Affairs-General, Housing, Municipalities/Towns, Rural Affairs, Safety, Urban & Community Affairs
Education: Agricultural Education, Colleges & Universities, Education Funds, Education-General, Private Education (Precollege), Student Aid

Health: Alzheimers Disease, Cancer, Emergency/ Ambulance Services, Health Organizations, Heart, Hospitals, Nursing Services, Public Health
Social Services: Animal Protection, Community Centers, Community Service Organizations, Recreation & Athletics, Scouts, Senior Services, Youth Organizations

Application Procedures

Initial Contact: Send request for application form.
Deadlines: March 1.

Restrictions

Limited to governmental subdivisions or charities in Hamilton County, NE.

Additional Information

Trust(s): Heritage Bank

Foundation Officials

James E. Koepke: trustee

Grants Analysis

Disclosure Period: calendar year ending 2001
Total Grants: $278,017
Number of Grants: 14
Average Grant: $11,787*
Highest Grant: $63,000
Lowest Grant: $1,500
Typical Range: $5,000 to $20,000
*Note: Average grant excludes two highest grants ($113,000).

Recent Grants

Note: Grants derived from 2001 Form 990.

General

63,000	Community Center of Hamilton County
50,000	Nebraska Vocational Aging Foundation, NE
26,575	Hamilton County Senior Center, Aurora, NE
25,000	Hamilton County Information Technology
23,988	Hamilton County Foundation Inc., Aurora, NE
19,516	Hamilton County Senior Center, Aurora, NE
17,678	Hamilton Community Foundation, Aurora, NE
15,000	ADC Foundation, Washington, DC
10,000	Edgerton Education Foundation
7,760	Memorial Hospital Foundation

DRUSILLA FARWELL FOUNDATION

Giving Contact

Leslie Wise, Treasurer
650 E. Big Beaver, Suite E
Troy, MI 48083
Phone: (248)619-6030

Description

Founded: 1937
EIN: 386082430
Organization Type: Private Foundation
Giving Locations: MI
Grant Types: General Support.

Financial Summary

Total Giving: $243,900 (fiscal year ending August 31, 2001); $232,000 (fiscal 2000); $152,175 (fiscal 1998)
Giving Analysis: Giving for fiscal 2000 includes: foundation grants to United Way ($2,000)
Assets: $3,695,069 (fiscal 2001); $4,221,840 (fiscal 2000); $3,810,656 (fiscal 1998)

Typical Recipients

Arts & Humanities: Arts Associations & Councils, Arts Funds, Arts Institutes, Community Arts, Arts & Humanities-General, History & Archaeology, Libraries, Museums/Galleries, Music, Opera, Performing Arts, Public Broadcasting, Theater
Civic & Public Affairs: Asian American Affairs, Civic & Public Affairs-General, Legal Aid, Municipalities/Towns, Professional & Trade Associations, Safety, Urban & Community Affairs, Women's Affairs
Education: Business Education, Colleges & Universities, Legal Education, Medical Education, Private Education (Precollege), Religious Education, Secondary Education (Private), Secondary Education (Public), Special Education
Health: Alzheimers Disease, Cancer, Children's Health/Hospitals, Clinics/Medical Centers, Clinics/Medical Centers, Diabetes, Emergency/Ambulance Services, Geriatric Health, Health Organizations, Heart, Hospices, Hospitals, Medical Research, Multiple Sclerosis, Public Health, Single-Disease Health Associations
International: Foreign Arts Organizations, Missionary/Religious Activities
Religion: Churches, Dioceses, Jewish Causes, Religious Organizations, Religious Welfare, Seminaries
Social Services: Child Welfare, Community Service Organizations, People with Disabilities, Shelters/Homelessness, Substance Abuse, United Funds/United Ways, Youth Organizations

Application Procedures

Initial Contact: Send brief letter describing program.
Deadlines: None.

Foundation Officials

Randolph Fields: treasurer
Helmuth Krave: secretary
Hugo Krave: president
Leslie Wise: treasurer

Grants Analysis

Disclosure Period: fiscal year ending August 31, 2001
Total Grants: $243,900
Number of Grants: 107
Average Grant: $2,279
Highest Grant: $10,000
Lowest Grant: $100
Typical Range: $1,000 to $5,000

Recent Grants

Note: Grants derived from 2000 Form 990.

Library-Related

5,000	Brother Rice High School, Bloomfield, MI

General

7,000	Catholic Central High School, Redford, MI
6,200	First Presbyterian Church, Orlando, FL
5,000	AFS Intercultural Programs USA, New York, NY
5,000	Alzheimer's Association, Southfield, MI
5,000	McLaren Regional Medical Center, Flint, MI
5,000	Orange County Historical Society, Orlando, FL
5,000	Our Lady of Loretto Bishop Church, Redford, MI
5,000	Philippine American Community Center of Michigan, Shelby Township, MI
5,000	St. Hugo of the Hills, Bloomfield Hills, MI
5,000	St. Paul Latvian Lutheran Church, Farmington Hills, MI

FASKEN FOUNDATION

Giving Contact

B. L. Jones, Trustee
PO Box 162786
Austin, TX 78716-2786
Phone: (512)708-1003

Description

Founded: 1955
EIN: 756023680
Organization Type: Private Foundation
Giving Locations: TX
Grant Types: General Support, Scholarship.

Donor Information

Founder: the late Andrew A. Fasken, the late Helen Fasken House, the late Vickie Mallison, the late Howard Marshall Johnson, the late Ruth Shelton

Financial Summary

Total Giving: $1,175,096 (2000); $566,746 (1999); $544,184 (1998)
Giving Analysis: Giving for 2000 includes: foundation scholarships ($131,696); foundation grants to United Way ($200,000); 1999: foundation grants to United Way ($15,000); foundation scholarships ($172,445); 1998: foundation grants to United Way ($15,000) foundation scholarships ($204,184)
Assets: $17,537,265 (2000); $19,055,497 (1999); $17,869,684 (1998)
Gifts Received: $50 (1994); $25,000 (1993); $125 (1992)

Typical Recipients

Arts & Humanities: Libraries
Civic & Public Affairs: Chambers of Commerce, Civic & Public Affairs-General, Hispanic Affairs, Housing, Rural Affairs, Safety
Education: Business Education, Colleges & Universities, Engineering/Technological Education, Faculty Development, Literacy, Medical Education, Public Education (Precollege), Special Education, Student Aid
Health: AIDS/HIV, Children's Health/Hospitals, Clinics/Medical Centers, Hospices, Single-Disease Health Associations
Religion: Ministries, Religious Welfare
Social Services: At-Risk Youth, Big Brother/Big Sister, Child Welfare, Community Service Organizations, Domestic Violence, Family Services, People with Disabilities, Scouts, Senior Services, Sexual Abuse, Substance Abuse, United Funds/United Ways, YMCA/YWCA/YMHA/YWHA, Youth Organizations

Application Procedures

Initial Contact: Send a brief letter of inquiry.
Application Requirements: list of governing board and proof of tax-exempt status. Grants are reviewed quarterly and awards are generally made in February and September.

Additional Information

Provides scholarships to graduates of Midland County, TX, public schools.
Publications: Application Guidelines

Foundation Officials

Andrew C. Elliott, Jr.: president
F. Andrew Fasken: vice president
Steven P. Fasken: trustee
William P. Franklin: trustee B Las Vegas, NM 1933. ED Texas A&M University (1955); University of Texas (1958). PRIM CORP EMPL president, chief executive officer: First City TX - Midland.
Tevis Herd: trustee
B. L. Jones: executive director
Thomas E. Kelly: trustee PRIM CORP EMPL chief financial officer: Cadence Design Systems, Inc.
Susan Fasken Martin: trustee

Grants Analysis

Disclosure Period: calendar year ending 2000
Total Grants: $843,400*
Number of Grants: 54
Average Grant: $10,450*
Highest Grant: $200,000
Lowest Grant: $500
Typical Range: $5,000 to $20,000
*Note: Average grant figure excludes two highest grants ($300,000). Giving excludes scholarships; United Way.

Recent Grants

Note: Grants derived from 1999 Form 990.

General

80,000	Midland Cerebral Palsy Center, Midland, TX
30,000	High Sky Children's Ranch, Midland, TX
27,301	Schriener College, Kerrville, TX
25,000	Casa de Amigos, Midland, TX
25,000	Texas A and M University Development Foundation, College Station, TX
15,000	Big Brothers/Big Sisters, Midland, TX
15,000	Midland College, Midland, TX -- nursing program
15,000	United Way, Midland, TX
15,000	YMCA, Midland, TX
11,328	Midland College, Midland, TX

MARIANNE G. FAULKNER TRUST

Giving Contact

Kenneth Gheno, Vice President
c/o JP Morgan Chase Bank
1211 Ave. of the Americas, 38th Floor
New York, NY 10036
Phone: (212)789-5263

Alternate Contact

Phone: (212)789-4159

Description

Founded: 1959
EIN: 136047458
Organization Type: Private Foundation
Giving Locations: VT: Northeast.
Grant Types: General Support, Operating Expenses.

Donor Information

Founder: the late Marianne Gaillard Faulkner

Financial Summary

Total Giving: $551,544 (2001); $309,506 (2000); $376,564 (1999)
Assets: $10,266,131 (2001); $11,235,196 (2000); $11,412,071 (1999)

Typical Recipients

Arts & Humanities: Arts Associations & Councils, Arts & Humanities-General, History & Archaeology, Libraries, Literary Arts, Public Broadcasting
Civic & Public Affairs: Civic & Public Affairs-General, Municipalities/Towns, Public Policy, Urban & Community Affairs
Education: Colleges & Universities, Education-General
Environment: Air/Water Quality, Environment-General, Resource Conservation
Health: Clinics/Medical Centers, Health Organizations, Home-Care Services, Hospitals
Religion: Churches, Ministries
Social Services: Child Welfare, Community Centers, Community Service Organizations, Food/Clothing Distribution, Homes, People with Disabilities, Recreation & Athletics, Senior Services, United Funds/ United Ways, Youth Organizations

Application Procedures

Initial Contact: Send a letter of application.
Application Requirements: Include description of project, financial data, and proof of tax-exempt status.
Deadlines: None.

Restrictions

Does not support individuals.

Additional Information

Trust(s): JP Morgan Chase Bank

Grants Analysis

Disclosure Period: calendar year ending 2001
Total Grants: $551,544
Number of Grants: 29
Average Grant: $12,498*
Highest Grant: $75,536
Lowest Grant: $3,000
Typical Range: $5,000 to $25,000 and $51,000 to $75,550
*Note: Average grant figure excludes three highest grants ($226,607).

Recent Grants

Note: Grants derived from 2001 Form 990.

General

75,536	Homestead, Inc., Woodstock, VT
75,536	Homestead, Inc., Woodstock, VT
75,535	Homestead, Inc., Woodstock, VT
57,502	Homestead, Inc., Woodstock, VT
57,502	Homestead, Inc., Woodstock, VT
25,000	North University
18,033	Homestead, Inc., Woodstock, VT
10,000	Vermont Council, Essex Junction, VT
10,000	Vermont Public Radio, Essex Junction, VT
9,000	Woodstock Associates, Woodstock Community Recreation Center, Woodstock, VT

FEAR NOT FOUNDATION

Giving Contact

Steven Russo, Director
1820 E. River Road, Suite 230
Tucson, AZ 85718
Phone: (520)529-1515

Description

Founded: 1991
EIN: 860647136
Organization Type: Private Foundation
Giving Locations: AZ: Tuscon
Grant Types: General Support.

Financial Summary

Total Giving: $117,500 (2001); $85,000 (2000); $70,000 (1999)
Assets: $1,356,469 (2001); $1,715,796 (2000); $1,818,276 (1999)
Gifts Received: $62,475 (1994); $220,179 (1992)

Typical Recipients

Arts & Humanities: Libraries
Civic & Public Affairs: Hispanic Affairs
Education: Arts/Humanities Education, Colleges & Universities, Education Funds, Education Reform, Education-General, Secondary Education (Private)
Environment: Environment-General
Health: Clinics/Medical Centers, Hospices
Religion: Religious Organizations
Social Services: Emergency Relief, Food/Clothing Distribution, People with Disabilities, Recreation & Athletics

Application Procedures

Initial Contact: Send a brief letter of inquiry.
Application Requirements: Include name of requestor, amount requested, purpose of funds sought, and why request is made.
Deadlines: None.

Foundation Officials

Ashley M. Dixon: director
Steven Russo: director
Ashley M. Willock: director
Katheryne Willock: director
Norman A. Willock: director
Scott Willock: director

Grants Analysis

Disclosure Period: calendar year ending 2001
Total Grants: $117,500
Number of Grants: 3
Highest Grant: $87,500
Lowest Grant: $10,000

Recent Grants

Note: Grants derived from 2000 Form 990.

General

40,000	University of Arizona Foundation, Tucson, AZ -- Heritage Center
25,000	Hillenbrand Aquatics
15,000	University of Arizona Foundation, Tucson, AZ -- Centennial Hall Dance Program
5,000	Kent Hospice Foundation, Inc., Chestertown, MD

FEDERATED MUTUAL INSURANCE CO.

Company Headquarters

121 E. Park Sq.
Owatonna, MN 55060
Web: http://www.federatedinsurance.com

Company Description

Assets: US$3.476 billion (2001)
Employees: 2,700
SIC(s): 6321 Accident & Health Insurance, 6331 Fire, Marine & Casualty Insurance.

Operating Locations

Federated Mutual Insurance Co. (AZ--Phoenix; GA--Atlanta; MN--Minneapolis, St. Paul)

Federated Mutual Insurance Foundation

Giving Contact

Brian Brose
121 E. Park Sq.
Owatonna, MN 55060
Phone: (507)455-5200

Description

EIN: 237173646
Organization Type: Corporate Foundation
Giving Locations: operating locations, mainly MN.
Grant Types: General Support, Project, Scholarship.

Financial Summary

Total Giving: $541,532 (2001); $360,345 (1999); $640,092 (1998)
Giving Analysis: Giving for 2001 includes: foundation scholarships ($17,100); foundation grants to United Way ($73,000); foundation ($451,432); 1998: foundation grants to United Way ($62,790) foundation ($577,302)

Assets: $225,037 (2001); $37,123 (1999); $124,447 (1998)
Gifts Received: $95,385 (2001); $46,878 (1999); $45,789 (1998)

Typical Recipients
Arts & Humanities: Arts Centers, Arts Festivals, Arts Institutes, Community Arts, Libraries, Music, Performing Arts, Theater
Civic & Public Affairs: Chambers of Commerce, Clubs, Community Foundations, Civic & Public Affairs-General, Housing, Municipalities/Towns, Parades/Festivals, Philanthropic Organizations, Professional & Trade Associations, Safety, Urban & Community Affairs, Women's Affairs, Zoos/Aquariums
Education: Afterschool/Enrichment Programs, Business Education, Business-School Partnerships, Colleges & Universities, Economic Education, Education Funds, Education-General, Public Education (Precollege), Science/Mathematics Education, Student Aid
Environment: Environment-General, Wildlife Protection
Health: Cancer, Children's Health/Hospitals, Emergency/Ambulance Services, Health-General, Geriatric Health, Health Policy/Cost Containment, Health Organizations, Heart, Home-Care Services, Medical Rehabilitation, Medical Research, Public Health
Religion: Religious Organizations, Religious Welfare
Social Services: At-Risk Youth, Big Brother/Big Sister, Camps, Community Service Organizations, Emergency Relief, Family Services, Food/Clothing Distribution, People with Disabilities, Recreation & Athletics, Scouts, Senior Services, Shelters/Homelessness, Social Services-General, Special Olympics, Substance Abuse, United Funds/United Ways

Application Procedures
Initial Contact: Send a brief letter of inquiry.
Deadlines: None.
Notes: The foundation has no formal grant application procedure or application form.

Restrictions
Does not support individuals, religious organizations, political or lobbying groups, or organizations outside operating areas.

Corporate Officials
Raymond R. Stawarz: chief financial officer PRIM CORP EMPL chief financial officer: Federated Mutual Insurance Co.

Foundation Officials
Rick Kraus: administrator NONPR AFFIL council member: City of Owatonna.
J. E. Meilahn: secretary, treasurer
Kirk N. Nelson: vice president
Raymond R. Stawarz: treasurer (see above)

Grants Analysis
Disclosure Period: calendar year ending 2001
Total Grants: $451,432*
Number of Grants: 144
Average Grant: $1,771*
Highest Grant: $100,000
Typical Range: $100 to $35,000 and $25,000 to $100,000
***Note:** Giving excludes scholarship, United Way.

Recent Grants
Note: Grants derived from 2001 Form 990.

Library-Related
4,500	Owatonna Public Library, Owatonna, MN

General
100,000	American Red Cross Disaster Relief Fund, New York, NY -- for victims of 9/11 attack
100,000	Big Brothers Big Sisters of New York City, New York, NY
50,000	Owatonna Foundation, Owatonna, MN
47,000	United Way Steele County, Owatonna, MN
30,000	Crossroads of Owatonna, Owatonna, MN
25,000	Riverland Community College Foundation, Austin, MN
8,500	Minnesota Private College Fund, St. Paul, MN
7,500	Minnesota State University Foundation, Mankato, MN
6,700	United Way Metropolitan Atlanta, Atlanta, GA
5,200	Valley of the Sun United Way, Phoenix, AZ

FRANK B. AND VIRGINIA V. FEHSENFELD CHARITABLE FOUNDATION

Giving Contact
H. Warren Smith, Vice President
1107 1st Avenue, No. 1404
Seattle, WA 98101
Phone: (206)621-7962

Description
Founded: 1989
EIN: 382775201
Organization Type: Private Foundation
Giving Locations: DC; MI
Grant Types: Emergency, General Support, Multiyear/Continuing Support.

Financial Summary
Total Giving: $119,500 (2001); $79,000 (1999); $101,900 (1998)
Assets: $1,789,320 (2001); $1,761,877 (1999); $1,503,418 (1998)
Gifts Received: $250,000 (1999); $250,000 (1995); $200,000 (1994). Note: In 1995 and 1999, contributions were received from Frank B. Fehsenfeld.

Typical Recipients
Arts & Humanities: Libraries, Museums/Galleries, Music
Civic & Public Affairs: Botanical Gardens/Parks, Civic & Public Affairs-General, Housing, Urban & Community Affairs
Education: Colleges & Universities, Education-General
Environment: Environment-General, Resource Conservation
Health: Children's Health/Hospitals, Emergency/Ambulance Services, Eyes/Blindness
International: International Environmental Issues
Religion: Religion-General, Ministries, Religious Welfare
Social Services: Camps, Community Centers, Crime Prevention, Emergency Relief, Family Planning, Scouts, United Funds/United Ways, YMCA/YWCA/YMHA/YWHA, Youth Organizations

Application Procedures
Initial Contact: Send a personal letter stating organization's name, address, exempt status, and needs.
Deadlines: None.

Restrictions
Limited to non-private IRC SEC 501 (C)(3) status organizations.

Foundation Officials
Frank B. Fehsenfeld: vice president, treasurer
John A. Fehsenfeld: trustee
Thomas V. Fehsenfeld: trustee
Virginia V. Fehsenfeld: president, secretary
William S. Fehsenfeld: trustee
Nancy Fehsenfeld Smith: trustee
H. Warren Smith: vice president

Grants Analysis
Disclosure Period: calendar year ending 2001
Total Grants: $119,500
Number of Grants: 48
Average Grant: $2,490
Highest Grant: $15,000
Typical Range: $500 to $5,000

Recent Grants
Note: Grants derived from 2001 Form 990.

Library-Related
2,000	Ryerson Library Foundation, Grand Rapids, MI -- annual support

General
15,000	Kent County Parks Foundation, Grand Rapids, MI -- annual support
10,000	St. Cecilia Music Society, Grand Rapids, MI -- annual support
6,500	Baxter Community Center, Grand Rapids, MI -- annual support
5,000	Conservation International Foundation, Washington, DC -- annual support
5,000	Eastern Michigan University, Ypsilanti, MI -- annual support
5,000	Grand Rapids Symphony, Grand Rapids, MI -- annual support
5,000	Land Conservancy of West Michigan, Grand Rapids, MI -- annual support
5,000	University of Michigan, Ann Arbor, MI -- annual support
5,000	Wedgwood Christian Youth and Family Services, Grand Rapids, MI -- annual support
4,000	YWCA, Grand Rapids, MI -- annual support

FEINSTEIN FOUNDATION

Giving Contact
Alan S. Feinstein, President
41 Alhambra Cir.
Cranston, RI 02905-3416
Phone: (401)467-5155
Web: http://www.feinsteinfoundation.com

Description
Founded: 1991
EIN: 223142312
Organization Type: Private Foundation
Giving Locations: NY; RI
Grant Types: Emergency, General Support.

Donor Information
Founder: Alan S. Feinstein

Financial Summary
Total Giving: $1,875,120 (2001); $1,509,816 (2000); $2,436,541 (1998)
Giving Analysis: Giving for 2001 includes: foundation grants to United Way ($7,500)
Assets: $32,010,979 (2001); $36,256,264 (2000); $38,961,104 (1998)
Gifts Received: $135,741 (2000); $226,429 (1998); $2,536 (1996). Note: In 1998 and 2000, contributions were received from Alan Shaw Feinstein. In 1994,

contributions were received from Alan Shawn Feinstein ($147,611).

Typical Recipients

Arts & Humanities: Libraries, Theater
Civic & Public Affairs: Community Foundations, Civic & Public Affairs-General, Municipalities/Towns, Philanthropic Organizations, Public Policy, Urban & Community Affairs
Education: Colleges & Universities, Education Funds, Education-General, Private Education (Precollege), Public Education (Precollege), Science/Mathematics Education, Secondary Education (Public), Student Aid
International: International Organizations
Religion: Religious Welfare
Social Services: Child Welfare, Community Centers, Community Service Organizations, Counseling, Family Services, Homes, People with Disabilities, Recreation & Athletics, Scouts, United Funds/United Ways, Youth Organizations

Application Procedures

Initial Contact: The foundation has no formal application procedure.
Application Requirements: Submit an application in any format.
Deadlines: None.

Foundation Officials

J. Troy Earhart: director
Alan Shawn Feinstein: president, director B Boston, MA 1931. ED Boston University BS (1952); Boston State College MS (1956); Johnson & Wales University PhD (1994); Providence College PhD (1995). NONPR AFFIL chairman: Cranston Crime Stoppers; founder: Providence College Institute Public Service.
David Goldman: director
Beverly Vale: director
Edward Walton: director

Grants Analysis

Disclosure Period: calendar year ending 2001
Total Grants: $1,867,620*
Number of Grants: 9
Lowest Grant: $10,000
*Note: Giving excludes United Way.

Recent Grants

Note: Grants derived from 2001 Form 990.

General

477,471	Johnson and Wales University, Providence, RI
409,000	University of Rhode Island, Kingston, RI
300,000	International Scholar Athletes
250,000	Chamber Education Program
125,068	Klein Foundation
100,000	University of Rhode Island, Kingston, RI -- Hunger Center
50,000	International Institute of Rhode Island, Providence, RI
10,000	United Way
7,500	Boy Scouts, Rochester, NY

FEINTECH FAMILY FOUNDATION

Giving Contact

Norman Feintech, President
321 South Beverly Drive, Suite K
Beverly Hills, CA 90212
Phone: (213)879-3262

Description

Founded: 1950
EIN: 956072287
Organization Type: Private Foundation

Giving Locations: CA
Grant Types: General Support.

Donor Information

Founder: Irving Feintech, Norman Feintech

Financial Summary

Total Giving: $313,050 (fiscal year ending September 30, 2001); $762,250 (fiscal 2000); $626,695 (fiscal 1998)
Assets: $2,374,087 (fiscal 2001); $3,081,180 (fiscal 2000); $4,850,300 (fiscal 1998)
Gifts Received: $84,841 (fiscal 2000); $350 (fiscal 1998); $750,000 (fiscal 1997). Note: In fiscal 2000, contributions were received from Irving Feintech.

Typical Recipients

Arts & Humanities: Arts Centers, Community Arts, Dance, Film & Video, History & Archaeology, Libraries, Museums/Galleries, Music, Public Broadcasting, Theater
Civic & Public Affairs: Civic & Public Affairs-General, Philanthropic Organizations, Safety
Education: Arts/Humanities Education, Colleges & Universities, Literacy, Medical Education, Preschool Education, Private Education (Precollege), Religious Education
Health: AIDS/HIV, Arthritis, Cancer, Clinics/Medical Centers, Diabetes, Emergency/Ambulance Services, Health Organizations, Heart, Hospitals, Medical Research, Mental Health, Multiple Sclerosis, Prenatal Health Issues, Research/Studies Institutes, Single-Disease Health Associations
International: Foreign Arts Organizations, Foreign Educational Institutions, Health Care/Hospitals, Missionary/Religious Activities
Religion: Jewish Causes, Religious Organizations, Religious Welfare, Social/Policy Issues, Synagogues/Temples
Social Services: Camps, Child Welfare, Community Service Organizations, Crime Prevention, Day Care, Family Planning, Family Services, Food/Clothing Distribution, People with Disabilities, YMCA/YWCA/YMHA/YWHA

Application Procedures

Initial Contact: Send a brief letter of inquiry.
Application Requirements: Include charitable purpose of organization.
Deadlines: None.

Foundation Officials

Evelyn M. Feintech: director
Irving Feintech: vice president
Norman Feintech: president
Celia Littenberg: director

Grants Analysis

Disclosure Period: fiscal year ending September 30, 2001
Total Grants: $313,050
Number of Grants: 37
Average Grant: $4,849*
Highest Grant: $93,325
Typical Range: $1,000 to $10,000
*Note: Average grant figure excludes two highest grants ($143,325).

Recent Grants

Note: Grants derived from fiscal 2000 Form 990.

General

331,750	Cedars-Sinai Medical Center, Los Angeles, CA -- support of medical research and health care
126,000	Hebrew Union College, Los Angeles, CA -- furtherance of social and religious activities
50,000	Anti - Defamation League, Los Angeles, CA -- furtherance of religious freedom
50,000	Shanes Inspiration, Valley Village, CA -- cancer research
30,000	Shoah Foundation, Pacific Palisades, CA -- overall charitable activities
26,900	Simon Weisenthal Center, Los Angeles, CA -- promote tolerance
25,000	University of Iowa Department of Ophthalmology, Iowa City, IA -- medical research
11,000	Foundation for the Junior Blind, Los Angeles, CA -- care and research
10,000	American Friends of Israel Philharmonic Orchestra, New York, NY -- furtherance of the arts
10,000	Discover Fund for Eye Research, Los Angeles, CA -- medical research

SAMUEL S. FELS FUND

Giving Contact

Helen Cunningham Newbold, Executive Director
1616 Walnut St., Suite 800
Philadelphia, PA 19103
Phone: (215)731-9455
Fax: (215)731-9457
Web: http://www.samfels.org

Description

Founded: 1935
EIN: 231365325
Organization Type: General Purpose Foundation
Giving Locations: PA: Philadelphia
Grant Types: General Support, Matching, Multiyear/Continuing Support, Operating Expenses, Project, Seed Money.

Donor Information

Founder: Samuel S. Fels established the fund in 1935. Mr. Fels, a Philadelphia philanthropist, civic leader, and president of a soap manufacturing company, was born in Yanceyville, NC, in 1860. He died in Philadelphia in 1950.

Financial Summary

Total Giving: $3,455,874 (2001); $2,239,673 (2000); $2,178,804 (1999)
Giving Analysis: Giving for 2001 includes: foundation grants to United Way ($25,000); 1999: foundation grants to United Way ($35,000); 1998: foundation grants to United Way ($3,442); international subsidiaries ($12,500) foundation ($1,913,316)
Assets: $49,017,145 (2001); $55,617,574 (2000); $62,928,347 (1999)
Gifts Received: GIV Civic Affairs, social services, arts, and education.

Typical Recipients

Arts & Humanities: Arts Associations & Councils, Arts Centers, Arts Festivals, Ballet, Community Arts, Dance, Ethnic & Folk Arts, Historic Preservation, History & Archaeology, Libraries, Museums/Galleries, Music, Opera, Performing Arts, Public Broadcasting, Theater, Visual Arts
Civic & Public Affairs: African American Affairs, Asian American Affairs, Botanical Gardens/Parks, Business/Free Enterprise, Civil Rights, Clubs, Economic Development, Economic Policy, Employment/Job Training, Ethnic Organizations, Gay/Lesbian Issues, Civic & Public Affairs-General, Hispanic Affairs, Housing, Inner-City Development, Law & Justice, Legal Aid, Legal Aid, Philanthropic Organizations, Public Policy, Urban & Community Affairs, Women's Affairs, Zoos/Aquariums
Education: Afterschool/Enrichment Programs, Arts/Humanities Education, Business Education, Colleges & Universities, Community & Junior Colleges, Continuing Education, Education Funds, Education Reform, Faculty Development, Education-General,

Literacy, Minority Education, Private Education (Pre-college), Public Education (Precollege), School Volunteerism, Social Sciences Education, Student Aid
Environment: Air/Water Quality, Energy, Environment-General
Health: Adolescent Health Issues, AIDS/HIV, Cancer, Children's Health/Hospitals, Clinics/Medical Centers, Diabetes, Emergency/Ambulance Services, Health Organizations, Health Organizations, Home-Care Services, Hospitals, Long-Term Care, Nutrition, Prenatal Health Issues, Public Health
International: Foreign Arts Organizations, International Affairs, International Organizations, International Relations
Religion: Churches, Jewish Causes, Ministries, Religious Organizations, Religious Welfare
Science: Science Museums, Scientific Centers & Institutes
Social Services: At-Risk Youth, Big Brother/Big Sister, Child Abuse, Child Welfare, Community Centers, Community Service Organizations, Crime Prevention, Day Care, Delinquency & Criminal Rehabilitation, Domestic Violence, Family Planning, Family Services, Food/Clothing Distribution, Homes, People with Disabilities, Recreation & Athletics, Refugee Assistance, Senior Services, Shelters/Homelessness, Social Services-General, United Funds/United Ways, Veterans, YMCA/YWCA/YMHA/YWHA, Youth Organizations

Application Procedures

Initial Contact: Organizations may call for further clarification as to whether a project falls within the foundation's priorities, and for a copy of the guidelines and proposal cover sheet. A preliminary letter or abbreviated proposal is not recommended; only complete proposals using the Delaware Valley Grantmakers Common Application Form will be accepted.
Application Requirements: Proposals should include the cover sheet, summary of the proposal (one page or less), and the actual proposal (five pages). In addition, a description of organization's purpose, history, goals, activities, and constituency is required. Funding plans and a program evaluation plan should also be included. The resumes of top staff, the addresses and occupations of the board of directors, budget, funding sources, financial statement, annual report, and proof of tax-exempt status are also required.
Deadlines: Deadlines for arts applications are January 15 and May 15. There are no deadlines for other applications.
Review Process: The board meets eight times a year. Proposals can usually be reviewed within two months. Notification is usually within two weeks after a decision.

Restrictions

The fund does not make grants to individuals, or for conferences, scholarships, fellowships or travel. Ordinarily, the fund also avoids making grants for major programs of large institutions, capital and equipment, endowment, and the routine or direct services of social service agencies. Individual day care and after school programs cannot be accommodated, although agencies that serve these fields may apply.

Additional Information

A written report is required on every grant received, to the satisfaction of the board. Organizations which do not fulfill this requirement will not be considered for subsequent grants.
The foundation allows its offices to be used as a meeting place for local nonprofit groups.
Publications: Annual Report; Guidelines; Application Form

Foundation Officials

Iso Briselli: board member OCCUPATION concert violinist. NONPR AFFIL member: Pennsylvania Council Arts.

Daniel W. Burke: board member B Pittsburgh, PA 1926. ED Catholic University America BA (1949); Catholic University America MA (1952); Catholic University America PhD (1957). PRIM CORP EMPL professor: LaSalle University. NONPR AFFIL member: Phi Beta Kappa; trustee emeritus: University Bethlehem; member: Modern Language Association; professor, art mus director: LaSalle University; trustee emeritus: Manhattan College; executive director: Catholic Commission on Cultural & Intellectual Affairs.
Ida K. Chen: board member
Helen Cunningham: executive director
Raymond K. Denworth, Jr.: vice president, director B Philadelphia, PA 1932. ED Wesleyan University BA (1954); University of Pennsylvania JD (1961). PRIM CORP EMPL partner: Drinker, Biddle & Reath. CORP AFFIL director: Keystone Insurance Co.; director: Shared Medical Systems Inc.; director: AAA Mid-Atlantic Inc. NONPR AFFIL director: United Way Southeast Pennsylvania; trustee, chairman: Wesleyan University. CLUB AFFIL Union League Philadelphia Club; Corinthian Yacht Club.
Sandra Featherman, PhD: vice president, director B Philadelphia, PA 1934. ED University of Pennsylvania BA (1955); University of Pennsylvania PhD (1978); University of Pennsylvania MA (1978). PRIM NONPR EMPL director, president: University New England. NONPR AFFIL president: Maine Independent Colleges Association; president: Pennsylvania Federation Chamber of Congress; director: Guild Maine Aquarium; director: Kennebec Girl Scout Council; member: American Political Science Association; member: Greater Portland Alliance Colleges Universitys; member: AAUW; board governors member executive committee: American Association Colleges Osteopathic Medicine.
Christine James-Brown: board member
David C. Melnicoff: board member
David Herschel Wice: board member B Petersburg, VA February 01, 1908. ED Washington & Lee University AB (1927); Washington & Lee University MA (1928); Hebrew Union College DHL (1933); Washington & Lee University DD (1948). OCCUPATION rabbi. NONPR AFFIL director: Jewish Community Relations; director: Union American Hebrew Congregations New Ams; co-chairman: Hebrew Union College; director: Family Services Association America; director: Federation Jewish Agencies; director: Council Jewish Education; member: Council Religion Independent Schools; member: Central Conference American Rabbis; rabbi emeritus: Congregation Rodeph Shalom, Philadelphia.

Grants Analysis

Disclosure Period: calendar year ending 2001
Total Grants: $3,430,874*
Number of Grants: 206
Average Grant: $6,217*
Highest Grant: $830,000
Lowest Grant: $1,000
Typical Range: $1,000 to $20,000
*Note: Giving excludes United Way. Amount excludes the eight largest grants.

Recent Grants

Note: Grants derived from 2001 Form 990.

General

200,000	Regional Performing Arts Center, Philadelphia, PA
200,000	Regional Performing Arts Center, Philadelphia, PA -- new orchestra concert hall
170,000	Franklin Institute, Philadelphia, PA -- renovate and modernize the Fels Planetarium
150,000	Trustees of the University of Pennsylvania, Philadelphia, PA -- MGA student scholarship
125,000	Temple University Fels Research Institute for Cancer, Philadelphia, PA -- support for new faculty
50,000	Hispanics in Philanthropy, Emeryville, CA -- funders collaborative for strong Latino communities
50,000	Public Education Network, Washington, DC -- financial reform
38,400	Asociacion de Musicos Latino Americanos, Philadelphia, PA
38,400	Asociacion de Musicos Latino Americanos, Philadelphia, PA -- fund booking agent position
33,821	Philadelphia Health Management Corporation, Philadelphia, PA -- evaluation study

FENTON FOUNDATION

Giving Contact

Frank M. Fenton, Treasurer & Director
310 W. 4th St.
Williamstown, WV 26187
Phone: (304)375-6122

Description

Founded: 1955
EIN: 556017260
Organization Type: Private Foundation
Giving Locations: OH: Washington County; WV: Wood County
Grant Types: General Support.

Financial Summary

Total Giving: $129,961 (2000); $144,824 (1999); $145,634 (1996)
Giving Analysis: Giving for 2000 includes: foundation grants to United Way ($14,091) 1999: foundation grants to United Way ($26,087)
Assets: $3,591,571 (2000); $3,782,414 (1999); $2,481,921 (1996)
Gifts Received: $62,559 (2000); $190,762 (1999); $62,465 (1996). Note: In 2000, contributions were received from Fenton Gift Shops, Inc. In 1999, contributions were received from Fenton Gift Shops ($62,452) and Fenton Art Glass Co. ($128,310). In 1996, contributions were received from Fenton Gift Shops ($23,935) and Fenton Art Glass Co. ($38,530).

Typical Recipients

Arts & Humanities: Arts Associations & Councils, Arts Centers, Film & Video, Arts & Humanities-General, Libraries, Museums/Galleries, Music, Performing Arts
Civic & Public Affairs: Clubs, Community Foundations, Economic Development, Civic & Public Affairs-General, Municipalities/Towns, Safety, Urban & Community Affairs, Women's Affairs
Education: Arts/Humanities Education, Business-School Partnerships, Colleges & Universities, Education Funds, Education Reform, Elementary Education (Public), Education-General, International Exchange, Medical Education, Private Education (Precollege), Public Education (Precollege), School Volunteerism, Science/Mathematics Education, Secondary Education (Public)
Health: Alzheimers Disease, Children's Health/Hospitals, Clinics/Medical Centers, Emergency/Ambulance Services, Health-General, Health Organizations, Hospices, Hospitals, Public Health, Research/Studies Institutes, Single-Disease Health Associations
International: Foreign Arts Organizations
Religion: Churches, Religious Organizations, Religious Welfare
Social Services: Child Welfare, Community Service Organizations, Homes, People with Disabilities, Recreation & Athletics, Scouts, Senior Services, Substance Abuse, United Funds/United Ways, Volunteer Services, YMCA/YWCA/YMHA/YWHA

Application Procedures
Initial Contact: Send a brief letter of inquiry.
Deadlines: None.

Restrictions
Does not support individuals.

Foundation Officials
Elinor P. Fenton: secretary, director
Frank M. Fenton: treasurer, director
Thomas K. Fenton: vice president, director
Wilmer C. Fenton: president, director

Grants Analysis
Disclosure Period: calendar year ending 2000
Total Grants: $115,870*
Number of Grants: 77
Average Grant: $1,196*
Highest Grant: $25,000
Typical Range: $500 to $3,000
*Note: Giving excludes United Way. Average grant excludes highest grant.

Recent Grants
Note: Grants derived from 2001 Form 990.

General
25,000	First United Methodist Church, Williamstown, WV
25,000	Marietta College, Marietta, OH
8,500	Williamstown United Way, Williamstown, WV
7,500	West Virginia Foundation for Independent Colleges, Charleston, WV
5,000	Williamstown High School, Williamstown, WV
4,500	Spring Heights Education Center, Charleston, WV
4,100	City of Williamstown, Williamstown, WV
4,000	Artsbridge, Parkersburg, WV
4,000	Artsbridge, Parkersburg, WV
3,500	Greater Marietta United Way, Marietta, OH

EUGENE AND ESTELLE FERKAUF FOUNDATION

Giving Contact
Barbara Dor, Trustee
67 Allenwood Rd.
Great Neck, NY 11023
Phone: (516)773-3269

Description
Founded: 1967
EIN: 132621094
Organization Type: Private Foundation
Grant Types: Multiyear/Continuing Support, Research.

Donor Information
Founder: Eugene Ferkauf, Estelle Ferkauf

Financial Summary
Total Giving: $289,800 (2000); $312,350 (1999); $236,000 (1998)
Assets: $5,727,560 (2000); $5,751,997 (1999); $5,574,974 (1998)

Typical Recipients
Arts & Humanities: Arts Funds, History & Archaeology, Libraries, Museums/Galleries, Music, Performing Arts, Public Broadcasting, Theater
Civic & Public Affairs: Botanical Gardens/Parks, Civil Rights, Civic & Public Affairs-General
Education: Colleges & Universities, Continuing Education, Private Education (Precollege), Religious Education, Special Education

Health: AIDS/HIV, Cancer, Children's Health/Hospitals, Health Organizations, Heart, Hospitals, Hospitals (University Affiliated), Long-Term Care, Medical Rehabilitation, Medical Research, Mental Health, Research/Studies Institutes, Single-Disease Health Associations
International: Foreign Educational Institutions, Health Care/Hospitals, International Relief Efforts, Missionary/Religious Activities
Religion: Religion-General, Religion-General, Jewish Causes, Religious Organizations, Synagogues/Temples
Social Services: Child Welfare, Community Centers, Community Service Organizations, Family Services, People with Disabilities, Social Services-General, Substance Abuse, YMCA/YWCA/YMHA/YWHA

Application Procedures
Initial Contact: Send a brief letter of inquiry describing program or project.
Deadlines: None.

Additional Information
Publications: Application Guidelines

Foundation Officials
Lenore Bronstein: trustee
Robert Bronstein: trustee
Richard M. Dicke, Esq.: trustee
Barbara Dor: trustee
Benny Dor: trustee
Estelle Ferkauf: trustee
Eugene Ferkauf: trustee
Amy Shapira: trustee
Israel Shapira: trustee

Grants Analysis
Disclosure Period: calendar year ending 2000
Total Grants: $289,800
Number of Grants: 51
Average Grant: $4,796*
Highest Grant: $50,000
Lowest Grant: $500
Typical Range: $1,000 to $10,000
*Note: Average grant figure excludes highest grant.

Recent Grants
Note: Grants derived from 2001 Form 990.

Library-Related
5,000	Standing Tall, Inc., New York, NY

General
40,000	Jewish Federation of Broward County, Inc., Ft. Lauderdale, FL
27,800	United Jewish Appeal Federation, New York, NY
27,750	Gift of Life, Boynton Beach, FL
20,650	Little Neck Jewish Center, Queens, NY
12,000	Chabad of Great Neck, Great Neck, NY
10,000	Project Judaica, Washington, DC
10,000	Sephardic Home for the Aged, Brooklyn, NY
9,000	Hill Crest Jewish Center, Flushing, NY
6,000	Tracy Fleisher Memorial Fund, Queens, NY
5,000	Aleph Society, New York, NY

FERRIDAY FUND CHARITABLE TRUST

Giving Contact
Douglas J. Boyle
c/o Bank of New York
1290 Ave. of the Americas, 5th Floor
New York, NY 10104
Phone: (212)635-1520

Description
Founded: 1991
EIN: 136967609
Organization Type: Private Foundation
Grant Types: General Support.

Donor Information
Founder: Established in 1991 by the late Carolyn Ferriday.

Financial Summary
Total Giving: $741,750 (fiscal year ending July 31, 2001); $558,250 (fiscal 2000); $420,750 (fiscal 1998)
Assets: $11,816,927 (fiscal 2001); $15,477,987 (fiscal 2000); $11,157,835 (fiscal 1998)
Gifts Received: $150,000 (fiscal 2001); $187,596 (fiscal 1994). Note: In 2001, contributions were received from Milena Knoll Unit-Trust.

Typical Recipients
Arts & Humanities: Arts Associations & Councils, Arts & Humanities-General, Historic Preservation, History & Archaeology, Libraries, Public Broadcasting, Theater
Civic & Public Affairs: African American Affairs, Civic & Public Affairs-General, Law & Justice, Native American Affairs, Public Policy
Education: Business Education, Colleges & Universities, Education Funds, Legal Education, Literacy, Medical Education, Private Education (Precollege), Secondary Education (Private)
Environment: Protection, Resource Conservation
Health: Clinics/Medical Centers, Health-General, Hospitals, Hospitals (University Affiliated), Single-Disease Health Associations
International: Health Care/Hospitals, International Relations
Religion: Churches, Jewish Causes, Religious Welfare
Social Services: At-Risk Youth, Child Welfare, People with Disabilities

Application Procedures
Initial Contact: Send a brief letter of inquiry.
Deadlines: None.

Additional Information
Trust(s): Bank of New York

Foundation Officials
Richard J. Carter, Jr.: trustee

Grants Analysis
Disclosure Period: fiscal year ending July 31, 2001
Total Grants: $741,750
Number of Grants: 103
Average Grant: $6,782*
Highest Grant: $50,000
Lowest Grant: $1,000
Typical Range: $1,000 to $10,000
*Note: Average grant figure excludes highest grant.

Recent Grants
Note: Grants derived from 2000 Form 990.

Library-Related
10,000	Westport Library

General
20,000	Antiquarian & Landmarks Society Inc, New York, NY
20,000	University of Notre Dame, Notre Dame, IN
15,000	Antiquarian & Landmarks Society Inc, New York, NY
10,000	Fordham University School of Law, New York, NY
10,000	Fordham University School of Law, New York, NY

10,000	Hope Worldwide
10,000	IGHL Foundation
10,000	Little Sisters of the Assumption, New York, NY
10,000	Student Conservation Association, Washington, DC
10,000	University of Notre Dame, Notre Dame, IN

FIDELITY INVESTMENTS

Company Headquarters
Boston, MA
Web: http://www.fidelity.com

Company Description
Employees: 7,000
SIC(s): 6719 Holding Companies Nec, 6722 Management Investment--Open-End.
Parent Company: FMR Corp., 82 Devonshire Street, Boston, MA, United States

Operating Locations
Fidelity Investments (KY--Covington; MA--Boston; OH--Cincinnati; TX--Dallas)

Fidelity Foundation

Giving Contact
Margaret H. Morton, Vice President, Program
Fidelity Foundation
82 Devonshire Street S3
Boston, MA 02109
Phone: (617)563-6806
Fax: (617)476-4234
Web: http://www.fidelityfoundation.org

Description
EIN: 046131201
Organization Type: Corporate Foundation
Former Name: Fidelity Investments Charitable Gift Fund Foundation, Inc.
Giving Locations: KY: Covington; MA: Boston, Marlborough; NH: Merrimack; NY: New York; RI: Smithfield; TX: Dallas, Ft. Worth; UT: Salt Lake City; Canada : Toronto, ON
Grant Types: Capital, Conference/Seminar, Employee Matching Gifts, Endowment, Fellowship, Matching, Project.
Note: Employee matching gift ratio: 2 to 1, up to $1,000; 1 to 1 for $1,000 to $3,500.

Donor Information
Founder: FMR Corp.

Financial Summary
Total Giving: $20,209,004 (2001); $18,314,415 (2000); $17,054,621 (1999). Note: Contributes through foundation only.
Giving Analysis: Giving for 2000 includes: foundation matching gifts ($2,138,240); foundation ($16,176,175); 1999: foundation grants to United Way ($50,000); foundation matching gifts ($1,849,469); foundation ($15,155,401); 1998: foundation grants to United Way ($165,000); foundation matching gifts ($1,551,869);
Assets: $306,283,121 (2001); $431,163,790 (2000); $554,870,380 (1999).
Gifts Received: $1,769,954 (2001); $38,692,968 (2000); $2,701,762 (1999). Note: Contributions are received from FMR Corp. and Fidelity Investors L.P.

Typical Recipients
Arts & Humanities: Art History, Arts Associations & Councils, Arts Centers, Arts Funds, Arts Institutes, Arts Outreach, Ballet, Arts & Humanities-General, Historic Preservation, History & Archaeology, Libraries, Museums/Galleries, Music, Opera, Performing Arts, Theater
Civic & Public Affairs: African American Affairs, Asian American Affairs, Business/Free Enterprise, Community Foundations, Economic Development, Economic Policy, Employment/Job Training, Gay/Lesbian Issues, Civic & Public Affairs-General, Housing, Legal Aid, Municipalities/Towns, Native American Affairs, Nonprofit Management, Parades/Festivals, Philanthropic Organizations, Public Policy, Urban & Community Affairs, Urban & Community Affairs, Women's Affairs, Zoos/Aquariums
Education: Arts/Humanities Education, Business Education, Colleges & Universities, Education Reform, Education-General, Leadership Training, Literacy, Preschool Education, Private Education (Precollege)
Environment: Environment-General, Resource Conservation
Health: Cancer, Children's Health/Hospitals, Clinics/Medical Centers, Health Organizations, Hospices, Hospitals, Medical Research, Mental Health, Nursing Services
International: Foreign Arts Organizations, Foreign Educational Institutions, International-General, International Environmental Issues, International Relations, International Relief Efforts
Religion: Churches, Religion-General, Religious Organizations, Religious Welfare
Science: Science Museums, Scientific Centers & Institutes, Scientific Labs
Social Services: At-Risk Youth, Camps, Child Abuse, Child Welfare, Community Service Organizations, Counseling, Family Services, Food/Clothing Distribution, People with Disabilities, Recreation & Athletics, Scouts, Senior Services, Shelters/Homelessness, Social Services-General, United Funds/United Ways, Volunteer Services, YMCA/YWCA/YMHA/YWHA, Youth Organizations

Application Procedures
Initial Contact: Send a letter of request.
Application Requirements: Include foundation's project summary form; itemized project budget; recent audited financial statements; IRS 501(c)(3) determination letter; history of organization, including objectives and programs; list of officers and directors and their affiliations; list of other funders and status of requests; current operating budget; and a description of request and rationale. Be evaluated?
Deadlines: March 30 to receive decision by August 1, and September 30 to receive decision by February 1.
Evaluative Criteria: The foundation seeks evidence of institutional commitment to the project on behalf of the organization's board; a realistic project budget; a thorough implementation plan, including a plan for performance measurement; net value to the organization and the community it serves; significant support from other funders; and other criteria. Also considered are the organization's financial health; the strength of its management team and board; and evidence of an overall strategic plan.
Notes: Contact the foundation to receive a project summary form. Applications should not be sent in folders, binders or packaging. Limit press clippings and background materials to five pages.

Restrictions
Foundation does not make multi-year grants or award grants to an organization in successive years.
Foundation does not make grants to individuals, sectarian or civic organizations, start-up organizations, public school systems, disease-specific organizations, for operating support, scholarships, video or film projects, sponsorships, benefit events or for memberships. Grants do not generally support an entire project's cost.

Additional Information
Fidelity Investments created the foundation in 1965 in order to represent the company's philanthropic interests in the communities where it does business.

Corporate Officials
Edward Crosby Johnson, III: chairman, president, chief executive officer, director B Boston, MA 1930. ED Harvard University AB (1954). PRIM CORP EMPL chairman, president, chief executive officer, director: FMR Corp. ADD CORP EMPL president: Fidelity Government Securities Fund; chairman: Fidelity Management Research Co.; president: Fidelity Management Trust Co.; president: Fidelity Cash Reserve Fund; director: Fidelity Distributors Corp.; chairman: Fidelity Magellan Fund; president: Fidelity Trend Fund OCCUPATION Fidelity Intermediate Bond Fund. NONPR AFFIL director: Center Neurologic Diseases; member: Massachusetts Historical Society; fellow: American Academy of Arts & Sciences; honorary trustee: Boston Museum Fine Arts.

Foundation Officials
Abigail P. Johnson: director
Edward Crosby Johnson, III: president (see above)
Margaret H. Morton: program officer
Ross E. Sherbrooke: trustee
Anne-Marie Soulliere: president, trustee

Grants Analysis
Disclosure Period: calendar year ending 2001
Total Grants: $18,017,155*
Number of Grants: 198
Average Grant: $57,934*
Highest Grant: $2,500,000
Lowest Grant: $500
Typical Range: $10,000 to $200,000
*Note: Giving excludes matching gifts; United Way. Average grant figure excludes three highest grants ($6,720,000).

Recent Grants
Note: Grants derived from 2001 Form 990.

Library-Related
| 300,000 | Boston Public Library Foundation, Boston, MA |

General
2,500,000	Frog Pond Foundation, Inc., Boston, MA
2,200,000	Peabody Essex Museum, Salem, MA
2,020,000	Boston Symphony Orchestra, Boston, MA
750,000	St. Paul's Cathedral Trust in America, New York, NY
500,000	Nashoba Brooks School of Concord, Inc., Concord, MA
450,000	Norman Rockwell Museum, Stockbridge, MA
300,000	Appalachian Mountain Club, Boston, MA
280,000	Salt Lake City Realty, Inc., Salt Lake City, UT
250,000	Carroll School, Lincoln, MA
250,000	Pine Street Inn, Boston, MA

FIELD FOUNDATION OF ILLINOIS

Giving Contact
Handy Lindsey, Jr., President
200 South Wacker Dr., Suite 3860
Chicago, IL 60606
Phone: (312)831-0910
Fax: (312)831-0961
E-mail: hlindsey@fieldfoundation.org
Web: http://www.fieldfoundation.org

Description
Founded: 1960
EIN: 366059408
Organization Type: General Purpose Foundation
Giving Locations: IL: Chicago including metropolitan area

Grant Types: Capital, Employee Matching Gifts, General Support, Matching, Operating Expenses, Project.

Donor Information

Founder: The foundation was established in 1960, with the late Marshall Field IV as donor.

Financial Summary

Total Giving: $1,000,000 (fiscal year ending April 30, 2002 approx); $1,900,088 (fiscal 2001); $1,782,203 (fiscal 2000)

Assets: $50,924,371 (fiscal 2001); $50,675,517 (fiscal 2000); $47,052,310 (fiscal 1999)

Typical Recipients

Arts & Humanities: Arts Associations & Councils, Arts Institutes, Dance, Ethnic & Folk Arts, Libraries, Museums/Galleries, Music, Opera, Public Broadcasting, Theater

Civic & Public Affairs: Asian American Affairs, Civil Rights, Clubs, Community Foundations, Economic Development, Employment/Job Training, Civic & Public Affairs-General, Housing, Law & Justice, Legal Aid, Municipalities/Towns, Nonprofit Management, Parades/Festivals, Philanthropic Organizations, Professional & Trade Associations, Public Policy, Urban & Community Affairs, Women's Affairs, Zoos/Aquariums

Education: Arts/Humanities Education, Colleges & Universities, Elementary Education (Private), Elementary Education (Public), Faculty Development, Education-General, Literacy, Medical Education, Preschool Education, Public Education (Precollege), Science/Mathematics Education, Secondary Education (Public), Social Sciences Education

Environment: Environment-General, Resource Conservation

Health: AIDS/HIV, Children's Health/Hospitals, Clinics/Medical Centers, Emergency/Ambulance Services, Health Organizations, Heart, Hospitals, Hospitals (University Affiliated), Medical Rehabilitation, Prenatal Health Issues, Public Health

Religion: Ministries, Religious Welfare

Science: Science Museums, Scientific Centers & Institutes, Scientific Organizations

Social Services: Child Welfare, Community Centers, Community Service Organizations, Crime Prevention, Day Care, Delinquency & Criminal Rehabilitation, Domestic Violence, Family Services, Family Services, Food/Clothing Distribution, People with Disabilities, Recreation & Athletics, Sexual Abuse, Shelters/Homelessness, Social Services-General, Substance Abuse, United Funds/United Ways, Volunteer Services, YMCA/YWCA/YMHA/YWHA, Youth Organizations

Application Procedures

Initial Contact: Written requests should be addressed to the foundation. The foundation has a prospective grantees checklist that organizations should request, which will aid in writing a proposal and in determining if the organization fits the criteria to apply.

Application Requirements: Proposal should be accompanied by a cover letter briefly describing the project, the proposed budget, and the history and background of the applicant. Applications should be accompanied by a copy of the organization's IRS determination letter of tax-exempt status, and a list of the membership of the board of directors and their affiliations.

Deadlines: January 15, May 15, September 15.

Review Process: The board meets three times per year, in May, September, and January; the grant evaluation process begins approximately four months before each meeting. A response to all inquiries is provided as quickly as possible.

Notes: For the general grant program, operating support generally is restricted from one to three years;

continuing operating support is not considered. Applications for grants from hospitals normally will be considered only if the applicant has a broad teaching and research program; conducts a comprehensive clinic service and provides a substantial amount of free care; has sufficient full-time clinicians in various specialties to secure good teaching and investigation; and if the specific project has distinctive importance or the promise of a unique cont ribution to medicine and/or medical education in Chicago.

Restrictions

Grants are not made to United Way of Chicago member agencies, or to member agencies of other United Ways in the metropolitan area for regular operating support; to endowments; to individuals; for medical research or national health agency appeals; for propaganda or to influence legislation; to fund conferences, seminars, or meetings; to cover costs of printed materials or video equipment; for elimination of accumulated operating deficit; for disease-specific voluntary associations; for theater programs other than outreach to disadvantaged students; for fund-raising events or advertising; for religious purposes; to other grantmaking agencies or foundations for ultimate distribution to agencies or programs of its own choosing; or for operating support of neighborhood health centers or clinics, day care centers for children, or small cultural groups. For the Primary and Secondary Education Grants Program, the foundation does not support scholarships, new building construction, centralized parenting training, city-wide advocacy efforts, endowment campaigns, degree-granting programs for teachers, repairs or improvements to public schools, or general operating needs of schools or of local school councils. An entity will be eligible to receive no more than one (1) grant from the Foundation during a fiscal year of the Foundarion.

Additional Information

In addition to its grant-making activities, the foundation also provides technical assistance to charitable organizations.

Publications: Grant Guidelines and Application Procedures; Grant Guidelines and Application Procedures: Primary and Secondary School Education; Annual Report; Self-Certification Checklist for Prospective Grantees

Foundation Officials

Berlean M. Burris: director

Milton Austin Davis: director PRIM CORP EMPL vice president, director: Shorebank Corp. CORP AFFIL partner: Williams Street Building Partnership.

Marshall Field, IV: director B Charlottesville, VA 1941. ED Harvard University BA (1963). PRIM CORP EMPL chairman: Field Corp. CORP AFFIL chairman, chief executive officer, senior director: Cabot Cabot & Forbes Investment Co. NONPR AFFIL chairman: Rush-Presbyterian-Saint Lukes Medical Center; director: World Wildlife Federation; member: Nature Conservancy; vice chairman, trustee: Field Museum Natural History; director: Lincoln Park Zoological Society; trustee: Chicago Public Library Foundation; director: Field Foundation; active: Chicago Orchestral Association; director: Atlantic Salmon Association; member advisory board: Brookfield Zoo; trustee: Art Institute of Chicago. CLUB AFFIL Shoreacres Club; Racquet Club; River Club; Jupiter Island Club; Onwentsia Club; Harvard Club; Chicago Club; Commercial Club.

Philip Wayne Hummer: director B 1931. PRIM CORP EMPL principal: Wayne Hummer Investments LLC.

Gary H. Kline: secretary

Handy L. Lindsey, Jr.: president

George A. Ranney, Jr.: director B Chicago, IL 1940. ED Harvard University BA (1962); University of Chicago JD (1966). PRIM CORP EMPL partner: Mayer, Brown & Platt PRIM NONPR EMPL president, chief executive officer: Chicago Metropolis 2020. CORP

AFFIL vice president, general counsel: Ryerson Tull Inc. NONPR AFFIL member: Commerce Counsel Network; trustee: University Chicago; member: Chicago Bar Association; member: American Bar Association.

Tina Tchen: director

Grants Analysis

Disclosure Period: fiscal year ending April 30, 2001

Total Grants: $1,900,088
Number of Grants: 253
Average Grant: $7,510
Highest Grant: $50,000
Lowest Grant: $4,000
Typical Range: $5,000 to $10,000

Recent Grants

Note: Grants derived from fiscal 2001 Form 990.

Library-Related

10,000	Chicago Public Library Foundation, Chicago, IL -- for Teacher in the Library

General

50,000	University of Chicago Hospitals, Chicago, IL -- for Arthur Queen Endowment for Health Administration Studies
36,500	Leadership Council for Metropolitan Open Communities, Chicago, IL -- for forum on CHA Transformation Plan
13,000	Robert Healy Elementary School, Chicago, IL -- for developing tools to deal with racism
12,500	Cambodian Association of Illinois, Chicago, IL -- for Cambodian Community Center
12,500	Cambodian Association of Illinois, Chicago, IL -- for Cambodian Community Center
12,500	Chicago Metropolis 2020, Chicago, IL -- for community forums
12,500	Chicago Metropolis 2020, Chicago, IL -- for community forums
12,500	Chicago Zoological Society, Brookfield, IL -- for Habitat Africa
12,500	Chicago Zoological Society, Brookfield, IL -- for Habitat Africa
12,500	Chicago Zoological Society, Brookfield, IL -- for Habitat Africa

FIFTH THIRD BANCORP

Company Headquarters

38 Fountain Square Plz.
Cincinnati, OH
Web: http://www.53.com

Company Description

Founded: 1900
Ticker: FITB
Exchange: NASDAQ
Acquired: Old Kent Financial Corp..
Assets: US$80.894 billion (2002)
Profit: US$1.634 billion (2002)
Employees: 18373 (2002)
Fortune Rank: 278, per FORTUNE Magazine's list of 500 Largest U.S. Corporations (2002).
SIC(s): 6022 State Commercial Banks, 6712 Bank Holding Companies.

Operating Locations

Fifth Third Bancorp (AZ--Scottsdale; FL--Naples; IN--Indianapolis; KY--Florence, Louisville; OH--Cincinnati, Cleveland, Columbus, Dublin, Hamilton, Hillsboro, Toledo)

Fifth Third Foundation

Giving Contact

Lawra Baumann, Foundation Officer
38 Fountain Square Plaza
Maildrop 1090D7
Cincinnati, OH 45263
Phone: (513)579-6034
Fax: (513)579-5461

Description

EIN: 316024135
Organization Type: Corporate Foundation
Giving Locations: OH: Cincinnati including metropolitan area
Grant Types: Capital, Conference/Seminar, Employee Matching Gifts, General Support, Project.
Note: Matches gifts to education.

Financial Summary

Total Giving: $6,715,761 (fiscal year ending September 30, 2001); $5,065,891 (fiscal 2000); $2,311,378 (fiscal 1999). Note: Contributes through foundation only.
Giving Analysis: Giving for fiscal 2001 includes: foundation matching gifts ($138,105); foundation grants to United Way ($1,445,004); foundation ($5,132,652); fiscal 2000: foundation grants to United Way ($965,929); foundation ($4,099,962); fiscal 1999: foundation ($2,311,378);
Assets: $43,334,782 (fiscal 2001); $44,660,611 (fiscal 2000); $38,421,863 (fiscal 1999)
Gifts Received: $1,050,000 (fiscal 1996); $1,800,000 (fiscal 1995); $1,800,000 (fiscal 1994). Note: Contributions are received from Fifth Third Bank.

Typical Recipients

Arts & Humanities: Arts Associations & Councils, Arts Centers, Arts Festivals, Arts Funds, Community Arts, Arts & Humanities-General, Historic Preservation, Museums/Galleries, Music, Opera, Performing Arts, Public Broadcasting, Theater
Civic & Public Affairs: African American Affairs, Botanical Gardens/Parks, Business/Free Enterprise, Chambers of Commerce, Civil Rights, Clubs, Community Foundations, Economic Development, Employment/Job Training, Civic & Public Affairs-General, Housing, Law & Justice, Minority Business, Municipalities/Towns, Parades/Festivals, Urban & Community Affairs, Zoos/Aquariums
Education: Arts/Humanities Education, Business Education, Colleges & Universities, Community & Junior Colleges, Community & Junior Colleges, Education Funds, Engineering/Technological Education, Education-General, Medical Education, Private Education (Precollege), Public Education (Precollege), Religious Education, Secondary Education (Public), Special Education, Student Aid
Health: Children's Health/Hospitals, Emergency/Ambulance Services, Health Funds, Health Organizations, Hospices, Hospitals, Medical Rehabilitation, Single-Disease Health Associations, Speech & Hearing
Religion: Jewish Causes, Religious Organizations, Religious Welfare
Science: Science-General
Social Services: Child Welfare, Community Centers, Community Service Organizations, Counseling, Family Services, Food/Clothing Distribution, People with Disabilities, Recreation & Athletics, Scouts, Senior Services, Shelters/Homelessness, United Funds/United Ways, YMCA/YWCA/YMHA/YWHA, Youth Organizations

Application Procedures

Initial Contact: Send a brief letter.
Application Requirements: Include a description of program.
Deadlines: None.

Additional Information

Trust(s): Fifth Third Bank

Corporate Officials

Paul Michael Brumm: executive vice president, chief financial officer B Cincinnati, OH 1947. ED University of Cincinnati BA (1969); University of Cincinnati MBA (1976). PRIM CORP EMPL executive vice president, chief financial officer: Fifth Third Bancorp. NONPR AFFIL trustee: Cath. Healthcare Partner; member: Delta Mu Delta; member: Bankers Roundtable; member: Banking & Finance Markets Committee. CLUB AFFIL Coldstream Country Club; University Club; Athletic Club.
Roger W. Dean: controller, chief administrative officer B 1963. PRIM CORP EMPL controller, chief administrative officer: Fifth Third Bancorp.
George A. Schaefer, Jr.: president B Cincinnati, OH 1945. ED United States Military Academy (1967); Xavier University (1974). PRIM CORP EMPL president: Fifth Third Bank. CORP AFFIL president, chief executive officer, chief operating officer, director: Fifth Third Bancorp. NONPR AFFIL vice chairman: Greater Cincinnati Chamber of Commerce.

Foundation Officials

Lawra Baumann: vice president

Grants Analysis

Disclosure Period: fiscal year ending September 30, 2001
Total Grants: $5,132,652*
Number of Grants: 428
Average Grant: $11,992
Highest Grant: $303,250
Typical Range: $1,000 to $10,000
*Note: Giving excludes matching gifts; United Way.

Recent Grants

Note: Grants derived from fiscal 2001 Form 990.

General

303,250	United Way, Cincinnati, OH -- for 2000-01 pledge
262,500	United Way, Cincinnati, OH -- for million dollar match campaign
262,500	United Way and Community Chest, Cincinnati, OH -- in support of United Home Health Care and Every Child Succeeds
250,000	Spirit of Cincinnati, Cincinnati, OH -- for the visitors center on Foundation Square
148,925	United Way, Cincinnati, OH -- for fulfillment of pledge
100,000	City of Cincinnati, Cincinnati, OH -- for Madisonville Community Center
100,000	Greater Cincinnati Chamber of Commerce, Cincinnati, OH -- for the partners for greater Cincinnati
100,000	Greater Cincinnati Chamber of Commerce, Cincinnati, OH -- for the partners for greater Cincinnati
100,000	Greater Cincinnati Housing Alliance, Cincinnati, OH -- toward the recapitalization of the alliance
100,000	Local Initiative Support Corporation, New York, NY -- to help with community development corps

FIGGIE EDUCATIONAL FOUNDATION

Giving Contact

Julie Brandow, care of Phillips Management
23550 Chagrin Boulevard, Suite 320
Beachwood, OH 44122
Phone: (216)622-8224

Description

Founded: 1992
EIN: 341199229
Organization Type: Private Foundation
Giving Locations: Nationally.
Grant Types: General Support.

Financial Summary

Total Giving: $55,510 (2000); $52,020 (1999)
Assets: $1,365,516 (2000); $1,141,317 (1999); $719,256 (1996)
Gifts Received: $35,000 (2000)

Typical Recipients

Arts & Humanities: History & Archaeology, Libraries, Museums/Galleries, Music
Civic & Public Affairs: Botanical Gardens/Parks, Civic & Public Affairs-General, Urban & Community Affairs
Education: Colleges & Universities, Education Funds, Education-General, Private Education (Precollege)
Religion: Churches
Science: Science-General

Application Procedures

Initial Contact: The foundation has no formal grant application procedure or application form. Send a brief letter of inquiry.
Deadlines: None.

Restrictions

Limited to educational organizations.

Foundation Officials

David Carpenter: secretary
Harry E. Figgie, Jr.: president, trustee B Cleveland, OH 1923. ED Case Institute of Technology (1947); Cleveland-Marshall College of Law (1953). CORP AFFIL chairman: Clark-Reliance.
Nancy F. Figgie: assistant secretary, trustee
Frances Rose: trustee
Richard S. Tomer: treasurer

Grants Analysis

Disclosure Period: calendar year ending 2000
Total Grants: $55,510
Number of Grants: 10
Average Grant: $2,779*
Highest Grant: $30,500
Lowest Grant: $100
Typical Range: $1,000 to $5,000
*Note: Average grant figure excludes highest grant.

Recent Grants

Note: Grants derived from 1999 Form 990.

Library-Related

500	Greenwich Library, Greenwich, CT

General

14,000	College of Wooster, Wooster, OH
5,100	USS Constitution Museum, Boston, MA
5,000	Gilmour Academy, Gates Mills, OH
5,000	St. Christopher's By-The-River
3,500	Baldwin-Wallace College, Berea, OH
3,500	McIntire School of Commerce
3,000	Holden Arboretum, Mentor, OH
3,000	Western Reserve Historical Society, Cleveland, OH
2,500	Northwestern University, Evanston, IL
2,000	LPS Alumni Association

FIGTREE FOUNDATION

Giving Contact

Jo Ann Morrison, President
PO Box 130843
Birmingham, AL 35213

Phone: (205)879-0712
Fax: (205)879-6382

Description
Founded: 1986
EIN: 630932247
Organization Type: General Purpose Foundation
Giving Locations: AL: Birmingham
Grant Types: General Support, Project.

Donor Information
Founder: The Figtree Foundation was established in 1986 by Jo Ann Morrison Myers.

Financial Summary
Total Giving: $436,687 (fiscal year ending November 30, 2000); $856,304 (fiscal 1998); $803,229 (fiscal 1997)
Giving Analysis: Giving for fiscal 2000 includes: foundation grants to United Way ($15,000) fiscal 1998: foundation grants to United Way ($15,000)
Assets: $99,082 (fiscal 2000); $1,434,424 (fiscal 1998); $1,873,847 (fiscal 1997)

Typical Recipients
Arts & Humanities: Arts Festivals, Arts Institutes, Community Arts, Dance, Arts & Humanities-General, History & Archaeology, Libraries, Literary Arts, Museums/Galleries, Music, Performing Arts, Public Broadcasting, Theater
Civic & Public Affairs: Civil Rights, Civic & Public Affairs-General, Housing, Legal Aid, Philanthropic Organizations, Public Policy, Safety
Education: Arts/Humanities Education, Colleges & Universities, Faculty Development, Minority Education, Private Education (Precollege), Religious Education, Student Aid
Health: Cancer, Health-General, Hospices, Medical Rehabilitation, Medical Research, Single-Disease Health Associations
International: Foreign Arts Organizations, Foreign Educational Institutions, Health Care/Hospitals, Human Rights, International Organizations, Missionary/Religious Activities
Religion: Religion-General, Jewish Causes, Religious Organizations, Social/Policy Issues, Synagogues/Temples
Science: Science Museums
Social Services: Camps, Community Service Organizations, Crime Prevention, People with Disabilities, Shelters/Homelessness, Social Services-General, Substance Abuse, United Funds/United Ways, YMCA/YWCA/YMHA/YWHA, Youth Organizations

Application Procedures
Initial Contact: Individual requests should be addressed to a trustee.
Deadlines: None.

Additional Information
Publications: Annual Report

Foundation Officials
Alan Engel: vice president B 1955. ED University of Colorado BS (1976-1977); Northwestern University MBA (1977-1978). PRIM CORP EMPL principal: Crowne Partners Inc. CORP AFFIL partner: Engel Associates.
Donald E. Hess: secretary-treasurer B 1948. ED Dartmouth College BS (1970). PRIM CORP EMPL president, chief executive officer: Parisian Inc. CORP AFFIL director: AmSouth Bancorp; director: Saks Inc.
Donald Marc Hess: secretary, treasurer B Bern, Switzerland 1936. PRIM CORP EMPL chairman, chief executive officer: Hess Holding PRIM NONPR EMPL chairman: Hess Collection Winery ADD CORP EMPL chairman: Blue Lake Ltd.; chairman: Hess International; chairman: Hess Ltd.; chairman: Valser

Mineral Water Ltd. CORP AFFIL director: Kambly Biscuits; director: Trubschachen CH. NONPR AFFIL cofounder: Kunst Heute Foundation; founder: Napa Contemporary Arts Foundation.
Jo Ann Morrison Myers: president

Grants Analysis
Disclosure Period: fiscal year ending November 30, 2000
Total Grants: $421,687*
Number of Grants: 23
Average Grant: $15,304*
Highest Grant: $85,000
Lowest Grant: $18
Typical Range: $5,000 to $30,000
*Note: Giving excludes United Way. Average grant figure excludes highest grant.

Recent Grants
Note: Grants derived from fiscal 2000 Form 990.

General
85,000	Birmingham Jewish Federation, Birmingham, AL
54,000	Nishmat
37,127	Chabad
30,000	Apple Hill Center for Chamber Music, East Sullivan, NH
30,000	Critical Illness Research Foundation, Birmingham, AL
26,000	Hebrew Union College
25,000	PAADC
18,000	Jewish Foundation of Memphis, Memphis, TN
18,000	Religious Zionist Forum
18,000	YWCA

LELAND FIKES FOUNDATION

Giving Contact
Nancy J. Solana, Vice President & Secretary
3050 Lincoln Plaza
500 North Akard, Suite 3050
Dallas, TX 75201-6696
Phone: (214)754-0144

Description
Founded: 1952
EIN: 756035984
Organization Type: General Purpose Foundation
Giving Locations: TX: Dallas
Grant Types: Capital, Department, Endowment, General Support, Matching, Multiyear/Continuing Support, Operating Expenses, Seed Money.

Donor Information
Founder: The Fikes Foundation was established in 1952 by Leland Fikes, a Texas oil producer and philanthropist. Mr. Fikes was also involved in many other business interests, including real estate. Family members are active in the foundation.

Financial Summary
Total Giving: $3,259,445 (2001); $4,085,900 (2000); $3,269,445 (1998)
Giving Analysis: Giving for 1998 includes: foundation scholarships ($10,000) foundation ($3,059,445)
Assets: $75,784,531 (2000); $69,725,714 (1998); $66,879,548 (1997)
Gifts Received: $180,000 (2000); $31,000 (1994); $182,000 (1993). Note: In 2000, contributions were received from the estate of Catherine Fikes.

Typical Recipients
Arts & Humanities: Arts Centers, Ethnic & Folk Arts, Film & Video, Arts & Humanities-General, Historic Preservation, Libraries, Museums/Galleries, Music, Public Broadcasting, Theater

Civic & Public Affairs: Botanical Gardens/Parks, Economic Development, Civic & Public Affairs-General, Housing, Nonprofit Management, Public Policy, Urban & Community Affairs, Women's Affairs, Zoos/Aquariums
Education: Colleges & Universities, Community & Junior Colleges, Education Associations, Education Funds, Education Reform, Elementary Education (Private), Education-General, Health & Physical Education, Literacy, Medical Education, Preschool Education, Private Education (Precollege), Public Education (Precollege), Science/Mathematics Education, Secondary Education (Private), Secondary Education (Private)
Environment: Environment-General, Wildlife Protection
Health: AIDS/HIV, Cancer, Children's Health/Hospitals, Clinics/Medical Centers, Diabetes, Eyes/Blindness, Health Organizations, Heart, Hospitals, Hospitals (University Affiliated), Medical Research, Mental Health, Nursing Services, Prenatal Health Issues, Public Health, Single-Disease Health Associations, Transplant Networks/Donor Banks, Trauma Treatment
International: Foreign Educational Institutions, Health Care/Hospitals, Human Rights, International Development, International Environmental Issues, International Organizations, International Peace & Security Issues, Missionary/Religious Activities
Religion: Churches, Jewish Causes, Ministries, Religious Organizations, Religious Welfare, Religious Welfare, Social/Policy Issues
Science: Observatories & Planetariums, Science Exhibits & Fairs, Science Museums, Scientific Organizations, Scientific Research
Social Services: At-Risk Youth, Camps, Child Welfare, Community Service Organizations, Counseling, Domestic Violence, Family Planning, Family Services, Food/Clothing Distribution, Homes, People with Disabilities, Scouts, Senior Services, Shelters/Homelessness, Substance Abuse, United Funds/United Ways, Volunteer Services, YMCA/YWCA/YMHA/YWHA, Youth Organizations

Application Procedures
Initial Contact: Applicants should submit concise and complete written proposals. The foundation does not have an application form.
Application Requirements: Proposals should contain a cover letter on organization letterhead (signed by the chief executive officer) describing the project, amount requested, and the date by which funds are needed; the names and affiliations of the board of directors or trustees; a brief history of the organization's work and purpose; a specific description of the program for which support is asked; a copy of the total budget showing projected income and expenses for the current year and, in the same format, the budget for the year immediately past with actual numbers; budget information pertaining to the p rogram or project; a statement of financial position (balance sheet); information about the principal staff or volunteers who will implement the program; the name and phone number of contact person for additional information; other funding sources that have responded favorably or are currently considering the project for funding; future funding plans of the program, project, or organization; plans for evaluating the effectiveness of the project; and a copy of letter determining tax-exempt status.
Deadlines: None.
Review Process: All grant requests are acknowledged. After the board of trustees has received proposal, it may request a meeting or additional information.

Restrictions
Grants are not made to individuals.

Additional Information
Publications: Application Guidelines

Foundation Officials

Amy L. Fikes: vice president, trustee
Lee Fikes: president, treasurer, trustee, chairman B 1943. PRIM CORP EMPL president: Bonanza Oil Co. CORP AFFIL president: Denton Hines Properties; president: Denton Hines Properties Inc.
Nancy Solana: vice president, secretary

Grants Analysis

Disclosure Period: calendar year ending 2001
Total Grants: $3,259,445
Number of Grants: 80
Average Grant: $40,499*
Highest Grant: $60,000
Lowest Grant: $1,000
Typical Range: $10,000 to $50,000 and $100,000 to $200,000
*Note: Average grant figure excludes highest grant.

Recent Grants

Note: Grants derived from 2000 Form 990.

Library-Related
50,000   Friends of the Dallas Public Library, Dallas, TX -- for eighth floor renovation

General
500,000   University of Texas Southwestern Medical Center, Dallas, TX -- for equipment for CBI and equipment for Computational Biology Program
400,000   Planned Parenthood of North Texas, Dallas, TX -- for debt forgiveness
300,000   University of Texas Southwestern Medical Center, Dallas, TX -- for start-up packages for three new research scientists
200,000   Communities Foundation of Texas, Inc., Dallas, TX -- for Leland Fikes Foundation Fund
200,000   Communities Foundation of Texas, Inc., Dallas, TX -- for Leland Fikes Foundation
200,000   St. Mark's School of Texas, Dallas, TX -- capital campaign
177,443   American Association for the Advancement of Science, Washington, DC -- for demonstration project
100,000   Dallas Symphony Association, Dallas, TX -- Vision 2000 campaign
100,000   Dallas Symphony Association, Dallas, TX -- for sustaining fund
100,000   East Dallas Community School, Dallas, TX -- to create charter school and for operating support of private school

DOAK FINCH FOUNDATION

Giving Contact

J. C. Dorety, Contact
10 Welloskie Dr.
Thomasville, NC 27360

Alternate Contact

c/o Bank of America
Bank of America Place NC1-002-11-18
Charlotte, NC 28255
Phone: (704)387-4562

Description

Founded: 1961
EIN: 566042823
Organization Type: Private Foundation
Giving Locations: NC: Thomasville including surrounding area
Grant Types: General Support.

Donor Information

Founder: the late Doak Finch

Financial Summary

Total Giving: $257,100 (fiscal year ending October 31, 2001); $247,000 (fiscal 2000); $235,000 (fiscal 1999)
Assets: $4,170,154 (fiscal 2001); $5,386,275 (fiscal 2000); $4,994,263 (fiscal 1999)

Typical Recipients

Arts & Humanities: Arts Associations & Councils, Libraries, Theater
Civic & Public Affairs: Community Foundations, Civic & Public Affairs-General, Housing, Municipalities/Towns, Urban & Community Affairs
Education: Community & Junior Colleges, Education-General, Private Education (Precollege), Public Education (Precollege), Secondary Education (Public)
Health: Emergency/Ambulance Services, Health-General, Hospices, Hospitals
Religion: Churches, Ministries, Religious Organizations, Religious Welfare
Social Services: Child Welfare, Community Service Organizations, Crime Prevention, Food/Clothing Distribution, Homes, People with Disabilities, Recreation & Athletics, Social Services-General, Substance Abuse, United Funds/United Ways, YMCA/YWCA/YMHA/YWHA, Youth Organizations

Application Procedures

Initial Contact: Send brief letter describing program, purpose of funds sought, amount requested, and proof of tax-exempt status.
Deadlines: None.

Additional Information

trustee
Trust(s): Bank of America NA

Foundation Officials

Mary Lola Cook: vice president

Grants Analysis

Disclosure Period: fiscal year ending October 31, 2001
Total Grants: $257,100
Number of Grants: 24
Average Grant: $4,550*
Highest Grant: $67,000
Lowest Grant: $1,000
Typical Range: $1,000 to $10,000
*Note: Average grant excludes two highest grants ($117,000).

Recent Grants

Note: Grants derived from 2000 Form 990.

General
60,000   Tom A. FINCHD YMCA, Thomasville, NC
50,000   Habitat for Humanity
50,000   Memorial United Methodist Church, Thomasville, NC
15,000   Community Schools of Thomasville, Thomasville, NC
11,000   Thomasville Community Foundation, Thomasville, NC
10,000   Arts Council of Davidson County, Lexington, NC
10,000   Community General Hospital Foundation, Thomasville, NC
10,000   Davidson County Community College, Lexington, KY
10,000   Pace Group, Thomasville, NC
10,000   Thomasville City Schools, Thomasville, NC

THOMAS AUSTIN FINCH FOUNDATION

Giving Contact

Linda G. Tilley, Administrator
c/o Wachovia Bank of North Carolina NA
PO Box 3099
Winston-Salem, NC 27150-7131
Phone: (336)732-5252

Description

Founded: 1944
EIN: 566037907
Organization Type: Private Foundation
Giving Locations: NC: Thomasville including surrounding area
Grant Types: Capital, Emergency, General Support, Matching, Multiyear/Continuing Support, Operating Expenses, Scholarship.

Donor Information

Founder: Ernestine L. Finch Mobley, Thomas Austin Finch, Jr.

Financial Summary

Total Giving: $689,539 (2001); $508,467 (2000); $468,093 (1999)
Giving Analysis: Giving for 2001 includes: foundation scholarships ($21,667); foundation matching gifts ($135,626); 2000: foundation scholarships ($29,667); foundation matching gifts ($215,947); 1999: foundation scholarships ($25,458) foundation matching gifts ($308,810)
Assets: $11,153,122 (2001); $13,535,090 (2000); $14,117,130 (1999)

Typical Recipients

Arts & Humanities: Arts Associations & Councils, History & Archaeology, Libraries
Civic & Public Affairs: Community Foundations, Civic & Public Affairs-General, Housing, Municipalities/Towns, Urban & Community Affairs
Education: Colleges & Universities, Community & Junior Colleges, Education-General, Private Education (Precollege), Public Education (Precollege), Secondary Education (Public), Student Aid
Health: Hospices, Hospitals
International: Health Care/Hospitals
Religion: Churches, Ministries, Religious Welfare
Social Services: Community Service Organizations, Crime Prevention, Domestic Violence, Family Services, Food/Clothing Distribution, Recreation & Athletics, Senior Services, Substance Abuse, United Funds/United Ways, YMCA/YWCA/YMHA/YWHA, Youth Organizations

Application Procedures

Initial Contact: Application form required.
Deadlines: None.

Restrictions

Limited to Thomasville, NC area.

Additional Information

Publications: Informational Brochure (including Application Guidelines)
Trust(s): Wachovia Bank NC NA

Foundation Officials

Kermit Cloniger: mem
Thomas Austin Finch, Jr.: manager
Ernestine L. Mobley: manager

Grants Analysis

Disclosure Period: calendar year ending 2000
Total Grants: $529,246*
Number of Grants: 24
Average Grant: $11,635*
Highest Grant: $250,000

Typical Range: $1,500 to $15,000
*Note:** Giving excludes matching gifts and scholarships. Average grant figure excludes highest grant.

Recent Grants

Note: Grants derived from 2001 Form 990.

General

250,000	Memorial United Methodist Church, Thomasville, NC
135,628	Tom A Finch Community YMCA, Thomasville, NC
100,000	Westchester Academy, High Point, NC
25,000	Memorial United Methodist Church, Thomasville, NC
25,000	Memorial United Methodist Church, Thomasville, NC
20,000	Thomasville Communities in School, Thomasville, NC
15,000	Piedmont School, High Point, NC
15,000	Thomasville Community Foundation, Thomasville, NC
13,667	Davidson County Education Foundation, Lexington, NC
10,000	City of Thomasville, Thomasville, NC

FINK FOUNDATION (NY)

Giving Contact

Romie Shapiro, President
501 5th Avenue, Rm. 1600
New York, NY 10017-7853
Phone: (212)687-8098

Description

Founded: 1956
EIN: 136135438
Organization Type: Private Foundation
Giving Locations: MD; NY: New York
Grant Types: General Support.

Donor Information

Founder: David Fink, Nathan Fink

Financial Summary

Total Giving: $334,500 (2001); $378,000 (2000); $256,150 (1999)
Assets: $1,479,658 (2001); $1,903,983 (2000); $2,233,295 (1999)
Gifts Received: $4,995 (1996)

Typical Recipients

Arts & Humanities: Film & Video, Libraries, Museums/Galleries, Music
Civic & Public Affairs: Civic & Public Affairs-General, Women's Affairs
Education: Arts/Humanities Education, Colleges & Universities, Community & Junior Colleges, Education Funds, Faculty Development, Education-General, Legal Education, Minority Education, Private Education (Precollege), Public Education (Precollege), Secondary Education (Private), Student Aid
Health: Geriatric Health, Health Organizations, Hospices, Hospitals, Long-Term Care, Research/Studies Institutes, Respiratory
International: Foreign Arts Organizations, Foreign Educational Institutions, International-General, Health Care/Hospitals, International Peace & Security Issues, Missionary/Religious Activities
Religion: Bible Study/Translation, Religion-General, Jewish Causes, Jewish Causes, Religious Organizations, Religious Welfare, Seminaries, Synagogues/Temples
Social Services: Camps, Community Service Organizations, Family Services, Homes, People with Disabilities, Scouts, Senior Services, YMCA/YWCA/YMHA/YWHA

Application Procedures

Initial Contact: Applicants should submit a brief resume of academic qualifications.
Application Requirements: For research grants, include an outline of the proposed investigation and budget.
Deadlines: None.

Foundation Officials

Stanley Dalneoff: treasurer
Harold Fink: secretary
David Maurice Levitan: vice president B Tver, Lithuania December 25, 1915. ED Northwestern University BS (1936); Northwestern University MA (1937); University of Chicago PhD (1940); Columbia University JD (1948). PRIM CORP EMPL counsel: Hahn & Hessen. NONPR AFFIL member: New York State Bar Association; chairman board zoning appeals: Village Roslyn Harbor; member: American Society International Law; member: New York City Bar Association; member: American Law Institute; member: American Political Science Association; member: American Bar Association; fellow: American College Trust & Estate Counsel.
Charles Shanok: treasurer
Romie Shapiro: president
Seymour Zises: director

Grants Analysis

Disclosure Period: calendar year ending 2001
Total Grants: $334,500
Number of Grants: 54
Average Grant: $6,194
Highest Grant: $40,000
Typical Range: $1,000 to $10,000

Recent Grants

Note: Grants derived from 2001 Form 990.

General

40,000	Friends of Bezalel Academy, New York, NY
35,000	Abraham Joshua Herschel School, New York, NY
25,000	American Friends Open University Israel, New York, NY
25,000	Charles E. Smith Jewish Day School, Rockville, MD
25,000	Hebrew High School of New England, Springfield, MA
25,000	Institute for Advancement in Education, Inc.
10,000	American Committee for Shaare Zedek Hospital, New York, NY
10,000	Hadassah The Womens Zionist Organization of America, Inc.
10,000	Hebrew Home for the Aged, Riverdale, NY
10,000	Jewish Theological Seminary, Broadway, NY

FIREMAN'S FUND INSURANCE CO.

Company Headquarters

777 San Marin Dr.
Novato, CA 94998
Web: http://www.firemansfund.com

Company Description

Founded: 1863
Parent Company: Allianz Life Insurance Company of North America, 5701 Golden Hill Dr., Minneapolis, MN, United States

Nonmonetary Support

Type: Donated Equipment; In-kind Services

Fireman's Fund Foundation

Giving Contact

Barbara Friede, Secretary & Director
Fireman's Fund Foundation
777 San Marin Drive
Novato, CA 94998-1406
Phone: (415)899-2757
Fax: (415)899-2012

Description

Founded: 1953
EIN: 946078025
Organization Type: Corporate Foundation
Giving Locations: CA: Marin and Sonoma Counties
Grant Types: Employee Matching Gifts, Project.
Note: Employee matching gift ratio: 1 to 1.

Donor Information

Founder: Fireman's Fund Insurance Co. & Subsidiaries

Financial Summary

Total Giving: $900,000 (2002 approx); $1,143,577 (2001); $970,541 (2000). Note: Contributes through foundation only.
Giving Analysis: Giving for 2000 includes: foundation grants to United Way ($69,330); foundation matching gifts ($169,577); foundation ($731,634); 1999: foundation grants to United Way ($131,227); foundation matching gifts ($157,521); foundation ($766,576); 1998: foundation matching gifts ($136,662); foundation grants to United Way ($139,225);
Assets: $136,017 (2001); $202,314 (2000); $191,562 (1999)
Gifts Received: $791,000 (2002 approx); $1,093,004 (2001); $1,023,223 (2000). Note: In 2001, contributions were received from Fireman's Fund Insurance Co. ($1,023,959) and miscellaneous contributions less than $5,000 each ($69,045).

Typical Recipients

Arts & Humanities: Arts Centers, Arts Institutes, Arts Outreach, Ballet, Community Arts, Dance, Ethnic & Folk Arts, Arts & Humanities-General, Historic Preservation, History & Archaeology, Libraries, Museums/Galleries, Music, Opera, Performing Arts, Public Broadcasting, Theater, Visual Arts
Civic & Public Affairs: Economic Development, Employment/Job Training, Gay/Lesbian Issues, Civic & Public Affairs-General, Housing, Legal Aid, Municipalities/Towns, Nonprofit Management, Parades/Festivals, Philanthropic Organizations, Safety, Urban & Community Affairs, Women's Affairs, Zoos/Aquariums
Education: Business Education, Colleges & Universities, Colleges & Universities, Community & Junior Colleges, Continuing Education, Education Funds, Education-General, Literacy, Preschool Education, Private Education (Precollege), Public Education (Precollege), Religious Education, Science/Mathematics Education, Secondary Education (Public)
Environment: Environment-General, Resource Conservation
Health: AIDS/HIV, Alzheimers Disease, Health Organizations, Home-Care Services, Hospitals, Medical Rehabilitation, Mental Health, Preventive Medicine/Wellness Organizations
Religion: Jewish Causes, Ministries, Religious Organizations, Religious Welfare, Social/Policy Issues
Science: Observatories & Planetariums, Science Exhibits & Fairs, Science Museums
Social Services: At-Risk Youth, Big Brother/Big Sister, Child Welfare, Community Centers, Community Service Organizations, Day Care, Domestic Violence, Emergency Relief, Family Services, Food/Clothing

Distribution, Homes, People with Disabilities, Recreation & Athletics, Senior Services, Shelters/Homelessness, Social Services-General, Substance Abuse, United Funds/United Ways, Volunteer Services, YMCA/YWCA/YMHA/YWHA, Youth Organizations

Application Procedures

Initial Contact: Send a brief letter of not more than two pages, plus attachments.
Application Requirements: Include a description of organization; constituency served; statement of mission, objectives and goals; amount requested, and an explanation of how funds will be used to support a specific program or project; program budget showing expenses and income sources; list of current contributors and amounts; recently audited financial statement; proof of tax-exempt status; and list of board members, executive director and other key staff members.
Deadlines: None.
Review Process: Foundation director reviews proposals prior to consideration by distribution committee.
Evaluative Criteria: Broad community support and proven track record; demonstration of how sustainable, positive change will be achieved; project meets community needs and targets a wide audience; projects have demonstrated impact in the community.
Decision Notification: Distribution committee meets four times a year; grants usually made within 90 days.

Restrictions

Grants are not made to individuals; religious, veterans', labor, or fraternal organizations; capital campaigns, endowment funds or operating expenses; fund-raising or sporting events; subscription fees or admission tickets; insurance premiums; medical research and health organizations; political candidates; political or lobbying groups; dinners or special events; trips or tours; advertisements; public sector services; or videos, films, or television productions.

Additional Information

Publications: Guidelines

Corporate Officials

Gary E. Black: president claims division, director actuary B 1945. PRIM CORP EMPL president claims division, director: Fireman's Fund Insurance Co. CORP AFFIL director: American Insurance Co. Inc.; director: Interstate National Corp.
David R. Pollard: officer PRIM CORP EMPL officer: Fireman's Fund Insurance Co. CORP AFFIL executive vice president: Associated Indemnity Corp.; officer: Interstate Fire & Casualty Co.
Jeffery H. Post: executive vice president, chief financial officer, chief actuary PRIM CORP EMPL executive vice president, chief financial officer, chief actuary: Fireman's Fund Insurance Co. ADD CORP EMPL chief financial officer: American Insurance Co. Inc.; vice president: Associated Indemnity Corp.

Foundation Officials

Gary E. Black: president, director (see above)
Bruce Friedberg: board member
Barbara Friede: director
Thomas Geillser: board member
Peter Huehne: board member
Janet S. Kloenhammer: director
H. David Lundgren: director
Harold N. Marsh, III: treasurer B 1948. ED Mitchell College AA (1972). PRIM CORP EMPL senior vice president, treasurer: Fireman's Fund Insurance Co. ADD CORP EMPL treasurer: American Insurance Co. Inc.; treasurer: National Surety Corp.; treasurer: Firemans Fund Insurance Co. Ohio; treasurer: Parkway Insurance Co.
David R. Pollard: director (see above)
Alastair Shore: president, board member

Grants Analysis

Disclosure Period: calendar year ending 2001
Total Grants: $919,773*
Number of Grants: 86
Average Grant: $9,409*
Highest Grant: $120,000
Lowest Grant: $500
Typical Range: $100 to $10,000
*Note: Giving excludes matching gifts and United Way. Average grant figure excludes highest grant.

Recent Grants

Note: Grants derived from 2001 Form 990.

General
120,000	Vector Theater Company
68,151	National Fallen Firefighters Foundation, Emmitsburg, MD
68,151	New York Fire 9-11 Disaster Relief Fund, Washington, DC
55,485	Marin Conservation Corps, Marin City, CA
50,000	Youth in Arts, San Rafael, CA
49,305	Volunteer Center of Sonoma County, Santa Rosa, CA
20,000	North Bay Children's Center, Novato, CA
17,500	Community Institute for Psychotherapy, San Rafael, CA
17,500	Marin Senior Coordination Council, Inc., San Rafael, CA
15,681	Volunteer Center of Marin County, San Rafael, CA

HARVEY FIRESTONE, JR. FOUNDATION

Giving Contact

Charles D'Arcy, Trust Officer
c/o Bank One Trust Co. NA
50 S. Main Street
PO Box 3547
Akron, OH 44308
Phone: (330)972-1872

Description

Founded: 1983
EIN: 341388254
Organization Type: Private Foundation
Giving Locations: east of the Mississippi River.
Grant Types: General Support.

Financial Summary

Total Giving: $1,250,000 (2000); $1,202,000 (1999); $1,089,000 (1998)
Giving Analysis: Giving for 2000 includes: foundation grants to United Way ($50,000); 1999: foundation grants to United Way ($50,000); foundation grants to United Way ($50,000); 1998: foundation grants to United Way ($50,000) foundation ($1,048,000)
Assets: $15,050,189 (2000); $27,024,506 (1999); $25,152,779 (1998)
Gifts Received: $8,001 (1995)

Typical Recipients

Arts & Humanities: Arts & Humanities-General, Historic Preservation, History & Archaeology, Libraries, Museums/Galleries, Music, Public Broadcasting, Theater
Civic & Public Affairs: Community Foundations, Employment/Job Training, Civic & Public Affairs-General, Philanthropic Organizations, Rural Affairs, Urban & Community Affairs
Education: Arts/Humanities Education, Colleges & Universities, Faculty Development, Private Education (Precollege), Science/Mathematics Education, Secondary Education (Public), Special Education
Environment: Resource Conservation

Health: Children's Health/Hospitals, Emergency/Ambulance Services, Health Organizations, Hospices, Hospitals, Nursing Services, Public Health
International: Foreign Arts Organizations, Foreign Educational Institutions
Religion: Churches, Dioceses, Religious Organizations, Religious Welfare, Seminaries
Science: Scientific Labs
Social Services: At-Risk Youth, Child Welfare, Community Centers, Community Service Organizations, Counseling, Family Services, People with Disabilities, Recreation & Athletics, Shelters/Homelessness, United Funds/United Ways, Youth Organizations

Application Procedures

Initial Contact: The foundation has no formal grant application procedure or application form.
Deadlines: None.

Foundation Officials

Anne F. Ball: trustee
Martha F. Ford: trustee

Grants Analysis

Disclosure Period: calendar year ending 2000
Total Grants: $1,200,000*
Number of Grants: 65
Average Grant: $12,444*
Highest Grant: $316,000
Typical Range: $5,000 to $30,000
*Note: Giving excludes United Way. Average grant excludes two highest grants ($416,000).

Recent Grants

Note: Grants derived from 1999 Form 990.

Library-Related
10,000	Greenwich Library, The, Greenwich, CT

General
463,500	Henry Ford Health System, Detroit, MI
141,500	Family Centers, Inc, Greenwich, CT
100,000	Archdiocese for Military Service, Washington, DC
77,000	Miss Porter's School, Farmington, CT
50,000	United Way of Greenwich, Greenwich, CT
45,500	Christ Church Grosse Pointe, Grosse Pte. Farms, MI
40,000	Vassar College, Poughkeepsie, NY
30,000	Greenwich Hospital, Greenwich, CT
20,000	Oakland University School of Health Sciences, Rochester, MI
15,000	Foxcroft School, Middleburg, VA

FIRMAN FUND

Giving Contact

Royal Firman, III, Trustee
1422 Euclid Ave., Suite 1030
Cleveland, OH 44115
Phone: (216)363-1035

Description

Founded: 1951
EIN: 346513655
Organization Type: Private Foundation
Giving Locations: CO: Denver; FL: Tallahassee; GA: Thomasville; KY: Lexington; OH: Cleveland
Grant Types: Capital, Endowment, General Support, Research.

Donor Information

Founder: Pamela H. Firman

Financial Summary

Total Giving: $50,000 (2002 approx); $458,700 (2001); $478,200 (2000)
Giving Analysis: Giving for 2001 includes: foundation grants to United Way ($20,000); 2000: foundation

grants to United Way ($20,000); 1999: foundation grants to United Way ($20,000);
Assets: $12,386,089 (2001); $13,449,474 (2000); $14,317,408 (1999)

Typical Recipients

Arts & Humanities: Arts Associations & Councils, Arts Centers, History & Archaeology, Libraries, Museums/Galleries, Music, Opera, Public Broadcasting, Theater
Civic & Public Affairs: Botanical Gardens/Parks, Employment/Job Training, Civic & Public Affairs-General, Municipalities/Towns, Women's Affairs
Education: Colleges & Universities, Education-General, Medical Education, Preschool Education, Private Education (Precollege), Science/Mathematics Education, Student Aid
Environment: Environment-General, Research, Resource Conservation, Wildlife Protection
Health: Cancer, Children's Health/Hospitals, Diabetes, Emergency/Ambulance Services, Eyes/Blindness, Hospitals (University Affiliated), Medical Rehabilitation, Mental Health, Nursing Services, Nursing Services, Speech & Hearing
Religion: Churches
Science: Science Museums, Scientific Centers & Institutes, Scientific Research
Social Services: Child Welfare, Community Service Organizations, People with Disabilities, Substance Abuse, United Funds/United Ways, Volunteer Services

Application Procedures

Initial Contact: Send a brief letter of inquiry.
Application Requirements: current income and expense statement, purpose of funds sought, projected budget, and proof of tax-exempt status. Board meetings are held during the first part of April and November. Requests for grants should be received at least six weeks prior to the meetings.

Restrictions

Does not give grants to individuals. Most grants are for educational and health care.

Foundation Officials

Neil A. Brown: secretary
Pamela H. Firman: president
Royal Firman: trustee
Stephanie Firman: trustee
Carole M. Nowak: treasurer
Cindy F. Webster: trustee
Robert C. Webster, Jr.: trustee

Grants Analysis

Disclosure Period: calendar year ending 2001
Total Grants: $438,700*
Number of Grants: 26
Average Grant: $12,835*
Highest Grant: $105,000
Lowest Grant: $500
Typical Range: $1,000 to $50,000
*Note: Giving excludes United Way. Average grant figure excludes highest grant.

Recent Grants

Note: Grants derived from 2001 Form 990.

General

105,000	Tall Timbers Research, Tallahassee, FL -- endowment
50,000	Cleveland Botanical Garden, Cleveland, OH -- for building campaign
50,000	Cleveland Museum of Natural History, Cleveland, OH -- for building campaign
50,000	Hathaway Brown School, Cleveland, OH -- for building campaign
50,000	Hotchkiss School, Lakeville, CA -- for endowment fund
25,000	American Red Cross, Cleveland, OH -- for NYC disaster
25,000	Tall Timbers Research, Tallahassee, FL -- research
20,000	United Way Services, Cleveland, OH -- annual fund
15,000	Colorado Academy, Denver, CO -- for annual fund
10,000	Colorado Conservation Trust, Denver, CO -- for annual fund

FIRST FINANCIAL BANK

Company Headquarters

1045 Clark St.
Stevens Point, WI 54481

Company Description

Employees: 1,283
SIC(s): 6035 Federal Savings Institutions.
Parent Company: First Financial Corp., 1 First Financial Plaza, Terre Haute, IN, United States

Operating Locations

First Financial Bank (WI--Stevens Point)

Associated Banc-Corp Foundation

Giving Contact

Jonathon Drayna
1305 Main Street
PO Box 13307
Stevens Point, WI 54481
Phone: (715)341-0400

Description

Founded: 1977
EIN: 391277461
Organization Type: Corporate Foundation
Former Name: First Financial Foundation (2002).
Giving Locations: IL: areas of business; WI: areas of business
Grant Types: Capital, Employee Matching Gifts, General Support.

Financial Summary

Total Giving: $64,000 (2001); $303,049 (1998); $224,383 (1997)
Giving Analysis: Giving for 1998 includes: foundation grants to United Way ($128,849); foundation ($174,200); 1997: foundation grants to United Way ($77,608) foundation ($146,775)
Assets: $763,893 (2001); $894,147 (1998); $1,153,175 (1997)
Gifts Received: $360,000 (1997); $90,000 (1996); $300,000 (1994). Note: In 1996, contributions were received from First Financial Bank.

Typical Recipients

Arts & Humanities: Arts & Humanities-General, Libraries, Museums/Galleries, Music, Opera, Performing Arts, Public Broadcasting, Theater
Civic & Public Affairs: Botanical Gardens/Parks, Chambers of Commerce, Clubs, Community Foundations, Economic Development, Civic & Public Affairs-General, Housing, Municipalities/Towns, Safety, Urban & Community Affairs, Women's Affairs
Education: Agricultural Education, Colleges & Universities, Economic Education, Education Reform, Literacy, Private Education (Precollege), Social Sciences Education, Student Aid, Vocational & Technical Education
Environment: Environment-General
Health: AIDS/HIV, Cancer, Children's Health/Hospitals, Clinics/Medical Centers, Geriatric Health, Health Funds, Hospitals, Medical Research, Nursing Services, Public Health, Single-Disease Health Associations

Religion: Missionary Activities (Domestic), Religious Organizations, Religious Welfare
Social Services: Child Welfare, Community Centers, Community Service Organizations, Domestic Violence, Family Planning, Food/Clothing Distribution, People with Disabilities, Recreation & Athletics, Scouts, Senior Services, Shelters/Homelessness, United Funds/United Ways, YMCA/YWCA/YMHA/YWHA, Youth Organizations

Application Procedures

Initial Contact: Request a contribution request form.
Deadlines: September 1.

Restrictions

The foundation does not make contributions to individuals, political or lobbying groups, labor organizations, or veterans' organizations. Contributions to religious organizations are limited to those facilities that offer higher education or hospital care to the general public.

Additional Information

Publications: Application Form

Corporate Officials

John C. Seramur: president, chief executive officer, director B 1943. PRIM CORP EMPL president, chief executive officer, director: First Financial Bank.

Foundation Officials

James O. Heinecke: director
Ignatius H. Robers: director

Grants Analysis

Disclosure Period: calendar year ending 2001
Total Grants: $64,000
Number of Grants: 1
Highest Grant: $64,000
Typical Range: $300 to $11,000

Recent Grants

Note: Grants derived from 2001 Form 990.

General

64,000	ABC Foundation Charitable, Green Bay, WI

FIRST HAWAIIAN, INC.

Company Headquarters

1111 S. Beretania St.
Honolulu, HI 96814
Web: http://www.fnb.com

Company Description

Employees: 3,384
SIC(s): 6022 State Commercial Banks, 6159 Miscellaneous Business Credit Institutions, 6719 Holding Companies Nec.

Operating Locations

First Hawaiian, Inc. (HI--Honolulu)

Nonmonetary Support

Volunteer Programs: Company supports employee volunteerism through the YesTeam.

First Hawaiian Foundation

Giving Contact

Lily K. Yao, President
First Hawaiian Foundation
999 Bishop Street, 29th Floor
Honolulu, HI 96813
Phone: (808)525-7766
Fax: (808)525-7750

Description

EIN: 237437822
Organization Type: Corporate Foundation
Giving Locations: HI
Grant Types: Capital, Employee Matching Gifts, General Support, Project.

Financial Summary

Total Giving: $1,637,351 (2001); $1,568,011 (2000); $1,500,000 (1999 approx)
Giving Analysis: Giving for 2000 includes: foundation grants to United Way ($346,000); foundation ($1,222,011); 1999: foundation grants to United Way ($314,500); foundation ($1,256,782); 1997: foundation scholarships ($10,000); foundation grants to United Way ($305,000); foundation ($850,249);
Assets: $18,387,932 (2001); $5,658,239 (2000); $8,060,435 (1998)
Gifts Received: $9,997,317 (2001); $2,004 (2000); $4,504 (1998). Note: In 2001, contributions were received from BancWest Corp. and First Hawaiian Bank. Prior to 2001, contributions were received from First Hawaiian Credit Corp., First Hawaiian Bank, and First Hawaiian Leasing.

Typical Recipients

Arts & Humanities: Arts Associations & Councils, Arts Centers, Arts Funds, Film & Video, Historic Preservation, History & Archaeology, Libraries, Museums/Galleries, Music, Public Broadcasting, Theater, Visual Arts
Civic & Public Affairs: Asian American Affairs, Business/Free Enterprise, Chambers of Commerce, Community Foundations, Civic & Public Affairs-General, Housing, Law & Justice, Parades/Festivals, Philanthropic Organizations, Urban & Community Affairs
Education: Agricultural Education, Arts/Humanities Education, Business Education, Colleges & Universities, Continuing Education, Economic Education, Education Funds, Elementary Education (Public), Education-General, Gifted & Talented Programs, International Studies, Literacy, Preschool Education, Private Education (Precollege), Public Education (Precollege), Religious Education, Science/Mathematics Education, Secondary Education (Private), Secondary Education (Public), Social Sciences Education, Special Education, Student Aid
Environment: Environment-General, Resource Conservation
Health: Cancer, Children's Health/Hospitals, Clinics/Medical Centers, Emergency/Ambulance Services, Health Organizations, Hospices, Hospitals, Medical Rehabilitation, Research/Studies Institutes, Single-Disease Health Associations
International: Foreign Educational Institutions, Health Care/Hospitals, Missionary/Religious Activities
Religion: Churches, Ministries, Missionary Activities (Domestic), Religious Organizations, Religious Welfare
Science: Science Museums, Scientific Centers & Institutes, Scientific Research
Social Services: Big Brother/Big Sister, Big Brother/Big Sister, Child Welfare, Community Centers, Community Service Organizations, Day Care, Domestic Violence, Family Services, Food/Clothing Distribution, Homes, People with Disabilities, Recreation & Athletics, Scouts, Senior Services, Shelters/Homelessness, Social Services-General, Substance Abuse, United Funds/United Ways, Volunteer Services, YMCA/YWCA/YMHA/YWHA, Youth Organizations

Application Procedures

Initial Contact: Send letter of request.
Application Requirements: Include a description of organization, amount requested, project budget, purpose of funds sought, recently audited financial statement, proof of tax-exempt status, income level of service area, and list of board members and officers.

Deadlines: None.
Review Process: Board meets quarterly.

Restrictions

Company will only fund organizations with tax-exempt status.

Corporate Officials

Lily K. Yao: director PRIM CORP EMPL director: First Hawaiian, Inc. CORP AFFIL secretary: First Hawaiian Bank. NONPR AFFIL chairman board regents: University Hawaii.

Foundation Officials

Robert Alm: president CORP AFFIL trustee: Liliuokalani Trust.
William E. Atwater: secretary, director
Anthony R. Guerrero, Jr.: executive vice president B Honolulu, HI 1945. ED University of Portland (1967). PRIM CORP EMPL executive vice president: First Hawaiian Bank. CORP AFFIL director: Oahu Transit Service Inc.
Gerald J. Keir: director
Gerald M. Pang: executive vice president B Honolulu, HI 1948. ED University of Hawaii (1970). PRIM CORP EMPL executive vice president, chief credit officer: First Hawaiian Bank.
Sheila M. Sumida: director
John K. Tsui: vice president, director B 1938. PRIM CORP EMPL president: First Hawaiian Bank. CORP AFFIL president: Bancwest Corp.; chief executive officer: First Hawaiian Leasing Inc.
Albert M. Yamada: director
Lily K. Yao: president, director (see above)

Grants Analysis

Disclosure Period: calendar year ending 2001
Total Grants: $1,286,351*
Number of Grants: 85
Average Grant: $15,134
Highest Grant: $268,750
Lowest Grant: $1,000
Typical Range: $5,000 to $20,000
*Note: Giving excludes United Way.

Recent Grants

Note: Grants derived from 2001 Form 990.

General

285,000	Aloha United Way Oahu, Oahu, HI -- corporate pledge
268,750	University of Hawaii Foundation, Honolulu, HI -- travel funds
70,000	Pacific International Center for High Technology Research, Honolulu, HI -- support of educational programs
50,000	Contemporary Museum, Honolulu, HI -- capital campaign
50,000	Washington Place Foundation, Honolulu, HI -- capital campaign
40,000	Iolani School, Honolulu, HI -- capital campaign
26,000	Hawaii Island United Way, Hilo, HI -- corporate pledge
25,000	Aloha Council Boy Scouts of America, Honolulu, HI -- capital campaign
25,000	Enterprise Honolulu, Honolulu, HI -- support Target 2005
25,000	Hawaii Community Foundation, Honolulu, HI -- to assist victims of national tragedy

FIRST TENNESSEE NATIONAL CORP.

Company Headquarters

Memphis, TN
Web: http://www.ftb.com

Company Description

Ticker: FTN
Exchange: OTC
Former Name: First Tennessee Bank.
Assets: US$22.81 billion (2002)
Employees: 9861 (2002)
SIC(s): 6021 National Commercial Banks, 6712 Bank Holding Companies.

Operating Locations

First Tennessee National Corp. (TN--Chattanooga, Cookeville, Dandridge, Dyersburg, Gallatin, Greeneville, Jackson, Johnson City, Knoxville, Maryville, Memphis, Morristown, Nashville)

Nonmonetary Support

Range: $5,000 - $15,000
Type: Donated Equipment; Donated Products; In-kind Services; Loaned Employees; Loaned Executives; Workplace Solicitation
Volunteer Programs: Company sponsors Volunteerbank.
Contact: Sue Jacks, Corporate Communications

First Tennessee Foundation

Giving Contact

J. Terrence Lee, Senior Vice President, Corporate Communications
First Tennessee National Corp.
165 Madison
Memphis, TN 38103
Phone: (901)523-4380
E-mail: jtlee@ftb.com

Description

EIN: 621533987
Organization Type: Corporate Foundation
Giving Locations: TN: headquarters and operating communities
Grant Types: Capital, Challenge, Endowment, General Support, Professorship, Project.

Financial Summary

Total Giving: $4,081,385 (2002); $1,731,485 (2001); $1,525,325 (2000). Note: Contributes through corporate direct giving program and foundation.
Giving Analysis: Giving for 2001 includes: foundation grants to United Way ($380,988) 2000: foundation ($1,525,325)
Assets: $12,609,200 (2001); $14,804,339 (2000)

Typical Recipients

Arts & Humanities: Arts Associations & Councils, Arts Centers, Arts Festivals, Arts Funds, Arts Institutes, Community Arts, Dance, Ethnic & Folk Arts, Historic Preservation, History & Archaeology, Libraries, Museums/Galleries, Music, Opera, Performing Arts, Public Broadcasting, Theater, Visual Arts
Civic & Public Affairs: Botanical Gardens/Parks, Business/Free Enterprise, Chambers of Commerce, Civil Rights, Community Foundations, Economic Development, Ethnic Organizations, Civic & Public Affairs-General, Professional & Trade Associations, Public Policy, Urban & Community Affairs, Zoos/Aquariums
Education: Business Education, Colleges & Universities, Economic Education, Education Reform, Elementary Education (Private), Faculty Development, Minority Education, Preschool Education, Private Education (Precollege), Public Education (Precollege)
Environment: Environment-General, Wildlife Protection
Health: Children's Health/Hospitals, Hospitals
Religion: Churches, Religion-General, Ministries
Social Services: Big Brother/Big Sister, Community Service Organizations, Emergency Relief, Recreation & Athletics, Scouts, Shelters/Homelessness,

United Funds/United Ways, Volunteer Services, Youth Organizations

Application Procedures

Initial Contact: a brief letter of inquiry to determine interest; proposal will be invited

Application Requirements: (after interest has been shown by First Tennessee Bank) a proposal that includes: name, address, telephone number and contact person of organization; brief a description of organization's history, accomplishments, and goals; objectives of program to be funded; amount sought in relation to total need; expected project outcomes; proposed evaluation method; geographic area and number of people served; current operating budget, expected project costs, and most recently audited financial statement; other funding sources, including government, individuals, foundations, corporations, and united funds; list of officers, board of directors, and other principles of the organization; involvement of volunteers in the organization; and proof of tax-exempt status volunteers in the organization; and proof of tax-exempt status

Deadlines: by the October prior to the year for which funding is requested

Review Process: after initial inquiry, notification within four weeks if written proposal is sought; complete review may take up to two months

Evaluative Criteria: relation to contributions policy objectives; extent to which project will prevent community problems or develop financial resources to respond to such problems; extent to which funding will promote self-sufficiency; community's need for program and lack of duplication of existing services; organization's record of accomplishment; community support; financial condition, management, and administrative costs of organization

Decision Notification: ongoing basis, with review process taking as long as two months; applicants notified in February of status of requests for that year **Notes:** The program is decentralized; apply to Memphis office for proposals with a statewide or Memphis area focus; apply to local bank president for proposals of a local or regional focus. Very few unsolicited requests are accepted.

Restrictions

Grants are not made to individuals; charities sponsored solely by a single civic organization; charities that redistribute funds to other organizations, except recognized united funds and arts funds; member agencies of the United Way or united arts funds; bank "clearinghouse" organizations; religious, veterans, social, athletic, or fraternal organizations; political organizations or other groups promoting a specific ideological point of view; trips or tours; operating budget deficits; multiyear commitments of four years or more; endowments; tickets to fund-raising benefits; goodwill advertising; or member agencies of united funds. tickets to fund-raising benefits; goodwill advertising; or member agencies of united funds.

Grants Analysis

Disclosure Period: calendar year ending 2001
Total Grants: $1,350,497*
Number of Grants: 107
Average Grant: $10,005*
Highest Grant: $200,000
Lowest Grant: $500
Typical Range: $5,000 to $20,000
*Note: Giving excludes United Way. Average grant figure excludes two highest grants ($300,000).

Recent Grants

Note: Grants derived from 2001 Form 990.

Library-Related

20,000	Foundation for the Memphis-Shelby County Public Library, Memphis, TN
11,250	Foundation for the Blount County Public Library, Maryville, TN

General

200,000	September 11th Fund, New York, NY
95,000	Memphis Arts Council, Memphis, TN
70,000	Memphis Chamber Foundation, Memphis, TN
50,000	Partners in Public Education, Memphis, TN
50,000	University of Memphis Foundation, Memphis, TN
45,000	United Way of the Mid-South, Memphis, TN
45,000	United Way of the Mid-South, Memphis, TN
30,000	Boy Scouts of America Great Smokey Run
25,000	American Battle Monuments Commission, Arlington, VA
25,000	Memphis Community Development Partnership, Memphis, TN

FIRSTAR BANK MILWAUKEE NA

Company Headquarters

777 E. Wisconsin Ave.
Milwaukee, WI 53202

Company Description

Former Name: First Wisconsin National Bank of Milwaukee.
Employees: 3,000
SIC(s): 6021 National Commercial Banks.

Operating Locations

Firstar Bank Milwaukee NA (AZ--Phoenix; FL--West Palm Beach; IL--Bolingbrook, Naperville, Northbrook, Park Forest; IA--Ames, Cedar Falls, Cedar Rapids, Council Bluffs, Davenport, Mount Pleasant, Ottumwa, Red Oak, Sioux City; MN--Bloomington, Brogan, Hugo, Minneapolis, Roseville, St. Anthony, Stillwater; WI--Brookfield, Cedarburg, Eldorado, Fond du Lac, Grantsburg, Green Bay, Madison, Manitowoc, Mayfair, Menasha, Milwaukee, Minocqua, Oshkosh, Portage, Racine, Rice Lake, Sheboygan, Two Rivers, Waunahee, Wausau, Wisconsin Rapids)

Nonmonetary Support

Volunteer Programs: The Company has an active employee volunteer program.

Firstar Foundation, Inc.

Giving Contact

Kathleen R. Toay, Foundation Director
Firstar Foundation
US Bank Place
225 South 6th Street
Minneapolis, MN 55402

Description

EIN: 396042050
Organization Type: Corporate Foundation
Former Name: Firstar Milwaukee Foundation.
Giving Locations: WI: Milwaukee
Grant Types: Capital, General Support, Multiyear/Continuing Support, Operating Expenses.

Financial Summary

Total Giving: $12,406,319 (2001); $15,215,561 (2000); $1,500,000 (1999 approx). Note: Contributes through corporate direct giving program and foundation.
Giving Analysis: Giving for 2001 includes: foundation grants to United Way ($1,037,492); foundation ($11,368,827); 2000: foundation ($15,215,561); 1998: foundation grants to United Way ($710,100); foundation ($1,658,998);

Assets: $61,761,597 (2001); $57,295,065 (2000); $26,581,413 (1998)
Gifts Received: $20,454,250 (2001); $35,120,581 (2000); $20,010,186 (1998). Note: Gifts were received from Firstar Bank, N.A.

Typical Recipients

Arts & Humanities: Arts Associations & Councils, Arts Centers, Arts Funds, Arts Institutes, Ballet, Dance, Historic Preservation, History & Archaeology, Libraries, Museums/Galleries, Music, Opera, Performing Arts, Public Broadcasting, Theater
Civic & Public Affairs: African American Affairs, Botanical Gardens/Parks, Business/Free Enterprise, Chambers of Commerce, Civil Rights, Economic Development, Employment/Job Training, Civic & Public Affairs-General, Hispanic Affairs, Housing, Municipalities/Towns, Nonprofit Management, Parades/Festivals, Urban & Community Affairs, Women's Affairs, Zoos/Aquariums
Education: Business Education, Colleges & Universities, Economic Education, Education Funds, Education Reform, Engineering/Technological Education, Education-General, Health & Physical Education, Leadership Training, Literacy, Medical Education, Minority Education, Secondary Education (Public), Social Sciences Education, Student Aid
Health: Children's Health/Hospitals, Clinics/Medical Centers, Emergency/Ambulance Services, Health-General, Health Organizations, Heart, Hospices, Hospitals, Nursing Services, Single-Disease Health Associations, Transplant Networks/Donor Banks
Religion: Jewish Causes, Religious Welfare
Social Services: Child Welfare, Community Centers, Community Service Organizations, Delinquency & Criminal Rehabilitation, Family Planning, Family Services, People with Disabilities, Recreation & Athletics, Scouts, Scouts, Senior Services, Shelters/Homelessness, Substance Abuse, United Funds/United Ways, Volunteer Services, YMCA/YWCA/YMHA/YWHA, Youth Organizations

Application Procedures

Initial Contact: Send a letter of request.
Application Requirements: Include name, address, and telephone number of the organization, any national organization with which affiliated, and dates each were established; proof of tax-exempt status; recently audited financial statement; purposes and activities of the organization, services provided, to whom, and how many served per year; names of administrative officers and governing board of organization; copy of most recent balance sheet and annual operating statement; percentage of budget received from United Way, federal or state funding, and other sources; percentage of program/services paid for by recipients; purpose of funds sought; and, if purpose is a specific project, a detailed budget.
Deadlines: None.

Restrictions

Contributions generally made only to institutions located in and providing services to the geographic areas in which Firstar does business. Foundation does give contributions to partisan political organizations; religious organizations for sectarian purposes; controversial social causes on which there are strong divergences of opinion; agencies which themselves receive a large portion of their annual budget from United Way and the Fine Arts Fund, drives to which the bank substantially contributes each year; direct support for individuals; general contributions will not be made to institutions supported principally by taxes, with the exception of specific programs at publicly funded educational institutions.

Corporate Officials

John A. Becker: director B Kenosha, WI 1942. ED Marquette University BS (1963); Marquette University MBA (1965). CORP AFFIL chairman, executive vice president: First Wisconsin National Bank Milwaukee.

NONPR AFFIL trustee: Marquette University; trustee: Wisconsin Bankers Association; member: Greater Madison Chamber of Commerce.

Foundation Officials

Roger Leon Fitzsimonds: chairman emeritus B Milwaukee, WI 1938. ED University of Wisconsin, Milwaukee BBA (1960); University of Wisconsin, Milwaukee MBA (1971). CORP AFFIL board directors: Firstar Bank Milwaukee NA. NONPR AFFIL member, director: Wisconsin Association Manufacturing & Commerce; director: Wisconsin Policy Research Institute; chairman advisory council: University Wisconsin School Business; director: Metropolitan Milwaukee Association Commerce; director: Milwaukee Boys & Girls Club; director: Competitive Wisconsin Inc.; director: Medical College Wisconsin; director: Columbia Health System Inc. CLUB AFFIL Milwaukee Country Club.

Sheldon B. Lubar: director B Milwaukee, WI 1929. ED University of Wisconsin BA (1951); University of Wisconsin LLB (1953); University of Wisconsin DSc (1988). PRIM CORP EMPL chairman: Christiana Companies, Inc. CORP AFFIL director: MGIC Investment Corp.; director: Weatherford International Inc.; director: Lubar & Co.; chairman: Massachusetts Mutual Life Insurance Co.; director: EVI Weatherford Inc.; director: Firstar Bank Corp.; director: Ameritech Corp.

Grants Analysis

Disclosure Period: calendar year ending 2001
Total Grants: $11,368,827*
Number of Grants: 1,602
Average Grant: $7,097
Highest Grant: $250,000
Typical Range: $1,000 to $10,000
*Note: Giving excludes United Way.

Recent Grants

Note: Grants derived from 2001 Form 990.

General

260,000	United Way of King County, Seattle, WA
250,000	St. Paul Riverfront Corp, St. Paul, MN
150,000	Regional Housing and Community Development Alliance, St. Louis, MO
150,000	St. Louis University, St. Louis, MO
100,000	Adams Park Community Center
100,000	City of St. Louis, St. Louis, MO
100,000	Dan Beard Council Boy Scouts of America, Cincinnati, OH
100,000	Greater Cincinnati Chamber of Commerce, Cincinnati, OH
100,000	National Underground Railroad Freedom Center, Cincinnati, OH
100,000	St. Louis Gateway Classic Sports Foundation, St. Louis, MO

FISCHBACH FOUNDATION

Giving Contact

Nancy Taubman, President & Treasurer
PO Box 224
Clinton, CT 06413
Phone: (860)669-0368

Description

Founded: 1944
EIN: 237416874
Organization Type: Private Foundation
Giving Locations: NY; Israel
Grant Types: General Support.

Donor Information

Founder: Established by members of the Fischbach family.

Financial Summary

Total Giving: $148,455 (2001); $255,066 (2000); $743,385 (1999)
Giving Analysis: Giving for 2000 includes: foundation scholarships ($5,000); 1998: foundation matching gifts ($19,085); foundation grants to United Way ($30,000); foundation ($740,114) 1997: foundation grants to United Way ($500)
Assets: $3,406,949 (2001); $3,971,907 (2000); $4,496,146 (1999)
Gifts Received: $2,210,611 (1998); $1,500 (1996); $1,500 (1995)

Typical Recipients

Arts & Humanities: Dance, Arts & Humanities-General, History & Archaeology, Libraries, Museums/Galleries, Music, Opera, Public Broadcasting
Civic & Public Affairs: Clubs
Education: Arts/Humanities Education, Colleges & Universities, Engineering/Technological Education, Education-General, Minority Education, Private Education (Precollege), Religious Education, Science/Mathematics Education
Health: AIDS/HIV, Cancer, Clinics/Medical Centers, Diabetes, Emergency/Ambulance Services, Eyes/Blindness, Health-General, Hospitals, Long-Term Care, Medical Rehabilitation, Medical Research, Single-Disease Health Associations
International: Foreign Arts Organizations, International-General, Health Care/Hospitals, International Peace & Security Issues, International Relief Efforts, Missionary/Religious Activities
Religion: Religion-General, Jewish Causes, Ministries, Religious Organizations, Religious Welfare, Synagogues/Temples
Social Services: Child Welfare, Community Centers, Community Service Organizations, Counseling, Food/Clothing Distribution, Shelters/Homelessness, United Funds/United Ways, Youth Organizations

Application Procedures

Initial Contact: Send written request.
Deadlines: None.

Restrictions

Grants are not made to individuals or political or lobbying groups.

Foundation Officials

Beatrice Fischbach: secretary
Beatrice Levenson: secretary
Nancy Taubman: president
Selwyn Taubman: treasurer

Grants Analysis

Disclosure Period: calendar year ending 2001
Total Grants: $148,455
Number of Grants: 38
Average Grant: $3,066*
Highest Grant: $35,000
Lowest Grant: $250
Typical Range: $1,000 to $5,000
*Note: Average grant figure excludes highest grant.

Recent Grants

Note: Grants derived from 2001 Form 990.

General

35,000	Gilda's Club Westchester, Purchase, NY -- for informational film
11,200	Congregation Beth Shalom, Deep River, CT -- capital fund
10,000	Project ALS, Inc., New York, NY
9,814	Congregation Beth Shalom, Deep River, CT -- capital fund

5,650	UJA Federation, New York, NY
5,250	Gilda's Club Westchester, Purchase, NY
5,000	American Red Cross, Washington, DC
5,000	American Red Cross, Washington, DC -- for El Salvador earthquake
5,000	Rensselaer Polytechnic Institute, Troy, NY -- for travel grant
5,000	Rensselaer Polytechnic Institute, Troy, NY -- scholarship fund

SONJA AND F. CONRAD FISCHER FOUNDATION

Giving Contact

F. Conrad Fischer, Trustee
c/o William Blair & Co.
222 W. Adams
Chicago, IL 60606
Phone: (312)236-1600

Description

Founded: 1991
EIN: 366941059
Organization Type: Private Foundation
Grant Types: General Support.

Financial Summary

Total Giving: $83,200 (2000); $75,750 (1999); $51,600 (1996)
Giving Analysis: Giving for 2000 includes: foundation grants to United Way ($1,000) 1999: foundation grants to United Way ($1,000)
Assets: $1,942,043 (2000); $1,544,066 (1999); $661,767 (1996)
Gifts Received: $207,271 (2000); $130,000 (1999); $93,136 (1996). Note: In 1996, 1999 and 2000, contributions were received from Sonja and F. Conrad Fischer.

Typical Recipients

Arts & Humanities: Libraries, Museums/Galleries, Music, Theater
Civic & Public Affairs: Botanical Gardens/Parks, Community Foundations, Civic & Public Affairs-General, Zoos/Aquariums
Education: Colleges & Universities, Education Associations, Education Funds, Public Education (Precollege), Secondary Education (Private)
Environment: Resource Conservation
Religion: Religious Organizations, Religious Welfare
Science: Science Museums
Social Services: Child Welfare, Community Service Organizations, Day Care, People with Disabilities, Recreation & Athletics, United Funds/United Ways

Application Procedures

Initial Contact: Send grant proposal with statement of purpose.
Deadlines: November 15.

Foundation Officials

F. Conrad Fischer: trustee
Sonja Fischer: trustee

Grants Analysis

Disclosure Period: calendar year ending 2000
Total Grants: $82,200*
Number of Grants: 17
Average Grant: $1,229*
Highest Grant: $20,000
Typical Range: $1,000 to $2,000
*Note: Giving excludes United Way. Average grant excludes three highest grants ($65,000).

Recent Grants

Note: Grants derived from 2000 Form 990.

Library-Related
25,000	Newbury Library

General
20,000	Chicago Botanic Garden, Chicago, IL
20,000	Chicago Child Care Society, Chicago, IL
4,000	Court Theatre
3,000	California Fresh Harvest, CA
2,500	Link Unlimited, Chicago, IL
1,000	Child Care Center, Evanston, IL
1,000	Greater Miami Tennis Association, Miami, FL
1,000	Harvard College, Cambridge, MA
1,000	Hazleton, Hazelton, PA
1,000	Salvation Army

FISERVE

Company Headquarters
West Des Moines, IA

Company Description
Employees: 85

Trust Foundation

Giving Contact
Greg Bentley, Chairman
Trust Foundation
Regency West 7
4400 Westown Parkway
West Des Moines, IA 50266-6751
Phone: (515)224-8013
Fax: (515)224-8186

Description
Founded: 1988
EIN: 421313172
Organization Type: Corporate Foundation
Former Name: Fiserve Foundation.
Giving Locations: IA: Des Moines
Grant Types: General Support.

Donor Information
Founder: Financial Information Trust

Financial Summary
Total Giving: $15,642 (2000); $12,733 (1999); $14,431 (1998)
Giving Analysis: Giving for 1999 includes: foundation ($2,733)
Assets: $3,108 (2000); $4,443 (1999); $2,213 (1998)
Gifts Received: $13,708 (2000); $14,976 (1999); $10,356 (1998)

Typical Recipients
Arts & Humanities: Arts Associations & Councils, Arts Centers, Historic Preservation, Libraries, Public Broadcasting
Civic & Public Affairs: Clubs, Civic & Public Affairs-General, Parades/Festivals, Public Policy, Urban & Community Affairs
Education: Colleges & Universities, Secondary Education (Public)
Environment: Wildlife Protection
Health: Alzheimers Disease, Cancer, Children's Health/Hospitals, Diabetes, Emergency/Ambulance Services, Heart, Hospices, Multiple Sclerosis, Respiratory, Single-Disease Health Associations
Religion: Religious Organizations, Religious Welfare
Science: Observatories & Planetariums, Scientific Centers & Institutes
Social Services: Animal Protection, At-Risk Youth, Big Brother/Big Sister, Child Welfare, Community Centers, Community Service Organizations, Family Services, Family Services, Food/Clothing Distribution, People with Disabilities, Shelters/Homelessness, Special Olympics, YMCA/YWCA/YMHA/YWHA

Application Procedures
Initial Contact: Send a brief letter of inquiry.
Application Requirements: history of organization, financial data, and contact person.
Deadlines: None.

Restrictions
Grants are not made to individuals.

Foundation Officials
Peter A. Anderson: treasurer
Greg Bentley: director
Kim Katch: secretary
Steve Willis: director
Edie C. Winkelman: chairman

Grants Analysis
Disclosure Period: calendar year ending 2000
Total Grants: $15,642
Number of Grants: 37
Average Grant: $423
Highest Grant: $1,500
Typical Range: $200 to $700

Recent Grants

Note: Grants derived from 2002 Form 990.

General
1,500	Blank Children's Hospital Foundation, Des Moines, IA
1,480	Make A Wish Foundation, Chicago, IL
1,214	Foodbank of Iowa, IA
1,162	Hospice of Central Iowa, Des Moines, IA
1,000	Civic Center, Des Moines, IA
750	Family Enrichment Center
683	Ronald McDonald House, Missoula, MT
600	Children's Convalescent Home, Des Moines, IA
520	Amanda the Panda, Des Moines, IA
500	Iowa College Foundation, Des Moines, IA

RAY C. FISH FOUNDATION

Giving Contact
Barbara F. Daniel, President
2001 Kirby Dr., Suite 1005
Houston, TX 77019
Phone: (713)522-0741
Fax: (713)529-4033

Description
Founded: 1957
EIN: 746043047
Organization Type: General Purpose Foundation
Giving Locations: TX: Galveston, Houston including metropolitan area, Kerrville
Grant Types: Capital, Challenge, Endowment, General Support, Matching, Multiyear/Continuing Support, Operating Expenses, Project, Research, Scholarship, Seed Money.

Donor Information
Founder: The late Raymond Clinton Fish established the foundation in Texas in 1957, five years before his death. Mr. Fish was board chairman of the Fish Engineering Corporation and president and director of numerous gas pipeline and petrochemical firms. He helped create the Transcontinental Gas Pipeline System (Transco), the Pacific Northwest Pipeline System, and the Texas-Illinois Pipeline Company. His wife, Mirtha Galvez Fish , chaired the foundation prior to her death in 1967. Large portions of their estates went to benefit the foundation.

Financial Summary
Total Giving: $1,400,000 (fiscal year ending June 30, 2003 approx); $1,400,000 (fiscal 2002 approx); $1,470,640 (fiscal 2001)
Assets: $27,000,000 (fiscal 2003 approx); $27,000,000 (fiscal 2002 approx); $27,061,427 (fiscal 2000)
Gifts Received: $68,676 (fiscal 1999); $60,643 (fiscal 1995); $43,419 (fiscal 1994). Note: The foundation has received contributions from the Ray C. and Martha G. Fish Trust in Houston, TX.

Typical Recipients
Arts & Humanities: Arts Associations & Councils, Arts Centers, Ballet, Dance, Ethnic & Folk Arts, Film & Video, Arts & Humanities-General, Historic Preservation, History & Archaeology, Libraries, Museums/Galleries, Music, Opera, Performing Arts, Public Broadcasting, Theater
Civic & Public Affairs: Botanical Gardens/Parks, Business/Free Enterprise, Clubs, Economic Development, Economic Policy, Employment/Job Training, Civic & Public Affairs-General, Hispanic Affairs, Housing, Inner-City Development, Parades/Festivals, Philanthropic Organizations, Professional & Trade Associations, Public Policy, Urban & Community Affairs, Zoos/Aquariums
Education: Business Education, Colleges & Universities, Education Reform, Engineering/Technological Education, Environmental Education, Faculty Development, Education-General, Legal Education, Literacy, Medical Education, Minority Education, Preschool Education, Private Education (Precollege), Public Education (Precollege), Science/Mathematics Education, Secondary Education (Private), Social Sciences Education, Special Education, Student Aid
Environment: Energy, Environment-General, Resource Conservation
Health: Alzheimers Disease, Cancer, Clinics/Medical Centers, Emergency/Ambulance Services, Health Organizations, Heart, Hospices, Hospitals, Hospitals (University Affiliated), Kidney, Medical Rehabilitation, Medical Research, Research/Studies Institutes, Single-Disease Health Associations, Single-Disease Health Associations
International: Health Care/Hospitals, Missionary/Religious Activities
Religion: Churches, Jewish Causes, Ministries, Religious Organizations, Religious Welfare, Social/Policy Issues
Science: Science Museums
Social Services: At-Risk Youth, Camps, Child Abuse, Child Welfare, Community Centers, Community Service Organizations, Counseling, Emergency Relief, Family Planning, Food/Clothing Distribution, Homes, People with Disabilities, Recreation & Athletics, Scouts, Senior Services, United Funds/United Ways, Volunteer Services, YMCA/YWCA/YMHA/YWHA, Youth Organizations

Application Procedures
Initial Contact: Proposals should be submitted in writing.
Deadlines: None.
Review Process: The foundation will review the proposal and respond as quickly as possible. The board of trustees may request an interview and supplementary information.

Additional Information
Publications: Guidelines

Foundation Officials
Robert J. Cruikshank: vice president, assistant secretary, trustee CORP AFFIL director: Reliant Energy Inc.; director: Texas Biotechnology Corp.; director:

MAXXAM Inc.; director: Kaiser Aluminum Corp.; director: KLU; director: Kaiser Aluminum & Chemical Corp.
Barbara Fish Daniel: president, trustee B 1935. PRIM CORP EMPL vice president: M.J. Daniel Co. Inc.
Christopher J. Daniel: vice president, treasurer, trustee
James L. Daniel, Jr.: vice president, trustee
Paula Hooton: executive administrator

Grants Analysis

Disclosure Period: fiscal year ending June 30, 2001
Total Grants: $1,470,640
Number of Grants: 168
Average Grant: $8,013*
Highest Grant: $132,500
Lowest Grant: $1,000
Typical Range: $1,000 to $25,000
***Note:** Average grant excludes highest grant.

HARMES C. FISHBACK FOUNDATION TRUST

Giving Contact

Katharine H. Stapleton, Trustee
8 Village Rd.
Englewood, CO 80110-4908
Phone: (303)789-1753

Description

Founded: 1972
EIN: 846094542
Organization Type: Private Foundation
Giving Locations: CO: Denver including metropolitan area
Grant Types: Endowment, Multiyear/Continuing Support, Scholarship.

Donor Information

Founder: the late Harmes C. Fishback

Financial Summary

Total Giving: $142,930 (2000); $182,960 (1999); $117,750 (1998)
Assets: $4,070,231 (2000); $3,870,079 (1999); $3,673,666 (1998)

Typical Recipients

Arts & Humanities: Arts Centers, Community Arts, Ethnic & Folk Arts, Historic Preservation, History & Archaeology, Libraries, Museums/Galleries, Music, Opera, Performing Arts, Theater
Civic & Public Affairs: Botanical Gardens/Parks, Economic Development, Civic & Public Affairs-General, Legal Aid, Public Policy, Urban & Community Affairs, Zoos/Aquariums
Education: Colleges & Universities, Continuing Education, Education-General, Gifted & Talented Programs, International Studies, Leadership Training, Private Education (Precollege), Student Aid
Environment: Environment-General
Health: AIDS/HIV, Arthritis, Cancer, Diabetes, Health-General, Health Organizations, Hospices, Hospices, Hospitals, Hospitals (University Affiliated), Medical Rehabilitation, Medical Research, Mental Health, Respiratory, Transplant Networks/Donor Banks
Religion: Churches, Dioceses, Religious Welfare
Science: Science Museums
Social Services: Child Welfare, Community Service Organizations, Day Care, Family Planning, Family Services, Food/Clothing Distribution, People with Disabilities, Senior Services, Social Services-General, United Funds/United Ways, YMCA/YWCA/YMHA/YWHA, Youth Organizations

Application Procedures

Initial Contact: Send brief letter describing program.
Deadlines: None.

Restrictions

Does not support individuals.

Foundation Officials

Katharine H. Stapleton: trustee

Grants Analysis

Disclosure Period: calendar year ending 2000
Total Grants: $142,930
Number of Grants: 40
Average Grant: $3,573
Highest Grant: $15,200
Typical Range: $1,000 to $5,000

Recent Grants

Note: Grants derived from 2000 Form 990.

General

15,200	Deb Ball County Symphony, Denver, CO
15,000	Children's Diabetes Foundation, Denver, CO
10,000	Denver University, Denver, CO
10,000	Dioceses of Colorado, Denver, CO
9,000	St. Joseph's Hospital, Denver, CO
7,500	Denver Art Museum, Denver, CO
5,500	Institute of Limb Repair, Denver, CO
5,000	Christ Episcopal Church, Denver, CO
5,000	Hospice of St. John, Lakewood, CO
5,000	Museum of Contemporary Art, Denver, CO

FISHER FOUNDATION

Giving Contact

Hinda N. Fischer, President & Treasurer
36 Brookside Boulevard
West Hartford, CT 06107
Phone: (860)232-2755

Description

Founded: 1959
EIN: 066039415
Organization Type: Private Foundation
Giving Locations: CT: Hartford including surrounding area
Grant Types: General Support.

Donor Information

Founder: Stanley D. Fisher Trust, FIP Corp.

Financial Summary

Total Giving: $397,100 (2000); $481,889 (1998); $449,185 (1997). Note: 1996 Giving includes scholarship (6,000); United Way ($2,000).
Giving Analysis: Giving for 2000 includes: foundation grants to United Way ($3,000) 1997: foundation grants to United Way ($3,000)
Assets: $9,913,525 (2000); $15,581 (1998); $38,259 (1997)
Gifts Received: $494,482 (1998); $460,100 (1997); $405,043 (1996). Note: In 1997 and 1998, contributions were received from the Stanley D. Fisher Trust. In 1995, contributions were received from the Stanley D. Fisher Trust.

Typical Recipients

Arts & Humanities: Arts Associations & Councils, Arts Centers, Ballet, Dance, Historic Preservation, Libraries, Literary Arts, Museums/Galleries, Music, Performing Arts, Public Broadcasting, Theater
Civic & Public Affairs: Botanical Gardens/Parks, Business/Free Enterprise, Community Foundations, Economic Development, Employment/Job Training,

Civic & Public Affairs-General, Hispanic Affairs, Housing, Municipalities/Towns, Nonprofit Management, Urban & Community Affairs, Women's Affairs
Education: Arts/Humanities Education, Colleges & Universities, Education Associations, Education Reform, Education-General, Literacy, Medical Education, Minority Education, Public Education (Precollege), Science/Mathematics Education, Special Education, Student Aid
Health: AIDS/HIV, Children's Health/Hospitals, Clinics/Medical Centers, Eyes/Blindness, Health Organizations, Home-Care Services, Hospices, Hospitals, Long-Term Care, Medical Rehabilitation, Mental Health, Multiple Sclerosis, Nursing Services, Public Health, Speech & Hearing
International: Human Rights, International Relief Efforts
Religion: Churches, Jewish Causes, Religious Organizations, Religious Welfare
Science: Scientific Centers & Institutes
Social Services: At-Risk Youth, Camps, Child Welfare, Community Centers, Community Service Organizations, Counseling, Day Care, Domestic Violence, Emergency Relief, Family Planning, Family Services, Food/Clothing Distribution, Homes, People with Disabilities, Recreation & Athletics, Senior Services, Shelters/Homelessness, Substance Abuse, United Funds/United Ways, YMCA/YWCA/YMHA/YWHA, Youth Organizations

Application Procedures

Initial Contact: The foundation has no formal grant application procedure or application form. Send a brief letter of inquiry.
Deadlines: None.

Foundation Officials

Diane Fisher Bell: vice president
Beverly Boyle: executive director
Michael Finkelstein: assistant treasurer
Hinda N. Fisher: president, treasurer
Nancy S. Freeman: secretary
Martha Newman: executive director
Lois Fisher Ruge: vice president

Grants Analysis

Disclosure Period: calendar year ending 2000
Total Grants: $397,100
Number of Grants: 80
Average Grant: $4,926
Highest Grant: $20,000
Typical Range: $1,000 to $10,000

Recent Grants

Note: Grants derived from 2000 Form 990.

General

20,000	Action in Education
14,000	Greater Hartford Interracial Scholarship, Hartford, CT
10,000	Bell School Reform Network, McLean, VA
10,000	Boundless Playgrounds, Inc
10,000	Camp Courant, Hartford, CT
10,000	Center City Churches, Hartford, CT
10,000	Children in Placement, Hartford, CT
10,000	Co-op Initiatives, Hartford, CT
10,000	Coon College, Coon Rapid, MN
10,000	CPEP

FLEETBOSTON FINANCIAL CORP.

Company Headquarters

100 Hundred Federal Street
Boston, MA 02110
Phone: (617)434-2629
Fax: (617)434-6072
Web: http://www.fleet.com

Company Description

Founded: 1999
Ticker: FBF
Exchange: NYSE
Former Name: Shawmut National Corp.; Fleet Bank of New York (1999); Fleet Financial Group (1999);
Formed by Merger of: BankBoston Corp. (1999).
Assets: US$190.453 billion (2002)
Profit: US$1.188 billion (2002)
Employees: 50000 (2002)
Fortune Rank: 115, per FORTUNE Magazine's list of 500 Largest U.S. Corporations (2002).
SIC(s): 6021 National Commercial Banks, 6712 Bank Holding Companies.

Operating Locations

AFSA Data Corp. (CA--Long Beach); BancBoston Capital (MA--Boston); Columbia Management Co. (OR--Portland); Fleet Bank, NA (NJ--Jersey City); Fleet Capital (CT--Glastonbury); Fleet Capital Leasing (RI--Providence); Fleet Credit Card Services, LP (PA--Horsham); Fleet Investment Advisors, Inc. (MA--Boston); Fleet Investment Services, Inc. (MA--Boston); Fleet Mortgage Group, Inc. (SC--Columbia); Fleet National Bank (MA--Boston); Fleet Private Equity (RI--Providence); Quick & Reilly/Fleet Securities, Inc. (NY--New York); Robertson Stephens (CA--San Francisco)

Nonmonetary Support

Type: Donated Equipment; Loaned Employees
Contact: Ronda Jackson, Senior Manager

FleetBoston Financial Foundation

Giving Contact

Gail Snowdon, President
100 Hundred Federal Street
Boston, MA 02110
Phone: (617)434-2629
Fax: (617)434-6072
Web: http://www.fleet.com

Description

Organization Type: Corporate Foundation
Giving Locations: CT; FL: in limited areas; ME; MA; NH; NJ; NY; RI
Grant Types: Employee Matching Gifts, Project, Seed Money.
Note: Matching gifts are restricted to higher education. Company also provides program support.

Financial Summary

Total Giving: $25,000,000 (2000 approx)

Typical Recipients

Arts & Humanities: Arts Associations & Councils, Arts Centers, Arts Funds, Arts Institutes, Community Arts, Dance, Ethnic & Folk Arts, Historic Preservation, History & Archaeology, Libraries, Museums/Galleries, Music, Opera, Performing Arts, Public Broadcasting, Theater, Visual Arts
Civic & Public Affairs: African American Affairs, Asian American Affairs, Business/Free Enterprise, Chambers of Commerce, Civil Rights, Economic Development, Economic Policy, Employment/Job Training, Civic & Public Affairs-General, Hispanic Affairs, Housing, Law & Justice, Native American Affairs, Nonprofit Management, Philanthropic Organizations, Public Policy, Safety, Urban & Community Affairs, Women's Affairs, Zoos/Aquariums
Education: Arts/Humanities Education, Business Education, Colleges & Universities, Community & Junior Colleges, Continuing Education, Economic Education, Education Associations, Engineering/Technological Education, Education-General, Health & Physical Education, Literacy, Minority Education,

Preschool Education, Public Education (Precollege), Social Sciences Education
Environment: Environment-General
Health: AIDS/HIV, Children's Health/Hospitals, Clinics/Medical Centers, Emergency/Ambulance Services, Heart, Hospices, Hospitals, Hospitals (University Affiliated), Medical Research, Nutrition, Prenatal Health Issues
Social Services: At-Risk Youth, Child Welfare, Community Centers, Community Service Organizations, Counseling, Day Care, Delinquency & Criminal Rehabilitation, Domestic Violence, Family Planning, Family Services, Food/Clothing Distribution, Homes, People with Disabilities, Recreation & Athletics, Refugee Assistance, Senior Services, Shelters/Homelessness, Substance Abuse, United Funds/United Ways, Volunteer Services, YMCA/YWCA/YMHA/YWHA, Youth Organizations

Application Procedures

Initial Contact: Submit a grant request in writing.
Application Requirements: Include a cover letter on the requesting organization's stationery that states the amount requested and the purpose of the grant, and clearly indicate the name and telephone number of the contact person; brief descriptions of the organization's purpose, history, and accomplishments; financial statements (audited if available) for the most recently completed fiscal year; most recent Form 990 (the combined federal and state charitable report); the current year's operating budget and next year's proposed budget for the organization and the specific project to be funded; a list of corporations and foundations that support the organization and the most recent amounts given; IRS determination letter of 501(c)(3) status and proof that the organization is not a private foundation under section 509(a) of the IRS Code; written agreement with the fiscal agent and a copy of its 501(c)(3), if a fiscal agent is to be used; names and affiliations of the board of directors; and a report on the last grant received from FleetBoston Financial Foundation or any of its legacy institutions, Fleet Financial Group or BankBoston.
Deadlines: None; proposals are accepted throughout the calendar year.
Review Process: Requests are reviewed quarterly by review committees.
Evaluative Criteria: The foundation prefers to fund new and innovative programs that promote positive, enduring social change and seek long-term solutions to economic and social problems.
Notes: The foundation accepts the Associated Grantmakers of Massachusetts Common Proposal Format.

Restrictions

Does not support individuals, national medical foundations, or political, religious, or fraternal organizations.

Additional Information

In October 1999, Fleet Financial Group, Inc. and BankBoston Corp. merged. The resulting company, FleetBoston Financial Corp., established the FleetBoston Financial Foundation.
Requests for grants and event support in Massachusetts should be sent to:
Grants Administrator, FleetBoston Financial Foundation, Mailstop: MA BOS 01-28-05, PO Box 2016, Boston, MA 02106 (617) 434-2804
Requests for all other regions should be addressed to: Community Relations Manager, FleetBoston Financial
Connecticut: Mailstop CT/MO/0395, 777 Main Street, Hartford, CT, 06115, (860) 986-5322
Rhode Island: Mailstop RI/MO/M18B, 111 Westminster Street, Providence, RI, 02903, (401) 278-6240
New Hampshire: Mailstop NH/NA/EO3A, 1155 Elm Street, Manchester, NH 03101 (603) 647,7611
Maine: Mailstop ME/PM/PO5B, 2 Portland Square, Portland, ME 04104, (207) 874-5102

NY - New York City/Westchester County: Mailstop NY/NY/A39B, 1133 Avenue of the Americas, 39th Floor, New York, NY 10036 (212) 703-1663
NY - Long Island: Mailstop NY/LI/MO3A, 300 Broad Hollow Road, Melville, NY 11747 (631) 547-7489
NY - Albany/Hudson Valley: Mailstop NY/KP/0302, Peter D. Kiernan Plaza, Albany, NY 12207 (518) 447-6145
NY - Buffalo/Rochester: Mailstop NY/FP/1000, 10 Fountain Plaza, 9th Floor, Buffalo, NY 14202 (716) 847-7245
NY Syracuse/Utica: Mailstop NY/SY/0495, One Clinton Square, Syracuse, NY 13202 (315) 426-4184
New Jersey: Mailstop NJ/SP/W03G, 1125 Route 22W, Bridgewater, NJ 08807 (908) 253-4570
Pennsylvania: Mailstop PA/SC/SO4G, One Fleet Way, Scranton, PA 18507 (570) 330-3708

Recent Grants

General
2,345   Fleet Charitable Trust

FLEISHHACKER FOUNDATION

Giving Contact

Christine Elbel, Executive Director
1016 Lincoln Blvd., No. 12
San Francisco, CA 94129
Phone: (415)561-5350
E-mail: info@fleishhackerfoundation.org
Web: http://www.fleishhackerfoundation.org

Description

Founded: 1947
EIN: 946051048
Organization Type: Private Foundation
Giving Locations: CA: San Francisco including Bay area; NY: New York
Grant Types: Capital, General Support, Project, Seed Money.

Donor Information

Founder: the late Mortimer Fleishhacker, Sr., Janet Fleishhacker Bates

Financial Summary

Total Giving: $111,000 (2002 approx); $600,700 (2001); $695,750 (2000)
Giving Analysis: Giving for 2001 includes: foundation gifts to individuals ($3,000); foundation grants to United Way ($54,200); 2000: foundation grants to United Way ($3,000) foundation fellowships ($70,917)
Assets: $13,354,633 (2001); $12,881,822 (2000); $11,419,788 (1998)
Gifts Received: $55,000 (1992). Note: In fiscal 1992, contributions were received from the Walter and Elise Haas Fund ($50,000) and Grants for the Arts ($5,000).

Typical Recipients

Arts & Humanities: Arts Appreciation, Arts Associations & Councils, Arts Centers, Arts Festivals, Arts Funds, Arts Institutes, Arts Outreach, Ballet, Community Arts, Dance, Ethnic & Folk Arts, Film & Video, Arts & Humanities-General, Historic Preservation, Libraries, Museums/Galleries, Music, Opera, Performing Arts, Theater
Civic & Public Affairs: Civic & Public Affairs-General, Nonprofit Management, Public Policy, Urban & Community Affairs, Zoos/Aquariums
Education: Arts/Humanities Education, Colleges & Universities, Education Reform, Faculty Development, Education-General, Literacy, Minority Education, Private Education (Precollege), Public Education (Precollege), School Volunteerism, Science/Mathematics Education, Secondary Education (Public), Social Sciences Education

Social Services: Family Services, United Funds/ United Ways

Application Procedures

Initial Contact: For grants, send a short letter proposal (2-6 pages) outlining the need for funding, how funds will be used, and the impact on the program's beneficiaries, and a summary of the financial parameters of the program.
Deadlines: January 15 and July 15.
Decision Notification: Decisions are made within two to five months.
Notes: Primarily supports preselected organizations.

Restrictions

Foundation supports arts and culture and precollegiate education in the greater Bay area. Does not provide funds for annual campaigns, deficit financing, matching gifts, financial aid, scholarships, or special events.

Additional Information

Publications: Application Guidelines

Foundation Officials

Delia Fleishhacker Ehrlich: director
Jodi Ehrlich: director
John Stephen Ehrlich, Jr.: vice president
Christine Elbel: executive director
David Fleishhacker: president B San Francisco, CA 1937. ED Princeton University AB (1959); University of California MA (1965). PRIM CORP EMPL president: Fleishhacker Foundation. NONPR AFFIL member: National Association Prin Girls Schools; director: Saint Josephs Hospital Queen Angels; member: Elementary School Heads Association.
Edie Fleishhacker: director
Mortimer Fleishhacker, III: treasurer
William Fleishhacker: director
Lois Gordon: director
Deborah Sloss Kelman: director
Sandra Fleishhacker Randall: director
Hillary Sloss: director
Laura Sloss: director

Grants Analysis

Disclosure Period: calendar year ending 2001
Total Grants: $543,500*
Number of Grants: 78
Average Grant: $6,968
Highest Grant: $50,000
Typical Range: $1,000 to $15,000
***Note:** Giving excludes United Way and gifts to individuals.

Recent Grants

Note: Grants derived from 2001 Form 990.

General

50,000	9th Street Media Consortium, San Francisco, CA -- capital campaign
32,500	Fine Arts Museum of San Francisco, San Francisco, CA -- capital campaign
25,000	Sonoma Valley Museum of Art, Sonoma, CA -- exhibit support
22,500	Intersection for the Arts, San Francisco, CA -- monthly jazz series
15,000	Earth Island Institute, San Francisco, CA -- annual prize for youth
15,000	Reading Tree, San Francisco, CA -- Book Giveaway Program
15,000	San Francisco Zoo, San Francisco, CA -- capital campaign
15,000	San Jose Repertory Theatre, San Jose, CA -- Playwright Festival
12,000	Hamlin School, San Francisco, CA -- capital campaign
11,000	Northern California Grantmakers, San Francisco, CA -- Summer Youth Project

ROBERT FLEMING AND JANE HOWE PATRICK FOUNDATION

Giving Contact

Adam B. Dantzscher, Executive Director
PO Box 234
Charlotte, VT 05445
Phone: (802)660-9447

Description

Founded: 1989
EIN: 030317962
Organization Type: Private Foundation
Giving Locations: VT
Grant Types: General Support.

Financial Summary

Total Giving: $87,830 (fiscal year ending June 30, 2001); $58,033 (fiscal 2000); $89,643 (fiscal 1999)
Assets: $1,976,128 (fiscal 2001); $1,831,320 (fiscal 2000); $2,023,227 (fiscal 1999)

Typical Recipients

Arts & Humanities: History & Archaeology, Libraries, Museums/Galleries, Performing Arts, Public Broadcasting
Civic & Public Affairs: Economic Development, Employment/Job Training, Civic & Public Affairs-General, Housing, Safety, Urban & Community Affairs, Women's Affairs
Education: Colleges & Universities, Education-General, Literacy, Social Sciences Education
Health: AIDS/HIV, Clinics/Medical Centers, Health Organizations, Heart, Hospices, Multiple Sclerosis, Single-Disease Health Associations
Religion: Churches
Social Services: Animal Protection, Child Abuse, Community Service Organizations, Domestic Violence, Emergency Relief, Family Planning, Food/Clothing Distribution, Homes, People with Disabilities, Shelters/Homelessness, YMCA/YWCA/YMHA/YWHA, Youth Organizations

Application Procedures

Initial Contact: Send a brief letter of inquiry.
Application Requirements: Include a description of organization and purpose of funds sought.
Deadlines: None.

Restrictions

Giving is limited to Vermont organizations.

Foundation Officials

Richard Cunningham: vice president, director
Adam B. Dantzscher: executive director
C. Dennis Hill: director
Harriet S. Patrick: president, director
Glen A. Wright: director

Grants Analysis

Disclosure Period: fiscal year ending June 30, 2001
Total Grants: $87,830
Number of Grants: 21
Average Grant: $3,142*
Highest Grant: $25,000
Lowest Grant: $1,000
Typical Range: $1,000 to $5,000
***Note:** Average grant figure excludes highest grant.

Recent Grants

Note: Grants derived from fiscal 2000 Form 990.

Library-Related

2,500	Brown Public Library, Northfield, VT

General

12,700	Burlington College, Burlington, VT
5,000	Flynn Theater, Burlington, VT
5,000	Vermont Foodbank, South Barre, VT -- operating support
5,000	Vermont Lions Charities, South Strafford, VT
3,500	Northern New England Tradeswomen, Barre, VT
3,333	Vermont Association for Blind and Visually Impaired, Burlington, VT
3,000	Vermont Museum and Gallery Alliance, Shelburne, VT -- operating support
2,500	Women Helping Battered Women, Burlington, VT
2,000	Vermont Foodbank, Barre, VT
2,000	Vermont Historical Society, Montpelier, VT

FLEMING FOUNDATION

Giving Contact

G. Malcolm Louden, CPA
500 W. 7th St., Suite 1007
Ft. Worth, TX 76102-4732
Phone: (817)335-3741
Fax: (817)338-4844

Description

Founded: 1936
EIN: 756022736
Organization Type: Family Foundation
Giving Locations: TX: Fort Worth including Tarrant County
Grant Types: Capital, General Support, Operating Expenses.

Donor Information

Founder: The late William Fleming, an oilman and philanthropist, established th Fleming Foundation in Texas in 1936. Mr. Fleming was interested in Baptist churches and schools.

Financial Summary

Total Giving: $546,500 (2001); $565,500 (2000); $214,450 (1999)
Giving Analysis: Giving for 1998 includes: foundation grants to United Way ($4,000); foundation ($1,258,450) 1997: foundation grants to United Way ($8,000)
Assets: $2,582,634 (2001); $2,796,015 (2000); $2,849,630 (1999)
Gifts Received: $1,000,000 (1997 approx); $1,000,000 (1996 approx); $665,000 (1995 approx)

Typical Recipients

Arts & Humanities: Arts Associations & Councils, Arts Centers, Arts Festivals, Ballet, Community Arts, Dance, History & Archaeology, Libraries, Museums/Galleries, Music, Opera, Performing Arts, Theater
Civic & Public Affairs: Botanical Gardens/Parks, Clubs, Economic Development, Civic & Public Affairs-General, Hispanic Affairs, Parades/Festivals, Philanthropic Organizations, Rural Affairs, Safety, Urban & Community Affairs, Women's Affairs, Zoos/Aquariums
Education: Colleges & Universities, Education Associations, Education Funds, Education-General, Private Education (Precollege), School Volunteerism, Special Education
Environment: Environment-General, Wildlife Protection
Health: AIDS/HIV, Alzheimers Disease, Cancer, Children's Health/Hospitals, Clinics/Medical Centers, Eyes/Blindness, Health Organizations, Heart, Hospitals, Medical Rehabilitation, Mental Health, Research/Studies Institutes, Single-Disease Health Associations

International: Foreign Educational Institutions, International Affairs, International Development, International Relief Efforts

Religion: Bible Study/Translation, Churches, Religion-General, Jewish Causes, Religious Welfare

Science: Science Museums

Social Services: Big Brother/Big Sister, Child Welfare, Community Centers, Community Service Organizations, Counseling, Crime Prevention, Family Planning, Family Services, Food/Clothing Distribution, Homes, People with Disabilities, Recreation & Athletics, Scouts, Shelters/Homelessness, Social Services-General, Substance Abuse, United Funds/United Ways, YMCA/YWCA/YMHA/YWHA, Youth Organizations

Application Procedures

Initial Contact: Applicants should submit a written proposal outlining intended use of funds.
Deadlines: None.
Review Process: The board of directors meets in January, April, July, and September.

Restrictions

The foundation does not give grants to individuals, or for capital or endowment funds, deficit financing, matching gifts, fellowships, scholarships, land acquisition, exchange programs, conferences, or publications.

Gives only to local organizations.

Additional Information

The foundation reports that it is closely affiliated with the Walsh Foundation, Ft. Worth, TX. The two foundations share many of the same officers and directors.

Foundation Officials

Gary F. Goble: assistant treasurer PRIM CORP EMPL secretary, treasurer, director: Walsh & Watts Inc.

G. Malcolm Louden: treasurer, secretary, general manager B 1945. ED Texas Christian University BBA (1969). PRIM CORP EMPL vice president, director: Walsh & Watts Inc. CORP AFFIL director: Overton Bank & Trust National Association; executive vice president, director: F Howard Walsh Jr Oper Co.; director: Overton Bancshares Inc.

F. Howard Walsh, Jr.: trustee B 1941. ED Texas Christian University BA (1963). PRIM CORP EMPL president, director: F Howard Walsh Jr Oper Co. ADD CORP EMPL owner: Walsh Oil Co.

Mary D. Fleming Walsh: president, trustee B Whitewright, TX October 29, 1913. ED Southern Methodist University BA (1934). CORP AFFIL partner: Walsh Co. NONPR AFFIL honorary director: Van Cliburn International Piano Competition; life member: YWCA; member: Texas League Composers; member: Texas Boys Club Auxilliary; member: Texas Christian University Fine Arts Foundation Guild; guarantor: Texas Boys Choir; charter member: Lloyd Shaw Foundation; member: Tarrant County Auxiliary Edna Gladney Home; guarantor: Scholar Cantorum; member: Rae Reimers Bible Study; member: Round Table International; member: National Association Cowbelles; member: Opera Guild; member: Jewel Charity Ball; member: Friends Texas Boys Choir; member: Goodwill Industries Auxiliary; guarantor: Fort Worth Theatre; guarantor: Fort Worth Opera Association; member: Fort Worth Pan Hellenic; member: Fort Worth Childrens Hospital; member: Fort Worth Ballet Association; member: Fort Worth Boys Club; guarantor, member: Fort Worth Art Council; guarantor, member: Fort Worth Ballet; member: Fort Worth Art Association; member: Childrens Hospital Women's Board; member: Colorado Springs Fine Arts Center; member: Child Study Center; member: Chi Omega Carousel; member: Chi Omega Mothers; member: Chi Omega; member: American Guild Organists; member: Big Brothers Tarrant County; member: American Automobile Association; co-founder:

American Field Service Fort Worth; member: American Association University Women. CLUB AFFIL Women's Club; Texas Christian University Women's Club; Ridglea Country Club; Shady Oaks Country Club; Garden of Gods Club; Colonial Country Club; Colorado Springs Country Club.

Grants Analysis

Disclosure Period: calendar year ending 2001
Total Grants: $546,500
Number of Grants: 15
Average Grant: $958*
Highest Grant: $210,000
Lowest Grant: $500
Typical Range: $500 to $1,000
*Note: Average grant figure excludes three highest grants ($535,000).

Recent Grants

Note: Grants derived from 2001 Form 990.

General

295,000	Dorothy Shaw Bell Choir, Ft. Worth, TX
210,000	Littlest Wiseman, Ft. Worth, TX
30,000	Texas Christian University, Ft. Worth, TX
2,500	Sister Cities, Ft. Worth, TX
1,000	Boys Scouts of America, Wichita Falls, TX
1,000	House of Prayer, Ft. Worth, TX
1,000	Interfaith Ministries, Wichita Falls, TX
1,000	Salvation Army, Wichita Falls, TX
1,000	Texas Rehab Center, Wichita Falls, TX
1,000	Wichita Falls Faith Mission, Inc., Wichita Falls, TX

FLETCHER FOUNDATION

Giving Contact

Warner S. Fletcher, Secretary, Treasurer & Trustee
370 Main St., 12th Fl.
Worcester, MA 01608
Phone: (508)798-8621
Fax: (508)791-1201
E-mail: wfletcher@ftwlaw.com

Description

Founded: 1981
EIN: 046470890
Organization Type: Private Foundation
Giving Locations: MA: Worcester
Grant Types: General Support.

Donor Information

Founder: the late Paris Fletcher

Financial Summary

Total Giving: $1,663,500 (1999); $1,382,500 (1998); $1,416,000 (1997)
Giving Analysis: Giving for 1999 includes: foundation grants to United Way ($20,000)
Assets: $31,882,373 (1999); $28,257,726 (1997); $26,583,360 (1996)
Gifts Received: $2,059,813 (1999); $176,612 (1995); $93,765 (1994). Note: In 1999, contributions were received from Warner S. Fletcher ($498,094), Patricia A. Fletcher ($1,082,813), and Allen W. Fletcher ($478,906). In 1995, contributions were received from the estate of Marion S. Fletcher.

Typical Recipients

Arts & Humanities: Arts Associations & Councils, Arts Festivals, Community Arts, Ethnic & Folk Arts, Historic Preservation, History & Archaeology, Libraries, Museums/Galleries, Music, Public Broadcasting, Theater

Civic & Public Affairs: Clubs, Community Foundations, Economic Development, Civic & Public Affairs-General, Hispanic Affairs, Housing, Law & Justice,

Legal Aid, Municipalities/Towns, Urban & Community Affairs, Women's Affairs

Education: Colleges & Universities, Education Associations, Education Funds, Education Reform, Education-General, Literacy, Medical Education, Private Education (Precollege), Science/Mathematics Education

Environment: Environment-General, Resource Conservation, Wildlife Protection

Health: Cancer, Children's Health/Hospitals, Clinics/Medical Centers, Diabetes, Emergency/Ambulance Services, Health Organizations, Medical Research, Nursing Services, Public Health

Science: Science Museums

Social Services: Animal Protection, At-Risk Youth, Child Welfare, Community Centers, Community Service Organizations, Counseling, Crime Prevention, Day Care, Family Planning, Homes, Senior Services, Shelters/Homelessness, Substance Abuse, United Funds/United Ways, YMCA/YWCA/YMHA/YWHA, Youth Organizations

Application Procedures

Initial Contact: Send brief letter describing program.
Application Requirements: Include proof of tax-exempt status.
Deadlines: None.

Restrictions

Must be listed in federal cumulative listings.

Foundation Officials

Allen W. Fletcher: chairman, trustee B 1948. PRIM CORP EMPL chairman, treasurer: Worcester Publishing Inc. CORP AFFIL chairman, treasurer: Worcester Business Journal; chairman, treasurer: Worcester Magazine; chairman, treasurer: Hartford Business Journal.

Mary F. Fletcher: trustee

Nina M. Fletcher: trustee

Patricia A. Fletcher: trustee

Warner S. Fletcher: secretary, treasurer, trustee B Worcester, MA 1945. ED Williams College BA (1967); Boston University JD (1973). PRIM CORP EMPL treasurer: Fletcher, Tilton & Whipple PC. CORP AFFIL director: Wyman-Gordon Co.

Elisabeth Rice: executive director

Grants Analysis

Disclosure Period: calendar year ending 1999
Total Grants: $1,643,500*
Number of Grants: 74
Average Grant: $20,049*
Highest Grant: $200,000
Typical Range: $1,000 to $50,000
*Note: Giving excludes United Way. Average grant excludes highest grant.

Recent Grants

Note: Grants derived from 1999 Form 990.

General

200,000	Worcester Art Museum, Worcester, MA -- toward handicapped access and visitor amenities
130,000	Greater Worcester Community Foundation, Inc., Worcester, MA -- for scholarship fund
125,000	Clark University, Worcester, MA -- toward funding an educational endowment program
100,000	Great Brook Valley Health Center, Inc., Worcester, MA -- for expansion
100,000	New England Science Center, Worcester, MA -- towards new otter habitat
100,000	Worcester County Mechanics Association, Worcester, MA -- towards 20th anniversary campaign renovations and endowment
50,000	Elm Park Center for Early Childhood Development, Worcester, MA -- towards

50,000	costs of new Burncoat Street Daycare facility
50,000	Great Brook Valley Health Center, Inc., Worcester, MA -- towards computers and equipment
40,000	Massachusetts College of Pharmacy and Allied Health Sciences, Boston, MA -- towards new facility in downtown Worcester
37,500	Guild of Saint Agnes Day Care Programs, Worcester, MA -- to support expansion of child care facilities

FLORIDA ROCK INDUSTRIES, INC.

Company Headquarters
127 Edgewood Ave., S
Jacksonville, FL 32254
Web: http://www.flarock.com

Company Description
Founded: 1945
Ticker: FRK
Exchange: NYSE
Revenue: US$723.7 million (2002)
Employees: 3092 (2002)
SIC(s): 1442 Construction Sand & Gravel, 3271 Concrete Block & Brick, 3273 Ready-Mixed Concrete.

Operating Locations
Florida Rock Industries (FL--Jacksonville)

Florida Rock Industries Foundation

Giving Contact
John D. Milton, Jr., Secretary
PO Box 4667
Jacksonville, FL 32201
Phone: (904)355-1781
Fax: (904)366-1866

Description
EIN: 592143326
Organization Type: Corporate Foundation
Giving Locations: FL
Grant Types: General Support.

Financial Summary
Total Giving: $315,251 (fiscal year ending September 30, 2001); $276,900 (fiscal 1999); $278,538 (fiscal 1998)
Giving Analysis: Giving for fiscal 2001 includes: foundation scholarships ($5,000); foundation grants to United Way ($41,500); foundation ($268,751); fiscal 1999: foundation grants to United Way ($22,400); foundation scholarships ($74,000); foundation ($180,500); fiscal 1998: foundation scholarships ($12,000); foundation grants to United Way ($31,600) foundation ($234,938)
Assets: $3,005,089 (fiscal 2001); $2,731,444 (fiscal 1999); $2,429,155 (fiscal 1998)
Gifts Received: $500,000 (fiscal 2001); $250,000 (fiscal 1999); $250,000 (fiscal 1998). Note: Contributions are received from Florida Rock Industries.

Typical Recipients
Arts & Humanities: Arts Associations & Councils, Historic Preservation, History & Archaeology, Libraries, Museums/Galleries, Music, Opera, Performing Arts, Public Broadcasting, Theater
Civic & Public Affairs: African American Affairs, Botanical Gardens/Parks, Community Foundations, Employment/Job Training, Civic & Public Affairs-General,

Public Policy, Urban & Community Affairs, Zoos/Aquariums
Education: Business Education, Colleges & Universities, Community & Junior Colleges, Continuing Education, Education Associations, Education-General, Minority Education, Public Education (Precollege), Student Aid, Vocational & Technical Education
Environment: Environment-General, Resource Conservation
Health: Alzheimers Disease, Cancer, Children's Health/Hospitals, Clinics/Medical Centers, Geriatric Health, Health Organizations, Medical Research, Multiple Sclerosis, Single-Disease Health Associations
International: Health Care/Hospitals, International Environmental Issues
Religion: Churches, Dioceses, Jewish Causes, Ministries, Religious Organizations, Religious Welfare
Science: Science Museums
Social Services: Animal Protection, At-Risk Youth, Camps, Child Welfare, Community Centers, Community Service Organizations, Family Planning, Family Services, Homes, People with Disabilities, Recreation & Athletics, Scouts, Senior Services, Shelters/Homelessness, United Funds/United Ways, YMCA/YWCA/YMHA/YWHA, Youth Organizations

Application Procedures
Initial Contact: Send brief letter describing program.
Application Requirements: Include recently audited financial statement, description of benefits or services provided, list of board members and leading contributors with amounts, whether activities qualify for "Community Contributions Tax Credit" under the Florida Corporation Tax Act, whether contributions will be for capital or operating funds, and proof of tax-exempt status.
Deadlines: None.

Corporate Officials
Edward L. Baker: chairman, director B 1935. PRIM CORP EMPL chairman, director: Florida Rock Industries. CORP AFFIL chairman, director: FRP Properties; director: Virginia Concrete Co. Inc.; director: Flowers Industries; chairman, director: Arundel Corp.; director: Cardinal Concrete Co.

Foundation Officials
Edward L. Baker: president (see above)

Grants Analysis
Disclosure Period: fiscal year ending September 30, 2001
Total Grants: $268,751*
Number of Grants: 51
Average Grant: $5,270
Highest Grant: $25,000
Lowest Grant: $250
Typical Range: $500 to $20,000
*Note: Giving excludes scholarships; United Way.

Recent Grants
Note: Grants derived from fiscal 2001 Form 990.

General

25,000	Florida Independent College Fund, St. Augustine, FL
20,000	First Coast Education Leadership Center, Jacksonville, MS
20,000	Greenwood School, Inc, Jacksonville, FL
20,000	Kesler Mentoring Connection, Jacksonville, FL
20,000	Police Athletic League, Jacksonville, FL
20,000	University of Florida Foundation, Gainesville, FL
16,000	United Way of Northeast Florida, Jacksonville, FL
15,000	United Way of Northeast Florida, Jacksonville, FL
15,000	Universal Studios Escape Foundation, Orlando, FL

10,000	Alliance for World Class Education

FLORIDA ROCK & TANK LINES

Company Headquarters
5714 Buffalo Ave.
Jacksonville, FL 32208
Web: http://www.patriottrans.com

Company Description
Employees: 537
SIC(s): 4200 Trucking & Warehousing.
Parent Company: Patriot Transportation Holding, Inc., 1801 Art MuseumDr., Jacksonville, FL, United States

Operating Locations
Florida Rock & Tank Lines (FL--Jacksonville)

Florida Rock & Tank Lines Foundation

Giving Contact
John D. Milton, Jr., Secretary
Florida Rock & Tank Lines Foundation
PO Box 4667
Jacksonville, FL 32201
Phone: (904)355-1781
Fax: (904)366-1866

Description
EIN: 593050577
Organization Type: Corporate Foundation
Giving Locations: FL
Grant Types: General Support.

Financial Summary
Total Giving: $38,565 (fiscal year ending September 30, 2001); $27,744 (fiscal 2000); $27,744 (fiscal 1999)
Giving Analysis: Giving for fiscal 2001 includes: foundation grants to United Way ($1,000) fiscal 1998: foundation grants to United Way ($1,000)
Assets: $645,720 (fiscal 2001); $731,124 (fiscal 2000); $731,124 (fiscal 1999)
Gifts Received: $100,000 (fiscal 1998); $100,000 (fiscal 1997); $100,000 (fiscal 1996). Note: Contributions were received from Florida Rock and Tank Lines.

Typical Recipients
Arts & Humanities: Libraries, Music, Performing Arts
Civic & Public Affairs: Civic & Public Affairs-General, Urban & Community Affairs
Education: Business Education, Colleges & Universities, Leadership Training
Environment: Forestry
Health: Health Organizations, Hospices, Single-Disease Health Associations
Religion: Ministries, Religious Organizations, Religious Welfare
Social Services: Community Service Organizations, Family Services, Recreation & Athletics, Scouts, Special Olympics, United Funds/United Ways, YMCA/YWCA/YMHA/YWHA, Youth Organizations

Application Procedures
Initial Contact: Send a brief letter of inquiry.
Application Requirements: Include a recently audited financial statement, description of benefits or services provided, list of board members and leading contributors and amount of such leading contributions/pledges, whether activities qualify for "Community Contributions Tax Credit" under the Florida Corporation Tax Act, whether contribution will be for

capital or operating funds, and proof of tax-exempt status.

Deadlines: None.

Corporate Officials

John Anderson: chairman, chief executive officer PRIM CORP EMPL chairman: Florida Rock & Tank Lines. CORP AFFIL president, chief executive officer: FRP Properties.

John R. Mabbett, III: president, chief executive officer PRIM CORP EMPL president, chief executive officer: Florida Rock & Tank Lines.

Foundation Officials

Edward L. Baker: president B 1935. PRIM CORP EMPL chairman, director: Florida Rock Industries. CORP AFFIL chairman, director: FRP Properties; director: Virginia Concrete Co. Inc.; director: Flowers Industries; chairman, director: Arundel Corp.; director: Cardinal Concrete Co.

Grants Analysis

Disclosure Period: fiscal year ending September 30, 2001

Total Grants: $37,565*

Number of Grants: 14

Average Grant: $1,351*

Highest Grant: $20,000

Lowest Grant: $187

Typical Range: $1,000 to $3,000

*Note: Giving excludes United Way. Average grant figure excludes highest grant.

Recent Grants

Note: Grants derived from fiscal 2001 Form 990.

General

20,000	Jacksonville University, Jacksonville, FL
5,500	Junior Achievement, Jacksonville, FL
3,500	Hospice of Baltimore, Baltimore, MD
2,000	Osmond Foundation for the Children, Salt Lake City, UT
1,000	Boy Scouts of America Flint River Council, Griffin, GA
1,000	Bridge of Northeast Florida, Carrollton, FL
1,000	Jacksonville Community Council, Jacksonville, FL
1,000	United Services Organization, Jacksonville, FL -- golf tournament
1,000	United Way Northeast Florida, Jacksonville, FL
780	Pine Castle, Jacksonville, FL

FLORSHEIM GROUP CO.

Company Headquarters

200 N. Lasalle Street
Chicago, IL 60601-1014
Web: http://www.florsheim.com

Company Description

Ticker: FLSQE

Exchange: OTC

Revenue: US$183.5 million (2001)

Employees: 2,810

SIC(s): 3100 Leather & Leather Products, 3143 Men's Footwear Except Athletic, 5600 Apparel & Accessory Stores, 5661 Shoe Stores.

Operating Locations

Florsheim Group Co. (IL--Chicago)

Florsheim Shoe Foundation

Giving Contact

Peter P. Corritori, President
200 N. LaSalle St.
Chicago, IL 60601
Phone: (312)458-7497
Fax: (312)458-7408
E-mail: john.diebold@florsheim.com

Description

EIN: 366108530

Organization Type: Corporate Foundation

Grant Types: General Support.

Financial Summary

Total Giving: $19,830 (2000); $30,047 (1999); $35,995 (1998)

Giving Analysis: Giving for 1999 includes: foundation ($30,047)

Assets: $1,362 (2000); $2,291 (1999); $8,785 (1998)

Gifts Received: $19,000 (2000); $23,575 (1999); $32,000 (1998). Note: In 1998, 1999 and 2000, contributions were received from the Florsheim Group. In 1996, contributions were received from the Florsheim Group.

Typical Recipients

Arts & Humanities: Arts Centers, Arts Institutes, Arts & Humanities-General, History & Archaeology, Libraries, Music, Opera, Theater, Visual Arts

Civic & Public Affairs: Clubs, Civic & Public Affairs-General, Zoos/Aquariums

Education: Business Education, Colleges & Universities, Education-General, Minority Education, Science/Mathematics Education, Student Aid

Environment: Resource Conservation

Health: AIDS/HIV, Cancer, Children's Health/Hospitals, Diabetes, Health Organizations, Heart, Hospices, Hospitals, Multiple Sclerosis, Prenatal Health Issues, Respiratory, Single-Disease Health Associations

International: Foreign Educational Institutions, International Organizations, International Relief Efforts

Religion: Churches, Jewish Causes, Ministries, Religious Welfare

Science: Science Museums

Social Services: At-Risk Youth, Camps, Community Service Organizations, Domestic Violence, Family Services, People with Disabilities, Recreation & Athletics, Scouts, United Funds/United Ways, YMCA/YWCA/YMHA/YWHA

Application Procedures

Initial Contact: Send brief letter describing organization and program.

Deadlines: None.

Corporate Officials

Richard Anglin: chief financial officer, president, chief executive officer PRIM CORP EMPL chief financial officer: Florsheim Group.

Charles J. Campbell: chairman, president, chief executive officer PRIM CORP EMPL chairman, president, chief executive officer: Florsheim Group.

Foundation Officials

Ronald J. Mueller: president B Chicago, IL 1935. CORP AFFIL director: Florsheim Shoe Co.; president, director: Hy Test Inc.; chairman, president: Florsheim S A de C V Mexico; president, director: Florsheim Canada; president, director: Florsheim Pacific Ltd.; president, director: Florsheim Australia Ltd.

Larry R. Solomon: secretary

James J. Tunney: vice president

Grants Analysis

Disclosure Period: calendar year ending 2000

Total Grants: $19,830

Number of Grants: 7

Highest Grant: $5,810

Lowest Grant: $150

Recent Grants

Note: Grants derived from 1999 Form 990.

General

6,000	Two/Ten Foundation, Watertown, MA -- 1999 Relief Fund Drive
5,000	Mt. Sinai Children's Center Foundation, New York, NY
5,000	Turn 2 Foundation -- Derek Jeter Sports Dinner
4,445	Two/Ten Foundation, Watertown, MA -- golf outing
4,300	Two/Ten Foundation, Watertown, MA -- 1999 Florsheim Challenge
2,500	Open Hand Holiday Brunch, Chicago, IL
1,603	Golf Dallas for Two/Ten Golf Outing, Dallas, TX
750	Dallas Can! Academy, Dallas, TX -- Dallas Mother of The Year luncheon
250	Duke Center for Living, Durham, NC -- Gene Bordeaux Memorial Fund
100	A.L.S. Association, MA -- Memorial William Gryder

ALBERT W. AND EDITH V. FLOWERS CHARITABLE TRUST

Giving Contact

Ron B. Tynan, Trust Officer
First Merit Bank, NA
121 South Main Street, Suite 200
Akron, OH 44308-1440
Phone: (330)384-7320

Description

Founded: 1968

EIN: 346608643

Organization Type: Private Foundation

Giving Locations: OH: Stark County

Grant Types: Capital, General Support, Operating Expenses, Scholarship.

Donor Information

Founder: the late Albert W. Flowers, the late Edith V. Flowers

Financial Summary

Total Giving: $197,430 (2001); $192,700 (2000); $162,943 (1999)

Giving Analysis: Giving for 2001 includes: foundation scholarships ($5,000); 2000: foundation scholarships ($5,000) 1999: foundation scholarships ($5,000)

Assets: $3,096,667 (2001); $3,859,049 (2000); $4,145,828 (1999)

Typical Recipients

Arts & Humanities: Arts Centers, Arts Outreach, Ballet, Arts & Humanities-General, Historic Preservation, History & Archaeology, Libraries, Museums/Galleries, Music, Performing Arts, Theater

Civic & Public Affairs: African American Affairs, Botanical Gardens/Parks, Clubs, Community Foundations, Economic Development, Employment/Job Training, Civic & Public Affairs-General, Housing, Minority Business, Municipalities/Towns, Urban & Community Affairs

Education: Colleges & Universities, Private Education (Precollege), Public Education (Precollege), Secondary Education (Private), Special Education, Student Aid

Environment: Environment-General, Resource Conservation

Health: Children's Health/Hospitals, Emergency/Ambulance Services, Prenatal Health Issues

International: Missionary/Religious Activities

Religion: Bible Study/Translation, Churches, Ministries, Religious Welfare

Social Services: Big Brother/Big Sister, Camps, Child Welfare, Community Centers, Community Service Organizations, Family Services, Food/Clothing Distribution, Recreation & Athletics, Scouts, Social Services-General, YMCA/YWCA/YMHA/YWHA, Youth Organizations

Application Procedures

Initial Contact: Send a brief letter of inquiry.

Application Requirements: Include amount requested and purpose of funds sought.

Deadlines: None.

Restrictions

Awards generally granted to qualifying organizations in Stark County.

Additional Information

Trust(s): First Merit Bank NA

Foundation Officials

F. E. McCullough: mem distribution comm
Albert Printz: mem distribution comm
Charles Tyburski: member distribution committee
Ronald B. Tynan: chairman

Grants Analysis

Disclosure Period: calendar year ending 2001
Total Grants: $192,430*
Number of Grants: 31
Average Grant: $6,207
Highest Grant: $12,200
Typical Range: $1,000 to $10,000
***Note:** Giving excludes scholarships.

Recent Grants

Note: Grants derived from 2001 Form 990.

General

15,000	Walsh University, North Canton, OH -- for phase II of capital campaign
12,200	Neo Christian Youth Camp, Lisbon, OH -- for Tafco walk-in cooler and freezer
10,000	Friends of Stark Parks, Canton, OH -- for Ohio and Erie Canal Heritage Corridor
10,000	St. John's Villa, Inc., Carrollton, OH -- for Sisters of Charity Foundation challenge
8,700	Lions Club of Massillon, Massillon, OH -- for Lincoln Theatre Restoration
8,300	Stark Christian Academy, Canton, OH -- for educational items
8,000	Great Trail Girl Scout Council, Canton, OH -- for capital campaign
6,500	Shrine Cripple Children Fund, Canton, OH -- for transportation fund
5,000	Bluecoats Drum and Bugle Corp, Canton, OH -- for 2001 horn fund drive
5,000	Canton Negro Oldtimers, Canton, OH -- for activity center construction

FLUOR CORP.

Company Headquarters

1 Enterprise Dr.
Aliso Viejo, CA 92656-2606
Web: http://www.fluor.com

Company Description

Founded: 1924
Ticker: FLR
Exchange: NYSE
Operating Revenue: US$9.959 billion (2002)
Profit: US$163.6 million (2002)
Employees: 44809 (2002)
Fortune Rank: 186, per FORTUNE Magazine's list of 500 Largest U.S. Corporations (2002).
SIC(s): 1221 Bituminous Coal & Lignite--Surface, 1241 Coal Mining Services, 1541 Industrial Buildings & Warehouses, 1629 Heavy Construction Nec.

Operating Locations

Fluor Corp. (AK--Anchorage; CA--Bakersfield, Irvine; CO--Denver; DC; IL--Chicago; KY; MO--Kansas City; NJ--Marlton; OH--Cincinnati, Dayton; OK--Tulsa; SC--Greenville; TN, Nashville; TX--Corpus Christi, Sugar Land; VA--Falls Church, Richmond; WI--Appleton)

Nonmonetary Support

Type: Donated Equipment; In-kind Services
Volunteer Programs: "The Fluor Community Involvement Team," is a corporate volunteer program in which employees, retirees, and their family and friends carry out service projects in local communities. Employees also volunteer for many education programs: Junior Achievement, school partnerships, mentoring, and classroom presentations.

Fluor Foundation

Giving Contact

Suzanne Huffmon Esber, Manager Community Relations
Fluor Foundation
One Enterprise Dr., F2C
Aliso Viejo, CA 92656-2606
Phone: (949)349-6797
E-mail: community.relations@fluordaniel.com
Web: http://fluor.com/community/involvement.asp

Description

EIN: 510196032
Organization Type: Corporate Foundation
Giving Locations: operating locations.
Grant Types: Capital, Employee Matching Gifts, Endowment, General Support, Matching, Operating Expenses, Project, Scholarship.
Note: Employee matching gift ratio: 1 to 1.

Financial Summary

Total Giving: $3,238,169 (2001); $60,815 (2000); $3,084,751 (1999). Note: Contributes through corporate direct giving program and foundation.
Giving Analysis: Giving for 2001 includes: foundation matching gifts ($215,070); foundation scholarships ($567,565); foundation grants to United Way ($961,917); foundation ($1,493,617); 2000: foundation scholarships ($29,815); foundation ($31,000); 1999: foundation fellowships ($60,000); foundation scholarships ($801,605); foundation grants to United Way ($837,163); foundation ($1,385,983);
Assets: $6,134,266 (2001); $5,708,299 (2000); $5,346,802 (1999)
Gifts Received: $3,245,714 (2001); $60,815 (2000); $3,093,537 (1999). Note: Contributions are received from Fluor Corp.

Typical Recipients

Arts & Humanities: Arts Associations & Councils, Arts Centers, Arts Funds, Dance, History & Archaeology, Museums/Galleries, Music, Opera, Performing Arts, Public Broadcasting, Theater
Civic & Public Affairs: Botanical Gardens/Parks, Community Foundations, Economic Development,

Employment/Job Training, Civic & Public Affairs-General, Hispanic Affairs, Housing, Nonprofit Management, Professional & Trade Associations, Public Policy, Safety, Urban & Community Affairs, Women's Affairs

Education: Business Education, Business-School Partnerships, Colleges & Universities, Education Associations, Education Funds, Education Reform, Engineering/Technological Education, Environmental Education, Education-General, International Studies, Literacy, Medical Education, Minority Education, Public Education (Precollege), Science/Mathematics Education, Student Aid

Environment: Environment-General

Health: AIDS/HIV, Cancer, Children's Health/Hospitals, Clinics/Medical Centers, Diabetes, Emergency/Ambulance Services, Hospitals

International: International Affairs, International Development

Religion: Religious Welfare

Science: Science Exhibits & Fairs, Scientific Centers & Institutes

Social Services: Child Welfare, Community Service Organizations, Emergency Relief, Scouts, Substance Abuse, United Funds/United Ways, Volunteer Services, YMCA/YWCA/YMHA/YWHA, Youth Organizations

Application Procedures

Initial Contact: Send a preliminary letter of request.
Application Requirements: Include a description of organization, amount requested, purpose of funds sought, recently audited financial statement, and proof of tax-exempt status.
Deadlines: None.
Review Process: After initial request is reviewed, additional information may be requested.
Decision Notification: Three to four months after receipt of request.

Restrictions

Does not provide funding directly to elementary or secondary schools, health initiatives or research, individual artists, film production, publishing activities, individuals, sports organizations, sports programs, veterans, fraternal, labor, religious organizations, lobbying organizations, or campaigns. Foundation prefers to limit operation support to two or three consecutive years, and capital support to one grant in a five-year period.

Additional Information

Giving figures for 2000 reflect a change in the foundation's fiscal year, and are for the period November 1, 2000 through December 31, 2000.

Corporate Officials

Alan L. Boeckmann: chairman, chief executive officer chief financial officer B 1948. ED University of Arizona. PRIM CORP EMPL chairman, chief executive officer: Fluor Corp. CORP AFFIL director: Burlington Northern Santa Fe Corp.; director: American Petroleum Institute. NONPR AFFIL director: Orange County Performing Arts Center.

John Robert Fluor, II: vice president corporate & public affairs B Orange, CA 1945. ED University of Southern California (1967). PRIM CORP EMPL vice president corporate & public affairs: Fluor Corp. NONPR AFFIL member: California Business Roundtable; member: United Way Orange County.

D. Michael Steuert: senior vice president, chief financial officer B Oklahoma City, OK 1948. ED Carnegie Mellon University (1971). PRIM CORP EMPL senior vice president, chief financial officer: Fluor Corp. NONPR AFFIL member: Leadership Akron Alumni Association; member: Private Sector Council; member: Carnegie Mellon Graduate School Council Finance.

Foundation Officials

Alan L. Boeckmann: trustee (see above)
Suzanne Huffmon Esber: manager, community relationss
John Robert Fluor, II: president, trustee (see above)
James L. Gardner: trustee PRIM CORP EMPL senior vice president, general counsel: AT Masset Coal Co. Inc.
Charles R. Oliver: trustee B Nashville, TN 1943. ED Auburn University (1967); California State Polytechnic University, Pomona (1996). PRIM CORP EMPL group president global sales: Fluor Daniel, Inc.

Grants Analysis

Disclosure Period: calendar year ending 2001
Total Grants: $1,493,617*
Number of Grants: 216
Average Grant: $6,915
Highest Grant: $104,207
Typical Range: $6,000 to $15,000
*Note: Giving excludes scholarships, matching gifts, and United Way.

Recent Grants

Note: Grants derived from 2001 Form 990.

General

503,015	Citizens Scholarship Foundation of America, St. Peter, MN -- for management fees and scholarship awards
222,391	United Way of Orange County, Irvine, CA -- corporate gift
158,618	United Way of Orange County, Irvine, CA -- for the Fluor Make a Difference Program
139,062	United Way of Orange County, Irvine, CA -- for the Flour Make a Difference Program
129,090	United Way of Orange County, Irvine, CA -- corporate gift
104,207	American Red Cross, Washington, DC -- for liberty disaster relief
68,762	American Red Cross, Washington, DC -- for liberty disaster relief
52,336	United Way Benton and Franklin Counties, Kennewick, WA -- for the Fluor Hanford Project
50,000	California State Polytechnical University, Pomona, CA -- for annual review
50,000	Points of Light Foundation, Washington, DC

FMC Corp.

Company Headquarters

Philadelphia, PA
Web: http://www.fmc.com

Company Description

Founded: 1928
Ticker: FMC
Exchange: NYSE
Revenue: US$1.852 billion (2002)
Employees: 5500 (2002)
SIC(s): 1041 Gold Ores, 1044 Silver Ores, 1479 Chemical & Fertilizer Mining Nec, 2819 Industrial Inorganic Chemicals Nec.

Operating Locations

FMC Corp. (AL--Anniston; AK--Anchorage; AZ--Yuma; CA--Anaheim, Fresno, Hacienda Heights, Hollister, Madera, Pomona, Richmond, Riverside, Santa Clara, Ventura, Woodland Hills; CO--Denver; DC--Washington; FL--Coral Gables, Jacksonville, Lakeland, Orlando; GA--Atlanta, Sparks; ID--Boise, Pocatello; IL--Champaign, Chicago, Downers Grove, Summit Argo, Wheeling, Wyoming; IA--Sergeant Bluff;

KS--Lawrence; LA--New Orleans, Opelousas; MD--Baltimore, Ridgely; MI--Howell, Warren; MN--Madison Lake; MS--Jackson; NE--Omaha; NV--Battle Mountain; NJ--Carteret, Princeton; NM--Hobbs; NY--Albany, Tonawanda; NC--Charlotte, Gastonia; OK--Lawton, Oklahoma City; PA--Bradford, Homer City, Lansdale, Philadelphia; SC--Aiken; SD--Aberdeen; TX--Austin, Corpus Christi, El Paso, Odessa, Pasadena; VA--Arlington, King George; WA--Vancouver, Walla Walla; WV--Institute, Nitro, South Charleston; WI--Columbus, Green Bay, Waukesha; WY--La Barge, Mills, Rock Springs)

Nonmonetary Support

Volunteer Programs: Through the Dollars for Doers program, the company matches up to $500 of employees' volunteer time at qualifying organizations.

FMC Foundation

Giving Contact

Judith Smeltzer
FMC Foundation
1735 Market Street
Philadelphia, PA 19103
Phone: (215)299-6000

Description

EIN: 946063032
Organization Type: Corporate Foundation
Giving Locations: nationally; operating locations.
Grant Types: Capital, Employee Matching Gifts, General Support.
Note: Employee matching gift ratio: 1 to 1 for qualifying educational and cultural institutions, up to $10,000 annually per employee. Company matches employee United Way contributions up to 60 percent on the dollar based on the percent of employee participation at each company site.

Financial Summary

Total Giving: $2,279,780 (fiscal year ending November 30, 2001); $2,146,793 (fiscal 2000); $2,000,000 (fiscal 1999 approx)
Giving Analysis: Giving for fiscal 2000 includes: foundation scholarships ($16,530); foundation matching gifts ($384,175); foundation grants to United Way ($430,153); fiscal 1998: foundation grants to United Way ($35,025); foundation matching gifts ($603,955) foundation ($1,202,276)
Assets: $422,096 (fiscal 2001); $423,069 (fiscal 2000); $499,446 (fiscal 1998)
Gifts Received: $2,400,000 (fiscal 2001); $2,020,000 (fiscal 2000); $1,350,000 (fiscal 1998)

Typical Recipients

Arts & Humanities: Arts Centers, Arts Festivals, Arts Institutes, Community Arts, Libraries, Museums/Galleries, Music, Opera, Theater
Civic & Public Affairs: African American Affairs, Business/Free Enterprise, Clubs, Economic Development, Economic Policy, Employment/Job Training, Civic & Public Affairs-General, Hispanic Affairs, Law & Justice, Philanthropic Organizations, Professional & Trade Associations, Public Policy, Rural Affairs, Urban & Community Affairs, Zoos/Aquariums
Education: Agricultural Education, Business Education, Colleges & Universities, Community & Junior Colleges, Economic Education, Education Funds, Education Reform, Engineering/Technological Education, Education-General, Gifted & Talented Programs, International Exchange, International Studies, Medical Education, Minority Education, Science/Mathematics Education, Student Aid
Environment: Air/Water Quality, Environment-General, Wildlife Protection
Health: Children's Health/Hospitals, Emergency/Ambulance Services, Health Policy/Cost Containment, Health Funds, Health Organizations, Heart, Hospitals,

Medical Rehabilitation, Public Health, Single-Disease Health Associations
International: Foreign Educational Institutions, International-General, International Affairs, International Environmental Issues, International Peace & Security Issues
Religion: Religious Welfare
Science: Science-General, Science Museums, Scientific Centers & Institutes, Scientific Organizations, Scientific Research
Social Services: Child Welfare, Community Service Organizations, Emergency Relief, Family Services, Family Services, Recreation & Athletics, United Funds/United Ways, Volunteer Services, YMCA/YWCA/YMHA/YWHA, Youth Organizations

Application Procedures

Initial Contact: Send a brief (no more than two pages) typewritten letter.
Application Requirements: Include a description of organization; statement of organization's activities and programs; specific amount of money requested; explanation of how funds will be used; project location; timetable; proof of tax-exempt status; and list of board of directors.
Deadlines: None; budget determined in fall quarter.
Review Process: If organization is local, request is forwarded for local management review and recommendation; if national, preliminary review by foundation committee, then review by foundation board.
Evaluative Criteria: Strong consideration given to organizations which count a number of FMC employees among their active supporters; emphasizes groups that strive to improve communities in which employees live and work and to improve environment in which company does business; organization must have proven effectiveness and a broad base of community support; priority given to organizations and institutions promoting the free enterprise system.
Decision Notification: Foundation board meets at least twice a year.
Notes: Foundation discourages submission of unsolicited and voluminous support materials. Based on application information listed above, if funding appears possible, foundation will request the following: audited financial report for most recently completed year of operation; organizational budget for current operating year, showing expenses and income by sources; copy of organization's IRS tax-exempt status ruling; and a sample donor list showing corporate and foundation contributors to the organization for the past 12 months.
Local contributions are determined by individual manufacturing plants and operating sites, and not through the foundation or corporate office.

Restrictions

Foundation does not support individuals, state or regional associations of independent colleges, elementary or secondary schools, organizations that receive or qualify for United Way support, dinners or special events, fraternal organizations, goodwill advertising, political or lobbying groups, or religious organizations for sectarian purposes.
Foundation also does not support national health agencies or hospitals for operating expenses, or medical research.
Grants are not pledged for a period longer than one year.
The foundation usually only gives in plant communities.

Additional Information

Requests for special programs at hospitals (for example, outpatient alcoholism programs, drug addiction, or prenatal care) are not given high priority, but are considered individually as funds become available.
Publications: Foundation Annual Report

Corporate Officials

William G. Walter: chairman, chief executive officer, director B 1946. ED Loras College BS (1968); Northwestern University MBA (1971). PRIM CORP EMPL president, chief executive officer, director: FMC Corp.

Grants Analysis

Disclosure Period: fiscal year ending November 30, 2001
Total Grants: $1,917,938*
Number of Grants: 177
Average Grant: $10,836
Highest Grant: $60,000
Typical Range: $1,000 to $30,000
*Note: Giving excludes matching gifts; United Way.

Recent Grants

Note: Grants derived from fiscal 2001 Form 990.

Library-Related
15,000	Newberry Library, Chicago, IL

General
204,291	Dollars for Doers, Chicago, IL
100,000	United Way of New York City, New York, NY -- September 11th Fund
60,000	Orchestral Association of Chicago, Chicago, IL
50,951	Dollars for Doers, Chicago, IL
40,000	Lyric Opera of Chicago, Chicago, IL
30,500	National FFA Foundation, Indianapolis, IN
30,000	Commercial Club Foundation, Chicago, IL
30,000	Houston Golf Association, Woodlands, TX
30,000	Orchestral Association of Chicago, Chicago, IL
30,000	Society of Hispanic Professional Engineers, Los Angeles, CA

FOELLINGER FOUNDATION

Giving Contact

Cheryl Taylor, President
520 East Berry Street
Ft. Wayne, IN 46802
Phone: (260)422-2900
Fax: (260)422-9436
E-mail: info@foelinger.org
Web: http://www.foellinger.org/

Description

Founded: 1958
EIN: 356027059
Organization Type: Family Foundation
Giving Locations: IN: Fort Wayne including Allen County
Grant Types: Capital, Challenge, Emergency, Matching, Operating Expenses, Project.

Donor Information

Founder: The Foellinger Foundation was established in Indiana in 1958 by the late Helene R. Foellinger (1910-1987) and her mother, the late Esther A. Foellinger (1890-1969). Helene Foellinger's father, Oscar G. Foellinger, was a prominent newspaper publisher and president of the *Ft. Wayne News-Sentinel*. After her father's death in 1936, Helene R. Foellinger served as president of the News Publishing Company until her retirement in November 1981. The foundation was also funded by profits from the News Publishing Company until the sale of the *News-Sentinel* in 1980.

Financial Summary

Total Giving: $7,416,280 (fiscal year ending August 31, 2001); $6,823,733 (fiscal 1999); $6,780,056 (fiscal 1998)

Giving Analysis: Giving for fiscal 2001 includes: foundation grants to United Way ($190,000); fiscal 1999: foundation grants to United Way ($100,000); fiscal 1998: foundation matching gifts ($50,000); foundation grants to United Way ($135,000);
Assets: $172,825,992 (fiscal 2001); $181,337,030 (fiscal 1999); $161,581,507 (fiscal 1998)
Gifts Received: $2,361 (fiscal 1992). Note: Prior to fiscal 1990, the foundation received contributions from the Helene R. Foellinger Trust. The remainder of funds from this trust have now been received.

Typical Recipients

Arts & Humanities: Arts Appreciation, Arts Associations & Councils, Arts Centers, Arts Funds, Ethnic & Folk Arts, Arts & Humanities-General, Historic Preservation, Libraries, Museums/Galleries, Music, Public Broadcasting, Theater
Civic & Public Affairs: Botanical Gardens/Parks, Business/Free Enterprise, Clubs, Community Foundations, Economic Development, Housing, Professional & Trade Associations, Urban & Community Affairs, Zoos/Aquariums
Education: Afterschool/Enrichment Programs, Business Education, Colleges & Universities, Continuing Education, Education Associations, Education Funds, Elementary Education (Public), Engineering/Technological Education, Education-General, Gifted & Talented Programs, Journalism/Media Education, Literacy, Private Education (Precollege), Public Education (Precollege), Science/Mathematics Education, Student Aid
Environment: Air/Water Quality, Protection, Resource Conservation
Health: AIDS/HIV, Clinics/Medical Centers, Health Organizations, Medical Rehabilitation, Preventive Medicine/Wellness Organizations, Public Health
Religion: Ministries, Religious Welfare
Science: Science Museums, Scientific Centers & Institutes
Social Services: Big Brother/Big Sister, Camps, Child Welfare, Community Centers, Community Service Organizations, Crime Prevention, Day Care, Domestic Violence, Family Services, Food/Clothing Distribution, Homes, People with Disabilities, Recreation & Athletics, Scouts, Shelters/Homelessness, Substance Abuse, United Funds/United Ways, YMCA/YWCA/YMHA/YWHA, YMCA/YWCA/YMHA/YWHA, Youth Organizations

Application Procedures

Initial Contact: Potential recipients should send a letter of intent to the foundation, after which grant-seekers will either be encouraged to submit a full grant application package, refine the current proposal, or explore other funding sources.
Application Requirements: The letter should include the following components, presented in order and under the headings listed: Goals Statement: include specific reasons as to why the proposed request is consistent with the foundation's grant guidelines. Issue Statement: a description of the issue that the proposed project/program will resolve or address, and the issue's relevance to the community. Proposed Project/Program: an outline of what will be done, and how and when it will be done. Cost Estimate: an estimate of the proposed total cost of the project/program and amount requested from the foundation. Collaboration: indicate the level of commitment from other agencies, and the level of commitment from other funders approached to support this project. An IRS letter indicating nonprofit status must accompany the letter of intent. If a grant application package is to be submitted, this should incude: the full legal name and address of the organization; a copy of the latest letter from the Internal Revenue Service verifying that the organization is tax-exempt under Section 501(c)(3) of the Internal Revenue Code, and is not a private foundation within the meaning of Section 509(a) of the code; a complete copy of the organization's latest financial statements, including a balance sheet and a revenue and expense statement, and a federal tax

return (Form 990) signed by an officer and the preparer. The package should also include a brief a description of organization and its mission; the names of the members of the board of trustees; the names and qualifications of the persons who will direct the program/project; a statement of other sources of support for the program; a narrative describing the program, including specific objectives and outcomes, time frames, and plans for ongoing support after the period of the requested grant.
Deadlines: Applications should be sent 90 days ahead of the committee meetings, held in February, May, August, and November.
Review Process: The foundation acknowledges the receipt of grant applications by mail and requests for any additional information. If the directors conclude that the application meets their guidelines, an interview or visit to the project site may be arranged.

Restrictions

Grants are not made to individuals, including scholarship or travel assistance; public or private elementary or secondary schools independent of their school systems; sectarian religious groups or causes; churches for their general operations; projects that taxpayers normally support; endowment purposes; the support of projects or programs that have begun or have been completed before the foundation receives a funding request; or to purchase advertising, tickets, or for special events or group trips.

Additional Information

The foundation reports that it also sponsors conferences and assists in planning grants and studies.
Publications: Grant Guidelines; Annual Report

Foundation Officials

Barbara Burt: president, treasurer
Walter Paul Helmke: vice president, secretary B Bloomington, IL 1948. PRIM CORP EMPL mayor: City Fort Wayne. CORP AFFIL director: Almet Inc.; secretary, director: Aalco Distributing. NONPR AFFIL president: United States Conference Mayors.
Joanne Baldwin Lantz: director B Defiance, OH 1932. ED University of Indianapolis BS (1953); Indiana University MS (1957); Michigan State University PhD (1969). CORP AFFIL director: Fort Wayne National Corp. NONPR AFFIL member: Sigma Xi; member: Southeast Psychological Association; member: Purdue University Alumni Society Fort Wayne; chancellor emeritus: Indiana University/Purdue University; member: Pi Lambda Theta; member: Indiana School Womens Club; member: Delta Kappa Gamma; director: Delta Kappa Gamma Education Foundation; member: American Psychological Association; member: American Association University Women.
Carl D. Rolfsen: chairman board B 1956. CORP AFFIL officer: Graphic Finishing Inc.
Don Wolf: director

Grants Analysis

Disclosure Period: fiscal year ending August 31, 2001
Total Grants: $7,226,280*
Number of Grants: 142
Average Grant: $44,513*
Highest Grant: $950,000
Typical Range: $20,000 to $75,000
*Note: Giving excludes United Way. Average grant excludes highest grant.

Recent Grants

Note: Grants derived from 2000 Form 990.

General
600,000	East Allen County Schools, Ft. Wayne, IN -- for Learning Perspectives Initiative
414,759	Fort Wayne Community Schools, Ft. Wayne, IN -- support summer programs
250,000	Fort Wayne Zoological Society, Ft. Wayne, IN -- capital support
250,000	Taylor University, Upland, IN -- capital

support for a new student commons on the Fort Wayne Campus

232,157	Fort Wayne Community Schools, Ft. Wayne, IN -- for summer program
212,500	Taylor University, Upland, IN -- support for Allen County Institute for Organizational Effectiveness
209,000	United Way Allen County, Inc., Ft. Wayne, IN -- program support
200,000	Indiana Institute of Technology, Ft. Wayne, IN -- capital campaign
179,596	Three Rivers Literacy Alliance, Ft. Wayne, IN -- program support for Families Learning Together
159,547	Community Partnership, Ft. Wayne, IN -- for case management initiative

FONDREN FOUNDATION

Giving Contact

Martie Herrick, Assistant Secretary-Treasurer
PO Box 2558
Houston, TX 77252-8037
Phone: (713)216-4513

Description

Founded: 1948
EIN: 746042565
Organization Type: Family Foundation
Giving Locations: TX: Houston nationally.
Grant Types: Capital, General Support, Project, Research.

Donor Information

Founder: Walter William Fondren , a Houston oilman, philanthropist, and founder of Humble Oil and Refining Co., established the Fondren Foundation in Texas in 1948.

Mrs. Walter Fondren administered his estate following his death and became the principal contributor to the foundation.

Financial Summary

Total Giving: $8,255,265 (fiscal year ending October 31, 2001); $8,932,724 (fiscal 2000); $9,077,000 (fiscal 1998)
Giving Analysis: Giving for fiscal 2001 includes: foundation scholarships ($38,250); fiscal 2000: foundation scholarships ($75,000); fiscal 1998: foundation matching gifts ($50,000); foundation scholarships ($265,000);
Assets: $149,652,569 (fiscal 2002); $172,674,279 (fiscal 2001); $206,245,751 (fiscal 2000)

Typical Recipients

Arts & Humanities: Art History, Arts Outreach, Ballet, Dance, Arts & Humanities-General, Historic Preservation, History & Archaeology, Libraries, Museums/Galleries, Music, Opera, Performing Arts, Public Broadcasting, Theater, Visual Arts
Civic & Public Affairs: Botanical Gardens/Parks, Economic Development, Employment/Job Training, Civic & Public Affairs-General, Hispanic Affairs, Housing, Philanthropic Organizations, Public Policy, Safety, Urban & Community Affairs, Women's Affairs, Zoos/Aquariums
Education: Arts/Humanities Education, Business Education, Colleges & Universities, Education Reform, Engineering/Technological Education, Faculty Development, Education-General, Education-General, Leadership Training, Legal Education, Literacy, Medical Education, Minority Education, Private Education (Precollege), Public Education (Precollege), Religious Education, Science/Mathematics Education, Secondary Education (Private), Social Sciences Education, Special Education, Student Aid
Environment: Environment-General, Resource Conservation, Wildlife Protection

Health: AIDS/HIV, Alzheimers Disease, Cancer, Children's Health/Hospitals, Clinics/Medical Centers, Emergency/Ambulance Services, Geriatric Health, Heart, Hospices, Hospitals, Medical Rehabilitation, Medical Research, Mental Health, Prenatal Health Issues, Public Health, Research/Studies Institutes, Single-Disease Health Associations, Speech & Hearing, Transplant Networks/Donor Banks
International: International Environmental Issues, International Relations
Religion: Churches, Jewish Causes, Ministries, Religious Welfare
Science: Science Museums, Scientific Centers & Institutes
Social Services: Animal Protection, At-Risk Youth, Camps, Child Welfare, Community Centers, Community Service Organizations, Family Planning, Family Services, Food/Clothing Distribution, People with Disabilities, Recreation & Athletics, Scouts, Senior Services, Substance Abuse, Volunteer Services, YMCA/YWCA/YMHA/YWHA, Youth Organizations

Application Procedures

Initial Contact: Applicants should send one copy of a concise proposal.
Application Requirements: Proposals should include a brief narrative history of the organization's purpose and work, specific description of the proposed program or project for which funds are requested, amount requested from the foundation as well as total amount needed, date by which funds are needed, proof of tax-exempt status, and a list of trustees or directors and principal staff.
Deadlines: Proposals should be submitted by the first day of the month preceding the month of a meeting, which are generally held in March, June, September, and December. Contact the foundation for the next scheduled meeting.
Review Process: The board of governors meets on a quarterly basis to consider grant proposals.

Restrictions

Grants are not made to individuals. The foundation does not award grants for annual fund drives.

Foundation Officials

Doris Fondren Allday: board of directors
R. Edwin Allday: board of directors
Ellanor Allday Beard: board of directors
Celia Whitfield Crank: board of directors
Bentley B. Fondren: board of directors
Leland T. Fondren: chairman
Robert E. Fondren: board of directors B 1962. PRIM CORP EMPL vice president, director: Trend Development. CORP AFFIL off: Lake Colony Four; off: Plantation Development Corp.; off: CNO Development; off: Companeros Development Co.
Walter W. Fondren, IV: board of directors
Walter W. Fondren, III: board of directors B 1935. PRIM NONPR EMPL chairman: Coastal Conservation Association.
Marie Fondren Hall: board of directors
Catherine Fondren Underwood Murray: secretary, treasurer
Carrie Trammell Sturges: board of directors
David M. Underwood, Jr: board of directors
David M. Underwood: board of directors B 1937. ED Yale University (1959). PRIM CORP EMPL president, director: Feliciana Corp.
Lynda Knapp Underwood: board of directors B 1937. PRIM CORP EMPL vice president, director: Feliciana Corp.
Sue Trammell Whitfield: board of directors
Susan T. Whitfield: board of directors
W. Trammell Whitfield: board of directors
William F. Whitfield, Jr.: board of directors
William F. Whitfield, Sr.: board of directors

Grants Analysis

Disclosure Period: fiscal year ending October 31, 2001
Total Grants: $8,961,750*

Number of Grants: 109
Average Grant: $77,588*
Highest Grant: $582,242
Typical Range: $40,000 to $150,000
***Note:** Giving excludes scholarships. Average grant figure excludes highest grants.

Recent Grants

Note: Grants derived from 2000 Form 990.

General

500,000	Episcopal High School of Houston, Bellaire, TX -- construction of student center and support endowment
340,000	Neighborhood Centers, Houston, TX -- emerging needs fund
333,000	Institute for Rehabilitation and Research Foundation, Houston, TX -- to fund Mission Connect
333,000	Rice University, Houston, TX -- enhancement of the Fondren Library
300,000	Southern Methodist University, Dallas, TX -- construction of gallery at Fondren Library
250,000	Houston Music Hall Foundation, Houston, TX -- reconstruction of Houston Music Hall
250,000	Trustees of Phillips Academy, Andover, MA -- establish new teaching foundation
250,000	YMCA of Greater Houston Area, Houston, TX -- capital campaign
249,750	KIPP Academy, Houston, TX -- to acquire new land and relocate temporary buildings to new site
207,500	Houston Foundation for Child Development, Houston, TX -- campaign to add neighborhood properties

FORD FAMILY FOUNDATION

Giving Contact

Norman J. Smith, President
1600 Northwest Stewart Parkway
Roseburg, OR 97470
Phone: (541)957-5574
Fax: (541)957-5720
Web: http://www.tfff.org

Description

Founded: 1957
EIN: 936026156
Organization Type: Private Foundation
Giving Locations: CA: Siskiyou County; OR: rural communities only with population of 30,000 or fewer people
Grant Types: Award, Capital, Challenge, Emergency, General Support, Multiyear/Continuing Support, Scholarship.

Donor Information

Founder: The foundation was established in 1957 by Kenneth and Hallie Ford , to give back to the timber communities of Southwest Oregon. (grant guidelines in 1998 Form 990).

Financial Summary

Total Giving: $15,319,855 (fiscal year ending April 30, 2001); $13,134,078 (fiscal 1999); $11,671,660 (fiscal 1998)
Giving Analysis: Giving for fiscal 2001 includes: foundation grants to United Way ($41,095); foundation scholarships ($10,699,427); fiscal 1999: foundation grants to United Way ($98,875); foundation scholarships ($3,346,884); fiscal 1998: foundation grants to United Way ($118,500) foundation scholarships ($2,574,049)
Assets: $483,138,339 (fiscal 2001); $396,545,212 (fiscal 1999); $369,675,159 (fiscal 1998)

Gifts Received: $5,251,710 (fiscal 2001); $5,376,000 (fiscal 1998); $71,487,474 (fiscal 1995). Note: Contributions are received from the estate of Kenneth Ford.

Typical Recipients

Arts & Humanities: Arts Appreciation, Arts Associations & Councils, Arts Centers, Community Arts, Libraries, Museums/Galleries, Music, Performing Arts, Theater

Civic & Public Affairs: Botanical Gardens/Parks, Economic Development, Employment/Job Training, Civic & Public Affairs-General, Housing, Municipalities/Towns, Parades/Festivals, Public Policy, Safety, Urban & Community Affairs

Education: Arts/Humanities Education, Colleges & Universities, Community & Junior Colleges, Education Funds, Elementary Education (Private), Elementary Education (Public), Education-General, Minority Education, Preschool Education, Private Education (Precollege), Public Education (Precollege), Religious Education, Science/Mathematics Education, Secondary Education (Private), Secondary Education (Public), Student Aid

Environment: Air/Water Quality, Environment-General

Health: Adolescent Health Issues, Cancer, Children's Health/Hospitals, Clinics/Medical Centers, Emergency/Ambulance Services, Health-General, Health Organizations, Hospices, Hospitals, Mental Health, Prenatal Health Issues

International: International Environmental Issues

Religion: Churches, Missionary Activities (Domestic), Religious Welfare

Science: Science-General, Science Museums, Scientific Centers & Institutes

Social Services: Animal Protection, At-Risk Youth, Child Abuse, Child Welfare, Community Centers, Community Service Organizations, Counseling, Crime Prevention, Day Care, Domestic Violence, Family Services, Food/Clothing Distribution, Homes, People with Disabilities, Recreation & Athletics, Scouts, Senior Services, Shelters/Homelessness, Social Services-General, Substance Abuse, United Funds/United Ways, Volunteer Services, YMCA/YWCA/YMHA/YWHA, Youth Organizations

Application Procedures

Initial Contact: Send a brief letter of inquiry.
Application Requirements: Applications should include a description of organization, project description, amount requested, purpose of funds sought, proof of tax-exempt status, list of board members, project timeline and budget, source and amount of committed and projected support, and who will benefit.
Deadlines: March 1.
Review Process: The foundation will respond within approximately four weeks to organizations submitting a pre-application letter. Final decisions may take as long as 12 months, but generally will occur within four months.

Restrictions

The Ford Family Foundation only provides funding to charitable organization, except for recipients of scholarships (see below). Funding will not be considered for endowments or reserve funds, general fund drives overhead expenses, debt reduction, Operating expenses, political or lobbying groups, purchase of art, nor environmental preservation which intends to deprive property owners use of their property. Unsolicited requests for funds are not accepted.

Additional Information

The Roseburg Forest Products Co. endowed the Ford Family Foundation.
Projects which have already secured at least 50% of funding needed to complete the project are eligible to apply.

Contact should be in written form; Foundation discourages phone calls.

Foundation Officials

Bart Howard: program officer Ford Scholars
David M. Mattocks, PhD: program officer general grants
Norman J. Smith: president

Grants Analysis

Disclosure Period: fiscal year ending April 30, 2001
Total Grants: $10,699,427*
Number of Grants: 244
Average Grant: $39,915*
Highest Grant: $1,000,000
Typical Range: $5,000 to $75,000 and $100,000 to $400,000
*Note: Giving excludes scholarships and United Way. Average grant figure excludes highest grant.

Recent Grants

Note: Grants derived from fiscal 2001 Form 990.

Library-Related

140,000	Coos County Library Service District, Coos Bay, OR -- Coos Connections
125,000	Jackson County Library Foundation, Medford, OR -- site acquisition
79,242	Jackson Education Service District, Medford, OR -- Southern Oregon Online School
65,100	Douglas County Library Foundation, Roseburg, OR -- national board certified teachers
42,000	Junior Achievement of Western Oregon, Eugene, OR -- program expansion

General

1,000,000	Oregon Food Bank, Portland, OR -- statewide distribution center
675,000	St. Mary's Home, Beaverton, OR -- community service center and gymnasium
600,000	City of Roseburg, Roseburg, OR -- City of Roseburg Community Park
500,000	Columbia River Maritime Museum, Astoria, OR -- charting a new course
500,000	Trillium Family Services, Portland, OR -- children's farm house
450,000	Phoenix Learning Center, Roseburg, OR -- school facility project
400,000	Northwest Medical Teams International, Portland, OR -- Douglas/Coos County Mobile Dental Care Clinic
400,000	Oregon Independent College Foundation, Portland, OR -- for Independent College support
341,340	Oregon Children's Foundation, Portland, OR -- rural county proposal
325,000	Oregon Garden Foundation, Portland, OR -- rediscovery Forest Education Center

FORD FOUNDATION

Giving Contact

Barron M. Tenny, Secretary
320 East 43rd Street
New York, NY 10017
Phone: (212)573-5000
Fax: (212)351-3677
E-mail: office-communications@fordfound.org
Web: http://www.fordfound.org

Description

Founded: 1936
EIN: 131684331
Organization Type: Private Foundation
Giving Locations: internationally, especially Asia, Latin America, and Africa; nationally.

Grant Types: Conference/Seminar, Endowment, Fellowship, General Support, Matching, Multiyear/Continuing Support, Project, Research, Seed Money.

Donor Information

Founder: Established in 1936 by Henry Ford , who founded Ford Motor Company in 1903, and his son, Edsel Ford. The late Henry Ford II (d. 1987), chairman of Ford Motor Company and a son of Edsel Ford, served on the foundation's board from 1943 until 1976. Under his tenure, the foundation evolved from a Michigan charity into a worldwide institutional philanthropy. Today, the foundation has no official ties to the Ford family or the Ford Motor Company.

Financial Summary

Total Giving: $827,695,000 (fiscal year ending September 30, 2001 approx); $683,715,497 (fiscal 2000 approx); $514,400,551 (fiscal 1999)
Giving Analysis: Giving for fiscal 2001 includes: foundation gifts to individuals (approx $1,907,865); foundation program-related investments (approx $31,289,859); foundation (approx $653,205,000); foundation (approx $860,688,135); fiscal 2000: foundation program-related investments (approx $30,510,497); fiscal 1999: foundation gifts to individuals ($1,633,954)
Assets: $10,548,500,000 (fiscal 2001 approx); $14,659,683,000 (fiscal 2000 approx); $11,960,279,629 (fiscal 1999)

Typical Recipients

Arts & Humanities: Arts Associations & Councils, Arts Centers, Dance, Ethnic & Folk Arts, Film & Video, Arts & Humanities-General, Historic Preservation, Libraries, Music, Performing Arts, Public Broadcasting, Theater

Civic & Public Affairs: African American Affairs, Business/Free Enterprise, Civil Rights, Community Foundations, Economic Development, Economic Policy, Employment/Job Training, First Amendment Issues, Civic & Public Affairs-General, Hispanic Affairs, Housing, Law & Justice, Legal Aid, Municipalities/Towns, Native American Affairs, Nonprofit Management, Philanthropic Organizations, Public Policy, Rural Affairs, Urban & Community Affairs, Women's Affairs

Education: Agricultural Education, Agricultural Education, Arts/Humanities Education, Business-School Partnerships, Colleges & Universities, Community & Junior Colleges, Continuing Education, Economic Education, Education Associations, Education Funds, Education Reform, Faculty Development, Education-General, Gifted & Talented Programs, International Studies, Leadership Training, Legal Education, Literacy, Minority Education, Public Education (Precollege), Science/Mathematics Education, Social Sciences Education, Student Aid

Environment: Air/Water Quality, Forestry, Environment-General, Resource Conservation

Health: AIDS/HIV, Health Organizations, Medical Research, Nutrition, Public Health

International: Foreign Arts Organizations, Foreign Educational Institutions, International-General, Health Care/Hospitals, Human Rights, International Affairs, International Development, International Environmental Issues, International Organizations, International Peace & Security Issues, International Relations, International Relief Efforts, Missionary/Religious Activities, Trade

Religion: Religious Organizations, Religious Welfare, Social/Policy Issues

Science: Science-General, Scientific Centers & Institutes, Scientific Organizations

Social Services: At-Risk Youth, Child Welfare, Community Service Organizations, Day Care, Delinquency & Criminal Rehabilitation, Domestic Violence, Family Planning, Family Services, Refugee Assistance, Substance Abuse, United Funds/United Ways, Volunteer Services, Youth Organizations

Application Procedures

Initial Contact: Before submitting any application, a brief letter of inquiry is recommended to determine whether the foundation's present interests and funds permit consideration of a proposal. Domestic applications and inquiries should be sent to the foundation's secretary. International applicants should direct their proposals to the nearest field office; field offices are listed in the foundation's annual report and on the foundation's Web site.

Application Requirements: The letter should include the purpose of the project for which funds are being requested; problems and issues the proposed project will address; information about the organization conducting the project; estimated project budget; period of time for which funds are requested; and qualifications of those who will be engaged in the project. After receiving the letter, the foundation may ask the applicant to submit a formal proposal. There is no grant application form. Proposals should include the organization's current budget; a description of the proposed work and how it will be conducted; the names and curriculum vitae of those engaged in the project; a detailed project budget; present means of support and status of applications to other funding sources; and legal and tax status.

Deadlines: None.

Review Process: Applications are considered throughout the year. Normally, applicants may expect to receive within six weeks an indication of whether their proposals are within the foundation's interests and budget limitations.

Restrictions

Activities supported by grants and program-related investments must be charitable, educational, or scientific, as defined under the U.S. Internal Revenue Code and Treasury Regulations. The foundation limits its grants to efforts likely to have wide effect. Support is not usually awarded for routine operating costs or for religious activities. Except in rare cases, funding is not available for construction or maintenance of buildings. The foundation does not award undergraduate scholarships or make grants for purely personal needs. Support for graduate fellowships is generally provided through grants to universities and other organizations, which are responsible for the selection of recipients. Grants to individuals are most often awarded either through publicly announced competitions or on the basis of nominations from universities and other nonprofit institutions.

Although the foundation also makes grants to individuals, they are few in number relative to demand and are limited to research, training, and other activities related to the foundation's interests.

Additional Information

The foundation publishes and distributes a variety of free publications and also disseminates foundation-supported videos and films. Videos may be purchased or rented. A catalog listing these publications and videos, along with video pricing and ordering information, is available free of charge. Requests for the catalog and other publications, or to be placed on the mailing list, should be sent to the Ford Foundation, Office of Communications, Dept. A, 320 E. 43rd St., New York, NY 10017.

Publications: Annual Report; Current Interests of the Ford Foundation; Ford Foundation Report; Videos and Films; Numerous Reports

Foundation Officials

Paul Arthur Allaire: trustee B Worcester, MA July 21, 1938. ED Worcester Polytechnic Institute BS (1960); Carnegie Mellon University MS (1966). CORP AFFIL director: Xerox Financial Services Inc.; director: SmithKline Beecham PLC; director: JP Morgan & Co. Inc.; director: Morgan Guaranty Trust Co. New York; director: Lucent Technologies Inc. NONPR AFFIL director: New York City Ballet; member: Tau Beta Pi; member: National Academy Engineering; member:

Council Foreign Relations; member: Eta Kappa Nu; member: Council Competitiveness; director: Catalyst for Women Inc.

Alain J. P. Belda: trustee B Morocco June 23, 1943. ED MacKenzie University BA (1969). PRIM CORP EMPL chairman, chief executive officer, director: Alcoa Inc. CORP AFFIL director: Cooper Industries Inc.; director: E.I. du Pont de Nemours & Co.; director: Citicorp.

Alison Bernstein: vice president, education, media, arts, & culture

Alison R. Bernstein: vice president, knowledge, creativity and freedom

Susan Vail Berresford: president B New York, NY 1943. ED Vassar College (1961-1963); Radcliffe College BA (1965). CORP AFFIL director: Chase Manhattan Corp.

Afsaneh M. Beschloss: trustee

Anke A. Ehrhardt: trustee

Nancy P. Feller: assistant secretary Assoc Gen Counc

Kathryn Scott Fuller: trustee B New York, NY 1946. ED Brown University BA (1968); University of Texas JD (1976); University of Maryland MS (1980-1982). PRIM NONPR EMPL president, chief executive officer: World Wildlife Fund. NONPR AFFIL member: World Bank Advisory Committee on Sustainable Development; honorary member: Zonta International; member: Texas Bar Association; member advisory committee: Trade Policy Negotiations; member: District of Columbia Bar Association; member advisory committee: President Commission Environmental Quality; director: Brown University.

Barry D. Gaberman: senior vice president

Nicholas M. Gabriel: treasurer, director financial services

Wilmot G. James: trustee

Yolanda Kakabadse: trustee

David Todd Kearns: trustee B Rochester, NY 1930. ED University of Rochester BS (1952). PRIM CORP EMPL chairman: New American Schools Development Corp. CORP AFFIL director: Chase Manhattan Bank NA; director: Ryder System Inc.

Wilma Pearl Mankiller: trustee B Stilwell, OK 1945. ED Skyline College; San Bruno College (1973); San Francisco State College (1973-1975); Union College BA (1977); University of Arkansas (1979).

Richard Moe: trustee

Yolanda T. Moses: trustee B Los Angeles, CA. ED California State College BS (1968); University of California MA (1976); University of California PhD (1976). PRIM NONPR EMPL president: City University of New York. NONPR AFFIL chairman: United Negro College Fund Advisory Board for Service Learning; member: Women's Forum; president, member: American Anthropological Association.

Luis Guerrero Nogales: trustee B Madera, CA 1943. ED San Diego State University BA (1966); Stanford University JD (1969). PRIM NONPR EMPL attorney, president: Nogales Partners. CORP AFFIL director: Southern California Edison Co.; director: Kaufman & Broad Home Corp.; director: Adolph Coors Co.; chairman, chief executive officer: Embarcadero Media Inc. NONPR AFFIL director: Edison International.

Melvin Oliver: vice president, asset building & community development

Deval Laurdine Patrick: trustee B Chicago, IL 1956. ED Harvard College AB (1978); Harvard College JD (1982). PRIM CORP EMPL executive vice president, general counsel: The Coca-Cola Co. CORP AFFIL director: UAL Corp. NONPR AFFIL member: Massachusetts Bar Association; member: Massachusetts Black Lawyers Association; Harvard Alumni Association; board overseers: Harvard University; member: American Bar Association; member: Boston Bar Association.

Bradford K. Smith: vice president, peace & social justice

Linda B. Strumpf: vice president, chief investment officer

Ratan Naval Tata: trustee B Bombay, MH India. ED Cornell University; Harvard University Graduate

School of Business Administration. PRIM CORP EMPL chairman: Tata Inc.

Barron M. Tenny: executive vice president, secretary, general counsel

Carl B. Weisbrod: trustee B New York, NY 1944. ED Cornell University BS (1965); New York University JD (1968). PRIM CORP EMPL chairman: National Income Realty Trust PRIM NONPR EMPL president: Alliance for Downtown New York.

W. Richard West, Jr.: trustee B San Bernardino, CA 1943. ED University of Redlands BA (1965); Harvard University AM (1968); Stanford University JD (1971). NONPR AFFIL honorary counselor: Wings America; member advisory committee: Winslow Foundation; trustee: University Redlands; national support committee: Native American Rights Fund; founding director: Smithsonian Institute National Museum American Indian; trustee: Education Foundation America; member, board trustees: Environmental Defense Fund; member: American Indian Bar Association; treasurer: American Indian Lawyer Training Program.

Alexander Wilde: vice president communications

Grants Analysis

Disclosure Period: fiscal year ending September 30, 2001

Total Grants: $862,596,000*

Number of Grants: 2,550

Average Grant: $120,000*

Highest Grant: $275,526,718

Typical Range: $10,000 to $2,000,000

*Note: Giving excludes program-related investments and funding for foundation-administered projects. Giving includes gifts to individuals. Grants analysis based upon grants approved in 2001. Average grant figure represents median grant size.

Recent Grants

Note: Grants derived from fiscal 2001 Form 990.

General

3,000,000   Bangladesh Freedom Foundation, Dhaka Bangladesh -- endowment support to ensure institutional sustainability and a financial base

2,500,000   Institute of International Education, New York, NY -- support for fellowship program to enhance Asian Scholarship and comparative study within the region

800,000   Shorebank Corporation, Chicago, IL -- recoverable grant to fund the purchase of equity and the extension of a subordinate loan to a finance subsidiary of Bhartiya Samrud

500,000   Gaitonde Medical, Educational and Research Foundation, Chennai India -- endowment support for YRG-Care to sustain and further strengthening HIV/AIDS related activities through it's project "Net Works"

480,000   Institute of International Education, New York, NY -- support for in-country graduate fellowships and partial funding of international scholarships in underserved disciplines

300,000   Anusandhan Trust, Mumbai India -- support to undertake activities to improve the reproductive health of women and address violence against them

300,000   Centre for Policy Dialogue, Raman Dhaka Bangladesh -- support for an independent, nongovernmental and nonprofit regional institution for building interstate cooperation in South Asia

300,000   Institute of Economic Growth, New Delhi India -- endowment support for chair and seed research funding for environmental and resources economics

300,000   Winrock International, New Delhi India -- support for a small grants program, publications, grassroots learning

259,000   exchanges, and information and administration support services

Ashoka Trust for Research in Ecology and the Environment, Bangalore India -- support for research on tribal-managed, forest product-based enterprise development in protected areas

WALTER AND JOSEPHINE FORD FUND

Giving Contact

David M. Hempstead, Secretary & Trustee
100 Renaissance Center, 34th Floor
Detroit, MI 48243
Phone: (313)259-7777
Fax: (313)393-7579

Description

Founded: 1951
EIN: 386066334
Organization Type: Family Foundation
Giving Locations: ME; MI: Detroit including metropolitan area; NY
Grant Types: General Support, Project.

Donor Information

Founder: The fund was established in 1951, with Walter B. Ford II, the fund's president, and his wife, Josephine F. Ford, the fund's vice president, as donors. Josephine Ford is the granddaughter of Ford Motor Company founder, Henry Ford, and the daughter of Eleanor and Edsel Ford. Walter B. Ford II, from an unrelated Detroit banking family, is chief executive of Ford & Earl Design Associates.

Financial Summary

Total Giving: $825,455 (2000); $511,250 (1998); $388,900 (1997)
Giving Analysis: Giving for 2000 includes: foundation grants to United Way ($16,000) 1998: foundation grants to United Way ($16,000)
Assets: $6,958,111 (2000); $8,041,764 (1998); $7,445,362 (1997)
Gifts Received: $258,041 (1997); $232,304 (1996); $194,175 (1995). Note: The fund receives gifts from a trust agreement between Josephine F. Ford and Comerica Bank of Detroit.

Typical Recipients

Arts & Humanities: Arts Associations & Councils, Arts Centers, Arts Funds, Arts Institutes, Historic Preservation, History & Archaeology, Libraries, Museums/Galleries, Music, Performing Arts, Public Broadcasting, Theater
Civic & Public Affairs: Botanical Gardens/Parks, Chambers of Commerce, Clubs, Community Foundations, Economic Development, Civic & Public Affairs-General, Housing, Municipalities/Towns, Nonprofit Management, Parades/Festivals, Philanthropic Organizations, Urban & Community Affairs, Zoos/Aquariums
Education: Arts/Humanities Education, Colleges & Universities, Education Associations, Education-General, Gifted & Talented Programs, Minority Education, Preschool Education, Private Education (Precollege), Public Education (Precollege), Public Education (Precollege), Science/Mathematics Education, Special Education, Student Aid
Environment: Forestry, Environment-General, Resource Conservation, Wildlife Protection
Health: Alzheimers Disease, Cancer, Clinics/Medical Centers, Health Organizations, Hospitals, Medical Research, Mental Health, Nursing Services, Public Health
International: Foreign Arts Organizations, Human Rights, International Organizations
Religion: Churches, Religious Organizations, Religious Welfare

Science: Scientific Centers & Institutes, Scientific Labs, Scientific Research
Social Services: Animal Protection, At-Risk Youth, Camps, Child Welfare, Community Service Organizations, Day Care, Family Planning, Family Services, People with Disabilities, Scouts, Social Services-General, Substance Abuse, United Funds/United Ways, YMCA/YWCA/YMHA/YWHA, Youth Organizations

Application Procedures

Initial Contact: Send a brief letter of inquiry.
Application Requirements: Include copy of financial statement and copy of IRS letter determining tax status, (unless already listed in cumulative list).
Deadlines: None.

Restrictions

The foundation does not support individuals.

Foundation Officials

Richard M. Cundiff: treasurer
Josephine Clay Ford: president, trustee, mem B 1923.
David M. Hempstead: secretary, trustee PRIM CORP EMPL secretary: Detroit Lions Inc. CORP AFFIL secretary: Higbie-Maxon Inc.
George A. Straitor: assistant treasurer

Grants Analysis

Disclosure Period: calendar year ending 2000
Total Grants: $809,553*
Number of Grants: 76
Average Grant: $8,101*
Highest Grant: $202,000
Lowest Grant: $100
Typical Range: $1,000 to $25,000
*Note: Giving excludes United Way. Average grant figure excludes highest grant.

Recent Grants

Note: Grants derived from 2000 Form 990.

General

202,000	Center for Creative Studies, Detroit, MI
50,000	Friends of Acadia, Bar Harbor, ME
50,000	International Design Conference, Aspen, CO
50,000	Philanthropic Collaborative, New York, NY
50,000	University of Michigan Dearborn, Dearborn, MI
48,405	Archbold Foundation, Thomasville, GA
26,500	Detroit Institute of Arts, Detroit, MI
25,250	Detroit Artists Market, Detroit, MI
25,000	Maine Maritime Academy, Castine, ME
25,000	Neighborhood House, Northeast Harbor, ME

WILLIAM AND MARTHA FORD FUND

Giving Contact

David M. Hempstead, Secretary, Trustee & Member
William and Martha Ford Fund
100 Renaissance Center, 34th Floor
Detroit, MI 48243
Phone: (313)259-7777

Description

Founded: 1953
EIN: 386066335
Organization Type: Private Foundation
Giving Locations: MI; NY; TX
Grant Types: General Support, Scholarship.

Donor Information

Founder: William Clay Ford, Martha Firestone Ford

Financial Summary

Total Giving: $1,255,250 (2000); $1,438,457 (1999); $1,341,300 (1998)
Giving Analysis: Giving for 2000 includes: foundation grants to United Way ($101,000) 1999: foundation grants to United Way ($176,000)
Assets: $10,385,822 (2000); $10,672,483 (1999); $12,134,156 (1998)
Gifts Received: $10,365,625 (1998); $3,940,821 (1996)

Typical Recipients

Arts & Humanities: Arts Centers, Arts Funds, Arts Institutes, Historic Preservation, History & Archaeology, Libraries, Museums/Galleries, Music, Performing Arts, Public Broadcasting
Civic & Public Affairs: Clubs, Community Foundations, Civic & Public Affairs-General, Housing, Municipalities/Towns, Parades/Festivals, Public Policy, Urban & Community Affairs, Women's Affairs, Zoos/Aquariums
Education: Colleges & Universities, Education-General, Minority Education, Private Education (Precollege), Science/Mathematics Education, Special Education, Student Aid
Environment: Environment-General, Resource Conservation
Health: Children's Health/Hospitals, Emergency/Ambulance Services, Health Organizations, Heart, Hospitals, Hospitals, Medical Research, Mental Health, Nursing Services, Public Health
International: Foreign Arts Organizations, Human Rights
Religion: Churches
Science: Scientific Centers & Institutes, Scientific Labs
Social Services: Child Welfare, Community Service Organizations, Delinquency & Criminal Rehabilitation, Family Planning, Homes, Recreation & Athletics, Scouts, Substance Abuse, United Funds/United Ways, Youth Organizations

Application Procedures

Initial Contact: Send a brief letter of inquiry.
Application Requirements: Include recently audited financial statement and proof of tax-exempt status.
Deadlines: None.

Restrictions

Awards are generally limited to charitable organizations already favorably known to and of interest to the substantial contributors of the foundation. Does not support individuals.

Foundation Officials

Richard M. Cundiff: treasurer
Martha F. Ford: trustee, mem
William Clay Ford, Sr.: president, trustee, mem B Detroit, MI 1925. ED Yale University BS (1949). CORP AFFIL director: Ford Motor Co.; owner, chairman: Detroit Lions Inc. NONPR AFFIL member: Psi Upsilon; associate member: Society Automotive Engineers; member: K. T. Phelps Association; chairman emeritus: Edison Institute; honorary life trustee: Eisenhower Medical Center; member: Automobile Old Timers. CLUB AFFIL Economic Club Detroit; Masons Club.
David M. Hempstead: secretary, trustee, member PRIM CORP EMPL secretary: Detroit Lions Inc. CORP AFFIL secretary: Higbie-Maxon Inc.
George A. Straitor: assistant treasurer

Grants Analysis

Disclosure Period: calendar year ending 2000
Total Grants: $1,154,250*
Number of Grants: 68
Average Grant: $9,765*
Highest Grant: $500,000

Typical Range: $1,000 to $25,000
*Note: Giving excludes United Way. Average grant figure excludes highest grant.

Recent Grants

Note: Grants derived from 2000 Form 990.

General

500,000	Edison Institute, Dearborn, MI
250,300	Henry Ford Health System, Detroit, MI
100,000	United Way Community Services, Detroit, MI
50,000	Boys and Girls Clubs of America, Atlanta, GA
50,000	Children's Center, Detroit, MI
50,000	Freedom Institute, New York, NY
30,000	St. Luke's Episcopal Hospital, Houston, TX
25,000	National Council on Alcoholism and Drug Dependence, New York, NY
15,600	University of Michigan Dearborn, Dearborn, MI
15,000	Children's Home, Grosse Pte. Woods, MI

EDSEL B. FORD II FUND

Giving Contact

David M. Hempstead, Secretary
100 Renaissance Center, 34th Fl.
Detroit, MI 48243-1006
Phone: (313)259-7777

Description

Founded: 1994
EIN: 383153050
Organization Type: Private Foundation
Giving Locations: MI: Detroit metro area some giving nationally.
Grant Types: General Support.

Financial Summary

Total Giving: $303,769 (2001); $251,100 (2000); $368,288 (1999)
Assets: $6,602,343 (2001); $7,330,443 (2000); $6,509,913 (1999)
Gifts Received: $5,051,922 (1998); $1,165,173 (1993). Note: Contributions were received from Edsel B. Ford II.

Typical Recipients

Arts & Humanities: Arts Institutes, Historic Preservation, History & Archaeology, Libraries, Museums/Galleries
Civic & Public Affairs: Botanical Gardens/Parks, Clubs, Housing, Zoos/Aquariums
Education: Arts/Humanities Education, Colleges & Universities, Faculty Development, Education-General, Private Education (Precollege), Public Education (Precollege), Secondary Education (Public)
Health: Children's Health/Hospitals, Diabetes, Health Organizations
Religion: Churches, Jewish Causes, Religious Welfare
Science: Scientific Centers & Institutes
Social Services: Camps, Child Welfare, Community Service Organizations, Family Planning, People with Disabilities

Application Procedures

Initial Contact: Send a brief letter of inquiry.
Application Requirements: Financial statement and proof of tax-exempt status.
Deadlines: None.

Restrictions

Awards are generally limited to charitable organizations already favorably known to, and of interest to, the substantial contributors of the foundation. Grants are not made to individuals.

Foundation Officials

Richard M. Cundiff: treasurer
Edsel B. Ford, II: president, director, member B 1949. PRIM CORP EMPL vice president, director: Ford Motor Co. CORP AFFIL vice chairman: Detroit Lions Inc.; director: Penske Motorsports Inc. NONPR AFFIL trustee: Henry Ford Museum; trustee: Greenfield Village; trustee: Edison Institute.
David M. Hempstead: secretary PRIM CORP EMPL secretary: Detroit Lions Inc. CORP AFFIL secretary: Higbie-Maxon Inc.

Grants Analysis

Disclosure Period: calendar year ending 2001
Total Grants: $303,769
Number of Grants: 36
Average Grant: $8,438
Highest Grant: $50,000
Lowest Grant: $250
Typical Range: $5,000 to $10,000

Recent Grants

Note: Grants derived from 2000 Form 990.

General

26,000	Juvenile Diabetes Foundation, Southfield, MI
25,450	Salvation Army, Southfield, MI
25,000	Detroit Institute for Children, Detroit, MI
15,000	Henry Ford Health System, Detroit, MI
15,000	Rollins College, Winter Park, FL
15,000	University Liggett School, Grosse Pte., MI
14,500	CATCH, Detroit, MI
12,000	Detroit Zoological Society, Royal Oak, MI
11,500	Grosse Pointe Memorial Church, Grosse Pte. Farms, MI
10,000	Dartmouth College, Hanover, ME

HENRY FORD II FUND

Giving Contact

David M. Hempstead, Secretary & Trustee
100 Renaissance Center, 34th Floor
Detroit, MI 48243
Phone: (313)259-7777
Fax: (313)393-7579

Description

Founded: 1953
EIN: 386066332
Organization Type: General Purpose Foundation
Giving Locations: MI: Detroit
Grant Types: General Support, Research, Scholarship.

Donor Information

Founder: The fund was established in 1953. The donor was the late Henry Ford II (d. 1987), a grandson of Ford Motor Company founder Henry Ford, and a chairman and chief executive of the automobile company.

Financial Summary

Total Giving: $1,743,500 (2000); $911,000 (1998); $646,500 (1997)
Giving Analysis: Giving for 2000 includes: foundation grants to United Way ($50,000); 1998: foundation grants to United Way ($50,000); foundation ($861,000) 1997: foundation grants to United Way ($55,000)
Assets: $31,446,968 (2000); $29,636,391 (1998); $24,775,598 (1997)
Gifts Received: $285,628 (1998); $262,434 (1997); $234,137 (1996). Note: In 1998, the fund received gifts from trust agreements between Henry Ford II and Comerica Bank.

Typical Recipients

Arts & Humanities: Arts Institutes, Arts & Humanities-General, Historic Preservation, History & Archaeology, Libraries, Museums/Galleries, Performing Arts, Public Broadcasting
Civic & Public Affairs: Clubs, Community Foundations, Civic & Public Affairs-General, Housing, Municipalities/Towns, Urban & Community Affairs
Education: Business-School Partnerships, Colleges & Universities, Community & Junior Colleges, Education Associations, Minority Education, Private Education (Precollege), Secondary Education (Public), Special Education, Student Aid
Health: Children's Health/Hospitals, Emergency/Ambulance Services, Eyes/Blindness, Health Organizations, Hospitals, Medical Rehabilitation, Medical Research
Religion: Churches, Religious Welfare
Science: Scientific Centers & Institutes
Social Services: Child Welfare, Child Welfare, Community Service Organizations, Food/Clothing Distribution, People with Disabilities, Recreation & Athletics, United Funds/United Ways, Volunteer Services, Youth Organizations

Application Procedures

Initial Contact: Send a brief letter of inquiry.
Application Requirements: Include recently audited financial statement and proof of tax-exempt status.
Deadlines: None.

Restrictions

Awards are generally limited to charitable organizations already favorably known to and of interest to the substantial contributors of this foundation. The purpose of each grant or contributions is to provide financial support to corporations, trust, community chests, funds or foundations, organized and operated solely for religious, charitable, scientific, literary or educational purposes, or for the prevention of cruelty to children or animals. The fund does not make grants to individuals.

Foundation Officials

Richard M. Cundiff: treasurer,
Edsel B. Ford, II: president, trustee, mem B 1949. PRIM CORP EMPL vice president, director: Ford Motor Co. CORP AFFIL vice chairman: Detroit Lions Inc.; director: Penske Motorsports Inc. NONPR AFFIL trustee: Henry Ford Museum; trustee: Greenfield Village; trustee: Edison Institute.
David M. Hempstead: secretary, trustee PRIM CORP EMPL secretary: Detroit Lions Inc. CORP AFFIL secretary: Higbie-Maxon Inc.

Grants Analysis

Disclosure Period: calendar year ending 2000
Total Grants: $1,693,500*
Number of Grants: 19
Average Grant: $89,132
Highest Grant: $300,000
Typical Range: $25,000 to $50,000 and $100,000 to $300,000
*Note: Giving excludes United Way.

Recent Grants

Note: Grants derived from 2000 Form 990.

General

300,000	Detroit 300, Inc., Detroit, MI
300,000	University Liggett School, Grosse Pte. Woods, MI
244,000	Children's Hospital of Michigan, Detroit, MI
150,000	Henry Ford Community College, Dearborn, MI

100,000	Edison Institute, Dearborn, MI
100,000	Focus HOPE, Detroit, MI
100,000	Salvation Army, Southfield, MI
75,000	Detroit Institute for Children, Detroit, MI
70,000	United Negro College Fund, Detroit, MI
50,000	Cornerstone Schools Association, Detroit, MI

FORD METER BOX CO.

Company Headquarters

775 Manchester Avenue
PO Box 443
Wabash, IN 46992-0443
Phone: (219)563-3171
Fax: (219)563-6781
Web: http://www.fordmeterbox.com

Company Description

Employees: 700
SIC(s): 3321 Gray & Ductile Iron Foundries, 3494 Valves & Pipe Fittings Nec, 3822 Environmental Controls, 3823 Process Control Instruments.

Operating Locations

Ford Meter Box Co. (IN--Wabash)

Ford Meter Box Foundation

Giving Contact

Marta D. Gidley, Secretary
PO Box 443
775 Manchester Avenue
Wabash, IN 46992
Phone: (0)563-3171

Description

Founded: 1988
EIN: 351253080
Organization Type: Corporate Foundation
Giving Locations: IN: Wabash County and surrounding area
Grant Types: General Support, Project, Scholarship.

Financial Summary

Total Giving: $1,259,318 (2002); $779,835 (2001); $315,709 (1999). Note: Contributes through foundation only.
Giving Analysis: Giving for 2001 includes: foundation scholarships ($1,000); foundation grants to United Way ($32,500) foundation ($746,335)
Assets: $3,959,005 (2002); $3,840,149 (2001); $3,941,954 (1999)
Gifts Received: $1,000,000 (2002); $500,000 (1998); $500,000 (1996). Note: Contributions are received from Ford Meter Box Co.

Typical Recipients

Arts & Humanities: Arts Associations & Councils, Community Arts, Dance, Film & Video, Historic Preservation, History & Archaeology, Libraries, Museums/Galleries, Music, Opera, Performing Arts, Theater
Civic & Public Affairs: Botanical Gardens/Parks, Business/Free Enterprise, Clubs, Community Foundations, Economic Development, Economic Policy, Employment/Job Training, Civic & Public Affairs-General, Housing, Law & Justice, Municipalities/Towns, Nonprofit Management, Parades/Festivals, Philanthropic Organizations, Professional & Trade Associations, Public Policy, Safety, Urban & Community Affairs, Zoos/Aquariums
Education: Agricultural Education, Arts/Humanities Education, Business Education, Business Education, Colleges & Universities, Education Associations, Education Funds, Elementary Education (Public), Education-General, International Studies, Leadership

Training, Preschool Education, Private Education (Precollege), Public Education (Precollege), Religious Education, Science/Mathematics Education, Secondary Education (Public), Student Aid
Health: Cancer, Children's Health/Hospitals, Emergency/Ambulance Services, Eyes/Blindness, Geriatric Health, Health Organizations, Heart, Hospices, Hospitals, Medical Research, Mental Health, Outpatient Health Care, Prenatal Health Issues, Single-Disease Health Associations
International: Foreign Arts Organizations, Health Care/Hospitals, Missionary/Religious Activities
Religion: Churches, Religious Welfare, Religious Welfare
Social Services: Animal Protection, At-Risk Youth, Big Brother/Big Sister, Child Abuse, Child Welfare, Community Service Organizations, Counseling, Crime Prevention, Domestic Violence, Emergency Relief, Family Services, Food/Clothing Distribution, Homes, Recreation & Athletics, Scouts, Senior Services, Substance Abuse, United Funds/United Ways, YMCA/YWCA/YMHA/YWHA, Youth Organizations

Application Procedures

Initial Contact: Send written request.
Application Requirements: Include amount requested and purpose for which funds will be used.
Deadlines: None.

Corporate Officials

Thomas W. Hodson: president, drcc
Christopher Shanks: vice president, director

Foundation Officials

Daniel Ford: vice chairman
Thomas Vanosdol: chairman

Grants Analysis

Disclosure Period: calendar year ending 2002
Total Grants: $1,259,318*
Number of Grants: 47
Average Grant: $6,426*
Highest Grant: $500,000
Typical Range: $200 to $5,000 and $25,000 to $50,000
***Note:** Giving excludes scholarship, United Way. Average grant figure excludes highest grant.

Recent Grants

Note: Grants derived from 2001 Form 990.

General

500,000	Community Foundation of Wabash County, Manchester, IN -- for endowment campaign
50,000	Community Foundation of Wabash County, Manchester, IN -- for Wabash County Historical Museum
50,000	Community Foundation of Wabash County, Manchester, IN -- for Wabash County Historical Museum
50,000	Community Foundation of Wabash County, Manchester, IN -- for Wabash County Historical Museum
32,500	Wabash County United Fund, Wabash, IN -- for annual fund drive
30,000	Independent Colleges of Indiana Foundation, Indianapolis, IN -- annual contribution
25,000	Community Foundation of Wabash County, Manchester, IN -- for Honeywell House Renovation Fund
5,000	Habitat for Humanity, Wabash, IN
5,000	Ivy Tech State College, Wabash, IN -- for computer lab
5,000	WEDCOR, Wabash, IN -- for Vision Program

FORD MOTOR CO.

Company Headquarters

1 American Rd.
Dearborn, MI 48126-2798
Web: http://www.ford.com

Company Description

Ticker: F
Exchange: NYSE
Revenue: US$134.425 billion (2002)
Employees: 350321 (2002)
Fortune Rank: 4, per FORTUNE Magazine's list of 500 Largest U.S. Corporations (2002).

Nonmonetary Support

Type: Donated Equipment; Donated Products
Volunteer Programs: Ford Motor Company offers every Ford salaried employee 16 hours of paid time off per year to volunteer in teams of co-workers at various agencies.
Contact: Ray Byers, Manager, Contributions Programs
Phone: (313)248-4745
Note: Company also donates land.

Ford Motor Co. Fund

Giving Contact

Sandra E. Ulsh, Vice President, Executive Director
Ford Motor Company Fund
One American Road
PO Box 1899
Dearborn, MI 48126
Phone: 888-313-0102
Web: http://www.ford.com/en/ourCompany/corporateCitizenship/fordMotorCompanyFund/default.htm

Alternate Contact

Shirly Durham, Contributions Manager

Description

EIN: 381459376
Organization Type: Corporate Foundation
Giving Locations: nationally; headquarters and operating communities; nationally.
Grant Types: Capital, Conference/Seminar, Department, Employee Matching Gifts, General Support, Multiyear/Continuing Support.
Note: Employee matching gift ratio: 1 to 1.

Financial Summary

Total Giving: $56,971,262 (2001); $83,749,284 (2000); $57,747,285 (1999). Note: Contributes through corporate direct giving program and foundation.
Giving Analysis: Giving for 2001 includes: foundation scholarships ($1,060,075); foundation matching gifts ($3,143,413); foundation grants to United Way ($12,488,806); foundation ($40,278,968); 1999: foundation matching gifts ($3,666,449); foundation ($49,897,759); 1998: nonmonetary support (approx $500,000); foundation matching gifts ($3,111,920); foundation grants to United Way ($4,432,811); corporate direct giving (approx $22,462,510); foundation ($27,792,759);
Assets: $144,907,832 (2001); $247,625,772 (2000); $97,789,429 (1999)
Gifts Received: $70,000,000 (2000); $245,008,771 (1999); $100,000,000 (1998). Note: Contributions are received from Ford Motor Company and Ford Holdings, Inc.

Typical Recipients

Arts & Humanities: Arts Associations & Councils, Arts Centers, Arts Festivals, Arts Institutes, Community Arts, Ethnic & Folk Arts, Arts & Humanities-General, Historic Preservation, History & Archaeology,

Libraries, Museums/Galleries, Music, Opera, Performing Arts, Public Broadcasting, Theater

Civic & Public Affairs: African American Affairs, Botanical Gardens/Parks, Business/Free Enterprise, Chambers of Commerce, Civil Rights, Community Foundations, Economic Development, Economic Policy, Employment/Job Training, Civic & Public Affairs-General, Hispanic Affairs, Housing, Law & Justice, Municipalities/Towns, Philanthropic Organizations, Professional & Trade Associations, Public Policy, Safety, Safety, Urban & Community Affairs, Women's Affairs, Zoos/Aquariums

Education: Agricultural Education, Arts/Humanities Education, Business Education, Colleges & Universities, Economic Education, Education Associations, Education Funds, Education Reform, Engineering/Technological Education, Faculty Development, Education-General, Gifted & Talented Programs, Health & Physical Education, Journalism/Media Education, Minority Education, Public Education (Precollege), Religious Education, Science/Mathematics Education, Secondary Education (Public), Student Aid

Environment: Environment-General, Wildlife Protection

Health: Cancer, Emergency/Ambulance Services, Health Policy/Cost Containment, Health Organizations, Hospices, Hospitals, Kidney, Prenatal Health Issues, Public Health

International: Foreign Arts Organizations, International Development, International Environmental Issues, International Organizations, International Peace & Security Issues, International Relations

Religion: Jewish Causes, Ministries

Science: Science Museums, Scientific Centers & Institutes

Social Services: Camps, Child Welfare, Community Service Organizations, Delinquency & Criminal Rehabilitation, People with Disabilities, Recreation & Athletics, Scouts, Substance Abuse, United Funds/United Ways, Volunteer Services, YMCA/YWCA/YMHA/YWHA, Youth Organizations

Application Procedures

Initial Contact: National organizations should submit a brief written proposal; organizations located in communities where Ford operates may submit requests to the fund or to the community relations committee at local plants. All organizations must complete the grant application enclosed in the Ford Fund annual report.

Application Requirements: Within two pages, the proposal should include a description of organization, amount requested, proposed use of the funds, and a brief description of the project or program, including goals and objectives. In addition, the proposal should include other sources of funding, a detailed budget and financial information, status of related projects previously supported by Ford Motor Company Fund, an explanation of how the Fund will be recognized, summary of past performance (if applicable), and proof of tax-exempt status.

Deadlines: None.

Decision Notification: The fund will send a postcard notifying applicant that proposal has been received. No further notification will occur if there is no interest in the proposal. If there is an interest in the request, applicant will receive notification of the disposition within six weeks of receiving initial acknowledgment card.

Restrictions

The Fund generally does not support animal rights organizations, beauty or talent contests, day-to-day business operations, debt reduction, vehicle donations, endowments, fraternal organizations, individual sponsorship related to fund-raising activities, individuals, labor groups, small business or program-related investment loans, general operating support to hospitals and health care institutions, non-U.S.-based charities, organizations without 501(c)(3) status, political

or lobbying groups, private schools, profit-making enterprises, religious organizations for sectarian purposes, species specific organizations, or organizations that may pose a conflict with Ford's mission, goals, programs, products, services, or employees.

Additional Information

Publications: Guidelines; Corporate Citizenship Report (annually); Ford Fund Annual Report (annually)

Corporate Officials

Elizabeth S. Acton: vice president, treasurer ED University of Minnesota BA (1973); Indiana University MBA (1976). PRIM CORP EMPL vice president, treasurer: Ford Motor Co.

W. Wayne Booker: vice chairman ED Purdue University BS. PRIM CORP EMPL vice chairman: Ford Motor Co.

William Clay Ford, Jr.: chairman, chief executive officer B Detroit, MI May 03, 1957. ED Princeton University BA (1979); Michigan Institute of Technology MS (1984). PRIM CORP EMPL chairman, chief executive officer: Ford Motor Co. CORP AFFIL treasurer: Detroit Lions Inc.; trustee: Henry Ford Health System. NONPR AFFIL trustee: Edison Institute; trustee: Michigan Nature Conservancy.

Allan Dana Gilmour: vice chairman, chief financial officer B Burke, VT June 17, 1934. ED Harvard University AB (1956); University of Michigan MBA (1959). PRIM CORP EMPL vice chairman, chief financial officer: Ford Motor Co. CORP AFFIL director: Prudential Financial; director: Whirlpool Corp.; trustee: Community Foundation Southeastern Michigan; director: DTE Energy Co. NONPR AFFIL member: Phi Kappa Phi; member vis committee grad sch business administration: University Michigan; member: Beta Gamma Sigma; trustee: Henry Ford Health Systems.

John M. Rintamaki: group vice president, chief of staff PRIM CORP EMPL group vice president, chief of staff: Ford Motor Co. ADD CORP EMPL assistant secretary: Ford Motor Credit Co.

Sir Nicholas Scheele: president, chief operating officer B Essex, United Kingdom January 03, 1944. PRIM CORP EMPL president, chief operating officer: Ford Motor Co.

Sandy Ulsh: vice president, executive director

Foundation Officials

Leo Joseph Brennan, Jr.: vice president, executive director B Hancock, MI 1930. ED University of Notre Dame BA (1951); University of Notre Dame MA (1952); Georgetown University (1953). NONPR AFFIL director: Michigan Bach Festival; member: Michigan Historical Society; member: Detroit Zoological Society; trustee: Michigan 4-H Council; director: Brother Rice High School; member founders society: Detroit Institute Arts. CLUB AFFIL Bloomfield Open Hunt Club; Otsego Ski Club.

Shirley Durham: contributions manager

Alfred B. Ford: trustee B 1934.

Sheila F. Hamp: trustee PRIM CORP EMPL trustee: Henry Ford Museum.

Malcolm S. McDonald: trustee

Jorge Piedrahita: assistant treasurer

John M. Rintamaki: secretary (see above)

Peter J. Sherry, Jr.: secretary

Dennis A. Tosh: assistant treasurer

Martin B. Zimmerman: trustee

Grants Analysis

Disclosure Period: calendar year ending 2001
Total Grants: $40,278,968*
Number of Grants: 1,610
Average Grant: $25,018
Highest Grant: $5,000,000
Typical Range: $1,000 to $100,000
*Note: Giving excludes matching gifts; scholarship; and United Way.

Recent Grants

Note: Grants derived from 2001 Form 990.

General

5,000,000 Conservation International Foundation, Washington, DC

3,500,000 National Audubon Society -- for complete Ford commitment

2,500,000 United Way Community Services, Detroit, MI -- for purchase and shipment of 125,000 seats

2,000,000 Georgia Institute of Technology, Atlanta, GA -- for Ford Motor Company Environmental Science and Technology

2,000,000 Northwestern University, Evanston, IL -- for Design Center grant

1,880,000 Berry College, Mt. Berry, VA -- restoration of Ford building

1,839,649 Employee Matching Gift Program, New York, NY

1,600,000 United Way Community Services, Detroit, MI -- for Boost America

1,500,000 United Way Community Services, Detroit, MI -- for Boost America Project

1,500,000 United Way Community Services, Detroit, MI -- capital fund

FOREST CITY ENTERPRISES, INC.

Company Headquarters

50 Public Sq.
Cleveland, OH 44113
Web: http://www.fceinc.com

Company Description

Founded: 1920
Ticker: FCEA
Exchange: NYSE
Revenue: US$906.6 million (2001)
Employees: 4515 (2001)
SIC(s): 1521 Single-Family Housing Construction, 1522 Residential Construction Nec, 1531 Operative Builders, 6531 Real Estate Agents & Managers.

Operating Locations

Forest City Enterprises, Inc. (AL--Homewood; CA--Los Angeles, Newport Beach; FL--Tampa; MN--Minneapolis; NH--Nashua; NY--New York; OH--Brook Park; OR--Beaverton, Bend, Portland; PA--Aliquippa)

Nonmonetary Support

Type: Loaned Employees; Loaned Executives

Forest City Enterprises Charitable Foundation, Inc.

Giving Contact

Allan C. Krulak, Vice President
Forest City Enterprises
50 Public Square, Suite 1100
Cleveland, OH 44113-2203
Phone: (216)621-6060
Fax: (216)263-6208

Description

Founded: 1976
EIN: 341218895
Organization Type: Corporate Foundation
Giving Locations: NY: New York including metropolitan area; OH, Cleveland including metropolitan area operating locations.
Grant Types: General Support, Scholarship.

Financial Summary

Total Giving: $3,117,317 (fiscal year ending January 31, 2002); $2,515,759 (fiscal 2000); $1,500,000 (fiscal 1999 approx). Note: Contributes through foundation only.

Giving Analysis: Giving for fiscal 2000 includes: foundation grants to United Way ($149,100); foundation ($2,366,659) fiscal 1998: foundation ($1,821,001)

Assets: $227,203 (fiscal 2002); $44,986 (fiscal 2000); $31,882 (fiscal 1998)

Gifts Received: $3,062,794 (fiscal 2002); $2,531,000 (fiscal 2000); $1,815,000 (fiscal 1998). Note: Contributions are received from Forest City Enterprises Inc.

Typical Recipients

Arts & Humanities: Arts Associations & Councils, Arts Institutes, Ballet, Arts & Humanities-General, History & Archaeology, Libraries, Museums/Galleries, Music, Opera, Performing Arts, Theater, Visual Arts

Civic & Public Affairs: African American Affairs, Business/Free Enterprise, Civil Rights, Clubs, Economic Development, Ethnic Organizations, Civic & Public Affairs-General, Housing, Municipalities/Towns, Parades/Festivals, Philanthropic Organizations, Public Policy, Safety, Urban & Community Affairs, Women's Affairs, Zoos/Aquariums

Education: Arts/Humanities Education, Colleges & Universities, Community & Junior Colleges, Education Funds, Education Reform, Engineering/Technological Education, Education-General, Private Education (Precollege), Religious Education, Student Aid

Environment: Forestry

Health: AIDS/HIV, Alzheimers Disease, Arthritis, Cancer, Children's Health/Hospitals, Clinics/Medical Centers, Diabetes, Emergency/Ambulance Services, Eyes/Blindness, Health-General, Health Organizations, Hospices, Hospitals, Multiple Sclerosis, Prenatal Health Issues, Public Health, Single-Disease Health Associations

International: International Peace & Security Issues, International Relations, International Relief Efforts, Missionary/Religious Activities

Religion: Churches, Dioceses, Religion-General, Jewish Causes, Ministries, Religious Organizations, Religious Welfare, Seminaries, Social/Policy Issues, Synagogues/Temples

Science: Scientific Centers & Institutes

Social Services: Animal Protection, Camps, Child Welfare, Community Service Organizations, Crime Prevention, Delinquency & Criminal Rehabilitation, Food/Clothing Distribution, Sexual Abuse, Substance Abuse, United Funds/United Ways, Volunteer Services, YMCA/YWCA/YMHA/YWHA, Youth Organizations

Application Procedures

Initial Contact: Send a brief letter or proposal.

Application Requirements: Include a description of organization, amount requested, purpose of funds sought, and proof of tax-exempt status.

Deadlines: None; grants committee meets as needed.

Restrictions

Grants are not made to individuals.

Corporate Officials

Allan C. Krulak: vice president corporate & public affairs, director PRIM CORP EMPL vice president corporate & public affairs, director: Forest City Enterprises, Inc.

Foundation Officials

Allan C. Krulak: vice president (see above)

Grants Analysis

Disclosure Period: fiscal year ending January 31, 2002

Total Grants: $2,914,897*

Number of Grants: 199

Average Grant: $7,962*

Highest Grant: $687,500

Lowest Grant: $100

Typical Range: $500 to $10,000

*****Note:** Giving excludes United Way. Average grant figure excludes three highest grants totaling ($1,354,420).

Recent Grants

Note: Grants derived from 2002 Form 990.

Library-Related

15,000	National First Ladies Library, Bethesda, MD

General

687,500	Jewish Community Federation of Cleveland, Cleveland, OH
464,500	Cleveland Orchestra, Cleveland, OH
202,420	United Way Services, Cleveland, OH
158,979	American Red Cross, Cleveland, OH
141,500	Cleveland Clinic Foundation, Cleveland, OH
130,000	United States Holocaust Memorial Council, Washington, DC
80,000	Hebrew Academy of Cleveland, Cleveland, OH
68,500	Cleveland State University, Cleveland, OH
63,888	Case Western Reserve University, Cleveland, OH
61,925	Cleveland Museum of Natural History, Cleveland, OH

FOREST FOUNDATION

Giving Contact

Frank D. Underwood, Executive Director
820 A Street, Suite 345
Tacoma, WA 98402
Phone: (253)627-1634
Fax: (253)627-6249

Description

Founded: 1962

EIN: 916020514

Organization Type: Family Foundation

Giving Locations: WA: southwestern Washington; especially Pierce County

Grant Types: Capital, Operating Expenses, Project.

Donor Information

Founder: Incorporated in 1962 by C. Davis Weyerhaeuser and William T. Weyerhaeuser.

Financial Summary

Total Giving: $2,305,513 (fiscal year ending October 31, 2001); $1,855,134 (fiscal 2000); $1,386,914 (fiscal 1998)

Giving Analysis: Giving for fiscal 2000 includes: foundation grants to United Way ($35,000) fiscal 1998: foundation grants to United Way ($25,000)

Assets: $29,251,996 (fiscal 2001); $31,860,252 (fiscal 2000); $30,053,334 (fiscal 1998)

Typical Recipients

Arts & Humanities: Arts Associations & Councils, Arts Outreach, Ballet, Dance, Ethnic & Folk Arts, Arts & Humanities-General, Historic Preservation, History & Archaeology, Libraries, Museums/Galleries, Music, Opera, Performing Arts, Public Broadcasting, Theater

Civic & Public Affairs: African American Affairs, Asian American Affairs, Business/Free Enterprise, Civil Rights, Clubs, Community Foundations, Economic Policy, Civic & Public Affairs-General, Housing, Municipalities/Towns, Native American Affairs, Parades/Festivals, Philanthropic Organizations, Public Policy, Safety, Urban & Community Affairs, Women's Affairs

Education: Arts/Humanities Education, Colleges & Universities, Colleges & Universities, Community & Junior Colleges, Continuing Education, Economic Education, Elementary Education (Public), Education-General, Health & Physical Education, Leadership Training, Medical Education, Minority Education, Private Education (Precollege), Public Education (Precollege), Religious Education, Secondary Education (Private), Special Education, Student Aid

Environment: Forestry, Environment-General, Resource Conservation, Watershed, Wildlife Protection

Health: AIDS/HIV, Cancer, Clinics/Medical Centers, Emergency/Ambulance Services, Health Funds, Health Organizations, Hospitals, Medical Research, Mental Health, Public Health, Single-Disease Health Associations, Transplant Networks/Donor Banks

International: International Relief Efforts

Religion: Churches, Religion-General, Ministries, Religious Organizations, Religious Welfare, Seminaries

Science: Scientific Centers & Institutes

Social Services: Animal Protection, Big Brother/Big Sister, Camps, Child Abuse, Child Welfare, Community Centers, Community Service Organizations, Counseling, Crime Prevention, Day Care, Domestic Violence, Family Planning, Family Services, Food/Clothing Distribution, Homes, People with Disabilities, Recreation & Athletics, Scouts, Senior Services, Sexual Abuse, Shelters/Homelessness, United Funds/United Ways, YMCA/YWCA/YMHA/YWHA, Youth Organizations

Application Procedures

Initial Contact: Submit five copies of a complete proposal, including cover letter that describes the project and amount of money requested, and a completed grant request summary sheet, which can be obtained from the foundation. Foundation does not accept faxed or emailed proposals. All proposals must clearly address one or more of the forest foundation outcomes provided in the guidelines.

Deadlines: Each of the program areas has specific deadlines. The Community Building and Development program, March 15 and July 15; Culture and the Arts program, May 15 and November 15; the Dependency to Self Sufficiency program, January 15, May 15 and September 15; the Environment program, March 15 and September 15; Children and Youth Development program, January 15, May 15, and September 15, and the Overcoming Adversity program May 15 and November 15. Contact the foundation to confirm the dates.

Review Process: The foundation meets six times a year. Decisions on complete proposals in each of the program areas are made at least twice annually. Action will be taken on proposals between 60 and 75 days from the deadline.

Restrictions

The foundation makes grants only to tax-exempt charitable organizations and generally does not support endowment funds; annual appeals; private foundations or operating foundations; individuals; production of films, videos or any publications; lobbying to influence elections or legislation; or school-related tours.

Additional Information

Grantmaker Consultants, Tacoma, WA, provides grant management services.

Publications: Program Policy Statement; Guidelines

Foundation Officials

Linda P. BeMiller: program officer

Nicholas C. Spika: secretary

Frank D. Underwood: executive director, member

Annette Thayer Black Weyerhaeuser: vice president, director, member

Gail T. Weyerhaeuser: president, treasurer, director

Dr. William Toycen Weyerhaeuser: director, member B Tacoma, WA 1943. ED Stanford University (1966); Fuller Graduate School of Psychology PhD

(1975). PRIM CORP EMPL owner, chairman: Yelm Telephone Co. CORP AFFIL director: Columbia Banking System Inc.; director: Potlatch Corp.

Grants Analysis
Disclosure Period: fiscal year ending October 31, 2001
Total Grants: $2,270,513*
Number of Grants: 73
Average Grant: $23,867*
Highest Grant: $552,100
Typical Range: $10,000 to $50,000
*Note: Giving excludes United Way. Average grant figure excludes highest grant.

Recent Grants
Note: Grants derived from 2001 Form 990.

General
552,100	Bellarmine Preparatory School, Tacoma, WA -- capital needs
200,000	Boys and Girls Clubs of Tacoma-Pierce County, Tacoma, WA -- capital needs
200,000	Tacoma Art Museum, Tacoma, WA -- capital needs
150,000	Mary Bridge Children's Foundation, Tacoma, WA -- capital needs
117,500	Boy Scouts of America Pacific Harbors Council, Tacoma, WA -- capital needs
80,000	People Organized to Operate Leisure Activities, Raymond, WA -- capital needs
54,000	Humane Society for Tacoma and Pierce County, Tacoma, WA -- capital needs
50,000	Tacoma Art Museum, Tacoma, WA -- operating budget
50,000	Tacoma Rescue Mission, Tacoma, WA -- capital needs
40,000	Port Townsend Marine Science Center, Port Townsend, WA -- capital needs

FOREST OIL CORP.

Company Headquarters
1600 Broadway, Suite 2200
Denver, CO
Web: http://www.forestoil.com

Company Description
Founded: 1916
Ticker: FST
Exchange: NYSE
Revenue: US$475.6 million (2002)
Employees: 500 (2002)
SIC(s): 1300 Oil & Gas Extraction.

Operating Locations
Forest Oil Corp. (PA--Bradford); NO SUBSIDIARIES (CO--Denver)
Note: List includes division location

Nonmonetary Support
Type: Donated Equipment; Workplace Solicitation

Glendorn Foundation

Giving Contact
William F. Higie, Secretary & Manager
Glendorn Foundation
78 Main St.
Bradford, PA 16701
Phone: (814)368-7171

Description
Founded: 1953
EIN: 251024349

Organization Type: Corporate Foundation
Giving Locations: nationally.
Grant Types: Capital, Endowment, General Support, Research.

Donor Information
Founder: Forest Oil Corp., Ruth H. Dorn

Financial Summary
Total Giving: $198,750 (2000); $181,250 (1999); $184,350 (1998)
Giving Analysis: Giving for 1999 includes: foundation ($181,250)
Assets: $3,703,212 (2000); $3,653,117 (1999); $3,597,979 (1998)
Gifts Received: $375 (2000); $895 (1999); $5,675 (1998). Note: Contributions were received from Forest Oil Corp.

Typical Recipients
Arts & Humanities: Arts Festivals, Dance, Historic Preservation, Libraries, Museums/Galleries, Music, Opera, Performing Arts, Theater
Civic & Public Affairs: Business/Free Enterprise, Economic Development, Civic & Public Affairs-General, Hispanic Affairs, Philanthropic Organizations, Zoos/Aquariums
Education: Colleges & Universities, Education-General, Literacy, Medical Education, Private Education (Precollege), Special Education, Student Aid
Health: Cancer, Clinics/Medical Centers, Hospices, Hospitals, Hospitals (University Affiliated), Medical Rehabilitation, Medical Research
International: International Development, Missionary/Religious Activities
Religion: Religious Welfare
Science: Science Museums
Social Services: Animal Protection, Child Welfare, Community Centers, Domestic Violence, Food/Clothing Distribution, People with Disabilities, Shelters/Homelessness, Substance Abuse, United Funds/United Ways, YMCA/YWCA/YMHA/YWHA

Application Procedures
Initial Contact: Due to the backlog of proposed gifts, no solicitations from grantees are desired at this time.

Corporate Officials
Bulent A. Berilgen: vice president, chief operating officer, director PRIM CORP EMPL vice president, chief operating officer, director: Forest Oil Corp.
Robert S. Boswell: president, chief executive officer, director B Tulsa, OK 1949. ED Vanderbilt University (1971); University of Texas (1973). PRIM CORP EMPL president, chief executive officer, director: Forest Oil Corp.
William L. Dorn: chairman, chief executive officer, director B San Antonio, TX 1948. ED University of Texas (1971). PRIM CORP EMPL chairman, chief executive officer, director: Forest Oil Corp.
David H. Keyte: vice president, chief financial officer PRIM CORP EMPL vice president, chief financial officer: Forest Oil Corp.

Foundation Officials
Clayton D. Chisum: trustee
David F. Dorn: trustee B 1924. PRIM CORP EMPL co-chairman, chairman executive committee, director: Forest Oil Corp.
Frederick M. Dorn: trustee
John C. Dorn: trustee B 1927. ED Yale University (1950).
Dale B. Grubb: trustee
William F. Higie: secretary, mgr B Bradford, PA 1926. ED Saint Bonaventure University (1949); Dickinson

School of Law (1952). PRIM CORP EMPL vice president, secretary, counsel, director: Forest Oil Corp. NONPR AFFIL vice chairman: Bradford Hospital.
Jeffrey W. Miller: trustee
Leslie D. Young: trustee

Grants Analysis
Disclosure Period: calendar year ending 2000
Total Grants: $198,750
Number of Grants: 11
Average Grant: $18,068
Highest Grant: $37,500
Typical Range: $7,500 to $25,000

Recent Grants
Note: Grants derived from 2000 Form 990.

General
37,500	University of Colorado Health Sciences Center, Denver, CO -- medical research
25,000	Johns Hopkins University, Baltimore, MD -- for medical research
25,000	YMCA, Bradford, PA -- for education/endowment
20,000	Tibetan Heritage Institute, Junction City, CA -- endowment
20,000	University of Pittsburgh, Bradford, PA -- for education
18,750	Burham Institute, La Jolla, CA -- cancer research
12,500	Denver Academy, Denver, CO -- endowment
12,500	Memorial Sloan-Kettering Cancer Center, New York, NY -- medical research
10,000	Denver Museum of Nature and Science, Denver, CO -- education
10,000	Enterprise Development International, Fairfax, VA -- educational

FORMOSA PLASTICS CORPORATION, USA

Company Headquarters
9 Peach Tree Hill Rd.
Livingston, NJ 07039-5702
Web: http://www.fpcusa.com

Company Description
Revenue: US$1.9 billion (2001)
Employees: 2,700 (2001)
SIC(s): 2800 Chemicals & Allied Products, 3000 Rubber & Miscellaneous Plastics Products.
Parent Company: Formosa Plastics Corp., 201 Tun Hwa North Rd., Taipei, Taiwan

Giving Contact
William H. Bauer, Jr., Trustee, Executive Advisory Committee
Formosa Plastics Religious Trust
First National Bank
PO Drawer 7
Port Lavaca, TX 77979
Phone: (361)552-6726

Description
Organization Type: Corporate Giving Program
Giving Locations: TX: Calhoun, Jackson, and Victoria counties
Grant Types: General Support.

Financial Summary
Total Giving: $55,005 (2001)
Giving Analysis: Giving for 2001 includes: foundation ($55,005)
Assets: $1,134,333 (2001)

Typical Recipients

Civic & Public Affairs: Civic & Public Affairs-General
Education: Colleges & Universities, Religious Education, Secondary Education (Private)
Health: Cancer
Religion: Churches, Religion-General, Ministries, Religious Organizations

Application Procedures

Initial Contact: Send for grant application.
Application Requirements: Include a description of organization and purpose of funds sought, benefits and costs of program, and evidence that the application is a qualified religious organization.
Deadlines: October 1.

Restrictions

Limited to commonly recognized religious organizations in a three-county area of the Formosa Plastics Corp. plant at Point Comfort, Texas (Calhoun, Jackson, and Victoria)

Corporate Officials

Robert P. H. Ho: chief financial officer, president B Taiwan 1949. ED National Taiwan University BA (1972). PRIM CORP EMPL chief financial officer: Formosa Plastics Corp. U.S.A. CORP AFFIL treasurer: Inteplast Corp.; treasurer: Nan Ya Plastics Corp. America; treasurer: Formosa Plastics Corp. America.
C. T. Lee: president PRIM CORP EMPL president: Formosa Plastics Corp. U.S.A.
Susan Wang: executive, president B 1960. PRIM CORP EMPL executive, president: Formosa Plastics Corp. U.S.A. ADD CORP EMPL executive, vice president: Formosa Plastics Corp. Delaware; executive, vice president: Formosa Plastics Corp. Texas.
Yung-ching Wang: chairman B Taiwan 1916. PRIM CORP EMPL chairman: Formosa Plastics Corp. U.S.A. CORP AFFIL chairman, director: Formosa Plastics Corp. USA; owner: Nan Ya Plastics Corp.; chairman, director: Formosa Plastics Corp. Texas; owner: Formosa Chemicals & Fibre Corp.; chairman, director: Formosa Plastics Corp. LA.

Grants Analysis

Disclosure Period: calendar year ending 2001
Total Grants: $55,005
Number of Grants: 12
Average Grant: $4,584
Highest Grant: $7,500
Lowest Grant: $1,000

Recent Grants

Note: Grants derived from 2001 Form 990.

General

7,500	First Christian Church, Victoria, TX -- video projection system
6,950	Calhoun County Ministerial Alliance, Victoria, TX -- outreach program to counsel married couples and strengthen existing marriages
6,825	Shiloh Missionary Baptist, Newark, OH -- after-school youth program
5,730	Texas Buddhist Association, Houston, TX -- lecture series and youth leadership development program
4,500	First English Lutheran Church, Victoria, TX -- conference to strengthen families
4,000	Jackson County Ministerial Alliance Industrial Commission, Vanderbilt, TX -- Speakers on substance abuse, sexual decisions, delinquent behavior, and related issues
4,000	St. Joseph High School, Victoria, TX -- spiritual retreat for seniors
4,000	Victoria College Library, Victoria, TX -- books on religion and theology
3,800	Faith Academy, Victoria, TX -- library tables and chairs
3,500	Seadrift Cemetery, Seadrift, TX -- construction of chapel at cemetery

JAMES W. AND ELLA B. FORSTER CHARITABLE TRUST

Giving Contact

Trust Officer
Frontier Bank
PO Box 549
Rock Rapids, IA 51246
Phone: (712)472-2567
Fax: (712)472-2620

Description

Founded: 1987
EIN: 421305882
Organization Type: Private Foundation
Giving Locations: IA
Grant Types: Department, General Support.

Donor Information

Founder: the late James W. Forster, the late Ella B. Forster

Financial Summary

Total Giving: $151,982 (fiscal year ending June 30, 2001); $172,556 (fiscal 2000); $175,211 (fiscal 1999)
Assets: $3,035,822 (fiscal 2001); $3,118,658 (fiscal 2000); $3,414,116 (fiscal 1999)

Typical Recipients

Arts & Humanities: Historic Preservation, History & Archaeology, Libraries, Music
Civic & Public Affairs: Clubs, Economic Development, Parades/Festivals, Safety
Education: Public Education (Precollege), Student Aid
Health: Clinics/Medical Centers, Emergency/Ambulance Services, Hospitals
Social Services: Community Centers, Day Care, Recreation & Athletics, Substance Abuse, Youth Organizations

Application Procedures

Initial Contact: Request application form.
Deadlines: September 30.

Additional Information

Publications: Application Form
Trust(s): Frontier Bank

Foundation Officials

John Appel: trustee
Edward Ladd: trustee

Grants Analysis

Disclosure Period: fiscal year ending June 30, 2001
Total Grants: $151,982
Number of Grants: 9
Average Grant: $10,873*
Highest Grant: $65,000
Lowest Grant: $1,751
Typical Range: $5,000 to $20,000
*****Note:** Average grant figure excludes highest grant.

Recent Grants

Note: Grants derived from fiscal 2000 Form 990.

Library-Related

6,000	Rock Rapids Public Library, Rock Rapids, IA -- establish "The Serendipity Club"

General

71,500	City of Rock Rapids, Rock Rapids, IA -- swimming pool renovation
38,500	Central Lyon Community School, Rock Rapids, IA -- paving projects
32,454	Lyon County Fair Board, Rock Rapids, IA -- new commercial exhibit building at fairgrounds
15,000	Commission of Veterans Affairs, Rock Rapids, IA -- West Side Park Veterans Memorial
5,429	Merrill Pioneer Community Hospital Kids Club, Rock Rapids, IA -- improve basement heating system, replace exterior doors, updating cribs, carpet front entry and car repair fund
2,673	Lyon County Historical Society, Rock Rapids, IA -- new computer
1,000	City of Rock Rapids, Rock Rapids, IA -- landscaping around new junior/senior high school

FORTIS HEALTH

Company Headquarters

501 W. Michigan St.
Milwaukee, WI 53203
Web: http://www.fortishealth.com

Company Description

Founded: 1892
Former Name: Time Insurance Co.
Employees: 2,000
SIC(s): 6311 Life Insurance, 6321 Accident & Health Insurance.
Parent Company: Fortis, Inc., One Chase Manhattan Plaza, New York, NY, United States
Parent Revenue: US$40,090,000,000 (2001)

Nonmonetary Support

Type: Donated Equipment; In-kind Services; Loaned Employees; Loaned Executives; Workplace Solicitation
Volunteer Programs: The foundation supports employee volunteer activities, with special consideration given to organizations where employees volunteer that fall within the foundation's focus areas. The foundation does consider grants to organizations where employees volunteer but are not within the foundation focus. However, grants of this nature are limited to $100 per organization, with priority given to programs providing education, training, and direct services.

Fortis Insurance Foundation

Giving Contact

Dawn Krautkramer, Secretary
501 West Michigan Avenue
Milwaukee, WI 53203-3050
Phone: (414)299-8557
Fax: (414)299-6900

Alternate Contact

Pat Cullen
Phone: (414)271-3011
Note: Pat Cullen may be reached at extension 6722.

Description

Founded: 1973
EIN: 237346436
Organization Type: Corporate Foundation
Former Name: Fortis Insurance Foundation.
Giving Locations: WI: Southeastern Wisconsin
Grant Types: Employee Matching Gifts, General Support.
Note: Employee matching gift ratio: 1 to 1 to social services, education, or cultural institutions, up to $500 annually. Also provides grants for specific organizational programs within the focus of the foundation.

Donor Information

Founder: Time Insurance Co.

Financial Summary

Total Giving: $368,039 (2001); $222,551 (2000); $277,007 (1999). Note: Contributes through foundation only.

Giving Analysis: Giving for 2001 includes: foundation scholarships ($1,000); foundation matching gifts ($96,511); foundation ($270,528); 2000: foundation matching gifts ($31,634); foundation grants to United Way ($44,160); foundation ($146,757); 1999: foundation grants to United Way ($32,000); foundation matching gifts ($35,055); foundation ($209,952);

Assets: $1,232,068 (2001); $1,116,979 (2000); $910,048 (1999)

Gifts Received: $480,000 (2001); $376,000 (2000); $182,000 (1999). Note: In 2001, 2000 and 1998, contributions were received from Fortis Insurance Co. (formerly known as the Times Industry Co.). In 1999, contributions were received from Fortis Insurance Co. ($181,000) and Diversified Pharmaceutical Services ($1,000).

Typical Recipients

Arts & Humanities: Arts Associations & Councils, Arts Funds, Libraries, Museums/Galleries, Music, Performing Arts, Public Broadcasting

Civic & Public Affairs: African American Affairs, Economic Development, Employment/Job Training, Civic & Public Affairs-General, Hispanic Affairs, Housing, Legal Aid, Minority Business, Nonprofit Management, Philanthropic Organizations, Public Policy, Safety, Urban & Community Affairs, Women's Affairs, Zoos/Aquariums

Education: Business Education, Economic Education, Health & Physical Education, Literacy, Minority Education, Public Education (Precollege), Science/Mathematics Education, Secondary Education (Public), Vocational & Technical Education

Environment: Environment-General

Health: AIDS/HIV, Alzheimers Disease, Alzheimers Disease, Children's Health/Hospitals, Clinics/Medical Centers, Geriatric Health, Health Policy/Cost Containment, Health Organizations, Hospitals, Medical Rehabilitation, Medical Research, Mental Health, Nutrition, Public Health, Respiratory, Single-Disease Health Associations

International: Health Care/Hospitals

Religion: Ministries, Religious Welfare

Science: Scientific Centers & Institutes

Social Services: Camps, Child Welfare, Community Centers, Community Service Organizations, Crime Prevention, Day Care, Domestic Violence, Family Planning, Family Services, Food/Clothing Distribution, People with Disabilities, Scouts, Social Services-General, Substance Abuse, United Funds/United Ways, Veterans, Volunteer Services, YMCA/YWCA/YMHA/YWHA, Youth Organizations

Application Procedures

Initial Contact: Send a letter requesting grant application form.

Application Requirements: Application form requests information on organization's background, its mission, size, and history; description of proposed program, its purpose, budget and goals; description of beneficiaries, including the approximate number of people who will be helped; and information on personnel, including qualifications for those personnel who play a key role in carrying out the objectives of the organization. Accompanying materials must include, financial statements for the past fiscal year, including IRS Form 990; a copy of the most recent IRS ruling under section 501(c)(3); list of officers and directors; actual income and expense statement for the past year, including sources of support; and projected income and expense budget for the current fiscal year.

Deadlines: One month prior to bi-monthly meetings.

Review Process: The board of directors will evaluate the proposal on its merits, its consistency with the foundation's policies, and the availability of funds.

Evaluative Criteria: A preference will be given to proposals that improve the quality, accessibility, and efficiency of health-care services.

Decision Notification: The trustees meet bi-monthly to consider grant applications, in February, April, June, August, October, and December; applicants receive written notice regarding the board's decision within 14 days after the meeting.

Notes: Foundation uses the Common Application Form of the Donors Forum of Wisconsin.

Restrictions

Grants are generally not made to organizations that are primarily political, fraternal, municipal, religious, or labor-related.

Generally does not provide grants for fund-raising events or multiyear grants, nor does it provide endowment grants.

Foundation will not individually support operational grant requests from organizations that receive a substantial amount of their funding from United Way or United Performing Arts Fund. Will not provide matching funds for food and clothing drives, sporting teams, payment for school or tuition expenses, alumni or membership dues, fees for services, unpaid pledges, bequests, subscription fees for publications, or insurance premium payments.

Additional Information

The foundation's grant programs include a Discretionary Grant program, a Community Cornerstone Grant program, and an Employee Matching Grant program. The Discretionary grant program awards grant monies to qualifying organizations addressing the priorities of the foundation: health issues, job creation and economic revitalization of its operating community, hunger/homelessness, long-term care, and other services for children, youth, elderly, and the family. Special consideration is given to organizations where company employees actively volunteer their services. Community Cornerstone grants are made for operational support to established community organizations providing equal and low-cost access to a variety of artistic, cultural, and scientific experiences. These grants are also made to support community-based fundraising initiatives such as the United Way and the United Performing Arts Fund. The Employee Matching Grant program provides for matching of personal employee contributions of $20 or more, to qualifying organizations, up to $500 per year per employee.

Publications: Community Annual Report; Application Guidelines; Application Form

Grants Analysis

Disclosure Period: calendar year ending 2001

Total Grants: $270,528*

Number of Grants: 33

Average Grant: $8,198

Highest Grant: $50,000

Lowest Grant: $1,500

Typical Range: $2,000 to $12,000

*Note: Giving excludes matching gifts; scholarship.

Recent Grants

Note: Grants derived from 2001 Form 990.

Library-Related

50,000	Library of Congress, Washington, DC -- special event fund
5,000	Milwaukee Public Library Foundation, Milwaukee, WI

General

25,000	Journey House, Milwaukee, WI
18,000	Children's Services Society, West Allis, WI
16,000	Scholes Middle School
12,500	YWCA Greater Milwaukee, Milwaukee, WI
12,000	YWCA Greater Milwaukee, Milwaukee, WI
10,000	16th Street Community Health Center, Milwaukee, WI
10,000	16th Street Community Health Center, Milwaukee, WI
8,500	American Lung Association, Duluth, MN
7,000	United Community Center, Milwaukee, WI
6,500	Alzheimer's Association, Philadelphia, PA

FORTIS, INC.

Company Headquarters

One Chase Manhattan Plaza
New York, NY 10005
Phone: (212)859-7000
Web: http://www.us.fortis.com

Company Description

Ticker: FTS

Exchange: Foreign

Former Name: Amev Holdings.

Employees: 6,000

SIC(s): 6211 Security Brokers & Dealers, 6719 Holding Companies Nec.

Parent Company: Fortis, Rue Royale 20, Brussels, Belgium

Operating Locations

American Security Group (GA--Atlanta); First Fortis Life Insurance Co. (NY--Syracuse); Fortis (NY--New York); Fortis Benefits Insurance Co. (AZ--Phoenix; CA--El Segundo, Sacramento, San Diego, San Francisco, Santa Ana; CO--Englewood; FL--Coral Gables, Tampa; GA--Atlanta; IL--Oakbrook Terrace; KS--Overland Park; MD--Annapolis; MA--Westborough; MI--Grand Rapids, Troy; MN--Minneapolis; MO--Kansas City, St. Louis; NJ--Parsippany; NY--New York, Pittsford; NC--Charlotte; OH--Cincinnati, North Olmsted; OR--Portland; PA--Bala-Cynwyd, Pittsburgh; TX--Austin, Dallas, Houston, Memphis; WI--Waukesha); Fortis Family (GA--Atlanta); Fortis Financial Group (MN--Woodbury); Fortis Health (WI--Milwaukee); Fortis Long Term Care (WI--Milwaukee)

Fortis Foundation

Giving Contact

Jackie Gentile, Directory
1 Chase Manhattan Plaza, 41st Floor
New York, NY 10005
Phone: (212)859-7000
Fax: (212)859-7010
Web: http://www.fortisfoundation.com

Description

Founded: 1982

EIN: 133156497

Organization Type: Corporate Foundation

Giving Locations: NY: nationally health-related organizations.

Grant Types: Award, Employee Matching Gifts, Matching, Scholarship.

Donor Information

Founder: AMEV Holdings

Financial Summary

Total Giving: $368,439 (2001); $321,615 (2000); $247,023 (1999). Note: Contributes through foundation only.

Giving Analysis: Giving for 2000 includes: foundation matching gifts ($6,490); foundation ($73,875); foundation grants to United Way ($85,844); foundation scholarships ($155,406); 1999: foundation matching gifts ($2,422); foundation ($53,838); foundation grants to United Way ($62,183); foundation scholarships ($128,580); 1996: foundation grants to United Way ($28,893) foundation ($139,534)

Assets: $1,010,405 (2001); $1,351,140 (2000); $817,161 (1999 approx)

Gifts Received: $244 (2001); $1,000,000 (2000); $500,000 (1999). Note: In fiscal 1999 and 2000, contributions were received from Fortis Benefits Insurance Company.

Typical Recipients

Arts & Humanities: Arts & Humanities-General, Libraries, Museums/Galleries, Music

Civic & Public Affairs: Civic & Public Affairs-General

Education: Arts/Humanities Education, Business Education, Colleges & Universities, Education Funds, Engineering/Technological Education, Education-General, Legal Education, Medical Education, Private Education (Precollege), Public Education (Precollege), Religious Education, Student Aid

Health: AIDS/HIV, Cancer, Children's Health/Hospitals, Emergency/Ambulance Services, Multiple Sclerosis, Single-Disease Health Associations, Transplant Networks/Donor Banks

International: Health Care/Hospitals

Religion: Jewish Causes

Social Services: Child Welfare, Community Service Organizations, Emergency Relief, Family Planning, Food/Clothing Distribution, Recreation & Athletics, Shelters/Homelessness, Social Services-General, Special Olympics, United Funds/United Ways, Youth Organizations

Application Procedures

Initial Contact: Request application form for scholarships, for employees' children only.

Application Requirements: For other requests, send a brief letter of inquiry; include a description of organization, amount requested, purpose of funds sought, and proof of tax-exempt status.

Deadlines: None.

Evaluative Criteria: Scholarship grants are based on the following criteria: prior academic performance, performance on tests designed to measure scholastic abilities and aptitudes, at least two recommendations from instructors, and conclusions from a personal interview as to motivation, character, ability and performance.

Restrictions

Fortis Inc. does not consider the following for charitable contributions: individuals, goodwill advertising, political or lobbying groups, religious organizations for sectarian purposes, or organizations outside NY operating area.

Corporate Officials

Jon Kerry Clayton: president, chief executive officer B Cincinnati, OH 1945. ED Georgia Institute of Technology BIE (1968); Harvard University MBA (1970). PRIM CORP EMPL president, chief executive officer: Fortis Inc.

Foundation Officials

Jon Kerry Clayton: trustee (see above)
Robert B. Pollock: trustee
J. G. Thomas: trustee

Grants Analysis

Disclosure Period: calendar year ending 2001
Total Grants: $14,800*
Number of Grants: 20
Average Grant: $740
Highest Grant: $2,750
Lowest Grant: $100
Typical Range: $100 to $1,000
*Note: Giving excludes matching gifts, scholarship, United Way.

Recent Grants

Note: Grants derived from 2001 Form 990.

General

32,006	United Way New York City, New York, NY
9,483	United Way New York City, New York, NY
5,500	New York Firefighters 9-11 Disaster Relief Fund, New York, NY
5,000	Educational Foundation, Atlanta, GA
5,000	University of South Carolina Education Foundation, Columbia, SC
4,000	Concordia College, St. Paul, MN
4,000	Hartwick College, Oneonta, NY
4,000	Marquette University, Milwaukee, WI
3,500	Wilson College, Chambersburg, PA
2,750	Make A Wish Foundation, Phoenix, AZ

FORTUNE BRANDS, INC.

Company Headquarters

300 Tower Parkway
Lincolnshire, IL 60069-3640
Web: http://www.fortunebrands.com

Company Description

Ticker: FO
Exchange: NYSE
Former Name: American Brands, Inc.
Revenue: US$5.366 billion (2002)
Profit: US$525.6 million (2002)
Employees: 28,000
Fortune Rank: 313, per FORTUNE Magazine's list of 500 Largest U.S. Corporations (2002).
SIC(s): 2085 Distilled & Blended Liquors, 2111 Cigarettes, 2121 Cigars, 6719 Holding Companies Nec.

Operating Locations

ACCO North America (IL--Deerfield); ACCO U.S.A. Inc. (NY--Long Island City); Acushnet Co. (MA--Fairhaven); Acushnet Rubber Co. (MA--New Bedford); Aristokraft Distribution Center (WA--Kent); Fortune Brands, Inc. (VA--Richmond; WI--Milwaukee); Jim Beam Brands (KY--Clermont; TX--Bedford); Master Lock Co. (WI--Milwaukee); Masterbrand Industries, Inc. (IL--Lincolnshire); Moen Inc. (NC--Sanford); Moen, Inc. (OH--Elyria); NHB Industries, Inc. (AL--Talladega); Schrock Cabinet Co. (IL--Arthur); Torco P/L (WA--Kalannie); Waterloo Industries Inc. (IA--Waterloo)

Note: Also has major operations in Weybridge, Surrey, England.

Nonmonetary Support

Value: $3,864,378 (1998)
Type: Donated Equipment; Donated Products; In-kind Services
Note: The company also reports that it donates the use of their facilities.

Giving Contact

Joan McGrath, Contributions Administrator
Fortune Brands, Inc. Contributions Program
1700 East Putnam Avenue
Old Greenwich, CT 06870
Fax: (203)698-5577

Description

Organization Type: Corporate Giving Program
Giving Locations: headquarters and operating communities.
Grant Types: Employee Matching Gifts, General Support, Multiyear/Continuing Support, Scholarship.
Note: Employee matching gift ratio: 2 to 1.

Financial Summary

Total Giving: $7,428,618 (1998); $4,298,448 (1997); $8,050,525 (1996). Note: Contributes through corporate direct giving program only. Giving includes corporate direct giving; domestic and international subsidiaries; nonmonetary support.

Giving Analysis: Giving for 1996 includes: foundation matching gifts ($180,912) foundation ($7,416,789)

Typical Recipients

Arts & Humanities: Arts Centers, Community Arts, Historic Preservation, Libraries, Museums/Galleries, Music, Opera, Performing Arts, Public Broadcasting, Theater

Civic & Public Affairs: Civil Rights, Economic Development, Employment/Job Training, Legal Aid, Urban & Community Affairs, Women's Affairs, Zoos/Aquariums

Education: Arts/Humanities Education, Business Education, Colleges & Universities, Community & Junior Colleges, Continuing Education, Economic Education, Education Associations, Elementary Education (Private), Literacy, Minority Education, Private Education (Precollege), Public Education (Precollege), Special Education

Environment: Environment-General

Health: Emergency/Ambulance Services, Health Organizations, Hospitals, Medical Research, Public Health, Single-Disease Health Associations

International: Health Care/Hospitals, International Peace & Security Issues, International Relations

Social Services: Child Welfare, Community Centers, Community Service Organizations, Day Care, Food/Clothing Distribution, People with Disabilities, Recreation & Athletics, Shelters/Homelessness, Substance Abuse, United Funds/United Ways, Volunteer Services, Youth Organizations

Application Procedures

Initial Contact: Send a brief letter of inquiry.

Application Requirements: Include organization's purpose, detailed description of project and amount of funding requested; list of other corporate contributors; and proof of tax-exempt status.

Deadlines: None.

Review Process: All requests are screened and approved by the corporate responsibility committee; operating companies administer local contributions programs.

Evaluative Criteria: Preference given to organizations close to company locations.

Decision Notification: Decisions are made as applications are received; final notification within one month.

Notes: The company reports that requests should be sent to the nearest company facility. The company's contributions program is highly decentralized.

Restrictions

Generally does not support individuals, political parties or candidates, fraternal organizations, member agencies of united funds, or religious organizations for sectarian purposes.

Additional Information

In 1997, American Brands, Inc. divided into two companies--Fortune Brands and Gallaher. Gallaher is based in the United Kingdom.

Corporate Officials

Thomas Chandler Hays: chairman, chief executive officer, director B Chicago, IL 1935. ED California Institute of Technology BS (1957); California Institute of Technology MS (1958); Harvard University Graduate School of Business Administration MBA (1963). PRIM CORP EMPL former chairman and chief executive officer; director: Fortune Brands, Inc. CORP AFFIL director: Master Lock Co.; director: Gallaher Ltd.; director: AC Nielsen Corp.; director: Acushnet Co.

NONPR AFFIL member: Conference Board & Economic; director: Southwest Area Commerce & Industry Association; member: Business Roundtable; director: Community Foundations Fairfield County; member: Ambassador Roundtable. CLUB AFFIL Economic Club; Tokeneke Club; Cincinnati Country Club; Darien Country Club; Bel-Air Bay Club.

Norman H. Wesley: president, chief operating officer PRIM CORP EMPL president, chief executive officer: Fortune Brands, Inc. ADD CORP EMPL chairman: ACCO World Corp.

Giving Program Officials
Joan S. McGrath: contributions administrator

Grants Analysis
Typical Range: $500 to $5,000

FOSTER CHARITABLE TRUST

Giving Contact
Bernard S. Mars, Trustee
681 Andersen Dr., Suite 300
Pittsburgh, PA 15220-2747
Phone: (412)928-8900

Description
Founded: 1962
EIN: 256064791
Organization Type: Private Foundation
Giving Locations: PA
Grant Types: General Support.

Donor Information
Founder: Foster Industries

Financial Summary
Total Giving: $413,940 (2000); $383,973 (1999); $345,223 (1998)
Giving Analysis: Giving for 2000 includes: foundation grants to United Way ($22,500); 1999: foundation grants to United Way ($32,200); 1998: foundation grants to United Way ($11,000)
Assets: $4,840,761 (2000); $5,443,314 (1999); $4,481,829 (1998)
Gifts Received: $161,100 (1999); $196,756 (1998); $327,023 (1996). Note: In 1999, contributions were received from Foster Investment Co. In 1998, contributions were received from Foster Industries, Inc. ($47,588) and Foster Investment Co. ($149,168). In 1992, contributions were received from Foster Industries, Inc.

Typical Recipients
Arts & Humanities: Arts Associations & Councils, Arts Festivals, Arts Funds, Ballet, Ethnic & Folk Arts, Libraries, Museums/Galleries, Music, Opera, Performing Arts, Public Broadcasting, Theater
Civic & Public Affairs: Civic & Public Affairs-General, Philanthropic Organizations
Education: Colleges & Universities, Health & Physical Education, Legal Education, Private Education (Precollege)
Health: AIDS/HIV, Alzheimers Disease, Clinics/Medical Centers, Eyes/Blindness, Hospitals, Medical Rehabilitation, Medical Research, Research/Studies Institutes, Single-Disease Health Associations
International: Foreign Educational Institutions, Missionary/Religious Activities
Religion: Jewish Causes, Religious Organizations, Religious Welfare, Synagogues/Temples
Science: Scientific Centers & Institutes
Social Services: Camps, Child Welfare, Community Centers, Community Service Organizations, People with Disabilities, Shelters/Homelessness, Substance Abuse, United Funds/United Ways, Youth Organizations

L.B. FOSTER CO.

Company Headquarters
PO Box 2806
Pittsburgh, PA 15230
Web: http://www.lbfoster.com

Company Description
Founded: 1902
Ticker: FSTR
Exchange: NASDAQ
Revenue: US$258 million (2002)
Employees: 686 (2002)
SIC(s): 3300 Primary Metal Industries, 3500 Industrial Machinery & Equipment.

Operating Locations
L.B. Foster Co. (PA--Pittsburgh)

L.B. Foster Co. Charitable Trust

Giving Contact
Monica Iurlano, Vice President, Human Resources
PO Box 2806
Pittsburgh, PA 15230
Phone: (412)928-3400

Application Procedures
Initial Contact: Send brief typed letter of inquiry.
Application Requirements: Include a description of organization and proof of tax-exempt status.
Deadlines: None.

Foundation Officials
J. R. Foster: trustee
Jay L. Foster: trustee
Lee B. Foster: trustee
Bernard S. Mars: trustee
Peter F. Mars: trustee
Kim Petracca: trustee

Grants Analysis
Disclosure Period: calendar year ending 2000
Total Grants: $319,450*
Number of Grants: 72
Average Grant: $4,189*
Highest Grant: $50,000
Typical Range: $1,000 to $10,000
*Note: Giving excludes United Way. Average grant figure excludes two highest grants ($98,240).

Recent Grants
Note: Grants derived from 1999 Form 990.

General
62,500	University of Pittsburgh - Creip Chair, Pittsburgh, PA
55,500	United Jewish Federation, Pittsburgh, PA
30,000	Temple Jeremiah, Northfield, IL
25,000	Trinity College, Hartford, CT
22,240	Camp Kon-O-Kwee/Spencer, Fombell, PA
20,000	United Way of Allegheny County, Pittsburgh, PA
11,500	Sarasota-Manatee Jewish Federation, Sarasota, FL
10,900	Carnegie Museums of Art, Pittsburgh, PA
10,100	Society for Contemporary Crafts, Pittsburgh, PA
10,000	Ben Gurion University of Negev, Lincolnwood, IL

Description
EIN: 256271616
Organization Type: Corporate Foundation
Giving Locations: PA: Pittsburgh
Grant Types: General Support, Matching, Multiyear/Continuing Support.

Financial Summary
Total Giving: $29,204 (fiscal year ending March 31, 1998 approx); $28,081 (fiscal 1997); $29,575 (fiscal 1996). Note: Fiscal 1997 Giving includes United Way ($6,640).
Assets: $493 (fiscal 1997); $5,314 (fiscal 1996); $6,105 (fiscal 1994)
Gifts Received: $23,500 (fiscal 1997); $35,000 (fiscal 1996); $30,340 (fiscal 1994). Note: In fiscal 1996, contributions were received from the L.B. Foster Co.

Typical Recipients
Arts & Humanities: Arts Associations & Councils, Arts Centers, Dance, Ethnic & Folk Arts, Arts & Humanities-General, History & Archaeology, Libraries, Museums/Galleries, Music, Performing Arts, Public Broadcasting, Theater
Civic & Public Affairs: Civic & Public Affairs-General, Housing, Safety, Women's Affairs, Zoos/Aquariums
Education: Afterschool/Enrichment Programs, Business Education, Education-General, Health & Physical Education, Leadership Training, Literacy, Minority Education, Public Education (Precollege), Student Aid
Environment: Resource Conservation
Health: AIDS/HIV, Cancer, Children's Health/Hospitals, Diabetes, Emergency/Ambulance Services, Health-General, Health Organizations, Heart, Hospices, Multiple Sclerosis, Nursing Services, Prenatal Health Issues, Public Health, Research/Studies Institutes, Respiratory, Single-Disease Health Associations, Speech & Hearing
Religion: Religious Welfare
Social Services: Big Brother/Big Sister, Camps, Community Service Organizations, Family Services, Food/Clothing Distribution, People with Disabilities, Senior Services, Social Services-General, Special Olympics, United Funds/United Ways

Application Procedures
Initial Contact: Send a full proposal. Include a description of organization, amount requested, purpose of funds sought, recently audited financial statement, and proof of tax-exempt status.
Deadlines: None.
Notes: The company discourages phone calls.

Restrictions
Does not support individuals, religious organizations for sectarian purposes, political or lobbying groups, or organizations outside operating areas.

Corporate Officials
Lee B. Foster: president, chief executive officer, director PRIM CORP EMPL president, chief executive officer, director: L.B. Foster Co.
Roger Nejes: senior vice president financial & administration, chief financial officer PRIM CORP EMPL senior vice president financial & administration, chief financial officer: L.B. Foster Co.
James William Wilcock: chairman, director B Dayton, OH September 02, 1917. ED University of Michigan BS (1938); Ohio Wesleyan University (1940). PRIM CORP EMPL chairman, director: Copperweld Corp. PRIM NONPR EMPL professor: University of Pittsburgh, Graduate Business School. CORP AFFIL chairman, president: Pace Industries; adjunct prof: University Pittsburgh Grad Business Sch; associate: Kolberg Kravis & Roberts Co.; chairman: LB Foster Co.; director: Joy Manufacturing Co.; chairman, chief executive officer: CEO Monitor Group; director: Michael Baker Corp. CLUB AFFIL Rivers Club; Johns Island Club; Allegheny Country Club; Duquesne Club.

Foundation Officials

Lee B. Foster: membership (see above)
Linda J. Moore: membership
Linda M. Terpenning: membership PRIM CORP EMPL vice president human resources: L.B. Foster Co.

Grants Analysis

Disclosure Period: fiscal year ending March 31, 1997
Total Grants: $21,441*
Number of Grants: 31
Average Grant: $692
Highest Grant: $5,128
Typical Range: $50 to $2,500
*Note: Giving excludes United Way. A more recent grants list was unavailable.

Recent Grants

Note: Grants derived from 1997 Form 990.

General

6,640	United Way Southwestern Pennsylvania, Pittsburgh, PA
5,128	Combined Health Appeal of Western Pennsylvania, Pittsburgh, PA
3,232	Pittsburgh Hearing, Speech, and Deaf Services, Pittsburgh, PA
2,500	Cultural Trust Campaign, Pittsburgh, PA
1,500	Margaret H.W. Watson Foundation, Sewickley, PA
1,000	National Multiple Sclerosis Society, Pittsburgh, PA
1,000	Salvation Army, Pittsburgh, PA
1,000	Women's Center and Shelter, Pittsburgh, PA
750	Cystic Fibrosis Foundation, Pittsburgh, PA
600	March of Dimes, Pittsburgh, PA

FOSTER FOUNDATION

Giving Contact

Jill Goodsell, Administrator
1929 43rd Avenue East, Suite 300
Seattle, WA 98112
Phone: (206)726-1815

Description

Founded: 1984
EIN: 911265474
Organization Type: Family Foundation
Giving Locations: WA: Seattle
Grant Types: Capital, Matching, Project, Research, Scholarship, Seed Money.

Donor Information

Founder: Established in 1984 by Evelyn W. Foster.

Financial Summary

Total Giving: $2,272,050 (2001); $1,924,500 (2000); $2,000,000 (1998)
Giving Analysis: Giving for 2001 includes: foundation grants to United Way ($35,000); 2000: foundation grants to United Way ($30,000); 1998: foundation grants to United Way ($35,000)
Assets: $39,205,096 (2001); $39,449,795 (2000); $39,368,378 (1998)

Typical Recipients

Arts & Humanities: Arts Associations & Councils, Arts Centers, History & Archaeology, Libraries, Museums/Galleries, Music, Opera, Performing Arts, Theater
Civic & Public Affairs: Employment/Job Training, Housing, Municipalities/Towns, Public Policy, Safety, Urban & Community Affairs, Women's Affairs
Education: Arts/Humanities Education, Business Education, Colleges & Universities, Education Reform,

Environmental Education, Literacy, Private Education (Precollege), Public Education (Precollege)
Environment: Environment-General, Resource Conservation
Health: AIDS/HIV, Cancer, Children's Health/Hospitals, Clinics/Medical Centers, Emergency/Ambulance Services, Geriatric Health, Health Organizations, Hospices, Hospitals, Medical Research, Nursing Services, Public Health, Research/Studies Institutes, Respiratory, Single-Disease Health Associations
International: Health Care/Hospitals
Religion: Churches, Missionary Activities (Domestic), Religious Organizations, Religious Welfare
Science: Scientific Centers & Institutes
Social Services: At-Risk Youth, Big Brother/Big Sister, Child Welfare, Community Centers, Community Service Organizations, Day Care, Emergency Relief, Family Planning, Family Services, Food/Clothing Distribution, Homes, People with Disabilities, Senior Services, Shelters/Homelessness, Social Services-General, United Funds/United Ways, YMCA/YWCA/YMHA/YWHA, Youth Organizations

Application Procedures

Initial Contact: Inquiries for funding should be described briefly in letter form. If the inquiry is deemed appropriate, a formal application will be requested.
Application Requirements: Inquiries should include a brief description of the project and its intended purpose. Formal applications must contain the name and address of the organization, proof of tax-exempt status, a list of officers and directors, a brief history of the program and its accomplishments, and financial reports including a budget for the current year. The formal application also must include a project plan defining the need and the methods for achieving the objectives and for evaluating the results, and a detailed budget for the project.
Deadlines: None.
Review Process: Applicants should allow three months for the board to make its decision.

Restrictions

Grants will be awarded to organizations for one year only. Grants to individuals will be made as scholarships through a school, college, or university. The foundation does not support endowment funds, fundraising activities, loans, or unrestricted operating funds.

Foundation Officials

Evelyn W. Foster: trustee
Michael G. Foster, Jr.: director
Michael G. Foster, Sr.: trustee PRIM CORP EMPL chief executive officer, director: Foster, Paulsell & Baker, Inc.
Jill Goodsell: admin, trustee PRIM CORP EMPL treasurer, director: Foster, Paulsell & Baker, Inc.

Grants Analysis

Disclosure Period: calendar year ending 2001
Total Grants: $2,237,050*
Number of Grants: 66
Average Grant: $27,262*
Highest Grant: $500,000
Typical Range: $10,000 to $40,000
*Note: Giving excludes United Way. Average grant figure excludes highest grant ($500,000).

Recent Grants

Note: Grants derived from 2001 Form 990.

Library-Related

500,000	Seattle Public Library Foundation, Seattle, WA
12,500	Seattle Public Library Foundation, Seattle, WA

General

160,000	University of Washington, Seattle, WA
100,000	Alliance for Education, Seattle, WA
100,000	Children's Hospital, Seattle, WA
100,000	YMCA Shelter, Seattle, WA
66,000	New Beginnings Women's Shelter, Seattle, WA
60,000	Seattle Symphony, Seattle, WA
54,000	Northwest Harvest/EMM (Eastern Mennonite Mission), Seattle, WA
50,000	Overlake School, Redmond, WA
50,000	Planned Parenthood of Western Washington, Seattle, WA
50,000	Seattle Art Museum, Seattle, WA

FOUNDATION FOR CHILD DEVELOPMENT

Giving Contact

Ruby Takanish, President
145 East 32nd Street
14th Floor
New York, NY 10016-6055
Phone: (212)213-8337
Fax: (212)213-5897
E-mail: inforequest@ffcd.org
Web: http://www.ffcd.org

Description

Founded: 1900
EIN: 131623901
Organization Type: Specialized/Single Purpose Foundation
Giving Locations: New York area.
Grant Types: Conference/Seminar, General Support, Multiyear/Continuing Support, Project, Research.

Donor Information

Founder: The foundation was incorporated as a voluntary agency in New York in 1900, and established as the Association for the Aid of Crippled Children in 1908. It was publicly supported by voluntary contributions until 1944 when substantial funds were received from the estate of Milo M. Belding Jr., as a testament to his wife, Annie K. Belding, who had devoted many years of service to the association. Mr. Belding (1865-1931) was president of Belding Brothers and Company, a firm established by his father, which became the largest silk manufacturer in the world. He was also president of Broadway Trust Company.
In its early years, the association was directly involved with the care of crippled children. In the 1950s, the foundation's focus shifted to the prevention of congenital disabilities, and until the 1970s, it primarily supported research into genetically based disorders and abnormalities of fetal development. In recognition of its evolving program and of its status as a grant-making organization, the association changed its name in 1972 to the Foundation for Child Development.

Financial Summary

Total Giving: $3,602,172 (fiscal year ending March 31, 2001); $2,095,280 (fiscal 1999); $2,411,703 (fiscal 1998)
Giving Analysis: Giving for fiscal 1998 includes: foundation grants to United Way ($10,000)
Assets: $101,462,405 (fiscal 2001); $98,284,309 (fiscal 1999); $97,379,665 (fiscal 1998)
Gifts Received: $3,000 (fiscal 2001); $716 (fiscal 1999); $350 (fiscal 1998). Note: In fiscal 1996, contributions were received from the estate of Kenneth Nussbaum.

Typical Recipients

Arts & Humanities: Arts & Humanities-General, Libraries, Museums/Galleries, Music, Public Broadcasting

Civic & Public Affairs: African American Affairs, Civil Rights, Community Foundations, Economic Development, Economic Policy, Employment/Job Training, Civic & Public Affairs-General, Hispanic Affairs, Law & Justice, Legal Aid, Nonprofit Management, Philanthropic Organizations, Professional & Trade Associations, Public Policy, Urban & Community Affairs, Women's Affairs

Education: Afterschool/Enrichment Programs, Arts/Humanities Education, Colleges & Universities, Education Associations, Education Funds, Education Reform, Engineering/Technological Education, Faculty Development, Education-General, Medical Education, Preschool Education, Public Education (Precollege), School Volunteerism, Social Sciences Education, Student Aid

Environment: Environment-General

Health: Children's Health/Hospitals, Geriatric Health, Health Funds, Hospitals, Medical Rehabilitation, Medical Research, Mental Health, Nutrition, Public Health, Research/Studies Institutes

International: International Relations

Religion: Religious Welfare

Science: Scientific Centers & Institutes, Scientific Organizations

Social Services: At-Risk Youth, Child Abuse, Child Welfare, Community Centers, Community Service Organizations, Counseling, Day Care, Delinquency & Criminal Rehabilitation, Domestic Violence, Family Planning, Family Services, Food/Clothing Distribution, People with Disabilities, Senior Services, Shelters/Homelessness, United Funds/United Ways, Volunteer Services, Youth Organizations

Application Procedures

Initial Contact: Send a one- or two-page letter of inquiry to the foundation. Contact the foundation for guidelines.

Application Requirements: Query letters should describe the proposed project, its objectives, and approximate level of funding required. If the project falls within the Foundation's scope of interest, a proposal will be invited and details regarding what the proposal should include will be provided.

Deadlines: None.

Review Process: The board of directors meets in June, September, December, and March to review invited proposals. The foundation replies quickly to query letters with an indication of whether a project fits its program interests.

Restrictions

The foundation does not consider requests for scholarships or grants to individuals, capital campaigns, or the purchase, construction, or renovation of buildings. The foundation does not make grants outside the United States.

Additional Information

The foundation indicates that future grant making will focus on the integration of research, policy, and advocacy or research and practice in the areas of availability and access to early childhood education and care programs and health care for children.

Publications: Annual Report; Guidelines

Foundation Officials

Ruth Ann Burns: director NONPR AFFIL vice president, director: Educational Broadcasting Corp.

P. Lindsay Chase-Lansdale: director, chairman nominating committee

Michael I. Cohen: director B Brooklyn, NY 1935. ED Columbia University BA (1956); Columbia University MD (1960). PRIM NONPR EMPL professor pediatrics, department chairman: Albert Einstein College of Medicine. NONPR AFFIL member: Society Adolescent Medicine; member: Society Pediatric Research; member: National Academy Sciences Institute Medicine; member: American Pediatric Society; member: American Psychosomatic Society; member: American Federation Clinical Research; member: American Gastrointestinal Association; member: American Academy Pediatrics; member: Alpha Omega Alpha; member: Ambulatory Pediatrics Association.

Claudia Conner: grant associate

John L. Furth: director, treasurer, chairman fin committee, mbr executive committee B 1931. PRIM CORP EMPL vice chairman, director: EM Warburg, Pincus & Co. Inc. CORP AFFIL vice chairman: Warburg EM Pincus Co. LLC. NONPR AFFIL president, director: Grand Street Settlement Inc.

Karen N. Gerard: vice chairman, director, vice chairman executive committee, mbr fin committee PRIM CORP EMPL vice president business locations division: Moran, Stahl & Boyer.

Eileen Mavis Hetherington: director B 1926. ED University of British Columbia BA (1947); University of British Columbia MA (1948); University of California at Berkeley PhD (1958). PRIM NONPR EMPL James M. Page Professor of Psychology: University of Virginia. NONPR AFFIL member: Social Research Adolescents; member: Society Research Child Development; member: American Psychological Association.

Edith Milberger: assistant treasurer

Julius Benjamin Richmond: director B Chicago, IL September 26, 1916. ED University of Illinois BS (1937); University of Illinois MS (1939); University of Illinois MD (1939). PRIM NONPR EMPL professor emeritus: Harvard University, School of Medicine. NONPR AFFIL member: Sigma Xi; member: Society Pediatric Research; associate member: New England Council Child Psychiatry; member: Phi Eta Sigma; professor health policy emeritus: Harvard University Medical School; member: National Academy Sciences Institute Medicine; member: American Public Health Association; advisor child health policy: Childrens Hospital Medical Center; fellow: American Psychiatric Association; member: American Psychosomatic Society; fellow: American Orthopsychiatric Association; member: American Pediatric Society; member: American Academy Pediatrics; member: American Medical Association; member: Alpha Omega Alpha.

Barbara Paul Robinson: chairman, chairman executive committee, member audit committee B 1941. ED Bryn Mawr College AB (1962); Yale University LLB (1965). PRIM CORP EMPL partner: Debevoise & Plimpton. NONPR AFFIL director: Yale Council; member: Yale Law School Association New York; member: Women's Forum; member advisory board, lecturer: Practicing Law Institute; director: Wave Hill Inc.; fellow: New York State Bar Foundation; director: Garden Conservancy; member: New York State Bar Association; director: Fund Modern Courts; member: Council Foreign Relations; trustee: William Nelson Cromwell Foundation; member: Association Bar New York City Fund; director: Catalyst for Women Inc.; president: Association Bar New York City; fellow: American College Trust & Estate Counsel; director: American Judicature Society; member: American Bar Association; fellow: American Bar Foundation; arbitrator, director: American Arbitration Association. CLUB AFFIL Washington Club; Yale Club.

Margaret Beale Spencer: director

Ruby Takanishi: president, member executive committee, director

Fasaha M. Traylor: senior program officer

Cathy Trost: director, member nonmonetary committee

Grants Analysis

Disclosure Period: fiscal year ending March 31, 2001

Total Grants: $3,602,172

Number of Grants: 52

Average Grant: $63,768*

Highest Grant: $350,000

Typical Range: $30,000 to $100,000

*Note: Average grant figure excludes highest grant.

Recent Grants

Note: Grants derived from 2000 Form 990.

Library-Related

350,000	University of Maryland Foundation, College Park, MD

General

228,418	Urban Institute, Washington, DC -- policy
209,963	Child Trends, Washington, DC
200,000	New York Academy of Medicine, New York, NY -- linking research policy and program
141,566	Economic Opportunity Institute, Seattle, WA
136,186	Northwestern University, Evanston, IL
135,000	Center for Law and Social Policy, Washington, DC
111,865	American Prospect, Cambridge, MA
100,000	American Forum, Washington, DC -- state-based media outreach on welfare reform
100,000	Center on Budget and Policy Priorities, Washington, DC
100,000	Center for the Child Care Workforce, Washington, DC

FOUNDATION FOR SEACOAST HEALTH

Giving Contact

Susan R. Bunting, President
100 Campus Dr., Suite 1
Portsmouth, NH 03801
Phone: (603)422-8200
Fax: (603)422-8207
E-mail: ffsh@communitycampus.org
Web: http://www.ffsh.org

Description

Founded: 1984

EIN: 020386319

Organization Type: General Purpose Foundation

Giving Locations: ME: Eliot, Kittery, York; NH: Greenland, New Castle, Newington, North Hampton, Portsmouth, Rye

Grant Types: Award, Challenge, General Support, Matching, Multiyear/Continuing Support, Project, Scholarship, Seed Money.

Donor Information

Founder: Incorporated in 1984 with private endowments and the proceeds from the sale of the Portsmouth Hospital franchise to Hospital Corporation of America.

Financial Summary

Total Giving: $1,650,000 (2002 approx); $1,996,419 (2001); $1,749,610 (2000)

Giving Analysis: Giving for 2000 includes: foundation grants to United Way ($10,000); foundation scholarships ($177,000); 1998: foundation scholarships ($139,500) foundation scholarships ($153,000)

Assets: $60,000,000 (2002 approx); $67,230,754 (2001); $73,974,141 (2000)

Gifts Received: $39,094 (2000); $200 (1998); $20,500 (1996). Note: In 2000, contributions were received from Portsmouth Regional Hospital. In 1998, contributions were received from the Wilder Fund.

Typical Recipients

Arts & Humanities: Arts Outreach, Museums/Galleries, Music, Public Broadcasting, Theater

Civic & Public Affairs: Employment/Job Training, Civic & Public Affairs-General, Municipalities/Towns, Nonprofit Management, Philanthropic Organizations, Professional & Trade Associations, Urban & Community Affairs, Women's Affairs

Education: Afterschool/Enrichment Programs, Arts/Humanities Education, Colleges & Universities, Community & Junior Colleges, Education Funds, Faculty Development, Education-General, Leadership Training, Literacy, Preschool Education, Private Education (Precollege), Public Education (Precollege), Religious Education, School Volunteerism, Special Education

Environment: Air/Water Quality, Environment-General, Resource Conservation

Health: Adolescent Health Issues, AIDS/HIV, Cancer, Cancer, Children's Health/Hospitals, Clinics/Medical Centers, Diabetes, Emergency/Ambulance Services, Health-General, Geriatric Health, Health Policy/Cost Containment, Health Funds, Health Organizations, Home-Care Services, Hospices, Hospitals, Medical Rehabilitation, Mental Health, Nursing Services, Prenatal Health Issues, Preventive Medicine/Wellness Organizations, Public Health, Single-Disease Health Associations, Trauma Treatment

Religion: Churches, Jewish Causes, Religious Organizations, Religious Welfare

Social Services: Child Welfare, Community Centers, Community Service Organizations, Counseling, Crime Prevention, Day Care, Domestic Violence, Family Planning, Family Services, Family Services, Food/Clothing Distribution, Homes, People with Disabilities, Recreation & Athletics, Scouts, Senior Services, Sexual Abuse, Shelters/Homelessness, Social Services-General, Substance Abuse, United Funds/United Ways, Volunteer Services, YMCA/YWCA/YMHA/YWHA, Youth Organizations

Application Procedures

Initial Contact: Applicants should write, e-mail, or call the foundation for a set of "request for proposals" brochures on the foundation's grant programs.

Application Requirements: Applicants should follow proposal instructions as set forth in the "request for proposals" brochures. Proof of tax-exempt status is required.

Deadlines: For the Scholarship Program, applications are due on February 1, and award notification is made in April. For the Infants, Children, and Adolescents Program, proposals are due on March 1 and grant notification is made in May. For discretionary fund requests, proposals are due on the last day of each month for grant notification the following month. For the Women's Health Initiative, proposals are due on October 1, with notification in November. For the Promoting Health and Preventing Disease Program, proposals are due June 1, with notification in August. For the discretionary fund, proposals are due on the last day of the month, for nonfiction the following month. for nonfiction the following month.

Review Process: Foundation staff, in researching a grant application, may find it necessary to review any and all of the information submitted with advisors of the foundation's choosing before presentation to the board of trustees.

Restrictions

The foundation does not consider requests for ongoing general expenses; elimination of deficits; support of political activities; grants to individuals other than through the Foundation for Seacoast Health's Scholarship Program; grants for travel, lodging and conferences; grants for bricks and mortar; general fundraising campaigns; capital expenditures; or equipment.

Additional Information

Grant recipients are required to submit quarterly narrative progress reports and an accounting of all funds. Demonstration of accountability by keeping the foundation informed is an important factor in future funding consideration.

In general, a one-time grant will be given the strongest consideration. Multiple-year proposals will only be considered for exceptional projects or programs that demonstrate special circumstances and can identify other resources or in-kind contributions to enhance

program stability and longevity. and can identify other resources or in-kind contributions to enhance program stability and longevity.

Publications: Annual Report; Newsletter; "Request for Proposals" Brochures for Each Program

Foundation Officials

Don Albertson, MD: trustee

Peter L. Bergeron: trustee ED University of New Hampshire (1974). PRIM CORP EMPL president: Simplex Technologies Inc.

Rodney G. Brock: trustee

Susan R. Bunting, EdD: president

Kenneth L. Chute: chairman, trustee B 1945. ED University of Massachusetts BA (1968); Rutgers University MBA (1969). PRIM CORP EMPL vice president: Sprague Energy Corp.

Nancy L. Cutter: admin assistant

Eileen D. Foley: trustee PRIM NONPR EMPL mayor: City of Portsmouth, New Hampshire.

Catherine R. Goodwin: trustee

William C. Henson: treasurer, trustee

Thomas M. Keane: vice chairman, trustee PRIM CORP EMPL partner: Taylor Keane Blanchard Lyons & Watson. CORP AFFIL secretary: Flooring Resources Inc.; secretary: Global Trade Group Inc.

Wendy A. McLaughlin, MD: trustee

J. Gregg Sanborn: trustee

Grants Analysis

Disclosure Period: calendar year ending 2000

Total Grants: $1,562,610*

Number of Grants: 38

Average Grant: $12,850*

Highest Grant: $600,000

Typical Range: $5,000 to $25,000

*Note: Giving excludes scholarships and United Way. Average grant figure excludes two highest grants ($1,100,000).

Recent Grants

Note: Grants derived from 2001 Form 990.

General

300,000	Seacoast Mental Health Center, Portsmouth, NH -- New Heights Program
286,000	Seacoast Mental Health Center, Portsmouth, NH -- New Heights Program
250,000	Families First of the Greater Seacoast, Portsmouth, NH -- family support/health services
225,000	Families First of the Greater Seacoast, Portsmouth, NH -- family support/health services
187,500	Portsmouth School Department, Portsmouth, NH -- Clipper Health Center
120,000	Community Child Care Center, Portsmouth, NH -- wage solutions
84,000	Community Child Care Center, Portsmouth, NH -- wage solutions
67,500	Lamprey Health Care, Newmarket, NH -- for medical financial assistance
50,000	Portsmouth School Department, Portsmouth, NH -- Clipper Health Center
45,000	Lamprey Health Care, Newmarket, NH -- for Information/Referral Program

JOHN EDWARD FOWLER MEMORIAL FOUNDATION

Giving Contact

Richard H. Lee, President
1725 K St. NW, Suite 1201
Washington, DC 20006
Phone: (202)728-9080
Fax: (202)728-9082
Web: http://fdncenter.org/grantmaker/fowler

Description

Founded: 1964

EIN: 516019469

Organization Type: General Purpose Foundation

Giving Locations: DC: Washington including immediate metropolitan area

Grant Types: Capital, General Support, Matching.

Donor Information

Founder: Created in 1964 by the late Pearl Gunn Fowler in memory of her husband, John Edward Fowler, who was a businessman and banker in Northern Virginia for forty years.

Financial Summary

Total Giving: $1,128,500 (2001); $1,313,500 (2000); $1,123,000 (1999)

Assets: $24,264,652 (2001); $18,509,658 (2000); $28,251,301 (1999)

Typical Recipients

Arts & Humanities: Arts Outreach, Ballet, Dance, Historic Preservation, Libraries, Literary Arts, Music, Performing Arts, Theater

Civic & Public Affairs: Botanical Gardens/Parks, Business/Free Enterprise, Civil Rights, Economic Development, Employment/Job Training, Hispanic Affairs, Housing, Legal Aid, Minority Business, Nonprofit Management, Philanthropic Organizations, Urban & Community Affairs, Women's Affairs

Education: Afterschool/Enrichment Programs, Arts/Humanities Education, Business Education, Colleges & Universities, Community & Junior Colleges, Education-General, Leadership Training, Literacy, Minority Education, Preschool Education, Private Education (Precollege), Religious Education, School Volunteerism, Secondary Education (Private), Secondary Education (Public), Special Education, Student Aid

Environment: Environment-General

Health: AIDS/HIV, Alzheimers Disease, Cancer, Children's Health/Hospitals, Clinics/Medical Centers, Emergency/Ambulance Services, Geriatric Health, Hospices, Hospitals, Hospitals (University Affiliated), Long-Term Care, Mental Health, Multiple Sclerosis, Outpatient Health Care, Prenatal Health Issues, Public Health

International: Health Care/Hospitals, International Development, Missionary/Religious Activities

Religion: Churches, Jewish Causes, Ministries, Missionary Activities (Domestic), Religious Organizations, Religious Welfare, Seminaries

Social Services: At-Risk Youth, Big Brother/Big Sister, Child Welfare, Community Centers, Community Service Organizations, Counseling, Day Care, Delinquency & Criminal Rehabilitation, Domestic Violence, Emergency Relief, Family Services, Food/Clothing Distribution, Homes, People with Disabilities, Scouts, Senior Services, Shelters/Homelessness, Volunteer Services, YMCA/YWCA/YMHA/YWHA, Youth Organizations

Application Procedures

Initial Contact: Send written request.

Application Requirements: The foundation accepts, but does not require, Washington Regional Association of Grantmakers' common grant application form. According to the foundation's guidelines, applicants should submit a concise (two-page) letter describing the project for which funding is sought. In addition, applicants should provide a brief statement (three pages) on the history of the organization, its purposes, its current activities, and evidence of its effectiveness. These letters and the foundation's application form should be submitted along with a copy of the organization's IRS determination letter; a budget for the project and the organization's current general operating budget; financial statements (balance sheet, income statements, and latest audit); and a list of the organization's board of directors and officers. Applicants

should also include any additional information which may be useful in evaluating the request.
Deadlines: None.
Review Process: Receipt of proposals will be acknowledged by postcard. Applicants will receive notification of the board's decision shortly after the board meets, but should expect the process to take at least four months. The foundation rarely conducts interviews or makes on-site visits. Applications outside the metropolitan Washington, DC, area are not accepted.

Restrictions

The foundation does not support individuals, medical research or government agencies. It does not make loans.

Additional Information

Initial grants are usually in the $5,000 range. First time applicants are advised not to make requests in excess of $10,000.
Publications: Application Guidelines; Grants Report; Application Form

Foundation Officials

Michael P. Bentzen: secretary, trustee
Jeffery P. Capron: treasurer, trustee
Richard H. Lee: president, trustee

Grants Analysis

Disclosure Period: calendar year ending 2001
Total Grants: $1,313,500
Number of Grants: 76
Average Grant: $14,849
Highest Grant: $75,000
Lowest Grant: $1,000
Typical Range: $10,000 to $25,000
Note: Grants analysis provided by foundation.

Recent Grants

Note: Grants derived from 2001 Form 990.

General

75,000	Boys and Girls Clubs of Greater Washington, Silver Spring, MD -- support of the eastern club
45,000	Junior Achievement of the National Capital Area, Washington, DC -- sponsorship of Elementary Economic Literacy Program in Prince George's County Public School
35,000	Bread for the City and Zacchaeus Free Clinic, Washington, DC -- campaign to build facility
30,000	House of Ruth, Washington, DC -- Family Services Program
25,000	Bethany, Washington, DC -- renovation of building
25,000	Christ Child Society, Inc., Washington, DC -- Inner City Counseling Program
25,000	Faith in the Family USA, Springfield, VA -- operating support
25,000	Montgomery Community College Foundation, Rockville, MD -- scholarship for economically disadvantaged students
25,000	So Others Might Eat (S.O.M.E), Washington, DC -- renovation of a warehouse for expansion of programs
25,000	Washington Ballet, Washington, DC -- DanceLinks

EMMA R. FOX CHARITABLE TRUST

Giving Contact

Frank Rizzo, Trustee
National City Bank
PO Box 5756
Cleveland, OH 44101
Phone: (216)575-2507

Description

Founded: 1959
EIN: 346511198
Organization Type: Private Foundation
Giving Locations: OH: northeastern region
Grant Types: General Support.

Donor Information

Founder: the late Emma R. Fox

Financial Summary

Total Giving: $343,800 (2001); $350,250 (2000); $353,000 (1998)
Giving Analysis: Giving for 2001 includes: foundation scholarships ($5,000); foundation grants to United Way ($9,000); 2000: foundation grants to United Way ($8,250) 1998: foundation grants to United Way ($7,000)
Assets: $9,440,966 (2001); $10,288,595 (2000); $9,779,116 (1998)

Typical Recipients

Arts & Humanities: Arts Associations & Councils, Arts Centers, Arts Outreach, Community Arts, History & Archaeology, Libraries, Museums/Galleries, Music, Opera, Performing Arts, Public Broadcasting, Theater, Visual Arts
Civic & Public Affairs: Botanical Gardens/Parks, Business/Free Enterprise, Civil Rights, Economic Development, Economic Policy, Employment/Job Training, Civic & Public Affairs-General, Legal Aid, Nonprofit Management, Parades/Festivals, Public Policy, Safety, Urban & Community Affairs, Women's Affairs
Education: Afterschool/Enrichment Programs, Arts/Humanities Education, Colleges & Universities, Community & Junior Colleges, Economic Education, Education Reform, Education-General, Education-General, Legal Education, Medical Education, Minority Education, Private Education (Precollege), Religious Education, Special Education, Student Aid
Environment: Environment-General
Health: Children's Health/Hospitals, Clinics/Medical Centers, Emergency/Ambulance Services, Eyes/Blindness, Geriatric Health, Health Funds, Health Organizations, Hospices, Hospitals, Long-Term Care, Medical Rehabilitation, Medical Research, Mental Health, Public Health, Research/Studies Institutes, Single-Disease Health Associations, Speech & Hearing
Religion: Churches, Jewish Causes, Ministries, Religious Organizations, Religious Welfare, Social/Policy Issues
Science: Science Museums, Scientific Centers & Institutes, Scientific Organizations
Social Services: Child Abuse, Child Welfare, Community Service Organizations, Crime Prevention, Day Care, Delinquency & Criminal Rehabilitation, Domestic Violence, Family Planning, Family Services, Food/Clothing Distribution, Homes, People with Disabilities, Senior Services, Shelters/Homelessness, Substance Abuse, United Funds/United Ways, Youth Organizations

Application Procedures

Initial Contact: Send a brief letter of inquiry and full proposal.
Application Requirements: Include a description of organization, amount requested, purpose of funds sought, recently audited financial statement, and proof of tax-exempt status.
Deadlines: May 15; November 15.

Restrictions

Support is not awarded to individuals, religious organizations for sectarian purposes, or political or lobbying groups.

Additional Information

Trust(s): National City Bank

Foundation Officials

Harold Edward Friedman: secretary B Cleveland, OH 1934. ED Ohio State University BS (1956); Case Western Reserve University LLB (1959). PRIM CORP EMPL partner: Ulmer & Berne. NONPR AFFIL member: Ohio Bar Association; director: YES; president: Metropolitan Health Foundation; president: National Association Jewish Vocational Services; director: Jewish Family Service Association; president: Jewish Vocational Services Cleveland; vice chairman endowment fund, director: Jewish Community Federation Cleveland; director: Jewish Convalesce & Rehabilitation Center; president: Cleveland Hillel Foundation; president: International Association Jewish Vocational Services; director: Bur Jewish Education; member: Cleveland Bar Association; director: Bellaire/Jewish Childrens Bureau; director: Big Brothers Greater Cleveland; member: American Bar Association. CLUB AFFIL Oakwood Country Club.
Nancy Friedman: trustee
Frank M. Rizzo: trustee PRIM CORP EMPL vice president: National City Bank.
Mrs. Edward Schweid: chairman

Grants Analysis

Disclosure Period: calendar year ending 2001
Total Grants: $329,800*
Number of Grants: 86
Average Grant: $3,835
Highest Grant: $23,000
Lowest Grant: $1,000
Typical Range: $1,000 to $10,000
*****Note:** Giving excludes United Way.

Recent Grants

Note: Grants derived from 2001 Form 990.

General

23,000	Jewish Community Federation of Cleveland, Cleveland, OH
10,500	American Civil Liberties, Cleveland, OH
10,000	Boys and Girls Club of Cleveland, Cleveland, OH
10,000	Food Rescue of Northeast Ohio, Cleveland, OH
10,000	Free Clinic of Greater Cleveland, Cleveland, OH
10,000	Metro Health Foundation, Cleveland, OH
9,000	United Way Services, Cleveland, OH
8,000	Cuyahoga Community College, Cleveland, OH
7,500	Hopewell Inn, Mesopotamia, OH
6,000	Cleveland Orchestra, Cleveland, OH

FRANCIS FAMILIES FOUNDATION

Giving Contact

Lyn A. Knox, Program Officer
800 West 47th Street, Suite 717
Kansas City, MO 64112
Phone: (816)531-0077
Fax: (816)531-8810
E-mail: lyn@francisfoundation.org
Web: http://www.francisfoundation.org

Description

Founded: 1989
EIN: 431492132
Organization Type: Specialized/Single Purpose Foundation
Giving Locations: MO: Kansas City nationally.
Grant Types: Capital, Fellowship, General Support, Operating Expenses, Project.

Donor Information

Founder: The Francis Families Foundation was formed in 1989 as the result of a merger between the Parker B. Francis Foundation and the Parker B. Francis III Foundation. The late Parker B. Francis and his wife, Mary B. Francis, established the Parker B. Francis Foundation as a trust in Missouri in 1951. Mr. Francis was a founder of the Puritan-Bennett Corporation, manufacturer and marketer of specialized hospital medical products and equipment for respiratory care.

As a result of the company's success, the research fellowship program was inaugurated in 1975. A major part of the foundation's income supported that program. In the interest of Mr. Francis and the Puritan Bennett Corporation, fellowship awards were made in fields related to pulmonary disease and anesthesiology.

The Parker B. Francis III Foundation was established in 1962. Its interest was in the principal education and cultural institutions in the metropolitan Kansas City area.

Financial Summary

Total Giving: $5,561,147 (2000); $4,870,326 (1998); $5,039,961 (1997)

Giving Analysis: Giving for 2000 includes: foundation grants to United Way ($375,000); foundation fellowships ($1,725,682) 1998: foundation fellowships ($1,457,023)

Assets: $124,172,018 (2000); $113,722,366 (1998); $90,689,000 (1997)

Typical Recipients

Arts & Humanities: Arts Associations & Councils, Arts Institutes, Ballet, Dance, Arts & Humanities-General, Historic Preservation, History & Archaeology, Libraries, Museums/Galleries, Music, Opera, Performing Arts, Public Broadcasting, Theater, Visual Arts

Civic & Public Affairs: Botanical Gardens/Parks, Community Foundations, Civic & Public Affairs-General, Public Policy, Zoos/Aquariums

Education: Arts/Humanities Education, Colleges & Universities, Community & Junior Colleges, Education Funds, Elementary Education (Private), Environmental Education, Faculty Development, Education-General, Medical Education, Minority Education, Preschool Education, Private Education (Precollege), Public Education (Precollege), Science/Mathematics Education, Science/Mathematics Education, Social Sciences Education, Special Education, Student Aid

Health: Children's Health/Hospitals, Clinics/Medical Centers, Health Organizations, Hospitals, Hospitals (University Affiliated), Medical Research, Prenatal Health Issues, Public Health, Research/Studies Institutes, Respiratory, Single-Disease Health Associations

International: Foreign Educational Institutions, Health Care/Hospitals

Religion: Religious Welfare

Social Services: At-Risk Youth, Child Welfare, Community Service Organizations, Counseling, Crime Prevention, Family Services, Social Services-General, United Funds/United Ways, Youth Organizations

Application Procedures

Initial Contact: Prospective applicants for educational and cultural funding should call or write the foundation to determine if their organization or project falls within foundation guidelines. Fellowship applicants should request a current-year brochure; fellowship application form. are available upon request.

Application Requirements: If an educational or cultural program falls within foundation guidelines, a written proposal will be requested. The proposal should include brief project summary; goals and plans; timetable with specific, measurable objectives; method of evaluation; plan to achieve financial stability during and after funding expiration; project budget; description of additional sources of support; recently audited

financial statement and IRS determination letter. Additional information may be requested during the review process.

Deadlines: Varies from year to year for fellowships, but is usually in mid-October. Late applications will not be accepted. Education and culture proposals must be submitted by August 1.

Review Process: The board reviews requests in January.

Restrictions

No grants are given to individuals or for loans. Applying organizations must be tax-exempt under the IRS code, and for grants to culture, education, child and youth development, must be located within the greater Kansas City, MO, area.

Capital campaigns are not a priority, but a limited number of solicited proposals will be considered.

Additional Information

In 1989, the Parker B. Francis Foundation and the Parker B. Francis III Foundation merged to form the Francis Families Foundation.

The director of any training program, pulmonary division, or research laboratory may apply on behalf of a candidate for fellowship. Only one application is accepted from a department at a time.

Publications: Annual Report; Guidelines; Application Form; Fellowship Brochure

Foundation Officials

Ann F. Barhoum: director, executive committee
Charles Curran: director
David V. Francis: director, executive committee
J. Scott Francis: director, executive committee
John B. Francis: director, honorary chairman
Mary Harris Francis: director, honorary vice chairman
Linda Jean French: secretary, treasurer B Newark, NY 1947. ED William Jewell College BA (1969); University of Missouri JD (1978). PRIM CORP EMPL partner: Blackwell, Sanders, Matheny, Weary & Lombardi LLP. CORP AFFIL director: Diastole. NONPR AFFIL director: University Missouri Kansas City Gallery Art; member: William Jewell Alumni Association; director: Trinity Lutheran Hospital Foundation; member: University Missouri Kansas City Alumni Association; director, president, secretary: Lawyers Association Kansas City; member: Missouri Bar Association; member: Kansas City Bar Association; member: American Society of Corporate Secretaries; member: Kansas City Association Women Lawyers; member: American Corporate Counsel Association; director, finance committee, executive committee: American Red Cross Greater Kansas City Chapter; member committee labor employment law, committee business law: American Bar Association. CLUB AFFIL Kansas City Club.
B. Spencer Heddens: director
Ramon Murguia: director
Susan Neves: director, executive committee
Ann Robertson: assistant secretary
James P. Sunderland: director B Springfield, MO 1928. ED Washington & Lee University BS (1950); Washington University LLB (1952). PRIM CORP EMPL chairman, director: Ash Grove Cement Co. CORP AFFIL chairman: Vinton Corp.; director: Ash Grove Aggregates Inc.; director: Boatmens First National Bank Kansas City. NONPR AFFIL director: Greater Kansas City Community Foundation.

Grants Analysis

Disclosure Period: calendar year ending 2000
Total Grants: $3,460,465*
Number of Grants: 66
Average Grant: $29,596*
Highest Grant: $725,000
Typical Range: $2,000 to $250,000
*Note: Giving excludes fellowships and United Way. Average grant figure excludes three highest grants ($1,595,929)

Recent Grants

Note: Grants derived from 2000 Form 990.

Library-Related

125,000	Truman Library Institute, Independence, MO

General

1,725,682	Parker B. Francis Fellowship Program
725,000	Greater Kansas City Community Foundation, Kansas City, MO
451,184	Francis Child Development Institute, Kansas City, MO
419,745	Francis Child Development Institute, Kansas City, MO
250,000	Heart of America United Way, Kansas City, MO
250,000	KCPT/Channel 19, Kansas City, MO
250,000	Nelson Atkins Museum of Art, Kansas City, MO
125,000	Heart of America United Way, Kansas City, MO
125,000	Kansas City Free Health Clinic, Kansas City, MO
100,000	Kansas City Art Institute, Kansas City, MO

A. J. FRANK FAMILY FOUNDATION

Giving Contact

Douglas Highberger
PO Drawer 79
Mill City, OR 97360
Phone: (503)897-2371

Description

Founded: 1959
EIN: 930523395
Organization Type: Private Foundation
Giving Locations: OR
Grant Types: General Support.

Donor Information

Founder: A. J. Frank, L. D. Frank, Frank Lumber Co., Inc., Frank Timber Products, Inc., members of the Frank family

Financial Summary

Total Giving: $372,321 (fiscal year ending September 30, 2000); $327,925 (fiscal 1998); $340,236 (fiscal 1997)

Assets: $7,487,619 (fiscal 2000); $7,524,899 (fiscal 1998); $7,296,514 (fiscal 1997)

Gifts Received: $13,000 (fiscal 2000); $48,000 (fiscal 1998); $50,000 (fiscal 1997)

Typical Recipients

Arts & Humanities: Libraries, Museums/Galleries, Music

Civic & Public Affairs: Botanical Gardens/Parks, Community Foundations, Housing, Municipalities/Towns, Safety, Urban & Community Affairs

Education: Agricultural Education, Colleges & Universities, Community & Junior Colleges, Economic Education, Elementary Education (Private), Private Education (Precollege), Secondary Education (Private), Secondary Education (Public)

Health: Cancer, Children's Health/Hospitals, Heart, Hospices, Hospitals, Long-Term Care, Medical Research, Multiple Sclerosis, Single-Disease Health Associations

International: International Affairs, International Environmental Issues, International Relations, International Relief Efforts, Missionary/Religious Activities

Religion: Churches, Dioceses, Religion-General, Ministries, Religious Organizations, Religious Welfare, Social/Policy Issues

Social Services: Animal Protection, Child Welfare, Community Service Organizations, Domestic Violence, Family Planning, Food/Clothing Distribution, Homes, People with Disabilities, Recreation & Athletics, Scouts, Special Olympics, Substance Abuse, United Funds/United Ways, Youth Organizations

Application Procedures

Initial Contact: Send a brief letter of inquiry.
Application Requirements: Include a description of organization, purpose of funds sought, budget of project, and proof of tax-exempt status.
Deadlines: August 15 and December 15.

Restrictions

Grants are not made to individuals.

Foundation Officials

C. M. Carey: director
Dennis D. Frank: director PRIM CORP EMPL president, chief executive officer: Frank Lumber Co.
J. T. Frank: director

Grants Analysis

Disclosure Period: fiscal year ending September 30, 2000
Total Grants: $372,321
Number of Grants: 62
Average Grant: $6,005
Highest Grant: $50,000
Typical Range: $1,000 to $10,000

Recent Grants

Note: Grants derived from fiscal 2000 Form 990.

General

50,000	Santiam Memorial Hospital, Stayton, OR
22,500	Immaculate Conception
20,000	St. Joseph's Parochial School
16,000	Salvation Army
15,000	Regis High School, New York, NY
15,000	St. Vincent de Paul, Oakland, CA
10,000	Benedictine Nursing Center, Mt. Angel, OR
10,000	City of Mill City
10,000	Epilepsy Foundation
10,000	Mt. Angel Abbey

EVAN FRANKEL FOUNDATION

Giving Contact

Nancy Wendell
PO Box 5072
East Hampton, NY 11937
Phone: (631)329-2833
E-mail: frankelfound@hamptons.com

Description

Founded: 1978
EIN: 132998402
Organization Type: Private Foundation
Giving Locations: NY: East Hampton including metropolitan area
Grant Types: Capital, Conference/Seminar, Department, Endowment, Fellowship, General Support, Matching, Multiyear/Continuing Support, Scholarship.

Donor Information

Founder: the late Evan M. Franbel

Financial Summary

Total Giving: $2,353,000 (fiscal year ending September 30, 2001); $2,285,120 (fiscal 2000); $2,272,065 (fiscal 1999)
Giving Analysis: Giving for fiscal 2000 includes: foundation scholarships ($49,270) fiscal 1999: foundation scholarships ($67,215)

Assets: $7,866,000 (fiscal 2001); $10,934,711 (fiscal 2000); $11,977,045 (fiscal 1999)
Gifts Received: $168,071 (fiscal 1997); $200,000 (fiscal 1995); $2,758,760 (fiscal 1994)

Typical Recipients

Arts & Humanities: Dance, Arts & Humanities-General, History & Archaeology, Libraries, Museums/Galleries, Music, Theater
Civic & Public Affairs: Botanical Gardens/Parks, Economic Development, Civic & Public Affairs-General, Legal Aid, Public Policy, Urban & Community Affairs, Women's Affairs
Education: Arts/Humanities Education, Colleges & Universities, Education-General, Legal Education, Secondary Education (Public), Special Education, Student Aid
Environment: Resource Conservation
Health: Cancer, Children's Health/Hospitals, Clinics/Medical Centers, Diabetes, Geriatric Health, Hospices, Public Health
International: International Environmental Issues, Missionary/Religious Activities
Religion: Jewish Causes
Science: Science Museums, Scientific Organizations
Social Services: Animal Protection, At-Risk Youth, Community Service Organizations, Crime Prevention, Day Care, Family Planning, Food/Clothing Distribution, Recreation & Athletics, Scouts, YMCA/YWCA/YMHA/YWHA

Application Procedures

Initial Contact: Request preliminary application guidelines in writing.
Deadlines: the 15th day of the first month of the quarter for action that quarter.

Restrictions

Grants are not made to individuals.

Foundation Officials

Ernest Frankel: president, director
C. Leonard Gordon: director
Joshua Murdock Pruzansky: secretary, director B New York, NY 1940. ED Columbia College BA (1960); Columbia College JD (1965). PRIM CORP EMPL partner: Greshin, Ziegler & Pruzansky. CORP AFFIL member advisory board: Ticor Title Guarantee Co.; member advisory board: Marine Midland Bank Long Island. NONPR AFFIL member executive council: New York State Conference Bar Leaders; member: Suffolk Bar Pac; fellow, director: New York State Bar Foundation; member: New York County Lawyers Association; vice president, executive committee del, member: New York State Bar Association; member: Nassau County Bar Association; member, director: Columbia University Law Alumni Associate Suffolk County; member Suffolk advisory board: Fund Modern Courts; member secondary sch advisory committee: Columbia University; member probate & real property section: American Bar Association.
Andrew E. Sabin: treasurer, director PRIM CORP EMPL president: Sabin Metal Corp.

Grants Analysis

Disclosure Period: fiscal year ending September 30, 2000
Total Grants: $2,235,850*
Number of Grants: 64
Average Grant: $19,601*
Highest Grant: $1,001,000
Typical Range: $5,000 to $40,000
*Note: Giving excludes scholarship. Average grant excludes highest grant.

Recent Grants

Note: Grants derived from fiscal 2000 Form 990.

General

1,600,000	Jewish Center of the Hampton's -- raised money for Jewish Community
1,000,000	University of California Los Angeles

	School of Law, Los Angeles, CA -- endowment fellowship
480,000	Columbia University Law School, New York, NY -- establish chair in environmental law
250,000	South Fork Natural History Society, Amagansett, NY
47,000	All People's Garden
12,500	College Scholarship Fund, Sacramento, CA -- paid to colleges

JOHN AND MARY FRANKLIN FOUNDATION INC.

Giving Contact

Dr. Marilu McCarty, Executive Secretary
NC1-002-11-18 Bank of America Plaza
Charlotte, NC 28255
Phone: (404)607-5209

Description

Founded: 1955
EIN: 586036131
Organization Type: General Purpose Foundation
Giving Locations: GA: Atlanta including metropolitan area
Grant Types: Award, Endowment, Fellowship, General Support, Professorship, Project, Research, Scholarship.

Donor Information

Founder: The John and Mary Franklin Foundation was established in Georgia in 1955 by John Leonard Franklin and his wife, Mary Owen Franklin. Mr. Franklin developed the Audichron equipment used by telephone companies to provide time-of-day telephone answering service to customers. The pattern of charitable giving established by the Franklins during their lives forms the basis of the foundation's grant program.

Financial Summary

Total Giving: $1,943,200 (2001); $2,000,000 (2000 approx); $1,947,900 (1999)
Giving Analysis: Giving for 2001 includes: foundation grants to United Way ($5,000); foundation matching gifts ($46,500); foundation scholarships ($85,500); 1999: foundation grants to United Way ($10,000); foundation matching gifts ($33,000); foundation scholarships ($218,500); 1998: foundation matching gifts ($1,300) foundation grants to United Way ($5,000)
Assets: $34,711,872 (2001); $42,000,000 (2000 approx); $42,049,118 (1999)

Typical Recipients

Arts & Humanities: Arts Centers, Ballet, Historic Preservation, History & Archaeology, Libraries, Museums/Galleries, Music, Performing Arts, Theater
Civic & Public Affairs: Botanical Gardens/Parks, Clubs, Civic & Public Affairs-General, Housing, Urban & Community Affairs, Zoos/Aquariums
Education: Agricultural Education, Business Education, Colleges & Universities, Community & Junior Colleges, Economic Education, Education Funds, Engineering/Technological Education, Environmental Education, Faculty Development, International Studies, Legal Education, Literacy, Medical Education, Minority Education, Private Education (Precollege), Religious Education, Science/Mathematics Education, Secondary Education (Private), Special Education, Student Aid
Environment: Environment-General, Resource Conservation
Health: Cancer, Children's Health/Hospitals, Clinics/Medical Centers, Emergency/Ambulance Services, Geriatric Health, Health Policy/Cost Containment,

Hospices, Hospitals, Long-Term Care, Medical Rehabilitation, Medical Research, Medical Training, Mental Health, Single-Disease Health Associations
International: Foreign Educational Institutions
Religion: Religious Organizations, Religious Welfare
Science: Science Museums
Social Services: At-Risk Youth, Child Welfare, Community Service Organizations, Family Planning, People with Disabilities, Recreation & Athletics, Scouts, Senior Services, Special Olympics, United Funds/United Ways, YMCA/YWCA/YMHA/YWHA, Youth Organizations

Application Procedures

Initial Contact: The foundation does not provide application forms. Initial contact should be a letter describing the program. Applications may be directed to the chairman, secretary, or any member of the board of trustees.
Application Requirements: The letter of application should include a description of the institution, its legal status, organization, officers, trustees or directors, and the purpose for which it was organized. Organizations that are not public institutions must also provide evidence of classification as a 501(c)(3) tax-exempt organization.
Deadlines: None.
Review Process: The board of trustees meets in January and July; the majority of funding decisions are made in January. The executive committee considers each application to determine whether it falls within the purposes of the foundation and whether funds are available for that type of project. The committee then forwards recommendations to the full board of trustees.

Restrictions

The foundation does not support religious denominations or political activities.

Additional Information

Bank South, N.A., in Atlanta, GA, provides administrative services for the foundation.
Publications: Annual Report (for trustees only)

Foundation Officials

Richard Winn Courts, II: trustee B Atlanta, GA. PRIM CORP EMPL chairman, director: Atlantic Investment Co. CORP AFFIL director: Southern Mills Inc.; director: SunTrust Bank Georgia Inc.; director: NAPA Distribution Center; director: Genuine Parts Co.; director: NAPA Auto Parts; director: Cousins Properties Inc.
George T. Duncan: trustee ED Army War College; Auburn University; United States Military Academy BS.
John B. Ellis: trustee B Columbus, GA 1924. ED Louisiana State University BS (1948); Indiana University MBA (1949). PRIM CORP EMPL director: Atlantic Investment Co. CORP AFFIL director: Interstate/Johnson Lane Inc.; director: UAP Inc.; director: Hughes Supply Inc.; director: Columbus Mills Inc.; director: Crystal Farms Inc.
Frank M. Malone, Jr.: trustee B 1936. ED University of North Carolina (1958). PRIM CORP EMPL senior vice president human resources: First Financial Management Corp.
Marilu H. McCarty: executive secretary ED Georgia Southern University BS; Georgia State University MA; Georgia State University PhD. NONPR AFFIL assistant dean: Georgia Institute Technology College Management.
L. Edmund Rast: trustee, member executive committee, chairman ED University of Georgia BCS. PRIM CORP EMPL chairman: Audichron Co.
Alexander Wyly Smith, Jr.: trustee, member executive committee B Atlanta, GA 1923. ED College of the Holy Cross (1941-1942); University of Georgia BBA (1947); University of Georgia LLB (1949). PRIM CORP EMPL partner retired: Smith Gambrell & Russell. NONPR AFFIL director: Our Lady Perpetual Help Free Cancer Home; member: Phi Delta Phi; director:

Marist School; member: Chi Phi; member: Georgia Bar Association; member: Atlanta Bar Association; director, planning developmental council: Catholic Archdiocese Atlanta. CLUB AFFIL Peachtree Golf Club; Piedmont Driving Club.
William Maurrelle Suttles: trustee B Ben Hill, GA July 25, 1920. ED Georgia State University BCS (1942); Yale University MDiv (1946); Emory University MTh (1947); Emory University MRE (1953); Auburn University EdD (1958). PRIM NONPR EMPL professor: Georgia State University. CORP AFFIL director: Georgia Federal Bank. NONPR AFFIL member: Sigma Tau Delta; trustee: George M Sparks Scholarship Fund; member: Sigma Nu; member, grand chaplain: Sigma Pi Alpha; member: Phi Eta Sigma; member: Phi Kappa Phi; member: Omicron Delta Kappa; member: Phi Delta Kappa; member: Kappa Phi Kappa; member: Mortar Board; director: John Mercer Foundation; member: Kappa Delta Phi; member: Georgia State University Athletic Association; trustee: Georgia State University Foundation; member: Georgia State University Alumni Association; trustee: Georgia Council Moral Civic Concerns; executive vice president, provost, professor: Georgia State University; trustee: Christian Council; trustee: Georgia Baptist Children's Homes & Families Ministries; member: Atlanta Chamber of Commerce; member: Beta Gamma Sigma; member: Alpha Lambda Delta; member: Alpha Kappa Psi. CLUB AFFIL Masons Club; Shriners Club; Commerce Club; Kiwanis Club; Blue Key Club.

Grants Analysis

Disclosure Period: calendar year ending 2001
Total Grants: $1,806,200*
Number of Grants: 185
Average Grant: $9,763*
Highest Grant: $85,000
Lowest Grant: $125
Typical Range: $1,000 to $15,000
*Note: Giving excludes scholarships, matching grants and United Way.

Recent Grants

Note: Grants derived from 2001 Form 990.

General

85,000	Auburn University, Auburn, AL -- arts and science lecture series
67,500	Georgia Institute of Technology, Atlanta, GA -- School of Electrical Engineering McCarty Chair
60,000	Auburn University, Auburn, AL -- Littleton Lecture Series
60,000	Georgia Institute of Technology, Atlanta, GA -- John and Marilu McCarty Chair
60,000	Georgia State University, Atlanta, GA -- child development and Suttles chair religious
60,000	University of Georgia Business School, Athens, GA -- L. Edmund Rast Chair
60,000	University of Georgia Foundation, Athens, GA -- School of Law
40,000	Georgia State University Foundation, Atlanta, GA -- scholarships and child development center
35,000	Emory University, Atlanta, GA -- Sports Hall of Fame
30,000	Auburn University, Auburn, AL -- environmental forum

MARY D. AND WALTER F. FREAR ELEEMOSYNARY TRUST

Giving Contact

Paula Boyce, Grants Administration Officer
c/o Pacific Century Trust
PO Box 3170
Honolulu, HI 96802

Phone: (808)538-4945
E-mail: pboyce@boh.com

Description

Founded: 1936
EIN: 996002270
Organization Type: Private Foundation
Giving Locations: HI
Grant Types: Capital, General Support, Multiyear/Continuing Support, Operating Expenses.

Donor Information

Founder: the late Mary D. Frear, Walter F. Frear

Financial Summary

Total Giving: $1,722,761 (2001); $678,315 (2000); $637,623 (1999)
Giving Analysis: Giving for 2000 includes: foundation matching gifts ($5,000); foundation scholarships ($127,950); 1999: foundation matching gifts ($5,000); foundation scholarships ($120,450); 1998: foundation matching gifts ($10,000); foundation scholarships ($25,200) foundation scholarships ($25,200)
Assets: $18,372,158 (2001); $21,739,132 (2000); $21,757,303 (1999)
Gifts Received: In 1991, contributions were received from Mary D. and Walter F. Frear Special Trust "A".

Typical Recipients

Arts & Humanities: Arts Festivals, Arts Funds, Community Arts, Dance, Arts & Humanities-General, Libraries, Museums/Galleries, Music, Opera, Public Broadcasting, Theater
Civic & Public Affairs: Botanical Gardens/Parks, Community Foundations, Civic & Public Affairs-General, Law & Justice, Women's Affairs
Education: Arts/Humanities Education, Business Education, Colleges & Universities, Economic Education, Faculty Development, Education-General, Literacy, Preschool Education, Private Education (Precollege), Secondary Education (Private), Special Education
Environment: Environment-General, Resource Conservation
Health: Alzheimers Disease, Clinics/Medical Centers, Hospices, Hospitals, Medical Rehabilitation, Mental Health
Religion: Churches, Ministries, Religious Organizations, Religious Welfare
Social Services: At-Risk Youth, Child Welfare, Community Centers, Community Service Organizations, Day Care, Family Planning, Family Services, Food/Clothing Distribution, People with Disabilities, Recreation & Athletics, Scouts, United Funds/United Ways, Veterans, YMCA/YWCA/YMHA/YWHA, Youth Organizations

Application Procedures

Initial Contact: Send full proposal signed by the presiding officer of the Board of Directors.
Application Requirements: board of directors, a description of organization. Include summary of proposed activity stating need, plan for distribution, population to be served, plan for evaluation effectiveness, total cost of project including other funding sources, both present and future, two or three letters of endorsement, amount requested, purpose of funds sought, recently audited financial statement, and proofs of tax-exempt status.
Deadlines: January 15, April 15, July 15, and October 15.

Restrictions

Does not support individuals or endowments.

Additional Information

The foundation reports that contributions are allocated in the following manner: 42% Health & Human Services; 40% Education; 13% Arts & Humanities,

5% Religion and Environment. PU/annual report (including application guidelines)
Trust(s): Pacific Century Trust

Grants Analysis

Disclosure Period: calendar year ending 2000
Total Grants: $545,365*
Number of Grants: 91
Average Grant: $5,993
Highest Grant: $25,000
Typical Range: $1,000 to $10,000
*Note: Giving excludes scholarships, matching gifts.

Recent Grants

Note: Grants derived from 2001 Form 990.

General

500,000	Honolulu Symphony Society, Honolulu, HI -- for capacity building and stabilization and establishment of trust fund for education programs
175,000	Hawaii Theatre Center, Honolulu, HI -- for restoration of a vertical sign
50,000	St. Francis Health Care Foundation of Hawaii, Honolulu, HI -- to purchase state of the art dual detector gamma camera
44,229	Boys and Girls Club of Hawaii, Honolulu, HI -- install gymnasium flooring for the Hawaii Ewa Beach Clubhouse
31,500	Hawaiian Island Ministries, Honolulu, HI -- for Honolulu 2002 Youth Night Program
25,000	Hawaii Alliance for Arts Education, Honolulu, HI -- for renovations
25,000	Honolulu Academy of Arts, Honolulu, HI -- for Ambassador Outreach Program
21,000	Modah Community Center, Honolulu, HI -- to purchase a 28 child seat school for the childcare program
20,000	Goodwill Industries, Honolulu, HI -- for Island Career Center Build Out on Britannia Street
20,000	Hawaii Nature Center, Honolulu, HI -- supplies for the Pouhala Project

FREAS FOUNDATION

Giving Contact

David M. Trout, Jr., Manager
c/o First Union National Bank
401 S. Tryon St., 4th Fl.
Charlotte, NC 28288-1159
Phone: (704)383-2885

Description

EIN: 221714810
Organization Type: Private Foundation
Giving Locations: CT; MD; PA; UT; WA
Grant Types: General Support.

Financial Summary

Total Giving: $461,048 (2001); $439,804 (2000); $395,212 (1999)
Giving Analysis: Giving for 1999 includes: foundation fellowships ($1,000)
Assets: $8,464,602 (2001); $8,983,465 (2000); $9,103,871 (1999)

Typical Recipients

Arts & Humanities: Arts Centers, Ballet, Historic Preservation, History & Archaeology, Libraries, Museums/Galleries, Opera, Performing Arts, Public Broadcasting, Theater
Civic & Public Affairs: Botanical Gardens/Parks, Community Foundations, Employment/Job Training, Civic & Public Affairs-General, Legal Aid, Urban & Community Affairs, Women's Affairs

Education: Arts/Humanities Education, Colleges & Universities, Health & Physical Education, Journalism/Media Education, Literacy, Medical Education, Private Education (Precollege), Public Education (Precollege), Religious Education, Secondary Education (Private), Secondary Education (Public), Student Aid
Health: Cancer, Emergency/Ambulance Services, Health Organizations, Hospices, Hospitals, Hospitals, Medical Rehabilitation, Nursing Services, Public Health
Religion: Churches, Religious Organizations, Religious Welfare, Seminaries
Social Services: Child Welfare, Community Centers, Community Service Organizations, Counseling, Day Care, Delinquency & Criminal Rehabilitation, Domestic Violence, Family Services, Food/Clothing Distribution, Homes, People with Disabilities, Scouts, Senior Services, Social Services-General, Substance Abuse, Volunteer Services, YMCA/YWCA/YMHA/YWHA, Youth Organizations

Application Procedures

Deadlines: None.

Additional Information

Trust(s): First Union National Bank

Foundation Officials

Arthur K. Freas: mgr
Margery H. Freas: mgr
David M. Trout, Jr.: mgr
Rebecca F. Trout: mgr

Grants Analysis

Disclosure Period: calendar year ending 2001
Total Grants: $461,048
Number of Grants: 83*
Average Grant: $3,555*
Highest Grant: $166,000
Lowest Grant: $100
Typical Range: $1,000 to $10,000
*Note: Average grant figure excludes highest grant.

Recent Grants

Note: Grants derived from 2001 Form 990.

Library-Related

5,000	Martin Library, York, PA

General

166,000	Bucknell University, Lewisburg, PA
22,200	Children's Center, Salt Lake City, UT
12,615	York County Heritage Trust, York, PA
12,000	York College of Pennsylvania, York, PA
11,000	Access York, Inc., York, PA
10,100	Strand Capitol Performing Arts Center, York, PA
8,500	Capon Bridge Middle School
6,750	Nine Months in York Town
5,998	York Hospital, York, ME
5,305	York Jewish Community Center

AMBROSE AND IDA FREDRICKSON FOUNDATION

Giving Contact

Tamara I. Morales, Trust Associate
c/o First Union Bank, NA
401 S. Tryon Street, 4th Fl.
Charlotte, NC 28288-1159
Phone: (704)383-5588

Alternate Contact

Phone: (908)598-3576

Description

Founded: 1989
EIN: 226422114
Organization Type: Private Foundation
Giving Locations: NJ: Millburn Township including organizations within a one-hundred mile radius; PA; VA
Grant Types: Capital, General Support, Project, Scholarship.

Financial Summary

Total Giving: $165,350 (2001); $148,586 (2000); $204,911 (1999)
Giving Analysis: Giving for 2001 includes: foundation scholarships ($85,500)
Assets: $2,623,506 (2001); $2,955,589 (2000); $3,127,103 (1999)

Typical Recipients

Arts & Humanities: Historic Preservation, History & Archaeology, Libraries, Museums/Galleries, Music, Opera, Performing Arts, Visual Arts
Civic & Public Affairs: Botanical Gardens/Parks, Economic Development, Civic & Public Affairs-General, Hispanic Affairs, Philanthropic Organizations
Education: Colleges & Universities, Elementary Education (Private), Education-General, Minority Education, Private Education (Precollege), Science/Mathematics Education, Secondary Education (Private), Special Education, Student Aid
Environment: Environment-General, Resource Conservation
Health: AIDS/HIV, Alzheimers Disease, Cancer, Children's Health/Hospitals, Health Organizations, Medical Rehabilitation
Religion: Religious Organizations, Religious Welfare
Social Services: At-Risk Youth, Child Welfare, Community Centers, Community Service Organizations, Family Services, People with Disabilities, Scouts, Youth Organizations

Application Procedures

Initial Contact: request Grant Proposal Format
Deadlines: December 1, March 1, June 1, and September 1.

Restrictions

Does not support political or lobbying groups.

Additional Information

The foundations primary funding concerns are human services, historic preservation and restoration, educational, conservation and restoration of woodland areas, and the arts.
Trust(s): First Union National Bank NA

Foundation Officials

Frederick A. Coombs: trustee
Andrew Davis: assistant vice president
Rosemary M. Karl: trustee
Hugo M. Pfaltz: trustee
Richard G. Ranck: trustee

Grants Analysis

Disclosure Period: calendar year ending 2001
Total Grants: $79,850*
Number of Grants: 22
Average Grant: $3,630
Highest Grant: $10,000
Typical Range: $2,000 to $10,000
*Note: Giving excludes scholarship.

Recent Grants

Note: Grants derived from 2001 Form 990.

General

20,000	Susquehanna University, Selinsgrove, PA

20,000	Susquehanna University, Selinsgrove, PA
20,000	Susquehanna University, Selinsgrove, PA
20,000	Susquehanna University, Selinsgrove, PA
10,000	Colonial Williamsburg Foundation, Williamsburg, VA -- support their efforts in rare breed conservation
10,000	Scholarship Fund for Inner-City Children, Newark, NJ -- for scholarships for needy elementary and secondary students
5,000	American Cancer Society -- for Reach to Recovery Program
5,000	Chad School Foundation, Newark, NJ -- for operating support
5,000	Girl Scout Council -- for renovation and capital campaign for Jockey Hollow Camp
5,000	Interfaith Council for the Homeless, Plainfield, NJ -- for Volunteers Shelter Program

FREED FOUNDATION

Giving Contact
Elizabeth Freed, President
1025 Thomas Jefferson St. NW, Suite 308E
Washington, DC 20007
Phone: (202)337-5487

Description
Founded: 1954
EIN: 526047591
Organization Type: General Purpose Foundation
Giving Locations: DC: Washington including metropolitan area; NJ; NY
Grant Types: General Support, Multiyear/Continuing Support, Operating Expenses, Project.

Donor Information
Founder: The foundation was incorporated in 1954 by the late Frances W. Freed and the late Gerald A. Freed .

Financial Summary
Total Giving: $900,130 (fiscal year ending May 31, 2001); $819,350 (fiscal 2000); $1,081,900 (fiscal 1999)
Assets: $24,215,934 (fiscal 2001); $26,327,010 (fiscal 2000); $23,915,357 (fiscal 1999)
Gifts Received: $156,261 (fiscal 2001); $186,254 (fiscal 2000); $186,254 (fiscal 1999). Note: Contributions were received from the estate of Gerald Freed.

Typical Recipients
Arts & Humanities: Arts Festivals, Arts Outreach, Film & Video, Historic Preservation, Libraries, Literary Arts, Museums/Galleries, Music, Public Broadcasting, Theater
Civic & Public Affairs: Botanical Gardens/Parks, Business/Free Enterprise, Community Foundations, Employment/Job Training, Civic & Public Affairs-General, Housing, Minority Business, Nonprofit Management, Professional & Trade Associations, Public Policy, Safety, Women's Affairs, Zoos/Aquariums
Education: Afterschool/Enrichment Programs, Arts/Humanities Education, Colleges & Universities, Continuing Education, Education Funds, Environmental Education, Education-General, International Studies, Literacy, Medical Education, Minority Education, Minority Education, Preschool Education, Religious Education, Science/Mathematics Education
Environment: Air/Water Quality, Environment-General, Protection, Resource Conservation, Wildlife Protection
Health: AIDS/HIV, Alzheimers Disease, Cancer, Children's Health/Hospitals, Clinics/Medical Centers,

Emergency/Ambulance Services, Eyes/Blindness, Health Policy/Cost Containment, Hospices, Hospitals, Medical Rehabilitation, Mental Health, Nutrition, Public Health, Research/Studies Institutes, Single-Disease Health Associations
Religion: Jewish Causes
Science: Science Museums, Scientific Centers & Institutes
Social Services: Animal Protection, At-Risk Youth, Big Brother/Big Sister, Camps, Child Abuse, Child Welfare, Community Service Organizations, Crime Prevention, Day Care, Domestic Violence, Emergency Relief, Family Planning, Family Services, Food/Clothing Distribution, People with Disabilities, Sexual Abuse, Shelters/Homelessness, Substance Abuse, United Funds/United Ways, Youth Organizations

Application Procedures
Initial Contact: Applicants should write to the foundation for an application form.
Application Requirements: Applicants should submit one copy of their proposal, a budget for the proposal, audited financial statements for the organization, and a copy of IRS tax ruling.
Deadlines: Rolling deadlines.

Restrictions
The foundation does not make grants to individuals, foreign organizations, international projects, conferences, or scholarships.

Additional Information
Publications: Annual Report

Foundation Officials
Lorraine Barnhart: director
Lloyd J. Derrickson: secretary, director
Elizabeth Ann Freed: president, director

Grants Analysis
Disclosure Period: fiscal year ending May 31, 2001
Total Grants: $850,130*
Number of Grants: 26
Average Grant: $26,005*
Highest Grant: $200,000
Lowest Grant: $2,000
Typical Range: $10,000 to $50,000
*Note: Giving excludes United Way. Average grant figure excludes highest grant.

Recent Grants
Note: Grants derived from 2001 Form 990.

General

200,000	Florida State University Foundation, Tallahassee, FL -- mental health professorship
50,000	AmeriCares Foundation, New Canaan, CT -- Heroes' Fund
50,000	Community Foundation of the National Capital Region, Washington, DC -- Survivors Fund
50,000	Discovery Creek Children's Museum of Washington, Washington, DC -- Science and Environmental Education Project
50,000	Ford's Theater, Washington, DC -- education programs
50,000	New York City Public Private Initiatives, New York, NY -- Twin Towers Fund
50,000	New York Firefighters 9-11 Disaster Relief Fund, New York, NY -- disaster relief
50,000	New York State Fraternal Order of Police Foundation, Hicksville, NY -- World Trade Center Disaster Relief Fund
50,000	United Way of New York City, New York, NY -- September 11th Fund
40,000	Washington AIDS Partnership, Washington, DC

SAMUEL FREEMAN CHARITABLE TRUST

Giving Contact
Linda Franciscouicif
c/o U.S. Trust Company of New York
114 West 47th Street
New York, NY 10036-1532
Phone: (212)852-3629
Fax: (212)852-3377

Description
Founded: 1981
EIN: 136803465
Organization Type: General Purpose Foundation
Giving Locations: mid-Atlantic region.
Grant Types: Challenge, Endowment, General Support.

Donor Information
Founder: Established in 1981 by the late Samuel Freeman .

Financial Summary
Total Giving: $2,424,953 (2000); $1,692,900 (1998); $1,581,630 (1996)
Assets: $48,726,663 (2000); $48,451,917 (1998); $37,950,000 (1997 approx)

Typical Recipients
Arts & Humanities: Arts Associations & Councils, Arts Festivals, Ballet, Dance, Arts & Humanities-General, History & Archaeology, Libraries, Museums/Galleries, Music, Opera, Performing Arts, Public Broadcasting, Theater
Civic & Public Affairs: Business/Free Enterprise, Clubs, Civic & Public Affairs-General, Municipalities/Towns, Philanthropic Organizations, Public Policy, Safety, Urban & Community Affairs, Zoos/Aquariums
Education: Arts/Humanities Education, Colleges & Universities, Education Associations, Engineering/Technological Education, Education-General, International Exchange, International Studies, Legal Education, Medical Education, Minority Education, Private Education (Precollege), Public Education (Precollege), Science/Mathematics Education, Student Aid
Environment: Environment-General, Resource Conservation
Health: AIDS/HIV, Cancer, Clinics/Medical Centers, Diabetes, Eyes/Blindness, Health-General, Hospitals, Medical Research, Multiple Sclerosis, Single-Disease Health Associations
International: Foreign Arts Organizations, Health Care/Hospitals, Human Rights, International Environmental Issues, International Organizations, International Relations, International Relief Efforts, Missionary/Religious Activities
Religion: Churches, Jewish Causes, Religious Welfare
Science: Scientific Centers & Institutes
Social Services: Big Brother/Big Sister, Community Service Organizations, Emergency Relief, Family Planning, People with Disabilities, Recreation & Athletics, Shelters/Homelessness, Social Services-General, Substance Abuse, YMCA/YWCA/YMHA/YWHA, Youth Organizations

Application Procedures
Initial Contact: The trust requests a two-page proposal.
Application Requirements: The proposal should include a budget, the most recent audit report, and an IRS determination letter.
Deadlines: None.

Restrictions

The trust does not make grants to individuals or private entities. Trust does not answer telephone inquiries.

Additional Information

Publications: Guidelines
Trust(s): US Trust Co.

Foundation Officials

William E. Murray: trustee B 1926. PRIM CORP EMPL chairman board, chief executive officer, director: East Bay Company Ltd.
Linda Stanciscovich: senior vice president

Grants Analysis

Disclosure Period: calendar year ending 2000
Total Grants: $2,424,953
Number of Grants: 115
Average Grant: $21,087
Highest Grant: $200,000
Typical Range: $1,000 to $25,000

Recent Grants

Note: Grants derived from 2000 Form 990.

Library-Related
20,000	New York Botanical Gardens, New York, NY

General
200,000	East West Institute, Germantown, MD
183,000	Cold Spring Harbor Laboratory, Cold Spring Harbor, NY
150,000	Cold Spring Harbor Laboratory, Cold Spring Harbor, NY
130,000	Marymount Manhattan College, New York, NY
125,000	St. James School
100,000	Cannon Street YMCA, Charleston, SC
100,000	Cannon Street YMCA, Charleston, SC
75,000	Adirondack Railway Preservation Society, Inc., Thendara, NY
75,000	College of Charleston, Charleston, SC
60,000	Saint Marguerite Bourgeoys, Brookfield, CT

FREEPORT BRICK CO.

Company Headquarters

Freeport, PA

Company Description

Employees: 40
SIC(s): 3500 Industrial Machinery & Equipment.
Parent Company: Freeport Refractories, PO Box F, Freeport, PA, United States

Operating Locations

Freeport Brick Co. (PA--Freeport)

Freeport Brick Co. Charitable Trust

Giving Contact

F. H. Laube, III, Secretary
Drawer F
Freeport, PA 16229-0306
Phone: (724)295-2111

Description

EIN: 256074334
Organization Type: Corporate Foundation
Giving Locations: PA: Freeport, Kittanning
Grant Types: General Support.

Financial Summary

Total Giving: $33,000 (2000); $46,500 (1999); $31,500 (1998)
Giving Analysis: Giving for 1999 includes: foundation grants to United Way ($500); foundation ($4,600); 1998: foundation grants to United Way ($500) 1997: foundation grants to United Way ($500)
Assets: $695,443 (2000); $675,353 (1999); $691,701 (1998)

Typical Recipients

Arts & Humanities: Historic Preservation, Libraries
Civic & Public Affairs: Botanical Gardens/Parks, Law & Justice, Municipalities/Towns, Safety, Urban & Community Affairs, Zoos/Aquariums
Education: Education-General, Student Aid
Health: Children's Health/Hospitals, Emergency/Ambulance Services, Health Organizations, Hospitals, Medical Research, Single-Disease Health Associations
Social Services: Community Service Organizations, Crime Prevention, Food/Clothing Distribution, Recreation & Athletics, Scouts, Senior Services, United Funds/United Ways, Volunteer Services, Youth Organizations

Application Procedures

Initial Contact: The foundation requests applications be made in writing.
Application Requirements: Include a description of organization, amount requested, and purpose of funds sought.
Deadlines: None.

Corporate Officials

Mildred Cook: chief financial officer, treasurer, secretary PRIM CORP EMPL chief financial officer, treasurer, secretary: Freeport Brick Co.
F. H. Laube, III: chairman, chief executive officer, president PRIM CORP EMPL chairman, chief executive officer, president: Freeport Brick Co.

Foundation Officials

F. H. Laube, III: secretary
Harry R. Laube: assistant secretary, assistant treasurer
J. Terry Medovitch: treasurer
J. C. Overholt: vchairman

Grants Analysis

Disclosure Period: calendar year ending 2000
Total Grants: $33,000
Number of Grants: 9
Highest Grant: $27,000
Lowest Grant: $500

Recent Grants

Note: Grants derived from 1999 Form 990.

General
40,000	Freeport Community Park Corp, Freeport, PA -- community recreation
1000	Freeport Area Library Association, Freeport, PA -- endowment fund
1000	Freeport Area Meals on Wheels, Freeport, PA -- senior citizens
1000	Freeport Historical Society, Freeport, PA -- historical preservation
1000	Freeport Volunteer Fire Department, Freeport, PA
1000	Pennsylvania State Police Camp Cadet, Kittanning, PA -- youth education
500	Pittsburgh Youth Golf Foundation, Pittsburgh, PA -- youth education
500	South Buffalo Volunteer Fire Department, Freeport, PA
500	United Way of Armstrong County, Kittanning, PA

FREEPORT-MCMORAN COPPER & GOLD, INC.

Company Headquarters

1615 Poydras St.
New Orleans, LA 70112
Web: http://www.fcx.com

Company Description

Founded: 1912
Ticker: FCX
Exchange: NYSE
Revenue: US$1.91 billion (2002)
Employees: 10107 (2002)
SIC(s): 1094 Uranium, Radium & Vanadium Ores, 1311 Crude Petroleum & Natural Gas, 1475 Phosphate Rock, 1479 Chemical & Fertilizer Mining Nec.

Operating Locations

Freeport-McMoRan Inc. (LA--New Orleans)

Nonmonetary Support

Type: Donated Equipment; Loaned Employees; Other

Freeport-McMoRan Foundation

Giving Contact

Nancy Adkerson, Executive Director
1615 Poydras St.
New Orleans, LA 70112
Phone: (504)582-4000
Fax: (504)582-4028

Alternate Contact

David B. Lowry, President
PO Box 61119
New Orleans, LA 70161

Description

EIN: 721316308
Organization Type: Corporate Foundation
Giving Locations: principally near operating locations and to national organizations.
Grant Types: Award, Emergency, Employee Matching Gifts, Endowment, General Support.
Note: Employee matching gift ratio: 2 to 1 up to $500; 1 to 1 after $500 and up to $20,000 per employee annually.

Financial Summary

Total Giving: $2,000,000 (2003 approx); $1,000,000 (2002 approx); $2,464,660 (2001). Note: Contributes through corporate direct giving program and foundation.
Giving Analysis: Giving for 2000 includes: foundation grants to United Way ($340,882); foundation ($1,246,764); 1999: foundation ($3,500,000); 1998: foundation ($5,700,000)
Assets: $1,331,878 (2001); $371,749 (2000)
Gifts Received: $2,347,000 (2001); $1,463,076 (2000). Note: In 2001, contributions were received from Freeport-McMoRan Copper & Gold Inc. ($1,842,973), Freeport -McMoRan Oil & Gas LLC ($504,027). In 2000, contributions were received from Freeport-McMoRan Copper & Gold Inc. ($1,003,557), Freeport-McMoRan Sulphur LLC ($191,719), and McMoRan Oil & Gas LLC ($267,801).

Typical Recipients

Arts & Humanities: Arts Appreciation, Arts Associations & Councils, Arts Centers, Arts Festivals, Arts Funds, Arts Institutes, Ballet, Community Arts, Dance, Ethnic & Folk Arts, Historic Preservation, History & Archaeology, Libraries, Museums/Galleries, Music, Opera, Performing Arts, Public Broadcasting, Theater

Civic & Public Affairs: African American Affairs, Asian American Affairs, Botanical Gardens/Parks, Business/Free Enterprise, Chambers of Commerce, Civil Rights, Clubs, Economic Development, Employment/Job Training, Civic & Public Affairs-General, Housing, Legal Aid, Minority Business, Municipalities/Towns, Native American Affairs, Professional & Trade Associations, Public Policy, Rural Affairs, Safety, Urban & Community Affairs, Women's Affairs, Zoos/Aquariums

Education: Agricultural Education, Business Education, Colleges & Universities, Community & Junior Colleges, Economic Education, Education Associations, Education Reform, Elementary Education (Private), Elementary Education (Public), Engineering/Technological Education, Education-General, Leadership Training, Legal Education, Literacy, Minority Education, Preschool Education, Private Education (Precollege), Public Education (Precollege), Science/Mathematics Education, Secondary Education (Private), Special Education, Student Aid

Environment: Environment-General, Resource Conservation, Wildlife Protection

Health: AIDS/HIV, Cancer, Cancer, Children's Health/Hospitals, Clinics/Medical Centers, Emergency/Ambulance Services, Eyes/Blindness, Health-General, Health Organizations, Heart, Hospitals, Medical Research, Mental Health, Nutrition, Prenatal Health Issues, Single-Disease Health Associations

International: Foreign Educational Institutions, International Affairs, International Organizations, International Relief Efforts

Science: Science Exhibits & Fairs, Science Museums, Scientific Centers & Institutes, Scientific Organizations

Social Services: Animal Protection, At-Risk Youth, Big Brother/Big Sister, Camps, Child Welfare, Community Service Organizations, Counseling, Crime Prevention, Delinquency & Criminal Rehabilitation, Domestic Violence, Emergency Relief, Family Services, Family Services, Food/Clothing Distribution, Homes, People with Disabilities, Recreation & Athletics, Scouts, Senior Services, Shelters/Homelessness, Social Services-General, Substance Abuse, United Funds/United Ways, Volunteer Services, YMCA/YWCA/YMHA/YWHA, Youth Organizations

Application Procedures

Initial Contact: Call or write foundation to ascertain foundation interest and request application form.

Application Requirements: Proposals should include: summary statement, with history, mission, and goals; description of project and organization; amount and specific purpose of request; need for the project in community; detailed report of how money will be spent; detailed annual operating budget; method of evaluation; list of board members; any collaborative efforts; list of other sources of support; financial statements; and proof of tax-exempt status.

Deadlines: November 30.

Review Process: The executive director and president of the foundation make recommendations to the board of trustees.

Evaluative Criteria: Efficiency of management and employee participation through contributions and volunteerism are considered when evaluating requests.

Decision Notification: A preliminary budget is drawn up in October and finalized in December; grants are announced by the end of February.

Restrictions

Does not support individuals; distributing foundations; national disease agencies; or religious, political, fraternal, labor, veterans, or tax-supported organizations (with the exception of public schools, colleges, and universities). The foundation also does not support sporting events, trips or festivals, organizations supported by the United Way, or discriminatory organizations.

Additional Information

Since 1996, the company has operated the Freeport-McMoRan Foundation and the Research, Environmental, and Corporate Fund.

Giving is based on 1% of pre-tax earnings; therefore the contributions budget varies from year to year. All contributions are suspended for 1999.

Publications: Giving Annual Report; Application Form

Foundation Officials

David B. Lowry: vice president PRIM CORP EMPL vice president social & development programs: Freeport-McMoRan Copper & Gold Inc.

Grants Analysis

Disclosure Period: calendar year ending 2001
Total Grants: $2,238,246*
Number of Grants: 338
Average Grant: $6,622
Highest Grant: $125,000
Lowest Grant: $50
Typical Range: $2,500 to $30,000
*Note: Giving excludes United Way.

Recent Grants

Note: Grants derived from 2001 Form 990.

Library-Related

33,333	Library of Congress, Washington, DC -- Kissinger chair

General

213,164	United Way of Greater Los Angeles, Los Angeles, CA -- Unrestricted
125,000	Unity for the Homeless, New Orleans, LA -- Unrestricted
95,000	University of New Orleans Foundation, New Orleans, LA -- Scholarship
90,000	Institute of Technology - Bandung Indonesia -- Endowed chair
81,500	Princeton University, Princeton, NJ -- Unrestricted
79,000	Horatio Alger Association of Distinguished Americans, Inc., Alexandria, VA -- Unrestricted
71,000	United States-Indonesia Society, Washington, DC -- Unrestricted
62,000	Crosier Fathers & Brothers Province, Inc., St Paul, MN -- Unrestricted
60,000	Teach for America, New Orleans, LA -- Unrestricted
50,600	St. Augustine High School, New Orleans, LA -- Unrestricted

D.E. FRENCH FOUNDATION

Giving Contact

J. Douglas Pedley, President & Director
D.E. French Foundation
120 Genesee Street, Suite 503
Auburn, NY 13021-3620
Phone: (315)253-9321

Description

Founded: 1955
EIN: 166052246
Organization Type: Private Foundation
Giving Locations: NY: Cayuga County
Grant Types: Capital, General Support.

Donor Information

Founder: the late Clara M. French, the late D. E. French

Financial Summary

Total Giving: $265,400 (2000); $220,340 (1999); $179,500 (1998)
Giving Analysis: Giving for 2000 includes: foundation scholarships ($22,000); foundation grants to United Way ($23,000); 1999: foundation scholarships ($20,000) 1998: foundation grants to United Way ($19,000)
Assets: $5,271,310 (2000); $5,272,757 (1999); $5,188,010 (1998)

Typical Recipients

Arts & Humanities: Arts Associations & Councils, Arts Centers, History & Archaeology, Libraries, Museums/Galleries, Performing Arts, Theater

Civic & Public Affairs: Botanical Gardens/Parks, Chambers of Commerce, Community Foundations, Employment/Job Training, Civic & Public Affairs-General, Housing, Municipalities/Towns, Safety, Urban & Community Affairs

Education: Colleges & Universities, Community & Junior Colleges, Elementary Education (Public), Medical Education, Private Education (Precollege), Secondary Education (Public), Special Education, Student Aid

Health: Emergency/Ambulance Services, Health Organizations, Heart, Hospitals, Long-Term Care, Medical Rehabilitation, Public Health

Religion: Churches, Religious Welfare

Social Services: Animal Protection, Camps, Child Welfare, Community Centers, Community Service Organizations, Day Care, People with Disabilities, Recreation & Athletics, Scouts, Senior Services, United Funds/United Ways, YMCA/YWCA/YMHA/YWHA, Youth Organizations

Application Procedures

Initial Contact: The foundation has no formal grant application procedure or application form.
Deadlines: None.

Foundation Officials

Caryl W. Adams: secretary
Frederick J. Atkins: director
James P. Costello: director
Walter M. Lowe: director
John P. McLane: director
J. Douglas Pedley: president, director
Ronald D. West: director

Grants Analysis

Disclosure Period: calendar year ending 2000
Total Grants: $265,400*
Number of Grants: 61
Average Grant: $3,613
Highest Grant: $20,000
Typical Range: $100 to $10,000
*Note: Giving excludes United Way and scholarships.

Recent Grants

Note: Grants derived from 2000 Form 990.

Library-Related

10,000	Seymour Library, Auburn, NY -- new books and periodical fund

General

20,000	Auburn Memorial Hospital, Auburn, NY -- east wing remodeling fund
20,000	United Way of Cayuga County, Auburn, NY
20,000	YMCA, WEIU -- capital improvement fund
15,000	Foundation Historical Association, Inc., Auburn, NY -- Seward House renovation fund
14,000	YMCA, WEIU -- capital improvement fund

10,000	Cayuga County Community College Foundation, Auburn, NY -- scholarship fund
10,000	Throop's Frank G. Sawyer Memorial Park -- playground fund
10,000	YMCA, WEIU -- capital improvement fund
5,000	American Red Cross Cayuga County Chapter, Auburn, NY
5,000	Cayuga County Community College Foundation, Auburn, NY -- nurses scholarship fund

FRENCH OIL MILL MACHINERY CO.

Company Headquarters

PO Box 920
Piqua, OH 45356
Web: http://www.frenchoil.com

Company Description

Revenue: US$9 million (2001)
Employees: 55 (2001)
SIC(s): 3500 Industrial Machinery & Equipment, 3554 Paper Industries Machinery, 3556 Food Products Machinery, 3559 Special Industry Machinery Nec.

Operating Locations

French Oil Mill Machinery Co. (OH--Piqua)

French Oil Mill Machinery Co. Charitable Trust

Giving Contact

Daniel P. French, Jr., President & Chief Executive Officer
French Oil Mill Machinery Co.
c/o Fifth Third Bank of Western Ohio
PO Box 630858
Cincinnati, OH 45263
Phone: (513)579-5310

Description

EIN: 316024511
Organization Type: Corporate Foundation
Giving Locations: OH: Dayton, Piqua
Grant Types: General Support, Seed Money.

Financial Summary

Total Giving: $28,420 (fiscal year ending November 30, 2001); $23,620 (fiscal 1999); $23,600 (fiscal 1998)
Giving Analysis: Giving for fiscal 2001 includes: foundation grants to United Way ($12,600); foundation ($15,820); fiscal 1999: foundation ($11,600) foundation grants to United Way ($21,000)
Assets: $662,871 (fiscal 2001); $741,500 (fiscal 1999); $678,344 (fiscal 1998)

Typical Recipients

Arts & Humanities: Arts Associations & Councils, Arts Centers, Arts Festivals, Community Arts, Arts & Humanities-General, Libraries, Performing Arts
Civic & Public Affairs: Chambers of Commerce, Clubs, Community Foundations, Economic Development, Economic Policy, Employment/Job Training, Civic & Public Affairs-General, Legal Aid, Public Policy
Education: Afterschool/Enrichment Programs, Arts/Humanities Education, Business-School Partnerships, Colleges & Universities, Community & Junior Colleges, Economic Education, Education Funds, Education-General, Religious Education, Science/Mathematics Education, Secondary Education (Public)
Environment: Environment-General

Health: Cancer, Emergency/Ambulance Services, Health-General, Heart, Hospices, Medical Rehabilitation, Medical Rehabilitation, Mental Health, Respiratory
Religion: Religious Organizations
Science: Science-General, Scientific Centers & Institutes
Social Services: Child Welfare, Community Service Organizations, Family Planning, Food/Clothing Distribution, People with Disabilities, Recreation & Athletics, Scouts, Senior Services, Social Services-General, United Funds/United Ways, YMCA/YWCA/YMHA/YWHA, Youth Organizations

Application Procedures

Initial Contact: The foundation has no formal grant application procedure or application form. Send a brief letter of inquiry.
Deadlines: None.

Restrictions

Does not support individuals or political or lobbying groups.

Additional Information

Trust(s): Fifth Third Bank Western OH

Corporate Officials

Dennis Bratton: vice president finance, treasurero, director PRIM CORP EMPL vice president finance, treasurer: French Oil Mill Machinery Co.
Daniel P. French: chairman, president, chief executive officer, director PRIM CORP EMPL chairman, president, chief executive officer, director: French Oil Mill Machinery Co.

Grants Analysis

Disclosure Period: fiscal year ending November 30, 2001
Total Grants: $15,820*
Number of Grants: 37
Average Grant: $428
Highest Grant: $1,175
Typical Range: $250 to $500
*Note: Giving excludes United Way.

Recent Grants

Note: Grants derived from fiscal 2001 Form 990.

General
12,600	Piqua Area United Fund, Piqua, OH
1,500	National Right to Work Legal Defense and Education Foundation, Springfield, VA
1,175	Piqua Community Foundation, Piqua, OH
1,000	American Legion Ambulance Fund, Moosup, CT
1,000	Edison State Community College, Edison, NJ
1,000	YMCA, Piqua, OH
975	Piqua Area Chamber of Commerce, Piqua, OH
800	Piqua Education Foundation, Piqua, OH
550	Planned Parenthood Association, Dayton, OH
500	Hipple Cancer Research Center, Dayton, OH

ARNOLD D. FRESE FOUNDATION

Giving Contact

James S. Smith, President & Treasurer
10 Rockefeller Plz., Suite 916
New York, NY 10020
Phone: (212)373-1960

Description

Founded: 1966
EIN: 136212507
Organization Type: Private Foundation
Giving Locations: , CA CT: Greenwich; DC: Washington; MA: Cambridge; NY, New York
Grant Types: General Support.

Donor Information

Founder: the late Arnold D. Frese

Financial Summary

Total Giving: $829,000 (2001); $948,500 (2000); $1,212,500 (1999)
Assets: $4,261,193 (2001); $5,964,416 (2000); $6,813,122 (1999)

Typical Recipients

Arts & Humanities: Arts Associations & Councils, Arts Festivals, Arts & Humanities-General, History & Archaeology, Libraries, Museums/Galleries, Music, Performing Arts
Civic & Public Affairs: Civic & Public Affairs-General, Women's Affairs
Education: Afterschool/Enrichment Programs, Colleges & Universities, Legal Education, Medical Education, Private Education (Precollege), Public Education (Precollege), School Volunteerism
Environment: Air/Water Quality, Environment-General
Health: Arthritis, Cancer, Clinics/Medical Centers, Diabetes, Emergency/Ambulance Services, Hospitals, Hospitals (University Affiliated), Long-Term Care, Prenatal Health Issues
International: Health Care/Hospitals, Human Rights, International Organizations, International Peace & Security Issues
Religion: Churches, Religious Welfare
Science: Scientific Centers & Institutes
Social Services: At-Risk Youth, Child Welfare, Community Centers, Day Care, Family Planning, Family Services, Food/Clothing Distribution, People with Disabilities, Recreation & Athletics, Shelters/Homelessness, United Funds/United Ways, Youth Organizations

Application Procedures

Initial Contact: Send a brief letter of inquiry.
Application Requirements: Include purpose of funds sought, amount requested, and proof of tax-exempt status.
Deadlines: None.

Foundation Officials

Hector G. Dowd: secretary
Ines Frese: chairman
Henry D. Mercer, Jr.: trustee
Emil Mosbacher, Jr.: trustee B White Plains, NY 1922. ED Dartmouth College BA (1943). CORP AFFIL director: Federal Insurance Co.; director: Vigilant Insurance Co.; director: Chubb Corp.; director: Avon Products Inc.; director: Chemical Bank; director: Amax Gold Inc. NONPR AFFIL member: U.S. Seniors Golf Association; member: U.S. Yacht Racing Association; member: Pilgrims U.S.; member: Independent Petroleum Association America; trustee: Lenox Hill Hospital; member, board overseers: Hoover Institute.
James S. Smith: president, treasurer
Laura Smith: trustee

Grants Analysis

Disclosure Period: calendar year ending 2001
Total Grants: $829,000
Number of Grants: 29
Average Grant: $2,724*
Highest Grant: $550,000
Lowest Grant: $1,000
Typical Range: $1,000 to $5,000
*Note: Average grant figure excludes two highest grants ($750,000).

Recent Grants

Note: Grants derived from 2001 Form 990.

General

550,000	Harvard College, Cambridge, MA
200,000	National Gallery of Art, Washington, DC
10,000	Lighthouse International, New York, NY
7,000	Westchester Association for Retarded Citizens, White Plains, NY
5,000	Family Center, Greenwich, CT
5,000	Fresh Air Fund, New York, NY
5,000	Girls, Incorporated, Greenwich, CT
5,000	Meals on Wheels, Pacific Grove, CA
5,000	Merry Go Round, Inc., Auburn, NY
5,000	Nathaniel Witherell Auxiliary

FRIBOURG FOUNDATION

Giving Contact

Susan McIntyre, Assistant Secretary
277 Park Ave., 50th Fl.
New York, NY 10172-0003
Phone: (212)207-5879

Description

Founded: 1953
EIN: 136159195
Organization Type: Private Foundation
Giving Locations: NY: New York
Grant Types: General Support.

Donor Information

Founder: Michel Fribourg, Lucienne Fribourg Arrow Steamship Co., Continental Grain Co.

Financial Summary

Total Giving: $577,400 (2001); $729,400 (2000); $716,000 (1999)
Giving Analysis: Giving for 1999 includes: foundation grants to United Way ($2,000) 1998: foundation grants to United Way ($2,000)
Assets: $99,197 (2001); $654,982 (2000); $1,298,153 (1999)
Gifts Received: $650,000 (1997); $600,000 (1996); $325,000 (1995)

Typical Recipients

Arts & Humanities: Arts Associations & Councils, Arts Centers, Arts Festivals, Arts Outreach, Ballet, Community Arts, Dance, Arts & Humanities-General, Historic Preservation, History & Archaeology, Libraries, Museums/Galleries, Music, Opera, Performing Arts, Public Broadcasting, Theater
Civic & Public Affairs: Botanical Gardens/Parks, Ethnic Organizations, Civic & Public Affairs-General, Housing, Public Policy, Urban & Community Affairs
Education: Arts/Humanities Education, Colleges & Universities, Education-General, International Studies, Legal Education, Medical Education, Private Education (Precollege), School Volunteerism, Social Sciences Education
Environment: Resource Conservation
Health: Cancer, Children's Health/Hospitals, Clinics/Medical Centers, Geriatric Health, Health Organizations, Hospitals, Medical Research, Single-Disease Health Associations, Transplant Networks/Donor Banks
International: Foreign Arts Organizations, Foreign Educational Institutions, Health Care/Hospitals, International Affairs, International Organizations, International Peace & Security Issues, International Relations, International Relief Efforts, Missionary/Religious Activities
Religion: Churches, Jewish Causes, Religious Organizations, Seminaries, Synagogues/Temples
Science: Science Museums
Social Services: Big Brother/Big Sister, Child Welfare, Community Service Organizations, Delinquency & Criminal Rehabilitation, Family Services, Recreation & Athletics, Shelters/Homelessness, United Funds/United Ways, YMCA/YWCA/YMHA/YWHA, Youth Organizations

Application Procedures

Initial Contact: Send brief letter describing program.
Application Requirements: Include purpose of funds sought and amount requested.
Deadlines: None.

Foundation Officials

Richard Anderson: treasurer
Dwight C. Coffin: secretary PRIM CORP EMPL vice president human resources: Continental Grain Co.
Gerald Frenchman: vice president
Charles Fribourg: director
Mary Ann Fribourg: mem, director
Paul J. Fribourg: vice president
David G. Friedman: assistant secretary
Susan McIntyre: assistant secretary
Bernard Steinweg: mem, director
Lawrence G. Weppler: vice president, director
Daniel J. Willet: treasurer

Grants Analysis

Disclosure Period: calendar year ending 2001
Total Grants: $577,400
Number of Grants: 66
Average Grant: $5,806*
Highest Grant: $200,000
Lowest Grant: $200
Typical Range: $1,000 to $10,000
***Note:** Average grant figure excludes highest grant.

Recent Grants

Note: Grants derived from 2000 Form 990.

General

200,000	New York University, New York, NY
100,000	New York Hospital Cornell Medical Center, New York, NY
60,000	New York University, New York, NY
50,000	Young Audiences, New York, NY
20,000	French Institute, Alliance Francaise, New York, NY
20,000	Weill Medical College of Cornell University, New York, NY
20,000	Young Audiences, New York, NY
15,000	Young Audiences, New York, NY
12,000	Musee Art Moderne, Geneva Switzerland
10,000	American Friends of Israel Philharmonic Orchestra, New York, NY

VIRGINIA FRIEDHOFER CHARITABLE TRUST

Giving Contact

Arnold Seidel, Trustee
8730 Wilshire Blvd., No. 530
Beverly Hills, CA 90211
Phone: (310)360-7541

Description

Founded: 1996
EIN: 956995937
Organization Type: Private Foundation
Giving Locations: CA
Grant Types: General Support.

Donor Information

Founder: Established in 1996 by the Virginia Friedhofer Trust.

Financial Summary

Total Giving: $181,500 (2000); $160,500 (1999); $147,700 (1998)
Assets: $4,623,808 (2000); $4,690,104 (1999); $4,419,007 (1998)
Gifts Received: $21,914 (1996); $2,675,534 (1995).
Note: In 1996, contributions were received from the estate of Virginia Friedhofer.

Typical Recipients

Arts & Humanities: Libraries, Music, Opera, Performing Arts
Civic & Public Affairs: Safety, Zoos/Aquariums
Education: Colleges & Universities, Education Funds, Engineering/Technological Education, Education-General, School Volunteerism
Health: Cancer, Clinics/Medical Centers, Eyes/Blindness, Heart, Multiple Sclerosis, Single-Disease Health Associations
International: Human Rights, Missionary/Religious Activities
Religion: Jewish Causes, Synagogues/Temples
Social Services: Child Welfare, Counseling, Domestic Violence, Family Planning, Food/Clothing Distribution, People with Disabilities, YMCA/YWCA/YMHA/YWHA, Youth Organizations

Application Procedures

Initial Contact: Send a written request.
Deadlines: None.

Foundation Officials

Arnold Seidel: trustee

Grants Analysis

Disclosure Period: calendar year ending 2000
Total Grants: $181,500
Number of Grants: 32
Average Grant: $5,672
Highest Grant: $20,000
Typical Range: $1,000 to $10,000

Recent Grants

Note: Grants derived from 1999 Form 990.

General

25,000	Cedars Sinai Medical Center, Los Angeles, CA
11,100	Discovery Fund Eye Research, Los Angeles, CA
10,500	Greater L.A. Zoo Association, Los Angeles, CA
10,000	Haven House, Los Angeles, CA
10,000	Regents of University of California, Los Angeles, CA
10,000	Zoological Society of San Diego, San Diego, CA
7,000	Wilshire Boulevard Temple, Los Angeles, CA
6,000	National Kertocunus Foundation
5,500	National Multiple Sclerosis, Los Angeles, CA
5,000	Amie Karen Cancer Fund, Los Angeles, CA

FRIEDMAN FAMILY FOUNDATION

Giving Contact

Lisa Kawahara, Program Director
PMB 719, 204 E. 2nd Ave.
San Mateo, CA 94401
Phone: (650)342-8750
Fax: (650)342-8750
E-mail: fffdn@aol.com
Web: http://www.friedmanfoundation.org

Description

Founded: 1964
EIN: 946109692
Organization Type: Private Foundation
Giving Locations: CA: San Francisco focus on Bay area

Grant Types: General Support, Operating Expenses, Project.

Donor Information
Founder: Established in 1964 by Phyllis K. Friedman and Howard Friedman.

Financial Summary
Total Giving: $1,345,300 (fiscal year ending February 28, 2001); $760,950 (fiscal 1999); $961,000 (fiscal 1998)
Assets: $21,919,550 (fiscal 2001); $22,306,524 (fiscal 1999); $22,306,524 (fiscal 1998)
Gifts Received: $12,000 (fiscal 1999); $850,000 (fiscal 1996); $804,602 (fiscal 1995). Note: In fiscal 1999, contributions were received from Mr. and Mrs. Ted Geballe. In fiscal 1996, contributions were received from Phyllis K. Friedman.

Typical Recipients
Arts & Humanities: Arts Associations & Councils, Arts Festivals, Community Arts, Film & Video, Libraries, Museums/Galleries, Music, Public Broadcasting, Theater
Civic & Public Affairs: African American Affairs, Asian American Affairs, Business/Free Enterprise, Economic Development, Employment/Job Training, Ethnic Organizations, Civic & Public Affairs-General, Hispanic Affairs, Housing, Law & Justice, Legal Aid, Native American Affairs, Nonprofit Management, Parades/Festivals, Professional & Trade Associations, Public Policy, Urban & Community Affairs, Women's Affairs
Education: Afterschool/Enrichment Programs, Business-School Partnerships, Colleges & Universities, Economic Education, Education-General, International Exchange, Preschool Education, Private Education (Precollege), Public Education (Precollege)
Environment: Environment-General
Health: AIDS/HIV, Children's Health/Hospitals, Clinics/Medical Centers, Emergency/Ambulance Services, Health Policy/Cost Containment, Health Organizations, Heart, Hospitals, Medical Research, Mental Health, Public Health, Single-Disease Health Associations
International: Foreign Educational Institutions, Health Care/Hospitals, Human Rights, International Development, International Organizations, International Relations, International Relief Efforts, Missionary/Religious Activities
Religion: Jewish Causes, Ministries, Religious Organizations, Religious Welfare, Synagogues/Temples
Science: Observatories & Planetariums
Social Services: Animal Protection, Camps, Child Abuse, Child Welfare, Community Centers, Community Service Organizations, Counseling, Domestic Violence, Emergency Relief, Family Services, Food/Clothing Distribution, People with Disabilities, Refugee Assistance, Senior Services, Shelters/Homelessness, Social Services-General, United Funds/United Ways, YMCA/YWCA/YMHA/YWHA, Youth Organizations

Application Procedures
Initial Contact: Letter of inquiry or request application procedures.
Application Requirements: In addition to the application, include the following: one or two client profiles; total project and organization budget for the current year; list of funding sources; list of board of directors with affiliations; proof of tax-exempt status; readily available printed materials describing the organization.
Deadlines: None. The deadlines vary each year.
Review Process: The Foundation board meets three times per year. Allow up to three months for the review process.

Restrictions
The foundation does not fund films, videos, conferences, seminars, capital grants, scholarships, research, individuals, or special or fundraising events.

Additional Information
Publications: Annual Report; Guidelines; Application Form

Foundation Officials
David A. Friedman: secretary PRIM CORP EMPL senior vice president: Heller Financial.
Eleanor Friedman: vice president
Phyllis K. Friedman: president B 1936. PRIM CORP EMPL president: Rochester Diet Inc.
Robert E. Friedman: treasurer

Grants Analysis
Disclosure Period: fiscal year ending February 28, 2001
Total Grants: $1,345,300*
Number of Grants: 151
Average Grant: $20,000
Highest Grant: $100,000
Lowest Grant: $500
Typical Range: $5,000 to $20,000
*****Note:** Grants analysis provided by foundation.

Recent Grants
Note: Grants derived from fiscal 2000 Form 990.

General
10,000	Access to Software for People
10,000	Arriba Juntos, San Francisco, CA
10,000	Ashoka, Arlington, VA
10,000	Asian Neighborhood Design, San Francisco, CA
10,000	Bar Association of San Francisco, San Francisco, CA
10,000	Bay Area Video Coalition, San Francisco, CA
10,000	Bay Area Women and Children's Center, San Francisco, CA
10,000	Building Opportunities for Self Sufficiency, Berkeley, CA
10,000	California ACORN, CA
10,000	California Association for Microenterprise Opportunity, Oakland, CA

FRIENDSHIP FUND

Giving Contact
Eleanor Millan
c/o Mellon Trust Co.
1 Boston Pl., AIM 024-002A
Boston, MA 02108
Phone: (617)722-3533

Description
Founded: 1918
EIN: 136089220
Organization Type: Private Foundation
Grant Types: Capital, General Support, Project, Scholarship.

Donor Information
Founder: the late Charles R. Crane

Financial Summary
Total Giving: $276,670 (fiscal year ending June 30, 2001); $253,060 (fiscal 2000); $255,010 (fiscal 1999)
Assets: $5,576,720 (fiscal 2001); $6,297,208 (fiscal 2000); $5,959,320 (fiscal 1999)

Typical Recipients
Arts & Humanities: Arts Centers, Film & Video, Historic Preservation, History & Archaeology, Libraries, Museums/Galleries, Music, Opera, Performing Arts, Public Broadcasting
Civic & Public Affairs: Civil Rights, Community Foundations, Civic & Public Affairs-General, Housing, Public Policy, Safety, Urban & Community Affairs, Women's Affairs

Education: Colleges & Universities, Education-General, Legal Education, Private Education (Precollege), Public Education (Precollege), Science/Mathematics Education, Social Sciences Education, Student Aid
Environment: Air/Water Quality, Forestry, Environment-General, Resource Conservation
Health: Clinics/Medical Centers, Diabetes, Emergency/Ambulance Services, Health Organizations, Hospitals, Mental Health, Nursing Services, Prenatal Health Issues
International: Foreign Educational Institutions, Health Care/Hospitals, International Affairs, International Development, International Environmental Issues, International Organizations, International Peace & Security Issues
Religion: Churches, Religious Organizations, Religious Welfare
Science: Scientific Centers & Institutes, Scientific Labs, Scientific Organizations
Social Services: Community Service Organizations, Family Planning, People with Disabilities, Sexual Abuse, Substance Abuse

Application Procedures
Initial Contact: Organizations seeking support may submit requests in writing.
Application Requirements: Include a concise statement of the purpose of funds sought, current year's operating budget, list of board members, recently audited financial statement, resumes of all key staff people, and proof of tax-exempt status. If a grant is for a specific program, the staff and budget of the program must be described.
Deadlines: April 1; for consideration at the annual meeting held during the first week of August.

Foundation Officials
Darby Bradley: trustee
Charles M. Crane: trustee
Diane Crane: trustee
Sylvia E. Crane: trustee
Thomas Crane: treasurer
Josephine DeGive: trustee
Elizabeth McLane-Bradley: trustee
Ellen D. B. F. Tully: president

Grants Analysis
Disclosure Period: fiscal year ending June 30, 2001
Total Grants: $276,670
Number of Grants: 131
Average Grant: $1,913*
Highest Grant: $28,000
Lowest Grant: $700
Typical Range: $1,000 to $2,000
*****Note:** Average grant figure excludes highest grant.

Recent Grants
Note: Grants derived from fiscal 2000 Form 990.

General
6,500	Vermont Community Foundation, Middlebury, VT
6,000	Tropical Forest Initiative
6,000	Upper Valley Habitat for Humanity, White River Junction, VT
6,000	Woods Hole Community Association, Woods Hole, MA
5,500	St. Michael's Church House
5,000	Aldo Leopold Foundation, Inc., Baraboo, WI
5,000	Center for Constitutional Rights, New York, NY
5,000	INFACT, Minneapolis, MN
5,000	James River Association, Richmond, VA
5,000	National Community Development Organization, Washington, DC

FRIST FOUNDATION

Giving Contact

Peter F. Bird, Jr., Executive Director
3319 West End Avenue, Suite 900
Nashville, TN 37203-1076
Phone: (615)292-3868
Fax: (615)292-5843
E-mail: askfrist@fristfoundation.org
Web: http://www.fristfoundation.org

Description

Founded: 1982
EIN: 621134070
Organization Type: General Purpose Foundation
Giving Locations: TN, Nashville
Grant Types: Capital, Emergency, Employee Matching Gifts, General Support, Multiyear/Continuing Support, Operating Expenses, Project, Seed Money.
Note: Award grants are given through foundation initiative programs.

Donor Information

Founder: The HCA Foundation was established in 1982 as a corporate foundation, sponsored by Hospital Corporation of America. The foundation became fully independent of the company in 1994. It adopted The Frist Foundation name in 1997 to honor the philanthropic influence and creative force of two of its founding directors, Dr. Thomas F. Frist, Jr., who continues as chairman, and Dr. Thomas F. Frist, Sr. , a gifted cardiologist, businessman, and philanthropist who died in 1998.

Financial Summary

Total Giving: $8,000,000 (2003 approx); $10,400,000 (2002 approx); $13,363,804 (2001)
Giving Analysis: Giving for 1998 includes: foundation matching gifts ($127,528) foundation grants to United Way ($296,000)
Assets: $151,733,000 (2002); $188,667,000 (2001); $211,433,000 (1999)

Typical Recipients

Arts & Humanities: Arts Appreciation, Arts Associations & Councils, Arts Centers, Arts Funds, Arts Institutes, Arts Outreach, Ballet, Dance, Arts & Humanities-General, Historic Preservation, History & Archaeology, Libraries, Literary Arts, Museums/Galleries, Music, Opera, Performing Arts, Public Broadcasting, Theater, Visual Arts
Civic & Public Affairs: Botanical Gardens/Parks, Business/Free Enterprise, Civil Rights, Clubs, Community Foundations, Economic Development, Economic Policy, Employment/Job Training, Civic & Public Affairs-General, Housing, Inner-City Development, Law & Justice, Nonprofit Management, Parades/Festivals, Public Policy, Rural Affairs, Safety, Urban & Community Affairs, Women's Affairs, Zoos/Aquariums
Education: Arts/Humanities Education, Business Education, Colleges & Universities, Community & Junior Colleges, Continuing Education, Economic Education, Education Associations, Education Funds, Education Reform, Faculty Development, Education-General, Health & Physical Education, Literacy, Medical Education, Minority Education, Preschool Education, Private Education (Precollege), Public Education (Precollege), Religious Education, Science/Mathematics Education, Social Sciences Education, Student Aid
Environment: Forestry, Environment-General
Health: Children's Health/Hospitals, Clinics/Medical Centers, Emergency/Ambulance Services, Health Policy/Cost Containment, Health Funds, Health Organizations, Medical Training, Mental Health, Nursing Services, Public Health, Speech & Hearing
Religion: Religious Organizations, Religious Welfare
Science: Science Exhibits & Fairs, Science Museums

Social Services: Animal Protection, Big Brother/Big Sister, Child Abuse, Child Welfare, Community Centers, Community Service Organizations, Day Care, Delinquency & Criminal Rehabilitation, Domestic Violence, Emergency Relief, Family Planning, Family Services, Food/Clothing Distribution, Homes, People with Disabilities, Recreation & Athletics, Scouts, Senior Services, Sexual Abuse, Shelters/Homelessness, Social Services-General, Special Olympics, Substance Abuse, United Funds/United Ways, Volunteer Services, YMCA/YWCA/YMHA/YWHA, Youth Organizations

Application Procedures

Initial Contact: Send a letter of inquiry or complete an online grant application, available on the foundation's website.
Application Requirements: The initial inquiry should describe in no more than two pages the organization, its record of accomplishments, objectives of program to be funded and who will benefit, amount sought from foundation in relation to total need, how foundation funds will be used, and proposed method of evaluating program's success. Also include an annual report, if available, and a copy of IRS determination letter. Foundation may also request copy of Form 990, budget, list of board members and their affiliations, list of current sources of support and amounts contributed, and list of other funding sources being approached for support.
Deadlines: For Internship Program, December 7; for Technology Program, April 1; for Building Cultures Program, August 1.
Review Process: Decisions on proposals are generally made within one month of submission, except for those requesting more than $50,000, which are scheduled for review at quarterly board of directors meetings. All proposals are acknowledged promptly. results of its effort; what plans the organization has for future funding. Foundation staff review proposals and conducts personal interviews or site visits, as necessary. Requests for more than $1,000 require review and approval by the board of directors.
Evaluative Criteria: Among the issues considered during the evaluation are the organization's history of success, including financial statements reflecting an ability to manage funds well; the program objectives and its intended beneficiaries; the proportion of funding sought from foundation to the total need; whether the program treats the causes of the problem or its effects; duplication of effort of other groups; the organization's efforts to collaborate with others; how the organization proposes to measure the results of its effort; what plans the organization has for future funding. Foundation staff review proposals and conducts personal interviews or site visits, as necessary.

Restrictions

With rare exception, grants are limited to organizations based in the greater Nashville area. Recipients must be tax-exempt under Section 501(c)(3) of the Internal Revenue Code. For legal reasons, the foundation does not support individuals or their projects, private foundations, political activities, advertising or sponsorships. As a matter of policy, the foundation does not ordinarily support disease-specific organizations seeking support for national projects and programs; biomedical or clinical research; hospitals; projects, programs, or organizations that serve a limited audience or a relatively small number of people; organizations whose principal impact is outside the United States; endowments; social events, telethons, or similar fundraising activities; organizations during their first three years of operation; or religious organizations for religious purposes.

Additional Information

Publications: Annual Report; Guidelines; Newsletter; Application Form

Corporate Officials

Dr. Thomas Fearn Frist, Jr.: chairman, chief executive officer B Nashville, TN 1938. ED Vanderbilt University BS (1961); Washington University MD (1966). PRIM CORP EMPL chairman, chief executive officer: Columbia/HCA Healthcare Corp. CORP AFFIL chairman, director: HCA Health Services Florida; chairman, director: HCA Health Services Louisiana. NONPR AFFIL member: Business Roundtable; vice chairman: International Medicine Group Pennsylvania; honorary fellow: American College Healthcare Executives; member: Business Council. CLUB AFFIL Belle Meade Country Club.

Foundation Officials

Peter F. Bird, Jr.: executive director, chief executive officer
Jack Oliver Bovender, Jr.: president, chief executive officer B Winston-Salem, NC 1945. ED Duke University AB (1967); Duke University MHA (1969). PRIM CORP EMPL president, chief operating officer: Hospital Corp. of America. CORP AFFIL president: Notami Hospital of California; president: Galen Health Care Inc.; president, director: HCA Health Services Virginia; president: Brigham City Community Hospital Inc.; president, chief operating officer: Columbia/HCA Healthcare Corp.; director: America Retirement Corp.; director: America Service Group Inc. NONPR AFFIL fellow: American College Healthcare Executives.
Robert C. Crosby: board member PRIM CORP EMPL chairman, chief executive officer: Long Term Care Physicians Inc.
Helen K. Cummings: board member
Hon. Frank F. Drowota, III: board member B Williamsburg, KY 1938. ED Vanderbilt University BA (1960); Vanderbilt University JD (1965). PRIM NONPR EMPL associate justice: Tennessee Supreme Court.
Dr. Thomas Fearn Frist, Jr.: chairman (see above)
Carolyn Griffin Hall: program officer
Regina F. Nash: administrative assistant
Kenneth Lewis Roberts: president, board member B Dungannon, VA 1932. ED Vanderbilt University BA (1954); Vanderbilt University LLB (1959). NONPR AFFIL member: Tennessee Bar Association; trustee: Vanderbilt University; member: Nashville Chamber of Commerce; trustee: Montgomery Bell Academy; member: Nashville Bar Association; director: Leadership Nashville; member: American Bar Association. CLUB AFFIL University Club; Ponte Vedra Inn Club; Belle Meade Country Club; Cumberland Club.

Grants Analysis

Disclosure Period: calendar year ending 2001
Total Grants: $12,951,804*
Number of Grants: 376
Average Grant: $34,446
Highest Grant: $200,000
Lowest Grant: $350
Typical Range: $5,000 to $60,000
***Note:** Giving excludes United Way.

Recent Grants

Note: Grants derived from 2001 Form 990.

General

5,000,000	First Center for the Visual Arts Foundation, Nashville, TN -- to strengthen the endowment of this organization
500,000	First Center for the Visual Arts Foundation, Nashville, TN -- operating expenses
350,000	United Way of Middle Tennessee, Nashville, TN -- support in connection with the 2000 campaign
200,000	Nashville Zoo, Inc., Nashville, TN -- to sustain the zoo during its transition to a balanced operating budget
132,300	Oasis Center, Nashville, TN -- support for Youth Pulse

125,000	Nashville Symphony Association, Nashville, TN -- support for a special campaign to strengthen the orchestra
100,000	Faith Family Medical Clinic of Nashville, Nashville, TN -- to help establish a medical clinic for low-income working people
100,000	Junior Achievement Middle Tennessee, Nashville, TN -- capital support
100,000	Nashville Civic Design Center, Nashville, TN -- to help establish Urban Design Center for Nashville
100,000	Nashville Symphony Association, Nashville, TN -- support for the 2001-2002 season

PAUL AND MAXINE FROHRING FOUNDATION

Giving Contact

R. A. Bumblis, CPA
Paul and Maxine Frohring Foundation
3200 National City Center
1900 E. 9th Street, Suite 3200
Cleveland, OH 44114-3485
Phone: (216)861-7976

Description

Founded: 1958
EIN: 346513729
Organization Type: Private Foundation
Giving Locations: FL; MD; MT; OH: Cleveland including northern Ohio; PA
Grant Types: Emergency, General Support.

Donor Information

Founder: Paul R. Frohring, the late Maxine A. Frohring

Financial Summary

Total Giving: $1,498,948 (2001); $1,303,484 (2000); $702,500 (1999)
Assets: $32,130,596 (2001); $34,370,933 (2000); $22,097,520 (1999)
Gifts Received: $242,500 (1993). Note: In 1993, contributions were received from Paul R. Frohring.

Typical Recipients

Arts & Humanities: Libraries, Museums/Galleries
Civic & Public Affairs: Botanical Gardens/Parks, Clubs, Employment/Job Training, Housing, Zoos/Aquariums
Education: Colleges & Universities, Engineering/Technological Education, Education-General, Minority Education, Private Education (Precollege)
Environment: Wildlife Protection
Health: Eyes/Blindness, Health-General, Hospices, Hospitals, Nursing Services, Public Health
International: Foreign Educational Institutions
Religion: Religious Welfare
Social Services: Community Service Organizations, Day Care, Family Planning, People with Disabilities, Senior Services, Substance Abuse, YMCA/YWCA/YMHA/YWHA, Youth Organizations

Application Procedures

Initial Contact: Send a written request.
Application Requirements: Include proof of tax-exempt status.
Deadlines: None.

Foundation Officials

William Wendell Falsgraf: secretary, trustee B Cleveland, OH 1933. ED Amherst College AB (1955); Case Western Reserve University JD (1958). PRIM CORP EMPL partner: Baker & Hostetler. NONPR AFFIL member: Ohio Bar Association; member: Ohio Bar Foundation; chairman board trustees: Hiram College;

member: Amherst College Alumni Association; member: Cleveland Bar Association; fellow: American Bar Foundation; president: American Bar Insurance Plans Consult; member: American Bar Association. CLUB AFFIL Country Club; Union Club.
Paul Robert Frohring: president, trustee B Cleveland, OH 1904. ED Ohio State University (1921-1922); Case Institute of Technology BS (1926). CORP AFFIL director: Newbury Industries; director: Horsburg & Scott; director: Irvin & Co.; director: Cleveland Machine Controls; director: Alco Standard Corp.; director: America Home Products Corp. NONPR AFFIL member: Ohio Society; member: Planned Parenthood; member: Newcomen Society; member: Ohio Academy Science; member: Navy League; fellow: New York Academy Sciences; trustee: John Cabot University; fellow: Garfield Society; trustee: Hiram College; trustee, honorary chairman: Cleveland Health Education Museum; trustee: Florida Zoological Society; member: American Oil Chemical Society; overseer: Case Western Reserve University; member: American Dairy Science Association; member: American Association Advancement Science; member: American Chemical Society; member: Alpha Chi Sigma. CLUB AFFIL Union Club; Commodore Club; Key Biscayne Yacht Club; Chagrin Valley Hunt Club.
Elmer Jagow: trustee B West Bend, WI 1922. ED Concordia University BS (1944); Northwestern University MBA (1955). CORP AFFIL director: Cleveland Machine Controls. NONPR AFFIL president emeritus: Hiram College; chairman: John Cabot University; member: Garfield Society. CLUB AFFIL Walden Golf & Tennis Club.
James Kushlan: director
Paula Frohring Kushlan: trustee
Jeffrey LaRich: trustee

Grants Analysis

Disclosure Period: calendar year ending 2001
Total Grants: $1,498,948
Number of Grants: 23
Average Grant: $38,947*
Highest Grant: $301,579
Typical Range: $5,000 to $100,000
*****Note:** Average grant figure excludes two highest grants ($603,158).

Recent Grants

Note: Grants derived from 2001 Form 990.

Library-Related
| 5,000 | Bainbridge Public Library, Chagrin Falls, OH |

General
301,579	Cleveland Botanical Garden, Cleveland, OH
301,579	Cleveland Health Museum, Cleveland, OH
260,000	John Cabot University, Rome Italy
250,000	Hiram College, Hiram, OH
150,790	Geauga YMCA at Heather Hill, Chardon, OH
35,000	Arundel Habitat for Humanity, Arnold, MD
35,000	Salvation Army, Annapolis, MD
30,000	McDonogh School, Owings Mills, MD
25,000	Hospice of Chesapeake, Millerville, MD
25,000	Planned Parenthood, Baltimore, MD

SAUL FROMKES FOUNDATION

Giving Contact

Otto Fromkes, Director
122 E. 42nd St., Rm. 4400
New York, NY 10168-0112
Phone: (212)447-8360

Description

Founded: 1993
EIN: 133682406
Organization Type: Private Foundation
Grant Types: General Support.

Financial Summary

Total Giving: $70,000 (2000); $70,000 (1999); $72,500 (1998)
Assets: $1,309,483 (2000); $1,305,643 (1999); $1,339,049 (1998)
Gifts Received: $2,860 (1996); $49,953 (1995); $1,230,350 (1994). Note: In 1994, contributions were received from the estate of Saul Fromkes.

Typical Recipients

Arts & Humanities: Dance, Libraries, Museums/Galleries
Civic & Public Affairs: Safety
Education: Colleges & Universities
Health: Cancer, Emergency/Ambulance Services
Religion: Jewish Causes, Religious Welfare

Application Procedures

Initial Contact: Send a brief letter of inquiry.
Application Requirements: Include a description of organization and purpose of funds sought.
Deadlines: None.

Foundation Officials

Otto Fromkes: director
Arthur Richenthal: director

Grants Analysis

Disclosure Period: calendar year ending 2000
Total Grants: $70,000
Number of Grants: 4
Average Grant: $17,500
Highest Grant: $25,000
Lowest Grant: $10,000
Typical Range: $10,000 to $25,000

Recent Grants

Note: Grants derived from 2000 Form 990.

Library-Related
| 10,000 | North Plain Field Library, Plainfield, NJ |

General
25,000	North Plainfield Fire Department, Plainfield, NJ
20,000	Brooklyn Museum of Art, Brooklyn, NY
15,000	Young Dance Makers

FROST NATIONAL BANK

Company Headquarters

100 W. Houston St.
San Antonio, TX 78205-1498
Web: http://www.frostbank.com

Company Description

Employees: 1,700
SIC(s): 6021 National Commercial Banks.
Parent Company: Cullen/Frost Bankers, Inc., 100 W. Houston St., No. 100, San Antonio, TX, United States

Operating Locations

Frost National Bank (TX--Austin, Corpus Christi, Houston, McAllen)

Nonmonetary Support

Type: Donated Equipment; Donated Products; In-kind Services; Loaned Employees; Loaned Executives

The Charitable Foundation of Frost National Bank of San Antonio

Giving Contact
William Clyborne, Executive Committee
Frost Bank
100 W. Houston St.
San Antonio, TX 78205
Phone: (210)220-4449
Fax: (210)220-5144

Description
Founded: 1981
EIN: 742058155
Organization Type: Corporate Foundation
Giving Locations: TX
Grant Types: Capital, General Support, Matching, Multiyear/Continuing Support, Scholarship.

Financial Summary
Total Giving: $559,418 (2001); $1,900,000 (2000 approx); $629,099 (1999). Note: Contributes through foundation only.
Giving Analysis: Giving for 2001 includes: foundation scholarships ($36,000); foundation grants to United Way ($176,000); 1999: foundation scholarships ($1,000); foundation grants to United Way ($206,000); foundation ($422,099); 1998: corporate direct giving (approx $650,000) foundation (approx $650,000)
Assets: $738,571 (2001); $2,240,980 (1999).
Gifts Received: $250,000 (2001). Note: Contributions were received from Frost National Bank.

Typical Recipients
Arts & Humanities: Arts Appreciation, Arts Associations & Councils, Arts Festivals, Arts Funds, Arts Institutes, Community Arts, Dance, Ethnic & Folk Arts, Historic Preservation, History & Archaeology, Libraries, Museums/Galleries, Music, Performing Arts, Public Broadcasting, Theater
Civic & Public Affairs: Botanical Gardens/Parks, Business/Free Enterprise, Economic Development, Employment/Job Training, Civic & Public Affairs-General, Housing, Minority Business, Nonprofit Management, Professional & Trade Associations, Zoos/Aquariums
Education: Agricultural Education, Arts/Humanities Education, Business Education, Colleges & Universities, Education Funds, Education Reform, Engineering/Technological Education, Faculty Development, Health & Physical Education, International Exchange, Literacy, Medical Education, Minority Education, Preschool Education, Private Education (Precollege), Public Education (Precollege), Science/Mathematics Education
Environment: Environment-General, Resource Conservation
Health: Cancer, Children's Health/Hospitals, Health Organizations, Hospices, Hospitals, Medical Rehabilitation, Medical Research, Mental Health, Public Health, Single-Disease Health Associations
International: International Relations
Religion: Churches, Religion-General, Ministries, Religious Organizations
Science: Scientific Organizations
Social Services: Child Welfare, Community Centers, Community Service Organizations, Counseling, Crime Prevention, Delinquency & Criminal Rehabilitation, Domestic Violence, Emergency Relief, Family Services, Food/Clothing Distribution, People with Disabilities, Recreation & Athletics, Senior Services, Social Services-General, Substance Abuse, United Funds/United Ways, Volunteer Services, Youth Organizations

Application Procedures
Initial Contact: Send a brief letter of inquiry.
Application Requirements: Provide a description of organization, amount requested, purpose of funds sought, recently audited financial statements, proof of tax-exempt status, deadline for project approval, and signature of authorization by organization's highest ranking officer. Also include a copy of the organization's charter and by-laws.
Deadlines: At least three weeks before funds are needed.
Decision Notification: Committee meets weekly.

Corporate Officials
Melissa J. Adams: corporate donations officer PRIM CORP EMPL corporate donations officer: Frost National Bank.
Richard W. Evans, Jr.: chairman, chief executive officer B 1946. ED Southwest Texas Junior College (1965-1966); University of Texas BA (1968). PRIM CORP EMPL chairman, chief executive officer: Frost National Bank.

Giving Program Officials
Melissa J. Adams: member (see above)

Grants Analysis
Disclosure Period: calendar year ending 2001
Total Grants: $347,418*
Number of Grants: 64
Average Grant: $5,428
Highest Grant: $25,000
Lowest Grant: $1,000
Typical Range: $1,000 to $10,000
*Note: Giving excludes scholarship; United Way.

Recent Grants
Note: Grants derived from 2001 Form 990.

Library-Related
5,000   El Progreso Memorial Library, Uvalde, TX -- for capital campaign

General
175,000   United Way of San Antonio and Bexar Counties, San Antonio, TX -- annual pledge
55,000   University of Texas at San Antonio, San Antonio, TX -- for Uteach Program
25,000   Neighborhood Housing Services, San Antonio, TX -- for Senior Partner contribution
25,000   San Antonio Symphony, San Antonio, TX -- for annual fund
20,000   San Antonio Education Partnership, San Antonio, TX -- for Scholarship Program
20,000   San Antonio Symphony, San Antonio, TX -- for 1998-2002 pledge
20,000   San Antonio Symphony, San Antonio, TX
15,000   White Museum, San Antonio, TX -- for Free Tuesday Program
10,000   Carver Development Board, San Antonio, TX -- for Camp Carver Complex
10,000   Ex-Students Association of the University of Texas, Austin, TX -- for Texas Leadership Scholarships

CHARLES A. FRUEAUFF FOUNDATION

Giving Contact
Sue M. Frueauff, Secretary
Three Financial Center
900 South Shackleford, Suite 300
Little Rock, AR 72211
Phone: (501)978-1078
Web: http://www.frueaufffoundation.com

Description
Founded: 1950
EIN: 135605371
Organization Type: General Purpose Foundation
Giving Locations: east of the Rocky Mountains.
Grant Types: Capital, Endowment, General Support, Matching, Operating Expenses, Project, Scholarship.

Donor Information
Founder: The foundation was established in 1950, with the late Charles A. Frueauff as donor.

Financial Summary
Total Giving: $4,844,960 (2001); $5,720,350 (2000); $5,208,000 (1999)
Giving Analysis: Giving for 2000 includes: foundation grants to United Way ($50,000); 1999: foundation grants to United Way ($100,000); 1998: foundation grants to United Way ($50,000)
Assets: $109,978,435 (2001); $118,547,522 (2000); $121,428,270 (1999)

Typical Recipients
Arts & Humanities: History & Archaeology, Libraries, Museums/Galleries, Music, Performing Arts, Public Broadcasting
Civic & Public Affairs: Economic Development, Economic Policy, Employment/Job Training, Civic & Public Affairs-General, Law & Justice, Legal Aid
Education: Business Education, Colleges & Universities, Education Funds, Engineering/Technological Education, Faculty Development, Education-General, Literacy, Medical Education, Minority Education, Private Education (Precollege), Public Education (Precollege), Science/Mathematics Education, Student Aid
Health: Children's Health/Hospitals, Clinics/Medical Centers, Emergency/Ambulance Services, Health Organizations, Hospices, Hospitals, Nursing Services, Public Health, Transplant Networks/Donor Banks
Religion: Religious Welfare
Social Services: At-Risk Youth, Child Welfare, Community Centers, Community Service Organizations, Counseling, Family Services, Food/Clothing Distribution, Homes, People with Disabilities, Recreation & Athletics, Scouts, Senior Services, Shelters/Homelessness, Substance Abuse, United Funds/United Ways, Veterans, YMCA/YWCA/YMHA/YWHA, Youth Organizations

Application Procedures
Initial Contact: Organizations should request application guidelines. Phone calls to the foundation are encouraged.
Application Requirements: Proposals should be in the letter form, and should include a history of the organization, project description, purpose of funds sought, objectives, time period, projected budget, evaluation plan, additional funding requested or received from other sources, a list of trustees or directors and key staff, most recent audited financial statements, and proof of tax-exempt status.
Deadlines: Submit the proposal for the May meeting by March 15 and submit the proposal for the November meeting by September 15. Any requests received after September 15 are reviewed at the following May meeting.
Review Process: The foundation notifies all applicants whether or not they receive a grant.
Notes: The foundation does not review incomplete applications. Pre-proposal letters, videos, and other special supplementary material are discouraged. All grant funds are distributed in December.

Restrictions
The foundation does not support individuals, multiyear grants, international projects, state supported colleges and universities, primary and secondary schools, churches, fundraising drives, or special events.

Additional Information

Grants to new agencies are generally limited to $15,000.

Publications: Informational Brochure

Foundation Officials

James P. Fallon: vice president, trustee
Karl P. Fanning: trustee
David Frueauff: president
Sue M. Frueauff: program officer, trustee
Anna Kay Frueauff-Grace: trustee
Charles T. Klein: vice president, trustee
Dr. A. C. McCully: trustee

Grants Analysis

Disclosure Period: calendar year ending 2001
Total Grants: $4,844,960
Number of Grants: 160
Average Grant: $30,281
Highest Grant: $100,000
Lowest Grant: $2,000
Typical Range: $2,000 to $100,000

Recent Grants

Note: Grants derived from 2001 Form 990.

General

100,000	Sweet Briar College, Sweet Briar, VA -- two scholarship endowed funds
100,000	Wickenburg Foundation for the Performing Arts, Wickenburg, AZ -- construction, equipment
60,000	Craig Hospital, Denver, CO -- housing project
55,000	Boys and Girls Club of the Arkansas River Valley, Russellville, AR -- program support, building campaign
55,000	City Harvest, New York, NY -- program support
55,000	Tallahassee Memorial Healthcare Foundation, Tallahassee, FL -- women's and Children's medical Services center, diabetes programs
50,000	Arkansas Children's Hospital, Little Rock, AR -- children life and education department endowment
50,000	Belmont University, Nashville, TN -- student center, music and business endowment
50,000	Big Bend Hospice, Tallahassee, FL -- endowment fund
50,000	Boys Clubs of New York, New York, NY -- program support

FRUEHAUF FOUNDATION

Giving Contact

Dian Stallings
100 Maple Park Blvd., Suite 106
St. Clair Shores, MI 48081
Phone: (810)774-5130
Fax: (810)774-1152

Description

Founded: 1968
EIN: 237015744
Organization Type: Private Foundation
Giving Locations: MI
Grant Types: General Support, Operating Expenses.

Donor Information

Founder: Angela Fruehauf

Financial Summary

Total Giving: $163,585 (2000); $117,500 (1999); $107,050 (1998)
Assets: $5,217,337 (2000); $6,785,067 (1999); $4,921,759 (1998)

Gifts Received: $21,753 (2000); $12,606 (1999); $191,000 (1996). Note: In 1999 and 2000, contributions were received from Barbara F. Bristol. In 1996, contributions were received from Barbara F. Bristol ($160,000) and Harvey C. Fruehauf, Jr. ($31,000).

Typical Recipients

Arts & Humanities: Arts Funds, Arts Institutes, Historic Preservation, History & Archaeology, Libraries, Music, Public Broadcasting
Civic & Public Affairs: Clubs, Economic Policy, Civic & Public Affairs-General, Law & Justice, Philanthropic Organizations, Public Policy, Safety, Urban & Community Affairs
Education: Business Education, Colleges & Universities, Education Funds, Medical Education, Private Education (Precollege), Public Education (Precollege), Religious Education, Student Aid
Environment: Resource Conservation
Health: AIDS/HIV, Cancer, Children's Health/Hospitals, Clinics/Medical Centers, Emergency/Ambulance Services, Eyes/Blindness, Health Funds, Health Organizations, Hospices, Hospitals, Long-Term Care, Medical Research, Mental Health, Nursing Services, Research/Studies Institutes, Single-Disease Health Associations
International: Foreign Educational Institutions, Health Care/Hospitals, International Organizations, International Relief Efforts
Religion: Churches, Ministries, Missionary Activities (Domestic), Religious Organizations, Religious Welfare, Seminaries, Social/Policy Issues
Science: Science Museums
Social Services: Animal Protection, Child Welfare, Community Service Organizations, Family Planning, Family Services, Homes, People with Disabilities, Recreation & Athletics, Scouts, Senior Services, Social Services-General, Substance Abuse, United Funds/United Ways, YMCA/YWCA/YMHA/YWHA, Youth Organizations

Application Procedures

Initial Contact: Send a brief letter of inquiry.
Deadlines: None.

Foundation Officials

Barbara F. Bristol: vice president
Harvey C. Fruehauf, Jr.: president B Grosse Pointe Park, MI 1929. ED University of Michigan (1952). PRIM CORP EMPL president, director: HCF Enterprises Inc. CORP AFFIL president, treasurer, director: HCF Realty Inc.; chairman, president: Miami Oil Producers Inc.; director: Georgia-Pacific Corp.
Robert B. Joslyn: trustee
Frederick R. Keydel: trustee
Julie Stranahan: trustee

Grants Analysis

Disclosure Period: calendar year ending 2000
Total Grants: $163,585
Number of Grants: 44
Average Grant: $2,409*
Highest Grant: $60,000
Typical Range: $500 to $5,000
*Note: Average grant figure excludes highest grant.

Recent Grants

Note: Grants derived from 2001 Form 990.

General

25,000	Church of Jesus Christ Disciples, Cameron, MO -- for Running Child Ministries
25,000	St. Lawrence University, Canton, NY -- for Linda's fund
25,000	Trinity Preparatory School, Winter Park, FL -- for operating expenses
20,000	Houston Museum of Natural Science, Houston, TX -- for mineral specimen
16,250	Lost Tree Chapel, North Palm Beach, FL -- for operating expenses
10,000	Hillsdale College, Hillsdale, MI -- for operating expenses
10,000	University of Texas M. D. Anderson Cancer Center, Houston, TX -- for cancer research
7,500	Lost Tree Chapel, North Palm Beach, FL -- for operating expenses
7,500	St. Francis Episcopal Day School, Houston, TX -- for permanent endowment
5,000	Billy Graham Evangelistic Association, Minneapolis, MN -- for operating expenses

LLOYD A. FRY FOUNDATION

Giving Contact

Jill C. Darrow-Seltzer, Executive Director
120 S LaSalle St., Suite 1950
Chicago, IL 60603
Phone: (312)580-0310
Fax: (312)580-0980
Web: http://www.fryfoundation.org

Description

Founded: 1983
EIN: 366108775
Organization Type: General Purpose Foundation
Giving Locations: IL: Chicago
Grant Types: Project, Seed Money.

Donor Information

Founder: Born in San Antonio, TX, in 1895, Lloyd A. Fry established a roofing business in Chicago in 1931. The Lloyd A. Fry Roofing Company grew into the world's largest producer of asphalt roofing products until its sale to Owens-Corning Fiberglas Corporation in 1977. Mr. Fry established the foundation in 1959. Upon his death in 1981, the foundation received a significant testamentary bequest which led to an increase in its philanthropic activity.

Financial Summary

Total Giving: $6,000,000 (fiscal year ending June 30, 2003 approx); $6,000,000 (fiscal 2002 approx); $6,399,477 (fiscal 2001)
Assets: $160,000,000 (fiscal 2003 approx); $160,000,000 (fiscal 2002 approx); $169,000,000 (fiscal 2001)
Gifts Received: $1,248,303 (fiscal 2000); $1,363,355 (fiscal 1999); $1,485,724 (fiscal 1997). Note: The foundation is a residual beneficiary of several trusts established by the estate of the founder.

Typical Recipients

Arts & Humanities: Arts Appreciation, Arts Centers, Arts Festivals, Arts Institutes, Dance, Ethnic & Folk Arts, Historic Preservation, Libraries, Museums/Galleries, Music, Opera, Performing Arts, Public Broadcasting, Theater
Civic & Public Affairs: African American Affairs, Clubs, Economic Development, Economic Policy, Employment/Job Training, Civic & Public Affairs-General, Housing, Law & Justice, Legal Aid, Nonprofit Management, Public Policy, Urban & Community Affairs, Zoos/Aquariums
Education: Afterschool/Enrichment Programs, Arts/Humanities Education, Business Education, Colleges & Universities, Continuing Education, Education Associations, Education Funds, Education Reform, Elementary Education (Private), Faculty Development, Education-General, International Exchange, Leadership Training, Literacy, Minority Education, Preschool Education, Private Education (Precollege), Public Education (Precollege), Science/Mathematics Education, Secondary Education (Private), Secondary Education (Public), Special Education, Student Aid
Environment: Environment-General
Health: AIDS/HIV, Children's Health/Hospitals, Clinics/Medical Centers, Geriatric Health, Health Policy/

Cost Containment, Health Organizations, Heart, Hospitals, Medical Rehabilitation, Mental Health, Nursing Services, Prenatal Health Issues, Public Health, Single-Disease Health Associations

International: Health Care/Hospitals, International Relations, International Relief Efforts, International Relief Efforts

Religion: Churches, Ministries, Religious Organizations, Religious Welfare, Seminaries

Science: Science Museums, Scientific Centers & Institutes, Scientific Labs

Social Services: At-Risk Youth, Child Abuse, Child Welfare, Community Centers, Community Service Organizations, Counseling, Day Care, Delinquency & Criminal Rehabilitation, Domestic Violence, Family Services, Food/Clothing Distribution, People with Disabilities, Refugee Assistance, Senior Services, Shelters/Homelessness, Social Services-General, Substance Abuse, United Funds/United Ways, Volunteer Services, YMCA/YWCA/YMHA/YWHA, Youth Organizations

Application Procedures

Initial Contact: Applicants may submit a brief inquiry before a full proposal. Inquiries should include a brief statement of the project and a project budget.

Application Requirements: Full proposals should include a brief history of the organization with functions and goals; brief proposal summary, including need to be addressed, budget, and an evaluation plan; most recent audited financial report and approved operating budget; other sources of support; list of board members and key personnel; and copy of IRS tax-exempt status letter.

Deadlines: December 1; March 1; June 1; and September 1.

Review Process: The board of directors meets in February, May, August, and November. Although the foundation considers requests for operating support and capital campaigns, it prefers to fund projects directed at the solution of specific problems. Priority is given to proposals for new programs rather than for support of ongoing direct service programs.

Restrictions

Grants rarely are made to organizations outside metropolitan Chicago. No grants are made to individuals, non-tax-exempt organizations, government agencies, fund-raising benefits, or tax-supported educational institutions for services that fall within their normal responsibilities.

Additional Information

Publications: Annual Report; Guidelines

Foundation Officials

Roger E. Anderson: vice chairman B Chicago, IL 1921. ED Northwestern University BA (1942).

Jill C. Darrow: executive director B Cheyenne, WY 1947. ED Mount Holyoke College BA (1969). CLUB AFFIL member: Fortnightly Chicago Club.

Lloyd A. Fry, III: vice president

Stephanie Pace Marshall, PhD: vice president PRIM NONPR EMPL president: Illinois Math & Science Academy. CORP AFFIL director: Tellabs Inc.

Howard McDowell McCue, III: vice president, secretary, director, chairman B Sumter, SC 1946. ED Princeton University AB (1968); Harvard University JD (1971). PRIM CORP EMPL partner: Mayer, Brown & Platt. NONPR AFFIL director: Lawrence Hall Youth Services; director, chairman board governors: Northwestern University Library Council; member: Illinois Bar Association; director: International Academy Estate & Trust Law; adj professor: Chicago Kent College Law; director: Harvard Law Society Illinois; director, member: Chicago Bar Foundation; director: Art Institute of Chicago; member federal tax committee: Chicago Bar Association; member: American College

Trust & Estate Counsel; member: American Bar Association; member: American College Tax Counsel. CLUB AFFIL Chicago Club.

M. James Termondt: president, treasurer

Grants Analysis

Disclosure Period: fiscal year ending June 30, 2000
Total Grants: $5,957,906
Number of Grants: 358
Average Grant: $16,642
Highest Grant: $125,000
Lowest Grant: $500
Typical Range: $5,000 to $50,000

Recent Grants

Note: Grants derived from fiscal 2000 Form 990.

General

125,000	Big Shoulders Fund, Chicago, IL
75,000	Providence-St. Mel School, Chicago, IL
65,000	Latin School of Chicago, Chicago, IL
62,689	Providence-St. Mel School, Chicago, IL
60,000	Erikson Institute for Early Childhood Education, Chicago, IL
60,000	Jobs for Youth, Chicago, IL
50,000	Center for New Horizons, Chicago, IL
50,000	Chicago Commons ETC, Chicago, IL
50,000	Chicago Commons ETC, Chicago, IL
50,000	Culver Educational Foundation, Culver, IN

GOTTFRIED AND MARY FUCHS FOUNDATION

Giving Contact

Gayleene Berry, Trust Officer
c/o Union Bank of California NA
1011 Pacific Ave.
Tacoma, WA 98402
Phone: (206)591-2548

Description

Founded: 1960
EIN: 916022284
Organization Type: Private Foundation
Giving Locations: WA: especially Tahoma and Pierce County, and the lower Puget Sound area
Grant Types: Capital, Emergency, General Support, Multiyear/Continuing Support, Operating Expenses, Project, Research, Scholarship.

Donor Information

Founder: the late Gottfried and Mary Fuchs

Financial Summary

Total Giving: $1,632,237 (2000); $1,388,074 (1999); $1,538,224 (1998)
Giving Analysis: Giving for 1999 includes: foundation scholarships ($20,000)
Assets: $25,882,736 (2000); $28,107,034 (1999); $29,500,874 (1998)

Typical Recipients

Arts & Humanities: Community Arts, Dance, Historic Preservation, History & Archaeology, Libraries, Museums/Galleries, Music, Opera, Theater

Civic & Public Affairs: African American Affairs, Asian American Affairs, Botanical Gardens/Parks, Clubs, Community Foundations, Employment/Job Training, Housing, Municipalities/Towns, Parades/Festivals, Urban & Community Affairs, Women's Affairs, Zoos/Aquariums

Education: Colleges & Universities, Community & Junior Colleges, International Studies, Private Education (Precollege), Public Education (Precollege), Religious Education, Special Education, Student Aid, Vocational & Technical Education

Environment: Environment-General, Wildlife Protection

Health: Children's Health/Hospitals, Clinics/Medical Centers, Emergency/Ambulance Services, Geriatric Health, Heart, Hospitals, Mental Health, Prenatal Health Issues, Transplant Networks/Donor Banks, Trauma Treatment

Religion: Churches, Ministries, Religious Organizations, Religious Welfare

Science: Scientific Centers & Institutes

Social Services: Animal Protection, Child Abuse, Child Welfare, Community Centers, Community Service Organizations, Crime Prevention, Day Care, Domestic Violence, Emergency Relief, Family Services, Food/Clothing Distribution, Homes, People with Disabilities, Recreation & Athletics, Refugee Assistance, Scouts, Senior Services, Shelters/Homelessness, Social Services-General, United Funds/United Ways, Volunteer Services, YMCA/YWCA/YMHA/YWHA, Youth Organizations

Application Procedures

Initial Contact: Return completed application form.
Application Requirements: Include proof of tax-exempt status, current financial statement, current budget pertinent to the grant request, resume of the director or person in charge of the program, and a list of board members.
Deadlines: None.

Restrictions

Does not support individuals.

Additional Information

Publications: Application Form; Guidelines
Trust(s): Union Bank CA NA

Grants Analysis

Disclosure Period: calendar year ending 2000
Total Grants: $1,632,237
Number of Grants: 99
Average Grant: $15,380*
Highest Grant: $125,000
Typical Range: $5,000 to $30,000
*Note: Average grant excludes highest grant.

Recent Grants

Note: Grants derived from 1999 Form 990.

General

290,000	Tacoma Art Museum, Tacoma, WA
72,000	Emergency Food Network, Tacoma, WA
50,000	First Assembly of God Church for Life Christian School, Tacoma, WA
50,000	Martin Luther King Housing Development Association, Tacoma, WA
50,000	Multicare Mary Bridge Hospital, Tacoma, WA
50,000	Washington State Historical Society, Tacoma, WA
40,000	Boys and Girls Clubs of Pierce County, Tacoma, WA
35,000	Associated Ministries, Tacoma, WA
35,000	Pierce College Foundation, Tacoma, WA
35,000	Tacoma Community College Foundation, Tacoma, WA

FUJITSU AMERICA

Company Headquarters

3055 Orchard Drive
San Jose, CA 95134
Web: http://www.fujitsu.com

Company Description

Former Name: Fujitsu American, Inc.
Revenue: US$4.33 billion (2002)
Employees: 188000 (2002)
SIC(s): 3571 Electronic Computers, 3661 Telephone & Telegraph Apparatus.

Parent Company: Fujitsu General America, Inc., 3900 NW 79th Ave., Ste. 320, Miami, FL, United States
Parent Revenue: US$42,239,100,000 (2002)

Operating Locations

Fujitsu America (CA--San Jose); Fujitsu America - Information Systems Group (CA--San Jose); Fujitsu America - Super Computer Group (CA--San Jose); Fujitsu Business Communication Systems (CA--Anaheim); Fujitsu Business Communication Systems - Sales & Marketing (AZ--Phoenix); Fujitsu Compound Semiconductor (CA--San Jose); Fujitsu Computer Packaging Technologies (CA--San Jose); Fujitsu Computer Products of America (CA--San Jose); Fujitsu Computer Products of America Manufacturing (OR--Hillsboro); Fujitsu Computer Products of America - Research & Development (CO--Longmont); Fujitsu General America Corp. (NJ--Fairfield); Fujitsu Laboratories of America (CA--San Jose); Fujitsu Ltd. (NY--New York); Fujitsu Microelectronics (CA--San Jose); Fujitsu Microelectronics - Manufacturing (OR--Gresham); Fujitsu Network Switching of America (NC--Raleigh); Fujitsu Network Transmission Systems (TX--Richardson); Fujitsu Networks Industries (CT--Stamford); Fujitsu Open Systems Solutions (CA--San Jose); Fujitsu Personal Systems (CA--Santa Clara); Fujitsu Systems of America (CA--La Jolla); Fujitsu Systems Business of America (CA--Santa Clara); Fujitsu Ten Corp. of America (CA--Torrance); HaL Computer Systems (CA--Campbell); ICL (CA--Irvine); Ross Technology (TX--Austin)

Giving Contact

George Tripshaw, Director, Marketing & Communications
3055 Orchard Dr.
San Jose, CA 95134
Phone: (408)432-1300

Description

Organization Type: Corporate Giving Program
Giving Locations: headquarters and operating communities.
Grant Types: General Support.

Typical Recipients

Arts & Humanities: Libraries, Museums/Galleries
Education: Colleges & Universities, Minority Education
Health: Hospitals, Single-Disease Health Associations
Social Services: Community Service Organizations, United Funds/United Ways

Application Procedures

Initial Contact: Submit a letter at any time, including a description of organization, amount and purpose of request, goals and objectives of the organization, and a list of the board of directors.

Restrictions

Value of monetary and nonmonetary support is not available. Nonmonetary support generally is in the form of donated computers and telecommunications equipment.

Corporate Officials

K. Kojima: chairman, chief executive officer chief financial officer PRIM CORP EMPL chairman, chief executive officer: Fujitsu America.
Motoyasu Matsuzaki: executive vice president, chief financial officer PRIM CORP EMPL executive vice president, chief financial officer: Fujitsu America.

Grants Analysis

Typical Range: $1,000 to $2,500

H.B. FULLER CO.

Company Headquarters

St. Paul, MN
Web: http://www.hbfuller.com

Company Description

Founded: 1887
Ticker: FULL
Exchange: NASDAQ
Revenue: US$1.256 billion (2002)
Employees: 4600 (2002)
SIC(s): 2842 Polishes & Sanitation Goods, 2851 Paints & Allied Products, 2891 Adhesives & Sealants.

Operating Locations

H.B. Fuller Co. (CA--La Mirada, Santa Fe Springs, Tulare, FL--Gainesville; GA--Atlanta; IL--Palatine, Tinley Park; IN; KY; MD--Baltimore; MA--Marlboro; MI--Detroit; MN--Minneapolis, St. Paul, Vadnais Heights; NY--Geneva; NC--Greensboro; OH--Blue Ash; OK; OR--Portland; TN--Memphis; TX--Houston, Mesquite; WA--Vancouver)

Nonmonetary Support

Value: $31,200 (2001); $44,960 (2000)
Type: Donated Equipment; Donated Products; In-kind Services; Loaned Employees

H.B. Fuller Co. Foundation

Giving Contact

Karen P. Muller, Director of Community Affairs
H.B. Fuller Co.
PO Box 64683
St. Paul, MN 55164-0683
Phone: (651)236-5207
Web: http://www.hbfuller.com/About_Us/Community/index.shtml

Alternate Contact

Naida Kissner, Community Affairs Assistant

Description

EIN: 363500811
Organization Type: Corporate Foundation
Giving Locations: internationally; headquarters and operating communities; nationally.
Grant Types: Employee Matching Gifts, General Support, Matching, Operating Expenses, Project.
Note: Employee matching gift ratio: 1 to 1 to education, 0.5 to 1 to the United Way. Company also has a matching gift program for employees serving on boards of community agencies.

Financial Summary

Total Giving: $750,755 (2001); $1,159,939 (2000); $1,750,437 (1998). Note: Contributes through corporate direct giving program and foundation.
Giving Analysis: Giving for 2001 includes: foundation matching gifts ($43,465); foundation grants to United Way ($138,083); corporate direct giving ($194,086); foundation ($375,121); 2000: foundation matching gifts ($44,412); international subsidiaries ($56,090); corporate direct giving ($186,848); foundation grants to United Way ($224,264); foundation ($648,325); 1998: corporate direct giving ($664,792); foundation ($1,085,645).
Assets: $1,002,789 (2000); $1,203,010 (1997); $1,037,844 (1995)
Gifts Received: $631,410 (2001); $1,000,757 (2000); $1,127,321 (1998). Note: Contributions received from H.B. Fuller Company.

Typical Recipients

Arts & Humanities: Arts Centers, Arts Funds, Arts Outreach, Dance, Libraries, Literary Arts, Museums/Galleries, Music, Opera, Performing Arts, Public Broadcasting, Theater
Civic & Public Affairs: African American Affairs, Asian American Affairs, Botanical Gardens/Parks, Economic Development, Employment/Job Training, Civic & Public Affairs-General, Hispanic Affairs, Housing, Legal Aid, Nonprofit Management, Philanthropic Organizations, Public Policy, Urban & Community Affairs, Women's Affairs
Education: Afterschool/Enrichment Programs, Arts/Humanities Education, Colleges & Universities, Economic Education, Education Funds, Education Reform, Elementary Education (Private), Elementary Education (Public), Education-General, Literacy, Minority Education, Preschool Education, Public Education (Precollege), Religious Education, Science/Mathematics Education, Secondary Education (Public), Social Sciences Education, Special Education
Environment: Air/Water Quality, Forestry, Environment-General
Health: Clinics/Medical Centers, Emergency/Ambulance Services, Health Organizations, Mental Health, Research/Studies Institutes
International: Foreign Educational Institutions, International-General, Health Care/Hospitals, Human Rights, International Environmental Issues, International Organizations, International Relief Efforts
Religion: Religion-General, Religious Organizations, Religious Welfare
Science: Science Museums
Social Services: At-Risk Youth, Big Brother/Big Sister, Camps, Child Abuse, Child Welfare, Community Centers, Community Service Organizations, Domestic Violence, Family Services, People with Disabilities, Recreation & Athletics, Refugee Assistance, Scouts, Shelters/Homelessness, Social Services-General, Special Olympics, Substance Abuse, United Funds/United Ways, Volunteer Services, YMCA/YWCA/YMHA/YWHA, Youth Organizations

Application Procedures

Initial Contact: Call or send a brief letter of inquiry. The Foundation is the central contact point for all new grant applicants.
Application Requirements: Include a description of organization, amount requested, current budget information, and proof of tax-exempt status.
Deadlines: February, June, and October.
Review Process: Decisions are made by local employee committees and by foundation contributions committee.
Evaluative Criteria: Includes organization's intention to address underlying causes of problems, not merely resulting problems; proximity of organization to company facilities; employee involvement with agency; effectiveness and impact of organization; urgency and need for organization, its leverage, and organizational strength; and multi-level approach to issue or problem.
Decision Notification: Local councils meet monthly and review proposals as they are received; foundation reviews applications three times a year.
Notes: Both foundation and company accept the Minnesota Common Grant Application. The H.B. Fuller Company and Foundation support a wide range of organizations and projects worldwide to reach the needs of the company's international communities. However, in Minnesota, the foundation only approves grants for organizations or programs that directly serve family literacy.

Restrictions

Foundation does not make grants to religious, fraternal, or veterans organizations except for programs that are of direct benefit to the community. Does not support individuals, political/lobbying organizations, basic or applied research, or travel. Does not give to disease-specific organizations, courtesy/public service advertising, or capital or endowment drives. Programs which are the responsibility of governments will not be supported unless the program is a community-based effort aimed at improving the delivery of government funded services.

Additional Information

Since 1987, H.B. Fuller's focus issue has been youth development. The company is committed to building strong communities which create economic and educational support for children and their families.

The foundation's primary areas of interest are social services organizations and organizations in which company employees are volunteers. Employees are encouraged to convey the needs of such organizations to the community affairs council for their location. Recipients of grants are required to submit complete financial reports.

H.B. Fuller allocates 3.5% of pre-tax profits to community affairs activities in the U.S.

In addition to company's community affairs budget, Community Affairs Councils operate in 33 communities in the United States, 23 in Latin America, and 11 in Europe. These councils contribute to over 270 local agencies and also provide nonmonetary support. A list of council chairpersons is available from the foundation.

Publications: Community Affairs Annual Report

Corporate Officials

Walter Kissling: chief financial officer B Limon, Costa Rica 1931. PRIM CORP EMPL director: H.B. Fuller Co. CORP AFFIL director: Pentair, Inc.

Foundation Officials

Naida Kissner: program assistant

Grants Analysis

Disclosure Period: calendar year ending 2001
Total Grants: $375,121*
Number of Grants: 78
Average Grant: $4,222*
Highest Grant: $50,000
Lowest Grant: $500
Typical Range: $1,000 to $10,000
*Note: Giving excludes matching gifts; United Way; and corporate contributions. Average grant figure excludes highest grant.

Recent Grants

Note: Grants derived from 2001 Form 990.

Library-Related
7,500	Friends of the St. Paul Public Library, St. Paul, MN -- for the Saint Paul Public Library's Summer Reading Program

General
93,291	Greater Twin Cities United Way, Minneapolis, MN -- for the United Way of the St. Paul Area
50,000	University of Minnesota Foundation, Minneapolis, MN -- for Elmer L. Andersen Library Endowment for Special Collections
40,000	Minnesota Public Radio, St. Paul, MN -- Minnesota Orchestra broadcast
20,000	Street Kids International Canada -- for the capacity building project
10,000	Asociacion de Empresarios para el Desarrollo -- for the development of a United Way of Costa Rica
10,000	Fundacion Hogar Manos Abiertas -- renovation of a home for disabled children and adults
10,000	Fundacion Sampedrana del Nino -- for Club House
10,000	Greater Twin Cities United Way, Minneapolis, MN -- for expansion and enhancement of the What's Up? Program
10,000	Greater Twin Cities United Way, Minneapolis, MN -- for expansion and enhancement of the What's Up? Program
10,000	Health Start, Inc., St. Paul, MN -- for operating support

FULLER FOUNDATION (DE)

Giving Contact

Nannette Barrigan, Executive Director
269 S. Beverly Dr., 469
Beverly Hills, CA 90212
Phone: (561)655-1980
Fax: (561)655-5677

Description

Founded: 1951
EIN: 756015942
Organization Type: Private Foundation
Giving Locations: nationally.
Grant Types: General Support.

Donor Information

Founder: Andrew P. Fuller, William M. Fuller

Financial Summary

Total Giving: $342,000 (2000); $287,500 (1999); $275,000 (1998)
Assets: $6,604,882 (2000); $7,416,492 (1999); $6,119,520 (1998)
Gifts Received: In 1991, contributions were received from Buffalo News/Berkshire Hathaway ($140) and William M. Fuller ($500).

Typical Recipients

Arts & Humanities: Arts Associations & Councils, Arts Funds, Community Arts, Film & Video, Historic Preservation, History & Archaeology, Libraries, Museums/Galleries, Music, Theater, Visual Arts
Civic & Public Affairs: Botanical Gardens/Parks, Employment/Job Training, Gay/Lesbian Issues, Civic & Public Affairs-General, Housing, Urban & Community Affairs, Zoos/Aquariums
Education: Arts/Humanities Education, Colleges & Universities, Education Funds, Education-General, Legal Education, Literacy, Medical Education, Private Education (Precollege), Science/Mathematics Education, Social Sciences Education
Environment: Environment-General, Resource Conservation
Health: AIDS/HIV, Arthritis, Cancer, Clinics/Medical Centers, Clinics/Medical Centers, Emergency/Ambulance Services, Health Organizations, Heart, Hospices, Hospitals, Hospitals (University Affiliated), Medical Rehabilitation, Medical Research, Mental Health, Multiple Sclerosis, Single-Disease Health Associations, Transplant Networks/Donor Banks
International: Health Care/Hospitals, Human Rights, International Environmental Issues, International Relief Efforts
Religion: Churches, Jewish Causes, Religious Organizations, Religious Welfare
Social Services: Animal Protection, Camps, Child Welfare, Community Centers, Domestic Violence, Family Planning, Food/Clothing Distribution, Recreation & Athletics, Social Services-General, Substance Abuse, YMCA/YWCA/YMHA/YWHA, Youth Organizations

Application Procedures

Initial Contact: Send proposal in any legible form containing all relevant information about organization.
Deadlines: None.

Foundation Officials

Kenneth S. Beall, Esq.: secretary
Fuller French: treasurer
Geraldine Fuller: president
Gillian Fuller: vice president

Grants Analysis

Disclosure Period: calendar year ending 2000
Total Grants: $342,000
Number of Grants: 36
Average Grant: $8,343*
Highest Grant: $50,000
Typical Range: $1,000 to $15,000
*Note: Average grant excludes highest grant.

Recent Grants

Note: Grants derived from 2001 Form 990.

General
50,000	Friendly Hand Foundation, Los Angeles, CA
31,500	MJ Fox Foundation, New York, NY
25,000	Children of Move, Los Angeles, CA
15,000	United World College, Montezuma, NM
10,000	Loyola Law School, Los Angeles, CA
10,000	St. John's Health Center Foundation, Santa Monica, CA
10,000	St. Joseph's Center, Venice, CA
10,000	Shakespearean Hobarts, Los Angeles, CA
10,000	Tuesday's Child, Culver City, CA
10,000	University of Southern California, Los Angeles, CA

GEORGE F. AND SYBIL H. FULLER FOUNDATION

Giving Contact

Russell E. Fuller, Chairman, Treasurer & Trustee
1B Central Street
Boylston, MA 01505
Phone: (508)869-6723
Fax: (508)869-2601

Description

Founded: 1955
EIN: 046125606
Organization Type: Family Foundation
Giving Locations: MA: Worcester County
Grant Types: Capital, Challenge, Loan.

Donor Information

Founder: Established in 1955 by the late George Freeman Fuller (d. 1962), who was an influential figure in the Worcester, MA area. Mr. Fuller served for many years as a trustee of Worcester Polytechnic Institute and worked with many charitable organizations. He was president and chairman of the board of the Wyman-Gordon Company, a leading industrial concern in the forging business. His wife, Sybil Harriet Flagg Fuller, died in 1955. The foundation received a considerable bequest from Mr. Fuller's estate at the time of his death.

Financial Summary

Total Giving: $3,500,000 (2002 approx); $3,500,000 (2001); $3,874,200 (2000)
Giving Analysis: Giving for 2000 includes: foundation grants to United Way ($75,000) 1998: foundation grants to United Way ($65,000)
Assets: $69,000,000 (2001); $71,965,151 (2000); $65,115,689 (1998)

Typical Recipients

Arts & Humanities: Arts Centers, Ethnic & Folk Arts, Arts & Humanities-General, Historic Preservation, History & Archaeology, Libraries, Museums/Galleries, Music, Performing Arts, Public Broadcasting, Theater

Civic & Public Affairs: African American Affairs, Business/Free Enterprise, Clubs, Community Foundations, Civic & Public Affairs-General, Housing, Professional & Trade Associations, Public Policy, Safety, Urban & Community Affairs
Education: Agricultural Education, Arts/Humanities Education, Colleges & Universities, Community & Junior Colleges, Education Reform, Engineering/Technological Education, Education-General, Literacy, Medical Education, Preschool Education, Private Education (Precollege), Public Education (Precollege), Science/Mathematics Education, Secondary Education (Private), Special Education, Student Aid
Environment: Environment-General, Protection, Resource Conservation
Health: Children's Health/Hospitals, Clinics/Medical Centers, Diabetes, Emergency/Ambulance Services, Health-General, Health Organizations, Hospices, Hospitals, Medical Research, Nursing Services, Public Health, Single-Disease Health Associations
International: Foreign Arts Organizations
Religion: Churches, Jewish Causes, Ministries, Religious Organizations, Religious Welfare
Science: Science Museums, Scientific Centers & Institutes, Scientific Research
Social Services: Big Brother/Big Sister, Child Welfare, Community Centers, Community Service Organizations, Counseling, Day Care, Family Services, Food/Clothing Distribution, People with Disabilities, Recreation & Athletics, Senior Services, Substance Abuse, United Funds/United Ways, YMCA/YWCA/YMHA/YWHA, Youth Organizations

Application Procedures
Initial Contact: The foundation has no formal application requirements or procedures. Initial contact should be a letter of inquiry mailed to the foundation.
Application Requirements: Applications should be made in a reasonably brief narrative form with an appropriate budget. The purpose to be achieved, reasons why the organization is fitted to achieve them, and how these purposes integrate with the existing activities of the institution are also of interest. In addition, included evidence of tax exempt status and the most recent annual report, including the audited financial report. Signature of the Chief Executive Officer is required.
Deadlines: None. The six-member board of trustees meets six times a year.
Review Process: If the foundation is interested in the project, one copy of a full proposal will be requested. The foundation occasionally acknowledges receipt of proposals. Applicants may arrange interviews.

Restrictions
No grants are made to individuals for scholarships or fellowships.

Foundation Officials
Joyce I. Fuller: assistant treasurer, trustee PRIM CORP EMPL executive vice president, clerk, director: REFCO Inc.
Lincoln E. Fuller: trustee PRIM CORP EMPL executive vice president, director: REFCO Inc.
Mark W. Fuller: vice chairman, trustee B 1949. ED Pennsylvania State University (1972). PRIM CORP EMPL president, treasurer, chief executive officer, director: REFCO Inc. CORP AFFIL president: Industrial & Tool Suppliers; president: Leen/Refco Co.
Russell E. Fuller: chairman, treasurer, trustee B 1925. PRIM CORP EMPL chairman, director: REFCO Inc. CORP AFFIL director: Wyman-Gordon Co.
David P. Hallock: trustee
Dianne Robbins: secretary, trustee

Grants Analysis
Disclosure Period: calendar year ending 2000
Total Grants: $3,799,200*
Number of Grants: 85
Average Grant: $41,437*

Highest Grant: $318,500
Typical Range: $1,000 to $25,000 and $100,000 to $200,000
*Note: Giving excludes United Way. Average grant figure excludes highest grant.

Recent Grants
Note: Grants derived from 2000 Form 990.

Library-Related
150,000	Worcester Public Library, Worcester, MA

General
318,500	YMCA Greater Worcester, Worcester, MA
250,000	Greater Worcester Community Foundation, Inc., Worcester, MA
220,000	Clark University, Worcester, MA
210,000	Worcester Polytechnic Institute, Worcester, MA
200,000	Worcester Art Museum, Worcester, MA
175,000	Seven Hills Foundation, Worcester, MA
152,000	Worcester Area Chamber of Commerce, Worcester, MA
150,000	American Antiquarian Society, Worcester, MA
125,000	YWCA of Central Massachusetts, Worcester, MA
115,000	University of Massachusetts, Boston, MA -- Memorial Health Care -- Memorial Campus

FULLER FOUNDATION (MA)

Giving Contact
John T. Bottomley, Executive Director & Trustee
PO Box 461
Rye Beach, NH 03871
Phone: (603)964-8998

Description
Founded: 1936
EIN: 042241130
Organization Type: Private Foundation
Giving Locations: MA: Boston; NH: seacoast area
Grant Types: Capital, General Support, Operating Expenses, Scholarship.

Donor Information
Founder: the late Alvan T. Fuller, Sr.

Financial Summary
Total Giving: $730,369 (2001); $666,200 (2000); $657,649 (1999)
Giving Analysis: Giving for 2001 includes: foundation grants to United Way ($500); foundation scholarships ($16,000); 2000: foundation grants to United Way ($7,500); foundation scholarships ($11,000); 1999: foundation grants to United Way ($10,000)
Assets: $15,833,289 (2001); $17,237,158 (2000); $16,547,526 (1999)

Typical Recipients
Arts & Humanities: Arts Associations & Councils, Arts Centers, Arts Festivals, Arts Institutes, Arts Outreach, Arts & Humanities-General, Historic Preservation, Libraries, Music, Performing Arts, Public Broadcasting
Civic & Public Affairs: Community Foundations, Economic Development, Employment/Job Training, Civic & Public Affairs-General, Philanthropic Organizations, Urban & Community Affairs, Zoos/Aquariums
Education: Colleges & Universities, Elementary Education (Public), Engineering/Technological Education, Leadership Training, Private Education (Precollege), Public Education (Precollege)

Environment: Environment-General, Resource Conservation
Health: AIDS/HIV, Cancer, Children's Health/Hospitals, Emergency/Ambulance Services, Health Organizations, Hospitals, Medical Research
International: International Relief Efforts
Religion: Churches, Jewish Causes, Ministries, Religious Organizations, Religious Welfare
Science: Scientific Centers & Institutes
Social Services: Big Brother/Big Sister, Child Welfare, Community Service Organizations, Crime Prevention, Day Care, Emergency Relief, Family Services, Food/Clothing Distribution, Recreation & Athletics, Scouts, Shelters/Homelessness, Social Services-General, Substance Abuse, United Funds/United Ways, Youth Organizations

Application Procedures
Initial Contact: Telephone foundation.
Deadlines: None.

Restrictions
Does not support individuals or provide funds for publications or conferences.

Additional Information
Publications: Application Guidelines

Foundation Officials
Mindy Bocko: trustee
Miranda Fuller Bocko: trustee
Mrs. George T. Bottomley: honorary trustee
John T. Bottomley: executive director, trustee
Lydia Fuller Bottomley: trustee
Stephen D. Bottomley: treasurer
Anne Fuller Donovan: trustee
Peter Fuller, Jr.: president
Peter D. Fuller, Sr.: trustee B Boston, MA 1923. ED Harvard University (1946). PRIM CORP EMPL chairman, president: Cadillac Automobile Co. Boston. CORP AFFIL president, director: Fuller Enterprises.
James D. Henderson: trustee
Susanne Fuller MacDonald: trustee
John Pierce: trustee
Sandra Scagliotti: program administrator
Mrs. Frederick W. Swasey: honorary trustee
Hope Halsey Swasey: trustee
Melinda F. vanden Henvel: trustee

Grants Analysis
Disclosure Period: calendar year ending 2001
Total Grants: $713,869*
Number of Grants: 138
Average Grant: $5,173
Highest Grant: $22,810
Typical Range: $1,000 to $10,000
*Note: Giving excludes United Way and scholarships.

Recent Grants
Note: Grants derived from 2001 Form 990.

General
22,810	Fuller Foundation of New Hampshire, Rye Beach, NH
20,000	Fuller Foundation of New Hampshire, Rye Beach, NH
20,000	Fuller Foundation of New Hampshire, Rye Beach, NH
15,000	Fuller Foundation of New Hampshire, Rye Beach, NH
15,000	Fuller Foundation of New Hampshire, Rye Beach, NH
14,000	Fuller Foundation of New Hampshire, Rye Beach, NH
10,000	Fuller Foundation of New Hampshire, Rye Beach, NH
10,000	Fuller Foundation of New Hampshire, Rye Beach, NH
10,000	Fuller Foundation of New Hampshire, Rye Beach, NH
10,000	Fuller Foundation of New Hampshire, Rye Beach, NH

FULLERTON FOUNDATION

Giving Contact
Walter E. Cavell, Executive Director
PO Box 2208
Gaffney, SC 29342-2208
Phone: (864)489-6678
Fax: (864)487-9946
E-mail: cjbonner@fullertonfoundation.org

Description
Founded: 1954
EIN: 570847444
Organization Type: Family Foundation
Giving Locations: NC; SC
Grant Types: Matching, Project, Scholarship, Seed Money.

Donor Information
Founder: Established in 1954 by the late Alma H. Fullerton .

Financial Summary
Total Giving: $2,005,000 (fiscal year ending November 30, 2001); $2,096,000 (fiscal 2000); $2,046,000 (fiscal 1999)
Giving Analysis: Giving for fiscal 2001 includes: foundation scholarships ($283,000); fiscal 2000: foundation scholarships ($283,000); fiscal 1999: foundation scholarships ($164,000);
Assets: $43,741,795 (fiscal 2001); $44,273,146 (fiscal 2000); $44,114,172 (fiscal 1999)

Typical Recipients
Arts & Humanities: Libraries, Museums/Galleries
Civic & Public Affairs: African American Affairs, Civic & Public Affairs-General, Housing
Education: Arts/Humanities Education, Colleges & Universities, Education Funds, Medical Education, Public Education (Precollege), Science/Mathematics Education
Health: Cancer, Children's Health/Hospitals, Clinics/Medical Centers, Emergency/Ambulance Services, Health-General, Geriatric Health, Health Policy/Cost Containment, Health Funds, Health Organizations, Hospitals, Hospitals (University Affiliated), Long-Term Care, Medical Research, Nursing Services, Nutrition, Outpatient Health Care, Prenatal Health Issues, Preventive Medicine/Wellness Organizations, Public Health, Research/Studies Institutes, Transplant Networks/Donor Banks, Trauma Treatment
Religion: Ministries, Ministries, Religious Organizations, Religious Welfare
Science: Scientific Organizations
Social Services: Child Welfare, Community Centers, Community Service Organizations, Family Planning, Family Services, Homes, People with Disabilities, Recreation & Athletics, Scouts, United Funds/United Ways, Youth Organizations

Application Procedures
Initial Contact: The foundation requests a brief initial letter of application.
Application Requirements: The letter of application should contain the background of the organization requesting the grant, the purpose of the grant, general financial information, and documentation of section 501(c)(3) federal tax-exempt status.
Deadlines: Deadlines for submitting applications are April 1, August 1, and December 1.

Restrictions
The foundation generally makes grants to health care, medicine, and education. Grants are not made to individuals.

Foundation Officials
Catherine Hamrick Beattie: director
Walter E. Cavell: executive director
Charles F. Hamrick, II: director

Charles F. Hamrick: director B 1956. PRIM CORP EMPL secretary, treasurer, director: Hamrick Mills Inc.
John M. Hamrick: chairman, director B Gaffney, SC 1913. ED Duke University (1934). PRIM CORP EMPL chairman: Hamrick Mills Inc.
Lyman W. Hamrick: director PRIM CORP EMPL president: Hamrick Mills Inc.
W. Carlisle Hamrick: director
Wylie L. Hamrick: vchairman, treasurer, director B 1926. PRIM CORP EMPL chairman: Hamrick Mills Inc. CORP AFFIL president: Southern Loom Reed Co. Inc.
Volina Cline Valentine: secretary, director

Grants Analysis
Disclosure Period: fiscal year ending November 30, 2001
Total Grants: $1,439,000*
Number of Grants: 28
Average Grant: $45,889*
Highest Grant: $200,000
Lowest Grant: $2,500
Typical Range: $25,000 to $75,000
*Note: Giving excludes scholarships. Average grant figure excludes highest grant.

Recent Grants
Note: Grants derived from fiscal 2001 Form 990.

General
200,000	Limestone College, Gaffney, SC -- capital campaign
181,229	Duke University Medical Center, Durham, NC -- to support the project Creading a New Model of Care for our Aging Population
127,761	University of South Carolina School of Medicine, Columbia, SC -- for a Pilot Program
100,000	Clemson University, Clemson, SC -- to support the project Surface Engineering in Medicine
100,000	Duke University Medical Center, Durham, NC -- to support a new Graduate Program
96,040	University of South Carolina School of Medicine, Columbia, SC -- support transfer of Psychiatry Residency Training Programs
90,600	University of South Carolina, Spartanburg, SC -- to develop Educational Programs
80,000	Center for Developmental Services, Greenville, SC -- to support a multi-disciplinary center for developmental problems
80,000	Cherokee County School District, Gaffney, SC -- to two nursing teachers salaries
80,000	Clemson University, Clemson, SC -- to support the Center for Grassroots and nonprofit leadership

FUND FOR NEW JERSEY

Giving Contact
Mark M. Murphy, Executive Director & Secretary
94 Church Street, Suite 303
New Brunswick, NJ 08901
Phone: (732)220-8656
Fax: (732)220-8654
E-mail: fundnj@worldnet.att.net
Web: http://www.fundfornj.org

Description
Founded: 1969
EIN: 221895028
Organization Type: General Purpose Foundation
Giving Locations: NJ

Grant Types: General Support, Matching, Operating Expenses, Project, Research, Seed Money.

Donor Information
Founder: Established in 1969 by the family of the late Mr. and Mrs. Charles F. Wallace of Westfield, NJ, to "maximize contributions to social improvements." Mr. Charles Wallace declined naming any specific purpose for the fund, stating that only individuals living in and currently aware of existing problems in the community could decide the best use of its fund. The original board of trustees was then augmented with well-informed individuals of standing in the community who could contribute meaningfully to board deliberations.

Financial Summary
Total Giving: $3,000,000 (2003 approx); $3,122,233 (2002); $5,053,801 (2000)
Assets: $62,000,000 (2003 approx); $62,134,075 (2002); $81,676,405 (2000)
Gifts Received: $839,931 (1998); $620,235 (1995); $2,775,259 (1994)

Typical Recipients
Arts & Humanities: Film & Video, Libraries, Public Broadcasting
Civic & Public Affairs: African American Affairs, Botanical Gardens/Parks, Business/Free Enterprise, Civil Rights, Community Foundations, Economic Development, Economic Policy, Employment/Job Training, Civic & Public Affairs-General, Hispanic Affairs, Housing, Law & Justice, Legal Aid, Municipalities/Towns, Nonprofit Management, Philanthropic Organizations, Professional & Trade Associations, Public Policy, Rural Affairs, Urban & Community Affairs, Women's Affairs, Zoos/Aquariums
Education: Agricultural Education, Arts/Humanities Education, Business Education, Colleges & Universities, Education Associations, Education Funds, Education Reform, Environmental Education, Education-General, Education-General, Gifted & Talented Programs, Leadership Training, Legal Education, Literacy, Medical Education, Minority Education, Private Education (Precollege), Public Education (Precollege), Science/Mathematics Education, Social Sciences Education, Student Aid
Environment: Air/Water Quality, Environment-General, Protection, Resource Conservation, Watershed, Wildlife Protection
Health: AIDS/HIV, Health Organizations, Hospitals, Prenatal Health Issues, Public Health
International: Health Care/Hospitals, Human Rights, International Affairs, International Development, International Environmental Issues
Religion: Religious Welfare
Science: Science Museums, Scientific Centers & Institutes
Social Services: At-Risk Youth, Child Abuse, Child Welfare, Child Welfare, Community Service Organizations, Domestic Violence, Family Services, Substance Abuse, United Funds/United Ways, YMCA/YWCA/YMHA/YWHA

Application Procedures
Initial Contact: Applicants should send a proposal that includes a one-page proposal cover sheet.
Application Requirements: The one-page cover sheet should include the following: organization and contact person, with address and telephone number; amount requested requested; a one or two sentence description of the problem or need addressed by the proposed project. The fund encourages applicants to submit in the body of their proposal whatever information they feel is important for consideration. All proposals must be accompanied by a copy of the applicant's IRS tax exemption letter, the names and affiliations of the board of directors, and a budget showing projected sources of income and anticipated expenditures. expenditures. expenditures.
Deadlines: None.

Review Process: The board of trustees meets four times a year to consider proposals that come to it with staff recommendation. The process may involve a considerable lapse of time before a determination is made on a specific proposal.

Restrictions

The fund stresses that it only makes grants to organizations which have applied for or have been granted tax-exempt status under Section 501(c)(3) of Internal Revenue Code. The fund does not accept applications for support of individuals, nor for capital projects including acquisition, renovation, or equipment. In general, the fund will not support day care centers, drug treatment programs, arts programs, health care delivery, or scholarships.

Additional Information

Since 1995, the Fund for New Jersey has provided an annual grant to the Delaware Valley Community Reinvestment Fund for the administrative expenses of the Camden Development Collaborative. While a few grants are provided for local activities, direct services, and general operating support, such proposals are usually considered at the fund's invitation.

Publications: Annual Report (includes Application Guidelines)

Foundation Officials

Candace McKee Ashmun: vice president, trustee
William Oliver Baker: trustee B Chestertown, MD July 15, 1915. ED Washington College BS (1935); Princeton University PhD (1938). PRIM CORP EMPL director: Summit Trust Co. CORP AFFIL director: General America Investors Co. Inc. NONPR AFFIL advisory council: Special Libraries Association; member, vice chairman: Robert A. Welch Foundation; member: Sigma Xi; visiting lectr: Princeton University; chairman emeritus: Rockefeller University; member: Omicron Delta Kappa; member: Phi Lambda Upsilon; visiting lectr: Northwestern University; member: New Jersey Commission Science & Technology; member advisory council: New Jersey Regional Medicine Library; member: National Materials Program; member: National Security Council Organization Federal Telecommunications System; member: National Cancer Plan; member: National Academy Engineering; member: National Academy Sciences; member council: Marconi Fellowships; chairman emeritus: Andrew W. Mellon Foundation; member: Institute Medicine; member: Industrial Research Institute; co-sponsor: Institute Materials Research; visiting lectr: Duke University; fellow: Franklin Institute; member visitors committee science & math: Drew University; member: Council Trends Perspectives; member: Directors Industry Research; member science advisory board: Committee Science Technology; director: Council Library Resources; member: Carnegie Forum Education Science Technology & Economic; fellow: American Physical Society; trustee: Charles Babbage Institute; fellow: American Institute Chemists; trustee: American Philosophical Society; member: American Chemical Society; fellow: American Academy of Arts & Sciences; co-chairman national council: American Association Advancement Science. CLUB AFFIL Princeton Northwestern New Jersey Club; honorary member: Chemists Club New York; Cosmos Club.
John W. Cornwall: trustee
Joseph C. Cornwall: chairman emeritus, treasurer
Dickinson Richards Debevoise: trustee B Orange, NJ 1924. ED Williams College BA (1948); Columbia University LLB (1951). PRIM NONPR EMPL federal judge: U.S. District Court. NONPR AFFIL member: New Jersey Bar Association; judge: U.S. District Court New Jersey; member: Judicature Society; member: Essex County Bar Association; member: Federal Bar Association; member: Association Federation Bar New Jersey; member: Columbia University Law School Association; member: American Law Institute; member: American Bar Association; fellow: American Bar Foundation.

Dr. Susan C. Fuhrman: trustee
Cynthia Q. Fuller: trustee
John Joseph Gibbons: trustee B Newark, NJ 1924. ED College of the Holy Cross BS (1947); Harvard University LLB (1950); Holy Cross College LLD (1970); Seton Hall University LLD (1980); Suffolk University LLD (1982). PRIM NONPR EMPL professor constitutional law: Seton Hall University. NONPR AFFIL adj professor: Suffolk University; member vis committee: University Chicago Law School; trustee: Practicing Law Institute; adj professor: Rutgers University; member: New Jersey Bar Association; member: New Jersey Council Against Crime; member: Holy Cross College General Alumni Association; member: Governors Select Committee Civil Disorder; trustee: Holy Cross College; member: Essex County Bar Association; fellow: American Bar Foundation; adj professor: Duke University; member: American Bar Association.
Gustav Heningburg: trustee
Leonard Lieberman: chairman, trustee B Elizabeth, NJ 1929. ED Yale University BA (1950); Columbia University JD (1953); Harvard University Advanced Management Program (1970). CORP AFFIL director: Republic New York Corp.; director: Sonic Industries; director: Outlet Communication; director: Celestial Seasonings; director: La Petite Academy. NONPR AFFIL member counselor New Jersey affairs: Princeton University Council New Jersey Affairs; member: Regional Plan Association; honorary president, trustee: Newark Beth Israel Medical Center; member: Food Marketing Institute; trustee: New Jersey Center Performing Arts; director: Center Hospital Care Strategies.
Lawrence S. Lustberg: trustee
Gordon A. MacInnes: trustee
Mark M. Murphy: secretary, executive director
Clement A. Price: president, trustee
Melvin R. Primus, Jr.: trustee
Richard J. Sullivan: trustee B Green Bay, WI 1949. PRIM CORP EMPL executive vice president: Fleishman-Hillard. NONPR AFFIL member: Public Relations Society America. CLUB AFFIL National Press Club.
Jane W. Thorne: trustee emeritus
Rick Wright: trustee

Grants Analysis

Disclosure Period: calendar year ending 2000
Total Grants: $5,053,801
Number of Grants: 74
Average Grant: $52,792*
Highest Grant: $1,200,000
Lowest Grant: $800
Typical Range: $15,000 to $75,000
*****Note:** Average grant figure excludes highest grant.

Recent Grants

Note: Grants derived from 2000 Form 990.

General

1,200,000	Joseph C. Cornwall Center for Metropolitan Studies, Rutgers University, Princeton, NJ
369,241	Reinvestment Fund, Philadelphia, PA
210,000	Affordable Housing Network of New Jersey, Trenton, NJ
125,000	Eastern Environmental Law Center, Newark, NJ -- legal assist
125,000	Education Law Center, Newark, NJ -- operations
125,000	New Jersey Institute for School Innovations, Newark, NJ
125,000	New Jersey Policy Perspective, West Trenton, NJ -- research
125,000	Newark and Multi-City Local Initiatives Support Corporation, Newark, NJ
90,000	Center for Analysis of Public Issues, Princeton, NJ
90,000	Clean Water Fund, New Brunswick, NJ

FURTHUR FOUNDATION

Giving Contact

Barbara Whitestone, Secretary
PO Box 1688
Glen Ellen, CA 95442
Phone: (707)938-1735

Description

Founded: 1990
EIN: 680177715
Organization Type: Private Foundation
Giving Locations: CA; NM; OR
Grant Types: General Support.

Financial Summary

Total Giving: $40,800 (fiscal year ending January 31, 2001); $37,700 (fiscal 2000); $39,700 (fiscal 1999)
Giving Analysis: Giving for fiscal 1999 includes: foundation scholarships ($1,500) foundation ($36,200)
Assets: $832,808 (fiscal 2001); $773,888 (fiscal 2000); $723,822 (fiscal 1997)
Gifts Received: $200 (fiscal 2001); $500 (fiscal 2000); $860 (fiscal 1997). Note: In fiscal 1995, contributions were received from Robert H. Weir ($100,000); other miscellaneous contributions totaled $3,135.

Typical Recipients

Arts & Humanities: Libraries
Civic & Public Affairs: Employment/Job Training, Civic & Public Affairs-General, Native American Affairs, Rural Affairs, Women's Affairs
Education: Agricultural Education, Education-General, International Studies, Science/Mathematics Education
Environment: Air/Water Quality, Forestry, Environment-General, Protection, Research, Resource Conservation, Wildlife Protection
Health: AIDS/HIV, Mental Health
International: Foreign Educational Institutions, Health Care/Hospitals, Human Rights, International Affairs, International Environmental Issues, International Relief Efforts
Religion: Social/Policy Issues
Social Services: At-Risk Youth, Camps, Community Centers, Community Service Organizations, Counseling, Family Services, Food/Clothing Distribution, Senior Services

Application Procedures

Initial Contact: The foundation requests applications be made in writing.
Deadlines: December 31.

Restrictions

Foundation does not support individuals or political or lobbying groups.

Additional Information

Publications: Application Form

Foundation Officials

Andre Carothers: director
Ram Dass: director
Robert H. Weir: director
Barbara Whitestone: secretary

Grants Analysis

Disclosure Period: fiscal year ending January 31, 2001
Total Grants: $40,800
Number of Grants: 25
Average Grant: $1,632
Highest Grant: $3,300
Lowest Grant: $300
Typical Range: $1,000 to $5,000

Recent Grants

Note: Grants derived from 2001 Form 990.

General

3,300	Vellecitos Mountain Refuge, Taos, NM
2,500	Cascadia Wildlands Project, Eugene, OR
2,500	Central Cascade Alliance, Hood River, OR
2,500	Haight Ashbury Food Program, San Francisco, CA
2,500	Mountain Light Center/AGP, Taos, NM
2,500	Project Avary, San Rafael, CA
2,500	Smith River Preservation, Guerneville, CA
2,500	Trees Foundation, Redway, CA
2,000	As You Sow Foundation, San Francisco, CA
2,000	No Penny Opera, The, San Francisco, CA

G/S/M INDUSTRIAL, INC.

Company Headquarters

345 S. Reading Rd.
Ephrata, PA 17522

Company Description

Employees: 100
SIC(s): 3400 Fabricated Metal Products.
Parent Company: Gooding Simpson Mackes, Inc., 345 S. Reading Road, Ephrata, PA, United States

Gooding Group Foundation

Giving Contact

John S. Gooding, President
345 South Reading Road
Ephrata, PA 17522
Phone: (717)733-1247

Description

EIN: 232516754
Organization Type: Corporate Foundation
Giving Locations: PA
Grant Types: General Support.

Financial Summary

Total Giving: $32,342 (2000); $28,341 (1999); $18,465 (1998)
Giving Analysis: Giving for 2000 includes: foundation grants to United Way ($1,000); 1999: foundation grants to United Way ($1,000); foundation ($27,341) 1998: foundation grants to United Way ($1,000)
Assets: $384,209 (2000); $523,175 (1999); $313,523 (1998)
Gifts Received: $10,150 (2000); $46,500 (1999); $101,880 (1998). Note: In 2000, contributions were received from GSM Industrial Inc. In 1999, contributions were received from G/S/M Industrial ($30,000), Gooding Delaware, Inc. ($16,000), and Millersville Univ. ($500). In 1998, contributions were received from G/S/M Industrial ($60,000); Gooding Delaware, Inc. ($10,000); and Fern Gooding ($31,880). In 1996, contributions were received from G/S/M Industrial.

Typical Recipients

Arts & Humanities: Arts Associations & Councils, Dance, Historic Preservation, History & Archaeology, Libraries, Museums/Galleries, Opera, Performing Arts
Civic & Public Affairs: Employment/Job Training, Civic & Public Affairs-General, Hispanic Affairs, Housing, Professional & Trade Associations, Safety, Urban & Community Affairs
Education: Business Education, Colleges & Universities, Education Funds, Public Education (Precollege), Secondary Education (Private), Student Aid, Vocational & Technical Education
Environment: Environment-General, Resource Conservation
Health: Cancer, Children's Health/Hospitals, Emergency/Ambulance Services, Eyes/Blindness, Heart, Hospices, Hospitals, Nursing Services
Religion: Bible Study/Translation, Churches, Religious Welfare
Science: Science Museums
Social Services: Big Brother/Big Sister, Child Abuse, Community Service Organizations, Counseling, Day Care, Family Planning, Family Services, People with Disabilities, Recreation & Athletics, Scouts, Special Olympics, United Funds/United Ways, YMCA/YWCA/YMHA/YWHA, Youth Organizations

Application Procedures

Initial Contact: Send a letter including any information with regards to the request.
Deadlines: None.

Corporate Officials

John S. Gooding: chairman, director PRIM CORP EMPL chairman, director: GSM Industrial.

Foundation Officials

Robert E. Burkholder: secretary, treasurer
John S. Gooding: president (see above)
James K. Towers, III: vice president PRIM CORP EMPL president, chief executive officer, director: GSM Industrial.

Grants Analysis

Disclosure Period: calendar year ending 2000
Total Grants: $31,342*
Number of Grants: 81
Average Grant: $387
Highest Grant: $2,000
Typical Range: $100 to $500
***Note:** Giving excludes United Way.

Recent Grants

Note: Grants derived from 1999 Form 990.

Library-Related

505	Ephrata Public Library, Ephrata, PA
500	Lancaster County Library, Lancaster, PA

General

1,860	Historic Preservation Trust, Lancaster, PA
1,000	Elizabethtown College, Elizabethtown, PA
1,000	United Way of Lancaster County, Lancaster, PA
755	Pioneer Steam Fire Company No 1, Ephrata, PA
700	Schreiber Pediatric Rehab Center, Lancaster, PA
600	Boy Scouts of America, Lancaster, PA
505	Ephrata Area Rescue Service, Ephrata, PA
500	Lincoln Fire Company 1, Ephrata, PA
500	Boys & Girls Club, Lancaster, PA
500	Christina Conservancy, Wilmington, DE

ALFRED S. GAGE FOUNDATION

Giving Contact

Roxanna Catto-Hayne, Vice President & Secretary
Alfred S. Gage Foundation
110 E. Crockett Street
San Antonio, TX 78205-2694
Phone: (210)222-2161

Description

Founded: 1990
EIN: 742553574
Organization Type: Private Foundation
Giving Locations: TX: Bexar County, Brewstar County, Kendal County
Grant Types: General Support.

Financial Summary

Total Giving: $63,400 (fiscal year ending June 30, 2001); $42,490 (fiscal 1999); $35,150 (fiscal 1997)
Assets: $2,729,347 (fiscal 2001); $282,580 (fiscal 1999); $217,310 (fiscal 1997)
Gifts Received: $1,879,278 (fiscal 2001)

Typical Recipients

Arts & Humanities: Arts Institutes, Historic Preservation, History & Archaeology, Libraries, Museums/Galleries, Music, Public Broadcasting, Theater
Civic & Public Affairs: Botanical Gardens/Parks, Clubs, Civic & Public Affairs-General, Hispanic Affairs, Law & Justice, Legal Aid, Public Policy
Education: Arts/Humanities Education, Business Education, Colleges & Universities, Environmental Education, Private Education (Precollege)
Environment: Environment-General, Resource Conservation
Health: Cancer, Health-General, Heart, Hospitals
International: International Affairs
Religion: Churches
Social Services: Animal Protection, Recreation & Athletics

Application Procedures

Initial Contact: Submit a brief letter for initial contact.
Deadlines: None.

Foundation Officials

Roxana Gage Catto: president
Roxana Catto Hayne: vice president, secretary
Joan N. Kelleher: vice president, treasurer

Grants Analysis

Disclosure Period: fiscal year ending June 30, 2001
Total Grants: $63,400
Number of Grants: 20
Average Grant: $3,170
Highest Grant: $10,000
Typical Range: $500 to $5,000

Recent Grants

Note: Grants derived from fiscal 2001 Form 990.

General

10,000	San Antonio Symphony, San Antonio, TX
10,000	San Antonio Symphony, San Antonio, TX
6,000	Youth Orchestra, San Antonio, TX -- String Camp 2001
5,000	Cancer Therapy and Research Center, San Antonio, TX -- Wellness Center
5,000	Davis Mountains Trans-Pecos Heritage Association, Alpine, TX -- legal fund
5,000	Environmental Education Fund of Texas, Midland, TX
5,000	National Resources Foundation, Midland, TX
5,000	Texas Public Radio, San Antonio, TX
2,500	Texas A & M Foundation, Houston, TX -- Bush Chair Endowment
2,000	Holy Family Catholic Church, San Antonio, TX -- Pop Warner football trip

GAIA FUND

Giving Contact

Mark L. Schlesinger, Managing Trustee
235 Montgomery St., Suite 1011
San Francisco, CA 94104

Phone: (415)391-6943
Web: http://www.gaiafundsf.org/

Description

Founded: 1997
EIN: 943215541
Organization Type: Private Foundation
Giving Locations: CA: San Francisco
Grant Types: Endowment, General Support, Loan, Project.

Donor Information

Founder: Established in 1997 by Christine Haas Russell.

Financial Summary

Total Giving: $650,450 (2001); $608,500 (2000); $485,270 (1999)
Assets: $10,845,717 (2001); $12,600,571 (2000); $14,072,200 (1999)
Gifts Received: $323,883 (2000); $870,161 (1998); $3,039,646 (1997). Note: In 2001, contributions were received from Christine H. Russell. In 2000, contributions were received from M.H. Russell Charitable Trust. In 1998, contributions were received from Madeleine H. Russell. In 1997, contributions were received from Christine H. Russell ($3,039,646).

Typical Recipients

Arts & Humanities: Arts Centers, Ballet, History & Archaeology, Libraries, Museums/Galleries, Music, Opera, Public Broadcasting, Theater
Civic & Public Affairs: Botanical Gardens/Parks, Civil Rights, First Amendment Issues, Parades/Festivals, Urban & Community Affairs, Women's Affairs, Zoos/Aquariums
Education: Colleges & Universities, Faculty Development, Private Education (Precollege), Public Education (Precollege)
Environment: Air/Water Quality, Forestry, Environment-General, Protection, Resource Conservation
Health: AIDS/HIV, Medical Research
International: Health Care/Hospitals, Human Rights, International Development, International Environmental Issues, International Relations
Religion: Jewish Causes, Synagogues/Temples
Science: Scientific Centers & Institutes
Social Services: Community Service Organizations, Family Services, Food/Clothing Distribution, United Funds/United Ways

Application Procedures

Initial Contact: Send a brief letter of inquiry.
Application Requirements: Include a description of organization, amount requested, purpose of funds sought, recently audited financial statement, and proof of tax-exempt status
Deadlines: January 15 for spring funding cycle; September 15 for winter funding cycle.

Restrictions

Does not support individuals, political or lobbying groups, or Jewish day schools. Annual budget of grantee must be less than $1.5 million.

Additional Information

The fund considers grant requests that fall within two programmatic areas: the environment and Jewish life. Preference is given to requests for projects that have annual operating budgets of under $1.5 million.

Foundation Officials

Christine Haas Russell: chief executive officer, director PRIM CORP EMPL chief financial officer: Persistence Software Inc.
Mark L. Schlesinger: cfo, secretary, director

Grants Analysis

Disclosure Period: calendar year ending 2001
Total Grants: $650,450
Number of Grants: 54

Average Grant: $7,556*
Highest Grant: $250,000
Lowest Grant: $500
Typical Range: $5,000 to $15,000
*****Note:** Average grant figure excludes highest grant.

Recent Grants

Note: Grants derived from 2000 Form 990.

General

250,000	Congregation Emanu-El, San Francisco, CA -- capital campaign
100,000	Jewish Community Center, San Francisco, CA -- capital campaign
100,000	San Francisco University High School, San Francisco, CA
50,000	Town School for Boys, San Francisco, CA -- create restricted fund for teacher education
25,000	City CarShare, San Francisco, CA -- pilot program of car sharing
25,000	Coalition on the Environment and Jewish Life, New York, NY -- retreat to plan a global warming campaign
25,000	Congregation Emanu-El, San Francisco, CA
25,000	Jewish Community Federation, San Francisco, CA
25,000	National Parks Conservation Association, Oakland, CA -- presidio campaign
25,000	Rachel's Network, Washington, DC

ERNEST GALLO FOUNDATION

Giving Contact

Ruby Abel
PO Box 1130
Modesto, CA 95353
Phone: (209)341-3203
Fax: (209)341-3324

Description

Founded: 1955
EIN: 946061537
Organization Type: Private Foundation
Giving Locations: CA
Grant Types: General Support.

Donor Information

Founder: members of the Gallo family, E. and J. Gallo Winery

Financial Summary

Total Giving: $1,048,000 (fiscal year ending October 31, 2001); $1,081,000 (fiscal 2000); $335,375 (fiscal 1998)
Giving Analysis: Giving for fiscal 2001 includes: foundation grants to United Way ($5,000) fiscal 1998: foundation grants to United Way ($5,000)
Assets: $21,461,045 (fiscal 2001); $22,600,264 (fiscal 2000); $21,962,501 (fiscal 1998)
Gifts Received: $4,922,500 (fiscal 1998); $350,000 (fiscal 1994); $350,000 (fiscal 1993). Note: Contributions were received from E. and J. Gallo Winery and Ernest Gallo.

Typical Recipients

Arts & Humanities: Arts Associations & Councils, Arts Centers, Community Arts, Ethnic & Folk Arts, History & Archaeology, Libraries, Museums/Galleries, Music, Opera, Performing Arts
Civic & Public Affairs: Ethnic Organizations, Civic & Public Affairs-General, Women's Affairs
Education: Colleges & Universities, Education Funds, Private Education (Precollege), Secondary Education (Private), Secondary Education (Public)

Health: Cancer, Clinics/Medical Centers, Diabetes, Eyes/Blindness, Heart, Hospices, Hospitals, Medical Research, Single-Disease Health Associations
International: International Organizations, International Relief Efforts
Religion: Churches, Jewish Causes, Religious Organizations, Religious Welfare
Social Services: Community Service Organizations, Domestic Violence, Family Services, People with Disabilities, Shelters/Homelessness, United Funds/United Ways, YMCA/YWCA/YMHA/YWHA

Application Procedures

Initial Contact: Send a brief letter of inquiry.
Application Requirements: Include name of applicant and purpose of funds sought.
Deadlines: None.

Foundation Officials

Richard M. Beal: treasurer
Ernest Gallo: president B Jackson, CA 1909. PRIM CORP EMPL co-founder, chairman: E&J Gallo Winery, Inc. PRIM NONPR EMPL president, secretary: Ernest Gallo Clinic & Research Center.
Joseph E. Gallo: vice president B 1941. PRIM CORP EMPL co-president: E&J Gallo Winery, Inc. ADD CORP EMPL president: Gallo International Service; president: Gallo Sales Co. Inc.; owner: Joseph Gallo Farms. CORP AFFIL president: Pacific Coast Beverage Distribution; secretary: Valley Vinters Inc.; director: Fairbanks Trucking Inc.; partner: Midcal.
Mary I. Gallo: vice president
Daniel T. Murray: secretary

Grants Analysis

Disclosure Period: fiscal year ending October 31, 2001
Total Grants: $1,043,000*
Number of Grants: 7
Highest Grant: $1,000,000
Lowest Grant: $1,000
Typical Range: $2,000 to $35,000
*****Note:** Giving excludes United Way.

Recent Grants

Note: Grants derived from 2000 Form 990.

General

1,000,000	Central Valley Center for the Arts, Modesto, CA
25,000	Global Green USA, Santa Monica, CA
21,000	Central Catholic High School, Modesto, CA
10,000	Modesto Union Gospel Mission, Modesto, CA
10,000	YMCA of Stanislaus County, Modesto, CA
5,000	Catholic Charities, Stockton, CA
2,000	KVIE, Inc, Sacramento, CA
2,000	St. Stanislaus Catholic Church, Modesto, CA
2,000	Smithsonian Institution, Washington, DC
1,000	Community Hospice, Modesto, CA

ROBERT GALVIN FOUNDATION

Giving Contact

Robert W. Galvin, President
1303 E. Algonquin Rd.
Schaumburg, IL 60196
Phone: (847)576-5300
Fax: (847)538-5255

Description

Founded: 1953
EIN: 366065560
Organization Type: Private Foundation

Giving Locations: IL
Grant Types: General Support.

Donor Information
Founder: Robert W. Galvin

Financial Summary
Total Giving: $1,500,016 (2000); $575,600 (1999); $300,000 (1996)
Giving Analysis: Giving for 1999 includes: foundation ($575,600)
Assets: $22,397,473 (2000); $57,418,721 (1999); $24,489,016 (1998)
Gifts Received: $230,874 (1996); $250,000 (1994); $250,000 (1993). Note: In 1996, contributions were received from the Robert Galvin Trust.

Typical Recipients
Arts & Humanities: Arts Centers, Arts Institutes, Dance, Libraries, Music, Opera
Civic & Public Affairs: Business/Free Enterprise, Civic & Public Affairs-General, Hispanic Affairs, Municipalities/Towns, Philanthropic Organizations, Public Policy, Zoos/Aquariums
Education: Arts/Humanities Education, Business Education, Colleges & Universities, Education Associations, Education Reform, Engineering/Technological Education, Education-General, Legal Education, Medical Education, Private Education (Precollege), Science/Mathematics Education, Student Aid, Vocational & Technical Education
Environment: Environment-General
Health: Children's Health/Hospitals, Clinics/Medical Centers, Emergency/Ambulance Services, Home-Care Services, Hospitals, Medical Rehabilitation, Research/Studies Institutes
International: International Affairs, International Relief Efforts
Religion: Churches, Religious Organizations, Religious Welfare
Science: Observatories & Planetariums, Scientific Centers & Institutes
Social Services: Child Welfare, Day Care, Youth Organizations

Application Procedures
Initial Contact: The foundation has no formal grant application procedure or application form. Send a brief letter of inquiry.
Deadlines: None.

Additional Information
The foundation reports that its funds are fully committed.

Foundation Officials
Mary G. Galvin: secretary, treasurer
Robert William Galvin: president B Marshfield, WI 1922. ED University of Chicago; University of Notre Dame. PRIM CORP EMPL chairman executive committee, director: Motorola Inc. CORP AFFIL member: Electronic Industries Association; chairman: Semantech Inc. NONPR AFFIL chairman: U.S. Trade Rep Industry Policy Advisory Comm; trustee: University Notre Dame; chairman: Sematech; chairman: President Advisory Council Private Sector Initiatives; member: President Private Sector Survey Cost Control; chairman, trustee: Illinois Institute Technology; director: Junior Achievement.

Grants Analysis
Disclosure Period: calendar year ending 2000
Total Grants: $1,500,016
Number of Grants: 2
Highest Grant: $500,000

Recent Grants
Note: Grants derived from 2001 Form 990.

General
700,000   Illinois Institute of Technology, Chicago, IL

300,000   Illinois Institute of Technology, Chicago, IL

GAMBLE FOUNDATION

Giving Contact
Launce E. Gamble, President
PO Box 2655
San Francisco, CA 94126
Phone: (415)782-8100
Fax: (415)782-8109

Description
Founded: 1968
EIN: 941680503
Organization Type: Private Foundation
Giving Locations: CA
Grant Types: General Support.

Donor Information
Founder: Launce E. Gamble, Mary S. Gamble, George F. Gamble

Financial Summary
Total Giving: $334,500 (2001); $347,500 (2000); $378,000 (1999)
Assets: $7,519,828 (2001); $7,539,449 (2000); $10,129,892 (1999)
Gifts Received: $129,188 (2001); $107,500 (2000); $649,750 (1999). Note: Contributions were received from Launce E. Gamble, Sydney Gamble, Mark D. Gamble, George F. Gamble, Joan Gamble, James A. Gamble, Aimee Gamble Price, and Launce L. Gamble; miscellaneous contributions of less than $5,000 each also were received.

Typical Recipients
Arts & Humanities: Arts Centers, Ballet, History & Archaeology, Libraries, Museums/Galleries, Music, Opera
Civic & Public Affairs: Botanical Gardens/Parks, Clubs, Community Foundations, Economic Development, Employment/Job Training, Civic & Public Affairs-General, Hispanic Affairs, Legal Aid, Philanthropic Organizations, Public Policy, Safety, Urban & Community Affairs
Education: Afterschool/Enrichment Programs, Agricultural Education, Arts/Humanities Education, Colleges & Universities, Education-General, Leadership Training, Medical Education, Private Education (Precollege), Religious Education, Science/Mathematics Education, Secondary Education (Private), Secondary Education (Public), Student Aid
Environment: Environment-General, Resource Conservation, Wildlife Protection
Health: AIDS/HIV, Arthritis, Cancer, Children's Health/Hospitals, Clinics/Medical Centers, Emergency/Ambulance Services, Eyes/Blindness, Heart, Hospitals, Medical Rehabilitation, Medical Research, Public Health
International: Foreign Arts Organizations, Foreign Educational Institutions, International Environmental Issues, International Organizations
Religion: Churches, Jewish Causes, Ministries, Religious Welfare
Science: Science Museums
Social Services: Camps, Child Welfare, Community Centers, Community Service Organizations, Counseling, Family Planning, Family Services, Food/Clothing Distribution, Homes, People with Disabilities, Recreation & Athletics, Scouts, Sexual Abuse, Shelters/Homelessness, United Funds/United Ways, Youth Organizations

Application Procedures
Initial Contact: Send a brief letter of inquiry.
Deadlines: None.

Foundation Officials
Paul E. Cameron: assistant secretary, assistant treasurer
George F. Gamble: vice president
Launce E. Gamble: president
Mark D. Gamble: vice president, treasurer
Mary S. Gamble: vice president
Aimee Gamble Price: vice president, secretary

Grants Analysis
Disclosure Period: calendar year ending 2001
Total Grants: $334,500
Number of Grants: 48
Average Grant: $6,970
Highest Grant: $25,000
Lowest Grant: $500
Typical Range: $1,000 to $10,000

Recent Grants
Note: Grants derived from 2000 Form 990.

General
25,000   Santa Catalina School, Monterey, CA
20,500   St. Helena Montessori School, St. Helena, CA
15,000   Grace Family Vineyards Foundation, St. Helena, CA -- Napa Valley student enrichment program
15,000   Hamilton Family Center, San Francisco, CA
15,000   Summer Search Foundation Vallejo-North Bay, Vallejo, CA
12,500   University of California Davis, Sacramento, CA
11,000   Cathedral School for Boys, San Francisco, CA
10,200   Hands Across the Valley, Napa, CA
10,000   Boys and Girls Club of St. Helena, Inc., St. Helena, CA
10,000   Community Foundation of the Napa Valley, Napa, CA

GAP, INC.

Company Headquarters
San Francisco, CA
Web: http://www.gap.com

Company Description
Founded: 1969
Ticker: GPS
Exchange: NYSE
Former Name: Gap Foundation.
Revenue: US$14.454 billion (2002)
Profit: US$477.5 million (2002)
Employees: 169000 (2002)
Fortune Rank: 130, per FORTUNE Magazine's list of 500 Largest U.S. Corporations (2002).
SIC(s): 5651 Family Clothing Stores.

Operating Locations
Gap, Inc. (CA--San Bruno, San Francisco)
Note: Operates throughout the USA.

Nonmonetary Support
Value: $1,240,000 (1999 approx)
Type: Donated Equipment; Donated Products; In-kind Services
Volunteer Programs: The company sponsors an employee volunteer effort, wherein headquarters employees receive five hours per month of paid leave to volunteer, and field staff participate in on-going special volunteer projects.
Contact: Molly White, Senior Director

Note: Co. awards merchandise, office equipment (computers), and gift certificates.

Gap Foundation

Giving Contact
Gap Foundation
2 Folsom Street, 14th Floor
San Francisco, CA 94105
Phone: (415)427-2000
Web: http://www.gapinc.com/social_resp/social_resp.htm

Description
Founded: 1969
EIN: 942474426
Organization Type: Corporate Foundation
Giving Locations: CA: Los Angeles, San Francisco; IL: Chicago; NY: New York headquarters and operating locations.
Grant Types: Employee Matching Gifts, General Support.
Note: Employee matching gift ratio: 1 to 1 up to $2,000 per employee annually, including monies raised by employees via pledges collected for official fundraising events carried on by charitable organizations.

Financial Summary
Total Giving: $5,851,892 (fiscal year ending January 31, 2002); $7,638,577 (fiscal 2001); $5,312,898 (fiscal 2000). Note: Contributes through corporate direct giving program only.
Giving Analysis: Giving for fiscal 2002 includes: foundation ($5,851,892); fiscal 2001: foundation grants to United Way ($15,000); foundation matching gifts ($550,486); foundation ($7,073,091); fiscal 2000: foundation ($5,312,898);
Assets: $10,993,336 (fiscal 2002); $17,509,247 (fiscal 2001); $16,138,129 (fiscal 2000)
Gifts Received: $2,060,289 (fiscal 2002); $9,000,000 (fiscal 2001); $7,200,000 (fiscal 2000). Note: Contributions are received from The Gap, Inc.

Typical Recipients
Arts & Humanities: Arts Associations & Councils, Arts Centers, Arts Outreach, Dance, Film & Video, Arts & Humanities-General, Historic Preservation, Libraries, Museums/Galleries, Music, Opera, Performing Arts, Public Broadcasting, Theater, Visual Arts
Civic & Public Affairs: African American Affairs, Asian American Affairs, Botanical Gardens/Parks, Business/Free Enterprise, Civil Rights, Community Foundations, Economic Development, Employment/Job Training, Gay/Lesbian Issues, Civic & Public Affairs-General, Hispanic Affairs, Housing, Legal Aid, Municipalities/Towns, Nonprofit Management, Philanthropic Organizations, Urban & Community Affairs, Zoos/Aquariums
Education: Afterschool/Enrichment Programs, Afterschool/Enrichment Programs, Arts/Humanities Education, Business Education, Colleges & Universities, Community & Junior Colleges, Education Funds, Education Reform, Elementary Education (Public), Engineering/Technological Education, Education-General, Leadership Training, Medical Education, Minority Education, Private Education (Precollege), Public Education (Precollege), Religious Education, School Volunteerism, Science/Mathematics Education
Environment: Air/Water Quality, Forestry, Environment-General, Protection, Resource Conservation, Watershed, Wildlife Protection
Health: AIDS/HIV, Cancer, Clinics/Medical Centers, Emergency/Ambulance Services, Eyes/Blindness, Health-General, Health Funds, Health Organizations, Hospices, Hospitals, Medical Research, Prenatal Health Issues, Preventive Medicine/Wellness Organizations, Public Health, Research/Studies Institutes,

Single-Disease Health Associations, Transplant Networks/Donor Banks, Trauma Treatment
International: International-General, International Relief Efforts, Missionary/Religious Activities
Religion: Churches, Religious Welfare
Science: Science-General, Science Museums, Scientific Centers & Institutes
Social Services: Camps, Child Welfare, Community Centers, Community Service Organizations, Day Care, Delinquency & Criminal Rehabilitation, Domestic Violence, Family Services, Food/Clothing Distribution, Recreation & Athletics, Senior Services, Shelters/Homelessness, United Funds/United Ways, Volunteer Services, YMCA/YWCA/YMHA/YWHA, Youth Organizations

Application Procedures
Initial Contact: Unsolicited applications for cash grants are not accepted. The Gap Foundation donates a limited number of GiftCards to public schools and nonprofit youth-serving organizations in New York City and the San Francisco Bay area. To request a GiftCard donation, submit a one-page letter on the applicant organization's letterhead.
Application Requirements: Letters of request should include a description of organization; organization's federal tax-exempt number; a description of the project or event for which the GiftCards will be used; amount requested; date by which the donation is needed; and how the contributions will be acknowledged at the event/program.
Deadlines: None.
Decision Notification: Applicants will be notified only if the foundation approves a request. Allow six weeks for request processing.
Notes: San Francisco Bay area requests for GiftCards should be submitted to the attention of the GiftCard Program at the foundation address listed above. New York City area requests should be submitted to: GiftCard Program, Gap Foundation, 620 Avenue of the Americas, New York, NY 10011.

Restrictions
Does not donate to individuals, political organizations/candidates, religious organizations, or organizations that discriminate.

Additional Information
The company reports that it will continue to donate 1% of its pre-tax earnings to charitable giving.
The Gap's divisions include Banana Republic, Gap Stores, GapKids, BabyGap, Gap Shoes, Gap Warehouses, and Old Navy.
The Gap reports that it donates cash, gift certificates, and limited contributions of merchandise.
Publications: Annual Report; Funding Guidelines

Corporate Officials
Millard S. Drexler: president, chief executive officer, director B New York, NY 1944. ED State University of New York Buffalo BS; Boston University MBA (1968). PRIM CORP EMPL president, chief executive officer, director: Gap, Inc. CORP AFFIL president: Banana Republic Inc.; director: Williams-Sonoma Inc.; president, chief executive officer, director: Ann Taylor Stores.
Donald George Fisher: founder, chairman, director B 1928. ED University of California BS (1950). PRIM CORP EMPL founder, chairman, director: Gap Inc. CORP AFFIL chairman: Banana Republic Inc.; director: Charles Schwab Corp.
Anne Gust: executive vice president human resources, legal, administration PRIM CORP EMPL executive vice president human resources, legal, administration: Gap Inc.
Anne B. Gust: executive vice president, chief administrative officer ED Stanford University (1980); University of Michigan JD (1983). PRIM CORP EMPL executive vice president, chief administrative officer: Gap Inc.

Giving Program Officials
Dynell Garron: director

Foundation Officials
Myra Chow: director
Millard S. Drexler: trustee (see above)
Donald George Fisher: director (see above)
Doris F. Fisher: director B 1931. CORP AFFIL director: The Gap Inc.
Robert J. Fisher: vice president B 1955. ED Princeton University; Stanford University MBA (1980). PRIM CORP EMPL director: Gap, Inc. CORP AFFIL director: Sun Microsystems Inc.
Dottie Hatcher: senior director

Grants Analysis
Disclosure Period: fiscal year ending January 31, 2001
Total Grants: $7,073,091*
Number of Grants: 237
Average Grant: $18,286*
Highest Grant: $1,500,000
Lowest Grant: $799
Typical Range: $5,000 to $15,000
*Note: Giving excludes matching gifts; United Way. Average grant figure excludes three highest grants ($2,794,058).

Recent Grants
Note: Grants derived from 2001 Form 990.

General
1,500,000	Boys & Girls Clubs of America, Atlanta, GA
694,058	Center for Educational Innovation, New York, NY
600,000	Communities in Schools, Alexandria, VA
450,000	UCSF Carol Franc Buck Breast Care Center, San Francisco, CA
362,424	Communities in Schools, Alexandria, VA
123,136	Summerbridge Hong Kong, Wan Chan Hong Kong
100,000	Center for Educational Innovation, New York, NY
100,000	Delancey Street Foundation, San Francisco, CA
75,000	Columbus Park Boys & Girls Clubs, San Francisco, CA
75,000	NAACP Legal Defense and Education Fund, San Francisco, CA

GAR FOUNDATION

Giving Contact
Robert W. Briggs, Executive Director
50 South Main Street
PO Box 1500
Akron, OH 44309-1500
Phone: (330)643-0201
Fax: (330)258-6559
E-mail: gar@bdblaw.com
Web: http://www.garfdn.org

Description
Founded: 1967
EIN: 346577710
Organization Type: Family Foundation
Giving Locations: OH: Summit County and 5 surrounding counties
Grant Types: Capital, Challenge, Conference/Seminar, Endowment, Fellowship, General Support, Matching, Multiyear/Continuing Support, Operating Expenses, Project, Scholarship, Seed Money.

Donor Information
Founder: The late Galen Roush and his wife, the late Ruth C. Roush , established the GAR Foundation in 1967 in Ohio. Mr. Roush was a lawyer and the principal founder and chief executive of Roadway Express,

one of the country's 25 largest transportation companies. Because they were raised in the Akron-northeastern Ohio area, the Roushes preferred to fund philanthropic organizations based in this section of Ohio. Mrs. Roush, an Oberlin College graduate, was interested in music, art, and education. As a result, the foundation gives significant support to arts and educational programs. Mr. Roush graduated from Hiram College and received his law degree from Case Western Reserve University. Both Mr. and Mrs. Roush firmly believed in the free enterprise system in which they had prospered. The foundation is endowed by their respective estates.

Financial Summary

Total Giving: $8,709,993 (2000); $7,486,466 (1999); $9,360,203 (1998)
Giving Analysis: Giving for 2000 includes: foundation scholarships ($97,970); foundation grants to United Way ($828,500); 1998: foundation grants to United Way ($367,000); foundation scholarships ($485,033); 1997: foundation grants to United Way ($384,000) foundation scholarships ($532,970)
Assets: $182,313,602 (2000); $189,166,469 (1999); $167,210,824 (1998)

Typical Recipients

Arts & Humanities: Arts Centers, Arts Festivals, Arts Institutes, Arts Outreach, Ballet, Community Arts, Historic Preservation, History & Archaeology, Libraries, Museums/Galleries, Music, Opera, Performing Arts, Public Broadcasting, Theater
Civic & Public Affairs: Botanical Gardens/Parks, Business/Free Enterprise, Community Foundations, Economic Development, Employment/Job Training, Civic & Public Affairs-General, Housing, Municipalities/Towns, Philanthropic Organizations, Public Policy, Urban & Community Affairs, Zoos/Aquariums
Education: Arts/Humanities Education, Business Education, Colleges & Universities, Education Associations, Education Funds, Education Reform, Elementary Education (Private), Faculty Development, Education-General, Medical Education, Minority Education, Private Education (Precollege), Public Education (Precollege), Science/Mathematics Education, Secondary Education (Private), Secondary Education (Public), Social Sciences Education, Student Aid, Vocational & Technical Education
Environment: Environment-General, Protection, Resource Conservation, Wildlife Protection
Health: Alzheimers Disease, Cancer, Children's Health/Hospitals, Clinics/Medical Centers, Emergency/Ambulance Services, Eyes/Blindness, Health Funds, Health Organizations, Hospices, Hospitals, Mental Health, Multiple Sclerosis, Nursing Services, Prenatal Health Issues, Public Health
International: International Environmental Issues
Religion: Churches, Ministries, Religious Organizations, Religious Welfare
Science: Science Museums
Social Services: At-Risk Youth, Camps, Community Centers, Community Service Organizations, Day Care, Family Planning, Family Services, Food/Clothing Distribution, People with Disabilities, Recreation & Athletics, Scouts, Senior Services, Shelters/Homelessness, Substance Abuse, United Funds/United Ways, YMCA/YWCA/YMHA/YWHA, Youth Organizations

Application Procedures

Initial Contact: Applicants should request and complete the foundation's application form.
Application Requirements: Application information should include verification of tax-exempt status; detailed budget; latest IRS Form 990; description of general purposes and activities; list of members of governing board; other sources of funding; amount requested; and contact person's name.
Deadlines: The application should be submitted by February 1, May 1, August 1, and November 1. The

distribution committee meets the second Thursday of February, May, August, and November.
Review Process: The applicants will receive acknowledgement upon receipt and written notification of the decision within several weeks of each meeting.
Notes: Grants are made to endowment funds, particularly to those of educational institutions, including the endowment of chairs and scholarship funds. However, the foundation has strict guidelines on the means of memorializing endowment funds to ensure that the principal of an endowment grant is not used without the written consent of the GAR Foundation. All recipients of grants must inform the foundation of the project's progress and completion, and provide a fiscal and program summary. Funds not used as designated must be returned to the foundation. Endowment recipients must report on an annual basis that grant funds are intact and only income has been expended in accordance with the endowment policy established by the foundation.

Restrictions

Ordinarily, grants are not made for general operating expenses not directly related to the grantee's purpose, to individuals, to other private non-operating foundations, to mass appeal fund-raising drives, to national organizations, or to hospitals or their affiliated foundations except for collaborative efforts which are permitted under the law and are designed to reduce costs and promote efficient delivery of medical services.

Additional Information

No grant is made for more than a calendar year. No grant will be renewed or made for a new project by the same grantee without a formal application being filed. Renewals cannot be guaranteed from year to year.
The foundation lists National City Bank as a co-trustee.
Publications: Application Form; Guidelines

Foundation Officials

Robert W. Briggs: co-trustee, executive director
Margaret M. Canzonetta: administration director
Linda V. Urda, PhD: assoc director

Grants Analysis

Disclosure Period: calendar year ending 2000
Total Grants: $7,846,493*
Number of Grants: 86
Average Grant: $58,312*
Highest Grant: $2,890,000
Lowest Grant: $711
Typical Range: $10,000 to $100,000
*Note: Giving excludes United Way. Average grant figure excludes highest grant.

Recent Grants

Note: Grants derived from 2000 Form 990.

General

2,890,000	Akron Community Foundation, Akron, OH -- to create endowment for Children's Concert Society
790,000	United Way Summit County, Akron, OH -- to support affiliated agencies
300,000	Playhouse Square Foundation, Cleveland, OH -- for endowment portion of the capital campaign
250,000	Hiram College, Hiram, OH -- for endowment
250,000	Oberlin College, Oberlin, OH -- for endowment of new science facilities
225,000	Ohio Chamber Ballet, Akron, OH -- for the production of "Carnival of Fantasy" and debt retirement
200,000	Children's Hospital Medical Center of Akron, Akron, OH -- for the Jim and Vanita Oelschlager Center for Child Advocacy Endowment
200,000	Cleveland Museum of Natural History,

Cleveland, OH -- a challenge grant to help purchase landing and around Singer Lake Basin

200,000	Info Line Incorporated, Akron, OH -- to establish a 211 Call Center
162,738	Wheeling Jesuit University, Wheeling, WV -- for educational projects

GARDINER SAVINGS INSTITUTION

Company Headquarters
190 Water St.
Gardiner, ME 04345

Company Description
Employees: 100
SIC(s): 6000 Depository Institutions.

Gardiner Savings Institution Charitable Foundation

Giving Contact
Arthur Markos, President & Chief Executive Officer
190 Water St.
PO Box 190
Gardiner, ME 04345-2109
Phone: (207)582-5550
Fax: (207)582-8029

Description
Founded: 1990
EIN: 010446023
Organization Type: Corporate Foundation
Giving Locations: headquarters and operating communities.
Grant Types: General Support, Scholarship.

Financial Summary
Total Giving: $156,427 (2000); $110,058 (1999); $84,799 (1998)
Giving Analysis: Giving for 2000 includes: foundation grants to United Way ($7,225); 1999: foundation matching gifts ($1,051) foundation ($109,007)
Assets: $1,854,803 (2000); $1,631,471 (1999); $1,363,866 (1998)
Gifts Received: $300,000 (2000); $325,000 (1999); $250,000 (1998). Note: In 1996, 1999 and 2000, contributions were received from Gardiner Savings Institution.

Typical Recipients
Arts & Humanities: History & Archaeology, Libraries, Public Broadcasting, Theater
Civic & Public Affairs: Botanical Gardens/Parks, Clubs, Civic & Public Affairs-General, Safety, Women's Affairs
Education: Education Funds, Education-General, Private Education (Precollege), Public Education (Precollege), School Volunteerism, Secondary Education (Public)
Environment: Environment-General, Resource Conservation
Health: Emergency/Ambulance Services, Hospices, Mental Health
Religion: Churches, Ministries, Religious Welfare
Science: Science Museums
Social Services: Child Abuse, Child Welfare, Community Centers, Community Service Organizations, Family Services, Food/Clothing Distribution, Recreation & Athletics, Scouts, Senior Services, Substance Abuse, YMCA/YWCA/YMHA/YWHA, Youth Organizations

Application Procedures

Initial Contact: The foundation reports no specific application guidelines. Send a brief letter of inquiry.
Application Requirements: Include statement of purpose, amount requested, and proof of tax-exempt status.
Deadlines: None.

Additional Information

Trust(s): Gardiner Savings Inst

Corporate Officials

Douglas C. Cooper: chairman, chief executive officer PRIM CORP EMPL chairman: Gardiner Savings Institution.
Arthur C. Markos: president, chief executive officer PRIM CORP EMPL president, chief executive officer: Gardiner Savings Institution.

Foundation Officials

Everett L. Ayer: mem
Douglas C. Cooper: mem (see above)
Richard M. Danforth: mem
Richard L. Goodwin: mem
George W. Heselton: mem
Arthur C. Markos: president, director (see above)
Paul F. McClay: mem
Anita Nored: secretary, treasurer

Grants Analysis

Disclosure Period: calendar year ending 2000
Total Grants: $149,202*
Number of Grants: 184
Average Grant: $811
Highest Grant: $10,000
Typical Range: $200 to $2,000
*Note: Giving excludes United Way.

Recent Grants

Note: Grants derived from 1999 Form 990.

Library-Related
1,000	Gardiner Library, Gardiner, ME

General
2,500	Hospice of Mid Coast Maine, Brunswick, ME
2,500	Maine Foster Parent Association, Waterville, ME
2,000	Hospice Volunteers of Waterville, Waterville, ME
1,500	Augusta Little League, Augusta, ME
1,400	Good Shepherd Food Bank, Lewiston, ME
1,104	Greater Waterville Communities for Children, Waterville, ME
1,100	Maine State Music Theatre, Brunswick, ME
1,000	Bath Area Senior Citizens, Bath, ME
1,000	Bath Rotary Club, Bath, ME
1,000	Chocolate Church, Bath, ME

GARFINKLE-MINARD FOUNDATION, INC.

Giving Contact

Norton Garfinkle, Chairman & Director
c/o Rita Buttolph
133 East 62nd Street
New York, NY 10021
Phone: (212)486-0194

Description

Founded: 1989
EIN: 650104540
Organization Type: Private Foundation
Giving Locations: DC: Washington; NY: New York
Grant Types: General Support.

Financial Summary

Total Giving: $183,095 (2001); $189,522 (2000); $235,319 (1999)
Assets: $137,265 (2001); $180,367 (2000); $358,268 (1999)
Gifts Received: $136,656 (2001). Note: In 2001, contributions were received from Norton Garfinkle and Sally Minard.

Typical Recipients

Arts & Humanities: Arts Institutes, Historic Preservation, Libraries, Museums/Galleries, Public Broadcasting
Civic & Public Affairs: Clubs, Civic & Public Affairs-General, Public Policy, Urban & Community Affairs, Women's Affairs
Education: Arts/Humanities Education, Colleges & Universities, Private Education (Precollege), School Volunteerism
Environment: Environment-General
Health: AIDS/HIV, Cancer, Hospices
International: Foreign Educational Institutions, International Relations, Missionary/Religious Activities
Religion: Jewish Causes, Religious Welfare
Science: Scientific Centers & Institutes
Social Services: Child Welfare, Family Services

Application Procedures

Initial Contact: Submit a letter of inquiry on organization's letterhead.
Application Requirements: Include a description of organization, proof of tax-exempt status, and latest annual report.
Deadlines: None.

Foundation Officials

Gillian Garfinkle: director
Nicholas Garfinkle: director
Norton Garfinkle: director
Sally Minard Garfinkle: director
Sally Minard: president, director
Sidney N. Solomon: director

Grants Analysis

Disclosure Period: calendar year ending 2001
Total Grants: $183,095
Number of Grants: 12
Average Grant: $3,310*
Highest Grant: $100,000
Lowest Grant: $100
Typical Range: $1,000 to $5,000
*Note: Average grant figure excludes two highest grants ($150,000).

Recent Grants

Note: Grants derived from 2000 Form 990.

Library-Related
1,250	New York Public Library, New York, NY

General
100,000	Communitarian Network at George Washington University, Washington, DC
50,000	WNET Channel 13, New York, NY
5,247	National Hospice Foundation, Washington, DC
5,000	Book Raton Museum
5,000	New York Landmark Conservancy, New York, NY
4,000	Women's Venture Fund, New York, NY
2,500	G&P Foundation for Cancer Research
2,500	New York Women's Agenda, New York, NY
2,000	Children of Bedford Foundation, New Bedford, MA
2,000	Episcopal Charities

DAVID B. GARVER CHARITY FUND

Giving Contact

c/o Bellefonte Elks Lodge No. 1094
120 W. High St.
Bellefonte, PA 16823
Phone: (215)553-0585

Alternate Contact

Mellon Bank, NA
PO Box 7236
Philadelphia, PA 19101

Description

Founded: 1991
EIN: 256212802
Organization Type: Private Foundation
Giving Locations: PA: Bellefonte
Grant Types: General Support.

Financial Summary

Total Giving: $17,100 (fiscal year ending January 31, 2000); $42,199 (fiscal 1999); $42,450 (fiscal 1997)
Assets: $1,027,600 (fiscal 2000); $1,035,977 (fiscal 1999); $867,018 (fiscal 1997)
Gifts Received: $14,338 (fiscal 1999); $2,000 (fiscal 1997)

Typical Recipients

Arts & Humanities: Arts Funds, History & Archaeology, Libraries, Music
Civic & Public Affairs: Clubs, Civic & Public Affairs-General, Municipalities/Towns, Safety, Urban & Community Affairs
Education: Public Education (Precollege), School Volunteerism, Science/Mathematics Education, Secondary Education (Public)
Health: Cancer, Emergency/Ambulance Services, Home-Care Services, Hospitals
Social Services: Community Service Organizations, Family Services, Recreation & Athletics, Scouts, YMCA/YWCA/YMHA/YWHA, Youth Organizations

Application Procedures

Initial Contact: Send a brief letter of inquiry.
Application Requirements: Include a description of organization, amount requested, reason for request, and proof of tax-exempt status.
Deadlines: Quarterly.

Restrictions

Provides grants for the needy and civic projects in Bellefonte and vicinity.

Additional Information

Trust(s): Mellon Bank NA

Grants Analysis

Disclosure Period: fiscal year ending January 31, 2000
Total Grants: $17,100
Number of Grants: 12
Average Grant: $1,425
Highest Grant: $2,500
Typical Range: $500 to $3,000

Recent Grants

Note: Grants derived from 2001 Form 990.

General
5,000	Snow Shoe Borough Council (Fire Company), Snow Shoe, PA
3,500	Centre County Historical Society, Bellefonte, PA
2,500	American Cancer Society, Baltimore, MD
2,500	Bellefonte Youth Football Association, Bellefonte, PA

EDWARD CHASE GARVEY MEMORIAL FOUNDATION

Giving Contact
Cindy Lewis
Commerce Bank
8000 Forsyth Blvd.
Clayton, MO 63105
Phone: (314)746-7332

Description
Founded: 1970
EIN: 436132744
Organization Type: Private Foundation
Giving Locations: MO: St. Louis
Grant Types: General Support.

Donor Information
Founder: the late Edward C. Garvey

Financial Summary
Total Giving: $320,000 (fiscal year ending September 30, 2001); $285,500 (fiscal 1999); $220,000 (fiscal 1998)
Assets: $5,749,535 (fiscal 2001); $6,811,086 (fiscal 1999); $5,959,838 (fiscal 1998)

Typical Recipients
Arts & Humanities: Arts Centers, Arts Outreach, Community Arts, Dance, Arts & Humanities-General, History & Archaeology, Libraries, Literary Arts, Museums/Galleries, Music, Opera, Performing Arts, Theater
Civic & Public Affairs: Botanical Gardens/Parks, Zoos/Aquariums
Education: Arts/Humanities Education, Colleges & Universities, Private Education (Precollege), Science/Mathematics Education, Secondary Education (Public), Special Education, Vocational & Technical Education
Environment: Environment-General, Wildlife Protection
Health: Eyes/Blindness
Science: Scientific Centers & Institutes
Social Services: Animal Protection, Child Welfare, Family Planning, People with Disabilities, Social Services-General, Youth Organizations

Application Procedures
Initial Contact: Send a brief letter of inquiry.
Application Requirements: Include proof of tax-exempt status and most recent budget.
Deadlines: None.

Restrictions
Does not support individuals.

Additional Information
Trust(s): Commerce Bank St Louis

Foundation Officials
Bliss Lewis Shands: trustee

Grants Analysis
Disclosure Period: fiscal year ending September 30, 2001
Total Grants: $320,000
Number of Grants: 45
Average Grant: $7,111
Highest Grant: $40,000
Typical Range: $1,000 to $15,000

Recent Grants
Note: Grants derived from fiscal 2000 Form 990.

Library-Related
12,000	Law Library Association of St. Louis, St. Louis, MO
8,500	Kirkwood Public Library Foundation, Kirkwood, MO

General
30,000	Stages St. Louis, St. Louis, MO
25,000	Stages St. Louis, St. Louis, MO
18,000	Missouri Botanical Garden, St. Louis, MO
18,000	Opera Theatre of St. Louis, St. Louis, MO
18,000	Webster University, St. Louis, MO
16,000	St. Louis Symphony Orchestra, St. Louis, MO
12,000	St. George's School
10,000	Central Institute for the Deaf, St. Louis, MO
10,000	Frank Lloyd Wright Conservancy -- for the Ruth and Russell Kraus House
8,500	Animal Protective Association

GARVEY TEXAS FOUNDATION

Giving Contact
Shirley F. Garvey, President
PO Box 9600
Ft. Worth, TX 76147-2600
Phone: (817)335-5881

Description
Founded: 1962
EIN: 756031547
Organization Type: Private Foundation
Giving Locations: CO; KS; NE; OK; TX
Grant Types: Capital, Research.

Donor Information
Founder: James S. Garvey, Shirley F. Garvey, Garvey Foundation

Financial Summary
Total Giving: $541,557 (2000); $479,043 (1999); $497,701 (1998)
Giving Analysis: Giving for 1999 includes: foundation grants to United Way ($10,000) 1998: foundation grants to United Way ($10,000)
Assets: $9,609,667 (2000); $9,937,199 (1999); $10,760,652 (1998)
Gifts Received: $32,374 (1998); $6,300 (1996); $5,500 (1995). Note: In 1998, contributions were received from Fifty Charitable Trust. In 1996, contributions were received from Fifty Charitable Trust ($1,800) and Garvey, Inc. ($4,500).

Typical Recipients
Arts & Humanities: Arts Associations & Councils, Arts Centers, Arts Festivals, Ballet, Dance, Historic Preservation, History & Archaeology, Libraries, Museums/Galleries, Music, Opera, Performing Arts, Public Broadcasting, Theater
Civic & Public Affairs: Clubs, Civic & Public Affairs-General, Hispanic Affairs, Housing, Municipalities/Towns, Parades/Festivals, Philanthropic Organizations, Public Policy, Safety, Urban & Community Affairs, Zoos/Aquariums
Education: Agricultural Education, Arts/Humanities Education, Colleges & Universities, Community & Junior Colleges, Education Funds, Education Reform, Education-General, Minority Education, Private Education (Precollege), Private Education (Precollege), Public Education (Precollege), Student Aid
Environment: Environment-General, Research, Resource Conservation
Health: Alzheimers Disease, Cancer, Children's Health/Hospitals, Emergency/Ambulance Services, Health Policy/Cost Containment, Health Organizations, Hospices, Hospitals, Medical Research, Public Health, Research/Studies Institutes, Respiratory, Single-Disease Health Associations, Speech & Hearing

International: International Relations
Religion: Churches, Religious Organizations, Religious Welfare
Science: Science Museums
Social Services: Big Brother/Big Sister, Child Welfare, Community Centers, Community Service Organizations, Counseling, Crime Prevention, Domestic Violence, Family Planning, Family Services, Food/Clothing Distribution, Homes, Recreation & Athletics, Scouts, Senior Services, Substance Abuse, United Funds/United Ways, YMCA/YWCA/YMHA/YWHA, Youth Organizations

Application Procedures
Initial Contact: Send a brief letter of inquiry. Include a description of organization, amount requested, and proof of tax-exempt status.
Deadlines: None.

Restrictions
Does not support individuals.

Foundation Officials
Bedford L. Burgher: treasurer
James Sutherland Garvey: vice president B Colby, KS 1922. ED Wichita State University BA (1947). PRIM CORP EMPL chairman, president, director: JaGee Corp. CORP AFFIL chairman: Service Oil Co.; chairman: Walnut Creek Milling Co.; president: Rafter J Ranch; chairman: Garvey Properties; president, director: Jim Garvey Ranches; director: Garvey Inc.; chairman, director: Garvey Enterprises; ptr: Garvey Farms Management Co.; chairman, director: Garvey Elevators; chairman: Garvey Center. CLUB AFFIL Exchange Club.
Richard F. Garvey: trustee PRIM CORP EMPL vice president: JaGee Corp. CORP AFFIL sec: Garvey Enterprises; secretary, director: Jim Garvey Ranches; secretary, director: Garvey Elevators.
Shirley F. Garvey: president
Carol G. Sweat: trustee

Grants Analysis
Disclosure Period: calendar year ending 2000
Total Grants: $541,557
Typical Range: $1,000 to $10,000
Note: No grants list available for 2000.

Recent Grants
Note: Grants derived from 2001 Form 990.

General
40,000	National Cowgirl Museum and Hall of Fame, Ft. Worth, TX
30,000	Texas Christian University, Ft. Worth, TX
29,500	Fort Worth Country Day School, Ft. Worth, TX
25,000	Colby United Methodist Church
25,000	Fort Worth Symphony Orchestra Association, Ft. Worth, TX
23,100	First United Methodist Church
20,000	Child Study Center Foundation, Ft. Worth, TX
15,860	Amon Carter Museum, Ft. Worth, TX
15,100	Warm Place, Ft. Worth, TX
12,000	Happy Hill Farm, Ft. Worth, TX

GATES FAMILY FOUNDATION

Giving Contact
Tom Kaesemeyer, Executive Director
3575 Cherry Creek North Drive, Suite 100
Denver, CO 80209
Phone: (303)722-1881
Fax: (303)316-3038
E-mail: info@gatesfamilyfoundation.org
Web: http://www.gatesfamilyfdn.org

Description

Founded: 1946
EIN: 840474837
Organization Type: Family Foundation
Giving Locations: CO
Grant Types: Capital, Matching, Multiyear/Continuing Support.

Donor Information

Founder: The Gates Foundation was established in Colorado in 1946 by the late Charles C. Gates Sr. , and members of the Gates family. Gates Corporation, an aircraft parts, instruments, and mechanical rubber goods company, was founded in 1911 by Mr. Gates. In 1961, he transferred the presidency of the company to his son, Charles C. Gates, Jr. The company is one of the largest privately-owned companies in the country, and Charles Gates, Jr., remains the chairman, president, and chief executive officer.

Financial Summary

Total Giving: $8,500,000 (2002 approx); $9,917,669 (2001); $9,367,517 (2000). Note: Giving for 2000 includes grants from Bernice Gates Hopper and Robert E. Hopper family funds.
Giving Analysis: Giving for 2000 includes: foundation grants to United Way ($135,000) 1998: foundation grants to United Way ($135,000)
Assets: $182,031,741 (2001); $217,398,029 (2000); $207,500,773 (1998)
Gifts Received: $1,000,000 (2001); $1,967,985 (1998). Note: In 2001, contributions were received from Bernice Gates Hopper. In 1998, contributions were received from Bernice Gates Hopper ($983,993) and Robert E. Hopper ($983,993).

Typical Recipients

Arts & Humanities: Arts Associations & Councils, Arts Centers, Arts Funds, Arts Outreach, Ballet, Dance, Ethnic & Folk Arts, Arts & Humanities-General, Historic Preservation, History & Archaeology, Libraries, Museums/Galleries, Music, Opera, Performing Arts, Public Broadcasting, Theater, Visual Arts
Civic & Public Affairs: Botanical Gardens/Parks, Business/Free Enterprise, Clubs, Community Foundations, Economic Development, Employment/Job Training, Civic & Public Affairs-General, Housing, Inner-City Development, Municipalities/Towns, Native American Affairs, Parades/Festivals, Public Policy, Rural Affairs, Urban & Community Affairs, Women's Affairs, Zoos/Aquariums
Education: Arts/Humanities Education, Business Education, Colleges & Universities, Continuing Education, Economic Education, Education Associations, Education Reform, Elementary Education (Private), Engineering/Technological Education, Faculty Development, Education-General, Gifted & Talented Programs, International Studies, Leadership Training, Literacy, Preschool Education, Private Education (Precollege), Public Education (Precollege), Science/Mathematics Education, Secondary Education (Private), Secondary Education (Public), Social Sciences Education, Student Aid
Environment: Environment-General, Resource Conservation
Health: Health-General, Health Policy/Cost Containment, Medical Rehabilitation
Religion: Bible Study/Translation, Dioceses, Religion-General, Jewish Causes, Ministries, Religious Welfare
Science: Science Museums, Scientific Centers & Institutes, Scientific Organizations, Scientific Research
Social Services: At-Risk Youth, Camps, Child Abuse, Child Welfare, Community Centers, Community Service Organizations, Crime Prevention, Day Care, Domestic Violence, Family Planning, Family Services, Food/Clothing Distribution, People with Disabilities, Recreation & Athletics, Scouts, Senior Services, Shelters/Homelessness, Social Services-General, Substance Abuse, United Funds/United Ways, YMCA/YWCA/YMHA/YWHA, Youth Organizations

Application Procedures

Initial Contact: Applicants may call a program officer before submitting a proposal. A letter of inquiry may also be submitted, including a brief narrative description of the proposed project. If interested the foundation will request a completed copy of the Common Grant Application.
Deadlines: January 15 for the April 1 meeting; April 1 for the June 15 meeting; July 1 for the October 1 meeting; and October 1 for the December 15 meeting.
Review Process: The foundation's staff acknowledges and reviews all applications, and notifies each applicant in writing regarding funding decisions within two weeks following each quarterly meeting. Highly specialized requests and proposals requiring on-site study or outside consultation may require even more time for review.
Evaluative Criteria: The Foundation attempts wherever possible to invest its funds in organizations that address root problems with substantive solutions; views as important sound management of an applying organization, with an effective board of trustees that has supported the project to the fullest financial extent possible; expects strong support for the project from the community; believes it is appropriate to support new organizations only when it is clear they will not become a financial burden on others.
Notes: Only one copy of proposal is requested. Trustees will initiate any meetings with applicants.

Restrictions

Generally the foundation does not make grants outside Colorado; to individuals or loans to organizations; for projects that have been completed prior to the next trustees' meeting; to conferences, meetings, or studies that are not initiated by trustees; to organizations engaged in grant making; to retire operating debt; for the purchase of vehicles or office equipment; directly to public schools or public school districts; for the construction of medical facilities or for medical research; or tickets for fundraising dinners, parties, benefits, balls or other social fundraising events. The foundation will not consider more than one application per organization per year. Grants are generally confined to campaigns for capital projects.

Additional Information

Occasionally, the foundation will conduct post-grant evaluation of completed projects; written reports must be submitted by all grantees.
Publications: Annual Report; Common Application Form

Foundation Officials

George B. Beardsley: trustee
Charles G. Cannon: trustee
Charles Cassius Gates, Jr.: trustee B Morrison, CO 1921. ED Massachusetts Institute of Technology (1939-1941); Stanford University BS (1943). PRIM CORP EMPL chairman, director: Cody Energy Co. CORP AFFIL chairman: Gates Capital Management LLC. NONPR AFFIL trustee: Denver Museum Natural History; trustee: Graland Country Day School Foundation; trustee: Denver Art Museum; trustee: California Institute Technology; Member: Conference Board. CLUB AFFIL Wigwam Club; Waialae Country Club; Roundup Riders Rockies Club; Shikar Safari International Club; Old Baldy Club; Outrigger Canoe Club; Ltd. Club; Country Club Colorado; Denver Country Club; Castle Pines Golf Club; Conquistadores del Cielo Club; Augusta National Golf Club; Boone & Crockett Club.
Valerie Gates: vice president

William West Grant, III: trustee B New York, NY 1932. ED Yale University BA (1954); New York University (1958); Columbia University School of Business Administration (1968); Harvard University Graduate School of Business Administration (1971). NONPR AFFIL trustee: Midwest Research Institute; director: Mountain Studies Employers Council; trustee: Denver Museum Natural History; member: Colorado Bankers Association; member: Denver Chamber of Commerce. CLUB AFFIL Denver Country Club.
Tom Kaesemeyer: executive director, secretary
Karen W. Mather: grants manager, program officer
Thomas C. Stokes: trustee, treasurer
Christina H. Turissini: comptroller
Diane Gates Wallach: vice president PRIM CORP EMPL director: Gates Rubber Co. CORP AFFIL director: The Gates Corp.

Grants Analysis

Disclosure Period: calendar year ending 2001
Total Grants: $9,917,669
Number of Grants: 104
Average Grant: $86,579*
Highest Grant: $1,000,000
Lowest Grant: $1,000
Typical Range: $5,000 to $100,000
*Note: Average grant figure excludes highest grant.

Recent Grants

Note: Grants derived from 2001 Form 990.

Library-Related
100,000	Pikes Peak Library District, Colorado Springs, CO
90,000	Hotchkiss Public Library, Hotchkiss, CO

General
1,000,000	Denver Museum of Nature and Science, Denver, CO
400,000	Girls, Inc., Denver, CO
400,000	YMCA/USO of the Pikes Peak Region, Colorado Springs, CO
350,000	Rocky Mountain Public Broadcasting, Denver, CO
330,000	Human Services, Inc., Denver, CO
300,000	Philanthropic Education Partnership, Denver, CO
280,000	Gold Crown Foundation, Denver, CO
250,000	Boys and Girls Club of Larimer County, Ft. Collins, CO
250,000	Fountain Valley School, Denver, CO
250,000	Kent Denver School, Englewood, CO

BILL AND MELINDA GATES FOUNDATION

Giving Contact

Grant Inquiry Coordinator
PO Box 23350
Seattle, WA 98102
Phone: (206)709-3140
Fax: (206)709-3280
E-mail: info@gatesfoundation.org
Web: http://www.gatesfoundation.org

Alternate Contact

Phone: (206)709-3400
Fax: (206)709-3252
E-mail: libraryinfo@gatesfoundation.org
Note: Contact for information about library programs.

Description

Founded: 1999
EIN: 911663695
Organization Type: Private Foundation
Formed by Merger of: William H. Gates Foundation (1999).
Formed by Merger of: Gates Learning Foundation (1999).

Giving Locations: Pacific Northwest; internationally; nationally.

Donor Information

Founder: The Bill & Melinda Gates Foundation was established in 1999 by William H. Gates III and Melinda French Gates to consolidate the efforts of the William H. Gates Foundation and the Gates Learning Foundation.

Bill Gates developed the programming language BASIC while attending Harvard University. He launched Microsoft Corp. in 1975 with partner Paul Allen to develop software to be used on personal computers. Bill Gates serves as chairman of Microsoft and continues to play an active role in both the management of the corporation and the development of its products. Melinda French Gates attended Duke University, where she earned a bachelor's degree in computer science and economics in 1986 and a master's degree from Duke's Fuqua School of Business in 1987. She played a role in developing many of Microsoft's multimedia and Web-based products, but retired two years after marrying Bill Gates in order to raise their children and contribute more fully to a number of philanthropic endeavors.

Financial Summary

Total Giving: $1,147,045,501 (2001); $994,875,079 (2000); $761,045,533 (1999 approx)

Giving Analysis: Giving for 2000 includes: foundation matching gifts ($184,667) foundation grants to United Way ($1,408,700)

Assets: $32,751,464,978 (2001); $21,149,088,035 (2000); $17,000,000,000 (1999 approx)

Gifts Received: $2,107,500,000 (2001). Note: In 2001, contributions were received from William H. Gates III.

Typical Recipients

Arts & Humanities: Libraries, Public Broadcasting

Civic & Public Affairs: Community Foundations, Civic & Public Affairs-General, Nonprofit Management, Urban & Community Affairs

Education: Colleges & Universities, Education Associations, Education Reform, Education-General, Medical Education, Minority Education, Public Education (Precollege)

Health: AIDS/HIV, Children's Health/Hospitals, Health-General, Health Policy/Cost Containment, Health Organizations, Medical Research, Public Health, Research/Studies Institutes

International: Foreign Arts Organizations, Foreign Educational Institutions, International-General, Health Care/Hospitals

Religion: Religious Welfare

Social Services: Child Welfare, Community Service Organizations

Application Procedures

Initial Contact: Submit a brief letter of inquiry not exceeding two pages in length.

Application Requirements: Letters of inquiry should include objectives, including the goals and charitable purpose of the project; information on how the organization will achieve the outlined goals and a project timeline; a brief statement of the organization's need for funding for the stated objectives; organizational information, including past projects, previous grants, the qualifications of those involved in the project, a list of board members (when applicable), the address for any organizational Web site, and a copy of the organization's IRS tax determination letter. Additional materials should not be sent with a letter of inquiry, as the foundation will not review supporting materials at this stage in the process and is unable to return items to the sender.

The foundation will accept letters of inquiry sent by mail or e-mail (info@gatesfoundation.org).

Deadlines: None.

Review Process: The foundation will review letters of inquiry and may invite those organizations whose goals coincide with the scope and mission of available funding to submit a full proposal.

Notes: The foundation does not generally consider unsolicited proposals. However, the foundation does accept letters of inquiry from tax-exempt, charitable organizations for the following program areas: Global Health, Pacific Northwest, and Public Access to Information.

Restrictions

The foundation cannot accept proposals benefiting individuals or that serve religious organizations for sectarian purposes.

Additional Information

Educational Programs: Gates Millennium Scholars Program, The goal of the scholars program is to increase the number of African-Americans, American Indians/Alaska Natives, Asian Pacific Americans, and Hispanic Americans attending and completing college/university programs, with an emphasis on students studying math, science, engineering, education, or library science. The Bill & Melinda Gates Foundation has committed $1 billion over the next two decades to provide 20,000 scholarships through the scholars program.. Application Procedure: Application is made by nomination of a student by a principal, teacher, counselor, or other education professional. Eligibility criteria and nomination instructions are available on the program's Web site: http://www.gmsp.org. EDU. Deadline: Gates Millennium Scholars Program.

Foundation Officials

Richard Akeroyd: executive director, libraries & public access to information ED University of Connecticut BA; University of Pittsburgh MS. NONPR AFFIL member: American Society Information Science; member: Coalition for Networked Information; member: American Library Association.

David Fleming, MD: director global health strategies program ED State University of New York Albany BS; State University of New York Medical Center MD. PRIM CORP EMPL deputy director public health: United States Centers for Disease Control.

Jaime Garcia: director, pac northwest giving ED University of New Mexico; University of Washington.

Melinda French Gates: co-founder B 1965. ED Duke University BS (1986); Duke University Fuqua School of Business MBA (1987). CORP AFFIL board member: Third Age Media. NONPR AFFIL board trustee: Duke University; technology committee member: Sacred Heart Catholic School (Bellevue, Washington).

William H. Gates, Sr.: co-chair, chief executive officer B Bremerton, WA 1925. ED University of Washington BS (1949); University of Washington School of Law (1949-1950). ADD CORP EMPL co-founder: Preston, Gates & Ellis LLP.

William Henry Gates, III: co-founder B Seattle, WA October 28, 1955. ED Harvard University (1975). PRIM CORP EMPL co-founder, chairman, chief software architect: Microsoft Corp. ADD CORP EMPL chairman: Corbis Corp. CORP AFFIL director: ICOS; director: Teledesic Corp.

Dr. Helene Gayle, MPH: director HIV, TB and reprod health program ED Barnard College BA; Johns Hopkins University MPH; University of Pennsylvania MD.

Allan C. Golston, CPA: chief financial officer, chief administrative officer ED Seattle University MBA; University of Colorado BA. NONPR AFFIL alumnus: INROADS Denver; trustee: Make-a-Wish Foundation; trustee: Artist Trust; fellow: British-American Project.

Richard D. Klausner, MD: executive director, global health ED Duke University MD; Yale University.

Sylvia M. Mathews: chief operating officer, executive director, libraries, pac northwest B Hinton, WV. ED Harvard University; Oxford University.

Gordon W. Perkin, MD: senior fellow, global health program

Dr. Regina Rabinovich, MPH: director, infectious disease program ED Southern Illinois University MD;

University of Iowa BA; University of North Carolina, Chapel Hill MPH.

Patty Stonesifer: co-chair, president PRIM CORP EMPL senior vice president Consumer division: Microsoft Corp. CORP AFFIL board member: Amazon.com; board member: Viacom Inc. NONPR AFFIL member: Seattle Foundation; member: YWCA King County (Washington).

Tom Vander Ark: executive director education NONPR AFFIL trustee: Western Governors University.

Grants Analysis

Disclosure Period: calendar year ending 2001

Total Grants: $1,147,045,501

Number of Grants: 2,050 (approx)

Average Grant: $559,534

Typical Range: $100,000 to $1,000,000

Recent Grants

Note: Grants derived from 2001 Form 990.

General

425,000,000 Vaccine Fund, Seattle, WA -- support immunization of children

60,000,000 PATH, Seattle, WA -- support the elimination of epidemic meningitis in sub-Saharan Africa

50,975,000 PATH, Seattle, WA -- support Children's Vaccine Program

45,254,679 United Negro College Fund, Fairfax, VA -- support Gates Millennium Scholars Program

41,325,000 Save the Children Federation, Westport, CT -- support the Global Neonatal Survival Initiative

30,000,000 Trustees of Columbia University in the City of New York, New York, NY -- reduce maternal deaths in developing countries by improving access to life saving treatment

20,000,000 American Friends of London School of Hygiene and Tropical Medicine, Inc., Washington, DC -- establish the Malaria Center

15,000,000 Northwest Educational Service District 189, Mt. Vernon, WA -- support Teacher Leadership Project

15,000,000 PATH, Seattle, WA -- support Malaria vaccine initiative

10,850,000 International Vaccine Institute Republic of Korea -- vaccines to prevent diseases of the most impoverished

GATX CORP.

Company Headquarters

Chicago, IL

Web: http://www.gatx.com

Company Description

Founded: 1916

Ticker: GMT

Exchange: NYSE

Operating Revenue: US$1.34 billion (2002)

Employees: 2800 (2002)

SIC(s): 4432 Freight Transportation on the Great Lakes, 4613 Refined Petroleum Pipelines, 4741 Rental of Railroad Cars, 6159 Miscellaneous Business Credit Institutions.

Operating Locations

GATX Corp. (CA--Carson, Compton, Richmond, San Francisco, Wilmington; FL--Jacksonville, Taft, Tampa; IL--Argo, Chicago; IN--East Chicago; LA--Good Hope; NY--Buffalo; OH--Youngstown; OR--Portland; PA; TX--Houston, Norco, Pasadena; UT; WA--Vancouver)

Nonmonetary Support

Value: $10,000 (2001); $125,000 (2000 approx); $100,000 (1999 approx)

Type: Donated Equipment; Donated Products; In-kind Services

Volunteer Programs: GATX employees nationwide are recognized for volunteer efforts from tutoring students to building playgrounds. GATX presents its Spirit of Volunteerism Award twice a year to honor those whose best exemplify principles of community service, teamwork, and good corporate citizenship. Unions service projects during work hours with work release time for eligible employees.

Giving Contact

Jesse Kane, Supervisor, Community Affairs
500 West Monroe Street
Chicago, IL 60661-3676
Phone: (312)621-6222
Fax: (312)621-6665
E-mail: communityaffairs@gatx.com
Web: http://www.gatx.com

Description

Organization Type: Corporate Giving Program
Giving Locations: IL: Chicago operating locations.
Grant Types: Award, Employee Matching Gifts, General Support, Multiyear/Continuing Support, Operating Expenses, Project, Seed Money.

Financial Summary

Total Giving: $991,000 (2002); $1,460,000 (2001 approx); $1,425,000 (2000 approx)
Giving Analysis: Giving for 2001 includes: nonmonetary support ($10,000); corporate direct giving ($1,460,000); 2000: nonmonetary support ($125,000) corporate direct giving ($1,300,000)

Typical Recipients

Arts & Humanities: Arts Associations & Councils, Arts Institutes, Arts Outreach, Community Arts, Dance, Ethnic & Folk Arts, Historic Preservation, Libraries, Museums/Galleries, Music, Opera, Performing Arts, Public Broadcasting, Theater, Visual Arts

Civic & Public Affairs: Botanical Gardens/Parks, Civil Rights, Economic Development, Employment/Job Training, Housing, Public Policy, Urban & Community Affairs, Women's Affairs, Zoos/Aquariums

Education: Afterschool/Enrichment Programs, Arts/Humanities Education, Colleges & Universities, Education Associations, Education Reform, Elementary Education (Private), Faculty Development, Education-General, Literacy, Minority Education, Preschool Education, Private Education (Precollege), Science/Mathematics Education, Special Education, Student Aid

Health: AIDS/HIV, Cancer, Clinics/Medical Centers, Geriatric Health, Health Organizations, Hospices, Hospitals, Medical Rehabilitation, Mental Health, Nutrition, Public Health, Single-Disease Health Associations

International: Human Rights
Religion: Religious Welfare
Science: Science Museums

Social Services: At-Risk Youth, Child Abuse, Child Welfare, Community Centers, Community Service Organizations, Counseling, Delinquency & Criminal Rehabilitation, Domestic Violence, Family Services, Food/Clothing Distribution, People with Disabilities, Senior Services, Shelters/Homelessness, Substance Abuse, United Funds/United Ways, Youth Organizations

Application Procedures

Initial Contact: Call or write for Chicago Area Grant Application Form, then submit a written proposal.
Application Requirements: Proposal should include: statement of purpose and history of organization; current program activities and goals, specifics regarding particular project to be funded; itemized budget for the organization, with both projected revenues and expenses for the current fiscal year; current program budget; current sources of revenue; audited financial statement or Form 990 for the most recently completed fiscal year; annual report; list of board members and affiliations; and proof of tax-exempt status.
Deadlines: By the 15th day of January, April, July, or October.
Review Process: The initial review is done by the supervisor; further review and decision is made by the contributions committee on a quarterly basis.
Evaluative Criteria: Evaluation is based on the involvement of company employees in organization; geographical area served; efficiency of structure and management; cost of fund-raising activities; existence or level of government funding; evidence of broad community support; proven effectiveness of organization in meeting community needs; potential of program to become self-sustaining; and the impact on the community.
Decision Notification: Completed applications will be acknowledged in writing; final decisions are made at meetings in March, June, September, and December, and as necessary.

Restrictions

Corporation does not support individuals; political organizations; religious organizations for sectarian purposes; trips, conferences, or tours; organizations which lack status as a 501(c)(3) organization or equivalent; land acquisition; deficit financing; member organizations of united funds for general operating support; organizations or programs which pose a potential conflict of interest; social, fraternal, athletic, labor, or veterans' groups serving a limited constituency.

Additional Information

Recipients must submit progress reports as a condition of funding.
Grant renewals are not automatic.
Publications: Guidelines; Grants List; Application Form

Corporate Officials

David M. Edwards: president, president, chief executive officer, chief operating officer B Berkeley, CA 1951. ED University of California, Davis AB (1973); University of California, Davis MA (1975). PRIM CORP EMPL president: GATX Corp. CORP AFFIL director: General American Transportation Corp.; director: GATX Capital Corp.; director: GATX Terminals Corp. NONPR AFFIL member: Finance Executive Institute.

Ronald H. Zech: chairman, president, chief executive officer, chief operating officer B Reedsburg, WI 1943. ED Valparaiso University BSEE (1965); University of Wisconsin MBA (1967). PRIM CORP EMPL chairman, president, chief executive officer, chief operating officer: GATX Corp. CORP AFFIL president, chief executive officer: GATX Capital Corp.; director: McGrath Rentcorp.

Grants Analysis

Disclosure Period: calendar year ending 2001
Total Grants: $1,460,000 (approx)*
Number of Grants: 75
Average Grant: $19,466
Highest Grant: $50,000
Lowest Grant: $10,000
Typical Range: $10,000 to $25,000
*Note: Giving excludes nonmonetary support. Grants analysis provided by the corporation. A more recent grants list was unavailable.

Recent Grants

Note: Grants derived from 1996 grants list.

General

50,000	Music and Dance Theater -- capital campaign
50,000	Music and Dance Theater -- capital campaign
45,000	Heartland Alliance for Human Needs and Human Rights, Chicago, IL -- for Neon Street Programs
45,000	Heartland Alliance for Human Needs and Human Rights, Chicago, IL -- for Neon Street Programs
25,000	Chicago Botanic Garden, Chicago, IL -- for Green Chicago Program
23,600	Robert Crown Center for Health Education, Hinsdale, IL -- for Farren School Family Life
20,000	Associated Colleges of Illinois, Chicago, IL -- for North Central College's Inner-City Tutoring Program, Rosary College's Tutoring Program with Farren School
20,000	Rainbow House/Arco Iris, Chicago, IL -- for Adolescent Services
20,000	Teen Living Programs, Chicago, IL -- for Belfort House
17,500	Big Shoulders Fund, Chicago, IL -- counseling services

GAULT-HUSSEY CHARITABLE TRUST

Giving Contact

Rudy Wrenick, Jr., Senior Vice President & Trust Officer
c/o Bank of America
PO Box 88
Topeka, KS 66601
Phone: (785)295-3463
Fax: (785)295-3450

Description

Founded: 1980
EIN: 486237061
Organization Type: Private Foundation
Giving Locations: KS
Grant Types: Capital, Endowment, General Support, Operating Expenses, Project.

Financial Summary

Total Giving: $144,500 (fiscal year ending November 30, 2001); $140,000 (fiscal 2000); $100,000 (fiscal 1999). Note: Fiscal 1997 Giving includes scholarship($23,500); United Way ($10,000).
Giving Analysis: Giving for fiscal 2001 includes: foundation grants to United Way ($14,500); fiscal 2000: foundation grants to United Way ($14,000); fiscal 1999: foundation grants to United Way ($10,000)
Assets: $2,733,928 (fiscal 2001); $3,019,777 (fiscal 2000); $3,174,406 (fiscal 1999)

Typical Recipients

Arts & Humanities: Arts Centers, Arts Funds, Historic Preservation, Libraries, Museums/Galleries, Performing Arts, Theater
Civic & Public Affairs: Community Foundations, Employment/Job Training, Civic & Public Affairs-General, Housing, Public Policy
Education: Business Education, Colleges & Universities, Economic Education, Education Funds, Elementary Education (Public), Medical Education, Public Education (Precollege), Student Aid, Vocational & Technical Education
Environment: Resource Conservation
Health: Alzheimers Disease, Cancer, Children's Health/Hospitals, Clinics/Medical Centers, Diabetes, Emergency/Ambulance Services, Health Organizations, Home-Care Services, Hospices, Hospitals, Medical Research, Mental Health, Mental Health, Prenatal Health Issues, Respiratory, Single-Disease Health Associations, Trauma Treatment
Religion: Religious Welfare
Social Services: Animal Protection, At-Risk Youth, Child Welfare, Community Service Organizations,

Day Care, Domestic Violence, Food/Clothing Distribution, People with Disabilities, Scouts, Senior Services, Shelters/Homelessness, United Funds/United Ways, YMCA/YWCA/YMHA/YWHA, Youth Organizations

Application Procedures

Initial Contact: The foundation has no formal grant application procedure or application form. Send a brief letter of inquiry.
Deadlines: January 1 and July 1.

Restrictions

Priority is given to organizations that seek to fill a community need and whose programs would be unlikely to receive adequate support from any other funding source. Does not support individuals.

Additional Information

Publications: Grant Guidelines
Trust(s): Bank of America

Grants Analysis

Disclosure Period: fiscal year ending November 30, 2001
Total Grants: $130,000*
Number of Grants: 18
Average Grant: $7,222
Highest Grant: $20,500
Lowest Grant: $1,000
Typical Range: $1,000 to $10,000
*Note: Giving excludes United Way.

Recent Grants

Note: Grants derived from fiscal 2000 Form 990.

General

30,000	Washburn University, Topeka, KS -- nursing scholarships
21,000	Capper Foundation, Topeka, KS -- services for disabled persons
17,625	Stormont Vail Regional Medical Center, Topeka, KS -- nursing scholarships
14,000	Kansas Independent College Fund, Topeka, KS -- scholarship for disadvantaged
14,000	United Way of Greater Topeka, Topeka, KS -- community services
12,500	YWCA, Topeka, KS -- youth programs and building fund
4,000	Menninger Foundation, Topeka, KS
3,500	Boy Scouts of America, Topeka, KS -- community service
3,500	Salvation Army of Topeka, Topeka, KS -- homeless
3,000	Kansas University Endowment Association, Lawrence, KS -- nursing ethics

GAZETTE CO.

Company Headquarters

Cedar Rapids, IA
Web: http://www.gazettecommunications.com

Company Description

Employees: 650
SIC(s): 2700 Printing & Publishing, 4800 Communications.

Operating Locations

Gazette Co. (IA--Cedar Rapids)

Gazette Foundation

Giving Contact

Joseph F. Hladky, III, President
Gazette Foundation
500 3rd Ave. SE
Cedar Rapids, IA 52401
Phone: (319)398-8280

Description

Founded: 1960
EIN: 426075177
Organization Type: Corporate Foundation
Giving Locations: IA: Cedar Rapids
Grant Types: Capital, General Support.

Donor Information

Founder: The Gazette Co.

Financial Summary

Total Giving: $149,236 (2000); $173,485 (1999); $190,956 (1998)
Giving Analysis: Giving for 2000 includes: foundation grants to United Way ($44,000); 1999: foundation grants to United Way ($46,400); foundation ($127,085) 1998: foundation grants to United Way ($44,200)
Assets: $1,109,774 (2000); $1,215,662 (1999); $1,225,556 (1998)
Gifts Received: $47,000 (2000); $60,000 (1999); $223,945 (1998). Note: In 2000, contributions were received from Cedar Rapids Television Co. ($12,000) and Gazette Communications Inc. ($35,000). In 1999, contributions were received from Cedar Rapids Television Co. ($12,000) and Gazette Communications Inc. ($48,000). Contributions were received from the Cedar Rapids Television Co., the Cedar Rapids Gazette, the Gazette Co., the Iowa Farmer Today, and Publications, Inc.

Typical Recipients

Arts & Humanities: Arts Associations & Councils, Ethnic & Folk Arts, History & Archaeology, Libraries, Literary Arts, Museums/Galleries, Music, Performing Arts, Theater
Civic & Public Affairs: African American Affairs, Botanical Gardens/Parks, Chambers of Commerce, Clubs, Community Foundations, Civic & Public Affairs-General, Housing, Municipalities/Towns, Philanthropic Organizations, Professional & Trade Associations, Public Policy, Safety, Urban & Community Affairs, Women's Affairs, Zoos/Aquariums
Education: Agricultural Education, Business Education, Colleges & Universities, Community & Junior Colleges, Education-General, Leadership Training, Literacy, Private Education (Precollege), Public Education (Precollege), Secondary Education (Private), Student Aid
Environment: Environment-General
Health: Cancer, Children's Health/Hospitals, Diabetes, Emergency/Ambulance Services, Health Organizations, Hospitals, Kidney, Multiple Sclerosis, Outpatient Health Care
Religion: Religious Welfare
Science: Science-General
Social Services: Animal Protection, Camps, Community Centers, Community Service Organizations, Counseling, Delinquency & Criminal Rehabilitation, Domestic Violence, Family Services, Food/Clothing Distribution, Scouts, Senior Services, Substance Abuse, United Funds/United Ways, YMCA/YWCA/YMHA/YWHA, Youth Organizations

Application Procedures

Initial Contact: Return completed application.
Application Requirements: Include a description of organization, proof of tax-exempt status, purpose of funds sought, financial information relating to the project, and project personnel.
Deadlines: None.
Review Process: Review process takes approximately three months.

Restrictions

Does not support individuals.

Additional Information

Publications: Guidelines Sheet

Corporate Officials

Joseph F. Hladky, III: president, chief executive officer, publisher, editor B Cedar Rapids, IA 1940. ED University of Iowa BA (1962). PRIM CORP EMPL president, chief executive officer, publisher, editor: Gazette Co. CORP AFFIL director: Banks IA; director: Merchants National Bank. NONPR AFFIL member: National Association Broadcasters; member: Shriners; member: Masons; member: Inland Daily Press Association; member: Iowa Newspaper Association; director: Coe College; member: American Society Newspaper Editors; director, member: Cedar Rapids Chamber of Commerce; director, member: American Newspaper Publishers Association. CLUB AFFIL Cedar Rapids Country Club.
Ken Slaughter: chief financial officer PRIM CORP EMPL chief financial officer: Gazette Co.

Foundation Officials

Elizabeth T. Barry: director PRIM CORP EMPL secretary: Gazette Co. Inc. ADD CORP EMPL secretary: Cedar Rapids Gazette Inc.; assistant secretary: Cedar Rapids Television Co.
John L. Donnelly: treasurer, director
Joseph F. Hladky, III: president, director (see above)
Ken Slaughter: vice president, director (see above)

Grants Analysis

Disclosure Period: calendar year ending 2000
Total Grants: $105,236*
Number of Grants: 42
Average Grant: $2,506
Highest Grant: $20,000
Typical Range: $1,000 to $5,000
*Note: Giving excludes United Way.

Recent Grants

Note: Grants derived from 2001 Form 990.

General

47,000	United Way of East Central Iowa, Cedar Rapids, IA -- annual campaign
20,000	Iowa Children's Museum, Iowa City, IA -- capital campaign
10,000	Kernels Foundation, Cedar Rapids, IA -- capital campaign
10,000	Kirkwood Community College, Cedar Rapids, IA -- capital campaign
7,000	St. Luke's Health Care Foundation, Cedar Rapids, IA -- capital campaign
6,500	YMCA, Cedar Rapids, IA -- capital campaign
6,000	Xavier Foundation, Cedar Rapids, IA -- capital campaign
5,000	City of Cedar Rapids, Cedar Rapids, IA -- SKATE Program
5,000	Coe College, Cedar Rapids, IA -- capital campaign
5,000	Science Station, Cedar Rapids, IA -- capital campaign

GE CAPITAL CORP.

Company Headquarters

260 Long Ridge Rd.
Stamford, CT 06927
Web: http://www.gecapital.com

Company Description

Acquired: Heller Financial Inc. (2001).
Employees: 1,250
SIC(s): 6141 Personal Credit Institutions, 6153 Short-Term Business Credit.
Parent Company: General Electric Co., 3135 Easton Turnpike, Fairfield, CT, United States

Operating Locations

Fuji Bank Atlanta (GA--Atlanta); Fuji Bank Chicago Branch (IL--Chicago); Fuji Bank Houston (TX--Houston); Fuji Bank International (CA--San Francisco); Fuji

Bank Los Angeles (CA--Los Angeles); Fuji Bank New York Branch (NY--New York); Fuji Bank San Francisco (CA--San Francisco); Fuji Bank & Trust Co. (NY--New York); Fuji Capital Holdings (NY--New York); Fuji Capital Markets Corp. (NY--New York); Fuji Securities - Chicago (IL--Chicago); Fuji Securities - New York (NY--New York); Fuji-Wolfensohn International (NY--New York); Fujilease Corp. (NY--New York); FWI Holdings (DE--Wilmington); Heller International Corp. (IL--Chicago); Miami Representative Office (FL--Miami); Seattle Representative Office (WA--Seattle); Washington, D.C. Representative Office (DC--Washington)

Nonmonetary Support

Type: Donated Equipment
Volunteer Programs: The company has a volunteer committee, an incentive program, and has adopted a public school.

Giving Contact

Leslie Krohn, Vice President Communications
500 West Monroe Street
Chicago, IL 60661
Phone: (312)441-6748
Fax: (312)441-7710

Description

Organization Type: Corporate Giving Program
Giving Locations: headquarters and operating communities.
Grant Types: Employee Matching Gifts, General Support.
Note: Matching gifts are for academic purposes only.

Financial Summary

Total Giving: $1,300,000 (2000 approx); $1,200,000 (1999 approx); $860,000 (1998 approx). Note: Contributes through corporate direct giving program only. Giving includes corporate direct giving; nonmonetary support.
Giving Analysis: Giving for 1998 includes: corporate direct giving (approx $1,200,000)

Typical Recipients

Arts & Humanities: Libraries, Music, Public Broadcasting
Civic & Public Affairs: Business/Free Enterprise, Professional & Trade Associations, Public Policy
Education: Colleges & Universities, Elementary Education (Private), Literacy, Minority Education, Private Education (Precollege), Public Education (Precollege)
Health: Mental Health
Social Services: United Funds/United Ways, Youth Organizations

Application Procedures

Initial Contact: brief letter of inquiry, then a full proposal
Application Requirements: a description of the organization, amount requested, purpose of funds sought, list of board of trustees or directors, percentage of budget used for administration and overhead, evidence of 501(c)(3) status, outcomes expected, method of evaluation, and list of funding from other organizations or government agencies
Deadlines: None.

Restrictions

Does not support individuals, organizations outside operating areas, political or lobbying groups, United Way-supported organizations, or religious organizations for sectarian purposes.

Additional Information

The majority of Heller Financial, Inc.'s charitable contributions is distributed by the corporate headquarters office in Chicago, IL, but a small percentage of funding is distributed through various regional offices.

Corporate Officials

Richard Almeida: chairman, chief executive officer B New York, NY 1942. ED George Washington University BA (1963); Syracuse University MA (1965). PRIM CORP EMPL chairman, chief executive officer: Heller Financial Inc. ADD CORP EMPL president: Heller Equity Capital Corp.; chief executive officer: Heller Interstate Inc.
Lauralee Martin: chief financial officer B Minneapolis, MN 1950. ED Oregon State University (1972); University of Connecticut (1979). PRIM CORP EMPL chief financial officer: Heller Financial. CORP AFFIL director: Gables Residental Trust.
Rick Wolfert: president, chief operating officer PRIM CORP EMPL president, chief operating officer: Heller Financial.

Giving Program Officials

Judy Korba: PRIM CORP EMPL contributions manager: Heller Financial.

Grants Analysis

Typical Range: $1,000 to $25,000

GEBBIE FOUNDATION

Giving Contact

Thomas M. Cardman, Executive Director
110 W 3rd Street, No. 308
Jamestown, NY 14701
Phone: (716)487-1062
Fax: (716)484-6401

Description

Founded: 1964
EIN: 166050287
Organization Type: General Purpose Foundation
Giving Locations: NY
Grant Types: Capital, Challenge, Matching, Multiyear/Continuing Support, Project, Research, Scholarship, Seed Money.

Donor Information

Founder: The foundation was established in 1964 and initially funded by the estates of the late Miss Marion Bertram Gebbie and the late Mrs. Geraldine Gebbie Bellinger in memory of their parents, Frank and Harriet Louise Hubbell Gebbie. Frank Gebbie was one of the developers (with Gail Borden) of condensed milk, and a founder of the Mohawk Condensed Milk Company in St. Johnsville, NY, in the late 1800s.
Geraldine, the older daughter, studied violin privately in Rochester, NY, but did not choose to have a professional career. In 1908, she married Earl J. Bellinger, a St. Johnsville area resident connected with the Mohawk Dairy. The young couple went to the western New York and northern Pennsylvania areas where they purchased farms and set up dairies. Mrs. Bellinger also managed the Mohawk Condensed Milk Company plant in Sherman. As time passed, Mrs. Bellinger became interested in Chautauqua Institution and was particularly close to the institution when it suffered setbacks in the early 1930s. She became a founding member of the Chautauqua Foundation, serving on its board until her death in 1963. She was also an active member of the Jamestown YWCA Board and the First Presbyterian Church.
Marion, the second daughter, graduated from the Wheaton Female Seminary, now Wheaton College, in 1901. Immediately after college, however, she chose to be helpful to her parents by remaining at home. She was one of the first women in New York to operate a motor car and she enjoyed driving for her parents. She also enjoyed traveling with her father on his business trips. After her mother's death in 1912, she remained with her father until his death in 1928. She eventually lived with her sister in Magnolia. Upon

joining Mrs. Bellinger in Chautauqua County, she became an active member of the WCA Hospital Board in Jamestown. She passed away in 1949. In 1952, Mrs. Bellinger and her daughter, Mrs. Parker, provided funds for setting up the WCA snack shop as a memorial to Marion.

Financial Summary

Total Giving: $4,018,226 (fiscal year ending September 30, 2002); $3,756,141 (fiscal 2001); $4,307,984 (fiscal 2000)
Giving Analysis: Giving for fiscal 2001 includes: foundation grants to United Way ($885,500); fiscal 1999: foundation scholarships ($8,000) foundation grants to United Way ($483,204)
Assets: $74,458,978 (fiscal 2002); $70,252,260 (fiscal 2001); $88,066,972 (fiscal 2000)

Typical Recipients

Arts & Humanities: Arts Associations & Councils, Arts Funds, Arts & Humanities-General, Historic Preservation, History & Archaeology, Libraries, Museums/Galleries, Music, Opera, Performing Arts, Public Broadcasting, Theater
Civic & Public Affairs: Botanical Gardens/Parks, Business/Free Enterprise, Community Foundations, Economic Development, Employment/Job Training, Civic & Public Affairs-General, Housing, Legal Aid, Municipalities/Towns, Nonprofit Management, Philanthropic Organizations, Professional & Trade Associations, Public Policy, Urban & Community Affairs
Education: Business-School Partnerships, Colleges & Universities, Community & Junior Colleges, Education Associations, Education Funds, Education Reform, Environmental Education, Education-General, Literacy, Medical Education, Minority Education, Private Education (Precollege), Public Education (Precollege), Student Aid
Environment: Air/Water Quality, Environment-General, Resource Conservation, Watershed
Health: Alzheimers Disease, Cancer, Children's Health/Hospitals, Emergency/Ambulance Services, Health-General, Heart, Hospices, Hospitals, Medical Rehabilitation, Medical Research, Mental Health, Nursing Services, Prenatal Health Issues, Public Health, Research/Studies Institutes, Speech & Hearing
Religion: Churches, Ministries, Religious Welfare
Science: Scientific Centers & Institutes
Social Services: Animal Protection, Camps, Child Welfare, Community Service Organizations, Community Service Organizations, Counseling, Day Care, Domestic Violence, Family Services, Food/Clothing Distribution, Homes, People with Disabilities, Scouts, Senior Services, Social Services-General, Substance Abuse, United Funds/United Ways, YMCA/YWCA/YMHA/YWHA, Youth Organizations

Application Procedures

Initial Contact: Send a letter of inquiry addressed to the executive director of the foundation.
Application Requirements: The letter should contain a brief statement of the need for funds and enough factual information to enable the staff to determine whether or not the application falls within the foundation's areas of preferred interest or warrants consideration as a special project.
If the request falls into the foundation's geographical and interest areas, further information will be solicited, including 13 copies of a formal proposal, IRS determination letter, most recent audited financial statements, most recent Form 990, and current and proposed budgets for the and organization and/or program.
Deadlines: Although proposals may be submitted at any time, they must reach the foundation by December 1 for the March meeting, April 1 for the July meeting, and August 1 for the November meeting.
Review Process: All inquiries and proposals are reported to the board, including those declined at the staff or committee level.

Restrictions

Grants are not made to individuals, or to sectarian or religious organizations; however, traditional support is an exception. Special projects may be supported, but funds are not usually available for general support, endowment purposes, or national appeals.

Additional Information

Progress reports on grants, and annual audits of the grant program or agency, are requested. The foundation also suggests that programs seek funding from other sources.
Publications: Annual Report

Foundation Officials

George Campbell: director
Thomas Cardman: executive director
Dianne L. Eisenhardt: assistant treasurer, assistant secretary, grants administrator
Charles T. Hall: vice president
Rhoe B. Henderson, III: director
Dr. Lillian V. Ney: president, director
Bertram B. Parker: director
Geraldine M. Parker: secretary, director
Paul W. Sandberg: treasurer, director B 1932. PRIM CORP EMPL president; C L Carnahan Corp. CORP AFFIL director: Carnahan's of Chautauqua Inc.; director: Dowcraft Corp.
Linda Swanson: director

Grants Analysis

Disclosure Period: fiscal year ending September 30, 2001
Total Grants: $2,870,641*
Number of Grants: 73
Average Grant: $39,324
Highest Grant: $600,000
Lowest Grant: $100
Typical Range: $1,000 to $50,000 and $100,000 to $300,000
*Note: Giving excludes United Way.

Recent Grants

Note: Grants derived from fiscal 2001 Form 990.

Library-Related

184,047	Chautauqua-Cattaraugus Library System, Chautauqua, NY -- Gates Foundation partnership
30,000	James Prendergast Free Library, Jamestown, NY -- purchase of books
27,763	Chautauqua-Cattaraugus Library System, Chautauqua, NY -- book plan and subscriptions
15,000	Chautauqua-Cattaraugus Library System, Chautauqua, NY -- Alexander Finley Library

General

600,000	Jamestown Center City Development Corporation, Jamestown, NY -- debt services
442,750	United Way Southern Chautauqua County, Jamestown, NY -- Success by 6
330,500	United Way Southern Chautauqua County, Jamestown, NY -- annual campaign
250,000	Chautauqua Institution, Chautauqua, NY -- main gate
250,000	Lutheran Social Services, Falconer, NY -- focus 2000 building
155,000	Resource Center, Jamestown, NY -- dental clinic
110,000	Funds for the Arts, Jamestown, NY
100,000	Jamestown Community Learning Council, Jamestown, NY -- community schools
75,000	Kids Promise, Jamestown, NY
68,161	YWCA, Jamestown, NY -- Team Program

GEIFMAN FAMILY FOUNDATION

Giving Contact

Stephen L. Geifman, President
57 W. Burton Pl.
Chicago, IL 60610
Phone: (312)732-6519

Description

Founded: 1964
EIN: 366123096
Organization Type: Private Foundation
Giving Locations: IL
Grant Types: Endowment, General Support.

Financial Summary

Total Giving: $196,510 (2000); $280,090 (1999); $211,525 (1998)
Giving Analysis: Giving for 1999 includes: foundation scholarships ($1,000) foundation grants to United Way ($4,000)
Assets: $4,375,267 (2000); $3,038,540 (1999); $5,193,673 (1998)

Typical Recipients

Arts & Humanities: Ballet, Community Arts, Dance, History & Archaeology, Libraries, Museums/Galleries, Music, Opera, Theater
Civic & Public Affairs: Botanical Gardens/Parks, Civic & Public Affairs-General, Urban & Community Affairs, Zoos/Aquariums
Education: Colleges & Universities, Legal Education, Private Education (Precollege), Student Aid
Health: Alzheimers Disease, Cancer, Emergency/Ambulance Services, Heart, Hospitals, Prenatal Health Issues, Public Health, Research/Studies Institutes, Respiratory, Single-Disease Health Associations
International: Foreign Educational Institutions, Health Care/Hospitals, Missionary/Religious Activities
Religion: Jewish Causes, Religious Organizations, Religious Welfare, Social/Policy Issues, Synagogues/Temples
Social Services: Community Centers, Community Service Organizations, Homes, People with Disabilities, Substance Abuse, United Funds/United Ways, Youth Organizations

Application Procedures

Initial Contact: Applications have no set format; however, they must be typewritten.
Deadlines: None.

Foundation Officials

Geraldine Geifman: secretary, director
Stephen L. Geifman: president
Terri Geifman: assistant treasurer, director
Cherie Handler: assistant secretary, director

Grants Analysis

Disclosure Period: calendar year ending 2000
Total Grants: $196,510
Typical Range: $100 to $5,000
Note: No grants list available for 2000.

Recent Grants

Note: Grants derived from 1999 Form 990.

General

22,000	Anshe Emet Synagogue, Chicago, IL
20,000	Hillels of Greater Washington, Washington, DC
16,000	Mesorah Heritage Foundation, New York, NY
15,000	Georgetown University Law School, Washington, DC
15,000	New York University School of Law, New York, NY
15,000	Washington University, St. Louis, MO
12,000	Lyric Opera of Chicago, Chicago, IL
10,500	Bernard Zell Anshe Emet Day School, Chicago, IL
10,000	Jewish Federation of Quad Cities, Rock Island, IL
10,000	Latin School, Chicago, IL

FRED GELLERT FAMILY FOUNDATION

Giving Contact

Fred Gellert, President
361 Third Street, Suite A
San Rafael, CA 94901
Phone: (415)256-5420
E-mail: foundation@fredgellert.com
Web: http://fdncenter.org/grantmaker/fredgellert/

Description

Founded: 1958
EIN: 946062859
Organization Type: Private Foundation
Giving Locations: CA: San Francisco including San Mateo and San Francisco counties
Grant Types: Capital, Endowment, General Support, Multiyear/Continuing Support, Operating Expenses, Project, Research.

Donor Information

Founder: the late Fred Gellert, Sr.

Financial Summary

Total Giving: $582,500 (fiscal year ending November 30, 2001); $1,208,155 (fiscal 2000); $1,093,700 (fiscal 1999)
Assets: $12,836,601 (fiscal 2001); $13,964,727 (fiscal 2000); $14,059,313 (fiscal 1999)

Typical Recipients

Arts & Humanities: Community Arts, Ethnic & Folk Arts, Historic Preservation, Libraries, Museums/Galleries, Opera, Performing Arts, Public Broadcasting, Theater
Civic & Public Affairs: Botanical Gardens/Parks, Civic & Public Affairs-General, Municipalities/Towns, Public Policy, Urban & Community Affairs, Women's Affairs
Education: Arts/Humanities Education, Colleges & Universities, Education-General, Literacy, Minority Education, Private Education (Precollege), Public Education (Precollege), School Volunteerism, Secondary Education (Public), Special Education
Environment: Air/Water Quality, Environment-General, Protection, Resource Conservation
Health: Adolescent Health Issues, Cancer, Clinics/Medical Centers, Eyes/Blindness, Health Organizations, Hospices, Hospitals, Medical Research, Public Health
International: Health Care/Hospitals, International Environmental Issues, International Organizations
Religion: Ministries, Religious Welfare, Social/Policy Issues
Science: Scientific Centers & Institutes
Social Services: Child Welfare, Community Centers, Community Service Organizations, Day Care, Family Planning, Family Services, Food/Clothing Distribution, People with Disabilities, Recreation & Athletics, Shelters/Homelessness, Volunteer Services, Youth Organizations

Application Procedures

Initial Contact: Request application guidelines.
Deadlines: None.

Restrictions

Grants are not made to individuals. Environmental grants have no geographical limitations. All other grants are limited to the San Francisco Bay area.

Additional Information

Publications: Application Guidelines

Foundation Officials

Annette Gellert: director
Fred Gellert, Jr.: chairman
John D. Howard: secretary

Grants Analysis

Disclosure Period: fiscal year ending November 30, 2001
Total Grants: $582,500
Number of Grants: 75
Average Grant: $7,767
Highest Grant: $50,000
Lowest Grant: $1,000
Typical Range: $2,000 to $15,000

Recent Grants

Note: Grants derived from fiscal 2000 Form 990.

General

30,000	KQED TV, San Francisco, CA
30,000	Sterne School, San Francisco, CA
25,000	Galef Institute, Los Angeles, CA
25,000	Menlo College, Atherton, CA
25,000	Rachel's Network, Washington, DC
25,000	Seton Foundation for Learning, Staten Island, NY
20,900	City of Daly City, Daly City, CA
20,000	Goodwill Industries
20,000	Yosemite Fund, San Francisco, CA
15,000	Bay Institute, San Francisco, CA

CARL GELLERT AND CELIA BERTA GELLERT FOUNDATION

Giving Contact

Peter J. Brusati, Secretary & Director
1169 Market St., Suite 808
San Francisco, CA 94103
Phone: (415)255-2829
Web: http://home.earthlink.net/~cgcbg/

Description

Founded: 1958
EIN: 946062858
Organization Type: Private Foundation
Giving Locations: CA: San Francisco Alamada, Contra Costa, Marin, Napa, San Mateo, Santa Clara, Solano, and Sonoma counties in CA
Grant Types: Capital, Endowment, General Support, Multiyear/Continuing Support, Operating Expenses, Project, Research, Scholarship.

Donor Information

Founder: the late Carl Gellert, Atlas Realty Co., Pacific Coast Construction Co., the late Gertrude E. Gellert

Financial Summary

Total Giving: $983,000 (fiscal year ending November 30, 2002); $4,209,940 (fiscal 2001); $909,500 (fiscal 2000)
Giving Analysis: Giving for fiscal 1998 includes: foundation scholarships ($155,500)

Assets: $50,164,865 (fiscal 2001); $22,762,317 (fiscal 2000); $14,470,978 (fiscal 1998)
Gifts Received: $33,693,318 (fiscal 2001); $10,840,544 (fiscal 2000); $315,000 (fiscal 1998). Note: In fiscal 2001, contributions were received from the Estate of Celia Ann Gellert. In fiscal 2000, contributions were received from Cecilia A. Gellert ($395,000) and Carl Gellert Trust ($10,445,544). In fiscal 1994 and in fiscal 1998, contributions were received from Celia A. Gellert.

Typical Recipients

Arts & Humanities: Community Arts, Historic Preservation, Libraries, Museums/Galleries, Music, Performing Arts
Civic & Public Affairs: Legal Aid, Municipalities/Towns, Zoos/Aquariums
Education: Afterschool/Enrichment Programs, Arts/Humanities Education, Colleges & Universities, Engineering/Technological Education, Private Education (Precollege), Religious Education, Science/Mathematics Education, Secondary Education (Private), Secondary Education (Public), Special Education, Student Aid
Health: Alzheimers Disease, Arthritis, Cancer, Clinics/Medical Centers, Emergency/Ambulance Services, Eyes/Blindness, Health Organizations, Home-Care Services, Hospitals, Long-Term Care, Medical Rehabilitation, Medical Research, Mental Health, Nursing Services
International: Health Care/Hospitals
Religion: Churches, Dioceses, Religion-General, Ministries, Religious Organizations, Religious Welfare, Seminaries
Social Services: Animal Protection, Big Brother/Big Sister, Child Welfare, Community Centers, Community Service Organizations, Family Planning, Family Services, Food/Clothing Distribution, Homes, People with Disabilities, Recreation & Athletics, Senior Services, Substance Abuse, Youth Organizations

Application Procedures

Initial Contact: Send a brief letter of inquiry of not more than five pages.
Application Requirements: Foundation's application, proof of tax-exempt status, documentation that the organization is not a private foundation, brief background information on organization, and a brief outline of program or project to be funded.
Deadlines: August 15.

Restrictions

Grants are not made to individuals. The foundation does not support organizations outside operating areas, loans, donations, multi-year commitments, sponsorships, fund raising events such as dinner, walk-a-thons, tournaments or fashion show.

Additional Information

Publications: Application Guidelines; Grant Request Application; Form 990; Financial Statements

Foundation Officials

Fred R. Bahrt: president, director
Maria C. Bentley: treasurer, director
Peter J. Brusati: executive director, secretary
Andrew A. Cresci: director
Lorraine D'Elia: director
Jack Fitzpatrick: director
Robert J. Grassilli: treasurer, director
Michael J. King: director
Robert L. Pauly: chairman
J. Malcolm Visbal: director

Grants Analysis

Disclosure Period: fiscal year ending November 30, 2002
Total Grants: $983,000
Number of Grants: 181
Average Grant: $5,431
Highest Grant: $50,000

Lowest Grant: $1,000
Typical Range: $1,000 to $10,000

Recent Grants

Note: Grants derived from fiscal 2000 Form 990.

General

55,000	Seton Medical Center, Daly City, CA -- patient bed replacement
25,000	College of Notre Dame, Belmont, CA -- financial aid
25,000	Little Sisters of the Poor, San Francisco, CA -- emergency power load additions
20,000	Immaculate Conception Academy, San Francisco, CA -- scholarship fund
20,000	Junipero Serra High School, San Mateo, CA -- financial aid
20,000	Mercy High School, Burlingame, CA -- tuition assistance
20,000	RCH, Inc, San Francisco, CA -- after school and summer day camp
20,000	RCH, Inc., San Francisco, CA -- After School and Summer Day Camp
20,000	Sacred Heart Cathedral Preparatory, San Francisco, CA -- technology classroom upgrade
20,000	Saint Ignatius College Preparatory, San Francisco, CA -- tuition assistance

GENAMERICA FINANCIAL CORP.

Company Headquarters

700 Market Street
St. Louis, MO 63101
Phone: (314)231-1700
Fax: (314)525-6444
Web: http://www.genamerica.com

Company Description

SIC(s): 6311 Life Insurance, 6321 Accident & Health Insurance.
Parent Company: Metropolitan Life Insurance Co., 1 Madison Avenue, New York, NY, United States

Operating Locations

GenAmerica Corp. (GA--Atlanta; MO--Clayton, St. Louis)

Nonmonetary Support

Type: In-kind Services
Note: NOT Nonmonetary support is provided by both the company and the foundation.
Volunteer Programs: Company executives and associates have assumed leadership roles in a variety of civic and charitable causes.

GenAmerican Foundation

Giving Contact

Cheryl Endicot, Contributions Specialist
700 Market Street
St. Louis, MO 63101
Phone: (314)444-0434
Fax: (314)444-0681
E-mail: cendicott@genam.com
Web: http://www.genamerica.com

Description

EIN: 431401687
Organization Type: Corporate Foundation
Former Name: General American Foundation (1999).
Giving Locations: MO: St. Louis

Grant Types: Capital, General Support, Multiyear/ Continuing Support, Professorship, Project, Research, Scholarship.

Financial Summary

Total Giving: $800,000 (fiscal year ending November 30, 2001); $845,546 (fiscal 2000); $1,016,468 (fiscal 1998). Note: Contributes through foundation, direct/ corporate giving, nonmonetary support, and domestic subsidiary giving.
Giving Analysis: Giving for fiscal 2001 includes: foundation grants to United Way ($340,000); foundation ($460,000); fiscal 2000: foundation grants to United Way ($344,896); foundation ($500,650); fiscal 1998: foundation grants to United Way ($378,248); foundation ($638,220);
Assets: $13,942,046 (fiscal 2000); $14,000,000 (fiscal 1999 approx); $13,293,030 (fiscal 1998)
Gifts Received: $8,151,125 (fiscal 1998); $500,000 (fiscal 1996); $428,000 (fiscal 1995)

Typical Recipients

Arts & Humanities: Arts Centers, Arts Funds, Arts Outreach, Community Arts, Dance, Ethnic & Folk Arts, History & Archaeology, Libraries, Museums/Galleries, Music, Opera, Performing Arts, Public Broadcasting, Theater
Civic & Public Affairs: African American Affairs, Botanical Gardens/Parks, Business/Free Enterprise, Chambers of Commerce, Employment/Job Training, Civic & Public Affairs-General, Minority Business, Municipalities/Towns, Nonprofit Management, Parades/ Festivals, Philanthropic Organizations, Professional & Trade Associations, Public Policy, Urban & Community Affairs, Women's Affairs, Zoos/ Aquariums
Education: Arts/Humanities Education, Business Education, Colleges & Universities, Economic Education, Economic Education, Education Associations, Education Funds, Education-General, Medical Education, Minority Education, Public Education (Precollege), Science/Mathematics Education, Secondary Education (Public), Special Education, Student Aid
Environment: Environment-General
Health: AIDS/HIV, Alzheimers Disease, Cancer, Children's Health/Hospitals, Clinics/Medical Centers, Diabetes, Emergency/Ambulance Services, Heart, Hospitals, Hospitals (University Affiliated), Medical Rehabilitation, Medical Research, Preventive Medicine/Wellness Organizations, Public Health, Single-Disease Health Associations
Religion: Churches, Dioceses, Jewish Causes, Ministries, Religious Organizations, Religious Welfare
Science: Scientific Centers & Institutes, Scientific Centers & Institutes
Social Services: At-Risk Youth, Child Welfare, Community Centers, Community Service Organizations, Counseling, Domestic Violence, Emergency Relief, Family Planning, Food/Clothing Distribution, Homes, People with Disabilities, Recreation & Athletics, Scouts, Senior Services, Substance Abuse, United Funds/United Ways, Volunteer Services, YMCA/ YWCA/YMHA/YWHA, Youth Organizations

Application Procedures

Initial Contact: Send a brief letter or proposal and request for application form.
Application Requirements: Include a brief history of the organization; list of officers and board of directors, including affiliations; a copy of the organization's most recent financial statement; and a copy of IRS Code Section 501(c)(3) tax-exempt letter.
Deadlines: October 1.
Evaluative Criteria: Priority is given to arts and education.
Decision Notification: Grants are approved in January for the following year.

Restrictions

Does not contribute to individuals or any individual benefit, political organizations, candidates for political office, religious organizations for non-secular purposes, social clubs, or labor organizations for political or organizational purposes.

Additional Information

GenAmerica Corporation was formerly known as General America Corporation.

Corporate Officials

Richard A. Liddy: chairman, president, chief executive officer B 1935. ED Iowa State University BS (1957). PRIM CORP EMPL chairman, president, chief executive officer: General American Life Insurance Co. ADD CORP EMPL chairman: General American Corp.; chairman: Cova Corp.; chairman: Reins Group America Inc.; chairman: Security Mutual Life Insurance New York. CORP AFFIL director: Ralston Purina Co.; director: Security Equity Life Insurance Co.; director: Ameren Corp.; director: Brown Shoe Co. Inc.

Grants Analysis

Disclosure Period: fiscal year ending November 30, 2001
Total Grants: $460,000*
Number of Grants: 27
Average Grant: $17,037
Highest Grant: $50,000
Lowest Grant: $500
Typical Range: $500 to $20,000
*Note: Giving excludes United Way. Grants analysis provided by foundation.

Recent Grants

Note: Grants derived from fiscal 2000 Form 990.

General

85,000	United Way of Greater St. Louis, St. Louis, MO
85,000	United Way of Greater St. Louis, St. Louis, MO
85,000	United Way of Greater St. Louis, St. Louis, MO
85,000	United Way of Greater St. Louis, St. Louis, MO
50,000	Webster University, St. Louis, MO
45,000	St. Louis 2004, St. Louis, MO
40,000	Missouri Historical Society, St. Louis, MO
30,000	St. Louis Symphony Orchestra, St. Louis, MO
20,000	St. Louis Symphony Orchestra, St. Louis, MO
18,750	State of St. Louis Foundation, St. Louis, MO

GENERAL ELECTRIC CO.

Company Headquarters

3135 Easton Turnpike
Fairfield, CT 06431-0001
Web: http://www.ge.com

Company Description

Ticker: GE
Exchange: NYSE
Revenue: US$130.685 billion (2002)
Profit: US$14.118 billion (2002)
Employees: 315000 (2002)
Fortune Rank: 5, per FORTUNE Magazine's list of 500 Largest U.S. Corporations (2002).

Nonmonetary Support

Type: Donated Equipment; Donated Products; Loaned Executives
Note: NOT The company provides nonmonetary support.

Volunteer Programs: GE supports the United Way and United Way-sponsored agencies where GE volunteers perform a variety of services, including agency clean-ups, refurbishing day care centers, and building houses through Habitat for Humanity. GE also supports Elfun, a global organization of GE employees and retirees who work to improve the company and communities through volunteerism, leadership, and camaraderie.
GE volunteer hours approach $500,000 in billable hours.
Note: For nonmonetary support contact nearest company office.

GE Foundation

Giving Contact

Marc Saperstein, President
3135 Easton Turnpike
Fairfield, CT 06828
Phone: (203)373-3216
Fax: (203)373-3029
E-mail: gefoundation@ge.com
Web: http://www.gefoundation.com

Alternate Contact

Gisele Hill, Secretary

Description

EIN: 222621967
Organization Type: Corporate Foundation
Former Name: GE Foundations.
Former Name: GE Fund (2003).
Giving Locations: headquarters and operating communities; international organizations; national organizations.
Grant Types: Award, Emergency, Employee Matching Gifts, General Support, Multiyear/Continuing Support, Project, Research.
Note: Employee matching gift ratio: 1 to 1 for education and health and human services.

Financial Summary

Total Giving: $75,000,000 (2002 approx); $51,924,088 (2001 approx); $39,925,221 (2000). Note: Contributes through corporate direct giving program and foundation.
Giving Analysis: Giving for 2001 includes: nonmonetary support (approx $700,000); international subsidiaries (approx $1,900,000); domestic subsidiaries (approx $21,200,000); corporate direct giving (approx $23,100,000); foundation (approx $52,700,000); 2000: foundation matching gifts ($17,170,764); foundation ($18,414,848); 1999: foundation grants to United Way ($4,093,575); foundation matching gifts ($14,714,093); foundation ($16,455,433);
Assets: $29,346,467 (2001); $18,827,392 (2000); $53,887,325 (1999)
Gifts Received: $59,800,007 (2001); $5,000,000 (2000); $78,024,702 (1999). Note: Contributions are received from General Electric Company.

Typical Recipients

Arts & Humanities: Arts Associations & Councils, Arts Centers, Arts Funds, Dance, Ethnic & Folk Arts, Historic Preservation, Libraries, Museums/Galleries, Music, Opera, Performing Arts, Public Broadcasting, Theater, Visual Arts
Civic & Public Affairs: African American Affairs, Business/Free Enterprise, Civil Rights, Community Foundations, Economic Development, Economic Policy, Employment/Job Training, Civic & Public Affairs-General, Housing, Law & Justice, Nonprofit Management, Professional & Trade Associations, Public Policy, Urban & Community Affairs, Women's Affairs, Zoos/Aquariums

Education: Afterschool/Enrichment Programs, Arts/
Humanities Education, Business Education, Colleges & Universities, Colleges & Universities, Continuing Education, Economic Education, Education Associations, Education Reform, Engineering/
Technological Education, Faculty Development, Education-General, International Exchange, International
Studies, Legal Education, Literacy, Medical Education, Minority Education, Public Education (Precollege), Science/Mathematics Education, Student Aid
Environment: Energy, Environment-General, Resource Conservation, Watershed, Wildlife Protection
Health: Clinics/Medical Centers, Emergency/Ambu-
lance Services, Health Policy/Cost Containment,
Health Organizations, Hospitals, Hospitals (University
Affiliated), Medical Research
International: Foreign Educational Institutions,
Health Care/Hospitals, International Affairs, Interna-
tional Development, International Environmental Is-
sues, International Organizations, International
Peace & Security Issues, International Relations, In-
ternational Relief Efforts, Missionary/Religious Activi-
ties, Trade
Religion: Ministries, Religious Welfare
Science: Scientific Centers & Institutes, Scientific Or-
ganizations
Social Services: Child Welfare, Community Centers,
Community Service Organizations, Family Services,
Food/Clothing Distribution, People with Disabilities,
Senior Services, Shelters/Homelessness, Social Ser-
vices-General, Substance Abuse, United Funds/
United Ways, Volunteer Services, Youth Organiza-
tions

Application Procedures

Initial Contact: Send letter requesting application to
Joyce Hergenhan, President, GE Fund, 3135 Easton
Turnpike, Fairfield, CT 06828, or telephone
(203)373-3216.
Deadlines: None.
Notes: Giving priorities are for pre-college and higher
education, arts education programs, international education programs and institutions, and public policy
organizations where GE has a presence. A community awards program supports local improvement efforts in selected locations overseas.

Restrictions

The Fund does not provide scholarships or other direct support to individuals, nor does it support capital
campaigns, endowments, endowed chairs, ongoing
operations, or institutional overhead/indirect costs;
capital investment, construction or renovation, solely
equipment purchases; grants to individuals and/or private elementary and secondary schools; projects that
directly benefit the GE company, employees, or customers; projects for political or religious purposes;
special events, such as conferences, sports competitions, and art exhibits; activities of organizations serving primarily their own membership; organizations or
projects in countries with which the U.S. government
restricts business dealings; recipients of funds
through the GE Fund More Gifts...More Givers matching gifts; or United Way agencies.

Additional Information

Company has operating locations in nearly all 50
states.
In 1994, GE combined its two charitable foundations,
the GE Foundation, a trust established in 1952 to
make grants in the US, and the GE Foundation, Inc.,
a corporation established in 1985 to make grants both
domestically and internationally. The combined entity
is known as the GE Fund and serves as the company's primary vehicle for philanthropic support.
Biographical information above covers the chairperson of each foundation committee. Complete list of
committee members is available upon request from
foundation office.
Publications: Annual Report

Corporate Officials

Dennis Dean Dammerman: vice chairman, director
B Fairfield, IA 1945. ED University of Dubuque BS
(1967). PRIM CORP EMPL vice chairman, director:
General Electric Co. ADD CORP EMPL chairman,
chief executive officer: Capital Services. CORP AFFIL
vice president: Monogram General Agency Texas;
director: General Electric Financial Services; director:
General Electric Capital Corp.; officer: General Electric Capital Services. NONPR AFFIL member: Officers Conference Group; director: University Dubuque; member: Financial Executives Institute;
trustee: Fairfield University; trustee: Financial Accounting Foundation; member: Council Financial Executives.
William P. Driscoll, Junior: vice president, officer
PRIM CORP EMPL vice president, officer: General
Electric Co.
Jeffrey R. Immelt: chairman, chief executive officer
B February 19, 1956. PRIM CORP EMPL chairman,
chief executive officer: General Electric Co.
Steven Kerr: vice president corporate leadership development ED City University of New York PhD. PRIM
CORP EMPL vice president corporate leadership de-
velopment: General Electric Co.
John D. Opie: vice chairman, executive officer, direc-
tor ED Michigan Technological Institute BS (1961).
PRIM CORP EMPL vice chairman, executive officer,
director: General Electric Co. CORP AFFIL director:
National Broadcasting Co. Inc.
Keith S. Sherin: senior vice president finance, chief
financial officer ED Columbia University MBA; University of Notre Dame BA. PRIM CORP EMPL senior
vice president finance, chief financial officer: General
Electric Corp.

Foundation Officials

William J. Conaty: chairperson, director B Johnson
City, NY 1945. ED Bryant College (1967). PRIM
CORP EMPL senior vice president human resources:
General Electric Co. NONPR AFFIL director: Labor
Policy Association; fellow: National Academy Human
Resources; director: Jobs for Americas Grads.
Michael J. Cosgrove: treasurer PRIM CORP EMPL
executive vice president: General Electric Investment
Corp. ADD CORP EMPL executive vice president: GE
Investment Management Inc. CORP AFFIL trustee:
General Electric S&S Long Term Fund; trustee: Gen-
eral Electric S&S Program.
Benjamin Walter Heineman, Jr.: director B Chicago,
IL 1944. ED Harvard University BA (1965); Oxford
University Balliol College (1967); Yale University JD
(1971). PRIM CORP EMPL senior vice president,
general counsel, secretary: General Electric Co. ADD
CORP EMPL director: General Electric Capital Corp.;
officer: General Electric Capital SVCs. NONPR AFFIL
member: American Law Institute; member: Phi Beta
Kappa; member: American Bar Association.
Joyce Hergenhan: director, president B Mount
Kisco, NY 1941. ED Syracuse University BA (1963);
Columbia University MBA (1978). PRIM CORP EMPL
vice president corporate & public relations: General
Electric Co.
Henry A. Hubschman: director B Newark, NJ 1947.
ED Rutgers University BA (1969); Harvard University
JD (1973). PRIM CORP EMPL president: GE Capital
Aviation Service Inc.
Keith S. Sherin: director (see above)
Lloyd G. Trotter: director PRIM CORP EMPL presi-
dent, chief executive officer: GE Industrial Systems
ADD CORP EMPL president: General Electric Co.

Grants Analysis

Disclosure Period: calendar year ending 2001
Total Grants: $28,459,000*
Number of Grants: 392
Average Grant: $47,210*
Highest Grant: $10,000,000
Typical Range: $5,000 to $100,000

*__Note:__ Grants analysis provided by the company. Giv-
ing excludes matching gifts, scholarships, United
Way. Average grant figure excludes highest grant.

Recent Grants

Note: Grants derived from 2001 Form 990.

General

1,000,000	College Board, New York, NY
891,930	Institute for International Education, New York, NY
306,716	Union College, Barbourville, KY
290,942	Princeton University, Princeton, NJ
275,472	Harvard University, Cambridge, MA
269,565	University of Pennsylvania, Philadelphia, PA
262,234	Pennsylvania State University, University Park, PA
250,000	Lowrides County Community-Based Coalition
250,000	NACM Educational Services, Phoenix, AZ
250,000	United Negro College Fund, Fairfax, VA

GENERAL MILLS, INC.

Company Headquarters

Minneapolis, MN
Web: http://www.generalmills.com

Company Description

Founded: 1928
Ticker: GIS
Exchange: NYSE
Revenue: US$7.949 billion (2002)
Profit: US$458 million (2002)
Employees: 29859 (2002)
Fortune Rank: 235, per FORTUNE Magazine's list
of 500 Largest U.S. Corporations (2002).
SIC(s): 2026 Fluid Milk, 2034 Dehydrated Fruits, Veg-
etables & Soups, 2037 Frozen Fruits & Vegetables,
2043 Cereal Breakfast Foods.

Operating Locations

General Mills, Inc. (AK--Anchorage; CA--Lodi, Los
Angeles, Orange; CO--Englewood, Henderson; DC--
Washington; FL--Orlando; HI--Waipahu; ID--Ameri-
can Falls, Idaho Falls, Newdale, Pocatello; IL--
Gurnee, Hoffman Estates, Lisle, Montgomery, West
Chicago; IA--Carlisle, Cedar Rapids, Iowa City; KS--
Shawnee Mission; MA--Franklin; MN--Bloomington,
Minneapolis; MO--Chesterfield, Kansas City; MT--
Broadview, Carter, Chester, Choteau, Cut Bank, Den-
ton, Fort Benton, Geraldine, Gilford, Harlowton, Ha-
vre, Hingham, Joplin, Plentywood, Stanford,
Sweetgrass, Wolf Point; NV, Winnemucca; OH--North
Olmsted, Toledo; OR, Lake Oswego; TN--Chatta-
nooga, Germantown; TX--Dallas, Fort Worth)

Nonmonetary Support

Value: $16,000,000 (2000)
Type: Donated Products; Loaned Employees;
Loaned Executives
Volunteer Programs: General Mills' Volunteer Con-
nection and Retirement PLUS programs promote em-
ployee volunteerism by matching volunteers with proj-
ects, and the Volunteer Advisory Board Steers
Company involvement in volunteer endeavors.
Contact: David Nasby, Vice President
Phone: (612)540-4351
Note: Co. donates a substantial amount of food prod-
ucts primarily through Second Harvest food banks.

General Mills Foundation

Giving Contact

Chris L. Shea, President and Executive Director
General Mills Foundation
PO Box 1113
Minneapolis, MN 55440
Phone: (612)540-2579
Fax: (612)540-4114
Web: http://www.generalmills.com/corporate/about/community/

Alternate Contact

Constance L. Schillings
General Mills Foundation
One General Mills Boulevard
Minneapolis, MN 55426
Note: Contact for volunteer questions and requests only.

Description

Founded: 1954
EIN: 416018495
Organization Type: Corporate Foundation
Giving Locations: nationally; operating locations.
Grant Types: Capital, Employee Matching Gifts, General Support, Multiyear/Continuing Support, Operating Expenses.
Note: Employee matching gift ratio: 1 to 1. Foundation makes a limited number of capital grants and only for special purposes that meet specific community needs within the foundation's funding focus.

Financial Summary

Total Giving: $15,000,157 (fiscal year ending May 31, 2001); $15,009,837 (fiscal 2000); $15,999,986 (fiscal 1999). Note: Contributes through corporate direct giving program and foundation.
Giving Analysis: Giving for fiscal 2000 includes: foundation scholarships ($603,688); foundation grants to United Way ($2,582,345); foundation matching gifts ($2,584,944); foundation ($9,229,181); fiscal 1999: foundation matching gifts ($3,857,948); foundation ($12,142,039); fiscal 1998: corporate direct giving ($5,600,000) foundation ($16,000,038)
Assets: $27,829,500 (fiscal 2001); $46,929,735 (fiscal 1996); $54,310,223 (fiscal 1995)
Gifts Received: $8,000,000 (fiscal 2001); $7,500,000 (fiscal 1996); $9,000,000 (fiscal 1995). Note: The foundation receives contributions from General Mills and its subsidiaries.

Typical Recipients

Arts & Humanities: Arts Associations & Councils, Arts Centers, Arts Funds, Arts Institutes, Dance, Film & Video, Arts & Humanities-General, Historic Preservation, History & Archaeology, Libraries, Literary Arts, Museums/Galleries, Music, Opera, Performing Arts, Public Broadcasting, Theater
Civic & Public Affairs: African American Affairs, Asian American Affairs, Business/Free Enterprise, Civil Rights, Community Foundations, Economic Development, Employment/Job Training, Civic & Public Affairs-General, Hispanic Affairs, Housing, Law & Justice, Legal Aid, Municipalities/Towns, Native American Affairs, Professional & Trade Associations, Public Policy, Urban & Community Affairs, Women's Affairs, Zoos/Aquariums
Education: Agricultural Education, Arts/Humanities Education, Business Education, Business-School Partnerships, Colleges & Universities, Community & Junior Colleges, Continuing Education, Economic Education, Education Associations, Education Funds, Education Reform, Elementary Education (Public), Engineering/Technological Education, Faculty Development, Education-General, Gifted & Talented Programs, International Exchange, International Studies,

Legal Education, Literacy, Medical Education, Minority Education, Preschool Education, Private Education (Precollege), Public Education (Precollege), Religious Education, Science/Mathematics Education, Secondary Education (Public), Social Sciences Education, Special Education, Student Aid
Environment: Environment-General
Health: Cancer, Children's Health/Hospitals, Clinics/Medical Centers, Emergency/Ambulance Services, Geriatric Health, Health Policy/Cost Containment, Health Organizations, Hospitals, Medical Rehabilitation, Medical Research, Mental Health, Nutrition
Religion: Churches, Religious Welfare, Social/Policy Issues
Science: Science Museums, Scientific Centers & Institutes
Social Services: At-Risk Youth, Big Brother/Big Sister, Child Welfare, Community Centers, Community Service Organizations, Counseling, Day Care, Delinquency & Criminal Rehabilitation, Domestic Violence, Emergency Relief, Family Planning, Family Services, Food/Clothing Distribution, Homes, People with Disabilities, Recreation & Athletics, Refugee Assistance, Scouts, Senior Services, Shelters/Homelessness, Social Services-General, Substance Abuse, United Funds/United Ways, Volunteer Services, YMCA/YWCA/YMHA/YWHA, Youth Organizations

Application Procedures

Initial Contact: Request grant application or download application from the foundation's web site.
Application Requirements: Completed application form; a description of organization and mission statement with a list of its officers and board members, including affiliations; proof of tax-exempt status; a recently audited financial statement; objectives for the current fiscal year; the previous year's major accomplishments; and a major donor list.
Deadlines: None; board meets periodically throughout the year.
Review Process: If proposal meets foundation criteria, application is assigned to a program officer for review; officer analyzes proposal and makes recommendation to foundation's Grants Committee; officer will contact organization if additional information is required.
Evaluative Criteria: Priority is given to organizations whose mission is closely related to the foundation's priorities; programs focus on the needs of families, children, and youth; services are direct and of high quality; programs or activities are based in communities with General Mills facilities and employees; programs or activities involve General Mills employees and retirees.
Decision Notification: Four to six weeks after recommendation to Grants Committee.
Notes: Send proposals to the Community Partnership Council in applicant's region; see foundation guidelines for list of councils.

Restrictions

Foundation does not support organizations without 501(c)(3) and 509(a) status; individuals; travel by groups; social, labor, veterans, alumni or fraternal organizations serving a limited constituency; political causes, candidates, or legislative lobbying efforts; recreational, sporting events or athletic associations; religious organizations for religious purposes; or organizations seeking underwriting for advertising or program sponsorship. Generally, the foundation also does not support: conferences, seminars and workshops; underwriting for program sponsorship; campaigns to eliminate or control specific diseases; or publications, films, or television programs. campaigns to eliminate or control specific diseases; or publications, films, or television programs.

Additional Information

Foundation funding takes four forms: grants to nonprofit organizations; gift-matching to education and arts and culture organizations; match of employee

and retiree contributions to annual United Way campaign; and scholarships for children of employees. Foundation grant amounts begin at $1,000 and can exceed $100,000 for a single project.
The foundation conducts both pre- and post-grant evaluations and seeks the participation of the nonprofit in this process. The foundation also keeps a confidential record of all grant requests that have been accepted in the past nine years. Records of grants requests that are declined are kept for three years.
Publications: Annual Report; Application Form

Corporate Officials

Stephen R. Demeritt: vice chairman PRIM CORP EMPL vice chairman: General Mills Inc.
James A. Lawrence: chief financial officer, executive vice president PRIM CORP EMPL chief financial officer, executive vice president: General Mills, Inc. CORP AFFIL director: Avnet Inc.
Siri M. Marshall: senior vice president, general counsel ED Harvard University BA (1970); Yale University JD (1974). PRIM CORP EMPL senior vice president, general counsel: General Mills Inc. CORP AFFIL director: Nova Care Inc. NONPR AFFIL member executive committee: Center Public; trustee: Minneapolis Institute Arts; American Arbitration Association.
Michael A. Peel: senior vice president human resources B 1950. PRIM CORP EMPL senior vice president human resources: General Mills, Inc.
Stephen W. Sanger: chairman, chief executive officer, director B April 10, 1946. ED DePauw University BA (1968); University of Michigan MBA (1970). PRIM CORP EMPL chairman, chief executive officer, director: General Mills, Inc. CORP AFFIL director: Dayton Hudson Corp.; director: Donaldson Co. Inc. NONPR AFFIL director: Conference Board Inc.; treasurer: Guthrie Theater Foundation.
Austin Padraic Sullivan, Junior: senior vice president corporate relations B Washington, DC 1940. ED Princeton University AB (1964). PRIM CORP EMPL senior vice president corporate relations: General Mills, Inc. NONPR AFFIL member: Grocery Manufacturer America; director: Minnesota Chamber of Commerce; member: Business Roundtable; board advisors: Democrat Leadership Council.
Raymond Viault: vice chairman, director B New York, NY 1944. ED Brown University (1967); Columbia University (1969). PRIM CORP EMPL vice chairman, director: General Mills, Inc. CORP AFFIL director: Willis Corroon Group LLC.

Foundation Officials

Siri M. Marshall: trustee (see above)
Michael A. Peel: trustee (see above)
Stephen W. Sanger: chairman, chief executive officer (see above)
Austin Padraic Sullivan, Junior: trustee (see above)
Cynthia A. Thelen: coordinator
David Van Benschoten: vice president, treasurer B 1955. ED University of Minnesota; Bethel College (1976). PRIM CORP EMPL vice president investment management: General Mills, Inc.

Grants Analysis

Disclosure Period: fiscal year ending May 31, 2001
Total Grants: $9,229,181*
Number of Grants: 557
Average Grant: $16,569
Highest Grant: $500,000
Typical Range: $5,000 to $30,000
*Note: Giving excludes matching gifts, scholarship, and United Way.

Recent Grants

Note: Grants derived from 2001 Form 990.

General

1,673,172 United Way of Minneapolis Area, Minneapolis, MN -- match of employee and retiree contributions

425,000	University of Minnesota Foundation, Minneapolis, MN -- for General Mills Genomics for Healthful Foods Chair and fellowship
300,000	Hawthorne Area Community Council, Minneapolis, MN -- for Hawthorne Homestead Program
271,177	Citizens Scholarship Foundation of America, St. Peter, MN -- scholarships
178,555	United Way East Central Iowa, Cedar Rapids, IA -- match of employee contributions
173,472	United Way San Joaquin County, Stockton, CA -- match of employee contributions
162,500	Minnesota Public Radio, St. Paul, MN -- for Saint Paul Sunday
146,200	Twin Cities Public Television, St. Paul, MN -- operating support
125,000	Dunwoody Industrial Institute, Minneapolis, MN -- Living the Promise... Fulfilling the Dream Campaign
125,000	Gustavus Adolphus College, St. Peter, MN -- post tornado recovery funding

GENERAL MOTORS CORP.

Company Headquarters

Detroit, MI
Web: http://www.gm.com

Company Description

Founded: 1908
Ticker: GM
Exchange: NYSE
Acquired: Hughes Electronics Corp..
Revenue: US$186.763 billion (2002)
Profit: US$1.736 billion (2002)
Employees: 349000 (2002)
Fortune Rank: 2, per FORTUNE Magazine's list of 500 Largest U.S. Corporations (2002).
SIC(s): 3663 Radio & T.V. Communications Equipment, 3711 Motor Vehicles & Car Bodies, 3743 Railroad Equipment, 3769 Space Vehicle Equipment Nec.

Operating Locations

General Motors Corp. (AL--Athens, Decatur; CA--Ontario, San Francisco; CT--Fairfield, Plainville; DE--Wilmington; FL--Fort Myers; GA--Norcross, Rome; IL--La Grange, Maywood, Morrisonville; IN--Bedford, Bloomington, Fort Wayne, Indianapolis, Marion, Mount Vernon; IA--West Burlington; KS--Arkansas City, Kansas City; KY--Bowling Green, Louisville; LA--Monroe, Shreveport; MD--Baltimore, Rockville; MA--Fitchburg, Lynn; MI--Adrian, Bay City, Coopersville, Detroit, Flint, Grand Blanc, Kalamazoo, Lake Orion, Lansing, Livonia, Orion, Pontiac, Saginaw, Three Rivers, Warren, Waterford, Ypsilanti; MS--Clinton; MO--Springfield; NH--Hooksett, Somersworth; NJ--Camden, Linden; NY--Lockport, Schenectady, Selkirk, Syracuse; NC--Hendersonville, Hickory, Mebane; OH--Bucyrus, Cincinnati, Circleville, Cleveland, Coshocton, Ravenna, Warren; OK--Oklahoma City; PA--Erie, Grove City, King of Prussia, Philadelphia; TN--Columbia; TX--Arlington, Richardson, Wichita Falls; VT--North Clarendon, Rutland; VA--Winchester; WV--Martinsburg, Parkersburg, Washington; WI--Janesville)

Nonmonetary Support

Value: $15,200,000 (1999); $15,500,000 (1998)
Type: Donated Equipment; Donated Products; In-kind Services; Loaned Employees
Volunteer Programs: The GM Volunteer PLU$ program recognizes and rewards employees for the time they spend volunteering with charities and allows employees to direct a monetary gift from the GM Foundation to local charities for which they regularly volunteer.

Note: Co. also donates real estate. Co. will not donate products for on-highway use.

General Motors Foundation

Giving Contact

Deborah I. Dingell, Vice Chairman
General Motors Foundation
300 Renaissance Center
MC 482-C16-D25
Detroit, MI 48265-3000
Phone: (313)665-4085
Fax: (313)665-0746
Web: http://www.gm.com/company/gmability/philanthropy/
Note: Address for general (non-local, non-education) applications. Local grants requests should be directed to the local GM Community Relations Committee.

Alternate Contact

General Motors Education Relations
300 Renaissance Center
MC 482-C09-D36
Detroit, MI 48265
Note: Address for education-related applications.

Description

EIN: 382132136
Organization Type: Corporate Foundation
Giving Locations: nationally; operating locations.
Grant Types: General Support, Project.

Financial Summary

Total Giving: $30,819,897 (2002 approx); $36,485,097 (2001); $43,280,242 (2000). Note: Corporate program-related investment indicated for 1999 reflects the company's participation in charity events.
Giving Analysis: Giving for 2000 includes: foundation matching gifts ($1,025,626); foundation ($40,636,066); 1999: foundation scholarships ($486,500); foundation matching gifts (approx $1,250,000); foundation grants to United Way ($3,115,770); corporate program-related investments (approx $6,200,000); nonmonetary support (approx $15,200,000); corporate direct giving (approx $17,100,000); foundation ($25,447,730); 1998: foundation grants to United Way ($175,000); foundation scholarships ($542,700); foundation matching gifts ($1,430,849); nonmonetary support ($15,500,000); corporate direct giving ($22,700,000) foundation ($25,534,644)
Assets: $322,837,455 (2001); $401,916,997 (2000); $155,059,576 (1999)
Gifts Received: $286,867,500 (2000); $43,300,000 (1999); $23,700,000 (1998). Note: In 1998, contributions were received from General Motors Corp.

Typical Recipients

Arts & Humanities: Arts Associations & Councils, Arts Centers, Arts Festivals, Arts Funds, Arts Institutes, Dance, Historic Preservation, History & Archaeology, Libraries, Museums/Galleries, Music, Opera, Performing Arts, Public Broadcasting, Theater, Visual Arts
Civic & Public Affairs: African American Affairs, Business/Free Enterprise, Chambers of Commerce, Civil Rights, Community Foundations, Economic Development, Economic Policy, Employment/Job Training, Ethnic Organizations, First Amendment Issues, Civic & Public Affairs-General, Hispanic Affairs, Housing, Law & Justice, Minority Business, Municipalities/Towns, Nonprofit Management, Professional & Trade Associations, Professional & Trade Associations, Public Policy, Rural Affairs, Safety, Urban & Community Affairs, Women's Affairs, Zoos/Aquariums
Education: Agricultural Education, Arts/Humanities Education, Business Education, Business-School Partnerships, Colleges & Universities, Community &

Junior Colleges, Continuing Education, Economic Education, Education Associations, Education Funds, Education Reform, Elementary Education (Private), Engineering/Technological Education, Faculty Development, Education-General, Health & Physical Education, International Exchange, International Studies, Legal Education, Literacy, Minority Education, Private Education (Precollege), Public Education (Precollege), Science/Mathematics Education, Student Aid
Environment: Environment-General, Resource Conservation, Resource Conservation
Health: Alzheimers Disease, Cancer, Children's Health/Hospitals, Clinics/Medical Centers, Emergency/Ambulance Services, Health Organizations, Hospices, Hospitals, Medical Rehabilitation, Medical Training, Mental Health, Public Health, Single-Disease Health Associations, Transplant Networks/Donor Banks
International: International Affairs, International Environmental Issues, International Peace & Security Issues, International Relations
Religion: Religious Welfare
Science: Science Exhibits & Fairs, Scientific Centers & Institutes, Scientific Organizations
Social Services: Child Welfare, Community Centers, Community Service Organizations, Emergency Relief, Family Services, Food/Clothing Distribution, Homes, People with Disabilities, Recreation & Athletics, Scouts, Senior Services, Shelters/Homelessness, Substance Abuse, United Funds/United Ways, Volunteer Services, YMCA/YWCA/YMHA/YWHA, Youth Organizations

Application Procedures

Initial Contact: Send a one-page cover letter and concept summary; only written requests will be given consideration.
Application Requirements: The cover letter should include the organization name; contact person; project purpose; specific funding, service, or in-kind request; time period; possible strategic link with GM; and total length of time GM support would be needed. The concept summary should include the following information, in bullet format and not exceeding two pages, using the following order and numeric identification: (1) date of application; (2) legal name of organization; (3) year founded; (4) current operating budget; (5) contact person, address, phone and fax; (6) project name; (7) purpose of grant (statement of requested support); (8) project time frame; (9) amount requested; (10) total project cost; (11)geographic area; (12) previous support and requests to GM or GM Foundation over the last five years; (13) other organizations to which requests are being submitted; (14) signature of chairperson and executive director; (15) attachment of latest IRS Form 990, including federal identification number and a copy of the IRS correspondence confirming the organization's tax-exempt status. Indicate if organization has submitted this or other proposals to other GM units (e.g., marketing divisions) or GM subsidiaries (e.g. GMAC, Hughes Electronics Corp.).
Deadlines: GM and the GM Foundation accept and screen proposals for grants on a continuous basis; however, proposals must be received no less than 45 days prior to the month of the quarterly Contributions Planning Board (CPB) meeting in order to be included in the next review.
Review Process: As of 2002, The GM Contributions Planning Board (CPB) has been eliminated and the Chairperson, Vice-Chairperson, and President of the Foundation have collectively assumed the responsibilities of the CPB and serve as the governing body for all contributions and memberships drawing on interactive staff and operating unit input to guide the overall philanthropic process. The CPB has recommended an annual budget and has set policies, guidelines, criteria, and strategic direction, and has approved major contributions. Under the oversight of the CPB, various contributions subcommittees -- centered on the Foundations identified program areas of education, health, public policy, environment and

energy, and community relations -- set strategic direction within their scope as well as review and evaluate proposals prior to submitting recommendations to Foundation. The GM Corporate Relations staff refers regional and local proposals for consideration and handling to the appropriate local committee.

Evaluative Criteria: Primary consideration is given to requests that exhibit a clear purpose and defined need in one of GM's areas of focus; recognize innovative approaches in addressing the defined need; demonstrate an efficient organization and detail the organization's ability to follow through on proposal; explain clearly the benefits to GM and plant city communities; and have a strong commitment to diversity.

Decision Notification: Inappropriate applicants are informed on a timely basis; if recommended, application will be reviewed by the CPB, which meets quarterly in March, June, September and December.

Notes: Based on the outcome of the concept evaluation, GM may request submission of a comprehensive proposal for additional evaluation, including: expanded project description, goals, and objectives; description of persons or groups who will benefit; relevant experience of the project's principal staff; history of organization (most recent annual report); detailed workplan, time frame, and action plan for expected outcome; evaluation plan including criteria for measuring effectiveness of the proposed project; all current and projected sources of funding (list amount requested of other corporations, foundations, and funding sources); detailed budget and long-term funding strategy beyond the initial grant period; current financial statements; current Board of Directors with affiliations. The CPB has been eliminated in 2002. The Chairperson, Vice-Chairperson, and the President of the Foundation have collectively assumed the responsibilities of the CPB.

Restrictions

Does not support organizations that discriminate on the basis of race, religion, creed, gender, age, veteran status, physical challenges, or national origin. In addition, contributions are generally not provided to individuals; religious organizations; political parties or candidates; U.S. hospitals and health care institutions (for general operating support); capital campaigns; endowment funds; or conferences, workshops, or seminars not directly related to GM's business interests. GM believes that giving to capital programs and endowment campaigns does not appropriately utilize the corporation's resources. Does not support multi-year grants; usually only the first year of multi-year requests will be considered and subsequent years will be evaluated annually for future support.

Additional Information

General Motors has established a nonprofit organization, the GM Cancer Research Foundation, which awards substantial prizes for outstanding individual achievement in cancer research. As an extension of the foundation's ongoing commitment in the fight against cancer, the foundation established an international science journalism awards program in 1989. This program recognizes excellence in reporting about biomedical research with application to cancer and cancer research. Three awards, one each for newspaper, magazine and book, and broadcast coverage, carry a $10,000 cash award and a limited-edition work of art.

In 1999, General Motors established the GM Global Aid program to enable the company to quickly direct funds from the GM Foundation to aid victims of natural disasters around the world. As part of this program, General Motors launched the www.WebHands.org web site which allows employees worldwide to identify nonprofit organizations needing assistance in their community and donate to disaster relief funds.

In addition to its philanthropic activities, General Motors provides funding for numerous educational and public interest programs as a corporate sponsor (an example is the Concept:Cure breast cancer research initiative which raises funds through a design collaboration with the Council of Fashion Designers of America, where fashion designers work with GM's design staff and brand teams to create one-of-a-kind GM vehicles).

Company actively works to increase educational opportunities for minorities and women inside the corporation and in the business community.

Publications: Philanthropic Annual Report

Corporate Officials

John M. Devine: vice chairman, chief financial officer ED Duquesne University BS (1967); University of Michigan MBA (1972). PRIM CORP EMPL vice chairman, chief financial officer: General Motors Corp.

Harry J. Pearce: vice chairman ED United States Air Force Academy BS (1964); Northwestern University JD (1967). PRIM CORP EMPL vice chairman: General Motors Corp.

John Francis Smith, Jr.: chairman B Worcester, MA 1938. ED University of Massachusetts BBA (1960); Boston University MBA (1965). PRIM CORP EMPL chairman: General Motors Corp. CORP AFFIL director: Procter & Gamble Co.; trustee: Hughes Electronics Corp.; director: Electronic Data Systems Corp.; drc: General Motors Acceptance Corp. NONPR AFFIL business council: Memorial Sloan-Kettering Cancer Center; member: U.S.-Japan Business Council; member: Business Roundtable Policy Comm; member, board: Detroit Renaissance Inc.; member: Beta Gamma Sigma; director: Boards Global Business Management Council; member: American Society Corporate Executives; member, director: American Automobile Manufacturers Association. CLUB AFFIL director: Economic Club Detroit.

G. Richard Wagoner, Jr.: president, chief executive officer, director B Wilmington, DE February 09, 1953. ED Duke University BA (1975); Harvard University MBA (1977). PRIM CORP EMPL president, chief executive officer, director: General Motors Corp.

Foundation Officials

K. W. Cobb: chief tax officer
Wallace W. Creek: chief financial funds officer, trustee B Kankakee, IL 1939. ED University of Illinois (1960); Michigan State University (1972). PRIM CORP EMPL comptroller: General Motors Corp.
Deborah I. Dingell: president, trustee
R. D. Gillum: chairperson
C. D. Hogan: director
K. A. Merkle: secretary
M. D. Mobley: treasurer
L. Utley: president

Grants Analysis

Disclosure Period: calendar year ending 2001
Total Grants: $36,485,097*
Number of Grants: 1108
Average Grant: $33,000
Highest Grant: $2,890,500
Lowest Grant: $50
Typical Range: $10,000 to $427,000 and $1,000 to $30,000
*Note: Giving excludes United Way.

Recent Grants

Note: Grants derived from 2001 Form 990.

General

2,890,500	Charities Funds Transfer, Alexandria, VA
2,000,000	National Safe Kids Campaign, Washington, DC
1,250,000	National Safe Kids Campaign, Washington, DC
1,000,000	American Red Cross, Denison, TX
1,000,000	Detroit 300, Inc., Detroit, MI
1,000,000	Detroit 300, Inc., Detroit, MI
1,000,000	General Motors Cancer Research Foundation, New York, NY
1,000,000	Inner City Games Foundation, New York, NY

905,000	Automotive Youth Educational Systems, Troy, MI
905,000	Automotive Youth Educational Systems, Troy, MI

ELIZABETH MORSE GENIUS CHARITABLE TRUST

Giving Contact

Charles Slamar, Jr., Trust Officer
c/o Bank of America
231 S. Lasalle St.
Chicago, IL 60697
Phone: (312)828-5554
Fax: (312)987-0806

Description

Founded: 1992
EIN: 367010559
Organization Type: Private Foundation
Giving Locations: IL: Chicago

Financial Summary

Total Giving: $2,627,479 (fiscal year ending November 30, 2002 approx); $3,322,639 (fiscal 2001); $2,876,428 (fiscal 1999)
Assets: $60,027,015 (fiscal 2001); $72,361,014 (fiscal 1999); $66,070,722 (fiscal 1998)
Gifts Received: $22,934,009 (fiscal 1994). Note: In fiscal 1994, contributions were received from the Richard M. Genius, Jr. Trust.

Typical Recipients

Arts & Humanities: Arts Associations & Councils, Arts Funds, Community Arts, Dance, Libraries, Museums/Galleries, Music, Opera, Public Broadcasting, Theater

Civic & Public Affairs: Asian American Affairs, Botanical Gardens/Parks, Community Foundations, Economic Development, Employment/Job Training, Civic & Public Affairs-General, Hispanic Affairs, Housing, Nonprofit Management, Public Policy, Safety, Urban & Community Affairs, Women's Affairs, Zoos/Aquariums

Education: Afterschool/Enrichment Programs, Arts/Humanities Education, Colleges & Universities, Education Reform, International Studies, Preschool Education, Private Education (Precollege), Public Education (Precollege), Student Aid

Environment: Environment-General

Health: AIDS/HIV, Cancer, Children's Health/Hospitals, Clinics/Medical Centers, Emergency/Ambulance Services, Hospitals, Long-Term Care, Mental Health, Public Health

International: Foreign Arts Organizations

Religion: Jewish Causes, Religious Welfare

Science: Science Museums, Scientific Centers & Institutes

Social Services: At-Risk Youth, Child Abuse, Child Welfare, Community Service Organizations, Counseling, Delinquency & Criminal Rehabilitation, Domestic Violence, Family Services, Food/Clothing Distribution, People with Disabilities, Recreation & Athletics, Senior Services, Shelters/Homelessness, Social Services-General, Youth Organizations

Application Procedures

Initial Contact: Send a brief letter of inquiry.
Deadlines: None.
Notes: The foundation has no formal grant application procedure or application form.

Additional Information
Trust(s): Bank Am IL

Foundation Officials
James Alexander: co-trustee

Grants Analysis
Disclosure Period: fiscal year ending November 30, 2001
Total Grants: $3,322,639
Number of Grants: 66
Average Grant: $44,937*
Highest Grant: $400,000
Typical Range: $20,000 to $75,000
*Note: Average grant figure excludes the highest grant.

Recent Grants
Note: Grants derived from fiscal 2001 Form 990.

Library-Related
75,000	Chicago Public Library, Chicago, IL

General
400,000	Association House of Chicago, Chicago, IL
214,546	SSI Coalition for a Responsible Safety Net, Chicago, IL
202,963	Mount Sinai Hospital Medical Center, Chicago, IL
165,000	Jobs for Youth, Chicago, IL
150,000	Greater Chicago Food Depository, Chicago, IL
125,000	Ravinia Association, Highland Park, IL
108,905	IT Resource Center, Chicago, IL
106,725	Children's Memorial Foundation, Chicago, IL
100,000	Brookfield Zoo, Brookfield, IL
75,000	Chicago Council on Planned Giving, Keinworth, IL

GEORGE FOUNDATION

Giving Contact
Roland Adamson, Executive Director
Private Mail Box
310 Morton Street - Suite C
Richmond, TX 77469
Phone: (281)342-6109
Fax: (281)341-7635
E-mail: radamson@thegeorgefoundation.org
Web: http://www.thegeorgefoundation.org

Description
Founded: 1945
EIN: 746043368
Organization Type: General Purpose Foundation
Giving Locations: TX: Fort Bend County and surrounding area
Grant Types: Capital, Endowment, General Support, Multiyear/Continuing Support, Project, Scholarship, Seed Money.

Donor Information
Founder: The George Foundation was established in Texas in 1945 with funds donated by A. P. George and Mamie E. George.

Financial Summary
Total Giving: $5,523,900 (2000); $2,178,201 (1999); $1,776,472 (1998)
Giving Analysis: Giving for 2000 includes: foundation grants to United Way ($50,000); foundation matching gifts ($289,377); foundation matching gifts ($1,896,333); 1998: foundation matching gifts ($108,000) foundation scholarships ($268,123)
Assets: $111,095,580 (2000); $113,244,478 (1999); $106,861,924 (1998)
Gifts Received: $288,373 (1993); $150,000 (1992)

Typical Recipients
Arts & Humanities: Arts Associations & Councils, Arts Festivals, Arts Institutes, Community Arts, Historic Preservation, History & Archaeology, Libraries, Museums/Galleries, Performing Arts, Public Broadcasting, Theater
Civic & Public Affairs: African American Affairs, Botanical Gardens/Parks, Community Foundations, Economic Development, Employment/Job Training, Civic & Public Affairs-General, Hispanic Affairs, Housing, Legal Aid, Municipalities/Towns, Nonprofit Management, Public Policy, Safety, Urban & Community Affairs, Women's Affairs, Zoos/Aquariums
Education: Business Education, Colleges & Universities, Community & Junior Colleges, Continuing Education, Education Associations, Education Funds, Education Reform, Elementary Education (Private), Elementary Education (Public), Education-General, Legal Education, Literacy, Medical Education, Preschool Education, Public Education (Precollege), Science/Mathematics Education, Special Education, Student Aid
Environment: Air/Water Quality, Resource Conservation, Wildlife Protection
Health: Adolescent Health Issues, AIDS/HIV, Alzheimers Disease, Cancer, Children's Health/Hospitals, Clinics/Medical Centers, Diabetes, Emergency/Ambulance Services, Eyes/Blindness, Geriatric Health, Health Organizations, Hospices, Hospitals, Long-Term Care, Medical Research, Mental Health, Multiple Sclerosis, Prenatal Health Issues, Research/Studies Institutes, Single-Disease Health Associations, Speech & Hearing, Transplant Networks/Donor Banks
Religion: Churches, Jewish Causes, Ministries, Religious Organizations, Religious Welfare, Social/Policy Issues
Science: Science-General, Observatories & Planetariums, Science Museums, Scientific Organizations
Social Services: At-Risk Youth, Big Brother/Big Sister, Camps, Child Abuse, Child Welfare, Community Centers, Community Service Organizations, Counseling, Day Care, Delinquency & Criminal Rehabilitation, Domestic Violence, Emergency Relief, Family Planning, Family Services, People with Disabilities, Recreation & Athletics, Scouts, Senior Services, Shelters/Homelessness, Special Olympics, Substance Abuse, United Funds/United Ways, United Funds/United Ways, YMCA/YWCA/YMHA/YWHA, Youth Organizations

Application Procedures
Initial Contact: Prospective applicants should submit a letter signed by the executive director and board chairman and fully setting forth the purposes and needs for the requested grant.
Application Requirements: The letter should clearly state the proposed objectives of the project and the need for the grant. It should also provide the organization's plan to achieve identified goals; the methods by which the goals will be reached; the methods, criteria, and plan to evaluate the project's effectiveness; an outline of specific, measurable objectives with a timetable for accomplishment; and the organization's plan to achieve self-sufficiency after the grant term. The grant packet should also include the following: a list of board of director and officers; specific amount requested; budget for the proposed project; list of funding sources for current and prior years; list of persons responsible for project; copy of organization's most recent financial statement; copies of the organization's two most recent IRS Form 990s; a list of organizations asked for support of the specific project, including their responses to date and amount committed; and a copy of the organization's qualifying letter from the Internal Revenue Service; and a statement on the organization's letterhead that there has been no change in IRS status since issuance of ruling letter.
Deadlines: Applications must be submitted ninety days prior to a grant request meeting: October 15, for the January meeting; January 15, for the April

meeting; April 15, for the July meeting; and July 15, for the October meeting.
Review Process: During the review process, interviews and site visits may be requested to better evaluate the proposal. When the review process is completed, a final decision will be made by the foundation's trustees at the appropriate quarterly grant meeting. Applicants will be notified within two weeks of the trustees' determination of their application.
Notes: Because the focus of the foundation may change as new areas of concern evolve within the community, previous grant commitments should not be taken as precedents for subsequent grants. The foundation will not consider a grant request, whether granted or denied, more than once in a twelve month period. The foundation encourages matching gifts proposals to leverage funds granted.

Restrictions
The foundation accepts projects which benefit Ft. Bend County, TX and its residents only. No grants are made to the following: individuals; loans; fundraising events; organizations that are not tax exempt; organizations that practice discrimination; proposals that commit the foundation to continued support; or political activities of any nature.

Additional Information
Publications: Application Guidelines

Foundation Officials
Roland Adamson: executive director ED Texas A&M University BS (1976).
Thomas E. Daniels: trustee
Charles Herder: trustee
William A. Little: trustee B Boston, MA 1929. ED Tufts University BA (1951); Trinity College LTCL (1952); Harvard University MA (1953); Harvard University PhD (1961). NONPR AFFIL visiting professor musicology: University Rochester; professor German & music emeritus: University Virginia; member: MLA; member: Organ Historic Society; registrar, archivist: American Guild Organists Central Florida Chapter; member: American Music Society; member: American Association Teachers German; member, national committee professional education: American Guild Organists.
James D. Sartwelle, Sr.: chairman B 1921. PRIM CORP EMPL chairman, director: Port City Stockyards Co. CORP AFFIL chairman, director: Sealy Livestock Auction.
Lane Ward: trustee PRIM CORP EMPL president, chief executive officer, director: Fort Bend Federal Savings & Loan Association.

Grants Analysis
Disclosure Period: calendar year ending 2000
Total Grants: $3,288,190*
Number of Grants: 63
Average Grant: $52,193
Highest Grant: $833,333
Lowest Grant: $75
Typical Range: $1,000 to $50,000 and $200,000 to $800,000
*Note: Giving excludes scholarships; matching gifts; United Way.

Recent Grants
Note: Grants derived from 2000 Form 990.

General
833,333	Wharton County Junior College, Wharton, TX -- scholarships for Fort Bend residents
833,000	Wharton County Junior College, Wharton, TX -- scholarships for Fort Bend residents
600,000	University of Houston System, Houston, TX -- for recruitment/retention of minorities of the School of Pharmacy

600,000	University of Houston System, Houston, TX
252,000	Memorial Hermann Foundation, Houston, TX -- to support Memorial Hermann Health Centers for schools initiative
200,000	University of Houston System, Houston, TX -- for recruitment/retention of minorities of the School of Pharmacy
200,000	University of Houston System, Houston, TX -- for recruitment/retention of minorities of the School of Pharmacy
200,000	University of Houston System, Houston, TX -- for recruitment/retention of minorities of the School of Pharmacy
200,000	University of Houston System, Houston, TX -- for recruitment/retention of minorities of the School of Pharmacy
118,320	Fort Bend County Women's Center, Richmond, TX -- second year of children's mentoring program

GEORGIA-PACIFIC CORP.

Company Headquarters

Georgia-Pacific Center
133 Peachtree St. NE
Atlanta, GA 30303
Web: http://www.gp.com

Company Description

Founded: 1927
Ticker: GP
Exchange: NYSE
Revenue: US$23.271 billion (2002)
Employees: 65000 (2002)

Nonmonetary Support

Type: Donated Equipment; Donated Products
Volunteer Programs: Employee volunteers serve such organizations as United Way, American Red Cross, Boy Scouts of America, Girl Scouts, Better Business Bureaus and councils, and Keep America Beautiful.

Georgia-Pacific Foundation

Giving Contact

Curley M. Dossman, Jr., President
133 Peachtree Street Northeast
Atlanta, GA 30303
Phone: (404)652-4000
Fax: (404)584-1470
Web: http://www.gp.com/center/community/index.html

Description

EIN: 936023726
Organization Type: Corporate Foundation
Giving Locations: operating locations.
Grant Types: Capital, Employee Matching Gifts, Endowment, General Support, Scholarship.
Note: Employee matching gift ratio: 2 to 1. Foundation matches employee gifts to approved educational institutions, cultural organizations, hospitals and other medical institutions, and public radio and television stations.

Financial Summary

Total Giving: $4,873,020 (2001); $3,579,390 (2000); $4,733,183 (1999). Note: Contributes through corporate direct giving program and foundation.
Giving Analysis: Giving for 2000 includes: foundation scholarships ($26,500); foundation grants to United Way ($371,696); foundation ($3,181,194); 1999: foundation scholarships ($158,207); foundation grants to United Way ($388,063); foundation

($4,186,913); 1998: foundation scholarships ($249,049); foundation grants to United Way ($336,403); corporate direct giving ($2,984,355); **Assets:** $899,640 (2001); $1,025,790 (1999); $1,025,790 (1998)
Gifts Received: $3,755,000 (2001); $3,650,000 (2000); $4,650,000 (1999). Note: Contributions are received from the Georgia-Pacific Corporation.

Typical Recipients

Arts & Humanities: Arts Associations & Councils, Arts Centers, Arts Festivals, Dance, Ethnic & Folk Arts, Historic Preservation, History & Archaeology, Libraries, Museums/Galleries, Music, Opera, Public Broadcasting, Theater
Civic & Public Affairs: African American Affairs, Botanical Gardens/Parks, Business/Free Enterprise, Chambers of Commerce, Civil Rights, Community Foundations, Economic Development, Employment/ Job Training, Ethnic Organizations, Civic & Public Affairs-General, Housing, Law & Justice, Municipalities/ Towns, Public Policy, Safety, Urban & Community Affairs, Zoos/Aquariums
Education: Arts/Humanities Education, Business Education, Colleges & Universities, Economic Education, Education Associations, Education Funds, Education Reform, Elementary Education (Public), Engineering/Technological Education, Environmental Education, Education-General, Leadership Training, Literacy, Medical Education, Minority Education, Private Education (Precollege), Public Education (Precollege), Science/Mathematics Education, Special Education, Student Aid
Environment: Air/Water Quality, Forestry, Environment-General, Protection, Resource Conservation, Wildlife Protection
Health: Children's Health/Hospitals, Emergency/Ambulance Services, Eyes/Blindness, Health-General, Health Funds, Health Organizations, Hospitals, Hospitals (University Affiliated), Medical Rehabilitation, Medical Research, Single-Disease Health Associations
Religion: Churches, Religion-General, Jewish Causes, Religious Welfare
Science: Science Exhibits & Fairs, Science Museums, Scientific Centers & Institutes
Social Services: At-Risk Youth, Big Brother/Big Sister, Camps, Child Abuse, Child Welfare, Community Centers, Community Service Organizations, Family Services, Food/Clothing Distribution, Homes, People with Disabilities, Recreation & Athletics, Scouts, Social Services-General, Substance Abuse, United Funds/United Ways, Volunteer Services, YMCA/ YWCA/YMHA/YWHA, Youth Organizations

Application Procedures

Initial Contact: Submit a brief letter or proposal.
Application Requirements: Include background information including name of organization and name of project, project's goal and objective, need project seeks to meet, priority area and company area project will affect, anticipated results, project budget, proof of tax-exempt status and list of board members and staff, including description of qualifications.
Deadlines: October 31.
Decision Notification: Written notification within 45 days of receipt of proposal.

Restrictions

Foundation does not support non-tax exempt organizations; organizations that discriminate on the basis of race, color, creed, nationality or gender; individuals; political causes; religious institutions or schools; social, labor, veterans, alumni or fraternal organizations; goodwill advertising or fundraising; sports; operating support for members of United Way; national groups whose local chapters already receive support; benefit tickets; operating support for colleges and universities; medical and nursing schools; academic chairs; organizations that channel funds; raffles, telethons, walk-a-thons and trips or tours. chairs; organizations

that channel funds; raffles, telethons, walk-a-thons and trips or tours.

Foundation Officials

Curley M. Dossman, Junior: president
Danny W. Huff: chairman
Phillip M. Johnson: treasurer
Kenneth F. Khoury: vice president B New York, NY 1951. ED Rutgers University Stonier Graduate School of Banking BA (1972); Fordham University School of Law JD (1977). PRIM CORP EMPL vice president, secretary, deputy general counsel: Georgia-Pacific Corp.

Grants Analysis

Disclosure Period: calendar year ending 2001
Total Grants: $3,726,237*
Number of Grants: 578
Average Grant: $6,447
Highest Grant: $138,053
Lowest Grant: $15
Typical Range: $200 to $25,000
*Note: Giving excludes scholarship; United Way.

Recent Grants

Note: Grants derived from 2001 Form 990.

General

138,055	Habitat for Humanity, Atlanta, GA
116,667	Atlanta Symphony Orchestra, Atlanta, GA
100,000	American Red Cross, Albany, NY
100,000	National Park Foundation, Washington, DC
86,000	United Way of Brown County, Green Bay, WI
85,241	United Way of Southeast Georgia, Statesboro, GA
54,855	United Way of South Wood, Wisconsin Rapids, WI
50,000	Augusta Foundation, Inc.
50,000	College Fund, Richmond, VA
50,000	Eastlake Community Foundation, Eastlake, OH

GEORGIA POWER CO.

Company Headquarters

Atlanta, GA
Web: http://www.georgiapowerco.com

Company Description

Assets: US$5 million (2001)
Employees: 8855 (2001)
SIC(s): 4911 Electric Services.
Parent Company: Southern Co., Atlanta, GA, United States

Operating Locations

Georgia Power Co. (AL--Valley; GA--Alma, Americus, Arlington, Ashburn, Atlanta, Augusta, Bainbridge, Baxley, Brunswick, Budford, Buena Vista, Butler, Cartersville, Caton, Cedar Springs, Cedartown, Chickamauga, Clarkesville, Claxton, Clayton, Cochran, Columbus, Comer, Cornelia, Cuthbert, Dahlonega, Dalton, Darien, Donalsonville, Douglas, Eastman, Eastonollee, Ellijay, Evans, Folkston, Forest Park, Fort Gaines, Gainesville, Glennville, Gordon, Gray, Greenville, Hahira, Hartwell, Hawkinsville, Hinesville, Homerville, Jasper, Jefferson, Juliette, Kingsland, La Grange, Lakeland, Lavonia, Lincolnton, Lithonia, Louisville, Madison, Manchester, Mc Rae, Metter, Millen, Montezuma, Moultrie, Nashville, Newnan, Ocilla, Pearson, Pelham, Pine Mountain, Rabun Gap, Reidsville, Richland, Rockmart, Rome, Royston, Soperton, St. Marys, St. Simons Island, Statesboro, Summerville, Swainsboro, Tallapoosa, Thomasville, Thomson, Tifton, Toccoa, Valdosta, Vidalia, Vienna, Villa Rica, Waycross, Waynesboro, West Point, Winder, Zebulon)

Nonmonetary Support

Value: $594,525 (2003); $80,000 (2002)
Type: In-kind Services
Note: Donated equipment, in-kind services, workplace solicitation.
Volunteer Programs: Company sponsors the Citizens of Georgia Power, a group of employees that volunteers with nonprofit groups throughout the state. The Ambassadors is the same type of program for retired employees. OrganizationS supported include Habitat for Humanity, the March of Dimes, and the American Red Cross.
Contact: Susan M. Carter, Executive Director, Georgia Power Foundation
Note: Annual Sponsorship Budget: $34,000 to $138,000.

Georgia Power Foundation

Giving Contact

Judy M. Anderson, Foundation President
Senior Vice President, Georgia Power Co.
Bin 10131
241 Ralph McGill Boulevard NE
Atlanta, GA 30308-3374
Phone: (404)506-6784
Fax: (404)506-1485

Alternate Contact

Jim Trupiano, Manager of Charitable Contributions
Phone: (404)506-2960

Description

Founded: 1930
EIN: 581709417
Organization Type: Corporate Foundation
Giving Locations: GA: operating locations and service area
Grant Types: Award, Capital, Conference/Seminar, Emergency, Employee Matching Gifts, Endowment, General Support, Matching, Multiyear/Continuing Support, Professorship, Project, Research.

Financial Summary

Total Giving: $9,100,000 (2002); $7,636,518 (2001); $7,764,923 (2000). Note: Contributes through corporate direct giving program and foundation.
Giving Analysis: Giving for 2002 includes: nonmonetary support ($80,000); 2001: corporate direct giving ($2,541,810); foundation ($7,672,448); 2000: foundation scholarships ($8,000); foundation grants to United Way ($1,822,740); foundation ($5,934,183).
Assets: $2,755,000 (2003 approx); $87,000,000 (2002); $103,127,952 (2001)
Gifts Received: $15,000,000 (2001); $7,000,000 (1996); $2,566,083 (1993). Note: Foundation receives contributions from Georgia Power Co.

Typical Recipients

Arts & Humanities: Arts Associations & Councils, Arts Centers, Arts Festivals, Arts Funds, Arts Institutes, Community Arts, Dance, Ethnic & Folk Arts, Arts & Humanities-General, Historic Preservation, Libraries, Museums/Galleries, Music, Performing Arts, Theater
Civic & Public Affairs: African American Affairs, Botanical Gardens/Parks, Chambers of Commerce, Civil Rights, Community Foundations, Economic Development, Economic Policy, Employment/Job Training, Ethnic Organizations, Civic & Public Affairs-General, Housing, Legal Aid, Municipalities/Towns, Parades/Festivals, Philanthropic Organizations, Professional & Trade Associations, Rural Affairs, Urban & Community Affairs, Women's Affairs, Zoos/Aquariums

Education: Agricultural Education, Arts/Humanities Education, Business Education, Colleges & Universities, Community & Junior Colleges, Economic Education, Education Associations, Education Funds, Education Reform, Elementary Education (Private), Engineering/Technological Education, Faculty Development, Education-General, Health & Physical Education, Journalism/Media Education, Leadership Training, Literacy, Medical Education, Minority Education, Private Education (Precollege), Public Education (Precollege), Science/Mathematics Education, Secondary Education (Public), Student Aid, Vocational & Technical Education
Environment: Environment-General, Resource Conservation, Wildlife Protection
Health: Alzheimers Disease, Cancer, Children's Health/Hospitals, Clinics/Medical Centers, Emergency/Ambulance Services, Eyes/Blindness, Geriatric Health, Health Organizations, Hospices, Hospitals, Medical Rehabilitation, Medical Research, Mental Health, Public Health, Single-Disease Health Associations
International: International Affairs, International Relations
Religion: Religious Welfare
Science: Science Museums, Scientific Centers & Institutes
Social Services: At-Risk Youth, Big Brother/Big Sister, Camps, Child Abuse, Child Welfare, Community Centers, Community Service Organizations, Day Care, Delinquency & Criminal Rehabilitation, Emergency Relief, Family Planning, Family Services, Food/Clothing Distribution, Homes, People with Disabilities, Recreation & Athletics, Scouts, Senior Services, Shelters/Homelessness, Social Services-General, Special Olympics, Substance Abuse, United Funds/United Ways, Volunteer Services, YMCA/YWCA/YMHA/YWHA, Youth Organizations

Application Procedures

Initial Contact: Send a brief letter or proposal.
Application Requirements: Include a brief a description of organization, list of officers and board members, amount requested, purpose for which funds are sought, sources of other support and the amounts assured or anticipated for the proposed project, audited financial statements detailing current position of organization, list (if any) of Georgia Power and Southern Company employees participating in the organization, and proof of tax-exempt status.
Deadlines: None, but grant proposals should arrive at least three weeks before quarterly board meetings held in March, June, September and December.
Review Process: Each request is organized by category (education, health, etc.) and set up in files as well as on the philanthropy system.
Evaluative Criteria: Must fit strategic focus area; past contributions, survey data, tax status, and support of similar or other corporate or foundation support issues.
Decision Notification: Grants are made quarterly.

Restrictions

Does not give to individuals, private elementary or secondary schools, religious organizations, or political campaigns or causes. Do not send videotapes or supplemental materials with initial inquiry.

Additional Information

The Georgia Power Foundation was established in December 1986 with a $10.5 million grant from Georgia Power Co., although the company also continues to give directly.
Southern Co., Georgia Power's parent company, does not administer a contributions program. However, several other subsidiaries administer direct giving programs: Alabama Power Co.; Gulf Power Company/Gulf Power Foundation, 500 Bayfront Parkway, PO Box 1151, Pensacola, FL 32520, 904-444-6325; and Mississippi Power Company/Mississippi Power Foundation. 32520, 904-444-6325; and Mississippi

Power Company/Mississippi Power Foundation (see separate entry for details).
Publications: Brochure

Corporate Officials

Judy M. Anderson: senior vice president charitable giving B Jay, FL 1948. ED Troy State University (1971); Atlanta Law School (1979). PRIM CORP EMPL senior vice president charitable giving: Georgia Power Co. ADD CORP EMPL secretary: Piedmont-Forrest Corp. NONPR AFFIL member: American Bar Association.
W. C. Archer, III: senior vice president external affairs
Ronnie L. Bates: sen vice president external affairs
Mickey A. Brown: senior vice president distribution
H. Allen Franklin: president, chief executive officer B 1945. ED University of Alabama BEE (1966). PRIM CORP EMPL president, chief executive officer: Georgia Power Co. CORP AFFIL director: Southern Energy Resources Inc.; director: SouthTrust Corp.; director: Southern Electric Generating Co.; director: SEI Holdings Inc.; executive vice president, director: Southern Co. Inc.
Allen L. Leverett: executive vice president, chief financial officer
David M. Ratcliffe: chief financial officer, treasurer, director B Tifton, GA 1948. ED Valdosta State College (1970); Woodrow Wilson College (1975). PRIM CORP EMPL chief financial officer, treasurer, director: Georgia Power Co. ADD CORP EMPL senior vice president external affairs: Southern Co.
Leslie R. Sibert: vice president transmission
Chris Womack: senior vice president

Foundation Officials

Judy M. Anderson: executive director, secretary, assistant treasurer (see above)
Ronnie L. Bates: director (see above)
Mickey A. Brown: director (see above)
Susan M. Carter: director, secretary, assistant treasurer
O. Ben Harris: director, assistant secretary
Robert H. Haubein, Jr.: director B 1940. ED University of Missouri BSEE (1981). PRIM CORP EMPL senior vice president: Georgia Power Co.
Gene R. Hodges: executive vice president B 1938. ED Georgia State University BBA (1963). PRIM CORP EMPL executive vice president customer operations: Georgia Power Co.
Allen L. Leverett: director (see above)
Charles O. Rawlins: treasurer, assistant secretary
Roger S. Steffens: treasurer
Chris Womack: director (see above)

Grants Analysis

Disclosure Period: calendar year ending 2002
Total Grants: $6,400,000*
Number of Grants: 1,082 (approx)
Average Grant: $8,400
Highest Grant: $1,081,037
Lowest Grant: $20
Typical Range: $1,000 to $15,000
*Note: Giving excludes scholarships and corporate giving. Grants analysis provided by foundation.

Recent Grants

Note: Grants derived from 2001 Form 990.

General

2,000,000	United Way of Metropolitan Atlanta, Atlanta, GA -- for operating support
2,000,000	United Way of Metropolitan Atlanta, Atlanta, GA
500,000	North Georgia Community Foundation, Gainesville, GA -- for project support
200,000	Nature Conservancy, Atlanta, GA -- for operating
200,000	Nature Conservancy, Atlanta, GA
200,000	Robert W. Woodruff Arts Center, Atlanta, GA -- for challenge grant

200,000	Robert W. Woodruff Arts Center, Atlanta, GA
100,000	Friends of Georgia State Park and Historic Sites, Inc., Warm Springs, GA -- capital fund support
100,000	Georgia State University, Atlanta, GA -- challenge grant
100,000	Georgia State University, Atlanta, GA -- for annual fund alumni challenge

GERBER PRODUCTS CO.

Company Headquarters

445 State St.
Fremont, MI 49412
Web: http://www.gerber.com

Company Description

Employees: 9,200
SIC(s): 2032 Canned Specialties, 2033 Canned Fruits & Vegetables, 2043 Cereal Breakfast Foods, 2341 Women's/Children's Underwear.
Parent Company: Novartis Corp., 608 Fifth Ave., New York, NY, United States
Parent Revenue: US$23,901,900,000 (2002)

Operating Locations

Biocine Co. (CA--Emeryville); Biotrack (CA--Mountain View); Chiron Diagnostics (CA--Emeryville); CIBA Corning Diagnostics Corp. (CA--Irvine); Ciba Corning Diagnostics Corp. (CA--Palo Alto; MA--East Walpole); CIBA Corning Diagnostics Corp. (MA--Medfield); Ciba Corning Diagnostics Corp. (OH--Oberlin); CIBA-GEIGY Formulated Systems Group (WI--Madison Heights); CIBA-GEIGY Pharmaceutical Production (NY--Suffern); CIBA Seeds (NC--Greensboro); CIBA Self-Medication (NJ--Woodbridge); CIBA Vision Corp. (GA--Duluth); EMS-Togo (MI--Taylor); Fredonia Seed Co. (MN--Golden Valley); Genetic Therapy (MD--Gaithersburg); Geneva Pharmaceuticals (CO--Broomfield); Gerber Finance Co. (MI--Fremont); Gerber Life Insurance Co. (NY--White Plains); Gerber Products Co. (AR--Fort Smith; CA--Anaheim, Fremont; CO--Englewood; GA--Norcross; HI--Honolulu; IL--Schaumburg; IN--Indianapolis; MA--Chelmsford; MI--Fremont, Southfield; NJ--Fort Lee; NC--Asheville, Skyland; OH--Akron; PR; WI--Reedsburg); Gerber Products, Div.-Baby Care (WI--Reedsburg); Gerber Products Overseas (MI--Fremont); Hi-Speed Checkweigher Co. (NY--Ithaca); Hilleshog Mono-Hy, Inc. (CO--Longmont); Ingold Electrodes (MA--Wilmington); International Forest Seed Co. (AL--Odenville); Maag Agrochemicals (FL--Vero Beach); McHutchinson Division (NJ--Ridgefield Park); NK Lawn & Garden (MN--Golden Valley); Northrup King Co. (MN--Golden Valley); Novartis Nutrition Corp. (MN--St. Louis Park); Novartis Pharmaceuticals (NJ--East Hanover); Novartis Seeds (IL--Downers Grove); Ohaus Corp. (NJ--Florham Park); Pedigree Seed Co. (MN--Golden Valley); Red Line Health Care Corp. (MN--Golden Valley); Reed Plastics (MI--Albion; TX--Grand Prairie); Repligen Sandoz Research Corp. (MN--St. Louis Park); Rogers Brothers Seed Co. (ID--Boise); Rogers NK Seed Co. (ID--Boise); Sandoz Agro, Inc. (IL--Des Plaines); Sandoz Argo Corp. (TX--Dallas); Sandoz Chemical Corp. (NC--Charlotte); Sandoz Chemical Corp. Purchasing (NJ--Fair Lawn); Sandoz Clinical & Nutrition Division (MN--Minneapolis); Sandoz Consumer Pharmaceutical (MD--Baltimore; TN--Chattanooga); Sandoz Corp. (NY--New York); Sandoz Food Service & Industrial Division (MN--Minneapolis); Sandoz Pharmaceutical Corp. (AZ--Scottsdale; DC--Washington; NJ--East Hanover); Sandoz Research Institute (NJ--East Hanover); Summit Plastic Co. (OH--Tallmadge); SyStemix (CA--Palo Alto)
Note: Operates in Canada and Costa Rica.

Nonmonetary Support

Type: Donated Products
Contact: Van Hinds, Director, Committee Affairs
Note: Company makes product donations to international relief organizations only.

Gerber Foundation

Giving Contact

Cathy Obits
Gerber Foundation
4747 W. 48th Street, Suite 153
Fremont, MI 49412
Phone: (231)924-3175
Fax: (231)924-7906
E-mail: tgf@ncisd.net
Web: http://www.gerberfoundation.org

Description

EIN: 386068090
Organization Type: Corporate Foundation
Giving Locations: nationally.
Grant Types: Award, Employee Matching Gifts, General Support, Matching, Research, Scholarship.
Note: Matching gifts program supports educational institutions and health and human services organizations.

Donor Information

Founder: Foundation was established in 1952 as the Gerber Baby Foods Fund by Dan Gerber and the Gerber Products Company.

Financial Summary

Total Giving: $4,070,000 (2002 approx); $4,017,746 (2001); $4,833,684 (2000). Note: Contributes through foundation.
Giving Analysis: Giving for 2001 includes: foundation matching gifts ($164,512); foundation scholarships ($222,806); foundation ($3,630,428); 2000: foundation scholarships ($208,500); foundation matching gifts ($265,287) foundation ($4,568,397)
Assets: $83,984,750 (2001); $94,427,720 (2000); $100,000,000 (1999 approx)
Gifts Received: $1,969 (1997); $40,292 (1996); $43,037 (1995)

Typical Recipients

Arts & Humanities: Arts Centers, Libraries, Museums/Galleries, Public Broadcasting
Civic & Public Affairs: African American Affairs, Clubs, Community Foundations, Economic Development, Employment/Job Training, Civic & Public Affairs-General, Hispanic Affairs, Housing, Legal Aid, Municipalities/Towns, Native American Affairs, Nonprofit Management, Parades/Festivals, Philanthropic Organizations, Professional & Trade Associations, Public Policy, Safety, Zoos/Aquariums
Education: Agricultural Education, Arts/Humanities Education, Business Education, Colleges & Universities, Community & Junior Colleges, Education Funds, Engineering/Technological Education, Education-General, Medical Education, Minority Education, Preschool Education, Private Education (Precollege), Private Education (Precollege), Public Education (Precollege), Science/Mathematics Education, Secondary Education (Public), Student Aid, Vocational & Technical Education
Environment: Environment-General
Health: AIDS/HIV, Arthritis, Cancer, Children's Health/Hospitals, Clinics/Medical Centers, Diabetes, Eyes/Blindness, Health-General, Health Policy/Cost Containment, Health Organizations, Heart, Hospices, Hospitals, Medical Rehabilitation, Medical Research, Medical Training, Mental Health, Nursing Services, Nutrition, Prenatal Health Issues, Preventive Medicine/Wellness Organizations, Public Health, Speech & Hearing
International: Health Care/Hospitals, International Relief Efforts

Religion: Churches, Religion-General, Religious Welfare, Seminaries
Science: Scientific Centers & Institutes, Scientific Organizations, Scientific Research
Social Services: At-Risk Youth, Child Abuse, Child Welfare, Community Service Organizations, Domestic Violence, Family Services, Food/Clothing Distribution, People with Disabilities, Recreation & Athletics, Social Services-General, Special Olympics, United Funds/United Ways, Volunteer Services, YMCA/YWCA/YMHA/YWHA, Youth Organizations

Application Procedures

Initial Contact: Call or write for guidelines and application, then submit written proposal.
Application Requirements: Cover letter, signed by senior administrative official, which describes the applicant organization and endorses the proposed project; completed application form; proposal narrative, including: description of organization, current programs, services, and population served, description of project, how it fits within organization, primary project audience, project schedule and anticipated outcomes, evaluation measures, description and status of any collaborations with other organizations, expected impact of the project nationally or regionally, potential for replication, plan of project funding, description of current or expected funding from other donors, plans for continuation of project after funding period; line-item project budget; most recent audited financial statement, or Form 990; board roster, including affiliations; proof of tax-exempt status; supporting information, such as: letters of support, news articles, annual report, newsletters, etc.
Deadlines: February 1, May 1 and August 1.
Review Process: Trustees review proposals in May, August, and November.
Evaluative Criteria: Specific projects with measurable national or regional impact.
Decision Notification: Up to three months after receipt.
Notes: Foundation staff is willing to discuss projects with applicants before a full proposal is submitted.

Restrictions

Grants are not made to agencies based outside of the United States.
Does not support dinners or special events, fraternal organizations, individuals, political or lobbying groups, religious organizations for sectarian purposes, or organizations not tax-exempt under the Internal Revenue Code.
Foundation does not generally support capital, endowment, or local projects.

Additional Information

Publications: Application Form; Guidelines

Corporate Officials

Frank Palantoni: chief executive officer PRIM CORP EMPL chief executive officer: Gerber Products Co.

Foundation Officials

Tracy A. Baker: trustee
Ted C. Davis: trustee
Michael G. Ebert: trustee
Fernando Flores-New: trustee
Barbara Getz: executive director
Barbara J. Ivens: president, trustee
John J. James, Esq.: trustee
Jane M. Jeannero: secretary, trustee
David C. Joslin: trustee
Carolyn R. Morby: trustee
Steven W. Poole: trustee
Randy A. Puff: vice president, trustee
Stan M. VanderRoest: treasurer, trustee B Kalamazoo, MI 1961. ED Calvin College (1983); University of Pittsburgh (1984). NONPR AFFIL member: American Institute CPAs.
Dr. William B. Weil, Jr.: trustee

Grants Analysis

Disclosure Period: calendar year ending 2001
Total Grants: $4,017,755*
Number of Grants: 100
Average Grant: $75,000*
Highest Grant: $688,000
Lowest Grant: $250
Typical Range: $10,000 to $100,000
*Note: Grants analysis provided by foundation. Giving includes United Way.

Recent Grants

Note: Grants derived from 2001 Form 990.

Library-Related

75,000	Hespena Library, Hespena, MI -- heritage giving
50,000	Fremont Area District Library, Fremont, MI

General

688,480	Bethany Christian Services, Fremont, MI -- Infant and Child Programs
320,040	Jumpstart, Boston, MA -- for education and training
210,000	Prevent Child Abuse America, Chicago, IL -- heritage giving
200,000	Lucille Packard Foundation, Palo Alto, CA
197,323	University of Michigan, Ann Arbor, MI -- for science and research
148,000	Children's National Medical Center, Washington, DC -- for science and research
140,000	Pediatric AIDS Foundation, Monica, CA -- for science and research
123,000	Children's Defense Fund, Washington, DC -- for Infant and Child Programs
106,211	Oregon Health Sciences University, Portland, OR -- for science and research
100,000	Local Initiatives Support Corp, Grand Rapids, MI

GERMAN PROTESTANT ORPHAN ASYLUM ASSOCIATION FOUNDATION

Giving Contact

Lisa M. Kaichan, Foundation Manager
German Protestant Orphan Asylum Association
PO Box 158
Mandeville, LA 70470-0158
Phone: (504)895-2361
Fax: (504)674-0490

Description

Founded: 1979
EIN: 720423621
Organization Type: Private Foundation
Giving Locations: LA
Grant Types: General Support, Operating Expenses.

Financial Summary

Total Giving: $635,846 (fiscal year ending November 30, 2001); $661,477 (fiscal 2000); $540,000 (fiscal 1999)
Assets: $13,097,029 (fiscal 2001); $14,191,418 (fiscal 2000); $14,915,536 (fiscal 1999)
Gifts Received: $16 (fiscal 2001); $170 (fiscal 2000); $65 (fiscal 1998)

Typical Recipients

Arts & Humanities: Libraries, Museums/Galleries, Public Broadcasting
Civic & Public Affairs: African American Affairs, Clubs, Employment/Job Training, Civic & Public Affairs-General, Housing, Philanthropic Organizations, Women's Affairs

Education: Arts/Humanities Education, Business Education, Colleges & Universities, Education Reform, Education-General, Private Education (Precollege), Public Education (Precollege), Science/Mathematics Education, Vocational & Technical Education
Health: Children's Health/Hospitals, Emergency/Ambulance Services, Health Organizations, Hospitals, Medical Rehabilitation, Research/Studies Institutes, Single-Disease Health Associations
Religion: Churches, Religion-General, Jewish Causes, Religious Organizations, Religious Welfare
Science: Scientific Centers & Institutes
Social Services: At-Risk Youth, Big Brother/Big Sister, Child Welfare, Community Centers, Community Service Organizations, Counseling, Day Care, Delinquency & Criminal Rehabilitation, Domestic Violence, Family Planning, Family Services, Homes, People with Disabilities, Scouts, Shelters/Homelessness, Social Services-General, Substance Abuse, Volunteer Services, YMCA/YWCA/YMHA/YWHA, Youth Organizations

Application Procedures

Initial Contact: Contact foundation for application guidelines.
Application Requirements: Proposals should be in the form of a letter signed by an authorized official of the agency and must indicate that the agency's governing body officially approved submitting the proposal. The letter should be sufficient to convey the basic elements of the proposal, but should not exceed three pages. Include the project's short title and the amount requested in the first paragraph; a concise description of the project; what the project hopes to accomplish; qualifications of the personnel involved in the project; estimate of the time involved in carrying out the project and a time chart; and financial requirements of the project, other sources of funding, and amounts to be contributed by other sources. Attachments should include a list of members of the governing body, proof of tax-exempt status, recently audited financial statement, and other appropriate material. Submit ten copies of the proposal.
Deadlines: February 1, May 1, August 1, November 1.

Restrictions

Grants are limited to organizations providing social services to children and youth Louisiana.

Additional Information

Publications: Annual Report (including Application Guidelines)

Foundation Officials

Charles Bennett: director
Phillip W. Bohne: director
Walter C. Flower, III: secretary
J. Gary Haller: president
John G. Haller: trustee
Robert L. Hattler: treasurer
Paul Haygood: trustee
Charles B. Mayer: vice president
George J. Mayer: director
Charles Monsied, III: trustee
Camilee Strachan: trustee

Grants Analysis

Disclosure Period: fiscal year ending November 30, 2001
Total Grants: $635,846
Number of Grants: 67
Average Grant: $8,876*
Highest Grant: $50,000
Lowest Grant: $700
Typical Range: $5,000 to $15,000
*Note: Average grant figure excludes highest grant.

Recent Grants

Note: Grants derived from fiscal 2000 Form 990.

General

171,000	Greater New Orleans Foundation, New Orleans, LA
25,200	Bossier Caddo Children's Advocacy Center, Shreveport, LA
25,000	CASA Services, Inc., Ponchatoula, LA
24,780	Youth Service Bureau, Covington, LA
22,000	Young Leader's Academy, The, Baton Rouge, LA
19,631	St. John Lutheran Church, New Orleans, LA
17,000	Family Service GNO, New Orleans, LA
16,500	Catholic Charities - GERT, New Orleans, LA
15,000	Boys and Girls Club of Baton Rouge, Baton Rouge, LA
15,000	CADA of Acadiana, Lafayette, LA

ROLLIN M. GERSTACKER FOUNDATION

Giving Contact

Gail E. Lanphear, President
PO Box 1945
Midland, MI 48641-1945
Phone: (989)631-6097
Fax: (989)832-8842
E-mail: lanphear@concentric.net
Web: http://www.mindnet.org/gf.htm

Alternate Contact

E. N. Brandt, Vice President and Assistant Secretary

Description

Founded: 1957
EIN: 386060276
Organization Type: Family Foundation
Giving Locations: MI: Midland; OH: Cleveland
Grant Types: Capital, Challenge, Endowment, General Support, Multiyear/Continuing Support, Operating Expenses, Project, Research, Seed Money.

Donor Information

Founder: The foundation was established by Mrs. Eda U. Gerstacker in 1957 in memory of her husband, Rollin M. Gerstacker . Its primary purpose is to continue financial support of charities of all types supported by Mr. and Mrs. Gerstacker. Mrs. Gerstacker died in 1975. Family members continue to serve as officers and trustees of the foundation, although a majority of the trustees are non-family. Assets consist primarily of Dow Chemical common stock.

Financial Summary

Total Giving: $9,737,400 (2001); $10,367,942 (2000); $9,139,304 (1999)
Giving Analysis: Giving for 2001 includes: foundation grants to United Way ($326,000); foundation ($9,411,726); 2000: foundation matching gifts ($27,000); foundation grants to United Way ($240,500); 1999: foundation grants to United Way ($245,175)
Assets: $188,845,151 (2001); $205,396,252 (2000); $237,650,186 (1999)
Gifts Received: $35,009,391 (1997); $14,083,000 (1996); $499,055 (1995). Note: Contributions were received from the estate of Carl A. Gerstacker.

Typical Recipients

Arts & Humanities: Arts Centers, History & Archaeology, Libraries, Music
Civic & Public Affairs: Business/Free Enterprise, Chambers of Commerce, Community Foundations, Economic Development, Economic Policy, Employment/Job Training, Civic & Public Affairs-General,

Housing, Legal Aid, Municipalities/Towns, Native American Affairs, Parades/Festivals, Philanthropic Organizations, Professional & Trade Associations, Public Policy, Safety, Urban & Community Affairs, Zoos/Aquariums

Education: Agricultural Education, Colleges & Universities, Community & Junior Colleges, Education Associations, Engineering/Technological Education, Education-General, Literacy, Minority Education, Public Education (Precollege), Religious Education, Science/Mathematics Education

Environment: Environment-General, Environment-General, Resource Conservation

Health: AIDS/HIV, Alzheimers Disease, Arthritis, Clinics/Medical Centers, Emergency/Ambulance Services, Eyes/Blindness, Geriatric Health, Hospitals, Medical Rehabilitation, Medical Research, Mental Health, Multiple Sclerosis, Nursing Services, Public Health, Research/Studies Institutes, Single-Disease Health Associations, Transplant Networks/Donor Banks

Religion: Churches, Religious Welfare, Seminaries
Science: Scientific Centers & Institutes, Scientific Organizations

Social Services: At-Risk Youth, Child Welfare, Community Centers, Community Service Organizations, Domestic Violence, Family Services, Food/Clothing Distribution, Homes, People with Disabilities, Recreation & Athletics, Recreation & Athletics, Scouts, Senior Services, Substance Abuse, United Funds/ United Ways, YMCA/YWCA/YMHA/YWHA, Youth Organizations

Application Procedures

Initial Contact: Applicants should write the foundation for guidelines, or send a brief letter outlining the project for which funding is sought.

Application Requirements: The application letter should provide a brief description of the program in need of funding, including an explanation of its importance and a clear statement of its goals. Include a budget for the proposed program, information about other potential sources of funding, the amount requested from the foundation, and evidence of tax-exempt status.

Deadlines: Applications should reach the foundation prior to June 1 or December 1.

Review Process: The board meets twice a year, in June and December, to review proposals.

Restrictions

The foundation does not provide funding for scholarships, for individuals, or to religious organizations for sectarian purposes.

Additional Information

Publications: Annual Report

Foundation Officials

Alexio R. Baum: trustee
E. N. Brandt: vice president, assistant secretary, trustee
Frank Gerace: trustee
Esther S. Gerstacker: vice president, trustee
Lisa J. Gerstacker: vice president, secretary, assistant treasurer, trustee
Gail E. Lanphear: president, trustee CORP AFFIL president, chief executive officer: Sysco Food Services-Albany.
Thomas L. Ludington: trustee
Paul Fausto Oreffice: trustee B Venice, Italy 1927. ED Purdue University BS (1949). CORP AFFIL director: Saratoga Race Track; director: Coca-Cola USA; director: Minute Maid Co.; director: CIGNA Corp.; director: Coca-Cola Co.; director: Aqueduct Race Track; director: Belmont Park. NONPR AFFIL director: New York Racing Association Inc.
Alan Wayne Ott: treasurer, trustee B Manistique, MI 1931. CORP AFFIL director, chairman: Chemical Bank West; chairman, director: Chemical Finance

Corp.; chairman: Chemical Bank & Trust Co.; chairman, director: Chemical Bank Michigan; chairman, director: Chemical Bank Thumb Area; director, chairman: Chemical Bank Huron.
Jean U. Popoff: trustee
William D. Schuette: vice president, trustee
William S. Stavropoulos: trustee B Bridgehampton, NY 1939. ED Fordham University BA (1961); University of Washington PhD (1966). PRIM CORP EMPL chairman, director, executive committee: Dow Chemical Co. CORP AFFIL director: Marion Merrell Dow Inc.; director: NCR Corp.; director: Dow Corning Corp.; director: Chemical Bank & Trust Co.; director: Chemical Finance Corp.; director: BellSouth Corp.

Grants Analysis

Disclosure Period: calendar year ending 2001
Total Grants: $9,411,726*
Number of Grants: 199
Average Grant: $42,314*
Highest Grant: $1,033,518
Typical Range: $2,000 to $50,000
*Note: Giving excludes United Way. Average grant figure excludes highest grant.

Recent Grants

Note: Grants derived from 2001 Form 990.

Library-Related
60,000	Houghton Lake Public Library

General
1,033,518	Midland Economic Development Council, Midland, MI
400,000	Midland County Council on Aging, Midland, MI
300,000	Midland Area Community Foundation, Midland, MI
300,000	Midland County Education Service Agency, Midland, MI
250,000	Homer Township Fire Department
240,000	Central Michigan University, Mt. Pleasant, MI
240,000	United Way of Bay and Saginaw Counties, MI
200,000	Detroit Area Pre-College Engineering Program, Detroit, MI
200,000	Michitario Friendship Games, MI
200,000	Northwood University, Midland, MI

CHARLES M. AND NANCY A. GESCHKE FOUNDATION

Giving Contact

Charles M. Geschke, President
220 University Avenue
Los Altos, CA 94022-3518
Phone: (650)961-4400

Description

Founded: 1987
EIN: 943052556
Organization Type: Private Foundation
Giving Locations: CA
Grant Types: General Support, Scholarship.

Donor Information

Founder: Charles W. and Nancy A. Geschke

Financial Summary

Total Giving: $686,548 (fiscal year ending September 30, 2001); $132,185 (fiscal 2000); $42,763 (fiscal 1999)
Giving Analysis: Giving for fiscal 2001 includes: foundation scholarships ($13,150)
Assets: $7,404,912 (fiscal 2001); $23,858,407 (fiscal 2000); $5,357,971 (fiscal 1999)
Gifts Received: $4,080,402 (fiscal 2000); $990,000 (fiscal 1995); $2,300 (fiscal 1993). Note: In fiscal

1995, 1997 and 2000, contributions were received from Charles M. and Nancy A. Geschke.

Typical Recipients

Arts & Humanities: History & Archaeology, Libraries, Music
Civic & Public Affairs: Civic & Public Affairs-General, Hispanic Affairs
Education: Arts/Humanities Education, Colleges & Universities, Public Education (Precollege), Secondary Education (Private), Social Sciences Education
Health: Emergency/Ambulance Services
Religion: Churches, Religious Welfare
Social Services: Emergency Relief, Senior Services

Application Procedures

Initial Contact: The foundation reports no specific application guidelines. Send a brief letter of inquiry, including statement of purpose, amount requested, and proof of tax-exempt status.
Deadlines: None.

Foundation Officials

Charles Matthew Geschke: president B Cleveland, OH 1939. ED Carnegie Mellon University PhD; Xavier University AB (1962); Xavier University MS (1963). PRIM CORP EMPL co-chairman: Adobe Systems. NONPR AFFIL member: Math Association America; member: National Academy Engineers; member: Association Computer Math.
Kathleen A. Geschke: director
Nancy A. Geschke: secretary, treasurer

Grants Analysis

Disclosure Period: fiscal year ending September 30, 2001
Total Grants: $673,398*
Number of Grants: 27
Average Grant: $7,073*
Highest Grant: $249,354
Lowest Grant: $1,000
Typical Range: $2,500 to $15,000
*Note: Giving excludes scholarship. Average grant figure excludes three highest grants ($503,648).

Recent Grants

Note: Grants derived from fiscal 2000 Form 990.

General
49,091	St. Mary's Church, Nantucket, MA
27,422	St. Nicholas Parish, Los Altos, CA
25,000	San Francisco Symphony, San Francisco, CA -- 1999-2000 annual fund
24,422	San Mateo County Community College Foundation, San Mateo, CA
3,250	Los Altos School District, Los Altos, CA -- history field trip grant

J. PAUL GETTY TRUST

Giving Contact

The Getty Grant Program
1200 Getty Center Dr., Suite 800
Los Angeles, CA 90049-1685
Phone: (310)440-7320
Fax: (310)440-7703
E-mail: enovotny@getty.edu
Web: http://www.getty.edu/grants

Description

Founded: 1953
EIN: 951790021
Organization Type: General Purpose Foundation
Giving Locations: internationally; nationally.
Grant Types: Fellowship, Matching, Project, Research.

Donor Information

Founder: "The Getty Grant Program is part of the J. Paul Getty Trust, a private operation foundation dedicated to the visual arts and the humanities. In addition to the Grant Program, the Trust has seven operating programs. The Trust's origins date to 1953 and the founding of the J. Paul Getty Museum as a California charitable trust. When most of Mr. Getty's personal estate passed to the Trust in 1992, the trustees decided that -- given the size of the endowment and Mr. Getty's purpose, stated in the trust indenture as 'the diffusion of artistic and general knowledge' -- the Trust should make a greater contribution to the visual arts than the museum could alone." Billionaire J. Paul Getty was the son of Oklahoma oilman George Franklin Getty, who founded the Getty Oil Company.

Financial Summary

Total Giving: $19,579,820 (fiscal year ending June 30, 2001); $15,658,090 (fiscal 2000); $14,591,859 (fiscal 1999)

Giving Analysis: Giving for fiscal 2001 includes: foundation matching gifts ($1,584,706); foundation gifts to individuals ($2,615,474); fiscal 1999: foundation matching gifts ($1,316,165); foundation gifts to individuals ($2,166,420); fiscal 1998: foundation matching gifts ($878,328) foundation scholarships ($1,108,352)

Assets: $8,793,485,757 (fiscal 2001); $10,929,809,811 (fiscal 2000); $8,066,293,000 (fiscal 1999)

Gifts Received: $3,071,442 (fiscal 2001); $1,573,357 (fiscal 2000); $1,539,337 (fiscal 1999). Note: The J. Paul Getty Trust occasionally receives works of art and reference materials from individuals, libraries, and other museums. These gifts are listed in terms of their fair market value. The Getty Grant program is the philanthropic arm of the J. Paul Getty Trust, a private operating foundation. Figures are for the Trust as a whole.

Typical Recipients

Arts & Humanities: Arts Associations & Councils, Arts Centers, Arts Funds, Arts Institutes, Ethnic & Folk Arts, Film & Video, Historic Preservation, History & Archaeology, Libraries, Literary Arts, Museums/Galleries, Visual Arts

Civic & Public Affairs: Botanical Gardens/Parks, Ethnic Organizations, Civic & Public Affairs-General, Municipalities/Towns, Nonprofit Management, Public Policy

Education: Arts/Humanities Education, Colleges & Universities, Education Funds, Education Reform, Engineering/Technological Education, Environmental Education, Education-General, International Exchange, Minority Education, Private Education (Precollege), Public Education (Precollege), Science/Mathematics Education, Social Sciences Education, Student Aid

Environment: Environment-General, Resource Conservation, Resource Conservation

Health: Adolescent Health Issues, Health-General

International: Foreign Arts Organizations, Foreign Educational Institutions, International-General, International Development, International Environmental Issues, International Organizations, International Peace & Security Issues, International Relations, Missionary/Religious Activities

Religion: Religious Organizations

Science: Observatories & Planetariums, Science Museums

Application Procedures

Initial Contact: Potential applicants should request the Getty Grant Program's funding priorities brochure for information about areas of support. The next step, in most cases, is to submit a preliminary letter. Applicants are welcome to contact the grant program office for assistance with applications. Initial inquiries can be faxed, but final applications must be mailed.

Deadlines: Varies according to grant category.

Review Process: All application materials must be received in the Grant Program Office before the review process can begin. Applications are reviewed by specialists in relevant fields. The Grant Program bases its final decisions on the recommendations of outside reviewers and committee members. Final notification is usually within six months of receipt of the complete application.

Restrictions

The Trust generally will not support operating expenses, indirect costs, endowment funds, building maintenance or construction, or production or acquisition of works of art.

Additional Information

The Getty Grant Program reports that most grants range between $3,000 and $300,000. The majority of grants are under $50,000. Grants also range from one to three years, and are not renewable.

Publications: Guidelines; Grant Program Description; Grants Awarded Report; Biennial Report; application form.

Foundation Officials

Lewis W. Bernard: trustee PRIM CORP EMPL chairman: Classroom Inc. CORP AFFIL director: Harvard Management Co.; director: Marsh & McLennan Companies Inc. NONPR AFFIL trustee, vice chairman: American Museum Natural History; director: Harvard University.

John Herron Biggs: trustee B Saint Louis, MO 1936. ED Harvard University AB (1958); Washington University PhD (1983). PRIM CORP EMPL chairman, chief executive officer, director: Teachers Insurance Annuity Association/College Retirement Equities Fund. CORP AFFIL director: Ralston Purina Co.; director: Boeing Co.; director: American Council of Life Insurance. NONPR AFFIL director: United Way New York City; trustee: Washington University; fellow: Society Actuaries; chairman: National Bureau Economic Affairs; member: New York City Partnership; member: Financial Accounting Foundation; emeritus trustee: Missouri Botanical Gardens; member: Business Higher Education Forum; member: American Academy of Arts & Sciences; member: Association Governing Board Higher Education; member: American Academy of Actuaries. CLUB AFFIL Westchester Country Club; Saint Louis Club; Sky Club; Harvard Club; Log Cabin Club.

Louise Henry Bryson: trustee PRIM CORP EMPL chairman: Community Television of Southern California.

John F. Cooke: executive vice president external affairs, trustee B 1942. PRIM CORP EMPL executive vice president, officer: Walt Disney Co. Inc. ADD CORP EMPL executive vice president: Disney Enterprises Inc.; president, director: Disney Channel Inc.

Ramon C. Cortines: trustee CORP AFFIL director: Scholastic Corp.

Peter C. Erichsen: vice president, general counsel, secretary

David I. Fisher: trustee B Bellmore, NY 1939. ED University of California (1961); University of Missouri (1965). PRIM CORP EMPL chairman: Capital Group Companies Inc.

David Pierpont Gardner: vice chairman, trustee B Berkeley, CA 1933. ED Brigham Young University BS (1955); University of California at Berkeley MA (1959); University of California at Berkeley PhD (1966). CORP AFFIL director: First Security Corp.; director: Fluor Corp. NONPR AFFIL fellow: American Academy of Arts & Sciences; member: American Philosophical Society.

Marilyn Gillette: director information technology services

Russell S. Gould: senior vice president finance investments PRIM CORP EMPL executive: Metropolitan West Securities.

Agnes Gund: trustee B Cleveland, OH 1938. ED Connecticut College; Harvard University AM (1980). PRIM NONPR EMPL president: Music of Modern Art.

Steve Juarez: director financial management

Helene L. Kaplan: vice chairman, trustee B New York, NY 1933. ED Barnard College AB (1953); New York University JD (1967). PRIM CORP EMPL of counsel: Skadden, Arps, Slate, Meagher & Flom. CORP AFFIL director: Metro Life Insurance Co.; director: Verizon Communications Inc.; director: Exxon-Mobil Corp.; director: May Department Stores Co.; director: Chase Manhattan Corp. NONPR AFFIL trustee: Olive Free Library; member: Women's Forum; member: New York State Bar Association; vice chairman, trustee: Mount Sinai Medical Center; vice chairman, trustee: Mount Sinai School of Medicine; member: Century Association; trustee: Institute Advanced Studies; trustee: Barnard College; member: American Philosophical Society; member: Association Bar New York City; member: American Bar Association; trustee, vice chairman: American Museum Natural History; member: American Academy of Arts & Sciences. CLUB AFFIL Cosmopolitan Club.

Herbert L. Lucas, Jr.: trustee B Winnetka, IL 1926. ED Princeton University (1950); Harvard University MBA (1952). CORP AFFIL director: Nutraceutix Inc.; director: Wellington Trust Co. Boston; director: Clean Age Minerals Inc.; director: Electronic Clearing House.

Deborah Marrow: director Getty Grant Program ED University of Pennsylvania BA (1970); Johns Hopkins University MA (1972); University of Pennsylvania PhD (1978). NONPR AFFIL member: Grantmakers in the Arts; member: International Council Museums; member: Art Table.

Barry Munitz: president, chief executive officer B 1941. ED Brooklyn College BA (1963); Princeton University MA (1965); Princeton University PhD (1968). PRIM NONPR EMPL chancellor: California State University System. CORP AFFIL director: SunAmerica Inc. NONPR AFFIL member: Phi Beta Kappa; member: Young President Organization; member: National Business Higher Education Forum; director: American Council Education; director: KCET-TV.

Stephen D. Rountree: executive vice president, chief operating officer

Lori Starr: director communications

John Walsh: vice president and director, J Paul Getty Museum B Mason City, WA 1937. ED Yale University BA (1961); Columbia University MA (1965); University of Leyden (1965-1966); Columbia University PhD (1971). PRIM NONPR EMPL director: J. Paul Getty Museum. NONPR AFFIL member government board: Smithsonian Council; member government board: Yale University Art Gallery; member: College Art Association; member, trustee: Association Art Museum Directors; board fellows: Claremont University Center Graduate School; member: American Association Museums; member: Archaeological Institute America; member: American Antiquarian Society. CLUB AFFIL Century Club.

Timothy P. Whalen: director Conservation Institute

Dr. Blenda Jacqueline Wilson: trustee B Woodbridge, NJ 1941. ED Cedar Crest College AB (1962); Seton Hall University AM (1965); Boston College PhD (1979). PRIM NONPR EMPL president, chief executive officer: Nellie Mae Education Foundation. CORP AFFIL director: Union Bancal Corp.; director: Union Bank; director: Alpha Capital Management. NONPR AFFIL member: Women Foundations; member: Women's Economic Club Detroit; member: Women Executives State Government; advisory board: University Southern California District 60 National Alliance; advisory board: Valley Cultural Center; chairman: University Corporate; director: University Detroit Jesuit High School; director: United Way Southeast Michigan; advisory board: Stanford Institute Higher Education Research; American delegate: United States-UK Dialogue About Quality Judgements Higher Education; visitors committee: PEW Forum K-12 Education Reform U.S.; member: Race Relations

Council Metropolitan Detroit; director: Nothridge Hospital Medical Center; member: Michigan Womens Forum; member: National Coalition 100 Black Women; director, vice chairman: Metropolitan Affairs Corp.; director: Metropolitan Center High Technology; member: International Womens Forum; visitors committee: Harvard College Division Continuing Education Faculty Arts Science; director: International Foundation Education & Self-Help; trustee: J. Paul Getty Music; member: Greater Detroit Interfaith Round Table NCCJ; director, trustee emeritus: Foundation Center; member: College Board; trustee: Sammy Davis Junior National Liver Institute; life trustee: Cambridge College; trustee: Clark University; member: Black Women Higher Education; member: Association Black Professionals & Administrations; member advisory council president: Association Government Boards; member higher education colloquium: American Council Education; director: Arab Community Center Economic Social Services; member: American Association University Women; director: Achievement Council; member: American Association State Colleges & Universities. CLUB AFFIL Economic Club; Rotary Club.

Ira E. Yellin: trustee PRIM CORP EMPL senior vice president: Catellus Development Corp.

Grants Analysis

Disclosure Period: fiscal year ending June 30, 2001
Total Grants: $17,995,114*
Number of Grants: 471
Average Grant: $38,206
Highest Grant: $150,000
Typical Range: $3,000 to $250,000
*Note: Giving excludes matching gifts. Giving includes gifts to individuals.

Recent Grants

Note: Grants derived from fiscal 2001 Form 990.

Library-Related
141,000	Library of Congress, Washington, DC -- education and training

General
500,000	Barnes Foundation, Merion, PA -- support of charitable activities
307,906	University College London, London United Kingdom -- education and training
300,000	Center for Advanced Study in the Behavioral Sciences, Stanford, CA -- collaborative research grants
300,000	Los Angeles County Museum of Natural History, Los Angeles, CA -- electronic cataloguing initiative
300,000	Teachers Documentary Project, Los Angeles, CA -- support for charitable activities
300,000	University of Southern California, Los Angeles, CA -- electronic cataloguing initiative
273,686	Staatliche Kunstsammlungen Dresden, Dresden Germany -- research resources
250,000	Autry Museum of Western Heritage, Los Angeles, CA -- electronic cataloguing initiative
250,000	Barnes Foundation, Merion, PA -- support of charitable activities
250,000	Harvard University, Cambridge, MA -- reference works

GHEENS FOUNDATION

Giving Contact

James N. Davis, Executive Director
One Riverfront Plaza, Suite 705
Louisville, KY 40202
Phone: (502)584-4650

Fax: (502)584-4652
E-mail: lindahw@aye.net

Description

Founded: 1957
EIN: 616031406
Organization Type: General Purpose Foundation
Giving Locations: KY: Louisville; LA: LaFourche Parish
Grant Types: Capital, Fellowship, General Support, Matching, Multiyear/Continuing Support, Operating Expenses, Project, Research, Scholarship.

Donor Information

Founder: The foundation was established in 1957, by the late C. Edwin Gheens and the late Mary Jo Gheens Hill . Mr. Gheens owned a successful candy manufacturing company in Louisville, KY. His family, which was successful in the wholesale grocery business, also owned a sugar cane plantation in the New Orleans, LA area. Mr. & Mrs. Gheens were leaders in their church and active in other philanthropic endeavors in Louisville, and founded the Gheens Foundation to continue their interests in education, religious programs and human services.

Financial Summary

Total Giving: $4,868,917 (fiscal year ending October 31, 2002 approx); $4,868,917 (fiscal 2001); $4,868,917 (fiscal 2000)
Giving Analysis: Giving for fiscal 2000 includes: foundation grants to United Way ($80,000)
Assets: $90,570,318 (fiscal 2002 approx); $90,570,318 (fiscal 2001); $90,570,318 (fiscal 2000)

Typical Recipients

Arts & Humanities: Arts Associations & Councils, Arts Centers, Arts Festivals, Arts Funds, Ballet, Community Arts, Historic Preservation, History & Archaeology, Libraries, Literary Arts, Museums/Galleries, Music, Opera, Public Broadcasting, Theater
Civic & Public Affairs: African American Affairs, Botanical Gardens/Parks, Clubs, Community Foundations, Economic Development, Civic & Public Affairs-General, Hispanic Affairs, Housing, Legal Aid, Municipalities/Towns, Philanthropic Organizations, Rural Affairs, Safety, Urban & Community Affairs, Women's Affairs, Zoos/Aquariums
Education: Afterschool/Enrichment Programs, Agricultural Education, Business Education, Colleges & Universities, Economic Education, Education Associations, Education Reform, Elementary Education (Private), Engineering/Technological Education, Education-General, Leadership Training, Legal Education, Literacy, Medical Education, Minority Education, Preschool Education, Private Education (Precollege), Public Education (Precollege), Religious Education, School Volunteerism, Science/Mathematics Education, Secondary Education (Private), Social Sciences Education, Special Education, Student Aid
Environment: Air/Water Quality, Environment-General, Resource Conservation, Wildlife Protection
Health: Cancer, Children's Health/Hospitals, Clinics/Medical Centers, Diabetes, Eyes/Blindness, Geriatric Health, Health Organizations, Hospices, Hospitals, Hospitals (University Affiliated), Medical Rehabilitation, Medical Research, Mental Health, Preventive Medicine/Wellness Organizations, Public Health, Single-Disease Health Associations
International: Foreign Educational Institutions
Religion: Churches, Dioceses, Religion-General, Jewish Causes, Ministries, Religious Organizations, Religious Welfare, Seminaries
Science: Science Museums
Social Services: At-Risk Youth, Child Welfare, Community Centers, Community Service Organizations, Day Care, Family Planning, Family Services, Food/Clothing Distribution, Homes, People with Disabilities, Recreation & Athletics, Scouts, Senior Services, Special Olympics, Substance Abuse, United Funds/United Ways, United Funds/United Ways, Volunteer

Services, YMCA/YWCA/YMHA/YWHA, Youth Organizations

Application Procedures

Initial Contact: The foundation provides an application form; ten copies of the completed application should be sent to the foundation.
Application Requirements: The application form requests the following information: name of organization, contact person and title, address, program summary describing the activities of the organization and the particular activity that the grant would fund; and a financial summary detailing the amount of the request, total annual budget of the organization, and the budget for the project which the grant would support. The foundation also requires copies of IRS letters confirming the organization's tax-exempt status, and that it is not a private foundation.
Deadlines: None.

Restrictions

Grants are not made to individuals.

Additional Information

Publications: Guidelines; Application Form

Foundation Officials

Morton Boyd: trustee B Louisville, KY 1936. ED University of Virginia BA (1958); Rutgers University Stonier Graduate School of Banking (1964). PRIM CORP EMPL chairman, chief executive officer: National City Bank Kentucky. CORP AFFIL executive vice president: National City Corp.; executive vice president, director: First Kentucky Trust Co.; vice chairman: First National Bank Louisville. NONPR AFFIL chairman: Louisville Central Area; member: Louisville Chamber of Commerce; director: Fund Arts; director: Kentucky Derby Museum Corp.; member: Association Reserve City Bankers.
Walter S. Coe: trustee
James N. Davis: executive director
Donald W. Doyle: vice president, trustee
William G. Duncan, Jr.: trustee
Michael B. Mountjoy: trustee, secretary, treasurer B 1942. ED University of Kentucky (1963). PRIM CORP EMPL managing director: Carpenter & Mountjoy PSC. CORP AFFIL secretary-treasurer, director: T-Shirts & More Inc.
Joseph E. Stopher: president, trustee B 1914. ED University of Louisville LLB (1938). PRIM CORP EMPL partner: Boehl Stopher & Graves.

Grants Analysis

Disclosure Period: fiscal year ending October 31, 2000
Total Grants: $4,788,917*
Number of Grants: 128
Average Grant: $37,413
Highest Grant: $500,000
Lowest Grant: $500
Typical Range: $10,000 to $25,000
*Note: Giving excludes United Way.

Recent Grants

Note: Grants derived from 2001 Form 990.

General .
950,000	University of Louisville, Louisville, KY -- Gheens Hall/Rauch Planetarium
500,000	University of Louisville, Louisville, KY -- medical research
133,000	National D-Day Museum, New Orleans, LA
125,000	Louisville Presbyterian Seminary, Louisville, KY
125,000	Tulane University Medical Center, New Orleans, LA
111,712	Loyola University New Orleans, New Orleans, LA
100,000	African American Heritage Foundation, Keokuk, IA

100,000	Bellarmine College, Louisville, KY
100,000	Cathedral Heritage Foundation, Louisville, KY
100,000	Home of the Innocents, Louisville, KY

GHIDOTTI FOUNDATION

Giving Contact
William Toms, Trustee
3961 De Sabla Rd.
Cameron Park, CA 95682
Phone: (530)677-3994

Description
Founded: 1969
EIN: 946181833
Organization Type: Private Foundation
Giving Locations: CA: Nevada County
Grant Types: General Support, Scholarship.

Donor Information
Founder: William Ghidotti, the late Marian Ghidotti

Financial Summary
Total Giving: $625,316 (2001); $745,331 (2000); $594,818 (1999). Note: 1997 Giving includes scholarship.
Giving Analysis: Giving for 2001 includes: foundation scholarships ($494,767); 2000: foundation scholarships ($465,966) 1999: foundation scholarships ($405,700)
Assets: $13,187,034 (2001); $9,760,461 (2000); $14,969,649 (1999)
Gifts Received: $184,916 (1994)

Typical Recipients
Arts & Humanities: Arts & Humanities-General, Historic Preservation, Libraries, Literary Arts, Music, Theater
Civic & Public Affairs: Clubs, Civic & Public Affairs-General, Rural Affairs
Education: Agricultural Education, Elementary Education (Private), Education-General, Literacy, Private Education (Precollege), Public Education (Precollege), Science/Mathematics Education, Secondary Education (Public), Special Education, Student Aid
Environment: Energy, Resource Conservation
Health: Alzheimers Disease, Home-Care Services, Hospices, Hospitals, Prenatal Health Issues
Religion: Religious Welfare
Social Services: At-Risk Youth, Big Brother/Big Sister, Child Welfare, Community Service Organizations, United Funds/United Ways, Volunteer Services, Youth Organizations

Application Procedures
Initial Contact: Send standard application form by February for new scholarships, August for renewals. Also send transcript of grades, student and family income, and personal resume.

Additional Information
Provides scholarships to graduating seniors residing in and attending Nevada County, CA, high schools.
Trust(s): Wells Fargo Bank

Foundation Officials
Mary Bouma: trustee
Erica Erickson: trustee
Frank Francis: trustee
William Toms: trustee
Ruth Halls Unger: trustee

Grants Analysis
Disclosure Period: calendar year ending 2001
Total Grants: $130,549*
Number of Grants: 21
Average Grant: $5,277*
Highest Grant: $25,000

Lowest Grant: $159
Typical Range: $1,000 to $10,000
*Note: Giving excludes scholarships. Average grant figure excludes highest grant.

Recent Grants
Note: Grants derived from 2000 Form 990.

Library-Related
15,000	Friends of the Library, Woodstock, NY

General
75,000	Music in the Mountains, New Paltz, NY
50,000	Miners Foundry Culture Preservation
30,000	Nevada County Theatre Company, Las Vegas, NV
23,641	Nevada County Fair, Las Vegas, NV
15,000	Hospice of the Foothills, Grass Valley, CA
14,826	Hennessy School
8,000	Foothill Theatre Company, The, Pasadena, CA
5,000	Nevada Union High School, NV
5,000	Sierra Nevada Memorial Hospital Alzheimer's, Las Vegas, NV
4,500	Sierra Nevada Memorial Hospital Foundation, Grass Valley, CA

GIANT EAGLE, INC.

Company Headquarters
Pittsburgh, PA
Web: http://www.gianteagle.com

Company Description
Revenue: US$5.943 billion (2002)
Employees: 35000 (2002)
SIC(s): 2032 Canned Specialties, 2033 Canned Fruits & Vegetables, 2051 Bread, Cake & Related Products, 5411 Grocery Stores.

Operating Locations
Giant Eagle Inc. (PA--Pittsburgh)

Giant Eagle Foundation

Giving Contact
Jody Clark, Administrator
101 Kappa Drive
Pittsburgh, PA 15238
Phone: (412)963-6200
Fax: (412)963-2540

Alternate Contact
Ray Huber, Scholarship Administrator

Description
EIN: 256033905
Organization Type: Corporate Foundation
Giving Locations: PA: Pittsburgh
Grant Types: General Support, Research.

Financial Summary
Total Giving: $3,162,273 (fiscal year ending August 31, 2001); $2,624,913 (fiscal 2000); $1,686,256 (fiscal 1998). Note: Contributes through corporate direct giving program and foundation.
Giving Analysis: Giving for fiscal 2000 includes: foundation scholarships ($46,500); foundation grants to United Way ($74,000); foundation ($2,504,413); fiscal 1998: foundation scholarships ($17,000); foundation grants to United Way ($73,000); foundation ($1,596,256); fiscal 1997: foundation grants to United Way ($1,000); foundation ($1,571,449);
Assets: $17,472,774 (fiscal 2001); $19,482,390 (fiscal 2000); $11,740,124 (fiscal 1998)
Gifts Received: $3,423,466 (fiscal 2001); $3,887,036 (fiscal 2000); $3,473,737 (fiscal 1998).

Note: Contributions are received from Giant Eagle, Inc.

Typical Recipients
Arts & Humanities: Arts Associations & Councils, Arts Centers, Arts Institutes, Ballet, Community Arts, Dance, Ethnic & Folk Arts, Arts & Humanities-General, History & Archaeology, Libraries, Museums/Galleries, Music, Opera, Performing Arts, Public Broadcasting, Theater
Civic & Public Affairs: African American Affairs, Civil Rights, Clubs, Economic Development, Economic Policy, Civic & Public Affairs-General, Law & Justice, Legal Aid, Municipalities/Towns, Philanthropic Organizations, Public Policy, Urban & Community Affairs, Women's Affairs, Zoos/Aquariums
Education: Business Education, Colleges & Universities, Education Funds, Elementary Education (Private), Faculty Development, Medical Education, Minority Education, Private Education (Precollege), Public Education (Precollege), Religious Education, Special Education, Student Aid
Environment: Environment-General, Resource Conservation, Wildlife Protection
Health: AIDS/HIV, Cancer, Children's Health/Hospitals, Diabetes, Emergency/Ambulance Services, Geriatric Health, Health Organizations, Heart, Hospitals, Kidney, Medical Rehabilitation, Medical Research, Mental Health, Prenatal Health Issues, Public Health, Single-Disease Health Associations
International: Health Care/Hospitals, International Organizations, International Relief Efforts, Missionary/Religious Activities
Religion: Dioceses, Religion-General, Jewish Causes, Jewish Causes, Religious Organizations, Religious Welfare, Social/Policy Issues, Synagogues/Temples
Science: Scientific Centers & Institutes, Scientific Research
Social Services: At-Risk Youth, Big Brother/Big Sister, Child Welfare, Community Centers, Community Service Organizations, Counseling, Delinquency & Criminal Rehabilitation, Domestic Violence, Family Services, Food/Clothing Distribution, People with Disabilities, Recreation & Athletics, Scouts, Senior Services, Sexual Abuse, Shelters/Homelessness, Substance Abuse, United Funds/United Ways, YMCA/YWCA/YMHA/YWHA, Youth Organizations

Application Procedures
Initial Contact: Send a written proposal.
Application Requirements: Include a description of organization, amount requested, purpose of funds sought, recently audited financial statement, and proof of tax-exempt status.
Deadlines: January 31 for grants; November 1 for scholarship applications.

Restrictions
Does not support individuals or non-501(c)(3) organizations.

Corporate Officials
David S. Shapira: chairman, chief executive officer, director B 1942. ED Oberlin College BA (1964); Stanford University MA (1966). PRIM CORP EMPL chairman, chief executive officer, director: Giant Eagle Inc. CORP AFFIL director: Mellon Bank Corp.; director: Mellon Bank NA; director: Equitable Resources Inc.

Foundation Officials
Gerald Chait: trustee CORP AFFIL director: Giant Eagle Inc.; director: Tamarkin Co. Inc.
Edward Moravitz: trustee B 1925. ED University of Pittsburgh (1948). CORP AFFIL director: Tamarkin Co. Inc.
David S. Shapira: trustee (see above)
Norman Weizenbaum: trustee B 1933. ED University of Pennsylvania (1955). CORP AFFIL director: Giant Eagle Inc.; director: Tamarkin Co. Inc.

Grants Analysis

Disclosure Period: fiscal year ending August 31, 2001
Total Grants: $3,069,273*
Number of Grants: 233
Average Grant: $6,669*
Highest Grant: $1,522,100
Lowest Grant: $250
Typical Range: $1,000 to $10,000
*Note: Giving excludes United Way and scholarships. Average grant figure excludes highest grant.

Recent Grants

Note: Grants derived from 2002 Form 990.

General

1,522,100	United Jewish Federation, Pittsburgh, PA
150,000	Carnegie Mellon University, Pittsburgh, PA
50,000	Food Marketing Institute Foundation, Washington, DC
36,667	Pittsburgh Zoo and Aquarium, Pittsburgh, PA
35,000	Allegheny Conference on Community Development, Pittsburgh, PA
35,000	Extra-Mile Education Foundation, Inc., Pittsburgh, PA
35,000	Jewish Learning Center, Pittsburgh, PA
35,000	Pittsburgh Symphony, Pittsburgh, PA
28,750	Pittsburgh Ballet Theater, Pittsburgh, PA
27,000	Hillel Academy, Pittsburgh, PA

GIANT FOOD, INC.

Company Headquarters

6300 Sheriff Rd.
Landover, MD 20785
Web: http://www.giantfood.com

Company Description

Revenue: US$5.289 billion (2001)
Employees: 35000 (2001)
SIC(s): 5411 Grocery Stores, 5912 Drug Stores & Proprietary Stores.

Operating Locations

Giant Food Inc. (CA--Fresno; DC--Washington; MD--Baltimore, Burtonsville, Gaithersburg, Jessup, Joppa Heights, Landover, Lutherville, Pikesville, Prince Frederick, Rockville, Silver Spring, Upper Marlboro, Westminster; VA--Annandale, Fredericksburg, Herndon, Lakeridge, McLean, Warrenton)

Nonmonetary Support

Range: $75,000 - $400,000
Type: Cause-related Marketing & Promotion; Donated Equipment; Donated Products; In-kind Services
Contact: Barry F. Scher, Vice President, Public Affairs

Giant Food Foundation

Giving Contact

Richard A. Baird, President
6300 Sheriff Road
Landover, MD 20785
Phone: (301)341-4171
Fax: (301)618-4972
Web: http://www.giantfood.com/community.htm

Alternate Contact

Barry Scher, Vice President of Public Affairs
PO Box 1804
Washington, DC 20013
Note: Contact for sponsorship, direct giving and nonmonetary support.

Description

Founded: 1950
EIN: 526045041
Organization Type: Corporate Foundation
Giving Locations: DE; DC; MD; NJ; VA
Grant Types: General Support.

Financial Summary

Total Giving: $503,266 (fiscal year ending January 31, 2001); $419,622 (fiscal 2000 approx); $410,817 (fiscal 1999). Note: Contributes through corporate direct giving program and foundation.
Giving Analysis: Giving for fiscal 2001 includes: foundation grants to United Way ($207,450); foundation ($295,816); fiscal 1999: corporate grants to United Way ($199,450) foundation ($211,367)
Assets: $715,544 (fiscal 2001); $901,665 (fiscal 1999); $712,905 (fiscal 1998 approx)
Gifts Received: $500,000 (fiscal 1999); $600,000 (fiscal 1996); $600,000 (fiscal 1995). Note: Contributions are received from Giant Food Inc.

Typical Recipients

Arts & Humanities: Arts Centers, Ballet, Community Arts, Dance, Historic Preservation, History & Archaeology, Libraries, Museums/Galleries, Music, Opera, Performing Arts, Public Broadcasting, Theater
Civic & Public Affairs: African American Affairs, Business/Free Enterprise, Chambers of Commerce, Economic Development, Employment/Job Training, Civic & Public Affairs-General, Housing, Law & Justice, Public Policy, Urban & Community Affairs, Women's Affairs, Zoos/Aquariums
Education: Afterschool/Enrichment Programs, Arts/Humanities Education, Colleges & Universities, Community & Junior Colleges, Education Associations, Education Funds, Education-General, Medical Education, Minority Education, Public Education (Precollege), Religious Education, Science/Mathematics Education, Special Education, Student Aid
Health: Alzheimers Disease, Cancer, Children's Health/Hospitals, Clinics/Medical Centers, Geriatric Health, Health Organizations, Heart, Hospices, Hospitals, Mental Health, Prenatal Health Issues, Single-Disease Health Associations
Religion: Dioceses, Jewish Causes, Religious Organizations, Religious Welfare, Social/Policy Issues
Social Services: Animal Protection, Big Brother/Big Sister, Child Welfare, Community Centers, Community Service Organizations, Counseling, Family Services, Food/Clothing Distribution, People with Disabilities, Recreation & Athletics, Scouts, Senior Services, Shelters/Homelessness, Substance Abuse, United Funds/United Ways, Youth Organizations

Application Procedures

Initial Contact: Submit a brief letter or proposal.
Application Requirements: Include a description of organization, amount requested, purpose of funds sought, recently audited financial statement, and proof of Internal Revenue Service Section 170(c) status
Deadlines: None.

Corporate Officials

Richard A. Baird: president B 1942. PRIM CORP EMPL president, chief executive officer: Giant Food Inc. CORP AFFIL senior vice president: Stop & Stop Co. Inc.
Mark H. Berey: senior vice president, chief financial officer, treasurer B 1951. ED Indiana University BA (1974); Northwestern University MBA (1975). PRIM CORP EMPL senior vice president, chief financial officer, treasurer: Giant Food Inc.
Michael J. Bush: vice president real estate B Phoenix, AZ 1943. ED Stanford University (1965); Harvard University (1968). PRIM CORP EMPL vice president real estate: Giant Food Inc. CORP AFFIL vice president: GFS Realty Inc.; executive vice president, chief operating officer, director: Movado Group Inc.

Russell B. Fair: vice president pharmacy operations B Nashua, NH 1948. ED Northeastern University (1971). PRIM CORP EMPL vice president pharmacy operations: Giant Food Inc. ADD CORP EMPL vice president: Giant Maryland Inc.
M. Davis Herriman, Junior: vice president, grocery operations B Washington, DC 1938. ED George Washington University (1961). PRIM CORP EMPL vice president, grocery operations: Giant Food Inc. ADD CORP EMPL vice president: Giant of Maryland Inc.
Odonna Mathews: vice president consumer affairs B Washington, DC 1950. ED University of Maryland (1972); University of Maryland (1981). PRIM CORP EMPL vice president consumer affairs: Giant Food Inc. ADD CORP EMPL vice president: Giant Maryland Inc. NONPR AFFIL member consumer affairs committee: Food Marketing Institute; member: Society of Consumer Affairs Professionals.
David W. Rutstein: senior vice president, general counsel, chief administrative officer B New York, NY 1944. ED University of Pennsylvania BA (1966); George Washington University JD (1969). PRIM CORP EMPL senior vice president, general counsel, chief administrative officer: Giant Food Inc. ADD CORP EMPL senior vice president: Giant Maryland Inc.; senior vice president: Giant of Maryland Inc. NONPR AFFIL member: Washington Metropolitan Area Corporate Counsel Association; treasurer, director: Washington Metropolitan Board Trade; trustee: Greater Washington Research Center; member: District of Columbia Bar Association; treasurer, director, member executive committee: Federal City Council.
Barry F. Scher: vice president public affairs B Richmond, VA 1942. ED College of William & Mary (1964); American University (1965). PRIM CORP EMPL vice president public affairs: Giant Food Inc. ADD CORP EMPL vice president: Giant Maryland Inc. NONPR AFFIL member: Public Relations Society America; director: Second Harvest; vice chairman: Maryland Retailers Association; member: Food Marketing Government Affairs & Communications Division; chairman food bank national task force: Food Marketing Institute.
Samuel E. Thurston: senior vice president distribution B New Haven, CT 1943. ED University of New Haven (1966). PRIM CORP EMPL senior vice president distribution: Giant Food Inc. CORP AFFIL senior vice president: Giant Maryland Inc.

Foundation Officials

David W. Rutstein: secretary (see above)

Grants Analysis

Disclosure Period: fiscal year ending January 31, 2001
Total Grants: $295,816*
Number of Grants: 89
Average Grant: $2,623*
Highest Grant: $65,000
Lowest Grant: $100
Typical Range: $100 to $5,000
*Note: Giving excludes United Way. Average grant figure excludes highest grant.

Recent Grants

Note: Grants derived from 2001 Form 990.

Library-Related

1,666	Kennedy Krieger Institute, Baltimore, MD

General

150,000	United Way National Capital Area, Washington, DC
65,000	United Jewish Appeal Federation of Greater Washington, New York, NY
50,000	DC College Access Program, Washington, DC
50,000	National Capital Foundation
50,000	United Way of Central Maryland, Baltimore, MD

35,000	Associated Jewish Community Federation of Baltimore, Baltimore, MD
10,000	Associated United Ways of Pennsylvania, New Jersey, Delaware
5,000	Fauquier Hospital Foundation, Warrenton, VA
5,000	John F. Kennedy Center for Performing Arts, Washington, DC
3,000	American Jewish Committee, New York, NY

GIANT FOOD STORES

Company Headquarters
1149 Harrisburg Pike
Carlisle, PA 17013
Web: http://www.giantpa.com

Company Description
Employees: 3,000
SIC(s): 5411 Grocery Stores.
Parent Company: Royal Ahold N.V., Albert Heijnweg 1, Zaandam, Netherlands

Operating Locations
BI-LO (SC--Greenville); Edwards Super Food Stores (PA--Carlisle); Edwards Super Foods Stores Long Island Division (NY--Garden City); FINAST (OH--Maple Heights); Giant Food Stores (MD, Landover; PA--Carlisle; VA; WV); Stop & Shop Cos. (MA--Quincy); Tops Markets (NY--Amherst)

Nonmonetary Support
Type: Donated Equipment; Donated Products

Giving Contact
Debra Stoven, Consumer Affairs
1149 Harrisburg Pike
Carlisle, PA 17013
Phone: (717)249-4000
Fax: (717)960-1920
Web: http://www.giantpa.com

Description
Organization Type: Corporate Giving Program
Giving Locations: headquarters and operating communities.
Grant Types: Capital, General Support, Seed Money.

Typical Recipients
Arts & Humanities: Arts Associations & Councils, Historic Preservation, Libraries, Public Broadcasting
Civic & Public Affairs: Business/Free Enterprise, Civil Rights, Economic Development, Law & Justice, Municipalities/Towns, Safety, Urban & Community Affairs, Women's Affairs
Education: Colleges & Universities, Literacy, Minority Education, Student Aid
Environment: Environment-General
Health: Health Funds, Health Organizations, Hospitals, Medical Research, Mental Health, Single-Disease Health Associations
Religion: Religious Organizations
Social Services: Child Welfare, Community Centers, Community Service Organizations, Domestic Violence, Family Services, People with Disabilities, Senior Services, Substance Abuse, United Funds/United Ways, Youth Organizations

Application Procedures
Initial Contact: Send a brief letter or proposal.
Application Requirements: Include a description of organization, amount requested, and purpose for which funds are sought; a recently audited financial statement and proof of tax-exempt status occasionally are requested.

Additional Information
Does not support political or lobbying groups. Giant Food Stores makes contributions to United Way agencies in each of the localities in which it does business. It also supports some capital campaigns for participating agencies, but generally does not support United Way member agencies. Giant's local stores are free to support local individual fund-raising activities at the store manager's discretion and as limited by the individual store's budget.

Corporate Officials
Jim Ferraro: chief financial officer, chief executive officer PRIM CORP EMPL chief financial officer: Giant Food Stores.
Anthony Schiano: president, chief executive officer PRIM CORP EMPL president, chief executive officer: Giant Food Stores Inc. ADD CORP EMPL vice president: May fair Super Markets Inc.

GIDDINGS & LEWIS

Company Headquarters
142 Doty St.
Fond du Lac, WI 54935

Company Description
Employees: 3,967
SIC(s): 3541 Machine Tools--Metal Cutting Types, 3625 Relays & Industrial Controls, 3825 Instruments to Measure Electricity.

Operating Locations
Giddings & Lewis (WI--Fond du Lac)

Giddings & Lewis Foundation

Giving Contact
Heike Franke, Treasurer
142 Doty Street
Fond du Lac, WI 54935
Phone: (920)921-9400

Alternate Contact
3155 W. Big Beaver Road
Suite 5084
Troy, MI 48007-5084
Phone: (248)643-3514

Description
Founded: 1952
EIN: 396061306
Organization Type: Corporate Foundation
Giving Locations: CA; MI; OH; WI
Grant Types: General Support.

Donor Information
Founder: Giddings & Lewis Machine Tool Co.

Financial Summary
Total Giving: $373,621 (2001); $433,254 (2000); $532,563 (1999)
Giving Analysis: Giving for 2000 includes: foundation scholarships ($10,000); foundation matching gifts ($66,329); foundation grants to United Way ($118,925); foundation ($238,000); 1999: foundation scholarships ($2,000); foundation matching gifts ($82,572); foundation grants to United Way ($108,800); foundation ($339,191); 1998: corporate scholarships ($2,000); corporate matching gifts ($20,730); corporate grants to United Way ($112,800) corporate direct giving ($397,201)
Assets: $2,384,643 (2001); $2,875,263 (2000); $3,044,217 (1999)

Gifts Received: $297,180 (1999); $250,000 (1993); $250,000 (1992). Note: In 1999, contributions were received from Giddings & Lewis, LLC.

Typical Recipients
Arts & Humanities: Arts Associations & Councils, Arts Centers, Community Arts, History & Archaeology, Libraries, Museums/Galleries, Music, Performing Arts, Public Broadcasting, Theater
Civic & Public Affairs: Botanical Gardens/Parks, Business/Free Enterprise, Clubs, Community Foundations, Economic Development, Civic & Public Affairs-General, Housing, Municipalities/Towns, Professional & Trade Associations, Safety, Urban & Community Affairs, Women's Affairs
Education: Business Education, Colleges & Universities, Community & Junior Colleges, Education Funds, Engineering/Technological Education, Faculty Development, Education-General, International Studies, Private Education (Precollege), Public Education (Precollege), Secondary Education (Private), Secondary Education (Public), Student Aid
Environment: Wildlife Protection
Health: AIDS/HIV, Cancer, Clinics/Medical Centers, Emergency/Ambulance Services, Heart, Hospices, Hospitals, Multiple Sclerosis, Nursing Services, Prenatal Health Issues, Single-Disease Health Associations, Transplant Networks/Donor Banks
Religion: Religious Organizations, Religious Welfare, Seminaries
Science: Science Museums, Scientific Organizations
Social Services: At-Risk Youth, Big Brother/Big Sister, Child Welfare, Community Centers, Community Service Organizations, Homes, People with Disabilities, Recreation & Athletics, Scouts, Senior Services, Social Services-General, Substance Abuse, United Funds/United Ways, YMCA/YWCA/YMHA/YWHA, Youth Organizations

Application Procedures
Initial Contact: Send brief letter describing program.
Application Requirements: Include written proof of tax-exempt status.
Deadlines: None.

Additional Information
The majority of the foundation's giving is through a matching gift program.

Corporate Officials
Joseph R. Coppola: chairman, president, chief executive officer, director PRIM CORP EMPL chairman, president, chief executive officer, director: Giddings & Lewis.

Foundation Officials
Robert D. Kamphuis: president PRIM CORP EMPL vice president, controller: Giddings & Lewis.

Grants Analysis
Disclosure Period: calendar year ending 2001
Total Grants: $210,112*
Number of Grants: 13
Average Grant: $3,465*
Highest Grant: $100,000
Lowest Grant: $12
Typical Range: $250 to $10,000
*Note: Giving excludes scholarships, matching gifts, and United Way. Average grant figure excludes two highest grants totaling $172,000.

Recent Grants
Note: Grants derived from 2001 Form 990.

General

2,335	University of Wisconsin Foundation, Madison, WI
2,000	Northwestern College, Chicago, IL
2,000	University of Wisconsin Madison, Madison, WI

2,000	University of Wisconsin Madison, Madison, WI
1,070	Sinnissippi Council, Boy Scouts of America, Janesville, WI
1,000	Dequesne University, Pittsburgh, PA
1,000	Marquette University, Milwaukee, WI
1,000	Milwaukee School of Engineering, Milwaukee, WI
1,000	Rotary Gardens, Janesville, WI
1,000	San Diego State University, San Diego, CA

ROSAMOND GIFFORD CHARITABLE CORP.

Giving Contact

Kathryn Goldfarb, Executive Director
518 James Street, Suite 280
Syracuse, NY 13203
Phone: (315)474-2489
Fax: (315)475-4983
E-mail: kgoldfarb@giffordfd.org
Web: http://www.giffordfd.org

Description

Founded: 1954
EIN: 150572881
Organization Type: General Purpose Foundation
Giving Locations: NY: Syracuse and Onondaga County
Grant Types: Award, Capital, Emergency, Endowment, General Support, Loan, Matching, Multiyear/Continuing Support, Project, Seed Money.

Donor Information

Founder: The foundation was incorporated in 1954 by the late Rosamond Gifford .

Financial Summary

Total Giving: $1,380,969 (2002 approx); $1,380,969 (2001); $1,480,636 (2000). Note: 1997 Giving includes United Way ($267,300).
Giving Analysis: Giving for 2000 includes: foundation grants to United Way ($125,000) 1998: foundation grants to United Way ($3,200)
Assets: $27,931,970 (2002 approx); $27,931,970 (2001); $33,583,452 (2000)

Typical Recipients

Arts & Humanities: Arts Associations & Councils, Historic Preservation, History & Archaeology, Libraries, Museums/Galleries, Music, Performing Arts, Public Broadcasting, Theater
Civic & Public Affairs: Botanical Gardens/Parks, Clubs, Community Foundations, Economic Development, Employment/Job Training, Ethnic Organizations, Civic & Public Affairs-General, Housing, Legal Aid, Municipalities/Towns, Nonprofit Management, Parades/Festivals, Rural Affairs, Urban & Community Affairs, Women's Affairs
Education: Arts/Humanities Education, Business Education, Colleges & Universities, Community & Junior Colleges, Education Funds, Education-General, Leadership Training, Literacy, Private Education (Precollege), Public Education (Precollege), Social Sciences Education, Student Aid
Environment: Environment-General
Health: Alzheimers Disease, Clinics/Medical Centers, Emergency/Ambulance Services, Health-General, Health Organizations, Heart, Hospices, Hospitals, Kidney, Long-Term Care, Medical Research, Mental Health, Nursing Services, Prenatal Health Issues, Public Health, Single-Disease Health Associations
Religion: Churches, Jewish Causes, Ministries, Religious Organizations, Religious Welfare, Social/Policy Issues
Science: Scientific Centers & Institutes, Scientific Organizations

Social Services: Animal Protection, Camps, Child Welfare, Community Centers, Community Service Organizations, Family Planning, Family Services, Food/Clothing Distribution, Homes, People with Disabilities, Recreation & Athletics, Scouts, Senior Services, Sexual Abuse, Shelters/Homelessness, Social Services-General, Special Olympics, Substance Abuse, United Funds/United Ways, Volunteer Services, YMCA/YWCA/YMHA/YWHA, Youth Organizations

Application Procedures

Initial Contact: Applicants should call or write to the corporation to request an application form.
Deadlines: February1; May1; August1; November1.

Restrictions

The corporation does not make grants to individuals, or for continuing support, deficit financing, land acquisition, matching gifts, scholarships, fellowships, or loans.

Additional Information

Publications: Application Guidelines; Program Policy Statement; Annual Report

Foundation Officials

Richard G. Case: assistant secretary
Charles A. Chappell, Jr.: secretary B Syracuse, NY 1924. ED Syracuse University BA (1949). PRIM CORP EMPL chairman: C. E. Chappell & Sons Inc.
Patricia Civil: treasurer
Robert F. Dewey: president, trustee
Bethaida C. Gonzalez: trustee
Edward S. Green: assistant treasurer
Amelia Greiner: trustee
Linda Hall: trustee
Bill Harper: trustee
Patrick A. Mannion: vice president, trustee PRIM CORP EMPL chief executive officer: Unity Mutual Life Insurance Co. CORP AFFIL director: Germantown Life Insurance Co.
Judith Mower: trustee
Sharon Northrup: trustee

Grants Analysis

Disclosure Period: calendar year ending 2000
Total Grants: $1,355,636*
Number of Grants: 35
Average Grant: $33,989*
Highest Grant: $200,000
Typical Range: $15,000 to $50,000
*Note: Giving excludes United Way. Average grant figure excludes highest grant.

Recent Grants

Note: Grants derived from 2001 Form 990.

General

250,000	United Way Central New York, Syracuse, NY -- to support various needs in Onondaga County
178,253	Youth Violence Program -- for medial and public relations regarding youth violence
150,000	Syracuse Partnership to Reduce Gun Violence, Syracuse, NY -- support staffing for outreach and case workers
90,000	LeMoyne College, Syracuse, NY -- create theatre for children to teach life skills
87,000	Syracuse University Theater Corp, Syracuse, NY -- to help create education programs for youth to discuss
75,000	Syracuse University School of Social Work, Syracuse, NY -- to support forums regarding violence, welfare, work and education
50,000	MOST -- to enhance science and technology education program for students
45,000	Dunbar Association, Syracuse, NY -- to redevelop day care facility for disadvantaged kids
35,290	Contract Syracuse, Inc, Syracuse, NY -- School-based Violence Prevention Program
35,000	Open Hand Theater, Syracuse, NY -- grant for purchase of building

PAUL AND OSCAR GIGER FOUNDATION

Giving Contact

Frank A. Blazek, President & Secretary
Paul and Oscar Giger Foundation
Care of Fraser Stryker Law Firm
500 Energy Plz.
409 S. 17th Street
Omaha, NE 68102
Phone: (402)341-6000

Description

Founded: 1985
EIN: 470682708
Organization Type: Private Foundation
Giving Locations: NE: Omaha including metropolitan area; OH
Grant Types: General Support.

Donor Information

Founder: the late Ruth Giger

Financial Summary

Total Giving: $119,700 (2001); $118,270 (2000); $118,400 (1999)
Assets: $2,691,095 (2001); $2,877,513 (2000); $2,878,525 (1999)

Typical Recipients

Arts & Humanities: Arts Associations & Councils, Ballet, Community Arts, Libraries, Museums/Galleries, Music, Opera, Performing Arts, Public Broadcasting, Theater
Civic & Public Affairs: Botanical Gardens/Parks, Civic & Public Affairs-General, Housing, Philanthropic Organizations, Urban & Community Affairs, Zoos/Aquariums
Education: Arts/Humanities Education, Colleges & Universities, Education-General, Health & Physical Education, Private Education (Precollege), Public Education (Precollege), Religious Education
Environment: Environment-General, Wildlife Protection
Health: Cancer, Emergency/Ambulance Services, Eyes/Blindness, Health Organizations, Nursing Services, Preventive Medicine/Wellness Organizations, Single-Disease Health Associations
International: Missionary/Religious Activities
Religion: Bible Study/Translation, Churches, Ministries, Religious Organizations, Religious Welfare
Social Services: Animal Protection, Child Welfare, Community Service Organizations, Emergency Relief, Family Services, Food/Clothing Distribution, Homes, Scouts, Senior Services, Volunteer Services, Youth Organizations

Application Procedures

Initial Contact: Contact foundation for application form.
Deadlines: May 15 and October 1.

Restrictions

Does not support individuals, private for-profit businesses, private nonoperating foundations, or building funds.

Additional Information

Publications: Application Form; Instructions

Foundation Officials

Janet Acker: secretary B 1951. PRIM CORP EMPL vice president: Airfield Plaza Inn Corp.
Frank A. Blazek: president, secretary
Beverly Ingram: vice president

Grants Analysis

Disclosure Period: calendar year ending 2001
Total Grants: $119,700
Number of Grants: 23
Average Grant: $3,819
Highest Grant: $18,000
Lowest Grant: $500
Typical Range: $500 to $10,000

Recent Grants

Note: Grants derived from 2001 Form 990.

Library-Related

5,000	Omaha Public Library, Omaha, NE

General

20,000	Fontanel Forest Association, Omaha, NE
20,000	Omaha Botanical Gardens, Omaha, NE
12,500	First Central Congregational Church, Omaha, NE
10,000	Omaha Symphony Association, Omaha, NE
10,000	Omaha Zoo Foundation, Omaha, NE
5,000	American Red Cross, Omaha, NE
5,000	Volunteer Intervening for Equity, Omaha, NE
4,500	Tuesday Musical Concert Series, Omaha, NE
4,000	Nebraska Humane Society, Omaha, NE
3,500	Salvation Army, Omaha, NE

GILLETTE CO.

Company Headquarters

Boston, MA
Web: http://www.gillette.com

Company Description

Founded: 1901
Ticker: G
Exchange: NYSE
Revenue: US$8.453 billion (2002)
Profit: US$1.216 billion (2002)
Employees: 30300 (2002)
Fortune Rank: 218, per FORTUNE Magazine's list of 500 Largest U.S. Corporations (2002).
SIC(s): 2844 Toilet Preparations, 3421 Cutlery, 3634 Electric Housewares & Fans, 3951 Pens & Mechanical Pencils.

Operating Locations

Gillette Co. (CA--Mission Viejo, Santa Monica, Thousand Oaks, Westlake Village; GA--Marietta; IL--Itasca, North Chicago, Schaumburg; MA--Boston, Lynnfield, Norwood; MN--St. Paul; OH--Cleveland)

Nonmonetary Support

Value: $10,500,000 (2000)
Type: Cause-related Marketing & Promotion; Donated Equipment; Donated Products; In-kind Services
Note: In-kind product donations are given to in-need recipients in the locations where the company has a major presence. Except in the event of a natural disaster, production donations are generally reviewed using the same priorities and criteria that are used to select grant recipients. Gillette also works with an international organization which serves as the company's agent in providing product donations. Product requests can be directed to Gifts in Kind International (703) 836-2121.

Volunteer Programs: Company employees volunteer with Making Strides for Breast Cancer, Walk for Hunger, and the AIDS Walk. The Gillette Retiree Outreach Program (GROUP) is a retiree managed program that administers a variety of volunteer activities ranging from literacy programs to blood drives.

Giving Contact

Royall Mack, Director, Civic Affairs
Gillette Corp.
Prudential Tower Bldg., 49th Floor
Boston, MA 02199-8004
Phone: (617)463-8608
Fax: (617)421-8484
E-mail: royall_mack@gillette.com
Web: http://www.gillette.com/community/corpcontributions.asp

Description

Organization Type: Corporate Giving Program
Giving Locations: MA: Boston operating locations.
Grant Types: Employee Matching Gifts, General Support, Operating Expenses, Scholarship.
Note: The company matches employee gifts to most 501(c)(3) charities.

Financial Summary

Total Giving: $21,000,000 (2000 approx); $3,200,000 (1999 approx); $352,348 (1998)
Giving Analysis: Giving for 2000 includes: corporate direct giving ($10,500,000); nonmonetary support ($10,500,000) 1998: foundation grants to United Way ($352,348)
Assets: $4,406,606 (1998); $4,016,893 (1996); $3,117,355 (1995)
Gifts Received: $500,000 (1995)

Typical Recipients

Arts & Humanities: Arts Centers, Dance, Libraries, Museums/Galleries, Music, Public Broadcasting
Civic & Public Affairs: Employment/Job Training, Urban & Community Affairs
Education: Business Education, Colleges & Universities
Health: Clinics/Medical Centers, Emergency/Ambulance Services, Hospitals
Religion: Jewish Causes
Social Services: United Funds/United Ways, Youth Organizations

Application Procedures

Initial Contact: After confirming that proposal falls within Gillette's priorities, submit a written request.
Application Requirements: The request must include responses to the following questions: What is the issue your organization is addressing? What is your organization's mission statement and how does it relate to The Gillette Company's areas of focus? What is your experience and capabilities in dealing with this issue? What is the scope of your program, including objectives, timelines and expected outcomes? What communities, audience or people are the beneficiaries of this program? What results do you expect for the program? How will you track and measure the results? How will you communicate those results to The Gillette Company? What is the time frame of the program? How is your program different from like programs that may also be addressing the issue you have identified? How will you sustain this program after Gillette support ends? Is this a single request of The Gillette Company or will you be seeking additional support? If so, please describe. Do you receive support from The United Way? Does the program or your organization have volunteer opportunities for Gillette employees? How will you acknowledge Gillette Company support? The following supporting documents must also be included with the request: annual report or other information about the applicant organization, its leadership, advisory board, current programs, budget, financial statement,

and a list of other current or proposed contributions, and proof of tax-exempt status.
Deadlines: December 31, for grants to be awarded in March; March 31, for grants to be awarded in June; June 30, for grants to be awarded in September; and September 30, for grants to be awarded in December.
Decision Notification: Within six to eight weeks.
Notes: Gillette support to an organization or program is limited to three consecutive years; previously funded organizations may reapply after a two-year hiatus.

Restrictions

Gillette does not fund projects or organizations that are not located within a Gillette community; endowments or capital campaigns; fundraising events; golf tournaments or sporting events; multi-year pledges or commitments; contributions for more than three years to a specific organization; organizations that conflict with Gillette's mission, goals, policies, or products; organizations without IRS 501(c)(3) tax exempt status; organizations that limit membership and services in a discriminatory manner; conferences, seminars, trips, tours or similar events; advertising for benefit or courtesy purposes; operating expenses of organizations supported by United Way; loans or debt retirement; religious or sectarian programs for religious purposes; churches, synagogues, or ministries unless for specific social programs that meet all other foundation criteria; and fraternities, sororities, individuals, scholarships, political action committees, or candidates for political office.

Additional Information

Scholarships provided only through the National Merit Scholarship Program.

Corporate Officials

Charles W. Cramb: senior vice president finance, chief financial officer ED Dartmouth College BA (1968); University of Chicago MBA (1970). PRIM CORP EMPL senior vice president finance, chief financial officer: The Gillette Co.
Edward F. DeGraan: president, chief operating officer, director ED Suffolk University. PRIM CORP EMPL president, chief operating officer, director: The Gillette Co. NONPR AFFIL trustee: National Urban League.
James M. Kilts: chairman, chief executive officer, director B February 10, 1948. ED Knox College BA (1970); University of Chicago MBA (1974). PRIM CORP EMPL chairman, chief executive officer, director: The Gillette Co.

Giving Program Officials

Cathleen Chizauskas: director civic affairs

Grants Analysis

Disclosure Period: calendar year ending 2000
Total Grants: $21,000,000 (approx)
Typical Range: $300,000 to $500,000

Recent Grants

Note: Grants derived from 1998 Form 990.

General

352,348	United Way New England, Providence, RI

HOWARD GILMAN FOUNDATION

Giving Contact

Jennifer Amis, Program Administrator
111 West 50th Street
New York, NY 10020
Phone: (212)307-1073
Fax: (212)262-4108
Web: http://www.howardgilman.org

Description

Founded: 1981
EIN: 133097486
Organization Type: Family Foundation
Giving Locations: NY: New York internationally; nationally.
Grant Types: General Support, Multiyear/Continuing Support, Operating Expenses, Project, Research.

Donor Information

Founder: The foundation was established in 1981 by Howard Gilman, former chairman of the board of the Gilman Paper Co. Three generations of the Gilman family have worked toward building its philanthropic legacy. Founded in 1884 by Howard Gilman's grandfather, the Gilman Paper Co. is the largest privately-owned paper company in the United States. The company has operations in New York, Florida, and Georgia. Howard Gilman died in 1998.

Financial Summary

Total Giving: $8,581,377 (2000); $5,018,346 (1999); $4,197,800 (1998)
Assets: $289,874,575 (2000); $29,000,000 (1999); $29,909,105 (1998)
Gifts Received: $500 (2000); $6,500,000 (1994); $1,500,000 (1993). Note: In fiscal 1994, contributions were received from Gilman Securities Corporation. In fiscal 1993, gifts were received from Gilman Investment Company.

Typical Recipients

Arts & Humanities: Arts Appreciation, Arts Associations & Councils, Arts Centers, Arts Funds, Arts Institutes, Arts Outreach, Ballet, Dance, Ethnic & Folk Arts, Film & Video, Arts & Humanities-General, Libraries, Literary Arts, Museums/Galleries, Music, Opera, Performing Arts, Public Broadcasting, Theater, Visual Arts

Civic & Public Affairs: African American Affairs, Civil Rights, Employment/Job Training, Gay/Lesbian Issues, Civic & Public Affairs-General, Municipalities/Towns, Philanthropic Organizations, Professional & Trade Associations, Public Policy, Urban & Community Affairs, Women's Affairs, Zoos/Aquariums

Education: Arts/Humanities Education, Colleges & Universities, Colleges & Universities, Education Funds, Environmental Education, Education-General, Literacy, Medical Education, Social Sciences Education

Environment: Environment-General, Protection, Resource Conservation, Wildlife Protection

Health: AIDS/HIV, Children's Health/Hospitals, Clinics/Medical Centers, Health-General, Health Organizations, Heart, Hospitals, Hospitals (University Affiliated), Medical Research, Public Health, Single-Disease Health Associations

International: Foreign Arts Organizations, International-General, Health Care/Hospitals, Human Rights, International Affairs, International Development, International Environmental Issues, International Organizations, International Peace & Security Issues, International Relations, International Relief Efforts, Missionary/Religious Activities, Missionary/Religious Activities

Religion: Jewish Causes, Religious Organizations, Religious Welfare, Synagogues/Temples

Science: Science-General, Science Museums, Scientific Labs

Social Services: Animal Protection, Child Welfare, Community Service Organizations, Crime Prevention, Family Services, Food/Clothing Distribution, Refugee Assistance, Shelters/Homelessness, Social Services-General, YMCA/YWCA/YMHA/YWHA

Application Procedures

Initial Contact: The foundation requests that prospective applicants check the foundation's web site for program guidelines, as updates are posted each program year.

Application Requirements: Applications are accepted in the Partners for Performing Arts and Training & Mentoring Young Talent program areas. Applications are not accepted for the Cardiovascular Research program area, as Foundation support is provided solely to the Howard Gilman Institute for Valvular Heart Diseases at Weill Medical College of Cornell University. The Foundation also operates the White Oak Plantation, which supports wildlife conservation and performing arts programs on-site. Unsolicited requests are not currently being accepted for the use of White Oak Plantation.
Deadlines: Deadlines vary by program area. Refer to the foundation's web site for details.

Restrictions

The foundation supports charitable organizations classified under IRS Code 509(a)(1),(2), or (3) and 501(c)(3) or private operating foundation under section 4942 (j)(3) only. It does not support political or religious activity, nor individuals. It also will not fund deficit operations, construction or renovation of buildings, capital investments, endowments, scholarships, fellowships, or foreign grantees not satisfying the requirements of the Foundation Tax Excise regulations. The animal program focuses on wildlife, not domesticated animals or humane societies. International AIDS programming is policy-oriented. Arts and Medical focused in NYC.

Additional Information

The foundation is particularly interested in trans-Atlantic cooperation.
In 1999, the Gilman Paper Co. was acquired by Group Industrial Durango of Mexico. The Gilman Paper Co. reported that assets from the acquisition would be given to the Howard Gilman Foundation.
Publications: Guidelines; Background Statement

Foundation Officials

Pierre Apraxine: director
Bernard D. Bergreen: president B 1923. ED New York University AB (1943); Columbia University LLB (1948).
Dr. Jeffrey Borer: director
Donald Bruce: director
Robert L. Burkett: director
Steve Cropper: director
Luigi Gasparinetti: director
Ambassador Marcello Guidi: director
John Lukas: director
Natalie Moody: director
Isabella Rossellini: director

Grants Analysis

Disclosure Period: calendar year ending 2000
Total Grants: $8,581,377*
Number of Grants: 108
Average Grant: $41,289*
Highest Grant: $1,646,000
Lowest Grant: $500
Typical Range: $1,500 to $25,000 and $100,000 to $500,000
*Note: Average grant figure excludes three highest grants ($4,246,000).

Recent Grants

Note: Grants derived from 2000 Form 990.

General

1,646,000	Museum of Modern Art, New York, NY
1,600,000	Weill Medical College of Cornell University, New York, NY
1,000,000	Brooklyn Academy of Music, Brooklyn, NY
450,000	New York University Medical Center, New York, NY
411,350	New York Presbyterian Hospital Community Health Center, New York, NY
333,000	City of St. Mary's, St. Mary's, GA
290,000	Baryshnikov Dance Foundation, Philadelphia, PA
260,000	Brooklyn Academy of Music, Brooklyn, NY
260,000	Howard Gilman Israel Culture Foundation, Tel Aviv Israel
250,000	Mark Morris Dance Group, New York, NY

Irving S. Gilmore Foundation

Giving Contact

Frederick W. Freund, Executive Director
136 East Michigan Avenue, Suite 900
Kalamazoo, MI 49007
Phone: (269)342-6411
Fax: (269)342-6465
E-mail: fritz@isgilmorefoundation.org
Web: http://www.isgilmorefoundation.org

Description

Founded: 1972
EIN: 237236057
Organization Type: General Purpose Foundation
Giving Locations: MI: Kalamazoo including greater metropolitan area
Grant Types: Capital, Conference/Seminar, Emergency, General Support, Matching, Multiyear/Continuing Support, Operating Expenses, Project, Seed Money.

Donor Information

Founder: The foundation was established in 1972 with an initial donation of $5,000 by the founder, Irving S. Gilmore of Kalamazoo, MI. Mr. Gilmore died in 1986 and through his will distributed assets valued at $67,010,041 to the foundation.

Financial Summary

Total Giving: $7,500,000 (2003 approx); $7,845,952 (2002); $10,052,363 (2000)
Giving Analysis: Giving for 2000 includes: foundation grants to United Way ($148,834); 1998: foundation scholarships ($17,150) foundation grants to United Way ($147,333)
Assets: $235,000,000 (2003 approx); $235,737,981 (2002); $235,763,035 (2000)

Typical Recipients

Arts & Humanities: Arts Associations & Councils, Arts Centers, Arts Festivals, Arts Funds, Arts Institutes, Arts Outreach, Ballet, Community Arts, Dance, Ethnic & Folk Arts, Arts & Humanities-General, Historic Preservation, History & Archaeology, Libraries, Museums/Galleries, Music, Performing Arts, Theater

Civic & Public Affairs: Botanical Gardens/Parks, Business/Free Enterprise, Clubs, Community Foundations, Economic Development, Civic & Public Affairs-General, Hispanic Affairs, Housing, Municipalities/Towns, Native American Affairs, Nonprofit Management, Parades/Festivals, Philanthropic Organizations, Professional & Trade Associations, Public Policy, Urban & Community Affairs, Urban & Community Affairs, Women's Affairs, Zoos/Aquariums

Education: Arts/Humanities Education, Business Education, Colleges & Universities, Community & Junior Colleges, Education Associations, Education Funds, Education Reform, Engineering/Technological Education, Education-General, Literacy, Medical Education, Public Education (Precollege), Science/Mathematics Education, Special Education, Student Aid

Environment: Environment-General

Health: AIDS/HIV, Clinics/Medical Centers, Emergency/Ambulance Services, Eyes/Blindness, Nursing Services, Public Health, Single-Disease Health Associations, Speech & Hearing

International: Foreign Arts Organizations

Religion: Churches, Dioceses, Ministries, Religious Organizations, Religious Welfare

Social Services: At-Risk Youth, Big Brother/Big Sister, Camps, Child Welfare, Community Centers, Community Service Organizations, Counseling, Day Care, Emergency Relief, Family Planning, Family Services, Food/Clothing Distribution, Homes, People with Disabilities, Recreation & Athletics, Scouts, Senior Services, Substance Abuse, United Funds/United Ways, YMCA/YWCA/YMHA/YWHA, Youth Organizations

Application Procedures

Initial Contact: Applicants should mail a proposal to the foundation.
Application Requirements: The proposal should be unbound, not more than 8-10 pages include the following: a brief history of the organization; description of the project; anticipated outcome; need for the program; amount requested; means by which outcome of project can be achieved; means for evaluating outcome and success; list of the board of directors or trustees and affiliations and occupations; the organization's past and present sourcs of support and a list of sources of support being sought for the present proposal, both prospective and received; a one-page, line-item project budget; latest audited financial statement including a balance sheet and income and expense statement; all interim and final reports from any grants previously received from the Foundation; and a copy of the IRS tax-exempt determination letter. A cover letter must also be sent, signed by the organizations's board president and chief executive officer.
Deadlines: June 1 for the July meeting; August 1 for the September meeting; October 1 for the November meeting; December 1 for the January meeting; February 1 for the March meeting; and April 1 for the May meeting.

Restrictions

Grants are not made to individuals. The foundation only gives to organization in the area of Kalamazoo, MI. No grant applications accepted via e-mail or via fax.

Additional Information

Publications: Annual Report; Application Guidelines

Foundation Officials

Julie Batts: secretary
Frederick W. Freund: executive director, trustee
Russell L. Gabier: secretary, trustee NONPR AFFIL director: Gilmore Music Festival.
Richard M. Hughey, Sr.: program officer
Richard M. Hughey, Jr.: program officer CORP AFFIL director: Spring Root Scraper Co.
Floyd L. Parks: vice president, treasurer, trustee
Kay Tomas: secretary

Grants Analysis

Disclosure Period: calendar year ending 2000
Total Grants: $9,903,529
Number of Grants: 99
Average Grant: $60,972*
Highest Grant: $2,000,000
Typical Range: $15,000 to $100,000
*Note:** Average grant figure excludes three highest grants ($4,050,200).

Recent Grants

Note: Grants derived from 2000 Form 990.

General

2,000,000	Western Michigan University Foundation, Kalamazoo, MI
1,038,700	Western Michigan University Foundation, Kalamazoo, MI
1,011,500	Irving S. Gilmore International Keyboard Festival, Kalamazoo, MI -- operations
944,500	Kalamazoo Regional Education Service Agency, Kalamazoo, MI -- operations and programming
477,600	Arts Council of Greater Kalamazoo, Kalamazoo, MI -- programming

360,000	Western Michigan University Foundation, Kalamazoo, MI
304,100	City of Kalamazoo, Kalamazoo, MI -- operations
300,000	Boys and Girls Club of Kalamazoo, Kalamazoo, MI -- programming
250,000	Western Michigan University Foundation, Kalamazoo, MI
200,000	Heritage Community of Kalamazoo, Kalamazoo, MI -- facilities

WILLIAM G. GILMORE FOUNDATION

Giving Contact

Faye C. Wilson, Secretary
120 Montgomery St., Suite 1880
San Francisco, CA 94104
Phone: (415)546-1400
Fax: (415)391-8732

Description

Founded: 1953
EIN: 946079493
Organization Type: Private Foundation
Giving Locations: CA: northern CA
Grant Types: General Support.

Donor Information

Founder: the late William G. Gilmore, Mrs. William G. Gilmore

Financial Summary

Total Giving: $958,470 (2000); $1,050,250 (1999); $781,875 (1996)
Giving Analysis: Giving for 2000 includes: foundation grants to United Way ($20,000) 1999: foundation grants to United Way ($25,000)
Assets: $22,365,003 (2000); $20,708,711 (1999); $17,250,498 (1996)

Typical Recipients

Arts & Humanities: Arts Associations & Councils, Arts Centers, Ethnic & Folk Arts, Arts & Humanities-General, History & Archaeology, Libraries, Museums/Galleries, Music, Opera, Performing Arts, Public Broadcasting
Civic & Public Affairs: Botanical Gardens/Parks, Community Foundations, Civic & Public Affairs-General, Hispanic Affairs, Legal Aid, Zoos/Aquariums
Education: Afterschool/Enrichment Programs, Colleges & Universities, Continuing Education, Education Funds, Education-General, Private Education (Precollege), Public Education (Precollege), Religious Education, Science/Mathematics Education, Secondary Education (Private), Student Aid
Environment: Resource Conservation, Wildlife Protection
Health: Cancer, Children's Health/Hospitals, Clinics/Medical Centers, Emergency/Ambulance Services, Health Organizations, Hospices, Hospitals, Medical Research, Nursing Services, Single-Disease Health Associations, Speech & Hearing, Trauma Treatment
International: Foreign Arts Organizations
Religion: Churches, Dioceses, Religious Organizations, Religious Welfare
Science: Science Museums, Scientific Centers & Institutes
Social Services: Animal Protection, At-Risk Youth, Camps, Community Centers, Community Service Organizations, Family Services, Food/Clothing Distribution, People with Disabilities, Scouts, Shelters/Homelessness, United Funds/United Ways, YMCA/YWCA/YMHA/YWHA, Youth Organizations

Application Procedures

Initial Contact: Send a brief letter of inquiry.
Application Requirements: Include a description of organization.

Deadlines: December 1.
Review Process: Decisions are made within two months.

Foundation Officials

Thomas B. Boklund: trustee
C. Lee Emerson: vice president, treasurer
V. Neil Fulton: assistant secretary
Patrice Gehrke: trustee
Robert C. Harris: president B San Francisco, CA 1916. ED Stanford University (1937); Harvard University (1940). PRIM CORP EMPL counsel: Heller, Ehrman, White & McAuliffe.
William R. Mackey: trustee
Faye C. Wilson: secretary

Grants Analysis

Disclosure Period: calendar year ending 2000
Total Grants: $938,470*
Number of Grants: 132
Average Grant: $7,110
Highest Grant: $50,000
Typical Range: $1,000 to $15,000
*Note:** Giving excludes United Way.

Recent Grants

Note: Grants derived from 1999 Form 990.

General

50,000	Historic Arkansas Riverwalk of Pueblo Foundation, AR
50,000	San Francisco Foundation, San Francisco, CA
40,000	Queen of Valley Hospital Foundation, Napa, CA
30,000	Project Open Hand, Atlanta, GA
25,000	Boy Scouts of America San Francisco Bay Area Council, San Francisco, CA
25,000	Children's Charity Ball
25,000	Oregon Graduate Institute of Science & Technology, Portland, OR
25,000	Oregon Public Broadcasting, Portland, OR -- NOVA sponsorship
25,000	Portland Art Museum, Portland, OR
25,000	Project Open Hand, Atlanta, GA

GLASER FOUNDATION

Giving Contact

R. Thomas Olson, Secretary
PO Box 6548
Bellevue, WA 98008-0548
Phone: (425)881-2485

Description

Founded: 1952
EIN: 916028694
Organization Type: Private Foundation
Giving Locations: WA: Puget Sound area
Grant Types: General Support, Project, Seed Money.

Donor Information

Founder: the late Paul F. Glaser

Financial Summary

Total Giving: $641,998 (fiscal year ending November 30, 2001); $687,505 (fiscal 2000); $651,533 (fiscal 1999)
Assets: $13,512,884 (fiscal 2001); $15,143,487 (fiscal 2000); $14,788,887 (fiscal 1999)

Typical Recipients

Arts & Humanities: Arts Associations & Councils, Arts Centers, Arts Outreach, Ballet, Community Arts, Dance, Ethnic & Folk Arts, Arts & Humanities-General, Libraries, Music, Performing Arts, Theater
Civic & Public Affairs: African American Affairs, Business/Free Enterprise, Economic Development,

Employment/Job Training, Civic & Public Affairs-General, Hispanic Affairs, Housing, Legal Aid, Professional & Trade Associations, Urban & Community Affairs, Women's Affairs, Zoos/Aquariums
Education: Afterschool/Enrichment Programs, Arts/Humanities Education, Colleges & Universities, Community & Junior Colleges, Education Reform, Elementary Education (Private), Engineering/Technological Education, Education-General, Literacy, Preschool Education, Private Education (Precollege), Public Education (Precollege), Science/Mathematics Education, Secondary Education (Public), Social Sciences Education, Special Education, Student Aid
Environment: Wildlife Protection
Health: AIDS/HIV, Cancer, Children's Health/Hospitals, Clinics/Medical Centers, Diabetes, Geriatric Health, Health Funds, Health Organizations, Hospices, Hospitals, Mental Health, Nursing Services, Nutrition, Prenatal Health Issues, Public Health, Single-Disease Health Associations, Speech & Hearing, Transplant Networks/Donor Banks
Religion: Ministries, Missionary Activities (Domestic), Religious Welfare
Science: Scientific Centers & Institutes
Social Services: Animal Protection, At-Risk Youth, Camps, Child Abuse, Child Welfare, Community Centers, Community Service Organizations, Counseling, Crime Prevention, Day Care, Domestic Violence, Family Planning, Family Services, Food/Clothing Distribution, Homes, People with Disabilities, Recreation & Athletics, Refugee Assistance, Senior Services, Sexual Abuse, Shelters/Homelessness, Substance Abuse, United Funds/United Ways, YMCA/YWCA/YMHA/YWHA, Youth Organizations

Application Procedures

Initial Contact: Application form in duplicate is required. Pacific Northwest Grantmakers Forum common grant application form is accepted. Phone calls are discouraged.
Deadlines: None.

Restrictions

Emphasis is on direct line services, mainly to children and the elderly in King County and immediately adjoining areas. Does not support individuals or provide loans.

Additional Information

Publications: Application Guidelines

Foundation Officials

R. N. Brandenburg: president
R. William Carlstrom: secretary
R. Thomas Olson: mem
Janet L. Politeo: vice president
Walt Smith: treasurer

Grants Analysis

Disclosure Period: fiscal year ending November 30, 2001
Total Grants: $641,998
Number of Grants: 79
Average Grant: $6,949*
Highest Grant: $100,000
Lowest Grant: $100
Typical Range: $1,000 to $10,000
*Note: Average grant figure excludes highest grant.

Recent Grants

Note: Grants derived from fiscal 2000 Form 990.

General

150,000	Health Housing and Human Services, Bainbridge Island, WA -- community connections for youth program
50,000	Children's Home Society of Washington, Seattle, WA -- capital campaign
25,000	Seabeck Christian Conference Center, Seabeck, WA -- restoration of the Seabeck Inn
25,000	YMCA of Greater Seattle, Seattle, WA
22,000	Olympic College Foundation, Bremerton, WA -- library capital campaign
20,000	Pike Market Community Clinic, Seattle, WA -- assistance to low income patients
20,000	Puget Sound Blood Center Program, Seattle, WA -- bloodmobile donor coach
16,000	Whidbey Dance Theatre, Freeland, WA -- nutcracker presentation and community theatre work
11,400	Pike Market Child Care and Preschool, Seattle, WA -- tuition assistance for low income families
10,000	Bailey Boushay House, Seattle, WA -- nutrition program, services to people with HIV/AIDS

GLAXOSMITHKLINE PLC

Company Headquarters

Berkeley Sq.
Greenford UB6 0NN, United Kingdom
Phone: ENG 20 89668000

Fax: ENG 20 89668330
Web: http://www.gsk.com

Company Description

Ticker: GSK
Exchange: OTC
Formed by Merger of: SmithKline Beecham;
Former Name: Glaxo Wellcome.
SIC(s): 2800 Chemicals & Allied Products, 5100 Wholesale Trade--Nondurable Goods.

Nonmonetary Support

Value: $15,000,000 (1998)
Type: Donated Equipment; Donated Products
Volunteer Programs: The company maintains an employee volunteering support scheme.
Contact: Jean Glenn, Manager, Community Partnership
E-mail: jean.glenn@sb.com
Note: Product donations are provided for humanitarian relief efforts at the request of government agencies and major charities. Such donations are made on a

Global Community Partnerships

Giving Contact

Doug Bauer, Director, Global Community Partnerships
GlaxoSmithKline
One Franklin Plaza
PO Box 7929
Philadelphia, PA 19101-7929
Phone: (215)751-4668
Fax: (215)751-7655
E-mail: community.partnership@gsk.com
Web: http://corp.gsk.com/community/

Description

Founded: 2001
EIN: 232120418
Organization Type: Corporate Foundation
Giving Locations: internationally; nationally.
Grant Types: Award, Employee Matching Gifts, General Support, Project.
Note: Employee matching gift ratio: 1 to 1 to education, health and human services organizations, and the arts.

Donor Information

Founder: GlaxoSmithKline

Financial Summary

Total Giving: $2,612,604 (2000); $27,597,050 (1999); $1,223,737 (1998). Note: Contributes through corporate direct giving program and foundation. Total giving figures represent SmithKline Beecham giving prior to the company's merger with Glaxo Wellcome.
Giving Analysis: Giving for 2000 includes: foundation ($612,786); foundation matching gifts ($1,990,818); 1998: foundation matching gifts ($1,156,591); foundation ($1,300,000); corporate direct giving ($4,430,187); international subsidiaries ($7,713,545); nonmonetary support ($15,000,000); 1997: foundation ($1,082,819); corporate direct giving ($4,144,598); international subsidiaries ($7,113,500) nonmonetary support ($15,060,000)
Assets: $3,401,675 (2000); $1,910,103 (1998); $1,627,051 (1996). Note: Asset figures are for the SmithKline Beecham Foundation, prior to SmithKline Beecham's merger with Glaxo Wellcome.
Gifts Received: $3,598,448 (2000); $1,335,268 (1998); $1,172,722 (1995). Note: Gifts received represent contributions received by the SmithKline Beecham Foundation prior to the company merger with Glaxo Wellcome. Contributions were received from SmithKline Beecham Corporation.

Typical Recipients

Arts & Humanities: Arts Associations & Councils, Arts Outreach, Ballet, Ethnic & Folk Arts, History & Archaeology, Libraries, Museums/Galleries, Music, Opera, Public Broadcasting, Theater
Civic & Public Affairs: Economic Policy, Employment/Job Training, Municipalities/Towns, Nonprofit Management, Philanthropic Organizations, Professional & Trade Associations, Public Policy, Urban & Community Affairs, Women's Affairs, Zoos/Aquariums
Education: Arts/Humanities Education, Business Education, Colleges & Universities, Community & Junior Colleges, Education Funds, Engineering/Technological Education, Faculty Development, Education-General, International Exchange, Literacy, Medical Education, Private Education (Precollege), Science/Mathematics Education, Science/Mathematics Education, Secondary Education (Private), Social Sciences Education, Student Aid
Environment: Environment-General
Health: AIDS/HIV, Cancer, Children's Health/Hospitals, Clinics/Medical Centers, Diabetes, Emergency/Ambulance Services, Health Funds, Health Organizations, Hospitals, Long-Term Care, Medical Research, Single-Disease Health Associations
International: Foreign Educational Institutions, Health Care/Hospitals, International Organizations, International Relations
Religion: Jewish Causes, Religious Welfare, Seminaries
Science: Scientific Centers & Institutes, Scientific Labs, Scientific Organizations
Social Services: Camps, Community Service Organizations, Crime Prevention, People with Disabilities, Substance Abuse, United Funds/United Ways, Volunteer Services, Youth Organizations

Application Procedures

Initial Contact: Send a one- to two-page letter of inquiry by mail or e-mail.
Application Requirements: Include a summary a description of organization of the organization; a summary of the proposed project or program with description of the problem to be addressed; the proposed solution; how it meets GlaxoSmithKline's support criteria; how GlaxoSmithKline volunteers (if appropriate) can be incorporated; the amount requested and the proposed project budget (with all other anticipated sources of income); a plan to measure and evaluate program results; an explanation of how the request and program relate to GlaxoSmithKline's focus on

health care; and a contact name, address, phone number, fax number and e-mail address if available.
Deadlines: None.
Evaluative Criteria: Proposals are screened to ensure that the proposed program identifies targets and possible barriers to success; includes a plan for self-sufficiency; measures and evaluates progress; and has the potential to be replicated.
Decision Notification: If the initial inquiry is unsuccessful, the applicant will be informed in writing with 30 days of receipt. A staff person will contact organization for full proposal if one is desired.
Notes: Company rarely supports unsolicited grant proposals, but prefers to initiate partnerships.

Restrictions

No grants are made to the following: deficit financing or debt retirement; capital campaigns, chairs, or endowments; individuals; political, labor, religious, fraternal, athletic or veterans' organizations; fund-raising events and associated advertising; conferences and symposia; lobbying groups; or universities or free-standing scientific research centers for research on GlaxoSmithKline projects or products. Ongoing general operating expenses are rarely funded. Commercial sponsorships and corporate hospitality opportunities are not funded. Multiple grants to the same organization are not made within a calendar year. Recipients must be exempt under IRS 501(c)(3) and do not receive substantial federal, state or local government funding.

Additional Information

A merger between SmithKline Beecham and Glaxo Wellcome was finalized in January 2001. The new company is known as GlaxoSmithKline plc. The Global Community Partnerships program was formed after the merger.
Publications: Guidelines Sheet; Annual Report

Corporate Officials

James Hill: senior vice president corporate affairs PRIM CORP EMPL senior vice president corporate affairs: SmithKline Beecham Corp.

Foundation Officials

Carol Ashe: secretary, general counsel
Robert Carr, MD: president

Grants Analysis

Disclosure Period: calendar year ending 2000
Total Grants: $612,786*
Average Grant: $799
Typical Range: $50 to $11,000
*Note: Giving excludes matching gifts. Above figures and recent grants are for the SmithKline Beecham Foundation. Sample grants were not yet available for the Global Community Partnerships program.

Recent Grants

Note: Grants derived from 2000 Form 990.

General

35,048	University of Pennsylvania Trustees of the University of Pennsylvania, Philadelphia, PA
13,044	Cornell University, Ithaca, NY
12,525	North Carolina State University, Raleigh, NC
12,500	Free Health Clinic of Montgomery County, Willow Grove, PA
12,000	Free Library of Philadelphia, Philadelphia, PA -- Science in the Summer programs
11,250	St. Peter's High School, New Brunswick, NJ
11,042	Wilson College, Chambersburg, PA
10,910	Duke University, Durham, NC
10,750	Lehigh University, Bethlehem, PA
10,206	State University of Iowa Foundation, Iowa City, IA

GLEASON FOUNDATION

Giving Contact

Ralph E. Harper, Secretary, Treasurer
1000 University Avenue
PO Box 22970
Rochester, NY 14692-2970
Phone: (585)241-4030
Fax: (585)241-4099
E-mail: susy.elniski@gleasonfoundation.org

Description

Founded: 1959
EIN: 166023235
Organization Type: General Purpose Foundation
Former Name: Gleason Memorial Fund.
Giving Locations: NY: Rochester
Grant Types: Capital, Challenge, General Support, Loan, Multiyear/Continuing Support, Operating Expenses, Scholarship.

Donor Information

Founder: Formerly known as the Emmet Blakeney Gleason Memorial Fund, the fund was incorporated in 1959 in New York by the late Miriam Blakeney Gleason in memory of her son. In 1961, it was merged with the J. E. and Eleanor Gleason Trust to form the Gleason Memorial Fund.

Financial Summary

Total Giving: $8,768,351 (2000); $7,200,000 (1999 approx); $11,866,354 (1998)
Giving Analysis: Giving for 2000 includes: foundation scholarships ($114,144) foundation grants to United Way ($280,000)
Assets: $136,271,738 (2000); $160,000,000 (1999 approx); $140,990,518 (1998)

Typical Recipients

Arts & Humanities: Arts Funds, Arts Outreach, Dance, Arts & Humanities-General, Historic Preservation, Libraries, Literary Arts, Museums/Galleries, Music, Public Broadcasting, Theater
Civic & Public Affairs: African American Affairs, Botanical Gardens/Parks, Business/Free Enterprise, Economic Development, Economic Policy, Employment/Job Training, Civic & Public Affairs-General, Hispanic Affairs, Housing, Law & Justice, Legal Aid, Public Policy, Urban & Community Affairs, Women's Affairs, Zoos/Aquariums
Education: Business Education, Colleges & Universities, Community & Junior Colleges, Continuing Education, Education Associations, Elementary Education (Private), Engineering/Technological Education, Education-General, Minority Education, Private Education (Precollege), Religious Education, Science/Mathematics Education, Secondary Education (Private), Special Education, Student Aid
Environment: Environment-General
Health: Children's Health/Hospitals, Clinics/Medical Centers, Emergency/Ambulance Services, Medical Rehabilitation, Medical Research, Nursing Services, Nutrition
International: Foreign Educational Institutions, Health Care/Hospitals, International Affairs
Religion: Churches, Religion-General, Religious Organizations
Science: Science Museums, Scientific Research
Social Services: At-Risk Youth, Child Abuse, Child Welfare, Community Centers, Community Service Organizations, Crime Prevention, Domestic Violence, Family Planning, Food/Clothing Distribution, People with Disabilities, Senior Services, Senior Services, Shelters/Homelessness, Social Services-General, United Funds/United Ways, Volunteer Services, Youth Organizations

Application Procedures

Initial Contact: Applicants should contact the foundation for an application form.
Application Requirements: The proposal should include a history and background of the organization; explanation of the project; amount requested; project budget and time schedule; names of board of directors and responsible staff; detailed financial statements for current and two previous years; a list of present funding sources; and a copy of IRS 501(c)(3) or 509(a) and 990 PF.
Deadlines: None.
Review Process: The board meets quarterly. Final notification occurs after board meetings.

Restrictions

Generally no funding is made for United Way-supported agencies. No grants are made to individuals. Grants are limited to greater Rochester or Monroe County, NY.

Additional Information

The foundation changed its name from the Gleason Memorial Fund to the Gleason Foundation.
Publications: Application Form

Foundation Officials

Dr. Edward C. Atwater: secretary, treasurer
James S. Gleason: director, chairman B 1934. ED Princeton University (1955); University of Rochester MBA (1973). PRIM CORP EMPL president, chief executive officer, chairman: Gleason Works ADD CORP EMPL chairman, president, chief executive officer, director: Gleason Corp.
Janis F. Gleason: director
Tracy R. Gleason: president, director
Ralph E. Harper: secretary, treasurer, director B Batavia, NY 1933. ED University of Rochester (1956); George Washington University JD (1966). PRIM CORP EMPL vice president, secretary, treasurer: Gleason Corp. CORP AFFIL secretary: Gleason Works.
Gary J. Kimmet: director PRIM CORP EMPL vice president engineering: Gleason Works.
Albert W. Moore: director B Norwood, MA 1934. ED Clarkson College of Technology (1959); University of Rochester (1970). CORP AFFIL director: Gleason Corp. NONPR AFFIL president, director: Association Manufacturing Technology.

Grants Analysis

Disclosure Period: calendar year ending 2000
Total Grants: $8,374,344*
Number of Grants: 137
Average Grant: $39,810*
Highest Grant: $2,000,000
Lowest Grant: $35
Typical Range: $25 to $1,500 and $10,000 to $50,000
*Note: Giving excludes scholarships and United Way. Average grant excludes two highest grants ($3,000,000).

Recent Grants

Note: Grants derived from 2000 Form 990.

General

2,000,000	University of Rochester Simon School, Rochester, NY
1,000,000	Al Sigl Center, Rochester, NY
1,000,000	Susan B. Anthony House, Rochester, NY
555,000	Center for Governmental Research, Rochester, NY
500,000	University of Rochester, Rochester, NY -- river campus libraries
350,000	Life Span, Rochester, NY
330,000	Rochester Philharmonic Orchestra, Rochester, NY

280,000   United Way, Rochester, NY
250,000   Foodlink, Rochester, NY
230,000   Rochester Institute of Technology, Rochester, NY

GLENCOE FOUNDATION

Giving Contact

Ellice McDonald, Jr., President & Director
Greenville Center
3801 Kennett Pke., Suite C-300
Greenville, DE 19807-2377
Phone: (302)654-9933
Fax: (302)429-8472

Description

Founded: 1975
EIN: 510164761
Organization Type: Private Foundation
Giving Locations: Scotland: Highland and Island regions of Scotland.
Grant Types: Capital, Emergency, General Support, Multiyear/Continuing Support, Operating Expenses, Scholarship.

Donor Information

Founder: Ellice McDonald, Jr., Rosa H. McDonald

Financial Summary

Total Giving: $1,049,195 (2001); $282,133 (2000); $422,201 (1999)
Giving Analysis: Giving for 2001 includes: foundation scholarships ($19,410); 2000: foundation scholarships ($23,767); 1999: foundation scholarships ($48,148)
Assets: $5,864,154 (2001); $7,345,483 (2000); $7,128,372 (1999)
Gifts Received: $1,000 (2001); $1,246,013 (2000); $681,975 (1999). Note: In 1997, 1999, 2000, and 2001, contributions were received from Ellice, Jr. & Rosa H. McDonald.

Typical Recipients

Arts & Humanities: Libraries, Museums/Galleries, Music
Education: Private Education (Precollege)
Health: Hospitals, Mental Health
International: Foreign Arts Organizations, Foreign Educational Institutions, International Development, International Environmental Issues, International Organizations, International Peace & Security Issues, International Relief Efforts

Application Procedures

Initial Contact: Send brief letter requesting application form.
Deadlines: None.

Restrictions

Limited to Scottish and American charitable organizations that promote Scottish-American traditions and culture.

Additional Information

Publications: Application Guidelines; Application Form

Foundation Officials

Gregory A. Inskip: director CLUB AFFIL Ocean Forest Golf Club; Wilmington Country Club.
Walter Jones Laird, Jr.: director B Philadelphia, PA 1926. ED Princeton University BS (1948); Massachusetts Institute of Technology MSCE (1950). PRIM CORP EMPL senior vice president: Dean Witter Reynolds Inc. CORP AFFIL director: Wentz Corp.; director: Meridian Asset Management; director: Sinkler Corp. NONPR AFFIL member: Wilmington Club;

chairman emeritus, trust: Winterthur Museum & Gardens; member: Financial Analysts Federation; gov: Society Colonial Wars; director: Delaware Trust Co.
Ellice McDonald, Jr.: president, director
Rosa H. McDonald: vice president, director
John C. Milner: secretary, treasurer
John P. Sinclair, Esq.: director

Grants Analysis

Disclosure Period: calendar year ending 2001
Total Grants: $1,029,785*
Number of Grants: 2
Highest Grant: $773,310
Lowest Grant: $256,475
*****Note:** Giving excludes scholarships.

Recent Grants

Note: Grants derived from 2000 Form 990.

General
257,304   Clan Donald Lands Trust United Kingdom -- operating grants
23,767   Lamond School, Helensburgh United Kingdom -- traditional music scholarship
1,062   Clan Donald Lands Trust United Kingdom -- projects grants

EUGENE AND MARILYN GLICK FOUNDATION

Giving Contact

Eugene Glick, President
Eugene and Marilyn Glick Foundation
PO Box 40177
Indianapolis, IN 46240
Phone: (317)469-5836
E-mail: info@glickco.com
Web: http://www.genebglick.com/about_foundation.asp

Description

Founded: 1982
EIN: 351549707
Organization Type: Private Foundation
Giving Locations: IN: Indianapolis
Grant Types: Capital, General Support, Operating Expenses, Project.

Donor Information

Founder: Eugene B. Glick, Marilyn K. Glick

Financial Summary

Total Giving: $2,665,009 (fiscal year ending November 30, 2001); $2,608,874 (fiscal 2000); $2,345,718 (fiscal 1999)
Giving Analysis: Giving for fiscal 2001 includes: foundation grants to United Way ($25,400); fiscal 2000: foundation grants to United Way ($25,000) fiscal 1998: foundation grants to United Way ($17,500)
Assets: $56,066,363 (fiscal 2001); $54,753,384 (fiscal 2000); $57,547,918 (fiscal 1999)
Gifts Received: $4,147,434 (fiscal 2001); $3,750,250 (fiscal 2000); $4,411,448 (fiscal 1998). Note: Contributions were received from Eugene B. and Marilyn K. Glick.

Typical Recipients

Arts & Humanities: Arts Associations & Councils, Arts Centers, Community Arts, Arts & Humanities-General, Historic Preservation, Libraries, Museums/Galleries, Music, Opera, Public Broadcasting, Theater
Civic & Public Affairs: African American Affairs, Botanical Gardens/Parks, Business/Free Enterprise, Civil Rights, Community Foundations, Employment/Job Training, Civic & Public Affairs-General, Nonprofit Management, Parades/Festivals, Philanthropic Organizations, Public Policy, Urban & Community Affairs, Women's Affairs, Zoos/Aquariums

Education: Business Education, Colleges & Universities, Education Funds, Engineering/Technological Education, Private Education (Precollege), Public Education (Precollege), Student Aid
Health: Cancer, Clinics/Medical Centers, Diabetes, Emergency/Ambulance Services, Health Organizations, Heart, Hospitals, Medical Research, Mental Health, Public Health, Single-Disease Health Associations
International: Foreign Arts Organizations, Health Care/Hospitals
Religion: Jewish Causes, Missionary Activities (Domestic), Religious Organizations, Religious Welfare, Seminaries, Synagogues/Temples
Social Services: Child Welfare, Community Service Organizations, Domestic Violence, Family Planning, Family Services, Recreation & Athletics, Scouts, Senior Services, United Funds/United Ways, YMCA/YWCA/YMHA/YWHA, Youth Organizations

Application Procedures

Initial Contact: Submit a brief letter of inquiry.
Application Requirements: Include a description of organization, amount requested, and purpose of funds sought.
Deadlines: None.

Foundation Officials

James T. Bisesi: director
Eugene B. Glick: president, trustee
Marilyn K. Glick: trustee, secretary, treasurer
Barbara Gunn: director
Sharon Kibbe: director

Grants Analysis

Disclosure Period: fiscal year ending November 30, 2001
Total Grants: $2,639,609*
Number of Grants: 167
Average Grant: $1,353*
Highest Grant: $2,415,000
Lowest Grant: $50
Typical Range: $1,000 to $5,000
*****Note:** Giving excludes United Way. Average grant excludes highest grant.

Recent Grants

Note: Grants derived from fiscal 2000 Form 990.

General
2,325,000   Central Indiana Community Foundation, Indianapolis, IN -- contribution to Gene and Marilyn Glick Foundation Fund
25,000   Indianapolis Symphony Orchestra, Indianapolis, IN -- in support of endowment campaign
21,566   Children's Bureau, Indianapolis, IN
21,565   Children's Bureau, Indianapolis, IN -- in support of PRO-100
21,565   Children's Bureau, Indianapolis, IN -- in support of PRO-100
17,000   United Way of Central Indiana, Inc., Indianapolis, IN -- annual contribution
10,000   Conner Prairie, Fishers, IN
10,000   Indianapolis Art Center, Indianapolis, IN -- in support of building campaign
9,000   Indiana Repertory Theater, Indianapolis, IN -- for current budget
8,000   United Way of Central Indiana, Inc., Indianapolis, IN -- in support of the Forever Fund

CHARLES B. GODDARD FOUNDATION

Giving Contact

William R. Goddard, Jr., Trustee
PO Box 1485
Ardmore, OK 73402
Phone: (580)226-6040

Description

Founded: 1958
EIN: 756005868
Organization Type: Private Foundation
Giving Locations: OK: southern OK; TX: northern TX
Grant Types: Capital, Emergency, General Support, Multiyear/Continuing Support, Operating Expenses, Research, Seed Money.

Donor Information

Founder: the late Charles B. Goddard

Financial Summary

Total Giving: $605,277 (fiscal year ending June 30, 2002); $561,510 (fiscal 2001); $727,220 (fiscal 2000)
Giving Analysis: Giving for fiscal 2002 includes: foundation grants to United Way ($10,000); fiscal 2001: foundation grants to United Way ($10,000); fiscal 2000: foundation grants to United Way ($10,000)
Assets: $11,253,226 (fiscal 2002); $12,509,451 (fiscal 2001); $11,432,384 (fiscal 2000)

Typical Recipients

Arts & Humanities: Arts Institutes, Historic Preservation, Libraries, Museums/Galleries, Performing Arts, Public Broadcasting, Theater
Civic & Public Affairs: Chambers of Commerce, Economic Development, Civic & Public Affairs-General, Law & Justice, Legal Aid, Parades/Festivals, Public Policy, Safety, Urban & Community Affairs, Zoos/Aquariums
Education: Colleges & Universities, Education Funds, Education Reform, Elementary Education (Private), Education-General, Literacy, Private Education (Precollege), Public Education (Precollege), Science/Mathematics Education, Student Aid
Environment: Wildlife Protection
Health: Children's Health/Hospitals, Clinics/Medical Centers, Diabetes, Health Policy/Cost Containment, Health Organizations, Hospices, Hospitals, Medical Rehabilitation, Medical Research, Public Health, Respiratory, Single-Disease Health Associations
International: International Affairs
Religion: Churches, Religious Welfare
Science: Science Museums, Scientific Centers & Institutes, Scientific Organizations
Social Services: Animal Protection, At-Risk Youth, Camps, Child Welfare, Community Service Organizations, Crime Prevention, Day Care, Domestic Violence, Family Services, Homes, People with Disabilities, Recreation & Athletics, Scouts, Shelters/Homelessness, Substance Abuse, United Funds/United Ways, YMCA/YWCA/YMHA/YWHA, Youth Organizations

Application Procedures

Initial Contact: Send a brief letter of inquiry.
Deadlines: None.

Foundation Officials

Elizabeth E. Cashman: trustee
Garland Clay: trustee
Ann G. Corrigan: trustee
William R. Goddard, Jr.: trustee
William M. Johns: trustee

Grants Analysis

Disclosure Period: fiscal year ending June 30, 2002
Total Grants: $595,277*
Number of Grants: 31
Average Grant: $14,665*
Highest Grant: $95,000
Lowest Grant: $300
Typical Range: $5,000 to $20,000
*Note: Giving excludes United Way. Average grant excludes two highest grants ($170,000).

Recent Grants

Note: Grants derived from fiscal 2000 Form 990.

General

216,000	Goddard Youth Foundation, Sulphur, OK -- for exhibits for children's museum
100,000	Children's Medical Center, Dallas, TX -- for ambulance dispatch center
61,250	Ardmore City Schools, Ardmore, OK -- for curriculum improvement
50,000	Oak Hall Episcopal School, Ardmore, OK -- for capital improvements
50,000	Oklahoma Medical Research Foundation, Oklahoma City, OK -- for capital campaign
25,000	Ardmore City Schools, Ardmore, OK -- for boys town training
25,000	Payne Education Center, Ardmore, OK -- for school therapists
25,000	Presbyterian Healthcare Foundation, Dallas, TX -- for capital campaign
25,000	Vogel Alcove Child Care, Dallas, TX -- to sponsorship art performance event
20,000	Ardmore Tiger Quarterback Club, Ardmore, OK -- for athletic field completion

GOEL FOUNDATION

Giving Contact

Prabhu Goel, Secretary
98 Ridgeview Dr.
Atherton, CA 94027-6464
Phone: (408)977-7092

Description

Founded: 1990
EIN: 770269072
Organization Type: Private Foundation
Giving Locations: no restrictions.
Grant Types: General Support.

Donor Information

Founder: Established in 1990 by Prabhu Goel and Poonam Goel.

Financial Summary

Total Giving: $390,033 (fiscal year ending March 31, 2002); $403,543 (fiscal 2001); $391,098 (fiscal 2000)
Assets: $7,617,778 (fiscal 2002); $8,161,133 (fiscal 2000); $8,241,823 (fiscal 1999)
Gifts Received: $17,500 (fiscal 1998); $372,500 (fiscal 1997)

Typical Recipients

Arts & Humanities: Ethnic & Folk Arts, Libraries
Civic & Public Affairs: Native American Affairs, Philanthropic Organizations
Education: Colleges & Universities, Private Education (Precollege), Science/Mathematics Education
Health: AIDS/HIV, Public Health
International: Foreign Arts Organizations, Foreign Educational Institutions, International Peace & Security Issues, International Relief Efforts, Missionary/Religious Activities
Religion: Religious Organizations, Synagogues/Temples
Science: Science Museums
Social Services: Community Service Organizations, Domestic Violence

Application Procedures

Initial Contact: Send a brief letter of inquiry.
Deadlines: None.

Foundation Officials

Poonam Goel: president
Prabhu Goel: secretary

Grants Analysis

Disclosure Period: fiscal year ending March 31, 2002
Total Grants: $390,033
Number of Grants: 1

Recent Grants

Note: Grants derived from 2000 Form 990.

General

403,543	Fidelity Investments Charitable Gift Fund, Boston, MA

DAVID B. GOLD FOUNDATION

Giving Contact

Elaine E. Gold, Executive Director
44 Montgomery Street, Suite 3750
Suite 3610
San Francisco, CA 94104
Phone: (415)288-9530
Fax: (415)288-9549

Description

Founded: 1993
EIN: 943169439
Organization Type: Private Foundation
Giving Locations: CA: San Francisco; NY: New York
Grant Types: General Support.

Financial Summary

Total Giving: $2,300,683 (fiscal year ending November 30, 2001); $1,944,213 (fiscal 2000); $2,500,459 (fiscal 1999)
Assets: $57,679,538 (fiscal 2001); $4,884,669 (fiscal 2000); $51,320,277 (fiscal 1999)
Gifts Received: $1,564,505 (fiscal 2001); $2,434,044 (fiscal 2000); $1,776,266 (fiscal 1999).
Note: In fiscal 1998, 1999, 2000, and 2001, contributions were received from David B. Gold Trust. In fiscal 1994 and fiscal 1995, contributions were received from the estate of David B. Gold.

Typical Recipients

Arts & Humanities: Arts Outreach, Libraries, Museums/Galleries, Music, Public Broadcasting, Theater
Civic & Public Affairs: African American Affairs, Botanical Gardens/Parks, Civil Rights, Civic & Public Affairs-General, Hispanic Affairs, Legal Aid, Municipalities/Towns, Public Policy, Safety
Education: Private Education (Precollege), Student Aid
Environment: Air/Water Quality, Environment-General, Protection, Resource Conservation
Health: Cancer, Heart, Medical Research, Prenatal Health Issues
International: Health Care/Hospitals
Religion: Jewish Causes, Religious Welfare
Science: Scientific Organizations
Social Services: Big Brother/Big Sister, Child Welfare, Community Centers, Community Service Organizations, Day Care, Domestic Violence, Family Planning, Family Services, Food/Clothing Distribution, Recreation & Athletics, Senior Services, Shelters/Homelessness, Youth Organizations

Application Procedures

Initial Contact: The foundation has no formal grant application procedure or application form.
Deadlines: None.

Foundation Officials

Elaine Gold: secretary, treasurer, director
Emily Gold: director
Steven A. Gold: director
Diane Gold-Bubier: director
Barbara Gold-Lurie: president

Grants Analysis

Disclosure Period: fiscal year ending November 30, 2001
Total Grants: $2,300,683
Number of Grants: 105
Average Grant: $17,314*
Highest Grant: $500,000
Lowest Grant: $500
Typical Range: $5,000 to $30,000
*Note: Average grant figure excludes highest grant.

Recent Grants

Note: Grants derived from fiscal 2001 Form 990.

General

500,000	San Francisco Conservatory of Music, San Francisco, CA -- capital campaign
150,000	Jewish Community Center of San Francisco, San Francisco, CA -- capital campaign
75,000	Cardiac Arrhythmia Center, Minneapolis, MN -- women at risk of sudden death
60,000	Earth Justice Legal Defense Fund, San Francisco, CA -- healthy cities, healthy wildlands
50,000	American Civil Liberties Union, San Francisco, CA -- Racial Justice Project
50,000	Bay Area Legal Aid, Oakland, CA
50,000	Union of Concerned Scientists, Cambridge, MA -- Food and Environment Program
40,000	Pesticide Action Network of North America, San Francisco, CA -- Database and Mapping Project
40,000	Planned Parenthood Golden Gate, San Mateo, CA -- specific project
35,000	Homeless Prenatal Program, San Francisco, CA -- Case Management Program

GOLDBERG FAMILY FOUNDATION

Giving Contact

Avram J. Goldberg, Trustee
225 Franklin St., Suite 2700
225 Franklin St., Suite 2700
Boston, MA 02110-2804
Phone: (617)695-1946

Description

Founded: 1961
EIN: 046039556
Organization Type: Private Foundation
Giving Locations: MA; NY; VT
Grant Types: General Support.

Donor Information

Founder: Avram J. and Carol R. Goldberg

Financial Summary

Total Giving: $820,518 (2001); $707,677 (2000); $631,612 (1999)
Giving Analysis: Giving for 2001 includes: foundation grants to United Way ($1,000,000); 2000: foundation grants to United Way ($101,250); 1999: foundation grants to United Way ($47,419);
Assets: $15,461,386 (2001); $17,388,687 (2000); $17,710,508 (1999)
Gifts Received: $25 (2000); $36,290 (1996); $236,272 (1995). Note: In 1995, contributions were received from Avram J. and Carol R. Goldberg. In 1996, contributions were received from Carol Goldberg.

Typical Recipients

Arts & Humanities: Arts Centers, Community Arts, History & Archaeology, Libraries, Museums/Galleries, Music, Performing Arts, Public Broadcasting, Theater
Civic & Public Affairs: Clubs, Economic Development, Civic & Public Affairs-General, Philanthropic Organizations, Public Policy
Education: Arts/Humanities Education, Business Education, Colleges & Universities, Education Funds, Elementary Education (Public), Education-General, Legal Education, Minority Education, Private Education (Precollege), Religious Education, Social Sciences Education
Environment: Environment-General
Health: Children's Health/Hospitals, Clinics/Medical Centers, Geriatric Health, Hospitals, Medical Rehabilitation, Medical Research, Public Health, Single-Disease Health Associations
International: Foreign Arts Organizations, International Organizations, International Relations, Missionary/Religious Activities
Religion: Jewish Causes, Religious Organizations, Synagogues/Temples
Science: Science Museums, Scientific Centers & Institutes
Social Services: Community Service Organizations, Family Planning, People with Disabilities, United Funds/United Ways

Application Procedures

Initial Contact: Send a brief letter of inquiry.
Deadlines: None.

Foundation Officials

Avram Jacob Goldberg: trustee B Brookline, MA 1930. ED Harvard University AB (1951); Harvard University JD (1954). PRIM CORP EMPL chairman: AVCAR Group. CORP AFFIL director: Boston Co. Inc.; director: Boston Safe Deposit & Trust Co.
Carol Rabb Goldberg: trustee B Newton, MA 1931. ED Tufts University BA (1955); Harvard University Graduate School of Business Administration (1969). PRIM CORP EMPL president: AVCAR Group. CLUB AFFIL Commercial Merchants Boston Club.
Deborah Beth Goldberg: trustee
Joshua Rabb Goldberg: trustee

Grants Analysis

Disclosure Period: calendar year ending 2001
Total Grants: $720,518*
Number of Grants: 215
Average Grant: $2,616*
Highest Grant: $158,000
Typical Range: $500 to $3,000
*Note: Giving excludes United Way. Average grant figure excludes highest grant.

Recent Grants

Note: Grants derived from 2001 Form 990.

General

158,000	Combined Jewish Philanthropies, Boston, MA
50,000	United Way of Massachusetts Bay, Boston, MA
50,000	United Way of Massachusetts Bay, Boston, MA
49,000	Center for Collaborative Education, New York, NY
37,500	Putney School, Putney, VT
37,000	Combined Jewish Philanthropies, Boston, MA
34,000	Congregation Kehilath Israel, New York, NY
32,000	Combined Jewish Philanthropies, Boston, MA
32,000	Combined Jewish Philanthropies, Boston, MA
31,000	Combined Jewish Philanthropies, Boston, MA

HERMAN GOLDMAN FOUNDATION

Giving Contact

Richard K. Baron, Executive Director
61 Broadway, 18th Floor
New York, NY 10006
Phone: (212)797-9090
Fax: (212)797-9162

Description

Founded: 1943
EIN: 136066039
Organization Type: General Purpose Foundation
Giving Locations: NY: New York including metropolitan area
Grant Types: Award, Capital, Conference/Seminar, Department, Endowment, Fellowship, General Support, Operating Expenses, Project, Research, Scholarship.

Donor Information

Founder: The Herman Goldman Foundation was established in 1943 by the late Herman Goldman , a New York City attorney, tax expert, and philanthropist. During his lifetime, Mr. Goldman was active in the affairs of a number of New York charitable undertakings. Included among his philanthropic interests were Beekman-Downtown, Mount Sinai, and North Shore Hospitals; Hebrew Home for the Aged; Fordham University; and Lincoln Center for the Performing Arts. In addition, he was one of the founders of the Albert Einstein College of Medicine.

Financial Summary

Total Giving: $2,117,200 (fiscal year ending February 28, 2001); $1,922,600 (fiscal 1999); $1,754,000 (fiscal 1998)
Assets: $36,520,252 (fiscal 2001); $37,000,000 (fiscal 2000 approx); $37,538,128 (fiscal 1999)

Typical Recipients

Arts & Humanities: Arts Centers, Arts Festivals, Arts Funds, Arts Outreach, Ballet, Community Arts, Dance, Libraries, Museums/Galleries, Music, Performing Arts, Public Broadcasting, Theater, Visual Arts
Civic & Public Affairs: Civil Rights, Clubs, Employment/Job Training, Civic & Public Affairs-General, Law & Justice, Legal Aid, Nonprofit Management, Philanthropic Organizations, Professional & Trade Associations, Public Policy, Urban & Community Affairs, Women's Affairs
Education: Arts/Humanities Education, Colleges & Universities, Education-General, Legal Education, Literacy, Medical Education, Private Education (Precollege), Public Education (Precollege), Religious Education, Special Education, Student Aid
Health: AIDS/HIV, Cancer, Clinics/Medical Centers, Geriatric Health, Health Funds, Health Organizations, Hospitals, Hospitals (University Affiliated), Long-Term Care, Medical Research, Mental Health, Multiple Sclerosis, Prenatal Health Issues, Single-Disease Health Associations
International: Foreign Educational Institutions, International Peace & Security Issues, International Relief Efforts, Missionary/Religious Activities
Religion: Churches, Jewish Causes, Religious Organizations, Religious Welfare, Seminaries, Synagogues/Temples
Science: Scientific Centers & Institutes
Social Services: Big Brother/Big Sister, Child Welfare, Community Service Organizations, Counseling, Crime Prevention, Family Services, Family Services, Homes, People with Disabilities, Recreation & Athletics, Senior Services, Shelters/Homelessness, Social Services-General, Veterans, YMCA/YWCA/YMHA/YWHA, Youth Organizations

Application Procedures

Initial Contact: Applicants should send a proposal in the form of a letter.

Application Requirements: Proposal should include: amount requested; a description of existing activities, intended activites and their expected impact; other sources if funding committed and anticipated; prospects for project's continuance; plans for future support; a budget, and a copy of a letter from the IRS exempting the applicant from Federal Income Tax.

Deadlines: None.

Restrictions

Grants are not given to individuals.

Additional Information

Publications: Annual Report

Foundation Officials

Jules M. Baron: director

Richard K. Baron: executive director

David A. Brauner: vice president, director B New York, NY 1942. ED Dickinson College AB (1963); Columbia University JD (1966). PRIM CORP EMPL partner: Baron Rosenzweig Klein & Brauner. NONPR AFFIL member: Maritime Law Association United States; member: New York County Lawyers Association; vice president, director: The Bridge Inc.

Robert N. Davies: director CLUB AFFIL Baltusrol Golf Club.

Michael L. Goldstein: director

David R. Kay: treasurer, director

Allan Nisselson: director

Elias Rosenzweig: director

Gail Schneider: director

Christopher C. Schwabacher: director B New York, NY 1941. ED Harvard University BA (1963); Harvard University LLB (1966); New York University LLM (1967).

Norman H. Sparber: director B Brooklyn, NY 1917. ED Saint John's University BBA (1942); Brooklyn Law School JD (1952). PRIM CORP EMPL attorney: Brauner Baron Rosenzweig Kligler Sparber & Bauman.

Roy M. Sparber: director PRIM CORP EMPL partner: Baron Rosenzweig Klein & Brauner.

Grants Analysis

Disclosure Period: fiscal year ending February 28, 2001

Total Grants: $2,117,200

Number of Grants: 136

Average Grant: $15,577

Highest Grant: $150,000

Typical Range: $5,000 to $30,000

Recent Grants

Note: Grants derived from fiscal 2001 Form 990.

General

150,000	United Jewish Appeal Federation of Jewish Philanthropies of New York, Inc., New York, NY
125,000	United Jewish Appeal Federation of Jewish Philanthropies of New York, Inc., New York, NY
75,000	Catholic Charities Diocese of Brooklyn, Brooklyn, NY
75,000	Catholic Charities Diocese of Brooklyn, Brooklyn, NY
75,000	Catholic Charities Diocese of Brooklyn, Brooklyn, NY
75,000	Catholic Charities Diocese of Brooklyn, Brooklyn, NY
75,000	Stanley M. Klein Foundation, Inc
75,000	Stanley M. Klein Foundation, Inc
75,000	Stanley M. Klein Foundation, Inc
60,000	American Friends of Maccabee Institute Foundation, New York, NY

RICHARD AND RHODA GOLDMAN FUND

Giving Contact

Robert Gamble, Executive Director
One Lombard Street, Suite 303
San Francisco, CA 94111
Phone: (415)788-1090
Fax: (415)788-7890
E-mail: info@goldmanfund.org
Web: http://www.goldmanfund.org

Description

Founded: 1951

EIN: 946064502

Organization Type: Family Foundation

Giving Locations: CA: San Francisco including metropolitan area

Grant Types: Capital, General Support, Multiyear/Continuing Support, Project.

Donor Information

Founder: The fund was incorporated in 1951 by Rhoda H. Goldman and Richard N. Goldman.

Financial Summary

Total Giving: $47,512,937 (2001); $32,540,477 (2000); $20,000,000 (1999 approx)

Assets: $394,822,720 (2002); $466,044,479 (2001); $430,000,000 (2000)

Gifts Received: $152,450,731 (1998); $109,096,827 (1992). Note: In 1998, contributions were received from the Goldman '96 Charitable Remainder Trust.

Typical Recipients

Arts & Humanities: Arts Centers, Arts Festivals, Arts Institutes, Ballet, Dance, Film & Video, Historic Preservation, History & Archaeology, Libraries, Museums/Galleries, Music, Opera, Public Broadcasting, Theater

Civic & Public Affairs: Asian American Affairs, Botanical Gardens/Parks, Business/Free Enterprise, Civil Rights, Economic Development, Employment/Job Training, Civic & Public Affairs-General, Law & Justice, Legal Aid, Native American Affairs, Nonprofit Management, Philanthropic Organizations, Public Policy, Urban & Community Affairs, Women's Affairs, Zoos/Aquariums

Education: Afterschool/Enrichment Programs, Arts/Humanities Education, Business Education, Colleges & Universities, Colleges & Universities, Education Funds, Environmental Education, Faculty Development, Education-General, Health & Physical Education, International Studies, Leadership Training, Literacy, Minority Education, Private Education (Precollege), Special Education

Environment: Air/Water Quality, Forestry, Environment-General, Protection, Resource Conservation, Watershed, Wildlife Protection

Health: AIDS/HIV, Alzheimers Disease, Cancer, Children's Health/Hospitals, Clinics/Medical Centers, Health-General, Health Policy/Cost Containment, Health Organizations, Heart, Hospices, Long-Term Care, Medical Research, Medical Training, Nursing Services, Public Health

International: International-General, Health Care/Hospitals, Human Rights, International Environmental Issues, International Peace & Security Issues, International Relations, Missionary/Religious Activities, Trade

Religion: Religion-General, Jewish Causes, Religious Welfare, Social/Policy Issues

Science: Science Museums

Social Services: Child Abuse, Community Service Organizations, Counseling, Crime Prevention, Day Care, Delinquency & Criminal Rehabilitation, Domestic Violence, Family Planning, Family Services, Food/Clothing Distribution, Recreation & Athletics, Senior Services, Shelters/Homelessness, United Funds/

United Ways, YMCA/YWCA/YMHA/YWHA, Youth Organizations

Application Procedures

Initial Contact: The foundation requests applications be made in writing.

Application Requirements: Letters of inquiry, no longer than two pages plus attachments, should include a one-paragraph executive summary describing the project for which funding is being sought, total project budget, amount requested, and short descriptive project title (proposals will not be accepted without the executive summary paragraph). Also include the name of the primary contact person along with his or her title, address, and phone number; description of project, including its necessity, objectives, significance, and plans for implementation; one-page itemized project budget; other sources or potential sources of funding; total annual budget; and a copy of the IRS letter verifying tax exempt status.

Deadlines: None.

Review Process: If the fund is interested in receiving a full proposal, applicant will be contacted and asked to submit additional information.

Restrictions

The fund does not accept unsolicited proposals for the support of arts organizations or institutions of primary, secondary or higher education, and generally does not accept applications for deficit budgets; endowments, or conferences; basic research; documentary films; and grants or scholarships to individuals.

Additional Information

Publications: Annual Report; Application Guidelines

Foundation Officials

Robert Gamble: executive director

Michael C. Gelman: director

Susan R. Gelman: director, member executive committee

Douglas E. Goldman: director, member executive committee

John D. Goldman: trustee, member executive committee CORP AFFIL president, director: Richard N Goldman & Co.; president, director: Goldman Insurance.

Lisa Goldman: trustee

Marcia L. Goldman: trustee NONPR AFFIL co-chairman: Theatreworks.

Richard Nathaniel Goldman: president, director, member executive committee B San Francisco, CA April 16, 1920. ED University of California at Berkeley Boalt Hall School of Law; University of California at Berkeley (1941). PRIM CORP EMPL chairman, chief executive officer: Richard N. Goldman & Co.

Donald H. Seller: director, member executive committee

Duane Silverstein: executive director

Grants Analysis

Disclosure Period: calendar year ending 2001

Total Grants: $47,512,937

Number of Grants: 775 (approx)

Average Grant: $61,307

Highest Grant: $1,000,000

Lowest Grant: $1,000

Typical Range: $25,000 to $200,000

Recent Grants

Note: Grants derived from 2001 Form 990.

Library-Related

211,000	Alameda County Library Foundation, Fremont, CA -- for the Reading for Life Program

General

2,000,000	Jewish Community Center of San Francisco, San Francisco, CA -- capital campaign
2,000,000	Richard and Rhoda Goldman School of

Public Policy, Berkeley, CA -- building
expansion

1,700,000 Friends of Recreation and Parks, San
Francisco, CA -- San Francisco Conservatory of Flowers

1,572,000 Jerusalem Foundation, Jerusalem Israel -- Richard and Rhoda Goldman
Promenade in Jerusalem

1,000,000 Birthright Israel North America, New
York, NY -- travel to Israel for Jewish
youth

1,000,000 Exploratorium, San Francisco, CA --
campaign for the future

1,000,000 KQED, San Francisco, CA -- campaign
for the future

1,000,000 National Geographic Society, Washington, DC -- for Sustainable Seas Expedi-
tions

1,000,000 Rhoda Goldman Plaza, San Francisco,
CA -- assisted living facility and school
service complex for seniors

1,000,000 Rhoda Goldman Plaza, San Francisco,
CA -- assisted living facility and school
service complex for seniors

MORRIS GOLDSEKER FOUNDATION OF MARYLAND

Giving Contact

Sally Scott, Program Officer
1040 Park Avenue, Suite 310
Baltimore, MD 21201
Phone: (410)837-5100
Fax: (410)837-7927
E-mail: sscott@goldsekerfoundation.org
Web: http://www.goldsekerfoundation.org

Description

Founded: 1974
EIN: 520983502
Organization Type: General Purpose Foundation
Giving Locations: MD: Baltimore
Grant Types: Award, Loan, Matching, Multiyear/Continuing Support, Professorship, Project, Seed Money.
Note: Also provides grants for evaluations, program development, and technical assistance.

Donor Information

Founder: The Morris Goldseker Foundation of Maryland was established in 1973 by the will of Morris Goldseker expressly to support programs directly benefiting the people of the Baltimore metropolitan area.

Financial Summary

Total Giving: $5,300,000 (2001 approx); $3,995,275 (2000); $3,726,070 (1999)
Assets: $100,174,901 (2001); $108,320,537 (2000); $108,012,418 (1999)
Gifts Received: $40,948 (1994). Note: In 1994, contributions were received from LISC.

Typical Recipients

Arts & Humanities: Arts Centers, History & Archaeology, Libraries, Literary Arts
Civic & Public Affairs: African American Affairs, Botanical Gardens/Parks, Business/Free Enterprise, Civil Rights, Community Foundations, Economic Development, Employment/Job Training, Civic & Public Affairs-General, Hispanic Affairs, Housing, Law & Justice, Nonprofit Management, Parades/Festivals, Philanthropic Organizations, Professional & Trade Associations, Public Policy, Urban & Community Affairs, Women's Affairs

Education: Colleges & Universities, Education Funds, Education-General, Literacy, Medical Education, Preschool Education, Private Education (Precollege), Special Education, Student Aid, Vocational & Technical Education
Environment: Environment-General
Health: Clinics/Medical Centers, Health Organizations, Mental Health, Research/Studies Institutes
International: International Development
Religion: Jewish Causes, Ministries, Religious Organizations, Religious Welfare
Social Services: Animal Protection, At-Risk Youth, Big Brother/Big Sister, Child Abuse, Child Welfare, Community Centers, Community Service Organizations, Counseling, Crime Prevention, Domestic Violence, Family Planning, Family Services, Food/Clothing Distribution, Homes, People with Disabilities, Recreation & Athletics, Scouts, Senior Services, Shelters/Homelessness, Substance Abuse, Youth Organizations

Application Procedures

Initial Contact: Applicants should submit a brief preliminary letter to the foundation. Telephone inquiries are also welcome.
Application Requirements: Applicants should include a description of organization, evidence of IRS tax-exempt status under sections 501(c)(3) and 509(a) of the Internal Revenue Code, background information, statement of need and objectives of the proposed project, methods for accomplishing objectives, projected program budget, and amount sought from the foundation. If foundation staff determine the request is within the foundation's interests and policies, they will send the applicant a proposal development form.
Deadlines: For full proposals: April 1; August 1; and December 1.
Review Process: The foundation's board meets three times a year, in March, June, and October, to consider proposals. Applicants are notified in writing of the outcome of their requests immediately after each meeting.
Because the foundation is not a long-term source of funds, applicants are encouraged to demonstrate how the proposed activity will be sustained. Applicants are expected to demonstrate adequate administrative capacity and financial stability, and to describe evaluation criteria and methods on their requests.

Restrictions

In order to be considered for funding, an organization must carry on its work and activities principally in the Baltimore metropolitan area.
The foundation does not make grants in support of religious programs or purposes, endowments, individuals, building campaigns, deficit financing, annual giving, or publications. The foundation reports it does not support arts and culture, ongoing operating budgets, political action groups, specific diseases or disabilities, or projects normally financed with public funds. In accordance with the donor's instruction, the foundation awards no more than five percent of its net income in any calendar year to any single recipient. Also, the foundation prefers not to award grants for longer than one year, but may consider requests for longer periods.

Additional Information

The foundation lists NationsBank Trust Company of Baltimore as a corporate trustee represented by Howard M. Weiss. The foundation is affiliated with the Baltimore Community Foundation. Also, the foundation is working with Johns Hopkins Health System, Johns Hopkins University, and the Kennedy Krieger Institute to establish a private community development bank in east and southeast Baltimore, to begin the long-term restoration of an inner-city neighborhood.
Publications: Annual Report; Program Guidelines

Foundation Officials

Timothy D. Armbruster: president PRIM NONPR EMPL president, director: Baltimore Community Foundation.
Sheldon Goldseker: chairman, trustee, member B 1940. PRIM CORP EMPL president: Multi-Properties Inc.
Simon Goldseker: vice chairman, trustee, member B 1939. PRIM CORP EMPL vice president, director: Multi-Properties Inc. CORP AFFIL partner: Maryland Apartments.
Catherine Gray: member investment committee
W. Wallace Lanahan, Jr.: member investment committee NONPR AFFIL trustee: Johns Hopkins Bayview Medical Center.
Sheila L. Purkey: secretary, treasurer
Sally Scott: program director
Ronald J. Staines: member investment committee PRIM CORP EMPL managing partner: Wolpoff & Co.
Semmes Guest Walsh: member investment committee B Annapolis, MD 1926. ED Yale University BE (1946); Harvard University MBA (1950). NONPR AFFIL director: J. L. Kernan Hospital Foundation.
Howard M. Weiss: corporate co-trustee, member investment committee PRIM CORP EMPL partner, attorney: Fletcher, Heald & Hildreth.

Grants Analysis

Disclosure Period: calendar year ending 2001
Total Grants: $5,300,000*
Number of Grants: 72
Average Grant: $73,611
Highest Grant: $256,250
Lowest Grant: $3,800
Typical Range: $25,000 to $125,000
*Note: Grants analysis provided by foundation.

Recent Grants

Note: Grants derived from 2000 Form 990.

General

235,500	Associated Jewish Charities, Baltimore, MD
235,500	Baltimore Community Foundation, Baltimore, MD
235,500	Johns Hopkins University, Baltimore, MD
235,500	Morgan State University, Baltimore, MD
225,000	Association of Baltimore Area Grantmaker, Baltimore, MD
225,000	Midtown Community Fund, Baltimore, MD
185,000	Citizens Planning and Housing Association, Baltimore, MD
150,000	Maryland Center for Arts and Technology, Baltimore, MD
125,000	Children's Scholarship Fund, Baltimore, MD
125,000	Greater Homewood Community Corporation, Baltimore, MD

GOLUB CORP.

Company Headquarters

Schenectady, NY
Web: http://www.pricechopper.com

Company Description

Revenue: US$2 billion (2001)
Employees: 19500 (2001)
SIC(s): 5411 Grocery Stores.

Operating Locations

Golub Corp. (MA; NY--Albany, Broom, Clinton, Delaware, Essex, Franklin Square, Fulton, Hamilton, Herkimer, Jefferson, Madison, Oneida, Onondaga, Orange, Oswego, Rensselaer, Saratoga Springs, Schenectady, Schoharie, Washington; PA; VT--Bennington)

Golub Foundation

Giving Contact

Melissa Pabis, Foundation Administrator
PO Box 1074
Schenectady, NY 12301
Phone: (518)356-9450

Alternate Contact

PO Box 1074
Schenectady, NY 12301
Phone: (518)356-9270
Note: Alternate phone number is for scholarship information only.

Description

Founded: 1981
EIN: 222341421
Organization Type: Corporate Foundation
Giving Locations: headquarters and operating communities.
Grant Types: Employee Matching Gifts, General Support, Scholarship.

Donor Information

Founder: Golub Corp., Jane Golub, Neil M. Golub

Financial Summary

Total Giving: $478,750 (fiscal year ending March 31, 2001); $219,718 (fiscal 2000); $448,443 (fiscal 1999). Note: Contributes through foundation only.
Giving Analysis: Giving for fiscal 2001 includes: foundation matching gifts ($2,895); corporate grants to United Way ($49,980); foundation scholarships ($51,000); foundation ($374,875); fiscal 1999: corporate gifts to individuals ($300); corporate direct giving ($1,500); foundation matching gifts ($2,131); foundation grants to United Way ($30,250); foundation scholarships ($41,750); foundation ($374,012); fiscal 1997: foundation matching gifts (approx $2,975); foundation grants to United Way (approx $32,300); foundation scholarships (approx $43,255) foundation (approx $347,864)
Assets: $477,299 (fiscal 2001); $4,575,177 (fiscal 2000); $70,628 (fiscal 1999)
Gifts Received: $962,265 (fiscal 2001); $300,000 (fiscal 1999); $445,000 (fiscal 1997). Note: Contributions are received from the Golub Corporation.

Typical Recipients

Arts & Humanities: Arts Associations & Councils, Arts Centers, Arts Institutes, Arts Outreach, Ethnic & Folk Arts, Historic Preservation, Libraries, Literary Arts, Museums/Galleries, Music, Performing Arts, Theater
Civic & Public Affairs: African American Affairs, Civic & Public Affairs-General, Housing, Professional & Trade Associations, Public Policy, Urban & Community Affairs
Education: Business Education, Colleges & Universities, Community & Junior Colleges, Engineering/Technological Education, Education-General, Literacy, Medical Education, Preschool Education, Public Education (Precollege), Science/Mathematics Education, Student Aid
Health: Arthritis, Cancer, Children's Health/Hospitals, Clinics/Medical Centers, Eyes/Blindness, Health Organizations, Hospices, Hospitals, Medical Rehabilitation, Prenatal Health Issues, Single-Disease Health Associations
Religion: Dioceses, Jewish Causes, Religious Organizations, Religious Welfare, Synagogues/Temples
Science: Science Museums
Social Services: Community Centers, Community Service Organizations, Counseling, Family Services, Food/Clothing Distribution, People with Disabilities, Recreation & Athletics, Scouts, Senior Services, United Funds/United Ways, YMCA/YWCA/YMHA/YWHA, Youth Organizations

Application Procedures

Initial Contact: Brief letter for general proposals; letter requesting application form for scholarship awards.
Application Requirements: For grant proposals, a description of organization, amount requested, purpose of funds sought, recently audited financial statement, and proof of tax-exempt status. Scholarship application packet must include applicant's educational history, including courses taken, ACT/SAT scores, class ranking, grades received; activity profile, including honors/awards and extracurricular activities; three reference letters; original essay; and completed application form.
Deadlines: for grant requests: None; for scholarship applications: March.
Notes: Scholarship applicants must plan to attend a school in NY, MA, PA, VT, CT, or NH.

Additional Information

Publications: Informational Brochure

Corporate Officials

Lewis Golub: chairman, chief executive officer, director B 1931. ED Michigan State University BS (1953). PRIM CORP EMPL chairman, chief executive officer, director: Golub Corp. CORP AFFIL director: Taylor Made Co.; chairman, chief executive officer: Price Chopper Oper Co. Massachusetts; chairman, chief executive officer: Price Chopper Oper Co. Pennsylvania; director: CIES; chairman, chief executive officer: Golub Service Stations Inc.; chairman: Central Distributors Inc.; member regional advisory board: Chase Bank; chairman: Cengo Construction Corp. NONPR AFFIL director: Saratoga Performing Arts Center; member advisory board: Union College; director: Proctor's Theater; advisor mba program: Russell Sage College; director: Food Marketing Institute; chairman: New York State Business Council; director: Empire State College Foundation.

Foundation Officials

Margaret Davenport: trustee PRIM CORP EMPL vice president: Golub Corp.
Mona Golub: trustee

Grants Analysis

Disclosure Period: fiscal year ending March 31, 1999
Total Grants: $374,875*
Number of Grants: 474
Average Grant: $791
Highest Grant: $77,500
Typical Range: $50 to $5,000
*Note: Giving excludes matching gifts; scholarships; United Way.

Recent Grants

Note: Grants derived from 2001 Form 990.

General

77,500	United Jewish Federation, Latham, NY
38,750	United Jewish Federation, Latham, NY
38,750	United Jewish Federation, Latham, NY
20,000	Siena College, Albany, NY -- for M. Dean Potts Memorial Scholarship
10,000	Empire State College Foundation, Saratoga Springs, NY
10,000	Jewish Community Center, Albany, NY -- pledge payment
10,000	Roman Catholic Diocese of Albany, Albany, NY
10,000	St. Claire's Hospital, Schenectady, NY
10,000	Saratoga Performing Arts Center, Saratoga Springs, NY
6,500	United Way Schenectady County, Schenectady, NY

GOOD SAMARITAN

Giving Contact

Edmund N. Carpenter, Jr., President
600 Center Mill Rd.
Wilmington, DE 19807
Phone: (302)654-7558
Fax: (302)654-2376

Description

Founded: 1938
EIN: 516000401
Organization Type: Private Foundation
Giving Locations: East Coast.
Grant Types: General Support.

Donor Information

Founder: the late Elias Ahuja

Financial Summary

Total Giving: $970,260 (2000); $1,454,340 (1999); $1,866,740 (1998). Note: 1996 Giving includes scholarship ($318,000).
Giving Analysis: Giving for 1999 includes: foundation scholarships ($25,700)
Assets: $34,622,627 (2000); $37,656,712 (1999); $32,589,538 (1998).

Typical Recipients

Arts & Humanities: Libraries, Museums/Galleries
Civic & Public Affairs: Community Foundations, Civic & Public Affairs-General, Housing, Law & Justice, Legal Aid, Public Policy, Urban & Community Affairs
Education: Colleges & Universities, Community & Junior Colleges, Education Funds, Elementary Education (Public), Engineering/Technological Education, Environmental Education, Faculty Development, Education-General, Minority Education, Private Education (Precollege), Public Education (Precollege), Religious Education, Science/Mathematics Education, Special Education, Student Aid
Environment: Environment-General, Protection, Resource Conservation, Wildlife Protection
Health: Cancer, Hospitals, Medical Research, Mental Health, Preventive Medicine/Wellness Organizations
International: Foreign Educational Institutions, International-General
Religion: Ministries
Social Services: At-Risk Youth, Child Welfare, Community Service Organizations, Day Care, Delinquency & Criminal Rehabilitation, Family Planning, People with Disabilities, Recreation & Athletics, YMCA/YWCA/YMHA/YWHA, Youth Organizations

Application Procedures

Initial Contact: Send a written narrative report.
Deadlines: Four weeks before first Thursday in June and four weeks before first Thursday in November.

Restrictions

Grants are not provided for building funds, other capital assets, or conferences.

Additional Information

Publications: Application Guidelines

Foundation Officials

Carroll M. Carpenter: vice president
Edmund Nelson Carpenter, II: secretary, treasurer B Philadelphia, PA 1921. ED Princeton University BA (1943); Harvard University LLB (1948). PRIM CORP EMPL director: Barclays Bank. CORP AFFIL director: Bank DE Corp. Wilmington. NONPR AFFIL trustee: Woodrow Wilson Foundation; trustee: Winterthur Museum; trustee: Wilmington Medical Center; member: Delaware Health Care Injury Insurance Study Commission; director: Good Samaritan; member: Delaware Bar Association; member: American Judicature

Society; member: American Trial Lawyers Association; fellow: American College Trial Lawyers; member: American Bar Association; fellow: American Bar Foundation.
Elizabeth Lee DuPont: vice president
Lea C. DuPont: vice president
Jeffrey M. Nielsen: secretary, treasurer
Rev. Edmund K. Sherrill, II: director
H. Sinclair Sherrill: director
Rev. Henry W. Sherrill: president

Grants Analysis

Disclosure Period: calendar year ending 2000
Total Grants: $970,260
Number of Grants: 19
Average Grant: $42,792*
Highest Grant: $200,000
Typical Range: $20,000 to $100,000
***Note:** Average grant figure excludes highest grant.

Recent Grants

Note: Grants derived from 1999 Form 990.

General

500,000	University of Delaware, Newark, DE -- renovation and expansion of P.S. Dupont Hall
125,000	Christina Care, Wilmington, DE -- support the creating of a cancer center
100,000	Wooster School, Danbury, CT -- Donald G. Schwartz scholarship
75,000	Angel Fund Lou Gehrig Disease, Charlestown, MA -- to strengthen the mission and scope of ALS research
75,000	CTAC, Hockessin, DE -- one time start up grant
75,000	Steppingstone Foundation, Boston, MA -- support of programs
50,000	Berkshire School, Sheffield, MA -- seed funds and challenge grant
37,000	Best Friends Foundation, Washington, DC -- develop a high school diamond girl curriculum
30,000	William T. and Mary McLaughlin Education Foundation, Wilmington, DE -- academic support economically and educationally disadvantaged students
25,000	Council of Court Excellence, Washington, DC -- support National Jury Pride project

GOODMAN FAMILY FOUNDATION

Giving Contact

Roy M. Goodman, Trustee
1035 5th Ave.
New York, NY 10028
Phone: (212)298-5524

Description

Founded: 1970
EIN: 136355553
Organization Type: Private Foundation
Giving Locations: NY: New York
Grant Types: General Support.

Donor Information

Founder: the late Israel Matz

Financial Summary

Total Giving: $196,278 (fiscal year ending June 30, 2001); $196,278 (fiscal 2000); $235,490 (fiscal 1999)
Assets: $5,018,845 (fiscal 2001); $5,018,845 (fiscal 2000); $5,782,783 (fiscal 1999)

Typical Recipients

Arts & Humanities: Arts Associations & Councils, Arts Centers, Arts Festivals, Arts Funds, Arts Outreach, Ballet, Community Arts, Dance, Libraries, Literary Arts, Museums/Galleries, Music, Opera, Performing Arts, Public Broadcasting, Theater
Civic & Public Affairs: Botanical Gardens/Parks, Clubs, Community Foundations, Civic & Public Affairs-General, Philanthropic Organizations, Professional & Trade Associations, Public Policy, Urban & Community Affairs, Women's Affairs
Education: Arts/Humanities Education, Business Education, Colleges & Universities, Faculty Development, International Studies, Medical Education, Minority Education, Private Education (Precollege), Science/Mathematics Education, Social Sciences Education, Special Education, Student Aid
Environment: Wildlife Protection
Health: AIDS/HIV, Cancer, Clinics/Medical Centers, Emergency/Ambulance Services, Hospitals, Hospitals (University Affiliated), Long-Term Care, Medical Research, Research/Studies Institutes
International: Health Care/Hospitals, International Affairs, International Relations, Missionary/Religious Activities
Religion: Churches, Dioceses, Jewish Causes, Religious Organizations, Religious Welfare, Synagogues/Temples
Science: Science Museums
Social Services: Camps, Child Welfare, Community Centers, Community Service Organizations, Crime Prevention, Day Care, Family Services, People with Disabilities, Recreation & Athletics, United Funds/United Ways, Youth Organizations

Application Procedures

Initial Contact: Send a brief letter of inquiry describing program.
Application Requirements: Include a written outline describing the special use of all contributions.
Deadlines: None.

Foundation Officials

Barbara F. Goodman: trustee
Roy Matz Goodman: trustee B New York, NY 1930. ED Harvard University BA (1951); Harvard University MBA (1953). PRIM CORP EMPL member: New York State Senate. NONPR AFFIL member: Omicron Delta Epsilon; trustee: Temple Emanu-El; sponsor: New York Philharmonic Society; member: New York Society Security Analysts; patron: Metropolitan Opera; member council advisor: New York Comm Young Audiences; fellow: Metropolitan Museum Art; trustee: Heart Research Foundation; member visitors committee: John F. Kennedy School Government Harvard University Overseers; member council advisor: Harvard Comm University Resources; member: Council Foreign Relations; member: Financial Analysts Federation; trustee: Carnegie Hall Society; member: Association Harvard Alumni; trustee: Carnegie Hall Corp.; member: Anti-Defamation League; member: American Young President Organization. CLUB AFFIL Senate New York Saint Club; Harvard Club; Fort Orange Club; Harvard Business School Club; Dutch Treat Club; Century Country Club; City Club; Century Association.

Grants Analysis

Disclosure Period: fiscal year ending June 30, 2001
Total Grants: $196,278
Number of Grants: 63
Average Grant: $1,714*
Highest Grant: $90,000
Lowest Grant: $100
Typical Range: $500 to $5,000
***Note:** Average grant excludes highest grant.

Recent Grants

Note: Grants derived from fiscal 2000 Form 990.

General

750,000	Harvard University, Cambridge, MA
12,700	Teachers College, Columbia University, New York, NY
10,000	Carnegie Hall Society Inc., New York, NY
10,000	Woodrow Wilson Center, Washington, DC
6,000	Congregation Emanu-El, New York, NY
5,000	American Museum of Natural History, New York, NY
5,000	Center for Jewish History, New York, NY
4,900	City Parks Foundation, New York, NY
3,000	Dalton School, New York, NY
3,000	Stephen Gaynor School, The, New York, NY

GOODNOW FUND

Giving Contact

Edward B. Goodnow, Trustee
36 Old Kings Highway South
Darien, CT 06820-4523
Phone: (203)655-6272
Fax: (203)655-7351

Description

Founded: 1994
EIN: 066395384
Organization Type: Private Foundation
Giving Locations: CT; MA; NY
Grant Types: General Support.

Donor Information

Founder: Established in 1994 by Edward B. Goodnow.

Financial Summary

Total Giving: $1,371,755 (2001); $621,575 (2000); $596,670 (1998)
Giving Analysis: Giving for 2000 includes: foundation grants to United Way ($23,000) 1998: foundation grants to United Way ($17,000)
Assets: $15,168,348 (2001); $15,003,151 (2000); $13,147,521 (1998)
Gifts Received: $1,500,000 (1995); $3,035,000 (1994); $3,000,100 (1993)

Typical Recipients

Arts & Humanities: History & Archaeology, Libraries, Literary Arts, Museums/Galleries
Civic & Public Affairs: Civic & Public Affairs-General, Housing, Philanthropic Organizations, Professional & Trade Associations, Safety, Urban & Community Affairs
Education: Colleges & Universities, Medical Education, Minority Education, Private Education (Precollege), School Volunteerism, Student Aid
Environment: Air/Water Quality, Protection, Resource Conservation, Wildlife Protection
Health: Cancer, Emergency/Ambulance Services, Hospitals, Medical Research, Public Health
International: International Relief Efforts
Religion: Churches, Religious Organizations, Religious Welfare
Social Services: Animal Protection, Camps, Child Welfare, Community Centers, Community Service Organizations, Family Services, Food/Clothing Distribution, People with Disabilities, Scouts, Senior Services,

Special Olympics, United Funds/United Ways, Volunteer Services, YMCA/YWCA/YMHA/YWHA, Youth Organizations

Application Procedures

Initial Contact: The foundation has no formal grant application procedure or application form. Send a brief letter of inquiry.
Deadlines: None.

Foundation Officials

Edward B. Goodnow: trustee

Grants Analysis

Disclosure Period: calendar year ending 2001
Total Grants: $1,371,755
Number of Grants: 23
Average Grant: $845*
Highest Grant: $1,353,155
Lowest Grant: $100
Typical Range: $100 to $1,000
*Note: Average grant excludes highest grant.

Recent Grants

Note: Grants derived from 2000 Form 990.

Library-Related

20,000	Friends of Darien Library, Darien, CT

General

250,000	Princeton University Trustees, Princeton, NJ
30,000	Salvation Army, Norristown, PA
25,000	Fairfield County Foundation, Fairfield, CT
20,000	Darien United Way, Darien, CT
20,000	Fresh Air Fund, New York, NY
20,000	Stamford Health Foundation, Inc, Stamford, CT
15,000	Jericho Project, The, New York, NY
15,000	Norwalk Hospital Foundation, Norwalk, CT
10,000	Catholic Relief Services
10,000	Hospital for Special Surgery, New York, NY

GOODRICH CORP.

Company Headquarters

4 Coliseum Centre
2730 W. Tyvola Rd.
Charlotte, NC 28217-4578
Web: http://www.goodrich.com

Company Description

Founded: 1870
Ticker: GR
Exchange: NYSE
Revenue: US$3.91 billion (2002)
Profit: US$117.9 million (2002)
Employees: 19200 (2002)
Fortune Rank: 385, per FORTUNE Magazine's list of 500 Largest U.S. Corporations (2002).

Nonmonetary Support

Type: Donated Equipment; In-kind Services; Loaned Employees; Loaned Executives; Workplace Solicitation
Volunteer Programs: Foundation sponsors a Bonus Volunteer Match program in addition to its Donors Match program. The foundation will make an extra 1 to 1 match of employee gifts to eligible organizations for which the employee volunteers, to a maximum of

$1,000. The company also sponsors a school partnership in Charlotte, NC.

B.F. Goodrich Foundation, Inc.

Giving Contact

Jan Locke, Manager, Community Affairs
B.F. Goodrich Foundation, Inc.
Four Coliseum Center
2730 W. Tyvola Road
Charlotte, NC 28217-4578
Phone: (704)423-7080
Fax: (704)423-7069
Web: http://www.goodrich.com/giving.asp

Description

EIN: 341601879
Organization Type: Corporate Foundation
Giving Locations: nationally; operating locations.
Grant Types: Award, Capital, Employee Matching Gifts, General Support, Multiyear/Continuing Support.
Note: Matching gifts are given to nonprofit organizations through its Partners in Giving Plan. Employee matching gift ratio: 1 to 1, from $50 to $2,500.

Donor Information

Founder: The Goodrich Corp. established the foundation with a contribution in 1988.

Financial Summary

Total Giving: $2,469,797 (2001); $1,858,726 (2000); $2,198,953 (1999). Note: Contributes through corporate direct giving program and foundation.
Giving Analysis: Giving for 2001 includes: domestic and international subsidiaries ($1,250,000); corporate direct giving ($2,400,000); 2000: foundation grants to United Way ($395,404); foundation ($1,463,322); 1998: foundation ($1,357,984);
Assets: $14,965,814 (2001); $16,302,708 (1998); $15,294,386 (1997)
Gifts Received: $2,000,000 (2001); $1,107,180 (1998); $218,680 (1997). Note: In 1997, contributions were received from Goodrich.

Typical Recipients

Arts & Humanities: Arts Associations & Councils, Arts Centers, Ballet, Community Arts, Dance, Historic Preservation, History & Archaeology, Libraries, Museums/Galleries, Music, Opera, Performing Arts, Public Broadcasting, Theater, Visual Arts
Civic & Public Affairs: Botanical Gardens/Parks, Business/Free Enterprise, Chambers of Commerce, Community Foundations, Economic Development, Economic Policy, Employment/Job Training, Civic & Public Affairs-General, Housing, Law & Justice, Municipalities/Towns, Parades/Festivals, Philanthropic Organizations, Professional & Trade Associations, Public Policy, Safety, Urban & Community Affairs, Women's Affairs
Education: Afterschool/Enrichment Programs, Business Education, Colleges & Universities, Community & Junior Colleges, Economic Education, Education Associations, Education Funds, Education Reform, Engineering/Technological Education, Education-General, Minority Education, Public Education (Precollege), Science/Mathematics Education, Student Aid
Health: Cancer, Children's Health/Hospitals, Emergency/Ambulance Services, Geriatric Health, Health Organizations, Hospices, Hospitals, Nursing Services
International: International Affairs
Religion: Religious Organizations, Religious Welfare
Science: Science Exhibits & Fairs, Science Museums, Scientific Centers & Institutes, Scientific Organizations

Social Services: Camps, Child Welfare, Community Centers, Community Service Organizations, Emergency Relief, People with Disabilities, People with Disabilities, Recreation & Athletics, Scouts, Senior Services, Social Services-General, Substance Abuse, United Funds/United Ways, YMCA/YWCA/YMHA/YWHA, Youth Organizations

Application Procedures

Initial Contact: Request an application form from the foundation or download an application from the foundation's web site: www.goodrich.com/giving.asp.
Application Requirements: Mail the completed application form and any supporting documentation outlining the project and its impact on the community.
Deadlines: None.
Review Process: Calendar budget cycle begins in February of each year.
Decision Notification: Funding decisions are made by the Foundation Contributions Committee.
Notes: Telephone and e-mail requests are not accepted.

Restrictions

Grants are not made for multi-year grants in excess of five years; individuals, private foundations, endowments, churches or religious programs, fraternal, social, labor, or veterans' organizations; groups with unusually high fundraising or administrative expenses; political parties, candidates, or lobbying activities; travel funds for tours, trips, or exhibitions by individuals or special interest groups; organizations that discriminate because of race, color, religion, national origin; local athletic or sports programs or equipment, courtesy advertising benefits, raffle tickets, and other fundraising events involving the purchase of tables, tickets, or advertisements; organizations that receive sizable portions of their support from government entities; individuals United Way agencies that already benefit from Goodrich contributions to the United Way Campaign; or international organizations. Contributions are made only to 501(c)(3) tax-exempt organizations.

Corporate Officials

David L. Burner: chairman, chief executive officer, director B Lodi, OH April 05, 1939. ED Ohio University BS (1962). PRIM CORP EMPL chairman: Goodrich Corp. ADD CORP EMPL officer: Jcair Inc.; chairman: Simmonds Precision Products. CORP AFFIL director: Brush Wellman Inc. NONPR AFFIL director: Salvation Army Greater Cleveland; director: Summit Education Initiative; director: Greater Cleveland Growth Association; board governor: Aerospace Institute America; director: Cleveland Scholarship Program Inc.
Gary L. Habegger: vice president human resources B Decatur, IN 1944. ED Seattle Pacific University (1966); University of Michigan (1978). PRIM CORP EMPL vice president human resources: B.F. Goodrich Co. ADD CORP EMPL vice president: Simmonds Precision Products.
Robert Jewell: vice president communications PRIM CORP EMPL vice president communications: B.F. Goodrich Co.
Scott E. Kuechle: vice president treasurer PRIM CORP EMPL vice president, treasurer: B.F. Goodrich Co.
Marshall O. Larsen: president, chief executive officer, director ED Purdue University MS. PRIM CORP EMPL president, chief executive officer, director: Goodrich Corp.
Les C. Vinney: senior vice president, chief financial officer B Cleveland, OH 1948. ED Cornell University BA (1970); Cornell University MBA (1972). PRIM CORP EMPL senior vice president, chief financial officer: B.F. Goodrich Co. CORP AFFIL president, director: Tremco Autobody Technologies; president: Tremco Inc.; treasurer: B.F. Performance Freedom Chem Co.

Foundation Officials

Gary L. Habegger: president (see above)
Scott E. Kuechle: treasurer (see above)
David B. Price, Jr.: vice president ED University of Missouri BS (1968); Harvard University MBA (1976). PRIM CORP EMPL executive vice president: BF Goodrich Co. CORP AFFIL president: B.F. Performance Freedom Chem Co.; president, chief operating officer: B.F. Performance Materials.

Grants Analysis

Disclosure Period: calendar year ending 2001
Total Grants: $2,136,342 (approx)*
Number of Grants: 686
Average Grant: $3,184
Highest Grant: $200,000
Lowest Grant: $50
Typical Range: $2,000 to $20,000
*Note: Giving excludes United Way.

Recent Grants

Note: Grants derived from 2001 Form 990.

Library-Related
20,125	Western Reserve Academy, Hudson, OH
20,000	Echo Foundation, Charlotte, NC

General
200,000	Cleveland Orchestra, Cleveland, OH
192,543	United Way of Central Carolinas, Charlotte, NC
125,361	Case Western Reserve University, Cleveland, OH
100,000	Advance Carolina, Charlotte, NC
100,000	American Red Cross Disaster Relief Fund, Charlotte, NC
100,000	Children's Learning Center, Charlotte, NC
84,000	Communities in School, Charlotte, NC
75,000	North Carolina Dance Theater, Charlotte, NC
71,161	United Way of Wayne County, Goldsboro, NC
60,000	Coltsville Heritage Park, Hartford, CT

GOODSTEIN FOUNDATION

Giving Contact

R. W. Miracle, President
PO Box 2773
Casper, WY 82602
Phone: (307)234-0821

Description

Founded: 1952
EIN: 836003815
Organization Type: Private Foundation
Giving Locations: CO; WY
Grant Types: General Support.

Donor Information

Founder: J. M. Goodstein

Financial Summary

Total Giving: $408,390 (fiscal year ending June 30, 2001); $196,291 (fiscal 1998); $258,079 (fiscal 1997). Note: Fiscal 1997 Giving includes United Way ($2,500).
Giving Analysis: Giving for fiscal 2001 includes: foundation grants to United Way ($2,500) fiscal 1998: foundation grants to United Way ($2,500)

Assets: $5,982,781 (fiscal 2001); $6,627,794 (fiscal 1998); $5,908,528 (fiscal 1997)

Typical Recipients

Arts & Humanities: Community Arts, Libraries, Museums/Galleries, Music, Opera, Public Broadcasting, Theater
Civic & Public Affairs: Botanical Gardens/Parks, Civic & Public Affairs-General, Urban & Community Affairs, Zoos/Aquariums
Education: Agricultural Education, Arts/Humanities Education, Colleges & Universities, Education Funds, Education-General, Legal Education, Private Education (Precollege), Science/Mathematics Education, Secondary Education (Private)
Environment: Environment-General
Health: Alzheimers Disease, Arthritis, Cancer, Children's Health/Hospitals, Clinics/Medical Centers, Diabetes, Health Funds, Health Organizations, Heart, Hospices, Hospitals, Medical Research, Nursing Services, Prenatal Health Issues, Respiratory, Speech & Hearing
International: Health Care/Hospitals, Missionary/Religious Activities
Religion: Churches, Religion-General, Jewish Causes, Religious Organizations, Religious Welfare
Science: Science Museums
Social Services: Animal Protection, Child Welfare, Community Service Organizations, Crime Prevention, Day Care, Emergency Relief, Family Planning, Food/Clothing Distribution, People with Disabilities, Senior Services, United Funds/United Ways, Youth Organizations

Application Procedures

Initial Contact: The foundation requests applications be made in writing. Clearly outline the purpose of funds sought.
Deadlines: None.

Restrictions

Primarily limited to colleges, universities, churches, hospitals, and like educational and health institutions.

Foundation Officials

Lucy M. Goodstein: vice president
Morris Massey: secretary
Robert Warren Miracle: president B Casper, WY. ED University of Wyoming BS (1951); Pacific Coast Banking School (1960). NONPR AFFIL member: Veterans Foreign Wars; member: Wyoming Bankers Association; trustee: Myra Fox Skelton Foundation; member: Newcomen Society North America; member: Rocky Mountain Oil & Gas Association; member: Masons; member: Casper Chamber of Commerce; member: Lions; member: American Management Association; member: American Bankers Association. CLUB AFFIL Casper Country Club.

Grants Analysis

Disclosure Period: fiscal year ending June 30, 2001
Total Grants: $405,890*
Number of Grants: 59
Average Grant: $4,412*
Highest Grant: $150,000
Typical Range: $1,000 to $10,000
*Note: Giving excludes United Way. Average grant figure excludes highest grant.

Recent Grants

Note: Grants derived from fiscal 2000 Form 990.

General
92,851	Wyoming Medical Center, Casper, WY
50,000	Cent. WY M/P Facility
12,655	Wyoming Medical Center Foundation, Casper, WY
10,000	Hebrew Educational Alliance, Denver, CO

10,000	University of Denver, Denver, CO
7,584	Life Steps Campus Foundation
5,000	Allied Jewish Apartments, Denver, CO
5,000	Allied Jewish Federation, Denver, CO
5,000	Children's Hospital
5,000	Congregational Emmanuel

PEGGY AND YALE GORDON CHARITABLE TRUST

Giving Contact

Sidney S. Sherr, Director, Trustee
3 Church Ln.
Pikesville, MD 21208
Phone: (410)484-6410

Description

Founded: 1980
EIN: 521174287
Organization Type: Private Foundation
Giving Locations: MD, Baltimore
Grant Types: Multiyear/Continuing Support.

Donor Information

Founder: The late Yale Gordon.

Financial Summary

Total Giving: $54,600 (2001); $374,105 (2000); $359,068 (1999)
Assets: $6,097,181 (2001); $6,825,177 (2000); $8,647,133 (1999)
Gifts Received: $38 (1998); $100 (1996); $11,088 (1995). Note: In 1996, contributions were received from Raymond and Alice Gordon.

Typical Recipients

Arts & Humanities: Arts Associations & Councils, Arts Funds, Arts Institutes, Arts Outreach, Community Arts, Historic Preservation, Libraries, Museums/Galleries, Music, Opera, Performing Arts, Public Broadcasting, Theater
Education: Arts/Humanities Education, Colleges & Universities, Private Education (Precollege)
International: Missionary/Religious Activities
Religion: Jewish Causes, Ministries, Religious Organizations, Synagogues/Temples

Application Procedures

Initial Contact: The foundation has no formal grant application procedure or application form. Submit a full proposal.
Application Requirements: Provide a description of organization, amount requested, purpose of funds sought, recently audited financial statement, proof of tax-exempt status.
Deadlines: None.

Restrictions

Does not support individuals, religious organizations for sectarian purposes, political or lobbying groups, or organizations outside operating areas.

Foundation Officials

Kenneth Battye: trustee
Loraine Bernstein: trustee, assistant director, concert coordinator
Judith A. Burke: trustee
Phyllis C. Friedman: trustee
Sherry B. Gill: trustee
Raymond J. Gordon: trustee, real estate mgr

Grants Analysis

Disclosure Period: calendar year ending 2001
Total Grants: $54,600*
Number of Grants: 4
Average Grant: $13,650*
Highest Grant: $50,000
*Note: Average grant figure excludes highest grant.

Recent Grants

Note: Grants derived from 2001 Form 990.

General

50,000	P and Y Gordan Performing Arts Center, Owings Mills, MD -- new construction and music
2,500	Baltimore Choral Arts Society, Baltimore, MD -- music
1,500	Towson State University, Towson, MD -- music
600	GBMC, Baltimore, MD -- music

THE FLORENCE GOULD FOUNDATION

Giving Contact

John R. Young, President
Cahill, Gordon, and Reindel
80 Pine St., Ste. 1701
New York, NY 10005-1702
Phone: (212)701-3400
Fax: (212)269-5420

Description

Founded: 1957
EIN: 136176855
Organization Type: General Purpose Foundation
Giving Locations: nationally; France
Grant Types: Conference/Seminar, Department, Endowment, General Support, Project, Research.

Donor Information

Founder: Established in 1957 by Florence J. Gould.

Financial Summary

Total Giving: $7,573,920 (2000); $7,966,313 (1999); $6,257,364 (1998)
Giving Analysis: Giving for 1999 includes: foundation scholarships ($5,000)
Assets: $120,924,657 (2000); $135,812,340 (1999); $124,681,146 (1998)
Gifts Received: $6,494 (1992). Note: The foundation receives contributions from trusts under the will of Florence J. Gould.

Typical Recipients

Arts & Humanities: Arts Associations & Councils, Arts Centers, Ballet, Dance, Ethnic & Folk Arts, Arts & Humanities-General, Historic Preservation, History & Archaeology, Libraries, Literary Arts, Museums/Galleries, Music, Opera, Performing Arts, Public Broadcasting, Theater, Visual Arts
Civic & Public Affairs: Botanical Gardens/Parks, Clubs, Civic & Public Affairs-General, Law & Justice, Philanthropic Organizations, Public Policy, Urban & Community Affairs
Education: Arts/Humanities Education, Colleges & Universities, Continuing Education, Engineering/Technological Education, Education-General, International Exchange, International Studies, Legal Education, Medical Education, Public Education (Precollege), Science/Mathematics Education
Environment: Environment-General
Health: AIDS/HIV, Alzheimers Disease, Children's Health/Hospitals, Clinics/Medical Centers, Geriatric Health

International: Foreign Arts Organizations, Foreign Educational Institutions, International-General, Health Care/Hospitals, International Affairs, International Development, International Organizations, International Peace & Security Issues, International Relations
Religion: Churches, Jewish Causes, Religious Organizations, Religious Welfare
Science: Science-General, Scientific Labs
Social Services: Community Service Organizations, People with Disabilities

Application Procedures

Initial Contact: No particular form of application is required.
Deadlines: None.

Foundation Officials

Walter Conway Cliff: assistant treasurer, secretary, director B Detroit, MI 1932. ED University of Detroit LLB (1955); University of Detroit BS (1955); New York University LLM (1956). PRIM CORP EMPL president: Walter C. Cliff PC PRIM NONPR EMPL partner: Cahill Gordon & Reindel. CORP AFFIL partner: Cahill Gordon & Reindel. NONPR AFFIL member collections committee: Harvard University Art Museum; member: New York State Bar Association; member: American Bar Association; member: Association Bar New York City. CLUB AFFIL Stockbridge Golf Club; Downtown Club.
Daniel Pomeroy Davison: vice president, treasurer, ast secretary, director B New York, NY 1925. ED Yale University BA (1949); Harvard University JD (1952).
Daniel Leopold Wildenstein: vice president, director B Verrieres-le-Buisson, France September 11, 1917. PRIM CORP EMPL chairman: Wildenstein & Co. Inc.
John R. Young: president B Milwaukee, WI 1934. ED University of Chicago AB (1953); University of Chicago JD (1956). PRIM CORP EMPL Cahill Gordon & Reindel.

Grants Analysis

Disclosure Period: calendar year ending 1999
Total Grants: $7,961,313*
Number of Grants: 194
Average Grant: $37,796*
Highest Grant: $666,666
Lowest Grant: $2,000
Typical Range: $3,000 to $50,000
*Note: Giving excludes scholarships. Average grant figure excludes highest grant.

Recent Grants

Note: Grants derived from 2000 Form 990.

Library-Related

200,000	New York Public Library, New York, NY

General

200,000	American Hospital of Paris Foundation, Paris France
200,000	Cold Spring Harbor Laboratory Association, Cold Spring Harbor, NY
200,000	Cold Spring Harbor Laboratory Association, Cold Spring Harbor, NY
200,000	New York City Ballet, New York, NY
175,000	Institut de France, Domaine de Chantilly, Chantilly France -- restoration of the "The Grand Ecuries"
175,000	Metropolitan Museum of Art, New York, NY
175,000	Metropolitan Museum of Art, New York, NY
170,000	Society for French American Cultural Services and Education Aid, New York, NY
150,000	French Institute Alliance Francaise, New York, NY
150,000	Friends of Vieilles Maisons Francaises, Phoenix, AZ

GRABLE FOUNDATION

Giving Contact

Susan H. Brownlee, Executive Director
650 Smithfield Street, Suite 240
Pittsburgh, PA 15222
Phone: (412)471-4550
Fax: (412)471-2267
E-mail: grable@grablefdn.org
Web: http://www.grablefdn.org

Description

Founded: 1977
EIN: 251309888
Organization Type: General Purpose Foundation
Giving Locations: PA: southwest region
Grant Types: General Support, Matching, Multiyear/Continuing Support, Operating Expenses, Project, Research, Seed Money.

Donor Information

Founder: Minnie K. Grable founded the Grable Foundation in 1976.

Financial Summary

Total Giving: $10,984,014 (2001); $11,750,000 (2000 approx); $11,346,957 (1999)
Giving Analysis: Giving for 1998 includes: foundation scholarships ($1,500); foundation grants to United Way ($123,000); foundation grants to United Way ($373,000) foundation ($9,257,128)
Assets: $234,656,940 (2001); $261,564,244 (1999); $253,016,718 (1998)
Gifts Received: $35,013,925 (1997); $27,592,274 (1996); $28,128,119 (1995). Note: In 1996 and 1997, contributions were received from the Minnie K. Grable Trust.

Typical Recipients

Arts & Humanities: Arts Centers, Community Arts, Arts & Humanities-General, History & Archaeology, Libraries, Museums/Galleries, Public Broadcasting
Civic & Public Affairs: African American Affairs, Business/Free Enterprise, Economic Development, Economic Policy, Employment/Job Training, Civic & Public Affairs-General, Law & Justice, Professional & Trade Associations, Public Policy, Urban & Community Affairs, Zoos/Aquariums
Education: Afterschool/Enrichment Programs, Arts/Humanities Education, Business Education, Colleges & Universities, Community & Junior Colleges, Economic Education, Education Associations, Education Funds, Education Reform, Elementary Education (Private), Elementary Education (Public), Environmental Education, Faculty Development, Education-General, International Exchange, Leadership Training, Leadership Training, Literacy, Minority Education, Private Education (Precollege), Public Education (Precollege), School Volunteerism, Science/Mathematics Education, Secondary Education (Public), Social Sciences Education, Special Education, Vocational & Technical Education
Environment: Forestry, Resource Conservation
Health: Children's Health/Hospitals, Health-General, Health Organizations, Hospitals, Mental Health, Prenatal Health Issues
Religion: Religious Welfare
Science: Scientific Centers & Institutes
Social Services: Big Brother/Big Sister, Child Welfare, Community Service Organizations, Day Care, Family Planning, Family Services, Shelters/Homelessness, Substance Abuse, United Funds/United Ways, Volunteer Services, YMCA/YWCA/YMHA/YWHA, Youth Organizations

Application Procedures

Initial Contact: Send a brief letter of inquiry describing program.
Application Requirements: If notified that the program is within foundation guidelines, applications

should include a one-page summary of proposal, a description of organization, description of project, statement of need, description of project supervisor and staff, project budget showing committed and anticipated funds, how project will be sustained after funding, organization's operating budget, description of anticipated outcomes of the project, list of board members, and a copy of IRS tax-exempt certification.
Deadlines: None. The board meets three times a year, usually in March, July, and November.
Notes: The Common Grant Application is also accepted.

Restrictions

Foundation does not support endorsement, capital campaigns, fundraisers or individuals.

Additional Information

Publications: Annual Report Guidelines

Foundation Officials

Susan Brownlee: executive director
Charles R. Burke, Jr.: associate director, board director
Charles R. Burke: chairman, director
Patricia G. Burke: director
Steven E. Burke: director, treasurer
Barbara N. McFadyen: director
Jan Nicholson: president
Marion G. Nicholson: director
William B. Nicholson: director
Merrilynn Young: comptroller

Grants Analysis

Disclosure Period: calendar year ending 2001
Total Grants: $10,809,014*
Number of Grants: 279
Average Grant: $38,742
Highest Grant: $385,000
Lowest Grant: $1,000
Typical Range: $10,000 to $100,000
***Note:** Giving excludes United Way.

Recent Grants

Note: Grants derived from 2001 Form 990.

Library-Related

200,000	Allegheny County Library, Pittsburgh, PA -- for eiNetwork

General

385,000	Pittsburgh Public Schools, Pittsburgh, PA -- for planning grant and support for the literacy plus
300,000	Carnegie Science Center, Pittsburgh, PA -- for SciQuest Exhibition
270,000	NARSAD, Great Neck, NY -- for investigators
250,000	Sports and Exhibition Authority of Pittsburgh and Allegheny County, Pittsburgh, PA -- for North Shore Riverfront Park
158,100	Beginning with Books, Inc., Pittsburgh, PA -- for Project Beacon
150,000	DePaul Institute, Pittsburgh, PA -- for Transition Program
150,000	Family Communications, Pittsburgh, PA -- for challenging child
150,000	Western Pennsylvania Conservancy, Mill Run, PA -- for school garden initiative
150,000	YMCA of Pittsburgh, Pittsburgh, PA -- capital campaign
140,000	Zoological Society of Pittsburgh, Pittsburgh, PA -- for Aquarium Project

GRAHAM ENGINEERING CORP.

Company Headquarters

1203 Eden Rd.
York, PA 17402
Web: http://www.grahammachinerygroup.com

Company Description

Revenue: US$41 million (2001)
Employees: 175 (2001)

Graham Foundation

Giving Contact

William H. Kerlin, Jr., Trustee
PO Box 1104
York, PA 17405
Phone: (717)849-4001

Description

Founded: 1986
EIN: 236805421
Organization Type: Corporate Foundation
Giving Locations: headquarters area only.
Grant Types: General Support.

Donor Information

Founder: Graham Engineering

Financial Summary

Total Giving: $1,735,485 (fiscal year ending June 30, 1999); $202,028 (fiscal 1998); $149,550 (fiscal 1996)
Giving Analysis: Giving for fiscal 1999 includes: foundation grants to United Way ($36,000); foundation ($1,699,485) fiscal 1998: foundation grants to United Way ($32,000)
Assets: $24,714,869 (fiscal 1999); $21,917,075 (fiscal 1998); $2,044,709 (fiscal 1996)
Gifts Received: $488,143 (fiscal 1999); $18,725,804 (fiscal 1998). Note: Contributions are received from Graham Capital Corp. In fiscal 1999, contributions were received from Donald C. Graham

Typical Recipients

Arts & Humanities: Arts Associations & Councils, Historic Preservation, History & Archaeology, Libraries, Museums/Galleries, Performing Arts, Theater
Civic & Public Affairs: Botanical Gardens/Parks, Business/Free Enterprise, Chambers of Commerce, Community Foundations, Civic & Public Affairs-General, Housing, Urban & Community Affairs
Education: Business Education, Colleges & Universities, Economic Education, Engineering/Technological Education, Education-General, Health & Physical Education, Preschool Education, Private Education (Precollege), Public Education (Precollege), Secondary Education (Private), Student Aid
Environment: Environment-General, Resource Conservation
Health: Cancer, Children's Health/Hospitals, Emergency/Ambulance Services, Health-General, Health Organizations, Heart, Home-Care Services, Hospices, Hospitals, Medical Research, Mental Health, Nursing Services, Public Health, Single-Disease Health Associations
Religion: Churches, Jewish Causes, Ministries, Religious Welfare
Science: Science Exhibits & Fairs
Social Services: Camps, Child Welfare, Community Service Organizations, Family Planning, Homes, People with Disabilities, Recreation & Athletics, Senior Services, Social Services-General, United Funds/United Ways, YMCA/YWCA/YMHA/YWHA, Youth Organizations

Application Procedures

Initial Contact: The foundation has no formal grant application procedure or application form.
Deadlines: None.

Restrictions

Grants are not made to individuals.

Corporate Officials

William H. Kerlin, Jr.: chairman PRIM CORP EMPL chairman: Graham Engineering Corp.

Foundation Officials

William H. Kerlin, Jr.: trustee (see above)

Grants Analysis

Disclosure Period: fiscal year ending June 30, 1999
Total Grants: $1,699,485*
Number of Grants: 51
Average Grant: $33,323
Highest Grant: $385,000
Typical Range: $10,000 to $50,000
***Note:** Giving excludes United Way.

Recent Grants

Note: Grants derived from fiscal 2001 Form 990.

Library-Related

2,000	Kaltreider Benfer Library, Red Lion, PA -- capital campaign

General

1,003,467	Burke Mountain Academy, East Burke, VT -- capital fund
365,000	Babson College, Babson Park, MA
168,671	Burke Mountain Academy, East Burke, VT -- scholarship fund
151,322	Burke Mountain Academy, East Burke, VT
100,000	University of Michigan, Ann Arbor, MI -- for Sam Graham Trust Fund
60,000	Strand Capital Performing Arts Center, York, PA
58,500	United Way of York County, York, PA
40,000	Penn State, York, PA -- for scholarship fund
25,000	Squam Lake Association, Holderness, NH -- capital campaign
12,850	Junior Achievement, York, PA

GRAHAM FOUNDATION FOR ADVANCED STUDIES IN THE FINE ARTS

Giving Contact

Richard Solomon, Director
4 West Burton Place
Chicago, IL 60610-1416
Phone: (312)787-4071
E-mail: info@grahamfoundation.org
Web: http://www.grahamfoundation.org

Description

Founded: 1956
EIN: 362356089
Organization Type: General Purpose Foundation
Giving Locations: internationally; nationally.
Grant Types: Award, Conference/Seminar, Fellowship, Project, Research.

Donor Information

Founder: The foundation was established in 1956 by a bequest from Ernest R. Graham (1866-1936), a Chicago architect. Under the guidance of Daniel Burnham, Mr. Graham was the principal assistant in overseeing construction of the 1893 World's Columbian Exhibition and later was associated with the D. H. Burnham & Co. architectural firm. After Mr. Burnham's death in 1912, Graham built the company into one of the nation's largest designers of railroad stations, banks, office buildings, museums, department stores, theaters, and post offices. Ernest Graham died during the Depression, leaving his estate severely undervalued. It took 20 years for his associate and executor, the late Charles F. Murphy, to rebuild the estate and begin the foundation.

Financial Summary

Total Giving: $1,345,845 (2001); $1,341,642 (2000); $940,247 (1998)

Giving Analysis: Giving for 2001 includes: foundation gifts to individuals ($459,185); 2000: foundation gifts to individuals ($454,465); 1998: foundation scholarships ($425,529) foundation ($514,718)

Assets: $35,000,000 (2002 approx); $38,186,292 (2001); $39,423,718 (2000)

Gifts Received: $5,000 (2001); $9,431 (1998); $15,000 (1992). Note: In 1998, contributions were received from Bright New City.

Typical Recipients

Arts & Humanities: Art History, Arts Appreciation, Arts Associations & Councils, Arts Centers, Arts Festivals, Arts Funds, Arts Institutes, Community Arts, Ethnic & Folk Arts, Film & Video, Arts & Humanities-General, Historic Preservation, History & Archaeology, Libraries, Literary Arts, Museums/Galleries, Performing Arts, Visual Arts

Civic & Public Affairs: African American Affairs, Botanical Gardens/Parks, Clubs, Economic Development, Civic & Public Affairs-General, Housing, Municipalities/Towns, Philanthropic Organizations, Professional & Trade Associations, Public Policy, Urban & Community Affairs, Women's Affairs

Education: Arts/Humanities Education, Business Education, Colleges & Universities, Continuing Education, Continuing Education, Engineering/Technological Education, Education-General, International Exchange, International Studies, Journalism/Media Education, Minority Education, Private Education (Precollege), Religious Education, Social Sciences Education, Student Aid

Environment: Environment-General

Health: Health Organizations

International: Foreign Arts Organizations, Foreign Educational Institutions, International Development, International Environmental Issues

Religion: Jewish Causes

Social Services: Senior Services, Social Services-General

Application Procedures

Initial Contact: A written proposal should be sent to the foundation. There is no formal application form.

Application Requirements: The application should succinctly specify the grant request's objectives and the applicant's qualifications. All applications should have a first-page summary sheet with the following information: project title; name, address, telephone number, and e-mail address of applicant and names of principal project participants; abstract of 150 words or less describing project; specific amount (in U.S. dollars) sought from foundation; anticipated final products of project; names of people from whom letters of support have been requested; and a list of other funding sources being approached and an indication of the status of those applications.

In addition to the summary sheet, applicants should supply the following: proposal succinctly describing purpose, audience, and outcome of project and addressing applicant's relevant background and capacity to accomplish project; career resumes of principal participants and background information on applying institution; work plan and schedule including applicant's plans for dissemination of completed work; budget, including cost components of total project and identifying other potential sources of support (do not include overhead or fringe benefits); letters from three

references knowledgeable in area of project (references should assess worthiness of applicant and project and submit letter in confidence directly to foundation); supplemental information, including visual information, when appropriate; and IRS determination letter.

Deadlines: Applications should be postmarked no later than January 15 and July 15. Only reference letters postmarked up to 15 days after application deadline will be accepted. Deadline for the Carter Manny Award is March 15.

Review Process: Applications are considered twice a year. Notification of the decision on the proposal is usually made within 150 days.

Notes: The foundation will not accept applications or letters by fax or e-mail. If possible, use type no smaller than 10 points in application material.

Restrictions

Typically, grants are not made for endowments, operating expenses, construction or other capital expenditures, architectural fees for construction or renovation, or direct scholarships to students in pursuit of a degree. (However, doctoral candidates are eligible for the Carter Manny Award.) Grants are typically reserved for the early stages of a project.

Additional Information

Grants to individuals do not exceed $10,000. If a large sum of money is requested, other sources of funding should be included. In addition to making grants, the foundation conducts lectures and exhibits. The foundation also reports that it makes its Madlener House available to other organizations, at a nominal fee, for activities that relate to the foundation's purposes and do not conflict with its schedule. Applicants seeking permission to use the house should apply in writing well in advance of the date desired and must comply with strict rules governing use of the building.

Publications: Annual Report; Guidelines

Foundation Officials

Irwin J. Askow: vice president, trustee PRIM CORP EMPL secretary, director: Allied World Travel Inc.

Thomas H. Beeby: trustee B 1941. ED Yale University MS (1962-1965). PRIM CORP EMPL partner: Hammond, Beeby Rupert, Ainge.

Miles Lee Berger: director B Chicago, IL 1930. ED Brown University (1952). PRIM CORP EMPL chairman: Berger Financial Services Corp. CORP AFFIL chairman: Midtown Bank Chicago; vice chairman: Heitman Finance Ltd.; director: Innkeepers, Inc.; vice chairman: Columbia National Bank Chicago; director: Franklin Holding. NONPR AFFIL member: Society Real Estate Appraisers; member: Society Real Estate Counsellors; member: American Institute of Real Estate Appraisers.

Sally A. Kitt Chappell: trustee PRIM NONPR EMPL professor: DePaul University.

Roberta Feldman: trustee PRIM NONPR EMPL assoc vice chancellor academic aff: University of Illinois, Chicago.

Henry Kuehn: trustee

Carter Hugh Manny, Jr.: director emeritus B Michigan City, IN November 16, 1918. ED Harvard University AB (1941); Illinois Institute of Technology BS (1948). NONPR AFFIL member advisory committee architecture: Art Institute of Chicago; member: Phi Beta Kappa; fellow: American Institute Architects. CLUB AFFIL Tavern Club; Michigan City Yacht Club; Pottawattomie Country Club; Arts Club; Cliff Dwellers Club.

James Nagle: trustee B 1933. ED University of Illinois BSME (1956). PRIM CORP EMPL president: Nagle Pumps Inc.

John I. Schlossman: trustee B Chicago, IL 1931. ED University of Minnesota BA (1953); University of Minnesota BArch (1955); Massachusetts Institute of Technology MArch (1956). PRIM CORP EMPL principal: Loebl, Schlossman & Hackl. NONPR AFFIL architectural Society of Art Institute Chicago; trustee: Merit

Music Program Inc.; fellow: American Institute Architects. CLUB AFFIL Arts Club; Tavern Club.

John James Schornack: trustee B Chicago, IL 1930. ED Loyola University BS (1951); Northwestern University MBA (1956); Harvard University Graduate School of Business Administration (1969). PRIM CORP EMPL chairman: Binks Sames Corp. CORP AFFIL director: Wintrust Finance Corp.; director: North Shore Bancorp Inc.; director: Binks James Corp. NONPR AFFIL chairman, member: Midwest-Japan Association; trustee: Saint Francis Hospital; trustee: Kohl Childrens Museum; member: Illinois Certified Public Accountant Society; member: Japan American Society; trustee: Chicago Symphony Orchestra; trustee: Graham Foundation; trustee: Catholic Theological Union; member: American Institute of Certified Public Accountants; chairman, trustee: Barat College; member: American Accounting Association. CLUB AFFIL Tavern Club; Glen View Golf Club; Ocean Club; Economic Club; 410 Club; Chicago Club.

Patricia Snyder: admin

Richard Solomon: director

Benjamin Horace Weese: president, trustee B Evanston, IL 1929. ED Harvard University BArch (1951); Ecole des Beaux Arts (1956); Harvard University MArch (1957). PRIM CORP EMPL principal: Weese Langley Weese Ltd. NONPR AFFIL co-founder, president: Glessner House; member: National Council Architectural Registration Boards; fellow: American Institute Architects; co-founder, president: Chicago Architects Foundation.

Robert A. Wislow: trustee B 1945. PRIM CORP EMPL chairman: U.S. Equities Realty Inc. CORP AFFIL chairman: Load Link Inc.

Grants Analysis

Disclosure Period: calendar year ending 2001

Total Grants: $886,660*

Number of Grants: 52

Average Grant: $15,425*

Highest Grant: $100,000

Lowest Grant: $2,500

Typical Range: $5,000 to $25,000

*Note: Giving excludes gifts to individuals. Average grant figure excludes highest grant.

Recent Grants

Note: Grants derived from 2001 Form 990.

General

100,000	Chicago Architecture Foundation, Chicago, IL
55,000	Society of Architectural Historians, Philadelphia, PA -- buildings of the state book series
50,000	Center for American Places -- center books on Chicago and Environs
46,500	2001 Carter Manny Awards, Chicago, IL -- Ph.D. dissertation assistance
46,000	N E A, washington, DC -- graham fellow in federal service
37,488	Graham Lectures and Exhibitions
30,000	Chicago Cultural Center Foundation, Chicago, IL -- book support
25,000	Archeworks, Chicago, IL -- investigation
25,000	Auburn University, Auburn, AL
25,000	Business and Professional People for the Public Interest, Chicago, IL -- Chicago public schools design competition

PHILIP L. GRAHAM FUND

Giving Contact

Candice C. Bryant, President
1150 15th Street, Northwest
Washington, DC 20071
Phone: (202)334-6640
Fax: (202)334-4498
E-mail: plgfund@washpost.com

Description

Founded: 1963
EIN: 526051781
Organization Type: General Purpose Foundation
Giving Locations: DC: Washington including metropolitan area
Grant Types: Award, Capital, Emergency, General Support, Project.

Financial Summary

Total Giving: $5,000,000 (2003 approx); $5,112,500 (2002); $5,033,000 (2001)
Giving Analysis: Giving for 1998 includes: foundation scholarships ($35,000)
Assets: $107,235 (2002); $98,000,000 (2001 approx); $106,604,466 (2000)

Typical Recipients

Arts & Humanities: Arts Associations & Councils, Arts Centers, Arts Festivals, Arts Funds, Arts Outreach, Ballet, Dance, Ethnic & Folk Arts, Arts & Humanities-General, History & Archaeology, Libraries, Museums/Galleries, Music, Opera, Performing Arts, Public Broadcasting, Theater, Visual Arts
Civic & Public Affairs: African American Affairs, Asian American Affairs, Botanical Gardens/Parks, Community Foundations, Economic Development, Economic Policy, Employment/Job Training, First Amendment Issues, Civic & Public Affairs-General, Hispanic Affairs, Housing, Municipalities/Towns, Nonprofit Management, Professional & Trade Associations, Public Policy, Urban & Community Affairs, Women's Affairs
Education: Afterschool/Enrichment Programs, Arts/Humanities Education, Business Education, Colleges & Universities, Education Associations, Education Reform, Elementary Education (Public), Environmental Education, Education-General, International Studies, Journalism/Media Education, Leadership Training, Legal Education, Literacy, Minority Education, Preschool Education, Private Education (Precollege), Public Education (Precollege), Science/Mathematics Education, Secondary Education (Private), Special Education, Student Aid, Vocational & Technical Education
Environment: Environment-General, Watershed
Health: AIDS/HIV, Cancer, Children's Health/Hospitals, Clinics/Medical Centers, Diabetes, Emergency/Ambulance Services, Geriatric Health, Health Organizations, Heart, Home-Care Services, Hospices, Hospitals, Long-Term Care, Mental Health, Outpatient Health Care, Prenatal Health Issues, Public Health, Transplant Networks/Donor Banks
International: Foreign Arts Organizations, Human Rights, International Affairs, International Development, International Organizations, International Relations
Religion: Churches, Jewish Causes, Ministries, Religious Organizations, Religious Welfare
Science: Science Museums, Scientific Centers & Institutes, Scientific Research
Social Services: Animal Protection, At-Risk Youth, Child Welfare, Community Centers, Community Service Organizations, Counseling, Day Care, Delinquency & Criminal Rehabilitation, Domestic Violence, Family Planning, Family Services, Food/Clothing Distribution, People with Disabilities, Recreation & Athletics, Scouts, Senior Services, Shelters/Homelessness, Social Services-General, Substance Abuse, United Funds/United Ways, Volunteer Services, YMCA/YWCA/YMHA/YWHA, Youth Organizations

Application Procedures

Initial Contact: Request recent summary of grants. If applicant's needs falls within the Fund's areas of interest, send an original and two copies of a proposal letter of ten pages or less.
Application Requirements: The letter of proposal should describe the organization, its purpose, and the people it benefits. Applicants should also include a description of the project, benefits, costs, amount requested, other funding sources, the organization's qualifications to accomplish its goals, potential future support (if relevant), and a summary of prior support received from the Fund. Applicants also should submit a recent audited financial statement or IRS Form 990 for the most recent fiscal year, a current budget, project budget (including expected sources of funding), a copy of the organization's IRS letter of tax-exempt status, and a list of the organization's board of directors. Proposals should not be bound. The Fund accepts, but does not require, the WRAG common grant application form.
Deadlines: Proposals must be received by February 1, May 1, August 1, and October 15 for review at the next meeting.
Review Process: The fund's trustees meet four times a year to make funding decisions.
Evaluative Criteria: Preference is given to proposals that address one-time needs of organizations rather than general operating or program support.
Decision Notification: Organizations will be notified of decisions within 120 days of each application deadline.

Restrictions

Grants are not made to individuals; political, religious, or lobbying activities; membership organizations; for advocacy or litigation; research; conferences, workshops, or seminars; travel expense; benefits or fundraising events; courtesy advertising; national or international organizations; medical care; production of films or publications; annual giving campaigns, independent schools; post-secondary education institutions; or event sponsorships. The Fund generally makes grants only to organizations in the Washington, DC metropolitan area, and only to organizations that have been ruled to be tax-exempt under Section 501(c)(3) of the Internal Revenue Code, and that are not private foundations.

Additional Information

The fund accepts but does not require the WRAG common grant application format. The fund prefers proposals that address specific, special, primarily one-time needs. Proposals should not be bound.
Publications: History and Proposal Guidelines; Summary of Grants

Foundation Officials

Mary Bellor: president, secretary
Martin Cohen: trustee, treasurer B New York, NY 1932. ED Brown University AB (1953); University of Pennsylvania Wharton School MBA (1957). PRIM CORP EMPL vice president, director: Washington Post Co. NONPR AFFIL president: Frenchmans Creek Country Club. CLUB AFFIL Woodmont Country Club.
Donald Edward Graham: trustee B Baltimore, MD 1945. ED Harvard University BA (1966). PRIM CORP EMPL chairman, chief executive officer, director, publisher: Washington Post Co. NONPR AFFIL member: American Antiquarian Society.
Theodore M. Lutz: trustee
Vincent Emory Reed: trustee B Saint Louis, MO 1928. ED West Virginia State College BS (1952); Howard University MA (1965); University of Pennsylvania Wharton School (1969); West Virginia State College HLD (1977). PRIM NONPR EMPL assistant secretary elementary & secondary education: U.S. Department of Education. CORP AFFIL director: Home Federal Savings & Loan Association. NONPR AFFIL volunteer: Southeast Youth Football Association; director: Washington YMCA; volunteer: Southeast Boys Club; member: National Education Association; member: Phi Delta Kappa; member: National Association School Security Officers; member: National Association Secondary School Principals; member: NAACP; staff member: District of Columbia Public Schools; member: Kappa Alpha Psi; member: District of Columbia Parent Teacher Association; member: District of Columbia PTA Washington Schools; director: District of Columbia Goodwill Industries; member: American Association School Administrations; member: American Society Business Officals; director: 12 Neediest Kids. CLUB AFFIL Kiwanis Club; Pigskin Club.

Grants Analysis

Disclosure Period: calendar year ending 2001
Total Grants: $5,033,000*
Number of Grants: 194
Average Grant: $25,943
Highest Grant: $300,000
Lowest Grant: $2,500
Typical Range: $5,000 to $50,000 and $100,000 to $150,000
*Note: Grants analysis provided by foundation.

Recent Grants

Note: Grants derived from 2001 Form 990.

General

300,000	District of Columbia College Access Program, Washington, DC -- operating support
100,000	Alfred Friendly Foundation, Washington, DC -- increase endowment
100,000	Bread for the City, Washington, DC -- build new comprehensive center
100,000	Federal City Council, Washington, DC -- District of Columbia School Leadership Project
100,000	Funds for the Capital Visitor Center, Washington, DC -- support cultural and educational programming
100,000	National Capital Area Council Boy Scouts of America, Bethesda, MD -- support construction of Marriott Scout Service Center
100,000	Round House Theater, Silver Spring, MD -- support "Scripting the Future" capital campaign
100,000	Wolftrap Foundation, Vienna, VA -- "The Campaign for Wolf Trap"
90,000	Community Foundation for the National Capital Region, Washington, DC -- Survivor's Fund
75,000	Boys and Girls Clubs of Greater Washington, Silver Springs, MD -- capital improvements

CHARLES M. AND MARY D. GRANT FOUNDATION

Giving Contact

Hildy J. Simmons, Vice President
c/o JP Morgan Chase Bank
60 Wall Street
New York, NY 10260
Phone: (212)648-9673

Description

Founded: 1967
EIN: 136264329
Organization Type: Private Foundation
Giving Locations: Southeastern U.S.A.
Grant Types: Capital, General Support, Operating Expenses, Project, Seed Money.

Donor Information

Founder: the late Mary D. Grant

Financial Summary

Total Giving: $510,000 (2001); $510,000 (2000); $450,000 (1999 approx)
Assets: $9,607,265 (2001); $10,492,573 (2000); $10,255,638 (1998)

Typical Recipients

Arts & Humanities: Libraries

Civic & Public Affairs: Botanical Gardens/Parks, Civil Rights, Economic Development, Civic & Public Affairs-General, Legal Aid, Nonprofit Management, Philanthropic Organizations, Public Policy, Rural Affairs, Urban & Community Affairs, Women's Affairs

Education: Afterschool/Enrichment Programs, Literacy

Environment: Environment-General

Health: Long-Term Care, Medical Research, Public Health

Social Services: Child Welfare, Community Centers, Community Service Organizations, Domestic Violence, Food/Clothing Distribution, Homes, Youth Organizations

Application Procedures

Initial Contact: Send a brief letter of inquiry with pertinent financial information.

Application Requirements: Include information on a description of organization, purpose of funds sought, recently audited financial statement, and proof of tax-exempt status.

Deadlines: None.

Restrictions

Grants are given for education, health, and welfare in the U.S. Does not support individuals or provide individual scholarships or loans.

Additional Information

Trust(s): JP Morgan Chase Bank

Grants Analysis

Disclosure Period: calendar year ending 2001

Total Grants: $510,000

Number of Grants: 17

Average Grant: $30,000

Highest Grant: $50,000

Lowest Grant: $10,000

Typical Range: $20,000 to $40,000

Recent Grants

Note: Grants derived from 2000 Form 990.

Library-Related

40,000	Yazoo Library Association, Yazoo City, MS -- restoration of the B.S. Ricks Memorial Library

General

50,000	Partnership for After School Education, New York, NY -- FAST PASE
40,000	ALT Consulting, Memphis, TN -- Technology Project
40,000	Handmade In American Foundation, Asheville, NC -- for the Stecoah Weavers and Trash to Treasures business incubators
40,000	World Wildlife Fund, Washington, DC -- Southeastern Rivers and Streams Program
35,000	Girls Incorporated, New York, NY -- economic literacy initiative
35,000	Madison County Children's Action Network, Berea, KY -- child care initiative
35,000	Quitman County Development Organization, Marks, MS -- Youth Development Program
30,000	Dekalb Economic Opportunity Authority, Inc., Decatur, GA -- expansion of Project Phoenix
30,000	Foundation for the Mid-South, Jackson, MS -- Mid South Collaborative for Nonprofit Development
30,000	Vanderbilt University Center for Health Services, Nashville, TN -- Maternal Infant Health Outreach Worker Project

GARLAND AND AGNES TAYLOR GRAY FOUNDATION

Giving Contact

Darcy Oman, President
7325 Beaufont Springs Drive, Suite 210
Richmond, VA 23225
Phone: (804)330-7400

Description

EIN: 546071867

Organization Type: Private Foundation

Giving Locations: VA: Waverly including surrounding area

Grant Types: Capital, Endowment, General Support, Multiyear/Continuing Support, Operating Expenses, Scholarship, Seed Money.

Donor Information

Founder: the late Garland Gray

Financial Summary

Total Giving: $1,025,759 (2001); $1,379,081 (1999); $1,100,583 (1998)

Giving Analysis: Giving for 2001 includes: foundation grants to United Way ($3,000) 1999: foundation grants to United Way ($13,000)

Assets: $20,600,068 (2001); $24,132,463 (1999); $22,058,292 (1998)

Gifts Received: $2,478 (1996); $3,577 (1994). Note: In 1996, contributions were received from Thomas C. Gordon, Jr.

Typical Recipients

Arts & Humanities: Arts Appreciation, Arts Centers, Historic Preservation, History & Archaeology, Libraries, Museums/Galleries

Civic & Public Affairs: Clubs, Community Foundations, Economic Development, Employment/Job Training, Civic & Public Affairs-General, Hispanic Affairs, Housing, Municipalities/Towns, Philanthropic Organizations, Urban & Community Affairs

Education: Agricultural Education, Colleges & Universities, Education Funds, Environmental Education, Education-General, Medical Education, Private Education (Precollege), Public Education (Precollege), Science/Mathematics Education, Student Aid

Environment: Environment-General

Health: Cancer, Clinics/Medical Centers, Health Organizations, Hospitals, Medical Research, Multiple Sclerosis, Research/Studies Institutes, Single-Disease Health Associations

International: International Organizations

Religion: Churches, Religious Welfare

Science: Science Museums

Social Services: Animal Protection, At-Risk Youth, Child Welfare, Community Centers, Community Service Organizations, Crime Prevention, Emergency Relief, Family Services, Homes, People with Disabilities, Recreation & Athletics, Scouts, United Funds/United Ways, YMCA/YWCA/YMHA/YWHA, Youth Organizations

Application Procedures

Initial Contact: Send a brief letter of inquiry.

Deadlines: None.

Restrictions

Foundation does not support individuals or "start-up" organizations.

Additional Information

The Garland and Agnes Taylor Gray Foundation has become a supporting organization of the Community Foundation, a public charity.

Foundation Officials

William Birch Douglass, III: secretary B Richmond, VA 1943. ED Hampden-Sydney College BA (1965); University of Richmond LLB (1968); Harvard University LLM (1969). PRIM CORP EMPL partner: McGuire, Woods, Battle & Boothe. CORP AFFIL director: Flippo Lumber Corp.; director: Ted Lansing Corp.; director: Air Conditioning Suppliers; director: Carpenter Co. NONPR AFFIL trustee: Hampden-Sydney College; associate: University Richmond; fellow: American College Tax Counsel; fellow: American College Trust & Estate Counsel.

Charles F. Duff: vice president, trustee

C. Taylor Everett: trustee

Thomas Christian Gordon, Jr.: assistant secretary, trustee B Richmond, VA July 14, 1915. ED University of Virginia BS (1936); University of Virginia LLB (1938). NONPR AFFIL trustee: Childrens Hospital Richmond; member: Virginia Bar Association; member: American Bar Association; fellow: American Bar Foundation.

Bruce B. Gray: assistant treasurer, trustee

Elmon T. Gray: president, treasurer, trustee

Garland Gray, II: assistant secretary, trustee

Wallace Stettinius: vice president, trustee B New York, NY 1933. ED University of Virginia BA (1955); University of Virginia MBA (1959). PRIM CORP EMPL chairman, chief executive officer, director: Cadmus Communications Corp. CORP AFFIL director: Chesapeake Corp.

Thomas H. Tullidge: vice president, trustee

Grants Analysis

Disclosure Period: calendar year ending 2001

Total Grants: $1,022,759*

Number of Grants: 56

Average Grant: $15,868*

Highest Grant: $150,000

Lowest Grant: $500

Typical Range: $1,000 to $10,000 and $20,000 to $50,000

*Note: Giving excludes United Way. Average grant excludes highest grant.

Recent Grants

Note: Grants derived from 2001 Form 990.

Library-Related

75,000	Friends of the Waverly Public Library, Waverly, VA

General

150,000	Suffolk Center for Cultural Arts, Suffolk, VA
107,259	Community Foundation, Richmond, VA
104,500	Stuart Hall School, Staunton, VA
87,000	Collegiate Schools, Richmond, VA
55,000	YMCA of Greater Richmond, Richmond, VA
50,000	Horizon Health Services, Ivor, VA
50,000	Virginia Home, Richmond, VA
49,500	Randolph-Macon College, Ashland, VA
40,000	Southeast 4-H Educational Center, Wakefield, VA
22,000	University of Richmond, Richmond, VA

GREAT-WEST LIFE AND ANNUITY INSURANCE CO.

Company Headquarters

PO Box 1700
Denver, CO 80201
Web: http://www.gwl.com

Company Description

Assets: US$28.811 billion (2002)

Employees: 8160 (2002)

SIC(s): 6311 Life Insurance, 6321 Accident & Health Insurance.

Parent Company: Great-West Life Assurance Co., 100 Osborne St. N., Winnipeg, MB, Canada

Operating Locations
Great-West Life & Annuity Insurance Co. (CO--Englewood); Great-West Life Assurance Co. (CO--Englewood); Great-West Realty Investments (CO--Englewood); GWL Properties (CO--Englewood)

Nonmonetary Support
Type: Donated Equipment; In-kind Services; Loaned Employees; Loaned Executives

Giving Contact
John Clayton, Vice President, Corporate Services
8515 East Orchard Road
Englewood, CO 80111
Phone: (303)737-3000

Description
Organization Type: Corporate Giving Program
Giving Locations: headquarters and operating locations.
Grant Types: General Support, Research, Scholarship.

Typical Recipients
Arts & Humanities: Arts Associations & Councils, Arts Centers, Community Arts, Dance, Libraries, Museums/Galleries, Music, Performing Arts
Civic & Public Affairs: Women's Affairs
Education: Business Education, Colleges & Universities, Economic Education, Minority Education, Student Aid
Health: Health Policy/Cost Containment, Hospitals, Medical Research, Mental Health
Social Services: Community Service Organizations, Domestic Violence, Family Services, People with Disabilities, Substance Abuse, United Funds/United Ways, Youth Organizations

Application Procedures
Initial Contact: Company does not have a formal application form, but requests must be made in writing.
Application Requirements: Include a brief description of organization and its purpose; amount requested; specific purpose for which funds are being solicited; the total cost of program or project and the amount that will be spent in the Denver area; list of current contributors and amounts; copy of IRS tax-exemption letter of determination; list of officers and directors; copy of organization's most recent financial statement and annual report; and reasons why you believe Great-West Life should support your organization.
Review Process: Request for support are normally processed within 2 to 3 months from the date of receipt.
Decision Notification: All applicants are notified of the company's decision.

Restrictions
Contributions are not made to political organizations, veterans organizations, labor or fraternal organizations, individuals, or religious organizations for purposes of religious advocacy.

Additional Information
Company gives approximately $125,000 in nonmonetary support each year. This amount is not included in the contributions budget or figures above.
Publications: Contributions Policy and Procedures Sheet

Corporate Officials
William T. McCallum: president, chief executive officer chief financial officer PRIM CORP EMPL president, chief executive officer: Great-West Life Assurance Co.

Douglas Wooden: senior vice president, chief financial officer PRIM CORP EMPL senior vice president, chief financial officer: Great-West Life Assurance Co.

Grants Analysis
Typical Range: $500 to $1,000

GREDE FOUNDRIES

Company Headquarters
1320 S. 1st St.
Milwaukee, WI 53204
Web: http://www.grede.com

Company Description
Revenue: US$591 million (2001)
Employees: 4500 (2001)
SIC(s): 3321 Gray & Ductile Iron Foundries, 3325 Steel Foundries Nec.

Grede Foundation

Giving Contact
Burleigh E. Jacobs, President
9898 West Bluemound Road
Milwaukee, WI 53226-0499
Phone: (414)257-3600

Description
EIN: 396042977
Organization Type: Corporate Foundation
Giving Locations: WI
Grant Types: General Support, Scholarship.

Financial Summary
Total Giving: $168,445 (2001); $205,077 (2000); $322,505 (1999)
Giving Analysis: Giving for 2001 includes: foundation scholarships ($22,000); foundation grants to United Way ($31,500); foundation ($114,945); 2000: foundation scholarships ($22,000); foundation grants to United Way ($38,000); foundation ($145,077); 1999: foundation scholarships ($23,050); foundation grants to United Way ($30,500); foundation ($268,955);
Assets: $205,617 (2001); $376,172 (2000); $392,738 (1999)
Gifts Received: $165,983 (2000); $118,000 (1999); $406,000 (1998). Note: Contributions received from Grede Foundries.

Typical Recipients
Arts & Humanities: Arts Associations & Councils, Libraries, Museums/Galleries, Performing Arts
Civic & Public Affairs: Clubs, Community Foundations, Economic Development, Economic Policy, Civic & Public Affairs-General, Hispanic Affairs, Housing, Legal Aid, Professional & Trade Associations, Public Policy, Urban & Community Affairs
Education: Arts/Humanities Education, Colleges & Universities, Community & Junior Colleges, Education Funds, Engineering/Technological Education, Education-General, Medical Education, Private Education (Precollege), Public Education (Precollege), Science/Mathematics Education, Secondary Education (Public), Student Aid, Vocational & Technical Education
Environment: Environment-General
Health: Cancer, Children's Health/Hospitals, Clinics/Medical Centers, Hospitals, Medical Research, Nursing Services, Single-Disease Health Associations, Speech & Hearing, Transplant Networks/Donor Banks
Religion: Religious Welfare
Science: Science Museums, Scientific Centers & Institutes
Social Services: Child Welfare, Community Centers, Community Service Organizations, Family Services,

People with Disabilities, Recreation & Athletics, Senior Services, United Funds/United Ways, YMCA/YWCA/YMHA/YWHA, Youth Organizations

Application Procedures
Initial Contact: Call or write to request materials. Request scholarship applications from Jan Winberg (414-257-3600).
Deadlines: Scholarship applications are due December 31 of the year prior to expected enrollment.

Restrictions
Scholarships are awarded only to high school seniors with a parent who is a regular employee of Grede Foundries, Inc or its subsidiaries, and has been employed as such for at least two years prior to application. Children and grandchildren of the Grede Foundation, Inc. board of directors are not eligible.

Additional Information
Publications: Application Form

Corporate Officials
Bruce E. Jacobs: president, chief executive officer B Milwaukee, WI 1947. ED University of Wisconsin (1969). PRIM CORP EMPL president, chief executive officer: Grede Foundries. CORP AFFIL owner: Watermark Press; owner: Watermark West Rare Books; owner: Watermark Books.

Foundation Officials
Bruce E. Jacobs: vice president, director (see above)

Grants Analysis
Disclosure Period: calendar year ending 2001
Total Grants: $114,945*
Number of Grants: 47
Average Grant: $2,446
Highest Grant: $10,000
Lowest Grant: $100
Typical Range: $100 to $10,000
*Note: Giving excludes scholarships, and United Way.

Recent Grants
Note: Grants derived from 2001 Form 990.

Library-Related

5,000	Milwaukee Public Library Foundation, Milwaukee, WI

General

25,000	Milwaukee Rescue Mission, Milwaukee, WI
20,000	United Way, Milwaukee, WI
10,000	Blood Center Research Foundation, Milwaukee, WI
7,000	YMCA Milwaukee Youth Village, Milwaukee, WI
6,000	Bruce Guadalupe Community School, Milwaukee, WI
6,000	Foundry Educational Foundation, Chicago, IL
6,000	United Way, WI
5,000	Kiwanis Club, Wauwatosa, WI
5,000	Salvation Army, Milwaukee, WI
5,000	Wittenbraker YMCA, New Castle, IN

ALLEN P. AND JOSEPHINE B. GREEN FOUNDATION

Giving Contact
Walter G. Staley, Jr., Secretary, Treasurer & Director
Allen P. and Josephine B. Green Foundation
PO Box 523
Mexico, MO 65265
Phone: (573)581-5568

E-mail: nrcox@greenfdn.org
Web: http://www.greenfdn.org

Description

Founded: 1941
EIN: 436030135
Organization Type: Private Foundation
Giving Locations: MO: Mexico including surrounding area
Grant Types: Capital, Conference/Seminar, Emergency, Endowment, Fellowship, Project, Scholarship, Seed Money.

Donor Information

Founder: the late Allen P. Green, the late Mrs. Allen P. Green

Financial Summary

Total Giving: $633,800 (2001); $730,000 (2000); $722,441 (1999)
Giving Analysis: Giving for 2001 includes: foundation scholarships ($5,000)
Assets: $12,978,458 (2001); $14,651,740 (2000); $15,960,747 (1999)

Typical Recipients

Arts & Humanities: Historic Preservation, History & Archaeology, Libraries, Museums/Galleries, Opera, Performing Arts, Public Broadcasting, Theater
Civic & Public Affairs: Botanical Gardens/Parks, Clubs, Community Foundations, Employment/Job Training, Housing, Safety, Urban & Community Affairs
Education: Agricultural Education, Colleges & Universities, Community & Junior Colleges, Elementary Education (Public), Environmental Education, Faculty Development, Education-General, Literacy, Medical Education, Preschool Education, Private Education (Precollege), Public Education (Precollege), Religious Education, Science/Mathematics Education, Special Education, Student Aid, Vocational & Technical Education
Environment: Environment-General, Resource Conservation
Health: Arthritis, Cancer, Children's Health/Hospitals, Clinics/Medical Centers, Diabetes, Eyes/Blindness, Hospices, Medical Rehabilitation, Mental Health, Preventive Medicine/Wellness Organizations, Public Health, Speech & Hearing
Religion: Bible Study/Translation, Churches, Religious Organizations, Religious Welfare
Science: Scientific Centers & Institutes
Social Services: Animal Protection, At-Risk Youth, Child Abuse, Child Welfare, Community Service Organizations, Day Care, Family Services, Food/Clothing Distribution, People with Disabilities, Recreation & Athletics, Scouts, Senior Services, Social Services-General, Substance Abuse, Veterans, YMCA/YWCA/YMHA/YWHA, Youth Organizations, Youth Organizations

Application Procedures

Initial Contact: Contact foundation for application guidelines.
Deadlines: Contact foundation for annual deadlines.

Restrictions

Does not support individuals, scholarships, or fellowships.

Additional Information

Publications: Annual Report

Foundation Officials

Arthur D. Bond, III: president, director
Senator Christopher Samuel Bond: director B Saint Louis, MO 1939. ED Princeton University BA (1960); University of Virginia LLB (1963). PRIM CORP EMPL senior ator: MO. NONPR AFFIL chairman: Midwestern Governments Conf; chairman: Rep Governments Association.
Rev. Robert R. Collins: director

Carl D. Fuemmeler: vice president, director
Judge James F. McHenry: director
Robert E. McIntosh: assistant secretary, assistant treasurer, director
Walter G. Staley, Jr.: secretary, treasurer, director
Nancy G. White: director
George C. Willson, III: president, director
Robert A. Wood: director
Elizabeth Wood Knight: director

Grants Analysis

Disclosure Period: calendar year ending 2001
Total Grants: $628,800*
Number of Grants: 69
Average Grant: $9,113
Highest Grant: $27,000
Lowest Grant: $400
Typical Range: $2,000 to $20,000
*Note: Giving excludes scholarship.

Recent Grants

Note: Grants derived from 2001 Form 990.

General

27,000	Moberly Area Community College, Moberly, MO -- for computer network lab
22,000	NBA Gateways, St. Louis, MO -- for sprinkler system
20,000	City Academy, St. Louis, MO -- for third grade classroom
20,000	Fire Fighters Foundation of Missouri, Mexico, MO -- for new memorial statue
20,000	Independence Center, St. Louis, MO -- programs for individuals with mental illness
20,000	Mexico Athletic Booster Club, Mexico, MO -- for portable concession stand
20,000	Partnership for Youth, St. Louis, MO -- for Americorps St. Louis Partners Program
20,000	St. Charles Regional Child Assessment Center, Wentzville, MO -- equipment for abused victims
17,000	Northeast Community Services Agency, Inc., Mexico, MO -- for Alternative Sentencing Program
15,500	Handi-Shop, Mexico, MO -- for 1997 GMC box van

ROBERT AND SUSAN GREEN FOUNDATION

Giving Contact

Robert L. Green, President
2601 Mariposa St., Suite 100
San Francisco, CA 94110
Phone: (415)865-1700
Fax: (415)865-1700

Description

EIN: 943025003
Organization Type: Private Foundation
Giving Locations: CA
Grant Types: General Support.

Financial Summary

Total Giving: $203,434 (2000); $304,428 (1999); $224,723 (1998). Note: In 1998 and 1996 Giving includes United Way ($25,000).
Giving Analysis: Giving for 1999 includes: foundation grants to United Way ($25,000) 1998: foundation grants to United Way ($25,000)
Assets: $301,573 (2000); $440,236 (1999); $658,705 (1998)
Gifts Received: $43,224 (2000); $91,186 (1999); $75,000 (1996). Note: In 2000, contributions were received from John Doerr ($18,224) and Robert

Green ($25,000). In 1999, contributions were received from Mr. John Doerr. In 1996, contributions were received from Fidelity.

Typical Recipients

Arts & Humanities: Arts Associations & Councils, Arts Centers, Arts Institutes, Ethnic & Folk Arts, Arts & Humanities-General, Historic Preservation, Libraries, Museums/Galleries, Music, Opera, Public Broadcasting, Theater
Civic & Public Affairs: Civic & Public Affairs-General, Philanthropic Organizations, Public Policy, Women's Affairs
Education: Afterschool/Enrichment Programs, Business Education, Colleges & Universities, Education Funds, Elementary Education (Public), Education-General, Leadership Training, Medical Education, Private Education (Precollege), Public Education (Precollege), School Volunteerism, Secondary Education (Private), Secondary Education (Public), Student Aid
Environment: Environment-General, Wildlife Protection
Health: Cancer, Children's Health/Hospitals, Clinics/Medical Centers, Eyes/Blindness, Geriatric Health, Hospitals, Long-Term Care, Prenatal Health Issues, Public Health
International: International Affairs, Missionary/Religious Activities
Religion: Churches, Religion-General, Jewish Causes, Religious Welfare
Social Services: Child Abuse, Child Welfare, Community Service Organizations, Food/Clothing Distribution, Recreation & Athletics, Senior Services, United Funds/United Ways, Volunteer Services, Youth Organizations

Application Procedures

Initial Contact: Send a brief letter of inquiry and a full proposal in writing.
Deadlines: None.

Foundation Officials

Robert L. Green: president

Grants Analysis

Disclosure Period: calendar year ending 2000
Total Grants: $203,434*
Number of Grants: 37
Average Grant: $4,262*
Highest Grant: $50,000
Typical Range: $1,000 to $10,000
*Note: Giving excludes United Way. Average grant figure excludes highest grant.

Recent Grants

Note: Grants derived from 1999 Form 990.

Library-Related

1,000	Friends and Foundation of San Francisco Public Library, San Francisco, CA

General

91,186	Garfield Elementary School
77,813	San Francisco Museum of Modern Art, San Francisco, CA
25,000	United Way
22,000	San Francisco Day School, San Francisco, CA
18,114	American Conservatory Theater, San Francisco, CA
15,000	John Kerner Foundation
10,000	Chronicle Season of Sharing, San Francisco, CA
7,500	San Francisco School Volunteers, San Francisco, CA
5,000	Jewish Community Federation, San Francisco, CA
4,750	Opera House Theatre, Napa Valley, CA

ALBERT M. GREENFIELD FOUNDATION

Giving Contact
Priscilla Luce, President
PO Box 30267
Philadelphia, PA 19103
Phone: (215)333-8949

Description
Founded: 1953
EIN: 236050816
Organization Type: Private Foundation
Giving Locations: PA: Philadelphia including metropolitan area
Grant Types: General Support.

Donor Information
Founder: the late Albert M. Greenfield, the late Etelka J. Greenfield

Financial Summary
Total Giving: $556,918 (fiscal year ending August 31, 2001); $371,650 (fiscal 2000); $443,000 (fiscal 1999)
Assets: $9,924,198 (fiscal 2001); $11,083,193 (fiscal 2000); $10,987,694 (fiscal 1999)

Typical Recipients
Arts & Humanities: Arts Associations & Councils, Arts Centers, Arts Institutes, Arts Outreach, Ballet, Community Arts, Dance, History & Archaeology, Libraries, Museums/Galleries, Music, Theater
Civic & Public Affairs: Botanical Gardens/Parks, Economic Policy, Employment/Job Training, Legal Aid, Urban & Community Affairs, Zoos/Aquariums
Education: Arts/Humanities Education, Colleges & Universities, Community & Junior Colleges, Environmental Education, Education-General, Private Education (Precollege), Public Education (Precollege), Secondary Education (Public), Student Aid
Religion: Jewish Causes
Science: Science Museums
Social Services: Camps, Community Service Organizations, Domestic Violence, Family Planning, Recreation & Athletics, Recreation & Athletics, Shelters/Homelessness, Social Services-General, United Funds/United Ways, Youth Organizations

Application Procedures
Initial Contact: The foundation has no formal grant application procedure or application form.
Deadlines: None.

Additional Information
All awards reviewed on an individual basis. Awards are generally given to tax-exempt organizations.

Foundation Officials
Gustave G. Amsterdam: trustee
Debra DeLauro: secretary
Albert M. Greenfield, III: trustee
Bruce Harold Greenfield: trustee B Philadelphia, PA March 12, 1917. ED Duke University BA (1938); Yale University JD (1941). NONPR AFFIL member: Phi Beta Kappa; lecturer: Tulane University; trustee: Albert M Greenfield Foundation; lecturer: New York University; director: American Jewish Committee; lecturer: American University Tax Institute. CLUB AFFIL Yale Club.
Bernard M. Guth: trustee
Janet Guth: trustee
Derek G. Howard: trustee
Priscilla Luce: chairperson
Sarah E. Mark: trustee
Elizabeth M. Petrie: trustee
Julie G. Six: treasurer
Susan Torrance: assistant secretary
Elizabeth G. Zeidman: trustee

Grants Analysis
Disclosure Period: fiscal year ending August 31, 2001
Total Grants: $556,918
Number of Grants: 17
Average Grant: $29,807*
Highest Grant: $80,000
Lowest Grant: $5,000
Typical Range: $10,000 to $50,000
*Note: Average grant figure excludes highest grant.

Recent Grants
Note: Grants derived from 2000 Form 990.

Library-Related
10,000	Athenaeum of Philadelphia, Philadelphia, PA -- for book fund

General
51,650	Interfaith Council on the Holocaust, Philadelphia, PA -- for facing history and ourselves
50,000	Arden Theatre Company, Philadelphia, PA -- for Arden children's theatre
50,000	Franklin Institute, Philadelphia, PA -- for cutting edge gallery and cyberzone
44,500	Fairmount Park Commission, Philadelphia, PA -- for summer beautification project
29,000	Philadelphia Committee to End Homelessness, Philadelphia, PA -- to conduct study on best practices for homelessness
25,000	Wilma Theater, Philadelphia, PA -- for Camp Wilma
20,000	Partners Program, Philadelphia, PA -- for outdoor team building days
20,000	Richie Ashburn Baseball Foundation, Blue Bell, PA -- for free clinics to underprivileged children
18,500	Abraham Lincoln High School, Philadelphia, PA -- for summer beautification project
18,500	Swenson Arts and Technology, Philadelphia, PA -- for summer beautification project

GREENTREE FOUNDATION

Giving Contact
Richard Schaffer, President
400 Madison Avenue, Suite 1001
New York, NY 10017
Phone: (212)888-7755
Fax: (212)888-1574
E-mail: rschaffer@greentreefdn.org

Description
Founded: 1982
EIN: 133132117
Organization Type: Family Foundation
Giving Locations: NY: New York including metropolitan area
Grant Types: Project.

Donor Information
Founder: Established in 1982 by Betsey C. Whitney.

Financial Summary
Total Giving: $1,491,900 (2000); $748,000 (1998); $947,000 (1997)
Assets: $286,496,400 (2000); $107,055,496 (1998); $30,646,755 (1997)
Gifts Received: $157,880,676 (2000); $72,198,379 (1998); $401,936 (1997). Note: In 2000, contributions were received from the estate of Betsey Cushing Whitney ($156,276,260); John Hay Whitney Charitable Trust ($1,387,944); Sara Wilford ($113,160); and Kate Whitney ($103,312). In 1998, contributions were received from the estate of Betsey C. Whitney-Greentree and John Hay Whitney Charitable Trust.

Typical Recipients
Arts & Humanities: Arts Associations & Councils, Arts Centers, Arts Outreach, Community Arts, Dance, Ethnic & Folk Arts, Arts & Humanities-General, History & Archaeology, Libraries, Museums/Galleries, Music, Performing Arts, Public Broadcasting, Theater
Civic & Public Affairs: African American Affairs, Botanical Gardens/Parks, Clubs, Economic Development, Employment/Job Training, Civic & Public Affairs-General, Hispanic Affairs, Public Policy, Urban & Community Affairs, Women's Affairs
Education: Afterschool/Enrichment Programs, Arts/Humanities Education, Business Education, Colleges & Universities, Community & Junior Colleges, Education Funds, Education Reform, Elementary Education (Private), Education-General, International Exchange, Literacy, Medical Education, Minority Education, Private Education (Precollege), Public Education (Precollege), School Volunteerism, Science/Mathematics Education, Special Education, Student Aid
Environment: Air/Water Quality, Environment-General, Resource Conservation
Health: Hospitals, Mental Health, Research/Studies Institutes
Religion: Religious Welfare
Science: Scientific Centers & Institutes
Social Services: At-Risk Youth, Child Abuse, Child Welfare, Community Centers, Community Service Organizations, Counseling, Family Planning, Family Services, Food/Clothing Distribution, Scouts, Senior Services, Shelters/Homelessness, Social Services-General, Volunteer Services, YMCA/YWCA/YMHA/YWHA, Youth Organizations

Application Procedures
Initial Contact: Contact the foundation to request a grant application form.
Application Requirements: The form should be completed and submitted with a grant proposal, which should include a proposal summary, a narrative of no more than five pages, and attachments.
The proposal summary should summarize in a short paragraph the purpose of the organization, explaining the purpose for requesting a grant, the proposed outcomes and achievements, and how the grant funds will be spent.
The narrative portion of the proposal should include organizational background, the grant proposal, and an evaluation. Background information should include a brief description of the organization's history and mission; the need or problem to be addressed; current programs and accomplishments; the population served by the organization, including geographic location, socioeconomic status, race, ethnicity, gender, sexual orientation, age, physical ability, and language; the number of paid full-time staff, number of paid part-time staff, and the number of volunteers; and the organization's relationships--both formal and informal--with other organizations working to meet the same needs or providing similar services, explaining how the organization differs from these other agencies.
The grant proposal should include a statement of the primary purpose and the need or problem that will be addressed; population the grant will serve and how population will benefit from project; strategies to implement project; names and qualifications of the individuals who will direct the project; anticipated length of project; how project contributes to organization's overall mission; and a list of foundations and corporations, and other sources that funds are being solicited from, and the status of each.
The evaluation section of the proposal should explain how the organization will measure the effectiveness of the activities. Further, describe the organization's criteria for a successful program and the expected results.

The supplemental attachments should be labeled and should include both financial information and other supporting materials. The financial documentation should include the most recent financial statement, audited if available, that reflects actual expenditures and funds received during the most recent fiscal year; the operating budgets (aligned side by side on one page) for the current and most recent fiscal year; a list of foundation and corporate supporters (aligned side by side on one page) and other sources of income, with amounts, for the current and most recent fiscal year; and a current budget for the project (list each staff line separately, include percentage of time spent on the project, and indicate the specific uses of the requested grant).

Other supporting materials should include a list of the board of directors and their affiliations; a copy of the most recent IRS letter indicating tax-exempt status; one paragraph resumes of key staff; the most recent annual report, if available; and no more than three examples of recent articles about, or evaluations of, the organization, if available.

Deadlines: None.

Review Process: The trustees meet to consider proposals in March, June, September, and December. The review of and decision on any pending application depends upon the number and nature of other applications and the availability of funds. The review process can take several months.

Notes: If it appears that the project has a reasonable chance for funding, the foundation will arrange a site visit.

Restrictions

Grants are not made to individuals.

Additional Information

Publications: Grant Application Form

Foundation Officials

Robert Carswell: secretary B Brooklyn, NY 1928. ED Harvard University AB (1949); Harvard University LLB (1952). CORP AFFIL director: Georgia-Pacific Corp.; chairman: Private Export Funding Corp. NONPR AFFIL member: Phi Beta Kappa; member: Saint Andrews Society State New York; member: Harvard University Law School Alumni Association New York; member: Law Council Foreign Relations; member: California State Bar Association; chairman: Carnegie Endowment International Peace; member: American Society International Law; member: Association Bar New York City; member: American Bar Association; member: American Law Institute. CLUB AFFIL The Links New York City Club; Metro Club; Century Association.

Kathryn A. Ritchie: assistant secretary
Richard Schaffer: president
Kate R. Whitney: president
Sara R. Wilford: vice president, treasurer

Grants Analysis

Disclosure Period: calendar year ending 2000
Total Grants: $1,491,900
Number of Grants: 72
Average Grant: $16,787*
Highest Grant: $300,000
Lowest Grant: $5,000
Typical Range: $5,000 to $25,000
*Note: Average grant figure excludes highest grant.

Recent Grants

Note: Grants derived from 2000 Form 990.

Library-Related

15,000	Brooklyn Public Library, Brooklyn, NY

General

300,000	Kingsborough Community College, Brooklyn, NY
82,500	Bank Street College of Education, New York, NY
50,000	After School Corporation, New York, NY
35,000	Manhattan Country School, New York, NY
33,500	Brooks School, North Andover, MA
33,000	Kingsborough Community College, Brooklyn, NY
25,000	East Harlem Tutorial Program, New York, NY
25,000	Nature Conservancy of Georgia, Atlanta, GA
25,000	Partnership for After School Education, New York, NY
25,000	Project Reach Youth, Brooklyn, NY

GREENVILLE FOUNDATION

Giving Contact

Virginia Hubbell, Program Director
Care of Conrad Business Services
1100 Main Street, Suite C
Sonoma, CA 95476
Phone: (707)938-9377
Web: http://www.greenville-foundation.org

Description

Founded: 1949
EIN: 954396319
Organization Type: Private Foundation
Giving Locations: AZ; CA; DC; MN; NM; ND; OR; TX; Canada : ON
Grant Types: General Support.

Donor Information

Founder: the late William Miles

Financial Summary

Total Giving: $967,750 (2001); $1,100,750 (2000); $953,730 (1999)
Giving Analysis: Giving for 1999 includes: foundation matching gifts ($10,000)
Assets: $18,317,499 (2001); $19,666,264 (2000); $20,291,777 (1999)
Gifts Received: $602,942 (1995); $723,927 (1993). Note: In 1995, contributions were received from the William Miles Charitable Trust.

Typical Recipients

Arts & Humanities: Arts Outreach, Film & Video, Libraries, Public Broadcasting
Civic & Public Affairs: Civil Rights, Economic Development, Employment/Job Training, First Amendment Issues, Civic & Public Affairs-General, Hispanic Affairs, Housing, Law & Justice, Native American Affairs, Public Policy, Rural Affairs, Urban & Community Affairs, Women's Affairs
Education: Colleges & Universities, Environmental Education, International Studies, Leadership Training, Minority Education, Preschool Education, Private Education (Precollege), Religious Education, Science/Mathematics Education, Special Education
Environment: Energy, Forestry, Environment-General, Resource Conservation, Watershed
Health: Public Health
International: International-General, Health Care/Hospitals, Human Rights, International Affairs, International Development, International Environmental Issues, International Peace & Security Issues, International Relations, Missionary/Religious Activities, Trade
Religion: Churches, Jewish Causes, Ministries, Religious Organizations, Religious Welfare
Science: Science Museums, Scientific Organizations
Social Services: Child Abuse, Child Welfare, Community Service Organizations, Domestic Violence, Family Services, Food/Clothing Distribution, People with Disabilities, Recreation & Athletics, Shelters/Homelessness, Social Services-General, Youth Organizations

Application Procedures

Initial Contact: Send a brief outline of proposal or project.
Deadlines: April1 and October1.

Restrictions

Does not provide funds for individuals, scholarship, venture capital, capital improvements, endowments, general classroom-based environmental education programs, individuals species preservation, health, food banks, or temporary shelter.

Foundation Officials

Donald W. Crew: treasurer, director
Herb Crew: director, chairman
John Crew: director, treasurer
Richard A. Crew: chairman, director
Brian Fish: director
Susanne Fish-Sadin: director, secretary
Virginia Hubbell: program director
Pat Miles: secretary, director
William Miles: director

Grants Analysis

Disclosure Period: calendar year ending 2001
Total Grants: $967,750
Number of Grants: 65
Average Grant: $14,888
Highest Grant: $25,000
Typical Range: $5,000 to $25,000

Recent Grants

Note: Grants derived from 2001 Form 990.

General

25,000	Arriba Juntos, San Francisco, CA -- to support a 17-week intensive training program
25,000	New Mexico Conference of Churches, Albuquerque, NM -- to support a part-time coordinator for Standing Together as Communities for Human Dignity and Respect
25,000	Rural Advancement Foundation International, Winnipeg, ON Canada -- to support a State of the World Farmers Report
25,000	Seattle University, Seattle, WA -- to support the School of Theology and Ministry Liturgical Institute's Summer Pilot Program
21,750	Project Alchemy FA Western States Center, Inc., Seattle, WA -- to support and build technology capacity civil rights organizations in the Pacific Northwest
21,000	Center for Ecoliteracy, Berkeley, CA -- to support the Food Systems Project
20,000	Arizona Center for Law in the Public Interest, Phoenix, AZ -- to support litigation challenging
20,000	Californians for Justice, Oakland, CA -- to support youth and parent leadership
20,000	Center for Victims of Torture, Minneapolis, MN -- to support traumatized refugees from Sierra Leone
20,000	Correct Help FA Tides Center, West Hollywood, CA -- to support CorrectHelp

GREENWALL FOUNDATION

Giving Contact

William C. Stubing, President
2 Park Avenue, 24th Floor
New York, NY 10016-9301
Phone: (212)679-7266
E-mail: admin@greenwall.org
Web: http://www.greenwall.org

Description

Founded: 1949
EIN: 136082277
Organization Type: General Purpose Foundation
Giving Locations: NY
Grant Types: Project, Research.

Donor Information

Founder: Frank Greenwall and his wife, Anna Alexander Greenwall , established the foundation in 1949. Anna Alexander Greenwall's father owned a company called National Gum and Mica. In 1920, Frank Greenwall joined the company, which became National Starch and Chemical Corporation in 1959. Mr. Greenwall was chairman and chief executive of the adhesives, resins, and specialty chemical business. The foundation was originally named the Susan Greenwall Foundation in memory of the Greenwall's daughter. Its focus was on bone cancer research, the disease which took Susan's life at age 16. Frank and Anna were joined as donors to the foundation by their daughter, Nancy Greenwall, and their close friends and colleagues, Alfred A. Halden and Elias D. Cohen. In 1981, after the deaths of both Anna and Nancy, the name of the foundation was changed to the Greenwall Foundation to honor the deceased family members. Frank Greenwall, the last surviving founder, died in 1985.

Financial Summary

Total Giving: $4,387,324 (2000); $3,838,194 (1998); $3,277,460 (1997)
Assets: $97,910,056 (2000); $96,546,313 (1998); $90,316,741 (1997)
Gifts Received: $2,750 (1998); $5,000 (1997); $3,500 (1996)

Typical Recipients

Arts & Humanities: Arts Associations & Councils, Arts Funds, Arts Outreach, Ballet, Dance, Ethnic & Folk Arts, Arts & Humanities-General, Historic Preservation, History & Archaeology, Libraries, Literary Arts, Museums/Galleries, Music, Opera, Performing Arts, Public Broadcasting, Theater, Visual Arts
Civic & Public Affairs: Botanical Gardens/Parks, Civic & Public Affairs-General, Law & Justice, Legal Aid, Municipalities/Towns, Nonprofit Management, Professional & Trade Associations, Public Policy, Zoos/Aquariums
Education: Arts/Humanities Education, Colleges & Universities, Education Associations, Education Funds, Education Reform, Engineering/Technological Education, Faculty Development, Faculty Development, Education-General, Health & Physical Education, Journalism/Media Education, Medical Education, Minority Education, Private Education (Precollege), Public Education (Precollege), School Volunteerism, Science/Mathematics Education
Environment: Environment-General
Health: Alzheimers Disease, Children's Health/Hospitals, Clinics/Medical Centers, Diabetes, Health Policy/Cost Containment, Health Organizations, Heart, Hospitals, Hospitals (University Affiliated), Long-Term Care, Medical Research, Public Health
International: Human Rights
Science: Science Museums, Scientific Centers & Institutes, Scientific Labs, Scientific Research
Social Services: Community Service Organizations, Volunteer Services, Youth Organizations

Application Procedures

Initial Contact: The foundation does not have an application form or a standard outline for proposals. Initial letter should describe the program, objectives, amount requested, and qualifications of organization and project directors.
Application Requirements: If interested, the foundation will request additional information such as financial statements, itemized budget, tax-exempt status letter, and other relevant material.

Deadlines: Applications must be received by February 1 for consideration at the spring board meeting, or by August 1 for the autumn meeting.
Review Process: The foundation gives special attention to proposals demonstrating innovative approaches.

Restrictions

The foundation generally will not fund private foundations, endowment campaigns, or individuals. Arts organizations that have received contributions from the foundation for three consecutive years are not eligible for renewals for at least one year after foundation support has ceased.

Additional Information

Publications: Annual Report

Foundation Officials

Dr. George Francis Cahill, Jr.: director B New York, NY 1927. ED Yale University BS (1949); Columbia University MD (1953); Harvard University MA (1966). PRIM NONPR EMPL professor biological science: Dartmouth College. NONPR AFFIL member: National Commission Diabetes; senior physician: Peter Bent Brigham Hospital; vice president, trustee: Hotchkiss School; overseer: C. Everett Koop Institute; member: Endocrine Society; professor medical emeritus: Harvard University; member: Association American Physicians; overseer: Dartmouth University School Medicine; member: American Physiological Society; member: American Society Clinical Investigation; member: American Clinical & Climatological Association; member: American Diabetes Association; fellow: American Academy of Arts & Sciences; fellow: American Association Advancement Science. CLUB AFFIL Siasconset Casino Club.
Christine Karen Cassel, MD: vice chairman B Minneapolis, MN 1945. ED University of Chicago AB (1967); University of Massachusetts MD (1976). PRIM CORP EMPL chairman geriatric department, professor geriatric medicine: Mount Sinai. NONPR AFFIL president, director: Physicians Social Responsibility; member: Society Health & Human Values; member: NAS Institute Medicine; fellow bioethics: Institute Health Policy Studies; member: Institute Medicine; fellow: American Geriatrics Society; director: American Society Law & Medicine; member: American Board Internal Medicine; fellow: American College Physicians.
John Edwin Craig, Jr.: director B Lancaster, SC 1944. ED Davidson College BA (1966); Princeton University MA (1968). NONPR AFFIL chairman investment committee: Social Science Research Council; member, board: US-Australia-New Zealand Council; member government council: Rockefeller Archives Center; chairman investment committee: Investment Fund Foundations; chairman: Nonprofit Coordinating Committee; member: Foundation Administration Group; member: Foundation Financial Officer Group; member, board visitors: Davidson College. CLUB AFFIL mem: University Club.
Harvey J. Goldschmid: director B New York, NY 1940. ED Columbia University AB (1962); Columbia University JD (1965). PRIM CORP EMPL general counsel: Securities & Exchange Commission. NONPR AFFIL member: Phi Beta Kappa; board visitors: University Arizona College Law; member: New York City Bar Association; member: Association American Law Schools; director: National Center Philanthropy & Law; member: American Bar Association; fellow: American Bar Foundation; director, secretary, treasurer: American Association International Committee Jurists. CLUB AFFIL member: Century Association; member: Riverdale Yacht Club.
Francis M. Greenwall: director
Rosmarie E. Homberger: corporate secretary
Matina Souretis Horner: director B Boston, MA 1939. ED Bryn Mawr College AB (1961); University of Michigan MS (1963); University of Michigan PhD (1968). CORP AFFIL director: Neiman Marcus Group

Inc.; executive vice president: TIAA-CREF New York City; director: BEC Energy; director: Boston Edison Co. NONPR AFFIL member advisory committee: Women's Leadership Conference National Security; member, board directors, chairman research committee: Women's Research Education Institute; trustee: Twentieth Century Fund; member: Phi Kappa Phi; president emerita: Radcliffe College; member: Phi Beta Kappa; member: Phi Delta Kappa; member: National Organization Women; member executive committee: New England Colleges Fund; trustee: Massachusetts General Hospital Institute Health Professions; member: National Institute Social Sciences; member: Council Foreign Relations; president: American Laryngol Voice Research Education Foundation; trustee: Committee for Economic Development.
Fredrica Jarcho: program officer
Ellen Condliffe Langemann, PhD: director
Edith Levett: secretary emeritus
Robert J. McMinn: grants administrator
Carl Braun Menges: director B Pleasantville, NY 1930. ED Hamilton College BA (1951); Harvard University MBA (1953). PRIM CORP EMPL vice chairman, managing director: Donaldson, Lufkin & Jenrette Inc. CLUB AFFIL Maidstone Club; National Golf Links America Club.
Gayle Pemberton: board member
Joseph George Perpich, MD, JD: director B Hibbing, MN 1941. ED University of Minnesota BA (1963); University of Minnesota MD (1966); Georgetown University JD (1974). PRIM NONPR EMPL vice president: Howard Hughes Medical Institute.
Roger Rosenblatt: director B New York, NY 1940. ED Harvard University PhD. CORP AFFIL contributing editor: Time Inc.; contributing editor: New Republic Inc. NONPR AFFIL essayist: PBS NewsHour with Jim Lehrer.
Oscar Melick Ruebhausen: chairman emeritus B New York, NY August 28, 1912. ED Dartmouth College AB (1934); Yale University LLB (1937). NONPR AFFIL member: Sigma Xi; member: Yale Law School Association; member national committee US-China relations: Rockefeller University Council; member: Sigma Phi Epsilon; member: Order Coif; member: Phi Beta Kappa; member: New York State Bar Association; member: Association Bar New York City; member: Council Foreign Relations; member: American Bar Association. CLUB AFFIL Rockefeller Center Club; Rancho Sante Fe Association; River Club; Century Club.
Richard L. Salzer, Jr, MD: director NONPR AFFIL treasurer, director: Jewish Home & Hospital Aged.
Stephen Stamas: chairman, director B Salem, MA 1931. ED Harvard University AB (1953); Oxford University BPhil (1955); Harvard University PhD (1957). PRIM CORP EMPL investment executive: Wincrest Partners. CORP AFFIL director: Seacor Holdings Inc.; director: BNY Hamilton Funds. NONPR AFFIL director: Philharmonic Symphony Society New York; trustee, vice chairman: Rockefeller University; chairman: Marlboro School Music; member: Phi Beta Kappa; member: Council Foreign Relations; vice chairman: Lincoln Center Performing Arts; president, trustee: American Ditchley Foundation; vice chairman, trustee: Columbia University; chairman: American Assembly; member: American Council Germany; member: Academy Political Science. CLUB AFFIL Manursing Island Club; Century Association; Harvard Club.
William C. Stubing: president, director
William S. Vaun, MD: vice president, director

Grants Analysis

Disclosure Period: calendar year ending 2000
Total Grants: $4,387,324
Number of Grants: 159
Average Grant: $27,593
Highest Grant: $268,927
Typical Range: $5,000 to $25,000 and $100,000 to $200,000

Recent Grants

Note: Grants derived from 2000 Form 990.

General

268,927	Johns Hopkins University, Baltimore, MD
187,500	Institute of Medicine National Academy of Sciences
171,250	University of California San Francisco, San Francisco, CA
158,866	Dartmouth College, Hanover, NH
122,500	Issues TV, LTD, Bedford Hills, NY
105,510	Hastings Center, Inc., Garrison, NY
97,951	University of California Berkeley, Berkeley, CA
94,736	Johns Hopkins University, Baltimore, MD
92,858	Mount Sinai School of Medicine, New York, NY
68,000	City College of the City University of New York, New York, NY

GREGG-GRANITEVILLE FOUNDATION

Giving Contact

Patricia H. Knight, Secretary-Treasurer
PO Box 418
Graniteville, SC 29829
Phone: (803)663-7552
Fax: (803)663-6435

Description

Founded: 1941
EIN: 570314400
Organization Type: General Purpose Foundation
Giving Locations: GA: Richmond County; SC: Aiken County
Grant Types: Award, Scholarship.

Donor Information

Founder: "The Gregg-Graniteville Foundation was established in 1941 in honor of William Gregg to carry out his philosophy of genuine concern for people, their betterment, and their well-being."

Financial Summary

Total Giving: $850,000 (2002 approx); $779,430 (2001); $578,550 (2000). Note: 1997 Giving includes scholarship ($72,400) and support for the Gregg Park Civic Center ($257,600).
Giving Analysis: Giving for 2000 includes: foundation scholarships ($65,900); 1998: foundation scholarships ($56,300); foundation ($175,700) 1997: foundation scholarships ($71,400)
Assets: $19,573,674 (2001); $21,830,831 (2000); $20,000,000 (1999 approx)
Gifts Received: $710 (1998). Note: In 1998, contributions were received from Triarc, Inc.

Typical Recipients

Arts & Humanities: Arts Associations & Councils, Arts Centers, Ballet, Community Arts, Dance, Libraries, Museums/Galleries, Music, Opera, Performing Arts
Civic & Public Affairs: Botanical Gardens/Parks, Clubs, Economic Development, Economic Policy, Civic & Public Affairs-General, Housing, Rural Affairs, Safety, Urban & Community Affairs, Women's Affairs
Education: Arts/Humanities Education, Business Education, Colleges & Universities, Community & Junior Colleges, Economic Education, Education Funds, Elementary Education (Private), Elementary Education (Public), Education-General, Health & Physical Education, Minority Education, Public Education (Precollege), Science/Mathematics Education, Secondary Education (Public), Student Aid, Vocational & Technical Education

Health: Cancer, Diabetes, Emergency/Ambulance Services, Geriatric Health, Health Organizations, Hospitals, Hospitals (University Affiliated), Medical Rehabilitation, Mental Health, Research/Studies Institutes, Single-Disease Health Associations
Religion: Churches, Ministries, Religious Organizations, Religious Welfare
Science: Science Museums, Scientific Organizations
Social Services: Camps, Community Centers, Community Service Organizations, Domestic Violence, Food/Clothing Distribution, People with Disabilities, Recreation & Athletics, Senior Services, Special Olympics, Youth Organizations

Application Procedures

Initial Contact: Contact the foundation for a grant application.
Application Requirements: A completed application and a full proposal, which includes a brief description of sponsoring organization, need to be addressed, financial resources available, constituency served by the grant, most recent audited financial statement or current operating budget, and a copy of the IRS tax exemption letter.
Deadlines: Grants None; scholarship June 15.
Review Process: Applications are reviewed at the foundation office before presentation to the board of directors. Applicants are notified of the board's decision following regular meetings, held bimonthly.

Restrictions

Other than scholarships, no grants are made to individuals. Grants are restricted to organizations operating in Georgia and South Carolina. The foundation does not provide grants for operating budgets. Scholarship are awarded to children of employees of Avondale Milles, formerly knowns as Graniteville CO or are residents of Graniteville, Warrenville, and Vacluse South Carolina areas or Augusta, Georgia.

Additional Information

Publications: Annual Report; Guidelines; Application Form

Foundation Officials

Robert Morrall Bell: president, director B Graniteville, SC 1936. ED University of South Carolina AB (1958); University of South Carolina LLB (1965). PRIM CORP EMPL senior partner: Bell & Surasky PRIM NONPR EMPL county attorney: Aiken County. NONPR AFFIL member: South Carolina Trial Lawyers Association; member: Tau Kappa Alpha; member: South Carolina Bar Association; member: Phi Delta Phi; member: Shriners; member: American Trial Lawyers Association; member: Kappa Sigma Kappa; member: American Bar Association; member: Aiken County Bar Association. CLUB AFFIL Masons Club.
Ira E. Coward: director, board member
John W. Cunningham: vice president, board member, director
Jerry Ray Johnson: board mem, director B Savannah, GA 1926. ED University of South Carolina BSME (1950).
Carl W. Littlejohn, Jr.: director, board mem
Joan F. Phibbs: director, member board
James A. Randall: director, board mem
J. Paul Reeves: vice president, board mem, director
Robert P. Timmerman: board mem, director B Warrenville, SC November 09, 1920. ED Clemson University BA (1941). PRIM CORP EMPL director: Graniteville Co. CORP AFFIL director: Textile Hall Corp.; director: McCampbell Co. Ltd. (Tokyo Japan); chairman: C H Patrick & Co.; chairman, chief executive officer: Graniteville International Sales. NONPR AFFIL chairman: Community Services.

Grants Analysis

Disclosure Period: calendar year ending 2000
Total Grants: $512,650*
Number of Grants: 26
Average Grant: $9,106*

Highest Grant: $285,000
Lowest Grant: $1,000
Typical Range: $5,000 to $20,000
***Note:** Giving excludes scholarships. Average grant figure excludes highest grant.

Recent Grants

Note: Grants derived from 2001 Form 990.

General

50,000	American Red Cross-Aiken County Chapter, Aiken, SC
35,000	Augusta State University, Augusta, GA
20,000	Aiken Community Playhouse, Aiken, SC
20,000	Aiken Partnership of the University of South Carolina Educational Foundation, Aiken, SC
20,000	Aiken Partnership of the University of South Carolina Educational Foundation, Aiken, SC
20,000	Newberry College, Newberry, SC
20,000	South Carolina Independent Colleges & Universities, Columbia, SC
18,000	Aiken Partnership of the University of South Carolina Educational Foundation, Aiken, SC
18,000	Aiken Partnership of the University of South Carolina Educational Foundation, Aiken, SC
17,000	Helping Hands, Aiken, SC

ROSA MAY GRIFFIN FOUNDATION

Giving Contact

Dan Phillips, Secretary & Treasurer
PO Box 1790
Kilgore, TX 75663
Phone: (903)983-2051

Description

Founded: 1960
EIN: 756011866
Organization Type: Private Foundation
Giving Locations: TX
Grant Types: Capital, Emergency, General Support, Multiyear/Continuing Support, Operating Expenses.

Donor Information

Founder: the late Rosa May Griffin

Financial Summary

Total Giving: $356,088 (2001); $445,535 (2000); $406,958 (1999)
Giving Analysis: Giving for 2001 includes: foundation grants to United Way ($500); 2000: foundation grants to United Way ($14,000); 1999: foundation grants to United Way ($1,000)
Assets: $6,593,156 (2001); $8,303,095 (2000); $9,528,920 (1999)

Typical Recipients

Arts & Humanities: Arts & Humanities-General, Historic Preservation, History & Archaeology, Libraries, Museums/Galleries, Theater
Civic & Public Affairs: Botanical Gardens/Parks, Clubs, Civic & Public Affairs-General, Housing, Safety, Urban & Community Affairs
Education: Arts/Humanities Education, Business Education, Colleges & Universities, Education-General, Literacy, Preschool Education, Private Education (Precollege), Public Education (Precollege), School Volunteerism, Science/Mathematics Education, Secondary Education (Private), Student Aid
Health: Children's Health/Hospitals, Diabetes, Emergency/Ambulance Services, Geriatric Health, Heart, Hospitals, Hospitals (University Affiliated), Long-Term Care, Medical Rehabilitation, Medical Research, Public Health, Research/Studies Institutes

Religion: Churches, Ministries, Religious Organizations, Religious Welfare, Seminaries, Synagogues/Temples

Social Services: Camps, Child Welfare, Community Service Organizations, Counseling, Crime Prevention, Family Services, Homes, People with Disabilities, Recreation & Athletics, Scouts, Senior Services, Substance Abuse, United Funds/United Ways, Youth Organizations

Application Procedures

Initial Contact: Send a brief letter of inquiry.
Application Requirements: Include amount requested, purpose of funds sought, and proof of tax-exempt status.
Deadlines: None.

Restrictions

Does not support individuals.

Additional Information

Publications: Program Policy Statement

Foundation Officials

E. B. Mobley: president
Ebb Mobley: vice president
O. N. Pederson: trustee
Dan Phillips: secretary, treasurer

Grants Analysis

Disclosure Period: calendar year ending 2001
Total Grants: $355,588*
Number of Grants: 27
Average Grant: $11,753*
Highest Grant: $50,000
Lowest Grant: $500
Typical Range: $5,000 to $20,000
*Note: Giving excludes United Way. Average grant excludes highest grant.

Recent Grants

Note: Grants derived from 2001 Form 990.

General

50,000	Laird Hospital Foundation, Kilgore, TX
35,000	Texas Shakespeare Festival, TX
25,000	East Texas Treatment Center, Kilgore, TX
24,850	Schreiner College, Kerrville, TX
20,000	All-Star Music Scholarships, Kilgore, TX
20,000	American Heart Association, Longview, TX
20,000	East Texas Council on Alcoholism and Drug Abuse, Longview, TX
18,571	Kilgore Historical Preservation Foundation, Kilgore, TX
16,667	Evergreen Presbyterian Ministries, Bossier City, LA
15,000	KISD-Baseball Booster Program, Kilgore, TX

GRIFFIS FOUNDATION

Giving Contact

Hughes Griffis, President & Director
c/o Waller, Smith & Palmer
52 Eugene O'Neill Drive
New London, CT 06320
Phone: (212)577-8400

Description

Founded: 1943
EIN: 135678764
Organization Type: Private Foundation
Giving Locations: CT; NY
Grant Types: General Support.

Donor Information

Founder: the late Stanton Griffis, Nixon Griffis

Financial Summary

Total Giving: $514,768 (2000); $1,652,907 (1999); $1,800 (1996)
Assets: $8,999,486 (2000); $11,216,556 (1999); $8,781,574 (1996)

Typical Recipients

Arts & Humanities: Arts Associations & Councils, Arts Centers, Arts Institutes, Dance, History & Archaeology, Libraries, Museums/Galleries, Music, Theater
Civic & Public Affairs: Botanical Gardens/Parks, Community Foundations, Civic & Public Affairs-General, Municipalities/Towns, Philanthropic Organizations, Zoos/Aquariums
Education: Arts/Humanities Education, Colleges & Universities, Education-General, Private Education (Precollege), Secondary Education (Private)
Health: Cancer, Children's Health/Hospitals, Clinics/Medical Centers, Emergency/Ambulance Services, Hospices, Hospitals, Medical Research, Single-Disease Health Associations
International: Human Rights
Religion: Religious Welfare
Social Services: Animal Protection, Camps, Family Services, Shelters/Homelessness, United Funds/United Ways, Youth Organizations

Application Procedures

Initial Contact: The foundation has no formal grant application procedure or application form.
Deadlines: None.

Additional Information

Publications: Program Policy Statement; Application Guidelines

Foundation Officials

Alexander Dmitrieff: director
Hughes Griffis: president, director
Elizabeth Nye: vice president, director
Patricia Morel Shippee: director B Brooklyn, NY 1940. ED Fordham University BA (1981). PRIM NONPR EMPL trustee: Griffis Art Center. NONPR AFFIL director: Connecticut Graphic Arts Center; trustee: Mondrian/Holtzman Trust.
Sharon Tripp: director

Grants Analysis

Disclosure Period: calendar year ending 2000
Total Grants: $514,768
Number of Grants: 72
Average Grant: $7,150
Highest Grant: $50,000
Lowest Grant: $35
Typical Range: $100 to $20,000

Recent Grants

Note: Grants derived from 2000 Form 990.

General

50,000	Institute of Nautical Archeology, College Station, TX
48,812	San Francisco Art Institute, San Francisco, CA
37,260	California College of Arts and Crafts
25,000	Animal Medical Center, New York, NY
25,000	Omega Institute, Hudson River Valley, NY
20,000	Griffis Art Center, New London, CT
20,000	Griffis Art Center, New London, CT
20,000	Hewitt School, The, New York, NY
16,125	New York Military Academy, New York, NY
14,500	Long Island University, Brooklyn, NY

W. C. GRIFFITH FOUNDATION

Giving Contact

Curt Farran
Trustee Contact
c/o National City Bank of Indiana
101 W. Washington Street
Indianapolis, IN 46255
Phone: (317)267-7290
Fax: (317)267-3786

Description

Founded: 1959
EIN: 356007742
Organization Type: Private Foundation
Giving Locations: IN: Indianapolis
Grant Types: General Support, Operating Expenses.

Donor Information

Founder: the late William C. and Ruth Perry Griffith

Financial Summary

Total Giving: $974,500 (fiscal year ending November 30, 2001); $798,500 (fiscal 2000); $782,000 (fiscal 1999)
Assets: $14,274,037 (fiscal 2001); $17,838,007 (fiscal 2000); $19,343,256 (fiscal 1999)

Typical Recipients

Arts & Humanities: Arts Associations & Councils, Arts Centers, Ballet, Community Arts, Ethnic & Folk Arts, Historic Preservation, History & Archaeology, Libraries, Museums/Galleries, Music, Opera, Performing Arts, Public Broadcasting, Theater
Civic & Public Affairs: Botanical Gardens/Parks, Economic Development, Employment/Job Training, Civic & Public Affairs-General, Housing, Municipalities/Towns, Parades/Festivals, Public Policy, Safety, Urban & Community Affairs, Zoos/Aquariums
Education: Business Education, Colleges & Universities, Education Funds, Education Reform, Faculty Development, Education-General, International Studies, Private Education (Precollege), Public Education (Precollege), Secondary Education (Private), Student Aid
Environment: Environment-General, Resource Conservation
Health: AIDS/HIV, Cancer, Clinics/Medical Centers, Emergency/Ambulance Services, Health Organizations, Hospitals, Medical Rehabilitation, Medical Research, Mental Health, Preventive Medicine/Wellness Organizations, Single-Disease Health Associations
International: International Organizations, International Relief Efforts
Religion: Churches, Ministries, Religious Organizations, Religious Welfare
Social Services: Animal Protection, At-Risk Youth, Big Brother/Big Sister, Child Welfare, Community Service Organizations, Counseling, Family Planning, Food/Clothing Distribution, People with Disabilities, Recreation & Athletics, Scouts, Social Services-General, Substance Abuse, United Funds/United Ways, YMCA/YWCA/YMHA/YWHA, Youth Organizations

Application Procedures

Initial Contact: Send a brief letter of inquiry.
Application Requirements: Include a description of organization and purpose of funds sought.
Deadlines: None.

Restrictions

Does not support individuals or organizations outside the United States.

Foundation Officials
Ruthelen Griffith Burns: adv
Charles P. Griffith, Jr.: adv
Walter S. Griffith: adv
William C. Griffith, III: adv
Wendy Griffith Kortepeter: adv

Grants Analysis
Disclosure Period: fiscal year ending November 30, 2001
Total Grants: $974,500
Number of Grants: 156
Average Grant: $6,247
Highest Grant: $50,000
Lowest Grant: $550
Typical Range: $1,000 to $10,000

Recent Grants
Note: Grants derived from fiscal 2000 Form 990.

General

75,000	First Baptist Church Athletic Department
50,000	James Whitcomb Riley Memorial Association, Indianapolis, IN
25,000	Ann's Angel of Hope
25,000	Boy Scouts of America, Indianapolis, IN
25,000	Children's Museum
25,000	Indiana State Museum Foundation, Indianapolis, IN
25,000	Indianapolis Museum of Art, Indianapolis, IN
20,000	Christamore House Guild
15,000	Brook's Place
15,000	Nova Southeastern University, Ft. Lauderdale, FL

MARY LIVINGSTON GRIGGS AND MARY GRIGGS BURKE FOUNDATION

Giving Contact
Marvin J. Pertzik, Secretary & Treasurer
55 East Fifth Street
1400 5th Street
St. Paul, MN 55101-1792
Phone: (651)227-7683
Fax: (651)602-2670

Description
Founded: 1966
EIN: 416052355
Organization Type: General Purpose Foundation
Giving Locations: MN: Minneapolis, St. Paul; NY: New York
Grant Types: Capital, Challenge, Department, Endowment, General Support, Professorship, Project.

Donor Information
Founder: The Mary Livingston Griggs and Mary Griggs Burke Foundation was established in 1966. The donor was Mary Livingston Griggs.

Financial Summary
Total Giving: $2,028,740 (fiscal year ending June 30, 2002); $2,479,610 (fiscal 2001); $1,216,428 (fiscal 1999)
Giving Analysis: Giving for fiscal 2001 includes: foundation grants to United Way ($42,000) fiscal 1999: foundation grants to United Way ($40,000)
Assets: $25,803,733 (fiscal 2002); $29,010,630 (fiscal 2001); $33,311,178 (fiscal 1999)

Typical Recipients
Arts & Humanities: Arts Associations & Councils, Arts Centers, Arts Funds, Arts Institutes, Arts Outreach, Ballet, Dance, Arts & Humanities-General, Historic Preservation, History & Archaeology, Libraries, Museums/Galleries, Music, Opera, Performing Arts, Public Broadcasting, Theater, Visual Arts
Civic & Public Affairs: African American Affairs, Botanical Gardens/Parks, Business/Free Enterprise, Employment/Job Training, Civic & Public Affairs-General, Municipalities/Towns, Nonprofit Management, Parades/Festivals, Philanthropic Organizations, Urban & Community Affairs, Zoos/Aquariums
Education: Arts/Humanities Education, Colleges & Universities, Environmental Education, Education-General, International Studies, Literacy, Minority Education, Private Education (Precollege), Science/Mathematics Education, Student Aid
Environment: Environment-General, Resource Conservation, Wildlife Protection
Health: AIDS/HIV, Clinics/Medical Centers, Heart, Hospitals, Medical Research
International: International Environmental Issues, International Peace & Security Issues, International Relations
Science: Science Museums, Scientific Organizations
Social Services: Child Welfare, Day Care, Family Planning, Shelters/Homelessness, United Funds/United Ways

Application Procedures
Initial Contact: Applicants should send a proposal that includes four copies of the cover letter.
Application Requirements: Proposals should include a copy of the IRS tax-exempt determination letter. If the letter is more than one-year old, the foundation requests a statement indicating that there has been no change in the applicant's tax-exempt status. The proposal should also describe, clearly and concisely, the purposes of the grant, amount needed, the budget for the project, and whether or not assistance is sought from any other foundation. The proposal should also include the latest audited financial statements.
Deadlines: None.

Restrictions
The foundation does not make contributions to individuals, for dinners or special events, to fraternal organizations, political or lobbying groups, religious organizations for sectarian purposes, or for goodwill advertising.

Foundation Officials
Eleanor Briggs: director
Mary Griggs Burke: president, director B Saint Paul, MN. ED Columbia University MA; New School for Social Research; Sarah Lawrence College BA. NONPR AFFIL William Beene fellow: New York Zoological Society; member visitors committee: Smithsonian Institute Freer Gallery Art; member visitors committee, member ed committee, member aquis: Metropolitan Museum Art; member international council: Museum Modern Art; director: Hobe Sound Nature Center; honorary life trustee: Japan House Gallery; honorary life trustee: Brooklyn Museum Art; honorary life trustee: Friends Asian Art Freer & Sackler Galleries.
Gale Lansing Davis: director
C. E. Bayliss Griggs: vice president, director
Marvin J. Pertzik: secretary, treasurer, director B 1929. PRIM CORP EMPL partner: Moore, Costello and Hart.

Grants Analysis
Disclosure Period: fiscal year ending June 30, 2002
Total Grants: $2,028,740

Number of Grants: 78
Average Grant: $22,062*
Highest Grant: $194,469
Lowest Grant: $500
Typical Range: $10,000 to $40,000
*Note: Average grant figure excludes two highest grants ($352,000).

Recent Grants
Note: Grants derived from fiscal 2002 Form 990.

Library-Related

30,000	Friends of the St. Paul Public Library, St. Paul, MN -- system renewal
15,000	New York Public Library, New York, NY -- for specific programs

General

200,000	Asia Society, Inc., New York, NY -- for capital campaign
200,000	International Crane Foundation, Baraboo, WI -- endowment
200,000	Northland College, Ashland, WI -- science building
200,000	Sarah Lawrence College, Washington, DC -- endowment fund
194,469	Mary and Jackson Burke Foundation, St. Paul, MN -- art acquisition
157,531	Mary and Jackson Burke Foundation, St. Paul, MN -- for administration
120,000	Central Park Conservancy, New York, NY -- Shakespeare Garden
55,450	Metropolitan Museum of Art, New York, NY -- for purchase of art
53,000	Central Park Conservancy, New York, NY
50,000	Minneapolis Society of Fine Arts, Minneapolis, MN

GRIMES FOUNDATION

Giving Contact
Lewis B. Moore, Trustee
166 Tanglewood Dr.
Urbana, OH 43078
Phone: (937)653-4865

Description
Founded: 1951
EIN: 346528288
Organization Type: Private Foundation
Giving Locations: FL; OH
Grant Types: Capital, General Support, Scholarship.

Donor Information
Founder: Warren G. Grimes

Financial Summary
Total Giving: $276,248 (2000); $264,400 (1999); $220,350 (1998)
Assets: $3,088,841 (2000); $3,315,449 (1999); $3,131,659 (1998)

Typical Recipients
Arts & Humanities: Arts Associations & Councils, Ethnic & Folk Arts, Libraries, Museums/Galleries, Theater
Civic & Public Affairs: Economic Development, Civic & Public Affairs-General, Municipalities/Towns, Safety, Urban & Community Affairs
Education: Colleges & Universities, Education Reform, Elementary Education (Private), Elementary Education (Public), Engineering/Technological Education, Faculty Development, Private Education (Precollege), Public Education (Precollege), Science/Mathematics Education, Secondary Education (Public)
Environment: Environment-General
Health: Cancer, Emergency/Ambulance Services, Health Organizations, Hospitals, Medical Research

---

Religion: Churches
Social Services: At-Risk Youth, Community Centers, Community Service Organizations, Day Care, Scouts, Senior Services, YMCA/YWCA/YMHA/YWHA, Youth Organizations

Application Procedures
Initial Contact: The foundation has no formal grant application procedure or application form.
Deadlines: None.

Foundation Officials
Clarence J. Brown, Jr.: trustee
James S. Mihori: trustee
Gregory Moore: trustee
Lewis B. Moore: trustee
Robert S. Oelman: trustee
Steven Posley: trustee

Grants Analysis
Disclosure Period: calendar year ending 2000
Total Grants: $276,248
Number of Grants: 37
Average Grant: $5,590*
Highest Grant: $75,000
Typical Range: $1,000 to $10,000
*Note: Average grant figure excludes highest grant.

Recent Grants
Note: Grants derived from 1999 Form 990.

General
50,000	Champaign Family YMCA, Urbana, OH
25,000	Urbana Main Street Project, Urbana, OH
10,000	Unity School, Delray Beach, FL
10,000	Urbana City Schools, Urbana, OH
10,000	Urbana University, Urbana, OH
8,000	Bethesda Hospital Association, Boynton Beach, FL
5,500	Morikami Museum, Delray Beach, FL
5,000	Adriel School, Urbana, OH
4,000	St. Mary's School, Urbana, OH
3,000	Champaign County Arts Council, Urbana, OH

GRIMSHAW-GUDEWICZ CHARITABLE FOUNDATION

Giving Contact
Anne Fazendeiro, Trustee
173 Auburn Street
New Bedford, MA 02740
Phone: (508)997-2297

Description
Founded: 1995
EIN: 046778721
Organization Type: Private Foundation
Giving Locations: MA; NH; RI
Grant Types: General Support.

Financial Summary
Total Giving: $1,250,000 (2000); $1,200,000 (1999); $1,000,000 (1998)
Giving Analysis: Giving for 1999 includes: foundation grants to United Way ($500); 1998: foundation grants to United Way ($500) foundation ($999,500); **Assets:** $27,172,626 (2000); $25,215,358 (1999); $26,598,413 (1998)

Typical Recipients
Arts & Humanities: Arts Centers, History & Archaeology, Libraries, Museums/Galleries, Music, Opera, Theater

Education: Colleges & Universities, Community & Junior Colleges, Continuing Education, Education-General, Literacy, Public Education (Precollege), Student Aid
Environment: Forestry
Health: Clinics/Medical Centers, Eyes/Blindness, Health Organizations, Heart, Hospitals, Medical Research, Public Health, Single-Disease Health Associations
International: Missionary/Religious Activities
Religion: Religion-General, Jewish Causes, Religious Welfare, Synagogues/Temples
Social Services: Community Service Organizations, Homes, People with Disabilities, Recreation & Athletics, Social Services-General, YMCA/YWCA/YMHA/YWHA

Application Procedures
Initial Contact: Send a letter indicating purpose of funds sought, and including proof of tax-exempt status and a statement that the organization is currently in good standing.
Deadlines: None.

Foundation Officials
Anne Fazendeiro: trustee
Arthur Parker: trustee
Barry Robbins: trustee
Andrew Shabshelowitz: trustee
Harold Shabshelowitz: trustee
Bernard A. G. Taradash: trustee

Grants Analysis
Disclosure Period: calendar year ending 2000
Total Grants: $1,250,000
Number of Grants: 73
Average Grant: $9,191*
Highest Grant: $125,000
Typical Range: $5,000 to $20,000
*Note: Average grant figures excludes five highest grants ($625,000).

Recent Grants
Note: Grants derived from 2002 Form 990.

General
115,000	Franklin Pierce College, Rindge, NH
115,000	Masonic Education and Charity Trust, Inc., Boston, MA
115,000	New Hampshire Association for the Blind, Concord, NH
115,000	Schepens Eye Research Institute, Boston, MA
110,000	Brown University, Providence, RI
64,000	Eastern Nazarene College, Quincy, MA
60,000	Dartmouth-Hitchcock Medical Clinic for Continuing Education, Lebanon, NH
55,000	St. Francis Xavier Foreign Mission, Inc., Wayne, NJ
40,000	Freetown Historical Society, Freetown, MA
30,000	Lown Cardiovascular Research Foundation, Brookline, MA

GRINNELL MUTUAL REINSURANCE CO.

Company Headquarters
4215 Hwy. 146
Grinnell, IA 50112

Company Description
Employees: 650
SIC(s): 6331 Fire, Marine & Casualty Insurance.

Grinnell Mutual Group Foundation

Giving Contact
Steph Meggers, Manager
4215 Highway 146
PO Box 790
Grinnell, IA 50112-0790
Phone: (641)236-6121
Fax: (641)236-6121

Description
EIN: 421308146
Organization Type: Corporate Foundation
Former Name: GMG Foundation (2002).
Giving Locations: IA: headquarters area only
Grant Types: Employee Matching Gifts, General Support, Scholarship.

Financial Summary
Total Giving: $78,897 (2001); $82,968 (2000 approx); $79,765 (1999)
Giving Analysis: Giving for 2001 includes: foundation scholarships ($6,000); foundation matching gifts ($11,670); foundation grants to United Way ($23,470); 2000: foundation scholarships ($6,644); foundation matching gifts ($8,000); foundation grants to United Way ($20,221); 1999: foundation grants to United Way ($1,986); foundation matching gifts ($5,965); foundation scholarships ($8,000); foundation ($63,814);
Assets: $13,072 (2001); $16,778 (2000); $29,186 (1999)
Gifts Received: $75,000 (2001); $70,000 (2000); $100,000 (1999). Note: Contributions were received from Ginnell Mutual Reinsurance Co.

Typical Recipients
Arts & Humanities: Film & Video, Libraries, Literary Arts, Museums/Galleries, Public Broadcasting, Theater
Civic & Public Affairs: Clubs, Community Foundations, Civic & Public Affairs-General, Parades/Festivals, Rural Affairs, Safety
Education: Agricultural Education, Business Education, Colleges & Universities, Community & Junior Colleges, Secondary Education (Public), Student Aid
Environment: Air/Water Quality, Forestry, Environment-General, Protection, Research, Resource Conservation
Health: Cancer, Clinics/Medical Centers, Emergency/Ambulance Services, Heart, Hospices, Hospitals, Multiple Sclerosis
Social Services: Animal Protection, Community Service Organizations, Day Care, Domestic Violence, Family Services, Recreation & Athletics, Social Services-General, United Funds/United Ways

Application Procedures
Initial Contact: Send a brief letter of inquiry and a full proposal.
Application Requirements: Include a description of organization, amount requested, purpose of funds sought, recently audited financial statement, and proof of tax-exempt status.
Deadlines: None.

Restrictions
Does not support individuals, religious organizations for sectarian purposes, political or lobbying groups, or organizations outside operating areas.

Corporate Officials
Dan F. Agnew: president, chief executive officer B Grinnell, IA 1944. ED University of Northern Iowa (1967). PRIM CORP EMPL president, chief executive officer: Grinnell Mutual Reinsurance Co. CORP AFFIL president, director: Grinnell Realty Co.; director: Grinnell Select Insurance Co.; director: Greater Grinnell

Development; director: Grinnell Infosystems Inc.; chairman: Big M Agency Inc. NONPR AFFIL member: Ancient Free Accepted Masons; member: Lions International.

Michael J. Fordyce: chairman, director PRIM CORP EMPL chairman, director: Grinnell Mutual Reinsurance Co.

Robert C. Latham: second vice chairman, director PRIM CORP EMPL second vice chairman, director: Grinnell Mutual Reinsurance Co.

Clifford L. Strovers: director PRIM CORP EMPL director: Grinnell Mutual Reinsurance Co.

Jerry Dean Woods: vice president financial B Osceola, IA 1948. ED University of Iowa (1971). PRIM CORP EMPL vice president financial: Grinnell Mutual Reinsurance Co. CORP AFFIL director: Grinnell Life Insurance Co.

Foundation Officials

Dan F. Agnew: president, director (see above)
Tom Bachmann: director
Michael J. Fordyce: director (see above)
Stacy Heinen: director
Larry Jansen: director B Marshalltown, IA 1947. ED University of Iowa (1969). PRIM CORP EMPL vice president: Grinnell Mutual Reinsurance Co. CORP AFFIL president, director: Grinnell Select Insurance Canada.
Brent Larsen: director
Shawn McKay: director
Steph Meggers: manager
Wendy Nelson Munyon: secretary PRIM CORP EMPL assistant general counsel: Grinnell Mutual Reinsurance Co.
Ray Spriggs: director
Phyllis Steffen: director
Clifford L. Strovers: vice president, director (see above)
Ralph LaSalle Thompson: treasurer B Hopkinton, IA 1927. PRIM CORP EMPL treasurer: Grinnell Inco Co. CORP AFFIL treasurer: Grinnell Select Insurance Co.; treasurer: Invest Manager Grinnell Mutual Reinsurance Co.; treasurer, manager: Grinnell Realty Co.; treasurer: Grinnell Infosystems Inc.; treasurer secretary: Grinnell Mutual Life Insurance Co.; treasurer: Big M Agency.
Jerry Dean Woods: treasurer (see above)

Grants Analysis

Disclosure Period: calendar year ending 2001
Total Grants: $35,758*
Number of Grants: 18
Average Grant: $926*
Highest Grant: $20,000
Lowest Grant: $200
Typical Range: $250 to $2,000
*Note: Giving excludes matching gifts, scholarships, United Way. Average grant excludes highest grant.

Recent Grants

Note: Grants derived from 2000 Form 990.

Library-Related
1,000 Stewart Library, Grinnell, IA

General
20,000 Grinnell Regional Medical Center, Grinnell, IA -- pledge donation
9,948 United Way of Grinnell, Grinnell, IA -- United Way employee match
6,000 Ahrens Family Center, Grinnell, IA -- pledge donation
6,000 Iowa College Foundation, Des Moines, IA -- scholarships
3,000 Farm Safety 4 Just Kids, Earlham, IA
3,000 Grinnell Middle School, Grinnell, IA -- GMS Campaign for Technology
2,000 Dordt College, Sioux Center, IA -- educational scholarship donation
2,000 Grinnell Production, Grinnell, IA -- pledge donation

2,000 Iowa 4-H Foundation, Ames, IA
1,885 Montezuma Community Fund -- united way employee match

JOHN C. GRISWOLD FOUNDATION

Giving Contact
Jacqueline G. Moore, President
201 E. 5th St.
Cincinnati, OH 45202
Phone: (312)857-7820

Description
Founded: 1978
EIN: 132978937
Organization Type: Private Foundation
Grant Types: General Support.

Donor Information
Founder: the late John C. Griswold

Financial Summary
Total Giving: $757,000 (fiscal year ending November 30, 2001); $762,000 (fiscal 2000); $618,000 (fiscal 1999)
Assets: $13,479,208 (fiscal 2001); $15,035,160 (fiscal 2000); $14,968,333 (fiscal 1999)
Gifts Received: $519,491 (fiscal 2001); $368,446 (fiscal 2000); $280,446 (fiscal 1999). Note: In 1998, 1996, fiscal 1999, 2000, and 2001, contributions were received from the John C. Griswold Charitable Lead Trust.

Typical Recipients
Arts & Humanities: Arts Centers, Arts Funds, Ballet, Historic Preservation, Libraries, Museums/Galleries, Performing Arts, Public Broadcasting, Theater
Civic & Public Affairs: Community Foundations, Civic & Public Affairs-General, Public Policy, Urban & Community Affairs
Education: Colleges & Universities, Education Associations, Education Reform, Education-General, Medical Education, Private Education (Precollege), Public Education (Precollege), School Volunteerism
Environment: Environment-General, Research, Wildlife Protection
Health: Cancer, Children's Health/Hospitals, Clinics/Medical Centers, Diabetes, Hospitals, Medical Rehabilitation, Medical Research, Mental Health, Prenatal Health Issues, Preventive Medicine/Wellness Organizations, Single-Disease Health Associations, Trauma Treatment
International: International Relief Efforts
Religion: Churches, Jewish Causes, Religious Organizations
Science: Scientific Centers & Institutes
Social Services: Child Welfare, Community Service Organizations, Counseling, Domestic Violence, People with Disabilities, Recreation & Athletics, Shelters/Homelessness, Social Services-General, Youth Organizations

Application Procedures
Initial Contact: Send brief letter describing program.
Deadlines: None.

Restrictions
Applicants must be personally known by directors.

Foundation Officials
James R. Donnelley: vice president, treasurer B Chicago, IL 1935. ED Dartmouth College BA (1957); University of Chicago MBA (1962). PRIM CORP EMPL vice chairman: R.R. Donnelley & Sons Co. CORP AFFIL director: Sierra Pacific Power Co.; director: Sierra Pacific Resources; director: Pacific Magazines & Printing Ltd.

Jeffrey W. Earls: vice president
Lynda Earls: secretary
D. Ross Griswold, Jr.: vice president
Henry Hobson: secretary
Jacqueline G. Moore: president

Grants Analysis
Disclosure Period: fiscal year ending November 30, 2001
Total Grants: $757,000
Number of Grants: 59
Average Grant: $10,810*
Highest Grant: $130,000
Lowest Grant: $1,000
Typical Range: $5,000 to $20,000
*Note: Average grant figure excludes highest grant.

Recent Grants
Note: Grants derived from fiscal 2000 Form 990.

General
130,000 Greater Cincinnati Foundation, Cincinnati, OH
60,000 Cincinnati Art Museum, Cincinnati, OH
36,000 Bethany Lutheran School, Long Beach, CA
35,000 Narsad Research Institute, Great Neck, NY
25,000 Cincinnati Ballet Company, Cincinnati, OH
25,000 Heart of America Shakespeare Festival, Kansas City, MO
20,000 American Center for Wine, Food and Art, Napa, CA
20,000 Friends of School for Creative and Performing Arts, Cincinnati, OH
20,000 John Magro Artist Development Fund, Cincinnati, OH
20,000 Prospect House, Cincinnati, OH

LILLIAN SHERWOOD GRISWOLD FOUNDATION

Giving Contact
c/o Griswold Management Co.
1701 Placentia
Costa Mesa, CA 92627
Phone: (949)496-1174

Description
Founded: 1995
EIN: 330668667
Organization Type: Private Foundation
Grant Types: General Support.

Financial Summary
Total Giving: $146,097 (2001); $111,527 (2000); $97,252 (1999)
Assets: $2,699,300 (2001); $2,942,654 (2000); $3,344,060 (1999)
Gifts Received: $300,000 (1999); $600,000 (1998); $1,412,444 (1995). Note: In 1998 and 1999, contributions were received from Griswold Industries.

Typical Recipients
Arts & Humanities: Libraries
Civic & Public Affairs: Civic & Public Affairs-General
Education: Colleges & Universities, Education-General
Health: Children's Health/Hospitals, Hospitals, Prenatal Health Issues
Religion: Churches, Religion-General, Religious Welfare
Social Services: Camps, Child Welfare, Homes, Social Services-General, Volunteer Services, Youth Organizations

Application Procedures

Initial Contact: The foundation has no formal grant application procedure or application form.
Deadlines: None.

Foundation Officials

Lois G. Ericson: off
David E. Griswold: off
Donalyn G. Kling: off

Grants Analysis

Disclosure Period: calendar year ending 2001
Total Grants: $146,097
Number of Grants: 29
Average Grant: $3,532*
Highest Grant: $47,201
Lowest Grant: $100
Typical Range: $1,000 to $5,000
*Note: Average grant figure excludes highest grant.

Recent Grants

Note: Grants derived from 2000 Form 990.

Library-Related

2,000	Child Help Village Library Fund

General

30,000	Noohra Foundation, The, Smyrna, GA
10,418	Cloverleaf Foundation, Greenbelt, MD
10,149	Berkley Foundation, New York, NY
10,149	Northern California Campfire Boys and Girls, CA
10,000	Dorris Volunteer Fire Department
9,000	Hoag Hospital Foundation, Newport Beach, CA
9,000	March of Dimes, Oklahoma City, OK
5,000	Klamath Adolescent Program, Klamath Falls, OR
5,000	University of California, Los Angeles, CA -- campaign for Tahoe
4,000	Christian Science Society

GROTTO FOUNDATION

Giving Contact

Sarah Marquardt, Grants Manager
W-1050 First National Bank Building
332 Minnesota Street
St. Paul, MN 55101
Phone: (651)225-0777
Fax: (651)225-0752
E-mail: info@grottofoundation.org
Web: http://www.grottofoundation.org

Description

Founded: 1964
EIN: 416052604
Organization Type: Private Foundation
Giving Locations: AK; MN
Grant Types: General Support, Project, Research, Scholarship, Seed Money.

Donor Information

Founder: Louis W. Hill, Jr.

Financial Summary

Total Giving: $712,993 (fiscal year ending April 30, 2002); $859,879 (fiscal 2001); $875,183 (fiscal 2000)
Giving Analysis: Giving for fiscal 2000 includes: foundation matching gifts ($5,000)
Assets: $23,982,631 (fiscal 2002); $27,319,413 (fiscal 2001); $33,939,162 (fiscal 2000)
Gifts Received: $5,000 (fiscal 2002); $65,000 (fiscal 2001)

Typical Recipients

Arts & Humanities: Arts Associations & Councils, Arts Outreach, Film & Video, History & Archaeology, Libraries, Literary Arts, Public Broadcasting, Visual Arts

Civic & Public Affairs: African American Affairs, Asian American Affairs, Civil Rights, Economic Development, Gay/Lesbian Issues, Civic & Public Affairs-General, Hispanic Affairs, Municipalities/Towns, Native American Affairs, Nonprofit Management, Philanthropic Organizations, Public Policy, Urban & Community Affairs, Women's Affairs

Education: Afterschool/Enrichment Programs, Colleges & Universities, Continuing Education, Faculty Development, Education-General, Legal Education, Minority Education, Private Education (Precollege), Public Education (Precollege), School Volunteerism, Special Education, Student Aid

Environment: Environment-General

Health: AIDS/HIV, Clinics/Medical Centers, Emergency/Ambulance Services, Health Organizations, Hospitals, Public Health

International: Foreign Arts Organizations, Human Rights, International Relations

Religion: Religious Organizations, Religious Welfare

Social Services: Community Service Organizations, Domestic Violence, Family Services, Homes, People with Disabilities, Refugee Assistance, Scouts, Senior Services, Substance Abuse, Youth Organizations

Application Procedures

Initial Contact: Application form required.
Application Requirements: Include in the grant application, organizational information, purpose of funds sought, and evaluation information regarding program effectiveness and criteria. Attachments to application form include an IRS SOI(c)(3) letter; current registration receipt from state attorney general's office; officers list; recent audited report; project financials; projected budget; and any additional information.
Deadlines: January15, March15, July15, November15.

Restrictions

The foundation does not support individuals; scholarships; capital fund programs; subsidies for writing or publishing; multiple years; outside Minnesota; for travel; graduate or under graduate research; general operating expense; government agencies.

Additional Information

Publications: Annual Report (including Application Guidelines)

Foundation Officials

Austin J. Baillon: director
Peter M. Baillon: director
Ellis F. Bullock: secretary, executive director, director
John E. Diehl: director
Louis Fors Hill: vice president
Louis Shea Hill: director
Michael Johnson: director
Mary Manuel: director
Malcolm W. McDonald: treasurer NONPR AFFIL director: Amherst H. Wilder Foundation.
Elizabeth Pegues: director
Elizabeth Pegues-Smart: 1st vice president, director
William B. Randall: president
Nancy Randall-Dana: director
Margaret Jean Thomas: executive director, secretary B Detroit, MI 1943. ED Michigan State University BS (1964); San Francisco Theological Seminary DMin (1971); Union Theological Seminary MDiv (1971). NONPR AFFIL director: Presbyterian Homes Minnesota; member: Religion Education Association; member: NOW; member: National Association Ecumenical Staff; member: North American Academy Ecumenists; officer: Ecumenical Networks; director: Franklin National Bank; director: Clearwater Forest; member: Amnesty International; member national planning committee: Christian Unity Workshop.
Scott Wisdom: member

Grants Analysis

Disclosure Period: fiscal year ending April 30, 2002
Total Grants: $712,993
Number of Grants: 50
Average Grant: $13,428*
Highest Grant: $55,000
Lowest Grant: $5,000
Typical Range: $5,000 to $20,000
*Note: Average grant figure excludes highest grant.

Recent Grants

Note: Grants derived from fiscal 2000 Form 990.

General

210,000	Little Earth Residents Association, Minneapolis, MN -- support programs that combine culture and technology to help families thrive in Native American inner cities
99,023	Model Cities of St. Paul, Inc., St. Paul, MN -- support organizational capacity building, accounts receivable upgrade, client tracking and planning
42,700	Model Cities of St. Paul, Inc., St. Paul, MN -- capacity building and accounts receivable upgrade
30,000	Little Earth Residents Association, Minneapolis, MN -- support youth as they develop programs that motivate kids to do well in school in Native American
20,000	Saint John's University, Collegeville, MN -- support program in the philosophy, practices and techniques of environmentally sound and sustainable pottery practices
20,000	St. Paul Area Council of Churches, St. Paul, MN -- support building of more usable space for American Indian community feasts and events
17,860	Blooming Prairie Center, Inc., Blooming Prairie, MN -- support a driver's education/functional English program to area Spanish speaking adults
17,860	Blooming Prairie Center, Inc., Blooming Prairie, MN -- support Spanish language outreach and services to rural children and their families
15,000	Asian American Renaissance, St. Paul, MN -- support multicultural activities to strengthen the Asian American Community
15,000	Lauj Youth Society of Minnesota, St. Paul, MN -- home tutoring

GRUNDY FOUNDATION

Giving Contact

Roland H. Johnson, Executive Director
680 Radcliffe Street
PO Box 701
Bristol, PA 19007
Phone: (215)788-5460
Fax: (215)788-0915

Description

Founded: 1961
EIN: 231609243
Organization Type: General Purpose Foundation
Giving Locations: PA: Bristol and Bucks County
Grant Types: Capital, Project.

Donor Information

Founder: The foundation was established in 1961 pursuant to the will of the late Joseph Ridgeway Grundy . Mr. Grundy was president of Grundy and Company (a linen manufacturer) and the Farmers

National Bank of Bucks County. He was also appointed by the governor of Pennsylvania to an unexpired term in the U.S. Senate (1929-1930).

Financial Summary

Total Giving: $1,226,666 (2002); $1,275,915 (2001); $1,279,206 (2000)

Giving Analysis: Giving for 1999 includes: foundation grants to United Way ($191,500); 1998: foundation ($180,000); 1997: foundation grants to United Way ($100,000) foundation ($100,000)

Assets: $53,000,000 (2002); $52,473,285 (2001); $58,253,033 (2000)

Gifts Received: $35,104 (1993). Note: In 1993, contributions were received from the Johnson Fund.

Typical Recipients

Arts & Humanities: Arts Centers, Arts Festivals, Arts Outreach, Ethnic & Folk Arts, Film & Video, Historic Preservation, History & Archaeology, Libraries, Museums/Galleries, Music, Opera, Performing Arts, Theater

Civic & Public Affairs: Botanical Gardens/Parks, Economic Development, Economic Policy, Civic & Public Affairs-General, Hispanic Affairs, Housing, Municipalities/Towns, Parades/Festivals, Safety, Urban & Community Affairs, Women's Affairs

Education: Colleges & Universities, Community & Junior Colleges, Education Funds, Education-General, International Exchange, Preschool Education, Public Education (Precollege), Science/Mathematics Education, Secondary Education (Public), Student Aid

Environment: Air/Water Quality, Forestry, Environment-General, Resource Conservation, Wildlife Protection

Health: Cancer, Children's Health/Hospitals, Clinics/Medical Centers, Emergency/Ambulance Services, Health-General, Hospitals, Long-Term Care, Mental Health, Public Health, Respiratory

International: International Affairs, International Relations

Social Services: Animal Protection, Big Brother/Big Sister, Camps, Child Welfare, Community Centers, Community Service Organizations, Crime Prevention, Day Care, Domestic Violence, Emergency Relief, Family Planning, Family Services, Food/Clothing Distribution, Homes, People with Disabilities, Recreation & Athletics, Scouts, Scouts, Senior Services, Sexual Abuse, Shelters/Homelessness, Social Services-General, Substance Abuse, United Funds/United Ways, YMCA/YWCA/YMHA/YWHA, Youth Organizations

Application Procedures

Initial Contact: The foundation has no specific application requirements. Submit a brief letter of inquiry.

Application Requirements: Include a description of organization, amount requested, purpose of funds sought, recently audited financial statement, and proof of tax-exempt status. report. of annual report.

Deadlines: None.

Review Process: Grants are reviewed throughout the year at board meetings. The foundation may request more information or make a site visit before reaching a decision. Applicants are notified by letter within a week of the board meeting at which the decision is made.

Notes: Telephone request for clarification of proposal requirements are accepted, but faxed proposals and videotapes are not.

Restrictions

The foundation does not make grants to nonpublic schools, individuals, religious organizations, or for endowments, loans, research or political activities. The foundation can not consider proposals for operating support from United Way member agencies.

Additional Information

The foundation operates a museum and a library.

Publications: Application Guidelines

Trust(s): First Union National Bank

Foundation Officials

James M. Gassaway: trustee

Roland H. Johnson: executive director

John Knoell: trustee B 1927. PRIM CORP EMPL president: John Knoell & Sons Inc.

Frederick J. M. La Valley: trustee ED Stanford University (1969); University of Pennsylvania (1972).

Leonard N. Snyder: trustee

Grants Analysis

Disclosure Period: calendar year ending 2001

Total Grants: $1,275,915*

Number of Grants: 70

Average Grant: $15,000*

Highest Grant: $100,000

Lowest Grant: $1,000

Typical Range: $1,000 to $30,000

*Note: Grants analysis provided by foundation.

Recent Grants

Note: Grants derived from 2001 Form 990.

Library-Related

| 25,000 | Friends of Southhampton Free Library, Southampton, PA |

General

100,000	Bristol Borough Recreation Authority, Bristol, PA
100,000	Bristol Borough School District, Bristol, PA -- construction of athletic field at Spurline Park
75,000	Bristol Riverside Theater, Bristol, PA -- support 2001-2 performance season
75,000	Bristol Riverside Theater, Bristol, PA -- support 2001-2 performance season
60,000	Bristol Riverside Theater, Bristol, PA -- for operating support
60,000	Bristol Riverside Theater, Bristol, PA -- for operating support
57,000	United Way Bucks County, Fairless Hills, PA -- support 2001-2 campaign
50,000	Bristol Riverside Theater, Bristol, PA -- endowment fund
50,000	Please Touch Museum, Philadelphia, PA -- capital campaign
25,000	American Cancer Society, Providence, RI

GUARANTY BANK & TRUST CO.

Company Headquarters

Cedar Rapids, IA

Web: http://www.guaranty-bank.com

Company Description

Employees: 56

SIC(s): 6022 State Commercial Banks.

Guaranty Bank and Trust Co. Charitable Trust

Giving Contact

Robert Becker, President
PO Box 1807
Cedar Rapids, IA 52406-1807
Phone: (319)286-6200
Fax: (319)362-1295
E-mail: becker@guaranty-bank.com

Description

EIN: 510182485

Organization Type: Corporate Foundation

Giving Locations: IA

Grant Types: General Support.

Financial Summary

Total Giving: $49,475 (2000); $52,415 (1999); $60,000 (1998)

Giving Analysis: Giving for 2000 includes: foundation grants to United Way ($3,750); 1999: foundation grants to United Way ($3,500) foundation ($48,915)

Assets: $131,362 (2000); $131,403 (1999); $86,217 (1996)

Gifts Received: $42,000 (2000); $60,000 (1999); $40,000 (1996). Note: Contributions were received from Guaranty Bank and Trust Co.

Typical Recipients

Arts & Humanities: Arts Festivals, Community Arts, Ethnic & Folk Arts, Historic Preservation, History & Archaeology, Libraries, Museums/Galleries, Music, Theater

Civic & Public Affairs: African American Affairs, Botanical Gardens/Parks, Chambers of Commerce, Clubs, Community Foundations, Civic & Public Affairs-General, Housing, Municipalities/Towns, Parades/Festivals, Professional & Trade Associations, Safety, Urban & Community Affairs, Women's Affairs, Zoos/Aquariums

Education: Business Education, Colleges & Universities, Community & Junior Colleges, Education Funds, Private Education (Precollege), Public Education (Precollege), Science/Mathematics Education

Environment: Environment-General

Health: AIDS/HIV, Alzheimers Disease, Cancer, Cancer, Children's Health/Hospitals, Diabetes, Emergency/Ambulance Services, Health Organizations, Hospitals, Kidney, Single-Disease Health Associations

Religion: Churches, Jewish Causes, Religious Welfare

Science: Science-General, Scientific Centers & Institutes

Social Services: Animal Protection, Camps, Community Centers, Community Service Organizations, Domestic Violence, Family Planning, Food/Clothing Distribution, People with Disabilities, Recreation & Athletics, Scouts, Senior Services, Social Services-General, Substance Abuse, United Funds/United Ways, YMCA/YWCA/YMHA/YWHA

Application Procedures

Initial Contact: Send brief letter describing program.

Deadlines: None.

Corporate Officials

Harold M. Becker: chairman, chief executive officer PRIM CORP EMPL chairman, chief executive officer: Guaranty Bank & Trust Co.

B. Larry Johnson: president PRIM CORP EMPL president: Guaranty Bank & Trust Co.

John Waters: chief financial officer PRIM CORP EMPL chief financial officer: Guaranty Bank & Trust Co.

Foundation Officials

Harold M. Becker: director (see above)

Robert D. Becker: director

Nancy H. Evans: director

Grants Analysis

Disclosure Period: calendar year ending 2000

Total Grants: $45,725*

Number of Grants: 66

Average Grant: $693*

Highest Grant: $6,000

Typical Range: $100 to $1,000

*Note: Giving excludes United Way.

Recent Grants

Note: Grants derived from 2001 Form 990.

General

4,000	United Way of East Central Iowa, Cedar Rapids, IA
3,750	Cedar Rapids Museum of Art, Cedar Rapids, IA
3,000	Cedar Rapids Symphony Orchestra, Cedar Rapids, IA
3,000	Linn County Historical Museum, Cedar Rapids, IA
3,000	Science Station, Cedar Rapids, IA
2,500	City Treasurer, City of Cedar Rapids, Cedar Rapids, IA
2,250	YMCA of Cedar Rapids, Cedar Rapids, IA
2,000	American Red Cross, Cedar Rapids, IA
1,650	National Czech and Slovak Museum and Library, Cedar Rapids, IA
1,600	Marion Historical Museum, Marion, IA

GUARDIAN LIFE INSURANCE COMPANY OF AMERICA

Company Headquarters

New York, NY
Web: http://www.theguardian.com

Company Description

Revenue: US$8.136 billion (2002)
Employees: 6000 (2001)
Fortune Rank: 232, per FORTUNE Magazine's list of 500 Largest U.S. Corporations (2002).
SIC(s): 6036 Savings Institutions Except Federal, 6311 Life Insurance, 6321 Accident & Health Insurance.

Operating Locations

Guardian Life Insurance Co. of America (PA; WA; WI)

Giving Contact

Karen Olvany, Assistant Corporate Secretary
7 Hanover Square
New York, NY 10004-2616
Phone: (212)598-7499
Fax: (212)919-2944
E-mail: karen_olvany@glic.com
Web: http://www.glic.com

Description

Organization Type: Corporate Giving Program
Giving Locations: PA: Bethlehem; WA: Spokane; WI: Appleton headquarters and operating communities.
Grant Types: General Support.

Financial Summary

Total Giving: $1,000,000 (2002 approx); $966,918 (2001); $898,200 (2000). Note: Contributes through corporate direct giving program only.
Giving Analysis: Giving for 2001 includes: foundation matching gifts ($131,225)
Assets: $33,900,000,000 (2000 approx); $31,700,000,000 (1999)

Typical Recipients

Arts & Humanities: Arts Centers, Community Arts, Historic Preservation, Libraries, Museums/Galleries, Music, Opera, Performing Arts, Public Broadcasting, Theater
Civic & Public Affairs: Business/Free Enterprise, Economic Development, Economic Policy, Law & Justice, Safety, Urban & Community Affairs, Zoos/Aquariums
Education: Arts/Humanities Education, Business Education, Colleges & Universities, Community & Junior Colleges, Economic Education, Education Funds, Literacy
Health: Health Policy/Cost Containment, Hospices, Medical Research, Single-Disease Health Associations
Social Services: Food/Clothing Distribution, Substance Abuse, United Funds/United Ways, Youth Organizations

Application Procedures

Initial Contact: Submit a brief letter of inquiry.
Application Requirements: A description of organization, amount requested and purpose of funds sought, recently audited financial statement, and proof of tax-exempt status.
Deadlines: None.

Restrictions

Does not support individuals, religious organizations for sectarian purposes, or political or lobbying groups.

Additional Information

In 1992, the company began a direct giving program. The Guardian Life Charitable Trust was terminated in December 1993.

Corporate Officials

Peter Lounsbery Hutchings: executive vice president, chief financial officerc B New York, NY 1943. ED Yale University BA (1964). PRIM CORP EMPL executive vice president, chief financial officer: Guardian Life Insurance Co. of America ADD CORP EMPL director: Family Service Lifeline Co.; president, director: First International; director: Guardian Insurance & Annuity Co. Inc.; director: Guardian Investors Services Corp.; president, director: Park Avenue Life; president, director: Sentinel American Life Insurance. NONPR AFFIL member: American Academy of Actuaries; fellow: Society Actuaries; member: Actuarial Society Greater New York; director: 14th Street Business Improvement District; director: 14th Street Union Square Local Development Corp.

Joseph Dudley Sargent: president, chief executive officer, director B Philadelphia, PA 1937. ED Fairfield University AB (1959). PRIM CORP EMPL president, chief executive officer, director: Guardian Life Insurance Co. of America ADD CORP EMPL director: Family Service Life Insurance Co.; president, chief executive officer: Guardian Insurance & Annuity Co. Inc. NONPR AFFIL member: National Association Life Underwriters; director: United Way New York City; director: Life Office Management Association; director: Discovery Museum Bridgeport; director: Life Insurance Marketing & Research Institute.

Giving Program Officials

Karen L. Olvany: contact PRIM CORP EMPL assistant corporate secretary: Guardian Life Insurance Co. of America.

Grants Analysis

Disclosure Period: calendar year ending 2001
Total Grants: $966,900*
Number of Grants: 322
Average Grant: $1,000
Highest Grant: $171,400
Lowest Grant: $250
Typical Range: $500 to $5,000
*Note: Giving includes matching gifts, United Way. Grants analysis provided by foundation.

HOMER AND MARTHA GUDELSKY FAMILY FOUNDATION

Giving Contact

Medda Gudelsky, Secretary & Director
11900 Tech Road
Silver Spring, MD 20904
Phone: (301)622-0100
Fax: (301)622-3507

Description

Founded: 1968
EIN: 520885969
Organization Type: Family Foundation
Giving Locations: DC: Washington; FL; MD
Grant Types: Capital, Project, Scholarship.

Donor Information

Founder: Established in 1968 by members of the Gudelsky family, Percontee, Inc., and Axcorp, Inc.

Financial Summary

Total Giving: $1,345,000 (2001); $1,173,550 (2000); $191,000 (1998)
Giving Analysis: Giving for 1998 includes: foundation gifts to individuals ($20,000)
Assets: $26,626,320 (2001); $27,754,949 (2000); $26,523,663 (1998)
Gifts Received: $8,888 (1993)

Typical Recipients

Arts & Humanities: Arts Centers, Arts Funds, History & Archaeology, Libraries, Museums/Galleries, Public Broadcasting, Theater
Civic & Public Affairs: Clubs, Civic & Public Affairs-General, Hispanic Affairs, Parades/Festivals, Public Policy, Safety, Urban & Community Affairs, Women's Affairs, Zoos/Aquariums
Education: Arts/Humanities Education, Colleges & Universities, Education-General, International Studies, Medical Education, Private Education (Precollege), Public Education (Precollege), Student Aid
Environment: Resource Conservation
Health: Cancer, Clinics/Medical Centers, Emergency/Ambulance Services, Hospitals, Long-Term Care, Research/Studies Institutes
Religion: Churches, Jewish Causes, Religious Organizations, Religious Welfare, Synagogues/Temples
Science: Science-General
Social Services: Child Welfare, Community Service Organizations, Homes, Shelters/Homelessness, Substance Abuse, Veterans

Application Procedures

Initial Contact: Submit a written proposal.
Application Requirements: Applications should include a detailed account of why funds are sought.
Deadlines: None.

Foundation Officials

John Gudelsky: secretary, director B 1956. PRIM CORP EMPL president: Gudelsky Materials Inc.
Martha Gudelsky: president, director B 1922.
Medda Gudelsky: secretary, director PRIM CORP EMPL vice president: Homer Properties Inc.
Rita Regino: vice president, director B 1958. PRIM CORP EMPL president: 495 Trucking Inc. CORP AFFIL officer: Homer Properties Inc.
Holly Stone: vice president, director CORP AFFIL director: Homer Properties Inc.
Joseph Yedlin: treasurer, director PRIM CORP EMPL treasurer, assistant secretary, director: Percontee Inc. CORP AFFIL secretary: Homer Properties Inc.

Grants Analysis

Disclosure Period: calendar year ending 2001
Total Grants: $1,345,000
Number of Grants: 25
Average Grant: $35,208*
Highest Grant: $500,000
Lowest Grant: $1,000
Typical Range: $5,000 to $25,000 and $100,000 to $500,000
*Note: Average grant figure excludes highest grant.

Recent Grants

Note: Grants derived from 2001 Form 990.

General

500,000	Howard County Conservancy, Woodstock, MD
100,000	Boca Raton Community Hospital Foundation, Boca Raton, FL
100,000	Capitol College, Laurel, MD
100,000	Round House Theater, Silver Spring, MD
100,000	University of Maryland, Baltimore, MD
100,000	University of Maryland Medical System, Baltimore, MD
35,000	Mobile Medical Care, Rockville, MD
20,000	School 33 Art Center, MD
10,000	Florence Fuller Child Development Center, Boca Raton, FL
10,000	Melwood Endowment Fund, Upper Marlboro, MD

HARRY FRANK GUGGENHEIM FOUNDATION

Giving Contact

Karen Colvard, Program Officer
527 Madison Avenue, 15th Floor
New York, NY 10022-4304
Phone: (212)644-4907
Fax: (212)644-5110
E-mail: hfgacf@aol.com
Web: http://www.hfg.org

Description

Founded: 1929
EIN: 136043471
Organization Type: General Purpose Foundation
Giving Locations: nationally and internationally.
Grant Types: Employee Matching Gifts, Fellowship, Project, Research.

Donor Information

Founder: The foundation was established in 1929 by the late Harry Frank Guggenheim .

Financial Summary

Total Giving: $1,400,000 (2003 approx); $1,500,000 (2002 approx); $1,800,000 (2001 approx)
Giving Analysis: Giving for 2000 includes: foundation matching gifts ($282,820); foundation gifts to individuals ($792,945); 1999: foundation grants to United Way ($1,000); foundation matching gifts ($78,540); foundation gifts to individuals ($945,363); 1998: foundation matching gifts ($72,740) foundation gifts to individuals ($773,597).
Assets: $71,000,000 (2003 approx); $72,000,000 (2002 approx); $78,000,000 (2001 approx)

Typical Recipients

Arts & Humanities: Ethnic & Folk Arts, History & Archaeology, Libraries, Literary Arts, Museums/Galleries, Music, Theater
Civic & Public Affairs: Chambers of Commerce, Community Foundations, Civic & Public Affairs-General, Nonprofit Management, Professional & Trade Associations, Public Policy, Safety, Urban & Community Affairs, Women's Affairs
Education: Arts/Humanities Education, Colleges & Universities, Education Reform, Education-General, International Studies, Leadership Training, Medical Education, Public Education (Precollege), Science/Mathematics Education, Social Sciences Education, Student Aid
Environment: Environment-General
Health: Alzheimers Disease, Children's Health/Hospitals, Eyes/Blindness, Health Funds, Hospitals, Kidney, Medical Research

International: Foreign Educational Institutions, International-General, Health Care/Hospitals, Human Rights, International Affairs, International Organizations, International Peace & Security Issues
Religion: Churches, Jewish Causes, Religious Organizations, Synagogues/Temples
Science: Scientific Centers & Institutes, Scientific Research
Social Services: Child Abuse, Crime Prevention, People with Disabilities, Substance Abuse, United Funds/United Ways, Youth Organizations

Application Procedures

Initial Contact: Request a title page and abstract form from the foundation. Submit four copies of a typewritten application in English.
Application Requirements: Applications for research grants should include the title page, the abstract including a description of the project in plain English and its relevance to human dominance, aggression, and violence; curricula vitae and lists of relevant publications for the principal investigator and all professional personnel; an IRS tax-exempt determination letter if proposal is submitted by an institution; a budget in U.S. dollars with justification of each item; a research plan discussing the specific aims, background, and significance of the project; a description of other sources of support; a discussion of how subjects used in the research will be protected; and referee's comments. Applications for dissertation fellowships should include the title page, abstract, advisor's letter, applicant's background, research plan, description of how subjects will be protected, and a list of facilities and resources already available for the proposed research.
Deadlines: New applications for research grants must be received by August 1 for consideration at the December board meeting; applications for continuation may be submitted by August 1 for a decision in December or February 1 for a decision at the June board meeting. Applications for dissertation fellowships must be received by February 1 for a decision in June.
Review Process: Applicants will be informed promptly by letter of the board's decision.
Notes: Faxed applications will not be accepted.

Restrictions

The foundation will not fund overhead costs of institutions, professional meetings and conferences, self-education, elaborate fixed equipment, travel costs, or support while completing the requirements for advanced degrees (apart from those indirectly involved in research assistantships or those awarded through the Dissertation Fellowship program).

Additional Information

The foundation generally gives about 30 research grants and 10 dissertation awards. The research grants range from $15,000 to $35,000; the dissertation awards are $15,000 each.
Publications: Biennial Report; Application Guidelines; Application Form

Foundation Officials

William Oliver Baker: director B Chestertown, MD July 15, 1915. ED Washington College BS (1935); Princeton University PhD (1938). PRIM CORP EMPL director: Summit Trust Co. CORP AFFIL director: General America Investors Co. Inc. NONPR AFFIL advisory council: Special Libraries Association; member, vice chairman: Robert A. Welch Foundation; member: Sigma Xi; visiting lectr: Princeton University; chairman emeritus: Rockefeller University; member: Omicron Delta Kappa; member: Phi Lambda Upsilon; visiting lectr: Northwestern University; member: New Jersey Commission Science & Technology; member advisory council: New Jersey Regional Medicine Library; member: National Materials Program; member: National Security Council Organization Federal Telecommunications System; member: National Cancer

Plan; member: National Academy Engineering; member: National Academy Sciences; member council: Marconi Fellowships; chairman emeritus: Andrew W. Mellon Foundation; member: Institute Medicine; member: Industrial Research Institute; co-sponsor: Institute Materials Research; visiting lectr: Duke University; fellow: Franklin Institute; member visitors committee science & math: Drew University; member: Council Trends Perspectives; member: Directors Industry Research; member science advisory board: Committee Science Technology; director: Council Library Resources; member: Carnegie Forum Education Science Technology & Economic; fellow: American Physical Society; trustee: Charles Babbage Institute; fellow: American Institute Chemists; trustee: American Philosophical Society; member: American Chemical Society; fellow: American Academy of Arts & Sciences; co-chairman national council: American Association Advancement Science. CLUB AFFIL Princeton Northwestern New Jersey Club; honorary member: Chemists Club New York; Cosmos Club.
Josiah Bunting, III: director CORP AFFIL director: Owens & Minor Inc. NONPR AFFIL superintendent: Virginia Military Institute.
Peyton S. Cochran, Jr.: director B 1916. ED University of Virginia BA (1950). PRIM CORP EMPL senior vice president, director: Rouse Co. of Saint Louis. CORP AFFIL senior vice president, director: Governors Square Inc.; senior vice president, director: Salem Mall Inc.; senior vice president: Charlottetown Inc.; senior vice president: Franklin Park Mall Inc.
Karen Colvard: program officer
Howard Graves: director
Donald Redfield Griffin: director B Southampton, NY August 03, 1915. ED Harvard University BS (1938); Harvard University MA (1940); Harvard University PhD (1942). NONPR AFFIL professor emeritus: Rockefeller University; member: Sigma Xi; member: Phi Beta Kappa; member: Ecological Society America; member: National Academy Sciences; member: Animal Behavior Society; member: American Physiological Society; member: American Society Zoologists; member: American Philosophical Society; member: American Academy of Arts & Sciences; member: American Ornithologists Union.
James McNaughton Hester: president, director B Chester, PA 1924. ED Princeton University BA (1945); Oxford University BA (1950); Oxford University PhD (1955). NONPR AFFIL director: Alliance Fund; member: Association American Rhodes Scholars. CLUB AFFIL University Club; Century Association; Pretty Brook Tennis Club.
Donald Charles Hood: director B North Merrick, NY 1942. ED State University of New York Harper College BA (1965); Brown University MSc (1968); Brown University PhD (1969). PRIM NONPR EMPL professor psychology: Columbia University. NONPR AFFIL trustee, vice chairman: Smith College; member: Society Experimental Psychology; member: Optical Society of America; James F. Bender professor psychology: Columbia University; member: Eastern Psychology Association; fellow: American Psychonomics Society; member: Association Research Vision & Opthalmology; member: American Association Advancement Science; member: American Association University Professors.
Joseph A. Koenigsberger: treasurer
Carol Langstaff: director
Lewis Lapham: director
Peter Orman Lawson-Johnston: chairman, director B New York, NY 1927. ED University of Virginia (1951). PRIM CORP EMPL senior partner: Guggenheim Brothers PRIM NONPR EMPL pres, trust: Lawrenceville School. CORP AFFIL chairman, director: Zemex Corp.; director: National Review; president, director: Elgerbar Corp.; director: Feldspar Corp. NONPR AFFIL president: Lawrenceville School.
Gillian Lindt: director
Theodore Davidge Lockwood: director B Hanover, NH 1924. ED Trinity College BA (1948); Princeton University MA (1950); Princeton University PhD (1952). NONPR AFFIL member: Phi Beta Kappa;

member: Pi Gamma Mu; member: Association American Colleges; member: Greater Hartford Chamber of Commerce.

Tania L-J. McCleery: trustee

Jeremiah Milbank, III: director ED Trinity College BA (1970); Stanford University MBA (1973); University of Virginia JD (1980). PRIM CORP EMPL chairman: Milbank Associate ADD CORP EMPL vice president: Cypress Woods Corp.; vice president: Turkey Hill Plantation; president: Winthrop Milbank & Co.

Alan Jay Parrish Pifer: director B Boston, MA 1921. ED Harvard University AB (1947); Emmanuel College (1947-1948). CORP AFFIL director: Techno-Serve Inc. NONPR AFFIL trustee: University Bridgeport; director: US-South Africa Leader Exchange Program; fellow: Royal Society Arts; member: American Association Higher Education; member: Century Association; fellow, founder: African Studies Association; fellow: American Academy of Arts & Sciences. CLUB AFFIL Harvard Club.

Lois Dickson Rice: director B Portland, ME 1933. ED Radcliffe College AB (1954); Columbia University (1954-1955). CORP AFFIL director: UNUM Corp.; director: International Multifoods Corp.; director: McGraw-Hill Inc.; director: Hartford Steam Boiler Inspection & Insurance Co.; director: Fleet Financial Group. NONPR AFFIL member: President Foreign Intelligence Advisory Board; director: Reading Is Fundamental; member: Phi Beta Kappa; guest scholar: Brookings Institute Program Economic Studies; trustee: CNA Corp. Public Agenda Foundation. CLUB AFFIL Cosmos Club.

Joan G. Van De Maele: director

Joel Wallman: program officer

William C. Westmoreland: director

Mary-Alice Yates: secretary

Grants Analysis

Disclosure Period: calendar year ending 2000
Total Grants: $232,001*
Number of Grants: 24
Average Grant: $9,667
Highest Grant: $50,000
Typical Range: $5,000 to $20,000
*Note: Giving excludes matching gifts, gifts to individuals. Total grants also excludes funds for programs, conferences and mailings conducted by the foundation ($22,332).

Recent Grants

Note: Grants derived from 2000 Form 990.

General

50,000	Friends for Long Island's Heritage, Muttontown, NY -- cradle of aviation museum exhibit
50,000	Temple Emanu-el, New York, NY
36,600	Universitetet I Bergen Fosswinckelsgate Norway -- globalization
35,002	Lehigh University, Bethlehem, PA -- testosterone, serotonin and aggression cellular markers
34,400	Northeastern University, Boston, MA -- "The Soviet struggle against banditry"
34,160	Center for AIDS Outreach and Prevention, New York, NY -- remembering violence and the transvaluation of public sphere
33,330	Centre for the Study of Violence and Reconciliation, Johannesburg Republic of South Africa -- farm killing
33,250	Afrika Study Centre -- transformation of aqro-pastoralist conflict and violence in northeastern Uganda
31,250	University of Missouri - St. Louis, St. Louis, MO -- "carjacker's perspective"
30,260	University of Texas, Austin, TX -- military history of East Africa

GULF COAST MEDICAL FOUNDATION

Giving Contact

Mr. Dee McElroy, Executive Vice President & Foundation Manager
135 West Elm
PO Box 30
Wharton, TX 77488
Phone: (979)532-0904
Web: http://www.gulfcoastmedical.com

Description

Founded: 1983
EIN: 741285242
Organization Type: Private Foundation
Giving Locations: CO: Jackson County, Matagorda County, Wharton County; TX: Brazoria County, Fort Bend County
Grant Types: General Support.

Financial Summary

Total Giving: $870,768 (2000); $804,400 (1998); $281,905 (1996)
Assets: $18,668,377 (2000); $19,105,514 (1998); $16,037,319 (1996)

Typical Recipients

Arts & Humanities: Arts Festivals, History & Archaeology, Libraries, Museums/Galleries, Music, Theater
Civic & Public Affairs: Botanical Gardens/Parks, Clubs, Civic & Public Affairs-General, Municipalities/Towns, Nonprofit Management, Parades/Festivals, Safety, Urban & Community Affairs
Education: Afterschool/Enrichment Programs, Agricultural Education, Community & Junior Colleges, International Exchange, Literacy, Medical Education, Public Education (Precollege), Science/Mathematics Education, Secondary Education (Public), Student Aid, Vocational & Technical Education
Health: Cancer, Children's Health/Hospitals, Clinics/Medical Centers, Diabetes, Emergency/Ambulance Services, Geriatric Health, Health Organizations, Hospices, Long-Term Care, Mental Health, Nursing Services, Nutrition, Preventive Medicine/Wellness Organizations, Public Health, Transplant Networks/Donor Banks
Religion: Churches, Ministries, Religious Welfare
Science: Scientific Centers & Institutes
Social Services: At-Risk Youth, Child Welfare, Community Centers, Community Service Organizations, Crime Prevention, Day Care, Emergency Relief, People with Disabilities, Recreation & Athletics, Senior Services, Shelters/Homelessness, YMCA/YWCA/YMHA/YWHA, Youth Organizations

Application Procedures

Initial Contact: Write a letter to the foundation requesting a grant application.
Deadlines: None.

Restrictions

Grants are made primarily for medically-related projects.

Additional Information

In 1995, foundation changed from a fiscal year ending May 31 to a calendar year.
Publications: Application Form; Guidelines

Foundation Officials

Laurance H. Armour, III: director
Laurance Hearne Armour, Jr.: director B Chicago, IL 1923. ED Princeton University AA (1945); Northwestern University (1947-1948). NONPR AFFIL member national board governors: Institute Living. CLUB AFFIL Shoreacres Club; New York Yacht Club; Onwentsia Club; Chicago Club; Chicago Yacht Club; Casino Club.

R. B. Caraway, MD: director
Charles Davis, Jr.: treasurer
Charles F. Drees: director
Kent Hill: president
Bert Huebner: director
Dee McElroy: executive vice president, foundation manager
Sylvan Miori: director
Irving Moore, Jr.: secretary B Wharton City, TX 1912. ED University of Texas LLB. CORP AFFIL director: Heritage Bank.
Jack Moore: vice president
Max Rotholz: director
Clive Runnells: director
Clive Runnells, III: director
David Stovall: director
Guy F. Stovall, III: director
C. E. Woodson, MD: director

Grants Analysis

Disclosure Period: calendar year ending 2000
Total Grants: $870,768
Number of Grants: 59
Average Grant: $14,759
Highest Grant: $100,000
Lowest Grant: $1,000
Typical Range: $500 to $50,000

Recent Grants

Note: Grants derived from 2000 Form 990.

Library-Related

15,000	Palacios Library, Palacios, TX -- for new roof

General

100,000	MD Anderson Cancer Center, Houston, TX -- for leukemia research and honor caraway
50,000	Depelchin Center, Houston, TX -- for replacements, renovation of buildings
50,000	Lifeline Chaplaincy, Houston, TX -- restricted for use in the compassionate touch program
50,000	Team Wharton, Wharton, TX -- for phase I of building program
50,000	Wharton County Junior College, Wharton, TX -- for telecom health courses
35,000	East Bernard Emergency Medical Services, East Bernard, TX
27,000	Colorado Valley Transit, Columbus, TX -- for wheel chair van
25,000	Blood Center, Houston, TX -- for bus and taps programs
25,000	East Fort Bend Human Needs Ministry, Inc., Stafford, TX -- for pantry
25,000	Fort Bend Literacy, Sugar Land, TX -- option/improve building

GULF POWER CO.

Company Headquarters

1 Energy Pl.
Pensacola, FL 32520
Web: http://www.gulfpower.com

Company Description

Assets: US$807 million (2001)
Employees: 1500 (2001)
SIC(s): 4911 Electric Services.
Parent Company: Southern Co., Atlanta, GA, United States

Nonmonetary Support

Volunteer Programs: Company reports that it supports, "Junior Achievement, (charity) runs and holiday shopping."

Gulf Power Foundation

Giving Contact

John E. Hodges, Jr., Chairman
1 Energy Place
Pensacola, FL 32520-0786
Phone: (850)444-6806

Alternate Contact

500 Bayfront Parkway
Pensacola, FL 32501
Phone: (850)444-6206

Description

Founded: 1987
EIN: 592817740
Organization Type: Corporate Foundation
Giving Locations: Northwest Florida.
Grant Types: Employee Matching Gifts, General Support, Scholarship.

Donor Information

Founder: Gulf Power Company

Financial Summary

Total Giving: $209,548 (2001); $227,905 (2000); $189,502 (1999)
Giving Analysis: Giving for 2001 includes: foundation matching gifts ($4,395); foundation scholarships ($12,000); foundation grants to United Way ($64,353); foundation ($128,800); 2000: foundation matching gifts ($6,050); foundation grants to United Way ($60,935); foundation ($160,920); 1999: foundation fellowships ($1,500); foundation matching gifts ($3,815); foundation scholarships ($12,500); foundation grants to United Way ($64,087); foundation ($107,600);
Assets: $770,295 (2001); $1,119,136 (2000); $1,323,537 (1999)
Gifts Received: $200 (1997); $1,082,484 (1993); $1,000,000 (1992). Note: In 1997, contributions were received from J. Lewis Davidson.

Typical Recipients

Arts & Humanities: Arts Associations & Councils, Arts & Humanities-General, Historic Preservation, History & Archaeology, Libraries, Museums/Galleries, Music
Civic & Public Affairs: African American Affairs, Botanical Gardens/Parks, Chambers of Commerce, Community Foundations, Civic & Public Affairs-General, Housing, Parades/Festivals, Safety, Urban & Community Affairs, Women's Affairs
Education: Agricultural Education, Business Education, Colleges & Universities, Community & Junior Colleges, Education Associations, Education Funds, Engineering/Technological Education, Education-General, Literacy, Student Aid
Environment: Environment-General, Resource Conservation, Wildlife Protection
Health: Cancer, Children's Health/Hospitals, Emergency/Ambulance Services, Health Organizations, Health Organizations, Hospices, Hospitals, Prenatal Health Issues, Public Health, Single-Disease Health Associations
Religion: Ministries, Religious Organizations, Religious Welfare, Social/Policy Issues
Social Services: At-Risk Youth, Child Welfare, Community Service Organizations, Counseling, Food/Clothing Distribution, Homes, People with Disabilities, Recreation & Athletics, Scouts, Senior Services, Shelters/Homelessness, Social Services-General, Substance Abuse, United Funds/United Ways, YMCA/YWCA/YMHA/YWHA, Youth Organizations

Application Procedures

Initial Contact: Contact the foundation to obtain a Grant Request Form.
Deadlines: None.

Restrictions

The foundation does not support individuals or organizations outside service area.

Corporate Officials

Travis J. Bowden: chairman, president, chief executive officer, director B Greenville, AL 1938. ED University of Alabama (1960). PRIM CORP EMPL chairman, president, chief executive officer, director: Gulf Power Co.
Arlan Earl Scarbrough: vice president financial B Carnes, MS 1936. ED University of Southern Mississippi (1958); East Carolina University (1962). PRIM CORP EMPL vice president financial: Gulf Power Co. NONPR AFFIL member: American Institute CPAs.

Foundation Officials

Francis M. Fisher, Jr.: trustee
John E. Hodges, Jr.: chairman PRIM CORP EMPL vice president: Gulf Power Co.
Ronnie R. Labrato: secretary B Pensacola, FL 1953. ED University of West Florida (1974). PRIM CORP EMPL controller: Gulf Power Co.
Robert Moore: trustee
Arlan Earl Scarbrough: trustee (see above)
Warren E. Tate: section, treasurer

Grants Analysis

Disclosure Period: calendar year ending 2001
Total Grants: $128,800*
Number of Grants: 51
Average Grant: $2,076*
Highest Grant: $25,000
Lowest Grant: $500
Typical Range: $200 to $10,000
*Note: Giving excludes matching gifts, scholarship, and United Way. Average grant figure excludes highest grant.

Recent Grants

Note: Grants derived from 2001 Form 990.

Library-Related
5,000	Washington County Public Library, Chipley, FL -- capital funds	
1,000	Friends of the Crestview Library, Crestview, FL	

General
36,996	United Way Escambia County, Pensacola, FL
25,000	Pensacola Junior College, Pensacola, FL
12,102	United Way Northwest Florida, Panama City, FL
10,000	Santa Rosa County Chamber of Commerce Foundation, Milton, FL
7,100	United Way Santa Rosa County, Milton, FL
7,058	United Way Okaloosa-Walton Counties, Ft. Walton Beach, FL -- capital funds
5,500	Junior Achievement Northwest Florida, Pensacola, FL
5,000	Arts Council of Northwest Florida, Pensacola, FL
5,000	Florida State University, Panama City, FL
5,000	Foundation of Greater Fort Walton Beach, Ft. Walton Beach, FL

JOSEPHINE GUMBINER FOUNDATION

Giving Contact

Julie Meenan, Executive Director
401 E. Ocean View Blvd., Suite 503
Long Beach, CA 90802
Phone: (562)437-2882

Description

Founded: 1989
EIN: 330345249
Organization Type: Private Foundation
Giving Locations: CA: Long Beach; FL; TX
Grant Types: General Support.

Donor Information

Founder: Established in 1989 by the late Josephine S. Gumbiner .

Financial Summary

Total Giving: $602,257 (2001); $746,278 (2000); $517,508 (1999)
Assets: $13,917,615 (2001); $15,654,898 (2000); $17,584,070 (1999)
Gifts Received: $9,855 (1999); $100,000 (1998); $250,000 (1996). Note: In 1998, contributions were received from the Gumbiner Family Foundation. In 1996, contributions were received from Josephine S. Gumbiner.

Typical Recipients

Arts & Humanities: Arts Appreciation, Arts Outreach, Ballet, Dance, Ethnic & Folk Arts, Libraries, Museums/Galleries, Music, Opera, Performing Arts, Theater
Civic & Public Affairs: Asian American Affairs, Botanical Gardens/Parks, Clubs, Economic Development, Employment/Job Training, Civic & Public Affairs-General, Hispanic Affairs, Housing, Legal Aid, Nonprofit Management, Urban & Community Affairs, Women's Affairs, Zoos/Aquariums
Education: Afterschool/Enrichment Programs, Arts/Humanities Education, Business Education, Colleges & Universities, Community & Junior Colleges, Education Reform, Elementary Education (Public), Faculty Development, Education-General, Literacy, Literacy, Preschool Education, Social Sciences Education, Special Education, Student Aid
Health: AIDS/HIV, Alzheimers Disease, Children's Health/Hospitals, Clinics/Medical Centers, Emergency/Ambulance Services, Heart, Hospices, Medical Research, Medical Training, Mental Health, Prenatal Health Issues, Respiratory
Religion: Churches, Jewish Causes, Religious Welfare
Social Services: At-Risk Youth, Big Brother/Big Sister, Child Welfare, Community Service Organizations, Counseling, Day Care, Domestic Violence, Emergency Relief, Family Planning, Family Services, Food/Clothing Distribution, People with Disabilities, Recreation & Athletics, Scouts, Sexual Abuse, Shelters/Homelessness, Social Services-General, Substance Abuse, Volunteer Services, YMCA/YWCA/YMHA/YWHA, Youth Organizations

Application Procedures

Initial Contact: Telephone contact person to request application and guidelines.
Application Requirements: In a complete proposal include the grant application; two-page proposal letter, containing history of organization, statement of need, current accomplishments, description of program, project strategies; one-page project budget; financial statements; operating budget; revenue; list of anticipated outcomes; one-paragraph resumes of staff; list of Board of Directors; list of volunteers; and a copy of recent IRS (c) (3) letter.
Deadlines: None.
Review Process: Board of Directors meets quarterly to consider new funding.

Restrictions

The foundation does not make grants to individuals, political or lobbying groups, or any organizations that discriminate on the basis of race, creed, sexual orientation, or national origin.

Additional Information

In 1998, the Gumbiner Family Foundation merged with the Josephine S. Gumbiner Foundation. The organization has an interest in women's and children's issues.

Publications: Application Form; Guidelines

Foundation Officials

Beth Campbell: director
Beth Campbell: director
Art Gottlieb: secretary
Alis Gumbiner: cfo, vp
Burke F. Gumbiner: chief financial officer
Lee Gumbiner: vice president
Julie Meenan: executive director
Dennis Rockway: director

Grants Analysis

Disclosure Period: calendar year ending 2001
Total Grants: $602,257*
Number of Grants: 55
Average Grant: $9,586*
Highest Grant: $37,500
Typical Range: $5,000 to $20,000
*Note: Average grant figure excludes two highest grants. ($75,000).

Recent Grants

Note: Grants derived from 2001 Form 990.

Library-Related

11,700	Long Beach Public Library Foundation, Long Beach, CA

General

37,500	Habitat for Humanity, Immokalee, FL
37,500	SCADD
25,000	Long Beach Nonprofit Partnership, Long Beach, CA
20,500	Boys & Girls Club, Pontiac, IL
20,000	Liberty Hill Foundation, Santa Monica, CA
18,750	Lutheran Social Services, Austin, TX
18,500	Robin Hood Foundation, New York, NY
15,000	Children's Clinic, Long Beach, CA
15,000	Harbor Area Halfway Houses
15,000	Jewish Family and Children's Service, Inc., Baltimore, MD

GEOFFREY GUND FOUNDATION

Giving Contact

Geoffrey Gund, Trustee
40 E. 94th St., Apt. 28-E
New York, NY 10128
Phone: (212)689-3075

Alternate Contact

8075 Leesburg Pike
Vienna, VA 22182

Description

Founded: 1991
EIN: 521509128
Organization Type: Private Foundation
Giving Locations: no restrictions.
Grant Types: Research, Scholarship.

Donor Information

Founder: Established in 1991 by Geoffrey and Felicity Gund.

Financial Summary

Total Giving: $974,140 (fiscal year ending June 30, 2000); $913,050 (fiscal 1999); $801,556 (fiscal 1998)
Giving Analysis: Giving for fiscal 2000 includes: foundation scholarships ($100,000) fiscal 1999: foundation scholarships ($100,000)

Assets: $30,302,340 (fiscal 2000); $18,173,466 (fiscal 1999); $18,618,785 (fiscal 1998)
Gifts Received: $150,000 (fiscal 1999); $256,521 (fiscal 1998); $1,300,000 (fiscal 1996). Note: In fiscal 1998 and 1999, contributions were received from Geoffrey Gund.

Typical Recipients

Arts & Humanities: Arts Associations & Councils, Ballet, Film & Video, Arts & Humanities-General, Historic Preservation, History & Archaeology, Libraries, Museums/Galleries, Music, Performing Arts
Civic & Public Affairs: Botanical Gardens/Parks, Civic & Public Affairs-General, Philanthropic Organizations, Public Policy, Women's Affairs
Education: Arts/Humanities Education, Colleges & Universities, Education Funds, Education-General, Minority Education, Private Education (Precollege), Student Aid
Environment: Environment-General, Resource Conservation, Wildlife Protection
Health: Emergency/Ambulance Services, Eyes/Blindness, Hospitals, Medical Research, Mental Health
International: Foreign Educational Institutions, Health Care/Hospitals
Religion: Churches, Religious Welfare
Social Services: Child Welfare, Community Service Organizations, Day Care, Family Planning, Food/Clothing Distribution, Recreation & Athletics, Senior Services

Application Procedures

Initial Contact: The foundation has no formal grant application procedure or application form. Send a brief letter of inquiry.
Deadlines: None.

Additional Information

Trust(s): Key Trust Co OH NA

Foundation Officials

Geoffrey de Conde Gund: trustee
Donald Kozusko: trustee
James O'Hara: trustee

Grants Analysis

Disclosure Period: fiscal year ending June 30, 2000
Total Grants: $874,140*
Number of Grants: 20
Average Grant: $23,563*
Highest Grant: $300,000
Typical Range: $10,000 to $50,000
*Note: Giving excludes scholarships. Average grant figure excludes two highest grants ($450,000).

Recent Grants

Note: Grants derived from fiscal 1999 Form 990.

General

300,000	Groton School, Groton, MA
150,000	Ethical Culture Fieldston School, New York, NY
150,000	Ethical Culture Fieldston School, New York, NY
100,000	Groton School, Groton, MA
100,000	Riverdale Presbyterian Church, Bronx, NY
25,000	Museum of Modern Art, New York, NY
16,500	Riverdale Presbyterian Church, Bronx, NY
15,000	RP Foundation Fighting Blindness, Princeton, NJ
13,800	Wave Hill, Bronx, NY
10,000	Cleveland Orchestra Musical Arts Association, Cleveland, OH

GEORGE GUND FOUNDATION

Giving Contact

David T. Abbott, Executive Director
45 Prospect Avenue West
1845 Guildhall Building
Cleveland, OH 44115
Phone: (216)241-3114
Fax: (216)241-6560
E-mail: dabbott@gundfdn.org
Web: http://www.gundfdn.org

Description

Founded: 1952
EIN: 346519769
Organization Type: General Purpose Foundation
Giving Locations: OH: Cleveland including northeastern Ohio region
Grant Types: General Support, Project, Seed Money.

Donor Information

Founder: Established in 1952 by the late George Gund (d. 1966), former chairman of the board of the Cleveland Trust Company. Mr. Gund was involved in banking and real estate in Seattle, military intelligence during World War I, the Kaffee-Hag Corporation in Cleveland, animal husbandry in Iowa, and ranching in Nevada. He was also devoted to the arts, serving as president of the Cleveland Art Institute; and education, serving as a trustee at several institutions of higher education.

Financial Summary

Total Giving: $19,556,406 (2002); $20,345,592 (2001); $23,448,518 (1998)
Giving Analysis: Giving for 1998 includes: foundation grants to United Way ($120,500) foundation scholarships ($226,500)
Assets: $397,593,000 (2002); $424,502,237 (2001); $476,737,798 (1998)

Typical Recipients

Arts & Humanities: Arts Associations & Councils, Arts Centers, Arts Institutes, Community Arts, Dance, Ethnic & Folk Arts, Film & Video, Arts & Humanities-General, Historic Preservation, History & Archaeology, Libraries, Museums/Galleries, Music, Opera, Performing Arts, Public Broadcasting, Theater
Civic & Public Affairs: African American Affairs, Botanical Gardens/Parks, Business/Free Enterprise, Civil Rights, Clubs, Community Foundations, Economic Development, Employment/Job Training, Civic & Public Affairs-General, Housing, Inner-City Development, Law & Justice, Legal Aid, Municipalities/Towns, Parades/Festivals, Public Policy, Urban & Community Affairs, Urban & Community Affairs, Women's Affairs
Education: Arts/Humanities Education, Colleges & Universities, Community & Junior Colleges, Education Funds, Education Reform, Engineering/Technological Education, Environmental Education, Faculty Development, Education-General, Leadership Training, Minority Education, Preschool Education, Public Education (Precollege), Science/Mathematics Education, Student Aid, Vocational & Technical Education
Environment: Air/Water Quality, Energy, Environment-General, Resource Conservation
Health: AIDS/HIV, Children's Health/Hospitals, Clinics/Medical Centers, Emergency/Ambulance Services, Eyes/Blindness, Hospitals, Single-Disease Health Associations
International: International Environmental Issues
Religion: Dioceses, Jewish Causes, Ministries, Religious Welfare
Science: Science Museums, Scientific Centers & Institutes
Social Services: Child Welfare, Community Centers, Community Service Organizations, Counseling,

Crime Prevention, Day Care, Family Planning, Family Services, Food/Clothing Distribution, People with Disabilities, Recreation & Athletics, Social Services-General, United Funds/United Ways, Veterans, YMCA/YWCA/YMHA/YWHA, Youth Organizations

Application Procedures

Initial Contact: Organizations should send a proposal addressed to the executive director.

Application Requirements: Applications must include a one-page cover letter describing the project and the amount being requested. The proposal should also include a one page summary of the project, name and telephone number of contact person, organizational background, need for project implementation, project objectives, project budget, anticipated income including information about other sources approached for funding, steps in implementation, time frame, qualifications of key personnel to be involved, and method of project evaluation. Also include list of current board of trustees, current budget, a proposed budget for the project year(s) showing both income and expenses, copy of IRS classification letter, recent audited financial statement, outline of sources of income, letters of support, and readily available printed material about the organization such as annual reports and brochures.

Deadlines: Submit requests by March 30, June 30, September 30, and December 30 for consideration at the next regularly scheduled meeting of the trustees in March, June, September, and December.

Review Process: Proposals are screened and evaluated by the staff before presentation at the trustees' meeting. Organizations submitting proposals outside of the foundation's priorities and guidelines will be notified promptly. Preference is given to pilot projects, innovative programs, and research endeavors which promise significant benefits and broad application. Grantees must be able to demonstrate administrative capabilities for programs funded and provide periodic reports and a financial account of how funds have been utilized.

Restrictions

No support is given to carry on propaganda, influence legislation and elections, or for voter registration drives; for endowments or capital needs, including renovation, equipment and construction; for debt reduction or to fund benefit events; for services to the physically, mentally or developmentally disabled or the elderly; to individuals; or for purposes and activities outside of the United States. Proposals sent electronically or by fax are not accepted.

Additional Information

Publications: Annual Report (including Application Guidelines)

Foundation Officials

David T. Abbott: executive director B Fremont, OH. ED Denison University BA; Columbia University MS (1975); Harvard University JD (1982).
Marjorie Carlson: trustee
Marcia Egbert: senior program officer
Deena M. Epstein: senior program officer
Geoffrey Glebocki: senior program officer
Ann Landreth Gund: secretary, trustee
Catherine Gund: trustee
Geoffrey de Conde Gund: president, treasurer, trustee
George Gund, III: trustee B Cleveland, OH 1937. ED Case Western Reserve University School of Business Administration. PRIM CORP EMPL chairman: Northstar Financial Corp. CORP AFFIL vice president hockey: Sun Valley Ice Skating Inc.; chairman: North Stars Metro Center Management Corp.; chairman, co-owner: San Jose Sharks; co-owner: Cleveland Cavaliers; vice chairman: Gund Investment Corp.; director: Ameritrust Cleveland; film producer: Caipirinha Productions. NONPR AFFIL director: Sundance Institute; director: University Nevada-Reno Foundation;

advisory council: Sierra Club Foundation; director: Sun Valley Center Arts & Humanities; chairman: San Francisco International Film Festival; director: San Francisco Museum Art; member sponsors council: Project Population Action; member international council: Museum Modern Art; collectors committee: National Gallery Art; director: Cleveland Health Museum; director: Cleveland International Film Festival; director: Bay Area Education Television Association; director: California Theatre Foundation. CLUB AFFIL University Club; Rowfant Club; Union Club; Olympic Club; Rainier Club; Cleveland Athletic Club; Kirtland Country Club; California Tennis Club.
Llura A. Gund: vice president, trustee
Robert Jaquay: associate director
Jon Mark Jensen: senior program officer B Norristown, PA 1953. ED Albright College BS (1975); Bucknell University MS (1980). PRIM CORP EMPL president, director: Intecon Inc.
Robert Davis Storey: trustee B Tuskegee, AL 1936. ED Harvard University AB (1958); Case Western Reserve University JD (1964). PRIM CORP EMPL partner: Thompson Hine LLP. CORP AFFIL director: Verizon Communications Inc.; director: Procter & Gamble Co.; treasurer: Allied Resinous Products Inc.; director: May Department Stores Co. NONPR AFFIL member: Society Benchers; trustee: Spelman College; member: Cleveland Bar Association; trustee: Great Lakes Science Center; trustee: Case Western Reserve University. CLUB AFFIL University Club; Rowfant Club; Union Club; Ponce de Leon Club.

Grants Analysis

Disclosure Period: calendar year ending 2002
Total Grants: $19,556,406*
Number of Grants: 493
Average Grant: $35,756*
Highest Grant: $2,000,000
Lowest Grant: $900
Typical Range: $5,000 to $200,000
*__Note:__ Giving includes United Way; scholarships. Average grant figure excludes highest grant.

Recent Grants

Note: Grants derived from 2001 Form 990.

General

1,000,000	Foundation Fighting Blindness, Hunt Valley, MD -- retinal degenerative disease research
1,000,000	Foundation Fighting Blindness, Hunt Valley, MD -- retinal degenerative disease research
500,000	Great Lakes Museum of Science, Environment, and Technology, Cleveland, OH -- leadership endowment grant
500,000	Neighborhood Progress, Cleveland, OH
500,000	Neighborhood Progress, Cleveland, OH -- neighborhood development organizations and project financing
250,000	Institute for Civil Society, Newton, MA -- building early learning systems
200,000	Community Partnership for Arts and Culture, Cleveland, OH
162,500	Cleveland Initiative for Education, Cleveland, OH -- operating and program support
162,500	Cleveland Initiative for Education, Cleveland, OH
152,625	Greater Cleveland Roundtable, Cleveland, OH -- Cleveland Summit on Education

STELLA AND CHARLES GUTTMAN FOUNDATION

Giving Contact

Elizabeth Olofson, Executive Director
445 Park Avenue, 19th Floor
New York, NY 10022

Phone: (212)371-7082
Fax: (212)371-8936
E-mail: info@guttmanfdn.org
Web: http://www.fdncenter.org/grantmaker/guttman/

Description

Founded: 1959
EIN: 136103039
Organization Type: General Purpose Foundation
Giving Locations: NY: New York including metropolitan area; Israel
Grant Types: General Support, Operating Expenses, Project.

Donor Information

Founder: Incorporated in 1959 by the late Charles Guttman and the late Stella Guttman .

Financial Summary

Total Giving: $2,198,150 (2000); $1,620,020 (1998); $1,797,470 (1997)
Giving Analysis: Giving for 2000 includes: foundation scholarships ($30,000); foundation grants to United Way ($30,000) 1998: foundation scholarships ($2,500)
Assets: $50,937,066 (2000); $47,364,995 (1998); $43,000,000 (1997 approx)

Typical Recipients

Arts & Humanities: Arts Associations & Councils, Dance, Arts & Humanities-General, Libraries, Museums/Galleries, Music, Public Broadcasting
Civic & Public Affairs: African American Affairs, Botanical Gardens/Parks, Community Foundations, Employment/Job Training, Civic & Public Affairs-General, Legal Aid, Public Policy, Safety, Urban & Community Affairs
Education: Afterschool/Enrichment Programs, Arts/Humanities Education, Colleges & Universities, Education Associations, Education Funds, Education Reform, Elementary Education (Public), Environmental Education, Education-General, Health & Physical Education, International Studies, Legal Education, Literacy, Medical Education, Minority Education, Preschool Education, Public Education (Precollege), Religious Education, Science/Mathematics Education, Social Sciences Education, Special Education, Student Aid
Environment: Air/Water Quality, Environment-General
Health: Adolescent Health Issues, AIDS/HIV, Alzheimers Disease, Cancer, Diabetes, Emergency/Ambulance Services, Geriatric Health, Health Policy/Cost Containment, Heart, Hospitals, Medical Research, Mental Health, Nutrition, Prenatal Health Issues, Public Health, Single-Disease Health Associations
International: Foreign Educational Institutions, Health Care/Hospitals, International Development, International Peace & Security Issues, International Relations, International Relief Efforts, Missionary/Religious Activities
Religion: Churches, Jewish Causes, Religious Organizations, Religious Welfare
Science: Scientific Centers & Institutes, Scientific Centers & Institutes, Scientific Research
Social Services: At-Risk Youth, Big Brother/Big Sister, Camps, Child Welfare, Community Centers, Community Service Organizations, Day Care, Delinquency & Criminal Rehabilitation, Family Planning, Family Services, Homes, People with Disabilities, Recreation & Athletics, Senior Services, Shelters/Homelessness, Social Services-General, Substance Abuse, United Funds/United Ways, Volunteer Services, YMCA/YWCA/YMHA/YWHA, Youth Organizations

Application Procedures

Initial Contact: Applicants should send a request for funding three to five pages in length.
Application Requirements: Request for funding should include; a statement of the need for the project

and population served; explanation of program that will meet need; description of intended results; amount requested; detailed project budget; other sources of support;; summary of staff and board qualifications; current financial statement; most recent IRS Form 990; IRS tax exempt letter; and signed statement by CEO or Chairman that proposal is accurate.
Deadlines: None.
Review Process: The Board of Directors meets at least three times a year to review proposals.
Notes: The Foundation also accepts the New York area common application form.

Restrictions

The foundation does not make grants to religious organizations for religious purposes, public interest litigation, anti-vivisectionist causes, individuals, organizations not qualified as charitable, or for foreign travel or study.

Additional Information

Publications: Funding Guidelines; Application Procedures

Foundation Officials

Charles S. Brenner: director
Edgar H. Brenner: president B New York, NY 1930. ED Carleton College BA (1951); Yale University JD (1954). PRIM NONPR EMPL national director: Behavioral Law Center. NONPR AFFIL codirector: International University Center Legal Studies; vis. res. professor. law: National Law Center; director: Institute Behavior Resources; fellow: College Problems Drug Dependency; senior counsel terrorism studies program: George Washington University; member: American Bar Association; president, chairman board: Americans Medical Progress. CLUB AFFIL member: Explorers Club; member: Yale Club.
Robert S. Gassman: treasurer, director
Peter A. Herbert: vice president, director
Elizabeth Olofson: executive director
Sonia Rosenberg: director
Ernest Rubenstein: secretary, director NONPR AFFIL director: Covenant House.

Grants Analysis

Disclosure Period: calendar year ending 2000
Total Grants: $2,138,150*
Number of Grants: 129
Average Grant: $15,064*
Highest Grant: $125,000
Typical Range: $5,000 to $30,000
*Note: Giving excludes scholarships and United Way. Average grant figure excludes two highest grants ($225,000).

Recent Grants

Note: Grants derived from 2000 Form 990.

General

125,000	United Jewish Appeal-Federation of Jewish Philanthropies of New York, Inc., New York, NY -- support of the NORC Supportive Services Fund, help senior service agencies develop NORC supportive service programs for the elderly & general support
100,000	United Jewish Appeal-Federation of Jewish Philanthropies of New York, Inc., New York, NY -- support of the Israel association of Community Centers PELE Program
60,000	University Settlement Society of New York, New York, NY -- support a pilot project with Henry Street and Grand Street Settlement Houses
30,000	Council of Senior Centers and Services of New York City, Inc., New York, NY -- support adult day services initiative
30,000	Grand Street Settlement, Inc, New York, NY -- support of a College Discovery

Center, which offers comprehensive college and career guidance and academic support for middle and high school students

30,000	United Neighborhood Houses of New York, Inc., New York, NY -- support the development of a family child care network at Kingsbridge Heights Community Center in the South Bronx
30,000	United Way of New York City, New York, NY -- support of child care and early education fund
25,000	After School Corporation, New York, NY -- to support Scholar Programs
25,000	Bank Street College of Education, New York, NY -- to support the Liberty Program
25,000	Big Brothers and Big Sisters of New York City, Inc., New York, NY -- to support the Borough Partnership Program, which expand will expand mentoring programs at community-based agencies in South Bronx and Queens

H. C. S. FOUNDATION

Giving Contact

L. Thomas Hiltz, Trustee
1801 East 9th Street, Suite 1035
Cleveland, OH 44114-3103
Phone: (216)781-3502
Fax: (216)781-3504

Description

Founded: 1959
EIN: 346514235
Organization Type: General Purpose Foundation
Giving Locations: MD; OH: Cincinnati
Grant Types: Capital, Challenge, Conference/Seminar, Operating Expenses.

Donor Information

Founder: Established in 1959 by the late Harold C. Schott .

Financial Summary

Total Giving: $4,309,333 (2000); $4,000,000 (1999 approx); $3,848,000 (1998)
Assets: $93,831,430 (2000); $96,768,843 (1998); $94,780,066 (1997)
Gifts Received: $2,800,000 (1997); $15,000 (1992)

Typical Recipients

Arts & Humanities: Arts Associations & Councils, Arts Centers, Arts & Humanities-General, Historic Preservation, History & Archaeology, Libraries, Museums/Galleries, Music, Opera, Public Broadcasting, Theater
Civic & Public Affairs: Botanical Gardens/Parks, Clubs, Economic Development, Employment/Job Training, Civic & Public Affairs-General, Legal Aid, Municipalities/Towns, Parades/Festivals
Education: Colleges & Universities, Legal Education, Literacy, Private Education (Precollege), Public Education (Precollege), Religious Education, Science/Mathematics Education, Secondary Education (Private), Special Education, Student Aid
Environment: Resource Conservation
Health: Cancer, Clinics/Medical Centers, Eyes/Blindness, Health Funds, Health Organizations, Heart, Hospitals, Long-Term Care, Medical Rehabilitation, Prenatal Health Issues, Speech & Hearing, Trauma Treatment
International: Foreign Arts Organizations, International Relations, International Relief Efforts
Religion: Churches, Dioceses, Religion-General, Ministries, Religious Organizations, Religious Welfare, Seminaries
Science: Scientific Centers & Institutes

Social Services: Animal Protection, At-Risk Youth, Child Welfare, Community Service Organizations, Family Planning, Family Services, Food/Clothing Distribution, People with Disabilities, Recreation & Athletics, Shelters/Homelessness, Social Services-General, Substance Abuse, United Funds/United Ways, YMCA/YWCA/YMHA/YWHA, Youth Organizations

Application Procedures

Initial Contact: The foundation has no formal grant application procedure or application form.
Application Requirements: Applications should be in writing and include detailed information about the project, the amount requested, and proof of the organization's tax-exempt status.
Deadlines: None.

Restrictions

Grants are not made to individuals.

Foundation Officials

Francie S. Hiltz: trustee
L. Thomas Hiltz: trustee CORP AFFIL director: Applied Industrial Technologies; director: Drees Co.
Betty Jane Mulcahy: trustee
William Dunne Saal: trustee B 1948. ED University of Cincinnati BA (1970). PRIM CORP EMPL principal: William D. Saal Real Estate. CORP AFFIL president, director: Hyde Park Associates Inc.
Milton B. Schott, Jr.: trustee

Grants Analysis

Disclosure Period: calendar year ending 2000
Total Grants: $4,309,333
Number of Grants: 24
Average Grant: $122,145*
Highest Grant: $1,500,000
Typical Range: $25,000 to $200,000
*Note: Average grant figure excludes highest grant.

Recent Grants

Note: Grants derived from 2000 Form 990.

General

1,500,000	Renaissance Village, Inc., Palm Beach Gardens, FL -- toward the construction of the Administration Building
350,000	St. Elizabeth Medical Center Foundation, Dayton, OH -- to provide nationally recognized care to the Northern Kentucky/Greater Cincinnati area
315,000	St. Joseph Infant Home, Cincinnati, OH -- toward campaign to heighten awareness
300,000	Cincinnati Zoo and Botanical Garden, Cincinnati, OH -- toward Events and Education Center
300,000	University of Cincinnati College of Law, Cincinnati, OH -- for faculty candidates
250,000	WCET - TV 48, Cincinnati, OH -- toward program for their conversation to digital broadcasting
200,000	Diocese of Columbus, Columbus, OH -- for the Challenge in Changing Times Campaign
200,000	Veterans Guest House, Cincinnati, OH -- funding for the construction of a Fisher House
150,000	Operation Smile, Norfolk, VA -- support of reconstructive surgery for disadvantaged children
100,000	Legal Aid Society of Greater Cincinnati, Cincinnati, OH -- for endowment campaign

H.J. HEINZ CO.

Company Headquarters

600 Grant Street
Pittsburgh, PA 15219
Web: http://www.heinz.com

Company Description

Founded: 1869
Ticker: HNZ
Exchange: NYSE
Revenue: US$9.431 billion (2002)
Profit: US$833.9 million (2002)
Employees: 46500 (2002)
Fortune Rank: 194, per FORTUNE Magazine's list of 500 Largest U.S. Corporations (2002).
SIC(s): 2032 Canned Specialties, 2033 Canned Fruits & Vegetables, 2038 Frozen Specialties Nec, 2099 Food Preparations Nec.

Operating Locations

Alden Merrell Desserts (MA--West Newburyport); Chef Francisco, Inc. (PA--King of Prussia); Escalon Premier Brands, Inc. (CA--Escalon); Heinz Frozen Food Co. (FL--Fort Myers; ID--Pocatello; OH--Massillon; OR--Ontario; PA--West Chester); H.J. Heinz Co. (AZ--Phoenix; CA, Chatsworth, Escalon, Irvine, Stockton; FL--Jacksonville; GA--Atlanta; IL--Northbrook; IA--Cedar Rapids, Muscatine; MA--Westburyport; MI--Holland; NJ--Pennsauken; OH--Fremont, Mason; PA--King of Prussia; TX--Dallas); Portion Pac, Inc. (CA--Chatsworth; FL--Jacksonville; GA--Atlanta; OH--Mason; TX--Dallas); Quality Chef Foods, Inc. (IA--Cedar Rapids); Thermo Pac, Inc. (GA--Stone Mountain); Todds (AZ--Phoenix; CA--Irvine)
Note: Heinz also has operating locations in Italy, India, Indonesia, Singapore, China, South Korea, Hong Kong and the Philippines.

H.J. Heinz Co. Foundation

Giving Contact

Loretta M. Oken, Program Director
H.J. Heinz Co. Foundation
PO Box 57
Pittsburgh, PA 15230-0057
Phone: (412)456-5772
Fax: (412)456-7868
E-mail: heinz_foundation@hjheinz.com
Web: http://www.heinz.com/jsp/foundation.jsp

Alternate Contact

Robert Hass
Mellon Bank NA
AIM 151-3725
Pittsburgh, PA 15230

Description

Founded: 1951
EIN: 256018924
Organization Type: Corporate Foundation
Giving Locations: principally near operating locations and to national organizations.
Grant Types: Capital, Challenge, Conference/Seminar, Employee Matching Gifts, Endowment, Fellowship, General Support, Project, Scholarship.
Note: Foundation gives to scholarship funds only and does not give individual scholarships.

Donor Information

Founder: H. J. Heinz Co.

Financial Summary

Total Giving: $5,699,101 (2001); $6,494,241 (2000); $6,249,022 (1999). Note: Contributes through foundation only.
Giving Analysis: Giving for 2000 includes: foundation grants to United Way ($494,332); foundation ($5,999,909); 1999: foundation matching gifts ($90,000); foundation grants to United Way ($119,333); foundation ($6,039,689); 1998: foundation ($6,690,018) foundation matching gifts ($6,690,018).
Assets: $1,153,903 (2001); $753,778 (2000); $1,113,438 (1999)

Gifts Received: $6,000,000 (2001); $6,000,000 (2000); $6,000,000 (1999). Note: Foundation receives contributions from the H.J. Heinz Company and various individuals.

Typical Recipients

Arts & Humanities: Arts Associations & Councils, Arts Centers, Arts Festivals, Arts Funds, Arts Outreach, Ballet, Dance, Film & Video, Arts & Humanities-General, Historic Preservation, History & Archaeology, Libraries, Literary Arts, Museums/Galleries, Music, Opera, Performing Arts, Public Broadcasting, Theater
Civic & Public Affairs: African American Affairs, Botanical Gardens/Parks, Business/Free Enterprise, Civil Rights, Community Foundations, Economic Development, Economic Policy, Employment/Job Training, Civic & Public Affairs-General, Housing, Law & Justice, Legal Aid, Philanthropic Organizations, Professional & Trade Associations, Public Policy, Rural Affairs, Safety, Urban & Community Affairs, Women's Affairs, Zoos/Aquariums
Education: Afterschool/Enrichment Programs, Agricultural Education, Arts/Humanities Education, Business Education, Colleges & Universities, Community & Junior Colleges, Continuing Education, Economic Education, Education Associations, Education Funds, Elementary Education (Private), Environmental Education, Education-General, Health & Physical Education, International Exchange, International Studies, Journalism/Media Education, Legal Education, Literacy, Medical Education, Minority Education, Private Education (Precollege), Public Education (Precollege), Religious Education, Science/Mathematics Education, Secondary Education (Private), Special Education, Student Aid
Environment: Environment-General
Health: AIDS/HIV, Cancer, Children's Health/Hospitals, Clinics/Medical Centers, Health Organizations, Heart, Home-Care Services, Hospices, Hospitals, Medical Rehabilitation, Medical Research, Nutrition, Public Health, Single-Disease Health Associations
International: Foreign Educational Institutions, Health Care/Hospitals, Human Rights, International Affairs, International Development, International Environmental Issues, International Organizations, International Peace & Security Issues, International Relations, International Relief Efforts
Religion: Religious Organizations, Religious Welfare
Science: Science-General, Scientific Centers & Institutes, Scientific Organizations
Social Services: Animal Protection, Child Welfare, Community Centers, Community Service Organizations, Counseling, Delinquency & Criminal Rehabilitation, Family Planning, Family Services, Food/Clothing Distribution, Homes, People with Disabilities, Recreation & Athletics, Senior Services, Substance Abuse, United Funds/United Ways, Volunteer Services, YMCA/YWCA/YMHA/YWHA, Youth Organizations

Application Procedures

Initial Contact: Submit a brief letter requesting guidelines or obtain guidelines from the foundation's web site.
Application Requirements: A formal proposal should be made in writing and must include five items: Program Information, Financial Information, Volunteers, Impact, and Policy Decisions. Program Information should provide an executive summary, a description of organization, including the organization's purposes, overall goals, and plans for the current year; project description; measurable goals and objectives; target demographic; and sustainability of the project after grant funding ends. Financial Information must include the organization's current operating budget; project budget; and recently audited financial statement with management letter. Requested Volunteers information includes a description of the extent to which Heinz employees, retirees, or directors are involved with the organization and an outline of volunteer opportunities available within the organization. Impact information describes how the program will be evaluated, which may include feedback from recipients, improvements made, attendance and/or participation at events, and independent evaluation. Policy Decision describes the organization's type of governing structure. The following Attachments are required: proof of tax-exempt status; a list of board members, with affiliations; most recent annual report; and requested financial information.
Deadlines: None; board meets quarterly.
Evaluative Criteria: Priority to United Ways, scholarship programs in food-related courses of study, grants for health-related facilities in geographic areas served by the company, and organizations receiving matching gifts.

Restrictions

The foundation does not provide loans and does not support individuals, equipment, conferences, travel, general scholarships, religious programs, political campaigns, or unsolicited research projects.

Additional Information

Publications: Grant Application Information

Corporate Officials

William R. Johnson: chairman, president, chief executive officer B 1949. ED University of California, Los Angeles BBA (1971); University of Texas MBA (1974). PRIM CORP EMPL chairman, president, chief executive officer: H.J. Heinz Co. CORP AFFIL director: Amerada Hess Corp.
S. Donald Wiley: director B Pittsburgh, PA 1926. ED Westminster College BA (1950); University of Pennsylvania School of Law LLB (1953). NONPR AFFIL director: Weighco Inc.; trustee: Westminister College; trustee: Carnegie Mellon University.
David R. Williams: executive vice president, director B London, United Kingdom 1943. ED Exeter University BA (1964). PRIM CORP EMPL executive vice president: H.J. Heinz Co. CORP AFFIL chief executive officer: StarKist Foods Inc. NONPR AFFIL member: Association Chartered Accts U.S.; member: Financial Executives Institute; member: Association Chartered Accts UK.

Foundation Officials

Tammy B. Aupperle: program director
Karyll A. Davis: trustee
Loretta M. Oken: program director
David R. Williams: trustee (see above)

Grants Analysis

Disclosure Period: calendar year ending 2001
Total Grants: $3,885,951*
Number of Grants: 146
Average Grant: $5,464
Highest Grant: $250,000
Lowest Grant: $115
Typical Range: $1,000 to $100,000
*Note: Giving excludes matching gifts, scholarship, and United Way.

Recent Grants

Note: Grants derived from 2001 Form 990.

General

485,000	United Way Allegheny County, Pittsburgh, PA -- for operating support
250,000	Hospital for Sick Children, North York, ON Canada -- in support of the SPRINKLES Research in Toronto
100,000	American Ireland Fund, San Francisco, CA -- in support of the Institute for Neuroscience at Trinity College
100,000	Carnegie Mellon University, Pittsburgh, PA -- for scholarships
100,000	Center for Environmental Science and Economics, Washington, DC -- for endowment support
100,000	Extra-Mile Education Foundation, Inc., Pittsburgh, PA -- funding to 4 inner-city parochial schools

100,000	Irish Educational Foundation, Cork Ireland -- in support of endowed research fellowship
100,000	National Underground Freedom Center, Cincinnati, OH -- for endow the Teacher Candidate's Summer Institute on Freedom
100,000	Robert Morris College, Moon Township, PA -- in support of the College's Communications Skills Program
100,000	United Way Allegheny County, Pittsburgh, PA -- funding to 4 inner-city parochial schools

H&R BLOCK, INC.

Company Headquarters
4400 Main St.
Kansas City, MO 64111
Web: http://www.hrblock.com

Company Description
Founded: 1955
Ticker: HRB
Exchange: NYSE
Operating Revenue: US$3.317 billion (2002)
Profit: US$434.4 million (2002)
Employees: 99100 (2002)
Fortune Rank: 462, per FORTUNE Magazine's list of 500 Largest U.S. Corporations (2002).
SIC(s): 7291 Tax Return Preparation Services, 8721 Accounting, Auditing & Bookkeeping.

Operating Locations
List includes headquarters offices for Personnel Pool of America, an H&R Block operating company.

Nonmonetary Support
Type: Donated Products; Loaned Employees; Loaned Executives
Volunteer Programs: Individual H&R Block associates actively participate in community programs such as Habitat for Humanity and United Way. The foundation provides strategic support, rewards, and recognition for volunteer efforts.
Contact: Marla Sutton, Volunteer & Community Program Coordinator
Note: Nonmonetary support is provided by the company and foundation.

H&R Block Foundation

Giving Contact
David P. Miles, President
4400 Main Street
Kansas City, MO 64111
Phone: 800-869-9220
Fax: (816)753-1585
E-mail: foundation@hrblock.com
Web: http://www.hrblockfoundation.org

Alternate Contact
Kay Pearson-Boyd
Phone: (816)932-8324
Note: For general inquiries and contributions requests for the Kansas City, MO area.

Description
Founded: 1974
EIN: 237378232
Organization Type: Corporate Foundation
Giving Locations: MO: Kansas City
Grant Types: Capital, Employee Matching Gifts, General Support, Multiyear/Continuing Support.
Note: Employee matching gift ratio: 1 to 1 for gifts to education institutions and the September 11 Fund.

Financial Summary
Total Giving: $3,177,017 (2001); $2,662,591 (2000); $2,033,376 (1999). Note: Contributes through corporate direct giving program and foundation.
Giving Analysis: Giving for 1999 includes: foundation matching gifts ($106,383); foundation ($1,926,996); 1998: corporate grants to United Way ($5,000); corporate scholarships ($139,560) corporate direct giving ($1,720,653).
Assets: $47,017,571 (2001); $50,377,297 (2000); $53,622,717 (1999)
Gifts Received: $1,800,000 (2001); $5,787,279 (1999); $3,311,138 (1998). Note: In 1999, contributions were received from HRB Management, Inc. In 1996, 1998, and 2001 contributions were received from H&R Block, Inc.

Typical Recipients
Arts & Humanities: Arts Appreciation, Arts Associations & Councils, Arts Centers, Arts Festivals, Arts Funds, Arts Institutes, Arts Outreach, Ballet, Community Arts, Dance, Ethnic & Folk Arts, Arts & Humanities-General, Libraries, Literary Arts, Museums/Galleries, Music, Opera, Performing Arts, Public Broadcasting, Theater, Visual Arts
Civic & Public Affairs: Botanical Gardens/Parks, Business/Free Enterprise, Civil Rights, Clubs, Community Foundations, Economic Development, Employment/Job Training, Civic & Public Affairs-General, Housing, Law & Justice, Legal Aid, Nonprofit Management, Public Policy, Safety, Urban & Community Affairs, Women's Affairs, Zoos/Aquariums
Education: Afterschool/Enrichment Programs, Agricultural Education, Arts/Humanities Education, Business Education, Colleges & Universities, Community & Junior Colleges, Continuing Education, Economic Education, Education Funds, Education Reform, Environmental Education, Education-General, Legal Education, Literacy, Medical Education, Minority Education, Preschool Education, Private Education (Precollege), Public Education (Precollege), Science/Mathematics Education, Social Sciences Education, Special Education, Student Aid
Environment: Environment-General, Watershed
Health: AIDS/HIV, Cancer, Children's Health/Hospitals, Clinics/Medical Centers, Geriatric Health, Health Funds, Health Organizations, Heart, Home-Care Services, Hospices, Hospitals, Medical Rehabilitation, Mental Health, Multiple Sclerosis, Prenatal Health Issues, Public Health, Research/Studies Institutes, Single-Disease Health Associations
International: International Relations
Religion: Religion-General, Jewish Causes, Ministries, Religious Organizations, Religious Welfare, Social/Policy Issues
Science: Science Exhibits & Fairs, Science Museums
Social Services: At-Risk Youth, Camps, Child Welfare, Community Centers, Community Service Organizations, Counseling, Crime Prevention, Day Care, Delinquency & Criminal Rehabilitation, Domestic Violence, Emergency Relief, Family Planning, Family Services, Food/Clothing Distribution, Homes, People with Disabilities, Recreation & Athletics, Refugee Assistance, Scouts, Senior Services, Shelters/Homelessness, Social Services-General, Special Olympics, Substance Abuse, United Funds/United Ways, Volunteer Services, YMCA/YWCA/YMHA/YWHA, Youth Organizations

Application Procedures
Initial Contact: Request guidelines, then submit a formal proposal.
Application Requirements: Information should include a cover letter detailing amount requested and grant period; project description (including an explanation of why the project is needed, who will be served and what will be accomplished during a specific time period); information on the sustainability of the project and its lasting benefits to the participants, organization and community; a specific plan for evaluating and reporting outcomes; budget and projected sources of funds for the grant period; recently audited financial statement; proof of tax-exempt status; and a description of organization (including staff, board of directors, history and accomplishments).
Deadlines: None.
Evaluative Criteria: Demonstrated need; relevance to foundation's funding categories; 501(c)(3) status; location within metropolitan areas of Kansas City, MO; stability of organization's management; financial planning; fiscal soundness; long- and short-range goals and objectives; and measurable evaluation.
Decision Notification: The board of directors considers requests at quarterly meetings in September (annual meeting), December, March, and June; written notification of grants awarded follows each meeting.
Notes: Organizations may be asked to submit additional information or to meet with a member of the foundation's board of directors or staff.

Restrictions
Foundation does not support individuals or businesses; publications; projects for which the Foundation must exercise expenditure responsibility; single-disease agencies; travel or conferences; historic preservation; telethons, dinners, advertising, or other fund-raising events.

Additional Information
Foundation favors making proportionately significant grants to relatively few activities, rather than relatively minor grants to a great many activities. Hands-on contributions have a special place within the foundation's priorities. Generally, grants of less than $500 are not made.

Foundation usually makes one-year grants but, in appropriate circumstances, will consider requests for up to five years for special project funding. Recipients may apply for additional funding after original grant has expired.

H&R Block is no longer affiliated with CompuServe.
Publications: Annual Report; Guidelines

Corporate Officials
Frank L. Salizzoni: chairman, director B 1938. ED Pennsylvania State University BS (1960); George Washington University MS (1964). PRIM CORP EMPL chairman, director: H&R Block Inc. CORP AFFIL director: Orbital Sciences Corp.; director: SKF U.S.A. Inc.; president: Block Financial Corp.; president: H & R Block.

Foundation Officials
Robert L. Bloch: secretary, program officer
Charles E. Curran: director
Barbara Lebedun: president
Frank L. Salizzoni: vice chairman, director (see above)

Grants Analysis
Disclosure Period: calendar year ending 2001
Total Grants: $2,920,917*
Number of Grants: 385
Average Grant: $6,974*
Highest Grant: $150,000
Lowest Grant: $66
Typical Range: $500 to $20,000
*Note: Giving excludes scholarships and United Way. Average grant figure excludes two highest grants totaling $250,000.

Recent Grants
Note: Grants derived from 2001 Form 990.

General
793,208	City Fountains Foundation, Kansas City, MO -- community development
156,400	Citizens Scholarship Foundation of America, St. Peter, MN -- for education
150,000	UMKC Block School of Business & Public Administration, Kansas City, MO -- for education

100,000	Nelson Gallery Foundation, Kansas City, MO -- arts and culture
75,000	Kansas City Area Life Sciences Foundation, Kansas City, MO -- for corporate social responsibility
75,000	Sunflower House, Inc., Overland Park, KS -- for high risk youth
64,500	Kaw Valley Habitat for Humanity, Kansas City, MO -- for Volunteer Program
50,000	Kansas City Free Health Clinic, Kansas City, MO -- for corporate social responsibility
50,000	KCPT/Channel 19, Kansas City, MO -- arts and culture
50,000	Rockhurst College, Kansas City, MO -- for education

MIRIAM AND PETER HAAS FUND

Giving Contact

Cheryl Polk, Executive Director & Secretary
201 Filbert Street, 5th Floor
San Francisco, CA 94133
Phone: (415)296-9249
Fax: (415)296-8842
E-mail: mphf@mphf.org

Description

Founded: 1982
EIN: 946064551
Organization Type: Family Foundation
Giving Locations: CA: San Francisco County
Grant Types: Capital, Endowment, General Support, Matching, Multiyear/Continuing Support, Operating Expenses, Project.

Donor Information

Founder: The fund was incorporated in 1982 in California by funds from Peter E. Haas Sr., his wife, Miriam Haas, and his mother, the late Elise Haas . Peter E. Haas, Sr., is the great-grandnephew of Levi Strauss, the founder of Levi Strauss & Company, the world's largest manufacturer of clothing. Mr. Haas, although retired, still operates as the company's chairman of its executive committee.

Financial Summary

Total Giving: $9,317,268 (fiscal year ending August 31, 2003 approx); $11,594,068 (fiscal 2002); $12,482,542 (fiscal 2000)
Giving Analysis: Giving for fiscal 1998 includes: foundation grants to United Way ($100,000)
Assets: $185,000,000 (fiscal 2003 approx); $190,145,600 (fiscal 2002); $265,612,590 (fiscal 2000)
Gifts Received: $142,434 (fiscal 1995); $12,947,831 (fiscal 1994); $63,035,667 (fiscal 1993). Note: In fiscal 1992 and 1994, contributions were received from the estate of Elise S. Haas. In fiscal 1993, contributions were received from the estate of Elise S. Hass ($60,000,000) and from Peter and Miriam Haas ($3,035,667).

Typical Recipients

Arts & Humanities: Arts Centers, Arts Funds, Arts Institutes, Ballet, Community Arts, Dance, Film & Video, Arts & Humanities-General, Historic Preservation, History & Archaeology, Libraries, Museums/Galleries, Music, Opera, Performing Arts, Public Broadcasting, Theater, Visual Arts
Civic & Public Affairs: African American Affairs, Asian American Affairs, Botanical Gardens/Parks, Business/Free Enterprise, Community Foundations, Economic Development, Employment/Job Training, Civic & Public Affairs-General, Hispanic Affairs, Housing, Nonprofit Management, Philanthropic Organizations, Professional & Trade Associations, Public Policy, Urban & Community Affairs, Women's Affairs, Zoos/Aquariums
Education: Afterschool/Enrichment Programs, Arts/Humanities Education, Business Education, Colleges & Universities, Continuing Education, Education Funds, Education Reform, Elementary Education (Public), Education-General, Preschool Education, Private Education (Precollege), Public Education (Precollege), Religious Education, Secondary Education (Private), Secondary Education (Public), Social Sciences Education, Vocational & Technical Education
Environment: Environment-General
Health: AIDS/HIV, Cancer, Children's Health/Hospitals, Clinics/Medical Centers, Hospitals, Long-Term Care, Medical Rehabilitation, Medical Research, Mental Health, Public Health, Research/Studies Institutes
International: Foreign Educational Institutions, Human Rights, International Organizations, International Peace & Security Issues, International Relations, Missionary/Religious Activities
Religion: Jewish Causes, Religious Organizations, Religious Welfare, Synagogues/Temples
Science: Science Museums, Scientific Centers & Institutes
Social Services: Child Welfare, Community Centers, Community Service Organizations, Day Care, Domestic Violence, Emergency Relief, Family Planning, Family Services, Food/Clothing Distribution, People with Disabilities, Recreation & Athletics, Refugee Assistance, Shelters/Homelessness, Substance Abuse, United Funds/United Ways, Youth Organizations

Application Procedures

Initial Contact: The foundation has no formal grant application procedure or application form.
Deadlines: None.

Restrictions

The fund does not support individuals.

Additional Information

The majority of grantmaking is staff and trustee initiated, and the fund works with other organizations to solicit proposals.
Publications: Annual Report

Foundation Officials

Miriam Lurie Haas: don, president, trustee
Cheryl Polk: executive director

Grants Analysis

Disclosure Period: fiscal year ending August 31, 2000
Total Grants: $12,482,542*
Number of Grants: 254
Average Grant: $24,335*
Highest Grant: $3,350,000
Typical Range: $100 to $5,000 and $25,000 to $300,000
*Note: Average grant figure excludes two highest grants ($6,350,000).

Recent Grants

Note: Grants derived from 2000 Form 990.

General

3,350,000	San Francisco Museum of Modern Art, San Francisco, CA
3,000,000	Museum of Modern Art, New York, NY
400,000	Jewish Family and Children's Services, San Francisco, CA

250,000	American Fund for the Tate Gallery, New York, NY
250,000	Council on Foreign Relations, New York, NY
200,000	City College of San Francisco, San Francisco, CA
200,000	KQED, San Francisco, CA
200,000	Low-Income Housing Fund, San Francisco, CA
200,000	San Francisco State University, San Francisco, CA
189,871	Duke University, Durham, NC

WALTER AND ELISE HAAS FUND

Giving Contact

Pamela H. David, Executive Director
1 Lombard Street, Suite 305
San Francisco, CA 94111-1130
Phone: (415)398-4474
Fax: (415)986-4779
E-mail: brendan@haassr.org
Web: http://www.haassr.org

Description

Founded: 1953
EIN: 946068564
Organization Type: Family Foundation
Giving Locations: CA: Alameda County, Marin County, San Mateo County, San Francisco the Bay area
Grant Types: Capital, Endowment, General Support, Multiyear/Continuing Support, Project.

Donor Information

Founder: The Walter and Elise Haas Fund was established in 1952 by Walter Abraham Haas and Elise Haas "to provide support for charitable and cultural purposes consistent with traditions and values which they held in regard. In creating the fund, Mr. and Mrs. Haas sought to return to the community benefits which they felt fortunate to have enjoyed as part of their active careers."
Walter Abraham Haas was head of Levi Strauss and Company from 1928 to 1955, during which time the company was developed into the world's largest apparel manufacturer. His wife, Elise Haas, was the daughter of Sigmund Stern, a nephew of Levi Strauss. Mrs. Haas was active in San Francisco cultural and civic life for many years and was involved in the establishment of the Museum of Modern Art, the San Francisco Symphony, the Stern Grove Festival, and Mount Zion Hospital. Mr. Haas died in 1979; Mrs. Haas continued to serve as vice president of the fund until her death in 1990.

Financial Summary

Total Giving: $10,697,970 (2001); $10,390,205 (2000); $11,776,346 (1999)
Giving Analysis: Giving for 2000 includes: foundation grants to United Way ($100,000) 1998: foundation grants to United Way ($50,000)
Assets: $213,128,308 (2001); $233,139,808 (2000); $239,711,061 (1999)
Gifts Received: $200,000 (1998); $200,000 (1997 approx); $500,000 (1996)

Typical Recipients

Arts & Humanities: Arts Associations & Councils, Arts Centers, Arts Institutes, Arts Outreach, Ballet, Dance, Ethnic & Folk Arts, Film & Video, Arts & Humanities-General, Historic Preservation, History & Archaeology, Libraries, Literary Arts, Museums/Galleries, Music, Opera, Performing Arts, Public Broadcasting, Theater, Visual Arts

Civic & Public Affairs: Asian American Affairs, Botanical Gardens/Parks, Business/Free Enterprise, Civil Rights, Community Foundations, Economic Development, Employment/Job Training, First Amendment Issues, Civic & Public Affairs-General, Hispanic Affairs, Housing, Legal Aid, Municipalities/Towns, Native American Affairs, Nonprofit Management, Parades/Festivals, Philanthropic Organizations, Public Policy, Urban & Community Affairs, Women's Affairs, Zoos/Aquariums

Education: Afterschool/Enrichment Programs, Arts/Humanities Education, Business Education, Colleges & Universities, Education Associations, Education Funds, Education Reform, Environmental Education, Faculty Development, Education-General, International Exchange, Literacy, Minority Education, Private Education (Precollege), Public Education (Precollege), Religious Education, School Volunteerism, Science/Mathematics Education, Secondary Education (Public), Social Sciences Education, Special Education, Student Aid

Environment: Energy, Environment-General, Resource Conservation, Wildlife Protection

Health: AIDS/HIV, Children's Health/Hospitals, Clinics/Medical Centers, Diabetes, Health-General, Health Organizations, Hospitals, Long-Term Care, Mental Health, Prenatal Health Issues, Public Health

International: Foreign Arts Organizations, Foreign Educational Institutions, International Affairs, International Relations, Missionary/Religious Activities

Religion: Religion-General, Jewish Causes, Religious Welfare

Science: Science Museums, Scientific Organizations

Social Services: At-Risk Youth, Child Welfare, Community Centers, Community Service Organizations, Counseling, Crime Prevention, Domestic Violence, Emergency Relief, Family Planning, Family Services, Food/Clothing Distribution, Homes, People with Disabilities, Recreation & Athletics, Recreation & Athletics, Senior Services, Shelters/Homelessness, Substance Abuse, United Funds/United Ways, Volunteer Services, YMCA/YWCA/YMHA/YWHA, Youth Organizations

Application Procedures

Initial Contact: "As discussed in our January, 2003 letter, the Walter & Elise Haas Fund is now in the midst of an intensive strategic planning project. The Board of Trustees and the staff are fully engaged in the iterative process of refining our founders' legacies and values, restating our Fund's vision and goals, and examining potential strategies. We've made a great deal of progress, but still have quite some distance to go before we have a fully developed plan in place. Receipt of applications is suspended until we have finished our strategic planning process."

Application Requirements: Proposals should include the organization name and description, names and addresses of contact persons, project name, and project summary. The following attachments should be included: total project budget; annual organization budget; list of other sources of financial support, including amounts of current and proposed funding; financial statement for the previous year; list of the organization's board of directors, proof of tax-exempt status, and a complete project description.

Deadlines: None, for general funding requests. Deadlines for the Creative Work Fund: February 3 and August 1.

Review Process: The directors meet quarterly.

Restrictions

No grants are made to individuals; for general fundraising benefits; or for video or film production or distribution. Applications for capital grants are considered if the projects are of interest to the fund. Outside of the San Francisco Bay area, only projects of unusual merit are considered; grants in the categories citizenship and Civic Education and Professional Ethics are awarded to national organizations.

Additional Information

The fund also is related through family membership to three other foundations in California: Evelyn and Walter A. Haas, Jr. Fund, Miriam and Peter Haas Fund, and Richard and Rhoda Goldman Fund.

Publications: Periodic Reports; Annual Reports; Guidelines; Application Forms

Foundation Officials

Elizabeth Haas Eisenhardt: trustee PRIM CORP EMPL partner: Oakland Athletics.

Douglas E. Goldman: trustee

John D. Goldman: trustee CORP AFFIL president, director: Richard N Goldman & Co.; president, director: Goldman Insurance.

Peter Edgar Haas, Jr.: president B San Francisco, CA 1947. ED Stanford University AB (1969); Harvard University MBA (1972). CORP AFFIL director: Levi Strauss & Co.

Peter Edgar Haas, Sr.: honorary president B San Francisco, CA December 20, 1918. ED University of California at Berkeley AB (1940); Harvard University MBA (1943). PRIM CORP EMPL chairman executive committee, director: Levi Strauss & Co. ADD CORP EMPL chairman executive committee, director: Levi Strauss Associates Inc. Holding Corp. CORP AFFIL director emeritus: AT&T Corp. NONPR AFFIL trustee: San Francisco Foundation; associate: Smithsonian Institute National Board; director: Northern California Grantmakers.

Grants Analysis

Disclosure Period: calendar year ending 2001
Total Grants: $10,577,970*
Number of Grants: 361
Average Grant: $23,262*
Highest Grant: $1,000,000
Lowest Grant: $50
Typical Range: $2,500 to $50,000
*Note: Giving excludes United Way. Average grant figure excludes three highest grants ($2,250,000).

Recent Grants

Note: Grants derived from 2001 Form 990.

Library-Related
75,000   Libraries for the Future, New York, NY -- for Bay Area Education ACCESS

General
1,000,000   Skirball Cultural Center, Los Angeles, CA -- for construction of the American Family Heritage Hall and Amphitheater
625,000   Jewish Community Center of San Francisco, San Francisco, CA -- for 2001 annual campaign
625,000   Jewish Community Center of San Francisco, San Francisco, CA -- for 2001 annual campaign
300,000   San Francisco Conservatory of Music, San Francisco, CA -- renovation of 50-70 Oak Street as a larger campus
250,000   Bay Area Discovery Museum, Sausalito, CA -- for "My Place by the Bay" capital campaign
250,000   Northern California Community Loan Fund, San Francisco, CA -- creation of the capital fund
240,000   San Francisco Unified School District, San Francisco, CA -- for the Office of Teacher Affairs and CARE
220,000   Tides Center, San Francisco, CA -- to provide fellowships to eight Jewish social entrepreneurs, ages 21-35
202,000   Regents of the University of California, Berkeley, CA -- for New Teacher Center
200,000   National Asian American Telecommunications Association, San Francisco, CA -- for 9th street media consortium

EVELYN AND WALTER HAAS, JR. FUND

Giving Contact

Clayton Juan, Grants Administrator
One Market Landmark, Suite 400
San Francisco, CA 94105
Phone: (415)856-1400
Fax: (415)856-1500
E-mail: info@haasjr.org
Web: http://www.haasjr.org

Description

Founded: 1953
EIN: 946068932
Organization Type: Family Foundation
Giving Locations: CA: Alameda County, San Francisco County
Grant Types: Challenge, Employee Matching Gifts, General Support, Multiyear/Continuing Support, Operating Expenses, Seed Money.

Donor Information

Founder: The Evelyn and Walter Haas, Jr. Fund was established in 1953 by Mr. and Mrs. Walter A. Haas Jr. . Walter A. Haas, Jr., who died in 1995, was the son of Walter A. Haas, the head of Levi Strauss & Company from 1928 to 1955. His mother, Elise Haas, was the daughter of Sigmund Stern, a nephew of Levi Strauss. When Walter Haas, Jr., became president, CEO, and board chair of Levi Strauss & Company, he helped develop the business into the world's largest apparel company. He was also honorary chairman and director of Levi Strauss Associates. He was a trustee of the Ford Foundation and was an early president of the Guardsmen, a group of young men involved in social welfare. A philanthropist with a strong commitment to the Bay Area, he was a leader in San Francisco Urban League inner-city activities, and he helped establish a Boys' Club at Hunter's Point. His wife, Evelyn Haas, serves on the board of the San Francisco Museum of Art and Children's Hospital of San Francisco.

Financial Summary

Total Giving: $21,769,070 (2001); $21,357,826 (2000); $17,778,150 (1999)
Giving Analysis: Giving for 1999 includes: foundation matching gifts ($13,655); foundation grants to United Way ($25,000); 1998: foundation matching gifts ($20,305) foundation grants to United Way ($150,000)
Assets: $488,632,860 (2001); $505,019,277 (2000); $512,894,532 (1999)
Gifts Received: $14,031,647 (1994); $110,000,000 (1992)

Typical Recipients

Arts & Humanities: Arts Centers, Arts Funds, Arts Institutes, Ballet, Film & Video, Arts & Humanities-General, Libraries, Museums/Galleries, Music, Opera, Performing Arts, Public Broadcasting

Civic & Public Affairs: Asian American Affairs, Botanical Gardens/Parks, Business/Free Enterprise, Civil Rights, Clubs, Community Foundations, Economic Development, Economic Policy, Employment/Job Training, Ethnic Organizations, Gay/Lesbian Issues, Civic & Public Affairs-General, Hispanic Affairs, Housing, Law & Justice, Legal Aid, Native American Affairs, Nonprofit Management, Philanthropic Organizations, Professional & Trade Associations, Public Policy, Safety, Urban & Community Affairs, Women's Affairs

Education: Afterschool/Enrichment Programs, Business Education, Business-School Partnerships, Colleges & Universities, Education Funds, Education Reform, Education-General, Gifted & Talented

Programs, Journalism/Media Education, Legal Education, Literacy, Minority Education, Private Education (Precollege), Public Education (Precollege), Religious Education, School Volunteerism, Science/Mathematics Education, Special Education
Environment: Environment-General, Resource Conservation
Health: Alzheimers Disease, Clinics/Medical Centers, Geriatric Health, Health Organizations, Home-Care Services, Hospices, Hospitals, Long-Term Care, Mental Health, Nursing Services, Nutrition, Research/Studies Institutes, Research/Studies Institutes
International: Foreign Educational Institutions, International Affairs
Religion: Churches, Religion-General, Jewish Causes, Religious Organizations, Religious Welfare
Social Services: Animal Protection, Camps, Child Abuse, Child Welfare, Community Centers, Community Service Organizations, Day Care, Domestic Violence, Family Services, Food/Clothing Distribution, Homes, People with Disabilities, Recreation & Athletics, Refugee Assistance, Senior Services, Shelters/Homelessness, Social Services-General, United Funds/United Ways, Volunteer Services, YMCA/YWCA/YMHA/YWHA, Youth Organizations

Application Procedures

Initial Contact: Applicants should submit a two- to three-page letter of inquiry. An applicant who knows a trustee should indicate the association in the inquiry letter, and staff will bring the application to the attention of the trustees.
Application Requirements: Letters of inquiry should include brief statement of organization's purpose and goals; if applicable, description of project, need, and target population; information about capability of leaders who will implement project; anticipated short- and long-term outcomes and plans for assessing achievements; grant amount requested; statement about total agency budget and project budget, if different; and statement about other funding sources for agency and/or project, specifying committed as well as projected sources of support.
Deadlines: None.
Review Process: Staff reviews the letter of inquiry within one month of receipt to determine whether the proposed effort fits within the fund's giving programs. If so, a staff member will call or write the applicant, requesting additional information or a full proposal. The fund will provide specific questions and a list of required attachments if it requests a full proposal. Staff members analyze each proposal for fit with the fund's program priorities and values, significance of the need being addressed, potential to add value and achieve significant and enduring impacts, capacity of the agency to accomplish its goals and objectives, appropriateness of the budget (cost efficiencies), and the capacity to track program progress and assess results. Staff members research each request through telephone inquiries, meetings, or site visits. Staff might speak with colleagues, board members, or outside experts. Staff will then submit a written grant recommendation to the trustees.
Applicants can expect a decision within four months of the date of full-proposal receipt. This time line may vary, depending on the dates of the trustee meetings and the number of proposals being considered. The board of trustees meets at least three times a year to discuss program strategies and make grant decisions.

Restrictions

The fund will not make grants for capital or endowment campaigns, major equipment, basic research, conferences, publications, films or videos, deficit or emergency funding, scholarships, direct-mail campaigns, fund-raising events, annual appeals, or aid to individuals. Exceptions may be made for requests that are a component of a larger effort in which the fund is engaged, or for an organization with a well-established relationship with the fund.
The fund supports organizations that are tax-exempt under Section 501(c)(3) of the IRS code and are not

classified as private foundations under Section 509(a) of the code. In selected cases, the fund might consider support for projects sponsored by governmental entities. Organizations also can submit applications through a sponsoring organization, if the sponsor has a 501(c)(3) status, is not a private foundation under 509(a), and provides written authorization confirming its willingness to act as the fiscal sponsor.

Additional Information

Publications: Annual Report; Guidelines

Foundation Officials

Elizabeth Haas Eisenhardt: trustee, secretary PRIM CORP EMPL partner: Oakland Athletics.
Evelyn Danzig Haas: don, co-chairman, trustee
Robert Douglas Haas: trustee B San Francisco, CA 1942. ED University of California at Berkeley BA (1964); Harvard University MBA (1968). PRIM CORP EMPL chairman: Levi Strauss & Co. ADD CORP EMPL chairman: Levi Strauss Associates Inc. NONPR AFFIL honorary director: San Francisco AIDS Foundation; member: Trilateral Commission; member: Phi Beta Kappa; member: Council Foreign Relations; director: Meyer Friedman Institute; member: California Business Roundtable; member: Conference Board; trustee: Brookings Institution; director: Bay Area Community; director: Bay Area Council.
Ira S. Hirschfield: president, trustee

Grants Analysis

Disclosure Period: calendar year ending 2001
Total Grants: $21,769,070*
Number of Grants: 339
Average Grant: $64,200*
Highest Grant: $4,000,000
Lowest Grant: $100
Typical Range: $5,000 to $75,000
*Note: Grants analysis provided by foundation.

Recent Grants

Note: Grants derived from 2001 Form 990.

Library-Related
4,000,000   Museum of Modern Art, New York, NY -- for a capital project

General
5,000,000   Youth Sports Connection, Oakland, CA -- to harness the power of youth sports as a vehicle for youth development in Alameda and San Francisco counties
4,000,000   San Francisco Museum of Modern Art, San Francisco, CA -- for a special project
4,000,000   San Francisco Museum of Modern Art, San Francisco, CA -- for a special project
2,500,000   Northern California Community Loan Fund, San Francisco, CA -- to assist in the creation of permanently affordable office and program space for nonprofits in San Francisco
2,000,000   University of California Berkeley Foundation, Berkeley, CA -- for a special project
1,000,000   Wheaton College, Wheaton, IL -- for a capital campaign
1,000,000   Youth Sports Connection, Oakland, CA -- to harness the power of youth sports as a vehicle for youth development in Alameda and San Francisco counties
500,000   Unity Council, The, Oakland, CA -- for the Fruitvale Transit Village
450,000   Creative Work Fund, San Francisco, CA -- to support creative collaborations between artists and community organizations
450,000   Creative Work Fund, San Francisco, CA -- to support creative collaborations

between artists and community organizations

HAFFNER FOUNDATION

Giving Contact

Charles C. Haffner, III, President, Treasurer & Director
35 E. Wacker Dr., Suite 2650
Chicago, IL 60601
Phone: (312)920-6020

Description

Founded: 1952
EIN: 366064770
Organization Type: Private Foundation
Giving Locations: IL; MA; WA
Grant Types: Capital, Emergency, Endowment, General Support, Seed Money.

Donor Information

Founder: the late Charles C. Haffner, Jr., the late Mrs. Charles C. Haffner, Jr., Charles C. Haffner III

Financial Summary

Total Giving: $261,000 (2000); $261,000 (1999); $229,000 (1998)
Giving Analysis: Giving for 2000 includes: foundation grants to United Way ($5,000); 1999: foundation grants to United Way ($5,000); 1998: foundation grants to United Way ($5,000) foundation ($224,000)
Assets: $5,295,100 (2000); $5,030,908 (1999); $5,025,117 (1998)

Typical Recipients

Arts & Humanities: Arts Institutes, Ballet, Community Arts, Arts & Humanities-General, History & Archaeology, Libraries, Museums/Galleries, Music, Public Broadcasting
Civic & Public Affairs: Botanical Gardens/Parks, Clubs, Community Foundations, Civic & Public Affairs-General, Native American Affairs, Professional & Trade Associations, Public Policy, Rural Affairs, Zoos/Aquariums
Education: Agricultural Education, Colleges & Universities, Medical Education, Private Education (Precollege), Public Education (Precollege), Secondary Education (Private), Secondary Education (Public)
Environment: Environment-General, Resource Conservation, Watershed, Wildlife Protection
Health: Children's Health/Hospitals, Clinics/Medical Centers, Hospitals, Medical Rehabilitation, Public Health
International: International Environmental Issues
Religion: Churches, Religious Welfare
Science: Observatories & Planetariums
Social Services: Community Service Organizations, Food/Clothing Distribution, People with Disabilities, United Funds/United Ways, Youth Organizations

Restrictions

Does not support individuals or provide funds for scholarships.

Foundation Officials

Phoebe Haffner Andrew: director CLUB AFFIL Brook Club.
Clarissa Haffner Chandler: vice president, secretary, director B 1928. ED Vassar College (1948). CLUB AFFIL Great Lakes Cruising Club; Onwentsia Club; Contemporary Club; Friday Club.
Frances Haffner Colburn: director ED Bryn Mawr College (1958). CLUB AFFIL Friday Club; Somerset Club; Chilton Club; Essex County Club.
Charles Christian Haffner, III: president, treasurer, director B Chicago, IL 1928. ED Yale University BA (1950). PRIM CORP EMPL treasurer, director: R.R. Donnelley & Sons Co. CORP AFFIL director: Protection Mutual Insurance Co.; director: Du Kane Corp.

NONPR AFFIL life trust: Nature Conservancy; chairman: Sprague Foundation; trustee: Lincoln Park Zoological Society; chairman: Morton Arboretum; trustee: Art Institute of Chicago; trustee: Chicago City Day School. CLUB AFFIL Racquet Club; Commercial Club; Commonwealth Club; Caxton Club; Chicago Club; Casino Club.

Grants Analysis

Disclosure Period: calendar year ending 2000
Total Grants: $256,000*
Number of Grants: 36
Average Grant: $7,111
Highest Grant: $35,000
Typical Range: $2,000 to $20,000
***Note:** Giving excludes United Way.

Recent Grants

Note: Grants derived from 1999 Form 990.

Library-Related

30,000	Newberry Library, Chicago, IL

General

40,750	Museum of Fine Arts, Boston, MA
35,000	Henry Gallery Association, University of Washington, Seattle, WA
20,000	Children's Memorial Hospital, Chicago, IL
18,000	Bush School, Seattle, WA
15,000	Nature Conservancy, Illinois Chapter, Chicago, IL
10,000	Chicago City Day School, Chicago, IL
8,000	Morton Arboretum, Lisle, IL
6,000	Marquette Community Foundation, Marquette, MI
5,000	Access Living, Chicago, IL
5,000	Greater Chicago Food Depository, Chicago, IL

HAFIF FAMILY FOUNDATION

Giving Contact

Herbert Hafif, Director
269 West Bonita Avenue
Claremont, CA 91711
Phone: (310)624-1671
Fax: (310)621-4851

Description

Founded: 1987
EIN: 954081964
Organization Type: Private Foundation
Giving Locations: CA: Los Angeles
Grant Types: General Support.

Donor Information

Founder: Herbert Hafif

Financial Summary

Total Giving: $487,607 (2000); $472,745 (1999); $531,892 (1998)
Giving Analysis: Giving for 2000 includes: foundation grants to United Way ($5,000) 1998: foundation grants to United Way ($3,000)
Assets: $7,728,930 (2000); $9,506,029 (1999); $8,336,362 (1998)
Gifts Received: $100 (1999); $4,289 (1998); $1,500,004 (1996)

Typical Recipients

Arts & Humanities: Libraries, Museums/Galleries, Music, Performing Arts
Civic & Public Affairs: Clubs, Community Foundations, Civic & Public Affairs-General, Hispanic Affairs, Law & Justice, Parades/Festivals, Professional & Trade Associations, Public Policy, Urban & Community Affairs

Education: Afterschool/Enrichment Programs, Colleges & Universities, Community & Junior Colleges, Education-General, Medical Education, Private Education (Precollege), Religious Education, Secondary Education (Private)
Health: Clinics/Medical Centers, Emergency/Ambulance Services, Health Organizations, Medical Rehabilitation, Medical Research, Mental Health, Nutrition, Prenatal Health Issues, Preventive Medicine/Wellness Organizations, Single-Disease Health Associations
International: International Organizations, International Peace & Security Issues, International Relations, Missionary/Religious Activities
Religion: Churches, Religious Organizations, Religious Welfare, Social/Policy Issues, Synagogues/Temples
Science: Scientific Organizations
Social Services: Community Centers, Community Service Organizations, Counseling, Crime Prevention, Emergency Relief, Family Services, People with Disabilities, Recreation & Athletics, Senior Services, Sexual Abuse, Shelters/Homelessness, Social Services-General, Substance Abuse, United Funds/United Ways, Volunteer Services, YMCA/YWCA/YMHA/YWHA, Youth Organizations

Application Procedures

Initial Contact: The foundation requests applications be made in writing.
Deadlines: None.

Foundation Officials

Herbert Hafif: director B Philadelphia, PA 1930. ED Pomona College BA; University of Southern California JD. OCCUPATION attorney.
Jay Rodriguez: president

Grants Analysis

Disclosure Period: calendar year ending 2000
Total Grants: $482,607*
Number of Grants: 107
Average Grant: $4,510
Highest Grant: $50,000
Typical Range: $1,000 to $10,000
***Note:** Giving excludes United Way.

Recent Grants

Note: Grants derived from 2001 Form 990.

General

50,000	University of La Verne, La Verne, CA
30,000	Center for Public Integrity, Washington, DC
30,000	State Fair Community College, Sedalia, MO
25,000	University Muslim Medical Association
20,000	Claremont School of Theology, Claremont, CA
17,950	Spanish Trails Girls Scouts, Montclair, CA
15,000	Lestonnac Clinic
13,000	Foothill Country Day School, Claremont, CA
12,500	Center for Public Integrity, Washington, DC
12,500	Pitzer College, Claremont, CA

HAGEDORN FUND

Giving Contact

Monica Neal, Vice President
c/o JP Morgan Chase Bank
345 Park Ave., 8th Fl.
New York, NY 10021
Phone: (212)464-0134
Web: http://fdncenter.org/grantmaker/hagedorn/

Description

Founded: 1953
EIN: 136048718
Organization Type: General Purpose Foundation
Giving Locations: OH: Cuyahoga County
Grant Types: General Support, Research, Scholarship.

Donor Information

Founder: Established in 1953 by the late William Hagedorn .

Financial Summary

Total Giving: $1,500,000 (2002 approx); $1,530,500 (2001); $1,605,000 (2000)
Giving Analysis: Giving for 2001 includes: foundation scholarships ($25,500)
Assets: $31,167,003 (2001); $35,088,895 (2000); $26,480,607 (1998)
Gifts Received: $11,286 (1998)

Typical Recipients

Arts & Humanities: Arts Associations & Councils, Historic Preservation, Libraries, Performing Arts, Public Broadcasting
Civic & Public Affairs: Botanical Gardens/Parks, Clubs, Community Foundations, Economic Development, Housing, Inner-City Development, Legal Aid, Urban & Community Affairs, Women's Affairs
Education: Afterschool/Enrichment Programs, Colleges & Universities, Community & Junior Colleges, Education Associations, Engineering/Technological Education, Education-General, Legal Education, Literacy, Medical Education, Minority Education, Private Education (Precollege), Religious Education, Special Education, Student Aid
Environment: Environment-General, Resource Conservation
Health: AIDS/HIV, Arthritis, Cancer, Children's Health/Hospitals, Clinics/Medical Centers, Diabetes, Emergency/Ambulance Services, Eyes/Blindness, Health Policy/Cost Containment, Health Organizations, Heart, Hospices, Hospitals, Medical Rehabilitation, Mental Health, Nursing Services, Respiratory
International: Health Care/Hospitals
Religion: Churches, Jewish Causes, Religious Organizations, Religious Welfare, Seminaries, Synagogues/Temples
Social Services: At-Risk Youth, Big Brother/Big Sister, Child Welfare, Community Centers, Community Service Organizations, Counseling, Family Planning, Family Services, Food/Clothing Distribution, Homes, People with Disabilities, Recreation & Athletics, Senior Services, Shelters/Homelessness, Shelters/Homelessness, Social Services-General, United Funds/United Ways, YMCA/YWCA/YMHA/YWHA, Youth Organizations

Application Procedures

Initial Contact: Letter of inquiry.
Deadlines: None.

Restrictions

The fund does not make grants to individuals, or for continuing support, seed money, emergency funds, deficit financing, endowment funds, matching gifts, fellowships, research, special projects, publications, conferences, or loans.

Additional Information

Chase Manhattan Bank is corporate trustee for the fund.

Giving Program Officials

Monica Neal: contact

Foundation Officials

John J. Kindred, III: trustee ED Washington & Lee University (1952); University of Virginia (1955). NONPR AFFIL Colonial Order Acorn; Saint Nicholas Society.
Charles B. Lauren: trustee

Grants Analysis

Disclosure Period: calendar year ending 2001
Total Grants: $1,505,000*
Number of Grants: 90
Average Grant: $15,955*
Highest Grant: $85,000
Lowest Grant: $1,000
Typical Range: $5,000 to $25,000
*Note: Giving excludes scholarships. Average grant figure excludes highest grant.

Recent Grants

Note: Grants derived from 2001 Form 990.

Library-Related
25,000	New York Public Library, New York, NY -- for research

General
85,000	Wells College, Aurora, NY -- Ruth M. Hagedorn Memorial Fund
35,000	Education Broadcasting Corp, New York, NY -- general support and antenna
35,000	Rockefeller University, New York, NY -- general operating support
35,000	St. Vincent Services, New York, NY -- for American Dream Scholarship
35,000	South Bronx Overall Economic Development Corporation, Bronx, NY -- grant for general operating support for capital campaign
25,000	Big Brothers and Big Sisters, New York, NY -- general operating support
25,000	Brooklyn Botanic Garden, Brooklyn, NY -- general operating support
25,000	Cancer Research Institute, New York, NY -- general operating support
25,000	Children's AIDS Society
25,000	Community Service Society, New York, NY -- general operating support

HAIGH-SCATENA FOUNDATION

Giving Contact

Ronald W. Clement, Executive Director
PO Box 4399
Davis, CA 95617-4399
Phone: (530)758-5327

Description

Founded: 1967
EIN: 941753746
Organization Type: Private Foundation
Giving Locations: CA: Northern part of state
Grant Types: Conference/Seminar, Loan, Project, Research, Seed Money.

Donor Information

Founder: the late Isabelle Simi Haigh, Vivien Haigh

Financial Summary

Total Giving: $41,000 (fiscal year ending August 31, 2002 approx); $274,850 (fiscal 2001); $339,350 (fiscal 2000)
Assets: $3,095,169 (fiscal 2001); $4,097,035 (fiscal 2000); $3,909,460 (fiscal 1999)
Gifts Received: $122,225 (fiscal 1997)

Typical Recipients

Arts & Humanities: Libraries, Museums/Galleries
Civic & Public Affairs: Business/Free Enterprise, Community Foundations, Economic Development, Employment/Job Training, Civic & Public Affairs-General, Law & Justice, Legal Aid, Native American Affairs, Nonprofit Management, Philanthropic Organizations, Public Policy, Urban & Community Affairs, Women's Affairs

Education: Afterschool/Enrichment Programs, Colleges & Universities, Continuing Education, Education-General, Public Education (Precollege), Science/Mathematics Education, Special Education, Student Aid
Health: Children's Health/Hospitals
Religion: Churches, Religious Organizations, Religious Welfare
Social Services: At-Risk Youth, Child Abuse, Child Welfare, Community Service Organizations, Counseling, Day Care, Delinquency & Criminal Rehabilitation, Domestic Violence, Family Planning, Family Services, Shelters/Homelessness, Youth Organizations

Application Procedures

Initial Contact: Contact executive director to determine whether foundation is interested in project.
Deadlines: None.
Review Process: Review process from first contact to a grant award is typically six months or more.

Restrictions

Limited to organizations that benefit children or youth. Foundation does not fund political or lobbying groups, organizations outside operating areas, individuals, capital campaigns, equipment purchases, endowments, direct services, academic scholarships, or media production and distribution.

Additional Information

Foundation prefers to support efforts that emphasize advocacy and organizing strategies and favors prevention approaches rather than intervention. The foundation welcomes collaboration with other grantmakers and favors grantseekers with multiple sources of support.
Publications: Informational Brochure (including Application Guidelines)

Foundation Officials

Jean Bacigalupi: president
Ronald W. Clement: executive director
Jeanette Maddux Dunckel: director
Andrew J. Eber: director
James J. Gallagher: director
Bruce D. Goldstein: secretary
Gloria S. Hom: director
Wayne Koike: treasurer
Jan Masaoka: treasurer
Arnold X. C. Perkins: director
Gary A. Templin: director
Caroline Tower: director
Joanna Uribe de Mena: vice president

Grants Analysis

Disclosure Period: fiscal year ending August 31, 2001
Total Grants: $274,850
Number of Grants: 19
Average Grant: $14,466
Highest Grant: $52,100
Typical Range: $1,000 to $30,000

Recent Grants

Note: Grants derived from 2002 Form 990.

General
52,100	Sierra Adoption Services, Nevada City, CA -- for technical assistance
30,000	Buena Vista United Methodist Church, Alameda, CA -- for a new non-profit organization
30,000	Center on Juvenile and Criminal Justice, San Francisco, CA -- for research, technical assistance and public education
30,000	Families in Self Help, West Sacramento, CA -- support of a new community-based organization assisting immigrant and refugee families in moving to self-efficiency
30,000	Sacramento Valley Organizing Community, Sacramento, CA -- support for the Solano County Organizing Community
28,000	Youth Empowerment Center, Oakland, CA -- support of a new organization providing leadership, technical assistance and sponsorship to youth-led organizations
25,000	Immigrant Legal Resource Center, San Francisco, CA -- for training, technical assistance and advocacy efforts
8,750	Families in Self Help, West Sacramento, CA -- support of a new community-based organization assisting immigrant and refugee families in moving to self-efficiency
7,500	Sacramento Valley Organizing Community, Sacramento, CA -- support for the Solano County Organizing Community
7,000	Northern California Grantmaker, San Francisco, CA -- for Summer Youth Project

CRESCENT PORTER HALE FOUNDATION

Giving Contact

Ulla Z. Davis, Executive Director
655 Redwood Highway, Suite 301
Mill Valley, CA 94941
Phone: (415)388-2333
Fax: (415)381-4799

Description

Founded: 1961
EIN: 946093385
Organization Type: General Purpose Foundation
Giving Locations: CA: San Francisco Bay area
Grant Types: Capital, General Support, Scholarship.

Donor Information

Founder: Incorporated in 1961 by the late Elwyn C. Hale and the late M. Eugenie Hale .

Financial Summary

Total Giving: $1,190,400 (2002 approx); $1,190,400 (2000); $1,100,000 (1999 approx)
Assets: $26,000,000 (2002 approx); $28,921,817 (2000); $30,000,000 (1999 approx)

Typical Recipients

Arts & Humanities: Arts Festivals, Arts Institutes, Arts Outreach, Ballet, Libraries, Museums/Galleries, Music, Opera, Performing Arts, Theater
Civic & Public Affairs: Botanical Gardens/Parks, Economic Development, Employment/Job Training, Civic & Public Affairs-General, Hispanic Affairs, Housing, Law & Justice, Municipalities/Towns, Native American Affairs, Urban & Community Affairs, Women's Affairs
Education: Afterschool/Enrichment Programs, Arts/Humanities Education, Business Education, Colleges & Universities, Education Funds, Education Reform, Elementary Education (Private), Environmental Education, Education-General, International Studies, Medical Education, Preschool Education, Private Education (Precollege), Private Education (Precollege), Public Education (Precollege), Religious Education, Science/Mathematics Education, Secondary Education (Private), Secondary Education (Public), Special Education
Environment: Environment-General
Health: AIDS/HIV, Arthritis, Cancer, Health Organizations, Hospices, Hospitals, Long-Term Care, Medical Research, Nursing Services, Research/Studies Institutes, Single-Disease Health Associations
International: Foreign Educational Institutions, International Development

Religion: Churches, Religion-General, Religious Organizations, Religious Welfare, Seminaries
Science: Science Museums
Social Services: At-Risk Youth, Big Brother/Big Sister, Camps, Child Welfare, Community Centers, Community Service Organizations, Day Care, Day Care, Family Planning, Family Services, Food/Clothing Distribution, Homes, People with Disabilities, Recreation & Athletics, Senior Services, Sexual Abuse, Shelters/Homelessness, Social Services-General, Substance Abuse, United Funds/United Ways, Volunteer Services, YMCA/YWCA/YMHA/YWHA, Youth Organizations

Application Procedures

Initial Contact: The foundation requests applications be made in writing.
Application Requirements: A concise letter of intent (up to two pages) should include the target population to be served; agency or project budget; amount requested from this foundation; purpose of funds sought; and other anticipated or committed sources of funding; and a brief statement of agency/project's history, goals and objectives.
Deadlines: None.
Review Process: The foundation will respond to inquiries within 30 days of receipt. Additional information will be requested from applicants invited to submit a full proposal. Eligibility is limited to organizations within the San Francisco Bay area.

Restrictions

No gifts will be made to individuals, for research for health projects, or to hospitals. Organizations must be tax exempt under Section 501(c)(3) of the IRS code. Grants are restricted to the San Francisco Bay area.

Additional Information

Publications: Application Guidelines; Application Letter

Foundation Officials

L. E. Alford: president
A. L. Ballard: secretary, treasurer B 1934. PRIM CORP EMPL president, director: Ballard Exploration Co.
Eugene Edmund Bleck, MD: director B Milwaukee, WI 1923. ED Northwestern University; Duke University (1948-1955); University of Southern California (1960); Marquette University MD (1977). NONPR AFFIL member: San Mateo County Medicine Association; member: Western Orthopedic Association; member: Piedmont Orthopedic Society; member advisor: Rehabilitation Engineering Society North America; director: Notre Dame High School Belmont California; member: Pediatric Orthopedic Society North American; member advisor: New York Academy Science; member: California Medicine Association; member: Medicine Advisory Group State Department Rehab; member: American Orthopaedic Association; member: American Academy Orthopedic Surgeons; member: American Academy Orthopedic Surgery; member: American Academy for Cerebral Palsy and Dev Medicine.
Ulla Z. Davis: executive director
Joan Withers Dinner: director
Rev. Charles Dullea, SJ: director NONPR AFFIL chancellor emeritus: University San Francisco.
Ephraim P. Engelman, MD: director
Lorraine Horn: director
Robert S. Kelling, Jr.: director
Hon. Thomas J. Mellon, Jr.: vice president
E. William Swanson: director

Grants Analysis

Disclosure Period: calendar year ending 2000
Total Grants: $1,190,400
Number of Grants: 209
Average Grant: $5,696
Highest Grant: $150,000

Lowest Grant: $1,000
Typical Range: $5,000 to $100,000

Recent Grants

Note: Grants derived from 2000 Form 990.

General
150,000	Family Aid Catholic Education, Oakland, CA
50,000	Archbishop Riordan High School, San Francisco, CA
50,000	Catholic Charities, San Francisco, CA
50,000	Marin Catholic High School, Kentfield, CA
50,000	Saint Vincent de Paul Society, San Francisco, CA
40,000	Central YMCA, San Francisco, CA
40,000	San Domenico School, San Anselmo, CA
30,000	Hamilton Family Center, San Francisco, CA
25,000	Catholic Youth Organization, San Rafael, CA
25,000	Dominican College of San Rafael, San Rafael, CA

W. B. HALEY FOUNDATION

Giving Contact

Eloise T. Haley, President
1612 Orchard Dr.
Albany, GA 31707
Phone: (229)435-3686

Description

Founded: 1973
EIN: 586113405
Organization Type: Private Foundation
Giving Locations: GA: Albany
Grant Types: General Support.

Donor Information

Founder: the late W. B. Haley, Jr.

Financial Summary

Total Giving: $190,000 (fiscal year ending February 28, 2002); $189,500 (fiscal 2001); $193,500 (fiscal 2000)
Giving Analysis: Giving for fiscal 2002 includes: foundation grants to United Way ($3,000); fiscal 2001: foundation grants to United Way ($3,000); fiscal 2000: foundation grants to United Way ($3,000)
Assets: $2,265,517 (fiscal 2002); $2,481,148 (fiscal 2001); $2,657,476 (fiscal 2000)

Typical Recipients

Arts & Humanities: Community Arts, Historic Preservation, History & Archaeology, Libraries, Museums/Galleries, Music, Opera, Theater
Civic & Public Affairs: Civic & Public Affairs-General, Housing, Women's Affairs
Education: Colleges & Universities
Health: Cancer, Heart, Hospitals, Medical Research, Public Health, Single-Disease Health Associations
International: International Affairs, International Relations
Religion: Religion-General, Religious Welfare
Social Services: Community Centers, Community Service Organizations, Family Services, People with Disabilities, Scouts, United Funds/United Ways, YMCA/YWCA/YMHA/YWHA, Youth Organizations

Application Procedures

Initial Contact: Send a brief letter of inquiry describing program.
Deadlines: None.

Foundation Officials

Stephen J. Byrne: director
Eloise T. Haley: president
Virginia Holman: director
Emily Jean H. McAfee: director
G. Edmund Nobles: director
Joseph B. Powell, Jr.: director
Stuart G. Watson: secretary
Harry Willson: director

Grants Analysis

Disclosure Period: fiscal year ending February 28, 2002
Total Grants: $187,000*
Number of Grants: 16
Average Grant: $1,800*
Highest Grant: $160,000
Lowest Grant: $500
Typical Range: $500 to $3,000
*Note: Giving excludes United Way. Average grant excludes highest grant.

Recent Grants

Note: Grants derived from fiscal 2000 Form 990.

General
160,000	Albany Museum of Art, Albany, GA
8,500	Salvation Army, Albany, GA
5,000	Albany YMCA, Albany, GA
3,000	Albany Symphony Association, Albany, NY
3,000	United Way of Southwest Georgia, Albany, GA
2,000	Girls Inc., Albany, GA
1,000	Carter Center, Atlanta, GA
1,000	Operalbany - Darton College, Albany, GA
1,000	St. Clare's Community, Albany, GA
6,00	Boys and Girls Club of Albany, Albany, GA

G. A. C. HALFF FOUNDATION

Giving Contact

Thomas F. Bibb, Vice President, Treasurer & Trustee
745 East Mulberry, Suite 400
San Antonio, TX 78212
Phone: (210)735-3300

Description

Founded: 1951
EIN: 746042432
Organization Type: Private Foundation
Giving Locations: TX: San Antonio
Grant Types: General Support, Research.

Donor Information

Founder: the late G. A. C. Halff

Financial Summary

Total Giving: $490,000 (fiscal year ending February 28, 2002); $437,340 (fiscal 2001); $466,900 (fiscal 2000)
Giving Analysis: Giving for fiscal 2002 includes: foundation grants to United Way ($30,000); fiscal 2001: foundation grants to United Way ($30,000); fiscal 2000: foundation grants to United Way ($30,000);
Assets: $7,773,369 (fiscal 2002); $9,251,577 (fiscal 2001); $11,300,891 (fiscal 2000)

Typical Recipients

Arts & Humanities: Arts Institutes, Ethnic & Folk Arts, Libraries, Museums/Galleries, Music, Public Broadcasting, Theater

Civic & Public Affairs: Employment/Job Training, Civic & Public Affairs-General, Nonprofit Management, Zoos/Aquariums
Education: Colleges & Universities, Education Funds, Education-General, Literacy, Private Education (Precollege)
Environment: Environment-General
Health: Cancer, Children's Health/Hospitals, Eyes/Blindness, Health Organizations, Hospices, Hospitals, Medical Rehabilitation, Medical Research, Nursing Services, Public Health, Single-Disease Health Associations
Religion: Dioceses, Religious Organizations, Religious Welfare
Social Services: At-Risk Youth, Big Brother/Big Sister, Camps, Child Welfare, Community Centers, Community Service Organizations, Counseling, Family Planning, Family Services, Food/Clothing Distribution, Homes, People with Disabilities, Scouts, Sexual Abuse, Shelters/Homelessness, Substance Abuse, United Funds/United Ways, YMCA/YWCA/YMHA/YWHA, Youth Organizations

Application Procedures

Initial Contact: Send a brief letter of inquiry describing program or project. Include proof of tax-exempt status.
Deadlines: May 15.

Restrictions

Does not support individuals.

Foundation Officials

Roland R. Arnold: trustee
Thomas F. Bibb: vice president, treasurer, trustee
Catherine H. Edson: trustee
Thomas H. Edson: trustee
Hugh Halff, Jr.: president B 1936. OCCUPATION investor. NONPR AFFIL member: McNay Friends Gallery Council; member: Order Alamo; member: Charity Ball Association. CLUB AFFIL San Antonio German Club; Giraud Club; San Antonio Country Club; Argyle Club.
Marie M. Halff: trustee
J. O. Street: trustee
S. H. Street: trustee

Grants Analysis

Disclosure Period: fiscal year ending February 28, 2002
Total Grants: $460,000*
Number of Grants: 62
Average Grant: $7,419
Highest Grant: $10,000
Lowest Grant: $2,000
Typical Range: $5,000 to $10,000
*Note: Giving excludes United Way.

Recent Grants

Note: Grants derived from fiscal 2000 Form 990.

Library-Related
10,000	San Antonio Public Library, San Antonio, TX

General
30,000	United Way, San Antonio, TX
10,000	Big Brothers & Sisters, San Diego, CA
10,000	Child Guidance Center of SA, San Antonio, TX
10,000	Episcopal Diocese of West Texas, San Antonio, TX
10,000	Family Service Association of Sa. Inc., San Antonio, TX
10,000	Family Violence Prevention Services, San Antonio, TX
10,000	Good Samaritan Center, San Antonio, TX
10,000	Judson Montessori School, San Antonio, TX

10,000	McNay Art Museum, San Antonio, TX
10,000	Nonprofit Resource Center of Texas, San Antonio, TX

THE HALL FAMILY FOUNDATION

Giving Contact

William A. Hall, President
PO Box 419580, Department 323
Kansas City, MO 64141-6580
Phone: (816)274-8515
Fax: (816)274-8547

Description

Founded: 1993
EIN: 446006291
Organization Type: Family Foundation
Giving Locations: MO: Kansas City metropolitan area
Grant Types: Capital, Endowment, General Support, Matching, Multiyear/Continuing Support, Project, Seed Money.

Donor Information

Founder: Joyce C. Hall was born in 1891, in David City, NE. In 1910, he went to Kansas City, MO, and built a business that eventually would become Hallmark Cards. With his wife, Elizabeth Ann Dilday, he began a foundation to aid and strengthen the Kansas City area.
In 1983, the Hallmark Educational Foundation of Kansas and the Hallmark Education Foundation merged into the Hall Family Foundation to reflect more accurately the source of funds and to avoid philanthropic confusion between Hallmark Cards and the Hall family.

Financial Summary

Total Giving: $39,012,000 (2002); $36,958,990 (2001); $39,174,044 (2000)
Giving Analysis: Giving for 2000 includes: foundation gifts to individuals ($236,250); foundation grants to United Way ($710,000); 1999: foundation gifts to individuals ($57,445); foundation scholarships ($217,500); foundation grants to United Way ($435,000); 1998: foundation scholarships ($20,000); foundation gifts to individuals ($259,250) foundation grants to United Way ($550,000)
Assets: $611,394,790 (2002); $741,132,396 (2001); $861,619,337 (2000)
Gifts Received: $90,000 (1998). Note: In 1998, contributions were received from Hallmark Cards.

Typical Recipients

Arts & Humanities: Arts Associations & Councils, Arts Institutes, Dance, Arts & Humanities-General, History & Archaeology, Libraries, Museums/Galleries, Music, Opera, Performing Arts, Public Broadcasting, Theater, Visual Arts
Civic & Public Affairs: Botanical Gardens/Parks, Business/Free Enterprise, Community Foundations, Economic Development, Employment/Job Training, Civic & Public Affairs-General, Hispanic Affairs, Housing, Inner-City Development, Minority Business, Municipalities/Towns, Nonprofit Management, Parades/Festivals, Philanthropic Organizations, Urban & Community Affairs, Zoos/Aquariums
Education: Arts/Humanities Education, Business Education, Colleges & Universities, Education Reform, Environmental Education, Environmental Education, Education-General, Health & Physical Education, Literacy, Medical Education, Minority Education, Preschool Education, Private Education (Precollege), Public Education (Precollege), School Volunteerism, Science/Mathematics Education, Vocational & Technical Education
Health: Children's Health/Hospitals, Clinics/Medical Centers, Health-General, Health Organizations,

Home-Care Services, Hospitals, Hospitals (University Affiliated), Medical Rehabilitation, Mental Health, Public Health
International: International Relations
Religion: Dioceses, Ministries, Religious Welfare
Science: Science Museums, Scientific Organizations
Social Services: At-Risk Youth, Big Brother/Big Sister, Camps, Child Abuse, Child Welfare, Community Centers, Community Service Organizations, Crime Prevention, Day Care, Domestic Violence, Emergency Relief, Family Services, Food/Clothing Distribution, Homes, Recreation & Athletics, Scouts, Senior Services, Sexual Abuse, Shelters/Homelessness, Social Services-General, Special Olympics, Substance Abuse, United Funds/United Ways, Volunteer Services, YMCA/YWCA/YMHA/YWHA, Youth Organizations

Application Procedures

Initial Contact: All requests must be submitted in writing. If the request falls within the foundation's areas of interest and meets the guidelines, a proposal will be requested. Only requests from the metropolitan Kansas City area are considered. Grant application guidelines are available from the foundation.
Application Requirements: If requested, proposals should contain the following information: a clear description of the project for which funds are being requested, including program goals and objectives, documentation, of need and expected outcomes; a brief background on the proposing organization or agency; a detailed expense budget for the project indicating how the funds would be spent and over what time period; an income statement showing other sources of project support, public and/or private, which have been or will be solicited, including a statement of funds which have been received or pledged to date; a financial plan showing how the project will be supported beyond the grant period; criteria and/or method by which effectiveness of the grant will measured; information on the staff responsible for managing the project; a list of the organization's current board of directors and their terms of office; a copy of the organization's most recent 501 (c)(3) tax-exempt ruling from the Internal Revenue Service; and the organization's most recent certified audit or audited financial statement, where applicable.
Deadlines: None. However, proposals must be submitted at least eight weeks prior to when the board meets to be considered at the meeting.
Review Process: The average period of preliminary review (before a proposal is presented to the board) is six to eight weeks. The board of directors meets in March, June, September, and December. The average period of initial review is six to eight weeks.
Notes: The foundation gives preference to programs which create long-term solutions, have a positive impact on the community, are innovative, have the likelihood of future support for on-going operating costs, are non-competing with the government, promote excellence, have the capacity to achieve the desired results, and cooperate with other community agencies.

Restrictions

Grants are not made to individuals. In addition, the foundation does not provide grants for dinners, special events, international or fraternal organizations, political and lobbying groups, international or religious organizations for sectarian purposes, goodwill advertising, past operating deficits, or travel/conference expenses.

Additional Information

Grant recipients are asked to make periodic written progress reports.
Publications: Annual Report; Guidelines and Procedures for Grant Applicants

Foundation Officials

Jeanne M. Bates: vice president, program officer PRIM CORP EMPL manager community development: Hallmark Cards Inc.

Richard C. Green: director

Donald Joyce Hall: chairman, director B Kansas City, MO 1928. ED Dartmouth College AB (1950). PRIM CORP EMPL chairman board, director: Hallmark Cards Inc. CORP AFFIL director: United Telecommunications Inc.; director: Mutual Benefit Life Insurance Co.; director: Target Corp.; director: Commerce Bank NA; director: William E Coutts Co. Ltd.; director: 1st National Bank Lawrence; director: Business Mens Assurance Co. NONPR AFFIL trustee: Midwest Research Institute; trustee: Nelson-Atkins Museum Art; director: Kansas City Minority Suppliers Development Council; director: Kansas City Symphony; director: Friends of Art; member: Kansas City Chamber of Commerce; director: American Royal Association; president: Civic Council Greater Kansas City; honorary member: American Institute Architects.

William A. Hall: president

Irvine O. Hockaday: director

Lucinda S. Hogle: assistant secretary

David H. Hughes: director

Robert Almy Kipp: director B Lincoln, NE 1932. ED University of Kansas BScE (1952); University of Kansas MPA (1956). PRIM CORP EMPL group vice president: Hallmark Cards Inc. CORP AFFIL officer: Culinary Concepts Ltd.; officer: Milano.

John Laney: vice president, program officer

John A. MacDonald: vice president, treasurer

John P. Mascotte: director

Terri R. Maybee: assistant treasurer

Margaret H. Pence: director

Danita M.H. Robinson: secretary

Morton I. Sosland: director

Grants Analysis

Disclosure Period: calendar year ending 2001

Total Grants: $36,933,990*

Number of Grants: 134

Average Grant: $257,076*

Highest Grant: $1,500,000

Lowest Grant: $2,500

Typical Range: $50,000 to $500,000

*Note: Giving excludes United Way. Average grant figure excludes two highest grants ($3,000,000).

Recent Grants

Note: Grants derived from 2001 Form 990.

Library-Related

1,800,000 Missouri Development Finance Board, Jefferson City, MO -- for Adult Rehabilitation Center

General

12,375,000 Children's Mercy Hospital, Kansas City, MO -- for capital expenditures on Hospital Hill

1,500,000 Kansas University Endowment Association, Lawrence, KS -- for multi-faceted program

1,500,000 Union Station Kansas City, Inc., Kansas City, MO -- for operating support and museum building modifications

1,000,000 Union Station Kansas City, Inc., Kansas City, MO -- for operating support and museum building modifications

903,128 Children's Mercy Hospital, Kansas City, MO -- for research and education collaboration

800,000 Greater Kansas City Community Foundation, Kansas City, MO -- capital project

639,407 University of Kansas Medical Center, Kansas City, KS -- for research and education collaboration

625,000 Truman Medical Center Charitable Foundation, Kansas City, MO -- for Women's Health and Homeless Support

567,000 Greater Kansas City Community Foundation, Kansas City, MO -- for initiative fund

500,000 City of Fountains Foundation, Kansas City, MO -- for Union Station Fountain

HALL-PERRINE FOUNDATION

Giving Contact

Jack B. Evans, President, Chief Executive Officer
115 3rd Street Southeast, Suite 803
Cedar Rapids, IA 52401-1222
Phone: (319)362-9079
Fax: (319)362-7220

Description

Founded: 1953

EIN: 426057097

Organization Type: Family Foundation

Giving Locations: IA: Linn County, Cedar Rapids

Grant Types: Capital, Challenge, General Support, Matching.

Donor Information

Founder: The foundation originally was organized by Howard Hall under the Iowa Nonprofit Corporation Act in 1953. The incorporators were the late Margaret L. Hall and Howard Hall , Margaret D. Hall (also deceased), Irene H. Perrine, and Beahl T. Perrine (deceased). Howard Hall (d. 1971) was born in Onslow, IA. Mr. Hall was founder of the Margaret and Howard Hall Radiation Center and president and chairman of Iowa Manufacturing Co., Iowa Steel and Iron Works, and the Amana Refrigeration Co. He also was director of Iowa Electric Light and Power Co., Quaker Oats Co., and the Square D Co. of Detroit.

Financial Summary

Total Giving: $5,000,000 (2002); $5,000,000 (2001); $5,601,659 (2000)

Giving Analysis: Giving for 2000 includes: foundation grants to United Way ($385,000); 1999: foundation grants to United Way ($350,000) 1998: foundation grants to United Way ($618,000)

Assets: $100,875,000 (2002); $115,192,242 (2000); $114,590,450 (1999)

Gifts Received: $535 (2000); $751 (1999); $573 (1998). Note: The above gifts were bequeathed from the estate of Irene H. Perrine, former chairman of the foundation.

Typical Recipients

Arts & Humanities: Ethnic & Folk Arts, History & Archaeology, Libraries, Museums/Galleries, Music, Opera, Theater

Civic & Public Affairs: Botanical Gardens/Parks, Business/Free Enterprise, Chambers of Commerce, Clubs, Community Foundations, Economic Development, Employment/Job Training, Civic & Public Affairs-General, Housing, Nonprofit Management, Urban & Community Affairs, Zoos/Aquariums

Education: Business Education, Colleges & Universities, Community & Junior Colleges, Leadership Training, Minority Education, Science/Mathematics Education, Student Aid

Environment: Environment-General, Resource Conservation

Health: Clinics/Medical Centers, Emergency/Ambulance Services, Geriatric Health, Health Organizations, Heart, Hospitals, Hospitals

Religion: Churches, Jewish Causes, Religious Welfare, Synagogues/Temples

Science: Science-General

Social Services: Animal Protection, Camps, Child Welfare, Community Centers, Community Service Organizations, Counseling, Domestic Violence, Emergency Relief, Family Planning, Family Services, Food/Clothing Distribution, Homes, People with Disabilities, Recreation & Athletics, Scouts, Senior Services, Shelters/Homelessness, Substance Abuse, United Funds/United Ways, Volunteer Services, YMCA/YWCA/YMHA/YWHA, Youth Organizations

Application Procedures

Initial Contact: Applicants should make a preliminary inquiry to determine the foundation's interest in their request. This inquiry should briefly describe the organization and its purposes, and outline the goal of the proposed project. A grant application form is available upon request.

Application Requirements: Formal written proposals should include a brief description of the organization (legal name, history, activities, purpose, and governing board); purpose for grant; amount requested; other sources of financial support; audited financial statement; IRS determination letter of 501(c)(3) status; and Form 990.

Deadlines: None.

Review Process: Grant proposals are thoroughly screened by the foundation staff. Those meeting the established criteria are then considered by the board of directors or its duly authorized committee. Proposals are reviewed by the board approximately four times per year.

When a decision is reached, the foundation promptly sends a written notice advising of either the approval or disapproval of the grant proposal.

For grants that are approved, it is essential that the grantee accept the grant and the conditions set forth in an Agreement of Donee which includes financial reporting and a summary of the results obtained. This procedure enables the foundation to periodically review and evaluate its performance.

Restrictions

No grants are made to individuals. The following types of support do not have high priority: deficit financing, scholarships, fellowships, loans, endowment, continuing operating support, and basic scholarly research. Funds also are restricted for churches, elementary and secondary schools, benefits, special events, and conferences. Serves only county organizations.

Additional Information

The foundation's original name was The Hall Foundation.

Publications: Guidelines; Application Form

Foundation Officials

Bethany Allsbrook: program officer

Dr. Dennis Boatman: director B 1939. ED University of Iowa MD (1965). NONPR AFFIL principal: PCI Urology.

Ernest J. Buresh: director PRIM CORP EMPL president: Citizens Savings Bank.

Jack B. Evans: president, director B 1948. ED University of Iowa MBA. PRIM CORP EMPL president, director: Sci Fin Group Inc. CORP AFFIL director: Cedar Rapids Gazette Inc.; director: United Fire Casualty Co.

George C. Foerstner: director

Carleen M. Grandon: director

John Gabrielson Lidvall: treasurer, director B 1924.

Joseph R. Loufek: director

Alex Alfred Meyer: director B Cedar Rapids, IA 1931. ED University of Iowa (1956). PRIM CORP EMPL president, chairman, chief executive officer: Amana Refrigeration. CORP AFFIL director: Toro Co.

Darrel Arle Morf: vice president, attorney, director B Fredericksburg, IA 1943. ED University of Iowa BA (1966); University of Iowa JD (1969). PRIM CORP EMPL partner: Simmons, Perrine, Albright. NONPR AFFIL member: Iowa Bar Association; member: Linn

County Bar Association; member: American Bar Association.
Iris Muchmore: director, secretary PRIM CORP EMPL partner: Simmons, Perrine, Albright.
William Perry Whipple: board chairman, director B Cedar Rapids, IA November 01, 1913. ED Coe College BA (1935). PRIM NONPR EMPL chairman, director: Hall-Perrine Foundation, Inc. NONPR AFFIL director: Linn County ARC; honorary director: Methwick Manor; chairman, trustee: Coe College; trustee: Cedar Rapids Public Library. CLUB AFFIL mem: Rotary Club; mem: Elks Club.

Grants Analysis

Disclosure Period: calendar year ending 2000
Total Grants: $6,521,825*
Number of Grants: 23
Average Grant: $191,515*
Highest Grant: $1,250,000
Typical Range: $30,000 to $400,000
***Note:** Giving excludes United Way. Average grant figure excludes two highest grants ($2,500,000).

Recent Grants

Note: Grants derived from 2000 Form 990.

General

2,250,000	Mount Mercy College, Cedar Rapids, IA -- to construct a learning resources center
1,500,000	City of Cedar Rapids, Cedar Rapids, IA -- for Paramount renovations
1,000,000	City of Cedar Rapids, Cedar Rapids, IA -- for construction of new stadium
750,000	Meth Wick Community, Cedar Rapids, IA
385,000	United Way East Central Iowa, Cedar Rapids, IA
350,000	Iowana Council of Camp Fire, Inc., Cedar Rapids, IA -- camp renovations
300,000	Boy Scouts of America Hawkeye Area Council, Central City, IA -- camp renovations
148,818	Cedar Rapids-Marion Chamber of Commerce Foundation, Cedar Rapids, IA -- for economic development
110,500	Cedar Valley Habitat for Humanity, Cedar Rapids, IA -- for 16 new homes "Genesis Park"
31,000	Cedar Rapids Symphony Orchestra Association, Cedar Rapids, IA -- operating support

E. L. AND R. F. HALLBERG FOUNDATION

Giving Contact

Virginia L. Winker, Co-Trustee
2705 S. Cooper St., Suite 300
Arlington, TX 76015
Phone: (817)884-4448

Description

Founded: 1986
EIN: 756356892
Organization Type: Private Foundation
Giving Locations: TX
Grant Types: General Support.

Financial Summary

Total Giving: $168,125 (fiscal year ending September 30, 2001); $149,775 (fiscal 2000); $151,308 (fiscal 1998)
Giving Analysis: Giving for fiscal 1998 includes: foundation scholarships ($23,000) foundation ($128,308)
Assets: $4,183,871 (fiscal 2001); $4,523,944 (fiscal 2000); $4,143,549 (fiscal 1998)

Typical Recipients

Arts & Humanities: Libraries, Museums/Galleries, Music, Performing Arts, Theater
Civic & Public Affairs: Clubs, Civic & Public Affairs-General, Hispanic Affairs, Housing, Philanthropic Organizations
Education: Colleges & Universities, Engineering/Technological Education, Environmental Education, Health & Physical Education, Journalism/Media Education, Literacy, Minority Education, Private Education (Precollege), Religious Education, School Volunteerism, Science/Mathematics Education, Student Aid
Environment: Wildlife Protection
Health: Alzheimers Disease, Hospices
International: International Organizations
Religion: Churches, Religious Welfare
Social Services: Child Welfare, Community Service Organizations, Food/Clothing Distribution, People with Disabilities, Shelters/Homelessness

Application Procedures

Initial Contact: Send a brief letter of inquiry.
Application Requirements: Include a description of organization, amount requested, purpose of funds sought, recently audited financial statement, and proof of tax-exempt status.
Deadlines: None.

Restrictions

Does not support individuals or political or lobbying groups.

Additional Information

Trust(s): Bank One TX NA

Foundation Officials

Virginia Winkler: co-trustee

Grants Analysis

Disclosure Period: fiscal year ending September 30, 2001
Total Grants: $168,125
Number of Grants: 30
Average Grant: $3,897*
Highest Grant: $34,000
Lowest Grant: $1,000
Typical Range: $1,000 to $5,000
***Note:** Average grant figure excludes two highest grants ($59,000).

Recent Grants

Note: Grants derived from fiscal 2000 Form 990.

General

25,000	Ferris Heights United Methodist Church, Waxahachie, TX
16,000	University of Texas - Austin, Austin, TX
12,000	First Baptist Church, El Paso, TX
11,325	Van Cliburn Foundation, Ft. Worth, TX
11,200	First Christian Church, Arlington, TX
9,000	First United Methodist Church, Mansfield, TX
8,750	Fort Worth Symphony Orchestra, Ft. Worth, TX
7,000	University of North Texas, Denton, TX
7,000	University of Texas at Austin, Austin, TX
5,000	Baylor University, Waco, TX

E. W. HALLETT CHARITABLE TRUST

Giving Contact

Duane Feragen, Trust Officer
c/o US National Bank
PO Box 64713
St. Paul, MN 55164
Phone: (612)973-4485

Description

Founded: 1984
EIN: 416261160
Organization Type: Private Foundation
Giving Locations: MN
Grant Types: General Support, Scholarship.

Financial Summary

Total Giving: $779,217 (fiscal year ending November 30, 2001); $811,200 (fiscal 2000); $1,084,977 (fiscal 1999)
Giving Analysis: Giving for fiscal 2001 includes: foundation scholarships ($18,000) fiscal 1999: foundation scholarships ($18,000)
Assets: $16,411,279 (fiscal 2001); $19,113,040 (fiscal 2000); $19,506,928 (fiscal 1999)

Typical Recipients

Arts & Humanities: History & Archaeology, Libraries
Civic & Public Affairs: Economic Development, Housing, Municipalities/Towns, Urban & Community Affairs
Education: Colleges & Universities, Education Funds, Public Education (Precollege), Religious Education, Science/Mathematics Education, Special Education, Student Aid
Health: Clinics/Medical Centers, Eyes/Blindness, Heart, Home-Care Services, Hospices, Hospitals, Medical Rehabilitation
Religion: Churches, Seminaries
Social Services: Camps, Child Welfare, Community Centers, Crime Prevention, Food/Clothing Distribution, Homes, People with Disabilities, Recreation & Athletics, Scouts, Youth Organizations

Application Procedures

Initial Contact: Send a brief letter of inquiry describing program or project.
Deadlines: None.

Restrictions

Does not support individuals.

Additional Information

Trust(s): US National Bank
Trust(s): US National Bank NA

Foundation Officials

A. C. Jensen: co-trustee
N. Jean Rude: co-trustee
Paul D. Schliesman: executive director
Osmon R. Springsted: co-trustee

Grants Analysis

Disclosure Period: fiscal year ending November 30, 2001
Total Grants: $761,217*
Number of Grants: 9
Highest Grant: $295,000
Lowest Grant: $5,000
***Note:** GEX scholarship.

Recent Grants

Note: Grants derived from fiscal 2000 Form 990.

Library-Related

80,000	Jessie F. Memorial Library -- second payment of year 2000 grant

General

600,000	Hallett Community Center, St. Paul, MN -- fiscal year 2000 grants
71,200	Independent School District 182 -- third year of three year commitment for technology
25,000	Crosby Ironton Presbyterian Church, Crosby, MN -- fiscal year 2000 grants
10,000	Second Harvest Food Bank, Youngstown, OH -- 2000 grant payment

HALLIBURTON CO.

Company Headquarters

3600 Lincoln Plaza
500 N. Akard Street
Dallas, TX 75201-3391
Phone: (214)978-2600
Fax: (214)978-2611
Web: http://www.halliburton.com

Company Description

Founded: 1919
Ticker: HAL
Exchange: NYSE
Revenue: US$12.572 billion (2002)
Employees: 83000 (2002)
Fortune Rank: 153, per FORTUNE Magazine's list of 500 Largest U.S. Corporations (2002).
SIC(s): 1389 Oil & Gas Field Services Nec, 1541 Industrial Buildings & Warehouses, 1629 Heavy Construction Nec, 1799 Special Trade Contractors Nec.

Operating Locations

Halliburton Co. (AL--Mobile; CA--Alhambra; DC--Washington; FL--St. Petersburg; MD--Gaithersburg; OK--Davis, Duncan; PA--Pittsburgh)

Nonmonetary Support

Type: Donated Equipment; Donated Products

Halliburton Foundation, Inc.

Giving Contact

Margaret E. Carriere, Vice President & Secretary
Halliburton Foundation
3600 Lincoln Plaza
500 N. Akard Street
Dallas, TX 75201
Phone: (214)978-2600
Fax: (214)978-2611
Web: http://www.halliburton.com/corp/about.asp
Note: Contact for foundation giving.

Alternate Contact

Community & Governmental Affairs Manager
Halliburton Co.
PO Box 3
Houston, TX 77001-0003
Note: Contact for corporate contributions.

Description

EIN: 751212458
Organization Type: Corporate Foundation
Giving Locations: TX: Southwest.
Grant Types: Employee Matching Gifts, General Support.
Note: Employee matching gift ratio: 2 to 1.

Financial Summary

Total Giving: $1,299,441 (2001); $1,746,644 (2000); $1,826,289 (1999). Note: Contributes through foundation only.
Giving Analysis: Giving for 2000 includes: foundation ($1,746,644); 1999: foundation fellowships (approx $25,000); foundation grants to United Way ($53,706); foundation scholarships ($264,225); foundation ($1,483,358) 1998: foundation ($1,435,592)
Assets: $16,326,786 (2001); $15,679,123 (2000); $17,312,052 (1999)
Gifts Received: $1,077,480 (2001); $1,406,603 (2000); $688,810 (1999). Note: Gifts are received from Halliburton Energy Services and Brown & Root Companies.

Typical Recipients

Arts & Humanities: Arts Centers, History & Archaeology, Libraries, Museums/Galleries, Music, Opera, Performing Arts
Civic & Public Affairs: Business/Free Enterprise, Employment/Job Training, Civic & Public Affairs-General, Philanthropic Organizations, Public Policy, Urban & Community Affairs, Women's Affairs, Zoos/Aquariums
Education: Agricultural Education, Business Education, Business-School Partnerships, Colleges & Universities, Community & Junior Colleges, Elementary Education (Public), Engineering/Technological Education, Faculty Development, Education-General, International Studies, Legal Education, Literacy, Medical Education, Minority Education, Private Education (Precollege), Religious Education, Science/Mathematics Education, Social Sciences Education, Student Aid, Student Aid
Environment: Energy, Environment-General
Health: Cancer, Hospitals
International: Foreign Educational Institutions
Religion: Religious Welfare, Seminaries
Science: Science Museums, Scientific Centers & Institutes
Social Services: Scouts, Social Services-General, Substance Abuse, United Funds/United Ways, YMCA/YWCA/YMHA/YWHA, Youth Organizations

Application Procedures

Initial Contact: Requests for corporate contributions (either cash or in-kind support) should be in the form of a written proposal. Requests for foundation funding should be in the form of a letter.
Application Requirements: Corporate contributions requests should include description of organization to be funded, expected outcomes, program objectives with target dates, evaluation plan, and strategy to secure full funding for program. Also include 501(c)3 determination letter; list of board of directors and their business or other affiliations; audited financial statement; and current list of supporters.
Letters requesting foundation support should include amount requested and purpose of funds sought.
Deadlines: None.
Review Process: Requests are reviewed throughout the year. Decisions are based on available resources and eligibility of applying organization. Full review may take up to three months.
Evaluative Criteria: The company reports that it evaluates applications based on their ability to demonstrate Halliburton employee involvement or interest; meet critical community needs; provide solutions to critical social issues that have a demonstrated impact on children and youth; serve as a catalyst for raising additional funds from other corporations and foundations; demonstrate a specific need for Halliburton support; demonstrate sound financial management; impact or benefit key communities around the world where Halliburton has an employee and business presence. In addition, the program or activity should be recognized as a model program and have potential for replication.

Restrictions

Support is not made for individuals, scholarships for individuals, advertising campaigns, travel expenses, sporting events, or film and video projects. Also does not support religious organizations or organizations whose fundraising/administrative expenses exceed 15% of their annual budget.

Additional Information

Halliburton Co. merged with Dresser Industries effective September 1998.

Corporate Officials

David J. Lesar: chairman, president, chief executive officer B 1953. ED University of Wisconsin MBA; University of Wisconsin BS. PRIM CORP EMPL chairman president, chief executive officer: Halliburton Co.

ADD CORP EMPL chairman: Kellogg Brown & Root Inc. CORP AFFIL director: Highlands Insurance Co.; director: Southern Co. Inc.; director: Cordant Technology Inc.

Foundation Officials

Margaret E. Carriere: vice president, secretary, trustee
Celeste Colgan: vice president, secretary B Lander, WY 1939. ED University of Wyoming (1961); University of Maryland (1973). PRIM CORP EMPL vice president human resources: Halliburton Co. CORP AFFIL vice president human resources: Brown & Root Inc.
D. L. Foshee: trustee
David J. Lesar: trustee (see above)
G. V. Morris: trustee

Grants Analysis

Disclosure Period: calendar year ending 1999
Total Grants: $1,483,358*
Number of Grants: 345
Average Grant: $4,300
Highest Grant: $150,000
Typical Range: $2,000 to $20,000
*Note: Giving excludes scholarships; fellowships; United Way.

Recent Grants

Note: Grants derived from 2001 Form 990.

General

100,000	Oklahoma Centennial Commission, Oklahoma City, OK
100,000	University of Texas M.D. Anderson Cancer Center, Houston, TX
65,108	Texas A&M International University, College Station, TX
50,000	Denver Museum of Nature and Science, Denver, CO
47,250	Rice University, Houston, TX
37,161	University of Texas Arlington, Arlington, TX
35,000	Junior Achievement of Southeast Texas, Houston, TX
33,000	Texas A&M International University, College Station, TX
30,000	Oklahoma State University Foundation, Stillwater, OK
30,000	University of Oklahoma Foundation, Inc., Norman, OK

EWING HALSELL FOUNDATION

Giving Contact

Gilbert M. Denman, Jr., Trustee, Chairman of the Board
711 Navarro, Suite 537
San Antonio, TX 78205
Phone: (210)223-2649
Fax: (210)271-9089

Description

Founded: 1957
EIN: 746063016
Organization Type: General Purpose Foundation
Giving Locations: TX: San Antonio
Grant Types: Capital, Challenge, Endowment, Matching, Operating Expenses, Project, Research, Scholarship.

Donor Information

Founder: Established in 1957 by the late Ewing Halsell and the late Grace Fortner Rider , who died in 1971. Mr. Halsell was a cattle rancher whose interests centered in Texas, Oklahoma, and Kansas.

Financial Summary

Total Giving: $2,839,888 (fiscal year ending June 30, 1999); $2,086,270 (fiscal 1997); $1,761,196 (fiscal 1996)

Giving Analysis: Giving for fiscal 1999 includes: foundation grants to United Way ($8,000)

Assets: $67,449,111 (fiscal 1999); $55,981,458 (fiscal 1997); $49,170,176 (fiscal 1996)

Typical Recipients

Arts & Humanities: Arts Associations & Councils, Arts Centers, Arts Festivals, Ballet, Dance, Ethnic & Folk Arts, History & Archaeology, Libraries, Literary Arts, Museums/Galleries, Music, Opera, Public Broadcasting, Theater

Civic & Public Affairs: Botanical Gardens/Parks, Community Foundations, Economic Development, Employment/Job Training, Civic & Public Affairs-General, Hispanic Affairs, Housing, Nonprofit Management, Philanthropic Organizations, Safety, Urban & Community Affairs, Zoos/Aquariums

Education: Afterschool/Enrichment Programs, Agricultural Education, Arts/Humanities Education, Colleges & Universities, Economic Education, Education Reform, Elementary Education (Public), Faculty Development, Education-General, Literacy, Minority Education, Private Education (Precollege), Religious Education, Science/Mathematics Education, Special Education, Student Aid, Vocational & Technical Education

Environment: Environment-General, Resource Conservation, Watershed, Wildlife Protection

Health: AIDS/HIV, Cancer, Children's Health/Hospitals, Clinics/Medical Centers, Emergency/Ambulance Services, Geriatric Health, Health Organizations, Heart, Hospitals, Medical Research, Nursing Services, Public Health, Single-Disease Health Associations

International: International Organizations

Religion: Churches, Ministries, Religious Organizations, Religious Welfare

Social Services: Camps, Child Welfare, Community Centers, Community Service Organizations, Day Care, Domestic Violence, Family Planning, Family Services, Food/Clothing Distribution, People with Disabilities, Scouts, Shelters/Homelessness, Substance Abuse, United Funds/United Ways, YMCA/YWCA/YMHA/YWHA, Youth Organizations

Application Procedures

Initial Contact: Applicants should submit a letter and a short summary of the proposed project.

Application Requirements: Proposals should include the history and purposes of the organization, proposed use of funds, anticipated results of expenditures, and explanation of financial need (including other sources of funds, if any, to be used for the project). Also include a copy of the IRS tax exemption letter and information clearly indicating that any contribution made by the foundation will be considered a qualifying distribution, not a taxable expenditure. Applications should be signed or approved in writing by the chief executive of the applicant organization.

Deadlines: None.

Review Process: The foundation's trustees meet three to four times a year. Applicants will be notified in writing of receipt of application. Interviews are conducted only at the foundation's initiative.

Notes: The foundation discourages expensive and elaborate presentations.

Restrictions

The foundation discourages proposals for general support, deficit reduction, or continuing or additional support for current or previous programs. Grants are not made to individuals.

Additional Information

Grant commitments may cover several years. Matching funding is encouraged. The foundation trustees also initiate grants, and may make challenge grants

to stimulate other financial participation. In fields of special foundation interest, the foundation's program includes support for undertaking these projects. In many cases, trustees take an active part in the formation and operation of these programs as well as their support.

Because of the periodic nature of the trustees' meetings and the foundation's long-range planning process, it is suggested that applicants needing immediate help should apply to private individuals or corporations who are in a better position to make such grants to municipal, state, federal, or other public agencies.

Denman, Franklin, Denman in San Antonio, TX, provides legal and administrative services.

Publications: Application Guidelines

Foundation Officials

Edward H. Austin, Jr.: trustee B 1941. ED New York University; University of Texas; Tulane University BBA (1961). PRIM CORP EMPL partner, treasurer: Austin, Calvert & Flavin Inc. CORP AFFIL director: KN Energy Inc.

Jean Deacy: trustee

Gilbert M. Denman, Jr.: trustee, chairman B San Antonio, TX 1921. ED University of Texas BA (1940); University of Texas LLB (1942). PRIM CORP EMPL attorney: Denman, Franklin & Denman.

Leroy G. Denman, Jr.: trustee B San Antonio, TX 1918. ED University of Texas LLB (1939); University of Texas BA (1939). PRIM CORP EMPL attorney: Denman, Franklin & Denman. CORP AFFIL vice president, director: King Ranch Saddle Shop Inc.; vice president, director: Running W Saddle Shop; director: King Ranch Holdings Inc.

Hugh A. Fitzsimmons, Jr.: trustee

Grants Analysis

Disclosure Period: fiscal year ending June 30, 1999

Total Grants: $2,831,888*

Number of Grants: 55

Average Grant: $34,564*

Highest Grant: $500,000

Lowest Grant: $500

Typical Range: $1,000 to $35,000

*Note: Giving excludes United Way. Average grant excludes two highest grants ($1,000,000).

Recent Grants

Note: Grants derived from fiscal 2000 Form 990.

Library-Related

60,000	Dimmit County Public Library, Carrizo Springs, TX -- contribution toward new library and museum construction
50,000	San Antonio Library Foundation, San Antonio, TX -- purchase of books

General

1,000,000	Trinity University, San Antonio, TX -- Trinity University Press
500,000	Cancer Therapy and Research Center, San Antonio, TX -- contribution toward oncology, chemotherapy suites
300,000	Trinity University, San Antonio, TX -- Trinity University Press
250,000	University of Texas at San Antonio, San Antonio, TX -- contribution toward neurotransmitter research laboratory
175,000	San Antonio Museum of Art, San Antonio, TX -- support Scythian gold exhibit
100,000	Daughters of the Republic of Texas, Inc. - Alamo Fund, San Antonio, TX -- new educational amphitheater
100,000	San Pedro Playhouse, San Antonio, TX
75,000	Alamo Area Council Boy Scouts of America, San Antonio, TX -- capital campaign for Bear Creek
60,000	Nature Conservancy of Texas, San Antonio, TX -- Edwards Aquifer Conservation

50,000	Good Samaritan Center, San Antonio, TX -- capital campaign

HAMAN FAMILY FOUNDATION

Giving Contact

Larry Markworth
Huntington National Bank
232 W. Third St.
Dover, OH 44622
Phone: (614)331-9539

Description

Founded: 1998

EIN: 316565640

Organization Type: Private Foundation

Giving Locations: OH: Tuscarawas County

Grant Types: Capital, Project.

Financial Summary

Total Giving: $56,891 (fiscal year ending March 31, 2002); $61,076 (fiscal 2001); $54,666 (fiscal 2000)

Assets: $1,188,421 (fiscal 2002); $1,208,567 (fiscal 2001); $1,262,914 (fiscal 2000)

Typical Recipients

Arts & Humanities: Libraries, Museums/Galleries

Civic & Public Affairs: Civic & Public Affairs-General, Safety

Education: Colleges & Universities, Elementary Education (Public), Public Education (Precollege)

Health: Emergency/Ambulance Services

Social Services: Emergency Relief, YMCA/YWCA/YMHA/YWHA, Youth Organizations

Restrictions

Grants must go to charitable organizations in and for the benefit of Tuscarawas County, Ohio.

Additional Information

Trust(s): Huntington National Bank

Foundation Officials

Ruth Goertz: committee member
Ruth Goertz: committee member
Mark Heil: committee member
Mark Heill: committee member
Wilford Miller: committee member
Wilford Miller: committee member

Grants Analysis

Disclosure Period: fiscal year ending March 31, 2002

Total Grants: $56,891

Number of Grants: 19

Average Grant: $2,994

Highest Grant: $10,000

Lowest Grant: $500

Typical Range: $2,500 to $5,000

Recent Grants

Note: Grants derived from 2001 Form 990.

Library-Related

2,500	Dover Public Library, Dover, OH -- building addition

General

10,000	Kent State University, Kent, OH -- science and technology facility
6,562	Tusky Valley Youth Services -- software and television for youth center
5,500	Port Washington Police Department -- video camera for cruiser
5,000	Bolivar Volunteer Fire Department -- for portable radios
5,000	Claymont High School Library -- for library reference material

5,000	East Elementary -- for PTA and school playground renovation
5,000	New Philadelphia Fire Department, Philadelphia, PA -- equipment for trench rescue team
3,333	TUSC County YMCA -- expansion of Wellness Center
3,163	Tri County Joint Ambulance Department -- for emergency medical equipment
2,518	Dennison Railroad Depot Museum, Dennison, OH -- for photographic archival supplies

HAMER FOUNDATION

Giving Contact

Diane M. Kerly, Trustee
Hamer Foundation
2470 Fox Hill Road
State College, PA 16803-1797
Phone: (814)355-8004

Description

Founded: 1989
EIN: 251610780
Organization Type: Private Foundation
Giving Locations: PA: Centre County
Grant Types: General Support.

Donor Information

Founder: Established in 1989 by Donald W. Hamer.

Financial Summary

Total Giving: $705,000 (2001); $919,750 (2000); $323,500 (1999)
Giving Analysis: Giving for 1999 includes: foundation grants to United Way ($12,500); foundation scholarships ($55,000) foundation ($300,000)
Assets: $4,903,128 (2001); $5,469,760 (2000); $1,698,389 (1996)
Gifts Received: $750,000 (2001); $1,040,440 (2000); $892,250 (1999). Note: In 1996 and 2001, contributions were received from Donald W. Hamer. In 1999, contributions were received from Donald W. Hamer and Diane M. Kerly.

Typical Recipients

Arts & Humanities: Libraries, Museums/Galleries
Civic & Public Affairs: Botanical Gardens/Parks, Community Foundations, Housing, Women's Affairs
Education: Business Education, Colleges & Universities, Education-General, Minority Education
Environment: Environment-General, Resource Conservation, Wildlife Protection
Health: Hospitals
Religion: Religion-General
Social Services: Community Service Organizations, Food/Clothing Distribution, Scouts, United Funds/United Ways

Application Procedures

Initial Contact: The foundation reports no specific application guidelines. Send a brief letter of inquiry.
Application Requirements: Include statement of purpose, amount requested, and proof of tax-exempt status.
Deadlines: None.

Restrictions

Focus is on environmental concerns and educational institutions in the Centre County, PA, area.

Foundation Officials

Donald W. Hamer: trustee
Diane M. Kerly: trustee
Edward J. Matosziuk: trustee

Grants Analysis

Disclosure Period: calendar year ending 2001
Total Grants: $705,000
Number of Grants: 21
Average Grant: $8,158*
Highest Grant: $500,000
Lowest Grant: $1,250
Typical Range: $1,000 to $12,500
*Note: Average grant figure excludes two highest grants ($550,000).

Recent Grants

Note: Grants derived from 2000 Form 990.

General

500,000	Penn State University-Campaign For Excellence, University Park, PA -- capital fund
200,000	Penn State University-Campaign For Excellence, University Park, PA -- capital fund
67,500	Penn State University-Campaign For Excellence, University Park, PA -- capital fund
55,000	Penn State University-Campaign For Excellence, University Park, PA -- capital fund
12,500	Centre County Community Foundation, State College, PA -- distribution fund
12,500	Nature Conservancy, Arlington, VA -- operating fund
10,000	Centre Community Hospital, State College, PA -- building fund
10,000	University of Chicago Graduate School of Business, Chicago, IL -- capital fund
6,500	Temporary Housing, Inc., State College, PA -- operating fund
5,000	Centre County Parks and Recreation Nature Center, State College, PA -- capital fund

HAMILTON CHARITABLE CORP.

Giving Contact

Harold Brown, President & Treasurer
39 Brighton Avenue
Allston, MA 02134-2301
Phone: (617)783-0039

Description

Founded: 1996
EIN: 043314367
Organization Type: Private Foundation
Giving Locations: MA
Grant Types: General Support, Scholarship.

Financial Summary

Total Giving: $174,559 (2001); $171,530 (2000); $177,690 (1999)
Assets: $2,361,671 (2001); $3,081,260 (2000); $2,721,574 (1999)
Gifts Received: $160,000 (2001); $80,000 (2000); $155,725 (1999). Note: Contributions were received from Harold Brown.

Typical Recipients

Arts & Humanities: Libraries, Theater
Civic & Public Affairs: Civic & Public Affairs-General, Philanthropic Organizations, Women's Affairs
Education: Colleges & Universities, Private Education (Precollege), Public Education (Precollege), Student Aid
Health: Cancer, Heart, Hospitals, Public Health
Religion: Jewish Causes
Social Services: Community Service Organizations, Recreation & Athletics, Senior Services

Application Procedures

Initial Contact: The foundation has no formal application procedure.
Deadlines: None.

Foundation Officials

Harold Brown: president, treasurer
Harold Brown: president, treasurer, director
Sally Starr: director
Sally Starr: clerk
Luci Daley Vincent: director

Grants Analysis

Disclosure Period: calendar year ending 2001
Total Grants: $174,559
Number of Grants: 23
Average Grant: $1,169*
Highest Grant: $100,000
Lowest Grant: $89
Typical Range: $500 to $2,500
*Note: Average grant excludes two highest grants ($150,000).

Recent Grants

Note: Grants derived from 2001 Form 990.

Library-Related

| 1,000 | Brookline Public Library, Brookline, MA |
| 1,000 | Brookline Public Library, Brookline, MA |

General

100,000	MIT Scholarship Fund, Cambridge, MA
50,000	Massachusetts General Hospital, Boston, MA
6,000	American Associates Ben-Gurion University, Los Angeles, CA
2,500	Anti-Defamation League, Boston, MA
2,000	Brookline Youth Hockey, Brookline, MA
1,500	Beaver Country Day School, Brookline, MA
1,500	Whittier Street Health Clinic, Roxbury, MA
1,000	Belmont Women's Club Preservation Fund, Belmont, MA
1,000	Brookline High School 21st Century Fund, Brookline, MA
1,000	Brookline Senior Citizens, Brookline, MA

GEORGE AND MARY JOSEPHINE HAMMAN FOUNDATION

Giving Contact

E. Alan Fritsche, Executive Director
3336 Richmond, Suite 310
Houston, TX 77098
Phone: (713)522-9891
Fax: (713)522-9693
E-mail: hammanfdn@aol.com
Web: http://www.hammanfoundation.org

Description

Founded: 1954
EIN: 746061447
Organization Type: Family Foundation
Giving Locations: TX: Houston
Grant Types: Capital, Challenge, Emergency, General Support, Operating Expenses, Project, Research, Scholarship.

Donor Information

Founder: Incorporated in 1954 by George Hamman and the late Mary Josephine Hamman .

Financial Summary

Total Giving: $2,700,000 (2002); $2,497,026 (2001); $2,709,000 (2000)
Assets: $57,000,000 (2002); $56,654,713 (2001); $55,151,636 (2000)

Typical Recipients

Arts & Humanities: Arts Centers, Ballet, Dance, History & Archaeology, Libraries, Museums/Galleries, Music, Performing Arts, Theater
Civic & Public Affairs: Botanical Gardens/Parks, Clubs, Economic Development, Civic & Public Affairs-General, Hispanic Affairs, Housing, Urban & Community Affairs, Zoos/Aquariums
Education: Colleges & Universities, Education Reform, Education-General, Health & Physical Education, Literacy, Medical Education, Minority Education, Private Education (Precollege), Public Education (Precollege), Religious Education, Science/Mathematics Education, Secondary Education (Private), Special Education, Student Aid
Environment: Air/Water Quality, Environment-General, Protection, Resource Conservation, Wildlife Protection
Health: Alzheimers Disease, Cancer, Children's Health/Hospitals, Clinics/Medical Centers, Emergency/Ambulance Services, Eyes/Blindness, Health Organizations, Heart, Hospices, Hospitals, Hospitals (University Affiliated), Medical Rehabilitation, Medical Research, Mental Health, Single-Disease Health Associations, Speech & Hearing
Religion: Churches, Religious Organizations, Religious Welfare
Science: Science Museums
Social Services: At-Risk Youth, Camps, Child Welfare, Community Centers, Community Service Organizations, Domestic Violence, Family Planning, Family Services, Food/Clothing Distribution, Homes, People with Disabilities, Scouts, Scouts, Senior Services, Shelters/Homelessness, Special Olympics, Substance Abuse, Volunteer Services, YMCA/YWCA/YMHA/YWHA, Youth Organizations

Application Procedures

Initial Contact: The foundation requests applications be made in writing. Applications for scholarships must be obtained from the foundation either by downloading forms from the website or request them in writing.
Deadlines: Monthly for grant applications; February 28 for scholarship applications.

Restrictions

The foundation does not support post-graduate education or individuals. Scholarship recipients must be Houston area high school seniors.

Additional Information

Publications: Guidelines; application form. for scholarships.

Foundation Officials

E. Alan Fritsche: executive director PRIM CORP EMPL chief financial officer: Looney & Co.
Henry R. Hamman: president, director B 1937. ED University of Texas BS (1959); University of Texas MA (1961). PRIM CORP EMPL president: Hamman Oil & Refining Co. CORP AFFIL director: Devon Energy Corp.; Hamman Aviation Inc.
Charles D. Milby, Jr.: treasurer
Ann H. Shepherd: secretary

Grants Analysis

Disclosure Period: calendar year ending 2001
Total Grants: $2,497,026*
Number of Grants: 313
Average Grant: $7,978*
Highest Grant: $100,000

Lowest Grant: $1,500
Typical Range: $5,000 to $15,000
*Note: Grants analysis provided by foundation.

Recent Grants

Note: Grants derived from 2000 Form 990.

General

75,000	Friends of Hermann Park, Houston, TX
50,000	Boy Scouts of America, Houston, TX -- for general support
50,000	Casa de Esperanza, Houston, TX
33,700	Aldine Y.O.U.T.H., Houston, TX
31,000	Stehlin Foundation for Cancer Research, Houston, TX -- for medical treatment and research
30,000	American Cancer Society, Houston, TX
30,000	Armand Bayou Nature Center, Houston, TX
30,000	Neuhaus Education Center, Houston, TX -- for general support
25,000	Boy Scouts of America, Houston, TX -- for general support
25,000	Houston Christian High School, Houston, TX

ARMAND HAMMER FOUNDATION

Giving Contact

Michael A. Hammer, President, Chief Executive Officer & Director
2425 Olympic Boulevard, Suite 140 E
Santa Monica, CA 90404
Phone: (713)951-3303

Description

Founded: 1968
EIN: 237010813
Organization Type: General Purpose Foundation
Giving Locations: broad geographic distribution.
Grant Types: Capital, General Support, Multiyear/Continuing Support, Project, Research.

Donor Information

Founder: the late Dr. Armand Hammer

Financial Summary

Total Giving: $2,261,800 (2001); $538,755 (2000); $695,486 (1995)
Assets: $1,403,658 (2001); $4,264,567 (2000); $6,858,457 (1995)
Gifts Received: $30,000 (2001); $295,500 (2000); $826,000 (1995). Note: In 1995, 2000, and 2001, contributions were received from the Armand Hammer Living Trust.

Typical Recipients

Arts & Humanities: Arts Associations & Councils, Arts Centers, Film & Video, Historic Preservation, History & Archaeology, Libraries, Museums/Galleries, Music, Opera, Public Broadcasting, Theater
Civic & Public Affairs: Clubs, Civic & Public Affairs-General, Parades/Festivals, Philanthropic Organizations, Public Policy
Education: Business Education, Colleges & Universities, Education-General, Medical Education, Private Education (Precollege), Public Education (Precollege), Religious Education, Student Aid, Vocational & Technical Education
Health: Cancer, Children's Health/Hospitals, Clinics/Medical Centers, Emergency/Ambulance Services, Health-General, Health Organizations, Heart, Hospices, Hospitals, Hospitals (University Affiliated), Medical Research, Medical Training, Multiple Sclerosis, Single-Disease Health Associations

International: Foreign Arts Organizations, Foreign Educational Institutions, Health Care/Hospitals, International Affairs, International Organizations, International Peace & Security Issues, Missionary/Religious Activities
Religion: Churches, Jewish Causes, Ministries, Missionary Activities (Domestic), Religious Organizations, Religious Welfare
Science: Scientific Centers & Institutes
Social Services: Child Welfare, Community Service Organizations, Crime Prevention, Day Care, Family Services, People with Disabilities, Recreation & Athletics, Scouts, Social Services-General, Volunteer Services, YMCA/YWCA/YMHA/YWHA, Youth Organizations

Application Procedures

Initial Contact: The foundation has no formal grant application procedure or application form.
Deadlines: None.

Restrictions

No grants are made to individuals.

Foundation Officials

Rex Alexander: director
G. Dwight Clayton: director
Scott R. Deitrick: vice president
Dru Hammer: cfo, secretary, director
Michael A. Hammer: president, chief executive officer, director
W. Dayton Pittman: director
David Sewell: director

Grants Analysis

Disclosure Period: calendar year ending 2001
Total Grants: $2,261,800
Number of Grants: 20
Average Grant: $13,779*
Highest Grant: $2,000,000
Lowest Grant: $900
Typical Range: $10,000 to $30,000
*Note: Average grant figure excludes highest grant.

Recent Grants

Note: Grants derived from 2000 Form 990.

General

175,000	San Diego Museum of Art, San Diego, CA
105,000	Armand Hammer United World College, Montezuma, NM
52,500	Pepperdine University, Malibu, CA
50,000	San Diego Museum of Art, San Diego, CA
50,000	UCLA Regents, Los Angeles, CA
30,000	Frick Museum, New York, NY
25,000	Heartland Film Festival, Chicago, IL
23,100	Stop Cancer, Los Angeles, CA
10,000	Adopt a Fire Station 71, Los Angeles, CA
8,055	Armand Hammer Museum of Art and Cultural Center, Los Angeles, CA

EDNA AND YU-SHAN HAN CHARITABLE FOUNDATION

Giving Contact

Robert Sung, Co-Trustee
c/o Sonderbeck
6151 W. Century Blvd., Suite 1112
Los Angeles, CA 90045
Phone: (310)670-5442

Description

Founded: 1983
EIN: 953823449
Organization Type: Private Foundation
Giving Locations: CA
Grant Types: General Support, Scholarship.

Financial Summary

Total Giving: $142,820 (2000); $119,951 (1999); $112,073 (1998)
Assets: $2,844,621 (2000); $3,218,076 (1999); $2,935,220 (1998)

Typical Recipients

Arts & Humanities: Libraries, Music, Performing Arts, Public Broadcasting
Civic & Public Affairs: Asian American Affairs, Civic & Public Affairs-General, Philanthropic Organizations
Education: Arts/Humanities Education, Colleges & Universities, International Studies, Student Aid
Health: Emergency/Ambulance Services
International: International Relations, Missionary/Religious Activities

Application Procedures

Initial Contact: Send financial statement, scholastic record, letter of admissions from an accredited college or university, and a short essay about applicants life goals and plans.
Deadlines: None.

Additional Information

Provides assistance to needy students without restriction as to race or ethnic background to study Chinese culture, art, or history. Assistance is also provided to needy students of Asian descent, with preference given to students of Chinese ancestry, who are of good character and high scholastic achievement to pursue any field of study.

Foundation Officials

Patsy Sung: co-trustee
Robert Sung: co-trustee

Grants Analysis

Disclosure Period: calendar year ending 2000
Total Grants: $142,820
Number of Grants: 15
Average Grant: $6,630*
Highest Grant: $50,000
Typical Range: $1,000 to $10,000
*Note: Average grant figure excludes highest grant.

Recent Grants

Note: Grants derived from 1999 Form 990.

General

30,000	Stanford University, Stanford, CA
20,000	UCLA East Asian Library, Los Angeles, CA
10,000	Curtis Institute of Music, Philadelphia, PA
10,000	UCLA Film Archive, Los Angeles, CA
10,000	UCLA School Of Arts & Architecture, Los Angeles, CA
10,000	University of California Los Angeles School of Theater, Film, and TV, Los Angeles, CA
10,000	USC Asian Pacific American Support Group Scholarship Fund, CA
5,000	Hong Kong School Alumni Federation Scholarship Hong Kong
5,000	UCLA Foundation, Los Angeles, CA -- chancellor's associates annual fund
4,720	UCLA Royce Center Circle, Los Angeles, CA

HANDY & HARMAN

Company Headquarters

555 Theodore Fremd Avenue
Rye, NY 10580
Web: http://www.handyharmon.com

Company Description

Employees: 2,567
SIC(s): 3300 Primary Metal Industries, 3400 Fabricated Metal Products.

Operating Locations

Handy & Harman (CT--Fairfield, South Windsor; MI--Auburn Hills; NJ--Willingboro; NY--Oriskany; OH--Dover; OK--Tulsa; WI--Cudahy)

Handy & Harman Foundation

Giving Contact

Paul E. Dixon, Trustee & Secretary
555 Theodore Fremd Avenue
Rye, NY 10580-1451
Phone: (914)921-5200

Description

EIN: 237408431
Organization Type: Corporate Foundation
Giving Locations: CT; IL; IN; ME; MA; NY; PA: principally near operating locations and to national organizations.
Grant Types: General Support.

Financial Summary

Total Giving: $125,205 (2001); $134,618 (2000); $149,584 (1999)
Giving Analysis: Giving for 2001 includes: foundation grants to United Way ($18,025); 2000: foundation grants to United Way ($25,050); 1999: foundation grants to United Way ($26,850); foundation ($122,734); foundation ($150,000);
Assets: $193,660 (2001); $295,704 (2000); $276,184 (1999)
Gifts Received: $150,000 (2000); $150,000 (1999); $150,000 (1998)

Typical Recipients

Arts & Humanities: Arts Centers, Community Arts, Arts & Humanities-General, Libraries, Museums/Galleries, Public Broadcasting
Civic & Public Affairs: Botanical Gardens/Parks, Business/Free Enterprise, Clubs, Community Foundations, Economic Development, Economic Policy, Employment/Job Training, Civic & Public Affairs-General, Inner-City Development, Law & Justice, Legal Aid, Municipalities/Towns, Professional & Trade Associations, Public Policy, Safety, Urban & Community Affairs, Women's Affairs, Zoos/Aquariums
Education: Arts/Humanities Education, Business Education, Colleges & Universities, Economic Education, Education Associations, Education Funds, Education Reform, Engineering/Technological Education, Education-General, Legal Education, Medical Education, Minority Education, Private Education (Precollege), Public Education (Precollege), Science/Mathematics Education, Secondary Education (Private), Secondary Education (Public), Student Aid
Health: Arthritis, Cancer, Children's Health/Hospitals, Clinics/Medical Centers, Diabetes, Emergency/Ambulance Services, Eyes/Blindness, Health-General, Health Organizations, Heart, Home-Care Services, Hospitals, Hospitals (University Affiliated), Medical Training, Mental Health, Nursing Services, Single-Disease Health Associations
International: Health Care/Hospitals, International Affairs, International Organizations, International Relations, International Relief Efforts

Religion: Dioceses, Religion-General, Jewish Causes, Religious Organizations, Religious Organizations
Science: Science Museums, Scientific Centers & Institutes
Social Services: Camps, Community Centers, Community Service Organizations, Crime Prevention, Domestic Violence, Emergency Relief, Recreation & Athletics, Shelters/Homelessness, Social Services-General, Substance Abuse, United Funds/United Ways, Veterans, YMCA/YWCA/YMHA/YWHA, Youth Organizations

Application Procedures

Initial Contact: Requests should be in writing on organizations letterhead.
Application Requirements: Include a description of organization, amount requested, purpose of funds sought, and proof of tax-exempt status.
Deadlines: None.

Restrictions

Does not support individuals, religious organizations for sectarian purposes, political or lobbying groups, or organizations outside operating areas.

Corporate Officials

Robert LeBlanc: president, chief operating officer PRIM CORP EMPL president, chief operating officer: Handy & Harman.

Foundation Officials

R. F. Burlinson: treasurer, trust
Paul Edward Dixon: secretary, trustee B Brooklyn, NY 1944. ED Villanova University BA (1966); Saint John's University JD (1972). PRIM CORP EMPL vice president, general counsel, secretary: Handy & Harman. CORP AFFIL chairman: Teeches Ltd. NONPR AFFIL member: New York State Bar Association; member: U.S. Supreme Court Historical Society; member: American Corporate Counsel Association; member: New York City Bar Association; member: American Bar Association. CLUB AFFIL Bedford Golf & Tennis Club.
D. C. Kelly: treasurer, trustee
D. P. Murphy, Jr.: president trustee

Grants Analysis

Disclosure Period: calendar year ending 2002
Total Grants: $107,180*
Number of Grants: 104
Average Grant: $838*
Highest Grant: $20,000
Typical Range: $100 to $2,000
*Note: Giving excludes United Way. Average grant excludes highest grant.

Recent Grants

Note: Grants derived from 2002 Form 990.

General

20,000	Alliance for Progress - National Roofing Foundation, Rosemont, IL
10,000	Boston College, Boston, MA
10,000	United Way Eastern Fairfield County, Fairfield, CT
5,000	American Lyme Disease Foundation, New York, NY
5,000	CLMB Foundation, Stockton Springs, ME
5,000	Mary Louis Academy, Jamaica Estates, NY
5,000	Mary Louis Academy, Jamaica Estates, NY
4,000	Avon Old Farms School, Avon, CT
4,000	Sisters of St. Joseph, Holyoke, MA
4,000	United Way Tri-State, New York, NY

JOHN WESLEY AND ANNA HODGIN HANES FOUNDATION

Giving Contact

Linda Tilley, Relationship Manager
c/o Wachovia Bank
100 North Main
PO Box 3099
Winston-Salem, NC 27150-7131
Phone: (336)732-5372
Fax: (336)732-6537

Description

Founded: 1947
EIN: 566037589
Organization Type: Family Foundation
Giving Locations: NC: Winston-Salem and Forsyth County area, Winston-Salem
Grant Types: Capital, General Support, Matching, Project, Research, Seed Money.

Donor Information

Founder: Established in 1947.

Financial Summary

Total Giving: $1,447,902 (2001); $1,496,100 (2000); $1,225,498 (1998)
Assets: $28,253,555 (2001); $31,179,351 (2000); $29,598,751 (1998)
Gifts Received: $284,831 (1996). Note: Contributions were received from C. Annelle Shillington.

Typical Recipients

Arts & Humanities: Arts Associations & Councils, Arts Centers, Arts Festivals, Arts Institutes, Community Arts, Historic Preservation, History & Archaeology, Libraries, Museums/Galleries, Music, Performing Arts, Theater
Civic & Public Affairs: Botanical Gardens/Parks, Chambers of Commerce, Community Foundations, Economic Development, Employment/Job Training, Civic & Public Affairs-General, Housing, Municipalities/Towns, Public Policy, Urban & Community Affairs, Zoos/Aquariums
Education: Afterschool/Enrichment Programs, Arts/Humanities Education, Colleges & Universities, Community & Junior Colleges, Education Associations, Education Funds, Elementary Education (Public), Education-General, Medical Education, Private Education (Precollege), Public Education (Precollege), Religious Education, Vocational & Technical Education
Environment: Air/Water Quality, Environment-General, Resource Conservation, Wildlife Protection
Health: AIDS/HIV, Alzheimers Disease, Clinics/Medical Centers, Emergency/Ambulance Services, Eyes/Blindness, Health Funds, Hospices, Hospitals, Medical Rehabilitation, Public Health, Single-Disease Health Associations, Transplant Networks/Donor Banks
International: International Development
Religion: Churches, Religion-General, Jewish Causes, Ministries, Religious Organizations, Religious Welfare
Science: Science Museums, Scientific Centers & Institutes
Social Services: Child Welfare, Community Service Organizations, Crime Prevention, Delinquency & Criminal Rehabilitation, Domestic Violence, Family Planning, Family Services, Family Services, Food/Clothing Distribution, Homes, People with Disabilities, Recreation & Athletics, Scouts, Senior Services, Shelters/Homelessness, Social Services-General, Substance Abuse, United Funds/United Ways, Volunteer Services, YMCA/YWCA/YMHA/YWHA, Youth Organizations

Application Procedures

Initial Contact: Write to the foundation for a formal application.
Application Requirements: The foundation's formal application includes the name and address of the organization requesting assistance; a contact person; a brief description of the organization, including a list of trustees; major goals and purposes; range and scope of programs; properties owned and rented; and date of founding. Applicants are also requested to attach a copy of the IRS certification indicating the organization's status as tax-exempt and as a private or public foundation. Information about the project should include a three-page outline of the project's scope and purpose, a description of the geographic area to be served, the project budget, other sources of funding, and plans for future funding of the project.
Deadlines: Deadlines for submitting applications are March 15, June 15, September 15, and December 15.
Review Process: The board reviews applications in January, April, July, and October. Requests received after the deadline will be carried over for consideration at the next meeting when appropriate. Each organization completing the application form for a grant will be notified of the decision of the trustees shortly after each meeting.

Restrictions

Grants are disbursed to IRS-designated tax-exempt section 501(c)(3) organizations only and must be public foundations. The foundation reports that in order for a request to receive adequate attention from the trustees, prospective applicants must complete an application form and adhere to foundation's established procedures. No grants are made to individuals or for operating expenses. Grants are not made for typical operational costs or maintenance-oriented purposes.

Additional Information

Wachovia Bank of North Carolina, is the foundation's corporate trustee.
Publications: Program Policy Statement; Application Guidelines; Application Form

Foundation Officials

Joyce T. Adger: manager PRIM CORP EMPL senior vice president: Wachovia Bank NA.
Frank Borden Hanes, Jr.: trustee B Winston-Salem, NC 1945. ED University of North Carolina BA (1942); Saint Andrew's Presbyterian College DHL (1992). CORP AFFIL member: P.E.N.; member: North Carolina Quarter Horse Association; member: North Carolina Writers Conference; director: Hanes Co.; director: Chatham Manufacturing Co. NONPR AFFIL member: Order Minotaur; member: Sigma Alpha Epsilon; member: Order Gimghoul. CLUB AFFIL Rotarian Club; Roaring Gap Club; Rainbow Springs Club; Rancheros Visitadores Club; Old Town Club.
Frank Borden Hanes, Sr.: trustee B Winston-Salem, NC January 21, 1920. ED University of North Carolina BA (1942). CORP AFFIL director: Hanes Co.; director: Chatham Manufacturing Co. NONPR AFFIL member: Sigma Alpha Epsilon; member, board governors: University North Carolina Press; member: Poets Playwrights Editors Essayists & Novelists; member: Order Gimghoul; member: Order Minotaur; member: North Carolina Writers Conference; director: North Carolina Zoological Society; member: North Carolina Quarter Horse Association; member, board: North Carolina Society; director: North Carolina Childrens Home Society. CLUB AFFIL Rotary Club; Rancheros Visitadores Club; Roaring Gap Club; Old Town Club; Rainbow Springs Club.
Ralph Philip Hanes, Jr.: trustee B Winston-Salem, NC 1926. ED University of North Carolina BA (1944-1946); Yale University BA (1949). NONPR AFFIL member: Wilderness Society; member: World Business Council; member: Walpole Society; member: Isaac Walton League; member: Trout Unlimited;

member: Utah Prosim Society; member: Royal Society Arts; member: Southeast Council Foundations; member: North American Mycological Association; member: Pennsylvania Academy Fine Arts; board government: National Committee for the New River; member: National Wildlife Federation; director: Jargon Society Inc.; trustee emeritus: Kennedy Center for the Arts; member: Appalachian Trail Conference; member: East African Wildlife Society; member: American League Anglers; member: Appalachian Consortium; executive committee: Ambs for the Arts. CLUB AFFIL Yale Club; Roaring Gap Club; Twin City Club; Piedmont Club; Potomac Appalachian Mountain Club; Metro Club; Peale Visual Arts Club; Currituck Club; Lotos Club; Cane River Club; Century Association; Bohemian Club.
Ralph H. Womble: trustee

Grants Analysis

Disclosure Period: calendar year ending 2001
Total Grants: $1,447,902
Number of Grants: 55
Average Grant: $19,383*
Highest Grant: $200,000
Lowest Grant: $1,000
Typical Range: $10,000 to $40,000
***Note:** Average grant figure excludes three highest grants ($440,000).

Recent Grants

Note: Grants derived from 2001 Form 990.

Library-Related
10,000   Friends of Boonville Library, Boonville, NC -- construction of Boonville library

General
333,333   Second Harvest Food Bank of Northwest North Carolina, Winston-Salem, NC -- fund expansion/add cold storage space/upgrade comp
200,000   Wake Forest University Baptist Medical Center-Nutrition Center, Winston-Salem, NC -- support the endowment fund
50,000   Arts Council Incorporated Winston-Salem Arts Council, Winston-Salem, NC -- downtown festival
50,000   Forsyth Technical Community College Foundation, Winston-Salem, NC -- to construct an addition to Bob Green Hall
50,000   Wake Forest University Baptist Medical Center-Nutrition Center, Winston-Salem, NC -- to support nutrition center
50,000   Winston-Salem Enrichment Center, Winston-Salem, NC -- help fund " Beyond Walls" capital campaign
50,000   YMCA of Greater Winston-Salem, Winston-Salem, NC -- ship support the V2000 capital campaign
40,000   Nature Conservancy, Arlington, VA -- North Carolina Chapter/ "Forever Wild" campaign
40,000   Southeastern Center for Contemporary Art, Winston-Salem, NC -- help support 5 exhibitions/programs/performances
37,500   Downtown Winston-Salem Foundation, Winston-Salem, NC -- revolving loan fund/revitalization of downtown

HANNAFORD BROTHERS CO.

Company Headquarters

Scarborough, ME
Web: http://www.hannaford.com

Company Description

Employees: 22,000
SIC(s): 5411 Grocery Stores, 5912 Drug Stores & Proprietary Stores.

Parent Company: Sobey, Inc., 115 King St., Stellarton, NS, Canada

Operating Locations

Hannaford Brothers Co. (ME--Bangor, Portland); Hannaford Brothers Co. (NC--Raleigh)

Nonmonetary Support

Type: Loaned Employees; Loaned Executives

Hannaford Charitable Foundation

Giving Contact

Donna J. Boyce, Secretary
PO Box 1000
Portland, ME 04104
Phone: (207)883-2911
Web: http://www.hannaford.com/community/charitable.htm

Alternate Contact

Hannaford Scholarship Program
Scholarship Management Services, CSFA
PO Box 297
St. Peter, MN 56082
Phone: (507)931-1682
Note: For scholarship program information only.

Description

Founded: 1994
EIN: 010483892
Organization Type: Corporate Foundation
Giving Locations: headquarters and operating communities.
Grant Types: Capital, General Support, Multiyear/Continuing Support, Project.
Note: Scholarships are for associates and their dependent children.

Financial Summary

Total Giving: $1,200,000 (2002 approx); $932,155 (2001); $1,028,483 (2000). Note: Contributes through corporate direct giving program and foundation.
Giving Analysis: Giving for 2001 includes: foundation scholarships ($200,000); foundation grants to United Way ($288,050); 2000: foundation scholarships ($100,000); foundation grants to United Way ($209,300); foundation ($719,183); 1999: foundation scholarships ($204,000); foundation grants to United Way ($322,550); foundation ($417,082);
Assets: $1,904,836 (2001); $1,969,264 (2000); $1,940,623 (1999)
Gifts Received: $1,018,000 (2001); $1,130,000 (2000); $1,036,000 (1998). Note: Contributions were received from Hannaford Brothers Co.

Typical Recipients

Arts & Humanities: Arts Associations & Councils, Arts Centers, Arts Institutes, Arts & Humanities-General, History & Archaeology, Libraries, Museums/Galleries, Music, Opera, Performing Arts, Theater
Civic & Public Affairs: Chambers of Commerce, Civic & Public Affairs-General, Nonprofit Management, Parades/Festivals, Urban & Community Affairs, Zoos/Aquariums
Education: Arts/Humanities Education, Business Education, Colleges & Universities, Environmental Education, Education-General, Leadership Training, Special Education, Student Aid
Environment: Environment-General, Resource Conservation
Health: AIDS/HIV, Alzheimers Disease, Cancer, Children's Health/Hospitals, Clinics/Medical Centers, Emergency/Ambulance Services, Health Organizations, Heart, Home-Care Services, Hospices, Hospitals, Hospitals (University Affiliated), Medical Research, Research/Studies Institutes
Religion: Religious Welfare

Science: Scientific Labs
Social Services: Animal Protection, Big Brother/Big Sister, Camps, Child Welfare, Community Centers, Day Care, Family Services, Food/Clothing Distribution, Scouts, Senior Services, Social Services-General, United Funds/United Ways, YMCA/YWCA/YMHA/YWHA, Youth Organizations

Application Procedures

Initial Contact: Submit an application form.
Application Requirements: Include name, address, and telephone number of organization; contact person and title; amount requested; population and geographic area served; a two- or three-sentence mission statement for your organization, with a brief description of its background; a two- or three-sentence description of the specific project or program for which you are seeking funding; a copy of your organization's tax-exemption letter indicating both Section 501(c)(3) and 509(a) status, and most recent Form 990 return, as well as a letter attesting that tax-exempt status is current; a list of current and potential funding sources; and a recent annual statement of revenues and expenses.
Deadlines: April 1 for scholarship.
Evaluative Criteria: Should have active and responsible boards of trustees, exhibit ethical publicity methods and solicitation of funds, provide for an appropriate audit to reveal income disbursements in reasonable detail, demonstrate long-term financial viability; preference given to programs that involve Hannaford associates and are located in Hannaford's marketing territory.
Notes: A member of the foundation may contact organization to request additional information.

Restrictions

The foundation will not contribute to institutions that, by virtue of their charters, programs, or policies, are open to a relatively small or restricted segment of the public; operations of veterans, fraternal, or religious organizations, except those that make their services fully available to the community on a nonsectarian basis; individuals; tax-supported institutions; or organizations that are not qualified as tax-exempt under IRS Section 501(c)(3).

The foundation will not give sales discounts or purchase advertisements in publications or programs.

Additional Information

Apart from its charitable foundation, Hannaford contributes to the community in many ways. Each Hannaford Store makes its own contributions to its local community through fundraising drives and sponsorships, as well as gift certificates and cash donations. All stores, distribution centers, and offices participate in the United Way's annual fund drive. Hannaford's promotions department sponsors nonprofit youth athletic leagues, school events, performing arts organizations, civic events, and environmental and health organizations. The company also is a major donor to local food banks, shelters, and soup kitchens. Sobey Inc. has a 26% investment in Hannaford Brothers.
Publications: Guidelines Sheet

Corporate Officials

Hugh G. Farrington: president, chief executive officer, director B 1945. ED Dartmouth College BA (1967); University of New Hampshire MA (1968). PRIM CORP EMPL president, chief executive officer, director: Hannaford Brothers Co. CORP AFFIL president: Progressive Distributors Inc.; president: Shop'n Save Massachusetts Inc.; president: Boney Wilson Sons Inc.; president: Martin's Foods of South Burlington Inc.

Giving Program Officials

Paul A. Fritzson: executive vice president , chief executive officer B 1953. PRIM CORP EMPL executive vice president , chief executive officer: Hannaford

Brothers Co. CORP AFFIL director: Hannaford Trucking Co.

Foundation Officials

Shelley Broader: director
Beth Newlands Campbell: director
Mark Doiron: director
Paul A. Fritzson: president, director (see above)
Ronald C. Hodge: director B 1947. PRIM CORP EMPL executive vice president sales northeast operation: Hannaford Brothers Co. CORP AFFIL director: Hannaford Trucking Co.
Andy Mayo: director
Bradford A. Wise: director

Grants Analysis

Disclosure Period: calendar year ending 2001
Total Grants: $444,105*
Number of Grants: 49
Average Grant: $6,127*
Highest Grant: $150,000
Lowest Grant: $271
Typical Range: $1,000 to $15,000
*Note: Giving excludes United Way and scholarship. Average grant figure excludes highest grant.

Recent Grants

Note: Grants derived from 2001 Form 990.

Library-Related
5,000	Auburn Public Library, Auburn, ME

General
200,000	Citizens Scholarship Foundation of America, St. Peter, MN
150,000	Nature Conservancy of Maine, ME
121,000	United Way of Greater Portland, Portland, ME
31,000	Maine Medical Center, Portland, ME
20,000	Good Shepherd Food Bank, Lewiston, ME
20,000	Maine Discovery Museum, Portland, ME
20,000	Portland Museum of Art, Portland, ME
20,000	United Way of Mid-Maine, Waterville, ME
15,000	United Way of York County, York, PA
13,333	Wilmington Family YMCA

HANOVER FOUNDATION

Giving Contact

Ralph J. Shapiro, Chairman
9401 Wilshire Blvd., Ste. 1201
Beverly Hills, CA 90212
Phone: (310)550-0960
Fax: (310)205-3879

Description

Founded: 1983
EIN: 953887151
Organization Type: Private Foundation
Giving Locations: CA
Grant Types: General Support.

Donor Information

Founder: Ralph J. Shapiro, Shirley Shapiro, Kihi Foundation, Knoll International Holdings, Inc.

Financial Summary

Total Giving: $1,284,550 (fiscal year ending January 31, 2002); $396,395 (fiscal 2001); $712,742 (fiscal 2000)
Giving Analysis: Giving for fiscal 2002 includes: foundation grants to United Way ($950,000); fiscal 2001: foundation grants to United Way ($176,000); fiscal 2000: foundation grants to United Way ($470,297);
Assets: $3,619,917 (fiscal 2002); $3,976,092 (fiscal 2001); $3,169,285 (fiscal 2000)

Gifts Received: $818,408 (fiscal 2002); $405,838 (fiscal 2001); $205,380 (fiscal 2000). Note: In fiscal 2001, contributions were received from Ralph & Shirley Shapiro ($485,351), Alison D. Shaprio ($87,295), Pete Kameron Living Trust ($150,000), and Raps Industries ($95,762). In fiscal 2001, contributions were received from Earl W. Kavanau ($5,000) and Ralph J. and Shirley Shapiro ($400,838). In fiscal 2000, contributions were received from Flavia Kavanau ($10,000) and Ralph J. and Shirley Shapiro ($195,380). In fiscal 1999, contributions were received from Earl W. Kavanau ($4,000), Lawrence N. Field ($55,000), and Ralph J. and Shirley Shapiro ($53,433). In fiscal 1997, contributions were received from Earl Kavanau ($7,200) and Ralph J. and Shirley Shapiro ($234,150).

Typical Recipients

Arts & Humanities: Arts & Humanities-General, Libraries, Museums/Galleries, Music, Opera, Public Broadcasting
Civic & Public Affairs: Botanical Gardens/Parks, Civil Rights, Community Foundations, Civic & Public Affairs-General, Housing, Law & Justice, Legal Aid, Public Policy, Urban & Community Affairs
Education: Colleges & Universities, Education Funds, Education Reform, Legal Education, Medical Education, Minority Education, Private Education (Precollege), Student Aid
Environment: Environment-General, Resource Conservation
Health: Alzheimers Disease, Cancer, Children's Health/Hospitals, Clinics/Medical Centers, Health-General, Heart, Hospitals (University Affiliated), Mental Health, Trauma Treatment
International: Foreign Arts Organizations, Health Care/Hospitals, International Organizations, Missionary/Religious Activities
Religion: Jewish Causes, Religious Welfare
Social Services: Child Welfare, Community Service Organizations, Family Planning, Recreation & Athletics, Special Olympics, United Funds/United Ways, Volunteer Services, YMCA/YWCA/YMHA/YWHA, Youth Organizations

Application Procedures

Initial Contact: The foundation has no formal grant application procedure or application form.
Deadlines: None.

Foundation Officials

Floyd P. Cook, Jr.: chief financial officer
Ava Coyne: secretary
Alison D. Shapiro: vice president, secretary
Peter W. Shapiro: vice president, treasurer
Ralph J. Shapiro: chairman
Shirley Shapiro: president

Grants Analysis

Disclosure Period: fiscal year ending January 31, 2002
Total Grants: $334,550*
Number of Grants: 100
Average Grant: $1,602*
Highest Grant: $176,000
Lowest Grant: $45
Typical Range: $500 to $5,000
*Note: Giving excludes United Way. Average grant figure excludes highest grant.

Recent Grants

Note: Grants derived from 2000 Form 990.

General

470,297	United Way, Los Angeles, CA
39,600	University of California Foundation, Los Angeles, CA
37,000	United Cerebral Palsy and Spastic Children's Foundation, Los Angeles, CA
15,000	Rails to Trails Conservancy, Washington, DC
10,000	Beverly Hills Y.M.C.A,, Beverly Hills, CA
6,000	Public Counsel Law Center, Los Angeles, CA
6,000	United Friends of Children, Los Angeles, CA
5,000	California Institute of Technology, Pasadena, CA
5,000	Sun Valley Writers Conference, Ketchum, ID
5,000	United States Holocaust Memorial Museum, Washington, DC

DANE G. HANSEN FOUNDATION

Giving Contact

Ross Beach, President & Trustee
110 West Main Street
PO Box 187
Logan, KS 67646
Phone: (785)689-4832
Fax: (785)689-4833
E-mail: hansentr@ruraltel.net

Description

Founded: 1965
EIN: 486121156
Organization Type: General Purpose Foundation
Giving Locations: KS: Northwestern part of state
Grant Types: General Support, Project, Scholarship.

Donor Information

Founder: The foundation was established in 1965, following the death of Dane G. Hansen , who left most of his estate to the foundation. Mr. Hansen, the son of Danish immigrants, was born in 1883, and grew up in Kansas. He entered the mercantile business with his parents and later developed interests in ranching, cattle raising, and road and bridge construction. In the 1930s, he went into oil development and became one of the largest independent oil producers in Kansas. Mr. Hansen served in the administration of President Eisenhower and later became a trustee of the Eisenhower Foundation. He was very active in civic organizations in Logan, KS, and wanted his foundation to continue his commitment to the Logan area. His charitable interests included children and education.

Financial Summary

Total Giving: $2,800,841 (fiscal year ending September 30, 2001); $2,347,305 (fiscal 1999); $1,557,176 (fiscal 1997)
Giving Analysis: Giving for fiscal 2001 includes: foundation scholarships ($371,756)
Assets: $53,785,422 (fiscal 2001); $33,968,685 (fiscal 1999); $53,408,475 (fiscal 1997)

Typical Recipients

Arts & Humanities: Arts Associations & Councils, Community Arts, Arts & Humanities-General, Libraries, Museums/Galleries, Music, Performing Arts, Public Broadcasting, Theater
Civic & Public Affairs: Business/Free Enterprise, Chambers of Commerce, Clubs, Community Foundations, Economic Development, Economic Policy, Employment/Job Training, Housing, Municipalities/Towns, Professional & Trade Associations, Public Policy, Rural Affairs, Safety, Urban & Community Affairs
Education: Agricultural Education, Arts/Humanities Education, Business Education, Colleges & Universities, Faculty Development, Education-General, Journalism/Media Education, Medical Education, Private Education (Precollege), Public Education (Precollege), Student Aid, Student Aid, Vocational & Technical Education
Environment: Environment-General, Resource Conservation

Health: Cancer, Children's Health/Hospitals, Clinics/Medical Centers, Emergency/Ambulance Services, Eyes/Blindness, Health-General, Health Organizations, Heart, Hospices, Hospitals, Long-Term Care, Medical Rehabilitation, Medical Research, Single-Disease Health Associations
Religion: Churches, Religious Welfare
Social Services: Animal Protection, At-Risk Youth, Community Centers, Community Service Organizations, Food/Clothing Distribution, People with Disabilities, Recreation & Athletics, Scouts, Senior Services, Social Services-General, Youth Organizations

Application Procedures

Initial Contact: Grant applicants should submit seven unfolded copies of a detailed proposal to the foundation. Application forms for the scholarship program are available from either the foundation or the office of the school counselor.
Application Requirements: Detailed proposals for grants should include the name, address, and phone number of the organization and the contact person; verification of 501(c)3 tax status; concise description of the project, its significance, benefits, and objectives; amount requested; detailed financial statement (preferably audited); detailed proposal budget; project timetable; list of other sources of potential funding; list of board members; qualifications of the organization and individuals with respect to project objectives; appropriate institution, organizational or individual letter of support; eva luation procedure for the project; and method and criteria for assessing the project's effectiveness.
Deadlines: None, for grant proposals. For scholarships, all applications and six semester grades (with GPA circled) must be completed and returned no later than October 9, reference questionnaires are due no later than October 29, and letters of acceptance of scholarship should be received within thirty days after graduation from high school.
Review Process: The foundation board meets monthly. Grant applicants will be notified within two weeks of receipt of proposal. Scholarship recipients are expected to enroll in appropriate institutions of higher learning without delay and in the fall term of the awarding year.
Notes: The following rules apply to scholarship applicants: only high school seniors who are graduating in the current academic year are eligible; students who have intentions of attending an out-of-state school should not apply; students interested in the Hansen Leader of Tomorrow, the Hansen Scholar, or Hansen Student scholarships must register with their school counselor or principal and take the qualifying test (no formal application is required); students interested in Vocational Education scholarships must complete the application form.

Restrictions

The foundation does not support political projects; normal organizational operating expenses; construction projects; endowment programs; degree programs; organizations without tax-exempt status; or organizations that practice discrimination by race, color, creed, sex, or national origin.

Additional Information

Publications: Application Guidelines

Foundation Officials

Dane G. Bales: president, trustee B 1918.
Ross Beach: trustee PRIM CORP EMPL chairman, president, director: Douglas County Bank.
Oscar F. Belin: trustee B El Reno, OK. ED University of Kansas LLB; University of Kansas BS. PRIM CORP EMPL partner: Bever Dye Mustard Belin Attorneys. NONPR AFFIL member: Kansas Bar Association; member: Wichita Bar Association.
F. Doyle Fair: trustee
Charles I. Moyer: trustee PRIM CORP EMPL president: First National Bank & Trust.

Doyle Dean Rahjes: trustee B Kirwin, KS 1930. PRIM CORP EMPL president: Farm Bureau Mutual Insurance Co. CORP AFFIL president: Kansas Farm Bureau Life Insurance Co.; president: Kansas Farm Bureau Services; partner: Gus Rahjes & Sons Farms; president: Kansas Farm Bureau Insurance Co. NONPR AFFIL member: Kansas Livestock Association; director: Western Agriculture Insurance Co.; president: Kansas Farm Bureau; president: Kansas Agricultural Marketing Association; member: Kansas Association Commerce Industry.

Grants Analysis

Disclosure Period: fiscal year ending September 30, 2001
Total Grants: $2,429,085*
Number of Grants: 84
Average Grant: $28,918
Highest Grant: $210,975
Typical Range: $15,000 to $50,000
*Note: Giving excludes scholarships.

Recent Grants

Note: Grants derived from fiscal 2001 Form 990.

General

210,975	City of Logan, Logan, KS -- for Hansen Plaza
160,000	Boys Scouts of America, Salina, KS -- Camp Hansen
150,000	Kansas State University, Manhattan, KS -- for discretion of the president
150,000	Kansas University Endowment, Lawrence, KS -- for chancellor's discretionary fund
117,433	Kansas State University, Manhattan, KS
100,000	Kansas University Endowment, Lawrence, KS -- Robert Dole Institute
100,000	Norton County Hospital, Norton, KS -- for addition and renovation
100,000	Philips County Hospital, Phillipsburg, KS -- for area wide telemedicine
75,000	City of Logan, Logan, KS -- Logan Manor
75,000	City of Phillipsburg, Phillipsburg, KS -- for land, renovation and operating

ELLEN KNOWLES HARCOURT FOUNDATION

Giving Contact

Paul Altermatt, President
51 Main St.
New Milford, CT 06776
Phone: (860)355-2631
Fax: (860)355-9460

Description

Founded: 1982
EIN: 061068025
Organization Type: Private Foundation
Giving Locations: CT: New Milford
Grant Types: General Support.

Donor Information

Founder: the late Ellen Knowles Harcourt

Financial Summary

Total Giving: $125,750 (2001); $213,299 (2000); $168,850 (1999)
Giving Analysis: Giving for 2001 includes: foundation grants to United Way ($4,000); foundation scholarships ($18,000); 2000: foundation grants to United Way ($500); foundation scholarships ($81,000); 1999: foundation scholarships ($57,550)
Assets: $4,172,340 (2001); $4,500,740 (2000); $4,093,759 (1999)

Typical Recipients

Arts & Humanities: Arts Associations & Councils, Historic Preservation, History & Archaeology, Libraries, Literary Arts, Museums/Galleries, Music, Performing Arts, Public Broadcasting
Civic & Public Affairs: Botanical Gardens/Parks, Clubs, Employment/Job Training, Civic & Public Affairs-General, Housing, Parades/Festivals, Professional & Trade Associations, Safety, Urban & Community Affairs
Education: Afterschool/Enrichment Programs, Agricultural Education, Arts/Humanities Education, Colleges & Universities, Environmental Education, Education-General, Minority Education, Private Education (Precollege), Public Education (Precollege), Science/Mathematics Education, Secondary Education (Public), Student Aid
Environment: Environment-General, Protection, Resource Conservation, Watershed
Health: Cancer, Children's Health/Hospitals, Home-Care Services, Hospitals, Medical Rehabilitation, Nursing Services
International: Health Care/Hospitals
Religion: Jewish Causes
Social Services: Animal Protection, Child Welfare, Community Centers, Community Service Organizations, Recreation & Athletics, Senior Services, Shelters/Homelessness, Social Services-General, United Funds/United Ways, Volunteer Services, YMCA/YWCA/YMHA/YWHA, Youth Organizations

Application Procedures

Initial Contact: Send a brief letter of inquiry.
Application Requirements: Include amount requested, purpose of funds sought, and proof of tax-exempt status.
Deadlines: None.

Foundation Officials

Paul B. Altermatt: president, director B New Haven, CT 1930. ED Wesleyan University BA (1951); Georgetown University LLB (1956). PRIM CORP EMPL partner: Cramer & Anderson.
Roger Chace: assistant treasurer
Barbara Chappuis: secretary, director
Adele F. Ghisalbert: director
Susan N. Kustosz: director
Nancy A. Miller: director B 1943. ED California State University; University of California; University of Nevada.
Leandro Pasqual: director
George Verenes: treasurer, director

Grants Analysis

Disclosure Period: calendar year ending 2001
Total Grants: $103,750*
Number of Grants: 23
Average Grant: $4,511
Highest Grant: $15,000
Lowest Grant: $500
Typical Range: $1,000 to $10,000
*Note: Giving excludes scholarships and United Way.

Recent Grants

Note: Grants derived from 2000 Form 990.

Library-Related

4,000	New Milford Public Library, New Milford, CT -- for dedication room for USA veteran

General

30,000	University of Connecticut Foundation, Storrs, CT -- matching fund for scholarship
30,000	Wesleyan University, Middletown, CT -- for scholarship fund
21,000	J.P. Memorial Scholarship, New Milford, CT -- scholarship fund
20,000	New Milford Historical Society, New Milford, CT -- for publication history of New Milford

18,500	Harrybrooke Park, New Milford, CT -- for park improvements
12,500	Watershed All. of South Kent, South Kent, CT -- preservation for pond and wetlands
10,000	Waterbury Foundation, Waterbury, CT -- for program support
6,935	New Milford High School, New Milford, CT -- for student scholarship and programs
6,314	Children's Center, The, New Milford, CT -- cultural program for pre-school
6,000	Cumberland College, Williamsburg, KY -- for program support

HARDEN FOUNDATION

Giving Contact

Joseph C. Grainger, Executive Director
PO Box 779
Salinas, CA 93902-0779
Phone: (831)442-3005
Fax: (831)443-1429
E-mail: jgrainger@hardenfoundation.org
Web: http://www.hardenfoundation.org

Alternate Contact

Patricia Tynan Chapman, Secretary

Description

Founded: 1963
EIN: 946098887
Organization Type: General Purpose Foundation
Giving Locations: CA: Monterey County, Salinas Valley
Grant Types: Capital, Emergency, General Support, Matching, Multiyear/Continuing Support, Operating Expenses, Project, Scholarship.

Donor Information

Founder: Established in 1963 by Eugene E. Harden and Ercia E. Harden , both deceased. Mr. Harden was born in Wyoming in 1892. He moved to California as a young man. In 1913, he married Ercia Swindle. The Hardens were active in the civic and social life of the Imperial Valley, where they formed the Zenos and Harden Farms.
In the 1930s, the Hardens moved to Salinas where Mr. Harden formed the E.E. Harden Packing Company (later known as Harden Farms of California) and Harden Farms, Inc. He also helped to found the Growers Ice and Development Company. Mr. Harden died in 1984.
Mrs. Harden was an active volunteer with local charitable and civic organizations, often bringing home grown flowers to patients' rooms at the Salinas Valley Memorial Hospital. She was also a founding member and volunteer of the Pink Lady in the Service League. Mrs. Harden died in 1986.

Financial Summary

Total Giving: $1,800,000 (fiscal year ending February 28, 2002 approx); $2,320,556 (fiscal 2001); $1,758,790 (fiscal 1999). Note: Figure for 1996 includes $773,500 in matching gifts.
Giving Analysis: Giving for fiscal 2001 includes: foundation matching gifts ($24,000) fiscal 1999: foundation matching gifts ($127,500)
Assets: $65,167,635 (fiscal 2001); $59,313,198 (fiscal 1999); $58,684,641 (fiscal 1998)

Typical Recipients

Arts & Humanities: Arts Associations & Councils, Arts Centers, Arts Outreach, Arts & Humanities-General, History & Archaeology, Libraries, Literary Arts, Museums/Galleries, Music, Theater
Civic & Public Affairs: Chambers of Commerce, Community Foundations, Economic Development, Civic & Public Affairs-General, Housing, Legal Aid,

Nonprofit Management, Philanthropic Organizations, Rural Affairs, Urban & Community Affairs, Zoos/Aquariums

Education: Agricultural Education, Arts/Humanities Education, Colleges & Universities, Education Funds, Environmental Education, Faculty Development, Literacy, Preschool Education, School Volunteerism, Student Aid

Environment: Environment-General, Resource Conservation

Health: AIDS/HIV, Alzheimers Disease, Children's Health/Hospitals, Clinics/Medical Centers, Emergency/Ambulance Services, Eyes/Blindness, Health Funds, Heart, Home-Care Services, Hospices, Hospitals, Long-Term Care, Medical Rehabilitation, Mental Health, Nursing Services, Nutrition, Outpatient Health Care, Prenatal Health Issues, Respiratory, Single-Disease Health Associations

International: Health Care/Hospitals, International Relief Efforts

Religion: Churches, Religious Welfare

Social Services: Animal Protection, At-Risk Youth, Big Brother/Big Sister, Child Abuse, Child Welfare, Community Service Organizations, Counseling, Crime Prevention, Day Care, Delinquency & Criminal Rehabilitation, Domestic Violence, Family Planning, Family Services, Food/Clothing Distribution, People with Disabilities, Recreation & Athletics, Scouts, Senior Services, Shelters/Homelessness, Social Services-General, Special Olympics, Substance Abuse, United Funds/United Ways, Veterans, Volunteer Services, YMCA/YWCA/YMHA/YWHA, Youth Organizations

Application Procedures

Initial Contact: Applicants should contact the foundation for application guidelines and procedures. Applicants are also encouraged to discuss proposals with the Executive Director before subbmitting an application.

Application Requirements: Applicants should keep a copy of the completed proposal for themselves and send two to the foundation. Proposal must have a cover letter which includes organization's name, address, contact, telephone and amount and purpose of funding being requested; brief history of organization including date established; number of full-time, part-time, and volunteer employees; list of officers and board memebers, including name, address, occupation and phone number; copies of state and federal tax-exempt letters; if an ongoing program, cite effectiveness or uni que achievement; need for project; how project relates to other programs, if any; major objectives accomplished, inlcuding a time frame for each objective; how results will be evaluated; project budget, include anticipated income and expense; other grant requests pending, showing funding source and amount requested; qualification and experience of staff to accomplish project; plan for future funding; and discuss alternate plans of support if funding is rejected.

Deadlines: March 1 and September 1.

Review Process: Grants are reviewed semi-annually in June and December.

Restrictions

The foundation will not make grants for the following: to support sectarian religious programs, to support education programs, other than special projects that are related to agriculture; to support operating foundations or associations established for the benefit of an organization which receives substantial tax support; to establish or add to endowments; or to support annual events, conferences, or fundraising events. Grant requests generally should not exceed $100,000. Multiyear grants will be considered only in exceptional cases. The foundation will consider one request per calendar year per organization.

Additional Information

The foundation allows 501(c)(3) charitable organizations to use the premises of the Harden Home for events. Contact the foundation for more information. The Harden Home now serves as the Harden Foundation's headquarters.

Publications: Guidelines; Annual Report; Application Form

Foundation Officials

William Elliot: vice president

Frank E. Ferrasci: treasurer

Joseph C. Grainger: executive director

Ralph L. Kokjer, Jr.: president, director PRIM CORP EMPL CPA: Bailey Kokjer & Berry.

Thomas M. Merrill: vice president, director B 1929. PRIM CORP EMPL president, chief executive officer: Merrill Farms. CORP AFFIL president: Growers Ice Co.

Pat Sais: assistant secretary

Patricia Tynan-Chapman: secretary, director ED University of California at Berkeley (1949). PRIM CORP EMPL chairwoman: Tynan Lumber Co. Inc.

Grants Analysis

Disclosure Period: fiscal year ending February 28, 2001

Total Grants: $2,296,556*

Number of Grants: 117

Average Grant: $24,970*

Highest Grant: $400,000

Typical Range: $10,000 to $50,000

*Note: Giving excludes matching gifts. Average grant figure excludes highest grant.

Recent Grants

Note: Grants derived from fiscal 2000 Form 990.

General

500,000	Boys & Girls Club of Monterey County -- restructuring program
400,000	Public Recreation Unlimited, Salinas, CA -- Salinas Sports Complex - phase II
300,000	Steinbeck Center Foundation, Salinas, CA -- Salinas Valley agricultural history and education center
250,000	Natividad Medical Foundation, Salinas, CA -- funding for the Family Center project
217,000	Steinbeck Center Foundation, Salinas, CA -- Salinas Valley agricultural history and education center
200,000	Steinbeck Center Foundation, Salinas, CA -- funding for design & construction of Steinbeck center
200,000	Steinbeck Center Foundation, Salinas, CA -- funding for design & construction of Steinbeck center
100,000	Ariel Theatrical, Inc
100,000	Boy Scouts of America Monterey Bay Council, Salinas, CA -- scouting in the 21st century
100,000	Public Recreation Unlimited, Salinas, CA -- Salinas Sports Complex - phase II

PHIL HARDIN FOUNDATION

Giving Contact

C. Thompson Wacaster, Vice President
PO Drawer 5533
Meridian, MS 39302-5533
Phone: (601)483-4282
Fax: (601)483-5665
E-mail: info@philhardin.org
Web: http://www.philhardin.org

Description

Founded: 1964

EIN: 646024940

Organization Type: General Purpose Foundation

Giving Locations: MS: nationally.

Grant Types: Award, Capital, Challenge, Conference/Seminar, Endowment, Fellowship, General Support, Loan, Matching, Multiyear/Continuing Support, Operating Expenses, Professorship, Project, Research, Scholarship, Seed Money.

Donor Information

Founder: Incorporated in 1964 by the late Philip Bernard Hardin and Hardin's Bakeries Corp. A remarkable marketing entrepreneur, Mr. Hardin built the Hardin Bakeries Corp. into a highly successful business operation. Mr. Hardin had a strong sense of the importance of the bakeries' corporation being a good corporate citizen and responsible member of the community.

Financial Summary

Total Giving: $1,565,980 (2003 approx); $1,746,523 (2002); $2,085,222 (2001)

Giving Analysis: Giving for 1998 includes: foundation scholarships ($121,458)

Assets: $43,783,715 (2001); $49,792,380 (2000); $52,415,735 (1998)

Typical Recipients

Arts & Humanities: Arts Associations & Councils, Arts Centers, Arts Institutes, Historic Preservation, History & Archaeology, Libraries, Literary Arts, Museums/Galleries, Opera, Public Broadcasting, Visual Arts

Civic & Public Affairs: Community Foundations, Economic Development, Economic Policy, Civic & Public Affairs-General, Hispanic Affairs, Nonprofit Management, Philanthropic Organizations, Professional & Trade Associations, Urban & Community Affairs, Women's Affairs

Education: Afterschool/Enrichment Programs, Arts/Humanities Education, Business Education, Colleges & Universities, Community & Junior Colleges, Education Associations, Education Funds, Education Reform, Elementary Education (Private), Faculty Development, Education-General, Gifted & Talented Programs, International Studies, Leadership Training, Literacy, Minority Education, Preschool Education, Private Education (Precollege), Public Education (Precollege), Religious Education, School Volunteerism, Science/Mathematics Education, Special Education, Student Aid

Environment: Resource Conservation

Health: Health Policy/Cost Containment, Hospitals (University Affiliated), Medical Rehabilitation, Medical Research, Outpatient Health Care, Speech & Hearing

International: Foreign Arts Organizations, International Environmental Issues

Religion: Jewish Causes, Religious Welfare

Science: Observatories & Planetariums, Science Museums

Social Services: Child Welfare, Community Centers, Community Service Organizations, Family Services, People with Disabilities, Volunteer Services, Youth Organizations

Application Procedures

Initial Contact: The foundation requests that grant applicants submit an application form, obtainable from the foundation, and a written proposal.

Application Requirements: Proposal summaries should include a brief summary of not more than one page describing the purpose of the organization, why the organization is requesting the grant and how the grant will be spent and the aspired outcomes. Proposals, of not more than five pages, should include a statement of need for the project, the project's goals, a calendar of the project's major activities and a description of each, the names of the persons planning and implementing the uses of the grant and their qualifications, a statement of approval for the project from the organizations's chief officer, a description of how the request relates to the organization's long-range planning and priorities, and how the organization will evaluate the effectiveness of the use of the grant. Also include a line-item budget, the most recent audit or financial statement, a statement of the organization's tax-exempt status and a copy of the tax exemption letter from the IRS. Submit a list of the members of the governing board of the organization and any optional materials to supplement the proposal, if appropriate. If the request is for partial support of a project, submit the entire project budget and show the projected amounts and sources of other financial and in-kind support for the project. If the project is to continue beyond the Hardin Foundation grant, describe future plans for project funding.

Deadlines: Submit proposals at least three months in advance of the date by which a funding decision is needed.

Review Process: The directors of the foundation meet monthly but do not consider proposals each month.

Restrictions

All grants are given for projects that directly benefit education of Mississippians. No grants are made for land acquisition or deficit financing.

Additional Information

Publications: Guidelines; Program Policy Statement; Application Form

Foundation Officials

Joe S. Covington, MD: director

R. B. Deen, Jr.: secretary, director

Edwin E. Downer: director CORP AFFIL director: MIS Power Co.

Archie R. McDonnell, Sr.: treasurer, director

Stephen O. Moore: director, vice president

Lynne Taleff: director

C. Thompson Wacaster: vice president B 1941. ED Yale University BS (1963); University of Virginia MA (1965); University of Oregon PhD (1973).

Robert F. Ward: president, director B Eden, NC 1949. ED North Carolina State University BS (1970-1974); North Carolina State University BS (1977). PRIM CORP EMPL senior vice president: Mantech Environmental Technology.

Sarah W. Wile: director B 1944. ED Vanderbilt University BA (1966); Mississippi State University MEd (1975). PRIM CORP EMPL secretary, treasurer, director: Southern Cast Product Inc.

Grants Analysis

Disclosure Period: calendar year ending 2001
Total Grants: $2,085,222*
Number of Grants: 22
Average Grant: $31,578*
Highest Grant: $380,000
Lowest Grant: $2,000
Typical Range: $2,500 to $100,000
***Note:** Giving excludes scholarships. Average grant amount excludes highest grant.

Recent Grants

Note: Grants derived from 1999 Form 990.

Library-Related
1,500	Foundation Center, The, New York, NY

General
221,350	Gulf Coast Community Foundation, Gulfport, MS -- local capacity endowment
150,000	DSUF/CCC, Cleveland, MS -- Educational Partnership Project
100,000	Holmes Community College Development Foundation, Goodman, MS -- Technology for Tomorrow's Workforce
100,000	Rust College, Holly Springs, MS -- endowment challenge for Chair in Elementary Education
90,000	Greater Jackson Foundation, Jackson, MS
85,047	Meridian Public School District, Meridian, MS -- implementation of education reform models
75,000	Mississippi Museum Natural Science Foundation, Jackson, MS -- Nature's Niche
65,400	Alcorn State University, Lorman, MS -- accelerated schools model in Claiborne County
5,4000	Jackson Servant Leadership Corps, Jackson, MS -- strategic planning outcomes
50,000	Audrey Cohen College, New York, NY -- develop a consortium

HARKNESS FOUNDATION FOR DANCE

Giving Contact

Theodore S. Bartwink, Treasurer
145 East 48th St., Suite 26C
New York, NY 10017-0025
Phone: (212)755-5540
Fax: (212)755-5542

Description

Founded: 1986
EIN: 131926551
Organization Type: Private Foundation
Giving Locations: NY: New York some giving nationally.
Grant Types: General Support, Scholarship.

Donor Information

Founder: In 1986, Rebekah Harkness founded the Harkness Ballet Foundation, now known as the Harkness Foundation for Dance.

Financial Summary

Total Giving: $1,300,000 (2003 approx); $1,400,000 (2002 approx); $1,433,100 (2001)
Assets: $21,700,000 (2003 approx); $21,700,000 (2002 approx); $21,740,615 (2001)
Gifts Received: $352 (2001); $437,402 (1994); $410,943 (1993)

Typical Recipients

Arts & Humanities: Arts Centers, Arts Festivals, Arts Funds, Ballet, Community Arts, Dance, Ethnic & Folk Arts, Film & Video, Music, Opera, Performing Arts, Theater
Civic & Public Affairs: Civic & Public Affairs-General, Public Policy, Urban & Community Affairs
Education: Arts/Humanities Education, Colleges & Universities
Health: AIDS/HIV, Cancer, Hospitals
International: Foreign Arts Organizations
Science: Scientific Organizations
Social Services: At-Risk Youth, Community Centers, Community Service Organizations, YMCA/YWCA/YMHA/YWHA, Youth Organizations

Application Procedures

Initial Contact: Send a brief letter of inquiry.
Application Requirements: Provide a description of the program or project, amount requested, purpose of funds sought, budget, and copy of IRS 501 (c)(3) determination.
Deadlines: None.

Restrictions

Grants are awarded to arts organizations qualified under IRC Section 501(c)(3).

Additional Information

Publications: Guidelines

Foundation Officials

Theodore S. Bartwink: treasurer, secretary

Etta Brandman: vice president, assistant treasurer, secretary

William Alan Perlmuth: president B New York, NY 1929. ED Wilkes College AB (1951); Columbia University LLB (1953). PRIM CORP EMPL partner: Stroock & Stroock & Lavan. CORP AFFIL director: Sentry Tech Corp. NONPR AFFIL trustee: School American Ballet; trustee: Wilkes University; trustee: New York University Medical Center; member: New York City Bar Association; member: New York State Bar Association; trustee: 55th Street Theater Foundation; trustee: Hospital Joint Diseases Orthopedic Institute. CLUB AFFIL Harmonie Club.

Grants Analysis

Disclosure Period: calendar year ending 2001
Total Grants: $1,433,100
Number of Grants: 203
Average Grant: $7,060
Highest Grant: $117,000
Lowest Grant: $500
Typical Range: $500 to $10,000

Recent Grants

Note: Grants derived from 2001 Form 990.

General
117,000	Brooklyn Academy of Music, Brooklyn, NY
112,000	92nd Street Y, New York, NY
110,000	Hospital for Joint Diseases, New York, NY
53,900	City Center, New York, NY
50,000	Lincoln Center, New York, NY
41,500	Discalced, Inc., New York, NY
39,250	Joyce Theater Foundation, New York, NY
35,000	School of American Ballet, New York, NY
35,000	Spoleto Festival, Charleston, SC
31,000	American Ballet Theatre, New York, NY

JOHN H. AND WILHELMINA D. HARLAND CHARITABLE FOUNDATION

Giving Contact

John A. Conant, Secretary
2 Piedmont Center, Suite 106
Atlanta, GA 30305
Phone: (404)264-9912
Fax: (404)266-8834
E-mail: harland@randomc.com

Description

Founded: 1972
EIN: 237225012
Organization Type: General Purpose Foundation
Giving Locations: GA: Atlanta metropolitan area
Grant Types: Capital, Endowment, General Support, Matching, Professorship, Project, Research.

Donor Information

Founder: Established in May 1972 by Mr. John Harland and his wife, Wilhelmina D. Harland through a gift of 125,000 shares of John H. Harland Company common stock. Mr. Harland, originally from Northern

Ireland, came to Atlanta in 1906. In 1923, he founded the John H. Harland Company which now operates 44 plants in the United States and Puerto Rico. Mrs. Harland was born in Atlanta, and she studied at the New England Conservatory of Music in Boston. She also offered voluntary service in France and Serbia during and immediately following World War I.

Financial Summary

Total Giving: $1,619,067 (2001); $1,554,416 (2000); $1,463,056 (1999)
Giving Analysis: Giving for 2001 includes: foundation grants to United Way ($20,000)
Assets: $28,856,882 (2001); $27,906,575 (2000); $27,931,284 (1999)
Gifts Received: $238,680 (2001); $214,425 (2000); $208,079 (1999). Note: In 2001, contributions were received from John A. & Miriam H. Conant.

Typical Recipients

Arts & Humanities: Arts Centers, Arts Festivals, Arts Outreach, Ballet, Film & Video, Historic Preservation, Libraries, Museums/Galleries, Opera, Performing Arts, Theater
Civic & Public Affairs: African American Affairs, Botanical Gardens/Parks, Community Foundations, Economic Development, Employment/Job Training, Ethnic Organizations, Civic & Public Affairs-General, Housing, Law & Justice, Legal Aid, Municipalities/Towns, Philanthropic Organizations, Professional & Trade Associations, Urban & Community Affairs
Education: Arts/Humanities Education, Colleges & Universities, Economic Education, Education Funds, Education-General, International Studies, Literacy, Medical Education, Preschool Education, Private Education (Precollege), Public Education (Precollege), Religious Education, Science/Mathematics Education, Special Education, Vocational & Technical Education
Environment: Environment-General, Resource Conservation
Health: Children's Health/Hospitals, Clinics/Medical Centers, Emergency/Ambulance Services, Geriatric Health, Health Organizations, Hospitals, Long-Term Care, Medical Rehabilitation, Mental Health, Nutrition, Public Health, Research/Studies Institutes, Single-Disease Health Associations, Speech & Hearing
International: Foreign Arts Organizations, International Organizations, International Relief Efforts
Religion: Churches, Jewish Causes, Ministries, Religious Organizations, Religious Welfare, Seminaries
Science: Science Museums, Scientific Centers & Institutes
Social Services: At-Risk Youth, At-Risk Youth, Big Brother/Big Sister, Camps, Child Abuse, Child Welfare, Community Centers, Community Service Organizations, Counseling, Day Care, Delinquency & Criminal Rehabilitation, Domestic Violence, Family Services, Food/Clothing Distribution, Homes, People with Disabilities, Recreation & Athletics, Scouts, Shelters/Homelessness, Social Services-General, Substance Abuse, United Funds/United Ways, Volunteer Services, YMCA/YWCA/YMHA/YWHA, Youth Organizations

Application Procedures

Initial Contact: Send a brief letter of inquiry requesting a Grant Applicant Questionnaire.
Application Requirements: Proposals should include a letter of request and a copy of the foundation's Grant Applicant Questionnaire.
Deadlines: Proposals may be submitted at any time, but the cut-off for new proposals to be considered at the Trustees' April and October meetings is no later than March 1 and September 1.
Notes: After the trustees have considered a grant proposal from an applicant organization, there is generally a 21-month waiting period before a new grant proposal will be eligible for consideration.

Restrictions

The foundation does not make grants to private primary or secondary schools except for those serving the disabled, to individual churches for operations or capital campaigns, or to individuals, annual funds, or special events.

Additional Information

The foundation requires a written report on the use of the grant at the end of the grant period.
Publications: Annual Report; Grant Application Questionnaire

Foundation Officials

John A. Conant: secretary B 1923. NONPR AFFIL chairman: Columbia Theological Seminary.
Miriam Harland Conant: president
Winifred S. Davis: trustee
Margaret C. Dickson: vice president, treasurer
Michael M. Dickson: trustee
James Malcolm Sibley: trustee B Atlanta, GA August 05, 1919. ED Princeton University AB (1941); Woodrow Wilson School of Law (1942); Harvard University Law School (1945-1946). CORP AFFIL director: Summit Industries; director: Rock-Tenn Co.; director: Ichauway Inc. NONPR AFFIL member: Georgia Bar Association; trustee: AG Rhodes Home; member: Atlanta Bar Association; member: American College Probate Counsel; member: American Law Institute; member: American Bar Foundation; member: American Bar Association. CLUB AFFIL Piedmont Driving Club; Commerce Club.
Allison F. Williams: trustee

Grants Analysis

Disclosure Period: calendar year ending 2001
Total Grants: $1,599,067*
Number of Grants: 70
Average Grant: $19,790*
Highest Grant: $153,225
Lowest Grant: $2,500
Typical Range: $10,000 to $30,000
*Note: Giving excludes United Way. Average grant figure excludes two highest grants ($253,371).

Recent Grants

Note: Grants derived from 2001 Form 990.

General
153,225	Hillside, Inc. -- improvements to the Conant school
151,544	Presbyterian Homes of Georgia, Inc., Quitman, GA -- capital campaign
151,130	Georgia Shakespeare Festival, Atlanta, GA -- setting the stage campaign
55,298	Georgia Foundation for Independent Colleges, Atlanta, GA -- challenge grant
50,372	Global Health Action, Atlanta, GA -- capital campaign
50,000	Carrie Steele-Pitts Home, Atlanta, GA -- construction costs of Life Learning Center
50,000	Grant Park Family Health Center, Chicago, IL -- new facility
38,928	Emory University Center for Ethics in Public Policy and Professions, Atlanta, GA -- ethics fellow
30,218	Families First, Atlanta, GA -- merger with capitol area mosaic
30,000	Boy Scouts of America Atlanta Area Council, Atlanta, GA -- Character in Action Campaign

HARLEY-DAVIDSON CO.

Company Headquarters
Milwaukee, WI
Web: http://www.harley-davidson.com

Company Description
Founded: 1903
Ticker: HDI
Exchange: NYSE
Revenue: US$4.091 billion (2002)
Profit: US$580.2 million (2002)
Employees: 8100 (2001)
Fortune Rank: 392, per FORTUNE Magazine's list of 500 Largest U.S. Corporations (2002).
SIC(s): 2389 Apparel & Accessories Nec, 3519 Internal Combustion Engines Nec, 3714 Motor Vehicle Parts & Accessories, 3751 Motorcycles, Bicycles & Parts.

Operating Locations
Harley-Davidson Co. (PA--York)

Nonmonetary Support
Type: Donated Products; In-kind Services

Harley-Davidson Foundation

Giving Contact
Mary Ann Martiny, Manager
3700 West Juneau Avenue
Milwaukee, WI 53208
Phone: (414)343-4001

Description
Founded: 1993
EIN: 391769946
Organization Type: Corporate Foundation
Giving Locations: AL, headquarters and operating communities; MO; PA: headquarters and operating communities; WI: headquarters and operating communities
Grant Types: Employee Matching Gifts, General Support, Operating Expenses, Project, Research, Scholarship.
Note: Foundation makes a small number of contributions for capital or operating support, but this is not the priority.

Financial Summary
Total Giving: $2,146,038 (2001); $1,841,864 (2000); $2,073,000 (1999)
Giving Analysis: Giving for 2000 includes: foundation grants to United Way ($228,040); foundation ($1,613,823); 1998: foundation grants to United Way ($189,140) foundation ($1,440,544)
Assets: $6,797,885 (2001); $7,007,915 (2000); $5,241,291 (1998)
Gifts Received: $2,468,778 (2001); $2,485,093 (2000); $1,800,000 (1998). Note: Contributions are received from the Harley-Davidson Motor Co.

Typical Recipients
Arts & Humanities: Arts Centers, Arts Institutes, Arts & Humanities-General, History & Archaeology, Libraries, Museums/Galleries, Music, Opera, Performing Arts, Public Broadcasting, Theater
Civic & Public Affairs: African American Affairs, Business/Free Enterprise, Chambers of Commerce, Civil Rights, Community Foundations, Economic Development, Economic Policy, Employment/Job Training, Civic & Public Affairs-General, Hispanic Affairs, Housing, Inner-City Development, Urban & Community Affairs, Women's Affairs, Zoos/Aquariums
Education: Arts/Humanities Education, Business Education, Colleges & Universities, Education Funds, Education Reform, Engineering/Technological Education, Education-General, Health & Physical Education, Minority Education, Private Education (Precollege), Public Education (Precollege), Secondary Education (Public)
Environment: Environment-General
Health: Cancer, Children's Health/Hospitals, Clinics/Medical Centers, Diabetes, Emergency/Ambulance

Services, Health Organizations, Mental Health, Nursing Services, Public Health, Single-Disease Health Associations
Science: Science Museums, Scientific Centers & Institutes
Social Services: Child Welfare, Community Centers, Community Service Organizations, Crime Prevention, Family Planning, Family Services, Food/Clothing Distribution, People with Disabilities, Scouts, Substance Abuse, United Funds/United Ways, Veterans, Volunteer Services, YMCA/YWCA/YMHA/YWHA, Youth Organizations

Application Procedures

Initial Contact: Send a complete proposal using the Milwaukee Area Funders common grant application form.
Application Requirements: For merchandise or table sponsorship, submit a letter describing the organization and how the event will benefit the community, including what percentage of the event's budget will result in a contribution to the organization; copy of 501(c)(3) letter and federal identification number.
Deadlines: February 9, April 13, June 9, August 17, October 26, and December 14.
Evaluative Criteria: Foundation looks closely for relevance to foundation's areas of interest; clarity in expected outcomes and strategy for achieving them; and a collaborative approach to solving problems.
Decision Notification: Bimonthly.
Notes: Call the foundation's information line for a list of current dates (414)343-8047.

Restrictions

The foundation does not make grants to individuals, political causes or candidates, athletic events or teams, conferences, or religious causes unless for a major project that benefits the greater community.

Additional Information

The Harley-Davidson family of employees, dealers, and customers has raised approximately $20 million for the Muscular Dystrophy Association in the last 16 years.
The foundation's emphasis is community revitalization and education. However, other areas of interest are arts and culture, medicine, and the environment. Because of the number of requests the foundation receives, only one request per year from an organization is considered. considered.
Publications: Guidelines

Corporate Officials

Dr. Jeffrey L. Bleustein: chief executive officer, chairman B 1939. ED Columbia University PhD; Columbia University MS; Cornell University BS. PRIM CORP EMPL chief executive officer, chairman: Harley-Davidson Inc. CORP AFFIL chairman, chief executive officer, director: Harley-Davidson Motor Co.; director: Holiday Holding Corp.; president: Harley-Davidson Holding Co.; director: Brunswick Corp.; chief executive officer: Buell Motorcycle Co.

Foundation Officials

James M. Brostowitz: treasurer B Milwaukee, WI 1952. ED Marquette University BS (1974). PRIM CORP EMPL vice president, treasurer: Harley-Davidson Motor Co. ADD CORP EMPL vice president, treasurer, controller: Harley-Davidson Inc.; treasurer: Harley-Davidson Transportation Co.
Mr. Gail A. Lione: secretary
Mary Anne Martiny: assistant secretary
James L. Ziemer: president B 1950. ED University of Wisconsin BA (1975); University of Wisconsin MBA (1986). PRIM CORP EMPL vice president, chief financial officer: Harley-Davidson Inc. CORP AFFIL vice president: Harley-Davidson Transportation Co.

Grants Analysis

Disclosure Period: calendar year ending 2001
Total Grants: $1,913,703*
Number of Grants: 359
Average Grant: $5,331
Highest Grant: $250,000
Lowest Grant: $13
Typical Range: $25 to $25,000
*Note: Giving excludes United Way.

Recent Grants

Note: Grants derived from 2001 Form 990.

Library-Related
10,000	Franklin Public Library -- program support

General
250,000	L&H Bradley Tech and Training -- program support
161,120	United Way of Greater Milwaukee, Milwaukee, WI -- program support
100,000	Strand Capitol Arts, York, PA -- program support
84,000	Boys and Girls Club of Greater Milwaukee, Milwaukee, WI -- program support
65,830	United Way of York County, York, PA -- program support
53,500	Hunger Task Force, Milwaukee, WI -- program support
50,000	American Battle Monuments Commission, Arlington, VA -- program support
50,000	Florentine Opera Company, Milwaukee, WI -- program support
50,000	Urban Day School, Milwaukee, WI -- program support
50,000	Veterans of Foreign Wars, Valley, NE -- program support

PEARL M. AND JULIA J. HARMON FOUNDATION

Giving Contact

George L. Hangs, Jr., Secretary & Treasurer
PO Box 52568
Tulsa, OK 74152-0568
Phone: (918)743-6191
Web: http://www.HarmonFoundation.com
Note: The foundation reported in 1997 that it is over-distributed in funding and is not currently accepting applications.

Description

Founded: 1962
EIN: 736095893
Organization Type: General Purpose Foundation
Giving Locations: AR; KS; NM; OK: Tulsa; TX
Grant Types: Endowment, General Support, Loan, Project.

Financial Summary

Total Giving: $59,870 (fiscal year ending May 31, 1999); $48,716 (fiscal 1997); $74,204 (fiscal 1996)
Assets: $31,788,455 (fiscal 1999); $29,485,395 (fiscal 1997); $27,900,196 (fiscal 1996)
Gifts Received: $4,684 (fiscal 1999); $11,790 (fiscal 1997); $500 (fiscal 1995)

Typical Recipients

Arts & Humanities: Arts Associations & Councils, Ballet, Arts & Humanities-General, History & Archaeology, Libraries, Museums/Galleries, Music, Opera, Theater
Civic & Public Affairs: Botanical Gardens/Parks, Business/Free Enterprise, Community Foundations, Employment/Job Training, Civic & Public Affairs-General, Hispanic Affairs, Housing, Legal Aid, Municipalities/Towns, Nonprofit Management, Parades/Festivals, Safety, Urban & Community Affairs

Education: Afterschool/Enrichment Programs, Colleges & Universities, Elementary Education (Private), Elementary Education (Public), Education-General, Leadership Training, Private Education (Precollege), Public Education (Precollege), Secondary Education (Private)
Environment: Resource Conservation
Health: Clinics/Medical Centers, Emergency/Ambulance Services, Health-General, Health Organizations, Medical Rehabilitation, Mental Health, Nursing Services, Prenatal Health Issues, Research/Studies Institutes
Religion: Churches, Dioceses, Ministries, Religious Organizations, Religious Welfare
Social Services: Big Brother/Big Sister, Child Welfare, Community Service Organizations, Crime Prevention, Domestic Violence, Emergency Relief, Family Planning, Family Services, Food/Clothing Distribution, People with Disabilities, Recreation & Athletics, Senior Services, Sexual Abuse, Shelters/Homelessness, Substance Abuse, Volunteer Services, Youth Organizations

Application Procedures

Initial Contact: Inquiry by one page letter.

Restrictions

The foundation is restricted by trust agreement to charitable organizations in Oklahoma, Kansas, Texas, Arkansas, and New Mexico. The foundation does not fund evangelism or research, and it will not make grants to individuals or foundations.

Additional Information

The foundation operates the Harmon Science Center, an interactive science museum in Tulsa, OK.
Publications: Guidelines

Foundation Officials

Catherine H. Frederick: trustee
George L. Hangs, Jr.: secretary, treasurer, trustee, directory
Jean M. Kuntz: trustee
Charlotte Kay Owens: trustee, officer mgr

Grants Analysis

Disclosure Period: fiscal year ending May 31, 1999
Total Grants: $59,870
Number of Grants: 39
Average Grant: $1,535
Highest Grant: $5,000
Lowest Grant: $100
Typical Range: $100 to $2,500

Recent Grants

Note: Grants derived from 2002 Form 990.

Library-Related
19,380	Nowata City-County Library, Nowata, OK -- maintain grounds, Nowata library
13,743	Nowata City County Library, Nowata, OK -- contribution
5,000	Tulsa City County Library, Tulsa, OK -- contribution Hardesty Library
5,000	Tulsa City County Library, Tulsa, OK -- contribution Hardesty Library
2,000	Nowata City County Library, Nowata, OK -- contribution
1,500	Nowata City County Library, Nowata, OK -- contribution

General
250,000	Big Brothers & Big Sisters, Tulsa, OK -- for Bartlesville/Nowata
104,989	Ambulance Service, Nowata, OK -- Ford Ambulance
8,468	Grand Lake Mental Health Center, Nowata, OK -- building maintenance and utilities
8,046	Ambulance Service, Nowata, OK -- equipment for new ambulance

6,480	City of Nowata, Nowata, OK -- purchase drug enforcement equipment
5,000	Living Word Family Church, Nowata, OK -- for construction
5,000	New Life Assembly of God Church, Nowata, OK -- renovation
5,000	Seventh Day Adventist Church, Nowata, OK -- renovation
5,000	Tulsa Opera, Inc., Tulsa, OK -- contribution
5,000	Tulsa Philharmonic, Tulsa, OK -- contribution

HARPER BRUSH WORKS

Company Headquarters
400 N. 2nd St.
Fairfield, IA 52556
Web: http://www.harper-brush.com

Company Description
Revenue: US$9 million (2001)
Employees: 75 (2001)
SIC(s): 3900 Miscellaneous Manufacturing Industries, 3991 Brooms & Brushes.

Harper Brush Works Foundation

Giving Contact
Wendall King, Director
Harper Brush Works Foundation
PO Box 608
Fairfield, IA 52556
Phone: (515)472-5186

Description
EIN: 421145331
Organization Type: Corporate Foundation
Giving Locations: headquarters area only.
Grant Types: Award, General Support, Scholarship.

Financial Summary
Total Giving: $29,050 (fiscal year ending August 31, 2001); $46,243 (fiscal 2000); $47,475 (fiscal 1999)
Giving Analysis: Giving for fiscal 2001 includes: foundation scholarships ($18,500); fiscal 2000: foundation scholarships ($22,500); fiscal 1999: foundation scholarships ($18,000) foundation ($29,475)
Assets: $95,043 (fiscal 2001); $74,158 (fiscal 2000); $65,238 (fiscal 1999)
Gifts Received: $49,825 (fiscal 2001); $49,291 (fiscal 2000); $63,185 (fiscal 1999). Note: In fiscal 2000 and 2001, contributions were received from Harper Brush Works, Inc. and Harper Corp. (d/b/a Texas Feathers). In fiscal 1999, contributions were received from Harper Brush Works ($30,800) and Texas Feathers ($32,385). In fiscal 1998, contributions were received from Harper Brush Works, Inc. and Harper Corp. (d/b/a Texas Feathers). In 1996 and 1997, contributions were received from Harper Brush Works ($9,760) and Texas Feathers.

Typical Recipients
Arts & Humanities: Libraries
Civic & Public Affairs: Botanical Gardens/Parks, Clubs, Civic & Public Affairs-General, Safety, Women's Affairs
Education: Business-School Partnerships, Colleges & Universities, Faculty Development, Education-General, Private Education (Precollege), Public Education (Precollege), Science/Mathematics Education, Student Aid
Health: Cancer, Hospitals
Religion: Religious Welfare

Social Services
Social Services: Community Centers, Day Care, Recreation & Athletics, Shelters/Homelessness, Social Services-General, Substance Abuse, Youth Organizations

Application Procedures
Initial Contact: The foundation has no formal grant application procedure or application form.
Deadlines: None.

Additional Information
Provides scholarships to IA residents for higher education.

Corporate Officials
Barry Harper: president, chief executive officer PRIM CORP EMPL president, chief executive officer: Harper Brush Works.
Dan Turtell: chief financial officer PRIM CORP EMPL chief financial officer: Harper Brush Works.

Foundation Officials
Wendall King: director
George Patten: director
Emily Reneker: director

Grants Analysis
Disclosure Period: fiscal year ending August 31, 2001
Total Grants: $8,050*
Number of Grants: 14
Average Grant: $575
Highest Grant: $2,000
Lowest Grant: $100
Typical Range: $100 to $1,000
*Note: Giving excludes scholarship.

Recent Grants
Note: Grants derived from 2000 Form 990.

General

2,000	Arlington ISD Foundation, Arlington, TX
2,000	City of Hope
1,360	Fairfield Police Department, Fairfield, CT
1,000	Arlington Quality of Life Foundation, Arlington, TX
1,000	Arlington Women's Shelter, Arlington, TX
1,000	Birdwell Riverside Center
1,000	Boys & Girls Club of Arlington, Arlington, TX
1,000	Boys & Girls Club of Brownwood, Brownwood, TX
1,000	Fairfield Christian School, Fairfield, IA
1,000	Fairfield Fire Department, Fairfield, CT

HARPERCOLLINS PUBLISHERS, INC.

Company Headquarters
10 E. 53rd Street
New York, NY 10022
Web: http://www.harpercollins.com

Company Description
Employees: 3,500
SIC(s): 2700 Printing & Publishing.
Parent Company: News Corporation Ltd., 2 Holt St., Sydney, Australia

Operating Locations
Ballinger Publishing Co. (MA--Cambridge); Basic Books, Inc. (NY--New York); Harper Audio (NY--New York); Harper Reference (NY--New York); HarperCollins Adult Trade Division (NY--New York); HarperCollins Junior Books Division (NY--New York); HarperCollins Publishers (NY--New York); HarperCollins San Francisco (CA--San Francisco); Scott Foresman/

Addison Wesley (IL--Glenview); Zondervan Corp. (MI--Grand Rapids)

Nonmonetary Support
Type: Donated Products; Workplace Solicitation
Note: Workplace solicitation is United Way only.

Giving Contact
Aimee Johnson, Corp. Communications, Asst. Director
10 E. 53rd St.
New York, NY 10022
Phone: (212)207-7555
Fax: (212)207-7909

Description
Organization Type: Corporate Giving Program
Giving Locations: principally near operating locations and to national organizations.
Grant Types: Employee Matching Gifts, General Support.

Financial Summary
Total Giving: Company does not disclose contributions figures.

Typical Recipients
Arts & Humanities: Ethnic & Folk Arts, Libraries, Literary Arts
Civic & Public Affairs: First Amendment Issues, Women's Affairs
Education: Education-General, Literacy, Minority Education
Social Services: Community Service Organizations, Family Services, Volunteer Services

Application Procedures
Initial Contact: Initial letter and proposal, addressed to Karen Berberich, may be submitted at any time and should include a description of organization, amount requested, purpose of funds sought, a recently audited financial statement, and proof of tax-exempt status.

Restrictions
Does not support fraternal organizations, individuals, member agencies of united funds, political or lobbying groups, or religious organizations for sectarian purposes.

Corporate Officials
Glenn D'Agnes: chief financial officer PRIM CORP EMPL chief financial officer: HarperCollins Publishers Inc.
Anthea Disney: president, chief executive officer B Dunstable, United Kingdom 1946. ED Queens College. PRIM CORP EMPL president, chief executive officer: HarperCollins Publishers. NONPR AFFIL editorial director: Murdoch Mags.

Grants Analysis
Note: Grant size varies.

GLADYS AND ROLAND HARRIMAN FOUNDATION

Giving Contact
William F. Hibberd, Secretary
63 Wall Street
140 Broadway, 4th Floor
New York, NY 10005-1101
Phone: (212)493-8182
Fax: (212)493-5570

Description
Founded: 1966
EIN: 510193915
Organization Type: General Purpose Foundation

Giving Locations: NY: New York nationally.
Grant Types: General Support.

Donor Information
Founder: Established in 1966 by the late Gladys Harriman and Roland Harriman. Their trusts continue to support the foundation.

Financial Summary
Total Giving: $8,321,772 (2000); $8,529,899 (1999); $7,538,340 (1998)
Giving Analysis: Giving for 1998 includes: foundation scholarships ($54,700)
Assets: $134,317,723 (2000); $149,508,165 (1999); $140,157,112 (1998)
Gifts Received: $600,000 (1994); $1,200,000 (1993); $1,200,000 (1992)

Typical Recipients
Arts & Humanities: Ballet, Arts & Humanities-General, Historic Preservation, History & Archaeology, Libraries, Literary Arts, Museums/Galleries, Music, Public Broadcasting
Civic & Public Affairs: Botanical Gardens/Parks, Business/Free Enterprise, Civil Rights, Economic Development, Employment/Job Training, Civic & Public Affairs-General, Public Policy, Urban & Community Affairs
Education: Afterschool/Enrichment Programs, Arts/Humanities Education, Business Education, Colleges & Universities, Community & Junior Colleges, Elementary Education (Public), Engineering/Technological Education, Education-General, Leadership Training, Medical Education, Minority Education, Private Education (Precollege), Public Education (Precollege), Secondary Education (Private), Student Aid
Environment: Air/Water Quality, Forestry, Forestry, Environment-General, Research, Resource Conservation, Wildlife Protection
Health: Cancer, Clinics/Medical Centers, Diabetes, Emergency/Ambulance Services, Geriatric Health, Health Organizations, Hospitals, Medical Research, Speech & Hearing
International: Foreign Educational Institutions, Health Care/Hospitals, International Relief Efforts
Religion: Churches, Religious Organizations, Seminaries
Science: Science Museums, Scientific Labs
Social Services: Animal Protection, At-Risk Youth, Big Brother/Big Sister, Camps, Child Abuse, Child Welfare, Community Service Organizations, Domestic Violence, Emergency Relief, Family Planning, Family Services, Scouts, Scouts, Social Services-General, Substance Abuse, United Funds/United Ways, Volunteer Services, YMCA/YWCA/YMHA/YWHA, Youth Organizations

Application Procedures
Initial Contact: Applicants should submit a written proposal.
Application Requirements: Proposals should be typed and include the organization's history and details of its program.
Deadlines: None.
Review Process: The directors meet twice a year.

Restrictions
There are no restrictions or limitations on grants.

Additional Information
The foundation shares office space and members of the board of directors with the Mary W. Harriman Foundation, New York, NY.

Foundation Officials
Cristin H. Connery: director
Thomas F. Dixon: vice president, director
Terrence Michael Farley: director B New York, NY 1930. ED City College of New York BBA (1955). PRIM CORP EMPL partner: Brown Brothers Harriman & Co. CORP AFFIL director: Atlantic Reinsurance Co.;

director: Centennial Insurance Co.; trustee: Atlantic Mutual Insurance Co. CLUB AFFIL Wianno Club; The Links Club; University Club; Echo Lake Country Club.
Elbridge Thomas Gerry: president B New York, NY November 22, 1908. ED Harvard University BA (1931). PRIM CORP EMPL general partner: Brown Brothers Harriman & Co. CORP AFFIL partner: Gerry Brothers & Co. NONPR AFFIL vice president: Boys Club New York; president: New York Society for Children; honorary trustee: American Museum Natural History. CLUB AFFIL Rittenhouse Club; Meadow Brook Club; Piping Rock Club; Colony Club; The Links Club.
Elbridge Thomas Gerry, Jr.: president, director B New York, NY 1933. ED Harvard University AB (1955). PRIM CORP EMPL general partner: Brown Brothers Harriman & Co. ADD NONPR EMPL vice president: Boys Club New York. CORP AFFIL director: Union Pacific Corp.
William F. Hibberd: secretary
Anna T. Korniczky: treasurer
Wilhem E. Northrup: director

Grants Analysis
Disclosure Period: calendar year ending 2000
Total Grants: $8,321,772
Number of Grants: 94
Average Grant: $88,529
Highest Grant: $525,000
Lowest Grant: $1,000
Typical Range: $1,000 to $50,000 and $100,000 to $500,000

Recent Grants
Note: Grants derived from 2001 Form 990.

Library-Related
50,000	Auburn Public Library, Auburn, ME
50,000	New York Public Library, New York, NY

General
550,000	American Red Cross in Greater New York, Washington, DC
504,500	American Red Cross, Washington, DC
500,000	University of Minnesota Medical School, Minneapolis, MN
470,000	American Museum of Natural History, New York, NY
250,000	Purnell School, Pottersville, NJ
250,000	Shelburne Museum, Shelburne, VT
250,000	United Way September 11th Fund, New York, NY
235,000	Columbia University, New York, NY
205,000	St. Thomas Episcopal Church, Washington, DC
175,000	Cold Spring Harbor Laboratory Association, Cold Spring Harbor, NY

MARY W. HARRIMAN FOUNDATION

Giving Contact
William F. Hibberd, Secretary
63 Wall Street, Suite 3101
New York, NY 10005
Phone: (212)493-8182
Fax: (212)493-5570

Description
Founded: 1925
EIN: 237356000
Organization Type: General Purpose Foundation
Giving Locations: NY: New York metropolitan area
Grant Types: Department, General Support, Project, Research.

Donor Information
Founder: The Mary W. Harriman Foundation was established in New York in 1925 and incorporated in 1973, with funds donated by the late Mary W. Harriman , wife of Union Pacific Railroad magnate and financier Edward Henry Harriman.

Financial Summary
Total Giving: $1,600,950 (2000); $1,557,200 (1999); $1,429,000 (1998)
Assets: $34,494,139 (2000); $38,235,271 (1999); $35,072,490 (1998)

Typical Recipients
Arts & Humanities: Arts Centers, Ballet, Film & Video, Historic Preservation, History & Archaeology, Libraries, Museums/Galleries, Music, Performing Arts, Public Broadcasting, Theater
Civic & Public Affairs: African American Affairs, Botanical Gardens/Parks, Clubs, Community Foundations, Civic & Public Affairs-General, Law & Justice, Municipalities/Towns, Native American Affairs, Public Policy, Urban & Community Affairs, Zoos/Aquariums
Education: Arts/Humanities Education, Business Education, Colleges & Universities, Education Associations, Faculty Development, Education-General, International Studies, Legal Education, Medical Education, Minority Education, Private Education (Precollege), Public Education (Precollege), Religious Education, School Volunteerism, Secondary Education (Private), Secondary Education (Public), Special Education
Environment: Air/Water Quality, Environment-General, Research, Resource Conservation, Wildlife Protection
Health: AIDS/HIV, Cancer, Children's Health/Hospitals, Emergency/Ambulance Services, Hospices, Hospitals, Medical Rehabilitation, Mental Health, Nursing Services
International: Foreign Educational Institutions, International Affairs, International Environmental Issues, International Relations, International Relief Efforts
Religion: Jewish Causes
Science: Science Museums
Social Services: Child Abuse, Child Welfare, Community Service Organizations, Counseling, Day Care, Emergency Relief, Family Planning, Family Services, People with Disabilities, Recreation & Athletics, Social Services-General, Volunteer Services, Youth Organizations

Application Procedures
Initial Contact: Applicants should submit a written proposal and include tax-exempt status.
Application Requirements: Proposals should be typed and include the organization's history and details of grants purposes.
Deadlines: Proposals should be submitted no later than February.
Review Process: The directors meet once a year.

Additional Information
The foundation shares office space and members of the board of directors with the Gladys and Roland Harriman Foundation.

Foundation Officials
Kathleen L.F. Ames: vice president
Marjorie N. Friedman: director
Elbridge Thomas Gerry: director B New York, NY November 22, 1908. ED Harvard University BA (1931). PRIM CORP EMPL general partner: Brown Brothers Harriman & Co. CORP AFFIL partner: Gerry Brothers & Co. NONPR AFFIL vice president: Boys Club New York; president: New York Society for Children; honorary trustee: American Museum Natural History. CLUB AFFIL Rittenhouse Club; Meadow Brook Club; Piping Rock Club; Colony Club; The Links Club.
William F. Hibberd: secretary
Anna T. Korniczky: treasurer

David H. Mortimer: president, director
Kathleen H. Mortimer: director

Grants Analysis

Disclosure Period: calendar year ending 2000
Total Grants: $1,600,950
Number of Grants: 118
Average Grant: $12,077*
Highest Grant: $101,000
Lowest Grant: $1,000
Typical Range: $5,000 to $25,000
*Note: Average grant figure excludes two highest grants ($200,000).

Recent Grants

Note: Grants derived from 2000 Form 990.

Library-Related
10,000	New York Public Library, New York, NY

General
101,000	Bennington College, Bennington, VT
99,000	Learning Leaders, Inc., New York, NY
65,000	School for Language and Communication Development, North Bellmore, NY
60,000	Concord Academy, Concord, MA
53,000	Yale University, New Haven, CT
50,000	American Assembly, New York, NY
50,000	New York City Ballet Company, New York, NY
50,000	Take the Field, New York, NY
45,000	World Wildlife Fund, Washington, DC
42,500	Weill Medical College of Cornell University, New York, NY

FRANCIS A. AND JACQUELYN H. HARRINGTON FOUNDATION

Giving Contact

Sumner B. Tilton, Jr., Trustee
370 Main St., 12th Fl.
Worcester, MA 01608
Phone: (508)798-8621
Fax: (508)791-6454

Description

Founded: 1965
EIN: 046125088
Organization Type: Private Foundation
Giving Locations: MA: Worcester
Grant Types: Capital, General Support, Project.

Donor Information

Founder: Francis A. Harrington, Charles A. Harrington Foundation

Financial Summary

Total Giving: $772,000 (2001); $919,500 (2000); $774,795 (1999)
Giving Analysis: Giving for 2001 includes: foundation grants to United Way ($4,000); foundation scholarships ($10,000); 2000: foundation grants to United Way ($4,000); foundation scholarships ($20,000); 1999: foundation grants to United Way ($4,000);
Assets: $13,626,489 (2001); $15,857,075 (2000); $17,131,502 (1999)

Typical Recipients

Arts & Humanities: Arts Centers, Historic Preservation, History & Archaeology, Libraries, Museums/Galleries, Music, Performing Arts, Public Broadcasting, Theater
Civic & Public Affairs: Botanical Gardens/Parks, Clubs, Community Foundations, Civic & Public Affairs-General, Housing, Municipalities/Towns, Native

American Affairs, Philanthropic Organizations, Public Policy, Rural Affairs, Urban & Community Affairs
Education: Arts/Humanities Education, Colleges & Universities, Community & Junior Colleges, Education Funds, Education Reform, Private Education (Precollege), Religious Education, Science/Mathematics Education, Secondary Education (Private), Student Aid
Environment: Environment-General, Resource Conservation, Wildlife Protection
Health: Cancer, Clinics/Medical Centers, Health-General, Health Organizations, Hospitals (University Affiliated), Medical Research, Nursing Services, Public Health
International: Foreign Arts Organizations
Religion: Churches, Jewish Causes
Science: Science Museums, Scientific Centers & Institutes, Scientific Organizations, Scientific Research
Social Services: Big Brother/Big Sister, Child Welfare, Community Centers, Community Service Organizations, Crime Prevention, Family Planning, Family Services, United Funds/United Ways, YMCA/YWCA/YMHA/YWHA, Youth Organizations

Application Procedures

Initial Contact: Send a brief letter of inquiry.
Application Requirements: Provide proof of tax-exempt status. Include goals and objectives and plan.
Deadlines: June 1.

Restrictions

The foundation provides grants to health, educational, and cultural organizations that are exempt under section 51(c)(3) of the IRC.

Foundation Officials

Francis A. Harrington, Jr.: trustee
James H. Harrington: trustee
Phyllis Harrington: trustee
Sumner B. Tilton, Jr.: trustee PRIM CORP EMPL clerk: New England Newspaper Supply Co. CORP AFFIL clerk: Whitinsville Water Co.; clerk: Whiteater Inc.; clerk: NDI Inc.; clerk: R H White Co. Inc.; officer: Fletcher, Tilton & Whipple PC. NONPR AFFIL president: Greater Worcester Community Foundation.

Grants Analysis

Disclosure Period: calendar year ending 2001
Total Grants: $758,000*
Number of Grants: 45
Average Grant: $12,977*
Highest Grant: $100,000
Lowest Grant: $1,000
Typical Range: $5,000 to $25,000
*Note: Giving excludes United Way and scholarships. Average grant figure excludes two highest grants ($200,000).

Recent Grants

Note: Grants derived from 2001 Form 990.

Library-Related
20,000	Friends of the Worcester Public Library, Worcester, MA -- expansion and renovation of library

General
100,000	Bancroft School, Worcester, MA -- building new lower middle school facility
100,000	Greater Worcester Community Foundation, Inc., Worcester, MA -- to fund F A & J H Harrington Human Service Fund
60,000	EcoTarium, Worcester, MA -- capital campaign
50,000	Clark University, Worcester, MA -- Traina Center for the Arts
40,000	Worcester Art Museum, Worcester, MA -- capital campaign
25,000	Greater Worcester Community Foundation, Inc., Worcester, MA -- December 3rd Fund

20,000	Greater Worcester Community Foundation, Inc., Worcester, MA -- United Way Endowment Fund
20,000	Massachusetts Audubon Society-Worcester, Worcester, MA -- Worcester county drive
20,000	Mechanics Hall of Worcester, Worcester, MA -- anniversary campaign
20,000	Quinsigamond Community College Foundation, Worcester, MA -- increase endowment

WILLIAM H. AND MATTIE WATTIS HARRIS FOUNDATION

Giving Contact

Marilyn Harris-Hite, Secretary
6655 W. Sahara, Suite B-118
Las Vegas, NV 89102
Phone: (702)253-1317

Description

Founded: 1960
EIN: 870405724
Organization Type: Private Foundation
Giving Locations: Western US.
Grant Types: General Support, Project.

Donor Information

Founder: the late Matte Wattis Harris, William H. Harris

Financial Summary

Total Giving: $459,680 (2000); $406,780 (1999); $327,500 (1998)
Giving Analysis: Giving for 2000 includes: foundation scholarships ($4,500) 1999: foundation scholarships ($8,000)
Assets: $9,342,422 (2000); $9,640,241 (1999); $9,405,387 (1998)

Typical Recipients

Arts & Humanities: Arts Associations & Councils, Arts Centers, Arts Festivals, Arts Institutes, Ballet, Community Arts, Dance, Ethnic & Folk Arts, Film & Video, Arts & Humanities-General, Historic Preservation, History & Archaeology, Museums/Galleries, Music, Opera, Public Broadcasting, Theater
Civic & Public Affairs: Community Foundations, Civic & Public Affairs-General, Professional & Trade Associations, Urban & Community Affairs, Zoos/Aquariums
Education: Arts/Humanities Education, Colleges & Universities, Environmental Education, Faculty Development, Education-General, Health & Physical Education, International Studies, Journalism/Media Education, Medical Education, Preschool Education, Private Education (Precollege), Science/Mathematics Education, Secondary Education (Private), Social Sciences Education, Student Aid
Environment: Air/Water Quality, Forestry, Environment-General, Protection, Research, Resource Conservation, Wildlife Protection
Health: AIDS/HIV, Eyes/Blindness, Health Organizations, Medical Research, Speech & Hearing
International: Foreign Arts Organizations, Health Care/Hospitals, International Environmental Issues, International Organizations, International Relations
Religion: Churches, Religious Welfare
Science: Science Museums, Scientific Centers & Institutes, Scientific Research
Social Services: Animal Protection, At-Risk Youth, Camps, Child Welfare, Community Centers, Community Service Organizations, Crime Prevention, Family Planning, Family Services, Food/Clothing Distribution, People with Disabilities, Recreation & Athletics, Senior Services, Shelters/Homelessness, Substance

Abuse, YMCA/YWCA/YMHA/YWHA, Youth Organizations

Application Procedures

Initial Contact: Request application guidelines, then send four copies of proposal.
Application Requirements: Include a description of organization, purpose of funds sought, and other funding sources.
Deadlines: February 1 and August 1.

Restrictions

Does not support individuals.

Additional Information

Publications: Program Policy Statement; Application Guidelines

Foundation Officials

Henry Hite: president
James W. Hite: vice president
Marilyn Harris Hite: secretary
Sharon Lewis: trustee
William Rohrback: trustee

Grants Analysis

Disclosure Period: calendar year ending 2000
Total Grants: $455,180*
Number of Grants: 90
Average Grant: $5,058
Highest Grant: $60,000
Typical Range: $1,000 to $10,000
*Note: Giving excludes scholarships.

Recent Grants

Note: Grants derived from 1999 Form 990.

General

50,000	Friends of the Earth, Seattle, WA -- Elwah River Restoration Project
50,000	Marine Conservation Biology Institute, Redmond, WA -- general fund/Marine Protected Areas
50,000	Westminster College, Salt Lake City, UT -- degree program in complementary healing
10,000	Punahou School, Honolulu, HI -- endowment fund
10,000	School of American Research, Santa Fe, NM -- Chief White Antelope Blanket
8,000	Billfish Foundation, Ft. Lauderdale, FL -- general fund/Spearfish
8,000	St. John's College, Santa Fe, NM -- Challenge Grant/tutor salary
8,000	University of Nevada Reno, Reno, NV -- Brown Scholarship Fund
7,000	World Wildlife Fund, Washington, DC -- Save the Tiger fund, TRAFFIC program
7,000	YMCA of Rome - Floyd County, Rome, GA -- soccer program

HARSCO CORP.

Company Headquarters

350 Poplar Church Rd.
Camp Hill, PA 17011
Web: http://www.harsco.com

Company Description

Founded: 1956
Ticker: HSC
Exchange: NYSE
Revenue: US$1.976 billion (2002)
Employees: 17500 (2002)
SIC(s): 2952 Asphalt Felts & Coatings, 3295 Minerals--Ground or Treated, 3494 Valves & Pipe Fittings Nec, 3743 Railroad Equipment.

Operating Locations

Harsco Corp. (AL--Birmingham, Leeds, Theodore; CA--Los Angeles, Pomona; CT--Hamden; FL--Plant City, Tampa; GA--Jesup; IL--Chicago; IN--Gary, Highland; IA--Bloomfield, Des Moines; KY--Drakesboro; LA--Crowley; MD--Baltimore; MN--Fairmont; NJ--Fort Lee, Union; NY--Lockport, Long Island City, New York; NC--Charlotte; OH--Cleveland, Columbus, Kenton, Lansing, Marysville, West Jefferson; OK--Tulsa; PA--Butler, Cheswick, East Stroudsburg, Harrisburg, York; TN--Nashville; TX--Channelview, Houston, Mineral Wells; WV--Moundsville)
Note: Also operates internationally.

Harsco Corp. Fund

Giving Contact

Robert G. Yocum, Chairman & Trustee
PO Box 8888
Camp Hill, PA 17001-8888
Phone: (717)763-7064
Web: http://www.harsco.com/about1/community.html

Description

EIN: 236278376
Organization Type: Corporate Foundation
Giving Locations: headquarters and operating communities.
Grant Types: Capital, Department, Employee Matching Gifts, General Support, Research, Scholarship.

Financial Summary

Total Giving: $1,832,268 (2002 approx); $1,319,930 (2001); $1,153,080 (2000). Note: Contributes through foundation only.
Giving Analysis: Giving for 2000 includes: foundation matching gifts ($49,345); foundation grants to United Way ($109,625); 1999: foundation matching gifts ($36,021); foundation grants to United Way ($107,495); foundation ($1,163,205); 1998: foundation matching gifts ($59,348); foundation grants to United Way ($75,305); foundation ($873,578);
Assets: $6,114,221 (2001); $8,775,067 (2000); $10,709,401 (1999)
Gifts Received: $210,000 (1997); $150,000 (1996); $150,000 (1995). Note: Fund receives contributions from the Harsco Corp and Sordoni Enterprises.

Typical Recipients

Arts & Humanities: Arts Associations & Councils, Arts Centers, Arts Festivals, Arts Funds, Community Arts, Dance, Historic Preservation, History & Archaeology, Libraries, Museums/Galleries, Music, Opera, Performing Arts, Public Broadcasting, Theater
Civic & Public Affairs: African American Affairs, Business/Free Enterprise, Chambers of Commerce, Civil Rights, Clubs, Economic Development, Economic Policy, Employment/Job Training, Ethnic Organizations, Civic & Public Affairs-General, Hispanic Affairs, Housing, Law & Justice, Legal Aid, Philanthropic Organizations, Professional & Trade Associations, Public Policy, Safety, Urban & Community Affairs
Education: Arts/Humanities Education, Business Education, Colleges & Universities, Community & Junior Colleges, Economic Education, Education Associations, Education Funds, Engineering/Technological Education, Education-General, International Exchange, International Studies, Leadership Training, Legal Education, Literacy, Medical Education, Minority Education, Public Education (Precollege), Religious Education, Science/Mathematics Education, Student Aid
Environment: Environment-General
Health: Cancer, Children's Health/Hospitals, Clinics/Medical Centers, Diabetes, Emergency/Ambulance Services, Health Organizations, Hospices, Hospitals, Medical Research, Mental Health, Public Health, Single-Disease Health Associations

International: Foreign Arts Organizations, Foreign Arts Organizations, International Relations
Religion: Jewish Causes, Missionary Activities (Domestic), Religious Welfare, Social/Policy Issues
Science: Science Museums, Scientific Centers & Institutes
Social Services: Big Brother/Big Sister, Child Welfare, Community Centers, Community Service Organizations, Crime Prevention, Day Care, Emergency Relief, Family Planning, Food/Clothing Distribution, Homes, People with Disabilities, Recreation & Athletics, Scouts, Sexual Abuse, Shelters/Homelessness, Social Services-General, Substance Abuse, United Funds/United Ways, Volunteer Services, YMCA/YWCA/YMHA/YWHA, Youth Organizations

Application Procedures

Initial Contact: Send a brief letter or proposal; organizations in company operating locations should contact local divisions directly.
Application Requirements: Include a description of organization, amount requested, purpose of funds sought, recently audited financial statement, and proof of tax-exempt status.
Deadlines: None. For US scholarship programs, January 1 of year preceding date of entrance into college.
Evaluative Criteria: Organization must be in area where corporation has business operations.
Decision Notification: Annually, usually in January or February.

Restrictions

Does not support dinners or special events, fraternal organizations, goodwill advertising, political or lobbying groups, religious organizations for sectarian purposes, or individuals.
The fund seldom makes grants to organizations with limited purposes or for special projects that do not receive wide public support.

Foundation Officials

Leonard A. Campanaro: treasurer B Philadelphia, PA 1948. ED Temple University BBA (1970). PRIM CORP EMPL senior vice president, chief operating officer director: Harsco Corp.
P. C. Coppock: trustee
Salvatore D. Fazzolari: treasurer, secretary, trustee
Malcolm W. Gambill: president, trustee B Crumpler, NC 1930. CORP AFFIL director: York International Corp.
D. C. Hathaway: trustee
Robert G. Yocum: secretary PRIM CORP EMPL treasurer, director: Harsco Corp.

Grants Analysis

Disclosure Period: calendar year ending 2001
Total Grants: $1,184,050*
Number of Grants: 118
Average Grant: $9,118*
Highest Grant: $117,236
Lowest Grant: $50
Typical Range: $1,000 to $20,000
*Note: Giving excludes matching gifts and United Way. Average grant figure excludes highest grant.

Recent Grants

Note: Grants derived from 2001 Form 990.

General

117,236	Institute of International Education, New York, NY
109,290	National Merit Scholarship Corporation, Chicago, IL
105,800	Goodwill Industries of Central Pennsylvania, Harrisburg, PA
97,245	WITF, Harrisburg, PA
58,333	Harrisburg Community Theater, Harrisburg, PA
51,000	State System of Higher Education, Inc., Harrisburg, PA

50,000	ALS Association, Ft. Washington, PA
50,000	Capital Center for the Arts, Science, and Education, Harrisburg, PA
50,000	Pinnacle Health Foundation, Harrisburg, PA
42,000	Messiah College, Grantham, PA

HARTFORD COURANT FOUNDATION

Giving Contact

Kate Miller, Executive Director
285 Broad Street
Hartford, CT 06115
Phone: (860)241-6472
Fax: (860)520-6988
E-mail: hcfoundation@courant.com
Web: http://www.hartfordcourantfoundation.org

Description

Founded: 1950
EIN: 060759107
Organization Type: General Purpose Foundation
Giving Locations: CT: Central Connecticut
Grant Types: Capital, Challenge, General Support, Matching, Operating Expenses, Project, Scholarship, Seed Money.

Donor Information

Founder: The foundation was established in 1950 by The Hartford Courant newspaper. When the newspaper was purchased by Times Mirror Corporation in 1979, The Hartford Courant Foundation was restructured as a private foundation independent of the company.

Financial Summary

Total Giving: $868,181 (2001); $886,140 (2000); $760,665 (1999)
Giving Analysis: Giving for 2001 includes: foundation matching gifts ($70,000); 1999: foundation matching gifts ($77,000) 1998: foundation matching gifts ($728,925)
Assets: $15,781,216 (2001); $17,191,047 (2000); $19,065,155 (1999)
Gifts Received: $111,699 (2001); $2,000 (1999); $12,000 (1998). Note: In 2001, contributions were received from Hartford Courant.

Typical Recipients

Arts & Humanities: Arts Associations & Councils, Arts Centers, Arts Outreach, Ballet, Dance, Arts & Humanities-General, Libraries, Literary Arts, Museums/Galleries, Music, Opera, Performing Arts, Public Broadcasting, Theater
Civic & Public Affairs: African American Affairs, Botanical Gardens/Parks, Community Foundations, Economic Development, Employment/Job Training, Civic & Public Affairs-General, Hispanic Affairs, Housing, Nonprofit Management, Philanthropic Organizations, Public Policy, Urban & Community Affairs, Women's Affairs
Education: Arts/Humanities Education, Colleges & Universities, Continuing Education, Education-General, Health & Physical Education, Literacy, Minority Education, Preschool Education, Private Education (Precollege), Public Education (Precollege), Science/Mathematics Education, Secondary Education (Private), Special Education, Student Aid, Vocational & Technical Education
Health: AIDS/HIV, Children's Health/Hospitals, Clinics/Medical Centers, Hospitals, Hospitals (University Affiliated), Medical Rehabilitation, Medical Research, Mental Health, Nursing Services, Prenatal Health Issues, Public Health
International: Health Care/Hospitals, International Development
Religion: Churches, Jewish Causes, Ministries, Religious Organizations, Religious Welfare

Science: Science Museums, Scientific Centers & Institutes
Social Services: At-Risk Youth, Big Brother/Big Sister, Camps, Child Abuse, Child Welfare, Community Service Organizations, Community Service Organizations, Counseling, Crime Prevention, Domestic Violence, Emergency Relief, Family Planning, Family Services, Food/Clothing Distribution, Homes, People with Disabilities, Recreation & Athletics, Scouts, Shelters/Homelessness, Social Services-General, Substance Abuse, United Funds/United Ways, YMCA/YWCA/YMHA/YWHA, Youth Organizations

Application Procedures

Initial Contact: Send full proposal, including completed application. Application form is available on the foundation's web site.
Application Requirements: Completed application form must be accompanied by the following attachments: proof of tax-exempt status; list of current funders and their levels of support; most recent income and expense statement (audited, if possible); program for the most recent year; and description of program for which funds are requested including evidence of need, measurable outcomes, program activities, detailed budget, timetable, evaluation plan, and plan for future funding.
Deadlines: December 15, March 15, June 15, and September 15.
Review Process: Foundation staff reviews requests prior to submitting applications to the board of trustees. Staff review may involve meeting with the applicant, site visits, and interviews with other agencies and individuals who are knowledgeable about the need the application addresses.
Notes: Applicants are expected to be able to demonstrate compliance with anti-discrimination legislation.

Restrictions

Does not make contributions to individuals, endowments, organizations which are not tax-exempt, organizations which have IRS private foundation designation, religious institutions other than for provision of non-sectarian community services, groups engaged in activities meant to influence either legislation or the outcome of elections, capital projects related to the arts, performances, conferences, trips, one-time events, and annual campaigns. Applicants must be located in Hartford, Middlesex, or Tolland County.

Additional Information

Publications: Annual Report; Application Guidelines; Informational Brochure

Corporate Officials

Raymond Koupal: vice president, chief financial officer PRIM CORP EMPL vice president, chief financial officer: Hartford Courant Co.
Worth Loomis: president, trustee B New York, NY 1923. ED Yale University BS (1947); New York University MBA (1955). PRIM CORP EMPL president, trustee: Hartford Graduate Center. CORP AFFIL director: Spencer Turbine Co.; director: Southern New England Telephone Co.; chairman: Life Techs Inc.; trustee: Mechanics Savings Bank; director: Covenant Mutual Insurance Co.; director: Colts Manufacturing Co.; director: Connecticut Natural Gas Corp.; president board trustees: Colt Bequest Inc.; director: Chemstone Corp.; director: CIGNA Funds Group; director: Capewell Components Co. NONPR AFFIL trustee: Trinity College; trustee: Yale-Berkeley Divinity School; member, board overseers: New York University Stern School Business; member: Society Cincinnati; trustee: Morehouse College; member: National Association Manufacturers; trustee: Kazanjian Economic Foundation; trustee: Hartford Courant Foundation; visiting professor, trustee: Hartford Seminary; trustee: Hartford College Women; member: Century Association; member: Connecticut Business & Industry Association; trustee: American Institute Managing Diversity; trustee: Alpha Center.

Millard H. Pryor, Jr.: managing director B Owosso, MI 1933. ED University of Michigan (1955-1957). PRIM CORP EMPL managing director: Pryor & Clark Co. CORP AFFIL chairman: Lydall; chairman: Wiremold Corp.; director: Hartford Fund; director: Hoosier Magnetics Inc.; director: Duro-Test Corp.; director: GEO International Corp.; vice chairman: Compudyne Corp.
George A. Scott: president PRIM CORP EMPL president: Hartford West Indian Bakeries.

Foundation Officials

Dr. Eddie L. Davis: trustee
Luis Diez-Morales: trustee
Bernard Michael Fox: trustee B New York, NY 1942. ED Manhattan College BSEE (1963); Rensselaer Polytechnic Institute MSEE (1964); Harvard University Graduate School of Business Administration (1979). PRIM CORP EMPL president, chief executive officer, director, chairman: Northeast Utilities. CORP AFFIL director: Shawmut Bank Connecticut; director: Shawmut National Corp.; director: Shawmut Bank; director: Connecticut Yankee Atomic Power Co.; director: Dexter Corp.; director: CIGNA Corp. NONPR AFFIL director: Institute Nuclear Power Operations; director: Mount Holyoke College; chairman: Institute Living; director: Connecticut Business & Industry Association; sr member: Institute Electrical & Electronics Engineers; member: American Leadership Forum.
Mary E. Junck: trustee PRIM CORP EMPL president, eastern newspapers: Times Mirror Co.
Raymond Koupal: trustee (see above)
Maura L. Melley: trustee PRIM CORP EMPL senior vice president public affairs: Phoenix Home Life Mutual Insurance Co.
Marty Petty: trustee PRIM CORP EMPL vice president sales: Hartford Courant Co.
Olcott D. Smith: hon trustee
Michael E. Waller: trustee
Efram Zimbalist, III: trustee ED Harvard University BA; Harvard University MBA. PRIM CORP EMPL president, chief executive officer: Times Mirror Magazines. NONPR AFFIL member national council: House Ear Institute; chairman emeritus, trustee: Robert Louis Stevenson School.

Grants Analysis

Disclosure Period: calendar year ending 2001
Total Grants: $798,181*
Number of Grants: 115
Average Grant: $6,941
Highest Grant: $70,000
Typical Range: $5,000 to $15,000 and $250 to $3,000
*Note: Giving excludes matching gifts.

Recent Grants

Note: Grants derived from 2001 Form 990.

General

70,000	Greater Hartford Arts Council, Hartford, CT -- challenge grant
40,000	Urban League of Greater Hartford, Hartford, CT -- annual fund
25,000	Girls Scouts -- annual fund
20,000	Northwest Catholic High School -- Hispanic Scholarship Program
15,000	Antiquarian and Landmark Society, Hartford, CT
15,000	Career Counseling Center, Hartford, CT -- Child Care Assistant Training Program
15,000	Connecticut Council for Philanthropy, Hartford, CT -- Connecticut Giving Project
15,000	Easter Seals Society of Connecticut, CT -- paving the way project
15,000	Greater Hartford YMCA, Hartford, CT -- Read to Succeed
15,000	HARC

HARTFORD FINANCIAL SERVICES GROUP, INC.

Company Headquarters

Hartford Plaza
690 Asylum Ave.
Hartford, CT 06115
Web: http://www.thehartford.com

Company Description

Founded: 1810
Ticker: HIG
Exchange: NYSE
Revenue: US$182.043 billion (2002)
Employees: 29000 (2002)

Nonmonetary Support

Value: $530,000 (2002)
Type: Donated Equipment; Loaned Employees; Loaned Executives
Volunteer Programs: The company sponsors a Reading Buddies Program with a local middle elementary school. Approximately 100 employees volunteer for this program.

Giving Contact

Jennifer Kasparian, Grants Program Specialist
The Hartford Financial Services Group, Inc.
Hartford Place
690 Asylum Avenue
T-12-56
Hartford, CT 06115
Phone: (860)547-4995
Fax: (860)547-6393
E-mail: Jennifer.Kasparian@thehartford.com
Web: http://www.thehartford.com/about/affairs.html

Alternate Contact

Darlene Leak, corporate relations
Phone: (860)547-3133

Description

Organization Type: Corporate Giving Program
Giving Locations: CT: Hartford Greater Hartford area principally near operating locations and to national organizations, grants are allocated based on the size of the operation in the.
Grant Types: Capital, Employee Matching Gifts, General Support, Project, Scholarship.
Note: Employee matching gift ratio: 1 to 1 up to $2,000 per employee annually for education.

Financial Summary

Total Giving: $5,000,000 (2003 approx); $5,108,893 (2002); $6,928,970 (2001). Note: Contributes through corporate direct giving program only. 2001 giving includes prepaid capital commitments and United Way contributions for 2002.
Giving Analysis: Giving for 2002 includes: corporate direct giving (approx $3,460,000); 2001: corporate direct giving ($6,928,970) 2000: corporate direct giving ($4,356,078)
Assets: $562,532 (1995); $469,766 (1994); $76,033 (1993)
Gifts Received: $1,136,066 (1997); $2,500,000 (1995); $2,200,000 (1994). Note: Contributions are received from Hartford Fire Insurance Co.

Typical Recipients

Arts & Humanities: Arts Associations & Councils, Arts Centers, Arts Funds, Community Arts, Dance, Arts & Humanities-General, History & Archaeology, Libraries, Literary Arts, Museums/Galleries, Music, Opera, Performing Arts, Public Broadcasting, Theater
Civic & Public Affairs: African American Affairs, Botanical Gardens/Parks, Business/Free Enterprise, Civil Rights, Economic Development, Employment/Job Training, Civic & Public Affairs-General, Hispanic Affairs, Housing, Law & Justice, Nonprofit Management, Parades/Festivals, Professional & Trade Associations, Public Policy, Safety, Urban & Community Affairs, Women's Affairs
Education: Agricultural Education, Arts/Humanities Education, Business Education, Colleges & Universities, Community & Junior Colleges, Continuing Education, Education Associations, Education Funds, Education-General, Health & Physical Education, International Studies, Journalism/Media Education, Legal Education, Literacy, Medical Education, Minority Education, Private Education (Precollege), Public Education (Precollege), Religious Education, Science/Mathematics Education, Special Education, Student Aid, Vocational & Technical Education
Environment: Environment-General
Health: AIDS/HIV, Children's Health/Hospitals, Clinics/Medical Centers, Eyes/Blindness, Geriatric Health, Health Policy/Cost Containment, Health Organizations, Hospices, Hospitals, Medical Rehabilitation, Medical Research, Prenatal Health Issues, Preventive Medicine/Wellness Organizations, Public Health
Religion: Ministries, Religious Welfare
Social Services: Big Brother/Big Sister, Camps, Child Welfare, Community Service Organizations, Crime Prevention, Day Care, Delinquency & Criminal Rehabilitation, Domestic Violence, Emergency Relief, Family Services, Food/Clothing Distribution, Homes, People with Disabilities, Recreation & Athletics, Senior Services, Shelters/Homelessness, Social Services-General, Substance Abuse, United Funds/United Ways, YMCA/YWCA/YMHA/YWHA, Youth Organizations

Application Procedures

Initial Contact: Organizations in Hartford should send a brief two-page letter requesting application form to headquarters; organizations near the company's regional offices should send requests to the local general manager for consideration, who may forward it to Hartford depending on the size of the grant requested. Application and guidelines may also be obtained on company's web site or by calling (810) 547-4998.
Application Requirements: Submit a completed application form and required attachments.
Deadlines: January 15, April 1, July 1, and September 15.
Review Process: Committee meets in March, June, September, and November for grant considerations. Decisions are generally based on written proposals, however, a periodic site visit by Hartford or a personal interview may be required.
Evaluative Criteria: Degree to which proposal meets company's guidelines, efficient management of program funds, human service value and practicality of objectives, nonduplication of existing programs, number of individuals served, fundraising stability of organization and range of support of program, organization's track record.
Decision Notification: Quarterly.

Restrictions

Excluded from consideration are endowments, health care issues or organizations, individualss, conferences and seminars, courtesy advertising, private foundations, religious purposes, athletic outings, reducing or eliminating a pre-existing debt, one-time events including testimonial and fund-raising dinners, environmental issues/organizations, or activities such as scouting band, and little league, etc. if they are not a part of programs that fall under the specified funding categories.
Capital support is generally limited to agencies in Greater Hartford. Organizations accepted for a capital grant may not also receive operating support in the same year.
Funding is generally not provided to agencies that receive United Way funding. Special programs can be an exception, but the agency must have the permission of the United Way before it solicits funding.

Individual applications for scholarships are not accepted.

Additional Information

In 1997, the foundation was integrated into the corporate giving program.
Generally seeks to support organizations that enable individuals to help themselves and that are supported by creative and ultimately self-supporting funding initiatives.
Where possible, the Hartford will try to leverage its funds through matching and challenge grants and consider awarding multiple-year grants if appropriate and where desirable. matching and challenge grants and consider awarding multiple-year grants if appropriate and where desirable.

Corporate Officials

Ramani Ayer: chairman, president, chief executive officer B Kerala, KE India 1947. ED Indian Institute of Technology BS (1969); Drexel University MS (1973). PRIM CORP EMPL chairman, president, chief executive officer: The Hartford. CORP AFFIL chairman: Trumball Insurance Co.; chairman: Twin City Fire Insurance Co.; director: New York Stock Exchange Inc.; president: Hartford Insurance Southeast; chairman: Hartford Life Accident Insurance Co.; chairman: Hartford Insurance Midwest; president: Hartford Index Fund Inc.; chairman: Hartford Insurance Co. Illinois; chairman, chief executive officer: Hartford Financial Services Group Inc.; chairman: Hartford Casualty Insurance Co.; president: Hartford Financial Group Inc.; chairman: Hartford Accident Indemnity Co.
Joseph H. Gareau: executive vice president, chief investment officer B Westfield, MA 1947. ED University of Massachusetts BBA (1973); University of Hartford MBA (1978). PRIM CORP EMPL executive vice president, chief investment officer: The Hartford Insurance Co. ADD CORP EMPL executive vice president: Hartford Financial Services Group Inc.; senior vice president, chief investment officer, director: Hartford Insurance Midwest; executive vice president: Hartford Insurance of the Southeast; executive vice president: Hartford Accident Indemnity Co.; executive vice president, director: Hartford Casualty Insurance Co.; president, chief invest officer: Hartford Investment Management Co.; vice president,chief investment officer: Pacific Industry Co. Inc. CORP AFFIL vice president, chief investment officer: Pacific Industry Co. Inc.
Edward L. Morgan: group senior vice president B Scranton, PA 1943. ED Gettysburg College (1965). PRIM CORP EMPL group senior vice president: The Hartford ADD CORP EMPL senior vice president: Hartford Financial Services Group Inc.; senior vice president: Hartford Fire Insurance Co.

Giving Program Officials

Ann D. De Raismes: member PRIM CORP EMPL senior vice president: Hartford Life Annuity Insurance Co.
Joseph H. Gareau: investment officer B Westfield, MA 1947. ED University of Massachusetts BBA (1973); University of Hartford MBA (1978). PRIM CORP EMPL executive vice president, chief investment officer: The Hartford Insurance Co. ADD CORP EMPL executive vice president: Hartford Financial Services Group Inc.; senior vice president, chief investment officer, director: Hartford Insurance Midwest; executive vice president: Hartford Insurance of the Southeast; executive vice president: Hartford Accident Indemnity Co.; executive vice president, director: Hartford Casualty Insurance Co.; president, chief invest officer: Hartford Investment Management Co.; vice president,chief investment officer: Pacific Industry Co. Inc. CORP AFFIL vice president, chief investment officer: Pacific Industry Co. Inc.
Helen G. Goodman: senior vice president B Bridgeport, CT 1941. ED Barnard College (1964); Columbia University (1979). PRIM CORP EMPL senior vice

president: The Hartford. CORP AFFIL treasurer, director: Hartford Action Plan Infant Health; senior vice president: Hartford Financial Services Group Inc.

David M. Klein: vice president B Brooklyn, NY 1946. ED University of Rhode Island (1968); Temple University (1970). PRIM CORP EMPL senior vice president: The Hartford ADD CORP EMPL senior vice president: Hartford Insurance Group; executive vice president: Hartford Financial Service Group; senior vice president: Hartford Insurance Midwest.

Edward L. Morgan: member contributions committee B Scranton, PA 1943. ED Gettysburg College (1965). PRIM CORP EMPL group senior vice president: The Hartford ADD CORP EMPL senior vice president: Hartford Financial Services Group Inc.; senior vice president: Hartford Fire Insurance Co.

Edna Negron: PRIM CORP EMPL director community affairs: The Hartford.

Michael Stephen Wilder: B New Haven, CT 1941. ED Yale University BA (1963); Harvard University JD (1966). PRIM CORP EMPL senior vice president, general counsel: The Hartford Financial Services Group Inc. CORP AFFIL senior vice president: Twin City Fire Insurance Co.; vice president: ITT Hartford Insurance Group; vice president: Property Casualty Insurance; secretary: Hartford Insurance Southeast; officer: Hartford Fire Insurance Co.; officer: Hartford Insurance Midwest; secretary: Hartford Equity Sales Co.; officer: Hartford Accident Indemnity Co.; secretary: Hartford Casualty Insurance Co. NONPR AFFIL director: American Arbitration Association; member: American Bar Association.

Grants Analysis

Disclosure Period: calendar year ending 2002
Total Grants: $5,108,893
Number of Grants: 2,396
Average Grant: $2,200
Highest Grant: $680,000
Lowest Grant: $10
Typical Range: $50 to $5,000
Note: Grants analysis was provided by the foundation.

Recent Grants

Note: Grants derived from 1997 Form 990.

Library-Related
88,000	Wadsworth Athenaeum, Hartford, CT

General
383,333	United Way Capital Area
110,000	Greater Hartford Arts Council, Hartford, CT
100,000	Connecticut Children's Medical Center, Hartford, CT
100,000	St. Francis Hospital and Medical Center
40,000	Disabled Sports USA, Rockville, MD
40,000	Mark Twain House
40,000	Salvation Army, Hartford, CT
25,000	Hartford Action Plan on Infant Health, Hartford, CT
25,000	West Middle School Committee, Hartford, CT
20,000	Child Council, Hartford, CT

THE JOHN A. HARTFORD FOUNDATION, INC.

Giving Contact

James F. O'Sullivan, Grants Manager
55 East 59th Street, 16th Fl.
New York, NY 10022-1178
Phone: (212)832-7788
Fax: (212)593-4913
E-mail: mail@jhartfound.org
Web: http://www.jhartfound.org

Description

Founded: 1929
EIN: 131667057
Organization Type: General Purpose Foundation
Giving Locations: nationally.
Grant Types: Employee Matching Gifts, Fellowship, Matching, Multiyear/Continuing Support, Project, Research.

Donor Information

Founder: The John A. Hartford Foundation was established in 1929 by the late John A. Hartford (d. 1951) and George L. Hartford Jr. (d. 1957). The donors were the sons of George Huntington Hartford who, with George F. Gilman, founded the Great Atlantic and Pacific Tea Company in 1869 (which became the A&P foodstore chain). Upon their father's death in 1917, George Hartford, Jr., became chairman of the company, and John Hartford, the president. The brothers left the bulk of their estates to the foundation. Although the foundation formerly held a great deal of A&P stock, its holdings have been diversified and its portfolio no longer contains A&P stock.

Financial Summary

Total Giving: $25,600,000 (2002 approx); $24,305,339 (2001); $24,763,861 (2000)
Giving Analysis: Giving for 2000 includes: foundation matching gifts ($436,389); 1998: foundation grants to United Way ($5,000); foundation grants to United Way ($5,000); foundation matching gifts ($541,775); foundation matching gifts ($541,775) foundation ($18,364,017)
Assets: $587,895,434 (2001); $623,590,336 (2000); $607,276,301 (1999)

Typical Recipients

Arts & Humanities: Arts Associations & Councils, Ethnic & Folk Arts, Libraries
Civic & Public Affairs: Housing, Nonprofit Management, Philanthropic Organizations, Professional & Trade Associations, Public Policy, Women's Affairs
Education: Colleges & Universities, Health & Physical Education, Medical Education, Minority Education, Private Education (Precollege)
Health: Arthritis, Cancer, Clinics/Medical Centers, Health-General, Geriatric Health, Health Policy/Cost Containment, Health Funds, Health Organizations, Home-Care Services, Hospitals, Long-Term Care, Medical Rehabilitation, Medical Research, Medical Training, Mental Health, Public Health, Research/Studies Institutes
Religion: Religious Welfare
Science: Science-General, Scientific Labs
Social Services: At-Risk Youth, Community Service Organizations, People with Disabilities, Senior Services, Volunteer Services, Youth Organizations

Application Procedures

Initial Contact: Submit a brief letter of inquiry which summarizes the prupose and activities of the grant, the qualifications of the applicant and institution, and an estimated cost and time frame for the project.
Deadlines: None.
Review Process: Although the foundation requires no formal application, it expects applicants to be familiar with the guidelines and interests of the foundation. Current program guidelines may be obtained by contacting the foundation. The proposed project will be reviewed by members of the foundation's staff and possibly by outside reviewers. Results of this review will be sent within approximately six weeks and may be asked to supply additional information.

Restrictions

Grants are made only to organizations with tax-exempt status under IRS section 501(c)(3) and which are not private foundations under sections 509(a) or 170(c)(1). No grants are given to individuals. Support is not provided for general research. Rarely will the foundation support projects for longer than three years.

Additional Information

Publications: Annual Report; Guidelines

Foundation Officials

Anson McCook Beard, Jr.: trustee B New York, NY 1936. ED Yale University BA (1958). PRIM CORP EMPL managing director: Morgan Stanley & Co., Inc. CORP AFFIL chairman: MS Securities Services Inc.
William Comfort: trustee
James Duncan Farley: chairman, trustee B Chicago, IL 1926. ED Georgetown University (1949). CORP AFFIL director: Davco; director: Moore Corp. CLUB AFFIL Wequetonsing Golf Club; Round Hill Club; Valley Club; Loblolly Pines Golf Club; Los Angeles Country Club; Birnham Wood Golf Club; Cypress Point Club.
Samuel R. Gische: fin director, controller B 1953. ED Queens College BA (1975); New York University MBA (1983).
James G. Kenan, III: trustee B Lexington, KY 1945. ED University of North Carolina (1968). PRIM CORP EMPL chairman: Flagler System Inc.
William B. Matteson: trustee B New York, NY 1928. ED Yale University BA (1950); Harvard University JD (1953). PRIM CORP EMPL partner: Debevoise & Plimpton. NONPR AFFIL member: New York Institute; member: New York State Bar Association; member: American Bar Association; member: New York City Bar Association. CLUB AFFIL Sky Club; Union Club; River Club; Sankaty Head Club.
Christopher T.H. Pell: trustee
Thomas A. Reynolds, Jr.: trustee B Chicago, IL 1928. ED Georgetown University AB (1948); University of Michigan JD (1951). PRIM CORP EMPL chairman emeritus: Winston & Strawn. CORP AFFIL director: Gannett Co. Inc.; director: Union Pacific Corp. NONPR AFFIL member: Chicago Bar Association; member: Illinois State Bar Association; member: American Bar Association.
Corrine H. Rieder, EdD: executive director, treasurer
Norman Hans Volk: president, trustee B New York, NY 1935. ED Valparaiso University BA (1957); Marquette University MA (1959). PRIM CORP EMPL president: Chamberlain & Steward Associates. CLUB AFFIL University Club; University Glee Club New York; Doubles Club.
Kathryn Dineen Wriston: secretary, trustee B Syracuse, NY. ED University of Geneva (1958-1959); Smith College BA (1960); University of Michigan LLB (1963). CORP AFFIL director: Waccamaw Corp.; chairman, director, member audit committee, member nomina: Santa Fe Energy Resources Inc.; director: Stanley Works Inc.; director, member audit committee, member invest fin p: Northwestern Mutual Life Insurance Co. NONPR AFFIL member: Practicing Law Institute; member visiting committee: University Michigan Law School; member: New York County Lawyers Association; member: New York State Bar Association; member: Independent Standards Board; member: National Association Accts; member: Finance Womens Association New York; member: Association Bar New York City; member executive committee: CPR Institute Dispute Resolution; member: American Bar Association.

Grants Analysis

Disclosure Period: calendar year ending 2001
Total Grants: $42,887,719
Number of Grants: 40
Average Grant: $107,219
Highest Grant: $5,244,254
Lowest Grant: $2,000
Typical Range: $75,000 to $300,000
Note: Grants analysis provided by foundation.

Recent Grants

Note: Grants derived from 2000 Form 990.

General

3,429,258 American Federation for Aging Research (AFAR), New York, NY -- Paul Beeson Physician Faculty Scholars in Aging

1,668,300 Gerontological Society of America, Washington, DC -- Hartford Geriatric Social work Faculty Scholars

984,000 American Academy of Nursing, Washington, DC -- nursing initiative coordinating center and scholar stipends

884,678 Association of American Medical Colleges, Washington, DC -- enhancing geriatrics in undergraduate medical education

879,317 New York University, New York, NY -- Johns A. Hartford Foundation Institute for the Advancement of Geriatric Nursing Practice

715,930 American Federation for Aging Research (AFAR), New York, NY -- fellowship cohort expansion

649,345 American Federation for Aging Research (AFAR), New York, NY -- medical student Geriatric Scholars program

564,383 Stanford University, Stanford, CA -- enhancing dissemination of innovations in geriatric education

508,192 American Geriatrics Society, Inc, New York, NY -- enhancing geriatric care through practicing physician education

473,501 New York University, New York, NY -- Geriatric Interdisciplinary Team Training Program

HARTMARX CORP.

Company Headquarters

101 N. Wacker Dr.
Chicago, IL 60606
Web: http://www.hartmarx.com

Company Description

Founded: 1983
Ticker: HMX
Exchange: NYSE
Revenue: US$601.6 million (2001)
Employees: 5000 (2001)
SIC(s): 2311 Men's/Boys' Suits & Coats, 2325 Men's/Boys' Trousers & Slacks, 2329 Men's/Boys' Clothing Nec, 6719 Holding Companies Nec.

Operating Locations

Hartmarx Corp. (AL--Anniston; AR--Rector; GA--Loganville, Norcross; IL--Des Plaines; IN--Michigan City; KY--Elizabethtown, Winchester; MO--Cape Girardeau, Chaffee, Farmington, St. Louis; NY--Buffalo, New York, Rochester; PA--Easton)

Hartmarx Charitable Foundation

Giving Contact

Kay C. Nalbach, President
101 North Wacker Drive, 23rd Floor
Chicago, IL 60606
Phone: (312)357-5331
Web: http://www.hartmarx.com

Description

EIN: 366152745
Organization Type: Corporate Foundation
Giving Locations: headquarters and operating communities.

Grant Types: Capital, Employee Matching Gifts, General Support, Research.
Note: Employee matching gift ratio: 1 to 1 up to $3,000 for each individual annually for gift amounts of at least $25. Matches gifts made to institutions of higher learning. Foundation will not match bequests, dues, tuition fees, subscription fees, loan payment, or contributions not made as direct donations.

Financial Summary

Total Giving: $326,593 (fiscal year ending November 30, 2001); $366,990 (fiscal 2000); $366,251 (fiscal 1999). Note: Contributes through corporate direct giving program and foundation.
Giving Analysis: Giving for fiscal 2000 includes: foundation matching gifts ($18,855); foundation grants to United Way ($136,800); foundation ($181,335); fiscal 1999: foundation matching gifts ($29,762); foundation grants to United Way ($125,925); foundation ($210,564); fiscal 1998: foundation matching gifts ($25,575); foundation grants to United Way ($134,200) foundation ($181,348)
Assets: $12,279 (fiscal 2001); $25,433 (fiscal 2000); $56,867 (fiscal 1999)
Gifts Received: $314,000 (fiscal 2001); $335,800 (fiscal 2000); $362,250 (fiscal 1999)

Typical Recipients

Arts & Humanities: Arts Associations & Councils, Arts Festivals, Arts Institutes, Dance, Arts & Humanities-General, Historic Preservation, History & Archaeology, Libraries, Museums/Galleries, Music, Opera, Performing Arts, Public Broadcasting, Theater
Civic & Public Affairs: African American Affairs, Botanical Gardens/Parks, Business/Free Enterprise, Clubs, Community Foundations, Economic Development, Ethnic Organizations, Civic & Public Affairs-General, Housing, Law & Justice, Legal Aid, Nonprofit Management, Professional & Trade Associations, Public Policy, Safety, Urban & Community Affairs, Women's Affairs, Zoos/Aquariums
Education: Arts/Humanities Education, Business Education, Business Education, Colleges & Universities, Community & Junior Colleges, Economic Education, Education Associations, Education Funds, Education Reform, Engineering/Technological Education, Faculty Development, Education-General, Literacy, Minority Education, Private Education (Precollege), Public Education (Precollege), Science/Mathematics Education, Social Sciences Education, Student Aid, Vocational & Technical Education
Environment: Air/Water Quality, Environment-General, Wildlife Protection
Health: AIDS/HIV, Arthritis, Cancer, Children's Health/Hospitals, Clinics/Medical Centers, Diabetes, Emergency/Ambulance Services, Health Organizations, Heart, Hospitals, Multiple Sclerosis, Nursing Services, Prenatal Health Issues, Prenatal Health Issues, Public Health, Respiratory, Single-Disease Health Associations
International: Foreign Arts Organizations
Religion: Jewish Causes, Ministries, Religious Organizations, Religious Welfare
Science: Science Museums
Social Services: Animal Protection, At-Risk Youth, Camps, Child Abuse, Child Welfare, Community Centers, Community Service Organizations, Crime Prevention, Domestic Violence, Family Planning, Family Services, Food/Clothing Distribution, People with Disabilities, Recreation & Athletics, Scouts, Senior Services, Sexual Abuse, Shelters/Homelessness, United Funds/United Ways, Volunteer Services, YMCA/YWCA/YMHA/YWHA, Youth Organizations

Application Procedures

Initial Contact: Submit a written request.
Application Requirements: Include legal name of organization, summary of specific project to be supported, amount requested, latest financial statements and budget, and proof of tax-exempt status.
Deadlines: None.

Review Process: Foundation president and contributions committee review requests over $2,500, which are then submitted to board of directors for approval; grants of less than $2,500 must be approved by foundation president and the subsidiary's chief executive officer before processing.
Decision Notification: Quarterly, for contributions over $2,500.

Restrictions

Does not support goodwill advertising, fundraising benefits, political or lobbying groups, individuals, or religious organizations for sectarian purposes.
In July 2002, the foundation president reported that the foundation is not accepting proposals from any organization that is not presently being funded.

Corporate Officials

Elbert O. Hand: chairman, chief executive officer, director B 1939. ED Hamilton College BA (1961). PRIM CORP EMPL chairman, chief executive officer, director: Hartmarx Corp. CORP AFFIL director: Jaymar-Ruby Inc.
Glenn R. Morgan: executive vice president, chief financial officer, treasurer, member B Chicago, IL 1947. ED Northwestern University BS (1968); Northwestern University MBA (1970). PRIM CORP EMPL executive vice president, chief financial officer: Hartmarx Corp. CORP AFFIL vice president: Hart Schaffner & Marx. NONPR AFFIL chairman financial managing committee: American Apparel Manufacturer Association; member: Financial Executives Institute.
Homi Burjor Patel: president, chief operating officer, director B Bombay, MH India 1949. ED University of Bombay BS (1973); Columbia University MBA (1975). PRIM CORP EMPL president, chief operating officer, director: Hartmarx Corp. CORP AFFIL chairman, director: M Wile & Co.; treasurer, director: Textile Clothing Tech Corp.; director: Jaymar-Ruby Inc.; chairman: Plaid Clothing Co. Inc.; vice president: Hart Schaffner & Marx; president: Hart Services Inc. DEL. NONPR AFFIL executive vice president, member, director: Clothing Manufacturer Association America. CLUB AFFIL Chicago Club; University Club New York.

Foundation Officials

Kay C. Nalbach: president B Moweaqua, IL. ED University of Illinois (1959). PRIM CORP EMPL assistant section: Hartmarx Corp. NONPR AFFIL member: American Society of Corporate Secretaries; member: Executive Women International.
Taras R. Proczko: secretary, director
Andrew A. Zahr: treasurer

Grants Analysis

Disclosure Period: fiscal year ending November 30, 2001
Total Grants: $203,335*
Number of Grants: 133
Average Grant: $1,529
Highest Grant: $15,000
Lowest Grant: $100
Typical Range: $100 to $5,000
*Note: Giving excludes matching gifts and United Way.

Recent Grants

Note: Grants derived from fiscal 2001 Form 990.

General

52,500 United Way Crusade of Mercy, Chicago, IL -- for program support

22,000 United Way Michigan City, Michiana Area, Michigan City, IN -- for program support

15,000 Fresh Air Fund, New York, NY -- for program support

15,000 Kellogg Graduate School of Management, Evanston, IL -- for program support

15,000	Music of the Baroque, Chicago, IL -- for program support
12,000	United Way Buffalo and Erie County, Buffalo, NY -- for program support
10,000	Lyric Opera of Chicago, Chicago, IL -- for program support
10,000	United Way Greater Rochester, Rochester, NY -- for program support
7,500	Robert T. Jones Memorial Scholarship Fund, New York, NY -- for program support
6,000	United Way Calhoun County, Anniston, AL -- for program support

C. Felix Harvey Foundation

Giving Contact
C. Felix Harvey, Vice President
PO Box 189
Kinston, NC 28502
Phone: (252)523-4103

Description
EIN: 237038942
Organization Type: Private Foundation
Grant Types: General Support.

Donor Information
Founder: Felix Harvey, Margaret B. Harvey

Financial Summary
Total Giving: $416,192 (fiscal year ending August 31, 2002); $421,575 (fiscal 1999); $426,075 (fiscal 1998)
Giving Analysis: Giving for fiscal 2002 includes: foundation grants to United Way ($500); foundation scholarships ($5,000); fiscal 1998: foundation scholarships ($7,550); foundation grants to United Way ($12,000) foundation ($402,025)
Assets: $10,005,705 (fiscal 2002); $9,449,650 (fiscal 1999); $276,761 (fiscal 1998)
Gifts Received: $263,781 (fiscal 2002); $770,757 (fiscal 1999); $260,000 (fiscal 1996). Note: In fiscal 2002, contributions were received from John O. & Leigh H. McNairy ($33,281) and Robert L. & Sunny H. Burrows Jr. ($35,500). In fiscal 1999, contributions were received from L. Harvey & Son ($100,000), Mallard Oil Co. ($10,000), Tidewater Transit Co. ($70,000), C. Felix Harvey ($321,000), John & Leigh McNairy ($169,845.75), and Sunny Burrows ($99,911.25).In fiscal 1998, contributions were received from L. Harvey & Son ($100,000), Mallard Oil Co. Tidewater Transit Co. ($70,000), L. Harvey, Inc. ($10,000), C. Felix Harvey ($321,000), John S. Leigh McNairy ($169,845.75), and Sunny Borrows ($99,911.25). North Carolina Natural Gas ($10,000), and Robert Lee Burrows ($50,000).

Typical Recipients
Arts & Humanities: Arts Associations & Councils, Arts Funds, Historic Preservation, History & Archaeology, Libraries, Museums/Galleries, Music, Performing Arts, Public Broadcasting
Civic & Public Affairs: Botanical Gardens/Parks, Community Foundations, Economic Development, Civic & Public Affairs-General, Housing, Rural Affairs, Safety, Urban & Community Affairs, Zoos/Aquariums
Education: Agricultural Education, Arts/Humanities Education, Business Education, Colleges & Universities, Community & Junior Colleges, Education Funds, Education-General, Private Education (Precollege), Science/Mathematics Education, Secondary Education (Public), Student Aid
Health: Cancer, Health Organizations, Single-Disease Health Associations, Trauma Treatment
International: International Relations, Missionary/Religious Activities
Religion: Churches, Religious Organizations, Religious Welfare, Seminaries

Science: Scientific Centers & Institutes
Social Services: Child Welfare, Community Service Organizations, Food/Clothing Distribution, Homes, Recreation & Athletics, Refugee Assistance, Scouts, Special Olympics, United Funds/United Ways, Veterans, Youth Organizations

Application Procedures
Initial Contact: The foundation has no formal grant application procedure or application form.
Deadlines: None.

Foundation Officials
Robert Lee Burrows, Jr.: vice president
Sunny Harvey Burrows: secretary, treasurer
Ann Harvey: director
C. Felix Harvey: vice president
Margaret B. Harvey: president
Ruth Heath: assistant secretary

Grants Analysis
Disclosure Period: fiscal year ending August 31, 2002
Total Grants: $410,692*
Number of Grants: 65
Average Grant: $5,167*
Highest Grant: $80,000
Lowest Grant: $250
Typical Range: $1,000 to $10,000
*Note: Giving excludes scholarships and United Way. Average grant figure excludes highest grant.

Recent Grants
Note: Grants derived from 2002 Form 990.

General
80,000	Global Transpark Foundation, Kinston, NC -- operating expenses
26,000	Mount Olive College, Mt. Olive, NC -- operating expenses
25,000	LaGrange Development Corporation, Toledo, OH -- operating expenses
25,000	Louisburg College, Louisburg, NC -- operating expenses
25,000	Mount Olive College, Mt. Olive, NC -- debt reduction
20,000	Charis Community Housing, Atlanta, GA -- operating expenses
20,000	North Avenue Presbyterian Church, Atlanta, GA -- for operating expenses
20,000	Salvation Army -- operating expenses
20,000	University of North Carolina Education Foundation, Chapel Hill, NC -- operating expenses
15,000	Westminster Schools, Atlanta, GA -- operating expenses

Hasbro, Inc.

Company Headquarters
1027 Neport Avenue
Pawtucket, RI 02861
Phone: (401)431-8697
Web: http://www.hasbro.com

Company Description
Founded: 1923
Ticker: HAS
Exchange: NYSE
Revenue: US$2.816 billion (2002)
Employees: 8000 (2002)
SIC(s): 3944 Games, Toys & Children's Vehicles.

Operating Locations
Hasbro Inc. (Rhode Island) (CA--San Diego; NJ--Northvale; NY--Amsterdam; SC--Easley; TX--El Paso)

Nonmonetary Support
Value: $3,500,000 (2000 approx)
Type: Donated Products; Loaned Employees; Loaned Executives; Workplace Solicitation
Note: The foundation has several toy donation programs, including hospital and shelter playrooms, the after-school programs of the United Neighborhood Centers and Boys & Girls Clubs, children whose lives have been affected by disaster, and holiday giving to needy children. Also donates toys yearly to the Appalachian areas and to Walking Shield, the agency handling all Native American Indian reservations west of the Mississippi River. The Hasbro Orphanage program works with World Vision, an international relief agency. Each year a different country is selected for toy donations and orphanage support. The Team Hasbro volunteer program allows eligible employees to donate up to four hours a month of volunteer time to organizations that work with children.
Note: Company donates toys nationally to direct service organizations that provide services around the clock for children (see "Other Things You Should Know")

Hasbro Charitable Trust Inc.

Giving Contact
Karen Davis, Director
1027 Newport Avenue
Pawtucket, RI 02862
Phone: (401)431-8151
Fax: (401)721-7275
Web: http://www.hasbro.org

Description
EIN: 222538470
Organization Type: Corporate Foundation
Giving Locations: headquarters and operating communities.
Grant Types: Capital, Employee Matching Gifts, General Support, Multiyear/Continuing Support, Project.
Note: Employee matching gift ratio: 1 to 1 for higher education.

Financial Summary
Total Giving: $1,482,663 (2000); $1,361,214 (1999); $1,046,334 (1998). Note: Contributes through corporate direct giving program and foundation.
Giving Analysis: Giving for 2000 includes: foundation matching gifts ($22,893); foundation grants to United Way ($179,000); foundation ($1,280,770); 1999: foundation grants to United Way ($203,297); foundation ($1,157,917); 1998: foundation matching gifts ($16,634); foundation grants to United Way ($170,000); foundation ($860,000);
Assets: $1,579,082 (2000); $1,384,453 (1999); $1,518,944 (1998)
Gifts Received: $1,650,000 (2000); $1,214,175 (1999); $1,000,000 (1998). Note: The trust receives contributions from Hasbro Inc. and miscellaneous donors.

Typical Recipients
Arts & Humanities: Arts Centers, Arts Funds, Arts Institutes, Community Arts, History & Archaeology, Libraries, Museums/Galleries, Music, Performing Arts
Civic & Public Affairs: African American Affairs, Business/Free Enterprise, Community Foundations, Economic Development, Economic Policy, Ethnic Organizations, Civic & Public Affairs-General, Hispanic Affairs, Housing, Law & Justice, Legal Aid, Minority Business, Municipalities/Towns, Public Policy, Urban & Community Affairs, Women's Affairs, Zoos/Aquariums

Education: Arts/Humanities Education, Business Education, Colleges & Universities, Economic Education, Education Funds, Education Reform, Elementary Education (Public), Education-General, Education-General, Literacy, Medical Education, Preschool Education, Private Education (Precollege), Public Education (Precollege), School Volunteerism, Student Aid

Environment: Air/Water Quality, Forestry, Environment-General

Health: AIDS/HIV, Alzheimers Disease, Cancer, Children's Health/Hospitals, Clinics/Medical Centers, Diabetes, Emergency/Ambulance Services, Eyes/Blindness, Geriatric Health, Health Organizations, Heart, Hospices, Hospitals, Hospitals (University Affiliated), Kidney, Medical Rehabilitation, Medical Research, Multiple Sclerosis, Nursing Services, Prenatal Health Issues, Public Health, Research/Studies Institutes, Single-Disease Health Associations, Single-Disease Health Associations, Transplant Networks/Donor Banks

International: Health Care/Hospitals, Human Rights, International Affairs, International Environmental Issues, International Organizations, International Peace & Security Issues, International Relations, International Relief Efforts

Religion: Jewish Causes, Religious Organizations, Religious Welfare

Science: Science Museums

Social Services: Big Brother/Big Sister, Child Abuse, Child Welfare, Community Centers, Community Service Organizations, Day Care, Emergency Relief, Family Planning, Family Services, Food/Clothing Distribution, People with Disabilities, Recreation & Athletics, Refugee Assistance, Scouts, Senior Services, Sexual Abuse, Shelters/Homelessness, Special Olympics, Substance Abuse, United Funds/United Ways, United Funds/United Ways, Volunteer Services, YMCA/YWCA/YMHA/YWHA, Youth Organizations

Application Procedures

Initial Contact: Request guidelines and application by phone.

Application Requirements: Include statement of purpose and objectives; history of organization's programs; list of board and staff, as well as record of financial commitment by board for proposed project; annual operating budget for organization and for year in which grant will occur; recently audited financial statement; description of program for which funds are requested, including its budget; amount requested; copy of tax-exempt determination letter; list of other corporations and foundations approached and level of financial support requested or received.

Deadlines: March 31 for annual review in June.

Notes: Foundation only reviews requests in communities where company has operations.

Restrictions

From time to time, unusual or special projects will alter the grant review process.

Cash contributions are limited to operating locations. Does not support religious organizations, individuals, political organizations, scholarships, loans, endowments, goodwill advertising, fund raisers, sponsorship of recreational activities, or research.

Additional Information

Hasbro also sponsors the Hasbro Children's Foundation, which contributes about $2,000,000 annually to health, social services, and educational programs for children under the age of 12. Contact is Eve Weiss, Executive Director, Hasbro Children's Foundation, 32 W 23rd Street, New York, NY 10010, (212) 645-2400. Toy requests should be submitted by October 1. If an organization receives toys for two consecutive years, company follows with a two year hiatus. No participation in fundraisers, give-a-ways, or incentives. Toys go to supervised playrooms in organizations which provide direct services to children, especially shelters

and child life departments of hospitals. Donates only to 501(c)(3) organizations within the U.S. Policy holds for Hasbro and its subsidiaries: Milton Bradley, Playskool, Tonka, Kenner, and Parker.

Corporate Officials

Cynthia Reed: senior vice president, general counsel ED Wellesley College AB (1977); Northeastern University JD (1980). PRIM CORP EMPL senior vice president, general counsel: Hasbro Inc.

Alfred J. Verrecchia: executive, director B Providence, RI 1943. ED University of Rhode Island BS (1967); University of Rhode Island MBA (1972). PRIM CORP EMPL executive, director: Hasbro Inc. CORP AFFIL president, director: Hasbro Inc. NONPR AFFIL director: Bradley Hospital.

Foundation Officials

Karen Davis: director

Cynthia Reed: assistant secretary (see above)

Alfred J. Verrecchia: treasurer, trustee (see above)

Grants Analysis

Disclosure Period: calendar year ending 2000

Total Grants: $1,280,770*

Number of Grants: 119

Average Grant: $10,763

Highest Grant: $175,000

Lowest Grant: $500

Typical Range: $1,000 to $10,000

*Note: Giving excludes matching gifts; United Way.

Recent Grants

Note: Grants derived from 2000 Form 990.

General

175,000	Boundless Playgrounds, Inc
166,000	United Way of Southeastern New England, Providence, RI
67,420	Toys 'R' Us Children's Fund Inc.
50,000	American Ballet Monuments Commission - WWI, Arlington, VA
50,000	Girl Scouts of Rhode Island, Providence, RI
50,000	Golf Foundation of Rhode Island, Providence, RI
50,000	University of Rhode Island Foundation, Providence, RI
42,000	United Appeal Community Chest - Red Cross of the Cincinnati Area, Cincinnati, OH
36,000	Waterfire Providence, Providence, RI
33,500	For All Kids Foundation, Ramsey, NJ

HASKELL FUND

Giving Contact

James Sekerak
1422 Euclid Avenue, Rm. 1010
Cleveland, OH 44115-2078
Phone: (216)363-6481

Description

Founded: 1955

EIN: 346513797

Organization Type: Private Foundation

Giving Locations: OH: Cleveland nationally.

Grant Types: Capital, Endowment, General Support, Multiyear/Continuing Support, Operating Expenses, Project, Scholarship.

Donor Information

Founder: the late Melville H. Haskell, Coburn Haskell, Melville H. Haskell, Jr., Mark Haskell

Financial Summary

Total Giving: $209,000 (2002); $311,000 (2000); $261,000 (1999)

Giving Analysis: Giving for 2002 includes: foundation scholarships ($16,000); 2000: foundation scholarships ($19,000) 1999: foundation scholarships ($23,000)

Assets: $3,502,626 (2002); $5,682,891 (2000); $6,704,033 (1999)

Typical Recipients

Arts & Humanities: Arts Associations & Councils, Arts Centers, Community Arts, History & Archaeology, Libraries, Literary Arts, Museums/Galleries, Music, Visual Arts

Civic & Public Affairs: Clubs, Civic & Public Affairs-General, Hispanic Affairs, Native American Affairs, Professional & Trade Associations, Urban & Community Affairs

Education: Arts/Humanities Education, Colleges & Universities, Education Funds, Engineering/Technological Education, International Studies, Medical Education, Minority Education, Private Education (Precollege), Public Education (Precollege), Student Aid, Vocational & Technical Education

Environment: Air/Water Quality, Environment-General, Resource Conservation, Wildlife Protection

Health: AIDS/HIV, Cancer, Children's Health/Hospitals, Clinics/Medical Centers, Emergency/Ambulance Services, Health Organizations, Hospitals, Hospitals (University Affiliated), Medical Research, Nursing Services, Public Health

International: Human Rights, International Environmental Issues, International Relief Efforts, Missionary/Religious Activities

Religion: Churches, Religion-General, Religious Organizations, Religious Welfare

Science: Scientific Centers & Institutes, Scientific Organizations

Social Services: Child Abuse, Child Welfare, Community Service Organizations, Day Care, Domestic Violence, Emergency Relief, Family Planning, Family Services, Food/Clothing Distribution, Recreation & Athletics, Shelters/Homelessness, Social Services-General, United Funds/United Ways, Youth Organizations

Application Procedures

Initial Contact: Send brief letter and proposal.

Application Requirements: Include statement of operations and proof of tax-exempt status.

Deadlines: None.

Restrictions

Does not support individuals.

Additional Information

Publications: Annual Report

Foundation Officials

Coburn Haskell: president, trustee

Eric T. Haskell: trustee

Mark Haskell: trustee

Mary E. Haskell: trustee

Melville H. Haskell, Jr.: trustee

Schuyler A. Haskell: vice president, trustee

Sarah Haskell-Green: trustee

Paulette F. Kitko: secretary, treasurer

James C. Sekerak: treasurer

Mary H. Walker: trustee

Grants Analysis

Disclosure Period: calendar year ending 2002

Total Grants: $193,000*

Number of Grants: 73

Average Grant: $2,644

Highest Grant: $16,000

Lowest Grant: $500

Typical Range: $1,000 to $5,000

*Note: Giving excludes scholarships.

Recent Grants

Note: Grants derived from 2002 Form 990.

General

16,000	University of Arizona, Tucson, AZ -- H.M. Hanna Scholarship

12,000	Hoag Hospital, Newport Beach, CA -- Women's Pavilion capital campaign
11,500	Arizona Sonora Desert Museum, Tucson, AZ -- endowment fund
7,500	Pacolet Area Conservancy, Columbus, NC
7,000	North Kohala Community Hospital, Inc.
6,600	Direct Relief International, Santa Barbara, CA -- endowment campaign
6,000	Scripps College, Claremont, CA -- French and humanities symposia
5,000	Cleveland Scholarship Programs, Cleveland, OH
5,000	Community Arts Music Association, Santa Barbara, CA -- endowment campaign
5,000	Maritime Museum, San Diego, CA -- Educational Programs

MARGARET MILLIKEN HATCH CHARITABLE TRUST

Giving Contact

Donna Daniels, Vice President & Trust Officer
c/o The Bank of New York
One Wall St., 28th Fl.
New York, NY 10286
Phone: (212)635-1520

Description

Founded: 1970
EIN: 136330533
Organization Type: Private Foundation
Giving Locations: CT; NY
Grant Types: Emergency, General Support.

Donor Information

Founder: the late Margaret Milliken Hatch

Financial Summary

Total Giving: $259,000 (fiscal year ending October 31, 2000); $29,000 (fiscal 1999); $15,000 (fiscal 1998)
Giving Analysis: Giving for fiscal 1999 includes: foundation ($29,000)
Assets: $399,676 (fiscal 2001); $393,127 (fiscal 2000); $632,041 (fiscal 1999)

Typical Recipients

Arts & Humanities: Arts & Humanities-General, Historic Preservation, Libraries, Museums/Galleries, Public Broadcasting
Civic & Public Affairs: Zoos/Aquariums
Education: Colleges & Universities, Education Funds, Medical Education, Minority Education, Science/Mathematics Education, Student Aid
Health: Cancer, Clinics/Medical Centers, Hospitals, Research/Studies Institutes
International: International Affairs, International Development
Religion: Churches, Religious Welfare
Social Services: Animal Protection, Child Welfare, People with Disabilities, Senior Services, United Funds/United Ways, YMCA/YWCA/YMHA/YWHA, Youth Organizations

Application Procedures

Initial Contact: The foundation has no formal grant application procedure or application form.
Deadlines: None.

Restrictions

Does not support individuals.

Additional Information

Trust(s): Bank NY

Foundation Officials

Rakia I. Hatch: trustee
Richard L. Hatch: trustee

Grants Analysis

Disclosure Period: fiscal year ending October 31, 2001
Note: No grants awarded in 2001.

Recent Grants

Note: Grants derived from 2000 Form 990.

General

150,000	Maine Medical Center, Portland, ME
50,000	Columbia Presbyterian Medical Center, New York, NY
25,000	Maine Public Broadcasting Corp, Lewiston, ME
25,000	Parkview Memorial Hospital, Brunswick, ME
9,000	Cancer Research Institute Of New York, New York, NY

HATHAWAY MEMORIAL CHARITABLE TRUST

Giving Contact

Augusta Haydock
c/o Fleet National Bank
PO Box 6767
Providence, RI 02940
Phone: (401)276-7239

Description

Founded: 1992
EIN: 046599655
Organization Type: Private Foundation
Giving Locations: MA: Somerset
Grant Types: General Support.

Financial Summary

Total Giving: $89,972 (fiscal year ending July 31, 2002); $74,800 (fiscal 2000); $53,500 (fiscal 1997)
Giving Analysis: Giving for fiscal 2000 includes: foundation scholarships ($10,000)
Assets: $1,700,675 (fiscal 2002); $2,115,411 (fiscal 2000); $1,836,357 (fiscal 1997)

Typical Recipients

Arts & Humanities: Dance, History & Archaeology, Libraries
Civic & Public Affairs: Civic & Public Affairs-General
Education: Afterschool/Enrichment Programs, Elementary Education (Public), Education-General, Private Education (Precollege), Public Education (Precollege), Student Aid
Health: Health Organizations, Hospices, Nursing Services
International: Missionary/Religious Activities
Religion: Churches, Ministries, Religious Organizations, Religious Welfare
Social Services: Day Care, Delinquency & Criminal Rehabilitation, Family Services, Social Services-General, YMCA/YWCA/YMHA/YWHA, Youth Organizations

Application Procedures

Initial Contact: Send a brief letter of inquiry.
Application Requirements: Include all pertinent information for review by the advisory committee.
Deadlines: None.

Restrictions

Limited to Somerset, MA.

Additional Information

Provides scholarships to deserving students from Somerset, MA.
Trust(s): Fleet National Bank

Foundation Officials

Eydie A. Furtado: adv
Rev. Susan Horgan-Baker: adv
Christopher Matte: adv
Charles E. Reed, Esq.: consultant

Grants Analysis

Disclosure Period: fiscal year ending July 31, 2002
Total Grants: $89,972*
Typical Range: $500 to $7,500
***Note:** Grants list not available for 2002.

Recent Grants

Note: Grants derived from 2000 Form 990.

Library-Related

1,800	Somerset Public Library, Somerset, MA

General

10,000	Citizens Scholarship Foundation of Somerset, Somerset, MA
7,500	St. Vincent's, Santa Barbara, CA
7,000	Hospice Outreach, Inc.
6,250	Somerset Children's Center, Somerset, MA
6,000	Somerset Historical Society, Somerset, MA
5,000	Congregational Christian Church
5,000	Historical Commission
4,950	Congregational Christian Church
4,000	Somerset Baptist Church, Somerset, MA
3,500	YMCA of Greater Fall River

A. JOHN AND BARBARA A. HAUPTLI CHARITABLE FOUNDATION

Giving Contact

Barbara A. Hauptli, Trustee
A. John and Barbara A. Hauptli Charitable Foundation
427 Upper Mill Heights Drive
Salina, KS 67401-3364
Phone: (785)827-7177

Description

Founded: 1996
EIN: 481173715
Organization Type: Private Foundation
Grant Types: General Support.

Financial Summary

Total Giving: $82,600 (fiscal year ending September 30, 2001); $51,421 (fiscal 2000); $39,638 (fiscal 1999)
Giving Analysis: Giving for fiscal 2000 includes: foundation grants to United Way ($1,000)
Assets: $1,147,192 (fiscal 2001); $1,400,990 (fiscal 2000); $1,277,332 (fiscal 1999)
Gifts Received: $1,896 (fiscal 2001); $1,556 (fiscal 1999); $919,600 (fiscal 1996). Note: In fiscal 2001, contributions were received from Barbara A. Hauptli. In fiscal 1996, contributions were received from A. John and Barbara A. Hauptli.

Typical Recipients

Arts & Humanities: Art History, Museums/Galleries, Public Broadcasting, Theater
Civic & Public Affairs: Civic & Public Affairs-General

Education: Arts/Humanities Education, Colleges & Universities
Health: Emergency/Ambulance Services, Multiple Sclerosis
Religion: Churches, Missionary Activities (Domestic), Religious Welfare
Social Services: Child Abuse, Counseling, Domestic Violence, Food/Clothing Distribution, Social Services-General, United Funds/United Ways, YMCA/YWCA/YMHA/YWHA

Application Procedures
Initial Contact: Send a letter of request.
Deadlines: None.

Foundation Officials
Barbara A. Hauptli: trust

Grants Analysis
Disclosure Period: fiscal year ending September 30, 2001
Total Grants: $82,600
Number of Grants: 32
Average Grant: $1,427*
Highest Grant: $20,000
Lowest Grant: $25
Typical Range: $500 to $2,000
***Note:** Average grant figure excludes two highest grants ($39,795).

Recent Grants
Note: Grants derived from fiscal 2000 Form 990.

General

20,000	Kansas Wesleyan University, Salina, KS
9,523	St. John's Lutheran Church, Salina, KS
6,100	Salina Community Theater, Salina, KS
5,000	GSCM, Salina, KS
2,500	Smoky Hills Public Television, Salina, KS
1,500	Salina Activity Center, Salina, KS
1,000	Salina Area United Way, Salina, KS
1,000	Wesleyan Library Art College, Salina, KS
530	Salina Young Women's Christian Association, Salina, KS
500	American Red Cross, Salina, KS

ROBERT Z. HAWKINS FOUNDATION

Giving Contact
William H. Wallace, Chairman
One East Liberty Street, Suite 509
Reno, NV 89501
Phone: (775)786-1105
Fax: (775)786-4886
E-mail: rzhawkins@aol.com

Description
Founded: 1980
EIN: 880162645
Organization Type: General Purpose Foundation
Giving Locations: CA; NV: Northern Nevada, Reno
Grant Types: Capital, Matching, Scholarship.
Note: Operating expenses includes equipment.

Donor Information
Founder: Robert Ziemer Hawkins was born in Boulder, CO., December 26, 1903, the eldest son of Prince A. Hawkins, Sr., and Myrtle Ziemer Hawkins.
Bob Hawkins was a lawyer and an investor. He was the dominant shareholder of Security National Bank of Nevada, where he served as a member of the Board and was Chairman of the Executive Committee.
He also became interested in, and acquired several large ranches in the Marysville area where he grew the first commercially successful wild rice.

Some years prior to his death, he decided to leave the bulk of his estate in trust, for charitable purposes. He died in September, 1979. The Robert Z. Hawkins Foundation was created by his will. The Foundation is a Testamentary Trust, established on March 3, 1980, by Decree of the Second Judicial District Court of the State of Nevada. The Trust is under the supervision of the Court and renders an annual account to the Court.

Financial Summary
Total Giving: $635,928 (2001); $916,033 (2000); $1,800,000 (1999)
Giving Analysis: Giving for 2000 includes: foundation grants to United Way ($10,000); foundation scholarships ($65,000) 1998: foundation grants to United Way ($10,000).
Assets: $22,403,419 (2001); $24,211,637 (2000); $25,000,000 (1999)
Gifts Received: In 1991, contributions were received from the trust fund of Kathryn Ackley Hawkins.

Typical Recipients
Arts & Humanities: Arts Funds, Ballet, Film & Video, Arts & Humanities-General, Libraries, Museums/Galleries, Music, Opera, Performing Arts, Public Broadcasting, Theater
Civic & Public Affairs: Botanical Gardens/Parks, Business/Free Enterprise, Chambers of Commerce, Clubs, Employment/Job Training, Civic & Public Affairs-General, Hispanic Affairs, Housing, Law & Justice, Legal Aid, Municipalities/Towns, Native American Affairs, Urban & Community Affairs
Education: Business Education, Colleges & Universities, Community & Junior Colleges, Education Reform, Elementary Education (Private), Elementary Education (Public), Engineering/Technological Education, Journalism/Media Education, Legal Education, Literacy, Medical Education, Private Education (Precollege), Public Education (Precollege), School Volunteerism, Secondary Education (Public), Student Aid
Environment: Research
Health: Cancer, Children's Health/Hospitals, Diabetes, Emergency/Ambulance Services, Health Organizations, Hospitals, Long-Term Care, Mental Health, Public Health, Single-Disease Health Associations, Transplant Networks/Donor Banks
Religion: Churches, Religion-General, Religious Organizations, Religious Welfare
Science: Science Museums, Scientific Labs, Scientific Research
Social Services: Animal Protection, At-Risk Youth, Child Welfare, Community Centers, Community Service Organizations, Counseling, Crime Prevention, Domestic Violence, Family Services, Family Services, Food/Clothing Distribution, People with Disabilities, Recreation & Athletics, Scouts, Senior Services, Shelters/Homelessness, Social Services-General, Special Olympics, Substance Abuse, United Funds/United Ways, Volunteer Services, YMCA/YWCA/YMHA/YWHA, Youth Organizations

Application Procedures
Initial Contact: The foundation requests that applicants call to obtain a request form.
Application Requirements: The grant request should include six copies of the request form, the amount and purpose of the request, a brief history of the organization, and a description of the need and how it will be met by the proposal. The applicant should also submit financial information, including a copy of the determination letter from the IRS, stating that the organization is exempt from taxation under Section 501(c)(3), or other identification to establish eligibility to receive charitable contributions; a copy of the last annual financial statement, current budget, an d most recent operating statement; a statement of the organization's major sources of financial support; and a statement of plans to secure continuing operating funds, if the program is of an ongoing nature.

In addition, the applicant should include personnel information, including biographical descriptions of those responsible for the project and a list of the directors or trustees. Also include in request any other foundations and sources which aid has been requested or received, with any reasons why grants from other sources have not been requested; and a statement t of how the applicant will judge the success of the project. Applicants are requested to report to the foundation upon completion of the project to evaluate the worth of the grant.
Deadlines: None.
Review Process: Applications received by the 30th day of any month will be considered at the board's meeting the following month, unless additional information is required. After a grant request has been initiated, a meeting, site visit or telephone discussion may be required before submitting a formal proposal.

Restrictions
The foundation reports that grants are exclusively for charitable purposes within, or directly related to, the state of Nevada. The foundation does not make grants to individuals except through its scholarship funds. The foundation does not approve requests that would require permanent or on-going support.

Additional Information
The Bank of America, Reno, NV, acts as a corporate trustee for the foundation.
The foundation generally favors projects with a recognizable and long lasting effect; projects that are not financed by public tax funds; projects that will become self-sustaining; and projects in which other donors or foundations participate.
Publications: Annual Report; Guidelines; Application Form

Foundation Officials
Carolyn K. Bernard: trustee
Prince A. Hawkins: trustee
Bill A. Ligon, Jr.: trustee
William H. Wallace: chairman B Senatobia, MS 1933. ED University of Mississippi BBA (1955); University of Mississippi MBA (1956); University of Illinois PhD (1962). PRIM NONPR EMPL professor finance: Old Dominion University College Business & Public Administration. CORP AFFIL president: Wallace Consulting Inc. NONPR AFFIL trustee: Dallas Historical Society; member executive committee: Greater Dallas Chamber of Commerce; member: Central Dallas Association; member: Dallas Committee Foreign Relations; member: American Economic Association; member: American Statistical Association. CLUB AFFIL Rotary Club.

Grants Analysis
Disclosure Period: calendar year ending 2001
Total Grants: $545,641*
Number of Grants: 71
Average Grant: $7,685
Highest Grant: $50,000
Lowest Grant: $200
Typical Range: $2,000 to $10,000
***Note:** Giving excludes United Way; scholarships.

Recent Grants
Note: Grants derived from 2001 Form 990.

General

50,000	University of Nevada Reno, Reno, NV -- for computer lab
45,000	KNPB - Channel 5, Reno, NV -- for civic and cultural
28,200	St. Mary's Foundation, Pierre, SD -- for emergency room equipment
26,000	Nevada Humane Society, Reno, NV -- spray/neuter program
24,000	University of Nevada Reno School of Medicine, Reno, NV -- research
20,000	Assistance League, Reno, NV -- food pantry

14,741	Washoe County Parks and Recreation, Washoe, NV -- support of community amphitheater
14,287	Stanford University, Stanford, CA -- scholarship
13,600	Lyon County School District, Yerington, NV -- for track and football complex
13,000	Casa De Vida, Reno, NV -- purchase furnishings

HAWN FOUNDATION

Giving Contact
Joe V. Hawn, Jr., President
5949 Sherry Lane, No. 775
Dallas, TX 75225-3553
Phone: (214)696-6595
Fax: (214)696-6596

Alternate Contact
Janey Bateman, Secretary

Description
Founded: 1962
EIN: 756036761
Organization Type: Family Foundation
Giving Locations: TX: Dallas
Grant Types: Endowment, Fellowship, General Support, Multiyear/Continuing Support, Operating Expenses, Project, Research, Scholarship, Seed Money.

Donor Information
Founder: Incorporated in 1962 by the late Mildred Hawn .

Financial Summary
Total Giving: $1,551,000 (fiscal year ending August 31, 2002); $1,400,000 (fiscal 2001); $1,401,500 (fiscal 2000)
Assets: $39,400,000 (fiscal 2002); $29,700,527 (fiscal 2000); $30,503,751 (fiscal 1998)
Gifts Received: $628,253 (fiscal 2000); $5,000 (fiscal 1998). Note: In fiscal 2000, contributions were received from the Mary C. Hawn Estate.

Typical Recipients
Arts & Humanities: Arts Associations & Councils, Arts Outreach, Community Arts, Dance, Historic Preservation, Libraries, Museums/Galleries, Music, Opera, Performing Arts, Theater
Civic & Public Affairs: Business/Free Enterprise, Hispanic Affairs, Housing, Professional & Trade Associations, Urban & Community Affairs
Education: Arts/Humanities Education, Colleges & Universities, Literacy, Minority Education, Private Education (Precollege), Religious Education, Secondary Education (Private), Special Education, Student Aid
Health: Alzheimers Disease, Arthritis, Cancer, Children's Health/Hospitals, Clinics/Medical Centers, Diabetes, Emergency/Ambulance Services, Eyes/Blindness, Health-General, Health Funds, Health Organizations, Heart, Hospitals, Hospitals (University Affiliated), Long-Term Care, Medical Rehabilitation, Medical Research, Mental Health, Multiple Sclerosis, Nursing Services, Public Health, Research/Studies Institutes, Respiratory, Single-Disease Health Associations
International: Health Care/Hospitals, Missionary/Religious Activities
Religion: Churches, Missionary Activities (Domestic), Religious Organizations, Religious Welfare
Science: Science Museums
Social Services: Animal Protection, At-Risk Youth, Camps, Child Abuse, Child Welfare, Community Centers, Community Service Organizations, Counseling, Emergency Relief, Family Services, People with Disabilities, Recreation & Athletics, Scouts, Shelters/Homelessness, Substance Abuse, United Funds/United Ways, Volunteer Services, YMCA/YWCA/YMHA/YWHA, Youth Organizations

Application Procedures
Initial Contact: Initial approach for a grant should be through a brief narrative letter.
Application Requirements: The letter should describe the project for which funds are asked, its justification, and the type and amount requested. Also include a copy of the organization's IRS 501(c)(3) letter and a written statement that no financial support will be donated to any political cause out of funds granted from the Hawn Foundation, Inc.
Deadlines: June 1.
Review Process: If the project falls within the areas of the foundation's interests, purposes, and current funding policies, the board may act directly upon the original request or ask for more detailed information before making a grant decision. The board may meet at any time of the year to consider applications and approve or reject applications at these meetings. The annual meeting is held in August prior to fiscal year-end date of August 31.
Notes: If a grant is approved, it will be with stipulations that accounting for the expenditures of such grant may be required.

Restrictions
Grants are not made to individuals. No grants are made outside the foundation's main focus. Under the present policy of the board of directors, the foundation does not make loans.

Additional Information
Publications: Guidelines

Foundation Officials
Janey Bateman: secretary, director
Edward Alvin Copley: director B Memphis, TN 1936. ED Southern Methodist University BA (1957); Southern Methodist University JD (1960). PRIM CORP EMPL managing partner: Akin Gump Strauss Hauer & Feld LLP.
J. Verne Hawn: director
Jim J. Hawn: director
Joe Verne Hawn, Jr.: director
W. A. Hawn, Jr.: president
William Russell Hawn, Jr.: director
Grady Jordan: director
Irby N. Taylor: director

Grants Analysis
Disclosure Period: fiscal year ending August 31, 2000
Total Grants: $1,401,500
Number of Grants: 67
Average Grant: $20,918
Highest Grant: $100,000
Typical Range: $1,000 to $50,000

Recent Grants
Note: Grants derived from 2000 Form 990.

General
100,000	M.D. Anderson Cancer Center, Houston, TX -- medical research
100,000	Salesmanship Club, Dallas, TX -- capital campaign
100,000	Texas Scottish Rite Hospital, Dallas, TX -- medical assistance
75,000	Arthritis Foundation, North Texas, Dallas, TX -- medical research
75,000	Multiple Sclerosis, Dallas Chapter, Dallas, TX -- medical aid
75,000	Southwestern Medical Foundation, Dallas, TX -- Alzheimer's disease research
50,000	Baylor Medical Foundation, Houston, TX -- medical research
50,000	Juvenile Diabetes Foundation, Dallas, TX -- medical research
50,000	Parkland Foundation, Dallas, TX -- medical services classrooms renovations
50,000	Presbyterian Health Care Foundation, Dallas, TX -- arthritis research

CHARLES HAYDEN FOUNDATION

Giving Contact
Kenneth D. Merin, President, Chief Executive Officer
130 Liberty Street, Suite 2707
New York, NY 10006-1196
Phone: (212)785-3677
Fax: (212)785-3689
Web: http://www.fdncenter.org/grantmaker/hayden/

Alternate Contact
Mary Phillips, Boston Program Officer
c/o Grants Management Associates
230 Congress Street, 3rd Floor
Boston, MA 02110-2109
Note: Organizations in the metropolitan Boston area should send second copies of requests to alternate contact.

Description
Founded: 1937
EIN: 135562237
Organization Type: General Purpose Foundation
Giving Locations: MA: Boston metropolitan area; NY: New York metropolitan area
Grant Types: Capital, Project, Seed Money.

Donor Information
Founder: Charles Hayden was born in Boston, MA, in 1870. He was the elder of the two sons of Emma A. Tirrell Hayden and Josiah Willard Hayden. After graduating from Massachusetts Institute of Technology in 1890 with an engineering degree, he began his business career as a clerk for the Boston brokerage firm of Clark, Ward and Co. Within two years he founded the Boston brokerage firm of Hayden, Stone and Company. In 1906, he opened a New York City office and later moved into the city. Charles Hayden was excellent at predicting the stock market's future, including foreseeing the stock market crash of 1929. At the time of his death, he was well known as an international businessman and was serving as a director of 58 different corporations.
During the Depression, Mr. Hayden contributed to many causes, often anonymously. In 1934, he was honored as the primary benefactor of the American Museum of Natural History's Hayden Planetarium in New York. The foundation was established in 1937 by a $45.8 million bequest from Charles Hayden.

Financial Summary
Total Giving: $15,500,000 (fiscal year ending June 30, 2002 approx); $16,851,508 (fiscal 2001); $15,483,696 (fiscal 2000)
Giving Analysis: Giving for fiscal 2000 includes: foundation grants to United Way ($5,000) fiscal 1999: foundation grants to United Way ($5,000)
Assets: $311,558,536 (fiscal 2001); $327,800,572 (fiscal 2000); $307,855,842 (fiscal 1999)

Typical Recipients
Arts & Humanities: Arts Outreach, Libraries, Museums/Galleries
Civic & Public Affairs: Botanical Gardens/Parks, Economic Development, Employment/Job Training, Civic & Public Affairs-General, Hispanic Affairs, Nonprofit Management, Public Policy, Urban & Community Affairs, Zoos/Aquariums
Education: Afterschool/Enrichment Programs, Arts/Humanities Education, Business Education, Colleges & Universities, Continuing Education, Education Associations, Education Funds, Education Reform, Elementary Education (Private), Elementary

Education (Public), Education-General, Health & Physical Education, Leadership Training, Literacy, Minority Education, Preschool Education, Private Education (Precollege), Public Education (Precollege), School Volunteerism, Science/Mathematics Education, Secondary Education (Private), Secondary Education (Public), Special Education, Vocational & Technical Education

Environment: Air/Water Quality, Wildlife Protection

Health: AIDS/HIV, Hospitals, Research/Studies Institutes

International: International Environmental Issues

Religion: Jewish Causes, Religious Welfare

Science: Science Museums, Scientific Centers & Institutes

Social Services: At-Risk Youth, Camps, Child Welfare, Community Centers, Community Service Organizations, Crime Prevention, Day Care, Family Planning, Family Services, Food/Clothing Distribution, Homes, People with Disabilities, Recreation & Athletics, Scouts, Social Services-General, Substance Abuse, Volunteer Services, YMCA/YWCA/YMHA/YWHA, Youth Organizations

Application Procedures

Initial Contact: Applicants should send a written request. The Foundation encourages applicants to use the New York area and AGM (Boston area) common application forms. Boston area agencies should send copies of proposals and all related follow-up correspondence to alternate contact as well as contact.

Application Requirements: Funding requests should include a concise description of the project and its goals, description of the youth population, including age and number of youth, to be served, total costs (based on professional estimates), sources for additional operating funds, operating budget (including breakdown of revenue sources and amounts, for current and previous years), most recent audited financial report, IRS letter stating that applicant has 501(c)(3) tax-exempt status, the project's expected outcomes, criteria the applicant prefers that the foundation apply in evaluating the completed project, and other printed material concerning the activities and history of the institution. If the request is for less than the total amount, explain the plans for raising the balance of those costs. If request is for full amount, describe how a lesser amount would be of assistance and how, in that event, the balance of funds could be raised from other sources.

Review Process: The board of trustees meets ten times a year. If the foundation has declined a grant request, reapplication can be made six months after the denial letter. The reapplication may be for the same project or a different one.

Restrictions

Capital grants generally are not made to groups that have received funds from the foundation within the past two years, unless the applicant is a large organization with distinctly separate facilities in different locations. In addition, the foundation does not fund individuals; theological institutions; projects to raise revenue to offset operating costs; hospitals; hospices; projects that are basically medical in nature; religious organizations, unless the program is community youth oriented; institutions of higher education, except for program support for work with pre-collegiate education; endowments; and arts exposure programs. Also, the foundation has restrictions on supporting dinners, special events, goodwill advertising, and fraternal organizations.

Additional Information

Publications: Annual Report (biennially); Application Guidelines

Foundation Officials

Maureen T. Fletcher: assistant secretary

Robert Howitt: treasurer, trustee PRIM NONPR EMPL officer: Door - A Center of Alternatives.

Kristen J. McCormack: vice president, trustee B 1955. PRIM NONPR EMPL executive director: Federated Dorchester.

Kenneth D. Merin: president, chief executive officer, trustee PRIM CORP EMPL partner: Purcell, Ries, Shannon, Mulcahy & O'Neill.

Dean H. Steeger: secretary, trustee

Carol Van Atten: assistant secretary

Howard Wachenfeld: trustee

Grants Analysis

Disclosure Period: fiscal year ending June 30, 2001

Total Grants: $16,851,508*

Number of Grants: 99

Average Grant: $74,706

Highest Grant: $2,500,000

Lowest Grant: $1,500

Typical Range: $10,000 to $150,000

*Note: Grants analysis provided by foundation.

Recent Grants

Note: Grants derived from fiscal 2000 Form 990.

Library-Related

150,000   Brooklyn Public Library, Brooklyn, NY -- toward construction of the Technology Loft in their new youth wind.

90,000   Replications, New York, NY -- toward replication of KIPP Academy in IS 148 in Community Schools District Nine

75,000   Mind-Builders Creative Arts Co., Inc., Bronx, NY -- toward renovation of basement and courtyard space at their Bronx facility

75,000   Queens Library Foundation, Jamaica, NY -- toward renovation of the second floor children's area of the Steinway Branch

General

1,550,000   Nonprofit Facilities Fund, New York, NY -- additional grant toward the implementation of their initiative, Building for the Future, to be offered to Boys & Girls Clubs in the NY & Boston area.

1,000,000   American Museum of Natural History, New York, NY -- toward one or more aspects of the expansion of the American Museum of Natural History or its programs.

1,000,000   Nonprofit Facilities Fund, New York, NY -- toward the implementation of Building for the Future, a 10-yr initiative to be offered to Boy & Girls Clubs in the NY & Boston area.

750,000   Fresh Air Fund, The, New York, NY -- toward their capital development program to upgrade their Campus Pioneer and ABC at Sharpe Reservation in Fishkill, NY

750,000   Good Shepherd Services, New York, NY -- toward construction of a new Good Shepherd Services Center in Red Hook, Brooklyn.

520,000   Fund for the City of New York Youth Development Institute, New York, NY -- toward the Beacon Academic Support and Enrichment Program grant initiative over three years..

450,000   Brooklyn Children's Museum, Brooklyn, NY -- towards their centennial campaign

450,000   Madison Square Boys and Girls Club, New York, NY -- toward renovation and construction needs at the South Queens Boys & Girls Club.

375,000   Children's Aid Society, New York, NY -- Wrap-Around Community School Program

200,000   Boston Plan for Excellence in the Public Schools, Boston, MA -- toward continued support of their 21st Century Schools Project for 1998-1999 and 1999-2000

JOHN RANDOLPH AND DORA HAYNES FOUNDATION

Giving Contact

Diane Cornwell, Administrative Director
888 West 6th Street, Suite 1150
Los Angeles, CA 90017-2737
Phone: (213)623-9151
Fax: (213)623-3951
E-mail: info@haynesfoundation.org
Web: http://www.haynesfoundation.org

Description

Founded: 1926

EIN: 951644020

Organization Type: Specialized/Single Purpose Foundation

Giving Locations: CA: Los Angeles metropolitan area

Grant Types: Award, Employee Matching Gifts, Fellowship, Research, Scholarship.

Donor Information

Founder: The Haynes Foundation was established in 1926 by Dr. John Randolph Haynes, "a distinguished physician, and his wife Dora Haynes, who were active and progressive citizens of Los Angeles during one of the city's most important developmental period (1887-1937)."

Financial Summary

Total Giving: $2,000,000 (fiscal year ending August 31, 2003 approx); $2,722,797 (fiscal 2002); $3,064,840 (fiscal 2001)

Giving Analysis: Giving for fiscal 2001 includes: foundation scholarships ($658,000); foundation fellowships ($1,028,500); fiscal 1998: foundation ($6,004); foundation scholarships ($552,000) foundation fellowships ($741,600)

Assets: $47,100,000 (fiscal 2002); $51,406,080 (fiscal 2001); $54,000,000 (fiscal 2000 approx)

Gifts Received: In fiscal 1990, the foundation received a gift from Edward Levonlan.

Typical Recipients

Arts & Humanities: Historic Preservation, History & Archaeology, Libraries, Museums/Galleries, Public Broadcasting

Civic & Public Affairs: Economic Development, Economic Policy, Civic & Public Affairs-General, Hispanic Affairs, Housing, Law & Justice, Legal Aid, Native American Affairs, Nonprofit Management, Philanthropic Organizations, Professional & Trade Associations, Public Policy, Urban & Community Affairs, Women's Affairs

Education: Arts/Humanities Education, Business Education, Colleges & Universities, Continuing Education, Economic Education, Education Reform, Environmental Education, Faculty Development, Education-General, International Studies, Medical Education, Minority Education, Religious Education, Science/Mathematics Education, Social Sciences Education, Social Sciences Education, Student Aid

Environment: Environment-General, Resource Conservation

Health: Children's Health/Hospitals, Geriatric Health, Health Policy/Cost Containment, Medical Research

International: International Affairs

Religion: Jewish Causes, Social/Policy Issues

Science: Science Museums

Social Services: At-Risk Youth, Crime Prevention, Delinquency & Criminal Rehabilitation, Senior Services, Shelters/Homelessness, Substance Abuse

Application Procedures

Initial Contact: The Foundation requests that applicants notify the Foundation of their intent to apply prior to submitting a proposal. When submitting a proposal, applicants should send 15 hard copies of the proposal and one copy electronically to info@-haynesfoundation.org.

Application Requirements: Proposals for Research Grants should include a main proposal that describes the project and includes objectives for the period of the proposed work, expected significance of the proposed work, problems to be dealt with and a detailed explanation of the methods which will be followed, explanation of how the proposed work relates to the present state of knowledge in the field, how the proposed work relates to the principal investigator's longer-term goals, other works in progress by the PI, other support being received by the PI for the proposed work and/or for other projects, and, if appropriate, plans for preservation, documentation, and sharing of data resulting from the project; a one-page summary of the proposed activity, written in third person in laymen's terms; a detailed budget and time-line for the project; the names and qualifications of the personnel involved; a cover letter from the college, university, or research institute, signed by an administrative officer or grants administrator; and copies of the institution's exemption letters from the IRS and California Franchise Tax Board.

Proposals for Archival Grants should include a statement of purpose for which the funds will be used; a detailed budget and time-line for the project; names and qualifications of the personnel involved; a cover letter on the institution's letterhead, signed by an administrative officer; and copies of the institution's exemption letters from the IRS and the California Franchise Tax Board.

Deadlines: January 18, March 29, May 17, September 6, and November 1.

Review Process: Grants are made quarterly. Requests for grants are considered first by the foundation's committee on research and grants, which then makes its recommendations to the foundation's board of trustees.

Notes: Applications for scholarships should be made directly to the educational institution and not to the foundation.

Restrictions

No grants are made to individuals. The foundation does not pay for equipment or for institutional overhead. Grants are made only to organizations within the United States whose endeavors are focused in or on Los Angeles.

Additional Information

Publications: Guidelines; Purposes and Program Brochure

Foundation Officials

Diane Cornwell: administrative director

Robert Ray Dockson: 1st vice president, trustee B Quincy, IL October 06, 1917. ED Springfield Junior College AB (1937); University of Illinois BS (1939); University of Southern California MS (1940); University of Southern California PhD (1946). CORP AFFIL director: CalFed Inc. NONPR AFFIL member: Phi Kappa Phi; member, board councils: University Southern California School Business Administration; board regents: Pepperdine University; member: Hugh O'Brian Youth Foundation; president, trustee: Orthopedic Hospital; member: Los Angeles Chamber of Commerce; member: Newcomen Society; trustee: Committee for Economic Development; trustee: California Council Economic Education; chairman housing task force: California Roundtable; member: Beta Gamma Sigma; member: California Chamber of Commerce; member: American Arbitration Association. CLUB AFFIL Thunderbird Country Club; California Club; Los Angeles Country Club; Bohemian Club; 100 Club; Birnham Wood Golf Club.

Philip Metschan Hawley: trustee B Portland, OR 1925. ED University of California at Berkeley BS (1946); Harvard University Advanced Management

Program (1967). CORP AFFIL chairman, chief executive officer: Krauses Furniture Inc.; director: Weyerhaeuser Co. NONPR AFFIL member: Phi Beta Kappa; trustee: University Notre Dame; trustee: California Institute Technology; chairman, member: California Retailers Association; member: Beta Alpha Psi; member: Beta Gamma Sigma. CLUB AFFIL Newport Harbor Yacht Club; Pacific-Union Club; Los Angeles Country Club; Multnomah Athletic Club; California Club; The Links Club; Beach Club; Bohemian Club.

Kent Kresa: trustee B New York, NY 1938. ED Massachusetts Institute of Technology BSAA (1959); Massachusetts Institute of Technology MSAA (1961); Massachusetts Institute of Technology EAA (1966). PRIM CORP EMPL chairman: Northrop Grumman Corp. CORP AFFIL director: Atlantic Richfield Co.; director: Daimler Chrysler. NONPR AFFIL member: Society Flight Test Engineers; director: John Tracy Clinic for the Hearing Impaired; member: Navy League; member (visiting committee): Massachusetts Institute Technology; member: Naval Aviation Museum Foundation; board governors: Los Angeles Music Center; member: Los Angeles World Affairs Council; member: DNA New Alternative Working Group; member: Defense Science Board; member: Department Aeronautics & Astronautics Corp.; member: Association U.S. Army; member: Chief Naval Operations Executive Panel Washington; fellow: American Institute Aeronautics & Astronautics; member: Aerospace Industries Association; member: American Defense Preparedness Association. CLUB AFFIL Los Angeles Country Club; National Space Club.

F. Haynes Lindley, Jr.: president emeritus, trustee B Los Angeles, CA 1945. ED Claremont Men's College BA (1967); Claremont Graduate School MFA (1972); Southwestern University JD (1976). NONPR AFFIL member board fellows: Claremont University Center Graduate School; member: Marin Agricultural Land Trust.

Daniel A. Mazmanian: trustee

Harry P. Pachon: trustee

Jane G. Pisano: chairman comm res & grants, trustee

Gilbert T. Ray: trustee B Mansfield, OH 1944. ED Ashland College BA (1966); University of Toledo MBA (1968); Howard University JD (1972). PRIM CORP EMPL partner: O'Melveny & Myers. CORP AFFIL director: Host Marriott Services Corp. NONPR AFFIL board directors: Automobile Club Southern California; board directors: Los Angeles Chamber of Commerce. CLUB AFFIL California Club; Louisiana Country Club.

Willis B. Wood, Jr.: trustee B Kansas City, MO 1934. ED University of Tulsa BS (1957); Harvard University (1983); Pepperdine University JD (1996). NONPR AFFIL director, member business council: Sustainable Energy Future; trustee: University Southern California; member: Society Petroleum Engineers; trustee: Southwest Museum; director: Pacific Council International Affairs; member: Pacific Energy Association; member: National Association Manufacturers; member: Pacific Coast Gas Association; trustee: Harvey Mudd College; director: Los Angeles World Affairs Council; chairman, trustee: California Medical Center Foundation; member: Chamber of Commerce California State; member: American Gas Association. CLUB AFFIL Hacienda Golf Club; California Club; Center Club.

Grants Analysis

Disclosure Period: fiscal year ending August 31, 2001

Total Grants: $1,378,340*

Number of Grants: 35

Average Grant: $39,381

Highest Grant: $97,628

Lowest Grant: $2,500

Typical Range: $5,000 to $100,000

*Note: Giving excludes fellowships and scholarships.

Recent Grants

Note: Grants derived from 2001 Form 990.

Library-Related

22,000	Huntington Library, Huntington, CA -- for history fellowships
16,712	Library Foundation of Los Angeles, Los Angeles, CA -- electronic neighborhood
10,000	Huntington Library, Huntington, CA -- to cataloging the papers of Edmund D Edelman papers

General

97,628	University of Southern California, Sacramento, CA -- toward urban participatory democracy
94,000	University of Southern California, Sacramento, CA -- new contours of racial diversity in Los Angeles
75,000	RAND Corporation, Santa Monica, CA -- private dollars and public schools
66,270	University of Southern California, Sacramento, CA -- toward a sustainable Los Angeles
65,104	Los Angeles Economic Roundtable, Los Angeles, CA -- working welfare parents
64,038	California Tomorrow, San Francisco, CA -- a new look at the majority
48,542	University of Southern California, Sacramento, CA -- civic/transnational roles of immigrant and ethnic congregations
41,647	University of Southern California, Sacramento, CA -- philanthropy and social capital
40,000	RAND Corporation, Santa Monica, CA -- anticipating effects of prop 36
37,638	Pepperdine University, Culver City, CA -- faith factors in Welfare Programs

EDWARD W. HAZEN FOUNDATION

Giving Contact

Barbara A. Taveras, President
309 Fifth Avenue, Suite 200-3
New York, NY 10016
Phone: (212)889-3034
Fax: (212)889-3039
E-mail: hazen@hazenfoundation.org
Web: http://www.hazenfoundation.org

Description

Founded: 1925
EIN: 060646671
Organization Type: General Purpose Foundation
Giving Locations: nationally.
Grant Types: General Support, Matching.

Donor Information

Founder: Incorporated in 1925 by the late Edward Warriner Hazen , the late Helen Russell Hazen , the late Lucy Abigail Hazen , and the late Mary Hazen Arnold .

Financial Summary

Total Giving: $1,987,452 (2001); $1,810,426 (2000); $1,589,635 (1999)
Giving Analysis: Giving for 2001 includes: foundation matching gifts ($1,460)
Assets: $34,888,534 (2001); $43,160,106 (2000); $48,279,620 (1999)

Typical Recipients

Arts & Humanities: Arts Funds, Arts Outreach, Libraries, Music, Public Broadcasting
Civic & Public Affairs: African American Affairs, Asian American Affairs, Botanical Gardens/Parks,

Civil Rights, Community Foundations, Economic Development, Economic Policy, Employment/Job Training, Ethnic Organizations, Gay/Lesbian Issues, Civic & Public Affairs-General, Hispanic Affairs, Housing, Law & Justice, Legal Aid, Municipalities/Towns, Native American Affairs, Nonprofit Management, Philanthropic Organizations, Professional & Trade Associations, Public Policy, Rural Affairs, Safety, Urban & Community Affairs, Women's Affairs, Zoos/Aquariums

Education: Afterschool/Enrichment Programs, Colleges & Universities, Education Associations, Education Funds, Education Reform, Elementary Education (Private), Education-General, Leadership Training, Legal Education, Minority Education, Private Education (Precollege), Public Education (Precollege), School Volunteerism, Science/Mathematics Education, Special Education, Vocational & Technical Education

Environment: Air/Water Quality, Environment-General, Protection, Resource Conservation

Health: AIDS/HIV, Medical Research, Mental Health, Public Health, Single-Disease Health Associations

International: Foreign Arts Organizations, Human Rights, International Affairs, International Environmental Issues, International Relations

Religion: Churches, Religion-General, Ministries, Religious Organizations, Religious Welfare

Science: Scientific Labs

Social Services: At-Risk Youth, Child Welfare, Community Centers, Community Service Organizations, Crime Prevention, Delinquency & Criminal Rehabilitation, Family Planning, Family Services, Food/Clothing Distribution, Homes, Refugee Assistance, Sexual Abuse, Shelters/Homelessness, Social Services-General, United Funds/United Ways, YMCA/YWCA/YMHA/YWHA, Youth Organizations

Application Procedures

Initial Contact: Applicants should send a brief letter of inquiry (1-2 pages) to the foundation.

Application Requirements: The letter should highlight the goals, objectives, activities target population, duration, and total cost of the project for which funding is sought. If the foundation staff feel that the goals of the project address the foundation's mission and the approach is a sound one, they will mail applicants a formal application. The application should be prepared in compliance with instructions supplied by the foundation. Two copies should be submitted.

Deadlines: Deadlines for applications are January 15 and July 15 for review at the spring and fall board meetings, respectively.

Review Process: All applicants will be notified of the status of their request two to three weeks after submission. The trustees meet twice each year to set foundation policy and make grants.

Notes: Do not send articles, letters of reference, videos, audio cassettes, books, or press kits unless they are specifically requested by foundation staff. The foundation does not accept letters of inquiry by fax.

Restrictions

The foundation does not make grants to individuals, schools, or school districts. It also does not provide funds toward ongoing operational expenses, endowments, building construction or maintenance, deficits, scholarships, or fellowships.

Additional Information

The foundation favors proposals from organizations which demonstrate a commitment to diversifying their boards and staff. In those cases where the demographics of the community served by the organization limit such diversity, the foundation encourages its grantees to collaborate with agencies or groups that work with people from other racial, ethnic, and cultural backgrounds.

Publications: Application Guidelines; Application Form; Newsletter

Foundation Officials

Arlene Adler: board chair PRIM CORP EMPL vice president: Citigroup NA.

Marsha Bonner: trustee

Madeline de Lone: trustee CLUB AFFIL Merion Cricket Club; Racquet & Tennis Club.

Beverly Divers-White: trustee

Earl Durham: vice chair, trustee

Edward Sermier: trustee NONPR AFFIL chief financial officer, director: Philharmonic Symphony Society New York.

Barbara Taveras: president

Arturo Vargas: trustee

Grants Analysis

Disclosure Period: calendar year ending 2001

Total Grants: $1,985,992*

Number of Grants: 115

Average Grant: $17,269

Highest Grant: $150,000

Lowest Grant: $500

Typical Range: $10,000 to $40,000

*Note: Giving excludes matching gifts.

Recent Grants

Note: Grants derived from 2001 Form 990.

General

70,000	Intercultural Development Research Association, San Antonio, TX
65,000	National Coalition of Advocates for Students, Boston, MA -- technical assistance and capacity building for education
50,000	Highbridge Community Life Center, Bronx, NY -- community collaborative to improve district 9 schools
50,000	South Central Los Angeles-Religious Sponsoring Committee, Los Angeles, CA -- Los Angeles Metro Alliance Schools Initiative
50,000	Temple University Center for Public Policy, Philadelphia, PA -- organizing for educational excellence training institute
50,000	Temple University Center for Public Policy, Philadelphia, PA -- organizing for educational excellence
45,000	Brooklyn ACORN, Brooklyn, NY -- Brooklyn Schools turnaround campaign
45,000	Chicago School Leadership Development Cooperative, Chicago, IL -- Cooperative's Organizing for Quality Leadership Training Program
45,000	Parents Organized for Westside Renewal, Santa Monica, CA -- Venice/Mar Vista School organizing campaign
45,000	People Acting for Community Together, Miami, FL -- parent organizing project

THE HEARST FOUNDATION, INC.

Giving Contact

Robert M. Frehse, Jr., Executive Director & Vice President
888 7th Avenue, 45th Floor
New York, NY 10106-0057
Phone: (212)586-5404
Fax: (212)586-1917
E-mail: hearst@fdn.org
Web: http://www.hearstfdn.org
Note: Applicants located east of the Mississippi River should mail appeals to the New York office.

Alternate Contact

Thomas Eastham, Western Director
Hearst Foundation
290 New Montgomery Street, Suite 1212
San Francisco, CA 94105
Phone: (415)543-0400

Note: Applicants located west of the Mississippi River should mail appeals to Western Director.

Description

Founded: 1945

EIN: 136161746

Organization Type: General Purpose Foundation

Giving Locations: nationally.

Grant Types: Endowment, General Support, Project, Research, Scholarship.

Financial Summary

Total Giving: $13,500,000 (2002 approx); $6,430,000 (2001 approx); $13,295,000 (2000)

Giving Analysis: Giving for 2000 includes: foundation scholarships ($50,000) 1998: foundation scholarships ($50,000)

Assets: $301,502,914 (2000); $322,007,000 (1999 approx); $283,685,795 (1998)

Typical Recipients

Arts & Humanities: Arts Centers, Arts Funds, Arts Institutes, Arts Outreach, Ballet, Ethnic & Folk Arts, Historic Preservation, History & Archaeology, Libraries, Museums/Galleries, Music, Opera, Performing Arts, Public Broadcasting, Theater

Civic & Public Affairs: Community Foundations, Employment/Job Training, Civic & Public Affairs-General, Hispanic Affairs, Housing, Native American Affairs, Nonprofit Management, Philanthropic Organizations, Public Policy, Safety, Urban & Community Affairs

Education: Arts/Humanities Education, Business Education, Colleges & Universities, Education Associations, Education Funds, Education Reform, Engineering/Technological Education, Faculty Development, Education-General, Health & Physical Education, International Studies, Journalism/Media Education, Literacy, Medical Education, Minority Education, Preschool Education, Private Education (Precollege), Public Education (Precollege), Religious Education, Science/Mathematics Education, Special Education, Student Aid

Environment: Environment-General, Resource Conservation

Health: AIDS/HIV, Cancer, Children's Health/Hospitals, Clinics/Medical Centers, Emergency/Ambulance Services, Heart, Home-Care Services, Hospitals, Hospitals (University Affiliated), Medical Rehabilitation, Medical Research, Mental Health, Nursing Services, Prenatal Health Issues, Public Health, Research/Studies Institutes, Single-Disease Health Associations

International: Health Care/Hospitals

Religion: Dioceses, Ministries, Religious Organizations, Religious Welfare, Seminaries

Science: Science Museums, Scientific Centers & Institutes, Scientific Labs

Social Services: Animal Protection, Child Welfare, Community Service Organizations, Counseling, Day Care, Family Services, Food/Clothing Distribution, People with Disabilities, Recreation & Athletics, Scouts, Senior Services, Shelters/Homelessness, Substance Abuse, United Funds/United Ways, Volunteer Services, YMCA/YWCA/YMHA/YWHA, Youth Organizations

Application Procedures

Initial Contact: The foundation does not have a formal application form. The foundation prefers applicants submit a one-page executive summary accompanied by a full proposal.

Application Requirements: The one-page proposal summary should describe the organization's mission and the purpose and dollar amount of the request. The expanded proposal narrative should not exceed five pages. Additionally, the following information is required: budget showing project costs and how funds will be used; current fiscal year's operating budget; most recent audited financial report; current and potential sources of support for proposed project and for organization in general; names and primary affiliations of officers and board members; IRS documentation certifying applicant is tax-exempt under section 501(c)(3) and "not a private foundation" under section 509(a). Organizations should be listed in the current IRS cumulative list of tax-exempt organizations (Publication 78). If an organization has been omitted from this publication, further documentation of its tax-exempt status will be required. Catholic organizations should be listed in the current official Catholic directory. Colleges and universities should include a current profile or fact sheet if available.

Deadlines: None.

Review Process: Board meetings on grant decisions are held in March, June, September, and December. Only fully documented appeals will be considered. Meetings are arranged between foundation staff and applicants only if serious consideration of their appeals is anticipated. A site visit is required prior to board review.

Restrictions

Except in rare cases, the following restrictions apply: Private sector organizations are favored over those financed through taxation. Organizations serving larger geographical areas are favored over those of a neighborhood or grassroots nature. The foundation does not fund on an annual basis or make multi-year grants. Grantee organizations must wait a minimum of three years from their grant award date before the foundation will consider another request. Only one proposal from an organization will be reviewed in a calendar year. Institutions with more than one department should coordinate proposals through a central office. The foundation does not support public policy, conferences, workshops, seminars, building projects, or requests for start-up/seed funding. The foundation will not consider requests for individuals, loans, funds for radio, film television or other media related projects, or special events, tickets, tables or advertising for fundraising events.

Additional Information

Please see the related entry for the William Randolph Hearst Foundation.

The Hearst Foundation and William Randolph Hearst Foundation are independent private philanthropies operating separately from the Hearst Corporation. Charitable goals of the two foundations are the same; they are administered as one, and only one proposal need be submitted.

Supplemental material should be held to a minimum necessary to ensure a basic understanding of the organization seeking support. Video tapes should not be sent unless specifically requested.

Publications: Application Guidelines

Foundation Officials

Frank Anthony Bennack, Jr.: director, board chairman B San Antonio, TX 1933. ED University of Maryland (1954-1956); Saint Mary's University (1956-1958). PRIM CORP EMPL chief executive officer, president, director: Hearst Corp. CORP AFFIL director: San Francisco Newspaper Printing Co.; director: Motor Information Systems Division; director: San Francisco Newspaper Agency; director: Manufacturers Hanover Trust Co.; director: Midland Publishing Co.; president, chief executive officer: Hearst Realties Division; president, chief executive officer, director: Down East Timberlands Division; director: Hearst Business Publishing Development Corp.; director: Chase Manhattan Corp.; director: Diversion Magazine Division; director: Chase Manhattan Bank NA; director: American Home Products Corp. NONPR AFFIL president: Texas Daily Newspaper Association; honorary trustee: Witte Memorial Museum; trustee: Our Lady Lake College; chairman: Museum Television & Radio; member, board governors: New York Hospital; director: American Newspaper Publishers Association; president: Greater San Antonio Chamber of Commerce. CLUB AFFIL Rotary Club.

Millicent Hearst Boudjakdji: director B 1940. CORP AFFIL director: King Features Syndicate Division; director: Sunical Land & Livestock Division; director: Hearst Realties Division; director: Down East Timberlands Division; director: Hearst Corp.

John G. Conomikes: director PRIM CORP EMPL vice president, director: Hearst Corp. Broadcasting Group. CORP AFFIL vice president: King Features Syndicate Division; vice president, director: Sunical Land & Livestock Division; vice president: Hearst Realties Division; vice president: Down East Timberlands Division; president, co-chief executive officer: Hearst-Argyle Television Inc.

Ralph Cuomo: treasurer

Richard Emmet Deems: director B New York, NY January 19, 1913. PRIM CORP EMPL director, consult: Hearst Corp. CORP AFFIL director: Sunical Land & Livestock Division; director: Omega Publishing Co.; director: King Features Syndicate Division; director: National Magazine Co. London; director: HMI France Inc.; director: Hearst Realties Division; director: HMI Espana Inc.; director: Down East Timberlands Division. NONPR AFFIL member: Magazine Publishers Association. CLUB AFFIL Bohemian Club; Everglades Club.

Thomas Eastham: western director B Attleboro, MA 1923. ED Northwestern University (1952).

Robert M. Frehse, Jr.: executive director NONPR AFFIL secretary: Interchurch Center.

Victor F. Ganzi: director B New York, NY 1947. ED Fordham University BS (1968); Harvard University JD (1971). PRIM CORP EMPL executive vice president: Hearst Books/Business Publications Group. CORP AFFIL director: PGA Tour Inc.; executive vice president, chief operating officer: Sunical Land & Livestock Division; director: Palm Management Corp.; executive vice president, chief operating officer: King Features Syndicate Division; president: Motor Information Systems Division; executive vice president, chief operating officer: Hearst Realties Division; director: IMI System Inc.; executive vice president, chief operating officer: Hearst Corp.; director: ESPN; president: Hearst Business Publishing Development Corp.; president: Diversion Magazine Division; executive vice president, chief operating officer: Down East Timberlands Division; president: America Druggist Division. NONPR AFFIL member: Council Future Law School; director: New York City Economic Development Corp.; member: Colorado Society of Certified Public Accountants; member: American Bar Association; member: American Institute of Certified Public Accountants. CLUB AFFIL Cherry Valley Country Club; Sky Club.

George Randolph Hearst, Jr.: president, director B San Francisco, CA 1927. PRIM CORP EMPL chairman: Hearst Corp. NONPR AFFIL member: Veterans Foreign Wars. CLUB AFFIL Riviera Club; Jonathan Club; Burlingame Country Club; California Club.

John Randolph Hearst, Jr.: director B 1934. CORP AFFIL director: Hearst Corp. NONPR AFFIL vice president: United Service Organization Metropolitan New York.

William R. Hearst, III: president B Washington, DC 1949. ED Harvard University AB (1972). PRIM CORP EMPL publisher: San Francisco Examiner. CORP AFFIL director: Sun Microsystems; director: Preview Travel Inc.; director: Hearst Corp.; general partner: Kleiner Perkins Caufiled Byers; director: At Home Network. NONPR AFFIL trustee: Carnegie Institute.

Jodie W. King: secretary B Birmingham, MI 1957. ED Mount Holyoke College AB (1979); University of Michigan JD (1982). PRIM CORP EMPL vice president, secretary, counsel: Hearst Corp. ADD CORP EMPL secretary: Hearst Business Publishing Development Corp.; secretary: Periodical Publishing Service Bureau.

Harvey L. Lipton: director B Brooklyn, NY 1925. ED New York University (1948); Saint John's University LLB (1951). PRIM CORP EMPL director: Hearst Corp. CORP AFFIL director: King Features Syndicate Division; director: Sunical Land & Livestock Division; secretary, director: Intellinet; secretary, director: Hearst

Entertainment Inc.; director: Hearst Realties Division; secretary, director: Edwardsville Publishing Co.; secretary, director: Eyeline; director: Down East Timberlands Division; secretary, director: Edwardsville Intelligencer.

Gilbert Charles Maurer: director B New York, NY 1928. ED Saint Lawrence University AB (1950); Harvard University MBA (1952). PRIM CORP EMPL executive vice president, chief operating officer, director: Hearst Corp. ADD CORP EMPL chief operating officer, director: Down East Timberlands Division; chief operating officer, director: Hearst Realties Division; chief operating officer, director: King Features Syndicate Division; chief operating officer, director: Sunical Land & Livestock Division. NONPR AFFIL member New York advisory board: Salvation Army; president, trustee: Whitney Museum American Art; member: Magazine Publishers Association; trustee: Norton Museum Art; director: Boys & Girls Clubs America. CLUB AFFIL Metro Club; Harvard Club New York.

Mark F. Miller: director PRIM CORP EMPL executive vice president, general manager, magazine division: Hearst Corp. CORP AFFIL director: Periodical Publishers Service Bureau.

Raymond Joseph Petersen: director B West Orange, NJ 1919. PRIM CORP EMPL executive vice president, director: Hearst Magazines. CORP AFFIL director: Sunical Land & Livestock Division; director: Hearst Realties Division; director: Down East Timberlands Division; director: Hearst Corp. NONPR AFFIL director, vice president: United Service Organization Metropolitan New York; director: U.S. National Comm Libs Info Science; member chairman committee: United Cerebral Palsy Campaign; honorary advisor: Children Alcoholics Foundation; director: National Crime Prevention Council; director: Boys & Girls Clubs Madison Square; member, director: American Advertising Federation.

Virginia H. Randt: director

Grants Analysis

Disclosure Period: calendar year ending 2000
Total Grants: $13,245,000*
Number of Grants: 186
Average Grant: $71,210
Highest Grant: $500,000
Lowest Grant: $10,000
Typical Range: $25,000 to $50,000
*Note: Giving excludes scholarships.

Recent Grants

Note: Grants derived from 2000 Form 990.

General

500,000	National World War II Memorial Fund, Arlington, VA
350,000	American Museum of Natural History, New York, NY
300,000	Weill Medical College of Cornell University, New York, NY
250,000	Founders Society Detroit Institute of Arts, Detroit, MI
200,000	House Ear Institute, Los Angeles, CA
200,000	Lincoln Center for the Performing Arts, New York, NY
150,000	Guthrie Theater Foundation, Minneapolis, MN
150,000	Mexican American Legal Defense and Education Fund, Los Angeles, CA
150,000	St. Jude Children's Research Hospital, Memphis, TN
150,000	Wake Forest University, Winston-Salem, NC

WILLIAM RANDOLPH HEARST FOUNDATION

Giving Contact

Robert M. Frehse, Jr., Executive Director & Vice President
888 7th Avenue, 45th Floor
New York, NY 10106-0057

Phone: (212)586-5404
Fax: (212)586-1917
Web: http://hearstfdn.org
Note: Applicants headquartered east of the Mississippi River should mail appeals to the New York office.

Alternate Contact

Thomas Eastham, Western Director
90 New Montgomery Street
Suite 1212
San Francisco, CA 94105
Phone: (415)543-0400
Fax: (415)243-0760
Note: Applicants located west of the Mississippi River should mail appeals to the Western Director.

Description

Founded: 1948
EIN: 136019226
Organization Type: General Purpose Foundation
Giving Locations: nationally.
Grant Types: Challenge, Endowment, General Support, Project, Research, Scholarship.

Financial Summary

Total Giving: $28,928,400 (2001); $21,755,000 (2000); $27,710,000 (1999)
Giving Analysis: Giving for 1998 includes: foundation scholarships ($180,200)
Assets: $624,456,279 (2001); $656,800,000 (2000); $703,444,000 (1999)

Typical Recipients

Arts & Humanities: Arts Associations & Councils, Arts Centers, Arts Institutes, Arts Outreach, Ballet, Community Arts, Ethnic & Folk Arts, Arts & Humanities-General, Historic Preservation, History & Archaeology, Libraries, Museums/Galleries, Music, Opera, Performing Arts, Theater, Visual Arts
Civic & Public Affairs: Business/Free Enterprise, Chambers of Commerce, Community Foundations, Employment/Job Training, Civic & Public Affairs-General, Hispanic Affairs, Native American Affairs, Nonprofit Management, Public Policy, Safety, Women's Affairs, Zoos/Aquariums
Education: Arts/Humanities Education, Business Education, Colleges & Universities, Continuing Education, Education Funds, Education Funds, Engineering/Technological Education, Faculty Development, Literacy, Medical Education, Minority Education, Private Education (Precollege), Religious Education, Science/Mathematics Education, Secondary Education (Private), Special Education, Student Aid
Environment: Resource Conservation
Health: Cancer, Children's Health/Hospitals, Clinics/Medical Centers, Emergency/Ambulance Services, Eyes/Blindness, Geriatric Health, Health Funds, Health Organizations, Home-Care Services, Hospitals, Hospitals (University Affiliated), Medical Rehabilitation, Medical Research, Medical Training, Prenatal Health Issues, Public Health, Research/Studies Institutes, Single-Disease Health Associations, Transplant Networks/Donor Banks
International: Health Care/Hospitals, International Affairs, International Development, International Environmental Issues
Religion: Churches, Dioceses, Religious Welfare, Seminaries
Science: Science Museums, Scientific Labs, Scientific Organizations, Scientific Research
Social Services: At-Risk Youth, Child Welfare, Community Service Organizations, Counseling, Family Services, People with Disabilities, Recreation & Athletics, Senior Services, Shelters/Homelessness, Substance Abuse, Volunteer Services, YMCA/YWCA/YMHA/YWHA, Youth Organizations

Application Procedures

Initial Contact: The Foundation does not have a formal application form. Applicants should submit a one-page executive summary accompanied by a proposal narrative and attachments.
Application Requirements: The proposal narrative should include: an executive summary summarizing key points of the proposal, purpose and relevance of the request, and amount requested; organizational history and capacity, including mission, governing structure, principal activities, and population served by organization; statement of need, identifying the needs that the proposal addresses, and how those needs coincide with the goals of the Foundation; program description, identifying the program's goals and objectives, activities, numbers served, facilities, timeline and staffing plan, and anticipated outcomes; evaluation, indicating how methods for evaluating program outcomes and effectiveness, including findings from previous evaluations, if available; and a conclusion, summarizing the proposal's main points and describing the purpose, relevance, and amount requested. The following attachments must be included with a proposal: current proof of tax-exempt status and non-private foundation status; names and primarily affiliations of officers and board members; most recent audited financial statements; organizational operating budget for the previous and current fiscal years; program budget for the previous and current fiscal years, if applicable; list of foundation and corporate grants for the previous and current fiscal years for both the organization and program or project, including dollar amounts; current fair market value of endowment, if applicable; and most recent annual report. Applicants should also check the foundation's guidelines for additional information required for proposals in the specific grant category for which they are applying.
Deadlines: None.
Review Process: Board meetings on grant decisions are held in March, June, September, and December. Only fully documented appeals will be considered. Meetings are arranged between foundation staff and applicants only if serious consideration of their appeals is anticipated. A site visit is required prior to board review.

Restrictions

Grants must be used for charitable purposes within the U.S. and its territories. Except in rare cases, the following restrictions apply: private sector organizations are favored over those financed through taxation; organizations serving larger geographical areas are favored over those of a neighborhood or grassroots nature; the foundation does not provide funding for building projects; the foundation does not make grants on an annual basis or make multi-year grants; organizations must wait three years from their award date before submitting another request; only one proposal will be considered from an organization within a calendar year; institutions with more than one department should coordinate grants through appropriate central office; the foundation does not support public policy, workshops, seminars, or requests for start-ups/seed funding. No grants are made to individuals, for loans, funds for radio, film, television or other related projects, publishing projects, equipment of any kind, special events, tickets, tables or advertising for an event. Proposals sent by fax or e-mail will not be accepted.

Additional Information

In addition to general grantmaking activities, the foundation provides funds and advisors for two operating programs: United States Senate Youth Program, which allows two students from each state to travel to Washington, DC for one week to observe the federal government in action and meet key officials. For more information contact Rita A. Almon, Program Director at the foundation's San Francisco office.

The Journalism Awards Program is designed to encourage excellence in journalism education. Prizes are awarded in writing, photography, television and radio news. For more information contact Jan C. Watten, Program Director at the foundation's San Francisco office.

The Hearst Foundation and William Randolph Hearst Foundation are independent private philanthropies operating separately from the Hearst Corporation. Because the charitable goals of the two foundations are the same, they are administered as one, and only one proposal need be submitted for review.

Supplemental material should be held to a minimum necessary to ensure a basic understanding of the organization seeking support. Videotapes should not be sent unless specifically requested.
Publications: Application Guidelines

Foundation Officials

James M. Asher: section
Frank Anthony Bennack, Jr.: vice president, director B San Antonio, TX 1933. ED University of Maryland (1954-1956); Saint Mary's University (1956-1958). PRIM CORP EMPL chief executive officer, president, director: Hearst Corp. CORP AFFIL director: San Francisco Newspaper Printing Co.; director: Motor Information Systems Division; director: San Francisco Newspaper Agency; director: Manufacturers Hanover Trust Co.; director: Midland Publishing Co.; president, chief executive officer: Hearst Realties Division; president, chief executive officer, director: Down East Timberlands Division; director: Hearst Business Publishing Development Corp.; director: Chase Manhattan Corp.; director: Diversion Magazine Division; director: Chase Manhattan Bank NA; director: American Home Products Corp. NONPR AFFIL president: Texas Daily Newspaper Association; honorary trustee: Witte Memorial Museum; trustee: Our Lady Lake College; chairman: Museum Television & Radio; member, board governors: New York Hospital; director: American Newspaper Publishers Association; president: Greater San Antonio Chamber of Commerce. CLUB AFFIL Rotary Club.
Millicent Hearst Boudjakdji: president, director B 1940. CORP AFFIL director: King Features Syndicate Division; director: Sunical Land & Livestock Division; director: Hearst Realties Division; director: Down East Timberlands Division; director: Hearst Corp.
John G. Conomikes: vice president, director PRIM CORP EMPL vice president, director: Hearst Corp. Broadcasting Group. CORP AFFIL vice president: King Features Syndicate Division; vice president, director: Sunical Land & Livestock Division; vice president: Hearst Realties Division; vice president: Down East Timberlands Division; president, co-chief executive officer: Hearst-Argyle Television Inc.
Ralph Cuomo: treasurer
Richard Emmet Deems: vice president, director B New York, NY January 19, 1913. PRIM CORP EMPL director, consult: Hearst Corp. CORP AFFIL director: Sunical Land & Livestock Division; director: Omega Publishing Co.; director: King Features Syndicate Division; director: National Magazine Co. London; director: HMI France Inc.; director: Hearst Realties Division; director: HMI Espana Inc.; director: Down East Timberlands Division. NONPR AFFIL member: Magazine Publishers Association. CLUB AFFIL Bohemian Club; Everglades Club.
Ronald J. Doefler: assistant treasurer
Thomas Eastham: vice president, executive director
Robert M. Frehse, Jr.: vice president, executive director NONPR AFFIL secretary: Interchurch Center.
Victor F. Ganzi: vice president, secretary B New York, NY 1947. ED Fordham University BS (1968); Harvard University JD (1971). PRIM CORP EMPL executive vice president: Hearst Books/Business Publications Group. CORP AFFIL director: PGA Tour Inc.; executive vice president, chief operating officer: Sunical Land & Livestock Division; director: Palm Management Corp.; executive vice president, chief operating officer: King Features Syndicate Division; president: Motor Information Systems Division; executive vice president, chief operating officer: Hearst Realties Division; director: IMI System Inc.; executive

vice president, chief operating officer: Hearst Corp.; director: ESPN; president: Hearst Business Publishing Development Corp.; president: Diversion Magazine Division; executive vice president, chief operating officer: Down East Timberlands Division; president: America Druggist Division. NONPR AFFIL member: Council Future Law School; director: New York City Economic Development Corp.; member: Colorado Society of Certified Public Accountants; member: American Bar Association; member: American Institute of Certified Public Accountants. CLUB AFFIL Cherry Valley Country Club; Sky Club.

George Randolph Hearst, Jr.: vice president, director B San Francisco, CA 1927. PRIM CORP EMPL chairman: Hearst Corp. NONPR AFFIL member: Veterans Foreign Wars. CLUB AFFIL Riviera Club; Jonathan Club; Burlingame Country Club; California Club.

John Randolph Hearst, Jr.: vice president, director B 1934. CORP AFFIL director: Hearst Corp. NONPR AFFIL vice president: United Service Organization Metropolitan New York.

William R. Hearst, III: vice president, director B Washington, DC 1949. ED Harvard University AB (1972). PRIM CORP EMPL publisher: San Francisco Examiner. CORP AFFIL director: Sun Microsystems; director: Preview Travel Inc.; director: Hearst Corp.; general partner: Kleiner Perkins Caufiled Byers; director: At Home Network. NONPR AFFIL trustee: Carnegie Institute.

Jodie W. King: assistant secretary B Birmingham, MI 1957. ED Mount Holyoke College AB (1979); University of Michigan JD (1982). PRIM CORP EMPL vice president, secretary, counsel: Hearst Corp. ADD CORP EMPL secretary: Hearst Business Publishing Development Corp.; secretary: Periodical Publishing Service Bureau.

Harvey L. Lipton: vice president, director B Brooklyn, NY 1925. ED New York University (1948); Saint John's University LLB (1951). PRIM CORP EMPL director: Hearst Corp. CORP AFFIL director: King Features Syndicate Division; director: Sunical Land & Livestock Division; secretary, director: Intellinet; secretary, director: Hearst Entertainment Inc.; director: Hearst Realties Division; secretary, director: Edwardsville Publishing Co.; secretary, director: Eyeline; director: Down East Timberlands Division; secretary, director: Edwardsville Intelligencer.

Gilbert Charles Maurer: vice president, director B New York, NY 1928. ED Saint Lawrence University AB (1950); Harvard University MBA (1952). PRIM CORP EMPL executive vice president, chief operating officer, director: Hearst Corp. ADD CORP EMPL chief operating officer, director: Down East Timberlands Division; chief operating officer, director: Hearst Realties Division; chief operating officer, director: King Features Syndicate Division; chief operating officer, director: Sunical Land & Livestock Division. NONPR AFFIL member New York advisory board: Salvation Army; president, trustee: Whitney Museum American Art; member: Magazine Publishers Association; trustee: Norton Museum Art; director: Boys & Girls Clubs America. CLUB AFFIL Metro Club; Harvard Club New York.

Mark F. Miller: vice president, director PRIM CORP EMPL executive vice president, general manager, magazine division: Hearst Corp. CORP AFFIL director: Periodical Publishers Service Bureau.

Raymond Joseph Petersen: vice president, director B West Orange, NJ 1919. PRIM CORP EMPL executive vice president, director: Hearst Magazines. CORP AFFIL director: Sunical Land & Livestock Division; director: Hearst Realties Division; director: Down East Timberlands Division; director: Hearst Corp. NONPR AFFIL director, vice president: United Service Organization Metropolitan New York; director: U.S. National Comm Libs Info Science; member chairman committee: United Cerebral Palsy Campaign; honorary advisor: Children Alcoholics Foundation; director: National Crime Prevention Council; director: Boys & Girls Clubs Madison Square; member, director: American Advertising Federation.

Virginia H. Randt: vice president, director

Jon D. Smith, Jr.: assistant treasurer
John P. Spisak: assistant treasurer

Grants Analysis

Disclosure Period: calendar year ending 2001
Total Grants: $28,502,800*
Number of Grants: 214
Average Grant: $125,014*
Highest Grant: $1,000,000
Lowest Grant: $25,000
Typical Range: $50,000 to $300,000
*Note: Giving excludes scholarship. Average grant figure excludes two highest grants ($2,000,000).

Recent Grants

Note: Grants derived from 2001 Form 990.

Library-Related
225,000	Friends of the Bancroft Library, Berkeley, CA

General
1,000,000	National Museum of the American Indian, Washington, DC
1,000,000	Wildlife Conservation Society, Bronx, NY
500,000	American Red Cross, Los Angeles, CA
500,000	Case Western Reserve University, Cleveland, OH
500,000	New York Presbyterian Hospital, New York, NY
500,000	New York University School of Education, New York, NY
500,000	Oregon Health and Science University Foundation, Portland, OR
500,000	University at Albany, Albany, NY
500,000	University of California Los Angeles School of Public Policy and Social Research, Los Angeles, CA
500,000	University of Houston, Houston, TX

ED AND MARY HEATH FOUNDATION

Giving Contact

W. R. Smith, Chairman
PO Box 338
Tyler, TX 75710
Phone: (903)597-7436

Description

Founded: 1954
EIN: 756021506
Organization Type: Private Foundation
Giving Locations: TX: Smith County
Grant Types: General Support.

Donor Information

Founder: the late J. E. Heath, the late Mary M. Heath

Financial Summary

Total Giving: $61,750 (2001); $63,200 (2000); $67,725 (1999)
Giving Analysis: Giving for 2001 includes: foundation grants to United Way ($250)
Assets: $2,188,101 (2001); $2,266,769 (2000); $2,264,695 (1999)

Typical Recipients

Arts & Humanities: Arts Outreach, History & Archaeology, Libraries, Museums/Galleries, Music, Public Broadcasting, Theater
Civic & Public Affairs: Economic Policy, Employment/Job Training, Civic & Public Affairs-General, Hispanic Affairs, Housing, Municipalities/Towns, Native American Affairs, Philanthropic Organizations, Public Policy, Urban & Community Affairs
Education: Agricultural Education, Colleges & Universities, Community & Junior Colleges, Elementary Education (Public), Environmental Education, Faculty Development, Education-General, Literacy, Minority Education, Private Education (Precollege), Public Education (Precollege), Religious Education, Special Education, Student Aid
Health: AIDS/HIV, Alzheimers Disease, Cancer, Children's Health/Hospitals, Clinics/Medical Centers, Emergency/Ambulance Services, Eyes/Blindness, Hospices, Medical Rehabilitation, Mental Health, Prenatal Health Issues, Respiratory, Single-Disease Health Associations, Speech & Hearing
International: Health Care/Hospitals
Religion: Churches, Ministries, Religious Organizations, Religious Welfare, Seminaries, Synagogues/Temples
Science: Science Museums, Scientific Centers & Institutes
Social Services: Animal Protection, Camps, Child Abuse, Child Welfare, Community Service Organizations, Day Care, Delinquency & Criminal Rehabilitation, Domestic Violence, Family Services, Food/Clothing Distribution, People with Disabilities, Recreation & Athletics, Scouts, Senior Services, Social Services-General, Substance Abuse, United Funds/United Ways, YMCA/YWCA/YMHA/YWHA, Youth Organizations

Application Procedures

Initial Contact: Send a brief letter of inquiry on organization letterhead.
Application Requirements: Include a description of organization and purpose of funds sought.
Deadlines: None.

Foundation Officials

Jack Jackson: vice chairman, secretary, treasurer
Mike Massar: director
Charlotte Schaeffers: program director, trustee
Margaret Smith: director
W. R. Smith: director
Charles H. White, Jr.: director

Grants Analysis

Disclosure Period: calendar year ending 2001
Total Grants: $61,500*
Number of Grants: 77
Average Grant: $799
Highest Grant: $6,000
Lowest Grant: $50
Typical Range: $200 to $1,000
*Note: Giving excludes United Way.

Recent Grants

Note: Grants derived from 2000 Form 990.

General
6,000	First Baptist Church, Tyler, TX
2,000	Marvin United Methodist Church, Tyler, TX -- for benevolence fund
2,000	People Attempting to Help (PATH), Tyler, TX
1,750	American Red Cross, Tyler, TX
1,750	ETYRC Charitable Trust, Tyler, TX
1,500	Children's Village, Tyler, TX
1,500	First Christian Church, Tyler, TX
1,500	First Presbyterian Church, Tyler, TX
1,500	Meals on Wheels, Tyler, TX
1,500	Young Audiences, Tyler, TX

MARY HEATH FOUNDATION

Giving Contact

Jimmy J. Rogers, Vice President
c/o Old National Trust Co.
PO Box 217
Oblong, IL 62449-0217
Phone: (618)544-2960

Description

Founded: 1994
EIN: 371330907
Organization Type: Private Foundation
Giving Locations: IL
Grant Types: General Support.

Donor Information

Founder: Established in 1994 by Mary Heath Morris.

Financial Summary

Total Giving: $61,900 (2001); $146,586 (2000); $167,545 (1999)
Giving Analysis: Giving for 1998 includes: foundation ($140,735)
Assets: $5,115,728 (2001); $5,472,090 (2000); $5,520,942 (1999)
Gifts Received: $1,824,105 (1996). Note: In 1996, contributions were received from the estate of Mary Heath Morris.

Typical Recipients

Arts & Humanities: Historic Preservation, History & Archaeology, Libraries, Museums/Galleries
Civic & Public Affairs: Botanical Gardens/Parks, Clubs, Community Foundations, Civic & Public Affairs-General, Housing, Municipalities/Towns, Safety, Urban & Community Affairs
Education: Education-General, Literacy, Private Education (Precollege), Public Education (Precollege), Science/Mathematics Education, Secondary Education (Public), Special Education
Environment: Air/Water Quality
Health: Emergency/Ambulance Services
Religion: Churches, Religious Welfare
Social Services: Animal Protection, Community Centers, Community Service Organizations, Crime Prevention, Emergency Relief, Food/Clothing Distribution, Recreation & Athletics, Senior Services, Social Services-General, Veterans, Youth Organizations

Application Procedures

Initial Contact: Request application form.
Application Requirements: Include six identical copies of the complete proposal. Include current financial information and tax exempt ruling determination from the Internal Revenue Service.
Deadlines: May 1 and November 1.
Evaluative Criteria: The Advisory Committee looks for applicants with a history of achievement and good management; with a current stable financial condition, supported by financial statements; whose programs and projects which encourage self-sufficiency; whose projects mean to accomplish a measurable impact in the area and for the purpose for which the applicant requests; and whose programs are consistent with the purpose of the Foundation.
Notes: Foundation will monitor the impact of all grants to help determine the Foundation's future program objectives. Committee does not permit individual contact regarding specific grant proposals.

Restrictions

Applying organizations must be located in the State of Illinois; must have received permanent, tax-exempt ruling from the IRS; and the organization's project must be for the benefit and enjoyment of the general public of the State of Illinois.

Grants are not made for individuals; organizations which use funds granted to support other organizations; endowments; deficit reductions; routine institutional expenses; general campaigns, including fundraising events, dinners, or mass mailings; efforts to carry out propaganda, or influence legislation; participation or intervention in political campaigns on behalf of any candidate for public office; or requests that do not fall within the Foundation's specific areas of interest.

Foundation Officials

Radford Burkett: adv board comm mem
Betty Cunningham: adv board comm mem
Thomas Eden: adv board committee member
Steve Holliday: adv board committee member
Myrl Littejohn: advisory board, committee member
Todd Musgrave: adv board committee member
Thomas Pearce: adv board comm mem
Gilbert Phillippe: adv board comm mem
Keith Waldrop: adv board committee member

Grants Analysis

Disclosure Period: calendar year ending 2001
Total Grants: $61,900
Number of Grants: 22
Average Grant: $2,814
Highest Grant: $9,000
Lowest Grant: $300
Typical Range: $1,000 to $5,000

Recent Grants

Note: Grants derived from 2001 Form 990.

Library-Related

2,000	Coffeen Community Library, Coffeen, IL -- purchase of books
400	Palestine Public Library District, Palestine, IL -- library lighting

General

9,000	Hutsonville Fire Protection District, Hutsonville, IL -- thermal imaging camera
7,500	Hutsonville Community Unit School District 1, Hutsonville, IL -- After School Teen Center
5,000	Oblong Community Unit School District 4, Oblong, IL -- school road extension and parking lot
4,000	Eastern Illinois Children's Home, Oblong, IL -- construction of new home
4,000	Summer Success Project, Robinson, IL -- programs for children
3,700	Illinois Oil Field Museum of Oblong, Oblong, IL -- Erect Old Wooden Derrick display
3,000	Goshen Preservation Alliance, Edwardsville, IL -- restoration of train depot
3,000	St. Michael Archangel School, Sigel, IL -- school roof repairs
2,500	Palestine Development Association, Palestine, IL -- soil and water conservation survey
2,500	Pioneer City Youth Baseball, Palestine, IL -- lights for baseball diamonds

HEBREW TECHNICAL INSTITUTE

Giving Contact

Anita Goldberg, Trust Officer
c/o REM Residential
118 East 17th Street
New York, NY 10003
Phone: (212)286-2600

Description

Founded: 1884
EIN: 135562240
Organization Type: Private Foundation
Giving Locations: NY
Grant Types: General Support, Scholarship.

Financial Summary

Total Giving: $354,000 (2000); $407,500 (1999); $318,000 (1998)
Giving Analysis: Giving for 2000 includes: foundation scholarships ($107,500) 1999: foundation scholarships ($17,500)

Assets: $3,532,429 (2000); $3,832,805 (1999); $3,990,042 (1998)
Gifts Received: $29,157 (2000); $18,644 (1999); $18,627 (1998). Note: In 1995, contributions were received from the Henry Stern Trust.

Typical Recipients

Arts & Humanities: Libraries, Museums/Galleries
Civic & Public Affairs: Botanical Gardens/Parks, Business/Free Enterprise, Housing, Women's Affairs
Education: Arts/Humanities Education, Colleges & Universities, Engineering/Technological Education, Environmental Education, Education-General, Private Education (Precollege)
Environment: Environment-General, Resource Conservation
International: Missionary/Religious Activities
Religion: Jewish Causes, Religious Organizations
Science: Science Museums, Scientific Centers & Institutes, Scientific Organizations
Social Services: Community Centers, Community Service Organizations, Refugee Assistance, Youth Organizations

Application Procedures

Initial Contact: Send a brief letter of inquiry describing program.
Deadlines: None.

Restrictions

Grants are limited to IRS approved public charities involved in vocational studies.

Foundation Officials

Catherine H. Behrend: director
Lawrence A. Benenson: director
Andrew Berkman: director
Seth Harris Dubin: director B New York, NY 1933. ED Amherst College BA (1954); Harvard University LLB (1957). PRIM CORP EMPL partner: Satterlee Stephens Burke & Burke. NONPR AFFIL trustee, president: New York Hall Science; member: New York State Bar Association; chairman: Hebrew Technology Institute; member: Council Foreign Relations; fellow: Foreign Political Association; trustee: Chatham House Foundation; member advisory council: Cooper Union School Engineering; member: Association Bar New York City. CLUB AFFIL Century Association.
Irving Lipkowitz: director
Jay J. Meltzer: director
John R. Menke: director
Sandra Priest Rose: director
Herbert A. Raisler: director
Hyman B. Ritchin: director
Robert Rosenthal, Esq.: director
Bruce D. Schlechter: director
Russell O. Vernon: director
Charles Weilman: director

Grants Analysis

Disclosure Period: calendar year ending 2000
Total Grants: $246,500*
Number of Grants: 12
Average Grant: $17,864*
Highest Grant: $50,000
Typical Range: $5,000 to $30,000
***Note:** Giving excludes scholarships. Average grant figure excludes highest grant.

Recent Grants

Note: Grants derived from 1999 Form 990.

Library-Related

50,000	New York Public Library, New York, NY
12,500	New York Public Library, New York, NY

General

75,000	New York Hall of Science, New York, NY

50,000	Cooper Union, New York, NY
25,000	B'Nai Zion
25,000	Brooklyn Children's Museum, Brooklyn, NY
25,000	New York Academy of Sciences, New York, NY
20,000	Brandeis University, Waltham, MA
20,000	Housing Conservation Coordinator
15,000	Mosholu Montefiore Community Center, Bronx, NY
15,000	Rockefeller University, New York, NY
15,000	Rockefeller University, New York, NY

HECHT-LEVI FOUNDATION

Giving Contact

Blanche Roche, Trust Officer
c/o Mercantile Safe Deposit and Trust Co.
2 Hopkins Plaza
Baltimore, MD 21201
Phone: (410)209-5454

Description

Founded: 1958
EIN: 526035023
Organization Type: Private Foundation
Giving Locations: MD: Baltimore metropolitan area
Grant Types: General Support.

Donor Information

Founder: the late Alexander Hecht, the late Selma H. Hecht, Robert H. Levi, Ryda H. Levi

Financial Summary

Total Giving: $748,667 (2000); $780,592 (1999); $527,000 (1998)
Giving Analysis: Giving for 1999 includes: foundation grants to United Way ($5,000); 1998: foundation grants to United Way ($5,000) foundation ($522,000)
Assets: $19,333,754 (2000); $16,791,064 (1999); $16,134,107 (1998)

Typical Recipients

Arts & Humanities: Arts Funds, Arts Institutes, Arts Outreach, Ballet, Dance, Historic Preservation, History & Archaeology, Libraries, Museums/Galleries, Music, Opera, Performing Arts, Public Broadcasting, Theater
Civic & Public Affairs: Civil Rights, Community Foundations, Civic & Public Affairs-General, Housing, Legal Aid, Philanthropic Organizations, Urban & Community Affairs, Zoos/Aquariums
Education: Arts/Humanities Education, Business Education, Colleges & Universities, Education Funds, Elementary Education (Public), Environmental Education, Education-General, Leadership Training, Private Education (Precollege), Religious Education, Student Aid
Environment: Environment-General, Resource Conservation
Health: Emergency/Ambulance Services, Health Organizations, Hospitals, Mental Health, Preventive Medicine/Wellness Organizations
Religion: Churches, Jewish Causes, Religious Organizations, Religious Welfare, Synagogues/Temples
Science: Science Museums, Scientific Centers & Institutes
Social Services: Child Welfare, Community Service Organizations, Family Planning, Food/Clothing Distribution, People with Disabilities, Recreation & Athletics, United Funds/United Ways, Youth Organizations

Application Procedures

Initial Contact: The foundation requests applications be made in writing.
Deadlines: None.

Additional Information

Trust(s): Mercantile Safe Deposit & Trust Co

Foundation Officials

Sandra L. Gerstung: president, director
Clementine Kaufman: officer
Alexander H. Levi: vice president, director
Richard H. Levi: vice president, treasurer, director
Ryda H. Levi: vice president, director
Blanche Roche: trust officer
Wilbert H. Sirota, Esq.: secretary, director

Grants Analysis

Disclosure Period: calendar year ending 2000
Total Grants: $748,667
Number of Grants: 58
Average Grant: $6,117*
Highest Grant: $400,000
Typical Range: $1,000 to $10,000
***Note:** Average grant figure excludes highest grant.

Recent Grants

Note: Grants derived from 2001 Form 990.

Library-Related

5,000	Enoch Pratt Free Library, Baltimore, MD

General

400,000	Johns Hopkins University, Baltimore, MD -- Bioethics Chair
60,000	Baltimore Symphony Orchestra, Baltimore, MD
50,000	Associated Jewish Charities, Baltimore, MD
50,000	Baltimore Symphony Orchestra, Baltimore, MD -- Sustaining Greatness Campaign
40,000	Baltimore Museum of Art, Baltimore, MD -- garden maintenance
25,000	American Civil Liberties Union -- Bill of Rights
10,000	Jewish Museum of Maryland, Baltimore, MD
10,000	Johns Hopkins University, Baltimore, MD -- Bioethics Institute
10,000	Marlboro Music School, Philadelphia, PA
10,000	Park School, Buffalo, NY

HECKSCHER FOUNDATION FOR CHILDREN

Giving Contact

Virginia Sloane, President
17 East 47th Street
New York, NY 10017
Phone: (212)371-7775
Fax: (212)371-7787

Description

Founded: 1921
EIN: 131820170
Organization Type: Specialized/Single Purpose Foundation
Giving Locations: NY: New York
Grant Types: Capital, General Support, Multiyear/Continuing Support, Project.

Donor Information

Founder: August Heckscher , who died in 1941, was the donor of the Heckscher Foundation for Children, which was established in 1921. Mr. Heckscher made his fortune in mining and New York City real estate. He first demonstrated his interest in the welfare of children in New York City in the early twentieth century, when he donated a building and the land on which it stood to a children's home.

Financial Summary

Total Giving: $4,087,301 (2000); $3,105,911 (1999); $2,172,944 (1998)
Giving Analysis: Giving for 1998 includes: foundation scholarships ($5,000)
Assets: $125,285,128 (2000); $121,323,392 (1999); $115,433,481 (1998)

Typical Recipients

Arts & Humanities: Arts Associations & Councils, Arts Centers, Arts Institutes, Arts Outreach, Ballet, Dance, Ethnic & Folk Arts, Historic Preservation, History & Archaeology, Libraries, Museums/Galleries, Music, Opera, Performing Arts, Public Broadcasting, Theater
Civic & Public Affairs: Botanical Gardens/Parks, Clubs, Economic Development, Employment/Job Training, Civic & Public Affairs-General, Hispanic Affairs, Housing, Municipalities/Towns, Philanthropic Organizations, Public Policy, Urban & Community Affairs, Women's Affairs, Zoos/Aquariums
Education: Afterschool/Enrichment Programs, Arts/Humanities Education, Colleges & Universities, Education Associations, Education Reform, Elementary Education (Private), Elementary Education (Public), Environmental Education, Leadership Training, Medical Education, Minority Education, Preschool Education, Private Education (Precollege), Public Education (Precollege), Special Education, Student Aid
Environment: Forestry, Environment-General
Health: Adolescent Health Issues, AIDS/HIV, Cancer, Children's Health/Hospitals, Clinics/Medical Centers, Emergency/Ambulance Services, Health Organizations, Hospitals, Medical Rehabilitation, Medical Research, Mental Health, Nursing Services, Preventive Medicine/Wellness Organizations, Single-Disease Health Associations, Speech & Hearing, Transplant Networks/Donor Banks
International: Health Care/Hospitals
Religion: Churches, Jewish Causes, Religious Welfare
Social Services: At-Risk Youth, Big Brother/Big Sister, Camps, Child Welfare, Community Centers, Community Service Organizations, Day Care, Delinquency & Criminal Rehabilitation, Family Planning, Family Services, People with Disabilities, Recreation & Athletics, Scouts, Shelters/Homelessness, Substance Abuse, Volunteer Services, YMCA/YWCA/YMHA/YWHA, Youth Organizations

Application Procedures

Initial Contact: Applicants should send a letter to the foundation.
Application Requirements: Include a concise statement of the program or project; amount requested; a brief background of the organization; a budget for the program/project; a list of officers, director, or trustees; donor list for the past twelve months, and a copy of the IRS tax-determination letter.
Deadlines: None.

Additional Information

Publications: Application Guidelines

Foundation Officials

John M. D'Mara: trustee
William D. Hart, Jr.: secretary, general counsel, trustee B 1918. ED Yale University AB (1940); Harvard University LLB (1943). PRIM CORP EMPL vice president, director: North Shore Corp. CORP AFFIL vice president, treasurer, director: Park Lexington Co.; partner: Whitman & Ransom.
Carole Landman: trustee
John D. MacNeary: trustee
Gail Meyers: trustee PRIM CORP EMPL senior vice president: Barnett Bank South Florida. NONPR AFFIL secretary: Greater Miami Jewish Federation.
George Noumair: trustee
Fred Obser: trustee
Howard Rosenbaum: assistant treasurer, trustee
Marlene Shyer: trustee

Howard Grant Sloane: chairman B 1922. PRIM CORP EMPL president, director: North Shore Corp. CORP AFFIL president: Anahma Realty; president: Okeechobee Inc.

Virginia Sloane: president, trustee PRIM CORP EMPL president: Anahma Realty.

Arthur J. Smadbeck: trustee B 1949. PRIM CORP EMPL vice president, director: Park Lexington Co. CORP AFFIL vice president: Okeechobee Inc.; vice president: Anahma Realty. NONPR AFFIL selectman: Town of Edgartown, Massachusetts.

Louis Smadbeck, Jr.: trustee

Mina Smadbeck: trustee

Paul Smadbeck: trustee PRIM CORP EMPL vice president, director: Park Lexington Co. CORP AFFIL vice president, director: North Shore Corp.

Grants Analysis

Disclosure Period: calendar year ending 2000
Total Grants: $4,087,301
Number of Grants: 232
Average Grant: $17,618
Highest Grant: $150,000
Typical Range: $2,500 to $25,000 and $50,000 to $80,000

Recent Grants

Note: Grants derived from 2000 Form 990.

General

150,000	Children's Aid Society, New York, NY
150,000	United Cerebral Palsy of New York, New York, NY
100,000	Jazz at Lincoln Center, New York, NY
100,000	Summer on The Hill, Mobile, AL
100,000	Take the Field, New York, NY
75,000	92nd Street YMHA, New York, NY
75,000	Enterprise Foundation, New York, NY
75,000	Friends of Karen, Croton Falls, NY
75,000	Good Shepherd Services, New York, NY
75,000	YMCA of Greater New York, New York, NY

HEDCO FOUNDATION

Giving Contact

Mary A. Goriup, Foundation Manager
1221 Broadway, 21st Fl.
1221 Broadway, 21st Fl.
Oakland, CA 94612
Phone: (925)283-3442

Description

Founded: 1972
EIN: 237259742
Organization Type: Private Foundation
Giving Locations: CA; MN
Grant Types: Capital, Project, Scholarship.

Donor Information

Founder: Herrick Corp., Catalina Associates

Financial Summary

Total Giving: $2,557,383 (fiscal year ending November 30, 2003 approx); $3,403,028 (fiscal 2002); $1,570,665 (fiscal 2000)
Assets: $22,080,129 (fiscal 2002); $12,832,420 (fiscal 2000); $14,694,620 (fiscal 1999)
Gifts Received: $14,308,768 (fiscal 2002); $200,000 (fiscal 2000); $3,507,256 (fiscal 1999). Note: In fiscal 1999 and 2000, contributions were received from Herrick-Pacific Corp. ($3,002,350) and David Dornsife ($504,906). In fiscal 1998, contributions were received from the Herrick Corp. ($100,000); Catalina Associates II ($2,500,000). In fiscal 1997, contributions were received from the Herrick Corp., Catalina Associates II, and Dorothy Jernstedt. In fiscal 2002, contributions were received from Herrick-Pacific Corp. ($4,000,000); The Herrick Corp. ($100,000);

Dorothy Jernstedt ($100,000); Dornsife Family Trust ($8,108,568); David Dornsife ($2,000,100) and James Appleton ($100).

Typical Recipients

Arts & Humanities: Libraries, Museums/Galleries
Civic & Public Affairs: Asian American Affairs, Civic & Public Affairs-General, Housing
Education: Arts/Humanities Education, Colleges & Universities, Education Reform, Minority Education, Private Education (Precollege), Religious Education, Science/Mathematics Education, Social Sciences Education, Student Aid
Environment: Environment-General, Resource Conservation
Health: Alzheimers Disease, Cancer, Children's Health/Hospitals, Clinics/Medical Centers, Health Organizations, Hospices, Hospitals, Medical Research, Research/Studies Institutes, Single-Disease Health Associations
International: International Relations, International Relief Efforts
Religion: Religious Welfare, Seminaries
Social Services: Community Service Organizations, Food/Clothing Distribution, Homes, Scouts, Senior Services, YMCA/YWCA/YMHA/YWHA, Youth Organizations

Application Procedures

Initial Contact: The foundation has no formal grant application procedure or application form.
Deadlines: None.

Foundation Officials

Laine Ainsworth: director
Dr. James Appleton: director
Rena Brantley: secretary, director
Allen L. Dobbins, EdD: director
David H. Dornsife: vice president, director
Ester M. Dornsife: president, director
Harold W. Dornsife: cfo, director B Mishawaka, IN 1915. ED University of Southern California (1939). PRIM CORP EMPL chairman: Peninsula Steel Product. CORP AFFIL chairman, chief executive officer: Herrick-Pacific Corp.; chairman: Peninsula Steel Products; chairman: Central Texas IW; chairman: Gillig Corp.
Mary A. Goriup: mgr
Tom Herman: director
Derek Jernstedt: director
Dorothy Jernstedt: secretary, director
James S. Little: director
Dr. William Picard: director
Roger Schwab: director

Grants Analysis

Disclosure Period: fiscal year ending November 30, 2002
Total Grants: $3,403,028
Number of Grants: 17
Average Grant: $53,872*
Highest Grant: $2,000,000
Typical Range: $25,000 to $150,000
*Note: Average grant excludes two highest grants ($2,487,200).

Recent Grants

Note: Grants derived from fiscal 2001 Form 990.

General

2,000,000	San Francisco Theological Seminary, San Francisco, CA
487,200	World Vision, Minneapolis, MN
256,000	Children's Hospital Oakland, Oakland, CA
154,515	St. Vincent's Day Home, Oakland, CA
129,053	Oregon Health Sciences University, Portland, OR
84,115	St. Vincent's Day Home, Oakland, CA
62,078	St. Luke's Hospital Foundation, San Francisco, CA
60,000	Alzheimer's Association
35,031	East Bay Conservation Corps, Oakland, CA
33,922	St. Luke's Hospital Foundation, San Francisco, CA

JULIUS W. HEGELER II FOUNDATION

Giving Contact

Madelle G. Hegeler, Manager
Julius W. Hegeler II Foundation
1521 N. Vermilion Street
Danville, IL 61832-2370
Phone: (217)442-1521

Description

Founded: 1993
EIN: 371302455
Organization Type: Private Foundation
Grant Types: General Support.

Financial Summary

Total Giving: $301,365 (fiscal year ending June 30, 2001); $31,835 (fiscal 1999); $13,990 (fiscal 1997)
Giving Analysis: Giving for fiscal 2001 includes: foundation grants to United Way ($3,500); fiscal 1999: foundation grants to United Way ($3,250) fiscal 1997: foundation grants to United Way ($2,750)
Assets: $11,694,506 (fiscal 2001); $7,976,071 (fiscal 1999); $7,020,204 (fiscal 1997)
Gifts Received: $1,000 (fiscal 1996)

Typical Recipients

Arts & Humanities: Arts Institutes, Historic Preservation, Libraries, Museums/Galleries, Music
Civic & Public Affairs: Clubs, Civic & Public Affairs-General
Education: Business Education, Colleges & Universities, Community & Junior Colleges, Education Funds
Environment: Resource Conservation
Health: Single-Disease Health Associations
Social Services: Community Centers, Recreation & Athletics, United Funds/United Ways, YMCA/YWCA/YMHA/YWHA

Application Procedures

Initial Contact: The foundation has no formal grant application procedure or application form.
Deadlines: None.

Foundation Officials

R. K. Bates: director
F. Jay Foster: acct
Alix S. Hegeler: director
Julius W. Hegeler, II: director
Madelle G. Hegeler: mgr
Dolores A. Roberts: director

Grants Analysis

Disclosure Period: fiscal year ending June 30, 2001
Total Grants: $297,865*
Number of Grants: 14
Average Grant: $17,143*
Highest Grant: $75,000
Typical Range: $5,000 to $20,000
*Note: Giving excludes United Way. Average grant figure excludes highest grant.

Recent Grants

Note: Grants derived from fiscal 2001 Form 990.

Library-Related

25,000	Westville Public Library, Westville, IL

General

75,000	Vermilion County Conservation District - Forest Glen, Danville, IL

55,000	YMCA, Danville, IL
50,000	YWCA, Danville, IL
25,000	Ambucs Playground for Everyone, Danville, IL
25,000	Cerebral Palsy Association, Chicago, IL
20,000	Vermilion Area Community Health Center, Danville, IL
6,300	Vermilion County Museum, Danville, IL
5,000	Danville Community Public School Fund, Danville, IL
5,000	Millikin University, Decatur, IL
5,000	USS LST Ship Memorial, Danville, IL

ANNA M. HEILMAIER CHARITABLE FOUNDATION

Giving Contact

Penny Berger, Vice President
c/o U. S. Bank
332 Minnesota Street
PO Box 64704
St. Paul, MN 55164-0704
Phone: (651)244-4513
Fax: (651)244-4172

Description

Founded: 1993
EIN: 411761632
Organization Type: Private Foundation
Giving Locations: MN: Dakota County, Saint Paul; WA: Ramsey
Grant Types: General Support.

Donor Information

Founder: Founded in 1993 by the late Anna M. Heilmaier.

Financial Summary

Total Giving: $408,500 (2000); $464,500 (1999); $302,000 (1998). Note: Giving includes scholarship ($8,000).
Giving Analysis: Giving for 1998 includes: foundation scholarships ($8,000)
Assets: $8,963,085 (2000); $8,791,845 (1999); $8,085,887 (1998)
Gifts Received: $4,039,850 (1994). Note: In 1994, contributions were received from the estate of Anna M. Heilmaier.

Typical Recipients

Arts & Humanities: Arts Associations & Councils, Arts Funds, Ballet, History & Archaeology, Libraries, Museums/Galleries, Music, Opera
Civic & Public Affairs: Clubs, Civic & Public Affairs-General
Education: Arts/Humanities Education, Colleges & Universities, Medical Education, Student Aid
Health: Cancer, Children's Health/Hospitals, Clinics/Medical Centers, Eyes/Blindness, Health Organizations, Hospices, Hospitals, Prenatal Health Issues, Speech & Hearing
Religion: Churches, Religious Welfare
Science: Science Museums
Social Services: Child Welfare, Community Service Organizations, Family Services, Social Services-General

Application Procedures

Initial Contact: Send a brief letter of inquiry.
Application Requirements: Include information on purpose of funds sought and proof of tax-exempt status.
Deadlines: None.

Restrictions

Does not support individuals, religious organizations for sectarian purposes, political or lobbying groups, or organizations outside operating areas.

Additional Information

Emphasis is on treatment of cancer, diseases of the eye, medical research, and support for chamber and classical music.
Trust(s): US Bank National Association Minnesota

Foundation Officials

Terence N. Doyle: co-trustee B Minneapolis, MN 1936. ED Saint Thomas College BA (1958); University of Minnesota JD (1961). NONPR AFFIL member: Minnesota Law Alumni Association; member: Order Coif; fellow: American College Trust & Estate Counsel; member: Minnesota Bar Association; director: AH South Foundation; member: American Bar Association. CLUB AFFIL Minnesota Club.

Grants Analysis

Disclosure Period: calendar year ending 2000
Total Grants: $408,500
Number of Grants: 24
Average Grant: $12,326*
Highest Grant: $125,000
Lowest Grant: $5,000
Typical Range: $5,000 to $25,000
*Note: Average grant excludes highest grant.

Recent Grants

Note: Grants derived from 2001 Form 990.

Library-Related

10,000	Friends of the St. Paul Public Library, St. Paul, MN

General

200,000	Schubert Club, St. Paul, MN -- for Raspberry Island Bandshell Project
62,500	Saint Paul Chamber Orchestra Society, St. Paul, MN
26,000	Minnesota Sinfonia, Minneapolis, MN
25,000	Gillette Children's Foundation, St. Paul, MN -- for focus on special children
25,000	State Services for the Blind, St. Paul, MN
20,000	Lifetrack Resources, St. Paul, MN -- support of rehabilitation therapies division services for low income and elderly
15,000	Healthstart, Inc., St. Paul, MN -- for support of school based clinics
10,000	Minnesota Historical Society, St. Paul, MN
10,000	Minnesota Opera, Minneapolis, MN
10,000	United Cambodian Association of Minnesota, Inc., St. Paul, MN

HOWARD HEINZ ENDOWMENT

Giving Contact

Maxwell King, Executive Director
30 Dominion Tower
625 Liberty Avenue
Pittsburgh, PA 15222-3199
Phone: (412)281-5777
Fax: (412)281-5788
E-mail: info@heinz.org
Web: http://www.heinz.org

Description

Founded: 1941
EIN: 251721100
Organization Type: General Purpose Foundation
Giving Locations: PA: Southwest Pennsylvania, Pittsburgh
Grant Types: General Support.

Donor Information

Founder: Howard Heinz was born near Sharpsburg, a suburb of Pittsburgh, on August 27, 1877, the son of Henry John and Sarah Young Heinz. After graduation from Shady Side Academy and then Yale University in 1900, he entered active service with the H.J. Heinz Company, where he successfully became advertising manager, sales manager, vice president and president.

He was a director and/or trustee of the Pennsylvania Railroad, Mellon Bank, N.A., National Industrial Conference Board, Pittsburgh Regional Planning Association, Pittsburgh Chamber of Commerce, University of Pittsburgh, Carnegie Institute, Shady Side Academy, Western Pennsylvania Hospital and the Pittsburgh Symphony Society. He was ruling elder of the Shadyside Presbyterian Church.

Mr. Heinz died on February 9, 1941. He bequeathed his residual estate to the Howard Heinz Endowment for philanthropic purposes.

Financial Summary

Total Giving: $55,398,822 (2001); $45,810,679 (2000); $27,286,031 (1998)
Giving Analysis: Giving for 2000 includes: foundation grants to United Way ($2,284,648); 1998: foundation scholarships ($100,000) foundation grants to United Way ($1,207,500)
Assets: $1,400,000,000 (2001); $1,028,810,621 (2000); $970,162,858 (1998)

Typical Recipients

Arts & Humanities: Arts Associations & Councils, Arts Festivals, Arts Funds, Arts Institutes, Arts Outreach, Ballet, Community Arts, Dance, Film & Video, Arts & Humanities-General, Historic Preservation, History & Archaeology, Libraries, Museums/Galleries, Music, Opera, Performing Arts, Public Broadcasting, Theater

Civic & Public Affairs: African American Affairs, Business/Free Enterprise, Clubs, Community Foundations, Economic Development, Economic Policy, Employment/Job Training, Civic & Public Affairs-General, Housing, Municipalities/Towns, Nonprofit Management, Philanthropic Organizations, Professional & Trade Associations, Public Policy, Urban & Community Affairs, Urban & Community Affairs, Zoos/Aquariums

Education: Afterschool/Enrichment Programs, Business Education, Colleges & Universities, Community & Junior Colleges, Economic Education, Education Associations, Education Funds, Education Reform, Elementary Education (Private), Elementary Education (Public), Environmental Education, Faculty Development, Education-General, Health & Physical Education, International Studies, Leadership Training, Legal Education, Literacy, Medical Education, Minority Education, Preschool Education, Private Education (Precollege), Public Education (Precollege), School Volunteerism, Science/Mathematics Education, Secondary Education (Public), Social Sciences Education, Student Aid, Vocational & Technical Education

Environment: Air/Water Quality, Energy, Forestry, Environment-General, Protection, Resource Conservation, Watershed, Wildlife Protection

Health: Children's Health/Hospitals, Clinics/Medical Centers, Health Policy/Cost Containment, Health Organizations, Heart, Hospitals, Medical Rehabilitation, Medical Research, Mental Health, Nursing Services, Nutrition, Prenatal Health Issues, Preventive Medicine/Wellness Organizations, Public Health, Research/Studies Institutes

International: International Affairs, International Organizations

Religion: Churches

Science: Scientific Centers & Institutes

Social Services: At-Risk Youth, Child Abuse, Child Welfare, Community Centers, Community Service Organizations, Day Care, Domestic Violence, Family

Planning, Family Services, Food/Clothing Distribution, Senior Services, Shelters/Homelessness, Substance Abuse, United Funds/United Ways, Volunteer Services, YMCA/YWCA/YMHA/YWHA, Youth Organizations

Application Procedures

Initial Contact: Applicants should request a copy of guidelines before sending letter of inquiry. If the proposed project meets the basic funding criteria of the grantmaking program, applicants are asked to submit a formal proposal.

Application Requirements: The letter of inquiry should be signed by the head of the applicant's organization and should address: the need for the proposed program; the nature of the program, including objectives, target population(s), and action plan; ways that the program is consistent with the endowment's strategy in this area; staff and organizational qualifications for carrying out program; how the program is distinguished from similar programs; estimated cost and amount of funding requested; and the method by which the project's effectiveness will be monitored and measured. The proposal should include: a list of the program's board of directors; the organization's budget, including projected income sources and average contribution per member for membership organizations; the organization's most recent audit and financial statement, IRS determination letter, and a line-item budget (revenues and expenses) for the proposed project.

Deadlines: None.

Review Process: The board of trustees meets twice annually to award grants. Written notification of decisions made on grants will be mailed within a few weeks of the meetings.

Notes: The Heinz Endowments has separate guideline brochures for each of the following program areas: Arts and Culture, Economic Opportunity, Education Environment and Health and Human Services. These are available in print format, or by accessing the website.

Restrictions

Individuals and for-profit organizations are not eligible for funding. Grants are awarded primarily to organizations in southwestern Pennsylvania, and exclusively for projects that benefit Pennsylvania and its residents.

Additional Information

The Howard Heinz Endowment operates jointly with the Vira I. Heinz Endowment.

A representative of Mellon Bank serves as a corporate trustee for the endowment.

Each program area is reviewed every five years; program guidelines are revised accordingly.

Publications: Annual Report; Guidelines; Newsletters; Special Report

Foundation Officials

Carol R. Brown: director

Frank Vondell Cahouet: director B Cohasset, MA 1932. ED Harvard University BA (1954); University of Pennsylvania Wharton School MBA (1959). PRIM CORP EMPL chairman, president, chief executive officer, director: Mellon Bank NA. CORP AFFIL director: Saint-Gobain Corp.; director: Allegheny Teledyne Inc.; director: Avery Dennison Corp.; chairman: Allegheny General Hospital. NONPR AFFIL trustee: Carnegie-Mellon University; trustee: University Pittsburgh.

Drue Heinz: director emeritus

H. John Heinz, IV: director

Teresa Heinz: chairwoman B Mozambique 1938. ED University of the Witwatersrand BA (1959). NONPR AFFIL cons: UN Trusteeship; trustee: Yale University Art Gallery; director trustee: Phillips Exeter Academy; director trustee: Saint Pauls School; trustee: National Gallery Art; director: Ovation Inc.; founder: National Council Families & Television; director trustee:

Georgetown University; chairman environ policy: John F. Kennedy School Government; vice chairman: Environmental Defense Fund; director: Family Communications Inc.; director: Carnegie Institute; member advisory board: Earth Committee Office; trustee emeritus: Brookings Institution.

Howard McClintic Love: director B Pittsburgh, PA 1930. ED Colgate University (1952); Harvard University Graduate School of Business Administration (1956). CORP AFFIL director: COMSAT Corp.; director: Monsanto Co.; director: AEA Investors Inc. CLUB AFFIL Pittsburgh Golf Club; Rolling Rock Club; The Links Club; Masons Club; Colony Club; Fox Chapel Golf Club.

Shirley M. Malcom: director PRIM NONPR EMPL head education and human resources programs: American Association for the Advancement of Science.

William H. Rea: director B Pittsburgh, PA 1912. PRIM CORP EMPL director: Colt Industries Inc.

Barbara K. Robinson: director

Frederick W. Thieman: director

Mallory Walker: director B Washington, DC 1939. ED University of Virginia (1958-1963). PRIM CORP EMPL president, director: Walker & Dunlop. CORP AFFIL director: Charles E Smith Residential Realty Inc. NONPR AFFIL member: Mortgage Bankers Association of America; member: Urban Land Institute; trustee: Greater Washington Research Center; member: American Society Real Estate Counsel; trustee: Federal City Council.

Grants Analysis

Disclosure Period: calendar year ending 2001

Total Grants: $54,308,822*

Number of Grants: 324

Average Grant: $149,563*

Highest Grant: $6,000,000

Lowest Grant: $1,000

Typical Range: $2,000 to $20,000 and $50,000 to $500,000

*Note: Giving excludes United Way. Average grant figure excludes highest grant.

Recent Grants

Note: Grants derived from 2001 Form 990.

General

3,750,000	Sports and Exhibition Authority of Pittsburgh and Allegheny County, Pittsburgh, PA -- To support Phase One of the North Shore Riverfront Park
1,000,000	Carnegie Mellon University, Pittsburgh, PA -- Operating and research support in medical robotics and information technology
1,000,000	Community Loan Fund of Southwestern Pennsylvania, Pittsburgh, PA -- For the green building loan fund
1,000,000	Pittsburgh Foundation, Pittsburgh, PA -- For the Frick Nine Mile Run Trust
1,000,000	University of Pittsburgh, Pittsburgh, PA -- To perform the management of the ECI model demonstration in two communities Braddock and Wilkinsburg
1,000,000	University of Pittsburgh, Pittsburgh, PA -- For University initiatives in International Studies, Environment Studies, and School Improvement
940,000	Sarah Heinz House Association, Pittsburgh, PA -- For operating support
850,000	Pittsburgh Cultural Trust, Pittsburgh, PA -- for operating support
794,140	United Way Allegheny County, Pittsburgh, PA -- CANCELLED $6,205,860 on 4/26/2001 to support the Early Childhood Initiative (ECI)
769,000	United Way Allegheny County, Pittsburgh, PA -- To support the 2000/2001 annual campaign

Vira I. Heinz Endowment

Giving Contact

Maxwell King, President
30 Dominion Tower
625 Liberty Avenue
Pittsburgh, PA 15222-3199
Phone: (412)281-5777
Fax: (412)281-5788
E-mail: info@heinz.org
Web: http://www.heinz.org

Description

Founded: 1986
EIN: 251762825
Organization Type: General Purpose Foundation
Giving Locations: PA: Southwest Pennsylvania
Grant Types: Capital, General Support, Multiyear/Continuing Support, Operating Expenses.

Donor Information

Founder: In a city known for its active and concerned civic leaders, Vira Ingham Heinz was among the foremost. Born Vira M. Ingham in what is now the Brighton Heights district of Pittsburgh, in 1932 she married Clifford S. Heinz, son of Henry J. Heinz, founder of the food processing company.

Mrs. Heinz actively engaged in the philanthropic and civic work for which she is now remembered. She was vice president of the World Council of Christian Education and an active supporter of its works in Africa. She was a founder of the Civic Light Opera, president and principal benefactor of the Pittsburgh Youth Symphony, and a member of the boards of the Pittsburgh Chamber Music Society, the Pittsburgh Opera, and the Pittsburgh Symphony Society.

Mrs. Heinz received the Chancellor's Medal from the University of Pittsburgh and honorary degrees from eleven colleges and universities. She was a trustee of Chatham College and the first woman trustee of Carnegie Mellon University. She served as a member of College Hospital Administrators. As a member of the Board of Directors of the H.J. Heinz Company, she was the first woman board member of a multinational corporation headquartered in Pittsburgh. In the spirit of the generosity that characterized her life, Vira I. Heinz's will provided for the establishment Vira I. Heinz Endowment in 1986.

Financial Summary

Total Giving: $18,506,696 (2001); $24,387,151 (2000); $22,621,276 (1998)
Giving Analysis: Giving for 1998 includes: foundation grants to United Way ($1,050,000) 1997: foundation grants to United Way ($1,100,000)
Assets: $468,932,556 (2001); $526,725,527 (2000); $500,921,314 (1998)

Typical Recipients

Arts & Humanities: Arts Associations & Councils, Arts Centers, Arts Funds, Arts Outreach, Ballet, Community Arts, Dance, Ethnic & Folk Arts, Arts & Humanities-General, Historic Preservation, History & Archaeology, Libraries, Museums/Galleries, Music, Opera, Performing Arts, Public Broadcasting, Theater, Visual Arts

Civic & Public Affairs: African American Affairs, Business/Free Enterprise, Community Foundations, Economic Development, Economic Policy, Employment/Job Training, Civic & Public Affairs-General, Housing, Legal Aid, Municipalities/Towns, Parades/Festivals, Philanthropic Organizations, Professional & Trade Associations, Public Policy, Urban & Community Affairs, Urban & Community Affairs, Zoos/Aquariums

Education: Afterschool/Enrichment Programs, Arts/Humanities Education, Business Education, Business-School Partnerships, Colleges & Universities,

Community & Junior Colleges, Economic Education, Education Associations, Education Funds, Education Reform, Elementary Education (Public), Engineering/ Technological Education, Environmental Education, Faculty Development, Education-General, International Studies, Leadership Training, Literacy, Medical Education, Minority Education, Preschool Education, Private Education (Precollege), Public Education (Precollege), Religious Education, School Volunteerism, Science/Mathematics Education, Secondary Education (Public), Student Aid, Vocational & Technical Education

Environment: Energy, Forestry, Environment-General, Environment-General, Protection, Research, Resource Conservation, Watershed, Wildlife Protection

Health: Adolescent Health Issues, Cancer, Children's Health/Hospitals, Geriatric Health, Health Policy/Cost Containment, Health Organizations, Hospitals, Medical Research, Mental Health, Single-Disease Health Associations

International: Foreign Arts Organizations, Health Care/Hospitals, International Affairs, International Environmental Issues, International Organizations, Missionary/Religious Activities

Religion: Churches, Jewish Causes, Ministries, Religious Organizations, Religious Welfare, Seminaries

Science: Scientific Centers & Institutes

Social Services: At-Risk Youth, Big Brother/Big Sister, Camps, Child Welfare, Community Service Organizations, Crime Prevention, Day Care, Delinquency & Criminal Rehabilitation, Domestic Violence, Emergency Relief, Family Planning, Family Services, Food/Clothing Distribution, Homes, Recreation & Athletics, Scouts, Senior Services, Sexual Abuse, Shelters/Homelessness, Social Services-General, Substance Abuse, United Funds/United Ways, Volunteer Services, YMCA/YWCA/YMHA/YWHA, Youth Organizations

Application Procedures

Initial Contact: Applicants should request a copy of the guidelines before sending a letter of inquiry. If the endowment feels the proposal merits further consideration, a full proposal will be requested.

Application Requirements: The letter of inquiry should be signed by the head of the applicant organization of its board and should address: the need for the proposed program; the objectives, target population(s), and action plan for the program; an explanation of how the program is consistent with the endowment's strategy for its area of significance; staff and organizational qualifications; how the program is distinguished from similar programs; the estimated cost and amount of funding requested; and the method by which the project's impact will be monitored and measured. The formal proposal should include: a list of the organization's board of directors; the organization's budget, including projected income sources, and average contribution per member for membership organizations; a recent financial statement and an independent auditor's report thereof; a letter from the IRS confirming tax exempt public charity status; and a line-item budget (revenues and expenses) for the proposed project. Proposal materials should not be included with the initial letter of inquiry.

Deadlines: None.

Review Process: The trustees meet twice annually to award grants. Written notification of decisions made on grants will be mailed within a few weeks of meeting.

Notes: Letters of inquiry will be presented to the Howard Heinz Endowment as well as the Vira I Heinz Endowment. There is no need for organizations to submit applications to each endowment separately.

Restrictions

Individuals and for-profit organizations are not eligible for funding.

Grants are awarded primarily to organizations in Southwestern Pennsylvania and exclusively for projects that benefit Pennsylvania and its residents.

Additional Information

The Vira I Heinz Endowment operates jointly with the Howard Heinz Endowment.

A representative of Mellon Bank serves as a corporate trustee for the endowment.

Publications: Annual Report

Foundation Officials

John Carter Brown: director B Providence, RI 1934. ED Harvard University AB (1956); Harvard University MBA (1958); University of Munich postgrad (1958). PRIM NONPR EMPL director emeritus: National Gallery Art. CORP AFFIL chairman: Ovation Inc.; director: Nordstern Insurance Co. America. NONPR AFFIL treasurer: White House Historical Association; trustee: World Monuments Fund; member, honorary trustee: Touro Synagogue National Heritage Trust; chairman: U.S. Commission of Fine Arts; member: State Hermitage Museum Advisory Board; trustee: Storm King Art Center; chairman: Pritzker Architecture Prize Jury; honorary fellow: Royal Academy Arts; trustee: National Geographic Society; member: Phi Beta Kappa; member: National Advisory Council Leonard Bernstein Center Education Arts; chairman: National Cultural Alliance; chairman: Leadership Council; fellow: National Academy Design; trustee: John F. Kennedy Center Performing Arts; trustee: Federal City Council; treasurer, member: Federal Council Arts & Humanities; board governors, trustee: Brown University; director, member: Committee Preservation White House; trustee: John Nicolas Brown Center Study American Civilization; board governors: John Carter Brown Library Association; chairman: Arts Network; member, honorary life trustee: Association Art Museum Directors; honorary member: American Institute Architects; member: American Philosophical Society; trustee: American Academy Rome; trustee: American Federation Arts; fellow: American Academy of Arts & Sciences.

Andre T. Heinz: director

Teresa Heinz: director B Mozambique 1938. ED University of the Witwatersrand BA (1959). NONPR AFFIL cons: UN Trusteeship; trustee: Yale University Art Gallery; director trustee: Phillips Exeter Academy; director trustee: Saint Pauls School; trustee: National Gallery Art; director: Ovation Inc.; founder: National Council Families & Television; director trustee: Georgetown University; chairman environ policy: John F. Kennedy School Government; vice chairman: Environmental Defense Fund; director: Family Communications Inc.; director: Carnegie Institute; member advisory board: Earth Committee Office; trustee emeritus: Brookings Institution.

Jack E. Kime: chief financial officer

Maxwell King: executive director

Wendy Jacobus McKenzie: director

William H. Rea: director B Pittsburgh, PA 1912. PRIM CORP EMPL director: Colt Industries Inc.

Franklin Tugwell: executive director

James Mellon Walton: chairman B Pittsburgh, PA 1930. ED Yale University BA (1953); Harvard University MBA (1958). PRIM CORP EMPL vice chairman, director: MMC Group Inc. NONPR AFFIL member sponsoring comm: Pennsylvania Southwest Association; director: World Affairs Council Pittsburgh; director: Irish Investment Fund Inc.; director: One Hundred Friends Pittsburgh Art; life trustee: Carnegie-Mellon University; member: Cultural District Development Committee; treasurer: Carnegie Hero Fund Commission.

Konrad M. Weis: director B Leipzig, Germany 1928. ED University of Bonn PhD (1955). PRIM CORP EMPL chairman, director: AGFA Division Miles. CORP AFFIL director: PNC Equity Management Corp.; director: Titan Pharmaceuticals; director: Dravo Corp.; director: Leipzig Trade Fair Corp.; honorary chairman: Bayer Corp.; director: Biological Detection Systems. NONPR AFFIL life trustee: The Carnegie Institute; life trustee: Carnegie-Mellon University.

Grants Analysis

Disclosure Period: calendar year ending 2001
Total Grants: $18,496,696*
Number of Grants: 200
Average Grant: $92,483
Highest Grant: $1,000,000
Lowest Grant: $1,000
Typical Range: $20,000 to $250,000
*Note: Giving excludes United Way.

Recent Grants

Note: Grants derived from 2001 Form 990.

Library-Related

1,000,000 Carnegie Library of Pittsburgh, Pittsburgh, PA -- for expansion of the eNetwork

General

1,307,385 H. John Heinz III Center for Science, Economics, and the Environment, Washington, DC -- to create a new independent institution that will do applied research on environmental issues

1,000,000 University of Pittsburgh, Pittsburgh, PA -- for University initiatives in International Studies

1,000,000 Western Pennsylvania Conservancy, Mill Run, PA -- for the restoration of Fallingwater

500,000 Elizabeth Glass Workshop, Inc., Pittsburgh, PA -- to support the Pittsburgh Glass Center Project

400,000 Carnegie Institute, Pittsburgh, PA -- for the school performance network

377,328 Mid-Atlantic Arts Foundation, Baltimore, MD -- for expansion of the PennPAT Program to the Mid Atlantic Region

300,000 Pittsburgh Opera, Inc., Pittsburgh, PA -- for the Artistic Excellence Project

300,000 Pittsburgh Regional Alliance, Pittsburgh, PA -- to support regional economic development activities

292,000 Pennsylvania Environmental Council, Philadelphia, PA -- for continued funding of the Council's Western Pennsylvania watershed protection and education efforts

250,000 Brookings Institution, Washington, DC -- for Smart Growth education and assistance in Southwestern Pennsylvania

HEINZ FAMILY FOUNDATION

Giving Contact

Teresa Heinz, Chairperson & Chief Executive Officer
32 Dominion Tower
625 Liberty Avenue
Pittsburgh, PA 15222
Phone: (412)497-5775

Description

Founded: 1984
EIN: 251689382
Organization Type: Private Foundation
Giving Locations: PA: some giving nationally.
Grant Types: Fellowship, General Support, Matching.

Donor Information

Founder: Teresa and H. John Heinz III Charitable Trust

Financial Summary

Total Giving: $6,375,393 (2000); $7,186,531 (1999); $6,585,123 (1998)

Giving Analysis: Giving for 2000 includes: foundation grants to United Way ($11,000); foundation gifts

to individuals ($1,083,192); 1999: foundation fellowships ($10,000); foundation grants to United Way ($11,000) foundation gifts to individuals ($1,119,021).
Assets: $76,299,076 (2000); $74,073,082 (1999); $81,339,192 (1998)
Gifts Received: $7,063,955 (2000); $6,663,955 (1998); $6,663,955 (1996). Note: Contributions were received from Teresa and H. John Heinz III Charitable Trust, H. John Heinz III Charitable and Family Trust and the Howard Heinz Endowment.

Typical Recipients

Arts & Humanities: Community Arts, Film & Video, Arts & Humanities-General, History & Archaeology, Libraries, Museums/Galleries, Music, Performing Arts, Public Broadcasting
Civic & Public Affairs: Botanical Gardens/Parks, Business/Free Enterprise, Economic Development, Economic Policy, Employment/Job Training, Civic & Public Affairs-General, Philanthropic Organizations, Professional & Trade Associations, Public Policy, Safety, Women's Affairs
Education: Arts/Humanities Education, Business Education, Colleges & Universities, Engineering/Technological Education, Environmental Education, Faculty Development, Education-General, Gifted & Talented Programs, International Studies, International Exchange, Literacy, Medical Education, Minority Education, Private Education (Precollege), Science/Mathematics Education, Social Sciences Education
Environment: Energy, Environment-General, Resource Conservation, Wildlife Protection
Health: AIDS/HIV, Cancer, Children's Health/Hospitals, Clinics/Medical Centers, Health Policy/Cost Containment, Medical Rehabilitation, Medical Research, Prenatal Health Issues, Public Health, Research/Studies Institutes
International: Foreign Educational Institutions, Human Rights, International Affairs, International Environmental Issues, International Relations, International Relief Efforts
Religion: Jewish Causes, Religious Welfare
Science: Scientific Centers & Institutes
Social Services: At-Risk Youth, Child Welfare, Family Services, Recreation & Athletics, United Funds/United Ways

Application Procedures

Initial Contact: The foundation has no formal grant application procedure or application form. Send a brief letter of inquiry.
Application Requirements: Include a description of organization, type and amount of funding, budget information, and proof of tax-exempt status.
Deadlines: None.

Foundation Officials

Rose Gibson: assistant secretary
Andre Heinz: director
Teresa Heinz: chairperson, chief executive officer B Mozambique 1938. ED University of the Witwatersrand BA (1959). NONPR AFFIL cons: UN Trusteeship; trustee: Yale University Art Gallery; director trustee: Phillips Exeter Academy; director trustee: Saint Pauls School; trustee: National Gallery Art; director: Ovation Inc.; founder: National Council Families & Television; director trustee: Georgetown University; chairman environ policy: John F. Kennedy School Government; vice chairman: Environmental Defense Fund; director: Family Communications Inc.; director: Carnegie Institute; member advisory board: Earth Committee Office; trustee emeritus: Brookings Institution.
Jack E. Kime: chief financial officer
Jeffrey R. Lewis: executive director, chief operating officer
Wendy Jacobus Mackenzie: secretary
Joan D. McCauley: director
John R. Taylor: investment officer

Grants Analysis

Disclosure Period: calendar year ending 2000
Total Grants: $5,281,201*
Number of Grants: 192
Average Grant: $27,506
Highest Grant: $1,000,000
Typical Range: $500 to $250,000
*Note: Giving excludes gifts to individuals and United Way.

Recent Grants

Note: Grants derived from 2000 Form 990.

General

1,000,000	Carnegie Mellon University, Pittsburgh, PA -- endowment purposes
500,000	Harvard University, Cambridge, MA -- Heinz Challenge Fund
340,000	St. Luke's Regional Medical Center, Boise, ID -- Wood River Valley EMS study
250,000	H. John Heinz III Center for Science, Economics, and Environment, Washington, DC -- endowment
250,000	Sun Valley Ski Education Foundation, Sun Valley, ID -- operating support
250,000	University of Arkansas Foundation, Little Rock, AR -- distinguished professorship
150,000	Environmental Defense Fund, New York, NY -- operating support
150,000	National Gallery of Art, Washington, DC -- educational endowment
125,000	Pennsylvania Public School Health Care Trust, Hermitage, PA -- operating support
100,000	Maryland Public Broadcasting Foundation, Owings Mills, MD -- continued production and distribution of HealthWeek

DRUE HEINZ TRUST

Giving Contact

Julia V. Shea, Foundation Manager
c/o Drue Heinz Office
PO Box 68
FDR Station
New York, NY 10150
Phone: (212)371-5757
Fax: (212)759-0479

Description

Founded: 1954
EIN: 256018930
Organization Type: General Purpose Foundation
Giving Locations: NY: New York; United Kingdom
Grant Types: Award, General Support, Multiyear/Continuing Support, Project.

Financial Summary

Total Giving: $2,322,696 (2001); $2,251,761 (2000); $2,371,584 (1998)
Assets: $34,708,794 (2001); $39,274,369 (2000); $46,639,354 (1998)
Gifts Received: $3,836 (1995); $1,686,244 (1994); $88,537 (1993)

Typical Recipients

Arts & Humanities: Arts Appreciation, Arts Associations & Councils, Arts Centers, Arts Funds, Arts Institutes, Arts Outreach, Ballet, Community Arts, Dance, Film & Video, Arts & Humanities-General, Historic Preservation, History & Archaeology, Libraries, Literary Arts, Museums/Galleries, Music, Opera, Performing Arts, Public Broadcasting, Theater, Visual Arts
Civic & Public Affairs: African American Affairs, Botanical Gardens/Parks, Ethnic Organizations, Civic & Public Affairs-General, Law & Justice, Philanthropic Organizations, Professional & Trade Associations,

Public Policy, Urban & Community Affairs, Women's Affairs, Zoos/Aquariums
Education: Afterschool/Enrichment Programs, Arts/Humanities Education, Colleges & Universities, Continuing Education, Education Reform, Elementary Education (Private), Education-General, International Studies, Literacy, Medical Education, Private Education (Precollege), Social Sciences Education, Student Aid
Environment: Air/Water Quality, Environment-General, Wildlife Protection
Health: AIDS/HIV, Cancer, Children's Health/Hospitals, Clinics/Medical Centers, Emergency/Ambulance Services, Eyes/Blindness, Geriatric Health, Hospitals, Medical Rehabilitation, Medical Research, Single-Disease Health Associations
International: Foreign Arts Organizations, Foreign Educational Institutions, International-General, Health Care/Hospitals, Human Rights, International Affairs, International Environmental Issues, International Organizations, International Peace & Security Issues, International Relations, Missionary/Religious Activities
Religion: Churches, Religious Organizations
Science: Scientific Centers & Institutes
Social Services: Child Welfare, Community Service Organizations, Emergency Relief, Family Planning, People with Disabilities, Scouts, Shelters/Homelessness, United Funds/United Ways, YMCA/YWCA/YMHA/YWHA, Youth Organizations

Application Procedures

Initial Contact: All requests should be submitted by letter.

Restrictions

The foundation generally limits funding to the London, England, and New York City geographic areas.

Additional Information

Trust(s): Mellon Bank NA

Foundation Officials

James F. Dolan: trustee
Drue Heinz: trustee

Grants Analysis

Disclosure Period: calendar year ending 2001
Total Grants: $2,322,696
Number of Grants: 76
Average Grant: $20,103*
Highest Grant: $815,000
Lowest Grant: $250
Typical Range: $5,000 to $50,000
*Note: Average grant figure excludes highest grant ($815,000).

Recent Grants

Note: Grants derived from 2001 Form 990.

Library-Related

20,000	Pierpont Morgan Library, New York, NY

General

815,000	Americans for Oxford, New York, NY
150,000	International Institute for Strategic Studies, London United Kingdom
100,000	American Academy in Rome, New York, NY
83,500	Royal Shakespeare Company America, Inc., New York, NY
75,000	Americans for Oxford, New York, NY
75,000	C A F America, Alexandria, VA
75,000	Pittsburgh Arts and Lectures, Pittsburgh, PA
70,000	Royal Oak Foundation, New York, NY -- support for Drue Heinz Lectures
50,000	Carnegie Museum of Art, Pittsburgh, PA
50,000	Charities Aid Foundation America, New York, NY

EVAN AND MARION HELFAER FOUNDATION

Giving Contact

Pat Denning, Co-Trustee & Administrator
735 North Water Street
Milwaukee, WI 53202
Phone: (414)287-7184
Fax: (414)276-0172

Description

Founded: 1971
EIN: 396238856
Organization Type: General Purpose Foundation
Giving Locations: WI: Milwaukee
Grant Types: Capital, General Support, Professorship, Research.

Donor Information

Founder: Established in 1971 by the late Evan P. Helfaer .

Financial Summary

Total Giving: $948,760 (fiscal year ending July 31, 2001); $1,898,500 (fiscal 1999); $1,139,622 (fiscal 1998)
Assets: $26,851,186 (fiscal 2001); $27,294,828 (fiscal 1999); $26,097,538 (fiscal 1998)

Typical Recipients

Arts & Humanities: Arts Centers, Arts Festivals, Community Arts, Dance, Libraries, Museums/Galleries, Music, Opera, Performing Arts, Theater
Civic & Public Affairs: Botanical Gardens/Parks, Employment/Job Training, Civic & Public Affairs-General, Hispanic Affairs, Municipalities/Towns, Parades/Festivals, Urban & Community Affairs, Zoos/Aquariums
Education: Arts/Humanities Education, Business Education, Colleges & Universities, Education Funds, Engineering/Technological Education, Faculty Development, Health & Physical Education, Leadership Training, Medical Education, Private Education (Precollege), Public Education (Precollege), Secondary Education (Private), Secondary Education (Public), Student Aid
Environment: Environment-General
Health: Cancer, Children's Health/Hospitals, Clinics/Medical Centers, Geriatric Health, Health Organizations, Heart, Hospitals, Medical Research, Mental Health, Nursing Services, Public Health, Single-Disease Health Associations, Transplant Networks/Donor Banks
International: Foreign Arts Organizations, Health Care/Hospitals, Trade
Religion: Churches, Jewish Causes, Religious Organizations, Religious Welfare
Social Services: Animal Protection, Child Abuse, Child Welfare, Community Centers, Community Service Organizations, Counseling, Family Services, Food/Clothing Distribution, Homes, People with Disabilities, Recreation & Athletics, Scouts, Social Services-General, Substance Abuse, United Funds/United Ways, United Funds/United Ways, YMCA/YWCA/YMHA/YWHA, Youth Organizations

Application Procedures

Initial Contact: Organizations should request the foundation's application form.
Deadlines: None.

Restrictions

Grants are not made to individuals. or to organizations outside Wisconsin.

Foundation Officials

Thomas L. Smallwood: co-trustee, admin

Grants Analysis

Disclosure Period: fiscal year ending July 31, 2001
Total Grants: $948,760
Number of Grants: 118
Average Grant: $6,400*
Highest Grant: $100,000
Lowest Grant: $100
Typical Range: $1,000 to $10,000
*Note: Average grant figure excludes hightes grant.

Recent Grants

Note: Grants derived from 2001 Form 990.

General

100,000	Marquette University, Milwaukee, WI -- for John P. Raynor Library
100,000	University of Wisconsin Foundation, Milwaukee, WI
100,000	University of Wisconsin Madison, Madison, WI -- for the School of Pharmacy
50,000	Great Circus Parade, Milwaukee, WI
50,000	Medical College of Wisconsin, Milwaukee, WI -- for the Cancer Care Center
50,000	Milwaukee Art Museum, Milwaukee, WI -- capital campaign
25,000	Milwaukee School of Engineering, Milwaukee, WI
20,000	Boys and Girls Club, Milwaukee, WI -- for the James Center at Whitcomb
20,000	Child Abuse Prevention Fund, Milwaukee, WI
20,000	Medical College of Wisconsin, Milwaukee, WI -- for Family House

CLARENCE E. HELLER CHARITABLE FOUNDATION

Giving Contact

Bruce A. Hirsch, Executive Director
1 Lombard St., Suite 305
San Francisco, CA 94111
Phone: (415)989-9839
Fax: (415)989-1909
Web: http://www.cerritos.edu/cerritos/development/funders_heller.html

Description

Founded: 1982
EIN: 942814266
Organization Type: Private Foundation
Giving Locations: CA
Grant Types: General Support, Research, Scholarship, Seed Money.

Donor Information

Founder: the late Clarence E. Heller

Financial Summary

Total Giving: $2,108,113 (2000); $1,739,794 (1999); $1,600,937 (1998)
Giving Analysis: Giving for 1996 includes: foundation scholarships ($35,800)
Assets: $45,198,847 (2000); $46,084,889 (1999); $42,039,507 (1998)
Gifts Received: $4,024,706 (1994); $6,596,349 (1993)

Typical Recipients

Arts & Humanities: Arts Centers, Arts Outreach, History & Archaeology, Libraries, Music, Theater
Civic & Public Affairs: Community Foundations, Employment/Job Training, Legal Aid, Nonprofit Management, Public Policy, Rural Affairs
Education: Agricultural Education, Arts/Humanities Education, Colleges & Universities, Elementary Education (Public), Environmental Education, Faculty Development, Literacy, Private Education (Precollege),

Public Education (Precollege), School Volunteerism, Science/Mathematics Education, Student Aid
Environment: Energy, Forestry, Environment-General, Protection, Research, Resource Conservation
Health: AIDS/HIV, Medical Research, Public Health, Research/Studies Institutes
International: International Development, International Environmental Issues, International Organizations, International Relations, Trade
Science: Scientific Organizations, Scientific Research
Social Services: Shelters/Homelessness

Application Procedures

Initial Contact: Send a brief letter of inquiry.
Application Requirements: Include project description, amount requested, both project and annual budgets, and a description of organization. Foundation will request a full proposal.
Deadlines: None; the board meets three times each year.

Foundation Officials

Anne Heller Anderson: secretary, trustee
Peter B. Harckham: secretary, trustee
Alfred E. Heller: president, trustee
Katherine Heller: secretary, trustee
Miranda Heller: vice president, trustee
Bruce A. Hirsch: executive director
Elizabeth H. Mandell: president, trustee
Sarah Coade Mandell: secretary, trustee

Grants Analysis

Disclosure Period: calendar year ending 2000
Total Grants: $2,108,113
Number of Grants: 48
Average Grant: $43,919
Highest Grant: $200,000
Typical Range: $20,000 to $100,000

Recent Grants

Note: Grants derived from 1999 Form 990.

General

200,000	Environmental Defense, Oakland, CA -- educate public about human health risks of toxic chemicals
100,000	Environmental Working Group, Washington, DC -- analyze and disseminate new information on the environmental health threats posed by toxic chemicals
80,000	Tides Center, San Francisco, CA -- research and public policy project aimed at developing a long-term agenda for sustainable agriculture in California
75,000	Early Childhood Resources, Corte Madera, CA -- for a project to extend developmentally appropriate practices to upper elementary classrooms
75,000	Pesticide Action Network, San Francisco, CA -- support Californians for Pesticide Reform
75,000	Sonoma State University Foundation, Rohnert Park, CA -- support of the California Interactive Mathematics Program
75,000	Sustainable Cotton Project, Oroville, CA -- support of on-farm advice for organic cotton farmers and a marketing program for organic cotton
70,000	Redefining Progress, San Francisco, CA -- policy research on the role of common assets in protecting and restoring ecosystem health and promoting sustainable agriculture
60,000	Developmental Studies Center, Oakland, CA -- for the Preserve Initiative to restructure teacher training at colleges and universities
55,000	Center for Ecoliteracy, Berkeley, CA -- project to implement a food policy that provides organic meals to public school

students and supports regional agriculture

HELMERICH FOUNDATION

Giving Contact
Walter H. Helmerich, III, Trustee
1579 East 21st Street
Tulsa, OK 74114
Phone: (918)742-5531

Description
Founded: 1965
EIN: 736105607
Organization Type: Family Foundation
Giving Locations: OK: Tulsa
Grant Types: Capital, Endowment, Scholarship.

Donor Information
Founder: Established in 1965 by the late W.H. Helmerich .

Financial Summary
Total Giving: $4,418,000 (fiscal year ending September 30, 2002; $4,535,000 (fiscal 2001); $4,280,500 (fiscal 2000). Note: Fiscal 1997 Giving includes scholarship ($65,000).
Giving Analysis: Giving for fiscal 2001 includes: foundation scholarships ($25,000)
Assets: $67,844,728 (fiscal 2002); $81,527,787 (fiscal 2001); $92,587,952 (fiscal 2000)

Typical Recipients
Arts & Humanities: Arts Centers, Ballet, Historic Preservation, History & Archaeology, Libraries, Literary Arts, Museums/Galleries, Music, Opera, Performing Arts
Civic & Public Affairs: African American Affairs, Botanical Gardens/Parks, Clubs, Community Foundations, Civic & Public Affairs-General, Housing, Parades/Festivals, Public Policy, Safety, Urban & Community Affairs, Women's Affairs, Zoos/Aquariums
Education: Business Education, Colleges & Universities, Education Funds, Education Reform, Elementary Education (Public), Education-General, International Studies, Literacy, Preschool Education, Private Education (Precollege), Public Education (Precollege), Religious Education, School Volunteerism, Science/Mathematics Education, Secondary Education (Private), Student Aid
Environment: Environment-General, Wildlife Protection
Health: AIDS/HIV, Cancer, Children's Health/Hospitals, Clinics/Medical Centers, Diabetes, Emergency/Ambulance Services, Eyes/Blindness, Health Organizations, Hospices, Mental Health, Nursing Services, Public Health, Respiratory
International: Foreign Educational Institutions
Religion: Bible Study/Translation, Ministries, Religious Organizations, Religious Welfare, Seminaries
Social Services: Child Welfare, Community Service Organizations, Crime Prevention, Day Care, Domestic Violence, Family Services, Food/Clothing Distribution, Homes, People with Disabilities, People with Disabilities, Recreation & Athletics, Scouts, Senior Services, Shelters/Homelessness, YMHA/YWCA/YMHA/YWHA, Youth Organizations

Application Procedures
Initial Contact: The foundation does not publish an official grant application form. Applicants should send request letters directly to the foundation.
Deadlines: None.

Restrictions
Grants are limited to the Tulsa, OK, area and will focus primarily on large capital needs. The foundation does not make grants to individuals, matching gifts,

fellowships, emergency funds, deficit financing, research, operating budgets, demonstration projects, conferences, publications, or loans.

Additional Information
Publications: Application Guidelines; Program Policy Statement

Foundation Officials
Walter Hugo Helmerich, III: trustee B Tulsa, OK 1921. ED University of Oklahoma BA (1948); Harvard University MBA (1950). PRIM CORP EMPL chairman, director: Helmerich & Payne Inc. ADD CORP EMPL chairman: Helmerich & Payne International Drilling; chairman: Helmerich & Payne Columbia Drilling Co.; chairman: Helmerich & Payne Trinidad Drilling; chairman: Helmerich & Payne de Venezuela. CORP AFFIL director: Atwood Oceanics Inc.

Grants Analysis
Disclosure Period: fiscal year ending September 30, 2002
Total Grants: $4,398,000*
Number of Grants: 52
Average Grant: $71,529*
Highest Grant: $750,000
Lowest Grant: $2,500
Typical Range: $20,000 to $100,000
*Note: Giving excludes scholarships. Average grant figure excludes highest grant.

Recent Grants
Note: Grants derived from fiscal 2002 Form 990.

General
750,000	Hillcrest Medical Center, Tulsa, OK -- capital improvements
522,500	Philbrook Museum of Art, Tulsa, OK -- for grounds and garden endowment
350,000	Monte Cassing School, Tulsa, OK -- for building campaign and renovations
250,000	Hospice and Visiting Nurse Association of the Florida Keys, Key West, FL -- operating support
250,000	Indian Nations Council Boy Scouts, Tulsa, OK -- for Scout Resource Center
250,000	Tulsa Day Center for the Homeless, Tulsa, OK -- for endowment funds
250,000	University of Oklahoma Foundation, Inc., Norman, OK -- for stadium
225,000	University of Tulsa, Tulsa, OK -- for athletic locker rooms
175,000	Salvation Army, Tulsa, OK -- building campaign
150,000	12 and 12 Corporation, Tulsa, OK -- for renovations

HENDERSON FOUNDATION

Giving Contact
Ernest Henderson, III, Trustee
PO Box 420
Sudbury, MA 01776
Phone: (978)449-4646

Description
Founded: 1947
EIN: 046051095
Organization Type: Private Foundation
Giving Locations: MA
Grant Types: General Support, Multiyear/Continuing Support.

Donor Information
Founder: the late Ernest Henderson, the late George B. Henderson, the late J. Brooks Fenno, Ernest Henderson III

Financial Summary
Total Giving: $852,000 (2000); $804,250 (1999); $785,000 (1998)
Giving Analysis: Giving for 2000 includes: foundation scholarships ($2,500); 1999: foundation scholarships ($2,500) 1998: foundation scholarships ($2,500)
Assets: $12,414,893 (2000); $14,951,298 (1999); $12,626,813 (1998)

Typical Recipients
Arts & Humanities: Ballet, Dance, Historic Preservation, History & Archaeology, Libraries, Literary Arts, Music, Public Broadcasting
Civic & Public Affairs: Botanical Gardens/Parks, Clubs, Civic & Public Affairs-General, Housing, Public Policy
Education: Business Education, Colleges & Universities, Economic Education, Education Funds, Education-General, Preschool Education, Private Education (Precollege), Student Aid
Health: Health-General, Hospitals, Medical Research, Nursing Services
International: Foreign Arts Organizations, International Peace & Security Issues, International Relations
Religion: Religious Welfare, Synagogues/Temples
Social Services: Child Welfare, Community Centers, Family Planning, Scouts, Scouts, Substance Abuse, United Funds/United Ways, Youth Organizations

Application Procedures
Initial Contact: Send a brief letter of inquiry.
Application Requirements: Include purpose of funds sought and proof of tax-exempt status.
Deadlines: None.

Restrictions
Does not support individuals or provide funds for scholarships or fellowships.

Foundation Officials
Barclay G. S. Henderson: trustee
Ernest Henderson, III: trustee B Boston, MA 1924. ED Harvard University SB (1944); Harvard University MBA (1949). PRIM CORP EMPL president, chief executive officer: Fidelity Product Corp. CORP AFFIL president: Henderson Houses Am; director: Boston Biotechnology Corp. NONPR AFFIL president: Sudbury Nursing Home; director: Wellesley Community Center; member: Chief Executives Organization; treasurer, director: Boston Biomedical Research Institute.
Joseph Carlton Petrone, Jr.: trustee

Grants Analysis
Disclosure Period: calendar year ending 2000
Total Grants: $849,500*
Number of Grants: 109
Average Grant: $7,794
Highest Grant: $50,000
Typical Range: $1,000 to $15,000
*Note: Giving excludes scholarships.

Recent Grants
Note: Grants derived from 1999 Form 990.

General
50,000	Bard College, Annandale-on-Hudson, NY
50,000	Boston Biomedical Research Institute, Boston, MA
50,000	New England Genealogical Society, Boston, MA
40,000	Northeastern University, Boston, MA
35,000	Better Homes Foundation, Newton Center, MA
27,000	Wellesley Community Center, Wellesley, MA
25,000	Dartmouth College, Hanover, NH
25,000	Massachusetts Committee for Children and Youth, Boston, MA

| 21,000 | Boy Scouts of America, Newton, MA |
| 20,000 | Harvard Business School, Cambridge, MA |

GEORGE B. HENDERSON FOUNDATION

Giving Contact
Brenda Taylor
c/o Palmer & Dodge LLP
111 Huntington Avenue
Boston, MA 02199
Phone: (617)239-0556

Description
Founded: 1964
EIN: 046089310
Organization Type: Private Foundation
Giving Locations: MA: Boston
Grant Types: Capital, General Support.

Donor Information
Founder: the late George B. Henderson

Financial Summary
Total Giving: $667,503 (2001); $607,483 (2000); $545,646 (1999)
Assets: $11,681,901 (2001); $13,460,065 (2000); $13,938,645 (1999)

Typical Recipients
Arts & Humanities: Arts Associations & Councils, Arts Centers, Historic Preservation, History & Archaeology, Libraries, Museums/Galleries, Music, Public Broadcasting, Theater, Visual Arts
Civic & Public Affairs: African American Affairs, Botanical Gardens/Parks, Clubs, Economic Development, Civic & Public Affairs-General, Housing, Municipalities/Towns, Urban & Community Affairs, Women's Affairs, Zoos/Aquariums
Education: Colleges & Universities, Education Funds, Education-General, Secondary Education (Private)
Environment: Environment-General, Resource Conservation
Health: Clinics/Medical Centers, Health Organizations
Religion: Churches
Social Services: Community Centers, Community Service Organizations, Recreation & Athletics, Veterans, Youth Organizations

Application Procedures
Initial Contact: Send letter requesting application form.
Deadlines: None. Applicants are usually notified within three months.

Restrictions
Does not support individuals, endowment funds, or operating expenses. Grants solely for enhancement of physical appearance of Boston city.

Additional Information
Publications: Application Form

Foundation Officials
Thomas B. Adams: mem
Valerie Burns: secretary board designators
Robert Cormier: ex-officio member NONPR AFFIL member: Boston Art Commission.
Margaret DePopolo: mem
Henry Rice Guild, Jr.: trustee B Boston, MA 1928. ED Harvard University (1950-1953). PRIM CORP EMPL president: Guild Monrad & Oates. CORP AFFIL director: Tampa Electric Co.; director: TECO Energy Inc.
Pauline Chase Harrell: mem

Ernest Henderson, III: trustee B Boston, MA 1924. ED Harvard University SB (1944); Harvard University MBA (1949). PRIM CORP EMPL president, chief executive officer: Fidelity Product Corp. CORP AFFIL president: Henderson Houses Am; director: Boston Biotechnology Corp. NONPR AFFIL president: Sudbury Nursing Home; director: Wellesley Community Center; member: Chief Executives Organization; treasurer, director: Boston Biomedical Research Institute.
Gerald C. Henderson: trustee
John K. Herbert, III: trustee
Carol R. Johnson: chairman
Jane C. Nylander: ex-officio mem

Grants Analysis
Disclosure Period: calendar year ending 2001
Total Grants: $667,503
Number of Grants: 18
Average Grant: $24,589*
Highest Grant: $125,000
Typical Range: $10,000 to $50,000
*Note: Average grant figure excludes two highest grants ($225,000).

Recent Grants
Note: Grants derived from 2001 Form 990.

General
125,000	Allston Congregational Church, Boston, MA
100,000	Massachusetts Audubon Society, Boston, MA
65,580	Light Boston, Inc., Boston, MA
64,000	Historic Boston, Inc., Boston, MA
57,800	Union United Methodist Church, Boston, MA
50,000	Shirley Eustis House, Shirley, MA
34,600	Women's Educational and Industrial Union, Boston, MA
31,037	Christ Episcopal Church, Hyde Park, MA
29,875	Gibson House Museum, Boston, MA
18,811	Concord Square Association, Concord, MA

HENKEL CORP.

Company Headquarters
2200 Renaissance Boulevard, Suite 200
King of Prussia, PA 19406
Phone: (610)270-8100
Fax: (610)270-8104
Web: http://www.henkelcorp.com

Company Description
Employees: 3,315
SIC(s): 2819 Industrial Inorganic Chemicals Nec, 2821 Plastics Materials & Resins, 2899 Chemical Preparations Nec, 5169 Chemicals & Allied Products Nec.

Operating Locations
Emery Group Henkel Corp. (CA--Los Angeles); Henkel Adhesives Corp. (CA--Hayward); Henkel Chemical Specialities Division (PA--Ambler); Henkel Corp. (PA--Gulph Mills); Henkel Corp. Chemicals Group (OH--Cincinnati); Henkel Corp. Fine Chemicals Division (PA--Gulph Mills); Henkel Corp. Functional Products Division (IL--La Grange); Henkel Corp. Minerals Industry Division (AZ--Tucson); Henkel Corp. Polymers Division (IL--La Grange); Henkel Corp. Process Chemicals (GA--Cedartown); Henkel Corp. Textile Chemicals (NC--Charlotte); Henkel Organic Products Division (PA--Ambler); Henkel Surface Technologies (WI--Madison Heights)

Subsidiary Companies
CT: Henkel Loctite, Rocky Hill

Giving Contact
William B. Read, Vice President, Human Resources Services
The Triad, Suite 200
2200 Renaissance Blvd.
King of Prussia, PA 19406
Phone: (610)270-8100
Fax: (610)270-8102
E-mail: bill.read@henkel-americas.com
Web: http://www.henkelcorp.com

Description
Organization Type: Corporate Giving Program
Giving Locations: headquarters and operating communities.
Grant Types: General Support.

Typical Recipients
Arts & Humanities: Arts Centers, Dance, Historic Preservation, Libraries, Museums/Galleries, Music, Public Broadcasting, Theater
Civic & Public Affairs: Business/Free Enterprise, Civil Rights, Law & Justice, Municipalities/Towns, Safety, Women's Affairs, Zoos/Aquariums
Education: Colleges & Universities
Health: Hospitals
International: International Relations
Social Services: United Funds/United Ways

Application Procedures
Initial Contact: Send a brief letter of inquiry and a full proposal. Include a description of organization, amount and purpose of funds sought, and proof of tax-exempt status.

Restrictions
Program does not support political or religious organizations. Member agencies of united funds also will not be considered. Henkel Corp. divisions in Arizona, Illinois, Michigan, North Caroline, New Jersey, and Pennsylvania have independent giving programs.

Corporate Officials
John E. Knudson, Jr.: vice president, chief financial officer PRIM CORP EMPL vice president, chief financial officer: Henkel Corp.
Robert Lurcott: president, chief executive officer PRIM CORP EMPL president, chief executive officer: Henkel Corp.
Hans Dietrich Winkhaus: chairman, director PRIM CORP EMPL chairman, director: Henkel Corp.

Grants Analysis
Typical Range: $2,500 to $5,000

KEITH HENNEY TRUST

Giving Contact
Lenora Hurley, Trust Officer
PO Box 2
Eaton Center, NH 03832
Phone: (401)438-1810

Description
Founded: 1992
EIN: 026065480
Organization Type: Private Foundation
Grant Types: General Support, Scholarship.

Financial Summary
Total Giving: $27,065 (2001); $22,315 (1999); $35,556 (1998)
Giving Analysis: Giving for 2001 includes: foundation scholarships ($15,315); 1999: foundation scholarships ($6,400) 1998: foundation scholarships ($8,000)

Assets: $619,543 (2001); $673,137 (1999); $666,736 (1998)
Gifts Received: $250 (2001); $233 (1992). Note: In 2001, contributions were received from Christopher Burns.

Typical Recipients

Arts & Humanities: Arts & Humanities-General, Historic Preservation, History & Archaeology, Libraries
Civic & Public Affairs: Municipalities/Towns, Urban & Community Affairs
Education: Colleges & Universities
Religion: Churches

Application Procedures

Initial Contact: Request application procedures.
Deadlines: April 10.

Additional Information

Provides scholarships to graduates of Kennett High School in Eaton, NH.
Trust(s): Fleet Bank NH

Grants Analysis

Disclosure Period: calendar year ending 2001
Total Grants: $11,750*
Number of Grants: 6
*Note: Giving excludes scholarship.

Recent Grants

Note: Grants derived from 2000 Form 990.

Library-Related
7,601   Conway Public Library

General
2,500   Sandwich Historical Society
2,000   Freedom Historical Society
750   Colby College, Waterville, ME
750   Dartmouth College, Hanover, NH
750   University of New Hampshire, Durham, NH
694   Conway Historical Society
500   The Brownfield Historical Society
500   University of Maine Orono, Orono, ME
500   University of Maryland/Baltimore County, Baltimore, MD
500   University of South Carolina, Columbia, SC

RICHARD A. HENSON FOUNDATION

Giving Contact

Donna Ashby, Executive Director
PO Box 151
Salisbury, MD 21803
Phone: (410)742-7057
Fax: (410)742-4036

Description

Founded: 1989
EIN: 521642558
Organization Type: Private Foundation
Giving Locations: MD: Eastern Shore area, Salisbury
Grant Types: Capital, General Support, Operating Expenses, Project.

Donor Information

Founder: Richard A. Henson

Financial Summary

Total Giving: $213,603 (2001); $169,140 (2000); $713,700 (1999)
Giving Analysis: Giving for 2001 includes: foundation grants to United Way ($1,000); 1999: foundation grants to United Way ($1,000); 1998: foundation grants to United Way ($1,000) foundation ($947,095)

Assets: $8,459,248 (2001); $9,329,258 (2000); $9,881,947 (1999)
Gifts Received: $868,332 (2001); $226,000 (2000); $1,164,162 (1999). Note: In 1998, 1999, 2000 and 2001, contributions were received from Richard A. Henson.

Typical Recipients

Arts & Humanities: Libraries, Museums/Galleries
Civic & Public Affairs: Botanical Gardens/Parks, Chambers of Commerce, Community Foundations, Civic & Public Affairs-General, Housing, Municipalities/Towns, Parades/Festivals, Professional & Trade Associations, Public Policy, Safety, Urban & Community Affairs, Zoos/Aquariums
Education: Business Education, Colleges & Universities, Community & Junior Colleges, Preschool Education, Private Education (Precollege), Public Education (Precollege), Science/Mathematics Education
Health: Alzheimers Disease, Arthritis, Cancer, Children's Health/Hospitals, Clinics/Medical Centers, Health Organizations, Hospices, Hospitals
Religion: Churches, Religious Welfare
Social Services: Child Welfare, Community Service Organizations, Domestic Violence, Domestic Violence, Recreation & Athletics, Scouts, Shelters/Homelessness, Social Services-General, Substance Abuse, United Funds/United Ways, YMCA/YWCA/YMHA/YWHA, Youth Organizations

Application Procedures

Initial Contact: Send a brief letter of inquiry.
Application Requirements: Include a summary of scope and acts.
Deadlines: None.

Foundation Officials

Thomas H. Evans: trustee
Gordon D. Gladden: trustee
Richard A. Henson: chairman, trustee
C. Brooks Hubbert: treasurer, trustee
Thomas F. McCarthy: chairman, trustee
Jon Sherwell: trustee
Thomas L. Trice, IV: treasurer, trustee

Grants Analysis

Disclosure Period: calendar year ending 2001
Total Grants: $212,603*
Number of Grants: 24
Average Grant: $2,775*
Highest Grant: $56,000
Lowest Grant: $250
Typical Range: $1,000 to $20,000
*Note: Giving excludes United Way. Average grant excludes three highest grants ($146,000).

Recent Grants

Note: Grants derived from 2001 Form 990.

General
56,000   Boy Scouts of America
56,000   Salisbury State University Foundation, Salisbury, MD
38,000   Dorchester County YMCA, Boston, MA
20,000   West Salisbury Youth Club, Salisbury, MD
19,000   University of Maryland Eastern Shore Foundation, Princess Office, MD
5,000   Life Crisis Center, Salisbury, MD
5,000   Salisbury Neighborhood Housing Services, Salisbury, MD
3,853   Junior Achievement of the Eastern Shore, Salisbury, MD
3,000   Salisbury Substance Abuse, Salisbury, MD
2,000   Christian Shelter, Inc., Salisbury, MD

BOB L. HERD FOUNDATION

Giving Contact

Janice Thompson, Secretary & Treasurer
3901 Manhattan
Tyler, TX 75701
Phone: (903)509-3456

Description

Founded: 1994
EIN: 752530305
Organization Type: Private Foundation
Giving Locations: TX: Tyler
Grant Types: General Support.

Donor Information

Founder: Established in 1994 by Bob L. Herd.

Financial Summary

Total Giving: $383,500 (2000); $306,350 (1999); $245,700 (1998)
Giving Analysis: Giving for 2000 includes: foundation grants to United Way ($20,000); 1999: foundation grants to United Way ($20,000); 1998: foundation grants to United Way ($15,000) foundation ($230,000)
Assets: $9,106,149 (2000); $8,622,364 (1999); $8,143,240 (1998)
Gifts Received: $4,106,149 (2000); $1,000,000 (1998); $1,000,000 (1996). Note: In 1998 and 2000, contributions were received from Bob L. Herd.

Typical Recipients

Arts & Humanities: Libraries, Museums/Galleries, Music
Civic & Public Affairs: Clubs, Economic Policy, Civic & Public Affairs-General, Housing
Education: Business Education, Colleges & Universities, Community & Junior Colleges, Engineering/Technological Education, Medical Education, Private Education (Precollege), Public Education (Precollege), Secondary Education (Public), Student Aid
Health: Cancer, Health-General, Heart, Hospices, Hospitals (University Affiliated), Respiratory, Single-Disease Health Associations
International: Health Care/Hospitals
Religion: Churches, Religion-General, Religious Welfare
Social Services: Camps, Child Welfare, Community Centers, Community Service Organizations, Counseling, Crime Prevention, Domestic Violence, Family Services, Food/Clothing Distribution, Recreation & Athletics, Substance Abuse, United Funds/United Ways, Youth Organizations

Application Procedures

Initial Contact: The foundation requests applications be made in writing. Include proof of tax-exempt status.
Deadlines: None.

Foundation Officials

Bob L. Herd: president
Patsy L. Herd: vice president
Janice Thompson: secretary, treasurer

Grants Analysis

Disclosure Period: calendar year ending 2000
Total Grants: $363,500*
Number of Grants: 55
Average Grant: $4,787*
Highest Grant: $105,000
Lowest Grant: $500
Typical Range: $1,000 to $10,000
*Note: Giving excludes United Way. Average grant excludes highest grant.

Recent Grants

Note: Grants derived from 2001 Form 990.

General

101,000	Good Shepherd Episcopal, Dallas, TX
50,000	Texas State History Museum Foundation, Austin, TX
15,000	Marvin Methodist Church, Tyler, TX
15,000	United Way of Tyler/Smith County, Tyler, TX
10,000	American Cancer Society, Tyler, TX
10,000	Junior League of Tyler, Inc., Tyler, TX
10,000	PATH, Tyler, TX
6,300	Azleway Boys Ranch, Tyler, TX
5,000	American Heart Association, Tyler, TX
5,000	Habitat for Humanity, Tyler, TX

GROVER HERMANN FOUNDATION

Giving Contact

Katheryn V. Rhoads, Executive Director
1000 Hillgrove, Suite 200
Western Springs, IL 60558
Phone: (708)246-8331
Fax: (708)246-8319

Alternate Contact

PO Box 596
Pebble Beach, CA 93953
Note: Organizations in Monterey County, CA should use the alternate address.

Description

Founded: 1955
EIN: 366064489
Organization Type: Family Foundation
Giving Locations: IL: Chicago
Grant Types: Capital, Challenge, Endowment, Fellowship, General Support, Project, Research, Scholarship.

Donor Information

Founder: The Grover Hermann Foundation was established in 1955. Its donors are Grover Hermann and Sarah T. Hermann.

Financial Summary

Total Giving: $871,000 (2001); $936,500 (2000); $1,000,000 (1999 approx)
Assets: $13,953,283 (2001); $16,069,183 (2000); $14,911,003 (1998)
Gifts Received: $11,027,026 (1998). Note: In 1998, contributions were received from the Estate of Sarah T. Hermann ($6,302,612); Trust A U/W Grover M. Hermann ($4,284,986); Harriet Thurmond CRAT U/W Sarah T. Hermann ($245,744); Harriet Thurmond CRAT U/W Grover Hermann ($112,627); and Ruth Pooley West CRAT ($81,057).

Typical Recipients

Arts & Humanities: Arts Institutes, Ballet, Historic Preservation, Libraries, Museums/Galleries, Music, Performing Arts, Theater
Civic & Public Affairs: Community Foundations, Economic Policy, Employment/Job Training, Civic & Public Affairs-General, Hispanic Affairs, Law & Justice, Legal Aid, Nonprofit Management, Philanthropic Organizations, Professional & Trade Associations, Public Policy, Women's Affairs, Zoos/Aquariums
Education: Arts/Humanities Education, Colleges & Universities, Continuing Education, Education Associations, Education Funds, Education Reform, Engineering/Technological Education, Faculty Development, Education-General, Health & Physical Education, Journalism/Media Education, Legal Education, Literacy, Medical Education, Minority Education, Preschool Education, Private Education (Precollege), Social Sciences Education, Special Education, Student Aid
Environment: Environment-General
Health: Children's Health/Hospitals, Emergency/Ambulance Services, Health-General, Health Policy/Cost Containment, Health Organizations, Hospices, Hospitals, Long-Term Care, Medical Rehabilitation, Medical Research, Mental Health, Nursing Services, Single-Disease Health Associations, Speech & Hearing
International: Health Care/Hospitals, International Affairs, International Organizations, International Relations
Religion: Ministries, Religious Organizations, Religious Welfare
Social Services: Animal Protection, Child Abuse, Child Welfare, Community Centers, Community Service Organizations, Domestic Violence, Emergency Relief, Family Services, Food/Clothing Distribution, People with Disabilities, Senior Services, Social Services-General, Youth Organizations

Application Procedures

Initial Contact: Organizations should submit a brief letter to the foundation. Telephone inquiries are not considered. The foundation has no formal application form.
Application Requirements: Requests for funds should provide, in triplicate, a concise description of the proposed project or other use for requested funds; a brief history of the organization, identity of board members and their affiliations; specific objectives to be accomplished; background and qualifications of the organization and the individuals involved; the methods by which the organization will evaluate the results of the proposed project; a budget, including amount requested; latest audited financial statement; and a copy of the organization's most recent evidence of its federal tax-exempt status, accompanied by a separate representation that no change in that status has occurred or is currently anticipated since it was issued. Also include a listing of major grants from corporate and foundation contributors during the past twelve months. The foundation discourages submission of extraneous materials such as brochures, marketing materials, and newspaper or magazine clippings or booklets containing the same.
Deadlines: None.
Review Process: The foundation's board normally meets in March, June, September, and December. Responses normally will be received from several weeks to two or three months following application.

Restrictions

The foundation will not provide funds for individuals, non-exempt organizations, general operating expenses, fraternal organizations, foreign organizations, athletic organizations, other private foundations, or political entities. Grantmaking confined to greater Chicago area.

Foundation Officials

John Hayes: director, secretary
Katheryn V. Rhoads: executive director
Paul Kelly Rhoads: president, director B La Grange, IL 1940. ED Washington & Lee University BA (1962); Loyola University JD (1967). PRIM CORP EMPL partner: Schiff Hardin & Waite. CORP AFFIL director: McKay Enterprises; director: Glen Ellyn III; director: Haymarsh Corp. NONPR AFFIL director: Philanthropy Roundtable; member: Union League; member: Illinois State Bar Association; member: Chicago Bar Association. CLUB AFFIL Salt Creek Club; Manistee Golf Club & Country Club; Portage Lake Yacht Club.

Grants Analysis

Disclosure Period: calendar year ending 2001
Total Grants: $871,000
Number of Grants: 45

Average Grant: $9,791*
Highest Grant: $250,000
Lowest Grant: $1,000
Typical Range: $5,000 to $20,000
*Note: Average grant figure excludes two highest grants ($450,000).

Recent Grants

Note: Grants derived from 2001 Form 990.

General

250,000	Community Foundation for Monterey County, Monterey, CA
200,000	Heritage Foundation
50,000	Intercollegiate Studies Institute, Inc,, Wilmington, DE
25,000	Alice Lloyd College, Grayson, KY
25,000	Cato Institute, Washington, DC
25,000	Philanthropy Roundtable, Washington, DC
24,000	Daniel Murphy Scholarship Foundation, Chicago, IL
20,000	Reason Foundation
15,000	Capital Research Center, Washington, DC
15,000	Cumberland College, Williamsburg, KY

HERRICK FOUNDATION

Giving Contact

Kenneth G. Herrick, Chairman, President, Treasurer, & Trustee
840 W. Long Lake Road, Suite 200
Troy, MI 48098
Phone: (248)267-3321
Fax: (248)879-2001

Description

Founded: 1949
EIN: 386041517
Organization Type: Family Foundation
Giving Locations: MI: Primarily Michigan, occasionally Washington, D.C., Indiana, Mississippi, Ohio, Tennesse, Oklahoma and Wisconsin
Grant Types: Capital, Emergency, Endowment, Fellowship, General Support, Matching, Multiyear/Continuing Support, Operating Expenses, Professorship, Research, Scholarship, Seed Money.

Donor Information

Founder: Established in 1949 by the late Ray Wesley Herrick and his wife, the late Hazel M. Herrick . In the early days of the automotive industry in Detroit, Mr. Herrick was in charge of production for the Ford Motor Company. In the early 1930s, he moved to Tecumseh, MI, where he founded and became chairman of the board of directors of the predecessor of the Tecumseh Products Company. Through the Herrick Foundation, he helped build Adrian College in Michigan and the Howe (Indiana) Military Academy. He also gave the city of Holland, MI, a public library now bearing his name. A majority of the foundation's assets consist of shares in the Tecumseh Products Company.

Financial Summary

Total Giving: $10,000,000 (fiscal year ending September 30, 2002 approx); $11,384,885 (fiscal 2001); $8,328,820 (fiscal 2000)
Giving Analysis: Giving for fiscal 2001 includes: foundation scholarships ($130,000); foundation grants to United Way ($135,000); fiscal 1999: foundation grants to United Way ($35,000); foundation scholarships ($315,500); fiscal 1998: foundation grants to United Way ($25,000) foundation scholarships ($116,000).
Assets: $209,098,025 (fiscal 2001); $235,555,981 (fiscal 2000); $227,516,127 (fiscal 1999)

Typical Recipients

Arts & Humanities: Arts Centers, Arts & Humanities-General, Historic Preservation, History & Archaeology, Libraries, Museums/Galleries, Music, Opera, Performing Arts, Public Broadcasting, Theater
Civic & Public Affairs: Botanical Gardens/Parks, Clubs, Community Foundations, Economic Development, Economic Policy, Civic & Public Affairs-General, Housing, Municipalities/Towns, Native American Affairs, Philanthropic Organizations, Public Policy, Safety, Urban & Community Affairs, Zoos/Aquariums
Education: Arts/Humanities Education, Business Education, Colleges & Universities, Community & Junior Colleges, Economic Education, Education Associations, Education Reform, Elementary Education (Private), Elementary Education (Public), Engineering/Technological Education, Faculty Development, Education-General, Health & Physical Education, Medical Education, Private Education (Precollege), Public Education (Precollege), Religious Education, Science/Mathematics Education, Secondary Education (Private), Secondary Education (Public), Student Aid
Environment: Resource Conservation
Health: Alzheimers Disease, Cancer, Children's Health/Hospitals, Clinics/Medical Centers, Diabetes, Emergency/Ambulance Services, Health-General, Health Funds, Health Organizations, Heart, Hospices, Hospitals, Hospitals (University Affiliated), Kidney, Long-Term Care, Medical Research, Nursing Services, Preventive Medicine/Wellness Organizations, Single-Disease Health Associations
International: Health Care/Hospitals, Missionary/Religious Activities
Religion: Churches, Ministries, Religious Organizations, Religious Welfare
Social Services: Animal Protection, At-Risk Youth, Child Welfare, Community Service Organizations, Crime Prevention, Delinquency & Criminal Rehabilitation, Emergency Relief, Family Services, Food/Clothing Distribution, Homes, People with Disabilities, Recreation & Athletics, Scouts, Senior Services, Special Olympics, Substance Abuse, United Funds/United Ways, YMCA/YWCA/YMHA/YWHA, Youth Organizations

Application Procedures

Initial Contact: The foundation has no formal application requirements and procedures. Prospective grantees should send the foundation a letter of request.
Application Requirements: The letter should include the amount requested, the goal to be accomplished, methods to be used, plans for evaluation, copy of the most current IRS 501(c)(3) tax-exempt ruling, name of the person to contact who will be administering the program, other organizations contributing to the project, specify name of organization and amount of contributions, and any other information that would aid the board of trustees in making their decision.
Deadlines: None.
Notes: The foundation prefers that applications be brief and to the point.

Restrictions

No grants for use outside the U.S.

Grants Analysis

Disclosure Period: fiscal year ending September 30, 2001
Total Grants: $11,119,885*
Number of Grants: 229
Average Grant: $46,578*
Highest Grant: $500,000
Lowest Grant: $500
Typical Range: $20,000 to $100,000
*Note: Giving excludes United Way and scholarships. Average grant figure excludes highest grant.

Recent Grants

Note: Grants derived from fiscal 2001 Form 990.

Library-Related
75,000   Sanilac District Library, Port Sanilac, MI -- for building expansion and renovation project

General
1,000,000   Bixby Hospital Community Health Care Endowment Fund, Adrian, MI -- for the Community Crusade Against Cancer
500,000   Howe Military School, Howe, IN -- for renovation and replacements of bathrooms
500,000   Michigan State University School of Music, East Lansing, MI -- for the Catherine Herrick Cobb Professorship in the School of Music
377,000   Sand Lake Volunteer Fire Department, Tipton, MI -- for replacement of fire truck and necessary equipment
375,000   Central American Ministries, Toledo, OH -- for its endowment fund
300,000   American Diabetes Association Research Foundation, Detroit, MI -- to fund Kidney Disease Research Project
300,000   Berea College, Berea, KY -- for the renovation of its Jesse Preston Draper Building
250,000   St. John's Jesuit High School, Toledo, OH -- for a new Fitness Center and Auxiliary Gym
250,000   Saline Christian School Association, Saline, MI -- for its campaign toward building a new pre-K-12th grade school building
250,000   University of Michigan Business School, Ann Arbor, MI -- for the Innovation Initiative Endowment

HERSHEY FAMILY FOUNDATION

Giving Contact

Barry J. Hershey, Trustee
1 International Place
Boston, MA 02110
Phone: (617)428-3414
Web: http://fdncenter.org/grantmaker/hershey

Description

Founded: 1988
EIN: 341574366
Organization Type: Private Foundation
Grant Types: General Support.

Donor Information

Founder: Barry J. Hershey

Financial Summary

Total Giving: $2,074,992 (2000); $2,941,816 (1999); $1,737,362 (1998)
Assets: $60,386,943 (2000); $57,439,816 (1999); $52,287,235 (1998)
Gifts Received: $36,235,950 (1996); $26,000 (1995); $602,000 (1994). Note: In 1996, contributions were received from Barry J. Hershey ($35,771,200) and Walden Woods Film Co. ($464,750).

Typical Recipients

Arts & Humanities: Arts Associations & Councils, Ballet, Film & Video, Arts & Humanities-General, Historic Preservation, Libraries, Literary Arts, Museums/Galleries, Music, Theater
Civic & Public Affairs: Botanical Gardens/Parks, Civic & Public Affairs-General, Housing, Urban & Community Affairs, Women's Affairs

Education: Arts/Humanities Education, Colleges & Universities, Continuing Education, Education Associations, Education Funds, Medical Education, Private Education (Precollege), Public Education (Precollege), Religious Education, Science/Mathematics Education, Student Aid
Environment: Resource Conservation
Health: Children's Health/Hospitals, Clinics/Medical Centers, Health Organizations, Hospitals
International: Foreign Arts Organizations, International-General, Human Rights, International Development, International Organizations, International Peace & Security Issues
Religion: Jewish Causes, Religious Organizations, Religious Welfare
Social Services: Child Welfare, Community Service Organizations, Food/Clothing Distribution

Application Procedures

Initial Contact: The foundation has no formal grant application procedure or application form.
Deadlines: None.

Foundation Officials

Barry J. Hershey: trustee
Connie Hershey: trustee

Grants Analysis

Disclosure Period: calendar year ending 2000
Total Grants: $2,074,992
Number of Grants: 24
Average Grant: $43,772*
Highest Grant: $600,000
Typical Range: $20,000 to $100,000
*Note: Average grant figure excludes two highest grants ($1,112,000).

Recent Grants

Note: Grants derived from 1999 Form 990.

General
1,512,000   Harvard University, Cambridge, MA
400,000   Beth Israel Deaconess, Boston, MA
300,000   University of Pennsylvania, Philadelphia, PA
100,000   Concord Land Conservation Trust, Concord, MA
100,000   Wisdom Publications, Inc, Somerville, MA
86,028   Institute of Tibetan Classics, Montreal, QC Canada
70,000   Hershey Montessori School, Concord Township, OH
50,000   American Repertory Theatre, Cambridge, MA
50,000   Huntington Theater, Boston, MA
38,000   Boston Film Video Foundation, Boston, MA

HERSHEY FOODS CORP.

Company Headquarters

Hershey, PA
Web: http://www.hersheys.com

Company Description

Founded: 1894
Ticker: HSY
Exchange: NYSE
Revenue: US$4.12 billion (2002)
Profit: US$403.6 million (2002)
Employees: 16000 (2002)
Fortune Rank: 390, per FORTUNE Magazine's list of 500 Largest U.S. Corporations (2002).
SIC(s): 2064 Candy & Other Confectionery Products, 2066 Chocolate & Cocoa Products, 2098 Macaroni & Spaghetti.

Operating Locations

Hershey Foods Corp. (CA--Fresno, Oakdale; CT--Naugatuck; KY--Louisville; NE--Omaha; NM--Farmington; PA--Hazleton, Lebanon, Reading; VA--Stuarts Draft, Winchester)

Nonmonetary Support

Type: Cause-related Marketing & Promotion; Donated Products; Loaned Executives
Contact: Harold Miller, Senior Account Representative, Customer Service
Note: Loaned executives are for United Way only.

Giving Contact

Jennifer Goss, Corporate Contributions Dept.
100 Crystal A Dr.
PO Box 810
Hershey, PA 17033-0810
Phone: (717)534-7880
Fax: (717)534-7015
Web: http://www.hersheys.com/about/contributions.shtml

Description

Organization Type: Corporate Giving Program
Giving Locations: limited to manufacturing site communities.
Grant Types: Capital, Employee Matching Gifts, Endowment, General Support, Operating Expenses, Project, Research.
Note: Employee matching gift ratio: 2 to 1 to colleges only.

Financial Summary

Total Giving: $2,300,000 (1999 approx); $2,300,000 (1998 approx); $2,358,534 (1995). Note: Contributes through corporate direct giving program only.
Assets: $244,447 (1993); $139,702 (1992)
Gifts Received: $2,400,000 (1993)

Typical Recipients

Arts & Humanities: Arts Associations & Councils, Libraries, Museums/Galleries, Theater
Civic & Public Affairs: Business/Free Enterprise, Community Foundations, Economic Development, Employment/Job Training, Civic & Public Affairs-General
Education: Colleges & Universities, Community & Junior Colleges, Economic Education, Engineering/Technological Education, Literacy, Science/Mathematics Education
Environment: Resource Conservation
Health: Clinics/Medical Centers, Hospitals, Nutrition
Science: Scientific Centers & Institutes, Scientific Organizations
Social Services: Community Service Organizations, Food/Clothing Distribution, People with Disabilities, Substance Abuse, United Funds/United Ways, Volunteer Services

Application Procedures

Initial Contact: Submit a written proposal.
Application Requirements: Requests for under $5,000 should provide a description of organization and its purpose; proof of tax-exempt status; list of organization's key management and board of directors; recently audited financial statement; amount requested; brief description and proposed timeline of the project for which funding is requested; list of other funding sources and support amounts for this project (including cash, in-kind, and volunteer services); and a list of Hershey Foods Corp. employees who currently volunteer for your organization.
Requests for $5,000 and over should complete the Common Funding Application Form, available on the company's web site.
Deadlines: None; decisions generally made monthly; 60-day lead time needed.
Notes: Organizations outside the Harrisburg, PA metropolitan area should direct requests for funding

to the local management of the Hershey Foods facility in their geographic area.
Organizations in the Harrisburg, PA metropolitan area, national organizations and statewide organizations should direct funding requests to the Corporate Contributions Department.

Restrictions

Does not support individuals; fraternal, veterans, or labor organizations; churches or religious organizations, including seminaries, bible colleges, and theological institutions; political contributions; organizations outside the immediate areas of Hershey Foods' manufacturing facilities, except for national and statewide organizations whose programs complement Hershey Foods' priorities; member agencies of the United Way of the Capital Region, Central Pennsylvania (Cumberland, Dauphin and Perry counties), and United Way of Lebanon County, Pennsylvania; affiliate organizations of the Allied Arts Fund in Central Pennsylvania; or organizations without 501(c)(3) non-profit, tax exempt status.

Additional Information

The Hershey Fund is defunct; giving is now done at the discretion of the corporation.
Publications: Biennial Report

Corporate Officials

William F. Christ: executive vice president, chief operating officer PRIM CORP EMPL executive vice president, chief operating officer: Hershey Foods Corp.
Richard H. Lenny: president, chief executive officer B 1951. ED Georgia State University; Northwestern University. PRIM CORP EMPL president, chief executive officer: Hershey Foods Corp.
Kenneth L. Wolfe: chairman, director B February 15, 1939. ED Yale University BA (1961); University of Pennsylvania MBA (1967). PRIM CORP EMPL chairman, director: Hershey Foods Corp. CORP AFFIL chairman: Henry Heide Inc.; director: Hershey Trust Co.; director: Bausch & Lomb Inc.; director: Carpenter Technology Corp.

Grants Analysis

Disclosure Period: calendar year ending 1995
Total Grants: $2,358,534
Number of Grants: 250
Average Grant: $9,434
Highest Grant: $125,000
Lowest Grant: $1,000
Typical Range: $5,000 to $20,000

HERSHEY FOUNDATION

Giving Contact

Debra H. Guren, President
10229 Prouty Rd.
Concord, OH 44077
Phone: (202)682-4780
Web: http://fdncenter.org/grantmaker/hershey/

Description

Founded: 1986
EIN: 341525626
Organization Type: Private Foundation
Giving Locations: OH: Northeastern Ohio
Grant Types: Capital, Project.

Donor Information

Founder: Jo Hershey Selden

Financial Summary

Total Giving: $818,000 (2001); $926,625 (2000); $786,580 (1999)
Giving Analysis: Giving for 1998 includes: foundation grants to United Way ($14,200) foundation ($701,375)

Assets: $16,762,673 (2001); $18,314,193 (2000); $18,555,421 (1999)
Gifts Received: $1,803,125 (1996); $214,375 (1994); $152,500 (1992). Note: In 1996, contributions were received from Debra H. Guren ($1,450,000) and Carole Walters ($353,125).

Typical Recipients

Arts & Humanities: Arts Centers, Arts Outreach, Ballet, Historic Preservation, History & Archaeology, Libraries, Museums/Galleries, Music, Opera, Performing Arts, Public Broadcasting, Theater, Visual Arts
Civic & Public Affairs: Botanical Gardens/Parks, Economic Development, Civic & Public Affairs-General, Nonprofit Management, Urban & Community Affairs, Women's Affairs, Zoos/Aquariums
Education: Arts/Humanities Education, Colleges & Universities, Community & Junior Colleges, Education Reform, Elementary Education (Private), Education-General, Leadership Training, Literacy, Minority Education, Preschool Education, Private Education (Precollege), Public Education (Precollege), Science/Mathematics Education, Special Education
Environment: Environment-General
Health: Emergency/Ambulance Services
Religion: Jewish Causes
Science: Science Museums, Scientific Centers & Institutes
Social Services: Animal Protection, Big Brother/Big Sister, Child Welfare, Community Service Organizations, Crime Prevention, Day Care, Family Planning, Family Services, People with Disabilities, Recreation & Athletics, Social Services-General, YMCA/YWCA/YMHA/YWHA, Youth Organizations

Application Procedures

Initial Contact: Send a brief letter of inquiry and a full proposal.
Application Requirements: Include a description of organization, amount requested, purpose of funds sought, recently audited financial statement, proof of tax-exempt status, and other funding sources.
Deadlines: None.

Restrictions

The foundation does not support individuals, religious organizations for sectarian purposes, political or lobbying groups, or organizations outside operating areas.

Foundation Officials

Georgia A. Froelich: treasurer
Debra S. Guren: president
Loren W. Hershey: chairman
Carole H. Walters: vice president

Grants Analysis

Disclosure Period: calendar year ending 2001
Total Grants: $818,000
Number of Grants: 38
Average Grant: $16,789*
Highest Grant: $100,000
Typical Range: $5,000 to $40,000
***Note:** Average grant excludes two highest grants ($180,000).

Recent Grants

Note: Grants derived from 2001 Form 990.

General

100,000	Cleveland Botanical Garden, Cleveland, OH -- Hershey Children's Garden
80,000	Hershey Montesorri School, Concord Township, OH -- capital and farm school
63,000	Montessori Development Partnerships, Cleveland, OH -- project support and farm project
50,000	Hiram House, Chagrin Falls, OH -- capital campaign for facilities

30,000	Cuyahoga Valley Scenic Railroad, Peninsula, OH -- for curriculum revision project
30,000	Parkworks, Cleveland, OH -- for Green School Environmental Education Program
26,000	WVIZ, Cleveland, OH -- for WVIZ/PBS Kids
25,000	Boys and Girls Clubs of Cleveland, Cleveland, OH -- capital campaign for Broadway Club facility
25,000	Cuyahoga County Board of Commissioners, Cleveland, OH -- for Early Childhood Initiative
25,000	Geauga Humane Society, Novelty, OH -- for Rescue Village Capital Campaign

ALBERT AND ETHEL HERZSTEIN CHARITABLE FOUNDATION

Giving Contact

L. Michael Hajtman, President
6131 Westview
Houston, TX 77055
Phone: (713)681-7868
Fax: (713)681-3652
E-mail: albertandethel@herzsteinfoundation.org
Web: http://www.herzsteinfoundation.org

Description

Founded: 1965
EIN: 746070484
Organization Type: Family Foundation
Giving Locations: TX: Houston
Grant Types: Capital, Emergency, Endowment, General Support, Multiyear/Continuing Support, Research, Scholarship, Seed Money.

Donor Information

Founder: The foundation was established in 1965 by the Herzstein family. The estate of Ms. Sadie R. Smith, Mr. Herzstein's sister, contributed to the foundation in 1985.

Financial Summary

Total Giving: $3,100,000 (2002 approx); $3,197,000 (2001 approx); $2,498,372 (2000)
Giving Analysis: Giving for 1998 includes: foundation (approx $1,788,000)
Assets: $69,231,000 (2001); $44,255,428 (2000); $38,912,000 (1999)
Gifts Received: $2,286,131 (2000); $383,570 (1998); $71,390 (1995). Note: Contributions were received from the Albert Herzstein Estate.

Typical Recipients

Arts & Humanities: Arts Associations & Councils, Arts Festivals, Arts Funds, Ballet, Historic Preservation, History & Archaeology, Libraries, Museums/Galleries, Music, Opera, Performing Arts, Public Broadcasting, Theater
Civic & Public Affairs: African American Affairs, Botanical Gardens/Parks, Chambers of Commerce, Clubs, Community Foundations, Economic Development, Economic Policy, Employment/Job Training, Civic & Public Affairs-General, Hispanic Affairs, Municipalities/Towns, Nonprofit Management, Parades/Festivals, Philanthropic Organizations, Public Policy, Urban & Community Affairs, Women's Affairs, Zoos/Aquariums
Education: Business Education, Colleges & Universities, Education Funds, Education Reform, Education-General, Medical Education, Private Education

(Precollege), Public Education (Precollege), Secondary Education (Private), Secondary Education (Public), Special Education, Student Aid, Vocational & Technical Education
Environment: Energy, Environment-General, Resource Conservation
Health: Adolescent Health Issues, AIDS/HIV, Alzheimers Disease, Cancer, Children's Health/Hospitals, Clinics/Medical Centers, Diabetes, Emergency/Ambulance Services, Eyes/Blindness, Health-General, Health Organizations, Heart, Hospitals, Medical Research, Mental Health, Multiple Sclerosis, Prenatal Health Issues, Respiratory, Single-Disease Health Associations
International: Health Care/Hospitals, International Organizations, Missionary/Religious Activities
Religion: Churches, Dioceses, Religion-General, Jewish Causes, Ministries, Religious Organizations, Religious Welfare, Social/Policy Issues, Synagogues/Temples
Science: Science Museums, Scientific Centers & Institutes
Social Services: Animal Protection, Camps, Child Welfare, Community Centers, Community Service Organizations, Crime Prevention, Food/Clothing Distribution, People with Disabilities, Recreation & Athletics, Scouts, Senior Services, Social Services-General, Special Olympics, Substance Abuse, United Funds/United Ways, Veterans, YMCA/YWCA/YMHA/YWHA, Youth Organizations

Application Procedures

Initial Contact: Applicants should send a written request.
Application Requirements: Include a brief description of the history and mission, and achievements of the organization; names of present officers and board members; IRS determination letter documenting tax-exempt status; and financial statements (preferably audited) and IRS Form 990 for most recent fiscal year. Also include information on the proposed project, including need for the program and population it will serve; goals and objectives for the program and timetable for their accomplishment; overall project cost and specific amount requested; project budget (revenue and expense); sources and amounts being solicited and/or received or pledged; and future funding plans, if the project is new and continuing. for which funding is sought and the amount of funding requested of the foundation; and a separate sheet showing the project budget, including projected revenue and expenses. The statement should further discuss how the project will continue to operate after the foundation's funding ceases. Also include names of present officers and board members, IRS determination letter, audited financial statements, Form 990 of the most recent fiscal year, and list of officers and board members.
Deadlines: None.
Notes: Organizations submitting proposals should limit their request to no more than one (1) in any twelve (12) month period. Lobbying of the individual Directors by grant applications may result in the adverse consideration of grant application.

Restrictions

Grants are made only to nonprofit organizations which are tax exempt under sections 501(c)(3) or 170(c) of the Internal Revenue Code. The foundation does not make grants to individuals or provide loans.

Additional Information

Publications: Foundation brochure

Foundation Officials

L. Michael Hajtman: president
Richard Loewenstern: director
George W. Strake, Jr.: director B Houston, TX 1935. ED University of Notre Dame AB (1957); Harvard University MBA (1961). PRIM CORP EMPL chairman, chief executive officer, founder: Strake Trading Group

Inc. CORP AFFIL principal: GW Strake Co. NONPR AFFIL director: Texas Independent Producers & Royalty Board; advisory council: University Notre Dame College Arts and Sciences; director: Task Force Public Education; director: Boy Scouts America; director: Interstate Oil Compact Commission.
Dr. Nathan Topek: director

Grants Analysis

Disclosure Period: calendar year ending 2001
Total Grants: $3,197,000*
Number of Grants: 126
Average Grant: $8,550*
Highest Grant: $300,000
Typical Range: $3,000 to $30,000
*Note: Grants analysis provide by foundation. Average grant excludes major grants.

Recent Grants

Note: Grants derived from 2000 Form 990.

General

500,000	New Houston Jewish School, Houston, TX -- for construction of the educational campus and facilities
400,000	Houston Museum of Natural Science, Houston, TX -- to create an endowment to support the Exhibition Hall on the Museum's second level
250,000	Neighborhood Centers, Houston, TX -- capital campaign
200,000	Boys and Girls Club of Greater Houston, Houston, TX -- capital campaign
150,000	Nature Conservancy of Texas, Houston, TX -- for the Texas City Prairie preserve located in Texas City
102,000	San Jacinto Museum, La Porte, TX -- to fully catalog, automate and computerize the library and collections at San Jacinto Museum of History
100,000	Houston Area Women's Center, Houston, TX -- in support of the new 125 bed emergency shelter for abused and sexually assaulted women and their children
99,472	Rice University, Houston, TX -- educational
30,000	Jewish Federation of Greater Houston, Houston, TX -- for the United Jewish Campaign
25,000	American Battle Monuments Commission, Arlington, VA -- in support of the first national memorial dedicated to all who served during WWII

BERNARD K. AND NORMA F. HEUERMANN FOUNDATION

Giving Contact

John B. Atkins, Treasurer & Director
c/o Wells Fargo Bank Nebraska
Private Client Services
10010 Regency Circle
Suite 300
Omaha, NE 68114

Alternate Contact

Charles L. Whitney, Secretary & Director
c/o Law Offices
Professional Building
PO Box 228
Aurora, NE 68818
Phone: (402)536-2470

Description

Founded: 1991
EIN: 470748466
Organization Type: Private Foundation

Giving Locations: NE
Grant Types: Capital, General Support, Project, Scholarship.

Donor Information
Founder: Bernard K. Heuermann, Norma F. Heuermann

Financial Summary
Total Giving: $559,692 (fiscal year ending July 31, 2002); $423,784 (fiscal 2001); $464,329 (fiscal 2000)
Giving Analysis: Giving for fiscal 2002 includes: foundation scholarships ($22,462)
Assets: $8,889,404 (fiscal 2002); $10,945,255 (fiscal 2001); $10,228,075 (fiscal 2000)
Gifts Received: $2,000,000 (fiscal 2001); $1,000 (fiscal 2000); $450,103 (fiscal 1998). Note: In fiscal 2001, contributions were received from Bernard K. and Norma F. Heuermann. In fiscal 1998, contributions were received from B. K. Heuermann.

Typical Recipients
Arts & Humanities: History & Archaeology, Libraries, Museums/Galleries, Public Broadcasting
Civic & Public Affairs: Chambers of Commerce, Clubs, Community Foundations, Economic Development, Civic & Public Affairs-General
Education: Agricultural Education, Colleges & Universities, Education-General, Private Education (Pre-college), Science/Mathematics Education, Student Aid
Health: Alzheimers Disease, Cancer, Children's Health/Hospitals, Hospitals, Public Health
Religion: Churches
Social Services: Child Welfare, Community Centers, Homes, People with Disabilities, Senior Services, Youth Organizations

Application Procedures
Initial Contact: Submit a proposal (limited to two pages). The foundation requests an original proposal and two copies.
Application Requirements: Identify a special need or project to which funds will be applied, including the objectives to be obtained, people or groups who will benefit, a timetable for achieving objectives, and other means of support. Include proof of tax-exempt status. Supporting documents such as a project budget, other resources and names of supporters, and background information about the organization may be attached to the proposal.
Deadlines: None.
Decision Notification: The trustees meet at least three times per year to review grant requests. All grant applicants are notified of the foundation's decision after the request has been reviewed.
Notes: Stapled proposals are preferred to bound ones.

Restrictions
The foundation does not support individuals, nor does it provide loans.

Additional Information
Publications: Grant Guidelines
Trust(s): Wells Fargo Bank NE NA

Foundation Officials
John B. Atkins: treasurer, director
Bernard K. Heuermann: president, director
Norma F. Heuermann: vice president, director
Charles L. Whitney: atty, secretary, director

Grants Analysis
Disclosure Period: fiscal year ending July 31, 2002
Total Grants: $537,230*
Number of Grants: 67
Average Grant: $8,018
Highest Grant: $41,420
Lowest Grant: $250

Typical Range: $1,000 to $25,000
***Note:** Giving excludes scholarships.

Recent Grants
Note: Grants derived from 2002 Form 990.

General

41,420	Nebraska Christian Schools, Central City, NE -- for improvements and equipment
35,000	Nebraska Wesleyan University, Lincoln, NE
33,000	Hamilton County Senior Center, Aurora, NE -- pledge
30,000	Memorial Hospital Foundation, Aurora, NE -- for endowment fund
29,000	University of Nebraska Foundation, Lincoln, NE -- for Agronomy Department
25,000	Hastings College Foundation, Omaha, NE
22,000	Hamilton County Foundation Inc., Aurora, NE -- for Nebraska Wesleyan tuition
21,542	Nebraska Wesleyan University, Lincoln, NE -- for annual insurance premium
21,000	Hamilton County Foundation Inc., Aurora, NE -- for scholarships
20,000	Plainsman Museum, Aurora, NE -- for endowment

HEWIT FAMILY FOUNDATION

Giving Contact
William D. Hewit, President, Treasurer & Director
Hewit Family Foundation
621 17th St., Suite 2555
Denver, CO 80293
Phone: (303)292-0697

Description
Founded: 1985
EIN: 742397040
Organization Type: Private Foundation
Giving Locations: CO: Denver
Grant Types: General Support.

Donor Information
Founder: members of the Hewit family

Financial Summary
Total Giving: $715,000 (fiscal year ending November 30, 2001); $1,457,500 (fiscal 2000); $762,500 (fiscal 1999)
Assets: $13,812,832 (fiscal 2001); $13,602,280 (fiscal 2000); $8,814,510 (fiscal 1999)
Gifts Received: $5,754,524 (fiscal 2000); $4,290,846 (fiscal 1998); $300,000 (fiscal 1997). Note: In fiscal 1998 and 2000, contributions were received from the estate of William E. Hewit. In fiscal 1995, contributions were received from William D. Hewit ($150,000) and Betty Ruth Hewit ($150,000).

Typical Recipients
Arts & Humanities: Historic Preservation, Libraries, Museums/Galleries, Public Broadcasting
Civic & Public Affairs: Botanical Gardens/Parks, Civic & Public Affairs-General, Philanthropic Organizations, Zoos/Aquariums
Education: Afterschool/Enrichment Programs, Education Funds, Education-General, Science/Mathematics Education
Health: Cancer, Children's Health/Hospitals, Health Policy/Cost Containment, Health Organizations, Hospitals, Hospitals (University Affiliated), Transplant Networks/Donor Banks
Science: Science Museums, Scientific Centers & Institutes

Social Services: Big Brother/Big Sister, Child Welfare, Community Service Organizations, Recreation & Athletics, Scouts, Youth Organizations

Application Procedures
Initial Contact: Send a brief letter of inquiry.
Application Requirements: Include a description of organization, amount requested, proof of tax-exempt status.
Deadlines: None.

Restrictions
Does not support individuals, religious organizations for sectarian purposes, political or lobbying groups, or organizations outside operating areas.

Foundation Officials
Christie F. Andrews: vice president, director
Richard J. Andrews: director
Robert S. Brown: director
Betty Ruth Hewit: vice president, director
William D. Hewit: president, treasurer, director
Jack E. Kennedy: director

Grants Analysis
Disclosure Period: fiscal year ending November 30, 2001
Total Grants: $715,000
Number of Grants: 20
Average Grant: $9,737*
Highest Grant: $530,000
Lowest Grant: $5,000
Typical Range: $5,000 to $20,000
***Note:** Average grant figure excludes highest grant.

Recent Grants
Note: Grants derived from fiscal 2000 Form 990.

Library-Related

5,000	Denver Public Library, Denver, CO

General

530,000	Children's Hospital Foundation, Denver, CO
500,000	PorterCare Foundation, Denver, CO
206,300	Billfish Foundation, Ft. Lauderdale, FL
43,700	Virginia Institute of Marine Science, Gloucester Point, VA
25,000	University of Colorado Health Science Center, Denver, CO
15,000	Denver Museum of Natural History, Denver, CO
15,000	Kempe Children's Foundation, Denver, CO
15,000	Make a Wish Foundation, Englewood, CO
10,000	Boy Scouts of America, Denver, CO
10,000	Boys and Girls Club of Metro Denver, Denver, CO

WILLIAM AND FLORA HEWLETT FOUNDATION

Giving Contact
Paul Brest, President
2121 Sand Hill Road
Menlo Park, CA 94025
Phone: (650)234-4500
Fax: (650)234-4501
E-mail: info@hewlett.org
Web: http://www.hewlett.org

Description
Founded: 1966
EIN: 941655673
Organization Type: General Purpose Foundation
Giving Locations: CA: San Francisco Bay area internationally; nationally.

Grant Types: Challenge, Department, Employee Matching Gifts, General Support, Matching, Multiyear/Continuing Support, Operating Expenses, Project.

Donor Information

Founder: The Hewlett Foundation was established in 1966 by William R. Hewlett; his late wife, Flora Lamson Hewlett; and their eldest son, Walter B. Hewlett. William Hewlett is a co-founder of the Hewlett-Packard Company, established in 1939 with his partner, David Packard. Mr. Hewlett is retired from the computer and electronics company and is chairman of the foundation. In 1977, the foundation's name changed to the William and Flora Hewlett Foundation, in memory of Mrs. Hewlett who died that year. She bequeathed $230 million in Hewlett-Packard stock to the foundation.

Financial Summary

Total Giving: $100,000,000 (2002 approx); $119,000,000 (2001); $135,298,270 (2000)
Giving Analysis: Giving for 2000 includes: foundation grants to United Way ($450,000)
Assets: $5,459,549,000 (2001); $3,930,366,990 (2000); $2,738,945,087 (1999)
Gifts Received: $394,835,000 (2000); $46,880,438 (1998); $84,910,000 (1995). Note: In 2000 and 1998, contributions were received from William R. Hewlett.

Typical Recipients

Arts & Humanities: Arts Associations & Councils, Arts Funds, Arts Institutes, Arts Outreach, Ballet, Dance, Ethnic & Folk Arts, Libraries, Museums/Galleries, Music, Opera, Performing Arts, Public Broadcasting, Theater
Civic & Public Affairs: Botanical Gardens/Parks, Chambers of Commerce, Community Foundations, Economic Development, Economic Policy, Employment/Job Training, Civic & Public Affairs-General, Housing, Law & Justice, Native American Affairs, Nonprofit Management, Philanthropic Organizations, Professional & Trade Associations, Public Policy, Urban & Community Affairs, Women's Affairs
Education: Afterschool/Enrichment Programs, Arts/Humanities Education, Business Education, Colleges & Universities, Colleges & Universities, Continuing Education, Economic Education, Education Associations, Education Reform, Engineering/Technological Education, Environmental Education, Faculty Development, Education-General, International Studies, Legal Education, Literacy, Minority Education, Science/Mathematics Education, Social Sciences Education, Student Aid, Vocational & Technical Education
Environment: Air/Water Quality, Energy, Environment-General, Resource Conservation
Health: Adolescent Health Issues, AIDS/HIV, Health Policy/Cost Containment, Health Organizations, Public Health, Research/Studies Institutes
International: Foreign Educational Institutions, International-General, Health Care/Hospitals, International Affairs, International Development, International Environmental Issues, International Organizations, International Peace & Security Issues, International Relations
Religion: Seminaries, Social/Policy Issues
Science: Scientific Centers & Institutes, Scientific Organizations
Social Services: Child Welfare, Community Service Organizations, Crime Prevention, Emergency Relief, Family Planning, Family Services, Shelters/Homelessness, Volunteer Services, Youth Organizations

Application Procedures

Initial Contact: Applicants should submit a letter of inquiry addressed to the president, containing a brief statement of need for funds and sufficient factual information to enable the staff to determine whether the proposal falls within the foundation's area of preferred interest. Applicants also should provide reasons and needs for support, taking into account other possible sources of funding.

Application Requirements: Applicants who receive a favorable response to their initial inquiry will be invited to submit a formal proposal. Special supporting materials may be requested in some cases, but normally the formal proposal should include: a statement of purpose; a budget and financial statement, including an indication of other prospective funding sources, the amount requested of each, and how they would continue a successful program once support from the Hewlett Foundation ceases; the identity and qualifications of key personnel; a list of governing members; evidence of tax-exempt status; and a statement that the proposal has been reviewed and approved by the applicant's governing body, and specifically approved for submission to the foundation.

Deadlines: Applications for music programs should be submitted by January 1, for review in April. Theater program applications should be submitted by April 1, for review in July. Applications from dance programs and film and video service organizations are due by July 1, for review in October. For the Conflict Resolution program, applications from theory organizations and international organizations are due January 1, for review in April; applications from training and promotional organizations and public policy decision making organizations are due July 1, for review in October; and applications from practitioner organizations are due October 1, for review in January. Although the foundation does not expect to be able to adhere rigidly to this schedule, it will make every effort to do so.

Review Process: Letters of application will be acknowledged briefly upon receipt. Grants must be reviewed by the Board of Directors, which meets quarterly. Because the foundation prefers to conduct its affairs with a small staff, a more detailed response will be delayed in some cases. Applicants who have not received a substantive reply after a reasonable period of time should make a follow-up inquiry. All inquiries initially are reviewed by the relevant program officer who will request further information, if needed. He or she, in consultation with the president, will either decline those requests which seem unlikely to result in a project the foundation can support, or present the request to the staff for discussion.

Restrictions

The foundation recognizes that significant programs require time to demonstrate their value, and is therefore willing to consider proposals covering several years of support. While the foundation will fund specific projects in its areas of interest and will occasionally provide general support for organizations of special interest, it expects to work primarily through support of organizations active in its main programs. One exception is the regional grants program, under which the foundation will fund specific projects that meet an immediate community need.

The foundation normally will not consider grants or loans to individuals, for basic research, capital construction funds, or medical or health-related fields. It will not support general fund-raising drives or make grants intended directly or indirectly to support candidates for political office or to influence legislation. The foundation does not accept proposals by fax or e-mail.

Additional Information

The foundation reports that "in its grantmaking decisions as well as in its interests and activities, the Hewlett Foundation is wholly independent of the Hewlett-Packard Company and the Hewlett-Packard Company Foundation."
Publications: Annual Report; Guidelines

Foundation Officials

Paul Brest: president ED Swarthmore College (1962); Harvard University JD (1965).
Robert F. Erburu: director B Ventura, CA 1930. ED University of Southern California BA (1952); Harvard University JD (1955). PRIM CORP EMPL director: The Times Mirror Co. CORP AFFIL director: Marsh & McLennan Companies Inc.; director: Tejon Ranch Co.; director: Cox Communications Inc. NONPR AFFIL chairman board trustee: H.E. Huntington Library Art Gallery; life director: Independent Colleges Southern California; member: American Bar Association.
James C. Gaither: director B Oakland, CA 1937. ED Princeton University BA (1959); Stanford University JD (1964). CORP AFFIL director: Stanford Management Co.; trustee: Rand Corp.; secretary: Siebel Systems Inc.; director: Levi Strauss International; director: Levi Strauss North America; director: Basic American Inc.; director: Levi Strauss & Co.; director: Amylin Pharmaceuticals Inc.; director: Basic American Food. NONPR AFFIL member: San Francisco Bar Association; member executive committee, board visitors, advisory board: Stanford University School Law; member: Phi Delta Phi; member executive committee, trustee, vice chairman: Carnegie Endowment International Peace; member: Order Coif; member: American Bar Association; member: California Bar Association; fellow: American Academy of Arts & Sciences.
Eleanor H. Gimon: director
Eleanor Hewlett Gimon: director NONPR AFFIL treasurer: Family Foundation North America.
H. Irving Grousbeck: director CORP AFFIL director: CIMA Capital Group.
Walter B. Hewlett: chairman
Mary Hewlett Jaffe: director
Herant Katchadourian, MD: director B Iskenderun, Turkey 1933. ED American University BA (1954); American University MD (1958); University of Rochester (1958-1961). PRIM NONPR EMPL member undergraduate studies: Stanford University. NONPR AFFIL trustee: Haigazian College; member corporate visitors committee: Massachusetts Institute Technology; member: Alpha Omega Alpha.
Richard C. Levin: director
William Ford Nichols, Jr.: treasurer B Palo Alto, CA 1934. ED Stanford University AB (1956); Stanford University MBA (1958). PRIM CORP EMPL controller: Saga Corp. NONPR AFFIL member: Institute of Management Accountants; trustee: Investment Fund Foundations; member: Financial Executives Institute; member: American Institute of Certified Public Accountants; member: California Society Certified Public Accountants.
Marianne Marguerite Pallotti: vice president, corp secretary B Hartford, CT 1937. ED New York University BA (1968); New York University MA (1972). NONPR AFFIL member: Women's Advisory Committee National Council; World Wildlife Fund; member: Peninsula Grantmakers; member: Women Foundations; member: Northern California Grantmakers; board director: Overseas Development Networks; board director: New York Theatre Ballet.
Jean G. Stromberg: director

Grants Analysis

Disclosure Period: calendar year ending 2001
Total Grants: $119,000,000
Number of Grants: 825 (approx)
Average Grant: $144,242
Highest Grant: $5,000,000
Typical Range: $50,000 to $300,000

Recent Grants

Note: Grants derived from 2001 Form 990.

General
5,000,000 San Diego State University Foundation, San Diego, CA -- reform initiatives
2,750,000 Massachusetts Institute of Technology, Cambridge, MA -- for the OpenCourseWare Project
2,600,000 Energy Foundation, San Francisco, CA -- for work on the Hewlett Foundation's Energy Initiative
1,600,000 Greater Washington Educational Telecommunications Association, Washington, DC -- The New Hour

1,356,000	Community Foundation Silicon Valley, San Jose, CA -- for the Mayfair Improvement Initiative
1,200,000	Achieve, Cambridge, MA -- for a project entitled Defining the Twenty First Century New Basic Skills
1,200,000	Carnegie Foundation for the Advancement of Teaching, Menlo Park, CA -- collaboration to build practical understanding of and commitment to the liberal arts
1,100,000	John F. Kennedy University, Orinda, CA -- for the capital campaign
1,000,000	Center for Reproductive Law and Policy, New York, NY
1,000,000	Coalition of Essential Schools, Oakland, CA

HEXCEL CORP.

Company Headquarters

2 Stamford Plaza
281 Tressor Boulevard
Stamford, CT 06901
Web: http://www.hexcel.com

Company Description

Founded: 1946
Ticker: HXL
Exchange: NYSE
Revenue: US$850.8 million (2002)
Employees: 4245 (2002)
SIC(s): 2200 Textile Mill Products, 2800 Chemicals & Allied Products, 3400 Fabricated Metal Products, 3728 Aircraft Parts & Equipment Nec.

Operating Locations

Hexcel Corp. (AZ--Casa Grande, Chandler; CA--Chatsworth, City of Industry, Livermore, Pleasanton, San Francisco; MI--Zeeland; OH--Lancaster; PA--Pottsville; TX--Graham, Seguin)
Note: Includes plant locations

Hexcel Foundation

Giving Contact

Michael Bacal, Treasurer
Hexcel Foundation
281 Tresser Blvd.
Stamford, CT 06901
Phone: (203)969-0666
Fax: (925)416-7756

Description

EIN: 942972860
Organization Type: Corporate Foundation
Giving Locations: CA
Grant Types: Employee Matching Gifts, General Support, Scholarship.

Financial Summary

Total Giving: $20,316 (fiscal year ending June 30, 2001); $66,332 (fiscal 2000); $28,093 (fiscal 1998)
Giving Analysis: Giving for fiscal 2000 includes: foundation matching gifts ($250); fiscal 1998: foundation grants to United Way ($12,500) foundation grants to United Way ($19,000)
Assets: $119,854 (fiscal 2001); $115,532 (fiscal 2000); $280,028 (fiscal 1998)
Gifts Received: $3,000 (fiscal 1993)

Typical Recipients

Arts & Humanities: Libraries, Museums/Galleries, Music, Opera
Civic & Public Affairs: Civic & Public Affairs-General, Urban & Community Affairs
Education: Business Education, Colleges & Universities, Community & Junior Colleges, Engineering/Technological Education, Education-General, Public

Education (Precollege), Religious Education, Science/Mathematics Education, Secondary Education (Public), Student Aid
Health: Cancer, Children's Health/Hospitals, Emergency/Ambulance Services, Eyes/Blindness, Health Organizations, Heart, Hospices, Hospitals, Mental Health, Prenatal Health Issues, Single-Disease Health Associations
International: International-General
Science: Science Exhibits & Fairs
Social Services: Community Service Organizations, Crime Prevention, Day Care, Food/Clothing Distribution, Homes, Recreation & Athletics, Senior Services, Shelters/Homelessness, Substance Abuse, United Funds/United Ways, YMCA/YWCA/YMHA/YWHA, Youth Organizations

Application Procedures

Initial Contact: Send a brief letter of inquiry.
Application Requirements: Include proof of tax-exempt status.
Deadlines: None.

Restrictions

Does not support individuals; religious organizations for sectarian purposes; political or lobbying groups; veterans, labor or other groups; or organizations which function only in and for the benefit of communities where Hexcel has no operations or employees.

Additional Information

Publications: Corporate Contributions Guidelines

Corporate Officials

Stephen C. Forsyth: senior vice president finance & administration, chief financial officer PRIM CORP EMPL senior vice president finance & administration, chief financial officer: Hexcel Corp.
Juergen Habermeier: vice chairman PRIM CORP EMPL vice chairman: Hexcel Corp.
John J. Lee: chairman, president, chief executive officer, director B 1933. PRIM CORP EMPL chairman, president, chief executive officer, director: Hexcel Corp. CORP AFFIL director: Playtex Products; chief executive officer: Seminole Fertilizer Corp.; director: Aviva Petroleum Co.

Foundation Officials

Michael Bacal: treasurer
William Christensen: vice president
Bruce Herman: treasurer
Rodney P. Jenks: secretary
John J. Lee: trustee (see above)
William P. Meehan: trustee

Grants Analysis

Disclosure Period: fiscal year ending June 30, 2001
Total Grants: $20,316*
Number of Grants: 13
Average Grant: $860*
Highest Grant: $10,000
Typical Range: $100 to $2,000
*Note: Average grant figure excludes highest grant.

Recent Grants

Note: Grants derived from fiscal 2000 Form 990.

General

250,000	Cal Poly Pomona Foundation, Pomona, CA
10,000	CSLA Foundation, Los Angeles, CA
10,000	Franklin S. Wimer '58 Memorial Fund, New Haven, CT
10,000	Yale University - Team Lux, New Haven, CT
7,500	Saint Vincent's Hospital and Medical Center, New York, NY
6,667	Decatur City Schools, Decatur, AL
5,000	David Wong Memorial Fund Canada
5,000	David Wong Memorial Fund Canada
3,500	Boys & Girls Clubs of America, New York, NY

| 2,500 | Child Care Action Campaign, New York, NY |

NAN AND MATILDA HEYDT FUND

Giving Contact

Thea Katsounakis, Trust Officer
PO Box 6767
PO Box 6767
Providence, RI 02940-6767
Phone: (401)276-7229

Description

Founded: 1966
EIN: 046136421
Organization Type: Private Foundation
Giving Locations: MA: Hampden County
Grant Types: Capital, Project, Seed Money.

Donor Information

Founder: the late Matilda L. Heydt

Financial Summary

Total Giving: $263,115 (2002); $253,840 (2000); $251,005 (1999)
Assets: $5,250,990 (2002); $6,873,665 (2000); $7,355,621 (1999)

Typical Recipients

Arts & Humanities: Arts Associations & Councils, Arts Institutes, Ethnic & Folk Arts, Film & Video, Historic Preservation, History & Archaeology, Libraries, Literary Arts, Museums/Galleries, Music, Opera, Public Broadcasting, Theater
Civic & Public Affairs: Asian American Affairs, Botanical Gardens/Parks, Business/Free Enterprise, Community Foundations, Employment/Job Training, Civic & Public Affairs-General, Hispanic Affairs, Housing, Legal Aid, Minority Business, Public Policy, Safety, Urban & Community Affairs
Education: Business-School Partnerships, Colleges & Universities, Community & Junior Colleges, Elementary Education (Public), Education-General, International Studies, Social Sciences Education, Special Education
Environment: Energy, Environment-General, Resource Conservation, Watershed
Health: AIDS/HIV, Alzheimers Disease, Children's Health/Hospitals, Clinics/Medical Centers, Health Funds, Hospices, Hospitals, Medical Rehabilitation, Medical Training, Mental Health, Nursing Services, Public Health
International: Human Rights, Missionary/Religious Activities
Religion: Churches, Seminaries
Science: Scientific Centers & Institutes
Social Services: At-Risk Youth, Camps, Child Welfare, Community Service Organizations, Counseling, Domestic Violence, Emergency Relief, Family Planning, Food/Clothing Distribution, People with Disabilities, Recreation & Athletics, Scouts, Senior Services, Social Services-General, United Funds/United Ways, Volunteer Services, YMCA/YWCA/YMHA/YWHA, Youth Organizations

Application Procedures

Initial Contact: Contact trust officer for application information and deadlines.

Additional Information

Publications: Informational Brochure (including Application Guidelines)
Trust(s): Fleet National Bank

Grants Analysis

Disclosure Period: calendar year ending 2002
Total Grants: $263,115
Number of Grants: 43

Average Grant: $6,119
Highest Grant: $31,000
Typical Range: $1,000 to $7,000

Recent Grants

Note: Grants derived from 2002 Form 990.

General

31,000	Hampshire Education Collaborative, Inc., Northampton, MA
10,000	Community Adolescent Resources and Education Center, Holyoke, MA
10,000	Cooperative Development Institute, Greenfield, MA
10,000	Hampshire Education Collaborative, Inc., Northampton, MA
10,000	Hampshire Education Collaborative, Inc., Northampton, MA
10,000	Holyoke Community Land Trust, Inc., Holyoke, MA
8,650	Community Foundation of Western Massachusetts, Springfield, MA
8,498	Community Foundation of Western Massachusetts, Springfield, MA
8,498	Community Foundation of Western Massachusetts, Springfield, MA
7,500	Community Adolescent Resources and Education Center, Holyoke, MA

DUBOSE AND DOROTHY HEYWARD MEMORIAL FUND

Giving Contact

Peter McDermott, Trust Officer
c/o The Bank of New York, Tax Dept.
1290 Ave. of the Americas, 5th Fl.
New York, NY 10104
Phone: (212)635-1520

Description

Founded: 1985
EIN: 136840999
Organization Type: Private Foundation
Giving Locations: NH; NY; SC
Grant Types: General Support.

Donor Information

Founder: the late Jenifer Heyward

Financial Summary

Total Giving: $478,500 (2002); $420,000 (2000); $587,500 (1999)
Assets: $6,719,738 (2002); $9,679,673 (2000); $10,451,587 (1999)
Gifts Received: $129,518 (1999); $35 (1995); $130,000 (1994). Note: In 1999, contributions were received from Patti Whitelaw Charitable Trust. In 1994, contributions were received from Elizabeth Miller Charitable Trust.

Typical Recipients

Arts & Humanities: Arts Associations & Councils, Arts Festivals, Arts Institutes, Ballet, Dance, Arts & Humanities-General, History & Archaeology, Libraries, Literary Arts, Museums/Galleries, Music, Opera, Performing Arts, Public Broadcasting, Theater
Civic & Public Affairs: Community Foundations, Civic & Public Affairs-General, Municipalities/Towns, Parades/Festivals, Urban & Community Affairs
Education: Arts/Humanities Education, Colleges & Universities, Medical Education
Health: Cancer, Hospitals, Single-Disease Health Associations
Social Services: Community Centers

Application Procedures

Initial Contact: Send a brief letter of inquiry.
Application Requirements: Include a description of organization.
Deadlines: None.

Restrictions

Provides grants for the promotion of the arts or for cancer research and treatment.

Additional Information

Trust(s): The Bank of New York

Foundation Officials

Albert J. Cardinali: trustee B New York, NY 1934. ED City College of New York BA (1955); Columbia University LLB (1958); New York University LLM (1965). PRIM CORP EMPL Partner: Thatcher Proffitt & Wood. NONPR AFFIL member: Association Bar New York City; member: New York State Bar Association; member: American Bar Association. CLUB AFFIL Shenorock Shore Club; University Club.

Grants Analysis

Disclosure Period: calendar year ending 2002
Total Grants: $478,500
Number of Grants: 41
Average Grant: $9,962*
Highest Grant: $50,000
Lowest Grant: $1,000
Typical Range: $5,000 to $20,000
*Note: Average grant figure excludes two highest grants ($90,000).

Recent Grants

Note: Grants derived from 2001 Form 990.

General

50,000	MacDowell Colony, New York, NY
40,000	MacDowell Colony, New York, NY
25,000	Carnegie Hall Society, New York, NY
25,000	Metropolitan Opera Association, New York, NY
25,000	Metropolitan Opera Association, New York, NY
25,000	Public Theatre New York Shakespeare Festival, New York, NY
20,000	City Center 55th Street Theater Foundation, New York, NY
20,000	Columbia University Cancer Center, New York, NY
20,000	Glimmerglass Opera, New York, NY
20,000	Jazz at Lincoln Center, New York, NY

HICKORY TECH CORP.

Company Headquarters

Mankato, MN
Web: http://www.hickorytech.com

Company Description

Founded: 1898
Ticker: HTCO
Exchange: NASDAQ
Revenue: US$106.6 million (2002)
Employees: 502 (2002)
SIC(s): 4813 Telephone Communications Except Radiotelephone, 4841 Cable & Other Pay Television Services.

Operating Locations

Hickory Tech Corp. (IA--Homestead; MN--St. Paul)

Hickory Tech Corp. Foundation

Giving Contact

Jane L. Rush, Administrator
221 E. Hickory St.
PO Box 3248
Mankato, MN 56002-3248
Phone: (507)387-1866
Fax: (507)625-9191

Description

Founded: 1963
EIN: 416034001
Organization Type: Corporate Foundation
Giving Locations: MN: Mankato
Grant Types: Capital, Employee Matching Gifts, General Support, Multiyear/Continuing Support, Scholarship.

Financial Summary

Total Giving: $192,560 (fiscal year ending February 28, 2000); $193,020 (fiscal 1999); $200,375 (fiscal 1998). Note: Contributes through foundation only.
Giving Analysis: Giving for fiscal 2000 includes: foundation matching gifts ($20,834); foundation grants to United Way ($31,786); foundation ($139,536); fiscal 1999: corporate scholarships ($22,667); corporate grants to United Way ($27,000) foundation ($143,353)
Assets: $3,465,857 (fiscal 2000); $3,510,123 (fiscal 1999); $3,100,000 (fiscal 1998 approx)
Gifts Received: $10,000 (fiscal 1996); $70,000 (fiscal 1994); $450,000 (fiscal 1993). Note: Gifts are received from Mankato Citizens Telephone Co.

Typical Recipients

Arts & Humanities: Arts Outreach, Arts & Humanities-General, Historic Preservation, Libraries, Music, Performing Arts, Public Broadcasting, Theater
Civic & Public Affairs: Botanical Gardens/Parks, Business/Free Enterprise, Chambers of Commerce, Clubs, Community Foundations, Economic Development, Economic Policy, Civic & Public Affairs-General, Housing, Municipalities/Towns, Parades/Festivals, Public Policy, Safety, Urban & Community Affairs, Women's Affairs
Education: Arts/Humanities Education, Business Education, Business-School Partnerships, Colleges & Universities, Community & Junior Colleges, Economic Education, Education Funds, Engineering/Technological Education, Faculty Development, Education-General, International Studies, Leadership Training, Minority Education, Private Education (Precollege), Public Education (Precollege), Religious Education, Science/Mathematics Education, Secondary Education (Private), Secondary Education (Public), Social Sciences Education, Student Aid, Vocational & Technical Education
Environment: Environment-General, Resource Conservation, Wildlife Protection
Health: Alzheimers Disease, Cancer, Children's Health/Hospitals, Clinics/Medical Centers, Emergency/Ambulance Services, Health-General, Heart, Hospitals, Medical Rehabilitation, Multiple Sclerosis, Prenatal Health Issues, Public Health, Trauma Treatment
International: International Organizations
Religion: Religious Welfare, Social/Policy Issues
Science: Observatories & Planetariums, Science Exhibits & Fairs
Social Services: At-Risk Youth, Camps, Community Service Organizations, Family Services, Food/Clothing Distribution, Recreation & Athletics, Scouts, Senior Services, Shelters/Homelessness, Social Services-General, United Funds/United Ways, Volunteer Services, YMCA/YWCA/YMHA/YWHA, Youth Organizations

Application Procedures

Initial Contact: by telephone, to request guidelines
Application Requirements: if project meets foundation's mission: a description of project, including specific goals and completion dates; amount requested and percentage of budget it represents; current budget; audited financial statement; list of other contributors, and funding levels; a list of board of directors with affiliations; letter of tax-exempt status; description of how support will be recognized; a plan to evaluate the project's success; and any descriptive brochures or materials
Deadlines: December 15 of each fiscal year.
Evaluative Criteria: foundation focuses on areas of Hickory Tech Corporation's subsidiaries in South Central Minnesota.

Restrictions

Does not support individuals; political activities or organizations; religious organizations for sectarian purposes; fraternal, veteran or labor groups; special occasion or goodwill advertising; general operating purposes, except United Way; loans; sports programs or events; cause-related marketing; organizations that discriminate; hospital operating funds or capital funds; and organizations without 501(c)(3) status.

Corporate Officials

Lyle T. Bosacker: director PRIM CORP EMPL director: Hickory Tech Corp.
Robert K. Else: director B 1935. ED University of Illinois MBA (1958); University of Chicago MBA (1959). PRIM CORP EMPL president: El Microcircuits Inc. CORP AFFIL director: Hickory Technology Corp.; director: Mankato Citizens Tel Co.
James H. Holdrege: director PRIM CORP EMPL director: Hickory Tech Corp. CORP AFFIL director: Mankato Citizens Tel Co.
R. Wynn Kearney, Jr.: director PRIM CORP EMPL director: Hickory Tech Corp. CORP AFFIL director: Hickory Technology Corp.
Starr J. Kirklin: director PRIM CORP EMPL director: Hickory Tech Corp. CORP AFFIL director: Mankato Citizens Tel Co.
Brett M. Taylor, Junior: director PRIM CORP EMPL director: Hickory Technology Corp. CORP AFFIL director: Mankato Citizens Tel Co.

Foundation Officials

Robert D. Alton, Jr.: trustee B 1948. ED Lindenwood University MBA; Iowa State University (1970). CORP AFFIL chairman: Minnesota Southern Wireless Co.
Lyle T. Bosacker: trustee (see above)
Robert K. Else: secretary (see above)
James H. Holdrege: trustee (see above)
Lyle Gordon Jacobson: treasurer B Duluth, MN 1941. ED University of Minnesota (1963); University of Minnesota MS (1965). PRIM CORP EMPL president, chief executive officer: Katolight Corp. ADD CORP EMPL vice president: Jones Metal Products Inc.; treasurer: Winnebago Manufacturing Co. CORP AFFIL director: Mankato Citizens Tel Co.; director: Hickory Technology Corp.; director, owner: JKW Management Corp. NONPR AFFIL Kiwanis International.
R. Wynn Kearney, Jr.: trustee (see above)
Starr J. Kirklin: trustee (see above)
Brett M. Taylor, Junior: president (see above)

Grants Analysis

Disclosure Period: fiscal year ending February 28, 2001
Total Grants: $139,536*
Number of Grants: 22
Average Grant: $6,343
Highest Grant: $20,000
Lowest Grant: $500
Typical Range: $4,000 to $15,000
***Note:** Giving excludes matching gifts and United Way.

Recent Grants

Note: Grants derived from fiscal 2001 Form 990.

General

31,786	Mankato Area United Way, Mankato, MN
20,000	Mankato State University Foundation, Mankato, MN
20,000	Twin Valley Council - BSA, Mankato, MN -- new building project
20,000	YWCA Renovation Campaign, Mankato, MN -- renovation project
11,500	Bethany Lutheran College, Mankato, MN
10,000	South Central Technical College, North Mankato, MN
7,500	Gustavus Adolphus College, St. Peter, MN -- Nobel Hall and Student Center renovation
5,000	Mankato Symphony Orchestra, Mankato, MN
5,000	Minnesota State University, Mankato, MN -- new building project
5,000	Minnesota State University, Mankato, MN -- partial funding for theatre production

JOHN W. AND CLARA C. HIGGINS FOUNDATION

Giving Contact

Sumner B. Tilton, Jr., President
370 Main St., 12th Fl.
Worcester, MA 01608
Phone: (508)798-8521
Fax: (508)794-1201

Description

Founded: 1956
EIN: 046026914
Organization Type: Private Foundation
Grant Types: Multiyear/Continuing Support, Project.

Financial Summary

Total Giving: $175,000 (2000); $150,000 (1999); $103,000 (1998)
Giving Analysis: Giving for 2000 includes: foundation grants to United Way ($500); 1999: foundation grants to United Way ($300); 1998: foundation grants to United Way ($500) foundation ($102,500)
Assets: $3,292,003 (2000); $3,408,784 (1999); $4,016,335 (1998)

Typical Recipients

Arts & Humanities: Arts Associations & Councils, Arts Institutes, Ethnic & Folk Arts, History & Archaeology, Libraries, Literary Arts, Museums/Galleries, Music, Opera
Civic & Public Affairs: Civil Rights, Community Foundations, Ethnic Organizations, Civic & Public Affairs-General, Native American Affairs
Education: Afterschool/Enrichment Programs, Colleges & Universities, Journalism/Media Education, Private Education (Precollege)
Health: Emergency/Ambulance Services
Religion: Churches, Religious Welfare, Synagogues/Temples
Social Services: Animal Protection, Food/Clothing Distribution, Senior Services, Social Services-General, Youth Organizations

Application Procedures

Initial Contact: Send a brief letter of inquiry.
Application Requirements: Include proof of tax-exempt status.
Deadlines: None.

Restrictions

Recipient must be eligible for listing in the IRS cumulative list. Grants are not made to individuals.

Foundation Officials

Richard Higgins: trustee
Mary Louise Wilding White: trustee
Philip Q. Wilding White: trustee

Grants Analysis

Disclosure Period: calendar year ending 2000
Total Grants: $174,500*
Number of Grants: 61
Average Grant: $2,861
Highest Grant: $20,000
Typical Range: $1,000 to $5,000
***Note:** Giving excludes United Way.

Recent Grants

Note: Grants derived from 1999 Form 990.

General

20,000	American Civil Liberties Union, New York, NY -- establishment of Dick Higgins Fund for Freedom of Artistic Expression
20,000	Higgins Armory Museum, Worcester, MA -- endowment
19,000	Dutchess County Arts Council, Poughkeepsie, NY -- left hand books
14,000	Higgins Armory Museum, Worcester, MA -- director's choice
8,000	Higgins Armory Museum, Worcester, MA -- operating
5,000	Institute for Publishing Arts, Barrytown, NY
5,000	University of Illinois, Chicago, IL -- gallery 400
5,000	University of Maine Foundation, Bangor, ME
5,000	Wesleyan University, Middletown, CT -- Olin Library
4,000	Greater Worcester Community Foundation, Inc., Worcester, MA -- for the benefit of John W. Higgins Museum

CORINA HIGGINSON TRUST

Giving Contact

Charles C. Abeles, Esq., Trustee
4449 Westover Place NW
Washington, DC 20016
Phone: (202)334-0553

Description

Founded: 1962
EIN: 526055743
Organization Type: Private Foundation
Giving Locations: DC: Washington
Grant Types: Emergency, General Support, Multiyear/Continuing Support, Operating Expenses, Project, Research, Seed Money.

Donor Information

Founder: the late Corina Higginson

Financial Summary

Total Giving: $466,800 (2000); $334,660 (1999); $224,500 (1998)
Assets: $8,907,201 (2000); $10,420,361 (1999); $6,425,703 (1998)
Gifts Received: $10,171 (1992)

Typical Recipients

Arts & Humanities: Arts Associations & Councils, Arts Centers, Arts Outreach, Ballet, Community Arts, Dance, Ethnic & Folk Arts, History & Archaeology,

Libraries, Museums/Galleries, Music, Opera, Performing Arts, Theater

Civic & Public Affairs: Community Foundations, Economic Development, Employment/Job Training, Civic & Public Affairs-General, Hispanic Affairs, Law & Justice, Nonprofit Management, Philanthropic Organizations, Professional & Trade Associations, Public Policy, Women's Affairs

Education: Afterschool/Enrichment Programs, Arts/Humanities Education, Environmental Education, Education-General, Gifted & Talented Programs, Literacy, Minority Education, Preschool Education, Private Education (Precollege), Private Education (Precollege), Science/Mathematics Education, Secondary Education (Public)

Environment: Forestry, Environment-General, Resource Conservation, Watershed, Wildlife Protection

Health: AIDS/HIV, Clinics/Medical Centers, Geriatric Health, Mental Health, Prenatal Health Issues

International: Health Care/Hospitals, International Environmental Issues

Religion: Churches, Jewish Causes, Religious Organizations, Religious Welfare, Social/Policy Issues

Social Services: Community Service Organizations, Counseling, Family Planning, Family Services, Food/Clothing Distribution, Recreation & Athletics, Refugee Assistance, Senior Services, Sexual Abuse, Shelters/Homelessness, Social Services-General, United Funds/United Ways, Volunteer Services, Youth Organizations

Application Procedures

Initial Contact: Send a concise, one-page statement summarizing the project. Submit the original and five copies.

Application Requirements: Include name and purpose of the organization, a summary of activities, names and qualifications of staff members, financial statements, amount requested, and proof of tax-exempt status.

Deadlines: March 1 and September 1.

Restrictions

Does not support individuals or provide funds for scholarships or endowments for individual schools, fixed assets, or medical or health-related programs or organizations.

Additional Information

Publications: Application Form; Guidelines

Foundation Officials

Charles Calvert Abeles: trustee B Norfolk, VA 1929. ED Harvard University AB (1952); University of Virginia JD (1958). CORP AFFIL director: D&D Ventures Corp. NONPR AFFIL member, officer: Transplant Recipients International Organization; member: Virginia Bar Association; member: District of Columbia Bar Association; trustee: Corina Higgins Trust. CLUB AFFIL Metropolitan Washington Club.

Wilton C. Corken, Jr.: trustee

Floretta Dukes McKenzie: trustee

Jean Head Sisco: trustee

Grants Analysis

Disclosure Period: calendar year ending 2000

Total Grants: $466,800

Number of Grants: 67

Average Grant: $6,967

Highest Grant: $50,000

Typical Range: $1,000 to $10,000

Recent Grants

Note: Grants derived from 1999 Form 990.

General

16,000	Grafton School, Washington, DC
15,000	Washington AIDS Partnership, Washington, DC
10,000	Capital Children's Museum, Washington, DC
10,000	Center City Consortium, Bethesda, MD
10,000	Environments Project, Washington, DC
10,000	Friends of Fort Dupont Ice Arena, Washington, DC
10,000	Friends of The United States National Arboretum, Washington, DC
10,000	Mentors, Inc., Washington, DC
10,000	Rachel's Women's Shelter, Washington, DC
10,000	Washington Ballet, Washington, DC

HIGH FOUNDATION

Giving Contact

Richard L. High, Trustee
831 Salisbury Ct.
Lancaster, PA 17601
Phone: (717)293-4444

Description

Founded: 1980
EIN: 232149972
Organization Type: Private Foundation
Grant Types: General Support, Scholarship.

Donor Information

Founder: High Industries

Financial Summary

Total Giving: $147,000 (fiscal year ending August 31, 2001); $150,000 (fiscal 2000); $156,000 (fiscal 1998)

Giving Analysis: Giving for fiscal 2001 includes: foundation scholarships ($19,000) fiscal 2000: foundation scholarships ($17,000)

Assets: $3,964,761 (fiscal 2001); $4,083,007 (fiscal 2000); $3,595,673 (fiscal 1998)

Gifts Received: $50,000 (fiscal 2001); $30,000 (fiscal 2000); $20,000 (fiscal 1998). Note: Contributions were received from High Industries.

Typical Recipients

Arts & Humanities: Arts Centers, Community Arts, Historic Preservation, Libraries, Music, Opera, Performing Arts, Theater

Civic & Public Affairs: Ethnic Organizations, Civic & Public Affairs-General, Housing, Parades/Festivals, Professional & Trade Associations, Urban & Community Affairs

Education: Arts/Humanities Education, Business Education, Colleges & Universities, Education Funds, Engineering/Technological Education, Education-General, Minority Education, Private Education (Precollege), Public Education (Precollege), Religious Education, Student Aid

Environment: Environment-General

Health: Children's Health/Hospitals, Clinics/Medical Centers, Heart, Hospices, Hospitals, Public Health, Single-Disease Health Associations

International: Health Care/Hospitals

Religion: Churches, Ministries, Religious Organizations, Religious Welfare

Social Services: Camps, Community Centers, Community Service Organizations, Family Services, Food/Clothing Distribution, People with Disabilities, Scouts, Substance Abuse, United Funds/United Ways, Youth Organizations

Application Procedures

Initial Contact: Request application form.
Deadlines: December 15.

Additional Information

Awards scholarships to dependent children of High Industries and related companies' employees.
Publications: Application Form

Foundation Officials

Calvin G. High: trustee
Gregory A. High: trustee
Janet C. High: trustee
Richard L. High: trustee

S. Dale High: trustee B Lancaster, PA 1942. ED Elizabethtown College BSBA (1963). PRIM CORP EMPL chairman, president: High Industries. CORP AFFIL partner: High Properties; director: Lancaster Alliance; director: High Hotels Ltd.; director: High Investors Ltd.; gen ptnr: High Empls Services Ltd; director: High Food Services Ltd.; director: Educators Mutual Life Insurance Co. NONPR AFFIL trustee, director: Pennsylvania Chamber Business & Industry; trustee: World President Organization; member: Lancaster Chamber of Commerce; trustee: Lancaster County Foundation; hon mem: Delta Mu Delta; trustee: Elizabethtown College. CLUB AFFIL Tuesday Club; Hamilton Club; Lancaster Country Club.

Sadie H. High: trustee
Steven D. High: trustee
Suzanne M. High: trustee
Chester A. Raber: trustee

Grants Analysis

Disclosure Period: fiscal year ending August 31, 2001

Total Grants: $128,000*

Number of Grants: 27

Average Grant: $3,520*

Highest Grant: $20,000

Lowest Grant: $500

Typical Range: $1,000 to $5,000

*****Note:** Giving excludes scholarships. Average grant figure excludes two highest grants ($40,000).

Recent Grants

Note: Grants derived from 2000 Form 990.

General

25,000	Thaddeus Stevens Foundation, Lancaster, PA -- capital campaign
20,000	Salvation Army, Lancaster, PA -- capital campaign
15,000	Arbor Place Christian Community Center, Lancaster, PA -- capital campaign
15,000	Penn Laurel Girl Scout Council, York, PA -- capital campaign
8,000	Locust Groove School, Smoketown, PA -- capital campaign
7,000	Samaritan Counseling Center, Lancaster, PA -- operating expenses
5,000	Drug and Alcohol Rehab, Lancaster, PA -- operating expenses
5,000	Mennonite Central Committee, Akron, PA -- capital campaign
5,000	Milagro House, Lancaster, PA -- operating expenses
4,500	Theatre of the Seventh Sister, Lancaster, PA -- operating expenses

HILL CREST FOUNDATION

Giving Contact

Charles R. Terry, Sr., Chairman
PO Box 530507
Birmingham, AL 35253
Phone: (205)870-0400
Fax: (205)870-0484

Description

Founded: 1988
EIN: 630516927
Organization Type: General Purpose Foundation
Giving Locations: AL: Birmingham metropolitan area
Grant Types: Capital, Operating Expenses, Project, Research, Scholarship.

Financial Summary

Total Giving: $1,636,700 (fiscal year ending June 30, 2001); $1,305,420 (fiscal 1999); $1,671,788 (fiscal 1998)

Giving Analysis: Giving for fiscal 2001 includes: foundation scholarships ($18,000)

Assets: $33,277,781 (fiscal 2001); $37,183,424 (fiscal 1999); $34,861,152 (fiscal 1998)

Typical Recipients

Arts & Humanities: Arts Associations & Councils, Arts Festivals, Arts Outreach, Ballet, Dance, History & Archaeology, Museums/Galleries, Music, Performing Arts, Theater

Civic & Public Affairs: Botanical Gardens/Parks, Clubs, Community Foundations, Economic Development, Civic & Public Affairs-General, Housing, Law & Justice, Municipalities/Towns, Public Policy, Urban & Community Affairs

Education: Colleges & Universities, Community & Junior Colleges, Education Associations, Education Funds, Education Reform, Elementary Education (Private), Elementary Education (Public), Education-General, Gifted & Talented Programs, International Studies, Leadership Training, Literacy, Medical Education, Minority Education, Private Education (Precollege), Public Education (Precollege), Social Sciences Education, Special Education, Student Aid, Vocational & Technical Education

Environment: Environment-General, Resource Conservation, Wildlife Protection

Health: AIDS/HIV, Alzheimers Disease, Cancer, Children's Health/Hospitals, Diabetes, Eyes/Blindness, Health Funds, Health Organizations, Hospitals, Hospitals (University Affiliated), Medical Rehabilitation, Mental Health, Nutrition, Prenatal Health Issues, Public Health, Respiratory, Single-Disease Health Associations, Trauma Treatment

Religion: Churches, Jewish Causes, Ministries, Religious Organizations, Religious Welfare, Social/Policy Issues

Science: Science Museums

Social Services: Animal Protection, At-Risk Youth, Camps, Child Welfare, Community Centers, Community Service Organizations, Counseling, Domestic Violence, Family Planning, Family Services, Food/Clothing Distribution, Homes, People with Disabilities, Recreation & Athletics, Scouts, Shelters/Homelessness, Social Services-General, Substance Abuse, YMCA/YWCA/YMHA/YWHA, Youth Organizations

Application Procedures

Initial Contact: Applicants should request guidelines prior to submitting a proposal. Organizations should submit a brief proposal of one to three pages in letter form.

Application Requirements: The proposal should contain the following: proof of IRS 501(c)(3) nonprofit status; a short history of the organization and its purpose; a description of the project goals and the qualifications of the staff involved; the amount of funding requested; and anticipated long- and short-term advantages of the project affecting the foundation as well as all others who stand to benefit.

Deadlines: None.

Restrictions

Grants are made only to tax-exempt organizations.

Additional Information

Publications: Annual Report; Guidelines

Foundation Officials

Peter G. Cowin: trustee B 1931. ED Oberlin College. PRIM CORP EMPL vice president, director: Cowin & Co. Inc. CORP AFFIL vice president, secretary: C & C Holding Inc.; chairman board, treasurer: Cowin Equipment Co. Inc.

Stanley E. Graham: trustee

Willard L. Hurley: trustee

Charles R. Terry, Sr.: chairman

Grants Analysis

Disclosure Period: fiscal year ending June 30, 2001

Total Grants: $1,618,700*

Number of Grants: 58

Average Grant: $23,433*

Highest Grant: $283,000

Lowest Grant: $1,000

Typical Range: $10,000 to $40,000

*Note: Giving excludes scholarships. Average grant figure excludes highest grant.

Recent Grants

Note: Grants derived from fiscal 2000 Form 990.

General

289,000	Exceptional Foundation, Birmingham, AL -- building fund
250,000	Mountain Brook Library Foundation, Mountain Brook, AL -- construction of new library
200,000	United Cerebral Palsy, Birmingham, AL -- construction child development center
100,000	Lakeshore Foundation, Birmingham, AL -- new handicapped facility
100,000	St. Vincent's Hospital, Birmingham, AL -- help construct lodging for patient's family
100,000	University of Alabama School of Medicine, Birmingham, AL -- help fund human genetic research building
100,000	University of Alabama School of Social Work, Tuscaloosa, AL -- fund chair
50,000	Birmingham Southern College, Birmingham, AL -- fund chair in psychology
50,000	Glenwood, Inc., Birmingham, AL -- mental health research
50,000	Theatre Tuscaloosa, Tuscaloosa, AL -- final construction costs

SANDY HILL FOUNDATION

Giving Contact

Floyd H. Rourke, Trustee
PO Box 30
Hudson Falls, NY 12839
Phone: (518)792-9314

Description

Founded: 1953

EIN: 146018954

Organization Type: Private Foundation

Giving Locations: NY: Hudson Falls including surrounding area

Grant Types: General Support.

Financial Summary

Total Giving: $443,743 (fiscal year ending August 31, 2000); $304,618 (fiscal 1998); $797,925 (fiscal 1997). Note: Fiscal 1997 Giving includes scholarships ($45,000) AND United Way ($12,000).

Giving Analysis: Giving for fiscal 2000 includes: foundation grants to United Way ($10,000); foundation scholarships ($55,000); fiscal 1998: foundation grants to United Way ($12,000) foundation scholarships ($45,000)

Assets: $10,579,828 (fiscal 2000); $9,472,411 (fiscal 1998); $9,431,895 (fiscal 1997)

Typical Recipients

Arts & Humanities: Arts Associations & Councils, History & Archaeology, Libraries, Literary Arts, Museums/Galleries, Music, Opera, Performing Arts, Theater

Civic & Public Affairs: Botanical Gardens/Parks, Chambers of Commerce, Clubs, Community Foundations, Civic & Public Affairs-General, Hispanic Affairs,

Municipalities/Towns, Native American Affairs, Parades/Festivals, Urban & Community Affairs

Education: Colleges & Universities, Education Funds, Literacy, Private Education (Precollege), Public Education (Precollege), Science/Mathematics Education, Student Aid

Environment: Environment-General, Wildlife Protection

Health: AIDS/HIV, Cancer, Clinics/Medical Centers, Emergency/Ambulance Services, Heart, Hospitals, Hospitals, Public Health

International: Foreign Arts Organizations

Religion: Churches, Ministries, Religious Welfare, Synagogues/Temples

Social Services: Animal Protection, Child Welfare, Community Centers, Community Service Organizations, Counseling, Day Care, Family Services, People with Disabilities, Recreation & Athletics, Scouts, United Funds/United Ways, Veterans, Volunteer Services, YMCA/YWCA/YMHA/YWHA, Youth Organizations

Application Procedures

Initial Contact: For scholarships: request application form from guidance department of high school. Return application with current academic records, letters of recommendation, and a written statement indicating academic and occupational career goals, interests and activities, and any other pertinent information.

Deadlines: April 1.

Additional Information

Provides scholarships to students from the greater Hudson Falls, NY, area.

Publications: Application Guidelines

Foundation Officials

Nancy Juckett Brown: trustee

Floyd H. Rourke: trustee

Grants Analysis

Disclosure Period: fiscal year ending August 31, 2000

Total Grants: $378,743*

Number of Grants: 124

Average Grant: $3,054

Highest Grant: $50,000

Typical Range: $100 to $15,000

*Note: Giving excludes scholarships; United Way.

Recent Grants

Note: Grants derived from 2000 Form 990.

General

50,000	Double H Hole in the Woods Ranch, Glens Falls, NY -- cap project
50,000	Prospect Child and Family Care Center, Queensbury, NY -- cap. Project
37,500	Salvation Army, Glens Falls, NY -- cap. Project
20,750	Hudson Falls Central School, Hudson Falls, NY -- special project
20,000	LARAC, Glens Falls, NY -- cap. Project
20,000	Saratoga Care Foundation, Saratoga, NY -- cap. Project
15,300	Glens Falls Hospital Foundation, Glens Falls, NY -- special project
13,823	Village of Hudson Falls, Hudson Falls, NY -- maintenance of Juckett Park
10,000	Double H Hole in the Woods Ranch, Glens Falls, NY -- special project
10,000	Skidmore College, Saratoga Springs, NY -- cap. Project

HILLCREST FOUNDATION

Giving Contact

Dan Kelly, Specialist
c/o Bank of America
901 Main, 19th Floor
Dallas, TX 75202

Phone: (214)209-1965
Fax: (214)209-1940

Description

Founded: 1959
EIN: 756007565
Organization Type: General Purpose Foundation
Giving Locations: TX: Dallas
Grant Types: Capital, Project.

Donor Information

Founder: The late Mrs. W. W. Caruth Sr. , (also known as Earle Clark Caruth) established the Hillcrest Foundation in 1959. The Caruth family, by the 1900s, had amassed some 30,000 acres of land in what is now North Dallas. The late W. W. Caruth, Jr., a former trustee of the Hillcrest Foundation, developed family land over the past four decades. He is succeeded by his widow, Mabel P. Caruth. Additionally, NationsBank and individuals named by the donor serve as trustees.

Financial Summary

Total Giving: $5,700,000 (fiscal year ending May 31, 2003 approx); $6,400,000 (fiscal 2002 approx); $6,995,533 (fiscal 2000)
Giving Analysis: Giving for fiscal 1998 includes: international subsidiaries ($80,000) foundation scholarships ($177,000)
Assets: $124,000,000 (fiscal 2003 approx); $138,000,000 (fiscal 2002 approx); $141,000,000 (fiscal 2001 approx)

Typical Recipients

Arts & Humanities: Arts Centers, Arts Outreach, Historic Preservation, History & Archaeology, Libraries, Literary Arts, Museums/Galleries, Performing Arts
Civic & Public Affairs: Business/Free Enterprise, Clubs, Economic Development, Employment/Job Training, Civic & Public Affairs-General, Hispanic Affairs, Housing, Law & Justice, Minority Business, Nonprofit Management, Public Policy, Safety, Urban & Community Affairs, Zoos/Aquariums
Education: Arts/Humanities Education, Business Education, Colleges & Universities, Community & Junior Colleges, Continuing Education, Elementary Education (Private), Engineering/Technological Education, Faculty Development, Education-General, International Studies, Legal Education, Literacy, Medical Education, Private Education (Precollege), Public Education (Precollege), School Volunteerism, Science/Mathematics Education, Secondary Education (Private), Social Sciences Education, Special Education, Student Aid
Environment: Environment-General
Health: Alzheimers Disease, Arthritis, Cancer, Children's Health/Hospitals, Clinics/Medical Centers, Diabetes, Emergency/Ambulance Services, Health Organizations, Heart, Hospitals, Long-Term Care, Medical Research, Mental Health, Nursing Services, Outpatient Health Care, Prenatal Health Issues, Public Health, Research/Studies Institutes, Respiratory, Single-Disease Health Associations
International: Foreign Educational Institutions
Religion: Bible Study/Translation, Churches, Jewish Causes, Ministries, Religious Welfare, Seminaries
Science: Science-General, Science Museums, Scientific Centers & Institutes
Social Services: At-Risk Youth, Camps, Child Abuse, Child Welfare, Community Centers, Community Service Organizations, Counseling, Crime Prevention, Day Care, Delinquency & Criminal Rehabilitation, Domestic Violence, Emergency Relief, Family Services, Food/Clothing Distribution, Homes, People with Disabilities, Recreation & Athletics, Scouts, Senior Services, Shelters/Homelessness, Substance Abuse, United Funds/United Ways, YMCA/YWCA/YMHA/YWHA, Youth Organizations

Application Procedures

Initial Contact: A formal application form, provided by the foundation, must be submitted. A copy of the full proposal is requested.
Application Requirements: The proposal should include a brief history of the organization, purpose of proposal, an explanation of how funds will be used, a list of other contributors, budget information, a copy of the organization's IRS tax-exemption letter, and a statement that the organization is not a private foundation.
Deadlines: March 31, August 31, and November 30.
Review Process: All applications are considered as long as they pertain to the purposes of the foundation. The trustees meet in January, May, and October.
Evaluative Criteria: Priority is given to organizations in the Dallas, Texas area and the majority of grants are made to organizations located in Dallas County.

Restrictions

The foundation does not fund individuals, propaganda, political campaigns, groups influencing legislation, or religious organizations. No loans are distributed. OrganizationS must be located in Texas and the purpose of the grant must be for the relief of poverty or furtherance of education or health.

Additional Information

Bank of America is the corporate trustee of the foundation.
Publications: Guidelines; Application Form
Trust(s): Bank of America

Foundation Officials

D. Harold Byrd, Jr.: trustee
Harry A. Shuford: trustee
Charles Porter Storey: trustee B Austin, TX 1922. ED University of Texas BA (1947); University of Texas LLB (1948); Southern Methodist University LLM (1952). CORP AFFIL secretary, director: Hargrove Electric Co. Inc.; director: Storey Armstrong Steger & Martin Professional Corp. NONPR AFFIL member: Texas Bar Association; fellow: Texas Bar Foundation; member: Philosophers Society Texas; trustee: Southwest Legal Foundation; member: Phi Delta Phi; member: Phi Delta Theta; fellow: American College Trial Lawyers; member: Dallas Bar Association; member: American Bar Association; fellow: American Bar Foundation. CLUB AFFIL Dallas Country Club; Idlewild Club; Crescent Club.

Grants Analysis

Disclosure Period: fiscal year ending May 31, 2000
Total Grants: $6,995,533
Number of Grants: 159
Average Grant: $43,997
Highest Grant: $200,000
Lowest Grant: $3,000
Typical Range: $25,000 to $50,000

Recent Grants

Note: Grants derived from 2000 Form 990.

Library-Related

100,000	Dallas Education Center, Dallas, TX -- equip and furnish virtual library
100,000	Friends of the Dallas Public Library, Dallas, TX -- renovate the J. Erik Jonsson Central Library's Genealogy Reference Collections
100,000	Friends of the Katy Trail, Inc., Dallas, TX -- support building of the Katy Trail

General

250,000	Goodwill Industries of Dallas, Inc., Dallas, TX -- construct new facility
200,000	YMCA, Dallas, TX -- construction of facility
166,666	Tyler Street Christian Academy, Dallas, TX -- construct science and technology wing at new school building
166,000	Frontiers of Flight Museum, Dallas,

	TX -- toward construction of a new frontiers of flight museum and to fund the Hillcrest foundation education center supporting educational tours
150,000	Baylor Health Care System Foundation, Dallas, TX -- purchase equipment/instruments for minimally invasive computer assisted robotics cardiac surgical system
150,000	Boys and Girls Clubs of Greater Dallas, Dallas, TX -- renovate West Dallas Boys and Girls Club
150,000	Hockaday School, Dallas, TX
150,000	Trinity Christian Academy, Addison, TX -- construct new kindergarten classrooms and computer stations
150,000	Trinity Ministry to the Poor, Dallas, TX -- build new facility
139,000	Food for the Poor, Dallas, TX -- annual grants

HILLIARD CORP.

Company Headquarters

PO Box 866
Elmira, NY 14902
Web: http://www.hilliardcorp.com

Company Description

Employees: 233
SIC(s): 3500 Industrial Machinery & Equipment, 3519 Internal Combustion Engines Nec, 3564 Blowers & Fans, 3568 Power Transmission Equipment Nec.

Operating Locations

Hilliard Corp. (NY--Elmira)

Hilliard Foundation

Giving Contact

Nelson Mooers van den Blink, President & Trustee
100 W. 4th St.
Elmira, NY 14901
Phone: (607)733-7121

Description

EIN: 161176159
Organization Type: Corporate Foundation
Giving Locations: NY: Elmira
Grant Types: General Support.

Financial Summary

Total Giving: $189,800 (fiscal year ending April 30, 2002); $160,000 (fiscal 2000); $108,650 (fiscal 1998)
Giving Analysis: Giving for fiscal 2002 includes: foundation grants to United Way ($9,000); fiscal 2000: foundation scholarships ($5,000); foundation grants to United Way ($8,500); foundation ($146,500) fiscal 1997: foundation grants to United Way ($8,500)
Assets: $1,134,803 (fiscal 2002); $1,573,630 (fiscal 2000); $1,171,832 (fiscal 1998)
Gifts Received: $200,000 (fiscal 2000); $200,000 (fiscal 1998); $150,000 (fiscal 1997). Note: Contributions were received from the Hilliard Corp.

Typical Recipients

Arts & Humanities: Arts Associations & Councils, Arts Centers, Community Arts, Historic Preservation, History & Archaeology, Libraries, Literary Arts, Museums/Galleries, Music, Performing Arts, Theater
Civic & Public Affairs: Community Foundations, Civic & Public Affairs-General, Housing, Urban & Community Affairs
Education: Business Education, Colleges & Universities, Education-General, Literacy
Environment: Environment-General

Health: AIDS/HIV, Cancer, Clinics/Medical Centers, Emergency/Ambulance Services, Health Organizations, Hospices, Hospitals, Multiple Sclerosis, Nursing Services
Religion: Religious Organizations, Religious Welfare
Science: Scientific Centers & Institutes
Social Services: Animal Protection, At-Risk Youth, Community Centers, Community Service Organizations, Delinquency & Criminal Rehabilitation, Family Planning, Family Services, Food/Clothing Distribution, People with Disabilities, Recreation & Athletics, Scouts, United Funds/United Ways, YMCA/YWCA/YMHA/YWHA, Youth Organizations

Application Procedures

Initial Contact: Send a brief letter of inquiry.
Application Requirements: Include a description of organization and program.
Deadlines: None.

Corporate Officials

Gerald F. Schichtel: president, chief operating officer, director PRIM CORP EMPL president, chief operating officer, director: Hilliard Corp.
Nelson Mooers van den Blink: chairman, chief executive officer, treasurer, director B Elmira, NY 1934. ED Smith College (1956). PRIM CORP EMPL chairman, chief executive officer, treasurer, director: Hilliard Corp. CORP AFFIL director: Chemung Canal Trust Co.; director: Southern Tier Econ Growth; president, director: Capabilities.
Gordon Webster: chief financial officer PRIM CORP EMPL chief financial officer: Hilliard Corp.

Foundation Officials

John R. Alexander: secretary, trustee PRIM CORP EMPL secretary: Hilliard Corp.
George L. Howell: trustee
Gerald F. Schichtel: trustee (see above)
Paul A. Schweizer: trustee B New York, NY 1913. ED New York University (1935). PRIM CORP EMPL director: Schweizer Aircraft Corp. CORP AFFIL director: Harris Hill Soaring Corp. NONPR AFFIL trustee: National Soaring Museum.
Allen C. Smith: trustee
Mary Welles Mooers Smith: vice president, trustee
Finley M. Steele: trustee
Richard W. Swan: trustee CORP AFFIL director: Hilliard Corp.
Jan van den Blink: trustee
Nelson Mooers van den Blink: president, trustee (see above)
Gordon Webster: treasurer, trustee

Grants Analysis

Disclosure Period: fiscal year ending April 30, 2002
Total Grants: $180,800*
Number of Grants: 25
Average Grant: $7,232
Highest Grant: $30,000
Lowest Grant: $500
Typical Range: $1,000 to $10,000
***Note:** Giving excludes United Way.

Recent Grants

Note: Grants derived from fiscal 2000 Form 990.

Library-Related
5,000	Steel Memorial Library

General
16,500	National Soaring Museum, Elmira, NY
16,500	Tanglewood Nature Center
11,000	Arnot Ogden Medical Center, Elmira, NY
10,000	Arnot Ogden Medical Center Foundation, Elmira, NY
10,000	Clemens Center, Elmira, NY
8,000	Elmira College, Elmira, NY
6,000	Arnot Art Museum, Elmira, NY
5,000	Arnot Art Museum, Elmira, NY
5,000	Chemung County Historical Society, Elmira, NY
5,000	Clemens Center, Elmira, NY

HILLMAN FOUNDATION

Giving Contact

Ronald W. Wertz, President
2000 Grant Building
Pittsburgh, PA 15219
Phone: (412)338-3466
Fax: (412)338-3463
E-mail: foundation@hillmanfo.com

Description

Founded: 1951
EIN: 256011462
Organization Type: General Purpose Foundation
Giving Locations: PA: Southwestern part of state, Pittsburgh
Grant Types: Capital, Endowment, General Support, Professorship, Scholarship, Seed Money.

Donor Information

Founder: The Hillman Foundation was established in 1951 by John Hartwell Hillman Jr. , a transportation and coal industrialist. The Hillman Company, a private corporation, is a major venture capital firm, with additional holdings in real estate and manufacturing. Mr. Hillman, who died in 1981, intended the foundation to benefit the city of Pittsburgh where his business interests were centered. The Hillmans had seven children, one of whom is chairman of the foundation.

Financial Summary

Total Giving: $6,462,400 (2001); $7,589,250 (2000); $5,653,200 (1998)
Giving Analysis: Giving for 2001 includes: foundation grants to United Way ($110,000) 2000: foundation grants to United Way ($100,000)
Assets: $133,410,036 (2001); $141,969,188 (2000); $115,958,383 (1998)
Gifts Received: $26,318 (1998). Note: In 1998, contributions were received from the John Hartwell Educational Trust.

Typical Recipients

Arts & Humanities: Arts Associations & Councils, Arts Centers, Ballet, Ethnic & Folk Arts, Film & Video, Arts & Humanities-General, History & Archaeology, Libraries, Museums/Galleries, Music, Opera, Public Broadcasting, Theater
Civic & Public Affairs: African American Affairs, Business/Free Enterprise, Clubs, Community Foundations, Economic Development, Employment/Job Training, Civic & Public Affairs-General, Housing, Minority Business, Urban & Community Affairs, Zoos/Aquariums
Education: Arts/Humanities Education, Business Education, Colleges & Universities, Community & Junior Colleges, Economic Education, Education Reform, Faculty Development, Education-General, Gifted & Talented Programs, Literacy, Medical Education, Minority Education, Preschool Education, Private Education (Precollege), Religious Education, Science/Mathematics Education, Social Sciences Education, Special Education, Student Aid
Environment: Environment-General, Wildlife Protection
Health: AIDS/HIV, Cancer, Children's Health/Hospitals, Eyes/Blindness, Health Organizations, Long-Term Care, Medical Rehabilitation, Medical Research, Mental Health, Nursing Services, Outpatient Health Care, Research/Studies Institutes, Single-Disease Health Associations, Speech & Hearing
International: International Relief Efforts
Religion: Jewish Causes, Religious Organizations, Religious Welfare, Seminaries
Science: Science Museums, Scientific Centers & Institutes

5,000	Clemens Center, Elmira, NY

Social Services: At-Risk Youth, Big Brother/Big Sister, Child Welfare, Community Centers, Community Service Organizations, Crime Prevention, Day Care, Delinquency & Criminal Rehabilitation, Domestic Violence, Family Planning, Food/Clothing Distribution, Homes, People with Disabilities, Recreation & Athletics, Scouts, Senior Services, Sexual Abuse, Shelters/Homelessness, Social Services-General, Substance Abuse, United Funds/United Ways, YMCA/YWCA/YMHA/YWHA, Youth Organizations

Application Procedures

Initial Contact: The foundation will accept the Common Grant Application Form of Grantmakers of Western Pennsylvania.
Application Requirements: The cover letter of the proposal should convey justification for the request and must be signed by an authorized official of the organization. The request should include an annual budget, a listing of the organization's directors or trustees, detailed information about costs of the project for which funds are sought, and a time schedule (if appropriate). Applications also must provide proof of tax-exempt status, and indicate that any grant received from the foundation will be considered a "qualifying distribution" as defined in the Internal Revenue Code Section 4942(g) rather than a "taxable expenditure" as defined in the Internal Revenue Code Section 4945(d).
Deadlines: None.
Review Process: The board meets quarterly to consider applications.

Restrictions

The foundation does not make grants to individuals, to organizations outside the United States, for travel expenses, or for conferences or seminars.

Additional Information

Recipients are expected to provide periodic written reports concerning the project or program funded. The foundation will specify the timetable and contents of the reports when each contribution is made.
Publications: Annual Report

Foundation Officials

H. Vaughan Blaxter, III: director, secretary B 1943. PRIM CORP EMPL vice president, secretary, director: Hillman Co. CORP AFFIL secretary: Emerald Holding Co. Inc. NONPR AFFIL treasurer: Childrens Center Pittsburgh.
Carl G. Grefenstette: director, vice president B Toledo, OH 1927. ED Duquesne University (1950). PRIM CORP EMPL chairman, chief executive officer, director: Hillman Co. NONPR AFFIL member: American Institute of Certified Public Accountants; director: Duquesne University.
Elsie Hilliard Hillman: director B 1925. ED Westminster Choir College (1944-1945). CORP AFFIL director: Hillman Co.; director: Hillman Manufacturing Co. NONPR AFFIL director: Westminster Choir College; director, vice president: WQED Public TV; vice president: Squirrel Hill Urban Coalition; director, vice president: Pittsburgh Oratorio Society; director, vice president: Pittsburgh Symphony Society; trustee: Carlow College; honorary board member: Ellis School.
Henry Lea Hillman, Jr.: chairman B Pittsburgh, PA December 25, 1918. ED Princeton University AB (1941). PRIM CORP EMPL chairman executive committee: Hillman Co. NONPR AFFIL member: Business Council; trustee: Carnegie Institute; emeritus member executive committee: Allegheny Conference Community Development. CLUB AFFIL Seminole Golf Club; Princeton Club; Rolling Rock Club; Pittsburgh Golf Club; The Links Club; Lyford Cay Club; Laurel Valley Golf Club; Duquesne Club; Fox Chapel Golf Club; Augusta National Golf Club.
Lisa R. Johns: assistant treasurer
Lawrence M. Wagner: treasurer, director B 1939. PRIM CORP EMPL president: Hillman Co.
Ronald W. Wertz: president B 1937.

Grants Analysis

Disclosure Period: calendar year ending 2001
Total Grants: $6,352,400*
Number of Grants: 59
Average Grant: $92,283*
Highest Grant: $1,000,000
Lowest Grant: $4,000
Typical Range: $50,000 to $150,000
*__Note:__ Giving excludes United Way. Average grant figure excludes highest grant.

Recent Grants

Note: Grants derived from 2000 Form 990.

Library-Related

100,000	Point Park College, Pittsburgh, PA -- towards project: teach designed to train K-12 teachers to meet anticipated teacher shortage

General

500,000	University of Pittsburgh, Pittsburgh, PA -- towards establishing endowed chair
500,000	UPMC Shadyside Auxiliary, Pittsburgh, PA -- towards construction
300,000	Duquesne University, Pittsburgh, PA -- towards establishing endowed chair
250,000	Ellis School, Pittsburgh, PA -- towards construction of Hillman Family Building
250,000	Ellis School, Pittsburgh, PA -- towards construction of Hillman Family Building
250,000	Pittsburgh Symphony Society, Pittsburgh, PA -- towards endowment to establish Henry and Elsie Hillman Principal Pops Conductor Chair
200,000	Allegheny Conference on Community Development, Pittsburgh, PA -- towards economic development activities to implement regional investment strategies
200,000	Carnegie Mellon University, Pittsburgh, PA -- towards endowment to establish The Hillman Entrepreneurship Fund
175,000	YMCA, Pittsburgh, PA -- towards renovation and expansion of Centre Avenue and Homewood Brushton Program Centers
175,000	Zoological Society of Pittsburgh, Pittsburgh, PA -- towards development of new aquarium

HILLSDALE FUND

Giving Contact

E. Eloy Doolan, Vice President
Hillsdale Fund
PO Box 20124
Greensboro, NC 27420
Phone: (336)274-5471

Description

Founded: 1963
EIN: 566057433
Organization Type: Family Foundation
Giving Locations: NC; U.S. Eastern Region.
Grant Types: General Support.

Donor Information

Founder: The fund was incorporated in 1963 by the L. Richardson family.

Financial Summary

Total Giving: $2,023,600 (2000); $1,750,800 (1998); $1,371,430 (1997)
Giving Analysis: Giving for 2000 includes: foundation grants to United Way ($5,000) 1998: foundation grants to United Way ($5,000)
Assets: $2,526,792 (2000); $42,656,238 (1998); $36,556,848 (1997)

Gifts Received: $1,556,478 (2000); $50,000 (1998); $50,000 (1997). Note: In 1998, contributions were received from Lunsford Richardson, Jr.

Typical Recipients

Arts & Humanities: Arts Associations & Councils, Arts Centers, Arts Festivals, Arts Funds, Ballet, Dance, Film & Video, Historic Preservation, History & Archaeology, Libraries, Literary Arts, Museums/Galleries, Music, Opera, Performing Arts, Public Broadcasting, Theater
Civic & Public Affairs: Botanical Gardens/Parks, Community Foundations, Economic Development, Ethnic Organizations, Civic & Public Affairs-General, Housing, Legal Aid, Municipalities/Towns, Nonprofit Management, Philanthropic Organizations, Public Policy, Rural Affairs, Safety, Urban & Community Affairs, Women's Affairs, Zoos/Aquariums
Education: Agricultural Education, Arts/Humanities Education, Colleges & Universities, Community & Junior Colleges, Economic Education, Elementary Education (Private), Engineering/Technological Education, Education-General, Health & Physical Education, Leadership Training, Legal Education, Literacy, Private Education (Precollege), Public Education (Precollege), Religious Education, Student Aid
Environment: Forestry, Environment-General, Resource Conservation
Health: AIDS/HIV, Alzheimers Disease, Cancer, Children's Health/Hospitals, Emergency/Ambulance Services, Health-General, Health Organizations, Hospices, Hospitals, Multiple Sclerosis, Preventive Medicine/Wellness Organizations, Public Health, Single-Disease Health Associations
International: Foreign Arts Organizations, Health Care/Hospitals, International Relief Efforts, International Relief Efforts, Missionary/Religious Activities
Religion: Churches, Ministries, Missionary Activities (Domestic), Religious Organizations, Religious Welfare, Seminaries
Science: Science Museums, Scientific Centers & Institutes, Scientific Labs
Social Services: Animal Protection, At-Risk Youth, Child Welfare, Community Service Organizations, Counseling, Family Planning, Family Services, Food/Clothing Distribution, Homes, People with Disabilities, Recreation & Athletics, Scouts, Senior Services, Shelters/Homelessness, Substance Abuse, United Funds/United Ways, YMCA/YWCA/YMHA/YWHA, Youth Organizations

Application Procedures

Initial Contact: Applicants should write for application form.
Application Requirements: Completed applications will include a copy of an IRS exemption letter with the application form, which asks for legal name of organization, name of contact person, summary description of project (not to exceed three double-spaced pages), total cost of project, amount requested, other principal funding sources, principal sources of funds for day-to-day operations, financial information, and signature of officer or chief staff person.
Deadlines: Set not less than two nor more than three months before the board meetings.
Review Process: The board of trustees meets twice each year--in the spring and fall. At each board meeting, the date of the next board meeting and the deadline for that meeting are established.

Restrictions

The fund does not maintain a discretionary fund nor make emergency grants. No grant funds will be made for indirect costs or overhead. Grants will not be made for routine, recurring operating expenses except in unusual circumstances, such as for pilot projects; where the need is temporary; or where more permanent funding is in sight. Pass-through grants from one organization to another will not be made unless the organizations are legally affiliated or in other unusual circumstances. Challenge grants will be limited to one year and will expire automatically after that time if the challenge is not met. Video tapes will not be accepted as part of the grant request. No grants will be made for conferences and seminars; for film or video production, or for travel for bands, sports teams, or other groups except in unusual circumstances. No grants will be made for travel and study. No grants will be made to individuals.

Additional Information

Publications: Application Form

Foundation Officials

Sion A. Boney, III: trustee B Goldsboro, NC 1923. ED University of North Carolina (1947); Harvard University Graduate School of Business Administration (1949). PRIM CORP EMPL vice president, secretary, treasurer, trustee: Hillsdale Fund Inc. CORP AFFIL director: Piedmont Finance Co.; director: Piedmont Management Co.
Sion A. Boney: trustee
Laurinda L. Douglas: trustee
Barbara Richardson Evans: trustee
J. Peter Gallagher: trustee
Margaret W. Gallagher: trustee
Louise Boney McCoy: trustee
Beatrix W. Richardson: trustee
Eudora L. Richardson: trustee
Lunsford Richardson, Jr.: president, trustee B Greensboro, NC 1924. ED Lehigh University (1946). PRIM CORP EMPL chairman: Richardson Corp. CORP AFFIL director: Chartwell Reinsurance Co.; director: Lexington Global Asset Management Co.
Lunsford Richardson Smith: trustee
Molly R. Smith: trustee
Richard G. Smith, III: trustee
Margaret R. White: trustee

Grants Analysis

Disclosure Period: calendar year ending 2000
Total Grants: $2,018,600*
Number of Grants: 91
Average Grant: $22,182
Highest Grant: $75,000
Lowest Grant: $2,000
Typical Range: $5,000 to $50,000
*__Note:__ Giving excludes United Way.

Recent Grants

Note: Grants derived from 2000 Form 990.

General

75,000	Edgecombe County, NC
75,000	Reynolda House, Inc., Winston-Salem, NC
60,000	Therapy Animals Means Equality, Breckenridge, CO
55,000	Fauquier Housing Corporation, Warrenton, VA
55,000	Gladney Fund, Ft. Worth, TX
53,000	Mercy Home, Brooklyn, NY
50,000	Andean Rural Health Corporation, Lake Junaluska, NC
50,000	Bishop McGuiness Memorial High School, Winston-Salem, NC
50,000	Corporation for Jefferson's Poplar Forest, Forest, VA
50,000	Cystic Fibrosis Foundation Headquarters, Los Angeles, CA

PAUL AND ANNETTA HIMMELFARB FOUNDATION

Giving Contact

Lillian Kronstadt, Executive Director
4545 42nd St. NW, Suite 203
Washington, DC 20016-4623
Phone: (202)966-3795

Description

Founded: 1947
EIN: 520784206
Organization Type: Private Foundation
Giving Locations: DC: Washington; MD; NY: New York
Grant Types: Emergency, General Support, Project, Research.

Donor Information

Founder: members of the Himmelfarb family

Financial Summary

Total Giving: $396,916 (2001); $379,166 (2000); $320,885 (1999)
Assets: $5,964,623 (2001); $6,534,623 (2000); $6,465,300 (1999)

Typical Recipients

Arts & Humanities: Arts Centers, Arts Outreach, Historic Preservation, Libraries, Museums/Galleries, Music, Opera, Performing Arts, Public Broadcasting, Theater
Civic & Public Affairs: Economic Development, Employment/Job Training, Civic & Public Affairs-General, Housing, Law & Justice, Urban & Community Affairs, Women's Affairs
Education: Arts/Humanities Education, Colleges & Universities, Preschool Education, Private Education (Precollege), Science/Mathematics Education, Secondary Education (Private), Student Aid, Vocational & Technical Education
Environment: Environment-General
Health: AIDS/HIV, Cancer, Children's Health/Hospitals, Clinics/Medical Centers, Diabetes, Emergency/Ambulance Services, Eyes/Blindness, Health-General, Heart, Hospices, Hospitals, Kidney, Long-Term Care, Medical Research, Mental Health, Research/Studies Institutes, Respiratory, Single-Disease Health Associations
International: Foreign Arts Organizations, Foreign Educational Institutions, Health Care/Hospitals, International Organizations, Missionary/Religious Activities
Religion: Churches, Religion-General, Jewish Causes, Religious Organizations, Religious Welfare, Synagogues/Temples
Science: Scientific Centers & Institutes
Social Services: Animal Protection, At-Risk Youth, Camps, Child Welfare, Community Service Organizations, Crime Prevention, Day Care, Delinquency & Criminal Rehabilitation, Domestic Violence, Emergency Relief, Family Services, Food/Clothing Distribution, Food/Clothing Distribution, Homes, People with Disabilities, Senior Services, Shelters/Homelessness, Substance Abuse, United Funds/United Ways, YMCA/YWCA/YMHA/YWHA, Youth Organizations

Application Procedures

Initial Contact: Send a brief letter describing program or project.
Application Requirements: Include annual report, proof of tax-exempt status, and amount requested.
Deadlines: None.

Restrictions

Does not provide grants to individuals.

Foundation Officials

Paul Himmelfarb: secretary, director
Annette Kronstadt: director
Lillian Kronstadt: executive director
Norma Lee Naiman: director
Carol Himmelfarb Parker: director
Carole Preston: director

Grants Analysis

Disclosure Period: calendar year ending 2001
Total Grants: $396,916
Number of Grants: 174

Average Grant: $2,218
Highest Grant: $16,666
Typical Range: $1,000 to $5,000

Recent Grants

Note: Grants derived from 2001 Form 990.

General

20,000	WETA, Washington, DC
16,666	Weizmann Institute of Science, Washington, DC
10,000	Gallaudet University, Washington, DC
10,000	Himmelfarb Mobile University - JSSA, Rockville, MD
7,500	Jewish Foundation for Group Homes, Rockville, MD
6,000	Lab School, Washington, DC
5,000	American Diabetes Association, Washington, DC
5,000	American Jewish World Services, New York, NY -- India earthquake
5,000	Bread for the City Zacchaeus Free Clinic, Washington, DC
5,000	Camp Holiday Trails, Charlottesville, VA

HINO DIESEL TRUCKS (U.S.A.)

Company Headquarters

25 Corporate Dr.
Orangeburg, NY 10962

Company Description

Employees: 44
SIC(s): 5012 Automobiles & Other Motor Vehicles.
Parent Company: Hino Motors, Ltd., 1-1 Hinadai 3-chome Hino-Shi, Tokyo, Japan

Operating Locations

Hino Diesel Trucks (U.S.A.) (NY--Orangeburg)

Giving Contact

Frank Merz, Vice President
25 Corporate Dr.
Orangeburg, NY 10962
Phone: (845)365-1400
Fax: (845)365-1409
E-mail: merz@hino.com

Description

Organization Type: Corporate Giving Program
Giving Locations: headquarters and operating communities.
Grant Types: Capital.

Typical Recipients

Arts & Humanities: Libraries
Social Services: Substance Abuse, Volunteer Services, Youth Organizations

Application Procedures

Initial Contact: Applications not encouraged.

Corporate Officials

Mr. Y. Hayakawa: chairman, president, chief executive officer treasurer PRIM CORP EMPL chairman, president, chief executive officer: Hino Diesel Trucks (USA).
N. Mukai: executive vice president, secretary, treasurer PRIM CORP EMPL executive vice president, secretary, treasurer: Hino Diesel Trucks (U.S.A.).

GILBERT M. AND MARTHA H. HITCHCOCK FOUNDATION

Giving Contact

Thomas R. Burke, Attorney
10306 Regency Pky. Dr.
Omaha, NE 68114
Phone: (402)397-7300

Description

Founded: 1943
EIN: 476025723
Organization Type: Private Foundation
Giving Locations: IA: Western part of state; NE: Omaha
Grant Types: Capital, Endowment, General Support, Scholarship.

Donor Information

Founder: the late Martha H. Hitchcock

Financial Summary

Total Giving: $808,000 (2001); $895,500 (2000); $709,000 (1999)
Giving Analysis: Giving for 2001 includes: foundation grants to United Way ($5,000); foundation scholarships ($40,000); 2000: foundation grants to United Way ($5,000); foundation scholarships ($10,000); 1999: foundation scholarships ($5,000); foundation grants to United Way ($5,000).
Assets: $17,675,166 (2001); $18,901,461 (2000); $18,497,580 (1999)

Typical Recipients

Arts & Humanities: Arts Associations & Councils, Community Arts, Dance, Historic Preservation, History & Archaeology, Libraries, Museums/Galleries, Music, Opera, Performing Arts, Public Broadcasting, Theater
Civic & Public Affairs: Botanical Gardens/Parks, Civic & Public Affairs-General, Safety, Zoos/Aquariums
Education: Colleges & Universities, Education Funds, Education-General, Legal Education, Private Education (Precollege), Public Education (Precollege), Special Education, Student Aid
Environment: Forestry, Environment-General, Resource Conservation
Health: Children's Health/Hospitals, Health Organizations, Hospices, Nursing Services
Religion: Churches, Religious Welfare
Science: Science Museums
Social Services: Child Welfare, Crime Prevention, Day Care, People with Disabilities, Scouts, United Funds/United Ways, Volunteer Services, Youth Organizations

Application Procedures

Initial Contact: Send a brief letter of inquiry requesting application form.
Application Requirements: Include a description of organization, amount requested, recently audited financial statement, printing, budget of project, purpose of funds sought and proof of tax-exempt status.
Deadlines: November 1.

Restrictions

Provides grants to private educational institutions, religious organizations, and arts organizations. Does not support individuals.

Additional Information

Foundation provides scholarships for newspaper carriers.
Publications: Application Guidelines; Application Form

Foundation Officials

Thomas R. Burke: secretary
Tyler B. Gaines: trustee
Charles Denman Kountze: trustee
Denman Kountze: president, trustee
Edward H. Kountze: trustee
Mary Kountze: trustee
Neely Kountze: trustee
Ronald R. Ruh: trustee
Paul V. Shirley, Jr.: trustee

Grants Analysis

Disclosure Period: calendar year ending 2001
Total Grants: $763,000*
Number of Grants: 34
Average Grant: $14,030*
Highest Grant: $300,000
Lowest Grant: $1,000
Typical Range: $5,000 to $30,000
*Note: Giving excludes United Way and scholarships. Average grant figure excludes highest grant.

Recent Grants

Note: Grants derived from 2001 Form 990.

Library-Related

10,000	Kountze Library, Kountze, TX

General

300,000	Omaha Botanical Gardens, Omaha, NE
50,000	Bellevue University Foundation, Bellevue, NE
50,000	Henry Doorly Zoo Farm Endowment Fund, Omaha, NE
50,000	Henry Doorly Zoo Farm Endowment Fund, Omaha, NE
45,000	Pottawattamie Conservation Foundation, Council Bluffs, IA
40,000	Brownell Talbot, Omaha, NE
25,000	Historical Society of Douglas County, Omaha, NE
25,000	Ross Film Theater
25,000	SAC Museum Memorial Society, Omaha, NE
25,000	Stephen Center, Omaha, NE

GEORGE HOAG FAMILY FOUNDATION

Giving Contact

Charles W. Smith, Secretary/Executive Director
11340 West Olympic Blvd., Ste. 300
Los Angeles, CA 90064
Phone: (310)473-9050
Fax: (310)473-9091

Description

Founded: 1940
EIN: 956006885
Organization Type: Family Foundation
Giving Locations: CA: Orange County
Grant Types: General Support, Project, Research.

Donor Information

Founder: The Hoag Foundation was established in 1940 with funds donated by the late George Grant Hoag and from bequests from his estate. His widow, Grace E. Hoag, and his son, George Grant Hoag II, also have supported the foundation with donations. George Grant Hoag was a prominent vice president and director of the J.C. Penney Company. The foundation sponsored the construction of the Hoag Memorial Hospital in Newport Beach, CA.

Financial Summary

Total Giving: $2,731,900 (2001); $2,058,400 (1998); $1,760,000 (1997)
Assets: $69,250,056 (2001); $62,445,007 (1998); $57,462,956 (1997)

Typical Recipients

Arts & Humanities: Arts Festivals, Ballet, Libraries, Literary Arts, Museums/Galleries, Music, Opera, Performing Arts, Public Broadcasting, Theater
Civic & Public Affairs: Civil Rights, Community Foundations, Employment/Job Training, Civic & Public Affairs-General, Hispanic Affairs, Housing, Law & Justice, Legal Aid, Municipalities/Towns, Public Policy, Urban & Community Affairs, Zoos/Aquariums
Education: Afterschool/Enrichment Programs, Agricultural Education, Arts/Humanities Education, Colleges & Universities, Education Associations, Education Reform, Elementary Education (Public), Education-General, Gifted & Talented Programs, Literacy, Preschool Education, Private Education (Precollege), Private Education (Precollege), Public Education (Precollege), Science/Mathematics Education, Secondary Education (Private), Secondary Education (Public), Special Education
Environment: Environment-General, Wildlife Protection
Health: Adolescent Health Issues, AIDS/HIV, Alzheimers Disease, Cancer, Children's Health/Hospitals, Clinics/Medical Centers, Diabetes, Emergency/Ambulance Services, Eyes/Blindness, Health-General, Health Organizations, Heart, Hospices, Hospitals, Medical Research, Outpatient Health Care, Prenatal Health Issues, Preventive Medicine/Wellness Organizations, Public Health, Research/Studies Institutes, Single-Disease Health Associations
International: International Environmental Issues, International Relations, International Relief Efforts, Missionary/Religious Activities
Religion: Churches, Religion-General, Religious Organizations, Religious Welfare
Science: Science Museums
Social Services: At-Risk Youth, Big Brother/Big Sister, Child Abuse, Child Welfare, Community Centers, Community Service Organizations, Counseling, Day Care, Domestic Violence, Family Services, Food/Clothing Distribution, Homes, People with Disabilities, Recreation & Athletics, Scouts, Senior Services, Shelters/Homelessness, Social Services-General, Substance Abuse, YMCA/YWCA/YMHA/YWHA, Youth Organizations

Application Procedures

Initial Contact: Written requests, not exceeding two pages, should be sent to the foundation to determine eligibility and to arrange for necessary forms and any additional information which may be needed.
Application Requirements: Requests should outline aims and specific needs. Finished applications (nine copies) must be accompanied by IRS determination letter of tax-exempt status, California Franchise Tax Board letter, Forms 4653 or 2218, and notification of status under section 509(a). Also include an audited financial statement; list of officers, directors, and trustees; detailed statement of request; budget; timetable; list of other funding sources; statement of how the project would benefit California and/or Orange County residents and the need served; statement specifying when the organization will report to the foundation on the disbursement of funds and the results obtained; and a declaration from the governing body of the organization authorizing the application.
Deadlines: March 31 for May meeting and September 30 for November meeting.
Review Process: The foundation's grant-making criteria include current need for proposed project and extent to which it duplicates existing services; reasonableness of budget; evidence of efficient, economical management and experienced, competent personnel; and assurance of practical results. Final decisions on each application are communicated to applicants in writing following the board meetings in May and November.

Restrictions

The foundation does not make grants to individuals for any purpose. It generally does not give to governmental agencies or organizations that receive substantial support from taxation; sectarian or religious organizations in which the principal activity benefits the members; or organizations soliciting funds in support of projects or programs operated by a party other than the applicant. The foundation usually does not make grants to any organization two years in succession, and prefers not to grant funds more often than once every three or four years.

Additional Information

Communications with individual directors of the foundation will not be of assistance to the applicant, and are discouraged.
The foundation was originally known as the HOAG Foundation.

Foundation Officials

Albert J. Auer: director B 1924. PRIM CORP EMPL president: Albert J. Auer Associates Inc. CORP AFFIL director: Kearney Mesa Bowl Inc.
John L. Curi: director CORP AFFIL general partner: Washington Plaza Associates.
W. Dickerson Milliken: secretary, director
Gwyn Parry: director
Melinda Hoag Smith: president, director
Del V. Werderman: treasurer

Grants Analysis

Disclosure Period: calendar year ending 2001
Total Grants: $2,731,900
Number of Grants: 74
Average Grant: $23,725*
Highest Grant: $1,000,000
Lowest Grant: $2,000
Typical Range: $10,000 to $50,000
*Note: Average grant figure excludes highest grant.

Recent Grants

Note: Grants derived from 2001 Form 990.

Library-Related

25,000	Library Foundation of Los Angeles, Los Angeles, CA -- Grandparents and Books reading enrichment program for children
10,000	Henry E. Huntington Library and Art Gallery, San Marino, CA -- design exhibition for the field lab station

General

1,000,000	Hoag Memorial Hospital Presbyterian Foundation, Newport Beach, CA -- construction of Women's Pavilion
75,000	Adult Day Services of Orange County, Costa Mesa, CA -- services to needy caregiving families of the Alzheimer's diagnosed elderly
75,000	All-American Boys Chorus, Costa Mesa, CA -- purchase a touring bus for travel throughout the United States and Canada
75,000	John Henry Foundation, Garden Grove, CA -- provide housing and employment opportunity for the mentally ill
75,000	Los Angeles Youth Programs, Los Angeles, CA -- after school program for youth
60,000	City of Hope, Los Angeles, CA -- Leukemia Research Program
55,000	Doheny Eye Institute, Los Angeles, CA -- purchase of ultrasound imaging equipment
50,000	Boys & Girls Club of Santa Monica, Santa Monica, CA -- restore and remodel the main branch facility
50,000	CHOC Foundation for Children, Orange, CA -- operational and capital support for healthy tomorrows mobile health clinic

50,000   Food Bank Coalition of San Luis Obispo County, Paso Robles, CA -- capital campaign for a larger food warehouse

HOBBY FAMILY FOUNDATION

Giving Contact

Jennifer Cole, Secretary
2131 San Felipe
Houston, TX 77019-5620
Phone: (713)521-4694
Fax: (713)521-3950

Description

Founded: 1945
EIN: 746026606
Organization Type: Family Foundation
Giving Locations: TX: Houston
Grant Types: General Support.

Donor Information

Founder: Incorporated in 1945 by Oveta Culp Hobby, the late W. P. Hobby , and the Houston Post Co.

Financial Summary

Total Giving: $1,300,000 (2001); $1,300,000 (1999 approx); $3,093,644 (1998)
Assets: $30,000,000 (2001); $30,992,749 (1998); $36,343,210 (1995)
Gifts Received: $100,000 (1993)

Typical Recipients

Arts & Humanities: Arts Associations & Councils, Arts Institutes, Ballet, Arts & Humanities-General, Historic Preservation, History & Archaeology, Libraries, Literary Arts, Museums/Galleries, Music, Opera, Theater
Civic & Public Affairs: African American Affairs, Botanical Gardens/Parks, Civic & Public Affairs-General, Hispanic Affairs, Housing, Legal Aid, Municipalities/Towns, Parades/Festivals, Philanthropic Organizations, Public Policy, Urban & Community Affairs, Women's Affairs, Zoos/Aquariums
Education: Arts/Humanities Education, Business Education, Colleges & Universities, Elementary Education (Public), Education-General, International Studies, Literacy, Minority Education, Private Education (Precollege), Private Education (Precollege), Science/Mathematics Education, Social Sciences Education, Special Education, Student Aid
Environment: Environment-General, Resource Conservation, Wildlife Protection
Health: AIDS/HIV, Alzheimers Disease, Cancer, Children's Health/Hospitals, Emergency/Ambulance Services, Eyes/Blindness, Health Funds, Health Organizations, Heart, Hospices, Hospitals, Mental Health, Single-Disease Health Associations
International: International Affairs, Missionary/Religious Activities
Religion: Churches, Ministries, Religious Organizations, Religious Welfare
Science: Observatories & Planetariums, Science Museums, Scientific Centers & Institutes, Scientific Organizations
Social Services: Animal Protection, Child Welfare, Community Centers, Community Service Organizations, Domestic Violence, Emergency Relief, Family Planning, Food/Clothing Distribution, People with Disabilities, Scouts, Shelters/Homelessness, United Funds/United Ways, Volunteer Services, YMCA/YWCA/YMHA/YWHA, Youth Organizations

Application Procedures

Initial Contact: Write a proposal letter or memorandum briefly describing the need for funds.
Application Requirements: The following information should be included in the proposal: a brief background of the organization; a description of the proposed project along with a concise statement of the project; an explanation of the proposed use of funds; evidence of tax-exempt status; and a statement of approval of the request for funds signed by the chief administrator of the organization.
Deadlines: None.

Restrictions

The foundation does not make grants or award scholarships to individuals. Majority of giving is limited to Houston area.

Additional Information

In 1996 the Hobby Foundation split into two seperate foundations: Catto Charitable Foundation in San Antonio, TX, and Hobby Family Foundation in Houston, TX.
Publications: Application Guidelines

Foundation Officials

Laura H. Beckworth: vice president
Pamela L. George: secretary
Diana P. Hobby: vice president
Paul W. Hobby: vice president B Houston, TX 1960. ED University of Virginia (1982); University of Texas JD (1985). PRIM CORP EMPL chairman: Hobby Media Services Inc. CORP AFFIL director: Coastal Bancorp Inc.; director: Stewart Information Services Corp.; director: Aronex Pharmaceuticals Inc.
William Pettus Hobby: president B Houston, TX 1932. ED Rice University BA (1953). CORP AFFIL director: Southwest Airlines Co. NONPR AFFIL professor: Rice University.
Cathy Leeson: treasurer

Grants Analysis

Disclosure Period: calendar year ending 1998
Total Grants: $691,704*
Number of Grants: 144
Average Grant: $4,804
Highest Grant: $100,000
Typical Range: $1,000 to $10,000
*Note: Giving excludes United Way and $2,396,940 in stock contributions to two organizations.

Recent Grants

Note: Grants derived from 1999 Form 990.

General

1,000,000	Baylor College of Medicine, Houston, TX -- for operating expenses
100,000	Harry Ransom Humanities Research Center, Austin, TX -- for endowment fund
60,000	St. John's School, Houston, TX -- for retirement of debt and building fund
50,000	Kinkaid School, Houston, TX -- capital campaign
37,500	Wake Forest University, Winston-Salem, NC -- for scholarship fund
35,000	Houston Symphony Society, Houston, TX -- for operating expenses
30,000	Lockhart Community Recreation Center, Lockhart, TX -- for operating expenses
30,000	Willie Mae Mitchell Community Opportunity Center, San Marcos, TX -- for operating expenses
25,000	Houston Ballet, Houston, TX -- for operating expenses
25,000	Houston Grand Opera, Houston, TX -- for operating expenses

HOBLITZELLE FOUNDATION

Giving Contact

Paul W. Harris, Executive Vice President
5956 Sherry Lane, Suite 901
Dallas, TX 75225-6522
Phone: (214)373-0462
Fax: (214)750-7412
E-mail: hoblitzelle@worldnet.att.net
Web: http://home.att.net/~hoblitzelle

Description

Founded: 1942
EIN: 756003984
Organization Type: General Purpose Foundation
Giving Locations: TX, Dallas
Grant Types: Capital, Matching, Multiyear/Continuing Support.

Donor Information

Founder: The foundation was established in 1942. The foundation's donors were the late Karl St. John Hoblitzelle and Esther Hoblitzelle. Karl Hoblitzelle (1879-1967) was president of Interstate Circuit, Texas Consolidated Theaters, and Hoblitzelle Properties. He was also chairman of Republic National Bank of Dallas and the Southwest Medical Foundation. In addition, he served as trustee of Texas A&M University and the Dallas Foundation.

Financial Summary

Total Giving: $5,178,882 (fiscal year ending April 30, 2002); $6,694,347 (fiscal 2001); $6,753,299 (fiscal 2000)
Giving Analysis: Giving for fiscal 2000 includes: foundation grants to United Way ($150,000) fiscal 1999: foundation grants to United Way ($350,000)
Assets: $116,000,000 (fiscal 2002); $131,795,263 (fiscal 2001); $144,961,778 (fiscal 2000)
Gifts Received: $30,140 (fiscal 2001); $27,924 (fiscal 2000); $27,093 (fiscal 1999). Note: In fiscal 2001, 2000 and 1999, contributions were received from the Karl Hoblitzelle Trust.

Typical Recipients

Arts & Humanities: Arts Festivals, Arts Outreach, Ballet, Community Arts, Ethnic & Folk Arts, Historic Preservation, History & Archaeology, Libraries, Museums/Galleries, Music, Opera, Public Broadcasting, Theater
Civic & Public Affairs: Botanical Gardens/Parks, Chambers of Commerce, Clubs, Economic Development, Employment/Job Training, Civic & Public Affairs-General, Hispanic Affairs, Housing, Native American Affairs, Nonprofit Management, Safety, Urban & Community Affairs, Women's Affairs, Zoos/Aquariums
Education: Afterschool/Enrichment Programs, Agricultural Education, Business Education, Colleges & Universities, Education Reform, Engineering/Technological Education, Education-General, Education-General, Literacy, Medical Education, Minority Education, Private Education (Precollege), Public Education (Precollege), Science/Mathematics Education, Secondary Education (Private), Special Education, Student Aid
Environment: Resource Conservation
Health: AIDS/HIV, Alzheimers Disease, Cancer, Children's Health/Hospitals, Clinics/Medical Centers, Diabetes, Emergency/Ambulance Services, Eyes/Blindness, Health-General, Health Funds, Health Organizations, Hospices, Hospitals, Hospitals (University Affiliated), Long-Term Care, Medical Research, Medical Training, Multiple Sclerosis, Nursing Services, Prenatal Health Issues, Public Health, Single-Disease Health Associations, Transplant Networks/Donor Banks, Trauma Treatment

Religion: Churches, Ministries, Missionary Activities (Domestic), Religious Organizations, Religious Welfare

Science: Science Exhibits & Fairs, Science Museums, Scientific Centers & Institutes

Social Services: Animal Protection, At-Risk Youth, Big Brother/Big Sister, Camps, Child Welfare, Community Centers, Community Service Organizations, Counseling, Crime Prevention, Day Care, Emergency Relief, Family Planning, Family Services, Food/Clothing Distribution, Homes, People with Disabilities, Recreation & Athletics, Scouts, Senior Services, Shelters/Homelessness, Substance Abuse, United Funds/United Ways, Volunteer Services, YMCA/YWCA/YMHA/YWHA, Youth Organizations

Application Procedures

Initial Contact: Applicants should send a letter to the foundation.

Application Requirements: The letter should include a brief narrative describing the project, its justification, cost based on reliable estimates, funding already realized or anticipated from other sources, proof of tax-exempt status, and the amount requested. If the project falls within the foundation's areas of interest, a more detailed proposal may be requested.

Deadlines: Submit requests before January 15, May 15, or September 15.

Review Process: The board meets to consider applications in the latter part of February, June, and October.

Restrictions

No grants are made for religious purposes or to individuals. Grants are not made for operating budgets, debt retirement, research, media productions or publications, scholarships, endowments, or loans. No grants are made outside of Texas.

Additional Information

The foundation lists Nations Bank as a corporate trustee.

Publications: Annual Report

Foundation Officials

Jerry S. Farrington: director B Burkburnett, TX 1934. ED North Texas State University BBA (1955); North Texas State University MBA (1958). PRIM CORP EMPL chairman emeritus, director: Texas Utilities Co. CORP AFFIL chairman emeritus: Texas Utilities Mining Co.; chairman: TXV Corp.

Gerald W. Fronterhouse: chairman, director B Ada, OK 1936. ED University of Oklahoma (1959); Harvard University MBA (1962). CORP AFFIL director: Texas Instruments; director: Employees Casualty Co. NONPR AFFIL member: Beta Theta Pi.

Paul W. Harris: executive vice president

Caren H. Prothro: treasurer, director

George A. Shafer: president, chief executive officer, director PRIM CORP EMPL president: Industrial Properties Corp. CORP AFFIL director: General Homes Corp.

William Tarver Solomon: director B Dallas, TX 1942. ED Southern Methodist University BScE (1965); Harvard University MBA (1967). PRIM CORP EMPL chairman, chief executive officer, director: Austin Industries. CORP AFFIL director: National Bank Texas; director: Chilton Corp.; director: Fidelity Union Life Insurance Co.; director: AH Belo Corp.; chairman: British American Insurance Co.; chairman: Austin Commercial Inc. NONPR AFFIL trustee: Southwest Medicine Foundation; member: Young President Organization; member: Salesmanship Club Dallas; trustee: Southern Methodist University; member: Dallas Chamber of Commerce; founder: Dallas Museum Art; director: Baylor University Medical Center Foundation; member: Dallas Assembly; member: American Society Civil Engineers.

Mary L. Stacy: corporate secretary

Grants Analysis

Disclosure Period: fiscal year ending April 30, 2001
Total Grants: $6,694,347
Number of Grants: 78
Average Grant: $74,926*
Highest Grant: $500,000
Typical Range: $30,000 to $150,000
*Note: Average grant figure excludes two highest grants ($1,000,000).

Recent Grants

Note: Grants derived from fiscal 2000 Form 990.

Library-Related

300,000	East Dallas Community School, Dallas, TX -- toward campus development
50,000	East Dallas Community School, Dallas, TX -- facility restoration

General

500,000	St. Mark's School, Dallas, TX -- toward new administration building
300,000	Family Place, The, Dallas, TX -- to help build a new residential campus
300,000	Southwestern Medical Foundation, Karl and Esther Hoblitzelle Fund, Dallas, TX -- assistant professor/scholar development program
250,000	Lutheran High School of Dallas, Dallas, TX -- campus improvements
250,000	University of Dallas, Irving, TX -- campus improvements
235,000	YMCA Of Metropolitan Dallas, Dallas, TX -- area wide campaign
200,000	Buckner Children and Family Services, Dallas, TX -- for new group living facility
150,000	Dallas CASA, Dallas, TX -- toward facility development
150,000	Katy Trail, Dallas, TX -- toward development of a urban hike/bike greenway
150,000	United Way of Metropolitan Dallas, Dallas, TX -- communications systems

CHARLES H. HOCH FOUNDATION

Giving Contact

Richard J. Hummel, President & Treasurer
1825 Lehigh Parkway N.
Allentown, PA 18103
Phone: (610)366-9934

Description

Founded: 1956
EIN: 236265016
Organization Type: Private Foundation
Giving Locations: PA: Allentown
Grant Types: General Support.

Financial Summary

Total Giving: $334,822 (2000); $316,500 (1999); $291,400 (1998)
Giving Analysis: Giving for 2000 includes: foundation scholarships ($34,000) 1999: foundation scholarships ($21,000)
Assets: $7,342,357 (2000); $7,115,362 (1999); $6,404,393 (1998)
Gifts Received: $619,044 (1994)

Typical Recipients

Arts & Humanities: Arts Outreach, History & Archaeology, Libraries, Museums/Galleries, Music, Public Broadcasting, Theater

Civic & Public Affairs: Community Foundations, Hispanic Affairs, Housing

Education: Arts/Humanities Education, Business Education, Colleges & Universities, Community & Junior Colleges, Private Education (Precollege), Secondary Education (Private), Special Education, Student Aid

Environment: Resource Conservation, Wildlife Protection

Health: Emergency/Ambulance Services, Eyes/Blindness, Health Organizations

International: International Peace & Security Issues

Religion: Churches, Ministries, Religious Welfare

Social Services: Animal Protection, Camps, Family Services, Food/Clothing Distribution, People with Disabilities, Recreation & Athletics, Scouts, Scouts, Senior Services, Shelters/Homelessness, Social Services-General, Special Olympics, YMCA/YWCA/YMHA/YWHA, Youth Organizations

Application Procedures

Initial Contact: Send a brief letter of inquiry.
Application Requirements: Include purpose of funds sought and proof of tax-exempt status.
Deadlines: None.

Restrictions

Grants are not made to individuals.

Foundation Officials

Alfred E. DeMott: director
James R. Feller: secretary, director
Richard J. Hummel: president, treasurer
Russell K. Laub: first vice president

Grants Analysis

Disclosure Period: calendar year ending 2000
Total Grants: $300,822*
Number of Grants: 69
Average Grant: $4,360
Highest Grant: $10,000
Typical Range: $2,000 to $10,000
*Note: Giving excludes scholarships.

Recent Grants

Note: Grants derived from 2001 Form 990.

General

15,000	Boys and Girls Club of Allentown, Allentown, PA -- Youth Program
12,000	Lehigh County Meals on Wheels, Allentown, PA -- Senior Citizens Programs
10,000	Allentown Rescue Mission, Allentown, PA -- building repairs
10,000	Allentown YMCA/ YWCA, Allentown, PA -- support Youth Programs
10,000	Cedar Crest College, Allentown, PA -- student scholarships
10,000	Lehigh County Historical Society, Allentown, PA -- new building program
10,000	Minsi Trails Boy Scouts of America, Allentown, PA -- Scouting Program
10,000	Muhlenberg College, Allentown, PA -- scholarship fund
10,000	Salvation Army, Allentown, PA -- charitable food bank
8,000	Allentown Art Museum, Allentown, PA -- educational project

HOCHE-SCOFIELD FOUNDATION

Giving Contact

Dorothy Dudley
c/o Fleet Bank
446 Main St.
Worcester, MA 01608-2302
Phone: (508)770-7292

Description

Founded: 1983
EIN: 222519554
Organization Type: Private Foundation
Giving Locations: MA: Worcester County, Worcester

Grant Types: Capital, General Support, Multiyear/ Continuing Support, Project, Seed Money.

Donor Information
Founder: the late William B. Scofield

Financial Summary
Total Giving: $865,647 (fiscal year ending June 30, 2002); $1,064,351 (fiscal 2001); $898,934 (fiscal 2000)
Giving Analysis: Giving for fiscal 1999 includes: foundation grants to United Way ($15,000) foundation grants to United Way ($27,000)
Assets: $17,156,541 (fiscal 2002); $20,155,873 (fiscal 2001); $21,207,153 (fiscal 2000)

Typical Recipients
Arts & Humanities: Arts Associations & Councils, Arts Outreach, Historic Preservation, History & Archaeology, Libraries, Museums/Galleries, Music, Theater
Civic & Public Affairs: Clubs, Economic Development, Civic & Public Affairs-General, Housing, Municipalities/Towns, Professional & Trade Associations, Urban & Community Affairs, Women's Affairs
Education: Arts/Humanities Education, Colleges & Universities, Community & Junior Colleges, Education Reform, Engineering/Technological Education, Preschool Education, Private Education (Precollege), Public Education (Precollege), Science/Mathematics Education, Secondary Education (Private)
Environment: Environment-General, Resource Conservation
Health: Cancer, Children's Health/Hospitals, Clinics/Medical Centers, Diabetes, Health Policy/Cost Containment, Health Organizations, Hospitals, Medical Research, Nursing Services, Public Health
International: Foreign Arts Organizations
Religion: Jewish Causes, Religious Welfare
Science: Scientific Centers & Institutes
Social Services: At-Risk Youth, Big Brother/Big Sister, Child Welfare, Community Service Organizations, Counseling, Crime Prevention, Domestic Violence, Family Planning, Food/Clothing Distribution, Senior Services, Sexual Abuse, Shelters/Homelessness, Substance Abuse, United Funds/United Ways, YMCA/YWCA/YMHA/YWHA, Youth Organizations

Application Procedures
Initial Contact: Request application and guidelines. Requests are reviewed four times per year.

Additional Information
Publications: Application Form; Guidelines
Trust(s): Fleet National Bank

Foundation Officials
Henry Bowen Dewey, Esq.: co-trustee B Worcester, MA 1924. ED Williams College BA (1948); Boston University LLB (1952). PRIM CORP EMPL vice president: Clark Art Institute. NONPR AFFIL overseer: UGBA; member, director: Worcester Youth Guidance Association; member: Massachusetts Historical Society; president: Rural Cemetery; fellow: American College Estate & Turst Council; trustee: Hoche Scofield Charitable Trust; member: American Antiquarian Society. CLUB AFFIL Worcester Club.
Lois B. Green: co-trustee
Paul S. Morgan: co-trustee PRIM CORP EMPL chairman, director: Morgan Construction Co.
John M. Nelson: co-trustee

Grants Analysis
Disclosure Period: fiscal year ending June 30, 2002
Total Grants: $865,647
Number of Grants: 115
Average Grant: $7,527
Highest Grant: $50,000
Lowest Grant: $1,000
Typical Range: $5,000 to $10,000

Recent Grants
Note: Grants derived from fiscal 2000 Form 990.

Library-Related
30,000	Worcester Public Library, Worcester, MA

General
114,781	Trustees of Clark University, Worcester, MA
111,227	Worcester Art Museum, Worcester, MA
111,227	Worcester Polytechnic Institute, Worcester, MA
92,673	City of Worcester, Worcester, MA
91,226	Music Worcester, Inc., Worcester, MA
19,000	American Antiquarian Society, Worcester, MA
15,000	United Way of Central Massachusetts, Worcester, MA
13,500	Worcester Municipal Research Bureau, Worcester, MA
13,000	Dynamy Inc., Worcester, MA
12,000	Tri - Community Young Men's Christian Association

BESS J. HODGES FOUNDATION

Giving Contact
Joyce Murchison, Executive Director
3780 Kilroy Airport Way, No. 820
Long Beach, CA 90806
Phone: (562)424-1040

Description
Founded: 1984
EIN: 330046140
Organization Type: Private Foundation
Giving Locations: CA
Grant Types: General Support.

Donor Information
Founder: the late Bess J. Hodges

Financial Summary
Total Giving: $203,627 (2001); $213,241 (1999); $209,443 (1998)
Assets: $4,849,941 (2001); $4,763,769 (1999); $4,765,268 (1998)

Typical Recipients
Arts & Humanities: Arts Centers, Arts Outreach, Community Arts, History & Archaeology, Libraries, Museums/Galleries, Music, Opera, Performing Arts, Public Broadcasting, Theater
Civic & Public Affairs: African American Affairs, Economic Development, Civic & Public Affairs-General, Hispanic Affairs, Law & Justice, Legal Aid, Urban & Community Affairs, Women's Affairs
Education: Colleges & Universities, Education-General, Private Education (Precollege), Religious Education, Secondary Education (Private), Student Aid
Health: Cancer, Children's Health/Hospitals, Clinics/Medical Centers, Health-General, Hospices, Hospitals, Medical Rehabilitation, Medical Research, Nursing Services
Religion: Religious Organizations, Religious Welfare, Social/Policy Issues
Social Services: At-Risk Youth, Child Welfare, Community Service Organizations, Day Care, Emergency Relief, Family Services, Food/Clothing Distribution, Recreation & Athletics, Scouts, Shelters/Homelessness, Substance Abuse, Volunteer Services, YMCA/YWCA/YMHA/YWHA, Youth Organizations

Application Procedures
Initial Contact: Proposals should be submitted in duplicate, with a cover letter typed on the organization's letterhead and signed by the chief executive officer.
Deadlines: March 31.

Restrictions
Government agencies are not encouraged to apply.

Additional Information
Publications: Application Guidelines

Foundation Officials
Pierre E. Auw: trustee
George M. Murchison: trustee

Grants Analysis
Disclosure Period: calendar year ending 2001
Total Grants: $203,627
Number of Grants: 38
Average Grant: $5,359
Highest Grant: $25,000
Lowest Grant: $650
Typical Range: $1,000 to $20,000

Recent Grants
Note: Grants derived from 2000 Form 990.

Library-Related
5,000	Long Beach Public Library Foundation, Long Beach, CA
5,000	St. Barnabas School Library, Long Beach, CA

General
26,327	Pathways Volunteer Hospice, Lakewood, CA
13,164	Trinity Broadcasting, Santa Ana, CA
12,500	Childnet, Long Beach, CA
10,000	CSULB Academic Council, Long Beach, CA
10,000	Long Beach City College Foundation, Long Beach, CA
10,000	Public Corporation for the Arts of the City of Long Beach, Long Beach, CA
8,000	Oral Roberts University, Tulsa, OK
7,000	National Conference of Christians, Long Beach, CA
6,250	Children's Clinic, Long Beach, CA
5,000	Boys & Girls Clubs of Long Beach, Long Beach, CA

H. LESLIE HOFFMAN & ELAINE S. HOFFMAN FOUNDATION

Giving Contact
J. Kristoffer Popovich, Trustee
225 South Lake Ave., Suite 1150
Pasadena, CA 91101
Phone: (626)793-0043
Fax: (626)793-0047

Description
Founded: 1952
EIN: 956048600
Organization Type: General Purpose Foundation
Giving Locations: CA: Los Angeles metro area
Grant Types: Employee Matching Gifts, General Support, Multiyear/Continuing Support.

Donor Information

Founder: Established in 1952 by the late H. Leslie Hoffman and the late Elaine S. Hoffman .

Financial Summary

Total Giving: $1,419,811 (2001); $1,185,741 (2000); $1,031,601 (1999)
Giving Analysis: Giving for 2000 includes: foundation grants to United Way ($10,000); 1999: foundation grants to United Way ($10,000); 1998: foundation grants to United Way ($10,000)
Assets: $37,875,884 (2001); $40,809,135 (2000); $37,578,850 (1999)

Typical Recipients

Arts & Humanities: Arts Associations & Councils, Arts Centers, Libraries, Museums/Galleries, Music, Opera, Performing Arts
Civic & Public Affairs: Business/Free Enterprise, Civil Rights, Clubs, Community Foundations, Employment/Job Training, Civic & Public Affairs-General, Law & Justice, Legal Aid, Nonprofit Management, Philanthropic Organizations, Professional & Trade Associations, Public Policy, Safety, Zoos/Aquariums
Education: Arts/Humanities Education, Business Education, Colleges & Universities, Education-General, Health & Physical Education, Medical Education, Minority Education, Preschool Education, Private Education (Precollege), Public Education (Precollege)
Environment: Environment-General, Protection
Health: Arthritis, Arthritis, Cancer, Children's Health/Hospitals, Clinics/Medical Centers, Diabetes, Emergency/Ambulance Services, Eyes/Blindness, Health-General, Health Organizations, Heart, Hospices, Hospitals, Medical Research
International: International Peace & Security Issues
Religion: Churches, Dioceses, Religious Organizations, Religious Welfare
Social Services: Camps, Child Welfare, Community Service Organizations, Crime Prevention, Emergency Relief, Family Services, Food/Clothing Distribution, Homes, People with Disabilities, Recreation & Athletics, Scouts, Senior Services, Special Olympics, Substance Abuse, United Funds/United Ways, Volunteer Services, YMCA/YWCA/YMHA/YWHA, Youth Organizations

Application Procedures

Initial Contact: The foundation has no formal grant application procedure or application form. Grant requests are received in any form.
Deadlines: None.

Restrictions

No grants are made to individuals.

Foundation Officials

J. Kristoffer Popovich: trustee PRIM CORP EMPL chief executive officer: Hoffman Video System.
Jane H. Popovich: trustee

Grants Analysis

Disclosure Period: calendar year ending 2001
Total Grants: $1,419,811
Number of Grants: 72
Average Grant: $11,263*
Highest Grant: $365,000
Lowest Grant: $500
Typical Range: $1,000 to $15,000
***Note:** Average grant figure excludes two highest grants ($631,400).

Recent Grants

Note: Grants derived from 2001 Form 990.

Library-Related

5,000	Huntington Library, San Marino, CA

General

365,000	University of Southern California School of Business Administration, Los Angeles, CA
266,400	Kidspace, Pasadena, CA
150,000	Children's Hospital Foundation, Los Angeles, CA
103,000	Widows and Children's Fund, New York, NY
102,000	Los Angeles Music Center, Los Angeles, CA
50,000	Archdioceses of Los Angeles, Los Angeles, CA
35,000	YMCA of Metro Los Angeles, Los Angeles, CA
32,000	Huntington Memorial Hospital, Los Angeles, CA
25,600	San Marino Schools Foundation, San Marino, CA
25,000	National Conference for Community and Justice, Los Angeles, CA

MAXIMILIAN E. AND MARION O. HOFFMAN FOUNDATION

Giving Contact

Doris C. Chaho, President
970 Farmington Avenue, Suite 203
West Hartford, CT 06107
Phone: (860)521-2949
Fax: (860)561-5082

Description

Founded: 1986
EIN: 222648036
Organization Type: General Purpose Foundation
Giving Locations: U.S. Northeastern Region.
Grant Types: Capital, Endowment, General Support, Project, Scholarship.

Donor Information

Founder: The foundation was established in 1986 in Connecticut as a successor foundation of the Maximilian E. and Marion O. Hoffman Foundation, which was established in New York in 1984 by Marion O. Hoffman.

Financial Summary

Total Giving: $2,194,853 (fiscal year ending June 30, 2002); $2,145,883 (fiscal 2001); $2,646,276 (fiscal 1999)
Assets: $38,019,247 (fiscal 2002); $52,593,918 (fiscal 2001); $49,481,091 (fiscal 1999)

Typical Recipients

Arts & Humanities: Arts Associations & Councils, Arts Centers, Ballet, Dance, Film & Video, Arts & Humanities-General, Historic Preservation, History & Archaeology, Libraries, Literary Arts, Museums/Galleries, Music, Opera, Performing Arts, Public Broadcasting, Theater
Civic & Public Affairs: Botanical Gardens/Parks, Clubs, Economic Policy, Employment/Job Training, Civic & Public Affairs-General, Housing, Law & Justice, Public Policy, Safety, Urban & Community Affairs, Women's Affairs
Education: Arts/Humanities Education, Colleges & Universities, Continuing Education, Education Funds, Elementary Education (Private), Engineering/Technological Education, Environmental Education, Education-General, Health & Physical Education, International Exchange, International Studies, Literacy, Medical Education, Minority Education, Private Education (Precollege), Public Education (Precollege), Science/Mathematics Education, Secondary Education (Private), Social Sciences Education, Special Education, Student Aid, Vocational & Technical Education
Environment: Air/Water Quality, Energy, Environment-General, Protection, Resource Conservation, Watershed

Health: Adolescent Health Issues, AIDS/HIV, Alzheimers Disease, Cancer, Children's Health/Hospitals, Clinics/Medical Centers, Diabetes, Emergency/Ambulance Services, Health-General, Geriatric Health, Health Organizations, Heart, Home-Care Services, Hospitals, Hospitals (University Affiliated), Kidney, Medical Rehabilitation, Mental Health, Nursing Services, Nutrition, Prenatal Health Issues, Research/Studies Institutes, Respiratory, Single-Disease Health Associations
International: Health Care/Hospitals, International Development, International Environmental Issues, International Organizations, International Relief Efforts, Missionary/Religious Activities
Religion: Churches, Dioceses, Religion-General, Jewish Causes, Ministries, Religious Organizations, Religious Welfare, Seminaries, Social/Policy Issues, Synagogues/Temples
Science: Scientific Centers & Institutes, Scientific Organizations, Scientific Research
Social Services: Camps, Child Abuse, Child Welfare, Community Service Organizations, Emergency Relief, Family Services, Food/Clothing Distribution, Homes, People with Disabilities, Scouts, Senior Services, Social Services-General, Substance Abuse, United Funds/United Ways, Volunteer Services, YMCA/YWCA/YMHA/YWHA, Youth Organizations

Application Procedures

Initial Contact: Send letter of request for application.
Application Requirements: Applications should include a copy of the IRS tax-exempt determination letter.
Deadlines: Applications should be received by the foundation a month before board meetings.
Review Process: The board meets three times a year.

Restrictions

Does not make grants for political purposes.

Foundation Officials

Bahij Chaho: treasurer, vice president
Doris C. Chaho: president

Grants Analysis

Disclosure Period: fiscal year ending June 30, 2002
Total Grants: $2,194,853
Number of Grants: 67
Average Grant: $32,759
Highest Grant: $250,000
Lowest Grant: $500
Typical Range: $15,000 to $50,000

Recent Grants

Note: Grants derived from fiscal 2002 Form 990.

Library-Related

10,000	Wadsworth Athenaeum, Hartford, CT -- for Docent Program

General

250,000	St. Francis Hospital and Medical Center, Hartford, CT -- for capital campaign
200,000	Saint Joseph College, West Hartford, CT -- for construction of center for arts and humanities
175,000	Saint Francis Hospital and Medical Center, Hartford, CT -- for equipment
110,000	Archdiocese of The Syrian Orthodox Church, Lodi, NJ
110,000	Connecticut Aeronautical Historical Association, Windsor Locks, CT -- for educational programs
100,000	CCARC, New Britain, CT -- for construction of new facility
100,000	Hundred Club, Glastonbury, CT -- for catastrophic injury assistance
100,000	Saint Dominic Church, Southington, CT -- for Information and Communications Center

| 100,000 | Salk Institute, La Jolla, CA -- for post-doctoral fellows |
| 87,700 | New Britain Museum of American Art, New Britain, CT -- for capital campaign |

HOFFMANN-LA ROCHE, INC.

Company Headquarters
Nutley, NJ
Web: http://www.roche.com

Company Description
Employees: 17,000
SIC(s): 2833 Medicinals & Botanicals, 2834 Pharmaceutical Preparations, 8071 Medical Laboratories.
Parent Company: Roche Group, Grenzacherstrasse 124, Basel, Switzerland

Operating Locations
American Roche International (NJ--Clifton); Genentech (CA--San Francisco); Givaudan-Roure Corp. (NJ--Clifton); Givaudan-Roure Corp. Flavors Division (NJ--Clifton); Givaudan-Roure Corp. Fragrances Division (NJ--Teaneck); Hoffmann-La Roche Inc. (NJ--Belleville, Belvidere, Montclair, Nutley, Paramus, Raritan, Totowa; NC--Burlington); Roche Biomedical Laboratories (NC--Burlington); Roche Diagnostic Systems (NJ--Somerville); Roche Molecular Systems (NJ--Somerville); Roche Professional Service Centers (NJ--Paramus); Syntex (CA--Palo Alto); Syntex Agribusiness (CA--Palo Alto); Syntex Chemicals (CO--Boulder)

Nonmonetary Support
Type: In-kind Services

Hoffmann-La Roche Foundation

Giving Contact
Vivian Beetle, Director Corporate Relations, Contributions/Community Affairs
PO Box 278
Nutley, NJ 07110-0278
Phone: (973)562-2055
Fax: (973)562-2999
Web: http://www.rocheusa.com

Alternate Contact
340 Kingsland Street
Nutley, NJ 07110-1199
Phone: (973)235-5000

Description
Founded: 1945
EIN: 226063790
Organization Type: Corporate Foundation
Giving Locations: NJ
Grant Types: Employee Matching Gifts, Fellowship, Research, Seed Money.

Donor Information
Founder: Hoffmann-La Roche Inc.

Financial Summary
Total Giving: $1,338,155 (2001); $687,500 (2000); $928,202 (1999). Note: Contributes through corporate direct giving program and foundation.
Giving Analysis: Giving for 2001 includes: foundation grants to United Way ($500,000); foundation ($838,155) 1999: foundation ($928,202)
Assets: $122 (1997); $22,678 (1996); $28 (1993)
Gifts Received: $1,338,405 (2001); $687,750 (2000); $953,452 (1999). Note: In 1999 and 2000, the foundation received funds from Hoffmann-La Roche and Roche Laboratories, Inc.

Typical Recipients
Arts & Humanities: Libraries, Museums/Galleries, Music, Opera, Performing Arts
Civic & Public Affairs: Community Foundations, Employment/Job Training, Civic & Public Affairs-General, Philanthropic Organizations, Professional & Trade Associations, Urban & Community Affairs, Zoos/Aquariums
Education: Arts/Humanities Education, Colleges & Universities, Economic Education, Education Funds, Education-General, International Exchange, Medical Education, Minority Education, Private Education (Precollege), Science/Mathematics Education, Secondary Education (Public), Vocational & Technical Education
Environment: Environment-General, Wildlife Protection
Health: AIDS/HIV, Cancer, Children's Health/Hospitals, Emergency/Ambulance Services, Health Policy/Cost Containment, Health Organizations, Hospices, Hospitals, Hospitals, Medical Research, Medical Training, Mental Health, Public Health, Single-Disease Health Associations, Transplant Networks/Donor Banks
International: Health Care/Hospitals, Human Rights, International Affairs, International Environmental Issues, International Relations
Religion: Churches, Religious Organizations
Science: Science Museums, Scientific Centers & Institutes, Scientific Labs, Scientific Organizations, Scientific Research
Social Services: Animal Protection, Community Service Organizations, People with Disabilities, Social Services-General, Substance Abuse, United Funds/United Ways, YMCA/YWCA/YMHA/YWHA

Application Procedures
Initial Contact: Send a letter of inquiry of not more than three pages.
Application Requirements: Include basic background on the organization including contact information, purpose, and mission; and a description of the program for which support is requested including proposed purpose, current status, professional personnel, anticipated length of program, and final results; and program budget information.
Deadlines: None.
Decision Notification: Applicants are notified of decisions within six to eight weeks of receipt of letter.

Restrictions
The foundation will not consider requests for: gifts to individuals; endowment or scholarship funds; international organizations or projects; political organizations, parties, candidates, or office holders; the purchase, construction, expansion or modification of facilities; equipment or other capital expenditures; goodwill advertising; sectarian groups, except for education and health programs which serve the general population without regard to religious affiliation; or labor or veterans' organizations, unless the project in question is for the general welfare of an entire community in which Roche is present or has a significant interest. Grants are focused on health and education programs with priority emphasis on health promotion (not medical delivery) and math and science education.

Additional Information
Preference is given to organizations located within the state of New Jersey and sites of Hoffmann-La Roche. Preference is also given to local chapters of national health organizations. National headquarters of health organizations are rarely funded.
Publications: Guidelines

Corporate Officials
Vivian Beetle: director community affairsrc PRIM CORP EMPL director community affairs: Hoffmann-La Roche Inc.
Frederick C. Kentz, III: vice president, secretary, general counsel B Summit, NJ 1952. ED Georgetown University (1974); Fordham University (1977). PRIM CORP EMPL vice president, secretary, general counsel: Hoffmann-La Roche Inc. CORP AFFIL officer: Roche Diagnostics System; officer: Roche Molecular System Inc.; officer: Roche Carolina Inc.
Patrick J. Zenner: president, chief executive officer, director B 1948. ED Creighton University BSBA; Fairleigh Dickinson University MBA (1969). PRIM CORP EMPL president, chief executive officer, director: Hoffmann-La Roche Inc. CORP AFFIL officer: Roche Carolina Inc.; officer: Roche Molecular System Inc.; president: HLR Service Corp.

Foundation Officials
George Abercrombie: trustee
Vivian Beetle: admin director (see above)
Frederick C. Kentz, III: trustee (see above)
Patrick J. Zenner: trustee (see above)

Grants Analysis
Disclosure Period: calendar year ending 2001
Total Grants: $838,155*
Number of Grants: 12
Average Grant: $30,741*
Highest Grant: $500,000
Lowest Grant: $3,155
Typical Range: $25,000 to $120,000
*Note: Giving excludes United Way. Average grant figure excludes highest grant.

Recent Grants
Note: Grants derived from 2001 Form 990.

General

500,000	Independent College Fund of New Jersey, Summit, NJ -- to establish September 11th victim assistance post-secondary education fund
500,000	United Way, Hudson, NJ -- to address the emerging environmental health issues related to the events of September 11
120,000	University of South Carolina School of Medicine, Columbia, SC -- for weight loss and weight management for rural communities
50,000	Hollings Cancer Center, Charleston, SC -- for non-capital community outreach programming and establishment of a Cancer Prevention and Control Access Network Program
30,000	Princeton Area Community Foundation, Princeton, NJ -- for AIDS partnership
25,000	American Society of Hospital Pharmacists Research and Education Foundation, Bethesda, MD -- support "The Joseph A. Oddis Endowment Fund"
25,000	Independent College Fund of New Jersey, Summit, NJ -- for distribution of funds to member colleges and universities in 2001
25,000	New Jersey Performing Arts Center, Newark, NJ -- for renewed support of New Jersey Performing Art Center's science and the arts program
20,000	United Negro College Fund, Newark, NJ -- support annual campaign
15,000	Technical Training Project, Newark, NJ -- support for 2001 training programs

HOGLUND FOUNDATION

Giving Contact
Kelly H. Compton, Executive Director
3729 Normandy
Dallas, TX 75205
Phone: (214)526-6522

E-mail: khc@hoglundfdtn.org
Web: http://www.hoglundfdtn.org/

Description

Founded: 1989
EIN: 752300978
Organization Type: Private Foundation
Giving Locations: TX
Grant Types: Capital, General Support, Project.

Donor Information

Founder: Established in 1989 by Forrest E. Hoglund.

Financial Summary

Total Giving: $1,862,514 (2000); $1,091,669 (1999); $1,089,800 (1998)
Giving Analysis: Giving for 2000 includes: foundation grants to United Way ($37,500)
Assets: $47,597,141 (2000); $30,355,392 (1999); $20,234,586 (1996)
Gifts Received: $4,576,563 (2000); $1,546,552 (1999); $250,000 (1996). Note: In 1996, 1999 and 2000, contributions were received from Forrest E. Hoglund.

Typical Recipients

Arts & Humanities: Arts Outreach, History & Archaeology, Libraries, Museums/Galleries, Performing Arts, Theater
Civic & Public Affairs: Economic Development, Women's Affairs, Zoos/Aquariums
Education: Business Education, Colleges & Universities, Education-General, Medical Education, Minority Education, Private Education (Precollege), Student Aid
Health: AIDS/HIV, Alzheimers Disease, Arthritis, Cancer, Children's Health/Hospitals, Clinics/Medical Centers, Emergency/Ambulance Services, Health Organizations, Hospices, Kidney, Long-Term Care, Nursing Services, Prenatal Health Issues, Single-Disease Health Associations, Transplant Networks/Donor Banks
International: Foreign Arts Organizations
Religion: Churches, Ministries, Ministries, Religious Welfare
Science: Science-General, Science Museums
Social Services: At-Risk Youth, Child Welfare, Community Centers, Community Service Organizations, Crime Prevention, Family Planning, Family Services, Food/Clothing Distribution, People with Disabilities, Recreation & Athletics, Senior Services, Shelters/Homelessness, Special Olympics, Substance Abuse, United Funds/United Ways, YMCA/YWCA/YMHA/YWHA, Youth Organizations

Application Procedures

Initial Contact: Send a brief letter of inquiry; request application guidelines
Application Requirements: a description of organization, amount requested, purpose of funds sought, recently audited financial statement, proof of tax-exempt status, list of current officers and board of trustees, current budget, budget for the proposed project (if applicable) and plans to support the project after the grant period.
Deadlines: None. Board meets quarterly to review grant applications.

Restrictions

The foundation does not support individuals.

Additional Information

Publications: Application guidelines.

Foundation Officials

Kelly Hoglund Compton: secretary, treasurer
Shelly Louise Hoglund Dee: trustee
Forrest Eugene Hoglund: don, president B Lawrence, KS 1933. ED University of Kansas BS (1956). PRIM CORP EMPL chairman, president, chief executive officer: Enron Oil & Gas Co. CORP AFFIL director:

Texas Commerce Bancshares; director: Western Transmission Corp.; director: Marathon Oil Co. NONPR AFFIL vice president: Kansas University Endowment Association; director: Texas Research League; member: American Petroleum Institute; member: Dallas Citizens Council.
Sally Sue Roney Hoglund: vice president
Kristy Kay Hoglund Robinson: trustee

Grants Analysis

Disclosure Period: calendar year ending 1999
Total Grants: $1,825,014*
Number of Grants: 123
Average Grant: $11,777*
Highest Grant: $200,000
Typical Range: $5,000 to $20,000
*Note: Giving excludes United Way. Average grant figure excludes two highest grants ($400,000).

Recent Grants

Note: Grants derived from 1999 Form 990.

General

200,000	Family Place, Dallas, TX -- for construction of new shelter
75,000	Houston Museum of Natural Science, Houston, TX -- for construction of Southwest Gallery in the Hall of the Americas
50,000	Dallas Zoological Society, Dallas, TX -- for construction of children's zoo
50,000	Salesmanship Club Youth and Family Centers, Dallas, TX -- for computer, math, and science labs
50,000	YMCA Of Metropolitan Dallas, Dallas, TX -- for construction of new gymnasium
49,650	Alzheimers Disease Resource Center, Dallas, TX -- operating support and underwrite education conference
43,000	University of Texas Houston, Houston, TX -- for capital campaign, student lounge and prevention of atherosclerosis
25,000	Goodwill Industries, Dallas, TX -- for construction of new facility
25,000	Shelter Ministries of Dallas, Inc., Dallas, TX -- for capital campaign and pathway house
25,000	Southern Methodist University, Dallas, TX -- for capital campaign and blanton student services building

HOLMBERG FOUNDATION

Giving Contact

Dr. Robert F. Wettingfeld, President
519 Washington St.
Jamestown, NY 14701
Phone: (716)483-0735

Description

Founded: 1992
EIN: 161426226
Organization Type: Private Foundation
Giving Locations: NY: Chautauqua County
Grant Types: Capital, Fellowship, General Support.

Financial Summary

Total Giving: $160,500 (fiscal year ending July 31, 2001); $174,500 (fiscal 2000); $165,000 (fiscal 1999)
Giving Analysis: Giving for fiscal 2001 includes: foundation grants to United Way ($7,500); fiscal 2000: foundation grants to United Way ($2,500); fiscal 1999: foundation grants to United Way ($2,500)
Assets: $3,632,816 (fiscal 2001); $3,733,544 (fiscal 2000); $3,621,860 (fiscal 1999)
Gifts Received: $500 (fiscal 2001); $600 (fiscal 2000); $500 (fiscal 1999). Note: In fiscal 2000, contributions were received from Robert F. Wettingfeld.

Typical Recipients

Arts & Humanities: Libraries
Civic & Public Affairs: Economic Development
Education: Community & Junior Colleges
Environment: Wildlife Protection
Health: Hospitals, Nursing Services
Religion: Missionary Activities (Domestic)
Social Services: Camps, United Funds/United Ways, Youth Organizations

Application Procedures

Initial Contact: Send a brief letter of inquiry.
Deadlines: None.

Foundation Officials

Mary T. Bessemer: director emeritus
Joseph C. Johnson: treasurer
Leslie A. Johnson: secretary
William J. Kelly: vice president, treasurer
Robert F. Wettingfeld, MD: president

Grants Analysis

Disclosure Period: fiscal year ending July 31, 2001
Total Grants: $155,500*
Number of Grants: 12
Average Grant: $6,864*
Highest Grant: $80,000
Typical Range: $2,000 to $15,000
*Note: Giving excludes United Way. Average grant figure excludes highest grant.

Recent Grants

Note: Grants derived from 2000 Form 990.

Library-Related

7,000	James Prendergast Library, Jamestown, NY -- educational
7,000	Ripley Free Library, Ripley, NY -- educational

General

90,000	Jamestown Community College, Jamestown, NY -- educational
15,000	Fredonia College Foundation, Fredonia, NY -- educational
11,500	Chautauqua Striders, Chautauqua, NY -- educational
10,000	YWCA -- educational
8,000	Boy's Jim Club of America -- educational
7,500	Chautauqua Institution, Jamestown, NY -- educational
5,000	Jamestown Community Learning Council, Jamestown, NY -- educational
5,000	Roger Tory Peterson Institute, Jamestown, NY -- educational
2,500	United Way of Southern Chautauqua County, Chautauqua, NY -- educational
2,000	Camp Mission Meadows -- educational

HOLNAM, INC.

Company Headquarters

6211 N. Ann Arbor Rd.
Dundee, MI 48131
Web: http://www.holcim.com/us

Company Description

Employees: 5,200
SIC(s): 3241 Cement--Hydraulic, 3273 Ready-Mixed Concrete, 3531 Construction Machinery, 6719 Holding Companies Nec.
Parent Company: Holderbank Financiere Glaris Ltd., Zurcherstrasse 156, Jona, Switzerland

Operating Locations

Braswell Concrete Products (LA--Shreveport); Braswell Industries (LA--Shreveport); Braswell Sand & Gravel Co. (AR--Wilton); Dundee Cement Co. (MI--Dundee); Graysonia, Nashville & Ashdawn Railroad

Co. (AR--Nashville); Holnam Inc. (MI--Dundee); Holnam Inc. (West Division) (CO--Lakewood); Ideal Concrete (TX--Houston); Kevaland Corp. (CO--Denver); Kevaland Texas Corp. (CO--Denver); Louisiana Nevada Transit Co. (CO--Denver); Northwestern States Portland Cement (IA--Mason City); Thorstenberg Materials Co. (CO--Denver); United Cement Co. (MS--Artesia)

Nonmonetary Support

Type: Cause-related Marketing & Promotion; Donated Equipment; Donated Products; Loaned Employees

Giving Contact

Linda McCormick, Public Affairs Administrator
6211 N. Ann Arbor Rd.
PO Box 122
Dundee, MI 48131
Phone: (734)529-2411
Fax: (734)529-5268

Description

Organization Type: Corporate Giving Program
Giving Locations: headquarters and operating communities.
Grant Types: Capital, Conference/Seminar, Emergency, Employee Matching Gifts, General Support, Multiyear/Continuing Support, Project, Scholarship.

Typical Recipients

Arts & Humanities: Arts Associations & Councils, Arts Festivals, Arts & Humanities-General, Historic Preservation, Libraries, Music, Performing Arts, Public Broadcasting
Civic & Public Affairs: Chambers of Commerce, Community Foundations, Economic Development, Civic & Public Affairs-General, Parades/Festivals, Professional & Trade Associations, Safety, Urban & Community Affairs
Education: Agricultural Education, Business Education, Business-School Partnerships, Colleges & Universities, Community & Junior Colleges, Continuing Education, Education-General
Environment: Environment-General, Wildlife Protection
Health: Health-General
Science: Science-General
Social Services: Social Services-General

Application Procedures

Initial Contact: Send a full proposal.
Application Requirements: Include a description of organization, amount requested, purpose of funds sought, and proof of tax-exempt status.

Restrictions

Does not support individuals, religious organizations for sectarian purposes, political or lobbying groups, or organizations outside operating areas.

Corporate Officials

Kent Jensen: chief financial officer, treasurer, director PRIM CORP EMPL chief financial officer, treasurer: Holnam.
Paul A. Yhouse: president, chief executive officer, director B Grand Rapids, MI 1949. ED University of Michigan BBA (1971). PRIM CORP EMPL president, chief executive officer, director: Holnam. NONPR AFFIL member: Michigan Association Certified Pub Accts; advisory board: University Michigan Paton Acct Center; member: American Institute CPA's; member: Financial Executives Institute.

Grants Analysis

Typical Range: $10 to $999

HOLT FAMILY FOUNDATION

Giving Contact

Leon C. Holt, Jr., Trustee
1611 Pond Road, Suite 300
Allentown, PA 18104-2256
Phone: (610)391-0377

Description

Founded: 1988
EIN: 236906143
Organization Type: Private Foundation
Giving Locations: PA: Allentown and Lehigh Valley Area
Grant Types: General Support.

Donor Information

Founder: Leon C. and June W. Holt, Jr.

Financial Summary

Total Giving: $234,500 (2001); $218,050 (2000); $202,600 (1999). Note: 1997 Giving includes United Way ($1,000).
Giving Analysis: Giving for 2001 includes: foundation grants to United Way ($2,000); 2000: foundation grants to United Way ($1,000); 1998: foundation grants to United Way ($1,000) foundation ($190,000)
Assets: $4,726,431 (2001); $5,026,638 (2000); $35,894 (1999)
Gifts Received: $142,814 (2000); $350,000 (1999); $905,274 (1998). Note: Contributions were received from Leon C. and June W. Holt.

Typical Recipients

Arts & Humanities: Ballet, History & Archaeology, Libraries, Museums/Galleries, Music, Theater
Civic & Public Affairs: Clubs, Economic Development, Civic & Public Affairs-General, Hispanic Affairs, Urban & Community Affairs
Education: Arts/Humanities Education, Colleges & Universities, Private Education (Precollege)
Environment: Environment-General, Resource Conservation, Wildlife Protection
Health: Prenatal Health Issues, Public Health
Religion: Churches, Religious Welfare
Science: Scientific Centers & Institutes
Social Services: Child Welfare, Community Service Organizations, Recreation & Athletics, United Funds/United Ways, YMCA/YWCA/YMHA/YWHA, Youth Organizations

Application Procedures

Initial Contact: Request funding guidelines, then send a brief letter of inquiry.
Application Requirements: Include a description of organization, amount requested, purpose of funds sought, proof of tax-exempt status, proposed project budget, including other sources of financial support, plan to measure and evaluate program results, and a summary of the proposed program along with a plan for accomplishing objectives.
Deadlines: None.

Restrictions

The foundation does not support individuals, religious organizations for sectarian purposes, political or lobbying groups, organizations outside operating areas, debt reduction, charitable or testimonial dinners, fundraising events or related advertising, or fraternal, social, or veterans organizations.

Additional Information

Publications: Funding Guidelines

Foundation Officials

June W. Holt: trustee
Leon Conrad Holt, Jr.: trustee B Reading, PA 1925. ED Lehigh University BS (1948); University of Pennsylvania JD (1951). CORP AFFIL director: VF Corp.;

director: Air Products & Chemicals. NONPR AFFIL member: Tunkhannock Creek Association; member advisory board: University Pennsylvania Institute Law & Economics; trustee: Pool (Dorothy Rider) Health Care Trust; director: Pennsylvanians Modern Courts; director: Pocono Lake Preserve; member: New York City Bar Association; member: Pennsylvania Society; member executive committee: Machinery & Allied Products Institute; director: Nature Conservancy Pennsylvania Chapter; trustee: Committee for Economic Development; director: Lehigh County United Fund; member: American Bar Association; member: Allentown Chamber of Commerce; member: Alpha Tau Omega; trustee: Allentown Art Museum. CLUB AFFIL Lehigh Country Club.
Richard W. Holt, Jr.: trustee
Deborah Holt Weil: trustee

Grants Analysis

Disclosure Period: calendar year ending 2001
Total Grants: $232,500*
Number of Grants: 48
Average Grant: $3,670*
Highest Grant: $60,000
Lowest Grant: $250
Typical Range: $1,000 to $5,000
*Note: Giving excludes United Way. Average grant figure excludes highest grant.

Recent Grants

Note: Grants derived from 2000 Form 990.

General

60,000	Allentown Art Museum, Allentown, PA
25,000	University of Pennsylvania, Philadelphia, PA
15,000	Episcopal Church of the Mediator, Allentown, MA
10,000	Allentown Symphony, Allentown, PA
10,000	Discovery Center of Science and Technology, Bethlehem, PA
10,000	Lehigh University, Bethlehem, PA
10,000	Lehigh Valley Hospital, Allentown, PA
10,000	Nature Conservancy, Philadelphia, PA
10,000	Wildlands Conservancy, Emmaus, PA
5,000	Baum School of Art, Allentown, PA

WILLIAM KNOX HOLT FOUNDATION

Giving Contact

George M. Malti, Director
300 Aztec Ave., Suite 200
Gallup, NM 87301
Phone: (505)863-6851

Description

Founded: 1967
EIN: 746084245
Organization Type: Private Foundation
Giving Locations: CA: Northern part of state; CO; NY; TX: Southern part of state
Grant Types: Capital, Endowment, General Support, Project, Research, Scholarship.

Donor Information

Founder: the late William Knox Holt

Financial Summary

Total Giving: $553,500 (2002); $775,729 (2000); $829,354 (1999)
Giving Analysis: Giving for 2002 includes: foundation scholarships ($20,000); 2000: foundation scholarships ($41,000); 1999: foundation scholarships ($55,000);
Assets: $8,396,923 (2002); $12,644,242 (2000); $16,672,407 (1999)

Typical Recipients

Arts & Humanities: Arts Associations & Councils, Arts Centers, Arts Outreach, Libraries, Museums/Galleries, Music, Theater

Civic & Public Affairs: Civic & Public Affairs-General, Hispanic Affairs, Native American Affairs, Zoos/Aquariums

Education: Arts/Humanities Education, Colleges & Universities, Education Funds, Education-General, Leadership Training, Legal Education, Private Education (Precollege), Public Education (Precollege), Science/Mathematics Education, Secondary Education (Public), Student Aid

Health: Cancer, Children's Health/Hospitals, Emergency/Ambulance Services, Health-General, Health Organizations, Multiple Sclerosis, Public Health

Religion: Religious Welfare

Science: Science Museums, Scientific Centers & Institutes, Scientific Labs

Social Services: At-Risk Youth, Child Welfare, Community Service Organizations, Crime Prevention, Domestic Violence, People with Disabilities, Recreation & Athletics, Scouts, Social Services-General, Youth Organizations

Application Procedures

Initial Contact: Send a brief letter of inquiry describing program or project.

Application Requirements: Include a description of organization and purpose of funds sought.

Deadlines: None.

Restrictions

Limited to science and education charities in CA, TX, CO, NM, and NY.

Foundation Officials

Judy S. Akin: assistant secretary
Geary Atherton: director
Holt Atherton: director
George M. Malti: director
Richard C. Perkins: director
Roberta S. Plummer: director

Grants Analysis

Disclosure Period: calendar year ending 2002
Total Grants: $533,500*
Number of Grants: 27
Average Grant: $16,673*
Highest Grant: $100,000
Lowest Grant: $2,500
Typical Range: $10,000 to $30,000
*Note: Giving excludes scholarships. Average grant figure excludes highest grant.

Recent Grants

Note: Grants derived from 2001 Form 990.

General

100,000	Lawrence Hall of Science, Berkeley, CA -- for interactive landscape experience
65,000	Haggin Museum, Stockton, CA -- for maintenance of Holt Hall and industrial archives
33,000	Central E Austin Community Organization, Austin, TX -- for youth and women's programs
33,000	Rehoboth McKinley/Christian Health Care Services, Gallup, NM -- for women's health services
30,000	Austin Symphony Orchestra, Austin, TX -- for young peoples' concerts
30,000	Navajo Nation, Window Rock, AZ -- for educational programs
25,000	Colorado Rocky Mountain School, Carbondale, CO -- for Scholarship Program
25,000	Monterey Bay Aquarium, Monterey, CA -- for educational programs
20,000	Cancer Therapy & Research Center, San Antonio, TX -- for Cancer Institute symposium
20,000	Crime Prevention Institute, Austin, TX -- for job and resource fairs

JACOB L. AND LILLIAN HOLTZMANN FOUNDATION

Giving Contact

Howard Holtzmann, Trustee
c/o Holtzmann, Wise & Shepard
630 5th Ave., Suite 2000
New York, NY 10111-0100

Description

Founded: 1958
EIN: 136174349
Organization Type: Private Foundation
Giving Locations: NY
Grant Types: General Support.

Donor Information

Founder: the late Jacob L. Holtzmann, the late Lillian Holtzmann, Howard M. Holtzmann

Financial Summary

Total Giving: $3,095,459 (2000); $476,592 (1999); $622,933 (1998)
Giving Analysis: Giving for 1996 includes: foundation ($252,848); 1995: foundation ($259,400) 1994: foundation ($247,569)
Assets: $11,026,064 (2000); $12,099,104 (1999); $11,510,315 (1998)
Gifts Received: $50,000 (2000); $50,000 (1999); $50,000 (1998). Note: Contributions received from Howard M. Holtzmann.

Typical Recipients

Arts & Humanities: Ballet, Libraries, Museums/Galleries, Music, Opera, Theater

Civic & Public Affairs: Botanical Gardens/Parks, Employment/Job Training, Civic & Public Affairs-General, Law & Justice, Legal Aid, Native American Affairs, Philanthropic Organizations, Public Policy, Women's Affairs

Education: Arts/Humanities Education, Colleges & Universities, Education Funds, Elementary Education (Private), Education-General, Legal Education, Medical Education, Private Education (Precollege), Public Education (Precollege), Religious Education

Environment: Environment-General

Health: Geriatric Health, Health Organizations, Hospitals, Medical Research, Single-Disease Health Associations

International: Foreign Arts Organizations, Foreign Educational Institutions, Health Care/Hospitals, International Affairs, International Organizations, International Relief Efforts, Missionary/Religious Activities

Religion: Churches, Jewish Causes, Missionary Activities (Domestic), Religious Organizations, Religious Welfare, Seminaries, Synagogues/Temples

Social Services: Community Centers, Community Service Organizations, People with Disabilities, Youth Organizations

Application Procedures

Initial Contact: The foundation requests applications be made in writing.

Deadlines: None.

Restrictions

Does not support individuals.

Foundation Officials

Howard Marshall Holtzmann, Esq.: trustee B New York, NY 1921. ED Yale University AB (1942); Yale University JD (1947); Saint Bonaventure University LittD (1952); Jewish Theological Seminary LLD (1990). NONPR AFFIL US del: UN Commission International Trade Law; member: World Peace Law; member: Society Professionals Dispute Resolution; director: Stockholm Arbitration Institute; trustee: Pace University School Law; trustee emeritus: Saint Bonaventure University; member: New York State Bar Association; member: New York County Lawyers Association; member: New York Law Institute; member: New York City Bar Association; vice chairman, member: Intl Council Commercial Arbitration; honorary chairman: Jewish Theological Seminary; member: International Law Association; member: International Bar Association; member, vice chairman arbitration commissioner: International Chamber of Commerce; trustee: Institute International Law; director: Bagrain Arbitration Center; member: Indus Relations Research Association; member: American Society International Law; member: American Foreign Law Association; member: American Judicature Society; member: American Bar Foundation; member: American Association International Comm Jurists; member: American Bar Association; member: American Arbitration Association.

Benjamin C. O'Sullivan, Esq.: trustee
Susan H. Richardson: trustee

Grants Analysis

Disclosure Period: calendar year ending 2000
Total Grants: $3,095,459
Number of Grants: 31
Average Grant: $7,849*
Highest Grant: $2,010,000
Typical Range: $1,000 to $15,000
*Note: Average grant figure excludes two highest grants ($2,860,000).

Recent Grants

Note: Grants derived from 2001 Form 990.

General

150,000	Jewish Theological Seminary, New York, NY
50,000	Ackerman Institute for the Family, New York, NY
50,000	United Jewish Appeal - Federation of Jewish Philanthropies of New York, Greenwich, CT
25,000	Environmental Law Institute, Washington, DC
20,000	Jewish Child Care Association of New York, New York, NY
19,900	Metropolitan Opera Association, New York, NY
10,000	Classic Stage Company, New York, NY
10,000	Student Advocacy, Elmsford, NY
9,600	American Ballet Theatre, New York, NY
6,000	Yale Alumni Fund, New Haven, CT

RICHARD H. HOLZER MEMORIAL FOUNDATION

Giving Contact

Vivian K. Holzer, President
120 Sylvan Ave.
Englewood Cliffs, NJ 07632
Phone: (201)947-8810

Description

Founded: 1969
EIN: 237014880
Organization Type: Private Foundation
Giving Locations: U.S. Northeast Region.
Grant Types: General Support.

Donor Information
Founder: Erich Holzer

Financial Summary
Total Giving: $342,590 (2000); $326,900 (1999); $333,100 (1998)
Assets: $5,841,908 (2000); $5,744,033 (1999); $5,069,975 (1998)
Gifts Received: $337,230 (2000); $311,788 (1999); $310,555 (1998). Note: In 1998 and 1999, contributions were received from Eva Holzer. In 1996, major contributions were received from Eva Holzer Charitable Lead Trust ($299,224), Chickmaster International Co. ($100,000), and Victor Koenig ($50).

Typical Recipients
Arts & Humanities: Arts Associations & Councils, Arts Centers, Ballet, Community Arts, Dance, Libraries, Museums/Galleries, Music, Opera, Performing Arts, Public Broadcasting, Theater
Civic & Public Affairs: Clubs, Civic & Public Affairs-General
Education: Agricultural Education, Arts/Humanities Education, Business Education, Colleges & Universities, Education Funds, Gifted & Talented Programs, Minority Education, Private Education (Precollege), Public Education (Precollege), Student Aid
Health: Cancer, Clinics/Medical Centers, Health Organizations, Hospitals, Medical Rehabilitation, Medical Research, Single-Disease Health Associations
International: Missionary/Religious Activities
Religion: Churches, Jewish Causes, Jewish Causes, Religious Organizations, Seminaries, Synagogues/Temples
Social Services: Child Welfare, Community Centers, Community Service Organizations, Counseling, Homes, People with Disabilities

Application Procedures
Initial Contact: a brief letter of inquiry
Application Requirements: a description of organization, purpose of funds sought
Deadlines: None.

Restrictions
Grants are not made to support individuals, political or lobbying groups, or organizations outside operating areas.

Foundation Officials
Wally Dietl: secretary
Erich Holzer: vice president
Robert Holzer: treasurer
Vivian Holzer: president

Grants Analysis
Disclosure Period: calendar year ending 2000
Total Grants: $342,590
Number of Grants: 53
Average Grant: $5,627*
Highest Grant: $50,000
Typical Range: $1,000 to $10,000
*Note: Average grant excludes highest grant.

Recent Grants
Note: Grants derived from 1999 Form 990.

General
50,000	Metropolitan Opera, New York, NY
25,000	Jewish Theological Seminary, New York, NY
25,000	University of Vermont, Burlington, VT
22,500	Solomon Schechter Day School Bergen Avenue, New Milford, NJ
20,000	Cornell University College of Agriculture, Ithaca, NY
20,000	John Harms Center for the Arts, Englewood, NJ
15,000	Carnegie Hall, New York, NY
15,000	Lincoln Center for the Performing Arts, New York, NY
15,000	PVH Foundation, Westwood, NJ
14,050	JCC on the Palisades, Tenafly, NJ

HOME FOR AGED MEN IN THE CITY OF BROCKTON

Giving Contact
John F. Creedon, President
c/o Silverstein and Creedon
71 Legion Parkway, 3rd Fl.
Brockton, MA 02301
Phone: (508)584-4088

Description
EIN: 042103796
Organization Type: Private Foundation
Giving Locations: MA
Grant Types: General Support, Operating Expenses.

Donor Information
Founder: the late Horace Howard

Financial Summary
Total Giving: $300,000 (fiscal year ending March 31, 2001); $15,000 (fiscal 1998); $232,000 (fiscal 1997)
Assets: $5,400,353 (fiscal 2001); $5,758,493 (fiscal 1998); $4,425,923 (fiscal 1997)
Gifts Received: $6,848 (fiscal 2001); $6,943 (fiscal 1997); $6,621 (fiscal 1996). Note: In fiscal 1997, contributions were received from the Daniel W. Field Trust.

Typical Recipients
Arts & Humanities: Libraries
Civic & Public Affairs: Economic Development, Civic & Public Affairs-General, Municipalities/Towns, Parades/Festivals
Education: Colleges & Universities, Community & Junior Colleges, Student Aid
Health: Cancer, Clinics/Medical Centers, Health Organizations, Hospices, Hospitals, Long-Term Care, Medical Rehabilitation
Religion: Dioceses, Religious Welfare
Social Services: Community Service Organizations, Counseling, Family Planning, Family Services, Homes, People with Disabilities, Recreation & Athletics, Senior Services, United Funds/United Ways, YMCA/YWCA/YMHA/YWHA, Youth Organizations

Application Procedures
Initial Contact: The foundation has no formal grant application procedure or application form.
Deadlines: None.

Foundation Officials
Ida Caggiano: clerk
John F. Creedon: president
Robert Prince: treasurer

Grants Analysis
Disclosure Period: fiscal year ending March 31, 2001
Total Grants: $300,000
Number of Grants: 20
Average Grant: $11,667*
Highest Grant: $50,000
Typical Range: $5,000 to $20,000
*Note: Average grant figure excludes two highest grants ($90,000).

Recent Grants
Note: Grants derived from 1999 Form 990.

General
40,000	St. Joseph's Manor, Trumbull, CT
35,000	Dana Farber Institute, Boston, MA
35,000	Old Colony Y, Brockton, MA
34,000	City of Brockton - Council on Aging
30,000	Helpline
26,500	Salvation Army
25,000	Brockton VNA, Brockton, MA
25,000	New England Sinai Hospital, Stoughton, MA
20,000	Good Samaritan, San Francisco, CA
20,000	Massasoit Community College, Brockton, MA

HOMECREST INDUSTRIES, INC.

Company Headquarters
PO Box 350
Wadena, MN 56482
Web: http://www.homecrest.com

Company Description
Revenue: US$72.1 million (2001)
Employees: 680 (2001)
SIC(s): 2500 Furniture & Fixtures, 2514 Metal Household Furniture.

Operating Locations
Homecrest Industries (MN--Wadena)

Homecrest Foundation

Giving Contact
Mark E. Bottemiller, Secretary & Treasurer
PO Box 350
Wadena, MN 56482
Phone: (218)631-1000
Fax: (218)631-2609

Description
Founded: 1986
EIN: 411550750
Organization Type: Corporate Foundation
Giving Locations: MN
Grant Types: General Support, Scholarship.

Donor Information
Founder: Homecrest Industries

Financial Summary
Total Giving: $20,000 (fiscal year ending July 31, 2001); $16,695 (fiscal 2000); $15,250 (fiscal 1998). Note: Giving includes scholarship ($8,400).
Giving Analysis: Giving for fiscal 2001 includes: foundation grants to United Way ($3,750); foundation scholarships ($6,600); fiscal 2000: foundation grants to United Way ($2,250); foundation scholarships ($6,800); foundation ($7,645); fiscal 1998: foundation scholarships ($4,800) foundation grants to United Way ($6,000)
Assets: $184,439 (fiscal 2001); $197,231 (fiscal 2000); $118,092 (fiscal 1998)
Gifts Received: $50 (fiscal 2001); $15,040 (fiscal 2000); $35,353 (fiscal 1998). Note: Contributions were received from Homecrest Industries.

Typical Recipients
Arts & Humanities: Arts Outreach, Arts & Humanities-General, History & Archaeology, Libraries, Museums/Galleries
Civic & Public Affairs: Chambers of Commerce, Clubs, Economic Development, Civic & Public Affairs-General, Housing, Parades/Festivals, Safety

Education: Arts/Humanities Education, Economic Education, Education Funds, Preschool Education, Public Education (Precollege)
Health: Cancer, Hospitals, Multiple Sclerosis
International: Health Care/Hospitals
Religion: Religious Welfare
Social Services: Animal Protection, Community Centers, Family Services, Recreation & Athletics, Scouts, Special Olympics, United Funds/United Ways

Application Procedures
Initial Contact: Request application guidelines.
Deadlines: None.

Additional Information
Provides employee-related scholarships.
Publications: Application Guidelines

Corporate Officials
Donald L. Bottemiller: president, treasurer, vice president finance PRIM CORP EMPL president: Homecrest Industries.
Lawrence E. Calhoun: secretary, treasurer, vice president finance PRIM CORP EMPL secretary, treasurer, vice president finance: Homecrest Industries.

Foundation Officials
Donald L. Bottemiller: trustee (see above)
Mark Bottemiller: secretary, treasurer
Nancy Bottemiller: trustee
Lawrence E. Calhoun: secretary, treasurer (see above)
John Miles: trustee PRIM CORP EMPL executive vice president marketing: Homecrest Industries.
Nancy Miles: trustee
Clayton A. White: trustee

Grants Analysis
Disclosure Period: fiscal year ending July 31, 2001
Total Grants: $9,650*
Number of Grants: 10
Average Grant: $965
Highest Grant: $5,000
Lowest Grant: $100
Typical Range: $500 to $1,000
*Note: Giving excludes scholarships and United Way.

Recent Grants
Note: Grants derived from 2000 Form 990.

General

2,250	Wadena United Way, Wadena, MN -- contribution
1,000	American Cancer Society, Wadena, MN -- donation "Relay for Life"
1,000	Business Economic Education Foundation, St. Paul, MN -- promote education
1,000	Habitat for Humanity, New York Mills, MN -- help build homes for poor
1,000	Wadena Community Center, Wadena, MN -- promote youth
550	Minnesota Private College Fund, St. Paul, MN -- promote education
550	Tri-County Hospital, Wadena, MN -- donation to foundation
500	American Furniture Hall of Fame, High Point, NC -- education and development
500	WDC German Club, Wadena, MN -- promote education
250	Minnesota Council on Economic Education, Minneapolis, MN -- promote education

HOMELAND FOUNDATION (NY)

Giving Contact
E. Lisk-Wyckoff, Jr., President
230 Park Avenue
PMB 359
New York, NY 10017

Phone: (212)888-5959
Fax: (212)949-0949

Description
Founded: 1938
EIN: 136113816
Organization Type: General Purpose Foundation
Giving Locations: NY: metropolitan area internationally; nationally.
Grant Types: General Support, Scholarship.
Note: Capital and endowment grants are made on the basis of special interest.

Donor Information
Founder: The foundation was incorporated in 1938. In fiscal 1990, the foundation's assets grew to more than $75 million under a trust established by the late Chauncey Stillman .

Financial Summary
Total Giving: $3,455,591 (fiscal year ending April 30, 2000); $3,609,592 (fiscal 1999); $4,167,117 (fiscal 1998)
Giving Analysis: Giving for fiscal 2000 includes: foundation scholarships ($250,000); fiscal 1999: foundation scholarships ($25,000); fiscal 1998: foundation scholarships ($25,000)
Assets: $99,287,771 (fiscal 2000); $102,231,939 (fiscal 1999); $103,319,907 (fiscal 1998)
Gifts Received: $803 (fiscal 1998); $599,098 (fiscal 1997); $2,853 (fiscal 1996). Note: In 1997, contributions were received from Anne G. Earhart. In 1995, contributions were received from the estate of Chauncey Stillman.

Typical Recipients
Arts & Humanities: Arts Centers, Arts Outreach, Dance, Arts & Humanities-General, Historic Preservation, History & Archaeology, Libraries, Literary Arts, Museums/Galleries, Music, Opera, Public Broadcasting
Civic & Public Affairs: Clubs, Employment/Job Training, Civic & Public Affairs-General, Philanthropic Organizations, Public Policy, Urban & Community Affairs
Education: Colleges & Universities, Education Funds, Faculty Development, Education-General, Legal Education, Private Education (Precollege), Public Education (Precollege), Religious Education, Secondary Education (Private), Secondary Education (Public), Social Sciences Education, Student Aid
Environment: Environment-General, Resource Conservation, Wildlife Protection
Health: Cancer, Clinics/Medical Centers, Emergency/Ambulance Services, Heart, Hospitals, Long-Term Care, Prenatal Health Issues
International: Foreign Arts Organizations, Foreign Educational Institutions, International-General, Health Care/Hospitals, Human Rights, International Environmental Issues, International Organizations, International Peace & Security Issues, International Relations, Missionary/Religious Activities
Religion: Churches, Dioceses, Religion-General, Jewish Causes, Ministries, Missionary Activities (Domestic), Religious Organizations, Religious Welfare, Seminaries, Social/Policy Issues
Social Services: Camps, Child Welfare, Community Service Organizations, Emergency Relief, Family Planning, Family Services, Food/Clothing Distribution, Recreation & Athletics, Shelters/Homelessness, Social Services-General, Youth Organizations

Application Procedures
Initial Contact: Send a brief letter of inquiry.
Application Requirements: Include a description of organization, amount requested, purpose of funds sought, proof of tax-exempt status, organization budget, project budget, list of board of directors, and of major donors.
Deadlines: None.

Review Process: The foundation requires a report on a grant made, indicating how the applicant used the grant together with dates and expenditure responsibility.

Restrictions
Grants are limited to support of religious, charitable, scientific, or literary purposes, or for the prevention of cruelty to children or animals. Grants are not made to individuals, private foundations, or governmental organizations. Grants for endowments, building funds, and capital development are made only on the basis of a special interest.

Foundation Officials
Rev. Rafael F. Caamano: trustee
Monsignor Eugene V. Clark: vice president, secretary, trustee
Lucy Fleming-McGrath: trustee
Carl Schmitt: trustee
Charles Scribner, III: vice president, trustee B Washington, DC 1951. ED Princeton University AB (1973); Princeton University MFA (1975); Princeton University PhD (1977). PRIM CORP EMPL editor: Charles Scribner's Sons. NONPR AFFIL trustee: Saint Pauls School; board advisors: Wethersfield Institute; member: Association Princeton University Press. CLUB AFFIL Piping Rock Club; Racquet & Tennis Club; Ivy Club.
Ed Lisk Wyckoff, Jr.: president, treasurer, trustee B Middletown, NJ 1934. ED Duke University BA (1955); University of Michigan JD (1960). PRIM CORP EMPL partner: Kramer, Levin, Naftalis, Nessen, Kamin & Frankel. NONPR AFFIL board advisors: Wildlife Conservation Society; president, director: Wyckoff House Association; trustee: Society Preservation Long Island Antiquities; member: New York State Bar Association; lecturer: Practicing Law Institute; member: International Fiscal Association; trustee: New York Historical Society; member: International Bar Association; member: Association Bar New York City; member: Concilium Sodalium to Vatican Museum; member: American Bar Association; fellow: American College Probate Counsel. CLUB AFFIL Saint Nicholas Society; Pine Plains New York Club; Racquet & Tennis Club; Knickerbocker Club; Mashomack Fish & Game Preserve Club; Essex Connecticut Yacht Club; Holland Society.

Grants Analysis
Disclosure Period: fiscal year ending April 30, 2000
Total Grants: $3,205,591*
Number of Grants: 57
Average Grant: $46,528*
Highest Grant: $600,000
Typical Range: $10,000 to $100,000
*Note: Giving excludes scholarships. Average grant figure excludes highest grant.

Recent Grants
Note: Grants derived from fiscal 2001 Form 990.

Library-Related

400,000	Morgan Library, New York, NY -- for digitalize collection of medieval and renaissance illuminated manuscripts

General

500,000	Governatorato Dello Stato dell Citta del Vaticano, Vatican City Italy -- for restoration work at Papal Academy of Science
250,000	Florence Griswold Museum, Old Lyme, CT -- for conservation of paintings
250,000	Inner-city Scholarship Fund, New York, NY -- for scholarships
250,000	St. Bernard's School, New York, NY -- for teaching of theater
250,000	University of Michigan School of Law, Ann Arbor, MI -- for the Chauncey Stillman chair for ethics, morality and the practice of law
200,000	St. Joseph's Seminary, Yonkers, NY --

for the Francis Cardinal Spellman Chair in Church History

125,000	St. Jean Baptist Church, New York, NY -- for purchase of an organ
115,000	Path to Peace Foundation, New York, NY -- to purchase a new building for Papal Nuncio
100,000	Homes for the Homeless, New York, NY -- for crisis nursery
100,000	Pius XII Youth & Family Services, New York, NY -- for scholarships

HON INDUSTRIES, INC.

Company Headquarters

Muscatine, IA
Web: http://www.honi.com

Company Description

Founded: 1944
Ticker: HNI
Exchange: NYSE
Also Known As: Home-O-Nize.
Revenue: US$1.692 billion (2002)
Employees: 8800 (2002)
SIC(s): 2521 Wood Office Furniture, 2522 Office Furniture Except Wood, 2678 Stationery Products, 3433 Heating Equipment Except Electric.

Operating Locations

HON Industries Inc. (CA--South Gate, Van Nuys; GA--Cedartown; IA--Mount Pleasant; KY--Owensboro; NY--Avon, Wayland; NC--Louisburg; PA--Williamsport; TX--Sulphur Springs; VA--Richmond; WA--Kent)

HON Industries Charitable Foundation

Giving Contact

Susan J. Cradick, Secretary-Treasurer
414 East Third Street
Muscatine, IA 52761-0071
Phone: (563)264-7400
Fax: (563)264-7217
Web: http://www.honi.com/CorporateResponsibility.htm

Description

Founded: 1985
EIN: 421246787
Organization Type: Corporate Foundation
Giving Locations: IA: Muscatine headquarters and operating communities.
Grant Types: Employee Matching Gifts, General Support, Matching, Project, Scholarship.

Financial Summary

Total Giving: $738,198 (2001); $1,249,183 (2000); $1,044,085 (1999). Note: Contributes through corporate direct giving program and foundation.
Giving Analysis: Giving for 2000 includes: foundation grants to United Way ($181,143); foundation ($1,068,040); 1999: foundation grants to United Way ($108,775); foundation ($935,310); 1997: foundation grants to United Way ($87,717) foundation ($575,405))
Assets: $2,322,644 (2001); $6,617,814 (2000); $6,296,082 (1999)
Gifts Received: $200,000 (2000); $2,000,000 (1999); $1,900,000 (1997). Note: Contributions are received from HON Industries Inc.

Typical Recipients

Arts & Humanities: Arts Associations & Councils, Arts Centers, Arts Outreach, Arts & Humanities-General, History & Archaeology, Libraries, Museums/Galleries, Music

Civic & Public Affairs: Business/Free Enterprise, Chambers of Commerce, Clubs, Community Foundations, Economic Development, Economic Policy, Civic & Public Affairs-General, Housing, Legal Aid, Minority Business, Municipalities/Towns, Public Policy, Safety, Urban & Community Affairs
Education: Afterschool/Enrichment Programs, Agricultural Education, Business Education, Colleges & Universities, Community & Junior Colleges, Education Funds, Education Reform, Engineering/Technological Education, Education-General, Preschool Education, Public Education (Precollege), Science/Mathematics Education, Secondary Education (Public), Student Aid
Environment: Environment-General, Resource Conservation
Health: Cancer, Children's Health/Hospitals, Emergency/Ambulance Services, Health Organizations, Hospitals, Preventive Medicine/Wellness Organizations, Public Health, Speech & Hearing
Religion: Churches, Religious Organizations, Religious Welfare
Science: Science Exhibits & Fairs, Scientific Centers & Institutes, Scientific Research
Social Services: Animal Protection, Camps, Community Centers, Community Service Organizations, Day Care, Domestic Violence, Emergency Relief, Family Services, Recreation & Athletics, Scouts, Shelters/Homelessness, United Funds/United Ways, Volunteer Services, YMCA/YWCA/YMHA/YWHA, Youth Organizations

Application Procedures

Initial Contact: The foundation has no specific format for applications.
Application Requirements: Requests should include tax status and any pertinent information.
Deadlines: None.
Evaluative Criteria: Preference is given to organizations located in geographical areas in which HON Industries, Inc. or its operating companies have a presence.

Corporate Officials

A. Mosby Harvey, Jr.: vice president, secretary, general counsel B Memphis, TN 1943. ED Dartmouth College (1965); University of Texas (1969). PRIM CORP EMPL vice president, secretary, general counsel: HON Industries Inc.
Jack D. Michaels: chairman, chief executive officer, director B 1937. ED University of Cincinnati BA. PRIM CORP EMPL chairman, chief executive officer, director: HON Industries Inc. CORP AFFIL president, director: Holga Inc.; director: Snap-On Inc.

Foundation Officials

Roger Behrens: vice president
Susan J. Cradick: secretary, treasurer
R. Michael Derry: vice president B Owosso, MI 1937. ED Western Michigan University BBA (1960). PRIM CORP EMPL senior vice president administration: HON Industries Inc.
Jeffrey D. Fick: vice president
A. Mosby Harvey, Jr.: secretary (see above)
Stanley M. Howe: president B Muscatine, IA 1924. ED Iowa State University (1946); Harvard University Graduate School of Business Administration (1948). CORP AFFIL director: Pella Corp. NONPR AFFIL trustee: Iowa Wesleyan College; member: National Association Manufacturers; member: Benevolent Protectorate Elks; member: Bus Institutional Furniture Manufacturer Association. CLUB AFFIL Rotary Club; 33 Club; Elks Club.
Jack D. Michaels: secretary (see above)

Grants Analysis

Disclosure Period: calendar year ending 2001
Total Grants: $449,069*
Number of Grants: 89
Average Grant: $5,046
Highest Grant: $92,150

Lowest Grant: $45
Typical Range: $200 to $25,000
*Note: Giving excludes scholarship and United Way.

Recent Grants

Note: Grants derived from 2001 Form 990.

General

181,000	Citizens Scholarship Fund, St. Peter, MN
92,150	American Red Cross, Muscatine, IA
50,000	Historic Muscatine, Muscatine, IA
30,000	Muscatine Center for Strategic Action, Muscatine, IA
25,750	United Way Muscatine, Muscatine, IA
25,000	Iowa College Foundation, Des Moines, IA
25,000	Youth Sports Foundation, Muscatine, IA
23,991	Iowa State University Foundation, Ames, IA
20,000	Great Rivers Americorp, Muscatine, IA
19,011	United Way of Greater Los Angeles, Los Angeles, CA

HONDA OF AMERICA MANUFACTURING, INC.

Company Headquarters

24000 Honda Parkway
Marysville, OH 43040
Web: http://www.ohio.honda.com

Company Description

Founded: 1979
Employees: 13,000
SIC(s): 3711 Motor Vehicles & Car Bodies.
Parent Company: Honda Motor Co. Ltd., 1-1, 2-chome, Minami-Aoyama, Minato-ku, Tokyo, Japan

Operating Locations

Honda of America Manufacturing (OH--Marysville)

Nonmonetary Support

Volunteer Programs: The company maintains the Honda Hero Volunteer program, through which the company will donate $200 to eligible organizations to which employees volunteer a minimum of 50 hours.

Honda of America Foundation

Giving Contact

Lourene Hoy, Administrative Coordinator, Company Communications
Honda of America Manufacturing
24000 Honda Pkwy.
Marysville, OH 43040-9251
Phone: (937)645-6883

Description

Founded: 1981
EIN: 311006130
Organization Type: Corporate Foundation
Giving Locations: OH: 15-county hiring area
Grant Types: General Support, Project, Research, Scholarship.

Donor Information

Founder: Honda of America Manufacturing

Financial Summary

Total Giving: $403,705 (2001); $464,083 (2000); $406,255 (1999). Note: Figures are for foundation only. Company gives directly, but does not release information on direct giving.
Assets: $6,863,027 (2001); $7,653,261 (2000); $8,141,527 (1999)

Typical Recipients

Arts & Humanities: Arts Associations & Councils, Ethnic & Folk Arts, Arts & Humanities-General, History & Archaeology, Libraries, Literary Arts, Theater, Visual Arts
Civic & Public Affairs: Employment/Job Training, Civic & Public Affairs-General
Education: Business Education, Colleges & Universities, Community & Junior Colleges, Education Funds, Education-General, International Exchange, International Studies, Literacy, Student Aid
Environment: Environment-General
Health: Health-General
International: Health Care/Hospitals, International Organizations, International Relations
Science: Science Museums
Social Services: Community Centers, Community Service Organizations, Delinquency & Criminal Rehabilitation, Family Services, People with Disabilities, YMCA/YWCA/YMHA/YWHA, Youth Organizations

Application Procedures

Initial Contact: Request a grant application form by writing to:
Honda of America Mfg., Inc.
Company Communications Dept.
24000 Honda Parkway
Marysville, OH 43040. Explain request and purpose of funds sought.
Application Requirements: Completed application forms should be accompanied by a copy of the organization's 501(c)(3) certification.
Deadlines: January 31, for applications to be considered for the current year. If an application is not received by that date, it will be considered for the next fiscal year.
Decision Notification: Grants are reviewed by a Senior Management Board on a three- to four-month cycle beginning in April. Applicants will be notified in writing of the Board's decision.

Restrictions

Does not support individuals or organizations outside operating areas.

Additional Information

Honda of America's giving priorities focus on the development of programs (with emphasis on education) and not on annual operating support budgets. The company's support of area United Way campaigns is taken into account when evaluating requests.
All grants listed were made by the Honda of America Foundation; information on direct giving recipients is not available.

Giving Program Officials

Sandra Fleming: PRIM CORP EMPL administration government & committee relations: Honda of America Manufacturing.

Foundation Officials

John Adams: director PRIM CORP EMPL senior vice president, general manager: Honda of America Manufacturing.
Wendell Bugg: director
Don English: director
Tony Hines: director
Kathy Jones: president
David Nelson: president, director

Grants Analysis

Disclosure Period: calendar year ending 2001
Total Grants: $403,705
Number of Grants: 15
Average Grant: $19,479
Highest Grant: $131,000
Lowest Grant: $1,000
Typical Range: $15,000 to $38,500

Recent Grants

Note: Grants derived from 2001 Form 990.

Library-Related
2,000	Mechanicsburg Public Library, Mechanicsburg, OH -- Support for general programming

General
131,000	COSI Columbus, Columbus, OH -- Support for programming
38,500	UNCF College Fund, Columbus, OH -- Support for general programming
38,095	The Wilds, Columbus, OH -- Support for general programming
32,000	International Friendship Center, Bellefontaine, OH -- Support for general programming
30,000	Washington Center, Washington, DC -- Support for general programming
26,315	Educators to Japan Program, Marysville, OH -- Education program for area teachers to travel to Japan for school visits
22,795	Art Space Lima Center for the Visual Arts, Lima, OH -- Support for general programming
20,000	Ohio Historical Foundation, Columbus, OH -- Support for general programming
15,000	Jobs for Columbus Graduates, Columbus, OH -- Support for general programming
15,000	Logan County Alternative Center, Lewistown, OH -- Support general programming

HERBERT W. HOOVER FOUNDATION

Giving Contact

Brian Hostettler
c/o Key Bank
126 Central Plaza
Canton, OH 44702
Phone: (330)489-5427

Description

Founded: 1989
EIN: 346905388
Organization Type: Private Foundation
Giving Locations: FL: Miami; OH: Stark County
Grant Types: Capital, General Support.

Donor Information

Founder: the Hoover Foundation

Financial Summary

Total Giving: $831,020 (2002); $902,811 (2001); $771,087 (2000)
Giving Analysis: Giving for 2002 includes: foundation grants to United Way ($20,000); 2000: foundation grants to United Way ($37,500); 1999: foundation grants to United Way ($37,500)
Assets: $20,294,250 (2002); $22,692,939 (2001); $23,488,793 (2000)
Gifts Received: $10,184 (2001). Note: In 2001, contributions were received from Elizabeth Hoover.

Typical Recipients

Arts & Humanities: Arts Centers, Arts Institutes, Libraries, Museums/Galleries, Music, Theater
Civic & Public Affairs: African American Affairs, Chambers of Commerce, Community Foundations, Economic Development, Civic & Public Affairs-General, Housing, Minority Business, Nonprofit Management, Safety, Urban & Community Affairs, Zoos/Aquariums

Education: Business Education, Colleges & Universities, Education Funds, Education Reform, Elementary Education (Public), Education-General, Medical Education, Private Education (Precollege), Public Education (Precollege), Secondary Education (Public), Student Aid, Vocational & Technical Education
Environment: Air/Water Quality, Environment-General, Resource Conservation
Health: Cancer, Clinics/Medical Centers, Health-General, Health Organizations, Single-Disease Health Associations
Religion: Ministries, Religious Organizations, Religious Welfare
Science: Scientific Centers & Institutes
Social Services: Animal Protection, Camps, Child Welfare, Community Centers, Community Service Organizations, Crime Prevention, Domestic Violence, Family Services, Food/Clothing Distribution, People with Disabilities, Recreation & Athletics, Scouts, United Funds/United Ways, YMCA/YWCA/YMHA/YWHA, Youth Organizations

Application Procedures

Initial Contact: Send a brief letter of inquiry.
Application Requirements: Include a description of organization, amount requested, purpose of funds sought, background information on organization, proof of tax-exempt status, and other organizations funding the project.
Deadlines: None.

Restrictions

Foundation does not support individuals, religious organizations for sectarian purposes, political or lobbying groups, or organizations outside operating areas.

Additional Information

Trust(s): Key Trust Co OH NA

Foundation Officials

Ruth H. Basner: mem
Mrs. Carl Good Hoover: member
Elizabeth Lacy Hoover: chairman
Robert S. O'Brien: mem
Blair C. Woodside, Jr.: member

Grants Analysis

Disclosure Period: calendar year ending 2002
Total Grants: $811,020*
Number of Grants: 35
Average Grant: $19,276*
Highest Grant: $100,000
Lowest Grant: $2,500
Typical Range: $10,000 to $50,000
*Note: Giving excludes United Way. Average grant figure excludes two highest grants ($175,000).

Recent Grants

Note: Grants derived from 2001 Form 990.

Library-Related
75,000	National First Ladies Library, Canton, OH
25,000	Minerva Public Library, Minerva, OH

General
75,000	North Canton Community Building, North Canton, OH
75,000	Walsh University, Canton, OH
50,000	Kent State University, Kent, OH
50,000	North Canton Medical Foundation, North Canton, OH
50,000	Spinal Cord Society, Fergus Falls, MN
49,740	Tropical Audubon Society, Miami, FL
42,750	Minority Development Services, Canton, OH
33,000	Stark State College Foundation, Canton, OH
30,000	Cultural Center for the Arts, Canton, OH
30,000	Neighbors For Neighbors, Miami, FL

THE HOOVER FOUNDATION

Giving Contact

Lawrence R. Hoover, Chairman
101 East Maple Street
North Canton, OH 44720
Fax: (216)497-5857

Description

Founded: 1945
EIN: 346510994
Organization Type: General Purpose Foundation
Giving Locations: OH: Stark County
Grant Types: Capital, Challenge, General Support, Multiyear/Continuing Support, Research, Scholarship, Seed Money.

Donor Information

Founder: Established in 1945 by members of the Hoover family.

Financial Summary

Total Giving: $3,557,400 (2000); $3,090,000 (1999); $2,797,059 (1998). Note: The figure for 1995 includes $62,400 in matching gifts and scholarships.
Giving Analysis: Giving for 2000 includes: foundation scholarships ($12,500); foundation grants to United Way ($175,900); 1998: foundation matching gifts ($9,100) foundation grants to United Way ($510,000)
Assets: $60,985,981 (2000); $61,700,000 (1999); $54,189,371 (1998)
Gifts Received: $332,500 (1993)

Typical Recipients

Arts & Humanities: Arts Centers, Arts Funds, Arts Institutes, Arts Outreach, Ballet, Arts & Humanities-General, Historic Preservation, History & Archaeology, Libraries, Museums/Galleries, Music, Opera, Performing Arts, Public Broadcasting, Theater
Civic & Public Affairs: African American Affairs, Botanical Gardens/Parks, Chambers of Commerce, Clubs, Economic Development, Employment/Job Training, Civic & Public Affairs-General, Housing, Minority Business, Municipalities/Towns, Philanthropic Organizations, Professional & Trade Associations, Safety, Urban & Community Affairs, Zoos/Aquariums
Education: Agricultural Education, Business Education, Colleges & Universities, Economic Education, Education Funds, Education Reform, Education-General, Leadership Training, Minority Education, Preschool Education, Private Education (Precollege), Public Education (Precollege), Religious Education, Science/Mathematics Education, Secondary Education (Public), Special Education, Student Aid
Environment: Forestry, Resource Conservation
Health: Children's Health/Hospitals, Emergency/Ambulance Services, Eyes/Blindness, Health Funds, Health Organizations, Heart, Hospitals, Medical Research, Multiple Sclerosis, Respiratory, Transplant Networks/Donor Banks
International: International Relations, Missionary/Religious Activities
Religion: Ministries, Missionary Activities (Domestic), Religious Organizations, Religious Welfare
Social Services: Animal Protection, At-Risk Youth, Camps, Child Welfare, Community Centers, Community Service Organizations, Counseling, Day Care, Delinquency & Criminal Rehabilitation, Domestic Violence, Family Planning, Family Services, Food/Clothing Distribution, Homes, People with Disabilities, Recreation & Athletics, Scouts, Senior Services, Shelters/Homelessness, Substance Abuse, United Funds/United Ways, YMCA/YWCA/YMHA/YWHA, Youth Organizations

Application Procedures

Initial Contact: Send a brief letter of inquiry.
Application Requirements: Include purpose for which grant is requested, amount requested, and proof of 501(c)(3) status.
Deadlines: None.

Restrictions

The foundation primarily supports organizations located in the Stark County, OH, area. It does not make grants to individuals.

Additional Information

The Key Trust of Ohio, N.A. acts as a corporate trustee for the foundation.
Trust(s): Key Trust Company; United National Bank

Foundation Officials

Ronald Kent Bennington: trustee B Circleville, OH 1936. ED Kenyon College BA (1958); Ohio State University JD (1961). PRIM CORP EMPL partner: Black McCuskey Souers & Arbaugh. CORP AFFIL director: United Hard Chrome Inc. NONPR AFFIL board associates: Union College; fund-raising director: United Way Fund Drive; trustee: Timken Mercy Medical Center; member: Stark County Bar Association; president: Stark County Law Library Association; member: Ohio State Bar Foundation; steering committee: Pro Football Hall of Fame; ambassador: Ohio Foundation Independent Colleges; trustee: Malone College; member: Ohio Bar Association; member advisory committee: Kenyon College; member: Leadership Canton; trustee: Greater Canton Chamber of Commerce; ofcl: Big Ten Football; president: Eastern Ohio Football Officials Association; member: American Bar Foundation; director: American Red Cross Canton; member: American Bar Association; board associate: Alliance.
Lawrence Richard Hoover: chairman, trustee B Canton, OH 1935. ED Massachusetts Institute of Technology (1957). PRIM CORP EMPL vice president: Ohio Power Co. CORP AFFIL vice president: Columbus Southern Power Co. NONPR AFFIL Free Accepted Masons:.
Thomas H. Hoover: trustee B 1921. ED Cornell University (1947). PRIM CORP EMPL president: Stark Co. Womens Clinic.
Joyce U. Niffenegger: trustee
Dr. Timothy D. Schiltz: trustee NONPR AFFIL president: North Canton Board Education.

Grants Analysis

Disclosure Period: calendar year ending 2000
Total Grants: $3,369,000*
Number of Grants: 83
Average Grant: $40,590
Highest Grant: $575,000
Typical Range: $1,000 to $50,000
***Note:** Giving excludes sch; United Way.

Recent Grants

Note: Grants derived from 2000 Form 990.

Library-Related

575,000	North Canton Library Association, Canton, OH
215,000	National First Ladies Library, Canton, OH
25,000	Minerva Public Library

General

500,000	North Canton Community Building, North Canton, OH -- maintenance fund
250,000	Walsh University, North Canton, OH -- annual campaign
150,000	J.R. Coleman Family Services Corp., Canton, OH -- annual campaign
100,000	Education Enhancement Partnership, Canton, OH -- funds for continuation of programs
95,000	Cultural Center for Arts, Canton, OH
75,000	North Canton Community Building, North Canton, OH -- maintenance fund
60,000	Family Services, Canton, OH -- assist needy families
51,000	Minority Development Services of Stark County, Canton, OH -- assist minorities in the community
50,000	Cleveland Museum of Natural History, Cleveland, OH
50,000	East Canton Community Sports Complex, Canton, OH -- community development

W. HENRY HOOVER TRUST FUND

Giving Contact

Kim Mayle
c/o Key Trust Co. OH NA
4495 Everhand Road North West
Canton, OH 44718
Phone: (330)497-3604

Description

Founded: 1945
EIN: 346573738
Organization Type: Private Foundation
Giving Locations: OH
Grant Types: General Support.

Donor Information

Founder: the late W. Henry Hoover

Financial Summary

Total Giving: $280,000 (2002); $308,000 (2001); $332,000 (2000)
Giving Analysis: Giving for 2002 includes: foundation grants to United Way ($50,000); 2000: foundation grants to United Way ($50,000) 1999: foundation grants to United Way ($50,000)
Assets: $4,831,008 (2002); $5,979,535 (2001); $6,209,004 (2000)
Gifts Received: $1,000 (1995)

Typical Recipients

Arts & Humanities: Arts Centers, Arts Funds, Arts Institutes, Arts & Humanities-General, Historic Preservation, History & Archaeology, Libraries, Museums/Galleries, Performing Arts, Theater
Civic & Public Affairs: Clubs, Civic & Public Affairs-General, Municipalities/Towns, Urban & Community Affairs
Education: Colleges & Universities, Education Funds, Education Reform, Engineering/Technological Education, Education-General, Minority Education, Private Education (Precollege), Student Aid
Environment: Resource Conservation
Health: Cancer, Emergency/Ambulance Services, Heart, Medical Research, Respiratory, Single-Disease Health Associations
International: Health Care/Hospitals, International Relations
Religion: Churches, Religious Organizations, Religious Welfare, Religious Welfare
Social Services: Animal Protection, At-Risk Youth, Child Welfare, Community Service Organizations, Family Planning, Family Services, People with Disabilities, Scouts, United Funds/United Ways, YMCA/YWCA/YMHA/YWHA, Youth Organizations

Application Procedures

Initial Contact: Send a brief letter of inquiry.
Application Requirements: Include amount requested and purpose of funds sought.
Deadlines: None.

Additional Information

Trust(s): Key Trust Co OH NA

Grants Analysis

Disclosure Period: calendar year ending 2002
Total Grants: $230,000*
Number of Grants: 30
Average Grant: $6,207*
Highest Grant: $50,000
Lowest Grant: $1,000
Typical Range: $1,000 to $10,000
*Note: Giving excludes United Way. Average grant figure excludes highest grant.

Recent Grants

Note: Grants derived from 2001 Form 990.

General

50,000	Cultural Center for the Arts, Canton, OH
50,000	Ohio Wesleyan University, Delaware, OH
50,000	United Way of Central Stark County, Canton, OH
15,000	Central American Medical, Orville, OH
15,000	United Arts Fund, Canton, OH
10,000	Goodwill Industries, Canton, OH
10,000	Pathway Caring for Children, Canton, OH
10,000	Pegasus Farm, Hartville, OH
10,000	Wilderness Center, Wilmot, OH
8,000	Museum Guild, Canton, OH

HOPEDALE FOUNDATION

Giving Contact

Dr. Vincent J. Arone, Treasurer & Trustee
43 Hope St.
PO Box 123
Hopedale, MA 01747
Phone: (508)473-2871

Description

Founded: 1946
EIN: 046044779
Organization Type: Private Foundation
Giving Locations: MA: Hopedale
Grant Types: Capital, General Support, Loan, Scholarship.

Donor Information

Founder: Draper Corp., the late Thomas H. West, the late John D. Gannett

Financial Summary

Total Giving: $415,405 (fiscal year ending October 31, 2001); $330,436 (fiscal 2000); $325,290 (fiscal 1999)
Giving Analysis: Giving for fiscal 2001 includes: foundation scholarships ($145,405); fiscal 2000: foundation scholarships ($125,775) fiscal 1999: foundation scholarships ($101,590)
Assets: $8,438,197 (fiscal 2001); $10,790,804 (fiscal 2000); $8,773,198 (fiscal 1999)

Typical Recipients

Arts & Humanities: Arts Associations & Councils, Historic Preservation, History & Archaeology, Libraries, Museums/Galleries, Music, Public Broadcasting, Theater
Civic & Public Affairs: Botanical Gardens/Parks, Economic Development, Civic & Public Affairs-General, Municipalities/Towns, Safety, Zoos/Aquariums
Education: Arts/Humanities Education, Colleges & Universities, Education Funds, Elementary Education (Private), Elementary Education (Public), Education-General, Medical Education, Science/Mathematics Education, Secondary Education (Public)

Health: Children's Health/Hospitals, Clinics/Medical Centers, Health Organizations, Hospitals, Hospitals (University Affiliated), Nursing Services
Religion: Religious Welfare
Science: Science Museums
Social Services: Child Welfare, Community Centers, Community Service Organizations, Crime Prevention, Food/Clothing Distribution, People with Disabilities, Recreation & Athletics, Scouts, Senior Services, United Funds/United Ways, Veterans, YMCA/YWCA/YMHA/YWHA, Youth Organizations

Application Procedures

Initial Contact: Send a written request.
Deadlines: June 1 for student loans; no deadline for other grants.
Review Process: Board meets in February, June, and October.

Restrictions

Grants to charitable organizations are restricted to those having an impact on the local area.

Additional Information

Provides student loans to graduates of Hopedale High School.

Foundation Officials

Dr. Vincent J. Arone: treasurer, director
W. Gregory Burrill: secretary, director
Peter S. Ellis: director
William B. Gannett: president, director
Alfred H. Sparling, Jr.: director
Thomas H. West, Jr.: director

Grants Analysis

Disclosure Period: fiscal year ending October 31, 2001
Total Grants: $270,000*
Number of Grants: 25
Average Grant: $4,130*
Highest Grant: $100,000
Lowest Grant: $1,000
Typical Range: $1,000 to $10,000
*Note: Giving excludes scholarships. Average grant excludes two highest grants ($175,000).

Recent Grants

Note: Grants derived from 2000 Form 990.

Library-Related

13,000	Bancroft Memorial Library, Hopedale, MA -- for historic renovations
2,000	Friends of the Hopedale Library, Hopedale, MA

General

75,000	Milford Whitinsville Regional Hospital, Milford, MA -- for fourth floor renovation project
25,000	Hopedale Community House, Hopedale, MA
25,000	Milford Whitinsville Regional Hospital, Milford, MA
18,421	Hopedale Park Commission, Hopedale, MA -- for playground restoration project and statue
10,000	New England College Fund, Woburn, MA
6,000	Visiting Nurse Association, Menton, MA
5,000	Boy Scouts of America - Knox Trail Council, Framingham, MA
2,500	Children's Hospital, Boston, MA
2,500	Museum of Science, Boston, MA
2,500	New England Aquarium, Boston, MA

JOSEPHINE LAWRENCE HOPKINS FOUNDATION

Giving Contact

Ivan Obolensky, President, Treasurer & Director
61 Broadway, Suite 2100
New York, NY 10006
Phone: (212)480-0400

Description

Founded: 1968
EIN: 136277593
Organization Type: Private Foundation
Giving Locations: NY
Grant Types: General Support.

Donor Information

Founder: the late Josephine H. Graeber

Financial Summary

Total Giving: $156,000 (2001); $157,600 (2000); $158,500 (1999)
Assets: $3,947,217 (2001); $4,020,369 (2000); $3,845,935 (1999)
Gifts Received: $100 (1995)

Typical Recipients

Arts & Humanities: Arts Centers, Community Arts, Libraries, Literary Arts, Music, Performing Arts, Public Broadcasting
Civic & Public Affairs: Clubs, Civic & Public Affairs-General, Municipalities/Towns, Philanthropic Organizations, Professional & Trade Associations, Zoos/Aquariums
Education: Colleges & Universities, Education-General, Medical Education, Private Education (Precollege), Science/Mathematics Education, Secondary Education (Private), Secondary Education (Public), Special Education
Environment: Air/Water Quality, Environment-General, Resource Conservation
Health: Cancer, Children's Health/Hospitals, Emergency/Ambulance Services, Geriatric Health, Health Organizations, Hospitals, Long-Term Care, Medical Research
International: Missionary/Religious Activities
Religion: Churches, Missionary Activities (Domestic), Religious Organizations, Religious Welfare
Social Services: Animal Protection, Child Welfare, Community Centers, Community Service Organizations, Counseling, Emergency Relief, People with Disabilities, Recreation & Athletics, YMCA/YWCA/YMHA/YWHA, Youth Organizations

Application Procedures

Initial Contact: Send written request.
Deadlines: None.
Notes: Foundation mainly supports pre-selected organizations and rarely chooses to fund unsolicited requests.

Restrictions

Foundation does not support individuals.

Foundation Officials

Vera L. Colage: vice president, director
Lee Harrison Corbin: assistant secretary, assistant treasurer, director
William P. Hurley: vice president, secretary, assistant treasurer, director
John G. Ledes: assistant treasurer, assistant secretary, director
Ivan Obolensky: president, treasurer, director B London, United Kingdom 1925. ED Yale University BA (1947). PRIM CORP EMPL senior vice president: Josephthal & Co. CORP AFFIL vice president: Shields & Co.; general partner: Astor Capital Management Associates. NONPR AFFIL director: Un Service Organization; member: West Point Society; director: Tolstoy

Foundation; member: Saint Elmo Society; president, director: Soldiers Sailors & Airmens Club; member: Military Order Loyal Museum Art; member: New England Society; member: Metropolitan Museum Art; director: Childrens Blood Foundation New York Hospital; grand treasurer, member: Masons; member: American Legion; director: Audubon Canyon Ranch. CLUB AFFIL Saint Georges Society; Navy League US; New York Yacht Club; Knickerbocker Club; Army-Navy Country Club; Explorers Club.

Gerald C. Tobin: assistant treasurer, assistant secretary, director

Grants Analysis

Disclosure Period: calendar year ending 2001
Total Grants: $156,000
Number of Grants: 26
Average Grant: $6,000
Highest Grant: $20,000
Lowest Grant: $1,000
Typical Range: $1,000 to $10,000

Recent Grants

Note: Grants derived from 2001 Form 990.

General

20,000	Archbishop of New York, New York, NY
10,000	American Red Cross, West Palm Beach, FL
10,000	American Red Cross, Ft. Lauderdale, FL
10,000	Audubon Canyon Ranch, Glen Ellen, CA
10,000	Children's Blood Foundation, New York, NY
10,000	Christopher Reeves Paralysis Foundation, Springfield, NJ
10,000	Inner-city Scholarship Fund, New York, NY
10,000	Soldiers', Sailors', Marines & Airmen's Club, Inc., New York, NY
10,000	Yale University Medical School, New Haven, CT
7,500	Cornell University, Ithaca, NY -- science - education

JOHN M. HOPWOOD CHARITABLE TRUST

Giving Contact

Bruce Bickel, Senior Vice President and Manager
c/o Charitable and Endowment Management
PNC Bank
2 PNC Plaza, 25th Floor
620 Liberty Ave.
Pittsburgh, PA 15222-2705
Phone: (412)762-3502
Fax: (412)705-1043
E-mail: bruce.bickel@pncbank.com

Description

Founded: 1948
EIN: 256022634
Organization Type: Family Foundation
Giving Locations: PA: Western part of state
Grant Types: Challenge, Endowment, Loan, Matching, Project, Research, Seed Money.

Donor Information

Founder: Established in 1948 by the late John M. Hopwood .

Financial Summary

Total Giving: $1,418,353 (2000); $1,274,349 (1998); $1,069,107 (1997)
Giving Analysis: Giving for 2000 includes: foundation grants to United Way ($18,000); foundation scholarships ($290,000); 1998: foundation grants to United Way ($3,500); foundation scholarships ($265,000)

Assets: $31,585,289 (2000); $29,877,741 (1998); $25,183,620 (1997)
Gifts Received: In 1990, contributions were received from Mary Hopwood.

Typical Recipients

Arts & Humanities: Arts Centers, Ballet, Dance, Arts & Humanities-General, History & Archaeology, Libraries, Museums/Galleries, Music, Opera, Public Broadcasting, Theater
Civic & Public Affairs: Botanical Gardens/Parks, Community Foundations, Employment/Job Training, Civic & Public Affairs-General, Housing, Parades/Festivals, Professional & Trade Associations, Public Policy, Urban & Community Affairs, Women's Affairs, Zoos/Aquariums
Education: Business Education, Colleges & Universities, Community & Junior Colleges, Education Funds, Education-General, Legal Education, Literacy, Medical Education, Private Education (Precollege), Public Education (Precollege), Science/Mathematics Education, Student Aid, Student Aid
Environment: Air/Water Quality, Energy, Environment-General, Resource Conservation
Health: Cancer, Children's Health/Hospitals, Clinics/Medical Centers, Emergency/Ambulance Services, Health Organizations, Hospices, Hospitals, Kidney, Long-Term Care, Medical Rehabilitation, Mental Health, Multiple Sclerosis, Nursing Services, Public Health, Single-Disease Health Associations, Speech & Hearing
International: Health Care/Hospitals
Religion: Churches, Religion-General, Ministries, Religious Organizations, Religious Welfare
Social Services: Big Brother/Big Sister, Camps, Child Welfare, Community Centers, Community Service Organizations, Day Care, Domestic Violence, Family Services, Homes, People with Disabilities, Recreation & Athletics, Scouts, Senior Services, Social Services-General, Substance Abuse, United Funds/United Ways, Veterans, YMCA/YWCA/YMHA/YWHA, Youth Organizations

Application Procedures

Initial Contact: The trust requests applications be made in writing.
Deadlines: None.

Restrictions

The trust reports grants are made only to corporations or associations organized operated exclusively for religious, charitable, scientific, literary, medical, or educational purposes. Funding is limited to southwestern Pennsylvania.

Additional Information

The PNC Bank acts as a corporate trustee for the John M. Hopwood Charitable Trust.
Publications: Guidelines

Foundation Officials

Bruce Bickel: senior vice president, manager CORP AFFIL vice president, general manager: PNC Bank.
William T. Hopwood: trustee

Grants Analysis

Disclosure Period: calendar year ending 2000
Total Grants: $1,110,354*
Number of Grants: 69
Average Grant: $16,092
Highest Grant: $135,000
Typical Range: $1,000 to $30,000
*Note: Giving excludes United Way; scholarships.

Recent Grants

Note: Grants derived from 2000 Form 990.

General

155,000	Citizen's Scholarship Foundation, Santa Ana, CA
135,000	Richardson Scholarship Foundation, Vero Beach, FL
100,000	Shadyside Hospital Foundation, Pittsburgh, PA
75,000	Washington Hospital, Washington, PA
50,000	Allegheny Valley School, Coraopolis, PA
50,000	National Aviary in Pittsburgh, Pittsburgh, PA
50,000	Ohio Valley General Hospital, McKees Rocks, PA
40,000	ARC Washington County, Meadow Lands, PA
36,000	St. Clair Hospital Foundation, Pittsburgh, PA
35,000	Western Pennsylvania Conservancy, Mill Run, PA

HENRY HORNBLOWER FUND

Giving Contact

Nathan N. Withington, President
PO Box 2365
Boston, MA 02107
Phone: (617)589-3286

Description

Founded: 1945
EIN: 237425285
Organization Type: Private Foundation
Giving Locations: MA: Boston
Grant Types: General Support, Research.

Donor Information

Founder: Hornblower and Weeks - Hemphill, Noyes

Financial Summary

Total Giving: $360,100 (2000); $303,565 (1999); $280,000 (1998 approx)
Giving Analysis: Giving for 2000 includes: foundation matching gifts ($2,600); 1999: foundation matching gifts ($2,625) foundation ($300,000)
Assets: $6,271,693 (2000); $6,120,027 (1999); $4,713,073 (1997)

Typical Recipients

Arts & Humanities: Community Arts, Arts & Humanities-General, Historic Preservation, History & Archaeology, Libraries, Museums/Galleries, Music, Public Broadcasting
Civic & Public Affairs: Community Foundations, Employment/Job Training, Civic & Public Affairs-General, Parades/Festivals, Philanthropic Organizations, Urban & Community Affairs, Women's Affairs
Education: Colleges & Universities, Private Education (Precollege), Secondary Education (Private), Secondary Education (Public), Special Education
Environment: Environment-General, Resource Conservation, Wildlife Protection
Health: Cancer, Children's Health/Hospitals, Clinics/Medical Centers, Hospices, Hospitals, Medical Research, Nursing Services, Single-Disease Health Associations, Trauma Treatment
International: Health Care/Hospitals
Religion: Religious Organizations, Religious Welfare
Science: Science Museums
Social Services: Child Welfare, Community Centers, Community Service Organizations, Emergency Relief, Homes, People with Disabilities, Recreation & Athletics, Scouts, United Funds/United Ways, Youth Organizations

Application Procedures

Initial Contact: Foundation requests applications be made in writing. Send a brief letter of inquiry.
Application Requirements: Include a description of organization, amount requested, purpose of funds sought, and proof of tax-exempt status.
Deadlines: None.

Restrictions

Does not support individuals, or political or lobbying groups.

Foundation Officials

Dudley H. Bradlee, II: director B Medford, MA 1915. ED Harvard University (1938). PRIM CORP EMPL consultant: Shearson American Express. CORP AF-FIL treasurer: Franklin Square House; director: Winchester Co-operative Bank; vice president, director: Charlesbank Homes.
Elaine Renzi: secretary
Nathan N. Withington: president

Grants Analysis

Disclosure Period: calendar year ending 2000
Total Grants: $357,500*
Number of Grants: 28
Average Grant: $5,833*
Highest Grant: $200,000
Typical Range: $100 to $10,000
*Note: Giving excludes matching gifts. Average grant excludes highest grant.

Recent Grants

Note: Grants derived from 2001 Form 990.

Library-Related
5,000	Plymouth Public Library, Plymouth, MA

General
100,000	Eel River Watershed, Redway, CA
25,000	Plimouth Plantation, Plymouth, MA
20,000	Jordan Hospital Club, Plymouth, MA
5,000	Children's Hospital, Boston, MA
5,000	Cura Visiting Nurse Association, Plymouth, MA
5,000	Eel River Watershed, Redway, CA
5,000	Friends of Cranberry Hospice, Kingston, MA
5,000	Governor Dummer Academy, Byfield, MA
5,000	Jimmy Fund, Brookline, MA
5,000	Kenyon College, Gambier, OH

ERVIN G. HOUCHENS FOUNDATION

Giving Contact

Suel Houchens, Director
Ervin G. Houchens Foundation
PO Box 90009
Bowling Green, KY 42102-9009
Phone: (270)843-3252

Description

Founded: 1954
EIN: 610623087
Organization Type: Private Foundation
Giving Locations: KY: Bowling Green
Grant Types: General Support.

Donor Information

Founder: Houchens Markets, Inc., B.G. Wholesale

Financial Summary

Total Giving: $326,994 (2001); $186,746 (2000); $115,298 (1998)
Giving Analysis: Giving for 2001 includes: foundation grants to United Way ($10,200)

Assets: $3,369,196 (2001); $3,654,026 (2000); $3,751,879 (1998)
Gifts Received: $16,236 (2001); $8,547 (2000); $13,994 (1996). Note: In 2001, contributions were received from E. G. Houchens Foundation Charitable Trust. In 1995 and 2000, contributions were received from the Houchens-Ervin G. Houchens Foundation.

Typical Recipients

Arts & Humanities: Arts Associations & Councils, Arts Centers, Arts Festivals, Arts Funds, Historic Preservation, History & Archaeology, Libraries, Museums/Galleries, Music, Theater
Civic & Public Affairs: Clubs, Employment/Job Training, Civic & Public Affairs-General, Housing, Parades/Festivals, Safety, Urban & Community Affairs, Women's Affairs
Education: Business Education, Colleges & Universities, Economic Education, Education Funds, Elementary Education (Public), Literacy, Private Education (Precollege), Secondary Education (Public), Student Aid
Environment: Environment-General
Health: Children's Health/Hospitals, Clinics/Medical Centers, Eyes/Blindness, Single-Disease Health Associations
Religion: Churches, Missionary Activities (Domestic), Missionary Activities (Domestic), Religious Organizations, Religious Welfare
Science: Science Museums
Social Services: At-Risk Youth, Big Brother/Big Sister, Child Welfare, Community Service Organizations, Homes, Recreation & Athletics, Scouts, United Funds/United Ways, YMCA/YWCA/YMHA/YWHA, Youth Organizations

Application Procedures

Initial Contact: Send a brief letter of inquiry with comprehensive details.
Deadlines: None.

Additional Information

Provides interest-free and low-interest rate loans to churches and public charities.

Foundation Officials

Lou Beckner: assistant secretary
Covella H. Biggers: treasurer
Erin Biggers: director
Gil E. Biggers: director
Gil M. Biggers: president
George Suel Houchens: director
C. Cecil Martin: director
Lois Lynne Martin: secretary
Tara Biggers Parker: director

Grants Analysis

Disclosure Period: calendar year ending 2001
Total Grants: $316,794*
Number of Grants: 53
Average Grant: $3,186*
Highest Grant: $151,119
Lowest Grant: $60
Typical Range: $500 to $10,000
*Note: Giving excludes United Way. Average grant figure excludes highest grant.

Recent Grants

Note: Grants derived from 2001 Form 990.

General
151,119	State Street United Methodist Church, Bowling Green, KY
25,000	Salvation Army, Bowling Green, KY
16,000	Big Brothers Big Sisters, Inc., Bowling Green, KY
14,365	Girls Inc., Bowling Green, KY
13,479	Western Kentucky University Foundation, Bowling Green, KY
10,200	United Way of Southern Kentucky, Bowling Green, KY
7,500	State Street United Methodist Church, Bowling Green, KY
5,000	Court Appointed Special Advocates of Warren County, Bowling Green, KY
5,000	Horse Cave Theatre, Bowling Green, KY
5,000	Lindsey Wilson College, Columbia, KY

MAY KAY HOUCK FOUNDATION

Giving Contact

John Germany
Holland & Knight
PO Box 1288
Tampa, FL 33601
Phone: (813)227-8500

Description

Founded: 1955
EIN: 590777857
Organization Type: Private Foundation
Giving Locations: FL: Sarasota, Tampa; NY: Albany, Genesee, Greenwich, Rochester
Grant Types: General Support.

Financial Summary

Total Giving: $97,000 (fiscal year ending April 30, 2001); $160,000 (fiscal 2000); $110,000 (fiscal 1999)
Assets: $2,725,916 (fiscal 2001); $3,216,337 (fiscal 2000); $3,095,246 (fiscal 1999)

Typical Recipients

Arts & Humanities: Arts Funds, History & Archaeology, Libraries, Museums/Galleries, Music, Public Broadcasting, Theater
Civic & Public Affairs: Botanical Gardens/Parks, Community Foundations, Housing, Philanthropic Organizations, Urban & Community Affairs
Education: Business Education, Education Funds, Public Education (Precollege)
Environment: Air/Water Quality, Resource Conservation
Science: Scientific Centers & Institutes
Social Services: Community Centers, Community Service Organizations, Counseling, Domestic Violence, Homes, People with Disabilities, Recreation & Athletics, Sexual Abuse, Shelters/Homelessness, United Funds/United Ways, YMCA/YWCA/YMHA/YWHA, Youth Organizations

Application Procedures

Initial Contact: Request Application Form.
Deadlines: None.

Foundation Officials

Karen Hargrave: trustee
F. Wesley Moffett, Jr.: trustee
David Robison: trustee
Earl F. Robison: trustee

Grants Analysis

Disclosure Period: fiscal year ending April 30, 2001
Total Grants: $97,000
Number of Grants: 7
Average Grant: $7,667*
Highest Grant: $51,000
Lowest Grant: $2,000
Typical Range: $2,000 to $10,000
*Note: Average grant excludes highest grant.

Recent Grants

Note: Grants derived from fiscal 2000 Form 990.

Library-Related
15,000	Germany Public Library, Tampa, FL -- for program services
5,000	Friends of the Library, Tampa, FL -- for program services

General

40,000	Junior Achievement International, Colorado Springs, CO -- for program services
28,000	Albany Symphony, Albany, NY -- for program services
11,000	Albany Institute of History and Art, Albany, NY -- for program services
10,000	American Rivers, Washington, DC -- for program services
10,000	Genesee Valley Conservancy, Geneseo, NY -- for program services
8,000	Battenkill Conservancy, Greenwich, NY -- for program services
6,250	Habitat for Humanity, Sarasota, FL -- for program services
6,250	Lighthouse for the Blind, Sarasota, FL -- for program services
6,250	Safe Place and Rape Crisis Center of Sarasota, Sarasota, FL -- for program services
6,250	Southeastern Guide Dogs, Sarasota, FL -- for program services

HOUSTON ENDOWMENT

Giving Contact

H. Joe Nelson, III, President
600 Travis, Suite 6400
Houston, TX 77002-3000
Phone: (713)238-8100
Fax: (713)238-8101
E-mail: sjohns@houstonendowment.org
Web: http://www.houstonendowment.org

Description

Founded: 1937
EIN: 746013920
Organization Type: General Purpose Foundation
Giving Locations: TX: some statewide giving, Harris County, Houston
Grant Types: Capital, Endowment, Fellowship, General Support, Operating Expenses, Professorship, Project, Scholarship.

Donor Information

Founder: The Houston Endowment was established in 1937 by the late Mr. and Mrs. Jesse H. Jones . Mr. Jones was a Houston financier, owner-publisher of the *Houston Chronicle*, and a builder and real estate developer. In addition to his local leadership in civic affairs, Mr. Jones was nationally prominent as head of the Reconstruction Finance Corporation during the Depression, and Secretary of Commerce from 1940 to 1945.

Financial Summary

Total Giving: $41,092,512 (2003 approx); $69,512,900 (2002); $76,264,325 (2001)
Giving Analysis: Giving for 2000 includes: foundation scholarships ($4,088,553) 1999: foundation scholarships ($4,233,500)
Assets: $1,340,803,428 (2001); $1,387,672,493 (2000); $1,500,000,000 (1999 approx)

Typical Recipients

Arts & Humanities: Arts Associations & Councils, Arts Outreach, Ballet, Ethnic & Folk Arts, Historic Preservation, History & Archaeology, Libraries, Literary Arts, Museums/Galleries, Music, Opera, Performing Arts, Public Broadcasting, Theater, Visual Arts
Civic & Public Affairs: African American Affairs, Asian American Affairs, Botanical Gardens/Parks, Economic Development, Employment/Job Training, Civic & Public Affairs-General, Hispanic Affairs, Housing, Law & Justice, Municipalities/Towns, Professional & Trade Associations, Public Policy, Safety,

Urban & Community Affairs, Women's Affairs, Zoos/Aquariums
Education: Afterschool/Enrichment Programs, Arts/Humanities Education, Business Education, Business Education, Colleges & Universities, Economic Education, Education Associations, Education Reform, Elementary Education (Public), Engineering/Technological Education, Environmental Education, Faculty Development, Education-General, Gifted & Talented Programs, Health & Physical Education, International Studies, Legal Education, Literacy, Medical Education, Minority Education, Preschool Education, Private Education (Precollege), Public Education (Precollege), Religious Education, Science/Mathematics Education, Secondary Education (Private), Social Sciences Education, Special Education, Student Aid, Vocational & Technical Education
Environment: Environment-General, Resource Conservation, Wildlife Protection
Health: AIDS/HIV, Alzheimers Disease, Cancer, Children's Health/Hospitals, Children's Health/Hospitals, Clinics/Medical Centers, Diabetes, Emergency/Ambulance Services, Geriatric Health, Health Policy/Cost Containment, Health Organizations, Heart, Hospices, Hospitals, Medical Rehabilitation, Medical Research, Medical Training, Mental Health, Nursing Services, Outpatient Health Care, Research/Studies Institutes, Single-Disease Health Associations, Transplant Networks/Donor Banks
Religion: Churches, Jewish Causes, Ministries, Religious Organizations, Religious Welfare
Science: Science Museums, Scientific Centers & Institutes
Social Services: Animal Protection, At-Risk Youth, Child Abuse, Child Welfare, Community Centers, Community Service Organizations, Counseling, Crime Prevention, Day Care, Domestic Violence, Family Planning, Family Services, Food/Clothing Distribution, Homes, People with Disabilities, Recreation & Athletics, Scouts, Shelters/Homelessness, Substance Abuse, United Funds/United Ways, Volunteer Services, YMCA/YWCA/YMHA/YWHA, Youth Organizations

Application Procedures

Initial Contact: An application for a grant should be presented in written form. A specific application form is not required.
Application Requirements: Applications should contain a cover letter signed by the chief executive officer of the organization stating that he or she has approved the request. The letter should provide the name, title, and telephone number of the contact person; amount requested; a statement that no change occurred in the tax exempt status, purpose, character, or method of the organization's operation since the organization received its tax-exempt status from the IRS; and a statement indicating whether the organization has in the past or is now operated under any name other than the name on the organization's IRS determination letter. In addition, an application should include a three- to five-page proposal that provides a description of organization, the nature of its work, its mission, and its achievements; a statement about the issue being addressed by the proposed project; a list of names and qualifications of the people who will be in charge of the project; a description of the proposed project, including answers to the following questions:
How will the project address the identified issues? Where will the project make a difference? Who will it target? How will it impact them? When will the project begin and end? If the project already is underway, what has been accomplished so far? How will the project be evaluated? What are the expected milestones and outcomes? How much will the project cost? How much does the organization need from Houston Endowment and over what period of time? If the project is ongoing, how will it be sustained after the Endowment's funding ends?

The following attachments should be provided: proof of tax-exempt status; recently audited financial statement; a complete copy of the organization's most recently filed IRS Form 990; a current list of the organization's board of directors or trustees; and the organization's current annual operating budget. If request is for a multi-year grant, also include the organization's projected annual operating budget for the years covered by the request. If request is for a specific project, include a project budget including the amounts and sources of committed and pending funds, including amounts. Also indicate the percentage of board members and/or trustees who financially supported the organization during the last fiscal year and the aggregate amount they donated. Budgets should include a narrative describing each major item in the budget and should explain how each was determined.
Deadlines: None.
Review Process: The review and decision process typically takes three to six months. The board of directors usually meet six times a year to consider grant requests. Applicant will be notified if additional information is requested, or an interview or site visit is planned. All applicants are notified in writing of the action taken by the directors on their requests.
Notes: Elaborate presentations are not necessary. Proposals should be unbound and on 8.5" by 11" paper.

Restrictions

The endowment does not make grants to individuals; for loans of any kind; galas or gala-like events, testimonial or fund raising luncheons or dinners, advertising in programs, or similar fund raising activity; organizations that in turn make grants to others; activities that promote or support a religion, a denomination or church; purchase of uniforms, equipment or trips for school-related organizations or amateur sports teams; honoraria for guest speakers; charities operated by service clubs; memorials to individuals; activities that are typically the responsibility of the government, including public schools; or a second request for a capital support that has been previously funded. No grants are made to organizations outside the U.S.

Additional Information

Publications: Annual Report; Guidelines

Foundation Officials

D. Kent Anderson: chairman
D. Kent Anderson: chairman, director
Audrey Jones Beck: director
Jack Sawtelle Blanton: chairman, director B Shreveport, LA 1927. ED University of Texas BA (1947); University of Texas LLB (1950). PRIM CORP EMPL president: Eddy Refining Co. CORP AFFIL director: Pogo Producing Co.; director: Burlington Northern Santa Fe Corp. NONPR AFFIL member: U.S. Lawn Tennis Association; member: University Texas Ex-Students Association; member: Texas Independent Oil Producers & Refiners; member: Phi Delta Phi; member: Sons Republic Texas; member: National Tennis Association; member: Phi Alpha Delta; member: Mid-Continent Oil Gas Association; member: National Petroleum Council; member: Houston Chamber of Commerce; member: Sam Houston Memorial Association; member: Greater Houston Partnership; member: Delta Kappa Epsilon. CLUB AFFIL River Oaks Country Club; Eldorado Country Club; Houston Club.
Milton Carroll: director PRIM CORP EMPL chairman, president, chief executive officer: Instrument Product Inc. CORP AFFIL director: Reliant Energy Inc.; director: Seagull Energy Corp.; director: Healthcare Benefits Inc.
Anthony W. Hall, Jr.: director
Anthony W. Hall, Jr.: director
Sheryl Lightfoot Johns: vice president, treasurer B Pasadena, TX 1956. ED University of Houston BS (1986).
Melissa A. Jones: director

Harold Metts: director
David L. Nelson: vice president, grant director
H. Joe Nelson, III: president, director
L. E. Simmons: director B Salt Lake City, UT 1946. PRIM CORP EMPL chairman: Tuboscope Inc. ADD CORP EMPL chairman: Tuboscope Vetco International. CORP AFFIL partner: L.E. Simmons Associates Inc.; director: Zion Bancorp; owner, partner: SCF Partner LP; partner: SCF-II LP; president: SCF-III LP; chairman: Drilex International Inc.; director: C.E. Franklin; president: Ceco Holdings Inc.; director: Continental Emsco Co.
Melissa Jones Stevens: director PRIM CORP EMPL partner: KISS Radio San Antonio Ltd. CORP AFFIL partner: KLUP.
Rosie Zamora-Cope: director B Elsa, TX 1935. ED Pan American University (1955); University of Texas, Austin (1955-1958). PRIM CORP EMPL president, treasurer, director: Telesurveys TX Inc. CORP AFFIL president, treasurer, director: Legal Strategies. NONPR AFFIL board member: United Way Texas Gulf Coast; advisory board member: University Houston College Law Health Law & Policy Institute; regent: Texas Southern University; president: Mental Health Association Houston & Harris County; board member: Texas Institute Arts Education; trustee: Houston Grand Opera; member TX advisory committee: John F. Kennedy Center Performing Arts; board member: Foundation Womens Resources; board member: American Institute Managing Diversity.

Grants Analysis

Disclosure Period: calendar year ending 2002
Total Grants: $64,540,094*
Number of Grants: 610 (approx)
Average Grant: $86,273*
Highest Grant: $12,000,000
Typical Range: $5,000 to $100,000 and $200,000 to $1,000,000
***Note:** Giving excludes scholarship, matching gifts, fellowship. Average grant figure excludes highest grant.

Recent Grants

Note: Grants derived from 2001 Form 990.

Library-Related

400,000   San Antonio Public Library, San Antonio, TX -- toward an innovative three-year pilot program to reduce the rate of illiteracy in the San Antonio community

General

4,000,000   William Marsh Rice University, Houston, TX -- toward capital campaign
2,000,000   Project Grad, Houston, TX -- toward expansion into four HISD feeder systems
2,000,000   Texas Children's Hospital, Houston, TX -- toward the Building for Children Campaign
2,000,000   University of Texas at Austin, Austin, TX -- toward construction of an art museum on campus
1,200,000   University of Texas Houston Health Science Center, Houston, TX -- toward construction of a new Nursing and Biomedical Sciences Building
1,083,000   Houston Independent School District, Houston, TX
1,000,000   Boys and Girls Clubs of Greater Houston Foundation, Houston, TX -- toward construction of a new club facility
1,000,000   Cultural Trust Council, The, Austin, TX -- toward an endowment fund designed to enrich the cultural arts for urban and rural populations in Texas equitably
1,000,000   Hospice at the Texas Medical Center, Houston, TX -- to establish and sustain the Texas Hospice Education Institute
1,000,000   Houston Area Women's Center Education and Outreach Program, Houston,

TX -- toward construction of a shelter facility for battered women and children

HOWARD AND BUSH FOUNDATION

Giving Contact

Deborah Byers
2 Bekke Avenue
Troy, NY 12180
Phone: (518)271-1134

Description

EIN: 066059063
Organization Type: General Purpose Foundation
Giving Locations: NY: Rensselaer County
Grant Types: Challenge, General Support, Project.

Donor Information

Founder: the late Edith Mason Howard, the late Julia Howard Bush

Financial Summary

Total Giving: $308,780 (2001); $376,536 (2000); $235,470 (1999)
Giving Analysis: Giving for 1998 includes: foundation ($356,320)
Assets: $4,063,371 (2001); $4,470,235 (2000); $4,752,377 (1999)
Gifts Received: $75,553 (1999); $97,855 (1995); $116,758 (1994)

Typical Recipients

Arts & Humanities: Arts Associations & Councils, Arts Centers, Dance, Arts & Humanities-General, Historic Preservation, History & Archaeology, Libraries, Museums/Galleries, Music, Performing Arts, Public Broadcasting, Theater, Visual Arts
Civic & Public Affairs: African American Affairs, Botanical Gardens/Parks, Business/Free Enterprise, Economic Development, Civic & Public Affairs-General, Hispanic Affairs, Housing, Law & Justice, Legal Aid, Municipalities/Towns, Public Policy, Safety, Urban & Community Affairs
Education: Afterschool/Enrichment Programs, Arts/Humanities Education, Colleges & Universities, Elementary Education (Private), Elementary Education (Public), Engineering/Technological Education, Education-General, Literacy, Medical Education, Minority Education, Private Education (Precollege), Public Education (Precollege), Secondary Education (Public), Student Aid
Environment: Environment-General, Resource Conservation
Health: AIDS/HIV, Emergency/Ambulance Services, Health Organizations, Hospices, Hospitals, Medical Rehabilitation, Nursing Services, Prenatal Health Issues
Religion: Churches, Ministries, Religious Organizations, Religious Welfare
Social Services: Camps, Child Welfare, Community Centers, Community Service Organizations, Family Planning, Family Services, Food/Clothing Distribution, Recreation & Athletics, Senior Services, Shelters/Homelessness, YMCA/YWCA/YMHA/YWHA, Youth Organizations

Application Procedures

Initial Contact: Send letter requesting application guidelines and the annual report, or call for information.
Deadlines: None.

Restrictions

The foundation ordinarily does not make grants to government agencies; churches or schools not associated with the founders, except for nondenominational community projects; organizations that have

received grants from the foundation within the past two years; operating deficits; endowment funds; municipalities or other tax-supported institutions; reserve or revolving funds; or to individuals.

Additional Information

In 1991, the foundation contributed approximately $4 million, about half of the foundation's assets, to the Hartford Foundation for Public Giving. The funds supported approximately 27 advised grants made by the Hartford Foundation's main fund and created two permanent funds--Tomlinson Fund for Philanthropy and Endowment Fund for Architecture Conservancy of Hartford. Both are administered by the Hartford Foundation.
Publications: Application Guidelines.

Foundation Officials

Judith A. Barnes: director
Donald C. Bowes: director
Sarah H. Catlin: president
David Sands Haviland: director B Rome, NY 1942. ED Rensselaer Polytechnic Institute BS (1964); Rensselaer Polytechnic Institute BArch (1965); Rensselaer Polytechnic Institute MArch (1967). PRIM CORP EMPL dean student life, professor architect: Rensselaer Polytechnic Institute. NONPR AFFIL trustee: Troy Music Hall; vis professor: University Reading United Kingdom; trustee: Rensselaer Newman Foundation; member: New York Saint Association Architects; member: Project Management Institute; member: Association Collegiate Schs; member: Council Education Facility Planners; treasurer: Architectural Research Centers Consortium; member facilities committee: Albany Medical Center; member: American Institute Architects.
Margaret Mochon: director
David W. Parmelee: trustee

Grants Analysis

Disclosure Period: calendar year ending 2001
Total Grants: $308,780
Number of Grants: 18
Average Grant: $15,222*
Highest Grant: $50,000
Lowest Grant: $2,500
Typical Range: $5,000 to $30,000
***Note:** Average grant figure excludes highest grant.

Recent Grants

Note: Grants derived from 2000 Form 990.

General

100,000   Rensselaer County Junior Museum, Troy, NY
32,175   Troy Cemetery Association, Troy, NY
30,000   Arts Center of the Capital Region
30,000   YMCA of Troy-Cohoes, Troy, NY
26,500   YMCA of Troy-Cohoes, Troy, NY
25,000   Jewish Family Services of Northeastern New York, NY
25,000   Joseph's House and Shelter, Troy, NY
24,200   YMCA of Troy-Cohoes, Troy, NY
21,016   Upper Hudson Planned Parenthood
13,000   Broadway Gallery Membership Group, Troy, NY

HOWARTH TRUST FUND

Giving Contact

Elizabeth Campbell, Secretary & Trustee
2000 43rd Avenue East, Suite 402
Seattle, WA 98112-5051
Phone: (206)325-9715

Description

Founded: 1960
EIN: 916053815
Organization Type: Private Foundation

Giving Locations: WA: Snohomish County
Grant Types: General Support.

Donor Information

Founder: the late Mrs. Hugh R. Cawsey

Financial Summary

Total Giving: $196,000 (2001); $146,000 (2000); $154,500 (1999)
Giving Analysis: Giving for 1999 includes: foundation ($148,000)
Assets: $3,387,303 (2001); $3,588,181 (2000); $3,327,987 (1999)
Gifts Received: $550 (2001); $2,100 (1994)

Typical Recipients

Arts & Humanities: Arts Associations & Councils, Community Arts, Libraries, Museums/Galleries, Music, Theater
Civic & Public Affairs: Botanical Gardens/Parks, Civic & Public Affairs-General, Housing
Education: Elementary Education (Public), Education-General, Literacy, Private Education (Precollege), Public Education (Precollege)
Health: Children's Health/Hospitals, Hospices, Hospitals, Mental Health, Nursing Services
Religion: Churches
Social Services: Camps, Child Welfare, Community Service Organizations, Day Care, Domestic Violence, Family Planning, Food/Clothing Distribution, People with Disabilities, Recreation & Athletics, Substance Abuse, Volunteer Services, YMCA/YWCA/YMHA/YWHA, Youth Organizations

Application Procedures

Initial Contact: Send a brief letter of inquiry and a full proposal.
Application Requirements: Include a description of organization, amount requested, purpose of funds sought, recently audited financial statement, proof of tax-exempt status, and percentage of other support.

Restrictions

The foundation does not support individuals, religious organizations for sectarian purposes, political or lobbying groups, or organizations outside operating areas.

Foundation Officials

Elizabeth Campbell: secretary, trustee
G. Paul Carpenter: president
Mary Ellen Denman: vice president
Dr. Harold Gunderson: president
William Howarth Meadowcroft: trustee ED University of Puget Sound; Harvard University MBA (1954). PRIM CORP EMPL assistant to chairman: Weyerhaeuser Co. NONPR AFFIL member: Virginia Mason Medicine Foundation; member: Washington State Games Foundation; trustee, vice chairman: University Puget Sound; board member: Museum Flight; trustee: Takoma Art Museum; member: Leukemia Society America. CLUB AFFIL Washington Athletic Club; Rainier Club; Tacoma Club.
H. Roy Yates: vice president

Grants Analysis

Disclosure Period: calendar year ending 2001
Total Grants: $196,000
Number of Grants: 18
Average Grant: $10,889
Highest Grant: $15,000
Lowest Grant: $5,000
Typical Range: $5,000 to $15,000

Recent Grants

Note: Grants derived from 2001 Form 990.

Library-Related
10,000   Tacoma Public Library, Tacoma, WA -- programs

General
15,000	Assistance League of Everett, Everett, WA -- build new facilities
15,000	Campfire Girls and Boys, Everett, WA -- capital contribution
15,000	Housing Hope, Everett, WA -- capital contribution
15,000	Providence General Foundation, Everett, WA -- capital contribution
15,000	Volunteers of America, Everett, WA -- capital contribution
15,000	YMCA of Snohomish County, Okanogan, WA -- capital campaign
11,000	Everett Public Schools, Everett, MA -- Summer School Programs
10,000	Boys and Girls Club, Everett, WA -- fund programs for teens
10,000	Everett Parks Foundation, Everett, WA -- renovate public park
10,000	Planned Parenthood, Everett, WA -- capital contribution

LUCILLE HORTON HOWE AND MITCHELL B. HOWE FOUNDATION

Giving Contact

Mitchell B. Howe, Jr., President & Treasurer
180 S. Lake Ave.
Pasadena, CA 91101
Phone: (626)792-2771

Description

Founded: 1964
EIN: 956081945
Organization Type: Private Foundation
Giving Locations: CA: Pasadena
Grant Types: General Support.

Donor Information

Founder: the late Mitchell B. Howe

Financial Summary

Total Giving: $109,000 (2001); $94,002 (2000); $116,000 (1999)
Assets: $1,894,222 (2001); $1,921,044 (2000); $1,784,038 (1999)

Typical Recipients

Arts & Humanities: Arts Centers, Historic Preservation, Libraries, Museums/Galleries, Music
Civic & Public Affairs: Employment/Job Training, Civic & Public Affairs-General, Law & Justice, Legal Aid, Municipalities/Towns
Education: Business Education, Colleges & Universities, Community & Junior Colleges, Private Education (Precollege), Public Education (Precollege), Secondary Education (Private), Student Aid, Vocational & Technical Education
Health: Children's Health/Hospitals, Health Organizations, Hospitals, Kidney, Medical Research, Prenatal Health Issues, Public Health, Research/Studies Institutes, Single-Disease Health Associations
Religion: Churches, Religious Organizations, Religious Welfare
Social Services: Animal Protection, Child Welfare, Community Service Organizations, Family Services, Family Services, Homes, People with Disabilities, Recreation & Athletics, Substance Abuse, United Funds/United Ways, Volunteer Services, YMCA/YWCA/YMHA/YWHA, Youth Organizations

Application Procedures

Initial Contact: Send brief letter describing program.
Application Requirements: Include purpose of funds sought, indicate whether the donee is a new applicant, and include proof of tax-exempt status.
Deadlines: February.

Restrictions

Does not support: individuals, political or lobbying groups, or organizations outside operating areas.

Foundation Officials

John C. Cushman: secretary
James J. Howe: director
Mitchell B. Howe, Jr.: president, treasurer
Hugh V. Hunter: director
Lynn Howe Myers: chairman, vice president
Mitchell C. Myers: director

Grants Analysis

Disclosure Period: calendar year ending 2001
Total Grants: $109,000
Number of Grants: 10
Average Grant: $5,444*
Highest Grant: $60,000
Lowest Grant: $1,000
Typical Range: $2,000 to $10,000
*Note: Average grant figure excludes highest grant.

Recent Grants

Note: Grants derived from 2001 Form 990.

General
60,000	Huntington Medical Research Institute, Pasadena, CA
12,000	Pasadena Guild Children's Hospital, Pasadena, CA
10,000	Maranatha High School, Sierra Madre, CA
10,000	Santa Fe Christian Schools, Solana Beach, CA
5,000	Azusa Pacific University, Azusa, CA
4,000	Door of Hope, Newark, DE
3,000	Los Angeles Philharmonic Association, Los Angeles, CA
2,000	Hillsides Home for Children, Pasadena, CA
2,000	Sam Schmidt Paralysis Foundation, Indianapolis, IN
1,000	Huntington Medical Research Institute, Pasadena, CA

HRK FOUNDATION

Giving Contact

Kathleen Fluegel, Foundation Director
345 Saint Peter Street, Suite 1200
St. Paul, MN 55102
Phone: (651)293-9001
Fax: (651)298-0551
E-mail: hrkfoundation@hrkgroup.com
Web: http://www.hrkfoundation.org

Description

Founded: 1962
EIN: 416020911
Organization Type: Family Foundation
Former Name: Mary Anderson Foundation MAHADH Foundation (1994).
Former Name: MAHADH Foundation to HRK Foundation (1998).
Giving Locations: MN: Twin Cities metropolitan area; WI: St. Croix Valley and Ashland and Bayfield Counties
Grant Types: Capital, Endowment, General Support, Matching, Operating Expenses, Project, Scholarship.

Donor Information

Founder: The HRK Foundation, formerly the MAHADH Foundation, began in 1962 as the Mary Anderson Hulings Foundation, established by members of the Anderson and Hulings families.

Financial Summary

Total Giving: $3,000,000 (2003 approx); $3,600,000 (2002 approx); $3,475,085 (2001)
Assets: $33,463,486 (2001); $30,512,000 (2000 approx); $28,768,412 (1999)
Gifts Received: $2,101,715 (1999); $2,460,000 (1998); $4,580,000 (1997)

Typical Recipients

Arts & Humanities: Arts Associations & Councils, Arts Centers, Arts Institutes, Arts & Humanities-General, Historic Preservation, History & Archaeology, Libraries, Museums/Galleries, Music, Opera, Performing Arts, Public Broadcasting
Civic & Public Affairs: Clubs, Community Foundations, Economic Development, Employment/Job Training, Civic & Public Affairs-General, Housing, Municipalities/Towns, Professional & Trade Associations, Women's Affairs
Education: Colleges & Universities, Community & Junior Colleges, Education Funds, Education-General, International Exchange, Medical Education, Minority Education, Private Education (Precollege), Public Education (Precollege), Religious Education
Environment: Environment-General, Resource Conservation, Wildlife Protection
Health: AIDS/HIV, Children's Health/Hospitals, Clinics/Medical Centers, Emergency/Ambulance Services, Health Funds, Health Organizations, Hospitals, Medical Rehabilitation, Mental Health, Public Health, Single-Disease Health Associations, Transplant Networks/Donor Banks
International: Health Care/Hospitals, International Environmental Issues, International Relief Efforts
Religion: Churches, Religious Welfare, Seminaries
Science: Science Museums
Social Services: Child Welfare, Community Service Organizations, Day Care, Family Planning, Family Services, Homes, People with Disabilities, Scouts, Social Services-General, Substance Abuse, United Funds/United Ways, Volunteer Services, YMCA/YWCA/YMHA/YWHA, Youth Organizations

Application Procedures

Initial Contact: Prior to submitting a proposal (at least two weeks before the deadline), call the Foundation's Director to discuss your request.
Application Requirements: The foundation requests that applicants include one copy of an unbound proposal of six pages or less exclusive of attachments. Include a cover sheet; copy of IRS 501(c)(3) determination letter; recently audited financial statement; and organizational or project budget; organizational information, including history, mission and goals, description of current programs and activities, service statistics, board members and key staff, and relationship with other organizations working to meet the same needs or providing similar services; brief summary highlighting the situation, specific activities, goals, and timeframe; summary of how you define success and who will be involved in evaluating the potential outcomes. specific activities, and impact of the activities; and methods of evaluation. Required attachments include a copy of most recent audit and/or IRS Form 990 and unaudited financial statements; organizational and/or project budget; description of any future plans your organization has for a capital or endowment campaign; one-paragraph description of key staff, including qualifications; a listing of the board of directors and affiliations; and a letter from your fiscal agent, if not a 501(c)(3), explaining that you have been incorporated as a program or project of the sponsoring organization and are governed by its board of directors. If the request is for capital support, include a projected operating budget which
Deadlines: March 15 and September 15.
Review Process: Requests are generally reviewed in May and November. Final funding decisions will be mailed within three weeks of board meeting.

Notes: The foundation also accepts the Minnesota Common Grant Form. The foundation will not consider videos.

Restrictions

The foundation does not support individuals or businesses. The foundation reports that most of its resources are committed to organizations that have received support in the past. New applicants will be considered for single-year funding in the areas of AIDS issues, children's health, and community-specific projects only.

Additional Information

The Foundation has a commitment to long-term relationships with grantees and accepts only a limited numbero fnew, capital, or project requests in each calendar year.
Publications: Annual Report (including Application Guidelines)

Foundation Officials

Arthur W. Kaemmer, MD: chairman, treasurer NONPR AFFIL chairman: National Medicine Fellowships.
Martha H. Kaemmer: vice president CORP AFFIL director: Andersen Corp.
Mary H. Rice: vice president

Grants Analysis

Disclosure Period: calendar year ending 2001
Total Grants: $3,475,085*
Number of Grants: 286
Average Grant: $12,151
Highest Grant: $100,000
Lowest Grant: $100
Typical Range: $3,000 to $25,000
***Note:** Grants analysis provided by foundation.

Recent Grants

Note: Grants derived from 2001 Form 990.

General

500,000	Northland College, Ashland, WI -- for capital
300,000	Minnesota Historical Society, St. Paul, MN -- for challenge
200,000	Minnesota Historical Society, St. Paul, MN -- for capital
100,000	Croixdale Residence and Apartments -- for capital
97,373	Ashland Area Development Corporation, Ashland, WI -- for programs
75,000	Olivet Congregational Church, Bridgeport, CT -- for GOS
75,000	People's Congregational Church
75,000	Plymouth Music Series, Minneapolis, MN -- for GOS
62,116	Northland College, Ashland, WI -- for programs
50,000	Lake Superior Big Top Chautauqua, Washburn, WI -- for GOS

HUBBARD BROADCASTING, INC.

Company Headquarters

3415 University Ave., W
St. Paul, MN 55114
Web: http://www.kstp.com

Company Description

Employees: 1,200
SIC(s): 4832 Radio Broadcasting Stations, 4833 Television Broadcasting Stations, 7812 Motion Picture & Video Production.

Operating Locations

Hubbard Broadcasting, Inc. (CA--Montego Bay; FL--Cyprus Gardens, Dade County, Miami Beach, Pinellas Park, St. Petersburg, Tampa; MN--Maplewood, Minneapolis, St. Croix, White Bear Lake; NM--Albuquerque; WA--Spokane)

Hubbard Foundation

Giving Contact

Kathryn Hubbard-Rominski, Executive Director
3415 University Avenue
St. Paul, MN 55114
Phone: (651)642-4305
Fax: (612)642-4103

Alternate Contact

Phone: (651)642-4300

Description

EIN: 416022291
Organization Type: Corporate Foundation
Giving Locations: nationally; principally near operating locations and to national organizations.
Grant Types: Capital, Operating Expenses.

Financial Summary

Total Giving: $1,179,690 (2001); $48,000 (2000); $3,255,165 (1999)
Giving Analysis: Giving for 1999 includes: foundation fellowships ($1,500); foundation scholarships ($6,000); foundation grants to United Way ($8,000); foundation ($3,239,665); 1998: foundation grants to United Way ($7,000); foundation ($914,600); 1997: foundation grants to United Way ($17,250); foundation ($916,360);
Assets: $23,053,819 (2001); $24,899,226 (2000); $22,499,347 (1999)

Typical Recipients

Arts & Humanities: Arts Associations & Councils, Arts Centers, Arts Funds, Arts Institutes, Arts Outreach, Ballet, Community Arts, Historic Preservation, History & Archaeology, Libraries, Museums/Galleries, Music, Opera, Performing Arts, Public Broadcasting, Theater, Visual Arts
Civic & Public Affairs: African American Affairs, Botanical Gardens/Parks, Civil Rights, Clubs, Economic Development, Civic & Public Affairs-General, Housing, Municipalities/Towns, Nonprofit Management, Philanthropic Organizations, Professional & Trade Associations, Public Policy, Safety, Zoos/Aquariums
Education: Arts/Humanities Education, Business Education, Colleges & Universities, Colleges & Universities, Economic Education, Education Funds, Engineering/Technological Education, Education-General, Journalism/Media Education, Legal Education, Literacy, Medical Education, Minority Education, Private Education (Precollege), Public Education (Precollege), Secondary Education (Private), Secondary Education (Public), Special Education, Student Aid, Vocational & Technical Education
Environment: Air/Water Quality, Environment-General, Research
Health: Arthritis, Cancer, Children's Health/Hospitals, Diabetes, Health Funds, Health Organizations, Heart, Hospitals, Kidney, Medical Rehabilitation, Medical Research, Mental Health, Preventive Medicine/Wellness Organizations, Research/Studies Institutes, Single-Disease Health Associations, Speech & Hearing
International: International Environmental Issues, International Organizations
Religion: Churches, Jewish Causes, Religious Organizations, Religious Welfare
Science: Science Museums
Social Services: Camps, Child Welfare, Community Centers, Community Service Organizations, Counseling, Day Care, Emergency Relief, Family Planning, Family Services, Food/Clothing Distribution, Homes, People with Disabilities, Recreation & Athletics,

Scouts, Social Services-General, Substance Abuse, United Funds/United Ways, Volunteer Services, YMCA/YWCA/YMHA/YWHA, Youth Organizations

Application Procedures

Application Requirements: Send a summary of history and a description of organization, copy of IRS section 501(c)(3) status letter, purpose of funds sought, and whether funds are intended to be used for operating or non-operating expenses.
Deadlines: November 30.
Decision Notification: Most foundation activity takes place before the end of the calendar year.

Restrictions

The foundation typically does not accept unsolicited proposals.

Corporate Officials

Stanley S. Hubbard: chairman, president, chief executive officer B Saint Paul, MN 1933. ED University of Minnesota BA (1955). PRIM CORP EMPL chairman, president, chief executive officer: Hubbard Broadcasting, Inc. ADD CORP EMPL vice president: F & F Productions LLC. CORP AFFIL director: Fingerhut Co. Inc.; chairman, president, chief executive officer, director: US Satellite Broadcasting Co. Inc. NONPR AFFIL director: University Saint Thomas; member: World Business Council; director: University Minnesota Foundation; member: Society Professional Journalists; member: Society Satellite Professionals International; member: Royal Television Society London; chairman: Saint Croix Valley Youth Center; director: Ramsey County Ice Arena Committee; chairman, president, chief executive officer: Minnesota Business Partnership; member: Minnesota Executives Organization; member: Metropolitan Airports Public Foundation Advisory Board; director: Minneapolis American Friends Jamaica; member: International Radio & Television Society; director: Broadcast Pioneers Library; member: Broadcasters Foundation; director: Baptist Hospital Fund Sponsor Board; member: Broadcast Pioneers; director: Association Maximum Service Telecasters.

Foundation Officials

Julia D. Coyte: director
Robert W. Hubbard: director
Stanley E. Hubbard: director
Stanley S. Hubbard: president (see above)
Ronald L. Lindwall: treasurer
Virginia H. Morris: director

Grants Analysis

Disclosure Period: calendar year ending 2001
Total Grants: $1,166,690*
Number of Grants: 258
Average Grant: $4,522
Highest Grant: $80,000
Lowest Grant: $100
Typical Range: $500 to $25,000 and $50,000 to $80,000
*Note: Giving excludes scholarship and United Way.

Recent Grants

Note: Grants derived from 2001 Form 990.

Library-Related

52,000	Friends of the St. Paul Public Library, St. Paul, MN

General

80,000	St. Croix Valley Youth Center, St. Croix, MN
75,000	Gillette Children's Hospital Foundation, St. Paul, MN
75,000	Hamline University, St. Paul, MN
50,000	Breck School, Minneapolis, MN
50,000	St. Ambrose of Woodbury, Woodbury, MN
50,000	St. Paul Academy and Summit School, St. Paul, MN

30,000	Gustavus Adolphus College, St. Peter, MN
28,500	William Mitchell College of Law, St. Paul, MN
25,000	EAA Aviation Foundation, Oshkosh, WI
25,000	Minneapolis Foundation, Minneapolis, MN

R. D. AND JOAN DALE HUBBARD FOUNDATION

Giving Contact

James A. Stoddard, Executive Director
PO Box 2498
Ruidoso, NM 88355-2498
Phone: (505)258-5919
Fax: (505)258-3749

Description

Founded: 1986
EIN: 752266308
Organization Type: Family Foundation
Giving Locations: CA; IL; KS; NE; NM; OK; TX
Grant Types: Challenge, Endowment, Fellowship, General Support, Matching, Multiyear/Continuing Support, Professorship, Research, Scholarship.

Donor Information

Founder: The foundation was founded by R. D. Hubbard and Joan Dale Hubbard of Ft. Worth, TX, in 1986. Today, Mr. Hubbard is chairman of the board of AFG Industries, the second largest glass manufacturer in North America. His primary business interest is an extensive involvement in the racing industry. In addition to his horse breeding operations in Kentucky and New Mexico, he is the owner or major stockholder in four race tracks. Mr. Hubbard is owner and chairman of Ruidoso Downs Racing, a quarterhorse track in Ruidoso, NM; majority owner and chairman of the Woodlands, a dual horse and dog racing operation in Kansas City, KS; chairman and chief executive officer of Hollywood Park, a thoroughbred racing facility in California; and owner and chairman of Multnomah Kennel Club, a greyhound track in Portland, OR.

Financial Summary

Total Giving: $1,000,000 (2002 approx); $1,560,551 (2000); $1,535,789 (1998)
Giving Analysis: Giving for 2000 includes: foundation matching gifts ($58,000); foundation scholarships ($167,998) 1998: foundation scholarships ($277,966)
Assets: $43,609,207 (2000); $33,082,848 (1998); $26,439,974 (1995)
Gifts Received: $1,000 (1998). Note: In 1998, contributions were received from David Shepherd.

Typical Recipients

Arts & Humanities: Arts Associations & Councils, Dance, Historic Preservation, History & Archaeology, Libraries, Museums/Galleries, Music, Theater
Civic & Public Affairs: Business/Free Enterprise, Chambers of Commerce, Clubs, Community Foundations, Civic & Public Affairs-General, Municipalities/Towns, Nonprofit Management, Philanthropic Organizations, Urban & Community Affairs, Women's Affairs
Education: Agricultural Education, Arts/Humanities Education, Business Education, Colleges & Universities, Community & Junior Colleges, Education Funds, Elementary Education (Private), Elementary Education (Public), Faculty Development, Education-General, Legal Education, Medical Education, Private Education (Precollege), Public Education (Precollege), Science/Mathematics Education, Secondary Education (Public), Social Sciences Education, Student Aid
Environment: Wildlife Protection
Health: AIDS/HIV, Alzheimers Disease, Cancer, Children's Health/Hospitals, Clinics/Medical Centers, Heart, Home-Care Services, Medical Research, Medical Training, Single-Disease Health Associations

International: Foreign Arts Organizations, Foreign Educational Institutions
Religion: Religion-General, Religious Organizations, Religious Welfare
Social Services: Animal Protection, At-Risk Youth, Big Brother/Big Sister, Community Centers, Community Service Organizations, Domestic Violence, People with Disabilities, Recreation & Athletics, Scouts, Senior Services, Social Services-General, Youth Organizations

Application Procedures

Initial Contact: Send a brief letter describing the organization.
Application Requirements: The specific program to be considered, budget summary, and amount requested.
Deadlines: None.
Review Process: Applicants are informed of the decision within two months.

Additional Information

Publications: Application Guidelines; Annual Report; Program Policy Statement

Foundation Officials

Edward A. Burger: secretary, treasurer, director CLUB AFFIL secretary-treasurer, director: Multnomah Kennel Club.
Joan Dale Hubbard: vice president, director
Randall Dee Hubbard: president, director B Smith Center, KS 1935. ED Butler County Community College BA (1956). PRIM CORP EMPL chairman board: AFG Industries Inc. CORP AFFIL president, chief executive officer, director: Turf Paradise Inc.; chief executive officer, director: Sunflower Racing Inc.; director: Hollywood Park Realty Enterprises; president, director, co-owner: Ruidoso Downs Racing Inc.; chief executive officer, director: Hollywood Park Inc.; chairman, director: Hollywood Park Operation Inc.; chief executive officer, director: Hollywood Park Food Service; director: America Flat Glass Distributors. NONPR AFFIL member: International Association Businessmen & Professionals Foundation. CLUB AFFIL chairman, director, co-owner: Multnomah Kennel Club.
Jennings Jay Newcom: assistant secretary, director B Saint Joseph, MO 1941. ED Graceland College BA (1964); Harvard University JD (1968). PRIM CORP EMPL partner: Shook Hardy & Bacon. NONPR AFFIL member: Kansas City Bar Association; member: Lawyers Association Kansas City; chairman board: Graceland College.
James A. Stoddard: executive director

Grants Analysis

Disclosure Period: calendar year ending 2000
Total Grants: $1,334,553*
Number of Grants: 54
Average Grant: $19,140*
Highest Grant: $320,155
Typical Range: $10,000 to $40,000
*Note: Giving excludes scholarships and matching gifts. Average grant excludes highest grant.

Recent Grants

Note: Grants derived from 2001 Form 990.

General

320,155	Hubbard Museum, Ruidoso Downs, NM -- education of the arts
150,000	Emporia State University, Emporia, KS -- sorority construction
125,000	California State University San Bernardino, San Bernardino, CA -- Coachella Valley campus
100,000	Kansas State University Foundation, Manhattan, KS -- golf facility
78,500	Smith Center Public School, Smith Center, KS -- scholarships

75,524	Lincoln County Medical Center, Ruidoso, NM -- blood chemistry analysis machine
60,000	Fort Hays State University, Hays, KS -- Lewis Field renovation
58,500	Marywood Country Day School, Rancho Mirage, CA -- matching grant challenge for capital campaign
50,000	Butler County Community College, El Dorado, KS -- telecommunications
50,000	CAP Cure, Santa Monica, CA -- cancer research

HUBER FOUNDATION

Giving Contact
Lorraine Barnhart, Executive Director
PO Box 277
Rumson, NJ 07760
Phone: (732)933-7700

Description
Founded: 1949
EIN: 210737062
Organization Type: Family Foundation
Giving Locations: nationally.
Grant Types: General Support, Project.

Donor Information
Founder: The Huber Foundation was established in 1949 in New Jersey. Since then, the foundation has received personal contributions from various members of the Huber family.

Financial Summary
Total Giving: $2,087,000 (2000); $3,907,000 (1999); $3,952,000 (1998)
Assets: $48,968,140 (2000); $46,049,336 (1999); $48,322,810 (1998)
Gifts Received: $864 (1999); $991,259 (1995); $270,000 (1994). Note: The foundation receives contributions from the estate of Catherine G. Huber.

Typical Recipients
Arts & Humanities: Libraries
Civic & Public Affairs: African American Affairs, Civil Rights, Civic & Public Affairs-General, Nonprofit Management, Philanthropic Organizations, Professional & Trade Associations, Public Policy, Urban & Community Affairs, Women's Affairs
Education: Colleges & Universities, Social Sciences Education
Environment: Environment-General
Health: Clinics/Medical Centers, Health Organizations, Hospitals, Public Health
International: Health Care/Hospitals, International Environmental Issues, International Peace & Security Issues
Religion: Social/Policy Issues
Social Services: Family Planning, Family Services, Youth Organizations

Application Procedures
Initial Contact: Applications should take the form of a typewritten letter.
Application Requirements: Letters of application should describe the proposed project, and include a project budget, and proof of the applicant's tax-exempt status. The foundation will request more information if needed.
Deadlines: None.
Review Process: The trustees meet four times a year. The dates for these meetings are not fixed.
Notes: The foundation's interest lies in funding organizations that will impact issues on a national level. Therefore, the foundation does not encourage proposal submission from projects that are local or regional in scope.

Restrictions
Grants are made only to tax-exempt organizations. The foundation does not consider grants to individuals, foreign organizations, capital campaigns, scholarships, research, international projects, or film productions.

Additional Information
Publications: Annual Report

Foundation Officials
Lorraine Barnhart: vice president, trustee
Jennifer Curry: trustee
Lisa Goodspeed: trustee
Hans A. Huber: president, trustee CORP AFFIL director: J M Huber Corp.
Michael W. Huber: secretary, trustee B 1926. PRIM CORP EMPL director: J.M. Huber Corp. CORP AFFIL director: Crompton & Knowles Corp.
Julia Ann Nagy: treasurer
Christopher W. Seely: trustee
Catherine Weiss: trustee

Grants Analysis
Disclosure Period: calendar year ending 2000
Total Grants: $2,087,000
Number of Grants: 32
Average Grant: $65,219
Highest Grant: $225,000
Typical Range: $40,000 to $400,000

Recent Grants
Note: Grants derived from 2000 Form 990.

General
225,000	Planned Parenthood Federation of America, Inc., New York, NY
200,000	American Civil Liberties Union Foundation, New York, NY -- Reproductive Rights Project
200,000	Center for Reproductive Law and Policy, New York, NY
200,000	NARAL Foundation, Washington, DC -- Choice for America Campaign
150,000	Pro-Choice Resource Center, Mamaroneck, NY -- Pro-Choice Education Project
100,000	Alan Guttmacher Institute, New York, NY
60,000	NAACP Legal Defense and Educational Fund, New York, NY -- Herbert Lehman Educational Fund and reproductive rights work
50,000	AVSC International, New York, NY -- National Programs
50,000	Catholics for a Free Choice, Washington, DC
50,000	Choice U.S.A., Washington, DC

HUDSON RIVER BANCORP, INC.

Company Headquarters
1 Hudson City Cir.
Hudson, NY 12534
Web: http://www.hudsonriver.com

Company Description
Founded: 1998
Ticker: HRBT
Exchange: NASDAQ
Assets: US$2.508 billion (2001)
Employees: 571 (2001)
SIC(s): 6036 Savings Institutions Except Federal, 6719 Holding Companies Nec.

Hudson River Bancorp Inc. Foundation

Giving Contact
Holly Rappleyea, Secretary & Treasurer
One Hudson City Centre
PO Box 76
Hudson, NY 12534
Phone: (518)828-4600
Web: http://www.hudsonriverbank.com/html/foundation_hrbt.html
Note: Ms. Rappleyea is available at extension 303.

Description
Founded: 1999
EIN: 223595668
Organization Type: Corporate Foundation
Giving Locations: NY
Grant Types: General Support.

Financial Summary
Total Giving: $328,642 (fiscal year ending 1, 2002); $251,055 (fiscal 2001); $95,006 (fiscal 1999)
Giving Analysis: Giving for fiscal 2002 includes: foundation grants to United Way ($3,447); foundation ($325,195); fiscal 2001: foundation ($251,055); fiscal 1999: foundation grants to United Way ($3,300) foundation ($91,706)
Assets: $12,500,915 (fiscal 2002); $6,839,775 (fiscal 2001); $5,611,561 (fiscal 1999)
Gifts Received: $888,814 (fiscal 2002); $5,200,120 (fiscal 1999). Note: In fiscal 2002, contributions were received from the Estate of Arthur L. Hegarty. In fiscal 1999, contributions were received from Hudson River Bank & Trust.

Typical Recipients
Arts & Humanities: Arts Centers, Film & Video, History & Archaeology, Libraries, Music, Opera, Theater
Civic & Public Affairs: Civic & Public Affairs-General, Safety, Women's Affairs
Education: Colleges & Universities, Legal Education, Literacy, Private Education (Precollege), Public Education (Precollege)
Health: Clinics/Medical Centers, Emergency/Ambulance Services, Health-General, Hospitals, Single-Disease Health Associations
Religion: Churches, Religious Welfare
Social Services: People with Disabilities, Recreation & Athletics, Social Services-General, United Funds/United Ways, YMCA/YWCA/YMHA/YWHA, Youth Organizations

Application Procedures
Initial Contact: Submit a letter to request a grant request for less than $1,000. Requests for more than $1,000 should be submitted using the New York/New Jersey Area Common Grant Application Format. A copy of this application may be obtained by contacting the foundation.
Application Requirements: Requests for less than $1,000 should include a cover letter on the applicant's letterhead which describes the amount requested, purpose of funds sought, and name and telephone number of the contact person. The following attachments should be included: a brief description of the organization's purpose, history and accomplishments; the current year's operating budget; a list of organizations and foundations that support the applicant organization, including the most recent amounts contributed; proof of tax-exempt status; a list of the names and affiliations of the board of directors; and the purpose and amount of the last grant received from Hudson River Bank & Trust Company or the Hudson City Savings Institution (if applicable).
Deadlines: None.

Restrictions

Does not typically support individuals; political organizations; debt liquidation; religious groups for sectarian purposes; or memberships for which the company receives a benefit.

Corporate Officials

Timothy Blow: chief financial officer
Carl A. Florio: president, chief executive officer
Tony Jones: chairman

Foundation Officials

Stanley Bardwell, M.D.: treasurer
Carl A. Florio: director (see above)
Marilyn A. Herrington: president
Marilyn A. Herrington: president
William H. Jones: vice president
William H. Jones: vice president
Holly Rappleyea: secretary, treasurer
Earl Schram: director
Earl Schram, Jr.: director

Grants Analysis

Total Grants: $325,195*
Number of Grants: 250
Average Grant: $1,301
Highest Grant: $25,000
Lowest Grant: $25
Typical Range: $250 to $2,000
*Note: Giving excludes United Way.

Recent Grants

Note: Grants derived from fiscal 2001 Form 990.

Library-Related

5,000	Hudson Area Association Library, Hudson, NY -- children's room improvement project
2,500	Hudson Day Care Center, Hudson, NY -- insulation of infant room
2,000	Albany Public Library, Albany, NY -- support library campaign
2,000	Albany Public Library, Albany, NY -- library donation
2,000	Hudson Area Association Library, Hudson, NY -- library donation
2,000	River Street Park, Valatie, NY -- preservation in the Village of Valatie
2,000	Troy Public Library, Troy, NY -- library donation
1,000	Castleton Public Library, Castleton, NY -- library donation
1,000	East Greenbush Community Library, Rensselaer, NY -- library donation
1,000	Nassau Free Library, Nassau, NY -- library donation

General

25,000	Columbia Greene Hospital Foundation, Hudson, NY -- renovations

HUDSON-WEBBER FOUNDATION

Giving Contact

David O. Egner, President
333 West Fort Street, Suite 1310
Detroit, MI 48226
Phone: (313)963-7777
Fax: (313)963-2818

Description

Founded: 1943
EIN: 386052131
Organization Type: General Purpose Foundation
Giving Locations: MI: Oakland County, Southeastern Michigan, Wayne County, Detroit

Grant Types: Award, Challenge, Employee Matching Gifts, General Support, Matching, Multiyear/Continuing Support, Project, Research, Seed Money.

Donor Information

Founder: The Hudson-Webber Foundation was organized in 1943, with funds donated by the J. L. Hudson Company and by Richard Webber, Joseph Webber, and Oscar Webber. Significant contributions also were provided by company employees and other members of the family. At the close of 1983, the foundation merged with two other foundations: the Eloise and Richard Webber Foundation (established in 1939, with Richard and Eloise Webber; their daughters, Jean Webber Sutphin and Mary Webber Parker; and Richard Webber's sister, Louise Webber O'Brien as donors) and the Richard H. and Eloise Jenks Webber Charitable Fund (established in 1960, with Richard and Eloise Webber; their daughters, Jean and Mary; and Richard Webber's brother, Joseph L. Webber, as donors).

Joseph L. Hudson, Jr., chairman of the foundation, and Gilbert Hudson, its president and chief executive, are grandnephews of Joseph L. Hudson (1846-1912), who founded J. L. Hudson Company (1881), a major Detroit merchandiser. Joseph L. Hudson was a generous benefactor of local charities and a leader of civic boards and committees. The Webber family's relationship to the company derives from the founder's sister, Mary, who married Joseph T. Webber. When Mr. Hudson died, his four nephews inherited the majority of the company's stock, and Richard Hudson Webber became president of J. L. Hudson Company.

Financial Summary

Total Giving: $7,898,594 (2000); $6,800,000 (1999 approx); $6,147,552 (1998). Note: Giving includes United Way, gifts to individuals.
Giving Analysis: Giving for 1998 includes: foundation grants to United Way ($199,000) foundation matching gifts ($346,240)
Assets: $165,198,337 (2000); $180,000,000 (1999 approx); $160,375,938 (1998)
Gifts Received: $1,000,000 (1999 approx); $55,031 (1996); $4,000 (1995)

Typical Recipients

Arts & Humanities: Arts Associations & Councils, Arts Centers, Arts Funds, Arts Institutes, Ethnic & Folk Arts, Arts & Humanities-General, Historic Preservation, History & Archaeology, Libraries, Museums/Galleries, Music, Opera, Performing Arts, Public Broadcasting, Theater
Civic & Public Affairs: African American Affairs, Business/Free Enterprise, Chambers of Commerce, Community Foundations, Economic Development, Economic Policy, Employment/Job Training, Civic & Public Affairs-General, Hispanic Affairs, Housing, Inner-City Development, Law & Justice, Minority Business, Municipalities/Towns, Nonprofit Management, Parades/Festivals, Safety, Urban & Community Affairs, Women's Affairs, Zoos/Aquariums
Education: Arts/Humanities Education, Business Education, Colleges & Universities, Continuing Education, Education Funds, Education Reform, Education-General, Legal Education, Minority Education, Private Education (Precollege), Public Education (Precollege), Secondary Education (Public), Social Sciences Education, Student Aid, Vocational & Technical Education
Environment: Environment-General
Health: Cancer, Children's Health/Hospitals, Clinics/Medical Centers, Health Organizations, Hospitals, Nursing Services, Prenatal Health Issues, Public Health, Transplant Networks/Donor Banks
International: International Development, International Peace & Security Issues
Religion: Churches, Dioceses, Religious Organizations, Religious Welfare, Social/Policy Issues
Science: Scientific Centers & Institutes, Scientific Centers & Institutes

Social Services: At-Risk Youth, Child Abuse, Community Service Organizations, Counseling, Crime Prevention, Delinquency & Criminal Rehabilitation, Domestic Violence, Family Planning, Family Services, Food/Clothing Distribution, People with Disabilities, Recreation & Athletics, Substance Abuse, United Funds/United Ways, Volunteer Services, YMCA/YWCA/YMHA/YWHA, Youth Organizations

Application Procedures

Initial Contact: Applicants should send a brief letter, signed by a senior officer of the requesting organization.
Application Requirements: The letter of request should include a brief a description of organization; description of the proposed program, including an explanation of its importance and a clear statement of its goals; detailed income and expense budget for the program; potential sources of other funding; and amount requested and time period during which the funds will be used. Proof of the organization's tax-exempt status is required.
Deadlines: Grant requests should be submitted by April 15, August 15, or December 15. Requests received after these dates are reviewed during the next period.
Notes: Only one copy of the proposal should be submitted.

Restrictions

The foundation does not make grants for endowments, fundraising social events, conferences, or exhibits. Also, the foundation does not fund individuals, except under the Hudson-Webber program for Hudsonians. Programs outside the foundation's geographical area of interest are not supported.

Additional Information

Publications: Annual Report (annually); Guidelines

Foundation Officials

William C. Brooks: trustee PRIM CORP EMPL chairman: Brooks Group International. CORP AFFIL director: Louisiana-Pacific Corp.; chairman: Brooks Group International; director: DTE Energy Co. NONPR AFFIL chairman: Greater Detroit Chamber of Commerce.
David O. Egner: president, trustee ED Western Michigan University MS.
Alfred Robinson Glancy, III: trustee, treasurer B Detroit, MI 1938. ED Princeton University BA (1960); Harvard University MA (1962). PRIM CORP EMPL chairman, president, chief executive officer: MCN Corp. CORP AFFIL vice chairman: UNICO Properties; chairman, president, chief executive officer: MCN Energy Group Inc.; director: Morton Industrial Group Inc. NONPR AFFIL chairman: Detroit Symphony Orchestra; director: New Detroit Inc.; chairman: Detroit Renaissance Inc.; chairman: Detroit Medical Center. CLUB AFFIL Princeton Michigan Club; Country Club Detroit; Detroit Club.
Frank Martin Hennessey: trustee B Lynn, MA 1938. ED Northeastern University BS (1964). PRIM CORP EMPL vice chairman, chief executive officer: MascoTech Inc. ADD CORP EMPL chairman: Emco Ltd.; chairman, director: Metcraft Inc. CORP AFFIL director: MCN Corp.; director: MCN Energy Group Inc.
Hudson Holland, Jr.: secretary, trustee B Springfield, MA 1939. ED Williams College BA (1961). NONPR AFFIL trustee: Cottage Hospital Massachusetts; president: Nantucket House. CLUB AFFIL Fontinalis Club; Nantucket Yacht Club.
Gilbert Hudson: chairman, trustee
Joseph L. Hudson, IV: trustee CORP AFFIL director: Masco Corp.
Joseph Lowthian Hudson, Jr.: trustee CORP AFFIL director: Masco Corp.
John E. Lobbia: trustee B Chicago, IL 1941. ED University of Detroit BSEE (1964). PRIM CORP

EMPL chairman, chief executive officer, director: Detroit Edison Co. CORP AFFIL chairman, chief executive officer, director: DTE Energy Co.; director: Rouge Steel Co.
Jennifer H. Parke: trustee

Grants Analysis

Disclosure Period: calendar year ending 2000
Total Grants: $7,880,015*
Number of Grants: 79
Highest Grant: $1,500,000
Lowest Grant: $5,000
Typical Range: $5,000 to $100,000
*Note: Average grant excludes highest grant. Giving excludes matching gifts and United Way.

Recent Grants

Note: Grants derived from 2001 Form 990.

General

500,000	Local Initiatives Support Corporation, New York, NY -- Detroit Community Development Funders' Collaborative
300,000	Wayne State University, Detroit, MI -- research and technology park
250,000	Detroit Institute of Arts, Detroit, MI -- program needs
250,000	Goodwill Industries of Greater Detroit, Detroit, MI -- reducing chronic unemployment initiative
250,000	YMCA of Metro Detroit, Detroit, MI -- capital development program
200,000	Community Foundation for Southeastern Michigan, Detroit, MI -- Green Ways Initiative
200,000	Detroit Institute of Arts, Detroit, MI -- building addition
200,000	Detroit Regional Chamber Foundation, Detroit, MI -- career start
200,000	Detroit Symphony Orchestra Hall, Detroit, MI -- Orchestra Place Project
200,000	Detroit Symphony Orchestra Hall, Detroit, MI -- program needs

GEOFFREY C. HUGHES FOUNDATION

Giving Contact

John R. Young, President & Director
c/o Cahill, Gordon & Reindel
80 Pine Street, Suite 1701
New York, NY 10005
Phone: (212)701-3400

Description

Founded: 1991
EIN: 133622255
Organization Type: Private Foundation
Giving Locations: CA; KY; NY: northeastern states.
Grant Types: General Support.

Donor Information

Founder: the late Geoffrey C. Hughes

Financial Summary

Total Giving: $2,218,072 (fiscal year ending March 31, 2001); $2,239,374 (fiscal 2000); $2,734,000 (fiscal 1999)
Assets: $35,464,221 (fiscal 2001); $39,932,203 (fiscal 2000); $48,506,229 (fiscal 1999)
Gifts Received: $47,481 (fiscal 2000); $60,573 (fiscal 1997); $642,663 (fiscal 1996). Note: In fiscal 1996 and 2000, contributions were received from the estate of Geoffrey C. Hughes.

Typical Recipients

Arts & Humanities: Ballet, Ethnic & Folk Arts, History & Archaeology, Music, Opera, Theater
Civic & Public Affairs: Urban & Community Affairs, Zoos/Aquariums
Education: Arts/Humanities Education, Colleges & Universities, Literacy, Medical Education
Environment: Environment-General, Resource Conservation, Wildlife Protection
International: Foreign Arts Organizations

Application Procedures

Initial Contact: Send a brief letter of inquiry.
Application Requirements: Include a description of organization, amount requested, purpose of funds sought, and proof of tax-exempt status.
Deadlines: None.

Restrictions

Awards are generally concentrated in the areas of environmental protection, opera, and ballet.

Foundation Officials

Ursula Cliff: director
Joan Murtagh Frankel: assistant secretary, assistant treasurer
June McCandless: director
O. Carlysle McCandless: executive vice president, assistant secretary, treasurer, director
John R. Young: president, director B Milwaukee, WI 1934. ED University of Chicago AB (1953); University of Chicago JD (1956). PRIM CORP EMPL Cahill Gordon & Reindel.
Mary K. Young: director

Grants Analysis

Disclosure Period: fiscal year ending March 31, 2001
Total Grants: $2,218,072
Number of Grants: 35
Average Grant: $63,373
Highest Grant: $226,938
Lowest Grant: $1,000
Typical Range: $5,000 to $400,000

Recent Grants

Note: Grants derived from 2001 Form 990.

General

226,938	Hancock Shaker Village, Pittsfield, MA -- for HSV New England Heritage Breeds Conservancy Collaborations
200,000	Nature Conservancy, Boston, MA
200,000	Nature Conservancy, Middletown, CT -- for GCH land preservation fund
200,000	New York City Ballet, New York, NY -- for artist in residence program
150,000	San Francisco Opera, San Francisco, CA -- for showcase performances by Adler Fellows
120,000	Engremont Environmental Action and Land Trust
100,000	American Friends of the Paris Opera and Ballet -- for San Francisco Ballet appearance in Paris
100,000	Long Island Sound Keeper Fund, Monterey, CA -- for Yankee Oyster Project
100,000	Nature Conservancy, Concord, NH -- for preserving lands
100,000	New York City Opera, New York, NY

HOWARD HUGHES MEDICAL INSTITUTE

Giving Contact

Office of Grants and Special Programs
4000 Jones Bridge Road
Chevy Chase, MD 20815-6789
Phone: (301)215-8500
Fax: (301)215-8888
E-mail: grantvpr@hhmi.org
Web: http://www.hhmi.org

Description

Founded: 1954
EIN: 590735717
Organization Type: Specialized/Single Purpose Foundation
Giving Locations: internationally; nationally.
Grant Types: Award, Fellowship, Multiyear/Continuing Support, Research, Scholarship.

Donor Information

Founder: The Howard Hughes Medical Institute was established as a medical research organization in 1953 by aviator-industrialist Howard R. Hughes . The institute was funded through its ownership of the Hughes Aircraft Company whose sole trustee was Mr. Hughes until his death in 1976. New trustees were appointed in 1984, and, in 1985, they sold Hughes Aircraft Company to General Motors Corporation. The proceeds of that sale represent the basis of the institute's present endowment.

Financial Summary

Total Giving: $600,000,000 (fiscal year ending August 31, 2003 approx); $582,000,000 (fiscal 2002 approx); $103,278,000 (fiscal 2001)
Assets: $10,291,341,000 (fiscal 2002); $15,811,093,000 (fiscal 2001); $15,601,980,000 (fiscal 2000)
Gifts Received: $47,481 (fiscal 2000)

Typical Recipients

Arts & Humanities: Arts Outreach, Ballet, Museums/Galleries, Opera, Theater
Civic & Public Affairs: Botanical Gardens/Parks, Nonprofit Management, Zoos/Aquariums
Education: Colleges & Universities, Engineering/Technological Education, Faculty Development, Education-General, Medical Education, Minority Education, Science/Mathematics Education, Student Aid
Environment: Environment-General, Resource Conservation, Wildlife Protection
Health: Arthritis, Cancer, Hospitals (University Affiliated), Medical Research
International: Foreign Arts Organizations
Science: Science Museums, Scientific Centers & Institutes, Scientific Organizations, Scientific Research

Application Procedures

Initial Contact: For Grants and Special Programs, each of the programs in graduate, undergraduate, and pre-college, and international research has individual eligibility requirements, criteria for support, and methods of application. Informational brochures, program announcements, and application forms should be consulted prior to contact. These materials are available upon request from the Office of Grants and Special Programs.
Deadlines: For Grants and Special Programs, deadlines vary according to the particular program. Program announcements should be consulted for the exact dates.
Review Process: Graduate fellowships, grants for undergraduate and pre-college science education, and grants for research in selected countries abroad are awarded on the basis of applications or proposals reviewed by outside panels of scientists and educators. The panels' evaluations are reviewed by an internal committee, which makes recommendations to the institute's trustees for authorization of funding. The trustees and institute management annually review current grants policies, initiatives, and possible directions for program development.

Restrictions

The institute does not award scholarships or funds to students directly. The grantee colleges and universities award and distribute the funds on their own. The institute does not award grants for research in the United States. It does not award institutional training grants or support conferences or publications.

Additional Information

Information on specific programs may be obtained from the following contact persons: Barbara Filner, PhD., graduate science education; Stephen A. Barkanic, undergraduate science education; Jill G. Conley, PhD, international and pre-college science education, as well as the international program; and Dennis WC. Liu, PhD., research resource and public science education.

Publications: Annual Report; Guidelines; Application Form; Directories; Fact Sheets

Foundation Officials

James Addison Baker, III: trustee B Houston, TX 1930. ED Princeton University BA (1952); University of Texas LLB (1957). PRIM CORP EMPL senior partner: Baker & Botts, LLP ADD CORP EMPL senior counselor: Carlyle Group. CORP AFFIL director: Electronic Data Systems Corp. NONPR AFFIL member: Texas Bar Association; trustee: Woodrow Wilson International Center Scholars Smithsonian Institute; director: Rice University; member: Phi Delta Phi; vice president: Professional Development Institute; member: Houston Bar Association; honorary chairman: James A. Baker III Institute Public Policy; member: American Judicature Society; member: American Bar Association.

Alexander Gordon Bearn, MD: trustee B Surrey, United Kingdom 1923. ED University of London BS (1945); University of London MB (1945); University of London MD (1951). PRIM NONPR EMPL adj professor: Rockefeller University, Rockefeller Institute. CORP AFFIL director: Biogen Inc. NONPR AFFIL member: Society Experimental Biology & Medicine; member: Union League Philadelphia; director: Royal Society Medicine Foundation; member: Sigma Xi; fellow: Royal College Physicians Edinburgh; fellow: Royal College Physicians London; professor: Rockefeller Institute; trustee: Rockefeller University; member: Medical Society London; foreign associate: Norwegian Academy Science Letters; member, board science overseers: Jackson Laboratory; member: Medical Research Society Great Britain; trustee: Howard Hughes Medical Institute; member: Institute Medicine NAS; member: Harveian Society London; member: Harvey Society; coun: Forgarty Center NIH; member: Genetics Society America; member: Century Association; professor emeritus, medicine: Cornell University; member: Association American Physicians; member: Association Physicians Great Britain & Ireland; member: American Society Clinical Investigation; member: American Society Human Genetics; executive officer: American Philosophical Society; member: American Society Biological Chemists; fellow: American Association Advancement Science. CLUB AFFIL Knickerbocker Club; Misquamicut Club; Crail Golf Club.

Stephen M. Cohen: vice president, chief financial officer B Harrisburg, PA 1952. ED Pennsylvania State University BA (1974); New York University MBA (1976). PRIM NONPR EMPL dean: Yale University, School of Medicine. NONPR AFFIL mem: Association American Medical Colleges; director: Medicine Centre Industry Co. Ltd.; mem: America Israel Public Affairs Committee.

William Maxwell Cowan, MD,PhD: vice president, chief scientific officer B Johannesburg, Republic of South Africa 1931. ED University of Witwatersrand BSc (1951); Oxford University DPhil (1956); Oxford University MB (1958); Oxford University MA (1959). PRIM NONPR EMPL vice president, chief scientific officer: Howard Hughes Medical Institute. CORP AFFIL editor: Annual Reviews Neurosciences. NONPR AFFIL member: Sigma Xi; member: Society Neuroscience; fellow: Royal Society London; foreign member: Royal Society South Africa; member: Phi Beta Kappa; member: Royal Microscopic Society; adj professor:

Johns Hopkins School Medicine; fgn member: Norwegian Academy Science; member: American Philosophical Society; member: Anatomical Society Great Britain Ireland; member: American Association Advancement Science; member: American Association Anatomists; member: Alpha Omega Alpha; fellow: American Academy of Arts & Sciences.

Frank William Gay: trustee B Provo, UT. ED Brigham Young University; Colorado College. PRIM CORP EMPL former president, former chief executive officer: Summa Corp.

James Howard Gilliam, Jr.: trustee B Baltimore, MD 1945. ED Morgan State University BA (1967); Columbia University JD (1970). CORP AFFIL director: Delmarva Power & Light Co. NONPR AFFIL member: Rotary International; member: Sigma Pi Phi; member: National Guardsmen Inc.; member: Kappa Alpha Psi; member: National Bar Association; member: Delaware Bar Association; member: Delaware Roundtable Inc.; member: American Bar Association; board visitors: Columbia University Law School; member: American Bankers Association. CLUB AFFIL Wilmington Country Club; Rodney Square Club; University & Whist Club; Monday Club; Rehoboth Beach Country Club; Brandywine Country Club; Knickerbocker Club.

Joseph L. Goldstein, MD: trustee

Hanna Holborn Gray, PhD: chairman B Heidelberg, Germany 1930. ED Bryn Mawr College AB (1950); Harvard University PhD (1957); Yale University MA (1971); Yale University LLD (1978). PRIM NONPR EMPL professor of history: University of Chicago. CORP AFFIL director: JP Morgan & Co. Inc.; director: Morgan Guaranty Trust Co. New York; director: Atlantic Richfield Co.; director: Cummins Engine Co. Inc.; director: Ameritech Corp. NONPR AFFIL member: Renaissance Society America; board regents: Smithsonian Institute; member: National Academy Education; member: Phi Beta Kappa; trustee: Harvard University; trustee: Marlboro School Music; fellow: Center Advanced Study Behavioral Science; director: Council Foreign Relations; fellow: American Academy of Arts & Sciences; member: American Philosophical Society.

Garnett L. Keith: trustee B Atlanta, GA 1935. ED Georgia Institute of Technology (1957); Harvard University Graduate School of Business Administration MA (1962). PRIM CORP EMPL chairman, chief executive officer: SeaBridge Investment Advisors. CORP AFFIL director: Xybernet Inc.; director: AEA Investors Inc.; director: Supervalu Inc. NONPR AFFIL trustee: Drew University.

Jeremy R. Knowles, PhD: trustee B Rugby, United Kingdom 1935. ED Balliol College BA; Oxford University BA (1958); Christ Church University DPhil (1961); Christ Church University MA (1961). PRIM NONPR EMPL dean arts & sciences, Amory Houghton professor: Harvard University. NONPR AFFIL member: Royal Chemistry Society London; member: Royale Society; member: Biochemistry Society London; member: NAS; member: American Philosophical Society; member: American Society Biological Chemists; fellow: American Academy of Arts & Sciences; member: American Chemical Society.

Joan S. Leonard, Esq.: vice president, general counsel PRIM NONPR EMPL secretary, general counsel: Howard Hughes Medical Institute.

William R. Lummis, Esq.: trustee B Houston, TX 1929. ED University of Texas BA (1951); University of Texas LLB (1953). PRIM CORP EMPL chairman: Summa Corp. CORP AFFIL director: Rouse Co. Inc.; director: Stewart & Stevenson Services Inc.; director: Hughes Corp.

Joseph George Perpich, MD, JD: vice president grants & special programs B Hibbing, MN 1941. ED University of Minnesota BA (1963); University of Minnesota MD (1966); Georgetown University JD (1974). PRIM NONPR EMPL vice president: Howard Hughes Medical Institute.

Anne M. Tatlock: trustee

Grants Analysis

Disclosure Period: fiscal year ending August 31, 2002

Total Grants: $582,000,000 (approx)*

Number of Grants: 1,000 (approx)

Average Grant: $557,000*

Highest Grant: $25,000,000

Lowest Grant: $35,000

Typical Range: $100,000 to $1,000,000

*Note: Average grant figure excludes highest grant. The typical range for the graduate program fellowships is $29,000 to $106,000, and for the institutional grants in the undergraduate program, $500,000 to $2,200,000.

Recent Grants

Note: Grants derived from 2000 Form 990.

General

4,000,000	University of California School of Medicine, Los Angeles, CA
4,000,000	University of Michigan Medical School, Ann Arbor, MI
4,000,000	Yale University School of Medicine, New Haven, CT
3,800,000	SUNY - Buffalo School of Medicine, Buffalo, NY
3,800,000	University of California San Francisco School of Medicine, San Francisco, CA
3,400,000	Dartmouth Medical School, Hanover, NH
3,000,000	Case Western Reserve University School of Medicine, Cleveland, OH
2,800,000	Baylor College of Medicine, Houston, TX
2,600,000	University of Iowa College of Medicine, Iowa City, IA
2,600,000	University of North Carolina Chapel Hill School of Medicine, Chapel Hill, NC

HUGOTON FOUNDATION

Giving Contact

Joan K. Stout, President
900 Park Ave.
New York, NY 10021
Phone: (212)734-5447
Fax: (212)734-5448

Description

Founded: 1981
EIN: 341351062
Organization Type: Family Foundation
Giving Locations: FL: Miami; NY: New York
Grant Types: Project, Research.
Note: The foundation also reports equipment contributions.

Donor Information

Founder: Established in 1981 by the late Wallace Gilroy .

Financial Summary

Total Giving: $2,100,000 (2002 approx); $1,941,100 (2001); $2,059,900 (2000)

Giving Analysis: Giving for 2000 includes: foundation fellowships ($300,000); 1999: foundation scholarships ($4,000); foundation fellowships ($175,000) 1998: foundation scholarships ($5,000)

Assets: $41,234,974 (2001); $44,416,460 (2000); $47,329,196 (1999)

Typical Recipients

Arts & Humanities: Historic Preservation, History & Archaeology, Libraries, Museums/Galleries, Music, Performing Arts

Civic & Public Affairs: Botanical Gardens/Parks, Clubs, Public Policy

Education: Business Education, Colleges & Universities, Education-General, Legal Education, Medical Education, Private Education (Precollege), Public Education (Precollege), Religious Education, Science/Mathematics Education, Secondary Education (Private), Student Aid
Environment: Resource Conservation
Health: Alzheimers Disease, Cancer, Children's Health/Hospitals, Clinics/Medical Centers, Emergency/Ambulance Services, Eyes/Blindness, Geriatric Health, Health Organizations, Heart, Hospitals, Medical Rehabilitation, Medical Research, Mental Health, Mental Health, Nursing Services, Research/Studies Institutes, Respiratory, Single-Disease Health Associations, Transplant Networks/Donor Banks
International: Foreign Educational Institutions, International Organizations
Religion: Churches, Dioceses, Religion-General, Religious Organizations, Religious Welfare
Science: Science Museums
Social Services: Animal Protection, Big Brother/Big Sister, Child Welfare, Community Service Organizations, Emergency Relief, Food/Clothing Distribution, Homes, People with Disabilities, Recreation & Athletics, Senior Services, YMCA/YWCA/YMHA/YWHA

Application Procedures

Initial Contact: The foundation requests applications be made in writing.
Application Requirements: Written request must include a description of organization, proof of tax-exempt status, brief statement of need, date request is needed by, and a detailed cost analysis. Requests should not exceed three pages.
Deadlines: None. Requests are received and reviewed throughout the calendar year.

Restrictions

Foundation mainly gives in the New York, NY area and in Miami, FL to improve health care.

Foundation Officials

Frank S. Fejes: director
Jean C. Stout: treasurer, director
Joan K. Stout: president, managing director
Joan M. Stout: secretary, director
John K. Stout: director
Ray E. Stout, III: vice president, director

Grants Analysis

Disclosure Period: calendar year ending 2001
Total Grants: $1,941,100
Number of Grants: 97
Average Grant: $20,011
Highest Grant: $140,000
Typical Range: $10,000 to $40,000

Recent Grants

Note: Grants derived from 2001 Form 990.

Library-Related
100,000	South Florida Center for Theological Studies, Miami, FL -- for library expansion
10,000	New York Public Library, New York, NY -- for business research libraries

General
140,000	St. John Medical Center, Tulsa, OK -- for medical equipment
130,000	New York University Medical Center, New York, NY -- for pain study
95,000	New York Blood Center, New York, NY -- for equipment
76,500	St. John's Riverside Hospital, Yonkers, NY -- for patient simulator
75,000	Lenox Hill Hospital, New York, NY -- for spine research and fellowship
75,000	Sigma Theta Tau International, Indianapolis, IN -- for career development and retention initiatives

50,000	American Museum of Natural History, New York, NY -- for Pearl Exhibit
50,000	American Red Cross of Greater New York, New York, NY -- disaster relief
50,000	Archdiocese of Miami, Miami, FL
50,000	Cardinal's Committee of the Laity, New York, NY -- for religious purposes

HUISKING FOUNDATION

Giving Contact

Frank R. Huisking, Treasurer & Director
PO Box 368
Botsford, CT 06404-0353
Phone: (203)426-8618

Description

Founded: 1946
EIN: 136117501
Organization Type: Private Foundation
Giving Locations: nationally.
Grant Types: Operating Expenses, Project, Research.

Donor Information

Founder: members of the Huisking family and family-related corporations

Financial Summary

Total Giving: $815,000 (2000); $747,365 (1999); $411,500 (1996)
Giving Analysis: Giving for 2000 includes: foundation grants to United Way ($2,000) 1998: foundation grants to United Way ($6,500)
Assets: $21,348,485 (2000); $15,610,774 (1999); $14,561,192 (1998)
Gifts Received: In 1991, contributions in the form of stocks were received from Charles A. Huisking.

Typical Recipients

Arts & Humanities: History & Archaeology, Libraries, Museums/Galleries, Music
Civic & Public Affairs: Botanical Gardens/Parks, Municipalities/Towns, Urban & Community Affairs
Education: Arts/Humanities Education, Colleges & Universities, Education Funds, Engineering/Technological Education, Education-General, Legal Education, Private Education (Precollege), Secondary Education (Private), Student Aid
Environment: Resource Conservation
Health: Cancer, Children's Health/Hospitals, Clinics/Medical Centers, Emergency/Ambulance Services, Hospices, Hospitals, Long-Term Care, Medical Research, Multiple Sclerosis, Nursing Services, Single-Disease Health Associations
International: International Relief Efforts, Missionary/Religious Activities
Religion: Churches, Dioceses, Religion-General, Jewish Causes, Religious Organizations, Religious Welfare, Seminaries, Social/Policy Issues
Social Services: Animal Protection, At-Risk Youth, Community Centers, Community Service Organizations, Day Care, Family Services, Homes, People with Disabilities, Social Services-General, United Funds/United Ways, YMCA/YWCA/YMHA/YWHA, Youth Organizations

Application Procedures

Initial Contact: Send brief letter describing program.
Deadlines: None.

Restrictions

Does not support individuals.

Foundation Officials

Helen Crawford: director
Robert P. Daly: director
John E. Haigney: president, director
Claire F. Hanavan: director

Taylor W. Hanavan: director
Frank R. Huisking: treasurer, director
Richard V. Huisking, Sr.: director
Richard V. Huisking, Jr.: secretary, director
William W. Huisking, Jr.: vice president, director
Jean M. Steinschneider: director

Grants Analysis

Disclosure Period: calendar year ending 2000
Total Grants: $813,000*
Number of Grants: 284
Average Grant: $2,608*
Highest Grant: $75,000
Typical Range: $1,000 to $5,000
*Note: Giving excludes United Way. Average grant figure excludes highest grant.

Recent Grants

Note: Grants derived from 2001 Form 990.

Library-Related
20,000	Larchmont Public Library, Larchmont, NY -- operating needs

General
60,000	St. Mary's College, Notre Dame, IN -- Tech Center construction
35,000	Sound Shore Medical Center, Larchmont, NY -- operating needs
31,700	University of Notre Dame, Notre Dame, IN -- operating needs
30,000	St. Augustine's Roman Catholic Church, Larchmont, NY -- operating needs
30,000	Spring Hill College, Mobile, AL -- library upgrade
25,000	Ringling Museum Foundation, Venice, FL -- operating needs
25,000	St. Mary's Roman Catholic Church, Manhasset, NY -- operating needs
20,000	Christ the King Monastery -- operating needs
20,000	Florida West Coast Symphony, Sarasota, FL -- operating needs
20,000	Vincent R. Saurino Fellowship -- scholarship

NILA B. HULBERT FOUNDATION

Giving Contact

Henry L. Hulbert, Trustee
6 Ford Avenue
Oneonta, NY 13820
Phone: (607)432-6720

Description

Founded: 1971
EIN: 237039996
Organization Type: Private Foundation
Giving Locations: NY: Oneonta
Grant Types: General Support.

Donor Information

Founder: Nila B. Hulbert

Financial Summary

Total Giving: $269,756 (2002); $257,358 (2001); $329,000 (2000)
Giving Analysis: Giving for 2002 includes: foundation grants to United Way ($1,000); foundation scholarships ($13,000); 2000: foundation grants to United Way ($1,000); foundation scholarships ($12,500); 1999: foundation grants to United Way ($1,000)
Assets: $5,753,699 (2002); $7,149,132 (2001); $7,120,972 (2000)
Gifts Received: $14,021 (1992)

Typical Recipients

Arts & Humanities: Historic Preservation, History & Archaeology, Libraries, Museums/Galleries, Music
Civic & Public Affairs: Housing, Philanthropic Organizations
Education: Colleges & Universities, Public Education (Precollege)
Health: Children's Health/Hospitals, Health Organizations, Hospices, Hospitals
Religion: Churches, Religious Organizations, Religious Welfare
Social Services: Family Services, Food/Clothing Distribution, Recreation & Athletics, Social Services-General, United Funds/United Ways, YMCA/YWCA/YMHA/YWHA, Youth Organizations

Application Procedures

Initial Contact: Send a brief letter of inquiry with supporting documentation.
Deadlines: September 30.

Foundation Officials

Henry L. Hulbert: trustee
J. Burton Hulbert: trustee
William H. Hulbert: trustee

Grants Analysis

Disclosure Period: calendar year ending 2002
Total Grants: $255,756*
Number of Grants: 20
Average Grant: $8,198*
Highest Grant: $100,000
Lowest Grant: $500
Typical Range: $5,000 to $10,000
*Note: Giving excludes United Way and scholarships. Average grant figure excludes highest grant.

Recent Grants

Note: Grants derived from 2001 Form 990.

General

100,000	Hartwick College, Oneonta, NY
25,000	A.O. Fox Memorial Hospital Foundation, Oneonta, NY
20,000	Catskill Symphony Orchestra, Oneonta, NY
16,458	Huntington Memorial Library Foundation, Oneonta, NY
10,000	Catskill Area Hospice, Oneonta, NY -- for operations
10,000	First United Presbyterian Society, Oneonta, NY -- annual operation
10,000	St. Lawrence University, Canton, NY -- for operation
10,000	Volunteers in Medicine, Hilton Head, SC -- annual operation
8,000	Morris Central School, Morris, NY -- for scholarships
7,500	Oneonta Family YMCA, Oneonta, NY -- annual operation

MILTON G. HULME CHARITABLE FOUNDATION

Giving Contact

519 Frick Bldg.
Pittsburgh, PA 15219
Phone: (412)281-2007

Description

Founded: 1960
EIN: 256062896
Organization Type: Private Foundation
Giving Locations: PA
Grant Types: General Support.

Donor Information

Founder: Glove, Inc. and MacGregor

Financial Summary

Total Giving: $415,000 (2000); $430,000 (1999); $400,000 (1998)
Giving Analysis: Giving for 2000 includes: foundation grants to United Way ($5,000); 1999: foundation grants to United Way ($10,000) 1998: foundation grants to United Way ($10,000)
Assets: $10,112,258 (2000); $9,175,043 (1999); $9,187,669 (1998)
Gifts Received: $417,000 (1999); $285,600 (1998). Note: In 1999, contributions were received from Jocelyn H. MacConnell ($137,500), Natalie H. Curry ($129,625), and Holiday H. Shoup ($149,875). In 1998, contributions were received from Helen C. Hulme.

Typical Recipients

Arts & Humanities: Arts Associations & Councils, Ballet, Community Arts, Historic Preservation, History & Archaeology, Libraries, Museums/Galleries, Music, Opera, Performing Arts, Public Broadcasting, Theater
Civic & Public Affairs: Business/Free Enterprise, Civic & Public Affairs-General, Urban & Community Affairs
Education: Colleges & Universities, Preschool Education, Private Education (Precollege), Special Education, Student Aid
Environment: Resource Conservation
Health: Children's Health/Hospitals, Emergency/Ambulance Services, Geriatric Health, Hospices, Hospitals, Medical Rehabilitation, Nursing Services, Single-Disease Health Associations
Religion: Churches, Ministries, Religious Organizations, Religious Welfare
Science: Scientific Centers & Institutes
Social Services: Child Welfare, Community Centers, Community Service Organizations, Family Planning, Family Services, Food/Clothing Distribution, Homes, People with Disabilities, Recreation & Athletics, Scouts, Senior Services, Shelters/Homelessness, United Funds/United Ways, Youth Organizations

Application Procedures

Initial Contact: Send a brief letter of inquiry.
Application Requirements: Include a description of organization, purpose of funds sought, and proof of tax-exempt status.
Deadlines: June 30.

Foundation Officials

Natalie H. Curry: trustee
Aura P. Hulme: trustee
Helen C. Hulme: trustee
Jocelyn H. MacConnell: trustee
Helen H. Shoup: trustee

Grants Analysis

Disclosure Period: calendar year ending 2000
Total Grants: $410,000*
Number of Grants: 45
Average Grant: $8,227*
Highest Grant: $48,000
Typical Range: $1,000 to $15,000
*Note: Giving excludes United Way. Average grant excludes highest grant.

Recent Grants

Note: Grants derived from 2001 Form 990.

Library-Related

12,000	Carnegie Second Century Fund, Pittsburgh, PA
12,000	Lauri Ann West Memorial Library, Pittsburgh, PA
10,000	Carnegie Library for the Blind and Physically Handicapped, Pittsburgh, PA

General

49,000	Shadyside Hospital Foundation, Pittsburgh, PA
34,000	Pittsburgh Cultural Trust, Pittsburgh, PA
25,000	Family Resources, Pittsburgh, PA
23,000	Salvation Army, Pittsburgh, PA
20,000	United Way of Southwestern Pennsylvania, Pittsburgh, PA
20,000	WQED & WQED-FM, Pittsburgh, PA
15,200	Coalition for Christian Outreach, Pittsburgh, PA
15,000	Shadyside Presbyterian Church, Pittsburgh, PA
15,000	Three Rivers Rowing Association, Pittsburgh, PA
13,500	Shadyside Academy, Pittsburgh, PA

HULTQUIST FOUNDATION

Giving Contact

Thomas J. Flowers, President
PO Box 1219
Jamestown, NY 14701
Phone: (716)664-5210

Description

Founded: 1965
EIN: 160907729
Organization Type: Private Foundation
Giving Locations: NY: Chautauqua County
Grant Types: General Support.

Financial Summary

Total Giving: $1,191,339 (fiscal year ending June 30, 2002); $640,145 (fiscal 2001); $1,061,223 (fiscal 2000). Note: Fiscal 1999 Giving includes.
Giving Analysis: Giving for fiscal 2002 includes: foundation grants to United Way ($22,000); fiscal 2000: foundation grants to United Way ($21,000); fiscal 1999: foundation grants to United Way ($17,000)
Assets: $13,783,958 (fiscal 2002); $16,299,991 (fiscal 2001); $18,396,192 (fiscal 2000)
Gifts Received: $71,359 (fiscal 1992)

Typical Recipients

Arts & Humanities: Arts Associations & Councils, Arts Funds, Arts & Humanities-General, Historic Preservation, History & Archaeology, Libraries, Music, Performing Arts
Civic & Public Affairs: Civic & Public Affairs-General, Urban & Community Affairs
Education: Arts/Humanities Education, Colleges & Universities, Community & Junior Colleges, Education Funds, Education-General, Literacy, Student Aid
Environment: Environment-General, Wildlife Protection
Health: Cancer, Children's Health/Hospitals, Hospitals
Religion: Religious Welfare
Social Services: Animal Protection, Child Welfare, Community Service Organizations, Family Services, Food/Clothing Distribution, Homes, Recreation & Athletics, Scouts, United Funds/United Ways, YMCA/YWCA/YMHA/YWHA, Youth Organizations

Application Procedures

Initial Contact: Send a written description of the capital improvement or replacement project including an estimate of the cost.
Deadlines: approximately June 1 and December 1.

Restrictions

Emphasis is on religious, charitable, and educational organizations in Chautauqua County, NY, which the Hultquist family supported during their lifetimes.

Foundation Officials
Thomas J. Flowers: president
Charles H. Price: vice president
Robert F. Rohm, Jr.: secretary, treasurer
William L. Wright: vice president

Grants Analysis
Disclosure Period: fiscal year ending June 30, 2002
Total Grants: $1,169,339*
Number of Grants: 18
Average Grant: $31,289*
Highest Grant: $250,000
Lowest Grant: $2,500
Typical Range: $20,000 to $50,000
*Note: Giving excludes United Way. Average grant figure excludes three highest grants ($700,000).

Recent Grants
Note: Grants derived from fiscal 2000 Form 990.

Library-Related
70,000	Chautauqua-Cattaraugus Library System, Chautauqua, NY

General
313,000	Chautauqua Institution, Jamestown, NY -- endowment
250,000	Lutheran Social Services, Jamestown, NY -- building fund
200,000	Jamestown Community College, Jamestown, NY -- building fund
60,000	YMCA - Jamestown, Jamestown, NY -- building operation
40,000	Chautauqua Striders, Chautauqua, NY -- educational
38,723	J. Predergast Library, Jamestown, NY -- literacy program
25,000	Roger Tory Peterson Institute, Jamestown, NY
20,000	Chautauqua Haz. Mat. Team, Inc., Chautauqua, NY
20,000	United Way South Chautauqua County, Jamestown, NY -- annual fund
20,000	University of Buffalo Foundation, Buffalo, NY

HUMANA, INC.

Company Headquarters
Louisville, KY
Web: http://www.humana.com

Company Description
Founded: 1961
Ticker: HUM
Exchange: NYSE
Assets: US$4.6 billion (2002)
Profit: US$142.8 million (2002)
Employees: 13500 (2002)
Fortune Rank: 169, per FORTUNE Magazine's list of 500 Largest U.S. Corporations (2002).
SIC(s): 6321 Accident & Health Insurance, 6324 Hospital & Medical Service Plans, 6411 Insurance Agents, Brokers & Service, 8062 General Medical & Surgical Hospitals.

Operating Locations
Humana, Inc. (AL; AZ; DC; FL--Jacksonville; KS; KY--Lexington, Louisville; MO; OH; TX--San Antonio)

Humana Foundation

Giving Contact
Virginia Kelly-Judd
500 West Main Street
Louisville, KY 40202
Phone: (502)580-3613
Fax: (502)580-1256

E-mail: BWright@Humana.com
Web: http://www.humanafoundation.org

Alternate Contact
PO Box 740026
Louisville, KY 40201-7426

Description
EIN: 611004763
Organization Type: Corporate Foundation
Giving Locations: AL: Birmingham; CA: Claremont; CO: Pine; CT: New Haven; DC: Washington; KY: Lexington, Louisville, Murray; MN: St. Peter; NJ: Princeton; NY: New York; NC: Chapel Hill; SC: Columbia; TN: Memphis; VT: Middlebury; WI: Green Bay principally near operating locations and to national organizations.
Grant Types: Capital, Conference/Seminar, Department, Employee Matching Gifts, Endowment, General Support, Project, Research, Scholarship.
Note: Employee matching gift ratio: 1 to 1 for contributions made by officers and board of directors members only.

Financial Summary
Total Giving: $4,770,747 (2001); $4,418,131 (2000); $4,374,755 (1999). Note: Contributes through corporate direct giving program and foundation.
Giving Analysis: Giving for 2000 includes: foundation grants to United Way ($192,000); foundation scholarships ($521,668); foundation ($3,704,463); 1999: foundation grants to United Way ($197,500); foundation scholarships ($810,150); foundation ($3,367,105); 1998: foundation grants to United Way ($308,000); foundation ($8,990,267);
Assets: $47,434,063 (2001); $55,011,694 (2000); $47,896,016 (1999)
Gifts Received: $4,500,000 (2000); $6,746,773 (1994); $1,804,184 (1993). Note: Gifts are received from Humana Inc.

Typical Recipients
Arts & Humanities: Arts Associations & Councils, Arts Centers, Arts Festivals, Arts Funds, Ballet, Community Arts, Dance, Historic Preservation, History & Archaeology, Libraries, Museums/Galleries, Music, Opera, Performing Arts, Public Broadcasting, Theater, Visual Arts
Civic & Public Affairs: African American Affairs, Asian American Affairs, Botanical Gardens/Parks, Business/Free Enterprise, Civil Rights, Clubs, Community Foundations, Economic Development, Civic & Public Affairs-General, Hispanic Affairs, Housing, Legal Aid, Nonprofit Management, Philanthropic Organizations, Professional & Trade Associations, Public Policy, Rural Affairs, Urban & Community Affairs, Women's Affairs, Zoos/Aquariums
Education: Business Education, Colleges & Universities, Community & Junior Colleges, Continuing Education, Education Associations, Education Funds, Education Reform, Elementary Education (Private), Education-General, Leadership Training, Legal Education, Literacy, Medical Education, Minority Education, Preschool Education, Private Education (Precollege), Public Education (Precollege), Science/Mathematics Education, Secondary Education (Private), Special Education, Student Aid
Environment: Environment-General, Resource Conservation
Health: AIDS/HIV, Cancer, Children's Health/Hospitals, Clinics/Medical Centers, Diabetes, Emergency/Ambulance Services, Eyes/Blindness, Health-General, Health Organizations, Heart, Hospitals, Medical Research, Mental Health, Nursing Services, Prenatal Health Issues, Public Health, Respiratory, Single-Disease Health Associations

International: Foreign Educational Institutions, Human Rights, International Relations, International Relief Efforts
Religion: Churches, Dioceses, Religious Organizations, Religious Welfare
Science: Science Museums, Scientific Centers & Institutes, Scientific Organizations
Social Services: Animal Protection, Child Welfare, Community Centers, Community Service Organizations, Emergency Relief, Family Planning, Family Services, Food/Clothing Distribution, Homes, People with Disabilities, Recreation & Athletics, Scouts, Senior Services, United Funds/United Ways, YMCA/YWCA/YMHA/YWHA, Youth Organizations

Application Procedures
Initial Contact: Request an application from the foundation or obtain one from the foundation's web site.
Application Requirements: Include a description of organization amount requested, purpose of funds sought, other funding commitments to date, and copy of IRS tax-exemption letter. Scholarship applications should be submitted directly to Citizens Scholarship Foundation of America Inc. and are available from the foundation.
Deadlines: None; except for February 1 application deadline for Humana Foundation Scholarship Program.
Evaluative Criteria: The foundation evaluates applicants on their ability to improve the quality of life in communities where Humana has a business presence and the organization's level of community support.
Decision Notification: The foundation responds promptly to applications, either rejecting them or requesting full proposals; final decisions are made by the contributions committee within about three months.
Notes: Applications from organizations in the Louisville, KY area should be directed to the foundation's corporate office in Louisville. Applications from organizations outside of the Louisville area should be submitted to a local Humana market office; a list of market office mailing addresses is available on the foundation's web site (www.humana.com/agent/localsales.asp).

Restrictions
Does not support requests for seed money; social, labor, political, veterans, or fraternal organizations; religious organizations, except for fully accredited public or private religious educational institutions that possess 501(c)(3) status; requests to be used solely for an organization's salary or other administrative costs; or lobbying efforts or political action committees.

Recipient organizations must be 501(c)3 according to IRS regulations.

Additional Information
Scholarships are awarded to children of full-time Humana employees.
Publications: Application Form

Corporate Officials
David Allen Jones: co-founder, chairman, director B Louisville, KY 1931. ED University of Louisville BS (1954); Yale University JD (1960). PRIM CORP EMPL co-founder, chairman, director: Humana, Inc. CORP AFFIL director: Abbott Laboratories. NONPR AFFIL member: Louisville Chamber of Commerce.

Foundation Officials
Michael E. Gellert: director
David A. Jones, Jr.: director

David Allen Jones: chairman, chief executive officer, director (see above)
Joan O. Lenahan: secretary
Brett J. McIntyre: vice president, treasurer
James E. Murray: chief operating officer ED University of Dayton BS (1975). PRIM CORP EMPL vice president, chief financial officer: Humana, Inc. CORP AFFIL vice president, controller, director: Humana Health Plan Inc.

Grants Analysis

Disclosure Period: calendar year ending 2001
Total Grants: $4,007,997*
Number of Grants: 72
Average Grant: $55,667
Highest Grant: $491,133
Lowest Grant: $650
Typical Range: $2,500 to $50,000 and $100,000 to $334,000
***Note:** Giving excludes scholarship and United Way.

Recent Grants

Note: Grants derived from 2001 Form 990.

Library-Related
15,000	Louisville Free Public Library Foundation, Louisville, KY -- for Youth Summer Reading Program

General
506,250	Citizen's Scholarship Foundation, Santa Ana, CA -- scholarships for children
491,133	American Red Cross, Washington, DC -- for liberty fund for NY, DC and PA disaster relief
333,333	Louisville Science Center, Louisville, KY -- capital campaign for the World Within Us Exhibit
311,000	University Pediatrics Foundation, Louisville, KY -- for Romania/Poland Projects
225,000	Greater Louisville Fund for the Arts, Louisville, KY
200,000	Owsley Brown Frazier Historical Arms Museum Foundation, Louisville, KY -- capital campaign for new arms museum
200,000	University of Kentucky, Lexington, KY -- for library
199,000	Metro United Way, Louisville, KY
120,000	University of Alabama at Birmingham, Birmingham, AL -- capital campaign
112,000	University of Louisville Foundation, Louisville, KY -- salary support for international projects

JAQUELIN HUME FOUNDATION

Giving Contact

Gisele Huff, Executive Director
600 Montgomery St., Suite 2800
San Francisco, CA 94111
Phone: (415)705-5115

Description

Founded: 1962
EIN: 946080099
Organization Type: Private Foundation
Giving Locations: CA: San Francisco Bay area
Grant Types: General Support, Operating Expenses, Project.

Donor Information

Founder: Jaquelin H. Hume, Caroline H. Hume

Financial Summary

Total Giving: $7,892,427 (2000); $4,604,454 (1999); $1,861,750 (1998)
Giving Analysis: Giving for 2000 includes: foundation grants to United Way ($4,000); 1999: foundation grants to United Way ($4,000) 1998: foundation grants to United Way ($3,600)
Assets: $36,101,738 (2000); $39,174,690 (1998); $25,247,040 (1996)
Gifts Received: $5,453,158 (2000); $80,000 (1994); $292,304 (1993). Note: In 1994 and 2000, contributions were received from Caroline H. Hume.

Typical Recipients

Arts & Humanities: Ballet, Community Arts, History & Archaeology, Libraries, Museums/Galleries, Music, Opera, Public Broadcasting, Theater
Civic & Public Affairs: Botanical Gardens/Parks, Business/Free Enterprise, Civil Rights, Economic Development, Economic Policy, Civic & Public Affairs-General, Law & Justice, Legal Aid, Municipalities/Towns, Nonprofit Management, Philanthropic Organizations, Professional & Trade Associations, Public Policy, Safety, Women's Affairs, Zoos/Aquariums
Education: Arts/Humanities Education, Colleges & Universities, Economic Education, Education Associations, Education Funds, Education Reform, Environmental Education, Faculty Development, Education-General, Education-General, Leadership Training, Private Education (Precollege), Public Education (Precollege), Secondary Education (Public), Social Sciences Education, Student Aid
Environment: Environment-General, Resource Conservation, Wildlife Protection
Health: AIDS/HIV, Alzheimers Disease, Diabetes, Emergency/Ambulance Services, Health Policy/Cost Containment, Hospices, Hospitals, Research/Studies Institutes, Speech & Hearing
International: Foreign Arts Organizations, Foreign Educational Institutions, Health Care/Hospitals, Human Rights, International Affairs, International Organizations, International Peace & Security Issues
Religion: Churches, Religious Organizations, Religious Welfare
Science: Observatories & Planetariums, Science Museums, Scientific Centers & Institutes
Social Services: Child Welfare, Community Service Organizations, Community Service Organizations, Family Services, Food/Clothing Distribution, People with Disabilities, Recreation & Athletics, Shelters/Homelessness, United Funds/United Ways, Youth Organizations

Application Procedures

Initial Contact: Send a preliminary one-page letter.
Application Requirements: Outline the objectives and significance of the proposed project, the design of the project, and the qualifications of the organization and its individuals. Include recently audited financial statement, a projected budget for the project, amount requested, and support sought from other funders.
Deadlines: None.

Additional Information

Publications: Program Guidelines

Foundation Officials

Claire M. Collette: assistant secretary, assistant treasurer
Gisele Huff: executive director, assistant secretary, assistant treasurer
Caroline H. Hume: president, trustee
George H. Hume: first vice president, secretary, trustee
William J. Hume: second vice president, treasurer, trustee
Edward A. Landry: assistant secretary, assistant treasurer B New Orleans, LA 1939. ED Louisiana State University BA (1961); University of California, Los Angeles JD (1964). PRIM CORP EMPL attorney: Musick, Peeler & Garrett.
Walter H. Sullivan, Jr.: trustee

Grants Analysis

Disclosure Period: calendar year ending 2000
Total Grants: $7,888,427*
Number of Grants: 41
Average Grant: $70,016*
Highest Grant: $4,646,250
Typical Range: $50,000 to $100,000
***Note:** Giving excludes United Way. Average grant figure excludes two highest grants

Recent Grants

Note: Grants derived from 2000 Form 990.

Library-Related
105,000	Intercollegiate Studies Institute, Wilmington, DE

General
429,519	Foundation for Teaching Economics, Davis, CA
250,000	Center for Education Reform, Washington, DC
200,000	Center for Equal Opportunity, Washington, DC
200,000	Center for Individual Rights, Washington, DC
150,000	Public Agenda, New York, NY
125,000	Federalist Society for Law and Public Policy Studies, Washington, DC
110,000	Institute for Human Studies, Fairfax, VA
100,000	American Academy for Liberal Education, Washington, DC
100,000	American Enterprise Institute, Washington, DC
100,000	CATO, Washington, DC

GEORGE M. AND PAMELA S. HUMPHREY FUND

Giving Contact

Jackie A. Horning, Secretary & Treasurer
c/o Advisory Services, Inc.
1422 Euclid Ave., Suite 1010
Cleveland, OH 44115-2078
Phone: (216)363-6483

Description

Founded: 1951
EIN: 346513798
Organization Type: Private Foundation
Giving Locations: FL; GA; MA; OH
Grant Types: Capital, Emergency, Endowment, General Support, Multiyear/Continuing Support, Operating Expenses, Professorship, Research.

Donor Information

Founder: George M. Humphrey, the late Pamela S. Humphrey

Financial Summary

Total Giving: $612,370 (2001); $726,450 (2000); $777,950 (1999)
Giving Analysis: Giving for 2001 includes: foundation grants to United Way ($36,000); 1999: foundation scholarships ($5,000); foundation grants to United Way ($40,000) 1997: foundation grants to United Way ($40,000)
Assets: $13,433,192 (2001); $14,805,106 (2000); $15,508,519 (1999)

Typical Recipients

Arts & Humanities: Arts Associations & Councils, Historic Preservation, History & Archaeology, Libraries, Museums/Galleries, Music, Opera, Public Broadcasting, Theater
Civic & Public Affairs: Botanical Gardens/Parks, Economic Development, Employment/Job Training,

Civic & Public Affairs-General, Housing, Municipalities/Towns, Parades/Festivals, Philanthropic Organizations, Urban & Community Affairs, Women's Affairs
Education: Arts/Humanities Education, Colleges & Universities, Education-General, Medical Education, Private Education (Precollege), Special Education, Student Aid
Environment: Forestry, Environment-General, Research, Resource Conservation, Wildlife Protection
Health: AIDS/HIV, Cancer, Children's Health/Hospitals, Children's Health/Hospitals, Emergency/Ambulance Services, Eyes/Blindness, Hospitals, Hospitals (University Affiliated), Long-Term Care, Medical Rehabilitation, Medical Research, Multiple Sclerosis, Nursing Services, Single-Disease Health Associations, Speech & Hearing
Religion: Churches, Jewish Causes, Religious Welfare
Science: Science Museums, Scientific Centers & Institutes, Scientific Research
Social Services: Camps, Child Welfare, Community Centers, Community Service Organizations, Family Planning, Family Services, Food/Clothing Distribution, People with Disabilities, Recreation & Athletics, Senior Services, Substance Abuse, United Funds/United Ways, Volunteer Services

Application Procedures

Initial Contact: Send a brief letter of inquiry.
Application Requirements: Include amount requested and purpose of funds sought.
Deadlines: Prior to meetings held in September each year.

Restrictions

Does not support individuals or provide loans.

Additional Information

Publications: Annual Report

Foundation Officials

Peter Webster Adams: trustee B Cleveland, OH 1939. ED Yale University (1961). PRIM CORP EMPL senior vice president: Alliance Capital Management Corp.
Alice B. Burnham: trustee
Carol H. Butler: president, trustee
Jackie A. Horning: secretary, treasurer
Pamela B. Keefe: trustee

Grants Analysis

Disclosure Period: calendar year ending 2001
Total Grants: $576,370*
Number of Grants: 28
Average Grant: $7,549*
Typical Range: $1,000 to $30,000
*****Note:** Giving excludes United Way. Average grant excludes two highest grants ($365,000).

Recent Grants

Note: Grants derived from 2001 Form 990.

General

275,000	Hathaway Brown School, Shaker Heights, OH -- capital campaign
90,000	Benjamin Rose Institute, Cleveland, OH -- capital campaign
50,000	Rainbow Babies and Children's Hospital, Cleveland, OH -- pediatric surgical facilities
35,000	Cleveland Botanical Garden, Cleveland, OH -- operating support
31,000	United Way Services, Cleveland, OH -- operating support
25,000	University Hospitals of Cleveland, Cleveland, OH -- Department of Ophthalmology
20,000	Cleveland Museum of Natural History, Cleveland, OH -- planetarium facility
10,000	Foundation Center, Cleveland, OH -- endowment fund
10,000	Miss Hall's School, Pittsfield, MA -- capital campaign
10,000	Tall Timbers Research, Tallahassee, FL -- quail research initiative

H. P. AND ANNE S. HUNNICUTT FOUNDATION

Giving Contact

William Stafford, Jr.
c/o First Community Bank
PO Box 309
Princeton, WV 24740
Phone: (304)425-9259

Description

Founded: 1987
EIN: 550670462
Organization Type: Private Foundation
Giving Locations: WV: Southern West Virginia
Grant Types: General Support.

Donor Information

Founder: the late H. P. Hunnicutt, the late Anne S. Hunnicutt

Financial Summary

Total Giving: $1,046,857 (fiscal year ending June 30, 2001); $1,052,216 (fiscal 2000); $2,194,420 (fiscal 1999)
Assets: $37,067,432 (fiscal 2001); $20,982,643 (fiscal 2000); $27,538,578 (fiscal 1999)
Gifts Received: $7,115,860 (fiscal 1995)

Typical Recipients

Arts & Humanities: Libraries, Performing Arts
Civic & Public Affairs: Employment/Job Training, Civic & Public Affairs-General, Municipalities/Towns, Safety, Urban & Community Affairs
Education: Education Funds, Private Education (Precollege), Public Education (Precollege), Science/Mathematics Education, Secondary Education (Private), Secondary Education (Public)
Health: Emergency/Ambulance Services, Medical Research, Public Health
Religion: Churches, Religious Welfare
Social Services: Community Service Organizations, Recreation & Athletics, Substance Abuse, Youth Organizations

Application Procedures

Initial Contact: Send a brief letter of inquiry describing program or project.
Deadlines: None.

Additional Information

Trust(s): First Community Bank

Foundation Officials

James H. Sarver, II: treasurer
James H. Sarver: vice president
William Stafford, II: secretary
William P. Stafford: president

Grants Analysis

Disclosure Period: fiscal year ending June 30, 2001
Total Grants: $1,046,857
Number of Grants: 22
Average Grant: $22,343*
Highest Grant: $350,000
Lowest Grant: $229
Typical Range: $10,000 to $40,000
*****Note:** Average grant figure excludes two highest grants ($600,000).

Recent Grants

Note: Grants derived from fiscal 2000 Form 990.

General

980,216	Mercer County Board of Education, Princeton, WV -- athletic facilities
50,000	First United Methodist Church, Princeton, WV -- charitable
10,000	Concord United Methodist Church, Athens, WV -- charitable
3,923	Princeton Senior High School, Princeton, WV -- project graduation
2,600	Pikeview High School, Princeton, WV -- project graduation
2,520	Bluefield High School, Bluefield, WV -- project graduation
2,000	Pisgah United Methodist Church -- charitable
717	Montcalm High School, Montcalm, WV -- project graduation
240	Mercer Christian Academy, Princeton, WV -- project graduation

C. GILES HUNT CHARITABLE TRUST

Giving Contact

c/o Wells Fargo Bank of Oregon NA
PO Box 53456
Eugene, OR 97401
Phone: (541)465-5952

Description

Founded: 1974
EIN: 237428278
Organization Type: Private Foundation
Giving Locations: OR: Douglas County
Grant Types: Capital, Endowment, General Support.

Donor Information

Founder: the late C. Giles Hunt

Financial Summary

Total Giving: $308,166 (2002); $305,934 (2001); $365,643 (2000)
Assets: $5,434,618 (2002); $6,375,935 (2001); $6,343,493 (2000)

Typical Recipients

Arts & Humanities: Arts Associations & Councils, Community Arts, Arts & Humanities-General, Historic Preservation, History & Archaeology, Libraries, Music, Theater
Civic & Public Affairs: Botanical Gardens/Parks, Clubs, Community Foundations, Economic Development, Civic & Public Affairs-General, Municipalities/Towns, Parades/Festivals, Safety, Urban & Community Affairs
Education: Afterschool/Enrichment Programs, Agricultural Education, Community & Junior Colleges, Elementary Education (Public), Education-General, Literacy, Private Education (Precollege), Public Education (Precollege), Science/Mathematics Education, Secondary Education (Private), Secondary Education (Public)
Environment: Forestry, Environment-General, Wildlife Protection
Health: AIDS/HIV, Clinics/Medical Centers, Emergency/Ambulance Services, Health Organizations, Hospitals, Mental Health, Prenatal Health Issues
International: International Environmental Issues
Religion: Churches, Missionary Activities (Domestic), Religious Welfare
Science: Science Museums
Social Services: Camps, Child Welfare, Community Centers, Community Service Organizations, Counseling, Crime Prevention, Day Care, Domestic Violence, Family Planning, Family Services, Food/Clothing Distribution, People with Disabilities, Recreation &

Athletics, Scouts, Senior Services, Shelters/Homelessness, Substance Abuse, Volunteer Services, YMCA/YWCA/YMHA/YWHA, Youth Organizations

Application Procedures

Initial Contact: Send letter requesting application form.
Deadlines: February 28.

Additional Information

Publications: Application Guidelines
Trust(s): Wells Fargo OR NA

Grants Analysis

Disclosure Period: calendar year ending 2001
Total Grants: $305,934
Number of Grants: 60
Average Grant: $5,099
Highest Grant: $15,000
Typical Range: $2,000 to $15,000

Recent Grants

Note: Grants derived from 2001 Form 990.

Library-Related

6,800	Winston Branch Library, Winston, OR
6,425	Glendale Library Branch of the Douglas County, Glendale, OR
6,000	Reedsport Branch Library, Reedsport, OR

General

15,000	Cobb Street Children's Learning Center, Roseburg, OR
15,000	Sutherlin Lions Club, Sutherlin, OR
11,232	Umpqua Community College, Roseburg, OR
10,750	Safarj Game Search Foundation, Winston, OR
10,000	South Umpqua School District 19, Roseburg, OR
10,000	Friendly Kitchen, Roseburg, OR
10,000	Myrtle Creek Volunteer Fire Department, Myrtle Creek, OR
8,000	Umpqua Valley Endowment Foundation, Winchester, OR
8,000	Wilani Council Camp Fire Boys and Girls, Roseburg, OR
7,500	Umpqua Discovery Center, Reedsport, OR

HUNT CORP.

Company Headquarters

1 Commerce Sq.
2005 Market St.
Philadelphia, PA 19103-7085
Web: http://www.hunt-corp.com

Company Description

Ticker: HUN
Exchange: OTC
Former Name: Hunt Manufacturing Co..
Revenue: US$160.9 million (2001)
Employees: 900 (2001)
SIC(s): 2522 Office Furniture Except Wood, 2679 Converted Paper Products Nec, 2893 Printing Ink, 3579 Office Machines Nec.

Operating Locations

Hunt Manufacturing Co. (AL--Florence; CA--Fresno; CT--Naugatuck; KY--Florence; PA--Philadelphia; TX--Laredo; WI--Cottage Grove)

Nonmonetary Support

Value: $5,000 (1998)
Type: Donated Products

Giving Contact

Cheryl M. Walmsley, Grant Administrator
1 Commerce Sq.
2005 Market St.
Philadelphia, PA 19103-7085
Phone: (215)841-2398
Fax: (215)656-3714
E-mail: cheryl_walmsley@Hunt-Corp.com

Description

Organization Type: Corporate Giving Program
Giving Locations: headquarters.
Grant Types: Capital, Employee Matching Gifts, General Support, Project, Seed Money.

Financial Summary

Total Giving: $200,000 (fiscal year ending November 30, 2000 approx); $200,000 (fiscal 1999 approx); $379,185 (fiscal 1995). Note: Contributes through corporate direct giving program only. Foundation became defunct as of 1997. 1995 Giving includes foundation($302,525); matching gifts ($70,660).
Assets: $444 (fiscal 1995)

Typical Recipients

Arts & Humanities: Arts Appreciation, Arts Associations & Councils, Arts Centers, Ballet, Community Arts, Dance, Arts & Humanities-General, Libraries, Museums/Galleries, Music, Opera, Performing Arts, Public Broadcasting, Theater, Visual Arts
Civic & Public Affairs: Clubs, Economic Development, Economic Policy, Employment/Job Training, Legal Aid, Safety, Urban & Community Affairs
Education: Afterschool/Enrichment Programs, Arts/Humanities Education, Business-School Partnerships, Colleges & Universities, Community & Junior Colleges, Elementary Education (Private), Literacy, Public Education (Precollege), Secondary Education (Public), Student Aid, Vocational & Technical Education
Health: AIDS/HIV, Children's Health/Hospitals
International: International Affairs
Religion: Ministries
Science: Scientific Centers & Institutes
Social Services: Big Brother/Big Sister, Child Abuse, Child Welfare, Counseling, Domestic Violence, Family Services, Food/Clothing Distribution, Senior Services, United Funds/United Ways, YMCA/YWCA/YMHA/YWHA, Youth Organizations

Application Procedures

Initial Contact: brief letter or proposal
Application Requirements: name of organization and contact person; a description of organization and its programs; copy of current year budget and most recently audited financial statements; copy of IRS determination letter; NAA number, if organization has received designation as a Neighborhood Assistance Act organization; and if requesting project support, include description of project including objectives, methodology, budget, key staff, sources of funding, and expected results
Deadlines: March 15 and September 15
Decision Notification: at Contributions Committee meetings held twice a year, usually during April and October
Notes: Does not make contributions in response to telephone solicitations. Grantees are required to submit applications on an annual basis.

Restrictions

Company generally does not provide general support, endowment funds or building funds to schools, colleges or universities. However, grants may be made to both educational institutions and non-profit educational organizations for specific educational programs.

Support for national appeals is minimal. Contributions to fund-raising dinners, testimonials, and courtesy advertising are not made to individuals or for religious, social, or political purposes. Grants for building and capital campaigns, general support for education and health care institutions, and endowments are made only in exceptional cases. No telephone or fax solicitations.

Additional Information

Company's goal is to donate 3% of pretax profits to charitable organizations.

Favors applications that leverage company funds with monies from other sources. Encourages proposals for specific projects instead of general operating support. In 1998, the company reported that the foundation is inactive.

The company only funds a project for three consecutive years. Organization must wait one year before reapplying for grants.

Corporate Officials

William Everett Chandler: senior vice president finance, secretary, chief financial officer B Chattanooga, TN 1943. ED University of Florida BSBA (1965); University of Florida (1966). PRIM CORP EMPL senior vice president finance, secretary, chief financial officer: Hunt Co. CORP AFFIL treasurer: Hunt Holdings Inc.; secretary: Hunt Graphics America Corp. NONPR AFFIL member: Financial Executives Institute.
Kathleen Essex: vice president human resources PRIM CORP EMPL vice president human resources: Hunt Manufacturing Co.
Donald L. Thompson: chairman, chief executive officer B 1941. ED University of Vermont (1962); State University of New Jersey (1971). PRIM CORP EMPL chairman, chief executive officer, president: Hunt Corp.

Giving Program Officials

William Everett Chandler: secretary B Chattanooga, TN 1943. ED University of Florida BSBA (1965); University of Florida (1966). PRIM CORP EMPL senior vice president finance, secretary, chief financial officer: Hunt Co. CORP AFFIL treasurer: Hunt Holdings Inc.; secretary: Hunt Graphics America Corp. NONPR AFFIL member: Financial Executives Institute.
Kathleen Essex: member PRIM CORP EMPL vice president human resources: Hunt Manufacturing Co.
Donald L. Thompson: B 1941. ED University of Vermont (1962); State University of New Jersey (1971). PRIM CORP EMPL chairman, chief executive officer, president: Hunt Corp.
Cheryl M. Walmsley: grant administrator

Grants Analysis

Disclosure Period: fiscal year ending November 30, 1999
Total Grants: $300,000*
Number of Grants: 30
Average Grant: $2,000
Highest Grant: $20,000
Typical Range: $1,000 to $5,000
*Note: Grants analysis provided by the co. A more recent grants list was unavailable.

Recent Grants

Note: Grants derived from fiscal 1996 Form 990.

General

9,000	United Way Southeastern Pennsylvania, Philadelphia, PA
4,000	Family Services, Philadelphia, PA
4,000	Village of Arts and Humanities, Philadelphia, PA
3,000	Philadelphia Futures, Philadelphia, PA
2,000	AIDS Law Project, Philadelphia, PA
2,000	Brandywine Workshop, Philadelphia, PA
2,000	Print Club, Philadelphia, PA
2,000	Settlement Music School, Philadelphia, PA

ROY A. HUNT FOUNDATION

Giving Contact

Torrence M. Hunt, Jr., President & Trustee
One Bigelow Square, Suite 630
Pittsburgh, PA 15219-3030
Phone: (412)281-8734
Fax: (412)255-0522
Web: http://www.rahuntfdn.org

Description

Founded: 1966
EIN: 256105162
Organization Type: Family Foundation
Giving Locations: MA: Boston; PA: Pittsburgh limited national giving.
Grant Types: Capital, General Support, Operating Expenses.

Donor Information

Founder: The Roy A. Hunt Foundation was established in 1966, with funds bequeathed by Roy A. Hunt, former president and chairman of the executive committee of Alcoa. Mr. Hunt was an alumnus of Shady Side Academy and Yale University, and a trustee of the Carnegie Institute of Technology (now Carnegie-Mellon University). Each of these institutions traditionally receives support from the foundation.

Mr. Hunt and his wife founded the Hunt Institute for Botanical Documentation at Carnegie-Mellon in 1961. This institute was formed to receive and supervise Mrs. Hunt's large botanical collections, and remains a substantial recipient of the foundation's annual grants. The late Mr. Hunt and members of his family also set up the Hunt Foundation in 1951.

Financial Summary

Total Giving: $3,790,039 (fiscal year ending May 31, 2002); $3,694,131 (fiscal 2001); $2,610,004 (fiscal 2000)
Giving Analysis: Giving for fiscal 2002 includes: foundation scholarships ($5,000); foundation grants to United Way ($35,500); fiscal 2000: foundation scholarships ($5,500) foundation grants to United Way ($30,500)
Assets: $83,224,914 (fiscal 2002); $94,754,273 (fiscal 2001); $85,632,613 (fiscal 2000)

Typical Recipients

Arts & Humanities: Arts Associations & Councils, Arts Centers, Arts Festivals, Dance, Film & Video, Historic Preservation, History & Archaeology, Libraries, Museums/Galleries, Music, Opera, Performing Arts, Public Broadcasting, Theater
Civic & Public Affairs: Botanical Gardens/Parks, Business/Free Enterprise, Clubs, Civic & Public Affairs-General, Native American Affairs, Philanthropic Organizations, Professional & Trade Associations, Urban & Community Affairs, Zoos/Aquariums
Education: Agricultural Education, Arts/Humanities Education, Colleges & Universities, Environmental Education, Education-General, International Exchange, International Studies, Private Education (Precollege), Public Education (Precollege), School Volunteerism, Science/Mathematics Education, Science/Mathematics Education, Social Sciences Education, Special Education
Environment: Environment-General, Resource Conservation, Wildlife Protection
Health: AIDS/HIV, Alzheimers Disease, Cancer, Children's Health/Hospitals, Clinics/Medical Centers, Health Organizations, Hospitals, Medical Rehabilitation, Mental Health, Single-Disease Health Associations
International: Foreign Arts Organizations, Foreign Educational Institutions, International Environmental Issues, International Relations
Religion: Churches, Ministries, Religious Welfare

Science: Science Museums, Scientific Centers & Institutes, Scientific Research
Social Services: Animal Protection, Big Brother/Big Sister, Camps, Child Welfare, Community Centers, Community Service Organizations, Family Planning, Recreation & Athletics, Shelters/Homelessness, Substance Abuse, United Funds/United Ways, YMCA/YWCA/YMHA/YWHA, Youth Organizations

Application Procedures

Initial Contact: Contact foundation for application guidelines and deadlines.

Restrictions

The foundation does not support gifts to individuals.

Foundation Officials

Dr. Helen Hunt Bouscaren: trustee
Susan Hunt Hollingsworth: trustee
Andrew McQ. Hunt: trustee PRIM CORP EMPL president: Fitness & Exercise Supply Co.
Cathryn J. Hunt: trustee
Christopher M. Hunt, MD: trustee
Daniel K. Hunt: trustee
John Bankson Hunt: trustee B Pittsburgh, PA 1956. ED Boston University BS (1979). CORP AFFIL treasurer: Micro Serve New England. NONPR AFFIL treasurer, director: Rindge Historical Society; chairman: Rindge Rep Town Budget Committee; member: New Hampshire State House Representatives.
Dr. Richard M. Hunt: trustee, donor son
Dr. Roy A. Hunt, III: trustee
Torrence M. Hunt, Jr.: president, trustee B 1948. ED University of North Carolina (1970). PRIM CORP EMPL vice president, director: Elmhurst Corp. CORP AFFIL treasurer: Dahlia Development Corp. CLUB AFFIL Rolling Rock Club; Fox Chapel Golf Club; Pittsburgh Club.
Torrence M. Hunt: trustee, donor son ED Williams College (1944). CORP AFFIL vice president, director: Allegheny Cemetery. CLUB AFFIL Rolling Rock Golf Club; Fox Chapel Golf Club; Pittsburgh Golf Club.
William Edwards Hunt: trustee B Columbus, OH 1921. ED Ohio State University BA (1943); Ohio State University MD (1945). PRIM NONPR EMPL mem attending staff: Ohio State University Hospitals. CORP AFFIL president: Elmhurst Corp. NONPR AFFIL member: Society International Chirurgie; member: Society Neuroscience; member: Royal Society Medicine; member: Sigma Xi; member: Ohio State Medicine Association; member: Phi Beta Kappa; member: Neurosurgical Society America; member: Ohio Saint Neurosurgical Society; member: American Surgical Association; member: Congress Neurological Surgeons; member: American College Surgeons; member: American Medical Association; member: Academy Medicine Columbus & Franklin County; member: Alpha Omega Alpha.
Marion Hunt Badiner: trustee
Rachel Hunt Knowles: trustee

Grants Analysis

Disclosure Period: fiscal year ending May 31, 2002
Total Grants: $3,623,631*
Number of Grants: 523
Average Grant: $6,929
Highest Grant: $150,000
Typical Range: $5,000 to $10,000
*Note: Giving excludes scholarships and United Way.

Recent Grants

Note: Grants derived from 2000 Form 990.

General

100,000	National Parks and Conservation Association, Washington, DC
50,000	Carnegie Institute, Pittsburgh, PA -- Aluminum Exhibit
30,000	Weekapaug Foundation for Conservation, Westerly, RI -- purchase of Noyes Neck Farm

25,000	Center for the Development of Teen Empowerment Programs, Boston, MA -- youth violence program
25,000	East End Cooperative Ministry, Pittsburgh, PA -- youth violence
25,000	Phipps Conservatory, Inc., Pittsburgh, PA -- capital campaign for New Visitor Center
25,000	Phipps Conservatory, Inc., Pittsburgh, PA -- capital campaign for New Visitor Center
25,000	Program for Young Negotiators, Cambridge, MA -- Youth Violence Program
25,000	Shady Side Academy, Pittsburgh, PA -- for Computer Center
25,000	Spirit Awakening Foundation, Santa Monica, CA -- Youth Violence Program

SAMUEL P. HUNT FOUNDATION

Giving Contact

Wall Street Tower, Suite 710
555 Canal Street
Manchester, NH 03101
Phone: (603)627-1121

Description

Founded: 1951
EIN: 026004471
Organization Type: Private Foundation
Giving Locations: NH: Manchester
Grant Types: Capital, Conference/Seminar, Emergency, General Support, Multiyear/Continuing Support, Project, Research, Seed Money.

Donor Information

Founder: the late Samuel P. Hunt

Financial Summary

Total Giving: $725,980 (fiscal year ending September 30, 2001); $742,819 (fiscal 1999); $563,108 (fiscal 1998)
Giving Analysis: Giving for fiscal 1999 includes: foundation grants to United Way ($25,000)
Assets: $14,067,287 (fiscal 2001); $16,188,641 (fiscal 1999); $13,838,512 (fiscal 1998)

Typical Recipients

Arts & Humanities: Arts Associations & Councils, Arts Centers, Arts Funds, Arts Institutes, Community Arts, Historic Preservation, History & Archaeology, Libraries, Museums/Galleries, Music, Opera, Performing Arts, Public Broadcasting, Theater, Visual Arts
Civic & Public Affairs: Community Foundations, Ethnic Organizations, Hispanic Affairs, Housing, Law & Justice, Municipalities/Towns, Parades/Festivals, Urban & Community Affairs
Education: Afterschool/Enrichment Programs, Agricultural Education, Arts/Humanities Education, Business Education, Colleges & Universities, Environmental Education, Education-General, International Studies, Leadership Training, Private Education (Precollege), Public Education (Precollege), Science/Mathematics Education, Secondary Education (Public)
Environment: Forestry, Environment-General, Resource Conservation, Watershed, Wildlife Protection
Health: AIDS/HIV, Alzheimers Disease, Cancer, Children's Health/Hospitals, Clinics/Medical Centers, Emergency/Ambulance Services, Health Organizations, Hospices, Hospitals, Hospitals (University Affiliated), Medical Rehabilitation, Medical Research, Mental Health, Nursing Services, Public Health, Respiratory, Single-Disease Health Associations
Religion: Churches, Religious Welfare
Science: Observatories & Planetariums, Science Museums, Scientific Centers & Institutes

Social Services: Animal Protection, At-Risk Youth, Child Welfare, Community Centers, Community Service Organizations, Domestic Violence, Family Services, Food/Clothing Distribution, Homes, People with Disabilities, Recreation & Athletics, Scouts, Senior Services, Social Services-General, Substance Abuse, United Funds/United Ways, YMCA/YWCA/YMHA/YWHA, Youth Organizations

Application Procedures

Initial Contact: Send a brief letter requesting guidelines and grant application.
Deadlines: February 15 and August 15.

Restrictions

Does not support individuals or provide funds for scholarships or fellowships.

Additional Information

Publications: Program Policy Statement; Application Guidelines; Application Form
Trust(s): Citizens Bank NH

Foundation Officials

Douglas A. McIninch: co-trustee
James C. Tyrie: co-trustee

Grants Analysis

Disclosure Period: fiscal year ending September 30, 2001
Total Grants: $725,980
Number of Grants: 63
Average Grant: $11,523
Highest Grant: $50,000
Typical Range: $5,000 to $20,000

Recent Grants

Note: Grants derived from fiscal 2000 Form 990.

Library-Related

100,000	University of New Hampshire at Manchester, Manchester, NH -- for new library
25,000	Concord Public Library Foundation, Concord, NH -- for children's room renovation

General

100,000	American Red Cross, Manchester, NH -- capital campaign
80,000	Canterbury Shaker Village, Canterbury, NH -- for visitor education center
75,000	Salvation Army, Manchester, NH -- capital campaign
35,000	Manchester Historic Association, Manchester, NH -- for archivist for library collection
34,000	Nature Conservancy of New Hampshire, Concord, NH -- for construction of trail network
34,000	NE Salem Children's Trust, Rumney, NH -- for upgrading children's home
25,000	Notre Dame College, Manchester, NH -- for art gallery
25,000	Way Home, Inc., The, Manchester, NH -- for building development campaign
23,300	New Hampshire Historical Society, Concord, NH -- for partitions for exhibition
20,000	New Hampshire Community Loan Fund, Concord, NH -- for CAN training program

HUNTINGTON BANCSHARES, INC.

Company Headquarters

Huntington Center
41 South High Street, 34th Floor
Columbus, OH 43287
Web: http://www.huntington.com

Company Description

Founded: 1866
Ticker: HBAN
Exchange: NASDAQ
Assets: US$27.578 billion (2002)
Employees: 8177 (2002)
SIC(s): 6021 National Commercial Banks, 6022 State Commercial Banks, 6035 Federal Savings Institutions, 6712 Bank Holding Companies.

Operating Locations

Huntington Bancshares Inc. (FL--Orlando; IN--Indianapolis; KY--Covington; MI--Grand Rapids)

Nonmonetary Support

Type: Cause-related Marketing & Promotion; Donated Equipment; In-kind Services; Loaned Employees; Loaned Executives

Giving Contact

Elfi DiBella, Executive Vice President, Director of Community Affairs
41 S. High St.
Columbus, OH 43215
Phone: (614)480-8300
Fax: (614)480-4970
E-mail: elfi.dibella@huntington.com

Description

Organization Type: Corporate Giving Program
Giving Locations: headquarters area only; States where company has business locations.
Grant Types: Award, Capital, Challenge, Emergency, Endowment, Multiyear/Continuing Support, Operating Expenses, Professorship, Project, Research, Scholarship, Seed Money.

Financial Summary

Total Giving: $4,000,000 (2001); $3,500,000 (1997). Note: Contributes through corporate direct giving program only. Total giving is approximately 2% of Huntington's annual pre-tax earnings.

Typical Recipients

Arts & Humanities: Arts Associations & Councils, Arts Institutes, Ballet, Ethnic & Folk Arts, Arts & Humanities-General, Libraries, Museums/Galleries, Opera, Performing Arts, Theater, Visual Arts
Civic & Public Affairs: African American Affairs, Asian American Affairs, Business/Free Enterprise, Chambers of Commerce, Community Foundations, Economic Development, Employment/Job Training, Ethnic Organizations, Civic & Public Affairs-General, Housing, Inner-City Development, Minority Business, Nonprofit Management, Parades/Festivals, Philanthropic Organizations, Urban & Community Affairs, Women's Affairs, Zoos/Aquariums
Education: Agricultural Education, Business Education, Business-School Partnerships, Colleges & Universities, Community & Junior Colleges, Economic Education, Elementary Education (Private), Education-General, Health & Physical Education, International Exchange, International Studies, Minority Education, Science/Mathematics Education, Student Aid, Vocational & Technical Education
Health: Alzheimers Disease, Arthritis, Cancer, Children's Health/Hospitals, Eyes/Blindness, Health-General, Geriatric Health, Heart, Hospices, Hospitals, Hospitals (University Affiliated), Long-Term Care, Medical Research, Multiple Sclerosis, Respiratory, Speech & Hearing
International: International Affairs, International Development, Trade
Religion: Jewish Causes
Science: Science-General, Science Museums
Social Services: Animal Protection, Camps, Homes, Shelters/Homelessness, Social Services-General, United Funds/United Ways, Volunteer Services, Youth Organizations

Application Procedures

Initial Contact: Send a brief letter of inquiry.
Application Requirements: Include a description of organization, amount requested, purpose of funds sought, recently audited financial statement, and proof of tax-exempt status.
Deadlines: None. Company prefers to receive requests in summer for fall consideration of the following year's budget.

Restrictions

Does not support individuals, religious organizations for sectarian purposes, political or lobbying groups, or organizations outside operating areas.

Corporate Officials

Frank Wobst: chairman, director B Dresden, Germany 1933. ED University of Erlangen (1956); University of Goettingen (1958); Rutgers University MBA (1964). PRIM CORP EMPL chairman, director: Huntington Bancshares Inc. CORP AFFIL director: Midland Mutual Life Insurance Co.; member: Robert Morris Associates; chairman: Huntington Trust Co. NONPR AFFIL member: Greater Columbus Chamber of Commerce; member: Newcomen Society; member: American Institute Banking; member: Association Reserve City Bankers. CLUB AFFIL Sciotto Country Club.

HUNTINGTON FOUNDATION

Giving Contact

Arlene Aurthor, Executive Secretary
Huntington Foundation
517 9th Street, Suite 203
Huntington, WV 25701
Phone: (304)522-0611

Description

Founded: 1988
EIN: 550370129
Organization Type: Private Foundation
Giving Locations: WV
Grant Types: General Support.

Financial Summary

Total Giving: $426,806 (2000); $178,217 (1998); $56,786 (1997)
Assets: $6,847,384 (2000); $7,032,108 (1998); $6,979,440 (1997)
Gifts Received: $4,208 (1998); $3,410 (1997); $8,033 (1995)

Typical Recipients

Arts & Humanities: Libraries, Museums/Galleries
Civic & Public Affairs: Civic & Public Affairs-General, Municipalities/Towns, Professional & Trade Associations, Safety
Education: Colleges & Universities, Education Funds, Education-General, Medical Education, Public Education (Precollege), Science/Mathematics Education
Environment: Environment-General
Health: Geriatric Health, Hospices, Hospitals, Research/Studies Institutes
Social Services: At-Risk Youth, Child Welfare, Community Service Organizations, Domestic Violence, Family Services, People with Disabilities, Shelters/Homelessness, Social Services-General, Special Olympics, Volunteer Services, YMCA/YWCA/YMHA/YWHA, Youth Organizations

Application Procedures

Initial Contact: Request application form.
Deadlines: None.

Additional Information

Publications: Application Form

Foundation Officials

Frank E. Hanshaw, Jr.: vice president
John E. Jenkins, Jr.: director
Dr. Winfield C. John: director
Kermit E. McGinnis: secretary, treasurer
C. H. McKown: director
Cecil H. Underwood: president B Josephs Mills, WV 1922. ED Salem College BA (1943); West Virginia University MA (1952). PRIM CORP EMPL president: Morgantown Industrial Park. CORP AFFIL chairman: West Virginia Council Vocational Education; chairman,director: West Virginia Foundation Independent Coll; member: Sigma Phi Epsilon; chairman,director: Salem Teikyo University; member: Shriners; member: Rotary; president,member: National Association State Council Vocational Education; member: Pi Kappa Delta; member: Masons; member: Elks; secretary,director: Huntington Federal Savings & Loan Association; chairman,director: Applachian Regional Hospital.

Grants Analysis

Disclosure Period: calendar year ending 2000
Total Grants: $426,806
Number of Grants: 12
Average Grant: $27,942*
Highest Grant: $119,442
Lowest Grant: $2,000
Typical Range: $2,000 to $6,000 and $50,000 to $100,000
***Note:** Average grant figure excludes highest grant.

Recent Grants

Note: Grants derived from 1998 Form 990.

General

100,000	Huntington City Mission, Huntington, WV -- purchase and renovate building
70,000	Green Acres Foundations, Inc, Huntington, WV -- renovations
5,717	West Virginia Special Olympics, Huntington, WV
2,500	Educational Alliance, Huntington, WV

HURST FOUNDATION

Giving Contact

Anthony P. Hurst, President
675 Robinson Rd.
Jackson, MI 49203
Phone: (517)788-8600

Description

Founded: 1955
EIN: 386089457
Organization Type: Private Foundation
Giving Locations: MI: Jackson County
Grant Types: Capital, Operating Expenses, Project.

Donor Information

Founder: the late Peter F. Hurst, Elizabeth S. Hurst

Financial Summary

Total Giving: $424,500 (2000); $350,000 (1999 approx); $415,750 (1998)
Giving Analysis: Giving for 2000 includes: foundation grants to United Way ($25,000); 1998: foundation grants to United Way ($2,800) 1996: foundation grants to United Way ($2,000)
Assets: $9,384,605 (2000); $8,376,825 (1998); $6,795,611 (1996)

Typical Recipients

Arts & Humanities: History & Archaeology, Libraries, Museums/Galleries, Music, Public Broadcasting
Civic & Public Affairs: Botanical Gardens/Parks, Business/Free Enterprise, Clubs, Community Foundations, Employment/Job Training, Civic & Public Affairs-General, Housing, Municipalities/Towns, Parades/Festivals, Philanthropic Organizations, Professional & Trade Associations, Public Policy, Safety, Urban & Community Affairs
Education: Arts/Humanities Education, Business Education, Business-School Partnerships, Colleges & Universities, Community & Junior Colleges, Education Funds, Education Reform, Elementary Education (Public), Environmental Education, Education-General, International Studies, Preschool Education, Private Education (Precollege), Public Education (Precollege), Secondary Education (Private)
Environment: Environment-General
Health: AIDS/HIV, Alzheimers Disease, Health-General, Health Organizations, Hospices, Prenatal Health Issues, Respiratory, Speech & Hearing
International: International Organizations
Religion: Churches, Religious Organizations, Religious Welfare
Science: Observatories & Planetariums
Social Services: Animal Protection, At-Risk Youth, Camps, Child Welfare, Community Centers, Community Service Organizations, Crime Prevention, Day Care, Family Services, Homes, People with Disabilities, Recreation & Athletics, Shelters/Homelessness, Substance Abuse, United Funds/United Ways, Youth Organizations

Application Procedures

Initial Contact: Send a brief letter of inquiry and full proposal (two copies).
Application Requirements: Include a description of organization, amount requested, purpose of funds sought, recently audited financial statement, and proof of tax-exempt status. Also list of directors.
Deadlines: October 1.

Restrictions

Does not support individuals or loans.

Foundation Officials

Anthony P. Hurst: president
Ronald F. Hurst: vice president

Grants Analysis

Disclosure Period: calendar year ending 2000
Total Grants: $399,500*
Number of Grants: 42
Average Grant: $9,512
Highest Grant: $65,000
Typical Range: $5,000 to $20,000
***Note:** Giving excludes United Way.

Recent Grants

Note: Grants derived from 2001 Form 990.

General

204,200	Lily Missionary Baptist Church, Jackson, MI -- building fund
50,000	Spring Arbor College, Spring Arbor, MI -- building project
44,000	Community Respite Center, Jackson, MI -- building project
30,000	Cascade Humane Society, Jackson, MI -- building project
25,000	United Way of Jackson County, Jackson, MI -- endowment fund raising
20,000	Jackson Intermediate School, Jackson, MI -- Beaman Art Project
15,000	Disability Connection, Jackson, MI -- remodel facilities
10,000	Columbia School District, Brooklyn, MI -- joint star
10,000	Columbia School District, Brooklyn, MI -- staffing enrichment
10,000	Great Sauk Trails Boy Scout Council, Jackson, MI -- Camp facilities maintenance

STEWART HUSTON CHARITABLE TRUST

Giving Contact

Scott G. Huston, Executive Director
Lukens Executive office Building
50 S. 1st Avenue, 2nd Floor
Coatesville, PA 19320
Phone: (610)384-2666
Fax: (610)384-3396
Web: http://www.stewarthuston.org

Description

Founded: 1989
EIN: 232612599
Organization Type: Family Foundation
Giving Locations: GA: Savannah; PA: Chester County
Grant Types: Capital, Challenge, General Support, Matching, Operating Expenses, Project, Seed Money.

Donor Information

Founder: The foundation was established in 1989 in accordance with provisions left by Stewart Huston (d. 1971) in his will. He was the great-grandson of Rebecca Lukens, member of the founding family of Lukens Iron and Steel, Inc., of Coatesville, PA. Mr. Huston was an executive at Lukens Steel, and active with numerous community goups, small local business, and his church. He also was interested in Savannah, GA, the birthplace of his mother, and home of his wife, Harriet Lawrence Huston, who was an artist and a poet. The Trust has allotted money specifically for Trinitarian Evangelical activites and for secular activities, primarily for programs in Chester County, PA, and in Savannah, GA.

Financial Summary

Total Giving: $1,250,000 (2002 approx); $1,183,610 (2001); $1,989,000 (2000)
Giving Analysis: Giving for 1997 includes: foundation matching gifts ($2,725) foundation grants to United Way ($3,700)
Assets: $20,829,418 (2002); $20,829,418 (2001); $24,000,000 (2000 approx)

Typical Recipients

Arts & Humanities: Arts Outreach, Dance, Ethnic & Folk Arts, Arts & Humanities-General, Historic Preservation, History & Archaeology, Libraries, Museums/Galleries, Music, Public Broadcasting, Theater
Civic & Public Affairs: Community Foundations, Economic Development, Economic Policy, Employment/Job Training, Civic & Public Affairs-General, Housing, Nonprofit Management, Philanthropic Organizations, Public Policy, Urban & Community Affairs, Women's Affairs, Zoos/Aquariums
Education: Arts/Humanities Education, Business Education, Colleges & Universities, Continuing Education, Elementary Education (Public), Education-General, International Studies, Literacy, Private Education (Precollege), Public Education (Precollege), Religious Education, Science/Mathematics Education, Special Education, Student Aid
Environment: Resource Conservation
Health: AIDS/HIV, Children's Health/Hospitals, Clinics/Medical Centers, Health-General, Geriatric Health, Medical Rehabilitation, Mental Health, Nursing Services, Trauma Treatment
International: International Peace & Security Issues, Missionary/Religious Activities
Religion: Bible Study/Translation, Churches, Religion-General, Ministries, Missionary Activities (Domestic), Religious Organizations, Religious Welfare, Seminaries, Social/Policy Issues

Science: Observatories & Planetariums, Scientific Centers & Institutes, Scientific Labs
Social Services: Animal Protection, Child Abuse, Child Welfare, Community Centers, Community Service Organizations, Crime Prevention, Delinquency & Criminal Rehabilitation, Emergency Relief, Family Planning, Family Services, Food/Clothing Distribution, Homes, People with Disabilities, Recreation & Athletics, Senior Services, Shelters/Homelessness, Social Services-General, Substance Abuse, Volunteer Services, YMCA/YWCA/YMHA/YWHA, Youth Organizations

Application Procedures

Initial Contact: Organizations should contact the trust to request a Grant Request form. Organizations are encouraged to discuss projects with trust staff before submitting an application.
Application Requirements: A completed Grant Request form should be accompanied by a brief summary (4-6 pages) of the proposal; charitable organization registration CPA only; by-laws; most recent financial audit; list of board of directors, with community and professional affiliations; current operating budget; annual report; other sources solicited for funds; detailed project budget; media reviews of the program; other sources of funds; and a copy of the applicant's IRS tax-exempt determination letter.
Deadlines: March 1 and September 1 for religious grants; January 15 for secular grants.
Review Process: Notices of approval, rejection, or requests for additional information are sent out semi-annually in June and December.

Restrictions

The trust does not make grants to individuals, for endowments, for purchases of tickets or advertising, for operating deficits, or for publications costs. Groups such as fraternal organizations, political parties or candidates, veterans labor or local civic groups, volunteer fire companies, and groups influencing legislation will not receive support.

Additional Information

Publications: Application Form

Foundation Officials

Samuel A. Cann: trustee
Charles Lukens Huston, III: trustee B Dayton, OH 1934. ED University of Virginia; Spring Garden College (1956).
Scott G. Huston: executive director
Louis N. Seltzer: trustee

Grants Analysis

Disclosure Period: calendar year ending 2001
Total Grants: $1,183,610
Number of Grants: 113
Average Grant: $10,474
Highest Grant: $45,000
Lowest Grant: $500
Typical Range: $5,000 to $15,000

Recent Grants

Note: Grants derived from 1999 Form 990.

General

125,000	Coatesville Bible Fellowship, Coatesville, PA -- for building repair
50,000	Calvary Baptist Day School, Savannah, GA -- for science technology lab
50,000	Graystone Society, Coatesville, PA -- operating support
50,000	Greater Deliverance Church, Coatesville, PA -- construction of elevator
48,000	Calvary Baptist Day School, Savannah, GA -- construction and equipping new health and physical development facility
42,000	Salvation Army, Savannah, GA -- purchase and install auger/compactor
40,000	Bridges for Peace, Tulsa, OK -- equipment for International Headquarters
40,000	Bridges for Peace, Tulsa, OK -- for continued funding for office furniture and equipment
40,000	Coatesville Cultural Society, Coatesville, PA -- capital campaign
32,000	Salvation Army, Savannah, GA -- lights for community service baseball field

HUSTON FOUNDATION

Giving Contact

Susan B. Heilman, Executive Assistant
1 Fayette Street, Suite 190
Conshohocken, PA 19428-2064
Phone: (610)832-4949
Fax: (610)832-4960
E-mail: hustonfndn@aol.com

Description

Founded: 1957
EIN: 236284125
Organization Type: General Purpose Foundation
Giving Locations: PA: Eastern Pennsylvania nationally.
Grant Types: Capital, General Support, Matching, Operating Expenses, Project, Seed Money.
Note: The foundation also makes officer and director matching gift grants.

Donor Information

Founder: The foundation was established in 1957 by the late Charles Lukens Huston Jr. and the late Ruth Huston , as a tribute to their parents, Charles Lukens Huston, a Protestant Evangelical Christian philanthropic industrialist, and Anne Stewart Huston, a Protestant Evangelical Christian community leader.

Financial Summary

Total Giving: $1,100,000 (2002); $1,515,777 (2001); $2,059,741 (2000)
Giving Analysis: Giving for 2001 includes: foundation matching gifts ($1,000); 1999: foundation matching gifts ($1,200) 1998: foundation matching gifts ($2,000))
Assets: $32,914,000 (2002); $34,698,636 (2001); $41,302,890 (2000)

Typical Recipients

Arts & Humanities: Arts Institutes, Arts Outreach, Film & Video, Arts & Humanities-General, Historic Preservation, Libraries, Museums/Galleries, Music, Performing Arts, Public Broadcasting, Theater
Civic & Public Affairs: Community Foundations, Economic Development, Employment/Job Training, Civic & Public Affairs-General, Hispanic Affairs, Housing, Law & Justice, Municipalities/Towns, Nonprofit Management, Philanthropic Organizations, Professional & Trade Associations, Public Policy, Urban & Community Affairs, Zoos/Aquariums
Education: Afterschool/Enrichment Programs, Colleges & Universities, Education Funds, Education Reform, Education-General, Health & Physical Education, Leadership Training, Legal Education, Literacy, Medical Education, Minority Education, Preschool Education, Private Education (Precollege), Religious Education, Social Sciences Education, Special Education, Student Aid
Environment: Environment-General
Health: Children's Health/Hospitals, Clinics/Medical Centers, Emergency/Ambulance Services, Eyes/Blindness, Health Organizations, Hospices, Hospitals, Medical Rehabilitation, Medical Research, Nursing Services, Public Health, Single-Disease Health Associations
International: Foreign Educational Institutions, Health Care/Hospitals, International Organizations, Missionary/Religious Activities

Religion: Bible Study/Translation, Churches, Religion-General, Ministries, Missionary Activities (Domestic), Religious Organizations, Religious Welfare, Seminaries
Science: Observatories & Planetariums, Scientific Centers & Institutes
Social Services: At-Risk Youth, Big Brother/Big Sister, Camps, Child Abuse, Child Welfare, Community Service Organizations, Counseling, Family Planning, Family Services, Food/Clothing Distribution, Homes, People with Disabilities, Sexual Abuse, Shelters/Homelessness, Social Services-General, United Funds/United Ways, YMCA/YWCA/YMHA/YWHA, Youth Organizations

Application Procedures

Initial Contact: Send a brief letter of inquiry outlining the request. Applicants are also encouraged to call the foundation office to discuss potential projects with a program executive, and to have a Request Packet sent.
Application Requirements: 2-4 page grant proposal; IRS 990PF tax exemption letter and employee identification number; a history of the organization; a statement of faith (Protestant Evangelical Christian missions only); names of supporting organizations providing public and private funding sources, in general or for this specific project; a list of the Board of Directors; the organization's current operating budget and a detailed project budget; most recent annual/financial report; statement verifying there has been no change in purpose, character, or method of operation since the latest IRS tax letter was issued; and, where applicable, present project goals in quantifiable objectives.
Deadlines: Applicants should submit proposals by April 1 and October 1.

Restrictions

The foundation reports grants are made to religious, charitable, scientific, literary, and educational organizations. No grants are made to individuals, or for multiyear projects, grant-making organizations, endowment funds, organizations for individual or group travel purposes, fraternal organizations, political candidates or parties, veterans organizations, labor groups, social clubs, coverage of continuing operating deficits, document publication costs, for ticket purchases or benefit advertising, research, fellowships, or loans.

Additional Information

Publications: Annual Report; Informational Brochure; Application Guidelines

Foundation Officials

Charles B. Chadwick: director
Gardner H. Hansen: director
Nancy Huston Hansen: vice president evangelical relations B 1936.
Susan B. Heilman: executive assistant
Charles L. Huston, IV: treasurer
Charles Lukens Huston, III: director operations, vice president community relations B Dayton, OH 1934. ED University of Virginia; Spring Garden College (1956).
Rebecca L. Huston: secretary
Elinor Huston Lashley: vice president ed and cultural rels

Grants Analysis

Disclosure Period: calendar year ending 2001
Total Grants: $1,514,777*
Number of Grants: 208
Average Grant: $7,283
Highest Grant: $125,000
Lowest Grant: $1,000
Typical Range: $1,000 to $10,000
***Note:** Giving excludes matching gifts.

Recent Grants

Note: Grants derived from 2000 Form 990.

General

125,000	Coatesville Bible Fellowship, Coatesville, PA -- the building repair and renovation project
38,000	Episcopal Academy, Merion, PA -- stained glass windows in Houston Chapel
25,000	Good Shepherd Ministries, Washington, DC
25,000	Kingdom Princess Centerpeace Ministries, Delray Beach, FL -- support administrative and overhead costs
25,000	Sentinel Group, Lynnwood, WA -- "The Road to Transformation-Core Principles Project" three video series
20,000	Biblical Theological Seminary, Hatfield, PA -- master of Divinity-Cohart Program
20,000	Chester County Community Foundation, West Chester, PA -- the seventy and eighth payments of ten towards a commitment
20,000	Citizens Education Foundation, Yorba Linda, CA -- pre-production expenses to develop children's programming for cable Television series
20,000	Damaris Project, Dallas, TX -- general support to present, defend and spread the Gospel to women on the leading edge of our culture
20,000	Haggai Institute, Atlanta, GA -- sponsorship for three National Christian leaders to attend Haggai Institute leadership training seminar

HUTHSTEINER FINE ARTS TRUST

Giving Contact

Terry Crenshaw, Vice President & Trust Officer
c/o Chase Bank, TX
PO Drawer 140
El Paso, TX 79980
Phone: (915)546-6515

Description

Founded: 1980
EIN: 746308412
Organization Type: Private Foundation
Giving Locations: TX: West Texas
Grant Types: Emergency, Endowment, General Support, Multiyear/Continuing Support, Operating Expenses.

Donor Information

Founder: Robert and Pauline Huthsteiner Trust

Financial Summary

Total Giving: $129,700 (fiscal year ending July 31, 1999); $115,000 (fiscal 1997); $120,000 (fiscal 1996)
Assets: $3,302,908 (fiscal 1999); $2,850,997 (fiscal 1997); $2,273,420 (fiscal 1996)
Gifts Received: $416 (fiscal 1999); $500 (fiscal 1996). Note: In fiscal 1996, contributions were received from Burton Patterson.

Typical Recipients

Arts & Humanities: Arts Associations & Councils, Arts Funds, Ballet, Community Arts, Dance, Arts & Humanities-General, Libraries, Literary Arts, Museums/Galleries, Music, Opera, Performing Arts, Public Broadcasting, Theater
Civic & Public Affairs: Professional & Trade Associations
Education: Arts/Humanities Education, Colleges & Universities
International: Foreign Arts Organizations

Religion: Churches
Social Services: Community Service Organizations, Youth Organizations

Application Procedures

Initial Contact: Send a brief letter of inquiry.
Application Requirements: a description of organization, amount requested, and proof of tax-exempt status.
Deadlines: None.

Restrictions

Grants awarded to support the fine arts.

Additional Information

Trust(s): Chase Bank TX

Grants Analysis

Disclosure Period: fiscal year ending July 31, 1999
Total Grants: $129,700
Number of Grants: 27
Average Grant: $4,804
Highest Grant: $15,000
Typical Range: $1,000 to $20,000

Recent Grants

Note: Grants derived from 2000 Form 990.

General

35,000	International Museum of Art -- purchase art work
25,000	UTEP Music Department, TX -- musical instruments
12,500	El Paso Opera, El Paso, TX
12,500	El Paso Symphony, El Paso, TX
10,000	El Paso Pro Musica, El Paso, TX
10,000	UTEP Music Department, TX
6,000	KRWG - Public TV, TX
5,000	El Paso Symphony, El Paso, TX
5,000	El Paso Wind Symphony, El Paso, TX
5,000	YMCA of El Paso, El Paso, TX -- music scholarship

HYDE AND WATSON FOUNDATION

Giving Contact

Hunter W. Corbin, President
437 Southern Boulevard
Chatham, NJ 07928
Phone: (973)966-6024
Fax: (973)966-6404
Web: http://www.fdncenter.org/grantmaker/hydeandwatson

Description

Founded: 1983
EIN: 222425725
Organization Type: General Purpose Foundation
Giving Locations: NJ: Essex County, Morris County, Union County; NY: New York metropolitan area
Grant Types: Capital, Research.
Note: Funds for research are very limited.

Donor Information

Founder: The Hyde and Watson Foundation was established in 1983 through the consolidation of The Lillia Babbitt Hyde Foundation and The John Jay and Eliza Jane Watson Foundation.
Lillia Babbitt Hyde (1856-1939) was the daughter of Benjamin Talbot Babbitt, a businessman and inventor who made his fortune in the chemical industry and with mechanical products. Upon his death, he left to Lillia one-half of his estate and controlling interest in B.T. Babbitt, Inc. Lillia's name is derived from her marriage to Clarence Hyde, a New York lawyer. Lillia established The Lillia Babbitt Hyde Foundation in 1924, served as its president until her death, and left the bulk of her estate to the foundation.

John Jay Watson (1874-1939) headed two subsidiaries of U.S. Rubber Co. and organized Lee Tire and Rubber Co., which he later merged with Republic Tire and Rubber. Later in his career he headed International Minerals and Chemicals Corp., where he established a potash mine in New Mexico, freeing the United States from dependence on foreign sources. Eliza Jane Watson, John's wife, created The John Jay and Eliza Jane Watson Foundation as a tribute to her husband upon his death. The bulk of Eliza Jane's estate was donated to the foundation upon her own death in 1957.

Financial Summary

Total Giving: $4,849,400 (2001); $4,176,700 (2000); $4,300,200 (1999)
Assets: $106,913,170 (2001); $111,228,409 (2000); $107,177,296 (1999)

Typical Recipients

Arts & Humanities: Arts Associations & Councils, Arts Funds, Ethnic & Folk Arts, Historic Preservation, History & Archaeology, Libraries, Literary Arts, Museums/Galleries, Music, Opera, Performing Arts, Public Broadcasting, Theater, Visual Arts
Civic & Public Affairs: African American Affairs, Botanical Gardens/Parks, Business/Free Enterprise, Clubs, Economic Development, Employment/Job Training, Civic & Public Affairs-General, Hispanic Affairs, Inner-City Development, Nonprofit Management, Philanthropic Organizations, Public Policy, Safety, Urban & Community Affairs
Education: Afterschool/Enrichment Programs, Arts/Humanities Education, Business Education, Colleges & Universities, Education Reform, Elementary Education (Private), Engineering/Technological Education, Education-General, International Studies, Literacy, Medical Education, Minority Education, Private Education (Precollege), Public Education (Precollege), Religious Education, Science/Mathematics Education, Secondary Education (Private), Special Education, Student Aid
Environment: Air/Water Quality, Forestry, Environment-General, Protection, Resource Conservation, Watershed, Wildlife Protection
Health: Adolescent Health Issues, Alzheimers Disease, Cancer, Children's Health/Hospitals, Clinics/Medical Centers, Emergency/Ambulance Services, Eyes/Blindness, Health-General, Geriatric Health, Health Organizations, Heart, Hospices, Hospitals, Hospitals (University Affiliated), Medical Rehabilitation, Medical Research, Nursing Services, Prenatal Health Issues, Public Health, Research/Studies Institutes, Respiratory, Single-Disease Health Associations, Speech & Hearing, Transplant Networks/Donor Banks, Trauma Treatment
International: International Affairs
Religion: Churches, Jewish Causes, Religious Organizations, Religious Welfare, Seminaries
Science: Science Museums, Scientific Labs
Social Services: At-Risk Youth, Camps, Child Welfare, Community Centers, Community Service Organizations, Counseling, Day Care, Domestic Violence, Emergency Relief, Family Services, Food/Clothing Distribution, Homes, People with Disabilities, Scouts, Senior Services, Shelters/Homelessness, Social Services-General, Substance Abuse, United Funds/United Ways, YMCA/YWCA/YMHA/YWHA, Youth Organizations

Application Procedures

Initial Contact: Acquire the Grant Application Information Sheet from foundation or the foundation website, then send a full proposal.
Application Requirements: Full proposals will include completed Grant Application Information Sheet; a brief narrative (no more than three pages), signed by an appropriate officer, summarizing the background or the organization and constituency served, purpose of funds sought, project total and amount requested, and anticipated timeframe; project budget

with line items, including amount raised and balance needed; operating budget for current fiscal year; list of supporters for the most recent fiscal year; list of board of directors/trustees, with affiliations; copy of most recent audited financial report or Form 990; proof of tax-exempt status. The foundation also accepts the New York/New Jersey Area Common Application Form.

Deadlines: February 15 for review during the spring meetings and September 15 for the fall meetings.

Review Process: The foundation attempts to respond to each application. Appeals are preliminarily evaluated on an ongoing basis; therefore, early submission of appeals is encouraged.

Restrictions

The foundation does not make grants to individuals nor to applicants located outside the United States. Requests for endowment or operating support or from fiscal agents are not likely to receive favorable responses.

Additional Information

The foundation reports that it also provides investment advice and board and volunteer services to nonprofit organizations.

The foundation reports that it is affiliated with the Charles E. and Joy C. Pettinos Foundation in New Jersey.

Publications: Annual Report; Grant Application Information Sheet

Foundation Officials

Nancy A. Allocco: grant administrator, assistant secretary

Loretta J. Becht: assistant secretary

Thomas W. Berry: director, treasurer

Jennifer Chandler-Haige: director

Hunter W. Corbin: director, president, principal officer

Elizabeth R. Curry: director

H. Corbin Day: director B Orange, NJ 1937. ED Brown University BA (1959); University of Pennsylvania MBA (1963). CORP AFFIL director: Jemison Steel Co. LLC; director: Schreiber Corp. Inc.; chairman, chief executive officer, director: Jemison Investment Co. Inc.; director: Altec Industries Inc.; director: Hughes Supply Inc.

William V. Engel, Esq.: director, assistant treasurer

John W. Holman, III: director

John W. Holman, Jr.: chairman, director PRIM CORP EMPL managing director: Triak Services Corp.

G. Morrison Hubbard, Jr.: director emeritus

Anke Lofrese: assistant secretary

Brunilda Moriarty: assistant secretary

Robert W. Parsons, Jr.: director, vice chairman, assistant treasurer, section

Roger B. Parsons: director, assistant treasurer

Kate B. Wood: director NONPR AFFIL vice chairman: New Jersey Historical Society.

Grants Analysis

Disclosure Period: calendar year ending 2001

Total Grants: $4,849,400*

Number of Grants: 311

Average Grant: $15,593

Highest Grant: $225,000

Lowest Grant: $4,400

Typical Range: $5,000 to $25,000

*Note: Grants analysis provided by foundation.

Recent Grants

Note: Grants derived from 2000 Form 990.

General

200,000	Pingry Corp, Martinsville, NJ -- essential alteration and modernization of Short Hills Campus to increase effectiveness of programs
100,000	Foundation of the University of Medicine and Dentistry of New Jersey, Newark,

NJ -- purchase equipment for Child Health Institute

100,000	Frost Valley YMCA, Montclair, NJ -- purchase of adjacent property to enable future expansion of its programs, conditional upon this amount being matched
75,000	Bonnie Brae, Millington, NJ -- construction of new recreation/activity and vocational/technical education buildings
75,000	YMCA Madison, Madison, NJ -- modernization and expansion of facilities and other related costs of major capital campaign
50,000	Covenant House of New Jersey, Newark, NJ
50,000	Hudson School, Hoboken, NJ -- alternation and modernization of newly-acquired school facility and related preconstruction costs
50,000	Public Health Research Institute, New York, NY -- purchase of fluorometer equipment for infectious disease research
50,000	Purnell School, Pottersville, NJ -- replacement of waste management treatment facilities
50,000	Rutgers Preparatory School, Somerset, NJ -- construct new facility for Lower School

HYDE MANUFACTURING CO.

Company Headquarters

54 Eastford Road
Southbridge, MA 01550
Web: http://www.hudetools.com

Company Description

Employees: 500

SIC(s): 3421 Cutlery, 3423 Hand & Edge Tools Nec, 3545 Machine Tool Accessories.

Operating Locations

Hyde Manufacturing Co. (MA--Southbridge)

Hyde Charitable Foundation

Giving Contact

Richard B. Hardy, Chairman & Chief Executive Officer
Hyde Charitable Foundation
54 Eastford Rd.
Southbridge, MA 01550-3604
Phone: (508)764-4344
Fax: (508)765-9929

Description

EIN: 042752893

Organization Type: Corporate Foundation

Giving Locations: MA: Worcester County

Grant Types: Capital, General Support.

Financial Summary

Total Giving: $184,250 (2001); $163,942 (2000); $154,700 (1999)

Giving Analysis: Giving for 2000 includes: foundation ($163,942) 1999: foundation ($154,700)

Assets: $3,558,189 (2001); $3,636,846 (2000); $3,399,246 (1999)

Gifts Received: $166,000 (2001); $138,500 (2000); $163,500 (1999). Note: In 2001, contributions were received from Hyde Manufacturing Co. ($74,500), Dexter-Russell Inc. ($86,300), and Wilson Machine Knife Co., Inc. ($5,200). In 2000, contributions were

received from Hyde Manufacturer ($54,600), Russell Harrington Cutlery ($78,500), and Wilson Machine Knife Co. ($5,400). In 1999, contributions were received from Hyde Manufacturer ($76,900), Russell Harrington Cutlery ($80,100), and Wilson Machine Knife Co. ($6,500). In 1998, contributions were received from Hyde Manufacturing Co. ($66,300), Russell Harrington Cutlery ($69,100), and Wilson Machine Knife Co. ($5,600). In 1996, contributions were received from Hyde Manufacturing Co. ($39,000), Russell Harrington Cutlery ($54,000), and Wilson Machine Knife Co. ($3,000).

Typical Recipients

Arts & Humanities: Arts Centers, Historic Preservation, History & Archaeology, Libraries, Public Broadcasting

Civic & Public Affairs: Business/Free Enterprise, Clubs, Civic & Public Affairs-General, Public Policy, Safety

Education: Business Education, Colleges & Universities, Education Funds, Education Reform, Engineering/Technological Education, Education-General, Private Education (Precollege), Science/Mathematics Education

Health: Health Organizations, Hospices, Hospitals

Religion: Churches

Science: Scientific Centers & Institutes

Social Services: Child Welfare, Community Service Organizations, Family Services, Scouts, YMCA/YWCA/YMHA/YWHA, Youth Organizations

Application Procedures

Initial Contact: The foundation requests applications be made in writing. Include a description of organization, purpose of funds sought, amount requested, budget, and tax status of the organization.

Application Requirements: Include a description of organization, purpose of funds sought, amount requested, budget, and tax status of the organization.

Deadlines: None.

Restrictions

Does not support individuals or organizations outside operating areas.

Additional Information

Company reports approximately 25% of contributions support arts and humanities; 40% to education; 5% to health and human services; and 30% to civic and public affairs.

Corporate Officials

Richard B. Hardy: chairman, chief executive officer, director B Worcester, MA 1932. ED Rice University (1954). PRIM CORP EMPL chairman, chief executive officer, director: Hyde Manufacturing Co. CORP AFFIL chairman: Russell Harrington Cutlery; director: Mechanics Bank; chairman: Gutmann Cutlery Co.; director: Load Controls. NONPR AFFIL member: Shriners.

Ralph Lawrence: president, chief operating officer PRIM CORP EMPL president, chief operating officer: Hyde Manufacturing Co.

Foundation Officials

Richard R. Clemence: trustee B Southbridge, MA 1939. PRIM CORP EMPL executive vice president, secretary, director: Hyde Manufacturing Co. CORP AFFIL vice chairman, director: Savers Cooperative Bank; president, director: Wilson Machine Knife Co.; clerk, director: Russell Harrington Cutlery Co.; secretary, director: Beaut-Ease; secretary, director: Gutmann Cutlery Co.

Robert C. Clemence: trustee

Richard B. Hardy: trustee (see above)

Thomas B. Hardy: trustee

Alan S. Peppel: trustee

John P. Rawls: trustee

Grants Analysis

Disclosure Period: calendar year ending 2001
Total Grants: $184,250
Number of Grants: 25
Average Grant: $7,000
Highest Grant: $27,000
Lowest Grant: $500
Typical Range: $1,000 to $10,000

Recent Grants

Note: Grants derived from 2000 Form 990.

Library-Related

15,250	Jacob Edwards Library -- educational

General

27,000	Nichols College, Dudley, MA -- educational
26,500	New England Science Center, Worcester, MA -- for arts and sciences - ecotarium
26,000	Tri-Community YMCA, Southbridge, MA -- for community service
15,992	Southbridge Town Common, Southbridge, MA -- for community service
14,500	Worcester Academy, Worcester, MA -- educational
5,000	Elm Street Congregational Church, Boston, MA -- religious
5,000	Federated Church -- religious
4,000	Harrington Hospital South County Teen Network -- for community service
3,500	Trinity Catholic Academy, Southbridge, MA -- educational
3,000	Old Sturbridge Village, Sturbridge, MA -- for arts and sciences

IBP

Company Headquarters

800 Stevens Port Dr.
Dakota Dunes, SD 57049
Web: http://www.ibpinc.com

Company Description

Employees: 30,000
SIC(s): 2011 Meat Packing Plants.
Parent Company: Tyson Foods Inc., Springdale, AR, United States

Operating Locations

IBP (NE--Dakota City)

Nonmonetary Support

Type: Donated Equipment; Donated Products; Loaned Executives

IBP Foundation

Giving Contact

Gene Leman, Chairman, Board of DirectorS
PO Box 515
Dakota City, NE 68731
Phone: (605)235-2061

Description

Founded: 1979
EIN: 476014039
Organization Type: Corporate Foundation
Giving Locations: ID: Boise; IL: Joslin; IN: Logansport; IA: Columbus Junction, Denison, Perry, Sioux City, Storm Lake, Waterloo; KS: Emporia, Garden City; NE: Dakota City, Lexington, Madison, South Sioux City, West Point; TX: Amarillo; WA: Pasco
Grant Types: Award, Capital, Challenge, General Support.

Donor Information

Founder: IBP, Inc.

Financial Summary

Total Giving: $314,545 (2000); $220,420 (1999); $380,807 (1998)
Giving Analysis: Giving for 2000 includes: foundation grants to United Way ($129,500); foundation ($185,045); 1999: foundation grants to United Way ($55,500); foundation ($269,850); 1998: foundation grants to United Way ($97,500) foundation ($283,307)
Assets: $4,219,488 (2000); $4,538,991 (1999); $3,462,324 (1998)
Gifts Received: $1,000,000 (1999); $1,000,000 (1994). Note: In 1999, contributions were received from IBP, Inc. In 1994, substantial contributions were received from IBP.

Typical Recipients

Arts & Humanities: Libraries, Public Broadcasting, Theater
Civic & Public Affairs: Employment/Job Training, Civic & Public Affairs-General, Housing, Municipalities/Towns, Native American Affairs, Philanthropic Organizations, Professional & Trade Associations, Rural Affairs, Safety, Urban & Community Affairs
Education: Afterschool/Enrichment Programs, Business Education, Community & Junior Colleges, Elementary Education (Public), Education-General, Preschool Education, Public Education (Precollege), Secondary Education (Public)
Health: Children's Health/Hospitals, Clinics/Medical Centers, Emergency/Ambulance Services, Hospitals, Prenatal Health Issues
International: International-General
Religion: Churches, Religious Welfare
Social Services: Community Centers, Community Service Organizations, Family Services, Recreation & Athletics, United Funds/United Ways, United Funds/United Ways, YMCA/YWCA/YMHA/YWHA, Youth Organizations

Application Procedures

Initial Contact: Contact the foundation to request an application form.
Deadlines: None.

Additional Information

Publications: Application Form

Corporate Officials

Robert L. Peterson: chairman, chief executive officer, director B NE 1932. ED University of Nebraska. PRIM CORP EMPL chairman, chief executive officer, director: IBP. CLUB AFFIL Sioux City Country Club.
Larry Shipley: chief financial officer PRIM CORP EMPL chief financial officer: IBP.

Foundation Officials

Donald E. Willoughby: executive director PRIM CORP EMPL manager government & industry affairs: IBP.

Grants Analysis

Disclosure Period: calendar year ending 2000
Total Grants: $185,045*
Number of Grants: 17
Average Grant: $5,315*
Highest Grant: $100,000
Lowest Grant: $500
Typical Range: $1,000 to $10,000
*Note: Giving excludes United Way. Average grant figure excludes highest grant.

Recent Grants

Note: Grants derived from 2001 Form 990.

Library-Related

1,000	Friends of Sioux City Public Library,

Sioux City, IA -- purchase bilingual children's books

General

129,500	United Way, Cleveland, OH -- support for multiple charities
100,000	Orpheum Theater -- preservation campaign
50,000	City of Denison, Denison, TX -- daycare
20,000	Dawson County Family United Network, Lexington, NE -- after school expansion project
20,000	Emporia Kansas Community Housing Organization, Emporia, KS -- rehabilitation single living homes
10,000	Perry High School Soccer, Perry, IA -- soccer field
10,000	Sangralea Valley Soccer League, Logansport, IN -- soccer field
6,000	City of Perry, Perry, IA -- purchase drug dog
5,080	Walla Walls County Sheriff's Department -- video camera for patrol car
5,000	YMCA, Norfolk, NE -- remodel exercise area

CARL C. ICAHN FOUNDATION

Giving Contact

Gail Golden-Icahn, Secretary & Vice President
767 5th Avenue, 47th Floor
New York, NY 10153-0023
Phone: (212)702-4300

Description

Founded: 1980
EIN: 133091588
Organization Type: Private Foundation
Giving Locations: NY: New York
Grant Types: General Support.

Donor Information

Founder: Carl C. Icahn

Financial Summary

Total Giving: $2,225,650 (fiscal year ending November 30, 2001); $102,000 (fiscal 2000); $746,435 (fiscal 1999)
Assets: $12,833,905 (fiscal 2001); $14,489,644 (fiscal 2000); $13,965,916 (fiscal 1999)
Gifts Received: $100 (fiscal 2000)

Typical Recipients

Arts & Humanities: Arts Associations & Councils, Ballet, Community Arts, Historic Preservation, History & Archaeology, Libraries, Museums/Galleries, Music, Opera, Performing Arts, Public Broadcasting
Civic & Public Affairs: Civil Rights, Clubs, Community Foundations, Ethnic Organizations, Civic & Public Affairs-General, Municipalities/Towns, Philanthropic Organizations, Safety, Urban & Community Affairs, Women's Affairs
Education: Arts/Humanities Education, Colleges & Universities, Education Funds, Education-General, Minority Education, Private Education (Precollege), Student Aid
Environment: Air/Water Quality, Environment-General
Health: Alzheimers Disease, Cancer, Children's Health/Hospitals, Clinics/Medical Centers, Clinics/Medical Centers, Diabetes, Health Organizations, Heart, Hospitals, Long-Term Care, Medical Rehabilitation, Medical Research, Mental Health, Multiple Sclerosis, Single-Disease Health Associations

International: Foreign Arts Organizations, Health Care/Hospitals, Human Rights, International Development, International Environmental Issues, International Organizations, International Relief Efforts, Missionary/Religious Activities
Religion: Jewish Causes, Religious Welfare
Science: Scientific Research
Social Services: Animal Protection, Big Brother/Big Sister, Child Welfare, Community Centers, Community Service Organizations, Counseling, Crime Prevention, Day Care, Domestic Violence, Food/Clothing Distribution, People with Disabilities, Recreation & Athletics, Refugee Assistance, Shelters/Homelessness, Social Services-General, Substance Abuse, United Funds/United Ways, Youth Organizations

Application Procedures

Initial Contact: Send a brief letter of inquiry describing program or project. Include basic budget and proof of tax-exempt status.
Deadlines: None.

Foundation Officials

Gail Golden: vice president
Susan Gordon: assistant treasurer
Carl Celian Icahn: president, director B Queens, NY 1936. ED New York University School of Medicine; Princeton University BA (1957). PRIM CORP EMPL owner, chairman, director: Icahn & Co. CORP AFFIL chairman, president, chief executive officer: Trans World Airlines; chairman, chief executive officer: Starfire Holding Corp.; president: Riverdale Investors Corp., Inc.; Samsonite Corp.; chairman, president: Icahn Holding Corp.; director: Fairchild Corp.; president: Foxfield Thoroughbreds Inc.; chairman: Bayswater Realty & Capital; chairman, chief executive officer; director: ACF Industries Inc.; chairman: American RE Holdings LP. NONPR AFFIL Jewish Guild for the Blind Inc.
Liba Icahn: treasurer, director
Robert T. Osborne: chief operating officer

Grants Analysis

Disclosure Period: fiscal year ending November 30, 2001
Total Grants: $2,225,650
Number of Grants: 25
Average Grant: $9,402*
Highest Grant: $2,000,000
Lowest Grant: $500
Typical Range: $5,000 to $25,000
***Note:** Average grant figure excludes highest grant.

Recent Grants

Note: Grants derived from fiscal 2000 Form 990.

General

15,000	New York University Child Study Center, New York, NY
10,000	Knox College, Galesburg, IL
10,000	Las Vegas Philharmonic, Las Vegas, NV
5,000	American-Israel Chamber of Commerce, New York, NY
5,000	Doe Fund, Inc., The, New York, NY
5,000	Guild Hall of East Hampton, Inc., East Hampton, NY
5,000	Huggy Bears
5,000	Joint Distribution Committee, New York, NY -- uncommon decency project
5,000	Lauri Strauss Leukemia Foundation, New York, NY
5,000	Lustgarten Foundation

IDEAL INDUSTRIES, INC.

Company Headquarters

1 Becker Place
Sycamore, IL 60178
Web: http://www.idealindustries.com

Company Description

Employees: 480
SIC(s): 3546 Power-Driven Handtools, 3548 Welding Apparatus, 3549 Metalworking Machinery Nec, 3569 General Industrial Machinery Nec.

Operating Locations

Ideal Industries (IL--Sycamore)

Ideal Industries Foundation

Giving Contact

Jim Pfotenhauer, Treasurer
Becker Place
Sycamore, IL 60178
Phone: (815)895-5181
Fax: (815)895-6973
E-mail: wjablow@wirenot.com

Description

Founded: 1987
EIN: 363449960
Organization Type: Corporate Foundation
Giving Locations: IL
Grant Types: General Support.

Financial Summary

Total Giving: $169,975 (2001); $197,887 (2000); $67,569 (1999)
Giving Analysis: Giving for 2001 includes: foundation grants to United Way ($5,000); 2000: foundation scholarships ($500); foundation matching gifts ($730); foundation grants to United Way ($18,831); 1999: foundation matching gifts ($215); foundation scholarships ($1,500); foundation grants to United Way ($21,185); foundation ($44,669);
Assets: $232,216 (2001); $281,488 (2000); $295,097 (1999)
Gifts Received: $152,000 (2001); $192,000 (2000); $115,000 (1999). Note: Contributions are received from Ideal Industries.

Typical Recipients

Arts & Humanities: Libraries, Public Broadcasting
Civic & Public Affairs: Clubs, Community Foundations, Economic Development, Civic & Public Affairs-General, Hispanic Affairs, Housing, Professional & Trade Associations, Safety, Urban & Community Affairs
Education: Business Education, Colleges & Universities, Economic Education, Education Associations, Engineering/Technological Education, Faculty Development, Education-General, Private Education (Precollege), Public Education (Precollege), Secondary Education (Public), Student Aid
Health: Cancer, Heart, Hospices, Public Health, Single-Disease Health Associations
International: International Organizations
Religion: Religious Welfare
Social Services: Big Brother/Big Sister, Child Welfare, Community Service Organizations, Day Care, Family Planning, Family Services, Food/Clothing Distribution, Recreation & Athletics, Scouts, Shelters/Homelessness, Social Services-General, Special Olympics, Substance Abuse, United Funds/United Ways, Volunteer Services, YMCA/YWCA/YMHA/YWHA, Youth Organizations

Application Procedures

Initial Contact: Initial inquiry should be a brief letter indicating the nature of the project for which support is sought.
Deadlines: None.

Corporate Officials

David W. Juday: chairman, director PRIM CORP EMPL chairman, director: Ideal Industries.
Robert Lane: president PRIM CORP EMPL president: Ideal Industries.
James Pfotenhauer: chief financial officer PRIM CORP EMPL chief financial officer: Ideal Industries.

Foundation Officials

Margaret Baack: vice president
Wendy Joblow: director
David W. Juday: president (see above)
Chris Lomb: director
James Pfotenhauer: treasurer (see above)

Grants Analysis

Disclosure Period: calendar year ending 2001
Total Grants: $164,975*
Number of Grants: 43
Average Grant: $3,837
Highest Grant: $20,000
Typical Range: $1,000 to $5,000
***Note:** Giving excludes United Way.

Recent Grants

Note: Grants derived from 2001 Form 990.

General

20,100	Northern Public Radio, DeKalb, IL
13,000	Kishwaukee Family YMCA, DeKalb, IL
13,000	Sycamore United Fund, Sycamore, IL
12,700	DeKalb County Community Foundation, DeKalb, IN
12,334	Sycamore Community Schools, Sycamore, IL
12,270	Northern Illinois University, DeKalb, IL
11,000	CASA, DeKalb, IN
10,000	Tri County Community Health, DeKalb, IL
7,500	DeKalb County Economic Development Corp., DeKalb, IL
7,500	Habitat for Humanity International, Bloomington, IL

ILLINOIS TOOL WORKS, INC.

Company Headquarters

3600 W. Lake Avenue
Glenview, IL 60025-5811
Phone: (847)724-7500
Fax: (847)657-4392
Web: http://www.itwinc.com

Company Description

Founded: 1912
Ticker: ITW
Exchange: NYSE
Acquired: Premark International (1999).
Revenue: US$9.467 billion (2002)
Profit: US$712.6 million (2002)
Employees: 48700 (2002)
Fortune Rank: 189, per FORTUNE Magazine's list of 500 Largest U.S. Corporations (2002).
SIC(s): 2899 Chemical Preparations Nec, 3082 Unsupported Plastics Profile Shapes, 3089 Plastics Products Nec, 3429 Hardware Nec.

Operating Locations

Illinois Tool Works, Inc. (AR--Pine Bluff; CA--Hawthorne; CO--Colorado Springs; CT--Waterbury; IL--Des Plaines, Downers Grove, Elk Grove Village, Elmhurst, Glenview, Itasca, Lincolnshire, Lincolnwood, Wood Dale; MA--Danvers; MI--Detroit, Ferndale; NJ--Piscataway; NY--Orangeburg; OH--Loveland; PA--Montgomeryville; TN--Erin; TX--Arlington, Irving; VA--Lynchburg)

Nonmonetary Support

Type: Donated Equipment; Donated Products; Loaned Employees

Illinois Tool Works Foundation

Giving Contact

Mary Ann Mallahan, Manager, Community Relations
3600 West Lake Avenue
Glenview, IL 60025
Phone: (847)657-4092
Fax: (847)657-4505
E-mail: mmallahan@itw.com
Web: http://itw.com/itw_foundation.html

Description

EIN: 366087160
Organization Type: Corporate Foundation
Giving Locations: IL: principally near operating locations and to national organizations.
Grant Types: Capital, Employee Matching Gifts, General Support, Multiyear/Continuing Support.
Note: Employee matching gift ratio: 3 to 1 for donations to nonprofit charitable organisation not already sponsored by company.

Financial Summary

Total Giving: $6,070,358 (fiscal year ending February 28, 2001); $7,000,000 (fiscal 2000 approx); $4,048,316 (fiscal 1999)
Giving Analysis: Giving for fiscal 2001 includes: foundation scholarships ($254,964); foundation grants to United Way ($1,139,276); foundation ($2,093,691); foundation matching gifts ($2,582,427); fiscal 2000: foundation ($2,717,000); fiscal 1999: foundation grants to United Way ($570,455); foundation ($1,324,253) foundation matching gifts ($2,153,608)
Assets: $5,524,801 (fiscal 2001); $13,000,000 (fiscal 2000 approx); $13,465,701 (fiscal 1999)

Typical Recipients

Arts & Humanities: Arts Associations & Councils, Arts Festivals, Arts Institutes, Dance, Historic Preservation, History & Archaeology, Libraries, Museums/Galleries, Music, Opera, Performing Arts, Public Broadcasting, Theater
Civic & Public Affairs: Botanical Gardens/Parks, Business/Free Enterprise, Civil Rights, Clubs, Economic Development, Employment/Job Training, Civic & Public Affairs-General, Hispanic Affairs, Housing, Law & Justice, Legal Aid, Nonprofit Management, Professional & Trade Associations, Public Policy, Urban & Community Affairs, Women's Affairs, Zoos/Aquariums
Education: Business Education, Colleges & Universities, Community & Junior Colleges, Economic Education, Education Associations, Education Funds, Engineering/Technological Education, Faculty Development, Education-General, Literacy, Minority Education, Private Education (Precollege), Science/Mathematics Education, Student Aid
Health: Cancer, Children's Health/Hospitals, Clinics/Medical Centers, Heart, Hospitals, Medical Rehabilitation, Medical Research, Mental Health, Nursing Services
Religion: Bible Study/Translation, Jewish Causes, Religious Welfare
Science: Observatories & Planetariums, Science Exhibits & Fairs, Science Museums, Scientific Centers & Institutes
Social Services: Child Welfare, Community Centers, Family Planning, Family Services, Homes, People with Disabilities, Scouts, Senior Services, Substance Abuse, United Funds/United Ways, Volunteer Services, YMCA/YWCA/YMHA/YWHA, Youth Organizations

Application Procedures

Initial Contact: Send a brief letter or proposal.
Application Requirements: Provide a description of organization; amount requested and purpose of funds sought; recently audited financial statement; and proof of tax-exempt status.
Deadlines: May and December 1.

Corporate Officials

W. James Farrell: chairman, chief executive officer B New York, NY 1942. ED University of Detroit BA (1965). PRIM CORP EMPL chairman, chief executive officer: IL Tool Works Inc. CORP AFFIL director: Quaker Oats Co.; director: Sears, Roebuck & Co.; director: Morton International Inc.; director: Premark International Inc.

Foundation Officials

John Carpin: director
Stewart Skinner Hudnut: director B Cincinnati, OH 1939. ED Princeton University AB (1961); Oxford University AB (1961); Harvard University JD (1965); Pace University (1991). PRIM CORP EMPL senior vice president, general counsel, secretary: Illinois Tool Works, Inc. NONPR AFFIL member: Illinois Bar Association; member: Phi Beta Kappa; member: American Bar Association; director: Guild Lyric Opera Chicago.
Michael Lynch: director
Mary Ann Mallahan: secretary
Michael J. Robinson: treasurer
Harold Byron Smith, Jr.: president
Stephen Byron Smith: director

Grants Analysis

Disclosure Period: fiscal year ending February 28, 2001
Total Grants: $2,093,691*
Number of Grants: 99
Average Grant: $15,789*
Highest Grant: $211,324
Typical Range: $1,000 to $50,000
*Note: Giving excludes matching gifts, scholarship, United Way. Average grant figure excludes three highest grants ($577,991).

Recent Grants

Note: Grants derived from fiscal 2001 Form 990.

Library-Related
50,000	Newberry Library, Chicago, IL

General
593,000	United Way Crusade of Mercy, Chicago, IL
211,324	Citizens Scholarship Foundation of America, St. Peter, MN -- for ITW Foundation Scholarship Program
200,000	Museum of Science and Industry, Chicago, IL
166,667	Northwestern University, Evanston, IL
57,504	Ralph Wilson Youth Club, Temple, TX
50,000	Adler Planetarium, Chicago, IL
50,000	Big Shoulder's Fund, Chicago, IL
50,000	Boys and Girls Club Fox Valley, Inc., Appleton, WI
50,000	Chicago Academy of Sciences, Chicago, IL
50,000	Chicago Children's Museum, Chicago, IL

INASMUCH FOUNDATION

Giving Contact

Jeanne H. Smith, Adv Committee Member
PO Box 2325
Oklahoma City, OK 73101
Phone: (405)235-1356
Fax: (405)235-2340
E-mail: inasmuchfdn@coxinet.net

Description

Founded: 1983
EIN: 731167188
Organization Type: Private Foundation
Giving Locations: CO; OK
Grant Types: General Support, Research, Seed Money.

Donor Information

Founder: Edith Gaylord Harper

Financial Summary

Total Giving: $179,500 (fiscal year ending June 30, 2001); $160,000 (fiscal 2000); $228,500 (fiscal 1999)
Giving Analysis: Giving for fiscal 2001 includes: foundation grants to United Way ($1,000)
Assets: $5,708,715 (fiscal 2001); $5,500,000 (fiscal 2000); $4,476,699 (fiscal 1999)
Gifts Received: $1,020,108 (fiscal 2001); $364,375 (fiscal 1997); $150,000 (fiscal 1996). Note: Contributions were received from the Edith G. Harper and Edith G. Harper Estate.

Typical Recipients

Arts & Humanities: Arts Associations & Councils, Arts Institutes, Arts Outreach, Ethnic & Folk Arts, History & Archaeology, Libraries, Literary Arts, Museums/Galleries, Music, Opera, Performing Arts, Public Broadcasting, Theater
Civic & Public Affairs: Community Foundations, Hispanic Affairs, Nonprofit Management
Education: Arts/Humanities Education, Colleges & Universities, Elementary Education (Public), Faculty Development, Education-General, Literacy, Preschool Education, Private Education (Precollege), Special Education, Student Aid
Environment: Environment-General, Resource Conservation, Wildlife Protection
Health: Clinics/Medical Centers, Diabetes, Health Organizations, Hospices, Mental Health, Preventive Medicine/Wellness Organizations, Speech & Hearing
Science: Science Museums
Social Services: At-Risk Youth, Child Abuse, Child Welfare, Community Service Organizations, Domestic Violence, Family Planning, Family Services, People with Disabilities, Scouts, Senior Services, Shelters/Homelessness, YMCA/YWCA/YMHA/YWHA, Youth Organizations

Application Procedures

Initial Contact: Submit a concept paper of no more than three pages.
Application Requirements: Include a description of the project and the specific expected outcomes. Also send a description of organization, proof of tax-exempt status, other sources of funding, proposed budget for project, amount requested, and a timetable for the project.
Deadlines: February 15 and August 15.

Restrictions

Contributions are not generally made to individuals or for regular operating expenses. Giving is limited to organizations in Oklahoma and Colorado Springs, CO.

Foundation Officials

David O. Hogan: trustee
Mary Holloway Richard: adv comm mem
Cathy O. Robbins: advisory committee member
John Hugh Roff, Jr.: trustee B Wewoka, OK 1931. ED University of Oklahoma AB (1954); University of Oklahoma LLB (1955). PRIM CORP EMPL chairman: PetroUnited Terminals. NONPR AFFIL member: Phi Beta Kappa; chairman advisory board: Salvation Army; member: Order Coif; member advisory board: Center Strategic & International Studies; member council overseers: Jones School Business Administration; trustee: Baylor College Medicine; member: Beta Theta Pi. CLUB AFFIL Houstonian Club; Coronado Club; Houston Country Club.

Patrick T. Rooney: advisory committee member
Robert J. Ross: advisory committee member
William Jarboe Ross: trustee B Oklahoma City, OK 1930. ED University of Oklahoma BBA (1952); University of Oklahoma LLB (1954). PRIM CORP EMPL partner: Rainey, Ross, Rice & Binns. CORP AFFIL member admissions & grievences committee: US District Court; director: PetroUnited Terminals. NONPR AFFIL member: Rotary; director: Saint Anthony Hospital Foundation; chairman education committee, member: OK Heritage Association; member: Phi Alpha Delta; member: Newcomen Society; member: OK Bar Association; member: Knights of Columbus; member: Beta Theta Phi; director: Harn Homestead. CLUB AFFIL Oklahoma City Golf & Country Club; Economic Club.
Jeanne H. Smith: adv comm mem
Barbara L. Yalich: advisory committee member

Grants Analysis

Disclosure Period: fiscal year ending June 30, 2001
Total Grants: $178,500*
Number of Grants: 41
Average Grant: $4,354
Highest Grant: $10,000
Typical Range: $1,000 to $10,000
*Note: Giving excludes United Way.

Recent Grants

Note: Grants derived from fiscal 2000 Form 990.

Library-Related
5,000	Pikes Peak Library District, Colorado Springs, CO -- to provide funds for restoration of 1095 Carnegie Library Building

General
10,000	Community Council of Central Oklahoma, Oklahoma City, OK -- neighborhood outreach worker
10,000	Rainbow Fleet, Oklahoma City, OK -- funds for BEST
9,900	Oklahoma Arts Institute, Oklahoma City, OK -- funding for scholarships for teachers
7,500	Cheyenne Village, Inc., Colorado Springs, CO -- help fund the conversion of administrative building into two affordable apartments
6,500	McCall's Chapel School, Ada, OK -- upgrade and re-finish cottages for the school for mentally handicapped
5,500	Salvation Army, Oklahoma City, OK -- funding for the family shelter enhancement project
5,000	Arts Council of Oklahoma City, Oklahoma City, OK -- help support the continuing series, "Stage Center Presents"
5,000	Calm Waters Center for Children and Families, Inc., Oklahoma City, OK -- provide funding for grief and divorce supports groups
5,000	Center for Children and Families, Inc., Norman, OK -- help support neighborhood theater project
5,000	Colorado Springs Chamber Foundation, Colorado Springs, CO -- scholarship

INDEPENDENCE FOUNDATION

Giving Contact

Susan E. Sherman, President
Offices at the Bellevue
200 South Broad Street, Suite 1101
Philadelphia, PA 19102
Phone: (215)985-4009
Fax: (215)985-3989
E-mail: ssherman@independencefoundation.org
Web: http://www.independencefoundation.org

Description

Founded: 1932
EIN: 231352110
Organization Type: Specialized/Single Purpose Foundation
Giving Locations: , Bucks County, PA , Chester County , Delaware County , Montgomery County, Philadelphia metropolitan area
Grant Types: Capital, Challenge, Fellowship, General Support, Matching, Multiyear/Continuing Support, Operating Expenses, Project, Scholarship.

Donor Information

Founder: The Independence Foundation was established in 1932 by William H. Donner, but was originally named the International Cancer Research Foundation. In 1962, the foundation was split to form the William H. Donner Foundation and the Independence Foundation. Mr. Donner (1864-1953) was chairman of the Pennsylvania Steel Company and the Otis Hidden Company, and president of Union Steel Company, Cambria Steel Company, and Donner Steel Company. He was also a founder of the towns of Donora and Monessen, PA.

Financial Summary

Total Giving: $7,000,000 (2003 approx); $7,480,779 (2002); $9,100,000 (2001 approx)
Giving Analysis: Giving for 1999 includes: foundation grants to United Way ($50,000); foundation fellowships ($428,837) 1997: foundation scholarships ($90,000)
Assets: $104,608,608 (2002); $153,767,100 (2000); $177,671,109 (1999)

Typical Recipients

Arts & Humanities: Arts Associations & Councils, Arts Centers, Arts Festivals, Arts Funds, Arts Institutes, Ballet, Film & Video, Arts & Humanities-General, Historic Preservation, History & Archaeology, Libraries, Museums/Galleries, Music, Opera, Performing Arts, Public Broadcasting, Theater
Civic & Public Affairs: Botanical Gardens/Parks, Business/Free Enterprise, Civil Rights, Clubs, Economic Development, Civic & Public Affairs-General, Hispanic Affairs, Housing, Law & Justice, Legal Aid, Public Policy, Rural Affairs, Urban & Community Affairs, Women's Affairs, Zoos/Aquariums
Education: Arts/Humanities Education, Colleges & Universities, Colleges & Universities, Community & Junior Colleges, Faculty Development, Education-General, Health & Physical Education, International Studies, Legal Education, Medical Education, Private Education (Precollege), Student Aid
Environment: Wildlife Protection
Health: AIDS/HIV, Children's Health/Hospitals, Clinics/Medical Centers, Emergency/Ambulance Services, Eyes/Blindness, Health Policy/Cost Containment, Health Organizations, Hospitals, Hospitals (University Affiliated), Medical Rehabilitation, Medical Research, Mental Health, Nursing Services, Prenatal Health Issues, Preventive Medicine/Wellness Organizations, Public Health
International: Human Rights, International Relations
Religion: Religious Welfare
Science: Science Museums, Scientific Centers & Institutes
Social Services: Child Welfare, Community Service Organizations, Community Service Organizations, Domestic Violence, Emergency Relief, Family Planning, Homes, People with Disabilities, Senior Services, United Funds/United Ways, YMCA/YWCA/YMHA/YWHA, Youth Organizations

Application Procedures

Initial Contact: Each year, the foundation sends out Request For Proposals packets under the following categories: Nurse Managed Primary Health Care Initiatives; Health and Human Services Initiatives; Legal Aid Initiatives; Culture and Arts Initiatives; the Public Interest Law Fellowship Program; and fellowships in the visual and performing arts. Please contact the foundation for RFP packets and submission deadlines.
Deadlines: Indicated in the Request for Proposal packets.
Review Process: If an application is within the scope of the foundation's interests, the board of directors may grant interviews.

Restrictions

The foundation generally does not give to individuals; building and development projects; or grants for travel, research, or publication.

Additional Information

The foundation requires grant recipients to submit annual written progress reports and financial statements. Site visits and presentations to the board may also be required.
Publications: Annual Report; Guidelines; Request for Proposal Packets; Application Form

Foundation Officials

Hon. Phyllis Whitman Beck: chairman B Bronx, NY 1927. ED Brown University AB (1949); Temple University JD (1967). PRIM NONPR EMPL judge: Pennsylvania Superior Court. NONPR AFFIL member, board consultors: Villanova Law School; member: Women in the Profession; director: Temple University Law School; member, board overseers: University Pennsylvania School Nursing; member: Pennsylvania Bar Association; member: Pennsylvanians Modern Courts; member: National Association Women Judges; director: Free Library Philadelphia; member: Joint State Government Committee Domestic Relations Law; president: Foundation Cognitive Therapy; member: American Judicature Society; member: American Law Institute; member: American Bar Foundation.
Andre L. Dennis, Esq.: director
Eugene C. Fish, Esq.: vice president B 1910. ED University of Pennsylvania Wharton School (1931); University of Pennsylvania School of Law (1934). PRIM CORP EMPL chairman, secretary, director: Eastern Foundry Co. CORP AFFIL chairman: Peerless Industries Inc.
Andre Mengel, PhD: director
Susan Elizabeth Sherman: president, chief executive officer B Salem, MA 1945. ED Rhode Island Hospital School of Nursing (1966); University of Rhode Island BSN (1969); New York University MA (1971). NONPR AFFIL member: Organization Advancement Adn; member: Sigma Theta Tau; consult: National League Nursing; head department nursing: Community College Philadelphia; instructor: Hunter College; member: American Society Aging; assistant professor: Bronx Community College; member: American Association Community College; member: American Gerontological Society Higher Education.
Atty. Theodore Kugler Warner, Jr.: secretary, treasurer B Philadelphia, PA September 13, 1909. ED University of Pennsylvania AB (1931); University of Pennsylvania LLB (1934). PRIM CORP EMPL counsel: Harper & Driver. NONPR AFFIL member: Pennsylvania Bar Association; member: Tau Kappa Epsilon; member: Order Coif; life member: American Law Institute; member: National Tax Association; member: American Bar Association. CLUB AFFIL Union League Club; Aronimink Golf Club; Masons Club.

Grants Analysis

Disclosure Period: calendar year ending 2001
Total Grants: $9,100,000*
Number of Grants: 325
Average Grant: $28,000
Highest Grant: $500,000
Typical Range: $5,000 to $100,000
*Note: Grants analysis provided by the foundation.

Recent Grants

Note: Grants derived from 2001 Form 990.

General

1,000,000	Regional Performing Arts Center, Philadelphia, PA
500,000	Lebanon Valley College, Lebanon Valley, PA -- Eugene C. Fish Professorship in business
200,000	Please Touch Museum, Philadelphia, PA
174,000	Mural Arts Advocates, Philadelphia, PA
125,000	Community College, Philadelphia, PA -- scholarships
125,000	LaSalle University, Philadelphia, PA
125,000	National Nursing Centers Consortium, Philadelphia, PA
125,000	Resources for Human Development, Philadelphia, PA -- temple health connection
125,000	Resources for Human Development, Philadelphia, PA -- family practice and counseling centers
125,000	University of Pennsylvania, Philadelphia, PA -- youth center

INDIANAPOLIS NEWSPAPERS, INC.

Company Headquarters

307 N. Pennsylvania St.
Indianapolis, IN 46204

Company Description

Employees: 1,400
SIC(s): 2700 Printing & Publishing.
Parent Company: Central Newspapers, Inc., 200 E. Van Buren Street, Phoenix, AZ, United States
Parent Revenue: US$6,422,200,000 (2002)

Operating Locations

Indianapolis Newspapers, Inc. (IN--Indianapolis)

Giving Contact

Jennifer Gombach, Marketing Communications Manager
307 N. Pennsylvania St.
Indianapolis, IN 46204
Phone: (317)444-7023

Description

Organization Type: Corporate Giving Program
Giving Locations: headquarters area only.
Grant Types: General Support, Operating Expenses, Project.

Typical Recipients

Arts & Humanities: Arts Centers, Arts Festivals, Arts Funds, Arts Institutes, Arts Outreach, Ballet, Community Arts, Arts & Humanities-General, Historic Preservation, Libraries, Museums/Galleries, Music, Opera, Performing Arts, Public Broadcasting, Theater, Visual Arts
Civic & Public Affairs: Botanical Gardens/Parks, Business/Free Enterprise, Chambers of Commerce, Economic Development, Employment/Job Training, First Amendment Issues, Civic & Public Affairs-General, Housing, Inner-City Development
Education: Afterschool/Enrichment Programs, Arts/Humanities Education, Education-General, Journalism/Media Education, Literacy, Minority Education, Preschool Education
Environment: Environment-General
Health: Alzheimers Disease, Eyes/Blindness, Public Health, Speech & Hearing
Social Services: At-Risk Youth, Camps, Child Welfare, Community Centers, Community Service Organizations, Counseling, Day Care, Delinquency & Criminal Rehabilitation, Domestic Violence, Family

Planning, Family Services, Food/Clothing Distribution, Homes, Recreation & Athletics, Refugee Assistance, Senior Services, Shelters/Homelessness, Social Services-General, Substance Abuse, United Funds/United Ways, Volunteer Services, Youth Organizations

Application Procedures

Initial Contact: send a brief leter of inquiry
Application Requirements: a description of organization, amount requested, purpose of funds sought, recently audited financial statement, and proof of tax-exempt status

Restrictions

Does not support religious organizations for sectarian purposes, political or lobbying groups, or organizations outside operating areas.

Corporate Officials

Eugene S. Pulliam: senior vice president, publisher PRIM CORP EMPL senior vice president, publisher: Indianapolis Newspapers Inc.
Jeffrey B. Rogers: chief financial officer PRIM CORP EMPL chief financial officer: Indianapolis Newspapers Inc.

Grants Analysis

Typical Range: $2,500 to $5,000

ING NORTH AMERICA INSURANCE CORP.

Company Headquarters

Atlanta, GA
Web: http://www.ing-usa.com

Company Description

Former Name: Life Insurance Co. of Georgia.
Employees: 3,600
SIC(s): 6081 Foreign Banks--Branches & Agencies, 6300 Insurance Carriers.
Parent Company: ING Americas, 57800 Powers Ferry Rd. NW, Atlanta, GA, United States
Parent Assets: US$759,978,700,000 (2001)

Operating Locations

ING North America Atlanta Operations (GA--Atlanta); ING North America Insurance Corp. (GA--Atlanta)

Nonmonetary Support

Type: In-kind Services; Loaned Executives

Giving Contact

Karen Burnsed, Manager
PO Box 105006
Atlanta, GA 30348-5006
Phone: (770)980-5100
Fax: (770)850-7608

Description

Organization Type: Corporate Giving Program
Giving Locations: GA: southeastern states.
Grant Types: Employee Matching Gifts, General Support, Operating Expenses, Project.

Typical Recipients

Arts & Humanities: Arts Associations & Councils, Arts Centers, Dance, Ethnic & Folk Arts, Historic Preservation, Libraries, Museums/Galleries, Music, Theater
Civic & Public Affairs: Business/Free Enterprise, Employment/Job Training, Professional & Trade Associations, Safety, Zoos/Aquariums
Education: Business Education, Colleges & Universities, Economic Education, Education Associations, Literacy, Minority Education, Science/Mathematics Education

Health: Health Policy/Cost Containment, Health Organizations, Medical Research, Mental Health, Single-Disease Health Associations
Religion: Religious Welfare
Social Services: Child Welfare, Community Service Organizations, Domestic Violence, Family Services, Senior Services, Substance Abuse, United Funds/United Ways, Youth Organizations

Application Procedures

Initial Contact: Send proposal any time, including a description and history of organization, amount and purpose of funds sought, a recently audited financial statement, proof of tax-exempt status, a list of directors and officers, and a budget breakdown including administrative expenses. The National Charities Information Bureau's review of organization will be heavily considered in determining soundness of contribution.

Additional Information

Company reports contributions level and value of non-monetary support are confidential.

Corporate Officials

Michael W. Cunningham: chief financial officer, chief executive officer PRIM CORP EMPL chief financial officer: ING North American Atlanta.
Robert Glenn Hilliard: chairman B Anderson, SC 1943. ED Clemson University (1965); George Washington University (1968). PRIM CORP EMPL chairman: ING North American Insurance Corp. CORP AFFIL chairman: Netherlands Insurance Co.; director: Liberty Corp.; president, director: Liberty Life Insurance Co.; director: Cosmos Broadcasting Corp.; chairman: ING North America Atlanta; director: Carolina First. NONPR AFFIL director: SC Life Health Insurance Guarantee Association; director, vice chairman: YMCA Camp Greenville Management Board; director: North Carolina Life Health Insurance Guarantee Association; member: SC Bar Association; director: Greenville Association Retarded Children; member: Greenville County Bar Association; st vice president: American Council Life Insurance; member: American Society of Corporate Secretaries; member: American Bar Association.
Jim Thompson: president, chief executive officer PRIM CORP EMPL president, chief executive officer: ING North American Atlanta.

Grants Analysis

Typical Range: $1,000 to $2,500

LOUISE H. AND DAVID S. INGALLS FOUNDATION

Giving Contact

Jane Watson
20600 Chagrin Boulevard, Suite 430
Shaker Heights, OH 44122
Phone: (216)921-6000
Fax: (216)921-7709
E-mail: wwwatson@visnet.com

Description

Founded: 1953
EIN: 346516550
Organization Type: General Purpose Foundation
Giving Locations: CT; NY; OH: Ohio, Connecticut, Virginia, and New York; VT
Grant Types: Capital, Project.

Donor Information

Founder: Incorporated in 1953 by Edith Ingalls Vignos, Louise Ingalls Brown, David S. Ingalls Jr., Jane I. Davison, Anne I. Lawrence, the late Louise H. Ingalls, and the late David S. Ingalls.

Financial Summary

Total Giving: $1,800,000 (2001); $2,122,000 (2000); $2,276,000 (1998)
Giving Analysis: Giving for 2000 includes: foundation scholarships ($80,000)
Assets: $34,116,554 (2000); $31,966,009 (1998); $28,050,469 (1997)

Typical Recipients

Arts & Humanities: Arts Centers, Arts Funds, Arts Institutes, Arts Outreach, Ballet, Film & Video, History & Archaeology, Libraries, Museums/Galleries, Music, Performing Arts, Public Broadcasting, Theater
Civic & Public Affairs: Botanical Gardens/Parks, Employment/Job Training, Civic & Public Affairs-General, Municipalities/Towns, Philanthropic Organizations, Public Policy, Urban & Community Affairs, Zoos/Aquariums
Education: Arts/Humanities Education, Colleges & Universities, Education Funds, Faculty Development, Education-General, International Studies, Legal Education, Medical Education, Private Education (Precollege), Public Education (Precollege), Student Aid
Environment: Forestry, Environment-General, Environment-General, Resource Conservation, Wildlife Protection
Health: Clinics/Medical Centers, Emergency/Ambulance Services, Eyes/Blindness, Health Organizations, Hospitals, Long-Term Care, Medical Rehabilitation, Nursing Services, Single-Disease Health Associations, Transplant Networks/Donor Banks
International: Foreign Educational Institutions
Religion: Churches
Science: Science Museums, Scientific Centers & Institutes, Scientific Labs, Scientific Research
Social Services: Camps, Child Welfare, Community Centers, Community Service Organizations, Counseling, Family Planning, Family Services, People with Disabilities, Recreation & Athletics, Senior Services, United Funds/United Ways, YMCA/YWCA/YMHA/YWHA, Youth Organizations

Application Procedures

Initial Contact: The foundation has no formal grant application procedure or application form.
Deadlines: None.

Restrictions

The foundation makes grants to public charities only. Grants are not made to individuals.

Foundation Officials

James R. Bright: assistant secretary
Barbara Brown: president
Endicott P. Davidson: trustee
Rebekah Ingalls: secretary, trustee
Anne I. Lawrence: vice president
John T. Lawrence, Jr.: treasurer CORP AFFIL director: America Annuity Group Inc.
Caren Sturges: trustee
Jane W. Watson: assistant secretary, assistant treasurer

Grants Analysis

Disclosure Period: calendar year ending 2000
Total Grants: $2,042,000
Number of Grants: 33
Average Grant: $47,594*
Highest Grant: $519,000
Typical Range: $10,000 to $50,000 and $100,000 to $300,000
*Note: Average grant excludes highest grant.

Recent Grants

Note: Grants derived from 2000 Form 990.

General

280,000	University School, Hunting Valley, OH -- capital
250,000	Cleveland Museum of Natural History, Cleveland, OH -- capital
200,000	Delta Society, Renton, WA -- unrestricted
100,000	Cleveland Botanical Garden, Cleveland, OH -- capital
100,000	Cleveland Orchestra, Cleveland, OH
100,000	Nature Conservancy, Brunswick, ME -- unrestricted
55,000	College of Veterinary Medicine (Argus), Ft. Collins, CO -- unrestricted
50,000	High Hopes Therapeutic, Old Lyme, CT -- scholarship
50,000	National Theater of the Deaf, Chester, CT -- capital
50,000	Portland Museum of Art, Portland, ME -- capital

INTEGRA BANK

Company Headquarters

201 N. Main Street
Bridgeport, IL 62417-1521
Web: http://www.integrabank.com

Company Description

Former Name: Gallatin National Bank.
Assets: US$16 million (2001)
Employees: 5 (2001)
SIC(s): 6000 Depository Institutions.
Parent Company: Integra Financial Group, 14901 Park Lake Dr., No. PH6, Fort Myers, FL, United States

Operating Locations

Integra Bank of Uniontown/National City (PA--Uniontown)

Nonmonetary Support

Type: Loaned Employees

Giving Contact

Leo Krantez, President & Chief Executive Officer
2 W. Main St.
Uniontown, PA 15401
Phone: (412)438-3551

Description

Organization Type: Corporate Giving Program
Giving Locations: headquarters area only.
Grant Types: Capital, Emergency, Employee Matching Gifts, General Support, Operating Expenses, Project, Seed Money.

Financial Summary

Total Giving: $55,000 (1997 approx); $55,000 (1996); $68,000 (1995)

Typical Recipients

Arts & Humanities: Arts & Humanities-General, Historic Preservation, Libraries, Performing Arts, Theater
Civic & Public Affairs: Botanical Gardens/Parks, Chambers of Commerce, Clubs, Economic Development, Employment/Job Training, Civic & Public Affairs-General, Housing
Education: Colleges & Universities, Community & Junior Colleges, Education Associations, Education-General
Health: Cancer, Health-General, Hospitals
Social Services: Community Centers, Community Service Organizations, Shelters/Homelessness, Social Services-General, United Funds/United Ways

Application Procedures

Initial Contact: Send a full proposal. Include a description of organization, amount requested, purpose of funds sought, and proof of tax-exempt status. Also, include a list of board members.

Restrictions

Does not support individuals, religious organizations for sectarian purposes, or political or lobbying groups.

Corporate Officials

Leo Krantez: president, chief executive officer PRIM CORP EMPL president, chief executive officer: Integra Bank of Uniontown/National City.

Grants Analysis

Typical Range: $1,000 to $2,500

INTERKAL, INC.

Company Headquarters

5981 E. Cork St.
PO Box 2107
Kalamazoo, MI 49003
Web: http://www.interkal.com

Company Description

Revenue: US$16.9 million (2001)
Employees: 160 (2001)
SIC(s): 2531 Public Building & Related Furniture.
Parent Company: Kotobuki Corp., 1-22-5 Sumitomo Seimei Bldg. 3F, Hamamatsu-cho, Minato-ku, Tokyo, Japan

Operating Locations

Interkal, Inc. (MI--Kalamazoo)

Nonmonetary Support

Type: Donated Equipment; Donated Products

Giving Contact

Dick Patterson, Pres./CEO
PO Box 2107
Kalamazoo, MI 49003
Phone: (616)349-1521
Fax: (616)349-6530
E-mail: dpatterson@interkal.com

Description

Organization Type: Corporate Giving Program
Giving Locations: headquarters and operating communities.
Grant Types: General Support.

Typical Recipients

Arts & Humanities: Arts Associations & Councils, Arts Centers, Community Arts, Libraries, Music, Performing Arts
Civic & Public Affairs: Economic Development
Education: Business Education, Colleges & Universities, International Exchange, International Studies
Social Services: Family Services, United Funds/United Ways

Application Procedures

Initial Contact: Send brief letter of inquiry, including a description of organization and purpose of funds sought.

Restrictions

Does not support dinners or special events, fraternal organizations, goodwill advertising, individuals, political or lobbying groups, or religious organizations for sectarian purposes.

Corporate Officials

Minoru Amemiya: chairman, chief executive officer B 1942. PRIM CORP EMPL president: GDS Seating Inc. ADD CORP EMPL chairman, chief executive officer: Interkal.
Brian Gould: controller, treasurer PRIM CORP EMPL controller, treasurer: Interkal.
Richard L. Patterson: president PRIM CORP EMPL president: Interkal.

Grants Analysis

Typical Range: $250 to $500

INTERMOUNTAIN GAS CO.

Company Headquarters

555 S. Cole Rd.
Boise, ID 83709

Company Description

Employees: 315
SIC(s): 4900 Electric, Gas & Sanitary Services, 4924 Natural Gas Distribution.
Parent Company: Intermountain Industries, Inc., 555 S. Cole Road, Boise, ID, United States

Operating Locations

Intermountain Gas Co. (ID--Boise)

Nonmonetary Support

Type: Donated Equipment; In-kind Services; Loaned Employees; Loaned Executives

Intermountain Gas Industries Foundation

Giving Contact

James E. Simmerman, Manager, Human Resources
PO Box 7608
Boise, ID 83707
Phone: (208)377-6000
Fax: (208)377-6097

Description

EIN: 820431608
Organization Type: Corporate Foundation
Giving Locations: headquarters and operating communities.
Grant Types: General Support.

Financial Summary

Total Giving: $211,897 (fiscal year ending September 30, 2001); $214,513 (fiscal 2000); $180,064 (fiscal 1998)
Giving Analysis: Giving for fiscal 2001 includes: foundation scholarships ($9,600); foundation grants to United Way ($19,250); fiscal 2000: foundation scholarships ($12,260); foundation grants to United Way ($19,250); fiscal 1998: foundation scholarships ($15,750); foundation grants to United Way ($17,450) foundation ($146,864)
Assets: $342,566 (fiscal 2001); $695,919 (fiscal 2000); $426,712 (fiscal 1998)
Gifts Received: $175,000 (fiscal 2001); $132,500 (fiscal 2000); $175,000 (fiscal 1998). Note: In fiscal 2001, contributions were received from Intermountain Gas Co. In fiscal 1996 and 2000, contributions were received from Intermountain Gas Co. ($150,000) and IGI Resources ($50,000).

Typical Recipients

Arts & Humanities: Arts Associations & Councils, Arts Centers, Libraries, Museums/Galleries, Music, Performing Arts, Public Broadcasting, Theater
Civic & Public Affairs: Business/Free Enterprise, Clubs, Community Foundations, Economic Development, Civic & Public Affairs-General, Housing, Legal Aid, Parades/Festivals, Public Policy, Rural Affairs, Urban & Community Affairs, Zoos/Aquariums
Education: Agricultural Education, Arts/Humanities Education, Colleges & Universities, Economic Education, Engineering/Technological Education, Private Education (Precollege), Public Education (Precollege), Secondary Education (Private), Student Aid, Vocational & Technical Education

Environment: Environment-General, Resource Conservation
Health: Clinics/Medical Centers, Diabetes, Emergency/Ambulance Services, Hospitals
International: Missionary/Religious Activities
Religion: Churches, Religious Welfare
Social Services: Animal Protection, Child Welfare, Community Service Organizations, Family Services, Recreation & Athletics, Scouts, Special Olympics, Substance Abuse, United Funds/United Ways, YMCA/YWCA/YMHA/YWHA, Youth Organizations

Application Procedures

Initial Contact: Request application form.
Deadlines: None.

Corporate Officials

William C. Glynn: president, chief executive officer, director administration, treasurer B Monticello, IA 1944. ED Loras College (1968); Boise State University (1979). PRIM CORP EMPL president, chief executive officer, director: Intermountain Gas Co. CORP AFFIL president: Intermountain Industries. NONPR AFFIL member: American Gas Association; director: Pacific Coast Gas Association.
N. Charles Hedemark: executive vice president, chief operating officer, director B Boise, ID 1942. ED College of Idaho (1964). PRIM CORP EMPL executive vice president, chief operating officer, director: Intermountain Gas Co. CORP AFFIL director: Home Federal Savings & Loan. NONPR AFFIL director: Blue Cross ID.
Richard Hokin: chairman, director PRIM CORP EMPL chairman, director: Intermountain Gas Co.
Jeffrey Kent Lebens: senior vice president financial & administration, treasurer B Minneapolis, MN 1944. ED University of Washington (1972). PRIM CORP EMPL senior vice president financial & administration, treasurer: Intermountain Gas Co. CORP AFFIL vice president,treasurer,chief financial officer: IGI Resources; vice president,treasurer,chief financial officer: Intermountain Industries.

Foundation Officials

William C. Glynn: director (see above)
N. Charles Hedemark: director (see above)
Richard Hokin: director (see above)
Jeffrey Kent Lebens: director (see above)
Paul Powell: director
Randy Schultz: director PRIM CORP EMPL executive vice president: IGI Resources Inc.

Grants Analysis

Disclosure Period: fiscal year ending September 30, 2001
Total Grants: $183,047*
Number of Grants: 98
Average Grant: $1,868
Highest Grant: $25,000
Lowest Grant: $50
Typical Range: $500 to $5,000
*Note: Giving excludes scholarships; United Way.

Recent Grants

Note: Grants derived from fiscal 2000 Form 990.

General

25,000	Boise State University School of Engineering, Boise, ID
15,000	University of Idaho College of Agriculture, Moscow, ID
12,900	Boise Philharmonic Association, Boise, ID
10,000	Boys and Girls Club of Ada County, Boise, ID
10,000	Idaho Community Foundation, Boise, ID
10,000	United Way of Ada County, Boise, ID
7,500	Idaho Governor's Challenge, Boise, ID
6,295	Idaho State University Foundation, Pocatello, ID
6,100	Greyhound Rescue of Idaho, Boise, ID
5,905	Idaho Public Television, Boise, ID

INTERNATIONAL BUSINESS MACHINES(IBM)

Company Headquarters

1133 Westchester Ave.
White Plains, NY 10604
Web: http://www.ibm.com

Company Description

Ticker: IBM
Exchange: NYSE
Acquired: Sequent Computer Systems (2001).
Revenue: US$83.132 billion (2002)
Profit: US$3.579 billion (2002)
Employees: 319,876 (2002)
Fortune Rank: 8, per FORTUNE Magazine's list of 500 Largest U.S. Corporations (2002).

Nonmonetary Support

Value: $86,700,000 (2000); $82,000,000 (1999); $79,000,000 (1998 approx)
Type: Donated Equipment; Donated Products; In-kind Services
Volunteer Programs: The IBM Fund for Community Service recognizes and encourages the involvement of IBM employees and their spouses as volunteers in their local communities. Through the Fund, IBM makes financial and IBM product grants to specific projects of eligible community organizations and schools, provided an employee, retiree or spouse is actively involved on a continuing basis.
Note: Contact for nonmonetary support: Corporate Community Relations local or corporate staff. Nonmonetary figures are calculated at retail value.

IBM International Foundation

Giving Contact

Stanley S. Litow, Vice President, Corporate Community Relations
IBM Corp.
New Orchard Road
Armonk, NY 10504
Phone: (914)765-1900
Fax: (914)499-7624
Web: http://www.ibm.com/ibm/ibmgives

Alternate Contact

Note: For local projects, contact the Corporate Relations Manager at the local IBM office.

Description

Founded: 1985
EIN: 133267906
Organization Type: Corporate Foundation
Former Name: IBM South Africa Project Fund.
Giving Locations: principally near operating locations and to national organizations.
Grant Types: Emergency, Employee Matching Gifts, Fellowship, General Support, Multiyear/Continuing Support.
Note: Matching Grant Program: There is a maximum of $5,000 cash per donor per institution, up to $10,000 in gifts annually. Cash match: Active employee 1 to 1; retirees 0.5 to 1. Equipment match for higher education: Active employees 3 to 1; retirees 1.5 to 1. Equipment match for hospitals, hospices, nursing homes, cultural and environmental institutions: active employees 2 to 1; retirees 1 to 1. The company also sponsors a K-12 Matching Grant Program for donation of equipment to K-12 schools.

Financial Summary

Total Giving: $126,000,000 (2002 approx); $11,292,796 (2001); $126,100,000 (2000). Note: 2000 figure given by foundation.

Giving Analysis: Giving for 2000 includes: foundation grants to United Way ($250,000); foundation fellowships ($1,608,440); foundation ($1,772,483); foundation matching gifts ($6,517,695); corporate direct giving ($30,300,000); 1999: foundation (approx $9,200,000); corporate direct giving ($43,000,000); nonmonetary support ($82,000,000); 1998: foundation ($1,144,880); foundation matching gifts ($5,425,052); corporate direct giving (approx $30,631,068);

Assets: $153,475,604 (2001); $146,630,946 (2000); $150,700,000 (1999 approx)

Gifts Received: $28,100,000 (2001); $10,614,843 (2000); $20,331,500 (1998). Note: Contributions are received from IBM Corp.

Typical Recipients

Arts & Humanities: Arts Associations & Councils, Arts Centers, Arts Funds, Arts Institutes, Community Arts, Dance, Ethnic & Folk Arts, Historic Preservation, Libraries, Museums/Galleries, Music, Opera, Performing Arts, Public Broadcasting, Theater, Visual Arts

Civic & Public Affairs: Civil Rights, Employment/Job Training, Civic & Public Affairs-General, Public Policy, Urban & Community Affairs, Women's Affairs, Zoos/Aquariums

Education: Afterschool/Enrichment Programs, Business Education, Colleges & Universities, Community & Junior Colleges, Education Associations, Engineering/Technological Education, Faculty Development, Education-General, Literacy, Minority Education, Private Education (Precollege), Public Education (Precollege), Science/Mathematics Education, Special Education

Environment: Environment-General

Health: Health Policy/Cost Containment, Health Organizations, Hospitals, Mental Health, Single-Disease Health Associations

International: Foreign Arts Organizations, Foreign Educational Institutions, International-General, Health Care/Hospitals, International Peace & Security Issues

Science: Science Exhibits & Fairs, Science Museums, Scientific Organizations

Social Services: Child Welfare, Community Service Organizations, Delinquency & Criminal Rehabilitation, Emergency Relief, Family Services, People with Disabilities, Senior Services, Substance Abuse, United Funds/United Ways, Veterans, Volunteer Services, Youth Organizations

Application Procedures

Initial Contact: Send a two-page letter.

Application Requirements: Send a brief statement fully describing the mission of the organization, the amount requested, and purpose of contribution; description of problem to be addressed, proposed solution and how IBM technology and volunteers will be incorporated (if appropriate); proof of tax-exempt status; name, address, and telephone number of the project contact; project budget with anticipated sources of income; past managerial experiences; controls to ensure funds are used as described; and a plan to measure results.

Deadlines: None.

Review Process: Unsolicited proposals are reviewed on an ongoing basis, but funding is limited. Notification is usually sent within one month.

Evaluative Criteria: Priority given to requests involving IBM technology or employee volunteers; consideration is also given to organizations currently receiving other types of company support.

Decision Notification: Rejections or additional information requests usually given within one month.

Notes: Majority of funding is initiated by IBM and does not stem from unsolicited proposals. Videotapes and supplemental materials are strongly discouraged at initial stage.

Restrictions

Does not support individuals; political, labor, religious, or fraternal organizations; sports groups; organizations without tax-exempt status; operating cost requests from United Way member organizations; raffles or telethons; auctions; capital campaigns; chairs; construction and renovation; endowments; scholarships; and company generally does not underwrite conferences, sports competitions, symposia, or controversial organizations or projects.

Additional Information

Publications: Corporate Support Programs Guidelines; Reinventing Education Guidelines

Corporate Officials

Paula W. Baker: director corporate support plans & programs PRIM CORP EMPL director corporate support plans & programs: International Business Machines Corp.

Nicholas M. Donofrio: senior vice president technology manufacturing PRIM CORP EMPL senior vice president technology manufacturing: International Business Machines Corp.

David B. Kalis: senior vice president communications PRIM CORP EMPL senior vice president communication: International Business Machines Corp.

Samuel J. Palmisano: president, chief operating officer, director PRIM CORP EMPL president, chief operating officer, director: International Business Machines Corp.

Giving Program Officials

Carol Cromwell: program manager

Robin Willner: member PRIM CORP EMPL director corporate social policy & programs: International Business Machines Corp.

Foundation Officials

Paula W. Baker: vice president (see above)

A. Bonzani: secretary

Cassio A. Calil: treasurer

R. J. Carroll: controller

Cliff Clifford: manager

Abby V. Kohnstamm: vice chairman, director

Stanley S. Litow: president PRIM CORP EMPL vice president community relations: International Business Machines Corp.

T. R. Stack: assistant treasurer

John Torkildsen: assistant controller

Gerard Vilcot: treasurer

Robert F. Woods: director

Grants Analysis

Disclosure Period: calendar year ending 2001

Total Grants: $2,548,972*

Highest Grant: $67,650

*Note: Giving excludes fellowships, matching gifts, United Way.

Recent Grants

Note: Grants derived from 2001 Form 990.

General

6,786,823	IBM International Foundation, Armonk, NY -- to support IBM employee directed gifts
1,644,327	IBM International Foundation, Armonk, NY -- funds for students pursuing PhDs in engineering and computer sciences
892,090	IBM International Foundation, Armonk, NY -- grant for organizations working in the areas of education, workforce diversity, health, human services, etc.
650,700	IBM Italy Foundation, Milan Italy -- support educational/cultural initiatives
495,789	IBM International Foundation, Armonk, NY -- for grants to present new uses of technology in raising teacher quality
355,300	KidSmart Early Learning Program -- for

Asia Pacific NGS's proficient in the delivery of cutting-edge technology to preschoolers

210,000	United Way - Canada, Ottawa, ON Canada -- support local/social voluntary initiatives
102,674	Humber College, Etobicoke, ON Canada
87,443	IBM International Foundation, Armonk, NY -- for housing construction
67,650	Reinventing Education Project, Washington, DC -- cash grants to enhance student achievement through improved teacher performance aided by technology

INTERNATIONAL MULTIFOODS CORP.

Company Headquarters

Minnetonka, MN

Web: http://www.multifoods.com

Company Description

Ticker: IMC

Exchange: OTC

Employees: 6,807

SIC(s): 2045 Prepared Flour Mixes & Doughs, 5145 Confectionery, 5149 Groceries & Related Products Nec.

Operating Locations

International Multifoods Corp. (CA--La Mirada, Los Angeles, Rialto, Riverside; CO--Denver; CT--East Windsor; FL--Orlando; GA--Atlanta; IL--Melrose Park, Woodridge; IN--Noblesville; KS--Bonner Springs; KY--Louisville; MA--Billerica, Malden; MI--Belleville; MN--Motley, Rice; MO--Carthage, Piedmont; NJ--Parsippany, Paulsboro; NM--Albuquerque; NY--Lockport, New Rochelle; NC--Greensboro; OH--Elyria, Twinsburg; TX--Dallas, Grand Prairie, Houston; WA--Seattle)

Nonmonetary Support

Type: Donated Products

Volunteer Programs: Company donates to nonprofit organizations where employees volunteer through its Employee Volunteer Bonus program. Additionally, the company sponsors the Employee Board Member Bonus where employees serve on nonprofit boards.

Note: Products are donated through the Second Harvest Food Bank network. Annual nonmonetary support approximately $100,000.

International Multifoods Charitable Foundation

Giving Contact

Karen Anderson, Foundation Administrator

110 Cheshire Ln., Suite 300

Minnetonka, MN 55305-1060

Phone: (952)594-3568

Fax: (952)594-3377

Description

EIN: 237064628

Organization Type: Corporate Foundation

Giving Locations: MN: Minneapolis, St. Paul Major principally near operating locations and to national organizations.

Grant Types: Capital, Employee Matching Gifts, General Support, Matching, Operating Expenses.

Note: Employee matching gift ratio: 1 to 1 for higher education only.

Financial Summary

Total Giving: $322,838 (fiscal year ending February 28, 2003); $221,600 (fiscal 2001); $129,083 (fiscal 2000)

Giving Analysis: Giving for fiscal 2002 includes: foundation ($240,150); fiscal 2001: foundation ($224,560); fiscal 2000: foundation scholarships ($5,930); corporate direct giving ($10,000); foundation ($18,680); foundation grants to United Way ($94,473)

Assets: $167,724 (fiscal 2003); $240,150 (fiscal 2002); $224,560 (fiscal 2001)

Gifts Received: $300,000 (fiscal 2003); $200,000 (fiscal 2000); $200,000 (fiscal 1998). Note: Foundation receives contributions from International Multifoods Corporation.

Typical Recipients

Arts & Humanities: Arts Institutes, Community Arts, Ethnic & Folk Arts, Libraries, Museums/Galleries, Music, Opera, Theater

Civic & Public Affairs: Botanical Gardens/Parks, Clubs, Civic & Public Affairs-General, Hispanic Affairs, Municipalities/Towns

Education: Agricultural Education, Business Education, Colleges & Universities, Economic Education, Education Funds, Elementary Education (Public), Faculty Development, Education-General, Leadership Training, Medical Education, Minority Education, Private Education (Precollege), Public Education (Precollege), Religious Education, Science/Mathematics Education, Special Education, Student Aid

Environment: Environment-General

Health: Diabetes

Religion: Churches

Science: Science Museums

Social Services: At-Risk Youth, Big Brother/Big Sister, Child Welfare, Community Service Organizations, Crime Prevention, Family Services, Food/Clothing Distribution, People with Disabilities, Recreation & Athletics, Scouts, Substance Abuse, United Funds/United Ways, Volunteer Services, YMCA/YWCA/YMHA/YWHA, Youth Organizations

Application Procedures

Initial Contact: Request guidelines from the foundation, then send written proposal.

Application Requirements: Include name, history, and purpose of organization; proof of tax-exempt status; statement of current objectives, priorities, how organization fits Multifoods' priorities, and summary of past two years' accomplishments; list of board of directors; copy of recent annual report; copy of IRS Form 990 and current year's operating budget.

Deadlines: May 31.

Review Process: Applications are screened by community affairs staff and reviewed by contributions committee.

Evaluative Criteria: Proximity of service area to company operating locations. For funding for a specific project, include a description of organization, including reasons for it, problem addressed, timetable and expected results; detailed budget including sources of income; method of evaluation; plans for sustaining project support; statement of how project fits company's giving priorities.

Decision Notification: Contributions committee meets biannually; notification usually within 90 days of receipt.

Restrictions

The company does not support religious groups for sectarian purposes; political or lobbying organizations; individuals; loans or investments; fundraisers such as luncheons, dinners, special events, or advertisements; industry, trade or professional association memberships; organizations receiving more than 25% of their support from the United Way or government agencies; or medical research, treatment, or equipment. No grants are made to endowment funds,

and no more than 10% to 12% of the annual contributions budget will be designated to capital grants. The company does not consider requests for support through telephone solicitation or form letters.

Additional Information

Grantees are required to provide periodic progress reports; site visits by company staff also may be requested. Company gives 2% of its pretax profits for charitable activities. No more than 10% to 12% of annual contributions budget will be designated to capital grants.

Publications: Multifoods Community Connection

Corporate Officials

Frank W. Bonvino: vice president, secretary, general counsel B Mount Vernon, NY 1941. ED Coe College BA (1963); William Mitchell College of Law JD (1968). PRIM CORP EMPL vice president, secretary, general counsel: International Multifoods Corp. CORP AFFIL secretary: Multifoods Distribution Group Inc. NONPR AFFIL member: American Bar Association; member: Minnesota State Bar Association.

John Byom: chief financial officer

Gary E. Costley: chairman, president, chief executive officer, director B 1943. ED Oregon State University PhD; Oregon State University MS (1970). PRIM CORP EMPL chairman, president, chief executive officer, director: International Multifoods Corp. CORP AFFIL director: Bush Brothers; chairman: Multifoods Distribution Group Inc.

Ralph Hargrow: senior vice president Human Resources

Jill W. Schmidt: vice president communications B 1958. PRIM CORP EMPL vice president communications: International Multifoods Corp.

Dan Swander: president, chief operating officer

Grants Analysis

Disclosure Period: fiscal year ending February 28, 2003

Total Grants: $322,838*

Number of Grants: 21

Average Grant: $15,370

Lowest Grant: $100

Typical Range: $500 to $5,000

*Note: Grants analysis provided by foundation.

Recent Grants

Note: Grants derived from fiscal 2000 Form 990.

General

53,306	United Way of Minneapolis Area, Minneapolis, MN
15,685	Sedalia-Pettis County United Way, Sedalia, MO
11,809	United Way of St. Cloud Area, St. Cloud, MN
4,908	Mile High United Way, Denver, CO
3,480	United Way of the Ozarks, Springfield, MO
2,546	Valley of the Sun United Way, Tempe, AZ
1,117	United Way of Gloucester County, Woodbury, NJ
1,048	Heart of America United Way, Kansas City, MO
1,000	Monmouth College, Monmouth, IL
1,000	St. John's University, Collegeville, MN

INTERNATIONAL PAPER CO.

Company Headquarters

400 Atlantic St.
Stamford, CT 06921
Web: http://www.ipaper.com

Company Description

Ticker: IP
Exchange: NYSE
Acquired: Champion International Corp..
Revenue: US$24.975 billion (2002)
Employees: 91000 (2002)
Fortune Rank: 64, per FORTUNE Magazine's list of 500 Largest U.S. Corporations (2002).

Nonmonetary Support

Value: $500,000 (2002 approx)
Type: Donated Equipment; Donated Products
Note: For nonmonetary support contact the local facility.

International Paper Co. Foundation

Giving Contact

Phyllis Epp, Executive Director
400 Atlantic Street
Stamford, CT 06921
Phone: (901)763-6000
Web: http://www.internationalpaper.com
Note: In communities where company maintains facilities, contact mill or plant manager, or communications, human resources, or public affairs manager.

Alternate Contact

Phyllis Epp, Executive Director
International Paper Co. Foundation
400 Atlantic Street
Stamford, CT 06921
Phone: (914)397-1500

Description

EIN: 136155080
Organization Type: Corporate Foundation
Giving Locations: nationally; principally near operating locations and to national organizations.
Grant Types: Award, Employee Matching Gifts, General Support.
Note: Employee matching gift ratio: 2 to 1 for employee gifts up to $200 each year; 1 to 1 for gifts over $200. Minimum gift foundation will match is $25, the maximum amount is $1,000 per employee annually. The foundation also supports specific educational and environmental programs.

Financial Summary

Total Giving: $7,341,973 (2002); $14,086,000 (2001); $7,506,373 (2000). Note: Contributes through corporate direct giving program and foundation.

Giving Analysis: Giving for 2001 includes: foundation ($6,897,000); corporate direct giving ($7,189,000); 2000: foundation grants to United Way ($5,000); foundation ($7,501,373); 1998: foundation grants to United Way ($11,000); corporate direct giving ($3,500,000); foundation ($4,629,905).

Assets: $38,766,263 (2002); $46,000,000 (2001 approx); $56,504,945 (2000)

Gifts Received: $5,343,492 (2002); $5,000,000 (2001 approx); $353,695 (2000). Note: Contributions are received from International Paper Co.

Typical Recipients

Arts & Humanities: Arts Associations & Councils, Arts Centers, Arts Festivals, Arts Funds, Dance, Historic Preservation, History & Archaeology, Libraries, Museums/Galleries, Music, Opera, Performing Arts, Public Broadcasting, Theater

Civic & Public Affairs: Botanical Gardens/Parks, Chambers of Commerce, Community Foundations, Civic & Public Affairs-General, Municipalities/Towns, Professional & Trade Associations, Public Policy, Urban & Community Affairs, Zoos/Aquariums

Education: Agricultural Education, Business Education, Colleges & Universities, Community & Junior Colleges, Economic Education, Education Reform,

Elementary Education (Private), Elementary Education (Public), Engineering/Technological Education, Environmental Education, Education-General, Education-General, Literacy, Minority Education, Private Education (Precollege), Public Education (Precollege), Science/Mathematics Education, Secondary Education (Public), Student Aid

Environment: Energy, Environment-General, Protection, Resource Conservation, Wildlife Protection

Health: Children's Health/Hospitals, Clinics/Medical Centers, Emergency/Ambulance Services, Health Organizations, Hospitals

Religion: Dioceses, Religious Organizations, Religious Welfare

Science: Science-General, Science Museums, Scientific Centers & Institutes, Scientific Labs

Social Services: Child Welfare, Community Centers, Community Service Organizations, Day Care, Emergency Relief, Family Services, Food/Clothing Distribution, Homes, Recreation & Athletics, Senior Services, Shelters/Homelessness, Social Services-General, Substance Abuse, United Funds/United Ways, Veterans, Volunteer Services, YMCA/YWCA/YMHA/YWHA, Youth Organizations

Application Procedures

Initial Contact: Request application form from local facility; send to manager of local International Paper Co. facility.

Application Requirements: Include a brief background of organization, including board of directors; concise description of program, budget, and objectives; audited financial statement; IRS tax-exemption letter; current funding sources and specific amounts; current annual report; including amount requested requested.

Deadlines: Check with local facilities for local deadlines; if submitting directly to foundation, applications are accepted from January 1 through November 30.

Decision Notification: Usually within two months of receipt.

Restrictions

Does not support individuals; programs for gifted students; general operating expenses; endowments; capital expenses; veterans or labor groups; athletic organizations; religious, political, or lobbying groups; organizations located outside or whose contributed funds are distributed outside the United States and its territories; tables at charitable functions or courtesy advertising; organizations which discriminate on the basis of sex, race, or creed; or groups that do not have 501(c)(3) tax-exempt status. Major emphasis is on communities where International Paper Company operates mills and plants, also in Memphis, Tennessee.

Corporate Officials

John T. Dillon: chairman, chief executive officer, director B Schroon Lake, NY 1938. ED University of Hartford (1965); Columbia University (1971). PRIM CORP EMPL chairman, chief executive officer, director: International Paper Co. CORP AFFIL director: Caterpillar Inc.; director: Capital Formation Inc.; director: Carter Holt Harvey Ltd. NONPR AFFIL trustee: Economic Education.

James Patrick Melican, Jr.: executive vice president B Worcester, MA 1940. ED Fordham University BA (1962); Harvard University JD (1965); Michigan State University MBA (1971). PRIM CORP EMPL executive vice president legal & external affairs: International Paper Co. CORP AFFIL director: Scitex Corp. Ltd. NONPR AFFIL member: Industries Sector Advisory Comm Paper Products for Trade Policy Matters; chairman finance & management policy committee: National Association Manufacturers; member: Association General Counsel; trustee: Fordham Prep School; member: American Law Institute; member: Association Bar New York City; member: American Bar Association.

Marianne M. Parrs: executive vice president B 1944. ED Brown University (1965). PRIM CORP EMPL executive vice president: International Paper Co.

Foundation Officials

Phyllis Epp: executive director
John V. Faraci: director
Marianne Parrs: director
Ken Reeves: vice president, administrator, director
Dennis Thomas: director
Carol Tusch: treasurer
Elizabeth Walenczyk: assistant secretary
Sandra C. Wilson: vice president administration, director B 1949.

Grants Analysis

Disclosure Period: calendar year ending 2002
Total Grants: $6,788,531*
Number of Grants: 1,063
Average Grant: $6,400
Highest Grant: $400,000
Lowest Grant: $85
Typical Range: $1,000 to $5,000
*Note: Giving includes matching gifts.

Recent Grants

Note: Grants derived from 2002 Form 990.

General

500,000	National Geographic Society, Washington, DC
400,000	Citizen's Scholarship Foundation, Santa Ana, CA
250,000	National Civil Rights Museum, Memphis, TN
200,000	Army Emergency Relief, Alexandria, VA
200,000	Navy Marine Corps Relief Society
100,000	Alliance for Downtown New York, Inc., New York, NY
100,000	Brooklyn Bureau of Community Grants, Brooklyn, NY
100,000	Paul D. Camp Community College, Franklin, VA
100,000	Rise Foundation, Richardson, TX
60,000	National Council on Economic Education, New York, NY

INTERSTATE/JOHNSON LANE

Company Headquarters

1 West Pack Sq.
Asheville, NC 28801
Phone: (828)255-8886
Web: http://www.ijl.com

Company Description

Former Name: Interstate/Johnson, Lane, Space, Smith & Co. Inc.
Employees: 1,400
SIC(s): 6211 Security Brokers & Dealers, 6282 Investment Advice.

Operating Locations

Interstate/Johnson Lane Corp. (GA--Savannah)

Johnson, Lane, Space, Smith Foundation

Giving Contact

David T. Johnson, Trustee
7391 Hodgson Memorial Dr.
Savannah, GA 31406
Phone: (912)921-3400

Alternate Contact

Jane Shumaker, Director, Corporate Communications & Chairperson, Gift Committee
PO Box 1012
Charlotte, NC 28201-1012
Phone: (704)379-9000
Note: Contact for direct giving program.

Description

Founded: 1984
EIN: 581550996
Organization Type: Corporate Foundation
Giving Locations: GA: Chatham County, Savannah
Grant Types: General Support, Operating Expenses.

Donor Information

Founder: Johnson, Lane, Space, Smith & Co., Inc.

Financial Summary

Total Giving: $18,250 (2001); $46,550 (2000); $30,500 (1999)
Giving Analysis: Giving for 2000 includes: foundation grants to United Way ($10,800); foundation ($35,750); 1999: foundation grants to United Way ($9,000); foundation ($21,500) 1998: foundation grants to United Way ($9,000)
Assets: $77,835 (2001); $141,522 (2000); $308,164 (1999)

Typical Recipients

Arts & Humanities: Ballet, History & Archaeology, Libraries, Museums/Galleries, Music, Performing Arts
Civic & Public Affairs: Clubs, Community Foundations, Civic & Public Affairs-General, Housing, Parades/Festivals, Urban & Community Affairs
Education: Arts/Humanities Education, Business Education, Preschool Education, Private Education (Precollege), Special Education
Environment: Environment-General, Resource Conservation
Health: Cancer, Heart, Hospices
Religion: Religious Welfare
Science: Science Museums
Social Services: Community Service Organizations, Family Planning, Family Services, Food/Clothing Distribution, Recreation & Athletics, Scouts, Substance Abuse, United Funds/United Ways

Application Procedures

Initial Contact: Send a letter outlining the need for which the request is made.
Deadlines: None.

Restrictions

Does not support individuals.

Additional Information

Foundation's primary focus is education, basic needs, capital expenditures, and the arts.

Corporate Officials

David T. Johnson: chairman emeritus PRIM CORP EMPL chairman emeritus: Interstate/Johnson Lane Corp.
James H. Morgan: chairman, president, chief executive officer, director PRIM CORP EMPL chairman, president, chief executive officer, director: Interstate/Johnson Lane Corp.
Edward C. Ruff: executive vice president, chief operating officer PRIM CORP EMPL executive vice president, chief operating officer: Interstate/Johnson Lane Corp.
Lee Semones: chief financial officer PRIM CORP EMPL chief financial officer: Interstate/Johnson Lane Corp.

Foundation Officials

David T. Johnson: trustee (see above)

Grants Analysis

Disclosure Period: calendar year ending 2001
Total Grants: $18,250
Number of Grants: 3
Highest Grant: $10,000
Lowest Grant: $3,250

Recent Grants

Note: Grants derived from 2000 Form 990.

General

10,800	United Way, Savannah, GA -- for operations
10,000	Church of the Cross Preschool -- for operations
10,000	Elaine Clark Center, Savannah, GA -- for operations
5,000	Hospice Savannah, Savannah, GA -- for operations
5,000	St. Joseph's Foundation, Savannah, GA -- for operations
2,500	Junior League, Savannah, GA -- for operations
2,000	Junior Achievement, Savannah, GA -- for operations
1,250	Telfair Academy of Arts, Savannah, GA -- for operations

IOWA SAVINGS BANK

Company Headquarters

118 5th Ave.
Coon Rapids, IA 50058

Company Description

Employees: 23

Operating Locations

Iowa Savings Bank (IA--Coon Rapids)

Iowa Savings Bank Charitable Foundation

Giving Contact

William C. Hess, Chief Executive Officer
PO Box 967
Carroll, IA 51401
Phone: (712)792-9772

Description

Founded: 1988
EIN: 421329826
Organization Type: Corporate Foundation
Giving Locations: IA
Grant Types: General Support, Scholarship.

Financial Summary

Total Giving: $81,455 (2000); $98,915 (1999); $110,255 (1998)
Giving Analysis: Giving for 1999 includes: foundation grants to United Way ($800) foundation ($98,115).
Assets: $150,735 (2000); $90,740 (1999); $365,510 (1998)
Gifts Received: $250,536 (2000); $72,740 (1999); $426,100 (1997). Note: Contributions received from Iowa Savings Bank.

Typical Recipients

Arts & Humanities: Arts Associations & Councils, History & Archaeology, Libraries, Music, Public Broadcasting
Civic & Public Affairs: Botanical Gardens/Parks, Business/Free Enterprise, Chambers of Commerce, Clubs, Community Foundations, Civic & Public Affairs-General, Municipalities/Towns, Parades/Festivals, Professional & Trade Associations, Rural Affairs, Safety, Urban & Community Affairs, Women's Affairs
Education: Agricultural Education, Colleges & Universities, Education Associations, Education Funds, Private Education (Precollege), Secondary Education (Private), Secondary Education (Public)
Environment: Environment-General, Resource Conservation, Wildlife Protection
Health: Cancer, Children's Health/Hospitals, Emergency/Ambulance Services, Heart, Hospices, Hospitals, Hospitals, Multiple Sclerosis, Public Health
Religion: Churches, Religion-General, Religious Organizations, Religious Welfare
Science: Scientific Centers & Institutes, Scientific Organizations
Social Services: Child Welfare, Community Service Organizations, Day Care, Family Planning, Food/Clothing Distribution, People with Disabilities, Recreation & Athletics, United Funds/United Ways

Application Procedures

Initial Contact: Send a brief letter with an explanation as to the purpose or need.
Deadlines: None.

Corporate Officials

John Chrystal: chairman PRIM CORP EMPL chairman: Iowa Savings Bank.
Richard Fulton: chief financial officer PRIM CORP EMPL chief financial officer: Iowa Savings Bank.
William C. Hess: chief executive officer PRIM CORP EMPL chief executive officer: Iowa Savings Bank.

Foundation Officials

John Chrystal: president, director (see above)
Tom Chrystal: director
Stephen Garst: director
William C. Hess: secretary, treasurer, director (see above)

Grants Analysis

Disclosure Period: calendar year ending 2000
Total Grants: $80,655*
Number of Grants: 51
Average Grant: $728*
Highest Grant: $25,000
Lowest Grant: $25
Typical Range: $250 to $2,000
*Note: Giving excludes United Way. Average grant excludes two highest grants ($45,000).

Recent Grants

Note: Grants derived from 1999 Form 990.

Library-Related

1,500	Glidden Public Library, Glidden, IA

General

50,025	St. Anthony's Foundation, Carroll, IA
20,000	Kuemper Capital Campaign, Carroll, IA
5,000	Carroll Depot Centre, Carroll, IA
1,875	Holy Spirit Parish, Carroll, IA
1,500	Friends of Kuemper Ball, Carroll, IA
1,325	St. Lawrence Church, Carroll, IA
1,000	Annunciation Church, Coon Rapids, IA
1,000	Iowa College Foundation, Des Moines, IA
1,000	John Ruan Multiple Sclerosis Charity, Des Moines, IA
1,000	Quakerdale Golf Outing, Carroll, IA

THE JAMES IRVINE FOUNDATION

Giving Contact

Ann L. Clarke, Director of Grants Administration
One Market, Steuart Tower, Suite 2500
San Francisco, CA 94105

Phone: (415)777-2244
Fax: (415)777-0869
Web: http://www.irvine.org

Alternate Contact

James Irvine Foundation
725 South Figueroa Street
Suite 3075
Los Angeles, CA 90017
Phone: (213)236-0552
Fax: (213)236-0537
Note: Above address provides contact information for the foundation's Los Angeles office.

Description

Founded: 1937
EIN: 941236937
Organization Type: General Purpose Foundation
Giving Locations: CA
Grant Types: Capital, Employee Matching Gifts, General Support, Multiyear/Continuing Support, Operating Expenses, Project, Seed Money, Dissemination of Technical Information.

Donor Information

Founder: Established by James Irvine in 1937 "to promote the general welfare of the people of California." Mr. Irvine (d. 1947) was president of the Irvine Land and Orchard Company, Napa Valley Railroad, and Moraga Land Company. The original trust property was a significant portion of Irvine Company stock, whose primary asset was approximately 100,000 acres of land in Orange County, CA, known as Irvine Ranch.

Financial Summary

Total Giving: $51,000,000 (2003 approx); $61,818,595 (2002); $58,223,073 (2000)
Giving Analysis: Giving for 2000 includes: foundation scholarships ($20,000); foundation grants to United Way ($106,500) 1998: foundation grants to United Way ($250,000)
Assets: $1,200,000,000 (2002 approx); $1,509,641,005 (2000); $1,605,121,505 (1999)
Gifts Received: $2,000 (1996)

Typical Recipients

Arts & Humanities: Arts Centers, Arts Institutes, Arts Outreach, Ballet, Community Arts, Dance, Ethnic & Folk Arts, Film & Video, Arts & Humanities-General, History & Archaeology, Libraries, Literary Arts, Museums/Galleries, Music, Opera, Performing Arts, Public Broadcasting, Theater
Civic & Public Affairs: African American Affairs, Asian American Affairs, Business/Free Enterprise, Community Foundations, Economic Development, Economic Policy, Employment/Job Training, Civic & Public Affairs-General, Hispanic Affairs, Housing, Law & Justice, Legal Aid, Native American Affairs, Nonprofit Management, Philanthropic Organizations, Professional & Trade Associations, Professional & Trade Associations, Public Policy, Rural Affairs, Urban & Community Affairs, Women's Affairs, Zoos/Aquariums
Education: Agricultural Education, Arts/Humanities Education, Business Education, Colleges & Universities, Education Associations, Education Reform, Engineering/Technological Education, Faculty Development, Education-General, International Studies, Journalism/Media Education, Leadership Training, Minority Education, Religious Education, Science/Mathematics Education, Student Aid, Vocational & Technical Education
Environment: Air/Water Quality, Forestry, Environment-General, Resource Conservation, Watershed, Wildlife Protection
Health: AIDS/HIV, Children's Health/Hospitals, Clinics/Medical Centers, Health-General, Health Policy/Cost Containment, Health Organizations, Hospitals, Hospitals (University Affiliated), Medical Research, Nursing Services, Prenatal Health Issues, Preventive

Medicine/Wellness Organizations, Public Health, Research/Studies Institutes

International: Foreign Arts Organizations, Human Rights, International Affairs, International Development, International Environmental Issues

Religion: Churches, Jewish Causes, Religious Welfare, Social/Policy Issues

Science: Science Museums, Scientific Centers & Institutes

Social Services: At-Risk Youth, Child Welfare, Community Service Organizations, Crime Prevention, Day Care, Domestic Violence, Family Planning, Family Services, People with Disabilities, Recreation & Athletics, Refugee Assistance, Shelters/Homelessness, United Funds/Ways, Volunteer Services, Volunteer Services, YMCA/YWCA/YMHA/YWHA, Youth Organizations

Application Procedures

Initial Contact: Send a two-page letter of inquiry or use online inquiry form, after reviewing the foundation's annual report and/or website.

Application Requirements: The letter should include a brief background of organization, amount requested and a one-sentence summary of the proposed project, overview of issue being addressed, summary of goals and objectives of proposed project.

Deadlines: None.

Review Process: Letters of inquiry are accepted year-round and are reviewed promptly. Applicants will receive a response within three to six weeks. The foundation then invites proposals from qualifying organizations. Following review of the proposals, the foundation conducts site visits and interviews. Final decisions may take up to six months.

Restrictions

The foundation only supports programs and organizations that benefit the State of California. The foundation does not fund agencies of the government, tax-supported organizations, or groups that primarily benefit public entities. The foundation primarily supports organizations that are classified as tax-exempt under section 501(c)(3) under the Internal Revenue Code. Grants are not made to individuals.

Additional Information

Publications: Annual Report; Guidelines

Foundation Officials

Samuel Henry Armacost: director B Newport News, VA 1939. ED Denison University BA (1961); Stanford University MBA (1964). CORP AFFIL director: Scios Inc.; director: SRI International; director: Chevron Corp.; director: Exponent Inc.

Martha S. Campbell: director of evaluation, program director

Mary Campbell: director program development and eval

James E. Canales: president, chief executive officer B San Francisco, CA 1966. ED Stanford University BA (1988); Stanford University MA (1989). CORP AFFIL vice chairman: BoardSource. NONPR AFFIL regent: Saint Ignatius College Prep; vice chair: Stanford Alumni Association; honorary director: Larkin Street Youth Center; member: Aspen Institute Nonprofit Sector Research Fund; chair: KQED Public Broadcasting.

Dennis Arthur Collins: president, director, chief executive officer B Yakima, WA 1940. ED Stanford University BA (1962); Stanford University MA (1963). NONPR AFFIL trustee: Aspen Institute Nonprofit Sector Research Fund; member: Council Foundations; trustee: American Farmland Trust Washington. CLUB AFFIL University Club; World Trade Center Club; California Club.

Frank H. Cruz: director ED University of Southern California BA; University of Southern California MS. PRIM CORP EMPL president: Cruz & Associates. NONPR AFFIL director: Corp. for Public Broadcasting; trustee: University of Southern California.

Larry R. Fies: chief financial officer, treasurer

James C. Gaither: director B Oakland, CA 1937. ED Princeton University BA (1959); Stanford University JD (1964). CORP AFFIL director: Stanford Management Co.; trustee: Rand Corp.; secretary: Siebel Systems Inc.; director: Levi Strauss International; director: Levi Strauss North America; director: Basic American Inc.; director: Levi Strauss & Co.; director: Amylin Pharmaceuticals Inc.; director: Basic American Food. NONPR AFFIL member: San Francisco Bar Association; member executive committee, board visitors, advisory board: Stanford University School Law; member: Phi Delta Phi; member executive committee, trustee, vice chairman: Carnegie Endowment International Peace; member: Order Coif; member: American Bar Association; member: California Bar Association; fellow: American Academy of Arts & Sciences.

Thomas L. Harris: chief administrative officer, director finance

John R. Jenks: treasurer, chief information officer

Joan Fletcher Lane: director B San Francisco, CA 1928. ED Smith College AB (1949). CORP AFFIL director: McClatchy Newspapers Inc.; director: McClatchy Co. Inc. NONPR AFFIL special assistant board trustee: Stanford University.

Cheryl White Mason: director ED Purdue University; University of Chicago Law School JD. NONPR AFFIL director: National Lawyers Committee for Civil Rights Under Law; director: Public Policy Institute California; director: Challengers Boys & Girls Club.

Davis Mas Masumoto: director ED University of California BA; University of California, Davis MS. OCCUPATION author.

Donn Biddle Miller: vice chairman, director B Gallipolis, OH 1929. ED Ohio Wesleyan University BA (1951); University of Michigan JD (1954); Harvard University (1974). PRIM CORP EMPL president, chief executive officer: Pearson-Sibert Oil Co. of Texas. CORP AFFIL director: Pacific Life Insurance Co. NONPR AFFIL vice chairman, director: Automobile Club Southern California.

Cora Mirikitani: senior program director

Molly Munger: director ED Harvard University Law School; Radcliffe College. PRIM CORP EMPL attorney: English, Munger & Rice. NONPR AFFIL member: Rand Corp. Committee on K-12 Education; member executive committee: Western Justice Center; director: Children Now; trustee: Occidental College.

Patricia S. Pineda: director PRIM CORP EMPL general counsel, assistant corporate secretary: New United Motor Manufacturing Inc. CORP AFFIL director: Levi Strauss International; director: Levi Strauss North America; director: Levi Strauss & Co.

Gary B. Pruitt: director

Toby Rosenblatt: director PRIM CORP EMPL president, general partner: Founders Investments Ltd PRIM NONPR EMPL board chairman: The Presidio Trust. CORP AFFIL director: Premier Pacific Vineyards; director: State Street Research Mutual Funds; director: Pherin Corp.; director: AP Pharma Inc.; director: MetLife Series Mutual Funds.

Forrest Nelson Shumway: director B Skowhegan, ME 1927. ED Stanford University BA (1950); Stanford University LLB (1952). CORP AFFIL director: ALCOA Inc.; director: TransAmerica Corp.

Peter William Stanley: board chairman B Bronxville, NY 1940. ED Harvard University BA (1962); Harvard University MA (1964); Harvard University PhD (1970). NONPR AFFIL member: Phi Beta Kappa; humanities & science council: Stanford University; national advisory council: National Foreign Language Center; member: Council Foreign Relations; director: National Association Latino Elected Officers Education Fund; member executive committee: Consortium Financing Higher Education; member: Association Asian Studies; vice chairman, trustee: College Board; member: American Historical Association; member: American Association University Professors; committee international education: American Council Education.

Peter J. Taylor: director

Kathryn Lillard Wheeler: honorary director NONPR AFFIL life member: Assistance League Santa Ana.

Edward Zapanta, MD: director CORP AFFIL director: Times Mirror Co.; director: Southern California Edison Co. NONPR AFFIL director: Edison International.

Grants Analysis

Disclosure Period: calendar year ending 2002
Total Grants: $61,818,595*
Number of Grants: 265
Average Grant: $233,277
Highest Grant: $2,000,000
Typical Range: $5,000 to $15,000 and $100,000 to $500,000
*Note: Giving includes United Way and scholarships.

Recent Grants

Note: Grants derived from 2001 Form 990.

General

2,250,000	Great Valley Center, Modesto, CA -- for core support
1,200,000	University of Southern California, Los Angeles, CA -- enhance campus diversity
1,000,000	Southern California Public Radio, Pasadena, CA -- start-up costs and core costs
700,000	California Center for Land Recycling, San Francisco, CA -- for start-up and core support
650,000	California Center for Regional Leadership, San Francisco, CA -- start up costs
579,120	Environmental Careers Organization, Boston, MA -- expand and enhance Sustainable Communities Leadership Program in California
500,000	Community Partners, Los Angeles, CA -- C2K Network Partners
500,000	Community Television of Southern California/KCET, Los Angeles, CA -- support "Life and Times Tonight"
500,000	Education Trust, Inc., Washington, DC -- raise student achievement and close academic achievement gaps
500,000	KQED, San Francisco, CA -- toward the production and related outreach activities "Bay Window"

WILLIAM G. IRWIN CHARITY FOUNDATION

Giving Contact

Michael R. Gorman, Executive Director
235 Montgomery Street, Suite 711
San Francisco, CA 94104
Phone: (415)362-6954

Description

Founded: 1919
EIN: 946069873
Organization Type: General Purpose Foundation
Giving Locations: CA; HI
Grant Types: Capital, General Support, Project, Research.

Donor Information

Founder: Established in 1919 by Mrs. Fannie M. Irwin. The foundation received contributions from Mrs. Fannie M. Irwin and Mrs. Helene Irwin Fagan , both deceased.

Financial Summary

Total Giving: $5,000,000 (2002 approx); $6,093,650 (2000); $4,000,000 (1999 approx)
Giving Analysis: Giving for 2000 includes: foundation grants to United Way ($40,000); 1998: foundation matching gifts ($20,000) foundation grants to United Way ($20,000)

Assets: $1,000,000 (2002 approx); $123,373,665 (2000); $115,000,000 (1999 approx)

Typical Recipients
Arts & Humanities: Ballet, Dance, Ethnic & Folk Arts, Historic Preservation, History & Archaeology, Libraries, Museums/Galleries, Music, Opera, Performing Arts
Civic & Public Affairs: Botanical Gardens/Parks, Civic & Public Affairs-General, Law & Justice, Urban & Community Affairs
Education: Arts/Humanities Education, Colleges & Universities, Education-General, Medical Education, Private Education (Precollege), Public Education (Precollege), Religious Education, Science/Mathematics Education, Secondary Education (Private), Secondary Education (Public)
Environment: Resource Conservation
Health: Alzheimers Disease, Arthritis, Cancer, Children's Health/Hospitals, Clinics/Medical Centers, Emergency/Ambulance Services, Eyes/Blindness, Geriatric Health, Health Organizations, Health Organizations, Heart, Hospitals, Long-Term Care, Medical Rehabilitation, Medical Research, Multiple Sclerosis, Research/Studies Institutes, Single-Disease Health Associations, Speech & Hearing, Transplant Networks/Donor Banks
Religion: Churches, Religious Organizations, Religious Welfare, Seminaries
Social Services: Animal Protection, Child Welfare, Community Service Organizations, Day Care, Food/Clothing Distribution, People with Disabilities, Scouts, Shelters/Homelessness, Social Services-General, United Funds/United Ways, YMCA/YWCA/YMHA/YWHA, Youth Organizations

Application Procedures
Initial Contact: The foundation has no application forms. Prospective applicants should submit a summary letter to the foundation.
Application Requirements: Grant proposals should include a summary letter, current financial information (audited, if possible, with a balance sheet and statement of revenue and expenses), budget, list of officers, directors and/or trustees, complete justification for request, history of organization, description of activities, and proof of federal and state tax-exempt status.
Deadlines: None. However, applications should be submitted approximately four to six weeks prior to a meeting date which are held every two months.
Review Process: Meetings are held approximately every two months.
Notes: The foundation does not accept video or audio tapes.

Restrictions
The foundation does not give grants for scholarships or to individuals, and limits grants to charitable uses in California and Hawaii.

Additional Information
A waiting period of twelve months is required between proposal submissions.

Foundation Officials
George T. Cronin: trustee
Michael R. Gorman: executive director
William Lee Olds, Jr.: president, trustee ED University of San Francisco (1970).
William Lee Olds, III: trustee ED Lewis & Clark College (1981).
Anthony Olds Zanze: trustee ED Dartmouth College (1982); University of Wisconsin (1988).
J. Zanze: trustee

Grants Analysis
Disclosure Period: calendar year ending 2000
Total Grants: $6,053,650*
Number of Grants: 41
Average Grant: $126,341*

Highest Grant: $1,000,000
Typical Range: $25,000 to $250,000
*****Note:** Giving excludes United Way. Average grant figure excludes highest grant.

Recent Grants
Note: Grants derived from 2000 Form 990.
General
1,000,000	University of California San Francisco, San Francisco, CA -- endowment academic chair
500,000	Asian Art Museum, San Francisco, CA -- capital campaign
500,000	Stanford University School of Medicine, Palo Alto, CA -- laboratory construction
250,000	Kapiolani Health, Honolulu, HI -- renovation project
250,000	St. Mary's College, Moraga, CA -- scientific equipment
250,000	St. Paul's Episcopal Church, Oakland, CA -- renovation project
250,000	Stuart Hall High School, San Francisco, CA -- new school campus
205,000	University of California San Francisco, San Francisco, CA -- laboratory renovation
200,000	Buck Institute for Research in Aging, Novato, CA -- laboratory equipment
200,000	Chaminade University, Honolulu, HI -- telecommunications wiring

ISCOL FAMILY FOUNDATION

Giving Contact
Jill Iscol, President, Treasurer & Director
63 Lyndel Road
Pound Ridge, NY 10576
Phone: (914)764-8477
Fax: (914)966-0639

Description
Founded: 1990
EIN: 061314468
Organization Type: Private Foundation
Giving Locations: New England.
Grant Types: General Support.

Donor Information
Founder: Established in 1990 by Kenneth Iscol.

Financial Summary
Total Giving: $610,925 (fiscal year ending June 30, 2001); $458,387 (fiscal 2000); $302,360 (fiscal 1998)
Assets: $4,212,790 (fiscal 2001); $5,241,008 (fiscal 2000); $5,208,761 (fiscal 1998)
Gifts Received: $1,000 (fiscal 1994); $5,700 (fiscal 1993); $55,249 (fiscal 1992)

Typical Recipients
Arts & Humanities: Historic Preservation, History & Archaeology, Libraries, Museums/Galleries, Music, Visual Arts
Civic & Public Affairs: Economic Development, Civic & Public Affairs-General, Rural Affairs
Education: Colleges & Universities, Literacy, Minority Education, Private Education (Precollege), Science/Mathematics Education, Student Aid
Environment: Environment-General, Resource Conservation, Wildlife Protection
Health: AIDS/HIV, Alzheimers Disease, Cancer, Clinics/Medical Centers, Diabetes, Emergency/Ambulance Services, Health Organizations, Hospices, Hospitals, Hospitals (University Affiliated), Medical Research, Respiratory, Single-Disease Health Associations, Speech & Hearing, Trauma Treatment

International: International Environmental Issues, International Peace & Security Issues, International Relief Efforts
Religion: Jewish Causes, Synagogues/Temples
Science: Science Museums
Social Services: Child Welfare, Community Service Organizations, Crime Prevention, Delinquency & Criminal Rehabilitation, Domestic Violence, Food/Clothing Distribution, Recreation & Athletics, Shelters/Homelessness, Youth Organizations

Application Procedures
Initial Contact: Send a brief letter of inquiry.
Application Requirements: Include amount requested, need, and purpose of funds sought.
Deadlines: None.

Foundation Officials
Samuel Hurwitz: assistant secretary
Jill Iscol: president, treasurer, director
Kenneth H. Iscol: vice president, secretary, director

Grants Analysis
Disclosure Period: fiscal year ending June 30, 2001
Total Grants: $610,925
Number of Grants: 92
Average Grant: $3,365*
Highest Grant: $304,750
Typical Range: $1,000 to $5,000
*****Note:** Average grant figure excludes highest grant.

Recent Grants
Note: Grants derived from fiscal 2000 Form 990.
General
66,250	Cornell University, Ithaca, NY
35,400	Bank Street College of Education, New York, NY
35,000	Facing History and Ourselves, Brookline, MA
34,752	Horizons, New Canaan, CT
34,100	Prep for Prep, New York, NY
30,000	Teachers College, Columbia University, New York, NY
20,000	Youth Service America, Washington, DC
10,075	Stand for Children, Washington, DC
10,000	Chilmark Town Affairs Council, Chilmark, MA
10,000	H.E.R.A. Foundation, Bronx, NY

ISHIYAMA FOUNDATION

Giving Contact
George I. Ishiyama, President & Director
465 California St., No. 800
San Francisco, CA 94104
Phone: (415)392-0800
Fax: (415)392-1268

Description
Founded: 1968
EIN: 941659373
Organization Type: Private Foundation
Giving Locations: CA; Japan
Grant Types: General Support.

Donor Information
Founder: George S. Ishiyama

Financial Summary
Total Giving: $2,643,822 (2000); $2,062,661 (1999); $2,712,255 (1998)
Giving Analysis: Giving for 2000 includes: foundation scholarships ($608,990)
Assets: $59,759,696 (2000); $52,703,443 (1999); $54,545,546 (1998)
Gifts Received: $1,000,000 (2000); $1,000,000 (1999); $1,000,000 (1998). Note: In 1998, 1999, and

2000, contributions were received from George Is-hiyama.

Typical Recipients

Arts & Humanities: Arts Centers, Ethnic & Folk Arts, Libraries, Museums/Galleries, Music
Civic & Public Affairs: Ethnic Organizations, Civic & Public Affairs-General, Philanthropic Organizations, Urban & Community Affairs
Education: Colleges & Universities, Education Associations, Education-General, International Studies, Legal Education, Private Education (Precollege), Public Education (Precollege), Religious Education, Science/Mathematics Education, Student Aid
Environment: Air/Water Quality, Environment-General, Resource Conservation, Wildlife Protection
Health: Children's Health/Hospitals, Clinics/Medical Centers, Health Organizations, Heart, Hospitals, Medical Rehabilitation, Research/Studies Institutes, Single-Disease Health Associations, Speech & Hearing
International: Foreign Arts Organizations, Foreign Educational Institutions, Foreign Educational Institutions, International Peace & Security Issues, International Relations
Religion: Jewish Causes, Religious Organizations
Science: Science Museums, Scientific Centers & Institutes
Social Services: Community Service Organizations, Delinquency & Criminal Rehabilitation, Family Services, Senior Services

Application Procedures

Initial Contact: The foundation has no formal grant application procedure or application form.
Deadlines: None.

Restrictions

Preference is given to educational institutions. Does not support individuals.

Foundation Officials

Ralph Bardoff: vice president, director
George I. Ishiyama: president, director
Jean Ishiyama: assistant secretary
Setsuko Ishiyama: secretary, treasurer, director
Margaret Raffin: director

Grants Analysis

Disclosure Period: calendar year ending 2000
Total Grants: $2,034,832*
Number of Grants: 25
Average Grant: $26,149*
Highest Grant: $608,990
Lowest Grant: $1,000
Typical Range: $1,000 to $25,000 and $100,000 to $500,000
***Note:** Giving excludes scholarship. Average grant figure excludes three highest grants ($1,459,559).

Recent Grants

Note: Grants derived from 2000 Form 990.

Library-Related
135,700   Friends of the Library, Woodstock, NY

General
608,990   Alaska Pulp Scholarship Fund
500,000   Health Services Toranomon Hospital
500,000   Scripps College, Claremont, CA
459,559   International University of Japan, Niigata Japan
106,000   Science Museum Exploratorium
35,000   National Fish and Wildlife Foundation, Washington, DC
25,000   Rehabilitation Center Family Services
22,573   Alaska Kai
10,000   Palo Alto Endowment Fund, Palo Alto, CA
5,000   Medical Foundation Cardiac Therapy Foundation

ISLAND FOUNDATION (MA)

Giving Contact

Julie Early, Executive Director
589 Mill Street
Marion, MA 02738-1553
Phone: (508)748-2809
Fax: (508)748-0991
E-mail: islandfdn@earthlink.net

Description

Founded: 1979
EIN: 042670567
Organization Type: General Purpose Foundation
Giving Locations: MA: New Bedford
Grant Types: General Support, Multiyear/Continuing Support, Project, Research.

Donor Information

Founder: The Island Foundation was founded in 1980 by Van Alan Clark and Mary Aland and is perhaps the strongest expression of their activism. Van Clark was dedicated to change. He was constantly rethinking and the range of his inquiry was truly impressive. In his life, he sought to affect fields as far ranging as tropical disease, higher education, art in inner city, electronics, oceanography, anti-submarine warfare, low speed aerodynamics, and postitive alternatives for troubled youth.
In her seventies, Mary Clark is anything but retiring. After Van's death in 1983, she led the Foundation through years of expanding vision and capacity. She no longer serves on the board yet dynamically pursues a wide variety of other interests.
Van's goal was always to change the ground rules. He ardently believed that one should never accept an unsatisfactory status quo if one has the means of changing it. This would be admirable in itself, but what made Van and Mary remarkable was their willingness to put ideas to the test. They were singularly courageous. They understood that it takes money, vision, hard work and endurance to make ideas into reality. Thus, the charge of the Island Foundation is to foster those visions and provide the capital, guidance, and support to bring about a better reality.

Financial Summary

Total Giving: $1,643,333 (1999); $1,518,774 (1998); $997,563 (1997)
Giving Analysis: Giving for 1999 includes: foundation grants to United Way ($45,000) 1998: foundation grants to United Way ($31,025)
Assets: $37,271,124 (1999); $32,539,373 (1998); $26,000,000 (1996 approx)
Gifts Received: $271,808 (1994); $5,490 (1993)

Typical Recipients

Arts & Humanities: Arts Associations & Councils, Arts Festivals, Arts & Humanities-General, Historic Preservation, Museums/Galleries, Music, Theater
Civic & Public Affairs: Business/Free Enterprise, Civil Rights, Community Foundations, Economic Development, Employment/Job Training, Civic & Public Affairs-General, Hispanic Affairs, Law & Justice, Municipalities/Towns, Nonprofit Management, Philanthropic Organizations, Professional & Trade Associations, Public Policy, Urban & Community Affairs, Women's Affairs, Zoos/Aquariums
Education: Afterschool/Enrichment Programs, Arts/Humanities Education, Business Education, Colleges & Universities, Economic Education, Education Reform, Elementary Education (Public), Environmental Education, Faculty Development, Education-General, Health & Physical Education, Leadership Training, Preschool Education, Private Education (Precollege), Public Education (Precollege), Science/Mathematics Education, Secondary Education (Private), Secondary Education (Public), Student Aid

Environment: Air/Water Quality, Environment-General, Protection, Research, Resource Conservation, Watershed, Wildlife Protection
Health: Adolescent Health Issues, AIDS/HIV, Kidney, Medical Rehabilitation
International: International Affairs, International Environmental Issues, International Relations, Trade
Religion: Religious Welfare, Social/Policy Issues
Science: Science Museums, Scientific Centers & Institutes, Scientific Research
Social Services: At-Risk Youth, Community Centers, Community Service Organizations, Counseling, Day Care, Delinquency & Criminal Rehabilitation, Domestic Violence, Emergency Relief, Family Planning, Family Services, People with Disabilities, Recreation & Athletics, Senior Services, Shelters/Homelessness, Substance Abuse, United Funds/United Ways, YMCA/YWCA/YMHA/YWHA, Youth Organizations

Application Procedures

Initial Contact: The foundation requests an initial letter or phone call to determine the interest and appropriateness of a full proposal.
Application Requirements: A formal proposal should include the following: a cover letter; a narrative of the specific goals, intended beneficiaries, timetable, procedure, and current status of the project; a history and background of the organization; methods of assessment and evaluation; an income and expense budget for the organization and the project for past, current and proposed years; an IRS tax-determination letter indicating section 501(c)(3) status; the most recent year-end fiscal statement or audit; the background of key personnel and a list of directors; and any supplementary materials. Research proposals should be formatted to include a one-page abstract summarizing the question(s) asked, methods used, results expected, and justification.
Deadlines: None.
Review Process: Decisions are made by the board on an ongoing basis. Site visits are often made by the foundation, and grantees are expected to submit semiannual reports.
Notes: The foundation accepts proposals that use the Common Proposal Format as developed by the Associated Grantmakers of Massachusetts. The foundation asks that proposals be submitted in an environmentally sensitive manner. One copy will suffice.

Restrictions

All applicants must be tax-exempt organizations. No grants are made to individuals, sectarian religious activities, or candidates for public office. Grants made only in the New Bedford Area.

Additional Information

Publications: Annual Report; Application Guidelines

Foundation Officials

Kim N. Clark: vice president
Stephen H. Clark: president, director B 1953. ED Cornell University BA (1975); Cornell University MA (1976). PRIM CORP EMPL chairman: Quartermoon Inc.
Julie A. Early: executive director
Hannah T. C. Moore: treasurer
Michael J. Moore: director
Peter J. Nesbeda: corporator B 1950. PRIM CORP EMPL chairman, president, chief executive officer, director: Xyplex Inc.
Christopher N. Tupper: corporator
JoAnn Watson: corporator

Grants Analysis

Disclosure Period: calendar year ending 1999
Total Grants: $1,598,333*
Number of Grants: 56
Average Grant: $19,970*
Highest Grant: $500,000

Typical Range: $10,000 to $40,000
*Note: Giving excludes United Way. Average grant figure excludes highest grant.

Recent Grants

Note: Grants derived from 2001 Form 990.

General

300,000	Thompson Island Outward Bound, Boston, MA -- Middle School Program - Choices
200,000	YMCA Southcoast, New Bedford, MA -- Wareham YMCA capital campaign
100,000	Save the Bay, Providence, RI -- bay experience initiative
60,000	PKR Foundation, Kansas City, MO -- research support
50,000	Community Foundation of Southeastern Massachusetts, New Bedford, MA -- operating support
50,000	New England Aquarium, Boston, MA -- to support right whale research
40,000	Center for Coastal Studies, Provincetown, MA -- capital campaign
30,000	ArtWorks!, New Bedford, MA -- studio and exhibition programming
30,000	Cape Cod Stranding Network, Buzzards Bay, MA -- Cape Cod Stranding Network
30,000	Coalition for Buzzards Bay, Buzzards Bay, MA

ITTLESON FOUNDATION

Giving Contact

Anthony C. Wood, Executive Director
15 East 67th Street
New York, NY 10021
Phone: (212)794-2008
Fax: (212)794-0351
Web: http://www.ittlesonfoundation.org

Description

Founded: 1932
EIN: 510172757
Organization Type: Family Foundation
Giving Locations: nationally.
Grant Types: Project, Seed Money.

Donor Information

Founder: The Ittleson Foundation was established in New York in 1932 by the late Henry Ittleson , founder and past chairman of C.I.T. Financial Corporation. After his death in 1948, the foundation received a substantial bequest from his estate. Mr. Ittleson's widow, Blanche F. Ittleson, former trustee of the foundation (until her death in 1975), directed the focus of the foundation toward health and welfare, particularly mental health care and research.

Financial Summary

Total Giving: $1,328,896 (2000); $1,009,031 (1998); $631,630 (1997). Note: 1998 Giving includes membership grants ($15,755) and miscellaneous grants totaling ($143,276). 1997 Giving includes membership grants totaling ($10,130). 1996 Giving includes memberships ($10,130).
Assets: $26,482,436 (2000); $24,380,613 (1998); $21,301,496 (1997)
Gifts Received: $3,000 (2000); $25,000 (1998); $175,000 (1992). Note: Contributions were received from the estate of Nancy S. Ittleson.

Typical Recipients

Arts & Humanities: Arts Associations & Councils, Arts Centers, Arts Outreach, Dance, Film & Video, Historic Preservation, History & Archaeology, Libraries, Museums/Galleries, Opera, Public Broadcasting, Theater

Civic & Public Affairs: Botanical Gardens/Parks, Chambers of Commerce, Civil Rights, Community Foundations, Economic Development, Employment/Job Training, Gay/Lesbian Issues, Civic & Public Affairs-General, Housing, Law & Justice, Legal Aid, Minority Business, Native American Affairs, Nonprofit Management, Philanthropic Organizations, Professional & Trade Associations, Public Policy, Safety, Urban & Community Affairs, Women's Affairs, Zoos/Aquariums

Education: Arts/Humanities Education, Business Education, Colleges & Universities, Education Associations, Education Reform, Elementary Education (Private), Environmental Education, Faculty Development, Education-General, Medical Education, Private Education (Precollege), Social Sciences Education

Environment: Air/Water Quality, Forestry, Environment-General, Protection, Resource Conservation, Watershed, Wildlife Protection

Health: AIDS/HIV, Cancer, Children's Health/Hospitals, Emergency/Ambulance Services, Geriatric Health, Health Organizations, Hospitals, Medical Research, Mental Health, Nutrition, Prenatal Health Issues, Preventive Medicine/Wellness Organizations, Public Health, Research/Studies Institutes, Single-Disease Health Associations

International: Health Care/Hospitals, Human Rights, International Affairs, International Environmental Issues, International Organizations, International Peace & Security Issues, International Relations, International Relief Efforts

Religion: Churches, Jewish Causes, Religious Welfare

Social Services: At-Risk Youth, Child Abuse, Child Welfare, Community Service Organizations, Counseling, Crime Prevention, Delinquency & Criminal Rehabilitation, Family Services, Food/Clothing Distribution, Homes, People with Disabilities, Senior Services, Shelters/Homelessness, Social Services-General, Substance Abuse, United Funds/United Ways, Volunteer Services, Youth Organizations

Application Procedures

Initial Contact: The foundation does not supply application forms. Applicants should send a brief letter.
Application Requirements: The letter should include a a description of organization and project for which funds are sought, organization's budget, an annual report, if available, and evidence of tax-exempt status.
Deadlines: April 1 for the spring meeting, and September 1 for the fall meeting.
Review Process: Grant requests are reviewed on a continuing basis. If the grant proposal fits within the foundation's current scope of interest, additional information will be required. If the foundation declines a proposal, applicants must wait at least one year before reapplying for any purpose.

Restrictions

The foundation generally does not provide funding for general support, capital building projects, endowments, grants to individuals, scholarships or internships (except as part of a program), biomedical research, or continuing support to existing programs. Support also is not given for direct service programs, especially when outside New York City, or for projects with a local focus or constituency. The foundation does not make international grants.

Additional Information

The foundation reports that it supports pilot programs or the start-up of new services when the service or project is truly innovative, there are practical plans for evaluation, there appears to be an audience for the results, and there is a credible plan for dissemination to those audiences.
In 1995, the foundation reported that it had dropped its crime and justice program area.
Publications: Annual Report

Foundation Officials

Henry Anthony Ittleson: chairman, president, director B New York, NY 1937. ED Brown University BA (1960). PRIM CORP EMPL chairman: Travent Ltd. NONPR AFFIL board fellows: Brown University; member: Phi Gamma Delta; trustee: Brooks School. CLUB AFFIL Regency Whist Club; Shinnecock Hills Golf Club; Long Island Wyandanch Club; Meadow Club; Links America; Brown University Club; Deepdale Golf Club.
Marianne S. Ittleson: director
Lionel Irwin Pincus: director B Philadelphia, PA 1931. ED University of Pennsylvania BA (1953); Columbia University School of Business Administration MBA (1956). PRIM CORP EMPL chairman, chief executive officer, director: EM Warburg, Pincus & Co. Inc. ADD CORP EMPL managing partner: Warburg Pincus Capital Partners LP; president: Warburg Pincus Asset Management; managing partner: Warburg Pincus Ventures Inc. CORP AFFIL managing partner: Warburg Pincus Investors LP. NONPR AFFIL member: New York City Partnership Chamber of Commerce; trustee: School American Ballet; director: National Park Foundation; member: Council Foreign Relations; trustee: Montefiore Hospital Medical Center; trustee, chairman emeritus: Columbia University; member, board overseers: Columbia University Graduate School Business. CLUB AFFIL Meadow Club; National Golf Links America Club.
Lawrence O. Sneag: treasurer
Pamela L. Syrmis: vice president, director
Victor P. Syrmis, MD: director B 1943.
Anthony C. Wood: executive director, secretary

Grants Analysis

Disclosure Period: calendar year ending 2000
Total Grants: $1,125,000*
Number of Grants: 30
Average Grant: $30,172*
Highest Grant: $250,000
Typical Range: $15,000 to $60,000
*Note: Giving excludes memberships and miscellaneous grants. Average grant figure excludes highest grant.

Recent Grants

Note: Grants derived from 2000 Form 990.

Library-Related

2,000	Foundation Center, New York, NY

General

250,000	Brown University, Providence, RI -- The Foundation's new statement of mental health priorities
100,000	Foundation for Integrative Medicine, Tucson, AZ
80,000	Addiction Treatment Alternatives, San Francisco, CA -- launch the Harm Reduction Therapy Center
60,000	Village Care of New York, New York, NY -- AIDS-specific Mental Health Program
55,000	Reuse Development Organization, Inc., Indianapolis, IN -- create and make operational a national large donations program
50,000	INCube, Inc., New York, NY -- to launch the Train-the-Trainer program
50,000	Memorial Sloan-Kettering Cancer Center, New York, NY -- to support, The Mind-Body-Spirit Program, a holistic model of psychological support for patients with cancer
40,000	Center for Preventive Psychiatry, White Plains, NY -- establish early childhood consultation service
40,000	Miriam Hospital Foundation, Providence, RI -- Project Prevent
40,000	Preventive Intervention Research Center for Child Health, Bronx, NY -- study

effects on children shouldering caregiving responsibilities due to single mother's HIV/AIDS illness

J&L SPECIALTY STEEL, INC.

Company Headquarters
PO Box 3373
Pittsburgh, PA 15230
Web: http://www.jlspecialty.com

Company Description
Former Name: J&L Specialty Products Corp.
Employees: 1,200
SIC(s): 3300 Primary Metal Industries.
Parent Company: Ugine Stainless & Alloys, Inc., 370 Franklin Turnpike, Mahwah, NJ, United States

Operating Locations
Edgcomb Metals (PA--Bensalem); Edgcomb Metals of New England (NH--Nashua); Francosteel Corp. (NY--New York); Hood & Co. (PA--Hamburg); Interstate Steel Co. (IL--Des Plaines); J&L Specialty Steel (PA--Pittsburgh); Metron Steel (IL--Chicago); Rahns Specialty Metals (PA--Collegeville); Techalloy Co. (NJ--Mahwah)

J&L Specialty Steel Charitable Foundation

Giving Contact
James Leonard, Director, Public Affairs
J&L Specialty Steel, Inc
1 PPG Pl.
PO Box 3373
Pittsburgh, PA 15230-3373
Phone: (412)338-1600

Description
Founded: 1989
EIN: 256311251
Organization Type: Corporate Foundation
Giving Locations: headquarters and operating communities.
Grant Types: Employee Matching Gifts, General Support, Scholarship.

Financial Summary
Total Giving: $185,498 (2000); $181,185 (1999); $169,330 (1998)
Giving Analysis: Giving for 2000 includes: foundation grants to United Way ($60,510); 1999: foundation grants to United Way ($62,710); foundation ($118,475) 1998: foundation grants to United Way ($55,750)
Assets: $2,172,709 (2000); $2,272,423 (1999); $2,352,604 (1998)
Gifts Received: $300,000 (1994). Note: In 1994, contributions were received from J&L Specialty Steel.

Typical Recipients
Arts & Humanities: Arts Centers, Arts Outreach, Libraries, Museums/Galleries, Music, Public Broadcasting, Theater
Civic & Public Affairs: Economic Development, Employment/Job Training, Civic & Public Affairs-General, Urban & Community Affairs, Zoos/Aquariums
Education: Business Education, Colleges & Universities, Education Reform, Education-General, Preschool Education, Public Education (Precollege), Secondary Education (Public), Student Aid
Health: Cancer, Children's Health/Hospitals, Diabetes, Emergency/Ambulance Services, Heart, Hospitals, Kidney, Mental Health, Single-Disease Health Associations

Religion: Religious Welfare
Social Services: At-Risk Youth, Big Brother/Big Sister, Child Welfare, Community Service Organizations, Community Service Organizations, Family Services, Homes, People with Disabilities, Recreation & Athletics, Scouts, Sexual Abuse, Shelters/Homelessness, United Funds/United Ways, YMCA/YWCA/YMHA/YWHA, Youth Organizations

Application Procedures
Initial Contact: Send a letter describing organization and program or project for which funding is requested. Include a copy of 501(c)(3) certification letter and recent financial statements.
Deadlines: Submission should be made in the calendar year in which funds are requested.

Restrictions
Does not support individuals, religious organizations for sectarian purposes, political or lobbying groups, or organizations outside operating areas.

Additional Information
Trust(s): Mellon Bank NA NA

Corporate Officials
Guy Dolle: chairman vice president PRIM CORP EMPL chairman: J&L Specialty Steel.
Eugene Anthony Salvadore: president, chief executive officer B Pittsburgh, PA 1949. ED Carnegie Mellon University (1970); University of Pittsburgh (1975). PRIM CORP EMPL president, chief executive officer: J&L Specialty Steel. CORP AFFIL director: Midland Terminal Co.
Kirk F. Vincent: executive vice president PRIM CORP EMPL executive vice president: J&L Specialty Steel.

Foundation Officials
Daryl K. Fox: admin
Eugene Anthony Salvadore: chairman, administrator (see above)

Grants Analysis
Disclosure Period: calendar year ending 2000
Total Grants: $124,988*
Number of Grants: 83
Average Grant: $1,506
Highest Grant: $20,000
Typical Range: $1,000 to $5,000
*Note: Giving excludes United Way.

Recent Grants
Note: Grants derived from 2001 Form 990.

General

21,000	Salvation Army, Pittsburgh, PA
12,600	Robert Morris University, Moon Township, PA
7,200	Midland Borough School District, Midland, PA
5,000	Carnegie Mellon University, Pittsburgh, PA
5,000	Carnegie Museums of Pittsburgh, Pittsburgh, PA
5,000	Louisville Area YMCA, Louisville, OH
5,000	University of Pittsburgh School of Engineering, Pittsburgh, PA
5,000	Zoological Society of Pittsburgh, Pittsburgh, PA
3,500	Midland Borough, Midland, PA
3,000	American Red Cross Pittsburgh Allegheny County Chapter, Pittsburgh, PA

J.P. MORGAN CHASE & CO.

Company Headquarters
270 Park Ave.
New York, NY 10017
Web: http://www.jpmorganchase.com

Company Description
Founded: 2000
Ticker: JPM
Exchange: NYSE
Formed by Merger of: Chase Manhattan Corp (2000); J.P. Morgan & Company (2000).
Assets: US$758.8 billion (2002)
Profit: US$1.663 billion (2002)
Employees: 94335 (2002)
Fortune Rank: 26, per FORTUNE Magazine's list of 500 Largest U.S. Corporations (2002).
SIC(s): 6000 Depository Institutions, 6021 National Commercial Banks, 6712 Bank Holding Companies.

Operating Locations
Chase Manhattan Bank, NA (AZ--Phoenix; CA--Los Angeles, San Diego, San Francisco; DE--Newark, Wilmington; FL--Boca Raton, Palm Beach, St. Petersburg, Tampa; IL--Chicago; MD--Baltimore; NY--Rochester; TX--Dallas, Houston); J.P. Morgan & Co. (CA--Los Angeles, San Francisco; DE--Wilmington; FL--Palm Beach)

Nonmonetary Support
Range: $300,000 - $400,000
Type: Donated Equipment; In-kind Services
Volunteer Programs: Several thousand company employees volunteer in programs serving the communities in which they live and work, in a diverse set of activities that range from serving as mentors for at-risk teenagers to working as "huggers" for hospital boarder babies, from delivering meals to the homebound elderly to serving on numerous nonprofit boards.
Note: Co. donates equipment and surplus furniture, and supplies *pro bono* printing.

J.P. Morgan Chase Foundation

Giving Contact
Steven W. Gelston, Secretary
J.P. Morgan Chase Foundation
Care of The Corporate Tax Department
245 Park Ave., 8th Floor
New York, NY 10167
Phone: (212)270-8055
Web: http://www.jpmorganchase.com/cm/cs?pagename=Chase/Href&urlname=jpmc/community

Description
EIN: 237049738
Organization Type: Corporate Foundation
Giving Locations: AZ; CA; CT; DE; FL; MA; NJ; NY; OH: internationally; nationally; primarily headquarters and operating communities.
Grant Types: Award, Capital, Challenge, Department, Employee Matching Gifts, Fellowship, General Support, Multiyear/Continuing Support, Operating Expenses, Professorship, Project.
Note: Employee matching gifts are made to educational and cultural institutions, and for health and human services, housing, and the environment.

Financial Summary
Total Giving: $64,209,919 (2001); $44,656,806 (2000); $35,237,873 (1999). Note: Contributes through corporate direct giving program and foundation.
Giving Analysis: Giving for 2001 includes: foundation grants to United Way ($5,852,050); foundation matching gifts ($15,191,397); foundation ($53,069,489); 1999: foundation grants to United Way ($5,000,733); foundation matching gifts ($8,798,964); foundation ($21,438,176); 1998: foundation grants to United Way ($4,280,500); foundation matching gifts ($7,720,736); foundation ($19,837,903);
Assets: $83,071,014 (2001); $137,439,675 (2000); $146,577,162 (1999)

Gifts Received: $16,680,882 (2001); $37,876,292 (2000); $113,300,905 (1999). Note: Foundation receives funds from Chemical Investments Inc., Glazier Food Company, and individual contributors.

Typical Recipients

Arts & Humanities: Arts Appreciation, Arts Associations & Councils, Arts Centers, Arts Festivals, Arts Funds, Community Arts, Dance, Ethnic & Folk Arts, Libraries, Literary Arts, Museums/Galleries, Music, Opera, Performing Arts, Public Broadcasting, Theater, Visual Arts

Civic & Public Affairs: African American Affairs, Asian American Affairs, Botanical Gardens/Parks, Business/Free Enterprise, Civil Rights, Community Foundations, Economic Development, Economic Policy, Employment/Job Training, Civic & Public Affairs-General, Hispanic Affairs, Housing, Law & Justice, Legal Aid, Municipalities/Towns, Nonprofit Management, Philanthropic Organizations, Professional & Trade Associations, Public Policy, Rural Affairs, Safety, Urban & Community Affairs, Women's Affairs

Education: Arts/Humanities Education, Business Education, Business-School Partnerships, Colleges & Universities, Community & Junior Colleges, Economic Education, Education Associations, Education Funds, Education Reform, Elementary Education (Private), Elementary Education (Public), Engineering/Technological Education, Faculty Development, Education-General, Health & Physical Education, International Studies, Leadership Training, Literacy, Medical Education, Minority Education, Preschool Education, Private Education (Precollege), Public Education (Precollege), School Volunteerism, Science/Mathematics Education, Secondary Education (Private), Special Education, Student Aid, Student Aid, Vocational & Technical Education

Environment: Environment-General, Wildlife Protection

Health: AIDS/HIV, Cancer, Children's Health/Hospitals, Clinics/Medical Centers, Diabetes, Emergency/Ambulance Services, Eyes/Blindness, Geriatric Health, Health Policy/Cost Containment, Health Organizations, Hospitals, Medical Rehabilitation, Mental Health, Prenatal Health Issues, Public Health, Transplant Networks/Donor Banks

International: Foreign Arts Organizations, Foreign Educational Institutions, International-General, Health Care/Hospitals, International Affairs, International Development, International Organizations, International Peace & Security Issues, International Relations, International Relief Efforts, Missionary/Religious Activities

Religion: Churches, Dioceses, Religion-General, Jewish Causes, Ministries, Religious Organizations, Religious Welfare, Seminaries

Science: Science Museums, Scientific Centers & Institutes, Scientific Organizations

Social Services: At-Risk Youth, Big Brother/Big Sister, Camps, Child Welfare, Community Centers, Community Service Organizations, Counseling, Day Care, Delinquency & Criminal Rehabilitation, Domestic Violence, Emergency Relief, Family Planning, Family Services, Food/Clothing Distribution, Homes, People with Disabilities, Recreation & Athletics, Scouts, Senior Services, Sexual Abuse, Shelters/Homelessness, Social Services-General, Substance Abuse, United Funds/United Ways, Volunteer Services, YMCA/YWCA/YMHA/YWHA, YMCA/YWCA/YMHA/YWHA, Youth Organizations

Application Procedures

Initial Contact: Send written requests to Steven W. Gelston, Secretary, JPMCF, 270 Park Avenue, 46th Floor, New York, New York 10017. Requests for funding in New York, New Jersey, or Connecticut contact (212)552-1112 or from Web site www.chase.com/cdg; requests in eight other states call (212)622-2025.

Application Requirements: Requests for funding from organizations in New York, New Jersey, or Connecticut should submitted on the application form, which lists additional materials requested; requests

from eight other states require one-page application which requires copy of applicant's IRS determination letter aka 501(c)(3), requests for funding programs for national programs or programs serving overseas locations should send a brief letter outlining project and amount sought, letter should include IRS determination letter as appropriate - additional information may be sought from organizations of interest.

Deadlines: Deadlines vary for different focus areas in New York, New Jersey and Connecticut, Committees in other states meet periodically, National programs are on a rolling deadline, and International grants are generally reviewed in early summer.

Decision Notification: Foundation board meets three times per year; final notification is within six months, or for competitive grants, within three or four months.

Restrictions

Focus areas include Community Development and Human Services, Pre-Collegiate Education, Arts and Culture, Public Issues, International Programs. Geographic limitations: Arizona, California, Connecticut, Delaware, Florida, Illinois, Louisiana, Massachusetts, New Jersey, New York, Ohio, and developing countries overseas where JPMorgan Chase has a significant presence. All organizations in the United States must have ruling from IRS showing them to be public charity under 501 (c)(3) ruling and not a private foundation.

Additional Information

In 2001, Chase Manhattan Bank and J.P. Morgan merged under the name JPMorgan Chase. The foundation was renamed the J.P. Morgan Chase Foundation. The Foundation announced that they would review all philanthropic activities in order to develop the most effective programs for the new firm.

In 1995, Chase Manhattan Bank and Chemical Bank merged under the name Chase Manhattan Bank. Contributions are made through several programs:

The Foundation makes grants through its signature programs of corporate social responsibility, with a focus on community revitalization, education, human services (specifically child care), and the arts and culture.

The Foundation contributes to organizations outside the tri-state area (New York, New Jersey, and Connecticut) in areas where the company maintains a significant business presence.

The corporate responsibility office provides philanthropic and technical support under the Competitive Grants Program to nonprofit organizations in the tri-state area (New York, New Jersey, Connecticut). Areas of concern include culture and art, community revitalization, and pre-college education. Contact: 600 5th Ave., 3rd Fl., New York, NY 10020, (212)332-4100, fax: (212)332-4080.

The community relations office develops programs to address community needs and provides assistance to community-based organizations.

Foundation may make grants to foreign-based organizations that have never applied for, or received, an IRS tax-exempt ruling if applicant organization provides information sufficient to prove that it is a charitable, educational, or scientific organization within the meaning of Section 501(c)(3).

Community-based nonprofit 501(c)(3) organizations located in New York City, Long Island, Duchess County, Orange County, Putnam County, Rockland County, or Westchester County are eligible for the Neighborhood Grants Program, which provides funds for projects in culture and the arts, education, health and human services, and housing and economic development. The application deadline is mid-February.

Corporate Officials

Donald L. Boudreau: executive vice president B White Plains, NY 1940. ED Pace University (1970). PRIM CORP EMPL executive vice president: Chase

Manhattan Bank, NA. NONPR AFFIL trustee: Marymount College; trustee: Pace University.

Thomas Goulet Labrecque: president, chief operating officer, director B Long Branch, NJ 1938. ED Villanova University BA (1960); American University (1962-1964); New York University (1965). PRIM CORP EMPL president, chief operating officer, director: Chase Manhattan Bank, NA ADD CORP EMPL president: Chase Bank Texas; president: Chase Manhattan Corp.; chief executive officer: Chase Manhattan National Holding. CORP AFFIL director: Federal Reserve Bank New York; director: Pfizer Inc.; director: Delphi Automotive Systems Corp. NONPR AFFIL member: Trilateral Commission; treasurer: United Negro College Fund; director: New Visions Public Schools; director: New York Clearing House Association; member: Council Foreign Relations; member board visitors: Duke University Fuqua School Business; trustee: Central Park Conservancy; member: Business Higher Education Forum; member: Business Roundtable; trustee: Brookings Institution; member: Business Council.

Arjun K. Mathruni: executive vice president, chief financial officer B 1945. PRIM CORP EMPL executive vice president, chief financial officer: Chase Manhattan Corp.

Michael Urkowitz: senior vice president B Bronx, NY 1943. ED City University of New York BE (1965); City University of New York MME (1967). PRIM CORP EMPL senior vice president: Chase Manhattan Bank, NA. CORP AFFIL credit card business executive: Chase InfoServ International; director: MasterCard United States; director: Cedel SA (Luxembourg). NONPR AFFIL member: Pi Tau Sigma; member: Tau Beta Pi; member advisory board: New York City Salvation Army.

James W. Zeigon: executive vice president PRIM CORP EMPL executive vice president: Chase Manhattan Bank, NA.

Giving Program Officials

Steven Gelston: PRIM CORP EMPL contributions officer: Chase Manhattan Bank, NA.

Foundation Officials

Donald L. Boudreau: vice president, trustee (see above)

Richard James Boyle: trustee B Brooklyn, NY 1943. ED College of the Holy Cross BA (1965); New York University MBA (1969). NONPR AFFIL director: Saint Vincent Hospital; director: YMCA Greater New York; director: Foundling Hospital. CLUB AFFIL Baltusrol Golf Club; Beacon Hill Club.

Robert Royal Douglass: trustee B Binghamton, NY 1931. ED Dartmouth College BA (1953); Cornell University LLB (1959). PRIM CORP EMPL counsel: Milbank, Tweed, Hadly & McCloy. CORP AFFIL director: HRE Properties; counsel: Melbank, Tweed, Hadly & McCloy; director: Gryphon Inc.; director: Home Insurance Co.; chairman: Cedel SA (Luxembourg); director: Gryphon Holdings Inc. NONPR AFFIL member, board editors: New York Law Journal; member: New York State Bar Association; member: Council Foreign Relations; chairman: Downtown-Lower Manhattan Association; member: Alliance for Downtown New York; member: American Bar Association. CLUB AFFIL Round Hill Club; Seal Harbor Club; Blind Brook Country Club; Century Association.

Anson Wright Elliott: vice president, trustee B New Orleans, LA 1935. ED Princeton University BA (1957); Cornell University MA (1964). PRIM CORP EMPL executive vice president corporate marketing & communications: Chase Manhattan Bank, NA. NONPR AFFIL member government relations council: American Bankers Association; director: Manhattan Institute Policy Research.

Michael Patrick Esposito, Jr.: trustee B Hackensack, NJ 1939. ED University of Notre Dame BBA (1961); New York University MBA (1967). PRIM CORP EMPL vice chairman: Inter Atlantic Capital Partners. CORP AFFIL director: Inter Atlantic Securities; director: Risk Capital Reinsurance Co.; director:

Forest City Enterprises Inc.; treasurer: Chase Manhattan Overseas Banking; chairman: Exel Ltd.

John B. Evans: assistant secretary, assistant treasurer CORP AFFIL officer: Chase Manhattan Overseas Banking.

Hughlyn F. Fierce: trustee B New York, NY 1935. ED Morgan State University BA (1961); New York University MBA (1967). PRIM CORP EMPL senior vice president: Chase Bank of Arizona. CORP AFFIL vice chairman: Chase Manhattan Overseas Banking. NONPR AFFIL member: American Chamber of Commerce.

Robert D. Hunter: trustee ED Columbia University; Manhattan College. PRIM CORP EMPL president: Standard & Poors ADD CORP EMPL chairman: Standard & Poors Securities Inc.

Thomas Goulet Labrecque: president (see above)

Maria Elena Lagomasino: trustee PRIM CORP EMPL senior managing director: Chase Manhattan Bank. CORP AFFIL director: Phillips-Van Heusen Corp.

Thomas C. Lynch: trustee PRIM CORP EMPL executive vice president: Chase Manhattan Bank, NA.

Arjun K. Mathruni: trustee (see above)

Arthur Frederick Ryan: trustee B Brooklyn, NY 1942. ED Providence College BA (1963). PRIM CORP EMPL chairman, chief executive officer, president: The Prudential Insurance Co. of America. CORP AFFIL director, member policy & planning committee, chairman: Depository Trust Co. NONPR AFFIL vice chairman operations division, vice chairman government relations council: American Bankers Association; program manager: CHIPS Same Day Settlement New York Clearing House.

Susan Wylie Schoon: trustee B Brooklyn, IA 1948. ED University of Iowa BA (1970); New York University MBA (1978).

John Vincent Scicutella: trustee B New York, NY 1949. ED Fordham University (1971); Columbia University (1979). PRIM CORP EMPL executive vice president operations: Chase Manhattan Bank, NA. CORP AFFIL chief executive officer: Prudential Insurance Co. America.

Deborah L. Talbot: trustee PRIM CORP EMPL executive vice president, treasurer: Chase Manhattan Bank, NA.

Michael Urkowitz: trustee (see above)

Mark A. Willis: president

James W. Zeigon: trustee (see above)

Grants Analysis

Disclosure Period: calendar year ending 2001
Total Grants: $53,069,480*
Number of Grants: 3,000 (approx)
Average Grant: $17,690
Highest Grant: $500,000
Typical Range: $1,000 to $10,000
*Note: Giving excludes matching gifts and volunteer grants, and United Way.

Recent Grants

Note: Grants derived from 2002 Form 990.

General

3,000,000	United Way Tri-State, New York, NY
1,500,000	United Way Tri-State, New York, NY
1,275,273	United Negro College Fund, Fairfax, VA
1,000,000	Aspen Institute, Washington, DC
1,000,000	Brandeis University, Boston, MA
750,000	Local Initiatives Support Corporation, New York, NY
732,166	Save the Children United Kingdom
660,000	Enterprise Foundation, New York, NY
585,320	United Way, New York, NY
500,000	Borough of Manhattan Community College, New York, NY

J.P. MORGAN CHASE & CO.

Company Headquarters

270 Park Ave.
New York, NY 10017
Web: http://www.jpmorganchase.com

Company Description

Founded: 2000
Ticker: JPM
Exchange: NYSE
Formed by Merger of: Chase Manhattan Corp (2000); J.P. Morgan & Company (2000).
Assets: US$758.8 billion (2002)
Profit: US$1.663 billion (2002)
Employees: 94335 (2002)
Fortune Rank: 26, per FORTUNE Magazine's list of 500 Largest U.S. Corporations (2002).
SIC(s): 6000 Depository Institutions, 6021 National Commercial Banks, 6712 Bank Holding Companies.

Operating Locations

Chase Manhattan Bank, NA (AZ--Phoenix; CA--Los Angeles, San Diego, San Francisco; DE--Newark, Wilmington; FL--Boca Raton, Palm Beach, St. Petersburg, Tampa; IL--Chicago; MD--Baltimore; NY--Rochester; TX--Dallas, Houston); J.P. Morgan & Co. (CA--Los Angeles, San Francisco; DE--Wilmington; FL--Palm Beach)

Nonmonetary Support

Type: Donated Equipment
Volunteer Programs: Employee volunteers work with social service agencies, educational institutions, arts organizations, and hospitals. Company administers two volunteer-support programs: "Volunteer Center," which assists employees in finding suitable volunteer work, and "Volunteer Involvement Fund," which enhances employee volunteer efforts with cash grants of $100 to $1,000.
Contact: Jeanne Collins, Associate
Note: Nonmonetary support is provided by the company.

J.P. Morgan Charitable Trust

Giving Contact

Hildy Simmons, Managing Director, Community Relations
60 Wall Street, 46th Floor
New York, NY 10260
Phone: (212)648-9673
Fax: (212)648-5082
Web: http://www.jpmorganchase.com/cm/cs?pagename=Chase/Href&urlname=jpmc/community/cdg/grants

Description

EIN: 136037931
Organization Type: Corporate Foundation
Giving Locations: NY: New York some funding internationally; some funding nationally.
Grant Types: Capital, Employee Matching Gifts, Endowment, General Support, Multiyear/Continuing Support, Project.
Note: Employee matching gift ratio: 1 to 1; J.P. Morgan matches contributions of its employees, retired employees, bank directors, and any eligible person's spouse dollar-for-dollar. Gifts of cash, securities, and real estate are matched in six categories of giving--culture, education, environmental concerns, health care, human services, and international affairs. Minimum gift matched is $25. Maximum combined giving total matched is $8,000 per calendar year.

Financial Summary

Total Giving: $6,104,767 (2001); $12,516,515 (2000); $16,446,217 (1999). Note: Contributes through corporate direct giving program and foundation.

Giving Analysis: Giving for 2000 includes: foundation grants to United Way ($296,000); foundation matching gifts ($3,678,630); foundation ($8,541,885); 1999: corporate grants to United Way ($250,000); international subsidiaries ($2,518,518); corporate matching gifts ($5,259,618); foundation ($8,418,081); 1998: foundation grants to United Way ($439,200); corporate matching gifts ($569,325); corporate direct giving ($749,692); international subsidiaries ($3,101,133) foundation ($12,650,845)

Assets: $202 (2001); $7,379,843 (2000); $12,393,668 (1998)

Gifts Received: $8,708,083 (2000); $7,000,000 (1998); $6,413 (1996). Note: Trust receives substantial contributions from J.P. Morgan & Co.

Typical Recipients

Arts & Humanities: Arts Associations & Councils, Arts Centers, Arts Funds, Arts Outreach, Ballet, Dance, Ethnic & Folk Arts, Arts & Humanities-General, History & Archaeology, Libraries, Museums/Galleries, Music, Opera, Performing Arts, Public Broadcasting, Theater, Visual Arts

Civic & Public Affairs: African American Affairs, Botanical Gardens/Parks, Business/Free Enterprise, Chambers of Commerce, Community Foundations, Economic Development, Employment/Job Training, Gay/Lesbian Issues, Civic & Public Affairs-General, Hispanic Affairs, Housing, Law & Justice, Legal Aid, Municipalities/Towns, Nonprofit Management, Philanthropic Organizations, Public Policy, Rural Affairs, Urban & Community Affairs, Women's Affairs, Zoos/Aquariums

Education: Afterschool/Enrichment Programs, Arts/Humanities Education, Business Education, Colleges & Universities, Education Reform, Faculty Development, Education-General, Leadership Training, Literacy, Medical Education, Minority Education, Public Education (Precollege), Science/Mathematics Education, Social Sciences Education, Student Aid, Vocational & Technical Education

Environment: Air/Water Quality, Forestry, Environment-General

Health: Cancer, Clinics/Medical Centers, Emergency/Ambulance Services, Geriatric Health, Health Policy/Cost Containment, Health Organizations, Hospitals, Medical Research, Public Health, Transplant Networks/Donor Banks

International: Foreign Arts Organizations, Foreign Educational Institutions, Human Rights, International Affairs, International Development, International Peace & Security Issues, International Relations, International Relief Efforts

Religion: Religious Welfare

Science: Science Museums

Social Services: At-Risk Youth, Big Brother/Big Sister, Child Welfare, Community Centers, Community Service Organizations, Counseling, Crime Prevention, Day Care, Domestic Violence, Family Planning, Family Services, Food/Clothing Distribution, People with Disabilities, Recreation & Athletics, Senior Services, Sexual Abuse, Shelters/Homelessness, Social Services-General, United Funds/United Ways, Volunteer Services, YMCA/YWCA/YMHA/YWHA, Youth Organizations

Application Procedures

Initial Contact: Request guidelines, then written proposal.

Application Requirements: Include goals of organization, need or problem to be addressed, and a statement on the segment of the population to which grant is to be directed; latest annual report, if available; brief history of organization; brief description of programs and accomplishments in last year; explanation of how success will be evaluated; list of directors or trustees and their affiliations; a list of senior staff members, number of full staff, part-time staff, and volunteers, including one-paragraph resumes on key personnel; recently audited financial statement; current budget, including sources of projected income; budget for next fiscal year, if available; list of foundation and corporate supporters and other sources of income; copy of 501(c)(3) letter; recent Form 990; an outline of any plans to enlarge base of support from potential sources; a brief description of the specific project for which funds are requested; include primary purpose and problem, population it will serve, individual who will direct it and their qualifications, how long it will take, budget, and when funds are needed; plan for measuring the effectiveness of project; and three examples of recent articles or evaluations of organization.

Deadlines: None.

Review Process: Contributions Committee meets six times a year, between February and November.

Decision Notification: Within three months of receipt of application information. Grants approved in the first half of the year are normally paid in June, those in the second half in December.

Notes: Also accepts the New York Common Application Form, as long as additional requested information is provided. Application must be complete within two months of trust acknowledgement.

Restrictions

Does not support individuals, religious organizations for sectarian purposes, chemical dependency programs, specific disability or single-disease health associations other than AIDS programs, scholarly research, scholarships, or fellowships.

Additional Information

The Trust rarely contributes outside of the New York area, except for higher education and international affairs. Grants made outside the New York area are usually to organizations that operate nationwide.

An applicant whose proposals denied may not apply again for one year. New York area are usually to organizations that operate nationwide.

An applicant whose proposals denied may not apply again for one year. New York area are usually to organizations that operate nationwide.

An applicant whose proposals denied may not apply again for one year.

Corporate Officials

Walter Gubert: vice chairman B 1947. PRIM CORP EMPL vice chairman: J.P. Morgan & Co. Inc. ADD CORP EMPL director: Morgan Guaranty Trust Co. of New York.

Michael E. Patterson: vice chairman B New York, NY 1942. ED Harvard University AB (1964); Columbia University LLB (1967). PRIM CORP EMPL vice chairman: J.P. Morgan & Co. Inc. ADD CORP EMPL director: J.P. Morgan Investment Management Inc.; director: Morgan Guaranty Trust Co. of New York.

Foundation Officials

Hildy J. Simmons: managing director

Grants Analysis

Disclosure Period: calendar year ending 2000
Total Grants: $8,541,885*
Number of Grants: 449
Average Grant: $19,024
Highest Grant: $325,000
Lowest Grant: $1,000
Typical Range: $5,000 to $25,000
*Note: Giving excludes corporate direct giving; domestic and international subsidiaries; matching gifts; United Way.

Recent Grants

Note: Grants derived from 2001 Form 990.

General
66,150   Earth Share, Washington, DC -- for environmental protection and conservation

ANN JACKSON FAMILY FOUNDATION

Giving Contact

PO Box 5580
Santa Barbara, CA 93150
Phone: (805)969-2258
Fax: (805)969-0315

Description

Founded: 1978
EIN: 953367511
Organization Type: Family Foundation
Giving Locations: CA: Santa Barbara and surrounding areas
Grant Types: Capital, General Support, Project.

Donor Information

Founder: The foundation was established in 1978 by Ann G. Jackson and the Ann Jackson Family Charitable Trust.

Financial Summary

Total Giving: $2,927,933 (fiscal year ending May 31, 2001); $1,940,100 (fiscal 1999); $1,532,100 (fiscal 1998)
Giving Analysis: Giving for fiscal 2001 includes: foundation grants to United Way ($15,000) fiscal 1999: foundation grants to United Way ($12,000)
Assets: $56,373,702 (fiscal 2001); $54,168,269 (fiscal 1999); $47,313,623 (fiscal 1998)
Gifts Received: $262,500 (fiscal 1999); $350,000 (fiscal 1998); $350,000 (fiscal 1997). Note: Contributions were received from the Ann Jackson Charitable Trust.

Typical Recipients

Arts & Humanities: Arts Associations & Councils, Arts Centers, Arts Institutes, Arts Outreach, Community Arts, Arts & Humanities-General, Historic Preservation, History & Archaeology, Libraries, Museums/Galleries, Music, Opera, Theater
Civic & Public Affairs: Botanical Gardens/Parks, Clubs, Community Foundations, Economic Development, Employment/Job Training, Hispanic Affairs, Nonprofit Management, Philanthropic Organizations, Professional & Trade Associations, Urban & Community Affairs, Zoos/Aquariums
Education: Agricultural Education, Arts/Humanities Education, Business Education, Colleges & Universities, Community & Junior Colleges, Education Funds, Education Reform, Education-General, Minority Education, Private Education (Precollege), Private Education (Precollege), Public Education (Precollege), Religious Education, Secondary Education (Private), Special Education, Student Aid, Vocational & Technical Education
Environment: Environment-General, Resource Conservation
Health: Cancer, Clinics/Medical Centers, Emergency/Ambulance Services, Eyes/Blindness, Geriatric Health, Health Organizations, Heart, Hospitals, Medical Rehabilitation, Medical Research, Mental Health, Multiple Sclerosis, Nursing Services, Prenatal Health Issues, Respiratory
International: Foreign Arts Organizations, Health Care/Hospitals, International Relief Efforts
Religion: Churches, Religious Organizations, Religious Welfare
Science: Science Museums
Social Services: Child Welfare, Community Service Organizations, Family Planning, Family Planning,

Family Services, People with Disabilities, Recreation & Athletics, Senior Services, Shelters/Homelessness, Special Olympics, Substance Abuse, United Funds/United Ways, Volunteer Services, YMCA/YWCA/YMHA/YWHA, Youth Organizations

Application Procedures

Initial Contact: Applications should be in the form of a letter.
Application Requirements: The letter should detail the grant request and its proposed uses. A copy of the State and Federal ruling under Section 509(a)(1), (2), or (3) must be included, as well as a statement from an officer of the organization that the IRS exempt ruling has not changed since its issuance and that a grant from the foundation will not change the applicant's public charity status.
Deadlines: None.
Review Process: Applications are reviewed by the board of trustees.

Restrictions

Grants are not made to individuals.

Foundation Officials

Palmer G. Jackson: cfo, director B 1930. PRIM CORP EMPL president, director: Alisal Properties. NONPR AFFIL chief financial officer, director: Santa Barbara Cottage Hospital.
Peter Jackson: vice president, director
Flora J. Ramsey: president, director

Grants Analysis

Disclosure Period: fiscal year ending May 31, 2001
Total Grants: $2,912,933*
Number of Grants: 178
Average Grant: $16,365
Highest Grant: $136,000
Typical Range: $5,000 to $30,000
*Note: Giving excludes United Way.

Recent Grants

Note: Grants derived from 2000 Form 990.

General
150,000	Cottage Hospital, Santa Barbara, CA -- for systems, technology and equipment
150,000	Santa Barbara Civic Light Opera, Santa Barbara, CA
136,000	Yale University, New Haven, CT
128,100	Stanford University, Stanford, CA
60,000	Westmont College, Santa Barbara, CA
55,000	Santa Barbara City College, Santa Barbara, CA -- scholarships
52,000	Santa Ynez Valley YMCA, Solvang, CA
51,000	Santa Barbara Botanic Garden, Santa Barbara, CA
50,000	Cate School, Carpinteria, CA -- construct new dormitory
50,000	Dunn School, Los Olivos, CA -- for building fund

JACKSON FOUNDATION (OR)

Giving Contact

Robert H. Depew, Trust Officer
c/o US National Bank of Oregon
PO Box 3168
Portland, OR 97208
Phone: (503)275-6574

Description

Founded: 1960
EIN: 936020752
Organization Type: General Purpose Foundation
Giving Locations: OR: Portland
Grant Types: Capital, Endowment, Matching, Multiyear/Continuing Support, Project, Research.

Donor Information
Founder: Maria C. Jackson

Financial Summary
Total Giving: $793,460 (fiscal year ending June 30, 2001); $726,188 (fiscal 1999); $712,025 (fiscal 1998)
Assets: $16,116,768 (fiscal 2001); $18,031,128 (fiscal 1999); $17,318,671 (fiscal 1998)

Typical Recipients
Arts & Humanities: Arts Associations & Councils, Arts Festivals, Arts Funds, Arts Institutes, Ballet, Dance, Historic Preservation, History & Archaeology, Libraries, Museums/Galleries, Music, Opera, Performing Arts, Public Broadcasting, Theater
Civic & Public Affairs: Botanical Gardens/Parks, Clubs, Community Foundations, Economic Development, Employment/Job Training, Civic & Public Affairs-General, Hispanic Affairs, Housing, Legal Aid, Urban & Community Affairs, Women's Affairs, Zoos/Aquariums
Education: Afterschool/Enrichment Programs, Arts/Humanities Education, Colleges & Universities, Community & Junior Colleges, Education-General, Medical Education, Preschool Education, Private Education (Precollege), Public Education (Precollege), Science/Mathematics Education, Student Aid
Environment: Environment-General, Resource Conservation, Wildlife Protection
Health: AIDS/HIV, Alzheimers Disease, Children's Health/Hospitals, Clinics/Medical Centers, Emergency/Ambulance Services, Health Funds, Health Organizations, Hospices, Hospitals, Long-Term Care, Medical Rehabilitation, Medical Research, Mental Health, Public Health, Speech & Hearing
International: Health Care/Hospitals
Religion: Jewish Causes, Religious Organizations, Religious Welfare
Science: Science Museums
Social Services: At-Risk Youth, Camps, Child Welfare, Community Centers, Community Service Organizations, Counseling, Day Care, Domestic Violence, Family Planning, Family Services, Food/Clothing Distribution, Homes, People with Disabilities, Recreation & Athletics, Scouts, Senior Services, Shelters/Homelessness, Social Services-General, Substance Abuse, United Funds/United Ways, Volunteer Services, YMCA/YWCA/YMHA/YWHA, Youth Organizations

Application Procedures
Initial Contact: A formal application is available upon request.
Deadlines: None; applications are reviewed at the spring, fall, and winter meetings.

Restrictions
Grants are not made to individuals or private businesses, and generally not to a K-12 school. Grants are made only to organizations whose exemption letter shows them to be Oregon organizations.

Additional Information
The foundation reports, "Funds requested for operating purposes, staff salaries and the like do not, generally, have the priority that funds for one-time, special projects or developmental projects enjoy."
Publications: Annual Report; Application Form
Trust(s): US Natl Bank OR

Foundation Officials
Milo E. Ormseth: co-trustee
Julie Vigeland: co-trustee

Grants Analysis
Disclosure Period: fiscal year ending June 30, 2001
Total Grants: $793,460
Number of Grants: 138
Average Grant: $5,750
Highest Grant: $25,000
Typical Range: $1,000 to $10,000

Recent Grants
Note: Grants derived from fiscal 1999 Form 990.

General

20,000	Portland Art Museum, Portland, OR
15,000	Edgefield Children's Center, Troutdale, OR
15,000	Friends of the Portland Children's Museum, Portland, OR
15,000	Oregon State University Foundation, Corvallis, OR
15,000	Portland Center Stage, Portland, OR
11,463	Journal Public Welfare Fund
11,000	Oregon Community Foundation, Portland, OR
10,000	Cascade AIDS Project, Portland, OR
10,000	Gales Creek Camp Foundation, Lake Oswego, OR
10,000	Haienda Community Development

MARGARET G. JACOBS CHARITABLE TRUST

Giving Contact
William R. Levy, Co-Trustee
PO Box 58910
6114 Ensley Drive
Flourtown, PA 19031
Phone: (215)587-6311

Description
Founded: 1994
EIN: 232743317
Organization Type: Private Foundation
Giving Locations: PA
Grant Types: General Support.

Donor Information
Founder: Established in 1994 by Margaret G. Jacobs.

Financial Summary
Total Giving: $139,050 (fiscal year ending June 30, 2000); $68,500 (fiscal 1997); $64,500 (fiscal 1996)
Assets: $2,703,443 (fiscal 2000); $2,298,874 (fiscal 1997); $1,870,980 (fiscal 1996)
Gifts Received: $1,459,214 (fiscal 1993). Note: In fiscal 1993, contributions were received from Margaret G. Jacobs.

Typical Recipients
Arts & Humanities: Libraries
Civic & Public Affairs: Botanical Gardens/Parks, Clubs, Civic & Public Affairs-General, Urban & Community Affairs, Women's Affairs
Education: Private Education (Precollege)
Health: Children's Health/Hospitals, Diabetes, Emergency/Ambulance Services, Hospices, Single-Disease Health Associations
International: International Relief Efforts
Religion: Churches, Jewish Causes, Religious Welfare
Social Services: Child Welfare, Community Service Organizations, Crime Prevention, Family Services, Food/Clothing Distribution, People with Disabilities, Shelters/Homelessness, Special Olympics, YMCA/YWCA/YMHA/YWHA

Application Procedures
Initial Contact: Send a brief letter of inquiry.
Deadlines: None.

Foundation Officials
Philip Brown: co-trustee
William R. Levy: co-trustee

Grants Analysis
Disclosure Period: fiscal year ending June 30, 2001
Total Grants: $139,050
Number of Grants: 43

Average Grant: $2,392*
Highest Grant: $27,500
Lowest Grant: $1,000
Typical Range: $1,000 to $5,000
***Note:** Average grant figure excludes two highest grants ($41,000).

Recent Grants
Note: Grants derived from fiscal 2001 Form 990.

Library-Related

2,500	William Jeanes Memorial Library, Lafayette Hill, PA

General

27,500	American Red Cross, Philadelphia, PA
13,500	Germantown Friends School, Philadelphia, PA
5,000	Carson Valley School, Flourtown, PA
5,000	Congregation Kol Ami, New York, NY
5,000	Green Tree School, Philadelphia, PA
5,000	Juvenile Diabetes Foundation, Philadelphia, PA
5,000	Salvation Army, Philadelphia, PA
5,000	Special Olympics, Norristown, PA
3,000	Academy of Notre Dame De Namur, Villanova, PA
3,000	St. Christopher's Hospital for Children, Philadelphia, PA

JACOBS FAMILY FOUNDATION

Giving Contact
Henry D. Jacobs, Jr., Chairman & Trustee
PO Box 1726
Spartanburg, SC 29304-1726
Phone: (864)573-9211

Description
Founded: 1994
EIN: 576154661
Organization Type: Private Foundation
Grant Types: General Support.

Financial Summary
Total Giving: $6,710 (2000); $3,000 (1999); $16,000 (1996)
Assets: $55,923 (2001); $58,194 (2000); $244,088 (1999)
Gifts Received: $1,500 (2001); $1,500 (2000); $53,819 (1996). Note: In 1996, contributions were received from Henry D. Jacobs, Jr.

Typical Recipients
Arts & Humanities: Arts Associations & Councils, Libraries
Civic & Public Affairs: Community Foundations, Civic & Public Affairs-General
Education: Student Aid
Health: Cancer, Children's Health/Hospitals
Religion: Jewish Causes, Ministries, Synagogues/Temples
Social Services: Animal Protection, Child Welfare, Community Service Organizations, Crime Prevention, Emergency Relief, Scouts

Application Procedures
Initial Contact: The foundation has no formal grant application procedure or application form. Send a letter with basic background information and federal identification number.
Deadlines: None.

Foundation Officials
Brett S. Jacobs: secretary, trustee
Clay S. Jacobs: treasurer, trustee
Henry D. Jacobs, Jr.: chairman, trustee

Susan C. Jacobs: trustee
Philip Mark Talbrook: board member

Grants Analysis

Disclosure Period: calendar year ending 2001
Total Grants: $0*
Typical Range: $100 to $2,500
*****Note:** No grants awarded in 2001.

Recent Grants

Note: Grants derived from 2000 Form 990.

General

2,500	New Day, Inc, Spartanburg, SC
2,500	Spartanburg Regional Foundation Society of 1921, Spartanburg, SC
1,000	Congregation B'nai Israel, Spartanburg, SC
200	Children's Advocacy Center, Spartanburg, SC
160	Cancer Association of Spartanburg and Cherokee Counties, Spartanburg, SC
150	Spartanburg Humane Society, Spartanburg, SC
100	Girls Scouts of the Piedmont Area Council, Spartanburg, SC
100	Total Ministries of Spartanburg County, Spartanburg, SC

BERNARD H. AND BLANCHE E. JACOBSON FOUNDATION

Giving Contact

John L. Ray, Trustee
1210 BB&T Square
300 Summers Street
Charleston, WV 25301
Phone: (304)342-1141

Description

Founded: 1952
EIN: 556014902
Organization Type: Private Foundation
Giving Locations: WV: Kanawha Valley, Charleston
Grant Types: General Support.

Donor Information

Founder: Bernard H. Jacobson, Blanche E. Jacobson

Financial Summary

Total Giving: $448,500 (2001); $452,400 (2000); $403,000 (1999). Note: 1997 Giving includes United Way (50,000).
Giving Analysis: Giving for 2001 includes: foundation grants to United Way ($50,000); 2000: foundation grants to United Way ($50,000); 1999: foundation grants to United Way ($50,000)
Assets: $7,427,208 (2001); $8,305,360 (2000); $8,600,000 (1999)

Typical Recipients

Arts & Humanities: Arts Associations & Councils, Arts Centers, Community Arts, Film & Video, Historic Preservation, History & Archaeology, Libraries, Museums/Galleries, Music, Opera, Public Broadcasting, Theater
Civic & Public Affairs: Chambers of Commerce, Community Foundations, Economic Development, Civic & Public Affairs-General, Housing, Philanthropic Organizations, Professional & Trade Associations, Urban & Community Affairs, Women's Affairs
Education: Arts/Humanities Education, Business Education, Colleges & Universities, Continuing Education, Education Funds, Education Reform, Faculty Development, Education-General, Literacy, Minority Education, Public Education (Precollege), Science/

Mathematics Education, Secondary Education (Private), Vocational & Technical Education
Environment: Environment-General, Research
Health: Clinics/Medical Centers, Emergency/Ambulance Services, Health Organizations, Hospices, Mental Health
International: International Affairs, Missionary/Religious Activities
Religion: Churches, Jewish Causes, Religious Organizations, Religious Welfare, Synagogues/Temples
Science: Science-General, Scientific Centers & Institutes, Scientific Research
Social Services: At-Risk Youth, Camps, Child Welfare, Community Service Organizations, Counseling, Family Services, Food/Clothing Distribution, Homes, Recreation & Athletics, Scouts, Shelters/Homelessness, United Funds/United Ways, Volunteer Services, YMCA/YWCA/YMHA/YWHA, Youth Organizations

Application Procedures

Initial Contact: The foundation has no formal grant application procedure or application form.
Application Requirements: Include description of project, budget, amount requested, other funding sources and amount requested from them, proof of tax-exempt status, name, address, and telephone number of contact person.
Deadlines: None.
Review Process: The trustees generally meet in March, June, September, and December to review applications.

Additional Information

Trust(s): Branch Banking & Trust Company

Foundation Officials

Charles W. Loeb: trustee
John L. Ray: trustee
L. Newton Thomas, Jr.: trustee

Grants Analysis

Disclosure Period: calendar year ending 2001
Total Grants: $398,500*
Number of Grants: 32
Average Grant: $9,468*
Highest Grant: $105,000
Lowest Grant: $500
Typical Range: $5,000 to $15,000
*****Note:** Giving excludes United Way. Average grant figure excludes highest grant.

Recent Grants

Note: Grants derived from 2000 Form 990.

Library-Related

15,000	Library Foundation of Kanawha County, Charleston, WV

General

100,000	Center for the Arts and Sciences
55,000	Community Council of Kanawha Valley, Charleston, WV
50,000	United Way of Kanawha Valley, Charleston, WV
45,000	University of Charleston, Charleston, WV
20,000	West Virginia State Museum Board, Charleston, WV
15,000	West Virginia Symphony Orchestra, Charleston, WV
12,500	Union Mission
11,000	Business and Industrial Development Corp, Pittsburgh, PA
10,000	Covenant House
10,000	National Youth Science Foundation

JAFFE FOUNDATION

Giving Contact

Holly Seagrove, Executive Secretary
PO Box 307
Stockbridge, MA 01262
Phone: (413)298-0000
Fax: (413)298-3199

Description

Founded: 1962
EIN: 046049261
Organization Type: Private Foundation
Giving Locations: MA
Grant Types: General Support.

Donor Information

Founder: the late Meyer Jaffe, Edwin A. Jaffe

Financial Summary

Total Giving: $453,734 (fiscal year ending June 30, 2001); $453,734 (fiscal 2000); $573,746 (fiscal 1999)
Giving Analysis: Giving for fiscal 2000 includes: foundation grants to United Way ($10,000) fiscal 1999: foundation grants to United Way ($1,000)
Assets: $4,314,493 (fiscal 2001); $4,314,493 (fiscal 2000); $5,167,955 (fiscal 1997)
Gifts Received: $250 (fiscal 1997); $15,371 (fiscal 1994). Note: In fiscal 1997, contributions were received from Edwin A. Jaffe.

Typical Recipients

Arts & Humanities: Arts Associations & Councils, Arts Centers, Arts Outreach, Dance, Arts & Humanities-General, Libraries, Museums/Galleries, Music, Opera, Public Broadcasting, Theater
Civic & Public Affairs: African American Affairs, Economic Policy, Civic & Public Affairs-General, Urban & Community Affairs
Education: Arts/Humanities Education, Colleges & Universities, Community & Junior Colleges, Education-General, International Studies, Private Education (Precollege)
Environment: Environment-General, Resource Conservation
Health: AIDS/HIV, Cancer, Children's Health/Hospitals, Health Organizations, Hospices, Hospitals, Medical Research, Nursing Services, Public Health, Single-Disease Health Associations
International: Foreign Arts Organizations, Foreign Arts Organizations, Foreign Educational Institutions, Health Care/Hospitals, Human Rights, International Peace & Security Issues, International Relations, International Relief Efforts, Missionary/Religious Activities
Religion: Jewish Causes, Religious Organizations, Religious Welfare, Synagogues/Temples
Social Services: Child Welfare, Community Centers, Community Service Organizations, Family Planning, Food/Clothing Distribution, People with Disabilities, Recreation & Athletics, Sexual Abuse, United Funds/United Ways, Youth Organizations

Application Procedures

Initial Contact: Send a brief letter of inquiry.
Application Requirements: amount requested and purpose of funds sought.
Deadlines: None.

Restrictions

Does not support individuals.

Additional Information

Publications: Mission Statement (including General Guidelines)

Foundation Officials

Donna Jaffe Fishbein: trustee
David S. Greer: trustee B Brooklyn, NY 1925. ED University of Notre Dame BS (1948); University of

Chicago MD (1953); Brown University MA (1975); Southeastern Massachusetts University LHD (1981). PRIM CORP EMPL professor community health: Brown University. NONPR AFFIL member: RI Governments Task Force Institute Mental Health; member: RI Medicine Society; founding director: International Physicians Prevention Nuclear War; member: International Society Rehabilitation Medicine; member: Institute Medicine; member: Institute Mental Health Rhode Island; member: American Congress Rehabilitation Medicine; director: Association Home Health Agencies.

Edwin A. Jaffe: chairman
Lola Jaffe: vchairman
Robert Jaffe: trustee

Grants Analysis

Disclosure Period: fiscal year ending June 30, 2001
Total Grants: $443,734*
Number of Grants: 78
Average Grant: $4,464*
Highest Grant: $100,000
Typical Range: $1,000 to $10,000
*Note: Giving excludes United Way. Average grant figure excludes highest grant.

Recent Grants

Note: Grants derived from fiscal 2000 Form 990.

General

100,000	Berkshire South Regional Community Center, Stockbridge, MA -- capital campaign building
51,000	Bristol Community College, Fall River, MA -- educational
27,500	Berkshire Taconic Community Foundation, Great Barrington, MA -- youth outreach programs
25,000	Massachusetts General Hospital, Boston, MA -- health
24,000	Jacob's Pillow, Becket, MA -- capital campaign building
20,000	Human Rights Watch, New York, NY -- humanitarian aid
10,000	America-Israel Cultural Foundation, New York, NY -- cultural exchange
10,000	American Friends of the Israel Philharmonic Orchestra, New York, NY -- arts/cultural
10,000	Berkshire Theater Festival, Stockbridge, MA -- youth outreach programs
10,000	Brown University, Providence, RI -- education/health

LEE AND JOSEPH D. JAMAIL FOUNDATION

Giving Contact

Robert L. Jamail, Secretary & Treasurer
1200 Smith St., Suite 1135
Houston, TX 77002
Phone: (713)650-8544

Description

Founded: 1986
EIN: 760181247
Organization Type: Private Foundation
Giving Locations: TX
Grant Types: General Support.

Donor Information

Founder: Joseph D. Jamail, Lillie H. Jamail

Financial Summary

Total Giving: $626,918 (2001); $337,000 (2000); $332,500 (1999)
Assets: $14,527,096 (2001); $14,483,282 (2000); $13,792,309 (1999)
Gifts Received: $34,724 (1998); $200,000 (1996)

Typical Recipients

Arts & Humanities: Arts Centers, History & Archaeology, Libraries, Museums/Galleries, Music, Theater, Visual Arts
Civic & Public Affairs: Botanical Gardens/Parks, Clubs, Civic & Public Affairs-General, Hispanic Affairs, Housing, Law & Justice, Municipalities/Towns, Parades/Festivals, Urban & Community Affairs, Women's Affairs, Zoos/Aquariums
Education: Agricultural Education, Arts/Humanities Education, Colleges & Universities, Education Reform, Education-General, Legal Education, Literacy, Medical Education, Minority Education, Preschool Education, Private Education (Precollege), Religious Education, Secondary Education (Private), Special Education, Student Aid
Environment: Environment-General
Health: AIDS/HIV, Cancer, Children's Health/Hospitals, Clinics/Medical Centers, Emergency/Ambulance Services, Eyes/Blindness, Heart, Hospices, Hospitals, Medical Rehabilitation, Mental Health, Multiple Sclerosis, Public Health, Single-Disease Health Associations, Speech & Hearing
International: International Environmental Issues, International Relief Efforts
Religion: Churches, Ministries, Religious Welfare
Science: Science Museums
Social Services: At-Risk Youth, Camps, Child Abuse, Child Welfare, Community Service Organizations, Domestic Violence, Family Planning, Family Services, People with Disabilities, Senior Services, Social Services-General, Special Olympics, Youth Organizations

Application Procedures

Initial Contact: Send a brief letter of inquiry on organization's letterhead.
Application Requirements: Include proof of tax-exempt status.
Deadlines: None.

Foundation Officials

Denise S. Davidson: secretary
Joseph D. Jamail, III: vice president
Lee H. Jamail: president
Randall Hage Jamail: vice president
Robert Lee Jamail: secretary, treasurer

Grants Analysis

Disclosure Period: calendar year ending 2000
Total Grants: $337,000
Number of Grants: 24
Average Grant: $9,870*
Highest Grant: $100,000
Typical Range: $1,000 to $15,000
*Note: Average grant excludes highest grant.

Recent Grants

Note: Grants derived from 1999 Form 990.

Library-Related

5,000	Rice University Friends of Fondren Library, Houston, TX

General

100,000	Houston Museum of Natural Science, Houston, TX -- origins and diversity galley and Hall of America
42,500	The Kinkaid School, Houston, TX
25,000	Salvation Army, Houston, TX
21,000	Post Oak Montessori, Bellaire, TX
20,000	Contemporary Arts Museum, Houston, TX
13,000	Planned Parenthood of Houston, Houston, TX
10,000	Caritas of Austin, Austin, TX
10,000	M D Anderson Cancer Center, Houston, TX
10,000	St. John's School, Houston, TX -- fine arts center
10,000	St. Thomas High School, Houston, TX

J. W. AND IDA M. JAMESON FOUNDATION

Giving Contact

Les M. Huhn, President
PO Box 397
Sierra Madre, CA 91024
Phone: (626)355-3020

Description

Founded: 1955
EIN: 956031465
Organization Type: Private Foundation
Giving Locations: CA
Grant Types: General Support, Research, Scholarship.

Donor Information

Founder: J. W. Jameson Corp., the late Ida May Jameson

Financial Summary

Total Giving: $855,000 (fiscal year ending June 30, 2001); $875,000 (fiscal 2000); $875,000 (fiscal 1999)
Giving Analysis: Giving for fiscal 2000 includes: foundation scholarships ($20,000)
Assets: $15,269,748 (fiscal 2001); $15,532,165 (fiscal 2000); $16,525,801 (fiscal 1998)
Gifts Received: $990,000 (fiscal 1996); $973,000 (fiscal 1995); $1,008,851 (fiscal 1994)

Typical Recipients

Arts & Humanities: Arts Associations & Councils, Community Arts, Arts & Humanities-General, Libraries, Museums/Galleries, Music, Public Broadcasting, Visual Arts
Civic & Public Affairs: Botanical Gardens/Parks, Civic & Public Affairs-General, Law & Justice, Legal Aid, Philanthropic Organizations, Public Policy, Safety, Zoos/Aquariums
Education: Colleges & Universities, Community & Junior Colleges, Education-General, Legal Education, Medical Education, Preschool Education, Private Education (Precollege), Public Education (Precollege), Religious Education, Secondary Education (Public), Special Education, Student Aid
Health: Children's Health/Hospitals, Emergency/Ambulance Services, Geriatric Health, Health Organizations, Hospitals, Long-Term Care, Medical Research, Preventive Medicine/Wellness Organizations, Research/Studies Institutes, Single-Disease Health Associations
International: International Peace & Security Issues
Religion: Churches, Religious Organizations, Religious Welfare
Social Services: Community Service Organizations, People with Disabilities, Recreation & Athletics, Senior Services, Substance Abuse, Youth Organizations

Application Procedures

Initial Contact: Send a brief letter of inquiry.
Application Requirements: Include a description of organization, purpose of funds sought, amount requested, and proof of tax-exempt status.
Deadlines: February 1.
Decision Notification: The Directors meet in March to decide grant recipients.

Foundation Officials

Bill B. Betz: director
William M. Croxton: vice president
Les M. Huhn: president
Frederick Leroy Leydorf: director B Toledo, OH 1930. ED University of Toledo (1948-1949); University of Michigan BBA (1953); University of California, Los Angeles JD (1958). NONPR AFFIL member: Phi Delta Theta; member: University California Los Angeles Law Alumni Association; member: Los Angeles World Affairs Council; member: Phi Delta

Phi; member: Los Angeles County Bar Association; member: Los Angeles County Bar Foundation; member: Life Insurance & Trust Council; member: California Bar Association; member: Intl Academy Estate & Trust Law; member: American Bar Association; member: American College Trust & Estate Counsel. CLUB AFFIL Jonathan Club; Laguna Hills Golf Club; Chancery Club.

Pauline Vetrovec: secretary, director

Grants Analysis

Disclosure Period: fiscal year ending June 30, 2001
Total Grants: $855,000
Number of Grants: 53
Average Grant: $14,804*
Highest Grant: $50,000
Typical Range: $5,000 to $30,000
*Note: Average grant figure excludes two highest grants ($100,000).

Recent Grants

Note: Grants derived from fiscal 2000 Form 990.

Library-Related
25,000	Henry E. Huntington Library and Art Gallery, San Marino, CA

General
50,000	University of Michigan, Ann Arbor, MI
50,000	University of Southern California School of Internal Medicine, Los Angeles, CA
40,000	UCLA Foundation, Los Angeles, CA -- J.W. & Ida M. Jameson Fund
40,000	World Institute of Disability, Oakland, CA
30,000	Huntington Medical Research Institute, Pasadena, CA
30,000	Union Station Foundation, Pasadena, CA
30,000	Zoological Society of San Diego, San Diego, CA
25,000	Paraclete Mission Group, Pasadena, CA
25,000	Pasadena City College, Pasadena, CA -- Sculpture Garden
20,000	Bakersfield Symphony Orchestra, Bakersfield, CA

OLEONDA JAMESON TRUST

Giving Contact

Malcolm McLane, Trustee
c/o Orr & Reno
1 Eagle Sq.
PO Box 3550
Concord, NH 03302-3550
Phone: (603)224-2381
Fax: (603)224-2318

Description

Founded: 1977
EIN: 026048930
Organization Type: Private Foundation
Giving Locations: NH: Concord and Merrimack County
Grant Types: General Support.

Financial Summary

Total Giving: $333,962 (2001); $367,347 (2000); $331,125 (1999)
Giving Analysis: Giving for 2001 includes: foundation grants to United Way ($30,000); 2000: foundation grants to United Way ($30,000); foundation scholarships ($64,500); 1999: foundation grants to United Way ($30,000) foundation scholarships ($40,000)
Assets: $6,189,490 (2001); $7,549,683 (2000); $6,591,093 (1999)

Typical Recipients

Arts & Humanities: Arts Appreciation, Arts Associations & Councils, Arts Centers, Arts Institutes, History & Archaeology, Libraries, Museums/Galleries, Music, Public Broadcasting
Civic & Public Affairs: Civil Rights, Community Foundations, Civic & Public Affairs-General, Housing, Law & Justice, Legal Aid, Municipalities/Towns, Parades/Festivals, Philanthropic Organizations, Professional & Trade Associations, Public Policy, Urban & Community Affairs, Women's Affairs, Zoos/Aquariums
Education: Arts/Humanities Education, Colleges & Universities, Medical Education, Minority Education, Private Education (Precollege), Public Education (Precollege), Science/Mathematics Education, Student Aid
Environment: Air/Water Quality, Environment-General, Resource Conservation
Health: AIDS/HIV, Clinics/Medical Centers, Hospitals, Mental Health, Nursing Services, Public Health, Respiratory, Single-Disease Health Associations
Religion: Churches, Religious Organizations, Religious Welfare
Social Services: Animal Protection, Child Welfare, Community Centers, Community Service Organizations, Day Care, Domestic Violence, Emergency Relief, Family Planning, Family Services, Food/Clothing Distribution, Homes, People with Disabilities, Recreation & Athletics, Scouts, United Funds/United Ways, YMCA/YWCA/YMHA/YWHA, Youth Organizations

Application Procedures

Initial Contact: Send a brief letter of inquiry.
Application Requirements: Include amount requested, purpose of funds sought, and a description of organization.
Deadlines: None.

Restrictions

Grantmaking is limited to charitable organizations or individuals in the Concord, NH area.

Foundation Officials

Charles F. Leahy: trustee
Malcolm McLane: trustee
Robert H. Reno: trustee
Ronald Snow: trustee

Grants Analysis

Disclosure Period: calendar year ending 2001
Total Grants: $303,962*
Number of Grants: 27
Average Grant: $11,258
Highest Grant: $30,000
Typical Range: $1,000 to $25,000
*Note: Giving excludes United Way.

Recent Grants

Note: Grants derived from 2001 Form 990.

Library-Related
20,000	Concord Public Library Foundation, Concord, NH -- children's Room Project

General
30,000	United Way of Merrimack County, Concord, NH -- provide community services
25,000	Bishop Brady High School, Concord, NH -- building improvements
25,000	Concord Community Music School, Concord, NH -- develop new music programs for community
25,000	New Hampshire Center Public Policy Study, Durham, NH -- study of issues affecting New Hampshire persons
25,000	New Hampshire Charitable Foundation, Concord, NH -- scholarship fund
20,000	Fellowship Housing Opportunities, Concord, NH -- rehabilitation of low income housing

20,000	Initiative for a 20/20 Vision for Concord, Concord, NH -- vision guidelines
13,667	Rolfz and Rumford Home, Concord, NH -- repairs
12,500	Canterbury Shaker Village, Canterbury, NH -- building restoration
12,000	Concord Area Trust for Community Housing, Concord, MA -- education center

JANIRVE FOUNDATION

Giving Contact

Charles Dyson, Chairman, Advisory Committee
One North Pack Square, Suite 416
Asheville, NC 28801
Phone: (828)258-1877
Fax: (828)258-1837

Description

Founded: 1964
EIN: 596147678
Organization Type: General Purpose Foundation
Giving Locations: FL: Palm Beach, West Palm Beach; NC: Western North Carolina
Grant Types: Capital, Challenge, General Support, Matching, Operating Expenses, Project.

Donor Information

Founder: Established in 1964 by the late Irving J. Reuter , a General Motors executive. Upon the death of his widow, Jeannett Reuter, in 1984, the foundation became active on a full-time basis.
In 1985, the foundation received $25 million from the estate of Irving and Jeannett Reuter . Financial records are kept in Palm Beach, FL, the location of the Reuter's residence. The grant-making office is located in Asheville, NC, where the Reuters kept a summer home.

Financial Summary

Total Giving: $8,373,665 (2000); $4,000,000 (1999 approx); $4,043,191 (1998)
Assets: $82,462,214 (2000); $75,240,112 (1998); $68,111,517 (1997)

Typical Recipients

Arts & Humanities: Arts Associations & Councils, Arts Centers, Ethnic & Folk Arts, Arts & Humanities-General, History & Archaeology, Libraries, Museums/Galleries, Music, Opera, Public Broadcasting, Theater
Civic & Public Affairs: Botanical Gardens/Parks, Business/Free Enterprise, Chambers of Commerce, Community Foundations, Employment/Job Training, Civic & Public Affairs-General, Housing, Law & Justice, Legal Aid, Philanthropic Organizations, Professional & Trade Associations, Public Policy, Urban & Community Affairs
Education: Afterschool/Enrichment Programs, Arts/Humanities Education, Colleges & Universities, Community & Junior Colleges, Education Associations, Education Reform, Education-General, Leadership Training, Literacy, Medical Education, Preschool Education, Private Education (Precollege), Public Education (Precollege), Special Education, Student Aid, Vocational & Technical Education
Environment: Air/Water Quality, Environment-General, Resource Conservation
Health: Adolescent Health Issues, Alzheimers Disease, Cancer, Children's Health/Hospitals, Clinics/Medical Centers, Emergency/Ambulance Services, Health-General, Geriatric Health, Health Organizations, Hospices, Hospitals, Long-Term Care, Medical Rehabilitation, Preventive Medicine/Wellness Organizations, Public Health, Single-Disease Health Associations, Transplant Networks/Donor Banks
International: Foreign Educational Institutions

Religion: Bible Study/Translation, Jewish Causes, Ministries, Religious Organizations, Religious Welfare

Science: Science Museums, Scientific Centers & Institutes

Social Services: Animal Protection, Big Brother/Big Sister, Camps, Child Abuse, Child Welfare, Community Centers, Community Service Organizations, Counseling, Day Care, Domestic Violence, Family Planning, Family Services, Food/Clothing Distribution, Homes, People with Disabilities, Scouts, Senior Services, Social Services-General, Special Olympics, YMCA/YWCA/YMHA/YWHA, Youth Organizations

Application Procedures

Initial Contact: Prospective applicants may call or write the foundation for an application.

Application Requirements: Applicants should send a written proposal, no longer than three single-spaced pages, including a detailed description of the organization's activities, amount requested, grant purpose, financial information, and a list of governing members. Four copies of the proposal, with a completed application form and IRS tax-exemption letter, should be sent to the foundation's office.

Deadlines: Proposals should be received by December 1 for the first quarter, by March 1 for the second quarter, by June 1 for the third quarter, and by September 1 for the fourth quarter.

Review Process: Proposals are considered quarterly by a five-person advisory committee. Applicants will be notified of the committee's decision following the final meeting of the quarter.

Restrictions

Grants are not made to individuals.

Additional Information

All accepted applicants are expected to furnish a progress report(s) as well as a project completion report accounting for the use of the Janirve Foundation grant. The foundation makes single-year grants as opposed to multiple-year awards. It gives low priority to projects proposed by government groups or those operated primarily with tax funds.

First National Bank in Palm Beach, a division of First Union National Bank is the corporate trustee of the foundation.

Publications: Guidelines; Application Form; Information Sheet for Applicants

Foundation Officials

E. Charles Dyson: member advisory committee
John W. Erichson: member advisory committee
Met R. Poston: chairman adv comm
James Woollcott: mem adv comm
Richard B. Wynne: mem adv comm

Grants Analysis

Disclosure Period: calendar year ending 2000
Total Grants: $8,373,665
Number of Grants: 82
Average Grant: $62,958*
Highest Grant: $1,400,000
Lowest Grant: $1,000
Typical Range: $5,000 to $100,000
*Note: Average grant figure excludes three highest grants ($3,400,000).

Recent Grants

Note: Grants derived from 2000 Form 990.

Library-Related
450,000	Friends of Madison County Library, Marshall, NC

General
1,400,000	Community Foundation of Western North Carolina, Inc., Asheville, NC
1,000,000	North Carolina Center Creative Retirement, Asheville, NC
1,000,000	Young Men's Christian Association of Western North Carolina, Asheville, NC
475,000	Warren Wilson College, Asheville, NC
250,000	Conservation Trust for North Carolina, Raleigh, NC
250,000	Mission St. Joseph's Healthcare Foundation, Hendersonville, NC
203,175	Quality Forward, Asheville, NC
200,000	Crossnore School, Crossnore, NC
200,000	Grove Arcade Public Market Foundation, Inc., Asheville, NC
175,000	MANNA Food Bank, Asheville, NC

JAQUA FOUNDATION

Giving Contact

Eli Hoffman, Chairman
100 Campus Drive
PO Box 944
Florham Park, NJ 07932
Phone: (973)593-7010
Fax: (973)593-7070

Description

Founded: 1977
EIN: 222086399
Organization Type: Private Foundation
Giving Locations: NJ; NY
Grant Types: Endowment, General Support, Scholarship.

Donor Information

Founder: the late George R. Jaqua

Financial Summary

Total Giving: $4,540,714 (2001); $3,515,217 (2000); $2,594,688 (1999)
Giving Analysis: Giving for 2001 includes: foundation scholarships ($220,000); 1999: foundation grants to United Way ($5,000) 1998: foundation scholarships ($120,000)
Assets: $11,466,113 (2001); $15,232,943 (2000); $18,376,047 (1999)
Gifts Received: $22,974 (1996); $21,500 (1995); $27,550 (1994)

Typical Recipients

Arts & Humanities: Historic Preservation, History & Archaeology, Libraries, Museums/Galleries, Music, Performing Arts

Civic & Public Affairs: Economic Development, Civic & Public Affairs-General, Housing, Professional & Trade Associations

Education: Arts/Humanities Education, Colleges & Universities, Education Associations, Engineering/Technological Education, Medical Education, Private Education (Precollege), Public Education (Precollege), Science/Mathematics Education, Student Aid

Environment: Resource Conservation

Health: Cancer, Children's Health/Hospitals, Clinics/Medical Centers, Emergency/Ambulance Services, Geriatric Health, Health Organizations, Heart, Hospitals, Hospitals (University Affiliated), Long-Term Care, Medical Research, Public Health, Single-Disease Health Associations, Speech & Hearing

International: Foreign Educational Institutions

Religion: Churches, Jewish Causes, Ministries, Religious Organizations, Religious Welfare, Synagogues/Temples

Social Services: Animal Protection, At-Risk Youth, Child Welfare, Community Service Organizations, Family Services, Food/Clothing Distribution, Homes, People with Disabilities, Recreation & Athletics, Scouts, United Funds/United Ways, Volunteer Services, YMCA/YWCA/YMHA/YWHA, Youth Organizations

Application Procedures

Initial Contact: Submit a brief letter of inquiry.
Application Requirements: Include a description of organization, amount requested, and purpose of funds sought.
Deadlines: None.

Restrictions

Does not support individuals or private foundations.

Foundation Officials

W. Fletcher Hock, Jr.: secretary
Eli Hoffman: chairman
John Minnema: vice president
Samuel Pollock: trustee

Grants Analysis

Disclosure Period: calendar year ending 2001
Total Grants: $4,320,714*
Number of Grants: 79
Average Grant: $41,291*
Highest Grant: $1,100,000
Lowest Grant: $500
Typical Range: $20,000 to $50,000
*Note: Giving excludes scholarship. Average grant figure excludes highest grant.

Recent Grants

Note: Grants derived from 2000 Form 990.

General
500,000	New Jersey Symphony Orchestra, Newark, NJ
300,000	Cornell University, Ithaca, NY -- scholarships
300,000	Lafayette College, Easton, PA -- scholarships
250,000	Valley Hospital, Ridgewood, NJ -- building fund
200,000	Animal Medical Center, New York, NY
128,000	New Jersey Performing Arts Center, Livingston, NJ
100,000	Kildonan School, Amenia, NY -- scholarships
100,000	Michigan State University, East Lansing, MI -- College of Veterinary Medicine
100,000	School in Rose Valley, Rose Valley, PA
85,000	United Cerebral Palsy Association, Trenton, NJ

JARSON KAPLAN FOUNDATION

Giving Contact

Stanley M. Kaplan, Trustee
9435 Waterstone Blvd., Suite 390
Cincinnati, OH 45249
Phone: (513)785-6060

Alternate Contact

Myron J. Kaplan

Description

Founded: 1955
EIN: 316033453
Organization Type: Private Foundation
Former Name: Isaac N. and Esther M. Jarson Charitable Trust.
Former Name: Isaac and Esther Jarson-Stanley and Mickey Kaplan Foundation (2000).
Giving Locations: OH: Cincinnati The greater Cincinnati area
Grant Types: General Support.

Financial Summary

Total Giving: $37,750 (2002); $91,431 (2000); $184,928 (1999)
Assets: $1,840,850 (2002); $2,275,270 (2000); $2,773,617 (1999)

Typical Recipients

Arts & Humanities: Arts Associations & Councils, Arts Centers, Arts Festivals, Arts Funds, Arts Institutes, Arts Outreach, Ballet, Community Arts, Dance, Arts & Humanities-General, Historic Preservation, Libraries, Museums/Galleries, Music, Opera, Performing Arts, Public Broadcasting, Theater

Civic & Public Affairs: African American Affairs, Botanical Gardens/Parks, Community Foundations, Civic & Public Affairs-General, Housing, Parades/Festivals, Philanthropic Organizations, Urban & Community Affairs, Women's Affairs

Education: Afterschool/Enrichment Programs, Arts/Humanities Education, Business Education, Colleges & Universities, Education Funds, Engineering/Technological Education, Literacy, Medical Education, Minority Education, Private Education (Precollege), Public Education (Precollege), Religious Education, Secondary Education (Public), Student Aid

Environment: Air/Water Quality

Health: AIDS/HIV, Cancer, Children's Health/Hospitals, Clinics/Medical Centers, Diabetes, Emergency/Ambulance Services, Health Organizations, Hospices, Hospitals, Kidney, Medical Rehabilitation, Medical Research, Mental Health, Prenatal Health Issues, Preventive Medicine/Wellness Organizations, Single-Disease Health Associations

International: Foreign Arts Organizations, Health Care/Hospitals

Religion: Churches, Religion-General, Jewish Causes, Religious Organizations, Religious Welfare, Synagogues/Temples

Science: Science Museums

Social Services: Animal Protection, At-Risk Youth, Child Welfare, Community Centers, Community Service Organizations, Emergency Relief, Food/Clothing Distribution, People with Disabilities, Recreation & Athletics, Senior Services, Shelters/Homelessness, Substance Abuse, United Funds/United Ways, YMCA/YWCA/YMHA/YWHA, Youth Organizations

Application Procedures

Initial Contact: Send a brief letter of inquiry.
Application Requirements: Include proof of tax-exempt status.
Deadlines: None.

Foundation Officials

Myran J. Kaplan: trustee
Stanley Meisel Kaplan, MD: trustee B Cincinnati, OH 1922. ED University of Cincinnati BS (1943); University of Cincinnati MD (1946); Institute of Psychoanalysis (1962-1967). PRIM NONPR EMPL professor, faculty department psychiatry: University of Cincinnati. CORP AFFIL chairman, director: G&J Pepsi Cola. NONPR AFFIL member: Sigma Xi; professor: University Cincinnati; director: Contemporary Arts Center Ohio; director: Friends College Conservatory Music; director: Cincinnati Art Museum; director: Cincinnati Ballet; director: Bonds Israel; member: American Psychoanalytic Association; member: American Psychosomatic Society; fellow: American Psychiatric Association; member: American Association University Professors; member: American Medical Association.

Grants Analysis

Disclosure Period: calendar year ending 2002
Total Grants: $37,750
Number of Grants: 5
Highest Grant: $18,000
Typical Range: $250 to $18,000

Recent Grants

Note: Grants derived from 2002 Form 990.

General
18,000	Adath Israel Congregation, Cincinnati, OH
10,000	Free Store Food Bank, Cincinnati, OH
6,500	Fine Arts Fund, Cincinnati, OH
3,000	Playhouse in the Park, Cincinnati, OH
250	WGUC, Cincinnati, OH

JAYDOR CORP.

Company Headquarters

16 Bleeker St.
Millburn, NJ 07041
Web: http://www.bevnetwork.com

Company Description

Employees: 350
SIC(s): 5100 Wholesale Trade--Nondurable Goods.

Operating Locations

Jaydor Corp. (NJ--Millburn)

Nonmonetary Support

Type: Cause-related Marketing & Promotion

Jaydor Foundation

Giving Contact

Michael D. Silverman, Trustee
600 Washington Avenue
Carlstadt, NJ 07072
Phone: (201)842-6200

Description

Founded: 1979
EIN: 226067078
Organization Type: Corporate Foundation
Giving Locations: NJ
Grant Types: Award, Capital, Endowment, General Support, Multiyear/Continuing Support, Scholarship.

Financial Summary

Total Giving: $40,763 (fiscal year ending August 31, 2002); $40,063 (fiscal 2000); $50,490 (fiscal 1998)
Giving Analysis: Giving for fiscal 2002 includes: foundation grants to United Way ($250); fiscal 2000: foundation scholarships ($5,070); foundation ($34,993); fiscal 1998: foundation scholarships ($70); foundation grants to United Way ($250) foundation ($50,170)
Assets: $5,733 (fiscal 2002); $12,496 (fiscal 2000); $10,394 (fiscal 1998)
Gifts Received: $34,000 (fiscal 2002); $45,000 (fiscal 2000); $56,000 (fiscal 1998). Note: In 2002, contributions were received from Silverman Hilding Corp. In fiscal 1996, 1997, and 2000, contributions were received from the Jay Dor Corp.

Typical Recipients

Arts & Humanities: Community Arts, Arts & Humanities-General, Libraries, Museums/Galleries, Music, Performing Arts, Theater

Civic & Public Affairs: African American Affairs, Chambers of Commerce, Ethnic Organizations, Civic & Public Affairs-General, Philanthropic Organizations, Professional & Trade Associations, Urban & Community Affairs

Education: Education-General, Minority Education, Private Education (Precollege), Student Aid

Environment: Environment-General, Research

Health: Cancer, Children's Health/Hospitals, Clinics/Medical Centers, Diabetes, Emergency/Ambulance Services, Health-General, Heart, Hospices, Hospitals, Medical Rehabilitation, Mental Health, Single-Disease Health Associations

International: Foreign Educational Institutions, International Peace & Security Issues, International Relief Efforts, Missionary/Religious Activities

Religion: Churches, Dioceses, Religion-General, Jewish Causes, Social/Policy Issues, Synagogues/Temples

Science: Science-General

Social Services: Recreation & Athletics, Scouts, Social Services-General, Special Olympics, United Funds/United Ways, Veterans, YMCA/YWCA/YMHA/YWHA, Youth Organizations

Application Procedures

Initial Contact: Send a brief letter of inquiry and a full proposal.
Application Requirements: Include a description of organization, amount requested, purpose of funds sought, and proof of tax-exempt status.
Deadlines: None.

Restrictions

Grants are not made to individuals.

Corporate Officials

Louis Healey: chief financial officer, director PRIM CORP EMPL chief financial officer: Jaydor Corp.
Barry S. Silverman: chairman, director PRIM CORP EMPL chairman, director: Jaydor Corp.
Michael David Silverman: president, chief executive officer, director B Newark, NJ 1946. ED Yale University BA (1968). PRIM CORP EMPL president, chief executive officer, director: Jaydor Corp. CORP AFFIL member: Heublein Distributor Advisor Council. NONPR AFFIL member: Wine and Spirit Wholesalers of America; member: Wine and Spirit Wholesalers Association; member: Seagram Family Association.

Foundation Officials

Barry S. Silverman: trustee (see above)
Jeffrey Silverman: trustee
Michael David Silverman: trustee (see above)

Grants Analysis

Disclosure Period: fiscal year ending August 31, 2002
Total Grants: $40,513*
Number of Grants: 42
Average Grant: $513*
Highest Grant: $10,000
Lowest Grant: $1
Typical Range: $100 to $1,000
*Note: Giving excludes United Way. Average grant figure excludes two highest grants ($20,000).

Recent Grants

Note: Grants derived from 2000 Form 990.

General
7,500	United Jewish Appeal of Metro West, Whippany, NJ
5,000	Givat Haviva Educational Foundation, New York, NY
5,000	Thurgood Marshall Scholarship Fund, New York, NY
2,500	Horatio Alger Awards, Washington, DC
2,000	United Jewish Appeal of Metro West, Whippany, NJ
1,525	Temple B'nai Abraham, Livingston, NJ
1,525	Temple B'nai Abraham, Livingston, NJ
1,000	National Jewish Medical and Research Center, New York, NY
1,000	World Jewish Congress, New York, NY
750	American Jewish Committee, Millburn, NJ

JELD-WEN, INC.

Company Headquarters

3250 Lakeport Blvd.
Klamath Falls, OR 97601
Web: http://www.jeld-wen.com

Company Description

Founded: 1960
SIC(s): 2431 Millwork, 3442 Metal Doors, Sash & Trim.

Jeld-wen Foundation

Giving Contact

Carol Chesnut
JELD-WEN Foundation
PO Box 1329
Klamath Falls, OR 97601
Phone: (541)882-3451
Fax: (541)885-7454

Description

EIN: 936054272
Organization Type: Corporate Foundation
Giving Locations: major principally near operating locations and to national organizations.
Grant Types: Capital, Challenge, General Support, Project, Scholarship, Seed Money.

Financial Summary

Total Giving: $7,496,346 (2001); $5,575,784 (2000); $4,074,474 (1999). Note: Contributes through foundation only. 1996 Giving includes scholarship ($117,600); United Way ($371,519).
Giving Analysis: Giving for 2000 includes: foundation scholarships ($118,400); foundation grants to United Way ($545,741); foundation ($4,911,643); 1999: foundation scholarships ($153,200); foundation grants to United Way ($535,200); foundation ($3,386,074); 1998: foundation scholarships ($102,600); foundation grants to United Way ($511,700) foundation ($3,329,754)
Assets: $37,976,455 (2001); $45,115,030 (2000); $47,384,148 (1999)
Gifts Received: $1,000,000 (2000); $2,989,000 (1998); $5,085,000 (1997). Note: Contributions are received from JELD-WEN Inc.

Typical Recipients

Arts & Humanities: Arts Associations & Councils, Arts Centers, Arts Festivals, Film & Video, Historic Preservation, History & Archaeology, Libraries, Museums/Galleries, Music, Opera, Public Broadcasting, Theater
Civic & Public Affairs: Botanical Gardens/Parks, Business/Free Enterprise, Chambers of Commerce, Community Foundations, Economic Development, Employment/Job Training, Civic & Public Affairs-General, Housing, Municipalities/Towns, Native American Affairs, Philanthropic Organizations, Public Policy, Safety, Urban & Community Affairs, Women's Affairs
Education: Arts/Humanities Education, Colleges & Universities, Community & Junior Colleges, Education Associations, Education Reform, Elementary Education (Public), Engineering/Technological Education, Environmental Education, Education-General, Preschool Education, Private Education (Precollege), Public Education (Precollege), Science/Mathematics Education, Student Aid, Vocational & Technical Education
Environment: Forestry, Environment-General, Wildlife Protection
Health: Children's Health/Hospitals, Clinics/Medical Centers, Emergency/Ambulance Services, Health-General, Health Policy/Cost Containment, Health Organizations, Hospices, Hospitals, Medical Rehabilitation, Medical Research, Prenatal Health Issues, Public Health
Religion: Ministries, Religious Organizations, Religious Welfare
Science: Science Museums
Social Services: Animal Protection, At-Risk Youth, Child Welfare, Community Centers, Community Service Organizations, Crime Prevention, Domestic Violence, People with Disabilities, Recreation & Athletics, Scouts, Senior Services, Social Services-General, Substance Abuse, United Funds/United Ways, Volunteer Services, YMCA/YWCA/YMHA/YWHA, Youth Organizations

Application Procedures

Initial Contact: Write to request funding application.
Application Requirements: Applicants are encouraged to meet with a company manager in the area to discuss proposal. The completed application form should be submitted to this manager, who will forward it to the foundation.
Deadlines: Write to request deadline dates.
Review Process: Foundation board generally meets on a quarterly basis; receipt is acknowledged, and proposal may be accepted, rejected, or referred for modification within two weeks; proposals accepted for consideration are then reviewed at trustees' meeting in March, June, September, or December; proposal contact persons are notified within two weeks after meeting.
Evaluative Criteria: Location of organization relative to company operating areas, value of project to company employees and families, involvement of employees in organization and project proposed, few previous requests, proposed project planning, sources and uses of funds, and tax exempt status.
Notes: Foundation meeting dates vary due to requests received and scheduling logistics of foundation trustees.

Restrictions

Foundation does not fund projects related to religious purposes; proposals which duplicate government or private agency programs; projects which serve a very narrow segment of the community; proposals that the foundation feels are not clearly defined, not feasible, not cost effective, or inappropriate to meet existing needs. Funds must be used within the United States. Foundation generally discourages requests for annual support outside of United Way giving. Rejected proposals may not be resubmitted during the same calendar year.

Additional Information

The foundation may fund an outstanding organization more than once in a short period of time, but is cautious not to let organizations become dependent on regular giving.

Corporate Officials

William Bernard Early: senior vice president, assistant secretary, director B Mexico, MO 1936. ED Stanford University (1958); Harvard University (1964). PRIM CORP EMPL senior vice president, assistant secretary, director: Jeld-Wen, Inc. CORP AFFIL vice president: Bend Millwork System Inc.
Richard L. Wendt: chief executive officer, chairman B 1931. PRIM CORP EMPL chief executive officer, chairman: Jeld-Wen, Inc. CORP AFFIL director: Columbia Forest Products Inc.; director: Windmill Inns America Inc.; chairman: Avanti Industries Inc.; chairman: Bend Millwork System Inc.
Roderick C. Wendt: president, director B 1954. ED Willamette University Law School JD (1980). PRIM CORP EMPL president, director: Jeld-Wen, Inc. CORP AFFIL president: Bend Millwork System Inc.; treasurer: Windmill Inns America Inc.; president: 3D Industries Inc.
Larry V. Wetter: vice chairman, director B Rockwell City, IA 1933. ED Iowa State University of Science & Technology (1955). PRIM CORP EMPL vice chairman, director: Jeld-Wen, Inc. CORP AFFIL executive vice president: Bend Millwork System Inc.

Foundation Officials

William Bernard Early: trustee (see above)
Nancy Wendt: trustee
Richard L. Wendt: trustee (see above)
Roderick C. Wendt: trustee (see above)
Larry V. Wetter: trustee (see above)

Grants Analysis

Disclosure Period: calendar year ending 2001
Total Grants: $6,162,235*
Number of Grants: 204

Average Grant: $26,298*
Highest Grant: $500,000
Lowest Grant: $250
Typical Range: $5,000 to $100,000
*Note: Giving excludes scholarship and United Way. Average grant figure excludes two highest grants ($850,000).

Recent Grants

Note: Grants derived from 2001 Form 990.

Library-Related

100,000	Rantoul Public Library, Rantoul, IL
50,000	Friends of the Bruce Public Library, Bruce, WI

General

500,000	Oregon Health Science, Portland, OR
350,000	High Desert Museum, Bend, OR
200,000	Klamath Ice Sports, Klamath Falls, OR
200,000	Klamath Ice Sports, Klamath Falls, OR
200,000	University of Oregon Foundation, Eugene, OR
176,400	Reach, Inc., Klamath Falls, OR
166,841	Klamath Community Youth Sports Complex, Klamath Falls, OR
166,666	Hosana Christian School, Klamath Falls, OR
150,971	Klamath Community Youth Sports Complex, Klamath Falls, OR
150,000	Klamath Ice Sports, Klamath Falls, OR

JENJO FOUNDATION

Giving Contact

Alan Alda, Trustee
c/o Morris Pliskow, PC
641 Lexington Ave., No. 1400
New York, NY 10022
Phone: (212)421-6161

Description

Founded: 1990
EIN: 136944768
Organization Type: Private Foundation
Giving Locations: NY: New York
Grant Types: General Support, Research.

Donor Information

Founder: Established in 1990 by Alan Alda.

Financial Summary

Total Giving: $64,010 (2001); $146,000 (2000); $132,000 (1999)
Assets: $1,845,453 (2001); $1,846,999 (2000); $1,893,914 (1999)

Typical Recipients

Arts & Humanities: Arts Outreach, Libraries, Public Broadcasting
Civic & Public Affairs: Business/Free Enterprise, Civil Rights, Civic & Public Affairs-General, Housing, Municipalities/Towns, Philanthropic Organizations, Public Policy, Urban & Community Affairs, Women's Affairs
Education: Education Reform, Education-General, Literacy, Private Education (Precollege), Public Education (Precollege)
Environment: Environment-General
Health: AIDS/HIV, Single-Disease Health Associations
International: Missionary/Religious Activities
Social Services: At-Risk Youth, Child Welfare, Community Centers, Community Service Organizations, Counseling, Crime Prevention, Day Care, Domestic Violence, Family Services, Food/Clothing Distribution, Recreation & Athletics, Youth Organizations

Application Procedures

Initial Contact: Send a brief letter of inquiry.
Application Requirements: proof of tax-exempt status.
Deadlines: None.

Restrictions

Grants will generally be given to causes relating to health, education, the environment, and other critical areas that affect the quality of life for all people.

Foundation Officials

Alan Alda: trustee B New York, NY 1936. ED Fordham University BS (1956). OCCUPATION actor, writer, director. NONPR AFFIL member: Screen Actors Guild; member: Writers Guild America; member: Directors Guild America; member: Actors Equity Association; member: American Federation Television & Radio Artists.
Arlene Alda: trustee
Beatrice Alda: trustee
Elizabeth Alda: trustee
Mark Caligiuri: trustee
Eve Alda Coffey: trustee
James Coffey: trustee

Grants Analysis

Disclosure Period: calendar year ending 2001
Total Grants: $64,010
Number of Grants: 1

Recent Grants

Note: Grants derived from 2001 Form 990.

General

64,010	Philanthropic Initiative, Boston, MA -- health, education and environment

MARTHA HOLDEN JENNINGS FOUNDATION

Giving Contact

William T. Hiller, Executive Director
The Halle Building
1228 Euclid Avenue, Suite 710
Cleveland, OH 44115
Phone: (216)589-5700
Fax: (216)589-5730
Web: http://www.mhjf.org

Description

Founded: 1958
EIN: 340934478
Organization Type: General Purpose Foundation
Giving Locations: OH: Cuyahoga County
Grant Types: Award, Conference/Seminar, General Support, Project, Research.

Donor Information

Founder: Martha Holden Jennings established the foundation bearing her name in 1959, three years before her death. Mrs. Jennings made her home in Cleveland after living for many years in Europe with her husband, Andrew R. Jennings. She was known for her love of children, art, animals, and traveling. She hoped that her foundation would "foster the development of individual capabilities of young people to the maximum extent through improving the quality of teaching in secular primary and secondary schools and by furnishing incentives thereto." She supported elementary and secondary education because, although various foundations were committed to higher education, less attention was being paid to the earlier stages of learning, especially in public schools.

Financial Summary

Total Giving: $10,885,188 (2001); $7,000,000 (2000 approx); $7,577,988 (1999)
Giving Analysis: Giving for 1999 includes: foundation scholarships ($155,000)
Assets: $95,000,000 (2002); $103,079,737 (2001); $135,000,000 (2000 approx)
Gifts Received: $3,800 (1993)

Typical Recipients

Arts & Humanities: Arts Associations & Councils, Arts Centers, Arts Institutes, Arts Outreach, Ballet, Dance, Arts & Humanities-General, Historic Preservation, History & Archaeology, Libraries, Literary Arts, Museums/Galleries, Music, Opera, Performing Arts, Public Broadcasting, Theater
Civic & Public Affairs: African American Affairs, Botanical Gardens/Parks, Civic & Public Affairs-General, Hispanic Affairs, Nonprofit Management, Parades/Festivals, Public Policy, Zoos/Aquariums
Education: Afterschool/Enrichment Programs, Arts/Humanities Education, Business Education, Colleges & Universities, Education Associations, Education Funds, Education Reform, Elementary Education (Private), Faculty Development, Faculty Development, Education-General, Gifted & Talented Programs, Health & Physical Education, International Studies, Leadership Training, Literacy, Minority Education, Preschool Education, Private Education (Precollege), Public Education (Precollege), School Volunteerism, Science/Mathematics Education, Secondary Education (Public), Special Education, Student Aid
Environment: Environment-General, Resource Conservation
Health: Adolescent Health Issues, Heart, Mental Health, Preventive Medicine/Wellness Organizations
International: Foreign Educational Institutions
Religion: Religious Welfare
Science: Science Museums, Scientific Centers & Institutes
Social Services: At-Risk Youth, Child Welfare, Community Centers, Community Service Organizations, Family Services, People with Disabilities, Substance Abuse, Youth Organizations, Youth Organizations

Application Procedures

Initial Contact: Application forms for grants to educators are available from the website. There are no forms for other grant applications.
Application Requirements: Submit an original proposal. Applications must include a cover letter signed by the chief executive of the organization requesting funds and a listing of all enclosures. A one-page summary of the proposed project, listing the amount requested, specific purpose of and need for the project, proposed plan of action and projected outcome, number of participants or schools to be involved, and other sources of funding, should be included. A detailed budget must be enclosed indicating how the requested funds will be used and the amount, if any, of other funds to be used to support the project. Applications also must include a copy of the organization's tax-exempt classification under IRS section 501(c)(3). Institutions which provide services to schools should enclose a letter indicating the need for such services, signed by the superintendent of schools.
A succinct (limited to 10 pages) proposal must be included. The proposal should indicate how the project will help elementary or secondary teachers and students attain a higher level of excellence; how the project is innovative or original; how the project will be evaluated; how the results will be disseminated to others; who will direct the project; what the project's immediate and long-term objectives are; what the projects timetable is; and, if the project is successful, what plans there are for funding it after the grant has ended.
Deadlines: None.
Review Process: Proposals must be received by the 20th of each month to be considered for the following

month's committee meeting (committee does not meet in July or December). Applicants are notified within two months of their submission.

Restrictions

The foundation does not make grants for capital improvements, equipment, travel, or graduate study. A grant must be spent solely for the purpose for which it was made.

Additional Information

Besides making grants, the foundation also supports conferences, seminars/workshops, and offers proposal writing assistance. Reports are required from the grantees on how the funds were spent and the results achieved.
Publications: Annual Report; Guidelines; Application Form; Pro Excellentia Bulletin

Foundation Officials

Dr. Jeanette Grasselli Brown: trustee B Cleveland, OH 1928. ED Ohio University BS (1950); Case Western Reserve University MS (1958). ADD CORP EMPL director corporate research: BP America. CORP AFFIL director: BDM International Inc.; director: USX Corp. NONPR AFFIL trustee: Musical Arts Association/Cleveland Orchestra; chairperson: Ohio Board Regents.
George B. Chapman, III: member
George B. Chapman, Jr.: member PRIM NONPR EMPL professor: Georgetown University Depart. of Biology.
Dr. William Hiller: executive director ED Indiana University of Pennsylvania BS (1969); Indiana University of Pennsylvania MS (1972); University of Pittsburgh PhD (1979). PRIM CORP EMPL superintendent: Mentor (Ohio) Board of Education.
Daniel M. Kalish: executive director

Grants Analysis

Disclosure Period: calendar year ending 2001
Total Grants: $10,800,000*
Number of Grants: 230
Average Grant: $18,000*
Highest Grant: $350,000
Lowest Grant: $500
Typical Range: $5,000 to $40,000
*Note: Giving excludes scholarships. Grants analysis provided by foundation.

Recent Grants

Note: Grants derived from 2001 Form 990.

General

961,199	University Partnership/Urban Initiative, Cleveland, OH -- improving urban school
541,409	University Partnership/Urban Initiative, Cleveland, OH
38,0000	Goodrich Gannet Neighborhood Center, Cleveland, OH -- early childhood services
302,221	Kent State University Foundation, Kent, OH -- Urban Fellows Program
230,251	Ohio Aerospace Institute, Cleveland, OH -- TIMMS Related Math and Science Initiative Program
200,705	Ohio Department of Education, Columbus, OH -- Early Childhood Initiative Program
200,631	Cleveland State University Foundation, Cleveland, OH -- Urban Fellows Program
200,000	Cleveland Botanical Garden, Cleveland, OH -- campaign for Cleveland's Garden
200,000	Ohio Aerospace Institute, Cleveland, OH -- SMART funding school district action plans
100,642	Ohio Department of Education, Columbus, OH -- community-based approach to improving literacy

MARY HILLMAN JENNINGS FOUNDATION

Giving Contact

Paul Euwer, Jr., Executive Director
2203 Allegheny Tower
Pittsburgh, PA 15222
Phone: (412)434-5606
Fax: (412)434-5907

Description

Founded: 1968
EIN: 237002091
Organization Type: General Purpose Foundation
Giving Locations: PA: Pittsburgh
Grant Types: Capital, Department, Emergency, Endowment, Fellowship, General Support, Multiyear/Continuing Support, Project, Seed Money.

Donor Information

Founder: The foundation was established in 1968 by the late Mary Hillman Jennings .

Financial Summary

Total Giving: $3,414,000 (2001); $3,408,000 (2000); $2,936,500 (1999)
Giving Analysis: Giving for 2001 includes: foundation grants to United Way ($15,000); 2000: foundation grants to United Way ($15,000); 1999: foundation grants to United Way ($15,000)
Assets: $41,320,932 (2001); $49,843,763 (2000); $57,866,189 (1999)

Typical Recipients

Arts & Humanities: Arts Associations & Councils, Ballet, Ethnic & Folk Arts, Film & Video, Arts & Humanities-General, Historic Preservation, History & Archaeology, Libraries, Museums/Galleries, Music, Opera, Public Broadcasting, Theater
Civic & Public Affairs: Business/Free Enterprise, Community Foundations, Economic Development, Employment/Job Training, Civic & Public Affairs-General, Housing, Parades/Festivals, Professional & Trade Associations, Urban & Community Affairs, Zoos/Aquariums
Education: Arts/Humanities Education, Business Education, Colleges & Universities, Community & Junior Colleges, Education Funds, Education Reform, Elementary Education (Public), Environmental Education, Faculty Development, Education-General, Literacy, Minority Education, Preschool Education, Private Education (Precollege), Public Education (Precollege), Science/Mathematics Education, Social Sciences Education, Special Education
Environment: Environment-General, Resource Conservation, Wildlife Protection
Health: Alzheimers Disease, Cancer, Children's Health/Hospitals, Clinics/Medical Centers, Diabetes, Emergency/Ambulance Services, Health Organizations, Hospices, Hospitals, Long-Term Care, Medical Rehabilitation, Medical Research, Nursing Services, Outpatient Health Care, Public Health, Single-Disease Health Associations, Trauma Treatment
Religion: Churches, Jewish Causes, Ministries, Religious Welfare
Science: Science-General, Science Museums, Scientific Centers & Institutes, Scientific Centers & Institutes
Social Services: At-Risk Youth, Camps, Child Welfare, Community Centers, Community Service Organizations, Delinquency & Criminal Rehabilitation, Domestic Violence, Emergency Relief, Family Planning, Family Services, Food/Clothing Distribution, Homes, People with Disabilities, Recreation & Athletics, Sexual Abuse, Shelters/Homelessness, Substance Abuse, United Funds/United Ways, YMCA/YWCA/YMHA/YWHA, Youth Organizations

Application Procedures

Initial Contact: Submit a letter of proposal or common grant application form.
Application Requirements: The application should describe the organization, amount requested, and the intended use of the grant.
Deadlines: May 31 and October 1.
Review Process: The foundation's board of trustees meets twice a year to consider grant applications.

Foundation Officials

Paul Euwer, Jr.: executive director NONPR AFFIL vice president-treasurer, director: Allegheny Valley School.
Christina W. Jennings: director
Cynthia Jennings: director
Evan D. Jennings, II: president
Irving A. Wechsler: treasurer PRIM CORP EMPL partner: Wechsler Myers & Wolsh. CORP AFFIL director: Merchandise Service Division; director: Music Network Division; director: Comcast Corp.; director: Cablevision Communication Division; director: Comcast Cellular Communication.
Andrew L. Weil: secretary ED Chatham College (1949).

Grants Analysis

Disclosure Period: calendar year ending 2001
Total Grants: $3,399,000*
Number of Grants: 122
Average Grant: $10,000
Highest Grant: $400,000
Lowest Grant: $1,000
Typical Range: $10,000 to $50,000
***Note:** Grants analysis provided by foundation. Giving excludes United Way.

Recent Grants

Note: Grants derived from 2000 Form 990.

Library-Related
40,000	Sewickley Public Library, Sewickley, PA -- community

General
402,000	Shadyside Hospital Foundation, Pittsburgh, PA
200,000	Allegheny Valley School, Coraopolis, PA
200,000	Baptist Hospital of Miami, Miami, FL -- medical
200,000	Lahey Clinic Foundation, Burlington, MA -- community
200,000	Latrobe Area Hospital, Latrobe, PA -- medical
200,000	Shady Side Academy Fund, Pittsburgh, PA -- educational
100,000	George Washington Mount Vernon, Mt. Vernon, VA
100,000	Outside In School, Greensburg, PA -- community
50,000	Eye and Ear Institute of Pittsburgh, Pittsburgh, PA -- educational
50,000	Juvenile Diabetes Foundation, Pittsburgh, PA -- medical

GEORGE FREDERICK JEWETT FOUNDATION

Giving Contact

Ann D. Gralnek, Senior Advisor
Russ Building
235 Montgomery Street, Suite 612
San Francisco, CA 94104
Phone: (415)421-1351
Fax: (415)421-0721
E-mail: tfbjewettf@aol.com

Description

Founded: 1957
EIN: 046013832
Organization Type: Family Foundation
Giving Locations: CA: San Francisco; WA: Eastern Washington, Spokane
Grant Types: Capital, Endowment, Fellowship, General Support, Multiyear/Continuing Support, Project.

Donor Information

Founder: The George Frederick Jewett Foundation was established on December 2, 1957, under the will of George Frederick Jewett (1896-1956), whose mother was the former Margaret Weyerhaeuser. Mr. Jewett was chairman of Potlatch Corporation and a trustee of the American University of Cairo.

Financial Summary

Total Giving: $1,560,500 (2001); $1,813,800 (2000); $1,500,000 (1999 approx)
Giving Analysis: Giving for 2000 includes: foundation grants to United Way ($25,000) 1998: foundation grants to United Way ($25,000)
Assets: $36,837,552 (2001); $35,326,672 (2000); $37,083,414 (1998)
Gifts Received: $289,644 (1998); $128,499 (1994); $7,944 (1992). Note: In 1998, contributions were received from W.G. & E.S. Cooper. The foundation receives gifts from Berkshire Hathaway, Omaha, NE, and M. J. Gaiser House, Spokane, WA.

Typical Recipients

Arts & Humanities: Arts Associations & Councils, Arts Centers, Arts Festivals, Arts Institutes, Arts Outreach, Ballet, Dance, Film & Video, Historic Preservation, History & Archaeology, Libraries, Literary Arts, Museums/Galleries, Music, Opera, Performing Arts, Public Broadcasting, Visual Arts
Civic & Public Affairs: Botanical Gardens/Parks, Community Foundations, Economic Development, Economic Policy, Civic & Public Affairs-General, Housing, Nonprofit Management, Philanthropic Organizations, Public Policy, Zoos/Aquariums
Education: Arts/Humanities Education, Business Education, Colleges & Universities, Economic Education, Elementary Education (Public), Faculty Development, Faculty Development, Education-General, International Studies, Medical Education, Minority Education, Private Education (Precollege), Public Education (Precollege), Religious Education, Science/Mathematics Education, Secondary Education (Private), Social Sciences Education, Special Education, Student Aid
Environment: Air/Water Quality, Forestry, Environment-General, Resource Conservation, Watershed
Health: Cancer, Clinics/Medical Centers, Diabetes, Emergency/Ambulance Services, Hospitals, Medical Rehabilitation, Nursing Services, Prenatal Health Issues, Public Health, Speech & Hearing
International: Foreign Arts Organizations, Foreign Educational Institutions, Health Care/Hospitals, International Affairs, International Environmental Issues, International Relations
Religion: Churches, Religious Organizations, Religious Welfare
Science: Science-General, Science Museums, Scientific Centers & Institutes, Scientific Labs
Social Services: Child Welfare, Community Service Organizations, Family Planning, Family Services, Food/Clothing Distribution, People with Disabilities, Recreation & Athletics, Scouts, Senior Services, Shelters/Homelessness, Substance Abuse, United Funds/United Ways, YMCA/YWCA/YMHA/YWHA, Youth Organizations

Application Procedures

Initial Contact: Verbal requests will not be accepted. Before making a formal proposal, however, an applicant is welcome to make written inquiries regarding foundation policies and programs.

Application Requirements: Proposals should include the name and address of applicant, names of chief administrative officers, statement of private foundation status, and a letter from an officer endorsing the proposal and agreeing that the applicant will assume full fiscal management and accounting responsibility for any funds received. The statement must be supported either by a copy of an IRS letter regarding private foundation status; a copy of completed form 4653, with a statement from a principal officer providing date filed and IRS response; a n opinion of legal status; or a copy of an IRS letter of tax exemption. An applicant should also provide a statement attesting that no portion of a Jewett grant will be used to employ, compensate, or benefit a government official.

The foundation also requires specific information for project proposals. Proposals must contain a brief description of the project, with background information; development plan; e valuation method; expected results; constituency served; and information on key personnel administering the project. Applicants must provide budgetary information on salaries, rent, supplies for technicians, clerical services, equipment, expendable supplies, and travel. They also must indicate amounts of "in-kind" or cash contributions, sources of income, and amounts received from other philanthropic agencies. The foundation prefers to have a three-year projected budget. Prospective grantees also should indicate start and completion dates, and whether or not the proposal has been submitted to other grant-making organizations, including federal and state agencies.

Deadlines: None.

Review Process: Proposals are reviewed quarterly, and many are held for final processing at the foundation's annual meeting at the end of the year. Staff notify, within a reasonable period, applicants whose proposals fall outside the foundation's scope. The foundation prefers to participate with other donors, and not to assume a major portion of the amount to be raised. A high priority is given to organizations receiving little or no support from public tax funds.

Restrictions

The foundation limits its grants largely to requests from eastern Washington and San Francisco, CA. No grants are made to individuals. Support occasionally may be given to scholarship, fellowship, or research programs of established institutions. Grants generally are not given to other private or operating foundations. While the foundation will not support activities that influence legislation, it may support research on and studies of problems of public concern. Emergency petitions are not favored except when they involve disaster and human suffering. It is the intent of the trustees to keep the foundation's program flexible at all times by making no long-term commitments. No uninvited proposals will be accepted. No funds will be given for the purchase of tickets or for the support of fundraising events.

Additional Information

The administrative officers of each recipient organization must agree in writing to administer the grant in accordance with its stated terms, to submit interim financial and progress reports, to advise the foundation of any changes, to request the termination of a project if the program as approved becomes impossible to carry out, and to refund any unused amounts. When grants are made to organizations in states that require annual reporting of receipts and expenditures by organizations soliciting general support, the foundation requires evidence that its grant has been reported properly.

No plaques or memorials relating to the foundation can be used without prior approval.

Publications: Annual Report; Application Guidelines

Foundation Officials

Ann D. Gralnek: senior advisor
Margaret Weyerhaeuser Jewett Greer: trustee ED Harvard University (1952).
William Hershey Greer, Jr.: trustee B Owensboro, KY 1928. ED Yale University BA (1951); Harvard University JD (1954).
George Frederick Jewett, Jr.: chairman B Spokane, WA 1927. ED Dartmouth College BA (1950); Harvard University MBA (1952). PRIM CORP EMPL vice chairman, director: Potlatch Corp.
Lucille Winifred McIntyre Jewett: trustee B Saint Louis, MO 1929.

Grants Analysis

Disclosure Period: calendar year ending 2001
Total Grants: $1,535,500*
Number of Grants: 85
Average Grant: $18,065
Highest Grant: $50,000
Lowest Grant: $300
Typical Range: $10,000 to $40,000
***Note:** Giving excludes United Way.

Recent Grants

Note: Grants derived from 2001 Form 990.

General

90,000	Spokane Symphony Society, Spokane, WA -- support of the orchestra's annual sustaining Fund for 2001-02 and restoration and renovation of the Fox Theatre
87,500	St. Luke's Chamber Ensemble, New York, NY -- support of Bach's Cantatas in Context in Mar 2001 & fall 2001 with portion of grant offsetting reduced ticket prices for seniors and students
75,000	San Francisco General Hospital Foundation, San Francisco, CA -- grant for improvements on the Emergency Department/Trauma Center
50,000	Grace Cathedral Restoration Campaign, San Francisco, CA -- 2nd and final payment on 2-yr commitment toward priority repairs to preserve and protect this historic community asset
50,000	Healthcare Foundation for Falmouth Hospital, Falmouth, MA -- support of capital campaign for expansion of operating room facilities, increased patient beds and cardiovascular cauterization lab
50,000	Inland Northwest Land Trust, Spokane, WA -- support of conservation organization's community outreach, education and land protection efforts in Spokane
50,000	Population Council, New York, NY -- in support of postdoctoral fellowships in Center for Biomedical Research
50,000	San Francisco Foundation, San Francisco, CA -- toward maintenance and enhancement of the City's Lyon Street Park
50,000	University of Arkansas for Medical Sciences, Little Rock, MI -- toward the Elizabeth Stanley Cooper endowed Chair in Oncology Nursing
50,000	Woods Hole Oceanographic Institute, Woods Hole, MA -- to support research and educational/operational programs at the Martha's Vineyard Coastal Observatory

JEWISH HEALTHCARE FOUNDATION

Giving Contact

Karen Wolk-Feinstein, President
Center City Tower, Suite 2330
650 Smithfield Street
Pittsburgh, PA 15222
Phone: (412)261-1400

Fax: (412)232-6240
E-mail: info@jhf.org
Web: http://www.jhf.org

Description

Founded: 1991
EIN: 251624347
Organization Type: Specialized/Single Purpose Foundation
Giving Locations: PA: Western Pennsylvania
Grant Types: Challenge, Conference/Seminar, General Support, Matching, Multiyear/Continuing Support, Project, Research, Seed Money.

Donor Information

Founder: In 1991, Presbyterian University Hospital in Pittsburgh, PA, endowed a $75 million foundation as a health care resource after assuming control of Montefiore Hospital, which was also located in Pittsburgh.

Financial Summary

Total Giving: $6,393,839 (2000); $6,700,000 (1999 approx); $5,907,263 (1998)
Assets: $133,463,348 (2000); $140,740,000 (1999); $136,581,091 (1998)
Gifts Received: $2,273,792 (2000); $1,868,964 (1998). Note: In 2000, contributions were received from the Commonwealth of Pennsylvania AIDS Grant ($1,743,609), the City of Pittsburgh AIDS Grant ($529,702), and miscellaneous donors.

Typical Recipients

Arts & Humanities: Arts Outreach, Arts & Humanities-General, Libraries, Public Broadcasting, Theater
Civic & Public Affairs: African American Affairs, Business/Free Enterprise, Community Foundations, Economic Development, Civic & Public Affairs-General, Housing, Public Policy, Urban & Community Affairs, Women's Affairs
Education: Colleges & Universities, Education Funds, Education Reform, Education-General, Leadership Training, Medical Education, Preschool Education, Private Education (Precollege), Public Education (Precollege), Science/Mathematics Education, Special Education
Environment: Air/Water Quality, Environment-General
Health: Adolescent Health Issues, AIDS/HIV, Alzheimers Disease, Cancer, Children's Health/Hospitals, Clinics/Medical Centers, Health-General, Health-General, Geriatric Health, Health Policy/Cost Containment, Health Funds, Health Organizations, Heart, Home-Care Services, Hospitals, Hospitals (University Affiliated), Kidney, Long-Term Care, Medical Research, Medical Training, Mental Health, Nursing Services, Nutrition, Prenatal Health Issues, Preventive Medicine/Wellness Organizations, Public Health, Single-Disease Health Associations, Transplant Networks/Donor Banks
International: Health Care/Hospitals, Missionary/Religious Activities, Trade
Religion: Jewish Causes, Religious Welfare, Social/Policy Issues
Social Services: At-Risk Youth, Child Welfare, Community Service Organizations, Crime Prevention, Day Care, Delinquency & Criminal Rehabilitation, Domestic Violence, Family Services, Food/Clothing Distribution, People with Disabilities, Scouts, Senior Services, Social Services-General, Substance Abuse, United Funds/United Ways, Volunteer Services, YMCA/YWCA/YMHA/YWHA, Youth Organizations

Application Procedures

Initial Contact: Applicants should send four copies of a preliminary letter of intent that does not exceed six pages.
Application Requirements: The letter should describe the problem and the program objectives, include a budget, list of board of directors, IRS tax-determination letter, name and address of contact

person, institutional and personnel qualifications, the most recent auditor's report (if available), and recent financial statements showing amounts and sources of current income. In addition, the letter should include information on partnerships; a timetable; proposed intervention; anticipated outcome; innovative aspects; likelihood of success; long-term plans; and community education, research, and/or evaluation components.

Deadlines: None.

Evaluative Criteria: The Foundation honors certain values: faculty for creation partnerships and building community awareness; going beyond individual program breakthroughs to systems, policy, and practice changes; skill and determination to translate medical and scientific advances into new protocols and best practices.

Restrictions

Generally, the foundation does not fund organizations without IRS tax-exempt status, organizations outside western Pennsylvania, programs without a health care component, general operations, capital needs, operating deficits, debt retirement, political campaigns, scholarships, fellowships, individual research, or individual travel.

Additional Information

Foundation also sponsors conferences, and provides proposal writing assistance, and technical assistance in planning.

Publications: Annual Report; Guidelines; Branches Newsletter

Foundation Officials

Robert J. Feidner: fin officer
Karen Wolk Feinstein, PhD: president B 1945.
Stephen Halpern: vchairman NONPR AFFIL treasurer, director: United Jewish Federation.
Eileen Lane: secretary
Leon Netzer: chairman B 1923. ED University of Pittsburgh. PRIM CORP EMPL president: Federation Alloy Corp. CORP AFFIL president, director: Nicroloy Co. Inc.
Robert Arthur Paul: treasurer B New York, NY 1937. ED Cornell University AB (1959); Harvard University JD (1962); Harvard University MBA (1964). PRIM CORP EMPL president, chief executive officer, director: Ampco-Pittsburgh Corp. CORP AFFIL partner: Romar Trading Co.; partner: National City Corp.; executive vice president, assistant secretary, director, trustee: Louis Berkman Co. NONPR AFFIL member: Massachusetts Bar Association; trustee: Presbyterian University Hospital; trustee: Cornell University; member: American Bar Association. CLUB AFFIL Pittsburgh Athletic Association; Harvard Club; Concordia Club; Duquesne Club.
Kenneth T. Segel: senior program officer
Nancy Zionts: sr program officer

Grants Analysis

Disclosure Period: calendar year ending 2000
Total Grants: $6,348,839*
Number of Grants: 229*
Average Grant: $27,724
Highest Grant: $565,000
Typical Range: $10,000 to $100,000
*Note: Giving excludes United Way. Number of grants is approximate.

Recent Grants

Note: Grants derived from 2001 Form 990.

General

900,000	United Jewish Federation, Pittsburgh, PA
585,000	JAA Renaissance Campaign, Pittsburgh, PA
365,000	Renaissance Center, Pittsburgh, PA
300,000	Strategic Investment Fund, Pittsburgh, PA
158,571	Pittsburgh Regional Alliance, Pittsburgh, PA
150,000	Pennsylvania Health Law Project, Philadelphia, PA
125,000	Duquesne University, Pittsburgh, PA
100,000	Carnegie Mellon Research Institute, Pittsburgh, PA
100,000	University of Pittsburgh School of Medicine, Pittsburgh, PA -- School of Medicine
95,000	Mental Health Platform, Pittsburgh, PA

JJJ FOUNDATION

Giving Contact

Keith W. Wegen, President & Director
287 Century Circle, Suite 100
Louisville, CO 80027-9439
Phone: (303)926-1111

Description

Founded: 1985
EIN: 133379770
Organization Type: Private Foundation
Giving Locations: CO
Grant Types: General Support, Project, Seed Money.

Donor Information

Founder: John R. Butler

Financial Summary

Total Giving: $76,450 (fiscal year ending September 30, 2001); $88,411 (fiscal 2000); $136,563 (fiscal 1999)
Assets: $1,772,526 (fiscal 2001); $2,490,040 (fiscal 2000); $2,798,030 (fiscal 1999)
Gifts Received: $1,000 (fiscal 1994); $1,000 (fiscal 1993); $1,000 (fiscal 1992)

Typical Recipients

Arts & Humanities: Arts Centers, Arts Festivals, Arts Outreach, Dance, Museums/Galleries, Music
Civic & Public Affairs: Community Foundations, Civic & Public Affairs-General, Housing, Philanthropic Organizations, Safety
Education: Afterschool/Enrichment Programs, Colleges & Universities, Environmental Education, Education-General, Minority Education, Preschool Education, Private Education (Precollege), Secondary Education (Public), Special Education, Student Aid
Environment: Environment-General, Resource Conservation, Wildlife Protection
Health: AIDS/HIV, Cancer, Children's Health/Hospitals, Health-General, Geriatric Health, Hospitals, Medical Rehabilitation, Multiple Sclerosis, Prenatal Health Issues, Single-Disease Health Associations
International: Foreign Educational Institutions, Missionary/Religious Activities
Religion: Churches, Ministries, Religious Welfare
Social Services: At-Risk Youth, Big Brother/Big Sister, Child Abuse, Child Welfare, Community Service Organizations, Day Care, Delinquency & Criminal Rehabilitation, Domestic Violence, Emergency Relief, Family Services, People with Disabilities, Shelters/Homelessness, Social Services-General, Substance Abuse, Veterans, YMCA/YWCA/YMHA/YWHA

Application Procedures

Initial Contact: Send a one-page letter of inquiry.
Application Requirements: Include amount requested, description of project, purpose of funds sought, annual budget, government support, and a description of organization.
Deadlines: None.

Restrictions

Foundation limits contributions to only one grant per year.

Foundation Officials

John R. Butler: chairman
Stuart Lemle: director
Jennifer A. Wegen: vice president, secretary, director
Keith W. Wegen: president, director

Grants Analysis

Disclosure Period: fiscal year ending September 30, 2001
Total Grants: $76,450
Number of Grants: 29
Average Grant: $2,636
Highest Grant: $11,800
Lowest Grant: $35
Typical Range: $1,000 to $5,000

Recent Grants

Note: Grants derived from fiscal 2000 Form 990.

General

9,000	Character Matters, Louisville, CO -- for character education program in pilot schools
8,000	WOW! Children's Museum, Louisville, CO -- to sponsor low-income and special needs children
5,000	Boulder Nursery Association, Boulder, CO -- for family resource program
5,000	Burbank Middle School, Boulder, CO -- for student union
5,000	Earth Walk, Denver, CO -- for environmental service learning program for youth
5,000	Rocky Ridge Music Center Foundation, Estes Park, CO -- for summer music institute for youth
4,576	Partners for Human Progress, Denver, CO -- for programs to enhance peace and respect in the community and environment
4,000	Cleo Parker Robinson Dance Ensemble, Denver, CO -- support for dance ensemble
3,500	I Have A Dream Foundation, Lafayette, CO -- for drop-out prevention program
3,000	Crossroads Ministry of Estes Park, Inc., Estes Park, CO -- for temporary and emergency support services to families in need

JM FOUNDATION

Giving Contact

Carl Helstrom, Associate Executive Director
60 East 42nd Street, Room 1651
New York, NY 10165
Phone: (212)687-7735
Fax: (212)697-5495

Description

Founded: 1936
EIN: 136068340
Organization Type: General Purpose Foundation
Grant Types: Project, Research.

Donor Information

Founder: Jeremiah Milbank was engaged, throughout his life, in philanthropic activities. Mr. Milbank was born in New York City on January 24, 1887. After graduating from Yale University in 1909, Mr. Milbank established his own investment firm in 1916. A believer in free enterprise, Mr. Milbank was a director of several companies and had long-term investments in private corporations.

Mr. Milbank's belief that persons with disabilities could lead independent and meaningful lives was to become a subject of major national importance. His conviction that the Red Cross was a viable organization led him to found the Red Cross Institution for Crippled Soldiers and Sailors in 1917. This was the first American organization to address the needs of physically disabled veterans. In 1919, he founded the Institute for the Crippled and Disabled (ICD). It was at this Institute that vocational education, medical service, and psychosocial support were integrated to form a new comprehensive rehabilitation approach for people with physical disabilities.

In 1928, Mr. Milbank founded and financed the International Committee for the Study of Infantile Paralysis. As a result of this active interest in the subject of polio, President Roosevelt asked him to be the acting chairman of the organization that preceded the National Foundation for Infantile Paralysis.

Mr. Milbank personally contributed to a collaborative effort with Metropolitan Life Insurance Company to finance a research project to combat diphtheria. In addition, he worked with President Hoover to form the Boys and Girls Clubs of America, and served as its treasurer for 25 years. Mr. Milbank also had personal interests in recovering and converting acres of swampland in South Carolina for agricultural use. His spiritual beliefs led to his financing the first film on the life of Jesus Christ, Cecil B. DeMille's "King of Kings." Mr. Milbank died on March 22, 1972.

Financial Summary

Total Giving: $1,000,000 (2003 approx); $1,000,000 (2002 approx); $1,072,270 (2001)

Giving Analysis: Giving for 2001 includes: foundation matching gifts ($79,270); 1999: foundation matching gifts ($79,971) 1998: foundation scholarships ($10,000)

Assets: $27,000,000 (2002 approx); $28,386,000 (2000 approx); $29,009,000 (1999 approx)

Typical Recipients

Arts & Humanities: Arts & Humanities-General, History & Archaeology, Libraries, Public Broadcasting, Theater

Civic & Public Affairs: African American Affairs, Business/Free Enterprise, Civil Rights, Economic Development, Economic Policy, Employment/Job Training, Civic & Public Affairs-General, Housing, Law & Justice, Legal Aid, Native American Affairs, Nonprofit Management, Philanthropic Organizations, Professional & Trade Associations, Public Policy, Safety, Urban & Community Affairs, Women's Affairs, Zoos/Aquariums

Education: Arts/Humanities Education, Business Education, Colleges & Universities, Education Associations, Education Funds, Education Reform, Environmental Education, Faculty Development, Education-General, Journalism/Media Education, Leadership Training, Legal Education, Medical Education, Minority Education, Preschool Education, Private Education (Precollege), Secondary Education (Public), Social Sciences Education

Environment: Forestry, Environment-General

Health: Cancer, Children's Health/Hospitals, Clinics/Medical Centers, Eyes/Blindness, Geriatric Health, Health Policy/Cost Containment, Health Organizations, Heart, Hospitals, Medical Rehabilitation, Medical Research, Prenatal Health Issues, Preventive Medicine/Wellness Organizations, Public Health, Research/Studies Institutes, Single-Disease Health Associations, Speech & Hearing, Trauma Treatment

International: International-General, Health Care/Hospitals, International Development

Religion: Religious Organizations, Religious Welfare, Social/Policy Issues

Social Services: Child Welfare, Community Centers, Community Service Organizations, Crime Prevention, Day Care, Family Planning, Family Services, People with Disabilities, Scouts, Senior Services, Social Services-General, Substance Abuse, Volunteer Services, Youth Organizations

Application Procedures

Initial Contact: The foundation invites written proposals. The foundation requests that applicants do not send video or audio tapes unless requested.

Application Requirements: Applications should contain a brief abstract of the proposed project (one page or less); proposal, outlining purpose of project, plan of action, board and staff involvement, financing, plans for evaluation, and anticipated results; vitae of authors, researchers, or project officers; project budget, current organizational budget, promotional brochure, and most recent annual report; most recent audited financial statements; list of governing and advisory board members; copy of IRS 501(c)(3) tax-exemption letter; list of organization's current donors, current funders of the proposed project, and grantmakers with whom proposals are pending.

Deadlines: None.

Review Process: The foundation does not have a printed application form or a rigid format for requests. Applicants will be notified of a decision within three to four weeks. Proposals that are consistent with the capacity and interests of the foundation are examined further, and forwarded to the directors who meet in early May and late October.

Restrictions

The foundation usually declines support to annual appeals, dinner events, endowments, or operating funds; arts, music, or theater; capital campaigns, renovations, or building funds; equipment, including computers and biomedical devices; government agencies or public schools; grants to individuals, including scholarships and financial aid; or international projects.

Additional Information

The foundation collaborates with like-minded foundations and is closely affiliated with the Milbank Foundation for Rehabilitation.

Publications: Application Guidelines; Annual Report

Foundation Officials

Jeremiah Milbank Bogert: member B New York, NY 1941. ED Yale University BA (1963); University of Connecticut MBA (1973). PRIM CORP EMPL chairman board, director: James C. Edwards & Co. Inc.

Margaret Milbank Bogert: vice president

William Lee Hanley, Jr.: treasurer ED Yale University (1964).

Jeremiah Milbank, III: mem ED Trinity College BA (1970); Stanford University MBA (1973); University of Virginia JD (1980). PRIM CORP EMPL chairman: Milbank Associate ADD CORP EMPL vice president: Cypress Woods Corp.; vice president: Turkey Hill Plantation; president: Winthrop Milbank & Co.

Jeremiah Milbank, Jr.: president B New York, NY March 24, 1920. ED Yale University BA (1942); Harvard University MBA (1948). PRIM CORP EMPL president: Cypress Woods Corp. ADD CORP EMPL president: Turkey Hill Corp. CORP AFFIL director: International Minerals & Chemicals Corp. NONPR AFFIL chairman emeritus: Boys & Girls Club Greenwich; honorary president: International Center Disabled. CLUB AFFIL Yale Club; River Club; Round Hill Club; Brook Club.

Peter C. Morse: member CORP AFFIL director: America Guardian Life Assurance Co.; director: PFG Inc.

Chris K. Olander: executive director, assistant treasurer

Michael Sanger: member

Daniel Gleason Tenney, Jr.: secretary B New York, NY 1913. ED Yale University BA (1935); Yale University LLB (1938).

Grants Analysis

Disclosure Period: calendar year ending 2001

Total Grants: $993,000*

Number of Grants: 48

Average Grant: $20,688

Highest Grant: $125,000

Typical Range: $10,000 to $25,000

*Note: Giving excludes matching gifts.

Recent Grants

Note: Grants derived from 1999 Form 990.

General

125,000	ICD-International Center for Disabled, New York, NY -- for strategic planning and transition costs
105,000	Boys and Girls Clubs of America, Atlanta, GA -- toward strategic planning and youth services
75,000	State Policy Network (SPN), Ft. Wayne, IN -- to revitalize state policy network
50,000	Philanthropy Roundtable, Washington, DC -- to expand services for foundations, corporations, and individual donors
25,000	Americans for Tax Reform Foundation, Washington, DC -- to enhance the work state-based think tanks and launch the American Shareholders Association
25,000	Cold Spring Harbor Laboratory, New York, NY -- for the Undergraduate Research Program
25,000	Community Options, Washington, DC -- to launch the fund for microenterprise development for persons with severe disabilities
25,000	Donors Trust, Alexandria, VA -- to launch the Trust as a national community foundation
25,000	Fund for American Studies, Washington, DC -- to launch the Institute on Philanthropy and Voluntary Service
25,000	Manhattan Institute, New York, NY -- to launch the Jeremiah Project

JOCKEY HOLLOW FOUNDATION

Giving Contact

Betsy S. Michel, President
PO Box 462
Bernardsville, NJ 07924
Phone: (973)425-3212

Description

Founded: 1960
EIN: 221724138
Organization Type: Private Foundation
Giving Locations: MA; NJ
Grant Types: General Support, Scholarship.

Donor Information

Founder: Carl Shirley, Mrs. Carl Shirley

Financial Summary

Total Giving: $1,078,271 (fiscal year ending March 31, 2001); $246,548 (fiscal 1998); $720,318 (fiscal 1996)

Giving Analysis: Giving for fiscal 2001 includes: foundation grants to United Way ($1,000); foundation scholarships ($50,000); fiscal 1998: foundation scholarships ($50,000) foundation ($196,547)

Assets: $23,890,904 (fiscal 2001); $22,360,837 (fiscal 1998); $14,807,684 (fiscal 1996)

Gifts Received: $206,000 (fiscal 1996); $206,000 (fiscal 1995); $206,000 (fiscal 1994)

Typical Recipients

Arts & Humanities: Arts Associations & Councils, Arts Funds, Ethnic & Folk Arts, Historic Preservation, History & Archaeology, Libraries, Museums/Galleries, Music, Performing Arts, Theater

Civic & Public Affairs: African American Affairs, Employment/Job Training, Civic & Public Affairs-General, Safety, Urban & Community Affairs
Education: Business Education, Colleges & Universities, Education Funds, Education-General, Medical Education, Minority Education, Private Education (Precollege), Secondary Education (Private), Student Aid
Environment: Air/Water Quality, Environment-General, Resource Conservation
Health: Clinics/Medical Centers, Emergency/Ambulance Services, Health Funds, Health Organizations, Hospitals, Medical Research, Nursing Services, Public Health, Trauma Treatment
Religion: Churches
Social Services: Child Welfare, Community Centers, Community Service Organizations, Domestic Violence, Family Planning, Family Services, Recreation & Athletics, Shelters/Homelessness, Social Services-General, United Funds/United Ways, Youth Organizations

Application Procedures

Initial Contact: Send a brief letter of inquiry.
Application Requirements: Include a description of organization, amount requested, purpose of funds sought, recently audited financial statement, and proof of tax-exempt status.
Deadlines: None.

Foundation Officials

Joanne S. Forkner: vice president
Betsy S. Michel: president CORP AFFIL director: Seligman Growth Fund Inc.; director: Seligman Income Fund Inc.; director: Seligman Cash Management Fund; director: Seligman Common Stock Fund.
Clifford Lloyd Michel: treasurer B New York, NY 1939. ED Princeton University AB (1961); Yale University JD (1964). PRIM CORP EMPL partner: Cahill Gordon & Reindel. CORP AFFIL director: Wenonah Development Co.; director: Placer Dome Inc.; director: Alliance Capital Management Mutual Funds; director: Faber-Castell Corp. NONPR AFFIL member: New York State Bar Association; director: Saint Marks School; member: New York County Lawyers Association; member: Fed Bar Association; director: Morristown Memorial Hospital; member: American Society International Law; member: American Bar Association.
Betsy B. Shirley: vice president

Grants Analysis

Disclosure Period: fiscal year ending March 31, 2001
Total Grants: $1,043,644*
Number of Grants: 145
Average Grant: $7,198
Highest Grant: $130,000
Typical Range: $1,000 to $10,000
*Note: Giving excludes scholarships and United Way.

Recent Grants

Note: Grants derived from 2000 Form 990.

Library-Related
52,000   Bernardsville Public Library, Bernardsville, NJ -- for books

General
75,000   Peabody Essex Museum, Essex, MA -- for museum
75,000   Yale University Library, New Haven, CT -- for education
70,000   Dimoch Community Health Center, Roxbury, MA -- for health
60,000   Big Tree Boating, Islesboro, ME -- for youth
50,000   Bernards Area Scholarship Assistance, Bernardsville, NJ -- for financial aid
50,000   Community Theatre of Morristown, Morristown, NJ -- for performing arts

50,000   Morristown Memorial Fund, Morristown, NJ -- for service
40,000   Morristown Neighborhood House, Morristown, NJ -- for service
35,000   Matheny School, Peapack, NJ -- for education
30,000   Greater Newark Conservancy, Newark, NJ -- for environment

JOCO FOUNDATION

Giving Contact

Raymond D. Smoot, Jr., Treasurer
c/o Virginia Tech
312 Burruss Hall, No. 0142
Blacksburg, VA 24061
Phone: (540)231-5751

Description

Founded: 1990
EIN: 541552388
Organization Type: Private Foundation
Giving Locations: VA: Bedford, Roanoke Valley
Grant Types: General Support.

Donor Information

Founder: Reid Jones, Jr.

Financial Summary

Total Giving: $390,000 (2001); $1,314,323 (2000); $1,225,045 (1999)
Giving Analysis: Giving for 1997 includes: foundation grants to United Way ($20,000) 1996: foundation grants to United Way ($50,000)
Assets: $2,387,229 (2001); $3,567,104 (2000); $5,925,373 (1999)
Gifts Received: $3,000 (2001); $683,636 (1997); $1,967,727 (1992). Note: In 1997, contributions were received from the estate of Reid Jones, Jr.

Typical Recipients

Arts & Humanities: Arts Funds, History & Archaeology, Libraries, Museums/Galleries
Civic & Public Affairs: Botanical Gardens/Parks, Clubs, Community Foundations, Civic & Public Affairs-General, Housing, Municipalities/Towns, Safety
Education: Agricultural Education, Colleges & Universities, Education Funds, Elementary Education (Public), Engineering/Technological Education, Literacy, Private Education (Precollege), Student Aid
Environment: Air/Water Quality, Environment-General, Wildlife Protection
Health: Cancer, Children's Health/Hospitals, Emergency/Ambulance Services, Multiple Sclerosis, Public Health
International: International Organizations
Religion: Churches, Religious Welfare, Social/Policy Issues
Social Services: Animal Protection, At-Risk Youth, Community Centers, Crime Prevention, Family Planning, Recreation & Athletics, Senior Services, United Funds/United Ways, Volunteer Services, YMCA/YWCA/YMHA/YWHA, Youth Organizations

Application Procedures

Initial Contact: Send a written application.
Application Requirements: Include description of charitable purpose and brief history of charitable activities.
Deadlines: None.

Restrictions

The foundation does not support individuals, religious organizations or political or lobbying groups.

Foundation Officials

Judy Jarrells: director
William Killinger: director
Diane E. H. Wilcox, Esq.: director

Grants Analysis

Disclosure Period: calendar year ending 2001
Total Grants: $390,000
Number of Grants: 2
Average Grant: $195,000
Highest Grant: $240,000
Typical Range: $1,000 to $5,000 and $100,000 to $400,000

Recent Grants

Note: Grants derived from 2001 Form 990.

General
240,000   Smith Mountain Lake 4 H Center, Inc., Wirtz, VA
150,000   Rescue Mission, Roanoke, VA

JOHN HANCOCK FINANCIAL SERVICES

Company Headquarters

Boston, MA
Web: http://www.jhancock.com

Company Description

Founded: 1862
Ticker: JHF
Exchange: NYSE
Former Name: John Hancock Mutual Life (2000).
Assets: US$97.864 billion (2002)
Profit: US$516.2 million (2002)
Employees: 7962 (2002)
Fortune Rank: 208, per FORTUNE Magazine's list of 500 Largest U.S. Corporations (2002).
SIC(s): 6311 Life Insurance.

Operating Locations

John Hancock Mutual Life Insurance Co. (MA--Boston)
Note: Operates throughout the USA.

Nonmonetary Support

Value: $2,300,000 (2000)
Type: Donated Equipment; Donated Products; Inkind Services
Note: Co. also provides nonmonetary support in the form of meeting space, printing and graphic services, public relations assistance, photography, special events planning.
Volunteer Programs: Supports HERO (Hancock Employees Reaching Out), a program which organizes group volunteer projects. Outreach programs include Community Sports Initiative; educational programs, such as Operation Math Corps, Adopt-a-Class, Summer of Opportunity, and Financial Wizard Program; and community service programs, including the Incredible Sandwich Making Event (for food banks), Habitat for Humanity building projects, and holiday relief efforts.

Giving Contact

Carol Fulp, Vice President of Community Relations
Box 111, T-58
Boston, MA 02117
Phone: (617)572-0451
Fax: (617)572-6290
E-mail: cfulp@jhancock.com

Description

Organization Type: Corporate Giving Program
Giving Locations: MA: Boston
Grant Types: Employee Matching Gifts, General Support, Project.
Note: Employee matching gift ratio: 1 to 1 for non-educational nonprofits and 0.5 to 1 for education institutions; program allows employees to give to non-educational nonprofits through payroll deductions and have these gifts matched.

Financial Summary

Total Giving: $6,100,000 (2002 approx); $6,100,000 (2001 approx); $6,125,000 (2000 approx). Note: Contributes through corporate direct giving program only.
Giving Analysis: Giving for 2000 includes: nonmonetary support (approx $2,300,000); corporate direct giving (approx $3,825,000) 1998: corporate direct giving (approx $3,600,000)

Typical Recipients

Arts & Humanities: Arts Appreciation, Arts Associations & Councils, Arts Centers, Arts Institutes, Community Arts, Dance, Ethnic & Folk Arts, Historic Preservation, Libraries, Museums/Galleries, Music, Opera, Performing Arts, Public Broadcasting, Theater
Civic & Public Affairs: Business/Free Enterprise, Civil Rights, Economic Development, Economic Policy, Employment/Job Training, Law & Justice, Professional & Trade Associations, Public Policy, Urban & Community Affairs, Women's Affairs
Education: Business Education, Continuing Education, Economic Education, Education Funds, Medical Education, Minority Education, Science/Mathematics Education, Special Education
Environment: Environment-General
Health: Health Policy/Cost Containment, Hospitals, Medical Research, Nutrition, Public Health, Single-Disease Health Associations
Social Services: Child Welfare, Community Centers, Community Service Organizations, Counseling, Delinquency & Criminal Rehabilitation, Family Services, Food/Clothing Distribution, Homes, People with Disabilities, Recreation & Athletics, Senior Services, Shelters/Homelessness, Substance Abuse, United Funds/United Ways, Volunteer Services, Youth Organizations

Application Procedures

Initial Contact: Send a brief letter or proposal.
Application Requirements: Include objectives, services, program activities, and accomplishments of organization; purpose for which funds are sought; proof of tax-exempt status; names and affiliations of officers, trustees, and members of the board of directors; population served and their socioeconomic composition; annual budget for the project or program to be assisted, agency budget, audited financial statements, and list of current and potential funds; and method for program evaluation.
Deadlines: None.
Evaluative Criteria: Project provides innovative solutions to significant social needs; stimulates additional giving by other institutions and individuals.
Notes: All organizations receiving company grants are requested to submit periodic reports on how funds are used.

Restrictions

Does not support fraternal or political organizations, religious organizations for sectarian purposes, individuals, goodwill advertising, scholarships, conferences, or trips.

Corporate Officials

Wayne A. Budd: executive vice president, general counsel
David F. D'Alessandro: president, chief operating officer

Giving Program Officials

Carol Bolling: 2nd vice president, community relations

Grants Analysis

Disclosure Period: calendar year ending 1998
Total Grants: $3,825,000 (approx)*
Number of Grants: 2,200
Average Grant: $10,000
Typical Range: $5,000 to $20,000
*****Note:** Grants analysis provided by the company. Giving excludes nonmonetary support.

JOHNS MANVILLE

Company Headquarters

PO Box 5108
Denver, CO 80217-5108
Web: http://www.johnsmanville.com

Company Description

Former Name: Schuller International.
Revenue: US$2 billion (2002)
Employees: 9000 (2002)
SIC(s): 1499 Miscellaneous Nonmetallic Minerals, 2952 Asphalt Felts & Coatings, 3296 Mineral Wool, 5039 Construction Materials Nec.
Parent Company: Berkshire Hathaway Inc., 1440 Kiewit Plaza, Omaha, NE, United States

Operating Locations

Johns Manville (AZ--Tucson; CA--Pittsburg, Santa Ana, Willows; IL--Rockdale, Waukegan; KS--McPherson; ME--Lewiston; NJ--Edison, Penbryn; NC--Laurinburg; OH--Defiance; TN--Etowah; TX--Cleburne, Ennis, Fort Worth; VA--Shenandoah Valley; WV--Parkersburg)

Nonmonetary Support

Type: Donated Equipment; Donated Products; In-kind Services; Loaned Executives; Workplace Solicitation

Johns Manville Fund

Giving Contact

PO Box 5108
Denver, CO 80217-5108
Phone: (303)978-3863
Fax: (303)978-3547
Web: http://www.jm.com/AboutUs/JMFund/default.asp

Description

Founded: 1952
EIN: 136034039
Organization Type: Corporate Foundation
Giving Locations: company operating locations.
Grant Types: Award, Challenge, Emergency, Employee Matching Gifts, General Support, Scholarship, Seed Money.

Donor Information

Founder: Manville Corp.

Financial Summary

Total Giving: $163,412 (2002); $138,821 (2000); $165,917 (1999). Note: Figures represent fund contributions for foundation only; company does not distribute direct giving information. 1997 Giving includes matching gifts ($20,957).
Giving Analysis: Giving for 2002 includes: foundation matching gifts ($17,190); 2000: foundation matching gifts ($20,091); 1999: foundation matching gifts ($18,217); foundation ($147,700)
Assets: $398,579 (2002); $659,146 (2000); $774,155 (1999)
Gifts Received: $300,000 (1997); $475,000 (1996); $475,000 (1995). Note: In 1997, contributions were received from Johns Manville International, Inc.

Typical Recipients

Arts & Humanities: Arts Associations & Councils, Arts Centers, Arts Outreach, Ballet, Community Arts, Arts & Humanities-General, Historic Preservation, History & Archaeology, Libraries, Literary Arts, Museums/Galleries, Opera, Performing Arts, Theater, Visual Arts
Civic & Public Affairs: Botanical Gardens/Parks, Clubs, Economic Development, Employment/Job

Training, Civic & Public Affairs-General, Housing, Inner-City Development, Legal Aid, Safety, Urban & Community Affairs, Women's Affairs, Zoos/Aquariums
Education: Business Education, Colleges & Universities, Community & Junior Colleges, Elementary Education (Public), Education-General, Literacy, Public Education (Precollege), Public Education (Precollege)
Environment: Environment-General, Wildlife Protection
Health: AIDS/HIV, Cancer, Children's Health/Hospitals, Emergency/Ambulance Services, Eyes/Blindness, Health Organizations, Heart, Hospitals, Medical Rehabilitation, Mental Health, Multiple Sclerosis, Respiratory, Single-Disease Health Associations, Transplant Networks/Donor Banks
Religion: Religion-General, Religious Welfare
Social Services: Animal Protection, At-Risk Youth, Child Abuse, Child Welfare, Community Centers, Community Service Organizations, Counseling, Crime Prevention, Domestic Violence, Emergency Relief, Family Services, Food/Clothing Distribution, Homes, People with Disabilities, Recreation & Athletics, Recreation & Athletics, Scouts, Senior Services, Sexual Abuse, Shelters/Homelessness, Social Services-General, Substance Abuse, United Funds/United Ways, Volunteer Services, YMCA/YWCA/YMHA/YWHA, Youth Organizations

Application Procedures

Initial Contact: Send letter requesting guidelines.
Deadlines: None.

Restrictions

The fund does not give to hospitals, organizations involved in private education, religious activities, organizations without 501(c)(3) tax-exempt status, special events, or organizations that receive more than 20% of their annual income from the United Way or similar community fund drives.

Organizations that have previously been awarded a grant from the fund may not reapply until two years after the application date of the funded request.

Additional Information

Religious institutions may receive funding for programs that are secular and not religious or ceremonial in nature.

In 1997, the Schuller Fund was renamed as the Johns Manville Fund. Its program description includes the following areas: (1) Community Grants: Supports a range of organizations involved with the arts, culture, and social service activities. Recent recipients include child recreation groups, training for the handicapped, and health organizations; (2) Education Grants: Grants are available to high school seniors with a parent or guardian who has been a company employee for at least one year; and (3) Matching Grants: The fund matches dollar-for-dollar personal donations of $50 to $249 by company employees or their families to colleges and universities.

Program details, including budgets, deadlines, procedures, and forms can be obtained from representatives at company sites or from headquarters in Denver, CO.

Fund officers give preference to proposals that reflect company's employee's volunteerism at all levels and all locations.

Priority will be given to applicants for matching funds, challenge grants, and proposals that yield some significant multiple effect.

Corporate Officials

C. L. Henry: chairman, president, chief executive officer PRIM CORP EMPL chairman, president, chief executive officer: Johns Manville.
Kenneth L. Jensen: chief financial officer PRIM CORP EMPL chief financial officer: Johns Manville.

Foundation Officials

R. Arant: vice president, trustee
Joni E. Baird: vice president, fund administrator PRIM CORP EMPL community relations manager: Johns Manville.
D. A. Forte: vice president
J. J. Gebert: vice president, treasurer, trustee
M. Mitchell: vice president, trustee
Dave E. Pullen: president
M. K. Rhinehart: treasurer PRIM CORP EMPL director finance & administration: Johns Manville.
William G. Spink: secretary

Grants Analysis

Disclosure Period: calendar year ending 2002
Total Grants: $146,222*
Number of Grants: 54
Average Grant: $2,708*
Highest Grant: $31,100
Lowest Grant: $250
Typical Range: $1,000 to $5,000
*Note: Giving excludes matching gifts. Average grant figure excludes highest grant.

Recent Grants

Note: Grants derived from 2002 Form 990.

General

10,000	American Red Cross Denver Chapter, Denver, CO -- for Colorado wild fires
10,000	Harbor House, Waterville, NH
10,000	JM Charity Christmas Fund, Etowah, GA -- 50th initial major grant
5,000	Habitat for Humanity, Richmond, VA
5,000	Lost Valley Handicapped Ski Association, Lewiston, ID
5,000	National Multiple Sclerosis Society, Denver, CO
4,000	Richmond Community Schools, Richmond, IN
3,000	Arbor House, Ann Arbor, MI
3,000	Auglaize Volunteer Firemen's Association, Defiance, OH
3,000	Interfaith Hospital Network, Indianapolis, IN

TERRY WAYNE AND SHERON B. JOHNSON CHARITABLE TRUST

Giving Contact

Terry W. Johnson, Trustee
2124 Christine Cove
Birmingham, AL 35244
Phone: (205)706-9445

Description

Founded: 1989
EIN: 570884953
Organization Type: Private Foundation
Giving Locations: AL
Grant Types: General Support.

Financial Summary

Total Giving: $72,200 (2001); $128,601 (2000); $299,032 (1999)
Assets: $2,162 (2001); $2,757 (2000); $112,560 (1999)
Gifts Received: $73,000 (2001); $32,800 (2000); $123,848 (1999). Note: CRF Terry Wayne Johnson.

Typical Recipients

Arts & Humanities: Arts Centers, Libraries
Civic & Public Affairs: Civic & Public Affairs-General
Education: Business Education, Colleges & Universities, Private Education (Precollege)
Health: AIDS/HIV, Cancer, Diabetes, Single-Disease Health Associations

Religion: Churches, Ministries, Religious Organizations
Social Services: Camps, Domestic Violence, Scouts, United Funds/United Ways, Youth Organizations

Application Procedures

Initial Contact: The foundation reports no specific application guidelines. Send a brief letter of inquiry, including statement of purpose, amount requested, and proof of tax-exempt status.
Deadlines: None.

Restrictions

Supports only IRC section 509 (a)(1), (2), or (3) entities.

Foundation Officials

Terry W. Johnson: trustee
Jean Morris: trustee

Grants Analysis

Disclosure Period: calendar year ending 2001
Total Grants: $72,200
Number of Grants: 4
Highest Grant: $60,000
Lowest Grant: $1,000

Recent Grants

Note: Grants derived from 2000 Form 990.

Library-Related

836	Children's Hospital

General

43,265	Grace House Ministries, Fairfield, AL
34,000	United Methodist Church
30,000	Boy Scouts of America, Birmingham, AL
10,000	Big Oak Boys Ranch, Gadsden, AL
6,000	American Cancer Society
2,000	Alabama State University, Birmingham, AL
1,000	Girl Scouts of America
500	Angel Ministries, Raleigh, NC
500	Junior Achievement
500	Muscular Dystrophy

JAMES HERVEY JOHNSON CHARITABLE EDUCATIONAL TRUST

Giving Contact

Kevin Munnelly, Trustee
James Hervey Johnson Charitable Educational Trust
PO Box 16160
San Diego, CA 92176
Phone: (619)283-8016

Description

Founded: 1989
EIN: 336081439
Organization Type: Private Foundation
Giving Locations: CA
Grant Types: General Support.

Financial Summary

Total Giving: $30,000 (fiscal year ending July 31, 2001); $434,207 (fiscal 2000); $507,432 (fiscal 1998)
Assets: $11,783,739 (fiscal 2001); $12,368,552 (fiscal 2000); $12,803,525 (fiscal 1998)

Typical Recipients

Arts & Humanities: Ethnic & Folk Arts, History & Archaeology, Libraries, Museums/Galleries
Civic & Public Affairs: Clubs, Community Foundations, First Amendment Issues, Gay/Lesbian Issues, Professional & Trade Associations, Public Policy

Education: Faculty Development, Education-General, Health & Physical Education, Religious Education
Health: Health-General, Health Organizations, Public Health, Respiratory
International: International Organizations
Religion: Jewish Causes, Religious Organizations, Religious Welfare, Social/Policy Issues
Social Services: Shelters/Homelessness, Substance Abuse

Application Procedures

Initial Contact: Request guidelines and application form.
Application Requirements: Include IRS 501(c)(3) status, an itemized breakdown of grant fund expenditures, annual budget, IRS Form 990.
Deadlines: April 15.

Additional Information

Publications: Application Form; Instructions

Foundation Officials

Lawrence Y. True: trustee

Grants Analysis

Disclosure Period: fiscal year ending July 31, 2001
Total Grants: $30,000
Number of Grants: 2

Recent Grants

Note: Grants derived from 2001 Form 990.

General

15,000	American Natural Hygiene Society, Inc. -- donate subscriptions to Health Science magazine to various public libraries
15,000	San Diego Museum of Man, San Diego, CA

KEITH WOLD JOHNSON CHARITABLE TRUST

Giving Contact

Robert W. Johnson, IV, Trustee
c/o Johnson Co.
630 5th Ave., Suite 1510
New York, NY 10111
Phone: (212)872-7903

Description

Founded: 1986
EIN: 112845826
Organization Type: Private Foundation
Giving Locations: CO; NJ; NY
Grant Types: General Support.

Donor Information

Founder: Betty Wold Johnson

Financial Summary

Total Giving: $285,000 (2002); $290,000 (2000); $243,000 (1999)
Assets: $3,332,504 (2002); $5,731,546 (2000); $6,892,155 (1999)

Typical Recipients

Arts & Humanities: Ballet, Dance, Libraries, Public Broadcasting
Civic & Public Affairs: Civic & Public Affairs-General, Zoos/Aquariums
Education: Colleges & Universities, Faculty Development, Private Education (Precollege)
Health: Clinics/Medical Centers, Health Organizations, Hospitals, Medical Rehabilitation, Nursing Services, Public Health, Single-Disease Health Associations

Religion: Religious Organizations, Religious Welfare
Social Services: Crime Prevention, Food/Clothing Distribution, People with Disabilities

Application Procedures

Initial Contact: The foundation has no formal grant application procedure or application form.
Deadlines: None.

Restrictions

OrganizationS must be listed under section 501 (C) (3) of The Internal Revenue Code.

Foundation Officials

Christopher W. Johnson: trustee
Elizabeth Ross Johnson: trustee
Robert Wood Johnson, IV: trustee

Grants Analysis

Disclosure Period: calendar year ending 2002
Total Grants: $285,000
Number of Grants: 4
Highest Grant: $200,000
Lowest Grant: $25,000

Recent Grants

Note: Grants derived from 2002 Form 990.

General

200,000	Autism Research Institute, San Diego, CA
30,000	New School University, New York, NY
30,000	Princeton Friends School, Princeton, NJ
25,000	Vail Valley Medical Center Foundation, Vail, CO

JOHNSON CONTROLS INC.

Company Headquarters

Milwaukee, WI
Web: http://www.johnsoncontrols.com

Company Description

Founded: 1885
Ticker: JCI
Exchange: NYSE
Revenue: US$20.103 billion (2002)
Profit: US$600.5 million (2002)
Employees: 112000 (2002)
Fortune Rank: 86, per FORTUNE Magazine's list of 500 Largest U.S. Corporations (2002).
SIC(s): 2531 Public Building & Related Furniture, 3081 Unsupported Plastics Film & Sheet, 3085 Plastics Bottles, 3822 Environmental Controls.

Operating Locations

Johnson Controls Inc. (AL--Tuscaloosa; AR--Texarkana; CA--City of Industry, Fullerton, Los Angeles, Milpitas, Modesto, Stockton; DE--Middletown, New Castle; FL--Cape Canaveral, Orlando; GA--Atlanta, Cumming; IL--Geneva, Itasca; IN--Franklin, Goshen, Greencastle, Ossian; KS--Lenexa; KY--Bardstown, Cadiz, Florence, Glasgow, Harrodsburg, Lexington, Louisville, Nicholasville; LA--Shreveport; MD--Belcamp; MA--East Longmeadow; MI--Ann Arbor, Lapeer, Madison Heights, Mount Clemens, Novi, Owosso, Plymouth, Saline, Whitmore Lake, Williamston; MO--Jefferson City, St. Joseph; NH--Merrimack; NJ--Edison, Pine Brook, Somerville; OH--Columbus, Greenfield, Strongsville, Toledo; OK--Poteau; OR--Canby; PA--Erie, Pittsburgh; SC--Oconee; TN--Athens, Lewisburg, Lexington, Murfreesboro, Pulaski; TX--Carrollton, Fort Worth, Garland, New Braunfels; VT--Bennington; WA--Tacoma; WI--Watertown).

Nonmonetary Support

Note: Co. provides nonmonetary support.

Johnson Controls Foundation

Giving Contact

Valerie Adisek, Foundation Coordinator
5757 N. Green Bay Avenue
PO Box 591
Milwaukee, WI 53201-0591
Phone: (414)524-2296
Fax: (414)524-3200
Web: http://www.johnsoncontrols.com/corpvalues/foundation.htmfoundation

Description

EIN: 396036639
Organization Type: Corporate Foundation
Giving Locations: in areas where company has a significant presence.
Grant Types: Capital, General Support, Multiyear/Continuing Support.
Note: Employee matching gift ratio: 1 to 1 for gifts to education, the arts, and the United Way.

Financial Summary

Total Giving: $5,500,000 (2002 approx); $5,958,094 (2001); $2,625,670 (2000). Note: Contributes through corporate direct giving program and foundation.
Giving Analysis: Giving for 2000 includes: foundation grants to United Way ($1,015,511) foundation ($1,610,159)
Assets: $39,043,033 (2001); $41,453,367 (2000); $36,439,406 (1998)
Gifts Received: $5,000,000 (2001); $4,500,000 (2000); $4,000,000 (1999). Note: Contributions are received from Johnson Controls, Inc.

Typical Recipients

Arts & Humanities: Arts Associations & Councils, Arts Centers, Arts Festivals, Arts Funds, Arts Institutes, Ballet, Dance, Historic Preservation, Libraries, Museums/Galleries, Music, Opera, Performing Arts, Public Broadcasting, Theater
Civic & Public Affairs: Botanical Gardens/Parks, Business/Free Enterprise, Civil Rights, Economic Development, Employment/Job Training, Civic & Public Affairs-General, Housing, Municipalities/Towns, Nonprofit Management, Parades/Festivals, Professional & Trade Associations, Urban & Community Affairs, Women's Affairs, Zoos/Aquariums
Education: Afterschool/Enrichment Programs, Agricultural Education, Arts/Humanities Education, Business Education, Colleges & Universities, Colleges & Universities, Community & Junior Colleges, Continuing Education, Economic Education, Education Associations, Education Funds, Education Reform, Elementary Education (Private), Engineering/Technological Education, Education-General, Literacy, Medical Education, Minority Education, Private Education (Precollege), Public Education (Precollege), Science/Mathematics Education, Student Aid, Vocational & Technical Education
Environment: Energy, Environment-General, Resource Conservation
Health: Cancer, Children's Health/Hospitals, Clinics/Medical Centers, Health Organizations, Heart, Hospices, Hospitals, Medical Research, Public Health, Single-Disease Health Associations, Transplant Networks/Donor Banks
International: International Relations
Religion: Religious Welfare, Religious Welfare
Science: Science Museums, Scientific Centers & Institutes
Social Services: Animal Protection, Camps, Child Welfare, Community Centers, Community Service Organizations, Counseling, Emergency Relief, Family Services, Food/Clothing Distribution, People with Disabilities, Recreation & Athletics, Scouts, Senior Services, Social Services-General, Substance Abuse, United Funds/United Ways, YMCA/YWCA/YMHA/YWHA, Youth Organizations

Application Procedures

Initial Contact: Send a clear, concise letter on organization letterhead.
Application Requirements: Include a description of the organization's structure, purpose, history, and programs; a list of current officers and governing board members, including their outside affiliations; summary of need for support and its intended use; geographic area served; current income and expense budget, and copy of most recent audited financial statement; statement of other funding sources, community support and involvement; copy of 501 (c)(3) status letter.
Deadlines: None.
Evaluative Criteria: Organization's general structure, objectives, management capacity, relationship to community, population to be served, position relative to other organizations performing similar functions.
Decision Notification: Advisory board meets approximately three times per year in March, September, and November; allow up to 120 days for decision.
Notes: In preliminary stage, personal visits, phone calls to the foundation, and video tapes are discouraged.

Restrictions

Foundation does not support organizations which are not tax-exempt; individuals; private foundations or endowment funds; political or lobbying groups; fraternal or veterans groups; or organizations based or located outside the United States. The foundation does not generally support precollege education; medical or scientific research; religious groups for sectarian purposes; testimonials, fundraising events, tickets to benefits or shows; or travel, tours, seminars, conferences, or publications. The foundation does not donate equipment, products or labor.

Additional Information

Grants are not automatically renewed.
Publications: Giving Guidelines

Corporate Officials

John Barth: president, chief executive officer
Denise M. Zutz: vice president corporate communications B Milwaukee, WI 1951. ED University of Wisconsin (1973). PRIM CORP EMPL vice president corporate communications: Johnson Controls Inc.

Foundation Officials

Valerie Adisek: admin secretary
John Barth: member advisory board (see above)
James Henry Keyes: advisor B LaCrosse, WI 1940. ED Marquette University BS (1962); Northwestern University MBA (1963). ADD CORP EMPL president: Johnson Controls International; president: Johnson Controls Battery Group; president: Johnson Controls Interiors Inc.; vice president: Johnson Controls World Services Inc.; president: Prince Holding Corp. CORP AFFIL director: Pitney Bowes Inc.; director: Universal Foods Corp.; director: Federal Reserve Bank Chicago. NONPR AFFIL member: Manufacturers Alliance; member: National Association Manufacturers; member: American Institute CPAs.
Blaine Rieke: member advisory board
R. Douglas Ziegler: advisor B Milwaukee, WI 1927. ED Northwestern University (1949). CORP AFFIL director: Johnson Controls Inc.; vice president: Ziegler Asset Management Co.
Denise M. Zutz: member advisory board (see above)

Grants Analysis

Disclosure Period: calendar year ending 2001
Total Grants: $4,269,550*
Number of Grants: 693
Average Grant: $4,725*
Highest Grant: $1,000,000
Typical Range: $1,000 to $10,000
*Note: Giving excludes United Way. Average grant figure excludes highest grant.

Recent Grants

Note: Grants derived from 2001 Form 990.

General

1,000,000	American Red Cross National Disaster Relief Fund
300,374	Plymouth Community United Way, Plymouth, MN
167,000	Detroit 300, Inc., Detroit, MI
166,503	United Way of Greater Milwaukee, Milwaukee, WI
143,145	United Way of Greater Milwaukee, Milwaukee, WI
143,145	United Way of Greater Milwaukee, Milwaukee, WI
143,145	United Way of Greater Milwaukee, Milwaukee, WI
100,000	Focus HOPE, Detroit, MI
100,000	Marquette University, Milwaukee, WI
100,000	Milwaukee Art Museum, Milwaukee, WI

CHRISTIAN A. JOHNSON ENDEAVOR FOUNDATION

Giving Contact

Julie J. Kidd, President
1060 Park Avenue
New York, NY 10128-1033
Phone: (212)534-6620
Fax: (212)410-0568
E-mail: clubin@cajef.org

Description

Founded: 1952
EIN: 136147952
Organization Type: Family Foundation
Giving Locations: U.S. Eastern Region.
Grant Types: Challenge, Endowment, General Support, Matching, Multiyear/Continuing Support, Operating Expenses, Professorship.

Donor Information

Founder: The late Christian Johnson donated funds to establish the Christian A. Johnson Endeavor Foundation in 1952. Mr. Johnson, a director of the American Natural Gas Company, was a financier with interests in education, medical research, youth development, and free-enterprise economics. The donor's widow, Charlotte Jean Johnson, served as president and chairperson of the foundation.

Financial Summary

Total Giving: $12,000,000 (fiscal year ending September 30, 2002 approx); $10,541,563 (fiscal 2001); $7,139,552 (fiscal 2000)
Giving Analysis: Giving for fiscal 2001 includes: foundation scholarships ($155,000); fiscal 2000: foundation scholarships ($400,018); fiscal 1998: foundation scholarships ($125,000).
Assets: $198,000,000 (fiscal 2002 approx); $191,167,107 (fiscal 2001); $261,748,915 (fiscal 2000)
Gifts Received: $421,864 (fiscal 2001); $615,913 (fiscal 2000); $245,743 (fiscal 1998). Note: In fiscal 2001, contributions were received from Charlotte Johnson Charitable Lead TrustIn fiscal 2000, contributions were received from the Klingenstein Fund, the Charlotte Johnson Article 10B Charitable Lead Trust 2, and Richard S. Wolfe.

Typical Recipients

Arts & Humanities: Arts Centers, Arts Festivals, Arts Funds, Arts Institutes, Arts Outreach, Ballet, Dance, Ethnic & Folk Arts, Arts & Humanities-General, Libraries, Museums/Galleries, Music, Opera, Performing Arts, Public Broadcasting, Theater

Civic & Public Affairs: Botanical Gardens/Parks, Native American Affairs, Nonprofit Management, Philanthropic Organizations, Professional & Trade Associations

Education: Arts/Humanities Education, Colleges & Universities, Continuing Education, Economic Education, Education Reform, Elementary Education (Public), Engineering/Technological Education, Faculty Development, Education-General, International Exchange, International Studies, Leadership Training, Minority Education, Private Education (Precollege), School Volunteerism, Science/Mathematics Education, Social Sciences Education, Special Education, Student Aid

Environment: Environment-General

Health: Eyes/Blindness, Heart

International: Foreign Arts Organizations, Foreign Educational Institutions, International Affairs, International Development

Social Services: Community Service Organizations, People with Disabilities, Youth Organizations

Application Procedures

Initial Contact: Applicants should send a brief letter of inquiry to the foundation.
Application Requirements: The letter of inquiry should describe the project, its purposes, and its potential impact on the program or service of the sponsoring institution. If the foundation subsequently requests a proposal, it will provide guidelines.
Review Process: The board generally makes final decisions by October 1.

Restrictions

No grants are made to individuals; to neighborhood or community projects; to any city, county, state, or federal government-affiliated agency; or to institutions controlled by religious groups. The foundation will no longer consider projects in the fields of health care and medical research.

Additional Information

Publications: Application Guidelines

Foundation Officials

Susan Kassouf: special projects director

Grants Analysis

Disclosure Period: fiscal year ending September 30, 2001
Total Grants: $10,386,563*
Number of Grants: 112
Average Grant: $85,581*
Highest Grant: $887,060
Typical Range: $40,000 to $150,000
*Note: Giving excludes scholarships. Average grant figure excludes highest grant.

Recent Grants

Note: Grants derived from fiscal 2000 Form 990.

General

500,021	Hamilton College, Clinton, NY -- endowment challenge for full and visiting professors
352,000	Center for International Management Education, Annapolis, MD -- Program in Ukraine
350,011	Colorado College, Colorado Springs, CO -- International Programs
300,032	Williams College, Williamstown, MA -- CAJEF Fund for Interdisciplinary Teaching
265,006	Colby College, Waterville, ME -- CAJ Professorship of Integrated Learning
250,027	Bowdoin College, Brunswick, ME -- endowment - curricular innovation fund
250,027	Furman University, Greenville, SC -- CAJ Center for Engaged Learning
250,018	Bates College, Lewiston, ME -- CAJ Professorship of Interdisciplinary Studies
250,018	Harvard - JFK School of Government,

Cambridge, MA -- endowment challenge for scholarships

250,018	Hobart and William Smith Colleges, Geneva, NY -- endowment challenge for faculty and circular development

JOHNSON FOUNDATION

Giving Contact

Barbara Schmidt, Program Secretary
33 E. Four Mile Rd.
Racine, WI 53402
Phone: (262)681-3343
Fax: (262)681-3325
E-mail: bschmidt@johnsonfdn.org
Web: http://www.johnsonfdn.org

Description

Founded: 1958
EIN: 390958255
Organization Type: Private Foundation
Grant Types: Conference/Seminar, General Support.

Donor Information

Founder: S. C. Johnson and Son, the late H. F. Johnson, and descendants of the late H. F. Johnson

Financial Summary

Total Giving: $39,500 (fiscal year ending June 30, 2000); $38,000 (fiscal 1999 approx); $88,600 (fiscal 1994)
Assets: $35,201,908 (fiscal 2001); $13,330,514 (fiscal 1994); $12,934,177 (fiscal 1992)
Gifts Received: $4,456,907 (fiscal 2001); $2,352,275 (fiscal 1994); $1,808,657 (fiscal 1992). Note: In fiscal 2001, contributions were received from S.C. Johnson & Son Inc. ($2,300,000), Mr. & Mrs. Samuel C. Johnson ($9,187), The David and Lucile Packard Foundation ($47,107), and S.C. Johnson & Son Commercial Markets Inc. ($500,000). In fiscal 1994, contributions were received from S. C. Johnson and Sons ($2,100,000), Mr. and Mrs. S. C. Johnson ($50,000), William and Flora Hewlett Fdn. ($43,588), Pew Charitable Trust ($89,156), Lilly Endowment ($65,381), and miscellaneous ($4,150).

Typical Recipients

Arts & Humanities: Arts Associations & Councils, Libraries, Museums/Galleries, Music

Civic & Public Affairs: Civil Rights, Hispanic Affairs, Minority Business, Nonprofit Management, Public Policy

Education: Business Education, Colleges & Universities, Community & Junior Colleges, Engineering/Technological Education, Education-General, Leadership Training, Medical Education, Preschool Education, Private Education (Precollege), Secondary Education (Private), Student Aid

International: International Development, International Relief Efforts

Social Services: Family Services

Application Procedures

Initial Contact: Send a brief letter of inquiry requesting application guidelines.
Deadlines: None.

Restrictions

Does not make grants to individuals.

Additional Information

Publications: Application Guidelines

Foundation Officials

Lois Berg: secretary
Boyd M. Gibbons, III: president
Patricia Albjerg Graham, PhD: vice president B Lafayette, IN 1935. ED Purdue University BS (1955);

Purdue University MS (1957); Columbia University PhD (1964). CORP AFFIL trustee: Northwestern Mutual Life Insurance Co. NONPR AFFIL member: Phi Beta Kappa; member: Science Research Associates; member: National Academy Education; council: American Association Advancement Science; member: American Historical Association.

Samuel Curtis Johnson: chairman emeritus B Racine, WI 1928. ED Cornell University BA (1950); Harvard University MBA (1952). PRIM CORP EMPL chairman emeritus: S.C. Johnson & Son. CORP AFFIL chairman: Johnson Wax Fund; chairman: Johnson Worldwide Associates Inc.; director: Johnson Bank; chairman: Johnson International Inc.; director: H.J. Heinz Co.; director: Deere & Co.; director: Exxon-Mobil Corp.; director: Cargill Inc. NONPR AFFIL founder, chairman emeritus: Prairie School; regent emeritus: Smithsonian Institute; member national board governors: Nature Conservancy; chairman advisory council: Cornell University Johnson Graduate School Management; trustee emeritus: Mayo Foundation; trustee emeritus: Cornell University; honorary member: Business Council; member: Chi Psi; trustee: American Museum Natural History. CLUB AFFIL University Club; Racine Country Club; America Club; Cornell Club.

Helen P. Johnson-Leipold: trustee
Janice C. Kreamer: trustee
Charles Selden McNeer: treasurer B Gilbert, WV 1926. ED Berea College (1947); Northwestern University BSEE (1950). CORP AFFIL chairman, chief executive officer, director: WI Natural Gas Co.; director: WI Electric Power Co.; director: WI Energy Co.; director: Metro Milwaukee Inc.; director: Universal Foods Corp.; chairman: Bradley Center Corp.; chairman: Federal Reserve Bank Chicago; director: Badger Service Co. NONPR AFFIL director: WI Utilities Association; director: YMCA Metropolitan Milwaukee; chairman executive committee: WI Upper Michigan Systems; director: WI Electric Utilities Research Foundation; member: WI Society Prof Engineers; member advisory council: University Wisconsin School Business Administration; director: WI Chapter Nature Conservancy; director: Sinai Samaritan Medical Center; member: Tau Beta Pi; member: Sigma Pi Sigma; member: Sigma Xi; member: Pi Mu Epsilon; director: Milwaukee Redevelopment Corp.; member: National Society Professional Engineers; member executive committee: Mid-American Interpool Network; director: Milwaukee Innovation Center; member council: Medical College Wisconsin; vice chairman (urban affairs): Metropolitan Milwaukee Association Commerce; director: Greater Milwaukee Comm; member: Kiwanis; director: Forward Wisconsin; member: Edison Electric Institute; member: Eta Kappa Nu; trustee: Berea College; director: Competitive Wisconsin; chairman: American Comm Radwaste Disposal.

William J. Raspberry: trustee
John M. Richman: trustee
Paula Wolff: trustee

Grants Analysis

Disclosure Period: fiscal year ending June 30, 2000
Total Grants: $39,500
Number of Grants: 12
Average Grant: $3,375
Highest Grant: $6,000
Lowest Grant: $1,000
Typical Range: $1,000 to $5,000

Recent Grants

Note: Grants derived from fiscal 2001 Form 990.

General

6,000	Arts Council of Metropolitan Kansas City, Kansas City, MO
6,000	Institute for the Transformation of Learning, Milwaukee, WI
6,000	Resources for the Future, Washington, DC

6,000	University of Chicago, Chicago, IL
3,000	Harvard University, Cambridge, MA
2,500	Foundation Center, New York, NY
2,000	Berea College Alumni Association, Berea, KY
2,000	Grantmakers for Children, Youth, and Families, Washington, DC
2,000	Medical College of Wisconsin, Milwaukee, WI
2,000	National Lighthouse Museum, Staten Island, NY

A.D. JOHNSON FOUNDATION

Giving Contact

Wayne J. Johnson, President & Treasurer
1 N. LaSalle St., Suite 3000
1 N. LaSalle St., Suite 3000
Chicago, IL 60602-4003
Phone: (312)782-7320
Fax: (312)782-7131

Description

Founded: 1965
EIN: 366124270
Organization Type: Private Foundation
Giving Locations: FL; IL
Grant Types: General Support, Research.

Donor Information

Founder: the late A. D. Johnson

Financial Summary

Total Giving: $110,000 (2001); $140,000 (2000); $140,000 (1999)
Giving Analysis: Giving for 2001 includes: foundation grants to United Way ($10,000)
Assets: $2,717,700 (2001); $2,813,014 (2000); $2,511,307 (1999)

Typical Recipients

Arts & Humanities: Arts Festivals, Arts Outreach, Community Arts, Libraries, Music
Civic & Public Affairs: Parades/Festivals
Education: Arts/Humanities Education, Colleges & Universities, Medical Education, Private Education (Precollege), Science/Mathematics Education
Health: Clinics/Medical Centers, Diabetes, Health-General, Hospices, Hospitals, Long-Term Care, Medical Research, Mental Health, Single-Disease Health Associations
Religion: Churches
Social Services: Animal Protection, Child Welfare, Community Service Organizations, People with Disabilities, Shelters/Homelessness, United Funds/United Ways, Youth Organizations

Application Procedures

Initial Contact: Send a brief letter of inquiry describing program.
Deadlines: None.

Restrictions

Does not support individuals or political or lobbying groups.

Foundation Officials

Diane T. Johnson: vice president, secretary
Wayne J. Johnson: president, treasurer
Herbert J. Theisen: assistant secretary, general counsel

Grants Analysis

Disclosure Period: calendar year ending 2001
Total Grants: $110,000*
Number of Grants: 8
Highest Grant: $20,000

Lowest Grant: $5,000
Typical Range: $5,000 to $20,000
*Note: Giving includes United Way.

Recent Grants

Note: Grants derived from 2001 Form 990.

General

25,000	Cystic Fibrosis Gold Coast, Ft. Lauderdale, FL
20,000	Evanston Northwestern Healthcare Corporation, Evanston, IL
15,000	Henderson Mental Health Center, Ft. Lauderdale, FL
15,000	Humane Society of Broward County, Ft. Lauderdale, FL
10,000	Ravinia Festival, Inc., Chicago, IL
10,000	Ravinia Festival Young Artist Endowment Fund, Chicago, IL
10,000	United Way of Skokie Valley, Skokie, IL
5,000	St. Mark's Episcopal School, Ft. Lauderdale, FL

BURDINE JOHNSON FOUNDATION

Giving Contact

Robert C. Giberson, Trustee
PO Box 1230
Buda, TX 78610-1230
Phone: (512)312-1336
Fax: (512)295-4773

Description

Founded: 1960
EIN: 746036669
Organization Type: Family Foundation
Giving Locations: TX
Grant Types: General Support.

Donor Information

Founder: Established in 1960 by Burdine C. Johnson and J. M. Johnson.

Financial Summary

Total Giving: $1,800,000 (2002 approx); $1,713,750 (2001); $1,778,750 (2000)
Assets: $35,295,400 (2001); $38,877,712 (2000); $34,365,213 (1998)

Typical Recipients

Arts & Humanities: Arts & Humanities-General, Historic Preservation, Libraries, Museums/Galleries, Performing Arts, Theater
Civic & Public Affairs: Community Foundations, Civic & Public Affairs-General, Municipalities/Towns, Women's Affairs, Zoos/Aquariums
Education: Arts/Humanities Education, Colleges & Universities, Community & Junior Colleges, Elementary Education (Public), Education-General, Literacy, Medical Education, Private Education (Precollege), Public Education (Precollege), Religious Education, Student Aid
Environment: Environment-General, Resource Conservation
Health: Cancer, Children's Health/Hospitals, Emergency/Ambulance Services, Medical Research, Multiple Sclerosis, Single-Disease Health Associations, Transplant Networks/Donor Banks
International: Health Care/Hospitals
Religion: Churches, Religion-General, Religion-General, Religious Welfare
Science: Scientific Centers & Institutes
Social Services: Animal Protection, Community Service Organizations, Domestic Violence, Emergency Relief, Family Planning, Family Services, Food/Clothing Distribution, Recreation & Athletics, Scouts, Senior Services, Sexual Abuse, Substance Abuse

Application Procedures

Initial Contact: The foundation has no formal grant application procedure or application form.
Application Requirements: Applicants must submit full details about the applying organization and the use of the proposed grant. The foundation also requests applicants attach a copy of the IRS ruling or determination letter.
Deadlines: None.

Restrictions

Grants made by the foundation are limited to religious, charitable, scientific, literary, or educational purposes.

Foundation Officials

Robert C. Giberson: trustee
William T. Johnson: trustee
Martha L. Mattox: trustee

Grants Analysis

Disclosure Period: calendar year ending 2001
Total Grants: $1,713,750
Number of Grants: 37
Average Grant: $25,404*
Highest Grant: $400,000
Lowest Grant: $500
Typical Range: $15,000 to $50,000
*Note: Average grant figure excludes three highest grants ($850,000).

Recent Grants

Note: Grants derived from 2001 Form 990.

Library-Related

2,500	Friends of Public Library of Buda, Texas, Buda, TX -- operating funds

General

400,000	Hays Consolidated Independent School District, Kyle, TX -- to bid theater arts complex
250,000	St. Stephen's Episcopal School, Austin, TX -- to expand parking in lower lot next to Clayton Gym
200,000	Hays Consolidated Independent School District, Kyle, TX -- to bid theater arts complex
150,000	James Dick Foundation for Performing Arts, Round Top, TX -- for continuation of work on Concert Hall
150,000	St. Stephen's School, Wimberley, TX -- for construction of gym
100,000	James Dick Foundation for Performing Arts, Round Top, TX -- for continuation of work on Concert Hall
65,000	Hays Consolidated Independent School District, Kyle, TX -- Kodaly Music Program
50,000	Children's Hospital Foundation of Austin, Austin, TX -- for Children's Healing Garden Project
50,000	Planned Parenthood of the Texas Capital Region, Inc., Austin, TX -- for ongoing programs
45,000	Hays Consolidated Independent School District, Kyle, TX -- for Certification Program

CHARLES AND ANN JOHNSON FOUNDATION

Giving Contact

Charles B. Johnson, Trustee
c/o Franklin Resources Inc.
One Franklin Pkwy., Bldg. 920, 4th Floor
San Mateo, CA 94403
Phone: (650)312-3000

Description

Founded: 1986
EIN: 943026398
Organization Type: Private Foundation
Giving Locations: CA
Grant Types: General Support.

Donor Information

Founder: Ann L. Johnson, Charles B. Johnson

Financial Summary

Total Giving: $1,530,623 (2002); $1,357,071 (2001); $1,282,373 (2000)
Giving Analysis: Giving for 2000 includes: foundation grants to United Way ($3,000); 1999: foundation grants to United Way ($3,000) 1998: foundation grants to United Way ($3,000)
Assets: $32,560,181 (2002); $27,292,913 (2001); $29,537,364 (2000)
Gifts Received: $6,016,885 (2002); $1,216,805 (2001); $1,502,630 (2000). Note: In 2000, 2001, and 2002, contributions were received from Charles and Ann Johnson. In 1994 and 1999, contributions were received from Charles Johnson.

Typical Recipients

Arts & Humanities: Historic Preservation, History & Archaeology, Libraries, Museums/Galleries, Music, Opera, Public Broadcasting
Civic & Public Affairs: Community Foundations, Civic & Public Affairs-General, Housing, Municipalities/Towns, Parades/Festivals, Public Policy, Urban & Community Affairs, Zoos/Aquariums
Education: Colleges & Universities, Education Reform, Education-General, International Exchange, Private Education (Precollege), Public Education (Precollege), Student Aid
Environment: Air/Water Quality, Environment-General
Health: Cancer, Clinics/Medical Centers, Health Funds, Hospices, Hospitals, Single-Disease Health Associations
International: International Affairs, International Peace & Security Issues
Religion: Churches, Religious Organizations, Religious Welfare
Science: Science-General, Scientific Centers & Institutes
Social Services: Community Service Organizations, Domestic Violence, Family Planning, People with Disabilities, Recreation & Athletics, United Funds/United Ways, Volunteer Services

Application Procedures

Initial Contact: Send a brief letter of inquiry.
Deadlines: Contact foundation for deadline information.

Foundation Officials

Ann L. Johnson: trustee
Charles Bartlett Johnson: trustee B Montclair, NJ 1933. ED Yale University BA (1954). PRIM CORP EMPL chairman, chief executive officer, president: Franklin Resources. CORP AFFIL director: Res Capital Fund; director: Res Equity Fund; director: General Host Corp.; director: Franklin Money Fund; director: Franklin Option Fund; director: Franklin California Tax Free Income Fund; director: Franklin Custodian Funds. NONPR AFFIL chairman board governors: National Association Securities Directors; director: San Francisco Symphony; trustee: Crystal Springs Uplands School; 97 board overseers: Hoover Institution. CLUB AFFIL Commonwealth Club California; director: Pacific-Union Club; Burlingame Country Club.

Grants Analysis

Disclosure Period: calendar year ending 2001
Total Grants: $1,357,071
Number of Grants: 56
Average Grant: $12,949*

Highest Grant: $230,166
Lowest Grant: $100
Typical Range: $5,000 to $25,000
*Note: Average grant figure excludes three highest grants ($670,782).

Recent Grants

Note: Grants derived from 2000 Form 990.

General

280,331	California Academy of Sciences, San Francisco, CA
189,350	Santa Catalina School
137,605	Hoover Institution, Stanford, CA
110,488	San Francisco Foundation Community Initiative Funds, San Francisco, CA
102,249	St. Lawrence University, Canton, OH
53,018	Parents Television Council
51,984	American Museum of Natural History, New York, NY
41,356	San Francisco Opera, San Francisco, CA
35,856	San Francisco Symphony, San Francisco, CA
30,296	Eisenhower Exchange Fellowships, Philadelphia, PA

HELEN K. AND ARTHUR E. JOHNSON FOUNDATION

Giving Contact

John H. Alexander, President & Executive Director
1700 Broadway, Suite 1100
Denver, CO 80290-1039
Phone: (303)861-4127
Fax: (303)861-0607
Web: http://www.johnsonfoundation.net

Alternate Contact

Phone: 800-232-9931

Description

Founded: 1948
EIN: 846020702
Organization Type: General Purpose Foundation
Giving Locations: CO
Grant Types: Capital, Challenge, General Support, Matching, Operating Expenses, Project, Scholarship.

Donor Information

Founder: Incorporated in 1948 as the Arthur E. Johnson Foundation, the foundation became the Helen K. and Arthur E. Johnson Foundation in 1975.

Financial Summary

Total Giving: $6,750,000 (2003 approx); $7,400,000 (2002 approx); $8,078,427 (2001)
Giving Analysis: Giving for 1998 includes: foundation grants to United Way ($40,000); foundation scholarships ($126,000) foundation ($5,441,981)
Assets: $134,000,000 (2002 approx); $168,432,125 (2001); $172,108,930 (2000)

Typical Recipients

Arts & Humanities: History & Archaeology, Libraries, Museums/Galleries, Music, Opera, Public Broadcasting
Civic & Public Affairs: Botanical Gardens/Parks, Business/Free Enterprise, Community Foundations, Employment/Job Training, Civic & Public Affairs-General, Hispanic Affairs, Housing, Inner-City Development, Native American Affairs, Urban & Community Affairs, Women's Affairs, Zoos/Aquariums
Education: Afterschool/Enrichment Programs, Colleges & Universities, Community & Junior Colleges, Economic Education, Elementary Education (Private), Faculty Development, Education-General,

Leadership Training, Literacy, Minority Education, Private Education (Precollege), Public Education (Precollege), Science/Mathematics Education, Secondary Education (Private), Student Aid, Vocational & Technical Education

Environment: Air/Water Quality, Environment-General, Resource Conservation, Wildlife Protection

Health: AIDS/HIV, Alzheimers Disease, Cancer, Children's Health/Hospitals, Clinics/Medical Centers, Eyes/Blindness, Health-General, Health Organizations, Hospices, Hospitals, Long-Term Care, Medical Rehabilitation, Medical Research, Medical Training, Multiple Sclerosis, Nursing Services, Public Health, Research/Studies Institutes, Single-Disease Health Associations, Speech & Hearing, Transplant Networks/Donor Banks

Religion: Churches, Religion-General, Religious Welfare, Seminaries

Science: Science Museums, Scientific Centers & Institutes

Social Services: Animal Protection, At-Risk Youth, Child Welfare, Community Centers, Community Service Organizations, Day Care, Emergency Relief, Family Planning, Family Services, Food/Clothing Distribution, Homes, People with Disabilities, Recreation & Athletics, Scouts, Senior Services, Sexual Abuse, Shelters/Homelessness, Social Services-General, Substance Abuse, United Funds/United Ways, Volunteer Services, YMCA/YWCA/YMHA/YWHA, Youth Organizations

Application Procedures

Initial Contact: Applicants should send a brief preliminary letter of no more than two pages outlining the project. If interested, the foundation will request a full proposal.

Application Requirements: A full proposal: a cover letter that states the amount requested and objective of the project, signed by the Chief Executive Officer and the Presdient of the Board; a narrative stating the relevance of project to others, timetable for accomplishing goals, history of organization; current board members; list of other funding agencies; operating and project budget; a description of organization's programs and those they serve; financial statements for last two years, including balance sheet and statement of revenue and expenses; proposed evaluation plan; plans for possible long-term funding; a completed Tax Exempt Status Certificate; a completed Board and Community Support Form; and IRS tax exemption letter.

Deadlines: January 1 for the spring meeting; April 1 for summer meeting; July 1 for fall meeting; and October 1 for winter meeting.

Restrictions

The foundation does not support organizations whose purpose is to influence the legislative or judicial process in any manner or for any cause; it does not contribute to loans; endowments; purchase of blocks of tickets; individual scholarships; grants that pass through the nominal grant recipient to another organization; or support for conferences. The foundation makes grants primarily to Colorado organizations. Reapplicants must wait a full twelve months after submitting a proposal to re-apply.

Additional Information

Publications: Annual Report; Application Guidelines

Foundation Officials

Ashley Campion: trustee
Berit Campion: trustee
Lynn H. Campion: vice president, treasurer, trustee
Thomas B. Campion, Jr.: trustee
Brigit Ann Davis: program manager
Barbara Hartley: chairperson
Charles R. Hazelrigg: trustee
Gerald R. Hillyard, Jr.: trustee
Stan Kamprath: president, executive director
Ronald L. Lehr: trustee

Stanley Duane Neeleman: trustee B Salt Lake City, UT 1943. ED Westminster College BA (1967); George Washington University MA (1969); University of Denver JD (1972). PRIM NONPR EMPL professor: Brigham Young University, J. Reuben Clark Law School. CORP AFFIL counsel: Holme Roberts Owen. NONPR AFFIL founder: Utah Lawyers Arts; member: Utah State Bar Association; member: Governors Task Force Income Tax Reform Utah; member: Utah Citizens Arts; fellow: American College Trust & Estate Counsel; trustee: Beren Foundation.

Grants Analysis

Disclosure Period: calendar year ending 2001
Total Grants: $8,078,427
Number of Grants: 251
Average Grant: $15,000
Highest Grant: $25,000
Lowest Grant: $2,700
Typical Range: $5,000 to $100,000

Recent Grants

Note: Grants derived from 2000 Form 990.

General

250,000	Denver Museum of Nature and Science, Denver, CO -- space science initiative
200,000	Conservation Fund, Arlington, VA -- Greenland Ranch project
200,000	Girls Incorporated of Metropolitan Denver, Denver, CO -- capital campaign
167,188	Colorado College, Colorado Springs, CO -- for Johnson Scholars
150,000	Goodwill Industries, Denver, CO -- capital improvement campaign
150,000	Northwest Colorado Visiting Nurse Association, Steamboat Springs, CO -- purchase new facility
145,510	University of Denver, Denver, CO -- for Johnson Scholars
130,504	Regis University, Denver, CO -- for Johnson Scholars
127,200	Denver Museum of Nature and Science, Denver, CO -- SHARE Program
120,000	Colorado State University, Ft. Collins, CO -- capital campaign

HOWARD JOHNSON FOUNDATION

Giving Contact

Lisa Franciscovich, Trustee Officer
c/o U.S. Trust Co. of New York
114 W. 47th St.
New York, NY 10036
Phone: (212)852-3834

Description

Founded: 1961
EIN: 046060965
Organization Type: Private Foundation
Giving Locations: AK; ID; LA; MT; OR; WV
Grant Types: General Support.

Donor Information

Founder: the late Howard D. Johnson

Financial Summary

Total Giving: $311,500 (2000); $256,450 (1999); $169,425 (1998)
Assets: $5,324,763 (2000); $5,942,779 (1999); $4,961,377 (1998)
Gifts Received: $9,225 (1999); $24,725 (1997); $9,000 (1996). Note: In 1998, contributions were received from Dorothy Johnson Henry.

Typical Recipients

Arts & Humanities: Historic Preservation, Museums/Galleries, Music
Civic & Public Affairs: Botanical Gardens/Parks, Civic & Public Affairs-General, Zoos/Aquariums
Education: Colleges & Universities, Elementary Education (Private), Gifted & Talented Programs, Medical Education, Minority Education, Private Education (Precollege), Public Education (Precollege), Religious Education
Environment: Air/Water Quality, Forestry, Environment-General, Resource Conservation, Wildlife Protection
Health: Cancer, Children's Health/Hospitals, Clinics/Medical Centers, Health Organizations, Hospitals, Hospitals (University Affiliated), Medical Research, Single-Disease Health Associations
International: International Environmental Issues
Religion: Churches, Religious Organizations, Seminaries
Social Services: Animal Protection, Community Service Organizations, Family Planning, People with Disabilities, Scouts, United Funds/United Ways, Youth Organizations

Application Procedures

Initial Contact: Send a brief letter of inquiry.
Deadlines: None.

Restrictions

Does not support individuals. Funds are committed for the foreseeable future. No unsolicited proposals are being accepted at this time.

Foundation Officials

Marissa J. Brock: trustee
Patricia Bates Crawford: trustee
Dorothy J. Henry: trustee
Howard Bates Johnson: trustee
Howard Brennan Johnson: trustee
Joshua J. Weeks: trustee
William H. Weeks: trustee

Grants Analysis

Disclosure Period: calendar year ending 2000
Total Grants: $311,500
Number of Grants: 51
Average Grant: $5,120*
Highest Grant: $55,500
Typical Range: $1,000 to $10,000
*Note: Average grant figure excludes highest grant.

Recent Grants

Note: Grants derived from 2000 Form 990.

General

55,500	Greens Farms Academy, Greens Farms, CT
28,000	Tabor Academy, Marion, MA
25,000	Friends Academy, Locust Valley, NY
20,000	Harvard Business School, Cambridge, MA
18,000	Milton Academy, Milton, MA
14,500	Fresh Air Fund, New York, NY
12,500	Foxcroft School, Middleburg, VA
12,000	Lenox Hill Hospital, New York, NY
12,000	New York Presbyterian Hospital, New York, NY
10,000	Episcopal School, New York, NY

M. G. AND LILLIE A. JOHNSON FOUNDATION

Giving Contact

Robert Halepeska, Executive Vice President
PO Box 2269
Victoria, TX 77902
Phone: (512)575-7970

Fax: (512)575-2264
E-mail: mgj@cox-internet.com

Description

Founded: 1958
EIN: 746076961
Organization Type: General Purpose Foundation
Giving Locations: TX: Gulf Coast between San Patricio and Wharton.
Grant Types: Capital, Challenge, Endowment, Matching, Project, Scholarship.

Donor Information

Founder: The foundation was established in 1958, with contributions from M. G. Johnson and Lillie A. Johnson.

Financial Summary

Total Giving: $2,400,000 (fiscal year ending November 30, 2003 approx); $2,433,387 (fiscal 2002); $2,781,905 (fiscal 2001)
Giving Analysis: Giving for fiscal 1999 includes: foundation scholarships ($300,000)
Assets: $48,000,000 (fiscal 2003 approx); $46,492,541 (fiscal 2002); $51,612,794 (fiscal 2001)
Gifts Received: $50,000 (fiscal 1999 approx); $1,800,000 (fiscal 1998 approx); $500,000 (fiscal 1997 approx)

Typical Recipients

Arts & Humanities: Historic Preservation, History & Archaeology, Libraries, Museums/Galleries
Civic & Public Affairs: Botanical Gardens/Parks, Chambers of Commerce, Community Foundations, Civic & Public Affairs-General, Municipalities/Towns, Parades/Festivals, Safety, Urban & Community Affairs
Education: Colleges & Universities, Community & Junior Colleges, Continuing Education, Literacy, Medical Education, Religious Education, Science/Mathematics Education, Student Aid, Vocational & Technical Education
Environment: Wildlife Protection
Health: Clinics/Medical Centers, Emergency/Ambulance Services, Eyes/Blindness, Health Funds, Heart, Hospices, Hospitals, Long-Term Care, Medical Rehabilitation, Mental Health, Nursing Services, Nutrition, Public Health, Research/Studies Institutes, Transplant Networks/Donor Banks, Trauma Treatment
Religion: Bible Study/Translation, Churches, Ministries, Religious Organizations, Religious Welfare
Science: Science-General, Science Museums, Scientific Centers & Institutes
Social Services: At-Risk Youth, Child Welfare, Community Centers, Community Service Organizations, Counseling, Day Care, Domestic Violence, Emergency Relief, Food/Clothing Distribution, Homes, People with Disabilities, Recreation & Athletics, Senior Services, Sexual Abuse, Social Services-General, Substance Abuse, YMCA/YWCA/YMHA/YWHA, Youth Organizations

Application Procedures

Initial Contact: Submit one copy of a detailed written proposal.
Application Requirements: Applications should include biographical information, proof of tax-exempt status, amount requested, purpose of funds sought, and anticipated length of time within which the funds will be expended.
Deadlines: None. Proposals should be received no later than one month prior to a meeting for consideration.
Review Process: The board of trustees usually meets in March, July and October. Applicants whose proposals are not approved will be informed only if the proposal conforms to the foundation's stated criteria.

Restrictions

Grants are seldom provided for operational expenses. The foundation does not fund national charities, fellowship programs, or organizations outside its geographic area of interest.

Additional Information

Publications: Application Guidelines

Foundation Officials

James A. Bouligny: trustee CORP AFFIL director: Prosperity Bancshares Inc.
M. H. Brock: president, trustee CORP AFFIL chairman: Maurco Corp.
Robert L. Halepeska: executive vice president CORP AFFIL director: First Victoria National Bank.
Dick W. Koop: trustee CORP AFFIL director: Jackson Electric Co-op.
Jack Morrison, Jr.: trustee PRIM CORP EMPL partner: Bumgardner Morrison & Co.
Terrell Mullins: trustee
Judge Lloyd Rust: trustee
M. Munson Smith: trustee, secretary PRIM CORP EMPL secretary, treasurer, director: Texas Concrete Co.

Grants Analysis

Disclosure Period: fiscal year ending November 30, 2002
Total Grants: $2,433,387*
Number of Grants: 50
Average Grant: $40,000
Highest Grant: $250,000
Lowest Grant: $6,500
Typical Range: $10,000 to $60,000 and $100,000 to $250,000
*Note: Grants analysis provided by foundation.

Recent Grants

Note: Grants derived from fiscal 2001 Form 990.

General

200,000	Brookwood Community, Houston, TX -- construction of continuing care dining room and kitchen
200,000	Jackson County Hospital District, Edna, TX -- purchase of a Helical CT scanner
200,000	Yoakum Community Hospital, Yoakum, TX -- purchase Helical scanner
195,000	El Campo Medical Foundation, El Campo, TX -- purchase helical scanner
125,000	Northside Center, Victoria, TX -- renovation of a building
112,000	Friends of the Texas Historical Commission, Austin, TX -- excavation of Fort St. Louis
100,000	Community Food Bank of Victoria, Victoria, TX -- expand freezer and cooling system
100,000	Dewitt Community Development Foundation, Inc. -- construct technology and small business incubator facility
100,000	Gulf Bend Center -- purchase computers and software
100,000	Lavaca Medical Center, Hallettsville, TX -- purchase of radiographic and fluoroscopic system

SAMUEL S. JOHNSON FOUNDATION

Giving Contact

Elizabeth Hill Johnson, President
PO Box 356
Redmond, OR 97756-0079
Phone: (541)548-8104
Fax: (541)548-8104
E-mail: ssjohnson@empnet.com

Description

Founded: 1995
EIN: 946062478
Organization Type: Private Foundation
Giving Locations: OR
Grant Types: General Support.

Financial Summary

Total Giving: $584,266 (fiscal year ending May 31, 2001); $521,263 (fiscal 2000); $521,263 (fiscal 1999)
Giving Analysis: Giving for fiscal 2001 includes: foundation grants to United Way ($3,250); foundation gifts to individuals ($3,506); fiscal 1999: foundation grants to United Way ($1,050); foundation gifts to individuals ($3,000); foundation scholarships ($4,313); fiscal 1997: foundation grants to United Way ($11,000) foundation scholarships ($27,970)
Assets: $11,374,391 (fiscal 2001); $11,480,683 (fiscal 2000); $11,480,683 (fiscal 1999)
Gifts Received: $16,985 (fiscal 2001); $17,000 (fiscal 1995); $61,267 (fiscal 1994). Note: In fiscal 1995, contributions were received from Elizabeth Hill Johnson.

Typical Recipients

Arts & Humanities: Historic Preservation, History & Archaeology, Museums/Galleries, Music, Public Broadcasting
Civic & Public Affairs: Community Foundations, Civic & Public Affairs-General, Public Policy, Safety
Education: Arts/Humanities Education, Colleges & Universities, Legal Education, Literacy, Medical Education, Preschool Education, Special Education
Health: Health-General, Home-Care Services, Hospices, Preventive Medicine/Wellness Organizations
International: Health Care/Hospitals
Religion: Religion-General, Religious Welfare
Social Services: Animal Protection, Camps, Domestic Violence, Emergency Relief, People with Disabilities, Scouts, Senior Services, Shelters/Homelessness, Volunteer Services, YMCA/YWCA/YMHA/YWHA, Youth Organizations

Application Procedures

Initial Contact: The foundation has no formal grant application procedure or application form. Send a brief letter of inquiry.
Application Requirements: Include a description of organization, amount requested, purpose of funds sought, recently audited financial statement, and proof of tax-exempt status.
Deadlines: January 15 and June 15. The Foundation Board of Directors meet twice a year, in mid-February and mid-July.
Decision Notification: Applicants are notified in writing of the action taken by the board of directors relative to grant proposals usually within two weeks of the meeting of the Board of Directors.

Restrictions

Does not fund individuals, political or lobbying groups, endowments, capital expenditures, large equipment purchases, or building funds.

Foundation Officials

Karen K. Creason: director
John Helm: director
Elizabeth Hill Johnson: president, director
Patricia C. Johnson: cfo, director
Elizabeth K. Johnson-Helm: vice president, director

Grants Analysis

Disclosure Period: fiscal year ending May 31, 2001
Total Grants: $577,510*
Number of Grants: 195
Average Grant: $2,526*
Highest Grant: $50,000
Typical Range: $1,000 to $5,000
*Note: Giving excludes scholarships, United Way. Average grant figure excludes two highest grants ($90,000).

Recent Grants

Note: Grants derived from 1999 Form 990.

General

15,000	High Desert Museum, Bend, OR -- in support of "Root Diggin Diorama"
10,000	Friends of the Metolius, Camp Sherman, OR -- in memory of Leonard Lundgren
10,000	High Desert Museum, Bend, OR -- in support of the "Pow Wow Regalia Display"
10,000	Linfield College, McMinnville, OR -- for area of greatest need
10,000	Union Gospel Mission, Portland, OR -- support lifechange program
8,400	Disabilities, Opportunities, Internetworking and Technology Scholars Program, Seattle, WA -- support of Oregon scholars
6,000	Oregon Health Sciences University, Portland, OR -- new shelter
5,000	Boys and Girls Aid Society of Oregon, Portland, OR -- for area of greatest need
5,000	Chandler Center for Community Leadership, Bend, OR -- toward work with elected officials and volunteers
5,000	Crook County Cadet Boy Choir, Prineville, OR -- support of concert trip to Japan

THOMAS PHILLIPS AND JANE MOORE JOHNSON FOUNDATION

Giving Contact

Thomas P. Johnson, Chairman & Trustee
1500 Oliver Building
Pittsburgh, PA 15222
Phone: (412)261-9008

Description

Founded: 1991
EIN: 256357015
Organization Type: Private Foundation
Giving Locations: CO; PA: nationally.
Grant Types: General Support.

Financial Summary

Total Giving: $585,900 (2001); $223,160 (2000); $82,500 (1999)
Assets: $51,438,098 (2001); $3,004,221 (2000); $3,148,229 (1999)
Gifts Received: $48,808,751 (2001); $43,660 (2000); $481,406 (1999). Note: In 2000 and 2001, contributions were received from the Estate of Thomas Johnson. In 1996 and 1999, contributions were received from Thomas P. Johnson.

Typical Recipients

Arts & Humanities: Film & Video, History & Archaeology, Libraries, Museums/Galleries, Music, Performing Arts, Public Broadcasting
Civic & Public Affairs: Community Foundations, Civic & Public Affairs-General, Housing, Public Policy
Education: Arts/Humanities Education, Colleges & Universities, Community & Junior Colleges, Faculty Development, Private Education (Precollege), Student Aid
Environment: Air/Water Quality, Environment-General
Health: AIDS/HIV, Health-General, Hospitals
Religion: Churches, Religious Welfare
Science: Scientific Centers & Institutes

Application Procedures

Initial Contact: Send a brief letter of inquiry.
Application Requirements: Include amount requested, purpose of funds sought, and proof of tax-exempt status.
Deadlines: None.

Foundation Officials

William L. Casey: assistant secretary
Winifred J. Clive: trustee
James M. Johnson: trustee
Jane M. Johnson: vchairman
Jesse D. Johnson: trustee
Thomas P. Johnson, Jr.: trustee
Thomas P. Johnson: chairman, trustee

Grants Analysis

Disclosure Period: calendar year ending 2001
Total Grants: $585,900
Number of Grants: 36
Average Grant: $16,275
Highest Grant: $80,000
Lowest Grant: $400
Typical Range: $5,000 to $20,000

Recent Grants

Note: Grants derived from 2000 Form 990.

General

43,660	Capital Hill Foundation, Bethesda, MD
30,000	International Film Seminars, New York, NY
30,000	National Gallery of Art, Washington, DC
25,000	Frick Art and Historical Center, Pittsburgh, PA
12,000	Westcap, Grand Junction, CO
10,000	Covenant Whosoever Will Church, Wikensburg, PA
10,000	GLAAD
10,000	San Miguel County PDR Program, Telluride, CO
10,000	Telluride Society for the Performing Arts, Inc., Telluride, CO
7,500	Teachers and Writers Collaborative, New York, NY

WILLARD T. C. JOHNSON FOUNDATION

Giving Contact

Neil J. Burmeister, President
630 5th Avenue, Suite 1510
New York, NY 10111
Phone: (212)332-7500
Fax: (212)332-7510
E-mail: tjici1@tjinc.com

Description

Founded: 1979
EIN: 132993310
Organization Type: Family Foundation
Giving Locations: DC: Washington; NJ; NY: New York
Grant Types: General Support.

Donor Information

Founder: Incorporated in 1979 by the late Willard T. C. Johnson and the late Keith W. Johnson .

Financial Summary

Total Giving: $3,362,000 (2001); $3,143,000 (2000); $2,804,000 (1999)
Assets: $63,364,979 (2001); $69,923,368 (2000); $66,716,217 (1999)
Gifts Received: $1,124,456 (1992)

Typical Recipients

Arts & Humanities: Libraries, Music, Opera, Public Broadcasting
Civic & Public Affairs: African American Affairs, Botanical Gardens/Parks, Business/Free Enterprise, Civic & Public Affairs-General, Parades/Festivals
Education: Afterschool/Enrichment Programs, Colleges & Universities, Continuing Education, Education Funds, Education Reform, Faculty Development, Private Education (Precollege)
Environment: Wildlife Protection
Health: AIDS/HIV, Arthritis, Diabetes, Emergency/Ambulance Services, Health Organizations, Hospitals, Long-Term Care, Medical Research, Single-Disease Health Associations
International: Health Care/Hospitals
Religion: Religious Organizations, Religious Welfare
Science: Scientific Centers & Institutes
Social Services: Community Service Organizations, Crime Prevention, Family Planning, Senior Services, Youth Organizations

Application Procedures

Initial Contact: Send a brief letter of inquiry and a full proposal.
Deadlines: None.

Restrictions

Grants are made to organizations listed under section 501(c)(3) of the IRS code. Grants are not made to individuals.

Foundation Officials

Betty Wold Johnson: chairman
Robert Wood Johnson, IV: president, director
Robert J. Mortimer: vice president, secretary

Grants Analysis

Disclosure Period: calendar year ending 2001
Total Grants: $3,362,000
Number of Grants: 9
Average Grant: $196,250*
Highest Grant: $1,792,000
Lowest Grant: $20,000
Typical Range: $75,000 to $500,000
*Note: Average grant figure excludes highest grant.

Recent Grants

Note: Grants derived from 2001 Form 990.

General

1,792,000	Special Alliance for Lupus Research, Inc.
500,000	Robin Hood Foundation, New York, NY
300,000	Central Park Conservancy, New York, NY
300,000	Juvenile Diabetes Foundation International, New York, NY
200,000	University of Wisconsin Foundation, Madison, WI
125,000	Princeton Day School, Princeton, NJ
75,000	Opera Festival of New York, New York, NY
50,000	Best Friends Foundation, Washington, DC
20,000	New York City Police Foundation, Inc., New York, NY

EDWARD C. JOHNSON FUND

Giving Contact

Anne-Marie Soulliere, Foundation Director
Fidelity Investments
82 Devonshire Street, S3
Boston, MA 02109
Phone: (617)563-6806
Web: http://www.fidelityfoundation.org

Description

Founded: 1964
EIN: 046108344
Organization Type: Family Foundation
Giving Locations: New England.
Grant Types: Capital, Endowment, Project.

Donor Information

Founder: The fund was established in 1964 by Edward C. Johnson III and the late Edward C. Johnson II .

Financial Summary

Total Giving: $20,987,524 (2001); $20,272,028 (2000); $11,993,500 (1999)
Giving Analysis: Giving for 1998 includes: international subsidiaries ($432,464) foundation ($7,918,563)
Assets: $280,101,038 (2001); $654,898,858 (1999); $23,012,292 (1998)
Gifts Received: $1,637,361 (2001); $7,089,866 (1999); $1,841,853 (1998). Note: In 2001, contributions were received from Fidelity Investors ($242,093), FMR Corp. ($749,911), the Edward C. Johnson II Charitable Lead Trust ($308,001), the Edward C. Johnson III Charitable Lead Trust ($313,200), and Abel Partners ($23,716). In 1999, contributions were received from the Edward C. Johnson II Charitable Lead Trust ($621,201) and FMR Corp. ($6,468,665). In 1998, contributions were received from the Edward C. Johnson III and Edward C. Johnson II Charitable Lead Trusts.

Typical Recipients

Arts & Humanities: Art History, Arts Associations & Councils, Ethnic & Folk Arts, Film & Video, Arts & Humanities-General, Historic Preservation, History & Archaeology, Libraries, Museums/Galleries, Music, Opera
Civic & Public Affairs: Botanical Gardens/Parks, Clubs, Economic Development, Economic Policy, Civic & Public Affairs-General, Municipalities/Towns, Native American Affairs, Parades/Festivals, Philanthropic Organizations, Public Policy, Urban & Community Affairs
Education: Arts/Humanities Education, Business Education, Colleges & Universities, Education-General, International Studies, Leadership Training, Medical Education, Private Education (Precollege), Public Education (Precollege), Science/Mathematics Education, Vocational & Technical Education
Environment: Environment-General, Resource Conservation
Health: Alzheimers Disease, Cancer, Clinics/Medical Centers, Emergency/Ambulance Services, Eyes/Blindness, Health Organizations, Home-Care Services, Hospitals, Medical Research, Mental Health, Nursing Services, Preventive Medicine/Wellness Organizations, Single-Disease Health Associations
International: Foreign Arts Organizations, Foreign Educational Institutions, Health Care/Hospitals, International Environmental Issues, International Organizations
Religion: Churches, Religious Organizations, Religious Welfare
Science: Science Museums, Scientific Centers & Institutes, Scientific Labs, Scientific Research
Social Services: Animal Protection, Camps, Child Welfare, Community Centers, Community Service Organizations, Family Services, Recreation & Athletics, Senior Services, Shelters/Homelessness, Social Services-General, YMCA/YWCA/YMHA/YWHA

Application Procedures

Initial Contact: Contact the fund for a summary of request form.
Application Requirements: A full application is made in a letter of request with supporting materials including the following: an organizational history and the organization's objectives; current audited financial statements; a project budget; a list of officers and directors; an IRS 501(c)(3) determination letter; reports on previous Edward C. Johnson Fund grants; and a brief development summary, including a list of other foundations and corporations receiving proposals.
Deadlines: Applications should be received by March 30 or October 30.
Review Process: Applications are considered in June or December, respectively.

Restrictions

The fund does not make multiyear pledges and does not normally award grants to any organization in successive years. No grants are made to individuals or for scholarships.
Applicants to the Edward C. Johnson Fund may not submit proposals simultaneously to the Fidelity Foundation, nor to the Fidelity Non-Profit Management Foundation.

Additional Information

Publications: Application Guidelines; Summary of Request Form

Foundation Officials

Donald E. Alhart: treasurer
Patricia R. Harley: secretary
Abigail P. Johnson: trustee B 1961. PRIM CORP EMPL executive vice president: Fidelity Investments.
Edward Crosby Johnson, IV: trustee
Edward Crosby Johnson, III: trustee B Boston, MA 1930. ED Harvard University AB (1954). PRIM CORP EMPL chairman, president, chief executive officer, director: FMR Corp. ADD CORP EMPL president: Fidelity Government Securities Fund; chairman: Fidelity Management Research Co.; president: Fidelity Management Trust Co.; president: Fidelity Cash Reserve Fund; director: Fidelity Distributors Corp.; chairman: Fidelity Magellan Fund; president: Fidelity Trend Fund OCCUPATION Fidelity Intermediate Bond Fund. NONPR AFFIL director: Center Neurologic Diseases; member: Massachusetts Historical Society; fellow: American Academy of Arts & Sciences; honorary trustee: Boston Museum Fine Arts.
Elizabeth L. Johnson: trustee
Anne-Marie Soulliere: director

Grants Analysis

Disclosure Period: calendar year ending 2000
Total Grants: $20,272,028
Number of Grants: 60
Average Grant: $119,593*
Highest Grant: $7,661,414
Lowest Grant: $500
Typical Range: $10,000 to $50,000 and $75,000 to $250,000
***Note:** Average grant excludes four highest grants ($7,661,414, $2,500,000, $2,500,000, and $1,000,000).

Recent Grants

Note: Grants derived from 2000 Form 990.

General

7,661,414	Peabody Essex Museum, Salem, MA -- acquisition and capital support
2,500,000	Harvard Center for Neurodegeneration and Repair, Boston, MA -- program support
1,935,020	Bermuda Underwater Exploration Institute, Bermuda -- program and capital support
1,000,000	Brookfield Arts Foundation -- capital support
865,000	Barnstable Land Trust, Cotuit, MA -- land acquisition support
786,395	Garrison Forest School, Owings Mills, MD -- campaign support
664,800	Museum of Fine Arts of Boston, Boston, MA -- acquisition support
510,000	Shady Hill School, Cambridge, MA -- capital support
435,500	Smithsonian Institution, New York, NY -- acquisition support
400,000	Alzheimer's Research Forum Foundation -- operating support

JOHNSON & JOHNSON

Company Headquarters

1 Johnson & Johnson Plaza
New Brunswick, NJ 08933
Phone: (732)524-0400
Fax: (732)524-3300
Web: http://www.jnj.com

Company Description

Founded: 1886
Ticker: JNJ
Exchange: NYSE
Revenue: US$36.298 billion (2002)
Profit: US$6.597 billion (2002)
Employees: 108300 (2002)
Fortune Rank: 34, per FORTUNE Magazine's list of 500 Largest U.S. Corporations (2002).
SIC(s): 2676 Sanitary Paper Products, 2834 Pharmaceutical Preparations, 2844 Toilet Preparations, 3842 Surgical Appliances & Supplies.

Operating Locations

Johnson & Johnson (CA--Baldwin Park, Irvine, Los Angeles; CT--Southington; FL--Miami, Tampa; GA--Royston; IL--Chicago, Oak Lawn, Orland Park, Wilmington; MA--Raynham; NJ--New Brunswick, Piscataway, Raritan, Skillman, Tutusville, Warren; NY--Rochester; OH--Cincinnati; PA--Spring House, Westchester; PR; TX--Dallas, Fort Worth, Jacksonville, Sherman)

Nonmonetary Support

Value: $135,000,000 (1999); $125,400,000 (1998)
Type: Cause-related Marketing & Promotion; Donated Products
Note: Product donations at retail value. Co. provides products for medical aid in underdeveloped countries and emergency disaster relief. Co. donates real estate.

Johnson & Johnson Family of Companies Contribution Fund

Giving Contact

Michael J. Bzdak, Director, Corporate Contributions
One Johnson & Johnson Plaza
New Brunswick, NJ 08933
Phone: (732)524-3255
Fax: (732)524-3300
Web: http://www.johnsonandjohnson.com/who_is_jnj/sr_index.html

Alternate Contact

Conrad Person, Manager of International Programs
Note: Contact for arts, volunteerism, and K-12 education.

Description

EIN: 226062811
Organization Type: Corporate Foundation
Giving Locations: internationally; nationally; principally near operating locations and to national organizations.
Grant Types: Emergency, Employee Matching Gifts, General Support, Project.
Note: Employee matching gift ratio: 2 to 1 to education, libraries, and cultural organisation. Maximum $12,500 per employee annually.

Financial Summary

Total Giving: $281,100,000 (2002); $217,600,000 (2000); $188,116,908 (1999). Note: Contributes through corporate direct giving program and foundation.

Giving Analysis: Giving for 1999 includes: foundation matching gifts ($6,216,908); corporate direct giving ($46,900,000); nonmonetary support ($135,000,000); 1998: international subsidiaries (approx $5,000,000); foundation matching gifts ($6,014,416); corporate direct giving (approx $45,800,000) nonmonetary support ($125,400,000)

Assets: $188,218 (2001); $355,770 (1999); $286,062 (1998)

Gifts Received: $7,911,718 (2001); $6,014,416 (1998); $5,170,636 (1997)

Typical Recipients

Arts & Humanities: Arts Centers, Arts Outreach, Community Arts, Dance, Arts & Humanities-General, Libraries, Museums/Galleries, Music, Opera, Performing Arts, Public Broadcasting, Theater

Civic & Public Affairs: Employment/Job Training, Civic & Public Affairs-General, Safety, Women's Affairs

Education: Arts/Humanities Education, Business Education, Colleges & Universities, Community & Junior Colleges, Engineering/Technological Education, Education-General, International Studies, Medical Education, Minority Education, Science/Mathematics Education

Environment: Resource Conservation

Health: Cancer, Clinics/Medical Centers, Diabetes, Geriatric Health, Health Organizations, Hospitals, Hospitals (University Affiliated), Hospitals (University Affiliated), Medical Research, Public Health, Single-Disease Health Associations

International: Health Care/Hospitals

Religion: Jewish Causes, Seminaries

Social Services: At-Risk Youth, People with Disabilities, Shelters/Homelessness, Social Services-General, Substance Abuse, United Funds/United Ways, Youth Organizations

Application Procedures

Initial Contact: Send a brief preliminary letter; organizations in communities where affiliate companies have a presence should direct requests to companies in those locations.

Application Requirements: Include amount requested; statement of purpose for request; organization's mission statement; demonstration that request meets company's guidelines and giving priorities; tax-exempt status; description of purposes and goals; budget for proposed project; and acknowledgment of other forms of support.

Deadlines: None.

Review Process: Staff responds to initial letter, either declining request or requesting full proposal; contributions committee at headquarters determines how most cash donations are allocated and monitors noncash donations; each affiliate company also makes independent judgments about cash support within corporate guidelines (most product and equipment gifts are made at affiliate company level).

Evaluative Criteria: 501(c)(3) status, effect on company's operating communities, method of evaluating project results, competency of organization's management.

Notes: Guidelines are for corporate program. Company cannot return supplemental materials sent with requests.

Restrictions

The company does not consider funding individuals; requests for unrestricted funds; loans; trips or tours; endowments of any kind; advertising for benefit purposes; sectarian and religious organizations that do not serve the general public on a nondenominational basis; capital requests; or political, fraternal, or athletic groups.

Additional Information

Donates up to 5% of Worldwide pre-tax income annually. Requests for specific projects or program support generally receive more favorable attention than proposals for unrestricted funding. Giving program also seek to be proactive in meeting objectives and priorities. Most Johnson & Johnson operating companies conduct separate cash giving programs and use these contributions programs guidelines to make their funding decisions.

The Johnson & Johnson Family of Companies Contribution Fund exists to provide employee matching gifts gifts. Therefore, the Fund does not accept unsolicited requests for funds.

Publications: Annual Report; Giving Guidelines

Corporate Officials

Aldrage B. Cooper: vice president community relationsrc PRIM CORP EMPL vice president community relations: Johnson & Johnson.

Robert W. Croce: group chairman PRIM CORP EMPL group chairman: Johnson & Johnson.

William D. Dearstyne, Jr.: group chairman PRIM CORP EMPL group chairman: Johnson & Johnson.

Ruth C. Edelson: director special projects PRIM CORP EMPL director special projects: Johnson & Johnson.

Roger Seth Fine: vice president, general counsel B Brooklyn, NY 1942. ED Columbia College BA (1963); New York University LLB (1966). PRIM CORP EMPL vice president, general counsel: Johnson & Johnson. NONPR AFFIL director: Robert Wood Johnson University Hospital; trustee: University Medicine Dentistry New Jersey; member: National Center State Courts; member: American Arbitration Association; member: American Bar Association.

Ronald G. Gelbman: chairman diagnostics group

Robert Zalmon Gussin, PhD: vice president science & technology B Pittsburgh, PA 1938. ED Duquesne University BS (1959); Duquesne University MS (1961); University of Michigan PhD (1965). NONPR AFFIL member: American Society Nephrology; member: American Society Pharmacology & Experimental Therapeutics; member: American Society Clinical Pharmacology & Therapeutics; member: American Federation Clinical Research; member: American Heart Association; member: American Academy of Arts & Sciences.

JoAnn Heffernan Heisen: vice president, chief information officer B Washington, DC 1950. ED Syracuse University BA (1972); New York University MBA (1978). PRIM CORP EMPL vice president, chief information officer, controller: Johnson & Johnson. NONPR AFFIL director: Women's First Healthcare; director: Women's Research Education Institute; trustee: Princeton Medical Center; director: Recordings for Blind; director visitors committee: Massachusetts Institute Technology Sloan School Management; director: Maxwell School Citizenship Public Affairs; member: Financial Womens Association. CLUB AFFIL Economic Club New York.

Willard D. Nielsen: vice president public affairs PRIM CORP EMPL vice president public affairs: Johnson & Johnson.

William C. Weldon: chairman, chief executive officer, director B November 26, 1948. ED Quinnipiac College BS (1971). PRIM CORP EMPL chairman, chief executive officer, director: Johnson & Johnson.

Foundation Officials

Michael J. Bzdak: director corporate contributions

Aldrage B. Cooper: member corporate contributions committee (see above)

Paulo F. Costa: member corporate contributions committee B 1950. PRIM CORP EMPL president, director: Janssen Pharmaceutica LP.

William D. Dearstyne, Jr.: member corporate contributions committee (see above)

R. Deyo: president, trustee

Ruth C. Edelson: member corporate contributions committee (see above)

Roger Seth Fine: president (see above)

Ronald G. Gelbman: member corporate contributions committee (see above)

Robert Zalmon Gussin, PhD: member corporate contributions committee (see above)

JoAnn Heffernan Heisen: treasurer (see above)

Helen M. Hughes: director corporate contributions B 1951. PRIM CORP EMPL senior administrator corp. contributions: Johnson & Johnson.

Wendy B. Logan: member corporate contributions committee

Alfred T. Mays: member corporate contributions committee PRIM CORP EMPL senior vice president corporate communication: Johnson & Johnson.

Willard D. Nielsen: member corporate contributions committee (see above)

Gerlad M. Ostrov: member corporate contributions committee

Conrad Person: manager international programs & product giving

Grants Analysis

Disclosure Period: calendar year ending 1999

Total Grants: $6,265,026*

Number of Grants: 1,680 (approx)

Average Grant: $3,729 (approx)

Highest Grant: $160,782

Typical Range: $1,000 to $10,000

*Note: Giving includes matching gifts.

Recent Grants

Note: Grants derived from 2001 Form 990.

General

204,646	Mount Saint Mary's College, Emmitsburg, MD
180,250	Rutgers University Foundation, New Brunswick, NJ
101,370	Messiah College, Grantham, PA
90,480	Pennsylvania State University, University Park, CA
87,106	BAPS Care International, Houston, TX
83,410	Rollins College, Winter Park, FL
78,280	Robert Wood Johnson University Hospital Foundation, New Brunswick, NJ
70,410	Georgetown College, Georgetown, KY
70,396	New Jersey Symphony Orchestra, Newark, NJ
66,800	University of Notre Dame Du Lac, Notre Dame, IN

JOHN ALFRED AND OSCAR JOHNSON MEMORIAL TRUST

Giving Contact

Carole W. Sellstrom, Foundation Coordinator
9-11 E. Fourth St.
PO Box 50
Jamestown, NY 14702
Phone: (716) 484-7190

Description

Founded: 1996
EIN: 166438291
Organization Type: Private Foundation
Giving Locations: NY: Jamestown
Grant Types: General Support.

Financial Summary

Total Giving: $438,104 (fiscal year ending January 31, 2002); $460,092 (fiscal 2001); $490,524 (fiscal 2000)

Giving Analysis: Giving for fiscal 2002 includes: foundation grants to United Way ($1,000); fiscal 2000: foundation grants to United Way ($1,000) fiscal 1999: foundation grants to United Way ($1,000)

Assets: $7,499,286 (fiscal 2002); $9,312,213 (fiscal 2001); $8,856,462 (fiscal 2000)
Gifts Received: $25 (fiscal 2000)

Typical Recipients

Arts & Humanities: Libraries, Music
Civic & Public Affairs: Urban & Community Affairs
Education: Environmental Education, Private Education (Precollege)
Environment: Environment-General
Health: Hospitals, Medical Research, Speech & Hearing
Social Services: Child Welfare, Family Services, Food/Clothing Distribution, Social Services-General, YMCA/YWCA/YMHA/YWHA, Youth Organizations

Application Procedures

Initial Contact: Submit a written request.
Application Requirements: Include a description of project; project budget; recently audited financial statement; proof of tax-exempt status; list of board members and officers and their names and telephone numbers; a report of the organization's public and private funding sources,a nd a copy of the organization's most recent IRS Form 990.
Deadlines: June 1 and December 1.

Restrictions

No grants to individuals.

Additional Information

Trust(s): M&T Trust Co.

Foundation Officials

John L. Sellstrom: co-trustee

Grants Analysis

Disclosure Period: fiscal year ending January 31, 2002
Total Grants: $437,104*
Number of Grants: 19
Average Grant: $12,728*
Highest Grant: $208,000
Lowest Grant: $100
Typical Range: $5,000 to $20,000
*Note: Giving excludes United Way. Average grant excludes highest grant.

Recent Grants

Note: Grants derived from 2001 Form 990.

Library-Related

14,500   James Prendergast Library, Jamestown, NY -- for computer resources and senior services

General

232,000   Salvation Army, Jamestown, NY -- for grant
47,000   Jamestown Center City Development Corporation, Jamestown, NY -- for Ice Arena Project
30,000   Jamestown New York YMCA, Jamestown, NY -- for Camp Scandinavia 2000 Program
23,592   Chautauqua Lake Association, Lakewood, NY -- purchase shore conveyor
14,000   Chautauqua Striders, Chautauqua, NY -- for Lighted Schoolhouse Program
12,000   Jamestown Audubon Society, Jamestown, NY -- for Rural pre-school Program and After School Nature
10,000   National Multiple Sclerosis Society, New York, NY -- for grant
10,000   Roger Tory Peterson Institute, Jamestown, NY -- for gift photographic exhibit
10,000   WBFO/FM 88, Jamestown, NY -- gift to improve area signal
9,000   Chautauqua Institute, Chautauqua, NY -- for underwriting Sunday amphitheater

S.C. JOHNSON & SON

Company Headquarters

Racine, WI
Web: http://www.scjohnsonwax.com

Company Description

Former Name: S.C. Johnson Wax Fun (1998).
Revenue: US$5.895 billion (2002)
Employees: 14000 (2002)
SIC(s): 2841 Soap & Other Detergents, 2842 Polishes & Sanitation Goods, 2844 Toilet Preparations, 2879 Agricultural Chemicals Nec.

Operating Locations

S.C. Johnson & Son (AR--Rogers; CA--Brea; GA--Atlanta; IL--Downers Grove; MD--Columbia, Millersville, Silver Spring; NJ--Hammonton; OH--Cleveland; TX--Dallas, Houston; WA--Issaquah)

Nonmonetary Support

Type: Donated Equipment; Donated Products; Inkind Services; Loaned Executives
Contact: Kari Iselin, Community Relations Administrator

S.C. Johnson Fund

Giving Contact

Colleen Cribari, Program Administrator
S.C. Johnson Fund
1525 Howe Street
Racine, WI 53403
Phone: (262)260-2119
Fax: (262)260-2652
Web: http://www.scjohnson.com/community/

Description

EIN: 396052089
Organization Type: Corporate Foundation
Former Name: S.C. Johnson Wax Fund, Inc. (1998).
Giving Locations: WI: Racine headquarters and operating communities.
Grant Types: Employee Matching Gifts, Fellowship, General Support, Project, Scholarship, Seed Money.
Note: Employee matching gift ratio: 1 to 1 for gifts to education and the United Way.

Financial Summary

Total Giving: $15,014,000 (fiscal year ending June 30, 2002); $15,947,000 (fiscal 2001); $13,946,000 (fiscal 2000). Note: Contributes through corporate direct giving program and foundation.
Giving Analysis: Giving for fiscal 2002 includes: foundation grants to United Way ($10,000); foundation matching gifts ($1,339,726); corporate direct giving (approx $4,879,227); foundation ($8,785,047); fiscal 2001: foundation matching gifts ($1,507,371); foundation ($6,632,654); corporate direct giving (approx $7,806,975); fiscal 2000: foundation scholarships ($486,589); foundation matching gifts ($904,983); foundation ($3,838,183); corporate direct giving (approx $8,716,244);
Assets: $7,781,185 (fiscal 2002); $6,523,783 (fiscal 2001); $6,452,782 (fiscal 2000)
Gifts Received: $11,301,798 (fiscal 2002); $7,992,066 (fiscal 2001); $5,906,676 (fiscal 2000). Note: In 2002, contributions were received from S.C. Johnson & Son and JohnsonDiversey, Inc. In 2001, contributions were received from S.C. Johnson & Son and S.C. Johnson Commercial Markets, Inc. In 2000, contributions were received from S.C. Johnson & Son.

Typical Recipients

Arts & Humanities: Arts Associations & Councils, Arts Centers, Arts Funds, Arts Institutes, Community Arts, Dance, Ethnic & Folk Arts, Arts & Humanities-General, Historic Preservation, History & Archaeology, Libraries, Museums/Galleries, Music, Performing Arts, Public Broadcasting, Theater
Civic & Public Affairs: Botanical Gardens/Parks, Business/Free Enterprise, Civil Rights, Community Foundations, Economic Development, Employment/Job Training, Civic & Public Affairs-General, Hispanic Affairs, Housing, Law & Justice, Minority Business, Municipalities/Towns, Professional & Trade Associations, Public Policy, Safety, Urban & Community Affairs, Women's Affairs, Zoos/Aquariums, Zoos/Aquariums
Education: Arts/Humanities Education, Business Education, Colleges & Universities, Economic Education, Education Associations, Education Funds, Engineering/Technological Education, Education-General, Health & Physical Education, International Exchange, International Studies, Leadership Training, Literacy, Medical Education, Minority Education, Private Education (Precollege), Public Education (Precollege), Religious Education, Science/Mathematics Education, Secondary Education (Private), Secondary Education (Public), Social Sciences Education, Special Education, Student Aid, Vocational & Technical Education
Environment: Air/Water Quality, Environment-General, Resource Conservation, Wildlife Protection
Health: AIDS/HIV, Cancer, Children's Health/Hospitals, Clinics/Medical Centers, Health Organizations, Hospitals, Medical Research, Medical Training, Nutrition, Single-Disease Health Associations
International: International Environmental Issues, International Relations
Religion: Religion-General, Ministries, Religious Welfare
Social Services: Animal Protection, Child Welfare, Community Service Organizations, Crime Rehabilitation, Day Care, Delinquency & Criminal Rehabilitation, Emergency Relief, Family Services, Homes, People with Disabilities, Recreation & Athletics, Scouts, Senior Services, Social Services-General, Substance Abuse, United Funds/United Ways, Veterans, Volunteer Services, YMCA/YWCA/YMHA/YWHA, Youth Organizations

Application Procedures

Initial Contact: Send a brief letter of inquiry.
Application Requirements: Include proof of tax-exempt status, statement of purpose and brief history of the organization, description of overall program, explanation regarding the specific request for support, itemized annual and project budget, copy of most recent audited financial statements, and list of other corporate and foundation donors.
Deadlines: March 1, July 1, and November 1.
Review Process: Process involves four advisory committees in program areas, who make recommendations to the trustees. Proposals are acknowledged upon receipt; if within guidelines and interest of fund, follow-up contact is made by the foundation.
Evaluative Criteria: Project reflects favorably on company's public image; employee involvement; nonduplication or overlap of services and programs provided by organizations already receiving funds or corporate support, either directly or indirectly through united funds; broad support within community; impacts a community where employees live and work. Most S.C. Johnson Fund grants are made to private organizations; contributions to tax-supported organizations are considered only for projects in which the Fund has a specific interest.
Decision Notification: Committees review proposals prior to each board meeting, which are held in February, June, and October. All grant seekers are informed of the board's decision on their applications.

Restrictions

The fund does not support individuals; social, athletic, veterans, labor, or fraternal organizations, or religious institutions. (A program may be considered if it is not restricted to organization members and is available to the community as a whole.) The fund also does not support political actions or lobbying efforts; national health fund drives or national health organizations; or salary or wage support. Fund does not make individual grants to United Way agencies for operating expenses, but will consider major capital requests. The fund should not be the only funding source for an organization. (Sole source funding may be given for special, one-time projects.) Grants are given for one year to discourage dependence of the recipient on this source, with the exception of major capital drives. The fund makes grants only to programs in the United States.

The Johnson Foundation, Inc., an entirely separate institution, operates the Wingspread Conference Center and also receives contributions from S.C. Johnson & Son, Inc. Therefore, the fund generally does not support conferences, workshops, or seminars.

Additional Information

Corporation contributes at least 5% of pre-tax profit to nonprofit organizations.

Publications: Social Responsibility Report; Application Form; Contributions Policy and Guidelines (Pamphlet)

Corporate Officials

James F. DiMarco: senior vice president B 1935. ED University of Minnesota BS (1959); University of Minnesota MA (1964). PRIM CORP EMPL senior vice president: S.C. Johnson & Son.

H. Fisk Johnson: chairman

Samuel Curtis Johnson: chairman emeritus B Racine, WI 1928. ED Cornell University BA (1950); Harvard University MBA (1952). PRIM CORP EMPL chairman emeritus: S.C. Johnson & Son. CORP AFFIL chairman: Johnson Wax Fund; chairman: Johnson Worldwide Associates Inc.; director: Johnson Bank; chairman: Johnson International Inc.; director: H.J. Heinz Co.; director: Deere & Co.; director: ExxonMobil Corp.; director: Cargill Inc. NONPR AFFIL founder, chairman emeritus: Prairie School; regent emeritus: Smithsonian Institute; member national board governors: Nature Conservancy; chairman advisory council: Cornell University Johnson Graduate School Management; trustee emeritus: Mayo Foundation; trustee emeritus: Cornell University; honorary member: Business Council; member: Chi Psi; trustee: American Museum Natural History. CLUB AFFIL University Club; Racine Country Club; America Club; Cornell Club.

William D. Perez: president, chief executive officer, director

Foundation Officials

Richard S. Hutchings: trustee
Jane M. Hutterly: executive vice president
H. Fisk Johnson: trustee (see above)
Samuel Curtis Johnson: chairman emeritus (see above)
Helen P. Johnson-Leipold: trustee
William D. Perez: vice chairman, trustee (see above)
J. Gary Raley: trustee
Thomas J. Reigle: vice president, executive director, secretary
Jeffrey M. Waller: treasurer, trustee
Thomas M. Wierzba: trustee

Grants Analysis

Disclosure Period: fiscal year ending June 30, 2002
Total Grants: $8,785,047*
Number of Grants: 76
Average Grant: $68,281*
Highest Grant: $1,512,500
Typical Range: $5,000 to $50,000

*Note: Giving excludes corporate direct giving; matching gifts; United Way. Average grant figure excludes three highest grants ($3,800,500).

Recent Grants

Note: Grants derived from fiscal 2002 Form 990.

General

1,512,500	Cornell University, Ithaca, NY
1,288,000	Racine Charter One, Inc., Racine, WI
1,000,000	Wustum Museum of Art Association, Racine, WI
450,000	Next Generation Now, Inc., Racine, WI
400,000	Mound Properties, Inc., Racine, WI
346,250	University of Wisconsin Parkside, Kenosha, WI
330,000	Sustainable Racine, Racine, WI
329,800	Citizens Scholarship Foundation of America, St. Peter, MN
292,858	YMCA of Racine, Racine, WI
250,000	Conservation International, Washington, DC

JOHNSTON-HANSON FOUNDATION

Giving Contact

Elizabeth J. Hanson, Chairperson & Secretary-Treasurer
5118 S. Perry St.
Spokane, WA 99223
Phone: (509)448-4708

Description

Founded: 1948
EIN: 943077091
Organization Type: Private Foundation
Giving Locations: CA; FL; ID; KY; NE; RI; WA: Spokane
Grant Types: Endowment, Multiyear/Continuing Support, Scholarship.

Donor Information

Founder: the late Eric Johnston

Financial Summary

Total Giving: $105,000 (2002 approx); $242,650 (2001); $235,120 (2000)
Giving Analysis: Giving for 2002 includes: foundation scholarships (approx $163,000); 2001: foundation scholarships ($128,950); 2000: foundation scholarships ($15,000); foundation scholarships ($124,220);
Assets: $4,739,031 (2001); $5,105,559 (2000); $5,020,698 (1999)

Typical Recipients

Arts & Humanities: Arts Associations & Councils, Ballet, Community Arts, Arts & Humanities-General, Historic Preservation, History & Archaeology, Museums/Galleries, Music, Opera, Performing Arts, Public Broadcasting, Theater
Civic & Public Affairs: Civic & Public Affairs-General, Housing, Urban & Community Affairs
Education: Arts/Humanities Education, Business Education, Colleges & Universities, Education-General, Private Education (Precollege), Religious Education, Secondary Education (Private), Student Aid
Religion: Churches, Dioceses, Religious Organizations, Religious Welfare
Science: Scientific Centers & Institutes
Social Services: Big Brother/Big Sister, Community Service Organizations, Food/Clothing Distribution, People with Disabilities, Scouts, United Funds/United Ways, YMCA/YWCA/YMHA/YWHA, Youth Organizations

Application Procedures

Initial Contact: The foundation has no formal grant application procedure or application form. Submit inquiry by phone or mail.
Application Requirements: Provide a description of organization, amount requested, purpose of funds sought, recently audited financial statement, and proof of tax-exempt status.
Deadlines: None.

Restrictions

Does not support individuals, public institutions, or the medical field. Grants are generally restricted to the Spokane, WA area.

Foundation Officials

Herbert Johnston Butler: director
Victoria Butler Carney: director
Elizabeth J. Hanson: chp, secretary, treasurer
Eric Hanson: director
Fred L. Hanson: vice president
Maage E. LaCounte: director
Scott Lukins: assistant treasurer, assistant secretary
Ann Hanson Scarborough: director
Gil A. Zwetsch: director

Grants Analysis

Disclosure Period: calendar year ending 2001
Total Grants: $113,700*
Number of Grants: 15
Average Grant: $4,580*
Highest Grant: $45,000
Typical Range: $1,000 to $10,000
*Note: Giving excludes Scholarship. Average grant figure excludes highest grant.

Recent Grants

Note: Grants derived from 2001 Form 990.

General

45,000	Museum of Arts and Culture, Miami, FL -- for the auditorium
32,000	Saint Georges School, Newport, RI -- for scholarships
25,000	Gonzaga University, Spokane, WA -- for scholarships
15,000	Habitat for Humanity, Spokane, WA -- to help people build homes and independence
15,000	MIT University -- for scholarships
15,000	Work for Education, Pedacah, KY -- for scholarships
12,950	Gonzaga Preparatory School, Spokane, WA -- for scholarships
10,000	Cathedral and the Arts, Spokane, WA
10,000	Whitworth College, Spokane, WA -- for scholarships
5,000	Cathedral of St. John the Evangelist, Spokane, WA

CYRUS W. AND AMY F. JONES AND BESSIE D. PHELPS FOUNDATION

Giving Contact

Aram H. Tellalian, Jr., President & Treasurer
c/o Tellalian & Tellalian
211 State St.
Bridgeport, CT 06604
Phone: (203)336-5566

Description

EIN: 060943204
Organization Type: Private Foundation
Giving Locations: CT: Bridgeport
Grant Types: General Support, Operating Expenses, Project.

Donor Information

Founder: the late Amy F. Jones

Financial Summary

Total Giving: $210,000 (fiscal year ending September 30, 2001); $237,500 (fiscal 2000); $187,500 (fiscal 1999)

Giving Analysis: Giving for fiscal 2000 includes: foundation scholarships ($2,000)

Assets: $4,862,997 (fiscal 2001); $5,880,275 (fiscal 2000); $5,405,817 (fiscal 1999)

Typical Recipients

Arts & Humanities: Arts Centers, Community Arts, Libraries, Museums/Galleries, Music, Opera, Performing Arts, Public Broadcasting, Theater

Civic & Public Affairs: Ethnic Organizations, Housing, Inner-City Development, Municipalities/Towns, Parades/Festivals, Philanthropic Organizations, Urban & Community Affairs

Education: Colleges & Universities, Education-General, Legal Education, Private Education (Precollege), Public Education (Precollege), Secondary Education (Private), Student Aid, Vocational & Technical Education

Environment: Environment-General

Health: Cancer, Children's Health/Hospitals, Clinics/Medical Centers, Heart, Hospices, Hospitals, Prenatal Health Issues, Research/Studies Institutes, Single-Disease Health Associations

International: International Affairs

Religion: Churches, Religious Welfare

Social Services: Big Brother/Big Sister, Child Welfare, Community Centers, Community Service Organizations, Family Planning, Family Services, Food/Clothing Distribution, People with Disabilities, Senior Services, YMCA/YWCA/YMHA/YWHA, Youth Organizations

Application Procedures

Initial Contact: Send brief letter describing program. Include history, current function, and needs as a tax exempt organization.

Deadlines: None.

Restrictions

Preference is given to local religious organizations.

Foundation Officials

Alexander R. Nestor: vice president, trustee
Aram H. Tellalian, Jr.: president, trustee
Robert S. Tellalian: secretary, trustee

Grants Analysis

Disclosure Period: fiscal year ending September 30, 2001
Total Grants: $210,000
Number of Grants: 44
Average Grant: $4,773
Highest Grant: $20,000
Lowest Grant: $1,000
Typical Range: $1,000 to $10,000

Recent Grants

Note: Grants derived from fiscal 2000 Form 990.

General

30,000	Greater Bridgeport Symphony, Bridgeport, CT -- for operations
20,000	Town of Trumbull, Trumbull, CT -- for community center project
18,000	Sacred Heart University, Fairfield, CT -- for graduate program in occupational therapy
10,000	Bridgeport Hospital Foundation, Bridgeport, CT -- for operations
10,000	Connecticut Grand Opera and Orchestra, Stamford, CT -- for operations
10,000	Goodwill Industries of Western Connecticut, Bridgeport, CT -- for operations
10,000	Olivet Congregational Church, Bridgeport, CT
10,000	St. Vincent's Medical Center Foundation, Bridgeport, CT -- for operations
7,500	American Cancer Society, Fairfield, CT -- for research and education
7,500	Armenian Church of the Holy Ascension, Trumbull, CT -- for operations

DAISY MARQUIS JONES FOUNDATION

Giving Contact

Roger L. Gardner, President & Trustee
1600 South Avenue, Suite 250
Rochester, NY 14620
Phone: (585)461-4950
Fax: (585)461-9752
E-mail: mail@dmjf.org
Web: http://www.dmjf.org

Description

Founded: 1968
EIN: 237000227
Organization Type: General Purpose Foundation
Giving Locations: NY: Monroe County, Yates County
Grant Types: Capital, Challenge, General Support, Matching, Project, Seed Money.

Donor Information

Founder: "The Daisy Marquis Jones Foundation is a not-for-profit, private foundation created in 1968 by the late Daisy Marquis Jones . Daisy Marquis Jones was born in Pennsylvania and came to Rochester around 1909. She married Nelson Jones, a Himrod dairy farmer in the 1940s. The years they operated the dairy farm together formed the basis for her special interest in Yates County. She gave her Himrod farmhouse to the fledgling volunteer fire department and continued to support them in building a firehouse and purchasing equipment. After her husband's death in 1961 she returned to Rochester. Daisy was a shrewd investor and an astute businesswoman. She had the admiration and respect of the bankers and brokers of the downtown area, but was little known in the community until after her death in 1971. She left a multi-million dollar estate to the Foundation she had set up three years before her death."

Financial Summary

Total Giving: $3,100,000 (2001); $3,255,855 (2000); $1,792,612 (1998)

Giving Analysis: Giving for 2000 includes: foundation grants to United Way ($10,000); foundation scholarships ($84,500); 1998: international subsidiaries ($15,000); foundation scholarships ($26,000) foundation ($1,751,612)

Assets: $48,000,000 (2001); $62,123,128 (2000); $44,764,658 (1998)

Gifts Received: $650,000 (1998); $3,754,757 (1997); $200,000 (1996). Note: In 1998, the foundation received gifts from Leo M. Lyons, its chairman.

Typical Recipients

Arts & Humanities: Arts Associations & Councils, Arts Outreach, Dance, Arts & Humanities-General, Historic Preservation, History & Archaeology, Libraries, Literary Arts, Museums/Galleries, Music, Opera, Performing Arts, Public Broadcasting, Visual Arts

Civic & Public Affairs: African American Affairs, Botanical Gardens/Parks, Civil Rights, Community Foundations, Economic Development, Employment/Job Training, Gay/Lesbian Issues, Civic & Public Affairs-General, Housing, Law & Justice, Legal Aid, Municipalities/Towns, Native American Affairs, Nonprofit Management, Philanthropic Organizations, Public Policy, Safety, Urban & Community Affairs, Women's Affairs, Zoos/Aquariums

Education: Arts/Humanities Education, Business Education, Colleges & Universities, Community & Junior Colleges, Continuing Education, Education-General, Health & Physical Education, Legal Education, Literacy, Medical Education, Preschool Education, Science/Mathematics Education, Secondary Education (Public), Special Education, Student Aid, Vocational & Technical Education

Environment: Environment-General

Health: Adolescent Health Issues, AIDS/HIV, Alzheimers Disease, Cancer, Children's Health/Hospitals, Clinics/Medical Centers, Emergency/Ambulance Services, Geriatric Health, Health Organizations, Hospices, Hospitals, Hospitals (University Affiliated), Long-Term Care, Medical Rehabilitation, Mental Health, Nursing Services, Nutrition, Outpatient Health Care, Prenatal Health Issues, Preventive Medicine/Wellness Organizations, Public Health, Research/Studies Institutes, Speech & Hearing

International: Foreign Arts Organizations, Health Care/Hospitals

Religion: Churches, Jewish Causes, Religious Organizations, Religious Welfare

Science: Science Museums, Scientific Centers & Institutes, Scientific Organizations

Social Services: Big Brother/Big Sister, Child Welfare, Community Centers, Community Service Organizations, Crime Prevention, Day Care, Delinquency & Criminal Rehabilitation, Domestic Violence, Family Planning, Family Services, Food/Clothing Distribution, Homes, People with Disabilities, Recreation & Athletics, Scouts, Senior Services, Shelters/Homelessness, Substance Abuse, United Funds/United Ways, United Funds/United Ways, Veterans, YMCA/YWCA/YMHA/YWHA, Youth Organizations

Application Procedures

Initial Contact: A short letter of inquiry should be sent to the foundation.

Application Requirements: The letter should describe the project, list the amount requested, and include an intended starting date. If the foundation is interested in the proposal, an application form will be sent. The form should include a detailed program description, work plan, qualifications of staff, itemized program budget, plans for evaluation, and coordination with related organizations and programs.

Deadlines: None. Early submission of requests is encouraged.

Review Process: A decision generally takes two to three months. The board meets monthly, except during July and August, to review proposals.

Restrictions

The foundation does not make grants in the following areas: arts, endowments, local chapters of national health-related organizations, private schools, religious projects, research, scholarships, and projects by or for individuals.

Additional Information

HSBC and M&T Bank, both of Rochester, NY, serve as corporate trustees for the foundation.

Publications: Annual Report; Guidelines

Foundation Officials

Roger L. Gardner: president, trustee
Pearl W. Rubin: trustee
Donald W. Whitney: chairman

Grants Analysis

Disclosure Period: calendar year ending 2000
Total Grants: $3,161,355*
Number of Grants: 72
Average Grant: $43,908
Highest Grant: $200,000
Lowest Grant: $250
Typical Range: $10,000 to $50,000
***Note:** Giving excludes scholarships, United Way,

Recent Grants

Note: Grants derived from 2000 Form 990.

General

200,000	Children's Institute, Livingston, NJ -- help expand the services of Rochester Early Enhancement Project
200,000	Lifespan, Rochester, NY -- increase the availability and accessibility of preventive services
200,000	Rochester Family Resource Network, Rochester, NY -- help relocate the Family Place
150,000	Al Sigl Center for Rehabilitation, Rochester, NY -- support the Gathering of Hearts Partnership campaign
150,000	Lifespan, Rochester, NY -- increase the availability and accessibility of preventive services
150,000	North East Area Development, Rochester, NY -- help renovate a three-story brick building
125,000	Keuka College, Keuka Park, NY -- support the modernization of the current Millspaugh Science Center
100,000	American Red Cross - Rochester Chapter, Rochester, NY -- help relocate Food and Nutrition Service Program
100,000	Children's Institute, Livingston, NJ -- continue to support RECAP
100,000	Foodlink, Rochester, NY -- help renovate and upgrade Foodlink's Shared Harvest Center

FLETCHER JONES FOUNDATION

Giving Contact

Christine W. Sisley, Executive Director
523 W. Sixth Street, Suite 301
Los Angeles, CA 90014
Phone: (213)943-4646
Fax: (213)943-4648
E-mail: chris@fletcherjonesfdn.org

Description

Founded: 1969
EIN: 237030155
Organization Type: General Purpose Foundation
Giving Locations: CA
Grant Types: Award, Challenge, Endowment, Fellowship, Loan, Matching, Scholarship.

Donor Information

Founder: In 1969, the Jones Foundation was established by the will of Fletcher Jones with a bequest of approximately $30 million. Mr. Jones was the co-founder, chairman, and chief executive officer of Computer Services Corporation, a computer software services company. He was a collector of fine art, and possessed a large collection of Impressionist paintings. He also assembled one of the West's preeminent stables of thoroughbred racehorses. Mr. Jones died in 1972 at the age of 41. The first distribution of funds from the Jones estate was given to the foundation in 1977; the final distribution of the estate was made in 1981. The foundation donated its first grants in 1974. In March of 1987, the Jones Foundation was renamed the Fletcher Jones Foundation.

Financial Summary

Total Giving: $7,000,000 (2002 approx); $6,800,000 (2001); $9,986,825 (2000)
Giving Analysis: Giving for 2000 includes: foundation scholarships ($390,000); foundation fellowships ($2,500,000); 1999: foundation scholarships ($310,000); foundation fellowships ($1,115,000); 1998: foundation scholarships ($169,000); foundation fellowships ($986,000)

Assets: $130,000,000 (2002 approx); $152,000,000 (2001); $164,458,913 (2000)

Typical Recipients

Arts & Humanities: Arts Institutes, Arts Outreach, Ballet, Arts & Humanities-General, History & Archaeology, Libraries, Museums/Galleries, Music, Opera, Performing Arts, Public Broadcasting
Civic & Public Affairs: Botanical Gardens/Parks, Community Foundations, Civic & Public Affairs-General, Law & Justice, Legal Aid, Professional & Trade Associations, Public Policy, Zoos/Aquariums
Education: Afterschool/Enrichment Programs, Arts/Humanities Education, Business Education, Colleges & Universities, Continuing Education, Education Funds, Engineering/Technological Education, Faculty Development, Education-General, International Studies, Leadership Training, Legal Education, Private Education (Precollege), Public Education (Precollege), Religious Education, Science/Mathematics Education, Secondary Education (Private), Social Sciences Education, Special Education, Student Aid, Vocational & Technical Education
Environment: Environment-General, Wildlife Protection
Health: Children's Health/Hospitals, Clinics/Medical Centers, Eyes/Blindness, Health-General, Health Organizations, Hospices, Hospitals, Medical Research, Nursing Services, Public Health, Research/Studies Institutes, Single-Disease Health Associations
International: International Affairs, International Development, International Peace & Security Issues, International Relations, International Relief Efforts
Religion: Religious Welfare
Science: Science Museums, Scientific Centers & Institutes, Scientific Research
Social Services: Child Welfare, Day Care, Domestic Violence, Food/Clothing Distribution, Homes, People with Disabilities, Recreation & Athletics, Scouts, Volunteer Services, Youth Organizations

Application Procedures

Initial Contact: The foundation urges organizations to read the application guidelines carefully to ensure that only qualified applicants apply. Organizations may submit a short "test letter" to the foundation before preparing a formal grant application. There is no special grant application format.
Application Requirements: For a full proposal, include a fact sheet summarizing significant statistics and background information about the organization's qualifications, objectives, current programs and services, sources of support, purpose, goals, expense budget, funding, and method of evaluation, and include most recent financial report, proof of nonprofit status, most recent IRS Form 990, list of officers with professional affiliations, and most recent annual report. Also include the name, address, and telephone number of the organization's attorney. A short cover letter summarizing the request should accompany the proposal. The foundation requests that proposals be typewritten on 8 1/2 x 11 white paper, and places no limit on the number of attachments.
Deadlines: None.
Review Process: Each test letter will be acknowledged with either a denial or an invitation to submit a formal application.
Decision Notification: Grant decisions are made once in each calendar quarter.

Restrictions

Grants are not made to individuals, political candidates; projects which are financed by government agencies, or K-12 schools; or for deficit financing, operating funds, contingencies; conferences, seminars, or workshops; travel exhibits or surveys; elections, campaigns, voter registration, or propaganda.

Additional Information

Publications: Annual Report

Foundation Officials

Samuel P. Bell: vice president, trustee
Robert F. Erburu: vice president, trustee B Ventura, CA 1930. ED University of Southern California BA (1952); Harvard University JD (1955). PRIM CORP EMPL director: The Times Mirror Co. CORP AFFIL director: Marsh & McLennan Companies Inc.; director: Tejon Ranch Co.; director: Cox Communications Inc. NONPR AFFIL chairman board trustee: H.E. Huntington Library Art Gallery; life director: Independent Colleges Southern California; member: American Bar Association.
Houston I. Flournoy: vice president B New York, NY 1929. ED Cornell University BA (1950); Princeton University MA (1952); Princeton University PhD (1956). CORP AFFIL director: Tosco Refining Co.; director: Tosco Corp.; director: Tosco Marketing Co.; director: Lockheed Martin Corp.; director: Lockheed Martin Financial Corp.; director: Fremont General Corp.; director: LFC. NONPR AFFIL special assistant president government affairs: University Southern California Sacramento.
Robert W. Kummer, Jr.: vice president, trustee B Pittsburgh, PA 1936. ED Oberlin College (1958); University of California (1960). PRIM CORP EMPL chairman, chief executive officer: First Business Bank. CORP AFFIL chairman, chief executive officer: First Business Corp.; chairman: Mellon First Business Corp.
Michael McKee: director
John Phleger Pollock: president B Sacramento, CA April 28, 1920. ED Stanford University AB (1942); Harvard University JD (1948). PRIM CORP EMPL officer counsel: Rodi, Pollock, Pettker, Galbraith & Phillips. NONPR AFFIL trustee: Good Hope Medicine Foundation; member: Los Angeles County Bar Association; member: American Bar Association; active: Boy Scouts America.
Dickinson C. Ross: vice president, trustee B Los Angeles, CA 1923. ED University of Southern California (1947). CORP AFFIL director: Westmark Realty Advisors; director: Xybernet Inc.; director: Assoc Travel Corp.; director: Fremont General Corp.
John W. Smythe: executive director, treasurer B 1925.

Grants Analysis

Disclosure Period: calendar year ending 2000
Total Grants: $7,096,825*
Number of Grants: 66
Average Grant: $65,029*
Highest Grant: $1,000,000
Typical Range: $200,000 to $500,000 and $2,000 to $10,000
*Note: Giving excludes scholarships and fellowships. Average grant figure excludes three highest grants ($3,000,000).

Recent Grants

Note: Grants derived from 2000 Form 990.

Library-Related

50,000	Huntington Library, Huntington, CA -- William Morris Collection

General

2,000,000	University of California, Oakland, CA -- graduate fellowship fund
1,000,000	Claremont Graduate University, Claremont, CA -- information science scholars
1,000,000	Stanford University, Stanford, CA -- memorial grant Rudy Munzer Business Center
1,000,000	University of Southern California, Los Angeles, CA -- scientific research

791,000	University of San Francisco, San Francisco, CA -- lab equipment
525,825	Dominican College, Orangeburg, NY -- technology
500,000	Azusa Pacific University, Azusa, CA -- technology and teacher education
500,000	Keck Graduate Institute, Claremont, CA -- fund staffing
500,000	University of Southern California, Los Angeles, CA -- Graduate Fellowship Program
400,000	Biola University, La Mirada, CA -- technology

HARVEY AND BERNICE JONES FOUNDATION

Giving Contact

Al Stehben
P.O. Box 2035
Springdale, AR 72765
Phone: (501)756-8090
Fax: (501)750-7444
Web: http://www.free-4u.com/
harvey_and_bernice_jones_foundation.htm

Description

Founded: 1956
EIN: 716057141
Organization Type: Private Foundation
Giving Locations: AR: Springdale
Grant Types: General Support, Scholarship.

Donor Information

Founder: Harvey Jones, Mrs. Harvey Jones, and their related companies

Financial Summary

Total Giving: $358,481 (fiscal year ending November 30, 1999); $9,156,738 (fiscal 1998); $1,390,766 (fiscal 1996)
Giving Analysis: Giving for fiscal 1999 includes: foundation grants to United Way ($10,000) foundation scholarships ($50,000)
Assets: $16,108,318 (fiscal 1998); $6,924,139 (fiscal 1996); $6,919,628 (fiscal 1994)
Gifts Received: $5,000 (fiscal 1994)

Typical Recipients

Arts & Humanities: Arts Centers, Libraries, Public Broadcasting
Civic & Public Affairs: Employment/Job Training, Civic & Public Affairs-General, Municipalities/Towns, Nonprofit Management, Safety
Education: Agricultural Education, Colleges & Universities, Engineering/Technological Education, Education-General, Private Education (Precollege), Public Education (Precollege), Religious Education, School Volunteerism, Student Aid
Health: AIDS/HIV, Alzheimers Disease, Eyes/Blindness, Health-General, Health Organizations, Heart, Multiple Sclerosis, Research/Studies Institutes, Single-Disease Health Associations
International: Missionary/Religious Activities
Religion: Churches, Ministries, Religious Organizations, Religious Welfare
Science: Scientific Centers & Institutes
Social Services: Child Welfare, Community Service Organizations, Community Service Organizations, Counseling, Day Care, Family Services, Food/Clothing Distribution, Homes, People with Disabilities, Recreation & Athletics, Senior Services, United Funds/United Ways, Youth Organizations

Application Procedures

Initial Contact: Send a brief letter of inquiry.
Deadlines: None.
Review Process: Board meets November 30.

Foundation Officials

Herbert G. Frost, Jr.: director B Little Rock, AR 1931. ED University of Arkansas (1952). PRIM CORP EMPL vice president: American Fuel Cell & Coated Fabrics Co. CORP AFFIL president, director: Jack Frost Management Co.nsult.
Bernice Jones: director
Hugh Means: director
Gene Thompson: director
William Walker: director

Grants Analysis

Disclosure Period: fiscal year ending November 30, 2000
Total Grants: $0*
*Note: No grants were awarded in 2000.

Recent Grants

Note: Grants derived from fiscal 1999 Form 990.

General

138,481	UAP Aging with Independence
50,000	Arkansas Baptist Boys Ranch, Harrison, AR
50,000	Arkansas Single Parent Scholarship Fund, Fayetteville, AR
50,000	Kids for Health
20,000	Salvation Army, Denver, CO
15,000	Educational Services for the Visually Impaired
10,000	Arkansas Midwives School and Services, AR
10,000	Community Marriage Policy
10,000	United Way of Washington County, Hagerstown, MD
3,000	Arkansas Athletes Outreach, Inc, AR

HELEN JONES FOUNDATION

Giving Contact

Louise Arnold, President & Director
4603 92nd St.
Lubbock, TX 79424
Phone: (806)794-8078

Description

Founded: 1984
EIN: 751977748
Organization Type: Private Foundation
Giving Locations: TX: Lubbock
Grant Types: General Support, Operating Expenses, Scholarship.

Donor Information

Founder: Helen DeVitt Jones

Financial Summary

Total Giving: $4,354,550 (2001); $3,891,500 (2000); $740,500 (1999)
Giving Analysis: Giving for 2001 includes: foundation grants to United Way ($30,000) 2000: foundation grants to United Way ($20,000)
Assets: $89,222,932 (2001); $95,815,138 (2000); $101,372,924 (1999)

Typical Recipients

Arts & Humanities: Arts Associations & Councils, Arts Centers, Ballet, Ethnic & Folk Arts, Historic Preservation, History & Archaeology, Libraries, Museums/Galleries, Music, Public Broadcasting, Theater

Civic & Public Affairs: Clubs, Civic & Public Affairs-General, Housing, Philanthropic Organizations
Education: Agricultural Education, Arts/Humanities Education, Colleges & Universities, Education Reform, Elementary Education (Private), Engineering/Technological Education, Journalism/Media Education, Preschool Education, Public Education (Precollege), Science/Mathematics Education, Secondary Education (Public), Social Sciences Education, Student Aid
Environment: Environment-General
Health: Alzheimers Disease, Hospitals, Medical Research
International: International Relations
Religion: Churches, Religious Welfare
Science: Science Museums, Scientific Centers & Institutes, Scientific Organizations
Social Services: Child Welfare, Community Service Organizations, Food/Clothing Distribution, Homes, People with Disabilities, Scouts, Shelters/Homelessness, Social Services-General, Substance Abuse, United Funds/United Ways, YMCA/YWCA/YMHA/YWHA, Youth Organizations

Application Procedures

Initial Contact: Send a brief letter of inquiry.
Application Requirements: Include amount requested and purpose of funds sought.
Deadlines: None.

Restrictions

Does not support individuals. Grantmaking is generally restricted to the Lubbock, TX area.

Foundation Officials

James C. Arnold: vice president
Louise Willson Arnold: president, executive secretary, director
Robert Neff Arnold: vice president, secretary, director
Helen DeVitt Jones: director
Marianna Markham: director
L. Edwin Smith: treasurer, director
Randy L. Wright: treasurer

Grants Analysis

Disclosure Period: calendar year ending 2001
Total Grants: $4,324,550*
Number of Grants: 65
Average Grant: $21,364*
Highest Grant: $1,000,000
Lowest Grant: $500
Typical Range: $15,000 to $50,000
*Note: Giving excludes United Way. Average grant figure excludes three highest grants ($3,000,000).

Recent Grants

Note: Grants derived from 2001 Form 990.

General

1,000,000	Museum of Texas Tech University, Lubbock, TX -- Curator of Art
1,000,000	Texas Tech University College of Education, Lubbock, TX
1,000,000	Texas Tech University, College of Human Sciences, Lubbock, TX
103,000	O.L. Slaton Junior High School, LISD, Lubbock, TX
100,000	San Angelo Museum of Fine Arts, San Angelo, TX
67,000	Ballet Lubbock, Lubbock, TX
62,500	Lubbock Regional Arts Center, Lubbock, TX
61,000	Museum Association of Texas Tech University, Lubbock, TX
57,000	Museum of Texas Tech University, Lubbock, TX
54,000	Lubbock Women's Club, Lubbock, TX

MARY RANKEN JORDAN AND ETTIE A. JORDAN CHARITABLE FOUNDATION

Giving Contact

Fred E. Arnold, Chairman, Advisory Committee
1 US BankPlaza, Suite 3500
St. Louis, MO 63101
Phone: (314)552-6000
Fax: (314)552-7000
E-mail: farnold@thompsoncoburn.com

Description

Founded: 1958
EIN: 436020554
Organization Type: General Purpose Foundation
Giving Locations: MO: emphasis on St. Louis area
Grant Types: Capital, Endowment, General Support.

Donor Information

Founder: Established in 1957 by the late Mary Ranken Jordan and Ettie A. Jordan.

Financial Summary

Total Giving: $1,100,000 (2003 approx); $1,236,120 (2002); $1,300,714 (2001 approx)
Giving Analysis: Giving for 1998 includes: foundation scholarships ($2,500) foundation grants to United Way ($10,000)
Assets: $23,431,233 (2001); $26,014,273 (2000); $26,867,220 (1999)
Gifts Received: $10,000 (1996)

Typical Recipients

Arts & Humanities: Arts Associations & Councils, Arts Centers, Arts Funds, Arts Outreach, Dance, Ethnic & Folk Arts, Arts & Humanities-General, Historic Preservation, History & Archaeology, Libraries, Literary Arts, Museums/Galleries, Music, Opera, Performing Arts, Public Broadcasting, Theater
Civic & Public Affairs: Botanical Gardens/Parks, Clubs, Employment/Job Training, Civic & Public Affairs-General, Hispanic Affairs, Urban & Community Affairs, Zoos/Aquariums
Education: Arts/Humanities Education, Colleges & Universities, Medical Education, Private Education (Precollege), Secondary Education (Private), Secondary Education (Public), Special Education, Vocational & Technical Education
Health: Children's Health/Hospitals, Clinics/Medical Centers, Clinics/Medical Centers, Diabetes, Emergency/Ambulance Services, Hospitals, Mental Health, Respiratory
International: International Relations
Religion: Churches, Jewish Causes, Ministries, Religious Welfare
Science: Scientific Centers & Institutes, Scientific Organizations
Social Services: Animal Protection, At-Risk Youth, Child Welfare, Community Centers, Community Service Organizations, Day Care, Family Services, Food/Clothing Distribution, Homes, People with Disabilities, Scouts, United Funds/United Ways, Volunteer Services, YMCA/YWCA/YMHA/YWHA, Youth Organizations

Application Procedures

Initial Contact: The foundation requests that applications be made in writing and that three copies be furnished.
Deadlines: December 31.
Review Process: Grants are made annually in the spring.

Restrictions

Grants are not made to individuals. The foundation makes grants only to charitable organizations.

Additional Information

The foundation lists the Mercantile Trust Co. NA as a corporate trustee.

Foundation Officials

Fred E. Arnold: chairman advisory committee B Mexico 1930. ED Harvard University AB (1960); Harvard University AB (1963). PRIM CORP EMPL partner: Thompson Coburn. NONPR AFFIL member board curators: Ctrl Meth College; member: Missouri Bar Association; member: American College Real Estate Lawyers; member: American Bar Association. CLUB AFFIL Racquet Club; Noonday Club.
W. Stanley Walch: mem adv comm B Sedalia, MO 1934. ED Kenyon College AB (1956); University of Michigan JD (1959). PRIM CORP EMPL partner: Thompson & Mitchell. CORP AFFIL director: Precision Stainless Co.; director: Orion Capital Corp.; director: Central Street Diversified Corp.; director: Morgan-Wrightmann Supply Co. NONPR AFFIL member: Saint Louis Bar Association; member campaign committee: United Way Saint Louis; member: Missouri Bar Association; member: American Law Institute; director: Downtown Saint Louis Inc.; member: American Bar Association; member: Algonquin Chamber of Commerce. CLUB AFFIL Noonday Club.
W. David Wells: mem adv comm

Grants Analysis

Disclosure Period: calendar year ending 2001
Total Grants: $1,300,714
Number of Grants: 79
Average Grant: $16,465
Highest Grant: $100,000
Lowest Grant: $800
Typical Range: $5,000 to $60,000
Note: Grants analysis provided by foundation.

Recent Grants

Note: Grants derived from 2000 Form 990.

General

75,000	Missouri Botanical Garden, St. Louis, MO
75,000	Washington University, St. Louis, MO
60,000	Ranken Jordan Home for Convalescent Crippled Children, St. Louis, MO
55,000	Ranken Technical College, St. Louis, MO
50,000	Central Institute for the Deaf, St. Louis, MO
50,000	Forest Park Forever, St. Louis, MO
50,000	Missouri Historical Society, St. Louis, MO
50,000	St. Louis Symphony Orchestra, St. Louis, MO
50,000	St. Louis Zoo, St. Louis, MO
30,000	Sheldon Arts Foundation, St. Louis, MO

JOSLIN-NEEDHAM FAMILY FOUNDATION

Giving Contact

Judy Gunnon
PO Box 324
Brush, CO 80723
Phone: (970)842-5101
Fax: (970)842-5105

Description

EIN: 846038670
Organization Type: Private Foundation
Giving Locations: CO: Brush
Grant Types: General Support.

Donor Information

Founder: the late Gladys Joslin

Financial Summary

Total Giving: $272,356 (2001); $278,541 (2000); $298,926 (1999)
Giving Analysis: Giving for 2001 includes: foundation grants to United Way ($2,000) 2000: foundation grants to United Way ($2,000)
Assets: $5,240,307 (2001); $5,684,852 (2000); $5,757,737 (1999)

Typical Recipients

Arts & Humanities: Libraries
Civic & Public Affairs: Clubs, Civic & Public Affairs-General, Municipalities/Towns, Parades/Festivals, Safety, Urban & Community Affairs
Education: Afterschool/Enrichment Programs, Agricultural Education, Public Education (Precollege), Secondary Education (Public)
Health: Clinics/Medical Centers, Emergency/Ambulance Services, Health Organizations, Hospitals, Long-Term Care
Religion: Churches, Ministries, Religious Organizations, Religious Welfare
Social Services: Camps, Community Service Organizations, Food/Clothing Distribution, Recreation & Athletics, Scouts, United Funds/United Ways, Volunteer Services, Youth Organizations

Application Procedures

Initial Contact: Send a brief letter of inquiry describing need and any pertinent information.
Deadlines: None.

Restrictions

Grantmaking is limited to the Brush, CO area.

Additional Information

Trust(s): Farmers State Bank

Foundation Officials

Robert V. Hansen: director
Robert Petteys: director

Grants Analysis

Disclosure Period: calendar year ending 2001
Total Grants: $270,356*
Number of Grants: 10
Average Grant: $27,036
Highest Grant: $60,000
Lowest Grant: $300
Typical Range: $5,000 to $60,000
***Note:** Giving excludes United Way.

Recent Grants

Note: Grants derived from 2001 Form 990.

Library-Related

43,800	East Morgan County Library, Brush, CO

General

60,000	East Morgan County Hospital Foundation, Brush, CO -- for challenge campaign
58,700	City of Brush, Brush, CO -- for recreation
57,046	Eben Ezer Lutheran Care Center, Brush, CO
39,650	East Morgan County Hospital Foundation, Brush, CO -- equipment
5,000	Brush High School, Brush, CO -- grants, summer workshops
3,000	Brush Area Churches, Brush, CO
3,000	Brush Boy Scout Troop 28, Brush, CO
2,260	Northeastern County Transportation Authority, Ft. Morgan, CO -- for van trip
2,000	Morgan County United Way, Ft. Morgan, CO -- 2001 campaign donation
600	Brush Girl Scouts, Brush, CO

JOSTENS, INC.

Company Headquarters
Minneapolis, MN
Web: http://www.jostens.com

Company Description
Founded: 1897
Ticker: JOSEA
Exchange: OTC
Revenue: US$756 million (2002)
Employees: 6100 (2002)
SIC(s): 2389 Apparel & Accessories Nec, 2741 Miscellaneous Publishing, 2752 Commercial Printing--Lithographic, 3911 Jewelry & Precious Metal.

Operating Locations
Jostens, Inc. (CA--Porterville, Visalia; IL--Princeton; KS--Topeka; MN--Burnsville, Owatonna, Red Wing; NY--Webster; PA--State College; SC--Laurens; TN--Clarksville, Shelbyville; TX--Denton)

Nonmonetary Support
Value: $40,000 (2001)
Type: Donated Products; In-kind Services
Note: Co. provides nonmonetary support.

The Jostens Foundation Inc.

Giving Contact
Lynda Michielutti, Executive Director
5501 Norman Center Dr.
Minneapolis, MN 55437
Phone: (612)830-8461
Fax: (612)897-4116
Web: http://www.jostens.com

Alternate Contact
Phone: (612)830-3229

Description
EIN: 411280587
Organization Type: Corporate Foundation
Giving Locations: principally near operating locations and to national organizations.
Grant Types: Emergency, Employee Matching Gifts, General Support, Multiyear/Continuing Support, Project.

Financial Summary
Total Giving: $500,000 (2002 approx); $489,875 (2001); $422,211 (2000). Note: Contributes through corporate direct giving program and foundation.
Giving Analysis: Giving for 2002 includes: foundation (approx $500,000); 2001: foundation (approx $500,000); 2000: corporate grants to United Way ($60,000); corporate matching gifts ($70,526); foundation ($269,850);
Assets: $399,875 (2001); $479,297 (2000); $380,650 (1998)
Gifts Received: $500,000 (2001); $500,000 (2000); $500,000 (1998). Note: Contributions made by Jostens, Inc.

Typical Recipients
Arts & Humanities: Arts Associations & Councils, Arts Centers, Arts Institutes, Dance, Ethnic & Folk Arts, Arts & Humanities-General, History & Archaeology, Libraries, Museums/Galleries, Music, Opera, Performing Arts, Public Broadcasting, Theater
Civic & Public Affairs: Asian American Affairs, Business/Free Enterprise, Community Foundations, Economic Development, Employment/Job Training, Civic & Public Affairs-General, Housing, Legal Aid, Nonprofit Management, Public Policy, Urban & Community Affairs, Women's Affairs, Zoos/Aquariums

Education: Arts/Humanities Education, Business Education, Colleges & Universities, Economic Education, Education Associations, Education Funds, Education Reform, Education Reform, Engineering/Technological Education, Education-General, Gifted & Talented Programs, International Studies, Leadership Training, Literacy, Medical Education, Minority Education, Private Education (Precollege), Public Education (Precollege), Science/Mathematics Education, Secondary Education (Public), Student Aid, Vocational & Technical Education
Environment: Environment-General
Health: AIDS/HIV, Arthritis, Cancer, Children's Health/Hospitals, Clinics/Medical Centers, Diabetes, Emergency/Ambulance Services, Eyes/Blindness, Health-General, Heart, Hospices, Hospitals, Mental Health, Multiple Sclerosis, Prenatal Health Issues, Public Health, Single-Disease Health Associations, Trauma Treatment
International: Foreign Educational Institutions
Religion: Religion-General, Religious Welfare
Science: Science Museums
Social Services: Animal Protection, At-Risk Youth, Big Brother/Big Sister, Camps, Child Abuse, Child Welfare, Community Centers, Community Service Organizations, Day Care, Family Services, Food/Clothing Distribution, Homes, People with Disabilities, Recreation & Athletics, Scouts, Senior Services, Social Services-General, Special Olympics, Substance Abuse, United Funds/United Ways, YMCA/YWCA/YMHA/YWHA, Youth Organizations

Application Procedures
Initial Contact: Submit a written application.
Application Requirements: Applicants may use the Minnesota Common Grant form or submit an application the includes the following information: Organizational Information, Purpose of Grant, Evaluation, and Financial Information. Organizational Information should include the history, mission and goals of the organization, current programs, activities, service statistics, and accomplishments; the organization's relationship with other organizations that provide similar services; the reason that your organization is appropriate to address the problem; and a list of board members and the number of full- and part-time paid staff and volunteers. The Purpose of Grant section should describe the community need the proposal addresses and how the focus was determined; the specific activities for which funding is sought and who will carry them out; the overall goals and how they will be met; and how the proposed activities will benefit the community, including a long-term plan for sustaining them. Evaluation should state how effectiveness of the activities will be measured and the results that are expected by the end of the funding period. Financial Information must include financial statements from the most recently completed fiscal year, organizational and/or project budget, and proof of tax-exempt status.
Deadlines: None for Jostens Community Grants; March 1 for Jostens Our Town Grants.
Review Process: The board of directors meets quarterly to review applications.
Evaluative Criteria: The foundation gives preference to organizations that provide services in communities where Jostens facilities and employees are located, and to nonprofit organizations that involve Jostens employees.

Restrictions
The foundation does not provide grants to schools or school districts; organizations involved in highly political or controversial issues; churches, religious groups, or programs primarily sponsored by religious organizations; individuals or groups for personal needs or travel expenses; political or lobbying groups; benefit fundraisers or tickets to fundraisers; recognition or testimonial events; fundraising campaigns to eliminate or control specific diseases; fraternal, veterans or professional associations; athletic scholarships

or activities; advertising sponsorships; or endowments.
Foundation gives grants only to 501(c)(3) organizations.

Additional Information
Jostens provides most of its funding through two programs: Jostens Our Town Award and Grant, and Jostens Community Grants.
The Our Town Grant is based on the foundation's current strategic direction. Over a five-year period beginning in 1999, the Foundation will award 10 extraordinary communities with $50,000 grants based on their past successes and future plans within the Search Institute's Healthy Communities-Healthy Youth (HC-HY) and Jostens' Our Town guidelines. Organizations that are currently using the HC-HY model may contact the Search Institute at 800-888-7828 or on the web at www.search-institute.org for more information.
Jostens Community Grants program offers funding to organizations that "enhance the lives of youth and promote educational opportunities that positively impact children from birth through college". Community Grants typically range from $500 to $10,000. Grants for this program should be sent directly to the Jostens Foundation.
Program grants generally made during the current year and not in installments for future years.
In 1987, Jostens organized GIVE employee contributions committees in several operating locations across the country. These committees make charitable grants for special community president within employees' local communities from dollars allocated by the foundation.
Publications: Annual Report; Application Form; Guidelines

Corporate Officials
Robert C. Buhrmaster: president, chief executive officer, chairman B Schenectady, NY 1947. ED Rensselaer Polytechnic Institute BS (1969); Dartmouth College MBA (1974). PRIM CORP EMPL president, chief executive officer, chairman: Jostens, Inc. ADD CORP EMPL president: American Yearbook Co.; president, director: Jostens Photography Inc. CORP AFFIL director: Toro Co.

Grants Analysis
Disclosure Period: calendar year ending 2001
Total Grants: $272,660*
Number of Grants: 49
Average Grant: $5,564
Highest Grant: $45,000
Lowest Grant: $100
Typical Range: $1,000 to $20,000
*Note: Giving excludes matching gifts, scholarship, and United Way.

Recent Grants
Note: Grants derived from 2001 Form 990.

Library-Related

5,000	Hennepin County Library Foundation, Minnetonka, MN

General

45,916	Jostens New York Relief Fund, Minneapolis, MN
45,000	United Way of Minneapolis Area, Minneapolis, MN
20,000	Alternatives, Inc., Chicago, IL
20,000	Essex Chips, Essex Junction, VT
20,000	Family Services of Warren County, North Warren, PA
20,000	Georgetown Project, Georgetown, TX
20,000	Prarie Ridge Addiction Treatment Services, Macon City, IA
20,000	Search Institute, Minneapolis, MN
20,000	Union County Friends of 4H, Creston, IA

20,000   United Way of Columbia Williamette,
          Portland, OR

JOUKOWSKY FAMILY FOUNDATION

Giving Contact
Nina Joukowsky-Koprulu, Director & President
410 Park Avenue, Suite 1610
New York, NY 10022
Phone: (212)355-3151
Fax: (212)355-3147
E-mail: info@joukowsky.org
Web: http://www.joukowsky.org

Description
Founded: 1981
EIN: 133242753
Organization Type: Family Foundation
Former Name: The Joukowsky Foundation.
Giving Locations: U.S. Northeast Region; internationally; nationally.
Grant Types: Award, Capital, Challenge, Conference/Seminar, Department, Endowment, Fellowship, General Support, Matching, Multiyear/Continuing Support, Operating Expenses, Project, Scholarship.

Financial Summary
Total Giving: $11,230,590 (fiscal year ending October 31, 2001); $5,073,048 (fiscal 2000); $4,776,051 (fiscal 1999)
Giving Analysis: Giving for fiscal 2001 includes: foundation fellowships ($9,750); foundation grants to United Way ($45,000); foundation scholarships ($149,297); fiscal 1999: foundation grants to United Way ($35,100); foundation scholarships ($96,504) fiscal 1997: foundation grants to United Way ($36,000)
Assets: $100,892,337 (fiscal 2001); $136,387,716 (fiscal 2000); $101,494,419 (fiscal 1999)
Gifts Received: $387,504 (fiscal 2001); $386,998 (fiscal 2000); $397,275 (fiscal 1999). Note: In fiscal 2001, contributions were received from Artemis W. Joukowsky.

Typical Recipients
Arts & Humanities: Arts Appreciation, Film & Video, Arts & Humanities-General, Historic Preservation, History & Archaeology, Libraries, Museums/Galleries, Music, Opera, Performing Arts, Theater
Civic & Public Affairs: Business/Free Enterprise, Chambers of Commerce, Community Foundations, Economic Development, Economic Policy, Civic & Public Affairs-General, Municipalities/Towns, Professional & Trade Associations, Public Policy, Urban & Community Affairs, Women's Affairs, Zoos/Aquariums
Education: Afterschool/Enrichment Programs, Arts/Humanities Education, Colleges & Universities, Education Funds, Engineering/Technological Education, Education-General, International Exchange, International Studies, Legal Education, Medical Education, Minority Education, Private Education (Precollege), Public Education (Precollege), Science/Mathematics Education, Secondary Education (Private), Student Aid
Environment: Air/Water Quality, Environment-General, Wildlife Protection
Health: Diabetes, Hospices, Hospitals, Medical Rehabilitation, Medical Research, Single-Disease Health Associations
International: Foreign Educational Institutions, International-General, Health Care/Hospitals, Human Rights, International Affairs, International Development, International Organizations, International Peace & Security Issues, International Relations, Missionary/Religious Activities
Religion: Churches, Jewish Causes, Religious Organizations, Religious Welfare, Seminaries

Social Services: Animal Protection, Big Brother/Big Sister, Camps, Community Service Organizations, Domestic Violence, Family Planning, Family Services, Food/Clothing Distribution, Homes, People with Disabilities, Scouts, Social Services-General, United Funds/United Ways, YMCA/YWCA/YMHA/YWHA, Youth Organizations

Application Procedures
Initial Contact: Send a brief letter of inquiry.
Application Requirements: Proposals should not be more than 10 pages in length and should include: a description of organization; information on your key personnel; purpose of funds sought; amount requested; audited financial statement including budget; balance sheet; statement of activities and statement of functional expense (if available); copies of 501(c)(3) determination letter; and current list of board of directors.
Deadlines: None.
Review Process: All requests will be answered by mail.

Restrictions
The foundation does not accept faxed proposals.

Additional Information
Publications: Guidelines

Foundation Officials
Randall G. Drain: director CORP AFFIL secretary: China America Insurance Co. Ltd.
Artemis A. W. Joukowsky: director B Shanghai, People's Republic of China 1930. ED Brown University AB (1955). NONPR AFFIL member: U.S. Chamber of Commerce; member: US-USSR Trade & Economic Council; trustee: Saint Croix Landmark Society; trustee: International Research Exchange Board; trustee: Lawrenceville School; member: Hungarian-American Trade & Economic Council; member advisory committee: Institute International Studies; founder, chairman: Brown University Sports Foundation; member, vice chairman board governors: John Carter Brown Library Association; trustee, vice chancellor: Brown University; chairman: Archaeological Institute America. CLUB AFFIL University Club; Saint Croix Yacht Club; Knickerbocker Club; Larchmont Yacht Club; Hope Club; India House Club; Hong Kong Club; Brown Club; Explorers Club.
Martha Content Joukowsky: director
Emily R. Kessler: executive director
Nina Joukowsky Koprulu: director

Grants Analysis
Disclosure Period: fiscal year ending October 31, 2001
Total Grants: $11,026,543*
Number of Grants: 167
Average Grant: $29,733*
Highest Grant: $4,371,837
Typical Range: $10,000 to $50,000
*Note: Giving excludes scholarships; fellowship, United Way. Average grant figure excludes two highest grants ($6,120,537).

Recent Grants
Note: Grants derived from 2001 Form 990.

General
4,371,837 Brown University, Providence, RI -- for the medical school and Watson Institute
1,748,700 Lawrenceville School, Lawrenceville, NJ -- for Noyes Building Renovation and Dawes House Restoration Project
600,000   Hampshire College, Amherst, MA
400,000   Brown University, Providence, RI -- for the School of Medicine
350,000   Lawrenceville School, Lawrenceville, NJ -- for financial aid
300,000   Families of Spinal Muscular Atrophy, Highland Park, IL

225,000   Gordon School, East Providence, RI -- for library improvement and expansion
200,000   Nightingale Bamford School, New York, NY -- for capital campaign
136,500   Limelight Theatre, St. Augustine, FL
125,000   Families of Spinal Muscular Atrophy, Highland Park, IL

JOURNAL-GAZETTE CO.

Company Headquarters
701 S. Clinton St., Ste. 104
Fort Wayne, IN 46802

Company Description
Employees: 600
SIC(s): 2711 Newspapers.

Journal-Gazette Foundation, Inc.

Giving Contact
Richard G. Inskeep, President
701 South Clinton Street
Ft. Wayne, IN 46802-1883
Phone: (260)424-5257
Fax: (219)426-0949

Description
Founded: 1985
EIN: 311134237
Organization Type: Corporate Foundation
Giving Locations: IN: Northeast Indiana; OH: Northwest Ohio
Grant Types: Capital, Operating Expenses.

Donor Information
Founder: Journal-Gazette Co., Richard G. Inskeep

Financial Summary
Total Giving: $545,782 (2001); $616,157 (2000); $500,000 (1999 approx). Note: Contributes through foundation only.
Giving Analysis: Giving for 2000 includes: foundation grants to United Way ($79,300); foundation ($534,557); 1998: foundation grants to United Way ($82,600); foundation ($560,905); 1997: foundation grants to United Way ($87,276) foundation ($402,837)
Assets: $8,620,941 (2001); $8,928,378 (2000); $8,887,846 (1998)
Gifts Received: $103,281 (2001); $174,334 (2000); $11,250 (1998). Note: in 2001, contributions were received from Richard G. Inskeep ($14,439), Harriet J. Inskeep ($5,164), and Journal Gazette Company ($83,678). In 2000, contributions were received from Journal-Gazette Co. ($122,049); Richard G. and Harriett J. Inskeep ($49,204); and Stephen S. Inskeep ($3,081).In 1998 and 1997, contributions were received from Richard G. Inskeep and Harriett J. Inskeep.

Typical Recipients
Arts & Humanities: Arts Appreciation, Arts Associations & Councils, Arts Funds, Arts Outreach, Historic Preservation, History & Archaeology, Libraries, Museums/Galleries, Music, Performing Arts, Public Broadcasting, Theater
Civic & Public Affairs: African American Affairs, Botanical Gardens/Parks, Business/Free Enterprise, Chambers of Commerce, Clubs, Community Foundations, Employment/Job Training, Civic & Public Affairs-General, Hispanic Affairs, Municipalities/Towns, Parades/Festivals, Public Policy, Rural Affairs, Urban & Community Affairs, Women's Affairs, Zoos/Aquariums

Education: Agricultural Education, Business Education, Colleges & Universities, Continuing Education, Education Associations, Education Funds, Education Funds, Engineering/Technological Education, Education-General, Journalism/Media Education, Literacy, Medical Education, Private Education (Precollege), Public Education (Precollege), Secondary Education (Private), Secondary Education (Public), Special Education, Student Aid
Environment: Air/Water Quality, Environment-General, Resource Conservation
Health: AIDS/HIV, Cancer, Children's Health/Hospitals, Clinics/Medical Centers, Emergency/Ambulance Services, Health-General, Geriatric Health, Health Organizations, Hospices, Hospitals, Kidney, Mental Health, Research/Studies Institutes, Single-Disease Health Associations
Religion: Churches, Jewish Causes, Ministries, Religious Organizations, Religious Welfare
Science: Science Museums, Scientific Centers & Institutes
Social Services: Animal Protection, At-Risk Youth, Camps, Child Abuse, Child Welfare, Community Service Organizations, Crime Prevention, Day Care, Family Planning, Family Services, Food/Clothing Distribution, People with Disabilities, Recreation & Athletics, Scouts, Senior Services, Shelters/Homelessness, Social Services-General, Substance Abuse, United Funds/United Ways, Volunteer Services, YMCA/YWCA/YMHA/YWHA, Youth Organizations

Application Procedures

Initial Contact: Send a brief letter.
Application Requirements: Include the need for financial assistance, timeframe and proof of tax-exempt status.
Deadlines: None.
Decision Notification: Committee meets quarterly.

Restrictions

Recipient organization must be in the general geographic area of northeast Indiana or northwest Ohio and qualify under the IRS code as a 501(c)(3) organization.

Corporate Officials

Richard G. Inskeep: owner, president, public B 1925. PRIM CORP EMPL owner: Journal-Gazette Co.
Craig Klugman: editor B Fargo, ND 1945. PRIM CORP EMPL editor: Journal-Gazette Co. NONPR AFFIL member: American Newspaper Editors.

Foundation Officials

Jerry D. Fox: secretary, treasurer, director B 1952. PRIM CORP EMPL secretary, treasurer, director: Journal-Gazette Co.
Harriet J. Inskeep: director
Richard G. Inskeep: president, director (see above)
Julie Inskeep Walda: director PRIM CORP EMPL vice president, director: Journal-Gazette Co.

Grants Analysis

Disclosure Period: calendar year ending 2001
Total Grants: $446,682*
Number of Grants: 83
Average Grant: $5,382
Highest Grant: $27,000
Lowest Grant: $100
Typical Range: $500 to $16,000
***Note:** Giving excludes United Way.

Recent Grants

Note: Grants derived from 2001 Form 990.

Library-Related

6,000	Allen County Public Library Foundation, Ft. Wayne, IN

General

98,600	United Way Allen County, Inc., Ft. Wayne, IN

27,000	Indiana University Foundation, Bloomington, IN
26,250	Allen County Courthouse Preservation Trust, Ft. Wayne, IN
25,000	YMCA, Ft. Wayne, IN
16,000	IP Foundation
15,400	Turnstone Center for Disabled Children and Adults, Ft. Wayne, IN
15,000	Fort Wayne Park Foundation, Ft. Wayne, IN
15,000	Fort Wayne Park Foundation, Ft. Wayne, IN
14,700	Arts United of Greater Fort Wayne, Ft. Wayne, IN
10,500	YMCA, Ft. Wayne, IN

JOY FAMILY FOUNDATION

Giving Contact

Marsha J. Sullivan, Exec. Dir.
5436 Main St.
Williamsville, NY 14221
Phone: (716)633-6600
E-mail: info@joyfamilyfoundation.org
Web: http://www.joyfamilyfoundation.org

Description

Founded: 1990
EIN: 166335211
Organization Type: Private Foundation
Giving Locations: NY: Erie County, Niagra County
Grant Types: Capital, Department, General Support, Matching.

Donor Information

Founder: Established in 1990 by Paul W. Joy.

Financial Summary

Total Giving: $452,685 (2002); $440,407 (2000); $490,116 (1999)
Giving Analysis: Giving for 2002 includes: foundation grants to United Way ($12,000); 2001: foundation grants to United Way ($10,000); 2000: foundation grants to United Way ($10,000); foundation matching gifts ($59,225);
Assets: $6,733,577 (2000); $7,996,539 (1999); $7,973,199 (1998)
Gifts Received: $29,904 (2002); $43,201 (2000); $115,552 (1998). Note: In 1998, 2000, and 2002 contributions were received from Paul Joy. In 1993, contributions were received from Paul W. Joy ($177,205) and miscellaneous ($4,670).

Typical Recipients

Arts & Humanities: Arts Associations & Councils, Arts Centers, Historic Preservation, Libraries, Music, Public Broadcasting
Civic & Public Affairs: Civic & Public Affairs-General, Housing, Law & Justice, Municipalities/Towns, Urban & Community Affairs, Women's Affairs, Zoos/Aquariums
Education: Afterschool/Enrichment Programs, Arts/Humanities Education, Business Education, Colleges & Universities, Community & Junior Colleges, Faculty Development, Education-General, Leadership Training, Literacy, Private Education (Precollege), Science/Mathematics Education, Secondary Education (Private), Secondary Education (Public), Special Education, Student Aid
Health: Alzheimers Disease, Cancer, Children's Health/Hospitals, Eyes/Blindness, Geriatric Health, Hospices, Hospitals, Medical Research, Nursing Services, Speech & Hearing
Religion: Churches, Religious Organizations, Religious Welfare, Seminaries
Social Services: Animal Protection, At-Risk Youth, Camps, Child Welfare, Community Centers, Community Service Organizations, Counseling, Day Care, Family Services, Food/Clothing Distribution, People

with Disabilities, Recreation & Athletics, Scouts, Substance Abuse, United Funds/United Ways, YMCA/YWCA/YMHA/YWHA, Youth Organizations

Application Procedures

Initial Contact: Request application form.
Deadlines: None.

Additional Information

Publications: Application Form

Foundation Officials

Joan H. Joy: trustee
Paul W. Joy: don, trustee
Stephen T. Joy: trustee
Paula Joy Reinhold: trustee
Marsha Joy Sullivan: trustee

Grants Analysis

Disclosure Period: calendar year ending 2002
Total Grants: $440,685*
Number of Grants: 98
Average Grant: $4,732
Highest Grant: $25,000
Typical Range: $1,000 to $10,000
***Note:** Giving excludes United Way.

Recent Grants

Note: Grants derived from 2002 Form 990.

General

25,000	Bison Fund, Buffalo, NY -- children's scholarship fund
25,000	Burchfield-Penney Art Center, Buffalo, NY -- building campaign
25,000	Catholic Charities of Buffalo New York, Buffalo, NY
25,000	Catholic Charities of Buffalo New York, Buffalo, NY
20,000	Alcohol and Drug Dependency Services Foundation, West Seneca, NY -- addition of two buildings
20,000	Center for Joy, Niagara Falls, MI -- annual support
17,000	Nardin Academy High School, Buffalo, NY -- scholarship
16,000	Foundation of the RC Diocese of Buffalo, Buffalo, NY -- construct a new catholic middle school
15,000	Buffalo Philharmonic Orchestra Society, Buffalo, NY
15,000	Heart and Soul, Inc., Niagara Falls, NY -- building fund

JOY GLOBAL, INC.

Company Headquarters

100 E. Wisconsin Avenue, Suite 2780
Milwaukee, WI 53201-0554
Web: http://www.harnischfeger.com

Company Description

Founded: 1884
Ticker: JOYG
Exchange: NASDAQ
Revenue: US$1.15 billion (2002)
Employees: 6800 (2002)
SIC(s): 3532 Mining Machinery, 3536 Hoists, Cranes & Monorails, 3554 Paper Industries Machinery, 3599 Industrial Machinery Nec.

Operating Locations

Harnischfeger Industries (WI--Milwaukee)

Harnischfeger Industries Foundation

Giving Contact

Sandy McKenzie, Executive Assistant
PO Box 554
Milwaukee, WI 53201-0554
Phone: (414)319-8506
Fax: (414)319-8520

Description

Founded: 1989
EIN: 391659070
Organization Type: Corporate Foundation
Giving Locations: AZ; DC; IL; MD; MI; MN; NY; PA; TX; VA; WI
Grant Types: Employee Matching Gifts, General Support, Operating Expenses, Project.

Donor Information

Founder: Established in 1989 by Harnishfeger Industries.

Financial Summary

Total Giving: $473,568 (fiscal year ending October 31, 2002); $644,135 (fiscal 2001); $773,155 (fiscal 2000)
Giving Analysis: Giving for fiscal 2002 includes: foundation (approx $750,000); fiscal 2001: foundation ($644,135); fiscal 2000: foundation grants to United Way ($100,000); foundation ($673,155);
Assets: $10,475,500 (fiscal 2002); $11,286,728 (fiscal 2000); $9,485,418 (fiscal 1999)
Gifts Received: $2,256,024 (fiscal 1992). Note: In fiscal 1992, major contributions were received from Harnischfeger Foundation.

Typical Recipients

Arts & Humanities: Arts Associations & Councils, Libraries, Museums/Galleries, Music, Opera, Performing Arts
Civic & Public Affairs: Botanical Gardens/Parks, Chambers of Commerce, Clubs, Economic Development, Civic & Public Affairs-General, Hispanic Affairs, Housing, Municipalities/Towns, Nonprofit Management, Parades/Festivals, Philanthropic Organizations, Professional & Trade Associations, Public Policy, Urban & Community Affairs, Women's Affairs, Zoos/Aquariums
Education: Arts/Humanities Education, Business Education, Colleges & Universities, Education Funds, Education Reform, Engineering/Technological Education, Education-General, Medical Education, Minority Education, Private Education (Precollege), Public Education (Precollege), Science/Mathematics Education, Secondary Education (Private)
Environment: Air/Water Quality, Energy, Environment-General
Health: AIDS/HIV, Cancer, Children's Health/Hospitals, Clinics/Medical Centers, Diabetes, Emergency/Ambulance Services, Health Organizations, Heart, Long-Term Care, Medical Research, Mental Health, Prenatal Health Issues, Single-Disease Health Associations
Religion: Dioceses, Religious Organizations, Religious Welfare
Science: Science Museums, Scientific Centers & Institutes
Social Services: Camps, Child Welfare, Community Centers, Community Service Organizations, Crime Prevention, Domestic Violence, Family Services, Food/Clothing Distribution, People with Disabilities, Recreation & Athletics, Social Services-General, United Funds/United Ways, United Funds/United Ways, YMCA/YWCA/YMHA/YWHA, Youth Organizations

Application Procedures

Initial Contact: Apply in writing, with proof of tax-exempt status attached.
Application Requirements: Requests for $1,000 or more should include a description of the organization's structure, purpose, history and programs; a list of current officers and directors and their affiliations; current income and expense budget; recently audited financial statement; summary of the proposed program(s) for which support is requested, including the specific objectives to be achieved, total amount to be raised, amount requested, and other anticipated sources of funding; population and geographic location to be served; and evidence of need for the programs to be funded.
Decision Notification: The foundation will communicate its funding decision in writing within 90 days of application receipt.
Notes: Do not submit videotapes unless requested to do so by the foundation. Phone calls and personal visits to the foundation are discouraged.

Restrictions

The foundation does not contribute to religious organizations or institutions primarily supported by taxes or public funds. Contributions are limited to 501(c)(3) organizations in communities where Joy Global Inc. has a significant employee presence. Contributions will not be made for use in foreign countries.

Additional Information

Publications: Guidelines; Grant Request Form

Corporate Officials

John Nils Hanson: chairman, president, chief executive officer treasurer ED Carnegie Mellon University PhD; Massachusetts Institute of Technology BS; Massachusetts Institute of Technology MS. PRIM CORP EMPL chairman, president, chief executive officer: Joy Global Inc. CORP AFFIL board member: Arrow Electronics Inc.
Donald C. Roof: executive vice president, chief financial officer, treasurer ED Eastern Michigan University BS. PRIM CORP EMPL executive vice president, chief financial officer, treasurer: Joy Global Inc.

Foundation Officials

Eric Fonstad: assistant secretary
John Nils Hanson: president (see above)

Grants Analysis

Disclosure Period: fiscal year ending October 31, 2001
Total Grants: $644,135
Number of Grants: 87
Average Grant: $7,403
Highest Grant: $100,000
Lowest Grant: $100
Typical Range: $50 to $1,000 and $5,000 to $20,000
Note: Grants analysis provided by foundation.

Recent Grants

Note: Grants derived from 2000 Form 990.

Library-Related
10,000	Milwaukee Public Library Foundation, Milwaukee, WI

General
100,000	United Way Greater Milwaukee, Milwaukee, WI
80,450	Milwaukee Women's Center, Milwaukee, WI
75,000	United Performing Arts Fund, Milwaukee, WI
50,000	St. Ann Center for Intergenerational Care, Milwaukee, WI
40,000	Boy and Girls Club of Greater Milwaukee, Milwaukee, WI
30,500	American Cancer Society, Wauwatosa, WI
25,000	Milwaukee Art Museum, Milwaukee, WI
22,500	Milwaukee Habitat for Humanity, Milwaukee, WI
15,000	Journey House, Milwaukee, WI
15,000	Milwaukee Public Museum, Milwaukee, WI

JOYCE FAMILY FOUNDATION

Giving Contact

Kim Williams, Trust Officer
Joyce Family Foundation
Care of SunTrust Bank Nashville NA
PO Box 305110
Nashville, TN 37230-5110
Phone: (615)748-5813

Description

Founded: 1991
EIN: 626225946
Organization Type: Private Foundation
Grant Types: General Support.

Financial Summary

Total Giving: $244,985 (2001); $223,300 (1999); $219,000 (1998)
Assets: $2,460,509 (2001); $2,171,848 (1999); $1,951,789 (1998)
Gifts Received: $344,982 (2001); $334,565 (1999); $312,925 (1998). Note: In 1998 and 1996, contributions were received from Margaret Henry Wood.

Typical Recipients

Arts & Humanities: Arts Centers, Historic Preservation, Libraries, Opera
Civic & Public Affairs: Botanical Gardens/Parks, Civic & Public Affairs-General, Public Policy, Safety, Zoos/Aquariums
Education: Colleges & Universities, Education-General, Private Education (Precollege)
Environment: Resource Conservation
Health: Cancer, Children's Health/Hospitals, Multiple Sclerosis, Speech & Hearing
Religion: Churches, Religion-General, Religious Organizations, Religious Welfare
Social Services: Community Service Organizations, Food/Clothing Distribution, Sexual Abuse, Social Services-General

Application Procedures

Initial Contact: Send a brief letter of inquiry.
Deadlines: None.

Additional Information

Trust(s): SunTrust Bank Nashville NA

Foundation Officials

Dr. Benjamin F. Byrd, Jr.: director
Douglas Henry: director
Margaret Henry Wood: chairperson
Richard D. Holton, Esq.: director
Alexis Jones Joyce: director

Grants Analysis

Disclosure Period: calendar year ending 2001
Total Grants: $244,985
Number of Grants: 18
Average Grant: $8,529*
Highest Grant: $100,000
Lowest Grant: $100
Typical Range: $1,000 to $15,000
***Note:** Average grant figure excludes highest grant.

Recent Grants

Note: Grants derived from 2001 Form 990.

Library-Related

50,000	Metropolitan Nashville Library, Nashville, TN

General

100,000	Vanderbilt Cancer Center, Nashville, TN
50,000	Second Harvest Food Bank, Allentown, PA
15,000	Wofford College, Spartanburg, SC
8,800	Woodberry Forest School, Woodberry Forest, VA
6,000	TJ Martell Foundation for Cancer, New York, NY
5,000	Bill Wilkerson Center, Nashville, TN
2,000	Percy Priest School
1,210	Cheekwood, Nashville, TN
1,000	All Saints Episcopal Church
1,000	Bethlehem House, El Dorado, KS

JSJ CORP.

Company Headquarters

700 Robbins Rd.
Grand Haven, MI 49417
Web: http://www.jsjcorp.com

Company Description

Employees: 2,000
SIC(s): 2522 Office Furniture Except Wood, 3089 Plastics Products Nec, 3364 Nonferrous Die-Castings Except Aluminum, 3469 Metal Stampings Nec.

Operating Locations

JSJ Corp. (MI--Grand Rapids; WI--La Crosse)

Nonmonetary Support

Value: $21,100 (2000)
Type: Donated Equipment; Workplace Solicitation
Note: Workplace solicitation is for United Way only.

JSJ Foundation

Giving Contact

Lynne Sherwood, Secretary & Trustee
700 Robbins Road
Grand Haven, MI 49417-2603
Phone: (616)842-6350
Fax: (616)847-3112
E-mail: sherwoodl@jsjcorp.com

Description

EIN: 382421508
Organization Type: Corporate Foundation
Giving Locations: CA: southern; FL; MI; TX; WI
Grant Types: Capital, General Support, Multiyear/Continuing Support, Operating Expenses.

Financial Summary

Total Giving: $357,900 (2001); $373,980 (2000); $275,386 (1999)
Giving Analysis: Giving for 2000 includes: domestic subsidiaries ($12,819); nonmonetary support ($21,115); foundation grants to United Way ($31,918); corporate direct giving ($40,112); foundation ($268,016); 1999: foundation grants to United Way ($26,211); foundation ($249,175); 1998: foundation grants to United Way ($28,335) foundation ($254,976)
Assets: $698,108 (2001); $795,264 (2000); $650,000 (1999 approx)
Gifts Received: $300,000 (2001); $275,000 (2000); $275,000 (1999). Note: Contributions received from JSJ Corp.

Typical Recipients

Arts & Humanities: Arts Associations & Councils, Arts Centers, Arts Festivals, Arts Funds, Arts Institutes, Community Arts, Arts & Humanities-General, Libraries, Museums/Galleries, Music, Opera, Performing Arts, Public Broadcasting, Theater
Civic & Public Affairs: Community Foundations, Economic Policy, Civic & Public Affairs-General, Housing, Municipalities/Towns, Public Policy, Urban & Community Affairs, Women's Affairs, Zoos/Aquariums
Education: Afterschool/Enrichment Programs, Arts/Humanities Education, Business Education, Colleges & Universities, Community & Junior Colleges, Continuing Education, Economic Education, Education Associations, Education Funds, Engineering/Technological Education, Education-General, Minority Education, Private Education (Precollege)
Health: Cancer, Health Policy/Cost Containment, Health Organizations, Hospices, Transplant Networks/Donor Banks
International: Foreign Arts Organizations
Religion: Churches, Ministries, Religious Organizations, Religious Welfare
Social Services: Child Welfare, Community Service Organizations, Counseling, Day Care, Family Services, Homes, Recreation & Athletics, Scouts, Shelters/Homelessness, Social Services-General, Substance Abuse, United Funds/United Ways, Volunteer Services, YMCA/YWCA/YMHA/YWHA, Youth Organizations

Application Procedures

Initial Contact: No specific format required.
Deadlines: None.
Decision Notification: Applicants are notified within 60 days.

Restrictions

Limited to the geographic areas where JSJ Corp. has facilities.

Corporate Officials

F. Martin Johnson: chairman, director PRIM CORP EMPL chairman, chief executive officer, director: JSJ Corp.
Michael D. Metzger: vice president, chief financial officer B Buchanan, MI 1947. ED Western Michigan University (1969); Seidman Graduate School MBA (1977). PRIM CORP EMPL vice president, chief financial officer: JSJ Corp. NONPR AFFIL member: Financial Executives Institute.
Edward L. Ozark: vice president administration, assistant secretary B Buffalo, NY 1944. ED Canisius College (1967); Aquinas College (1994). PRIM CORP EMPL vice president, treasurer, assistant secretary: JSJ Corp. NONPR AFFIL director: Priority Health; member: Risk & Insurance Management Society.
Lynne Sherwood: corporate secretary PRIM CORP EMPL secretary: JSJ Corp.
Philip E. Taylor: president, chief executive officer ED Ball State University BS (1968); University of Wisconsin MBA (1980). PRIM CORP EMPL president: JSJ Corp.

Foundation Officials

Donald A. Johnson: chairman
F. Martin Johnson: trustee (see above)
Lynne Sherwood: secretary, treasurer, trustee (see above)

Grants Analysis

Disclosure Period: calendar year ending 2001
Total Grants: $241,900*
Number of Grants: 45
Average Grant: $5,376
Highest Grant: $30,000
Lowest Grant: $500
Typical Range: $1,000 to $10,000
***Note:** Giving excludes scholarship, United Way.

Recent Grants

Note: Grants derived from 2001 Form 990.

Library-Related

25,000	Warner Baird District Library, Spring Lake, MI -- capital campaign
3,000	Riverfront, Inc., La Crosse, WI -- capital campaign

General

60,000	Tri-Cities Area United Fund, Grand Haven, MI -- support for operations
30,000	Grand Rapids Community College Foundation, Grand Rapids, MI -- Ottawa Area Advance Technology Training Center
20,000	Citizens Research Council of Michigan, Livonia, MI -- endowment
20,000	Grand Valley State University Foundation, Grand Rapids, MI -- Grand Rapids Campus
15,000	Center for Women in Transition, Holland, MI -- capital campaign
15,000	Michigan Colleges Foundation, Inc., Southfield, MI -- scholarships
13,415	United Way Volusia County, Daytona Beach, FL -- support of operations
10,000	City of Grand Haven, Grand Haven, MI -- Sinage Program
10,000	Grand Rapids Symphony, Grand Rapids, MI -- support for operations
10,000	Lakeshore Ethnic Diversity Coalition, Grand Haven, MI -- support of operations

ALFRED JURZYKOWSKI FOUNDATION

Giving Contact

Bluma D. Cohen, Executive Director & Vice President
15 East 65th Street
New York, NY 10021
Phone: (212)535-8930

Description

Founded: 1960
EIN: 136192256
Organization Type: Family Foundation
Giving Locations: NY: New York metropolitan area; Brazil; Poland
Grant Types: General Support, Operating Expenses, Project.

Donor Information

Founder: Incorporated in 1960 by the late Alfred Jurzykowski .

Financial Summary

Total Giving: $2,650,243 (2001); $2,459,558 (2000); $1,516,167 (1999)
Giving Analysis: Giving for 2000 includes: foundation scholarships ($95,000); foundation fellowships ($233,600); 1999: foundation scholarships ($15,000) 1998: foundation gifts to individuals ($66,000)
Assets: $39,202,860 (2001); $44,361,606 (2000); $45,524,040 (1999)

Typical Recipients

Arts & Humanities: Arts Associations & Councils, Arts Outreach, Ethnic & Folk Arts, Arts & Humanities-General, Libraries, Museums/Galleries, Music, Performing Arts, Public Broadcasting, Theater, Visual Arts
Civic & Public Affairs: Botanical Gardens/Parks, Community Foundations, Employment/Job Training, Ethnic Organizations, Civic & Public Affairs-General, Nonprofit Management, Philanthropic Organizations, Public Policy, Women's Affairs, Zoos/Aquariums

Education: Afterschool/Enrichment Programs, Arts/Humanities Education, Colleges & Universities, Education Funds, Environmental Education, Faculty Development, International Exchange, International Studies, Journalism/Media Education, Literacy, Medical Education, Minority Education, Private Education (Precollege), Science/Mathematics Education, Secondary Education (Public), Student Aid
Environment: Environment-General, Resource Conservation
Health: AIDS/HIV, Cancer, Children's Health/Hospitals, Clinics/Medical Centers, Health Organizations, Home-Care Services, Hospices, Hospitals
International: Foreign Arts Organizations, Foreign Educational Institutions, Health Care/Hospitals, Human Rights, International Affairs, International Development, International Environmental Issues, International Organizations, International Relations, International Relief Efforts, Missionary/Religious Activities
Religion: Religion-General, Jewish Causes, Religious Organizations, Religious Welfare, Social/Policy Issues, Synagogues/Temples
Science: Science Museums, Scientific Centers & Institutes
Social Services: Big Brother/Big Sister, Child Welfare, Child Welfare, Community Centers, Community Service Organizations, Delinquency & Criminal Rehabilitation, Family Planning, Family Services, Food/Clothing Distribution, People with Disabilities, Shelters/Homelessness, United Funds/United Ways, Youth Organizations

Application Procedures

Initial Contact: The foundation requests applications be made in writing.
Application Requirements: Applications must include a statement of the purposes and objectives of the organization, an explanation of the current financial needs of the organization and any special projects requiring aid, a project budget and any other sources of support, a copy of the most recent audited financial statement, and a formal statement from the IRS as to the organization's tax-exempt status and that it is not a private foundation. Applicants are encouraged to include any other information that might be helpful in processing the application.
Deadlines: None.

Restrictions

The foundation does not make grants for endowment funds or loans.

Additional Information

The foundation's awards program has been discontinued.
Publications: Application Guidelines

Foundation Officials

Bluma D. Cohen: vice president, executive director, foundation manager, trustee
Karin Falencki: trustee
M. Christine Jurzykowski: secretary, treasurer, trustee B New York, NY 1952. ED Boston University BA (1968). PRIM NONPR EMPL president: Fossil Rim Wildlife Center. NONPR AFFIL president: Conservation Connection.
Yolande L. Jurzykowski: executive vice president, trustee

Grants Analysis

Disclosure Period: calendar year ending 2001
Total Grants: $2,627,413*
Number of Grants: 37
Average Grant: $39,864*
Highest Grant: $666,112
Lowest Grant: $3,500
Typical Range: $20,000 to $50,000
*Note: Giving excludes fellowship. Average grant figure excludes three highest grants ($1,272,046).

Recent Grants

Note: Grants derived from 2001 Form 990.

Library-Related
15,000 New York Public Library, New York, NY -- support of the research libraries

General
666,112 Ashoka, Arlington, VA -- support for Public Entrepreneurship Program in Brazil
355,934 Ashoka, Arlington, VA -- support of promoting public entrepreneurship in Poland
250,000 Youth Venture, Arlington, VA -- support of expanding from a prototype to a national movement
235,000 Kosciusko Foundation, New York, NY -- Polish exchange grant
194,700 Ashoka, Arlington, VA -- support for Public Entrepreneurship Program in the United States
130,000 Conservation International Foundation, Washington, DC -- support of ecosystem conservation in Brazil
99,167 Cornell University, Ithaca, NY -- support the Polish component of their International Agriculture Program
90,000 Kosciusko Foundation, New York, NY -- establishment of a Department of Environmental Sciences at the University of Mining and Metallurgy International School of Technology in Krakow
60,000 Tides Foundation, San Francisco, CA -- Global Greengrants Fund
50,000 ACCION International, Cambridge, MA -- support of microenterprise initiative in Brazil

EDITH C. JUSTUS TRUST

Giving Contact

Stephen P. Kosak
PO Box 374
Oil City, PA 16301
Phone: (814)677-5085

Description

Founded: 1931
EIN: 256031057
Organization Type: Private Foundation
Giving Locations: PA: Oil City Venango County
Grant Types: General Support.

Donor Information

Founder: the late Edith C. Justus

Financial Summary

Total Giving: $216,293 (1999); $159,921 (1998); $166,685 (1996)
Giving Analysis: Giving for 1999 includes: foundation grants to United Way ($24,500)
Assets: $7,170,766 (1999); $6,513,696 (1998); $4,833,079 (1996)

Typical Recipients

Arts & Humanities: Arts Appreciation, Arts Associations & Councils, Arts Centers, Film & Video, Historic Preservation, History & Archaeology, Libraries, Museums/Galleries, Music, Opera, Theater
Civic & Public Affairs: Botanical Gardens/Parks, Community Foundations, Economic Development, Employment/Job Training, Civic & Public Affairs-General, Housing, Municipalities/Towns, Safety, Urban & Community Affairs
Education: Agricultural Education, Arts/Humanities Education, Colleges & Universities, Education-General, Literacy, Private Education (Precollege), Public Education (Precollege), Vocational & Technical Education
Environment: Environment-General

Health: Clinics/Medical Centers, Health-General, Health Organizations, Mental Health, Nursing Services
Religion: Churches, Religious Organizations, Religious Welfare
Science: Science Museums
Social Services: Child Welfare, Community Service Organizations, Day Care, Family Services, Food/Clothing Distribution, People with Disabilities, Recreation & Athletics, Senior Services, Shelters/Homelessness, United Funds/United Ways, Volunteer Services, YMCA/YWCA/YMHA/YWHA, Youth Organizations

Application Procedures

Initial Contact: Send a brief letter of inquiry.
Application Requirements: Include purpose of funds sought and proof of tax-exempt status.
Deadlines: None.

Additional Information

Trust(s): National City Bank of PA

Grants Analysis

Disclosure Period: calendar year ending 1999
Total Grants: $191,793*
Number of Grants: 37
Average Grant: $3,479*
Highest Grant: $66,539
Typical Range: $1,000 to $10,000
*Note: Giving excludes United Way. Average grant excludes highest grant.

Recent Grants

Note: Grants derived from 2001 Form 990.

Library-Related
20,000 Oil City Library, Oil City, PA

General
38,750 Oil City YMCA, Oil City, PA
32,500 Family Service and Children's Aid Society, Oil City, PA
27,250 Community Services of Venango County, Oil City, PA
22,000 Salvation Army, Oil City, PA
17,490 Oil City Civic Center, Inc., Oil City, PA
16,667 City of Oil City, Oil City, PA
15,845 Youth Alternatives, Oil City, PA
15,000 Venango Museum of Art Science, Oil City, PA
13,000 Oil Valley Center for the Arts, Oil City, PA
11,000 Venango Center for Creative Development, Franklin, PA

KAHN, LUCAS-LANCASTER, INC. CHILDREN'S WEAR

Company Headquarters

100 W. 33rd St., Ste. 921
New York, NY 10001

Company Description

Employees: 940
SIC(s): 2300 Apparel & Other Textile Products.

Operating Locations

Kahn-Lucas-Lancaster (NY--New York; PA--Columbia)

Kahn Foundation

Giving Contact

Andrew Kahn, Director
100 West 33rd Street, Suite 921
New York, NY 10001
Phone: (717)684-6911

Description

Founded: 1987
EIN: 236343794
Organization Type: Corporate Foundation
Grant Types: General Support.

Financial Summary

Total Giving: $10,550 (2000); $10,201 (1999); $36,016 (1997)
Giving Analysis: Giving for 1999 includes: foundation ($10,201)
Assets: $36,138 (2000); $36,496 (1999); $54,519 (1997)
Gifts Received: $44,153 (2000); $12,000 (1997); $5,000 (1996). Note: In 2000, contributions were received from Andrew Kahn. In 1997, contributions were received from Kahn-Lucas-Lancaster.

Typical Recipients

Arts & Humanities: Community Arts, Libraries
Civic & Public Affairs: Civic & Public Affairs-General, Urban & Community Affairs
Education: Business Education, Colleges & Universities, Literacy, Private Education (Precollege), Public Education (Precollege), Science/Mathematics Education, Secondary Education (Public)
Environment: Environment-General
Health: AIDS/HIV, Cancer, Children's Health/Hospitals, Diabetes, Emergency/Ambulance Services, Geriatric Health, Heart, Hospices, Hospitals (University Affiliated), Prenatal Health Issues, Single-Disease Health Associations
Religion: Churches, Jewish Causes, Religious Organizations
Social Services: Crime Prevention, Food/Clothing Distribution, People with Disabilities, Recreation & Athletics, United Funds/United Ways

Application Procedures

Initial Contact: The foundation requests applications be made in writing.
Deadlines: None.

Corporate Officials

Andrew Kahn: chief executive officer PRIM CORP EMPL chief executive officer: Kahn-Lucas-Lancaster.
Donald E. McKonly: chief financial officer PRIM CORP EMPL chief financial officer: Kahn-Lucas-Lancaster.
Stanley Silver: president PRIM CORP EMPL president: Kahn-Lucas-Lancaster.

Foundation Officials

Andrew Kahn: director (see above)
Peggy Anne Kahn: director
Donald E. McKonly: director (see above)

Grants Analysis

Disclosure Period: calendar year ending 2000
Total Grants: $10,550
Number of Grants: 19
Average Grant: $555
Typical Range: $100 to $1,000

Recent Grants

Note: Grants derived from 1999 Form 990.

Library-Related

200	Columbia Public Library, Washington, DC

General

3,750	National Jewish Medicine and Research Center, Tulsa, OK
1,500	UJA-Federation, New York, NY
1,150	Rye County Day School, Rye, NY -- spring benefit
1,000	Faculty and Friends Campaign - New York University Medical Center, NY
1,000	Sephardic Bikar Hoim and Maoz Larebgon, Brooklyn, NY
560	American Jewish Congress, Philadelphia, PA
250	AHA/New York City, New York, NY
250	Crohn's & Colitis Foundation, St. Louis, MO
250	Sid Jacobson Jewish Community Center, New York, NY
100	Oxalises & Hperoxaluria Foundation

KAJIMA ENGINEERING AND CONSTRUCTION, INC.

Company Headquarters

901 Corporate Center Dr., Ste. 201
Monterey Park, CA 91754

Company Description

Founded: 1984
SIC(s): 6552 Subdividers & Developers Nec.
Parent Company: Kajima Corp., 2-7, Motoakasaka 1-chome, Minato-ku, Tokyo, Japan

Giving Contact

Itsuko Kosai, Office Manager
901 Corporate Center Dr., Suite 104
Monterey Park, CA 91754
Phone: (323)262-8484
Fax: (323)262-8893

Description

Organization Type: Corporate Giving Program
Giving Locations: CA: Monterey Park

Financial Summary

Total Giving: $59,447 (1993)
Assets: $941,590 (1993)
Gifts Received: $4,246 (1993)

Typical Recipients

Arts & Humanities: Ballet, Historic Preservation, Libraries, Museums/Galleries, Music, Opera, Performing Arts
Civic & Public Affairs: Housing, Urban & Community Affairs, Zoos/Aquariums
Education: Colleges & Universities, Engineering/Technological Education, International Studies, Minority Education, Secondary Education (Public), Student Aid, Vocational & Technical Education
Health: AIDS/HIV, Cancer, Children's Health/Hospitals, Emergency/Ambulance Services, Multiple Sclerosis, Single-Disease Health Associations
International: Foreign Educational Institutions
Social Services: Big Brother/Big Sister, Child Welfare, Community Service Organizations, Recreation & Athletics, Scouts, United Funds/United Ways, YMCA/YWCA/YMHA/YWHA

Corporate Officials

Eiichi Motoshige: chairman, president, chief executive officer PRIM CORP EMPL chairman, president, chief executive officer: Kajima Development Corp.

Recent Grants

Library-Related

2,500	Museum of Modern Art, New York, NY

General

5,000	Princeton in Asia, Princeton, NJ -- for internships
5,000	University of Michigan, Ann Arbor, MI -- for scholarships
2,500	Cancer Care, Inc., New York, NY -- to provide guidance, information and referrals
2,500	New Jersey Institute of Technology, Newark, NY -- for scholarship
2,500	Ohio Wesleyan University, Delaware, OH -- for a conference
2,000	Habitat for Humanity, Stone Mountain, GA -- to provide funds to construct single family residences
2,000	Long Beach Junior Crew, Long Beach, CA -- for equipment and scholarships
2,000	Long Island University, Brookville, NY
1,500	Cystic Fibrosis Foundation, New York, NY
1,000	Boy Scouts of America Northeast Georgia Council, Athens, GA -- to continue and expand programs

KAJIMA INTERNATIONAL, INC.

Company Headquarters

Englewood Cliffs, NJ
Web: http://www.kajimausa.com

Company Description

Employees: 457
SIC(s): 1542 Nonresidential Construction Nec, 1711 Plumbing, Heating & Air-Conditioning, 7812 Motion Picture & Video Production.
Parent Company: Kajima Corp., 2-7, Motoakasaka 1-chome, Minato-ku, Tokyo, Japan

Operating Locations

Kajima Engineering & Construction (CA--Pasadena); Kajima International (GA; IL; NJ--Englewood Cliffs; NY; TX); Kajima U.S.A. (NY--New York)

Kajima Foundation

Giving Contact

Kent Stolzman
395 W. Passaic St.
Rochelle Park, NJ 07662
Phone: (201)518-2100

Description

EIN: 521675796
Organization Type: Corporate Foundation
Giving Locations: headquarters and operating communities.
Grant Types: Emergency, Employee Matching Gifts, Multiyear/Continuing Support, Project, Research.

Financial Summary

Total Giving: $50,000 (2001); $48,275 (2000); $44,500 (1999)
Giving Analysis: Giving for 2001 includes: foundation scholarships ($7,500) 1999: foundation ($44,500)
Assets: $894,994 (2001); $923,957 (2000); $926,014 (1999)
Gifts Received: $4,246 (1993); $3,650 (1992)

Typical Recipients

Arts & Humanities: Ballet, Historic Preservation, Libraries, Literary Arts, Museums/Galleries, Music, Opera, Performing Arts
Civic & Public Affairs: Chambers of Commerce, Community Foundations, Civic & Public Affairs-General, Housing, Zoos/Aquariums
Education: Colleges & Universities, Community & Junior Colleges, Economic Education, Engineering/Technological Education, Faculty Development, International Exchange, International Studies, Leadership Training, Minority Education, Private Education (Precollege), Science/Mathematics Education, Secondary Education (Public), Student Aid
Health: AIDS/HIV, Cancer, Heart, Hospitals
International: Foreign Arts Organizations, Foreign Educational Institutions, International Relations, International Relief Efforts
Religion: Jewish Causes, Religious Welfare

Social Services: At-Risk Youth, Big Brother/Big Sister, Child Welfare, Emergency Relief, Family Services, Recreation & Athletics, Scouts, United Funds/United Ways, Volunteer Services, YMCA/YWCA/YMHA/YWHA, Youth Organizations

Application Procedures

Initial Contact: Application form required. Send a brief letter of inquiry and a full proposal. Include a description of organization, amount requested, purpose of funds sought, recently audited financial statement, and proof of tax-exempt status.
Deadlines: on a bimonthly basis.

Restrictions

Contributions are limited to the 40 states in which Kajima International conducts business. Major U.S. headquarters for Kajima operating companies are listed above. Contributions also are restricted to organizations in which employees volunteer.

Corporate Officials

Hiroaki Hoshino: president, chief executive officer PRIM CORP EMPL president, chief executive officer: Kajima International.
Kiyoshi Sugasawa: chief financial officer PRIM CORP EMPL chief financial officer: Kajima International ADD CORP EMPL treasurer: Commercial Development International East Inc.; chief financial officer: Kajima Construction Services; vice president: Kajima Real Estate Development; vice president: Kajima United States of America Inc.

Foundation Officials

Hiroaki Hoshino: treasurer, trustee (see above)
Ayao Katayama: president, trustee
Marvin J. Suomi: secretary

Grants Analysis

Disclosure Period: calendar year ending 2001
Total Grants: $42,500*
Number of Grants: 23
Average Grant: $1,848
Highest Grant: $5,000
Typical Range: $1,000 to $5,000
*Note: Giving excludes scholarship.

Recent Grants

Note: Grants derived from 2001 Form 990.

General

5,000	Japanese Community World Trade Center Relief, New York, NY -- aid victims of World Trade Center attacks
5,000	Long Beach Aquarium, Long Beach, CA -- aquarium fundraising
5,000	University of Michigan College of Literature, Science and the Arts, Ann Arbor, MI -- Kajima Dean's Merit Scholarship
5,000	William Paterson University of New Jersey Foundation Inc., Wayne, NJ -- needy student in the College of Education
4,000	Jewish Federation of Southern New Jersey, Cherry Hill, NJ -- early literacy conference
3,000	Habitat for Humanity, Stone Mountain, GA -- construct single family residences
3,000	Woodrow Wilson National Fellowship Foundation, Princeton, NJ -- support ongoing programs
2,500	California State University, Long Beach, CA -- scholarships for National Merit Scholars and Valedictorians
2,500	Emmaus House, Atlanta, GA -- "The Study Hall"
2,000	Avon Breast Cancer 3-Day Walk, Chicago, IL -- Breast Health Programs

KALKUS FOUNDATION

Giving Contact

Lara Purchase, Vice President
Kalkus Foundation
Care of Lamar Companies
365 South Street
Morristown, NJ 07960
Phone: (973)285-0010

Description

Founded: 1992
EIN: 650258064
Organization Type: Private Foundation
Grant Types: General Support.

Financial Summary

Total Giving: $96,140 (2001); $115,867 (2000); $75,125 (1999)
Assets: $1,094,465 (2001); $1,264,990 (2000); $1,577,344 (1999)
Gifts Received: $4,000 (1996); $85,000 (1994)

Typical Recipients

Arts & Humanities: Libraries, Music, Opera, Theater
Civic & Public Affairs: Community Foundations, Civic & Public Affairs-General, Public Policy, Safety, Urban & Community Affairs, Zoos/Aquariums
Education: Colleges & Universities, Education Funds, Education-General, Private Education (Precollege), Student Aid
Environment: Air/Water Quality, Environment-General
Health: Cancer, Clinics/Medical Centers, Health Organizations, Hospitals, Medical Research, Single-Disease Health Associations
International: International-General
Religion: Churches
Social Services: Child Welfare, Community Service Organizations, Domestic Violence, People with Disabilities, Recreation & Athletics, Social Services-General, United Funds/United Ways

Application Procedures

Initial Contact: The foundation requests applications be made in writing.
Application Requirements: Include a description of organization.
Deadlines: None.

Foundation Officials

June Kalkus: vice president
Mark Kalkus: secretary
Peter Kalkus: president B 1959. CORP AFFIL vice president, treasurer, director: Cyprus Foote Mineral Co.
Lara Purchase: vice president

Grants Analysis

Disclosure Period: calendar year ending 2001
Total Grants: $96,140
Number of Grants: 36
Average Grant: $2,175*
Highest Grant: $20,000
Lowest Grant: $100
Typical Range: $1,000 to $5,000
*Note: Average grant figure excludes highest grant.

Recent Grants

Note: Grants derived from 2001 Form 990.

General

20,000	St. Clare of Assisi Parish, Edwards, CO
14,190	Metropolitan Opera Association, Vail, CO
12,500	Vail Valley Foundation, Vail, CO
10,000	Eisenhower Medical Center, Rancho Mirage, CA
10,000	Morristown Memorial Hospital, Morristown, NJ
8,000	Bravo Colorado, Vail, CO
5,000	Betty Ford Center, Rancho Mirage, CA
2,700	Vail Valley Medical Center, Vail, CO
2,350	CASA of the Continental Divide, Vail, CO
2,000	American Friends of Czech Republic

KANSAS CITY SOUTHERN RAILWAY

Company Headquarters

114 W. 11th Street
Kansas City, MO 64105-1804
Web: http://www.kcsi.com

Company Description

Revenue: US$512 million (2002)
Employees: 2711 (2002)
SIC(s): 4000 Railroad Transportation, 6700 Holding & Other Investment Offices.

Operating Locations

Kansas City Southern Industries (LA--Shreveport; MS--Jackson; MO--Kansas City)

Nonmonetary Support

Type: Donated Equipment; In-kind Services; Loaned Employees; Loaned Executives

Giving Contact

Jan Armstrong, Director, Community Relations
114 West 11th Street
Kansas City, MO 64105
Phone: (816)983-1303
Fax: (816)983-1192

Description

Organization Type: Corporate Giving Program
Giving Locations: headquarters and operating communities.
Grant Types: Capital, Challenge, Emergency, Employee Matching Gifts, Endowment, General Support, Multiyear/Continuing Support, Operating Expenses, Project.

Financial Summary

Total Giving: Company does not disclose contributions figures.

Typical Recipients

Arts & Humanities: Arts Associations & Councils, Arts Centers, Arts Festivals, Arts Funds, Arts Institutes, Arts Outreach, Ballet, Community Arts, Dance, Ethnic & Folk Arts, Film & Video, Arts & Humanities-General, Historic Preservation, History & Archaeology, Libraries, Literary Arts, Museums/Galleries, Music, Opera, Performing Arts, Public Broadcasting, Theater, Visual Arts
Civic & Public Affairs: African American Affairs, Asian American Affairs, Botanical Gardens/Parks, Business/Free Enterprise, Chambers of Commerce, Civil Rights, Community Foundations, Economic Development, Economic Policy, Ethnic Organizations, Civic & Public Affairs-General, Hispanic Affairs, Housing, Inner-City Development, Municipalities/Towns, Native American Affairs, Nonprofit Management, Parades/Festivals, Philanthropic Organizations, Public Policy, Safety, Urban & Community Affairs, Women's Affairs, Zoos/Aquariums
Education: Afterschool/Enrichment Programs, Agricultural Education, Arts/Humanities Education, Business Education, Business-School Partnerships, Colleges & Universities, Community & Junior Colleges, Continuing Education, Economic Education, Education Funds, Elementary Education (Public), Education-General, Literacy, Minority Education, Preschool

Education, Private Education (Precollege), Public Education (Precollege), Science/Mathematics Education, Secondary Education (Private), Secondary Education (Public), Social Sciences Education, Special Education

Environment: Environment-General, Resource Conservation, Wildlife Protection

Health: Adolescent Health Issues, AIDS/HIV, Alzheimers Disease, Arthritis, Cancer, Children's Health/Hospitals, Clinics/Medical Centers, Diabetes, Eyes/Blindness, Health-General, Geriatric Health, Health Organizations, Heart, Home-Care Services, Hospices, Hospitals, Hospitals (University Affiliated), Long-Term Care, Medical Rehabilitation, Nursing Services, Single-Disease Health Associations

Science: Science-General, Science Exhibits & Fairs, Science Museums, Scientific Centers & Institutes, Scientific Research

Social Services: Animal Protection, At-Risk Youth, Camps, Child Welfare, Community Centers, Community Service Organizations, Counseling, Day Care, Delinquency & Criminal Rehabilitation, Domestic Violence, Emergency Relief, Family Planning, Family Services, Food/Clothing Distribution, Homes, People with Disabilities, Recreation & Athletics, Refugee Assistance, Senior Services, Sexual Abuse, Shelters/Homelessness, Social Services-General, Substance Abuse, United Funds/United Ways, Volunteer Services, YMCA/YWCA/YMHA/YWHA, Youth Organizations

Application Procedures

Initial Contact: Send a brief letter of inquiry and a full proposal.

Application Requirements: Include a description of organization, amount requested, purpose of funds sought, recently audited financial statement, proof of tax-exempt status, and a list of the board of directors.

Restrictions

Does not support individuals, religious organizations for sectarian purposes, political or lobbying groups, or organizations outside operating areas.

Corporate Officials

Joseph D. Monello: vice president financeo, director B New York, NY 1945. ED Trenton State College (1973). PRIM CORP EMPL vice president finance: Kansas City Southern Industries.

Landon Hill Rowland: president, chief executive officer, director B Fuquay Springs, NC 1937. ED Dartmouth College BA (1959); Harvard University LLB (1962). PRIM CORP EMPL president, chief executive officer, director: Kansas City Southern Industries. CORP AFFIL chairman: Kansas City Southern Railway Co.; chief executive officer: Louisiana & Northwest Railroad Co.; chairman: DST Systems. NONPR AFFIL member: Phi Beta Kappa; chairman board director: Swope Ridge Health Care Center; trustee: Midwest Research Institute; member: Missouri Bar Association; director: Lyric Opera Kansas City; chairman: Metropolitan Performing Arts Fund; director: Jacob L & Ella C Loose Foundation; member: American Bar Association; director: American Royal Association. CLUB AFFIL River Club; Kansas City Country Club.

Grants Analysis

Typical Range: $1,000 to $2,500

KANSAS HEALTH FOUNDATION

Giving Contact

Nancy Claassen, Grants Manager
309 East Douglas
Wichita, KS 67202-3405
Phone: (316)262-7676
Fax: (316)262-2044

E-mail: nclaassen@khf.org
Web: http://www.kansashealth.org

Alternate Contact

Phone: 800-373-7681

Description

Founded: 1978
EIN: 480873431
Organization Type: Private Foundation
Giving Locations: KS
Grant Types: Award, Conference/Seminar, Employee Matching Gifts, Endowment, General Support, Matching, Multiyear/Continuing Support, Project, Research.

Financial Summary

Total Giving: $15,151,145 (2003 approx); $13,762,000 (2002); $16,300,000 (2001)
Assets: $374,652,000 (2002); $438,900,000 (2001); $467,555,588 (2000)
Gifts Received: $183,843 (2000); $39,828 (1999); $1,056,828 (1998). Note: In 1998, contributions were received from the George E. and Blanche Sterling Trust ($38,828), the Mrs. H.C. Wear Charitable Remainder Annuity Trust 1 ($1,000,00), and the Turner Investment Partners, Inc ($18,000).

Typical Recipients

Arts & Humanities: Arts Centers, Arts Outreach, Libraries, Public Broadcasting

Civic & Public Affairs: African American Affairs, Botanical Gardens/Parks, Community Foundations, Nonprofit Management, Parades/Festivals, Safety

Education: Afterschool/Enrichment Programs, Colleges & Universities, Elementary Education (Public), Faculty Development, Education-General, Health & Physical Education, Literacy, Medical Education, Preschool Education, Public Education (Precollege), Religious Education, Secondary Education (Public), Social Sciences Education, Special Education, Student Aid

Environment: Air/Water Quality, Environment-General

Health: Adolescent Health Issues, AIDS/HIV, Alzheimers Disease, Cancer, Children's Health/Hospitals, Clinics/Medical Centers, Emergency/Ambulance Services, Geriatric Health, Health Policy/Cost Containment, Health Organizations, Heart, Home-Care Services, Hospices, Hospitals, Hospitals (University Affiliated), Medical Rehabilitation, Medical Research, Medical Training, Nursing Services, Nutrition, Prenatal Health Issues, Preventive Medicine/Wellness Organizations, Public Health, Research/Studies Institutes, Respiratory

International: International Relief Efforts
Religion: Churches, Ministries, Religious Welfare
Science: Science Museums, Scientific Centers & Institutes

Social Services: At-Risk Youth, Big Brother/Big Sister, Camps, Child Abuse, Child Welfare, Community Service Organizations, Crime Prevention, Domestic Violence, Emergency Relief, Family Services, Food/Clothing Distribution, People with Disabilities, Scouts, Senior Services, Sexual Abuse, Social Services-General, Substance Abuse, Volunteer Services, YMCA/YWCA/YMHA/YWHA, Youth Organizations

Application Procedures

Initial Contact: Applications are available for the Recognition Grant program, and can be obtained by visiting www.kansashealth.org.

Application Requirements: Letters of inquiry should include summary of need, explanation of plan and address that need, and estimated cost.

Deadlines: March 15 and September 15 for the Recognition Grants.

Notes: The foundation reports that, with the exception of the Recognition Grant program, relatively few grants are awarded through unsolicited requests.

Restrictions

Grants are not made to individuals., clinical research, capital campaigns, operating deficits, endowments, construction, or vehicle purchases. Grants typically made only to preselected organizations.

Additional Information

Publications: Annual Report; Guidelines for Making Grants (Brochure); Newsletter

Foundation Officials

Charles Q. Chandler: chairman B Wichita, KS 1926. ED Kansas State University (1949). PRIM CORP EMPL chairman: Intrust Financial Corp. CORP AFFIL director: Western Resources Inc.

Jack Focht: mem B Denver, CO 1934. ED Southwestern College AB (1957); Washburn University JD (1960). PRIM CORP EMPL special counsel: Foulston & Seifkin. NONPR AFFIL member: State Board Law Examiners; member: Wichita Bar Association; trustee, chairman: Southwestern College; fellow: Kansas Bar Association; member: National Association Criminal Defense Lawyers; member: Kansas Association Criminal Defense Lawyers; member: Association Professional Responsibility Lawyers; member: Kansas Action Children; member: American Trial Lawyers Association; fellow: American Bar Foundation; fellow: American College Trial Lawyers.

Jane E. Henney, MD: member PRIM NONPR EMPL vice president, health sciences: University New Mexico Health Sciences Center. NONPR AFFIL president: United States Pharmacopeial Conventions.

Bishop Kenneth W. Hicks: member ED York College BA (1947); Iliff School of Theology MTh (1953). PRIM NONPR EMPL bishop: United Methodist Church, Kansas.

Eric T. Knorr: director CORP AFFIL director: Intrust Bank Park.

Jana L. Konek: grants manager

Timothy E. McKee: director PRIM CORP EMPL partner: Triplett Woolf & Garretson.

Evan A. Meyers: vice president, chief financial officer

Judge Deanell Reece Tacha: director B 1946. ED University of Kansas BA (1968); University of Michigan JD (1971). PRIM NONPR EMPL judge: U.S. Court Appeals Denver. NONPR AFFIL member: United States Sentencing Commission.

John T. Stewart, III: chairman PRIM CORP EMPL chairman: First National Bank. CORP AFFIL director: Intrust Finance Corp.

Marni Vliet: president, chief executive officer

Kermit Wedel, MD: vice chairman PRIM CORP EMPL partner: Wedel Barker & Burnett Medical Practice.

Rev. Charles E. Winkler: director

Grants Analysis

Disclosure Period: calendar year ending 2001
Total Grants: $16,300,000*
Number of Grants: 194
Average Grant: $84,021
Highest Grant: $1,650,000
Lowest Grant: $100
Typical Range: $10,000 to $25,000 and $100,000 to $450,000
*Note: Grants analysis provided by foundation.

Recent Grants

Note: Grants derived from 2001 Form 990.

General

3,250,000 Kansas Health Institute, Topeka, KS -- develop and maintain a health policy and research institute for Kansas

2,600,000 Wichita State University, Wichita, KS -- to establish a health communication program for children

1,549,365 Kansas Health Institute, Topeka, KS -- to expand evaluation to refine the review of individual grants as well as assessing the overall impact of Kansas Health Foundation

1,275,000	Wichita State University, Wichita, KS -- to establish a health communication program for children
616,177	Kansas University Endowment Association, Lawrence, KS -- to enhance the education of primary care physicians to meet the needs of all Kansans
500,000	Wichita Community Foundation, Wichita, KS -- to provide temporary funds to the Wichita Community Foundation
400,000	Wichita State University, Wichita, KS -- to provide funding for a three year project that will facilitate and support intentional networks of individuals
305,000	Kansas Health Institute, Topeka, KS -- to expand the Kansas Integrated Public Health System
298,905	Kansas Action for Children, Topeka, KS -- plan and implement a statewide report card reflecting the health status of Kansas children
294,530	Kansas Action for Children, Topeka, KS -- to plan and implement a statewide report card reflecting the health status of Kansas children

KANTZLER FOUNDATION

Giving Contact

Robert D. Sarow, Secretary
900 Center Ave.
Bay City, MI 48708
Phone: (989)892-4549

Description

Founded: 1974
EIN: 237422733
Organization Type: Private Foundation
Giving Locations: MI: Bay City including the greater Bay City area
Grant Types: Capital, General Support, Operating Expenses, Seed Money.

Donor Information

Founder: Leopold I. Kantzler

Financial Summary

Total Giving: $297,514 (2002); $329,166 (2001); $338,949 (2000)
Assets: $4,943,712 (2002); $5,828,542 (2001); $5,634,109 (2000)
Gifts Received: $19,263 (1998)

Typical Recipients

Arts & Humanities: Arts Associations & Councils, Community Arts, Historic Preservation, History & Archaeology, Libraries, Performing Arts, Theater, Visual Arts
Civic & Public Affairs: Botanical Gardens/Parks, Chambers of Commerce, Community Foundations, Civic & Public Affairs-General, Housing, Municipalities/Towns, Nonprofit Management, Urban & Community Affairs, Women's Affairs
Education: Colleges & Universities, Public Education (Precollege), Science/Mathematics Education, Student Aid
Environment: Environment-General, Resource Conservation, Wildlife Protection
Health: Health Funds, Health Organizations, Hospitals
Religion: Ministries
Science: Observatories & Planetariums
Social Services: Big Brother/Big Sister, Community Service Organizations, Day Care, Family Services, People with Disabilities, Recreation & Athletics, Scouts, Senior Services, United Funds/United Ways, YMCA/YWCA/YMHA/YWHA, Youth Organizations

Application Procedures

Initial Contact: Request application guidelines.
Deadlines: two weeks prior to each scheduled board meeting.

Additional Information

Publications: Application Guidelines

Foundation Officials

Meade A. Gougeon: trustee
Linda R. Heemstra: trustee
Ruth M. Jaffe: trustee
D. Brian Law: trustee
D. Brian Law: trustee
Mr. Dominic Monastiere: president
Robert D. Sarrow: secretary
Joseph Sasiela: vice president
Clifford D. Van Dyke: vice president B Fort Madison, IA 1929. ED Knox College BA (1951); Harvard University MBA (1955). PRIM CORP EMPL senior vice president: First American Bank of Mid Michigan. NONPR AFFIL director: Delta College Foundation; trustee: Kantzler Foundation; president, director: Bay County Growth Alliance; member: Bay Area Chamber of Commerce. CLUB AFFIL Saginaw Valley Torch Club; Rotary Club; Saginaw Bay Yacht Club; Bay City Country Club; Elks Club.
Jerome Yantz: treasurer

Grants Analysis

Disclosure Period: calendar year ending 2002
Total Grants: $297,514
Number of Grants: 14
Average Grant: $16,468*
Highest Grant: $50,000
Lowest Grant: $1,000
Typical Range: $5,000 to $30,000
***Note:** Average grant figure excludes two highest grants ($100,000).

Recent Grants

Note: Grants derived from 2001 Form 990.

General

100,000	Studio 23, Bay City, MI -- to renovate art gallery
75,000	Bay County Women's Center, Bay City, MI -- to construct a women's shelter
50,000	Saginaw Valley State University, University Center, MI -- to endow scholarship funds
25,000	County of Bay City, Bay City, MI -- to construct skate park
20,000	Saginaw Basin Land Conservation, Bay City, MI -- to purchase shoreline land
16,666	Bay Area Community Foundation, Bay City, MI -- for construction of ice arena
12,500	Bay Sail, Bay City, MI -- sails for schooner appledore
10,000	Hidden Harvest, Saginaw, MI -- to expand food program
7,500	Bay Area Chamber Commerce, Bay City, MI -- to fund family support program
7,500	Bay Sail, Bay City, MI -- to fund environmental scholarship

J. M. KAPLAN FUND

Giving Contact

Peter Davidson, Chairman
261 Madison Avenue, 19th Floor
New York, NY 10016
Phone: (212)767-0630
Fax: (212)767-0639
E-mail: info@jmkfund.org
Web: http://www.jmkfund.org

Description

Founded: 1945
EIN: 136090286
Organization Type: Family Foundation
Giving Locations: NY: New York
Grant Types: General Support, Multiyear/Continuing Support, Operating Expenses, Project, Research, Seed Money.

Donor Information

Founder: Jacob Merrill Kaplan (1891-1987) established the fund in 1945 with proceeds from the Welch Grape Juice Company, which he headed for many years. His daughter, Joan K. Davidson, was president of the fund between 1977 and 1993. Mr. Kaplan worked imaginatively in responding to human need and the improvement of American social service institutions. Today, Mr. Kaplan's ideas and values govern the work of the fund, as they have for over fifty years.

Financial Summary

Total Giving: $6,606,219 (2000); $6,737,450 (1999); $7,236,580 (1998)
Assets: $160,118,875 (2000); $150,645,100 (1999); $134,342,052 (1998)
Gifts Received: $4,627,454 (2000)

Typical Recipients

Arts & Humanities: Arts Associations & Councils, Arts Festivals, Arts Funds, Arts Outreach, Ethnic & Folk Arts, Film & Video, Historic Preservation, History & Archaeology, Libraries, Literary Arts, Museums/Galleries, Performing Arts, Public Broadcasting, Theater
Civic & Public Affairs: Asian American Affairs, Botanical Gardens/Parks, Business/Free Enterprise, Civil Rights, Clubs, Community Foundations, Economic Development, Economic Policy, Employment/Job Training, Civic & Public Affairs-General, Hispanic Affairs, Housing, Law & Justice, Legal Aid, Municipalities/Towns, Nonprofit Management, Public Policy, Rural Affairs, Urban & Community Affairs, Women's Affairs, Women's Affairs
Education: Afterschool/Enrichment Programs, Arts/Humanities Education, Business Education, Colleges & Universities, Economic Education, Education Funds, Education Reform, Elementary Education (Public), Education-General, International Studies, Leadership Training, Literacy, Minority Education, Private Education (Precollege), Science/Mathematics Education, Secondary Education (Private), Secondary Education (Public), Social Sciences Education, Student Aid
Environment: Air/Water Quality, Environment-General, Resource Conservation
Health: AIDS/HIV, Cancer, Children's Health/Hospitals, Health Organizations, Respiratory
International: Foreign Arts Organizations, International-General, Human Rights, International Development, International Environmental Issues, International Relief Efforts
Religion: Churches, Jewish Causes
Science: Scientific Labs
Social Services: At-Risk Youth, Child Welfare, Community Centers, Community Service Organizations, Day Care, Family Planning, Family Services, Food/Clothing Distribution, Senior Services, Shelters/Homelessness

Application Procedures

Initial Contact: Applicants are strongly encouraged to complete the pre-application questionnaire which can be obtained from the fund, or send a clear, concise letter (two to three pages) describing the organization and project for which support is requested.
Application Requirements: Proposals should include a one-page summary and be fewer than ten pages. They should include a history of the organization, its mission, current programs and accomplishments, statement of purpose, beneficiaries served

Morris J. and Betty Kaplun Foundation

and how they will be involved, what qualities or advantages the organization has to be successful in purpose, planned approach and strategy, time frame for project, results anticipated, how program will be evaluated, recent annual report, IRS tax exemption letter, latest financial statement or 990 Form, operating budget including year-to-date income and expenses as source of income, list of Board and staff members, and, if funding is for a specific project, include a description and project budget.

Deadlines: None, however proposals received after October 1 may be carried over to the next year.

Review Process: All requests are acknowledged. A request for further information or a decision in writing is generally made within three months. A site visit or meeting is often helpful.

Notes: Fund accepts the New York Area Common Grant Application.
Fund asks that applicants do not send audio or video tapes unless requested to do so.

Restrictions

The fund generally does not contribute to: operating budgets of educational and medical, institutions; endowment funds, building programs or construction; individuals; films or video; individual scholarships or fellowships; and/or for the personal sponsorship of books, dances, plays or works of art.

Additional Information

Applicants should not fax proposals.
Applicants for the fund's Furthermore program should submit applications to: Furthermore, PO Box 667, Hudson, NY 12534, (518) 828-8900.

Foundation Officials

Brad Davidson: trustee
Elizabeth Davidson: trustee
John Matthew Davidson: trustee
Peter W. Davidson: chairman B Portland, OR 1959. ED Stanford University BA (1981); Harvard University MBA (1986). PRIM CORP EMPL founder, chief executive officer, president: Latin Community Group.
William Falahee: controller
Caio Fonseca: trustee
Elizabeth K. Fonseca: trustee
Isabel Fonseca: trustee
Quina Fonseca: trustee
Mary E. Kaplan: trustee
Richard D. Kaplan: trustee

Grants Analysis

Disclosure Period: calendar year ending 2000
Total Grants: $6,606,219
Number of Grants: 246
Average Grant: $26,855
Highest Grant: $750,000
Typical Range: $5,000 to $100,000

Recent Grants

Note: Grants derived from 2000 Form 990.

Library-Related
150,000	Brooklyn Public Library, Brooklyn, NY
110,000	Queens Library Foundation, Queens, NY
40,000	Queens Library Foundation, Queens, NY

General
750,000	City College of New York, New York, NY
500,000	Trust for Public Land, San Francisco, CA -- for Stewardship Fund for development of community gardens
250,000	Trust for Public Land, San Francisco, CA -- for Stewardship Fund for development of community gardens
200,000	New York Foundation For The Arts, New York, NY -- for the Artists' Fund
150,000	Manhattan Institute for Policy Research,

	New York, NY -- support for the Social Entrepreneurship Initiative
150,000	New York City Public and Private Initiatives, New York, NY -- for Shelter Family Literacy Program
127,250	New York Foundation For The Arts, New York, NY -- for the BUILD (Building Up Infrastructure Levels for Dance) Program
100,000	City Parks Foundation, New York, NY
100,000	Essential Information, Washington, DC
100,000	George Mason University Foundation, Arlington, VA -- support for Project for New Inquiry into Social Research

KAPLEN FOUNDATION

Giving Contact
Wilson R. Kaplen, Trustee
Kaplen Foundation
PO Box 792
Tenafly, NJ 07670-0792
Phone: (201)227-0722

Description
Founded: 1963
EIN: 226048152
Organization Type: Private Foundation
Giving Locations: NJ
Grant Types: General Support.

Donor Information
Founder: Wilson R. Kaplen

Financial Summary
Total Giving: $6,018,239 (fiscal year ending July 31, 2001); $6,487,851 (fiscal 2000); $1,749,943 (fiscal 1999)
Assets: $133,943,900 (fiscal 2001); $135,918,882 (fiscal 2000); $127,728,968 (fiscal 1999)
Gifts Received: $1,000 (fiscal 2001); $4,500 (fiscal 2000); $54,725,391 (fiscal 1998). Note: In 1998, contributions were received from Wilson R. Kaplan ($54,723,392), Andrew V. Schnurr ($1,000), Alexander Kaplan ($500), and Lawrence Kaplan ($500). In fiscal 1996, contributions were received from Wilson R. Kaplen ($1,000,000) and Evelyn Surloff ($100).

Typical Recipients
Arts & Humanities: Arts Centers, Libraries, Literary Arts, Public Broadcasting, Theater
Civic & Public Affairs: Civic & Public Affairs-General, Legal Aid, Women's Affairs
Education: Colleges & Universities, Community & Junior Colleges, Education-General, Legal Education, Medical Education, Private Education (Precollege), Special Education
Environment: Air/Water Quality, Environment-General
Health: Children's Health/Hospitals, Clinics/Medical Centers, Emergency/Ambulance Services, Hospitals, Medical Rehabilitation, Medical Research, Mental Health, Public Health, Single-Disease Health Associations
International: Foreign Educational Institutions, International Relations, International Relief Efforts
Religion: Jewish Causes, Religious Organizations, Seminaries, Synagogues/Temples
Social Services: Community Centers, Community Service Organizations, Day Care, Food/Clothing Distribution, Homes, People with Disabilities, Recreation & Athletics, Scouts, Senior Services, Shelters/Homelessness, Substance Abuse, United Funds/United Ways, Youth Organizations

Application Procedures
Initial Contact: The foundation requests applications be made in writing.
Application Requirements: Include a description of organization, amount requested, purpose of funds

sought, recently audited financial statement, and proof of tax-exempt status.
Deadlines: None.

Foundation Officials
Alexander Kaplen: trustee
Lawrence Kaplen: trustee
Margaret Kaplen: fdn mgr, trustee
Wilson R. Kaplen: trustee
Andrew V. Schnurr, Jr.: trustee

Grants Analysis
Disclosure Period: fiscal year ending July 31, 2001
Total Grants: $6,018,239
Number of Grants: 127
Average Grant: $16,850*
Highest Grant: $400,000
Lowest Grant: $100
Typical Range: $10,000 to $30,000
***Note:** Average grant figure excludes six highest grants ($3,979,363).

Recent Grants
Note: Grants derived from 2000 Form 990.

General
1,313,400	WNYC, New York, NY
1,304,418	Jewish Home and Rehabilitation Center, Rockleigh, NJ
1,207,500	Englewood Healthcare Foundation, Englewood, NJ
651,000	United Jewish Community, River Edge, NJ
304,071	Temple Sinai of Bergen County, Tenafly, NJ
265,350	JCC on the Palisades, Tenafly, NJ
250,000	Roundabout Theater Company, New York, NY
200,000	American Red Cross, Bergen Crossroads Chapter, Ridgewood, NJ
135,000	Community School of Bergen County, Teaneck, NJ
107,500	National Yiddish Book Center, Amherst, MA

MORRIS J. AND BETTY KAPLUN FOUNDATION

Giving Contact
Zvi Levavy, President
225 W. 34th St., Suite 320
New York, NY 10122
Phone: (212)594-8155

Description
Founded: 1955
EIN: 136096009
Organization Type: Private Foundation
Giving Locations: NY: New York
Grant Types: General Support, Research.

Donor Information
Founder: the late Morris J. Kaplun

Financial Summary
Total Giving: $201,912 (fiscal year ending August 31, 2001); $201,912 (fiscal 2000); $202,461 (fiscal 1999)
Giving Analysis: Giving for fiscal 1998 includes: foundation scholarships ($1,000) foundation ($216,944)
Assets: $3,722,445 (fiscal 2001); $3,722,445 (fiscal 2000); $4,162,274 (fiscal 1999)
Gifts Received: $18 (fiscal 2001); $18 (fiscal 2000)

Typical Recipients
Arts & Humanities: Film & Video, Libraries, Literary Arts, Performing Arts, Public Broadcasting, Theater
Civic & Public Affairs: Civil Rights, Civic & Public Affairs-General, Public Policy, Women's Affairs

The Big Book of Library Grant Money 2004-2005

757

Education: Arts/Humanities Education, Colleges & Universities, Education Funds, Education-General, Literacy, Medical Education, Private Education (Precollege), Religious Education

Health: AIDS/HIV, Cancer, Children's Health/Hospitals, Eyes/Blindness, Health Organizations, Hospitals, Medical Research, Prenatal Health Issues, Public Health, Single-Disease Health Associations

International: Foreign Educational Institutions, Health Care/Hospitals, International Peace & Security Issues, International Relations, International Relief Efforts, Missionary/Religious Activities

Religion: Religion-General, Jewish Causes, Religious Organizations, Religious Welfare

Social Services: At-Risk Youth, Child Welfare, Community Service Organizations, Crime Prevention, Delinquency & Criminal Rehabilitation, Family Services, Homes, People with Disabilities, Refugee Assistance, Senior Services, United Funds/United Ways, Youth Organizations

Application Procedures

Initial Contact: The foundation has no formal grant application procedure or application form.
Deadlines: None.

Foundation Officials

Glorie Isakower: vice president
Zvi Levavy: president
Lawrence Marin: vice president
Aaron Seligson: vice president
Moshe Sheinbaum: vice president

Grants Analysis

Disclosure Period: fiscal year ending August 31, 2001
Total Grants: $201,912
Number of Grants: 75
Average Grant: $2,201*
Highest Grant: $39,052
Typical Range: $1,000 to $5,000
*Note: Average grant figure excludes highest grant.

Recent Grants

Note: Grants derived from 2000 Form 990.

General

32,606	Essay Contest
10,000	Tel Aviv University, New York, NY
6,000	Yeshiva Torah Mitzion, North Merrick, NY -- educational
5,500	P.E.F. Israel Endowment Funds, Inc., New York, NY
5,000	American Friends of the Open University of Israel, New York, NY -- educational
5,000	Anti - Defamation League, New York, NY -- social
5,000	Jewish Book Council, New York, NY -- educational
5,000	Jewish Federation of Greater Middlesex County, South River, NJ -- educational
5,000	J.I.T.R American Friends of The Jerusalem Institute Machon Yerushalayim, Jerusalem Israel -- social
5,000	Sanz Medical Center Laniado Hospital, New York, NY -- medical

SAMUEL AND REBECCA KARDON FOUNDATION

Giving Contact

David Kitter, President & Trustee
c/o MAJ
16 Sentry Park West, Suite 310
Blue Bell, PA 19422-2240
Phone: (215)643-3900

Description

Founded: 1952
EIN: 236278123
Organization Type: Private Foundation
Giving Locations: PA
Grant Types: General Support.

Donor Information

Founder: Emanuel S. Kardon, American Bag and Paper Corp.

Financial Summary

Total Giving: $551,430 (2000); $510,895 (1999); $440,106 (1996)
Giving Analysis: Giving for 2000 includes: foundation grants to United Way ($10,000) 1999: foundation grants to United Way ($10,000)
Assets: $9,020,471 (2000); $9,089,197 (1999); $8,705,781 (1996)

Typical Recipients

Arts & Humanities: Arts Associations & Councils, Arts Outreach, Libraries, Museums/Galleries, Music, Opera

Civic & Public Affairs: Civic & Public Affairs-General, Professional & Trade Associations

Education: Arts/Humanities Education, Colleges & Universities, Legal Education, Medical Education, Private Education (Precollege)

Health: Alzheimers Disease, Cancer, Health-General, Heart, Hospitals, Medical Rehabilitation, Medical Research, Nursing Services

International: International Affairs, Missionary/Religious Activities

Religion: Jewish Causes, Religious Welfare, Synagogues/Temples

Social Services: Community Service Organizations, People with Disabilities, Scouts, Social Services-General, United Funds/United Ways, Volunteer Services, YMCA/YWCA/YMHA/YWHA

Application Procedures

Initial Contact: Send a brief letter of inquiry.
Application Requirements: Include a description of organization and purpose of funds sought.
Deadlines: None.

Foundation Officials

Emanuel S. Kardon: president, trustee
David Kittner: president, trustee

Grants Analysis

Disclosure Period: calendar year ending 2000
Total Grants: $541,430*
Number of Grants: 55
Average Grant: $8,165*
Highest Grant: $100,500
Typical Range: $1,000 to $20,000
*Note: Giving excludes United Way. Average grant figure excludes highest grant.

Recent Grants

Note: Grants derived from 1999 Form 990.

General

100,000	Alzheimer Disease Association, Chicago, IL
86,000	Jewish Federation of Greater Philadelphia, Philadelphia, PA
65,000	Museum of American Folk Art, New York, NY
57,000	Kardon Institute of the Arts, Philadelphia, PA
55,250	Settlement Music School, Philadelphia, PA
27,500	Philadelphia Chamber Music Society, Philadelphia, PA
12,500	Holy Family College, Philadelphia, PA
10,000	Inglis House, Philadelphia, PA
10,000	Philadelphia Museum of the Arts, Philadelphia, PA
10,000	United Way, Philadelphia, PA

KATZ FAMILY FOUNDATION

Giving Contact

Cheryl Kurz, Grants Administrator
409 Summit
Mill Valley, CA 94941
Phone: (415)381-4800

Description

Founded: 1986
EIN: 042947276
Organization Type: Private Foundation
Grant Types: General Support.

Donor Information

Founder: Bruce R. Katz

Financial Summary

Total Giving: $283,000 (fiscal year ending November 30, 2001); $640,100 (fiscal 2000); $239,300 (fiscal 1998). Note: Fiscal 1997 Giving includes United Way ($1,000).
Assets: $4,444,823 (fiscal 2001); $6,939,126 (fiscal 2000); $4,936,795 (fiscal 1998)
Gifts Received: $2,194,695 (fiscal 2000); $52,350 (fiscal 1998); $50,000 (fiscal 1997). Note: In fiscal 2000, contributions were received from Bruce R. Katz. In 1998, contributions were received from Steve Mayer.

Typical Recipients

Arts & Humanities: Ballet, Film & Video, Historic Preservation, Libraries, Music, Opera

Civic & Public Affairs: Botanical Gardens/Parks, Community Foundations, Economic Development, Civic & Public Affairs-General, Housing, Native American Affairs, Public Policy, Safety, Urban & Community Affairs

Education: Afterschool/Enrichment Programs, Agricultural Education, Arts/Humanities Education, Colleges & Universities, Private Education (Precollege), Public Education (Precollege), Science/Mathematics Education

Environment: Environment-General, Resource Conservation, Wildlife Protection

Health: AIDS/HIV, Clinics/Medical Centers, Hospices, Hospitals, Mental Health, Preventive Medicine/Wellness Organizations

International: Human Rights, International Environmental Issues, International Organizations, International Peace & Security Issues, International Relations, International Relief Efforts

Religion: Churches, Religious Organizations

Social Services: Camps, Child Welfare, Community Service Organizations, Day Care, Family Services, Food/Clothing Distribution, Special Olympics, United Funds/United Ways, Youth Organizations

Application Procedures

Initial Contact: Send a brief letter of inquiry, including statement of purpose, amount requested, and proof of tax-exempt status.
Deadlines: None.

Foundation Officials

Tracy Barbutes: executive director
Bruce Katz: trustee B 1948.
Roger Katz: trustee
Saul Katz: trustee

Grants Analysis

Disclosure Period: fiscal year ending November 30, 2001
Total Grants: $283,000
Number of Grants: 21

Average Grant: $9,632*
Highest Grant: $50,000
Lowest Grant: $1,000
Typical Range: $1,000 to $20,000
***Note:** Average grant figure excludes two highest grants ($100,000).

Recent Grants

Note: Grants derived from fiscal 2000 Form 990.

Library-Related
25,000   Zen Library Project, San Francisco, CA

General
102,000   Camphill, CA
100,000   FIRST, White Plains, NY
65,000   Kudiat Initiative for Democracy
50,000   Link Foundation, Binghamton, NY
28,000   California Pacific Medical Center, San Francisco, CA
25,000   Camp Winnarainbow, Berkeley, CA
25,000   Film Odyssey, Washington, DC
25,000   Operation USA, Los Angeles, CA
25,000   San Francisco Ballet, San Francisco, CA
25,000   San Francisco Opera, San Francisco, CA

KATZENBERGER FOUNDATION

Giving Contact

Abner J. Golieb, President, Director & Member
200 Park Avenue S, Suite 1700
New York, NY 10003
Phone: (212)315-5575

Description

Founded: 1952
EIN: 136094434
Organization Type: Private Foundation
Giving Locations: IL: IL, MA, NJ, and NY; MA; NJ; NY
Grant Types: General Support.

Donor Information

Founder: the late Walter B. Katzenberger, the late Helen Katherine Katzenberger, The Advertising Checking Bureau

Financial Summary

Total Giving: $655,000 (fiscal year ending November 30, 2001); $806,000 (fiscal 2000); $806,000 (fiscal 1999)
Assets: $17,749,496 (fiscal 2001); $18,685,039 (fiscal 2000); $18,685,039 (fiscal 1999)

Typical Recipients

Arts & Humanities: Arts Associations & Councils, Arts Funds, Arts Institutes, Arts Outreach, Community Arts, Libraries, Museums/Galleries, Performing Arts
Civic & Public Affairs: Community Foundations, Economic Development, Civic & Public Affairs-General, Hispanic Affairs, Housing, Inner-City Development, Philanthropic Organizations
Education: Arts/Humanities Education, Business Education, Colleges & Universities, Community & Junior Colleges, Education-General, Minority Education, Private Education (Precollege), Special Education, Vocational & Technical Education
Environment: Resource Conservation
Health: Children's Health/Hospitals, Mental Health
Religion: Churches, Religious Organizations, Religious Welfare
Science: Science Museums
Social Services: Animal Protection, Camps, Child Abuse, Child Welfare, Community Service Organizations, Counseling, Domestic Violence, Food/Clothing Distribution, People with Disabilities, Recreation &

Athletics, Scouts, Shelters/Homelessness, United Funds/United Ways, YMCA/YWCA/YMHA/YWHA, Youth Organizations

Application Procedures

Initial Contact: Send a brief letter of inquiry describing program or project.
Deadlines: September 1.

Restrictions

Does not support individuals or provide scholarships, grants or awards.

Foundation Officials

Margaret G. Axelrod: treasurer, director, mem
Edward Davis: secretary, director, mem PRIM CORP EMPL president: Advertising Checking Bur.
Richard Eason: director, mem
Abner J. Golieb: president, director, mem
George Haibloom: director, member
Earl Swanson: director, member

Grants Analysis

Disclosure Period: fiscal year ending November 30, 2001
Total Grants: $655,000
Number of Grants: 40
Average Grant: $12,632*
Highest Grant: $100,000
Lowest Grant: $1,000
Typical Range: $5,000 to $30,000
***Note:** Average grant figure excludes two highest grants ($175,000).

Recent Grants

Note: Grants derived from fiscal 2000 Form 990.

General
130,000   Chicago Junior School, Chicago, IL
100,000   First Church of Christ, Scientist, Boston, MA
80,000   Lincoln Center for Performing Arts, New York, NY
80,000   Salvation Army
36,000   Juilliard School, The, New York, NY
35,000   United Negro College Fund, New York, NY
30,000   New York University, New York, NY
25,000   Lighthouse
22,000   Smithsonian Institute, Washington, DC
20,000   Asher Student Foundation

EWING MARION KAUFFMAN FOUNDATION

Giving Contact

Sharon Cohen, Vice President
4801 Rockhill Road
Kansas City, MO 64110-2046
Phone: (816)932-1000
Fax: (818)932-1440
E-mail: info@emkf.org
Web: http://www.emkf.org

Alternate Contact

Web: http://www.entreworld.org

Description

Founded: 1966
EIN: 436064859
Organization Type: Private Foundation
Giving Locations: MO: Kansas City
Grant Types: Award, Employee Matching Gifts, Fellowship, General Support, Multiyear/Continuing Support, Operating Expenses, Project, Research.

Donor Information

Founder: The foundation was established in 1966 by the late Ewing Marion Kauffman , who died in August 1993 of bone cancer. Kauffman's wealth was estimated at $2 billion, with more than half to be awarded to the foundation upon his death.
Kauffman, born on a southern Missouri farm, began his career as a pharmaceutical salesman. In 1950, he started his own pharmaceutical company, Marion Laboratories. The company merged in 1989 with Merrell Dow Pharmaceuticals. He served on the board of the Merrell Dow subsidiary Marion Merrell Dow as chairman emeritus and director until his death.
Kauffman devoted many of his later years to major league baseball and the foundation. He owned the Kansas City Royals, and in 1993 created a trust to keep his team in Kansas City after his death. Kauffman was too ill to attend a July 1993 ceremony to rename the Royals Stadium as Kauffman Stadium.

Financial Summary

Total Giving: $81,865,000 (fiscal year ending June 30, 2002 approx); $90,652,000 (fiscal 2001 approx); $61,831,143 (fiscal 2000)
Giving Analysis: Giving for fiscal 2000 includes: foundation matching gifts ($50,000); foundation scholarships ($300,000); foundation grants to United Way (approx $310,000); foundation grants to United Way ($468,746) foundation fellowships ($1,324,076)
Assets: $1,681,328,000 (fiscal 2002); $2,034,722,000 (fiscal 2001); $2,473,651,998 (fiscal 2000)
Gifts Received: $135,000 (fiscal 2001 approx); $193,283 (fiscal 2000); $986,261 (fiscal 1999)

Typical Recipients

Civic & Public Affairs: Business/Free Enterprise, Clubs, Community Foundations, Employment/Job Training, Civic & Public Affairs-General, Hispanic Affairs, Housing, Nonprofit Management, Professional & Trade Associations, Public Policy, Urban & Community Affairs, Women's Affairs
Education: Afterschool/Enrichment Programs, Agricultural Education, Business Education, Colleges & Universities, Community & Junior Colleges, Education Associations, Elementary Education (Private), Faculty Development, Education-General, Leadership Training, Literacy, Preschool Education, Public Education (Precollege), Science/Mathematics Education, Special Education, Student Aid, Vocational & Technical Education
Environment: Resource Conservation
Health: Clinics/Medical Centers, Health Policy/Cost Containment, Mental Health, Prenatal Health Issues
Religion: Dioceses, Jewish Causes, Religious Welfare
Science: Science Museums
Social Services: At-Risk Youth, Child Welfare, Community Service Organizations, Counseling, Day Care, Family Services, Scouts, Social Services-General, Substance Abuse, United Funds/United Ways, Volunteer Services, YMCA/YWCA/YMHA/YWHA, Youth Organizations

Application Procedures

Initial Contact: Applicants should request the foundation's Guidelines for Grantseekers, either in writing or via email (info@emkf.org).
Application Requirements: Proposals should describe how the proposed project complements the missions and goals of the foundation and its youth development projects and entrepreneurship, describe the organization, and indicate the level of support requested. The letter should be on the organization's letterhead, and contain the following information: a brief description of the problem or opportunity to be addressed; a brief statement of the project's primary goals; a brief statement of the rationale for the project and how it fits within the foundation's focus areas; a time estimate for the project, and the project's expected outcome; a compressed budget estimate for

the project, including the amount requested from the foundation and other anticipated sources of support; a brief statement describing how the program will be sustained after grant funding expires; the name of the primary contact person for follow-up; and verification that the applicant organization has a tax-exempt status under the Internal Revenue Code.

Deadlines: None.

Review Process: Acknowledgments of all grant requests are sent within four weeks of their receipt. When the foundation needs additional information for thorough consideration of a request, the foundation will contact the organization.

Restrictions

The foundation does not make grants to individuals, secular or fraternal organizations, political organizations or campaigns, social clubs, or organizations which do not have 501(c)(3) tax-exempt status. The foundation also does not make grants for endowments, capital campaigns, or special events. The foundation generally does not seek unsolicited proposals. Most grants develop out of relationships with key partners who are pursuing mutual goals.

Additional Information

The foundation is primarily an operating foundation which uses its research for education of at-risk youth to become self-sufficient and productive members of society and to support the understanding of the free enterprise system and the spirit of entrepreneurship for future generations.

Publications: Annual Report; Guidelines

Foundation Officials

Gene Arthur Budig: board member B McCook, NE 1939. ED University of Nebraska BS (1962); University of Nebraska MEd (1963); University of Nebraska EdD (1967); Illinois State University LLD (1982); University of Nebraska LHD (1989); Baker University LHD (1995). PRIM CORP EMPL president: American Baseball League. CORP AFFIL director: Western Resources Inc. NONPR AFFIL director: Harry South Truman Library Institute; director: University Field Staff International; trustee: Nelson-Atkins Museum Art; director: Midwest Research Institute.

Paul Carttar: chief operating officer ED Stanford University Graduate School of Business Administration MBA; University of Kansas (1976).

Patricia M. Cloherty: director

Sharon Cohen: chief communications officer ED University of Wisconsin. NONPR AFFIL senior fellow: The Philanthropic Initiative; board member: Women for Women International; board member: Count Me In.

Robert A. Compton: board member

David C. Lady: administration

John A. "Tony" Mayer, Jr.: board member

Dr. Anne Hodges Morgan: board member

Michael F. Morrissey: chairman, director ED Temple University MBA; University of Notre Dame BA.

Kurt H. Mueller: Kansas City new economy PRIM CORP EMPL partner: Ernst & Young, LLP.

Brian O'Connell: director B Worcester, MA 1930. ED Tufts University BA (1953); Maxwell School of Citizenship & Public Affairs (1953-1954). NONPR AFFIL professor: Tufts University; trustee: Tufts University Alumni Council; director emeritus: National Association Mental Health; fellow: National Committee Patients Rights; founding president: Independent Sector; fellow: National Academy Public Administration; fellow trustee: American Public Health Association.

Carl J. Schramm: president, chief executive officer, director ED Georgetown University JD; Le Moyne College BA; University of Wisconsin PhD; University of Wisconsin MA.

Michie P. Slaughter: director

Eugene R. Wilson: senior vice president development B Findlay, OH 1938. ED Bowling Green State University BA (1960); Syracuse University MS (1961).

NONPR AFFIL visitor: Center Philanthropy; member: Omicron Delta Kappa; member: Bowling Green State University National Alumni Association. CLUB AFFIL Gnome Athenaeum Club.

Grants Analysis

Disclosure Period: fiscal year ending June 30, 2002

Total Grants: $57,001,000*

Number of Grants: 575*

Average Grant: $52,175*

Highest Grant: $27,000,000

Lowest Grant: $100

Typical Range: $25,000 to $100,000

*Note: Giving excludes United Way, scholarships, matching gifts, and fellowships. Totals are approximate. Average grant figure excludes highest grant. Giving includes gifts to individuals.

Recent Grants

Note: Grants derived from fiscal 2001 Form 990.

General

31,825,567 Kauffman Center for Entrepreneurial Leadership, Kansas City, MO -- to support the Kauffman Center for Entrepreneurial Leadership's grants and programs

15,000,000 Kauffman Center for Entrepreneurial Leadership, Kansas City, MO -- to support grants and programs which are directed toward entrepreneurship education at all levels

5,000,000 Stanford University, Palo Alto, CA -- funding toward endowment of the Gardner Center for Children and Communities

2,300,000 Georgetown University, Washington, DC -- for creation of Waldemar A. Nielsen Chair in Philanthropy

1,000,000 Greater Kansas City Community Foundation and Affiliated Trusts, Kansas City, MO -- for program enhancement, outreach and state the art technology to "feed" all other public library branches

1,000,000 Greater Kansas City Community Foundation and Affiliated Trusts, Kansas City, MO -- to support grantmaking by the Kauffman Fund

1,000,000 Union Station Kansas City, Inc., Kansas City, MO -- funding to enable the transition to sustainable financial operation

800,000 Boys and Girls Club of Greater Kansas City, Kansas City, MO -- to support increased organizational development of four of the Boys and Girls Club hub sites

700,000 Kansas City, Kansas Unified School District 500, Kansas City, MO -- to provide support for Phase 2 of the First Things First Initiative

566,667 Greater Kansas City Community Foundation and Affiliated Trusts, Kansas City, MO -- to support the Kansas Community Development Initiative

LOUIS G. KAUFMAN ENDOWMENT FUND

Giving Contact

Jim Duranceau, Vice President & Trust Officer
c/o Wells Fargo
101 West Washington
PO Box 580
Marquette, MI 49855
Phone: (906)228-1243
Fax: (906)228-1479

Description

Founded: 1927

EIN: 386048505

Organization Type: Private Foundation

Giving Locations: MI: Marquette

Grant Types: Emergency, General Support, Operating Expenses, Project, Scholarship, Seed Money.

Donor Information

Founder: L. G. Kaufman Trust

Financial Summary

Total Giving: $132,902 (fiscal year ending December 01, 2001); $163,286 (fiscal 2000); $127,450 (fiscal 1999)

Giving Analysis: Giving for fiscal 2001 includes: foundation scholarships ($62,000) fiscal 1999: foundation scholarships ($57,200)

Assets: $3,252,695 (fiscal 2001); $3,379,928 (fiscal 2000); $3,507,941 (fiscal 1999)

Typical Recipients

Arts & Humanities: Arts & Humanities-General, History & Archaeology, Museums/Galleries, Music, Public Broadcasting

Civic & Public Affairs: Municipalities/Towns, Safety

Education: Afterschool/Enrichment Programs, Private Education (Precollege), Public Education (Precollege), Science/Mathematics Education, Secondary Education (Public), Student Aid

Environment: Resource Conservation

Health: Health Organizations, Public Health

Science: Scientific Centers & Institutes

Social Services: Camps, Community Service Organizations, Crime Prevention, Family Planning, Family Services, Recreation & Athletics, Scouts, Substance Abuse, United Funds/United Ways, YMCA/YWCA/YMHA/YWHA, Youth Organizations

Application Procedures

Initial Contact: Send a brief letter of inquiry.

Application Requirements: Include the history and purpose of requesting organization, statement of financial condition, proof of tax-exempt status, purpose of funds sought, and amount requested.

Deadlines: April 30.

Restrictions

Limited to the advancements of the moral, physical, and mental development of youth.

Additional Information

Trust(s): Wells Fargo

Foundation Officials

Henry J. Bothwell: fund comm mem

Don Grisham: fund committee member

Harold N. Herlich, Jr.: secretary

Ann K. Jordan: fund comm mem

Michael Kaufman: fund committee member

Peter Kaufman: chairman, fund comm mem

Ellwood Mattson: fund comm mem

Donald Parsons, Esq.: director

Melvin Rossway: fund comm mem

Grants Analysis

Disclosure Period: fiscal year ending December 01, 2001

Total Grants: $70,902*

Number of Grants: 18

Average Grant: $1,818*

Highest Grant: $40,000

Lowest Grant: $400

Typical Range: $500 to $5,000

*Note: Giving excludes scholarships. Average grant figure excludes highest grant.

Recent Grants

Note: Grants derived from 2001 Form 990.

General

40,000	Marquette Area Public Schools, Marquette, MI -- high school scholarship program
40,000	Peter White Public Library, Marquette, MI
11,000	Marquette Area Public Schools, Marquette, MI -- middle school scholarship program
7,000	Marquette Junior Hockey, Marquette, MI -- scholarship programs
5,000	Bay Cliff Health Camp, Marquette, MI
5,000	City of Marquette, Marquette, MI -- Sesquicentennial Pavilion Project
4,152	Marquette Area Public Schools, Marquette, MI -- Lyceum Program
4,000	Marquette Area Public Schools, Marquette, MI -- special incentive programs
3,000	YMCA of Marquette County, Marquette, MI -- strong kids scholarship program
2,000	YMCA of Marquette County, Marquette, MI

KAUFMAN FOUNDATION

Giving Contact

Richard Kaufman, Trustee
297 West Clay Avenue, Suite 106
Muskegon, MI 49440
Phone: (231)727-3415

Description

Founded: 1959
EIN: 386091556
Organization Type: Private Foundation
Grant Types: General Support.

Financial Summary

Total Giving: $172,790 (fiscal year ending October 31, 2002); $195,086 (fiscal 2001); $271,105 (fiscal 2000)
Giving Analysis: Giving for fiscal 2002 includes: foundation grants to United Way ($1,000) fiscal 2000: foundation grants to United Way ($2,000)
Assets: $2,905,812 (fiscal 2002); $3,139,373 (fiscal 2001); $3,403,630 (fiscal 2000)
Gifts Received: $25,000 (fiscal 1994). Note: In fiscal 1994, contributions were received from Amstore Corp.

Typical Recipients

Arts & Humanities: Arts Associations & Councils, Arts Centers, Arts Institutes, Dance, Arts & Humanities-General, Libraries, Museums/Galleries, Music, Public Broadcasting, Theater
Civic & Public Affairs: Community Foundations, Employment/Job Training, Civic & Public Affairs-General, Nonprofit Management, Philanthropic Organizations, Public Policy, Women's Affairs
Education: Arts/Humanities Education, Business Education, Colleges & Universities, Education Funds, Environmental Education, Education-General, Minority Education, Private Education (Precollege), Religious Education, Secondary Education (Public), Special Education
Health: Children's Health/Hospitals, Heart, Hospices, Medical Research
International: Foreign Educational Institutions, International Affairs, International Relief Efforts, Missionary/Religious Activities
Religion: Churches, Religion-General, Jewish Causes, Religious Organizations, Religious Welfare, Synagogues/Temples
Science: Scientific Centers & Institutes
Social Services: Child Welfare, Community Service Organizations, Family Planning, Scouts, United Funds/United Ways, YMCA/YWCA/YMHA/YWHA

Application Procedures

Initial Contact: Send a brief letter of inquiry.
Deadlines: None.

Foundation Officials

Richard F. Kaufman: trustee
Sylvia C. Kaufman: trustee

Grants Analysis

Disclosure Period: fiscal year ending October 31, 2002
Total Grants: $171,790*
Number of Grants: 72
Average Grant: $954*
Highest Grant: $80,000
Lowest Grant: $50
Typical Range: $100 to $3,000
*Note: Giving excludes United Way. Average grant figure excludes two highest grants ($105,000).

Recent Grants

Note: Grants derived from 2001 Form 990.

General

8,333	Grand Valley State University, Allendale, MI
7,500	Cleveland Clinic Foundation, Cleveland, OH
2,394	Aspen Museum of Art, Aspen, CO
1,667	Aspen Museum of Art, Aspen, CO
1,000	Blossoming Rose, Cedar Springs, MI
1,000	Congregation B'nai Israel, Northampton, MA
1,000	United Way of Muskegon County, Muskegon, MI
550	Aitz Chayim Synagogue
250	Abraham Fund, New York, NY
250	Amherst Parent's Fund, Amherst, OH

HENRY KAUFMANN FOUNDATION

Giving Contact

Philip J. Hirsch, President & Director
c/o Proskauer, Rose, Goetz & Mendelsohn
1585 Broadway
New York, NY 10036
Phone: (212)969-3299

Description

Founded: 1928
EIN: 136034179
Organization Type: Private Foundation
Giving Locations: NY: New York and greater area; PA: Pittsburgh and greater area
Grant Types: General Support.

Donor Information

Founder: the late Henry Kaufmann

Financial Summary

Total Giving: $400,000 (1999 approx); $284,500 (1998); $281,000 (1997)
Assets: $441,114 (1998); $721,380 (1997); $972,384 (1996)

Typical Recipients

Arts & Humanities: Arts Centers, Arts Outreach, Libraries, Museums/Galleries, Theater
Civic & Public Affairs: Community Foundations, Housing, Municipalities/Towns, Urban & Community Affairs
Education: Arts/Humanities Education, Colleges & Universities, Education Associations, Education Reform, Legal Education, Literacy, Medical Education, Private Education (Precollege), Public Education (Precollege)
Environment: Forestry, Environment-General

Health: AIDS/HIV, Cancer, Clinics/Medical Centers, Hospices, Hospitals, Long-Term Care, Medical Research, Mental Health, Prenatal Health Issues, Single-Disease Health Associations
International: International Affairs, International Organizations
Religion: Jewish Causes, Religious Organizations, Religious Welfare
Social Services: Camps, Child Welfare, Community Centers, Community Service Organizations, Counseling, Crime Prevention, Family Planning, Family Services, Homes, People with Disabilities, Senior Services, Social Services-General, United Funds/United Ways, YMCA/YWCA/YMHA/YWHA, Youth Organizations

Application Procedures

Initial Contact: Send a brief letter of inquiry.
Deadlines: None.

Additional Information

Publications: Annual Report

Foundation Officials

Leonard Nathan Block: vice president, director B Brooklyn, NY December 21, 1911. ED University of Pennsylvania BS (1933). PRIM CORP EMPL senior chairman: Block Drug Co. NONPR AFFIL director: Federation Jewish Philanthropies. CLUB AFFIL Ocean Beach Club; Harmonie Club; Hollywood Golf Club.
Mitchell A. Drossman: assistant secretary
William T. Golden: treasurer, director B New York, NY October 25, 1909. ED University of Pennsylvania AB (1930); Harvard University (1930-1931); Columbia University MA (1979). CORP AFFIL director: Verde Exploration Ltd. Inc.; chairman emeritus: General America Investors Co. Inc.; chairman: Black Rock Forest Consortium; director: Block Drug Co. Inc. NONPR AFFIL member: New York Academy Medicine; member, board governors: New York Academy Science; trustee emeritus: National Humanities Center; vice chairman: Mount Sinai Medical Center; member: National Academy Public Administration; director: International University Exchange Inc.; treasurer, trustee: Hebrew Free Loan Society; member: History Science Society; member: Downtown Association; secretary, trustee: Carnegie Institute; member: Council Foreign Relations; trustee, emeritus: Barnard College; chairman emeritus: American Museum Natural History; member: American Philosophical Society; treasurer, director: American Association Advancement Science; trustee: The After School Corp. CLUB AFFIL Cosmos Club; Army-Navy Country Club; Century Association.
Philip J. Hirsch: president, director
Jeffrey A. Horwitz: secretary
Arnold N. Levine: director
Charles Looker: director
Frederick Phineas Rose: director B New York, NY 1923. ED Yale University BCE (1944). PRIM CORP EMPL chairman: Rose Associates. CORP AFFIL member publs committee: Commentary Magazine; director: Olympia & York Inc.; trustee: Asia Society. NONPR AFFIL director: Rockefeller University; member: Union League New York; trustee: Philharmonic Symphony Society; director: Metropolitan Museum Art; government: New York Real Estate Board; director: Lincoln Center Performing Arts; trustee: Manhattan Institute; member: Council Foreign Relations; honorary chairman: Federation Jewish Philanthropies New York; trustee: American Museum Natural History; member: Century Association. CLUB AFFIL Yale Club; Beach Point Yacht Club; Century Country Club.
John M. Wolf, Sr.: director

Grants Analysis

Disclosure Period: calendar year ending 1998
Total Grants: $284,500
Number of Grants: 8
Average Grant: $35,563

Highest Grant: $70,000
Typical Range: $1,000 to $70,000

Recent Grants

Note: Grants derived from 1999 Form 990.

General

103,242	Hebrew Home for the Aged at Riverdale, Riverdale, NY
103,242	Jewish Board of Family & Children's Services, New York, NY
103,242	Jewish Community Center of Pittsburgh, Pittsburgh, PA
103,242	Jewish Community Center of Upper West Side, New York, NY
500	Hospice and Home Care B/T Sea, Inc.

HUGH KAUL FOUNDATION TRUST

Giving Contact

Karla Gayle, Vice President & Trust Officer
Care of AmSouth Bank
PO Box 11426
Birmingham, AL 35202
Phone: (205)326-4696
Fax: (205)581-7433

Description

Founded: 1990
EIN: 636158725
Organization Type: Family Foundation
Giving Locations: AL: Coosa County, Jefferson County, Birmingham Clay County
Grant Types: Capital, Fellowship, General Support, Matching, Multiyear/Continuing Support, Research.

Donor Information

Founder: Established in 1990 by the late Mr. Hugh Kaul .

Financial Summary

Total Giving: $3,339,483 (2000); $2,882,600 (1998); $1,756,550 (1997)
Assets: $68,280,294 (2000); $64,042,367 (1998); $53,258,709 (1997)
Gifts Received: $7,176,129 (1998); $21,212,494 (1992). Note: The foundation received contributions from the estate of Hugh Kaul.

Typical Recipients

Arts & Humanities: Arts Associations & Councils, Arts Festivals, Arts Funds, Ballet, History & Archaeology, Libraries, Museums/Galleries, Music, Opera, Public Broadcasting, Theater
Civic & Public Affairs: Asian American Affairs, Botanical Gardens/Parks, Clubs, Community Foundations, Civic & Public Affairs-General, Housing, Nonprofit Management, Philanthropic Organizations, Public Policy, Urban & Community Affairs, Women's Affairs, Zoos/Aquariums
Education: Arts/Humanities Education, Business Education, Colleges & Universities, Economic Education, Education Reform, Environmental Education, Education-General, Gifted & Talented Programs, Leadership Training, Literacy, Medical Education, Minority Education, Preschool Education, Private Education (Precollege), Public Education (Precollege), Religious Education, Special Education, Student Aid
Environment: Air/Water Quality, Environment-General, Resource Conservation, Wildlife Protection
Health: Cancer, Children's Health/Hospitals, Eyes/Blindness, Hospitals, Medical Research, Mental Health, Public Health, Single-Disease Health Associations, Speech & Hearing
International: International Organizations
Religion: Churches, Ministries, Missionary Activities (Domestic), Religious Organizations, Religious Welfare

Science: Science Museums, Scientific Centers & Institutes
Social Services: Child Welfare, Community Centers, Community Service Organizations, Crime Prevention, Family Planning, Family Services, Recreation & Athletics, Scouts, Senior Services, Shelters/Homelessness, Social Services-General, Substance Abuse, United Funds/United Ways, YMCA/YWCA/YMHA/YWHA, Youth Organizations

Application Procedures

Initial Contact: Applicants should submit grant requests to the foundation in written form.
Application Requirements: Grant requests should include a one-page cover letter, with the name and address of the organization which is requesting funds, as well as a designation of the individual filing the request and his/her relationship to the organization, amount requested, and succinct summary of project (no more than one paragraph); a full proposal of no more than four pages, with agency's history including major programs and accomplishments, links with similar organizations, need or issue project addresses, total cost of program and amount requested, goals and objectives, activities that will be carried out, qualifications of key personnel, and other organizations involved in project. Documentation of the tax-exempt status of the organization is also required.
Deadlines: Requests must be received by March 15 and September 15 in order to be considered at the June and December meetings of the trustees.
Review Process: Applicants are notified within a reasonable period following the meeting of the trustees.

Additional Information

Trust(s): AmSouth Bank, NA

Foundation Officials

William Houston Blount: trustee B Union Springs, AL 1922. ED Harvard University; University of Alabama (1942). PRIM CORP EMPL chairman emeritus: Vulcan Materials Co. CORP AFFIL director: VF Corp.; director: Blount International Inc. NONPR AFFIL Rotary International. CLUB AFFIL member: Rotary Club of Birmingham; member: Shoal Creek; member: Mountain Brook Country Club; member: National Golf Club; member: The Club; member: Elk River Club.
Karla Gayle: vice president, trust officer
John K. Greene: trustee B Birmingham, AL 1929. ED Yale University (1951). PRIM CORP EMPL special principal: William Blair & Co. LLC. CORP AFFIL director: Vulcan Materials Co.
Beverly P. Head, III: trustee PRIM CORP EMPL chairman: Giles & Kendall Inc. CORP AFFIL vice president: Mantlecraft; chairman: Pacific Rim Manufacturing.

Grants Analysis

Disclosure Period: calendar year ending 2000
Total Grants: $3,339,483
Number of Grants: 73
Average Grant: $45,746
Highest Grant: $650,000
Lowest Grant: $1,000
Typical Range: $5,000 to $50,000

Recent Grants

Note: Grants derived from 2000 Form 990.

Library-Related

25,000	Birmingham Public Library, Birmingham, AL

General

650,000	University of Alabama at Birmingham, Birmingham, AL
500,000	Children's Hospital of Alabama, Birmingham, AL
200,000	Altamont School, Birmingham, AL
200,000	Birmingham Museum of Art, 2000, Birmingham, AL
200,000	Community Foundation of Greater Birmingham, Birmingham, AL
200,000	University of Alabama at Birmingham, Birmingham, AL
200,000	Vulcan Park Foundation, Birmingham, AL
75,000	Nature Conservancy of Alabama, Birmingham, AL
60,000	McWane Center, Birmingham, AL
50,000	Alabama Symphonic Association, Birmingham, AL

T. JAMES KAVANAGH FOUNDATION

Giving Contact

Brenda S. Brooks, Principal Manager
PO Box 609
Broomall, PA 19008
Phone: (610)356-0743
Fax: (610)356-4606

Description

Founded: 1968
EIN: 236442981
Organization Type: Private Foundation
Giving Locations: NJ: southern NJ; PA, Philadelphia PA, Sharon
Grant Types: Capital, Emergency, General Support, Multiyear/Continuing Support, Project, Research.

Donor Information

Founder: T. James Kavanagh

Financial Summary

Total Giving: $303,101 (2000); $405,611 (1999); $358,923 (1998)
Giving Analysis: Giving for 2000 includes: foundation grants to United Way ($3,000); 1999: foundation grants to United Way ($3,000); 1998: foundation grants to United Way ($3,000) foundation ($355,923)
Assets: $15,529,312 (2000); $14,679,206 (1999); $15,626,960 (1998)

Typical Recipients

Arts & Humanities: Ballet, Historic Preservation, Libraries, Music, Opera, Performing Arts, Theater
Civic & Public Affairs: Safety
Education: Arts/Humanities Education, Colleges & Universities, Elementary Education (Private), Elementary Education (Public), Literacy, Medical Education, Private Education (Precollege), Religious Education, Science/Mathematics Education, Secondary Education (Private), Student Aid, Vocational & Technical Education
Environment: Environment-General
Health: Emergency/Ambulance Services, Health Organizations, Hospices, Hospitals, Long-Term Care, Medical Research, Nursing Services, Single-Disease Health Associations
Religion: Churches, Missionary Activities (Domestic), Religious Organizations, Religious Welfare, Synagogues/Temples
Social Services: Camps, Community Service Organizations, Day Care, Family Services, Food/Clothing Distribution, Recreation & Athletics, Shelters/Homelessness, United Funds/United Ways, YMCA/YWCA/YMHA/YWHA, Youth Organizations

Application Procedures

Initial Contact: Applications must be accompanied by proper identification and proof of tax-exempt status.
Deadlines: None.

Restrictions

Grants are not made to individuals.

Additional Information

Publications: Application Guidelines

Foundation Officials

Frank J. Brooks: trustee
Louis J. Esposito: trustee
Thomas E. Kavanagh: trustee

Grants Analysis

Disclosure Period: calendar year ending 2000
Total Grants: $300,101*
Number of Grants: 95
Average Grant: $3,159
Highest Grant: $25,000
Typical Range: $1,000 to $10,000
*Note: Giving excludes United Way.

Recent Grants

Note: Grants derived from 1999 Form 990.

Library-Related

5,000	Newtown Public Library, Newtown Square, PA

General

20,000	Notre Dame Church, Hermitage, PA
20,000	Prince of Peace Center, Farrell, PA
13,000	St. Joseph's School, Sharon, PA
10,000	Camilla Hall Nursing Home, Immaculata, PA
10,000	Discalced Carmelite Monastery, Loretto, PA
10,000	St. Francis College, Loretto, PA
10,000	St. Francis Xavier Church, Cresson, PA
10,000	Sister Servants of the Sacred Heart of Jesus, Cresson, PA
9,000	St. Anastasia Church, Newtown Square, PA
7,500	Cabrini College, Radnor, PA

KAWABE MEMORIAL FUND

Giving Contact

Margaret Liu, Trust Officer
Kawabe Memorial Fund
Care of Bank of America
PO Box 24565
Seattle, WA 98124
Phone: (206)358-3144

Description

Founded: 1972
EIN: 916116549
Organization Type: Private Foundation
Giving Locations: WA: Seattle including metropolitan area
Grant Types: Capital, Emergency, Multiyear/Continuing Support, Operating Expenses, Seed Money.

Donor Information

Founder: the late Tomo Kawabe, the late Harry Kawabe

Financial Summary

Total Giving: $208,000 (2001); $186,500 (2000); $158,600 (1999)
Giving Analysis: Giving for 2001 includes: foundation scholarships ($6,000); 2000: foundation scholarships ($11,000); 1999: foundation scholarships ($8,000)
Assets: $4,140,101 (2001); $4,777,751 (2000); $4,851,981 (1999)
Gifts Received: $200 (1999)

Typical Recipients

Arts & Humanities: Libraries, Museums/Galleries, Opera
Civic & Public Affairs: Asian American Affairs, Civic & Public Affairs-General, Housing, Urban & Community Affairs, Women's Affairs
Education: Colleges & Universities, International Studies, Minority Education, Religious Education, Student Aid
Health: AIDS/HIV, Children's Health/Hospitals, Clinics/Medical Centers, Emergency/Ambulance Services, Geriatric Health, Health Organizations, Long-Term Care, Nursing Services, Nutrition, Trauma Treatment
International: International Relations, International Relief Efforts
Religion: Churches, Jewish Causes, Ministries, Religious Organizations, Religious Welfare, Synagogues/Temples
Social Services: Community Centers, Community Service Organizations, Domestic Violence, Family Services, Food/Clothing Distribution, Homes, People with Disabilities, Refugee Assistance, Senior Services, Shelters/Homelessness, Substance Abuse, United Funds/United Ways, Youth Organizations

Application Procedures

Initial Contact: Send a brief project proposal.
Application Requirements: Include expenses, income summary, and proof of tax-exempt status.
Deadlines: None.
Review Process: Requests are reviewed quarterly.

Restrictions

Support is given to institutions and social service agencies devoted to the care of children, the indigent, and aged people, and for capital grants to churches for improvement of physical facilities.

Additional Information

Provides scholarships to graduating students of Seward High School, AK.
Publications: Application Guidelines
Trust(s): Bank of America

Foundation Officials

Yasue Brevig: mem allocations comm NONPR AFFIL member: Permian Basin Petroleum Association.
Rev. Donald Castro: mem allocations comm
Tsuyoshi Horike: mem allocations comm
Ruth S. Iwata: mem allocations comm
Aizo Kosai: mem allocations comm
Takashi Matsui: mem allocations comm
Tsuyoshi Nakano: mem allocations comm
Rev. Sadamori Ouichi: mem allocations comm
Toru Sakahara: mem allocations comm
Chiyoko Yasutake: member allocations committee
Webster T. Yasutake: member allocations committee

Grants Analysis

Disclosure Period: calendar year ending 2001
Total Grants: $202,000*
Number of Grants: 38
Average Grant: $4,316
Highest Grant: $40,500
Lowest Grant: $500
Typical Range: $1,000 to $10,000
*Note: Giving excludes scholarships.

Recent Grants

Note: Grants derived from 2000 Form 990.

Library-Related

10,000	Seattle Public Library, Seattle, WA -- for program fund

General

25,500	Seattle Betsuin Buddhist Temple, Seattle, WA -- for repairs and maintenance projects

20,000	Seattle Japanese Language School, Seattle, WA -- building renovations
10,000	Make a Wish Foundation
10,000	Providence Mount St. Vincent, Seattle, WA -- to purchase a bus
6,000	Seattle Koyasan Buddhist Temple, Seattle, WA -- for building renovations
5,500	Children's Hospital and Medical Center, Seattle, WA
5,000	Asian Counseling and Referral Service, Seattle, WA -- for food bank
5,000	In A Pinch -- operations for crisis nursery
5,000	Jubilee Women's Center, Seattle, WA -- for Learning and Technology Center
5,000	Kawabe Memorial House, Seattle, WA -- for garden project

KAWASAKI MOTORS MANUFACTURING CORPORATION U.S.A.

Company Headquarters

Lincoln, NE
Web: http://www.kawasaki.com

Company Description

Employees: 800
SIC(s): 3751 Motorcycles, Bicycles & Parts, 3799 Transportation Equipment Nec.
Parent Company: Kawasaki Heavy Industries, Ltd., Kobe Crystal Tower, 1-3 Higashikawasaki-cho 1-chome, Chuo-ku, Kobe, Japan

Operating Locations

Kawasaki Heavy Industries U.S.A. (NY--New York); Kawasaki Loaders Manufacturing Corp. U.S.A. (GA--Newnan); Kawasaki Motors Manufacturing Corp. U.S.A. (CA--Irvine); Kawasaki Rail Car (NY--Yonkers); Kawasaki Robotics U.S.A. (MI--Farmington Hills)

Kawasaki Good Times Foundation

Giving Contact

Steve Becker
PO Box 81469
Lincoln, NE 68501
Phone: (402)476-6600
Fax: (402)476-4735

Description

Founded: 1993
EIN: 363879896
Organization Type: Corporate Foundation
Giving Locations: DC: Washington; GA: Atlant; MO: Maryville; NE: Lincoln; NJ: New Brunswick; NY: New York, Yonkers; PA: Warrendale

Financial Summary

Total Giving: $55,500 (1999); $88,500 (1998); $68,500 (1997)
Giving Analysis: Giving for 1999 includes: foundation ($55,000)
Assets: $2,138,041 (1999); $1,903,188 (1998); $1,812,391 (1997)
Gifts Received: $241,000 (1999); $69,000 (1998); $55,000 (1997). Note: In 1999, contributions were received from Kawasaki Motors Manufacturing Corporation ($70,000), Kawasaki Robotics ($15,000), Kawasaki Motors Corp ($117,000), Kawasaki Heavy Industries ($9,000) and Kawasaki Loaders Mfg. Corp. ($30,000). In 1998, contributions were received from Kawasaki Motors Manufacturing Corporation ($60,000) and Kawasaki Robotics ($9,000).

Typical Recipients

Arts & Humanities: Arts Associations & Councils, Arts Centers, Ethnic & Folk Arts, History & Archaeology, Libraries, Museums/Galleries, Music
Civic & Public Affairs: Professional & Trade Associations, Zoos/Aquariums
Education: Colleges & Universities, Engineering/Technological Education
Health: Cancer
International: Foreign Arts Organizations, International Relief Efforts
Science: Scientific Organizations, Scientific Research

Application Procedures

Initial Contact: Send proposal in written form.
Application Requirements: Include amount requested, purpose of funds sought, time needed, expected benefits to the public, and any other information related to the request.
Deadlines: None.

Corporate Officials

Steve Becker: chief executive officer, chief financial officer PRIM CORP EMPL chief executive officer, chief financial officer: Kawasaki Motors Manufacturing Corp. U.S.A.
Stan Hanson: vice president PRIM CORP EMPL vice president: Kawasaki Motors Manufacturing Corp. U.S.A.
Takehiko Saeki: president PRIM CORP EMPL president: Kawasaki Motors Manufacturing Corp. U.S.A.

Foundation Officials

Terry (Terunori) Kitajima: vice president PRIM CORP EMPL vice president finance, chief financial officer: Kawasaki Motors Manufacturing Corp. U.S.A.
Takeshi Miyakoshi: president, director
Hiroshi Noda: director
Takehiko Saeki: director (see above)
Takeshi Suzaki: secretary, treasurer

Grants Analysis

Disclosure Period: calendar year ending 1999
Total Grants: $55,500
Typical Range: $500 to $5,000

Recent Grants

Note: Grants derived from 1998 Form 990.

Library-Related

5,000	Maryville Public Library, Maryville, MO

General

30,000	University of Nebraska (NE), Lincoln, NE
20,000	George Washington University, Washington, DC
10,000	The Metropolitan Museum of Art, New York, NY
5,000	The Jane Voorhees Zimmerli Art Museum, New Brunswick, NJ
5,000	The New York Pops, Inc., New York, NY
5,000	United States Committee for UNICEF, New York, NY
3,500	The New York Transit Museum, Yonkers, NY
2,500	Inoue Chamber Ensemble, New York, NY
1,000	Memorial Sloan-Kettering Cancer Center, New York, NY
1,000	Woodruff Arts Center, Atlanta, GA

KAYSER FOUNDATION

Giving Contact

R. Bruce LaBoon, President
600 Travis, Suite 3500
Houston, TX 77002
Phone: (713)226-1393

Description

Founded: 1961
EIN: 746050591
Organization Type: Private Foundation
Giving Locations: DC; SC; TX
Grant Types: Emergency, General Support, Research.

Donor Information

Founder: Paul Kayser, Mrs. Paul Kayser

Financial Summary

Total Giving: $267,189 (2001); $243,689 (2000); $228,439 (1999)
Giving Analysis: Giving for 2001 includes: foundation scholarships ($5,000)
Assets: $4,886,127 (2001); $5,712,815 (2000); $5,990,053 (1999)

Typical Recipients

Arts & Humanities: Arts Outreach, Ballet, History & Archaeology, Libraries, Museums/Galleries, Music, Performing Arts, Theater
Civic & Public Affairs: Botanical Gardens/Parks, Employment/Job Training, Law & Justice, Safety, Women's Affairs
Education: Afterschool/Enrichment Programs, Business Education, Colleges & Universities, Education-General, Legal Education, Medical Education, Private Education (Precollege), Public Education (Precollege), Secondary Education (Private), Student Aid
Environment: Forestry, Environment-General, Wildlife Protection
Health: AIDS/HIV, Alzheimers Disease, Arthritis, Cancer, Children's Health/Hospitals, Clinics/Medical Centers, Diabetes, Emergency/Ambulance Services, Eyes/Blindness, Health Organizations, Heart, Hospices, Hospitals, Hospitals (University Affiliated), Medical Rehabilitation, Medical Research, Mental Health, Multiple Sclerosis, Prenatal Health Issues, Public Health, Single-Disease Health Associations
International: Health Care/Hospitals
Religion: Religion-General, Jewish Causes, Ministries, Religious Organizations, Religious Welfare, Social/Policy Issues
Social Services: Animal Protection, At-Risk Youth, Child Abuse, Child Welfare, Community Service Organizations, Crime Prevention, Day Care, Emergency Relief, Family Planning, Family Services, Food/Clothing Distribution, Homes, People with Disabilities, Scouts, Shelters/Homelessness, Special Olympics, Substance Abuse, United Funds/United Ways, YMCA/YWCA/YMHA/YWHA, Youth Organizations

Application Procedures

Initial Contact: Send a brief letter of inquiry.
Application Requirements: Outline the purpose of funds sought.
Deadlines: None.

Restrictions

Does not support individuals. Must be organized under IRS Section 501(c) (3).

Foundation Officials

Robert Bruce La Boon: vice president B Saint Louis, MO 1941. ED Texas Christian University BSc (1963); Southern Methodist University LLB (1965). PRIM CORP EMPL partner: Liddell, Sapp, Zivley, Hill & LaBoon. CORP AFFIL director: Texas Commerce Bankshares; director: Texas Med Center Board; director: Gamma Biological; director: Big Three Industries. NONPR AFFIL member: Texas State Bar; member, board visitors: University Cancer Foundation Maryland Anderson Cancer Center; trustee: Texas Christian University; advisor director: Retina Research Foundation; fellow: Texas Bar Foundation; trustee: Kayser Foundation; director: Institute Rehabilitation & Research; director: International Center Arbitration; director: Houston International Festival; director: Greater Houston Partnership & Community

Schools Houston; member: Houston Bar Association; member: Association Bank Counsel; director: Greater Houston Community Foundation; member: American Law Institute; member: American Bar Association; fellow: American College Probate Counsel. CLUB AFFIL Houston River Oaks Country Club.
Jeff Love: vice president
Charles Sapp: vice president
Kenneth Simon: secretary, treasurer
Henry O. Weaver: president

Grants Analysis

Disclosure Period: calendar year ending 2001
Total Grants: $262,189*
Number of Grants: 36
Average Grant: $5,894*
Highest Grant: $50,000
Typical Range: $2,000 to $10,000
*Note: Giving excludes scholarship. Average grant figure excludes highest grant.

Recent Grants

Note: Grants derived from 2001 Form 990.

General

50,000	Retina Research Foundation, Houston, TX -- for research on vision related items
25,000	American Red Cross, Denison, TX -- for disaster assistance services
21,689	University of Texas at Austin, Austin, TX -- for law school
10,000	Boys and Girls Club of America, Richardson, TX -- for community services to less fortunate youth
10,000	Dallas Bar Foundation, Dallas, TX -- for legal assistance to the poor
10,000	Houston Eye Associates Foundation, Houston, TX -- for research on vision related items
10,000	Kent Waldrep National Paralysis Foundation, Dallas, TX -- for research on paralysis related items
10,000	University of Houston Law Foundation, Houston, TX -- for law school
7,500	Hobby Center for the Performing Arts, Houston, TX -- for the arts
5,000	American Judicature Society, Washington, DC -- for legal assistance to the poor

W. M. KECK FOUNDATION

Giving Contact

Dr. Maria Pellegrini, Program Director
550 South Hope Street, Suite 2500
Los Angeles, CA 90071
Phone: (213)680-3833
Fax: (213)614-0934
E-mail: info@wmkeck.org
Web: http://www.wmkeck.org
Note: Contact person handles requests concerning higher education in science, engineering, and liberal arts.

Alternate Contact

Roxanne Ford, Program Director, medical research.

Description

Founded: 1954
EIN: 956092354
Organization Type: General Purpose Foundation
Giving Locations: CA: southern CA nationally.
Grant Types: Capital, Challenge, Project, Research.

Donor Information

Founder: The W. M. Keck Foundation was established in 1954 by William M. Keck, founder of Superior Oil Company, one of the nation's largest independent producers of oil and gas. He also established the W.

M. Keck Trust for the sole benefit of the foundation. In 1984, the W. M. Keck Foundation and the W. M. Keck Trust benefited from the sale of Superior Oil stock to Mobil Corporation. The sale produced combined assets for the trust and foundation of more than $500 million, and raised its ranking nationwide to twenty-first by asset size in 1991. Mr. Keck also established within his will charitable trusts for the benefit of several colleges and his family church.

Mr. Keck's son, Howard B. Keck, was chairman of the foundation until his death in 1996, and several of Mr. Keck's grandchildren are officers and directors of the foundation. Mr. Keck died in 1964.

Financial Summary

Total Giving: $70,626,000 (2001); $81,745,562 (2000); $67,698,000 (1999)

Giving Analysis: Giving for 2000 includes: foundation grants to United Way ($17,500) 1998: foundation grants to United Way ($51,000)

Assets: $1,263,938,000 (2001); $1,533,720,277 (2000); $1,789,949,000 (1999)

Gifts Received: $7,024,808 (1998). Note: Gifts received from W.M. Keck Trust.

Typical Recipients

Arts & Humanities: Arts Associations & Councils, Arts Centers, Arts Institutes, Dance, Libraries, Museums/Galleries, Music, Performing Arts, Public Broadcasting

Civic & Public Affairs: Civil Rights, Housing, Inner-City Development

Education: Agricultural Education, Arts/Humanities Education, Business Education, Colleges & Universities, Education Reform, Engineering/Technological Education, Faculty Development, Education-General, Gifted & Talented Programs, International Studies, Legal Education, Literacy, Medical Education, Private Education (Precollege), Science/Mathematics Education, Secondary Education (Private), Social Sciences Education, Student Aid

Environment: Research, Resource Conservation

Health: Clinics/Medical Centers, Geriatric Health, Hospitals, Medical Rehabilitation, Medical Research, Speech & Hearing

Religion: Churches

Science: Observatories & Planetariums, Science Museums, Scientific Centers & Institutes, Scientific Labs, Scientific Organizations, Scientific Research

Social Services: Child Welfare, Community Service Organizations, Day Care, Family Services, People with Disabilities, Scouts, Social Services-General, Substance Abuse, Youth Organizations

Application Procedures

Initial Contact: Applicants should call or write the foundation for detailed application instructions.

Application Requirements: The application process is divided into two phases. After reviewing the foundation's materials, organizations may submit a letter of inquiry, which must contain a narrative, no longer than three pages, with a description of the project; statement of the amount sought from the foundation; brief statement of the institution's background; cost summary of the project or program for which funds are sought; current, certified, audited financial statement; and copy of the organization's IRS determination letter showing 501(c)(3) and not 509(a) status. If the institution is located within the state of California, or is operating in the state, evidence is required showing that the institution is tax-exempt under Section 23701(d) of the California Revenue and Taxation Code. Both federal and California tax exemptions must be permanent.

Phase II involves submitting a full proposal upon invitation from the foundation. Unsolicited proposals are never accepted. The foundation will provide all necessary guidelines and materials.

Deadlines: Phase I inquiries are due by May 15 for consideration in the December grant cycle, and by November 15 for consideration in the June grant cycle; full proposals, if invited, are due by September 15 for consideration at the December board meeting, and by March 15 for consideration at the June board meeting.

Review Process: The foundation will reply to initial inquiries within six weeks. Grants are made in June and December.

Restrictions

Funding will not be considered for the following purposes: routine institutional or general operating expenses, general endowments, deficit reduction, or general or administrative overhead expenses; general and federated campaigns, including fundraising events, dinners, or mass mailings; direct aid to individuals; support for conduit organizations, unified funds, or organizations that use grant funds to support other organizations or individuals; sponsorship for conferences or seminars; publication of books or the production of films or theater; public policy research or activities of any kind; organizations or projects to be undertaken outside the United States; or requests that do not fall within the foundation's areas of interest.

Additional Information

Publications: Annual Report; Statement of Policies & Procedures

Foundation Officials

Dr. Lew Allen, Jr.: director, member directors grant program committee B Miami, FL 1925. ED United States Military Academy BS (1946); University of Illinois MS (1952); University of Illinois PhD (1954). NONPR AFFIL member: National Academy Engineering; member: Sigma Xi; fellow: American Physical Society; member: Council Foreign Relations; member: American Geophysical Union. CLUB AFFIL Sunset Club; Alfalfa Club.

Norman Barker, Jr.: director, member audit committee, member grant committee B San Diego, CA 1922. ED University of Chicago BA (1947); University of Chicago MBA (1953). CORP AFFIL director: SPI Pharmaceutical; director: TCW Convertible Securities Fund Inc.; director: Southern California Edison Co.; director: Pacific America Income Shares Inc.; director: Pacific Telesis Group; director: First Executive Corp.; director: ICN Pharmaceuticals Inc.; director: Fidelity Federal Bank FSB; director: America Health Properties; director: Carter Hawley Hale Stores Inc.

Peter Keefe Barker: treasurer, director, member executive committee, member grant B Chicago, IL 1948. ED Colgate University (1966-1968); Claremont McKenna College (1968-1969); University of Chicago MBA (1971). PRIM CORP EMPL partner: Goldman Sachs & Co.

John E. Bryson: director, member executive committee, member grant committee B New York, NY 1943. ED Stanford University BA (1965); Freie University Berlin (1965-1966); Yale University JD (1969). PRIM CORP EMPL chairman, chief executive officer: Edison International. CORP AFFIL chairman, chief executive officer: Southern California Edison Co.; director: Times Mirror Co.; director: Mission Group Inc.; director: Pacific America Income Shares Inc.; director: Boeing Co.; chairman: Edison Mission Energy. NONPR AFFIL director: World Resources Institute; member, board editors, associate editor: Yale University Law Journal; member: Phi Beta Kappa; member: Stanford University Alumni Association; member: District of Columbia Bar Association; member: Oregon Bar Association; member: California Water Rights Law Review Committee; trustee: Claremont University Center; member: California Bar Association; member: California Pollution Control Financing Authority.

Marsh Alexander Cooper: vice president, director, member grant program committee B Toronto, ON Canada October 08, 1912. ED University of Toronto BSc (1935); University of Toronto MSc (1935); Harvard University (1938-1939). PRIM CORP EMPL

president, chief executive officer: M.A. Cooper Consultants Inc. NONPR AFFIL member: Engineering Institute Canada; member: Society Economic Geologists; member: Canadian Institute Mining & Metallurgy; member: American Institute Mining Metallurgical Petroleum Engineers; member: Association Professional Engineers Ontario.

Howard M. Day: vice president, director, member director grant program committee PRIM CORP EMPL general partner: Crescent Investment Co.

Robert A. Day, Jr.: chairman, president, chief executive officer B 1945. ED Claremont McKenna College (1965). PRIM CORP EMPL founder, chairman, chief executive officer: TCW Asset Management Co. CORP AFFIL chairman, chief executive officer, director: Trust Co. West; chairman, chief executive officer: TCW Capital Investment Corp.; chairman, director: TCW Group Inc.; director: Freeport-McMoRan Copper Gold Inc.; chairman, director: Oakmont Corp.; general partner: Crescent Investment Co.; director: Fisher Scientific International Inc. NONPR AFFIL chairman investments committee, trustee: Claremont McKenna College.

Tammis M. Day: director PRIM CORP EMPL general partner: Crescent Investment Co.

Theodore J. Day: director, member audit committee PRIM CORP EMPL general partner: Crescent Investment Co.

Bob Rawls Dorsey: director emeritus B Rockland, TX August 27, 1912. ED University of Texas BSChE (1940).

Richard N. Foster: director

Lucinda Fournier: director

Walter Bland Gerken: vice president, director, chairman audit comm B New York, NY 1922. ED Wesleyan University BA (1948); Syracuse University MPA (1958). CORP AFFIL chairman equity board: PIMCO Advisors LP; director: Times Mirror Co.; director: Mullin Consulting Inc.; director, senior advisor: Boston Consulting Group. NONPR AFFIL trustee emeritus: Occidental College; trustee emeritus: Wesleyan University; director: Nature Conservancy California; director: Hoag Memorial Presbyterian Hospital; member: Maxwell School Citizenship & Public Affairs; director: Edison International; director: Executive Service Corps; member: California Commission Higher Education; member: California Citizens Budget Commission; member: California Commission Campaign Finance Reform. CLUB AFFIL Pauma Valley Country Club; California Club; Dairymens Country Club; director: Automobile Club Southern California; Balboa Bay Yacht Club.

Jonathan D. Jaffrey: vice president, chief admin officer

Erin A. Keck: director, member directors grant program committee

Howard B. Keck, Jr.: vice president, director, member audit & executive committees

William M. Keck, III: director

William M. Keck, II: vice president, director, membership audit & executive committee B 1942. PRIM CORP EMPL president, director: Coalinga Corp.

John E. Kolb: director, mem executive committee, chairman legal committee B Argenta, TX 1928. ED University of Texas BBA (1949); University of Texas LLB (1955).

Kent Kresa: director, member executive committee, member grant committee B New York, NY 1938. ED Massachusetts Institute of Technology BSAA (1959); Massachusetts Institute of Technology MSAA (1961); Massachusetts Institute of Technology EAA (1966). PRIM CORP EMPL chairman: Northrop Grumman Corp. CORP AFFIL director: Atlantic Richfield Co.; director: Daimler Chrysler. NONPR AFFIL member: Society Flight Test Engineers; director: John Tracy Clinic for the Hearing Impaired; member: Navy League; member (visiting committee): Massachusetts Institute Technology; member: Naval Aviation Museum Foundation; board governors: Los Angeles Music Center; member: Los Angeles World Affairs Council; member: DNA New Alternative Working Group;

member: Defense Science Board; member: Department Aeronautics & Astronautics Corp.; member: Association U.S. Army; member: Chief Naval Operations Executive Panel Washington; fellow: American Institute Aeronautics & Astronautics; member: Aerospace Industries Association; member: American Defense Preparedness Association. CLUB AFFIL Los Angeles Country Club; National Space Club.

Max R. Lents: director, chairman medical research committee CORP AFFIL director: Miller & Lents Ltd.

James Paul Lower: director, mem legal comm B Los Angeles, CA 1943. ED Claremont McKenna College BA (1965); Loyola University JD (1968). PRIM CORP EMPL partner: Hanna & Morton.

Judith A. Lower: secretary

Michael Terry Masin: director, chairman legal committee, member executive committee B Montreal, QC Canada 1945. ED Dartmouth College BA (1966); University of California, Los Angeles JD (1969). PRIM CORP EMPL vice chairman, president: Verizon Communications Inc. ADD CORP EMPL managing partner: O'Melveny & Myers. CORP AFFIL director: Trust Co.; director: Compania Anonima Nacional Telefonos de Venezuela; director: Travelers Group Inc.; director: Citigroup Inc.; director: British Columbia Telecommunications. NONPR AFFIL member deans advisory committee: Dartmouth College; member business committee, board trustee: Museum Modern Art; board member: China American Society; member: Council Foreign Relations; member: American Bar Association; trustee: Carnegie Hall. CLUB AFFIL California Club; Brook Club.

Kerry K. Mott: director

Maria Pellegrini: director science engineering and lib arts programs

Dr. Simon Ramo: director, member executive committee, member grant committee B Salt Lake City, UT May 07, 1913. ED University of Utah BS (1933); California Institute of Technology PhD (1936). CORP AFFIL consult, director: TRW Inc.; member advisory council: Chartwell Investments; member advisory council: General Atomics Corp.; member advisory council: Aurora Capital Partners; chairman: Allenwood Ventures; director: ARCO Power Techs. NONPR AFFIL member: Pacific Council International Policy; member: Theta Tau; member: New York Academy Science; member: National Academy Engineering; member: National Academy Sciences; member: International Academy Astronautics; member: Institute Advancement Engineering; fellow: Institute Electrical & Electronics Engineers; member: Eta Kappa Nu; life trustee, visiting professor: California Institute Technology; member: Council Foreign Relations; member: American Philosophical Society; member: American Physics Society; member: American Academy Political Science; fellow: American Academy of Arts & Sciences.

Stephen J. Ryan: director, member executive committee, member grant committee NONPR AFFIL director: Pasadena Hospital Association.

Edward Carroll Stone, Jr.: director, chairman science engineering liberal arts committee B Knoxville, IA 1936. ED Burlington Junior College AA (1956); University of Chicago MS (1959); University of Chicago PhD (1964). NONPR AFFIL member, board governors: National Space Club; scientist: Voyager; fellow: International Astronomical Union; member: National Academy Sciences; member: California Council Science & Technology; member: International Academy Astronautics; honorary member: Astronomical Society Pacific; member: California Association Research Astronomy; member: American Philosophical Society; fellow: American Physics Society; fellow: American Geophysical Union; fellow: American Institute Aeronautics & Astronautics; member: American Association Physics Teachers; member: American Astronomical Society; fellow: American Association Advancement Science.

David A. Thomas: director, member legal committee PRIM CORP EMPL chief executive officer, director: Execusoft Inc.

Brendan Thorpe: secretary

James R. Ukropina: director, member legal committee B Fresno, CA 1937. ED Stanford University (1959); University of Southern California Law School (1965). PRIM CORP EMPL partner: O'Melveny & Myers. CORP AFFIL director: Pacific Mutual; director: Lockheed Martin Corp.; director: Pacific Life Insurance Co. NONPR AFFIL member: Los Angeles County Bar Association; trustee: Stanford University; member: Beta Theta Pi; member: American Bar Association. CLUB AFFIL Annandale Golf Club; California Club.

C. William Verity, Jr.: director emeritus CORP AFFIL director: Encor Tech Inc.; director, principal: Leaver Corp.; director: Encor & Compression Engineering.

Julian Onesime von Kalinowski: director, member legal committee B Saint Louis, MO May 19, 1916. ED Mississippi College BA (1937); University of Virginia JD (1940). PRIM CORP EMPL attorney, advisor partner: Gibson, Dunn & Crutcher. CORP AFFIL chairman emeritus: Dispute Dynamics. NONPR AFFIL member: Phi Kappa Psi; member: University Virginia Law School Alumni Association; member: Los Angeles County Bar Association; member: Phi Alpha Delta; fellow: American College Trial Lawyers; member: California Bar Association; fellow: American Bar Foundation; member: American Bar Association. CLUB AFFIL member: Sky Club; member: La Jolla Beach & Tennis Club; member: Los Angeles Country Club; member: California Club.

Grants Analysis

Disclosure Period: calendar year ending 2001
Total Grants: $70,626,000
Number of Grants: 200 (approx)
Average Grant: $353,130
Highest Grant: $10,000,000
Lowest Grant: $1,000
Typical Range: $100,000 to $1,000,000

Recent Grants

Note: Grants derived from 2000 Form 990.

Library-Related

954,391 Performing Arts Center of Los Angeles, Los Angeles, CA -- to fund construction of the Children's Amphitheater at the new Disney Concert Hall

General

10,000,000 Keck Graduate Institute of Applied Life Sciences, Claremont, CA -- founding grant to establish a new school for Applied Life Sciences in the Claremont Colleges Group

6,000,000 University of Southern California, Los Angeles, CA -- for support of a Neurogentic Initiative

4,800,000 Rice University, Houston, TX -- challenge grant to modernize an historic building for bioengineering research

4,375,000 Saint John's Health Center, Los Angeles, CA -- to support construction of a new state-of-the-art health care facility

2,000,000 University of California, Davis, CA -- to establish a cellular and molecular neuroscience imaging center and central database for the study of neuropsychiatric disorders

2,000,000 University of California, Irvine, CA -- to establish an accelerator mass spectrometry facility dedicated to carbon cycle research

2,000,000 University of California, San Diego, CA -- to fund a 4T large bore NMR for the MRI Center

1,500,000 Columbia University, New York, NY -- to create a laboratory for the study of electrons under extreme conditions

1,500,000 Cornell University, Ithaca, NY -- to establish an integrated research and training

program in membrane biology and biophysics to study signaling complexes at the cellular level

1,500,000 University of Alabama at Birmingham, Birmingham, AL -- to support a center for functional neuroimaging

WILLIAM M. KECK, JR. FOUNDATION

Giving Contact

Hilda Avanesian
12575 Beatrice St.
Los Angeles, CA 90066-7001
Phone: (310)578-5900
Fax: (310)578-5900

Description

Founded: 1958
EIN: 136097874
Organization Type: Private Foundation
Giving Locations: CA: southern California area
Grant Types: General Support.

Donor Information

Founder: William M. Keck, Jr.

Financial Summary

Total Giving: $755,000 (2001); $1,250,000 (2000); $950,000 (1999)
Assets: $14,772,600 (2001); $17,399,030 (2000); $19,837,960 (1999)
Gifts Received: $175,000 (2001); $175,000 (2000); $175,000 (1999). Note: In 1995, 1997, 1999, and 2001, contributions were received from the trust for the benefit of W. M. Keck, Jr. Foundation.

Typical Recipients

Arts & Humanities: Arts Centers, Libraries, Music, Theater
Civic & Public Affairs: Economic Policy, Civic & Public Affairs-General, Zoos/Aquariums
Education: Arts/Humanities Education, Colleges & Universities, Education Funds, Education Reform, Education-General, Legal Education, Minority Education, Private Education (Precollege), Public Education (Precollege), School Volunteerism, Secondary Education (Private), Secondary Education (Public)
Environment: Environment-General
Health: Clinics/Medical Centers, Emergency/Ambulance Services, Health-General, Public Health
International: International Development, International Relations
Religion: Churches, Religious Welfare
Social Services: Child Welfare, Counseling, Family Planning, Food/Clothing Distribution, People with Disabilities, Shelters/Homelessness, Substance Abuse, United Funds/United Ways

Application Procedures

Initial Contact: Send a brief letter of inquiry. Include a description of organization.
Deadlines: November 30.

Foundation Officials

Carl D. Hasting: vice president, secretary, treasurer, director
William M. Keck, II: president, director B 1942. PRIM CORP EMPL president, director: Coalinga Corp.

Grants Analysis

Disclosure Period: calendar year ending 2001
Total Grants: $755,000
Number of Grants: 4
Highest Grant: $490,000
Lowest Grant: $15,000

Recent Grants

Note: Grants derived from 2000 Form 990.

General

1,100,000	Institute of International Economics, Washington, DC -- for economics research
50,000	Midnight Mission, Los Angeles, CA -- for Homeless Programs
50,000	Student Health Services, Los Angeles, CA -- for Student Health Programs
50,000	United Negro College Fund, Fairfax, VA -- for education

KEEL FOUNDATION

Giving Contact

Diane Gilchrist, Executive Director
c/o Testa, Hurwitz & Thibeault
125 High Street
Boston, MA 02110-2725
Phone: (617)248-7412

Description

Founded: 1992
EIN: 043166698
Organization Type: Private Foundation
Giving Locations: MA
Grant Types: General Support.

Donor Information

Founder: Established in 1992 by Kenneth H. Olsen.

Financial Summary

Total Giving: $380,000 (2001); $380,000 (2000); $310,000 (1999)
Assets: $5,010,820 (2001); $5,391,057 (2000); $5,752,747 (1999)
Gifts Received: $3,500,000 (1992)

Typical Recipients

Arts & Humanities: Libraries, Literary Arts
Civic & Public Affairs: Zoos/Aquariums
Education: Colleges & Universities, Education-General, Minority Education, Preschool Education
Health: Cancer
Social Services: Community Service Organizations, Youth Organizations

Application Procedures

Initial Contact: Application may be requested of the executive director.
Deadlines: None.

Restrictions

Limited to tax-exempt organizations other than religious and political organizations.

Foundation Officials

Kenneth Harry Olsen: trustee B Bridgeport, CT 1926. ED Massachusetts Institute of Technology BSEE (1950); Massachusetts Institute of Technology MS (1952). CORP AFFIL director: Polaroid Corp.; chairman: Advanced Modular Solutions Inc. NONPR AFFIL director: Corporate MIT.
Richard J. Testa: trustee B Marlboro, MA 1939. ED Assumption College AB (1959); Harvard University LLB (1962). PRIM CORP EMPL managing partner: Testa Hurwitz & Thibeault ADD CORP EMPL vice president: Granite State Phoenix Co. NONPR AFFIL member: American Bar Association.
Peter A. Wilson: trustee PRIM CORP EMPL senior vice president: Shawmut Bank Boston. NONPR AFFIL treasurer, director MA division: American Cancer Society.

Grants Analysis

Disclosure Period: calendar year ending 2001
Total Grants: $380,000
Number of Grants: 4
Average Grant: $95,000
Highest Grant: $200,000
Lowest Grant: $30,000
Typical Range: $30,000 to $200,000

Recent Grants

Note: Grants derived from 2001 Form 990.

General

200,000	Assumption College, Worcester, MA
100,000	Connecticut College, New London, CT
50,000	A Different September, Boston, MA
30,000	Teen Ink

KEELER FOUNDATION

Giving Contact

Miner S. Keeler, Jr., Trustee
200 Monroe Ave. NW, Suite 340
Grand Rapids, MI 49503
Phone: (616)774-0422

Alternate Contact

Mary Ann Keeler

Description

Founded: 1985
EIN: 382625402
Organization Type: Private Foundation
Former Name: Miner S. and Mary Ann Keeler Fund.
Giving Locations: MI
Grant Types: General Support.

Donor Information

Founder: Keeler Fund

Financial Summary

Total Giving: $988,073 (fiscal year ending July 31, 2001); $462,196 (fiscal 2000); $327,822 (fiscal 1998)
Giving Analysis: Giving for fiscal 2001 includes: foundation grants to United Way ($20,000); fiscal 2000: foundation grants to United Way ($20,000); fiscal 1998: foundation grants to United Way ($20,000) foundation ($307,822)
Assets: $3,996,447 (fiscal 2001); $3,523,246 (fiscal 2000); $3,940,457 (fiscal 1998)
Gifts Received: $43,799 (fiscal 2001); $47,926 (fiscal 1994). Note: In fiscal 2001, contributions were received from Miner S. Keeler II & Mary Ann Keller. In fiscal 1994, contributions were received from M. S. Keeler, II.

Typical Recipients

Arts & Humanities: Arts Associations & Councils, Historic Preservation, History & Archaeology, Libraries, Museums/Galleries, Music, Opera, Public Broadcasting, Theater, Visual Arts
Civic & Public Affairs: Botanical Gardens/Parks, Chambers of Commerce, Clubs, Community Foundations, Economic Policy, Law & Justice, Nonprofit Management, Parades/Festivals, Philanthropic Organizations, Urban & Community Affairs, Zoos/Aquariums
Education: Business Education, Colleges & Universities, Environmental Education, Private Education (Precollege), Science/Mathematics Education, Secondary Education (Public)
Environment: Environment-General, Resource Conservation, Wildlife Protection
Health: Eyes/Blindness, Health Organizations, Hospices, Hospitals, Medical Rehabilitation, Single-Disease Health Associations
International: Foreign Arts Organizations, International Affairs
Religion: Churches, Religious Welfare

Social Services: Camps, Community Service Organizations, Family Services, Food/Clothing Distribution, Recreation & Athletics, Scouts, Senior Services, United Funds/United Ways, YMCA/YWCA/YMHA/YWHA, Youth Organizations

Application Procedures

Initial Contact: Send a brief letter of inquiry.
Deadlines: None.

Restrictions

Contributions generally are artistic or scholastic in nature.

Foundation Officials

Issac S. Keeler: trustee
Mary Ann Keeler: trustee
Miner S. Keeler, II: trustee

Grants Analysis

Disclosure Period: fiscal year ending July 31, 2001
Total Grants: $968,073*
Number of Grants: 52
Average Grant: $5,450*
Highest Grant: $350,000
Lowest Grant: $250
Typical Range: $1,000 to $10,000
***Note:** Giving excludes United Way. Average grant figure excludes three highest grants ($701,000).

Recent Grants

Note: Grants derived from 2000 Form 990.

Library-Related

84,186	Ryerson Library Foundation, Grand Rapids, MI

General

75,000	Catholic Diocese of Grand Rapids, Grand Rapids, MI
50,000	Greater Grand Rapids Chamber Foundation, Grand Rapids, MI
38,000	Frederick Meijer Gardens, Grand Rapids, MI
20,000	United Way of West Michigan, Grand Rapids, MI
13,500	Grand Rapids Art Museum, Grand Rapids, MI
13,000	St. Stephens Parish, Grand Rapids, MI
12,150	Grand Rapids Symphony Orchestra, Grand Rapids, MI
11,000	North American Choral Company, Grand Rapids, MI
10,400	Opera Grand Rapids, Grand Rapids, MI
10,000	Bright Horizons, Jenison, MI

KELLER FAMILY FOUNDATION

Giving Contact

Mary K. Zervigon, President
PO Box 13625
New Orleans, LA 70185-3625
Phone: (504)861-3391

Description

Founded: 1949
EIN: 726027426
Organization Type: Private Foundation
Giving Locations: LA: New Orleans
Grant Types: General Support.

Donor Information

Founder: Charles Keller, Jr., Rosa F. Keller

Financial Summary

Total Giving: $992,743 (2000); $1,019,967 (1999); $841,000 (1998)
Assets: $19,338,687 (2000); $20,510,439 (1999); $20,166,028 (1998)

Gifts Received: $1,156,892 (1999); $140,475 (1996). Note: In 1996 and 1999, contributions were received from the estate of Charles Keller, Jr.

Typical Recipients

Arts & Humanities: Arts Centers, Ballet, Community Arts, Historic Preservation, Libraries, Museums/Galleries, Music, Public Broadcasting

Civic & Public Affairs: Botanical Gardens/Parks, Clubs, Community Foundations, Economic Development, Civic & Public Affairs-General, Housing, Philanthropic Organizations, Public Policy, Urban & Community Affairs, Women's Affairs, Zoos/Aquariums

Education: Afterschool/Enrichment Programs, Arts/Humanities Education, Colleges & Universities, Education Reform, Education-General, Minority Education, Private Education (Precollege), Science/Mathematics Education, Special Education, Student Aid

Environment: Environment-General, Resource Conservation

Health: Geriatric Health, Hospitals

International: International Peace & Security Issues

Religion: Churches, Ministries, Religious Organizations, Religious Welfare, Seminaries

Social Services: Camps, Child Welfare, Community Service Organizations, Food/Clothing Distribution, Recreation & Athletics, Scouts, United Funds/United Ways, YMCA/YWCA/YMHA/YWHA, Youth Organizations

Application Procedures

Initial Contact: Send two copies of a two-page proposal on letter size paper or 2 copies of the Common application form. of the Southeast Louisiana Association of grantmakers.

Application Requirements: Include the legal name and address of the organization, the name of the contact person including a telephone number, purpose of funds sought, amount requested, total cost of the program or project, other sources of funding, and references. Also attach recently audited fianancial statement, the first two pages of organizations Form 990, and proof of tax-exempt status.

Deadlines: Between January 1 and October 1.

Restrictions

Preference is given to organizations devoted to education, civic affairs, and social services. Grants are not made to individuals.

Additional Information

Publications: Application Guidelines

Foundation Officials

Julie F. Breitmeyer: trustee
Caroline K. Loughlin: treasurer, trustee
Elizabeth M. Loughlin: director
Luis C. Zervigon: secretary, director
Mary K. Zervigon: secretary, trustee

Grants Analysis

Disclosure Period: calendar year ending 2000
Total Grants: $992,743
Number of Grants: 1

Recent Grants

Note: Grants derived from 2001 Form 990.

Library-Related

12,500	Grand Rapids Public Library, Grand Rapids, MI

General

15,750	United Methodist Community House, Grand Rapids, MI
15,500	St. Cecilia Music Society, Grand Rapids, MI
15,000	Grand Rapids Symphony, Grand Rapids, MI
12,500	Camp Blodgett, Grand Rapids, MI
12,500	YMCA, Grand Rapids, MI
10,250	Gilda's Club, Grand Rapids, MI
10,000	Garrett Evangelical Seminary, Evanston, IL
10,000	Grand Rapids Ballet, Grand Rapids, MI
10,000	In the Image, Grand Rapids, MI
9,700	Delta Strategy, Grand Rapids, MI

KELLER FOUNDATION

Giving Contact

Anne Williamson, Executive Director
5225 33rd St. SE
Grand Rapids, MI 49512
Phone: (616)949-2220
Fax: (616)949-2796

Description

Founded: 1985
EIN: 382331693
Organization Type: Private Foundation
Giving Locations: MI: Grand Rapids

Donor Information

Founder: Cascade Engineering Co., Paragon Die & Engineering Co.

Financial Summary

Total Giving: $217,050 (fiscal year ending June 30, 2002); $533,350 (fiscal 1999); $271,046 (fiscal 1998)
Assets: $4,508,920 (fiscal 2002); $4,320,362 (fiscal 1999); $3,847,175 (fiscal 1997)
Gifts Received: $360,741 (fiscal 1999); $379,698 (fiscal 1997); $397,554 (fiscal 1996). Note: In fiscal 1999, contributions were received from Paragon Die & Engineering ($76,741) and Fred and Bernedine Keller ($284,000). In fiscal 1997, contributions were received from Paragon Die & Engineering and David Muir. In fiscal 1996, contributions were received from Paragon Die & Engineering.

Typical Recipients

Arts & Humanities: Arts Associations & Councils, Ballet, Libraries, Museums/Galleries, Music, Opera, Performing Arts, Theater

Civic & Public Affairs: Botanical Gardens/Parks, Clubs, Civic & Public Affairs-General, Housing, Urban & Community Affairs, Zoos/Aquariums

Education: Business Education, Colleges & Universities, Community & Junior Colleges, Education-General, Public Education (Precollege), Special Education

Health: AIDS/HIV, Health Organizations, Long-Term Care

Religion: Churches, Ministries, Religious Organizations, Religious Welfare, Seminaries

Social Services: Camps, Child Welfare, Community Service Organizations, Counseling, Family Planning, Food/Clothing Distribution, People with Disabilities, Scouts, Senior Services, Youth Organizations

Application Procedures

Initial Contact: Send a brief letter of inquiry.
Application Requirements: Include a description of organization; a brief description of the program to be funded, including its importance and goals; amount requested and the time period in which funds would be used; a detailed income and expense budget for the proposed program; and proof of tax-exempt status.
Deadlines: None.
Review Process: Grant requests are reviewed quarterly in March, June, September, and December.

Restrictions

Grants are not made to individuals.

Additional Information

Trust(s): Fifth-Third Bank

Foundation Officials

Bernedine J. Keller: vice president
Fred M. Keller: president
Frederick P. Keller: treasurer
Linn Maxwell Keller: director
Lorissa K. Keller: director
Susan Keller: director
David F. Muir: director
Elizabeth M. Muir: director
Kathleen K. Muir: secretary
William M. Muir: director
William W. Muir, Jr.: director B Grand Rapids, MI 1936. ED Bowling Green State University (1958). PRIM CORP EMPL chairman, president, director: Grand Rapids Label Co. CORP AFFIL director: First America Bank West Michigan; director: Paragon Die & Engineering; director: Alpena Power Co.; secretary, treasurer, director: Cascade Sales Associates.
Anne Williamson: executive director

Grants Analysis

Disclosure Period: fiscal year ending June 30, 2002
Total Grants: $217,050
Number of Grants: 65
Average Grant: $3,339
Highest Grant: $15,300
Typical Range: $250 to $10,000

Recent Grants

Note: Grants derived from fiscal 2002 Form 990.

General

15,300	Gilda's Club of Grand Rapids, Grand Rapids, MI
15,000	Grand Rapids Symphony, Grand Rapids, MI
11,250	United Methodist Community House, Grand Rapids, MI
10,000	Garrett-Evangelical Seminary, Evanston, IL
10,000	Grand Rapids Ballet, Grand Rapids, MI
10,000	In the Image, Grand Rapids, MI
10,000	Progressions, Grand Rapids, MI
10,000	Spectrum Health Care Foundation, Grand Rapids, MI
6,050	First United Methodist Church, Grand Rapids, MI
5,100	John Ball Zoo Society, Grand Rapids, MI

EDWARD BANGS KELLEY AND ELZA KELLEY FOUNDATION

Giving Contact

Henry L. Murphy, Jr., President & Director
243 Station Street
PO Box M
Hyannis, MA 02601
Phone: (508)775-3117
Fax: (508)775-3720

Description

Founded: 1954
EIN: 046039660
Organization Type: Private Foundation
Giving Locations: MA: Barnstable County
Grant Types: Capital, Emergency, General Support, Operating Expenses, Project, Research, Scholarship.

Donor Information

Founder: the late Edward Bangs Kelley, the late Elza deHorvath Kelley

Financial Summary

Total Giving: $214,000 (2002); $236,771 (2001); $234,260 (2000). Note: 1997 Giving includes scholarship ($53,375).

Giving Analysis: Giving for 1999 includes: foundation scholarships ($54,250)

Assets: $4,863,002 (2002); $5,376,699 (2001); $5,678,588 (2000)

Gifts Received: $7,500 (2002); $16,715 (2001); $16,000 (2000). Note: In 2002, contributions were received from Harriett Schluter. In 2001, contributions were received from Harriett Schluter ($5,000) and Ann Renner Trust ($10,615). In 2000, contributions were received from Harriett Schluter ($5,000) and Ann Renner Trust ($10,000). In 1998, contributions were received from Christmas Tree Shops. In 1996, contributions were received from the Carlotta Casey Coyne Trust.

Typical Recipients

Arts & Humanities: Arts Centers, Arts Festivals, Arts Funds, Arts Institutes, Arts Outreach, Community Arts, Arts & Humanities-General, Historic Preservation, History & Archaeology, Libraries, Literary Arts, Museums/Galleries, Music, Performing Arts, Theater
Civic & Public Affairs: Civic & Public Affairs-General, Housing, Legal Aid, Philanthropic Organizations, Professional & Trade Associations, Urban & Community Affairs
Education: Arts/Humanities Education, Colleges & Universities, Community & Junior Colleges, Private Education (Precollege), Secondary Education (Private), Student Aid, Vocational & Technical Education
Environment: Air/Water Quality, Environment-General, Resource Conservation, Wildlife Protection
Health: AIDS/HIV, Alzheimers Disease, Cancer, Emergency/Ambulance Services, Eyes/Blindness, Hospices, Hospitals, Medical Rehabilitation, Medical Research, Mental Health, Nursing Services, Prenatal Health Issues, Preventive Medicine/Wellness Organizations, Public Health, Research/Studies Institutes, Single-Disease Health Associations
International: International Organizations
Religion: Churches, Religious Welfare
Science: Science Museums, Scientific Centers & Institutes
Social Services: Animal Protection, Big Brother/Big Sister, Child Welfare, Community Service Organizations, Day Care, Family Services, Homes, Recreation & Athletics, Senior Services, Substance Abuse, Youth Organizations

Application Procedures

Initial Contact: Send letter requesting application form.
Deadlines: April 30 for scholarships; no deadline for grants.
Review Process: The Executive Committee meets once or twice each quarter to interview grant applications and the Board of DirectorS meets quarterly to act on Executive Committee recommendations.

Additional Information

Publications: Annual Report (includes Application Guidelines)

Foundation Officials

Adm. John F. Aylmer: director
Doreen Bilezikian: director
Jocelyn Bowman: director
Palmer Davenport: director
R. Bruce Hammatt, Jr.: clerk, director
Robert B. Hirschman: director
Townsend Hornor: director
John M. Kayajan: director
Ruth B. Kelley: hon director
Kenneth S. MacAffer, Jr.: director

Stephen W. Malaquias, MD: director
Mary Louise Montgomery: clerk, director
Henry L. Murphy, Jr.: vice president, admin mgr, director
E. Carlton Nickerson: hon director
Frank L. Nickerson: hon director
Joshua A. Nickerson, Jr.: director
Thomas S. Olsen: treasurer, director
Milton L. Penn: president, director
Charles N. Robinson: director
Walter G. Robinson: hon director
Barbara H. Sheaffer: director
Hamilton N. Shepley: director

Grants Analysis

Disclosure Period: calendar year ending 2002
Total Grants: $214,000
Number of Grants: 26
Average Grant: $7,208*
Highest Grant: $25,000
Lowest Grant: $150
Typical Range: $1,000 to $15,000
***Note:** Average grant figure excludes two highest grants ($41,000).

Recent Grants

Note: Grants derived from 2001 Form 990.

Library-Related
6,850	Hyannis Public Library Association -- air conditioning of the facility

General
25,000	Hospice Foundation of Cape Cod, Yarmouth Port, MA -- campaign for Hospice House
15,000	Cape Cod Community College Educational Foundation, Inc., Barnstable, MA -- Smart Classroom
12,500	Rehabilitation Hospital of Cape and Islands -- capital gift
12,500	Sandwich Historical Society -- renovation, expansion
12,500	Three Bays Preservation, Inc, Osterville, MA -- Volunteer Monitoring Program
12,000	Cape Cod Symphony Orchestra Association, Inc., Yarmouth Port, MA -- education and access plan
10,000	Dennis Memorial Library -- library expansion
10,000	Latham Centers, Inc., Brewster, MA -- renovation of Latham Schoolhouse
7,500	Cape Cod Museum of Natural History, Brewster, MA -- A Naturalist in the Schools
7,000	Big Brothers and Big Sisters of Cape Cod and the Islands, MA -- health and human services, community development

KELLY FOUNDATION

Giving Contact

Scott G. Nichols, Treasurer
3610 American River Dr., Suite 190
PO Box 255868
Sacramento, CA 95864
Phone: (916)978-4892

Description

Founded: 1989
EIN: 680175739
Organization Type: Private Foundation
Grant Types: General Support, Scholarship.

Financial Summary

Total Giving: $280,000 (fiscal year ending September 30, 2001); $170,618 (fiscal 2000); $124,723 (fiscal 1998)

Giving Analysis: Giving for fiscal 2001 includes: foundation scholarships ($7,400); foundation fellowships ($45,000); fiscal 2000: foundation scholarships ($5,500); fiscal 1998: foundation scholarships ($11,667) foundation ($113,056)

Assets: $5,392,648 (fiscal 2001); $6,756,804 (fiscal 2000); $3,166,140 (fiscal 1998)

Gifts Received: $2,685,000 (fiscal 2000); $387,488 (fiscal 1996); $525,000 (fiscal 1995). Note: In fiscal 2000, contributions were received from G.G. Kelly, LLC and J.S. Kelly, LLC.

Typical Recipients

Arts & Humanities: Arts Outreach, Ballet, Libraries
Civic & Public Affairs: Housing, Urban & Community Affairs
Education: Afterschool/Enrichment Programs, Business Education, Education Funds, Education Reform, Education-General, Literacy, Preschool Education, Private Education (Precollege), Public Education (Precollege), School Volunteerism, Science/Mathematics Education, Student Aid
Environment: Wildlife Protection
Health: Alzheimers Disease, Heart, Hospices, Mental Health
Religion: Bible Study/Translation, Religious Welfare
Science: Scientific Centers & Institutes
Social Services: At-Risk Youth, Child Welfare, Community Service Organizations, Crime Prevention, Food/Clothing Distribution, People with Disabilities, Recreation & Athletics, Senior Services, Social Services-General, Special Olympics, Volunteer Services, Youth Organizations

Application Procedures

Initial Contact: Send a a brief letter of inquiry. Request application form.
Application Requirements: Submit application form.; proof of tax-exempt status; budget; recently audited financial statement; and list of Board of Directorss.
Deadlines: October 15; January 15; April 15; July 15 for foundation.

Restrictions

Foundation does not support religious organizations for religious activities, as distinguished from social or educational activities; political or lobbying groups; fraternal organizations, labor, societies or orders, telephone societies, or national fundraising efforts. An organization may only apply once a year. Primarily funds preselected organizations.

Foundation Officials

Jon S. Kelly: chief executive officer, director
Robert E. Kelly: director
Scott G. Nichols: secretary, treasurer

Grants Analysis

Disclosure Period: fiscal year ending September 30, 2001
Total Grants: $227,600*
Number of Grants: 21
Average Grant: $10,838
Highest Grant: $25,000
Lowest Grant: $2,400
Typical Range: $5,000 to $20,000
***Note:** Giving excludes scholarships and fellowship.

Recent Grants

Note: Grants derived from fiscal 2000 Form 990.

Library-Related
5,000	Sacramento Public Library Foundation, Sacramento, CA -- to update computers in branches

General
25,000	Jesuit High School, Sacramento, CA -- for men for others
25,000	Mercy Foundation, Rancho Cordova, CA -- operational support

10,000	Alzheimer's Association, Sacramento, CA -- to purchase art supplies for Gala
10,000	Ducks Unlimited, Inc., Memphis, TN -- research
10,000	Optimist Foundation, Sacramento, CA -- to repair water system and for handicapped camping
10,000	Sacramento Area Congregation Together, Sacramento, CA -- public safety program
10,000	Sacramento Start, Sacramento, CA -- after school programs
8,700	Natomas Youth Baseball, Sacramento, CA -- to construct two baseball fields
5,000	Asian Pacific Rim Foundation, Sacramento, CA -- scholarships
5,000	Christmas in April, Sacramento, CA

WILLIAM T. KEMPER FOUNDATION

Giving Contact

Michael D. Fields, Executive Director
Care of Commerce Bank
PO Box 13095
Kansas City, MO 64199-3095
Phone: (816)234-2985
Fax: (816)234-8690

Description

Founded: 1989
EIN: 436345116
Organization Type: General Purpose Foundation
Giving Locations: MO
Grant Types: Capital, Challenge, Conference/Seminar, General Support, Matching, Multiyear/Continuing Support, Operating Expenses, Project.

Donor Information

Founder: The foundation was established in 1989, following the death of William T. Kemper . Kemper was associated with the former First National Bank of Independence, as their president, chairman, chairman of the executive committee, and director. He was involved in the development and improvement of downtown Kansas City and was active in social service and community organizations like the American Red Cross, Boy Scouts of America, and American Royal Association. He was an avid art collector and he founded the Charlotte Crosby Kemper Gallery at the Kansas City Art Institute, in memory of his mother. Kemper was associated with Commerce Bank of Kansas City by family ties, and gave the majority of his estate to the William T. Kemper Foundation, with Commerce Bank as co-trustee, at his death.

Financial Summary

Total Giving: $13,267,045 (fiscal year ending October 31, 2001); $13,476,139 (fiscal 2000); $12,172,682 (fiscal 1999)
Giving Analysis: Giving for fiscal 2000 includes: foundation grants to United Way ($9,000); fiscal 1999: foundation grants to United Way ($9,000) fiscal 1998: foundation grants to United Way ($60,000)
Assets: $240,896,887 (fiscal 2001); $291,978,087 (fiscal 2000); $270,022,764 (fiscal 1999)
Gifts Received: $89,546 (fiscal 2000); $625,000 (fiscal 1999); $1,654,508 (fiscal 1998). Note: Receives funding from the William T. Kemper Trust.

Typical Recipients

Arts & Humanities: Arts Associations & Councils, Arts Centers, Arts Institutes, Ballet, Libraries, Museums/Galleries, Music, Opera, Public Broadcasting, Theater
Civic & Public Affairs: Botanical Gardens/Parks, Chambers of Commerce, Clubs, Community Foundations, Economic Development, Employment/Job Training, Civic & Public Affairs-General, Housing,
Law & Justice, Municipalities/Towns, Nonprofit Management, Philanthropic Organizations, Rural Affairs, Urban & Community Affairs, Zoos/Aquariums
Education: Agricultural Education, Arts/Humanities Education, Business Education, Colleges & Universities, Education Associations, Elementary Education (Public), Education-General, Medical Education, Private Education (Precollege), Private Education (Precollege), Public Education (Precollege), Secondary Education (Public), Vocational & Technical Education
Environment: Environment-General, Resource Conservation
Health: Cancer, Children's Health/Hospitals, Clinics/Medical Centers, Eyes/Blindness, Health Organizations, Hospitals, Hospitals (University Affiliated), Medical Research, Mental Health, Nursing Services, Research/Studies Institutes
International: International Development, International Relations
Religion: Churches, Dioceses, Jewish Causes, Religious Organizations, Religious Welfare
Science: Science Museums
Social Services: At-Risk Youth, Big Brother/Big Sister, Camps, Child Welfare, Community Centers, Community Service Organizations, Domestic Violence, Family Planning, Homes, Scouts, Sexual Abuse, United Funds/United Ways, YMCA/YWCA/YMHA/YWHA, Youth Organizations

Application Procedures

Initial Contact: All proposals must be submitted in writing; guidelines available on request.
Application Requirements: A complete proposal must include a clear statement of the problem or need, what will be accomplished by a particular date, background of organization and staff, general plan for evaluation, proof of tax-exempt status, amount requested, program budget, recently audited financial statement, and letter from chairman or chief administrative officer indicating endorsement of proposal.
Deadlines: None.
Evaluative Criteria: Preference is given to projects in the Midwest, with particular emphasis on the state of Missouri and surrounding areas.

Restrictions

The foundation does not fund private foundations, individuals, tickets for benefits, exhibits, or other event activities, advertisements, endowment funds, politically partisan purposes, loans or investment funds, fraternal or veteran organizations, or research unrelated to current priorities. Although the foundation typically makes one-year grants, requests for up to five years of funding for special projects may be considered.

Additional Information

Publications: Application Guidelines; Brochure
Trust(s): Commerce Bank, N.A. trustee

Foundation Officials

Jonathan McBride Kemper: co-trustee, contributions committee B Kansas City, MO 1953. ED Harvard University AB (1975); Harvard University MBA (1979). PRIM CORP EMPL vice chairman, chief executive officer, director: Commerce Bank, NA ADD CORP EMPL vice chairman: Commerce Bancshares Inc.; president, chief executive officer, director: Commerce Bank Kansas City. NONPR AFFIL director: Greater Kansas City Community Foundation.
Sheila K. Rice: program mgr NONPR AFFIL finance director: YMCA Springfield Missouri.

Grants Analysis

Disclosure Period: fiscal year ending October 31, 2001
Total Grants: $13,476,139*
Number of Grants: 407
Average Grant: $33,110
Typical Range: $396 to $1,000,000

*Note: Giving excludes United Way. Grants analysis provided by foundation.

Recent Grants

Note: Grants derived from 2000 Form 990.

Library-Related

62,500	Harry S. Truman Library Institute for National and International Affairs, Independence, MO

General

1,000,000	Nelson Gallery Foundation, Kansas City, MO
600,000	Nelson Gallery Foundation, Kansas City, MO
400,000	Archdiocese of Saint Louis, St. Louis, MO
400,000	Exploration Place, Wichita, KS
400,000	Exploration Place, Wichita, KS
400,000	Kansas City Art Institute, Kansas City, MO
400,000	Pembroke Hill School, Kansas City, MO
390,000	Kansas City Museum Association, Kansas City, MO
356,000	Harvard University, Cambridge, MA
300,000	Washington University, St. Louis, MO

KEMPER NATIONAL INSURANCE COMPANIES

Company Headquarters

Long Grove, IL
Web: http://www.kemperinsurance.com

Company Description

Former Name: Kemper Corp.
Employees: 9,000
SIC(s): 6331 Fire, Marine & Casualty Insurance.

Operating Locations

Kemper National Insurance Companies (CA--Los Angeles, Menlo Park, Pasadena; CO--Denver; IL--Chicago; OH--Cleveland; WI--Milwaukee)

Nonmonetary Support

Type: In-kind Services
Note: Company contributes printing and creative support in the way of writing and design.

James S. Kemper Foundation

Giving Contact

Thomas Hellie, Executive Director
One Kemper Drive
Long Grove, IL 60049-0001
Phone: (847)320-2000
Fax: (847)320-7996
E-mail: thellie@kemperinsurance.com
Web: http://jskemperfoundation.org

Alternate Contact

Charles W. Meinhardt, Corp. Contributions Coordinator
Note: Contact for direct giving program only.

Description

EIN: 366007812
Organization Type: Corporate Foundation
Giving Locations: IL: Chicago including metropolitan area nationally.
Grant Types: Fellowship, Multiyear/Continuing Support, Professorship, Research, Scholarship, Seed Money.

Financial Summary

Total Giving: $2,000,000 (fiscal year ending July 31, 2001 approx); $1,873,322 (fiscal 2000); $1,750,000 (fiscal 1999 approx). Note: Contributes through corporate direct giving program and foundation.

Giving Analysis: Giving for fiscal 2000 includes: foundation fellowships ($20,000); foundation scholarships ($487,327); foundation ($1,365,995); fiscal 1998: foundation fellowships ($24,996); foundation scholarships ($439,255) foundation ($1,191,253)

Assets: $47,000,000 (fiscal 2001 approx); $47,943,185 (fiscal 2000 approx); $45,781,174 (fiscal 1998)

Gifts Received: $230 (fiscal 2000); $6,256,515 (fiscal 1998); $7,705 (fiscal 1995). Note: Contributions are received from James S. Kemper, Jr.

Typical Recipients

Arts & Humanities: Arts Festivals, Arts Funds, Arts Outreach, Community Arts, Dance, Libraries, Museums/Galleries, Music, Opera, Public Broadcasting, Theater

Civic & Public Affairs: Business/Free Enterprise, Parades/Festivals, Public Policy

Education: Afterschool/Enrichment Programs, Arts/Humanities Education, Business Education, Colleges & Universities, Community & Junior Colleges, Continuing Education, Economic Education, Education Associations, Engineering/Technological Education, Faculty Development, Education-General, International Studies, Legal Education, Medical Education, Minority Education, Science/Mathematics Education, Student Aid

Health: Emergency/Ambulance Services, Hospitals, Medical Rehabilitation, Medical Research, Single-Disease Health Associations

International: International Affairs

Science: Science Museums

Social Services: People with Disabilities, Recreation & Athletics, Substance Abuse, YMCA/YWCA/YMHA/YWHA, Youth Organizations

Application Procedures

Initial Contact: Send a brief letter.

Application Requirements: Include a concise description of project, realistic time-frame, mission statement, detailed project budget, statement of how future funding needs will be met, amount needed to complete project, amount requested, information about personnel involved, and method of evaluation.

Deadlines: Applications must be received by November 1.

Decision Notification: Decisions are made annually, in late February or early March.

Notes: The foundation identifies colleges and universities and invites them to participate in the Kemper Scholars program. If they choose to do so, the institution conducts a selection process which leads to the identification of individuals from the freshman class who are the institutional nominees for the program. The foundation then selects one of the nominees as a Kemper Scholar.

Restrictions

Does not support dinners or special events, fraternal organizations, good-will advertising, member agencies of united funds, political or lobbying groups, or religious organizations for sectarian purposes.
The foundation rarely supports multi-year grants.

Additional Information

Publications: Foundation Annual Report

Corporate Officials

General John T. Chain, Junior: president PRIM CORP EMPL president: Quarterdeck Equity Partners Inc. CORP AFFIL director: RJR Nabisco Inc.; director: Thomas Group Inc.; director: RJR Nabisco Holdings Corp.; director: Nabisco Inc.; director: Northrop Grumman Corp.; director: American Motorists Insurance Co.

Foundation Officials

General John T. Chain, Junior: trustee (see above)

J. Reed Coleman: trustee CORP AFFIL director: Regal-Beloit Corp.

John K. Conway: secretary

Robert A. Daniel: assistant treasurer

Peter Bannerman Hamilton: trustee B Philadelphia, PA 1946. ED Princeton University AB (1968); Yale University JD (1971). PRIM CORP EMPL vice president, president: Brunswick Corp. CORP AFFIL director: Fidelity Life Association; director: Kemper National Insurance Companies; director: American Motorists Insurance Co.

Thomas L. Hellie: executive director NONPR AFFIL trustee: Lenoir-Rhyne College.

Roberta S. Karmel: trustee B Chicago, IL 1937. ED Radcliffe College BA; New York University LLB (1962). PRIM CORP EMPL partner: Kelly, Drye & Warren LLP PRIM NONPR EMPL professor: Brooklyn Law School. CORP AFFIL director: Mallinckrodt Inc. NONPR AFFIL member: Financial Womens Association; trustee: Practicing Law Institute; member: Association Bar New York City; co-director: Center Study International Business Law; fellow: American Bar Foundation; member: American Law Institute; member: American Bar Association.

George Ralph Lewis: trustee B Burgess, VA 1941. ED Hampton University BS (1963); Iona College MBA (1966). CORP AFFIL director: Ceridian Corp.

Katharine Culbert Lyall: trustee B Lancaster, PA 1941. ED Cornell University BA (1963); New York University MBA (1965); Cornell University PhD (1969). PRIM NONPR EMPL president: University of Wisconsin System. CORP AFFIL director: Kemper National Insurance Companies; director: Marshall & Ilsley Corp.; director: Heartland Development Corp.; director: Interstate Energy Corp. NONPR AFFIL member: Phi Beta Kappa; professor: University Wisconsin Madison; member board: Carnegie Foundation Advancement Teaching; member: American Economic Association; member: Association American Universities.

David B. Mathis: chief executive officer, chairman B Atlanta, GA 1938. ED Lake Forest College BA (1960). PRIM CORP EMPL chairman, chief executive officer: Kemper Insurance Companies. CORP AFFIL director: TMC Global Inc.; chairman: Lumbermens Mutual Casualty Co.; chairman, chief executive officer: Kemper Corp.; director: Kemper Income Capital Prese; director: Fidelity Life Association; director: IMC Global Inc.; chief executive officer: American Manufacturer Mutual Insurance Co.; chairman: American Motorists Insurance Co. NONPR AFFIL director: Evanston Hospital Corp.

William D. Smith: chief executive officer

Grants Analysis

Disclosure Period: fiscal year ending July 31, 2000

Total Grants: $1,365,995*

Number of Grants: 59

Average Grant: $21,828*

Highest Grant: $100,000

Lowest Grant: $5,000

Typical Range: $15,000 to $25,000

*Note: Giving excludes scholarship and fellowships.

Recent Grants

Note: Grants derived from 2001 Form 990.

General

100,000	Boys and Girls Clubs of America, Atlanta, GA -- support for the James S. Kemper Foundation
75,000	Baylor University, Waco, TX -- support for ethics in undergraduate business education
75,000	Coe College, Cedar Rapids, IA -- funding for smart classrooms
50,000	Lake Forest College, Lake Forest, IL -- support educational projects
41,597	La Salle University School of Business

	Administration, Philadelphia, PA -- Kemper Scholars National Conference
35,000	Insurance Education Foundation, Indianapolis, IN -- support educational workshops for high school teachers
34,000	Lake Forest College, Lake Forest, IL -- support of Chicago Outreach Program
25,000	Bradley University, Peoria, IL -- support the International Insurance Scholars Program
25,000	College of Insurance, New York, NY -- enhance quality of MBA Program
25,000	Drake University College of Business and Public Administration, Des Moines, IA -- to support technology-based learning

HARRIS AND ELIZA KEMPNER FUND

Giving Contact

Elaine Perachio, Executive Director
2201 Market Street, Suite 601
Galveston, TX 77550-1529
Phone: (409)762-1603
Fax: (409)762-5435
E-mail: information@kempnerfund.org
Web: http://kempnerfund.org

Description

Founded: 1946

EIN: 746042458

Organization Type: Family Foundation

Giving Locations: TX: Galveston county

Grant Types: Award, Capital, Challenge, Conference/Seminar, Endowment, Fellowship, General Support, Matching, Multiyear/Continuing Support, Operating Expenses, Project, Research, Seed Money.

Note: Also provides family matching gifts.

Donor Information

Founder: The Kempner family established the "Galveston Fund" in 1946 with an initial donation of $38,500. In 1950 the name was changed to the Harris and Eliza Kempner Fund to honor the family's first American generation and founder of the family's business interests.

Harris Kempner, a Jewish refugee from Poland, served in the Confederate Army and shortly after the war he started a general mercantile business in Galveston, TX. The following generations developed extensive interests in banking, farming, ranching, cotton, and sugar refining. In the early 1900s, the family bought a bank, which today is known as the United States National Bank in Galveston. The bank is a subsidiary of Cullen/Frost Bankers located in San Antonio, TX. Harris L. Kempner, Jr., and Isaac Herbert Kempner III, both serve on the boards of directors of Cullen/Frost and the Imperial Holly Corporation, which contributed $75,000 to the foundation in 1990. Isaac H. Kempner III, also serves as the chairman of the Imperial Holly Corporation.

Financial Summary

Total Giving: $1,500,000 (2002); $1,000,000 (2001); $1,680,131 (2000). Note: 1995 Giving includes matching gifts and scholarship ($246,765).

Giving Analysis: Giving for 2000 includes: foundation grants to United Way ($110,000); foundation scholarships ($129,402); foundation fellowships ($150,000); foundation matching gifts ($226,515); 1999: foundation grants to United Way ($150,000); foundation matching gifts ($239,048); 1997: foundation grants to United Way ($69,350); foundation scholarships ($132,500) foundation matching gifts ($210,723)

Assets: $35,590,000 (2002); $40,000,000 (2001); $42,982,322 (2000)

Gifts Received: $84,947 (2000); $500 (1999); $50,000 (1998). Note: Foundation receives gifts from Daniel K. Thorne.

Typical Recipients

Arts & Humanities: Arts Associations & Councils, Arts Centers, Historic Preservation, History & Archaeology, Libraries, Literary Arts, Museums/Galleries, Music, Opera, Public Broadcasting, Theater, Visual Arts

Civic & Public Affairs: Botanical Gardens/Parks, Chambers of Commerce, Civil Rights, Community Foundations, Economic Development, Employment/Job Training, Civic & Public Affairs-General, Law & Justice, Municipalities/Towns, Public Policy, Urban & Community Affairs, Zoos/Aquariums

Education: Colleges & Universities, Elementary Education (Public), Engineering/Technological Education, Environmental Education, Faculty Development, International Exchange, Legal Education, Literacy, Medical Education, Preschool Education, Preschool Education, Private Education (Precollege), Public Education (Precollege), Religious Education, Science/Mathematics Education, Student Aid, Vocational & Technical Education

Environment: Environment-General, Resource Conservation

Health: Adolescent Health Issues, AIDS/HIV, Alzheimers Disease, Cancer, Children's Health/Hospitals, Clinics/Medical Centers, Emergency/Ambulance Services, Health Organizations, Heart, Hospices, Mental Health, Nursing Services, Prenatal Health Issues, Research/Studies Institutes, Single-Disease Health Associations

International: Health Care/Hospitals, International Development, International Environmental Issues, International Relations, International Relief Efforts

Religion: Churches, Jewish Causes, Religious Welfare, Synagogues/Temples

Social Services: Big Brother/Big Sister, Big Brother/Big Sister, Child Abuse, Child Welfare, Community Centers, Community Service Organizations, Crime Prevention, Domestic Violence, Emergency Relief, Family Planning, People with Disabilities, Recreation & Athletics, Scouts, Special Olympics, Substance Abuse, United Funds/United Ways, Youth Organizations

Application Procedures

Initial Contact: Applicants should send a grant proposal to the fund.

Application Requirements: Include a cover letter signed by the executive directory and the board chair or president that includes a brief description of organization of need and amount requested. Project or program information should include name and telephone number of contact person, a description of organization, timeline budget (income and expenses), list of sources and amounts solicited and/or pleged, future funding plans if program is new and continuing, and plans for evaluation. Organizational information should include statement of purpose and brief history; list of current officers and board members; operating budget (revenue and expenses) for year for which funds are sought; financial statements, audit, and/or 990 for most recent fiscal year; proof of tax-exempt status; and statement on organization letterhead that there has been no change in IRS status since issuance of ruling letter.

Deadlines: March 15, June 15, October 15, for primary grant programs; December 1 for grants regarding the environment and population control; March 31 for student loan program.

Review Process: Proposals are reviewed three times a year at trustee meetings in April, July, and December. Requests of a national/international nature related to the areas of education, environment, population control, and Third World development will be reviewed at the April meeting.

Restrictions

The Kempner Fund does not participate in fund-raising benefits, direct-mail solicitations, or make grants to individuals, or organizations not based in the United States.

Additional Information

Publications: Biennial Report (includes Application Guidelines)

Foundation Officials

John Thornton "Jack" Currie: vice chairman, trustee B Houston, TX 1928. ED University of Texas BA (1949); University of Texas BBA (1950). CORP AFFIL director: Triflex Fund; director: American Indemnity Financial Corp.; director: Stewart & Stevenson Services Inc.; director: America National Growth Fund; director: America National Income Fund. NONPR AFFIL member devel board: University Texas Medicine Branch; member chancellors council: University Texas System. CLUB AFFIL Krewe Momus Galveston Club; Galveston Artillery Club; Houston Country Club.

Hetta Ellen Towler Kempner: trustee

Isaac Herbert Kempner, III: trustee B Houston, TX 1932. ED Stanford University BA (1955); Stanford University MBA (1959). PRIM CORP EMPL chairman, director: Imperial Holly Corp. CORP AFFIL president: Foster Farms Inc. NONPR AFFIL trustee: Methodist Health Care System; trustee: U.S. Cane Sugar Refiners Association; trustee: H. Kempner Trust Association; trustee, treasurer: Contemporary Art Museum; chairman, director: Federal Reserve Bank Dallas-Houston. CLUB AFFIL Coronado Club; Bayou Club; Camden Ale & Quail Club.

Rabbi James Lee Kessler: trustee B Houston, TX 1945. ED University of Texas BA (1967); Hebrew Union College MA (1972); Hebrew Union College (1988). PRIM NONPR EMPL rabbi: Temple B'nai Israel. NONPR AFFIL member: Texas Jewish Historical Society; member rev board: University Texas Medicine Board; member: Siebel Loan Fund; member: Kallah Texas Rabbis; chairman: Lipson Scholarship Fund; member: Central Conference American Rabbis; advisor: Handbook Texas; member: B'nai B'rith. CLUB AFFIL member: Masons Club.

Robert L. K. Lynch: chairman CORP AFFIL director: Imperial Holly Corp.

Elaine Perachio: executive director

Barbara Weston Sasser: secretary B 1953. ED University of Texas, Galveston Medical School PhD. PRIM CORP EMPL manager: XVI Ltd. Co. CORP AFFIL secretary: ABA/Zack Inc.; manager: EMZ Ltd.

Lyda Ann Quinn Thomas: trustee

Leonora Kempner Thompson: chairman emeritus

Peter K. Thompson, MD: treasurer

Daniel Kempner Thorne: trustee PRIM CORP EMPL president: Star Lake Cattle Co. ADD CORP EMPL president: Star Lake Properties. CORP AFFIL director: Imperial Holly Corp.; director: Imperial Sugar Co.

Grants Analysis

Disclosure Period: calendar year ending 2000
Total Grants: $1,064,214*
Number of Grants: 182
Average Grant: $5,847
Highest Grant: $37,500
Typical Range: $2,500 to $10,000
*Note: Giving excludes United Way, scholarships, fellowship, matching gifts.

Recent Grants

Note: Grants derived from 1999 Form 990.

General

100,000	Galveston College Foundation, Galveston, TX -- Universal Access Program
75,000	University of Texas Medical Branch, Galveston, TX -- Jeane B. Kempner Fellowship Program
75,000	University of Texas Medical Branch, Galveston, TX -- Jeane B. Kempner Fellowship Program
60,000	United Way of Galveston, Galveston, TX -- operations
58,000	City of Galveston, Galveston, TX -- water truck purchase
37,500	Grand 1894 Opera House, Galveston, TX -- operations support
30,000	Galveston College Foundation, Galveston, TX -- Harris L. Kempner Award for Universal Access Endowment
30,000	United Way of Galveston, Galveston, TX -- operations
30,000	United Way of Galveston, Galveston, TX -- operations
30,000	United Way of Galveston, Galveston, TX -- operations

HENRY P. KENDALL FOUNDATION

Giving Contact

Theodore M. Smith, Executive Director
176 Federal Street
Boston, MA 02110
Phone: (617)951-2525
Fax: (617)443-1977
Web: http://www.kendall.org

Description

Founded: 1957
EIN: 046029103
Organization Type: Family Foundation
Giving Locations: AK; New England and the Pacific Northwest; Canada: maritime provinces; western Canada.
Grant Types: General Support.

Donor Information

Founder: The foundation was established in 1957. Donors to the foundation are members of the Henry P. Kendall family.

Financial Summary

Total Giving: $3,322,395 (2001); $3,492,293 (2000); $3,013,485 (1998)
Assets: $79,448,455 (2001); $92,170,575 (2000); $85,668,689 (1998)
Gifts Received: $5,890,000 (2000)

Typical Recipients

Arts & Humanities: Arts & Humanities-General, Historic Preservation, History & Archaeology, Libraries, Museums/Galleries, Public Broadcasting

Civic & Public Affairs: Botanical Gardens/Parks, Community Foundations, Civic & Public Affairs-General, Public Policy, Urban & Community Affairs, Zoos/Aquariums

Education: Colleges & Universities, Environmental Education, Journalism/Media Education, Legal Education, Medical Education, Private Education (Precollege), Secondary Education (Public)

Environment: Air/Water Quality, Energy, Forestry, Environment-General, Protection, Research, Resource Conservation, Watershed, Wildlife Protection

International: Foreign Educational Institutions, Health Care/Hospitals, International Affairs, International Environmental Issues, International Peace & Security Issues, International Relations, Trade

Science: Science Museums, Scientific Centers & Institutes, Scientific Labs, Scientific Organizations

Social Services: Food/Clothing Distribution

Application Procedures

Initial Contact: Brief proposals of no more than two pages should be sent to the foundation.

Application Requirements: Proposals should include amount and purpose of funds sought in the first paragraph; background of the issue to be addressed, the strategy being employed, the timetable, and the budget; organization's mission statement; organization's total annual budget; other sources of financing sought; staff personnel and a list of board members, including the curriculum vitae of the chief executive; and a copy of the organization's IRS determination letter of tax-exempt status.

Deadlines: February1; May 1; October 1.

Review Process: Decisions are made in three cycles, requests postmarked by February 1 made in March; by May 1 made in June; by October 1 in November. Requests are usually acknowledged within two to three weeks.

Restrictions

The foundation does not fund the following: waste clean-ups, toxics or air/water pollution prevention or pollution monitoring initiatives, land trusts, or species-specific preservation efforts; endowments or capital fund campaigns; building construction/operation; capital equipment; routine institutional operating costs; conference participation/travel unrelated to current foundation institutional grants; debt reduction; basic research; or individual fellowships. E-mail requests and audio/video tapes are not acceptable.

Additional Information

The foundation admits to a preference for concise, well-organized, jargon-free letters printed on high post-consumer content recycled paper. Grants are usually given for a two-year period.

Publications: Annual Report; Guidelines

Foundation Officials

Salvatore Battinelli: finance manager

Michael M. Davis: trustee B 1939. PRIM CORP EMPL partner: Sullivan & Worcester.

Henry Way Kendall: trustee B Boston, MA 1926. ED Amherst College BA (1950); Massachusetts Institute of Technology PhD (1955). PRIM NONPR EMPL JA Stratton professor: Massachusetts Institute of Technology. CORP AFFIL chairman: Union Concerned Scientists Inc. NONPR AFFIL fellow: American Physics Society; fellow: National Academy Sciences; fellow: American Academy of Arts & Sciences.

John P. Kendall: trustee PRIM CORP EMPL officer: Faneuil Hall Associates Inc. CORP AFFIL director: Colgate-Palmolive Co.

Anne W. Plimpton: trustee

Theodore M. Smith: executive director

Grants Analysis

Disclosure Period: calendar year ending 2001

Total Grants: $3,322,395

Number of Grants: 70

Average Grant: $38,806*

Highest Grant: $644,781

Lowest Grant: $5,000

Typical Range: $10,000 to $50,000

*Note: Average grant figure excludes highest grant.

Recent Grants

Note: Grants derived from 2001 Form 990.

General

644,781	Kendall Whaling Museum, Sharon, MA
150,000	Clean Air - Cool Planet, Portsmouth, NH
150,000	Franklin Institute, Boston, MA
150,000	International Council for Local Environmental Initiatives, Brattleboro, VT
150,000	New England Forestry Foundation, Cambridge, MA
145,000	Canadian Parks and Wilderness Society, Toronto, ON Canada -- for the Northern Rockies campaign
106,000	St. Francis Xavier University-Center for Community-Based Management, Antigonish, NS Canada
75,000	Coast Range Association, Newport, OR
75,000	Nature Conservancy of Montana, Helena, MT

74,000	Tufts University, Medford, MA

ETHEL AND W. GEORGE KENNEDY FAMILY FOUNDATION

Giving Contact

Kathleen Kennedy-Olsen, President
1550 Madruga Ave., Suite 225
Coral Gables, FL 33146
Phone: (305)666-6226
Fax: (605)666-2441
E-mail: admin@kennedyfamilyfdn.org
Web: http://www.kennedyfamilyfdn.org

Description

Founded: 1968

EIN: 596204880

Organization Type: Private Foundation

Giving Locations: FL: Miami

Grant Types: Capital, Endowment, General Support, Matching, Multiyear/Continuing Support.

Donor Information

Founder: the late W. George Kennedy

Financial Summary

Total Giving: $1,192,667 (2001); $2,133,398 (2000); $1,058,632 (1999)

Assets: $26,462,585 (2001); $31,046,125 (2000); $30,631,239 (1999)

Typical Recipients

Arts & Humanities: Arts Associations & Councils, Arts Centers, Arts Festivals, Ballet, Arts & Humanities-General, History & Archaeology, Libraries, Museums/Galleries, Opera, Performing Arts, Theater

Civic & Public Affairs: Botanical Gardens/Parks, Chambers of Commerce, Community Foundations, Civic & Public Affairs-General, Nonprofit Management, Safety, Zoos/Aquariums

Education: Arts/Humanities Education, Colleges & Universities, Community & Junior Colleges, Education Funds, Education-General, Medical Education, Private Education (Precollege), Public Education (Precollege), Secondary Education (Public), Student Aid

Environment: Wildlife Protection

Health: Cancer, Children's Health/Hospitals, Emergency/Ambulance Services, Hospices, Hospitals, Long-Term Care, Medical Research, Preventive Medicine/Wellness Organizations, Single-Disease Health Associations, Speech & Hearing, Transplant Networks/Donor Banks

International: International Organizations

Religion: Churches, Religion-General, Jewish Causes, Missionary Activities (Domestic), Religious Welfare, Synagogues/Temples

Science: Science Museums, Scientific Centers & Institutes

Social Services: Child Welfare, Community Service Organizations, Emergency Relief, Food/Clothing Distribution, People with Disabilities, Recreation & Athletics, Sexual Abuse, Social Services-General, Special Olympics, Youth Organizations

Application Procedures

Initial Contact: Send a brief letter of inquiry outlining program for which funding is sought.

Application Requirements: For a full proposal, include 8 copies of proposal on 3 hole punches lettersized paper. Proposals not to exceed five pages in length. Include a description of organization, amount requested, purpose of funds sought, recently audited financial statement, list of Board of Directors, project and organization budgets, plan for sustaining project after the grant funding expires, and proof of tax-exempt status.

Deadlines: February 1 for March meeting and September 15 for October meeting.

Review Process: Board meets to consider requests in March and October.

Notes: Video material not to exceed ten minutes in length. Provide self-addressed stamped manila envelope for the return of supporting documents or visual aids.

Restrictions

Foundation Officials

Alvena Allen: director

Kendal Kennedy Dobkin: director

Karen Kennedy Herterich: director

Kimberly Kennedy: director

Wayne G. Kennedy: president, director

William Kennedy: director

Kathleen P. Kennedy Olsen: director

Forrest I. Mulcahey: director

Martin Nash: director

Guy Rizzo: director

Grants Analysis

Disclosure Period: calendar year ending 2001

Total Grants: $1,192,667

Number of Grants: 87

Average Grant: $9,255*

Highest Grant: $194,000

Lowest Grant: $250

Typical Range: $1,000 to $20,000

*Note: Average grant figure excludes three highest grants ($415,250).

Recent Grants

Note: Grants derived from 2001 Form 990.

General

194,000	Miami City Ballet, Miami, FL
110,650	Bay Point Schools, Miami, FL
110,600	American Red Cross, Idaho Falls, ID
70,000	University of Miami Pediatric Mobile Clinic, Miami, FL
48,000	House of Hope, Anaheim, CA
43,240	PACE Center for Girls, Orlando, FL
30,775	Blowing Rock Stage Company, Blowing Rock, NC
30,000	Neat Stuff, Miami, FL
30,000	Temple Emanu EL, Palm Beach, FL
25,500	Shake-A-Leg, Miami, FL

ETHEL KENNEDY FOUNDATION

Giving Contact

Ethel K. Marran, President & Treasurer
271 Johns Island Dr.
Vero Beach, FL 32963
Phone: (561)231-2971

Description

Founded: 1986

EIN: 112768682

Organization Type: Private Foundation

Giving Locations: NY

Grant Types: General Support.

Financial Summary

Total Giving: $538,972 (2000); $565,700 (1999); $365,700 (1996)

Assets: $12,036,447 (2000); $13,203,712 (1999); $9,874,326 (1996)

Typical Recipients

Arts & Humanities: Arts Centers, Arts & Humanities-General, History & Archaeology, Libraries, Museums/Galleries, Music, Public Broadcasting, Theater

Civic & Public Affairs: Economic Development, Employment/Job Training, Ethnic Organizations, Civic & Public Affairs-General, Housing, Legal Aid, Urban & Community Affairs, Women's Affairs

Education: Business Education, Colleges & Universities, Education Funds, Faculty Development, Medical Education, Minority Education, Private Education (Precollege), Public Education (Precollege), School Volunteerism, Science/Mathematics Education, Student Aid

Environment: Air/Water Quality, Environment-General, Resource Conservation

Health: Alzheimers Disease, Arthritis, Cancer, Clinics/Medical Centers, Clinics/Medical Centers, Health Organizations, Hospices, Hospitals, Medical Research, Single-Disease Health Associations

International: Health Care/Hospitals, Human Rights, International Relief Efforts

Religion: Religious Organizations, Religious Welfare

Social Services: Animal Protection, At-Risk Youth, Camps, Child Welfare, Community Centers, Community Service Organizations, Domestic Violence, Family Planning, Family Services, Food/Clothing Distribution, Homes, People with Disabilities, Recreation & Athletics, Senior Services, Shelters/Homelessness, Social Services-General, Special Olympics, United Funds/United Ways, Youth Organizations

Application Procedures

Initial Contact: The foundation requests applications be made in writing. Include proof of tax-exempt status, purpose of funds sought, a description of organization, and activities in general.
Deadlines: None.

Restrictions

Does not support individuals.

Foundation Officials

Elizabeth Marran: vice president
Ethel K. Marran: president, treasurer
Laura Marran: secretary

Grants Analysis

Disclosure Period: calendar year ending 2000
Total Grants: $538,972
Number of Grants: 46
Average Grant: $5,441*
Highest Grant: $105,000
Typical Range: $1,000 to $10,000
*Note: Average grant figure excludes three highest grants ($305,000).

Recent Grants

Note: Grants derived from 2001 Form 990.

General

150,000	Habitat of Vero Beach, Vero Beach, CA
100,000	Hanne Fenishil Center for Child Development
50,000	Coalition for the Homeless, New York, NY
25,000	Buckingham Browne and Nichols School, Cambridge, MA
20,000	Brigham and Women's Hospital, Boston, MA -- Department of Urology
20,000	Buckingham Browne and Nichols School, Cambridge, MA
20,000	Dollars for Scholars
20,000	Exeter Academy
20,000	Hamilton College Scholarship, Clinton, NY
20,000	Hampton Day School, Bridgehampton, NY

JOSEPH P. KENNEDY, JR. FOUNDATION

Giving Contact

Lucille Zeph, Executive Director
1325 G Street, Northwest, Suite 500
Washington, DC 20005-4709

Phone: (202)393-1250
Fax: (202)824-0351
E-mail: sswenson@specialolympics.org
Web: http://www.jpkf.org

Description

Founded: 1946
EIN: 136083407
Organization Type: Family Foundation
Giving Locations: nationally.
Grant Types: Project, Seed Money.

Donor Information

Founder: Joseph P. Kennedy, Jr., the oldest son of Joseph P. Kennedy and Rose Kennedy , was born in Massachusetts on July 28, 1915. He graduated from Choate School in Connecticut and attended the London School of Economics for one year before entering Harvard Law School in 1934. Joseph P. Kennedy Jr. left Harvard before his final year to volunteer as a Navy flyer. In May 1942, he was awarded his wings, and in 1943, was sent to England with the first naval squadron to fly B-24s with the British Naval Command. He died on August 12, 1944.

The Joseph P. Kennedy, Jr. Foundation was established in 1946 by Ambassador and Mrs. Joseph P. Kennedy, in honor of their son.

Financial Summary

Total Giving: $2,379,854 (fiscal year ending June 30, 2001); $2,675,716 (fiscal 2000); $1,051,860 (fiscal 1998)
Assets: $24,135,253 (fiscal 2001); $30,199,183 (fiscal 2000); $26,182,637 (fiscal 1998)
Gifts Received: $912,004 (fiscal 2000); $34,439 (fiscal 1998); $1,720 (fiscal 1997). Note: In fiscal 2000, contributions were received from Simon Grimault.

Typical Recipients

Arts & Humanities: Arts Outreach, Ballet, Community Arts, History & Archaeology, Libraries
Civic & Public Affairs: Botanical Gardens/Parks, Economic Development, Employment/Job Training, Civic & Public Affairs-General, Nonprofit Management, Philanthropic Organizations, Public Policy, Women's Affairs
Education: Colleges & Universities, Education Reform, Faculty Development, Education-General, Medical Education, Private Education (Precollege), Public Education (Precollege), Social Sciences Education, Special Education, Student Aid, Vocational & Technical Education
Environment: Environment-General, Watershed
Health: Children's Health/Hospitals, Clinics/Medical Centers, Health Policy/Cost Containment, Hospitals, Medical Research, Medical Training, Mental Health, Prenatal Health Issues, Preventive Medicine/Wellness Organizations
International: Foreign Educational Institutions, Health Care/Hospitals, Human Rights
Religion: Churches, Missionary Activities (Domestic), Religious Welfare
Social Services: Child Welfare, Counseling, Day Care, Family Planning, People with Disabilities, Recreation & Athletics, Shelters/Homelessness, Special Olympics, Substance Abuse, Youth Organizations

Application Procedures

Initial Contact: The foundation solicits its own grantees and also accepts applications from others. Applicants should direct letters of interest to Jill Sosse, Grants Manager.
Application Requirements: The proposal should include a five-page description of the project including description of problem, relevance of the proposal to the subject population, its goal, identify collaboration with other systems, and a statement of how the project will advance the present state of knowledge. Other items to include are the following: plan of work, including timelines, work methodology, and the identification of target population; training activities for various audiences (e.g., people with mental retardation, their families, caregivers, etc.); dissemination of results; description of organization and management, including qualifications of the personnel involved (full curriculum vitae of each person affiliated with the proposal are to be filed) and explanation of how the program builds on existing services; references including any literature discussed in the proposals and future funding; and budget information.
Deadlines: Short concept letters of intent can be accepted at any time. Proposals are accepted from July 1 through December 1.
Review Process: All applicants undergo initial screening; those suitable for further consideration are requested to prepare a more detailed proposal based on consultation with foundation staff. Scientific applications are reviewed by the Scientific Advisory Board and other applications are reviewed by experts in an area related to the grant proposal. Recommendations for funding are presented to the board of trustees, which makes the final funding decisions. Final decisions are made by July 1.

Restrictions

The foundation only works in the area of mental retardation and is only interested in innovative projects that are not supported elsewhere by public funds. The foundation does not fund capital costs or equipment for projects, nor does it pay for ongoing support or operations of existing programs.

Additional Information

The foundation also provides technical assistance and consultation services, including policy consultation, to assist in writing local and governmental policies for health and education programs for adolescents; operational consultation, to help schools and agencies access and develop supportive, caring environments for students, clients, and staff; financial consultation, to aid in fund raising, grant writing, and management; and program evaluation, to provide expert assistance in assessing community needs and program effectiveness.

Responding to the pressing need for change in the area of physical education for persons with mental retardation, the foundation created the Special Olympics program as a model for greatly expanded sports and recreation opportunities in schools, communities, and institutions throughout the world. Sanctioned by the United States Olympic Committee, recognized by the International Olympic Committee, and endorsed by most major organizations of special educators, recreation specialists, coaches, and athletes, Special Olympics International is the largest year around sports organization in the world for children and adults with mental retardation.

Publications: Grant Policy Statement; Grant Guidelines; Brochures

Foundation Officials

Joseph E. Hakim: treasurer B 1951. ED University of Pennsylvania Wharton School MBA (1971). PRIM CORP EMPL president, chief executive officer: Merchandise Mart Properties.

George Jesien, PhD: executive director

Hon. Edward Moore Kennedy: president, trustee B Boston, MA 1932. ED Harvard University AB (1956); The Hague Academy of International Law (1958); University of Virginia LLB (1959). PRIM NONPR EMPL senator: U.S. Senate. NONPR AFFIL member: NAACP; member: Technology Assessment Board; member: Martin Luther King Junior Federal Holiday Commission; trustee: Massachusetts General Hospital; trustee: John F. Kennedy Library; trustee: Robert F. Kennedy Memorial Foundation; trustee: John F. Kennedy Center Performing Arts; member: Commission Bicentennial U.S. Constitution; member: Congressional Friends Ireland; trustee emeritus: Boston Symphony Orchestra; trustee: Childrens Hospital Medical Center; member: Biomedical Ethics Board;

trustee: Boston College; member: Arms Control Observer Group.

Patricia Kennedy Lawford: trustee

Eunice Kennedy Shriver: executive vice president, trustee B Brookline, MA 1921. ED Manhattanville College of Sacred Heart; Stanford University BS (1943). NONPR AFFIL founder: Special Olympics International.

R. Sargent Shriver: officer B Westminster, MD November 09, 1915.

Jean Kennedy Smith: trustee B Brookline, MA 1927. ED Manhattanville College BA. NONPR AFFIL ambassador to Ireland: U.S. Department State; founder, director, chairman: Very Special Arts; trustee: John F. Kennedy Center Performing Arts.

Grants Analysis

Disclosure Period: fiscal year ending June 30, 2001
Total Grants: $2,379,854
Number of Grants: 38
Average Grant: $44,555*
Highest Grant: $275,000
Lowest Grant: $4,640
Typical Range: $25,000 to $75,000
*****Note:** Average grant figures excludes four highest grants ($865,000).

Recent Grants

Note: Grants derived from fiscal 2001 Form 990.

Library-Related

200,000	John F. Kennedy Library, Boston, MA
200,000	John F. Kennedy Library, Boston, MA

General

275,000	Community of Caring, Washington, DC -- conduct educational programs and activities for the prevention and care of adolescent pregnancy
190,000	Park Foundation, New York, NY -- support charitable activities
118,138	University of Maine, Orono, ME
78,000	ARC of Anne Arundel Co, Annapolis, MD -- education projects
72,921	University of Massachusetts Boston, Boston, MA -- education project
72,000	Family Voices, Algodones, NM -- Public Policy Leadership Program
69,780	University of Colorado Health Sciences Center, Aurora, CO -- education/development projects
66,000	Teacher's College, New York, NY -- education/development projects
65,000	Advocacy Center, New Orleans, LA -- Public Policy Leadership Program
65,000	Disability Rights Center, Inc., Concord, NH -- Public Policy Leadership Program

KENRIDGE FUND

Giving Contact

Paulette F. Kitko, Secretary & Treasurer
c/o Advisory Services
1422 Euclid Ave., Rm. 1010
Cleveland, OH 44115-2078
Phone: (216)363-6485

Description

Founded: 1989
EIN: 341616683
Organization Type: Private Foundation
Giving Locations: AL; FL; GA; IL; KY; ME; MA; NJ; OH; VA
Grant Types: Emergency, General Support, Operating Expenses, Research.

Donor Information

Founder: Established in 1989 by Fanny H. Bolton and Claire H. B. Jonklass.

Financial Summary

Total Giving: $164,000 (2001); $329,000 (2000); $230,000 (1999). Note: 1997 Giving includes United Way ($5,000).
Giving Analysis: Giving for 2001 includes: foundation grants to United Way ($3,000); foundation scholarships ($9,000); 2000: foundation grants to United Way ($3,000); foundation scholarships ($4,000); 1999: foundation grants to United Way ($3,000); foundation scholarships ($7,000)
Assets: $3,741,622 (2001); $4,340,460 (2000); $5,164,717 (1999)
Gifts Received: $40 (1996)

Typical Recipients

Arts & Humanities: Arts Centers, History & Archaeology, Museums/Galleries, Music
Civic & Public Affairs: Civic & Public Affairs-General
Education: Colleges & Universities, Faculty Development, Medical Education, Minority Education, Private Education (Precollege), Public Education (Precollege), Science/Mathematics Education, Special Education, Student Aid
Environment: Forestry, Environment-General, Research, Resource Conservation
Health: Cancer, Emergency/Ambulance Services, Hospitals, Medical Rehabilitation, Medical Research, Nursing Services, Prenatal Health Issues, Public Health, Respiratory, Single-Disease Health Associations
International: Foreign Arts Organizations, International Environmental Issues
Religion: Churches, Religious Welfare
Science: Science-General, Scientific Research
Social Services: Child Welfare, Emergency Relief, Recreation & Athletics, Scouts, Shelters/Homelessness, Substance Abuse, United Funds/United Ways, YMCA/YWCA/YMHA/YWHA, Youth Organizations

Application Procedures

Initial Contact: The foundation requests applications be made in writing.
Application Requirements: Include proof of tax-exempt status.
Deadlines: None.

Restrictions

Grants are not made to individuals.

Foundation Officials

Kenneth G. Hochman: vice president
Jackie A. Horning: assistant secretary
Anthony Jonklaas: trustee
Clair Hanna B. Jonklaas: president, trustee
Paulette F. Kitko: secretary, treasurer

Grants Analysis

Disclosure Period: calendar year ending 2001
Total Grants: $152,000*
Number of Grants: 31
Average Grant: $3,935*
Highest Grant: $30,000
Lowest Grant: $1,000
Typical Range: $1,000 to $10,000
*****Note:** Giving excludes United Way, scholarships. Average grant figure excludes highest grant.

Recent Grants

Note: Grants derived from 2001 Form 990.

General

30,000	Friends of the Bermuda Aquarium, Ltd, Wharton, NJ -- Bermuda Biodiversity Project
25,000	YMCA of Thomasville, Thomasville, GA -- Remington Park Project
6,000	Halcyon Home, Thomasville, GA -- child abuse counseling
5,000	American Red Cross - Thomas County Chapter -- operations
5,000	Auburn University Foundation, Auburn University, AL -- Scott Richey Research Center - sports medicine one day program
5,000	Christian Children's Fund, Richmond, VA -- United States aid
5,000	Cradle Society, Evanston, IL -- operations
5,000	Dana Hall School, Wellesley, MA -- operations
5,000	Hanna Perkins School, Cleveland, OH
5,000	Hearts Adaptive Riding Program, Santa Barbara, CA -- current operations

KENT-LUCAS FOUNDATION

Giving Contact

Elizabeth K. Van Alen, President, Treasurer & Trustee
101 Springer Bldg.
3411 Silverside Rd.
Wilmington, DE 19810
Phone: (302)478-4383

Description

Founded: 1968
EIN: 237010084
Organization Type: Private Foundation
Giving Locations: FL; ME; PA: Philadelphia including metropolitan area
Grant Types: Capital, General Support, Multiyear/Continuing Support, Operating Expenses.

Donor Information

Founder: Atwater Kent Foundation

Financial Summary

Total Giving: $87,125 (2000); $61,000 (1999); $137,200 (1998)
Assets: $3,243,670 (2000); $3,290,195 (1999); $3,106,280 (1998)

Typical Recipients

Arts & Humanities: Arts Associations & Councils, Historic Preservation, History & Archaeology, Libraries, Museums/Galleries, Public Broadcasting, Theater
Civic & Public Affairs: Botanical Gardens/Parks, Clubs, Employment/Job Training, Civic & Public Affairs-General, Municipalities/Towns, Philanthropic Organizations, Public Policy, Safety, Urban & Community Affairs
Education: Arts/Humanities Education, Colleges & Universities, Education-General, International Exchange, International Studies, Medical Education, Private Education (Precollege), Religious Education, Special Education, Student Aid
Environment: Environment-General, Resource Conservation
Health: Cancer, Children's Health/Hospitals, Clinics/Medical Centers, Emergency/Ambulance Services, Eyes/Blindness, Heart, Hospices, Hospitals, Medical Research, Nursing Services
International: Foreign Educational Institutions, International Environmental Issues, International Organizations, International Relief Efforts
Religion: Churches, Religion-General, Religious Organizations, Religious Welfare
Science: Scientific Centers & Institutes, Scientific Labs
Social Services: Animal Protection, Child Welfare, Community Service Organizations, Crime Prevention,

Family Services, Food/Clothing Distribution, Recreation & Athletics, Shelters/Homelessness, Youth Organizations

Application Procedures

Initial Contact: Send a full proposal. Describe the general activities of the organization and the specific need for and purpose of the requested grant. Include the complete legal name and address of the organziation, proof of tax-exempt status, most recent annual report and certified financial statements, and a detailed project budget.

Application Requirements: Describe the general activities of the organization and the specific need for and purpose of the requested grant. Include the complete legal name and address of the organziation, proof of tax-exempt status, most recent annual report and certified financial statements, and a detailed project budget.

Deadlines: None.

Restrictions

Does not support individuals.

Additional Information

Publications: Application Procedures

Foundation Officials

Cassandra V. A. Ludington: trustee
Elizabeth K. Van Alen: president, treasurer, trustee
James L. Van Alen, II: trustee
William L. Van Alen: vice president, trustee
James R. Weaver: secretary
Stella R. Williams: assistant secretary

Grants Analysis

Disclosure Period: calendar year ending 2000
Total Grants: $87,125
Number of Grants: 33
Average Grant: $1,773*
Highest Grant: $30,400
Typical Range: $500 to $5,000
*Note: Average grant excludes highest grant.

Recent Grants

Note: Grants derived from 2001 Form 990.

General

30,450	Children's Hospital of Philadelphia, Philadelphia, PA
19,550	University of Pennsylvania, Philadelphia, PA
15,000	Bascom Palmer Eye Institute, Miami, FL
5,400	Willistown Conservation Trust, Newtown Square, PA
5,000	Lost Tree Charitable Foundation, North Palm Beach, FL
3,500	Fellowship Christians University, West Tisbury, CT
1,250	Dream Chasers, Inc.
1,250	O'Gorman Garden Center, New York, NY
1,000	Barry Telecommunications, West Palm Beach, FL
1,000	Community Television Foundation of South Florida, Miami, FL

KERN FOUNDATION TRUST

Giving Contact

Dale Rudy, Contact
Northern Trust Co.
50 S. LsSalle St., L-5
Chicago, IL 60675
Phone: (312)630-6000
Fax: (312)444-4122
E-mail: dgr@ntrs.com

Note: Dale Rudy can also be reached at (312)444-3796.

Description

Founded: 1959
EIN: 366107250
Organization Type: Specialized/Single Purpose Foundation
Giving Locations: CA; IL
Grant Types: Fellowship, General Support, Project, Scholarship.
Note: The foundation reports that scholarships and fellowships are made to qualified persons interested in utilizing the theosophical world view and paid through their universities/colleges.

Donor Information

Founder: Established in 1959 by the late Herbert A. Kern , who felt that the basic theosophical concepts such as the essential unity of all in manifestation was a critical starting point for changing peoples' attitudes about race, culture, responsibility towards one another and the environment. It became operational in 1966 and is not affiliated with or related to any other charitable trust or foundation.

Financial Summary

Total Giving: $1,454,894 (2001); $1,000,000 (1999 approx); $1,105,849 (1998)
Giving Analysis: Giving for 1998 includes: foundation matching gifts ($5,126)
Assets: $11,383,185 (2001); $28,000,000 (1999 approx); $27,534,792 (1998)

Typical Recipients

Arts & Humanities: Libraries, Museums/Galleries
Education: Arts/Humanities Education, Colleges & Universities, Continuing Education, Private Education (Precollege), Public Education (Precollege)
Religion: Religious Organizations, Religious Welfare
Social Services: Child Welfare, People with Disabilities

Application Procedures

Initial Contact: The foundation has no formal grant application procedure or application form.
Deadlines: None.
Review Process: Upon receipt of a proposal which includes sufficient detail to make a case for support, the proposal is routed to a qualified professional to evaluate it.

Restrictions

The foundation reports that it limits grantmaking to religious foundations chartered to advance the cause of theosophy. Grants are not made to individuals.

Additional Information

The Northern Trust Company of Chicago operates as a corporate trustee.

The foundation reports that it provides all types of services to its principal theosophical organizations receiving grants. It gives only financial support to universities and colleges to which a grant has been made to assist a graduate student or faculty member.

Publications: Program Policy Statement

Foundation Officials

John C. Kern: trustee
Dale Rudy: corporate trustee rep

Grants Analysis

Disclosure Period: calendar year ending 2001
Total Grants: $1,454,894
Number of Grants: 5
Highest Grant: $1,253,184
Lowest Grant: $4,710
Typical Range: $5,000 to $75,000

Recent Grants

Note: Grants derived from 2001 Form 990.

General

1,253,184	Theosophical Society in America, Wheaton, IL
120,000	Krotona Institute of Theosophy, Ojai, CA
72,000	Happy Valley School, Ojai, CA
5,000	Theosophical Book Gift Institute, Wheaton, IL
4,710	Shimer College, Waukegan, IL

KERR FOUNDATION, INC.

Giving Contact

Robert S. Kerr, Jr., Chairman of Board
12501 North May Avenue
Oklahoma City, OK 73120
Phone: (405)749-7991
Fax: (405)749-2877
E-mail: aholz@thekerrfoundation.org
Web: http://www.thekerrfoundation.org

Description

Founded: 1963
EIN: 731256122
Organization Type: General Purpose Foundation
Giving Locations: OK
Grant Types: Capital, Challenge, Project, Research, Seed Money.

Donor Information

Founder: The foundation was established in 1963, with the late Grayce B. Kerr Flynn as donor.

Financial Summary

Total Giving: $768,860 (2001); $792,069 (2000); $1,549,158 (1999 approx)
Assets: $27,870,754 (2001); $30,387,430 (2000); $30,126,191 (1998)
Gifts Received: $1,344 (1995); $6,480 (1994); $6,565 (1993)

Typical Recipients

Arts & Humanities: Arts Associations & Councils, Arts Centers, Arts Festivals, Arts Funds, Arts Institutes, Arts Outreach, Ballet, Dance, Ethnic & Folk Arts, Film & Video, Arts & Humanities-General, Historic Preservation, History & Archaeology, Libraries, Museums/Galleries, Music, Opera, Performing Arts, Public Broadcasting, Theater
Civic & Public Affairs: Botanical Gardens/Parks, Community Foundations, Economic Development, Economic Policy, Employment/Job Training, Civic & Public Affairs-General, Housing, Native American Affairs, Nonprofit Management, Philanthropic Organizations, Professional & Trade Associations, Public Policy, Safety, Urban & Community Affairs, Women's Affairs, Zoos/Aquariums
Education: Arts/Humanities Education, Business Education, Business-School Partnerships, Colleges & Universities, Community & Junior Colleges, Education Funds, Engineering/Technological Education, Environmental Education, Faculty Development, Education-General, Legal Education, Literacy, Medical Education, Private Education (Precollege), Public Education (Precollege), School Volunteerism, Science/Mathematics Education, Secondary Education (Private), Secondary Education (Public), Social Sciences Education, Special Education, Student Aid
Environment: Energy, Forestry, Environment-General, Resource Conservation, Wildlife Protection
Health: Cancer, Children's Health/Hospitals, Clinics/Medical Centers, Emergency/Ambulance Services, Health-General, Geriatric Health, Health Organizations, Hospitals (University Affiliated), Mental Health, Prenatal Health Issues, Public Health, Single-Disease Health Associations

International: Foreign Arts Organizations, Health Care/Hospitals, International Affairs, International Development, International Environmental Issues
Religion: Ministries, Religious Welfare
Science: Science Museums, Scientific Organizations
Social Services: At-Risk Youth, Child Welfare, Community Service Organizations, Counseling, Delinquency & Criminal Rehabilitation, Domestic Violence, Emergency Relief, Family Planning, Family Services, Food/Clothing Distribution, People with Disabilities, Scouts, Senior Services, Shelters/Homelessness, Social Services-General, Substance Abuse, Veterans, Youth Organizations

Application Procedures

Initial Contact: Applicants should request the foundation's application forms.
Application Requirements: Requests for funding should include a cover letter with summary request, completed institutional profile and proposal summary forms, copy of the IRS determination letter of tax-exempt status, a proposal, and other documentation appropriate to the request. The foundation asks that applicants send an original and two duplicates.
Deadlines: None, but the foundation should receive applications at least forty-five days prior to quarterly trustee meetings to allow time for review for consideration at the meetings. Meetings are generally held in the third month of the quarter. Applicants should contact the foundation for specific dates.
Review Process: Upon acceptance of a proposal, the applicant will be informed as to when action by the trustees may be anticipated. Grant awards will be made contingent upon signing a grant contract which includes provision for project evaluation. Foundation trustees and/or staff often conduct site visits to organizations being considered for a grant.
Notes: Favorable consideration of a proposal will normally be in the form of a challenge grant.

Restrictions

The foundation does not make grants to individuals or provide operating dollars.

Additional Information

Publications: Annual Report; Guidelines; Application Form

Foundation Officials

Royce Mitchell Hammons: treasurer B Hallettsville, TX 1945. ED University of Oklahoma BBA (1969); Southern Methodist University (1976); Stanford University (1990). PRIM CORP EMPL president, chairman, chief executive officer: UMB Oklahoma Bank. CORP AFFIL director: UMB Financial Corp. NONPR AFFIL trustee: Oklahoma City University; trustee: University Oklahoma Associate Council; member: Oklahoma Bankers Association; trustee: Arthritis Foundation; financial committee: City Nichols Hills. CLUB AFFIL Whitehall Club; Oklahoma City Golf & Country Club; Galveston Country Club; Oklahoma City Dinner Club.
Cody T. Kerr: trustee
Lou C. Kerr: vice president, secretary
Robert Samuel Kerr, Jr.: president B Ada, OK 1926. ED University of Oklahoma (1951); University of Oklahoma (1955). PRIM CORP EMPL attorney, chairman: Kerr, Irvine & Rhodes. CORP AFFIL director: Kerr-McGee Corp.; director: Bank Oklahoma Tulsa. NONPR AFFIL member: American Bar Association.
Sharon Kerr: trustee
Steven Kerr: assistant treasurer, trustee
Ray Klein: trustee
Laura Kerr Ogle: trustee
Elmer Boyd Staats: trustee B Richfield, KS June 06, 1914. ED McPherson College AB (1935); University of Kansas MA (1936); University of Minnesota PhD (1939). PRIM NONPR EMPL chairman: Harry S Truman Scholarship Foundation. CORP AFFIL director: Computer Data System; emeritus member: Metro Life

Insurance Co. NONPR AFFIL member visiting committee: University California Los Angeles Graduate School Management; member: University Chicago Comm Public Policy Studies; member: Pi Sigma Alpha; member: National Academy Public Administration; member: Phi Beta Kappa; chairman: Federal Accounting Standards Advisory Board; director: George C. Marshall Foundation; member: Association Government Accountants; member: Beta Gamma Sigma; member: American Management Association; member: American Society Public Administration; member: Alpha Kappa Psi; member, director: American Academy Political & Social Science. CLUB AFFIL Chevy Chase Club; Cosmos Club.

Grants Analysis

Disclosure Period: calendar year ending 2001
Total Grants: $768,860
Number of Grants: 73
Average Grant: $9,463*
Highest Grant: $87,500
Lowest Grant: $1,500
Typical Range: $5,000 to $10,000
*Note: Average grant figure excludes highest grant.

Recent Grants

Note: Grants derived from 2000 Form 990.

General
200,000	Carl Albert, Jr. College Development Foundation -- Kerr Country Mansion and Conference Center facility
75,000	University of Oklahoma Foundation, Inc., Norman, OK -- build an addition to the College of Law
65,000	Lyric Theater, Oklahoma City, OK -- funds for renovation of 16th Street Plaza Theatre Project
50,000	Oklahoma School of Science and Math, Oklahoma City, OK -- fund teaching laboratory
35,000	Tulsa Ballet, Tulsa, OK -- support the acquisition and production Lady of the Camellias
30,000	India Shriners -- funds to purchase van
25,000	Centers for Youth and Families, Little Rock, AR -- construction of a new kitchen
25,000	Central Missouri State University Foundation, Inc., MO -- construction of James C. Kirkpatrick Library
25,000	Choctaw Library Guild, Inc. -- help provide funds to construct a permanent branch library
25,000	Music Associates of Aspen, Aspen, CO -- 3:1 challenge for donors

GRAYCE B. KERR FUND

Giving Contact

Heather Brady Masone, contact
117 Bay Street
Easton, MD 21601
Phone: (410)822-6652
Fax: (410)822-4546
E-mail: gbkf@bluecrab.org

Description

Founded: 1986
EIN: 731256124
Organization Type: Family Foundation
Grant Types: Award, Capital, Challenge, Employee Matching Gifts, Endowment, Matching, Multiyear/Continuing Support, Project, Research.

Donor Information

Founder: Established in 1986 by Breene M. Kerr and the late Grayce B. Kerr Flynn . Grayce Flynn was the widow of Robert S. Kerr, a former govenor of Oklahoma and a former U.S. Senator. The Grayce B.

Kerr Fund is one of the four successor foundations of the Kerr Foundation managed by Mrs. Kerr's children after her death in 1965.

Financial Summary

Total Giving: $1,068,630 (2001); $1,320,599 (2000); $1,050,000 (1999)
Giving Analysis: Giving for 1998 includes: foundation matching gifts ($32,464)
Assets: $33,266,100 (2002); $35,724,250 (2001); $10,304,883 (2000)
Gifts Received: $2,767 (1998); $1,344 (1995); $6,480 (1994)

Typical Recipients

Arts & Humanities: Arts Associations & Councils, Arts Institutes, Arts Outreach, Community Arts, Historic Preservation, History & Archaeology, Libraries, Museums/Galleries, Music, Performing Arts, Theater
Civic & Public Affairs: Asian American Affairs, Botanical Gardens/Parks, Community Foundations, Employment/Job Training, Civic & Public Affairs-General, Hispanic Affairs, Housing, Law & Justice, Municipalities/Towns, Nonprofit Management, Professional & Trade Associations, Public Policy, Safety, Urban & Community Affairs
Education: Arts/Humanities Education, Business-School Partnerships, Colleges & Universities, Education Funds, Elementary Education (Public), Engineering/Technological Education, Faculty Development, Education-General, Gifted & Talented Programs, International Studies, Legal Education, Literacy, Private Education (Precollege), Public Education (Precollege), Science/Mathematics Education, Secondary Education (Private), Social Sciences Education
Environment: Air/Water Quality, Forestry, Environment-General, Resource Conservation, Wildlife Protection
Health: Cancer, Children's Health/Hospitals, Hospices, Hospitals, Medical Research, Mental Health, Public Health
International: Human Rights
Religion: Churches, Religious Organizations
Science: Science Museums, Scientific Centers & Institutes, Scientific Research
Social Services: At-Risk Youth, Camps, Community Service Organizations, Counseling, Crime Prevention, Day Care, Family Planning, Family Services, Recreation & Athletics, United Funds/United Ways, Youth Organizations

Application Procedures

Initial Contact: Applicants should submit a letter of inquiry.

Restrictions

Proposals which commit the fund to continued support of operations generally are not approved. The fund does not award grants to individuals.

Additional Information

Publications: Annual Report; Application Guidelines; Application Form

Foundation Officials

Candace Carlucci Backus: secretary, trustee, program officer
Heather Brady: administrative assistant
Breene M. Kerr: chairman, treasurer, life trustee B 1929. ED Massachusetts Institute of Technology MA (1951). CORP AFFIL director: Chesapeake Energy Corp.; vice chairman: Seven Seas Petroleum Inc.
Marcy S. Kerr: adv trustee
Sheryl V. Kerr: president, life trustee B 1953. PRIM CORP EMPL executive vice president: Kerr Consolidated Inc.
James F. Moffitt: trustee
Collin Wesley Scarborough: life trustee
John R. Valliant: trustee
Margaret Van den Berg: administration assistant

Grants Analysis

Disclosure Period: calendar year ending 2001
Total Grants: $1,068,630
Number of Grants: 20

Recent Grants

Note: Grants derived from 1999 Form 990.

General

561,662	Chesapeake Bay Maritime Museum, St. Michael's, MD
229,191	Washington College, Chestertown, MD
100,000	Memorial Sloan-Kettering Cancer Center, New York, NY
75,000	Central Park Conservation, New York, NY
68,866	Mental Health Association - Talbot County, Easton, MD
50,000	Chesapeake Bay Foundation, Annapolis, MD
50,000	Mystic Seaport Museum, Mystic, CT
49,015	Talbot County Public Schools, Easton, MD
40,000	Habitat for Humanity
30,464	Bay Street Ponds

KETROW FOUNDATION

Giving Contact

Thomas H. Graber, Jr., Trustee
507 S. Broadway
Greenville, OH 45331
Phone: (937)548-1157

Description

Founded: 1991
EIN: 341667300
Organization Type: Private Foundation
Giving Locations: OH: Darke County
Grant Types: General Support, Scholarship.

Financial Summary

Total Giving: $18,000 (fiscal year ending September 30, 2001); $18,500 (fiscal 2000); $20,000 (fiscal 1998)
Assets: $458,602 (fiscal 2001); $472,525 (fiscal 2000); $467,392 (fiscal 1998)

Typical Recipients

Arts & Humanities: Arts Centers, Arts Outreach, Historic Preservation, History & Archaeology, Libraries, Music
Civic & Public Affairs: Botanical Gardens/Parks, Employment/Job Training, Housing, Parades/Festivals
Education: Arts/Humanities Education, Elementary Education (Private), Elementary Education (Public), Medical Education, Private Education (Precollege)
Health: Hospitals, Mental Health
Religion: Religious Welfare
Social Services: Community Service Organizations, Emergency Relief, Recreation & Athletics, Senior Services, Shelters/Homelessness, Substance Abuse, YMCA/YWCA/YMHA/YWHA, Youth Organizations

Application Procedures

Initial Contact: Send a brief letter of inquiry.
Application Requirements: Include purpose of funds sought and charitable purpose of organization.
Deadlines: None.

Restrictions

Restricted to Darke County, OH.

Foundation Officials

Thomas H. Graber, II: trustee

Grants Analysis

Disclosure Period: fiscal year ending September 30, 2001
Total Grants: $18,000

Number of Grants: 9
Average Grant: $2,000
Highest Grant: $3,300
Lowest Grant: $500
Typical Range: $1,000 to $3,000

Recent Grants

Note: Grants derived from fiscal 2000 Form 990.

General

6,000	Ansonia Area Emergency Service, Inc., Ansonia, OH -- purchase of defibrillator
5,000	Greenville Girls Softball Association, Greenville, OH -- improvements to new complex
3,000	Greenville Vocal Music Boosters, Greenville, OH -- purchase a new sound system
2,000	DeColores Montessori School, Greenville, OH -- purchase materials for music program
1,500	Drake County Center for the Arts, Greenville, OH -- presentation of the arts
1,000	Drake County Park District, Greenville, OH -- purchase a new sound system

KETTERING FUND

Giving Contact

Judy Thompson, Executive Director
1560 Kettering Tower
Dayton, OH 45423
Phone: (937)228-1021
Fax: (937)449-7239
E-mail: ketteringfund@aol.com

Description

Founded: 1958
EIN: 316027115
Organization Type: General Purpose Foundation
Giving Locations: OH: especially Dayton
Grant Types: General Support.

Donor Information

Founder: Established in 1958 by Charles F. Kettering who died in the same year. Mr. Kettering was a principal stockholder in General Motors Corporation, which acquired his automotive engineering laboratory. Mr. Kettering's inventions include the modern automotive ignition system and the electric cash register. He worked with National Cash Register Company and General Motors, and organized Dayton Engineering Laboratories Company (Delco), Dayton Metal Products Company, and the Dayton-Wright Airplane Company. He was president of the Thomas A. Edison Foundation; co-founder of Moraine Park School; a trustee of Ohio State University, Antioch College, College of Wooster (OH), Miami University (OH), and Southern Research Institute; and a director of the Memorial Sloan-Kettering Institute of Cancer Research.

Financial Summary

Total Giving: $5,245,952 (fiscal year ending June 30, 2000); $4,468,568 (fiscal 1998); $3,851,000 (fiscal 1997)
Assets: $93,884,453 (fiscal 2000); $100,000,000 (fiscal 1999 approx); $94,794,183 (fiscal 1998)
Gifts Received: $8,492 (fiscal 2000)

Typical Recipients

Arts & Humanities: Arts Associations & Councils, Arts Centers, Arts Festivals, Arts Funds, Arts Institutes, Ballet, Community Arts, Dance, Historic Preservation, History & Archaeology, Libraries, Museums/Galleries, Music, Performing Arts, Public Broadcasting, Theater, Visual Arts
Civic & Public Affairs: African American Affairs, Botanical Gardens/Parks, Clubs, Community Foundations, Economic Development, Employment/Job Training, Civic & Public Affairs-General, Hispanic Affairs, Housing, Law & Justice, Municipalities/Towns, Nonprofit Management, Parades/Festivals, Professional & Trade Associations, Rural Affairs, Urban & Community Affairs, Women's Affairs, Women's Affairs, Zoos/Aquariums
Education: Business Education, Colleges & Universities, Education Associations, Education Funds, Education Reform, Engineering/Technological Education, Faculty Development, Education-General, International Studies, Journalism/Media Education, Literacy, Medical Education, Private Education (Precollege), Student Aid
Environment: Environment-General, Resource Conservation
Health: Arthritis, Children's Health/Hospitals, Clinics/Medical Centers, Emergency/Ambulance Services, Health Organizations, Hospices, Hospitals, Long-Term Care, Nursing Services, Public Health, Transplant Networks/Donor Banks
International: Health Care/Hospitals, International Affairs, International Development
Religion: Churches, Religious Welfare, Synagogues/Temples
Science: Science Museums
Social Services: Animal Protection, At-Risk Youth, Big Brother/Big Sister, Child Welfare, Community Centers, Community Service Organizations, Crime Prevention, Family Planning, Family Services, Food/Clothing Distribution, Homes, People with Disabilities, Scouts, Senior Services, YMCA/YWCA/YMHA/YWHA, Youth Organizations

Application Procedures

Initial Contact: Proposals should be sent to the fund. No specific application form is required.
Application Requirements: The proposal should include the amount requested, reason for request, a brief description of project or program, description and dates of previous Kettering Fund support, names of other foundations which have given support, project and organization budget, brief statement of the organization's long-range plans, a copy of IRS tax-exempt letter, and an audited financial statement.
Deadlines: Applications should be submitted by April 1 and October 1.
Review Process: The Distribution Committee meets in May and November.

Restrictions

The fund does not support individuals, partisan political causes or candidates, elementary or secondary schools. No scholarships are awarded directly through grants or loans. No travel for any purpose is funded. Organizations must be located in Ohio.

Additional Information

The Kettering Fund is affiliated with the Kettering Family Foundation, which is located at the same address.
The fund lists Bank One Trust Company, NA, as a corporate trustee.

Foundation Officials

Susan K. Beck: member distribution committee, trustee
Terri Hurd: administrator
Virginia W. Kettering: trustee CORP AFFIL director emeritus: Bank One Dayton NA; director: C F Kettering.
Jane K. Lombard: mem distribution comm, trustee
Susan K. Williamson: mem distribution comm, trustee

Grants Analysis

Disclosure Period: fiscal year ending June 30, 2000
Total Grants: $5,245,952
Number of Grants: 49

Average Grant: $88,457*
Highest Grant: $1,000,000
Lowest Grant: $1,250
Typical Range: $5,000 to $60,000 and $100,000 to $600,000
*Note: Average grant amount excludes highest grant.

Recent Grants

Note: Grants derived from fiscal 2001 Form 990.

General

1,000,000	Dayton Foundation, Dayton, OH
575,000	University of Dayton, Dayton, OH
500,000	Wright State University, Dayton, OH
380,000	Kettering University, Flint, MI
300,000	Ohio State University, Columbus, OH
279,000	Dayton Ballet, Dayton, OH
250,000	Kettering Medical Center, Dayton, OH
200,000	Dakota Center, Dayton, OH
200,000	Downtown Dayton Riverscape Fund, Dayton, OH
200,000	Hathaway Brown School, Shaker Heights, OH

KEY BANK NA

Company Headquarters

127 Public Sq.
Cleveland, OH 44114
Web: http://www.keybank.com

Company Description

Former Name: Society National Bank.
Assets: US$75.032 billion (2001)
Employees: 19285 (2001)
SIC(s): 6021 National Commercial Banks.
Parent Company: KeyCorp, 127 Public Square, Cleveland, OH, United States

Operating Locations

Key Bank of Cleveland (OH--Ahtabula, Akron, Canton, Celina, Columbus, Dayton, Defiance, Mansfield, Mentor, Sandusky, Springfield, Youngstown)

Nonmonetary Support

Type: In-kind Services
Volunteer Programs: Company employees volunteer at Neighbors Make The Difference Day, a program where key closes its office for one afternoon and send its employees to perform volunteer services.

Key Foundation

Giving Contact

Margot Copeland
KeyBank of Cleveland
127 Public Square
Mailcode OH-01-27-1305
Cleveland, OH 44114-1306
Phone: (216)689-4517
E-mail: key_foundation@keybank.com
Web: http://keybank.com/templates/t-ak2.jhtml?no-deID=A-12

Description

EIN: 237036607
Organization Type: Corporate Foundation
Giving Locations: primarily service area.
Grant Types: Capital, Conference/Seminar, Employee Matching Gifts, General Support, Matching, Multiyear/Continuing Support, Operating Expenses.

Financial Summary

Total Giving: $16,639,981 (2001); $13,239,555 (2000); $19,500,000 (1999 approx). Note: Contributes through corporate direct giving program and foundation.

Giving Analysis: Giving for 2000 includes: foundation matching gifts ($521,868); foundation grants to United Way ($2,722,729) foundation ($9,994,958)
Assets: $38,127,646 (2001); $47,591,488 (2000)
Gifts Received: $16,137 (2001). Note: Contributions received from KeyBank National Association ($10,291,003) and individuals (under $2,000 each).

Typical Recipients

Arts & Humanities: Arts Associations & Councils, Arts Funds, Ballet, Libraries, Museums/Galleries, Opera, Performing Arts, Public Broadcasting, Theater
Civic & Public Affairs: African American Affairs, Business/Free Enterprise, Economic Development, Civic & Public Affairs-General, Housing, Municipalities/Towns, Urban & Community Affairs
Education: Arts/Humanities Education, Business Education, Colleges & Universities, Community & Junior Colleges, Engineering/Technological Education, Leadership Training, Minority Education, Private Education (Precollege), Student Aid
Health: Alzheimers Disease, Cancer, Children's Health/Hospitals, Hospitals, Mental Health, Multiple Sclerosis, Prenatal Health Issues
Religion: Churches, Dioceses, Religious Welfare
Social Services: Child Welfare, Community Centers, Community Service Organizations, Emergency Relief, People with Disabilities, United Funds/United Ways

Application Procedures

Initial Contact: Submit a written proposal.
Application Requirements: Include history and purpose of the organization; amount requested and purpose of funds sought; budget information; list of officers, directors, or trustees; complete budget for the project period; last annual financial statement; proof of tax-exempt status; and any additional information that will aid the foundation in making its decision.
Deadlines: None.
Review Process: Local contributions committees review requests throughout the year; annual budget is approved in December.
Evaluative Criteria: Programs and objectives must benefit communities served by the company. The organization should enhance the civic, cultural, or educational goals of the community, or provide for the health and welfare of its citizens. The organization must demonstrate sound fiscal management, nonduplication of services, and evidence of broad community support.
Decision Notification: Decisions are made locally.
Notes: Requests should be directed to the nearest KeyBank office.

Restrictions

Company does not support political organizations or programs that are sensitive, controversial, harmful, or which pose a potential conflict of interest; churches or religious programs, preschool or primary educational institutions, fraternal, social, labor or veterans organizations unless for a significant project of benefit to the entire community regardless of race, religion, or sex; individualss, private foundations, trade or professional associations or organizations whose primary purpose is the support of athletic activities; international or foreign organizations.

Additional Information

In 1994, Society Corp. merged with KeyCorp and changed its name to Society National Bank Society National Bank changed its name to Key Bank of Cleveland in 1995.
Publications: Guidelines for Giving

Grants Analysis

Disclosure Period: calendar year ending 2001
Total Grants: $12,004,038*
Number of Grants: 2,099
Average Grant: $5,700
Highest Grant: $250,000

Lowest Grant: $500
Typical Range: $1,000 to $10,000
*Note: Giving excludes matching gifts, scholarships, and United Way.

Recent Grants

Note: Grants derived from 2001 Form 990.

Library-Related

50,000	East Cleveland Public Library, Cleveland, OH -- capital campaign

General

1,360,750	United Way Services, Cleveland, OH -- operating support
617,149	American Red Cross Disaster Liberty Fund, Cleveland, OH -- Operating Support
250,000	Cuyahoga Community College Foundation, Cleveland, OH -- Capital Campaign
250,000	University Hospitals of Cleveland, Cleveland, OH -- capital campaign
200,000	Case Western Reserve University, Cleveland, OH -- capital campaign
200,000	Musical Arts Association, Cleveland, OH -- Capital Campaign
145,000	United Way of Dayton Area, Dayton, OH -- Operating Support
120,000	United Way of Greater Toledo, Toledo, OH -- operating support
117,503	United Way September 11th Fund, New York, NY -- Operating Support
105,280	New York Fire Fighters 9/11 Distaster Relief Fund, Washington, DC -- Operating Support

KEY BANK OF MAINE

Company Headquarters

1 Canal Plz., No. 1
Portland, ME 04101

Company Description

Employees: 1,231
SIC(s): 6000 Depository Institutions.
Parent Company: KeyCorp, 127 Public Square, Cleveland, OH, United States

Key Bank of Maine Foundation

Giving Contact

Key Bank of Maine
800 Superior, Trust Tax
Cleveland, OH 44114
Phone: (216)828-9536

Description

EIN: 016017321
Organization Type: Corporate Foundation
Giving Locations: ME
Grant Types: Capital, General Support, Scholarship.

Financial Summary

Total Giving: $55,000 (fiscal year ending November 30, 1999); $43,090 (fiscal 1995); $41,000 (fiscal 1994). Note: Company gives directly and through the foundation. Figures for 1994 and 1995 represent foundation contributions.
Assets: $1,060,535 (fiscal 2000); $822,684 (fiscal 1999); $494,459 (fiscal 1995)

Typical Recipients

Arts & Humanities: Libraries, Museums/Galleries
Civic & Public Affairs: Economic Development, Civic & Public Affairs-General

Education: Arts/Humanities Education, Colleges & Universities, Medical Education, Private Education (Precollege), Student Aid
Environment: Environment-General
Health: Children's Health/Hospitals, Clinics/Medical Centers, Health Organizations, Hospitals, Mental Health, Prenatal Health Issues
Social Services: Big Brother/Big Sister, Child Welfare, Community Centers, Community Service Organizations, Recreation & Athletics, Scouts, Youth Organizations

Application Procedures

Initial Contact: The foundation requests applications be made in writing.
Deadlines: None.

Restrictions

Does not support religious organizations for sectarian purposes.

Additional Information

Trust(s): KeyBank NA

Corporate Officials

Michael William McNamara: chairman, president, chief executive officer, director B Saint Stephen, NB Canada 1945. ED University of Maine (1967). PRIM CORP EMPL chairman, president, chief executive officer, director: Key Bank of Maine.
Richard A. Molyneux: chairman, director PRIM CORP EMPL chairman, director: Key Bank of Maine.

Grants Analysis

Disclosure Period: fiscal year ending November 30, 2000
Total Grants: $0*
*Note: No grants were awarded in 2000.

KEYCORP

Company Headquarters

127 Public Square
Cleveland, OH 44114-1306
Phone: (216)689-3000
Web: http://www.key.com

Company Description

Founded: 1849
Ticker: KEY
Exchange: NYSE
Acquired: McDonald Investments.
Assets: US$85.202 billion (2002)
Profit: US$976 million (2002)
Employees: 20437 (2002)
Fortune Rank: 285, per FORTUNE Magazine's list of 500 Largest U.S. Corporations (2002).

Subsidiary Companies

OH: Key Bank NA, Cleveland

Nonmonetary Support

Type: Donated Equipment; Donated Products; In-kind Services; Loaned Employees; Loaned Executives
Note: Company provides nonmonetary support, but this is not the preferred method of giving.

McDonald Investments Foundation

Giving Contact

Karen A. White, Administrator
800 Superior Avenue
Cleveland, OH 44114-2603
Phone: (216)443-2981
Fax: (216)689-3865

E-mail: karen_a_white@keybank.com
Web: http://www.key.com

Alternate Contact

Phone: 800-553-2240

Description

EIN: 341386528
Organization Type: Corporate Foundation
Giving Locations: headquarters and operating communities.
Grant Types: Capital, General Support, Matching, Multiyear/Continuing Support, Operating Expenses, Project, Scholarship.

Financial Summary

Total Giving: $750,000 (fiscal year ending 6, 2001 approx); $991,970 (fiscal 1999); $700,000 (fiscal 1997 approx). Note: Contributes through corporate direct giving program and foundation.
Giving Analysis: Giving for fiscal 2001 includes: foundation ($750,000); fiscal 1998: foundation grants to United Way ($30,839) foundation ($961,131)
Assets: $1,098,352 (fiscal 1999); $1,000,000 (fiscal 1996 approx); $1,005,016 (fiscal 1995)
Gifts Received: $528,000 (fiscal 1999); $181,338 (fiscal 1995); $463,000 (fiscal 1994). Note: Contributions were received from McDonald & Company Securities, Inc., and McDonald Investments, Inc.

Typical Recipients

Arts & Humanities: Arts Associations & Councils, Arts Centers, Arts Festivals, Ballet, Community Arts, Ethnic & Folk Arts, Historic Preservation, Libraries, Museums/Galleries, Music, Opera, Performing Arts, Public Broadcasting, Theater, Visual Arts
Civic & Public Affairs: African American Affairs, Asian American Affairs, Business/Free Enterprise, Civil Rights, Clubs, Community Foundations, Economic Development, Economic Policy, Employment/Job Training, Ethnic Organizations, Civic & Public Affairs-General, Hispanic Affairs, Housing, Inner-City Development, Law & Justice, Municipalities/Towns, Parades/Festivals, Philanthropic Organizations, Professional & Trade Associations, Professional & Trade Associations, Public Policy, Urban & Community Affairs, Women's Affairs, Zoos/Aquariums
Education: Afterschool/Enrichment Programs, Business Education, Colleges & Universities, Community & Junior Colleges, Economic Education, Education Funds, Education Reform, Elementary Education (Public), Education-General, Literacy, Minority Education, Public Education (Precollege), Student Aid
Environment: Environment-General, Wildlife Protection
Health: AIDS/HIV, Alzheimers Disease, Cancer, Children's Health/Hospitals, Diabetes, Emergency/Ambulance Services, Eyes/Blindness, Health-General, Health Organizations, Hospices, Hospitals, Medical Research, Mental Health, Multiple Sclerosis, Nursing Services, Prenatal Health Issues, Single-Disease Health Associations, Speech & Hearing
International: Trade
Religion: Bible Study/Translation, Dioceses, Jewish Causes, Religious Organizations, Religious Welfare, Social/Policy Issues
Science: Science Museums, Scientific Centers & Institutes
Social Services: Animal Protection, At-Risk Youth, Camps, Child Welfare, Community Centers, Community Service Organizations, Counseling, Day Care, Delinquency & Criminal Rehabilitation, Domestic Violence, Emergency Relief, Family Planning, Family Services, Food/Clothing Distribution, People with Disabilities, Recreation & Athletics, Scouts, Senior Services, Sexual Abuse, Shelters/Homelessness, Social Services-General, Substance Abuse, United Funds/United Ways, Volunteer Services, YMCA/YWCA/YMHA/YWHA, Youth Organizations

Application Procedures

Initial Contact: Send a brief letter of inquiry, followed by a brief proposal.
Application Requirements: Include a description of organization, amount requested, purpose of funds sought, and proof of tax-exempt status.
Deadlines: None.
Evaluative Criteria: Requests must conform to either the Greater Cleveland Growth Association or Better Business Bureau guidelines; organizations must be nonprofit and tax-exempt; preference is given to regional rather than national projects.
Notes: Requests from branch offices which follow guidelines will also be considered.

Restrictions

Does not support individuals; community attractions that draw primarily from their immediate area or are nature-related; religious organizations for sectarian purposes; political or lobbying groups; organizations outside operating areas; athletic and sport related civic or national events such as the Olympics; causes that use tickets/lunches for fundraising; any subcommittee or auxiliary group of an organization to which a donation has already been made; individual colleges or secondary schools, both for annual support and capital programs.

Higher education is supported only through contributions to the Ohio Foundation for Independent Colleges and colleges not affiliated with OFIC.

Religious and welfare grants will be restricted to local arms of United Way, United Jewish Welfare Fund, and Catholic Charities.

Additional Information

Publications: Guidelines

Corporate Officials

Robert T. Clutterbuck: vice president, chief executive officer, president PRIM CORP EMPL president: McDonald & Co. Securities, Inc. CORP AFFIL treasurer: McDonald Co. Investments.
William B. Summers, Jr.: chairman, chief executive officer, president PRIM CORP EMPL chairman, chief executive officer, president: McDonald & Co. Securities, Inc. CORP AFFIL president: McDonald Co. Investments Delaware.

Foundation Officials

Margot Copeland: non-voting trustee
Jonathan Crane: trustee
William Grove: trustee
Robert G. Jones: trustee
Thomas McDonald: trustee
Mark Summers: trustee
William B. Summers, Jr.: trustee (see above)
Rebecca Talley: trustee
Karen White: secretary, treasurer

Grants Analysis

Total Grants: $750,000*
Number of Grants: 200
Average Grant: $3,750
Highest Grant: $20,000
Lowest Grant: $250
Typical Range: $250 to $5,000
*Note: Grants analysis provided by foundation.

Recent Grants

Note: Grants derived from fiscal 2001 Form 990.

Library-Related
2,500   Indianapolis-Marion County Public Library Foundation, Indianapolis, IN

General
20,000   Catholic Diocese of Cleveland, Cleveland, OH
15,000   Achievement Center For Children, Cleveland, OH

15,000	Musical Arts Association, Cleveland, OH
10,000	Business Volunteers Unlimited
10,000	Jewish Community Federation of Cleveland, Cleveland, OH
10,000	Law Enforcement Foundation, Columbus, OH
10,000	Musical Arts Association, Cleveland, OH
10,000	Musical Arts Association, Cleveland, OH
5,000	Cleveland Academy of Finance, Cleveland, OH
5,000	Cleveland Museum of Art, Cleveland, OH

KEYSPAN CORP.

Company Headquarters

1 MetroTech Center
Brooklyn, NY 11201
Web: http://www.keyspanenergy.com

Company Description

Founded: 1998
Ticker: KSE
Exchange: NYSE
Revenue: US$6.086 billion (2002)
Profit: US$377.7 million (2002)
Employees: 13,000 (2002)
Fortune Rank: 290, per FORTUNE Magazine's list of 500 Largest U.S. Corporations (2002).
SIC(s): 4911 Electric Services.

KeySpan Foundation

Giving Contact

Executive Director
52 Second Avenue
Waltham, MA 02451
Phone: (781)466-5101
Fax: (781)290-4899
E-mail: foundation@keyspanenergy.com
Web: http://www.keyspanenergy.com/corpinfo/community/index_all_all.jsp

Description

Founded: 1998
EIN: 113466416
Organization Type: Corporate Foundation
Grant Types: Challenge, General Support, Matching, Project.

Donor Information

Founder: Established in 1998 by KeySpan Corp.

Financial Summary

Total Giving: $712,000 (2003 approx); $911,000 (2002); $2,029,023 (2001)
Giving Analysis: Giving for 2000 includes: foundation grants to United Way ($462,000); foundation ($1,497,500) 1999: foundation grants to United Way ($225,000)
Assets: $24,913,152 (2001); $29,249,561 (2000); $20,803,327 (1999)
Gifts Received: $51,033 (2001); $10,000,000 (2000). Note: In 2000, contributions were received from KeySpan Corp.

Typical Recipients

Arts & Humanities: Historic Preservation, Libraries, Literary Arts, Museums/Galleries, Music, Performing Arts, Public Broadcasting, Theater
Civic & Public Affairs: Botanical Gardens/Parks, Economic Development, Civic & Public Affairs-General, Housing, Legal Aid, Nonprofit Management, Philanthropic Organizations, Zoos/Aquariums
Education: Business-School Partnerships, Colleges & Universities, Education Funds, Environmental Education, Education-General, Literacy, Public Education (Precollege), Special Education

Environment: Air/Water Quality, Forestry, Environment-General, Resource Conservation
Health: Cancer, Health Organizations, Heart, Hospices, Hospitals, Kidney, Mental Health, Prenatal Health Issues, Single-Disease Health Associations
Social Services: Community Service Organizations, Emergency Relief, Family Services, People with Disabilities, Recreation & Athletics, Scouts, Social Services-General, United Funds/United Ways, YMCA/YWCA/YMHA/YWHA

Application Procedures

Initial Contact: Submit a letter of request.
Application Requirements: Include purpose for which funds are requested and how the funds will be appropriated for the specific venture; project objectives and anticipated outcomes; detailed project budget, including a cost estimate for each item for which funds are requested; a description of organization, including geographic reach, number of clients served, and existing programs; a list of other potential sources of funding; proof of tax-exempt status; most current audited financial statements and/or Form 990; list of the organization's board of directors and affiliations; and the organization's annual report or brochures, if applicable. The foundation reports that they will also accept the New York/New Jersey Common Application Form in place of the above outline.
Deadlines: None.
Review Process: The board of directors meets on a quarterly basis to review requests.
Evaluative Criteria: Organization's mission should directly support one of the foundation's main focus areas (health and human services, education, environment, community development, or arts and culture). Organization should provide services within KeySpan's service territory or in areas where the company plans to operate in the future. Only one grant proposal request per organization will be evaluated in each calendar year.
Decision Notification: Proposal review is generally completed within 60 days.

Restrictions

Grants generally will not be made to individuals; to sectarian and religious organizations that do not serve the general public on a non-denominational basis; to organizations requesting funds for capital or endowment campaigns; to organizations requesting funds for advertisements, tables or tickets at dinners or other functions; to political, fraternal, social or other membership organizations providing services mainly to their own constituencies; or to organizations whose combined administrative, management and fundraising expenses exceed 30% of the organization's total operating budget.

Corporate Officials

Robert Barry Catell: chairman, chief executive officer B Brooklyn, NY February 01, 1937. ED City University of New York BME (1958); City University of New York MME (1964). PRIM CORP EMPL chairman, chief executive officer: KeySpan Corp. CORP AFFIL chairman, chief executive officer, director: MarketSpan Corp.; director: Star Energy Inc.; director: The Houston Exploration Co.; trustee: Independence Savings Bank; director: Fuel Resources Inc.; director: Gas Energy Inc.; director: Alberta Northeast Inc.; chairman: Boundary Gas Inc. NONPR AFFIL member: New York State Business Council; member: Society Gas Lighting; member: New York Serda Board; director: New York Energy Research & Development Authority; member executive committee: New York Gas Group; director: Gas Research Institute; member: New York City Partnership; director: American Gas Association; chairman: Business Council for a Sustainable Energy Future.

Grants Analysis

Disclosure Period: calendar year ending 2000
Total Grants: $1,497,500*
Number of Grants: 119

Average Grant: $12,584
Highest Grant: $100,000
Typical Range: $2,500 to $25,000
*__Note:__ Giving excludes United Way.

Recent Grants

Note: Grants derived from 2000 Form 990.

Library-Related
12,500	Brooklyn Public Library, Brooklyn, NY

General
387,000	United Way, New York, NY
100,000	Salvation Army of Massachusetts Divisional Headquarters, Boston, MA
75,000	Brooklyn Philharmonic Orchestra, Brooklyn, NY
75,000	Long Island United Way, Long Island, NY
63,000	Brooklyn Academy of Music, Brooklyn, NY
50,000	Brooklyn Information and Culture, Inc., Brooklyn, NY
30,000	American Heart Association, Bohemia, NY
30,000	Maurer Foundation, New York, NY
30,000	Research Foundation of the City University of New York, New York, NY
25,000	Breast Cancer Help, Inc., West Islip, NY

J. W. KIECKHEFER FOUNDATION

Giving Contact

Eugene P. Polk, Administrative Officer, Trustee
PO Box 1151
Prescott, AZ 86302
Phone: (928)445-4010
Fax: (928)445-4012

Description

Founded: 1953
EIN: 866022877
Organization Type: General Purpose Foundation
Giving Locations: AZ: nationally.
Grant Types: Capital, Emergency, Endowment, General Support, Multiyear/Continuing Support, Project, Research, Seed Money.

Donor Information

Founder: The foundation was established in 1953, with funds provided by John W. Kieckhefer, the founder of Kieckhefer Container Company. In 1957, the family firm and its affiliate, Eddy Paper Corporation, were merged into Weyerhaeuser Company.

Financial Summary

Total Giving: $891,250 (2001); $859,150 (2000); $1,204,250 (1999)
Giving Analysis: Giving for 2000 includes: foundation matching gifts ($5,000); foundation scholarships ($39,700); 1999: foundation scholarships ($1,500); foundation matching gifts ($10,000); 1998: foundation matching gifts ($4,500) foundation scholarships ($17,500)
Assets: $18,742,863 (2001); $20,425,967 (2000); $25,422,689 (1999)
Gifts Received: $58,090 (2001). Note: In 2001, contributions were received from Robert H. Kieckhefer Charitable Remainder Trust.

Typical Recipients

Arts & Humanities: Arts Associations & Councils, Arts Centers, Ballet, Community Arts, Film & Video, Arts & Humanities-General, Historic Preservation, History & Archaeology, Libraries, Literary Arts, Museums/Galleries, Music, Performing Arts, Public Broadcasting, Visual Arts

Civic & Public Affairs: Botanical Gardens/Parks, Community Foundations, Economic Development, Economic Policy, Civic & Public Affairs-General, Hispanic Affairs, Housing, Law & Justice, Legal Aid, Philanthropic Organizations, Public Policy, Women's Affairs, Zoos/Aquariums

Education: Agricultural Education, Business Education, Colleges & Universities, Continuing Education, Environmental Education, Education-General, Education-General, Literacy, Medical Education, Preschool Education, Private Education (Precollege), Public Education (Precollege), Science/Mathematics Education, Student Aid

Environment: Environment-General, Resource Conservation, Wildlife Protection

Health: Alzheimers Disease, Cancer, Children's Health/Hospitals, Clinics/Medical Centers, Eyes/Blindness, Geriatric Health, Health Funds, Health Organizations, Heart, Hospices, Hospitals, Kidney, Medical Rehabilitation, Medical Research, Prenatal Health Issues, Preventive Medicine/Wellness Organizations, Public Health, Research/Studies Institutes, Respiratory, Single-Disease Health Associations

International: Health Care/Hospitals, International Environmental Issues, International Organizations, International Peace & Security Issues

Religion: Churches, Missionary Activities (Domestic), Religious Welfare

Science: Science Museums, Scientific Centers & Institutes

Social Services: Animal Protection, At-Risk Youth, Camps, Child Abuse, Child Welfare, Community Centers, Community Service Organizations, Counseling, Day Care, Domestic Violence, Emergency Relief, Family Planning, Family Services, Food/Clothing Distribution, People with Disabilities, Recreation & Athletics, Senior Services, Shelters/Homelessness, Special Olympics, Substance Abuse, Volunteer Services, YMCA/YWCA/YMHA/YWHA, Youth Organizations

Application Procedures

Initial Contact: Send a brief letter of inquiry and a full proposal.

Application Requirements: The letter should include a description of the problem addressed, nature of the project, and objectives of the program. A copy of tax-exempt ruling also should be enclosed.

Deadlines: The foundation prefers to receive applications from May to November.

Review Process: The foundation acknowledges the receipt of all proposals and grants interviews with applicants during the secondary stage of the application process.

Notes: Final notification is made within six months.

Restrictions

Grants or loans are not made to individuals. Internally initiated grants are usually all of the current grant making of the foundation. Informal letters will be accepted, but may not be responded to.

Foundation Officials

John I. Kieckhefer: trustee PRIM CORP EMPL president, chief executive officer; Kieckhefer Associatess Inc. CORP AFFIL director: Weyerhaeuser Co.

Robert H. Kieckhefer: trustee B 1918.

Eugene P. Polk: admin off, trustee

Grants Analysis

Disclosure Period: calendar year ending 2001
Total Grants: $865,250*
Number of Grants: 65
Average Grant: $12,582*
Highest Grant: $60,000
Lowest Grant: $150
Typical Range: $5,000 to $25,000
*Note: Giving excludes scholarships and matching gifts. Average grant figure excludes highest grant.

Recent Grants

Note: Grants derived from 2001 Form 990.

General

60,000	Harmony Ranch, Camp Verde, AZ -- towards establishment of a new residential care
50,000	Foundation for Blind Children, Phoenix, AZ -- toward a new facility
50,000	Sharlot Hall Museum, Prescott, AZ
50,000	West Valley Child Crisis Center, Glendale, AZ -- toward construction of the new kid's campus
40,000	Museum of Northern Arizona, Flagstaff, AZ -- support of publication
30,000	Arizona Friends of Foster Children Foundation, Phoenix, AZ -- endowment fund
30,000	Mayo Foundation, Rochester, MN -- support of cancer research
25,000	Adult Care Services, Inc., Prescott, AZ -- adult day care
25,000	American Enterprise Institute for Public Policy Research, Washington, DC
25,000	Catholic Social Services of Yavapai, Prescott, AZ -- towards purchase of property

PETER KIEWIT FOUNDATION

Giving Contact

Lyn Wallin Ziegenbein, Executive Director
8805 Indian Hills Drive, Suite 225
Omaha, NE 68114
Phone: (402)344-7890
Fax: (402)344-8099

Description

Founded: 1980
EIN: 476098282
Organization Type: General Purpose Foundation
Giving Locations: CA: Rancho Mirage; IA: the portion of Iowa which is within a 100-mile radius of Omaha, NE; NE, Omaha; WY: Sheridan
Grant Types: Capital, Professorship, Project, Scholarship, Seed Money.

Donor Information

Founder: Established in Nebraska in 1975 by the late Peter Kiewit (1900-1979), president of Peter Kiewit Sons, a construction company. He successively worked as a mason tender, hod carrier, and bricklayer for his family business during his summer vacations and throughout high school. He completed one year of study at Dartmouth College before entering the construction business full-time at the age of 19. After he joined the business, Mr. Kiewit began buying company stock from his brothers. When Mr. Kiewit assumed leadership in 1931, the company's total assets were less than $125,000. Hard work, dedication to the principle of good relations with owners and their representatives, the ability to recognize contracting opportunities, and a farsighted plan of rewarding key employees with stock ownership in the company made Peter Kiewit Sons a multi-million dollar firm and one of the largest construction companies in the world. The present foundation is the result of Mr. Kiewit's personal philanthropy, and has no affiliation with the Kiewit Company.

Mr. Kiewit was committed to "building the character of men and good things for a better, more meaningful world." His commitment extended to civil rights, as he believed that "the competitive construction business allows no room for prejudice in employment practices." In 1963, he headed the employment subcommittee of the Mayors Bi-Racial Committee in Omaha, and in 1967, the National Conference of Christians and Jews presented him with its Brotherhood Award.

Peter Kiewit was also committed to philanthropy. At the time of his death, he had contributed $15 million to various causes, and had pledged an additional $5 million. The foundation which bears his name is a continuing reflection of Peter Kiewit's philanthropic interests.

Financial Summary

Total Giving: $25,656,429 (fiscal year ending June 30, 2002); $28,735,420 (fiscal 2001); $19,438,984 (fiscal 2000)

Giving Analysis: Giving for fiscal 2001 includes: foundation gifts to individuals ($127,356); foundation grants to United Way ($450,000); foundation scholarships ($2,480,638); fiscal 2000: foundation gifts to individuals ($116,588); foundation grants to United Way ($400,000); foundation scholarships ($1,608,011); fiscal 1999: foundation grants to United Way ($234,300) foundation scholarships ($3,403,696)

Assets: $349,247,678 (fiscal 2002); $462,612,397 (fiscal 2001); $540,459,172 (fiscal 2000)

Gifts Received: $275,751 (fiscal 1997); $2,800 (fiscal 1992). Note: Fiscal 1997 contributions consist of scholarship refunds, endowment refunds, and registration fees for fundraising seminars.

Typical Recipients

Arts & Humanities: Arts Appreciation, Arts Associations & Councils, Arts Centers, Arts Funds, Arts Outreach, Historic Preservation, History & Archaeology, Libraries, Museums/Galleries, Music, Opera, Performing Arts, Theater

Civic & Public Affairs: Botanical Gardens/Parks, Chambers of Commerce, Community Foundations, Economic Development, Employment/Job Training, Civic & Public Affairs-General, Housing, Municipalities/Towns, Native American Affairs, Parades/Festivals, Philanthropic Organizations, Safety, Urban & Community Affairs, Zoos/Aquariums

Education: Agricultural Education, Colleges & Universities, Community & Junior Colleges, Faculty Development, Education-General, International Studies, Journalism/Media Education, Literacy, Minority Education, Preschool Education, Public Education (Precollege), Science/Mathematics Education, Special Education, Student Aid

Environment: Environment-General, Resource Conservation

Health: AIDS/HIV, Cancer, Clinics/Medical Centers, Emergency/Ambulance Services, Health Organizations, Hospitals, Medical Rehabilitation, Nutrition, Trauma Treatment

International: International Peace & Security Issues

Religion: Religious Organizations, Religious Welfare

Science: Science Museums

Social Services: Animal Protection, Child Welfare, Community Centers, Community Service Organizations, Crime Prevention, Day Care, Family Planning, Family Services, Food/Clothing Distribution, Homes, People with Disabilities, Recreation & Athletics, Scouts, Senior Services, Shelters/Homelessness, United Funds/United Ways, Volunteer Services, YMCA/YWCA/YMHA/YWHA, Youth Organizations

Application Procedures

Initial Contact: Contact the foundation office to obtain standard application forms. Personal interviews are not a part of the normal application process, and are not encouraged.

Deadlines: April 1 and October 1 for general grants in excess of $10,000; March 1, June 1, September 1, and December 1 for small grants. Nebraska Teacher Achievement Awards applications are due February 1; scholarship applications are due March 1.

Review Process: The board of trustees meets in March, June, September, and December.

Notes: Organizations whose applications have been denied must wait one full year before resubmitting.

Grants are made only on a matching fund basis, except in situations involving dire need where matching funds cannot be made available. The foundation will also consider granting seed money for innovative programs. Priority consideration is given to organizations which are not tax-supported. At least equal matching funds are required of organizations which are not tax-supported, and at least a three-to-one match is required of organizations which receive tax support. Any grants made for the purposes of capital construction are conditioned upon the actual completion of such improvement. Applicants are encouraged to develop other sources of support for a particular project prior to approaching the foundation.

Restrictions

The foundation does not make grants to individuals or private, non-operating foundations. The foundation generally does not consider support for endowment funds; elementary and secondary schools; churches and similar groups; or construction, renovation, or operations of normally tax-supported public facilities. A low priority is given to applications for normal operating budgets or contributions to annual fund-raising campaigns. No more than two applications from the same organization will be considered in any calendar year.

Additional Information

Trust(s): U.S. Bank National Association

Foundation Officials

Mogens C. Bay: trustee
Michael L. Gallagher: trustee
John W. Hancock: vice chairman, trustee
Eve Kiewit: trustee
Peter Kiewit, Jr.: chairman, trustee B 1926. ED University of Arizona JD; University of Arizona BS. PRIM CORP EMPL of counsel: Gallagher & Kennedy. CORP AFFIL director: Peter Kiewit Sons Inc.
G. Richard Russell: chairman, trustee
Lyn Wallin Ziegenbein: executive director, secretary B 1952. ED University of Kansas BS (1974); Creighton University JD (1977). CORP AFFIL director: Aliant Communications Inc.; director: Woodmen Accident & Life Co.

Grants Analysis

Disclosure Period: fiscal year ending June 30, 2002
Total Grants: $21,845,512*
Number of Grants: 168
Average Grant: $83,407*
Highest Grant: $5,000,000
Lowest Grant: $534
Typical Range: $10,000 to $250,000
*Note: Giving excludes scholarships, gifts to individuals, and United Way. Average grant figure excludes two highest grants ($8,000,000).

Recent Grants

Note: Grants derived from fiscal 2002 Form 990.

General

5,000,000	City of Omaha, Omaha, NE -- for Convention Center and arena
3,000,000	University of Nebraska Foundation, Lincoln, NE -- for the Institute of Information, Science, Technology and Engineering
1,949,769	University of Nebraska, Lincoln, NE
1,929,408	Nebraska Game and Parks Foundation, Lincoln, NE -- for capital construction
1,500,000	Community Alliance, Omaha, NE -- for capital construction
875,000	Bellevue University, Bellevue, NE -- for capital construction
750,000	Nature Conservancy, Omaha, NE -- for capital construction
553,478	University of Nebraska Omaha, Omaha, NE
500,000	Omaha Zoological Society, Omaha, NE -- for an aquarium

500,000	University of Nebraska Foundation, Lincoln, NE -- for the College of Journalism

KIKKOMAN FOODS

Company Headquarters

PO Box 69
Walworth, WI 53184
Web: http://www.kikkoman.com

Company Description

Revenue: US$60.4 million (2001)
Employees: 145 (2001)
SIC(s): 2035 Pickles, Sauces & Salad Dressings.
Parent Company: Kikkoman Corp., 250 Noda, Chiba, Japan

Kikkoman Foundation

Giving Contact

Robert V. Conover, Director
11 North Wisconsin Street
Elkhorn, WI 53121
Phone: (414)723-3220

Description

Founded: 1993
EIN: 391763633
Organization Type: Corporate Foundation
Giving Locations: WI: internationally; nationally.
Grant Types: General Support.

Financial Summary

Total Giving: $160,380 (2000); $170,778 (1999); $141,028 (1998)
Giving Analysis: Giving for 2000 includes: foundation grants to United Way ($22,300); 1999: foundation grants to United Way ($2,000); foundation scholarships ($21,700) foundation ($147,078)
Assets: $5,528,797 (2000); $4,098,177 (1999); $3,276,548 (1998)
Gifts Received: $1,400,000 (2000); $600,000 (1999); $700,000 (1997). Note: In 1996, 1999, and 2000, contributions were received from Kikkoman Foods.

Typical Recipients

Arts & Humanities: Arts Festivals, History & Archaeology, Libraries, Performing Arts
Civic & Public Affairs: Asian American Affairs, Botanical Gardens/Parks, Business/Free Enterprise, Community Foundations, Economic Development, Employment/Job Training, Civic & Public Affairs-General, Municipalities/Towns, Urban & Community Affairs
Education: Business Education, Colleges & Universities, Education Funds, Education Reform, Engineering/Technological Education, Minority Education, Public Education (Precollege), Secondary Education (Public), Student Aid
Environment: Air/Water Quality
Health: Cancer
International: International-General, International Development, Trade
Social Services: Recreation & Athletics, YMCA/YWCA/YMHA/YWHA

Application Procedures

Initial Contact: Request application form in writing.
Application Requirements: Include the following information: organization's name, address, and phone number along with the name of the contact person familiar with the details of the program; the type of program being funded, the target population, amount requested, and the date by which funds are needed; a budget specifically outlining when and how the funding will be spent; the expected long-term and short-term results of the program; information on amounts

committed or pending from other sources for the program; a brief overview of the organization, including its history, purpose, number of members, the constituents it serves, geographic service area, volunteers, and general accomplishments to date; and a copy of the organization's determination letter from the IRS proving tax-exemption. If necessary, the foundation may request more detailed information about the organization, its proposal, and overall objectives of the project.
Review Process: Proposals are reviewed and evaluated by the foundation's board of directors.

Restrictions

Does not support individual persons one private organizations; raffle tickets, product purchases, etc.; political organizations, campaign committees, or lobbying groups; religious or sectarian organizations; performing or graphic art associations not in the state of Wisconsin; athletic events outside the foundation's interests; scientific or developmental research outside the food area; travel or lodging for individuals or groups; promotional events; organizations without 501(c)(3) status; organizations that discriminate on the basis of color, sex, religion, national origin, age, handicap, or veteran's status; or organizations or purposes that might in any way be inconsistent with the company's goals, programs, products, or employees.

Additional Information

Publications: Guidelines Sheet

Corporate Officials

Kuniki Hatayama: chief financial officer PRIM CORP EMPL chief financial officer: Kikkoman Foods.
Yozaburo Mogi: chairman, president, chief executive officer PRIM CORP EMPL chairman, president, chief executive officer: Kikkoman Foods.

Foundation Officials

Robert V. Conover: director
Hiroshi Futamura: director
Thomas Godfrey: director
Kuniki Hatayama: director (see above)
Dr. Kazuya Hayashi: director PRIM CORP EMPL executive vice president: Kikkoman Foods.
Michio Kiuchi: director
Yozaburo Mogi: director (see above)
William E. Nelson: director PRIM CORP EMPL vice president: Kikkoman Foods.
Milton E. Neshek: director
Malcolm Pennington: director
Kaichiro Someya: director
Kitsuo Someya: director
Hiroshi Takamatsu: director

Grants Analysis

Disclosure Period: calendar year ending 2000
Total Grants: $138,080*
Number of Grants: 46
Average Grant: $3,002
Highest Grant: $20,000
Typical Range: $1,000 to $5,000
*Note: Giving excludes scholarships.

Recent Grants

Note: Grants derived from 1999 Form 990.

Library-Related

25,000	California State Library Foundation, Sacramento, CA

General

16,000	Wisconsin Foundation for Independent Colleges, Milwaukee, WI
15,000	University of Wisconsin Foundation - Chancellor's Fun, Madison, WI
10,000	Institute for International Economics, Washington, DC
10,000	Institute for International Economics, Washington, DC -- study of international economic policy

7,500	University of Wisconsin Foundation - Chancellor's Fun, Madison, WI
6,000	Big Foot High School, Walworth, WI
6,000	Folsom High School, Folsom, CA
5,000	United Negro College Fund, Fairfax, MA
4,440	WMC Foundation, Madison, WI -- scholarship for WMC's Business World Program
3,700	WMC Foundation, Madison, WI -- scholarship for WMC's Business World Program

WILLIAM H. KILCAWLEY FUND

Giving Contact
Myra Vito
c/o National City Bank
PO Box 450
Youngstown, OH 44501
Phone: (330)742-4289

Description
Founded: 1946
EIN: 346515643
Organization Type: Private Foundation
Giving Locations: OH
Grant Types: Capital, General Support.

Financial Summary
Total Giving: $2,003,795 (2001); $101,000 (2000); $160,000 (1999)
Giving Analysis: Giving for 2000 includes: foundation grants to United Way ($5,000); 1998: foundation grants to United Way ($8,000) foundation ($125,000)
Assets: $1,679,037 (2001); $3,513,925 (2000); $3,366,784 (1999)

Typical Recipients
Arts & Humanities: Arts Centers, Arts Institutes, Arts & Humanities-General, History & Archaeology, Libraries, Music, Performing Arts, Public Broadcasting
Civic & Public Affairs: Botanical Gardens/Parks, Business/Free Enterprise, Civic & Public Affairs-General, Municipalities/Towns, Urban & Community Affairs
Education: Business Education, Colleges & Universities, Community & Junior Colleges, Education Funds, Private Education (Precollege)
Health: AIDS/HIV, Children's Health/Hospitals, Health Organizations, Home-Care Services, Hospices, Research/Studies Institutes, Speech & Hearing
Religion: Churches, Religious Organizations, Religious Welfare
Social Services: Animal Protection, Child Welfare, Community Service Organizations, Food/Clothing Distribution, People with Disabilities, Senior Services, United Funds/United Ways, YMCA/YWCA/YMHA/YWHA, Youth Organizations

Application Procedures
Initial Contact: The foundation requests applications be made in writing.
Deadlines: None.

Restrictions
Does not support individuals.

Additional Information
Trust(s): Natl City Bank

Foundation Officials
Anne K. Christman: trustee

Grants Analysis
Disclosure Period: calendar year ending 2001
Total Grants: $2,003,795
Number of Grants: 1

Recent Grants
Note: Grants derived from 2002 Form 990.

General
2,003,796	Youngstown Foundation, Cleveland, OH -- for distribution per governing document

CONSTANCE KILLAM TRUST

Giving Contact
Thomas P. Jalkut, Trustee
Constance Killam Trust
Care of Nutter, McClennen & Fish
1 International Pl.
Boston, MA 02110-2699
Phone: (617)439-2000
Fax: (617)973-9748

Description
Founded: 1977
EIN: 046420685
Organization Type: Private Foundation
Giving Locations: MA
Grant Types: Multiyear/Continuing Support, Scholarship.

Donor Information
Founder: the late Constance Killam

Financial Summary
Total Giving: $222,322 (fiscal year ending April 30, 2001); $332,500 (fiscal 2000); $193,700 (fiscal 1999)
Assets: $6,330,585 (fiscal 2001); $6,265,914 (fiscal 2000); $6,876,299 (fiscal 1999)
Gifts Received: $79,377 (fiscal 1995). Note: In fiscal 1995, contributions were received from the Constance Killam Trust.

Typical Recipients
Arts & Humanities: Libraries, Museums/Galleries, Music
Civic & Public Affairs: Native American Affairs, Zoos/Aquariums
Education: Arts/Humanities Education, Colleges & Universities, Health & Physical Education, Science/Mathematics Education
Environment: Environment-General

Application Procedures
Initial Contact: Send brief letter describing program and proposed use of funds requested.
Deadlines: None.

Foundation Officials
Thomas P. Jalkut: trustee
John Breed Newhall: trustee B Salem, MA 1932. ED Harvard University (1954); Harvard University JD (1959). CORP AFFIL chairman: D B Gurney Co. NONPR AFFIL member: American Bar Association.

Grants Analysis
Disclosure Period: fiscal year ending April 30, 2001
Total Grants: $222,322
Number of Grants: 9
Average Grant: $9,286*
Highest Grant: $100,000
Typical Range: $5,000 to $10,000
***Note:** Average grant figure excludes two highest grants ($157,322).

Recent Grants
Note: Grants derived from fiscal 2001 Form 990.

Library-Related
10,000	Boston Athenaeum, Boston, MA

General
100,000	Brown University, Providence, RI
57,322	Massachusetts Audubon Society, Lincoln, MA
10,000	Appalachian Mountain Club, Boston, MA
10,000	Boston Symphony Orchestra, Boston, MA
10,000	Bowdoin College, Bowdoin, ME
10,000	Harvard College, Cambridge, MA
10,000	Peabody Museum of Salem and Essex Institute, Salem, MA
5,000	Trustees of Reservations, Beverly, MA

KILMARTIN INDUSTRIES

Company Headquarters
Walton St.
Attleboro, MA 02703

Company Description
Employees: 100
SIC(s): 3900 Miscellaneous Manufacturing Industries.

Kilmartin Industries Charitable Foundation

Giving Contact
David F. Kilmartin, Chairman, President & Chief Executive Officer
247 Farnum Road
Glocester, RI 02814
Phone: (401)949-1166

Description
EIN: 222727613
Organization Type: Corporate Foundation
Giving Locations: headquarters area only.
Grant Types: General Support.

Financial Summary
Total Giving: $48,150 (fiscal year ending February 28, 2000); $39,047 (fiscal 1999); $27,620 (fiscal 1997)
Giving Analysis: Giving for fiscal 2000 includes: foundation ($48,150)
Assets: $839,983 (fiscal 2000); $706,178 (fiscal 1999); $531,059 (fiscal 1997)
Gifts Received: $32,252 (fiscal 2000); $3,000 (fiscal 1997); $40,000 (fiscal 1996). Note: In fiscal 2000, contributions were received from David Kilmartin. In fiscal 1997, contributions were received from Kilmartin Industries.

Typical Recipients
Arts & Humanities: Ballet, History & Archaeology, Libraries, Music, Public Broadcasting
Civic & Public Affairs: Zoos/Aquariums
Education: Arts/Humanities Education, Colleges & Universities, Legal Education, Medical Education, Private Education (Precollege), Student Aid, Vocational & Technical Education
Health: Cancer, Children's Health/Hospitals, Diabetes, Mental Health, Single-Disease Health Associations
Religion: Churches, Dioceses, Religious Organizations, Religious Welfare
Social Services: Animal Protection, Community Service Organizations, Scouts, Social Services-General

Application Procedures
Initial Contact: Send typed, double-spaced letter containing statement of need.
Deadlines: None.

Corporate Officials

David F. Kilmartin: chairman, president, chief executive officer, director PRIM CORP EMPL chairman, president, chief executive officer, director: Kilmartin Industries.

Foundation Officials

Vivianne V. Degrange: secretary, clerk
David F. Kilmartin: president, director (see above)

Grants Analysis

Disclosure Period: fiscal year ending February 28, 2000
Total Grants: $48,150
Number of Grants: 20
Average Grant: $1,797*
Highest Grant: $14,000
Typical Range: $250 to $5,000
*Note: Average grant excludes highest grant.

Recent Grants

Note: Grants derived from fiscal 1998 Form 990.

Library-Related

500	Harmony Library, Harmony, RI

General

7,000	Cardinal Cushing School, Hanover, MA
3,000	Mary's House, Providence, RI
3,000	St. Mary Academy Bay View, Providence, RI
3,000	Society of St. James, Brookline, MA
2,000	University of the South, Sewanee, TN
2,000	Washington and Lee University, NH
1,500	St. Thomas' Church, Greenville, RI
1,000	Mental Health Association, Pawtucket, RI
1,000	New England Old English Sheepdog, Lincoln, MA
1,000	St. Stephen's Church, Providence, RI

WILLIAM S. AND LORA JEAN KILROY FOUNDATION

Giving Contact

Lora Jean Kilroy, Jr., Trustee
3700 Buffalo Speedway, Ste. 750
Houston, TX 77098
Phone: (713)621-8221

Description

Founded: 1985
EIN: 760169904
Organization Type: Private Foundation
Giving Locations: CA; CT; TX
Grant Types: Capital, Endowment, Multiyear/Continuing Support, Operating Expenses, Research.

Donor Information

Founder: William S. Kilroy, Lora Jean Kilroy

Financial Summary

Total Giving: $478,192 (2001); $477,780 (2000); $485,709 (1999)
Giving Analysis: Giving for 1999 includes: foundation matching gifts ($148,998)
Assets: $10,499,132 (2001); $11,916,628 (2000); $11,018,288 (1999)
Gifts Received: In 1991, contributions were received from W. S. and L. J. Kilroy.

Typical Recipients

Arts & Humanities: Arts Funds, Community Arts, Dance, Historic Preservation, History & Archaeology, Libraries, Museums/Galleries
Civic & Public Affairs: Municipalities/Towns, Professional & Trade Associations, Public Policy, Urban & Community Affairs, Women's Affairs, Zoos/Aquariums
Education: Colleges & Universities, Elementary Education (Public), Medical Education, Private Education (Precollege), Religious Education, Science/Mathematics Education, Special Education, Student Aid
Environment: Resource Conservation
Health: Children's Health/Hospitals, Eyes/Blindness, Heart, Hospitals, Medical Rehabilitation, Medical Research, Mental Health, Single-Disease Health Associations
International: Health Care/Hospitals
Religion: Religious Organizations, Religious Welfare
Science: Science Museums
Social Services: Animal Protection, Child Abuse, Child Welfare, Community Service Organizations, Day Care, Family Services, People with Disabilities, Senior Services, YMCA/YWCA/YMHA/YWHA, Youth Organizations

Application Procedures

Initial Contact: Send a brief letter of inquiry.
Application Requirements: any information relevant to the request. There are no deadlines.

Foundation Officials

Lora Jean Kilroy: trustee
Mari Angela Kilroy: trustee
William S. Kilroy: trustee

Grants Analysis

Disclosure Period: calendar year ending 2001
Total Grants: $478,192
Number of Grants: 20
Average Grant: $11,228*
Highest Grant: $153,630
Typical Range: $5,000 to $20,000
*Note: Average grant figure excludes two highest grants ($253,630).

Recent Grants

Note: Grants derived from 2001 Form 990.

General

153,630	University School, Hunting Valley, OH -- for faculty excellence fund and the annual fund
100,000	Museum of Fine Arts, Houston, TX -- capital campaign pledge
75,000	Brookwood Community, Brookshire, TX -- to fund endowment of Kilroy House
44,462	Kinkaid School, Houston, TX -- for computer lab equipment
20,000	Texas Heart Institute, Houston, TX -- for pledge in honor of Denton Cooley
20,000	Texas Heart Institute, Houston, TX
10,000	Texas Children's Hospital, Houston, TX -- building for children capital campaign
10,000	University of Texas Houston Health Science Center, Houston, TX -- donor funds
10,000	University of Texas Medical School, Houston, TX -- for lung disease cellular research
10,000	Yale University, New Haven, CT -- for Trumbull fund

FLORENCE B. KILWORTH CHARITABLE TRUST

Giving Contact

Michael W. Steadman, Assistant Vice President & Trust Officer
c/o Key Trust Co., NW
800 Superior, 4th Fl.
Cleveland, OH 44114
Phone: (216)828-9535

Description

Founded: 1977
EIN: 916221495
Organization Type: Private Foundation
Giving Locations: WA: Tacoma and Pierce counties and surrounding area
Grant Types: Capital, Emergency, General Support, Project, Research, Scholarship.

Financial Summary

Total Giving: $296,000 (2001); $404,000 (2000); $338,600 (1999)
Giving Analysis: Giving for 1999 includes: foundation grants to United Way ($20,000) 1998: foundation grants to United Way ($20,000)
Assets: $5,957,120 (2001); $6,780,991 (2000); $7,354,540 (1999)

Typical Recipients

Arts & Humanities: Arts Associations & Councils, Ballet, Community Arts, History & Archaeology, Libraries, Museums/Galleries, Music, Opera, Performing Arts, Public Broadcasting, Theater
Civic & Public Affairs: African American Affairs, Botanical Gardens/Parks, Clubs, Community Foundations, Employment/Job Training, Civic & Public Affairs-General, Hispanic Affairs, Housing, Public Policy, Urban & Community Affairs, Women's Affairs, Zoos/Aquariums
Education: Arts/Humanities Education, Colleges & Universities, Community & Junior Colleges, Faculty Development, Literacy, Minority Education, Private Education (Precollege), Public Education (Precollege), Religious Education, Science/Mathematics Education, Secondary Education (Public), Special Education
Environment: Environment-General, Wildlife Protection
Health: Arthritis, Cancer, Children's Health/Hospitals, Clinics/Medical Centers, Emergency/Ambulance Services, Health-General, Health Policy/Cost Containment, Health Organizations, Hospitals, Mental Health, Single-Disease Health Associations, Transplant Networks/Donor Banks, Trauma Treatment
International: Missionary/Religious Activities
Religion: Churches, Religion-General, Ministries, Religious Organizations, Religious Welfare
Social Services: At-Risk Youth, Child Welfare, Community Service Organizations, Crime Prevention, Day Care, Family Planning, Family Services, Food/Clothing Distribution, People with Disabilities, Recreation & Athletics, Scouts, Senior Services, Shelters/Homelessness, Social Services-General, United Funds/United Ways, YMCA/YWCA/YMHA/YWHA, Youth Organizations

Application Procedures

Initial Contact: The foundation requests applications be made in writing.
Deadlines: None.

Additional Information

Trust(s): KeyBank N.A.

Foundation Officials

Michael W. Steadman: assistant vice president

Grants Analysis

Disclosure Period: calendar year ending 2001
Total Grants: $296,000
Number of Grants: 73
Average Grant: $4,055
Highest Grant: $15,000
Typical Range: $1,000 to $10,000

Recent Grants

Note: Grants derived from 2001 Form 990.

General

15,000	Tacoma Symphony Orchestra, Tacoma, WA

12,500	Tacoma Art Museum, Tacoma, WA
10,000	Annie Wright School, Tacoma, WA
10,000	Associated Ministries, Tacoma, WA
10,000	Boys and Girls Clubs of Pierce County, Tacoma, WA
10,000	Emergency Food Network, Tacoma, WA
10,000	Pacific Lutheran University, Tacoma, WA
10,000	Tacoma Actors Guild, Tacoma, WA
10,000	Tacoma Art Museum, Tacoma, WA
10,000	University of Puget Sound, Tacoma, WA

HORACE A. KIMBALL AND S. ELLA KIMBALL FOUNDATION

Giving Contact
Thomas F. Black, III, President
130 Woodville Rd.
Hope Valley, RI 02832
Phone: (401)364-3565
Fax: (401)364-3565
Web: http://www.hkimballfoundation.org

Description
Founded: 1956
EIN: 056006130
Organization Type: Private Foundation
Giving Locations: RI
Grant Types: Capital, General Support, Operating Expenses.

Donor Information
Founder: the late H. Earle Kimball

Financial Summary
Total Giving: $289,897 (fiscal year ending September 30, 2001); $284,950 (fiscal 2000); $424,105 (fiscal 1999)
Giving Analysis: Giving for fiscal 2001 includes: foundation scholarships ($20,000); foundation matching gifts ($60,660) fiscal 2000: foundation scholarships ($44,000)
Assets: $6,937,338 (fiscal 2001); $7,225,740 (fiscal 2000); $6,947,495 (fiscal 1999)
Gifts Received: $100 (fiscal 2001); $1,180 (fiscal 2000)

Typical Recipients
Arts & Humanities: Arts Centers, Arts Funds, Arts & Humanities-General, Historic Preservation, History & Archaeology, Libraries, Museums/Galleries, Performing Arts, Theater
Civic & Public Affairs: Botanical Gardens/Parks, Civic & Public Affairs-General, Municipalities/Towns, Safety, Urban & Community Affairs, Women's Affairs
Education: Afterschool/Enrichment Programs, Colleges & Universities, International Studies, Literacy, Preschool Education, Private Education (Precollege), School Volunteerism, Science/Mathematics Education, Secondary Education (Private), Student Aid
Environment: Environment-General, Resource Conservation, Watershed
Health: Children's Health/Hospitals, Clinics/Medical Centers, Emergency/Ambulance Services, Health Organizations, Hospitals, Long-Term Care, Medical Rehabilitation, Medical Research, Nursing Services, Public Health, Single-Disease Health Associations
International: International Peace & Security Issues
Religion: Religious Organizations, Religious Welfare
Social Services: Animal Protection, Big Brother/Big Sister, Camps, Child Welfare, Community Service Organizations, Crime Prevention, Day Care, Food/Clothing Distribution, Recreation & Athletics, Scouts, Senior Services, Shelters/Homelessness, Volunteer Services, YMCA/YWCA/YMHA/YWHA, Youth Organizations

Application Procedures
Initial Contact: Send a brief letter of inquiry. or apply online at the website.
Deadlines: None.

Foundation Officials
Norman D. Baker, Jr.: secretary, treasurer, trustee PRIM CORP EMPL senior vice president: Allendale Insurance.
Thomas F. Black, III: president, trustee
F. Thomas Lenihan, Esq.: trustee

Grants Analysis
Disclosure Period: fiscal year ending September 30, 2001
Total Grants: $219,277*
Number of Grants: 23
Average Grant: $9,534
Highest Grant: $36,000
Lowest Grant: $100
Typical Range: $2,000 to $15,000
*Note: Giving excludes scholarships and matching gifts.

Recent Grants
Note: Grants derived from fiscal 2000 Form 990.

General

28,000	Granite Theatre, Inc., Westerly, RI -- capital expenses and web site
26,100	Granite Theatre, Inc., Westerly, RI
25,000	Granite Theatre Corporation, The, Westerly, RI
15,000	Heritage Harbor Museum
15,000	South County Hospital, Wakefield, RI -- capital campaign
15,000	Westerly Senior Citizens Center, Westerly, MA -- circus tickets
10,000	Community Preparatory School, Providence, RI -- scholarship funds
10,000	Edmundite Society
10,000	Feinstein Challenge Grant
10,000	Rhode Island State Police Museum Fund, RI

KIMBERLY-CLARK CORP.

Company Headquarters
Dallas, TX
Web: http://www.kimberly-clark.com

Company Description
Founded: 1872
Ticker: KMB
Exchange: NYSE
Revenue: US$13.566 billion (2002)
Profit: US$1.674 billion (2002)
Employees: 63900 (2002)
Fortune Rank: 143, per FORTUNE Magazine's list of 500 Largest U.S. Corporations (2002).
SIC(s): 2621 Paper Mills, 2676 Sanitary Paper Products.

Operating Locations
Kimberly-Clark Corp. (AL--Aliceville, Birmingham, Boligee, Calvert, Coosa Pines, Excel, Gilbertown, Goodwater, Heflin, Huxford, Jacksons Gap, Lineville, Mobile, Monroeville, Oxford, Pine Hill, Quinton, Saraland, Weogufka, Westover; AZ--Scottsdale; AR--Little Rock, Maumelle; CA--Dublin, Fullerton; CO--Englewood, Golden, Littleton; DE--Dover; DC--Washington; FL--Jacksonville; GA--Dunwoody, Roswell; HI--Waipahu; ID--Santa; IL--Des Plaines; ME--Guilford; MD--Woodstock; MA--Feeding Hills; MI--Munising; MS--Corinth, Dennis, Hattiesburg, Pearlington, State Line, Waynesboro; MO--Chesterfield; NJ--Kirkwood Vrhes, Spotswood; NY--Ancram, Melville; NC--Charlotte, Hendersonville, Lexington; OH--Chagrin Falls,

Columbus; OK--Jenks; PA--Gibsonia, Media, Newtown Square; SC--Jackson; TN--Collierville, Knoxville, Loudon; TX--Dallas, Irving, Paris; UT--Ogden; WA--Everett; WI--Appleton, Elm Grove, Marinette, Oconto Falls, Oshkosh)

Nonmonetary Support
Type: Donated Products
Volunteer Programs: Foundation makes grants to organizations where employees and their spouses volunteer through the Community Partners program.
Note: Co. provides nonmonetary support in the form of donated products for disaster relief only.

Kimberly-Clark Foundation

Giving Contact
Carolyn Mentesana, Vice President
Kimberly-Clark Foundation
PO Box 619100
Dallas, TX 75261-9100
Phone: (972)281-1200
Fax: (972)281-1490
Web: http://www.kimberly-clark.com/aboutus/comm_involvement.asp
Note: Contact local plant manager for information on corporate direct giving.

Description
EIN: 396044304
Organization Type: Corporate Foundation
Giving Locations: nationally; operating locations.
Grant Types: Capital, Employee Matching Gifts, General Support, Operating Expenses, Project.
Note: Employee matching gift ratio: 1 to 1.

Financial Summary
Total Giving: $7,765,116 (2001); $6,496,851 (2000); $5,730,313 (1999). Note: Contributes through corporate direct giving program and foundation.
Giving Analysis: Giving for 2000 includes: foundation grants to United Way ($146,297); foundation matching gifts ($589,880); foundation scholarships ($1,790,000); foundation ($3,970,674); 1998: foundation grants to United Way ($160,231); foundation matching gifts ($529,023); corporate direct giving ($3,929,290); foundation ($5,881,456); 1997: foundation grants to United Way ($114,738); foundation matching gifts ($240,800); foundation ($6,053,450);
Assets: $6,019,856 (2001); $6,470,270 (2000); $2,743,366 (1999). Note: Assets pertain to Foundation only.
Gifts Received: $7,398,694 (2001); $10,335,947 (2000); $5,575,755 (1999). Note: The foundation receives contributions from Kimberly-Clark Corporation.

Typical Recipients
Arts & Humanities: Arts Appreciation, Arts Associations & Councils, Arts Centers, Arts Funds, Community Arts, Dance, Arts & Humanities-General, Historic Preservation, History & Archaeology, Libraries, Museums/Galleries, Music, Opera, Performing Arts, Public Broadcasting, Theater
Civic & Public Affairs: African American Affairs, Botanical Gardens/Parks, Business/Free Enterprise, Chambers of Commerce, Civil Rights, Clubs, Community Foundations, Economic Development, Economic Policy, Civic & Public Affairs-General, Law & Justice, Legal Aid, Municipalities/Towns, Parades/Festivals, Philanthropic Organizations, Public Policy, Safety, Urban & Community Affairs, Urban & Community Affairs, Women's Affairs, Zoos/Aquariums
Education: Arts/Humanities Education, Business Education, Colleges & Universities, Community & Junior Colleges, Economic Education, Education Associations, Education Funds, Education Reform, Engineering/Technological Education, Faculty Development, Education-General, International Studies,

Leadership Training, Legal Education, Literacy, Medical Education, Minority Education, Private Education (Precollege), School Volunteerism, Science/Mathematics Education, Special Education, Student Aid

Environment: Air/Water Quality, Environment-General, Resource Conservation

Health: Adolescent Health Issues, Cancer, Children's Health/Hospitals, Clinics/Medical Centers, Diabetes, Emergency/Ambulance Services, Health-General, Geriatric Health, Health Funds, Health Organizations, Hospitals, Hospitals (University Affiliated), Medical Research, Multiple Sclerosis, Nursing Services, Public Health, Single-Disease Health Associations

International: International-General, International Relations, International Relief Efforts

Religion: Religious Welfare

Science: Scientific Research

Social Services: Child Welfare, Community Centers, Community Service Organizations, Counseling, Delinquency & Criminal Rehabilitation, Domestic Violence, Emergency Relief, Family Services, Food/Clothing Distribution, People with Disabilities, Recreation & Athletics, Senior Services, Shelters/Homelessness, Substance Abuse, United Funds/United Ways, Volunteer Services, YMCA/YWCA/YMHA/YWHA, Youth Organizations, Youth Organizations

Application Procedures

Initial Contact: Send a written proposal.

Application Requirements: Include amount requested, purpose of grant, and proof of tax-exempt 501(c)(3) status.

Deadlines: None; proposals reviewed as received.

Restrictions

The foundation does not make grants to sports or athletic activities; dinners or special events; individuals; fraternal organizations; state or secondary schools (except through matching gifts); religious organizations; goodwill advertising; member agencies of united funds; or political parties or candidates.

Additional Information

Kimberly-Clark Corp. annually budgets 1% of pretax domestic income averaged from preceding three years for charitable contributions, which may be given directly to qualified recipients or to the Kimberly-Clark Foundation for distribution. Since 1952, the foundation has served as the principal means through which the corporation supports tax-exempt charitable organizations.

In 1995, Kimberly-Clark Corp. acquired Scott Paper Co. currently being considered by the Kimberly-Clark Foundation.

Publications: Annual Report

Corporate Officials

Tina S. Barry: vice president corporate communications PRIM CORP EMPL vice president corporate communications: Kimberly-Clark Corp.

Mark A. Buthman: senior vice president, chief financial officer

Thomas J. Falk: chairman, president, chief executive officer

Wayne R. Sanders: chairman B Chicago, IL 1947. ED Illinois Institute of Technology BS (1969); Marquette University MBA (1972). PRIM CORP EMPL chairman: Kimberly-Clark Corp. ADD CORP EMPL chairman: Durafab Inc. CORP AFFIL director: Texas Instruments Inc.; director: Adolph Coors Co.; director: Chase Bank Texas. NONPR AFFIL chairman: Marquette University.

Foundation Officials

Tina S. Barry: president, director (see above)

O. George Everbach: director

W. Anthony Gamron: treasurer, director B Seymour, IN 1948. ED Indiana State University BS (1971); Indiana University MBA (1976). PRIM CORP EMPL vice president, treasurer: Kimberly-Clark Corp. ADD

CORP EMPL treasurer: Kimberly Clark Tissue Co.

CORP AFFIL treasurer: Avent Inc.

Ron McCray: secretary

Grants Analysis

Disclosure Period: calendar year ending 2001

Total Grants: $6,616,333*

Number of Grants: 71

Average Grant: $40,527*

Highest Grant: $1,740,000

Lowest Grant: $200

Typical Range: $10,000 to $80,000

*Note: Giving excludes corporate direct giving, matching gifts, and United Way. Average grant figure excludes three highest grants ($3,860,500).

Recent Grants

Note: Grants derived from 2001 Form 990.

General

1,740,000	Bright Futures College Scholarship Program, Dallas, TX
1,120,500	Community Partners, Houston, TX
1,000,000	American Red Cross Liberty Disaster Relief Fund, New York, NY
800,000	Community Foundation for the Fox Valley Region, Inc., Appleton, WI
252,500	Marquette University, Milwaukee, WI
200,000	Southwestern Medical Foundation, Dallas, TX
200,000	Visiting Nurses Association, Dallas, TX
132,035	United Way of Metropolitan Dallas, Dallas, TX
125,000	Texans Can, Dallas, TX
100,000	Dallas County Community College District Foundation, Dallas, TX

KINDER MORGAN

Company Headquarters

1301 McKinney, Suite 3400

Houston, TX 77010

Phone: (713)844-9500

Web: http://www.kindermorgan.com

Company Description

Founded: 1936

Ticker: KMI

Exchange: NYSE

Former Name: KN Energy Co. (1999).

Assets: US$10.102 billion (2002)

Employees: 5390 (2002)

SIC(s): 4900 Electric, Gas & Sanitary Services, 4923 Gas Transmission & Distribution, 5172 Petroleum Products Nec, 5983 Fuel Oil Dealers.

Operating Locations

KN Energy (CO--Lakewood; NE--Hastings; WY--Casper)

Nonmonetary Support

Type: Donated Equipment

Note: NOTE: Company provides nonmonetary support.

Volunteer Programs: The Foundation funds the KM for Kids program, through which youth programs throughout Kinder Morgan's retail communities receive funding and volunteer support.

Kinder Morgan Foundation

Giving Contact

Maureen Bulkley, Foundation Administrator

370 Van Gordon Street

Lakewood, CO 80228-8304

Phone: (303)989-1740

Fax: (303)984-3306

E-mail: maureen_bulkley@kindermorgan.com

Web: http://www.kindermorgan.com/community/km_foundation.cfm

Description

Founded: 1990

EIN: 841148161

Organization Type: Corporate Foundation

Giving Locations: AR; CO; IL; IA; KS; LA; MO; MT; NE; NM; ND; OK; TX; UT; WY

Grant Types: Capital, Employee Matching Gifts, Project.

Note: Employee matching gift ratio: 1 to 1, up to $1,000 per employee each year.

Donor Information

Founder: KN Energy, Inc.

Financial Summary

Total Giving: $750,000 (2003 approx); $811,000 (2002); $755,752 (2001)

Giving Analysis: Giving for 2001 includes: foundation grants to United Way ($6,941); foundation matching gifts ($23,692); 2000: foundation grants to United Way ($19,775); foundation matching gifts ($25,080) foundation ($708,831)

Assets: $2,250,000 (2003 approx); $2,978,000 (2002); $4,216,599 (2001)

Typical Recipients

Arts & Humanities: Arts Associations & Councils, Arts Centers, Arts Funds, Arts & Humanities-General, Historic Preservation, History & Archaeology, Libraries, Museums/Galleries, Music, Opera, Performing Arts, Public Broadcasting, Theater

Civic & Public Affairs: African American Affairs, Botanical Gardens/Parks, Business/Free Enterprise, Chambers of Commerce, Clubs, Community Foundations, Economic Development, Civic & Public Affairs-General, Housing, Municipalities/Towns, Parades/Festivals, Rural Affairs, Safety, Urban & Community Affairs, Women's Affairs

Education: Agricultural Education, Business Education, Colleges & Universities, Community & Junior Colleges, Economic Education, Education Associations, Elementary Education (Private), Engineering/Technological Education, Education-General, Leadership Training, Minority Education, Private Education (Precollege), Public Education (Precollege), Secondary Education (Private), Secondary Education (Public), Special Education, Student Aid

Environment: Air/Water Quality, Environment-General

Health: Children's Health/Hospitals, Clinics/Medical Centers, Emergency/Ambulance Services, Health-General, Health Organizations, Hospices, Hospitals, Multiple Sclerosis, Public Health

Religion: Jewish Causes, Religious Welfare, Seminaries

Science: Science-General, Science Museums

Social Services: Big Brother/Big Sister, Camps, Child Welfare, Community Centers, Community Service Organizations, Delinquency & Criminal Rehabilitation, Emergency Relief, Family Planning, Family Services, Homes, People with Disabilities, Recreation & Athletics, Scouts, Senior Services, Social Services-General, United Funds/United Ways, YMCA/YWCA/YMHA/YWHA, Youth Organizations

Application Procedures

Initial Contact: Request guidelines and organization summary form from the foundation. Send a brief letter of inquiry. not more than three pages in length.

Application Requirements: Proposals should include a completed organization summary form, and a cover letter/proposal narrative of three pages or less. Include a description of organization, amount requested and total amount sought in campaign, and purpose of funds sought; statement of rationale for proposal including an indication of its goal, the need for such a program, any unique element, population

benefited, and geographical reach; list of other collaborative agencies, and their role in the program to be funded; timeline for implementation; expected goals, objectives, and tactics; plans for project evaluation; itemized budget for the program or project; list of officers and directors, with affiliations; detailed organizational budget for the current year, with income and expenses; recently audited financial statement, and proof of tax-exempt status.
Deadlines: None.
Decision Notification: Awards are typically announced on a quarterly basis.

Restrictions

Foundation will not fund individuals; political causes, candidates, or lobbying efforts; programs or organizations outside of the U.S.; operating expenses; projects of religious denominations; advertising; athletic team sponsorships; or elementary or secondary schools (unless submitted through an educational foundation).
Applicants must have 501(c)(3) status and proposals must reflect the purpose of the Kinder Morgan Foundation.

Foundation Officials

Maureen Bulkley: foundation administrator
Michael C. Morgan: director
Larry S. Pierce: director
James E. Street: director
Daniel E. Watson: director

Grants Analysis

Disclosure Period: calendar year ending 2001
Total Grants: $725,119*
Number of Grants: 378 (approx)
Average Grant: $1,720*
Highest Grant: $30,000
Lowest Grant: $50
Typical Range: $500 to $3,000
*Note: Giving excludes matching gifts and United Way. Average grant figure excludes three highest grants ($80,000).

Recent Grants

Note: Grants derived from 2001 Form 990.

General

30,000	Young Americans Education Foundation, Denver, CO
25,000	Spirit of Texas Flood Relief, Houston, TX
25,000	Tropical Storm Allison Flood Relief, Houston, TX
16,152	Montrose Youth and Community Foundation, Montrose, CO
13,150	New York Firefighters 9-11 Disaster Relief Fund, Washington, DC
11,880	North Jersey Disaster Relief Fund, Morristown, NJ
10,000	Lakewood Legacy Foundation, Lakewood, CO
8,333	United Way of the Texas Gulf Coast, Houston, TX
7,800	September 11th Fund, New York, NY
7,500	Ronald McDonald House of Houston, Houston, NY

CHARLES AND LUCILLE KING FAMILY FOUNDATION

Giving Contact

Karen Kennedy, Assistant Educational Director
366 Madison Avenue, 10th Floor
New York, NY 10017-3122
Phone: (212)682-2459
Fax: (212)949-0728

E-mail: info@kingfoundation.org
Web: http://www.kingfoundation.org

Description

Founded: 1988
EIN: 133489257
Organization Type: Private Foundation
Giving Locations: nationally.
Grant Types: Scholarship.

Donor Information

Founder: Diana King

Financial Summary

Total Giving: $385,762 (2001); $295,450 (2000); $227,918 (1999)
Giving Analysis: Giving for 2001 includes: foundation grants to United Way ($12,500); foundation scholarships ($74,850) 1999: foundation scholarships ($227,918)
Assets: $5,366,741 (2001); $6,133,577 (2000); $7,978,093 (1999)
Gifts Received: $155,220 (2001); $57,305 (2000); $87,869 (1999). Note: In 2001, contributions were received from Diana King ($95,200) and Karen Rabe ($60,000). In 1999, contributions were received from Diana King.

Typical Recipients

Arts & Humanities: Film & Video, Arts & Humanities-General, History & Archaeology, Libraries, Museums/Galleries, Performing Arts, Theater
Civic & Public Affairs: Civic & Public Affairs-General, Safety
Education: Arts/Humanities Education, Colleges & Universities, Journalism/Media Education, Minority Education, Special Education, Student Aid
Environment: Watershed, Wildlife Protection
Health: Cancer, Children's Health/Hospitals, Diabetes, Emergency/Ambulance Services, Home-Care Services, Hospitals, Public Health
International: International Affairs, International Organizations
Religion: Churches, Religious Organizations, Religious Welfare
Social Services: Child Welfare, Crime Prevention, Food/Clothing Distribution, Recreation & Athletics, Shelters/Homelessness, Special Olympics, United Funds/United Ways, Veterans, Youth Organizations

Application Procedures

Initial Contact: Request application form.
Deadlines: April 15.

Restrictions

Student applicants must be currently enrolled in a four-year university in the United States.

Additional Information

Provides scholarships to television and film undergraduate students.
Publications: Application Form

Foundation Officials

Charles J. Brucia: vice president, treasurer, director
Michael Collyer, Esq.: director
Diana King: president, director B 1949. PRIM CORP EMPL vice president, secretary, director: King World Productions.
Eugene V. Kokot: secretary, director

Grants Analysis

Disclosure Period: calendar year ending 2001
Total Grants: $298,412*
Number of Grants: 73
Average Grant: $4,088
Highest Grant: $60,000
Typical Range: $500 to $10,000
*Note: Giving excludes scholarships; United Way.

Recent Grants

Note: Grants derived from 2001 Form 990.

General

60,000	Blairsden Association, New York, NY
50,000	New York University, New York, NY -- millennium grant
15,000	New York University, New York, NY -- Heinemann grant
13,000	American Red Cross, Morristown, NJ
12,500	United Way, New York, NY
10,000	Columbia College-Chicago, Chicago, IL
10,000	International Council of Natas Foundation, New York, NY
10,000	Kips Bay Boys and Girls Club, Bronx, NY
10,000	Salvation Army, New York, NY
10,000	University of California Los Angeles, Los Angeles, CA

CARL B. AND FLORENCE E. KING FOUNDATION

Giving Contact

Board of Directors
5956 Sherry Lane, Suite 620
Dallas, TX 75225
Phone: (214)750-1884
Fax: (214)750-1651

Description

Founded: 1966
EIN: 756052203
Organization Type: General Purpose Foundation
Giving Locations: TX: Dallas including metropolitan area
Grant Types: Capital, Multiyear/Continuing Support, Project.

Donor Information

Founder: Incorporated in 1966 by the late Carl B. King and the late Florence E. King . Mr. King formed the Carl B. King Drilling Company during the oil boom in Oklahoma. The foundation was created a year before his death in 1967.

Financial Summary

Total Giving: $1,907,429 (2000); $1,500,000 (1999 approx); $1,308,437 (1998). Note: 1996 Giving includes scholarship ($39,500); 1995 scholarship ($15,500).
Giving Analysis: Giving for 2000 includes: foundation scholarships ($331,500); 1998: foundation scholarships ($263,667) foundation ($1,044,770)
Assets: $49,127,096 (2000); $48,186,371 (1998); $39,449,221 (1996)
Gifts Received: $484,377 (1995). Note: In 1995, contributions were received from the D.E. King estate.

Typical Recipients

Arts & Humanities: Arts Associations & Councils, Arts Festivals, Arts Institutes, Arts Outreach, Ballet, Ethnic & Folk Arts, Historic Preservation, History & Archaeology, Libraries, Museums/Galleries, Music, Opera, Public Broadcasting
Civic & Public Affairs: Botanical Gardens/Parks, Clubs, Community Foundations, Employment/Job Training, Civic & Public Affairs-General, Hispanic Affairs, Law & Justice, Municipalities/Towns, Nonprofit Management, Philanthropic Organizations, Professional & Trade Associations, Public Policy, Rural Affairs, Safety, Urban & Community Affairs, Women's Affairs, Zoos/Aquariums
Education: Afterschool/Enrichment Programs, Agricultural Education, Arts/Humanities Education, Colleges & Universities, Colleges & Universities, Education Reform, Engineering/Technological Education, Faculty Development, Education-General, Literacy, Medical Education, Private Education (Precollege),

Public Education (Precollege), Science/Mathematics Education, Secondary Education (Private), Social Sciences Education, Student Aid

Environment: Environment-General, Resource Conservation, Wildlife Protection

Health: Cancer, Children's Health/Hospitals, Clinics/Medical Centers, Diabetes, Emergency/Ambulance Services, Eyes/Blindness, Health Funds, Health Organizations, Hospices, Hospitals, Medical Rehabilitation, Medical Research, Nursing Services, Prenatal Health Issues

Religion: Churches, Jewish Causes, Religious Organizations, Religious Welfare, Religious Welfare

Science: Science Museums, Scientific Organizations

Social Services: Animal Protection, Camps, Child Welfare, Community Service Organizations, Counseling, Crime Prevention, Delinquency & Criminal Rehabilitation, Family Planning, Family Services, People with Disabilities, Recreation & Athletics, Scouts, Shelters/Homelessness, Substance Abuse, United Funds/United Ways, Veterans, Volunteer Services, YMCA/YWCA/YMHA/YWHA, Youth Organizations

Application Procedures

Initial Contact: The foundation welcomes introductory inquiries.

Application Requirements: Formal grant proposals should include an IRS tax-exempt form; a description of the applicant organization, a history of the organization's activities, and its purpose; a summary of the proposed program, its goals and objectives, and plans for implementation; the purpose of the grant; the specific amount requested from the foundation, as well as all other sources of funding; a financial statement and proposed budget a copy of the IRS determination letters; and a statement of approval, signed by the organization's chief administrator, for requesting funds.

Deadlines: None.

Review Process: Once the application has been received and reviewed, the foundation may call upon the applicant for additional information. The directors will then study the request and convey their decision directly to the applicant.

Notes: The foundation accepts no responsibility for keeping any part of a request confidential and reserves the right to discuss a proposal with outside consultants.

Restrictions

As a general policy, the foundation refrains from extending grants for individuals, organisation outside Texas, organization which are not tax-exempt, religious organizations for sectarian purposes, deficit financing or ongoing operating expenses, and loan financing. Scholarship are awarded to Texas High School graduates and/or to college students majoring in science, math, or english education. (1998 Form 990)

Additional Information

Publications: Program Policy Statement; Brochure and Guidelines

Foundation Officials

Thomas W. Vett: secretary, treasurer
Carl Yeckel: president, director

Grants Analysis

Disclosure Period: calendar year ending 2000
Total Grants: $1,575,929*
Number of Grants: 55
Average Grant: $26,036*
Highest Grant: $170,000
Lowest Grant: $400
Typical Range: $10,000 to $50,000
*Note: Giving excludes scholarships. Average grant excludes highest grant. Number of grants is approximate.

Recent Grants

Note: Grants derived from 2000 Form 990.

General

170,000	KERA Channel 13, Dallas, TX
50,000	Yale University Press, New Haven, CT
35,000	Galveston Historical Foundation, Galveston, TX
30,000	Barbara Bush Foundation for Family Literacy, Houston, TX
30,000	Fellowship of Christian Athletes, Dallas, TX
30,000	Salesmanship Club of Dallas, Dallas, TX
25,000	Boys Scouts of America, Dallas, TX -- youth at risk
25,000	Midland Memorial Foundation, Midland, TX
25,000	Notre Dame School of Dallas, Dallas, TX
25,000	Texas Scottish Rite Hospital, Dallas, TX

KENNETH KENDAL KING FOUNDATION

Giving Contact

Robert Sweeney, President & Director
Kenneth Kendal King Foundation
900 Pennsylvania Street
Denver, CO 80203-3163
Phone: (303)832-3200
Fax: (303)832-4176
E-mail: info@kennethkingfoundation.org
Web: http://www.kennethkingfoundation.org

Description

Founded: 1990
EIN: 841148157
Organization Type: Private Foundation
Grant Types: Capital, Emergency, General Support, Matching, Project, Research.

Donor Information

Founder: Established in 1990 by the late Kenneth Kendal King .

Financial Summary

Total Giving: $1,330,240 (2002); $1,500,000 (2001 approx); $2,537,795 (2000)
Giving Analysis: Giving for 1999 includes: foundation scholarships ($6,000); foundation matching gifts ($85,000) foundation scholarships ($182,000)
Assets: $40,266,998 (2002); $64,198,965 (2001); $65,972,296 (2000)
Gifts Received: $500 (2002); $500 (1999); $2,494 (1997)

Typical Recipients

Arts & Humanities: Arts Centers, Libraries, Museums/Galleries, Opera

Civic & Public Affairs: African American Affairs, Botanical Gardens/Parks, Employment/Job Training, Civic & Public Affairs-General, Housing, Women's Affairs, Zoos/Aquariums

Education: Arts/Humanities Education, Colleges & Universities, Community & Junior Colleges, Economic Education, Engineering/Technological Education, Education-General, Gifted & Talented Programs, Private Education (Precollege), Religious Education, Secondary Education (Private), Special Education, Student Aid, Vocational & Technical Education

Environment: Environment-General, Resource Conservation

Health: Cancer, Children's Health/Hospitals, Eyes/Blindness, Hospices, Hospitals, Mental Health, Multiple Sclerosis, Research/Studies Institutes, Speech & Hearing, Transplant Networks/Donor Banks

International: Health Care/Hospitals

Religion: Churches, Religious Welfare

Science: Science Museums

Social Services: At-Risk Youth, Child Welfare, Community Centers, Community Service Organizations, Counseling, Family Services, Food/Clothing Distribution, People with Disabilities, Recreation & Athletics, Refugee Assistance, Senior Services, YMCA/YWCA/YMHA/YWHA, Youth Organizations

Application Procedures

Initial Contact: Request application.
Application Requirements: Complete application will include proof of tax-exempt status and last two years balance sheet and income and expense statement are mandatory.
Deadlines: March 1.

Additional Information

Publications: Application Form; Annual Report

Foundation Officials

Matthew R. Banner, III: director
Bernice A. Bettis: secretary, director
Peter Hoke: director
Joseph Kelly: director
Minnie P. Lundberg: treasurer, director
Eaton Smith: director
Robert Sweeney: president, director
T. E. Welker: director

Grants Analysis

Disclosure Period: calendar year ending 2002
Total Grants: $1,330,240
Number of Grants: 233
Average Grant: $4,027*
Highest Grant: $200,000
Lowest Grant: $300
Typical Range: $1,000 to $10,000
*Note: Average grant figure excludes two highest grants.

Recent Grants

Note: Grants derived from 2002 Form 990.

Library-Related

20,000	Auraria Library, Denver, CO -- for purchasing additional equipment for the computer commons area

General

200,000	Auraria Foundation, Denver, CO -- for King Center multi year commitment
200,000	University of Colorado Foundation, Boulder, CO -- for multi year commitment
56,000	Iliff School of Technology, Denver, CO -- for operating support
25,000	Goodwill Industries of Denver, Denver, CO -- for School to Work Program
25,000	Little Voice Productions, Denver, CO -- for operating support
25,000	Metropolitan State College Denver, Denver, CO -- for purchasing specialized hardware and software
25,000	Sigma Chi Foundation, Evanston, IL -- commitment
18,000	Sigma Chi Foundation, Evanston, IL -- commitment
16,000	Sigma Chi Foundation, Evanston, IL -- for operating support
15,000	Liberty Day Colorado, Centennial, CO -- to support Liberty Day

KINGSBURY CORP.

Company Headquarters

80 Laurel St.
Keene, NH 03431
Web: http://www.kingsburycorp.com

Company Description

Revenue: US$47.2 million (2001)
Employees: 260 (2001)
SIC(s): 3541 Machine Tools--Metal Cutting Types, 3542 Machine Tools--Metal Forming Types.

Operating Locations

Kingsbury Corp. (NH--Keene)

Nonmonetary Support

Type: Donated Equipment; Donated Products; In-kind Services; Loaned Employees

Kingsbury Fund

Giving Contact

James E. O'Neil, Executive Trustee
Kingsbury Fund
Box 2020
80 Laurel Street
Keene, NH 03431-7020
Phone: (603)352-5212
Fax: (603)357-1955
Web: http://www.kingsburycorp.com

Description

Founded: 1952
EIN: 026004465
Organization Type: Corporate Foundation
Giving Locations: ME; MA; NH: especially Cheshire County; VT
Grant Types: Capital, Multiyear/Continuing Support, Operating Expenses, Project, Scholarship, Seed Money.
Note: Matches gifts to educational institutions.

Donor Information

Founder: Kingsbury Corp., Kingsbury Manufacturing Co., Fitchburg Foundry

Financial Summary

Total Giving: $154,590 (2001); $141,319 (2000); $201,642 (1999). Note: Contributes through foundation only.
Giving Analysis: Giving for 2000 includes: foundation matching gifts ($1,345); foundation scholarships ($19,000); foundation grants to United Way ($32,608); foundation ($88,366); 1998: foundation matching gifts ($2,830); foundation scholarships ($19,325); foundation grants to United Way ($37,266) foundation ($164,687)
Assets: $3,555,626 (2001); $4,019,272 (2000); $3,880,274 (1999)
Gifts Received: $10,000 (1998); $88,105 (1997); $20,000 (1996). Note: In 1998, contributions were received from an anonymous donor. In 1997, contributions were received from Kingsbury Corp.

Typical Recipients

Arts & Humanities: Arts Appreciation, Arts Associations & Councils, Arts Centers, Arts Festivals, Arts Funds, Ballet, Community Arts, Dance, Ethnic & Folk Arts, Arts & Humanities-General, Historic Preservation, History & Archaeology, Libraries, Museums/Galleries, Music, Opera, Performing Arts, Public Broadcasting, Theater, Visual Arts
Civic & Public Affairs: Botanical Gardens/Parks, Chambers of Commerce, Clubs, Economic Development, Civic & Public Affairs-General, Housing, Parades/Festivals, Safety, Urban & Community Affairs, Women's Affairs
Education: Arts/Humanities Education, Business Education, Colleges & Universities, Community & Junior Colleges, Continuing Education, Education Funds, Elementary Education (Public), Engineering/Technological Education, Education-General, International Studies, Private Education (Precollege), Public Education (Precollege), School Volunteerism, Science/

Mathematics Education, Student Aid, Vocational & Technical Education
Environment: Air/Water Quality, Environment-General, Resource Conservation
Health: AIDS/HIV, Cancer, Children's Health/Hospitals, Clinics/Medical Centers, Emergency/Ambulance Services, Health Organizations, Heart, Hospices, Medical Research
Religion: Religious Welfare
Science: Observatories & Planetariums
Social Services: Animal Protection, Camps, Child Welfare, Community Centers, Community Service Organizations, Crime Prevention, Day Care, Emergency Relief, Family Services, Food/Clothing Distribution, Homes, Recreation & Athletics, Scouts, Senior Services, Social Services-General, Special Olympics, Substance Abuse, United Funds/United Ways, Volunteer Services, YMCA/YWCA/YMHA/YWHA, Youth Organizations

Application Procedures

Initial Contact: Request application guidelines for scholarship grants. Submit a brief letter of inquiry for grant requests.
Application Requirements: Scholarship application forms include contact information, high school or college background, transcripts, estimated budget, evaluation form, and financial statement.
Deadlines: April 28.
Notes: There are no formal application procedures or deadlines for grant requests.

Additional Information

Provides scholarships for higher education to the children of Kingsbury Machine employees.
Trust(s): State Street Bank & Trust Co. of New Hampshire

Corporate Officials

James E. O'Neil: vice president technology PRIM CORP EMPL vice president corporate relations: Kingsbury Corp.

Foundation Officials

James E. O'Neil: executive trustee (see above)

Grants Analysis

Disclosure Period: calendar year ending 2001
Total Grants: $105,323*
Number of Grants: 141
Average Grant: $747
Highest Grant: $20,000
Typical Range: $25 to $5,000
***Note:** Giving excludes matching gifts; scholarships; United Way.

Recent Grants

Note: Grants derived from 2001 Form 990.

General

20,000	Cheshire County YMCA, Keene, NH
10,000	Cedarcrest Foundation, Keene, NH
10,000	Home Healthcare Hospice and Community Services, Nashua, NH
10,000	Keene State College, Keene, NH -- Safety Center
8,207	Monadnock United Way, Keene, NH -- matching gift
8,207	Monadnock United Way, Keene, NH -- matching gift
8,207	Monadnock United Way, Keene, NH -- matching gift
8,207	Monadnock United Way, Keene, NH -- matching gift
7,500	Adoption Learning Center
6,500	Westport Slate Bridge

KINNEY-LINDSTROM FOUNDATION

Giving Contact

Lowell K. Hall, Secretary/Treasurer
PO Box 520
Mason City, IA 50401
Phone: (515)896-3888

Description

Founded: 1957
EIN: 426037351
Organization Type: General Purpose Foundation
Giving Locations: IA
Grant Types: Capital, General Support, Scholarship.

Donor Information

Founder: the late Ida Lindstrom Kinney

Financial Summary

Total Giving: $212,651 (2001); $239,763 (2000); $208,740 (1999)
Giving Analysis: Giving for 2001 includes: foundation scholarships ($4,000); foundation grants to United Way ($30,000); 2000: foundation scholarships ($6,000); foundation grants to United Way ($30,000) 1999: foundation scholarships ($8,000)
Assets: $4,206,229 (2001); $4,187,380 (2000); $5,203,863 (1999)

Typical Recipients

Arts & Humanities: Arts Associations & Councils, Arts Festivals, Historic Preservation, History & Archaeology, Libraries, Museums/Galleries, Music, Performing Arts, Public Broadcasting, Theater
Civic & Public Affairs: Botanical Gardens/Parks, Community Foundations, Employment/Job Training, Civic & Public Affairs-General, Municipalities/Towns, Parades/Festivals, Safety, Urban & Community Affairs
Education: Agricultural Education, Colleges & Universities, Community & Junior Colleges, Public Education (Precollege), Science/Mathematics Education, Special Education, Student Aid
Environment: Environment-General, Resource Conservation
Health: Cancer, Children's Health/Hospitals, Emergency/Ambulance Services, Health-General, Heart
International: International Environmental Issues
Religion: Churches, Churches, Religious Welfare
Science: Science Museums
Social Services: Camps, Community Service Organizations, Counseling, Day Care, Emergency Relief, People with Disabilities, Recreation & Athletics, Scouts, Senior Services, Substance Abuse, United Funds/United Ways, YMCA/YWCA/YMHA/YWHA, Youth Organizations

Application Procedures

Initial Contact: Send a brief letter of inquiry.
Deadlines: None.

Foundation Officials

John H. Greve: trustee
Lowell K. Hall: secretary
Everett J. Hermanson: trustee
Thor J. Jenson: trustee

Grants Analysis

Disclosure Period: calendar year ending 2001
Total Grants: $178,651*
Number of Grants: 30
Average Grant: $4,436*
Highest Grant: $50,000
Lowest Grant: $250
Typical Range: $1,000 to $10,000
***Note:** Giving excludes scholarship and United Way. Average grant figure excludes highest grant.

Recent Grants

Note: Grants derived from 2001 Form 990.

General

50,000	Iowa College Foundation, Des Moines, IA -- library challenge
30,000	United Way of North Central Iowa, Mason City, IA -- annual fund drive
20,000	Iowa College Foundation, Des Moines, IA -- Net Library
12,000	Clear Lake, Clear Lake, IA -- public library
10,000	American Red Cross, Idaho Falls, ID -- New York Disaster Fund
8,500	Boy Scouts of America - Winnebago Council-- log cabin
8,000	Francis Lauer Youth Services, Mason City, IA -- equipment
7,500	Fertile Fire Department, Fertile, IA -- new fire truck funds
7,200	Pioneer Museum and Historical Society, IA -- museum repairs
6,000	Mason City, Mason City, IA -- trees forever plantings

KINNEY MEMORIAL FOUNDATION

Giving Contact

Thomas W. Bindert, Vice President & Trust Officer
c/o Bank of New York, Tax Dept.
1290 Ave. of the Americas
New York, NY 10104
Phone: (212)635-1520

Description

Founded: 1992
EIN: 136968427
Organization Type: Private Foundation
Giving Locations: no restrictions.
Grant Types: General Support.

Financial Summary

Total Giving: $243,143 (2002); $258,496 (2000); $234,461 (1999)
Assets: $3,780,134 (2002); $5,779,069 (2000); $6,278,176 (1999)
Gifts Received: $100 (1992)

Typical Recipients

Arts & Humanities: Arts & Humanities-General, Historic Preservation, History & Archaeology, Libraries, Theater
Civic & Public Affairs: Botanical Gardens/Parks, Clubs, Civic & Public Affairs-General, Housing, Law & Justice, Public Policy, Safety, Urban & Community Affairs
Education: Arts/Humanities Education, Colleges & Universities, Community & Junior Colleges, International Studies, Legal Education, Minority Education, Preschool Education, Private Education (Precollege), Science/Mathematics Education, Secondary Education (Private), Special Education
Environment: Environment-General, Resource Conservation
Health: AIDS/HIV, Clinics/Medical Centers, Diabetes, Eyes/Blindness, Heart, Hospitals, Medical Research, Mental Health
International: Foreign Educational Institutions, International Relief Efforts
Religion: Churches, Religion-General, Religious Organizations, Religious Welfare
Social Services: At-Risk Youth, Child Welfare, Community Service Organizations, Crime Prevention, Emergency Relief, Food/Clothing Distribution, People with Disabilities, Recreation & Athletics, Senior Services, Youth Organizations

Application Procedures

Initial Contact: Send a brief letter of inquiry.
Deadlines: None.

Additional Information

Trust(s): The Bank New York

Foundation Officials

Edward Holloway, Jr.: trustee
George R. Kinney: trustee
Josephine J. Kinney: trustee

Grants Analysis

Disclosure Period: calendar year ending 2002
Total Grants: $243,143
Number of Grants: 25
Average Grant: $6,754*
Highest Grant: $81,048
Lowest Grant: $1,000
Typical Range: $1,000 to $10,000
*Note: Average grant figure excludes highest grant.

Recent Grants

Note: Grants derived from 2002 Form 990.

General

81,047	Flatbush Tompkins Congregation Church of Brooklyn, Brooklyn, NY
25,000	Estes Park Volunteer Fire Department, Inc., Estes Park, CO
10,000	Bucknell University, Lewisburg, PA
10,000	Canadensis United Methodist Church
10,000	Carroll College, Milwaukee, WI
10,000	Estes Park Medical Center Foundation, Inc., Estes Park, CO
10,000	Estes Park Senior Citizen Center, Inc., Estes Park, CO
10,000	Freedom From Hunger, Davis, CA
10,000	Lucille Packard Children's Fund, Stanford, CA
10,000	Presbyterian Church of Sunnydale

KIPLINGER FOUNDATION

Giving Contact

Andrea Wilkes, Secretary
1729 H Street, Northwest
Washington, DC 20006
Phone: (202)887-6559
Fax: (202)496-1817

Description

Founded: 1948
EIN: 520792570
Organization Type: Family Foundation
Giving Locations: DC: Washington including metropolitan area
Grant Types: Capital, Challenge, Employee Matching Gifts, Endowment, General Support, Multiyear/Continuing Support, Project.

Donor Information

Founder: The foundation was incorporated in 1948 by the late Willard M. Kiplinger .

Financial Summary

Total Giving: $1,670,970 (2001); $2,241,529 (2000); $2,500,000 (1999 approx). Note: 1997 Giving includes matching gifts ($86,603).
Giving Analysis: Giving for 2000 includes: foundation grants to United Way ($30,000); foundation matching gifts ($105,064) 1998: foundation matching gifts ($94,359)
Assets: $19,598,144 (2001); $22,309,250 (2000); $22,039,635 (1998)
Gifts Received: $250,000 (1993). Note: Contributions were received from the Kiplinger Washington Editors, Inc.

Typical Recipients

Arts & Humanities: Arts Associations & Councils, Arts Centers, Arts Institutes, Ballet, Arts & Humanities-General, Historic Preservation, History & Archaeology, Libraries, Literary Arts, Museums/Galleries, Music, Opera, Performing Arts, Public Broadcasting, Theater
Civic & Public Affairs: Business/Free Enterprise, Civil Rights, Community Foundations, Economic Development, Employment/Job Training, Civic & Public Affairs-General, Hispanic Affairs, Housing, Law & Justice, Legal Aid, Nonprofit Management, Philanthropic Organizations, Professional & Trade Associations, Public Policy, Safety, Urban & Community Affairs, Women's Affairs
Education: Arts/Humanities Education, Business Education, Business Education, Colleges & Universities, Community & Junior Colleges, Education Funds, Elementary Education (Public), Engineering/Technological Education, Faculty Development, Education-General, International Exchange, Journalism/Media Education, Literacy, Minority Education, Private Education (Precollege), Public Education (Precollege), Science/Mathematics Education, Secondary Education (Private), Secondary Education (Public), Student Aid
Environment: Environment-General
Health: Cancer, Children's Health/Hospitals, Emergency/Ambulance Services, Health Organizations, Hospices, Hospitals, Medical Rehabilitation, Mental Health, Nursing Services, Public Health, Research/Studies Institutes
International: Foreign Arts Organizations, International Relations
Religion: Churches, Dioceses, Religion-General, Jewish Causes, Religious Welfare
Science: Science Exhibits & Fairs, Science Museums
Social Services: Child Welfare, Community Centers, Community Service Organizations, Family Planning, Family Services, Food/Clothing Distribution, Homes, People with Disabilities, Recreation & Athletics, Senior Services, Sexual Abuse, Shelters/Homelessness, Substance Abuse, United Funds/United Ways, Volunteer Services, Youth Organizations

Application Procedures

Initial Contact: The foundation requests applications be made in writing.
Application Requirements: Written proposals must state the purpose and the background of the organization, and provide proof of tax-exempt status.
Deadlines: None.
Review Process: The board meets four to five times a year. Decisions are made within three to six months.

Restrictions

Grants are limited to education, health, welfare, civic, and cultural organizations. No grants or scholarships are made to individuals.

Additional Information

The foundation reported that it was not considering any new proposals at the end of 1997.
On-going obligations and proposals from organizations that have been funded in the past have priority over applications for new programs.
Publications: Application Guidelines

Foundation Officials

David M. Daugherty: treasurer
Lucinda P. Janke: trustee
Austin Huntington Kiplinger: president, trustee B Washington, DC September 19, 1918. ED Cornell University AB (1939); Harvard University (1939-1940). PRIM CORP EMPL chairman, director: Kiplinger Washington Editors Inc. CORP AFFIL chairman: Fairview Properties; director: Outlook Inc.; chairman, director: Editors Press Service Inc.
Knight Austin Kiplinger: trustee B Washington, DC 1948. ED Cornell University BA (1969); Princeton University (1969-1970). PRIM CORP EMPL president,

publisher, director: Kiplinger Washington Editors Inc. CORP AFFIL director: Fairview Properties. NONPR AFFIL member: Society American Business Editors & Writers; member: Society Professional Journalists; member advisory board: Mount Vernon Ladies Association; director: Oratorio Society; trustee: Greater Washington Research Center; member advisory board: Levine School Music. CLUB AFFIL National Press Club.

Todd Lawrence Kiplinger: trustee PRIM CORP EMPL vice chairman, director: Kiplinger Washington Editors Inc.

Andrea Wilkes: secretary, trustee

Grants Analysis

Disclosure Period: calendar year ending 2001
Total Grants: $1,565,980*
Number of Grants: 103
Average Grant: $12,902*
Highest Grant: $250,000
Lowest Grant: $100
Typical Range: $5,000 to $25,000
*Note: Giving excludes matching gifts and United Way. Average grant figure excludes highest grant.

Recent Grants

Note: Grants derived from 2001 Form 990.

General

250,000	Historical Society of Washington, Washington, DC
100,000	Cornell University, Ithaca, NY -- ornithology lab
100,000	Saint Andrew's Episcopal School, Bethesda, MD
100,000	Stone Ridge School of the Sacred Heart, Bethesda, MD
91,500	National Press Foundation, Washington, DC
75,000	Tudor Place Foundation, Washington, DC
50,000	Lab School of Washington, Washington, DC
50,000	Ohio State University Kiplinger Fellows, Columbus, OH
50,000	Saint Stephen's & St. Agnes Schools, Alexandria, VA
42,500	National Symphony Orchestra, Washington, DC

KIPLINGER WASHINGTON EDITORS, INC.

Company Headquarters

1729 H Street NW
Washington, DC 20006
Web: http://www.kiplinger.com

Company Description

Revenue: US$34.5 million (2001)
Employees: 150 (2001)
SIC(s): 2700 Printing & Publishing, 7300 Business Services.

Operating Locations

Kiplinger Washington Editors (DC--Washington; MD--Hyattsville)

Giving Contact

Todd Kiplinger, Vice Chairman and Director
1729 H St. NW
Washington, DC 20006
Phone: (202)887-6400
Fax: (202)887-6655
E-mail: tkiplinger@kiplinger.com

Description

Organization Type: Corporate Giving Program
Giving Locations: DC: Washington metro area
Grant Types: Employee Matching Gifts, Project.

Financial Summary

Total Giving: $25,000 (1999 approx); $25,000 (1998 approx); $50,000 (1997 approx)

Application Procedures

Initial Contact: Send a brief letter of inquiry.
Application Requirements: Include a description of organization, amount requested, purpose of funds sought, and proof of tax-exempt status.

Restrictions

Does not fund individuals, religious organizations for sectarian purposes, political or lobbying groups, or organizations outside operating areas.

Additional Information

Company gives through the Kiplinger Foundation.

Corporate Officials

Austin Huntington Kiplinger: chairman, director B Washington, DC September 19, 1918. ED Cornell University AB (1939); Harvard University (1939-1940). PRIM CORP EMPL chairman, director: Kiplinger Washington Editors Inc. CORP AFFIL chairman: Fairview Properties; director: Outlook Inc.; chairman, director: Editors Press Service Inc.

Knight Austin Kiplinger: president, publisher, director B Washington, DC 1948. ED Cornell University BA (1969); Princeton University (1969-1970). PRIM CORP EMPL president, publisher, director: Kiplinger Washington Editors Inc. CORP AFFIL director: Fairview Properties. NONPR AFFIL member: Society American Business Editors & Writers; member: Society Professional Journalists; member advisory board: Mount Vernon Ladies Association; director: Oratorio Society; trustee: Greater Washington Research Center; member advisory board: Levine School Music. CLUB AFFIL National Press Club.

Todd Lawrence Kiplinger: vice chairman, director PRIM CORP EMPL vice chairman, director: Kiplinger Washington Editors Inc.

James Otis Mayo: vice chairman, secretary, director B Philadelphia, MS 1920. ED Mississippi State University (1941); George Washington University (1961). PRIM CORP EMPL vice chairman, secretary, director: Kiplinger Washington Editors. CORP AFFIL director: Outlook; president: Shadow Lake Groves; director: May Properties Inc.; director: Fairview Properties; director: Magazine Services.

Corbin M. Wilkes: vice president finance B Washington, DC 1946. ED Hampden-Sydney College (1968); Rutgers University (1972). PRIM CORP EMPL vice president finance: Kiplinger Washington Editors. CORP AFFIL chairman: Magazine Services; treasurer: Outlook; treasurer: KCMississippi Inc.; treasurer: Editors Press; treasurer: Fairview Properties.

Grants Analysis

Typical Range: $100 to $1,000

F. M. KIRBY FOUNDATION

Giving Contact

S. Dillard Kirby, Executive Director
17 DeHart Street
PO Box 151
Morristown, NJ 07963-0151
Phone: (973)538-4800
Web: http://fdncenter.org/grantmaker/kirby/

Description

Founded: 1931
EIN: 516017929
Organization Type: Family Foundation

Giving Locations: NJ: Morristown; NC: Hillsborough; PA: Wilkes-Barre some giving nationally.
Grant Types: Capital, Conference/Seminar, Endowment, Fellowship, General Support, Project.

Donor Information

Founder: Established in 1931 by the late Fred M. Kirby (1861-1940). In 1912, Mr. Kirby merged his interest in a chain of variety stores with F. W. Woolworth Company. He was a trustee of Lafayette College and a director of Wilkes-Barre Hospital, Wilkes-Barre YMCA, and the Wyoming Seminary. Mr. Kirby's son, Allan P. Kirby , was also a major contributor to the foundation, endowing it with approximately $10 million in Alleghany Corporation stock through his will in 1973. The Kirby family's fortune also stems from holdings in such companies as Alleghany Corporation, Investors Diversified Services, and Pittston Company.

Financial Summary

Total Giving: $19,866,828 (2002); $21,871,720 (2001); $26,358,521 (2000)
Giving Analysis: Giving for 1999 includes: foundation fellowships ($15,000); foundation grants to United Way ($417,500); 1998: foundation grants to United Way ($310,000); 1997: foundation grants to United Way ($225,000)
Assets: $465,996,621 (2001); $529,489,116 (2000); $550,964,930 (1999)

Typical Recipients

Arts & Humanities: Arts Associations & Councils, Arts Festivals, Community Arts, Ethnic & Folk Arts, History & Archaeology, Libraries, Museums/Galleries, Opera, Performing Arts, Public Broadcasting, Theater
Civic & Public Affairs: African American Affairs, Botanical Gardens/Parks, Civil Rights, Economic Policy, Civic & Public Affairs-General, Philanthropic Organizations, Professional & Trade Associations, Public Policy, Urban & Community Affairs, Zoos/Aquariums
Education: Business Education, Colleges & Universities, Education Associations, Education Funds, Education Reform, Elementary Education (Private), Education-General, International Exchange, International Studies, Journalism/Media Education, Medical Education, Private Education (Precollege), Religious Education, Science/Mathematics Education, Special Education, Student Aid
Environment: Air/Water Quality, Environment-General, Resource Conservation
Health: AIDS/HIV, Alzheimers Disease, Arthritis, Cancer, Children's Health/Hospitals, Emergency/Ambulance Services, Eyes/Blindness, Health-General, Geriatric Health, Health Funds, Health Organizations, Heart, Hospices, Hospitals, Medical Rehabilitation, Medical Research, Nursing Services, Public Health, Respiratory, Single-Disease Health Associations, Transplant Networks/Donor Banks
International: Health Care/Hospitals, International Affairs, International Organizations
Religion: Churches, Missionary Activities (Domestic), Religious Organizations, Religious Welfare, Seminaries
Science: Science Museums, Scientific Centers & Institutes
Social Services: Animal Protection, At-Risk Youth, Child Welfare, Community Centers, Community Service Organizations, Domestic Violence, Emergency Relief, Family Planning, Family Services, Food/Clothing Distribution, People with Disabilities, Recreation & Athletics, Shelters/Homelessness, Substance Abuse, United Funds/United Ways, YMCA/YWCA/YMHA/YWHA, Youth Organizations

Application Procedures

Initial Contact: Applications must be in written form, signed by an official, and addressed to the foundation. There is no formal application form.
Application Requirements: Proposals should include a report on the use of previous grants, if applicable; a report on current activities; a declaration of the

amount sought; a full description of the reasons for the current solicitation; an assertion as to whether it is for general operations, a specific project, capital needs, or endowment; a roster of directors (trustees) and principal officers; a copy of the audited financial statement; and a copy of the valid IRS tax exemption letter.

Deadlines: Proposals are considered throughout the year. Proposals received after October 31 are filed for consideration in the following year.

Review Process: The foundation does not grant interviews to grant applicants. Unsuccessful applicants do not receive notification.

Restrictions

The foundation does not fund organizations which have applied for tax-exempt status, but have not as yet received it; organizations outside the IRS regulations; or public foundations. No grants are made to individuals, fund-raising or underwriting of events such as benefits, charitable dinners, or sporting events. No loans are made.

Additional Information

Grants usually are reflective of personal interest by one or more members of the Kirby family.
Publications: Information Brochure

Foundation Officials

Thomas J. Bianchini: secretary, treasurer
Alice Kirby Horton: director
Fred M. Kirby, III: director
Fred Morgan Kirby: president, director B Wilkes-Barre, PA November 23, 1919. ED Lafayette College BA (1942); Harvard University (1947); Saint Joseph's University LLD (1981); Lafayette College LLD (1984). PRIM CORP EMPL chairman, member executive committee, director: Alleghany Corp. CORP AFFIL director: World Minerals Inc.; director: Celite Corp. NONPR AFFIL director: United Cerebal Palsy Research & Education Foundation Inc.; member: Zeta Psi; director: National Football Foundation; vice chairman: College Hall Fame Inc. CLUB AFFIL Westmoreland Country Club; Treyburn Country Club; Morris County Golf Club; Spring Valley Hunt Club.
Jefferson Walker Kirby: director B Summit, NJ 1961. ED Lafayette College BA (1984); Duke University MBA (1987). PRIM CORP EMPL vice president: Alleghany Corp. CORP AFFIL director: Sentius Corp.; director: Eldorado Bancshares; director: Connecticut Surety Corp.; director: Covenant Group Inc.; director: Alleghany Asset Management; director: Commerce Security Bancorp Inc. NONPR AFFIL trustee: The Peck School; member: Zeta Psi; volunteer: Green Village Volunteer Fire Department; director: National Football Foundation; director: College Hall Fame Inc. CLUB AFFIL Morris County Golf Club; University Club; Mendham Valley Gun Club.
S. Dillard Kirby: vice president, director
Walker D. Kirby: vice president, director
Paul B. Mott, Jr.: executive director

Grants Analysis

Disclosure Period: calendar year ending 2001
Total Grants: $21,265,720*
Number of Grants: 362
Average Grant: $46,571*
Highest Grant: $2,500,000
Lowest Grant: $1,500
Typical Range: $5,000 to $75,000
*Note: Giving excludes United Way and fellowship. Average grant figure excludes two highest grants ($4,500,000).

Recent Grants

Note: Grants derived from 2001 Form 990.

General

2,500,000 Wake Forest University, Winston-Salem, NC -- Support and name the F M Kirby Wing of Colloway Hall

2,000,000 Children's Hospital, Boston, MA -- Further support of the FM Kirby Director of the Division of Neuroscience

1,600,000 Kennedy Krieger Institute, Baltimore, MD -- Toward the new 3 0 Telsa machine within the F. M. Kirby Center for Functional Brain Imaging

1,000,000 Lawrenceville School, Lawrenceville, NJ -- reserved for future decision

750,000 Lafayette College, Easton, PA -- Athletics Enhancement Endowment Funds

673,000 Lafayette College, Easton, PA -- Reserved for future decision number two account

500,000 Alzheimer's Disease and Related Disorders Association, Inc, Chicago, IL -- Alzheimer's research

500,000 American Cancer Society Foundation, Atlanta, GA -- Cancer Research

500,000 Zachary and Elizabeth M Fisher Center for Alzheimer's Research Foundation, New York, NY -- New Research initiatives in Alzheimer's and Parkinson diseases

484,000 Scheie Eye Institute, Philadelphia, PA -- To fund the purchase of the Zeiss LSM 510

KIRKPATRICK FOUNDATION, INC.

Giving Contact

Susan Shaw-McCalmont, Executive Director
1200 N.W. 63rd, Suite 500
PO Box 268822
Oklahoma City, OK 73126-8822
Phone: (405)840-2882
Fax: (405)840-2946
E-mail: kfi@compuserve.com

Description

Founded: 1955
EIN: 730701736
Organization Type: Family Foundation
Former Name: Kirkpatrick Foundation.
Giving Locations: OK: Oklahoma City including metropolitan area
Grant Types: General Support, Matching, Project, Seed Money.

Donor Information

Founder: Incorporated in 1955 by Eleanor B. Kirkpatrick, John E. Kirkpatrick, and Joan E. Kirkpatrick.

Financial Summary

Total Giving: $1,635,240 (2002); $2,452,670 (2001); $1,000,905 (2000)
Assets: $26,844,013 (2002); $34,601,964 (2001); $40,333,460 (2000)
Gifts Received: $9,931,250 (1999); $159,557 (1998); $10,305,625 (1997)

Typical Recipients

Arts & Humanities: Arts Associations & Councils, Arts Centers, Arts Festivals, Arts Funds, Arts Institutes, Ballet, Dance, Ethnic & Folk Arts, Film & Video, Arts & Humanities-General, Historic Preservation, History & Archaeology, Libraries, Museums/Galleries, Music, Opera, Performing Arts, Public Broadcasting, Theater
Civic & Public Affairs: Asian American Affairs, Community Foundations, Economic Development, Civic & Public Affairs-General, Housing, Legal Aid, Municipalities/Towns, Public Policy, Urban & Community Affairs, Zoos/Aquariums
Education: Arts/Humanities Education, Colleges & Universities, Education-General, Gifted & Talented Programs, International Studies, Literacy, Medical

Education, Private Education (Precollege), Public Education (Precollege), Science/Mathematics Education, Secondary Education (Private)
Environment: Environment-General, Resource Conservation
Health: Children's Health/Hospitals, Clinics/Medical Centers, Emergency/Ambulance Services, Heart, Hospitals, Medical Research, Public Health, Single-Disease Health Associations
International: International Relations, Missionary/Religious Activities
Religion: Churches, Religion-General, Ministries, Religious Organizations, Religious Welfare, Synagogues/Temples
Science: Science Museums, Scientific Centers & Institutes
Social Services: Animal Protection, Camps, Child Welfare, Community Centers, Community Service Organizations, Crime Prevention, Domestic Violence, Family Planning, Family Services, Food/Clothing Distribution, People with Disabilities, Recreation & Athletics, Senior Services, Social Services-General, United Funds/United Ways, Youth Organizations

Application Procedures

Initial Contact: For assistance, contact Ms. Teresa Brekke, Program Officer, or Ms. Susan McCalmont, Executive Director, at 405/840-2882, or e-mail kfi@compuserve.com.
Application Requirements: Grant proposals should include the following information: a two-page preliminary letter summarizing the request is required no later than 5:00 p.m. on January 15, April 15, and July 15. The preliminary letter must include the amount to be requested, a brief summary of the project or program for which funding is needed, and your e-mail address if applicable. All mailed proposals must be sent to the Post Office Box.
Deadlines: Grant proposals are due on the 15th of February, May, and August for consideration in March, June, and September, respectively.
Review Process: The foundation's board of trustees makes funding decisions at quarterly meetings.

Restrictions

Grants are not made to individuals. Health care, mental health, social welfare, lobbying organizations, and school trips.

Additional Information

The foundation reports an affiliation with the Oklahoma City Community Foundation.
Faxed requests are not accepted.
Publications: Annual Report; Application Guidelines

Foundation Officials

Nancy Anthony: advisor
Donald Balaban: director B Caldwell, KS 1932. ED Kansas State University (1953); Oklahoma City University (1961). PRIM CORP EMPL senior vice president, senior trustee officer: Liberty Bank & Trust Oklahoma City NA. NONPR AFFIL director: Lyric Theatre; trustee: Omniplex; member: Lions International; member: American Bar Association; director: Goodwill Industries.
John L. Belt: director PRIM CORP EMPL secretary: Capital Mortgage Co. CORP AFFIL treasurer: Kirkpatrick Oil Co. Inc.; director: Texas Guaranty National Bank.
Douglas R. Cummings: honorary director B 1929. PRIM CORP EMPL chairman: Cummings Oil Co.
Dan Hogan: director B 1933. PRIM CORP EMPL chairman, director: Hogan Publishing Co. CORP AFFIL chairman: Hogan Information Services.
Joe Howell: director
Christian Kirkpatrick Keesee: vice president, director B Oklahoma City, OK 1961. ED Menlo College AA (1983); Harvard University (1985); Pepperdine

University (1984-1985); University of Central Oklahoma BS (1991). PRIM CORP director, director: American Bancorp Oklahoma. CORP AFFIL chairman, director: American Bank & Trust.

Joan E. Kirkpatrick: chairman PRIM CORP EMPL chairman, president, chief executive officer, director: Kirkpatrick Oil Co. Inc.

John Elson Kirkpatrick: honorary chairman, director B Oklahoma City, OK February 13, 1908. ED United States Military Academy (1925-1926); United States Naval Academy BS (1931); Harvard University Graduate School of Business Administration (1935-1936); Oklahoma City University LLD (1963); Bethany Nazarene College HHD (1967). PRIM CORP EMPL chairman: Kirkpatrick Oil Co. Inc. NONPR AFFIL honorary chairman board director: Presbyterian Home; honorary consult: Republic of Korea; honorary director: Oklahoma State Fair; life trustee: Oklahoma Zoological Society; member: Oklahoma Heritage Association; director emeritus: Oklahoma Historical Society; member advisory board: Oklahoma Health Sciences Center; founder, director: Oklahoma City Community Foundation; member: Oklahoma County Historical Society; life director: Oklahoma City Chamber of Commerce; director, president: Oklahoma Center Science & Arts; member, life board member: Oklahoma City Art Museum; director emeritus, honorary life trustee: National Cowboy Hall of Fame Western Heritage Center; director: Kirkpatrick Science Air Space Museum Omniplex; honorary chairman: Lyric Theatre Oklahoma; member: Industrial Petroleum Association; trustee: Falcon Foundation; member: Harvard Area Group; member: Asia Society Oklahoma; honorary life director: 45th Infantry Division Museum; member: Allied Arts Foundation. CLUB AFFIL Rotary Club; Men's Dinner Club; Oklahoma City Petroleum Club; Economic Club.

Linda P. Lambert: director

Eleanor Johnson Maurer: treasurer, director B Milan, MO 1914. ED Stephens College (1930-1931); Southwestern University (1932); Draughons Business College (1933). NONPR AFFIL director Oklahoma City chapter: English Speaking Union. CLUB AFFIL member: Rotary Club.

Susan McCalmont: executive director

Kathy McCord: secretary

Dr. Anne Hodges Morgan: vice president, director

Marilyn B. Myers: adv

Charles E. Nelson: chairman, director B 1944. ED Oklahoma State University (1965). PRIM CORP EMPL chairman emeritus: Bank One Oklahoma.

George Jeffrey Records: director B Saint Louis, MO 1934. ED Dartmouth College (1956). PRIM CORP EMPL chairman: Midland Mortgage. CORP AFFIL director: Wilson Foods Corp.; chairman: Midfirst Bank; chairman: Midland Financial Co.; director: Bonray Energy Corp. NONPR AFFIL director: Sunbeam Family Services Association; director: United Way Greater Oklahoma City; director: Oklahoma Chamber of Commerce.

Robert E. Torray: director PRIM CORP EMPL president: Robert E. Torray & Co. Inc.

Max Weitzenhoser: director

Grants Analysis

Disclosure Period: calendar year ending 2001
Total Grants: $2,452,670*
Number of Grants: 77
Average Grant: $31,853*
Highest Grant: $215,000
Lowest Grant: $1,000
Typical Range: $5,000 to $20,000
*Note: Grants analysis provided by foundation.

Recent Grants

Note: Grants derived from 2000 Form 990.

General

75,000	Oklahoma City Art Museum, Oklahoma City, OK
74,860	University of Central Oklahoma Foundation, Edmond, OK
60,000	Oklahoma City University, Oklahoma City, OK
57,332	Allied Arts Foundation, Oklahoma City, OK
50,000	Ballet Oklahoma, Oklahoma City, OK
50,000	Oklahoma Baptist University, Shawnee, OK
50,000	Oklahoma Cultural Coalition, Oklahoma City, OK
46,000	Oklahoma Zoological Society, Oklahoma City, OK
34,000	Oklahoma Philharmonic Society, Oklahoma City, OK
25,000	Community Council - Central Oklahoma, Oklahoma City, OK

KITZMILLER/BALES TRUST

Giving Contact

Robert U. Hansen, Trustee
PO Box 96
Wray, CO 80758
Phone: (970)332-3484

Description

Founded: 1984
EIN: 846178085
Organization Type: Private Foundation
Giving Locations: CO: East Yuma County School District
Grant Types: Capital, Operating Expenses, Project.

Donor Information

Founder: the late Edna B. Kitzmiller

Financial Summary

Total Giving: $431,003 (2001); $455,962 (2000); $537,597 (1999)
Assets: $9,578,910 (2001); $10,687,181 (2000); $11,469,540 (1999)

Typical Recipients

Arts & Humanities: Arts Associations & Councils, History & Archaeology, Libraries, Museums/Galleries, Performing Arts
Civic & Public Affairs: Civic & Public Affairs-General, Municipalities/Towns, Safety, Urban & Community Affairs
Education: Elementary Education (Public), Education-General, Literacy, Public Education (Precollege), Science/Mathematics Education, Secondary Education (Public)
Environment: Environment-General
Health: Emergency/Ambulance Services, Eyes/Blindness, Health Organizations, Hospices, Hospitals, Medical Rehabilitation
Social Services: Child Welfare, Community Centers, Community Service Organizations, Family Services, Recreation & Athletics, Scouts, Senior Services, Substance Abuse, Youth Organizations

Application Procedures

Initial Contact: Send a brief letter of inquiry and a full proposal in writing.
Deadlines: None.

Restrictions

Benefit vicinity of Yuma County within East Yuma County S.D. RJ-2.

Additional Information

Trust(s): Farmers State Bank

Foundation Officials

Duard Fix: trustee
Robert U. Hansen: trustee

Grants Analysis

Disclosure Period: calendar year ending 2001
Total Grants: $431,003
Number of Grants: 10

Highest Grant: $123,290
Lowest Grant: $2,000

Recent Grants

Note: Grants derived from 2001 Form 990.

General

123,290	City of Wray, Wray, CO -- for improvements and projects
91,492	Wray Rehabilitation and Public Activities Center, Wray, CO -- for improvements and projects
87,145	Wray Community District Hospital, Wray, CO -- equipment
83,963	East Yuma County School District, Wray, CO -- for improvements and projects
25,000	Renotta Health Care Systems, Inc., Wray, CO -- furniture
5,113	Baby Bear Hugs, Inc., Wray, CO -- Visitor Program
5,000	Hospice of the Plains, Inc., Wray, CO -- operating funds
5,000	Yuma County Fire Protection District, Wray, CO -- vehicle purchase
3,000	Yuma County Youth Center, Wray, CO -- improvements
2,000	Northeast Colorado Bookmobile Services, Wray, CO -- books

ROBERT J. KLEBERG, JR. AND HELEN C. KLEBERG FOUNDATION

Giving Contact

Robert L. Washington, Grants Coordinator
700 North Saint Mary's Street, Suite 1200
San Antonio, TX 78205
Phone: (210)271-3691
Fax: (210)271-9089

Description

Founded: 1950
EIN: 746044810
Organization Type: Family Foundation
Giving Locations: TX: nationally.
Grant Types: Capital, General Support, Multiyear/Continuing Support, Operating Expenses, Project, Research.

Donor Information

Founder: The foundation was established in Texas in 1950 with funds donated by Robert J. Kleberg Jr. , and his wife, Helen C. Kleberg . Mr. Kleberg was the grandson of Richard King, the founder of King Ranch, and he served as executive officer of the ranch for 56 years. He originated the Santa Gertrudis breed of beef cattle, bred horses, championed wildlife conservation, and initiated worldwide agricultural research. His wife shared these interests, and she participated in a variety of cultural and civic activities.

Financial Summary

Total Giving: $9,985,828 (2000); $8,061,147 (1998); $7,857,305 (1997)
Assets: $208,987,899 (2000); $205,280,834 (1998); $193,591,250 (1997)

Typical Recipients

Arts & Humanities: Arts Associations & Councils, Ballet, Ethnic & Folk Arts, Arts & Humanities-General, Historic Preservation, History & Archaeology, Libraries, Museums/Galleries, Music, Performing Arts, Public Broadcasting, Theater, Visual Arts
Civic & Public Affairs: Botanical Gardens/Parks, Economic Development, Housing, Nonprofit Management, Rural Affairs, Urban & Community Affairs, Zoos/Aquariums

Education: Agricultural Education, Arts/Humanities Education, Business Education, Colleges & Universities, Engineering/Technological Education, Faculty Development, International Studies, Literacy, Medical Education, Private Education (Precollege), Public Education (Precollege), Science/Mathematics Education, Special Education

Environment: Environment-General, Resource Conservation, Wildlife Protection

Health: Alzheimers Disease, Cancer, Children's Health/Hospitals, Clinics/Medical Centers, Emergency/Ambulance Services, Eyes/Blindness, Health-General, Health Organizations, Heart, Hospitals, Kidney, Medical Rehabilitation, Medical Research, Nursing Services, Research/Studies Institutes, Respiratory, Speech & Hearing, Transplant Networks/Donor Banks, Trauma Treatment

International: Health Care/Hospitals

Religion: Religious Welfare

Science: Observatories & Planetariums, Scientific Centers & Institutes, Scientific Research

Social Services: Camps, Community Centers, Counseling, Crime Prevention, Domestic Violence, Family Planning, Family Services, Food/Clothing Distribution, People with Disabilities, Recreation & Athletics, Scouts, Shelters/Homelessness, Social Services-General, Youth Organizations

Application Procedures

Initial Contact: Send a brief letter of inquiry full proposal on organization's letterhead.

Application Requirements: A full proposal should include a brief history of the organization, profile of the proposed project illustrating the need for such a project, outline of how the funds will be used and the specific amount requested, proof of tax-exempt status, a letter of approval signed by the organization's chief administrator, and a copy of the organizations exemption letter from the I.R.S.

Deadlines: None.

Review Process: The board meets in June and December.

Restrictions

The governing instrument directs that contributions be made to support biomedical research, veterinary science, and wildlife. Grants for other purposes favor organizations in south Texas. The foundation does not fund individuals, endowments, deficit financing, ongoing operating expenses, community organizations outside of Texas, organizations limited by race or religion, or groups that are not tax-exempt. The Foundation does not fund indirect costs or overhead for research projects.

Additional Information

Recipients must submit periodic progress reports and a financial record to the foundation.

Publications: Information Brochure; Annual Report

Foundation Officials

Helen C. Alexander: vice president, director

John D. Alexander, Jr.: secretary, vice president B 1954. PRIM CORP EMPL president: Alexander Production Co.

John Boyd Carter, Jr.: director B Fort Worth, TX 1924. ED Kemper Military School (1941-1943); University of Texas (1943-1946); Babson College (1946-1947). CORP AFFIL director: Sterling Bancshares; president, director: High Prairie Ranch Co.; director: Pogo Producing Co.; chairman: BCM Tech Inc. NONPR AFFIL member: Sigma Alpha Epsilon; member: U.S. Seniors Golf Association; member: Houston Society Financial Analysts; director: Private Enterprise Research Corp. Texas A&M University; trustee: Baylor College Medicine Howard Florey Institute; member: Houston Committee Foreign Relations. CLUB AFFIL Pilgrims Club; Brook Club; Houston Country Club; Bayou Club.

Henrietta A. George: director

Emory A. Hamilton: vice president, treasurer

Dorothy A. Matz: director PRIM NONPR EMPL assistant secretary, director: U.S. Equestrian Team.

Hugh Virgil Sherrill: director B Long Beach, CA 1920. ED Yale University (1942); Yale University JD (1948). PRIM CORP EMPL senior director: Prudential Securities Inc.

Grants Analysis

Disclosure Period: calendar year ending 2000

Total Grants: $9,985,828

Number of Grants: 51

Average Grant: $122,621*

Highest Grant: $2,100,000

Lowest Grant: $2,500

Typical Range: $10,000 to $50,000 and $250,000 to $500,000

*Note: Average grant excludes 3 highest grant.

Recent Grants

Note: Grants derived from 2000 Form 990.

General

2,100,000	Baylor College of Medicine, Houston, TX -- rat genome sequencing project
1,000,000	Foxcroft School, Middleburg, VA -- capital campaign
1,000,000	Vanderbilt Ingram Cancer Center, Nashville, TN -- genetics/genomic project
980,000	University of Texas M.D. Anderson Cancer Center, Houston, TX -- molecular genetics laboratory
500,000	Memorial Sloan-Kettering Cancer Center, New York, NY -- induced differentiation project
400,000	Memorial Sloan-Kettering Cancer Center, New York, NY -- cancer vaccine development
350,000	Salk Institute, La Jolla, CA -- neuropeptide research continuation
267,426	University of Pennsylvania, Philadelphia, PA -- veterinary research projects
262,000	Southwest Foundation for Biomedical Research, San Antonio, TX -- melanoma research continuation
250,000	Howard Florey Biomedical Foundation, San Antonio, TX -- Neuroendocrinology Research Programs

CONRAD AND VIRGINIA KLEE FOUNDATION

Giving Contact

Clayton M. Axtell, Jr., President
700 Security Mutual Bldg.
80 Exchange St.
Binghamton, NY 13901
Phone: (607)754-2504

Description

Founded: 1957

EIN: 156019821

Organization Type: Private Foundation

Giving Locations: NY: especially Broome County and Guilford

Grant Types: General Support, Operating Expenses.

Donor Information

Founder: the late Conrad C. Klee, the late Virginia Klee

Financial Summary

Total Giving: $919,693 (2002); $992,318 (2001); $1,168,145 (2000)

Giving Analysis: Giving for 2002 includes: foundation grants to United Way ($115,566); 2000: foundation grants to United Way ($110,000); 1999: foundation grants to United Way ($100,446)

Assets: $15,950,372 (2002); $18,289,283 (2001); $24,125,631 (1999)

Gifts Received: $1,017,130 (1992). Note: In 1992, contributions were received from Elise Coons ($791,184) and Margaret Bratton ($225,946).

Typical Recipients

Arts & Humanities: Arts Associations & Councils, Arts Centers, Historic Preservation, History & Archaeology, Libraries, Museums/Galleries, Music, Opera, Public Broadcasting

Civic & Public Affairs: Clubs, Economic Development, Civic & Public Affairs-General, Housing, Municipalities/Towns, Public Policy, Rural Affairs, Safety, Urban & Community Affairs, Zoos/Aquariums

Education: Arts/Humanities Education, Colleges & Universities, Education Funds, Education-General, Health & Physical Education, Religious Education, Science/Mathematics Education

Health: Emergency/Ambulance Services, Health-General, Health Organizations, Hospices, Hospitals, Public Health

Religion: Churches, Religious Organizations, Religious Welfare

Science: Science Museums, Scientific Centers & Institutes

Social Services: Animal Protection, Community Centers, Community Service Organizations, Counseling, Crime Prevention, Family Planning, Family Services, Food/Clothing Distribution, Homes, People with Disabilities, Recreation & Athletics, Scouts, Shelters/Homelessness, Social Services-General, United Funds/United Ways, YMCA/YWCA/YMHA/YWHA, Youth Organizations

Application Procedures

Initial Contact: Send a brief letter of inquiry and a full proposal.

Application Requirements: Include a description of organization, amount requested, purpose of funds sought, and proof of tax-exempt status.

Deadlines: None.

Restrictions

Does not support individuals.

Foundation Officials

Wells Allen, Jr.: director

Clayton M. Axtell, III: director

Clayton M. Axtell, Jr.: president

Linda Biemer: director

David Birchenough: vice president

John E. Gwyn: director

Floyd Lawson: director

Robert Nash: director

David K. Patterson: secretary

Grants Analysis

Disclosure Period: calendar year ending 2002

Total Grants: $804,127*

Number of Grants: 52

Average Grant: $12,558*

Highest Grant: $90,533

Lowest Grant: $1,263

Typical Range: $1,000 to $20,000

*Note: Giving excludes United Way. Average grant figure excludes two highest grants ($176,244).

Recent Grants

Note: Grants derived from 2001 Form 990.

General

113,300	Broome County United Way, Binghamton, NY -- operations
83,333	WSKG, Binghamton, NY -- capital project
60,000	Our Lady of Lourdes Hospital, Norfolk, NE -- capital project
50,000	Broome County of Churches, Binghamton, NY -- capital projects
50,000	Center for Health and Healing, Inc., New York, NY -- create a positive place for those touched by AD/HD

50,000	Phelps Mansion Foundation, Binghamton, NY -- capital projects
50,000	Roberson Museum and Science Center, Binghamton, NY -- building expansion
50,000	Sheltered Workshop for The Disabled -- operations
50,000	Tri-Cities Opera, Binghamton, NY -- expansion of set and costume construction and rental department
39,286	Samaritan Counseling Center -- operations

CHARLES AND FIGA KLINE FOUNDATION

Giving Contact
Fabian I. Fraenkel, Director
626 N. Main St.
Allentown, PA 18104
Phone: (610)437-4077

Description
Founded: 1957
EIN: 236262315
Organization Type: Private Foundation
Giving Locations: PA: Allentown
Grant Types: General Support.

Donor Information
Founder: the late Charles Kline, the late Figa Cohen Kline

Financial Summary
Total Giving: $385,840 (fiscal year ending October 31, 2001); $411,348 (fiscal 2000); $411,920 (fiscal 1999)
Giving Analysis: Giving for fiscal 2001 includes: foundation grants to United Way ($10,000); fiscal 2000: foundation grants to United Way ($10,000); fiscal 1999: foundation grants to United Way ($10,000)
Assets: $8,462,768 (fiscal 2001); $9,080,259 (fiscal 2000); $9,105,823 (fiscal 1999)

Typical Recipients
Arts & Humanities: Libraries, Museums/Galleries
Civic & Public Affairs: Civil Rights
Education: Arts/Humanities Education, Colleges & Universities, International Studies, Private Education (Precollege), Religious Education
Health: Hospitals, Medical Rehabilitation
International: Missionary/Religious Activities
Religion: Churches, Religion-General, Jewish Causes, Religious Organizations, Religious Welfare, Synagogues/Temples
Social Services: Community Centers, Community Service Organizations, People with Disabilities, Scouts, United Funds/United Ways, Youth Organizations

Application Procedures
Initial Contact: The foundation has no formal grant application procedure or application form.
Deadlines: September 30.

Restrictions
Does not support individuals.

Foundation Officials
Fabian I. Fraenkel: director
Stewart Furmansky: director
Leonard Rapoport: director

Grants Analysis
Disclosure Period: fiscal year ending October 31, 2001
Total Grants: $375,840*
Number of Grants: 21
Average Grant: $5,727*

Highest Grant: $210,000
Lowest Grant: $320
Typical Range: $1,000 to $10,000
*Note: Giving excludes United Way. Average grant excludes two highest grants ($267,020).

Recent Grants
Note: Grants derived from 2000 Form 990.

General
210,000	Jewish Federation of Lehigh Valley, Lehigh Valley, PA
65,481	Jewish Community Center, Allentown, PA
31,000	Jewish Day School, Allentown, PA
22,000	Congregational Sons of Israel
10,447	Jewish Family Services, Philadelphia, PA
10,000	United Way of Lehigh Valley, PA
7,500	Girls Club, Allentown, PA
6,500	Congregation Keneseth Israel, Allentown, PA
5,000	Anti-Defamation League of B'nai B'rith
5,000	Sacred Heart Foundation

JOSIAH W. AND BESSIE H. KLINE FOUNDATION

Giving Contact
John A. Obrock, Secretary
515 S. 29th St.
Harrisburg, PA 17104
Phone: (717)561-4373
Fax: (717)561-0826

Description
Founded: 1952
EIN: 236245783
Organization Type: General Purpose Foundation
Giving Locations: PA
Grant Types: Capital, Challenge, General Support, Loan, Matching, Multiyear/Continuing Support.

Donor Information
Founder: Incorporated in 1952 by the late Josiah W. Kline and the late Bessie H. Kline .

Financial Summary
Total Giving: $1,276,290 (2001); $1,287,628 (2000); $1,202,200 (1999)
Giving Analysis: Giving for 2000 includes: foundation grants to United Way ($50,000); 1999: foundation scholarships ($2,000); foundation grants to United Way ($100,000); 1998: foundation grants to United Way ($50,000)
Assets: $23,580,713 (2001); $25,650,712 (2000); $26,358,189 (1999)

Typical Recipients
Arts & Humanities: Arts Associations & Councils, Arts Centers, Historic Preservation, History & Archaeology, Libraries, Museums/Galleries, Music, Opera, Performing Arts, Public Broadcasting, Theater
Civic & Public Affairs: Botanical Gardens/Parks, Business/Free Enterprise, Clubs, Economic Policy, Employment/Job Training, Civic & Public Affairs-General, Hispanic Affairs, Housing, Professional & Trade Associations, Public Policy, Safety
Education: Afterschool/Enrichment Programs, Business Education, Colleges & Universities, Community & Junior Colleges, Education Funds, Education Reform, Environmental Education, Education-General, Legal Education, Literacy, Minority Education, Public Education (Precollege), Public Education (Precollege), Religious Education, Science/Mathematics Education, Student Aid
Environment: Forestry, Environment-General, Resource Conservation

Health: Alzheimers Disease, Arthritis, Cancer, Children's Health/Hospitals, Clinics/Medical Centers, Diabetes, Emergency/Ambulance Services, Health-General, Health Organizations, Heart, Hospices, Hospitals, Kidney, Medical Rehabilitation, Medical Research, Mental Health, Multiple Sclerosis, Nursing Services, Outpatient Health Care, Public Health, Single-Disease Health Associations
International: Foreign Arts Organizations
Religion: Churches, Jewish Causes, Ministries, Religious Welfare
Science: Science Museums
Social Services: Animal Protection, Big Brother/Big Sister, Camps, Child Welfare, Community Centers, Community Service Organizations, Emergency Relief, Family Planning, Family Services, Food/Clothing Distribution, People with Disabilities, Recreation & Athletics, Scouts, Shelters/Homelessness, Social Services-General, Special Olympics, Substance Abuse, United Funds/United Ways, Volunteer Services, YMCA/YWCA/YMHA/YWHA, Youth Organizations

Application Procedures
Initial Contact: The foundation requests applications be made in writing.
Application Requirements: Written applications should include the name, location, and purpose of the organization requesting assistance, qualifications of requesting organization budget, any support that will be received from other sources, amount requested and dates of need, and proof of tax-exempt status.
Deadlines: None.
Review Process: Board of Directors review requests in May and November.

Restrictions
The foundation only makes grants to tax-exempt charities; organization must provide documentation of IRS 501(c)(3) status. The foundation does not support individuals, endowment funds, operating budgets, special projects, publications, conferences, fellowships, or loans. Normally, grants are not made to State or Federal affiliated Schools, Colleges, or Universities.

Additional Information
Publications: Guidelines

Foundation Officials
Jeffrey John Burdge: director B London, United Kingdom 1922. ED Youngstown State University. PRIM CORP EMPL director: Harsco Corp.
Derek C. Hathaway: director B 1944. ED Aston University BS (1965). PRIM CORP EMPL chairman, chief executive officer: Harsco Corp.
William Joseph King: vice president, treasurer, director B Philadelphia, PA 1929. ED University of Pennsylvania Wharton School (1954); LaSalle University MBA (1979). PRIM CORP EMPL chairman, chief executive officer: Dauphin Deposit Bank & Trust Co. CORP AFFIL director: Hempt Brothers; director: Millers Mutual Insurance Co.
James Earl Marley: director B Marietta, PA 1935. ED Pennsylvania State University BS (1957); Drexel Institute of Technology MS (1963). PRIM CORP EMPL chairman, director: AMP Inc. CORP AFFIL director: Harsco Corp.; director: Armstrong World Industries Inc. NONPR AFFIL member: Institute Electrical & Electronics Engineers; member: Manufacturing Council Machinery & Allied Products Institute; member: American Society Mechanical Engineers; member: Harrisburg Chamber of Commerce; member: American Management Association. CLUB AFFIL Harrisburg Country Club.
Robert F. Nation: president, director B 1926. ED Elizabethtown College (1947). PRIM CORP EMPL former president, director: Penn Harris Co. CORP AFFIL treasurer: Sun Enterprises Inc.; treasurer: Sun

Motor Cars Inc.; director: Phico Insurance Co.; director: Phico Service Co.; treasurer: Mansun North Inc.; director: Phico Group Inc.; director: Harsco Corp.
Samuel D. Ross, Jr.: trustee B 1933. ED Susquehanna University. PRIM NONPR EMPL president, chief executive officer, director: Medical Service Association of Pennsylvania. CORP AFFIL chairman: Highmark Inc.
John A. Russell: director
David A. Smith: director

Grants Analysis

Disclosure Period: calendar year ending 2001
Total Grants: $1,276,290
Number of Grants: 54
Average Grant: $18,775*
Highest Grant: $200,000
Lowest Grant: $500
Typical Range: $10,000 to $40,000
*Note: Average grant figure excludes two highest grants ($300,000).

Recent Grants

Note: Grants derived from 2001 Form 990.

Library-Related

50,000	Dauphin County Library System, Harrisburg, PA -- support construction
50,000	Lebanon Valley College, Carlisle, PA -- finish and equip classroom
2,000	Marysville - Rye Library Association, Marysville, PA -- painting improvements to main floor

General

200,000	Pinnacle Health Foundation, Harrisburg, PA -- commitment to caring campaign
100,000	Harrisburg Area YMCA, Harrisburg, PA -- project to renovate and improve YMCA facilities
50,000	Boy Scouts of America Keystone Area Council, Mechanicsburg, PA -- Camp Hidden Valley improvements
50,000	Goodwill Industries of Central Pennsylvania, Harrisburg, PA -- Building Program
50,000	Messiag College, Grantham, PA -- student union
50,000	Susquehanna University, Selinsgrove, PA -- support equipment and technology
50,000	Tri-County United Way, Harrisburg, PA -- 2001 campaign
50,000	Wilson College, Chambersburg, PA -- library automation project
49,700	Whitaker Center for Science and the Arts, Harrisburg, PA -- learning posts
40,000	Dickinson College, Carlisle, PA -- Kline Center Annex, building addition

Esther A. And Joseph Klingenstein Fund, Inc.

Giving Contact

John Klingenstein, President
787 Seventh Avenue, 6th Floor
New York, NY 10019-6016
Phone: (212)492-6181
Fax: (212)492-7007

Description

Founded: 1946
EIN: 136028788
Organization Type: Family Foundation
Giving Locations: nationally.
Grant Types: Fellowship, General Support, Multiyear/Continuing Support, Operating Expenses, Project, Research, Scholarship.

Donor Information

Founder: The Esther A. and Joseph Klingenstein Fund was established in 1946 with the late Esther Adler Klingenstein and Joseph Klingenstein as donors. Mr. and Mrs. Klingenstein were contributors to Mount Sinai Hospital, with gifts including a chair in psychiatry and contributions toward a clinical center. They were also founding sponsors of the Mount Sinai School of Medicine. Mr. Klingenstein was chairman emeritus of the Mount Sinai Medical Center and was a senior partner in the investment banking firm of Wertheim and Company.

Financial Summary

Total Giving: $6,943,318 (fiscal year ending September 30, 2000); $6,964,060 (fiscal 1999); $6,137,512 (fiscal 1998)
Giving Analysis: Giving for fiscal 2000 includes: foundation scholarships ($3,000); foundation fellowships ($1,080,000); fiscal 1999: foundation fellowships ($1,230,000) fiscal 1998: foundation fellowships ($1,370,000)
Assets: $159,039,612 (fiscal 2000); $140,576,947 (fiscal 1999); $133,063,974 (fiscal 1997)
Gifts Received: $16,819 (fiscal 2000); $271,869 (fiscal 1997); $107,766 (fiscal 1992)

Typical Recipients

Arts & Humanities: History & Archaeology, Libraries, Museums/Galleries
Civic & Public Affairs: Botanical Gardens/Parks, Business/Free Enterprise, Civil Rights, First Amendment Issues, Gay/Lesbian Issues, Civic & Public Affairs-General, Philanthropic Organizations, Public Policy, Urban & Community Affairs, Women's Affairs
Education: Colleges & Universities, Education Associations, Education Funds, Education Reform, Engineering/Technological Education, Environmental Education, Faculty Development, Education-General, Health & Physical Education, Medical Education, Minority Education, Private Education (Precollege), Public Education (Precollege), Science/Mathematics Education
Environment: Environment-General, Protection
Health: Adolescent Health Issues, Cancer, Children's Health/Hospitals, Clinics/Medical Centers, Hospitals, Hospitals (University Affiliated), Medical Research, Mental Health, Preventive Medicine/Wellness Organizations, Public Health, Research/Studies Institutes, Single-Disease Health Associations
International: Foreign Educational Institutions, International Environmental Issues
Religion: Churches, Jewish Causes, Religious Organizations, Religious Welfare, Social/Policy Issues
Science: Science Museums, Scientific Centers & Institutes, Scientific Labs, Scientific Organizations
Social Services: Child Welfare, Family Planning, People with Disabilities, Youth Organizations

Application Procedures

Initial Contact: The fund has no specific application form. The proposal should be in writing. For the annual Klingenstein Fellowship Awards in the Neurosciences, contact the fund for application form and brochure.
Application Requirements: Proposals should include the following: a description of the proposed project or program its purpose, desired outcome, and how these outcomes will be evaluated; amount requested; project and/or organizational budget and other sources of support received or being sought; information about the organization, its latest audited financial statement, and a copy of its IRS tax-exemption letter.
Deadlines: None for general grants; December for Klingenstein neuroscience fellowships.
Review Process: The fund's directors meet four or five times a year to review proposals.
Notes: All applicants are informed in writing of the action taken by the fund, whether the proposal is approved or not.

Restrictions

The fund rarely contributes to endowments, buildings, or other types of capital projects.

Additional Information

Recipients must submit substantive and financial reports annually and at the conclusion of the grant period, and maintain a systematic record of payments and receipts, available to the fund on request.
Publications: Descriptive Brochure; Application for Fellowship Program

Foundation Officials

Frederick A. Klingenstein: first vice president, secretary, director B New York, NY 1931. ED Yale University BA (1953); Harvard University Graduate School of Business Administration (1953-1954); Saint Lawrence University LHD (1986). PRIM CORP EMPL chairman, partner: Klingenstein Fields & Co. LP ADD CORP EMPL president: Sherry-Netherland Inc. CORP AFFIL director: Whitley Products Inc.; director: Arch Petroleum Inc.; director: Pogo Producing Co. NONPR AFFIL trustee: American Museum Natural History; chairman: Mount Sinai Medical Center.
John Klingenstein: president, treasurer, director PRIM CORP EMPL general partner: Klingenstein Fields & Co. LP.

Grants Analysis

Disclosure Period: fiscal year ending September 30, 2000
Total Grants: $5,860,318*
Number of Grants: 120
Average Grant: $49,940*
Highest Grant: $1,000,468
Lowest Grant: $1,000
Typical Range: $5,000 to $40,000 and $100,000 to $500,000
*Note: Giving excludes fellowships. Scholarships.

Recent Grants

Note: Grants derived from fiscal 2000 Form 990.

Library-Related

500,000	New York Public Library, New York, NY

General

1,000,468	Teachers College Columbia University, New York, NY
500,000	Mt. Sinai Medical Center, New York, NY
500,000	Teachers College Columbia University, New York, NY
400,000	Deerfield Academy, Deerfield, MA
300,000	American Museum of Natural History, New York, NY
200,000	Yale University School of Medicine, New Haven, CT
187,500	UJA-Federation, New York, NY
100,000	Cold Spring Harbor Laboratory Association, Cold Spring Harbor, NY -- Watson School
100,000	Jewish Home and Hospital for the Aged, New York, NY
75,000	American Jewish Committee, New York, NY

Klingestein Fund

Giving Contact

Lee P. Klingenstein, President
31 Oxford Rd.
Scarsdale, NY 10583
Phone: (212)476-9000

Description

Founded: 1940
EIN: 136077894
Organization Type: Private Foundation
Giving Locations: CA; CO; CT; MA; NJ; NY; NC; VT

Grant Types: Emergency, Fellowship, General Support, Multiyear/Continuing Support, Project, Research.

Donor Information

Founder: Lee Paul Klingestein, Paul H. Klingestein

Financial Summary

Total Giving: $910,430 (2001); $392,394 (2000); $296,710 (1999)
Giving Analysis: Giving for 1998 includes: foundation grants to United Way ($3,750)
Assets: $5,618,606 (2001); $7,775,968 (2000); $7,722,446 (1999)
Gifts Received: $540,490 (2001); $438,688 (1999); $1,462,316 (1998). Note: In 2001, contributions were received from direct public support. In 1999, contributions were received from Paul H. Klingestein. In 1998, contributions were received from Lee P. Klingenstein ($1,321,938) and Frances Klingenstein ($140,377). In 1996, contributions were received from Paul H. Klingestein.

Typical Recipients

Arts & Humanities: Arts Associations & Councils, Arts Institutes, Ballet, History & Archaeology, Libraries, Museums/Galleries, Music, Public Broadcasting
Civic & Public Affairs: Botanical Gardens/Parks, Civic & Public Affairs-General, Legal Aid, Philanthropic Organizations, Public Policy, Urban & Community Affairs, Women's Affairs
Education: Afterschool/Enrichment Programs, Colleges & Universities, Leadership Training, Minority Education, Preschool Education, Private Education (Precollege), Public Education (Precollege)
Environment: Environment-General, Resource Conservation, Wildlife Protection
Health: AIDS/HIV, Cancer, Children's Health/Hospitals, Clinics/Medical Centers, Hospices, Hospitals, Long-Term Care, Medical Research
International: International Environmental Issues, International Peace & Security Issues, International Relief Efforts
Religion: Churches, Jewish Causes, Religious Welfare
Social Services: Camps, Child Welfare, Community Service Organizations, Delinquency & Criminal Rehabilitation, Family Planning, Family Services, United Funds/United Ways, Veterans, YMCA/YWCA/YMHA/YWHA

Application Procedures

Initial Contact: Submit a letter stating charitable purpose and proof of tax-exempt status.
Deadlines: None.

Additional Information

The Klingestein Fund primarily supports a private school and a wilderness program. In addition, the fund gives support for universities and other education and Jewish organizations.

Foundation Officials

Alan L. Klingestein: treasurer
Lee P. Klingestein: president
Paul H. Klingestein: vice president
Joanne K. Ziesing: secretary

Grants Analysis

Disclosure Period: calendar year ending 2001
Total Grants: $914,430
Number of Grants: 188
Average Grant: $1,859*
Highest Grant: $250,000
Typical Range: $500 to $5,000
*Note: Average grant figure excludes three highest grants ($565,000).

Recent Grants

Note: Grants derived from 2001 Form 990.

General
250,000	Juma Ventures, San Francisco, CA
215,000	Outward Bound, Asheville, NC
100,000	Taft School, Watertown, CT
50,000	Juma Ventures, San Francisco, CA
25,000	African Elephant Conservation Trust
25,000	Outward Bound, Asheville, NC
25,000	Vermont Academy, Saxtons River, VT
15,000	Harbor Schools, Newbury, MA
15,000	Princeton University, Princeton, NJ
11,000	Vail Valley Institute, Vail Valley, CO

ERNEST CHRISTIAN KLIPSTEIN FOUNDATION

Giving Contact

Marion C. White, Secretary
Village Rd.
PO Box 278
New Vernon, NJ 07976
Phone: (973)538-4445

Description

Founded: 1954
EIN: 226028529
Organization Type: Private Foundation
Giving Locations: CA; CT; IL; MA; NJ
Grant Types: Emergency, General Support, Project.

Donor Information

Founder: Kenneth H. Klipstein

Financial Summary

Total Giving: $178,045 (2001); $152,293 (2000); $200,835 (1999)
Assets: $3,792,562 (2001); $4,500,985 (2000); $4,540,580 (1999)

Typical Recipients

Arts & Humanities: Arts Associations & Councils, Arts Centers, Arts Funds, Community Arts, Libraries, Museums/Galleries, Music, Opera, Performing Arts, Public Broadcasting, Theater
Civic & Public Affairs: Community Foundations, Civic & Public Affairs-General, Public Policy, Safety, Urban & Community Affairs
Education: Business Education, Colleges & Universities, Education Reform, Engineering/Technological Education, Education-General, Legal Education, Private Education (Precollege), Public Education (Precollege), School Volunteerism, Science/Mathematics Education, Secondary Education (Public), Student Aid
Environment: Air/Water Quality, Environment-General, Resource Conservation, Watershed
Health: AIDS/HIV, Cancer, Children's Health/Hospitals, Clinics/Medical Centers, Emergency/Ambulance Services, Health Funds, Health Organizations, Hospitals, Medical Rehabilitation, Medical Research, Nursing Services, Prenatal Health Issues, Public Health, Research/Studies Institutes
International: International Environmental Issues, International Organizations
Religion: Churches, Jewish Causes, Religious Organizations
Science: Scientific Centers & Institutes, Scientific Labs
Social Services: Animal Protection, Camps, Community Centers, Community Service Organizations, Domestic Violence, Family Planning, Homes, Recreation & Athletics, Scouts, United Funds/United Ways, YMCA/YWCA/YMHA/YWHA, Youth Organizations

Application Procedures

Initial Contact: The foundation has no formal grant application procedure or application form.
Deadlines: None.

Restrictions

Does not support individuals.

Foundation Officials

David C. Klipstein: vice president
David H. Klipstein: president
Pamela Klipstein: treasurer
Pamela Klipstein Smith: vice president
Marion C. White: secretary

Grants Analysis

Disclosure Period: calendar year ending 2001
Total Grants: $178,045
Number of Grants: 67
Average Grant: $2,135*
Highest Grant: $35,000
Lowest Grant: $100
Typical Range: $500 to $5,000
*Note: Average grant figure excludes highest grant.

Recent Grants

Note: Grants derived from 2001 Form 990.

General
35,000	Women's Crisis Services, Flemington, NJ
30,000	Earth Justice Legal Defense Fund, San Francisco, CA
25,000	MIT, Cambridge, MA
25,000	Princeton University, Princeton, NJ
10,525	Rutgers Preparatory School, Somerset, NJ
5,200	Rutgers University Foundation, New Brunswick, NJ
5,000	Community Coalition, Chester Springs, PA
3,000	Upper Raritan Watershed Association, Gladstone, NJ
2,600	San Diego State University, San Diego, CA -- KPBS
2,500	Far Hills Country Day School, Far Hills, NJ

JAY E. KLOCK AND LUCIA KLOCK KINGSTON FOUNDATION

Giving Contact

Meri Beth Cummings, Assistant Vice President
c/o Key Trust Co.
2637 Wall St.
Kingston, NY 12401
Phone: (914)339-6752

Description

Founded: 1966
EIN: 146038479
Organization Type: Private Foundation
Giving Locations: NY: Kingston and Ulster counties
Grant Types: General Support.

Financial Summary

Total Giving: $295,500 (2000); $176,100 (1999); $210,000 (1995)
Giving Analysis: Giving for 2000 includes: foundation grants to United Way ($6,000); 1999: foundation matching gifts ($2,550) foundation grants to United Way ($10,500)
Assets: $5,545,555 (2000); $5,589,250 (1999); $4,381,558 (1995)

Typical Recipients

Arts & Humanities: Libraries, Music, Performing Arts

Civic & Public Affairs: Civic & Public Affairs-General, Philanthropic Organizations

Education: Business Education, Community & Junior Colleges, Education-General, Literacy, Student Aid

Health: Cancer, Children's Health/Hospitals, Health-General, Health Organizations, Heart, Hospices, Hospitals, Medical Research, Mental Health

Science: Science Museums, Scientific Centers & Institutes

Social Services: Child Welfare, Community Service Organizations, Family Services, Homes, People with Disabilities, Scouts, Social Services-General, Substance Abuse, United Funds/United Ways, YMCA/YWCA/YMHA/YWHA, Youth Organizations

Application Procedures

Initial Contact: Send a brief letter of inquiry. with a full proposal.

Application Requirements: Include a description of organization, amount requested, purpose of funds sought, recently audited financial statement, and proof of tax-exempt status.

Deadlines: Applications are due at the end of each calendar quarter.

Restrictions

Does not fund administrative purposes or expenses.

Additional Information

Trust(s): KeyBank NA

Grants Analysis

Disclosure Period: calendar year ending 2000
Total Grants: $289,500*
Number of Grants: 91
Average Grant: $3,181*
Highest Grant: $10,000
Typical Range: $1,000 to $10,000
*Note: Giving excludes United Way.

Recent Grants

Note: Grants derived from 1999 Form 990.

Library-Related

8,000	Kingston Area Library, Kingston, NY

General

10,000	UCCC Foundation
8,000	United Way, Dubuque, IA
5,000	Benedictine Health Foundation, Kingston, NY
5,000	Benedictine Health Foundation, Kingston, NY
5,000	Benedictine Health Foundation, Kingston, NY
5,000	Benedictine Health Foundation, Kingston, NY
5,000	Kingston Hospital Foundation, Kingston, NY
5,000	Kingston Hospital Foundation, Kingston, NY
5,000	Kingston Hospital Foundation, Kingston, NY
5,000	YMCA

ROSE AND LOUIS KLOSK FUND

Giving Contact

Nathan R. Cooper, co-Trustee
PO Box 31412 S-5
Rochester, NY 14603
Phone: (716)258-5330

Description

Founded: 1970
EIN: 136328994
Organization Type: Private Foundation
Giving Locations: CT; NM; NY; NC
Grant Types: Emergency, General Support, Multiyear/Continuing Support, Research.

Donor Information

Founder: the late Louis Klosk

Financial Summary

Total Giving: $320,000 (2001); $304,000 (2000); $345,000 (1999)
Assets: $6,558,628 (2001); $6,992,798 (2000); $7,377,144 (1999)

Typical Recipients

Arts & Humanities: Arts Associations & Councils, Libraries, Music, Opera

Civic & Public Affairs: Community Foundations, Civic & Public Affairs-General, Women's Affairs

Education: Colleges & Universities, Medical Education, Private Education (Precollege), Science/Mathematics Education

Health: Cancer, Children's Health/Hospitals, Clinics/Medical Centers, Geriatric Health, Health Organizations, Home-Care Services, Hospitals, Kidney, Long-Term Care, Medical Research, Multiple Sclerosis, Single-Disease Health Associations

International: International-General, Health Care/Hospitals, International Relations, Missionary/Religious Activities

Religion: Jewish Causes, Religious Organizations, Synagogues/Temples

Social Services: Child Abuse, Community Service Organizations, Domestic Violence, Homes, People with Disabilities, Senior Services, United Funds/United Ways

Application Procedures

Initial Contact: The foundation has no formal grant application procedure or application form.
Deadlines: None.

Additional Information

Trust(s): JPMorgan Chase Bank

Foundation Officials

Barry Cooper: trustee
Nathan Cooper: trustee

Grants Analysis

Disclosure Period: calendar year ending 2001
Total Grants: $320,000
Number of Grants: 38
Average Grant: $8,421
Highest Grant: $35,000
Lowest Grant: $1,000
Typical Range: $1,000 to $15,000

Recent Grants

Note: Grants derived from 2001 Form 990.

General

35,000	Columbia University College of Physicians and Surgeons, New York, NY
35,000	United Jewish Appeal, New York, NY
35,000	Weill Medical College of Cornell University, New York, NY
25,000	Sid Jacobson Jewish Community Center, New York, NY
20,000	Hadassah, New York, NY
20,000	Hebrew Home for the Aged in Riverdale, Riverdale, NY
20,000	Laura Rosenberg Foundation, Hewlett, NY
18,000	Women's League for Israel, New York, NY
15,000	Bar-Ilan University, New York, NY
10,000	Hebrew Hospital Home, Inc., West Hartford, CT

KNAPP FOUNDATION (CA)

Giving Contact

Janis Minton, Senior Program Advisor
10100 Santa Monica Blvd., Suite 2000
Los Angeles, CA 90067-4003
Phone: (310)553-7810
Fax: (310)553-7688

Description

Founded: 1993
EIN: 954416658
Organization Type: Private Foundation
Giving Locations: CA; MA; NM; NY
Grant Types: General Support.

Donor Information

Founder: Established in 1993 by Cleon T. Knapp.

Financial Summary

Total Giving: $3,755,649 (fiscal year ending September 30, 2001); $449,133 (fiscal 2000); $510,700 (fiscal 1999)
Assets: $4,171,294 (fiscal 2001); $9,837,191 (fiscal 2000); $9,257,122 (fiscal 1999)
Gifts Received: $461,272 (fiscal 1996); $1,365,000 (fiscal 1993)

Typical Recipients

Arts & Humanities: Ethnic & Folk Arts, Libraries, Museums/Galleries, Music, Opera

Education: Arts/Humanities Education, Colleges & Universities, Education Funds, Education-General, Health & Physical Education, Private Education (Precollege)

Environment: Forestry

Health: Alzheimers Disease, Cancer, Children's Health/Hospitals, Clinics/Medical Centers, Health-General, Kidney, Medical Research, Prenatal Health Issues

Religion: Religious Welfare

Social Services: Child Welfare, Community Service Organizations

Application Procedures

Initial Contact: Send a brief letter of inquiry.
Application Requirements: Include purpose of organization, geographic area and population served, brief description of project, amount requested, budget, and proof of tax-exempt status.
Deadlines: August

Restrictions

Foundation does not support individuals, religious activities, political or lobbying groups, publiclic policy research, fund-raising, or general endowments.

Foundation Officials

H. Stephen Cranston: secretary
Cleon Talboys Knapp: president B Los Angeles, CA 1937. ED University of California, Los Angeles (1955-1958). PRIM CORP EMPL president: Talwood Corp. NONPR AFFIL director, trustee: Sante Fe Opera; board visitors: University California Los Angeles John E Anderson Graduate School Management; director, trustee: Museum Contemporary Art; director, trustee: Fulfillment Fund; director, trustee: Los Angeles County Museum; chairman, trustee: Craft & Folk Art Museum; chairman, trustee: Art Center College Design. CLUB AFFIL Regency Club; Eagle Springs Golf Club; Bel-Air Country Club; Country Club Rockies.
Elizabeth W. Knapp: vice president
Karl H. Loring, CPA: chief financial officer

Grants Analysis

Disclosure Period: fiscal year ending September 30, 2001
Total Grants: $3,755,649
Number of Grants: 10
Highest Grant: $1,422,885
Lowest Grant: $1,370
Typical Range: $300,000 to $1,000,000

Recent Grants

Note: Grants derived from fiscal 2000 Form 990.

General

212,375	Santa Fe Opera, Santa Fe, NM -- arts
100,658	Wellesley College, Wellesley, MA -- education
50,000	Art Center College of Design, Pasadena, CA -- education
50,000	Fulfillment Fund, Los Angeles, CA -- education
25,000	Young Black Scholars, Inglewood, CA -- education
5,000	UCLA Athletic Fund, Los Angeles, CA -- education
5,000	UCLA Foundation, Los Angeles, CA -- education
1,000	Native Forest Council, Eugene, OR -- education
100	Pan Mass Challenge, Wellesley, MA -- medicine

KNAPP FOUNDATION, INC. (MD)

Giving Contact

Antoinette P. Vojvoda, President
PO Box O
St. Michaels, MD 21663
Phone: (410)745-5660

Description

Founded: 1929
EIN: 136001167
Organization Type: General Purpose Foundation
Giving Locations: East-coast states.
Grant Types: Matching.

Donor Information

Founder: Incorporated in 1929 by the late Joseph Palmer Knapp .

Financial Summary

Total Giving: $490,923 (2001); $928,313 (1999); $600,161 (1997)
Assets: $25,694,413 (2001); $27,856,300 (1999); $24,955,424 (1997)

Typical Recipients

Arts & Humanities: Film & Video, Historic Preservation, History & Archaeology, Libraries, Museums/Galleries

Civic & Public Affairs: Botanical Gardens/Parks, Civil Rights, Civic & Public Affairs-General, Municipalities/Towns, Public Policy, Safety, Urban & Community Affairs, Zoos/Aquariums

Education: Arts/Humanities Education, Colleges & Universities, Elementary Education (Public), Engineering/Technological Education, Environmental Education, Education-General, Health & Physical Education, Legal Education, Literacy, Medical Education, Private Education (Precollege), Public Education (Precollege), Religious Education, Science/Mathematics Education, Secondary Education (Public), Social Sciences Education, Special Education, Student Aid, Vocational & Technical Education

Environment: Environment-General, Research, Resource Conservation, Watershed, Wildlife Protection

Health: Cancer, Children's Health/Hospitals, Emergency/Ambulance Services, Hospitals, Research/

Studies Institutes, Single-Disease Health Associations

Science: Science-General, Science Museums, Scientific Centers & Institutes, Scientific Labs

Social Services: Child Welfare, Community Service Organizations, People with Disabilities, United Funds/United Ways, Youth Organizations

Application Procedures

Initial Contact: The foundation requests detailed letters of application.
Deadlines: Quarterly.

Restrictions

The foundation does not support individuals or international organizations, or provide funds for loans, scholarships, fellowships, research, endowment or building funds, or operating budgets. The foundation reports that giving to arts and humanities, civic and public affairs, and health and social services organizations is done so by a predetermined list of recipients for annual contribution purposes only.

Additional Information

Publications: Guidelines

Foundation Officials

Ruth M. Capranica: vice president
Steven F. Capranica: treasurer
Krista L. Hodgkin: trustee
Margaret P. Newcombe: trustee
Sylvia V. Penny: trustee PRIM CORP EMPL secretary: George L. Penny Inc.
Antoinette P. Vojvoda: president

Grants Analysis

Disclosure Period: calendar year ending 2001
Total Grants: $490,923
Number of Grants: 31
Average Grant: $16,380*
Highest Grant: $99,530
Lowest Grant: $2,000
Typical Range: $10,000 to $20,000
*Note: Average grant figure excludes highest grant.

Recent Grants

Note: Grants derived from 2001 Form 990.

Library-Related

10,000	American Foundation for Blind, New York, NY -- educational material for special library services
6,000	Currituck County Library, Barco, NC -- for computer equipment

General

99,530	St. Michael's Volunteer Fire Department, St. Michael's, MD -- for equipment acquisition
50,000	St. Mary's College Foundation, St. Mary's City, MD -- for digital database purchases
50,000	University of North Carolina at Chapel Hill, Chapel Hill, NC -- equipment and medical journal acquisitions
25,000	Virginia Living Museum, Newport News, VA -- curriculum resource material multimedia projector
20,000	Maine Coastal Heritage Trust, Topsham, ME -- for computer workstations
20,000	Tufts University School of Veterinary Medicine, North Grafton, MA -- equipment acquisition
15,000	North Carolina Coastal Federation, Newport, NC -- for Learning Center equipment acquisition
11,235	Delaware Nature Society, Hockessin, DE -- equipment acquisition for Education Programs
10,000	American Museum of Natural History, New York, NY
10,000	Boys Club of New York, New York, NY

JOHN S. AND JAMES L. KNIGHT FOUNDATION

Giving Contact

Hodding Carter, III, President & Chief Executive Officer
Wachovia Financial Center, Suite 3300
200 Biscayne Boulevard
Miami, FL 33131
Phone: (305)908-2600
Fax: (305)908-2698
E-mail: publications@knightfdn.org
Web: http://www.knightfdn.org
Note: Grant proposals should be addressed: Attn: Grant Request.

Description

Founded: 1950
EIN: 650464177
Organization Type: Private Foundation
Giving Locations: nationally.
Grant Types: Award, Capital, Challenge, Emergency, Endowment, Fellowship, Matching, Multiyear/Continuing Support, Operating Expenses, Project.
Note: The foundation also funds program-related investments.

Donor Information

Founder: The John S. and James L. Knight Foundation was established in Akron, OH, on December 29, 1950. Its forerunner was the Charles Landon Knight Memorial Education Fund. Upon the death of John S. Knight in 1981, his brother James was elected chairman of the foundation and served in that capacity until his death in February 1991. Foundation funds have been provided by the estates of John S. and James L. Knight and their mother, Clara I. Knight.

Financial Summary

Total Giving: $85,000,000 (2001 approx); $62,500,000 (2000); $53,142,772 (1999)
Assets: $1,900,829,942 (2001); $2,198,985,122 (2000); $1,888,543,168 (1999)
Gifts Received: $300,000 (2001 approx); $400,000 (2000 approx); $699,449 (1996). Note: Since 1991, the foundation has received almost $200,000,000 from the estate of James L. Knight.

Typical Recipients

Arts & Humanities: Arts Associations & Councils, Arts Centers, Arts Funds, Arts Institutes, Arts Outreach, Ballet, Community Arts, Dance, Ethnic & Folk Arts, Film & Video, Arts & Humanities-General, Historic Preservation, History & Archaeology, Libraries, Museums/Galleries, Music, Opera, Performing Arts, Public Broadcasting, Theater

Civic & Public Affairs: African American Affairs, Botanical Gardens/Parks, Clubs, Community Foundations, Economic Development, Employment/Job Training, First Amendment Issues, Civic & Public Affairs-General, Hispanic Affairs, Housing, Municipalities/Towns, Nonprofit Management, Philanthropic Organizations, Professional & Trade Associations, Public Policy, Urban & Community Affairs, Women's Affairs, Zoos/Aquariums

Education: Afterschool/Enrichment Programs, Arts/Humanities Education, Business Education, Colleges & Universities, Community & Junior Colleges, Education Associations, Education Funds, Education Reform, Elementary Education (Public), Engineering/Technological Education, Environmental Education, Faculty Development, Education-General, International Exchange, International Studies, Journalism/Media Education, Legal Education, Literacy, Minority Education, Public Education (Precollege), Science/Mathematics Education, Social Sciences Education, Student Aid, Vocational & Technical Education

Environment: Air/Water Quality

Health: Cancer, Children's Health/Hospitals, Emergency/Ambulance Services, Health Organizations, Hospices, Hospitals, Medical Research, Mental Health, Prenatal Health Issues

International: Foreign Educational Institutions, Human Rights, International Organizations, International Relations, International Relief Efforts

Religion: Ministries, Religious Welfare, Seminaries

Science: Observatories & Planetariums, Science Museums, Scientific Centers & Institutes, Scientific Labs

Social Services: At-Risk Youth, Child Welfare, Community Service Organizations, Day Care, Delinquency & Criminal Rehabilitation, Family Services, Food/Clothing Distribution, Recreation & Athletics, Refugee Assistance, Shelters/Homelessness, Social Services-General, Substance Abuse, United Funds/United Ways, Volunteer Services, YMCA/YWCA/YMHA/YWHA, Youth Organizations

Application Procedures

Initial Contact: Submit a brief letter of inquiry (two pages or less).

Application Requirements: All letters of inquiry should include a description of organization; contact information; amount requested and over what time period the funds are needed; purpose of funds sought and how it fills a public need; the organization's total income and expenditures for the most recent year; and proof of tax-exempt status. In addition to the above information, inquiries submitted to the National Venture Fund or the Knight Community Partners Program should describe the community need(s) addressed; the relationship of the project to the Foundation's funding priorities for the specific community; anticipated results and how they will benefit people in need; the organization's qualifications to carry out the project; the project's relation to the applicant's mission and programmatic goals; the role of any other organizations in planning the project and the nature of their participation.

Deadlines: None, with the exception of special initiatives. Proposals are accepted throughout the year and are reviewed on a rolling basis. If a proposal is considered appropriate and complete, it will be scheduled for board review.

Review Process: Organizations will be contacted if their inquiry has been approved for development into a proposal. Generally, it is approximately six months between proposal submission and board review, but the times may vary depending on the circumstances and timing of a proposal. The board of trustees meets quarterly in March, June, September, and December. Applicants are usually notified of the foundation's decisions in writing within two weeks after the trustees' meeting.

Restrictions

The Foundation prefers not to support fundraising events; operating deficits; charities operated by service clubs; activities that are normally the responsibility of government; medical research, single-disease associations, or hospitals (unless for a community-wide capital campaign with a stated goal and beginning and ending dates, or for specific projects that meet Foundation goals); religious organizations for sectarian purposes; political candidates; memorials; international programs and organizations, except U.S.-based organizations supporting a free press around the world; and conferences, group travel, or honoraria for distinguished guests (except in Foundation initiatives). The Foundation will not generally accept a second request for a capital campaign for which the Foundation has previously approved a grant, or a second proposal from an organization that has applied for support in the last twelve months.

Applications for the National Venture Fund and Knight Community Parters Program must benefit one or more of the Foundation's 26 communities located in the states of California, Colorado, Florida, Georgia, Indiana, Kansas, Kentucky, Minnesota, Mississippi, North Carolina, North Dakota, Ohio, Pennsylvania, South Carolina, and South Dakota. A complete list of the communities is available on the Foundation's web site. needed.

Additional Information

A major portion of the proposals are rejected because they fail to meet published criteria.

Education and Arts and Culture programs award grants nationally and locally (27 communities). Although the journalism program is national in focus, U.S. organizations funded by the foundation may support international journalism organizations.

Publications: Annual Report; Guidelines; Application Form; Quarterly Newsletter

Foundation Officials

Cesar Alvarez: trustee PRIM CORP EMPL president, chief executive officer: Greenberg Traurig.

W. Gerald Austen, MD: chairman, trustee B Akron, OH 1930. ED Massachusetts Institute of Technology BS (1951); Harvard University MD (1955). CORP AFFIL director: Abiomed Inc. NONPR AFFIL fellow: Royal College Surgeons; member: Society University Surgeons; member: New England Cardiovascular Society; life member: Massachusetts Institute Technology; member: National Academy of Sciences Institute Medicine; president, chief executive officer: Massachusetts General Physicians Organization; member: Massachusetts Heart Association; chief surgical services: Massachusetts General Hospital; professor surgery: Harvard University Medical School; trustee: Massachusetts Eye & Ear Infirmary; member: American Heart Association; member: Association Academy of Surgery; member, residency review surgery: American College Surgeons; member: American Board Surgery; director, member: American Board Thoracic Surgery; fellow: American Academy of Arts & Sciences; member: American Association Thoracic Surgery; member: Accreditation Council Graduate Medicine Education.

John Bare: director evaluation ED University of North Carolina BA; University of North Carolina MA; University of North Carolina PhD (1995). PRIM CORP EMPL free-lance columnist: Chapel Hill Herald Sun.

Creed Carter Black: trustee B Harlan, KY 1925. ED Northwestern University BS (1949); University of Chicago MA (1952). PRIM CORP EMPL president, chief executive officer: Knight Ridder Inc. NONPR AFFIL member: Newspapers Association America; president, member: Southern Newspaper Publishers Association; member: Lambda Chi Alpha; member: National Conference Editorial Writers; member: Kappa Tau Alpha. CLUB AFFIL member: Riviera Country Club; member: Bankers Club.

Robert Briggs: trustee

Gary Burger: co-director community partners program

Hodding Carter, III: president, chief executive officer, trustee ED Princeton University (1957). CORP AFFIL director: Dreyfus Strategic Municipals. NONPR AFFIL director: Twentieth Century Fund.

Alvah Herman Chapman, Jr.: trustee B Columbus, GA 1921. ED Citadel BS (1942). PRIM CORP EMPL executive committee, director: Knight-Ridder Inc. CORP AFFIL director: Philadelphia Newspapers Inc.; director: Wichita Eagle & Beacon Publishing Co.; director: RW Page Corp.; director: Northwest Publications Inc.; director: Observer Transportation Co.; director: Detroit Free Press Inc. NONPR AFFIL member: Newspaper Association America; member: Southern Newspaper Publishers Association; chairman emeritus: Florida International University Foundation; director: Miami Coalition Drug-Free Community; chairman: Community Anti-Drug Coalitions America; chairman: Community Partnership Homeless Inc.; member: American Newspaper Publishers Association.

Jill Kathryn Ker Conway: vice chairman, trustee B NW Australia 1934. ED University of Sydney BA (1958); Harvard University PhD (1969). PRIM NONPR AFFIL president emeritus: Smith Colorado. CORP AFFIL director: Nike Inc.; director: Merrill Lynch & Co. Inc.; director: Colgate-Palmolive Co.;

director: Arthur D Little Inc. NONPR AFFIL visiting scholar: Massachusetts Institute Technology.

Marjorie Knight Crane: trustee

Timothy J. Crowe: vice president, chief financial officer

Joe Ervin: co-director community partners program

Paul Grogan: trustee PRIM NONPR EMPL vice president government community & public affairs: Harvard University.

Gordon Emory Heffern: trustee B Utica, PA 1924. ED Stevens Institute of Technology (1944); University of Virginia (1949). CORP AFFIL director: Pioneer-Standard Electronics Inc.; director: A Schulman Inc.; director: Keybank National Assoc.

Scott D.A. Jones: grants administration assistant

Belinda Turner Lawrence: director administration

Michael Maidenberg: trustee

Jorge Martinez: director information NONPR AFFIL member: Foundation Information Systems Managers; member: Hispanics in Philanthropy; technology affinity group: Council on Foundations.

J. Bryan McCullar: manager grants administrator

Penelope McPhee: vice president, chief program officer

Lawrence H. (Bud) Meyer: commun director

Rolfe Neill: trustee B Mount Airy, NC 1932. ED University of North Carolina AB (1954). PRIM CORP EMPL chairman, publisher: Charlotte Observer ADD CORP EMPL chairman, publ: Knight Publishing Co. Inc.

Mariam C. Noland: trustee

Beverly Knight Olson: trustee

John Doyle Ong: trustee B Uhrichsville, OH 1933. ED Ohio State University MA (1954); Ohio State University BA (1954); Harvard University LLB (1957); Kent State University LHD (1982); Ohio State University H (1996); University of Akron H (1996). CORP AFFIL director: TRW Inc.; director: Marsh & McLennan Companies Inc.; director: Geon Co.; chairman emeritus: Goodrich Corp.; director: Cooper Industries Inc.; director: ASARCO Inc. NONPR AFFIL member: Rubber Manufacturers Association; trustee: University Chicago; member: Phi Beta Kappa; chairman: Ohio Historic Society; member: Phi Alpha Theta; member: Ohio Bar Association; member: Chemical Manufacturers Association; member: Conference Board; chairman: Business Roundtable Ohio; member: Business Council. CLUB AFFIL Union League Club; Union Club; Portage Country Club; Rolling Rock Club; Ottawa Shooting Club; The Links Club; Metro Club; Castalia Trout Club.

John W. Rogers, Jr.: trustee

Grants Analysis

Disclosure Period: calendar year ending 2001

Total Grants: $85,337,450*

Number of Grants: 286

Average Grant: $282,482*

Highest Grant: $4,830,000

Typical Range: $5,000 to $50,000 and $100,000 to $250,000

***Note:** Grants analysis based on grants approved in 2001. Giving excludes United Way. Average grant figure excludes highest grant.

Recent Grants

Note: Grants derived from 2001 Form 990.

General

3,000,000 Collins Center for Public Policy, Miami, FL -- for the Civic Partnership and Design center

2,500,000 Trust for Public Land, San Francisco, CA -- for the construction of the pedestrian friendly greenways in Miami's Overtown and East Little Havana neighborhoods

2,500,000 University of Akron, Akron, OH -- to implement the University Park Revitalization Plan

2,000,000 Local Initiatives Support Corporation,

New York, NY -- to strengthen the community development system in Miami's Overtown neighborhood

1,858,000 Child Care Resources, Charlotte, NC -- for Curriculum Matters

1,500,000 Performing Arts Center Trust, Miami, FL -- for five resident companies to move to the new center

1,000,000 Early Childhood Initiative Foundation, Miami, FL -- to launch a community wide child readiness media campaign addressing the needs of children ages 5 and younger

1,000,000 Miami Children's Museum, Miami, FL -- for a capital and endowment campaign for a new 53,000 square foot on Watson Island

1,000,000 Museum of Science, Miami, FL -- to secure public funding and anchor a community capital campaign

1,000,000 United Way of Miami-Dade, Miami, FL -- for the proposed Center of Excellence

MARION I. AND HENRY J. KNOTT FOUNDATION

Giving Contact

M. Gregory Contori, Exec. Dir.
3904 Hickory Avenue
Baltimore, MD 21211-1834
Phone: (410)235-7068
Fax: (410)889-2577
E-mail: knott@knottfoundation.org
Web: http://www.knottfoundation.org

Description

Founded: 1986
EIN: 521517876
Organization Type: Family Foundation
Giving Locations: CA; MD
Grant Types: Capital, Challenge, Endowment, General Support, Matching, Operating Expenses, Project.

Donor Information

Founder: Established in 1978 by Marion I. Knott and Henry J. Knott Sr.

Financial Summary

Total Giving: $1,866,000 (2002 approx); $2,377,520 (2000); $1,675,665 (1998)
Giving Analysis: Giving for 1998 includes: foundation matching gifts ($38,085); 1997: foundation matching gifts ($26,837) 1996: foundation matching gifts ($6,671)
Assets: $49,803,399 (2000); $47,037,416 (1998); $41,070,361 (1997)
Gifts Received: $281,090 (1997)

Typical Recipients

Arts & Humanities: Arts Centers, Arts Festivals, Arts Outreach, History & Archaeology, Libraries, Museums/Galleries, Music, Opera, Public Broadcasting, Theater
Civic & Public Affairs: African American Affairs, Botanical Gardens/Parks, Business/Free Enterprise, Economic Development, Employment/Job Training, Civic & Public Affairs-General, Housing, Legal Aid, Native American Affairs, Parades/Festivals, Professional & Trade Associations, Urban & Community Affairs, Women's Affairs, Zoos/Aquariums
Education: Afterschool/Enrichment Programs, Arts/Humanities Education, Business Education, Colleges & Universities, Continuing Education, Elementary Education (Public), Education-General, Health & Physical Education, Literacy, Medical Education, Minority Education, Preschool Education, Private Education (Precollege), Religious Education, Science/Mathematics Education, Secondary Education (Private), Special Education, Student Aid

Environment: Environment-General
Health: AIDS/HIV, Alzheimers Disease, Cancer, Children's Health/Hospitals, Clinics/Medical Centers, Eyes/Blindness, Health Funds, Health Organizations, Hospices, Medical Rehabilitation, Mental Health, Multiple Sclerosis, Nutrition, Prenatal Health Issues, Preventive Medicine/Wellness Organizations, Public Health, Single-Disease Health Associations, Trauma Treatment
Religion: Churches, Dioceses, Religion-General, Ministries, Religious Organizations, Religious Welfare
Science: Scientific Centers & Institutes
Social Services: At-Risk Youth, Big Brother/Big Sister, Child Welfare, Community Centers, Community Service Organizations, Counseling, Day Care, Delinquency & Criminal Rehabilitation, Family Services, Food/Clothing Distribution, People with Disabilities, Recreation & Athletics, Senior Services, Shelters/Homelessness, Special Olympics, Substance Abuse, YMCA/YWCA/YMHA/YWHA, Youth Organizations

Application Procedures

Initial Contact: The foundation requests that applicants call or write the foundation for formal application guidelines. The request must be presented by telephone to the foundation's executive director before submitting a fully developed written proposal.
Application Requirements: Two copies of the full proposal must be submitted as a formal application. The proposal should include: a cover letter including amount requested; purpose of the program, and a contact name and phone number; concise history, mission statement, current programs, description of volunteers (number and duties); funding request/purpose of grant, statement of need, target population, project outcomes, impact, timetable, project budget, list of key staff, expected results, outcomes and how measured, description of project evaluation, cost effectiveness, funding sources (anticipated, pending, and awarded); list of Board of Directors, description of organizational structure; current IRS Form 990, budget for previous two years, current annual operating budget, two-year projections, current audited financial statement including income expenses, and balance sheet; copy of IRS determination letter; and directions to organization.
Deadlines: February 1 and August 1.
Review Process: The board meets in June and December. Onsite visits are performed for all proposals.
Notes: Foundation does not accept proposals by fax or e-mail. Organizations are required to complete post-grant report one year after receipt of funding.

Restrictions

The foundation does not support individuals, public education, scholarships for education, "pro-choice activities," reproductive health, or political organizations. It does not support organizations that have not been in operation for at least one year, annual giving, one-time only events/seminars/workshops, legal services, the environment, medical research, day care centers, endowment funds for arts/humanities, national/local chapters for specific diseases, agencies that redistribute grants to other nonprofits, or government agencies that form 501 (c)(3) nonprofits to fund public sector projects. Multi-year grants are generally not awarded. awarded.

Additional Information

There are no extensions of the grant deadlines, under any circumstances.
Publications: Annual Report; Application Guidelines

Foundation Officials

Daniel J. Gallagher: treasurer PRIM CORP EMPL vice president, director: Liberty Federal Savings & Loan Association. CORP AFFIL treasurer, director: Gallagher Asphalt Corp.

Lindsay R. Gallagher: trustee
Marty Voelkel Hanssen: trustee, secretary
Kelly L. Harris: trustee
Lindsay Harris: trustee
Thomas K. Harris: trustee
Carlisle V. Hashim: trustee
David L. Knott: trustee
Henry Joseph Knott, Jr: president, chairman, director B Baltimore, MD November 02, 1906. ED College of Notre Dame; Loyola College; Mount Saint Mary's College. CORP AFFIL director: First National Bank Maryland Inc.; director: E I Kane Inc.; director: First Maryland Bancorp.
Marion I. Knott: chairman
Martin G. Knott: trustee B 1949. PRIM CORP EMPL president, director: Martin G. Knott & Associates.
Patty L. Knott: trustee
Teresa A. Knott: trustee B 1949. ED Johns Hopkins University (1971). PRIM CORP EMPL vice president: Martin G. Knott & Associates.
Robin Platts: executive director
Joann O. Porter: trustee
Martin S. Porter: trustee
Margaret K. Riehl: trustee B 1934. CORP AFFIL partner: Northern Village Apartments; partner: Riehl Estate Management Co.; partner: Beechfield Apartments.
Geralynn D. Smyth: trustee
John C. Smyth: vice president, director
Patricia K. Smyth: trustee NONPR AFFIL chairman, director: Good Samaritan Hospital Maryland.
Alice K. Voelkel: trustee

Grants Analysis

Disclosure Period: calendar year ending 2000
Total Grants: $2,377,126
Number of Grants: 103
Average Grant: $21,344*
Highest Grant: $200,000
Lowest Grant: $5
Typical Range: $15,000 to $50,000
*Note: Average grant excludes highest grant.

Recent Grants

Note: Grants derived from 2000 Form 990.

Library-Related
43,000 Enoch Pratt Free Library, Baltimore, MD

General
200,000 St. Bernadines Head Start Center, Baltimore, MD
100,000 Mount De Sales Academy, Catonsville, MD
100,000 MSGR O'Dwyer Retreat House
80,000 Faith Community of St. Casimir Parish
76,427 St. Vincent De Paul Society, Baltimore, MD
71,720 Literacy Works, Baltimore, MD
69,790 WJHU Radio
67,000 SESHI, Baltimore, MD
60,000 Woodmont Academy, Woodstock, MD
56,970 Salvation Army

SEYMOUR H. KNOX FOUNDATION

Giving Contact

James F. Wendel, Assistant Secretary & Assistant Treasurer
1 HSBC Center Suite 3840
Buffalo, NY 14203
Phone: (716)854-6811
Fax: (716)856-0517
E-mail: kbojw@aol.com

Description

Founded: 1945
EIN: 160839066
Organization Type: Family Foundation
Giving Locations: NY: Buffalo nationally.
Grant Types: General Support.

Donor Information

Founder: Incorporated in 1945 by the late Seymour H. Knox , the late Marjorie K. C. Klopp , and the late Dorothy K. G. Rogers .

Financial Summary

Total Giving: $703,969 (2001); $1,160,847 (1999); $780,911 (1998)
Giving Analysis: Giving for 1999 includes: foundation grants to United Way ($42,100) 1998: foundation grants to United Way ($42,100)
Assets: $21,197,169 (2001); $26,968,978 (1999); $24,838,812 (1998)
Gifts Received: $1,089,474 (1994)

Typical Recipients

Arts & Humanities: Arts Associations & Councils, Arts Centers, Arts Institutes, Arts & Humanities-General, Historic Preservation, History & Archaeology, Libraries, Museums/Galleries, Music, Performing Arts, Public Broadcasting, Theater
Civic & Public Affairs: Botanical Gardens/Parks, Business/Free Enterprise, Clubs, Economic Development, Civic & Public Affairs-General, Municipalities/Towns, Nonprofit Management, Philanthropic Organizations, Professional & Trade Associations, Urban & Community Affairs
Education: Arts/Humanities Education, Colleges & Universities, Education Funds, Environmental Education, Education-General, Medical Education, Private Education (Precollege), Public Education (Precollege), Secondary Education (Private), Student Aid
Environment: Air/Water Quality, Forestry, Environment-General, Resource Conservation, Wildlife Protection
Health: Alzheimers Disease, Cancer, Children's Health/Hospitals, Health Funds, Hospices, Hospitals, Medical Rehabilitation, Medical Research, Speech & Hearing, Trauma Treatment
International: International Organizations
Religion: Churches, Religious Organizations, Religious Welfare, Seminaries
Science: Scientific Centers & Institutes, Scientific Organizations
Social Services: Animal Protection, Community Service Organizations, Day Care, Family Planning, Family Services, Food/Clothing Distribution, Homes, People with Disabilities, Recreation & Athletics, Substance Abuse, United Funds/United Ways, YMCA/YWCA/YMHA/YWHA, Youth Organizations

Application Procedures

Initial Contact: Send a letter of inquiry to the foundation.
Deadlines: None.

Restrictions

Grants are not made to individuals.

Foundation Officials

Benjamin K. Campbell: vice president, treasurer
Hazard K. Campbell: chairman, treasurer
Northrup Rand Knox, Jr.: president ED Yale University (1984).
Seymour Horace Knox, IV: vice president, secretary B 1920. CORP AFFIL chairman: Buffalo Sabres Hockey Club.
Randolph A. Marks: director B Rome, NY 1935. ED Lehigh University (1957). CORP AFFIL director: Computer Task Group Inc.; director: Modern-Tek Shops; director: America Brass Co.; director: Columbus McKinnon Corp.

Henry Zellar Urban: director B Buffalo, NY July 11, 1920. ED Yale University BS (1943). NONPR AFFIL member: Buffalo Chamber of Commerce; member: New York State Publishers Association. CLUB AFFIL Tennis & Squash Club; Sankaty Head Golf Club; Saturn Club; Nantucket Yacht Club; Pack Club; Mid-Day Club; Buffalo Club; Buffalo Country Club.
James F. Wendell: assistant secretary, assistant treasurer

Grants Analysis

Disclosure Period: calendar year ending 2001
Total Grants: $661,469*
Number of Grants: 105
Average Grant: $5,476*
Highest Grant: $92,000
Lowest Grant: $250
Typical Range: $1,000 to $10,000
***Note:** Giving excludes United Way. Average grant figure excludes highest grant.

Recent Grants

Note: Grants derived from 2001 Form 990.

General

92,000	Ducks Unlimited, Memphis, TN
55,000	Elmwood Franklin School, Buffalo, NY
42,000	United Way Buffalo and Erie County, Buffalo, NY
30,000	United Court Tennis Preservation Foundation, Philadelphia, PA
27,000	Buffalo and Erie County Historical Society, Buffalo, NY
27,000	YMCA Greater Buffalo, Buffalo, NY
26,000	Buffalo Seminary, Buffalo, NY
25,000	Salvation Army, Buffalo, NY
24,250	St. Paul's School, Buffalo, NY
21,500	Yale University, New Haven, CT

ROBERT W. KNOX, SR., AND PEARL WALLIS KNOX CHARITABLE FOUNDATION

Giving Contact

Jacky Ducote, Trust Officer
c/o Bank of America
PO Box 2518
Houston, TX 77252-2518
Phone: (713)247-7411

Description

Founded: 1964
EIN: 746064974
Organization Type: Private Foundation
Giving Locations: TX: Galveston, Houston
Grant Types: General Support, Scholarship.

Donor Information

Founder: Robert W. Knox, Jr.

Financial Summary

Total Giving: $282,925 (fiscal year ending August 31, 2001); $299,330 (fiscal 2000); $250,086 (fiscal 1998)
Giving Analysis: Giving for fiscal 2001 includes: foundation grants to United Way ($5,000); foundation scholarships ($7,500); fiscal 2000: foundation grants to United Way ($5,000) foundation scholarships ($7,500)
Assets: $5,434,479 (fiscal 2001); $6,147,670 (fiscal 2000); $5,007,524 (fiscal 1998)

Typical Recipients

Arts & Humanities: Arts Associations & Councils, Arts Centers, Arts Institutes, Community Arts, Ethnic & Folk Arts, Historic Preservation, History & Archaeology, Libraries, Museums/Galleries, Music, Opera, Theater, Visual Arts
Civic & Public Affairs: Asian American Affairs, Botanical Gardens/Parks, Clubs, Civic & Public Affairs-General, Hispanic Affairs, Housing, Law & Justice, Municipalities/Towns, Parades/Festivals, Urban & Community Affairs, Women's Affairs, Zoos/Aquariums
Education: Business Education, Colleges & Universities, Education-General, Literacy, Medical Education, Minority Education, Private Education (Precollege)
Health: AIDS/HIV, Alzheimers Disease, Alzheimers Disease, Cancer, Children's Health/Hospitals, Clinics/Medical Centers, Emergency/Ambulance Services, Heart, Hospices, Mental Health, Prenatal Health Issues, Trauma Treatment
International: International Environmental Issues, International Relations
Religion: Churches, Ministries, Religious Organizations, Religious Welfare
Science: Science Museums
Social Services: Big Brother/Big Sister, Camps, Child Abuse, Child Welfare, Community Centers, Community Service Organizations, Crime Prevention, Day Care, Delinquency & Criminal Rehabilitation, Family Services, Food/Clothing Distribution, People with Disabilities, Scouts, Senior Services, Shelters/Homelessness, Substance Abuse, United Funds/United Ways, United Funds/United Ways, Volunteer Services, YMCA/YWCA/YMHA/YWHA, Youth Organizations

Application Procedures

Initial Contact: Send a brief letter of inquiry and a full proposal.
Application Requirements: Include a description of organization, amount requested, purpose of funds sought, recently audited financial statement, and proof of tax-exempt status.
Deadlines: None.

Additional Information

Trust(s): Bank of America

Grants Analysis

Disclosure Period: fiscal year ending August 31, 2001
Total Grants: $270,425*
Number of Grants: 86
Average Grant: $3,144
Highest Grant: $30,000
Lowest Grant: $500
Typical Range: $1,000 to $5,000
***Note:** Giving excludes scholarships and United Way.

Recent Grants

Note: Grants derived from 2000 Form 990.

General

20,000	Goodwill Industries, Miami, FL -- purchase equipment Houston Zoo work crews
15,000	Miller Outdoor Theatre, Houston, TX -- construction of new facility
13,000	Goodwill Industries, Miami, FL -- achievement
10,500	Galveston Historical Foundation, Galveston, TX -- U/W plankowners party and support historic homes
10,000	Galveston Historical Foundation, Galveston, TX -- U/W night of remembrance
10,000	Grand 1894 Opera House, Galveston, TX -- replace building elevator
8,000	Sam Houston Area Council Boy Scouts, Houston, TX

6,000	AIDS Foundation Houston, Houston, TX -- Red Ribbon toy drive
5,000	Austin College, Sherman, TX -- medical student scholarships
5,000	First Presbyterian Church, Dallas, TX

EARL KNUDSEN CHARITABLE FOUNDATION

Giving Contact

Judith D. Morrison, Secretary
PO Box 22070
Pittsburgh, PA 15222

Description

Founded: 1975
EIN: 256062530
Organization Type: Private Foundation
Giving Locations: PA
Grant Types: General Support.

Donor Information

Founder: the late Earl Knudsen

Financial Summary

Total Giving: $406,000 (2000); $492,000 (1999); $343,500 (1998)
Giving Analysis: Giving for 1999 includes: foundation grants to United Way ($5,000) 1998: foundation grants to United Way ($5,000)
Assets: $6,781,688 (2000); $6,871,921 (1999); $6,797,886 (1998)
Gifts Received: $1,000 (1995); $2,765 (1994); $1,638 (1993)

Typical Recipients

Arts & Humanities: Arts Centers, Ballet, Community Arts, Arts & Humanities-General, Historic Preservation, Libraries, Museums/Galleries, Music
Civic & Public Affairs: Community Foundations, Employment/Job Training, Civic & Public Affairs-General, Municipalities/Towns, Urban & Community Affairs, Women's Affairs
Education: Colleges & Universities, Education Funds, Education-General, Preschool Education, Private Education (Precollege), Science/Mathematics Education, Special Education, Student Aid
Health: Children's Health/Hospitals, Clinics/Medical Centers, Emergency/Ambulance Services, Eyes/Blindness, Health-General, Hospices, Hospitals, Hospitals (University Affiliated), Long-Term Care, Medical Rehabilitation, Mental Health, Public Health, Research/Studies Institutes, Single-Disease Health Associations
Religion: Churches, Ministries, Religious Organizations, Religious Welfare
Social Services: Big Brother/Big Sister, Child Welfare, Community Centers, Community Service Organizations, Crime Prevention, Day Care, Family Services, Food/Clothing Distribution, People with Disabilities, Scouts, Senior Services, United Funds/United Ways, YMCA/YWCA/YMHA/YWHA, Youth Organizations

Application Procedures

Initial Contact: Send brief letter describing program.
Application Requirements: Include purpose of funds sought and proof of tax-exempt status.
Deadlines: None.

Additional Information

Trust(s): National City Bank of PA, Clark & Peelor.

Foundation Officials

Roy Thomas Clark, Esq.: co-trustee
Pamela K. Peelor, Esq.: co-trustee

Grants Analysis

Disclosure Period: calendar year ending 2000
Total Grants: $406,000
Number of Grants: 67
Average Grant: $6,060
Highest Grant: $25,000
Typical Range: $1,000 to $10,000

Recent Grants

Note: Grants derived from 2001 Form 990.

General

30,000	Pittsburgh Leadership Foundation, Pittsburgh, PA
25,000	Wells College, Aurora, NY
20,000	Extra-Mile Education Foundation, Inc., Pittsburgh, PA
20,000	Family Hospice, Pittsburgh, PA
15,000	Coalition for Christian Outreach, Pittsburgh, PA
15,000	DePaul Institute, Pittsburgh, PA
15,000	Family House, Pittsburgh, PA
10,000	Baptist Homes of Western Pennsylvania, Pittsburgh, PA
10,000	Focus on Renewal, McKees Rocks, PA
10,000	Intervarsity Christian Fellowship, Lexington, KY

KOCH FOUNDATION, INC.

Giving Contact

Michael A. Marconi, Executive Director
2830 Northwest 41st Street, Suite H
Gainesville, FL 32606
Phone: (352)373-7491
Fax: (352)337-1548

Description

Founded: 1979
EIN: 591885997
Organization Type: Family Foundation
Giving Locations: internationally; nationally.
Grant Types: Capital, Conference/Seminar, Matching, Project, Seed Money.

Donor Information

Founder: The Koch Foundation was established in 1979 with funds donated by Carl Koch and Paula Koch.

Financial Summary

Total Giving: $11,126,958 (fiscal year ending March 31, 2002); $10,756,718 (fiscal 2001); $11,795,505 (fiscal 2000)
Assets: $130,799,599 (fiscal 2002); $128,812,214 (fiscal 2001); $126,519,855 (fiscal 2000)
Gifts Received: $2,350,001 (fiscal 2001); $15,946 (fiscal 1993)

Typical Recipients

Arts & Humanities: Film & Video, Libraries, Public Broadcasting
Civic & Public Affairs: Civic & Public Affairs-General, Hispanic Affairs
Education: Colleges & Universities, Education Associations, Elementary Education (Private), Education-General, Minority Education, Private Education (Precollege), Religious Education
Health: Prenatal Health Issues

International: Foreign Educational Institutions, International-General, Health Care/Hospitals, International Development, International Relief Efforts, Missionary/Religious Activities
Religion: Churches, Dioceses, Religion-General, Ministries, Missionary Activities (Domestic), Religious Organizations, Religious Welfare, Seminaries
Social Services: Child Welfare, Community Service Organizations, Shelters/Homelessness, Social Services-General

Application Procedures

Initial Contact: Prospective applicants should submit a brief letter describing the project and requesting an application form.
Application Requirements: Provide a budget and statement of the impact on evangelization that the project would accomplish. If the program is outside the United States, include the country or diocese where it will take place and a verification letter from a U.S. fiscal stating that they will be assisting in the distribution of funds. If the funds are for a continuing project, include a report describing the progress of the project with the application.
Deadlines: Requests for application forms are received from January 1 to May 31. Letters of request for an application must be postmarked no later than May 31. Completed applications must be returned within 90 days of the date of the application cover letter.
Review Process: All applications are reviewed by the grant committee on a regular basis. Final decisions are made by the board at the annual meeting, and applicants will be notified by late March.
Notes: All requests must be made in English and may not be faxed.

Restrictions

Koch Foundation grants are limited to Roman Catholic activities that propagate the faith. Financial support is not provided to individuals or for individual scholarships.

Additional Information

Applicants are encouraged to seek matching or collaborative funding.
Publications: Annual Report; Guidelines

Foundation Officials

Carolyn L. Bomberger: president
Dorothy C. Bomberger: assistant treasurer, director
Matthew A. Bomberger: director
Michelle H. Bomberger: director
Rachel A. Bomberger: secretary, board member
William A. Bomberger: assistant secretary, board member
Maura J. Branly: director
Charlotte Spacinsky: director
Inge Vraney: vice president, board member
Lawrence Vraney: treasurer

Grants Analysis

Disclosure Period: fiscal year ending March 31, 2001
Total Grants: $10,756,718*
Number of Grants: 581
Average Grant: $18,500
Highest Grant: $1,000,000
Lowest Grant: $860
Typical Range: $10,000 to $30,000
***Note:** Grants analysis provided by foundation.

Recent Grants

Note: Grants derived from 2000 Form 990.

General

300,000	Society for the Propagation of the Faith, New York, NY -- funds to support African seminaries
75,000	Catholic Television of San Antonio, San Antonio, TX -- funds to be used to support Catholic television programming

75,000	Paulist National Catholic Evangelization Association, Washington, DC -- funds to support the Paulist diocesan and parish evangelization program
60,000	Diocese of St. Augustine, Office of Educational Services, Jacksonville, FL -- funds to support the salary of religious women in inner-city Catholic schools
50,000	Carmelite Communion, Disealed Carmelite Nuns, Beacon, NY
40,000	Alliance for Catholic Education, Notre Dame, IN -- funds to form a lay apostolic movement within Catholic school teachers
35,000	Archdiocese of Newark, Newark, NJ
35,000	Christian Renewal Center, Houston, TX -- funds to expand and renovate a Christian Renewal Center
35,000	Passionists, Province Pastoral Center, South River, NJ -- funds to support an evangelization outreach to a federal agency
35,000	St. Jude Media Ministry, Passaic, NJ

KOCH INDUSTRIES, INC.

Company Headquarters
Wichita, KS
Web: http://www.kochind.com

Company Description
Revenue: US$38.93 billion (2002)
Employees: 11000 (2002)
SIC(s): 0212 Beef Cattle Except Feedlots, 1311 Crude Petroleum & Natural Gas, 1321 Natural Gas Liquids, 2911 Petroleum Refining.

Operating Locations
Koch Industries, Inc. (KS--Wichita)

Nonmonetary Support
Type: Donated Equipment; In-kind Services
Note: The company provides nonmonetary support to schools, community groups, emergency response agencies, and charitable organizations near company facilities.

Fred C. and Mary R. Koch Foundation, Inc.

Giving Contact
Roger Ramseyer, Director, Community Relations
Koch Industries, Inc.
PO Box 2256
Wichita, KS 67201
Phone: (316)828-7483
Fax: (316)828-5739
E-mail: ramseyer@kochind.com
Web: http://www.kochind.com/community/default.asp
Note: Visit company website for further giving contact information.

Description
EIN: 486113560
Organization Type: Corporate Foundation
Giving Locations: KS
Grant Types: Capital, Endowment, General Support, Operating Expenses, Project, Scholarship.
Note: Also provides grants for special needs.

Financial Summary
Total Giving: $887,500 (2001); $925,500 (2000); $1,073,500 (1999). Note: Contributes through foundation only.
Giving Analysis: Giving for 2000 includes: foundation scholarships ($100,000); foundation ($825,500);

1999: foundation scholarships ($53,000); foundation ($1,020,500); 1998: foundation scholarships ($30,000); foundation ($846,000);
Assets: $20,735,423 (2001); $17,276,847 (2000); $18,580,566 (1999)
Gifts Received: $481,000 (2001); $370,000 (2000); $453,000 (1999). Note: In 2000 and 2001, contributions were received from Koch Industries, Inc. and the Charles G. Koch Charitable Foundation.

Typical Recipients
Arts & Humanities: Arts Associations & Councils, Arts Centers, Ballet, Dance, Ethnic & Folk Arts, Historic Preservation, Libraries, Museums/Galleries, Music, Opera, Performing Arts
Civic & Public Affairs: Botanical Gardens/Parks, Clubs, Economic Development, Employment/Job Training, Philanthropic Organizations, Rural Affairs
Education: Arts/Humanities Education, Business Education, Colleges & Universities, Education-General, Legal Education, Special Education, Student Aid
Environment: Environment-General
Health: Cancer, Children's Health/Hospitals, Hospices, Mental Health, Preventive Medicine/Wellness Organizations, Single-Disease Health Associations
Science: Science-General, Science Museums
Social Services: Big Brother/Big Sister, Child Welfare, Community Service Organizations, Family Services, Food/Clothing Distribution, People with Disabilities, Scouts, Senior Services, Social Services-General, United Funds/United Ways, YMCA/YWCA/YMHA/YWHA, Youth Organizations

Application Procedures
Initial Contact: Send a brief letter describing project.
Application Requirements: Include a list of board of directors, tax status, project budget, and annual report or audited financial statements.
Deadlines: None.

Restrictions
Grants limited to tax-exempt organizations. Scholarships are limited to children of Koch Industries employees. Does not support individuals, religious organizations for sectarian purposes, political or lobbying groups, or organizations outside operating areas.

Corporate Officials
Charles de Ganahl Koch: chairman, chief executive officer, director B Wichita, KS 1935. ED Massachusetts Institute of Technology BSE (1957); Massachusetts Institute of Technology MSME (1958); Massachusetts Institute of Technology MSChE (1959). PRIM CORP EMPL chairman, chief executive officer, director, president: Koch Industries, Inc. ADD CORP EMPL chairman: Koch Microelectronic Service Co.; principal: Koch Pipelines Co. LP. CORP AFFIL chairman: Koch Industries Inc.; director: Intrust Financial Corp.; director: Intrust Bank NA; director: Intrust Finance Corp. NONPR AFFIL chairman: Institute Humane Studies.
Joseph W. Moeller: president, chief operating officer
Roger Ramseyer: director community relations

Foundation Officials
Tye Darland: secretary
Richard H. Fink: director PRIM CORP EMPL executive vice president, director: Koch Industries, Inc.
Vonda Holliman: treasurer
David Hamilton Koch: trustee B Wichita, KS 1940. ED Massachusetts Institute of Technology BS (1962); Massachusetts Institute of Technology MS (1963). PRIM CORP EMPL executive vice president: Koch Industries, Inc. ADD CORP EMPL executive vice president: Koch Industries Chemical Technology Group. CORP AFFIL overseers: WGBH Channel 2; director: Koch Engineering Company Inc. NONPR AFFIL trustee: New York University Hospital Medical Center Fund; member: Whitehead Institute; trustee: Memorial Sloan Kettering Hospital; governor, chairman development committee: New York University

Downtown Hospital; trustee: Guggenheim Museum; director: Institute Human Origins; director: Citizens for Sound Economy; director: Earthwatch; director: Aspen Institute; director: Cato Institute; director: American Museum Natural History. CLUB AFFIL River Club; Explorers Club; Racquet & Tennis Club.
Elizabeth B. Koch: president, director
Michael Morgan: director
Roger Ramseyer: vice president (see above)

Grants Analysis
Disclosure Period: calendar year ending 2001
Total Grants: $803,500*
Number of Grants: 23
Average Grant: $22,886*
Highest Grant: $300,000
Lowest Grant: $1,000
Typical Range: $10,000 to $70,000
***Note:** Giving excludes scholarships. Average grant figure excludes highest grant.

Recent Grants
Note: Grants derived from 2001 Form 990.

General
300,000	Youth Entrepreneurs of Kansas, Inc., Wichita, KS -- program support
100,000	Big Brothers and Big Sisters of Sedgwick County, Wichita, KS -- support for program expansion
100,000	YMCA, Wichita, KS -- for Aquatic Programs
97,000	University of Kansas Endowment Association, Lawrence, KS -- for Educational Program Support
37,000	Wichita Center for Arts, Wichita, KS -- for program support
20,000	Rainbows United, Wichita, KS -- for Early Childhood Accelerated Program
17,500	Friends University, Wichita, KS -- for Ballet Program
15,000	Center for Health and Wellness, Wichita, KS -- for education program support
15,000	Washburn University, Topeka, KS -- for Scholarship Program
10,000	Communities in Schools, Wichita, KS -- for education program support

MARCIA AND OTTO KOEHLER FOUNDATION

Giving Contact
Jerry A. Higginson, Jr., Vice President & Trust Officer
Bank of America
PO Box 831041
Dallas, TX 75283-1041
Phone: (214)508-2422

Description
Founded: 1980
EIN: 742131195
Organization Type: Private Foundation
Giving Locations: TX: San Antonio
Grant Types: Capital, General Support, Operating Expenses, Research.

Donor Information
Founder: the late Marcia Koehler

Financial Summary
Total Giving: $522,100 (fiscal year ending July 31, 2002); $625,000 (fiscal 2000); $526,244 (fiscal 1997)
Giving Analysis: Giving for fiscal 2002 includes: foundation grants to United Way ($25,000) fiscal 2000: foundation grants to United Way ($25,000)
Assets: $7,503,952 (fiscal 2002); $13,055,902 (fiscal 2000); $9,130,132 (fiscal 1997)

Typical Recipients

Arts & Humanities: Arts Associations & Councils, Arts Centers, Arts Institutes, Arts Outreach, Community Arts, Ethnic & Folk Arts, Arts & Humanities-General, Libraries, Museums/Galleries, Music, Opera, Performing Arts, Public Broadcasting, Theater

Civic & Public Affairs: Botanical Gardens/Parks, Clubs, Economic Development, Hispanic Affairs, Municipalities/Towns, Nonprofit Management, Urban & Community Affairs, Zoos/Aquariums

Education: Arts/Humanities Education, Business Education, Business-School Partnerships, Colleges & Universities, Community & Junior Colleges, Education Funds, Education Reform, Literacy, Private Education (Precollege), Public Education (Precollege), Student Aid

Health: Children's Health/Hospitals, Children's Health/Hospitals, Geriatric Health, Health Organizations, Hospitals, Hospitals (University Affiliated), Medical Research, Mental Health, Single-Disease Health Associations

Religion: Jewish Causes, Religious Welfare

Social Services: Big Brother/Big Sister, Child Welfare, Community Centers, Community Service Organizations, Day Care, Family Services, Homes, People with Disabilities, Recreation & Athletics, Senior Services, Substance Abuse, United Funds/United Ways, YMCA/YWCA/YMHA/YWHA, Youth Organizations

Application Procedures

Initial Contact: The foundation has no formal grant application procedure or application form.
Deadlines: None.

Restrictions

Does not support individuals.

Additional Information

The purpose of the foundation is to award charitable and education grants.
Trust(s): Bank of America

Grants Analysis

Disclosure Period: fiscal year ending July 31, 2002
Total Grants: $497,100*
Number of Grants: 34
Average Grant: $14,621
Highest Grant: $30,000
Lowest Grant: $5,000
Typical Range: $5,000 to $25,000
***Note:** Giving excludes United Way.

Recent Grants

Note: Grants derived from 2000 Form 990.

General

60,000	McNay Art Museum, San Antonio, TX
40,000	Santa Rosa Children's Hospital, San Antonio, TX
35,000	San Antonio Symphony, San Antonio, TX
25,000	Centro Alameda Inc, SAAF, San Antonio, TX
25,000	Family Service Association, San Antonio, TX
25,000	Laity Renewal Foundation, San Antonio, TX
25,000	St. Mary's University, San Antonio, TX
25,000	San Antonio Children's Museum, San Antonio, TX
25,000	San Antonio Golf Association, San Antonio, TX
25,000	San Antonio Museum of Art, San Antonio, TX

KOHLER FOUNDATION

Giving Contact

Terri Yohoi, Executive Director
725 Woodlake Road, Suite X
Kohler, WI 53044
Phone: (920)458-1972
Fax: (920)458-4280
E-mail: Terri.Yoho@kohler.com
Web: http://www.kohlerfoundation.org

Description

Founded: 1940
EIN: 390810536
Organization Type: Specialized/Single Purpose Foundation
Giving Locations: CA; CO; IL; IN; MN; NJ; NY; NC; WI
Grant Types: Award, Conference/Seminar, Endowment, Fellowship, Matching, Multiyear/Continuing Support, Project, Scholarship.

Donor Information

Founder: Incorporated in 1940 by the late Herbert V. Kohler , the late Marie C. Kohler , the late Evangeline Kohler , the late Lillie B. Kohler , and the late O. A. Kroos .

Financial Summary

Total Giving: $4,355,716 (2000); $3,600,000 (1999 approx); $2,439,376 (1998)
Giving Analysis: Giving for 2000 includes: foundation scholarships ($175,791); 1998: foundation scholarships ($131,872) nonmonetary support ($1,956,767)
Assets: $335,742,465 (2000); $74,000,000 (1999 approx); $65,598,212 (1998)

Typical Recipients

Arts & Humanities: Arts Associations & Councils, Arts Centers, Arts Festivals, Arts Funds, Arts Institutes, Arts Outreach, Ballet, Community Arts, Dance, Ethnic & Folk Arts, Film & Video, Arts & Humanities-General, Historic Preservation, History & Archaeology, Libraries, Literary Arts, Museums/Galleries, Music, Opera, Performing Arts, Theater

Civic & Public Affairs: Asian American Affairs, Chambers of Commerce, Civic & Public Affairs-General, Hispanic Affairs, Municipalities/Towns, Rural Affairs, Urban & Community Affairs, Women's Affairs

Education: Arts/Humanities Education, Business Education, Colleges & Universities, Continuing Education, Education Reform, Elementary Education (Private), Elementary Education (Public), Engineering/Technological Education, Environmental Education, Education-General, Medical Education, Preschool Education, Private Education (Precollege), Public Education (Precollege), Science/Mathematics Education, Secondary Education (Private), Secondary Education (Public), Student Aid

Environment: Forestry, Environment-General

Health: Children's Health/Hospitals, Medical Rehabilitation, Nursing Services

Religion: Religious Organizations

Social Services: At-Risk Youth, Big Brother/Big Sister, Child Abuse, Community Service Organizations, Family Planning, Family Services, People with Disabilities, Recreation & Athletics, Scouts, Social Services-General, YMCA/YWCA/YMHA/YWHA, Youth Organizations

Application Procedures

Initial Contact: The foundation requests applications be made in writing.
Application Requirements: Copies of two designations of organization: 501(c) and 509(a) 1, 2 or 3. Also include a description of the project including why the grant is needed and how many people will benefit from the grant; a budget of how much the project will cost, other funding sources, and a timetable of when

the money is actually needed; and credentials of the project manager.
Deadlines: May 1 and November 1.
Review Process: The Grants Committee convenes in June and December to review grant requests.

Restrictions

The foundation does not make grants to individuals, except for scholarships in Sheboygan County, WI. No grants are made for health care or medical programs, operating budgets, or annual fundraising drives. The foundation does not make loans.

Additional Information

Publications: Application Guidelines

Foundation Officials

Natalie A. Black: vice president, director B Bakersfield, CA 1949. ED Stanford University AB (1972); Marquette University JD (1978). PRIM CORP EMPL general counsel, secretary, vice president: Kohler Co. CORP AFFIL secretary, director: Sterling Plumbing Group Inc.; secretary, director, vice chairman: McGuire Furniture Co.; vice president: Kohler Ltd.; secretary, director: Kohler Sanimex; vice president, secretary, director: Kohler of France; president, director: Kohler Interiors Group Ltd.; director: Johnson Controls Inc.; vice chairman, chief executive officer, director, secretary, president: Baker, Knapp & Tubbs Inc.; president, secretary, director: Dapha Ltd. NONPR AFFIL member: American Bar Association.

Jeffrey P. Cheney: vice president, treasurer ED Marquette University MBA; University of Wisconsin. NONPR AFFIL director: Friendship House.

Sam H. Davis: director B Gracemont, OK 1921. ED University of Texas BS (1949). CORP AFFIL director: Firstar Bank Sheboygan NA. NONPR AFFIL member: American Ceramic Society.

Ruth DeYoung Kohler, II: president, chief operating officer, director B Chicago, IL 1941. ED Smith College; University of Hamburg; University of Wisconsin. NONPR AFFIL principal: Sheboygan Arts Foundation Inc.

Paul H. Ten Pas: secretary, director

Grants Analysis

Disclosure Period: calendar year ending 2000
Total Grants: $4,179,925*
Number of Grants: 132
Average Grant: $3,908*
Highest Grant: $2,022,631
Lowest Grant: $358
Typical Range: $1,000 to $10,000
***Note:** Giving excludes scholarships. Average grant figure excludes highest grantS.

Recent Grants

Note: Grants derived from 2000 Form 990.

General

326,628	Sheboygan Arts Foundation, Sheboygan, WI
12,300	University of Wisconsin, Madison, WI
10,000	Duke University, Durham, NC
10,000	Hamline University, St. Paul, MN
10,000	Princeton University, Princeton, NJ
7,500	Stanford University, Stanford, CA
7,500	University of Notre Dame, Notre Dame, IN
6,018	Wade House
5,000	Florentine Opera Company, Milwaukee, WI
5,000	Northwestern College, Orange City, IL

KOHN-JOSELOFF FOUNDATION

Giving Contact

Bernhard L. Kohn, Sr., President
125 LaSalle Rd., Rm. 200
West Hartford, CT 06107
Phone: (860)521-7010

Description

Founded: 1936
EIN: 136062846
Organization Type: Private Foundation
Giving Locations: CT; DC: Washington; IL; NY
Grant Types: General Support.

Donor Information

Founder: the late Lillian L. Joseloff, Morris Joseloff Foundation Trust

Financial Summary

Total Giving: $222,230 (2000); $2,345,753 (1999); $6,695,021 (1998)
Giving Analysis: Giving for 2000 includes: foundation grants to United Way ($12,500); 1998: foundation grants to United Way ($12,500) foundation ($6,682,521)
Assets: $14,806,465 (2000); $13,276,936 (1999); $15,329,980 (1998)

Typical Recipients

Arts & Humanities: Arts Associations & Councils, History & Archaeology, Libraries, Literary Arts, Museums/Galleries, Music, Opera, Performing Arts, Public Broadcasting, Theater
Civic & Public Affairs: Botanical Gardens/Parks, Clubs, Civic & Public Affairs-General, Native American Affairs, Women's Affairs, Zoos/Aquariums
Education: Arts/Humanities Education, Colleges & Universities, Faculty Development, Minority Education, Private Education (Precollege), Public Education (Precollege), Special Education, Student Aid
Environment: Environment-General, Watershed
Health: Cancer, Children's Health/Hospitals, Emergency/Ambulance Services, Health Organizations, Home-Care Services, Hospices, Hospitals, Medical Research, Nursing Services, Respiratory, Single-Disease Health Associations
International: Health Care/Hospitals
Religion: Jewish Causes, Religious Organizations, Religious Welfare
Social Services: Camps, Child Welfare, Community Service Organizations, Family Services, People with Disabilities, Scouts, Senior Services, United Funds/United Ways, Youth Organizations

Application Procedures

Initial Contact: The foundation has no formal grant application procedure or application form.
Deadlines: None.

Restrictions

Does not support individuals. Awards limited to organizations qualifying under IRC SEC 501(c)(3).

Foundation Officials

Bernhard L. Kohn, Jr.: vice president
Bernhard L. Kohn, Sr.: president
Joan J. Kohn: secretary, treasurer
Kathryn K. Rieger: vice president

Grants Analysis

Disclosure Period: calendar year ending 2000
Total Grants: $209,730*
Number of Grants: 71
Average Grant: $2,268*
Highest Grant: $51,000
Typical Range: $100 to $10,000
*Note: Giving excludes United Way. Average grant figure excludes highest grant.

Recent Grants

Note: Grants derived from 2000 Form 990.

Library-Related

11,000	Wadsworth Athenaeum, Hartford, CT

General

51,000	Jewish Federation, Hartford, CT
25,000	Fidelco Guide Dog Foundation, Bloomfield, CT
20,000	Connecticut Historical Society, Hartford, CT
12,500	United Way, Hartford, CT
8,050	Loomis Chaffee School, Windsor, CT
7,600	Westminster School, Simsbury, CT
5,800	Easter Seal Society, Hartford, CT
5,000	American Cancer Society, Bloomfield, CT
5,000	Georgetown University, Washington, DC
5,000	Naples Philharmonic, Naples, FL

KONGSGAARD-GOLDMAN FOUNDATION

Giving Contact

Anna Agee, Administration
1932 1st Avenue, Suite 602
Seattle, WA 98101-1040
Phone: (206)448-1874
E-mail: kgf@kongsgaard-goldman.org
Web: http://www.kongsgaard-goldman.org

Description

Founded: 1989
EIN: 943088217
Organization Type: Private Foundation
Giving Locations: AK; ID; MT; OR; WA; Canada : BC
Grant Types: General Support.

Financial Summary

Total Giving: $885,698 (2001); $987,833 (2000); $1,139,391 (1999)
Assets: $86,291 (2001); $75,693 (2000); $33,521 (1999)
Gifts Received: $1,002,142 (2001); $1,131,839 (2000); $1,174,177 (1999). Note: Contributions were received from Peter Goldman and Martha Kongsgaard.

Typical Recipients

Arts & Humanities: Arts & Humanities-General, Libraries, Museums/Galleries, Music
Civic & Public Affairs: Community Foundations, Civic & Public Affairs-General, Law & Justice, Urban & Community Affairs, Women's Affairs, Zoos/Aquariums
Education: Education Reform, Legal Education, Private Education (Precollege)
Environment: Air/Water Quality, Environment-General, Resource Conservation, Wildlife Protection
International: Health Care/Hospitals, International Environmental Issues, International Peace & Security Issues, Missionary/Religious Activities
Religion: Jewish Causes, Religious Organizations
Social Services: Community Service Organizations, Domestic Violence, Recreation & Athletics, Youth Organizations

Application Procedures

Initial Contact: Send a preliminary letter of no more than two pages. The organization and the proposed project. Include amount requested, purpose of funds sought, proof of tax-exempt status, and budget.
Deadlines: March 16 and September 16.

Restrictions

Does not support individuals, religious organizations for sectarian purposes, or organizations outside operating areas.

Foundation Officials

Peter Goldman: president
Martha Kongsgaard: vice president

Grants Analysis

Disclosure Period: calendar year ending 2001
Total Grants: $885,698
Number of Grants: 112
Average Grant: $7,908
Highest Grant: $33,334
Lowest Grant: $400
Typical Range: $1,000 to $10,000

Recent Grants

Note: Grants derived from 2000 Form 990.

General

333,333	Earthjustice Legal Defense Fund, Seattle, WA
33,333	ArtsWest, Seattle, WA
30,000	Philanthropy Northwest, Seattle, WA
25,000	Bicycle Alliance of Washington, Seattle, WA
25,000	Earth Day Network, Seattle, WA
25,000	Northwest Jewish Environmental Project, Seattle, WA -- The Tides Foundation
25,000	Rails to Trails Conservancy, Washington, DC
25,000	Seattle Foundation, Seattle, WA
22,916	Fremont Public Association, Fremont, WA
22,916	Fremont Public Association, Seattle, WA

KOOPMAN FUND

Giving Contact

Georgette Koopman, President
17 Brookside Blvd.
West Hartford, CT 06107
Phone: (860)232-6406

Description

Founded: 1963
EIN: 066050431
Organization Type: Private Foundation
Giving Locations: CT
Grant Types: Capital, Emergency, Endowment, General Support, Multiyear/Continuing Support, Scholarship.

Donor Information

Founder: the late Richard Koopman, Georgette Koopman

Financial Summary

Total Giving: $856,655 (2002); $1,206,939 (2001); $749,832 (2000)
Giving Analysis: Giving for 2000 includes: foundation grants to United Way ($15,000); 1999: foundation grants to United Way ($17,500) 1998: foundation grants to United Way ($15,750)
Assets: $9,559,687 (2002); $11,480,985 (2001); $12,401,705 (2000)

Typical Recipients

Arts & Humanities: Arts Centers, Community Arts, Dance, Historic Preservation, History & Archaeology, Libraries, Museums/Galleries, Music, Public Broadcasting, Theater
Civic & Public Affairs: Civil Rights, Community Foundations, Economic Development, Civic & Public Affairs-General, Hispanic Affairs, Housing, Nonprofit Management, Philanthropic Organizations, Safety, Urban & Community Affairs, Women's Affairs, Zoos/Aquariums
Education: Agricultural Education, Arts/Humanities Education, Colleges & Universities, Engineering/

Technological Education, Education-General, Leadership Training, Preschool Education, Private Education (Precollege), Secondary Education (Private), Special Education, Student Aid

Environment: Environment-General, Resource Conservation

Health: AIDS/HIV, Clinics/Medical Centers, Emergency/Ambulance Services, Health Organizations, Hospices, Hospitals, Long-Term Care, Medical Rehabilitation, Medical Research, Nursing Services, Prenatal Health Issues, Preventive Medicine/Wellness Organizations, Public Health, Single-Disease Health Associations

International: International Affairs, International Peace & Security Issues, International Relations

Religion: Jewish Causes, Religious Organizations, Religious Welfare, Synagogues/Temples

Science: Scientific Centers & Institutes, Scientific Organizations

Social Services: At-Risk Youth, Camps, Child Welfare, Community Service Organizations, Crime Prevention, Emergency Relief, Family Planning, Family Services, Food/Clothing Distribution, Homes, People with Disabilities, United Funds/United Ways, YMCA/YWCA/YMHA/YWHA, Youth Organizations

Application Procedures

Initial Contact: The foundation has no formal grant application procedure or application form. Send a brief letter of inquiry detailing purpose of funds sought and proof of tax-exempt status.

Deadlines: None.

Foundation Officials

Beatrice F. Koopman: trustee
Dorothy B. Koopman: trustee
Georgette A. Koopman: president, trustee
Rena B. Koopman: secretary, trustee
Richard Koopman, Jr.: trustee

Grants Analysis

Disclosure Period: calendar year ending 2002
Total Grants: $856,655
Number of Grants: 103
Average Grant: $466*
Highest Grant: $809,089
Lowest Grant: $35
Typical Range: $100 to $2,000
*Note: Average grant figure excludes highest grant.

Recent Grants

Note: Grants derived from 2001 Form 990.

Library-Related

1,000	Alexandria Library, Alexandria, VA

General

4,100	Tripod School, Burbank, CA
3,000	Kenyon College, Gambler, OH
2,000	Kingswood Oxford School, West Hartford, CT
1,200	Deaf West Theatre Company, Los Angeles, CA
1,150	Hartford Art School, Hartford, CT -- HAS, Inc.
1,000	Alexandria United Way Community Services Fund, Alexandria, VA -- annual fund
1,000	American Red Cross Mile High Chapter, Denver, CO
1,000	Anderson Ranch Arts Center, Snowmass Village, CO
1,000	Boulder Community Hospital Foundation, Boulder, CO
1,000	Boulder County Safe House, Boulder, CO

KORET FOUNDATION

Giving Contact

33 New Montgomery Street, Suite 1090
San Francisco, CA 94105-4509
Phone: (415)882-7740
Fax: (415)882-7775
E-mail: info@koretfoundation.org
Web: http://www.koretfoundation.org

Description

Founded: 1966
EIN: 941624987
Organization Type: General Purpose Foundation
Giving Locations: CA: San Francisco including Bay area
Grant Types: Award, Capital, Challenge, Endowment, General Support, Multiyear/Continuing Support, Operating Expenses, Professorship, Project, Research, Scholarship, Seed Money.

Donor Information

Founder: The Koret Foundation was established in 1966, with the late Stephanie Koret and the late Joseph Koret as donors.

Financial Summary

Total Giving: $16,699,871 (2001); $17,131,797 (2000); $15,752,940 (1999 approx)
Giving Analysis: Giving for 1998 includes: foundation grants to United Way ($81,668)
Assets: $315,112,125 (2001); $320,284,438 (2000); $304,276,641 (1999)
Gifts Received: $2,500 (2001); $892 (1995); $100,000 (1993)

Typical Recipients

Arts & Humanities: Arts Centers, Arts Funds, Ballet, Ethnic & Folk Arts, History & Archaeology, Libraries, Museums/Galleries, Opera, Performing Arts, Public Broadcasting, Theater, Visual Arts

Civic & Public Affairs: Asian American Affairs, Botanical Gardens/Parks, Community Foundations, Economic Development, Economic Policy, Ethnic Organizations, Civic & Public Affairs-General, Housing, Public Policy, Urban & Community Affairs, Zoos/Aquariums

Education: Afterschool/Enrichment Programs, Colleges & Universities, Continuing Education, Economic Education, Education Funds, Environmental Education, Education-General, Gifted & Talented Programs, International Exchange, International Studies, Literacy, Medical Education, Preschool Education, Public Education (Precollege), Religious Education, Science/Mathematics Education, Secondary Education (Private), Student Aid

Environment: Resource Conservation

Health: Emergency/Ambulance Services, Geriatric Health, Hospitals (University Affiliated), Long-Term Care, Research/Studies Institutes

International: Foreign Educational Institutions, International-General, Health Care/Hospitals, International Affairs, International Development, International Environmental Issues, International Organizations, International Peace & Security Issues, Missionary/Religious Activities

Religion: Jewish Causes

Science: Science Museums

Social Services: Animal Protection, Camps, Child Welfare, Community Service Organizations, Family Services, Food/Clothing Distribution, Recreation & Athletics, Senior Services, Shelters/Homelessness, Social Services-General, United Funds/United Ways, Volunteer Services, Youth Organizations

Application Procedures

Initial Contact: Applicants must first submit a one-to three-page preliminary letter to the foundation's executive director or program officer.

Application Requirements: The preliminary letter should include a description of the project for which support is requested; information about the applicant organization, including experience, programs or services, and population and geographic area served; summary budget for the proposed project, including amount sought from the foundation and other sources; a list of the board of directors with professional affiliations; an evaluation plan; and copy of the IRS determination letter of tax-exempt status. If the foundation is interested, an application for funding package will be sent; if not, the applicant will be notified in writing within 90 days.

Deadlines: None.

Review Process: Completed applications for funding are reviewed by a program officer, who may request additional information, an interview, or a visit. The review process may take up to six months. All grants are subject to the approval of the foundation's board of directors. Once a grant is awarded, a grantee is required to provide narrative and financial reports at specified times detailing accomplishments, problems, and the use of funds.

Restrictions

The foundation reports that it will only make grants to organizations which have proof of tax-exempt status under Section 501(c)(3) of the IRS Code and which are not private foundations as described in Section 509(a). No grants will be made to fiscal agents soliciting funds in support of programs which are not conducted by the applicant, for propaganda or lobbying activities, or to organizations which have not fulfilled all the terms of a previous grant. Grants generally will not be made for a request in which there are no other sources of funding; for deficit funding, endowments, or emergency funding; for general fund-raising campaigns; for the purchase of equipment or furnishings; or to sectarian, veterans, fraternal, military, religious, or similar groups whose principal activity is for the benefit of their own membership.

Foundation Officials

Michael J. Boskin: director B New York, NY 1945. ED University of California at Berkeley AB (1967); University of California at Berkeley MA (1968); University of California at Berkeley PhD (1971). PRIM NONPR EMPL professor: Stanford University. CORP AFFIL director: First Health Group; director: Oracle Corp.; president, chief executive officer: Boskin & Co.; director: ExxonMobil Corp. NONPR AFFIL research associate: National Bureau Economic Research; professor: Stanford University; fellow: National Association Business Economists; scholar: American Enterprise Institute; chairman: Congressional Advisory Commission Consumer Price Index.

William Kraemer Coblentz: director B San Francisco, CA 1922. ED University of California at Berkeley BA (1943); Yale University (1947). PRIM CORP EMPL senior partner: Coblentz, Cahen, McCabe & Breyer. CORP AFFIL director: Pacific Telesis Group; director: Sacramento Bee; director: Modesto Bee; director: Pacific Bell; director: McClatchy Co. Inc.; director: McClatchy Newspapers Inc.; director: Fresno Bee.

Jeff Fearn: section, treasurer

Eugene L. Friend: vice chairman, director B 1916. PRIM CORP EMPL chairman, director: Kutler Clothiers Inc.

Richard L. Greene: director

Stanley Herzstein: director CORP AFFIL director: Software Logistics Corp.

Susan Koret: chairman, director

Thaddeus N. Taube: president, director B 1931. ED Stanford University BS (1954); Stanford University MS (1957). PRIM CORP EMPL chairman, director: Woodmont Companies.

Grants Analysis

Disclosure Period: calendar year ending 2001
Total Grants: $16,699,871
Number of Grants: 342

Average Grant: $36,873*
Highest Grant: $2,100,000
Lowest Grant: $508
Typical Range: $20,000 to $50,000
***Note:** Average grant figure excludes three highest grants ($4,200,000).

Recent Grants

Note: Grants derived from 2001 Form 990.

Library-Related

100,000	Berkeley Public Library Foundation, Berkeley, CA

General

2,000,000	University of California San Francisco, San Francisco, CA
1,100,000	University of San Francisco, San Francisco, CA
1,000,000	Jewish Community Center of San Francisco, San Francisco, CA
700,000	Fine Arts Museums of San Francisco, San Francisco, CA
650,000	Alameda County Health Care Foundation, Oakland, CA
500,000	Exploratorium, Des Moines, IA
500,000	Jewish Community Federation of San Francisco, San Francisco, CA
500,000	San Francisco Zoological Society, San Francisco, CA
500,000	San Jose State University, San Jose, CA
400,000	Jewish Community Federation of San Francisco, the Peninsula, Marin and Sonoma Counties, San Francisco, CA

EMILY DAVIE AND JOSEPH S. KORNFELD FOUNDATION

Giving Contact

Karen R. Berry, Secretary
Patterson Belknap Webb & Tyler LLP
1133 Avenue. of the Americans, Suite 2200
New York, NY 10036-6710
Phone: (212)336-2000
E-mail: office@kornfeldfdn.org
Web: http://fdncenter.org/grantmaker/kornfeld

Description

Founded: 1979
EIN: 133042360
Organization Type: Private Foundation
Giving Locations: NY
Grant Types: General Support.

Donor Information

Founder: the late Emily Davie Kornfeld

Financial Summary

Total Giving: $2,113,289 (2000); $1,887,806 (1999); $1,776,001 (1998)
Giving Analysis: Giving for 2000 includes: foundation fellowships ($325,352) 1999: foundation fellowships ($242,801)
Assets: $43,193,243 (2000); $48,048,037 (1999); $41,355,678 (1998)

Typical Recipients

Arts & Humanities: Arts Outreach, Arts & Humanities-General, Libraries, Museums/Galleries, Music
Civic & Public Affairs: Botanical Gardens/Parks, Economic Development, Civic & Public Affairs-General, Philanthropic Organizations, Professional & Trade Associations, Public Policy, Urban & Community Affairs

Education: Afterschool/Enrichment Programs, Arts/Humanities Education, Colleges & Universities, Education Funds, Education Reform, Environmental Education, Faculty Development, Education-General, Leadership Training, Literacy, Medical Education, Minority Education, Private Education (Precollege), Public Education (Precollege), Special Education
Health: Adolescent Health Issues, AIDS/HIV, Cancer, Clinics/Medical Centers, Geriatric Health, Health Organizations, Hospitals, Hospitals (University Affiliated), Medical Research, Mental Health, Public Health
International: International-General, Human Rights, Missionary/Religious Activities
Religion: Jewish Causes
Social Services: At-Risk Youth, Child Welfare, Community Centers, Community Service Organizations, People with Disabilities

Application Procedures

Initial Contact: Send a brief letter of inquiry.
Deadlines: None.

Restrictions

Emphasis is on research and other activities concerning the right of the individual to choose the time and manner of his or her death without undue interference by doctors, hospitals, courts, churches, families, or society and the advancement of the understanding of physical pain in human beings and, in particular, chronic and intractable pain, including the mechanism, causes, control, treatment, and prevention of such pain. The foundation also supports programs that teach reading, writing, and other subjects to students who attend New York City public schools. Grants are not awarded to individuals or for scholarships.

Foundation Officials

Christopher C. Angell: president, director
Karen R. Berry: secretary
Peter Bokor: director
Emme Levin Deland: director
Patricia Llosa: director
Morris S. Roberts: treasurer, director
William J. Welch: vice president, director
John P. White: chairman, director

Grants Analysis

Disclosure Period: calendar year ending 2000
Total Grants: $1,787,937*
Number of Grants: 20
Average Grant: $55,637*
Highest Grant: $730,832
Typical Range: $25,000 to $100,000
***Note:** Giving excludes fellowships. Average grant figure excludes highest grant.

Recent Grants

Note: Grants derived from 1999 Form 990.

General

297,878	Fund for Public Schools, Inc., Long Island, NY
200,000	Partnership for After School Education, New York, NY
180,000	Outward Bound - USA, Garrison, NY
150,000	REACH School of the Bronx, New York, NY
110,000	Henry Street Settlement, New York, NY
71,595	Columbia University College of Physicians and Surgeons, New York, NY
64,410	Learning Project, New York, NY
50,000	Multicare Health Systems, Tacoma, WA
50,000	Neighborhood Initiatives Development Corporation, Bronx, NY
50,000	New Visions for Public Schools, New York, NY

KORTE CONSTRUCTION CO.

Company Headquarters

12441 US Hwy. 40
PO Box 146
Highland, IL 62249
Web: http://www.korteco.com

Company Description

Employees: 300
SIC(s): 1500 General Building Contractors, 6700 Holding & Other Investment Offices.

Operating Locations

Korte Construction Co. (IL--Highland; MO--St. Louis)

Ralph and Donna Korte Family Charitable Foundation

Giving Contact

William Boudouris, Chief Financial Officer
700 St. Louis Union Station
St. Louis, MO 63103
Phone: (314)241-3327

Description

Founded: 1989
EIN: 431475774
Organization Type: Corporate Foundation
Giving Locations: IL; MO
Grant Types: Employee Matching Gifts, Endowment, General Support.

Financial Summary

Total Giving: $629,866 (2001); $116,674 (2000); $351,246 (1999)
Giving Analysis: Giving for 2001 includes: foundation grants to United Way ($10,000); 1999: foundation grants to United Way ($20,000) foundation ($331,246)
Assets: $725,263 (2001); $1,260,222 (2000); $1,620,219 (1999)
Gifts Received: $365,309 (1999); $125,500 (1998); $395,000 (1997). Note: In 1996, 1998 and 1999, contributions were received from Ralph Korte.

Typical Recipients

Arts & Humanities: Arts Associations & Councils, History & Archaeology, Libraries, Museums/Galleries, Theater
Civic & Public Affairs: Botanical Gardens/Parks, Business/Free Enterprise, Clubs, Civic & Public Affairs-General, Municipalities/Towns, Urban & Community Affairs, Women's Affairs, Zoos/Aquariums
Education: Business Education, Business-School Partnerships, Colleges & Universities, Continuing Education, Environmental Education, Education-General, Private Education (Precollege), Public Education (Precollege), Secondary Education (Public), Special Education
Environment: Forestry
Health: Geriatric Health, Hospitals, Prenatal Health Issues
International: Missionary/Religious Activities
Religion: Churches, Dioceses, Religion-General, Religious Organizations, Religious Welfare
Social Services: Big Brother/Big Sister, Child Welfare, Community Service Organizations, Family Services, Homes, Scouts, Social Services-General, Special Olympics, United Funds/United Ways, YMCA/YWCA/YMHA/YWHA, Youth Organizations

Corporate Officials

William Boudouris: chief financial officer PRIM CORP EMPL chief financial officer: Korte Construction Co.

Vernon Eardley: president, chief executive officer PRIM CORP EMPL president, chief executive officer: Korte Construction Co.

Ralph F. Korte: chairman PRIM CORP EMPL chairman: Korte Construction Co.

Foundation Officials

Susan D. Bowman: secretary, treasurer, director
Greg O. Korte: director
Ralph F. Korte: president, director (see above)
Todd J. Korte: vice president, director
Vicki Korte Solheim: director

Grants Analysis

Disclosure Period: calendar year ending 2001
Total Grants: $619,866*
Number of Grants: 32
Average Grant: $9,120*
Highest Grant: $328,000
Lowest Grant: $100
Typical Range: $1,000 to $20,000
*Note: Giving excludes United Way. Average grant figure excludes highest grant.

Recent Grants

Note: Grants derived from 2001 Form 990.

General

328,000	Siue Foundation, Edwardsville, IL
54,690	School Sisters of Notre Dame, St. Louis, MO
44,800	AIMM Management Association, St. Louis, MO
30,000	Diocese of Springfield, Springfield, MA
25,000	Faith Countryside Homes, Highland, IL
25,000	Pregnancy Resource Center, St. Louis, MO
20,000	Jackie Joyner-Kersee Youth Center Foundation, St. Louis, MO
15,000	Regional Business Council, St. Louis, MO
10,000	Alexis De Tocqueville Society, St. Louis, MO
10,000	Missouri Botanical Garden, St. Louis, MO

HENRY P. KOVARIK FOUNDATION FOR POETRY

Giving Contact

Lawrence J. Holt, Director
Henry P. Kovarik Foundation for Poetry
810 Middle Country Road
Selden, NY 11784
Phone: (631)732-6600

Description

Founded: 1988
EIN: 112781923
Organization Type: Private Foundation
Grant Types: General Support, Scholarship.

Financial Summary

Total Giving: $4,950 (fiscal year ending April 30, 2001); $6,000 (fiscal 1998); $5,956 (fiscal 1997)
Giving Analysis: Giving for fiscal 2001 includes: foundation scholarships ($1,000) fiscal 1997: foundation scholarships ($2,000)
Assets: $163,798 (fiscal 2001); $157,559 (fiscal 1997); $157,242 (fiscal 1996)

Typical Recipients

Arts & Humanities: Libraries
Education: Secondary Education (Public)

Application Procedures

Initial Contact: Contact foundation for scholarship application.
Deadlines: April 1.

Additional Information

Provides scholarships for higher education to graduates of Longwood High School in Middle Island, NY.
Publications: Scholarship Application

Foundation Officials

Eugene Dooley: director
Lawrence J. Holt: director
Karen Mouzakas: director

Grants Analysis

Disclosure Period: fiscal year ending April 30, 2001
Total Grants: $3,950*
Number of Grants: 1
*Note: Giving excludes scholarships.

Recent Grants

Note: Grants derived from fiscal 2001 Form 990.

Library-Related

3,950	Longwood Public Library, Middle Island, NY

SIDNEY AND JUDITH KRANES CHARITABLE TRUST

Giving Contact

Thomas J. Sweeney, Co-Trustee
420 Lexington Avenue
Suite 626
New York, NY 10170
Phone: (212)599-1892

Description

Founded: 1993
EIN: 136981197
Organization Type: Private Foundation
Giving Locations: NY: New York
Grant Types: General Support.

Financial Summary

Total Giving: $57,500 (2001); $141,500 (2000); $145,500 (1999)
Assets: $2,667,212 (2001); $2,740,427 (2000); $2,675,926 (1999)

Typical Recipients

Arts & Humanities: Arts Outreach, Historic Preservation, History & Archaeology, Libraries, Music, Opera
Civic & Public Affairs: Botanical Gardens/Parks, Law & Justice, Legal Aid, Urban & Community Affairs
Education: Colleges & Universities, Science/Mathematics Education, Special Education
Environment: Air/Water Quality, Environment-General
Health: Clinics/Medical Centers, Emergency/Ambulance Services, Health-General, Geriatric Health, Health Organizations, Hospitals, Speech & Hearing
Religion: Religion-General, Jewish Causes, Religious Welfare
Science: Scientific Centers & Institutes
Social Services: Community Service Organizations, Emergency Relief, Food/Clothing Distribution, People with Disabilities, Senior Services, Shelters/Homelessness, Substance Abuse, Youth Organizations, Youth Organizations

Application Procedures

Initial Contact: Send a brief letter of inquiry.
Application Requirements: Include an outline of the proposed project, a statement of its significance, and the proposed budget.
Deadlines: None.

Foundation Officials

Thomas J. Hubbard, Esq.: co-trustee
Thomas Joseph Sweeney, Jr.: co-trustee B New York, NY 1923. ED New York University BA (1947); Columbia University JD (1949). PRIM CORP EMPL partner: Decker, Hubbard, Welden & Sweeney. CORP AFFIL chairman inst trustee & investment committee: Morgan Guaranty Trust Co. New York. NONPR AFFIL director: WR Kenan Fund; member: New York State Bar Association.

Grants Analysis

Disclosure Period: calendar year ending 2001
Total Grants: $57,500
Number of Grants: 20
Average Grant: $2,875
Highest Grant: $5,000
Lowest Grant: $1,000
Typical Range: $1,000 to $10,000

Recent Grants

Note: Grants derived from 2001 Form 990.

Library-Related

5,000	New York Public Library, New York, NY -- support of public libraries in Greenwich Village area

General

5,000	Center for Applied Special Technology, Peabody, MA
5,000	Madison Square Boys & Girls Club, New York, NY -- for Summer Youth Development Program
5,000	Metropolitan Opera Guild, New York, NY -- for New York City School Children Programs
5,000	New York Botanical Gardens, Bronx, NY -- for Children's Education Program
5,000	St. Vincent's Hospital, New York, NY -- Care for the Frail Elderly of Greenwich Village
3,000	Coalition for the Homeless, New York, NY
3,000	New York Genealogical and Biographical Society, New York, NY -- Immigration Research and Library Technology Center
2,500	New York Landmark Conservancy, New York, NY
2,000	Clarke School for the Deaf, Northampton, MA
2,000	Doctors Without Borders, New York, NY

KREITLER FOUNDATION

Giving Contact

Hobart C. Kreitler, President
2960 Post Rd.
Southport, CT 06490-1242
Phone: (203)259-8585

Description

Founded: 1991
EIN: 061311676
Organization Type: Private Foundation
Giving Locations: CT
Grant Types: General Support.

Donor Information

Founder: Established in 1991 by Hobart C. Kreitler and Sally S. Kreitler.

Financial Summary

Total Giving: $233,655 (2000); $211,199 (1999); $217,005 (1998)

Giving Analysis: Giving for 2000 includes: foundation grants to United Way ($2,750); foundation scholarships ($6,400); 1999: foundation grants to United Way ($2,500); foundation scholarships ($30,470) 1998: foundation grants to United Way ($2,700)

Assets: $5,129,106 (2000); $5,464,312 (1999); $5,024,065 (1998)

Gifts Received: $9,884 (1999). Note: In 1991 and 1999, contributions were received from Hobart C. and Sally S. Kreitler.

Typical Recipients

Arts & Humanities: Arts Outreach, Arts & Humanities-General, Historic Preservation, History & Archaeology, Libraries, Museums/Galleries, Performing Arts

Civic & Public Affairs: Community Foundations, Employment/Job Training, Civic & Public Affairs-General, Housing, Public Policy, Rural Affairs, Safety, Urban & Community Affairs, Women's Affairs, Zoos/Aquariums

Education: Afterschool/Enrichment Programs, Arts/Humanities Education, Business Education, Colleges & Universities, Community & Junior Colleges, Education Funds, Education-General, Private Education (Precollege), Public Education (Precollege), Student Aid

Environment: Environment-General

Health: Children's Health/Hospitals, Diabetes, Home-Care Services, Hospices, Hospitals, Long-Term Care, Medical Rehabilitation, Prenatal Health Issues

International: Health Care/Hospitals, International Relief Efforts

Religion: Churches, Ministries, Religious Organizations, Religious Welfare

Science: Science Museums, Scientific Centers & Institutes

Social Services: Child Welfare, Community Centers, Community Service Organizations, Crime Prevention, Family Services, Food/Clothing Distribution, People with Disabilities, Recreation & Athletics, Senior Services, Shelters/Homelessness, United Funds/United Ways, YMCA/YWCA/YMHA/YWHA, Youth Organizations

Application Procedures

Initial Contact: Send a summary of grant request including proof of tax-exempt status.

Deadlines: None.

Foundation Officials

Katherine K. Hodge: treasurer
Hobart C. Kreitler: president
James S. Kreitler: director
John M. Kreitler: director
Karen R. Kreitler: director
Sally S. Kreitler: secretary
Thomas S. Kreitler: vice president

Grants Analysis

Disclosure Period: calendar year ending 2000
Total Grants: $224,505*
Number of Grants: 60
Average Grant: $3,292*
Highest Grant: $30,300
Typical Range: $1,000 to $5,000

*Note: Giving excludes United Way; scholarships. Average grant figure excludes highest grant.

KRESGE FOUNDATION

Giving Contact

John E. Marshall, III, President & Chief Executive Officer
3215 West Big Beaver Road
PO Box 3151
Troy, MI 48007-3151
Phone: (248)643-9630
Fax: (248)643-0588
Web: http://www.kresge.org

Description

Founded: 1924
EIN: 381359217
Organization Type: Private Foundation
Giving Locations: nationally; Canada; England; Republic of South Africa
Grant Types: Capital, Challenge, Scholarship.

Donor Information

Founder: The foundation was established in 1924 by Sebastian S. Kresge (1867-1966), the founder of the Kresge chain of retail stores now known as the Kmart Corporation. As owner of S. S. Kresge Company, Mr. Kresge amassed a fortune of $100 million by 1924. He established the foundation with an initial personal contribution of almost $2 million. Family representation is continued on the board of trustees through Dr. Bruce A. Kresge. The charity is an independent, private foundation and has never been affiliated with Kmart Corporation.

Financial Summary

Total Giving: $123,292,500 (2001); $131,669,426 (2000); $112,710,216 (1999)

Giving Analysis: Giving for 2001 includes: foundation matching gifts ($299,590); foundation grants to United Way ($1,500,000); 1999: foundation scholarships ($250,000); foundation matching gifts ($297,788) foundation grants to United Way ($1,100,000)

Assets: $2,415,971,841 (2001); $2,770,530,895 (2000); $2,575,424,556 (1999)

Typical Recipients

Arts & Humanities: Arts Centers, Arts Festivals, Arts Institutes, Arts Outreach, Ballet, Historic Preservation, History & Archaeology, Libraries, Museums/Galleries, Music, Opera, Performing Arts, Public Broadcasting, Theater, Visual Arts

Civic & Public Affairs: African American Affairs, Botanical Gardens/Parks, Clubs, Community Foundations, Economic Development, Gay/Lesbian Issues, Civic & Public Affairs-General, Housing, Nonprofit Management, Professional & Trade Associations, Public Policy, Zoos/Aquariums

Education: Agricultural Education, Arts/Humanities Education, Business Education, Colleges & Universities, Education Associations, Education Reform, Engineering/Technological Education, Faculty Development, International Studies, Journalism/Media Education, Legal Education, Medical Education, Minority Education, Preschool Education, Private Education (Precollege), Religious Education, Science/Mathematics Education, Social Sciences Education, Special Education, Student Aid

Environment: Air/Water Quality, Forestry, Environment-General, Resource Conservation, Wildlife Protection

Health: AIDS/HIV, Alzheimers Disease, Cancer, Children's Health/Hospitals, Clinics/Medical Centers, Diabetes, Emergency/Ambulance Services, Eyes/Blindness, Health Organizations, Hospices, Hospitals, Long-Term Care, Medical Rehabilitation, Medical Research, Mental Health, Nursing Services, Outpatient Health Care, Preventive Medicine/Wellness Organizations, Research/Studies Institutes, Single-Disease Health Associations, Trauma Treatment

International: Foreign Arts Organizations, Foreign Educational Institutions, Health Care/Hospitals, International Environmental Issues, International Relations, International Relief Efforts

Religion: Jewish Causes, Ministries, Religious Organizations, Religious Welfare, Seminaries

Science: Science Museums, Scientific Centers & Institutes

Social Services: Animal Protection, At-Risk Youth, Camps, Child Abuse, Child Welfare, Community Centers, Community Service Organizations, Domestic Violence, Family Planning, Family Services, Food/Clothing Distribution, People with Disabilities, Recreation & Athletics, Scouts, Senior Services, Sexual Abuse, Shelters/Homelessness, Substance Abuse, YMCA/YWCA/YMHA/YWHA, Youth Organizations

Application Procedures

Initial Contact: The foundation accepts telephone calls or meetings from grantseekers prior to sending an application. Applicants should submit a completed proposal after reviewing application guidelines.

Application Requirements: Submit a type-written, double-spaced cover letter (signed by the senior administrative official) describing the project's purpose, impact, and priority; proposal narrative including a Fact Sheet form (provided by foundation); a brief history of the organization; description of the services provided and persons served, along with external evidence of their quality and distinctiveness; a description of major affiliations with other nonprofit organizations; extent to which organization demonstrates through governance, staff and individuals served, a commitment to serving a diverse population; policy for maintaining the current facilities; and a listing of the governing board with professional affiliations. Project information should include a description of the project; expected impact on the organization; status of architectural plans; project cost estimates; effect of completed project on organization's budget; and photograph or drawing of project (no blueprints). Fundraising information should include a brief a description of organization's previous fund-raising track record; total dollar goal for each category listed on Fact Sheet; Identification of the five largest gifts shown on Fact Sheet; amount of fund raising expected while the four to six months that the proposal is under consideration by foundation; description of constituencies likely to respond to a challenge grant; description of campaign committee and role of volunteers; how a successfully completed campaign will strengthen on-going fundraising programs; and if project is part of a larger campaign, outline campaign goals and priorities. The proposal should include the following attachments: a most recent audit; description of any long-term financing for project shown on Fact Sheet; a copy of the most recent accreditation and/or licensure report; and IRS ruling letter indicating tax-exempt status. The Science Initiative is a challenge grant program to upgrade and endow scientific equipment and laboratories in colleges and universities, teaching hospitals, medical schools, and research institutions. The Science Initiative application and the proposal for the capital projects program should be considered two separate and unique applications.

Deadlines: None.

Review Process: A decision is made within five to six months after submission.

Notes: The foundation does not accept videos or architectural renderings. Limit one proposal per institution in any twelve-month period. Foundation encourages grant recipients to wait two years from payment before submitting another proposal.

Restrictions

The foundation does not give grants to religious organizations, elementary and secondary schools, community colleges, private foundations, or individuals. The foundation does not make grants toward projects that are substantially completed at the time of application, or toward the retirement of long-term debt. Minor equipment, furnishings, operating/program support, and endowment by themselves are not eligible (but may be funded as part of an eligible project). Projects that are eligible for funding include: construction and renovation of facilities, purchase of major equipment or an integrated system at a cost of at least $300,000, and the purchase of real estate.

Additional Information

Publications: Annual Report; Informational Pamphlets

Foundation Officials

Sandra McAlister Ambrozy: senior program officer
Leslie M. Bernard: program officer
Lee C. Bollinder: trustee
Jill Kathryn Ker Conway: chairwoman B NW Australia 1934. ED University of Sydney BA (1958); Harvard University PhD (1969). PRIM NONPR EMPL president emeritus: Smith Colorado. CORP AFFIL director: Nike Inc.; director: Merrill Lynch & Co. Inc.; director: Colgate-Palmolive Co.; director: Arthur D Little Inc. NONPR AFFIL visiting scholar: Massachusetts Institute Technology.
Jane L. Delgado: trustee B Havana, Cuba 1953. ED State University of New York College New Paltz BA (1973); New York University MA (1975); State University of New York College Stony Brook PhD (1981); W Averell Harriman School MS (1981). PRIM CORP EMPL president, chief executive officer: COSSHMO PRIM NONPR EMPL chief executive officer: National Coalition for Hispanic Health & Human Services. NONPR AFFIL president, chief executive officer, director: National Coalition Hispanic Health & Human Services; director: National Health Council; director: Carter Center Mental Health Task Force; member: Hispanics Philanthropy.
Richard Lowell Dunlap: senior program officer B Passaic, NJ 1950. ED Southern Methodist University BA (1972); Southern Methodist University MFA (1974). ADD NONPR EMPL music director: Presbyterian Church Utica. NONPR AFFIL member, trustee: Detroit Department Cultural Affairs Advisory Committee; member: Sterling Heights Cultural Community; director: Art Center Mount Clemens; member: Concerned Citizens Arts Michigan.
Ernest B. Gutierrez: sr program officer
Steve Hamp: trustee
Irene Y. Hirano: trustee
Edward Mark Hunia: sr vice president, treasurer, secretary B Sharon, PA 1946. ED Carnegie Mellon University BSME (1967); Carnegie Mellon University MSME (1968); University of Pittsburgh MBA (1971). NONPR AFFIL member: Association Investment Management & Research; member: Financial Analysts Society Detroit.
Bruce Anderson Kresge, MD: vice president, trustee B Detroit, MI 1931. ED Albion College BA (1953); Wayne State University MD (1956). OCCUPATION physician. NONPR AFFIL member: American Medical Association; trustee: Crittenton Hospital; trustee: Albion College.
George Dorland Langdon, Jr.: trustee B Putnam, CT 1933. ED Harvard University AB (1954); Amherst College MA (1957); Yale University PhD (1961). NONPR AFFIL president emeritus: Colgate University; trustee: Saint Lukes Roosevelt Hospital Center; president: American Museum Natural History.
Robert C. Larson: trustee
John Elbert Marshall, III: president, chief executive officer, trustee B Providence, RI 1942. ED Brown University BA (1964). NONPR AFFIL director: Detroit Symphony Orchestra Hall Inc.; director: United Way Community Services; member, board directors: Council Michigan Foundations.
Deborah E. McDowell: trustee
Carlotta R. Mills: program officer ED Case Western Reserve University MBA.
William F. L. Moses: program officer
David Keith Page: trustee B Detroit, MI 1933. ED Dartmouth College AB (1955); Harvard University LLB (1958). PRIM CORP EMPL senior partner: Honigman, Miller, Schwartz & Cohn.

Marlies H. Parenti: senior program officer
Gregory M. Smith: investment analyst
Robert Davis Storey: trustee B Tuskegee, AL 1936. ED Harvard University AB (1958); Case Western Reserve University JD (1964). PRIM CORP EMPL partner: Thompson Hine LLP. CORP AFFIL director: Verizon Communications Inc.; director: Procter & Gamble Co.; treasurer: Allied Resinous Products Inc.; director: May Department Stores Co. NONPR AFFIL member: Society Benchers; trustee: Spelman College; member: Cleveland Bar Association; trustee: Great Lakes Science Center; trustee: Case Western Reserve University. CLUB AFFIL University Club; Rowfant Club; Union Club; Ponce de Leon Club.
Elizabeth C. Sullivan: vice president program ED Michigan State University MA; Michigan State University BA. PRIM NONPR EMPL chairman development council: New Steps. NONPR AFFIL vice chairman board director: Family Services Detroit.
Alfred Hendricks Taylor, Jr.: trustee B Evanston, IL 1930. ED Williams College BA (1952). CORP AFFIL director: Comerica Bank.

Grants Analysis

Disclosure Period: calendar year ending 2001
Total Grants: $121,792,500*
Number of Grants: 205
Average Grant: $594,110
Highest Grant: $3,164,000
Typical Range: $50,000 to $2,000,000
*****Note:** Giving excludes matching gifts and United Way.

SAMUEL H. KRESS FOUNDATION

Giving Contact

Lisa M. Ackerman, Vice President
174 East 80th Street
New York, NY 10021
Phone: (212)861-4993
Fax: (212)628-3146
Web: http://www.kressfoundation.org

Description

Founded: 1929
EIN: 131624176
Organization Type: Specialized/Single Purpose Foundation
Giving Locations: nationally.
Grant Types: Conference/Seminar, Employee Matching Gifts, Fellowship, General Support, Matching, Multiyear/Continuing Support, Research, Scholarship.

Donor Information

Founder: The Samuel H. Kress Foundation was established in 1929, with three brothers, Samuel H. Kress (1863-1955), Claude W. Kress (1876-1940), and Rush H. Kress (1877-1963), as donors. Samuel H. Kress, a native Pennsylvanian, was the founder of the S. H. Kress and Company stores. Although Samuel was known for his extensive collection of Italian Renaissance art, the brothers expanded the Kress Collection to contain works of European masters in a variety of mediums. This vast collection of more than 3,000 pieces was eventually donated to 50 museums in 38 states. Samuel was a trustee of the Metropolitan Museum of Art and the National Gallery of Art, which received a significant portion of his art collection and named him as a Founding Benefactor.

Financial Summary

Total Giving: $5,000,000 (fiscal year ending June 30, 2002 approx); $4,873,012 (fiscal 2001); $5,489,035 (fiscal 2000)

Giving Analysis: Giving for fiscal 2000 includes: foundation matching gifts ($185,679); foundation fellowships ($1,906,000); fiscal 1999: foundation scholarships ($1,000); foundation matching gifts ($181,291) foundation fellowships ($1,022,750)
Assets: $110,000,000 (fiscal 2002 approx); $103,691,174 (fiscal 2001); $117,968,948 (fiscal 2000)

Typical Recipients

Arts & Humanities: Art History, Arts Associations & Councils, Arts Centers, Arts Funds, Arts Institutes, Ethnic & Folk Arts, Film & Video, Arts & Humanities-General, Historic Preservation, History & Archaeology, Libraries, Museums/Galleries, Music, Visual Arts
Civic & Public Affairs: Botanical Gardens/Parks, Ethnic Organizations, Civic & Public Affairs-General, Professional & Trade Associations, Public Policy, Urban & Community Affairs
Education: Arts/Humanities Education, Colleges & Universities, International Exchange, International Studies
International: Foreign Arts Organizations, Foreign Educational Institutions, International-General, International Development, International Environmental Issues, International Organizations, International Peace & Security Issues, Missionary/Religious Activities, Trade
Religion: Religious Organizations, Religious Welfare
Social Services: Community Service Organizations

Application Procedures

Initial Contact: Applicants should contact the foundation by letter. Fellowship applicants require an application form.
Application Requirements: Letters should include a description of the project, its budget, curriculum vitae of the principal investigator, an IRS determination letter, and the funds to be requested.
Deadlines: None. Proposals for projects within the standard funding programs may be submitted any time. Contact the foundation for specific program deadlines.

Restrictions

The foundation awards grants to U.S. charitable organizations only. The foundation does not support art history programs below the predoctoral level or the purchase of works of art. No grants are given to artists, operating budgets, annual campaigns, endowments, deficit financing, capital funds, films, or loans. The foundation does not accept applications via fax or e-mail.

Additional Information

Application forms for fellowships in art history and conservation are required. Applications are to be addressed: Kress Fellowship Program, Samuel H. Kress Foundation, 174 E 80th Street, New York, NY 10021. The foundation does not accept applications by fax or email.
Publications: Annual Report; Guidelines

Foundation Officials

Lisa Marilyn Ackerman: vice president B Danville, PA 1960. ED Middlebury College BA (1982); New York University MBA (1986). NONPR AFFIL member: Middlebury College Alumni Association; member: Museum Modern Art Education Department; member: College Art Association; member: Jewish Heritage Council.
Frederick William Beinecke: trustee B Stamford, CT 1943. ED Yale University BA (1966); University of Virginia JD (1972); Harvard University PMD (1977). PRIM CORP EMPL president, director: Antaeus Enterprises Inc.
Daniel N. Belin: vice chairman, trustee B 1938. PRIM CORP EMPL partner: Belin Rawling & Badal.
John C. Fontaine: chairman, trustee B 1932. ED University of Michigan BA (1953); Harvard University

LLB (1956). CORP AFFIL director: Twin Cities Newspaper Service; director: Wichita Eagle & Beacon Publishing Co.; director: State Newspaper; director: State-Record Co. Inc.; director: Pioneer Press Inc.; director: Saint Paul Pioneer Press; director: Northwest Publications Inc.; director: Miami Herald; director: Nittany Printing & Publishing Co. Inc.; partner: Hughes Hubbard & Reed LLP; president: Knight-Ridder Inc.; director: Columbia Newspaper; director: Detroit Free Press Inc.; director: Centre Daily Times.

Marilyn Perry: president, trustee B 1940. ED University of North Carolina (1970).

Inmaculada von Habsburg-Lothringen: trustee

Walter L. Weisman: trustee B Chicago, IL 1935. ED Stanford University BA (1956); Stanford University JD (1959). PRIM NONPR EMPL president, chief executive officer: American Medicine International Inc.

Grants Analysis
Disclosure Period: fiscal year ending June 30, 2001
Total Grants: $4,873,012*
Number of Grants: 300
Average Grant: $10,000*
Highest Grant: $250,000
Lowest Grant: $1,000
Typical Range: $1,000 to $25,000
*Note: Grants analysis provided by foundation.

VERNON K. KRIEBLE FOUNDATION

Giving Contact
Helen E. Krieble, President
6017 N. Villard Ct.
Parker, CO 80134

Description
Founded: 1985
EIN: 222538914
Organization Type: Private Foundation
Giving Locations: DC: Washington nationally.
Grant Types: General Support.

Donor Information
Founder: Established by Gladys V. K. Delmas.

Financial Summary
Total Giving: $1,083,800 (2001); $714,238 (2000); $341,500 (1999)
Assets: $8,888,045 (2001); $11,481,721 (2000); $14,914,983 (1999)

Typical Recipients
Arts & Humanities: Arts Institutes, Ballet, Historic Preservation, Libraries, Museums/Galleries, Music, Performing Arts, Public Broadcasting, Theater
Civic & Public Affairs: Business/Free Enterprise, Civil Rights, Economic Policy, Civic & Public Affairs-General, Law & Justice, Legal Aid, Professional & Trade Associations, Public Policy, Safety, Urban & Community Affairs
Education: Arts/Humanities Education, Colleges & Universities, Economic Education, Education Associations, Education Funds, Education-General, Journalism/Media Education, Legal Education, Private Education (Precollege), Science/Mathematics Education, Student Aid
Environment: Environment-General
Health: Hospitals
International: Foreign Educational Institutions, International Affairs, International Peace & Security Issues, International Relations
Science: Scientific Organizations
Social Services: Child Welfare, Community Service Organizations, Recreation & Athletics, United Funds/United Ways, Youth Organizations

Application Procedures
Initial Contact: Send a brief letter of inquiry.
Application Requirements: Include a summary of the project, project budget, amount requested, qualifications of individuals involved, and proof of tax-exempt status.
Deadlines: None.

Restrictions
Awards are made only to 501(c)(3) organizations.

Foundation Officials
Amanda Fusscas: director
Christopher Fusscas: director
Frederick Fusscas: director
Helen K. Fusscas: president
Collette C. Krieble: vice president
Frederick B. Krieble: director
Frederick K. Krieble: vice president B Camden, NJ 1941. ED Yale University (1967). PRIM CORP EMPL chairman financial committee, director: Loctite Corp. CORP AFFIL president: Management I Ltd.; president: Management II Ltd.
Helen E. Krieble: president
Nancy B. Krieble: secretary

Grants Analysis
Disclosure Period: calendar year ending 2001
Total Grants: $1,083,800
Number of Grants: 57
Average Grant: $8,589*
Highest Grant: $602,800
Lowest Grant: $500
Typical Range: $1,000 to $15,000
*Note: Average grant excludes highest grant ($602,800).

Recent Grants
Note: Grants derived from 2000 Form 990.

General
150,000	Young American Broadcaster, Alexandria, VA
95,000	Radio America, Washington, DC
70,988	Center for Security and Social Progress, Inc., Newton, MA
50,000	National Center for Policy Analysis, Dallas, TX
50,000	Visions for America, Inc., Pasadena, MD
30,000	Intercollegiate Studies Institute, Inc,, Wilmington, DE
25,000	America's Survival, Inc., Owings, MD
25,000	Greater Educational Opportunities Foundation, Indianapolis, IN
25,000	Republican Leadership Program, Greenwood Village, CO
15,000	High Frontier, Arlington, VA

KROGER CO.

Company Headquarters
Cincinnati, OH
Web: http://www.kroger.com

Company Description
Founded: 1883
Ticker: KR
Exchange: NYSE
Revenue: US$51.759 billion (2002)
Profit: US$1.204 billion (2002)
Employees: 288000 (2002)
Fortune Rank: 18, per FORTUNE Magazine's list of 500 Largest U.S. Corporations (2002).
SIC(s): 2000 Food & Kindred Products, 5300 General Merchandise Stores, 5400 Food Stores, 5900 Miscellaneous Retail.

Operating Locations
Kroger Co. (AZ--Phoenix; CO--Denver; GA--Atlanta; IN--Indianapolis; MI--Detroit; OH--Cincinnati, Columbus; TN--Memphis; TX--Dallas, Houston; VA--Roanoke)

Nonmonetary Support
Note: For nonmonetary support contact local store manager.

The Kroger Co. Foundation

Giving Contact
Janet Ausdenmoore, Administrator
1014 Vine Street
Cincinnati, OH 45202-1100
Phone: (513)762-4000
Fax: (513)762-1295
Web: http://www.kroger.com/corpnewsinfo_charitablegiving.htm

Description
EIN: 311192929
Organization Type: Corporate Foundation
Former Name: Kroger Co. Foundation.
Giving Locations: headquarters and operating communities.
Grant Types: Award, Capital, General Support, Operating Expenses, Seed Money.

Financial Summary
Total Giving: $3,167,322 (2001); $3,266,708 (2000); $3,122,214 (1999). Note: Contributes through foundation only.
Giving Analysis: Giving for 2001 includes: foundation ($3,167,322); 2000: foundation ($3,266,708); 1999: foundation matching gifts ($3,000); foundation scholarships ($27,150); foundation ($1,968,638)
Assets: $11,638,184 (2001); $12,957,218 (2000); $14,581,757 (1999)

Typical Recipients
Arts & Humanities: Arts Associations & Councils, Arts Centers, Arts Festivals, Arts Funds, Ballet, Dance, Historic Preservation, History & Archaeology, Libraries, Museums/Galleries, Music, Opera, Performing Arts, Public Broadcasting, Theater, Visual Arts
Civic & Public Affairs: Botanical Gardens/Parks, Business/Free Enterprise, Chambers of Commerce, Civil Rights, Community Foundations, Economic Development, Employment/Job Training, Civic & Public Affairs-General, Housing, Minority Business, Municipalities/Towns, Parades/Festivals, Philanthropic Organizations, Professional & Trade Associations, Public Policy, Rural Affairs, Safety, Urban & Community Affairs, Women's Affairs, Zoos/Aquariums
Education: Agricultural Education, Business Education, Colleges & Universities, Community & Junior Colleges, Economic Education, Education Associations, Education Funds, Elementary Education (Private), Education-General, Literacy, Medical Education, Minority Education, Private Education (Precollege), Public Education (Precollege), Science/Mathematics Education, Student Aid
Environment: Environment-General
Health: Arthritis, Cancer, Children's Health/Hospitals, Diabetes, Emergency/Ambulance Services, Eyes/Blindness, Health-General, Health Organizations, Hospices, Hospitals, Medical Rehabilitation, Medical Research, Nutrition, Prenatal Health Issues, Single-Disease Health Associations
International: Foreign Arts Organizations, International Relations
Religion: Churches, Religious Organizations, Religious Welfare
Science: Science Exhibits & Fairs

Social Services: Animal Protection, Big Brother/Big Sister, Camps, Child Welfare, Community Centers, Community Service Organizations, Day Care, Delinquency & Criminal Rehabilitation, Emergency Relief, Food/Clothing Distribution, Homes, People with Disabilities, Recreation & Athletics, Scouts, Senior Services, Shelters/Homelessness, Social Services-General, Special Olympics, Substance Abuse, United Funds/United Ways, YMCA/YWCA/YMHA/YWHA, Youth Organizations

Application Procedures

Initial Contact: Submit a brief letter or proposal.
Application Requirements: Include a description of organization, statement of goals and objectives, amount requested, purpose of funds sought, recently audited financial statement, proof of tax-exempt status, list of board of trustees.
Deadlines: None.
Review Process: Requests are reviewed by foundation trustees on a monthly basis.
Evaluative Criteria: Ability to address an identified need in the community; clearly defined goals and objectives; strong base of community support.
Decision Notification: Decisions usually made within four to six weeks.

Restrictions

The foundation does not assist religious institutions or organizations for sectarian purposes; individuals; endowment campaigns; program or journal advertisements; event sponsorships; medical research national organizations.

Additional Information

Certain national and regional groups are supported, but an important part of evaluating grant requests is the extent to which agency provides services to areas where the company operates.
The foundation was created in 1987.

Corporate Officials

David Brian Dillon: chief executive officer B Hutchinson, KS 1951. ED University of Kansas BS (1973); Southern Methodist University JD (1976). PRIM CORP EMPL chief executive officer: The Kroger Co. CORP AFFIL director: Jackson Ice Cream Co. Inc.; director: First National Hutchinson; director: Fry's Food Stores Arizona Inc.; director: City Market Inc. NONPR AFFIL board: University Kansas Business School; trustee: University Kansas Endowment Association; member: University Kansas Alumni Association; member: Sigma Chi; trustee: University Circle Foundation; member: Order Coif; director: Bethesda Hospital; den board council: Boy Scouts America.
Joseph A. Pichler: chairman B Saint Louis, MO 1939. ED University of Notre Dame BBA (1961); University of Chicago MBA (1963); University of Chicago PhD (1966). PRIM CORP EMPL chairman: Kroger Co. CORP AFFIL president: Pace Dairy Foods Co.; director: Federated Department Stores Inc.; director: Milacron Inc.; director: BF Goodrich Co. NONPR AFFIL chairman national board: National Alliance Business; director: Tougaloo College; director: Cincinnati Opera; national board director: Boys Hope; member: Business Roundtable. CLUB AFFIL Commercial Club Cincinnati; Queen City Club.

Foundation Officials

Lynn Marmer: president

Grants Analysis

Disclosure Period: calendar year ending 2001
Total Grants: $3,167,322*
Number of Grants: 989
Average Grant: $3,203
Highest Grant: $50,000
Lowest Grant: $250
Typical Range: $500 to $5,000
***Note:** Grants analysis provided by foundation.

Recent Grants

Note: Grants derived from 2001 Form 990.

General

106,250	United Way Community Chest, Cincinnati, OH -- campaign pledge
106,250	United Way Community Chest, Cincinnati, OH -- campaign pledge
106,250	United Way Community Chest, Cincinnati, OH -- campaign pledge
106,250	United Way Community Chest, Cincinnati, OH -- campaign pledge
56,000	United Way Franklin County, Columbus, OH -- annual campaign
50,000	Buckeye Ranch, Columbus, OH -- capital campaign
42,972	United Way - Mile High, Denver, CO -- support of annual campaign
40,000	Indianapolis Public Schools, Indianapolis, IN -- for scholarships for kids to attend college
35,000	Fulton County Parks and Recreation Department, Atlanta, GA -- for underwriting support of seven recreational events for children
30,000	Memphis Redbirds Baseball Foundation, Memphis, TN -- inner-city youth baseball program

CHARLES W. KUHNE FOUNDATION TRUST

Giving Contact

Alice Kopfer
c/o Norwest Bank
MAL N8622-031
PO Box 960
Ft. Wayne, IN 46801
Phone: (219)461-6451

Description

EIN: 356011137
Organization Type: Private Foundation
Giving Locations: IN: Allen City
Grant Types: Capital, General Support, Project.

Financial Summary

Total Giving: $185,858 (fiscal year ending July 31, 1999); $169,974 (fiscal 1998); $203,662 (fiscal 1997). Note: Fiscal 1997 Giving includes United Way ($60,500).
Giving Analysis: Giving for fiscal 1999 includes: foundation grants to United Way ($33,100)
Assets: $7,977,037 (fiscal 1999); $7,197,579 (fiscal 1998); $6,465,989 (fiscal 1997)

Typical Recipients

Arts & Humanities: Arts Associations & Councils, Arts Funds, Historic Preservation, History & Archaeology, Libraries, Museums/Galleries, Music, Public Broadcasting, Theater
Civic & Public Affairs: African American Affairs, Botanical Gardens/Parks, Community Foundations, Economic Development, Ethnic Organizations, Civic & Public Affairs-General, Hispanic Affairs, Urban & Community Affairs, Zoos/Aquariums
Education: Business Education, Colleges & Universities, Education Funds, Engineering/Technological Education, Education-General, Literacy, Private Education (Precollege), Public Education (Precollege), Science/Mathematics Education, Student Aid, Vocational & Technical Education
Environment: Air/Water Quality, Resource Conservation
Health: Children's Health/Hospitals, Health Funds, Health Organizations, Health Organizations, Mental Health, Public Health, Single-Disease Health Associations

Religion: Churches, Ministries, Religious Organizations, Religious Welfare
Social Services: Child Welfare, Community Service Organizations, Day Care, Family Services, Food/Clothing Distribution, Homes, People with Disabilities, Recreation & Athletics, Scouts, Senior Services, Shelters/Homelessness, Substance Abuse, United Funds/United Ways, YMCA/YWCA/YMHA/YWHA, Youth Organizations

Application Procedures

Initial Contact: Send a brief letter of inquiry.
Application Requirements: Include a description of organization, amount requested, purpose of funds sought, recently audited financial statement, and proof of tax-exempt status.
Deadlines: None.

Restrictions

Does not fund individuals, political or lobbying groups, religious organizations for sectarian purposes, or organizations outside operating areas.

Additional Information

Trust(s): Norwest Bank

Grants Analysis

Disclosure Period: fiscal year ending July 31, 1999
Total Grants: $152,758*
Number of Grants: 19
Average Grant: $8,040
Highest Grant: $25,000
Typical Range: $1,000 to $25,000
***Note:** Giving excludes United Way.

Recent Grants

Note: Grants derived from 2000 Form 990.

General

50,000	Old Fort YMCA, Ft. Wayne, IN
35,000	Fort Wayne Zoological Society, Ft. Wayne, IN
25,000	Anthony Wayne Council, Ft. Wayne, IN
25,000	Project Renew, Ft. Wayne, IN
25,000	United Way of Allen County, Ft. Wayne, IN
24,450	Arts United, Ft. Wayne, IN
20,000	Early Childhood Alliance, Ft. Wayne, IN
20,000	Turnstone, Ft. Wayne, IN
12,500	SCAN, Ft. Wayne, IN
10,000	Allen County Historical Society, Ft. Wayne, IN

JOHN CRAIN KUNKEL FOUNDATION

Giving Contact

Nancy W. Berget, Trustee
PO Box 658
Camp Hill, PA 17001-0658
Phone: (717)763-1284

Description

Founded: 1965
EIN: 237026914
Organization Type: Private Foundation
Giving Locations: PA
Grant Types: General Support, Project.

Financial Summary

Total Giving: $630,000 (2002 approx); $444,010 (2001); $626,800 (2000)
Giving Analysis: Giving for 2001 includes: foundation grants to United Way ($20,000); 1999: foundation grants to United Way ($15,000) 1998: foundation grants to United Way ($5,000)
Assets: $13,052,337 (2001); $13,890,362 (2000); $14,485,884 (1999)

Typical Recipients

Arts & Humanities: Arts Associations & Councils, Arts Centers, Arts Funds, Ballet, Community Arts, Historic Preservation, History & Archaeology, Libraries, Museums/Galleries, Public Broadcasting, Theater

Civic & Public Affairs: Botanical Gardens/Parks, Clubs, Civic & Public Affairs-General, Housing, Municipalities/Towns, Safety, Urban & Community Affairs, Zoos/Aquariums

Education: Colleges & Universities, Community & Junior Colleges, Medical Education, Preschool Education, Private Education (Precollege), Public Education (Precollege), Secondary Education (Private)

Health: Alzheimers Disease, Cancer, Clinics/Medical Centers, Emergency/Ambulance Services, Health Organizations, Hospitals, Kidney, Long-Term Care, Mental Health, Public Health, Single-Disease Health Associations

Religion: Churches, Religious Welfare

Social Services: Community Service Organizations, Family Planning, Family Services, Substance Abuse, United Funds/United Ways, YMCA/YWCA/YMHA/YWHA, Youth Organizations

Application Procedures

Initial Contact: The foundation requests applications be made in writing. Include specific requests.
Deadlines: None.

Foundation Officials

Nancy W. Bergent: trustee
Elizabeth K. Davis: trustee
Deborah L. Facini: trustee
John C. Kunkel, II: trustee
Paul A. Kunkel: trustee
W. Minster Kunkel, MD: trustee
Jay W. Stark: trustee
John K. Stark: trustee
K. R. Stark: trustee
Hasbrouck S. Wright: executive trustee
William T. Wright, II: trustee

Grants Analysis

Disclosure Period: calendar year ending 2001
Total Grants: $424,010*
Number of Grants: 13
Average Grant: $15,155*
Highest Grant: $120,000
Lowest Grant: $4,000
Typical Range: $5,000 to $50,000
*Note: Giving excludes United Way. Average grant figure excludes two highest grants ($227,000).

Recent Grants

Note: Grants derived from 2001 Form 990.

Library-Related

50,000	Fredrickson Public Library, Camp Hill, PA -- for building fund

General

120,000	Pinnacle Health Foundation, Harrisburg, PA
107,000	National Civil War Museum, Harrisburg, PA
50,000	Whitaker Center for the Arts, Harrisburg, PA
30,000	Allied Arts, Harrisburg, PA
20,000	United Way, Harrisburg, PA
15,000	Harrisburg Cemetery Association, Harrisburg, PA
12,000	Planned Parenthood, Harrisburg, PA
10,000	American Red Cross, Harrisburg, PA
10,000	Gaudenzia, Harrisburg, PA
10,000	Theatre Harrisburg, Harrisburg, PA

KURZ FAMILY FOUNDATION

Giving Contact

69 Lydecker St.
Nyack, NY 10960
Phone: (845)358-2300

Description

Founded: 1992
EIN: 133680855
Organization Type: Private Foundation
Grant Types: General Support.

Donor Information

Founder: Established in 1992 by Herbert Kurz.

Financial Summary

Total Giving: $341,250 (2002); $345,463 (2001); $548,473 (2000)
Assets: $7,160,672 (2002); $13,702,394 (2001); $9,699,559 (2000)
Gifts Received: $496,500 (2002); $525,500 (2001); $1,000,000 (1994). Note: In 1994, 2001, and 2002, , contributions were received from Herbert Kurz.

Typical Recipients

Arts & Humanities: Libraries, Music, Opera, Theater
Civic & Public Affairs: African American Affairs, Civil Rights, Economic Development, Economic Policy, Civic & Public Affairs-General, Law & Justice, Philanthropic Organizations, Professional & Trade Associations, Public Policy, Urban & Community Affairs, Women's Affairs
Education: Arts/Humanities Education, Colleges & Universities, Education Associations, Education Reform, Environmental Education, Education-General, Medical Education, Private Education (Precollege), Public Education (Precollege), Student Aid
Environment: Environment-General, Resource Conservation
Health: Cancer, Clinics/Medical Centers, Health-General, Health Organizations, Heart, Hospitals
International: International Affairs, International Peace & Security Issues, Trade
Religion: Jewish Causes
Social Services: Child Welfare, Community Service Organizations, Family Planning, Family Services, Food/Clothing Distribution, Recreation & Athletics

Application Procedures

Initial Contact: Send a written request including amount requested and a brief summary of the purpose of funds sought.
Deadlines: None.

Foundation Officials

Ellen Kurz: director
Herbert Kurz: president B New York, NY 1920. ED City University of New York (1941). PRIM CORP EMPL chairman, president, chief executive officer, director: Presidential Life Insurance Co. CORP AFFIL president, director: Presidential Life Corp.
Leonard Kurz: director
Brenda Noel: director
Lewis Wechsley: director

Grants Analysis

Disclosure Period: calendar year ending 2002
Total Grants: $341,250
Number of Grants: 184
Average Grant: $1,855
Highest Grant: $12,000
Lowest Grant: $36
Typical Range: $500 to $5,000

Recent Grants

Note: Grants derived from 2001 Form 990.

General

30,000	Alaska Wilderness League, Anchorage, AK
30,000	Center for Environmental Citizenship, Washington, DC
30,000	ProChoice Resource Center, Mamaroneck, NY
15,000	Public Policy and Education Fund, New York, NY
10,000	Westchester Jewish Community Center, Westchester, NY
5,000	Althea Gibson Foundation, Newark, NJ
5,000	CAP Cure, Santa Monica, CA
5,000	Children's Defense Fund
5,000	FIVF
5,000	Inner City Scholarship Fund, New York, NY

MILTON AND HATTIE KUTZ FOUNDATION

Giving Contact

Executive Director
Jewish Federation of Delaware
100 West 10th Street
Suite 301
Wilmington, DE 19801-1628
Phone: (302)427-2100

Description

Founded: 1955
EIN: 510187055
Organization Type: Private Foundation
Giving Locations: DE
Grant Types: Capital, Emergency, General Support, Operating Expenses, Project, Scholarship, Seed Money.

Donor Information

Founder: Milton Kutz, Hattie Kutz

Financial Summary

Total Giving: $148,100 (fiscal year ending June 30, 2000); $131,600 (fiscal 1999); $118,375 (fiscal 1998). Note: 1997 Giving includes scholarships ($7,500).
Giving Analysis: Giving for fiscal 2000 includes: foundation scholarships ($20,000); fiscal 1998: foundation scholarships ($20,000); fiscal 1997: foundation scholarships ($7,500) foundation scholarships ($20,000)
Assets: $3,378,749 (fiscal 2000); $3,642,603 (fiscal 1999); $3,715,958 (fiscal 1998)

Typical Recipients

Arts & Humanities: Libraries
Civic & Public Affairs: Botanical Gardens/Parks, Community Foundations, Economic Development, Employment/Job Training, Housing, Urban & Community Affairs
Education: Colleges & Universities, Literacy, Medical Education, Preschool Education, Private Education (Precollege), Secondary Education (Private), Student Aid
Environment: Resource Conservation
Health: Clinics/Medical Centers
International: Missionary/Religious Activities
Religion: Churches, Jewish Causes, Missionary Activities (Domestic), Religious Organizations, Religious Welfare, Synagogues/Temples
Social Services: At-Risk Youth, Child Welfare, Community Service Organizations, Crime Prevention, Day Care, Family Planning, Family Services, Food/Clothing Distribution, Homes, People with Disabilities, Scouts, Senior Services, Social Services-General, YMCA/YWCA/YMHA/YWHA, Youth Organizations

Application Procedures

Initial Contact: Send a brief letter of inquiry.
Application Requirements: Include a description of organization, amount requested, purpose of funds sought, proof of tax-exempt status, individuals served, program planning mechanism, budget, other funding sources, and program evaluation.
Deadlines: March 31.

Restrictions

Individual scholarships are no longer given. Funds go directly to Delaware colleges for distribution. No grants made outside Delaware. Grants made to Delaware nonsectarian not-for-profit organizations for educational and/or social projects.

Additional Information

Publications: Application Form

Foundation Officials

John A. Elzufon, Esq.: director
Dr. Bennett N. Epstein: secretary
Rolf F. Eriksen: treasurer
Clara Hollander: director
Dr. Barry Kayne: director
Donald Parsons: director
Barbara H. Schoenberg: director
Jeremiah Patrick Shea: vice president B Philadelphia, PA 1926. ED Yale University BA (1946); Catholic University America MA (1950). PRIM CORP EMPL chairman, chief executive officer, director: Bank of Delaware Wilmington. CORP AFFIL assistant secretary, treasurer: Santa Fe Natural Resources; president: Wilmington Financial Co.; chairman: Bank DE Corp. Wilmington; treasurer, director: Santa Fe Industries. NONPR AFFIL director: Saint Marks High School; vice president: United Way; member: Robert Morris Associates; member: American Bankers Association; member: National Alliance Businessmen.
Bernard L. Siegel: president
Judy B. Wortman: executive secretary
Toni P. Young: director
Dr. Leo Zeftel: director

Grants Analysis

Disclosure Period: fiscal year ending June 30, 2000
Total Grants: $128,100*
Number of Grants: 17
Average Grant: $4,256*
Highest Grant: $60,000
Lowest Grant: $1,000
Typical Range: $1,000 to $10,000
*Note: Giving excludes scholarships. Average grant figure excludes highest grant.

Recent Grants

Note: Grants derived from fiscal 1999 Form 990.

General

40,000	Jewish Federation of Delaware, Wilmington, DE -- grant
12,500	Albert Einstein Academy, Wilmington, DE -- grant
10,000	Hillel Center, Newark, DE -- grant
10,000	Lutheran Senior Services, Wilmington, DE -- grant
10,000	University of Delaware, Newark, DE -- scholarship
5,000	Delaware Gratz Hebrew High School, Wilmington, DE -- grant
5,000	Food Bank of Delaware, Newark, DE -- grant
5,000	St. Francis Health Care Services Foundation, Wilmington, DE -- grant
4,600	Jewish Family Services, Wilmington, DE -- grant
3,000	Salesianum School, Wilmington, DE -- grant

PETER H. AND E. LUCILLE GAASS KUYPER FOUNDATION

Giving Contact

Mary Van Zante, Secretary & Treasurer
c/o Pella Corp.
102 Main St.
Pella, IA 50219
Phone: (641)628-6224

Description

Founded: 1970
EIN: 237068402
Organization Type: Private Foundation
Giving Locations: IA: Pella
Grant Types: General Support.

Donor Information

Founder: Peter H. Kuyper, E. Lucille Gaass Kuyper

Financial Summary

Total Giving: $698,551 (2001); $777,404 (2000); $787,478 (1999)
Giving Analysis: Giving for 2001 includes: foundation scholarships ($185,000); foundation matching gifts ($222,915); 2000: foundation matching gifts ($153,700); foundation scholarships ($185,000); 1999: foundation matching gifts ($99,334) foundation scholarships ($210,000)
Assets: $11,638,422 (2001); $12,367,192 (2000); $12,823,258 (1999)

Typical Recipients

Arts & Humanities: Arts Associations & Councils, Arts Centers, Ballet, Historic Preservation, History & Archaeology, Libraries, Museums/Galleries, Music, Opera, Public Broadcasting
Civic & Public Affairs: Botanical Gardens/Parks, Chambers of Commerce, Clubs, Community Foundations, Civic & Public Affairs-General, Municipalities/Towns, Parades/Festivals, Urban & Community Affairs, Women's Affairs, Zoos/Aquariums
Education: Arts/Humanities Education, Colleges & Universities, Private Education (Precollege), Public Education (Precollege), Religious Education, Secondary Education (Public), Student Aid
Environment: Environment-General, Research, Resource Conservation
Health: Children's Health/Hospitals, Emergency/Ambulance Services, Health Organizations, Hospices, Hospitals, Public Health, Single-Disease Health Associations
Religion: Churches, Religion-General, Ministries, Religious Organizations, Religious Welfare, Seminaries
Social Services: At-Risk Youth, Child Welfare, Community Centers, Community Service Organizations, Day Care, Family Services, People with Disabilities, Recreation & Athletics, Special Olympics, United Funds/United Ways, Youth Organizations

Application Procedures

Initial Contact: The foundation has no formal grant application procedure or application form.
Deadlines: None.

Restrictions

Does not support individuals, religious organizations for sectarian purposes, political or lobbying groups, or organizations outside operating areas.

Additional Information

In 1996, the foundation changed from a fiscal year ending April 30 to a calendar year.

Foundation Officials

William J. Anderson: treasurer B Fort Dodge, IA 1946. ED Northeast Missouri State University (1969).
Charles Farver: vice president
Joan Kuyper Farver: president, director B 1919. ED Grinnell College BA (1941). PRIM CORP EMPL chairman emeritus, director: Pella Corp.
Chip Griffith: vice president
Mary Griffith: vice president
Ann Lennartz: vice president
Mary Van Zante: secretary, treasurer

Grants Analysis

Disclosure Period: calendar year ending 2001
Total Grants: $290,636*
Number of Grants: 33
Average Grant: $6,582*
Highest Grant: $80,000
Typical Range: $1,000 to $10,000
*Note: Giving excludes matching gifts and scholarships. Average grant figure excludes highest grant.

Recent Grants

Note: Grants derived from 2001 Form 990.

General

175,000	Central College, Pella, IA -- scholarship fund
80,000	Pella Historical Society, Pella, IA -- Windmill Project
39,056	Central College, Pella, IA -- scholarship fund
25,000	Nature Conservancy, St. Louis, MO
25,000	Pella Opera House, Pella, IA -- programming
20,012	Community Health Service of Marion County, Knoxville, IA -- van service
20,000	Carbondale Clay Center, Carbondale, CO
15,000	All Seasons Center, Sioux Center, IA -- expansion project
15,000	Aspen Country Day School, Aspen, CO
15,000	Kuemper High School, Carroll, IA -- expansion project

L AND L FOUNDATION

Giving Contact

Mildred C. Brinn, President, Treasurer & Director
570 Park Ave.
New York, NY 10021
Phone: (212)758-7764

Description

Founded: 1963
EIN: 136155758
Organization Type: Private Foundation
Giving Locations: NY
Grant Types: General Support.

Donor Information

Founder: Lawrence E. Brinn

Financial Summary

Total Giving: $495,850 (2001); $527,500 (2000); $539,450 (1999)
Assets: $9,628,975 (2001); $11,430,613 (2000); $13,185,687 (1999)

Typical Recipients

Arts & Humanities: Arts Appreciation, Arts Associations & Councils, Arts Centers, Ballet, Dance, Ethnic & Folk Arts, Arts & Humanities-General, Historic Preservation, History & Archaeology, Libraries, Literary Arts,

Museums/Galleries, Music, Opera, Performing Arts, Theater, Visual Arts
Civic & Public Affairs: Botanical Gardens/Parks, Civic & Public Affairs-General, Safety, Urban & Community Affairs, Women's Affairs
Education: Arts/Humanities Education, Colleges & Universities, Medical Education, Private Education (Precollege), Religious Education, School Volunteerism
Health: AIDS/HIV, Cancer, Children's Health/Hospitals, Health-General, Health Organizations, Heart, Hospices, Hospitals, Kidney, Long-Term Care, Single-Disease Health Associations
International: Foreign Educational Institutions, International Affairs, International Organizations, International Relations
Religion: Churches, Jewish Causes, Religious Organizations, Religious Welfare, Seminaries
Social Services: Animal Protection, Child Welfare, Community Service Organizations, Counseling, Crime Prevention, Homes, People with Disabilities, Recreation & Athletics, Veterans, Volunteer Services, Youth Organizations

Application Procedures

Initial Contact: Send a brief letter of inquiry.
Application Requirements: a description of organization and purpose of funds sought.
Deadlines: None.

Restrictions

Does not support individuals.

Foundation Officials

Mildred Cunningham Brinn: president, treasurer, director
Peter F. DeGaetano: secretary, director

Grants Analysis

Disclosure Period: calendar year ending 2001
Total Grants: $495,850
Number of Grants: 34
Average Grant: $7,121*
Highest Grant: $150,000
Typical Range: $1,000 to $15,000
***Note:** Average grant figure excludes two highest grants ($253,750).

Recent Grants

Note: Grants derived from 2001 Form 990.

General

150,000	Parrish Art Museum, New York, NY
103,750	Ballet Theatre Foundation, New York, NY
100,000	St. Bartholomew's Church, New York, NY
50,000	Lenox Hill Hospital, New York, NY
10,100	Skowhegan School of Painting and Sculpture, New York, NY
10,000	Cat Macrae Fund, New York, NY
8,000	St. John's Episcopal Church
7,000	Metropolitan Opera Association, New York, NY
5,000	God's Love We Deliver, New York, NY
5,000	Harlem School of the Arts, New York, NY

LA-Z-BOY, INC.

Company Headquarters

1284 N. Telegraph Road
Monroe, MI 48162-3390
Web: http://www.lazyboy.com

Company Description

Founded: 1928
Ticker: LZB
Exchange: NYSE
Former Name: La-Z-Boy Chair Co.

Revenue: US$2.154 billion (2002)
Employees: 17850 (2002)
SIC(s): 2512 Upholstered Household Furniture, 2514 Metal Household Furniture, 2521 Wood Office Furniture, 2522 Office Furniture Except Wood.

Operating Locations

La-Z-Boy Inc. (AR--Siloam Springs; CA--Redlands; MI--Grand Rapids, Monroe; MS--Leland, Newton; NC--Hudson, Lenoir; SC--Florence; TN--Dayton; UT--Tremonton)

La-Z-Boy Foundation

Giving Contact

Donald E. Blohm, Administrator/Treasurer
La-Z-Boy Foundation
1284 N. Telegraph Road
Monroe, MI 48162
Phone: (734)242-1444
Fax: (734)457-2005
Note: Mr. Blohm's extension is 3680.

Description

Founded: 1953
EIN: 386087673
Organization Type: Corporate Foundation
Giving Locations: AR: Siloam Springs; CA: Redlands; MI: Monroe; MS: Leland, Newton; MO: Neosho; NC: Lincolnton; SC: Florence; TN: Dayton; UT: Tremonton operating locations.
Grant Types: General Support.

Donor Information

Founder: E. M. Knabusch, the late Edwin J. Shoemaker, H. F. Gertz, and La-Z-Boy Chair Co.

Financial Summary

Total Giving: $974,850 (2002); $1,019,480 (2001); $1,049,750 (2000). Note: Contributes through foundation only.
Giving Analysis: Giving for 2000 includes: foundation grants to United Way ($231,000); foundation ($818,750); 1998: foundation scholarships ($73,200) foundation ($849,050)
Assets: $17,225,954 (2002); $19,760,434 (2001); $20,256,309 (2000)

Typical Recipients

Arts & Humanities: Arts Associations & Councils, Arts Centers, Community Arts, Historic Preservation, History & Archaeology, Libraries, Museums/Galleries, Music, Public Broadcasting, Theater
Civic & Public Affairs: Business/Free Enterprise, Community Foundations, Economic Development, Civic & Public Affairs-General, Housing, Municipalities/Towns, Safety, Urban & Community Affairs, Women's Affairs
Education: Business Education, Colleges & Universities, Community & Junior Colleges, Education Funds, Elementary Education (Public), Education-General, Public Education (Precollege), Religious Education, Science/Mathematics Education, Secondary Education (Public), Special Education
Environment: Resource Conservation
Health: Children's Health/Hospitals, Clinics/Medical Centers, Diabetes, Emergency/Ambulance Services, Health Organizations, Hospices, Hospitals, Single-Disease Health Associations
Religion: Churches, Ministries, Religious Welfare
Social Services: Animal Protection, At-Risk Youth, Community Centers, Community Service Organizations, Crime Prevention, Day Care, Emergency Relief, Family Services, Senior Services, Social Services-General, United Funds/United Ways, Veterans, YMCA/YWCA/YMHA/YWHA, Youth Organizations

Application Procedures

Initial Contact: Send a letter of request.
Application Requirements: Briefly describe the basic need; include a description of organization, amount requested, purpose of funds sought, recently audited financial statement, the organization's budget, and list of directors, proof of 501(c)(3) tax-exempt status, project time span and estimated costs, and benefits of the project to the community.
Deadlines: February 15, May 15, August 15, November 15.
Decision Notification: The board of trustees meets quarterly in March, June, September, and December.
Notes: Personal interviews are arranged upon the foundation's initiative only. Sufficient funding must be assured for successful completion of the project.

Restrictions

Foundation does not make direct grants to individuals; or for loans, travel or conferences, nor does it provide startup funds or seed money. The geographic areas for grant consideration are normally limited to the communities where La-Z-Boy Inc. production plants are located, and within a fifteen mile radius of corporate headquarters.

Corporate Officials

David K. Hehl: director B 1947. ED Michigan State University BA. PRIM CORP EMPL partner: Cooley, Hehl, Wohlgamuth & Carlton. CORP AFFIL director: La-Z-Boy Chair Co.; director: La-Z-Boy Inc.
James W. Johnston: director
Gerald L. Kiser: president, chief executive officer, director ED Western Carolina University BBA (1969). PRIM CORP EMPL president, chief executive officer, director: La-Z-Boy Inc.
Dr. H. George Levy: director PRIM CORP EMPL director: La-Z-Boy Inc.
Patrick H. Norton: chairman, director B 1923. PRIM CORP EMPL chairman, director: La-Z-Boy Inc. CORP AFFIL director: Culp Inc.; director: England/Corsair Inc.
Lorne G. Stevens: director
John F. Weaver: director PRIM CORP EMPL vice chairman: Monroe Bank & Trust Co.

Foundation Officials

Donald E. Blohm: administrator
Gene M. Hardy: director B Selma, AL 1937. ED University of Alabama (1959). PRIM CORP EMPL secretary, treasurer, director: La-Z-Boy Inc. NONPR AFFIL member: Financial Executives Institute.

Grants Analysis

Disclosure Period: calendar year ending 2002
Total Grants: $974,850*
Number of Grants: 169
Average Grant: $5,768
Highest Grant: $50,000
Lowest Grant: $250
Typical Range: $250 to $5,000
***Note:** Grants analysis provided by foundation.

Recent Grants

Note: Grants derived from 2001 Form 990.

Library-Related

7,500	Yucaipa Branch Library
6,000	St. Mary Catholic Central High
5,000	Rhea County Department of Education
5,000	Rhea County Department of Education

General

50,000	Monroe County Opportunity Program, Monroe, OH
50,000	Southwest Family YMCA
42,000	United Way of Lincoln County
40,000	Neosho United Fund
30,000	United Way of Greensboro, Greensboro, NC
27,000	Mississippi Delta Community College, Moorhead, MS

25,000	Chilhowie Fire Department
25,000	Mercy Memorial Hospital Foundation, Monroe, OH
25,000	United Way Northern Utah, Ogden, UT
25,000	United Way of Rhea County

HELEN AND GEORGE LADD CHARITABLE CORP.

Giving Contact

Charles A. Rosebrock, Director
c/o Nutter, McClennen & Fish
PO Box 51400
Boston, MA 02205
Phone: (617)439-2498
Fax: (617)973-9748
E-mail: car@nutter.com

Description

Founded: 1984
EIN: 042767890
Organization Type: Private Foundation
Giving Locations: ME
Grant Types: General Support.

Donor Information

Founder: George E. Ladd, Jr. Charitable Trust

Financial Summary

Total Giving: $559,095 (2002); $566,751 (2001); $437,820 (2000)
Giving Analysis: Giving for 2002 includes: foundation grants to United Way ($500); 2000: foundation grants to United Way ($500) 1999: foundation grants to United Way ($500)
Assets: $9,894,124 (2002); $11,363,726 (2001); $12,721,003 (2000)
Gifts Received: $167,500 (2001); $420,188 (2000); $420,188 (1999). Note: In 1999, 2000, and 2001, contributions were received from George E. Ladd Jr. Charitable Trust. In 1998 contributions were received from George E. Ladd, Jr. ($420,188) and Helen F. Ladd Charitable Trust ($84,699). In 1996, contributions were received from George E. Ladd, Jr. ($420,188) and the Helen F. Ladd Charitable Trust ($100,000).

Typical Recipients

Arts & Humanities: Community Arts, History & Archaeology, Libraries, Literary Arts, Music, Performing Arts, Public Broadcasting, Theater
Civic & Public Affairs: African American Affairs, Economic Development, Employment/Job Training, Civic & Public Affairs-General, Municipalities/Towns, Nonprofit Management, Parades/Festivals, Public Policy, Rural Affairs, Safety, Urban & Community Affairs, Women's Affairs, Zoos/Aquariums
Education: Colleges & Universities, Elementary Education (Public), Faculty Development, Leadership Training, Literacy, Minority Education, Private Education (Precollege), Special Education
Environment: Forestry, Environment-General, Resource Conservation
Health: Arthritis, Clinics/Medical Centers, Hospices, Hospitals, Mental Health, Public Health, Single-Disease Health Associations
International: International Affairs
Religion: Churches, Ministries, Religious Welfare
Social Services: Big Brother/Big Sister, Child Welfare, Community Centers, Community Service Organizations, Counseling, Crime Prevention, Domestic Violence, Family Planning, Food/Clothing Distribution, People with Disabilities, Recreation & Athletics, Social Services-General, Veterans, YMCA/YWCA/YMHA/YWHA, Youth Organizations

Application Procedures

Initial Contact: Send brief letter describing program. Include purpose of funds sought.
Deadlines: None.

Foundation Officials

George E. Ladd, III: director
Lincoln F. Ladd: director
Robert M. Ladd: director
Charles A. Rosebrock: director

Grants Analysis

Disclosure Period: calendar year ending 2002
Total Grants: $558,595*
Number of Grants: 64
Average Grant: $5,973*
Highest Grant: $80,235
Lowest Grant: $50
Typical Range: $1,000 to $10,000
*Note: Giving excludes United Way. Average grant figure excludes three highest grants ($194,235).

Recent Grants

Note: Grants derived from 2001 Form 990.

Library-Related

10,000	Lubec Memorial Library

General

62,000	Skidmore College, Saratoga Springs, NY
57,000	Bates College, Lewiston, ME
53,175	Town of Wayne, ME
27,500	Rural Action Community Ministry, Athens, OH
25,000	Kennebec Valley Mental Health Center, Waterville, ME
22,500	Opportunity Farm, New Gloucester, ME
20,000	Russell Medical Center
18,350	Maine Public Broadcasting Corp, Lewiston, ME
17,500	YMCA of Central Maine, ME
15,000	Good Shepherd Food Bank

LAFFEY-MCHUGH FOUNDATION

Giving Contact

Arthur G. Connolly, Jr., President
PO Box 2286
Wilmington, DE 19899
Phone: (302)654-1680
Fax: (302)654-1681

Alternate Contact

Sandy McCracken
Phone: (302)888-6215

Description

Founded: 1949
EIN: 516015095
Organization Type: General Purpose Foundation
Giving Locations: DE; NY; PA
Grant Types: Capital, General Support, Project, Scholarship.

Donor Information

Founder: The principal donor of the Laffey-McHugh Foundation was Frank A. McHugh, who died in 1949. Mr. McHugh was secretary to Pierre S. duPont at the E. I. duPont de Nemours Company. Other donors to the foundation included the late Alice L. McHugh and the late Marie Louise McHugh.

Financial Summary

Total Giving: $4,000,000 (2003 approx); $4,500,000 (2002 approx); $4,198,500 (2000)
Giving Analysis: Giving for 2000 includes: foundation scholarships ($100,000); foundation grants to United Way ($150,000); 1998: foundation grants to United Way ($235,000) 1997: foundation grants to United Way ($210,000)
Assets: $95,169,054 (2000); $88,353,636 (1998); $83,821,327 (1997)
Gifts Received: $23,736 (1997)

Typical Recipients

Arts & Humanities: Arts Centers, Arts Funds, Ballet, Historic Preservation, History & Archaeology, Libraries, Museums/Galleries, Public Broadcasting, Visual Arts
Civic & Public Affairs: Botanical Gardens/Parks, Clubs, Community Foundations, Employment/Job Training, Civic & Public Affairs-General, Housing, Law & Justice, Legal Aid, Public Policy, Urban & Community Affairs, Zoos/Aquariums
Education: Arts/Humanities Education, Business Education, Colleges & Universities, Education Associations, Education Funds, Elementary Education (Private), Elementary Education (Public), Education-General, Leadership Training, Legal Education, Minority Education, Private Education (Precollege), Public Education (Precollege), Science/Mathematics Education, Secondary Education (Private), Student Aid
Environment: Environment-General, Resource Conservation
Health: Alzheimers Disease, Cancer, Children's Health/Hospitals, Clinics/Medical Centers, Geriatric Health, Heart, Hospices, Hospitals, Long-Term Care, Nursing Services, Outpatient Health Care, Preventive Medicine/Wellness Organizations, Public Health, Single-Disease Health Associations
Religion: Churches, Dioceses, Jewish Causes, Ministries, Religious Organizations, Religious Welfare, Seminaries, Social/Policy Issues
Social Services: Animal Protection, At-Risk Youth, Camps, Child Abuse, Child Welfare, Community Centers, Community Service Organizations, Counseling, Counseling, Day Care, Emergency Relief, Family Planning, Family Services, Food/Clothing Distribution, Homes, People with Disabilities, Recreation & Athletics, Scouts, Senior Services, Shelters/Homelessness, Special Olympics, Substance Abuse, United Funds/United Ways, YMCA/YWCA/YMHA/YWHA, Youth Organizations

Application Procedures

Initial Contact: There are no application forms. Applicants should send a succinct two-page letter.
Application Requirements: Application letters should include background information on the organization and project, goals of the project, amount requested, listing of other funding sources, and indication of IRS tax-exempt status. The foundation will request any additional information.
Deadlines: Applications should be submitted by April 1 or October 1.
Review Process: The directors normally meet in May and November.

Restrictions

Grants are not made to individuals.

Additional Information

Trustees prefer capital investments/improvements rather than studies or projects.

Foundation Officials

Arthur Gould Connolly, Jr.: president B Wilmington, DE. ED Georgetown University BSS (1959); Georgetown University LLB (1962). PRIM CORP EMPL attorney: Connolly, Bove, Lodge & Hutz.
Arthur Guild Connolly, Sr.: vice president B Boston, MA November 08, 1905. ED Massachusetts Institute of Technology BS (1927); Harvard University LLB (1930). PRIM CORP EMPL partner emeritus: Connolly, Bove, Lodge & Hutz. NONPR AFFIL fellow: American College Trial Lawyers; member: Delaware Bar Association; member: American Bar Association.

CLUB AFFIL Lago Mar Golf & Country Club; Wilmington Country Club; Harvard Club Delaware.
Marie L. McHugh: vice president, director

Grants Analysis

Disclosure Period: calendar year ending 2000
Total Grants: $3,948,500*
Number of Grants: 123
Average Grant: $34,134
Highest Grant: $150,000
Lowest Grant: $2,000
Typical Range: $5,000 to $50,000
***Note:** Giving excludes United Way and Scholarship.

Recent Grants

Note: Grants derived from 2000 Form 990.

General

150,000	Christiana Care, Wilmington, DE -- capital campaign
150,000	United Way of Delaware, Wilmington, DE -- 2000 campaign
145,000	Ministry of Caring, Wilmington, DE -- building renovations
125,000	Children's Hospital Foundation, Philadelphia, PA -- Endowed Chair in Pediatric Nephrology
112,500	Salesianum School, Wilmington, DE -- capital campaign
100,000	Massachusetts Institute of Technology, Cambridge, MA -- general operations support
100,000	Thomas A. Edison Charter School, Wilmington, DE -- capital campaign
90,000	Catholic Relief Services, Baltimore, MD -- disaster funds
90,000	Neighborhood House, Wilmington, DE -- for Summer Day Camp programs
90,000	United Cerebral Palsy Association, Wilmington, DE -- building renovations and program development

LAKE PLACID EDUCATION FOUNDATION

Giving Contact

John S. Lansing, Executive Director
157 Saranac Avenue
Lake Placid, NY 12946
Phone: (518)523-4433

Description

Founded: 1922
EIN: 510243919
Organization Type: Private Foundation
Giving Locations: NY
Grant Types: Fellowship, General Support, Matching, Scholarship.

Donor Information

Founder: the late Melvil Dewey

Financial Summary

Total Giving: $2,392,110 (fiscal year ending June 30, 2001); $375,610 (fiscal 1999); $236,430 (fiscal 1997)
Giving Analysis: Giving for fiscal 2001 includes: foundation scholarships ($5,500); fiscal 1999: foundation fellowships ($10,000); foundation matching gifts ($12,025); foundation scholarships ($77,130); foundation ($276,455) fiscal 1997: foundation scholarships ($148,880)
Assets: $6,572,237 (fiscal 2001); $9,482,036 (fiscal 1999); $6,825,279 (fiscal 1997)
Gifts Received: $1,000 (fiscal 2001); $6,200 (fiscal 1997); $152,315 (fiscal 1996). Note: In fiscal 1997, contributions were received from various individuals for SL Youth AA.

Typical Recipients

Arts & Humanities: Arts Associations & Councils, Arts Centers, Arts Outreach, History & Archaeology, Libraries, Museums/Galleries, Music
Civic & Public Affairs: Clubs, Economic Development, Civic & Public Affairs-General, Philanthropic Organizations, Public Policy
Education: Arts/Humanities Education, Colleges & Universities, Faculty Development, Education-General, Literacy, Private Education (Precollege), Public Education (Precollege), Science/Mathematics Education, Student Aid
Religion: Churches
Social Services: Camps, Counseling, Day Care, Shelters/Homelessness

Application Procedures

Initial Contact: The foundation has no formal grant application procedure or application form. Send a brief letter of inquiry.
Deadlines: November 1.

Restrictions

Grants are generally limited to educational purposes.

Foundation Officials

Henry M. Bonner: director
Fred E. Brown: director
William J. Bumsted: director
Frederick C. Calder: vice president
Walter W. Curley: president
W. John Friedlander: director
George G. Hart: secretary
John S. Lansing: executive director
Meredith Prime: director
Peter F. Roland: director

Grants Analysis

Disclosure Period: fiscal year ending June 30, 2001
Total Grants: $2,386,610*
Number of Grants: 35
Average Grant: $8,577*
Highest Grant: $2,095,000
Typical Range: $1,000 to $25,000
***Note:** Giving excludes scholarships. Average grant figure excludes highest grant.

Recent Grants

Note: Grants derived from fiscal 2001 Form 990.

Library-Related

25,500	Lake Placid Public Library, Lake Placid, NY -- debt servicing
20,000	New York Library Association, Albany, NY -- library purposes and fellowships
7,410	Long Lake Library, Long Lake, NY -- education

General

2,095,000	Adirondack Community Crestview Plaza, Lake Placid, NY -- Dewey Endowment
50,000	National Sports Academy, Lake Placid, NY -- education
40,000	Northwood School, Lake Placid, NY -- education
35,000	Lake Placid Center for Arts, Lake Placid, NY -- arts and humanities
20,000	North Country School, Lake Placid, NY -- education
10,000	Adirondack Explorer, Saranac Lake, NY -- operations
10,000	Lake Placid Institute, Lake Placid, NY -- arts and humanities
10,000	Samaritan Family Counseling, Keene, NY -- social service
9,080	Lake Placid Central School, Lake Placid, NY -- education
9,050	Saranac Lake Central School, Saranac Lake, NY -- education

LAMB FOUNDATION

Giving Contact

Frank Lamb, Director
PO Box 1705
Lake Oswego, OR 97035-0575
Phone: (503)635-8010

Description

Founded: 1971
EIN: 237120564
Organization Type: Private Foundation
Giving Locations: OR
Grant Types: Emergency, General Support, Project, Seed Money.

Donor Information

Founder: members of the Lamb family

Financial Summary

Total Giving: $242,400 (2002); $180,110 (2001); $185,779 (2000)
Giving Analysis: Giving for 1999 includes: foundation fellowships ($2,000) foundation scholarships ($25,000)
Assets: $4,713,649 (2002); $5,618,838 (2001); $6,007,074 (2000)

Typical Recipients

Arts & Humanities: Arts Associations & Councils, Arts Festivals, Ballet, Community Arts, History & Archaeology, Libraries, Literary Arts, Museums/Galleries, Music, Public Broadcasting, Theater
Civic & Public Affairs: Botanical Gardens/Parks, Clubs, Economic Development, Civic & Public Affairs-General, Hispanic Affairs, Housing, Municipalities/Towns, Native American Affairs, Public Policy, Urban & Community Affairs
Education: Afterschool/Enrichment Programs, Arts/Humanities Education, Business Education, Colleges & Universities, Community & Junior Colleges, Continuing Education, Economic Education, Education-General, Literacy, Private Education (Precollege), Religious Education, Student Aid
Environment: Air/Water Quality, Air/Water Quality, Forestry, Environment-General, Resource Conservation, Wildlife Protection
Health: Cancer, Children's Health/Hospitals, Clinics/Medical Centers, Diabetes, Emergency/Ambulance Services, Health Organizations, Hospices, Hospitals
Religion: Religious Welfare
Social Services: Animal Protection, At-Risk Youth, Camps, Child Welfare, Community Centers, Community Service Organizations, Crime Prevention, Day Care, Delinquency & Criminal Rehabilitation, Family Planning, Family Services, Food/Clothing Distribution, People with Disabilities, Recreation & Athletics, Shelters/Homelessness, Social Services-General, Youth Organizations

Application Procedures

Initial Contact: Send a brief letter of inquiry.
Application Requirements: Include amount requested, purpose of funds sought and any additional information or brochures applicable.
Deadlines: None.

Restrictions

Does not support individuals.

Additional Information

Publications: Annual Report

Foundation Officials

Anita Lamb Bailey: director
Ben Bailey: director
Toff Bailey: director
Barbara Lamb: director
Carl Lamb: director

Dorothy Lamb: director
Frank Lamb: chairman
Greg Lamb: director
Helen Lamb: director
Maryann Lamb: treasurer
Paula L. Lamb: vchairman
Peter Lamb: director

Grants Analysis

Disclosure Period: calendar year ending 2002
Total Grants: $242,400
Number of Grants: 82
Average Grant: $2,956
Highest Grant: $12,500
Lowest Grant: $250
Typical Range: $1,000 to $5,000

Recent Grants

Note: Grants derived from 2001 Form 990.

General

7,500	Caldera
5,000	Center for Watershed and Community Health, Springfield, OR
5,000	Eastern Oregon Regional Arts Council, La Grande, OR
5,000	Heart of Oregon Corps, OR
5,000	Jackson Bottom Wetland Preservation
5,000	Mother Oak's Child
5,000	Nature Conservancy of Oregon, Portland, OR
5,000	Portland House of Umoja, Portland, OR
5,000	Pregnancy Centers
5,000	Shangri-La Corporation, Salem, OR

LAMCO COMMUNICATIONS

Company Headquarters

Williamsport, PA

Operating Locations

Lamco Communications (PA--Williamsport)

Lamco Foundation

Giving Contact

Andrew Stabler, Jr., Relationship Banking Leader
460 Market Street., Suite 310
Williamsport, PA 17701

Description

EIN: 246012727
Organization Type: Corporate Foundation
Giving Locations: PA
Grant Types: Award, Capital, Emergency, Employee Matching Gifts, Endowment, Fellowship, General Support, Operating Expenses, Project, Scholarship.

Financial Summary

Total Giving: $13,733 (2000); $20,034 (1999); $36,000 (1998)
Giving Analysis: Giving for 1999 includes: foundation grants to United Way ($5,200) foundation ($14,834)
Assets: $499,652 (2000); $493,546 (1999); $478,224 (1998)
Gifts Received: $25,000 (1998). Note: In 1989, contributions were received from LamCo. Communications.

Typical Recipients

Arts & Humanities: Art History, Arts Appreciation, Community Arts, Arts & Humanities-General, History & Archaeology, Libraries, Museums/Galleries, Music, Public Broadcasting
Civic & Public Affairs: Business/Free Enterprise, Chambers of Commerce, Community Foundations, Economic Development, Civic & Public Affairs-General, Housing, Inner-City Development, Urban & Community Affairs, Women's Affairs
Education: Business Education, Colleges & Universities, Economic Education, Education Funds, Education-General, Medical Education
Environment: Air/Water Quality
Health: Alzheimers Disease, Cancer, Diabetes, Emergency/Ambulance Services, Eyes/Blindness, Health-General, Hospitals, Medical Research, Preventive Medicine/Wellness Organizations
International: Health Care/Hospitals, Missionary/Religious Activities
Religion: Churches, Religion-General, Ministries, Religious Organizations, Religious Welfare
Science: Science-General, Science Museums, Scientific Centers & Institutes
Social Services: Animal Protection, Camps, Child Welfare, Community Centers, Community Service Organizations, Emergency Relief, Family Services, Homes, Shelters/Homelessness, Social Services-General, United Funds/United Ways, YMCA/YWCA/YMHA/YWHA, Youth Organizations

Application Procedures

Initial Contact: Send a full proposal. Include a description of organization, amount requested, and purpose of funds sought.
Deadlines: None.

Restrictions

Does not support organizations outside operating areas.

Additional Information

Trust(s): M & T Trust Co.

Corporate Officials

Frank Concino, Jr.: president, chief executive officer
PRIM CORP EMPL president, chief executive officer: Lamco Communications.

Foundation Officials

Howard Lamade: adv comm
J. Robert Lamade: adv comm
James S. Lamade: adv comm
Andrew Stabler: adv comm

Grants Analysis

Disclosure Period: calendar year ending 2000
Total Grants: $13,733
Number of Grants: 4
Highest Grant: $5,000
Lowest Grant: $400

Recent Grants

Note: Grants derived from 1999 Form 990.

Library-Related

2,000	James V. Brown Library, Williamsport, PA

General

5,200	Lycoming United Way, Williamsport, PA
3,334	Lycoming County Historical Society, Williamsport, PA
2,500	American Red Cross of Lycoming County, Williamsport, PA
2,000	Williamsport Symphony Orchestra, Williamsport, PA
1,500	Lycoming College, Williamsport, PA
1,000	Hemlock Girl Scout Council, Williamsport, PA
1,000	Hope Enterprises, Williamsport, PA
500	Children's Discovery Workshop, Williamsport, PA
500	Shepherd of the Street, Williamsport, PA
500	WVIA TV/FM, Williamsport, PA

LAND O'LAKES, INC.

Company Headquarters

4001 Lexington Ave. N.
St. Paul, MN 55126
Web: http://www.landolakesinc.com

Company Description

Founded: 1921
Revenue: US$5.847 billion (2002)
Employees: 8,600 (2001)
Fortune Rank: 297, per FORTUNE Magazine's list of 500 Largest U.S. Corporations (2002).
SIC(s): 2021 Creamery Butter, 5143 Dairy Products Except Dried or Canned, 5451 Dairy Products Stores.

Operating Locations

Land O'Lakes, Inc. (CA--Orland; FL--Orange City; ID; IA--Audubon; MN--Browerville, Luverne, Minneapolis; MT; NE--Hardy, Reynolds, Superior; OR; SD--Sioux Falls, Volga; UT; WA; WI--Kiel, Pulaski, Spencer; WY)

Nonmonetary Support

Value: $450,000 (1998)
Type: Donated Products; Loaned Executives
Volunteer Programs: Supports a Dollars for Doers program, which provides cash donations to organizations where employees volunteer. At many company plants and offices, Community Involvement Councils organize and coordinate community activities for employees. The company also supports Expanding Community and Horizon Outreach for Seniors (ECHOS), a volunteer program for company retirees.
Note: Food donations are made only through Second Harvest Foodbank Network.

Land O'Lakes Foundation

Giving Contact

Bonnie Bassett, Executive Director
Land O'Lakes Foundation
PO Box 64150
St. Paul, MN 55164-0150
Phone: (651)481-2212
Fax: (651)481-2000
E-mail: bbbass@landolakes.com
Web: http://foundation.landolakes.com

Description

EIN: 411864977
Organization Type: Corporate Foundation
Giving Locations: AR; CA; CO; ID; IN; IA; MD; MI; MN; MT; NE; ND; OH; OR; PA; SD; VA; WA; WI
Grant Types: Capital, Employee Matching Gifts, Endowment, General Support, Operating Expenses, Professorship, Project, Seed Money.
Note: Employee matching gift ratio: 1 to 1 for gifts to post-secondary education, ranging from $25 to $500 annually. Also offers a cooperative match program (for member cooperatives).

Financial Summary

Total Giving: $1,200,000 (2003 approx); $1,600,000 (2002); $1,368,958 (2001)
Giving Analysis: Giving for 2001 includes: foundation matching gifts ($77,913); foundation ($1,443,260); 2000: foundation matching gifts ($364,645); foundation ($985,893); 1999: foundation scholarships ($650); foundation grants to United Way ($169,360); foundation matching gifts ($221,082); foundation ($538,104);
Assets: $2,000,000 (2004 approx); $2,400,000 (2003 approx); $2,400,000 (2002)
Gifts Received: $1,145,165 (2001); $1,455,000 (2000); $493,750 (1999). Note: Contributions received are from Land O'Lakes, Inc.

Typical Recipients

Arts & Humanities: Arts Associations & Councils, Arts Centers, Arts Institutes, Community Arts, Ethnic & Folk Arts, Arts & Humanities-General, History & Archaeology, Libraries, Literary Arts, Museums/Galleries, Music, Performing Arts, Public Broadcasting, Theater

Civic & Public Affairs: Business/Free Enterprise, Clubs, Economic Policy, Employment/Job Training, Civic & Public Affairs-General, Housing, Municipalities/Towns, Native American Affairs, Parades/Festivals, Professional & Trade Associations, Public Policy, Rural Affairs, Safety, Urban & Community Affairs, Zoos/Aquariums

Education: Agricultural Education, Business Education, Colleges & Universities, Continuing Education, Elementary Education (Public), Elementary Education (Public), Faculty Development, Education-General, Minority Education, Private Education (Precollege), Public Education (Precollege), Secondary Education (Public), Social Sciences Education, Student Aid

Environment: Environment-General, Resource Conservation, Wildlife Protection

Health: Children's Health/Hospitals, Clinics/Medical Centers, Emergency/Ambulance Services, Geriatric Health, Health Organizations

International: International-General, International Development, International Relief Efforts

Religion: Religious Welfare

Science: Science Museums, Scientific Centers & Institutes

Social Services: Child Welfare, Community Centers, Crime Prevention, Day Care, Domestic Violence, Family Services, Food/Clothing Distribution, People with Disabilities, Recreation & Athletics, Senior Services, Shelters/Homelessness, Social Services-General, Special Olympics, United Funds/United Ways, Volunteer Services, YMCA/YWCA/YMHA/YWHA, Youth Organizations

Application Procedures

Initial Contact: For direct company grants toward programs of local interest, send a brief letter on organization's stationery to facility manager at nearest Land O'Lakes facility; for other corporate grants and for foundation grants, write or see website for application form.

Application Requirements: Include completed application, a copy of the most recent annual report with financial information included, or a brief history and current activities of the organization; a current operating budget and proposed budget; a copy of the organization's tax-exempt ruling, or description of organization's ownership and/or management.

Deadlines: April 1, July 1, September 1, and December 1 for general grants; for arts grants over $5,000, April 1.

Review Process: For direct company giving: operating locations are responsible for budgeting contributions strictly benefiting their communities; requests with broad applications are submitted to headquarters. For foundation giving: requests will be reviewed by foundation board for grants of over $5,000, and by the foundation staff for grants of less than $5,000.

Evaluative Criteria: The foundation looks for quality delivery of a needed service; potential benefit to a substantial segment of community; results which are predictable and can be evaluated; broad-based community support; competent, qualified staff and board; fiscal and management capability to carry out program.

Decision Notification: The foundation board meets in January, May, August, and October.

Restrictions

Does not support individuals; lobbying, political, or religious organizations; veteran, fraternal, or labor organizations; advertising; fund-raising events, dinners, or benefits; scholarships, or private colleges or universities; travel expenses; disease/medical research or treatment; or racing/sports sponsorships.

Additional Information

Because Land O'Lakes is a farmer-owned cooperative, rural and agriculture-related programs receive special consideration. About 80% of donations are made to rural areas, and 20% to urban communities. Special consideration also is given to organizations in which company employees are involved.

In December 1996, "Land O'Lakes, Inc., officially created and endowed the Land O'Lakes Foundation...with an initial donation of $2,000,000. The foundation continues Land O'Lakes' well-established corporate giving program and focuses on improving the quality of life in rural America."

Land O'Lakes dedicates 2% of pre-tax earnings to charitable giving, with 1.5% going to the Foundation and .5% into direct corporate giving.

The company and the foundation continue to focus on the North Central, Northwest and Eastern United States, where most of their operating facilities are located; also on rural areas.

The Foundation also matches dollar for dollar grants made by member co-operatives. Organizations should apply directly to the local co-op, which can request a match from the foundation.

Publications: Community Grants Program Guidelines

Corporate Officials

Lydia Botham: director test kitchens PRIM CORP EMPL director test kitchens: Land O'Lakes, Inc.

John E. Gherty: president, chief executive officer B New Richmond, WI 1944. ED University of Wisconsin BBA (1965); University of Wisconsin MA (1970); University of Wisconsin JD (1970). PRIM CORP EMPL president, chief executive officer: Land O'Lakes, Inc. CORP AFFIL member executive committee: CF Industries, Inc.; director: Recovery Engineering Inc.; director: Alpine Lace Brands Inc.; director: Cenex/Land O Lakes Agronomy Co. NONPR AFFIL member, director: National Council Farmer Coops; director: National Parenting Association; director: Minnesota Business Partnership; member: American Bar Association; director: Graduate Institute Coop Leadership.

Foundation Officials

Lydia Botham: vice chairman, secretary (see above)

Judy Kahler: director PRIM CORP EMPL human resources & building services supervisor: Land O'Lakes, Inc.

Bonnie Neuenfeldt: executive director PRIM CORP EMPL director community relations: Land O'Lakes, Inc.

Larry Wojchik: chairman PRIM NONPR EMPL general manager: Equity Cooperative of Amery Lake Wisconsin. CORP AFFIL director: Land O'Lakes Inc.

Grants Analysis

Disclosure Period: calendar year ending 2002
Total Grants: $1,600,000
Number of Grants: 600
Average Grant: $3,325
Highest Grant: $75,000
Lowest Grant: $100

Recent Grants

Note: Grants derived from 2001 Form 990.

Library-Related

5,000	Friends of the St. Paul Public Library, St. Paul, MN -- renewal capital campaign

General

97,200	Greater Twin Cities United Way, Minneapolis, MN -- for employee/leadership match of cash donations made to the September 11 fund
75,000	University of California Davis, Tulare, CA -- for California Dairy Technology Center
75,000	University of Wisconsin, Madison, WI -- capital campaign
60,000	National FFA Foundation, Madison, WI -- National Chapter Award Program
50,000	Pennsylvania State University College of Agricultural Sciences, University Park, PA -- food science capital campaign
37,640	American Red Cross, Washington, DC -- for September 11 American national tragedy relief efforts
32,058	American Red Cross, Washington, DC -- for September 11 American national tragedy relief efforts
30,000	Nature Conservancy, Minneapolis, MN -- Great Plains Conservation Campaign
28,000	Sharing Help Awareness United Network, Harlan, IA -- for Sowing Seeds of Hope Pilot Project
25,515	United Way of Tulare County, Tulare, CA -- operating support

LANDEGGER CHARITABLE FOUNDATION

Giving Contact

Jewell L. Fair, Secretary
2090 S. Nova Rd., Suite B-221
South Daytona, FL 32119
Phone: (386)763-9220

Description

Founded: 1975
EIN: 510180544
Organization Type: Private Foundation
Giving Locations: DC: Washington
Grant Types: General Support, Multiyear/Continuing Support.

Financial Summary

Total Giving: $783,500 (fiscal year ending October 31, 2001); $897,510 (fiscal 2000); $964,041 (fiscal 1999)
Assets: $13,322,229 (fiscal 2001); $14,924,115 (fiscal 2000); $14,944,570 (fiscal 1999)

Typical Recipients

Arts & Humanities: Arts Centers, Dance, Historic Preservation, Libraries, Museums/Galleries

Civic & Public Affairs: Civic & Public Affairs-General, Urban & Community Affairs

Education: Colleges & Universities, Community & Junior Colleges, Education-General, International Studies, Literacy, Private Education (Precollege), Religious Education, Secondary Education (Private), Student Aid

Health: Clinics/Medical Centers, Hospitals

International: Foreign Educational Institutions, International Affairs, International Relief Efforts, Missionary/Religious Activities

Religion: Churches, Religion-General, Jewish Causes, Religious Welfare

Social Services: Child Welfare, Community Service Organizations, Family Services, Recreation & Athletics

Application Procedures

Initial Contact: Send a brief letter of inquiry describing program or project.
Deadlines: None.

Foundation Officials

John F. Bolt: secretary
Jewell L. Fair: secretary
Carl Clement Landegger: treasurer, director B Vienna, Austria 1930. ED Georgetown University BS

(1951). PRIM CORP EMPL chairman, director: Black Clawson Co. CORP AFFIL vice chairman: Parsons & Whittemore; chairman: Saint Anne Nackawic Pulp & Paper Co.; chairman: AlabamaRiver Pulp Co.; director: Downingtown Manufacturing Co. NONPR AFFIL director: Georgetown University; trustee: New York Historical Society. CLUB AFFIL Explorers Club; Road Runners Club.

George Francis Landegger: president, director B 1938. PRIM CORP EMPL chairman, chief executive officer, director: Parsons & Whittemore Enterprises Corp.

Arthur L. Schwartz: vice president PRIM CORP EMPL president, director: Parsons & Whittemore Enterprises Corp.

Grants Analysis

Disclosure Period: fiscal year ending October 31, 2001
Total Grants: $783,500
Number of Grants: 76
Average Grant: $5,493*
Highest Grant: $277,000
Lowest Grant: $250
Typical Range: $1,000 to $10,000
***Note:** Average grant figure excludes two highest grants ($377,000).

Recent Grants

Note: Grants derived from 2001 Form 990.

General

277,000	Georgetown University, Washington, DC
100,000	Association of Jesuit Colleges and Universities, Washington, DC
54,000	Americares Foundation
50,000	Gregorian University Foundation
27,500	Interaid, Inc., Washington, DC
27,500	Taft School, Watertown, CT
25,000	Lifewater International, Arcadia, CA
25,000	Louise H & Arthur Schwartz Foundation, Inc.
22,500	Lenox Hill Neighborhood House, New York, NY
20,000	Abraham House

LANDMARK COMMUNICATIONS, INC.

Company Headquarters

150 W. Brambleton Ave.
Norfolk, VA 23510
Web: http://www.landmarkcom.com

Company Description

Revenue: US$732 million (2002)
Employees: 5000 (2002)
SIC(s): 2711 Newspapers, 2752 Commercial Printing--Lithographic, 2759 Commercial Printing Nec, 4833 Television Broadcasting Stations.

Operating Locations

Landmark Communications Inc. (NV--Las Vegas; NC--Greensboro; VA--Norfolk, Roanoke)

Nonmonetary Support

Type: Cause-related Marketing & Promotion; In-kind Services; Loaned Executives

Landmark Communications Foundation

Giving Contact

Linda Hyatt, Executive Director
150 W. Brambleton Avenue
Norfolk, VA 23510

Phone: (757)446-2016
Fax: (757)446-2489
E-mail: Lhyatt@Lcimedia.com

Description

EIN: 546038902
Organization Type: Corporate Foundation
Giving Locations: MD; NV: Las Vegas; NC: Greensboro; TN; VA
Grant Types: Capital, Conference/Seminar, Emergency, Endowment, Fellowship, Matching, Multiyear/Continuing Support.
Note: Also offers leadership gifts.

Financial Summary

Total Giving: $2,401,361 (2001); $2,739,555 (2000); $2,939,384 (1999). Note: Contributes through corporate direct giving program and foundation.
Giving Analysis: Giving for 2000 includes: foundation grants to United Way ($360,845); foundation ($2,378,710); 1999: foundation grants to United Way ($324,412); foundation ($2,614,972); 1998: foundation grants to United Way ($335,245); foundation ($1,651,605);
Assets: $53,481,734 (2001); $56,416,970 (1999); $51,813,107 (1998)
Gifts Received: $786,423 (2001); $1,048,505 (1999); $1,098,514 (1998). Note: Foundation receives contributions from Landmark Communications, Inc., and its subsidiaries.

Typical Recipients

Arts & Humanities: Arts Associations & Councils, Arts Centers, Arts Funds, Ballet, Ethnic & Folk Arts, Arts & Humanities-General, Historic Preservation, History & Archaeology, Museums/Galleries, Music, Opera, Public Broadcasting, Theater
Civic & Public Affairs: African American Affairs, Asian American Affairs, Clubs, Civic & Public Affairs-General, Housing, Nonprofit Management, Philanthropic Organizations, Professional & Trade Associations, Public Policy, Urban & Community Affairs, Zoos/Aquariums
Education: Business Education, Colleges & Universities, Community & Junior Colleges, Education Funds, Faculty Development, Education-General, Journalism/Media Education, Literacy, Minority Education, Preschool Education, Public Education (Precollege), Science/Mathematics Education, Student Aid
Environment: Resource Conservation
Health: Emergency/Ambulance Services, Health-General, Hospitals, Research/Studies Institutes
Religion: Bible Study/Translation, Ministries, Religious Welfare
Science: Science Museums, Scientific Centers & Institutes
Social Services: Child Welfare, Community Service Organizations, Crime Prevention, Day Care, Family Services, Food/Clothing Distribution, People with Disabilities, Scouts, Shelters/Homelessness, Social Services-General, United Funds/United Ways, Volunteer Services, YMCA/YWCA/YMHA/YWHA, Youth Organizations

Application Procedures

Initial Contact: Send one-page letter to the president of the nearest subsidiary.
Application Requirements: Include a description of organization, amount requested, purpose of funds sought, impact foundation funds would have on the program and community, evidence of other support, program timetable, expected sources of future revenue, program budget, and proof of tax-exempt status.
Deadlines: None.
Review Process: Applications are screened by local company and, if approved, forwarded to the foundation for further screening and possible inclusion in the foundation's annual budget.

Evaluative Criteria: Priority given to projects that reach a broad section of the community; yield substantial benefits to the community for costs involved; promote cooperation among agencies within their fields of interest; project seeks funds for new innovative programs, or to expand an innovative program to other parts of the community; demonstrates major support from other donors and can use foundation support to attract greater community support; is part of a capital campaign; demonstrates in-kind services; has not received foundation funding for a similar program.

Restrictions

Foundation does not make grants to organizations not tax-exempt under IRS standards, individuals, or any organization that has received a capital pledge from the foundation within the preceding two years. Foundation does not give for religious or political purposes; fundraising events; deficit financing; projects normally the responsibility of a government agency; health care; or medical education or research.

Additional Information

Individual budgets from participating Landmark companies are submitted to corporate headquarters in November each year, where they are reviewed and receive final approval during the month of January. Capital pledges are made with the provision that a campaign meets its goal and that the project goes forward as proposed.
Programs supportive of the broadcasting and publishing industries on a national scale occasionally receive grants from corporate headquarters.
Publications: Foundation Guidelines

Corporate Officials

Frank Batten, Sr.: chairman vice president B Norfolk, VA 1927. ED University of Virginia BA (1950); Harvard University MBA (1952). PRIM CORP EMPL chairman: Landmark Communications Inc. CORP AFFIL chairman: Roanoke Times; chairman, founder: Weather Channel; chairman: Norfolk Virginian-Pilot & Ledger Star; chairman: Greensboro Daily News & Record; chairman: KLAS-TV Las Vegas; director: Capital Gazette Communication Inc. NONPR AFFIL trustee: U.S. Naval Academy Foundation; trustee: University Virginia Colgate Business School; trustee: Southern Newspaper Publishers Association Foundation; member: Delta Kappa; member: Newspaper Association America; trustee: Culver Education Foundation.
Frank Batten, Jr.: executive vice president B 1958. PRIM CORP EMPL executive vice president: Landmark Communications Inc. ADD CORP EMPL president: Commonwealth Printing Co.

Foundation Officials

Frank Batten, Sr.: chairman, director (see above)
Linda S. Hyatt: vice president, executive director

Grants Analysis

Disclosure Period: calendar year ending 2001
Total Grants: $1,963,286*
Number of Grants: 194
Average Grant: $10,120
Highest Grant: $113,000
Lowest Grant: $100
Typical Range: $500 to $50,000
***Note:** Giving excludes matching gifts; scholarship; United Way.

Recent Grants

Note: Grants derived from 2001 Form 990.

General

177,000	United Way of South Hampton Roads, Norfolk, VA -- annual support
113,000	Business Consortium for Arts Support, Norfolk, VA -- annual arts support
75,000	Apple Ridge Farm, Roanoke, VA -- for special initiative capital campaign
75,000	Hampton Roads Maritime Heritage

	Foundation, Norfolk, VA -- for Schooner Virginia Project
75,000	YMCA of Middle Tennessee, Nashville, TN -- for Joe C. Davis YMCA Outdoor Center
70,000	United Way of Roanoke Valley, Roanoke, VA -- for annual support
61,500	Portsmouth Schools Foundation, Portsmouth, VA
60,000	Ferrum College, Ferrum, VA -- for academic change initiative
50,000	Hollins University, Roanoke, VA -- for Moody Student Center Renovation
50,000	New Century Council, Roanoke, VA -- for the Center for Innovative Leadership

LANE FAMILY CHARITABLE TRUST

Giving Contact

R&J Lane
Lane Family Charitable Trust
500 Almer Rd., No. 301
Burlingame, CA 94010
Phone: (415)348-4026

Description

EIN: 946585396
Organization Type: Private Foundation
Giving Locations: CA: San Francisco, San Mateo
Grant Types: General Support.

Financial Summary

Total Giving: $478,075 (fiscal year ending June 30, 2001); $493,500 (fiscal 2000); $424,600 (fiscal 1997)
Assets: $4,310,910 (fiscal 2001); $5,268,139 (fiscal 2000); $3,392,366 (fiscal 1997)
Gifts Received: $510,150 (fiscal 2000); $648,595 (fiscal 1997); $150,000 (fiscal 1996). Note: In fiscal 1996 and 2000, contributions were received from Ralph and Joan Lane.

Typical Recipients

Arts & Humanities: Arts Associations & Councils, Film & Video, Libraries, Literary Arts, Theater
Civic & Public Affairs: Community Foundations, Economic Development, Employment/Job Training, Civic & Public Affairs-General, Hispanic Affairs, Law & Justice, Philanthropic Organizations, Urban & Community Affairs
Education: Colleges & Universities, Community & Junior Colleges, Preschool Education, Public Education (Precollege), Religious Education, Secondary Education (Private), Student Aid
Environment: Environment-General, Resource Conservation
Health: AIDS/HIV, Cancer, Clinics/Medical Centers, Health Organizations
International: International Affairs
Religion: Churches, Religion-General, Religious Organizations, Religious Welfare, Social/Policy Issues
Social Services: Child Abuse, Child Welfare, Community Service Organizations, Counseling, Domestic Violence, Family Planning, Family Services, Food/Clothing Distribution, Recreation & Athletics, Shelters/Homelessness,   YMCA/YWCA/YMHA/YWHA, Youth Organizations

Application Procedures

Initial Contact: Send a brief letter of inquiry.
Application Requirements: Include purpose of funds sought and manner of expending funds.

Foundation Officials

Joan Lane: trustee
Ralph Lane: trustee

Grants Analysis

Disclosure Period: fiscal year ending June 30, 2001
Total Grants: $478,075
Number of Grants: 33
Average Grant: $12,196*
Highest Grant: $50,000
Typical Range: $5,000 to $25,000
*Note: Average grant figure excludes two highest grants ($100,000).

Recent Grants

Note: Grants derived from fiscal 2000 Form 990.

General

100,000	Peninsula Community Foundation, San Mateo, CA
35,000	San Mateo County Community College, San Mateo, CA
25,000	El Pajaro Community Development Corporation, Watsonville, CA
25,000	San Mateo Community College District Foundation, San Mateo, CA
25,000	Stonestown YMCA, San Francisco, CA
25,000	Sunset Youth Services, San Francisco, CA
20,000	Sierra Pac Soroptimists, Stockton, CA
15,000	Jefferson Elementary School, San Francisco, CA
15,000	Peninsula Interfaith Action, San Carlos, CA
15,000	Peninsula Interfaith Action, San Carlos, CA

MINNIE AND BERNARD LANE FOUNDATION

Giving Contact

R. L. Short, Trustee
414 Washington Street
Altavista, VA 24517
Phone: (804)369-6663

Alternate Contact

Bernard Lane, Trustee

Description

EIN: 546052404
Organization Type: Private Foundation
Giving Locations: VA
Grant Types: General Support.

Donor Information

Founder: Bernard B. Lane, Minnie B. Lane

Financial Summary

Total Giving: $815,590 (fiscal year ending March 31, 2001); $856,322 (fiscal 2000); $284,003 (fiscal 1997)
Giving Analysis: Giving for fiscal 2001 includes: foundation grants to United Way ($500) fiscal 1997: foundation grants to United Way ($100)
Assets: $8,719,109 (fiscal 2001); $12,290,156 (fiscal 2000); $7,343,601 (fiscal 1997)
Gifts Received: $270,880 (fiscal 2001); $294,371 (fiscal 2000); $5,994 (fiscal 1997). Note: In fiscal 2001, contributions were received from Crestar Bank ($262,924) and Bernard B. Lane, Jr. ($7,956). In fiscal 2000, contributions were received from Crestar Bank. In fiscal 1997, contributions were received from Bernard B. Lane, Jr.

Typical Recipients

Arts & Humanities: Arts & Humanities-General, Historic Preservation, Libraries, Music, Public Broadcasting

Civic & Public Affairs: Employment/Job Training, Civic & Public Affairs-General, Municipalities/Towns, Philanthropic Organizations, Professional & Trade Associations, Urban & Community Affairs
Education: Arts/Humanities Education, Colleges & Universities, Community & Junior Colleges, Education Funds, Engineering/Technological Education, International Exchange, Minority Education, Private Education (Precollege), Public Education (Precollege)
Environment: Forestry
Health: Clinics/Medical Centers, Emergency/Ambulance Services, Eyes/Blindness, Health Organizations, Hospitals, Medical Research, Prenatal Health Issues, Single-Disease Health Associations
International: Health Care/Hospitals, International Relief Efforts, Missionary/Religious Activities
Religion: Churches, Religion-General, Ministries, Missionary Activities (Domestic), Religious Organizations, Religious Welfare, Seminaries
Social Services: Animal Protection, Community Centers, Community Service Organizations, Emergency Relief, Food/Clothing Distribution, People with Disabilities, Scouts, Shelters/Homelessness, United Funds/United Ways, YMCA/YWCA/YMHA/YWHA, Youth Organizations

Application Procedures

Initial Contact: Send a brief letter of inquiry.
Application Requirements: Include applicant's name and address, a description of organization, amount requested, and purpose of funds sought.
Deadlines: None.

Restrictions

Does not support individuals.

Foundation Officials

Cindy Jester: administrative assistant
Bernard Bell Lane: director B Lynchburg, VA 1928. ED United States Naval Academy BS (1950). NONPR AFFIL member: Board Project Concern International; member: Virginia Manufacturers Association.
Minnie B. Lane: director

Grants Analysis

Disclosure Period: fiscal year ending March 31, 2001
Total Grants: $815,090*
Number of Grants: 142
Average Grant: $5,740
Highest Grant: $84,000
Typical Range: $100 to $25,000
*Note: Giving excludes United Way.

Recent Grants

Note: Grants derived from 2001 Form 990.

General

84,000	Altavista Area YMCA, Altavista, VA
58,350	Lane Memorial Methodist Church, Altavista, VA
50,000	Randolph Macon Academy, Front Royal, VA
46,000	New Covenant School, Lynchburg, VA
45,170	Project Concern International, San Diego, CA
40,000	Food for the Hungry, Scottsdale, AZ
25,000	Hickory Christian Academy, Hickory, NC
25,000	Princeton University, Princeton, NJ
25,000	SEMILLA, Chesapeake, VA
25,000	United Methodist Foundation, Richmond, VA

EUGENE M. LANG FOUNDATION

Giving Contact

Eugene Lang, Contact
535 5th Avenue, Suite 906
New York, NY 10017

Phone: (212)949-4100
Fax: (212)286-8964

Description

Founded: 1963
EIN: 136153412
Organization Type: General Purpose Foundation
Giving Locations: NY: New York internationally; nationally.
Grant Types: General Support, Scholarship.

Donor Information

Founder: The foundation was established in 1968 by Eugene M. Lang. Mr. Lang is the founder and president of REFAC Technology Development Corporation, which licences and promotes new technologies. He is most well-known for his offer to pay college tuition for a sixth-grade class at New York City's P.S. 121, which he attended as a youth. The I Have a Dream Foundation offers programs to motivate disadvantaged grade school students to attend college by offering scholarships, reading materials, support groups, and counseling services.

Financial Summary

Total Giving: $6,150,759 (2000); $4,064,096 (1998); $2,618,493 (1996)
Giving Analysis: Giving for 2000 includes: foundation scholarships ($1,000)
Assets: $50,156,012 (2000); $41,211,212 (1998); $31,438,754 (1996)
Gifts Received: $150,000 (2000); $5,489,896 (1998); $5,648,386 (1996). Note: In 1998, stock contributions were received from Eugene M. Lang. In 1996, the foundation received contributions from Eugene M. Lang. In previous years, the foundation received contributions from Susan Safer.

Typical Recipients

Arts & Humanities: Arts Festivals, Libraries, Museums/Galleries, Music, Opera, Performing Arts, Public Broadcasting, Theater
Civic & Public Affairs: African American Affairs, Botanical Gardens/Parks, Civic & Public Affairs-General, Law & Justice, Legal Aid, Philanthropic Organizations, Public Policy, Urban & Community Affairs, Women's Affairs, Zoos/Aquariums
Education: Arts/Humanities Education, Business Education, Colleges & Universities, Community & Junior Colleges, Education Funds, Education Reform, Elementary Education (Public), Education-General, Legal Education, Literacy, Minority Education, Private Education (Precollege), Public Education (Precollege), Science/Mathematics Education, Secondary Education (Private), Social Sciences Education, Student Aid
Health: AIDS/HIV, Cancer, Children's Health/Hospitals, Clinics/Medical Centers, Health Organizations, Hospitals, Medical Rehabilitation, Mental Health
International: Foreign Arts Organizations, International Organizations, International Peace & Security Issues, International Relations, International Relief Efforts, Missionary/Religious Activities
Religion: Churches, Jewish Causes, Religious Welfare, Synagogues/Temples
Science: Science Museums
Social Services: Child Welfare, Community Service Organizations, Family Services, Recreation & Athletics, Shelters/Homelessness, Social Services-General, Youth Organizations

Application Procedures

Initial Contact: The foundation does not have a formal application. Grant requests should be submitted in letter form.
Deadlines: None.

Foundation Officials

David Lang: trustee
Eugene Michael Lang: donor, trustee B New York, NY March 16, 1919. ED Swarthmore College BA (1938); Columbia University School of Business Administration MS (1940); Polytechnic Institute Brooklyn (1941-1942). PRIM CORP EMPL founder, chairman: Refac Technology Development Corp. ADD CORP EMPL chairman emeritus: Refac International Ltd. CORP AFFIL director: Gough Econ Inc. NONPR AFFIL vice chairman, trustee: New School Social Research; chairman emeritus: Swarthmore College; director: Mannes College Music; director: Columbia University Graduate School Business; member: Licensing Executive Society; advisor director: Carnegie-Mellon University Graduate School Business Administration. CLUB AFFIL Yale Club; University Club; Century Country Club; Golden Key Club.
Jane Lang: trustee B 1947. ED Swarthmore College BA (1967); University of Pennsylvania JD (1970). PRIM CORP EMPL partner, attorney: Sprenger & Lang. NONPR AFFIL member: District of Columbia Bar Association; member: Minnesota State Bar Association.
Stephen Lang: trustee
Theresa Lang: trustee B Hochhausen, Germany 1952. ED Fordham University BA (1974); University of California, Los Angeles MBA (1982). PRIM CORP EMPL senior vice president, treasurer: Merrill Lynch & Co., Inc. ADD CORP EMPL president, treasurer: Merrill Lynch Group Inc. CORP AFFIL president, treasurer: Merrill Lynch Group Inc.
Paul Sprenger: member B 1940. ED University of Michigan BBA (1962); University of Michigan JD (1965). PRIM CORP EMPL partner, attorney: Sprenger & Lang. NONPR AFFIL member: District of Columbia Bar Association; member: Minnesota Bar Association.

Grants Analysis

Disclosure Period: calendar year ending 2000
Total Grants: $6,149,759*
Number of Grants: 138
Average Grant: $10,453*
Highest Grant: $1,500,000
Lowest Grant: $50
Typical Range: $1,000 to $50,000
*Note: Giving excludes Scholarship. Average grant excludes four highest grants totaling $4,750,000.

Recent Grants

Note: Grants derived from 2000 Form 990.

Library-Related

5,000	New York Public Library, New York, NY

General

1,250,000	New York Hospital Medical Center, Queens, NY
1,000,000	Columbia Business School, New York, NY
1,000,000	Columbia Business School, New York, NY
250,000	American Museum of Natural History, New York, NY
100,000	Symphony Space, New York, NY
65,000	Levine School of Music, Washington, DC
30,000	Columbia Business School, New York, NY
25,000	College of New Rochelle, New Rochelle, NY
25,000	George School, Newtown, PA
25,000	Project Pericles Inc.

STANLEY S. LANGENDORF FOUNDATION

Giving Contact

Richard J. Guggenhime, President
3701 Sacramento Street
PMB377
San Francisco, CA 94118
Phone: (415)263-0780

Description

Founded: 1982
EIN: 942861512
Organization Type: Private Foundation
Giving Locations: CA: San Francisco
Grant Types: Fellowship, Operating Expenses, Project.

Donor Information

Founder: the late Stanley S. Langendorf

Financial Summary

Total Giving: $377,500 (2002 approx); $610,333 (2001); $616,333 (2000)
Giving Analysis: Giving for 2001 includes: foundation scholarships ($40,000)
Assets: $16,448,948 (2001); $16,549,432 (2000); $15,297,181 (1999)
Gifts Received: $443,007 (1995)

Typical Recipients

Arts & Humanities: Arts Associations & Councils, Ballet, Community Arts, Dance, Ethnic & Folk Arts, History & Archaeology, Libraries, Museums/Galleries, Music, Opera, Performing Arts, Theater
Civic & Public Affairs: Botanical Gardens/Parks, Civic & Public Affairs-General, Housing, Public Policy, Urban & Community Affairs, Zoos/Aquariums
Education: Afterschool/Enrichment Programs, Colleges & Universities, International Studies, Leadership Training, Literacy, Minority Education, Private Education (Precollege), Secondary Education (Private), Secondary Education (Public), Student Aid
Health: Cancer, Geriatric Health, Health Organizations, Hospitals
International: International Affairs
Science: Science Museums, Scientific Centers & Institutes
Social Services: Big Brother/Big Sister, Camps, Child Welfare, Community Service Organizations, Family Services, Food/Clothing Distribution, People with Disabilities, Recreation & Athletics, Senior Services, Veterans, YMCA/YWCA/YMHA/YWHA, Youth Organizations

Application Procedures

Initial Contact: Submit a one-page letter.
Application Requirements: Include a description of the organization, amount requested, purpose of funds sought, project budget, organization budget. Send six sets. Send one copy of recently audited financial statement and proof of tax-exempt status.
Deadlines: March 1, and October 1.

Restrictions

Does not support individuals. Limits funding primarily to the city and county of San Francisco

Additional Information

Publications: Application Guidelines

Foundation Officials

Charles H. Clifford, Jr.: director
Charles H. Clifford: treasurer
Richard Johnson Guggenhime: president, trustee B San Francisco, CA 1940. ED Stanford University AB (1961); Harvard University JD (1964). PRIM CORP EMPL partner: Heller, Ehrman, White & McAuliffe. CORP AFFIL director, member: North America Trust Co. NONPR AFFIL trustee: Saint Ignatius College Prep School; director, member: San Francisco Opera Association; member: American College Probate Counsel. CLUB AFFIL Wine & Food Society Club; Olympic Club; Thunderbird Country Club; Bohemian Club; Chevaliers du Tastevin Club.
Lisa G. Hauswirth: director
Ann Wagner: secretary, trustee

Grants Analysis

Disclosure Period: calendar year ending 2001
Total Grants: $570,333*
Number of Grants: 61
Average Grant: $7,984*
Highest Grant: $83,333
Typical Range: $5,000 to $25,000
*Note: Giving excludes scholarship. Average grant figure excludes highest grant.

Recent Grants

Note: Grants derived from 2001 Form 990.

General

83,333	San Francisco Zoological Society, San Francisco, CA -- for new amphitheater for educational programs
40,500	Marin Academy, San Rafael, CA -- for building campaign
30,000	Lick-Wilmerding High School, San Francisco, CA -- for scholarships
26,000	Coro Foundation, San Francisco, CA -- for Fellow Program
25,000	John Wayne Cancer Institute, Santa Monica, CA -- for operations
25,000	Marin City Children's Program, Marin City, CA -- for operations
25,000	San Francisco General Hospital, San Francisco, CA -- for Women's Imaging Center
25,000	San Francisco Opera Association, San Francisco, CA -- for In-school Program and performance attendance
25,000	World Affairs Council of Northern California, San Francisco, CA -- for Asilomar Conference
20,000	California Pacific Medical Center, San Francisco, CA -- for children with developmental disabilities

WALTER LANTZ FOUNDATION

Giving Contact

Edward A. Landry, Trustee
4444 Lakeside Dr., Ste. 310
Burbank, CA 91505
Phone: (818)842-1616
Fax: (818)842-1943

Description

Founded: 1984
EIN: 953994420
Organization Type: Private Foundation
Giving Locations: CA
Grant Types: General Support.

Donor Information

Founder: the late Grace T. Lantz, the late Walter Lantz

Financial Summary

Total Giving: $1,468,130 (fiscal year ending November 30, 2001); $1,452,283 (fiscal 2000); $1,119,116 (fiscal 1999)
Assets: $17,613,582 (fiscal 2001); $24,229,501 (fiscal 2000); $23,899,329 (fiscal 1999)
Gifts Received: $568,904 (fiscal 1997); $301,634 (fiscal 1996); $11,634,067 (fiscal 1995). Note: In fiscal 1994, contributions were received from Walter Lantz.

Typical Recipients

Arts & Humanities: Arts Associations & Councils, Arts Funds, Arts Institutes, Film & Video, Arts & Humanities-General, Libraries, Opera, Public Broadcasting
Civic & Public Affairs: Botanical Gardens/Parks, Civic & Public Affairs-General, Parades/Festivals, Philanthropic Organizations

Education: Arts/Humanities Education, Business Education, Colleges & Universities, Economic Education, Education Reform, Education-General, Private Education (Precollege), Special Education
Health: AIDS/HIV, Children's Health/Hospitals, Clinics/Medical Centers, Emergency/Ambulance Services, Eyes/Blindness
Religion: Religious Welfare
Social Services: Child Abuse, Child Welfare, Community Service Organizations, Crime Prevention, People with Disabilities, Recreation & Athletics, Special Olympics, Veterans, YMCA/YWCA/YMHA/YWHA

Application Procedures

Initial Contact: Send a brief letter of inquiry.
Deadlines: None.

Restrictions

Does not support individuals, religious organizations for sectarian purposes, political or lobbying groups, or organizations outside area.

Foundation Officials

Susan J. Hazard: trustee
Peggy E. Jackson: trustee
Edward A. Landry: trustee B New Orleans, LA 1939. ED Louisiana State University BA (1961); University of California, Los Angeles JD (1964). PRIM CORP EMPL attorney: Musick, Peeler & Garrett.

Grants Analysis

Disclosure Period: fiscal year ending November 30, 2001
Total Grants: $1,468,130
Number of Grants: 49
Average Grant: $14,875*
Highest Grant: $250,000
Lowest Grant: $1,000
Typical Range: $5,000 to $30,000
*Note: Average grant figure excludes eight highest grants ($858,263).

Recent Grants

Note: Grants derived from fiscal 2000 Form 990.

Library-Related

53,333	Huntington Library, Huntington, CA
25,000	Library Foundation, Los Angeles, CA

General

250,000	University of California Los Angeles Foundation, Los Angeles, CA
148,000	Assistance League of Southern California, Los Angeles, CA
125,000	Cathedral Building Foundation
121,584	Harvey Mudd College, Claremont, CA
108,333	Doheny Eye Institute, Los Angeles, CA
50,000	Baseballers Against Drugs
50,000	Teach for America, Los Angeles, CA
50,000	University of California Los Angeles Regents, Los Angeles, CA
50,000	Western Fund of Vertebrate Zoological
35,000	National Philanthropy

MARY POTISHMAN LARD TRUST

Giving Contact

Walker C. Friedman, Co-Trustee
Mary Potishman Lard Trust
500 W. Seventh, Suite 700
Ft. Worth, TX 76102
Phone: (817)884-4448

Description

Founded: 1968
EIN: 756210697
Organization Type: Private Foundation

Giving Locations: TX: especially Fort Worth area
Grant Types: General Support, Research.

Donor Information

Founder: the late Mary P. Lard

Financial Summary

Total Giving: $598,750 (2001); $493,500 (2000); $557,000 (1999)
Giving Analysis: Giving for 2001 includes: foundation grants to United Way ($10,000); 2000: foundation scholarships ($10,000); foundation grants to United Way ($10,000); foundation ($473,500) 1996: foundation ($541,000)
Assets: $13,057,077 (2001); $13,903,157 (2000); $13,791,684 (1999)

Typical Recipients

Arts & Humanities: Arts Associations & Councils, Arts Centers, Arts Festivals, Ballet, Dance, Ethnic & Folk Arts, Libraries, Museums/Galleries, Music, Opera, Performing Arts
Civic & Public Affairs: Business/Free Enterprise, Clubs, Civic & Public Affairs-General, Hispanic Affairs, Parades/Festivals, Philanthropic Organizations, Urban & Community Affairs, Women's Affairs, Zoos/Aquariums
Education: Business Education, Colleges & Universities, Education Reform, Private Education (Precollege), Public Education (Precollege), Special Education, Student Aid
Environment: Air/Water Quality
Health: AIDS/HIV, Alzheimers Disease, Cancer, Emergency/Ambulance Services, Health Organizations, Heart, Hospitals, Medical Research, Medical Training, Mental Health, Nursing Services, Prenatal Health Issues, Public Health, Research/Studies Institutes, Respiratory, Single-Disease Health Associations
International: Foreign Arts Organizations
Religion: Churches, Jewish Causes, Social/Policy Issues
Social Services: Child Welfare, Community Centers, Community Service Organizations, Counseling, Crime Prevention, Family Planning, Family Services, Food/Clothing Distribution, People with Disabilities, Recreation & Athletics, Scouts, Substance Abuse, United Funds/United Ways, Volunteer Services, YMCA/YWCA/YMHA/YWHA, Youth Organizations

Application Procedures

Initial Contact: Send a brief letter of inquiry describing program or project.
Application Requirements: Include name and location of organization, its purpose and the purpose of funds sought, and amount requested.
Deadlines: None.

Restrictions

Does not support individuals.

Additional Information

Trust(s): Bank One TX NA

Foundation Officials

Alan D. Friedman: co-trustee
Bayard H. Friedman: co-trustee CORP AFFIL director: Texas Utilities Co.; director: Tradewinds Technologies; director: ACME Brick; director: Justin Industries Inc.
Walker C. Friedman: co-trustee

Grants Analysis

Disclosure Period: calendar year ending 2001
Total Grants: $588,750*
Number of Grants: 69
Average Grant: $8,533
Highest Grant: $50,000
Lowest Grant: $500
Typical Range: $5,000 to $10,000
*Note: Giving excludes United Way.

Recent Grants

Note: Grants derived from 2000 Form 990.

General

50,000	Amon G. Carter Museum, Ft. Worth, TX
50,000	Texas Christian University, Ft. Worth, TX
25,000	All Saints Health Foundation, Ft. Worth, TX
25,000	All Saints Health Foundation, Ft. Worth, TX
25,000	Fort Worth Zoological Association, Ft. Worth, TX
25,000	Performing Arts, Ft. Worth, TX
20,000	Van Cliburn Foundation, Ft. Worth, TX
20,000	Warm Place, Ft. Worth, TX
15,000	Salesmanship Club, Dallas, TX
10,000	Child Study Center Foundation, Ft. Worth, TX

LARSEN FUND

Giving Contact

Patricia S. Palmer, Grants Administrator
2537 Post Road, Suite 224
Southport, CT 06490
Phone: (203)255-5318
Fax: (203)255-6206

Description

Founded: 1941
EIN: 136104430
Organization Type: Private Foundation
Giving Locations: CT; MA; MN: Minneapolis including metropolitan area; NY: New York including metropolitan area
Grant Types: Capital, Conference/Seminar, Endowment, Fellowship, General Support, Project, Research, Scholarship.

Donor Information

Founder: the late Roy E. Larsen

Financial Summary

Total Giving: $693,233 (2001); $787,419 (2000); $725,437 (1999)
Assets: $12,869,339 (2001); $15,103,944 (2000); $15,503,127 (1999)
Gifts Received: $3,904 (2000). Note: In 2000, contributions were received from Margaret Z. Larsen.

Typical Recipients

Arts & Humanities: Arts Centers, Arts Institutes, History & Archaeology, Libraries, Museums/Galleries, Music, Performing Arts, Theater
Civic & Public Affairs: Civic & Public Affairs-General, Professional & Trade Associations, Urban & Community Affairs, Zoos/Aquariums
Education: Colleges & Universities, Education-General, Journalism/Media Education, Minority Education, Private Education (Precollege), Science/Mathematics Education, Secondary Education (Public)
Environment: Air/Water Quality, Environment-General, Resource Conservation, Wildlife Protection
Health: Health Organizations, Hospitals, Hospitals (University Affiliated), Outpatient Health Care, Single-Disease Health Associations
International: Health Care/Hospitals, International Affairs, International Organizations
Religion: Churches, Seminaries
Science: Science Museums, Science Museums, Scientific Centers & Institutes
Social Services: Camps, Child Welfare, Community Centers, Community Service Organizations, Family Planning, Recreation & Athletics, YMCA/YWCA/YMHA/YWHA, Youth Organizations

Application Procedures

Initial Contact: Send a brief letter of inquiry accompanied by a brief proposal.
Application Requirements: Include history of project, project goals, methods, budget, and schedule for implementation. Attach a copy of organization's most recent annual financial statement, list board members, current grants, and proof of tax-exempt status.
Deadlines: None.
Review Process: Grant applications are circulated quarterly to board members. Board members advise the grants administrator which applications should be considered at the upcoming board meeting. Those who submitted an application that will not be considered will be notified at least three weeks prior to the board meeting. Board meetings are generally held in June and December.
Decision Notification: Applicants whose proposals are considered at a board meeting will be notified by mail of the board's decision within three weeks of the meeting.

Restrictions

Does not support individuals.

Additional Information

Publications: Annual Report (including Application Guidelines)

Foundation Officials

David L. Johnson: treasurer
Christopher Larsen: second vice president
Jonathan Zerbe Larsen: secretary B New York, NY 1940. ED Harvard University BA (1961); Harvard University MAT (1963). PRIM CORP EMPL editor in chief: Village Voice. NONPR AFFIL trustee: Cambridge College; trustee: Natural Resources Defense Council.
Robert R. Larsen: president
Patricia S. Palmer: grants admin
Anne Larsen Simonson: first vice president

Grants Analysis

Disclosure Period: calendar year ending 2001
Total Grants: $693,233
Number of Grants: 98
Average Grant: $6,002*
Highest Grant: $67,000
Lowest Grant: $500
Typical Range: $1,000 to $10,000
*Note: Average grant figure excludes two highest grants ($117,000).

Recent Grants

Note: Grants derived from 2000 Form 990.

Library-Related

10,000	Wadsworth Athenaeum, Hartford, CT -- annual fund

General

50,000	University of Hartford, Hartford, CT -- capital campaign
43,000	Hartford Symphony Orchestra, Hartford, CT -- capital campaign
40,000	Allen Chase Foundation, Deerfield, MA -- annual fund
40,000	Cambridge College, Cambridge, MA -- annual fund
40,000	Fairfield Country Day School, Fairfield, CT -- capital campaign
35,000	Natural Resources Defense Council, New York, NY -- annual fund
33,250	Council on the Environment of New York City, New York, NY -- to Christopher Larsen Segment
33,000	Science Museum of Minnesota, St. Paul, MN -- paleontology project
25,000	Nantucket Historical Association, Nantucket, MA -- capital campaign
25,000	Sarah Lawrence College, Bronxville, NY -- annual fund

WILLIAM AND MILDRED LASDON FOUNDATION

Giving Contact

Nanette L. Laitman, Trustee
575 Madison Avenue, Suite 1006
New York, NY 10022-2588
Phone: (212)935-3916

Description

Founded: 1947
EIN: 237380362
Organization Type: Private Foundation
Giving Locations: NY.
Grant Types: General Support.

Donor Information

Founder: Jacob S. Lasdon, William S. Lasdon, Mildred D. Lasdon, Nanetta L. Leitman

Financial Summary

Total Giving: $1,781,469 (2000); $1,269,493 (1999); $1,096,615 (1998)
Assets: $35,450,169 (2000); $32,418,722 (1999); $31,128,123 (1998)
Gifts Received: $4,283,813 (1998); $10,000 (1996); $10,000 (1995). Note: In 1998, contributions were received from N.L. Laitman ($383,813) and Estate of M.D. Lasdon ($3,900,000). In 1995, contributions were received from Mildred D. Lasdon.

Typical Recipients

Arts & Humanities: Arts Associations & Councils, Ballet, Dance, Ethnic & Folk Arts, Film & Video, Historic Preservation, Libraries, Museums/Galleries, Music, Opera, Performing Arts, Public Broadcasting, Theater
Civic & Public Affairs: Botanical Gardens/Parks, Civic & Public Affairs-General
Education: Arts/Humanities Education, Colleges & Universities, Leadership Training, Medical Education
Environment: Resource Conservation
Health: Cancer, Clinics/Medical Centers, Health-General, Hospitals, Nursing Services
International: Foreign Arts Organizations, International Organizations, Missionary/Religious Activities
Religion: Jewish Causes, Seminaries, Synagogues/Temples
Social Services: People with Disabilities, Youth Organizations

Application Procedures

Initial Contact: Send a brief letter of inquiry.
Application Requirements: current financial statements and purpose of funds sought.
Deadlines: None.

Foundation Officials

Bonnie Eletz: trustee
Nanette L. Laitman: trustee
Mildred D. Lasdon: trustee
Cathy Sorkin Seligman: trustee

Grants Analysis

Disclosure Period: calendar year ending 2000
Total Grants: $1,781,469
Number of Grants: 116
Average Grant: $6,795*
Highest Grant: $1,000,000
Typical Range: $1,000 to $10,000
*Note: Average grant figure excludes high grant.

Recent Grants

Note: Grants derived from 1999 Form 990.

Library-Related

5,000	New York Public Library, New York, NY

General

750,000	American Craft Museum, New York, NY
115,933	Weill Medical College
100,000	American Craft Museum, New York, NY
50,000	American Craft Museum, New York, NY
25,000	American Craft Museum, New York, NY
25,000	UJA Federation of New York, New York, NY
25,000	United Jewish Appeal, New York, NY
20,000	Yeshiva University, New York, NY
10,000	New York Presbyterian Hospital Community Health Center, New York, NY
8,750	Central Park Conservancy, New York, NY

HERBERT AND GERTRUDE LATKIN CHARITABLE FOUNDATION

Giving Contact

John Berryhill, Co-Trustee
1505 E. Valley Road, Suite B
Santa Barbara, CA 93150

Alternate Contact

Janice Gibbons
Care of Santa Barbara Bank & Trust
PO Box 2340
Santa Barbara, CA 93120-2340
Phone: (805)899-8407
Note: Applications may be submitted to either address.

Description

Founded: 1992
EIN: 776070540
Organization Type: Private Foundation
Giving Locations: CA: Santa Barbara
Grant Types: General Support, Scholarship.

Donor Information

Founder: Established in 1992 from the Herbert and Gertrude Latkin Trust.

Financial Summary

Total Giving: $434,545 (2001); $434,632 (2000); $379,038 (1999)
Giving Analysis: Giving for 2001 includes: foundation scholarships ($20,500) 1999: foundation scholarships ($16,000)
Assets: $7,253,373 (2001); $8,593,395 (2000); $9,383,729 (1999)
Gifts Received: $3,544,205 (1992)

Typical Recipients

Arts & Humanities: Libraries
Civic & Public Affairs: Urban & Community Affairs, Women's Affairs
Education: Minority Education, Student Aid
Health: AIDS/HIV, Alzheimers Disease, Cancer, Children's Health/Hospitals, Health Organizations, Hospitals, Medical Rehabilitation, Multiple Sclerosis, Nursing Services
Religion: Jewish Causes, Religious Organizations, Religious Welfare
Social Services: Animal Protection, At-Risk Youth, Camps, Child Abuse, Community Service Organizations, Day Care, Family Planning, Family Services, Food/Clothing Distribution, Senior Services, Sexual Abuse, Shelters/Homelessness, Youth Organizations

Application Procedures

Initial Contact: Send a brief letter of inquiry.
Application Requirements: Include organization's name and purpose, and describe how the grant would be used.
Deadlines: April 1 and October 1.

Additional Information

Trust(s): Santa Barbara Bank & Trust

Foundation Officials

John Berryhill: co-trustee

Grants Analysis

Disclosure Period: calendar year ending 2001
Total Grants: $414,045*
Number of Grants: 61
Average Grant: $6,788
Highest Grant: $20,000
Lowest Grant: $2,500
Typical Range: $1,000 to $10,000
*Note: Giving excludes scholarship.

Recent Grants

Note: Grants derived from 2000 Form 990.

Library-Related

8,654	Friends of the Guadalupe Public Library, Guadalupe, CA -- to assist the following the Guadalupe Public Library

General

20,000	Scholarship Foundation of Santa Barbara, Santa Barbara, CA -- to provide scholarships for higher education ten economically disadvantaged and deserving students
15,000	Friendship Adult Day Care Center, Santa Barbara, CA -- providing partial funding for a part-time nurse
15,000	Santa Barbara Jewish Federation, Santa Barbara, CA -- to provide funds for Sabbath and Holiday lunches for seniors
15,000	Villa Majella of Santa Barbara, Santa Barbara, CA -- to provide for the operation of the maternity home providing care for single pregnant women in crisis and their infants
10,000	Cornerstone House of Santa Barbara, Santa Barbara, CA -- to help purchase the residential facility for severally developmentally and physically disabled young adults'
10,000	Food Bank of Santa Barbara County, Santa Barbara, CA -- to provide a "Brown Bag Program" to purchase food that is not available through donations and program operating expenses
10,000	Long Term Care Ombudsman Services, Santa Barbara, CA -- for the "Stop Abuse Now" projects that seeks to aggressively stop elder abuse in our long term care facilities
10,000	National Multiple Sclerosis Society, Santa Barbara, CA -- to update and expand the MS Resource lending library available to the 150 people affected by MS
10,000	Noah's Anchorage, Inc., Santa Barbara, CA -- to support youth crisis shelter for homeless and runaway youth
10,000	The Pacific Pride Foundation, Inc., Santa Barbara, CA -- to support Project Food Chain, a home delivered hot meals program for low income people w/HIV and AIDS

FORREST C. LATTNER FOUNDATION

Giving Contact

Susan L. Lloyd, President & Secretary
777 East Atlantic Avenue, Suite 317
Delray Beach, FL 33483
Phone: (561)278-3781

Alternate Contact

Martha L. Connelly, Chairman

Description

Founded: 1982
EIN: 592147657
Organization Type: General Purpose Foundation
Giving Locations: FL: midwest.
Grant Types: General Support.

Donor Information

Founder: Incorporated in 1981 by Mrs. Forrest C. Lattner, Mrs. Frances H. Lattner, and the late Forrest C. Lattner .

Financial Summary

Total Giving: $7,185,200 (2001); $8,365,900 (2000); $7,333,250 (1998)
Giving Analysis: Giving for 2000 includes: foundation grants to United Way ($4,000)
Assets: $156,635,067 (2001); $168,254,973 (2000); $153,413,350 (1998)
Gifts Received: $2,690,497 (1998). Note: In 1998, contributions were received from the Francis H. Lattner Trust.

Typical Recipients

Arts & Humanities: Arts Associations & Councils, Community Arts, Arts & Humanities-General, Historic Preservation, Libraries, Museums/Galleries, Music, Performing Arts, Public Broadcasting, Theater
Civic & Public Affairs: African American Affairs, Botanical Gardens/Parks, Clubs, Community Foundations, Employment/Job Training, Civic & Public Affairs-General, Housing, Municipalities/Towns, Philanthropic Organizations, Professional & Trade Associations, Public Policy, Women's Affairs, Zoos/Aquariums
Education: Afterschool/Enrichment Programs, Arts/Humanities Education, Business Education, Colleges & Universities, Community & Junior Colleges, Education Associations, Education Reform, Elementary Education (Public), Education-General, Leadership Training, Literacy, Medical Education, Private Education (Precollege), Public Education (Precollege), Science/Mathematics Education, Special Education, Student Aid, Vocational & Technical Education
Environment: Air/Water Quality, Environment-General, Research, Resource Conservation, Wildlife Protection
Health: AIDS/HIV, Alzheimers Disease, Cancer, Children's Health/Hospitals, Clinics/Medical Centers, Emergency/Ambulance Services, Eyes/Blindness, Health-General, Health Funds, Heart, Home-Care Services, Hospices, Hospitals, Medical Research, Mental Health, Public Health, Research/Studies Institutes, Single-Disease Health Associations, Trauma Treatment
International: Health Care/Hospitals
Religion: Churches, Ministries, Ministries, Religious Organizations, Religious Welfare
Science: Science Museums, Scientific Centers & Institutes
Social Services: Big Brother/Big Sister, Child Welfare, Community Service Organizations, Counseling, Crime Prevention, Day Care, Domestic Violence, Family Planning, Family Services, Food/Clothing Distribution, Homes, People with Disabilities, Recreation & Athletics, Scouts, Senior Services, Shelters/Homelessness, Social Services-General, Substance Abuse, YMCA/YWCA/YMHA/YWHA, Youth Organizations

Application Procedures

Initial Contact: Send an initial letter of request to the foundation.
Application Requirements: Initial proposal should include the applicant's name, address, and phone number; the name of person to be contacted, with title; a brief statement of the history of the applicant

and the purpose of the grant request; and supplemental information about the applicant, including a list of officers and directors, an audited financial statement (receipts and disbursements and a balance sheet) for the most recent fiscal year, a budget for the current fiscal year, and an IRS tax-exempt letter.

Deadlines: Grant proposals are accepted in May and October.

Review Process: If the request falls within the foundation's guidelines, it will be acknowledged. If necessary, supplemental information will be requested. The foundation's grant review committee meets to consider final proposals. If the request is approved and a grant is awarded, the applicant will be notified in June or December following the grant review committee's meeting.

Foundation Officials

Forrest C. Brown, MD: trustee B 1940.
Martha L. Connelly: chairman, trustee
Richard M. Harris: trustee
Douglas W. Hollenbeck: trustee
Susan L. Lloyd: president, secretary, trustee

Grants Analysis

Disclosure Period: calendar year ending 2001
Total Grants: $7,185,200
Number of Grants: 288
Average Grant: $20,927*
Highest Grant: $710,000
Lowest Grant: $1,000
Typical Range: $5,000 to $40,000
*Note: Average grant amount excludes two highest grants ($1,200,000).

Recent Grants

Note: Grants derived from 2001 Form 990.

Library-Related
29,000   Delray Beach Library, Delray Beach, FL

General
710,000   Highland Academy, Flagstaff, AZ
500,000   Westerly Hospital, Westerly, RI
500,000   Wichita Art Museum, Wichita, KS
250,000   Wichita Art Museum, Wichita, KS
200,000   Via Christi Foundation, Wichita, KS
150,000   Bethesda Memorial Hospital, Boynton Beach, FL
150,000   YMCA of Wichita, Wichita, KS
130,000   Surfrider Foundation, Huntington, CA
110,000   Organic Farming Research Foundation, Santa Cruz, CA
100,000   Barton's Boosters, Boca Raton, FL

LAUDER FOUNDATION

Giving Contact

Barbara E. Capri, Administrator
767 5th Ave., 40th Fl.
New York, NY 10153
Phone: (212)572-4426

Description

Founded: 1962
EIN: 136153743
Organization Type: Family Foundation
Giving Locations: NY: New York
Grant Types: General Support.

Donor Information

Founder: The Lauder Foundation was incorporated in New York in 1962, with funds donated by the Lauder family. Estee Lauder and her husband, Joseph H. Lauder, founded the cosmetics firm, Estee Lauder, in 1946. Most of the company stock is still owned by members of the Lauder family, including Estee Lauder's two sons, Ronald S. Lauder and Leonard A. Lauder.

Financial Summary

Total Giving: $6,165,305 (fiscal year ending November 30, 2001); $47,857,240 (fiscal 2000); $6,355,577 (fiscal 1999)
Assets: $18,096,216 (fiscal 2001); $24,504,818 (fiscal 2000); $80,738,771 (fiscal 1999)
Gifts Received: $2,400,000 (fiscal 2001); $2,400,000 (fiscal 2000); $2,718,261 (fiscal 1998). Note: In fiscal 2001 and fiscal 2000, contributions were received from Estee Lauder. In fiscal 1996, contributions were received from Estee Lauder and Leonard Lauder.

Typical Recipients

Arts & Humanities: Art History, Arts Associations & Councils, Arts Centers, Arts Institutes, Ballet, Dance, Historic Preservation, History & Archaeology, Libraries, Museums/Galleries, Music, Theater, Visual Arts
Civic & Public Affairs: Botanical Gardens/Parks, Employment/Job Training, Ethnic Organizations, Civic & Public Affairs-General, Professional & Trade Associations, Public Policy, Urban & Community Affairs, Zoos/Aquariums
Education: Arts/Humanities Education, Colleges & Universities, Leadership Training, Literacy, Private Education (Precollege), Science/Mathematics Education, Social Sciences Education, Student Aid
Environment: Environment-General
Health: Cancer, Clinics/Medical Centers, Eyes/Blindness, Health Funds, Heart, Hospices, Hospitals, Hospitals (University Affiliated), Medical Research, Multiple Sclerosis, Public Health, Research/Studies Institutes
International: Foreign Arts Organizations, International Peace & Security Issues, International Relations, International Relief Efforts, Missionary/Religious Activities
Religion: Jewish Causes, Religious Welfare
Science: Science Museums
Social Services: Child Welfare, Community Service Organizations, Crime Prevention, Family Services, Homes, People with Disabilities, Recreation & Athletics, Senior Services, Substance Abuse, YMCA/YWCA/YMHA/YWHA, Youth Organizations

Application Procedures

Initial Contact: Prospective applicants should send a letter to the foundation describing the organization and the project for which funds are sought.
Deadlines: None.

Restrictions

No grants are given to individuals.

Foundation Officials

Estee Lauder: president B Queens, NY July 01, 1908. PRIM CORP EMPL founder, chairman board: Estee Lauder Co.
Leonard Alan Lauder: secretary-treasurer B New York, NY 1933. ED University of Pennsylvania BS (1954). PRIM CORP EMPL president, chief executive officer, director: Estee Lauder Co. NONPR AFFIL board governors: Joseph H Lauder Institute Management International Studies; president: Whitney Museum American Art; member: French-American Chamber of Commerce U.S.; trustee: Aspen Institute Humanistic Studies; member: Chief Executives Organization.
Ronald Stephen Lauder: vice president B New York, NY 1944. ED University of Paris (1964); University of Pennsylvania BS (1965). PRIM CORP EMPL chairman: Clinique Laboratorys Inc. CORP AFFIL founder, chairman: Central European Development Co.; chairman, president: Lauder Investments. NONPR AFFIL

trustee: Mt Sinai Medical Center; trustee: Museum Modern Art.

Grants Analysis

Disclosure Period: fiscal year ending November 30, 2000
Total Grants: $47,857,240
Number of Grants: 196
Average Grant: $16,358*
Highest Grant: $38,190,000
Typical Range: $5,000 to $30,000
*Note: Average grant figure excludes two highest grants ($44,683,850).

Recent Grants

Note: Grants derived from fiscal 1999 Form 990.

General
3,685,273 Wildlife Conservation Society, Seattle, WA -- to promote the work of the organization
1,000,000 Breast Cancer Research Foundation, New York, NY -- to promote the work of the foundation
125,000   United Jewish Appeal, New York, NY -- to promote the work of the organization
115,000   National Gallery of Art, Washington, DC -- to promote the work of the organization
108,500   Music Associates of Aspen, Aspen, CO -- to promote the work of the organization
105,000   Central Park Conservancy, New York, NY -- to promote the work of the organization
100,000   Children's Scholarship Fund, Spokane, WA -- to promote the work of the foundation
93,930   Aspen Institute, Aspen, CO -- to promote the work of the organization
80,000   Mid-Peninsula Community Day School, Palo Alto, CA -- to promote the work of the organization
60,000   Bronx High School of Science, Bronx, NY -- to promote the work of the organization

LAUREL FOUNDATION

Giving Contact

Donna M. Panazzi, Vice President
Two Gateway Center, Suite 1800
Pittsburgh, PA 15222
Phone: (412)765-2400
Fax: (412)765-2407

Description

Founded: 1951
EIN: 256008073
Organization Type: General Purpose Foundation
Giving Locations: PA: Pittsburgh including southwestern PA
Grant Types: General Support, Matching, Operating Expenses, Project.

Donor Information

Founder: Incorporated in 1951 by Cordelia S. May.

Financial Summary

Total Giving: $1,900,000 (2002 approx); $1,842,343 (2001); $1,895,045 (2000)
Giving Analysis: Giving for 1999 includes: foundation grants to United Way ($1,000)
Assets: $39,230,870 (2001); $42,617,104 (2000); $42,299,618 (1999)

Typical Recipients

Arts & Humanities: Arts Associations & Councils, Arts Festivals, Arts Funds, Arts Institutes, Arts Outreach, Community Arts, Dance, Ethnic & Folk Arts, Film & Video, Historic Preservation, History & Archaeology, Libraries, Literary Arts, Museums/Galleries, Music, Opera, Performing Arts, Public Broadcasting, Theater

Civic & Public Affairs: Botanical Gardens/Parks, Business/Free Enterprise, Civil Rights, Clubs, Economic Development, Employment/Job Training, Civic & Public Affairs-General, Nonprofit Management, Philanthropic Organizations, Professional & Trade Associations, Public Policy, Rural Affairs, Urban & Community Affairs, Women's Affairs, Zoos/Aquariums, Zoos/Aquariums

Education: Arts/Humanities Education, Business Education, Colleges & Universities, Community & Junior Colleges, Education Associations, Education Funds, Environmental Education, Faculty Development, Education-General, Journalism/Media Education, Literacy, Medical Education, Private Education (Precollege), Public Education (Precollege), School Volunteerism, Science/Mathematics Education, Secondary Education (Private), Secondary Education (Public), Social Sciences Education, Student Aid

Environment: Air/Water Quality, Energy, Environment-General, Resource Conservation, Watershed, Wildlife Protection

Health: Alzheimers Disease, Children's Health/Hospitals, Clinics/Medical Centers, Emergency/Ambulance Services, Health Funds, Hospitals, Medical Research, Nursing Services, Public Health

International: Foreign Educational Institutions, Health Care/Hospitals, International Affairs, International Development, International Environmental Issues, International Relations

Religion: Churches, Ministries, Religious Welfare

Science: Scientific Centers & Institutes

Social Services: Animal Protection, At-Risk Youth, Big Brother/Big Sister, Child Welfare, Community Service Organizations, Counseling, Day Care, Delinquency & Criminal Rehabilitation, Emergency Relief, Family Planning, Family Services, Homes, People with Disabilities, Senior Services, Shelters/Homelessness, Social Services-General, Substance Abuse, United Funds/United Ways, Volunteer Services, YMCA/YWCA/YMHA/YWHA, Youth Organizations

Application Procedures

Initial Contact: Applicants are encouraged to carefully review the annual report to gauge whether their project is likely to be funded.

Application Requirements: The foundation accepts the common Grant Application of the Grantmakers of Western Pennsylvania. With the complete application, include a narrative of less than 300 words and a proposal summary stating the specific purpose of the requested grant and the amount requested; a brief description of the applying organization and its mission, and a brief summary of the project and goals for the period of time during which the funds will be used; and the key staff who will be involved. The full proposal should also include a list of the board of directors with affiliations; a current operating budget and annual financial statements for the past two years; a list of any major contributors, with amounts, and a summary of the balance of contributions; the names of the organization's executive staff and the total number of paid staff; an annual report, if available; and an IRS determination letter.

Deadlines: Formal submission deadlines are April 1 and October 1 for consideration at trustee meetings held in June and December, respectively. Applicants are encouraged to submit applications early, however, as applications received late in the cycle necessarily receive less intensive review.

Review Process: Proposals are acknowledged promptly and applicants are advised of the meeting at which their request will be considered. Every effort is made to consider all proposals which have been timely submitted, but occasionally it is necessary to defer until the following meeting. If this occurs, applicants are promptly advised and given an opportunity to revise or withdraw their request, as appropriate.

Restrictions

Cultural organizations whose service areas fall outside the Greater Pittsburgh area ordinarily are not funded. The foundation does not accept proposals from individuals or from for-profit organizations. Multi-year grants are not usually approved.

Additional Information

Special preference is given to financially responsible organizations, i.e. those that direct 70% or more of funds to client services and limit administrative costs to less than 30%. The trustees also favor collaborations between art organizations and social service groups that pool resources to address common problems and programs.

Publications: Annual Report

Foundation Officials

Nancy C. Fales: trustee
Timothy M. Inglis: treasurer
Cordelia Scaife May: chairman, trustee, donor B Pittsburgh, PA 1928. ED University of Pittsburgh.
Roger F. Meyer: president B 1939. PRIM CORP EMPL treasurer, director: Commercial Electric Product Corp.
Donna M. Panazzi: vice president, secretary
Curtis S. Scaife: trustee ED University of Arizona (1956).
Thomas Mellon Schmidt: chairman, trustee B Pittsburgh, PA 1940. ED Princeton University AB (1962); Harvard University JD (1965). PRIM NONPR EMPL sr vice president law: Fallingwater & Urban Conservation. NONPR AFFIL vice chairman: Pittsburgh Historical Review Commission; trustee: Saint Barnabas Health Systems; trustee: Morris Arboretum; trustee: Carnegie Museum Natural History; advisor: Land Conservation Law Institute; member: American Bar Association; member: Allegheny County Bar Association; member: American Association Museums. CLUB AFFIL Rolling Rock Club; Anglers New York Club; Pittsburgh Golf Club.

Grants Analysis

Disclosure Period: calendar year ending 2000
Total Grants: $1,841,343*
Number of Grants: 92
Average Grant: $20,015
Highest Grant: $50,000
Lowest Grant: $1,000
Typical Range: $10,000 to $40,000
*Note: Giving excludes United Way.

Recent Grants

Note: Grants derived from 2000 Form 990.

General

50,000	Family Communications, Pittsburgh, PA
50,000	National Aviary in Pittsburgh, Pittsburgh, PA -- capital support
50,000	National Flag Foundation, Pittsburgh, PA
50,000	Pennsylvania Environmental Council, Philadelphia, PA -- program development
50,000	Pittsburgh Parks Conservancy, Pittsburgh, PA -- Park stewards program
50,000	Three Rivers Employment Service, Pittsburgh, PA -- video teleconferencing
50,000	Western Pennsylvania Conservancy, Mill Run, PA -- Downtown Greening Initiative
50,000	Westmoreland Museum of American Art, Greensburg, PA
50,000	Women's Health Services, Pittsburgh, PA
48,000	Mountain Watershed Association, Melcroft, PA -- Indian Creek watershed restoration

RICHARD AND RUTH LAVINE FAMILY FOUNDATION

Giving Contact

Ruth J. Lavine, President & Director
121 S. Beverly Drive
Beverly Hills, CA 90212
Phone: (310)275-5132

Description

Founded: 1991
EIN: 954300271
Organization Type: Private Foundation
Giving Locations: CA: Beverly Hills, Los Angeles
Grant Types: General Support.

Financial Summary

Total Giving: $188,625 (fiscal year ending June 30, 2001); $120,500 (fiscal 1999); $13,500 (fiscal 1997)
Giving Analysis: Giving for fiscal 2001 includes: foundation grants to United Way ($2,000)
Assets: $4,841,295 (fiscal 2001); $3,863,920 (fiscal 1999); $3,394,501 (fiscal 1997)
Gifts Received: $2,912,506 (fiscal 1997). Note: In fiscal 1997, contributions were received from Ruth J. Lavine.

Typical Recipients

Arts & Humanities: Arts Centers, Arts Festivals, Libraries, Music, Public Broadcasting, Theater
Civic & Public Affairs: Civic & Public Affairs-General, Law & Justice, Legal Aid, Minority Business, Philanthropic Organizations, Professional & Trade Associations
Education: Colleges & Universities, Education Funds, Legal Education
Health: Arthritis, Cancer, Medical Research
Religion: Jewish Causes, Religious Organizations, Synagogues/Temples
Social Services: Family Planning, Recreation & Athletics, Senior Services, United Funds/United Ways, Youth Organizations

Application Procedures

Initial Contact: Send a brief letter of inquiry.
Application Requirements: Include proof of tax-exempt status.
Deadlines: None.
Notes: The foundation reports that its funds are committed for the foreseeable future and it is therefore not soliciting proposals at this time.

Restrictions

Grants are not made to individuals.

Foundation Officials

Ruth J. Lavine: president, director
Leonard Unger: secretary, treasurer, director

Grants Analysis

Disclosure Period: fiscal year ending June 30, 2001
Total Grants: $186,625*
Number of Grants: 17
Average Grant: $6,775*
Highest Grant: $50,000
Lowest Grant: $250
Typical Range: $500 to $10,000
*Note: Giving excludes United Way. Average grant figure excludes two highest grants ($85,000).

Recent Grants

Note: Grants derived from fiscal 2001 Form 990.

General

50,000	University of Southern California Law School, Los Angeles, CA
35,000	KCET, Los Angeles, CA
28,000	Planned Parenthood, Los Angeles, CA
20,000	Arthritis Foundation Southern California Chapter, Los Angeles, CA
10,000	Women Lawyers Association of Los Angeles, Los Angeles, CA
9,500	American Jewish Committee, Los Angeles, CA
8,500	United Jewish Fund, Los Angeles, CA
7,000	Los Angeles Philharmonic, Los Angeles, CA
5,000	Jewish Family Service, Los Angeles, CA
3,000	Benefactors of the Jewish Club of 1933, Inc., Los Angeles, CA

LAZARUS CHARITABLE TRUST

Giving Contact

Charles Lazarus, Trustee
c/o Toys 'R' Us
461 From Road
Paramus, NJ 07652
Phone: (212)773-3000

Description

Founded: 1986
EIN: 133360876
Organization Type: Private Foundation
Giving Locations: DC: Washington; NY
Grant Types: General Support.

Donor Information

Founder: Charles Lazarus

Financial Summary

Total Giving: $263,388 (fiscal year ending May 31, 2001); $194,334 (fiscal 2000); $233,729 (fiscal 1999)
Assets: $3,618,681 (fiscal 2001); $3,042,309 (fiscal 2000); $3,599,982 (fiscal 1999)
Gifts Received: $1,938,600 (fiscal 1995). Note: In fiscal 1995, contributions were received from Charles P. Lazarus.

Typical Recipients

Arts & Humanities: Arts Associations & Councils, Ballet, Community Arts, Dance, Arts & Humanities-General, History & Archaeology, Libraries, Literary Arts, Museums/Galleries, Music, Performing Arts, Public Broadcasting
Civic & Public Affairs: Botanical Gardens/Parks, Clubs, Civic & Public Affairs-General, Municipalities/ Towns, Public Policy, Urban & Community Affairs, Women's Affairs
Education: Colleges & Universities, Education-General, Medical Education, Private Education (Precollege), Science/Mathematics Education, Student Aid
Environment: Environment-General, Resource Conservation
Health: AIDS/HIV, Cancer, Children's Health/Hospitals, Clinics/Medical Centers, Diabetes, Emergency/ Ambulance Services, Health Organizations, Hospices, Hospitals, Kidney, Medical Research, Mental Health, Multiple Sclerosis, Single-Disease Health Associations
International: Foreign Educational Institutions, Health Care/Hospitals, Human Rights, International Peace & Security Issues, Missionary/Religious Activities
Religion: Churches, Jewish Causes, Religious Organizations, Religious Welfare
Science: Scientific Centers & Institutes

Social Services: At-Risk Youth, Child Welfare, Community Centers, Community Service Organizations, Family Planning, Family Services, Food/Clothing Distribution, Recreation & Athletics, Scouts, YMCA/ YWCA/YMHA/YWHA, Youth Organizations

Application Procedures

Initial Contact: Send brief letter describing program.
Deadlines: None.

Foundation Officials

Charles P. Lazarus: trustee B Washington, DC 1923. PRIM CORP EMPL chairman, director: Toys R Us. CORP AFFIL director: Automatic Data Processing Corp.; director: Wal Mart Stores.

Grants Analysis

Disclosure Period: fiscal year ending May 31, 2001
Total Grants: $263,388
Number of Grants: 41
Average Grant: $3,941*
Highest Grant: $59,270
Lowest Grant: $100
Typical Range: $1,000 to $5,000
***Note:** Average grant figure excludes two highest grants ($109,680).

Recent Grants

Note: Grants derived from 2000 Form 990.

General

85,835	Dalton School, New York, NY -- educational
47,590	Sidwell Friends School, Washington, DC -- educational
28,900	New Museum, New York, NY
21,500	Alvin Ailey America, New York, NY
10,000	Facing History and Ourselves, Brookline, MA
5,000	East End Hospice, Quoque, NY
5,000	Weill Medical College -- educational
2,000	Jewish Arts Foundation, Palm Beach, FL
2,000	New York Child Study Center, New York, NY
1,500	Tate Museum, New York, NY

HELEN SPERRY LEA FOUNDATION

Giving Contact

Sperry Lea, President & Director
3534 Fulton Street NW
Washington, DC 20036
Phone: (202)337-5448
Fax: (202)337-6722

Description

Founded: 1940
EIN: 136161749
Organization Type: Private Foundation
Giving Locations: DC: Washington
Grant Types: General Support.

Donor Information

Founder: the late Helen Sperry Lea

Financial Summary

Total Giving: $200,920 (2000); $248,137 (1999); $197,546 (1998)
Assets: $3,743,965 (2000); $4,708,387 (1999); $4,736,812 (1998)

Typical Recipients

Arts & Humanities: Ballet, Dance, Film & Video, Historic Preservation, History & Archaeology, Libraries, Museums/Galleries, Music, Opera, Performing Arts, Public Broadcasting, Theater

Civic & Public Affairs: Ethnic Organizations, Civic & Public Affairs-General, Nonprofit Management, Philanthropic Organizations, Public Policy, Urban & Community Affairs
Education: Afterschool/Enrichment Programs, Arts/ Humanities Education, Colleges & Universities, Education Reform, International Exchange, International Studies, Legal Education, Private Education (Precollege), School Volunteerism, Secondary Education (Private), Secondary Education (Public)
Environment: Environment-General, Protection
Health: Hospitals
International: Foreign Educational Institutions, International Affairs, International Organizations, International Peace & Security Issues, International Relations
Religion: Religious Welfare
Science: Scientific Labs
Social Services: Community Service Organizations, Shelters/Homelessness

Application Procedures

Initial Contact: The foundation has no formal grant application procedure or application form.
Deadlines: None.

Foundation Officials

Anna L. Lea: vice president, treasurer, director
Helena A. Lea: vice president, director
R. Brooke Lea, II: vice president, director
Sperry Lea: president, director
Carol A. Rhees: secretary

Grants Analysis

Disclosure Period: calendar year ending 2000
Total Grants: $200,920
Number of Grants: 27
Average Grant: $7,441
Highest Grant: $22,495
Lowest Grant: $200
Typical Range: $500 to $15,000

Recent Grants

Note: Grants derived from 2000 Form 990.

General

22,495	Sidwell Friends School Chinese Student Exchange, Washington, DC
20,500	Society for the Preservation of the Greek Heritage, Washington, DC
16,000	Benaki Museum, Athens Greece
16,000	Inform, Washington, DC
11,500	Focus, Washington, DC
11,000	Washington Chamber Symphony, Washington, DC
10,650	Growing Together, Washington, DC
10,000	Arena Stage, Washington, DC
10,000	College Year in Athens, Cambridge, MA
10,000	Living State Theater, Washington, DC

THOMAS AND DOROTHY LEAVEY FOUNDATION

Giving Contact

Kathleen McCarthy, President
10100 Santa Monica Boulevard, Suite 610
Los Angeles, CA 90067
Phone: (310)551-9936
Fax: (310)551-9938

Description

Founded: 1952
EIN: 956060162
Organization Type: Family Foundation
Giving Locations: CA: Southern California
Grant Types: Capital, Endowment, General Support, Research, Scholarship.

Donor Information

Founder: The Thomas and Dorothy Leavey Foundation was established in California in 1952 by Thomas E. Leavey and his wife, Dorothy Leavey.

Financial Summary

Total Giving: $15,643,429 (2000); $29,023,844 (1999); $12,391,109 (1998)
Giving Analysis: Giving for 2000 includes: foundation scholarships ($356,919); 1998: foundation scholarships ($267,245) 1997: foundation scholarships ($377,417)
Assets: $267,729,622 (2000); $252,620,651 (1998); $207,501,323 (1997)
Gifts Received: $1,566,594 (1997). Note: Foundation receives contributions from Dorothy E. Leavey.

Typical Recipients

Arts & Humanities: Arts Associations & Councils, Arts Outreach, Ballet, History & Archaeology, Libraries, Music, Performing Arts, Public Broadcasting
Civic & Public Affairs: Clubs, Economic Policy, Civic & Public Affairs-General, Hispanic Affairs, Legal Aid, Philanthropic Organizations, Professional & Trade Associations, Public Policy, Women's Affairs
Education: Agricultural Education, Arts/Humanities Education, Colleges & Universities, Education Associations, Education Funds, Faculty Development, Education-General, International Exchange, Legal Education, Medical Education, Minority Education, Private Education (Precollege), Public Education (Precollege), Religious Education, Science/Mathematics Education, Secondary Education (Private), Special Education, Student Aid, Vocational & Technical Education
Environment: Resource Conservation
Health: AIDS/HIV, Cancer, Children's Health/Hospitals, Clinics/Medical Centers, Emergency/Ambulance Services, Health Funds, Health Organizations, Hospitals, Long-Term Care, Medical Research, Nursing Services, Prenatal Health Issues, Public Health, Respiratory, Single-Disease Health Associations
International: Foreign Educational Institutions, Health Care/Hospitals, International Organizations, International Peace & Security Issues, Missionary/Religious Activities
Religion: Churches, Dioceses, Religion-General, Ministries, Religious Organizations, Religious Welfare, Social/Policy Issues
Science: Science Museums
Social Services: At-Risk Youth, Camps, Child Abuse, Child Welfare, Community Service Organizations, Domestic Violence, Family Planning, Family Services, Food/Clothing Distribution, People with Disabilities, Recreation & Athletics, Senior Services, Shelters/Homelessness, Special Olympics, Substance Abuse, Volunteer Services, YMCA/YWCA/YMHA/YWHA, Youth Organizations

Application Procedures

Initial Contact: Applicants should submit a letter to the foundation.
Application Requirements: The letter should include descriptions of the organization and the project for which funds are sought, and proof of tax-exempt status.
Deadlines: None.
Review Process: If the application is accepted, a full proposal will be requested. Grants are made quarterly.

Restrictions

The foundation reports that scholarships are provided only to children of employees of agents of Farmers Insurance Group and its subsidiaries.

Foundation Officials

Louis M. Castruccio: trustee
Joseph James Leavey: trustee B Oakland, CA 1930. ED University of San Francisco AB (1952); Stanford

University LLB (1955). PRIM CORP EMPL attorney: Early Maslach Leavey & Nutt.
Kathleen Leavey McCarthy: acting chairman B Beverly Hills, CA 1935. ED University of Southern California BS (1957).
Kenneth Tyler: trustee

Grants Analysis

Disclosure Period: calendar year ending 2000
Total Grants: $15,286,510*
Number of Grants: 78
Average Grant: $146,578*
Highest Grant: $4,000,000
Lowest Grant: $1,000
Typical Range: $5,000 to $50,000 and $100,000 to $1,000,000
*****Note:** Giving excludes scholarships. Average grant figure excludes highest grant.

Recent Grants

Note: Grants derived from 2000 Form 990.

General

4,000,000	Archdiocese of Los Angeles, Los Angeles, CA
2,000,000	Georgetown University, Washington, DC
2,000,000	Santa Clara University, Santa Clara, CA
1,000,000	Santa Clara University, Santa Clara, CA
1,000,000	Sisters of Social Service, Los Angeles, CA
1,000,000	University of South Carolina Library Landscape Project, SC
1,000,000	University of Southern California Trustee's Chair in Law
500,000	Gregorian University, New York, NY
500,000	Loretto High School, Sacramento, CA
250,000	Marymount College, Los Angeles, CA

LEBANON MUTUAL INSURANCE CO.

Company Headquarters

137 W. Penn Ave.
Cleona, PA 17042

Company Description

Employees: 31
SIC(s): 6300 Insurance Carriers.

Operating Locations

Lebanon Mutual Insurance Co. (PA--Cleona)

Lebanon Mutual Foundation

Giving Contact

Rollin Rissinger, Jr., Director
137 W. Penn Ave.
PO Box 2005
Cleona, PA 17042
Phone: (717)272-6655

Description

EIN: 222521649
Organization Type: Corporate Foundation
Giving Locations: PA: Lebanon
Grant Types: General Support.

Financial Summary

Total Giving: $16,025 (2000); $14,500 (1999); $11,220 (1998). Note: 1997 Giving includes United Way ($2,300).
Giving Analysis: Giving for 2000 includes: foundation grants to United Way ($2,500); 1999: foundation grants to United Way ($2,500); foundation ($12,050) 1998: foundation grants to United Way ($2,600)

Assets: $304,264 (2000); $293,425 (1999); $256,744 (1998)
Gifts Received: $50,000 (1999). Note: In 1991 and 1999, contributions were received from Lebanon Mutual Insurance Company.

Typical Recipients

Arts & Humanities: Historic Preservation, Libraries, Performing Arts, Public Broadcasting
Civic & Public Affairs: Clubs, Civic & Public Affairs-General, Parades/Festivals, Philanthropic Organizations, Public Policy, Safety
Education: Colleges & Universities, Community & Junior Colleges, Education Associations, Education-General, Health & Physical Education, Secondary Education (Public), Student Aid
Environment: Environment-General
Health: Cancer, Children's Health/Hospitals, Hospitals, Public Health
Religion: Churches, Ministries
Social Services: Community Service Organizations, Crime Prevention, United Funds/United Ways, YMCA/YWCA/YMHA/YWHA

Application Procedures

Initial Contact: Send a written request specifying purpose of funds sought and affirmation of tax-exempt status.
Deadlines: None.

Corporate Officials

Samuel G. Kurtz: chairman, director PRIM CORP EMPL chairman, director: Lebanon Mutual Insurance Co.
Rollin Rissinger: president, director PRIM CORP EMPL president, director: Lebanon Mutual Insurance Co.

Foundation Officials

Milton Garrison: director B Doylesville, VA 1933. PRIM CORP EMPL senior vice president, secretary: Lebanon Mutual Insurance Co. NONPR AFFIL member: Lions; member: Masons.
Darwin Glick: director
Samuel B. Kurtz: director
Joseph Lauck: director
Warren Lewis: director
Rollin Rissinger, Jr.: director
William Schadler: director
Mark Randolph Tice: director B Harrisburg, PA 1941. ED Pennsylvania State University (1963); Pennsylvania State University (1969). PRIM CORP EMPL president: APR Supply Co. CORP AFFIL director: Lebanon Valley National Bank; director: Lebanon Mutual Insurance Co. NONPR AFFIL member: American Institute Heating Refrigeration & Air Conditioning Engineers.

Grants Analysis

Disclosure Period: calendar year ending 2000
Total Grants: $13,525*
Number of Grants: 13
Average Grant: $710*
Highest Grant: $5,000
Typical Range: $100 to $1,000
*****Note:** Giving excludes United Way. Average grant excludes highest grant.

Recent Grants

Note: Grants derived from 1999 Form 990.

Library-Related

500	Annville Free Library, Annville, PA

General

5,000	Lebanon Valley College Heilman Physical Therapy, Annville, PA
3,000	Harrisburg Area Community College, Harrisburg, PA
2,500	United Way of Lebanon County, Lebanon, PA
1,000	Lebanon Valley College Partnership, Annville, PA

500	Cleona Fire Department, Cleona, PA
500	Gravel Hill Church, Palmyra, PA
500	Keystone Prep Hoops Association, Lebanon, PA
500	Lebanon Valley Family YMCA, Lebanon, PA
250	Children's Miracle Network, Hershey, PA
100	Candlelighters Childhood Cancer Foundation, Bethesda, MD

LEBOVITZ FUND

Giving Contact

Herbert C. Lebovitz, President & Treasurer
3050 Tremont St.
Allentown, PA 18104
Phone: (610)820-5053

Description

Founded: 1944
EIN: 236270079
Organization Type: Private Foundation
Giving Locations: MI
Grant Types: General Support, Scholarship.

Donor Information

Founder: Peter Lebovitz

Financial Summary

Total Giving: $204,400 (fiscal year ending July 31, 2001); $192,847 (fiscal 2000); $165,871 (fiscal 1999)
Giving Analysis: Giving for fiscal 2001 includes: foundation scholarships ($1,000); fiscal 1999: foundation scholarships ($1,000) foundation ($164,871)
Assets: $4,026,204 (fiscal 2001); $3,806,650 (fiscal 2000); $3,950,757 (fiscal 1999)
Gifts Received: $70,000 (fiscal 2001); $21,150 (fiscal 2000); $12,285 (fiscal 1999). Note: In fiscal 2001, contributions were received from Beth Ann Segal Trust. In fiscal 1995 and 2000, contributions were received from Peter Lebovitz.

Typical Recipients

Arts & Humanities: Arts Associations & Councils, Arts Centers, Arts Institutes, Community Arts, Libraries, Museums/Galleries, Music, Opera, Public Broadcasting, Theater
Civic & Public Affairs: Botanical Gardens/Parks, Civic & Public Affairs-General, Municipalities/Towns, Public Policy, Safety, Women's Affairs
Education: Arts/Humanities Education, Business Education, Colleges & Universities, Engineering/Technological Education, Legal Education, Private Education (Precollege), Science/Mathematics Education, Secondary Education (Private), Student Aid
Environment: Environment-General, Resource Conservation, Wildlife Protection
Health: Children's Health/Hospitals, Health-General, Health Organizations, Home-Care Services, Hospitals, Long-Term Care, Medical Research, Single-Disease Health Associations
International: Human Rights
Religion: Religion-General, Jewish Causes, Ministries, Religious Organizations, Religious Welfare, Synagogues/Temples
Science: Science Museums
Social Services: Camps, Child Welfare, Community Service Organizations, Family Services, Food/Clothing Distribution, People with Disabilities, Recreation & Athletics, Social Services-General, United Funds/United Ways, YMCA/YWCA/YMHA/YWHA, Youth Organizations

Application Procedures

Initial Contact: Send brief letter describing program.
Deadlines: None.

Foundation Officials

Jonathan Javitch: director
Herbert C. Lebovitz: president, treasurer
James Lebovitz: director
Beth Ann Segal: vice president, secretary

Grants Analysis

Disclosure Period: fiscal year ending July 31, 2001
Total Grants: $203,400*
Number of Grants: 91
Average Grant: $1,593*
Highest Grant: $60,000
Lowest Grant: $25
Typical Range: $100 to $3,000
*****Note:** Giving excludes scholarships. Average grant figure excludes highest grant.

Recent Grants

Note: Grants derived from 2000 Form 990.

General

70,000	Trustees of Columbia University, New York, NY
18,500	Allentown Art Museum, Allentown, PA
15,000	Amos Tuck School of Business, Hanover, NH
10,000	Outback, The, New Canaan, CT
10,000	Wheaton College, Norton, MA
8,000	Federation of Jewish Services, Minneapolis, MN
5,000	Jewish Federation of Lehigh Valley, Allentown, PA
5,000	Nursing and Home Care, Wilton, CT
5,000	Salvation Army, Baltimore, MD
2,575	Baldwin School, Bryn Mawr, PA

FRANCIS L. LEDERER FOUNDATION

Giving Contact

Robert I. Ury, Vice President, Secretary & Director
120 S. Riverside Plz., Suite 1200
Chicago, IL 60606-3913
Phone: (312)876-7100
Fax: (312)876-0277

Description

Founded: 1966
EIN: 362594937
Organization Type: Private Foundation
Giving Locations: IL: Chicago
Grant Types: Endowment, General Support, Operating Expenses, Scholarship.

Financial Summary

Total Giving: $1,580,000 (2002 approx); $842,000 (2001); $665,500 (2000)
Giving Analysis: Giving for 2002 includes: foundation scholarships ($750,000); 2001: foundation scholarships ($250,000); 2000: foundation matching gifts ($25,000) foundation fellowships ($25,000)
Assets: $6,211,685 (2001); $7,284,853 (2000); $7,374,005 (1999)

Typical Recipients

Arts & Humanities: Arts Institutes, Arts Outreach, Historic Preservation, History & Archaeology, Libraries, Museums/Galleries, Music, Opera, Performing Arts, Public Broadcasting, Theater
Civic & Public Affairs: Botanical Gardens/Parks, Housing, Native American Affairs, Professional & Trade Associations, Public Policy, Urban & Community Affairs

Education: Colleges & Universities, Education Funds, Medical Education, Private Education (Precollege), Religious Education, Science/Mathematics Education, Student Aid
Health: AIDS/HIV, Alzheimers Disease, Cancer, Children's Health/Hospitals, Clinics/Medical Centers, Health Organizations, Medical Research, Multiple Sclerosis, Prenatal Health Issues, Public Health, Single-Disease Health Associations, Speech & Hearing
International: Foreign Arts Organizations
Religion: Religion-General, Jewish Causes, Religious Organizations, Synagogues/Temples
Science: Science-General, Science Museums
Social Services: At-Risk Youth, Child Abuse, Child Welfare, Community Service Organizations, Crime Prevention, Domestic Violence, Family Planning, Family Services, Homes, People with Disabilities, Scouts, Shelters/Homelessness, YMCA/YWCA/YMHA/YWHA, Youth Organizations

Application Procedures

Initial Contact: Send a brief letter of inquiry.
Application Requirements: Include a description of organization, purpose of funds sought, and proof of tax-exempt status.
Deadlines: None.

Foundation Officials

Adrienne Lederer: president, director
Lawrence D. Silverman: treasurer, director
Robert I. Ury: vice president, secretary, director

Grants Analysis

Disclosure Period: calendar year ending 2001
Total Grants: $592,000*
Number of Grants: 32
Average Grant: $12,250*
Highest Grant: $200,000
Typical Range: $8,000 to $40,000
*****Note:** Giving excludes scholarship. Average grant excludes highest grant.

Recent Grants

Note: Grants derived from 2001 Form 990.

General

250,000	University of Chicago School of Medicine, Chicago, IL -- scholarship endowment
200,000	Millennium Park, Inc., Chicago, IL -- Founders' Program
50,000	National Community for Prevention of Child Abuse, Chicago, IL
40,000	Chicago Opera Theater, Chicago, IL
40,000	Jewish United Fund of Metropolitan Chicago, Chicago, IL
25,000	Emanuel Congregation, Chicago, IL -- building renovation
25,000	Goodman Theatre, Chicago, IL -- campaign for new Goodman Theatre
20,000	Art Institute of Chicago, Chicago, IL
20,000	Chicago Children's Museum, Chicago, IL -- Dinosaur Discovery Program
20,000	Museum of Contemporary Art, Chicago, IL

LEE ENDOWMENT FOUNDATION

Giving Contact

Bill Feller, Trust Officer
c/o First Citizens Trust Co. NA
2601 4th Street SW
PO Box 1708
Mason City, IA 50402-1708
Phone: (641)423-1600
Fax: (641)423-4600
Web: http://www.firstcitizens.com

Alternate Contact

Dr. David L. Buettner, Chairman, Nominating
Committee, Muse Scholar
N. Iowa Area Community College
500 College Dr.
Mason City, IA 50401
Phone: (641)422-4050

Description

Founded: 1978
EIN: 421074052
Organization Type: Private Foundation
Giving Locations: IA
Grant Types: General Support, Scholarship.

Donor Information

Founder: the late Elizabeth Norris

Financial Summary

Total Giving: $1,168,572 (2000); $1,197,775 (1999);
$1,088,433 (1998)
Giving Analysis: Giving for 2000 includes: foundation scholarships ($193,527); 1999: foundation grants
to United Way ($8,749); foundation grants to United
Way ($8,749); foundation scholarships ($198,790);
foundation scholarships ($198,790) 1998: foundation
scholarships ($339,333)
Assets: $22,971,545 (2000); $25,411,440 (1999);
$25,828,684 (1998)

Typical Recipients

Arts & Humanities: Arts Festivals, Community Arts,
Libraries, Museums/Galleries, Music, Performing
Arts, Theater
Civic & Public Affairs: Botanical Gardens/Parks,
Clubs, Community Foundations, Economic Develop-
ment, Employment/Job Training, Civic & Public Af-
fairs-General, Housing, Municipalities/Towns, Pa-
rades/Festivals, Rural Affairs, Safety, Urban &
Community Affairs
Education: Arts/Humanities Education, Colleges &
Universities, Community & Junior Colleges, Minority
Education, Preschool Education, Private Education
(Precollege), Public Education (Precollege)
Environment: Environment-General
Health: Emergency/Ambulance Services, Health Or-
ganizations, Hospices, Hospitals, Public Health
Religion: Churches, Religious Organizations
Social Services: Camps, Child Welfare, Community
Service Organizations, Counseling, Delinquency &
Criminal Rehabilitation, Family Services, Food/Cloth-
ing Distribution, People with Disabilities, Recreation &
Athletics, Scouts, Senior Services, United Funds/
United Ways, Youth Organizations

Application Procedures

Initial Contact: Application form required for scholarships.
Deadlines: March 1. There are no deadlines for charitable fund applications, but funds are usually awarded
once a year in February.

Additional Information

Provides scholarships for residents of IA for higher
education.

Foundation Officials

Donald G. Harrer: president
Lloyd Loers: vice president
Robert D. Ross: vice president
Mr. Douglas F. Sherwin: vice president
J. Martin Wolman: vice president, treasurer B Elizabeth, NJ March 08, 1919. ED University of Wisconsin
(1937-1942). CORP AFFIL director: Madison Newspapers Inc. NONPR AFFIL member: WI Daily Newspaper League; member: WI Newspaper Association;
director, trustee: WI Clinical Cancer Center; member:
Madison Art Association; trustee: University Wisconsin Hospital & Clinic; member: Island Daily Press Association; trustee: Children & Youth Services; member: Edgewood College; member: Chamber of

Commerce Madison; member: B'nai B'rith; member:
Central Madison Comm.

Grants Analysis

Disclosure Period: calendar year ending 2000
Total Grants: $975,045*
Number of Grants: 69
Average Grant: $10,075*
Highest Grant: $200,000
Typical Range: $1,000 to $20,000
*Note: Giving excludes scholarships. Average grant
figure excludes two highest grants ($300,000).

Recent Grants

Note: Grants derived from 1999 Form 990.

Library-Related

50,000	Clear Lake Public Library, Clear Lake, IA

General

200,000	Mason City Foundation, Mason City, IA
100,000	NIACC, Mason City, IA
50,000	Francis Lauer Youth Services, Mason City, IA
50,000	MC Instrumental Music Boosters
44,991	Francis Lauer Youth Services, Mason City, IA
40,000	Windsor Theatre Development, Hampton, IA
25,000	NIACC Leadership Series, Mason City, IA
25,000	NIACC Performing Arts, Mason City, IA
25,000	Opportunity Village, Clear Lake, IA
24,000	Newman Catholic Schools

LEE ENTERPRISES, INC.

Company Headquarters

215 N. Main Street
Davenport, IA 52801-1924
Phone: (563)383-2100
Fax: (563)323-9609
Web: http://www.lee.net

Company Description

Founded: 1890
Ticker: LEE
Exchange: NYSE
Revenue: US$525.9 million (2002)
Employees: 6700 (2002)
SIC(s): 2711 Newspapers, 4813 Telephone Commu-
nications Except Radiotelephone, 4833 Television
Broadcasting Stations.

Operating Locations

Lee Enterprises (AZ--Tucson; CA--San Marcos; HI--
Honolulu; IL--Carbondale, Decatur; IA--Mason City,
Ottumwa, Rapid City; MN--Winona; MT--Billings,
Butte, Helena; NE--Lincoln, Omaha; NM--Albuquer-
que; ND--Bismarck; OR--Portland; WV--Huntington;
WI--La Crosse, Racine)

Lee Foundation

Giving Contact

Carl Schmidt, Secretary & Director
215 North Main Street
Davenport, IA 52801
Phone: (319)383-2102
Fax: (319)326-2972

Description

Founded: 1962
EIN: 426057173
Organization Type: Corporate Foundation
Giving Locations: IL; IA; MT; ND; OR; WI
Grant Types: Capital, Endowment, General Support.

Donor Information

Founder: Lee Enterprises

Financial Summary

Total Giving: $534,372 (fiscal year ending Septem-
ber 30, 2001); $399,201 (fiscal 1999); $383,201 (fiscal
1998). Note: Contributes through foundation only.
Giving Analysis: Giving for fiscal 2001 includes:
foundation scholarships ($22,500); foundation grants
to United Way ($40,039) foundation grants
($471,833)
Assets: $6,461,121 (fiscal 2001); $7,300,131 (fiscal
1999); $6,392,877 (fiscal 1998)
Gifts Received: $500,000 (fiscal 1992). Note: Contri-
butions were received from Lee Enterprises, Inc.

Typical Recipients

Arts & Humanities: Arts Centers, Arts & Humanities-
General, Historic Preservation, History & Archaeol-
ogy, Libraries, Literary Arts, Museums/Galleries, Mu-
sic, Public Broadcasting, Theater, Visual Arts
Civic & Public Affairs: Botanical Gardens/Parks,
Business/Free Enterprise, Clubs, Community Foundations, Economic Development, Employment/Job
Training, Civic & Public Affairs-General, Law & Justice, Municipalities/Towns, Nonprofit Management,
Parades/Festivals, Philanthropic Organizations, Professional & Trade Associations, Public Policy, Rural
Affairs, Urban & Community Affairs, Women's Affairs,
Zoos/Aquariums
Education: Afterschool/Enrichment Programs, Busi-
ness Education, Colleges & Universities, Community & Junior Colleges, Economic Education, Educa-
tion Funds, Environmental Education, Education-
General, International Studies, Journalism/Media Ed-
ucation, Literacy, Medical Education, Minority Educa-
tion, Private Education (Precollege), Public Education
(Precollege), Science/Mathematics Education, Sec-
ondary Education (Private), Secondary Education
(Public), Social Sciences Education, Student Aid, Vocational & Technical Education
Environment: Environment-General, Resource Conservation, Wildlife Protection
Health: Children's Health/Hospitals, Clinics/Medical
Centers, Emergency/Ambulance Services, Health-
General, Geriatric Health, Hospitals, Nursing Services, Public Health, Single-Disease Health Associa-
tions
International: Human Rights
Religion: Religion-General, Jewish Causes, Reli-
gious Welfare
Science: Science Museums, Scientific Organizations
Social Services: Big Brother/Big Sister, Child Wel-
fare, Community Centers, Community Service Orga-
nizations, Day Care, Emergency Relief, Family Plan-
ning, Family Services, Food/Clothing Distribution,
Homes, Recreation & Athletics, Scouts, Senior Services, Social Services-General, Special Olympics,
United Funds/United Ways, YMCA/YWCA/YMHA/
YWHA, Youth Organizations

Application Procedures

Initial Contact: Send a brief letter of inquiry.
Application Requirements: Include a description of
organization and purpose of funds sought.
Deadlines: None.
Notes: The foundation has no formal grant application
procedure or application form.

Restrictions

Foundation does not support individuals or outside of
geographic area of Lee Enterprises, Inc.

Corporate Officials

Larry L. Bloom: chief financial officer B 1949. ED
DePaul University BS. PRIM CORP EMPL senior vice
president finance, treasurer, chief financial officer:
Lee Enterprises Inc.

Foundation Officials

Russel R. Kennel: secretary, director
Ronald L. Rickman: vice president, director B 1939. PRIM CORP EMPL president newspapers, director: Lee Enterprises Inc.
George C. Wahlig: treasurer, director PRIM CORP EMPL vice president finance, chief administrative officer: Lee Enterprises Inc.

Grants Analysis

Disclosure Period: fiscal year ending September 30, 2001
Total Grants: $471,833*
Number of Grants: 108
Average Grant: $3,942*
Highest Grant: $50,000
Lowest Grant: $100
Typical Range: $500 to $30,000
*Note: Giving excludes scholarship and United Way. Average grant figure excludes highest grant.

Recent Grants

Note: Grants derived from fiscal 2001 Form 990.

General

50,000	Davenport One, Davenport, IA
31,639	United Way of the Quad Cities Area, Davenport, IA
20,000	Dakota Zoo Discovery, Bismarck, ND -- for 2000 Capital Campaign
12,500	Lincoln Children's Museum, Lincoln, NE
12,000	C.A.S.I., Davenport, IA
10,000	Friends of Brady Street Stadium, Davenport, IA
10,000	Iowa College Foundation, Des Moines, IA
10,000	Mid America Press Institute, Madison, WI
10,000	Muscatine Beyond 2000, Muscatine, IA
10,000	New Art Center Campaign, Billings, MT

WHILMA B. LEE SCHOLARSHIP FUND TRUST

Giving Contact

Donald R. France, Trustee
PO Box 247
Marcellus, MI 49067-0247
Phone: (616)646-5345

Description

Founded: 1989
EIN: 386547465
Organization Type: Private Foundation
Giving Locations: MI: Cass County, Kalamazoo County, St. Joseph County, Van Buren County
Grant Types: Scholarship.

Financial Summary

Total Giving: $12,075 (fiscal year ending , 2001); $9,300 (fiscal 2000); $15,000 (fiscal 1999)
Giving Analysis: Giving for fiscal 2001 includes: foundation scholarships ($12,075); fiscal 2000: foundation scholarships ($9,300); fiscal 1999: foundation scholarships ($15,000)
Assets: $146,227 (fiscal 2001); $152,380 (fiscal 2000); $153,778 (fiscal 1999)
Gifts Received: $2,000 (fiscal 1994); $2,000 (fiscal 1993). Note: In 1994, contributions were received from Jack and Rita Bradtke.

Typical Recipients

Education: Colleges & Universities, Education-General, Medical Education, Minority Education, Special Education, Student Aid
Social Services: Child Welfare, Community Service Organizations, Counseling, Family Services, Food/Clothing Distribution, United Funds/United Ways, YMCA/YWCA/YMHA/YWHA

Application Procedures

Initial Contact: Request application form.
Deadlines: April 15.

Additional Information

Provides scholarships for higher education to high school graduates from Van Buren, Cass, Kalamazoo, and St. Joseph counties, MI.

Foundation Officials

Donald R. France: trustee

Grants Analysis

Total Grants: $12,075*
Number of Grants: 21
Average Grant: $575
Highest Grant: $1,275
Typical Range: $300 to $1,000
*Note: Giving includes scholarships.

Recent Grants

Note: Grants derived from fiscal 1997 Form 990.

Library-Related

3,000	Atlanta Fulton Public Library, Atlanta, GA

General

40,000	Woodruff Arts Center, Atlanta, GA
30,000	Foundation of Public Broadcasting
25,000	Scottish Rite Children's Hospital
20,000	Harris College
20,000	Shorter College
12,500	Eagle Ranch, Chestnut Mountain, GA
12,500	United Way, Atlanta, GA
10,000	Juvenile Diabetes Foundation, New York, NY
10,000	State YMCA, Atlanta, GA
7,500	Devereaux Center, GA

LEF FOUNDATION

Giving Contact

Marina Drummer, Grants Administrator
LEF Foundation
1095 Lodi Lane
St. Helena, CA 94574
Phone: (707)963-9591
Fax: (707)963-2109
E-mail: marina@lef-foundation.org
Web: http://www.lef-foundation.org

Alternate Contact

Lyda Kuth, Director
PO Box 382866
Cambridge, MA 02238-2866
Phone: (617)492-5333
Fax: (617)868-5603

Description

Founded: 1985
EIN: 680070194
Organization Type: Private Foundation
Giving Locations: CA: New England.
Grant Types: General Support, Project, Scholarship, Seed Money.

Donor Information

Founder: Lyda Ebert Trust

Financial Summary

Total Giving: $1,332,250 (fiscal year ending June 30, 2002); $1,240,700 (fiscal 2001); $1,110,650 (fiscal 1999)
Giving Analysis: Giving for fiscal 2002 includes: foundation scholarships ($25,000); fiscal 2000: foundation fellowships ($10,000) foundation scholarships ($33,000)
Assets: $13,784,123 (fiscal 2002); $15,330,239 (fiscal 2001); $13,858,917 (fiscal 1997)
Gifts Received: $400,008 (fiscal 2002); $413,439 (fiscal 1997); $70,017 (fiscal 1994). Note: In fiscal 2002, contributions were received from Lyda Kuth. In fiscal 1994, contributions were received from Lyda Kuth ($50,034) and Marion Green ($19,983).

Typical Recipients

Arts & Humanities: Arts Associations & Councils, Arts Centers, Arts Festivals, Arts Funds, Dance, Ethnic & Folk Arts, Film & Video, Arts & Humanities-General, History & Archaeology, Libraries, Museums/Galleries, Music, Opera, Performing Arts, Theater, Visual Arts
Civic & Public Affairs: African American Affairs, Asian American Affairs, Clubs, Economic Development, Civic & Public Affairs-General, Native American Affairs, Urban & Community Affairs, Women's Affairs
Education: Arts/Humanities Education, Colleges & Universities, Engineering/Technological Education, Education-General, Private Education (Precollege), Public Education (Precollege)
Environment: Environment-General, Wildlife Protection
Health: AIDS/HIV, Emergency/Ambulance Services
International: Foreign Arts Organizations, International Organizations
Religion: Churches, Religious Organizations
Social Services: Camps, Community Service Organizations, Family Services, Recreation & Athletics, Youth Organizations

Application Procedures

Initial Contact: Telephone the foundation and submit a brief letter of inquiry.
Application Requirements: Include a description of organization, amount requested, purpose of funds sought.
Deadlines: Check website for current deadlines.
Review Process: Announcements made within two months of application deadlines.

Restrictions

The foundation funds projects, programs, and services that encourage a positive interchange between the arts and the natural and urban environment.

Additional Information

"Past grantees may reapply for one funding cycle per year, Spring or Fall, for two additional years, provided all final reports have been filed. After a third year of funding, the Foundation requests that grantees allow a two-year hiatus prior to reapplication." Guidelines.
Publications: Application Guidelines

Foundation Officials

Laurey Finneran: trustee
Marion E. Greene: president
Byron Kuth: vice president
Lyda Ebert Kuth: cfo, secretary

Grants Analysis

Disclosure Period: fiscal year ending June 30, 2002
Total Grants: $1,307,250*
Number of Grants: 155
Average Grant: $8,434
Highest Grant: $35,000
Lowest Grant: $500
Typical Range: $3,000 to $15,000
*Note: Giving excludes scholarships.

Recent Grants

Note: Grants derived from fiscal 2002 Form 990.

General

35,000	Center for Land Use Interpretation, Culver City, CA -- in support of the development of CLUI's Interactive Landscape Environment
25,000	Spoleto Festival USA, Charleston, SC -- in support of six artists
20,000	African Services Committee, New York, NY -- in support of Global AIDS Alliance Medication for All Initiative
20,000	Center for Independent Documentary Inc., Sharon, MA -- in support of Project Touched
20,000	Drawing Center, New York, NY -- in support of your joint exhibition
20,000	President and Fellows of Harvard, Cambridge, MA -- in support of Robb Moss's project The Same River Twice
20,000	Puppet Showplace Theater, Brookline, MA -- in support of Puppets at Night
20,000	Theater Offensive, Boston, MA -- in support of Plays at Work Laboratory
18,000	Trustees of Phillips Academy, Andover, MA -- in support of Art on Main Program
15,000	California College of Arts and Crafts, San Francisco, CA -- in support of a residency and installation at the Capp Street Project

AL PAUL LEFTON CO.

Company Headquarters

100 Independence Mall W.
Philadelphia, PA 19106-2399
Web: http://www.lefton.com

Company Description

Revenue: US$70 million (2001)
Employees: 60 (2001)
SIC(s): 7300 Business Services.

Al Paul Lefton Co. Foundation

Giving Contact

Al Paul Lefton, Jr.
100 Independence Mall W., 4th Fl.
Philadelphia, PA 19106
Phone: (215)923-9600
Fax: (215)351-4298

Description

EIN: 236298693
Organization Type: Corporate Foundation
Giving Locations: PA: Philadelphia
Grant Types: General Support.

Financial Summary

Total Giving: $22,270 (2000); $22,494 (1999); $15,959 (1995)
Giving Analysis: Giving for 2000 includes: foundation grants to United Way ($1,700) 1999: foundation grants to United Way ($3,660)
Assets: $39,486 (2000); $39,158 (1999); $7,548 (1995)
Gifts Received: $20,000 (2000); $15,000 (1999); $20,000 (1995)

Typical Recipients

Arts & Humanities: Arts Associations & Councils, Arts Centers, Arts Institutes, Arts & Humanities-General, History & Archaeology, Libraries, Museums/Galleries, Music, Opera

Civic & Public Affairs: Botanical Gardens/Parks, Civic & Public Affairs-General, Parades/Festivals, Public Policy, Urban & Community Affairs, Zoos/Aquariums
Education: Arts/Humanities Education, Business Education, Colleges & Universities, Student Aid
Environment: Resource Conservation
Health: Hospitals, Hospitals (University Affiliated), Multiple Sclerosis
Religion: Churches, Jewish Causes
Social Services: United Funds/United Ways, Youth Organizations

Application Procedures

Initial Contact: Send a brief letter of inquiry.
Deadlines: None.

Corporate Officials

Al Paul Lefton, Jr.: president, chief executive officer, director B Wilmington, DE 1928. ED Yale University BA (1950). PRIM CORP EMPL president, chief executive officer, director: Al Paul Lefton Co. CORP AFFIL member: Mayors Comm Culture Arts; director: University Arts; director: Mann Music Center.
Raymond D. Scanlon: vice president, chief financial officer, director PRIM CORP EMPL vice president, chief financial officer, director: Al Paul Lefton Co.

Foundation Officials

Al Paul Lefton, Jr.: trustee (see above)
Raymond D. Scanlon: trustee (see above)

Grants Analysis

Disclosure Period: calendar year ending 2000
Total Grants: $20,570*
Number of Grants: 20
Average Grant: $1,029
Highest Grant: $5,000
Typical Range: $500 to $2,600
*Note: Giving excludes United Way.

Recent Grants

Note: Grants derived from 2001 Form 990.

General

7,500	University of the Arts, Philadelphia, PA -- annual fund drive
5,600	Institute of Contemporary Art, Philadelphia, PA -- annual benefit fund
1,800	Union for Traditional Judaism, Teaneck, NJ -- for Ad in dinner journal
1,700	United Way of Southeastern Pennsylvania, Philadelphia, PA -- annual fund drive
1,050	Yale University, New Haven, CT -- for alumni fund
1,000	Main Line Art Center, Haverford, PA -- annual operating fund
750	Sconset Trust, Siasconset, MA -- for annual conservation
400	Japan America Society of Philadelphia, Philadelphia, PA -- annual sponsorship
170	Philadelphia Museum of Art, Philadelphia, PA -- for Craft Show and subscriber

LEHIGH CEMENT CO.

Company Headquarters

7660 Imperial Way, 4th Fl
Allentown, PA 18195

Company Description

Employees: 2,300
SIC(s): 3241 Cement--Hydraulic, 3272 Concrete Products Nec.
Parent Company: HeidelbergCement A.G., Berliner Strasse 6, Heidelberg, Germany

Operating Locations

Lehigh Cement Co. (AL--Birmingham; CA--Los Angeles; IN--Glastonbury; MN; VA--Mannassas, Norfolk); Lehigh Portland Cement Co. (PA--Allentown)

Nonmonetary Support

Type: Donated Products; In-kind Services; Loaned Employees

Giving Contact

Corliss Hirst, communications coordinator
7660 Imperial Way
Allentown, PA 18195
Phone: (610)366-4764
Fax: (610)366-4684
E-mail: chirst@lehighcement.com
Web: http://www.lehighcement.com

Description

Organization Type: Corporate Giving Program
Former Name: Lehigh Portland Cement Co. (1999).
Giving Locations: headquarters and operating communities.
Grant Types: Employee Matching Gifts, General Support, Project, Scholarship.

Financial Summary

Total Giving: $200,000 (2003 approx); $200,000 (2002); $700,000 (1999 approx). Note: The Co.'s corporate office location has a funding budget of approximately $200,000. Each economic base unit, or sales office location, has a funding budget of $50,000 to $100,000.
Giving Analysis: Giving for 1999 includes: corporate direct giving (approx $700,000) 1996: foundation matching gifts ($90,000)
Assets: $1,821 (1998); $737 (1997); $31,807 (1996)
Gifts Received: $225,000 (1995)

Typical Recipients

Arts & Humanities: Arts Funds, Historic Preservation, History & Archaeology, Libraries, Museums/Galleries, Music, Performing Arts, Public Broadcasting, Theater
Civic & Public Affairs: Business/Free Enterprise, Community Foundations, Employment/Job Training, Civic & Public Affairs-General, Municipalities/Towns, Native American Affairs, Professional & Trade Associations, Urban & Community Affairs, Zoos/Aquariums
Education: Business Education, Business-School Partnerships, Colleges & Universities, Community & Junior Colleges, Continuing Education, Economic Education, Education Associations, Education Funds, Elementary Education (Public), Engineering/Technological Education, Education-General, Literacy, Preschool Education, Private Education (Precollege), Public Education (Precollege), Science/Mathematics Education, Secondary Education (Public), Special Education, Student Aid, Vocational & Technical Education
Environment: Environment-General
Health: Cancer, Children's Health/Hospitals, Emergency/Ambulance Services, Health-General, Health Organizations, Heart, Hospices, Hospitals, Prenatal Health Issues, Transplant Networks/Donor Banks
Religion: Churches
Science: Scientific Organizations
Social Services: At-Risk Youth, Camps, Child Welfare, Community Service Organizations, Counseling, Day Care, Domestic Violence, Emergency Relief, Family Services, People with Disabilities, Recreation & Athletics, Scouts, Sexual Abuse, Shelters/Homelessness, Social Services-General, Substance Abuse, United Funds/United Ways, YMCA/YWCA/YMHA/YWHA, Youth Organizations

Application Procedures

Initial Contact: Send a brief letter of inquiry.
Deadlines: None.

Restrictions

Funding is provided to organization's in operating locations only. Tax exempt only.

Additional Information

The Lehigh Portland Cement Co. Charitable Trust dissolved in 1999.

Corporate Officials

Jeffry H. Brozyna: vice president, general counsel B Schenectady, NY 1952. ED Hobart College (1974); Albany Law School (1977). PRIM CORP EMPL vice president, general counsel: Lehigh Portland Cement Co. CORP AFFIL secretary: Addiment Inc. NONPR AFFIL director: American Portland Cement Alliance.
Helmut Erhard: president, chief executive officer

Foundation Officials

Jeffry H. Brozyna: trustee (see above)

Grants Analysis

Disclosure Period: calendar year ending 1996
Total Grants: $149,485*
Number of Grants: 250 (approx)
Average Grant: $598
Highest Grant: $19,755
Typical Range: $50 to $1,000
*Note: Giving excludes matching gifts.

Recent Grants

Note: Grants derived from 1999 Form 990.

General

8,138	Habitat for Humanity, Allentown, PA
500	United Way of Greater Lehigh, Bethlehem, PA

OTTO W. LEHMANN FOUNDATION

Giving Contact

Richard J. Peterson, Trustee
680 Lake Shore Dr.
420 Tower Res.
Chicago, IL 60611
Phone: (312)587-0762

Description

Founded: 1967
EIN: 366160836
Organization Type: Private Foundation
Giving Locations: IL: Chicago
Grant Types: General Support.

Donor Information

Founder: the late Otto W. Lehmann

Financial Summary

Total Giving: $200,000 (fiscal year ending July 31, 2002); $200,000 (fiscal 2001); $200,000 (fiscal 2000 approx)
Giving Analysis: Giving for fiscal 2002 includes: foundation scholarships ($47,000); fiscal 2001: foundation scholarships ($47,000); fiscal 1999: foundation scholarships ($30,000)
Assets: $1,970,507 (fiscal 2002); $2,212,827 (fiscal 2001); $2,364,011 (fiscal 1999)

Typical Recipients

Arts & Humanities: Arts Institutes, History & Archaeology, Libraries, Music, Opera
Civic & Public Affairs: Clubs, Employment/Job Training, Zoos/Aquariums

Education: Colleges & Universities, Engineering/Technological Education, Private Education (Precollege), Special Education, Student Aid
Health: Alzheimers Disease, Cancer, Children's Health/Hospitals, Emergency/Ambulance Services, Eyes/Blindness, Health Organizations, Hospitals, Medical Rehabilitation, Medical Research, Nursing Services, Outpatient Health Care, Single-Disease Health Associations
Religion: Religious Organizations, Religious Welfare
Science: Observatories & Planetariums, Science Museums
Social Services: Child Welfare, Community Service Organizations, Domestic Violence, Food/Clothing Distribution, Homes, People with Disabilities, Shelters/Homelessness, United Funds/United Ways, Youth Organizations

Application Procedures

Initial Contact: Send brief letter describing program.
Application Requirements: Include a description of organization, amount requested, purpose of funds sought, recently audited financial statement, and proof of tax-exempt status.
Deadlines: June 15.

Restrictions

Does not support individuals, religious organizations for sectarian purposes, political or lobbying groups, or organizations outside operating areas.

Foundation Officials

David W. Peterson: trustee
Lucille S. Peterson: trustee
Mary E. Peterson: officer
Richard J. Peterson: trustee
Orris Seng: trustee

Grants Analysis

Disclosure Period: fiscal year ending July 31, 2002
Total Grants: $113,000*
Number of Grants: 48
Average Grant: $2,354
Highest Grant: $8,000
Lowest Grant: $1,000
Typical Range: $1,000 to $5,000
*Note: Giving excludes scholarships.

Recent Grants

Note: Grants derived from 2000 Form 990.

General

6,0000	Museums of Science & Industry, Chicago, IL
15,000	Loyola University Chicago, Chicago, IL
15,000	Northwestern University, Evanston, IL
8,000	Lincoln Park Zoological Society, Chicago, IL
7,000	DePaul University, Chicago, IL
6,000	Chicago Zoological Society, Brookfield, IL
6,000	Field Museum of Natural History, Chicago, IL
6,000	Shedd Aquarium, Chicago, IL
5,000	Art Institute of Chicago, Chicago, IL
5,000	Boys & Girls Club of Chicago, Chicago, IL

JOHN J. LEIDY FOUNDATION

Giving Contact

W. Michel Pierson, President
201 E. Baltimore St., Suite 1420
Baltimore, MD 21202
Phone: (410)727-4136
E-mail: leidyfd@attglobal.net

Description

Founded: 1957
EIN: 526034785
Organization Type: Private Foundation
Giving Locations: MD: Baltimore including metropolitan area
Grant Types: General Support, Scholarship.

Donor Information

Founder: the late John J. Leidy

Financial Summary

Total Giving: $603,679 (2001); $603,359 (2000); $513,019 (1999)
Giving Analysis: Giving for 2001 includes: foundation scholarships ($125,540); 2000: foundation grants to United Way ($30,000); foundation scholarships ($115,400); 1999: foundation scholarships ($71,400);
Assets: $12,429,603 (2001); $13,893,380 (2000); $15,045,641 (1999)

Typical Recipients

Arts & Humanities: Arts Institutes, Community Arts, Historic Preservation, Libraries, Museums/Galleries, Music, Opera
Civic & Public Affairs: Clubs, Economic Development, Employment/Job Training, Civic & Public Affairs-General, Housing, Legal Aid, Philanthropic Organizations, Public Policy, Urban & Community Affairs
Education: Arts/Humanities Education, Colleges & Universities, Education Reform, Elementary Education (Private), Education-General, Legal Education, Literacy, Private Education (Precollege), Special Education, Student Aid
Health: AIDS/HIV, Clinics/Medical Centers, Emergency/Ambulance Services, Health Organizations, Heart, Hospitals, Medical Research, Public Health, Single-Disease Health Associations
Religion: Churches, Jewish Causes, Ministries, Religious Organizations, Religious Welfare
Science: Science Museums, Scientific Research
Social Services: Big Brother/Big Sister, Child Welfare, Community Service Organizations, Emergency Relief, Family Services, Food/Clothing Distribution, People with Disabilities, Senior Services, United Funds/United Ways, Veterans, Youth Organizations

Application Procedures

Initial Contact: Send full proposal.
Application Requirements: Include an original and four copies which contains complete details of need and amount requested, proof of tax-exempt status, budget, a description of organization and its activities in general, list of board members, and an explanation of whether the applicant is controlled by, related to, connected with, or sponsored by another organization.
Deadlines: None.

Restrictions

Preference is given to educational and health care organizations. Does not support individuals.

Foundation Officials

Henry E. Pear: treasurer
Ruth C. Pear: vice president
Robert L. Pierson: secretary
W. Michel Pierson: president

Grants Analysis

Disclosure Period: calendar year ending 2001
Total Grants: $478,139*
Number of Grants: 73
Average Grant: $6,550*
Highest Grant: $27,500
Lowest Grant: $500
Typical Range: $1,000 to $10,000
*Note: Giving excludes scholarships.

Recent Grants

Note: Grants derived from 2001 Form 990.

Library-Related

25,000	Enoch Pratt Free Library, Baltimore, MD

General

50,000	Maryland Institute College of Art, Baltimore, MD
50,000	Walters Art Museum, Baltimore, MD
27,500	Associated Jewish Charities, Baltimore, MD
20,000	Maryland Center for Veterans, Baltimore, MD
19,000	Preservation Society, Newport, RI
15,000	American Red Cross, Baltimore, MD
15,000	Govans Ecumenical Development, Baltimore, MD
12,500	Edward A. Myerberg Northwest Senior Center, Inc., Baltimore, MD
11,000	Baltimore Symphony Orchestra, Baltimore, MD
10,000	American Red Cross, Baltimore, MD

LEMBERG FOUNDATION

Giving Contact

John Usdan, Treasurer
60 E. 42nd St., Rm. 1814
New York, NY 10165
Phone: (212)682-9595

Description

Founded: 1945
EIN: 136082064
Organization Type: Private Foundation
Giving Locations: NY: New York
Grant Types: Capital, Endowment, Fellowship, Project, Research, Scholarship.

Donor Information

Founder: the late Samuel Lemberg

Financial Summary

Total Giving: $770,480 (2001); $1,485,877 (2000); $1,124,841 (1998)
Giving Analysis: Giving for 2001 includes: foundation scholarships ($40,500)
Assets: $32,208,117 (2001); $31,227,340 (2000); $26,308,537 (1998)
Gifts Received: $75,000 (2000)

Typical Recipients

Arts & Humanities: Arts Associations & Councils, Arts Centers, Arts Funds, Community Arts, Dance, Film & Video, Historic Preservation, Libraries, Museums/Galleries, Music, Opera, Performing Arts, Public Broadcasting, Theater, Visual Arts
Civic & Public Affairs: Botanical Gardens/Parks, Economic Development, Civic & Public Affairs-General, Professional & Trade Associations, Public Policy
Education: Arts/Humanities Education, Colleges & Universities, Economic Education, Education Funds, Education-General, Health & Physical Education, Literacy, Minority Education, Private Education (Precollege), Public Education (Precollege), Religious Education, Science/Mathematics Education, Student Aid
Health: Cancer, Clinics/Medical Centers, Health Organizations, Hospitals, Hospitals (University Affiliated), Medical Research, Multiple Sclerosis, Single-Disease Health Associations
International: Foreign Arts Organizations, Human Rights
Religion: Jewish Causes, Religious Organizations, Seminaries, Synagogues/Temples
Social Services: Animal Protection, Child Welfare, Community Service Organizations, Family Services, People with Disabilities, United Funds/United Ways, YMCA/YWCA/YMHA/YWHA

Application Procedures

Initial Contact: Send a brief letter of inquiry describing program or project.
Deadlines: None.

Restrictions

No grants for matching gifts.

Foundation Officials

Adam Usdan: vice president
John Usdan: treasurer
Suzanne Usdan: president

Grants Analysis

Disclosure Period: calendar year ending 2001
Total Grants: $729,980*
Number of Grants: 155
Average Grant: $4,710
Highest Grant: $75,000
Lowest Grant: $50
Typical Range: $100 to $50,000
***Note:** Giving excludes scholarships.

Recent Grants

Note: Grants derived from 2001 Form 990.

General

75,000	United Jewish Appeal Federation, New York, NY
65,600	Lincoln Center Institute, New York, NY
55,000	WNET/Channel 13, New York, NY
50,000	Multiple Sclerosis Research Fund
50,000	Usdan Center for Performing Arts, New York, NY
44,550	92nd Street "Y", New York, NY
40,500	Samuel Lemberg Scholarship Loan Fund, New York, NY
33,700	WNYC, New York, NY
28,000	Carnegie Hall Society, New York, NY
25,000	Bronx House, Bronx, NY

REGINALD A. AND ELIZABETH S. LENNA FOUNDATION

Giving Contact

Elizabeth S. Lenna, President
Reginald A. and Elizabeth S. Lenna Foundation
PO Box 407
Lakewood, NY 14750
Phone: (716)484-2402

Description

Founded: 1985
EIN: 112800733
Organization Type: Private Foundation
Giving Locations: NY: Jamestown
Grant Types: General Support.

Donor Information

Founder: Reginald A. Lenna

Financial Summary

Total Giving: $230,000 (2001); $265,000 (2000); $15,000 (1999)
Assets: $9,448,550 (2001); $11,315,686 (2000); $11,307,199 (1999)
Gifts Received: $8,681,017 (1998)

Typical Recipients

Arts & Humanities: Arts Associations & Councils, Arts Funds, Ballet, Arts & Humanities-General, History & Archaeology, Libraries, Music, Performing Arts, Public Broadcasting
Civic & Public Affairs: Community Foundations, Economic Development, Employment/Job Training, Civic & Public Affairs-General, Public Policy, Safety, Urban & Community Affairs
Education: Arts/Humanities Education, Colleges & Universities, Community & Junior Colleges, Education-General, Public Education (Precollege)
Environment: Environment-General, Wildlife Protection
Health: Emergency/Ambulance Services, Hospices, Hospitals
Religion: Churches, Religious Welfare
Science: Science Museums
Social Services: Animal Protection, Community Centers, Food/Clothing Distribution, Homes, Recreation & Athletics, Scouts, United Funds/United Ways, YMCA/YWCA/YMHA/YWHA, Youth Organizations

Application Procedures

Initial Contact: Send a brief letter of inquiry and a full proposal.
Application Requirements: Include purpose of funds sought, amount requested, a description of organization, and proof of tax-exempt status.
Deadlines: None.

Foundation Officials

John Dayton Hamilton: director B Pavilion, NY. ED Hamilton College AB (1922). NONPR AFFIL trustee: Chautauqua Institute; trustee: Jamestown Community College.
Elizabeth S. Lenna: director
Reginald A. Lenna: director
Samuel P. Price: director

Grants Analysis

Disclosure Period: calendar year ending 2001
Total Grants: $230,000
Number of Grants: 4
Highest Grant: $120,000
Lowest Grant: $25,000

Recent Grants

Note: Grants derived from 2000 Form 990.

General

250,000	YMCA, Jamestown, NY -- capital campaign
15,000	WCA Home, Fredonia, NY -- expansion project

MARTHA, DAVID AND BAGBY LENNOX FOUNDATION

Giving Contact

William P. Streng, President & Treasurer
228 6th St. SE
Paris, TX 75460
Phone: (903)784-4316

Description

Founded: 1985
EIN: 760157945
Organization Type: Private Foundation
Giving Locations: TX: northeast area
Grant Types: General Support, Scholarship.

Donor Information

Founder: the late Martha Lennox, the late David Lennox, the late Bagby Lennox

Financial Summary

Total Giving: $791,625 (2002); $807,416 (2000); $718,142 (1999)
Giving Analysis: Giving for 2002 includes: foundation scholarships ($22,500); 2000: foundation scholarships ($71,000); 1999: foundation scholarships ($155,000)

Assets: $11,612,662 (2002); $17,116,430 (2000); $17,843,873 (1999).
Gifts Received: $2,500 (1999); $3,514,610 (1994). Note: In 1994, contributions were received from the estate of Martha Lennox.

Typical Recipients

Arts & Humanities: History & Archaeology, Libraries, Museums/Galleries
Civic & Public Affairs: African American Affairs, Community Foundations, Civic & Public Affairs-General, Legal Aid, Municipalities/Towns, Public Policy, Urban & Community Affairs
Education: Agricultural Education, Colleges & Universities, Education-General, Gifted & Talented Programs, Science/Mathematics Education, Special Education, Student Aid
Environment: Resource Conservation
Health: Arthritis, Mental Health
International: International Organizations
Religion: Churches, Ministries, Religious Welfare
Social Services: Animal Protection, Camps, Child Welfare, Crime Prevention, Family Services, Scouts, Shelters/Homelessness, Youth Organizations

Application Procedures

Initial Contact: Send a brief letter of inquiry.
Deadlines: None.

Restrictions

Grants are not made to individuals.

Foundation Officials

Mary W. Clark: director
Sam L. Hocker: director
Hardy Moore: president
William Paul Streng: secretary, treasurer B Sterling, IL 1937. ED Wartburg College BA (1959); Northwestern University JD (1962). PRIM CORP EMPL law professor: Vision & Elkins. CORP AFFIL lecturer: Practicing Law Institute; lecturer: World Trade Institute; consult: Braceurell & Patterson; lecturer: International Fiscal Association; lecturer: America Law Institute. NONPR AFFIL member: American Bar Association; member: Texas State Bar.

Grants Analysis

Disclosure Period: calendar year ending 2002
Total Grants: $769,125*
Number of Grants: 28
Average Grant: $22,824*
Highest Grant: $100,000
Lowest Grant: $1,000
Typical Range: $10,000 to $50,000
*Note: Giving excludes scholarships. Average grant figure excludes two highest grants ($175,700).

Recent Grants

Note: Grants derived from 2002 Form 990.

Library-Related
15,000   Civil War Preservation Trust, Arlington, TX -- support for the Land and Water Conservation Fund

General
100,000   Christus St. Joseph's Health System, Paris, TX -- support for Lennox Health Resource Center
100,000   Nature Conservancy of Texas, Houston, TX -- support for acquisition of the Hancock land
75,700   Clarksville Independent School District, Clarksville, TX -- support towards implementing an electronic curriculum system
45,000   Red River County Firefighters Association, Detroit, TX -- to promote fire prevention
32,800   Avery Independent School District, Avery, TX -- to support the Laptop Learning Project

32,144   City of Detroit, Detroit, MI -- for construction of a new ball field
31,644   Rivercrest Independent School District, Bogata, TX -- for foreign language lab and technology upgrade to the high school library
30,000   Family Haven Crisis & Resource Center, Inc., Paris, TX -- to establish Crisis Center Programs
25,000   Detroit Independent School District, Detroit, TX -- for media center materials
21,715   City of Clarksville, Clarksville, TX -- support for the Historic Creek Walk Project

DEAN AND MARGARET LESHER FOUNDATION

Giving Contact

Kathleen Odne, Executive Director
Dean and Margaret Lesher Foundation
1333 N. California Boulevard, Suite 510
Walnut Creek, CA 94596
Phone: (925)935-9988
Fax: (925)935-7459

Description

Founded: 1994
EIN: 680208980
Organization Type: Private Foundation
Giving Locations: CA: Contra Costa County
Grant Types: General Support, Matching, Scholarship.

Donor Information

Founder: Established in 1994 by Dean S. Lesher.

Financial Summary

Total Giving: $1,959,525 (2000); $3,056,675 (1999); $688,966 (1995)
Assets: $44,668,207 (2000); $43,927,266 (1999); $29,714,512 (1995)
Gifts Received: $914,652 (2000); $10,207,579 (1995); $17,487,890 (1994). Note: In 1995, contributions were received from the estate of Dean S. Lesher.

Typical Recipients

Arts & Humanities: Arts Associations & Councils, Arts Centers, Ballet, Arts & Humanities-General, History & Archaeology, Libraries, Museums/Galleries, Music, Theater, Visual Arts
Civic & Public Affairs: Clubs, Housing, Municipalities/Towns, Parades/Festivals, Urban & Community Affairs, Women's Affairs
Education: Arts/Humanities Education, Colleges & Universities, Community & Junior Colleges, Education Funds, Elementary Education (Public), Private Education (Precollege), Public Education (Precollege), Secondary Education (Public)
Environment: Resource Conservation
Health: AIDS/HIV, Children's Health/Hospitals, Emergency/Ambulance Services, Heart, Mental Health, Prenatal Health Issues, Preventive Medicine/Wellness Organizations
Religion: Religious Organizations, Religious Welfare, Religious Welfare
Social Services: Animal Protection, Big Brother/Big Sister, Child Welfare, Community Centers, Community Service Organizations, Counseling, Day Care, Domestic Violence, Family Services, Food/Clothing Distribution, Homes, People with Disabilities, Recreation & Athletics, Scouts, Sexual Abuse, Shelters/Homelessness, Substance Abuse, Volunteer Services, YMCA/YWCA/YMHA/YWHA

Application Procedures

Initial Contact: Return completed application form with a brief letter of inquiry.
Application Requirements: Include a description of organization, amount requested, purpose of funds

sought, recently audited financial statement, and proof of tax-exempt status.
Deadlines: None.

Restrictions

Foundation does not support individuals, political or lobbying groups, or organizations outside operating areas.

Foundation Officials

Wendi Alves: director
Stephen P. Blanding: secretary, treasurer
Roxanne Gibson: director
Jill Heidt: director
Cynthia Lesher: director
Margaret L. Lesher: president, director
Melinda Lesher: director
Stephen Lesher: vice president
Patricia Ryan Simmonds: director
Linda Tatum: secretary, treasurer

Grants Analysis

Disclosure Period: calendar year ending 2000
Total Grants: $1,959,525
Number of Grants: 76
Average Grant: $25,783
Highest Grant: $250,000
Typical Range: $5,000 to $50,000

Recent Grants

Note: Grants derived from 2001 Form 990.

General
250,000   Battered Women's Alternatives, San Francisco, CA
244,000   Contra Costa County Office of Education, Contra Costa, CA
200,000   City of Walnut Creek, Walnut Creek, CA -- arts endowment grant
100,000   Cambridge Community Center, Concord, CA
100,000   Concord Pavilion Association, Concord, CA
100,000   Contra Costa Community College District, Contra Costa, CA
70,000   New Connections, Concord, CA
50,000   Diablo Ballet, Walnut Creek, CA
50,000   East Bay Habitat for Humanity, Oakland, CA
50,000   Rape Crisis Center, Beaufort, SC

LEVITT FOUNDATION (NY)

Giving Contact

Stephen J. Mathes, Secretary
Levitt Foundation
1650 Market St., Suite 4900
Philadelphia, PA 19103
Phone: (212)476-9000

Description

Founded: 1949
EIN: 136128226
Organization Type: Private Foundation
Giving Locations: NY: Suffolk and Nassau counties, New York
Grant Types: General Support.

Donor Information

Founder: Levitt and Sons, the late Abraham Levitt, the late Alfred Levitt, William Levitt

Financial Summary

Total Giving: $707,449 (fiscal year ending April 30, 2001); $668,989 (fiscal 2000); $700,000 (fiscal 1999 approx)
Giving Analysis: Giving for fiscal 2000 includes: foundation scholarships ($2,000)

Assets: $18,607,783 (fiscal 2001); $19,758,576 (fiscal 2000); $12,848,120 (fiscal 1997)

Typical Recipients

Arts & Humanities: Arts Appreciation, Arts Funds, Arts Outreach, Dance, History & Archaeology, Libraries, Museums/Galleries, Music, Opera, Performing Arts

Civic & Public Affairs: African American Affairs, Botanical Gardens/Parks, Business/Free Enterprise, Civil Rights, Economic Development, Gay/Lesbian Issues, Civic & Public Affairs-General, Hispanic Affairs, Housing, Legal Aid, Municipalities/Towns, Philanthropic Organizations, Urban & Community Affairs

Education: Afterschool/Enrichment Programs, Arts/Humanities Education, Colleges & Universities, Elementary Education (Public), International Studies, Leadership Training, Preschool Education, Private Education (Precollege)

Environment: Air/Water Quality, Environment-General

Health: Clinics/Medical Centers, Geriatric Health, Hospitals (University Affiliated), Mental Health, Prenatal Health Issues

International: International Relations, International Relief Efforts

Religion: Dioceses, Jewish Causes, Ministries, Religious Organizations

Science: Science Museums, Scientific Centers & Institutes

Social Services: At-Risk Youth, Child Welfare, Community Centers, Community Service Organizations, Day Care, Domestic Violence, Family Planning, Family Services, United Funds/United Ways

Application Procedures

Initial Contact: Send brief letter describing program.
Deadlines: None.

Restrictions

Does not support individuals.

Foundation Officials

Robert J. Appel: treasurer
Prudence Brown: trustee
Dr. Farrell Jones: president
Stephen Jon Mathes, Esq.: secretary B New York, NY 1945. ED University of Pennsylvania BA (1967); University of Pennsylvania JD (1970). NONPR AFFIL member: Philadelphia Bar Association; member: Thanatopsis Society; member: American Bar Association; member: Pennsylvania Bar Association; director: Academy Vocal Arts. CLUB AFFIL Racquet Club; Germantown Cricket Club.
May W. Newburger: trustee

Grants Analysis

Disclosure Period: fiscal year ending April 30, 2001
Total Grants: $707,449
Number of Grants: 47
Average Grant: $12,997*
Highest Grant: $109,606
Typical Range: $5,000 to $20,000
*Note: Average grant figure excludes highest grant.

Recent Grants

Note: Grants derived from fiscal 2000 Form 990.

General

119,000	Citizens Campaign Fund
78,970	Heckscher Museum of Art, Long Island, NY
51,177	Council on the Environment of New York City, New York, NY
50,000	Trust for Public Land, New York, NY
48,742	Group for the South Fork, Bridgehampton, NY
40,000	Point Community Development Corporation, Bronx, NY
35,000	Citizens Committee for New York, New York, NY
35,000	Crenulated Company, LTD, Bronx, NY
25,000	American Littoral Society, Broad Channel, NY
25,000	New York Restoration Project, New York, NY

JUNE ROCKWELL LEVY FOUNDATION

Giving Contact

Jonathan Loring, President
Sherry Trust Co.
175 Federal Street
Boston, MA 02110
Phone: (617)482-5270

Description

Founded: 1947
EIN: 046074284
Organization Type: General Purpose Foundation
Giving Locations: MA; RI
Grant Types: Capital, General Support, Research, Scholarship, Seed Money.

Donor Information

Founder: Incorporated in 1947 by the late Austin T. Levy .

Financial Summary

Total Giving: $1,301,999 (2001); $1,492,562 (1998); $958,288 (1997)
Giving Analysis: Giving for 1998 includes: foundation grants to United Way ($48,000)
Assets: $29,129,634 (2001); $32,010,978 (1998); $28,303,395 (1997)

Typical Recipients

Arts & Humanities: Arts Associations & Councils, Dance, Historic Preservation, History & Archaeology, Libraries, Museums/Galleries, Music, Opera, Performing Arts, Public Broadcasting, Theater

Civic & Public Affairs: African American Affairs, Economic Development, Civic & Public Affairs-General, Hispanic Affairs, Housing, Legal Aid, Municipalities/Towns, Nonprofit Management, Philanthropic Organizations, Public Policy, Safety, Urban & Community Affairs, Women's Affairs, Zoos/Aquariums

Education: Afterschool/Enrichment Programs, Agricultural Education, Arts/Humanities Education, Colleges & Universities, Engineering/Technological Education, Education-General, Health & Physical Education, Leadership Training, Medical Education, Medical Education, Minority Education, Private Education (Precollege), Public Education (Precollege), Secondary Education (Private), Secondary Education (Public), Special Education

Environment: Air/Water Quality, Environment-General, Resource Conservation

Health: AIDS/HIV, Cancer, Children's Health/Hospitals, Clinics/Medical Centers, Diabetes, Emergency/Ambulance Services, Geriatric Health, Health Funds, Health Organizations, Home-Care Services, Hospices, Hospitals, Long-Term Care, Medical Rehabilitation, Medical Research, Mental Health, Nursing Services, Public Health, Single-Disease Health Associations

International: International Affairs, International Organizations, International Relations

Religion: Religious Welfare, Social/Policy Issues

Science: Science Museums

Social Services: Animal Protection, At-Risk Youth, Camps, Child Welfare, Community Centers, Community Service Organizations, Domestic Violence, Family Planning, Family Services, Food/Clothing Distribution, Homes, People with Disabilities, Recreation & Athletics, Scouts, Senior Services, Sexual Abuse, Substance Abuse, United Funds/United Ways, Volunteer Services, YMCA/YWCA/YMHA/YWHA, Youth Organizations

Application Procedures

Initial Contact: The foundation requests applications be made in letter form.
Application Requirements: The application should include any materials the organization feels are necessary for a complete review.
Deadlines: None.

Restrictions

The foundation does not make grants for religious purposes or to individuals.

Foundation Officials

James K. Edwards: trustee
Paul F. Greene: trustee
George T. Helm: trustee
Raymond G. Leveille, Jr.: trustee
Jonathan B. Loring: president, trustee
Raymond N. Menard: trustee
James W. Noonan: secretary, trustee
Edward H. Osgood: trustee B Wenham, MA 1916. ED Harvard University (1938). CORP AFFIL director: Fiduciary Trust Co. International.
Nancy DuVergne Smith: treasurer, trustee B Meridian, MS 1951. ED Tulane University BFA (1973); Harvard University MA (1989). PRIM NONPR EMPL education director, public affairs office: Wellesley College. NONPR AFFIL member: National Writers Union; member: National Writers Union Services Organization; member: Council Advancement & Support Education; director: Artists Foundation; member: Boston Women Communicators.
James M. White, Jr.: trustee NONPR AFFIL assistant clerk, director: Nebraska Health Services.

Grants Analysis

Disclosure Period: calendar year ending 2001
Total Grants: $1,236,999*
Number of Grants: 88
Average Grant: $14,057
Highest Grant: $50,000
Lowest Grant: $1,000
Typical Range: $10,000 to $20,000
*Note: Giving excludes United Way.

Recent Grants

Note: Grants derived from 2001 Form 990.

Library-Related

10,000	Providence Athenaeum, Providence, RI -- architects' fees
10,000	Providence Public Library, Providence, RI -- support for a new program called Teen Power

General

65,000	United Way of Southeastern New England, Providence, RI
50,000	Massachusetts General Hospital, Boston, MA
50,000	Medical Foundation, Boston, MA
50,000	Memorial Hospital of Rhode Island, Pawtucket, RI
50,000	Nature Conservancy, Providence, RI
50,000	Stadium Theatre Foundation, Woonsocket, RI
30,000	Bryant College, Smithfield, RI
30,000	Miriam Hospital, Providence, RI
30,000	Rhode Island Hospital Foundation, Providence, RI
25,000	Boy Scouts of America Narraganset Council, Providence, RI

LG&E ENERGY CORP.

Company Headquarters

Louisville, KY
Web: http://www.lgeenergy.com

Company Description

Assets: US$2.707 billion (2001)
Employees: 5403 (2001)
SIC(s): 4911 Electric Services, 4922 Natural Gas Transmission, 6719 Holding Companies Nec.

Operating Locations

LG&E Energy Corp. (KY--Louisville)

LG&E Energy Foundation

Giving Contact

Elaine Ashcraft, Grants Administrator
LG&E Energy Foundation
PO Box 32030
Louisville, KY 40232
Phone: (502)627-2000
Fax: (502)217-2672
Web: http://lgeenergy.com/communityrelations/lge-support.htm

Description

Founded: 1994
EIN: 611257368
Organization Type: Corporate Foundation
Giving Locations: KY: Louisville headquarters and operating communities.
Grant Types: Award, Capital, Employee Matching Gifts, Endowment, General Support, Matching, Multiyear/Continuing Support, Scholarship.

Donor Information

Founder: Established in 1994 by Louisville Gas and Electric Co.

Financial Summary

Total Giving: $2,300,000 (2002 approx); $2,206,912 (2001); $2,274,941 (2000)
Giving Analysis: Giving for 2000 includes: foundation scholarships ($83,400); foundation matching gifts ($85,938); foundation grants to United Way ($750,650); foundation ($1,354,953); 1999: foundation scholarships ($71,600); foundation matching gifts ($538,421); foundation ($1,547,333); 1998: foundation scholarships ($15,600); foundation matching gifts ($99,152); foundation grants to United Way ($402,063); foundation ($744,230);
Assets: $17,541,353 (2001); $19,902,257 (2000); $19,902,471 (1999)
Gifts Received: $4,882 (1997); $15,000,000 (1994)

Typical Recipients

Arts & Humanities: Arts Associations & Councils, Arts Centers, Arts Funds, Ballet, Ethnic & Folk Arts, History & Archaeology, Libraries, Museums/Galleries, Music, Public Broadcasting, Theater
Civic & Public Affairs: African American Affairs, Botanical Gardens/Parks, Economic Development, Civic & Public Affairs-General, Housing, Law & Justice, Urban & Community Affairs, Women's Affairs, Zoos/Aquariums
Education: Agricultural Education, Business Education, Colleges & Universities, Education Reform, Engineering/Technological Education, Environmental Education, Education-General, Literacy, Minority Education, Private Education (Precollege), Public Education (Precollege), Religious Education, Science/Mathematics Education, Special Education, Special Education, Student Aid

Environment: Environment-General, Resource Conservation
Health: Children's Health/Hospitals, Emergency/Ambulance Services, Geriatric Health, Heart
Religion: Religious Organizations, Religious Welfare
Science: Science Exhibits & Fairs, Scientific Centers & Institutes
Social Services: At-Risk Youth, Child Welfare, Community Centers, Community Service Organizations, Day Care, Emergency Relief, Family Services, Food/Clothing Distribution, Homes, Recreation & Athletics, Scouts, Social Services-General, United Funds/United Ways, YMCA/YWCA/YMHA/YWHA, Youth Organizations

Application Procedures

Initial Contact: Request a corporate contributions application form.
Application Requirements: Include a description of organization, amount requested, purpose of funds sought, recently audited financial statement, proof of tax-exempt status, and list of board of directors.
Deadlines: None.

Restrictions

Does not support individuals, religious organizations for sectarian purposes, political or lobbying groups, or organizations outside operating areas. Applicant must be a 501(c)(3) organization.

Additional Information

Publications: Application Form; Guidelines

Corporate Officials

Roger W. Hale: chairman, chief executive officer, director B Baltimore, MD 1943. ED University of Maryland BA (1965); Massachusetts Institute of Technology MS (1979). PRIM CORP EMPL chairman, chief executive officer, director: LG&E Energy Corp. CORP AFFIL director: PNC Bank Corp.; director: H & R Block. NONPR AFFIL director: Edison Electric Institute.
Charles A. Markel, III: vice president finance, treasurer PRIM CORP EMPL vice president finance, treasurer: LG&E Energy Corp.
Stephen R. Wood: president

Foundation Officials

Roger W. Hale: president (see above)
Rudolph W. Keeling: vice president
Charles A. Markel, III: vice president, treasurer (see above)
John McCall: vice president
S. Bradford Rives: vice president, treasurer, director
Victor A. Staffieri: vice president

Grants Analysis

Disclosure Period: calendar year ending 2001
Total Grants: $1,543,338
Number of Grants: 86
Average Grant: $16,392*
Highest Grant: $150,000
Lowest Grant: $155
Typical Range: $5,000 to $25,000
*Note: Average grant figure excludes highest grant.

Recent Grants

Note: Grants derived from 2001 Form 990.

Library-Related

15,000	Louisville Free Public Library, Louisville, KY

General

478,900	Metro United Way, Louisville, NY
150,000	Lend-A-Hand, Louisville, KY -- for science forum
89,000	Fund for the Arts, Louisville, KY
84,000	Energy Conservation Associates, Inc., Louisville, KY -- for project warm

83,243	Energy Conservation Associates, Inc., Louisville, KY -- for project warm
75,000	Louisville Zoo, Louisville, KY -- for Gorilla Forest
68,948	United Way of Henderson County, Hendersonville, NC -- 2001 campaign and employee match
66,535	LG&E College Relations, Louisville, KY -- for Matching Gift Programs
60,000	Kentucky Independent College Foundation, Frankfort, KY -- for KICF Scholars Program
55,000	Kentucky Derby Festival Foundation, Louisville, KY

BERTHA AND ISAAC LIBERMAN FOUNDATION

Giving Contact

Jeffrey Klein, President
480 Park Avenue
New York, NY 10022

Description

Founded: 1947
EIN: 136119056
Organization Type: Private Foundation
Giving Locations: NY: New York City
Grant Types: General Support.

Donor Information

Founder: the late Isaac Liberman

Financial Summary

Total Giving: $278,550 (fiscal year ending June 30, 2001); $278,550 (fiscal 2000); $255,750 (fiscal 1998)
Giving Analysis: Giving for fiscal 2000 includes: foundation scholarships ($5,000) fiscal 1999: foundation scholarships ($265,000)
Assets: $7,225,857 (fiscal 2001); $7,225,857 (fiscal 2000); $265,000 (fiscal 1999 approx)
Gifts Received: $19,504 (fiscal 1998); $910,606 (fiscal 1997). Note: In fiscal 1997, contributions were received from the Estate of Seymour Klein and the from the Estate of Ruth Klein.

Typical Recipients

Arts & Humanities: Arts Centers, Libraries, Museums/Galleries, Music, Opera, Theater
Civic & Public Affairs: Inner-City Development, Law & Justice, Philanthropic Organizations, Urban & Community Affairs
Education: Business Education, Colleges & Universities, Education-General, Private Education (Precollege), Science/Mathematics Education, Secondary Education (Private)
Environment: Environment-General
Health: Cancer, Clinics/Medical Centers, Hospitals, Prenatal Health Issues, Single-Disease Health Associations
Religion: Jewish Causes, Religious Organizations
Social Services: Community Service Organizations, Crime Prevention, Delinquency & Criminal Rehabilitation, Food/Clothing Distribution, Scouts, YMCA/YWCA/YMHA/YWHA, Youth Organizations

Application Procedures

Initial Contact: Send a brief letter of inquiry describing program or project. Include purpose of funds sought and proof of tax-exempt status.
Deadlines: None.

Restrictions

Does not support individuals.

Foundation Officials

Donald Klein: vice president
Jeffrey Klein: president

Grants Analysis

Disclosure Period: fiscal year ending June 30, 2001
Total Grants: $278,550
Number of Grants: 53
Average Grant: $5,256
Highest Grant: $40,000
Lowest Grant: $250
Typical Range: $1,000 to $10,000

Recent Grants

Note: Grants derived from fiscal 2000 Form 990.

Library-Related

5,000	New York Public Library, New York, NY

General

35,000	Museum of Modern Art, New York, NY
32,000	DIA Center for the Arts, New York, NY
25,000	Lab School of Washington, Washington, DC
25,000	New York Chamber Symphony, New York, NY
20,000	Hebrew Association
15,000	Hundred Year Association, The, New York, NY
10,000	Collegiate School
10,000	New York City Opera, New York, NY
9,000	Whitney Museum of American Art, New York, NY
5,000	Children's Museum of Manhattan, New York, NY

LIBERTY CORP.

Company Headquarters

Greenville, SC
Web: http://www.libertycorp.com

Company Description

Founded: 1968
Ticker: LC
Exchange: NYSE
Revenue: US$206.4 million (2002)
Employees: 1300 (2002)
SIC(s): 4833 Television Broadcasting Stations, 6311 Life Insurance, 6321 Accident & Health Insurance, 6552 Subdividers & Developers Nec.

Operating Locations

Liberty Corp. (AL--Montgomery; AR--Jonesboro; IN--Evansville; KY--Louisville; OH--Toledo; SC--Columbia, Greenville)

Nonmonetary Support

Type: Donated Equipment; Loaned Executives

Liberty Corp. Foundation

Giving Contact

Sophia Vergas, Secretary
PO Box 789
Greenville, SC 29602
Phone: (864)609-8398
Fax: (864)241-5401
E-mail: svergas@libertycorp.com

Description

EIN: 570468195
Organization Type: Corporate Foundation
Giving Locations: SC: nationally.
Grant Types: Award, Capital, General Support, Multiyear/Continuing Support, Scholarship.

Financial Summary

Total Giving: $289,684 (fiscal year ending August 31, 2000); $429,350 (fiscal 1999); $306,704 (fiscal 1998). Note: Contributes through foundation only.

Giving Analysis: Giving for fiscal 2000 includes: foundation grants to United Way ($100,000); foundation ($189,684); fiscal 1999: foundation matching gifts ($13,075); foundation grants to United Way ($80,000); foundation ($336,275); fiscal 1998: foundation matching gifts ($17,287); foundation grants to United Way ($100,050);
Assets: $79,766 (fiscal 2000); $262,551 (fiscal 1999); $70,927 (fiscal 1998)
Gifts Received: $100,000 (fiscal 2000); $635,000 (fiscal 1999); $371,650 (fiscal 1998). Note: Contributions are received from Liberty Corporation; and Cosmos Broadcasting Corp.

Typical Recipients

Arts & Humanities: Arts Centers, Arts Festivals, Arts Funds, Community Arts, Arts & Humanities-General, History & Archaeology, Libraries, Museums/Galleries, Music, Performing Arts, Theater
Civic & Public Affairs: African American Affairs, Botanical Gardens/Parks, Business/Free Enterprise, Chambers of Commerce, Community Foundations, Economic Development, Employment/Job Training, Civic & Public Affairs-General, Housing, Legal Aid, Municipalities/Towns, Philanthropic Organizations, Professional & Trade Associations, Urban & Community Affairs, Women's Affairs, Zoos/Aquariums
Education: Arts/Humanities Education, Business Education, Colleges & Universities, Education Associations, Education Funds, Education Reform, Engineering/Technological Education, Education-General, Leadership Training, Literacy, Private Education (Precollege), Public Education (Precollege), Science/Mathematics Education, Special Education, Student Aid
Environment: Environment-General, Resource Conservation, Wildlife Protection
Health: Cancer, Children's Health/Hospitals, Clinics/Medical Centers, Emergency/Ambulance Services, Health Organizations, Hospitals, Research/Studies Institutes, Single-Disease Health Associations
International: Foreign Educational Institutions, International Relations
Religion: Churches, Religious Welfare
Science: Scientific Centers & Institutes
Social Services: Child Welfare, Community Centers, Community Service Organizations, Emergency Relief, Family Services, People with Disabilities, Recreation & Athletics, Scouts, Shelters/Homelessness, United Funds/United Ways, United Funds/United Ways, YMCA/YWCA/YMHA/YWHA, Youth Organizations

Application Procedures

Initial Contact: Send a brief letter.
Application Requirements: Include proof of tax-exempt status of organization.
Deadlines: None.

Restrictions

Awards are not made to individuals.
Contributions are made only to organizations exempt from Federal income tax under 501(c)(3).

Additional Information

Matching gifts program discontinued in 1999.
Publications: Policies Fact Sheet

Corporate Officials

Mary Anne Bunton: vice president public relations PRIM CORP EMPL vice president: Liberty Corp. treasurer: Press Printing International.
William Hayne Hipp: president, chief executive officer, director B Greenville, SC 1940. ED Washington & Lee University BA (1962); University of Pennsylvania Wharton School MBA (1965). PRIM CORP EMPL president, chief executive officer, director: Liberty Corp. CORP AFFIL director: SCANA Corp.; director: Wachovia Corp.; director: American Council Life Insurance; chairman: Pierce National Life Insurance Co. NONPR AFFIL member: Greenville Chamber of

Commerce; director: South Carolina Research Authority; chairman, trustee: Alliance for Quality Education; trustee: Communication Economic Development New York.
Kenneth W. Jones: controller PRIM CORP EMPL controller: Liberty Corp.
Carry Price: director public relations PRIM CORP EMPL director public relations: Liberty Corp.

Foundation Officials

Mary Anne Bunton: vice president (see above)
William Hayne Hipp: chairman, president, director (see above)
Kenneth W. Jones: controller, treasurer (see above)
Martha R. Rainey: assistant treasurer
Sophia Vergas: secretary, administrator
Martha G. Williams: director

Grants Analysis

Disclosure Period: fiscal year ending August 31, 2000
Total Grants: $189,684*
Number of Grants: 19*
Average Grant: $9,983
Highest Grant: $25,000
Lowest Grant: $1,000
Typical Range: $1,000 to $15,000
*****Note:** Giving excludes United Way. Number of grants excludes miscellaneous contributions of less than $1,000.

Recent Grants

Note: Grants derived from 2000 Form 990.

General

100,000	United Way Greenville County, Greenville, SC
25,000	Center for Development Services
25,000	Upstate Forever, Greenville, SC
20,000	Independent Colleges and Universities of South Carolina, Columbia, SC
20,000	University of South Carolina Hipp Chair of Insurance, Columbia, SC
12,500	African American History Monument, Columbia, SC
12,500	Brookgreen Gardens, Murrells Inlet, SC
12,500	Southern Environmental Law Center, Charlottesville, VA
10,000	Wofford College, Spartanburg, SC -- for science building
8,334	Greater Greenville YMCA, Greenville, SC -- capital campaign

LIED FOUNDATION TRUST

Giving Contact

Christina M. Hixson, Trustee
3907 West Charleston Boulevard
Las Vegas, NV 89102
Phone: (702)878-1559
Fax: (702)878-6469

Description

Founded: 1972
EIN: 237282946
Organization Type: General Purpose Foundation
Giving Locations: CA; IA; KS; NE; NV
Grant Types: Capital, General Support, Operating Expenses, Scholarship.

Financial Summary

Total Giving: $12,453,897 (2000); $25,934,039 (1997); $17,986,551 (1996)
Assets: $112,214,201 (2000); $78,978,632 (1997); $117,655,800 (1996)
Gifts Received: $459,090 (1994); $19,027,367 (1993); $96,088,670 (1992)

Typical Recipients

Arts & Humanities: Arts Centers, Arts Institutes, Ballet, Dance, History & Archaeology, Libraries, Museums/Galleries, Performing Arts, Public Broadcasting
Civic & Public Affairs: Economic Development, Employment/Job Training, Housing, Law & Justice, Municipalities/Towns, Parades/Festivals, Zoos/Aquariums
Education: Business Education, Colleges & Universities, Community & Junior Colleges, Faculty Development, Education-General, Private Education (Precollege), Public Education (Precollege), School Volunteerism, Science/Mathematics Education, Secondary Education (Private), Special Education, Student Aid
Environment: Forestry, Environment-General
Health: Health Organizations, Hospitals (University Affiliated), Research/Studies Institutes, Speech & Hearing, Speech & Hearing, Transplant Networks/Donor Banks
Religion: Bible Study/Translation, Churches, Religious Organizations, Religious Welfare
Science: Science-General, Science Museums
Social Services: Animal Protection, Child Welfare, Community Centers, Community Service Organizations, Day Care, Family Services, People with Disabilities, Recreation & Athletics, Senior Services, Youth Organizations

Application Procedures

Initial Contact: The foundation has no formal grant application procedure or application form.
Deadlines: None.

Grants Analysis

Disclosure Period: calendar year ending 2000
Total Grants: $11,453,896*
Number of Grants: 22
Average Grant: $147,621*
Highest Grant: $5,000,000
Lowest Grant: $2,500
Typical Range: $25,000 to $1,000,000
*Note: Giving excludes scholarships. Average grant excludes four highest grants (totaling $8,944,336).

Recent Grants

Note: Grants derived from 2000 Form 990.

Library-Related

75,000	Osmond Public Library, Osmond, NE -- for book shelves, computers and furniture for library
36,000	Tilden Library Foundation, Tilden, NE -- furnishings and equipment for auditorium in new library

General

5,000,000	University of Nebraska Foundation, Lincoln, NE -- for Christina M. Hixson-Lied Foundation
1,707,546	Nebraska Humane Society, Omaha, NE -- construction of new animal shelter
1,236,790	Animal Foundation, Las Vegas, NV -- for construction of animal shelter
1,000,000	Creighton University, Omaha, NE -- scholarships
1,000,000	Kansas University Endowment Association, Lawrence, KS -- Lied Performance Fund
500,000	Clark County Legal Services Program, Inc., Las Vegas, NV -- for reduce mortgage on building
500,000	House Ear Institute, Los Angeles, CA -- for the Children's Center
333,333	Lincoln Children's Museum, Lincoln, NE -- for exhibits for museum
200,000	Nevada Ballet Theatre, Las Vegas, NV -- for Future Dance Program
160,688	Iowa School for the Deaf Foundation, Council Bluffs, IA -- for construction of Lied Multipurpose Complex

LILLY ENDOWMENT

Giving Contact

Program Office
2801 North Meridian Street
PO Box 88068
Indianapolis, IN 46208-0068
Phone: (317)924-5471
Fax: (317)926-4431
Web: http://www.lilly.com/about/community/foundation/endowment.html

Description

Founded: 1937
EIN: 350868122
Organization Type: Family Foundation
Giving Locations: IN: statewide, Indianapolis nationally.
Grant Types: Award, Capital, Challenge, Conference/Seminar, Emergency, Endowment, Fellowship, General Support, Matching, Multiyear/Continuing Support, Operating Expenses, Project, Research.

Donor Information

Founder: The endowment was created in Indianapolis in 1937 with gifts of Eli Lilly and Company stock from the personal holdings of the late Josiah Kirby Lilly Sr. and his two sons, the late Eli Lilly and the late Josiah Kirby Lilly Jr. J. K. Lilly, Sr., was the son of Colonel Eli Lilly who, in 1876, founded what became one of the world's largest pharmaceutical firms. J. K. Lilly, Sr., strongly supported the YMCA, the Episcopal Church, and the Red Cross. His son, Eli Lilly, contributed large amounts of money to the Episcopal Church, the United Way, and colleges in Indiana. He left a majority of his estate to charity. J. K. Lilly, Jr., was especially interested in museums, libraries, and historical societies. The foundation still owns about 18 percent of Eli Lilly and Company stock, and its board of directors includes one family member.

Financial Summary

Total Giving: $598,001,582 (2001); $542,173,736 (2000); $558,287,507 (1999)
Giving Analysis: Giving for 2000 includes: foundation fellowships ($1,588,000); foundation scholarships ($35,226,375); foundation grants to United Way ($65,437,850); 1999: foundation matching gifts ($15,000); foundation fellowships ($520,690) foundation grants to United Way ($36,875,316)
Assets: $12,814,397,581 (2001); $15,591,737,808 (2000); $10,418,127,226 (1999)
Gifts Received: $137,468 (2001); $369,163 (1999). Note: In 2001, contributions were received from Voris Lyons Trust. In 1999, contributions were received from the Estate of Phoebe B. Comer ($221,695) and the Voris Lyons Trust ($137,468).

Typical Recipients

Arts & Humanities: Arts Associations & Councils, Arts Centers, Arts Festivals, Community Arts, Dance, Ethnic & Folk Arts, Historic Preservation, History & Archaeology, Libraries, Museums/Galleries, Music, Opera, Performing Arts, Public Broadcasting, Theater, Visual Arts
Civic & Public Affairs: African American Affairs, Asian American Affairs, Botanical Gardens/Parks, Community Foundations, Economic Development, Economic Policy, Employment/Job Training, Civic & Public Affairs-General, Housing, Nonprofit Management, Philanthropic Organizations, Public Policy, Rural Affairs, Urban & Community Affairs, Women's Affairs, Zoos/Aquariums
Education: Arts/Humanities Education, Business Education, Colleges & Universities, Economic Education, Education Associations, Education Funds, Education Reform, Elementary Education (Private), Engineering/Technological Education, Environmental Education, Faculty Development, Education-General,

Leadership Training, Literacy, Minority Education, Private Education (Precollege), Public Education (Precollege), Religious Education, Science/Mathematics Education, Secondary Education (Public), Social Sciences Education, Student Aid
Environment: Environment-General, Resource Conservation, Wildlife Protection
Health: Emergency/Ambulance Services, Health Organizations
International: Foreign Educational Institutions, International Development, Trade
Religion: Churches, Dioceses, Jewish Causes, Religious Organizations, Religious Welfare, Seminaries, Seminaries, Social/Policy Issues
Science: Science-General
Social Services: Child Welfare, Community Centers, Community Service Organizations, Crime Prevention, Day Care, Delinquency & Criminal Rehabilitation, Emergency Relief, Family Planning, Family Services, Homes, People with Disabilities, Recreation & Athletics, Scouts, Social Services-General, Substance Abuse, United Funds/United Ways, YMCA/YWCA/YMHA/YWHA, Youth Organizations

Application Procedures

Initial Contact: Applicants should submit a preliminary letter of no more than two pages describing the organization, project, and amount requested.
Application Requirements: Preliminary letter should include description of organization and project, and amount requested. The Endowment responds to all preliminary inquiries, and will request a full proposal if appropriate.
Deadlines: None.
Review Process: Grant proposals are reviewed by a program director. Proposals meeting the criteria for consideration are reviewed by the appropriate division or committee, then by the corporate officers, and finally by members of the board of directors. The process generally takes from three to six months; all grantseekers receive written notification of decisions. Grants are considered in February, March, May, June, July, September, November, and December.
Decision Notification: All requests receive written notification of decision.

Restrictions

The endowment generally will not make loans or grants to individuals; for healthcare projects; mass media projects; endowments or endowed chairs; libraries; or outside Indiana.

Additional Information

The endowment's concentration on Indianapolis and Indiana applies primarily to grants for community development and elementary/secondary education. The endowment's interest in higher education extends to Indiana colleges, and historically to black colleges nationwide. Religious and philanthropic support is given nationally.
Publications: Annual Report; Grant Guidelines; Progressions Magazine

Foundation Officials

David D. Biber: secretary, treasurer
Otis R. Bowen, MD: director B Rochester, IN February 26, 1918. ED Indiana University AB (1939); Indiana University MD (1942).
Daniel P. Carmichael: director
Sara B. Cobb: vice president education
Rev. Craig Richard Dykstra: vice president rel B Detroit, MI 1947. ED University of Michigan AB (1969); Princeton Theological Seminary MDiv (1973); Princeton Theological Seminary PhD (1978). NONPR AFFIL member: Phi Kappa Phi; member: Religion Education Association; lectr: Austin Theological Seminary, Texas; member: American Academy Religion; member: Association Professors Research Religious Education.

Rev. William Gerald Enright: director B Peoria, IL 1935. ED Wheaton College BA (1958); Fuller Theological Seminary MDiv (1961); McCormick Theological Seminary ThM (1965); University of Edinburgh PhD (1968). PRIM NONPR EMPL pastor: 2nd Presbyterian Church of Indianapolis. NONPR AFFIL director: Wishard Hospital Foundation; director: YMCA Indianapolis; member: Society Science Study Religion; director: Saint Vincent Hospital; member: Society American Church History; trustee: McCormick Theological Seminary; member: Police Chiefs Advisor Board; director: Indiana Center Advanced Research; chairman task force on ethics & values: City of Indianapolis. CLUB AFFIL member: Rotary Club.

William Maxwell Goodwin: vice president commun devel B Muncie, IN 1939. ED Indiana University AB (1961); Indiana University MBA (1966). NONPR AFFIL director: Greater Indianapolis Progress Committee; member: Indiana Association Certified Public Accountants; member: Delta Phi Alpha; member: American Institute of Certified Public Accountants; member: Beta Gamma Sigma.

Earl Binkley Herr, Jr.: director B Lancaster, PA 1928. ED Franklin and Marshall College BS (1948); University of Delaware MS (1950); University of Delaware PhD (1953); Cornell University (1953-1955). CORP AFFIL director: Ipalco Enterprises; director: Lilly Research Laboratories; director: Indianapolis Power & Light Co. NONPR AFFIL director: Indiana Science Education Foundation; member: Sigma Xi; member: American Association Advancement Science; member: American Chemical Society.

Eli Lilly, II: director

Mary K. Lisher: director

Thomas M. Lofton: chairman B Indianapolis, IN 1929. ED Indiana University BS (1951); Indiana University JD (1954). NONPR AFFIL member, board visitors: Indiana University Law School; member: Order Coif; member: Beta Gamma Sigma. CLUB AFFIL Masons Club.

Eugene F. Ratliff: director

N. Clay Robbins: president, director B Indianapolis, IN 1957. ED Wabash College BA (1979); Vanderbilt University JD (1982). NONPR AFFIL member: Indiana State Bar Association; vice chairman: United Way Central Indiana; member: Corporate Community Council.

Grants Analysis

Disclosure Period: calendar year ending 2001
Total Grants: $471,352,656*
Number of Grants: 739
Average Grant: $603,936*
Highest Grant: $25,647,959
Lowest Grant: $500
Typical Range: $25,000 to $250,000 and $500,000 to $2,000,000
***Note:** Giving excludes fellowships; scholarships, and United Way. Average grant figure excludes highest grant.

Recent Grants

Note: Grants derived from 2001 Form 990.

General

25,647,959 Purdue Research Foundation, West Lafayette, IN -- Purdue Discovery Park
21,998,984 Indiana University Foundation, Bloomington, IN
20,134,620 Ball State University, Muncie, IN -- Media Design Initiative
20,000,000 DePauw University, Greencastle, IN -- National eLearning Center
19,990,744 Alliance Initiatives Fund, Inc, Evansville, IN
16,443,200 Indianapolis Public Schools, Indianapolis, IN
15,000,000 Children's Museum of Indianapolis, Inc., Indianapolis, IN -- Development of a major permanent dinosaur project
14,995,648 University of Indianapolis, Indianapolis,

IN -- Center of Excellence in Leadership of Learning
13,009,051 Phi Delta Kappa, Inc, Bloomington, IN -- Community Alliances to Promote Education
10,411,617 Indiana Symphony Society, Indiana, PA

RICHARD COYLE LILLY FOUNDATION

Giving Contact

Jeffrey T. Peterson, Secretary & Treasurer
c/o US Bank NA
101 E. Fifth Street
St. Paul, MN 55101
Phone: (651)466-8735

Description

Founded: 1941
EIN: 416038717
Organization Type: Private Foundation
Giving Locations: MN: St. Paul
Grant Types: Capital, Endowment, General Support, Multiyear/Continuing Support, Project, Research, Seed Money.

Donor Information

Founder: the late Richard C. Lilly

Financial Summary

Total Giving: $441,300 (2002); $625,050 (2001); $669,800 (2000)
Giving Analysis: Giving for 2002 includes: foundation matching gifts ($2,000); foundation grants to United Way ($22,000); 2000: foundation matching gifts ($5,000); foundation grants to United Way ($22,500); foundation fellowships ($23,000) 1999: foundation grants to United Way ($20,000)
Assets: $8,902,992 (2002); $10,265,962 (2001); $10,095,454 (2000)

Typical Recipients

Arts & Humanities: Arts Associations & Councils, Arts Centers, Arts Institutes, Community Arts, Dance, Arts & Humanities-General, Historic Preservation, History & Archaeology, Libraries, Literary Arts, Museums/Galleries, Music, Opera, Public Broadcasting, Theater, Visual Arts
Civic & Public Affairs: Botanical Gardens/Parks, Business/Free Enterprise, Clubs, Economic Development, Civic & Public Affairs-General, Municipalities/Towns, Urban & Community Affairs, Women's Affairs, Zoos/Aquariums
Education: Arts/Humanities Education, Colleges & Universities, Education Funds, Education Reform, Elementary Education (Private), Faculty Development, Preschool Education, Private Education (Precollege), Public Education (Precollege), Student Aid
Environment: Environment-General, Resource Conservation
Health: Hospitals
International: Human Rights, International Peace & Security Issues
Religion: Churches, Religious Welfare
Social Services: Camps, Child Welfare, Community Centers, Community Service Organizations, Day Care, Family Planning, Family Services, Food/Clothing Distribution, United Funds/United Ways, YMCA/YWCA/YMHA/YWHA, Youth Organizations

Application Procedures

Initial Contact: Submit full proposal
Application Requirements: Include proof of tax-exempt status and any other supporting materials necessary to consider the request
Deadlines: None.

Restrictions

Does not make grants to individuals, for scholarships, or to organizations that would require expenditure responsibility.

Foundation Officials

Suzanne Lilly Hutcheson: director
Bruce A. Lilly: director
David M. Lilly, Jr.: president
David M. Lilly: president
Elizabeth M. Lilly: vice president
Jeffrey T. Peterson: secretary, treasurer

Grants Analysis

Disclosure Period: calendar year ending 2002
Total Grants: $417,300*
Number of Grants: 67
Average Grant: $6,228
Highest Grant: $35,000
Lowest Grant: $500
Typical Range: $1,000 to $10,000
***Note:** Giving excludes United Way; matching gifts.

Recent Grants

Note: Grants derived from 2001 Form 990.

General

50,000 Guthrie Theatre, Minneapolis, MN -- capital campaign
50,000 Minnesota Public Radio, St. Paul, MN
40,000 Family and Children's Services of Minneapolis, Minneapolis, MN -- capital campaign
35,000 St. Paul Academy, St. Paul, MN
30,000 St. Paul Foundation, St. Paul, MN
25,000 Compatible Technology International, St. Paul, MN -- capital campaign
25,000 Nantucket Maria Mitchell Association, Nantucket, MA -- new aquarium
25,000 Planned Parenthood of Minnesota and South Dakota, St. Paul, MN
22,000 University of Minnesota, Minneapolis, MN
20,000 United Way Twin Cities, Minneapolis, MN

T. Y. LIN FOUNDATION

Giving Contact

Robert B. Yee, Treasurer
T. Y. Lin Foundation
315 Bay St.
San Francisco, CA 94133
Phone: (415)989-3100

Description

Founded: 1991
EIN: 943107208
Organization Type: Private Foundation
Grant Types: General Support.

Financial Summary

Total Giving: $20,100 (2001); $24,201 (2000); $2,100 (1999)
Assets: $431,410 (2001); $519,452 (2000); $446,627 (1999)
Gifts Received: $17,000 (1999); $88,511 (1998); $41,226 (1996). Note: In 1999, contributions were received from T. Y. and Margaret Lin. In 1998, contributions were received from Y.C. and 1/a-Chen Yang ($60,000), U. and Margaret Lin ($26,000), and James and Alice Tai ($2,500). In 1996, contributions were received from T. Y. Lin-Taiwan ($2,500), T. Y. and Margaret Lin ($33,500), and T. Y. Lin-Hong Kong ($5,000).

Typical Recipients

Arts & Humanities: Ballet, Libraries
Education: Colleges & Universities, Engineering/Technological Education
International: Foreign Educational Institutions, International Peace & Security Issues
Science: Science Museums

Application Procedures

Initial Contact: Send a brief letter of inquiry.
Application Requirements: a description of organization, amount requested, and proof of tax-exempt status.
Deadlines: None.

Foundation Officials

Claudia Berger: secretary
Philip Chow: director
Y. C. Yang: chairman
Robert B. Yee: treasurer

Grants Analysis

Disclosure Period: calendar year ending 2001
Total Grants: $20,100
Number of Grants: 1

Recent Grants

Note: Grants derived from 2000 Form 990.

Library-Related
10,000   Bancroft Library, Berkeley, CA

General
14,201   University of California, Berkeley, CA

LINGNAN FOUNDATION

Giving Contact

Jane S. Permaul, Chairman & Trustee
PO Box 208340
New Haven, CT 06520
Phone: (203)432-1066
E-mail: mary.chang@yale.edu
Web: http://www.lingnanfoundation.org/

Description

Founded: 1893
EIN: 136400470
Organization Type: Private Foundation
Giving Locations: People's Republic of China; Hong Kong
Grant Types: Conference/Seminar, General Support, Operating Expenses, Professorship, Research, Seed Money.

Financial Summary

Total Giving: $1,349,850 (fiscal year ending June 30, 2001); $1,218,418 (fiscal 2000); $782,150 (fiscal 1998)
Assets: $22,404,957 (fiscal 2001); $27,243,540 (fiscal 2001); $19,093,516 (fiscal 1998)
Gifts Received: $94,465 (fiscal 2001); $1,972,795 (fiscal 2000); $505,004 (fiscal 1998). Note: In fiscal 2000 and 2001, contributions were received from the estate of Yue Shuen Lee. In fiscal 1998, contributions were received from Yi-Faai Laai Bequest and Ying-Lam Lee Foundation. In fiscal 1997, contributions were received from Joseph Lai, Max Saffiath and Marshall Sanders. In fiscal 1996, contributions were received from the estate of J. Ackerman Coles ($828,239) and from the estate of King Y. Laai ($160,000); miscellaneous contributions totaling $100 also were received.

Typical Recipients

Arts & Humanities: Libraries
Civic & Public Affairs: Civic & Public Affairs-General
Education: Arts/Humanities Education, Colleges & Universities, International Studies, Minority Education

International: Foreign Educational Institutions, International Peace & Security Issues, International Relations

Application Procedures

Initial Contact: Send a brief letter of inquiry.
Deadlines: None.

Restrictions

Grants are made to institutions contributing to the advancement of the formal education of Chinese students. As a general rule, grants are limited to selected colleges and universities in the People's Republic of China and in Hong Kong and to similar organizations in the U.S. that are engaged in cooperative programs with these colleges and universities. Does not support individuals or provide loans.

Additional Information

Publications: Program Policy Statement

Foundation Officials

Tung Au: trustee B Hong Kong, People's Republic of China 1923. ED Saint John's University BS (1943); University of Illinois MS (1948); University of Illinois PhD (1951); University of Michigan MS (1954). PRIM CORP EMPL ed consult: Carnegie Mellon University. NONPR AFFIL member: Phi Kappa Phi; member: Tau Beta Pi; member: American Society Engineering Education; member: Chi Epsilon.
Lo-Yi Cheung Yuen Chan: trustee B Canton, People's Republic of China 1932. ED Dartmouth College BA (1954); Harvard University MA (1959). NONPR AFFIL member: New York Saint Council Arts; member: Phi Beta Kappa; member: New York City Art Commission; member: Berkshire School; trustee: Henry Saint Settlement; fellow: American Institute Architects.
Frederic C. Chang, MD: trustee
Nancy Chapman: trustee PRIM CORP EMPL president: Yale China Association.
Jonathan E. Colby: trustee
Frances S. Connick: trustee
John Dykstra Eusden: trustee B Holland, MI 1922. ED Harvard University AB (1943); Harvard University (1946); Yale University BD (1949); Yale University PhD (1954). NONPR AFFIL member: National Association College & University Chaplains; member: Social Values Higher Education; minister: First Congregational Church; member: American Society Christian Ethics; member: American Society Church History; member: American Academy Religion; member: American Associate University Prof. CLUB AFFIL Appalachian Mountain Club; Randolph Mountain Club.
James V. Feinerman: trustee
Jerome B. Grieder: trustee
Terrill E. Lautz: trustee
Ralph E. Lerner: secretary, trustee B New York, NY 1943. ED Bucknell University BS (1964); Boston University JD (1967); New York University LLM (1969). PRIM CORP EMPL assistant professor paralegal studies: New York University. NONPR AFFIL member: New York State Bar Association; adj assistant professor: New York University; member: Intl Bar Association; member: American Bar Association; member: Association New York City Bar.
Karl Lo: trustee PRIM CORP EMPL director international programs: University CA San Diego.
William F. McCalpin: trustee
Douglas P. Murray: president, trustee
Jane S. Permaul: trustee PRIM CORP EMPL assistant vice chancellor student affairs administration: University CA.
Russell Alexander Phillips, Jr.: trustee B Charlotte, NC 1937. ED Duke University AB (1959); Yale University LLB (1962). NONPR AFFIL member: North Carolina Bar Association; member: Phi Beta Kappa; member: Council Foreign Relations; member: District of Columbia Bar Association; trustee, vice president, secretary: Asian Cultural Council. CLUB AFFIL University Club; Century Association.

Edward Rhoads: trustee
Gene Szutu: hon trustee
Stuyvesant Wainwright, III: treasurer, trustee

Grants Analysis

Disclosure Period: fiscal year ending June 30, 2001
Total Grants: $1,349,850
Number of Grants: 15
Average Grant: $89,990
Highest Grant: $192,500
Typical Range: $50,000 to $150,000

Recent Grants

Note: Grants derived from fiscal 2000 Form 990.

General
500,000   Lingnan University -- Y.S. Lee Bequest
150,000   Zhongshan University, Zhongshan People's Republic of China -- network student dorms
90,000   Trustees of the Board of L(U)C
87,000   Zhongshan University, Guangzhou People's Republic of China -- Martin Hall
72,000   Lingnan University -- scholarship fund
70,000   Lingnan University
41,000   Zhongshan University, Zhongshan People's Republic of China -- foreign language and literature
40,000   University of Hong Kong -- American studies
39,917   GX Trade, Inc -- foreign journals subscription
25,000   University of Connecticut, Storrs, CT -- China Bridges International

GEORGE LINK, JR. FOUNDATION

Giving Contact

Michael Cantanzaro, Vice President & Director
Bank of New York
1290 Avenue of the Americas, 5th Floor
New York, NY 10104
Phone: (201)846-8481

Description

Founded: 1980
EIN: 133041396
Organization Type: General Purpose Foundation
Giving Locations: NJ; NY: Northeast.
Grant Types: Capital, Endowment, Fellowship, General Support, Scholarship.

Donor Information

Founder: The foundation was established in 1980 by the late George Link Jr.

Financial Summary

Total Giving: $2,625,575 (2001); $1,976,000 (1998); $1,925,200 (1997)
Assets: $40,488,172 (2001); $44,063,893 (1998); $38,104,492 (1997)
Gifts Received: $142,797 (2001); $14,088 (1995); $55,273 (1994). Note: In 2001, contributions were received from the estate of Eleanor Link.

Typical Recipients

Arts & Humanities: Arts Associations & Councils, Arts Centers, Ethnic & Folk Arts, Historic Preservation, Libraries, Museums/Galleries, Performing Arts, Theater
Civic & Public Affairs: Community Foundations, Economic Development, Civic & Public Affairs-General, Housing, Philanthropic Organizations
Education: Arts/Humanities Education, Business Education, Colleges & Universities, Community & Junior Colleges, Education Funds, Education Reform, Elementary Education (Public), Education-General, Legal Education, Medical Education, Private Education

(Precollege), Public Education (Precollege), Religious Education, Secondary Education (Private), Secondary Education (Public), Special Education, Student Aid
Health: Cancer, Children's Health/Hospitals, Clinics/Medical Centers, Health Funds, Health Organizations, Heart, Hospitals, Long-Term Care, Medical Rehabilitation, Medical Research, Mental Health, Public Health, Single-Disease Health Associations
International: Health Care/Hospitals, International Affairs, International Development, International Organizations, Missionary/Religious Activities
Religion: Churches, Dioceses, Religion-General, Ministries, Missionary Activities (Domestic), Religious Organizations, Religious Welfare, Seminaries
Social Services: At-Risk Youth, Big Brother/Big Sister, Child Welfare, Community Service Organizations, Counseling, Family Services, Homes, People with Disabilities, Scouts, Senior Services, Shelters/Homelessness, Social Services-General, Volunteer Services, Youth Organizations

Application Procedures
Initial Contact: A letter of inquiry should be sent to the foundation.
Application Requirements: Letter should include a brief description of the project objective and the area(s) for which assistance is being requested.
Deadlines: None.

Foundation Officials
Michael J. Catanzaro: vice president, treasurer, director
Coleman F. Clougherty: vice president, director
Bernard F. Joyce: vice president, secretary, director
Eleanor Irene Higgins Link: chairman, director
Robert Emmett Link: vchairman, director

Grants Analysis
Disclosure Period: calendar year ending 2001
Total Grants: $2,625,575
Number of Grants: 239
Average Grant: $10,986
Highest Grant: $100,000
Lowest Grant: $250
Typical Range: $5,000 to $20,000

Recent Grants
Note: Grants derived from 2001 Form 990.

General
100,000	Catholic Relief Services, Baltimore, MD
62,500	New York City Partnership Foundation, New York, NY
59,200	Borough of Manhattan Community College, New York, NY
55,000	Renew International, Plainfield, NJ
55,000	St. Peter's Prep, Jersey City, NJ
50,000	Academy of Mount St. Ursula, Bronx, NY
50,000	Convent of Sacred Heart, New York, NY
50,000	Mercy Center Ministries, Asbury Park, NJ
50,000	Neighborhood Housing of New York, New York, NY
50,000	New York University Downtown Hospital, New York, NY

LIPTON CO.

Company Headquarters
Englewood Cliffs, NJ
Web: http://www.unilever.com

Company Description
Former Name: Thomas J. Lipton Co.
Employees: 7,400
SIC(s): 2034 Dehydrated Fruits, Vegetables & Soups, 2035 Pickles, Sauces & Salad Dressings, 2099 Food Preparations Nec.

Parent Company: Unilever PLC, Unilever House, Blackfriars, London, United Kingdom

Operating Locations
Lipton Co. (CA--Los Angeles, Santa Cruz; FL--Jacksonville; IA--Sioux City; NJ--Englewood Cliffs, Fairfield, Flemington, Moonachie; PA--Harrisburg; VA--Suffolk)

Lipton Foundation

Giving Contact
Suzanne Cuff, Contact
800 Sylvan Avenue
Englewood Cliffs, NJ 07632
Phone: (201)894-7405
Fax: (201)871-8198

Description
Founded: 1952
EIN: 226063094
Organization Type: Corporate Foundation
Giving Locations: primarily near corporate headquarters and plant locations.
Grant Types: Employee Matching Gifts, General Support.

Donor Information
Founder: Thomas J. Lipton Inc., Calvin Klein Cosmetics

Financial Summary
Total Giving: $400,000 (1996); $346,986 (1995); $462,732 (1994). Note: Contributes through foundation only. 1995 Giving includes foundation ($300,135); matching gifts ($23,351); United Way ($23,500).
Assets: $167,710 (1995); $61,932 (1994); $73,175 (1992)
Gifts Received: $443,795 (1995); $402,296 (1994); $993,750 (1992). Note: In 1995, the foundation received contributions from value of Colgate stock ($351,006) and from Conopco Inc. ($92,789).

Typical Recipients
Arts & Humanities: Arts Associations & Councils, Arts Centers, Arts Festivals, Dance, Historic Preservation, Libraries, Museums/Galleries, Music, Performing Arts, Public Broadcasting, Theater
Civic & Public Affairs: Business/Free Enterprise, Civil Rights, Economic Development, Civic & Public Affairs-General, Law & Justice, Legal Aid, Philanthropic Organizations, Public Policy, Safety, Urban & Community Affairs, Women's Affairs, Zoos/Aquariums
Education: Business Education, Colleges & Universities, Community & Junior Colleges, Economic Education, Education Associations, Education Funds, Education Reform, Health & Physical Education, Legal Education, Literacy, Medical Education, Minority Education, Private Education (Precollege), Public Education (Precollege), Science/Mathematics Education, Student Aid
Environment: Environment-General
Health: Cancer, Children's Health/Hospitals, Clinics/Medical Centers, Diabetes, Health Funds, Health Organizations, Heart, Hospices, Hospitals, Medical Rehabilitation, Medical Research, Medical Training, Mental Health, Multiple Sclerosis, Nutrition, Prenatal Health Issues, Single-Disease Health Associations
International: International Organizations, International Relations
Religion: Missionary Activities (Domestic), Religious Organizations, Religious Welfare
Science: Scientific Organizations
Social Services: At-Risk Youth, Big Brother/Big Sister, Community Centers, Community Service Organizations, Emergency Relief, Family Planning, Food/

Clothing Distribution, People with Disabilities, Recreation & Athletics, Scouts, Special Olympics, Substance Abuse, United Funds/United Ways, Volunteer Services, Youth Organizations

Application Procedures
Initial Contact: write for guidelines; then a letter or proposal
Application Requirements: description of the organization and its purpose, amount requested, purpose of funds sought, recently audited financial statement, proof of tax-exempt status, list of current sponsors and amount each contributes, past record of support, description of programs offered and their geographical scope, annual report, name of agency executive and phone number, methods to be used for evaluating program or project
Deadlines: to be included in next year's budget, no later than December; some late applications are approved if proposal meets requirements and funds are available; many are held over to the next year
Notes: Currently funded organizations wishing continued support should send letter by end of year with updated information.

Restrictions
Does not support individuals, dinners, tours, or special events.
Restricted from supporting international giving where funds will be spent overseas.

Additional Information
Publications: Guidelines

Corporate Officials
Patrick Cescau: president, chief executive officer
PRIM CORP EMPL president, chief executive officer: Lipton Co.

Grants Analysis
Disclosure Period: calendar year ending 1995
Total Grants: $300,135*
Number of Grants: 65
Average Grant: $4,617
Highest Grant: $75,000
Typical Range: $100 to $5,000 and $10,000 to $20,000
***Note:** Giving excludes matching gifts; United Way.

LISLE CORP.

Company Headquarters
807 E. Main St.
Clarinda, IA 51632
Web: http://www.lislecorp.com

Company Description
Revenue: US$32.2 million (2001)
Employees: 246 (2001)
SIC(s): 3400 Fabricated Metal Products, 3700 Transportation Equipment.

Operating Locations
Lisle Corp. (IA--Clarinda)

Lisle Foundation

Giving Contact
John C. Lisle, Trustee
PO Box 89
Clarinda, IA 51632
Phone: (712)542-5101

Description
EIN: 426056080
Organization Type: Corporate Foundation
Giving Locations: IA: Clarinda, Des Moines
Grant Types: General Support.

Donor Information
Founder: Lisle Corp.

Financial Summary
Total Giving: $14,225 (fiscal year ending November 30, 2001); $22,835 (fiscal 2000); $22,835 (fiscal 1999)
Assets: $219,653 (fiscal 2001); $213,474 (fiscal 2000); $213,474 (fiscal 1999)

Typical Recipients
Arts & Humanities: Historic Preservation, History & Archaeology, Libraries, Music, Theater
Civic & Public Affairs: Business/Free Enterprise, Community Foundations, Civic & Public Affairs-General, Housing, Municipalities/Towns, Parades/Festivals, Safety
Education: Colleges & Universities, Community & Junior Colleges, Education-General, Minority Education, Preschool Education, Secondary Education (Public)
Environment: Environment-General, Resource Conservation, Wildlife Protection
Health: Cancer, Children's Health/Hospitals, Clinics/Medical Centers, Diabetes, Emergency/Ambulance Services, Eyes/Blindness, Heart, Prenatal Health Issues, Single-Disease Health Associations
International: Health Care/Hospitals
Religion: Churches, Religious Welfare
Social Services: Community Centers, Community Centers, Community Service Organizations, Family Planning, Family Services, Food/Clothing Distribution, People with Disabilities, Scouts, Veterans

Application Procedures
Initial Contact: The foundation requests applications be made in writing.
Deadlines: None.

Restrictions
Grants are not made to individuals.

Corporate Officials
Edwin Lisle: chairman PRIM CORP EMPL chairman: Lisle Corp.
John C. Lisle: president, chief executive officer PRIM CORP EMPL president, chief executive officer: Lisle Corp.
Marty Williams: chief financial officer PRIM CORP EMPL chief financial officer: Lisle Corp.

Foundation Officials
Edwin Lisle: trustee (see above)
John C. Lisle: trustee (see above)

Grants Analysis
Disclosure Period: fiscal year ending November 30, 2001
Total Grants: $14,225
Number of Grants: 17
Average Grant: $306*
Highest Grant: $9,325
Lowest Grant: $100
Typical Range: $100 to $500
*Note: Average grant figure excludes highest grant.

Recent Grants
Note: Grants derived from fiscal 2000 Form 990.

General

10,550	Iowa Western Community College, Clarinda, IA
6,600	United Methodist Church, Clarinda, IA
1,000	Clarinda School to Work, Clarinda, IA
900	Iowa College Foundation, Des Moines, IA
600	Cardinal Theatre, Clarinda, IA
500	American Cancer Society, Clarinda, IA
350	Iowa Association of Business and Industry, Des Moines, IA
250	Clarinda Fire and Rescue, Clarinda, IA
250	Clarinda Foundation, Clarinda, IA
250	Nodaway Valley Historical Society, Clarinda, IA

ALBERT A. LIST FOUNDATION

Giving Contact
Vikki Laura List, President
1328 Broadway, Suite 524, PMB 117
New York, NY 10001-2121
Phone: (212)631-0065
Fax: 888-826-1402
E-mail: listdn@earthlink.net
Web: http://fdncenter.org/grantmaker/listfdn

Description
Founded: 1953
EIN: 510188408
Organization Type: Family Foundation
Giving Locations: nationally and regionally.
Grant Types: General Support, Project.

Donor Information
Founder: The Albert A. List Foundation was established in 1953 with funds donated by Albert A. List and Vera G. List. The List family still plays a major role in the foundation, with four family members among the officers and directors.

Financial Summary
Total Giving: $3,007,000 (2000); $2,941,435 (1999); $145,000 (1998)
Assets: $11,419,169 (2000); $15,463,161 (1999); $17,122,128 (1998)
Gifts Received: $2,400 (1994); $39,818 (1993)

Typical Recipients
Arts & Humanities: Arts Associations & Councils, Arts Institutes, Film & Video, Arts & Humanities-General, Libraries, Literary Arts, Museums/Galleries, Performing Arts, Public Broadcasting
Civic & Public Affairs: Business/Free Enterprise, Civil Rights, Community Foundations, Economic Development, Economic Policy, Employment/Job Training, First Amendment Issues, Gay/Lesbian Issues, Civic & Public Affairs-General, Housing, Law & Justice, Legal Aid, Native American Affairs, Nonprofit Management, Philanthropic Organizations, Professional & Trade Associations, Public Policy, Urban & Community Affairs, Women's Affairs
Education: Arts/Humanities Education, Community & Junior Colleges, Engineering/Technological Education, Education-General, Journalism/Media Education
Environment: Energy, Environment-General, Resource Conservation
Health: Clinics/Medical Centers, Long-Term Care, Public Health
International: Human Rights, International Development, International Peace & Security Issues, Missionary/Religious Activities, Trade
Religion: Jewish Causes, Religious Organizations, Religious Welfare, Social/Policy Issues, Synagogues/Temples
Science: Scientific Centers & Institutes
Social Services: At-Risk Youth, Community Service Organizations, Crime Prevention, Family Planning, Family Services, United Funds/United Ways, Youth Organizations

Application Procedures
Initial Contact: Send a brief letter of inquiry that includes the organization's mission, request for funding, amount requested, time period grant will cover, and how the request is consistent with the goals of the Foundation.

Application Requirements: As additional enclosures, include an organizational budget for the current and prior fiscal year; detailed soures of income for organization; and, if applicable, sources of income for the project and a project budget. Optional materials such as brochures, newsletters, or newspaper articles are permitted.
Deadlines: For full proposals: September 1 for consideration in January, January 1 for consideration in May, and May 1 for consideration in September.
Review Process: The foundation sends a note acknowledging receipt of inquiry letters, which are reviewed within one month. The foundation will contact organizations regarding the next step in the process.
Notes: To ensure eligibility for consideration, letters of inquiry should be sent four months in advance of the meeting at which you wish to be considered for funding. Meetings are held in January, May and September.

Restrictions
The foundation funds only organizations that are tax-exempt under 501(c)(3). The foundation does not fund medical grants, museum acquisitions, endowments, debt reduction, building or capital funds, grants to individuals, electoral or lobbying activities, scholarships or fellowships not initiated by the foundation, annual giving, local community fund drives, ongoing programs which are not essentially innovative, organizations which enjoy broad-based popular support, or activities outside the United States, not initiated by the foundation.

Additional Information
The foundation funds organizations which demonstrate the ability to translate their values and goals into strategically designed and executed activities politically, programmatically, and administratively. Within the organization and its program activities, the foundation seeks racial, ethnic, and cultural diversity; innovative and proactive strategies; and aggressive use of coalitions and cross-issue activity.
Publications: Guidelines

Foundation Officials
Jo List: treasurer
Viki List: president
Olga List Mack: secretary
Carol List Schwartz: director

Grants Analysis
Disclosure Period: calendar year ending 2000
Total Grants: $3,007,000
Number of Grants: 132
Average Grant: $22,780
Highest Grant: $125,000
Typical Range: $10,000 to $35,000

Recent Grants
Note: Grants derived from 2000 Form 990.

General

125,000	New Israel Fund, Washington, DC -- promoting religious freedom in Israel
100,000	Creative Capital Fund, New York, NY
50,000	Center for Jewish History, New York, NY -- staff person for outreach
50,000	Civil Rights Forum, Washington, DC
50,000	National Indian Telecommunications Institute, Santa Fe, NM
50,000	New Museum of Contemporary Art, New York, NY -- Visible Knowledge Program
50,000	New Press, Rego Park, NY -- Media Program
50,000	Progressive Technology Project, Washington, DC
50,000	Real Art Ways, Hartford, CT -- Micro-Radio and Digital Skills Development Pilot Project

50,000   Real Art Ways, Hartford, CT -- Micro-Radio and Digital Skills Development Pilot Project

LUCIUS N. LITTAUER FOUNDATION

Giving Contact

William Lee Frost, President
60 East 42nd Street, Suite 2910
New York, NY 10165
Phone: (212)697-2677

Alternate Contact

Pamela Ween Brumberg, Program Officer

Description

Founded: 1929
EIN: 131688027
Organization Type: General Purpose Foundation
Giving Locations: NY: New York internationally; nationally.
Grant Types: Challenge, Conference/Seminar, Employee Matching Gifts, Endowment, Fellowship, General Support, Project, Research, Scholarship.
Note: The foundation also supports the production of publications.

Donor Information

Founder: The foundation was established by Lucius N. Littauer in 1929. The late Mr. Littauer was president of Littauer Brothers, a family-owned glove manufacturing company, and president or director of several public utilities, and transportation and banking firms. He also served as a U.S. congressman.
Mr. Littauer was an active philanthropist. Aside from the charitable activities of the Littauer Foundation, he donated over $2.25 million to Harvard University for the Littauer Center and Graduate School in Public Administration, and established the Nathan Littauer Hospital in Gloversville, NY.

Financial Summary

Total Giving: $1,300,000 (2002 approx); $1,337,396 (2001); $1,288,210 (2000)
Giving Analysis: Giving for 2001 includes: foundation grants to United Way ($4,000); foundation scholarships ($21,666) 1997: foundation grants to United Way ($10,950).
Assets: $39,600,000 (2002 approx); $41,011,478 (2001); $39,634,584 (2000)
Gifts Received: $3,332,084 (2001); $944,350 (1998); $2,649,235 (1997)

Typical Recipients

Arts & Humanities: Arts Outreach, Ethnic & Folk Arts, Historic Preservation, History & Archaeology, Libraries, Literary Arts, Museums/Galleries, Music
Civic & Public Affairs: Botanical Gardens/Parks, Employment/Job Training, Ethnic Organizations, Civic & Public Affairs-General, Philanthropic Organizations
Education: Arts/Humanities Education, Colleges & Universities, Education Funds, Education Reform, Engineering/Technological Education, Education-General, International Exchange, International Studies, Journalism/Media Education, Legal Education, Literacy, Medical Education, Private Education (Precollege), Religious Education, School Volunteerism, Social Sciences Education, Student Aid
Environment: Forestry, Environment-General
Health: Clinics/Medical Centers, Geriatric Health, Geriatric Health, Health Policy/Cost Containment, Health Organizations, Hospitals, Hospitals (University Affiliated)

International: Foreign Arts Organizations, Foreign Educational Institutions, Health Care/Hospitals, International Environmental Issues, International Organizations, International Relations, Missionary/Religious Activities
Religion: Bible Study/Translation, Churches, Religion-General, Jewish Causes, Missionary Activities (Domestic), Religious Organizations, Religious Welfare, Seminaries
Science: Scientific Centers & Institutes, Scientific Research
Social Services: Community Centers, Family Services, People with Disabilities, Recreation & Athletics, Senior Services

Application Procedures

Initial Contact: Send a brief proposal.
Application Requirements: Include description of project, budget request, timetable for completion, curriculum vitae of key personnel, and proof of tax exempt status. Requests for a Book Fund should include a description of the library and its collections, details about any existing book fund program, current budget for Judaica, a list of holdings in Judaica as well as projected needs, and background information about the institution and the Jewish Studies program on campus.
Deadlines: None. The officers and directors meet as needed to decide on grants.
Notes: All grants must be administered without deductions for overhead and/or administration.

Restrictions

Grants are seldom made for endowments (except for book funds), operating budgets, or capital projects.

Additional Information

The foundation awards grants for travel purposes.
Publications: Guidelines

Foundation Officials

Charles Berlin, PhD: director B Boston, MA 1936. ED Hebrew College (1956); Harvard University AB (1958); Hebrew College (1959); Harvard University PhD (1963); Simmons College MLS (1964). NONPR AFFIL consult: University Florida; consult: University Texas; trustee: Hebrew College; member, executive secretary: Association Jewish Studies; head Judaica division: Harvard College; member: Association Jewish Libraries.
Berthold Bilski: director PRIM CORP EMPL officer: Lepercq De Neuflize & Co. Inc. CORP AFFIL director: Lepercq 99 First Management.
Pamela Ween Brumberg: program officer
Robert D. Frost: director
William Lee Frost: president, treasurer, director B Larchmont, NY 1926. ED Harvard University BA (1947); Yale University LLB (1951); Harvard University MPA (1958). OCCUPATION private law practice. CORP AFFIL director: Overseas Shipholding Group. NONPR AFFIL member: New York County Bar Association; member: New York State Bar Association; member: Harvard University Alumni Association; member: New York City Bar Association. CLUB AFFIL Yale Club; Harvard Club.
George Harris: assistant secretary, assistant treasurer, director
Henry A. Lowet: vice president, secretary, director
Mark Milski: director
Peter J. Solomon: director B New York, NY 1938. ED Harvard University BA (1960); Harvard University MBA (1963). PRIM CORP EMPL chairman, chief executive officer: Peter J Solomon Co. Ltd. CORP AFFIL director: Office Depot Inc.; director: Phillips-Van Heusen Corp.

Grants Analysis

Disclosure Period: calendar year ending 2001
Total Grants: $1,313,230*
Number of Grants: 147
Average Grant: $8,934

Highest Grant: $125,000
Typical Range: $1,000 to $15,000
*Note: Giving excludes scholarships and United Way.

Recent Grants

Note: Grants derived from 2001 Form 990.

Library-Related
10,000   American Friends of the Medem Library, Inc., New York, NY -- archives project
10,000   John Carter Brown Library, Providence, RI -- addition to endowment

General
75,000   United Jewish Appeal - Federation of Jewish Philanthropies of New York, New York, NY -- domestic activities
50,000   Harvard University College Library, Cambridge, MA -- addition to endowment
50,000   Stanford University, Stanford, CA -- Stanford University Libraries
50,000   United Jewish Appeal - Federation of Jewish Philanthropies of New York, New York, NY -- absorption of immigrants
40,000   Brooklyn College B'nai B'rith Hillel Foundation, Brooklyn, NY -- Center for Russian Jewish Life at Brooklyn Hillel
30,000   New York University Medical Center, New York, NY -- Palliative Care Program, Rabbinical Bereavement Counselor
27,500   Center for Judaic Studies, Brooklyn, NY -- Lucius N. Littauer Fellow
27,000   Cornell University - Weill Medical College, New York, NY -- Department of Public Health
25,000   American Friends of Hebrew University, New York, NY -- library support
25,000   Arizona State University, Tempe, AZ -- endowment

IDA BALLOU LITTLEFIELD MEMORIAL TRUST

Giving Contact

Joachim A. Weissfeld, Trustee
1500 Fleet Center
Providence, RI 02903
Phone: (401)274-2000

Description

Founded: 1989
EIN: 223022799
Organization Type: Private Foundation
Grant Types: Capital, Conference/Seminar, General Support, Scholarship.

Financial Summary

Total Giving: $406,531 (1998); $343,599 (1997); $340,035 (1996)
Assets: $11,487,416 (1998); $10,103,222 (1997); $8,363,381 (1996)

Typical Recipients

Arts & Humanities: Arts Outreach, Historic Preservation, History & Archaeology, Libraries, Museums/Galleries, Music, Performing Arts, Theater
Civic & Public Affairs: Municipalities/Towns, Women's Affairs, Zoos/Aquariums
Education: Arts/Humanities Education, Colleges & Universities, Education-General, Literacy, Private Education (Precollege), Secondary Education (Public), Special Education, Student Aid
Environment: Air/Water Quality, Environment-General
Health: Alzheimers Disease, Cancer, Children's Health/Hospitals, Clinics/Medical Centers, Diabetes, Emergency/Ambulance Services, Eyes/Blindness, Geriatric Health, Health Policy/Cost Containment,

Health Organizations, Heart, Hospitals, Long-Term Care, Medical Rehabilitation, Medical Research, Nursing Services, Prenatal Health Issues, Preventive Medicine/Wellness Organizations, Public Health
International: Health Care/Hospitals, International Affairs, International Relations
Religion: Churches, Religious Welfare
Science: Science Museums
Social Services: Animal Protection, Camps, Child Welfare, Community Centers, Community Service Organizations, Day Care, Family Services, Food/Clothing Distribution, Homes, People with Disabilities, Scouts, Senior Services, Shelters/Homelessness

Application Procedures
Initial Contact: Send a brief letter of inquiry.
Deadlines: None.

Additional Information
Trusts: Fleet Bank of RI.
Publications: Annual Report
Trust(s): Citizens Trust Co

Foundation Officials
William A. Viall: trustee
Joachim A. Weissfeld: trustee B Wuppertal, Germany 1927. ED Brown University AB (1950); Harvard University JD (1953). PRIM NONPR EMPL ptnr: Hinckley Allen Providence. NONPR AFFIL member: Phi Beta Kappa; member: RI Bar Association; member: Harvard Law School Association; fellow: American College Trust & Estate Counsel; member: Estate Planning Council Rhode Island; member: American Bar Association.

Grants Analysis
Disclosure Period: calendar year ending 1998
Total Grants: $406,531
Number of Grants: 35
Average Grant: $11,615
Highest Grant: $50,000
Typical Range: $3,000 to $20,000

Recent Grants
Note: Grants derived from 1998 Form 990.

General
50,000	Rhode Island School of Design, Providence, RI -- for renovations
20,000	Amos House, Providence, RI -- for eyeglass and RX program
20,000	Diabetes Foundation of Rhode Island, RI -- for statewide screening project
20,000	Rhode Island Community Food Bank, Providence, RI -- for operation and educational expenses
16,766	Women and Infants Hospital, Providence, RI -- for hearing assessment program
15,000	Clara Barton Diabetes Center, North Oxford, MA -- for building projects
15,000	Cranston Arc -- for school environment
15,000	Foundation Fighting Blindness, New York, NY -- for research
15,000	Nickerson House Community Center, Providence, RI -- for housing renovations
15,000	Rhode Island Philharmonic, Providence, RI -- for music gateways program

MILTON S. AND CORINNE N. LIVINGSTON FOUNDATION

Giving Contact
Yale Richards, Executive Director
11605 Miracle Hills Dr., Suite 300
Omaha, NE 68154-4487

Phone: (402)492-9800
Fax: (402)492-9336

Description
Founded: 1948
EIN: 476027670
Organization Type: Private Foundation
Giving Locations: DC; NE: Omaha; NJ; NY
Grant Types: Capital, General Support, Multiyear/Continuing Support.

Donor Information
Founder: the late Milton S. Livingston

Financial Summary
Total Giving: $537,625 (2001); $530,274 (2000); $701,951 (1999)
Giving Analysis: Giving for 2001 includes: foundation grants to United Way ($5,000); 2000: foundation grants to United Way ($5,000); 1999: foundation grants to United Way ($5,000);
Assets: $4,059,157 (2001); $4,372,544 (2000); $4,136,458 (1999)
Gifts Received: $2,200 (1993)

Typical Recipients
Arts & Humanities: Arts Funds, Ballet, Libraries, Museums/Galleries, Music, Opera
Civic & Public Affairs: Civic & Public Affairs-General, Municipalities/Towns, Philanthropic Organizations, Public Policy
Education: Colleges & Universities, Education Funds, Education-General, International Studies, Medical Education, Minority Education, Public Education (Precollege), Special Education, Student Aid
Health: AIDS/HIV, Cancer, Health Organizations, Nursing Services, Public Health
International: Foreign Educational Institutions, International-General, Missionary/Religious Activities
Religion: Jewish Causes, Religious Organizations, Social/Policy Issues, Synagogues/Temples
Social Services: Big Brother/Big Sister, Child Welfare, Family Planning, Family Planning, Food/Clothing Distribution, People with Disabilities, Scouts, Social Services-General, United Funds/United Ways, Youth Organizations

Application Procedures
Initial Contact: Send a brief letter of inquiry describing program or project.
Application Requirements: Include a description of organization, amount requested, purpose of funds sought, recently audited financial statement, and proof of tax-exempt status.
Deadlines: None.
Review Process: Board meets in 2lMay and 2lDecember.

Restrictions
Does not support individuals.

Foundation Officials
Gerald A. Hoberman: trustee
Robert I. Kully: president, trust
Murray H. Newman: vice president, trust
Dr. Patricia Newman: trustee
Yale Richards: asst secy
Suzanne Singer: secretary, trust
Stanley J. Slosburg: trust

Grants Analysis
Disclosure Period: calendar year ending 2001
Total Grants: $532,625*
Number of Grants: 34
Average Grant: $8,250*
Highest Grant: $252,125
Typical Range: $1,000 to $20,000
***Note:** Giving excludes United Way. Average grant figure excludes highest grant.

Recent Grants
Note: Grants derived from 2001 Form 990.

General
252,125	Jewish Federation Foundation, Omaha, NE
73,000	Jewish Federation, Omaha, NE
60,500	Temple Israel, Omaha, NE
20,000	Omaha Schools Foundation, Omaha, NE
17,500	Nebraska Jewish Historical Society, Omaha, NE
12,500	Chabad of Nebraska, Omaha, NE
11,500	National Conference For Community & Justice, Omaha, NE
10,000	Anti-Defamation League of B'Nai B'Rith, New York, NY
10,000	Girl Scouts, Omaha, NE
10,000	Planned Parenthood of Omaha/Council Bluffs, Omaha, NE

LIZ CLAIBORNE, INC.

Company Headquarters
New York, NY
Web: http://www.lizclaiborne.com

Company Description
Founded: 1976
Ticker: LIZ
Exchange: NYSE
Revenue: US$3.717 billion (2002)
Profit: US$231.2 million (2002)
Employees: 10400 (2001)
Fortune Rank: 429, per FORTUNE Magazine's list of 500 Largest U.S. Corporations (2002).
SIC(s): 2331 Women's/Misses' Blouses & Shirts, 2335 Women's/Misses' Dresses, 2337 Women's/Misses' Suits & Coats, 2339 Women's/Misses' Outerwear Nec.

Operating Locations
Liz Claiborne, Inc. (CA--Los Angeles; GA--Atlanta; NJ--Carlstadt, North Bergen; TX--Dallas)

Nonmonetary Support
Type: Donated Products
Note: Support is very limited, and products are only donated in support of significant employee volunteer involvement.

Liz Claiborne Foundation

Giving Contact
Melanie Lyons, Director
1441 Broadway Avenue
New York, NY 10018
Phone: (212)626-5767
Fax: (212)626-8060
Web: http://www.lizclaiborne.com/lizinc/foundation

Description
Founded: 1981
EIN: 133060673
Organization Type: Corporate Foundation
Giving Locations: AL: Montgomery; NJ: Hudson County; NY: New York; PA: Mount Pocono
Grant Types: Challenge, Employee Matching Gifts, General Support, Multiyear/Continuing Support, Project.
Note: Cash gifts of $25 or more will be matched, up to a total of $10,000 per associate in each calendar year. The maximum amount of match to a single institution for any associate is $2,000 per year. Groups not eligible for matching gifts include fraternal organizations, clubs, professional associations, programs,

or teams, and any organization not designated by the U.S. Department of the Treasury as a qualified charity.

Financial Summary

Total Giving: $1,742,182 (2001); $1,571,645 (2000); $1,301,823 (1999). Note: Contributes through foundation only.

Giving Analysis: Giving for 2000 includes: foundation scholarships ($1,000); foundation grants to United Way ($40,000); foundation ($1,530,645); 1999: foundation scholarships ($1,000) foundation ($1,300,823)

Assets: $26,140,954 (2001); $30,274,909 (2000); $31,527,317 (1999)

Gifts Received: $915,483 (1996); $1,171,218 (1995); $1,006,303 (1994). Note: In 1996, contributions were received from Liz Claiborne Inc.

Typical Recipients

Arts & Humanities: Arts Associations & Councils, Arts Centers, Community Arts, Ethnic & Folk Arts, Arts & Humanities-General, History & Archaeology, Libraries, Museums/Galleries, Music, Opera, Public Broadcasting, Theater

Civic & Public Affairs: Asian American Affairs, Botanical Gardens/Parks, Clubs, Community Foundations, Employment/Job Training, Gay/Lesbian Issues, Civic & Public Affairs-General, Housing, Inner-City Development, Law & Justice, Urban & Community Affairs, Women's Affairs, Zoos/Aquariums

Education: Arts/Humanities Education, Colleges & Universities, Education Funds, Education Reform, Elementary Education (Public), Education-General, Literacy, Medical Education, Minority Education, Preschool Education, Private Education (Precollege), Public Education (Precollege), Science/Mathematics Education, Secondary Education (Private)

Environment: Air/Water Quality, Environment-General

Health: AIDS/HIV, Cancer, Clinics/Medical Centers, Eyes/Blindness, Health Organizations, Hospitals, Long-Term Care, Prenatal Health Issues, Public Health, Single-Disease Health Associations

International: Human Rights

Religion: Jewish Causes, Religious Welfare

Science: Science Museums, Scientific Centers & Institutes

Social Services: Big Brother/Big Sister, Camps, Child Abuse, Child Welfare, Community Centers, Community Service Organizations, Crime Prevention, Day Care, Delinquency & Criminal Rehabilitation, Domestic Violence, Emergency Relief, Family Services, Family Services, Food/Clothing Distribution, Recreation & Athletics, Senior Services, Shelters/Homelessness, Social Services-General, United Funds/United Ways, Volunteer Services, YMCA/YWCA/YMHA/YWHA, Youth Organizations

Application Procedures

Initial Contact: Call or write for guidelines, then full written proposal.

Application Requirements: Include a statement of goals, history, and accomplishments; statement of purpose or objective; description of how the program or project is to be implemented and the qualifications of the staff involved; the number of clients to be served; plans to evaluate project's success; amount requested; current organization budget and proposed project budget, showing expenses and income, and following year's budgets if the proposal is submitted within three months of new fiscal year; most recent audited financial statements; list of funding sources and amounts contributed in current and previous year; funding pending approval for current year; amount of funding for project supplied by the organization's general budget; number of professional and support staff, with titles; list of board members, with affiliations; and proof of tax-exempt status.

Deadlines: None.

Review Process: Initial staff review, final review, and funding decision by grant-making committee.

Evaluative Criteria: Preference given to direct services; relevance to foundation's priorities and geographic focus; strength of project or program; managerial, planning, and financial capability of organization; other funding sources; employee involvement.

Decision Notification: Board meets in April, July, October, and December.

Notes: The foundation does not accept unsolicited proposals for the arts or the environment.

Restrictions

Contributions are not made to programs and projects based and/or operating outside the United States; religious, fraternal, or veterans' organizations; individuals; research; professional meetings, conferences, or symposia; building funds or equipment; endowments; hospital-based programs or single-disease organizations; film, video, television, or radio projects; courtesy advertising or fundraising events; or for sponsorship of events, performances, or exhibits.

Corporate Officials

Robert Bernard: senior vice president international sales PRIM CORP EMPL senior vice president international sales: Liz Claiborne, Inc.

Harvey L. Falk: president, vice chairman B 1934. ED New York University (1955). PRIM CORP EMPL president, vice chairman: Liz Claiborne, Inc. CORP AFFIL vice chairman: Liz Claiborne Cosmetics Inc.; vice chairman: Liz Claiborne Foreign Holdings Inc.

Foundation Officials

Robert Bernard: member grantmaking committee (see above)

Harvey L. Falk: member grantmaking committee (see above)

Melanie Lyons: director, member grant committee

Nancy Rogers: member grantmaking committee

Grants Analysis

Disclosure Period: calendar year ending 2001
Total Grants: $1,700,157*
Number of Grants: 511
Average Grant: $2,353*
Highest Grant: $500,000
Lowest Grant: $25
Typical Range: $25 to $50,000

*Note: Giving excludes United Way. Giving includes matching gifts. Average grant figure excludes highest grant.

Recent Grants

Note: Grants derived from 2001 Form 990.

General

500,000	Twin Tower Fund, New York, NY
500,000	Twin Tower Fund, New York, NY
62,402	American Red Cross New York City Disaster Fund, New York, NY
52,405	Educational Broadcasting Corporation, New York, NY
50,234	American Red Cross New York City Disaster Fund, New York, NY
50,000	Educational Broadcasting Corps, New York, NY
50,000	Girls, Incorporated, New York, NY
50,000	Girls, Incorporated, New York, NY
50,000	New Destiny Housing Corp, New York, NY
50,000	New Destiny Housing Corp, New York, NY

LOCKHART VAUGHAN FOUNDATION

Giving Contact

John B. Powell, Jr., Executive Director
2 E. Read Street, Suite 100
Baltimore, MD 21202
Phone: (410)837-9400

Description

EIN: 521693184
Organization Type: Private Foundation
Giving Locations: MD
Grant Types: General Support.

Financial Summary

Total Giving: $1,346,250 (2002); $1,479,300 (2000); $1,031,850 (1999)

Giving Analysis: Giving for 2000 includes: foundation grants to United Way ($11,000); foundation fellowships ($50,000); foundation scholarships ($80,000); 1999: foundation grants to United Way ($11,000); foundation scholarships ($25,000); foundation fellowships ($50,000) 1998: foundation grants to United Way ($10,000)

Assets: $26,411,756 (2002); $26,878,342 (2000); $29,497,184 (1999)

Typical Recipients

Arts & Humanities: Dance, Libraries, Theater

Civic & Public Affairs: Botanical Gardens/Parks, Community Foundations, Economic Development, Employment/Job Training, Civic & Public Affairs-General, Housing, Inner-City Development, Legal Aid, Philanthropic Organizations, Public Policy, Urban & Community Affairs, Women's Affairs, Zoos/Aquariums

Education: Afterschool/Enrichment Programs, Colleges & Universities, Education Funds, Elementary Education (Public), Faculty Development, Education-General, Leadership Training, Legal Education, Literacy, Medical Education, Preschool Education, Private Education (Precollege), Science/Mathematics Education, Social Sciences Education

Environment: Air/Water Quality, Forestry, Environment-General, Protection, Resource Conservation

Health: Cancer, Children's Health/Hospitals, Clinics/Medical Centers, Emergency/Ambulance Services, Health-General, Health Organizations, Hospitals, Medical Research, Mental Health, Public Health, Speech & Hearing

Religion: Churches, Ministries, Religious Welfare

Science: Science Museums, Scientific Centers & Institutes

Social Services: At-Risk Youth, Big Brother/Big Sister, Camps, Child Abuse, Child Welfare, Community Centers, Community Service Organizations, Crime Prevention, Family Planning, Family Services, Food/Clothing Distribution, People with Disabilities, Recreation & Athletics, Scouts, Shelters/Homelessness, Social Services-General, Substance Abuse, United Funds/United Ways, YMCA/YWCA/YMHA/YWHA, Youth Organizations

Application Procedures

Initial Contact: Submit a completed grant application. The foundation accepts the Association of Baltimore Area Grantmakers (ABAG) Common Grant Application Format, which can be obtained at www.abagmd.org.

Application Requirements: The application should be submitted in duplicate, and should include a cover letter, proposal narrative, and attachments as outlined in the ABAG Application Format.

Deadlines: February 20, June 20, and October 20.

Decision Notification: Applicants will be notified of the foundation's decision within approximately 60 days.

Restrictions

The foundation does not support organizations involved in the arts.

Additional Information

Publications: Application Procedures

Foundation Officials

Benjamin M. Baker, III: director
Julia Baker Menzies: director
Julia P. O'Brien: trustee

Brentnall M. Powell: trustee
John Brentnall Powell, Jr.: director
Susan Baker Powell: director
Julia B. Schnupp: trustee
Kevin A. Schnupp: trustee

Grants Analysis

Disclosure Period: calendar year ending 2002
Total Grants: $1,346,250
Number of Grants: 66
Average Grant: $20,398
Highest Grant: $150,000
Typical Range: $5,000 to $30,000

Recent Grants

Note: Grants derived from 2002 Form 990.

Library-Related
40,000	Roland Park Library Initiative, Inc., Baltimore, MD -- for community development

General
150,000	Maryland Zoological Society, Baltimore, MD -- for community development and capital campaign for Baltimore Zoo
100,000	Maryland Zoological Society, Baltimore, MD -- for community development and capital campaign for Baltimore Zoo
55,000	Hearing and Speech Agency, Baltimore, MD -- for health care and capital campaign
50,000	Baltimore Community Foundation, Baltimore, MD -- for Youth Program and A-Teams
50,000	Rice University, Houston, TX -- for education
35,000	Environmental Defense, Inc., Baltimore, MD -- for Community Development Baltimore Regional Partnership for Vision
30,000	Midtown Community Fund, Baltimore, MD -- for community development and operation of vacuum vehicle
30,000	St. Vincent de Paul, Baltimore, MD -- for community development
30,000	Shepherd's Clinic, Baltimore, MD -- for capital campaign and health care
25,000	Baltimore Museum of Industry, Baltimore, MD -- for Youth Program Afterschool and Weekend Educational Programs

LOEWS CORP.

Company Headquarters

667 Madison Ave.
New York, NY 10021-8087
Web: http://www.loews.com

Company Description

Ticker: LTR
Exchange: NYSE
Revenue: US$16.898 billion (2002)
Profit: US$940.9 million (2002)
Employees: 27820 (2001)
Fortune Rank: 107, per FORTUNE Magazine's list of 500 Largest U.S. Corporations (2002).

Nonmonetary Support

Type: Donated Products

Loews Foundation

Giving Contact

Peter Keegan, Senior Vice President & Chief Financial Officer
Loews Corp.
667 Madison Avenue
New York, NY 10021

Phone: (212)521-2950
Fax: (212)521-2329

Alternate Contact

John J. Kenny, Trustee
Loews Foundation
655 Madison Avenue
New York, NY 10021-8043
Phone: (212)521-2650

Description

Founded: 1957
EIN: 136082817
Organization Type: Corporate Foundation
Giving Locations: NY: operating locations.
Grant Types: Employee Matching Gifts, General Support, Matching, Scholarship.

Financial Summary

Total Giving: $1,824,476 (2001); $1,704,164 (2000); $1,782,597 (1999). Note: Contributes through foundation only.
Giving Analysis: Giving for 2000 includes: foundation grants to United Way ($10,000); foundation scholarships ($36,755); foundation matching gifts ($62,819); foundation ($1,594,590); 1998: foundation grants to United Way ($25,000); foundation scholarships ($31,965); foundation matching gifts ($61,527); foundation ($1,323,817); 1997: foundation scholarships ($9,660); foundation grants to United Way ($25,000); foundation matching gifts ($53,725);
Assets: $1,662,345 (2001); $1,324,637 (2000); $13,233 (1999)
Gifts Received: $2,119,390 (2001); $2,986,383 (2000); $1,735,000 (1999). Note: Foundation receives contributions from Loews Corporation and its subsidiaries.

Typical Recipients

Arts & Humanities: Arts Associations & Councils, Arts Festivals, Arts Funds, Arts Outreach, Dance, Historic Preservation, Libraries, Museums/Galleries, Music, Opera, Performing Arts, Public Broadcasting, Theater
Civic & Public Affairs: African American Affairs, Botanical Gardens/Parks, Business/Free Enterprise, Chambers of Commerce, Clubs, Economic Development, Employment/Job Training, Ethnic Organizations, Civic & Public Affairs-General, Housing, Law & Justice, Legal Aid, Municipalities/Towns, Parades/Festivals, Philanthropic Organizations, Professional & Trade Associations, Public Policy, Safety, Urban & Community Affairs, Women's Affairs, Zoos/Aquariums
Education: Afterschool/Enrichment Programs, Arts/Humanities Education, Business Education, Colleges & Universities, Education Funds, Education Reform, Education-General, International Studies, Legal Education, Literacy, Medical Education, Minority Education, Public Education (Precollege), Secondary Education (Private), Social Sciences Education, Special Education, Student Aid
Environment: Forestry, Environment-General, Resource Conservation, Wildlife Protection
Health: AIDS/HIV, Cancer, Children's Health/Hospitals, Clinics/Medical Centers, Diabetes, Emergency/Ambulance Services, Health-General, Geriatric Health, Health Organizations, Hospitals, Hospitals (University Affiliated), Medical Rehabilitation, Medical Research, Medical Research, Mental Health, Multiple Sclerosis, Nutrition, Prenatal Health Issues, Public Health, Research/Studies Institutes, Single-Disease Health Associations, Speech & Hearing
International: Foreign Arts Organizations, Health Care/Hospitals, Human Rights, International Organizations, International Peace & Security Issues, International Relations, International Relief Efforts, Missionary/Religious Activities
Religion: Jewish Causes, Religious Welfare
Science: Science Museums

Social Services: Animal Protection, Camps, Child Welfare, Community Centers, Community Service Organizations, Delinquency & Criminal Rehabilitation, Family Planning, People with Disabilities, Recreation & Athletics, Scouts, United Funds/United Ways, Volunteer Services, YMCA/YWCA/YMHA/YWHA, Youth Organizations

Application Procedures

Initial Contact: Contact foundation by letter; foundation does not accept phone calls.
Application Requirements: Include a description of organization and project, budget, and proof of tax exemption.
Deadlines: None.
Notes: Applications for employee-related sponsorships are available from the foundation. Scholarships are provided only for children of Loews Corporation through the National Merit Scholarship Corp.

Restrictions

Foundation does not make grants to individuals.

Additional Information

All charitable giving is through the foundation. Subsidiaries do not make contributions independent of Loews Foundation, except for CNA Insurance Co., which is affiliated with CNA Financial Corp., a Loews Corp. joint venture.

Corporate Officials

John J. Kenny: treasurer, chief executive officer, director B Jersey City, NJ 1938. ED New York University (1965); Saint John's University School of Law (1972). PRIM CORP EMPL treasurer: Loews Corp. ADD CORP EMPL treasurer, director: 48th Street & 8th Avenue Corp.; treasurer: Lowes Hotels Inc. NONPR AFFIL trustee: Loews Foundation.
James S. Tisch: president, chief executive officer, director B Atlantic City, NJ January 02, 1953. ED Cornell University BS (1975); University of Pennsylvania Wharton School MBA (1976). PRIM CORP EMPL president, chief executive officer, director: Loews Corp. CORP AFFIL chairman: Diamond Offshore Drilling Inc.; director: Vail Resorts Inc.; director: CNA Financial Corp. NONPR AFFIL trustee: Mount Sinai Medical Center New York; president elect: United Jewish Appeal Federation New York; trustee: Dalton School New York; director: Federation Employment & Guidance Service.
Laurence Alan Tisch: co-chairman, director B New York, NY March 05, 1923. ED New York University BS (1942); University of Pennsylvania MA (1943); Harvard University Law School (1946). PRIM CORP EMPL co-chairman, director: Loews Corp. ADD CORP EMPL chief executive officer: Continental Loss Adjusting Service. CORP AFFIL director: Petrie Stores Corp.; director: Transcontinental Insurance Co. New York; director: CNA Financial Corp.; director: Automatic Data Processing Inc.; director: Bulova Corp. NONPR AFFIL chairman board trustees: New York University; director: United Jewish Appeal Federation; trustee: New York Public Library; member: Council Foreign Relations; trustee: Metropolitan Museum Art.
Preston Robert Tisch: co-chairman, director B Brooklyn, NY 1926. ED Bucknell University (1943-1944); University of Michigan BA (1948). PRIM CORP EMPL co-chairman, director: Loews Corp. ADD CORP EMPL owner, chief executive officer, chairman: New York Football Giants Inc. CORP AFFIL director: Transcontinental Insurance Co. New York; director: Hasbro Inc.; director: Rite Aid Corp.; director: CNA Financial Corp.; director: Bulova Corp. NONPR AFFIL trustee: New York University; member: Sigma Alpha Mu; chairman emeritus: New York Convention & Visitor Bureau; president: Citymeals Wheels; member: Governments Business Advisory Council New York. CLUB AFFIL Rye Racquet Club; Century Country Club.

Foundation Officials

Peter Keegan: senior vice president B Providence, RI 1944. ED Brown University BA (1966); Columbia University MBA (1970). PRIM CORP EMPL senior vice president, chief financial officer: Loews Corp.
John J. Kenny: secretary, treasurer, trustee (see above)
Andrew H. Tisch: trustee
Laurence Alan Tisch: trustee (see above)
Preston Robert Tisch: trustee (see above)

Grants Analysis

Disclosure Period: calendar year ending 2001
Total Grants: $1,701,755*
Number of Grants: 72
Average Grant: $13,405*
Highest Grant: $750,000
Typical Range: $1,000 to $50,000
*Note: Giving excludes matching gifts, scholarships, and United Way. Average grant figure excludes highest grant.

Recent Grants

Note: Grants derived from 2001 Form 990.

General

750,000	United Jewish Appeal - Federation of Jewish Philanthropies of New York, New York, NY
200,000	New York City 2012, New York, NY
150,000	Take the Field, Inc., New York, NY
50,000	American Friends of Livnot U'Lehibanot, New York, NY
50,000	NARAL Foundation, New York, NY
40,000	Ronald H. Brown Center for Politics and Commercial Diplomacy
25,000	American Museum of Natural History, New York, NY
25,000	Camp Heartland, Wauwatosa, WI
25,000	Council on Foreign Relations, New York, NY
25,000	Special Operations Warrior Foundation, Tampa, FL

LOEWY FAMILY FOUNDATION

Giving Contact

John P. Reiner, Treasurer & Director
80 Wall Street, Suite 1018
New York, NY 10005-3601
Phone: (212)269-2466

Description

Founded: 1966
EIN: 136225288
Organization Type: Private Foundation
Giving Locations: NY: New York
Grant Types: General Support.

Donor Information

Founder: the late Alfred Loewy, the late Edna Loewy Butler

Financial Summary

Total Giving: $505,000 (fiscal year ending June 30, 2001); $490,000 (fiscal 2000); $585,012 (fiscal 1999)
Giving Analysis: Giving for fiscal 2001 includes: foundation scholarships ($25,000) fiscal 2000: foundation scholarships ($15,000)
Assets: $10,328,814 (fiscal 2001); $10,735,614 (fiscal 2000); $10,951,070 (fiscal 1999)

Typical Recipients

Arts & Humanities: Arts Associations & Councils, Libraries, Performing Arts, Public Broadcasting, Theater

Education: Colleges & Universities, Education Funds, Medical Education, Minority Education, Private Education (Precollege), Science/Mathematics Education
Health: Hospitals, Medical Research, Mental Health, Transplant Networks/Donor Banks
Social Services: Child Welfare, Youth Organizations

Application Procedures

Initial Contact: Send proposal in letter form.
Deadlines: None.

Restrictions

No grants to individuals.

Foundation Officials

Michael Green: vice president, director
Erik A. Hanson: vice president, director
Andrew Linz: president, director
John P. Reiner: secretary, treasurer, director
Mischa A. Zabotin: secretary, director

Grants Analysis

Disclosure Period: fiscal year ending June 30, 2001
Total Grants: $480,000*
Number of Grants: 6
Highest Grant: $200,000
Lowest Grant: $15,000
*Note: Giving excludes scholarships.

Recent Grants

Note: Grants derived from fiscal 2000 Form 990.

Library-Related

40,000	Lake Placid Public Library, Placid, NY -- building fund

General

200,000	Columbia University, New York, NY -- advancement of transplant medicine
100,000	Lehigh University, Bethlehem, PA -- Loewy visiting professorship endowment
75,000	St. Luke's Roosevelt Hospital, New York, NY -- support of medical ethics conference center
50,000	Georgetown University, Washington, DC -- lectureship program in science and technology
15,000	Native American Scholarship Fund, Albuquerque, NM -- provide scholarship assistance
10,000	Association for Development of Dramatic Arts Inc.,, New York, NY -- grant for student matinee series

GEORGE A. AND GRACE LONG FOUNDATION

Giving Contact

Marjorie Alexander Davis, Co-Trustee
Care of Fleet Bank
777 Main Street
Providence, RI 02904-5703
Phone: (203)728-2274

Description

Founded: 1960
EIN: 066030953
Organization Type: Private Foundation
Giving Locations: CT: Hartford greater Hartford
Grant Types: General Support, Project, Scholarship.

Donor Information

Founder: George A. Long, the late Grace L. Long

Financial Summary

Total Giving: $620,766 (2002); $612,316 (2000); $415,155 (1999)
Giving Analysis: Giving for 2002 includes: foundation scholarships ($20,300); 2000: foundation scholarships ($7,000); 1999: foundation scholarships ($2,500)
Assets: $9,601,127 (2002); $12,364,600 (2000); $12,492,634 (1999)

Typical Recipients

Arts & Humanities: Arts Centers, Community Arts, Dance, History & Archaeology, Libraries, Museums/Galleries, Music, Opera, Performing Arts, Public Broadcasting, Theater
Civic & Public Affairs: Botanical Gardens/Parks, Clubs, Community Foundations, Economic Development, Employment/Job Training, Civic & Public Affairs-General, Hispanic Affairs, Housing, Parades/Festivals, Professional & Trade Associations, Public Policy, Rural Affairs, Urban & Community Affairs, Women's Affairs
Education: Agricultural Education, Arts/Humanities Education, Colleges & Universities, Education Associations, Education Reform, Engineering/Technological Education, Leadership Training, Literacy, Minority Education, Preschool Education, Private Education (Precollege), Public Education (Precollege), Special Education, Student Aid, Vocational & Technical Education
Environment: Environment-General, Resource Conservation
Health: Adolescent Health Issues, AIDS/HIV, Alzheimers Disease, Children's Health/Hospitals, Clinics/Medical Centers, Emergency/Ambulance Services, Home-Care Services, Hospitals, Long-Term Care, Nursing Services, Prenatal Health Issues, Single-Disease Health Associations
International: International Relief Efforts
Religion: Churches, Ministries, Religious Organizations, Religious Welfare
Science: Scientific Centers & Institutes
Social Services: Animal Protection, At-Risk Youth, Big Brother/Big Sister, Camps, Child Welfare, Community Centers, Community Service Organizations, Counseling, Domestic Violence, Emergency Relief, Family Planning, Family Services, Food/Clothing Distribution, Homes, People with Disabilities, Recreation & Athletics, Scouts, Senior Services, Shelters/Homelessness, Social Services-General, United Funds/United Ways, YMCA/YWCA/YMHA/YWHA, Youth Organizations

Application Procedures

Initial Contact: Request application form.
Deadlines: March 15 and September 15.

Restrictions

Does not support individuals.

Additional Information

Publications: Application Form; Guidelines
Trust(s): Fleet National Bank

Foundation Officials

Charles R. Moore, Jr.: trustee

Grants Analysis

Disclosure Period: calendar year ending 2002
Total Grants: $600,466*
Number of Grants: 161
Average Grant: $3,730
Highest Grant: $10,000
Lowest Grant: $750
Typical Range: $1,000 to $5,000
*Note: Giving excludes scholarships.

Recent Grants

Note: Grants derived from 2002 Form 990.

General

10,000	Almada Lodge Times Farm Camp Corporation, Andover, CT
10,000	Connecticut Children's Medical Center Foundation, Hartford, CT
8,627	Hartford Camp Courant, Hartford, CT
8,000	Connecticut Humane Society, Newington, CT
7,500	Equistrides Therapeutic Riding Center, Inc.
6,000	City Slicker Farm Program
6,000	Community Foundation of Southeastern Connecticut, New London, CT
6,000	Connecticut Forum, Hartford, CT
6,000	Hartford Interval House, Hartford, CT
5,800	Trinity College Community Child Center, Hartford, CT

J. M. Long Foundation

Giving Contact

Robert M. Long, President & Trustee
2700 Ygnacio Valley Rd., Suite 172
Walnut Creek, CA 94598
Phone: (925)935-4138

Description

Founded: 1966
EIN: 941643626
Organization Type: Private Foundation
Giving Locations: CA
Grant Types: General Support, Scholarship.

Donor Information

Founder: the late Joseph M. Long

Financial Summary

Total Giving: $2,274,283 (2002); $1,764,600 (2001); $2,340,800 (2000)
Giving Analysis: Giving for 2000 includes: foundation scholarships ($350,000); 1999: foundation scholarships ($176,000) foundation scholarships ($176,000)
Assets: $47,993,889 (2002); $37,254,412 (2001); $37,677,456 (2000)
Gifts Received: $13,745,127 (2002); $1,388,243 (1993); $8,066,684 (1992). Note: In 2002, contributions were received from Joseph M. Long Marital Trust.

Typical Recipients

Arts & Humanities: Arts Associations & Councils, Historic Preservation, History & Archaeology, Libraries, Museums/Galleries, Music, Performing Arts
Civic & Public Affairs: Botanical Gardens/Parks, Economic Development, Employment/Job Training, Municipalities/Towns, Safety, Urban & Community Affairs, Women's Affairs, Zoos/Aquariums
Education: Agricultural Education, Arts/Humanities Education, Business Education, Colleges & Universities, Community & Junior Colleges, Education Funds, Education Reform, Elementary Education (Public), Environmental Education, Education-General, Health & Physical Education, Medical Education, Private Education (Precollege), Public Education (Precollege), School Volunteerism, Science/Mathematics Education, Secondary Education (Public), Social Sciences Education, Student Aid
Environment: Environment-General, Research, Resource Conservation, Wildlife Protection
Health: Arthritis, Cancer, Children's Health/Hospitals, Clinics/Medical Centers, Diabetes, Emergency/Ambulance Services, Health-General, Health Funds, Health Organizations, Hospices, Hospitals, Medical Rehabilitation, Medical Research, Mental Health,

Nursing Services, Preventive Medicine/Wellness Organizations, Public Health, Single-Disease Health Associations
Religion: Jewish Causes, Religious Organizations, Religious Welfare
Science: Science Museums, Scientific Centers & Institutes, Scientific Research
Social Services: Camps, Community Centers, Community Service Organizations, Counseling, Day Care, Family Services, Food/Clothing Distribution, People with Disabilities, Recreation & Athletics, Scouts, Senior Services, Social Services-General, Veterans, YMCA/YWCA/YMHA/YWHA, Youth Organizations

Application Procedures

Initial Contact: Send letter requesting application and guidelines. Deadline information is listed in the guidelines.

Restrictions

Grants are not awarded to individuals.

Foundation Officials

W. G. Combs: vice president, trustee
O. D. Jones: trustee
Milton Long: trustee
Robert Merrill Long: president, trustee B Oakland, CA 1938. ED Brown University (1956-1958); Claremont Men's College BA (1960). PRIM CORP EMPL chairman, chief executive officer, director: Longs Drug Stores Corp. NONPR AFFIL director: National Association Chain Drug Stores.
S. D. Roath: trustee PRIM CORP EMPL president, director: Longs Drug Stores Corp.
M. J. Souyoultzis: trustee
C. Tessler: secretary

Grants Analysis

Disclosure Period: calendar year ending 2002
Total Grants: $2,274,283
Number of Grants: 153
Average Grant: $9,771*
Highest Grant: $418,182
Typical Range: $1,000 to $20,000
*Note: Average grant figure excludes five highest grants ($828,182).

Recent Grants

Note: Grants derived from 2001 Form 990.

General

250,000	University of the Pacific School of Pharmacy and Health Sciences, Stockton, CA
50,000	City of Hope, Los Angeles, CA
50,000	John Muir Memorial Association, Martinez, CA
38,800	Isla Vista School, Isla Vista, CA
38,100	Milestones of Development, Vallejo, CA
35,000	Enloe Medical Center, Chico, CA
28,000	Community Action Marin, San Rafael, CA
25,000	Alameda Hospital Foundation, Alameda, CA
25,000	Arthritis Foundation
25,000	California Waterfowl Association, San Francisco, CA

John F. Long Foundation

Giving Contact

John F. Long, Director
5035 W. Camelback Rd.
Phoenix, AZ 85031
Phone: (602)272-0421
Fax: (602)846-7208
E-mail: webmaster@jflong.com
Web: http://www.jflong.com/foundation.htm

Description

Founded: 1959
EIN: 866052431
Organization Type: Private Foundation
Giving Locations: AZ
Grant Types: General Support.

Donor Information

Founder: John F. Long

Financial Summary

Total Giving: $370,915 (fiscal year ending April 30, 2002); $266,528 (fiscal 2001); $212,212 (fiscal 2000)
Assets: $6,190,500 (fiscal 2002); $6,216,000 (fiscal 2001); $6,112,795 (fiscal 2000)
Gifts Received: $76,057 (fiscal 2001); $1,565 (fiscal 1994)

Typical Recipients

Arts & Humanities: History & Archaeology, Libraries, Music, Public Broadcasting, Theater, Visual Arts
Civic & Public Affairs: Botanical Gardens/Parks, Clubs, Community Foundations, Civic & Public Affairs-General, Inner-City Development, Municipalities/Towns, Parades/Festivals, Urban & Community Affairs, Women's Affairs, Zoos/Aquariums
Education: Colleges & Universities, Education Reform, Elementary Education (Public), Education-General, Medical Education, Preschool Education, Private Education (Precollege), Public Education (Precollege), School Volunteerism, Secondary Education (Public)
Environment: Air/Water Quality, Environment-General
Health: AIDS/HIV, Cancer, Children's Health/Hospitals, Clinics/Medical Centers, Health Organizations, Research/Studies Institutes, Single-Disease Health Associations
International: International Environmental Issues, International Organizations
Religion: Churches, Jewish Causes, Ministries, Religious Organizations, Religious Welfare
Science: Science Museums
Social Services: Child Welfare, Community Centers, Crime Prevention, Family Planning, Food/Clothing Distribution, Homes, People with Disabilities, Recreation & Athletics, Scouts, Shelters/Homelessness, Social Services-General, Substance Abuse, Youth Organizations

Application Procedures

Initial Contact: Send a brief letter of inquiry.
Application Requirements: Include purpose of funds sought and Better Business Bureau approval.
Deadlines: None.

Foundation Officials

Jacob F. Long: trustee
John F. Long: director
Mary P. Long: director
Bonnie O'Hara: admin

Grants Analysis

Disclosure Period: fiscal year ending April 30, 2002
Total Grants: $370,915
Number of Grants: 156
Average Grant: $1,748*
Highest Grant: $100,000
Lowest Grant: $100
Typical Range: $500 to $3,000
*Note: Average grant figure excludes highest grant.

Recent Grants

Note: Grants derived from fiscal 2000 Form 990.

Library-Related

5,000	U.M.C.A. Library, Desert Hot Springs, CA

General

36,794	Cartwright School District, Phoenix, AZ
26,140	Friends of Channel 8, Tempe, AZ
15,000	Phoenix Parks & Preserve Initiative, Phoenix, AZ
8,000	Alhambra School District 68, Phoenix, AZ
5,000	Longhaven West Mobile Home Park Activities Committee/ Blockwatch, Phoenix, AZ
4,000	West Valley Child Crisis Center, Glendale, AZ
3,500	Phoenix Union School District, Phoenix, AZ
3,500	Planned Parenthood, Phoenix, AZ
3,000	Southampton College Wild Dolphin Project, Kihai, AZ
3,000	Xavier Scholarship Fund/ Mother-Daughter Fashion Show

Long Island Lighting Co.

Company Headquarters

600 Doctors Path
Riverhead, NY 11901

Company Description

Employees: 5,403
SIC(s): 4900 Electric, Gas & Sanitary Services.

Operating Locations

Long Island Lighting Co. (NY--Hicksville)

Nonmonetary Support

Type: Donated Equipment; In-kind Services; Loaned Employees; Loaned Executives; Workplace Solicitation

Giving Contact

James M. Cunningham, Public Affairs
175 E. Old Country Rd.
Hicksville, NY 11801
Phone: (516)755-6650

Description

Organization Type: Corporate Giving Program
Giving Locations: service area.

Typical Recipients

Arts & Humanities: Arts Associations & Councils, Arts Centers, Arts Festivals, Arts Funds, Community Arts, Ethnic & Folk Arts, Historic Preservation, Libraries, Literary Arts, Museums/Galleries, Music, Opera, Performing Arts, Public Broadcasting, Theater, Visual Arts
Civic & Public Affairs: Economic Development, Employment/Job Training, Nonprofit Management, Professional & Trade Associations, Safety, Urban & Community Affairs, Women's Affairs, Zoos/Aquariums
Education: Business Education, Colleges & Universities, Community & Junior Colleges, Continuing Education, Elementary Education (Private), Engineering/Technological Education, Faculty Development, Literacy, Minority Education, Public Education (Precollege), Science/Mathematics Education, Social Sciences Education, Special Education
Environment: Environment-General
Health: Geriatric Health, Nutrition, Single-Disease Health Associations
Science: Science Exhibits & Fairs, Scientific Centers & Institutes, Scientific Organizations
Social Services: Community Centers, Family Services, Food/Clothing Distribution, People with Disabilities, Senior Services, Shelters/Homelessness, United Funds/United Ways, Volunteer Services, Youth Organizations

Application Procedures

Initial Contact: Send inquiry letter.

Corporate Officials

James T. Flynn: executive vice president, chief operating officer chief financial officer PRIM CORP EMPL executive vice president, chief operating officer: Long Island Lighting Co.
Anthony Nozzolillo: senior vice president financial, chief financial officer B Marcone, Italy 1948. ED Brooklyn Polytechnic Institute (1972); Long Island University (1978). PRIM CORP EMPL senior vice president financial, chief financial officer: Long Island Lighting Co.

LONGWOOD FOUNDATION

Giving Contact

Peter C. Morrow, Executive Director
100 West 10th Street, Suite 1109
Wilmington, DE 19801
Phone: (302)654-2489
Fax: (302)654-2323

Alternate Contact

Phone: (302)654-2477

Description

Founded: 1937
EIN: 510066734
Organization Type: General Purpose Foundation
Giving Locations: DE; PA: Southern Chester County
Grant Types: Capital, Challenge, Multiyear/Continuing Support, Seed Money.

Donor Information

Founder: The Longwood Foundation was created in 1937 by Pierre Samuel du Pont and became the principal beneficiary of his estate upon his death in 1954.

Financial Summary

Total Giving: $39,872,605 (fiscal year ending September 30, 2002); $33,128,076 (fiscal 2001); $43,774,000 (fiscal 2000 approx)
Giving Analysis: Giving for fiscal 2001 includes: foundation grants to United Way ($416,000)
Assets: $600,786,854 (fiscal 2002); $651,327,269 (fiscal 2001); $815,559,000 (fiscal 1999)
Gifts Received: $919,510 (fiscal 1997); $552,560 (fiscal 1996)

Typical Recipients

Arts & Humanities: Arts Centers, Arts Funds, Dance, Arts & Humanities-General, Historic Preservation, History & Archaeology, Libraries, Museums/Galleries, Music, Opera, Public Broadcasting, Theater, Visual Arts
Civic & Public Affairs: Botanical Gardens/Parks, Clubs, Community Foundations, Economic Development, Employment/Job Training, Civic & Public Affairs-General, Housing, Municipalities/Towns, Nonprofit Management, Parades/Festivals, Public Policy, Rural Affairs, Safety, Urban & Community Affairs, Women's Affairs, Zoos/Aquariums
Education: Business Education, Colleges & Universities, Education Reform, Environmental Education, Education-General, Education-General, Literacy, Minority Education, Preschool Education, Private Education (Precollege), Public Education (Precollege), Religious Education, Science/Mathematics Education, Secondary Education (Private), Special Education, Student Aid
Environment: Air/Water Quality, Forestry, Environment-General, Resource Conservation, Wildlife Protection
Health: AIDS/HIV, Cancer, Children's Health/Hospitals, Clinics/Medical Centers, Emergency/Ambulance Services, Geriatric Health, Health Organizations,

Hospices, Hospitals, Long-Term Care, Medical Research, Preventive Medicine/Wellness Organizations, Public Health
Religion: Religion-General, Jewish Causes, Ministries, Religious Welfare
Science: Science Museums, Scientific Centers & Institutes, Scientific Organizations
Social Services: Animal Protection, At-Risk Youth, Camps, Child Welfare, Community Centers, Community Service Organizations, Counseling, Day Care, Family Planning, Family Services, Food/Clothing Distribution, Homes, People with Disabilities, Recreation & Athletics, Scouts, Senior Services, Shelters/Homelessness, Special Olympics, Substance Abuse, United Funds/United Ways, Veterans, YMCA/YWCA/YMHA/YWHA, Youth Organizations

Application Procedures

Initial Contact: Prospective applicants should send a two-page letter to the foundation.
Application Requirements: The letter of inquiry should include reason for the grant, pertinent financial statements, and a copy of the IRS 501(c)(3) tax-exempt status letter.
Deadlines: Proposals should be submitted by March 15 and September 15.

Restrictions

Grants are generally not made to fraternal organizations or to political or lobbying groups, or for special projects and/or events. Limited to the Delaware and Southern Chester County, PA area.

Additional Information

About 10% of the grantees in any given year are first-time recipients of foundation aid.

Foundation Officials

Gerret van Sweringen Copeland: trustee
David Leigh Craven: trustee B Winston-Salem, NC 1953. ED Davidson College BA (1975); Wake Forest University JD (1978). PRIM CORP EMPL senior vice president: BB & T Corp. CORP AFFIL senior vice president, secretary: Southern National Bank NC.
Edward Bradford du Pont: vice president, trustee B Wilmington, DE 1934. ED Yale University ED (1956); Harvard University MBA (1959). PRIM CORP EMPL chairman, director: Atlantic Aviation Corp. CORP AFFIL director: Wilmington Trust Co.; treasurer: Christiana Care Health Services; director: E.I. du Pont de Nemours & Co. NONPR AFFIL president: Eleutherian Mills-Hagley Foundation; treasurer: Wilmington Institute.
Stephen A. Martinenza: assistant secretary, assistant treasurer
Irenee du Pont May, Jr.: secretary, trustee
Peter C. Morrow: executive director PRIM CORP EMPL manager corporate contributions, executive secretary contributions committee: E.I. du Pont de Nemours & Co.
Hugh Rodney Sharp, III: president, trustee CORP AFFIL director: E.I. du Pont de Nemours & Co.
Henry Harper Silliman, Jr.: treasurer, trustee

Grants Analysis

Disclosure Period: fiscal year ending September 30, 2001
Total Grants: $32,712,076*
Number of Grants: 103 (approx)
Average Grant: $252,253*
Highest Grant: $6,982,300
Typical Range: $100,000 to $250,000
*Note: Giving excludes United Way. Average grant figure excludes highest grant.

Recent Grants

Note: Grants derived from fiscal 2001 Form 990.

Library-Related

100,000	Friends of the Milton Public Library, Milton, MA

General

6,982,300	Longwood Gardens, Kennett Square, PA
3,000,000	Sanford School, Hockessin, DE
2,000,000	Delaware Art Museum, Wilmington, DE
2,000,000	St. Anne's Episcopal School, Wilmington, DE
1,650,000	Campus Community School, Dover, DE
1,500,000	Jewish Federation of Delaware, Wilmington, DE
1,500,000	St. Francis Hospital, Wilmington, DE
1,500,000	Wilmington College, New Castle, DE
1,000,000	Chester County Hospital, West Chester, PA
1,000,000	Police Athletic League of Wilmington, Inc., Wilmington, DE

HARRY WILSON LOOSE TRUST

Giving Contact

Dalene Dradford
c/o Greater Kansas City Community Foundation
1010 Broadway, Suite 130
Kansas City, MO 64105
Phone: (816)842-0944
Fax: (816)842-0944
Web: http://www.gkccf.org

Description

Founded: 1927
EIN: 446009245
Organization Type: Private Foundation
Giving Locations: MO: Kansas City
Grant Types: Project, Research.

Donor Information

Founder: the late Harry Wilson Loose

Financial Summary

Total Giving: $250,602 (2000); $239,209 (1999); $226,121 (1998)
Giving Analysis: Giving for 1998 includes: foundation matching gifts ($10,000) foundation ($216,121)
Assets: $6,756,168 (2000); $7,417,105 (1999); $6,651,632 (1998)

Typical Recipients

Arts & Humanities: Arts Outreach, Libraries, Music
Civic & Public Affairs: Community Foundations, Economic Development, Nonprofit Management, Urban & Community Affairs, Zoos/Aquariums
Education: Business Education, Colleges & Universities, Community & Junior Colleges, Education Funds, Faculty Development, Education-General, International Exchange, Minority Education, Public Education (Precollege)
Environment: Environment-General
Health: Cancer, Clinics/Medical Centers, Health Organizations, Hospitals, Kidney, Public Health
Religion: Religious Welfare
Social Services: Child Welfare, Community Centers, Community Service Organizations, Day Care, Family Services, Recreation & Athletics, United Funds/ United Ways, Youth Organizations

Application Procedures

Initial Contact: Request grant guidelines.
Deadlines: Applications must be received four months prior to full board meetings.
Review Process: Board meets in March, June, September, and December.
Decision Notification: Decisions are made within two weeks of board meeting.

Restrictions

Does not support individuals or provide funds for general support, matching gifts, or scholarships.

Additional Information

Publications: Annual Report; Application Guidelines
Trust(s): Bank of America, N.A.

Foundation Officials

Donald Herbert Chisholm: trustee B Kansas City, MO September 25, 1917. ED Kansas City Junior College AA (1935); University of Missouri JD (1938); Park College LLD (1979). PRIM CORP EMPL officer counsel: Stinson, Mag & Fizzell PC. CORP AFFIL director: Kansas City Bridge Co. NONPR AFFIL director: Truman Medical Center; trustee: University Kansas City; trustee: Harry South Truman Library Institute; trustee: Saint Lukes Hospital Foundation; trustee: Victor East & Caroline East Schuttle Foundation; trustee emeritus: Park College; trustee: Midwest Research Institute; member: Order Coif; trustee: Mag Foundation; trustee: Illa C & Jacob Loose Foundation; trustee: Harry Wilson Loose Trust; member: Kansas City Bar Association; member: Lawyers Association Kansas City; chairman: Childrens Mercy Hospital; fellow: American College Trust & Estate Counsel; member: American Judicature Society; member: American Bar Association; fellow: American Bar Foundation. CLUB AFFIL Mission Hills Country Club; University Club.

Grants Analysis

Disclosure Period: calendar year ending 2000
Total Grants: $250,602
Number of Grants: 7
Highest Grant: $30,000
Lowest Grant: $5,000
Typical Range: $10,000 to $20,000

Recent Grants

Note: Grants derived from 2001 Form 990.

General

100,000	Swope Parkway Health Center, Kansas City, MO
82,804	Greater Kansas City Community Foundation, Kansas City, MO
10,000	Greater Kansas City Sports Commission and Foundation, Kansas City, MO -- national events and membership
10,000	Learning Exchange, Kansas City, MO -- support charter school evaluation study

L'OREAL U.S.A.

Company Headquarters

575 5th Avenue, Suite 14
New York, NY 10017
Web: http://www.lancome.com

Company Description

Employees: 585
SIC(s): 2844 Toilet Preparations.
Parent Company: L'Oreal SA, 41 rue Martre, Clichy, France

Operating Locations

Bivona (IN--Gary); Cosmair, Inc. (NY--New York); Cosmair, Ralph Lauren Fragrance Division (NY--New York); ELA Medical (MN--Minnetonka); Galderma Laboratories (TX--Fort Worth); Maybelline (TN--Memphis); Parbel (FL--Miami); Sylamerica (NY--Tarrytown); Yardley of London (TN--Memphis)

Nonmonetary Support

Type: Donated Products

Giving Contact

Susan Davidowitz, Vice President, Corporate Public Relations
575 5th Ave., 33rd Floor
New York, NY 10017
Phone: (212)984-4105
Fax: (212)984-4150

Description

Organization Type: Corporate Giving Program
Giving Locations: NY: New York including metropolitan area and New Jersey

Financial Summary

Total Giving: Company does not disclose contributions figures.

Typical Recipients

Arts & Humanities: Dance, Ethnic & Folk Arts, Arts & Humanities-General, Historic Preservation, Libraries, Literary Arts, Museums/Galleries, Music, Opera, Performing Arts, Public Broadcasting, Theater, Visual Arts
Civic & Public Affairs: Civic & Public Affairs-General, Housing, Philanthropic Organizations, Urban & Community Affairs
Education: Education-General
Health: Health-General, Hospitals, Medical Research, Nursing Services, Single-Disease Health Associations
Religion: Churches, Religion-General, Missionary Activities (Domestic), Religious Organizations, Synagogues/Temples
Science: Science-General
Social Services: Animal Protection, Child Welfare, Emergency Relief, Senior Services, Shelters/Homelessness, Social Services-General, Substance Abuse, United Funds/United Ways, Volunteer Services, Youth Organizations

Application Procedures

Initial Contact: Send a brief letter of inquiry.
Application Requirements: Include a description of organization, amount requested, and purpose of funds sought.

Restrictions

Does not support individuals or political or lobbying groups.

Corporate Officials

Jean-Paul Agon: president, chief executive officer, director PRIM CORP EMPL president, chief executive officer, director: L'Oreal USA Inc.
Roger Dolden: chief financial officer PRIM CORP EMPL chief financial officer: Cosmair.
Mr. Lindsay Owen-Jones: chairman, director PRIM CORP EMPL chairman, director: Cosmair.
Michel Somnolet: chief operating officer, director, executive, vice president B Chateaurenault, France 1940. ED Faculte de Droit et Science Economique; Paris Law School (1963); Hautes Etudes Commerciales MBA (1964). PRIM CORP EMPL chief operating officer, director, executive, vice president: Cosmair Inc. CORP AFFIL director: France-Growth Fund. NONPR AFFIL member: French Chamber of Commerce New York; member: French Reserve Officers United States of America; director: Chevalier de la Legion d'Honneur. CLUB AFFIL Millbrook Country Club; Paris American Club; CYCL de Saint Briac; Mashomack Club.

Grants Analysis

Typical Range: $1,000 to $5,000

MARY AND DANIEL LOUGHRAN FOUNDATION

Giving Contact
F. William Burke, Executive Director & Secretary
NationsBank Trust Co.
601 13th St. NW, Ste. 1000
Washington, DC 20005
Phone: (202)434-7005
Fax: (202)347-4866

Alternate Contact
Tawawna Williams, Grant Coordinator

Description
Founded: 1967
EIN: 521095883
Organization Type: General Purpose Foundation
Giving Locations: DC; MD; VA
Grant Types: Operating Expenses.

Donor Information
Founder: Incorporated in 1967 by the late John Loughran .

Financial Summary
Total Giving: $883,900 (fiscal year ending July 31, 2002); $819,900 (fiscal 2001); $754,650 (fiscal 1999)
Giving Analysis: Giving for fiscal 1999 includes: foundation matching gifts ($5,000) foundation scholarships ($162,500)
Assets: $12,937,202 (fiscal 2002); $17,010,011 (fiscal 2001); $17,165,678 (fiscal 1999)

Typical Recipients
Arts & Humanities: Arts Centers, Dance, Historic Preservation, History & Archaeology, Libraries, Museums/Galleries, Music, Performing Arts, Theater
Civic & Public Affairs: Community Foundations, Civic & Public Affairs-General, Housing, Law & Justice, Nonprofit Management, Philanthropic Organizations, Public Policy, Safety, Urban & Community Affairs, Women's Affairs
Education: Agricultural Education, Arts/Humanities Education, Business Education, Colleges & Universities, Education Funds, Elementary Education (Public), Engineering/Technological Education, Education-General, International Studies, Legal Education, Medical Education, Minority Education, Private Education (Precollege), Religious Education, Science/Mathematics Education, Secondary Education (Private), Special Education, Student Aid
Health: Adolescent Health Issues, Cancer, Children's Health/Hospitals, Clinics/Medical Centers, Emergency/Ambulance Services, Eyes/Blindness, Heart, Hospitals, Long-Term Care, Medical Rehabilitation, Medical Research, Prenatal Health Issues, Single-Disease Health Associations
International: International Affairs
Religion: Churches, Dioceses, Religious Welfare, Seminaries
Science: Scientific Centers & Institutes
Social Services: At-Risk Youth, Community Service Organizations, Crime Prevention, Family Planning, Family Services, Food/Clothing Distribution, Homes, People with Disabilities, Recreation & Athletics, Scouts, Senior Services, Sexual Abuse, Shelters/Homelessness, Youth Organizations

Application Procedures
Initial Contact: Applicants should submit a brief letter
Application Requirements: The letter should state the purpose of your organization, the specific amount requested, the use of the grant, IRS certification of tax-exempt status, financial reports, and list of directors and officers.
Deadlines: May 1.
Review Process: All grant requests are considered by the board during the July meeting.

Restrictions
The foundation does not make grants to individuals or for capital, endowment funds, or loans.

Additional Information
Trust(s): NationsBank Trust Co.

Foundation Officials
Richard K.A. Becker: assistant secretary PRIM CORP EMPL executive vice president: James Madison Mortgage.
F. William Burke: director, secretary
Walter Robert Fatzinger, Jr.: director B Northampton, PA 1942. ED George Washington University (1965); American University (1970). PRIM CORP EMPL president: Security Trust Co. NA.
Carl L. Gell: director
John T. Hazel, Jr.: director B 1930. ED Harvard University BA (1951); University of Virginia (1951-1952); Harvard University LLB (1954). PRIM CORP EMPL chairman, partner: Hazel & Thomas ADD CORP EMPL president: Flint Hill School.
A. Linwood Holton, Jr.: director B Big Stone Gap, VA 1923. ED Washington & Lee University BA (1944); Harvard University LLB (1949); Virginia State College LLD (1971); Virginia Union University LLD (1972); Washington & Lee University LLD (1972); College of William & Mary LLD (1973). PRIM CORP EMPL partner: Mezzulo & McCandlish. CORP AFFIL director: Interstate Railroad Co. NONPR AFFIL member: Virginia Bar Association; member: Virginia State Bar; member: Roanoke Bar Association; chairman: University Virginia Burket Miller Center Public Affairs; member: District of Columbia Bar Association; member: Omicron Delta Kappa; member: American Bar Association.
M. Langhorne Keith: assistant secretary B Washington, DC 1936. ED University of Virginia BA (1958); University of Virginia JD (1970). PRIM CORP EMPL lawyer: Hogan & Hartson. NONPR AFFIL member: Raven Society; member: Virginia Bar Association; member: District of Columbia Bar Association. CLUB AFFIL member: Omicron Delta Kappa.
R. Robert Linowes: director
Joseph L. Whyte: director

Grants Analysis
Disclosure Period: fiscal year ending July 31, 2002
Total Grants: $883,900
Number of Grants: 85
Average Grant: $10,399
Highest Grant: $40,000
Lowest Grant: $2,500
Typical Range: $5,000 to $20,000

Recent Grants
Note: Grants derived from 2001 Form 990.

General
40,000	Corcoran, Washington, DC -- for the Gallery of Art
30,000	University of Maryland Foundation, Adelphi, MD -- for financial aid to Historically Black Institutions
30,000	University of Virginia Fund, Charlottesville, VA -- for scholarship fund
20,000	Children's National Medical Center, Washington, DC -- for New Horizons program
20,000	Community Foundation for the National Capital Region, Washington, DC -- support for Community Foundation National Capital Region
20,000	Paramount Theater Community Center, Charlottesville, VA
20,000	Phillips Collection, Washington, DC -- for special exhibitions, lecturers, concerns, etc.
15,000	Keswick Equestrian Foundation, Keswick, VA -- to help provide medical care to individuals who do not have medical insurance coverage
15,000	Randolph Macon Academy, Front Royal, VA -- to support this school which promotes a moral character, discipline and leadership training
10,000	American University Washington College of Law, Washington, DC -- for video server

LOUISIANA-PACIFIC CORP.

Company Headquarters
111 Southwest 5th Ave., Ste. 4200
Portland, OR 97204

Company Description
Ticker: LPX
Exchange: OTC
Employees: 12,000 (1999)
SIC(s): 2421 Sawmills & Planing Mills--General, 2431 Millwork, 2435 Hardwood Veneer & Plywood, 2436 Softwood Veneer & Plywood.

Operating Locations
Louisiana-Pacific Corp. (AL--Clayton, Evergreen, Hanceville, Lockhart; CA, Chino, Cloverdale, Fort Bragg, Ontario, Oroville, Red Bluff, Rocklin, Samoa, Santa Rosa, Willits; CO--Kremmling; FL--Baker, Cypress, Panama City, Port St. Joe; GA--Athens, Eatonton, Greensboro, Statesboro; ID--Hayden, Moyie Springs, Post Falls, Priest River, Sandpoint; IL--Schaumburg; LA--Alexandria, Bernice, Logansport, Urania; ME--New Limerick; MI--Newberry; MS--Philadelphia, Purvis; MT--Belgrade, Deer Lodge, Missoula; NV--Fernley; NC--Henderson, Nashville, Pittsboro, Wilmington; OH--Bucyrus, Orrville, Winesburg, Youngstown; OR--Hillsboro, Lake Oswego; PA--Hanover; RI--East Providence; SC--West Union; TX; WA--Walla Walla; WI--Hayward, Mellen, Tomahawk)

Nonmonetary Support
Type: Donated Equipment; Donated Products
Note: Co. provides some nonmonetary support.

Louisiana-Pacific Foundation

Giving Contact
Kim Miller
111 Southwest Fifth Avenue
Portland, OR 97204
Phone: (503)221-0800
Fax: (503)821-5322

Alternate Contact
Phone: (503)821-5326

Description
EIN: 237268660
Organization Type: Corporate Foundation
Giving Locations: primarily headquarters and operating communities.
Grant Types: Capital, Emergency, General Support, Project, Scholarship.
Note: Scholarships are for dependents of employees.

Financial Summary
Total Giving: $116,325 (2000); $173,275 (1998); $459,909 (1997). Note: Contributes through corporate direct giving program and foundation. Giving includes foundation.
Giving Analysis: Giving for 2000 includes: foundation scholarships ($116,325)
Assets: $33,709 (2000); $13,951 (1998); $42,603 (1997)

Gifts Received: $150,000 (2000); $150,000 (1998); $475,000 (1997). Note: In 1997, contributions were received from Louisiana-Pacific Corp. ($475,000). In 1994, the foundation received contributions from Louisiana-Pacific Corp. and Ketchikan Pulp Co.

Typical Recipients

Arts & Humanities: Arts Centers, Ballet, History & Archaeology, Libraries, Museums/Galleries, Music, Opera, Performing Arts, Theater

Civic & Public Affairs: Botanical Gardens/Parks, Business/Free Enterprise, Community Foundations, Civic & Public Affairs-General, Housing, Municipalities/Towns, Public Policy, Urban & Community Affairs, Zoos/Aquariums

Education: Afterschool/Enrichment Programs, Business Education, Colleges & Universities, Community & Junior Colleges, Education Funds, Education-General, Leadership Training, Literacy, Minority Education, Private Education (Precollege), Public Education (Precollege), Religious Education, Science/Mathematics Education, Secondary Education (Private), Secondary Education (Public), Student Aid

Environment: Forestry, Environment-General, Wildlife Protection

Health: Cancer, Children's Health/Hospitals, Emergency/Ambulance Services, Health Organizations, Heart, Hospices, Hospitals, Medical Research, Prenatal Health Issues, Public Health, Single-Disease Health Associations

International: Foreign Educational Institutions, Health Care/Hospitals, International Development, International Environmental Issues, International Organizations, International Relief Efforts

Religion: Ministries, Religious Organizations, Religious Welfare

Science: Science Exhibits & Fairs, Science Museums

Social Services: At-Risk Youth, Child Welfare, Community Service Organizations, Emergency Relief, Family Services, Food/Clothing Distribution, Homes, People with Disabilities, Recreation & Athletics, Scouts, Shelters/Homelessness, Special Olympics, Substance Abuse, United Funds/United Ways, YMCA/YWCA/YMHA/YWHA, Youth Organizations

Application Procedures

Initial Contact: Send a brief letter or for scholarships complete an application form.

Application Requirements: Include a description of organization, amount requested, purpose of funds sought, recently audited financial statement, and proof of tax-exempt status. For scholarship include a transcript of grades.

Deadlines: None, for grants; April 15 for scholarships.

Review Process: Trustees review all applications at quarterly meetings.

Evaluative Criteria: For scholarships: academic achievement and potential; specific aptitudes, as indicated by special interests and as appraised by faculty members; desire to continue education; character and promise of future contribution to society; record of leadership in extracurricular and school affairs; use of spare time after school, on Saturday and during summer vacation periods; and financial need; applicant must be a dependent of an employee of Louisiana-Pacific, who has worked at the company for at least three years.

Decision Notification: Applicants will be notified by June.

Foundation Officials

Mark A. Suwyn: chairman, president B Denver, CO 1942. ED Hope College BS (1964); Washington State University PhD (1967). PRIM CORP EMPL chairman, chief executive officer, director: Louisiana - Pacific Corp. CORP AFFIL director: Scitex Corp. Ltd.; Shareholder Fitness Mania Inc.

Grants Analysis

Disclosure Period: calendar year ending 2000
Total Grants: $116,325*
Number of Grants: 83

Average Grant: $1,401
Highest Grant: $2,250
Lowest Grant: $750
Typical Range: $500 to $15,000
*Note: Giving includes scholarship.

Recent Grants

Note: Grants derived from 2000 Form 990.

General

2,250	Pacific University, Forest Grove, OR
2,250	Walsh University, Canton, OH
1,500	Alabama A & M University, Birmingham, AL
1,500	Alma College, Alma, MI
1,500	Alpena Community College, Alpena, MI
1,500	Alpena Community College, Alpena, MI
1,500	California State University, Los Angeles, CA
1,500	Georgia Southern University, Statesboro, GA
1,500	Humboldt State University, Arcata, CA
1,500	Humboldt State University, Arcata, CA

LOUTIT FOUNDATION

Giving Contact

c/o Michigan National Bank
PO Box 1707
Grand Rapids, MI 49501-1707
Phone: (616)451-7736

Description

Founded: 1957
EIN: 386053445
Organization Type: Private Foundation
Giving Locations: MI
Grant Types: Capital, Emergency, Endowment, General Support, Project, Seed Money.

Donor Information

Founder: the late William R. Loutit

Financial Summary

Total Giving: $250,802 (fiscal year ending June 30, 2001); $250,802 (fiscal 2000); $149,480 (fiscal 1999)
Assets: $1,124,195 (fiscal 2001); $1,124,195 (fiscal 2000); $1,222,472 (fiscal 1999)
Gifts Received: $136,265 (fiscal 2001); $136,265 (fiscal 2000); $126,100 (fiscal 1999). Note: In fiscal 1996, 1999, 2000, and 2001, contributions were received from the William Loutit Memorial.

Typical Recipients

Arts & Humanities: Arts Associations & Councils, Libraries, Museums/Galleries, Music, Public Broadcasting, Theater

Civic & Public Affairs: Community Foundations, Economic Development, Civic & Public Affairs-General, Housing, Municipalities/Towns, Parades/Festivals, Philanthropic Organizations, Urban & Community Affairs

Education: Colleges & Universities, Community & Junior Colleges, Education Associations, Education Funds, Education-General, Medical Education, Minority Education, Private Education (Precollege), Public Education (Precollege)

Health: Cancer, Emergency/Ambulance Services, Health Policy/Cost Containment, Health Organizations, Hospices, Hospitals, Public Health

International: International Relief Efforts

Religion: Churches, Ministries, Religious Organizations, Religious Welfare

Social Services: Animal Protection, Camps, Child Welfare, Community Centers, Community Service Organizations, Scouts, Senior Services, United Funds/United Ways, YMCA/YWCA/YMHA/YWHA, Youth Organizations

Application Procedures

Initial Contact: Send brief letter describing program. Include any information deemed relevant to the request, amount requested, and proof of tax-exempt status. Further information may be requested.
Deadlines: None.

Restrictions

Does not support individuals.

Additional Information

Publications: Biennial Report
Trust(s): MI Natl Bank

Foundation Officials

Thomas Boven: vice president
Kennard Creason: trustee
Jon W. Eshleman: president
Bari Johnson: trustee
Bonnie Kopp: secretary, treasurer
C. Christopher Worfel: secretary, treasurer

Grants Analysis

Disclosure Period: fiscal year ending June 30, 2001
Total Grants: $250,802
Number of Grants: 52
Average Grant: $3,937*
Highest Grant: $50,000
Typical Range: $1,000 to $10,000
*Note: Average grant figure excludes highest grant.

Recent Grants

Note: Grants derived from fiscal 2000 Form 990.

General

36,500	Tri - Cities Area Habitat for Humanity, Grand Haven, MI
25,000	Ottawa Area/ Intermediate School District, MI
17,500	Tri - Cities Area United Fund, Grand Haven, MI
10,000	Michigan Colleges Foundation, Southfield, MI
10,000	Olivet College, Olivet, MI
5,000	Civic Theatre, Grand Rapids, MI
5,000	Council of Michigan Foundations, Lansing, MI
5,000	South Haven Maritime Museum, South Haven, MI
5,000	Spring Lake Presbyterian Church, Spring Lake, MI
4,200	Grand Haven Area Community Foundation, Grand Haven, MI

GEORGE H. AND MARGARET MCCLINTIC LOVE FOUNDATION

Giving Contact

Helen Collins, Trust Officer
c/o Mellon Bank NA
1 Mellon Bank Center, Rm. 3815
Pittsburgh, PA 15258
Phone: (412)234-4695

Description

Founded: 1952
EIN: 256018655
Organization Type: Private Foundation
Giving Locations: nationally.
Grant Types: Capital, General Support.

Donor Information

Founder: George H. Love

Financial Summary

Total Giving: $712,500 (2001); $667,500 (2000); $1,032,500 (1999)
Giving Analysis: Giving for 2001 includes: foundation grants to United Way ($30,000) 1999: foundation grants to United Way ($35,000)
Assets: $6,186,986 (2001); $7,206,573 (2000); $7,515,301 (1999)
Gifts Received: $52,558 (2001); $56,967 (2000); $56,967 (1996). Note: In 1996, 2000, and 2001, contributions were received from the Charitable Trust No. 2.

Typical Recipients

Arts & Humanities: Arts Associations & Councils, Community Arts, Libraries, Music, Opera
Civic & Public Affairs: Civic & Public Affairs-General, Urban & Community Affairs, Women's Affairs
Education: Arts/Humanities Education, Colleges & Universities, Education Funds, Education-General, Private Education (Precollege), Public Education (Precollege), Religious Education, Science/Mathematics Education
Environment: Environment-General
Health: Children's Health/Hospitals, Clinics/Medical Centers, Hospices, Hospitals, Medical Research, Mental Health, Nursing Services, Single-Disease Health Associations
International: International Relations, International Relief Efforts
Religion: Churches, Religious Welfare
Social Services: Camps, Child Welfare, Community Service Organizations, Domestic Violence, Emergency Relief, Family Services, Food/Clothing Distribution, People with Disabilities, Shelters/Homelessness, Substance Abuse, United Funds/United Ways, YMCA/YWCA/YMHA/YWHA, Youth Organizations

Application Procedures

Initial Contact: Send a brief letter of inquiry describing program.
Deadlines: None.

Additional Information

Trust(s): Mellon Bank NA

Foundation Officials

Howard McClintic Love: director B Pittsburgh, PA 1930. ED Colgate University (1952); Harvard University Graduate School of Business Administration (1956). CORP AFFIL director: COMSAT Corp.; director: Monsanto Co.; director: AEA Investors Inc. CLUB AFFIL Pittsburgh Golf Club; Rolling Rock Club; The Links Club; Masons Club; Colony Club; Fox Chapel Golf Club.

Grants Analysis

Disclosure Period: calendar year ending 2001
Total Grants: $682,500*
Number of Grants: 26
Average Grant: $16,630*
Highest Grant: $200,000
Lowest Grant: $2,000
Typical Range: $7,500 to $30,000
*Note: Giving excludes United Way. Average grant excludes two highest grants ($300,000).

Recent Grants

Note: Grants derived from 2001 Form 990.

General

200,000	Shady Lane School, Pittsburgh, PA -- educational
38,000	Phillips Exeter Academy, Exeter, NH -- educational
35,000	Pittsburgh Opera, Pittsburgh, PA -- for public assistance

34,000	Little Sisters of the Assumption Family Center, New York, NY -- for family counseling
34,000	Westminister Choir College, Princeton, NJ -- religious
30,000	Greater Pittsburgh Chapter of National Parkinson Foundation, Pittsburgh, PA -- medical
30,000	Horizon Hospice, Chicago, IL -- for medical assistance
30,000	United Way of Allegheny County, Pittsburgh, PA -- for public assistance
25,000	Pitzer College, Claremont, CA -- educational
25,000	Winnie Palmer Nature Rescue, Latrobe, PA -- for public assistance

LOWE FAMILY FOUNDATION

Giving Contact

John W. Yates, CPA
228 East Primrose
Springfield, MO 65807-5206
Phone: (417)883-8176

Description

Founded: 1999
EIN: 431799494
Organization Type: Private Foundation
Grant Types: General Support.

Financial Summary

Total Giving: $116,840 (fiscal year ending September 30, 2001); $313,558 (fiscal 2000); $65,000 (fiscal 1999)
Assets: $878,267 (fiscal 2001); $1,313,699 (fiscal 2000); $1,255,356 (fiscal 1999)
Gifts Received: $38,000 (fiscal 2000). Note: In 2000, contributions were received from Derrick and Sonja Lowe.

Typical Recipients

Arts & Humanities: Libraries, Public Broadcasting
Environment: Air/Water Quality
International: International Environmental Issues, International Peace & Security Issues, Missionary/Religious Activities
Religion: Churches, Missionary Activities (Domestic), Religious Organizations, Religious Welfare
Social Services: Child Welfare, Family Planning, Food/Clothing Distribution, Homes

Foundation Officials

Derrick C. Lowe: vice president
Kimberly Lowe Root: secretary

Grants Analysis

Disclosure Period: fiscal year ending September 30, 2001
Total Grants: $116,840
Number of Grants: 12
Average Grant: $8,804*
Highest Grant: $20,000
Lowest Grant: $540
Typical Range: $5,000 to $15,000
*Note: Average grant figure excludes highest grant.

Recent Grants

Note: Grants derived from fiscal 2000 Form 990.

Library-Related

10,000	Lebanon Public Library, Lebanon, MO -- library project

General

50,000	Life Outreach International, Ft. Worth, TX -- Sudan crisis

34,000	New Tribes Mission, Sanford, FL -- support of missionaries
25,200	Life Outreach International, Ft. Worth, TX -- to provide fresh water wells for seven people in Africa
25,000	Baptist Charities St. Louis, Bridgeton, MO -- Missouri Baptist Children's Home water tower project
25,000	Special Care Homes, Lee's Summit, MO -- providing housing for unwed mothers
20,658	First Baptist Church, Lebanon, MO -- missionary work in Ethiopia Amhara and gulf Arab countries
20,000	Fellowship Christian Athletes, Springfield, MO
15,000	Vitae Society, The, Jefferson City, MO -- benefit of children
14,000	First Baptist Church, Lebanon, MO -- missionary couple in Chicago
13,000	First Baptist Church, Lebanon, MO

JOE AND EMILY LOWE FOUNDATION

Giving Contact

Ellen Liman, President
249 Royal Palm Way, Suite 502
Palm Beach, FL 33480
Fax: (561)655-7130

Description

Founded: 1949
EIN: 136121361
Organization Type: Family Foundation
Giving Locations: FL: Palm Beach; NY: New York metropolitan area
Grant Types: Challenge, Conference/Seminar, General Support, Matching, Multiyear/Continuing Support, Operating Expenses, Project, Research.

Financial Summary

Total Giving: $1,800,000 (1999); $1,802,000 (1998); $1,499,600 (1997)
Assets: $32,500,659 (1999); $33,514,906 (1998); $29,496,332 (1997)

Typical Recipients

Arts & Humanities: Arts Associations & Councils, Arts Centers, Arts Funds, Arts Outreach, Ballet, Dance, Ethnic & Folk Arts, Film & Video, History & Archaeology, Libraries, Museums/Galleries, Music, Opera, Performing Arts, Public Broadcasting, Theater, Visual Arts
Civic & Public Affairs: Civil Rights, Civic & Public Affairs-General, Legal Aid, Professional & Trade Associations, Safety, Urban & Community Affairs, Women's Affairs
Education: Arts/Humanities Education, Business Education, Colleges & Universities, Community & Junior Colleges, Education Reform, Faculty Development, Education-General, Legal Education, Literacy, Medical Education, Minority Education, Private Education (Precollege), Public Education (Precollege), Special Education, Student Aid
Environment: Environment-General, Resource Conservation
Health: Cancer, Children's Health/Hospitals, Clinics/Medical Centers, Emergency/Ambulance Services, Eyes/Blindness, Heart, Hospices, Hospitals, Kidney, Medical Rehabilitation, Mental Health, Single-Disease Health Associations
International: Foreign Arts Organizations, Foreign Educational Institutions, Human Rights
Religion: Jewish Causes, Religious Welfare, Social/Policy Issues, Synagogues/Temples
Social Services: Animal Protection, Child Welfare, Community Service Organizations, Emergency Relief, Family Planning, Family Services, Food/Clothing

Distribution, Homes, People with Disabilities, Social Services-General, Substance Abuse, YMCA/YWCA/YMHA/YWHA, Youth Organizations

Application Procedures

Initial Contact: Applicants should submit a letter.
Application Requirements: A brief description and need for the proposed project or activity; objectives; timetable; overall costs; amount requested from the foundation; the status of additional support; a project budget, including projected revenue and expenses; current annual operating budget; list of governing body and officers; IRS letter determining tax-exempt status; most recent audited financial statements; and any relevant promotional publications.
Deadlines: None.
Review Process: Letters are generaly acknowledged within two months.

Restrictions

The foundation does not give grants to individuals or award scholarships, fellowships, loans, prizes, or similar benefits.

Additional Information

The foundation has a revolving presidency.

Foundation Officials

David Hauben: vice president, treasurer
Ellen Liman: president ED Barnard College BA (1957); New York School Interior Design (1959).
Henry Stern: vice president, secretary

Grants Analysis

Disclosure Period: calendar year ending 1999
Total Grants: $1,800,000
Number of Grants: 206
Average Grant: $8,738
Highest Grant: $100,000
Lowest Grant: $500
Typical Range: $1,000 to $35,000

Recent Grants

Note: Grants derived from 1999 Form 990.

Library-Related
12,500	Randall Library, Stow, MA
10,000	Darien Library, Darien, CT

General
100,000	United Jewish Appeal of South Palm Beach, New York, NY
50,000	Bascom Palmer Eye Institute, Miami, FL
50,000	Beth Israel Deaconess Medical Center, Boston, MA
50,000	Boca Raton Community Hospital, Boca Raton, FL
50,000	Creative Capital Foundation, New York, NY
50,000	United Jewish Appeal of Bergen County, River Edge, NJ
35,000	WGBH Educational Foundation, Boston, MA
30,000	American Federation of the Arts, New York, NY
30,000	Jewish Museum, New York, NY
25,000	Ascent Funding Organization, Inc., Muttontown, NY

LEON LOWENSTEIN FOUNDATION

Giving Contact

Robert Austin Bendheim, President
126 East 56th Street, 28th Floor
New York, NY 10022
Phone: (212)319-0670
Fax: (212)319-0670

Description

Founded: 1941
EIN: 136015951
Organization Type: General Purpose Foundation
Giving Locations: NY: New York metropolitan area
Grant Types: General Support.

Donor Information

Founder: The foundation was established in 1941, with the late Leon Lowenstein as donor. Mr. Lowenstein's fortune stemmed from M. Lowenstein Corporation, a textile firm, now a subsidiary of Springs Industries.

Financial Summary

Total Giving: $9,631,592 (2000); $7,400,000 (1999 approx); $5,986,250 (1998)
Giving Analysis: Giving for 2000 includes: foundation grants to United Way ($25,000)
Assets: $181,026,560 (2000); $174,000,000 (1999 approx); $175,623,211 (1998)
Gifts Received: $2,441,585 (1992)

Typical Recipients

Arts & Humanities: Arts Associations & Councils, History & Archaeology, Libraries, Museums/Galleries, Music, Performing Arts, Public Broadcasting
Civic & Public Affairs: Botanical Gardens/Parks, Economic Development, Civic & Public Affairs-General, Housing, Municipalities/Towns, Nonprofit Management, Philanthropic Organizations, Public Policy, Zoos/Aquariums
Education: Arts/Humanities Education, Business Education, Colleges & Universities, Community & Junior Colleges, Education Reform, Elementary Education (Private), Elementary Education (Public), Engineering/Technological Education, Faculty Development, Education-General, International Studies, Leadership Training, Literacy, Medical Education, Minority Education, Private Education (Precollege), Public Education (Precollege), Special Education, Student Aid
Environment: Air/Water Quality, Wildlife Protection
Health: Arthritis, Cancer, Children's Health/Hospitals, Clinics/Medical Centers, Emergency/Ambulance Services, Eyes/Blindness, Health Organizations, Hospitals, Medical Rehabilitation, Medical Research, Mental Health, Nursing Services, Single-Disease Health Associations
International: Health Care/Hospitals, International Development, International Peace & Security Issues
Religion: Jewish Causes, Religious Welfare
Science: Science Museums
Social Services: At-Risk Youth, Big Brother/Big Sister, Child Welfare, Community Centers, Community Service Organizations, Emergency Relief, Family Services, Food/Clothing Distribution, People with Disabilities, Recreation & Athletics, Scouts, Social Services-General, Substance Abuse, United Funds/United Ways, Volunteer Services, YMCA/YWCA/YMHA/YWHA, Youth Organizations

Application Procedures

Initial Contact: Applications should be in letter form.
Deadlines: None.
Evaluative Criteria: Applications from the New York City area are given preference.

Foundation Officials

John M. Bendheim, Jr.: director
John M. Bendheim: vice president, director B New York, NY June 18, 1918. PRIM CORP EMPL director: M. Lowenstein Corp.
Robert Austin Bendheim: president, director B New York, NY August 05, 1916. ED Princeton University AB (1937); Harvard University (1942). PRIM CORP EMPL director: M. Lowenstein Corp. NONPR AFFIL member national campaign committee: Princeton University; director: United Way New York City; member education committee: New York City Partnership; trustee: Mount Sinai Hospital. CLUB AFFIL Union

League Club; Round Hill Club; Stanwich Club; Princeton Club; Century Club; Lyford Cay Club.
Lynn Bendheim-Thoman: director
Bernard R. Rapaport: secretary, treasurer B New York, NY 1919. ED Cornell University (1939); Cornell University JD (1941). PRIM CORP EMPL secretary, treasurer, general counsel, director: M. Lowenstein Corp.
John Frederic Van Gorder: executive director B Jacksonville, FL 1943. ED Dover College (1961); Dartmouth College AB (1965); United States Air Force Institute of Technology (1967-1968); George Washington University MS (1973); Fordham University School of Law JD (1981). NONPR AFFIL advisory committee: Toshiba American Foundation; member: U.S. Jaycees; member: Society Mayflower Descendants; member: Sons American Revolution; member: New Jersey Bar Association; member: New York City Jaycees; member: International Jaycees; member: American Bar Association; member: District of Columbia Jaycees; member: Alpha Delta Phi. CLUB AFFIL Masons Club; Toastmasters Club; Lions Club.

Grants Analysis

Disclosure Period: calendar year ending 2000
Total Grants: $9,606,592*
Number of Grants: 175
Average Grant: $39,778*
Highest Grant: $1,750,000
Lowest Grant: $400
Typical Range: $1,000 to $50,000
*Note: Giving excludes United Way. Grant figure excludes highest grant.

Recent Grants

Note: Grants derived from 2000 Form 990.

Library-Related
130,000	Greenwich Library, Greenwich, CT

General
1,750,000	Princeton University, Princeton, NJ
1,000,000	Mount Sinai Medical Center, New York, NY
500,000	Columbia University, New York, NY
500,000	Spence School, New York, NY
450,000	North Shore Long Island Jewish Health System Foundation, Great Neck, NY
250,000	Memorial Sloan-Kettering Cancer Center, New York, NY
250,000	University of Pennsylvania, Philadelphia, PA
150,000	Mount Sinai Medical Center, New York, NY
100,000	Columbia University Teachers College, New York, NY
100,000	Family Center, New York, NY

LOWE'S COMPANIES

Company Headquarters

North Wilkesboro, NC
Web: http://www.lowes.com

Company Description

Founded: 1957
Ticker: LOW
Exchange: NYSE
Revenue: US$26.491 billion (2002)
Profit: US$1.471 billion (2002)
Employees: 123000 (2002)
Fortune Rank: 60, per FORTUNE Magazine's list of 500 Largest U.S. Corporations (2002).
SIC(s): 5211 Lumber & Other Building Materials, 5251 Hardware Stores.

Operating Locations

Lowe's Companies (NC--North Wilkesboro)
Note: Company has 303 stores in 290 communities in 20 southeastern states.

Lowe's Charitable and Educational Foundation

Giving Contact

Marlowe Foster
Lowe's Companies
PO Box 1111
North Wilkesboro, NC 28656
Phone: (336)658-4221

Description

EIN: 566061689
Organization Type: Corporate Foundation
Giving Locations: headquarters and operating communities.
Grant Types: General Support.

Donor Information

Founder: Lowe's Companies, Inc.

Financial Summary

Total Giving: $1,177,996 (2001); $720,694 (2000); $912,953 (1998). Note: Fiscal 1997 Giving includes United Way ($2,000).
Giving Analysis: Giving for 2000 includes: foundation grants to United Way ($4,500); foundation ($716,194); 1998: foundation grants to United Way ($2,000) foundation ($910,952)
Assets: $1,168,433 (2001); $1,520,188 (2000); $845,222 (1998)
Gifts Received: $792,381 (2001); $1,414,249 (2000); $639,162 (1998). Note: In fiscal 2001, contributions were received from Lowe's Companies and Wilkes Educational Foundation. In fiscal 1998, contributions were received from Lowe's Companies and Thomas E. Whiddon.

Typical Recipients

Arts & Humanities: Arts & Humanities-General, Historic Preservation, Libraries
Civic & Public Affairs: Asian American Affairs, Clubs, Community Foundations, Economic Development, Civic & Public Affairs-General, Housing, Municipalities/Towns, Philanthropic Organizations, Public Policy, Safety, Urban & Community Affairs, Women's Affairs
Education: Arts/Humanities Education, Business Education, Colleges & Universities, Community & Junior Colleges, Elementary Education (Public), Engineering/Technological Education, Education-General, Medical Education, Public Education (Precollege), Secondary Education (Private), Secondary Education (Public), Student Aid, Vocational & Technical Education
Environment: Resource Conservation
Health: Cancer, Children's Health/Hospitals, Emergency/Ambulance Services, Health-General, Hospices, Hospitals
International: International Relief Efforts
Religion: Religion-General, Ministries, Religious Welfare
Social Services: At-Risk Youth, Big Brother/Big Sister, Community Service Organizations, Domestic Violence, Food/Clothing Distribution, People with Disabilities, Social Services-General, Special Olympics, Substance Abuse, United Funds/United Ways, YMCA/YWCA/YMHA/YWHA, Youth Organizations

Application Procedures

Initial Contact: All applications must be in written form.
Deadlines: None.
Notes: Grants will only be considered for qualified charitable and educational purposes.

Restrictions

Does not support individuals, religious organizations for sectarian purposes, political or lobbying groups, or organizations outside operating areas.

Corporate Officials

Robert L. Tillman: chairman, president, chief executive officer PRIM CORP EMPL chairman, president, chief executive officer: Lowes Companies.

Foundation Officials

Darryl K. Henderson: trustee
Leonard Gray Herring: vice president B Snow Hill, NC 1927. ED University of North Carolina BS (1948). CORP AFFIL member: Lowe's Companies Employee Stock Ownership Plan; director: First Union Corp. NONPR AFFIL trustee: Pfeiffer College; member, board visitors: University North Carolina; member board visitors: Davidson College; member: Chi Psi.
Perry G. Jennings: trustee
Petro Kulynych: chairman, treasurer B Smithmills, PA 1921. ED United States Merchant Marine Academy (1943); Kings Business College (1946). PRIM CORP EMPL founding director: Lowes Companies. CORP AFFIL director: Wachovia Bank & Trust Co. CLUB AFFIL mem: Shriners Club; mem: Elks Club.
N. Brian Peace: secretary
Dale C. Pond: trustee
Larry W. Stanley: treasurer
Larry D. Stone: chairman
Robert Louis Strickland: vice president B Florence, SC 1931. ED University of North Carolina BA (1952); Harvard University MBA (1957). PRIM CORP EMPL director, chairman: Lowes Companies. CORP AFFIL director: Summit Communication; director: Hannaford Brothers; director: T Rowe Price Associates. NONPR AFFIL member: Scabbard & Blade; trustee: University North Carolina Chapel Hill; member: Republican Senatorial Inner Circle; member: Phi Beta Kappa; member: Pi Kappa Alpha; member: National Association Over-the-Counter Companies; member: Newcomen Society; member: Employee Stock Ownership Association. CLUB AFFIL Roaring Gap Club; Twin City Club; Hound Ears Club; Piedmont City Club; Elk River Club; Forsyth Club.
William C. Warden, Jr.: secretary B Winchester, VA 1952. ED Wake Forest University (1974); Wake Forest University (1976). PRIM CORP EMPL senior vice president, secretary, general counsel: Lowes Companies.

Grants Analysis

Disclosure Period: calendar year ending 2001
Total Grants: $1,175,996*
Number of Grants: 175
Average Grant: $3,200*
Highest Grant: $372,105
Lowest Grant: $500
Typical Range: $1,000 to $10,000
*Note: Giving excludes United Way. Average grant figure excludes two highest grants ($622,105).

Recent Grants

Note: Grants derived from 2001 Form 990.

General

372,105	Town of Princeville, Princeville, QC Canada
250,000	YMCA of Greater Winston-Salem, Winston-Salem, NC
62,500	Wilkes Community College, Wilkesboro, NC
37,500	Wilkes Vision 20/20, Wilkes-Barre, PA
35,452	Town of Princeville, Princeville, QC Canada
25,000	Town of Princeville, Princeville, QC Canada
25,000	Winston-Salem Foundation, Winston-Salem, NC
20,000	Global Transpark Foundation, Kinston, NC
20,000	Ivy Tech Foundation, Indianapolis, IN
14,992	R.O. Nelson Elementary School

LSR FUND

Giving Contact

Clayton W. Frye, Jr., Trustee
LSR Fund
Care of Rockefeller Trust Co.
30 Rockefeller Plz., Rm. 5600
New York, NY 10112
Phone: (212)649-5979

Description

Founded: 1994
EIN: 137039108
Organization Type: Private Foundation
Giving Locations: nationally.
Grant Types: General Support.

Donor Information

Founder: Established in 1994 by Laurance S. Rockefeller.

Financial Summary

Total Giving: $1,963,933 (2001); $4,458,000 (1999); $1,055,137 (1997)
Assets: $27,390,633 (2001); $34,643,938 (1999); $23,103,458 (1997)
Gifts Received: $1,887,500 (1999); $1,000,000 (1997); $630,000 (1996). Note: In 1997 and 1999, contributions were received from from Laurance S. Rockefeller.

Typical Recipients

Arts & Humanities: Arts Associations & Councils, Ethnic & Folk Arts, Historic Preservation, History & Archaeology, Libraries, Public Broadcasting
Civic & Public Affairs: Civic & Public Affairs-General, Nonprofit Management, Parades/Festivals
Education: Arts/Humanities Education, Colleges & Universities, Education Reform, Legal Education
Environment: Environment-General, Protection, Resource Conservation, Wildlife Protection
Health: Health-General, Hospitals, Public Health, Single-Disease Health Associations
International: Foreign Arts Organizations
Religion: Religion-General
Science: Scientific Centers & Institutes
Social Services: Youth Organizations

Application Procedures

Initial Contact: Send a brief letter of inquiry.
Deadlines: None.

Foundation Officials

Clayton Wesley Frye, Jr.: trustee B Los Angeles, CA 1930. ED Stanford University AB (1953); Stanford University MBA (1959). PRIM CORP EMPL senior associate: Laurance S. Rockefeller. CORP AFFIL chairman: Woodstock Resort Corp.; director: Times Mirror Co.; partner: Rockefeller & Associates Realty; director: Tejon Ranch Co.; partner: Pacific Property Services; director: Colonial Williamsburg Hotel Properties Inc.; director: King Ranch Inc. NONPR AFFIL member: Urban Land Institute; trustee: White House Historical Association; trustee, chairman: Jackson Hole Preserve Inc.; trustee: Historic Hudson Valley.
Donal Clare O'Brien, Jr.: trustee B New York, NY 1934. ED Williams College BA (1956); University of Virginia LLB (1959). PRIM CORP EMPL partner: Milbank, Tweed, Hadley & McCloy. NONPR AFFIL trustee: Wendell Gilley Museum; trustee: Winthrop Rockefeller Charitable Trust; trustee: Trust Mutual Understanding; trustee: Waterfowl Research Foundation; chairman: Quebec Labrador Foundation; member council: Rockefeller University; trustee: North American Wildlife Foundation; trustee: JDR 3rd Fund; chairman: National Audubon Society; member: Council Environmental Quality; board directors: Greenacre Foundation; trustee: American Bird Conservancy;

chairman board directors: Atlantic Salmon Federation. CLUB AFFIL mem: Century Association Anglers Club.

Ellen R.C. Pomeroy: trustee

Laurance Spelman Rockefeller: trustee B New York, NY 1910. ED Princeton University BA (1932). CORP AFFIL chairman: Woodstock Resort Corp.; director: SKI Realty Inc. NONPR AFFIL life trustee: Wildlife Conservation Society; honorary director: Woodstock Foundation; trustee emeritus: Princeton University; honorary director: National Wildflower Center; commissioner emeritus: Palisades Interstate Park Comm; honorary trustee: National Geographic Society; life member: Massachusetts Institute Technology; honorary chairman: Memorial Sloan-Kettering Cancer Center; trustee, chairman emeritus: Jackson Hole Preserve Inc.; honorary chairman: American Conservation Association; chairman: Historic Hudson Valley. CLUB AFFIL University Club; Sleepy Hollow Country Club; Princeton Club; River Club; Lotos Club; Knickerbocker Club; The Links Club; Capitol Hill Club; Boone & Crockett Club; Brook Club.

James S. Sligar: trustee

Grants Analysis

Disclosure Period: calendar year ending 2001
Total Grants: $1,963,933
Number of Grants: 38
Average Grant: $31,292*
Highest Grant: $260,000
Lowest Grant: $5,000
Typical Range: $10,000 to $50,000
*Note:** Average grant figure excludes four highest grants ($860,000).

Recent Grants

Note: Grants derived from 2001 Form 990.

Library-Related

75,000	Norman Williams Public Library, Woodstock, VT

General

260,000	Hawaii Community Foundation, Honolulu, HI
200,000	Center for Special Studies
200,000	Mind Brain Body and Health Initiative, Chicago, IL
200,000	Vermont Institute of Natural Science, Woodstock, VT
100,000	Center for Special Studies
100,000	Council on the Environment, New York, NY
60,000	Henry M. Jackson Foundation, Rockville, MD
60,000	New York Hall of Science, Corona Park, NY
50,000	Central Park Conservancy, New York, NY
50,000	Classroom, Inc., New York, NY

HENRY LUCE FOUNDATION

Giving Contact

Michael Gilligan, President & Director
111 West 50th Street, Suite 4601
New York, NY 10020-1202
Phone: (212)489-7700
Fax: (212)581-9541
Web: http://www.hluce.org

Description

Founded: 1936
EIN: 136001282
Organization Type: General Purpose Foundation
Giving Locations: nationally; East and Southeast Asia.

Grant Types: Capital, Challenge, Conference/Seminar, Fellowship, General Support, Professorship, Project, Research, Seed Money.

Donor Information

Founder: The Henry Luce Foundation was established in 1936 by the late Henry R. Luce , co-founder and editor-in-chief of *Time Magazine*. Mr. Luce created the foundation as a tribute to his parents, the Reverend Dr. Henry Winters Luce and Elizabeth Root Luce. Dr. Luce, a Presbyterian minister, went to China as a missionary and educator in the late nineteenth century. He helped found Yenching University in 1916 and served as its vice president. His name is still linked to several sites on the campus of what is now the University of Beijing. Upon the death of Henry R. Luce in 1967, the foundation was a major beneficiary of his estate. The founder's son, Henry Luce III, has been chairman of the foundation since 1958.

Financial Summary

Total Giving: $54,275,009 (2001); $29,593,580 (1999); $27,040,428 (1997)
Assets: $905,305,357 (2001); $1,043,898,536 (1999); $692,888,311 (1997)
Gifts Received: $1,995,493 (1996); $199,910 (1994); $205,775 (1993)

Typical Recipients

Arts & Humanities: Art History, Arts Associations & Councils, Arts Institutes, Ethnic & Folk Arts, Film & Video, Arts & Humanities-General, Historic Preservation, History & Archaeology, Libraries, Literary Arts, Museums/Galleries, Music, Public Broadcasting, Visual Arts

Civic & Public Affairs: Asian American Affairs, Botanical Gardens/Parks, Civic & Public Affairs-General, Law & Justice, Philanthropic Organizations, Public Policy

Education: Arts/Humanities Education, Business Education, Colleges & Universities, Economic Education, Education Associations, Education Reform, Engineering/Technological Education, Environmental Education, Faculty Development, Education-General, International Exchange, International Studies, Legal Education, Medical Education, Medical Education, Minority Education, Private Education (Precollege), Religious Education, Science/Mathematics Education, Secondary Education (Private), Social Sciences Education, Student Aid

Environment: Environment-General, Wildlife Protection

Health: Geriatric Health, Public Health

International: Foreign Arts Organizations, Foreign Educational Institutions, Health Care/Hospitals, Human Rights, International Affairs, International Development, International Environmental Issues, International Organizations, International Peace & Security Issues, International Relations, Missionary/Religious Activities

Religion: Bible Study/Translation, Churches, Religion-General, Jewish Causes, Ministries, Religious Organizations, Religious Welfare, Seminaries, Social/Policy Issues, Synagogues/Temples

Science: Science Museums, Scientific Centers & Institutes, Scientific Organizations

Social Services: Crime Prevention, Recreation & Athletics

Application Procedures

Initial Contact: Contact foundation for guidelines or visit the website.
Deadlines: November 1 for the Henry R. Luce Professorship Program; the first Monday in December for Luce Scholarship Program institutional nominations. The Henry Luce III Fellows in Theology are selected through the Association of Theological Schools in Pittsburgh. Individual scholars should contact the ATS for application information.

Review Process: Awards for grants are determined by the board of directors, which meets three times a year.

Restrictions

The foundation does not provide funds for endowments, capital campaigns, construction projects, general operating support or annual fund drives. Outside of specifically designated programs, no grants are made to individuals.

Additional Information

Terrill E. Lautz is the Secretary and Program Director for Asia and Higher Education Programs.
Evelyn Benjamin is the Program Director for the Clare Boothe Luce and Public Affairs Programs.
Ellen Holtzman is the Program Director for the Arts.
Helene E. Redell is the Program Director for the Luce Scholars Program.
Michael Gilligan is the Program Directory for the Theology Program.
H. Christopher Luce is the Program Directory for Public Policy and the Environment Program.
Publications: Annual Report (biennially)

Foundation Officials

Robert E. Armstrong: director, new programs and major grants member B Omaha, NE 1932. ED University of Illinois BA (1954); Princeton University (1955). NONPR AFFIL member: National Theatre Deaf.

John W. Cook: president B 1946. ED State University of New York Oneonta (1967-1968). PRIM CORP EMPL president, director: Stamford Bank Corp.

Anne d'Harnoncourt: director, administration committee ED Radcliffe College BA (1965); University of London Courtauld Institute of Art MA (1967). PRIM NONPR EMPL George D. Widener director: Philadelphia Music of Art. NONPR AFFIL member: Pennsylvania Council Arts; member advisory committee: Stuart Foundation; member: Mayor's Cultural Advisory Council Philadelphia; trustee: Fairmont Park Art Association; member visitors committee: J Paul Getty Museum; member: Association Art Museum Directors; member: The Fabric Workshop; fellow: American Academy of Arts & Sciences; member: American Philosophical Society.

John C. Evans: director, compensation committee B 1943. CORP AFFIL president, director: Hauser Communication Inc. NONPR AFFIL treasurer; director: DIA Center Arts.

Margaret Boles Fitzgerald: nomations and chairwoman audit committee

Claire L. Gaudiani: director

Jane G. Irwin: director, chairman compensation committee

Kenneth T. Jackson: director

James Thomas Laney: director, chairman nominations committee B Wilson, AR 1927. ED Yale University BA (1950); Yale University BD (1954); Yale University PhD (1966). CORP AFFIL director: Trust Co. Georgia; director: Coca-Cola Co. NONPR AFFIL president: Society Values Higher Education; member tercentenary steering committee: Yale University; member: Phi Beta Kappa; member: Council Foreign Relations; member: Omicron Delta Kappa; trustee: Atlanta Symphony Orchestra; member: American Society Christian Ethics; trustee: Atlanta Chamber of Commerce. CLUB AFFIL Commerce Club.

Terrill E. Lautz: vice president, secretary,

H. Christopher Luce: director, finance, new programs and grants committee

Henry Luce, III: chairman, chief executive officer B New York, NY 1925. ED Yale University BA (1945). PRIM CORP EMPL chairman: American Security System. CORP AFFIL member: Fishers Island Development Co.; director: Applied Technology Investors Inc.; director: Applied Tech Investors. NONPR AFFIL trustee: New York History Society; trustee: Union Board Christian Higher Education Asia; chairman, chief executive officer: New Museum Contemporary

Art; trustee: Eisenhower Exchange Fellowships; president council: General Theological Union; trustee: Christian Ministry National Parks; trustee: College Wooster; trustee: Center Theological Inquiry; member: American Russian Young Artists Orchestra; trustee: Brooklyn Museum Art; member: American Council United Nations University. CLUB AFFIL University Club; Hay Harbor Club; Pilgrims Club; Fishers Island Country Club New York; Brook Club; Explorers Club New York.

Thomas Leffingwell Pulling: director, finance, nominations committee member B New York, NY 1939. ED Princeton University BA (1961). PRIM CORP EMPL managing director: Smith Barney Inc. CORP AFFIL chief executive officer: Smith Barney Investment Advisors. NONPR AFFIL trustee: South Street Seaport Museum; director: Woodlawn Cemetery; member: Pilgrims U.S.; member: Council Foreign Relations; trustee: Long Island University; member: Century Association. CLUB AFFIL University Club; Piping Rock Club; Surf Club.

Dr. David Vincent Ragone: director B New York, NY 1930. ED Massachusetts Institute of Technology SB (1951); Massachusetts Institute of Technology SM (1952); Massachusetts Institute of Technology ScD (1953). PRIM CORP EMPL lecturer: Cambridge PRIM NONPR EMPL senior lecturer u.s. department of of materials science: Massachusetts Institute of Technology. CORP AFFIL trustee: Mitre Corp.; director: Sifco Industry Inc.; partner: Ampersand Ventures; director: Cabot Corp.; general partner: Ampersand Specialty Materials Ventures. NONPR AFFIL member: Sigma Xi; member: Tau Beta Pi; senior lecturer: Massachusetts Institute Technology. CLUB AFFIL Longwood Cricket Club; University Club.

Grants Analysis

Disclosure Period: calendar year ending 2001
Total Grants: $54,275,009
Number of Grants: 234
Average Grant: $231,944
Highest Grant: $3,000,000
Typical Range: $25,000 to $500,000

Recent Grants

Note: Grants derived from 2001 Form 990.

Library-Related

220,000	Council on Library and Information Resources, Washington, DC -- distance learning initiative
185,000	Library of Congress, Washington, DC -- support acquisition and fellowship

General

3,500,000	Smithsonian American Art Museum, Washington, DC -- Luce Foundation Center for American Art
2,000,000	Brooklyn Museum of Art, Brooklyn, NY -- support to reinstall American art collection
1,000,000	Union Theological Seminary, New York, NY -- for the professorship in reformation history
540,926	Luce Scholar Stipends, New York, NY -- for the Cost of Living Master Record
500,000	Long Island University, Brookville, NY -- support to establish a Center for Urban Educators at the Brooklyn School of Education
500,000	Madison Avenue Presbyterian Church, New York, NY -- comprehensive renovation
500,000	Wesley Theological Seminary, Washington, DC -- to endow programs of the Center for Arts and Religion
400,000	Brown University, Providence, RI -- "Catalyzing the Flow of North-South Environmental Knowledge"
400,000	Stanford University, Stanford, CA -- "Interdisciplinary Environmental Studies Graduate Program"
400,000	Yale China Association, New Haven,

CT -- collaborative industrial ecology Asia

LUDWICK FAMILY FOUNDATION

Giving Contact

Arthur J. Ludwick, Chief Financial Officer, Director
PO Box 1796
Glendora, CA 91740
Phone: (626)852-0092
E-mail: ludwickfndn@ludwick.org
Web: http://www.ludwick.org

Description

Founded: 1990
EIN: 954296315
Organization Type: Private Foundation
Giving Locations: CA: nationally.
Grant Types: Capital, General Support.

Donor Information

Founder: Arthur J. Ludwick, Sarah Lynne Ludwick, Rain Bird Corporate Services

Financial Summary

Total Giving: $550,900 (2000); $430,000 (1999); $375,000 (1998)
Assets: $19,743,350 (2000); $19,325,614 (1999); $7,926,718 (1996)
Gifts Received: $1,562,683 (2000); $1,310,403 (1999); $805,063 (1996). Note: In 2000, contributions were received from Arthur J. and Sarah L. Ludwick. In 1996, contributions were received from Arthur J. and Sarah L. Ludwick ($505,063) and Rain Bird Corporate Services ($300,000).

Typical Recipients

Arts & Humanities: Arts Centers, Film & Video, Historic Preservation, History & Archaeology, Libraries, Museums/Galleries, Music, Opera, Theater
Civic & Public Affairs: Clubs, Economic Development, Employment/Job Training, Civic & Public Affairs-General, Hispanic Affairs, Housing, Legal Aid, Women's Affairs
Education: Business Education, Colleges & Universities, Education Reform, Education-General, School Volunteerism, Special Education, Vocational & Technical Education
Environment: Air/Water Quality, Environment-General, Resource Conservation, Wildlife Protection
Health: AIDS/HIV, Clinics/Medical Centers, Emergency/Ambulance Services, Hospitals, Prenatal Health Issues, Research/Studies Institutes
International: Health Care/Hospitals
Religion: Missionary Activities (Domestic), Religious Organizations
Science: Scientific Labs
Social Services: Animal Protection, At-Risk Youth, Child Welfare, Community Centers, Community Service Organizations, Day Care, Domestic Violence, Family Services, Food/Clothing Distribution, People with Disabilities, Recreation & Athletics, Senior Services, Substance Abuse, Volunteer Services, YMCA/YWCA/YMHA/YWHA, Youth Organizations

Application Procedures

Initial Contact: Send a brief letter of inquiry.
Application Requirements: Include a description of organization, amount requested, purpose of funds sought, and proof of tax-exempt status.
Deadlines: None.

Restrictions

Does not support individuals or political or lobbying groups.

Foundation Officials

Arthur J. Ludwick: cfo, director
Erik Arthur Ludwick: director
Heidi Ann Ludwick: director
Sarah Lynne Ludwick: president, director
Sharon Lynne Ludwick Warner: secretary, director

Grants Analysis

Disclosure Period: calendar year ending 2000
Total Grants: $550,900
Number of Grants: 20
Average Grant: $27,545
Highest Grant: $50,000
Typical Range: $10,000 to $50,000

Recent Grants

Note: Grants derived from 1999 Form 990.

General

48,000	American Red Cross - Black Hills Area Chapter, Rapid City, SD -- purchase upgraded technology for disaster communication for regional disaster response organization
46,400	Women's Connection, Inc, Rapid City, SD -- grant to purchase computers
39,500	National Food Foundation, Inc., Covina, CA
30,000	YWCA of San Gabriel Valley, West Covina, CA
27,000	Bonnie Bergin Assistance Dog Institute, Rohnert Park, CA
26,500	Casas por Cristo, El Paso, TX -- grant to purchase van to transport volunteers to sites where homes and community facilities are being constructed
25,000	East Valley Community Health Center, Inc., West Covina, CA -- grant to construct and furnish a medical examination room
25,000	Tucson Children's Museum, Inc., Tucson, AZ -- grant to improve museum signage and multimedia equipment for this program
25,000	Young Musicians Foundation, Beverly Hills, CA -- grant to purchase musical instruments for loan to children in this organization
21,600	Claremont McKenna/Mary B. Eyre Children's School, Claremont, CA

CHRISTOPHER LUDWICK FOUNDATION

Giving Contact

Christopher Ludwick Foundation
First Union National Bank
Broad and Walnut Sts., PA 1308
Philadelphia, PA 19109-1199
Phone: (215)985-8930
Web: http://www.ludwickfoundation.org/

Description

Founded: 1899
EIN: 236256408
Organization Type: Private Foundation
Giving Locations: PA: Philadelphia
Grant Types: Project, Scholarship.

Donor Information
Founder: Christopher Ludwick

Financial Summary
Total Giving: $250,000 (fiscal year ending April 30, 2001); $241,000 (fiscal 2000); $225,000 (fiscal 1999)
Assets: $5,541,736 (fiscal 2001); $5,207,156 (fiscal 2000); $3,891,274 (fiscal 1997)

Typical Recipients
Arts & Humanities: Arts & Humanities-General, History & Archaeology, Museums/Galleries, Theater
Civic & Public Affairs: Civic & Public Affairs-General, Hispanic Affairs, Urban & Community Affairs, Zoos/Aquariums
Education: Arts/Humanities Education, Colleges & Universities, Private Education (Precollege), Public Education (Precollege), Science/Mathematics Education, Secondary Education (Public), Special Education
Religion: Churches, Religious Welfare
Science: Scientific Centers & Institutes

Application Procedures
Initial Contact: Contact foundation for application form.
Deadlines: March 31

Restrictions
Does not support individuals, religious organizations for sectarian purposes, political or lobbying groups, organizations outside operating areas.

Additional Information
Supports the Voyager Program in the Philadelphia School District.
Publications: Application Form
Trust(s): First Union National Bank

Foundation Officials
Susan Williams Catherwood: vice president, mgr CORP AFFIL director: PECO Energy Co. NONPR AFFIL chairman: University Pennsylvania Health System.
Alan Crawford, Jr.: mgr
Henry E. Crouter: mgr
William M. Davidson, IV: treasurer, mgr
Dr. Roger Moss, Jr.: secretary, mgr
Hugh A. A. Sargent, Esq.: president, mgr
Dr. L. Wilbur Zimmerman: office, vice president, mgr

Grants Analysis
Disclosure Period: fiscal year ending April 30, 2001
Total Grants: $250,000
Number of Grants: 40
Average Grant: $6,250
Highest Grant: $50,000
Typical Range: $5,000 to $10,000

Recent Grants
Note: Grants derived from fiscal 2001 Form 990.

General

50,000	School District, Philadelphia, PA
7,500	Academy of Natural Sciences, Philadelphia, PA
7,500	Academy of Natural Sciences, Philadelphia, PA
7,500	Academy of Natural Sciences, Philadelphia, PA
7,500	Academy of Natural Sciences, Philadelphia, PA
7,500	Episcopal Community Services, Philadelphia, PA
7,500	Historic Bartram's Gardens, Philadelphia, PA
7,500	Wagner Free Institute of Science, Philadelphia, PA
7,500	William Penn Charter School, Philadelphia, PA
6,250	School District, Philadelphia, PA

LUNDA CHARITABLE TRUST

Giving Contact
Carl Holmquist, Trustee
620 Gebhardt Rd.
PO Box 669
Black River Falls, WI 54615-0669
Phone: (715)284-9491

Description
Founded: 1988
EIN: 396491037
Organization Type: Private Foundation
Giving Locations: WI: Jackson County and surrounding area
Grant Types: General Support, Scholarship.

Donor Information
Founder: Milton Lunda

Financial Summary
Total Giving: $475,691 (2001); $581,822 (2000); $517,964 (1999)
Giving Analysis: Giving for 2001 includes: foundation scholarships ($4,000); foundation matching gifts ($176,283) 2000: foundation matching gifts ($97,500)
Assets: $9,243,936 (2001); $9,423,452 (2000); $9,417,405 (1999)
Gifts Received: $128,547 (2000); $229,673 (1999); $1,004,340 (1998). Note: In 2000, contributions were received from Larry Lunda. In 1999, contributions were received from Larry Lunda ($139,673) and Marlee Slifka ($90,000). In 1998,, contributions were received from Milton Lunda ($463,500), Larry Lunda ($99,150), and Marlee Slifka ($200,000). In 1996, contributions were received from Milton Lunda ($880,849), Larry Lunda ($100,000), and Marlee Slifka ($104,500).

Typical Recipients
Arts & Humanities: History & Archaeology, Libraries
Civic & Public Affairs: Botanical Gardens/Parks, Clubs, Civic & Public Affairs-General, Housing, Municipalities/Towns, Rural Affairs, Safety, Urban & Community Affairs
Education: Agricultural Education, Arts/Humanities Education, Education-General, Student Aid, Vocational & Technical Education
Environment: Environment-General
Health: Health-General, Hospitals, Long-Term Care
Religion: Religion-General
Social Services: Animal Protection, Camps, Child Welfare, Community Service Organizations, Day Care, Emergency Relief, People with Disabilities, Recreation & Athletics, Scouts, Social Services-General

Application Procedures
Initial Contact: a brief letter of inquiry
Application Requirements: Include purpose of funds sought, amount requested, and proof of tax-exempt status.
Deadlines: July 31.

Restrictions
Foundation supports tax-exempt educational, scientific, and other charitable institutions, as the trustees select.

Additional Information
The foundation reports no specific application guidelines.
Trust(s): Firstar Bank

Foundation Officials
Carl Holmquist: trustee
Larry Lunda: trustee
Lydia Lunda: trustee
Milton Lunda: trustee
Marlee Slifka: trustee
Mary Van Gorden: trustee
Bill Waughtal: trustee

Grants Analysis
Disclosure Period: calendar year ending 2001
Total Grants: $295,408*
Number of Grants: 95
Average Grant: $3,110
Highest Grant: $25,000
Lowest Grant: $100
Typical Range: $1,000 to $5,000
*Note: Giving excludes matching gifts; scholarships.

Recent Grants
Note: Grants derived from 2001 Form 990.

General

176,283	City of Black River Falls, Black River Falls, WI -- Park Project
25,000	Black River Youth Hockey, Black River Falls, WI -- ice arena improvements and upkeep
15,000	Hixton Volunteer Fire Department, Hixton, WI -- equipment update and replacement
14,257	Pine View Home Health, Black River Falls, WI -- EZ stand and food service heating systems
10,444	Pine View Nursing Home, Black River Falls, WI -- Parker tub
10,000	Alma Center Play Ground Committee -- playground equipment upgrade
10,000	Jackson County Habitat for Humanity, Black River Falls, WI -- house with contingency
9,852	City of Black River Falls, Black River Falls, WI -- Karner Blue Garden Club 2000 operations
6,685	Partners of Black River Memorial Hospital, Black River Falls, WI
6,420	City of Black River Falls, Black River Falls, WI -- bleachers

GEORGES LURCY CHARITABLE AND EDUCATIONAL TRUST

Giving Contact
Seth E. Frank, Trustee
125 W. 55th St.
New York, NY 10019

Description
EIN: 136372044
Organization Type: Specialized/Single Purpose Foundation
Giving Locations: nationally.
Grant Types: Fellowship.

Donor Information
Founder: the late Georges Lurcy

Financial Summary

Total Giving: $1,968,100 (fiscal year ending June 30, 2000); $820,360 (fiscal 1997); $1,645,645 (fiscal 1996)
Assets: $34,995,748 (fiscal 2000); $28,242,031 (fiscal 1997); $23,322,326 (fiscal 1996)

Typical Recipients

Arts & Humanities: Arts Centers, Ballet, Libraries, Museums/Galleries, Music, Opera, Public Broadcasting, Theater
Civic & Public Affairs: Civic & Public Affairs-General, Public Policy
Education: Arts/Humanities Education, Colleges & Universities, Continuing Education, Engineering/Technological Education, Education-General, International Exchange, International Studies, Minority Education, Private Education (Precollege), Science/Mathematics Education, Student Aid
Environment: Environment-General
Health: Cancer, Hospitals, Single-Disease Health Associations
International: Foreign Arts Organizations, Foreign Educational Institutions, International Organizations, International Relations, Missionary/Religious Activities
Religion: Jewish Causes, Religious Welfare, Synagogues/Temples
Science: Science-General
Social Services: Camps, Community Service Organizations

Application Procedures

Initial Contact: Universities are requested to recommend a candidate for its fellowship. Applicants from France must apply to the FrancoAmerican Commission for Educational Exchange. Applicants cannot apply directly to the foundation.
Deadlines: None.

Additional Information

Provides fellowship grants to outstanding American students to study in French colleges and universities, and fellowships to outstanding French students to study in American colleges and universities.
Publications: Application Guidelines

Foundation Officials

Alan S. Bernstein: trustee
Daniel Lewis Bernstein: trustee B Durham, NC 1937. ED Amherst College BA (1959); Harvard University LLB (1962). CORP AFFIL pntr: Law Office Daniel L Bernstein. NONPR AFFIL member: International Bar Association; trustee: Georges Lucy Charitable & Education Trust; member: Bar Association New York City; director: Collegeeen Giblin Endowment Fund Child Neurology Research; member: American Bar Association; director: Arts & Sciences Foundation.
George Lurcy Bernstein: trustee PRIM NONPR EMPL associate professor: Tulane University, Department History.
Seth E. Frank: trustee
Sidney O. Friedman: trustee

Grants Analysis

Disclosure Period: fiscal year ending June 30, 2000
Total Grants: $1,968,100*
*Note: No grants list available for 2000.

Recent Grants

Note: Grants derived from fiscal 2000 Form 990.

Library-Related
25,000	Folger Shakespeare Library, Washington, DC

General
666,000	Amherst College, Amherst, MA
419,500	University of North Carolina, Greensboro, NC
103,500	Louis August Jonas Foundation, Inc
85,000	Tulane University, New Orleans, LA
65,300	Stanford University, Stanford, CA
61,000	Wave Hill, Inc., Bronx, NY
47,000	University of Chicago, Chicago, IL
30,000	Advocate for Science & Mathematics
30,000	Harvard University, Boston, MA
25,000	The Brookings Institution, Washington, DC

LOUIS R. LURIE FOUNDATION

Giving Contact

Robert A. Lurie, President
555 California Street, Suite 5100
San Francisco, CA 94104
Phone: (415)392-2470
Fax: (415)421-8669
Web: http://fdncenter.org/grantmaker/lurie/

Description

Founded: 1948
EIN: 946065488
Organization Type: General Purpose Foundation
Giving Locations: CA: San Francisco metropolitan area; IL: Chicago
Grant Types: General Support, Multiyear/Continuing Support, Operating Expenses.

Donor Information

Founder: Established in 1948 with donations from the late Louis R. Lurie , the late George S. Lurie , and Robert A. Lurie. Louis R. Lurie made his fortune in real estate and as a producer in the entertainment field. Robert A. Lurie, his son and president of the foundation, owns the San Francisco Giants baseball team.

Financial Summary

Total Giving: $2,614,205 (2001); $1,937,800 (2000); $1,027,167 (1999 approx)
Giving Analysis: Giving for 2000 includes: foundation matching gifts ($23,000)
Assets: $19,920,285 (2001); $23,332,152 (2000); $22,281,342 (1998)
Gifts Received: $353,534 (1998); $353,534 (1997); $353,534 (1996). Note: Contributions were received from the Charitable Trust under the will of Louis R. Lurie.

Typical Recipients

Arts & Humanities: Arts Associations & Councils, Arts Centers, Ballet, Community Arts, Ethnic & Folk Arts, Arts & Humanities-General, Libraries, Literary Arts, Museums/Galleries, Music, Opera, Performing Arts, Public Broadcasting, Theater
Civic & Public Affairs: Asian American Affairs, Botanical Gardens/Parks, Community Foundations, Employment/Job Training, Civic & Public Affairs-General, Hispanic Affairs, Housing, Law & Justice, Legal Aid, Philanthropic Organizations, Professional & Trade Associations, Public Policy, Urban & Community Affairs, Zoos/Aquariums
Education: Arts/Humanities Education, Colleges & Universities, Economic Education, Education Associations, Education Funds, Education Reform, Engineering/Technological Education, Education-General, Health & Physical Education, International Studies, Literacy, Medical Education, Minority Education, Preschool Education, Private Education (Precollege), Public Education (Precollege), Religious Education, School Volunteerism, Science/Mathematics Education, Secondary Education (Private), Secondary Education (Public), Social Sciences Education, Student Aid
Environment: Environment-General
Health: AIDS/HIV, Alzheimers Disease, Cancer, Children's Health/Hospitals, Clinics/Medical Centers, Emergency/Ambulance Services, Geriatric Health, Health Funds, Health Organizations, Hospitals, Medical Rehabilitation, Medical Research, Mental Health, Prenatal Health Issues, Public Health, Research/Studies Institutes, Single-Disease Health Associations, Speech & Hearing
International: Foreign Educational Institutions, Missionary/Religious Activities
Religion: Churches, Jewish Causes, Ministries, Religious Organizations, Religious Welfare
Science: Science Museums, Scientific Centers & Institutes
Social Services: At-Risk Youth, Camps, Child Abuse, Child Welfare, Community Centers, Community Service Organizations, Crime Prevention, Day Care, Delinquency & Criminal Rehabilitation, Domestic Violence, Family Planning, Family Services, Food/Clothing Distribution, People with Disabilities, Recreation & Athletics, Senior Services, Shelters/Homelessness, Social Services-General, Substance Abuse, United Funds/United Ways, YMCA/YWCA/YMHA/YWHA, Youth Organizations

Application Procedures

Initial Contact: Send a brief letter of inquiry.
Deadlines: None.

Restrictions

All grants go to organizations in the San Francisco and Chicago areas only.

Foundation Officials

Patricia R. Fay: director
James L. Hunt: secretary B Chicago, IL 1942. ED DePauw University BA (1964); Northwestern University JD (1967). PRIM CORP EMPL attorney: McCutchen Doyle Brown Enersen. CORP AFFIL director: Lurie Co. Inc. NONPR AFFIL member: Phi Beta Kappa; director: San Francisco Giants; Order Coif; member: American College Trial Lawyers; board visitors: Northwestern University Law School.
H. Michael Kurzman: vice president, director B 1939. PRIM CORP EMPL executive vice president, director: Lurie Co. Inc.
Robert Alfred Lurie: president, donor, director B 1929. ED Northwestern University BA (1951). PRIM CORP EMPL president, director: Lurie Co. Inc.
Eugene L. Valla: cfo, director CORP AFFIL vice president, director: Lurie Co. Inc.

Grants Analysis

Disclosure Period: calendar year ending 2001
Total Grants: $2,590,955*
Number of Grants: 104
Average Grant: $20,703*
Highest Grant: $250,000
Lowest Grant: $1,000
Typical Range: $10,000 to $40,000
*Note: Giving excludes matching gifts. Average grant figure excludes three highest grants ($500,000).

Recent Grants

Note: Grants derived from 2001 Form 990.

General
250,000	Jewish Community Federation, San Francisco, CA
150,000	Jewish Community Federation, San Francisco, CA
100,000	Jewish Community Center, San Francisco, CA
60,000	Exploratorium, Des Moines, IA
60,000	National Center for International Schools, San Francisco, CA
50,000	Asian Art Museum, San Francisco, CA
50,000	KQED, San Francisco, CA
50,000	Scott Street Senior Housing Complex, San Francisco, CA
40,000	Bay Area Community Resources, San Francisco, CA
40,000	Compass Community Services, San Francisco, CA

W. P. AND BULAH LUSE FOUNDATION

Giving Contact
Bill Arrington, Trust Officer
c/o Bank of America, NA
PO Box 831041
Dallas, TX 75283-1041
Phone: (214)209-1989

Description
Founded: 1947
EIN: 756007639
Organization Type: Private Foundation
Giving Locations: TX
Grant Types: General Support.

Financial Summary
Total Giving: $313,500 (2000); $229,590 (1999); $187,000 (1998)
Assets: $6,851,346 (2000); $7,049,528 (1999); $6,388,452 (1998)
Gifts Received: $839 (2000); $888 (1999); $928 (1998). Note: In 1999 and 2000, contributions were received from W. P. Luse Employees Trust.

Typical Recipients
Civic & Public Affairs: Civic & Public Affairs-General, Housing, Women's Affairs, Zoos/Aquariums
Education: Colleges & Universities, Education Reform, Engineering/Technological Education, Education-General, Literacy, Medical Education, Preschool Education, Private Education (Precollege), Special Education
Environment: Environment-General
Health: Cancer, Diabetes, Eyes/Blindness, Health-General, Health Organizations, Medical Research, Mental Health, Nursing Services, Public Health, Single-Disease Health Associations
Religion: Religious Welfare
Social Services: Big Brother/Big Sister, Camps, Child Welfare, Counseling, Family Planning, Family Services, Food/Clothing Distribution, People with Disabilities, Scouts, Senior Services, Shelters/Homelessness, Volunteer Services, Youth Organizations

Application Procedures
Initial Contact: The Foundation has no formal grant application procedure or application form. Send a brief letter of inquiry and a full proposal.
Application Requirements: Include a description of organization, amount requested, purpose of funds sought, and proof of tax-exempt status.
Deadlines: None. Requests are reviewed at the end of each year.

Restrictions
Request must be for educational or medical purposes or for the alleviation of poverty. Does not support individuals.

Additional Information
Trust(s): Bank of America NA

Foundation Officials
Jack Burrell: co-trustee
Jack L. Burrell, Jr.: co-trustee
George Wilkin: co-trustee

Grants Analysis
Disclosure Period: calendar year ending 2000
Total Grants: $313,500
Number of Grants: 34
Average Grant: $9,221
Highest Grant: $20,000
Typical Range: $5,000 to $20,000

Recent Grants
Note: Grants derived from 1999 Form 990.

General
20,460	Texas A and M University Development Foundation, College Station, TX -- education
13,640	Camp John Marc Myers, Dallas, TX -- education
13,640	Dallas Lighthouse for the Blind, Dallas, TX -- health
13,640	Family Place, Dallas, TX -- health/education
13,640	Presbyterian Healthcare Foundation, Dallas, TX -- health
13,640	Salvation Army, Dallas, TX -- relief of poverty
13,640	Senior Citizens of Greater Dallas, Dallas, TX -- health
13,640	Visiting Nurse Association, Dallas, TX -- health
10,910	Boy Scouts of America, Dallas, TX -- education
10,000	Episcopal School of Dallas, Dallas, TX -- education

MIRANDA LUX FOUNDATION

Giving Contact
Kenneth J. Blum, Executive Director
57 Post St., Suite 510
San Francisco, CA 94104
Phone: (415)981-2966
E-mail: admin@mirandalux.org
Web: http://www.mirandalux.org/

Description
Founded: 1908
EIN: 941170404
Organization Type: Private Foundation
Giving Locations: CA: San Francisco
Grant Types: Fellowship, General Support, Multiyear/Continuing Support, Operating Expenses, Project, Scholarship, Seed Money.

Donor Information
Founder: the late Miranda W. Lux

Financial Summary
Total Giving: $474,300 (fiscal year ending June 30, 2002); $521,800 (fiscal 2001); $455,058 (fiscal 2000)
Giving Analysis: Giving for fiscal 2002 includes: foundation scholarships ($10,000); fiscal 2001: foundation scholarships ($25,810) fiscal 2000: foundation scholarships ($27,560)
Assets: $9,348,861 (fiscal 2002); $10,478,366 (fiscal 2001); $10,448,942 (fiscal 2000)

Typical Recipients
Arts & Humanities: Film & Video, Arts & Humanities-General, Libraries, Music, Opera, Performing Arts, Public Broadcasting, Theater
Civic & Public Affairs: Asian American Affairs, Botanical Gardens/Parks, Business/Free Enterprise, Employment/Job Training, Hispanic Affairs, Nonprofit Management, Zoos/Aquariums
Education: Afterschool/Enrichment Programs, Arts/Humanities Education, Business Education, Business-School Partnerships, Colleges & Universities, Education Funds, Education-General, Journalism/Media Education, Leadership Training, Literacy, Preschool Education, Private Education (Precollege), Public Education (Precollege), Science/Mathematics Education, Secondary Education (Private), Secondary Education (Public), Student Aid, Vocational & Technical Education
Environment: Forestry, Resource Conservation

Health: Children's Health/Hospitals, Clinics/Medical Centers, Health Organizations, Mental Health
Religion: Jewish Causes, Religious Organizations, Religious Welfare
Science: Science Museums, Scientific Centers & Institutes
Social Services: At-Risk Youth, Child Welfare, Community Centers, Community Service Organizations, Counseling, Family Services, People with Disabilities, Recreation & Athletics, Shelters/Homelessness, Social Services-General, YMCA/YWCA/YMHA/YWHA, Youth Organizations

Application Procedures
Initial Contact: Send a full proposal.
Application Requirements: Include a description of organization; amount requested; purpose of funds sought; total project budget; other funding sources; number of participants; age range and distribution of participants; term and goals of the project; staff, and apartments.
Deadlines: None.

Restrictions
Foundation supports promising proposals for preschool through junior college in the fields of prevocational and vocational training in San Francisco. Does not support individuals or provide funds for annual campaigns, deficit financing, land acquisition, loans, renovations, publications, or conferences.

Additional Information
Publications: Annual Report

Foundation Officials
Beatrice Bowles: secretary, treasurer
Robert Cappelloni: trustee
Betsy Keller: trustee
Lawrence I. Kramer, Jr.: executive director
Philip F. Spalding: vice president
David Wisnom, Jr.: president

Grants Analysis
Disclosure Period: fiscal year ending June 30, 2002
Total Grants: $464,300*
Number of Grants: 35
Average Grant: $13,266
Highest Grant: $34,000
Lowest Grant: $1,500
Typical Range: $5,000 to $25,000
*Note: Giving excludes scholarships.

Recent Grants
Note: Grants derived from fiscal 2000 Form 990.

General
25,000	Bay Area Video Coalition, San Francisco, CA -- to support the youth link program
25,000	California Academy of Sciences, San Francisco, CA -- to support teen internships
20,000	Jewish Vocational Services, San Francisco, CA -- to support the work lab program
20,000	San Francisco Arts Education Project, San Francisco, CA -- to support the one to see pilot program
20,000	Society For Art Publications of The Americas -- to support Meridian Interns program
20,000	Youth for Service, San Rafael, CA -- to support the computer repair and maintenance program
15,120	Potrero Hill Neighborhood House, San Francisco, CA -- to support the peer counseling program
15,000	Exploratorium, San Francisco, CA -- to support the Children's Educational Outreach Program
15,000	Japanese Community Youth Council,

15,000 | San Francisco, CA -- to support the compass program
Jobs for Youth, Chicago, IL -- to support the promotion of youth employment opportunities

LYDALL, INC.

Company Headquarters
PO Box 151
Manchester, CT 06045-0151
Web: http://www.lydall.com

Company Description
Founded: 1879
Ticker: LDL
Exchange: NYSE
Revenue: US$253.5 million (2002)
Employees: 0 (2002)
SIC(s): 3900 Miscellaneous Manufacturing Industries.

Operating Locations
Lydall, Inc. (NH--Rochester; NY--Green Island; NC--Hamptonville; VA--Richmond)

Nonmonetary Support
Type: Donated Equipment; Loaned Employees; Loaned Executives

Giving Contact
Charlene Cefarattir, Executive Assistant
PO Box 151
Manchester, CT 06045-0151
Phone: (860)646-1233
Fax: (860)646-8847

Description
Organization Type: Corporate Giving Program
Giving Locations: headquarters and operating communities.
Grant Types: Capital, Emergency, Employee Matching Gifts, General Support, Multiyear/Continuing Support, Operating Expenses, Project, Research, Scholarship.

Financial Summary
Total Giving: $115,500 (1999); $130,024 (1998); $155,073 (1997)

Typical Recipients
Arts & Humanities: Arts Associations & Councils, Arts Centers, Arts Funds, Arts Institutes, Ballet, Community Arts, Arts & Humanities-General, Historic Preservation, Libraries, Literary Arts, Museums/Galleries, Music, Opera, Performing Arts, Public Broadcasting, Theater
Civic & Public Affairs: Chambers of Commerce, Economic Development, Civic & Public Affairs-General, Housing, Nonprofit Management, Philanthropic Organizations, Urban & Community Affairs
Education: Business Education, Business-School Partnerships, Colleges & Universities, Community & Junior Colleges, Continuing Education, Economic Education, Education-General, Literacy
Environment: Air/Water Quality, Resource Conservation
Health: Alzheimers Disease, Arthritis, Cancer, Children's Health/Hospitals, Eyes/Blindness, Health-General, Health Policy/Cost Containment, Health Organizations, Heart, Hospices, Hospitals, Medical Rehabilitation, Medical Research, Mental Health, Multiple Sclerosis, Nursing Services, Nutrition, Public Health, Single-Disease Health Associations
Social Services: Child Welfare, Community Centers, Community Service Organizations, Counseling, Domestic Violence, Emergency Relief, Family Services,

Food/Clothing Distribution, Homes, People with Disabilities, Shelters/Homelessness, Social Services-General, Special Olympics, Substance Abuse, United Funds/United Ways, Youth Organizations

Application Procedures
Initial Contact: Send a brief letter of request. Include a description of organization, amount requested, purpose of funds sought, recently audited financial statement, and proof of tax-exempt status.
Deadlines: September/October for the following year.

Restrictions
Does not support individuals, religious organizations for sectarian purposes, or political or lobbying groups.

Corporate Officials
John E. Hanley: chief financial officer, vice president finance, treasurerc PRIM CORP EMPL chief financial officer, vice president finance, treasurer: Lydall.
Leonard R. Jaskol: chairman, president, chief executive officer, director B New Rochelle, NY 1937. ED American University (1958); City University of New York (1969). PRIM CORP EMPL chairman, president, chief executive officer, director: Lydall.

Grants Analysis
Typical Range: $500 to $1,000

Recent Grants
Note: Grants derived from 1998 Form 990.

General
American Cancer Society, Hartford, CT
Connecticut Association for Human Services, Hartford, CT
Connecticut Special Olympics, Hartford, CT
Habitat for Humanity, Hartford, CT
Hartford College for Women, Hartford, CT
Jimmy Fund, Hartford, CT
Lutz Children's Museum, Manerostoe, CT
Manchester Symphony Orchestra and Chorale, Manchester, CT
United Way, Hartford, CT
Greater Hartford Arts Council, Hartford, CT

LYNDHURST FOUNDATION

Giving Contact
Jack Murrah, President
517 East Fifth Street
Chattanooga, TN 37403-1826
Phone: (423)756-0767
Fax: (423)756-0770
Web: http://www.lyndhurstfoundation.org

Description
Founded: 1938
EIN: 626044177
Organization Type: General Purpose Foundation
Giving Locations: TN: Chattanooga Southeastern USA.
Grant Types: Employee Matching Gifts, General Support, Matching, Multiyear/Continuing Support, Operating Expenses.

Donor Information
Founder: The Lyndhurst Foundation was established in Delaware in 1938 as the Memorial Welfare Foundation, with funds donated by the late Thomas Cartter Lupton and the Central Shares Corporation. Mr. Lupton was a pioneer in the development of the Coca-Cola bottling industry. The estate of Mr. Lupton transferred about $45 million to the foundation from 1977 to 1979.

Financial Summary
Total Giving: $6,000,000 (2002 approx); $10,000,000 (2001 approx); $10,822,959 (2000)
Giving Analysis: Giving for 2000 includes: foundation grants to United Way ($50,000); foundation matching gifts ($50,000); 1999: foundation grants to United Way ($5,000); foundation matching gifts ($26,209); foundation scholarships ($50,000); foundation gifts to individuals ($240,000); 1998: foundation gifts to individuals ($240,000).
Assets: $170,000,000 (2002 approx); $165,000,000 (2001 approx); $159,124,201 (2000)

Typical Recipients
Arts & Humanities: Arts Associations & Councils, Arts Centers, Arts Festivals, Arts Funds, Arts Institutes, Community Arts, Ethnic & Folk Arts, Film & Video, Arts & Humanities-General, Historic Preservation, Libraries, Literary Arts, Museums/Galleries, Music, Performing Arts, Public Broadcasting, Theater, Visual Arts
Civic & Public Affairs: Botanical Gardens/Parks, Chambers of Commerce, Community Foundations, Economic Development, Civic & Public Affairs-General, Housing, Municipalities/Towns, Nonprofit Management, Parades/Festivals, Professional & Trade Associations, Public Policy, Rural Affairs, Urban & Community Affairs, Zoos/Aquariums
Education: Arts/Humanities Education, Colleges & Universities, Colleges & Universities, Education Funds, Education Reform, Elementary Education (Private), Environmental Education, Education-General, Leadership Training, Private Education (Precollege), Public Education (Precollege), School Volunteerism, Student Aid
Environment: Air/Water Quality, Energy, Forestry, Environment-General, Protection, Resource Conservation, Sanitary Systems, Watershed, Wildlife Protection
Health: Clinics/Medical Centers, Mental Health
International: International Environmental Issues
Religion: Churches, Religious Welfare
Social Services: Animal Protection, Child Abuse, Community Centers, Community Service Organizations, Day Care, Family Services, Food/Clothing Distribution, Homes, Recreation & Athletics, Sexual Abuse, Substance Abuse, Volunteer Services, Youth Organizations

Application Procedures
Initial Contact: The foundation does not have an application form. Applicants should submit a letter of not more than three pages describing the project for which the grant is being sought.
Application Requirements: An application and a letter a description of organization, list of directors and staff, copy of the organization's annual budget, copy of the organization's tax-exempt ruling from the IRS, and an estimated project budget with tentative line items.
Deadlines: Proposals are considered on a quarterly basis. Contact the foundation for specific deadlines.
Review Process: All grant requests are reviewed and researched by the foundation's staff before presentation to the board of trustees. Applicants will be notified of the board's decision following regular meetings, generally held in January, April, July, and October.

Restrictions
The foundation reports that it does not award grants to individuals except under the Lyndhurst Prize. The Lyndhurst Prizes are given solely at the initiative of the board of trustees, never in response to applications, requests, or nominations.
The foundation generally does not accept unsolicited requests for funds. The only category the foundation does accept unsolicited requests for grants supporting environmental improvement programs in the southern Appalachian Mountain region of Tennessee, North Carolina, South Carolina, Georgia, Alabama, and Mississippi.

Additional Information

Publications: Annual Report; Guidelines

Foundation Officials

Nelson D. Campbell: trustee

Charles Benjamin Chitty: treasurer B Albany, GA 1942. ED United States Military Academy (1966); University of South Carolina (1973). PRIM CORP EMPL vice president finance planning, treasurer: Springs Industries, Inc.

Benic M. Clark, III: vice president

George R. Fontaine: trustee

Margaret L. Gerber: trustee

Katherine L. Juett: trustee

T. Cartter Lupton, II: trustee

Allen L. McCallie: secretary

Jack Murrah: president, trustee

Alice Smith: chairman, trustee

Grants Analysis

Disclosure Period: calendar year ending 2000

Total Grants: $10,722,959*

Number of Grants: 42

Average Grant: $76,471*

Highest Grant: $5,220,000

Lowest Grant: $2,500

Typical Range: $10,000 to $100,000

***Note:** Grants analysis provided by foundation. Giving excludes United Way, matching gifts, and scholarships. Average grant figure excludes highest grants.

Recent Grants

Note: Grants derived from 2000 Form 990.

General

5,220,000	Center for Documentary Studies, Durham, NC -- final distribution of $10 million commitment
900,000	Chattanooga Neighborhood Enterprise, Chattanooga, TN -- for challenge grant
661,362	Allied Arts of Greater Chattanooga, Chattanooga, TN -- for challenge grant
500,000	Conservation Fund, Arlington, VA -- in support of establishment of a Southeast Revolving Loan Fund
500,000	Rural School and Community Trust, Washington, DC -- for first payment of $1.5 million commitment
500,000	Tennessee Aquarium, Chattanooga, TN -- for second and final payment of $1 million commitment
450,000	Community Foundation of Greater Chattanooga, Chattanooga, TN -- for Lyndhurst Fund II, which covers 2000 staffing costs of the Community Impact Fund
300,000	Lula Lake Land Trust, Chattanooga, TN -- in support of land acquisition to advance the Cloudland Connector Project
206,000	Trust for Public Land, Chattanooga, TN -- in support of the Chattanooga Greenways Fund
106,000	Community Foundation of Greater Chattanooga, Chattanooga, TN -- for 1999 staffing costs of the Community Impact Fund

LYON FOUNDATION

Giving Contact

James W. Connor, President
PO Box 546
Bartlesville, OK 74005
Phone: (918)336-0066

Description

Founded: 1975
EIN: 237299980
Organization Type: General Purpose Foundation

Giving Locations: OK: Bartlesville

Grant Types: Capital, Scholarship.

Donor Information

Founder: Established in 1975 by the late E. H. Lyon and the late Melody Lyon .

Financial Summary

Total Giving: $945,527 (2000); $918,005 (1999); $826,959 (1998)

Giving Analysis: Giving for 2000 includes: foundation scholarships ($30,651) 1999: foundation scholarships ($66,151)

Assets: $22,107,229 (2000); $21,749,540 (1999); $21,361,771 (1998)

Gifts Received: $378,167 (2000); $376,719 (1999); $337,370 (1998). Note: In 2000, 1999, and 1998, contributions were received from from E. H. Lyon Trust.

Typical Recipients

Arts & Humanities: Arts Festivals, Ballet, Community Arts, Arts & Humanities-General, Historic Preservation, History & Archaeology, Libraries, Museums/Galleries, Music, Visual Arts

Civic & Public Affairs: Botanical Gardens/Parks, Clubs, Community Foundations, Civic & Public Affairs-General, Legal Aid, Municipalities/Towns, Native American Affairs, Nonprofit Management, Parades/Festivals, Public Policy, Safety

Education: Colleges & Universities, Faculty Development, Education-General, Medical Education, Private Education (Precollege), Public Education (Precollege), Special Education, Vocational & Technical Education

Health: Alzheimers Disease, Clinics/Medical Centers, Emergency/Ambulance Services, Geriatric Health, Health Organizations, Hospitals, Medical Rehabilitation, Mental Health, Nutrition, Public Health

Religion: Churches, Ministries, Religious Welfare

Social Services: Animal Protection, Big Brother/Big Sister, Child Welfare, Community Centers, Community Service Organizations, Family Services, Homes, People with Disabilities, Recreation & Athletics, Scouts, Senior Services, Substance Abuse, YMCA/YWCA/YMHA/YWHA, Youth Organizations

Application Procedures

Initial Contact: Submit a written application of no more than four double-spaced pages.

Application Requirements: An application should contain the following information about the project: formal name of organization; a brief description of organization of history and purpose; address and phone number; name and title of person responsible for grant application; amount of grant requested; period for which grant is requested; purpose of grant; copy of most current IRS determination letter; copy of most recently filed IRS Form 990; applicant's budget for current year and year(s) for which grant is requested; identification of other organizations solicited for same purpose; names, titles, and affiliations of officers and members of governing body; and certification that applicant's exempt status has not changed since initial IRS determination letter.

Deadlines: None.

Review Process: After reviewing the application, foundation staff may request additional information.

Restrictions

Policy guidelines established by the board of directors normally preclude grants for ongoing general operating expenses or existing deficits, endowment funds, direct support to individuals, and projects or programs outside the Bartlesville area. In addition, no grants will be made for computers or computer-related items. (However, grants in the past have been made for endowment funds and computers.)

Foundation Officials

Walter W. Allison: vice president, assistant treasurer PRIM NONPR EMPL chief accountant: City of Norman, Oklahoma.

James W. Connor: president

Don Donaldson: vice president, assistant secretary PRIM CORP EMPL president: Community Bank. CORP AFFIL director: Community State Bank.

John F. Kane: treasurer

Larry G. Markel, MD: assistant secretary PRIM CORP EMPL director: Weststar Bank.

Charles W. Selby: secretary, director

Grants Analysis

Disclosure Period: calendar year ending 2000

Total Grants: $914,876*

Number of Grants: 25

Average Grant: $36,595

Highest Grant: $181,760

Typical Range: $1,000 to $50,000

***Note:** Giving excludes scholarships.

Recent Grants

Note: Grants derived from 2000 Form 990.

General

181,760	City of Bartlesville, Bartlesville, OK -- Adams Golf Course improvements
150,000	Bartlesville Wesleyan College, Bartlesville, OK -- Vision 2000
100,000	Bartlesville History Museum, Bartlesville, OK -- preparation of 5th floor of City Hall
80,000	Bartlesville Community Center, Bartlesville, OK -- improvements to Lyon Gallery
53,625	Bartlesville Pony League, Bartlesville, OK -- fence, lighting
50,000	Bartlesville Wesleyan College, Bartlesville, OK -- vision 2000 campaign
37,570	City of Bartlesville, Bartlesville, OK -- Lyon Park
30,651	Bartlesville Wesleyan College, Bartlesville, OK -- nursing scholarships
30,285	YMCA, Bartlesville, OK -- various improvements and equipment
30,000	Family Care Services, Bartlesville, OK

BERTHA RUSS LYTEL FOUNDATION

Giving Contact

George Hindley, Manager
PO Box 893
Ferndale, CA 95536
Phone: (707)786-4682

Description

Founded: 1974
EIN: 942271250
Organization Type: Private Foundation
Giving Locations: CA: Humboldt County
Grant Types: Capital, General Support, Multiyear/Continuing Support, Operating Expenses, Scholarship, Seed Money.

Donor Information

Founder: the late Bertha Russ Lytel, L. D. O'Rourke

Financial Summary

Total Giving: $802,526 (fiscal year ending September 30, 2001); $738,883 (fiscal 2000); $723,395 (fiscal 1998)

Assets: $17,091,191 (fiscal 2001); $18,008,553 (fiscal 2000); $15,530,704 (fiscal 1998)

Gifts Received: $823,991 (fiscal 2000); $82,628 (fiscal 1998); $115 (fiscal 1992). Note: In fiscal 1998, contributions were received from the late Bertha Lytel.

Typical Recipients

Arts & Humanities: Arts Associations & Councils, Libraries, Museums/Galleries, Public Broadcasting, Theater

Civic & Public Affairs: Civil Rights, Clubs, Employment/Job Training, Civic & Public Affairs-General, Municipalities/Towns, Nonprofit Management, Parades/Festivals, Safety, Urban & Community Affairs

Education: Agricultural Education, Colleges & Universities, Education Associations, Engineering/Technological Education, Preschool Education, Private Education (Precollege), Public Education (Precollege), Science/Mathematics Education, Secondary Education (Public)

Environment: Environment-General, Resource Conservation

Health: Arthritis, Children's Health/Hospitals, Clinics/Medical Centers, Emergency/Ambulance Services, Health Organizations, Heart, Home-Care Services, Hospitals, Long-Term Care, Long-Term Care, Nursing Services, Public Health

Religion: Churches, Religious Welfare

Science: Scientific Organizations

Social Services: Child Welfare, Community Service Organizations, Family Planning, Family Services, Food/Clothing Distribution, People with Disabilities, Recreation & Athletics, Scouts, Senior Services, Special Olympics, Substance Abuse, Veterans, Volunteer Services, Youth Organizations

Application Procedures

Initial Contact: Send a letter requesting an application form for scholarships or grants.
Deadlines: April 1.

Restrictions

Does not provide funds for annual campaigns, emergency or deficit financing, land acquisition, loans, renovations, demonstration projects, or publications. Grants are awarded to organizations in Humboldt County that generally support programs that deal with the elderly.

Additional Information

Awards scholarships to students entering a four-year agricultural college. Priority is given to graduates of Ferndale High School. If no Ferndale High School graduates apply, graduates of Fortuna High School are given consideration. Applicants are judged on grade point average; rigor of course of study in high school; letters of recommendation; non-academic activities including leadership activities, age-related activities and work experience and an essay.
Publications: Application Guidelines; Application Form

Foundation Officials

Gerald R. Becker: vice president, treasurer
Betty Diehl: director
George Hindley: mgr
Charles Lakin: director
Charles M. Lawrence: president
James K. Morrison: secretary
Tom Renner: director
Jack Russ: director
Jack Smith: director

Grants Analysis

Disclosure Period: fiscal year ending September 30, 2001
Total Grants: $802,526
Number of Grants: 42
Average Grant: $16,891*
Highest Grant: $110,000
Lowest Grant: $750
Typical Range: $5,000 to $30,000
*Note: Average grant figure excludes highest grant.

Recent Grants

Note: Grants derived from fiscal 2000 Form 990.

Library-Related
12,786 Ferndale Library, Ferndale, CA

General
115,000	Humboldt Senior Resource Center
80,000	Congregational Church
79,994	Lutheran Home for the Aging, Wauwatosa, WI
59,630	Redwoods United, Inc
45,000	Humboldt Home Health Services
42,850	Vector Health Program, Inc., Eureka, CA
35,875	Retired Senior Volunteer Program
30,000	Cal Poly State University, San Luis Obispo, CA
25,000	City of Ferndale, Ferndale, CA
25,000	Easter Seals Society, Humboldt County

M/A-COM, INC.

Company Headquarters

PO Box 3295
Lowell, MA 01853-3295
Web: http://www.macom.com

Company Description

Employees: 3,932
SIC(s): 3679 Electronic Components Nec, 3699 Electrical Equipment & Supplies Nec.

Operating Locations

M/A-COM (MA--Waltham); M/A-COM Inc. (CA--Torrance; MD--Hunt Valley; MA--Amesbury, Burlington, Waltham)
Note: 12 different company names are listed as a division of either M/A-COM Inc. or Adams-Russell Inc.

M/A-COM Foundation

Giving Contact

Jan Barry, Administrator
1011 Pawtucket Blvd.
Lowell, MA 01854
Phone: (508)442-5000

Description

Founded: 1967
EIN: 046169568
Organization Type: Corporate Foundation
Giving Locations: MA
Grant Types: Employee Matching Gifts, General Support, Scholarship.
Note: Employee matching gift ratio: 1 to 1. Scholarships awarded to children of employees only.

Donor Information

Founder: M/A-COM, Inc.

Financial Summary

Total Giving: $82,784 (1999); $89,968 (1996); $200,423 (1995)
Giving Analysis: Giving for 1999 includes: foundation scholarships ($34,500) foundation ($48,284)
Assets: $2,144 (1999); $7,495 (1996); $27,117 (1995)
Gifts Received: $70,000 (1999); $70,000 (1996); $200,000 (1995). Note: In 1995 and 1999, contributions were received from M/A-COM, Inc.

Typical Recipients

Arts & Humanities: Arts Associations & Councils, Ballet, Libraries, Museums/Galleries, Music, Performing Arts, Public Broadcasting, Theater

Civic & Public Affairs: African American Affairs, Economic Development, Civic & Public Affairs-General, Legal Aid, Municipalities/Towns, Parades/Festivals, Safety, Urban & Community Affairs

Education: Business Education, Colleges & Universities, Education Funds, Engineering/Technological Education, Education-General, Legal Education, Minority Education, Private Education (Precollege), Religious Education, Secondary Education (Private), Secondary Education (Public), Student Aid

Health: AIDS/HIV, Arthritis, Cancer, Emergency/Ambulance Services, Health Organizations, Hospitals, Single-Disease Health Associations

Religion: Jewish Causes, Seminaries

Science: Science Museums

Social Services: Camps, Child Welfare, Community Service Organizations, Family Services, Homes, People with Disabilities, Recreation & Athletics, United Funds/United Ways, Youth Organizations

Application Procedures

Initial Contact: For scholarships, provide SAT scores. For other grants, send a complete description of activities and a determination letter. Deadline for scholarships is April 1. There is no deadline for other grants.

Restrictions

Does not support individuals, religious organizations for sectarian purposes, or political or lobbying groups.

Additional Information

The foundation switched from a fiscal to a calendar year in 1995.

Corporate Officials

Richard P. Clark: president, chief executive officer
PRIM CORP EMPL president, chief executive officer: M/A-COM Inc.

Foundation Officials

Ralph V. G. Bakkensen: secretary
J. Craig Barrows: assistant secretary, trustee PRIM CORP EMPL general counsel, secretary: New England Business Service.
Philip A. Orlando: assistant vice president taxation
Stephen P. Zezima: vice president taxation

Grants Analysis

Disclosure Period: calendar year ending 1999
Total Grants: $48,284*
Number of Grants: 108
Average Grant: $447
Highest Grant: $3,000
Typical Range: $100 to $500
*Note: Giving excludes scholarships.

Recent Grants

Note: Grants derived from 1998 Form 990.

General
5,500	Harvard University, Boston, MA -- scholarship
4,000	Massachusetts Institute of Technology, Cambridge, MA -- scholarship
3,000	Lowell Folk Festival, The, Lowell, MA
3,000	Town of Lexington - Trustees of Public Trust, Lexington, MA
3,000	Trustees of Tufts College, Boston, MA -- scholarship
3,000	Tufts University, Boston, MA -- scholarships
2,500	Georgetown University, Washington, DC -- scholarship
2,500	Lowell Association for the Blind, Lowell, MA
2,500	Lowell Philharmonic Orchestra, Lowell, MA
2,500	Lowell Plan, Lowell, MA

M.E. FOUNDATION

Giving Contact
Grace McCrane, Administrative Assistant
PO Box 20266
Washington, DC 20041
Phone: (703)478-0100

Description
Founded: 1966
EIN: 136205356
Organization Type: Private Foundation
Giving Locations: nationally.
Grant Types: General Support.

Donor Information
Founder: Margaret Brown Trimble, Frances Carroll Brown

Financial Summary
Total Giving: $2,607,929 (2000); $2,098,793 (1999); $1,378,978 (1998)
Assets: $17,442,583 (2000); $20,694,412 (1999); $20,676,284 (1998)
Gifts Received: $440 (1993)

Typical Recipients
Arts & Humanities: Libraries, Music, Public Broadcasting
Civic & Public Affairs: Economic Development, Civic & Public Affairs-General
Education: Colleges & Universities, International Exchange, Private Education (Precollege), Religious Education, Special Education, Student Aid
Health: Health-General, Health Organizations
International: Foreign Educational Institutions, International Development, International Organizations, International Peace & Security Issues, International Relations, International Relief Efforts, Missionary/Religious Activities
Religion: Churches, Ministries, Missionary Activities (Domestic), Religious Organizations, Religious Welfare, Seminaries, Social/Policy Issues
Social Services: At-Risk Youth, Community Service Organizations, Family Services, Homes, People with Disabilities, Social Services-General, Substance Abuse, Youth Organizations

Application Procedures
Initial Contact: Submit a statement describing how organization has participated in the furtherance of educational and religious beliefs and studies.
Deadlines: None.

Foundation Officials
Dr. Sharon Berry: director
Frances Carroll Brown: vice president, treasurer, director
Charles Wendell Colson: acting president B Boston, MA 1931. ED Brown University AB (1953); George Washington University JD (1959). NONPR AFFIL member: Order Coif; associate: Prison Fellowship; member: Beta Theta Pi.
Dr. Carl F.H. Henry: director
Calvin E. Howe: director

Grants Analysis
Disclosure Period: calendar year ending 2000
Total Grants: $2,607,929*
Typical Range: $1,000 to $25,000
*Note: No grant list available for 2000.

Recent Grants
Note: Grants derived from 2001 Form 990.

General
309,000	Prison Fellowship International, Washington, DC
130,000	Prison Fellowship International, Washington, DC

60,000	Fleming-Hunter Foundation, Inc., Randallstown, MD
60,000	Gordon Conwell Theological Seminary, South Hamilton, MA
53,000	Campus Crusade for Christ International, Orlando, FL
52,000	Walter Hoving Home, Garrison, NY
50,000	LeTourneau University, Longview, TX
48,000	World Reach, Birmingham, AL
41,000	Truth Ministries, Baltimore, MD
40,000	Spanish World Gospel Mission, Winona Lake, IN

J. E. AND L. E. MABEE FOUNDATION, INC.

Giving Contact
John H. Conway, Jr., Vice Chairman, Secretary-Treasurer & Trustee
401 South Boston Avenue, Suite 3000
Tulsa, OK 74103-4017
Phone: (918)584-4286
Fax: (918)584-5540

Description
Founded: 1948
EIN: 736090162
Organization Type: Family Foundation
Giving Locations: AR; KS; MO; NM; OK; TX
Grant Types: Capital.
Note: Most of the foundation's grants are made for building construction, renovations, and to purchase major medical capital equipment. Normally, capital grants are made on a challenge or conditional basis for leveraging purposes. The challenge is to raise the balance needed to assure complete project funding within the challenge period. There is no set rule to determine what percentage of the total project cost may be the subject of a challenge grant.

Donor Information
Founder: The J. E. and L. E. Mabee Foundation was established in 1948 by Mr. and Mrs. J. E. Mabee (both deceased), who lived in the southwestern United States and made their fortune in oil. The foundation formed its grant-making policies to reflect the interests of the founders.

Financial Summary
Total Giving: $28,759,122 (fiscal year ending August 31, 2002); $28,550,263 (fiscal 2001); $34,751,655 (fiscal 2000)
Giving Analysis: Giving for fiscal 2001 includes: foundation grants to United Way ($275,000); fiscal 1999: foundation grants to United Way ($125,000); fiscal 1998: foundation grants to United Way ($125,000)
Assets: $696,114,826 (fiscal 2002); $735,208,451 (fiscal 2001); $788,437,761 (fiscal 2000)

Typical Recipients
Arts & Humanities: Art History, Arts Associations & Councils, Arts Centers, Ethnic & Folk Arts, History & Archaeology, Libraries, Museums/Galleries, Opera, Performing Arts, Public Broadcasting, Theater
Civic & Public Affairs: Botanical Gardens/Parks, Clubs, Civic & Public Affairs-General, Hispanic Affairs, Housing, Minority Business, Urban & Community Affairs
Education: Business Education, Colleges & Universities, Education-General, Medical Education, Private Education (Precollege), Public Education (Precollege), Religious Education, Science/Mathematics Education, Special Education, Student Aid
Health: Alzheimers Disease, Cancer, Children's Health/Hospitals, Clinics/Medical Centers, Diabetes, Health-General, Health-General, Health Funds, Health Organizations, Heart, Hospices, Hospitals,

Long-Term Care, Medical Rehabilitation, Medical Research, Mental Health, Nursing Services, Preventive Medicine/Wellness Organizations, Public Health, Research/Studies Institutes, Single-Disease Health Associations
Religion: Churches, Dioceses, Religion-General, Jewish Causes, Ministries, Religious Organizations, Religious Welfare, Seminaries
Science: Science Museums, Scientific Centers & Institutes
Social Services: At-Risk Youth, Big Brother/Big Sister, Camps, Child Welfare, Community Centers, Community Service Organizations, Day Care, Domestic Violence, Family Services, Family Services, Food/Clothing Distribution, Homes, People with Disabilities, Recreation & Athletics, Scouts, Senior Services, Shelters/Homelessness, Social Services-General, Substance Abuse, United Funds/United Ways, Volunteer Services, YMCA/YWCA/YMHA/YWHA, Youth Organizations

Application Procedures
Initial Contact: The foundation does not require a standard application form.
Application Requirements: To be evaluated by the foundation, all proposals must contain the legal name and address of the applicant; name, title, address, and phone number of the appropriate contact person; a brief description of the organization, including a summary of its qualifications and background in the field in which funds are sought; a description of the project with its goals, significance, and benefiting population; substantiation of the extent of need for those benefits; and comments on past or present attempts by the applicant or others to meet this need. Applicants also should submit a detailed expenditure budget for the project which explains how major portions were estimated, and how and when the funds will be spent; description of other possible sources of support which have been or will be solicited, including funds previously received or pledged for the project; amount requested from the foundation; time schedule for the construction and commencement of the project; and an explanation of how the project will be sustained after the requested support period. If a challenge grant is requested, the period of time within which the challenge must be met needs to be included (not in excess of one year).
In addition to the proposal, the foundation requires an applicant to include copies of the most recent IRS 501(c)(3) tax-exempt status letter (if there is any variance between the name on the IRS letter and the applicant's letter, this must be fully explained and documented); a statement on organization letterhead, signed by its chief executive officer, that there has been no change in the purpose, character, or method of operation subsequent to the IRS ruling letter(s); a copy of the organization's audited financial statement for the most recently completed fiscal year (if not audited, include a copy of the latest IRS Form 990); and an interim financial statement for the current fiscal period. Applicants also should include a listing of names of the primary professional affiliations, members of the applicant's governing body, and names and titles of the officers.
Deadlines: December 1; March 1; June 1; and September 1.
Review Process: Applications should be as brief as possible, but must contain all the required information. The trustees send a written decision on the proposal usually within one week of their meeting.

Restrictions
The foundation ordinarily does not make grants for deficit financing, initial funds, total project costs, operating funds, annual fundraising campaigns, reserve purposes, dinners or special events, fraternal organizations, individuals, political or lobbying groups, goodwill advertising, projects that are likely to be delayed, endowments, religious organizations for sectarian purposes, tax supported organizations, government-owned or operated institutions and facilities (such as

state universities, municipal parks, and libraries), or precollege educational institutions. The foundation requests that only one proposal be submitted per twelve month period, unless a tremendous change in circumstances has occurred. If a grant has been previously issued to an applicant, there should be a two year period between the final payment for the previous grant and the request for another. New proposals must include all required information without relying on previously submitted information.

Additional Information

The foundation prefers to participate with other donors, so it is suggested that the applicant seek support from other foundations and donors before submitting a proposal. The typical recipient has previously raised some funds before applying and has outlined a fundraising strategy which incorporates the use of a Mabee Foundation challenge grant for securing the balance of funds needed to complete the project. Challenge grants are paid after the foundation is supplied with substantiation that the applicant has raised the balance of funds required to complete the project by the challenge deadline. A list of principal contributors is needed. If building is involved, construction must have begun and the foundation notified of project costs; these costs must be within the available resources. If asset acquisition is involved, the purchase order or similar information must be executed.
Publications: Application Guidelines

Foundation Officials

Thomas R. Brett: trustee B Oklahoma City, OK 1931. ED University of Oklahoma BBA (1953); University of Oklahoma LLB (1957); University of Oklahoma JD (1971). PRIM NONPR EMPL federal judge: U.S. District Court, Tulsa. NONPR AFFIL member: Tulsa County Bar Association; director: University Oklahoma College Law Alumni Association; advisory board: Salvation Army; member: Order Coif; member: Phi Delta Alpha; member: Oklahoma Bar Association; trustee: Oklahoma Bar Foundation; member: American Judicature Society; fellow: American Bar Foundation; fellow: American College Trial Lawyers.
John H. Conway, Jr.: vice chairman
Joseph A. Hogard: assistant secretary PRIM CORP EMPL controller, assistant treasurer, assistant secretary: Mabee Petroleum Corp.
James L. Houghton: trustee
Joe Mabee: vice chairman, trustee PRIM CORP EMPL president, director: Mabee Petroleum Corp. NONPR AFFIL president: Hillander School.
Joseph Guy Mabee, Jr.: trustee
William J. Teague: trustee
Raymond L. Tullius, Jr.: trustee

Grants Analysis

Disclosure Period: fiscal year ending August 31, 2002
Total Grants: $28,459,122*
Number of Grants: 81
Average Grant: $308,673*
Highest Grant: $1,000,000
Lowest Grant: $20,000
Typical Range: $50,000 to $500,000
*Note: Giving excludes United Way. Average grant figure excludes five highest grants ($5,000,000).

Recent Grants

Note: Grants derived from 2002 Form 990.

General

1,000,000 Drury University, Springfield, MO -- for science building
1,000,000 Evangel University, Springfield, MO -- for building
1,000,000 Gladney Center, Ft. Worth, TX -- for building
1,000,000 Hardin-Simmons University, Abilene, TX -- for building
1,000,000 St. Lawrence Catholic Campus Center, Lawrence, KS -- for building

924,622 Sterling College, Sterling, KS -- for building renovation and academic classroom building
900,000 Hendrick Medical Center, Abilene, TX -- for building and hospital
750,000 Boy Scouts of America, Sam Houston Area, Houston, TX -- for building
750,000 Boys and Girls Club of Deep East Texas, Inc., Nacogdoches, TX -- for building
750,000 Family and Children's Services, Tulsa, OK -- for building

JOHN D. AND CATHERINE T. MACARTHUR FOUNDATION

Giving Contact

Richard J. Kaplan, Assistant Vice President
140 South Dearborn Street
Chicago, IL 60603-5285
Phone: (312)726-8000
Fax: (312)920-6258
E-mail: 4answers@macfound.org
Web: http://www.macfound.org
Note: In Chicago metropolitan area.

Alternate Contact

John D. and Catherine T. MacArthur Foundation
550 Heritage Drive, Suite 160
Jupiter, FL 33458
Phone: (561)626-4800
Fax: (561)624-4948
Note: In the Palm Beach County area.

Description

Founded: 1970
EIN: 237093598
Organization Type: General Purpose Foundation
Giving Locations: FL: Palm Beach County: human and community development grants; IL: Chicago education reform grants, human and community development grants; internationally; nationally; Brazil: global security and sustainability grants; India: global security and sustainability grants; Mexico: global security and sustainability grants; Nigeria: global security and sustainability grants.
Grant Types: Fellowship, General Support, Matching, Multiyear/Continuing Support, Project, Research.

Donor Information

Founder: The foundation was incorporated in 1970 in Illinois, with funds donated by John D. MacArthur . Mr. MacArthur, who died in 1978, built his fortune through the Bankers Life and Casualty Company of Chicago, of which he was the sole owner. He also owned an array of related companies and over 100,000 acres of land, primarily in the Palm Beach, FL, area. He left the assets of his insurance fortune and real estate holdings, ultimately valued at more than $3 billion, to the foundation. His wife, Catherine T. MacArthur, was a board member of both Bankers Life and Casualty and the foundation prior to her death in 1981. Mr. MacArthur left the selection of areas of interest, programs, and guidelines for the foundation entirely up to its board of trustees.

Financial Summary

Total Giving: $175,000,000 (2003 approx); $226,600,000 (2001); $164,022,738 (2000)
Giving Analysis: Giving for 2000 includes: foundation matching gifts ($2,563,034); foundation gifts to individuals ($5,044,670); foundation fellowships ($6,624,500); 1998: foundation matching gifts ($2,307,874) foundation fellowships ($8,524,615)
Assets: $4,200,000,000 (2003 approx); $4,479,153,951 (2000); $4,720,044,000 (1999)

Typical Recipients

Arts & Humanities: Arts Associations & Councils, Arts Centers, Arts Festivals, Arts Funds, Arts Institutes, Community Arts, Dance, Ethnic & Folk Arts, Film & Video, Historic Preservation, History & Archaeology, Libraries, Literary Arts, Museums/Galleries, Music, Opera, Performing Arts, Public Broadcasting, Theater, Visual Arts
Civic & Public Affairs: African American Affairs, Business/Free Enterprise, Civil Rights, Economic Development, Economic Policy, Employment/Job Training, Civic & Public Affairs-General, Hispanic Affairs, Housing, Law & Justice, Legal Aid, Minority Business, Municipalities/Towns, Nonprofit Management, Philanthropic Organizations, Professional & Trade Associations, Public Policy, Safety, Urban & Community Affairs, Women's Affairs, Zoos/Aquariums
Education: Arts/Humanities Education, Business Education, Colleges & Universities, Economic Education, Education Associations, Education Reform, Environmental Education, Faculty Development, Education-General, Health & Physical Education, International Exchange, International Studies, Journalism/Media Education, Legal Education, Literacy, Medical Education, Minority Education, Public Education (Precollege), Science/Mathematics Education, Social Sciences Education
Environment: Air/Water Quality, Energy, Environment-General, Resource Conservation, Wildlife Protection
Health: Clinics/Medical Centers, Geriatric Health, Health Policy/Cost Containment, Health Organizations, Medical Research, Mental Health, Preventive Medicine/Wellness Organizations, Public Health, Research/Studies Institutes
International: Foreign Educational Institutions, Health Care/Hospitals, Human Rights, International Affairs, International Development, International Environmental Issues, International Organizations, International Peace & Security Issues, International Relations, Missionary/Religious Activities
Religion: Religious Welfare, Seminaries, Social/Policy Issues
Science: Observatories & Planetariums, Scientific Centers & Institutes, Scientific Organizations, Scientific Research
Social Services: Child Welfare, Community Service Organizations, Crime Prevention, Family Planning, Family Services, Senior Services, United Funds/United Ways, Volunteer Services, Youth Organizations

Application Procedures

Initial Contact: Submit a one-page summary accompanied by a two- to three-page letter of inquiry.
Application Requirements: The summary should include information regarding who will carry out the work; name of the organization (and acronym if commonly used); name of parent organization, if applicable; name of chief executive officer or similar person; organization's address, phone number, fax number, and e-mail address; name and title of principal contact person; and web address, if any.
Although the foundation has no set format for letters of inquiry, they should generally include the name or topic of the proposed project; a brief statement (two or three sentences) of the purpose and nature of the proposed work; the significance of the issue addressed and how it relates to a MacArthur program strategy; how the work will address the issue; how the issue relates to the applicant organization; why applicant organization is qualified to undertake the project; geographic area or country where the work will take place; time period for which funding is requested; information about those who will be helped by and interested in the work and how you will communicate with them; amount requested; and total estimated cost. The foundation welcomes attachments that the applicant feels will help the foundation understand the proposal.

Deadlines: None for most grant programs. However, the Special Grant Competitions do have varying deadlines; contact the Office of Grants Management for further information.
Review Process: Applicants will be acknowledged promptly.
Notes: Letters of Inquiry may be submitted by mail or may be emailed to: LOI@macfound.org. Faxed inquiries are not accepted.

Restrictions

The foundation does not support political activities or attempts to influence action on specific legislation, nor does it provide scholarships. Annual fundraising drives, institutional benefits, honorary functions, or similar projects are not supported.

Additional Information

Although not a prerequisite, the Foundation explores the possibility of including support for communications as part of the consideration of all proposals and welcomes proposals that have incorporated communication plans.
Publications: Annual Report; Programs and Policies; Individual Booklets Concerning Each Program as Well as Program-Related Investments

Foundation Officials

Lloyd Axworthy: director PRIM NONPR EMPL director Liu Centre Study Global Issues: University of British Columbia.
Carmen Barroso: director population, new partnerships
Kennette Benedict: director peace & international cooperation
Herman Brewer: director Chicago working group
John Seely Brown: director
Diane E. Carr: grant administrator
Drew Saunders Days, III: director B 1941. ED Hamilton College BA (1963); Yale University LLB (1966). PRIM NONPR EMPL Alfred M. Rankin Professor of Law: Yale University, Law School. NONPR AFFIL member: U.S. Citizen Committee Monitor Helsinki Accords; solicitor general: U.S. Department Justice; member: American Law Institute; director, member executive committee: Lawyers Committee Civil Rights Under Law.
Robert E. Denham: director PRIM CORP EMPL attorney: Munger, Tolles & Olson LLP.
Ignacio Estrada: grant administrator
Jonathan Foster Fanton: president, chief executive officer B Mobile, AL 1943. ED Yale University BA (1965); Yale University MA (1977); Yale University PhD (1978). CORP AFFIL co-chair: 14th Street Union Square Local Development Corp. NONPR AFFIL trustee: New York Commission Inc. Colleges & Universities; co-chairman: Taynbee Foundation; co-chairman: International Committee Academic Freedom; board directors: Foundation Civil Society; chairman: Helsinki Watch Committee; member: American Historical Association; member: Council Foreign Relations; board directors: American Ditchley Foundation. CLUB AFFIL Economic Club.
Mark D. Fitzsimmons: associate director fellows program
William H. Foege, MD: director B Decorah, IA 1936. ED Pacific Lutheran University BA (1957); University of Washington MA (1961); Harvard University MPh (1965). PRIM NONPR EMPL distinguished professor: Emory University, Rollins School Public Health. NONPR AFFIL director: Kaiser Permanente; executive director: Task Force for Child Survival and Development; director: Kaiser Foundation Hospitals; department field coord: International Red Cross Joint Relief Action; director: Kaiser Foundation Health Plan.
Jamie Shona Gorelick: director B New York, NY 1950. PRIM CORP EMPL vice chair: Fannie Mae. CORP AFFIL member: Local Initiatives Support Corp. NONPR AFFIL member: Washington Legal Clinic for

Homeless; member: Women's Bar Association; member: National Park Foundation; member: National Women's Law Center; member: National Community Support Law Enforcement; member: National Legal Center Public Interest; member: District of Columbia College Access; member: Carnegie Endowment; member: Council Foreign Relations; member: American Promise - Alliance for Youth; member: Bazelon Center Mental Health Law; follow: American Bar Foundation; member: American Law Institute.
Mary Graham: director PRIM NONPR EMPL research fellow: Harvard University, Kennedy School Government.
Judith F. Helzner: director population & reprod health
John Paul Holdren: director B Sewickley, PA 1944. ED Massachusetts Institute of Technology SB (1965); Massachusetts Institute of Technology SM (1966); Stanford University PhD (1970). NONPR AFFIL member: President Committee Advisory Science & Technology; chairman, member executive committee: Pugwash Conference Science & World Affairs; member: National Academy Sciences; professor envir policy: Harvard University; consult: Lawrence Livermore National Laboratory; member: California Academy Sciences; member: Federation American Scientists; member: American Physics Society; fellow: American Academy of Arts & Sciences; fellow: American Association Advancement Science.
Richard J. Kaplan: director grants mgmt, res and info CORP AFFIL president: Coastal Managed Healthcare. CLUB AFFIL pres: Standard Club.
Sara Lawrence Lightfoot: chairman ED Harvard University EdD. PRIM NONPR EMPL professor: Harvard University, Graduate School of Education. NONPR AFFIL director: Bright Horizons Childrens Centers.
Paul Eugene Lingenfelter: vice president human and community dev B Duncansville, PA 1945. ED Wheaton College BA (1967); Michigan State University MA (1968); University of Michigan PhD (1974). NONPR AFFIL member: America Evaluation Association; vice president: Program on Human and Community Development.
Susan E. Manske: vice president, chief investment officer ED Marquette University MBA; University of Wisconsin, Milwaukee.
Dan M. Martin: director world resources & population programs
Mario J. Molina: director PRIM NONPR EMPL institute professor: Massachusetts Institute Technology.
Mary E. Petrites: grant administrator
George A. Ranney, Jr.: director B Chicago, IL 1940. ED Harvard University BA (1962); University of Chicago JD (1966). PRIM CORP EMPL partner: Mayer, Brown & Platt PRIM NONPR EMPL president, chief executive officer: Chicago Metropolis 2020. CORP AFFIL vice president, general counsel: Ryerson Tull Inc. NONPR AFFIL member: Commerce Counsel Network; trustee: University Chicago; member: Chicago Bar Association; member: American Bar Association.
Elspeth Revere: director general program
J. Stephen Richards: grant department administrator
Daniel J. Socolow: director fellows program
Thomas Charles Theobald: director B Cincinnati, OH 1937. ED College of the Holy Cross AB (1958); Harvard University MBA (1960). PRIM CORP EMPL partner: Blair Capital Partners, LLC. CORP AFFIL director: Xerox Corp.; director: Stein Roe Funds; director: United States Timberlands Co.; director: RxRemedy; director: Mony Life Insurance Co.; director: Mutual Life Insurance Co. New York; director: Mony Group Inc.; director: LaSalle Printings Inc.; director: LaSalle United States Realty Income Growth Fund; director: Anixter International Inc. NONPR AFFIL director: Associates Harvard Business School; trustee: Northwestern University; member commission architecture: Art Institute of Chicago.
Woodward A. Wickham, Jr.: vice president general program B Jackson, MI 1942. ED Harvard University

BA (1964); Harvard University MA (1969). PRIM CORP EMPL senior vice president: Jan Krukowski Associates Inc.
Marc P. Yanchura: treasurer

Grants Analysis

Disclosure Period: calendar year ending 2001
Total Grants: $214,900,000*
Number of Grants: 1,514
Average Grant: $141,942
Highest Grant: $25,000,000
Lowest Grant: $2,500
Typical Range: $50,000 to $500,000
*Note: Giving excludes fellowship.

Recent Grants

Note: Grants derived from 2000 Annual Report.

General

1,050,000	World Federalist Movement, Institute for Global Policy, New York, NY
991,666	Stanford University, Stanford, CA
966,666	Human Rights Watch, New York, NY
800,000	Educational Foundation for Nuclear Science, Chicago, IL -- in support of the Bulletin of the Atomic Scientists
569,000	Foundation for Peace and Democracy, San Jose Costa Rica
513,600	Georgetown University, Institute for the Study of International Migration, Washington, DC
400,000	Moscow Public Science Foundation, Moscow Russia
400,000	Moscow Public Science Foundation, Moscow Russia
400,000	University of Maryland at College Park, Center for International and Security Studies, College Park, MD
370,000	Beijer International Institute of Ecological Economics, Stockholm Sweden

JOSIAH MACY, JR. FOUNDATION

Giving Contact

Martha Wolfgang, Vice President
44 East 64th Street
New York, NY 10021
Phone: (212)486-2424
Fax: (212)644-0765
Web: http://www.josiahmacyfoundation.org/jmacy1.html

Description

Founded: 1930
EIN: 135596895
Organization Type: General Purpose Foundation
Giving Locations: nationally.
Grant Types: Conference/Seminar, Project.

Donor Information

Founder: Established in 1930 by Mrs. Kate Macy Ladd (1863-1945) in honor of her father. The Macy family made its fortune in the whaling industry, shipping (both coastal and transoceanic), and oil. Mrs. Ladd directed the foundation to devote its attention to the advancement of medicine and health in the United States and abroad.

Financial Summary

Total Giving: $7,251,917 (fiscal year ending June 30, 2001); $7,906,573 (fiscal 2000); $7,245,479 (fiscal 1999)
Giving Analysis: Giving for fiscal 2001 includes: foundation matching gifts ($273,045)
Assets: $164,169,681 (fiscal 2001); $189,143,753 (fiscal 2000); $184,948,057 (fiscal 1999)

Typical Recipients

Arts & Humanities: Film & Video, Historic Preservation, Libraries, Museums/Galleries, Public Broadcasting

Civic & Public Affairs: Economic Policy, Civic & Public Affairs-General, Law & Justice, Nonprofit Management, Philanthropic Organizations, Women's Affairs

Education: Business Education, Colleges & Universities, Education Reform, Faculty Development, Gifted & Talented Programs, Health & Physical Education, Medical Education, Minority Education, Public Education (Precollege), Science/Mathematics Education, Social Sciences Education, Student Aid

Health: AIDS/HIV, Cancer, Children's Health/Hospitals, Clinics/Medical Centers, Health-General, Health Policy/Cost Containment, Health Funds, Health Organizations, Hospitals, Hospitals (University Affiliated), Medical Research, Medical Research, Medical Training, Nursing Services, Public Health, Single-Disease Health Associations

International: Foreign Educational Institutions, Health Care/Hospitals, Human Rights, International Development, International Relief Efforts

Religion: Social/Policy Issues

Science: Scientific Centers & Institutes, Scientific Labs

Social Services: Family Planning, Family Services, Substance Abuse

Application Procedures

Initial Contact: Send a full proposal.

Application Requirements: Brief summary should include the name of the sponsoring organization or institution, description of the project, names and qualifications of the persons in charge of the project, expected costs and duration of the project (including an itemized budget), letter of endorsement from the head of the sponsoring organization, and proof of current tax-exempt status.

Deadlines: None.

Review Process: Proposals are evaluated on their relevance to the foundation's current programs, the likelihood of the project's continued success after foundation support ceases, and the grantee's record of achievement in the proposed area of endeavor.

Restrictions

Grants are not made to individuals. The foundation does not fund medical research, general support, or construction or renovation projects.

Additional Information

The foundation also sponsors conferences and seminars/workshops.

Publications: Annual Report; Occasional Monographs

Foundation Officials

Lawrence Kimball Altman, MD: director B Quincy, MA 1937. ED Harvard University AB (1958); Tufts University MD (1962). PRIM CORP EMPL medicine corr columnist: New York Times Co. PRIM NONPR EMPL associate professor medicine: New York University. NONPR AFFIL fellow: New York Academy of Medicine; member: Society Epidemiology; associate professor medicine: New York University; member: American Society Tropical Medicine Hygiene; member: National Academy of Sciences Institute Medicine; fellow: American College Epidemiology; fellow: American College Physicians; member: American Board Medicine Specialties. CLUB AFFIL Century Club; Harvard Club.

Lou Stanton Auchincloss: honorary director B Lawrence, NY September 27, 1917. ED Yale University (1939); University of Virginia LLB (1941). NONPR AFFIL member: Century Association; chairman: Museum City New York; member: American Academy of Arts & Letters; member: Association Bar New York City.

John Carter Bacot: director B Utica, NY 1933. ED Hamilton College AB (1955); Cornell University LLB (1958). CORP AFFIL director: Time Warner Inc.; director: Venator Group Inc.; director: Centennial Insurance Co.; director: Phoenix Home Life Mutual Insurance Co.; director: Atlantic Reinsurance Co.; director: Associates First Capital Corp.; trustee: Atlantic Mutual Insurance Co. NONPR AFFIL member: New York State Bar Association; member: Pilgrims U.S.; chairman, trustee: New York Clearing House Association; director: Federal Reserve Bank New York; chairman board trustees: Hamilton College; member: Association Reserve City Bankers; member: Council Foreign Relations. CLUB AFFIL Montclair Golf Club; Union Club; Economic Club New York; The Links Club.

Alexander Gordon Bearn, MD: director honorary B Surrey, United Kingdom 1923. ED University of London BS (1945); University of London MB (1945); University of London MD (1951). PRIM NONPR EMPL adj professor: Rockefeller University, Rockefeller Institute. CORP AFFIL director: Biogen Inc. NONPR AFFIL member: Society Experimental Biology & Medicine; member: Union League Philadelphia; director: Royal Society Medicine Foundation; member: Sigma Xi; fellow: Royal College Physicians Edinburgh; fellow: Royal College Physicians London; professor: Rockefeller Institute; trustee: Rockefeller University; member: Medical Society London; foreign associate: Norwegian Academy Science Letters; member, board science overseers: Jackson Laboratory; member: Medical Research Society Great Britain; trustee: Howard Hughes Medical Institute; member: Institute Medicine NAS; member: Harveian Society London; member: Harvey Society; coun: Forgarty Center NIH; member: Genetics Society America; member: Century Association; professor emeritus, medicine: Cornell University; member: Association American Physicians; member: Association Physicians Great Britain & Ireland; member: American Society Clinical Investigation; member: American Society Human Genetics; executive officer: American Philosophical Society; member: American Society Biological Chemists; fellow: American Association Advancement Science. CLUB AFFIL Knickerbocker Club; Misquamicut Club; Crail Golf Club.

Rina Forlini: secretary

John W. Frymoyer, MD: director PRIM CORP EMPL dean: University of Vermont College Medicine. CORP AFFIL president, chief executive officer, director: Medical Center Hospital Vermont; president, chief executive officer, director: University Health Center; president, chief executive officer, director: Fanny Allen Hospital; president, chief executive officer, director: Fletcher Allen Health Care.

S. Parker Gilbert: advisory director B New York, NY 1933. ED Yale University BA (1956). CORP AFFIL director: Taubman Centers Inc.; director: Morgan Stanley Group Inc.; director: Burlington Resources Inc.; director, chairman audit committee: ITT Industries Inc. NONPR AFFIL president board trustee: Pierpont Morgan Library.

Bernard Warren Harleston, PhD: director, senior associates, B New York, NY 1930. ED Howard University BS (1951); University of Rochester PhD (1955). PRIM NONPR EMPL president: City College of City University of New York.

Dr. Arthur H. Hayes, Jr.: director B Highland Park, MI 1933. ED University of Santa Clara AB (1955); Oxford University MA (1957); Georgetown University (1957-1960); Cornell University MD (1964). PRIM CORP EMPL president: MediSci Associates. CORP AFFIL director: Myriad Genetics Inc.; director: Napro Biotherapeutics Inc.; director: Celgene Corp. NONPR AFFIL board regents: Santa Clara University; member: Sigma Xi; member editorial board: Prescribers Newsletter; fellow: Royal Society Medicine; director: Peace Foundation; member: Phi Beta Kappa; professor: New York Medicine College; fellow: New York Academy Medicine; member: New York Academy Science; member: Medical Society New York State; fellow: College Physicians Philadelphia; member:

Harvey Society; member, council deans, council academic socs: Association American Medical Colleges; honorary member: American Pharmacological Association; member: American Society Clinical Pharmacology & Therapeutics; member: American Federation Clinical Research; member: American Medical Association; fellow: American College Cardiology; fellow: American College Chest Physicians; fellow: American Academy Pharmacy Physicians; member: Alpha Omega Alpha; member: Alpha Sigma Nu; fellow: Academy Pharmacology Scientists.

Lawrence Smith Huntington: chairman emeritus B New York, NY 1935. ED Harvard University BA (1957); New York University LLB (1964). PRIM CORP EMPL chairman, chief executive officer, chairman executive committee, director: Fiduciary Trust Co. International. CORP AFFIL director: Princeton Packet Inc. NONPR AFFIL director: Woods Hole Research Center; director: World Wildlife Fund; vice chairman, treasurer, trustee: South Street Seaport Museum; director: Trinity Church; trustee: Saint Lukes Roosevelt Hospital Center; trustee: Santa Fe Institute; member advisory board: New York State Common Retirement Fund; trustee: Opsail; member advisory board: NASD International Markets; chairman: New York Law School; director: Business Executives National Security; trustee: Citizens Budget Committee. CLUB AFFIL trust: New York Yacht Club; American Alpine Club; Century Association.

John Jay Iselin, PhD: director B Greenville, SC 1933. ED Harvard University AB (1956); Cambridge University Corpus Christi College BA (1958); Cambridge University Corpus Christi College MA (1963); Harvard University PhD (1965). PRIM CORP EMPL president: Cooper Union for the Advancement of Science & Art. NONPR AFFIL member: Ventures Education; member: Waterford Institute; trustee: Public Education Association; member: Council Foreign Relations; member: National Geographic Society; member: Academy Political Science; member: American Friends University Cambridge. CLUB AFFIL Metro District of Columbia Club; Century Club; Harvard Club New York.

David Lincoln Luke, III: retired chairman board, B Tyrone, PA 1923. ED Yale University AB (1945). NONPR AFFIL trustee emeritus: Cold Spring Harbor Laboratory; trustee emeritus: Hotchkiss School. CLUB AFFIL River Club; Megantic Fish & Game Club; Piping Rock Club; Johns Island Club.

Mary Patterson McPherson, PhD: director B Abington, PA 1935. ED Smith College AB (1957); University of Delaware MA (1960); Bryn Mawr College PhD (1969). NONPR AFFIL member: American Philosophical Society; director: Philadelphia Contributionship. CLUB AFFIL Cosmopolitan Club.

Clarence F. Michalis: chairman B New York, NY 1922. ED Harvard University BS (1944). CORP AFFIL director: Schroeder Capital Funds. NONPR AFFIL trustee: Cooper Union; honorary chairman, trustee: Saint Lukes Roosevelt Hospital Center. CLUB AFFIL Masons Club.

June Elaine Osborn, MD: president B Endicott, NY 1937. ED Oberlin College BA (1957); Case Western Reserve University MD (1961). PRIM NONPR EMPL professor: University of Michigan. NONPR AFFIL member: National Vaccine Advisory Centre; professor emerita: University Michigan School Public Health & Medical School; member: National Institute on Drug Abuse; fellow: Infectious Diseases Society America; member: Institute Medicine; member: American Association Immunologists; director: Corporate Supportive Housing; fellow: American Academy Pediatrics; fellow: American Academy of Arts & Sciences; fellow: American Academy Microbiology.

Walter N. Rothschild, Jr.: hon director B New York, NY 1920. ED Harvard University (1942). CORP AFFIL honorary trustee, director: US Trust Co. New York. NONPR AFFIL director: Union Hospital Fund New York.

Grants Analysis

Disclosure Period: fiscal year ending June 30, 2001
Total Grants: $6,978,872*
Number of Grants: 55
Average Grant: $100,911*
Highest Grant: $880,600
Typical Range: $50,000 to $200,000
*Note: Giving excludes matching gifts. Average grant figure excludes two highest grants ($1,630,600).

Recent Grants

Note: Grants derived from fiscal 2002 Form 990.

General

765,492	New York University Medical Center, New York, NY
453,400	University of California School of Medicine, Los Angeles, CA
380,955	Columbia University Mailman School of Public Health, New York, NY
317,052	Case Western Reserve University, Cleveland, OH
317,052	University of Massachusetts at Boston, Boston, MA
298,388	University of Washington, Seattle, WA
224,273	Massachusetts Institute of Technology, Cambridge, MA
164,230	Ambulatory Pediatric Association, McLean, VA
131,840	University of Michigan School of Nursing, Ann Arbor, MI
125,558	National Public Health and Hospital Institute, Washington, DC

MACY'S EAST, INC.

Company Headquarters

151 W. 34th St.
New York, NY 10001
Web: http://www.macys.com

Company Description

Revenue: US$4.943 billion (2001)
Employees: 33200 (2001)
SIC(s): 5311 Department Stores.
Parent Company: Federated Department Stores, Inc., 7 W. Seventh St., Cincinnati, OH, United States

Operating Locations

Bloomingdale's (NY--New York); Bon Marche (WA--Seattle); Burdines (FL--Miami); Federated Department Stores, Inc. (OH--Cincinnati); Macy's East Inc. (CA--Los Angeles, Newark, San Francisco, San Jose, Sunnyvale; GA--Decatur; KS--Mission; NJ--Cranford, Lawrenceville, Paramus; NY--Bay Shore, Brooklyn); Rich's/Lazarus/Goldsmith's (GA--Atlanta); Stern's Department Stores (NJ--Paramus)

Giving Contact

Tom Zapf, Director, Consumer Affairs & Charitable Contributions
151 West 34th Street, Room 1825
New York, NY 10001
Phone: (212)494-4342
Web: http://www.macys.com

Description

Organization Type: Corporate Giving Program
Giving Locations: company operating locations.
Grant Types: Employee Matching Gifts, General Support, Project.

Financial Summary

Total Giving: Contributes through corporate direct giving program only.

Typical Recipients

Arts & Humanities: Arts Associations & Councils, Arts Centers, Arts Festivals, Arts Funds, Arts Institutes, Community Arts, Dance, Historic Preservation, Libraries, Literary Arts, Museums/Galleries, Music, Opera, Performing Arts, Public Broadcasting, Visual Arts
Civic & Public Affairs: Business/Free Enterprise, Civil Rights, Economic Policy, Employment/Job Training, Law & Justice, Legal Aid, Professional & Trade Associations, Public Policy, Safety, Urban & Community Affairs, Women's Affairs, Zoos/Aquariums
Education: Business Education, Colleges & Universities, Community & Junior Colleges, Continuing Education, Economic Education, Education Funds, Legal Education, Medical Education, Minority Education, Private Education (Precollege), Social Sciences Education, Special Education
Health: Emergency/Ambulance Services, Health Funds, Health Organizations, Hospitals, Medical Rehabilitation, Medical Research, Medical Training, Mental Health, Public Health
Social Services: Child Welfare, Community Centers, Community Service Organizations, Counseling, Delinquency & Criminal Rehabilitation, Emergency Relief, Homes, People with Disabilities, Recreation & Athletics, Senior Services, Substance Abuse, United Funds/United Ways, Volunteer Services, Youth Organizations

Application Procedures

Initial Contact: letter and proposal
Application Requirements: a description of organization, amount requested, purpose of funds sought, recently audited financial statement, last year's operating budget, list of major corporate contributors, copy of IRS determination letter
Deadlines: None.
Decision Notification: notification of funding decision will be made in writing
Notes: The company is unable to provide a status report on applications.

Restrictions

No merchandise, fashion shows, individuals, per answering machine message.

Additional Information

Although the company is now in Chapter 11, it is continuing its contributions. However, requests are being reviewed more carefully.
The company's objective is to donate 1% of pretax earnings to charitable activities.

Corporate Officials

James E. Gray: president, chief operating officer PRIM CORP EMPL president, chief operating officer: Macy's East Inc.

Giving Program Officials

Edward Jay Goldberg: vice president PRIM CORP EMPL vice president consumer affairs: R.H. Macy & Co. Inc.

J. F. MADDOX FOUNDATION

Giving Contact

Robert J. Reid, Executive Director, Secretary
PO Box 2588
Hobbs, NM 88241-2588
Phone: (505)393-6338
Fax: (505)397-7266
E-mail: bobreid@leaco.net
Web: http://www.jfmaddox.org/

Description

Founded: 1963
EIN: 756023767
Organization Type: General Purpose Foundation
Giving Locations: NM: Southeast New Mexico; TX: West Texas

Grant Types: Capital, Emergency, Loan, Matching, Project, Scholarship.
Note: Preference to capital programs and one-time programs.

Donor Information

Founder: The foundation was established in 1963 by the late J. F. Maddox and the late Mabel S. Maddox .

Financial Summary

Total Giving: $5,937,343 (2001); $7,379,143 (2000); $3,263,542 (1999)
Assets: $156,103,571 (2001); $155,595,342 (2000); $144,181,481 (1999). Note: NOT In 1998 the foundation moved from a fiscal year ending on June 30 to a calendar year.

Typical Recipients

Arts & Humanities: Arts & Humanities-General, Libraries, Museums/Galleries, Music, Opera, Performing Arts, Public Broadcasting, Theater
Civic & Public Affairs: Botanical Gardens/Parks, Community Foundations, Employment/Job Training, Civic & Public Affairs-General, Hispanic Affairs, Housing, Law & Justice, Legal Aid, Municipalities/Towns, Nonprofit Management, Professional & Trade Associations, Safety, Zoos/Aquariums
Education: Arts/Humanities Education, Colleges & Universities, Education Reform, Engineering/Technological Education, Education-General, Leadership Training, Literacy, Private Education (Precollege), Public Education (Precollege), Science/Mathematics Education, Student Aid
Environment: Environment-General, Resource Conservation
Health: Alzheimers Disease, Cancer, Diabetes, Emergency/Ambulance Services, Hospices, Hospitals, Hospitals (University Affiliated), Nutrition
International: Missionary/Religious Activities
Religion: Churches, Jewish Causes, Ministries, Religious Organizations, Religious Welfare
Social Services: At-Risk Youth, Child Abuse, Child Welfare, Community Centers, Community Service Organizations, Counseling, Crime Prevention, Day Care, Domestic Violence, Family Services, Food/Clothing Distribution, Homes, People with Disabilities, Recreation & Athletics, Scouts, Senior Services, Shelters/Homelessness, Social Services-General, Substance Abuse, United Funds/United Ways, United Funds/United Ways, Youth Organizations

Application Procedures

Initial Contact: Potential applicants should request guidelines before making formal proposals.
Application Requirements: The foundation will request further information if the proposal is considered to fall within the scope of the foundation. Include description of agency, list of agency's directors, officers, and key managers, description of proposed project, proof of tax-exempt status, and the agency's prior years Form 990
Deadlines: None.

Restrictions

The foundation does not ordinarily approve grants for individuals, operating budgets, other foundations, or endowment funds. Funding is restricted to Southeast New Mexico and Texas. The student loan and scholarship programs are limited to students in Lea County, New Mexico.

Additional Information

The foundation reports that projects which are ongoing must have a high probability of self-sustaining capability within a defined time frame in order to be funded.
Publications: Application Guidelines; Annual Report; Student Loan application form.

Foundation Officials

Harry H. Lynch: director B 1939. PRIM CORP EMPL principal: Sun Valley Partners Ltd. ADD CORP EMPL president: Lynch Properties Inc.; chairman, director: Sun Valley Fruit Co. Inc. CORP AFFIL director: Fleetwood Transportation Services.

Don Maddox: president PRIM CORP EMPL director: Maddox Law Firm PC. CORP AFFIL director: Southwest Public Service Co.

James M. Maddox: vice president

Thomas M. Maddox: director

Robert J. Reid: executive director, secretary

Ann M. Utterback: director

Grants Analysis

Disclosure Period: calendar year ending 2000
Total Grants: $7,106,551*
Number of Grants: 152
Average Grant: $23,086*
Highest Grant: $2,413,555
Lowest Grant: $500
Typical Range: $10,000 to $50,000
*Note: Giving excludes United Way and scholarships. Average grant figure excludes two highest grants ($3,643,700).

Recent Grants

Note: Grants derived from 2000 Form 990.

General

2,413,555	College of the Southwest, Hobbs, NM -- capital campaign
1,230,145	College of the Southwest, Hobbs, NM
813,516	City of Hobbs, Hobbs, NM -- for Teen Center
651,329	Hobbs Municipal Schools, Hobbs, NM -- core knowledge
438,720	Estacado Library Information Network, Hobbs, NM
146,310	United Way Lea County, Hobbs, NM
124,800	City of Jal, Jal, NM -- parks project
100,000	Artesia Main Street Beautification Project, Artesia, NM
98,732	College of the Southwest, Hobbs, NM -- for distinguished lecture series
90,000	New Mexico Junior College, Hobbs, NM -- college weekend event

MAGNA INTERNATIONAL OF AMERICA, INC.

Company Headquarters

600 Wilshire Drive
Troy, MI 48084
Web: http://www.magnaint.com

Company Description

Former Name: Douglas & Lomason Co.
Revenue: US$120 million (2001)
Employees: 400 (2001)
SIC(s): 3465 Automotive Stampings, 3714 Motor Vehicle Parts & Accessories.
Parent Company: Magna International, Inc., 337 Magna Dr., Aurora, ON, Canada

Operating Locations

Bloomington-Normal Seating Co. (IL--Normal); Chantland Co. Division (IA--Humboldt); Douglas & Lomason Co. (AR--Marianna; GA--Carrollton; IA--Red Oak; MO--Excelsior Springs, Troy; NE--Columbus; TN--Milan; TX--Del Rio); Magna International of America (MI--Southfield); Magna Lomason Corp. (AR--Marianna; GA--Carrollton, Columbus, La Grange; IL--Normal; IA--Humboldt, Red Oak; MI--Farmington Hills; MS--Amory; MO--Kansas City, Troy; NE--Columbus; TX--Del Rio)

Nonmonetary Support

Type: Donated Products; Workplace Solicitation

Giving Contact

Dick Banfield, President
24600 Hallwood Ct.
Farmington Hills, MI 48335-1671
Phone: (248)478-7800

Description

Organization Type: Corporate Giving Program
Giving Locations: MI
Grant Types: Capital, Challenge, Emergency, General Support, Operating Expenses, Project, Research, Scholarship.

Financial Summary

Total Giving: $91,000 (fiscal year ending September 30, 1997 approx); $91,000 (fiscal 1996); $108,000 (fiscal 1995)

Typical Recipients

Arts & Humanities: Arts Associations & Councils, Arts Institutes, Arts & Humanities-General, Historic Preservation, Libraries, Museums/Galleries, Music, Opera, Public Broadcasting, Theater
Civic & Public Affairs: Business/Free Enterprise, Economic Development, Civic & Public Affairs-General, Professional & Trade Associations, Public Policy, Safety, Urban & Community Affairs, Zoos/Aquariums
Education: Business Education, Colleges & Universities, Community & Junior Colleges, Education Associations, Engineering/Technological Education, Education-General, Minority Education
Health: Eyes/Blindness, Health-General, Hospices, Hospitals, Medical Research, Mental Health, Single-Disease Health Associations
Science: Science Exhibits & Fairs
Social Services: Animal Protection, Child Welfare, Community Centers, Community Service Organizations, Family Services, Recreation & Athletics, United Funds/United Ways, Volunteer Services, Youth Organizations

Application Procedures

Initial Contact: Send a full proposal. Include a description of organization, amount requested, purpose of funds sought, recently audited financial statements, proof of tax-exempt status, and how support benefits company associates.
Deadlines: None.

Restrictions

Does not support individuals, religious organizations for sectarian purposes, or political or lobbying groups.

Corporate Officials

Dick Banfield: president PRIM CORP EMPL president: Magna Lomason Corp.

Grants Analysis

Typical Range: $500 to $1,000
Note: A more recent grants list was unavailable.

Recent Grants

Note: Grants derived from fiscal 1996 grants list.

General

Boy Scouts of America, Detroit, MI
Detroit Historical Society, Detroit, MI
Detroit Institute of Arts, Detroit, MI
Detroit Institute for Children, Detroit, MI
Detroit Symphony Orchestra, Detroit, MI
Farmington Philharmonic, Farmington, MI
Girl Scouts Council of Michigan, Pontiac, MI
Michigan Opera Theater, Detroit, MI
YMCA Farmington, Farmington, MI
Concerned Citizens for Arts, Detroit, MI

CHESLEY G. MAGRUDER FOUNDATION

Giving Contact

Board of Trustees
c/o SunTrust
PO Box 3838
Orlando, FL 32802
Phone: (407)237-5319
Fax: (407)237-5346

Description

Founded: 1979
EIN: 591920736
Organization Type: Private Foundation
Giving Locations: FL: emphasis is on central FL
Grant Types: General Support, Multiyear/Continuing Support.

Donor Information

Founder: Chesley G. Magruder Trust

Financial Summary

Total Giving: $785,200 (fiscal year ending June 30, 2001); $833,635 (fiscal 2000); $728,980 (fiscal 1998)
Assets: $14,791,092 (fiscal 2001); $15,457,644 (fiscal 2000); $15,107,286 (fiscal 1998)

Typical Recipients

Arts & Humanities: Arts Associations & Councils, Dance, Historic Preservation, History & Archaeology, Libraries, Museums/Galleries, Opera, Public Broadcasting, Theater
Civic & Public Affairs: Clubs, Employment/Job Training, Civic & Public Affairs-General, Housing, Safety, Zoos/Aquariums
Education: Business Education, Colleges & Universities, Community & Junior Colleges, Literacy, Preschool Education, Private Education (Precollege), Vocational & Technical Education
Environment: Resource Conservation
Health: Alzheimers Disease, Cancer, Eyes/Blindness, Health Organizations, Hospices, Hospitals, Kidney, Single-Disease Health Associations
Religion: Churches, Religious Organizations, Religious Welfare, Religious Welfare
Science: Scientific Centers & Institutes
Social Services: Child Welfare, Community Centers, Community Service Organizations, Counseling, Crime Prevention, Day Care, Emergency Relief, Family Planning, Family Services, Food/Clothing Distribution, Scouts, YMCA/YWCA/YMHA/YWHA, Youth Organizations

Application Procedures

Initial Contact: Request application guidelines and grant proposal form.

Restrictions

Does not support individuals.

Additional Information

Publications: Application Guidelines; Grant Proposal Form
Trust(s): Suntrust Bank, Central Florida, NA

Foundation Officials

Robert N. Blackford: trustee
Leon Hunter Handley: trustee B Lakeland, FL 1927. ED University of Florida BSBA (1949). PRIM CORP EMPL president: Gurney & Handley. CORP AFFIL director: Claude H Wolfe; director: Mine & Mill Supply Co.; director: Southern Industries Savings Bank; chairman, director: Beneficial Savings Bank. NONPR AFFIL member: Trial Attorneys America; chairman, trustee: WMFE-TV; membere: Shriners; member: Rotary; member: Scottish Rite; member: Phi Kappa Phi; member: Press Society; director: Orlando/Tampa; member: Phi Delta Phi; member: Masons; member:

Orange County Bar Association; member: Intl Associate Defense Counsel; member: Florida Bar Association; member: Florida Blue Key; director: Cracker Groves; member: Fed Insurance & Corp. Counsel; member: Beta Gamma Sigma; general counselor, life director: Central Florida Fair; member: American Judicature Society; member: Association Defense Trial Attys; fellow: American College Trial Lawyers; nen: American Board Trial Advocates; member: American Board Trial Attys; member: Alpha Tau Omega; member: American Bar Association; member: Alpha Kappa Psi. CLUB AFFIL University Club; Orlando Country Club; Travelers Club; Century Club; Citrus Club.

Dr. Allen R. Holcomb: trustee
Ernest M. Kelly: trustee
Dr. G. Brock Magruder: trustee

Grants Analysis

Disclosure Period: fiscal year ending June 30, 2001
Total Grants: $785,200
Number of Grants: 64
Average Grant: $12,269
Highest Grant: $50,000
Lowest Grant: $3,657
Typical Range: $5,000 to $25,000

Recent Grants

Note: Grants derived from fiscal 2000 Form 990.

General

54,000	St. John Evangelical Lutheran Church
50,000	Orange County Historical Society, Orlando, FL
45,000	Orlando Science Center, Orlando, FL
25,000	Central Florida YMCA, Orlando, FL
25,000	Christ School
25,000	Lake Highland Preparatory School, Orlando, FL
25,000	University of Central Florida Foundation, Orlando, FL
21,000	Boy Scouts of America Central Florida Council, Orlando, FL
20,000	Beta Center Inc, Orlando, FL
20,000	Boys & Girls Club of Central Florida, FL

A. L. MAILMAN FAMILY FOUNDATION

Giving Contact

Luba H. Lynch, Executive Director
707 Westchester Avenue
White Plains, NY 10604
Phone: (914)683-8089
Fax: (914)686-5519
E-mail: almf@mailman.org
Web: http://www.mailman.org

Description

Founded: 1980
EIN: 510203866
Organization Type: Family Foundation
Giving Locations: nationally.
Grant Types: Project, Research.

Donor Information

Founder: The foundation was created by the late Abraham L. Mailman and the Mailman Foundation, Inc. A. L. Mailman was a financier from Hollywood, FL, who had a lifelong commitment to philanthropy. In 1943, with his brother Joseph, A. L. Mailman established the Mailman Foundation, which supported universities, hospitals, and Jewish causes in the United States and Israel. The brothers also contributed to the Mailman Child Development Center at the University of Miami, The Mailman Family Center at Nova Southeastern University, and the Mailman Research Center at McLean Hospital.

The A. L. Mailman Family Foundation was established in 1980 when the assets of the original Mailman Foundation were divided between the families of the two brothers. Marilyn M. Segal, A. L. Mailman's daughter, then became the chairman of the foundation and continued her father's philanthropic tradition.

Financial Summary

Total Giving: $1,532,569 (2001); $1,687,131 (2000); $1,095,640 (1999)
Assets: $25,869,540 (2001); $30,000,000 (2000); $31,180,616 (1999)
Gifts Received: $5,052 (1993); $15,000 (1992)

Typical Recipients

Arts & Humanities: Arts Centers, History & Archaeology, Libraries, Museums/Galleries, Music, Performing Arts, Public Broadcasting
Civic & Public Affairs: African American Affairs, Civil Rights, Community Foundations, Economic Development, Economic Policy, Civic & Public Affairs-General, Hispanic Affairs, Housing, Law & Justice, Philanthropic Organizations, Professional & Trade Associations, Public Policy, Urban & Community Affairs, Women's Affairs, Zoos/Aquariums
Education: Colleges & Universities, Continuing Education, Education Associations, Education Reform, Education-General, Health & Physical Education, International Studies, Leadership Training, Medical Education, Preschool Education, Public Education (Precollege), Religious Education, Social Sciences Education, Vocational & Technical Education
Environment: Environment-General
Health: Alzheimers Disease, Cancer, Children's Health/Hospitals, Clinics/Medical Centers, Health Organizations, Mental Health, Nutrition, Prenatal Health Issues, Public Health, Research/Studies Institutes
International: Health Care/Hospitals, International Development, International Relief Efforts
Religion: Jewish Causes, Religious Welfare, Social/Policy Issues
Social Services: At-Risk Youth, Camps, Child Welfare, Community Service Organizations, Counseling, Crime Prevention, Day Care, Delinquency & Criminal Rehabilitation, Domestic Violence, Family Planning, Family Services, Food/Clothing Distribution, People with Disabilities, Shelters/Homelessness, United Funds/United Ways, United Funds/United Ways, Youth Organizations

Application Procedures

Initial Contact: All potential applicants are encouraged to write a two- to three-page letter of inquiry before writing a full proposal. The letter should include a summary of the project's goals and target audience, its fit with the foundation's objectives, an estimated budget and timeframe, and plans for evaluation and dissemination of results. If the proposed project is of interest to the foundation, the applicant will be invited to send a full proposal.
Application Requirements: The full proposal should include the following: full contact information; a two-page executive summary; statement of need; description of the project and rationale for the approach; workplan, including a timeline and staffing plan; anticipated outcomes, benchmarks, products, and long-term impact; evaluation plan; plans for disseminating the product or communicating lessons learned to key constituencies; a description of organization and staff qualifications, including past performance on similar projects; project budget, showing committed and anticipated funds; organization's current operating budget; list of board members and/or advisors; letters of support from board and collaborating organizations; proof of tax-exempt status; and reasons for seeking partnership with a national funder (for state-focused proposals).
Deadlines: Proposals are due by January 15 for April review and by June 15 for October review. Letters of inquiry should be submitted at least four weeks prior to the proposal deadline.

Review Process: The directors of the foundation meet twice a year in April and October to set policy and to authorize grants.
Notes: Applicants are encouraged to submit letters of inquiry and proposals by e-mail rather than by hard copy, and to fax or mail the requested attachments. The foundation does not accept unsolicited proposals for health-related grants under The Love Jen Fund.

Restrictions

The foundation does not give grant support for ongoing direct services, general operating expenses, individual support, capital expenditures, or endowment campaigns. The foundation does not fund local services or programs.

Additional Information

The foundation reports that they conduct seminars and workshops.
The foundation is interested in projects that extend knowledge, make linkages between research and improved practice and policies, and communicate knowledge gained through research and practice to the broader public.
Publications: Annual Report (including Application Guidelines)

Foundation Officials

Betty S. Bardige: chairman, director PRIM CORP EMPL stockholder, director: Puritan Investment Corp.
Jonathan R. Gordon: director
Jay B. Langner: director B 1930. ED University of Pennsylvania BS; University of Pennsylvania Wharton School (1950). PRIM CORP EMPL chairman, president, chief executive officer, director: Hudson General Corp. CORP AFFIL president, director: Hudson Aviation Services Delaware.
Patricia S. Leiberman: vice chair PRIM CORP EMPL stockholder, director: Puritan Investment Corp.
Luba H. Lynch: executive director, secretary B Regensburg, Germany 1947. ED Royal Conservatory of Music (Toronto) AA (1967); University of Toronto BA (1968). NONPR AFFIL member: National Association Education Young Children; board member: New York Regional Association Grantmakers; board member: Family Resource Coalition; member: American Orthopsychiatric Association; board member: Viola W Bernard Foundation.
Wendy S. Masi: vice president PRIM CORP EMPL stockholder, director: Puritan Investment Corp.
Marilyn Mailman Segal: chairman emeritus B Utica, NY 1927. ED Wellesley College BA (1948); McGill University BS (1949); Nova University PhD (1970). CORP AFFIL stockholder, director: Puritan Investment Corp. NONPR AFFIL trustee: University Miami; chairman national visiting committee: University Miami School Nursing; dean: Nova University Family School Center; member: Society Research Child Development; member: American Psychological Association; member: Delta Kappa Gamma.
Richard D. Segal: president, director PRIM CORP EMPL stockholder, director: Puritan Investment Corp.
Donna Tookmanian: treasurer PRIM CORP EMPL controller: Seavest Partners.

Grants Analysis

Disclosure Period: calendar year ending 2001
Total Grants: $1,502,569*
Number of Grants: 64
Average Grant: $19,247*
Highest Grant: $290,000
Lowest Grant: $250
Typical Range: $5,000 to $50,000
*Note: Giving excludes United Way. Average grant figure excludes highest grant.

Recent Grants

Note: Grants derived from 2001 Form 990.

General

290,000	Nova Southeastern University, Ft. Lauderdale, FL -- capital

63,175	Florida Children's Forum, Tallahassee, FL -- educational
45,000	Parent Services Project, Inc., San Rafael, CA -- educational
45,000	Self Reliance Foundation, Washington, DC -- education
43,000	Pacific Oaks, Pasadena, CA -- educational
40,000	University of Rochester, Rochester, NY -- educational
35,000	Education Commission of States, Denver, CO -- educational
35,000	Nova Southeastern University, Ft. Lauderdale, FL -- educational
35,000	Publicolor, New York, NY -- educational
30,696	Chicago Health Connection, Chicago, IL -- educational

MANAGEMENT COMPENSATION GROUP/ DULWORTH, INC.

Company Headquarters
Los Angeles, CA

Company Description
Employees: 135
SIC(s): 8700 Engineering & Management Services.

Operating Locations
Management Compensation Group/Dulworth Inc. (TX--Houston)

Nonmonetary Support
Type: Donated Equipment

Giving Contact
Pat Bratcher, Office Manager
1021 Main St. Suite 1300
Houston, TX 77002
Phone: (713)222-8383
Fax: (713)222-8831
E-mail: pbratcher@mcghouston.com

Description
Organization Type: Corporate Giving Program
Giving Locations: headquarters area only.
Grant Types: Award, Employee Matching Gifts, Multiyear/Continuing Support.
Note: Also provides officer discretionary gifts.

Typical Recipients
Arts & Humanities: Arts Appreciation, Arts Associations & Councils, Arts Centers, Arts Funds, Arts Institutes, Ballet, Community Arts, Arts & Humanities-General, Libraries, Museums/Galleries, Music, Performing Arts, Public Broadcasting, Theater, Visual Arts
Civic & Public Affairs: Business/Free Enterprise, Civil Rights, Ethnic Organizations, Civic & Public Affairs-General, Inner-City Development, Philanthropic Organizations, Professional & Trade Associations
Education: Arts/Humanities Education, Business Education, Colleges & Universities, Education-General
Health: Cancer, Health-General, Geriatric Health, Multiple Sclerosis
Religion: Jewish Causes
Social Services: Animal Protection, At-Risk Youth, Camps, Family Planning, Social Services-General, United Funds/United Ways, Youth Organizations

Application Procedures
Initial Contact: Send a brief letter of inquiry.
Application Requirements: Include a description of organization, purpose of funds sought, and proof of tax-exempt status.

Restrictions
Does not support political or lobbying groups, fraternal or social organizations, or organizations outside operating areas.

Corporate Officials
Chuck Bracht: president PRIM CORP EMPL president: Management Compensation Group/Dulworth.
James Phillips: chief executive officer PRIM CORP EMPL chief executive officer: Management Compensation Group/Dulworth.

Grants Analysis
Typical Range: $10 to $1,000

JACK N. AND LILYAN MANDEL FOUNDATION

Giving Contact
Jack N. Mandel, Trustee
2829 Euclid Avenue
Cleveland, OH 44115
Phone: (216)875-6500
Fax: (216)875-6580

Description
Founded: 1963
EIN: 346546418
Organization Type: Private Foundation
Giving Locations: OH
Grant Types: General Support.

Donor Information
Founder: Jack N. Mandel and the late Lilyan Mandel

Financial Summary
Total Giving: $10,363,688 (2000); $11,042,839 (1999); $10,238,977 (1998)
Giving Analysis: Giving for 2000 includes: foundation grants to United Way ($25,000) 1999: foundation grants to United Way ($25,000)
Assets: $190,064,870 (2000); $240,227,924 (1999); $200,931,829 (1998)
Gifts Received: $4,735,700 (2000); $857,852 (1998); $131,709,375 (1996). Note: In 1998, contributions were received from John N. Mandel ($801,038) and Sheldon Mandel ($56,814). In 1996, contributions were received from John N. Mandel ($97,500,000), Courtland Associates ($33,509,375) and Lilyan Mandel Irrevocable Trust ($700,000). In 1993, contributions were received from Courtland Associates ($9,595,846) and Lilyan Mandel Trust ($500,000.)

Typical Recipients
Arts & Humanities: Arts Outreach, Ballet, Dance, History & Archaeology, Libraries, Museums/Galleries, Music, Opera, Performing Arts, Public Broadcasting, Theater
Civic & Public Affairs: Civil Rights, Economic Development, Ethnic Organizations, Civic & Public Affairs-General, Housing, Municipalities/Towns, Nonprofit Management, Professional & Trade Associations, Public Policy, Safety, Urban & Community Affairs, Women's Affairs
Education: Arts/Humanities Education, Business-School Partnerships, Colleges & Universities, Education-General, International Studies, Literacy, Private Education (Precollege), Student Aid
Health: AIDS/HIV, Alzheimers Disease, Children's Health/Hospitals, Clinics/Medical Centers, Diabetes, Emergency/Ambulance Services, Eyes/Blindness, Geriatric Health, Heart, Multiple Sclerosis, Public Health, Single-Disease Health Associations
International: Foreign Arts Organizations, Health Care/Hospitals, International Organizations, International Peace & Security Issues, Missionary/Religious Activities

Religion: Bible Study/Translation, Churches, Dioceses, Religion-General, Jewish Causes, Religious Organizations, Religious Welfare, Social/Policy Issues, Synagogues/Temples
Social Services: Child Welfare, Community Service Organizations, Food/Clothing Distribution, Homes, People with Disabilities, Recreation & Athletics, United Funds/United Ways, Volunteer Services, Youth Organizations

Application Procedures
Initial Contact: The foundation has no formal grant application procedure or application form. Send written request.
Application Requirements: Include description of project and justification for grant, amount requested and term of grant, pertinent financial information, proof of tax-exempt status, and an appraisal of the requesting organization by a standard-setting organization, if available.
Deadlines: None.

Foundation Officials
Jack N. Mandel: trustee B Austria July 16, 1911. ED Cleveland College; Fenn College (1930-1933). PRIM CORP EMPL director: Premier Farnell PLC. CORP AFFIL founder, chairman finance committee: Premier Industries Corp. NONPR AFFIL trustee: Tel Aviv University Museum Diaspora; trustee: Temple Woodruff Foundation; member executive committee: National Conference Christians & Jews; life trustee: South Broward Jewish Federation; honorary trustee: Hebrew University; president: Montefiore Home Aged; member executive committee: Florida Society Blind; life trustee: Cleveland Jewish Welfare Foundation; trustee: Cleveland Playhouse; president advisory board: Barry University. CLUB AFFIL Commede Club; Emerald Hills Country Club; Beachmont Country Club.

Grants Analysis
Disclosure Period: calendar year ending 2000
Total Grants: $10,338,688*
Number of Grants: 61
Average Grant: $8,569*
Highest Grant: $8,700,000
Lowest Grant: $17
Typical Range: $100 to $25,000
*Note: Giving excludes United Way. Average grant figure excludes highest grant.

Recent Grants
Note: Grants derived from 2000 Form 990.

Library-Related
| 1,000 | National First Ladies Library, Canton, OH |

General
8,700,000	Mandel Supporting Foundations, Cleveland, OH
833,333	Brandeis University, Waltham, MA
333,333	Jewish Community Federation of Cleveland, Cleveland, OH
61,000	Cleveland Clinic Foundation, Cleveland, OH
47,222	PEF Israel Endowment Funds, New York, NY
42,551	Case Western Reserve University, Cleveland, OH
37,251	Federation for Community Planning, Cleveland, OH
25,000	New Cleveland Opera Company dba Cleveland Opera, Cleveland, OH
25,000	United Way of Greater Cleveland, Cleveland, OH
22,000	Temple, Beachwood, OH

MANDEVILLE FOUNDATION

Giving Contact

Hubert T. Mandeville, President, Treasurer & Director
60 East 42nd St.
Suite 843
New York, NY 10165
Phone: (212)697-4785

Description

Founded: 1963
EIN: 066043343
Organization Type: Private Foundation
Giving Locations: CT; NY
Grant Types: General Support.

Donor Information

Founder: Ernest W. Mandeville

Financial Summary

Total Giving: $28,536 (2001); $62,529 (2000); $64,199 (1999)
Giving Analysis: Giving for 1998 includes: foundation scholarships ($250) foundation ($43,339)
Assets: $673,059 (2001); $1,169,068 (2000); $1,335,425 (1999)
Gifts Received: $22,000 (1995). Note: In 1995, contributions were received from the Ernest W. Mandeville Trust.

Typical Recipients

Arts & Humanities: Arts Associations & Councils, Community Arts, Ethnic & Folk Arts, Arts & Humanities-General, Historic Preservation, History & Archaeology, Libraries, Museums/Galleries, Music, Theater
Civic & Public Affairs: Botanical Gardens/Parks, Chambers of Commerce, Employment/Job Training, Civic & Public Affairs-General, Nonprofit Management, Public Policy, Safety, Urban & Community Affairs
Education: Colleges & Universities, Education Associations, Environmental Education, Faculty Development, Medical Education, Minority Education, Preschool Education, Private Education (Precollege), Public Education (Precollege), Student Aid
Environment: Air/Water Quality, Environment-General, Resource Conservation
Health: Cancer, Clinics/Medical Centers, Emergency/Ambulance Services, Heart, Hospitals, Medical Research, Single-Disease Health Associations
International: Foreign Educational Institutions, International Organizations, International Relations
Religion: Churches, Ministries
Social Services: Animal Protection, Camps, Child Welfare, Community Centers, Community Service Organizations, Recreation & Athletics, Youth Organizations

Application Procedures

Initial Contact: The foundation has no formal grant application procedure or application form.
Deadlines: None.
Decision Notification: Replies are usually made in 90 days.

Foundation Officials

Maurice Coleman Greenbaum: secretary, director B Detroit, MI April 03, 1918. ED Wayne State University BA (1938); University of Michigan JD (1941); New York University LLM (1948). PRIM CORP EMPL counsel: Rosenman & Colin. CORP AFFIL director: Scrambler Inc.; member advisory committee: Great Neck Senior Citizens Center. NONPR AFFIL member: Village Justice; director: World Rehabilitation Fund; member visitors committee: University Miami School Marine & Atmospheric Science; associate trustee: North Shore University Hospital.

Meredith H. Hollis: director
Hubert T. Mandeville: president, treasurer, director
Matthew T. Mandeville: director
P. Kempton Mandeville: vice president, director

Grants Analysis

Disclosure Period: calendar year ending 2001
Total Grants: $28,536
Number of Grants: 13
Average Grant: $828*
Highest Grant: $18,600
Lowest Grant: $100
Typical Range: $500 to $5,000
*Note: Average grant figure excludes highest grant.

Recent Grants

Note: Grants derived from 2001 Form 990.

General

18,600	Westover School, Middleburg, CT
2,600	Sherman Chamber Ensemble, Sherman, TX
2,377	Andrew Glover Youth Program, Inc., New York, NY
1,250	Yale University, New Haven, CT
1,000	Hotchkiss School, Lakeville, CT
1,000	Ridley College, St. Catharines, ON Canada
500	Holland Society of New York, NY
500	Sherman Soccer, Sherman, CT
250	Jewish Community Center, Sherman, CT
134	Naromi Land Trust, Inc.

MANEELY FUND

Giving Contact

James E. O'Donnell, Vice President & Treasurer
900 Haddon Ave., Suite 432
Collingswood, NJ 08108
Phone: (856)854-5400
Fax: (856)854-5578

Description

Founded: 1952
EIN: 231569917
Organization Type: Private Foundation
Giving Locations: PA: limited grantmaking nationally.
Grant Types: General Support.

Donor Information

Founder: the late Edward F. Maneely

Financial Summary

Total Giving: $220,805 (2001); $254,625 (2000); $214,615 (1999)
Giving Analysis: Giving for 2001 includes: foundation grants to United Way ($19,500); 2000: foundation scholarships ($9,850); foundation grants to United Way ($19,150); 1999: foundation scholarships ($16,200); foundation grants to United Way ($19,650);
Assets: $3,487,162 (2001); $3,944,418 (2000); $4,218,428 (1999)

Typical Recipients

Arts & Humanities: Arts Associations & Councils, Ballet, Historic Preservation, History & Archaeology, Libraries, Museums/Galleries, Music, Opera, Public Broadcasting
Civic & Public Affairs: African American Affairs, Botanical Gardens/Parks, Business/Free Enterprise, Clubs, Economic Development, Economic Policy, Employment/Job Training, Ethnic Organizations, Civic & Public Affairs-General, Housing, Public Policy, Safety
Education: Arts/Humanities Education, Business Education, Colleges & Universities, Education Funds, Elementary Education (Public), Education-General,

---

Legal Education, Preschool Education, Private Education (Precollege), Religious Education, Secondary Education (Private), Student Aid, Vocational & Technical Education
Health: AIDS/HIV, Cancer, Children's Health/Hospitals, Emergency/Ambulance Services, Geriatric Health, Health Organizations, Hospices, Hospitals, Long-Term Care, Medical Rehabilitation, Medical Research, Nursing Services, Single-Disease Health Associations
International: International Relief Efforts, Missionary/Religious Activities
Religion: Churches, Dioceses, Missionary Activities (Domestic), Religious Organizations, Religious Welfare
Social Services: At-Risk Youth, Child Welfare, Community Service Organizations, Delinquency & Criminal Rehabilitation, Domestic Violence, Family Planning, Family Services, Homes, People with Disabilities, United Funds/United Ways, Youth Organizations

Application Procedures

Initial Contact: Send a letter of request on organization's letterhead.
Application Requirements: Include a description of organization, purpose of funds sought, and proof of tax-exempt status.
Deadlines: None.

Foundation Officials

Elizabeth J. Boylan: vice president
Betty DiPilla: secretary
Marie E. Dooner: secretary
James E. O'Donnell: president, treasurer

Grants Analysis

Disclosure Period: calendar year ending 2001
Total Grants: $201,305*
Number of Grants: 169
Average Grant: $1,191
Highest Grant: $14,000
Typical Range: $500 to $5,000
*Note: Giving excludes United Way.

Recent Grants

Note: Grants derived from 2001 Form 990.

General

14,000	United Way of Mercer County, Sharon, PA -- annual campaign
10,000	Project H.O.M.E., Philadelphia, PA -- operating expenses
5,000	Archdiocese of Philadelphia, Philadelphia, PA -- Catholic Heritage Center
5,000	Christopher Dock Mennonite High School, Lansdale, PA -- capital campaign
5,000	Holy Redeemer Health System, Huntington Valley, PA -- Drueding Center
5,000	Mercy Hospice, Philadelphia, PA -- operating expenses
5,000	Mount Tamalpais School, Mill Valley, CA -- annual giving and building fund and faculty endowment
5,000	Penn Northwest Development Corp., Mercer, PA -- economic development marketing and industrial outreach
5,000	Philadelphia Museum of Art, Philadelphia, PA -- operating expenses
5,000	Philadelphia Museum of Art, Philadelphia, PA -- operating expenses

MARBROOK FOUNDATION

Giving Contact

Conley Brooks, Jr., Trustee
730 Second Ave. S., Suite 1450
Minneapolis, MN 55402
Phone: (612)752-1783

Description

Founded: 1948
EIN: 416019899
Organization Type: Private Foundation
Giving Locations: MN: Minneapolis, St. Paul
Grant Types: Capital, Conference/Seminar, Emergency, Endowment, General Support, Multiyear/Continuing Support, Operating Expenses, Professorship, Project, Research, Seed Money.

Donor Information

Founder: the late Edward Brooks, the late Markell C. Brooks, Markell C. Brooks Charitable Trust

Financial Summary

Total Giving: $778,500 (2002); $860,000 (2001); $850,000 (2000)
Giving Analysis: Giving for 2002 includes: foundation grants to United Way ($17,500); 2000: foundation grants to United Way ($5,000); 1999: foundation grants to United Way ($17,500).
Assets: $17,192,046 (2002); $13,055,675 (2001); $21,070,615 (2000)
Gifts Received: $1,600 (2001); $1,298,443 (2000); $150,380 (1999). Note: In 2001, contributions were received from Katherine S. Brooks. In 2000, contributions were received from the Dwight F. Brooks Estate. In 1999, contributions were received from Corey Gibson. In 1997, contributions were received from Markell Brooks.

Typical Recipients

Arts & Humanities: Arts Centers, Arts Institutes, Community Arts, History & Archaeology, Libraries, Museums/Galleries, Music, Public Broadcasting, Theater
Civic & Public Affairs: African American Affairs, Botanical Gardens/Parks, Business/Free Enterprise, Community Foundations, Economic Policy, Employment/Job Training, Civic & Public Affairs-General, Native American Affairs, Nonprofit Management, Philanthropic Organizations, Public Policy, Urban & Community Affairs, Zoos/Aquariums
Education: Colleges & Universities, Economic Education, Education Funds, Leadership Training, Private Education (Precollege)
Environment: Air/Water Quality, Environment-General, Resource Conservation
Health: Cancer, Hospitals
Religion: Religious Organizations, Seminaries, Seminaries
Science: Science Museums, Scientific Centers & Institutes
Social Services: Child Welfare, Community Service Organizations, Day Care, Family Planning, Family Services, Recreation & Athletics, Social Services-General, United Funds/United Ways, YMCA/YWCA/YMHA/YWHA, Youth Organizations

Application Procedures

Initial Contact: full proposal
Application Requirements: Includes a description of organization, amount requested, budget, other possible sources of support, purpose of funds sought, and proof of tax-exempt status.
Deadlines: None.
Review Process: Trustee meetings are generally held in June/July and November/ December.

Restrictions

Grants are not made to support individuals, political or lobbying groups, or organizations outside operating areas.

Additional Information

Publications: Annual Report (including Application Guidelines)

Foundation Officials

John E. Andrus, III: trustee B Fergus Falls, MN 1909. ED Wesleyan University BA (1933). NONPR AFFIL director: John E. Andrus Memorial Inc.

Conley Brooks, Sr.: trustee
Conley Brooks, Jr.: trustee
Markell Brooks: trustee
William R. Humphrey, Jr.: trustee

Grants Analysis

Disclosure Period: calendar year ending 2002
Total Grants: $761,000*
Number of Grants: 123
Average Grant: $6,187
Highest Grant: $25,000
Lowest Grant: $1,000
Typical Range: $1,000 to $10,000
*Note: Giving excludes United Way.

Recent Grants

Note: Grants derived from 2001 Form 990.

General

30,000	Guthrie Theater, Minneapolis, MN
30,000	Minnesota Parks and Trails Council, St. Paul, MN
25,000	Minneapolis Foundation, Minneapolis, MN
25,000	University of Minnesota, St. Paul, MN
18,000	National Center for Social Entrepreneurs, Minneapolis, MN
17,500	Greater Twin Cities United Way, Minneapolis, MN
15,000	Amherst College, Amherst, MA
15,000	Minnesota Historical Society, St. Paul, MN
15,000	Minnetonka Center for the Arts, Minneapolis, MN
15,000	St. Paul Academy and Summit School, St. Paul, MN

MARCUS CORP.

Company Headquarters

Milwaukee, WI
Web: http://www.marcuscorp.com

Company Description

Founded: 1935
Ticker: MCS
Exchange: NYSE
Operating Revenue: US$389.8 million (2002)
Employees: 7800 (2002)
SIC(s): 5812 Eating Places, 7011 Hotels & Motels, 7832 Motion Picture Theaters Except Drive-In.

Operating Locations

Marcus Corp. (CT; FL; IL; IN; IA; KY; MA; MI; MN; MO; NE; NM; NC; OH; SC; TN; TX; WI--Milwaukee)

Marcus Corp. Foundation

Giving Contact

Stephen H. Marcus, President
250 East Wisconsin Avenue, Suite 1700
Milwaukee, WI 53202-4209
Phone: (414)905-1503

Description

EIN: 396046268
Organization Type: Corporate Foundation
Giving Locations: WI: Milwaukee
Grant Types: General Support, Project, Research.

Financial Summary

Total Giving: $595,755 (2001); $550,505 (2000); $786,874 (1998). Note: Contributes through foundation only.
Giving Analysis: Giving for 2000 includes: foundation grants to United Way ($45,000); foundation

($505,505); 1998: corporate scholarships ($930); corporate grants to United Way ($56,850); foundation ($729,094); 1997: foundation grants to United Way ($58,955) foundation ($541,009)
Assets: $1,623,792 (2001); $1,558,966 (2000); $1,970,892 (1998)
Gifts Received: $606,323 (2001); $326,668 (2000); $1,068,619 (1998). Note: Contributions were received from the Marcus Corporation.

Typical Recipients

Arts & Humanities: Arts Centers, Arts Festivals, Arts Institutes, Ballet, Community Arts, Dance, Film & Video, Arts & Humanities-General, Historic Preservation, History & Archaeology, Libraries, Museums/Galleries, Music, Opera, Performing Arts, Theater
Civic & Public Affairs: African American Affairs, Clubs, Economic Development, Employment/Job Training, Civic & Public Affairs-General, Hispanic Affairs, Housing, Municipalities/Towns, Parades/Festivals, Philanthropic Organizations, Professional & Trade Associations, Public Policy, Urban & Community Affairs, Zoos/Aquariums
Education: Arts/Humanities Education, Business Education, Colleges & Universities, Education Associations, Education Funds, Engineering/Technological Education, Faculty Development, Education-General, Leadership Training, Medical Education, Minority Education, Private Education (Precollege)
Environment: Wildlife Protection
Health: AIDS/HIV, Alzheimers Disease, Arthritis, Cancer, Children's Health/Hospitals, Clinics/Medical Centers, Diabetes, Health Organizations, Heart, Hospitals, Kidney, Medical Research, Multiple Sclerosis, Prenatal Health Issues, Public Health, Respiratory, Single-Disease Health Associations, Transplant Networks/Donor Banks, Trauma Treatment
International: Foreign Arts Organizations, Foreign Educational Institutions, International Development
Religion: Jewish Causes, Religious Organizations, Religious Welfare, Religious Welfare
Social Services: Child Abuse, Child Welfare, Community Centers, Community Service Organizations, Crime Prevention, Day Care, Domestic Violence, Family Services, People with Disabilities, Recreation & Athletics, Scouts, Shelters/Homelessness, United Funds/United Ways, Volunteer Services, YMCA/YWCA/YMHA/YWHA, Youth Organizations

Application Procedures

Initial Contact: The foundation requests applications be made in writing.
Application Requirements: Include name, address, project/program objectives, and reason for the request.
Deadlines: None.
Decision Notification: Late May and late November

Corporate Officials

Stephen Howard Marcus: chairman, chief executive officer B Minneapolis, MN 1935. ED University of Wisconsin BBA (1957); University of Michigan LLB (1960). PRIM CORP EMPL chairman, chief executive officer: Marcus Corp. ADD CORP EMPL president: Centre Theatres Corp.; president: Marcus Restaurants Inc.; president: Marcus Cinemas Inc.; president: Vending Corp. CORP AFFIL chairman: Budgetel Inns Inc.; trustee: Marc Plz Corp.; chairman: Baymont Inns Suites.

Foundation Officials

Diane M. Gershowitz: director
Thomas F. Kissinger: secretary, director
Stephen Howard Marcus: president, director (see above)

Grants Analysis

Disclosure Period: calendar year ending 2001
Total Grants: $480,805*
Number of Grants: 110
Average Grant: $3,356*

Highest Grant: $115,000
Lowest Grant: $25
Typical Range: $250 to $25,000
*Note: Giving excludes United Way. Average grant figure excludes highest grant.

Recent Grants

Note: Grants derived from 2001 Form 990.

Library-Related
5,600	Milwaukee Public Library Foundation, Milwaukee, WI -- program support

General
115,000	Milwaukee Art Museum, Milwaukee, WI -- community education
56,500	United Way of Greater Milwaukee, Milwaukee, WI -- community betterment
50,000	Great Circus Parade, Milwaukee, WI -- for community betterment
30,600	United Way, Milwaukee, WI -- Miller Park Gala
25,000	Florentine Opera Club, Milwaukee, WI -- program support
25,000	Marcus Center for the Performing Arts, Milwaukee, WI -- building fund
25,000	Polycystic Kidney Research Foundation, Kansas City, MO -- medical research
25,000	United Performing Arts Fund, Milwaukee, WI -- for community betterment
20,000	Milwaukee Repertory Theater, Milwaukee, WI -- program support
20,000	Sinai Samaritan, Milwaukee, WI -- community education

MARDAG FOUNDATION

Giving Contact

Paul A. Verret, President
600 5th Street Center
St. Paul, MN 55101-1797
Phone: (651)224-5463
Fax: (651)224-8123
E-mail: inbox@mardag.org
Web: http://www.mardag.org/

Description

Founded: 1969
EIN: 411698990
Organization Type: General Purpose Foundation
Giving Locations: MN
Grant Types: Capital, Challenge, General Support, Matching, Multiyear/Continuing Support, Project.

Donor Information

Founder: The Mardag Foundation was established in 1969. Originally known as the Ober Charitable Foundation, it was created by the estate of Agnes E. Ober . Mrs. Ober, who died at the age of eighty-two in 1969, was interested in the education of youth and in securing the welfare of the elderly. She served on the boards of trustees of several charitable foundations in St. Paul. Much of her estate was left to benefit charitable foundations in Minnesota.
The Mardag Foundation continues to distribute grants that reflect the philanthropic interests of Mrs. Ober.

Financial Summary

Total Giving: $1,703,725 (2001); $2,081,772 (1998); $2,245,577 (1997)
Assets: $52,236,978 (2001); $57,144,951 (1998); $50,425,881 (1997)

Typical Recipients

Arts & Humanities: Arts Associations & Councils, Arts Centers, Historic Preservation, History & Archaeology, Libraries, Literary Arts, Museums/Galleries, Music, Opera, Public Broadcasting, Theater
Civic & Public Affairs: African American Affairs, Asian American Affairs, Botanical Gardens/Parks, Business/Free Enterprise, Community Foundations, Economic Development, Employment/Job Training, Civic & Public Affairs-General, Hispanic Affairs, Housing, Legal Aid, Municipalities/Towns, Native American Affairs, Nonprofit Management, Philanthropic Organizations, Public Policy, Rural Affairs, Urban & Community Affairs, Women's Affairs, Zoos/Aquariums
Education: Colleges & Universities, Continuing Education, Education Funds, Education Reform, Elementary Education (Private), Faculty Development, Education-General, Literacy, Minority Education, Preschool Education, Private Education (Precollege), Public Education (Precollege), School Volunteerism, Special Education
Environment: Air/Water Quality, Environment-General
Health: Alzheimers Disease, Emergency/Ambulance Services, Geriatric Health, Health Organizations, Hospices, Hospitals, Long-Term Care, Mental Health, Public Health, Single-Disease Health Associations
International: International Environmental Issues
Religion: Jewish Causes, Religious Welfare
Science: Science Museums
Social Services: Animal Protection, Camps, Child Abuse, Child Welfare, Community Centers, Community Service Organizations, Counseling, Crime Prevention, Day Care, Delinquency & Criminal Rehabilitation, Domestic Violence, Emergency Relief, Family Planning, Family Services, Food/Clothing Distribution, Homes, People with Disabilities, Refugee Assistance, Senior Services, Sexual Abuse, Shelters/Homelessness, Substance Abuse, United Funds/United Ways, Volunteer Services, YMCA/YWCA/YMHA/YWHA, Youth Organizations

Application Procedures

Initial Contact: The foundation has a full set of application requirements available upon request. Applicants may wish to submit a brief summary (three to four pages, and less detailed than a full proposal) of their projects to determine whether or not they meet the interests of the foundation.
Application Requirements: A full proposal should include the name and address of the applicant, amount requested, project objective, proof of tax-exempt status, and (if applicable) the estimated number of Minnesota citizens who will benefit from the project. Applicants should also include the position of the individual signing the application, detailed budget, other sources of funding, statement that applicant will spend the funds awarded solely for the purpose stated, length of time for which support will be needed, detailed income statement, and a description of each staff member assigned to the project.
Deadlines: None. Generally proposals must be received approximately three and one-half months prior to the scheduled meeting date.
Review Process: The board meets in April, August, and November.
Notes: Proposals will not be returned to the applicant.

Restrictions

Normally, the foundation will not make grants for the west metro area of Minnesota; make grants to individuals; make annual grants; support sectarian religious programs; make grants for federated campaigns; or make grants for events, development offices or officers, medical research, conservation, or scholarship programs.

Additional Information

Publications: Annual Report

Foundation Officials

James E. Davidson: director
Delores Henderson: director
Katherine V. Lilly: vice president, director
Gayle M. Ober: president
Richard B. Ober: director
Timothy M. Ober: treasurer, director

Edward G. Pendergast: director B Springfield, MA 1938. ED University of Hartford BA (1973); University of Hartford MBA (1977). PRIM CORP EMPL vice president: Saint Paul Companies. CORP AFFIL vice president: Saint Paul Fire Marine Insurance Co.; director: Seabord Surety Co.
Paul A. Verret: secretary B 1941. PRIM NONPR EMPL president: Saint Paul Foundation.

Grants Analysis

Disclosure Period: calendar year ending 2001
Total Grants: $1,703,725
Number of Grants: 71
Average Grant: $21,793*
Highest Grant: $100,000
Lowest Grant: $500
Typical Range: $10,000 to $35,000
*Note: Average grant figure excludes two highest grants ($200,000).

Recent Grants

Note: Grants derived from 2001 Form 990.

General
100,000	Como Zoo and Conservatory Society, St. Paul, MN -- help finance Visitor and Education Center
100,000	Minnesota Historical Society, St. Paul, MN -- "Sounds Good to Me"
75,000	Dale Warland Singers, Minneapolis, MN -- help finance program and expansion and capacity building
75,000	St. Paul Foundation, St. Paul, MN -- help finance Children's Literacy Initiative
60,000	Saint Paul Riverfront Corporation, St. Paul, MN -- operating budget
50,000	Children's Home Society of Minnesota, St. Paul, MN -- capital campaign
50,000	Emma Norton Residence, St. Paul, MN -- capital campaign
50,000	Friends of the St. Paul Farmers' Market, Shoreview, MN -- capital campaign
50,000	Minnesota Public Radio, St. Paul, MN -- help finance construction of new facilities
50,000	Pioneerland Library System, Willmar, MN -- operating budget of adaptive technology

MARITZ, INC.

Company Headquarters

Fenton, MO
Web: http://www.maritz.com

Company Description

Revenue: US$15 billion (2001)
Employees: 6000 (2001)
SIC(s): 8740 Management & Public Relations.

Operating Locations

Maritz Inc. (IL--Chicago; KS--Kansas City; MI--Detroit; MO--St. Louis; NY--New York; TX--Dallas)

Nonmonetary Support

Type: Donated Equipment; Donated Products; In-kind Services; Loaned Employees; Loaned Executives

Giving Contact

Tom Tener, Senior Vice President, Corporate Communications
1375 North Highway Drive
Fenton, MO 63099
Phone: (636)827-4000
Fax: (636)827-5505
E-mail: tom.tener@maritz.com
Web: http://www.maritz.com/maritz-community-involvement.html

Description

Organization Type: Corporate Giving Program
Giving Locations: headquarters and operating communities.
Grant Types: Award, Capital, Conference/Seminar, Emergency, Employee Matching Gifts, General Support, Matching, Multiyear/Continuing Support.
Note: Employee matching gift ratio: 1 to 1. The company also awards one-time grants.

Financial Summary

Total Giving: $900,000 (1999 approx); $900,000 (1998 approx); $900,000 (1996 approx). Note: Contributes through corporate direct giving program and foundation.
Giving Analysis: Giving for 1998 includes: corporate direct giving (approx $450,000) foundation (approx $450,000)

Typical Recipients

Arts & Humanities: Arts Associations & Councils, Arts Funds, Arts Institutes, Community Arts, Dance, Ethnic & Folk Arts, Historic Preservation, Libraries, Museums/Galleries, Music, Opera, Performing Arts, Public Broadcasting, Theater, Visual Arts
Civic & Public Affairs: Business/Free Enterprise, Civil Rights, Economic Development, Employment/Job Training, Municipalities/Towns, Philanthropic Organizations, Public Policy, Women's Affairs, Zoos/Aquariums
Education: Colleges & Universities, Community & Junior Colleges, Economic Education, Elementary Education (Private), Literacy, Minority Education, Preschool Education, Public Education (Precollege)
Environment: Environment-General
Health: Health-General, Hospitals, Mental Health
Social Services: Child Welfare, Delinquency & Criminal Rehabilitation, Domestic Violence, Emergency Relief, Food/Clothing Distribution, People with Disabilities, Shelters/Homelessness, Social Services-General, Substance Abuse, United Funds/United Ways, Youth Organizations

Application Procedures

Initial Contact: Send a brief letter of inquiry and a full proposal.
Application Requirements: Include a description of organization, amount requested, purpose of funds sought, and recently audited financial statement.
Deadlines: None.

Restrictions

Does not support individuals or religious organizations for sectarian purposes.

Corporate Officials

James W. Kienker: senior vice president, chief financial officer
W. Stephen Maritz: president, chief executive officer B 1958. PRIM CORP EMPL president, chief executive officer: Maritz Inc.
Jeffrey D. Reinberg: senior vice president

Grants Analysis

Disclosure Period: calendar year ending 1999
Total Grants: $900,000 (approx)
Typical Range: $500 to $2,000

JOHN C. MARKEY CHARITABLE FUND

Giving Contact

John C. Markey, Jr., Treasurer
PO Box 623
Bryan, OH 43506
Phone: (419)633-1424

Description

Founded: 1966
EIN: 346572724
Organization Type: Private Foundation
Giving Locations: OH: nationally
Grant Types: General Support.

Donor Information

Founder: the late John C. Markey

Financial Summary

Total Giving: $150,550 (fiscal year ending June 30, 2001); $150,550 (fiscal 2000); $149,250 (fiscal 1999)
Assets: $3,565,392 (fiscal 2001); $3,565,392 (fiscal 2000); $4,067,140 (fiscal 1999)

Typical Recipients

Arts & Humanities: Arts Associations & Councils, Arts Centers, Community Arts, History & Archaeology, Libraries, Museums/Galleries, Music, Opera, Public Broadcasting, Theater
Civic & Public Affairs: Clubs, Community Foundations, Civic & Public Affairs-General, Parades/Festivals, Public Policy, Safety, Urban & Community Affairs, Women's Affairs
Education: Colleges & Universities, Elementary Education (Public), Engineering/Technological Education, Education-General, Medical Education, Private Education (Precollege), Public Education (Precollege), Secondary Education (Public), Student Aid
Environment: Wildlife Protection
Health: Alzheimers Disease, Cancer, Clinics/Medical Centers, Diabetes, Emergency/Ambulance Services, Heart, Hospices, Hospitals, Medical Research, Multiple Sclerosis, Nursing Services, Preventive Medicine/Wellness Organizations, Public Health
International: Health Care/Hospitals, International Peace & Security Issues, Missionary/Religious Activities
Religion: Churches, Religion-General, Ministries, Religious Organizations
Social Services: Animal Protection, Community Centers, Community Service Organizations, Crime Prevention, Domestic Violence, Emergency Relief, Family Planning, Homes, People with Disabilities, Recreation & Athletics, United Funds/United Ways, YMCA/YWCA/YMHA/YWHA, Youth Organizations

Application Procedures

Initial Contact: Send a brief letter of inquiry.
Application Requirements: Include a description of organization and proof of tax-exempt status.
Deadlines: None.

Foundation Officials

Carl T. Anderson: secretary
Larry D. Lisle: trustee
Lorance W. Lisle: trustee
John Clifton Markey, II: trustee
John R. Markey: president, treasurer

Grants Analysis

Disclosure Period: fiscal year ending June 30, 2001
Total Grants: $150,550
Number of Grants: 46
Average Grant: $3,273
Highest Grant: $20,000
Lowest Grant: $500
Typical Range: $1,000 to $5,000

Recent Grants

Note: Grants derived from fiscal 2000 Form 990.

Library-Related

3,000	Fullerton Public Library, Fullerton, NE

General

120,300	Wesley United Methodist Church, Bryan, OH
20,000	St. James School, Los Angeles, CA
17,500	Bryan Athletic Boosters, Bryan, OH
15,000	Menlo School, Atherton, CA
10,000	Westmont College, Santa Barbara, CA
10,000	Westside Christian Church, Long Beach, CA
6,000	Los Angeles Philharmonic Association, Los Angeles, CA
5,000	Music Theater Academy of Orange County, Costa Mesa, CA
5,000	Music Theater of Southern California, San Gabriel, CA
5,000	Orange County Children's Theater, Fountain Valley, CA

JOHN AND MARY R. MARKLE FOUNDATION

Giving Contact

10 Rockefeller Plaza, 16th Floor
New York, NY 10020
Phone: (212)713-7600
Fax: (212)765-9690
E-mail: info@markle.org
Web: http://www.markle.org

Description

Founded: 1927
EIN: 131770307
Organization Type: General Purpose Foundation
Giving Locations: nationally.
Note: The foundation reports that it makes demonstration project grants.

Donor Information

Founder: The founder, John Markle (1858-1933), was born in Hazleton, PA, and graduated from Lafayette College in 1880 with a degree in mining engineering. When he returned home after college, John Markle took over his father's mining operations (G. B. Markle and Company) in Hazleton, and implemented technical improvements. His achievements culminated in a $1 million investment in a drainage tunnel that opened up the flooded Jeddo Coal Fields, which Mr. Markle had the foresight to acquire when they were nearly worthless.

In 1902, Mr. Markle moved to New York, where he engaged in a variety of business enterprises that substantially increased his fortune. In later years, he engaged in philanthropic activities. He built a dormitory for the McAuley Water Street Mission, and a hotel for working women in Greenwich Village. Mr. Markle also made a gift of $900,000 to the department of mining engineering at his alma mater, Lafayette College, of which he was also a trustee.

He established the foundation in 1927 with an initial endowment of $3 million, which later increased to approximately $16 million by the terms of his will.

Financial Summary

Total Giving: $3,741,693 (fiscal year ending June 30, 2000); $5,952,247 (fiscal 1997); $5,142,338 (fiscal 1996)
Assets: $195,634,549 (fiscal 1998); $172,414,903 (fiscal 1997); $143,646,313 (fiscal 1996)

Typical Recipients

Arts & Humanities: Film & Video, Arts & Humanities-General, Historic Preservation, Libraries, Literary Arts, Performing Arts, Public Broadcasting
Civic & Public Affairs: Business/Free Enterprise, Economic Policy, Civic & Public Affairs-General, Nonprofit Management, Philanthropic Organizations, Professional & Trade Associations, Public Policy
Education: Colleges & Universities, Continuing Education, Engineering/Technological Education, Education-General, Journalism/Media Education, Legal Education, Student Aid

International: Foreign Arts Organizations, Foreign Educational Institutions, International Affairs, International Organizations, International Relations
Social Services: Senior Services

Application Procedures

Initial Contact: Applicants should complete initial one page application available at web site.

Restrictions

Grants are not made outside the area of mass communications or for general operations, equipment, capital campaigns, projects within formal educational institutions, endowments, buildings, or individual scholarships. Funds are not awarded for publications or for production of films, radio, or television programs. Grants are rarely made outside of the United States. The foundation also does not fund web sites or conferences (not integral to specific projects in which it is active). Few unsolicited proposals are funded.

Additional Information

Publications: Annual Report; Information Brochure

Foundation Officials

Zoe Baird: president NONPR AFFIL senior visiting scholar, research associate: Yale Law School.
Lewis W. Bernard: chairman PRIM CORP EMPL chairman: Classroom Inc. CORP AFFIL director: Harvard Management Co.; director: Marsh & McLennan Companies Inc. NONPR AFFIL trustee, vice chairman: American Museum Natural History; director: Harvard University.
Edith Cameron Bjornson: vice president, senior program officer B Orlando, FL 1937. ED University of Florida BA (1953); University of Florida MA (1956). CORP AFFIL director: Pro Natura United States of America New York; vice president: Maryland Marine Inc. NONPR AFFIL life trustee: Health Care Chaplaincy; director: New York New Media Association; member: Delta Gamma. CLUB AFFIL member: Ocean Reef Club; member: International Association Culinary Professionals; member: Mortar Board Club.
Karen D. Byers: chief financial officer
Raymond C. Clevenger, III: director B Topeka, KS 1937. ED Yale University BA (1959); Yale University LLB (1966). PRIM NONPR EMPL judge: U.S. Court Appeals. NONPR AFFIL member: American Bar Association; member: District of Columbia Bar Association.
David Ronald Daniel: director B Hartford, CT 1930. ED Wesleyan University BA (1952); Harvard University MBA (1954). CORP AFFIL director: Taco Bell; director: Tricon Global Restaurants Inc.; director: McKinsey & Co. (NY); director: Pizza Hut; director: KFC. NONPR AFFIL trustee: Thirteen/WNET; chairman emeritus: Wesleyan University; trustee: National Trust Historic Preservation; trustee: Rockefeller University; member corporate board overseers: Harvard University; chairman board fellows: Harvard University Medical School; chairman: Harvard Management Co.; board directors, member executive committee: Brookings Institute; member: Council Foreign Relations.
Stephen W. Fillo: director CORP AFFIL director: LCIT; director: Vanstar Corp.; director: LCIM; director: LCI International Management Services; director: LCI International Telecommunication.
Joel Lawrence Fleishman: director B Fayetteville, NC 1934. ED University of North Carolina AB (1955); University of North Carolina MA (1959); University of North Carolina JD (1959); Yale University LLM (1960); Methodist College LiHD (1986). PRIM CORP EMPL president: Atlantic Philanthropic Service Co. Inc. NONPR AFFIL professor law & policy services: Duke University; chairman board trustees: Urban Institute; director: Boston Science Corp.
Ellen Condliffe Lagemann: director B New York, NY 1945. PRIM NONPR EMPL professor: New York University. NONPR AFFIL director: Russell Sage

Foundation; director: Urban Institute; member: Organization American Historians; director government council: Rockefeller Archives Center; member: National Academy Education; director: Nonprofits and Philanthropy; member: History Education Society; member: Century Association; director: Greenwall Foundation; director: Center Advanced Study Behavioral Science; member: American Education Research Association; member: American Historical Association. CLUB AFFIL Cosmopolitan Club.
Gertrude Geraldine Michelson: director B Jamestown, NY 1925. ED Pennsylvania State University BA (1945); Columbia University LLB (1947). CORP AFFIL director, member executive committee: RH Macy & Co. Inc.; director: National Broadcasting Co. Inc.; director: Goodyear Tire & Rubber Co.; director: Federal Insurance Co.; director: General Electric Co. NONPR AFFIL board overseers: Teachers Insurance Annuity Association American College Ret Equities Fund; member: Women's Forum; vice chairman, member: New York City Partnership; life trustee: Spelman College; chairman emeritus board trustee: Columbia University; member, executive committee, vice chairman, board director: New York City Chamber of Commerce; governor: American Stock Exchange Inc. CLUB AFFIL Economic Club.
Dolores E. Miller: secretary
Diana T. Murray: director
Stanley S. Shuman: director B Cambridge, MA 1935. ED Harvard University BA (1956); Harvard University JD (1959); Harvard University MBA (1961). PRIM CORP EMPL executive vice president, managing director: Allen & Co. ADD CORP EMPL director: Allen Holdings Inc. CORP AFFIL director: Hudson General Corp.; director: News America Holdings Inc.; director: Bayou Steel Corp.; stockholder, director: GHS Inc.
George Bernard Weiksner: director B Boulder, CO 1944. ED Princeton University BS (1966); Stanford University MBA (1970); Stanford University JD (1970). PRIM CORP EMPL managing director: CS First Boston Corp.

Grants Analysis

Disclosure Period: fiscal year ending June 30, 2000
Total Grants: $3,741,693
Number of Grants: 56
Average Grant: $66,816
Highest Grant: $300,000
Typical Range: $10,000 to $75,000 and $125,000 to $225,000

Recent Grants

Note: Grants derived from fiscal 2000 Form 990.

General

666,875	Oxygen MarklePlus LLC
423,500	Web White and Blue 2000
400,000	Internew/Worldlink
393,400	Public Education
377,200	Freedom Channel.com
362,024	Public Education
219,520	Ad Council
207,500	WNET Channel 13
200,000	Understanding USA
198,506	Internet Governance Project

MARMOT FOUNDATION

Giving Contact

Charles F. Gummey, Jr., Secretary (For Delaware OrganizationS)
1100 N. Market Street
Wilmington, DE 19890
Phone: (302)651-1000

Alternate Contact

Willis H. duPont, Chairman (For Florida OrganizationS)
Marmot Foundation
PO Box 2468
Palm Beach, FL 33480

Description

Founded: 1968
EIN: 516022487
Organization Type: General Purpose Foundation
Giving Locations: DE; FL
Grant Types: Capital, Matching, Research.

Donor Information

Founder: Established in 1968 by the Margaret F. duPont Trust.

Financial Summary

Total Giving: $1,978,000 (2001); $1,800,500 (1998); $1,599,000 (1997)
Giving Analysis: Giving for 1998 includes: foundation grants to United Way ($70,000) 1997: foundation grants to United Way ($70,000)
Assets: $33,185,646 (2001); $36,249,800 (1998); $37,642,069 (1997)

Typical Recipients

Arts & Humanities: Arts Associations & Councils, Arts Centers, Arts Funds, Ballet, Arts & Humanities-General, Historic Preservation, History & Archaeology, Libraries, Museums/Galleries, Opera, Performing Arts, Visual Arts
Civic & Public Affairs: Community Foundations, Economic Development, Employment/Job Training, Civic & Public Affairs-General, Housing, Philanthropic Organizations, Professional & Trade Associations, Public Policy, Safety, Urban & Community Affairs, Zoos/Aquariums
Education: Arts/Humanities Education, Business Education, Colleges & Universities, Elementary Education (Public), Education-General, Medical Education, Preschool Education, Private Education (Precollege), Public Education (Precollege), Religious Education, Science/Mathematics Education, Secondary Education (Private), Social Sciences Education, Special Education, Vocational & Technical Education
Environment: Air/Water Quality, Environment-General, Resource Conservation
Health: Arthritis, Cancer, Children's Health/Hospitals, Clinics/Medical Centers, Diabetes, Emergency/Ambulance Services, Eyes/Blindness, Health Funds, Health Organizations, Heart, Hospices, Hospitals, Hospitals (University Affiliated), Mental Health, Outpatient Health Care, Preventive Medicine/Wellness Organizations, Public Health, Research/Studies Institutes, Trauma Treatment
Religion: Churches, Dioceses, Religion-General, Jewish Causes, Ministries, Religious Organizations, Religious Welfare
Science: Science Museums, Science Museums, Scientific Centers & Institutes
Social Services: Child Welfare, Community Centers, Community Service Organizations, Day Care, Emergency Relief, Family Planning, Family Services, Food/Clothing Distribution, Homes, People with Disabilities, Recreation & Athletics, Scouts, Senior Services, Social Services-General, Special Olympics, Substance Abuse, United Funds/United Ways, YMCA/YWCA/YMHA/YWHA, Youth Organizations

Application Procedures

Initial Contact: The foundation has no formal grant application procedure or application form.
Deadlines: April 30 and October 31.
Review Process: The board meets in May and November to review Delaware grants, and only in November to review Florida grants. Decisions are reported within two weeks after the board meeting. Applicants should have established track records of meeting objectives. Appeals should be summarized in cover letter not longer than two pages.

Restrictions

The foundation does not support individuals, operating budgets, or scholarships, and does not make loans. No support is given to religious organizations.

Foundation Officials

Lammot Joseph du Pont: trustee
Miren de Amezola du Pont: trustee
Willis Harrington du Pont: president, trustee B Wilmington, DE 1936. ED Wesleyan University (1958); Cornell University (1960). NONPR AFFIL trustee: Miami Science Museum.
George S. Harrington: trustee

Grants Analysis

Disclosure Period: calendar year ending 2001
Total Grants: $1,908,000*
Number of Grants: 121
Average Grant: $15,769
Highest Grant: $60,000
Lowest Grant: $2,000
Typical Range: $10,000 to $25,000
*Note: Giving excludes United Way.

Recent Grants

Note: Grants derived from 2001 Form 990.

Library-Related

15,000	Friends of the Concord Pike Library, Wilmington, DE

General

70,000	Rollins College, Winter Park, FL
60,000	American Red Cross of Florida, West Palm Beach, FL
60,000	Baptist Health Systems of South Florida, Coral Gables, FL
60,000	Society of Memorial Sloan-Kettering Cancer Center, New York, NY
60,000	United Way of Delaware, Wilmington, DE
51,000	Winterthur Museum, Winterthur, DE
50,000	Bascom Palmer Eye Institute, Miami, FL
50,000	Boys and Girls Club, Wilmington, DE
50,000	St. Michael's School and Nursery, Inc., Stuart, FL
40,000	University of Delaware, Newark, DE

MARPAT FOUNDATION

Giving Contact

Joan Follin Hughes-Koven, Secretary, Treasurer & Director
Marsh & Foster
2001 L St. NW, Suite 400
Washington, DC 20036
Phone: (202)822-8888
E-mail: JKoven@aol.com
Web: http://fdncenter.org/grantmaker/marpat/

Description

Founded: 1985
EIN: 521358159
Organization Type: Private Foundation
Giving Locations: DC: Washington metropolitan area
Grant Types: General Support, Operating Expenses, Research.

Donor Information

Founder: Marvin Breckinridge Patterson

Financial Summary

Total Giving: $849,600 (2000); $1,357,300 (1999); $1,263,780 (1997)
Assets: $13,753,087 (2000); $14,580,064 (1999); $14,464,260 (1996)
Gifts Received: $119,978 (2000). Note: In 2000, contributions were received from Marvin B. Patterson Unitrust.

Typical Recipients

Arts & Humanities: Arts Associations & Councils, Arts Outreach, Ethnic & Folk Arts, Arts & Humanities-General, Historic Preservation, History & Archaeology, Libraries, Literary Arts, Museums/Galleries, Music, Public Broadcasting, Theater
Civic & Public Affairs: Asian American Affairs, Botanical Gardens/Parks, Employment/Job Training, Civic & Public Affairs-General, Law & Justice, Safety, Women's Affairs
Education: Arts/Humanities Education, Colleges & Universities, Education Reform, Environmental Education, International Exchange, International Studies, Private Education (Precollege), Science/Mathematics Education, Special Education
Environment: Air/Water Quality, Environment-General, Protection, Research, Resource Conservation, Watershed
Health: Adolescent Health Issues, AIDS/HIV, Children's Health/Hospitals, Clinics/Medical Centers, Health-General, Health Organizations, Home-Care Services, Hospitals, Long-Term Care, Nursing Services, Prenatal Health Issues, Preventive Medicine/Wellness Organizations, Public Health
International: International-General, International Organizations
Science: Science Museums, Scientific Centers & Institutes, Scientific Labs, Scientific Organizations
Social Services: At-Risk Youth, Child Abuse, Child Welfare, Community Service Organizations, Domestic Violence, Family Planning, Food/Clothing Distribution, Homes, Scouts, Senior Services, Shelters/Homelessness, Volunteer Services, YMCA/YWCA/YMHA/YWHA

Application Procedures

Initial Contact: Send a brief, one or two page letter. Include the completed summary sheet provided by the foundation, the correct legal name and address of the organization, a description of the need to be addressed by the program and how the need will be met, who will be served, amount requested, project budget, other sources of funding, plans for future funding, list of officers and directors, staff involved in the project and their qualifications, proof of tax-exempt status, and most recent annual report.
Deadlines: September 15.

Restrictions

Does not make grants to individuals, projects or organizations involved in weapons development, or to establish or add to endowment funds.

Additional Information

Publications: Informational Brochure (including Summary Sheet); Application Guidelines (annually)

Foundation Officials

Charles Thomas Akre: vice president, director B Washington, DC 1942. ED American University (1968). PRIM CORP EMPL vice president, director: Johnston, Lemon & Co.
Mrs. William H. Bozman: vice president, director
Isabella Breckinridge: director
Joan Follin Hughes Koven: secretary, treasurer, director B Washington, DC 1937. ED Scarritt College (1959); West Virginia University BS (1959); University of Salisbury (1961); Sorbonne University (1962-1963); American University (1973); George Washington University (1979). PRIM CORP EMPL director, treasurer, secretary: Marpat Foundation. NONPR AFFIL member: Society Women Geographers; member: Women & Fisheries Network; member: Sea Plane Pilots Association; member: Pacific Science Association; member: Phi Upsilon Omicron; researchcollaborator: National Museum Natural History; member: Omicron Nu; member: Intl Society Reef Studies; director: Marine Environmental Institute; member: Conchologists America; president coral reef res: Fiji Islands Astrolabe; member: American Malacological

Union; member: American Institute Biological Sciences; member: American Litoral Society; member: Aircraft Owners & Pilots Association; member: American Academy Underwater Research Scientists. CLUB AFFIL Hawaiian Shell Club; National Capital Shell Club.
Mrs. Joseph Krakora: vice president, director
Christine Minter-Dowd: vice president
Marvin Breckinridge Patterson: president, director
Thomas W. Richards: vice president
Mrs. John Farr Simons: director
Samuel N. Stokes: vice president

Grants Analysis

Disclosure Period: calendar year ending 2000
Total Grants: $849,600
Number of Grants: 112
Average Grant: $7,586
Highest Grant: $17,500
Typical Range: $1,000 to $15,000

Recent Grants

Note: Grants derived from 1999 Form 990.

Library-Related

20,000	Folger Shakespeare Library, Washington, DC

General

23,000	Friends of the Jefferson Patterson Park and Museum, St. Leonard, MD
20,000	Association for the Preservation of Civil War Sites, Inc., Hagerstown, MD
20,000	Calvary Bilingual Multicultural Learning Center, Washington, DC
20,000	Columbia Road Health Services, Washington, DC
20,000	DC Central Kitchen, Washington, DC
20,000	DC Children's Advocacy Center, Washington, DC
20,000	DC Primary Care Association, Washington, DC
20,000	La Clinica Del Pueblo, Washington, DC -- to provide primary care medical services to the low- income Latino community
20,000	National Trust for Historic Preservation in the U.S., Washington, DC -- to support the rural heritage program
20,000	Planned Parenthood of Metropolitan Washington, DC, Washington, DC

MARSHALL FOUNDATION

Giving Contact

Ron Mumford
PO Box 3306
Tucson, AZ 85722
Phone: (520)622-8613

Description

Founded: 1930
EIN: 860102198
Organization Type: Private Foundation
Giving Locations: AZ: Tuscon and Pima County
Grant Types: General Support.

Donor Information

Founder: the late Louise F. Marshall

Financial Summary

Total Giving: $263,545 (2001); $343,032 (2000); $790,947 (1999)
Assets: $18,393,246 (2001); $14,851,917 (2000); $13,050,444 (1999)

Typical Recipients

Arts & Humanities: Arts Associations & Councils, Historic Preservation, History & Archaeology, Libraries, Literary Arts, Museums/Galleries, Music

Civic & Public Affairs: Botanical Gardens/Parks, Civic & Public Affairs-General, Hispanic Affairs, Housing, Law & Justice, Legal Aid, Parades/Festivals, Philanthropic Organizations, Urban & Community Affairs
Education: Business Education, Colleges & Universities, Community & Junior Colleges, Continuing Education, Education Funds, Elementary Education (Public), Education-General, Health & Physical Education, Public Education (Precollege), Science/Mathematics Education, Student Aid
Environment: Resource Conservation
Health: AIDS/HIV, Clinics/Medical Centers, Diabetes, Health Organizations, Heart, Hospitals, Medical Research, Public Health, Single-Disease Health Associations
Religion: Churches, Religion-General, Jewish Causes, Ministries, Religious Welfare
Social Services: At-Risk Youth, Camps, Child Welfare, Community Service Organizations, Family Services, Food/Clothing Distribution, Homes, Recreation & Athletics, Scouts, Shelters/Homelessness, Social Services-General, Special Olympics, United Funds/United Ways, Veterans, YMCA/YWCA/YMHA/YWHA, Youth Organizations

Application Procedures

Initial Contact: a brief letter of inquiry
Application Requirements: a description of organization, purpose of funds sought, and proof of tax-exempt status
Deadlines: February 1, May 1, August 1, November 1. Board meets in March, June, September and December.

Restrictions

Grants are not made to support individuals, religious organizations for sectarian purposes, political or lobbying groups, or organizations outside operating areas.

Foundation Officials

Mr. Charles Jackson: president
Anne Nelson: secretary, treasurer
Jonathan Schmitt: vice president
George Steele: vice president
Elizabeth Sugges: student board mem
Christine Thompson: secretary

Grants Analysis

Disclosure Period: calendar year ending 2001
Total Grants: $263,545
Number of Grants: 20
Average Grant: $4,607*
Highest Grant: $176,012
Lowest Grant: $100
Typical Range: $1,000 to $10,000
*Note: Average grant figure excludes highest grant.

Recent Grants

Note: Grants derived from 2000 Form 990.

Library-Related
4,100	Make Way for Book

General
143,932	University of Arizona, Tucson, AZ
30,000	Primavera Services, Tucson, AZ
25,000	El Pueblo Clinic, Tucson, AZ
20,000	Angel Charity For Children, Tucson, AZ
20,000	Tucson Urban League, Tucson, AZ
15,000	League of United Latin American Citizens, San Antonio, TX
12,000	Arizona Friends of Foster Children Foundation, Phoenix, AZ
10,000	Parent Connection, Tucson, AZ
6,000	Community Food Bank, Tucson, AZ
5,000	Boy Scouts of America, Phoenix, AZ

MARSHALL & ILSLEY CORP.

Company Headquarters

770 N. Water St.
Milwaukee, WI 53202
Web: http://www.micorp.com

Company Description

Founded: 1847
Ticker: MI
Exchange: NYSE
Also Known As: Marshall & Ilsley Bank;
Acquired: National City Bancorporation.
Assets: US$26.37 billion (2001)
Employees: 11657 (2001)
SIC(s): 6021 National Commercial Banks, 6712 Bank Holding Companies.

Operating Locations

Marshall & Ilsley Corp. (WI--Adams, Beloit, Cambridge, Coloma, Dodgeville, Green Bay, Lancaster, Madison, Marshfield, Mayville, Merrill, Middleton, New Holstein, Racine, Rhinelander, Ripon, Stevens Point, Watertown, Wauwatosa, West Bend, Westfield)

Marshall & Ilsley Foundation, Inc.

Giving Contact

Rebecca Lonergan, Assistant Secretary
Marshall & Ilsley Foundation
770 North Water Street
Milwaukee, WI 53202
Phone: (414)765-7805
Fax: (414)765-7899

Description

Founded: 1958
EIN: 396043185
Organization Type: Corporate Foundation
Giving Locations: WI: emphasis on Milwaukee
Grant Types: Capital, General Support, Scholarship.

Financial Summary

Total Giving: $1,900,250 (2001); $1,756,000 (2000); $1,972,500 (1999). Note: Contributes through foundation only.
Giving Analysis: Giving for 2001 includes: foundation scholarships ($47,000); foundation grants to United Way ($280,000); foundation ($1,573,250); 2000: foundation scholarships ($49,500); foundation grants to United Way ($255,000); foundation ($1,451,500); 1999: foundation scholarships ($49,000); foundation grants to United Way ($240,000); foundation ($1,683,500);
Assets: $123,285 (2001); $118,186 (2000); $74,508 (1999)
Gifts Received: $1,900,000 (2001); $1,800,000 (2000); $397,355 (1999). Note: Contributions were received from M&I Corp. and M&I Bank.

Typical Recipients

Arts & Humanities: Arts Associations & Councils, Arts Centers, Arts Festivals, Arts Funds, Arts Institutes, Film & Video, Historic Preservation, History & Archaeology, Libraries, Museums/Galleries, Music, Performing Arts, Public Broadcasting, Theater, Visual Arts
Civic & Public Affairs: Botanical Gardens/Parks, Economic Development, Employment/Job Training, Civic & Public Affairs-General, Hispanic Affairs, Housing, Professional & Trade Associations, Urban & Community Affairs, Women's Affairs, Zoos/Aquariums

Education: Arts/Humanities Education, Business Education, Colleges & Universities, Community & Junior Colleges, Education Associations, Education Funds, Education Reform, Elementary Education (Private), Engineering/Technological Education, Engineering/Technological Education, Education-General, Leadership Training, Literacy, Medical Education, Minority Education, Private Education (Precollege), Secondary Education (Private), Secondary Education (Public), Student Aid
Environment: Environment-General, Wildlife Protection
Health: Cancer, Children's Health/Hospitals, Clinics/Medical Centers, Health Organizations, Hospitals, Long-Term Care, Medical Research, Medical Training, Mental Health, Multiple Sclerosis, Nursing Services, Research/Studies Institutes, Single-Disease Health Associations, Transplant Networks/Donor Banks, Trauma Treatment
International: International Relations
Religion: Religious Organizations, Religious Welfare
Science: Science Museums
Social Services: Animal Protection, Child Welfare, Community Centers, Community Centers, Community Service Organizations, Day Care, Family Planning, Family Services, Food/Clothing Distribution, People with Disabilities, Recreation & Athletics, Senior Services, Shelters/Homelessness, Social Services-General, United Funds/United Ways, Volunteer Services, YMCA/YWCA/YMHA/YWHA, Youth Organizations

Application Procedures

Initial Contact: Send a brief letter or proposal.
Application Requirements: Include a a description of organization, amount requested, purpose of funds sought, recently audited financial statement, and proof of tax-exempt status.
Deadlines: None.

Restrictions

Scholarships are for sons and daughters of permanent, full-time employees of M&I Corp.

Corporate Officials

Dennis J. Kuester: president, director B 1942. ED University of Milwaukee BBA (1966). PRIM CORP EMPL president, director: Marshall & Ilsley Corp. CORP AFFIL director: Modine Manufacturing Co.; director: Super Steel Products Corp.; president: Marshall & Ilsley Bank; director: Krueger International Inc.; chairman, chief executive officer: M & I Data Services Inc.
James B. Wigdale: chairman, director B 1936. PRIM CORP EMPL chairman, director: Marshall & Ilsley Corp. CORP AFFIL chairman, chief executive officer: Marshall & Ilsley Bank; chairman: M & I Marshall & Ilsley Bank; director: M & I Mortgage Corp.; director: M & I Capital Markets Group; director: M & I First National Leasing; director: Columbia Health System Inc.; director: Green Bay Packaging Inc. NONPR AFFIL chairman: Medical College Wisconsin; vice chairman: Metropolitan Milwaukee Association.

Foundation Officials

Dennis J. Kuester: vice president, director (see above)
James B. Wigdale: president, director (see above)

Grants Analysis

Disclosure Period: calendar year ending 2001
Total Grants: $1,573,250*
Number of Grants: 122
Average Grant: $12,895
Highest Grant: $120,000
Typical Range: $1,000 to $25,000
*Note: Giving excludes scholarships and United Way.

Recent Grants

Note: Grants derived from 2001 Form 990.

General

120,000	United Performing Arts Fund, Milwaukee, WI
67,500	United Way of Greater Milwaukee, Milwaukee, WI
67,500	United Way of Greater Milwaukee, Milwaukee, WI
67,500	United Way of Greater Milwaukee, Milwaukee, WI
67,500	United Way of Greater Milwaukee, Milwaukee, WI
50,000	Alverno College, Milwaukee, WI
50,000	Brookfield Academy, Brookfield, WI
50,000	Children's Hospital Foundation, Milwaukee, WI
50,000	Medical College of Wisconsin, Milwaukee, WI
50,000	Milwaukee Art Museum, Milwaukee, WI

MARGARET LEE MARTIN CHARITABLE TRUST

Giving Contact

James M. Floyd, Sr., Trustee
c/o Bank of America
PO Box 9626
Savannah, GA 31412
Phone: (912)651-8272

Description

Founded: 1995
EIN: 586305150
Organization Type: Private Foundation

Financial Summary

Total Giving: $295,000 (2001); $362,468 (1999); $254,822 (1998)
Giving Analysis: Giving for 2001 includes: foundation grants to United Way ($10,400); foundation scholarships ($165,000); 1999: foundation grants to United Way ($8,335) foundation scholarships ($158,283)
Assets: $10,325,011 (2001); $12,060,057 (1999); $11,192,055 (1998)
Gifts Received: $23,949 (1998); $1,470,000 (1996). Note: In 1998, contributions were received from the estate of Margaret L. Martin.

Typical Recipients

Arts & Humanities: Arts Associations & Councils, History & Archaeology, Libraries, Museums/Galleries
Civic & Public Affairs: Botanical Gardens/Parks
Education: Student Aid
Religion: Churches
Social Services: Scouts, United Funds/United Ways, Youth Organizations

Application Procedures

Initial Contact: Applications should be submitted on the forms provided to the high school guidance counselors. Also, counselors should provide a transcript, class ranking, and verification of S.A.T. or A.C.T. scores.
Deadlines: May 1.

Additional Information

Provides scholarships to residents of Liberty County, GA, who are in the top 10% of his or her class, score a minimum of 1,000 on the SAT or equivalent on the ACT, and have been accepted by a regionally accredited college, university, or nursing school.
Trust(s): Bank of America

Foundation Officials

James M. Floyd, Sr.: trustee

Grants Analysis

Disclosure Period: calendar year ending 2001
Total Grants: $119,600*
Number of Grants: 9
Average Grant: $13,289
Highest Grant: $26,000
Lowest Grant: $2,600
Typical Range: $2,600 to $26,000
*Note: Giving excludes United Way; scholarships.

Recent Grants

Note: Grants derived from 2000 Form 990.

Library-Related

20,714	Liberty County Public Library, Hinesville, GA -- operating support

General

155,000	Bank of America, Charlotte, NC -- for disbursement of scholarships
20,714	Flemington Presbyterian Church, Hinesville, GA -- for operations
20,714	Hinesville Arts Council, Hinesville, GA -- operating support
8,285	Liberty County Historical Society, Hinesville, GA -- operating support
8,285	Midway Church and Society, Hinesville, GA -- operating support
8,285	Midway Museum, Midway, GA -- operating support
8,285	United Way Liberty County, Hinesville, GA -- operating support
4,143	Leconte-Woodmanston Foundation, Midway, GA -- operating support
2,071	Coastal Empire Council Boy Scouts of America, Savannah, GA -- for operations
2,071	Girl Scout Council of Savannah, Savannah, GA -- for operations

MARTIN FOUNDATION

Giving Contact

Gerladine Martin, President
Castillo Square
5051 Castillo Drive, Suite 204
Naples, FL 34103

Description

Founded: 1954
EIN: 351070929
Organization Type: Family Foundation
Giving Locations: nationally.
Grant Types: Challenge, Conference/Seminar, Endowment, General Support, Matching, Professorship, Project, Research, Scholarship, Seed Money.

Donor Information

Founder: Incorporated in 1953 by Lee Martin, Geraldine F. Martin, the late Ross Martin, the late Esther Martin, and NIBCO, Inc.

Financial Summary

Total Giving: $2,758,420 (fiscal year ending June 30, 2001); $2,620,555 (fiscal 2000); $2,208,375 (fiscal 1999)
Giving Analysis: Giving for fiscal 2001 includes: foundation scholarships ($16,500); foundation fellowships ($1,490,000); fiscal 2000: foundation fellowships ($30,000) foundation scholarships ($112,500)
Assets: $68,901,780 (fiscal 2001); $58,068,654 (fiscal 2000); $62,062,417 (fiscal 1999)

Typical Recipients

Arts & Humanities: Arts Appreciation, Arts Associations & Councils, Arts Centers, Arts Institutes, Ethnic & Folk Arts, Historic Preservation, History & Archaeology, Libraries, Museums/Galleries, Music, Performing Arts, Public Broadcasting, Theater
Civic & Public Affairs: Botanical Gardens/Parks, Clubs, Community Foundations, Economic Development, Civic & Public Affairs-General, Hispanic Affairs, Housing, Law & Justice, Legal Aid, Municipalities/Towns, Public Policy, Safety, Urban & Community Affairs, Women's Affairs, Zoos/Aquariums
Education: Agricultural Education, Arts/Humanities Education, Colleges & Universities, Community & Junior Colleges, Continuing Education, Engineering/Technological Education, Environmental Education, Legal Education, Literacy, Medical Education, Minority Education, Preschool Education, Private Education (Precollege), Public Education (Precollege), Special Education, Student Aid
Environment: Air/Water Quality, Energy, Forestry, Environment-General, Protection, Resource Conservation, Wildlife Protection
Health: AIDS/HIV, Alzheimers Disease, Cancer, Clinics/Medical Centers, Emergency/Ambulance Services, Health-General, Hospices, Hospitals, Medical Research, Medical Training, Mental Health, Nursing Services, Public Health, Single-Disease Health Associations
International: Health Care/Hospitals, International Development, International Environmental Issues, International Environmental Issues, International Peace & Security Issues, International Relations, Missionary/Religious Activities
Religion: Churches, Ministries, Missionary Activities (Domestic), Religious Organizations, Religious Welfare, Social/Policy Issues
Science: Science Museums, Scientific Centers & Institutes, Scientific Organizations, Scientific Research
Social Services: Animal Protection, At-Risk Youth, Child Abuse, Child Welfare, Community Centers, Community Service Organizations, Crime Prevention, Day Care, Delinquency & Criminal Rehabilitation, Domestic Violence, Family Planning, Family Services, Food/Clothing Distribution, Homes, People with Disabilities, Recreation & Athletics, Scouts, Senior Services, Shelters/Homelessness, Social Services-General, Substance Abuse, United Funds/United Ways, YMCA/YWCA/YMHA/YWHA, Youth Organizations

Application Procedures

Initial Contact: Send a brief letter of inquiry and a full proposal.
Application Requirements: A written proposal should include the following: the legal name, address and telephone number of the organization; a copy of the IRS tax exempt determination letter; a brief description of the history of the organization including goals, objectives and activities; a statement describing in detail the project or activities for which grant was requested; a copy of the latest annual report and an audited financial statement or Form 990 for the most recent fiscal year; a list of other funding sources contacted and results; an itemized budget for the organization and project showing both projected revenue and expenses for the current fiscal year; time frame of the project and future funding plans; and a list of names of the current Board of Directors.
Deadlines: None.
Review Process: Proposals are reviewed by the board approximately four to six times a year.

Restrictions

The foundation does not support gifts to individuals.

Foundation Officials

Casper Martin: treasurer, secretary, director CORP AFFIL officer: NIBCO Inc.
Elizabeth Martin: co-president
Geraldine F. Martin: chairman

Lee Martin: director B Elkhart, IN February 07, 1920. ED Massachusetts Institute of Technology (1942). PRIM CORP EMPL vice chairman, director: NIBCO. CLUB AFFIL Pelican Bay Club; Union League Club.
Rex Martin: director B Elkhart, IN 1951. ED Indiana University BS (1974); Massachusetts Institute of Technology (1983). PRIM CORP EMPL chairman, president, chief executive officer: NIBCO. CORP AFFIL director: First Source Bank; director: First Source Corp.; director: Eriez Magnetics.
Jennifer Martin-Brown: co-president

Grants Analysis
Disclosure Period: fiscal year ending June 30, 2001
Total Grants: $1,251,920*
Number of Grants: 68
Average Grant: $16,696*
Highest Grant: $150,000
Lowest Grant: $500
Typical Range: $5,000 to $25,000
*Note: Giving excludes scholarship; fellowships. Average grant figures excludes highest grant.

Recent Grants
Note: Grants derived from fiscal 2000 Form 990.

General
950,000	Massachusetts Institute of Technology, Cambridge, MA -- support for commitment of graduate fellows
300,000	Boys and Girls Club, Goshen, IN
250,000	Philharmonic Center for Arts of Naples, Naples, FL -- payment to support new fine arts building
100,000	Goshen College, Goshen, IN -- Martin Foundation Scholarship in Environmental Science
100,000	Philharmonic Center for Arts of Naples, Naples, FL -- payment to support new fine arts building
60,000	Surface Transportation Policy Project, Washington, DC
50,000	Belgrade Regional Conservation Alliance, Belgrade, ME -- support programs
50,000	Red Cross Capital Campaign, Elkhart, IN -- promote capital campaign
31,000	Lacasa of Goshen, Goshen, IN
30,000	Elkhart YMCA/YWCA, Elkhart, IN

NICHOLAS MARTINI FOUNDATION

Giving Contact
777 Passaic Avenue
Clifton, NJ 07012
Phone: (973)594-1899

Description
Founded: 1986
EIN: 222756049
Organization Type: Private Foundation
Giving Locations: NJ: Bergen County, Essex County, Passaic County
Grant Types: General Support.

Donor Information
Founder: the late Nicholas Martini

Financial Summary
Total Giving: $365,850 (2001); $430,150 (2000); $437,600 (1999)
Giving Analysis: Giving for 2001 includes: foundation grants to United Way ($4,000); 2000: foundation grants to United Way ($4,000) 1998: foundation grants to United Way ($1,000)
Assets: $13,345,465 (2001); $14,495,460 (2000); $15,322,979 (1999)

Gifts Received: $295,000 (1995); $3,550,961 (1993). Note: In 1995, contributions were received from the estate of Nicholas Martini.

Typical Recipients
Arts & Humanities: Arts Associations & Councils, Dance, Ethnic & Folk Arts, Film & Video, History & Archaeology, Libraries, Museums/Galleries, Music, Performing Arts, Public Broadcasting
Civic & Public Affairs: Clubs, Economic Development, Ethnic Organizations, Civic & Public Affairs-General, Hispanic Affairs, Housing, Parades/Festivals, Public Policy, Safety
Education: Arts/Humanities Education, Colleges & Universities, Education Funds, Elementary Education (Private), Education-General, Gifted & Talented Programs, Journalism/Media Education, Legal Education, Medical Education, Preschool Education, Private Education (Precollege), Public Education (Precollege), Secondary Education (Private), Secondary Education (Public), Student Aid, Student Aid, Vocational & Technical Education
Environment: Air/Water Quality
Health: Cancer, Clinics/Medical Centers, Emergency/Ambulance Services, Health Organizations, Heart, Hospices, Hospitals, Hospitals (University Affiliated), Long-Term Care, Mental Health, Prenatal Health Issues, Single-Disease Health Associations
International: International Relief Efforts, Missionary/Religious Activities
Religion: Churches, Dioceses, Religious Organizations, Religious Welfare, Synagogues/Temples
Science: Scientific Centers & Institutes
Social Services: At-Risk Youth, Camps, Child Welfare, Community Service Organizations, Crime Prevention, Day Care, Family Services, Homes, People with Disabilities, Recreation & Athletics, Scouts, Scouts, Senior Services, Social Services-General, United Funds/United Ways, YMCA/YWCA/YMHA/YWHA, Youth Organizations

Application Procedures
Initial Contact: Send a brief letter of inquiry.
Application Requirements: Include a description of organization, qualifications of the people involved, the nature and scope of the proposed project and the anticipated results, a preliminary timetable, proposed budget, recently audited financial statement, proof of tax-exempt status, and a list of board members.
Deadlines: None.

Restrictions
Does not provide grants to individuals.

Foundation Officials
Gloria Martini: vice president
William J. Martini: trustee B Passaic, NJ. ED Villanova University (1968); Rutgers University JD (1972). PRIM CORP EMPL congressman: U.S. House Reps. NONPR AFFIL trustee: Center Italian American Culture; trustee: United Way Passaic County; trustee: Boy Scouts America Passaic Valley Council.
Fannie Rosta: trustee
Marie Salanitri: trustee

Grants Analysis
Disclosure Period: calendar year ending 2001
Total Grants: $361,850*
Number of Grants: 70
Average Grant: $5,169
Highest Grant: $30,200
Typical Range: $1,000 to $10,000
*Note: Giving excludes United Way.

Recent Grants
Note: Grants derived from 2001 Form 990.

General
30,200	Hackensack University Medical Center Foundation, Hackensack, NJ
25,350	NIAF, Washington, DC
25,000	John Cabot University, DE
25,000	Rutgers University Law School, New Brunswick, NJ
22,500	Boys & Girls Club of Clifton, Clifton, NJ
15,000	Montclair Art Museum, Montclair, NJ
15,000	Scholarship Fund for Inner-City Children, New York, NY
15,000	Tri-County Scholarship Fund, Paterson, NJ
12,500	Ripon Education Fund, Washington, DC
10,000	Boy Scouts of America Northern New Jersey Council, Fair Lawn, NJ

VIRGINIA AND LEONARD MARX FOUNDATION

Giving Contact
Jennifer Gruenberg, Secretary
708 Third Avenue
New York, NY 10017
Phone: (212)557-1400

Description
Founded: 1959
EIN: 136162557
Organization Type: Private Foundation
Giving Locations: NY: New York
Grant Types: General Support.

Donor Information
Founder: The late Leonard Marx, Virginia Marx.

Financial Summary
Total Giving: $491,300 (2001); $2,298,698 (2000); $883,800 (1999)
Giving Analysis: Giving for 2001 includes: foundation grants to United Way ($5,000); 2000: foundation grants to United Way ($5,000) 1999: foundation grants to United Way ($5,000)
Assets: $35,716,416 (2001); $33,000,402 (2000); $17,278,808 (1999)
Gifts Received: $1,233,768 (2001); $15,172,810 (2000); $1,082,046 (1999). Note: In 2001, contributions were received from Leonard Marx ($500,000); Dollar Land ($274,749); Rier Realty Co. ($140,850); and miscellaneous other donors who contributed less than $100,000 each. In 2000, contributions were received from the estate of Virginia Marx ($14,227,637), Leonard Marx ($500,000), Dollar Land Syndicate ($167,188), and miscellaneous other donors who contributions less than $100,000 each. Marx Co., Inc. ($79,325), Kesmar Realty Co., ($5,088), Leonard Marx ($500,000), Merchants National Properties, Inc. ($31,488), Promar Realty Co., Inc. ($46,081), Rier Realty Co., Inc. ($47,050), and Virginia Marx ($500,000). In 1996, contributions were received from 17 West Orange Realty Co. ($9,600), 26 East Realty Co. ($27,881), Argin Realty Co. ($21,900), Darb Realty Co. ($35,000), Dollar Land Syndicate ($267,385), Guest Realty Co. ($80,000), Joseph E. Marx Co. ($37,750), Kesmar Realty Co. ($6,138), Leonard Marx ($500,000), Merchants National Properties ($31,318), Promar Realty Co. ($60,437), Rier Realty Co. ($46,850), and Virginia Marx ($500,000).

Typical Recipients
Arts & Humanities: Arts Associations & Councils, Arts Funds, Historic Preservation, History & Archaeology, Libraries, Museums/Galleries, Music, Performing Arts, Public Broadcasting, Theater
Civic & Public Affairs: Civic & Public Affairs-General, Legal Aid, Philanthropic Organizations, Women's Affairs
Education: Arts/Humanities Education, Colleges & Universities, Community & Junior Colleges, Education Associations, Education-General, Minority Education, Public Education (Precollege)
Environment: Environment-General

Health: Alzheimers Disease, Cancer, Clinics/Medical Centers, Hospitals, Medical Research, Mental Health, Public Health, Research/Studies Institutes, Single-Disease Health Associations
Religion: Jewish Causes, Religious Organizations, Religious Welfare
Social Services: Camps, Child Welfare, Counseling, Crime Prevention, Family Planning, Family Services, United Funds/United Ways, YMCA/YWCA/YMHA/YWHA, Youth Organizations

Application Procedures

Initial Contact: Send a brief letter of inquiry describing program or project.
Application Requirements: Include complete information regarding grant requested.
Deadlines: None.

Foundation Officials

Jennifer Gruenberg: director
Leonard Marx, Jr.: treasurer
Leonard Marx: vice president B New York, NY 1932. ED Yale University (1954); Harvard University (1956). PRIM CORP EMPL president, director: Merchants National Properties.
Virginia Marx: president
John E. Tuchler: president

Grants Analysis

Disclosure Period: calendar year ending 2001
Total Grants: $491,300
Number of Grants: 43
Average Grant: $11,426
Highest Grant: $100,000
Lowest Grant: $200
Typical Range: $5,000 to $25,000

Recent Grants

Note: Grants derived from 2001 Form 990.

Library-Related
10,000   White Plains Public Library Foundation, White Plains, NY

General
100,000   UJA Federation, New York, NY
55,000   Jewish Board of Family and Children's Services, New York, NY
45,000   Westchester Jewish Community Services, Westchester, NY
25,000   American Jewish Committee
25,000   Thirteen-WNET, Brooklyn, NY
25,000   White Plains Hospital, White Plains, NY
25,000   Yale University Child Study Center, New Haven, CT
20,000   Mental Health Association of Westchester, Westchester, NY
16,000   Yale Alumni Fund, New Haven, CT
10,000   Hypertension Education Foundation, Inc.

Mascoma Savings Bank

Company Headquarters

67 N. Park St.
Lebanon, NH 03766

Company Description

Employees: 85
SIC(s): 6000 Depository Institutions.

Nonmonetary Support

Type: Donated Equipment

Mascoma Savings Bank Foundation

Giving Contact

Thomas F. Terry, Trustee
Mascoma Savings Bank Foundation
PO Box 435
Lebanon, NH 03766

Description

EIN: 222816632
Organization Type: Corporate Foundation
Giving Locations: operating communities.
Grant Types: Capital, General Support, Project.

Financial Summary

Total Giving: $104,405 (2001); $104,030 (2000); $106,325 (1999)
Giving Analysis: Giving for 2001 includes: foundation grants to United Way ($1,500); foundation ($102,905) 1999: foundation ($106,325)
Assets: $2,327,121 (2001); $2,369,776 (2000); $2,319,844 (1999)
Gifts Received: $153,625 (2001); $162,698 (2000); $155,275 (1999). Note: In 2000 and 2001, contributions were received from Mascoma Savings Bank. In 1999, contributions were received from Mascoma Savings Bank ($155,025) and Stephen Christy ($250).

Typical Recipients

Arts & Humanities: Arts & Humanities-General, Historic Preservation, History & Archaeology, Libraries, Museums/Galleries, Music, Opera, Public Broadcasting
Civic & Public Affairs: Botanical Gardens/Parks, Business/Free Enterprise, Clubs, Community Foundations, Civic & Public Affairs-General, Housing, Municipalities/Towns, Parades/Festivals, Safety, Urban & Community Affairs, Women's Affairs
Education: Colleges & Universities, Education Associations, Elementary Education (Public), Faculty Development, Education-General, Medical Education, Preschool Education, Private Education (Precollege), Public Education (Precollege), Science/Mathematics Education, Special Education, Student Aid
Environment: Air/Water Quality, Energy, Environment-General, Protection, Resource Conservation
Health: AIDS/HIV, Cancer, Emergency/Ambulance Services, Health-General, Health Funds, Health Organizations, Hospices, Medical Rehabilitation, Nursing Services, Public Health
International: International Affairs
Religion: Churches
Science: Science Museums
Social Services: Animal Protection, Camps, Child Welfare, Community Centers, Community Service Organizations, Crime Prevention, Day Care, Delinquency & Criminal Rehabilitation, Family Planning, Family Services, Food/Clothing Distribution, Recreation & Athletics, Scouts, Senior Services, Social Services-General, Substance Abuse, United Funds/United Ways, Veterans, Volunteer Services, Volunteer Services, YMCA/YWCA/YMHA/YWHA, Youth Organizations

Application Procedures

Initial Contact: Send a one- to three-page letter describing the organization and the program for which grant is sought.
Application Requirements: Include name, address, and phone number of contact person, amount requested, annual report, recently audited financial statement, proof of tax-exempt status, details of current sources of support, and plans for future funding.
Deadlines: April 1 and October 1.

Restrictions

Does not support individuals, religious organizations for sectarian purposes, political or lobbying groups, or organizations outside operating areas.

Corporate Officials

Stephen Christy: president, chief executive officer PRIM CORP EMPL president, chief executive officer: Mascoma Savings Bank.
Clark A. Griffiths: chairman PRIM CORP EMPL chairman: Mascoma Savings Bank.

Foundation Officials

Elizabeth L. Crory: trustee
Charles M. Harrington: trustee
Raymond A. Lagasse: chairman
Joseph M. Longacre: trustee
Barry E. McCabe: executive vice president, chief operating officer
Thomas T. Terry: trustee

Grants Analysis

Disclosure Period: calendar year ending 2001
Total Grants: $102,905*
Number of Grants: 88
Average Grant: $1,169
Highest Grant: $5,000
Typical Range: $500 to $2,000
*Note: Giving excludes United Way.

Recent Grants

Note: Grants derived from 2001 Form 990.

Library-Related
2,300   Fairlee Public Library, Fairlee, VT -- for renovations

General
5,000   Cooperative Preschool of Lebanon, Lebanon, OH -- for renovations
4,500   Friends of Veterans -- for Veteran's Aid and Assistance Programs
3,000   Northern Stage, White River Junction, VT -- for new rehearsal hall
3,000   Thompson Senior Center, Woodstock, VT -- for new computers
2,500   Saint Barnabas Church of Central Vermont Community Action, VT -- for the Good Wheels Program
2,150   Windsor School District, Boston, MA -- for LCD projector and laptop computer
2,000   Hampshire Cooperative Nursery School -- for facility improvements
2,000   Opera North, Hanover, NH -- for Opera Scenes Program
2,000   Wolf and Wild Canine Sanctuary, Inc., White River Junction, VT -- for upgrade to kennel roof
1,750   Child and Family Services -- for Mascoma Student Assistance Program

Maurice H. Masland Trust No. 2

Giving Contact

Phyllis W. Smith, Trustee
3932 Druid Hills Rd.
Louisville, KY 40207
Phone: (502)721-8982

Description

Founded: 1994
EIN: 237733774
Organization Type: Private Foundation
Giving Locations: CO; FL; IL; MI; PA
Grant Types: General Support.

Financial Summary

Total Giving: $128,000 (2001); $437,770 (2000); $731,610 (1999)
Assets: $22,685 (2001); $151,204 (2000); $638,859 (1999)

Typical Recipients

Arts & Humanities: Arts & Humanities-General, Libraries
Civic & Public Affairs: Civic & Public Affairs-General
Education: Colleges & Universities, Education-General, Leadership Training, Religious Education
Health: Clinics/Medical Centers, Health Organizations
International: Foreign Arts Organizations, Foreign Educational Institutions, International Development, Missionary/Religious Activities
Religion: Bible Study/Translation, Churches, Religion-General, Ministries, Missionary Activities (Domestic), Religious Organizations, Religious Welfare

Application Procedures

Initial Contact: Send a brief letter of inquiry.
Application Requirements: State project, funds requested, and background information.
Deadlines: None.

Foundation Officials

Phyllis W. Smith: trustee

Grants Analysis

Disclosure Period: calendar year ending 2001
Total Grants: $128,000
Number of Grants: 8
Average Grant: $9,000*
Highest Grant: $65,000
Lowest Grant: $3,000
Typical Range: $5,000 to $15,000
*Note: Average grant figure excludes highest grant.

Recent Grants

Note: Grants derived from 2001 Form 990.

General

65,000	Church of the Nazarene International Board of Education, Kansas City, MO
15,000	Philadelphia College of Bible, Langhorne, PA
10,000	Adelaide College of Ministries, Doyleston, PA
10,000	Christar, Reading, PA
10,000	SEND International, Farmington, MI
10,000	Stephen's Children Ministries, Atlanta, GA
5,000	ACMC, Atlanta, GA
3,000	Campus Crusade for Christ, Orlando, FL

MASSACHUSETTS MUTUAL LIFE INSURANCE CO.

Company Headquarters

1295 State Street
Springfield, MA 01111
Web: http://www.massmutual.com

Company Description

Revenue: US$20.247 billion (2002)
Profit: US$1.43 billion (2002)
Employees: 9000 (2001)
Fortune Rank: 84, per FORTUNE Magazine's list of 500 Largest U.S. Corporations (2002).
SIC(s): 6311 Life Insurance, 6321 Accident & Health Insurance.

Operating Locations

Massachusetts Mutual Life Insurance Co. (CT--Hartford)

Subsidiary Companies

NY: Oppenheimer Fund, Rochester

Nonmonetary Support

Type: Donated Equipment; Donated Products
Volunteer Programs: Company sponsors volunteer activities, such as Junior Achievement, literacy, and tutor/mentor programs. Supports the volunteers in Action Program, which awards cash grants to organizations where employees actively volunteer.
Contact: Portia Allen, Administrative Assistant, Corporate Communications
Note: Company provides nonmonetary support.

The MassMutual Foundation for Hartford, Inc.

Giving Contact

Ronald A. Copes, Executive Director
140 Garden Street
ATTN: H356
Hartford, CT 06154
Phone: (860)987-2085
Fax: (860)987-2493
E-mail: rcopes@massmutual.com
Web: http://massmutual.com/mmfg/about/community.html

Description

EIN: 510192500
Organization Type: Corporate Foundation
Giving Locations: CT: Hartford and surrounding area
Grant Types: Capital, General Support, Multiyear/Continuing Support, Scholarship.
Note: Employee matching gift ratio: 1 to 1, up to $1,000 for employees and up to $2,500 for directors.

Financial Summary

Total Giving: $1,900,000 (2002 approx); $1,418,203 (2001); $3,700,000 (2000 approx). Note: Contributes through corporate direct giving program and foundation.
Giving Analysis: Giving for 1999 includes: foundation matching gifts ($39,640); foundation grants to United Way ($268,000); corporate matching gifts ($500,000); foundation ($982,666); corporate direct giving ($1,903,640); 1998: foundation grants to United Way ($2,750); foundation matching gifts ($38,409); foundation ($1,336,605); corporate direct giving ($2,222,236); 1997: foundation matching gifts ($31,770); foundation grants to United Way ($255,000); foundation ($967,104);
Assets: $8,412,720 (2001); $10,599,282 (2000); $10,904,195 (1999)
Gifts Received: $3,400 (2000); $153,213 (1998).
Note: Contributions are received from Massachusetts Mutual Life Insurance Company.

Typical Recipients

Arts & Humanities: Arts Associations & Councils, Dance, Arts & Humanities-General, History & Archaeology, Libraries, Literary Arts, Museums/Galleries, Music, Opera, Performing Arts, Public Broadcasting, Theater
Civic & Public Affairs: African American Affairs, Botanical Gardens/Parks, Community Foundations, Economic Development, Employment/Job Training, Civic & Public Affairs-General, Parades/Festivals, Public Policy, Urban & Community Affairs
Education: Afterschool/Enrichment Programs, Business Education, Colleges & Universities, Community & Junior Colleges, Education Funds, Elementary

Education (Public), Education-General, Legal Education, Public Education (Precollege), Student Aid, Vocational & Technical Education
Environment: Environment-General
Health: AIDS/HIV, Children's Health/Hospitals, Clinics/Medical Centers, Hospitals, Medical Research, Multiple Sclerosis
Religion: Religious Welfare
Social Services: Animal Protection, At-Risk Youth, Big Brother/Big Sister, Camps, Child Welfare, Community Service Organizations, Food/Clothing Distribution, Homes, People with Disabilities, Social Services-General, Substance Abuse, United Funds/United Ways, Volunteer Services, YMCA/YWCA/YMHA/YWHA, Youth Organizations

Application Procedures

Initial Contact: Request copies of application and contribution guidelines, then submit a written proposal.
Application Requirements: Include a description of organization or program to be funded, including a clear statement of goals and objectives; budget; proof of tax-exempt status; a list of the organization's board of directors. tax-exemption letter. tax-exemption letter.
Deadlines: None.
Review Process: Applications are reviewed quarterly.
Decision Notification: Applicants are generally notified of the foundation's decision within two months of application.
Notes: The foundation prefers that applicants use the common grant application form developed by the Coordinating Council for Foundations in Hartford.

Restrictions

Contributions will not be made for: individuals; operating costs and expenses, such as transportation, refreshments and promotional items; deficit reduction campaigns; fraternal societies, labor organizations and veterans' groups; independent fundraising activities of United Way agencies, other than selected capital fund campaigns; organizations which are not tax-exempt; religious or political organizations; or fundraising activities such as golf tournaments, auctions, walkathons, etc.

Additional Information

Company has operations in nearly all 50 states.
Mass Mutual merged with Connecticut Mutual in 1996. The Connecticut Mutual Foundation became the MassMutual Foundation for Hartford; the Massachusetts Mutual Contributions Program continues its support for the Springfield, MA area.
Those organizations which receive support are required to provide a status report of the program funded at the end of the grant period, usually within six months of funding. A MassMutual report form will be provided for this purpose when the grant is awarded. Any future support will be contingent on MassMutual's receipt of this information in a timely manner.
Publications: Social Report; Guidelines; Application Form

Corporate Officials

Frances Emerson: senior vice president, Corporate Communications MassMutual

Foundation Officials

Eustis Walcott: vice president

Grants Analysis

Disclosure Period: calendar year ending 2001
Total Grants: $1,426,703*
Number of Grants: 189
Average Grant: $6,110*
Highest Grant: $278,000
Lowest Grant: $500
Typical Range: $1,000 to $20,000

*Note: Giving excludes scholarships; United Way; corporate direct giving. Average grant figure excludes highest grant.

Recent Grants

Note: Grants derived from 2001 Form 990.

General

278,250	United Way of the Capital Area, Hartford, CT -- capital campaign
100,000	Oppenheimer Funds, Inc. Legacy Program, Denver, CO -- World Trade Center relief fund
65,000	Greater Hartford Arts Council, Hartford, CT -- United Arts campaign
50,000	Riverfront Recapture, Inc., Hartford, CT -- for community boathouse capital campaign
50,000	Saint Francis Hospital and Medical Center, Hartford, CT -- renovation of emergency trauma center
50,000	Saint Joseph College, West Hartford, CT -- capital campaign
35,000	Mark Twain House, Hartford, CT -- capital campaign
31,171	Bushnell Park Foundation, Hartford, CT -- MassMutual Read Aloud Literacy Enrichment Project
25,000	Hartford Action Plan on Infant Health, Hartford, CT -- Teen Pregnancy Prevention Program
25,000	Hartford Camp Courant, Hartford, CT -- 2000 Master Plan

MASSEY CHARITABLE TRUST

Giving Contact

Walter J. Carroll, Executive Director & Trustee
PO Box 1178
Coraopolis, PA 15108
Phone: (412)262-5992

Description

Founded: 1968
EIN: 237007897
Organization Type: Family Foundation
Giving Locations: PA: emphasis on Southwest Pennsylvania, Pittsburgh
Grant Types: General Support, Research.

Donor Information

Founder: The trust was established in 1968 by Doris J. Massey, the late H. B. Massey, and Massey Rental.

Financial Summary

Total Giving: $2,116,580 (2001); $2,141,531 (2000); $2,015,036 (1998)
Assets: $38,433,065 (2001); $41,671,434 (2000); $40,299,400 (1998)

Typical Recipients

Arts & Humanities: Arts Associations & Councils, Arts Centers, Ballet, Historic Preservation, History & Archaeology, Libraries, Museums/Galleries, Music, Opera, Performing Arts, Public Broadcasting, Theater, Visual Arts
Civic & Public Affairs: Botanical Gardens/Parks, Clubs, Employment/Job Training, Civic & Public Affairs-General, Legal Aid, Professional & Trade Associations, Public Policy, Urban & Community Affairs, Zoos/Aquariums
Education: Colleges & Universities, Continuing Education, Education Funds, Education-General, Literacy, Medical Education, Minority Education, Private Education (Precollege), Public Education (Precollege), Science/Mathematics Education, Special Education
Environment: Resource Conservation

Health: Alzheimers Disease, Arthritis, Cancer, Children's Health/Hospitals, Clinics/Medical Centers, Diabetes, Emergency/Ambulance Services, Eyes/Blindness, Health Funds, Health Organizations, Hospices, Hospitals, Hospitals (University Affiliated), Kidney, Long-Term Care, Medical Rehabilitation, Medical Research, Nursing Services, Public Health, Single-Disease Health Associations
International: Foreign Arts Organizations, International Peace & Security Issues, International Relations
Religion: Churches, Dioceses, Ministries, Religious Organizations, Religious Welfare
Science: Scientific Centers & Institutes, Scientific Research
Social Services: At-Risk Youth, Big Brother/Big Sister, Child Welfare, Community Centers, Community Service Organizations, Counseling, Family Planning, Family Services, Food/Clothing Distribution, Homes, People with Disabilities, Scouts, Senior Services, Sexual Abuse, Shelters/Homelessness, Substance Abuse, United Funds/United Ways, Volunteer Services, YMCA/YWCA/YMHA/YWHA, Youth Organizations

Application Procedures

Initial Contact: The trust has no formal grant application procedure or application form.
Application Requirements: Applications should include the amount requested and purpose, and documentation of exempt and non-private foundation status.
Deadlines: None.

Restrictions

Grants are not made to individuals.

Foundation Officials

Daniel B. Carroll: trustee
Walter J. Carroll: executive director, trustee
Robert M. Connolly: trustee
Joe B. Massey: trustee

Grants Analysis

Disclosure Period: calendar year ending 2001
Total Grants: $2,116,580
Number of Grants: 135
Average Grant: $15,680
Highest Grant: $125,000
Lowest Grant: $2,000
Typical Range: $5,000 to $30,000

Recent Grants

Note: Grants derived from 2001 Form 990.

General

125,000	Robert Morris College, Moon Township, PA
90,000	High Museum of Art, Atlanta, GA
70,000	Pittsburgh Leadership Foundation, Pittsburgh, PA
60,000	Atlanta Symphony Orchestra, Atlanta, GA
50,000	Atlanta Historical Society, Atlanta, GA
50,000	Carlow College, Pittsburgh, PA
50,000	Carlow College, Pittsburgh, PA
40,000	Carnegie Museum of Pittsburgh, Pittsburgh, PA
35,000	Manchester Youth Development, Pittsburgh, PA
30,000	Georgia Justice Project, Atlanta, GA

DAVID MEADE MASSIE TRUST

Giving Contact

PO Box 41
Chillicothe, OH 45601
Phone: (740)772-5070

Description

EIN: 316022292
Organization Type: Private Foundation
Giving Locations: OH: Chillicothe County, Ross County
Grant Types: General Support.

Financial Summary

Total Giving: $290,176 (2001); $148,101 (2000); $159,148 (1999)
Assets: $5,262,183 (2001); $5,527,885 (2000); $5,353,892 (1999)

Typical Recipients

Arts & Humanities: Historic Preservation, History & Archaeology, Libraries, Music, Performing Arts, Theater
Civic & Public Affairs: African American Affairs, Botanical Gardens/Parks, Clubs, Civic & Public Affairs-General, Housing, Law & Justice, Municipalities/Towns, Parades/Festivals, Professional & Trade Associations, Rural Affairs, Safety, Urban & Community Affairs
Education: Agricultural Education, Arts/Humanities Education, Business Education, Colleges & Universities, Education Funds, Elementary Education (Private), Elementary Education (Public), Education-General, Private Education (Precollege), Public Education (Precollege), School Volunteerism, Science/Mathematics Education, Secondary Education (Public), Student Aid, Vocational & Technical Education
Health: Cancer, Cancer, Children's Health/Hospitals, Clinics/Medical Centers, Emergency/Ambulance Services, Health-General, Health Organizations, Heart, Home-Care Services, Hospitals, Medical Research, Mental Health, Public Health, Respiratory, Single-Disease Health Associations, Speech & Hearing
International: International Relations
Religion: Churches, Religious Organizations, Religious Welfare
Social Services: Animal Protection, At-Risk Youth, Camps, Child Welfare, Community Centers, Community Service Organizations, Day Care, Delinquency & Criminal Rehabilitation, Domestic Violence, Emergency Relief, Food/Clothing Distribution, Homes, People with Disabilities, Recreation & Athletics, Senior Services, Substance Abuse, Veterans, Volunteer Services, YMCA/YWCA/YMHA/YWHA, Youth Organizations

Application Procedures

Initial Contact: Request application form.
Application Requirements: Return completed application form along with proof of tax-exempt status, an itemization of the cost breakdown of the project, a copy of the minutes of executive committee meeting stating that the organization authorizes the filing of the application and assumes responsibility for the grant if it is awarded, and current financial statements. Application materials must be submitted in quadruplicate.
Deadlines: March 1, June 1, September 1, and December 1.

Restrictions

Grants are made to educational, charitable, and community service organizations to be used exclusively for the purpose of helping to provide for the health, happiness, and welfare of the citizens of Chillicothe and Roso County, OH.

Additional Information

Publications: Program Policy Statement; Application Form; Guidelines

Foundation Officials

Joseph G. Kear: trustee
Thomas M. Spetnagel: trustee
Joseph P. Sulzer: trustee B Chillicothe, OH 1947. ED Ohio University BGS (1972); Capital University JD (1982). PRIM CORP EMPL state rep: Ohio House

of Representatives. CORP AFFIL member environmental advisor board: Martin Marietta Energy Systems; member environmental advisor board: Goodyear Atomic Corp. NONPR AFFIL trustee: Juvenile Detention Center. CLUB AFFIL Kiwanis; KofC.

Grants Analysis

Disclosure Period: calendar year ending 2001
Total Grants: $290,176
Number of Grants: 37
Average Grant: $6,271*
Highest Grant: $64,424
Typical Range: $2,000 to $5,000 and $10,000 to $25,000
*Note: Average grant figure excludes highest grant.

Recent Grants

Note: Grants derived from 2001 Form 990.

General

64,424	YMCA, Chillicothe, OH -- for sidewalks and sewer repairs
26,982	Bishop Flaget Schools, Chillicothe, OH -- for heating system
25,000	Chillicothe Education Foundation, Chillicothe, OH -- for scholarships
16,517	Frontier Community Service, Chillicothe, OH -- for electronic communications and voice mail system
10,000	City of Chillicothe Community Affairs, Chillicothe, OH -- for Manor Park Project
5,000	Adena Local Schools, Frankfort, OH -- to equip science lab and junior high school
5,000	American Red Cross, Chillicothe, OH -- for manikins for training CPR
5,000	Chillicothe Area Artist Series, Inc, Chillicothe, OH -- for concert in October
5,000	City of Chillicothe Community Affairs, Chillicothe, OH -- for Chautauqua performance
5,000	God's Community Church, Chillicothe, OH -- for hymnals and screen

MASTERPOOL FOUNDATION

Giving Contact

James M. Hughes, Trustee
1432 Post Rd.
Fairfield, CT 06430
Phone: (203)256-1977

Description

Founded: 1989
EIN: 066323079
Organization Type: Private Foundation
Grant Types: General Support.

Financial Summary

Total Giving: $75,925 (fiscal year ending July 31, 2000); $48,425 (fiscal 1998); $3,250 (fiscal 1996)
Assets: $423,816 (fiscal 2001); $522,265 (fiscal 2000); $487,153 (fiscal 1998)
Gifts Received: $5,000 (fiscal 1994); $10,000 (fiscal 1993). Note: In fiscal 1994, contributions were received from Michael D. Masterpool.

Typical Recipients

Arts & Humanities: Arts Centers, Libraries, Museums/Galleries, Music, Opera, Performing Arts, Theater
Civic & Public Affairs: Civic & Public Affairs-General, Native American Affairs
Education: Colleges & Universities, Education Funds, Education-General, Student Aid
Environment: Environment-General

Health: Diabetes, Health Organizations, Medical Research, Single-Disease Health Associations
Religion: Churches, Religion-General, Religious Organizations, Religious Welfare
Science: Scientific Centers & Institutes
Social Services: Child Welfare, Community Service Organizations, Family Services, People with Disabilities, Substance Abuse, Youth Organizations

Application Procedures

Initial Contact: Send a brief letter of inquiry.
Application Requirements: EIN number and financial data.
Deadlines: None.

Foundation Officials

James M. Hughes: trustee

Grants Analysis

Disclosure Period: fiscal year ending July 31, 2001
Total Grants: $0*
Typical Range: $1,000 to $5,000
*Note: No grants awarded.

Recent Grants

Note: Grants derived from 2000 Form 990.

General

15,000	Rose Hill Center, Rosehill, MI
13,000	Metropolitan Opera Association, New York, NY
11,000	Lockwood Mathews Museum Foundation
7,500	St. Bartholomew's Church, New York, NY
5,000	Catholic Relief Fund
3,500	Maritime Center at Norwalk, South Norwalk, CT
3,500	McKinley Enrichment
3,500	Stratford Festival Theatre
2,500	Music and Arts Center
2,500	Senior Marion Rielly Memorial Foundation

MASTERS FAMILY FOUNDATION

Giving Contact

Micky Jo Masters, Chairman
433 E. Las Colinas Blvd., No. 1290
Irving, TX 75039
Phone: (972)556-1190

Description

Founded: 1991
EIN: 752323131
Organization Type: Private Foundation
Grant Types: General Support, Scholarship.

Financial Summary

Total Giving: $58,933 (1999); $59,033 (1996); $3,866 (1995)
Assets: $185,711 (1999); $244,661 (1996); $289,892 (1995)
Gifts Received: $250 (1995); $10,513 (1993). Note: In 1993, contributions were received from James L. Masters.

Typical Recipients

Arts & Humanities: Libraries
Health: Cancer, Children's Health/Hospitals, Emergency/Ambulance Services, Hospitals
Religion: Churches, Ministries, Religious Organizations, Religious Welfare
Social Services: Community Service Organizations, Food/Clothing Distribution, Homes, Substance Abuse, Youth Organizations

Application Procedures

Initial Contact: Request application guidelines.
Deadlines: March 14.

Additional Information

Provides scholarships to Hopkins County seniors who maintain a 3.0 grade point average and show financial need.
Publications: Application Form

Foundation Officials

James L. Masters, IV: president
Mickey Jo Masters: chairman
Chad Young: director

Grants Analysis

Disclosure Period: calendar year ending 1999
Total Grants: $58,933
Number of Grants: 2
Highest Grant: $58,333

Recent Grants

Note: Grants derived from 1999 Form 990.

General

58,333	Hopkins County Medical Hospital, Sulphur Springs, TX
600	St. James Catholic Church, IL

ELIZABETH RING MATHER AND WILLIAM GWINN MATHER FUND

Giving Contact

James D. Ireland, III, President
1111 Superior Ave., Suite 1000
Cleveland, OH 44114
Phone: (216)696-4200

Description

Founded: 1954
EIN: 346519863
Organization Type: Private Foundation
Giving Locations: OH: emphasis on the greater Cleveland area
Grant Types: Capital, Endowment, General Support.

Donor Information

Founder: the late Elizabeth Ring Mather

Financial Summary

Total Giving: $1,088,644 (2001); $1,040,513 (2000); $829,319 (1999)
Giving Analysis: Giving for 2001 includes: foundation grants to United Way ($10,000); 2000: foundation grants to United Way ($15,000) 1999: foundation grants to United Way ($15,000)
Assets: $9,711,729 (2001); $11,389,130 (2000); $10,436,344 (1999)
Gifts Received: $315,713 (2001); $532,511 (2000); $651,906 (1999). Note: Contributions are made by James D. Ireland III, Lucy I. Weller, Cornelia I. Hallinan, George R. Ireland, and the United States Trust Co.

Typical Recipients

Arts & Humanities: Arts Associations & Councils, Arts Centers, Arts Institutes, Ballet, Community Arts, Historic Preservation, History & Archaeology, Libraries, Museums/Galleries, Music, Opera, Performing Arts, Public Broadcasting
Civic & Public Affairs: Botanical Gardens/Parks, Business/Free Enterprise, Clubs, Community Foundations, Civic & Public Affairs-General, Municipalities/Towns, Nonprofit Management, Parades/Festivals, Philanthropic Organizations, Professional & Trade

Associations, Urban & Community Affairs, Women's Affairs, Zoos/Aquariums

Education: Arts/Humanities Education, Colleges & Universities, Economic Education, Education Funds, Environmental Education, Faculty Development, Education-General, Leadership Training, Legal Education, Medical Education, Private Education (Precollege), Public Education (Precollege), Science/Mathematics Education, Social Sciences Education, Student Aid

Environment: Air/Water Quality, Forestry, Environment-General, Resource Conservation, Wildlife Protection

Health: Cancer, Children's Health/Hospitals, Health Organizations, Hospitals, Medical Rehabilitation, Medical Research, Mental Health, Nursing Services, Public Health

Religion: Churches

Science: Science Museums, Scientific Centers & Institutes

Social Services: Child Welfare, Community Service Organizations, Day Care, Domestic Violence, Family Planning, Food/Clothing Distribution, People with Disabilities, Senior Services, United Funds/United Ways, Youth Organizations

Application Procedures

Initial Contact: Send a brief letter of inquiry.
Application Requirements: Include a description of organization, amount requested, purpose of funds sought, recently audited financial statement, and proof of tax-exempt status.
Deadlines: None.

Restrictions

Does not support individuals or provide scholarships or loans.

Foundation Officials

Cornelia I. Hallinan: secretary
Cornelia W. Ireland: trustee
George R. Ireland: treasurer
James D. Ireland, III: president CORP AFFIL director: Cleveland-Cliffs Inc.
Jane J. Masters: assistant secretary, assistant treasurer
Kathleen K. Riley: assistant secretary, assistant treasurer
Lucy I. Weller: vice president

Grants Analysis

Disclosure Period: calendar year ending 2001
Total Grants: $1,078,644*
Number of Grants: 43
Average Grant: $15,759*
Highest Grant: $416,760
Lowest Grant: $50
Typical Range: $10,000 to $30,000
*Note: Giving excludes United Way. Average grant figure excludes highest grant.

Recent Grants

Note: Grants derived from 2001 Form 990.

Library-Related
12,500	Cleveland Health Science Library

General
416,760	University Circle Incorporated, Cleveland, OH -- operations
132,000	Musical Arts, Cleveland, OH
100,000	Cleveland Botanical Garden, Cleveland, OH
100,000	Kenyon College, Gambier, OH
50,000	Hathaway Brown School, Cleveland, OH
50,000	Phillips Academy, Andover, MA
35,833	Great Lakes Science Center, Cleveland, OH

25,000	Hopewell Inn, Cleveland, OH
15,000	Saginaw Art Museum, Saginaw, MI
15,000	University Circle Incorporated, Cleveland, OH

S. LIVINGSTON MATHER CHARITABLE TRUST

Giving Contact

Nancy Zambie, Secretary
ONe Corporate Exchange
25825 Science Park Dr., Suite 110
Beachwood, OH 44122
Phone: (216)828-9770

Description

Founded: 1953
EIN: 346505619
Organization Type: Private Foundation
Giving Locations: OH: Northeastern Ohio
Grant Types: General Support.

Donor Information

Founder: the late S. Livingston Mather

Financial Summary

Total Giving: $285,000 (2000); $280,300 (1999); $212,500 (1998)
Giving Analysis: Giving for 1999 includes: foundation grants to United Way ($38,000); 1998: foundation grants to United Way ($32,000) foundation ($158,250)
Assets: $5,822,436 (2000); $6,270,382 (1999); $5,861,470 (1998)
Gifts Received: $1,766 (1993)

Typical Recipients

Arts & Humanities: Arts Associations & Councils, Arts Centers, Arts Institutes, Arts Outreach, Arts & Humanities-General, Historic Preservation, History & Archaeology, Libraries, Museums/Galleries, Music, Opera, Performing Arts, Public Broadcasting, Theater

Civic & Public Affairs: Botanical Gardens/Parks, Clubs, Employment/Job Training, Parades/Festivals, Urban & Community Affairs

Education: Afterschool/Enrichment Programs, Arts/Humanities Education, Colleges & Universities, Education Funds, Education Reform, Environmental Education, Faculty Development, Education-General, Medical Education, Minority Education, Private Education (Precollege), Public Education (Precollege), Student Aid

Environment: Environment-General, Resource Conservation

Health: AIDS/HIV, Clinics/Medical Centers, Emergency/Ambulance Services, Health Organizations, Hospices, Medical Rehabilitation, Mental Health

Science: Science Museums, Scientific Centers & Institutes

Social Services: Camps, Child Abuse, Child Welfare, Community Centers, Community Service Organizations, Day Care, Domestic Violence, Family Planning, Family Services, Food/Clothing Distribution, Homes, Sexual Abuse, Substance Abuse, United Funds/United Ways, Volunteer Services, Youth Organizations

Application Procedures

Initial Contact: Submit a a brief letter of inquiry.
Application Requirements: Submit a statement defining the purpose of funds sought, the project's significance to the community, sponsorship, budget for the project, other sources of support in hand and solicited, and staffing.
Deadlines: None.
Review Process: The Distribution Committee meets as needed, at least four times during the year.

Restrictions

Grants are made for operating support, building funds, and special purposes, but not ordinarily for scientific and medical programs or research, or in areas appropriately supported by the government and the United Way. Does not support individuals, provide deficit financing or loans, or award grants in response to mass mailings or telephone solicitations.

Additional Information

Publications: Biennial Report (including Application Guidelines)
Trust(s): Key Trust Co OH NA

Foundation Officials

Katharine M. Jeffrey: member
Elizabeth H. McMillan, M.D.: member
Elizabeth Mather McMillan: member
S. Sterling McMillan, PhD: member
S. Sterling McMillan, III: member
Thomas W. Offutt, III: secretary

Grants Analysis

Disclosure Period: calendar year ending 2000
Total Grants: $248,000*
Number of Grants: 43
Average Grant: $5,905
Highest Grant: $45,000
Typical Range: $1,000 to $10,000
*Note: Giving excludes United Way.

Recent Grants

Note: Grants derived from 1999 Form 990.

General
50,000	Cleveland Botanical Gardens, Cleveland, OH
45,000	Hathaway Brown School
38,000	United Way
22,000	Yellowstone Park Foundation, Bozeman, MT
15,000	Camp Ho Mita Koda, Cleveland, OH
15,000	Hiram House, OH
10,000	Great Lakes Science Center, Cleveland, OH
7,500	Cleveland Museum of Art, Cleveland, OH
5,000	American Red Cross, Texarkana, TX
5,000	Case Western Reserve University, Cleveland, OH

RICHARD MATHER FUND

Giving Contact

Michele Draper
Care of M&T Bank
101 S. Salina St.
Syracuse, NY 13202
Phone: (716)842-5506

Description

Founded: 1955
EIN: 156018423
Organization Type: Private Foundation
Giving Locations: NY: Central New York, Syracuse
Grant Types: Endowment, General Support, Project.

Donor Information

Founder: the late Flora Mather Hosmer, the late R. C. Hosmer, Jr., Hosmer Descendants Trust

Financial Summary

Total Giving: $333,300 (2001); $328,600 (2000); $234,200 (1999)
Giving Analysis: Giving for 2001 includes: foundation grants to United Way ($16,000); 2000: foundation grants to United Way ($15,000); 1999: foundation grants to United Way ($14,000)

Assets: $4,335,333 (2001); $4,896,597 (2000); $5,580,418 (1999)
Gifts Received: $10,438 (2000); $10,067 (1999); $10,837 (1998). Note: In 1994, 1999 and 2000, contributions were received from Hosmer Trust.

Typical Recipients
Arts & Humanities: Arts Associations & Councils, Community Arts, Arts & Humanities-General, History & Archaeology, Libraries, Museums/Galleries, Music, Opera, Performing Arts, Public Broadcasting, Theater
Civic & Public Affairs: Community Foundations, Civic & Public Affairs-General, Municipalities/Towns, Nonprofit Management, Public Policy, Urban & Community Affairs, Women's Affairs, Zoos/Aquariums
Education: Arts/Humanities Education, Colleges & Universities, Literacy, Private Education (Precollege), School Volunteerism
International: International Development, International Organizations
Religion: Missionary Activities (Domestic), Religious Welfare
Science: Science Museums, Scientific Centers & Institutes
Social Services: Camps, Child Welfare, Community Centers, Community Service Organizations, Family Planning, Family Services, United Funds/United Ways, Youth Organizations

Application Procedures
Initial Contact: Send a brief letter of inquiry in writings.
Application Requirements: Include proof of tax-exempt status.
Deadlines: None.

Restrictions
Limited to central NY cultural fields.

Additional Information
Publications: Informational Brochure (including Application Guidelines)

Foundation Officials
Stephen E. Chase: trustee
S. Sterling McMillan, PhD: trustee
Gay M. Pomeroy: trustee
Elizabeth H. Schaefer: trustee

Grants Analysis
Disclosure Period: calendar year ending 2001
Total Grants: $317,300*
Number of Grants: 20
Average Grant: $11,700*
Highest Grant: $95,000
Lowest Grant: $600
Typical Range: $5,000 to $20,000
*Note: Giving excludes United Way. Average grant figure excludes highest grant.

Recent Grants
Note: Grants derived from 2001 Form 990.

Library-Related
2,000	Syracuse Children's Chorus, Inc., Syracuse, NY

General
95,000	Syracuse Symphony Orchestra, Syracuse, NY
50,000	Everson Museum of Art, Syracuse, NY
32,500	Syracuse Symphony Foundation, Syracuse, NY
29,750	Syracuse Symphony Orchestra, Syracuse, NY
25,000	Syracuse Stage, Syracuse, NY
16,000	United Way of Central New York, Syracuse, NY
15,000	International Center of Syracuse, Syracuse, NY
15,000	Syracuse Opera, Syracuse, NY
10,000	Boys and Girls Club of Syracuse, Syracuse, NY
10,000	Cazenovia College, Cazenovia, NY

G. HAROLD AND LEILA Y. MATHERS CHARITABLE FOUNDATION

Giving Contact
James H. Handelman, Executive Director
118 N. Bedford Rd., Suite 203
Mt. Kisco, NY 10549-2555
Phone: (914)242-0465
Fax: (914)242-0665
E-mail: jhandelman@mathersfoundation.org
Web: http://www.mathersfoundation.org

Description
Founded: 1975
EIN: 237441901
Organization Type: Specialized/Single Purpose Foundation
Giving Locations: nationally.
Grant Types: Research.

Donor Information
Founder: The G. Harold and Leila Y. Mathers Charitable Foundation was established in 1975.

Financial Summary
Total Giving: $10,000,000 (2002 approx); $9,900,000 (2001); $10,539,461 (2000)
Assets: $176,000,000 (2001); $177,728,323 (2000); $176,885,088 (1999)

Typical Recipients
Arts & Humanities: Libraries, Theater
Civic & Public Affairs: Economic Development
Education: Business Education, Colleges & Universities, Education-General, Health & Physical Education, Medical Education, Science/Mathematics Education
Environment: Environment-General
Health: Cancer, Children's Health/Hospitals, Clinics/Medical Centers, Emergency/Ambulance Services, Health-General, Heart, Hospitals, Hospitals (University Affiliated), Medical Research, Public Health, Research/Studies Institutes, Single-Disease Health Associations
International: Foreign Educational Institutions, International-General, Health Care/Hospitals, International Relief Efforts
Science: Scientific Centers & Institutes, Scientific Labs, Scientific Research
Social Services: Emergency Relief, Family Services, Social Services-General

Application Procedures
Initial Contact: There is no formal application form. Initial contact should be in the form of a concise query letter.
Application Requirements: Letters should describe the research to be pursued; place the proposed research in a context of the current or historical efforts by other researchers addressing the problem; indicate the individuals conducting the research (with credentials); state whether the request has been, or is being submitted elsewhere, and if so, its status; and detail the funds required in the form of a simple budget statement.
Deadlines: None.
Review Process: Applications are reviewed initially by the foundation's executive director and, subsequently, by the executive committee. Additionally, applications often are examined by outside reviewers. A response, in the form of approval, rejection, or request for additional information, can be expected within ninety days. A request should state that an earlier response is desired if circumstances so require.

Restrictions
The foundation makes contributions only to organizations having tax-exempt status under section 501(c)(3) of the Internal Revenue Code and to those that are not private foundations within section 509(a) of the Code, or in the absence of such a determination, to a state or any political subdivision thereof within the meaning of section 170(c)(1) of the Code, or a state college or university. The foundation does not make grants to individuals, and rarely provides support for longer than three years.

Foundation Officials
Don Fizer: secretary, director
Donald E. Handelman: president, director B 1927. ED New York University MBA (1950). PRIM CORP EMPL partner: Meyer Handelman Co.
James H. Handelman: executive director
Joseph W. Handelman: treasurer, assistant secretary B 1930. ED New York University MBA; Princeton University (1952). PRIM CORP EMPL partner: Meyer Handelman Co.
William R. Handelman: vice president, director PRIM CORP EMPL partner: Meyer Handelman Co.
John R. Young: director B Milwaukee, WI 1934. ED University of Chicago AB (1953); University of Chicago JD (1956). PRIM CORP EMPL Cahill Gordon & Reindel.

Grants Analysis
Disclosure Period: calendar year ending 2000
Total Grants: $10,539,461
Number of Grants: 60
Average Grant: $175,659
Highest Grant: $509,300
Typical Range: $100,000 to $500,000 and $5,000 to $10,000

Recent Grants
Note: Grants derived from 2000 Form 990.

General
509,300	University of California San Francisco, San Francisco, CA
500,000	Dana Farber Cancer Institute, Boston, MA -- general support
495,000	Memorial Sloan-Kettering Cancer Center, New York, NY
385,000	Columbia University, New York, NY
384,918	University of Southern California, Los Angeles, Los Angeles, CA
375,000	Stanford University Beckman Center, Stanford, CA
371,875	Baylor College of Medicine, Houston, TX
365,834	Tufts University, New England Medical Center, Boston, MA
360,000	Salk Institute, La Jolla, CA
326,000	Rockefeller University, New York, NY -- general support

MATHIS-PFOHL FOUNDATION

Giving Contact
James M. Pfohl, President
5-46 46th Ave.
Long Island City, NY 11101
Phone: (718)784-4800

Description
Founded: 1947
EIN: 116013764
Organization Type: Private Foundation

Giving Locations: IA; MA; NY; NC
Grant Types: General Support, Scholarship.

Donor Information
Founder: members of the Pfohl family and associated companies

Financial Summary
Total Giving: $433,170 (fiscal year ending November 30, 1999); $355,725 (fiscal 1998); $272,370 (fiscal 1997)
Assets: $9,933,087 (fiscal 1999); $9,272,980 (fiscal 1998); $8,096,410 (fiscal 1997)
Gifts Received: $41,900 (fiscal 1994); $15,000 (fiscal 1993); $22,543 (fiscal 1992). Note: In fiscal 1994, contributions were received from William J. Kirby ($40,400) and miscellaneous ($1,500).

Typical Recipients
Arts & Humanities: Ballet, Community Arts, Historic Preservation, History & Archaeology, Libraries, Museums/Galleries, Music, Opera, Public Broadcasting
Civic & Public Affairs: Civic & Public Affairs-General, Municipalities/Towns, Urban & Community Affairs, Zoos/Aquariums
Education: Arts/Humanities Education, Colleges & Universities, Continuing Education, Education Funds, Education Reform, Education-General, Legal Education, Private Education (Precollege), Public Education (Precollege), Science/Mathematics Education, Secondary Education (Private), Secondary Education (Public), Special Education, Student Aid
Environment: Air/Water Quality
Health: Alzheimers Disease, Cancer, Clinics/Medical Centers, Health Organizations, Hospitals, Mental Health, Nursing Services, Public Health, Single-Disease Health Associations
International: International Relations, International Relief Efforts
Religion: Churches, Religious Organizations, Religious Welfare
Science: Science Museums, Scientific Organizations
Social Services: At-Risk Youth, Child Welfare, Community Centers, Community Service Organizations, Homes, Social Services-General, YMCA/YWCA/YMHA/YWHA, Youth Organizations

Application Procedures
Initial Contact: Send a brief letter of inquiry describing program or project.
Deadlines: None.

Foundation Officials
James M. Pfohl: president

Grants Analysis
Disclosure Period: fiscal year ending November 30, 1998
Total Grants: $355,725
Number of Grants: 127
Average Grant: $1,765*
Highest Grant: $50,000
Typical Range: $100 to $15,000
*Note: Average grant figure excludes highest grant.

Recent Grants
Note: Grants derived from fiscal 2000 Form 990.

General
50,000	Alive in Hope
34,000	Duke University, Durham, NC
25,000	Duke University, Durham, NC
20,000	Harvard Law School, Cambridge, MA
10,000	CNEWA, New York, NY
10,000	Harvard College, Cambridge, MA
10,000	Harvard Law School, Cambridge, MA
10,000	Harvard Law School, Cambridge, MA
10,000	Inner City Schools
10,000	Neuroscience Institute

MATTEL INC.

Company Headquarters
333 Continental Avenue
El Segundo, CA 90245-3802
Web: http://www.mattelmedia.com

Company Description
Founded: 1944
Ticker: MAT
Exchange: NYSE
Revenue: US$4.885 billion (2002)
Profit: US$230.1 million (2002)
Employees: 27000 (2002)
Fortune Rank: 337, per FORTUNE Magazine's list of 500 Largest U.S. Corporations (2002).
SIC(s): 3942 Dolls & Stuffed Toys, 3944 Games, Toys & Children's Vehicles.

Operating Locations
Mattel Inc. (CA--City of Industry; IL--Des Plaines; NY--East Aurora, New York; TX--Fort Worth)

Nonmonetary Support
Value: $500,000 (1998)
Type: In-kind Services
Volunteer Programs: Employees may apply for Employee Volunteer Grants. Grants amounts are linked to the length of service of requesting employee, and by number of other Mattel employees volunteering within the organization.
The Foundation coordinates more than 30 volunteer activities annually to encourage employee volunteerism.
Contact: Regina Rodman, Toy Donations Coordinator

Mattel Foundation

Giving Contact
Paul R. Millman, Foundation Directory
333 Continental Blvd.
Mail Stop M1-1418
El Segundo, CA 90245-5012
Phone: (310)252-3530
Fax: (310)252-3802
Web: http://www.mattel.com

Description
EIN: 953263647
Organization Type: Corporate Foundation
Giving Locations: CA: Los Angeles Southern California and Western New York.
Grant Types: Capital, Employee Matching Gifts, General Support, Matching, Scholarship.
Note: Employee matching gift ratio: 1 to 1 up to $5,000 per employee annually.

Financial Summary
Total Giving: $4,966,638 (2001); $3,922,556 (2000); $4,127,483 (1998). Note: Contributes through corporate direct giving program and foundation.
Giving Analysis: Giving for 2000 includes: foundation grants to United Way ($161,000); foundation matching gifts ($202,062); foundation ($3,559,494); 1998: corporate scholarships ($25,000); corporate grants to United Way ($177,000); corporate matching gifts ($215,653); corporate direct giving (approx $340,000); nonmonetary support (approx $500,000); foundation ($3,709,830); foundation ($3,837,177); 1996: corporate matching gifts ($144,260); corporate grants to United Way ($211,000) foundation ($3,212,130)
Assets: $707,767 (2001); $586,220 (2000); $899,138 (1998)
Gifts Received: $5,095,439 (2001); $3,997,000 (2000); $3,915,000 (1998). Note: Foundation receives contributions from Mattel, Inc.

Typical Recipients
Arts & Humanities: Arts Funds, Arts Institutes, Arts Outreach, Ballet, Dance, Libraries, Museums/Galleries, Music, Performing Arts, Theater
Civic & Public Affairs: African American Affairs, Botanical Gardens/Parks, Business/Free Enterprise, Civil Rights, Clubs, Community Foundations, Economic Development, Economic Policy, Employment/Job Training, Gay/Lesbian Issues, Civic & Public Affairs-General, Housing, Philanthropic Organizations, Public Policy, Urban & Community Affairs, Women's Affairs
Education: Afterschool/Enrichment Programs, Business Education, Colleges & Universities, Economic Education, Education Funds, Education Reform, Elementary Education (Private), Elementary Education (Public), Engineering/Technological Education, Education-General, Leadership Training, Literacy, Medical Education, Minority Education, Private Education (Precollege), Public Education (Precollege), Science/Mathematics Education, Secondary Education (Public), Special Education, Student Aid
Environment: Air/Water Quality, Forestry, Environment-General
Health: AIDS/HIV, Cancer, Children's Health/Hospitals, Clinics/Medical Centers, Diabetes, Geriatric Health, Health Funds, Health Organizations, Heart, Hospitals, Medical Rehabilitation, Multiple Sclerosis, Prenatal Health Issues, Public Health, Single-Disease Health Associations
International: Health Care/Hospitals, International Development, International Relief Efforts
Religion: Religious Welfare, Religious Welfare
Science: Scientific Centers & Institutes, Scientific Organizations
Social Services: Animal Protection, Big Brother/Big Sister, Camps, Child Welfare, Community Centers, Community Service Organizations, Crime Prevention, Day Care, Delinquency & Criminal Rehabilitation, Emergency Relief, Family Services, People with Disabilities, Recreation & Athletics, Scouts, Social Services-General, Special Olympics, Substance Abuse, United Funds/United Ways, Volunteer Services, YMCA/YWCA/YMHA/YWHA, Youth Organizations

Application Procedures
Initial Contact: For toy donations, send a written request.
Application Requirements: Application must be on the organization's letterhead and include a mission statement, contact person, and mailing address (no Post Office boxes); include proof of tax-exempt status. For silent auction items, include description of the event and the date that the item must arrive.
Deadlines: September 30 for holiday toy donation requests.
Evaluative Criteria: Ability of program to alleviate hardships, provide opportunities for better lives for children, or strengthen family life.
Decision Notification: Quarterly; meetings are in February, May, August, and November.
Notes: The foundation has a large commitment to the Mattel Children's Hospital at UCLA; because of this commitment, applications for grant support will not be accepted through 2004.

Restrictions
Foundation generally does not support capital facilities; religious activities; research activities; endowments; individuals; religious, fraternal, political, athletic, social, or veterans organizations; labor groups; programs receiving substantial financial support; federal, state, or local government agencies; or courtesy advertising. Toys will not be donated to third-party requests or to schools.
Only gives to nonprofit organizations that benefit children.

Additional Information

Fischer-Price is now part of Mattel, Inc.

Corporate Officials

Robert A. Eckert: chairman, chief executive officer B August 14, 1954. ED University of Arizona BS (1976); Northwestern University MBA (1977). PRIM CORP EMPL chairman, chief executive officer: Mattel Inc.

Foundation Officials

Harold Brown, PhD: chairman B New York, NY September 19, 1927. ED Columbia University AB (1945); Columbia University AM (1946); Columbia University PhD (1949). PRIM CORP EMPL chairman: Warburg, Pincus & Co. PRIM NONPR EMPL counsel: Center Strategic International Studies. CORP AFFIL partner: Warburg Pincus & Co. Inc.; trustee: Rand Corp.; trustee: Trilateral Community; director: Evergreen Holdings INC; director: Mattel Inc.; director: Alumax Inc.; director: Cummins Engine Co. Inc.; director: Altria Group Inc. NONPR AFFIL member: National Academy Sciences; member: Phi Beta Kappa; member: American Physical Society; member: National Academy Engineering; member: American Academy of Arts & Sciences. CLUB AFFIL River Club; Bohemian Club; Metro Club.

Paul Millman: director

William Stavro: vice president

Grants Analysis

Disclosure Period: calendar year ending 2001
Total Grants: $4,555,675*
Number of Grants: 106
Average Grant: $5,292*
Highest Grant: $4,000,000
Lowest Grant: $500
Typical Range: $1,000 to $10,000
*Note: Giving excludes matching gifts, United Way, and scholarships. Average grant figure excludes highest grant.

Recent Grants

Note: Grants derived from 2001 Form 990.

General

4,000,000	Mattel Children's Hospital at UCLA, Los Angeles, CA -- for operating support
100,000	United Way, Los Angeles, CA -- operating budget
50,000	Foundation for Technology Access, San Rafael, CA -- for operating support
50,000	United Fund of Buffalo and Erie County, Buffalo, NY -- operating support
37,500	Children Affected by AIDS Foundation, El Segundo, CA -- operating support
31,045	American Red Cross
30,000	Citizens Scholarship Foundation, St. Peter, MN -- support of scholarship awards for Mattel Employee children
25,000	Every Person Influences Children, Inc. (EPIC), Buffalo, NY -- for operating support
23,635	United Way of New York, New York, NY
21,310	NYCPPI, New York, NY

KATHARINE MATTHIES FOUNDATION

Giving Contact

Marjorie Alexander Davis, Trust Officer
c/o Fleet Bank
777 Main St., CT EH 40222B
Hartford, CT 06115
Phone: (860)952-7405
Web: http://electronicvalley.org/matthies/

Description

Founded: 1987
EIN: 066261860
Organization Type: Private Foundation
Giving Locations: CT: Ansonia, Beacon Falls, Derby, Oxford, Seymour
Grant Types: General Support.

Donor Information

Founder: the late Katharine Matthies

Financial Summary

Total Giving: $856,760 (2002); $788,563 (2001); $744,363 (2000)
Giving Analysis: Giving for 2002 includes: foundation grants to United Way ($45,000); 2000: foundation grants to United Way ($70,174) 1999: foundation grants to United Way ($26,850)
Assets: $18,352,334 (2001); $19,945,872 (2000); $19,778,871 (1999)
Gifts Received: $71,375 (1999)

Typical Recipients

Arts & Humanities: Arts Outreach, Arts & Humanities-General, History & Archaeology, Libraries, Music, Theater
Civic & Public Affairs: Botanical Gardens/Parks, Chambers of Commerce, Community Foundations, Economic Development, Civic & Public Affairs-General, Housing, Legal Aid, Municipalities/Towns, Nonprofit Management, Safety, Urban & Community Affairs, Zoos/Aquariums
Education: Afterschool/Enrichment Programs, Business Education, Environmental Education, Faculty Development, Education-General, Literacy, Student Aid
Environment: Environment-General, Resource Conservation, Wildlife Protection
Health: Adolescent Health Issues, Emergency/Ambulance Services, Health Organizations, Hospitals, Long-Term Care, Medical Rehabilitation, Public Health
International: Missionary/Religious Activities
Religion: Churches, Religious Organizations, Religious Welfare
Science: Scientific Centers & Institutes
Social Services: Child Welfare, Community Service Organizations, Crime Prevention, Day Care, People with Disabilities, Recreation & Athletics, Scouts, Senior Services, Social Services-General, Substance Abuse, United Funds/United Ways, Veterans, YMCA/YWCA/YMHA/YWHA, Youth Organizations

Application Procedures

Initial Contact: The foundation has no formal grant application procedure or application form. Applications are reviewed quarterly.

Additional Information

Trust(s): Fleet Bank

Grants Analysis

Disclosure Period: calendar year ending 2002
Total Grants: $811,760*
Number of Grants: 50
Average Grant: $14,866*
Highest Grant: $83,333
Lowest Grant: $2,500
Typical Range: $5,000 to $30,000
*Note: Giving excludes United Way. Average grant figure excludes highest grant.

Recent Grants

Note: Grants derived from 2001 Form 990.

General

95,333	Griffin Hospital, Derby, CT
57,189	Boys and Girls Club of Lower Naugatuck Valley, Shelton, CT -- for two vans and expenses
50,000	Lower Naugatuck Valley Parent Child Resource, Shelton, CT -- support capital campaign project
39,900	Catholic Family Services of Ansonia, Ansonia, CT -- to implement Stop it Now Youth Violence
39,125	Valley United Way, Ansonia, CT
35,000	Seymour Ambulance Association -- purchase of a safekids vehicle van
30,000	St. Joseph Parish -- for salary of coordinator
27,119	Southern Connecticut State University, New Haven, CT -- to provide violence prevention and serve the middle schools
24,850	Hewitt Foundation, Inc., Shelton, CT -- implement Clinical Education Program
24,365	TEAM, Wheaton, IL -- to deliver home meals and homemaking visits

JAMES AND EVA MAYER FOUNDATION

Giving Contact

Gene V. Owen, Trustee
PO Box 328
Plainview, TX 79073-0328
Phone: (806)296-6304

Description

Founded: 1988
EIN: 756360908
Organization Type: Private Foundation
Giving Locations: TX
Grant Types: Capital, Matching, Project.

Donor Information

Founder: the late Eva H. Mayer

Financial Summary

Total Giving: $24,500 (2001); $105,000 (2000); $203,600 (1999)
Assets: $4,884,337 (2001); $4,704,860 (2000); $4,566,167 (1999)

Typical Recipients

Arts & Humanities: Community Arts, Libraries, Music
Civic & Public Affairs: Clubs, Civic & Public Affairs-General
Education: Colleges & Universities, Legal Education, Literacy, Science/Mathematics Education, Secondary Education (Public)
Health: Cancer, Children's Health/Hospitals, Diabetes, Health Organizations, Hospices, Hospitals, Public Health, Single-Disease Health Associations
Religion: Religious Welfare
Social Services: Child Welfare, Community Centers, Community Service Organizations, Day Care, Recreation & Athletics, Senior Services, United Funds/United Ways, Youth Organizations

Application Procedures

Initial Contact: Send a brief letter of inquiry, not more than two pages.
Application Requirements: Include the nature and brief history of the organization; the circumstances leading to the need for the grant; amount requested; intended use/purpose of funds sought; date that funds are needed and when they will be expended; and what public recognition, if any, would be given to the Mayer Foundation. Requests should include proof of tax-exempt status.
Deadlines: None.

Restrictions

Does not support individuals, religious organizations for sectarian purposes, political or lobbying groups, or organizations outside operating areas.

Additional Information

Grants are made only to organizations operated exclusively for religious, charitable, educational, literary, or scientific purposes, no substantial part of the activities of which is carrying on propaganda, or otherwise attempting to influence legislation or the election of public officials. Grants are made only for use within the United States or its possessions.
Publications: Application Guidelines

Foundation Officials

Paul Lyle: trustee
Gene V. Owen: trustee
David Wilder: trustee

Grants Analysis

Disclosure Period: calendar year ending 2001
Total Grants: $24,500
Number of Grants: 5
Average Grant: $4,900
Highest Grant: $6,000
Lowest Grant: $3,500
Typical Range: $3,500 to $5,000

Recent Grants

Note: Grants derived from 2001 Form 990.

General

6,000	American Heart Association, Lubbock, TX -- implement CPR training in schools
5,000	Share A Warm Hug, Plainview, TX -- purchase winter coats for elementary school children
5,000	Soroptimist, Plainview, TX -- purchase shoes for needy school children
5,000	Southwest Diabetic Foundation, Gainesville, TX -- build activity center
3,500	Ronald McDonald House, Lubbock, TX -- furnish and decorate television room

MANUEL D. AND RHODA MAYERSON FOUNDATION

Giving Contact

Dr. Neal H. Mayerson, President
Manuel D. and Rhoda Mayerson Foundation
312 Walnut Street, Suite 3600
Cincinnati, OH 45202
Phone: (513)621-7500
E-mail: contact@mayersonfoundation.org
Web: http://www.mayersonfoundation.org/

Description

Founded: 1986
EIN: 311310431
Organization Type: Private Foundation
Giving Locations: OH: Cincinnati
Grant Types: Capital, Emergency, General Support, Project, Seed Money.

Donor Information

Founder: Manuel D. Mayerson, Rhoda Mayerson

Financial Summary

Total Giving: $2,423,028 (fiscal year ending October 31, 2001); $1,617,073 (fiscal 2000); $758,919 (fiscal 1999)
Giving Analysis: Giving for fiscal 2001 includes: foundation grants to United Way ($31,000); fiscal 2000: foundation grants to United Way ($11,814) fiscal 1999: foundation grants to United Way ($11,000)
Assets: $20,919,827 (fiscal 2001); $20,444,466 (fiscal 2000); $17,500,947 (fiscal 1999)
Gifts Received: $7,528,774 (fiscal 2001); $1,399,168 (fiscal 2000); $716,696 (fiscal 1999).
Note: In fiscal 2001, contributions were received from the Manuel D. Mayerson Charitable Lead Trust

($200,000), Rhoda & Manuel Mayerson Charitable Lead Trust ($303,714), and Manuel and Rhoda Mayerson ($7,025,060). In 2000, contributions were received from Manuel D. Mayerson ($213,886) and Rhoda & Manuel Mayerson ($1,185,282). In 1999, contributions were received from Manuel D. Mayerson ($568,896) and Rhoda Mayerson ($147,800). In fiscal 1998, contributions were received from the Manuel D. Mayerson Charitable Lead Trust ($200,000) and Rhoda Mayerson ($597,832).

Typical Recipients

Arts & Humanities: Arts Associations & Councils, Arts Centers, Arts Funds, Ballet, History & Archaeology, Museums/Galleries, Music, Performing Arts, Public Broadcasting, Theater, Visual Arts
Civic & Public Affairs: Civil Rights, Community Foundations, Employment/Job Training, Civic & Public Affairs-General, Legal Aid, Professional & Trade Associations, Public Policy, Urban & Community Affairs
Education: Arts/Humanities Education, Colleges & Universities, Education-General, Private Education (Precollege), Public Education (Precollege), Religious Education, Science/Mathematics Education, Secondary Education (Public), Student Aid
Environment: Environment-General
Health: Children's Health/Hospitals, Clinics/Medical Centers, Hospices, Hospitals, Medical Research, Multiple Sclerosis, Preventive Medicine/Wellness Organizations, Speech & Hearing
International: International Relations, Missionary/Religious Activities
Religion: Jewish Causes, Religious Organizations, Social/Policy Issues, Synagogues/Temples
Social Services: At-Risk Youth, Camps, Child Welfare, Community Service Organizations, Counseling, Domestic Violence, Family Planning, Family Services, Food/Clothing Distribution, People with Disabilities, Recreation & Athletics, Refugee Assistance, Senior Services, Shelters/Homelessness, Social Services-General, United Funds/United Ways, Youth Organizations

Application Procedures

Initial Contact: The foundation requests applications be made in writing.
Application Requirements: Include a description of organization, amount requested, purpose of funds sought, recently audited financial statement, and proof of tax-exempt status.
Deadlines: None.
Evaluative Criteria: Responsive to strategic planning, grantee stability and leadership ability, creativity, entrepreneurial visioning, leveraging of resources, and collaboration and empowerment of people.

Restrictions

Preference to improving the lives of children and people with disabilities, important community institutions and efforts aimed at preserving cultural heritage.

Additional Information

Publications: Application Guidelines

Foundation Officials

Arlene B. Mayerson: vice president
Donna Mayerson: secretary
Fred Mayerson: trust
Manuel D. Mayerson: trustee
Neal H. Mayerson: president, treasurer
Rhoda Mayerson: trustee

Grants Analysis

Disclosure Period: fiscal year ending October 31, 2001
Total Grants: $2,392,028*
Number of Grants: 179
Average Grant: $7,647*
Highest Grant: $432,667
Lowest Grant: $26

Typical Range: $1,000 to $10,000
*Note: Giving excludes United Way. Average grant figure excludes four highest grants ($1,053,773).

Recent Grants

Note: Grants derived from 2000 Form 990.

General

250,000	Children's Hospital Medical Center, Cincinnati, OH -- for Mayerson Center for Safe and Healthy Children
182,333	Values in Action Institute, Cincinnati, OH -- to support strand 1 of the Telos Project
170,000	Hebrew Union College - Jewish Institute of Religion, Cincinnati, OH -- gift
82,000	Jewish Federation of Cincinnati, Cincinnati, OH
53,334	Cinergy Children's Museum, Cincinnati, OH -- to access Museum Center Project
51,689	Ackermann Institute, The, New York, NY -- for Howard Weiss Consultant
50,000	Northern Kentucky University, Highland Heights, KY -- for the Mayerson Student Philosophy Program
42,500	Values in Action Institute, Cincinnati, OH -- for Dr. Martin E.P. Seligman
38,750	Cincinnati Art Museum, Cincinnati, OH -- for capital campaign
36,000	Mayerson Academy, Cincinnati, OH -- for Echostar

OLIVER DEWEY MAYOR FOUNDATION

Giving Contact

Philip S.L. McKinzie, Governor
c/o Bank of Texas Trust Co. NA
PO Box 1088
Sherman, TX 75091-1088
Phone: (903)813-5105

Description

Founded: 1983
EIN: 751864630
Organization Type: Private Foundation
Giving Locations: OK: Mayes County; TX: Grayson County
Grant Types: General Support.

Donor Information

Founder: the late Oliver Dewey Mayor

Financial Summary

Total Giving: $854,380 (fiscal year ending June 30, 2001); $474,102 (fiscal 2000); $591,533 (fiscal 1998)
Giving Analysis: Giving for fiscal 2000 includes: foundation grants to United Way ($3,200) fiscal 1998: foundation grants to United Way ($1,200)
Assets: $18,793,637 (fiscal 2001); $15,878,310 (fiscal 2000); $14,133,966 (fiscal 1998)

Typical Recipients

Arts & Humanities: Community Arts, Historic Preservation, History & Archaeology, Libraries, Museums/Galleries, Music, Performing Arts, Theater
Civic & Public Affairs: Chambers of Commerce, Clubs, Community Foundations, Economic Development, Civic & Public Affairs-General, Legal Aid, Municipalities/Towns, Native American Affairs, Parades/Festivals, Rural Affairs, Safety, Urban & Community Affairs
Education: Arts/Humanities Education, Colleges & Universities, Community & Junior Colleges, Continuing Education, Education Reform, Leadership Training, Literacy, Medical Education, Public Education (Precollege), Science/Mathematics Education, Secondary Education (Public), Student Aid

Health: Cancer, Children's Health/Hospitals, Clinics/ Medical Centers, Emergency/Ambulance Services, Hospices, Hospitals, Medical Rehabilitation, Nursing Services, Nutrition, Prenatal Health Issues, Public Health, Speech & Hearing, Transplant Networks/Donor Banks

Religion: Religious Welfare

Social Services: At-Risk Youth, Community Centers, Community Service Organizations, Crime Prevention, Family Services, Recreation & Athletics, Scouts, Senior Services, Shelters/Homelessness, United Funds/ United Ways, Youth Organizations

Application Procedures

Initial Contact: The foundation requests applications be made in writing.

Application Requirements: Include purpose of funds sought.

Deadlines: None.

Restrictions

Does not support individuals.

Additional Information

Publications: Application Guidelines

Foundation Officials

Monty M. Curry: gov
Samuel W. Graber: gov
M. Steve Jones: gov
Dana Lamb: gov
Tony J. Lyons: gov
Darius Maggi: gov
Philip S. L. McKinzie: gov

Grants Analysis

Disclosure Period: fiscal year ending June 30, 2001
Total Grants: $854,380
Number of Grants: 36
Average Grant: $23,733
Highest Grant: $50,000
Typical Range: $10,000 to $50,000

Recent Grants

Note: Grants derived from fiscal 2000 Form 990.

General

303,222	Grayson County, Denison, TX -- grants
170,880	Mayes County, OK -- grants

MAYS FOUNDATION

Giving Contact

Troy M. Mays, Director
914 S. Tyler St.
Amarillo, TX 79101
Phone: (806)376-5417

Description

Founded: 1965
EIN: 751213346
Organization Type: Private Foundation
Giving Locations: AR; TX
Grant Types: General Support.

Donor Information

Founder: W. A. Mays

Financial Summary

Total Giving: $338,924 (fiscal year ending July 31, 2002); $461,286 (fiscal 2001); $277,754 (fiscal 2000)
Giving Analysis: Giving for fiscal 2002 includes: foundation grants to United Way ($1,000); fiscal 2001: foundation grants to United Way ($1,350); fiscal 2000: foundation grants to United Way ($1,000)
Assets: $7,360,347 (fiscal 2002); $7,317,137 (fiscal 2001); $7,320,268 (fiscal 2000)
Gifts Received: $79,895 (fiscal 2002); $3,844 (fiscal 2001); $49,271 (fiscal 1997). Note: In fiscal 2002,

contributions were received from the Mays Trusts. In fiscal 1997, contributions were received from the W. A. and Agnes Mays Trust No. 2. In fiscal 1996, contributions were received from Mays Trusts ($1,298) and the W. A. and Agnes Mays Trust No. 2 ($79,861).

Typical Recipients

Arts & Humanities: Ballet, History & Archaeology, Libraries, Music, Public Broadcasting

Civic & Public Affairs: Botanical Gardens/Parks, Business/Free Enterprise, Community Foundations, Civic & Public Affairs-General, Urban & Community Affairs

Education: Colleges & Universities, Community & Junior Colleges, Elementary Education (Public), Engineering/Technological Education, Education-General, Private Education (Precollege), Public Education (Precollege), Religious Education, Secondary Education (Public), Student Aid

Health: Alzheimers Disease, Cancer, Clinics/Medical Centers, Health Organizations, Hospitals, Prenatal Health Issues, Public Health, Single-Disease Health Associations

International: Missionary/Religious Activities

Religion: Bible Study/Translation, Churches, Ministries, Religious Welfare, Social/Policy Issues

Science: Science Museums

Social Services: Child Welfare, Community Centers, Community Service Organizations, Day Care, Food/ Clothing Distribution, Recreation & Athletics, Scouts, Senior Services, United Funds/United Ways, YMCA/ YWCA/YMHA/YWHA, Youth Organizations

Application Procedures

Initial Contact: The foundation requests applications be made in writing. Send a full proposal.

Deadlines: None.

Restrictions

Does not support individuals, religious organizations for sectarian purposes, political or lobbying groups, or organizations outside operating areas.

Foundation Officials

Karra Mays Hill: director
Armon Mays: director
Troy M. Mays: director

Grants Analysis

Disclosure Period: fiscal year ending July 31, 2002
Total Grants: $337,924*
Number of Grants: 80
Average Grant: $1,963*
Highest Grant: $103,000
Lowest Grant: $125
Typical Range: $500 to $5,000
*Note: Giving excludes United Way. Average grant figure excludes two highest grants ($184,783).

Recent Grants

Note: Grants derived from 2000 Form 990.

Library-Related

3,600	Newton County Library, Jasper, AK
3,600	Searcy County Library, Marshall, AK
3,333	Canyon Library, Canyon, TX

General

83,785	Wayland Baptist University, Plainview, TX
76,700	Baylor University, Waco, TX
26,000	Hawaii Baptist Academy, Honolulu, HI
7,000	Trinity Fellowship Church, Amarillo, TX
5,000	KACV TV, Amarillo, TX
4,333	High Plains Food Bank, Amarillo, TX
4,000	Newton County Special Services Corporation, Jasper, AK
3,333	Panhandle-Plains Historical Museum, Canyon, TX
2,650	Boys Scouts of America - Golden Spread Council, Amarillo, TX
2,500	Amarillo College, Amarillo, TX

FRED MAYTAG FAMILY FOUNDATION

Giving Contact

Ellen Bergeron, Foundation Administrator
PO Box 366
Newton, IA 50208
Phone: (641)791-1133
Fax: (415)241-2973

Description

Founded: 1945
EIN: 426055654
Organization Type: General Purpose Foundation
Giving Locations: IA: Des Moines, Newton
Grant Types: Capital, Conference/Seminar, Department, Emergency, Endowment, General Support, Matching, Operating Expenses, Professorship, Project, Research, Scholarship, Seed Money.

Donor Information

Founder: Established in 1945 by the late Fred Maytag II .

Financial Summary

Total Giving: $3,468,217 (2000); $2,520,589 (1998); $1,714,000 (1997 approx)
Giving Analysis: Giving for 2000 includes: foundation grants to United Way ($9,660); 1998: foundation grants to United Way ($7,755) foundation scholarships ($12,000)
Assets: $67,852,161 (2000); $58,000,000 (1998 approx); $55,380,738 (1997)
Gifts Received: $1,447,863 (1998). Note: In 1998, contributions were received from the Ellen Pray Maytag Madsen Trust.

Typical Recipients

Arts & Humanities: Arts Centers, Ballet, Dance, Film & Video, Arts & Humanities-General, Historic Preservation, History & Archaeology, Libraries, Museums/Galleries, Music, Opera, Performing Arts, Public Broadcasting, Theater

Civic & Public Affairs: Botanical Gardens/Parks, Civil Rights, Clubs, Employment/Job Training, Civic & Public Affairs-General, Law & Justice, Municipalities/ Towns, Nonprofit Management, Public Policy, Zoos/ Aquariums

Education: Agricultural Education, Arts/Humanities Education, Colleges & Universities, Community & Junior Colleges, Education Associations, Education Reform, Education-General, Medical Education, Minority Education, Private Education (Precollege), Private Education (Precollege), Public Education (Precollege), Science/Mathematics Education, Student Aid

Environment: Forestry, Environment-General, Resource Conservation

Health: Cancer, Children's Health/Hospitals, Clinics/ Medical Centers, Emergency/Ambulance Services, Health Organizations, Heart, Hospices, Hospitals, Medical Rehabilitation, Medical Research, Mental Health, Single-Disease Health Associations

International: Health Care/Hospitals, International Peace & Security Issues, International Relations

Religion: Churches, Religion-General, Religious Organizations, Religious Welfare

Science: Science-General

Social Services: Big Brother/Big Sister, Child Abuse, Child Welfare, Community Centers, Community Service Organizations, Family Planning, Family Services, People with Disabilities, Recreation & Athletics, Scouts, Senior Services, Shelters/Homelessness, Social Services-General, Substance Abuse, United Funds/United Ways, Volunteer Services, YMCA/ YWCA/YMHA/YWHA, Youth Organizations

Application Procedures

Initial Contact: Applicants should call or submit a written request to the foundation for guidelines.

Application Requirements: The proposal should include a description of organization's mission; the project budget; financial information from the past two years; a copy of the organization's 501 (c)(3); and a list of the board of directors. Three copies of each should be submitted to the foundation.

Deadlines: Applications are accepted any time, preferably by April or May.

Additional Information

Publications: Application Guidelines

Foundation Officials

Frederick L. Maytag, III: trustee B 1937. PRIM CORP EMPL president, treasurer: Anchor Brewing Co.

Kenneth P. Maytag: trustee PRIM CORP EMPL vice president: Maytag Dairy Farms.

Grants Analysis

Disclosure Period: calendar year ending 2000
Total Grants: $3,458,557*
Number of Grants: 106
Average Grant: $22,919*
Highest Grant: $575,000
Lowest Grant: $100
Typical Range: $10,000 to $40,000
*Note: Giving excludes United Way. Average grant figure excludes two highest grants ($1,075,000).

Recent Grants

Note: Grants derived from 1999 Form 990.

General

1,500,000	City of Scottsdale -- toward purchase of McDowell Sonoran Preserve
139,352	St. Stephen's Episcopal Church, Phoenix, AZ -- grant toward restoration campaign
100,000	Camp Fire Boys & Girls, San Francisco, CA -- funding of new swimming pool
100,000	Easter Seals Society of Iowa, IA
100,000	Iowa College Foundation, Des Moines, IA
75,000	Nature Conservancy, Des Moines, IA
60,850	Central College, Pella, IA
55,600	Berea College, Berea, KY
50,305	California Exotic Pest Plant Council, Davis, CA
50,000	American Red Cross National Capital Chapter, Washington, DC

JACOB AND RUTH MAZER FOUNDATION

Giving Contact

David Mazer, Vice President & Treasurer
66 Mooreland Road
Greenwich, CT 06831
Phone: (203)661-9733

Description

Founded: 1961
EIN: 136115875
Organization Type: Private Foundation
Giving Locations: CT; NY: New York metro area
Grant Types: General Support.

Donor Information

Founder: Abraham Mazer Foundation

Financial Summary

Total Giving: $222,635 (2001); $235,430 (2000); $189,645 (1999)
Giving Analysis: Giving for 2001 includes: foundation grants to United Way ($7,500); 2000: foundation grants to United Way ($7,500); 1999: foundation grants to United Way ($5,500)
Assets: $1,499,741 (2001); $1,667,589 (2000); $1,871,176 (1999)

Typical Recipients

Arts & Humanities: Arts Centers, History & Archaeology, Libraries, Museums/Galleries, Music, Opera, Public Broadcasting

Civic & Public Affairs: Business/Free Enterprise, Civil Rights, Economic Development, Civic & Public Affairs-General, Philanthropic Organizations, Public Policy, Urban & Community Affairs

Education: Colleges & Universities, Education-General, Medical Education, Minority Education, Private Education (Precollege), Religious Education

Health: Cancer, Clinics/Medical Centers, Geriatric Health, Health Organizations, Hospitals, Medical Research, Research/Studies Institutes, Single-Disease Health Associations

International: Foreign Arts Organizations, International Peace & Security Issues, Missionary/Religious Activities

Religion: Jewish Causes, Religious Organizations, Synagogues/Temples

Social Services: Animal Protection, Community Service Organizations, Counseling, Family Planning, United Funds/United Ways, YMCA/YWCA/YMHA/YWHA, Youth Organizations

Application Procedures

Initial Contact: The foundation requests applications be made in writing.
Deadlines: None.

Restrictions

Does not give grants to individuals, religious organizations for sectarian purposes, or political or lobbying groups.

Foundation Officials

David Mazer: vice president, treasurer
Richard Mazer: vice president, secretary

Grants Analysis

Disclosure Period: calendar year ending 2001
Total Grants: $215,135*
Number of Grants: 72
Average Grant: $2,523*
Highest Grant: $36,000
Lowest Grant: $160
Typical Range: $500 to $5,000
*Note: Giving excludes United Way. Average grant figure excludes highest grant.

Recent Grants

Note: Grants derived from 2001 Form 990.

General

36,000	United Jewish Appeal of Greenwich, Greenwich, CT
25,000	United Jewish Appeal of Greenwich, Greenwich, CT
25,000	United Jewish Appeal of Greenwich, Greenwich, CT
10,000	Academy for Jewish Religion, New York, NY
10,000	Yale University, New Haven, CT
7,500	Connecticut Civil Liberties Union Foundation, Hartford, CT
7,500	Connecticut Civil Liberties Union Foundation, Hartford, CT
7,500	United Way of Greenwich, Greenwich, CT
7,000	Chamah, New York, NY
6,000	Beth Israel Deaconess Medical Center, Boston, MA

MBIA, INC.

Company Headquarters

Armonk, NY
Web: http://www.mbia.com

Company Description

Founded: 1974
Ticker: MBI
Exchange: NYSE
Assets: US$18.852 billion (2002)
Employees: 694 (2002)
SIC(s): 6399 Insurance Carriers Nec.

Nonmonetary Support

Type: Donated Equipment; In-kind Services
Note: The company also offers the use of its auditorium.

Giving Contact

Susan Voltz, Director
113 King Street
Armonk, NY 10504
Phone: (914)273-4545
Fax: (914)765-3375
E-mail: sue.voltz@mbia.com

Description

Organization Type: Corporate Giving Program
Giving Locations: generally in tri-state area where employees live.
Grant Types: Emergency, Employee Matching Gifts, Endowment.
Note: Employee matching gift ratio: 2 to 1 up to $1,000; 1 to 1 from $1,001 to $1,500. Employee matching gifts are for higher education only.

Financial Summary

Total Giving: $800,000 (2001); $800,000 (2000); $800,000 (1999 approx). Note: Contributes through corporate direct giving program only.

Typical Recipients

Arts & Humanities: Arts Associations & Councils, Arts & Humanities-General, Historic Preservation, Libraries, Museums/Galleries, Performing Arts

Civic & Public Affairs: Employment/Job Training, Civic & Public Affairs-General, Housing, Municipalities/Towns, Women's Affairs

Education: Business Education, Colleges & Universities, Elementary Education (Private), Education-General, Legal Education

Health: Health-General, Geriatric Health, Health Organizations, Medical Research, Single-Disease Health Associations

Social Services: Community Centers, Community Service Organizations, Counseling, Day Care, Family Planning, Family Services, Food/Clothing Distribution, Homes, People with Disabilities, Recreation & Athletics, Senior Services, Shelters/Homelessness, Social Services-General, Substance Abuse, Volunteer Services, Youth Organizations

Application Procedures

Initial Contact: Call or write for application, then full proposal

Application Requirements: a description of organization, program description, budget information, needs assessment, amount requested, purpose of funds sought, audited financial statements and Form 990's for past three years, and proof of tax-exempt status

Deadlines: None.

Review Process: requests reviewed by the Charitable Contributions Committee

Evaluative Criteria: employee volunteer involvement; impact on the trio-state area; focus on the cause of a problem; organization serves society's neediest; project improves quality of life; highest priority to organizations that will benefit most from contribution

Restrictions

The company does not support individuals, religious organizations for sectarian purposes, umbrella agencies, for general operating support, or for sponsorships or table purchases (unless there is a clear business reason).

Additional Information

Publications: Guidelines; Application Form

Corporate Officials

Joseph Warner Brown, Jr.: chairman, chief executive officer B Evanston, IL 1949. ED Northern Illinois University (1974). PRIM CORP EMPL chairman, chief executive officer: MBIA Inc. ADD CORP EMPL chairman: Industries Indemnity Holdings Inc.; chairman: Apprise Corp.; chairman: Constitution Re corp.; chairman: Coregis Group Inc.; chairman: Crum & Forster Holdings Inc.; chairman: Enuision Claims Management Corp.; chairman: Resolution Group Inc.; chairman, president, chief executive officer: Viking Insurance Holdings Inc.; chairman: Westchester SPLty Group Inc. CORP AFFIL director: First Quadrant Corp. NONPR AFFIL trustee: Ins Institute America; member: Society Chartered Property & Casualty Underwriters; trustee: American Institute Chartered Property & Casualty Underwriters; member: American Academy of Actuaries.

Gary C. Dunton: president, chief operating officer B 1955. ED Northeastern University BA (1978); Harvard University MBA (1980). PRIM CORP EMPL vice president, chief financial officer: MBIA Inc. CORP AFFIL director: MBIA Inc.; president: USF&G Corp.

Grants Analysis

Typical Range: $2,500 to $7,500

MBNA CORP.

Company Headquarters

1100 N. King St.
Wilmington, DE 19884-0341
Web: http://www.mbnainternational.com

Company Description

Founded: 1990
Ticker: KRB
Exchange: NYSE
Assets: US$52.856 billion (2002)
Employees: 28000 (2002)
SIC(s): 6712 Bank Holding Companies.

Nonmonetary Support

Type: In-kind Services; Loaned Executives
Volunteer Programs: The Community Partnership Program matches MBNA businesses with charitable organizations and schools for volunteer opportunities. The company provides financial contributions to nonprofit organizations for which MBNA employees have volunteered more than 40 hours of their personal time during a calendar year. MBNA also sponsors the Francis X. Norton Community Service award to recognize outstanding volunteerism among MBNA employees.

The MBNA Foundation

Giving Contact

W. Craig Schroeder, Executive Director
MBNA Foundation
1100 N. King St.
Wilmington, DE 19884
Phone: 800-441-7048
Web: http://www.mbnafoundation.org
Note: Dial ext. 25205 for information on the Community Grants Program and volunteer programs; dial ext.

25288 for information on Helen F. Graham Grants program.

Description

Founded: 2000
EIN: 522191136
Organization Type: Corporate Foundation
Giving Locations: DE; ME; OH: Cleveland
Grant Types: General Support, Scholarship.

Financial Summary

Total Giving: $46,740,190 (2001); $23,610,936 (2000)
Giving Analysis: Giving for 2001 includes: foundation grants to United Way ($172,250); foundation scholarships ($5,301,280) foundation ($41,266,660)
Assets: $69,529,857 (2001); $55,303,935 (2000)
Gifts Received: $63,978,715 (2001); $43,792,056 (2000). Note: Substantial contributions are received from MBNA America Bank, NA; The Cawley Family Foundation.

Typical Recipients

Arts & Humanities: Libraries, Music, Opera
Civic & Public Affairs: Employment/Job Training, Civic & Public Affairs-General, Municipalities/Towns
Education: Colleges & Universities, Education-General, Private Education (Precollege)
Environment: Environment-General
Health: Children's Health/Hospitals, Health Organizations, Hospitals, Long-Term Care
Religion: Dioceses, Ministries
Social Services: Community Service Organizations, Counseling, YMCA/YWCA/YMHA/YWHA, Youth Organizations

Application Procedures

Initial Contact: To apply to the Community Grants Program, call (302) 432-5205 or (800) 441-7048, ext. 25205. To apply to the Helen F. Graham Grants Program, download a grant application from the foundation's web site. To apply for either a grant through the Excellence in Education program or a college scholarship from the Scholars Program, download the appropriate application form for your geographic area from the foundation's web site.
Deadlines: None for the Helen F. Graham Grants program and the Excellence in Education program. Scholarship deadlines vary by region.

Restrictions

The Community Grants Program does not support organizations located outside of MBNA operating communities; travel for individuals or groups; sports-related sponsorships; sectarian activities of religious groups; or political causes or candidates. The Helen F. Graham Grants Program does not support salaries for additional staff, benefits, or tuition reimbursement for required courses or professional accreditation; capital projects, major repairs to buildings or equipment, and routine operating expenses; housing costs, tuition assistance, or other financial aid for individuals; private-employer work programs; or research projects. Excellence in Education Grants are not made to fund salaries for additional permanent staff, benefits, or tuition reimbursements for required courses or professional accreditation programs; capital projects and repairs to school buildings or equipment; large purchases of personal computers, networks, or upgrades in hardware and operating software (smaller purchases will be considered if they are an integral part of a well-developed program); routine school operating expenses and maintenance; or new or replacement textbooks, uniforms, band instruments, sports equipment, and other school supplies generally provided by school budgets.

Corporate Officials

Charles M. Cawley: chief executive officer, president, director
John R. Cochran, III: president & chief operating officer MBNA America Bank
Randolph D. Lerner, Esq.: chairman, director
Lance L. Weaver: executive vice chairman, chief administrative officer
Vernon H.C. Wright: executive vice chairman, chief financial officer

Foundation Officials

Nancy Beck: trustee
Kenneth F. Boehl: treasurer, trustee
Claire Z. Carey, PhD: trustee
C. Michael Cawley: trustee
Charles M. Cawley: chief executive officer, trustee (see above)
John R. Cochran, III: trustee (see above)
Phillip W. Conkling: trustee
William B. DeLauder: trustee
Lanny Edelson, MD: trustee
Michael C. Ford: trustee
David Ley Hamilton, Esq.: trustee
Vaughn C. Hardin: trustee
Frederick E. Hutchinson, PhD: trustee
David B. Kedash: chief financial officer
Rev. Edwin D. Leahy, OSB: trustee
Elizabeth A. Moran: trustee
Frank H. Murphy: trustee
Tern C. Murphy: trustee
David P. Roselle, PhD: trustee
John W. Scheflen: secretary
W. Craig Schroeder: executive director, trustee
David W. Spartin: trustee
Penelope J. Taylor: trustee
Lance L. Weaver: president, trustee (see above)

Grants Analysis

Disclosure Period: calendar year ending 2001
Total Grants: $41,266,660*
Number of Grants: 2,730
Average Grant: $12,254*
Highest Grant: $1,000,000
Lowest Grant: $25
Typical Range: $5,000 to $25,000
*Note: Giving excludes scholarships and United Way. Average grant figure excludes seven highest grants ($7,900,000).

Recent Grants

Note: Grants derived from 2001 Form 990.

Library-Related
600,000   George Bush Presidential Library Foundation, College Station, NY

General
1,500,000   Penobscot Bay YMCA, Camden, ME
1,400,000   Christiana Care Health System, Newark, DE
1,000,000   Loyola College in Maryland, Baltimore, MD
1,000,000   Maine Medical Center, Portland, ME
1,000,000   St. Benedict's Prep, Newark, NJ
1,000,000   St. Benedict's Preparatory School, Newark, NJ
1,000,000   University of Delaware, Newark, DE
600,000   Save Our Schools, Searsport, ME
550,000   Christiana Care Health System, Newark, DE
500,000   America's Promise, Alexandria, VA

HAROLD MCALISTER CHARITABLE FOUNDATION

Giving Contact

4801 Wilshire Boulevard, Suite 232
Los Angeles, CA 90010

Phone: (323)937-0927
Fax: (323)937-4727

Description

Founded: 1959
EIN: 956050036
Organization Type: Family Foundation
Giving Locations: CA: Los Angeles
Grant Types: General Support.

Donor Information

Founder: The foundation was incorporated in 1959 by Fern Smith McAlister and the late Harold McAlister.

Financial Summary

Total Giving: $1,647,018 (fiscal year ending May 31, 2002); $1,745,000 (fiscal 2001); $1,670,000 (fiscal 2000 approx)
Assets: $30,843,346 (fiscal 2002); $34,538,157 (fiscal 2001); $36,520,000 (fiscal 2000 approx)
Gifts Received: $50,000 (fiscal 1992)

Typical Recipients

Arts & Humanities: Arts Associations & Councils, Arts Outreach, Arts & Humanities-General, Libraries, Museums/Galleries, Music
Civic & Public Affairs: Civic & Public Affairs-General, Nonprofit Management, Public Policy, Urban & Community Affairs
Education: Colleges & Universities, Education Funds, Education-General, Private Education (Precollege), Science/Mathematics Education, Special Education, Student Aid
Environment: Environment-General, Wildlife Protection
Health: Arthritis, Cancer, Children's Health/Hospitals, Clinics/Medical Centers, Emergency/Ambulance Services, Geriatric Health, Health Organizations, Heart, Hospitals, Kidney, Long-Term Care, Medical Research, Nutrition, Public Health, Research/Studies Institutes, Research/Studies Institutes, Respiratory, Single-Disease Health Associations, Speech & Hearing
International: Health Care/Hospitals, International Relief Efforts
Religion: Churches, Religious Organizations, Religious Welfare
Social Services: Animal Protection, Camps, Child Welfare, Community Centers, Community Service Organizations, Counseling, Day Care, Family Services, Food/Clothing Distribution, Homes, People with Disabilities, Recreation & Athletics, Sexual Abuse, Substance Abuse, YMCA/YWCA/YMHA/YWHA, Youth Organizations

Application Procedures

Initial Contact: The foundation does not require a formal application form. Applicants should request funding by writing a letter to the board of trustees.
Application Requirements: The letter should detail the amount requested and for what purpose the money will be used. Any other information will be considered, but is not necessary.
Deadlines: None.
Review Process: Priority is given to organizations located in the Los Angeles area.

Restrictions

Grants are not made to individuals.

Foundation Officials

David B. Heyler, Jr.: trustee
Fern Smith McAlister: vice president, trustee
James P. McAlister: president

Grants Analysis

Disclosure Period: fiscal year ending May 31, 2002
Total Grants: $1,647,018
Number of Grants: 46
Average Grant: $24,934*
Highest Grant: $525,000
Lowest Grant: $18
Typical Range: $10,000 to $50,000
***Note:** Average grant figure excludes highest grant.

Recent Grants

Note: Grants derived from 2001 Form 990.

Library-Related

15,000	Carmel Public Library, Carmel, CA

General

585,000	St. John's Hospital and Health Center, Los Angeles, CA
150,000	Los Angeles Heart Institute, Los Angeles, CA
130,000	Stanford University, Stanford, CA
130,000	University of California Los Angeles Foundation, Los Angeles, CA
125,000	University of Southern California, Los Angeles, CA
110,000	Assistance League of Southern California, Hollywood, CA
100,000	Children's Hospital of Los Angeles, Los Angeles, CA
60,000	House Ear Institute, Los Angeles, CA
60,000	John Wayne Cancer Institute, Santa Monica, CA
35,000	Menlo College, Atherton, CA

ALLETTA MORRIS McBEAN CHARITABLE TRUST

Giving Contact

Charlene Kleiner, Assistant Secretary
400 S. El Camino Real, Suite 777
San Mateo, CA 94402
Phone: (650)558-8480
Fax: (650)558-8481
E-mail: mcbeancharitabletrust@att.net

Description

Founded: 1986
EIN: 943019660
Organization Type: General Purpose Foundation
Giving Locations: RI: Aquidneck Island, Newport
Grant Types: Capital, Challenge, Endowment, General Support, Multiyear/Continuing Support, Operating Expenses, Project.

Donor Information

Founder: Established in 1986 by the late Alletta Morris McBean.

Financial Summary

Total Giving: $2,593,500 (2001); $6,404,157 (2000); $3,355,500 (1999)
Assets: $55,196,085 (2001); $63,960,156 (2000); $82,709,322 (1999)

Typical Recipients

Arts & Humanities: Arts Associations & Councils, Arts Centers, Historic Preservation, History & Archaeology, Libraries, Museums/Galleries
Civic & Public Affairs: Economic Development, Civic & Public Affairs-General, Professional & Trade Associations, Urban & Community Affairs, Zoos/Aquariums

Education: Arts/Humanities Education, Colleges & Universities, Environmental Education, Private Education (Precollege), Public Education (Precollege)
Environment: Air/Water Quality, Environment-General, Resource Conservation
Health: Emergency/Ambulance Services, Health-General, Home-Care Services, Hospices, Hospitals, Mental Health, Nursing Services
Religion: Churches, Religious Organizations, Religious Welfare
Social Services: Animal Protection, Community Service Organizations, Family Services, Recreation & Athletics, Senior Services, Senior Services, Youth Organizations

Application Procedures

Initial Contact: The trust requests that applications be made in writing.
Application Requirements: Written proposals should thoroughly explain the program and the project for which the organization is seeking funding. Proposals should include budget information, along with other sources of funding, list of board of directors, and proof of 501 (c)(s) status. The board meets in May and October.
Deadlines: February 28 and July 31.

Restrictions

The trust does not make grants to individuals.

Additional Information

Publications: Application Guidelines

Foundation Officials

Donald Christ: secretary, trustee
Noreen Drexel: president, trustee
Hariett Reed: trustee
John A. van Beuren: trustee

Grants Analysis

Disclosure Period: calendar year ending 2000
Total Grants: $6,404,157
Number of Grants: 32
Average Grant: $120,139*
Highest Grant: $1,800,000
Lowest Grant: $2,500
Typical Range: $10,000 to $70,000 and $25,000 to $500,000
***Note:** Average grant figure excludes two highest grants ($2,800,000).

Recent Grants

Note: Grants derived from 2000 Form 990.

Library-Related

400,000	Redwood Library Athenaeum, Newport, RI -- restoration and renovation of the library
200,000	Newport Public Library, Newport, RI -- renovation and construction project

General

1,800,000	Newport Hospital Foundation, Newport, RI
1,000,000	Newport Public Schools, Newport, RI -- Facade preservation and Interior Refurbishing of the Townsend Building
500,000	Preservation Society of Newport, Newport, RI -- for Breakers roof repairs
440,000	Aquidneck Island Land Trust, Middletown, RI -- land preservation
250,000	Newport Art Museum, Newport, RI -- creative studies center
250,000	Salve Regina University, Newport, RI
200,000	Aquidneck Island Land Trust, Middletown, RI -- land preservation
200,000	Seaman's Church Institute of Newport, Newport, RI
200,000	Society of Friends Touro Synagogue, Newport, RI
166,362	Boys Clubs and Girls Clubs, Newport, RI -- for capital improvement plan

MCBEAN FAMILY FOUNDATION

Giving Contact
Charlene Kleiner, Secretary
400 S. El Camino Real, Suite 777
San Mateo, CA 94402
Phone: (650)558-8480
Fax: (605)558-8481
E-mail: mcbeanfamilyfoundation@att.net

Description
Founded: 1955
EIN: 946062239
Organization Type: Private Foundation
Giving Locations: CA: San Francisco Bay area
Grant Types: Capital, Endowment, General Support, Multiyear/Continuing Support.

Donor Information
Founder: Established in 1955 by the late Atholl McBean .

Financial Summary
Total Giving: $1,200,000 (2004 approx); $1,000,000 (2003 approx); $1,557,390 (2001)
Assets: $16,000,000 (2004 approx); $15,000,000 (2003 approx); $19,110,064 (2001)

Typical Recipients
Arts & Humanities: Arts Centers, Arts Institutes, Community Arts, Arts & Humanities-General, Historic Preservation, History & Archaeology, Libraries, Museums/Galleries, Music, Opera, Performing Arts
Civic & Public Affairs: Botanical Gardens/Parks, Business/Free Enterprise, Community Foundations, Civic & Public Affairs-General, Nonprofit Management, Philanthropic Organizations, Public Policy, Urban & Community Affairs, Zoos/Aquariums
Education: Colleges & Universities, Education Associations, Faculty Development, Education-General, Medical Education, Minority Education, Private Education (Precollege), Public Education (Precollege), Religious Education, Science/Mathematics Education, Special Education, Student Aid
Environment: Resource Conservation, Wildlife Protection, Wildlife Protection
Health: AIDS/HIV, Alzheimers Disease, Cancer, Clinics/Medical Centers, Eyes/Blindness, Health Organizations, Hospices, Hospitals, Long-Term Care, Medical Research, Prenatal Health Issues, Speech & Hearing
International: International Relations, Missionary/Religious Activities
Religion: Churches, Religion-General, Ministries, Religious Welfare
Science: Science Museums, Scientific Centers & Institutes, Scientific Organizations
Social Services: At-Risk Youth, Big Brother/Big Sister, Child Abuse, Child Welfare, Community Service Organizations, Family Services, Food/Clothing Distribution, People with Disabilities, Recreation & Athletics, Scouts, Sexual Abuse, Shelters/Homelessness, Social Services-General, United Funds/United Ways, Youth Organizations

Application Procedures
Initial Contact: The foundation decided in 1999 to no longer accept unsolicited proposals from organizations that have been previously received support from the foundation. Proposals are accepted, however, from previously supported organizations and from organizations which have been researched and endorsed by a board member prior to proposal submission.
Application Requirements: Proposals should include a description of organization, amount requested, purpose of funds sought, recently audited financial statement, proof of tax-exempt status, and list of Board of Directors.
Deadlines: September 1.

Restrictions
Does not support individuals or fund scholarships, fellowships, or loans.

Foundation Officials
Judith McBean Cosper: vice president, director
Peter Folger: director
Deidra Head: director
Sheila McBean Head: director
Natasha Hunt: director
Charlene Kleiner: secretary
Nancy H. McBean: director
Clark Nelson: treasurer
Edith McBean Newberry: president, director
Henry K. Newhall: director

Grants Analysis
Disclosure Period: calendar year ending 2001
Total Grants: $1,557,390
Number of Grants: 37
Average Grant: $42,092
Highest Grant: $200,000
Lowest Grant: $10,000
Typical Range: $10,000 to $50,000

Recent Grants
Note: Grants derived from 2001 Form 990.

Library-Related
10,000   National Sporting Library, Middleburg, VA -- acquisition fund endowment

General
200,000   Exploratorium, San Francisco, CA -- 30th Anniversary Capital Campaign Webcast Programming Endowment
177,000   Grace Cathedral, San Francisco, CA -- the last window- design, production, promotion, installation, video production
100,000   Corporation of the Fine Arts Museums of San Francisco, San Francisco, CA -- New de Young construction
100,000   Regents of the University of California, Davis, CA -- McBean Fellowship in Alzheimer's Disease Research
100,000   United Religions Initiative, San Francisco, CA
60,000   Asian Art Museum Foundation of San Francisco, San Francisco, CA -- New Astan capital campaign
58,730   San Francisco Zoological Society, San Francisco, CA -- zoo crew- Lake Merced Project
50,000   Autry Museum of Western Heritage, Los Angeles, CA -- Acquisition of California Ranching Life Materials
50,000   Friends of Recreation and Parks, San Francisco, CA -- development of Plant Collections and Interpretive Stations within the Restored Conservatory of Flowers
50,000   Friends of the Recreation and Parks Corporation, San Francisco, CA -- development of plant collection and interpretive stations within the restored conservatory of flowers

FAYE MCBEATH FOUNDATION

Giving Contact
Sarah M. Dean, Executive Director
1020 North Broadway
Milwaukee, WI 53202
Phone: (414)272-6262
Fax: (414)272-6235
E-mail: info@fayemcbeath.org
Web: http://www.fayemcbeath.org

Description
Founded: 1964
EIN: 396074450
Organization Type: General Purpose Foundation
Giving Locations: WI: particularly the Milwaukee metropolitan area
Grant Types: Capital, General Support, Operating Expenses, Project.

Donor Information
Founder: Faye McBeath was born in Milwaukee, WI, in 1882. She graduated from the University of Wisconsin in 1913, and taught in a local school for three years. In 1916, her uncle Lucius W. Nieman, founder of The Milwaukee Journal, invited her to join the Journal staff. She worked there for the next twenty years, and upon her uncle's death in 1935, inherited half of his estate. Throughout the last thirty years of her life, Miss McBeath became involved in a variety of local causes. In 1964, she created the Faye McBeath Foundation which received the bulk of her estate upon her death in 1967.

Financial Summary
Total Giving: $1,683,830 (2001); $2,024,700 (2000); $1,484,643 (1999)
Giving Analysis: Giving for 2000 includes: foundation grants to United Way ($12,500)
Assets: $15,001,253 (2001); $17,806,915 (2000); $18,858,272 (1999)
Gifts Received: $2,000 (2001); $2,000 (2000); $2,000 (1999)

Typical Recipients
Arts & Humanities: Arts Centers, Arts Festivals, Libraries, Museums/Galleries, Music
Civic & Public Affairs: Botanical Gardens/Parks, Business/Free Enterprise, Community Foundations, Economic Development, Employment/Job Training, Civic & Public Affairs-General, Hispanic Affairs, Housing, Inner-City Development, Law & Justice, Legal Aid, Minority Business, Native American Affairs, Nonprofit Management, Public Policy, Urban & Community Affairs, Women's Affairs
Education: Arts/Humanities Education, Colleges & Universities, Continuing Education, Education Funds, Education Reform, Elementary Education (Private), Faculty Development, Education-General, Health & Physical Education, Leadership Training, Literacy, Medical Education, Minority Education, Private Education (Precollege), Public Education (Precollege), Science/Mathematics Education, Secondary Education (Private), Social Sciences Education, Special Education
Environment: Environment-General
Health: AIDS/HIV, Alzheimers Disease, Children's Health/Hospitals, Clinics/Medical Centers, Eyes/Blindness, Geriatric Health, Health Policy/Cost Containment, Health Organizations, Hospices, Hospitals, Long-Term Care, Medical Rehabilitation, Mental Health, Nursing Services, Public Health, Single-Disease Health Associations, Speech & Hearing, Transplant Networks/Donor Banks
Religion: Dioceses, Jewish Causes, Ministries, Religious Welfare, Social/Policy Issues
Science: Scientific Centers & Institutes
Social Services: At-Risk Youth, Big Brother/Big Sister, Child Abuse, Child Welfare, Community Centers, Community Service Organizations, Counseling, Crime Prevention, Day Care, Delinquency & Criminal Rehabilitation, Domestic Violence, Family Planning, Family Services, Food/Clothing Distribution, People with Disabilities, Recreation & Athletics, Scouts, Senior Services, Shelters/Homelessness, Social Services-General, Substance Abuse, United Funds/United Ways, Volunteer Services, YMCA/YWCA/YMHA/YWHA, Youth Organizations

Application Procedures

Initial Contact: Applicants must complete a letter of intent application form, which can be obtained from the foundation offices.

Application Requirements: The preliminary application form should include basic information about the applying organization and its tax-exempt status; summary of the proposed project, its objectives, significance, and anticipated costs. If the proposed project falls within the scope of the foundation's activities, a formal proposal will be requested. At that time, a formal grant application and review schedule will be provided. When submitting a formal application, applicants must use the Milwaukee Area Common Grant Application. The formal proposal must include specific objectives and measures for assessing the project's success; detailed budget, including total costs and amount sought; a description of the agency qualifications and of key personnel; a statement that the request is made by the organization's governing body; and support statements from planning agencies underscoring the need for the project and the capability of the organization to complete it.

Deadlines: The board of trustees meet 5 times each year to consider proposals, with application deadlines in January (preliminary applications only), April, June, September, and November (formal applications only). Contact foundation for exact deadlines.

Review Process: Applicants are notified in writing within ten days of the trustee meeting. The following guidelines are used in considering grant proposals: the relevance of the proposal to the foundation's areas of interest; clearly-stated project or program outcomes and the strategy for achieving them; commitment to continue successful programs after the foundation's support ceases; the extent to which the proposal involves the people being served and other organizations in a collective approach to solve a problem or address an issue; the ability of the organization, its leadership, and staff to carry out the project; and the clarity and completeness of the grant application.

Notes: Proposals must be received by noon on the deadline date. General solicitation letters are not considered. Grants are paid out four times each year during the last week of each calendar quarter.

Restrictions

Grants are made to nonprofit, federally tax-exempt organizations created under the laws of Wisconsin. In any year, no more than 20 percent of grants will support construction or other capital programs. Grants are not made for annual fund drives, endowment funds, individuals, scholarships, specific scientific or medical research inquiries, emergency assistance, or operating expenses of established agencies. Grants will be made only within Wisconsin and principally to support projects having primary focus on the welfare of the residents of the greater Milwaukee community. Grants made to agencies located in other regions of the state will be limited to the support of projects which clearly have a state-wide focus. Capital grant awards will not be released until the construction or renovation project is about to get underway. Commitments will not be undertaken by the foundation for payment of grants beyond a period of three years from the time the grant was originally approved.

Additional Information

In 1997, the foundation modified its capital giving policy. Trustees will consider capital grant requests, but only for projects with significant community-wide impact. Few capital grants will be awarded each year. The Nonprofit Management Fund, established in 1993 in collaboration with the Milwaukee and Helen Bader Foundations, awards small grants to improve the management capabilities and provide technical assistance to Milwaukee County nonprofit organizations.

In 1991, the foundation began an awards program to "recognize excellence and leadership among nonprofit organizations" which have been recipients of foundation funds within the past five years. The purpose of this program is "to stimulate all nonprofits to strive for a greater degree of excellence in programming and management" and also to provide agencies with "unencumbered operating dollars." Admission to the awards program is by nomination. Final decision for the annual award, which will be in the range of $25,000 to $50,000, is made by the trustees.

Publications: Annual Report

Trust(s): US Bank NA

Foundation Officials

Sarah M. Dean: executive director

Joan J. Hardy: trustee PRIM CORP EMPL vice president: Hardy & Co. Inc.

Charles A. Krause: vice chairman, trustee PRIM CORP EMPL president: Krause Consultants Ltd.

William Lovis Randall: chairman, trustee B Milwaukee, WI 1930. ED Dartmouth College BA (1952); University of Michigan LLB (1956). PRIM CORP EMPL chairman emeritus: First Bank Milwaukee. NONPR AFFIL first chairman: United Performing Arts Fund Milwaukee; chairman: War Mem Development Committee; member: Study Arts Wisconsin Ad Hoc Committee; member: Museum for Youth; director: Private Industry Council; trustee: Milwaukee Boys Club; trustee: Medical College; member: Milwaukee Art Foundation; member: Governments Commission on University Systems Compensation; trustee: Community Milwaukee Foundation; member: Donors Forum; trustee: Alverno College.

Steve C. Smith: trustee B Hutchinson, MN 1949. ED University of Minnesota BA (1972); Oklahoma City University JD (1975). PRIM NONPR EMPL legislator: State of Minnesota.

Bonnie R. Weigell: trustee

Grants Analysis

Disclosure Period: calendar year ending 2001

Total Grants: $1,683,830

Number of Grants: 98

Average Grant: $15,297*

Highest Grant: $200,000

Lowest Grant: $500

Typical Range: $5,000 to $30,000

*Note: Average grant figure excludes highest grant.

Recent Grants

Note: Grants derived from 2001 Form 990.

Library-Related

25,000	Milwaukee Public Library Foundation, Milwaukee, WI -- technical assistance grant McBeath Community Partners

General

200,000	Greater Milwaukee Foundation, Milwaukee, WI -- Community Partners Endowment Project
75,000	St. John's Home of Milwaukee, Milwaukee, WI -- renovation/expansion of the health care center
70,000	Greater Milwaukee Foundation, Milwaukee, WI -- Nonprofit management fund
50,000	Marquette University, Milwaukee, WI -- Wisconsin nursing redesign
50,000	Marquette University, Milwaukee, WI -- capital support for Dental School Advanced Care Clinic
50,000	Milwaukee Art Museum, Milwaukee, WI -- children's tour
50,000	University of Wisconsin Milwaukee, Milwaukee, WI -- Core Operating Support for Helen Bader Institute
49,570	Older Adult Service, Milwaukee, WI -- strategic plan implementation
37,500	Medical College of Wisconsin, Milwaukee, WI -- expanding points of access through Metplex Health Center
35,000	YWCA of Greater Milwaukee, Milwaukee, WI -- girls and youth leadership project

McCann Foundation

Giving Contact

John J. Gartland, Jr., Trustee
35 Market Street
Poughkeepsie, NY 12601
Phone: (245)452-3085
Fax: (245)452-3093

Description

Founded: 1969

EIN: 146050628

Organization Type: General Purpose Foundation

Giving Locations: NY: Dutchess County, Poughkeepsie

Grant Types: Capital, Fellowship, Multiyear/Continuing Support.

Donor Information

Founder: The McCann Foundation was established in New York in 1969 following the death of James J. McCann , the foundation's benefactor. Mr. McCann, a grain merchant, was a lifetime resident of Poughkeepsie, NY. He owned and operated a feed and grain store; however, he amassed his fortune through shrewd understanding of and success with the stock market. His deep ties with the Catholic Church underlie one of the main focuses of the McCann Foundation.

Financial Summary

Total Giving: $800,000 (2002 approx); $914,766 (2001); $607,042 (2000). Note: Figure for 1996 represents the combined giving of both the McCann Foundation and the James J. McCann Trust.

Assets: $33,000,000 (2002 approx); $33,308,891 (2001); $33,483,987 (2000)

Typical Recipients

Arts & Humanities: Arts Associations & Councils, Arts Centers, Film & Video, Arts & Humanities-General, Historic Preservation, History & Archaeology, Libraries, Music, Opera, Performing Arts, Public Broadcasting

Civic & Public Affairs: Botanical Gardens/Parks, Community Foundations, Economic Development, Employment/Job Training, Civic & Public Affairs-General, Housing, Law & Justice, Legal Aid, Municipalities/Towns, Nonprofit Management, Philanthropic Organizations, Professional & Trade Associations, Public Policy, Safety, Urban & Community Affairs, Zoos/Aquariums

Education: Colleges & Universities, Community & Junior Colleges, Continuing Education, Education Funds, Elementary Education (Public), Engineering/Technological Education, Environmental Education, Legal Education, Private Education (Precollege), Public Education (Precollege), Religious Education, Secondary Education (Private), Student Aid

Environment: Air/Water Quality, Environment-General, Research, Resource Conservation

Health: Cancer, Children's Health/Hospitals, Emergency/Ambulance Services, Hospices, Hospitals, Trauma Treatment

International: Foreign Arts Organizations, Missionary/Religious Activities

Religion: Churches, Dioceses, Religion-General, Jewish Causes, Religious Organizations, Religious Welfare, Seminaries, Synagogues/Temples

Science: Science Exhibits & Fairs

Social Services: Animal Protection, Child Welfare, Community Centers, Community Service Organizations, Crime Prevention, Day Care, Delinquency & Criminal Rehabilitation, Emergency Relief, Food/Clothing Distribution, Homes, People with Disabilities, Recreation & Athletics, Senior Services, Shelters/Homelessness, United Funds/United Ways, Volunteer Services, YMCA/YWCA/YMHA/YWHA, Youth Organizations

Application Procedures

Initial Contact: The foundation has no formal application guidelines or forms.
Application Requirements: All applications for grants must be made in writing and addressed to the trustees, who meet regularly every January and July.
Deadlines: None. Applications should be received as far in advance as possible before trustees' meetings.

Restrictions

The foundation makes no grants to individuals or for operating budgets, emergency funds, endowment funds, deficit financing, matching gifts, or loans.

Additional Information

The McCann Foundation and the James J. McCann Charitable Trust are separate legal entities which act as a single unit. Most of the assets are held in the trust. For convenience, the activities of both organizations are referred to as the McCann Foundation.

Foundation Officials

Richard V. Corbally: secretary, director
John J. Gartland, Jr.: president, director B 1914. ED Georgetown University BA (1935); Fordham University LLB (1939); Saint John's University JSD (1941). PRIM CORP EMPL partner: Corbally Gartland & Rappleyea.
Michael G. Gartland: assistant secretary, director ADD CORP EMPL partner: Corbally Gartland & Rappleyea.

Grants Analysis

Disclosure Period: calendar year ending 2001
Total Grants: $914,766
Number of Grants: 58
Average Grant: $11,306*
Highest Grant: $181,651
Lowest Grant: $104
Typical Range: $1,000 to $20,000
*Note: Average grant figure excludes two highest grants ($281,651).

Recent Grants

Note: Grants derived from 2001 Form 990.

Library-Related

50,000	Millbrook Library, Millbrook, NY
1,000	Town of Clinton Library, Salt Point, NY

General

181,651	Bard College, Hudson, NY
100,000	St. Francis Hospital, Poughkeepsie, NY
86,069	Marist College, Poughkeepsie, NY
70,680	Our Lady of Lourdes, Poughkeepsie, NY
55,297	Lord's Place, West Palm Beach, FL
50,000	Catholic Charities Archdiocese of New York, New York, NY
50,000	Hudson Valley Philharmonic, Poughkeepsie, NY
50,000	Locust Grove, Poughkeepsie, NY
36,000	Patrons of the Arts in the Vatican Museums Italy
20,000	Vassar College, Poughkeepsie, NY

MCCARTHY CHARITIES

Giving Contact

Robert P. McCarthy, Treasurer
PO Box 1090
Troy, NY 12181
Phone: (518)273-6037

Description

Founded: 1917
EIN: 146019064
Organization Type: Private Foundation

Giving Locations: NY: Albany, Troy
Grant Types: General Support, Scholarship.

Donor Information

Founder: Robert H. McCarthy, the late Lucy A. McCarthy

Financial Summary

Total Giving: $957,220 (1999); $679,060 (1998); $499,708 (1996)
Assets: $18,326,844 (1999); $18,428,645 (1998); $10,810,058 (1996)
Gifts Received: $100 (1992)

Typical Recipients

Arts & Humanities: Arts Centers, Arts Institutes, Community Arts, History & Archaeology, Libraries, Museums/Galleries, Music, Theater
Civic & Public Affairs: Community Foundations, Civic & Public Affairs-General
Education: Arts/Humanities Education, Colleges & Universities, Community & Junior Colleges, Education Funds, Education Reform, Medical Education, Private Education (Precollege), Secondary Education (Private), Student Aid
Environment: Environment-General, Resource Conservation
Health: AIDS/HIV, Alzheimers Disease, Children's Health/Hospitals, Clinics/Medical Centers, Eyes/Blindness, Health Organizations, Hospices, Hospitals, Medical Research, Prenatal Health Issues, Public Health, Respiratory
Religion: Churches, Ministries, Religious Organizations, Religious Welfare
Social Services: Camps, Child Welfare, Community Centers, Community Service Organizations, Day Care, Family Services, Food/Clothing Distribution, Homes, People with Disabilities, Recreation & Athletics, Shelters/Homelessness, United Funds/United Ways, YMCA/YWCA/YMHA/YWHA, Youth Organizations

Application Procedures

Initial Contact: Send a brief letter of inquiry.
Application Requirements: Include a description of organization, purpose of funds sought, and list of staff and managers.
Deadlines: None.

Restrictions

Emphasis on Catholic organizations.

Foundation Officials

Pamela McCarthy Beauvais: president
Denis McCarthy: vice president B New York, NY 1935. ED Cooper Union (1963); Yale University BFA (1966); Yale University MFA (1966). PRIM CORP EMPL professor: Hunter College.
Robert P. McCarthy: treasurer

Grants Analysis

Disclosure Period: calendar year ending 1999
Total Grants: $957,220
Typical Range: $1,500 to $15,000
Note: A more recent grants list was unavailable.

Recent Grants

Note: Grants derived from 1997 Form 990.

Library-Related

25,000	Troy Public Library Foundation, Troy, NY

General

100,000	RCCA Arts Center
100,000	Siena College, Loudonville, NY
20,000	St. Ambrose School -- capital campaign fund
15,000	Doane Stuart School
15,000	Our Lady of Victory Roman Catholic Church
15,000	Rensselaer Newman Foundation
12,000	Community Foundation of the Capital Region, Albany, NY
10,000	BOCKS, Pines Bridge Playground
10,000	Catholic Central High School -- capital campaign
10,000	Friends of Dyken Pond Center -- support for Phase II

CATHERINE MCCARTHY MEMORIAL TRUST FUND

Giving Contact

PO Box 898
Lawrence, MA 01842
Phone: (978)435-7256

Description

Founded: 1984
EIN: 222549008
Organization Type: Private Foundation
Giving Locations: MA: and surrounding areas
Grant Types: General Support.

Donor Information

Founder: the late John J. McCarthy

Financial Summary

Total Giving: $143,419 (fiscal year ending June 30, 2002); $316,119 (fiscal 2001); $219,350 (fiscal 2000). Note: Fiscal 1997 Giving includes United Way ($2,000).
Giving Analysis: Giving for fiscal 1998 includes: foundation grants to United Way ($2,000)
Assets: $4,896,871 (fiscal 2002); $5,235,243 (fiscal 2001); $5,622,611 (fiscal 2000)

Typical Recipients

Arts & Humanities: Arts Associations & Councils, Arts Centers, Ethnic & Folk Arts, Arts & Humanities-General, History & Archaeology, Libraries, Museums/Galleries, Music
Civic & Public Affairs: Botanical Gardens/Parks, Chambers of Commerce, Clubs, Community Foundations, Civic & Public Affairs-General, Hispanic Affairs, Housing, Municipalities/Towns, Philanthropic Organizations, Safety, Urban & Community Affairs, Women's Affairs
Education: Arts/Humanities Education, Colleges & Universities, Legal Education, Private Education (Precollege), Public Education (Precollege), Secondary Education (Private), Student Aid
Health: Cancer, Geriatric Health, Health Organizations, Hospitals, Mental Health, Prenatal Health Issues, Public Health
Religion: Churches, Dioceses, Jewish Causes, Ministries, Religious Organizations, Religious Welfare, Synagogues/Temples
Social Services: Child Welfare, Community Centers, Community Service Organizations, Day Care, Family Services, Food/Clothing Distribution, Homes, People with Disabilities, Recreation & Athletics, Shelters/Homelessness, United Funds/United Ways, YMCA/YWCA/YMHA/YWHA, Youth Organizations

Application Procedures

Initial Contact: The foundation has no formal grant application procedure or application form.
Deadlines: None.

Additional Information

Trust(s): Fleet National Bank

Foundation Officials

Thomas F. Caffrey, Esq.: co-trustee

Grants Analysis

Disclosure Period: fiscal year ending June 30, 2002
Total Grants: $143,419
Number of Grants: 42
Average Grant: $3,415
Highest Grant: $10,000
Lowest Grant: $500
Typical Range: $1,000 to $5,000

Recent Grants

Note: Grants derived from fiscal 2000 Form 990.

Library-Related

7,550	Brooks School, North Andover, MA

General

25,500	Merrimack Valley Community Foundation, North Andover, MA
21,500	St. Mary Immaculate Conception, Lawrence, MA
12,500	Essex Art Center, Essex, MA
10,000	St. Augustine Parish, Lawrence, MA
10,000	St. Michael's Parish, Litchfield, CT
10,000	Summer in Greater Lawrence, Lawrence, MA
7,500	Addison Gallery of American Art, Andover, MA
7,500	Lawrence Boys and Girls Club, Lawrence, MA
7,500	Massachusetts Caring for Children Foundation, Boston, MA
5,000	American Textile History Museum, Lowell, MA

JOHN AND MARGARET MCCARTY FOUNDATION

Giving Contact

William H. Cheney, Sr., President
4435 Northside Pkwy., Suite 242
Atlanta, GA 30327
Phone: (404)760-0018

Description

Founded: 1989
EIN: 581867301
Organization Type: Private Foundation
Grant Types: General Support.

Donor Information

Founder: Established in 1989 by the late John McCarty and the late Margaret McCarty.

Financial Summary

Total Giving: $396,900 (2002); $556,150 (2001); $592,050 (2000)
Assets: $8,914,620 (2002); $9,357,405 (2001); $10,173,635 (2000)

Typical Recipients

Arts & Humanities: Film & Video, Historic Preservation, History & Archaeology, Libraries, Museums/Galleries, Music, Public Broadcasting
Civic & Public Affairs: Civil Rights, Community Foundations, Civic & Public Affairs-General, Housing, Law & Justice, Municipalities/Towns, Native American Affairs, Public Policy, Urban & Community Affairs
Education: Colleges & Universities, Education-General, Private Education (Precollege), Religious Education, Secondary Education (Private), Student Aid
Environment: Resource Conservation

Health: Alzheimers Disease, Children's Health/Hospitals, Health Organizations, Hospitals, Mental Health, Nursing Services, Single-Disease Health Associations
International: International Organizations, Missionary/Religious Activities
Religion: Churches, Dioceses, Dioceses, Religion-General, Ministries, Religious Organizations, Religious Welfare, Seminaries
Social Services: Camps, Community Service Organizations, Family Services, Social Services-General, United Funds/United Ways, YMCA/YWCA/YMHA/YWHA

Application Procedures

Initial Contact: Send a brief letter of inquiry.
Application Requirements: Include purpose of funds sought and proof of tax-exempt status.
Deadlines: None.

Foundation Officials

Eleanor M. Cheney: secretary
William H. Cheney, Sr.: president

Grants Analysis

Disclosure Period: calendar year ending 2002
Total Grants: $396,900
Number of Grants: 13
Average Grant: $16,408*
Highest Grant: $200,000
Lowest Grant: $1,000
Typical Range: $5,000 to $25,000
***Note:** Average grant figure excludes highest grant.

Recent Grants

Note: Grants derived from 2001 Form 990.

General

200,000	Visiting Nurse Association, Atlanta, GA -- Alzheimer's care
154,500	Community Bible Church, Highlands, NC
50,000	Heritage School, Newnan, GA -- for capital campaign
25,000	Capital Area YMCA, Arapahoe, NC -- for Camp Seagull
25,000	Highlands Cashiers Hospital Foundation, Highlands, NC
25,000	Kennesaw State University, Kennesaw, GA -- for building fund
25,000	Northwest Georgia Community Foundation, Dalton, GA -- for Alzheimer's issues
15,000	Raleigh MCCBG, Raleigh, NC
8,500	Atlanta Classic Foundation, Inc., Atlanta, GA
7,950	Anglican Mission in America

MCCASLAND FOUNDATION

Giving Contact

Barbara Braught, Executive Director
PO Box 400
Duncan, OK 73534
Phone: (580)252-5580
Fax: (580)252-5791

Description

Founded: 1952
EIN: 736096032
Organization Type: General Purpose Foundation
Giving Locations: OK: primarily Oklahoma
Grant Types: Challenge, Endowment, Operating Expenses, Professorship, Scholarship.

Donor Information

Founder: The foundation was established in 1952. The donors include members of the McCasland family as well as Mack Oil Company, where Thomas H. McCasland, Jr, a foundation trustee, serves as chairman and chief executive officer.

Financial Summary

Total Giving: $2,175,300 (2001); $2,307,199 (2000); $2,116,141 (1998)
Giving Analysis: Giving for 2000 includes: foundation grants to United Way ($20,000); foundation scholarships ($319,750); 1998: foundation matching gifts ($1,776); foundation grants to United Way ($32,508) foundation scholarships ($218,283)
Assets: $47,095,706 (2001); $50,758,427 (2000); $46,291,391 (1998)

Typical Recipients

Arts & Humanities: Arts Associations & Councils, Arts Centers, Arts Funds, Arts Institutes, Arts Outreach, Ethnic & Folk Arts, Arts & Humanities-General, Historic Preservation, History & Archaeology, Libraries, Museums/Galleries, Music, Public Broadcasting, Theater
Civic & Public Affairs: Botanical Gardens/Parks, Business/Free Enterprise, Clubs, Community Foundations, Economic Development, Employment/Job Training, Civic & Public Affairs-General, Housing, Municipalities/Towns, Native American Affairs, Nonprofit Management, Parades/Festivals, Philanthropic Organizations, Public Policy, Urban & Community Affairs
Education: Arts/Humanities Education, Business Education, Business-School Partnerships, Colleges & Universities, Community & Junior Colleges, Education Associations, Education Funds, Education Reform, Faculty Development, Education-General, Literacy, Medical Education, Private Education (Precollege), Public Education (Precollege), Religious Education, Science/Mathematics Education, Special Education, Student Aid, Vocational & Technical Education
Environment: Environment-General, Research, Wildlife Protection
Health: Alzheimers Disease, Cancer, Children's Health/Hospitals, Clinics/Medical Centers, Emergency/Ambulance Services, Health Organizations, Heart, Hospices, Hospitals, Long-Term Care, Medical Rehabilitation, Medical Research, Single-Disease Health Associations
International: Foreign Educational Institutions
Religion: Churches, Religion-General, Ministries, Religious Organizations, Religious Welfare
Science: Science Exhibits & Fairs, Science Museums, Scientific Centers & Institutes, Scientific Organizations
Social Services: At-Risk Youth, Camps, Child Welfare, Community Centers, Community Service Organizations, Emergency Relief, Family Services, Food/Clothing Distribution, Homes, People with Disabilities, Recreation & Athletics, Scouts, Senior Services, Shelters/Homelessness, Social Services-General, Substance Abuse, United Funds/United Ways, Veterans, Volunteer Services, YMCA/YWCA/YMHA/YWHA, Youth Organizations

Application Procedures

Initial Contact: The foundation requests applications be made in writing.
Application Requirements: The letter should include brief a description of organization, the amount and purpose of the grant, names of contact persons, and proof of tax-exempt status.
Deadlines: None.
Review Process: The board of trustees generally meets on a quarterly basis. Applicants receive notification following the board meeting.
Notes: An application form is available, but the foundation reports that use of the form is optional.

Foundation Officials

Barbara Braught: executive director
Thomas H. McCasland, Jr.: trustee B Duncan, OK 1933. ED University of Oklahoma BPOE (1956). PRIM CORP EMPL chairman, chief executive officer: Mack Energy Co. ADD CORP EMPL vice president, director: M&M Supply Co.; vice president, director: Mack Oil Co.; vice president, director: Thomas Drilling Co. CORP AFFIL president, director: Investors Trust Co.; chairman: AmQuest Bank Co.; manager: Enerwest Trading Co. NONPR AFFIL member: Benevolent Protectorate Elks.
Mary F. Michaelis: trustee
W. H. Phelps: trustee

Grants Analysis

Disclosure Period: calendar year ending 2001
Total Grants: $2,155,300*
Number of Grants: 101
Average Grant: $21,340*
Highest Grant: $181,500
Typical Range: $5,000 to $30,000 and $100,000 to $200,000
*Note: Giving excludes United Way.

Recent Grants

Note: Grants derived from 2001 Form 990.

General

181,500	On The Chisholm Trail Association, Duncan, OK -- 2 of 2 capital projects
170,000	On The Chisholm Trail Association, Duncan, OK
168,000	Communities Fund of Oklahoma, Oklahoma City, OK -- class of 2001 scholarships
150,000	University of Oklahoma Foundation, Inc., Norman, OK -- capital expense
125,000	Oklahoma University Foundation, Norman, OK -- botanical garden and arboretum
100,000	Cameron University Foundation, Lawton, OK -- capital for building renovation
100,000	Communities Fund of Oklahoma, Oklahoma City, OK -- October endowment fund
100,000	National Cowboy Hall of Fame, Oklahoma City, OK -- general operations
100,000	Oklahoma Medical Research Foundation, Oklahoma City, OK
62,471	Duncan Public Schools Foundation, Duncan, OK -- school grants

MCCAUSLAND FOUNDATION

Giving Contact

Bonnie McCausland, President
PO Box 6675
Radnor, PA 19087-8675
Phone: (610)687-5253

Description

Founded: 1994
EIN: 232776475
Organization Type: Private Foundation
Giving Locations: MA: Nantucket; PA: Philadelphia
Grant Types: General Support.

Financial Summary

Total Giving: $56,000 (2001); $101,000 (2000); $82,640 (1999)
Giving Analysis: Giving for 2000 includes: foundation scholarships ($500)
Assets: $80,693 (2001); $79,603 (2000); $264,365 (1999)
Gifts Received: $4,482 (1995); $1,500,032 (1994).
Note: In 1995, contributions were received from Peter McCausland.

Typical Recipients

Arts & Humanities: Libraries, Museums/Galleries, Music
Civic & Public Affairs: Botanical Gardens/Parks, Economic Development, Employment/Job Training
Education: Community & Junior Colleges, Education-General, International Exchange, Private Education (Precollege)
Environment: Environment-General, Resource Conservation, Wildlife Protection
Health: Cancer, Clinics/Medical Centers, Hospices, Hospitals, Public Health
Social Services: Child Welfare, Family Planning, Social Services-General

Application Procedures

Initial Contact: Send a brief letter of inquiry.
Application Requirements: a description of organization and purpose of funds sought.
Deadlines: None.

Foundation Officials

Cornelia B. Gross: secretary, treasurer
Gordon L. Keen, Jr.: director
Bonnie McCausland: president
Peter McCausland: vice president

Grants Analysis

Disclosure Period: calendar year ending 2001
Total Grants: $56,000
Number of Grants: 17
Average Grant: $2,250*
Highest Grant: $20,000
Lowest Grant: $500
Typical Range: $1,000 to $5,000
*Note: Average grant figure excludes highest grant.

Recent Grants

Note: Grants derived from 2000 Form 990.

Library-Related

500	Nantucket Athenaeum, Nantucket, MA

General

25,000	Independence Seaport Museum, Philadelphia, PA -- program support
24,000	Fox Chase Cancer Center, Philadelphia, PA -- program support
15,000	Eisenhower Exchange Fellowships, Philadelphia, PA
10,000	Springside School, Philadelphia, PA -- annual fund
5,000	National Council for Adoption, Washington, DC -- computer system
3,000	Central Piedmont Community College, Charlotte, NC -- The Jim Turner Center for Welding Technology
3,000	Chestnut Hill Healthcare, Philadelphia, PA -- program support
3,000	Fairmount Park Foundation, Philadelphia, PA -- program support
3,000	Morris Arboretum of the University of Pennsylvania, Philadelphia, PA
1,000	Fox Chase Cancer Center, Philadelphia, PA

MCCLATCHY CO.

Company Headquarters

2100 Q Street
Sacramento, CA 95816
Phone: (916)321-1846
Fax: (916)321-1964
Web: http://www.mcclatchy.com

Company Description

Founded: 1857
Ticker: MNI
Exchange: NYSE
Former Name: Cowles Media Co.

Revenue: US$1.08 billion (2001)
Employees: 9570 (2001)
SIC(s): 2711 Newspapers, 2721 Periodicals.

Operating Locations

McClatchy Media Co. (AZ--Scottsdale; CT--Stamford; MN--Minneapolis; PA--Harrisburg)

Subsidiary Companies

MN: Star Tribune Co., Minneapolis

Star Tribune Foundation

Giving Contact

Sandra K. Fleitman, Assistant Secretary
Star Tribune Foundation
425 Portland Avenue
Minneapolis, MN 55488-0002
Phone: (612)673-7314
Fax: (612)673-7020
E-mail: sfleitman@startribune.com
Web: http://startribune.com/company/ic/home/community/foundation.htm

Alternate Contact

Phone: (612)673-7051

Description

EIN: 416031373
Organization Type: Corporate Foundation
Former Name: Cowles Media Foundation.
Giving Locations: MN: Minneapolis-St. Paul
Grant Types: Capital, Employee Matching Gifts, Endowment, General Support.
Note: Employee matching gift ratio: 1 to 1 for schools, colleges, and civic and cultural organisation.

Financial Summary

Total Giving: $3,000,000 (2001); $3,000,000 (2000); $3,000,000 (1999 approx). Note: Contributes through corporate direct giving program and foundation.
Giving Analysis: Giving for 2001 includes: foundation scholarships ($17,500); foundation matching gifts ($202,510); foundation grants to United Way ($355,000); foundation ($2,424,990); 2000: foundation matching gifts ($175,818); foundation grants to United Way ($330,000); foundation ($2,494,182); 1998: foundation ($3,049,701);
Assets: $19,644,790 (2001); $23,891,593 (2000); $25,288,230 (1998)
Gifts Received: $200 (2001); $10,089,651 (1998); $1,359,500 (1996). Note: In 1998, contributions were received from Cowles Media Co.

Typical Recipients

Arts & Humanities: Arts Associations & Councils, Arts Centers, Arts Festivals, Arts Funds, Arts Institutes, Arts Outreach, Community Arts, Dance, Ethnic & Folk Arts, Arts & Humanities-General, Historic Preservation, History & Archaeology, Libraries, Literary Arts, Museums/Galleries, Music, Opera, Performing Arts, Public Broadcasting, Theater, Visual Arts
Civic & Public Affairs: African American Affairs, Chambers of Commerce, Civil Rights, Community Foundations, Economic Development, Employment/Job Training, First Amendment Issues, Civic & Public Affairs-General, Housing, Law & Justice, Native American Affairs, Nonprofit Management, Professional & Trade Associations, Public Policy, Urban & Community Affairs, Women's Affairs, Zoos/Aquariums
Education: Arts/Humanities Education, Business Education, Colleges & Universities, Community & Junior Colleges, Continuing Education, Economic Education, Education Associations, Education Funds, Education Reform, Elementary Education (Private), Engineering/Technological Education, Faculty Development, Education-General, Journalism/Media

Education, Leadership Training, Literacy, Minority Education, Private Education (Precollege), Public Education (Precollege), Science/Mathematics Education, Social Sciences Education, Vocational & Technical Education

Environment: Air/Water Quality, Resource Conservation

Health: AIDS/HIV, Emergency/Ambulance Services, Medical Rehabilitation

International: Foreign Educational Institutions, Human Rights

Religion: Churches, Jewish Causes, Missionary Activities (Domestic), Religious Welfare

Science: Science Exhibits & Fairs, Science Museums

Social Services: At-Risk Youth, Child Welfare, Community Centers, Community Service Organizations, Crime Prevention, Day Care, Delinquency & Criminal Rehabilitation, Domestic Violence, Emergency Relief, Family Planning, Family Services, Food/Clothing Distribution, People with Disabilities, Recreation & Athletics, Refugee Assistance, Shelters/Homelessness, Social Services-General, Substance Abuse, United Funds/United Ways, Volunteer Services, YMCA/YWCA/YMHA/YWHA, Youth Organizations

Application Procedures

Initial Contact: Request application guidelines, then send a brief letter or proposal.

Application Requirements: Include purpose of funds being sought; total project budget; a description of organization, its objectives, and how program will be administered; information about organization's officers and directors, current finances, and current contributors; and copy of current IRS tax-exempt ruling.

Deadlines: For general grants, None; for annual operating grants, January.

Review Process: General support is committed at the beginning of the fiscal year (April); large grants and capital requests are considered at the quarterly meetings of the board of directors.

Evaluative Criteria: The proposal must meet company objectives in one of the funding categories.

Decision Notification: Applications are considered on a quarterly basis; a response is made generally within three months.

Notes: Preliminary inquiries by phone or fax may be useful in determining the extent to which a proposed project relates to guidelines and existing commitments. The foundation now accepts the Minnesota Common Grant Application Form.

Restrictions

Generally does not support organizations principally related to medicine and specific diseases, substance abuse, rehabilitation, and related research; religious or international programs; development of low-income housing; dinners or special events; publications or films; recreation, athletic groups and sporting events; individuals, including travel; conferences and writing or performing; fund raising events; or political or lobbying groups. Preference is given to Minnesota charitable organizations.

Additional Information

A stipulation of the 1998 merger between McClatchy and Cowles Media provided for an annual contribution of at least $3 million to Twin Cities community causes for at least 10 years.

Publications: Contributions Report

Corporate Officials

Randy Miller Lebedoff: vice president, general counsel B Washington, DC 1949. ED Smith College BA (1971); Indiana University JD (1975). PRIM CORP EMPL vice president, general counsel: Star Tribune. CORP AFFIL assistant secretary: Star Tribune Cowles Media Co. NONPR AFFIL director: Minnesota Newspapers Association; member: Newspaper Association America.

John R. Schueler: publisher, president PRIM CORP EMPL publisher, president: Star Tribune Co.

Robert J. Weil: vice president operations ED Indiana University. PRIM CORP EMPL vice president operations: The McClatchy Co. ADD CORP EMPL vice president operations: McClatchy Newspapers Inc.

Foundation Officials

Craig Eiter: member PRIM CORP EMPL vice president finance: Star Tribune Co. Inc.

Randy Miller Lebedoff: secretary (see above)

Franklin Joseph Parisi: chairman B Elmhurst, NY 1945. ED Ohio University BS (1968). PRIM CORP EMPL vice president corporate communications: Cray Research Inc. NONPR AFFIL member: National Journalism Society; member: Public Relations Seminar.

Evelyn Piano: president, vice president community affairs

Robert J. Weil: member (see above)

Grants Analysis

Disclosure Period: calendar year ending 2001
Total Grants: $2,424,990*
Number of Grants: 200
Average Grant: $12,125
Highest Grant: $200,000
Typical Range: $1,000 to $25,000
*Note: Giving excludes matching gifts, scholarships, and United Way.

Recent Grants

Note: Grants derived from 2001 Form 990.

General

355,000	United Way of Minneapolis Area, Minneapolis, MN -- Annual Campaign Pledge
200,000	Children's Theatre Company, Minneapolis, MN -- First payment of five-year grant
200,000	Guthrie Theater, Minneapolis, MN -- First payment
100,000	American Red Cross, St. Paul, MN -- Second year of three year pledge
100,000	Committee to Protect Journalists, New York, NY -- Operating support
100,000	Goodwill/Easter Seals, Minneapolis, MN -- First payment
100,000	Minneapolis Urban League, Minneapolis, MN -- Second payment
100,000	Minnesota High Technology Foundation, Rosemount, MN -- Computers for school program
75,000	Minnesota Historical Society, St. Paul, MN -- Renovate flour towers
50,000	East Side Neighborhood Service, St. Paul, MN -- Second payment

MCCONNELL FOUNDATION

Giving Contact

Lee W. Salter, President & Executive Director
PO Box 492050
Redding, CA 96049-2050
Phone: (530)226-6200
Fax: (530)226-6210
E-mail: info@mcconnellfoundation.org
Web: http://www.mcconnellfoundation.org

Description

Founded: 1964
EIN: 946102700
Organization Type: General Purpose Foundation
Giving Locations: CA: Shasta County, Siskiyou County
Grant Types: Project, Scholarship.

Donor Information

Founder: The McConnell Foundation was established in 1964 by Carl R. McConnell and Leah F. McConnell.

Financial Summary

Total Giving: $1,500,000 (2002 approx); $3,650,773 (2001); $9,421,205 (2000)

Giving Analysis: Giving for 2000 includes: foundation matching gifts ($110,505); foundation scholarships ($140,050); 1999: foundation grants to United Way ($750); foundation scholarships ($150,050); 1998: foundation scholarships ($42,800); foundation matching gifts ($59,486); foundation matching gifts ($59,486); foundation scholarships ($172,150);

Assets: $350,000,000 (2001); $370,112,590 (2000); $375,163,303 (1999)

Gifts Received: $72,020 (2000); $315,871 (1998); $11,315,311 (1994). Note: In 2000, contributions were received from Myrle and Peggy Lema. In 1998, contributions were received from from Leah F. McConnell 1992 Trust.

Typical Recipients

Arts & Humanities: Arts Festivals, Arts & Humanities-General, Historic Preservation, History & Archaeology, Libraries, Museums/Galleries, Music, Performing Arts, Public Broadcasting, Theater

Civic & Public Affairs: Botanical Gardens/Parks, Clubs, Community Foundations, Economic Development, Employment/Job Training, Civic & Public Affairs-General, Housing, Law & Justice, Municipalities/Towns, Nonprofit Management, Parades/Festivals, Philanthropic Organizations, Public Policy, Safety, Urban & Community Affairs, Women's Affairs

Education: Arts/Humanities Education, Colleges & Universities, Education Funds, Environmental Education, Education-General, Literacy, Minority Education, Preschool Education, Private Education (Precollege), Public Education (Precollege), Science/Mathematics Education, Secondary Education (Private), Secondary Education (Public), Student Aid

Environment: Air/Water Quality, Forestry, Environment-General, Research, Resource Conservation, Wildlife Protection

Health: Clinics/Medical Centers, Emergency/Ambulance Services, Hospices, Hospitals, Medical Rehabilitation, Medical Research, Medical Training, Nutrition, Public Health

Religion: Religious Welfare

Social Services: Child Welfare, Community Centers, Community Service Organizations, Crime Prevention, Day Care, Domestic Violence, Family Planning, Family Services, People with Disabilities, Recreation & Athletics, Senior Services, Substance Abuse, Volunteer Services, YMCA/YWCA/YMHA/YWHA

Application Procedures

Initial Contact: Send an application letter of not more than five pages. Applicants should contact the foundation to obtain a grant application cover sheet.

Application Requirements: Applicants should include the following: the grant application cover sheet; the history and purpose of the organization; the amount requested and specific use of the proposed grant; description of why this project is needed and how it would make a difference; the project's goals and how progress will be measured; description of how volunteers will be utilized; the project timeline, including a projected completion date; personnel responsible for carrying out the project; and a list of board members. The following attachments are also required (in addition to the five page maximum proposal): for nonprofits, a copy of the organization's IRS determination letter (a letter from the State of California will not satisfy this requirement) and a current Income and Expense Statement and Balance Sheet; for schools and government agencies, a department budget; an itemized total project budget; a list of anticipated project funds and/or in-kind services, including all sources which applicant has approached or intends to approach (or an explanation of why your organization has not applied for other funding sources); for proposals requesting purchase of equipment, vehicles or services, list brand names, model numbers, specifications and name and address of vendors.

Deadlines: Foundation must receive the letter of intent and cover sheet by February 3; May 4; August 2; and November 1.

Review Process: Letters of intent will be reviewed and all applicants will be notified by mail on or before March 31. Successful applicants will be invited to submit a full proposal.

Restrictions

The foundation does not make grants to individuals, endowment funds, annual fund drives, sectarian religious purposes, construction or purchase of buildings, for salaries, administrative costs, operating costs or budget deficits.

Additional Information

The foundation reports that the distribution of funds in the Foundation's areas of interest changes from year to year depending on the number of suitable proposals received and favorably reviewed by the Board of Directors

Publications: Annual Report; Grant Policies and Procedures

Foundation Officials

Doreta Domke: director
Robert Lankenship: director
John A. Mancasola: executive vice president, secretary, treasurer
Leonard B. Nelson: director
William B. Nystrom: board chairman
Lee W. Salter: president, chief executive officer

Grants Analysis

Disclosure Period: calendar year ending 2000
Total Grants: $9,310,700*
Number of Grants: 54
Average Grant: $99,304*
Highest Grant: $2,346,894
Typical Range: $10,000 to $50,000 and $100,000 to $200,000
*Note: Giving excludes matching gifts. Average grant figure excludes two highest grants ($4,146,894).

Recent Grants

Note: Grants derived from 2000 Form 990.

Library-Related

41,617	Siskiyou County Public Library, Yreka, CA -- expansion and remodeling

General

2,346,894	Alliance of Redding Museums, Redding, CA -- capital campaign
1,800,000	Alliance of Redding Museums, Redding, CA -- capital campaign
750,000	Shasta Community Health Center, Redding, CA -- for Telemedicine
250,000	Alliance of Redding Museums, Redding, CA -- capital campaign
193,765	Shasta County, Redding, CA -- Mobile data computers
150,000	North State Institute for Sustainable Communities, Redding, CA -- start up costs
102,592	Siskiyou Golden Fair, Yreka, CA -- Livestock/equestrian complex at fairgrounds
100,000	Shasta County, Redding, CA -- Sacramento River Trail Extension
95,900	Shasta, Siskiyou, Modoc, Trinity & Big Valley H.S., Shasta, CA -- scholarships
67,473	City of Etna, Etna, CA -- new filtration system for Scott Valley Swimming Pool

MARGARET OGILVIE MCCORMICK CHARITABLE TRUST

Giving Contact

Larry A. Hartman, Trust Officer
Allfirst Bank
PO Box 2961
Harrisburg, PA 17105
Phone: (717)255-2046

Description

Founded: 1991
EIN: 236216167
Organization Type: Private Foundation
Giving Locations: PA: Harrisburg and surrounding area
Grant Types: General Support.

Financial Summary

Total Giving: $201,220 (2001); $212,500 (2000); $308,326 (1999). Note: 1997 Giving includes United Way ($7,560).
Giving Analysis: Giving for 1998 includes: foundation grants to United Way ($5,000) foundation ($113,403)
Assets: $3,629,599 (2001); $4,034,156 (2000); $4,128,571 (1999)

Typical Recipients

Arts & Humanities: Arts Associations & Councils, History & Archaeology, Libraries, Music, Public Broadcasting, Theater
Civic & Public Affairs: Civic & Public Affairs-General, Municipalities/Towns
Education: Colleges & Universities, Private Education (Precollege), Science/Mathematics Education
Health: Cancer, Hospices, Kidney, Mental Health, Public Health
Religion: Churches
Science: Science Museums
Social Services: Camps, Community Service Organizations, Family Services, Food/Clothing Distribution, Senior Services, Social Services-General, Special Olympics, United Funds/United Ways, YMCA/YWCA/YMHA/YWHA, Youth Organizations

Application Procedures

Initial Contact: Send a letter stating purpose or scope of project.
Deadlines: None.

Additional Information

Trust(s): Allfirst Bank

Grants Analysis

Disclosure Period: calendar year ending 2001
Total Grants: $201,220
Number of Grants: 10
Average Grant: $12,653*
Highest Grant: $50,000
Lowest Grant: $2,500
Typical Range: $1,000 to $15,000
*Note: Average grant figure excludes two highest grants ($100,000).

Recent Grants

Note: Grants derived from 2001 Form 990.

General

50,000	Allfirst Charitable Gift Fund, Inc., Harrisburg, PA
50,000	Messiah College, Grantham, PA
38,220	Pinnacle Health Hospice, Harrisburg, PA
17,000	Historical Society of Dauphin County, Harrisburg, PA

15,000	WITF TV-33, Harrisburg, PA
10,000	Military Heritage Foundation, Carlisle, PA
10,000	Project SHARE, Harrisburg, PA
5,000	Jump Street, Harrisburg, PA
3,500	Area M Special Olympics, Harrisburg, PA
2,500	Kidney Foundation of Central Pennsylvania, Harrisburg, PA

MCCORMICK & COMPANY, INC.

Company Headquarters

Sparks, MD
Web: http://www.mccormick.com

Company Description

Founded: 1889
Ticker: MKC
Exchange: NYSE
Revenue: US$2.32 billion (2002)
Employees: 9000 (2002)
SIC(s): 2079 Edible Fats & Oils Nec, 2087 Flavoring Extracts & Syrups Nec, 2099 Food Preparations Nec, 3085 Plastics Bottles.

Operating Locations

McCormick & Co. Inc. (AZ--Chandler; CA--Arbuckle, City of Industry, Irvine, Salinas, Stockton; CT--Bristol; FL--Tampa; IL--Aurora, Elmhurst; IN--South Bend; KS--Shawnee Mission; MD--Hunt Valley; MI--Belmont; MO--St. Louis; NJ--Rochelle Park; PA--Camp Hill; RI--North Providence; TX--Dallas, Salt Lake City, San Antonio, Spring; VT--Bradford; VA--Richmond; WA--Bellevue)

Nonmonetary Support

Type: Donated Products

Giving Contact

Allen M. Barrett, Jr., Vice President, Corporate Communications
18 Loveton Circle
Sparks, MD 21152-6000
Phone: (410)771-7310
Fax: (410)527-8289

Description

Organization Type: Corporate Giving Program
Giving Locations: headquarters and operating communities.
Grant Types: Capital, Employee Matching Gifts, Scholarship.
Note: Employee matching gift ratio: 1 to 1 for education institutions and cultural organisation.

Financial Summary

Total Giving: $1,175,000 (2002); $1,500,000 (2001); $1,500,000 (2000 approx). Note: Company gives directly through the McCormick Fund.

Typical Recipients

Arts & Humanities: Historic Preservation, Libraries, Museums/Galleries, Music, Public Broadcasting, Theater
Civic & Public Affairs: Business/Free Enterprise, Economic Development, Law & Justice, Professional & Trade Associations, Urban & Community Affairs
Education: Business Education, Colleges & Universities, Economic Education, Minority Education, Science/Mathematics Education, Student Aid
Environment: Environment-General
Health: Health Organizations, Medical Research, Nutrition
Science: Scientific Organizations

Social Services: Community Service Organizations, Family Planning, Family Services, Food/Clothing Distribution, United Funds/United Ways, Volunteer Services, Youth Organizations

Application Procedures

Initial Contact: call or write for guidelines, then written proposal

Application Requirements: a one-page, written summary statement, including: amount requested and funding periods, key deadline dates, program/project needs, organization's goals and objectives, mission statement, project fit with McComick's business operations; organization's name, address, phone number, and name of contact; current operating budget and project budget; sources of financial support; amounts committed or pending; statement of administrative, fundraising, and general expenses; audited financial statements; annual report; proof of tax-exempt status; and list of officers and board members, with affiliations

Deadlines: None.

Review Process: Charitable Donations Committee allocates donations from the fund and makes recommendations to the company; personal interviews are often requested

Evaluative Criteria: priority given to food-related causes, projects in communities with company operations, and McCormick representation on board of directors

Restrictions

Company does not support individuals; fraternal, veterans', or labor organizations; religious and sectarian organizations; political or lobbying groups; secondary schools; travel funds; organizations that might pose a conflict with company goals; or promotional activities, such as goodwill advertising or benefit events.

Additional Information

The McCormick Fund is a vehicle through which the company makes direct contributions.

Publications: Guidelines

Corporate Officials

Allen M. Barrett, Jr.: vice president corporate communications B Baltimore, MD 1949. ED Dartmouth College (1971); Loyola College (1983). PRIM CORP EMPL vice president corporate communications: McCormick & Co. Inc. NONPR AFFIL member: Public Relations Society America.

Francis A. Contino: executive vice president, chief financial officer B 1944. PRIM CORP EMPL executive vice president, chief financial officer: McCormick & Co. Inc.

Robert J. Lawless: chairman, president, chief executive officer, chief operating officer, director B Guelph, ON Canada 1946. ED University of Windsor. PRIM CORP EMPL chairman, president, chief executive officer, chief operating officer, director: McCormick & Co. Inc. CORP AFFIL director: Carpenter Technology Corp. NONPR AFFIL director: Grocery Manufacturers America Inc.; director: Kennedy Krieger Institute.

Carroll D. Nordhoff: executive vice president

Giving Program Officials

Allen M. Barrett, Jr.: chairman (see above)

Grants Analysis

Typical Range: $5,000 to $10,000

CHAUNCEY AND MARION DEERING MCCORMICK FOUNDATION

Giving Contact

Lawson E. Whitesides, Jr., President
410 North Michigan Avenue, Room 590
Chicago, IL 60611

Phone: (312)644-6720
Fax: (312)644-7555

Description

Founded: 1957
EIN: 366054815
Organization Type: General Purpose Foundation
Giving Locations: IL: Chicago metropolitan area
Grant Types: Capital, Endowment, General Support, Project, Scholarship.

Donor Information

Founder: The Chauncey and Marion Deering McCormick Foundation was established in 1957 by Brooks McCormick (b. 1917), and named after his parents. Mr. McCormick was the last member of his family to run International Harvester; he stepped down in 1977. International Harvester was formed through the merger of the McCormick and Deering Harvester Companies. The McCormick Company was founded in 1831 by Cyrus McCormick, inventor of the reaper.

Financial Summary

Total Giving: $3,682,167 (fiscal year ending July 31, 2001); $2,423,166 (fiscal 1999); $2,399,334 (fiscal 1998)

Giving Analysis: Giving for fiscal 2001 includes: foundation grants to United Way ($5,000) fiscal 1999: foundation grants to United Way ($5,000)

Assets: $71,461,331 (fiscal 2001); $73,948,318 (fiscal 1999); $67,486,192 (fiscal 1998)

Gifts Received: $30,000 (fiscal 2001); $50,000 (fiscal 1999); $2,908,437 (fiscal 1997). Note: In fiscal 2001, contributions were received from Fiona Hunt. In 1999, contributions were received from Nancy H. McCormick. In 1997, $2,908,437 was given by the Miami Corp.

Typical Recipients

Arts & Humanities: Arts Funds, Arts Institutes, Dance, Ethnic & Folk Arts, Historic Preservation, History & Archaeology, Libraries, Museums/Galleries, Music, Opera, Performing Arts, Public Broadcasting, Theater, Visual Arts

Civic & Public Affairs: Botanical Gardens/Parks, Community Foundations, Economic Development, Civic & Public Affairs-General, Philanthropic Organizations, Public Policy, Rural Affairs, Urban & Community Affairs, Women's Affairs, Zoos/Aquariums

Education: Agricultural Education, Business Education, Colleges & Universities, Education Associations, Education Funds, Faculty Development, Education-General, Medical Education, Minority Education, Private Education (Precollege), Private Education (Precollege), Public Education (Precollege), Secondary Education (Public)

Environment: Air/Water Quality, Forestry, Environment-General, Resource Conservation, Wildlife Protection

Health: Cancer, Clinics/Medical Centers, Emergency/Ambulance Services, Health Organizations, Hospices, Hospitals, Hospitals (University Affiliated), Medical Rehabilitation, Medical Research, Mental Health, Single-Disease Health Associations

International: Foreign Educational Institutions, Health Care/Hospitals, International Environmental Issues, Trade

Religion: Churches, Ministries, Religious Welfare, Seminaries

Science: Observatories & Planetariums, Science Museums, Scientific Centers & Institutes

Social Services: Animal Protection, Child Welfare, Family Planning, Homes, Scouts, United Funds/United Ways, YMCA/YWCA/YMHA/YWHA, Youth Organizations

Application Procedures

Initial Contact: The foundation has no formal application procedure.

Deadlines: None.

Restrictions

Grants, scholarships, fellowships loans, etc. are generally not made based upon an application. Recipients are limited to organizations described in Section 170(c) IRS Code and are determined by the foundation's board of directors.

Additional Information

In addition to giving grants, the foundation owns a 500-acre plot of land that is made available to various charitable organizations for conferences and meetings.

Foundation Officials

Brooks McCormick: chairman, director B Chicago, IL 1917. ED Yale University BA (1940). CORP AFFIL stockholder: Megabyte International Corp. CLUB AFFIL Racquet & Tennis Club; Casino Club; Chicago Club.

Charlotte Deering McCormick: vice president

Charles Edgar Schroeder: president, director B Chicago, IL 1935. ED Dartmouth College BA (1957); Dartmouth College Amos Tuck Graduate School of Business Administration MBA (1958). PRIM CORP EMPL president, director: Miami Corp. CORP AFFIL president, director: Cutler Oil & Gas Corp.; director: National Standard Co. NONPR AFFIL member: Financial Analysts Society Chicago; trustee: Northwestern University. CLUB AFFIL Glen View Golf Club; Michigan Shores Club; Chicago Club; Commercial Club.

Grants Analysis

Disclosure Period: fiscal year ending July 31, 2001
Total Grants: $3,677,167*
Number of Grants: 72
Average Grant: $37,707*
Highest Grant: $1,000,000
Lowest Grant: $1,000
Typical Range: $15,000 to $50,000
***Note:** Giving excludes United Way. Average grant figure excludes highest grant.

Recent Grants

Note: Grants derived from 2001 Form 990.

Library-Related

20,000   Newberry Library, Chicago, IL

General

1,000,000 Art Institute of Chicago, Chicago, IL -- sustaining fellows
213,000 Rush Presbyterian St. Luke's Medical Center, Chicago, IL -- Neurobehavioral Center
150,000 Music and Dance Theater, Chicago, IL
125,000 Lyric Opera of Chicago, Chicago, IL
115,000 Lawson House YMCA, Chicago, IL
110,000 College of the Atlantic, Bar Harbor, ME
110,000 Lincoln Park Zoological Society, Chicago, IL
100,000 DuPage Community Foundation, Wheaton, IL
100,000 Holton-Arms School, Bethesda, MD
100,000 Northwestern University, Evanston, IL -- medical school

ROBERT R. MCCORMICK TRIBUNE FOUNDATION

Giving Contact

Communications Department
435 North Michigan Avenue, Suite 770
Chicago, IL 60611
Phone: (312)222-3512
Fax: (312)222-3523
E-mail: rrmtf@tribune.com
Web: http://www.rrmtf.org

Description

Founded: 1990
EIN: 363689171
Organization Type: General Purpose Foundation
Former Name: Robert R. McCormick Charitable Trust.
Giving Locations: IL: Chicago metropolitan area varies by program area.
Grant Types: Award, Employee Matching Gifts, General Support, Matching.

Donor Information

Founder: The foundation was funded out of income from the estate of Colonel Robert R. McCormick (d. 1955), editor, publisher, and principal owner of the Chicago Tribune. The foundation was established, as directed in his will, for "religious, charitable, scientific, literary or educational purposes or for the prevention of cruelty to children or animals."

Financial Summary

Total Giving: $100,000,000 (2003 approx); $98,851,665 (2002); $112,048,773 (2001)
Giving Analysis: Giving for 1999 includes: foundation grants to United Way ($10,000)
Assets: $2,000,000,000 (2003 approx); $2,000,000,000 (2002 approx); $1,599,796,701 (2001)
Gifts Received: $41,639,215 (1998); $24,226 (1997); $16,079,628 (1996)

Typical Recipients

Arts & Humanities: Historic Preservation, History & Archaeology, Libraries, Museums/Galleries, Music, Opera, Performing Arts, Public Broadcasting, Theater
Civic & Public Affairs: African American Affairs, Asian American Affairs, Botanical Gardens/Parks, Clubs, Community Foundations, Economic Development, Economic Policy, Employment/Job Training, Ethnic Organizations, First Amendment Issues, Civic & Public Affairs-General, Hispanic Affairs, Housing, Law & Justice, Legal Aid, Municipalities/Towns, Native American Affairs, Nonprofit Management, Philanthropic Organizations, Professional & Trade Associations, Public Policy, Urban & Community Affairs, Women's Affairs, Zoos/Aquariums
Education: Afterschool/Enrichment Programs, Arts/Humanities Education, Business Education, Colleges & Universities, Economic Education, Education Associations, Education Funds, Education Reform, Engineering/Technological Education, Faculty Development, Education-General, Health & Physical Education, Journalism/Media Education, Literacy, Medical Education, Minority Education, Preschool Education, Private Education (Precollege), Public Education (Precollege), Special Education, Student Aid, Vocational & Technical Education
Health: AIDS/HIV, Cancer, Children's Health/Hospitals, Clinics/Medical Centers, Emergency/Ambulance Services, Eyes/Blindness, Health Organizations, Heart, Hospices, Hospitals, Medical Rehabilitation, Medical Research, Mental Health, Multiple Sclerosis, Nursing Services, Prenatal Health Issues, Public Health, Respiratory, Single-Disease Health Associations
International: Human Rights, International Affairs, International Organizations, International Relations
Religion: Churches, Jewish Causes, Ministries, Religious Organizations, Religious Welfare
Science: Science Museums, Scientific Centers & Institutes
Social Services: Animal Protection, At-Risk Youth, Camps, Child Welfare, Community Service Organizations, Crime Prevention, Day Care, Delinquency & Criminal Rehabilitation, Domestic Violence, Emergency Relief, Family Services, Food/Clothing Distribution, Homes, People with Disabilities, Recreation & Athletics, Refugee Assistance, Scouts, Senior Services, Shelters/Homelessness, Social Services-General, Special Olympics, Substance Abuse, United Funds/United Ways, Volunteer Services, YMCA/YWCA/YMHA/YWHA, Youth Organizations

Application Procedures

Initial Contact: The foundation suggests visiting their website prior to initiating a grant inquiry. Inquiries and proposals should then be addressed to the foundation.
Application Requirements: Guidelines for grant applications under the communities program may be obtained from participating corporate entities or from the McCormick Tribune Foundation. To initiate a grant request for the journalism, education, or citizenship programs, send a short letter describing the proposal.

Additional Information

Foundation trustees are active or retired officers of the Tribune Company and Chicago Tribune Company, with the exception of certain officers of the Society of the First Division, who are also board members of the Cantigny First Division Foundation.
Besides making grants, the foundation also conducts seminars for the benefit of nonprofit organizations.
Publications: Annual Report; Information Reports on Contingency Conferences

Foundation Officials

Richard A. Behrenhausen: president, chief executive officer ED George Washington University MS; United States Military Academy BS. NONPR AFFIL vice president, secretary, chief operating officer: Cantigny Foundation.
Catherine Brown: director communities programs
Charles T. Brumback: director B Toledo, OH 1928. ED Princeton University BA (1950); University of Toledo (1953-1954). PRIM CORP EMPL director: Tribune Co. CORP AFFIL director: Avid Technology Inc.; director: Spyglass Inc. NONPR AFFIL trustee: Northwestern Memorial Hospital; life trustee: Northwestern University; member: Florida Press Association; member: Newspaper Association America; trustee: Chicago Symphony Orchestra; trustee: Culver Education Foundation; trustee: Chicago Historical Society; member: American Institute of Certified Public Accountants; trustee: American Newspaper Publishers Association. CLUB AFFIL member: Commercial Club Chicago; member: Tavern Club; member: Chicago Club.
James C. Dowdle: director B 1934. ED University of Notre Dame BA (1956). PRIM CORP EMPL executive vice president, director: Tribune Co.
Dennis J. FitzSimons: director
Jack W. Fuller: director B Chicago, IL 1946. ED Northwestern University BS (1968); Yale University JD (1973). PRIM CORP EMPL president, chief executive officer, publisher: Tribune Publishing Co. NONPR AFFIL member: Pulitzer Prize Board; trustee: University Chicago; member: Newspaper Association America; member: International American Dialogue; director: International American Press Association; member: American Society Newspaper Editors; director: Field Museum Natural History; fellow: American Academy of Arts & Sciences. CLUB AFFIL Commercial Club Chicago.
Nicholas Goodban: senior vice president philanthropy
David L. Grange: executive vice president, chief operating officer
John W. Madigan: chairman, director B Chicago, IL 1937. ED University of Michigan BBA (1958); University of Michigan MBA (1959). PRIM CORP EMPL president, chief executive officer, director: Tribune Co. NONPR AFFIL trustee: Rush-Presbyterian-Saint Lukes Medical Center; member visiting committee: University Michigan School Business Administration; trustee: Northwestern University Medill School Journalism; trustee: Museum Television & Radio New York; director: Newspaper Association America; member, trustee, executive committee: Chicago Council Foreign Relations; trustee: Illinois Institute Technology; director: Associated Press. CLUB AFFIL Commercial Club Chicago; Economic Club Chicago.
Louis J. Marsico, Jr.: vice president finance and administration
Wanda Y. Newell: director education programs
John Sirek: director citizenship programs
Vivian Vahlberg: director journalism program B Oklahoma City, OK 1948. NONPR AFFIL member: Donors Forum; member: Society Professional Journalists. CLUB AFFIL member: National Press Club.

Grants Analysis

Disclosure Period: calendar year ending 2002
Total Grants: $98,851,665
Number of Grants: 1,900 (approx)
Average Grant: $52,027
Highest Grant: $2,500,000
Typical Range: $10,000 to $50,000 and $150,000 to $450,000

Recent Grants

Note: Grants derived from 2001 Form 990.

General

2,500,000	Millennium Park Incorporated, Chicago, IL -- skating rink
2,000,000	Big Shoulders Fund, Chicago, IL -- Act of Faith campaign
2,000,000	University of Chicago, Chicago, IL -- Program for Urban and Community Leadership
1,775,000	Voices for Illinois Children, Chicago, IL
1,250,000	Northwestern University Medill School of Journalism, Evanston, IL -- for construction, renovation and equipping of journalism buildings
1,000,000	Loyola University of Chicago, Chicago, IL -- for Center for Urban Research and Learning (CURL)
1,000,000	Partnership for Child Care Accreditation, Chicago, IL
798,000	University of Chicago Center for Early Childhood Research, Chicago, IL -- for the new Center on Early Childhood Research
625,000	YMCA of Metropolitan Chicago, Chicago, IL -- for the construction of new YMCA facilities in Logan Square and Pilsen
600,000	Civitas Initiative, Chicago, IL -- production and distribution of grandparent videos and companion book

ANNE MCCORMICK TRUST

Giving Contact

Larry A. Hartman, Trust Officer
c/o All First Bank
3607 Derry Street
Harrisburg, PA 17111
Phone: (717)565-2672

Description

Founded: 1989
EIN: 236471389
Organization Type: Private Foundation
Giving Locations: PA: Dauphin, Cumberland, Perry and Franklin counties
Grant Types: General Support.

Donor Information

Founder: Established in 1989 by the late Anne McCormick.

Financial Summary

Total Giving: $447,500 (2000); $662,700 (1999); $342,334 (1998). Note: 1997 Giving includes United Way ($2,000).
Giving Analysis: Giving for 2000 includes: foundation grants to United Way ($50,000)
Assets: $9,225,658 (2000); $9,098,978 (1999); $9,136,800 (1998)

Typical Recipients

Arts & Humanities: Arts Associations & Councils, Arts Funds, Arts Outreach, Community Arts, Dance, Arts & Humanities-General, History & Archaeology, Libraries, Literary Arts, Museums/Galleries, Music, Opera, Public Broadcasting, Theater
Civic & Public Affairs: Botanical Gardens/Parks, Civic & Public Affairs-General, Municipalities/Towns
Education: Business Education, Colleges & Universities, Community & Junior Colleges, Education Funds, Education-General, Medical Education, Public Education (Precollege), Religious Education, Science/Mathematics Education
Environment: Environment-General
Health: Arthritis, Cancer, Children's Health/Hospitals, Clinics/Medical Centers, Emergency/Ambulance Services, Eyes/Blindness, Heart, Hospices, Hospitals, Medical Research, Multiple Sclerosis, Public Health, Single-Disease Health Associations
Religion: Churches, Religious Welfare
Social Services: Big Brother/Big Sister, Child Welfare, Community Service Organizations, Counseling, Crime Prevention, Emergency Relief, Family Services, Food/Clothing Distribution, People with Disabilities, Special Olympics, Substance Abuse, United Funds/United Ways, YMCA/YWCA/YMHA/YWHA, Youth Organizations

Application Procedures

Initial Contact: Send a brief letter of inquiry.
Application Requirements: Include recently audited financial statement and proof of tax-exempt status.
Deadlines: None.

Restrictions

Support is limited to Dauphin, Cumberland, Pery, and Franklin counties of Pennsylvania.

Additional Information

Trust(s): Allfirst Bank

Grants Analysis

Disclosure Period: calendar year ending 2000
Total Grants: $447,500*
Number of Grants: 18
Average Grant: $11,618*
Highest Grant: $250,000
Lowest Grant: $2,000
Typical Range: $1,000 to $20,000
*Note: Giving excludes United Way. Average grant excludes highest grant.

Recent Grants

Note: Grants derived from 2000 Form 990.

General

250,000	Pinnacle Health, Harrisburg, PA
50,000	United Way Capital Region, Harrisburg, PA
31,000	Goodwill Industries of Central Harrisburg, Harrisburg, PA
15,000	Allied Arts Fund, Harrisburg, PA
15,000	Theatre Harrisburg, Harrisburg, PA
10,000	Dickinson College, Carlisle, PA
10,000	Perry County Council of the Arts, Newport, PA
7,500	YMCA, Carlisle, PA
6,000	Big Brothers and Big Sisters of the Capital Region, Harrisburg, PA
5,000	American Red Cross, Harrisburg, PA

MARSHALL L. AND PERRINE D. MCCUNE CHARITABLE FOUNDATION

Giving Contact

Frances R. Sowers, Associate Director
345 E. Alameda St.
Santa Fe, NM 87501-2229
Phone: (505)983-8300
Fax: (505)983-7887
E-mail: fsowers@swcp.com
Web: http://www.nmmccune.org

Description

Founded: 1988
EIN: 850375622
Organization Type: Private Foundation
Giving Locations: NM
Grant Types: General Support, Project.

Donor Information

Founder: the late Perrine Dixon McCune

Financial Summary

Total Giving: $6,761,674 (1999); $5,090,941 (1998 approx); $7,047,742 (1997)
Assets: $152,344,923 (1999); $133,250,360 (1998); $99,042,753 (1995)
Gifts Received: $2,600 (1993)

Typical Recipients

Arts & Humanities: Arts Associations & Councils, Ethnic & Folk Arts, Libraries, Literary Arts, Museums/Galleries, Music, Opera, Public Broadcasting
Civic & Public Affairs: Business/Free Enterprise, Community Foundations, Economic Development, Civic & Public Affairs-General, Hispanic Affairs, Housing, Legal Aid, Municipalities/Towns, Native American Affairs, Urban & Community Affairs, Women's Affairs
Education: Afterschool/Enrichment Programs, Colleges & Universities, Community & Junior Colleges, Faculty Development, Education-General, International Studies, Leadership Training, Preschool Education, Public Education (Precollege), Science/Mathematics Education, Secondary Education (Public), Student Aid, Vocational & Technical Education
Environment: Forestry, Environment-General, Resource Conservation
Health: AIDS/HIV, Children's Health/Hospitals, Clinics/Medical Centers, Diabetes, Hospices, Hospitals, Nursing Services, Prenatal Health Issues, Preventive Medicine/Wellness Organizations, Public Health
Religion: Churches, Religious Organizations, Religious Welfare
Science: Science Museums
Social Services: At-Risk Youth, Big Brother/Big Sister, Child Welfare, Community Centers, Community Service Organizations, Crime Prevention, Family Services, Food/Clothing Distribution, Sexual Abuse, Shelters/Homelessness, United Funds/United Ways, Volunteer Services, Youth Organizations

Application Procedures

Initial Contact: Request current application guideline since deadlines vary.

Restrictions

Does not support: individuals, religious organizations for sectarian purposes, political or lobbying groups, organizations outside operating areas, or deficits.

Foundation Officials

James M. Edwards: member ED University of Illinois BA (1953); Institute des Sciences Politiques (1955); Yale University (1960). CORP AFFIL director: Lockhart Chemical; director: Lockhart. NONPR AFFIL director: Childrens Hospital Pittsburgh.
Owen Lopez: executive director
Sarah McCune Losinger: chairman
John R. McCune, VI: member
Frances Sowers: associate director

Grants Analysis

Disclosure Period: calendar year ending 1999
Total Grants: $6,761,674
Note: No grants list available for 1999.

JOHN R. MCCUNE CHARITABLE TRUST

Giving Contact

James M. Edwards, Executive Director
6 PPG Place
Pittsburgh, PA 15222
Phone: (412)644-7796
Fax: (412)644-8059

Description

Founded: 1972
EIN: 256160722
Organization Type: General Purpose Foundation
Giving Locations: PA: Pittsburgh including western Pennsylvania
Grant Types: Capital, General Support, Project.

Donor Information

Founder: The trust was established in 1972 with funds donated by the late John R. McCune IV . The trust reports that it is affliated with the McCune Foundation, which is also located in Pittsburgh, PA.

Financial Summary

Total Giving: $6,000,000 (fiscal year ending November 30, 2003 approx); $7,500,000 (fiscal 2002 approx); $6,000,000 (fiscal 2001)
Giving Analysis: Giving for fiscal 2000 includes: foundation scholarships ($12,000) fiscal 1999: foundation scholarships ($11,000)
Assets: $140,000,000 (fiscal 2001); $180,910,159 (fiscal 2000); $181,407,966 (fiscal 1999)

Typical Recipients

Arts & Humanities: Arts Associations & Councils, Arts & Humanities-General, History & Archaeology, Libraries, Museums/Galleries, Music, Public Broadcasting
Civic & Public Affairs: Business/Free Enterprise, Community Foundations, Economic Development, Employment/Job Training, Civic & Public Affairs-General, Nonprofit Management, Philanthropic Organizations, Public Policy, Urban & Community Affairs, Women's Affairs
Education: Afterschool/Enrichment Programs, Arts/Humanities Education, Colleges & Universities, Education Funds, Education Reform, Elementary Education (Public), Education-General, Journalism/Media Education, Minority Education, Preschool Education, Private Education (Precollege), Public Education (Precollege), Religious Education, Secondary Education (Private), Social Sciences Education, Special Education, Vocational & Technical Education
Environment: Environment-General, Resource Conservation, Wildlife Protection
Health: Alzheimers Disease, Cancer, Children's Health/Hospitals, Clinics/Medical Centers, Diabetes, Geriatric Health, Health Funds, Health Organizations, Hospitals, Medical Research, Mental Health, Multiple

Sclerosis, Prenatal Health Issues, Public Health, Research/Studies Institutes, Single-Disease Health Associations, Transplant Networks/Donor Banks
International: Health Care/Hospitals, International Relations
Religion: Jewish Causes, Ministries, Religious Organizations, Religious Welfare, Seminaries
Science: Science Museums, Scientific Centers & Institutes, Scientific Research
Social Services: Animal Protection, Camps, Child Abuse, Child Welfare, Child Welfare, Community Service Organizations, Counseling, Crime Prevention, Delinquency & Criminal Rehabilitation, Family Services, Food/Clothing Distribution, Homes, People with Disabilities, Recreation & Athletics, Senior Services, Shelters/Homelessness, Substance Abuse, Volunteer Services, YMCA/YWCA/YMHA/YWHA, Youth Organizations

Application Procedures
Initial Contact: Applicants should submit a brief proposal no more than two pages.
Application Requirements: The inquiry should include the following: project description, including budget; amount of funding requested; copy of IRS tax-determination letter verifying the applicant's status as a nonprofit organization, and an annual report.
Deadlines: May 1.
Review Process: The dispensing committee meets annually in June to authorize grants.

Restrictions
The trust does not make grants to individuals nor pledges beyond one year.

Additional Information
Integra Trust Company, N.A., serves as a corporate trustee of the foundation.
Although the John R. McCune Charitable Trust and the McCune Foundation are co-housed, share staff and have overlapping board members, they operate as separate organizations with unique missions.

Foundation Officials
Janet McCune Edwards Anti: member dispensing committee
Molly McCune Cathey: member dispensing committee
David L. Edwards: chairman
James M. Edwards: executive director ED University of Illinois BA (1953); Institute des Sciences Politiques (1955); Yale University (1960). CORP AFFIL director: Lockhart Chemical; director: Lockhart. NONPR AFFIL director: Childrens Hospital Pittsburgh.
John H. Edwards: member dispensing committee
Michael M. Edwards: member dispensing committee
Carrie McCune Katigan: member dispensing committee
Laurie M. Lewis: member dispensing committee
Sarah McCune Losinger: member dispensing committee
John R. McCune, VI: member dispensing committee

Grants Analysis
Disclosure Period: fiscal year ending November 30, 2000
Total Grants: $8,551,359*
Number of Grants: 187
Average Grant: $45,729
Highest Grant: $250,000
Typical Range: $10,000 to $250,000
*Note: Giving excludes scholarships.

Recent Grants
Note: Grants derived from fiscal 2000 Form 990.

General
250,000	Ellis School, Pittsburgh, PA
125,000	Greater Oklahoma Hunter Jumper Association, Norman, OK

125,000	Jews for Jesus, San Francisco, CA
125,000	Oklahoma Medical Research Foundation, Oklahoma City, OK
125,000	Project Women Coalition, Oklahoma City, OK
125,000	School of the Plains, Oklahoma City, OK
125,000	Winchester Thurston School, Pittsburgh, PA
115,500	Grove City College, Grove City, PA
105,000	Children's Hospital of Pittsburgh, Pittsburgh, PA
100,000	Alzheimer's Disease and Related Disorders Association, Chicago, IL

MCCUNE FOUNDATION

Giving Contact
Henry S. Beukema, Executive Director
750 Six PPG Place
Pittsburgh, PA 15222
Phone: (412)644-8779
Fax: (412)644-8059
E-mail: info@mccune.org
Web: http://www.mccune.org

Description
Founded: 1979
EIN: 256210269
Organization Type: General Purpose Foundation
Giving Locations: CT; NM; OK; PA: Southwestern Pennsylvania, Pittsburgh
Grant Types: Capital, Endowment, Fellowship, Multiyear/Continuing Support, Project, Research, Scholarship, Seed Money.

Donor Information
Founder: The McCune Foundation was established in 1979 by the will of Charles Lockhart McCune (1895-1979) in memory of his parents, Janet Lockhart McCune and John Robison McCune. The Charles L. McCune Charitable Trust was absorbed into the McCune Foundation in 1980. Charles L. McCune was president of Union National Bank of Pittsburgh (which was founded by his grandfather in 1857) from 1945 to 1972, and then served as chairman of the board until his death. Mr. McCune also was an oilman and a corporate director of such companies as Texaco, Armstrong Cork Co., Sharon Steel Corp., Cyclops Steel Corp., and Joseph Horne Co.
The foundation became fully funded in 1984. According to terms of the donor's will, the foundation will terminate in 2029. The foundation is governed by a three-member distribution committee which meets at least twice a year.

Financial Summary
Total Giving: $22,500,000 (fiscal year ending September 30, 2003 approx); $25,375,494 (fiscal 2002); $28,391,003 (fiscal 2000)
Assets: $497,804,987 (fiscal 2002); $564,422,495 (fiscal 2001); $618,703,906 (fiscal 2000)

Typical Recipients
Arts & Humanities: Arts Associations & Councils, Arts Centers, Arts Festivals, Arts Funds, Arts Institutes, Arts Outreach, Ballet, Community Arts, Dance, Ethnic & Folk Arts, Film & Video, Arts & Humanities-General, Historic Preservation, History & Archaeology, Libraries, Museums/Galleries, Music, Opera, Performing Arts, Public Broadcasting, Theater
Civic & Public Affairs: African American Affairs, Business/Free Enterprise, Community Foundations, Economic Development, Employment/Job Training, Civic & Public Affairs-General, Housing, Municipalities/Towns, Nonprofit Management, Philanthropic Organizations, Professional & Trade Associations, Public Policy, Rural Affairs, Urban & Community Affairs, Women's Affairs, Zoos/Aquariums

Education: Afterschool/Enrichment Programs, Arts/Humanities Education, Business Education, Colleges & Universities, Economic Education, Education Funds, Education Reform, Engineering/Technological Education, Environmental Education, Faculty Development, Education-General, Health & Physical Education, International Studies, Literacy, Medical Education, Minority Education, Preschool Education, Private Education (Precollege), Religious Education, Social Sciences Education, Special Education, Student Aid, Vocational & Technical Education
Environment: Energy, Environment-General, Protection, Resource Conservation
Health: AIDS/HIV, Cancer, Children's Health/Hospitals, Clinics/Medical Centers, Geriatric Health, Health Policy/Cost Containment, Health Funds, Health Organizations, Hospices, Hospitals, Hospitals (University Affiliated), Medical Rehabilitation, Medical Research, Medical Training, Mental Health, Nursing Services, Nutrition, Prenatal Health Issues, Public Health, Single-Disease Health Associations
International: Health Care/Hospitals, Human Rights, International Relations
Religion: Churches, Dioceses, Jewish Causes, Ministries, Religious Organizations, Religious Welfare, Seminaries
Science: Science Museums, Scientific Centers & Institutes, Scientific Research
Social Services: Animal Protection, Camps, Child Welfare, Community Centers, Community Service Organizations, Community Service Organizations, Counseling, Crime Prevention, Day Care, Delinquency & Criminal Rehabilitation, Domestic Violence, Emergency Relief, Family Services, Food/Clothing Distribution, Homes, People with Disabilities, Recreation & Athletics, Scouts, Senior Services, Shelters/Homelessness, Social Services-General, Substance Abuse, United Funds/United Ways, YMCA/YWCA/YMHA/YWHA, Youth Organizations

Application Procedures
Initial Contact: Applicants should send a brief letter of inquiry addressed to the foundation's Executive Director. Contact foundation for detailed application guidelines.
Application Requirements: The summary should provide an overview of and rationale for the project along with a description of the constituencies served, the total cost of the project, the amount sought from the McCune Foundation, and the anticipated income from and information about other funders. A copy of the organization's IRS 501(c)(3) letter should also be included with the brief proposal.
Deadlines: Proposals should be submitted at least 90 days prior to scheduled Distribution Committee meetings, usually held in March, July, September, and December.
Review Process: If the proposal meets the foundation's current funding criteria, a request for a meeting at the foundation's office will be arranged to discuss the project. After a site visit, if necessary, the organization will receive further guidance regarding additional information needed for a formal proposal.
Evaluative Criteria: Potential for high impact on the health, growth and prosperity of the region; organizational capacity to render key services and programs in an increasingly complex environment; or research development, and experimental aspects to influence and improve the operation of individual organizations as well as clusters of related organizations.
Notes: The foundation requests that recipients make no public acknowledgement of grants from the foundation.

Restrictions
No grants are made to individuals. No pledges are made for more than one year. An applicant should have a realistic strategy for financing the project following foundation support. The foundation does not consider grants intended to support operations, special projects, or programs that rely on future support from the foundation.

Additional Information

Unsolicited proposals from outside the foundation's geographical focus area are rarely considered.

National City Bank serves as a corporate trustee for the foundation.

Publications: Annual Report; Guidelines

Foundation Officials

Henry S. Beukema: executive director

Michael M. Edwards: member distribution committee

Richard D. Edwards: member distribution committee

John R. McCune, VI: member distribution committee

Martha J. Perry: mng director

Grants Analysis

Disclosure Period: fiscal year ending September 30, 2002

Total Grants: $25,375,494*

Number of Grants: 189

Average Grant: $124,338*

Highest Grant: $2,000,000

Lowest Grant: $1,000

Typical Range: $10,000 to $250,000

*Note: Average grant figure excludes highest grants.

Recent Grants

Note: Grants derived from fiscal 2001 Form 990.

Library-Related

250,000   Carnegie Library, Pittsburgh, PA -- to improve building systems in the Homewood Branch

General

1,500,000   Westminster College, New Wilmington, PA -- to renovate and refurbish Thompson Hall

1,250,000   YMCA, Pittsburgh, PA -- capital campaign

1,000,000   University of Pittsburgh School of Medicine, Pittsburgh, PA -- to endow the McGowan Center for Artificial Organs

800,000   Manchester Youth Development Center, Manchester, CT -- for construction of new classroom building

750,000   United World College of the American West, Montezuma, NM -- to assist in the restoration of the Montezuma

500,000   Carnegie Mellon University, Pittsburgh, PA -- for development of new internet curricula

500,000   Chatham College, Pittsburgh, PA -- for institutional technology plan

500,000   Coordinated Care Network, Pittsburgh, PA -- to hire coordinators and begin marketing new products

500,000   Grove City College, Grove City, PA -- construction of new academic building

500,000   Phipps Conservatory, Inc., Pittsburgh, PA -- capital campaign

THE EUGENE MCDERMOTT FOUNDATION

Giving Contact

Mary McDermott Cook, President
3808 Euclid
Dallas, TX 75205
Phone: (214)521-2924

Alternate Contact

Patricia Brown, Assistant Secretary

Description

Founded: 1972

EIN: 237237919

Organization Type: General Purpose Foundation

Giving Locations: TX: Dallas

Grant Types: Award, Capital, Challenge, Endowment, General Support, Matching, Operating Expenses, Professorship, Project, Research, Scholarship.

Donor Information

Founder: Founded by Eugene McDermott (d. 1973), a geophysicist and a founder of Texas Instruments.

Financial Summary

Total Giving: $5,361,043 (fiscal year ending August 31, 2003 approx); $8,009,790 (fiscal 2002 approx); $8,991,902 (fiscal 2001 approx). Note: 1999 Giving includes United Way ($15,000). 1996 Giving includes scholarship ($521,000).

Giving Analysis: Giving for fiscal 1998 includes: foundation grants to United Way ($15,000) foundation scholarships ($255,000)

Assets: $110,362,338 (fiscal 2000); $110,836,016 (fiscal 1999); $81,145,348 (fiscal 1998)

Typical Recipients

Arts & Humanities: Arts Associations & Councils, Arts Centers, Arts Festivals, Arts Funds, Arts Institutes, Arts Outreach, Ballet, Dance, Ethnic & Folk Arts, Film & Video, Arts & Humanities-General, Historic Preservation, History & Archaeology, Libraries, Museums/Galleries, Music, Opera, Public Broadcasting, Theater, Visual Arts

Civic & Public Affairs: Asian American Affairs, Botanical Gardens/Parks, Chambers of Commerce, Economic Development, Civic & Public Affairs-General, Housing, Municipalities/Towns, Nonprofit Management, Parades/Festivals, Philanthropic Organizations, Professional & Trade Associations, Urban & Community Affairs, Women's Affairs, Zoos/Aquariums, Zoos/Aquariums

Education: Arts/Humanities Education, Business Education, Colleges & Universities, Community & Junior Colleges, Education Reform, Engineering/Technological Education, Education-General, Health & Physical Education, Literacy, Medical Education, Preschool Education, Private Education (Precollege), Public Education (Precollege), Religious Education, Secondary Education (Private), Student Aid

Environment: Environment-General, Research, Resource Conservation, Wildlife Protection

Health: AIDS/HIV, Cancer, Children's Health/Hospitals, Clinics/Medical Centers, Emergency/Ambulance Services, Hospitals, Hospitals (University Affiliated), Prenatal Health Issues, Preventive Medicine/Wellness Organizations, Public Health, Single-Disease Health Associations, Transplant Networks/Donor Banks

International: Foreign Arts Organizations, Health Care/Hospitals, International Organizations

Religion: Churches, Ministries, Religious Organizations, Religious Welfare

Science: Science Museums, Scientific Centers & Institutes

Social Services: Child Abuse, Child Welfare, Community Centers, Community Service Organizations, Counseling, Domestic Violence, Family Planning, Family Services, Food/Clothing Distribution, People with Disabilities, Recreation & Athletics, Scouts, Senior Services, Shelters/Homelessness, Substance Abuse, United Funds/United Ways, Volunteer Services, YMCA/YWCA/YMHA/YWHA, Youth Organizations

Application Procedures

Initial Contact: The foundation has no set application form or guidelines. Applicants should send a letter of inquiry and submit one copy of a proposal.

Application Requirements: The proposal should include a copy of the organization's 501(c)(3) letter.

Deadlines: None.

Review Process: The board of trustees meets quarterly.

Notes: The foundation will acknowledge letters of inquiry and provide applicants with an initial assessment of the likelihood of its consideration for a grant. The applicant will be notified approximately three months after the application is received.

Restrictions

Grants are not made to individuals.

Additional Information

NationsBank of Texas, N.A. serves as an agent to the foundation.

Foundation Officials

Patricia Brown: assistant secretary

Mary McDermott Cook: president

Charles Cullum: vice president, trustee B Dallas, TX August 26, 1916. ED Southern Methodist University BS (1936); Texas College LLD (1982). PRIM CORP EMPL chairman executive committee, director: Cullum Companies.

Margaret M. McDermott: trustee

Vincent Prothro: secretary, treasurer

C. J. Thomsen: trustee

Grants Analysis

Disclosure Period: fiscal year ending August 31, 2000

Total Grants: $4,973,725*

Number of Grants: 110

Average Grant: $24,534*

Highest Grant: $1,275,000

Lowest Grant: $1,000

Typical Range: $1,000 to $50,000 and $100,000 to $500,000

*Note: Giving excludes scholarships United Way. Average grant figure excludes two highest grants ($1,275,000 and $1,000,000).

Recent Grants

Note: Grants derived from 2001 Form 990.

Library-Related

400,000   Friends of the Dallas Public Library, Dallas, TX -- renovation of The J Erik Jonsson Library

General

1,275,000   Dallas Center for the Performing Arts, Dallas, TX -- capital campaign

1,000,000   Dallas Opera Guild, Dallas, TX -- endowment

500,000   Southern Methodist University, Dallas, TX -- for the Cullum Family Fund for Student Enrichment

200,000   Dallas County Community College District Foundation, Dallas, TX -- Rising Star Scholarship program

125,000   University of Texas at Dallas, Richardson, TX -- for the Eugene McDermott Library Enhancement

100,000   Dallas Black Dance Theater, Dallas, TX -- capital campaign

100,000   Dallas Theater Center, Dallas, TX -- for debt elimination and purchase new equipment

100,000   Trinity Works, Dallas, TX -- for programs benefiting the homeless

75,000   Connemara Conservancy Foundation, Dallas, TX -- endowment of executive directorship

75,000   North Texas Public Broadcasting, Inc., Dallas, TX -- for documentary

ARMSTRONG MCDONALD FOUNDATION

Giving Contact
Laurie L. Bouchard, President
PO Box 900
Cortaro, AZ 85652-0900
Phone: (602)949-0974

Description
Founded: 1987
EIN: 363458711
Organization Type: Private Foundation
Giving Locations: nationally.
Grant Types: Emergency, General Support, Research.

Financial Summary
Total Giving: $1,098,355 (2001); $1,250,000 (2000); $772,000 (1999)
Giving Analysis: Giving for 2001 includes: foundation grants to United Way ($35,000) 1999: foundation grants to United Way ($30,000)
Assets: $19,800,768 (2001); $23,073,889 (2000); $21,653,166 (1999)

Typical Recipients
Arts & Humanities: Ballet, Libraries, Museums/Galleries, Music, Public Broadcasting
Civic & Public Affairs: Botanical Gardens/Parks, Employment/Job Training, Civic & Public Affairs-General, Housing, Zoos/Aquariums
Education: Colleges & Universities, Education Associations, Education-General, Private Education (Precollege), Secondary Education (Private), Special Education, Student Aid
Environment: Protection
Health: Cancer, Children's Health/Hospitals, Clinics/Medical Centers, Emergency/Ambulance Services, Health-General, Health Organizations, Hospices, Hospitals, Long-Term Care, Medical Research, Prenatal Health Issues, Respiratory, Single-Disease Health Associations
Religion: Jewish Causes, Religious Organizations, Religious Welfare
Science: Observatories & Planetariums, Scientific Research
Social Services: Animal Protection, At-Risk Youth, Camps, Child Welfare, Community Service Organizations, Domestic Violence, Family Services, Food/Clothing Distribution, Homes, People with Disabilities, Senior Services, Substance Abuse, Youth Organizations

Application Procedures
Initial Contact: Send a brief letter of inquiry.
Application Requirements: Include purpose of funds sought, budget, time frame, future findings, and other sources of income.
Deadlines: April 15 and September 15.

Restrictions
Grants are not made to individuals.

Foundation Officials
Mike Bouchard: secretary, treasurer
Ryan Bouchard: vice president
Laurie Bourchard: vice president
James McDonald, IV: vice president
James M. McDonald, III: president
Katherine McDonald: secretary, treasurer

Grants Analysis
Disclosure Period: calendar year ending 2001
Total Grants: $1,063,355*
Number of Grants: 52
Average Grant: $18,526*
Highest Grant: $100,100
Lowest Grant: $2,500

Typical Range: $5,000 to $50,000
*Note: Giving excludes UNW. Average grant figure excludes highest grant.

Recent Grants
Note: Grants derived from 2001 Form 990.

General
100,000	National Jewish Research and Medical Center, Denver, CO
60,000	College of St. Mary, Omaha, NE
50,000	Hastings College Foundation, Hastings, NE
50,000	Radio Talking Book Services, Omaha, NE
30,000	Bellevue University Foundation, Bellevue, NE
30,000	San Diego Zoo Center for the Reproduction of Endangered Species, San Diego, CA
28,000	Easter Seals Arizona, AZ
25,000	Arizona's Children Foundation, Phoenix, AZ
25,000	Canine Companions
25,000	Esperanza, Phoenix, AZ

J. M. MCDONALD FOUNDATION

Giving Contact
Donald R. McJunkin, President
PO Box 3219
Evergreen, CO 80439
Phone: (303)674-9300
Fax: (303)674-9216

Description
Founded: 1952
EIN: 471431059
Organization Type: Family Foundation
Giving Locations: Northeast USA; primarily upstate NY.
Grant Types: Capital, General Support, Operating Expenses, Project.

Donor Information
Founder: James M. McDonald Sr. , founder of the J. M. McDonald Company, a department store chain, incorporated the foundation in 1952. The foundation received several gifts from Mr. McDonald during his lifetime and a bequest from his estate at the time of his death in 1956. Mr. McDonald's home was in Cortland, NY, where several of the foundation's recipients are located.

Financial Summary
Total Giving: $1,300,300 (2001); $1,110,000 (2000); $850,000 (1999)
Assets: $24,378,215 (2001); $26,952,284 (2000); $23,778,976 (1999)

Typical Recipients
Arts & Humanities: Ethnic & Folk Arts, Arts & Humanities-General, Libraries, Museums/Galleries, Opera, Public Broadcasting, Theater
Civic & Public Affairs: Community Foundations, Civic & Public Affairs-General, Women's Affairs, Zoos/Aquariums
Education: Afterschool/Enrichment Programs, Arts/Humanities Education, Business Education, Colleges & Universities, Education-General, Leadership Training, Literacy, Medical Education, Private Education (Precollege), Public Education (Precollege), Science/Mathematics Education, Special Education, Student Aid, Vocational & Technical Education
Environment: Air/Water Quality, Environment-General, Resource Conservation
Health: Cancer, Children's Health/Hospitals, Clinics/Medical Centers, Emergency/Ambulance Services,

Geriatric Health, Health Organizations, Heart, Hospices, Hospitals, Medical Rehabilitation, Medical Research, Mental Health, Outpatient Health Care, Public Health, Research/Studies Institutes, Single-Disease Health Associations, Speech & Hearing
International: International Affairs
Religion: Churches, Ministries, Religious Organizations, Religious Welfare
Science: Scientific Centers & Institutes, Scientific Research
Social Services: At-Risk Youth, Camps, Child Abuse, Child Welfare, Community Centers, Community Service Organizations, Delinquency & Criminal Rehabilitation, Domestic Violence, Emergency Relief, Family Planning, Family Services, Food/Clothing Distribution, Homes, People with Disabilities, Recreation & Athletics, Scouts, Scouts, Senior Services, Shelters/Homelessness, Social Services-General, Substance Abuse, United Funds/United Ways, YMCA/YWCA/YMHA/YWHA, Youth Organizations

Application Procedures
Initial Contact: Prospective applicants should send a letter to the foundation.
Application Requirements: The letter should include purpose of funds sought, budget, time frame, future funding and sources of income, and IRS Form 509A.
Deadlines: April 15 and September 15.
Review Process: Applicants may call the foundation to check on their status.

Restrictions
No grants are made to individuals or to organizations outside the United States. No grants can be made to projects that influence legislation or elections. No grants are awarded for conferences, seminars, workshops, travel or exhibits.

Additional Information
Grant payments are made only during October and May.
Publications: Guidelines

Foundation Officials
Donald C. Berry, Jr.: treasurer, trustee
Donald R. McJunkin: president, trustee
Eleanor F. McJunkin: vice president, trustee
Reed L. McJunkin: secretary, trustee

Grants Analysis
Disclosure Period: calendar year ending 2001
Total Grants: $1,300,300
Number of Grants: 44
Average Grant: $29,552
Highest Grant: $130,000
Lowest Grant: $300
Typical Range: $10,000 to $50,000

Recent Grants
Note: Grants derived from 2001 Form 990.

Library-Related
25,000	Ulysses Philmathic Library, Trumansburg, NY
15,000	Tompkins County Public Library, Ithaca, NY

General
130,000	Cortland Memorial Hospital, Cortland, NY
100,000	American Red Cross Disaster Relief Fund
100,000	Keuka College, Keuka Park, NY
100,000	Northwood School, Lake Placid, NY
100,000	September 11th Fund, New York, NY
50,000	Paul Smith's College, Paul Smiths, NY
50,000	St. Lawrence University, Canton, NY
50,000	Sciencenter, Ithaca, NY
50,000	Wells College, Aurora, NY
50,000	YWCA, Cortland, NY

A.Y. McDonald Manufacturing Co.

Company Headquarters

PO Box 508
Dubuque, IA 52004
Web: http://www.aymcdonald.com

Company Description

Founded: 1856
Revenue: US$28 million (2001)
Employees: 350 (2001)
SIC(s): 3432 Plumbing Fixtures Fittings & Trim, 3494 Valves & Pipe Fittings Nec, 3561 Pumps & Pumping Equipment, 5074 Plumbing & Hydronic Heating Supplies.

A.Y. McDonald Manufacturing Co. Charitable Foundation

Giving Contact

A. J. Wilherding, Chairman & Chief Executive Officer
PO Box 508
Dubuque, IA 52004-0508
Phone: (563)583-7311

Description

EIN: 426119514
Organization Type: Corporate Foundation
Giving Locations: IA: Dubuque and Eastern IA
Grant Types: General Support.

Financial Summary

Total Giving: $193,361 (2001); $152,785 (2000); $155,648 (1999)
Giving Analysis: Giving for 1999 includes: foundation scholarships ($1,500); foundation grants to United Way ($22,700); foundation ($131,448); 1998: foundation grants to United Way ($21,822) foundation ($82,650).
Assets: $2,613,315 (2001); $2,914,465 (2000); $2,538,392 (1999)
Gifts Received: $50,000 (2001); $50,000 (2000); $25,000 (1999). Note: In 1994, 2000, and 2001, contributions were received from A.Y. McDonald Industries.

Typical Recipients

Arts & Humanities: Arts Associations & Councils, Community Arts, Historic Preservation, History & Archaeology, Libraries, Museums/Galleries, Music, Opera, Performing Arts, Theater, Visual Arts
Civic & Public Affairs: Business/Free Enterprise, Chambers of Commerce, Employment/Job Training, Civic & Public Affairs-General, Municipalities/Towns, Urban & Community Affairs
Education: Business Education, Colleges & Universities, Community & Junior Colleges, Education-General, Leadership Training, Science/Mathematics Education, Secondary Education (Public), Student Aid
Environment: Resource Conservation
Health: Cancer, Clinics/Medical Centers, Emergency/Ambulance Services, Health Organizations, Hospices, Medical Research, Multiple Sclerosis, Nursing Services, Public Health
Religion: Seminaries
Social Services: Animal Protection, Camps, Community Service Organizations, Family Services, People with Disabilities, Recreation & Athletics, Scouts, United Funds/United Ways, YMCA/YWCA/YMHA/YWHA, Youth Organizations

Application Procedures

Initial Contact: Send brief letter describing program.
Application Requirements: Include amount requested and purpose of funds sought.
Deadlines: None.

Corporate Officials

John M. McDonald, III: chairman, president, director PRIM CORP EMPL chairman, president, director: A.Y. McDonald Manufacturing Co.
Mike McDonald: chief financial officer PRIM CORP EMPL chief financial officer: A.Y. McDonald Manufacturing Co.
Robert Delos McDonald: chairman, chief executive officer B Dubuque, IA 1931. ED University of Iowa (1953). PRIM CORP EMPL chairman, chief executive officer: A.Y. McDonald Manufacturing Co. CORP AFFIL chairman, president: A Y M; director: Dubuque Bank & Trust Co.; director: AY McDonald Supply Co.; director: Brock McVey Co.; chief executive officer: AY McDonald Industries. NONPR AFFIL director: Stonehill Care Center; trustee: United Way Dubuque; member: Sigma Alpha Epsilon; member: National Association of Manufacturers; director: Save IAS Civil War Monument Restoration Fund; director: Dubuque Boys Club; director: Dubuque County Historical Society; member: American Supply Association; member: American Water Works Association; member: American Management Association. CLUB AFFIL Dubuque Shooting Society; American Legion Club; Dubuque Golf & Country Club.
LeRoy J. Sherman: president, chief operating officer PRIM CORP EMPL president, chief operating officer: A.Y. McDonald Manufacturing Co.

Foundation Officials

William A. Knapp: vice president
John M. McDonald, III: vice president (see above)
M. B. McDonald: secretary
Robert Delos McDonald: president (see above)
LeRoy J. Sherman: vice president (see above)

Grants Analysis

Disclosure Period: calendar year ending 2001
Total Grants: $193,361
Number of Grants: 44
Average Grant: $4,395
Highest Grant: $24,550
Lowest Grant: $100
Typical Range: $1,000 to $10,000

Recent Grants

Note: Grants derived from 2000 Form 990.

General

23,610	United Way Services
20,000	Mississippi River Discovery Center, MS
15,000	Clarke College, Dubuque, IA
15,000	University of Dubuque, Dubuque, IA
10,500	Finley Health Foundation, Dubuque, IA
10,000	Loras College, Dubuque, IA
8,000	Grand Opera House, Oshkosh, WI
6,000	YMCA/YWCA, Burlington, IA
5,000	Dubuque Museum of Art, Dubuque, IA
4,500	Dubuque Symphony Orchestra, Dubuque, IA

Bernard McDonough Foundation

Giving Contact

James T. Wakley, President & Director
311 Fourth Street
Parkersburg, WV 26101
Phone: (304)424-6280
Fax: (304)424-6281
E-mail: jwakley@marmac.net

Description

Founded: 1961
EIN: 556023693
Organization Type: Private Foundation
Giving Locations: WV
Grant Types: Capital, Emergency, General Support, Multiyear/Continuing Support, Operating Expenses, Project.

Donor Information

Founder: Established in 1961 by the late Bernard P. McDonough .

Financial Summary

Total Giving: $1,456,643 (2001); $2,099,888 (2000); $2,061,000 (1999 approx)
Giving Analysis: Giving for 2000 includes: foundation scholarships ($17,150); foundation matching gifts ($21,650); foundation grants to United Way ($71,800); 1997: foundation matching gifts ($6,750); foundation scholarships ($10,000) foundation grants to United Way ($50,450)
Assets: $35,788,904 (2001); $38,617,461 (2000); $40,700,000 (1999 approx)

Typical Recipients

Arts & Humanities: Arts Associations & Councils, Arts Centers, History & Archaeology, Libraries, Museums/Galleries, Music, Theater
Civic & Public Affairs: Business/Free Enterprise, Chambers of Commerce, Community Foundations, Civic & Public Affairs-General, Hispanic Affairs, Housing, Minority Business, Municipalities/Towns, Zoos/Aquariums
Education: Agricultural Education, Colleges & Universities, Education Funds, Education-General, Legal Education, Medical Education, Minority Education, Preschool Education, Private Education (Precollege), Public Education (Precollege), Secondary Education (Public), Student Aid
Environment: Environment-General, Protection, Resource Conservation, Wildlife Protection
Health: Alzheimers Disease, Cancer, Cancer, Children's Health/Hospitals, Clinics/Medical Centers, Emergency/Ambulance Services, Health-General, Health Organizations, Heart, Hospices, Hospitals, Hospitals (University Affiliated), Mental Health, Multiple Sclerosis, Research/Studies Institutes
International: Foreign Educational Institutions, Health Care/Hospitals
Religion: Dioceses, Religious Welfare
Science: Science Museums
Social Services: At-Risk Youth, Child Welfare, Community Centers, Community Service Organizations, Day Care, Emergency Relief, Family Services, Food/Clothing Distribution, Homes, People with Disabilities, Recreation & Athletics, Scouts, Senior Services, Shelters/Homelessness, Social Services-General, Special Olympics, Special Olympics, United Funds/United Ways, Volunteer Services, YMCA/YWCA/YMHA/YWHA, Youth Organizations

Application Procedures

Initial Contact: Send a brief letter describing the program.
Deadlines: None.

Restrictions

The foundation does not support religious activities or individuals.

Foundation Officials

Robert E. Evans: director B 1935. PRIM CORP EMPL vice chairman: TCF Financial Corp.
Dale Knight: director
Mark C. Kury: executive vice president, director
Francis C. McCusker: director B Pittsburgh, PA 1937. ED Gannon University (1961). PRIM CORP EMPL senior vice president, chief financial officer: McDonough Corp.
George Partridge, Jr.: director

Mary Riccobene: vice president, director
Katrina Valentine: secretary
James T. Wakley: president, director B Springfield, OH 1921. NONPR AFFIL trustee: Ohio Valley Improvement Association; trustee: West Virginia Foundation Indiana Colleges; trustee: Marietta College; member: National Sand & Gravel Association.
T. J. Wilson: director

Grants Analysis

Disclosure Period: calendar year ending 2001
Total Grants: $1,383,243*
Number of Grants: 168
Average Grant: $8,234
Highest Grant: $154,460
Lowest Grant: $50
Typical Range: $5,000 to $20,000
*Note: Giving excludes United Way.

Recent Grants

Note: Grants derived from 2001 Form 990.

General

154,460	Ohio Valley College, Parkersburg, WV
69,036	Salvation Army, Parkersburg, WV -- Opportunity House
62,000	United Way of the Mid-Ohio Valley, Parkersburg, WV
54,000	Smoot Theater, Parkersburg, WV
45,000	West Virginia Independent Colleges and Universities, Charleston, WV
40,000	Marietta College, Marietta, OH
40,000	Mayo Foundation, Rochester, MN
30,000	American Red Cross, Parkersburg, WV
28,500	Boys and Girls Club
26,242	McDonough Wildlife Park, Vienna, WV

RUTH CAMP MCDOUGALL CHARITABLE TRUST

Giving Contact

Donald E. Koonce, First Vice President & Trust Officer
c/o Bank of America
PO Box 26903
Richmond, VA 23261
Phone: (804)788-2573

Description

Founded: 1976
EIN: 546162697
Organization Type: Private Foundation
Giving Locations: VA
Grant Types: General Support.

Donor Information

Founder: the late Ruth Camp McDougall

Financial Summary

Total Giving: $746,800 (2001); $930,325 (2000); $895,765 (1999)
Giving Analysis: Giving for 2001 includes: foundation scholarships ($95,500); 2000: foundation scholarships ($91,100); 1999: foundation grants to United Way ($3,500); foundation scholarships ($67,500)
Assets: $12,338,255 (2001); $15,470,831 (2000); $17,455,919 (1999)
Gifts Received: $17,000 (2000); $1,000 (1998); $3,953 (1996). Note: In fiscal 1992, contributions were received from the Ruth Camp McDougall Charitable Trust.

Typical Recipients

Arts & Humanities: Arts Associations & Councils, Arts Centers, Arts Funds, Ethnic & Folk Arts, Arts & Humanities-General, Historic Preservation, History & Archaeology, Libraries, Museums/Galleries, Opera, Performing Arts, Theater

Civic & Public Affairs: Botanical Gardens/Parks, Business/Free Enterprise, Community Foundations, Civic & Public Affairs-General, Housing, Municipalities/Towns, Parades/Festivals, Philanthropic Organizations, Public Policy, Safety, Urban & Community Affairs
Education: Agricultural Education, Business Education, Colleges & Universities, Community & Junior Colleges, Education Funds, Faculty Development, Education-General, Gifted & Talented Programs, Medical Education, Private Education (Precollege), Public Education (Precollege), Science/Mathematics Education, Student Aid
Environment: Resource Conservation, Wildlife Protection
Health: Cancer, Children's Health/Hospitals, Emergency/Ambulance Services, Heart, Hospices, Hospitals, Nursing Services
International: International Development
Religion: Churches, Dioceses, Missionary Activities (Domestic), Religious Welfare, Seminaries
Science: Science Museums, Scientific Centers & Institutes
Social Services: Child Welfare, Community Service Organizations, Family Services, Homes, Recreation & Athletics, Scouts, Volunteer Services, YMCA/YWCA/YMHA/YWHA, Youth Organizations

Application Procedures

Initial Contact: The foundation requests applications be made in writing.
Deadlines: None.

Restrictions

The majority of funds are limited to charitable organizations in Virginia.

Additional Information

Trust(s): Bank of America

Foundation Officials

John M. Camp, Jr.: director
Paul D. Camp, III: director
Paul Camp Marks: director
Harry Webster Walker, II: director B Bridgeport, CT 1921. PRIM CORP EMPL president, chief executive officer, director: Sunsweet Fruit Inc. CORP AFFIL president: Indian River Elite Citrus Inc.; director: Walker Group Inc.; director: Carpenter Technology Corp. NONPR AFFIL director: Vero Beach YMCA; devel board: Yale University; member: United States Yacht Racing Union; chairman: Piedmont College; member: Rotary Club; chairman: Olympic International Star Class Yacht Racing Association; director: Blue Ridge Assemblies, Inc.; member: National Boating Safety; member: Association Yale University Alumni.

Grants Analysis

Disclosure Period: calendar year ending 2001
Total Grants: $651,300*
Number of Grants: 69
Average Grant: $6,475*
Highest Grant: $211,000
Lowest Grant: $1,000
Typical Range: $1,000 to $10,000
*Note: Giving excludes scholarship. Average grant figure excludes highest grant.

Recent Grants

Note: Grants derived from 2000 Form 990.

Library-Related

12,000	Ruth Camp Campbell Memorial Library, Franklin, VA

General

121,500	Southampton Academy, Courtland, VA
61,700	Southampton County, Virginia County Administration, Courtland, VA
50,000	Paul D. Camp Community College, Franklin, VA

37,000	Virginia Foundation for Independent Colleges, Lynchburg, VA
35,000	Rawls Museum of Arts, Courtland, VA
30,000	St. John's Museum of Art, Wilmington, NC
27,500	Southampton County Historical Society, Newsoms, VA
24,500	Southeast 4-H Educational Center, Wakefield, VA
21,500	Virginia Beach Foundation, Virginia Beach, VA
21,000	College of William and Mary, Williamsburg, VA -- scholarships

R. J. MCELROY TRUST

Giving Contact

Linda L. Klinger, Executive Director
500 KWWL Building
Suite 318
Waterloo, IA 50703
Phone: (319)287-9102
Fax: (319)287-9105
E-mail: mcelroy@cedarnet.org
Web: http://www.cedarnet.org/mcelroy

Description

Founded: 1965
EIN: 426173496
Organization Type: General Purpose Foundation
Giving Locations: IA: Black Hawk County and rural counties in the Waterloo area, Waterloo
Grant Types: Capital, Challenge, Endowment, Fellowship, General Support, Project, Scholarship, Seed Money.

Donor Information

Founder: The trust was founded in 1965 with funds from the estate of Ralph J. McElroy , the owner of Black Hawk Broadcasting. McElroy's company included television and radio stations throughout Iowa and southern Minnesota.

McElroy started his career at the age of thirteen, when he left home, took off on a freight train, and worked the wheat fields. In 1935, McElroy became a salesman and air personality for WMT in Waterloo, IA. Twelve years later, he founded the Black Hawk Broadcasting Company.

McElroy died in 1965 and his will established a trust fund, the proceeds of which are to be used for the educational benefit of deserving youth. "It is ironic that McElroy's own accomplishments were achieved without the benefit of higher education, and he had no natural children of his own. Yet his strong commitment to youth and education has extended far beyond his lifetime to the enormous benefit of many, many young people."

Financial Summary

Total Giving: $2,599,964 (2001); $2,684,099 (2000); $2,719,383 (1999)
Giving Analysis: Giving for 2000 includes: foundation gifts to individuals ($26,000); foundation fellowships ($44,057); foundation scholarships ($243,668); 1999: foundation grants to United Way ($6,300); foundation gifts to individuals ($20,000); foundation fellowships ($46,264); foundation scholarships ($244,830); 1998: foundation fellowships ($36,707); foundation scholarships ($469,636);
Assets: $46,886,215 (2001); $49,906,049 (2000); $50,633,387 (1999)
Gifts Received: $26,099 (1998); $60,000 (1996). Note: In 1998, contributions were received from the estate of T.H. Williams. In 1996, gifts were given by T.H. Williams Family Trust.

Typical Recipients

Arts & Humanities: Arts Associations & Councils, Arts Centers, Arts Outreach, Historic Preservation, Libraries, Museums/Galleries, Music, Performing Arts, Public Broadcasting, Theater

Civic & Public Affairs: Botanical Gardens/Parks, Chambers of Commerce, Community Foundations, Employment/Job Training, Civic & Public Affairs-General, Municipalities/Towns, Philanthropic Organizations, Rural Affairs, Urban & Community Affairs, Women's Affairs

Education: Afterschool/Enrichment Programs, Arts/Humanities Education, Business Education, Colleges & Universities, Community & Junior Colleges, Economic Education, Education Funds, Elementary Education (Private), Faculty Development, Education-General, Gifted & Talented Programs, Health & Physical Education, International Exchange, Journalism/Media Education, Leadership Training, Literacy, Medical Education, Minority Education, Preschool Education, Private Education (Precollege), Public Education (Precollege), School Volunteerism, Science/Mathematics Education, Secondary Education (Public), Student Aid

Environment: Environment-General, Resource Conservation, Wildlife Protection

Health: AIDS/HIV, Children's Health/Hospitals, Clinics/Medical Centers, Hospices, Hospitals, Medical Training, Prenatal Health Issues, Research/Studies Institutes

Religion: Ministries, Religious Welfare

Science: Science Museums

Social Services: Big Brother/Big Sister, Child Welfare, Community Service Organizations, Crime Prevention, Day Care, Domestic Violence, Family Planning, Family Services, Food/Clothing Distribution, People with Disabilities, Recreation & Athletics, Scouts, Substance Abuse, Volunteer Services, YMCA/YWCA/YMHA/YWHA, Youth Organizations

Application Procedures

Initial Contact: Applicants should send a proposal to the trust.

Application Requirements: Proposals should contain general information including the following: name of organization and project, address, names and qualifications of persons who will administer the grant, contact person including title and phone number, a copy of 501(c)(3) determination letter, and the articles of incorporation. Background information should include a statement of purpose and a description of organization of the organization and its activities. A project description should explain community need and benefits to be derived by the community, long-term goals of the project, specific short-term measurable objectives, specific activities planned, number of young people to be served and from what age group, timetable for the project, and project evaluation plan. Financial information should include a copy of the organization's most recently audited financial statement, a copy of project budget including: payroll (hourly rate), payroll taxes and fringes, materials and supplies, taxes, rent, transportation, utilities, and miscellaneous; amount requested from McElroy Trust and desired timing of grant payment; amount requested from all other funding sources; and plans for ongoing funding.

Deadlines: Applications should be received on or before March 1, June 1, September 1, and December 1.

Review Process: Requests for funds are voted upon by the board; the trust will send written notice of the trustees' decision. Decisions are made by the first of May, August, November and February.

Restrictions

The trust does not make grants to individuals.

Additional Information

Publications: Application Guidelines

Foundation Officials

Raleigh D. Buckmaster: trustee

Ross D. Christensen: trustee B 1940. ED University of Iowa. PRIM CORP EMPL vice president, director: Heartland Midwest Management OCCUPATION orthodontist. CORP AFFIL partner: Jo Ro General Partnership; director: MidAmerican Energy Holdings Co.

Linda L. Klinger: executive director

James B. Waterbury: trustee, chairman B Waterloo, IA 1947. ED Princeton University (1969). PRIM CORP EMPL general manager: KWWL TV.

Richard C. Young: trustee B 1948. ED University of Colorado (1970). PRIM CORP EMPL president: Young Plumbing & Heating. CORP AFFIL principal: Park Avenue Plumbing & Heating; principal: Young Development.

Grants Analysis

Disclosure Period: calendar year ending 2001
Total Grants: $2,323,464*
Number of Grants: 138
Average Grant: $16,837
Highest Grant: $200,000
Typical Range: $10,000 to $40,000
*Note: Giving excludes scholarships; fellowships; gifts to individuals; and United Way.

Recent Grants

Note: Grants derived from 2001 Form 990.

Library-Related

25,000	Allison Public Library, Allison, IA -- new library and community room
15,000	Anamosa Public Library, Anamosa, IA -- Anamosa Library and Learning Center

General

200,000	University of Northern Iowa, Cedar Falls, IA -- Early Childhood Education Program
186,000	Northeast Iowa Area High Schools, IA -- scholarships
134,000	America's Agricultural/Industrial Heritage Landscape, Waterloo, IA -- Pilot Strategic Investment Area
100,000	Bremwood Lutheran Children's Home, Waverly, IA -- Alternative Education Center
100,000	Community Foundation of Waterloo, Waterloo, IA -- Museum of Art
70,000	Greater Denver Activities Board, Denver, IA -- Denver Library, community center and athletic fields
60,000	Greater Oelwein Area Chamber of Commerce, Oelwein, IA -- Greater Oelwein Area Performance and Wellness Center
53,500	Hawkeye Community College, Waterloo, IA -- African-American Scholarships
51,000	Luther College, Decorah, IA -- environmental college for young leaders in middle schools
50,000	Allen College of Nursing, Waterloo, IA -- RJ McElroy Professorship

MILDRED H. MCEVOY FOUNDATION

Giving Contact

Sumner B. Tilton, Jr., Trustee
370 Main Street
12th Floor
Worcester, MA 01608
Phone: (508)798-8621
Fax: (508)791-1201

Description

Founded: 1963
EIN: 046069958
Organization Type: General Purpose Foundation

Giving Locations: ME: Boothbay Harbor
Grant Types: Capital, General Support.

Donor Information

Founder: Established in 1963 by the late Mildred H. McEvoy .

Financial Summary

Total Giving: $1,480,663 (2001); $1,456,500 (2000); $1,000,000 (1999 approx)
Giving Analysis: Giving for 2000 includes: foundation scholarships ($45,500); foundation matching gifts ($49,500); 1997: foundation matching gifts ($14,328) foundation scholarships ($32,000)
Assets: $25,715,494 (2001); $30,473,911 (2000); $25,000,000 (1999 approx)

Typical Recipients

Arts & Humanities: Arts Appreciation, Arts Associations & Councils, Ethnic & Folk Arts, Film & Video, Historic Preservation, History & Archaeology, Libraries, Museums/Galleries, Music, Performing Arts, Public Broadcasting

Civic & Public Affairs: Botanical Gardens/Parks, Clubs, Community Foundations, Economic Development, Employment/Job Training, Civic & Public Affairs-General, Housing, Municipalities/Towns, Rural Affairs, Safety, Urban & Community Affairs

Education: Arts/Humanities Education, Colleges & Universities, Community & Junior Colleges, Education Reform, Engineering/Technological Education, Education-General, Medical Education, Private Education (Precollege), Public Education (Precollege), Science/Mathematics Education, Secondary Education (Private), Secondary Education (Public), Student Aid

Environment: Environment-General

Health: Cancer, Children's Health/Hospitals, Clinics/Medical Centers, Emergency/Ambulance Services, Hospitals, Hospitals (University Affiliated), Long-Term Care, Medical Research, Nursing Services, Public Health, Single-Disease Health Associations

International: Foreign Arts Organizations, International Environmental Issues

Religion: Bible Study/Translation, Churches, Jewish Causes, Missionary Activities (Domestic), Religious Organizations, Religious Welfare

Science: Science Museums, Scientific Centers & Institutes, Scientific Research

Social Services: Big Brother/Big Sister, Camps, Child Welfare, Community Centers, Community Service Organizations, Day Care, Emergency Relief, Family Planning, Family Services, Senior Services, Social Services-General, Substance Abuse, United Funds/United Ways, YMCA/YWCA/YMHA/YWHA, Youth Organizations

Application Procedures

Initial Contact: Submit a proposal in letter form.

Application Requirements: Proposals should include the goals and objectives of the request. It should include the project plan and budget and a copy of the organization's federal determination letter.

Deadlines: Requests should be received prior to June 1.

Review Process: The trustees meet twice a year, once in late summer to review requests received to date and to make tentative allocation of the funds, and again in December to review requests and confirm or reject tentative grants made at their summer meeting. If a request gains tentative approval it will be moved to the December agenda for further action at that time.

Restrictions

The foundation does not make grants for general operating expenses or for individual scholarship assistance. Grantees must qualify for federal cumulative listing. Grants made in the Boothbay area only.

Additional Information

The latest annual report is available for inspection at the offices of Fletcher, Tilton & Whipple, P.C., 370 Main Street, Worchester, MA.

Foundation Officials

George H. McEvoy: trustee
Paul Robert Rossley: trustee B Worcester, MA 1938. ED Clark University BSBA (1960). PRIM CORP EMPL State Mutual Life Assurance Co. America. CORP AF-FIL trustee: Leicester Savings Bank.
Sumner B. Tilton, Jr.: trustee PRIM CORP EMPL clerk: New England Newspaper Supply Co. CORP AFFIL clerk: Whitinsville Water Co.; clerk: Whiteater Inc.; clerk: NDI Inc.; clerk: R H White Co. Inc.; officer: Fletcher, Tilton & Whipple PC. NONPR AFFIL president: Greater Worcester Community Foundation.

Grants Analysis

Disclosure Period: calendar year ending 2001
Total Grants: $1,430,663*
Number of Grants: 52
Average Grant: $27,513
Highest Grant: $220,000
Typical Range: $10,000 to $50,000
*Note: Giving excludes matching gifts.

Recent Grants

Note: Grants derived from 2001 Form 990.

General

220,000	Boothbay Railway Village Museum, Boothbay, ME -- operations
170,000	Grand Banks Schooner Museum Trust, Boothbay, ME -- operations
100,000	Worcester Academy, Worcester, MA -- further the goals and mission of the Academy
85,000	Grand Banks Schooner Museum Trust, Boothbay, ME -- repairs
80,000	Worcester Art Museum, Worcester, MA -- support centennial campaign
60,000	Ecotarium North East Science Center, Worcester, MA -- capital campaign
60,000	Maine Maritime Museum, Bath, ME -- capital campaign
50,000	Clark University, Worcester, MA -- Traina Center for the Arts
50,000	Maine Maritime Museum, Bath, ME -- challenge grant
50,000	Maine Public Broadcasting, Lewiston, ME -- capital campaign

H. RICHARD MCFARLAND CHARITABLE TRUST

Giving Contact

Gail S. McLain, Trust Officer
c/o Fountain Trust Co.
PO Box 8
Covington, IN 47932
Phone: (765)793-2237

Description

Founded: 1989
EIN: 356479692
Organization Type: Private Foundation
Grant Types: Capital, General Support, Scholarship.

Financial Summary

Total Giving: $70,000 (2001); $70,000 (2000); $70,000 (1999)
Giving Analysis: Giving for 2001 includes: foundation scholarships ($70,000) 1998: foundation scholarships ($150,000)
Assets: $1,285,375 (2001); $1,348,116 (2000); $1,405,991 (1999)

Typical Recipients

Arts & Humanities: Libraries
Education: Colleges & Universities, Student Aid
Religion: Churches, Seminaries

Application Procedures

Initial Contact: Request application form.
Deadlines: None.

Additional Information

Provides scholarships for students primarily attending colleges and universities in Indiana and Illinois.
Trust(s): Fountain Trust Co.

Foundation Officials

H. Richard McFarland: trustee
Sarah F. McFarland: trustee

Grants Analysis

Disclosure Period: calendar year ending 2001
Total Grants: $70,000*
Number of Grants: 1
*Note: Giving includes scholarships.

Recent Grants

Note: Grants derived from 2001 Form 990.

General

70,000	University of Illinois, Bloomington, IL

L. SISLER MCFAWN-THE SISLER MCFAWN FOUNDATION

Giving Contact

Charlotte M. Stanley-Jowers, Grants Manager
PO Box 149
Richfield, OH 44286-0149
Phone: (216)828-9770

Description

Founded: 1956
EIN: 346508111
Organization Type: Private Foundation
Giving Locations: OH: Summit County, Akron
Grant Types: Capital, Endowment, General Support, Operating Expenses, Project.

Donor Information

Founder: Lois Sisler McFawn

Financial Summary

Total Giving: $1,020,904 (2001); $1,445,619 (2000); $1,084,187 (1999)
Giving Analysis: Giving for 2001 includes: foundation grants to United Way ($150,000); 2000: foundation grants to United Way ($150,000) 1999: foundation grants to United Way ($105,000)
Assets: $20,345,715 (2001); $22,441,814 (2000); $22,829,428 (1999)

Typical Recipients

Arts & Humanities: Arts Associations & Councils, Arts Outreach, Ballet, Community Arts, Dance, Arts & Humanities-General, Historic Preservation, History & Archaeology, Libraries, Museums/Galleries, Music, Performing Arts, Public Broadcasting, Theater
Civic & Public Affairs: Business/Free Enterprise, Clubs, Economic Development, Employment/Job Training, Civic & Public Affairs-General, Housing, Nonprofit Management, Parades/Festivals, Professional & Trade Associations, Urban & Community Affairs, Women's Affairs, Zoos/Aquariums
Education: Business Education, Colleges & Universities, Education Funds, Environmental Education,

Education-General, Literacy, Private Education (Pre-college), Science/Mathematics Education, Secondary Education (Private), Special Education, Student Aid
Health: AIDS/HIV, Arthritis, Cancer, Children's Health/Hospitals, Clinics/Medical Centers, Emergency/Ambulance Services, Eyes/Blindness, Hospices, Hospitals, Medical Research, Mental Health, Nursing Services, Prenatal Health Issues, Public Health
International: International Development
Religion: Ministries
Science: Science Museums, Scientific Centers & Institutes
Social Services: Big Brother/Big Sister, Camps, Child Welfare, Community Centers, Community Service Organizations, Counseling, Domestic Violence, Family Planning, Family Services, Food/Clothing Distribution, People with Disabilities, Refugee Assistance, Scouts, Scouts, Senior Services, Shelters/Homelessness, United Funds/United Ways, Volunteer Services, YMCA/YWCA/YMHA/YWHA, Youth Organizations

Application Procedures

Initial Contact: Send a brief letter of inquiry and one copy of an unbound 199 on agency letterhead (4-6 numbered pages) including Executive summary or a proposal letter (4-6 pages) including an Executive summary as an advertising.
Application Requirements: Include a description of organization, history, missions, operating expenses, sources of income, budget, and IRS determinations letter.
Deadlines: March 15; July 15; and October 15.

Restrictions

Does not support individuals, church, general units of government, private foundations, annual campaigns, special events, or provide loans.

Additional Information

The foundation has no formal grant application form.
Publications: Application Guidelines
Trust(s): KeyBank National Association

Grants Analysis

Disclosure Period: calendar year ending 2001
Total Grants: $870,904*
Number of Grants: 80
Average Grant: $10,886
Highest Grant: $100,000
Typical Range: $5,000 to $25,000
*Note: Giving excludes United Way.

Recent Grants

Note: Grants derived from 2001 Form 990.

General

100,000	Akron Art Museum, Akron, OH -- capital campaign for new museum
75,000	Musical Arts Association, Cleveland, OH -- capital campaign
75,000	United Way of Summit County, Akron, OH -- annual campaign
75,000	United Way of Summit County, Akron, OH -- leadership challenge grant
75,000	University of Akron, Akron, OH -- music and dance
65,000	Ohio Foundation of Independent Colleges, Columbus, OH -- Scholarship Program
25,000	Walsh Jesuit High School, Cleveland, OH -- capital campaign
21,000	Ohio Federation of Independent Colleges, Columbus, OH
15,000	Ashland University, Ashland, OH -- capital campaign
15,000	Battered Women's Shelter, Akron, OH -- operating

MCFEELY-ROGERS FOUNDATION

Giving Contact

James R. Okonak, Executive Director, Secretary & Trustee
PO Box 110
Latrobe, PA 15650-0110
Phone: (724)537-5588

Description

Founded: 1953
EIN: 251120947
Organization Type: Private Foundation
Giving Locations: PA: Latrobe including surrounding area, Pittsburgh metropolitan area
Grant Types: Capital, Emergency, Endowment, General Support, Multiyear/Continuing Support, Operating Expenses, Scholarship.

Donor Information

Founder: the late James H. Rogers, the late Nancy K. McFeely, the late Nancy M. Rogers

Financial Summary

Total Giving: $894,245 (2001); $1,260,210 (2000); $949,085 (1999)
Giving Analysis: Giving for 2001 includes: foundation grants to United Way ($4,900); 2000: foundation grants to United Way ($3,900); 1999: foundation grants to United Way ($3,700) foundation scholarships ($133,000)
Assets: $20,910,497 (2001); $23,683,228 (2000); $26,616,255 (1999)

Typical Recipients

Arts & Humanities: Arts Funds, Ballet, Libraries, Museums/Galleries, Music, Theater
Civic & Public Affairs: African American Affairs, Chambers of Commerce, Civic & Public Affairs-General, Municipalities/Towns, Nonprofit Management, Philanthropic Organizations, Professional & Trade Associations, Urban & Community Affairs, Women's Affairs, Zoos/Aquariums
Education: Arts/Humanities Education, Colleges & Universities, Education Funds, Education-General, Literacy, Minority Education, Private Education (Precollege), Public Education (Precollege), Science/Mathematics Education, Student Aid
Environment: Environment-General, Resource Conservation, Watershed
Health: Cancer, Children's Health/Hospitals, Clinics/Medical Centers, Emergency/Ambulance Services, Health-General, Health Organizations, Hospices, Hospitals, Single-Disease Health Associations
Religion: Churches, Religion-General, Religious Organizations, Religious Welfare
Social Services: At-Risk Youth, Camps, Community Service Organizations, Crime Prevention, Delinquency & Criminal Rehabilitation, Domestic Violence, Family Services, Homes, People with Disabilities, Recreation & Athletics, Scouts, Senior Services, United Funds/United Ways, YMCA/YWCA/YMHA/YWHA, Youth Organizations

Application Procedures

Initial Contact: Send a brief letter of inquiry and a full proposal.
Application Requirements: a description of organization, amount requested, purpose of funds sought, recently audited financial statement, proof of tax-exempt status and a list of names on the Board of Directors.
Deadlines: April 15 and November 1

Restrictions

Does not support individuals.

Additional Information

Publications: Application Guidelines

Foundation Officials

William P. Barker: trustee
Daniel G. Crozier, Jr.: trustee
James Brooks Crozier: trustee
Nancy R. Crozier: vice president, trustee
Catherine G. Keefe: assistant secretary, treasurer
Douglas R. Nowicki: trustee
James R. Okonak: executive director, secretary, trustee
Fred McFeely Rogers: president, trustee B Latrobe, PA 1928. ED Rollins College MusB (1951); Pittsburgh Theological Seminary MDiv (1962); Thiel College DHL (1969); Christian Theological Seminary DD (1973); Eastern Michigan University HHD (1973); Saint Vincent College LiHD (1973); Yale University LHD (1974). PRIM CORP EMPL executive producer, host: Mister Rogers' Neighborhood. NONPR AFFIL member: Luxor Ministerial Association; chairman child devel & mass media forum: White House Conference on Children; member: Esther Island Preserve Association.
James B. Rogers: trustee
John F. Rogers: trustee

Grants Analysis

Disclosure Period: calendar year ending 2001
Total Grants: $889,345*
Number of Grants: 87
Average Grant: $7,818*
Highest Grant: $217,000
Lowest Grant: $245
Typical Range: $1,000 to $15,000
*Note: Giving excludes United Way. Average grant figure excludes three highest grants ($530,350).

Recent Grants

Note: Grants derived from 2001 Form 990.

Library-Related
59,200	Adams Memorial Library, Latrobe, PA

General
217,000	Latrobe Foundation, Latrobe, PA
71,100	Greater Latrobe School District, Latrobe, PA
55,300	Saint Vincent College, Latrobe, PA -- scholarship fund
55,000	Rollins College, Winter Park, FL
40,500	American Red Cross Chestnut Ridge Chapter, Latrobe, PA
35,000	Latrobe Area Hospital Charitable Foundation, Latrobe, PA
30,000	Saint Vincent Archabbey, Latrobe, PA
25,250	Roanoke College, Salem, VA
25,000	Pittsburgh Youth Symphony Orchestra Association, Pittsburgh, PA
20,000	Family Communications, Pittsburgh, PA

MCGEE FOUNDATION (MO)

Giving Contact

Thomas R. McGee, Jr., President
709 W. 50th St.
Kansas City, MO 64112
Phone: (816)421-0050

Description

Founded: 1951
EIN: 446006285
Organization Type: Private Foundation
Giving Locations: MO: Kansas City metropolitan area

Grant Types: Capital, General Support, Multiyear/Continuing Support, Operating Expenses, Project, Scholarship.

Donor Information

Founder: the late Joseph J. McGee, the late Mrs. Joseph I. McGee, the late Frank McGee, the late Mrs. Frank McGee, the late Louis B. McGee, Old American Insurance Co., Thomas McGee and Sons, Joseph I. McGee, Jr.

Financial Summary

Total Giving: $429,300 (2001); $398,400 (2000); $647,500 (1999)
Assets: $12,725,082 (2001); $12,407,768 (2000); $11,362,475 (1999)
Gifts Received: $2,000 (2001); $2,720 (2000); $3,000 (1998)

Typical Recipients

Arts & Humanities: Libraries, Museums/Galleries
Civic & Public Affairs: Clubs, Civic & Public Affairs-General, Hispanic Affairs, Native American Affairs, Nonprofit Management, Public Policy, Urban & Community Affairs, Zoos/Aquariums
Education: Business Education, Colleges & Universities, Education Funds, Education Reform, Elementary Education (Public), Education-General, International Exchange, Private Education (Precollege), Religious Education, Science/Mathematics Education, Secondary Education (Public), Special Education, Student Aid
Health: AIDS/HIV, Cancer, Children's Health/Hospitals, Clinics/Medical Centers, Geriatric Health, Health Organizations, Home-Care Services, Hospices, Hospitals, Medical Rehabilitation, Mental Health, Prenatal Health Issues, Trauma Treatment
International: Missionary/Religious Activities
Religion: Churches, Missionary Activities (Domestic), Religious Organizations, Religious Welfare
Social Services: Camps, Child Welfare, Community Service Organizations, Emergency Relief, Food/Clothing Distribution, Homes, People with Disabilities, Senior Services, Shelters/Homelessness, Youth Organizations

Application Procedures

Initial Contact: Send a brief letter of inquiry. Include a description of organization, amount requested, purpose of funds sought, recently audited financial statement, and proof of tax-exempt status., one or two pages.
Deadlines: None.

Restrictions

Primary support to greater metropolitan Kansas City area. Does not support visual and performing arts, preservation of historic places, or with exception of applied research, scholarly research projects and programs.

Additional Information

Publications: Annual Report (including Application Guidelines)

Foundation Officials

Mrs. Bernard J. Duffy, Jr.: mem
Robert A. Long: mem
Joseph John McGee, Jr.: president, chairman, mem, director B Kansas City, MO 1919. ED Georgetown University; Rockhurst College. NONPR AFFIL director: Harry S Truman Library Institute; director: Truman Medical Center; director: Menorah Medical Center; trustee: Rockhurst College.
Thomas F. McGee, Sr.: vchairman, mem, director
Thomas R. McGee, Jr.: mem
Thomas R. McGee: treasurer, mem, director PRIM CORP EMPL Old American Insurance Co.
Edward J. Reardon: secretary, mem, director

Grants Analysis

Disclosure Period: calendar year ending 2001
Total Grants: $429,300
Number of Grants: 33
Average Grant: $7,907*
Highest Grant: $50,000
Lowest Grant: $1,000
Typical Range: $1,000 to $15,000
*****Note:** Average grant figure excludes four highest grants ($200,000).

Recent Grants

Note: Grants derived from 2000 Form 990.

General

50,000	Kansas City - St. Joseph Diocese, Kansas City, MO -- scholarship and tuition assistance for disadvantaged
50,000	Rockhurst High School, Kansas City, MO -- complete renovation of Jesuit Wing
50,000	Rockhurst University, Kansas City, MO -- purchase scientific teaching equipment
50,000	St. Teresa's Academy, Kansas City, MO -- upgrade lighting and sound system in auditorium
20,000	Gardner Institute, Kansas City, KS -- scholarships and tuition assistance for disadvantaged
19,000	Duchesne Clinic, Kansas City, KS
15,000	Avila College, Kansas City, MO -- scholarships
15,000	Redemptorist Retirement Home, Kansas City, MO -- relocate center and enlarge operations
10,000	Bishop Sullivan Center, Inc., Kansas City, MO -- purchase cargo van
10,000	De La Salle Education Center, Kansas City, MO -- implement new program

DEXTRA BALDWIN MCGONAGLE FOUNDATION

Giving Contact

Jonathan G. Spanier, President & Chief Executive Officer
PO Box 709
South Salem, NY 10590
Phone: (914)694-3493

Description

Founded: 1967
EIN: 136219236
Organization Type: Private Foundation
Giving Locations: CA; NY
Grant Types: Capital, Endowment, General Support, Research, Seed Money.

Donor Information

Founder: the late Mrs. Dextra Baldwin McGonagle

Financial Summary

Total Giving: $617,028 (2001); $566,661 (2000); $522,275 (1999)
Giving Analysis: Giving for 2001 includes: foundation grants to United Way ($1,000); 2000: foundation grants to United Way ($1,000); 1999: foundation grants to United Way ($1,000)
Assets: $12,375,372 (2001); $11,873,374 (2000); $11,235,431 (1999)

Typical Recipients

Arts & Humanities: Art History, Arts Associations & Councils, Community Arts, Historic Preservation, History & Archaeology, Libraries, Museums/Galleries, Music, Opera, Performing Arts, Public Broadcasting

Civic & Public Affairs: Botanical Gardens/Parks, Civic & Public Affairs-General, Legal Aid, Municipalities/Towns, Nonprofit Management, Philanthropic Organizations, Public Policy, Safety, Urban & Community Affairs, Zoos/Aquariums
Education: Colleges & Universities, Education Funds, Education-General, Legal Education, Medical Education, Preschool Education, Private Education (Precollege), Science/Mathematics Education, Student Aid
Environment: Environment-General
Health: Cancer, Children's Health/Hospitals, Clinics/Medical Centers, Clinics/Medical Centers, Emergency/Ambulance Services, Health-General, Geriatric Health, Hospices, Hospitals, Hospitals (University Affiliated), Long-Term Care, Medical Research, Mental Health, Prenatal Health Issues, Research/Studies Institutes, Single-Disease Health Associations, Speech & Hearing
International: Foreign Educational Institutions, International Environmental Issues, International Organizations, International Relations, Missionary/Religious Activities
Religion: Jewish Causes, Religious Organizations, Religious Welfare, Synagogues/Temples
Science: Science Museums, Scientific Centers & Institutes, Scientific Labs
Social Services: Child Welfare, Community Service Organizations, Family Services, People with Disabilities, Senior Services, Social Services-General, United Funds/United Ways, Youth Organizations, Youth Organizations

Application Procedures

Initial Contact: The foundation has no formal grant application procedure or application form. Submit a one-page summary of request.
Deadlines: None.
Review Process: The foundation will request additional information if interested in the proposal.

Foundation Officials

David B. Spanier: president
Helen G. Spanier: vice president
Jonathan Spanier: president, chief executive officer
Maury L. Spanier: chairman B New York, NY August 13, 1916. ED City University of New York (1936). PRIM CORP EMPL chairman emeritus: Un Aircraft Product. CORP AFFIL chairman executive committee: Baldwin Investment Co.

Grants Analysis

Disclosure Period: calendar year ending 2001
Total Grants: $616,028*
Number of Grants: 93
Average Grant: $5,881*
Highest Grant: $75,000
Lowest Grant: $15
Typical Range: $1,000 to $10,000
*****Note:** Giving excludes United Way. Average grant figure excludes highest grant.

Recent Grants

Note: Grants derived from 2001 Form 990.

Library-Related

75,000	South Salem Library Association, South Salem, NY

General

52,500	Columbia University School of Law, New York, NY
50,000	Purchase College Foundation, Purchase, NY
45,000	Young Adult Institute and Workshop, New York, NY
40,000	Tahoe Tallac Association, South Lake Tahoe, CA
35,000	Beth Israel Medical Center Foundation, New York, NY
35,000	Montefiore Medical Center, Bronx, NY
25,000	Central Synagogue, New York, NY
20,000	Federation of Jewish Philanthropies, New York, NY
15,000	American Lyme Disease Foundation, Somers, NY
15,000	Camphill Village, Copake, NY

JOHN P. MCGOVERN FOUNDATION

Giving Contact

Dr. John P. McGovern, President
2211 Norfolk, Suite 900
Houston, TX 77098-4044
Phone: (713)524-5255
Fax: (713)661-3031

Alternate Contact

Gay Collette, Secretary

Description

Founded: 1961
EIN: 746053075
Organization Type: General Purpose Foundation
Giving Locations: TX: Houston some giving nationally.
Grant Types: General Support, Research, Scholarship.

Donor Information

Founder: The foundation was established in 1961 by John P. McGovern M.D.

Financial Summary

Total Giving: $9,361,525 (fiscal year ending August 31, 2002); $9,451,286 (fiscal 2001); $8,350,000 (fiscal 1999)
Giving Analysis: Giving for fiscal 1999 includes: foundation grants to United Way ($30,000)
Assets: $193,043,587 (fiscal 2002); $197,269,019 (fiscal 2001); $180,094,718 (fiscal 1999)
Gifts Received: $2,560,653 (fiscal 2001); $4,410,914 (fiscal 1999); $12,979,109 (fiscal 1997). Note: Contributions were received from John P. McGovern, MD.

Typical Recipients

Arts & Humanities: Arts & Humanities-General, History & Archaeology, Libraries, Museums/Galleries, Music, Theater
Civic & Public Affairs: Botanical Gardens/Parks, Clubs, Economic Development, Civic & Public Affairs-General, Municipalities/Towns, Professional & Trade Associations, Public Policy, Women's Affairs, Zoos/Aquariums
Education: Colleges & Universities, Education Funds, Environmental Education, Education-General, International Studies, Literacy, Medical Education, Private Education (Precollege), Social Sciences Education, Student Aid
Environment: Environment-General
Health: Cancer, Children's Health/Hospitals, Clinics/Medical Centers, Eyes/Blindness, Health-General, Health Funds, Health Organizations, Heart, Hospitals, Medical Rehabilitation, Medical Research, Mental Health, Public Health, Research/Studies Institutes
International: Health Care/Hospitals
Religion: Religion-General, Jewish Causes, Ministries, Religious Welfare
Social Services: At-Risk Youth, Camps, Child Abuse, Child Welfare, Community Centers, Community Service Organizations, Domestic Violence, Emergency Relief, Family Services, Food/Clothing Distribution, Scouts, Social Services-General, Substance Abuse, United Funds/United Ways, Volunteer Services

Application Procedures

Initial Contact: Applicants should submit a letter to the foundation.

Application Requirements: There is no particular application form. Applicants should include information concerning the type of research to be conducted.

Deadlines: None.

Restrictions

The foundation reports no specific restrictions or limitations on giving to organizations. No grants are made to individuals, except for research purposes and honorariums. Generally, grants are foundation-initiated.

Foundation Officials

Gay Collette: secretary
Kathrine G. McGovern: vice president, treasurer

Grants Analysis

Disclosure Period: fiscal year ending August 31, 2001

Total Grants: $9,451,286

Number of Grants: 372

Average Grant: $17,436*

Highest Grant: $2,000,000

Typical Range: $5,000 to $30,000

*****Note:** Average grant figure excludes two highest grants ($3,000,000).

Recent Grants

Note: Grants derived from 2001 Form 990.

Library-Related

30,000	Friends of the Texas Medical Center Library, Houston, TX
30,000	George Bush Presidential Library, College Station, TX

General

1,000,000	John P. McGovern Museum of Health and Medical Science, Houston, TX -- permanent endowment fund
600,000	John P. McGovern Museum of Health and Medical Science, Houston, TX
300,000	The Medical Institute for Sexual Health, Austin, TX
200,000	Cosmos Club Historic Preservation Foundation, Washington, DC
152,075	Institute for Behavior and Health, Inc., Rockville, MD -- McGovern Lecture series
150,000	The DeLay Foundation, Sugar Land, TX
150,000	Houston Academy of Medicine, Houston, TX -- Texas Medical Center Library
120,000	ABC Recovery Center, Indio, CA
110,000	Drug Free American Foundation, New York, NY
100,000	American Red Cross, Houston, TX

MCGOVERN FUND

Giving Contact

Dr. John P. McGovern, President
2211 Norfolk, Suite 900
Houston, TX 77098
Phone: (713)524-5255

Description

Founded: 1979
EIN: 742086867
Organization Type: Private Foundation
Giving Locations: TX
Grant Types: Capital, General Support, Multiyear/Continuing Support.

Donor Information

Founder: the John P. McGovern Foundation

Financial Summary

Total Giving: $461,200 (fiscal year ending November 30, 2001); $6,198,500 (fiscal 2000); $5,310,668 (fiscal 1998)

Giving Analysis: Giving for fiscal 1998 includes: foundation grants to United Way ($28,000) foundation scholarships ($42,000)

Assets: $745,000 (fiscal 2001); $1,208,704 (fiscal 2000); $7,948,498 (fiscal 1998)

Gifts Received: $277,000 (fiscal 2000); $6,992,000 (fiscal 1998); $3,835,500 (fiscal 1996). Note: In fiscal 1998 and 2000, contributions were received from John P. McGovern, M.D.

Typical Recipients

Arts & Humanities: Arts & Humanities-General, Libraries, Museums/Galleries, Music

Civic & Public Affairs: Botanical Gardens/Parks, Clubs, Community Foundations, Economic Development, Employment/Job Training, Civic & Public Affairs-General, Hispanic Affairs, Municipalities/Towns, Nonprofit Management, Philanthropic Organizations, Public Policy, Safety, Urban & Community Affairs, Zoos/Aquariums

Education: Arts/Humanities Education, Colleges & Universities, Engineering/Technological Education, Environmental Education, Education-General, Health & Physical Education, Medical Education, Private Education (Precollege), Public Education (Precollege), Religious Education, Social Sciences Education, Special Education, Student Aid

Environment: Environment-General

Health: Cancer, Clinics/Medical Centers, Clinics/Medical Centers, Emergency/Ambulance Services, Eyes/Blindness, Health Organizations, Hospices, Hospitals, Hospitals (University Affiliated), Medical Rehabilitation, Medical Research, Public Health, Single-Disease Health Associations, Speech & Hearing

International: Foreign Educational Institutions, Health Care/Hospitals, International Organizations, International Relations

Religion: Churches, Religious Organizations, Religious Welfare

Science: Science Museums, Scientific Centers & Institutes, Scientific Labs, Scientific Organizations

Social Services: At-Risk Youth, Big Brother/Big Sister, Camps, Child Welfare, Community Service Organizations, Day Care, Domestic Violence, Scouts, Shelters/Homelessness, Substance Abuse, United Funds/United Ways, Volunteer Services, Youth Organizations

Application Procedures

Initial Contact: Send a brief letter of inquiry.
Application Requirements: Include purpose of funds sought.
Deadlines: None.

Foundation Officials

Gay Collette: secretary

John Phillip McGovern, MD: president B Washington, DC 1921. ED Duke University MD (1945); Duke University BS (1945). NONPR AFFIL professor: University Texas; professor: University Texas School Public Health; member: Southern Medicine Association; member: Texas Pediatric Society; honorary member: Sociedad de Algeria y Ciencias Afines; member: Society Experimental Biology & Medicine; member: Sigma Xi; member: Sigma Kappa Alpha; member: Sigma Pi Sigma; editor: Psychosomatics Headaches International Corresponding Society Allergists; member: Royal College Physicians; member: Phi Beta Kappa; member: Pi Kappa Alpha; member: Osler Club London; diplomate: National Board Medicine Examiners; consult: National Library Medicine;

director: McGovern Fund Behavioral Sciences; member: National Advisory Council Alcohol Abuse; honorary member: La Sociedad Mexicana de Alergia e Immunologia; regional consult: Lackland Air Force Base; adj professor: Kent State University; fellow: Green College; associate editor: Journal Asthma Research; member: Duke University Medicine Alumni Association; honorary member: Canadian Allergy Socs; editorial board: The Classics Medicine Libraries; adj professor: Baylor College Medicine; member: Association Research Nervous & Mental Diseases; regional consult, national medical advisory council: Asthmatic Childrens Foundation; honorary member: Asociacion Argentina de Alergia e Inmunologia; member: Association Convalescent Homes & Hospitals Asthmatic Children; member: American School Health Association; adj professor: Maryland Anderson Hospital & Tumor Institute; member: American Osler Society; member: American Medical Association; member: American Medicine Writers Association; member: American College Physicians; fellow: American College Allergy & Immunology; fellow: American College Chest Physicians; diplomate: American Board Pediatrics; fellow: American Association Study Headaches; diplomate: American Board Allergy & Immunology; member: American Association History Medicine; member: American Association Immunologists; fellow: American Academy Pediatrics; member: American Association Certified Allergists; fellow: American Academy Allergy & Immunology; member: Alpha Omega Alpha. CLUB AFFIL Westchester Club; Vintage Club; Cosmos Club; Osler Club; Army-Navy Country Club.

Kathrine G. McGovern: vice president, treasurer

Grants Analysis

Disclosure Period: fiscal year ending November 30, 2001

Total Grants: $461,200

Number of Grants: 44

Average Grant: $9,563*

Highest Grant: $50,000

Lowest Grant: $200

Typical Range: $1,000 to $20,000

*****Note:** Average grant figure excludes highest grant.

Recent Grants

Note: Grants derived from fiscal 2000 Form 990.

Library-Related

1,600,000	Stella Link Redevelopment Association, Houston, TX -- contribution for campus park

General

550,000	University of Oxford Chancellor, Masters, and Scholars, Oxford United Kingdom -- for the purchase of 13 Norham Gardens
500,000	Children's Museum, Houston, TX -- for kid's hall
500,000	Cosmos Club Historic Preservation Foundation, Washington, DC -- contribution
500,000	Texas Medical Center, Houston, TX -- for John P. McGovern Texas Medical Center Commons
500,000	University of Houston, Houston, TX -- for honors college capital campaign
300,000	Texas Medical Center, Houston, TX -- for John P. McGovern Texas Medical Center Commons
200,000	Houston Academy of Medicine, Houston, TX -- for research center and endowment fund
170,000	Houston Academy of Medicine, Houston, TX -- for research center endowment fund
100,000	Houston Music Hall Foundation, Houston, TX -- for the performing arts center
100,000	University of Texas Foundation, Austin, TX -- for fellowship program

WILLIAM G. MCGOWAN CHARITABLE FUND

Giving Contact

Bernard A. Goodrich, Executive Director
PO Box 40515
Washington, DC 20016-0515
Phone: (202)364-5030
Fax: (202)364-3382
E-mail: goodric@aol.com
Web: http://www.mcgowanfund.org

Description

Founded: 1992
EIN: 521829785
Organization Type: Private Foundation
Giving Locations: CA: Central, North of San Luis; DC: Washington; IL: Chicago; KS: Kansas City; MD: Baltimore; NY: Western; PA: Northern; TX: Dallas, Houston, San Antonio
Grant Types: Matching, Project, Research, Scholarship.

Donor Information

Founder: Established in 1992 by the late William G. McGowan .

Financial Summary

Total Giving: $7,358,735 (fiscal year ending June 30, 2000); $7,231,377 (fiscal 1999); $6,100,000 (fiscal 1998)
Giving Analysis: Giving for fiscal 1999 includes: foundation grants to United Way ($2,500); foundation matching gifts ($123,852) foundation scholarships ($201,000)
Assets: $152,000,000 (fiscal 2000 approx); $162,906,029 (fiscal 1999); $120,583,624 (fiscal 1997)
Gifts Received: $171,065 (fiscal 1996); $1,089,179 (fiscal 1994). Note: In fiscal 1996, contributions were received from the estate of William G. McGowan.

Typical Recipients

Civic & Public Affairs: Civic & Public Affairs-General, Housing
Education: Business Education, Colleges & Universities, Education Associations, Environmental Education, Faculty Development, International Studies, Medical Education, Minority Education, Preschool Education, Private Education (Precollege), Public Education (Precollege), School Volunteerism, Science/Mathematics Education, Secondary Education (Private), Special Education, Student Aid
Health: Cancer, Diabetes, Health-General, Heart, Public Health, Speech & Hearing, Transplant Networks/Donor Banks
International: International Peace & Security Issues, International Relief Efforts
Religion: Religious Welfare
Social Services: Child Welfare, Domestic Violence, Food/Clothing Distribution, Homes, People with Disabilities, Youth Organizations, Youth Organizations

Application Procedures

Initial Contact: The foundation requests applications be made in writing.
Application Requirements: Submit two (2) copies of the following (should be attached) in support of your application: Grant proposal, not more than five pages in length, including: program summary, reason why the problems to be addressed were selected, description of how the program was developed, list of specific objectives for the program and brief discussion of how each will be realized, and how the program will be evaluated; detailed budget for project and current agency budget, to include projected sources of income as well as expense; qualifications of personnel assigned to project, if special talents or skills are required; audited financial statements for latest fiscal year, list of principal officers and directors; and copy of Internal Revenue Service determination that applicant is an exempt organization under Section 501(c)(3) of the IRS Code name of applying organization must be identical with that on exemption letter.
Deadlines: February 1, May 1, August 1, November 1.

Additional Information

Publications: Application Guidelines; Informational Brochure

Foundation Officials

Kenneth Cox: trustee
Sue Gin McGowan: president

Grants Analysis

Disclosure Period: fiscal year ending June 30, 1999
Total Grants: $6,904,025*
Number of Grants: 106
Average Grant: $56,229*
Highest Grant: $1,000,000
Typical Range: $5,000 to $60,000 and $250,000 to $600,000
*Note: Giving excludes United Way; scholarships; matching gifts. Average grant figure excludes highest grant.

Recent Grants

Note: Grants derived from fiscal 2000 Form 990.

General

700,000	McGowan Center for Artificial Organ Development, Pittsburgh, PA -- for future research and operating expenses for the McGowan Center for Organ Development
600,000	Capitol College, Laurel, MD -- for the McGowan Academic Center on High Technology Campus
500,000	DePaul University, Chicago, IL -- for McGowan Biological and Environmental Sciences Center
417,000	Mount St. Mary's College and Seminary, Emmitsburg, MD -- to fund WGM Student Center
416,000	Mount St. Mary's College and Seminary, Emmitsburg, MD -- final contribution toward McGowan Student Center
250,000	College Misericordia, Dallas, PA -- for McGowan Center in new Library
250,000	Stanford University School of Medicine, Stanford, CA -- to continue support of scientific research into the future treatment of Alzheimer's disease
125,000	National Capital Poison Center, Washington, DC -- for operating support for the center
115,620	Catholic University of America, Washington, DC -- research on using electromagnetic exposure to increase chance of survival after heart attacks
100,000	Big Shoulder's Fund, Chicago, IL -- to support the Fund's Superintendents Scholarship Fund

MCGRAW-HILL COMPANIES, INC.

Company Headquarters

1221 Avenue of the Americas
New York, NY 10020
Web: http://www.mcgraw-hill.com

Company Description

Founded: 1925
Ticker: MHP
Exchange: NYSE
Revenue: US$4.787 billion (2002)
Profit: US$576.8 million (2002)
Employees: 17135 (2002)
Fortune Rank: 343, per FORTUNE Magazine's list of 500 Largest U.S. Corporations (2002).
SIC(s): 2721 Periodicals, 2731 Book Publishing.

Nonmonetary Support

Type: Donated Products

Giving Contact

Susan A. Wallman, Manager, Corporate Contributions
1221 Avenue of the Americas, 47th Floor
New York, NY 10020-1095
Phone: (212)512-6480
Fax: (212)512-3611
E-mail: swallman@mcgraw-hill.com
Web: http://www.mcgraw-hill.com/community/community/html

Description

Organization Type: Corporate Giving Program
Giving Locations: NY: New York nationally; primarily headquarters and operating communities.
Grant Types: Employee Matching Gifts, General Support.
Note: Employee matching gift ratio: 2 to 1.

Financial Summary

Total Giving: $3,600,000 (2002 approx); $3,600,000 (2001); $3,600,000 (2000). Note: Contributes through corporate direct giving program only, as of 1997. 1996 Giving includes foundation ($761,749); matching gifts ($1,198,505); United Way ($479,840).
Assets: $893,426 (1996); $840,524 (1995); $596,638 (1994)
Gifts Received: $2,400,000 (1996); $2,300,000 (1995); $2,650,000 (1994)

Typical Recipients

Arts & Humanities: Arts Centers, Dance, Libraries, Museums/Galleries, Music, Performing Arts, Public Broadcasting
Civic & Public Affairs: African American Affairs, Business/Free Enterprise, Civil Rights, Economic Development, Employment/Job Training, First Amendment Issues, Hispanic Affairs, Housing, Law & Justice, Professional & Trade Associations, Public Policy, Women's Affairs
Education: Business Education, Colleges & Universities, Education Associations, Education Funds, Education Reform, Engineering/Technological Education, Education-General, Journalism/Media Education, Literacy, Minority Education, Private Education (Precollege), Student Aid
Environment: Air/Water Quality
Health: AIDS/HIV, Clinics/Medical Centers, Eyes/Blindness, Health Organizations, Hospitals, Hospitals (University Affiliated), Transplant Networks/Donor Banks
International: International Development
Religion: Religious Welfare
Social Services: Community Service Organizations, Family Services, People with Disabilities, Substance Abuse, United Funds/United Ways, Volunteer Services, YMCA/YWCA/YMHA/YWHA

Application Procedures

Initial Contact: Send preliminary proposal letter.
Application Requirements: Brief background of your organization, including its goals and objectives, staff, and board of directors; a concise description of the program and objectives for which funds are sought; a copy of most recent audited financial statement and annual report; current year's budget and the sources of funding; the budget for the program for which you support is sought, and the sum requested; and evidence of your public charity status under the U.S. Internal Revenue Code.
Deadlines: None.

Review Process: If request fits current priorities, meeting may be arranged and on-site visits conducted.

Evaluative Criteria: Organization staffed by people with demonstrated competence and experience in the field; project addresses problems affecting communities the company serves; contribution supports projects that can be evaluated and serve as models elsewhere; project extends reach globally, and utilizes unique applications of new and developing technologies.

Decision Notification: Corporate Contributions and Community Relations Committee meets quarterly.

Restrictions

The organization does not support political activities or groups established to influence legislation; individuals; publication of books, magazines, videos, or films; member organizations of United Way funds; sectarian or religious organizations; endowment funds; loans; or institutions and agencies clearly outside McGraw-Hill's primary geographic concerns and interests.

McGraw-Hill does not subscribe to tables or tickets for charitable events, sponsor courtesy advertisements, or pledge support for walk-a-thons or similar activities.

Additional Information

Grants are not renewed automatically; new requests must be submitted each year.

Recipients are asked to submit periodic reports on, and evaluation of, progress and an annual financial report.

Foundation ceased operations in 1997; all contributions are now made through Corporate Contributions and Community Relations.

Publications: Giving Guidelines

Corporate Officials

Barbara A. Munder: senior vice president new initiatives B New York, NY 1945. ED Elmira College (1967); New York University Leonard N. Stern School of Business MBA (1980). PRIM CORP EMPL senior vice president new initiatives: McGraw-Hill Companies, Inc. NONPR AFFIL member: Information Industry Association; director: Lighthouse.

Louise Raymond: director corporate contributions

Donald S. Rubin: senior vice president investor relations B Chicago, IL 1934. ED Columbia University; University of Miami AB (1956). PRIM CORP EMPL senior vice president investor relations: McGraw-Hill Companies, Inc.

Susan A. Wallman: manager corporate contributions

Grants Analysis

Disclosure Period: calendar year ending 1996
Total Grants: $761,749*
Number of Grants: 174
Average Grant: $4,378
Highest Grant: $109,710
Typical Range: $1,000 to $20,000
***Note:** Giving excludes matching gifts; United Way. A more recent grants list was unavailable.

Recent Grants

Note: Grants derived from 1996 Form 990.

Library-Related
25,000	New York Public Library, New York, NY
10,000	Library Foundation, San Francisco, CA

General
361,680	United Way Tri-State Area, New York, NY
109,710	National Merit Scholarship Corporation, Evanston, IL
50,000	National Organization on Disability, Washington, DC
50,000	National Organization on Disability, Washington, DC
50,000	Salvation Army, New York, NY
30,400	United Way Burlington County, Mt. Holly, NJ
30,000	Cornell University Knight-Baghot Fellowship, New York, NY
25,000	A Better Chance, New York, NY
25,000	Lincoln Center for Performing Arts, New York, NY
20,000	Hartley House, New York, NY

THOMAS AND FRANCES MCGREGOR FOUNDATION

Giving Contact

Robert W. Smith
Thomas and Frances McGregor Foundation
PO Box 40
York, AL 36925
Phone: (601)485-8305

Description

Founded: 1961
EIN: 526041498
Organization Type: Private Foundation
Giving Locations: DC: Washington metropolitan area
Grant Types: General Support.

Donor Information

Founder: Thomas W. McGregor, McGregor Printing Corp.

Financial Summary

Total Giving: $203,719 (fiscal year ending February 28, 2001); $241,169 (fiscal 2000); $89,688 (fiscal 1996)
Giving Analysis: Giving for fiscal 2000 includes: foundation grants to United Way ($500)
Assets: $1,963,848 (fiscal 2001); $4,822,265 (fiscal 2000); $3,763,944 (fiscal 1996)
Gifts Received: $300,000 (fiscal 1992). Note: In 1992, contributions were received from McGregor Printing Corporation.

Typical Recipients

Arts & Humanities: Arts Associations & Councils, Arts Centers, Arts Institutes, Arts Outreach, Ballet, Libraries, Museums/Galleries, Music, Public Broadcasting, Theater

Civic & Public Affairs: African American Affairs, Botanical Gardens/Parks, Business/Free Enterprise, Clubs, Community Foundations, Economic Development, Employment/Job Training, Civic & Public Affairs-General, Hispanic Affairs, Housing, Municipalities/Towns, Public Policy, Urban & Community Affairs, Zoos/Aquariums

Education: Arts/Humanities Education, Colleges & Universities, Education Funds, Education Reform, Education-General, Private Education (Precollege), Secondary Education (Private)

Environment: Environment-General, Wildlife Protection

Health: AIDS/HIV, Cancer, Children's Health/Hospitals, Clinics/Medical Centers, Diabetes, Emergency/Ambulance Services, Health Organizations, Heart, Hospitals, Medical Rehabilitation, Medical Research, Multiple Sclerosis, Prenatal Health Issues, Research/Studies Institutes, Single-Disease Health Associations

International: Health Care/Hospitals, Missionary/Religious Activities

Religion: Churches, Jewish Causes, Religious Organizations, Religious Welfare, Synagogues/Temples

Social Services: Camps, Child Welfare, Community Service Organizations, Emergency Relief, Family Planning, Family Services, Food/Clothing Distribution, Refugee Assistance, Scouts, Shelters/Homelessness, United Funds/United Ways, YMCA/YWCA/YMHA/YWHA, Youth Organizations

Application Procedures

Initial Contact: No specific form of application is required.
Deadlines: None.

Foundation Officials

Victor Krakower: mgr

Grants Analysis

Disclosure Period: fiscal year ending February 28, 2001
Total Grants: $203,719*
Typical Range: $1,000 to $10,000
***Note:** No grants list available for 2001.

Recent Grants

Note: Grants derived from fiscal 2000 Form 990.

Library-Related
1,500	Hitower Library

General
72,244	Helen Keller
60,000	Helen Keller
16,000	University of North Caroline Arts & Sciences, NC
12,000	University of North Carolina Education Foundation, Chapel Hill, NC
10,000	NL Missions
10,000	University of North Carolina Education Foundation, Chapel Hill, NC
5,000	American Cancer Society
5,000	Cathedral Fund
5,000	Hazelton Foundation
5,000	Lewisburg College

MCGREGOR FUND

Giving Contact

C. David Campbell, President & Assistant Secretary
333 West Fort Street, Suite 2090
Detroit, MI 48226-3134
Phone: (313)963-3495
Fax: (313)963-3512
E-mail: info@mcgregorfund.org
Web: http://www.mcgregorfund.org

Description

Founded: 1925
EIN: 380808800
Organization Type: General Purpose Foundation
Giving Locations: MI: Detroit metropolitan area
Grant Types: Capital, Emergency, Endowment, General Support, Multiyear/Continuing Support, Operating Expenses, Project.

Donor Information

Founder: The McGregor Fund was established in 1925 by the late Tracy W. McGregor , and it was funded by Mr. McGregor and his wife, Katherine Whitney McGregor . Tracy McGregor was president of Whitney Realty Company, LaSalle Land Company, Provident Loan and Savings, Merrill-Palmer School, Detroit Community Fund, and the Training School of the Feeble Minded, as well as trustee of the Goodwill Farm School. The McGregors were dedicated "to relieving the misfortunes and promoting the well-being of mankind." Among their specific interests were the McGregor Institute (for homeless men), the McGregor Home (for children), Bay Court (for underprivileged mothers), and the Detroit Community Fund (a forerunner of the United Foundation). Mr. McGregor was also a member of the "Thursday Group" of influential men in Detroit who gathered to find solutions to the problems of their time. The McGregors' gifts to the fund from their estates totaled approximately $10 million.

Financial Summary

Total Giving: $7,429,552 (fiscal year ending June 30, 2002); $9,112,985 (fiscal 2001); $9,270,123 (fiscal 1999)

Giving Analysis: Giving for fiscal 2001 includes: foundation matching gifts ($85,007); foundation grants to United Way ($166,500); foundation scholarships ($225,000); fiscal 1999: foundation grants to United Way ($37,400); foundation matching gifts ($67,638); foundation scholarships ($400,000) fiscal 1997: foundation grants to United Way ($82,500)

Assets: $159,265,246 (fiscal 2002); $180,252,951 (fiscal 2001); $199,691,866 (fiscal 1999)

Typical Recipients

Arts & Humanities: Arts Associations & Councils, Arts Centers, Arts Institutes, Ethnic & Folk Arts, Historic Preservation, History & Archaeology, Libraries, Museums/Galleries, Music, Opera, Performing Arts, Public Broadcasting, Theater

Civic & Public Affairs: Chambers of Commerce, Community Foundations, Economic Development, Employment/Job Training, Civic & Public Affairs-General, Hispanic Affairs, Housing, Inner-City Development, Municipalities/Towns, Philanthropic Organizations, Professional & Trade Associations, Urban & Community Affairs, Zoos/Aquariums

Education: Afterschool/Enrichment Programs, Arts/Humanities Education, Business Education, Colleges & Universities, Education Reform, Elementary Education (Public), Engineering/Technological Education, Environmental Education, Faculty Development, Education-General, Minority Education, Private Education (Precollege), Public Education (Precollege), Science/Mathematics Education, Secondary Education (Private), Social Sciences Education, Student Aid

Health: AIDS/HIV, Children's Health/Hospitals, Emergency/Ambulance Services, Health Organizations, Hospitals, Long-Term Care, Mental Health, Nursing Services, Prenatal Health Issues

Religion: Churches, Dioceses, Religious Welfare, Seminaries, Social/Policy Issues

Science: Scientific Centers & Institutes, Scientific Research

Social Services: At-Risk Youth, Big Brother/Big Sister, Child Welfare, Community Service Organizations, Counseling, Delinquency & Criminal Rehabilitation, Emergency Relief, Family Planning, Family Services, Family Services, Food/Clothing Distribution, People with Disabilities, Recreation & Athletics, Scouts, Senior Services, Shelters/Homelessness, Substance Abuse, United Funds/United Ways, Volunteer Services, Youth Organizations

Application Procedures

Initial Contact: Applicants should request grant guidelines from the fund's office. Separate guidelines for private schools, colleges, and universities are available from the fund office. After reviewing the information, applicants are encouraged to speak with the staff of the Fund to discuss eligibility and purpose.

Application Requirements: Each grant request should include a brief cover letter signed by the chief executive officer, stating the specific purpose, time period, amount of request, proof of tax-exempt status under Internal Revenue Code Section 501(c)(3) and classification under Section 509(a) of the code. Also, please include a copy of Form 4653, an audited financial statement and balance sheet of income and expenses, detailed budget statement for the proposed project, and an explanation about the reasonable financial potential to achieve and sustain the project. The organization's most recent IRS Form 990 and a listing of the organization's officers and directors should also be included. If the organization is classified as a public charity, a written statement that the requested grant will not result in the loss of such organization's classification must be signed and submitted by an officer. A description of organization, including history, current programs, and future plans,

is required as well. Include details of the request, including: name and description of the proposed program or project, indicating whether it is a new program or part of an ongoing activity; description of the purpose of the program and the need it addresses; an indication of other known organizations offering such a program; amount of request; geographic area and target population to be served; description of the work plan and timeline to carry out the activity; expected measurable results, and how they will be evaluated; details about other sources of funding; whether any other funding sources have declined a request for support of this activity, and identify those sources; a plan for proceeding if only part of the funding sought is granted; an outline of a plan to secure continued support for the program after the conclusion of McGregor Fund support; and the names and qualifications of the individuals who will implement the program or project (resumes are acceptable). A copy of an annual report, if available, should be included.

Deadlines: None. Applications may be submitted anytime. Trustee meetings are scheduled four times a year, in February, May, September, and November. Applicants are encouraged to submit proposals well in advance of the trustee meeting where the proposal is to be considered, as proposals may take up to 3 months for staff review.

Restrictions

The fund does not provide loans; direct grants to students for scholarships; grants for travel, conferences, seminars, or workshops; or grants to individuals. The principal interest of the fund is the Detroit metropolitan area, although requests will be considered from organizations located elsewhere for programs or projects significantly benefiting the Detroit metropolitan area. The geographic area for educational programs at the private college level is limited to the states of Michigan and Ohio. Occasional grants are made as individual trustee selections to higher educational institutions elsewhere in the United States. National and local chapters of disease-specific organizations are no longer funded.

Additional Information

The Matching Gifts Program of the McGregor fund matches trustee and employee contributions to nonprofit organizations dollar-for-dollar with certain conditions and limitations. Matching gifts totaling $69,168 were paid during the 1998 fiscal year.

Publications: Annual Report; Guidelines

Foundation Officials

Dave Bing: trustee B Washington, DC 1943. ED Syracuse University BA (1966). PRIM CORP EMPL chief executive officer, chairman: Bing Group. CORP AFFIL owner: Heritage 21; chief executive officer, chairman: Superb Manufacturing; director: Detroit Edison Co.; founder: Alpha Capital Management; chairman, president: Bing Steel.

C. David Campbell: president, assistant secretary

Cynthia N. Ford: trustee

Ruth R. Glancy: trustee

Ira J. Jaffe: trustee

Eugene A. Miller: chairman, trustee B Detroit, MI 1937. ED Detroit Institute of Technology BBA (1964); University of Wisconsin School of Bank Administration (1968). CORP AFFIL director: Detroit Edison Co.; director: DTE Energy Co.; director: Amerisure Companies; chairman, chief executive officer: Comerica Bank. NONPR AFFIL director: Detroit Medical Center; director: Detroit Symphony Orchestra Hall Inc.; member: Bankers Roundtable; vice chairman, tru: Cranbrook Educational Community.

William W. Shelden, Jr.: trustee

Bruce W. Steinhauer, MD: trustee, vice chairman B 1933. ED Amherst College BS (1955); Harvard University Medical School MD (1959). CORP AFFIL director: Analogic Corp. NONPR AFFIL chief executive officer, director: Lahey-Hitchcock Clinic.

Peter Palms Thurber: trustee B Detroit, MI 1928. ED Williams College BA (1950); Harvard University Law School JD (1953). PRIM CORP EMPL council: Miller, Canfield, Paddock & Stone. NONPR AFFIL trustee: Council Michigan Foundations; member: Michigan Bar Association; trustee: Community Foundation Southeast Michigan; member: American Bar Association; fellow: American Bar Foundation. CLUB AFFIL mem: Country Club Detroit.

Grants Analysis

Disclosure Period: fiscal year ending June 30, 2002

Total Grants: $6,878,114*

Number of Grants: 79

Average Grant: $87,065

Highest Grant: $533,333

Typical Range: $25,000 to $150,000

*Note: Giving excludes matching gifts, scholarships, United Way.

Recent Grants

Note: Grants derived from fiscal 2001 Form 990.

General

534,583	Detroit Symphony Orchestra Hall, Detroit, MI -- support the Orchestra Place campaign
502,000	Community Foundation for Southeastern Michigan, Detroit, MI -- to support the Hope Fund
500,000	Local Initiative Support Corporation, Detroit, MI -- support program to revitalize neighborhoods
500,000	Wayne State University, Detroit, MI
400,000	Alternatives for Girls, Detroit, MI
307,000	Founders Society Detroit Institute of Arts, Detroit, MI -- to support operating and capital support
250,000	Schools of the 21st Century Corporation, Detroit, MI -- develop a school-based student performance accountability
200,000	Coalition on Temporary Shelter, Detroit, MI -- to support general operations at the Peterboro facility
200,000	Lighthouse of Oakland County, Pontiac, MI -- to support Keepers of Hope campaign
150,000	Children's Center of Wayne County, Detroit, MI -- support a new center and make improvements to link all facilities

McINERNY FOUNDATION

Giving Contact

c/o Pacific Century Trust
PO Box 3170
Honolulu, HI 96802-3170
Phone: (808)538-4540
Fax: (808)538-4647

Description

Founded: 1937

EIN: 996002356

Organization Type: General Purpose Foundation

Giving Locations: HI

Grant Types: Capital, Challenge, Matching, Project, Seed Money.

Donor Information

Founder: The McInerny Foundation was established in 1937, by William H. McInerny and James D. McInerny and their sister, Ella McInerny. They were descendants of Patrick Michael McInerny who arrived in the Hawaiian Islands from Ireland during the mid-nineteenth century whaling period. The first distribution committee of the McInerny Foundation consisted of James and William McInerny. After the death of James in 1945, William constituted the distribution committee until his death in 1947. Since then, as provided in the trust indenture, the distribution committee has consisted of three members appointed by the board of directors of Pacific Century Trust, corporate trustee of the foundation.

Financial Summary

Total Giving: $2,997,811 (fiscal year ending September 30, 2001); $2,798,461 (fiscal 2000); $2,562,202 (fiscal 1999)

Giving Analysis: Giving for fiscal 2000 includes: foundation grants to United Way ($15,000); fiscal 1999: foundation grants to United Way ($51,175); fiscal 1998: foundation grants to United Way ($71,556); foundation scholarships ($117,000);

Assets: $59,686,036 (fiscal 2001); $73,130,517 (fiscal 2000); $62,814,040 (fiscal 1999)

Typical Recipients

Arts & Humanities: Arts Centers, Arts Festivals, Arts Funds, Arts Institutes, Community Arts, Dance, Arts & Humanities-General, Historic Preservation, History & Archaeology, Libraries, Literary Arts, Museums/Galleries, Music, Opera, Performing Arts, Public Broadcasting, Theater, Visual Arts

Civic & Public Affairs: Asian American Affairs, Botanical Gardens/Parks, Community Foundations, Economic Development, Employment/Job Training, Civic & Public Affairs-General, Housing, Legal Aid, Nonprofit Management, Parades/Festivals, Rural Affairs, Women's Affairs

Education: Afterschool/Enrichment Programs, Arts/Humanities Education, Colleges & Universities, Economic Education, Education Reform, Elementary Education (Private), Elementary Education (Public), Environmental Education, Faculty Development, Education-General, Gifted & Talented Programs, International Studies, Literacy, Medical Education, Minority Education, Preschool Education, Private Education (Precollege), Public Education (Precollege), Science/Mathematics Education, Secondary Education (Private), Social Sciences Education, Special Education, Student Aid, Vocational & Technical Education

Environment: Environment-General, Resource Conservation

Health: AIDS/HIV, Cancer, Children's Health/Hospitals, Clinics/Medical Centers, Emergency/Ambulance Services, Health Organizations, Home-Care Services, Hospices, Hospitals, Long-Term Care, Medical Rehabilitation, Mental Health, Prenatal Health Issues, Public Health, Single-Disease Health Associations

International: Foreign Arts Organizations, Foreign Educational Institutions, International Affairs

Religion: Jewish Causes, Ministries, Religious Welfare

Science: Science Museums, Scientific Centers & Institutes

Social Services: Animal Protection, At-Risk Youth, Child Welfare, Community Centers, Community Service Organizations, Day Care, Domestic Violence, Family Planning, Family Services, Food/Clothing Distribution, People with Disabilities, Recreation & Athletics, Scouts, Senior Services, Shelters/Homelessness, Substance Abuse, United Funds/United Ways, Veterans, Volunteer Services, YMCA/YWCA/YMHA/YWHA, Youth Organizations

Application Procedures

Initial Contact: Applicants seeking capital grants, tuition aid, or scholarship programs (schools only) should contact the foundation to obtain required questionnaires. Organizations requesting general support should submit a written proposal.

Application Requirements: The proposal should include a letter of not more than three pages, signed by the presiding officer of the board of directors, containing a description of organization; summary of the proposed activity, including a statement of need or problem to be addressed, how the activity is to be carried out, population to be served, and plan for evaluating the activity's effectiveness; total cost of the project/program, amount requested from the McInerny Foundation and from other funding sources, and plans for future support; statement regarding the qualifications of personnel responsible for carrying out the project; statement as to active participation by board members; and name and telephone number of board members. The letter should be accompanied by a project/program budget and an organizational budget showing projected income and expenditures; a list of the governing board members and their professional of business affiliations; and two or three letters of endorsement for the proposed activity. Applicants should submit an original and six copies of the proposal, avoiding elaborate or bulky binding.

Additionally, one copy of the following should be included with the proposal: proof of tax-exempt status, organization's financial statements for its last accounting period (preferably audited); the organization's charter and bylaws; and any other information and material pertinent to the request.

Deadlines: None, for applications for general support; July 15 for major capital projects; and January 15 for scholarship programs.

Review Process: The distribution committee meets frequently to consider grant proposals. Requests for capital fund drives are considered only at the committee's September meetings. Requests from schools for tuition aid and scholarships are considered only at the committee's March meetings.

Sixty days are required to process proposals, allowing for a possible visit to the site and for studying the proposal in relation to other foundation activities.

Decision Notification: Applicants are notified in writing of the distribution committee's decision.

Restrictions

Under the deed of trust, the foundation does not give grants or scholarships to individuals, nor does it provide grants for deficit funding or endowments, or to religious organizations.

Additional Information

Grantees are required to submit narrative and financial reports to the foundation.

The foundation will consider one grant request per organization per year, with the exception of scholarship/tuition aid requests.

Publications: Annual Report (including Guidelines)

Foundation Officials

Gerry Ching: member distribution committee
Henry Benjamin Clark, Jr.: member distribution committee B Chevy Chase, MD October 08, 1915. ED Northwestern University BCS (1937); Harvard University MBA (1940). NONPR AFFIL chairman emeritus: Honolulu Academy Arts.
Mark H. Fukunaga: alternate mem distribution comm B Honolulu, HI. ED Pomona College (1978); University of Chicago JD (1982). PRIM CORP EMPL chief executive officer, chairman: Servco Pacific Inc. CORP AFFIL chairman, chief executive officer: Pola Cosmetics; chairman, chief executive officer: Service Motors; chairman, chief executive officer: Film Services Hawaii; chairman, chief executive officer: Motor Imports.
Lois C. Loomis: contact PRIM CORP EMPL vice president, secretary charitable foundations officer: Hawaiian Trust Co. Ltd.
Michael A. O'Brien: chairman
Thurston Twigg-Smith: alternate member B Honolulu, HI 1921. ED Yale University BA (1942). PRIM CORP EMPL chairman, chief executive officer, director: Persis Corp. CORP AFFIL director: Horvitz Newspaper Inc.; chairman: Northwest Media Inc.; director: Atlanta/Sosnoff Capital Corporate; chairman, chief executive officer: ASA Properties Inc.; director: Atlanta Capital. NONPR AFFIL member: Honolulu Chamber of Commerce; trustee: Yale University Art Gallery; trustee: Contemporary Museum, Hawaii; trustee: Honolulu Academy Arts. CLUB AFFIL Pacific Club; Waialae Country Club; Oahu Country Club; Outrigger Canoe Club; Honolulu Country Club.
Jenai Sullivan Wall: alternate member B 1950. PRIM CORP EMPL president: Foodland Super Market Ltd. CORP AFFIL officer: First Hawaiian Bank; officer: First Hawaiian Inc.

Grants Analysis

Disclosure Period: fiscal year ending September 30, 2001

Total Grants: $2,972,311*

Number of Grants: 196

Average Grant: $15,165

Highest Grant: $150,000

Typical Range: $5,000 to $25,000

*Note: Giving excludes United Way.

Recent Grants

Note: Grants derived from fiscal 2001 Form 990.

General

150,000	Honolulu Academy of Arts, Honolulu, HI -- Renaissance Campaign
100,000	Hawaii Community Foundation, Honolulu, HI -- Partnership in Community-Building Initiatives Program
58,000	Punahou School, Honolulu, HI -- tuition aid program
50,000	Oahu Economic Development Board, Honolulu, HI -- phase one target 2005 business plan budget
40,000	Daughters of Hawaii, Honolulu, HI -- renovation and expansion of the Kuakini building at Hulihe'e Palace
40,000	Hamakua Diversified Agricultural, Paauilo, HI -- capital campaign
40,000	University of Hawaii Foundation, Honolulu, HI -- challenge grant for alumni giving
40,000	University of Hawaii Foundation, Honolulu, HI -- scholarships in College of Education
37,500	Catholic Charities, Honolulu, HI -- economic relief to families and individuals with financial hardship
37,500	Institute for Human Services, Honolulu, HI -- economic relief to families and individuals with financial hardship

MCKAY FAMILY FOUNDATION

Giving Contact

C. Bruce Kilen, Trustee
2350 Oakmont Way, Rm. 206
PO Box 70313
Eugene, OR 97401-0117
Phone: (541)686-5963

Description

Founded: 1986
EIN: 930935036
Organization Type: Private Foundation
Giving Locations: OR: Lane County
Grant Types: Capital, General Support, Scholarship.

Donor Information

Founder: the late Miles E. McKay, the late Eleanor P. McKay

Financial Summary

Total Giving: $177,189 (2002); $169,820 (2001); $171,000 (2000)

Giving Analysis: Giving for 2002 includes: foundation scholarships ($10,000); 1998: foundation scholarships ($5,000) foundation ($166,965)

Assets: $3,900,639 (2002); $3,742,403 (2001); $3,675,143 (2000)

Gifts Received: $553 (2000); $550 (1999); $595 (1997)

Typical Recipients

Arts & Humanities: Arts & Humanities-General, Libraries, Museums/Galleries, Opera
Civic & Public Affairs: Botanical Gardens/Parks, Civic & Public Affairs-General, Housing, Women's Affairs
Education: Business Education, Engineering/Technological Education, Education-General, Leadership Training, Science/Mathematics Education, Student Aid
Health: Children's Health/Hospitals, Clinics/Medical Centers, Emergency/Ambulance Services, Heart, Mental Health, Prenatal Health Issues
Religion: Religious Welfare
Science: Scientific Centers & Institutes
Social Services: At-Risk Youth, Camps, Child Abuse, Child Welfare, Community Service Organizations, Counseling, Day Care, Emergency Relief, Family Services, Food/Clothing Distribution, People with Disabilities, Senior Services, Shelters/Homelessness, Youth Organizations

Application Procedures

Initial Contact: Send a brief letter of inquiry.
Application Requirements: Include a description of organization, amount requested, proof of tax-exempt status, list of board of governors.
Deadlines: March 15 and September 15.

Foundation Officials

Philip F. Baird, Jr.: trustee
C. Bruce Kilen: trustee
Tracie M. Shojai: trustee
Kelly L. Thakkar: trustee
Dale Williams: trustee

Grants Analysis

Disclosure Period: calendar year ending 2002
Total Grants: $167,189*
Number of Grants: 25
Average Grant: $6,688
Highest Grant: $20,000
Lowest Grant: $1,000
Typical Range: $1,000 to $10,000
*Note: Giving excludes scholarships.

Recent Grants

Note: Grants derived from 2001 Form 990.

General

15,000	Relief Nursery, Eugene, OR -- Outreach Connections Program
15,000	St. Vincent de Paul Society, Eugene, OR -- The Boy's Group Program
10,000	American Red Cross, Eugene, OR -- capital grant for renovation
10,000	Casa of Lane County, Eugene, OR -- Capacity Building Project
10,000	Cottage Grove Habitat for Humanity -- acquisition of land
10,000	Eugene Mission, Eugene, OR -- upgrading shelter building
10,000	Lane County Legal Aid Service, Inc., Eugene, OR -- Supervised Parenting Time Program
10,000	Looking Glass Youth and Family Services, Eugene, OR -- Violence Intervention Project
10,000	Pearl Buck Center, Eugene, OR -- Family with Special Needs program
7,500	Food for Lane County, Eugene, OR -- Youth Farm Project

THOMAS M. MCKEE CHARITABLE TRUST

Giving Contact

Lynn A. Hammond, Trustee
200 E. 7th St., Suite 418
Loveland, CO 80537-4871
Phone: (970)667-1023
Fax: (970)669-9380

Description

Founded: 1992
EIN: 846228546
Organization Type: Private Foundation
Giving Locations: CO: Loveland
Grant Types: General Support, Project.

Financial Summary

Total Giving: $309,345 (2001); $150,700 (2000); $136,230 (1999)
Assets: $3,902,308 (2001); $4,117,807 (2000); $3,916,106 (1999)

Typical Recipients

Arts & Humanities: Arts Centers, Libraries
Civic & Public Affairs: Employment/Job Training, Housing, Municipalities/Towns
Education: Colleges & Universities, Community & Junior Colleges, Education-General, Preschool Education, Public Education (Precollege)
Health: Clinics/Medical Centers, Heart, Hospices, Medical Rehabilitation, Public Health
Religion: Churches
Social Services: Community Service Organizations, Counseling, Day Care, Food/Clothing Distribution, People with Disabilities, Recreation & Athletics, Substance Abuse, Volunteer Services

Application Procedures

Initial Contact: Send a brief letter of inquiry.
Application Requirements: Include supporting financial information, purpose of funds sought, and proof of tax-exempt status.
Deadlines: None.

Restrictions

Grants limited to Loveland, CO and Colorado College.

Foundation Officials

Lynn A. Hammond: trustee
Clare W. White: trustee

Grants Analysis

Disclosure Period: calendar year ending 2001
Total Grants: $309,345
Number of Grants: 5
Highest Grant: $250,000
Lowest Grant: $5,000
Typical Range: $18,115 to $18,115

Recent Grants

Note: Grants derived from 2000 Form 990.

General

35,000	Hospice of Larimer County, Ft. Collins, CO -- medical
20,000	Colorado College, Colorado Springs, CO -- educational
20,000	Foothills - Gateway Foundation, Ft. Collins, CO -- educational
20,000	McKee Medical Center Foundation, Loveland, CO -- medical
12,500	P.O.P.S Program, Loveland, CO -- educational
10,000	Hearts and Horses, Loveland, CO -- therapeutic riding
8,700	Namaqua Center, Loveland, CO -- abuse rehabilitation

7,500	Thompson Education Foundation, Loveland, CO -- educational
7,000	Thompson Education Foundation, Loveland, CO -- educational
5,000	Mountain View Presbyterian Church, Loveland, CO -- religious

ROBERT E. AND EVELYN MCKEE FOUNDATION

Giving Contact

Louis B. McKee, President, Treasurer & Trustee
PO Box 220599
El Paso, TX 79913-2599
Phone: (915)581-4025
E-mail: McKee_Foundation@msn.com
Web: http://www.mckeefoundation.org

Description

Founded: 1952
EIN: 746036675
Organization Type: Private Foundation
Giving Locations: TX: emphasis on El Paso
Grant Types: Capital, Emergency, General Support, Multiyear/Continuing Support, Operating Expenses, Research, Scholarship, Seed Money.

Donor Information

Founder: the late Robert E. McKee, the late Evelyn McKee, Robert E. McKee, Inc., the Zia Co.

Financial Summary

Total Giving: $506,221 (2000); $448,927 (1999); $366,564 (1998)
Giving Analysis: Giving for 2000 includes: foundation grants to United Way ($15,000); foundation scholarships ($52,000) 1999: foundation scholarships ($177,942)
Assets: $8,122,280 (2000); $7,570,797 (1999); $6,660,077 (1996)
Gifts Received: $10,075 (1996); $10,000 (1995); $196,244 (1994). Note: In 1996, contributions were received from Elizabeth McKee Lund ($10,000) and Michael and Lillian Bidal ($75).

Typical Recipients

Arts & Humanities: Arts & Humanities-General, History & Archaeology, Libraries, Museums/Galleries, Music, Public Broadcasting
Civic & Public Affairs: Clubs, Civic & Public Affairs-General, Hispanic Affairs, Parades/Festivals, Urban & Community Affairs, Women's Affairs, Zoos/Aquariums
Education: Afterschool/Enrichment Programs, Agricultural Education, Business Education, Colleges & Universities, Education Funds, Elementary Education (Public), Engineering/Technological Education, Health & Physical Education, Medical Education, Private Education (Precollege), Public Education (Precollege), Science/Mathematics Education, Secondary Education (Public), Student Aid
Health: Alzheimers Disease, Cancer, Children's Health/Hospitals, Clinics/Medical Centers, Emergency/Ambulance Services, Eyes/Blindness, Heart, Hospices, Hospitals, Medical Rehabilitation, Medical Research, Mental Health, Nursing Services, Single-Disease Health Associations, Trauma Treatment
International: Health Care/Hospitals
Religion: Churches, Religious Welfare
Science: Science Museums
Social Services: Animal Protection, Camps, Child Abuse, Child Welfare, Community Centers, Community Service Organizations, Counseling, Crime Prevention, Domestic Violence, Food/Clothing Distribution, People with Disabilities, Scouts, Senior Services, Shelters/Homelessness, Substance Abuse, United Funds/United Ways, YMCA/YWCA/YMHA/YWHA, Youth Organizations

Application Procedures

Initial Contact: Send a brief letter of inquiry.
Application Requirements: Include a description of organization, purpose of funds sought, list of governing board and chief administrator of organization, recently audited financial statement, and proof of tax-exempt status.
Deadlines: December 15.

Restrictions

Does not support individuals.

Additional Information

Publications: Annual Report; Application Guidelines

Foundation Officials

Charlotte McKee Cohen: vice president, trustee
Frances McKee Hays: senior vice president
Robert L. Hazelton: senior vice president
Sharon Hays Herrera: vice president, trustee
Margaret McKee Lund: senior vice president
C. Steven McKee: trustee
David C. McKee: secretary, assistant treasurer, trustee
John S. McKee: senior vice president
Louis B. McKee: president-treasurer, trustee
Nelson D. McKee: vice president, trustee
Philip Russell McKee: vice president, trustee
R. Brian McKee: trustee
Robert E. McKee, III: trustee, treasurer ED Colorado School of Mines; Massachusetts Institute of Technology. PRIM CORP EMPL executive vice president corporate strategy & development: Conoco, Inc. CORP AFFIL senior vice president corporate strategy & development: El du Pont de Nemours & Co. NONPR AFFIL director: American Petroleum Institute; member: Society Petroleum Engineers.
Susan J. McKee: vice president, trustee
H.A. (Al) Woods: trustee
Helen Lund Yancey: vice president, trustee

Grants Analysis

Disclosure Period: calendar year ending 2000
Total Grants: $439,221*
Number of Grants: 140
Average Grant: $3,137
Highest Grant: $40,425
Typical Range: $1,000 to $5,000
*Note: Giving excludes scholarship; United Way.

Recent Grants

Note: Grants derived from 2001 Form 990.

General

149,534	XII Travelers Memorial of the Southwest, El Paso, TX
25,000	University of Texas at El Paso, El Paso, TX -- for Centennial Museum
15,990	El Paso Lighthouse for the Blind, El Paso, TX
15,000	New Mexico State University, Las Cruces, NM -- electric utility management program
15,000	University of Texas at El Paso, El Paso, TX -- for women's basketball
13,200	EPISD Fund, El Paso, TX
12,442	Carlos Rivera Elementary School, El Paso, TX
12,400	YMCA of Greater El Paso, El Paso, NM
12,000	Candlelighters of El Paso Area, El Paso, NM
11,000	Hospice of El Paso, El Paso, TX

KATHERINE MABIS MCKENNA FOUNDATION

Giving Contact

Linda M. Boxx, Chairman
Mellon Bank NA
PO Box 185
Latrobe, PA 15650

Phone: (724)537-6900
Fax: (724)537-6906

Description

Founded: 1969
EIN: 237042752
Organization Type: Family Foundation
Giving Locations: PA: Eastern Westmoreland County
Grant Types: Capital, Endowment, General Support, Operating Expenses, Project, Scholarship, Seed Money.

Donor Information

Founder: Incorporated in 1969 by the late Katherine M. McKenna .

Financial Summary

Total Giving: $3,717,750 (2000); $3,721,593 (1998); $3,234,850 (1997)
Giving Analysis: Giving for 1998 includes: foundation grants to United Way ($20,000); 1997: foundation grants to United Way ($15,000) foundation scholarships ($75,000)
Assets: $85,335,916 (2000); $79,326,591 (1998); $72,101,410 (1997)
Gifts Received: $25,881,829 (1993). Note: In 1991, contributions were received from the estate of Katherine Mabis McKenna. In 1993, contributions were also received from this estate as well as from property transferred from agency account for Alex McKenna, executor for Kathryn Mabis McKenna.

Typical Recipients

Arts & Humanities: Arts Associations & Councils, Arts Festivals, Ethnic & Folk Arts, Arts & Humanities-General, Historic Preservation, History & Archaeology, Libraries, Museums/Galleries, Music, Opera, Performing Arts, Public Broadcasting
Civic & Public Affairs: Botanical Gardens/Parks, Business/Free Enterprise, Chambers of Commerce, Civil Rights, Clubs, Community Foundations, Economic Development, Economic Policy, Civic & Public Affairs-General, Housing, Law & Justice, Legal Aid, Municipalities/Towns, Nonprofit Management, Parades/Festivals, Philanthropic Organizations, Public Policy, Safety, Urban & Community Affairs, Women's Affairs, Zoos/Aquariums
Education: Arts/Humanities Education, Business Education, Colleges & Universities, Community & Junior Colleges, Economic Education, Education Associations, Education Funds, Education Reform, Environmental Education, Education-General, Legal Education, Literacy, Minority Education, Private Education (Precollege), Public Education (Precollege), Religious Education, Science/Mathematics Education, Social Sciences Education, Student Aid
Environment: Environment-General, Resource Conservation, Watershed
Health: Arthritis, Cancer, Emergency/Ambulance Services, Hospitals, Medical Rehabilitation, Research/Studies Institutes, Single-Disease Health Associations
International: International Affairs, International Organizations
Religion: Bible Study/Translation, Churches, Religion-General, Religious Welfare, Religious Welfare, Social/Policy Issues
Science: Science Exhibits & Fairs, Scientific Centers & Institutes
Social Services: Big Brother/Big Sister, Community Service Organizations, Crime Prevention, Family Services, People with Disabilities, Recreation & Athletics, Scouts, Social Services-General, United Funds/United Ways, Volunteer Services, YMCA/YWCA/YMHA/YWHA, Youth Organizations

Application Procedures

Initial Contact: The foundation does not have a specific application form.
Application Requirements: All requests should briefly describe the requesting organization and the

particular project for which funding is sought. Foundation will provide requirements for a full proposal after initial inquiry. Proposals should include budgets for both the organization and the project, a list of donors and trustees or directors, the organization's IRS tax-exempt letter, and its most recent audited financial statements.
Deadlines: Contact the foundation for deadlines.

Restrictions

The foundation does not support individuals, matching funds, or loans.

Additional Information

Mellon Bank, NA, Pittsburgh, PA, is corporate agent. In 1993, the foundation made a non-cash gift of $1,500 in tangible property to the Westmoreland Symphony Orchestra.
Publications: Program Policy Statement

Foundation Officials

Linda McKenna Boxx: director
T. William Boxx: chairman
Wilma F. McKenna: vchairman, director
Zan McKenna Rich: director

Grants Analysis

Disclosure Period: calendar year ending 2000
Total Grants: $3,717,750*
Number of Grants: 70
Average Grant: $48,508
Highest Grant: $500,000
Lowest Grant: $1,000
Typical Range: $1,000 to $50,000 and $100,000 to $500,000
*Note: Giving excludes United Way.

Recent Grants

Note: Grants derived from 2000 Form 990.

Library-Related

25,000	Ligonier Valley Library, Ligonier, PA

General

500,000	Seton Hill College, Greensburg, PA -- general
500,000	University of Pittsburgh, Greensburg, PA -- capital campaign
325,000	Philip M. McKenna Foundation, Inc., Latrobe, PA -- public policy support
250,000	Westmoreland Trust, Greensburg, PA -- Palace Theatre - Capital
225,000	Westmoreland Trust, Greensburg, PA -- capital campaign
170,000	Loyalhanna Watershed Association, Ligonier, PA -- land acquisition
150,000	Fay-Penn Economic Development Council, Uniontown, PA -- Center at Fort Necessity
125,000	Bucknell University, Lewisburg, PA -- McKenna Internship Program
125,000	Bushy Run Battlefield Heritage Society, Inc., Harrison City, PA -- land acquisition
100,000	Greater Uniontown Heritage Consortium, Uniontown, PA -- Restoration - State Theatre

PHILIP M. MCKENNA FOUNDATION

Giving Contact

T. William Boxx, Chairman
PO Box 186
Latrobe, PA 15650
Phone: (724)537-6901
Fax: (724)537-6906

Description

Founded: 1967
EIN: 256082635
Organization Type: General Purpose Foundation
Giving Locations: PA: Southwestern Pennsylvania for community and civic programs nationally for public policy.
Grant Types: Capital, Operating Expenses, Research, Scholarship, Seed Money.

Donor Information

Founder: Incorporated in 1967 by the late Philip M. McKenna .

Financial Summary

Total Giving: $1,101,000 (2003 approx); $1,101,000 (2002 approx); $1,300,000 (2001)
Giving Analysis: Giving for 1997 includes: foundation grants to United Way ($5,000); foundation scholarships ($59,000) foundation fellowships ($70,000)
Assets: $20,000,000 (2001 approx); $19,682,099 (2000); $21,000,000 (1999 approx)
Gifts Received: $325,000 (2000); $325,000 (1998); $300,000 (1997). Note: Contributions were received from Katherine M. McKenna Foundation.

Typical Recipients

Arts & Humanities: Arts Centers, Libraries, Museums/Galleries, Public Broadcasting, Theater
Civic & Public Affairs: Business/Free Enterprise, Civil Rights, Economic Policy, Civic & Public Affairs-General, Law & Justice, Legal Aid, Philanthropic Organizations, Professional & Trade Associations, Public Policy
Education: Business Education, Colleges & Universities, Continuing Education, Economic Education, Education Associations, Education Funds, Education Reform, Environmental Education, Education-General, Journalism/Media Education, Legal Education, Minority Education, Religious Education, Science/Mathematics Education, Social Sciences Education, Student Aid
Environment: Environment-General, Watershed
Health: Health Policy/Cost Containment, Hospitals, Research/Studies Institutes
International: Foreign Educational Institutions, Health Care/Hospitals, International Relations
Religion: Religious Welfare, Social/Policy Issues
Science: Science Museums, Scientific Centers & Institutes, Scientific Research
Social Services: Animal Protection, Community Service Organizations, Emergency Relief, Family Services, Food/Clothing Distribution, Recreation & Athletics, United Funds/United Ways, Youth Organizations

Application Procedures

Initial Contact: Send a letter to the chairman explaining grant request and copy of 501(c).
Application Requirements: Include description of the organization, purpose of funds sought, operating budget, project budget, annual report, list of members of the governing board with affiliations, list of major donors, recently audited financial statement, and proof of tax-exempt status.
Deadlines: April1 and October 1.

Restrictions

The foundation does not make grants to individuals, foreign organizations, or for matching gifts or loans.

Foundation Officials

T. William Boxx: secretary, treasurer, officer
Zan McKenna Rich: director
Norbert Tail: secretary, director

Grants Analysis

Disclosure Period: calendar year ending 2000
Total Grants: $1,234,495
Number of Grants: 50
Average Grant: $24,690

Highest Grant: $105,000
Typical Range: $10,000 to $50,000

Recent Grants

Note: Grants derived from 1999 Form 990.

General

130,000	Intercollegiate Studies Institute, Philadelphia, PA -- operations
100,000	Heritage Foundation, The, Washington, DC -- McKenna senior fellow in political economy
95,000	Commonwealth Foundation for Public Policy Alternatives, Harrisburg, PA -- operations
60,500	St. Vincent College, Latrobe, PA -- for AGM Economics Education Series and George Washington program
50,000	Morley Institute, Washington, DC -- for catholic voters research
40,000	Claremont Institute for Study of Statesmanship and Political Philosophy, Claremont, CA -- operations
40,000	Pacific Research Institute for Public Policy, San Francisco, CA -- operating support
38,000	Pennsylvanians for Effective Government Education Committee, Harrisburg, PA -- support internships, educational projects
37,000	Capital Research Center, Washington, DC -- operating support
35,000	Federalist Society for Law and Public Policy Studies, Washington, DC -- support Pennsylvania and nationwide programs

CARL AND ALLEEN MCKINNEY CHARITABLE TRUST

Giving Contact

c/o Arvest Trust Co., NA
PO Box 1229
Bentonville, AR 72712-1229
Phone: (479)271-1254

Description

Founded: 1997
EIN: 716167536
Organization Type: Private Foundation
Giving Locations: AR
Grant Types: General Support, Scholarship.

Financial Summary

Total Giving: $250,108 (2001); $138,918 (2000); $95,428 (1999)
Giving Analysis: Giving for 2001 includes: foundation scholarships ($10,397); 1999: foundation scholarships ($1,556) 1998: foundation scholarships ($699)
Assets: $3,764,392 (2001); $3,858,879 (2000); $3,735,860 (1999)
Gifts Received: $49,952 (1998); $2,909,669 (1997). Note: In 1998, contributions were received from the McKinney Charitable Trust.

Typical Recipients

Civic & Public Affairs: Clubs, Housing
Education: Colleges & Universities, Elementary Education (Public), Education-General, Preschool Education, Student Aid, Vocational & Technical Education
Religion: Churches
Social Services: Child Welfare, Emergency Relief, Senior Services, Shelters/Homelessness, Social Services-General

Application Procedures

Initial Contact: Request scholarship application from NWACC Financial Aid Office.
Application Requirements: Include application, essay, letters of recommendation, copy of transcripts or GED test scores and/or grade transcript from post-secondary schools.

Additional Information

Trust(s): Arvest Trust Company

Foundation Officials

Joni C. Brake: board
Ed Clifford: trustee
Gary Compton: board
Morgan Cox: board
Doylene Fuqua: board
Lewis Holloway: board
Blaine Jackson: trustee
Carolyn F. Jines: trustee
Kurt Loyd: trustee
Charles H. Mullins: trustee
Stephen Pelphrey: trustee
Jim Reynolds: board
Donna Scanlan: trustee
Alice Stephens: trustee
T. Diane Wells: trustee

Grants Analysis

Disclosure Period: calendar year ending 2001
Total Grants: $239,711*
Number of Grants: 12
Average Grant: $19,976
Highest Grant: $35,559
Lowest Grant: $2,300
Typical Range: $5,000 to $32,000
*Note: Giving excludes scholarships.

Recent Grants

Note: Grants derived from 2001 Form 990.

General

35,559	Helen R. Walton Children's Center, Bentonville, AR -- for classroom repairs and furniture purchases
31,795	Northwest Arkansas Children's Shelter, Bentonville, AR -- to purchase storage building and 2 freezers
30,200	Youth Bridge, Inc., Centerton, AR -- for van and furnishings for shelter and recreation
28,582	Boys and Girls Club of Benton County, Bentonville, AR -- to replace gym floors
25,000	First United Methodist Church, Bentonville, AR -- for youth and children's building
25,000	Rocky Creek Horses Help, Rogers, AR -- for 50 riding scholarships
23,325	Bella Vista Leadership Class, Bentonville, AR -- for construction of state park in Bentonville
20,000	Our Farm, Inc., Rogers, AR -- for new windows for May House for Boys
7,000	Havenwood, Bentonville, AR -- for therapy and activity equipment and dental fund
5,650	Boys and Girls Club of Benton County, Bentonville, AR -- to replace bathroom stalls at McKinney Unit

MCLEAN CONTRIBUTIONSHIP

Giving Contact

Sandra L. McLean, Executive Director
945 Haverford Road
Bryn Mawr, PA 19010-3814
Phone: (610)527-6330

Fax: (610)527-9733
Web: http://fdncenter.org/grantmaker/mclean

Description

Founded: 1951
EIN: 236396940
Organization Type: General Purpose Foundation
Giving Locations: PA: primarily metropolitan Philadelphia
Grant Types: Capital, Endowment, Multiyear/Continuing Support.

Donor Information

Founder: Established in 1951 by the late Robert McLean , the late William L. McLean Jr. , and Bulletin Co.

Financial Summary

Total Giving: $2,269,240 (2001); $2,494,815 (2000); $2,148,010 (1999)
Assets: $47,265,519 (2001); $51,258,803 (2000); $48,776,634 (1999)
Gifts Received: $89,457 (2001); $177,222 (2000); $176,322 (1999). Note: In 2001, contributions were received from Independence Communications, Inc. ($80,000); William & Elizabeth McLean, III ($6,527); William McLean, IV ($2,048); and miscellaneous donors. In 1999 and 2000, substantial contributions were received from from Independence Communications, Inc. and William McLean, III.

Typical Recipients

Arts & Humanities: Arts Associations & Councils, Arts Centers, Ballet, Dance, Arts & Humanities-General, Historic Preservation, History & Archaeology, Libraries, Museums/Galleries, Music, Opera, Performing Arts, Theater
Civic & Public Affairs: Botanical Gardens/Parks, Business/Free Enterprise, Civil Rights, Clubs, Economic Development, Employment/Job Training, Civic & Public Affairs-General, Housing, Urban & Community Affairs, Women's Affairs, Zoos/Aquariums
Education: Agricultural Education, Arts/Humanities Education, Colleges & Universities, Continuing Education, Education Funds, Education Reform, Environmental Education, Education-General, Health & Physical Education, Journalism/Media Education, Journalism/Media Education, Literacy, Medical Education, Minority Education, Private Education (Precollege), Science/Mathematics Education, Social Sciences Education, Special Education, Student Aid, Vocational & Technical Education
Environment: Air/Water Quality, Environment-General, Resource Conservation, Watershed, Wildlife Protection
Health: AIDS/HIV, Cancer, Children's Health/Hospitals, Diabetes, Emergency/Ambulance Services, Eyes/Blindness, Health-General, Geriatric Health, Hospitals, Long-Term Care, Medical Rehabilitation, Medical Research, Mental Health, Nursing Services, Prenatal Health Issues, Public Health, Single-Disease Health Associations, Transplant Networks/Donor Banks
International: International Affairs, International Environmental Issues
Religion: Churches, Religious Welfare
Science: Science Museums, Scientific Centers & Institutes, Scientific Organizations
Social Services: Animal Protection, Camps, Child Welfare, Community Centers, Community Service Organizations, Day Care, Domestic Violence, Family Planning, Family Services, Food/Clothing Distribution, Homes, People with Disabilities, Recreation & Athletics, Scouts, Senior Services, Social Services-General, United Funds/United Ways, YMCA/YWCA/YMHA/YWHA, Youth Organizations

Application Procedures

Initial Contact: The foundation requests applications be made in writing.
Application Requirements: The Contributionship accepts the Delaware Valley Grantmakers Association Common Grant Application Form. Application may also be made by letter, including a project description and justification, budget and timetable, and strategy for securing funding. Applications should be accompanied by a financial statement for the most recent fiscal year, interim operating statements or budgets for future periods (if appropriate), proof of tax-exempt status, and a list of officers and directors.
Deadlines: None. Proposals are accepted throughout the year.
Review Process: The foundation reports that trustees meet three or four times per year.
Notes: The recipient of the grant is expected to submit periodic reports.

Restrictions

The Contributionship does not fund the costs or expenses of existing staff allocated to a project.

Additional Information

Publications: Application Guidelines

Foundation Officials

Jean Bodine: trustee
John Henry Buhsmer: trustee emeritus B Wilkes-Barre, PA 1932. ED King's College BA (1956). PRIM CORP EMPL vice president, director: Independent Publications Inc. ADD CORP EMPL president, chief executive officer: Newsnet Inc.
Charles E. Catherwood: treasurer B 1946. ED Pennsylvania State University BS (1969). PRIM CORP EMPL secretary, director: Finger Lakes Printing Co.
Leila Gordon Dyer: advisory trustee
Hunter R. Gordon: advisory trustee
Joseph K. Gordon: trustee B Philadelphia, PA 1925. ED Princeton University (1948); University of Pennsylvania School of Law (1951). PRIM CORP EMPL attorney: Montgomery, McCracken, Walker & Rhoads LLP. CORP AFFIL director: Independent Publications Inc.; chairman, director: Main Line Health Inc.
Sandra L. McLean: executive drc, advisory trustee
William L. McLean, IV: vice chairman, trustee PRIM CORP EMPL secretary: Independent Publications Inc.
William L. McLean, III: chairman, trustee B Philadelphia, PA 1927. ED Princeton University BA (1949). PRIM CORP EMPL president, director: Finger Lakes Printing Co. ADD CORP EMPL president, director: Independent Publications Inc.; president: Finger Lakes Times; president: Telegraph.
Carolyn M. Raymond: trustee

Grants Analysis

Disclosure Period: calendar year ending 2001
Total Grants: $2,269,240
Number of Grants: 83
Average Grant: $27,340
Highest Grant: $150,000
Lowest Grant: $425
Typical Range: $2,000 to $75,000

Recent Grants

Note: Grants derived from 2001 Form 990.

Library-Related

150,000	Library Company of Philadelphia, Philadelphia, PA -- towards the creation of a Conservation Endowment Fund
57,900	Lower Merion Library Foundation, Ardmore, PA -- collection development project
10,000	Abington Township Public Library, Abington, PA -- library renovation and automation project

General

150,000	Nature Conservancy, Inc., Philadelphia,

	PA -- funding for science and stewardship endowment
150,000	Williamson Free School of Mechanical Trades, Media, PA -- towards renovation the Townsend Cottage Dormitory
100,000	Lankenau Hospital, Wynnewood, PA -- renovation and development of new emergency room services
100,000	Morris Arboretum and Gardens, Philadelphia, PA -- endowment support for Natural Areas Land Management Program
100,000	National Constitution Center, Philadelphia, PA -- endowment
75,000	Delaware Nature Society, Hockessin, DE -- towards capital campaign
75,000	Jenkins Arboretum, Devon, PA -- endowment fund
55,000	Philadelphia Protestant Home, Philadelphia, PA -- renovation of Midway Manor
50,000	Bryn Mawr Rehabilitation Hospital, Malvern, PA -- construction of new stroke unit
50,000	Historic Bartram's Garden, Philadelphia, PA -- toward design and construction costs

CATHERINE L. AND ROBERT O. MCMAHAN FOUNDATION

Giving Contact

Neal W. McMahan, Executive Director
PO Box 221580
Carmel, CA 93922
Phone: (831)625-6444

Description

EIN: 946061273
Organization Type: Private Foundation
Giving Locations: CA: primarily Monterey County
Grant Types: Capital, General Support, Matching, Scholarship.

Donor Information

Founder: Robert O. McMahan

Financial Summary

Total Giving: $389,700 (2000); $381,900 (1999 approx); $346,500 (1998)
Giving Analysis: Giving for 2000 includes: foundation scholarships ($15,000); 1999: foundation matching gifts ($7,500) foundation scholarships ($14,500)
Assets: $8,507,878 (2000); $7,864,698 (1999); $7,579,375 (1998)

Typical Recipients

Arts & Humanities: Arts Centers, Arts & Humanities-General, History & Archaeology, Libraries, Museums/Galleries, Music, Public Broadcasting, Theater
Civic & Public Affairs: Clubs, Community Foundations, Civic & Public Affairs-General, Housing, Legal Aid, Municipalities/Towns, Parades/Festivals, Public Policy, Rural Affairs, Urban & Community Affairs, Zoos/Aquariums
Education: Colleges & Universities, Education-General, International Studies, Private Education (Precollege), Public Education (Precollege), School Volunteerism, Student Aid
Environment: Forestry, Resource Conservation, Wildlife Protection
Health: AIDS/HIV, Alzheimers Disease, Clinics/Medical Centers, Emergency/Ambulance Services, Eyes/Blindness, Heart, Home-Care Services, Medical Rehabilitation, Mental Health, Multiple Sclerosis, Nursing Services, Respiratory
Religion: Religious Welfare
Science: Science Museums

Social Services: Animal Protection, At-Risk Youth, Big Brother/Big Sister, Child Welfare, Community Service Organizations, Counseling, Emergency Relief, Family Planning, Family Services, Food/Clothing Distribution, People with Disabilities, Recreation & Athletics, Senior Services, Sexual Abuse, Shelters/Homelessness, Social Services-General, Substance Abuse, Volunteer Services, YMCA/YWCA/YMHA/YWHA, Youth Organizations

Application Procedures

Initial Contact: Send a brief letter of inquiry.
Application Requirements: Include a description of organization, current budget, list of board members, proof of tax-exempt status, purpose of funds sought, amount requested.
Deadlines: March 31 and September 30

Restrictions

Preference is given to education and healthcare organizations. No grants are made to individuals, religious purposes, religious organizations, or public schools.

Foundation Officials

Michael L. McMahan: chief financial officer
Neal W. McMahan: executive director
Nicki Wilson McMahan: director
Marsha Zelus: director

Grants Analysis

Disclosure Period: calendar year ending 2000
Total Grades: $374,700*
Number of Grants: 58
Average Grant: $4,905*
Highest Grant: $50,000
Typical Range: $1,000 to $10,000
*Note: Giving excludes scholarships. Average grant figure excludes two highest grants ($100,000).

Recent Grants

Note: Grants derived from 2001 Form 990.

General

50,000	Campaign for Sunset, Carmel, CA -- expansion and enhancement of Sunset Theater
30,000	Big Sur Land Trust, Carmel, CA -- Notley's Landing
25,000	York School, Monterey, CA -- capital campaign
15,000	Food Bank for Monterey County, Salinas, CA -- expand distribution center
10,000	Boys and Girls Club of Monterey County, Seaside, CA -- fund the intercession period
10,000	Central Coast YMCA, Salinas, CA -- Alisal Community Friends Program
10,000	Coalition of Homeless Services Providers, Marina, CA -- develop programs
10,000	Community Partnership for Youth, Monterey, CA -- after-school mentor/tutor program
10,000	Landwatch Monterey County, Monterey, CA
10,000	Planned Parenthood Mar Monte, Monterey, CA -- Expanded Service Program

MCMAHON FOUNDATION

Giving Contact

James F. Wood, Director
PO Box 2156
Lawton, OK 73502
Phone: (580)355-4622
Fax: (580)357-3248

Description

Founded: 1940
EIN: 730664314
Organization Type: General Purpose Foundation

Giving Locations: OK: Comanche County, only Oklahoma, Lawton
Grant Types: Capital, General Support, Matching, Multiyear/Continuing Support, Project, Scholarship.

Donor Information

Founder: The McMahon Foundation was established in Oklahoma in 1940, with funds donated by the estate of the late Eugene D. McMahon . The purpose of the foundation is to benefit the city of Lawton and Comanche County, OK.

Financial Summary

Total Giving: $2,882,584 (fiscal year ending March 31, 2002); $2,976,431 (fiscal 2001); $2,720,650 (fiscal 2000). Note: Figure for 1996 includes $157,200 in scholarships.
Giving Analysis: Giving for fiscal 1999 includes: foundation grants to United Way ($12,500) foundation scholarships ($156,339)
Assets: $56,383,430 (fiscal 2002); $56,383,430 (fiscal 2001); $56,760,517 (fiscal 2000)

Typical Recipients

Arts & Humanities: Arts Associations & Councils, Arts Festivals, Arts Institutes, Community Arts, Dance, Ethnic & Folk Arts, Historic Preservation, History & Archaeology, Libraries, Museums/Galleries, Music, Public Broadcasting, Theater
Civic & Public Affairs: Botanical Gardens/Parks, Community Foundations, Civic & Public Affairs-General, Housing, Municipalities/Towns, Parades/Festivals, Professional & Trade Associations, Safety, Urban & Community Affairs
Education: Arts/Humanities Education, Business-School Partnerships, Colleges & Universities, Education Reform, Education-General, Gifted & Talented Programs, Journalism/Media Education, Literacy, Public Education (Precollege), Secondary Education (Private), Special Education, Student Aid, Student Aid, Vocational & Technical Education
Environment: Wildlife Protection
Health: Emergency/Ambulance Services, Hospices, Nursing Services
Religion: Religion-General, Religious Welfare
Social Services: Child Welfare, Community Service Organizations, Crime Prevention, Food/Clothing Distribution, Homes, Recreation & Athletics, Substance Abuse, United Funds/United Ways, YMCA/YWCA/YMHA/YWHA, Youth Organizations

Application Procedures

Initial Contact: The foundation does not issue specific guidelines for applications. Send an initial letter of inquiry.
Application Requirements: The initial letter should describe the nature of the organization and the purpose of the grant requested.
Deadlines: None.
Review Process: The board meets on the first Monday of each month.

Restrictions

The foundation does not make grants to recipients outside of Oklahoma. Primary consideration in Comanche County, Oklahoma. No grants to individuals.

Foundation Officials

Kenneth Bridges: trustee
Ronald E. Cagle, MD: trustee
Kenneth Easton: trustee PRIM CORP EMPL secretary, director: Easton's Inc. CORP AFFIL secretary, director: Easton's Ace Hardware; secretary, director: Easton's Marine.
Charles S. Graybill, MD: chairman, trustee
Manville Redman: vchairman
Gale Sadler: secretary, treasurer PRIM CORP EMPL secretary, treasurer, director: Sunnyside Farm Store Inc.
Orville D. Smith: trustee
James F. Wood: director

Grants Analysis

Disclosure Period: fiscal year ending March 31, 2002
Total Grants: $2,738,918*
Number of Grants: 23
Average Grant: $60,246*
Highest Grant: $620,000
Lowest Grant: $3,000
Typical Range: $25,000 to $100,000
*Note: Giving excludes scholarships and United Way. Average grant excludes three highest grants totaling ($1,534,000).

Recent Grants

Note: Grants derived from 2002 Form 990.

General

620,000	Lawton Public Schools, Lawton, OK -- support special programs and purchase technology equipment
500,000	McMahon-Tomlinson Nursing, Lawton, OK -- building addition
414,000	Museum of the Great Plains, Lawton, OK -- support historical education, centennial sculpture, renovate classroom
267,250	Salvation Army of Lawton, Lawton, OK -- building expansion
242,941	City of Lawton, Lawton, OK -- building expansion, park improvements
236,212	J. Roy Dunning Children's Shelter, Lawton, OK -- building expansion
70,000	Roadback, Inc., Lawton, OK -- building grant
60,000	Wichita Mountains Easter Sunrise Service Association, Lawton, OK -- facility improvements
53,000	Cameron University, Lawton, OK -- scholarships
51,000	United Way Lawton, Lawton, OK -- annual support

HAROLD AND HELEN MCMASTER FOUNDATION

Giving Contact

Scott Savage, Trust Officer
6711 Monroe St., Building 4 Suite A
Sylvania, OH 43560-2538
Phone: (419)885-2626

Description

Founded: 1988
EIN: 341576110
Organization Type: Private Foundation
Giving Locations: OH
Grant Types: General Support.

Donor Information

Founder: Harold A. McMaster, Helen E. McMaster

Financial Summary

Total Giving: $1,505,282 (fiscal year ending November 30, 2001); $1,800,282 (fiscal 2000); $794,832 (fiscal 1998)
Giving Analysis: Giving for fiscal 2001 includes: foundation gifts to individuals ($3,600); foundation grants to United Way ($10,000); foundation scholarships ($20,000); fiscal 2000: foundation grants to United Way ($10,000); foundation scholarships ($20,000); foundation gifts to individuals ($43,200); fiscal 1998: foundation gifts to individuals ($3,300); foundation scholarships ($20,000);
Assets: $7,478,855 (fiscal 2001); $8,949,297 (fiscal 2000); $9,678,960 (fiscal 1998)
Gifts Received: $416,432 (fiscal 1998); $4,058,640 (fiscal 1997); $10,000 (fiscal 1996). Note: In 1997 and 1998, contributions were received from Harold and Helen McMaster. In 1996, contributions were received

from Harold A. McMaster Trust. In 1993, contributions were received from Harold and Helen McMaster.

Typical Recipients

Arts & Humanities: Arts Associations & Councils, Libraries, Museums/Galleries, Music, Public Broadcasting
Civic & Public Affairs: Business/Free Enterprise, Civic & Public Affairs-General
Education: Colleges & Universities, Education Funds, Education Reform, Education-General, Private Education (Precollege), Religious Education, Science/Mathematics Education, Secondary Education (Private), Student Aid, Vocational & Technical Education
Health: Hospices, Prenatal Health Issues
Religion: Ministries, Religious Welfare
Science: Scientific Centers & Institutes
Social Services: Community Centers, Family Planning, Recreation & Athletics, United Funds/United Ways, YMCA/YWCA/YMHA/YWHA, Youth Organizations

Application Procedures

Initial Contact: Send a brief letter of inquiry.
Application Requirements: Include explanation of needs and wants.
Deadlines: None.

Additional Information

Provides grants to individuals.

Foundation Officials

Frank D. Jacobs: assistant secretary
Harold A. McMaster: president, treasurer
Helen E. McMaster: vice president, secretary
Ronald A. McMaster: trustee

Grants Analysis

Disclosure Period: fiscal year ending November 30, 2001
Total Grants: $1,471,682*
Number of Grants: 31
Average Grant: $16,867*
Highest Grant: $300,000
Lowest Grant: $1,000
Typical Range: $5,000 to $30,000
*Note: Giving excludes scholarships, United Way, and gifts to individuals. Average grant figure excludes six highest grants ($1,050,000).

Recent Grants

Note: Grants derived from fiscal 2000 Form 990.

Library-Related
200,000   Library Legacy Foundation, Toledo, OH

General
200,000   Defiance College, Defiance, OH -- McMaster Institute
170,000   University of Toledo, Toledo, OH -- biomedical
150,000   Bowling Green State University, Bowling Green, KY
100,000   COSI, Toledo, OH
100,000   Defiance College, Defiance, OH -- Serrick Center
100,000   Defiance College, Defiance, OH -- annual fund
100,000   Defiance College, Defiance, OH -- science center
100,000   University of Arizona, Tucson, AZ -- telescope
100,000   Westside Montessori School, Sylvania, OH
60,000   WGTE, Toledo, OH -- Star Date

BRUCE MCMILLAN, JR. FOUNDATION

Giving Contact

Ralph Ward, Jr., President, Treasurer & Director
PO Box 9
Overton, TX 75684
Phone: (903)834-3148
Fax: (903)834-3947

Description

Founded: 1951
EIN: 750945924
Organization Type: Family Foundation
Giving Locations: TX: emphasis on the Overton area
Grant Types: Endowment, General Support, Scholarship.

Donor Information

Founder: Established in 1951 by the late V. Bruce McMillan M.D. and the late Mary Moore McMillan .

Financial Summary

Total Giving: $1,050,191 (fiscal year ending June 30, 2001); $997,128 (fiscal 1999); $959,559 (fiscal 1998). Note: 1997 Giving includes scholarship ($126,267).
Giving Analysis: Giving for fiscal 2001 includes: foundation scholarships ($70,648); fiscal 1999: foundation scholarships ($146,622) fiscal 1998: foundation scholarships ($119,902)
Assets: $20,306,968 (fiscal 2001); $23,849,949 (fiscal 1999); $22,030,033 (fiscal 1998)

Typical Recipients

Arts & Humanities: Film & Video, Libraries, Museums/Galleries
Civic & Public Affairs: Business/Free Enterprise, Economic Development, Housing, Legal Aid, Municipalities/Towns, Public Policy, Rural Affairs, Urban & Community Affairs
Education: Afterschool/Enrichment Programs, Agricultural Education, Arts/Humanities Education, Business Education, Colleges & Universities, Economic Education, Education Reform, Elementary Education (Private), Engineering/Technological Education, Faculty Development, Minority Education, Private Education (Precollege), Public Education (Precollege), Religious Education, Science/Mathematics Education, Special Education, Student Aid
Environment: Resource Conservation
Health: Cancer, Children's Health/Hospitals, Emergency/Ambulance Services, Health Organizations, Heart, Heart, Prenatal Health Issues, Public Health, Single-Disease Health Associations, Transplant Networks/Donor Banks
Religion: Churches, Missionary Activities (Domestic), Religious Organizations, Religious Welfare, Seminaries
Social Services: Child Abuse, Child Welfare, Crime Prevention, Domestic Violence, Family Planning, Family Services, Food/Clothing Distribution, Scouts, Sexual Abuse, Substance Abuse, Youth Organizations

Application Procedures

Initial Contact: Applicants for grants and scholarships should contact the foundation for a formal application.
Deadlines: June 15. For scholarships is March 1. For churches and noneducational institutions is May.
Review Process: All other applications are reviewed in June and October.

Restrictions

Scholarship awards are generally limited to applications from the following high schools; West Rusk, Overton, Henderson, Leverett Chapel, Kilgore, Troup, Arp, Troup Hill and Carlisle.
Grants are limited to Overton, TX.

Additional Information

Publications: Application Guidelines

Foundation Officials

Drew R. Heard: chairman B Lockhart, TX 1950. ED Baylor University BA (1972); Baylor University JD (1975). PRIM CORP EMPL attorney: Jenkens Gilchrist PC. NONPR AFFIL member: Phi Eta Sigma; member: State Bar Texas; member: Phi Alpha Theta; member: Dallas Bar Association; member: Phi Alpha Delta; member: American Bar Association.
Pamela M. Merritt: secretary
John Rogers Pope: vice chairman
Ralph Ward, Jr.: president, treasurer B 1947. ED Austin College (1968-1970); Texas A&M University (1970-1973).

Grants Analysis

Disclosure Period: fiscal year ending June 30, 2001
Total Grants: $979,543*
Number of Grants: 55
Average Grant: $14,048*
Highest Grant: $125,000
Typical Range: $5,000 to $25,000
*Note: Giving excludes scholarships. Average grant figure excludes two highest grants ($235,000).

Recent Grants

Note: Grants derived from fiscal 1999 Form 990.

Library-Related
32,000   Rusk County Library System, Henderson, TX -- literary endowment program

General
130,000   Baylor University, Waco, TX
100,250   Kilgore College, Kilgore, TX
50,000   Presbyterian Children's Home, Austin, TX
45,000   East Texas Baptist University, Marshall, TX
40,000   LeTourneau University, Longview, TX
36,000   University Cancer Foundation UT-M.D. Anderson Cancer Center, Houston, TX
30,000   Buckner Children and Family Services, Longview, TX
25,000   Austin College, Sherman, TX
25,000   Austin Presbyterian Theological Seminary, Austin, TX
20,000   Centenary College, Shreveport, LA

MCMILLEN FOUNDATION

Giving Contact

John F. McMillen, President
6610 Mutual Drive
Ft. Wayne, IN 46825
Phone: (260)484-8631
Fax: (260)483-0474

Description

Founded: 1947
EIN: 356021003
Organization Type: Family Foundation
Giving Locations: IN: Allen County, Ft. Wayne
Grant Types: Capital.

Donor Information

Founder: Incorporated in 1947 by the late Dale W. McMillen and members of the McMillen family.

Financial Summary

Total Giving: $1,000,000 (2003 approx); $1,000,000 (2002 approx); $1,016,529 (2001)
Giving Analysis: Giving for 1998 includes: foundation scholarships ($210,000)
Assets: $30,000,000 (2003 approx); $30,000,000 (2002 approx); $28,000,000 (2001 approx)

Typical Recipients

Arts & Humanities: Arts Associations & Councils, Arts Funds, Historic Preservation, Music, Theater
Civic & Public Affairs: Botanical Gardens/Parks, Business/Free Enterprise, Chambers of Commerce, Community Foundations, Economic Development, Civic & Public Affairs-General, Municipalities/Towns, Public Policy, Women's Affairs, Zoos/Aquariums
Education: Business Education, Colleges & Universities, Continuing Education, Education Funds, Engineering/Technological Education, Education-General, Health & Physical Education, International Exchange, Literacy, Private Education (Precollege), Public Education (Precollege), Religious Education, Secondary Education (Private), Student Aid
Environment: Air/Water Quality
Health: AIDS/HIV, Clinics/Medical Centers, Health-General, Geriatric Health, Health Organizations, Hospices, Public Health
Religion: Ministries, Religious Organizations, Religious Welfare
Science: Scientific Centers & Institutes
Social Services: Big Brother/Big Sister, Child Welfare, Community Centers, Community Service Organizations, Day Care, Delinquency & Criminal Rehabilitation, Domestic Violence, Emergency Relief, Family Planning, Family Services, Food/Clothing Distribution, Homes, People with Disabilities, Recreation & Athletics, Scouts, Sexual Abuse, Shelters/Homelessness, Substance Abuse, United Funds/United Ways, YMCA/YWCA/YMHA/YWHA, Youth Organizations

Application Procedures

Initial Contact: The foundation requests applications be made in writing. To be eligible for support, organizations must be operated for public purposes and qualify as non-for-profit and tax-exempt status under the regulations of the United States Internal Revenue Services 501 (c) (3). The Foundation does not use a specific form. Written request should include: A description of the organization and its history. The purpose, objective and the amount of the request. A list of officers and directors of the organization. Proof tax-exempt status under Section 501 (c) (3) of the IRS Code. A recent annual report, audited financial statement and operating budget. A three-year history of donors and funding sources and the amount of grants received (detail by donor $1,000 and over) plus grants and outstanding grant requests for current project request.

Foundation Officials

Harold L. Donelson: assistant secretary, assistant treasurer
Dale W. McMillen, III: director
John F. McMillen: president, director B 1945. PRIM CORP EMPL chairman: DuCharme McMillen & Associates.
Thomas Mitchell Shoaff: director B Fort Wayne, IN 1941. ED Williams College BA (1964); Vanderbilt University JD (1967). PRIM CORP EMPL partner: Baker & Daniels. CORP AFFIL director: Weaver Popcorn Co. Inc.; director: Fort Wayne National Bank; director: Fort Wayne National Corp.; director: America Steel Investment Corp.; director: Dreibelbiss Title Co. NONPR AFFIL director: Fort Wayne Park Foundation; member: Indiana Bar Association; member: American Bar Association; member: Allen County Bar Association.
Linda Crowe Tate: vice president, director

Grants Analysis

Disclosure Period: calendar year ending 2001
Total Grants: $1,016,529*
Number of Grants: 24
Average Grant: $28,800*
Highest Grant: $353,358
Lowest Grant: $2,000
Typical Range: $5,000 to $100,000
*Note: Giving excludes scholarships. Average grant figure excludes highest grant. Grants anaylsis provided by foundation.

Recent Grants

Note: Grants derived from 2000 Form 990.

General

358,682	Wildcat Recreation Association, Ft. Wayne, IN -- operating expenses
200,000	Fort Wayne Children's Zoo, Ft. Wayne, IN -- for heart of the zoo campaign
137,500	Fort Wayne YMCA, Ft. Wayne, IN -- capital campaign
113,126	Harold W. McMillen Center for Health Education, Ft. Wayne, IN -- challenge pledge
75,000	Anthony Wayne Area Council Boy Scouts of America, Ft. Wayne, IN -- capital campaign
50,000	Fort Wayne YWCA, Ft. Wayne, IN -- capital campaign
50,000	Girl Scouts of Limberlost Council, Inc. -- for Camp McMillen renovation
50,000	Indiana Institute of Technology, Ft. Wayne, IN -- renovation; library, lobby entrance
50,000	Indiana-Purdue Foundation, IN -- soccer field bleachers
50,000	SCAN, Ft. Wayne, IN -- for new facility capital campaign

MCNEELY FOUNDATION

Giving Contact

Karen Reynolds, Foundation Manager
444 Pine St.
St. Paul, MN 55101-2453
Phone: (651)228-4500
E-mail: kreynolds@meritexenterprises.com

Description

Founded: 1981
EIN: 411392221
Organization Type: Private Foundation
Giving Locations: MN: Minneapolis metropolitan area, St. Paul metropolitan area
Grant Types: General Support.

Donor Information

Founder: Lee and Rose Warner Foundation

Financial Summary

Total Giving: $1,333,946 (2001); $868,051 (2000); $744,507 (1999)
Giving Analysis: Giving for 2001 includes: foundation grants to United Way ($18,796); 2000: foundation grants to United Way ($12,076); 1999: foundation grants to United Way ($16,286);
Assets: $18,156,157 (2001); $22,624,978 (2000); $23,966,142 (1999)
Gifts Received: $252,810 (2000); $150,000 (1999); $833,444 (1998). Note: In 1999, contributions were received from Meritex Enterprises Inc. In 1998, contributions were received from Center Enterprises ($700,000), Armor Archbold ($99,728), and Shannon McNeely Whitaker ($33,716).

Typical Recipients

Arts & Humanities: Arts Associations & Councils, Community Arts, Libraries, Museums/Galleries, Music, Public Broadcasting, Theater
Civic & Public Affairs: Asian American Affairs, Botanical Gardens/Parks, Business/Free Enterprise, Community Foundations, Economic Development, Employment/Job Training, Civic & Public Affairs-General, Native American Affairs, Urban & Community Affairs
Education: Business Education, Colleges & Universities, Economic Education, Education Funds, Environmental Education, Education-General, Legal Education, Minority Education, Private Education (Precollege), Public Education (Precollege), Special Education
Environment: Environment-General, Resource Conservation, Wildlife Protection
Health: Children's Health/Hospitals, Health Organizations
International: International-General
Religion: Churches, Religious Organizations, Religious Welfare
Social Services: At-Risk Youth, Camps, Child Welfare, Community Centers, Community Service Organizations, Day Care, Delinquency & Criminal Rehabilitation, Domestic Violence, Family Services, People with Disabilities, Recreation & Athletics, United Funds/United Ways, YMCA/YWCA/YMHA/YWHA, Youth Organizations

Application Procedures

Initial Contact: The foundation requests applications be made in writing.
Application Requirements: Include a description of organization, amount requested, purpose of funds sought, recently audited financial statement, and proof of tax-exempt status.
Deadlines: None.

Restrictions

Grants are not made to individuals.

Additional Information

Meritex Foundation has been merged with McNeely Foundation.

Foundation Officials

Armar A. Archbold: trustee
W. E. Bye Barsness: vice chairman, trustee B 1941. ED Northwestern University MBA (1969). PRIM CORP EMPL president, chief executive officer, director: Pink Supply Corp. CORP AFFIL director: Faribault Woolen Mill Co.; president: Pink Business Interiors.
Malcolm W. McDonald: secretary, treasurer, trustee NONPR AFFIL director: Amherst H. Wilder Foundation.
Gregory McNeely: trustee
Harry G. McNeely, III: trustee
Harry G. McNeely, Jr.: chairman, trustee PRIM CORP EMPL president: Meritex.
Karen M. Reynolds: manager
Shannon McNeely Whitaker: trustee

Grants Analysis

Disclosure Period: calendar year ending 2001
Total Grants: $1,315,150*
Number of Grants: 72
Average Grant: $8,741*
Highest Grant: $450,000
Typical Range: $1,000 to $15,000
*Note: Giving excludes United Way. Average grant figure excludes three highest grants ($712,000).

Recent Grants

Note: Grants derived from 2001 Form 990.

General

450,000	Children's Hospital and Clinic Foundation, Minneapolis, MN

150,000	University of Saint Thomas, St. Paul, MN	
112,000	Saint Peter Claver Catholic School, St. Paul, MN	
50,000	Amherst H. Wilder Foundation, St. Paul, MN	
30,000	Friends of the Saint Paul Public Library, St. Paul, MN	
30,000	Wilderness Inquiry, Minneapolis, MN	
25,000	Goodwill/Easter Seals, St. Paul, MN	
25,000	YMCA of Greater Saint Paul, St. Paul, MN	
20,000	Minnesota Business Academy, Minneapolis, MN	
17,500	Minnesota Children's Museum, St. Paul, MN	

AMY SHELTON MCNUTT CHARITABLE TRUST

Giving Contact

Carol Bruehler, Trust Secretary
153 Treeline Park, Suite 300
San Antonio, TX 78209-1880
Phone: (210)829-1800

Description

Founded: 1983
EIN: 742298675
Organization Type: Private Foundation
Giving Locations: TX: Corpus Christi, San Antonio
Grant Types: General Support, Operating Expenses.

Donor Information

Founder: the late Amy Shelton McNutt

Financial Summary

Total Giving: $724,816 (fiscal year ending September 30, 2002); $829,866 (fiscal 2000); $379,753 (fiscal 1999)
Giving Analysis: Giving for fiscal 2002 includes: foundation grants to United Way ($27,000); fiscal 2000: foundation grants to United Way ($27,000); foundation scholarships ($31,905); fiscal 1999: foundation scholarships ($5,500); foundation grants to United Way ($27,000);
Assets: $11,067,115 (fiscal 2002); $17,418,411 (fiscal 2000); $14,854,967 (fiscal 1999)

Typical Recipients

Arts & Humanities: Arts Associations & Councils, Arts Centers, Ethnic & Folk Arts, Historic Preservation, History & Archaeology, Libraries, Museums/Galleries, Music, Performing Arts, Public Broadcasting, Theater
Civic & Public Affairs: Botanical Gardens/Parks, Clubs, Community Foundations, Economic Development, Economic Policy, Civic & Public Affairs-General, Hispanic Affairs, Philanthropic Organizations, Professional & Trade Associations, Public Policy, Urban & Community Affairs, Women's Affairs, Zoos/Aquariums
Education: Agricultural Education, Arts/Humanities Education, Business Education, Colleges & Universities, Education Reform, Engineering/Technological Education, Private Education (Precollege), Public Education (Precollege), Science/Mathematics Education, Secondary Education (Private), Social Sciences Education, Student Aid
Environment: Environment-General, Wildlife Protection
Health: Alzheimers Disease, Cancer, Emergency/Ambulance Services, Eyes/Blindness, Geriatric Health, Health Organizations, Hospices, Hospitals, Medical Rehabilitation, Medical Research, Mental Health, Nursing Services, Single-Disease Health Associations
International: Human Rights, International Peace & Security Issues, Missionary/Religious Activities

Religion: Churches, Ministries, Religious Organizations, Religious Welfare
Science: Scientific Centers & Institutes, Scientific Research
Social Services: Animal Protection, Community Centers, Community Service Organizations, Counseling, Day Care, Family Planning, Family Services, Homes, People with Disabilities, Recreation & Athletics, Senior Services, Substance Abuse, United Funds/United Ways, YMCA/YWCA/YMHA/YWHA, Youth Organizations

Application Procedures

Initial Contact: Submit a letter of application not exceeding three pages.
Application Requirements: Include purpose of funds sought, proof of tax-exempt status, and an indication of whether any of the organization's activities are considered lobbying activities under the Internal Revenue Code (and, if so, include copies of the past three years' tax returns).
Deadlines: February 28 and July 31 to ensure that proposal arrives prior to trustee meetings in March and August.
Decision Notification: Applicants are notified of the board of trustee's decisions after each meeting.
Notes: Newsletters and other supporting materials should not be submitted and will not be reviewed by the foundation.

Restrictions

Does not support individuals.

Foundation Officials

Carol Bruehler: secretary
Randall Brower Cutlip: trustee B Clarksburg, WV October 01, 1916. ED Bethany College BA (1940); East Texas State University MA (1949); University of Houston EdD (1953); Bethany College LLD (1965); Drury College LHD (1975); Southwestern Baptist University ScD (1978); Columbia College LLD (1980); William Woods College LittD (1981). NONPR AFFIL member: Phi Delta Kappa; trustee: William Woods College; member: Kappa Delta Pi; elder emeritus: Life Christian Church; member: Alpha Sigma Phi; member: American Personal Guidance Association; member: Alpha Chi.
Jack Egon Guenther: trustee B San Antonio, TX 1934. ED University of Texas, Austin BBA (1956); Saint Mary's University LLB (1959); New York University LLM (1960). CORP AFFIL chairman: Volvo & Porcshe Center; chairman: Rivergate Toyota; chairman: Performance Toyota; chairman: Performance Toyota Plano; chairman: Lexus Nashville; chairman: BMW Center; of coun: Cox & Smith; chairman: Bell Ford LP. NONPR AFFIL member: Texas Bar Association; member: Texas Society CPA's; member: Phi Delta Phi; member: Sigma Chi; member: American Bar Association.
Edward D. Muir: trustee
Courtney Johnson Walker: trustee

Grants Analysis

Disclosure Period: fiscal year ending September 30, 2002
Total Grants: $697,816*
Number of Grants: 125
Average Grant: $4,821
Highest Grant: $100,000
Typical Range: $1,000 to $5,000
*Note: Giving excludes United Way.

Recent Grants

Note: Grants derived from fiscal 2002 Form 990.

General

100,000	National Center for American Western Art, Kerrville, TX -- for building project	
55,000	William Woods University, Fulton, MO -- for renovation project	

50,000	Alamo Public Telecommunications Council, San Antonio, TX -- for digital conversion campaign	
50,000	Texas State Aquarium, Corpus Christi, TX -- for environmental discovery component of Dolphin Bay Project	
36,000	Wildlife Rescue and Rehabilitation, Inc., Boerne, TX -- for construction	
25,000	South Texas Public Broadcasting System, Corpus Christi, TX -- for digital conversion campaign	
25,000	United Way of San Antonio and Bexar Counties, San Antonio, TX	
25,000	University of Texas at San Antonio, San Antonio, TX -- for San Antonio Center for Water Research	
25,000	USS Lexington Museum Association, Corpus Christi, TX	
20,000	Cancer Therapy & Research Center, San Antonio, TX -- for campaign to purchase nuclear gamma camera	

ADELINE AND GEORGE MCQUEEN FOUNDATION

Giving Contact

Robert Lansford, Trust Officer
c/o Bank One Texas NA
PO Box 2050
Ft. Worth, TX 76113
Phone: (817)884-4448

Description

Founded: 1960
EIN: 756014459
Organization Type: Private Foundation
Giving Locations: TX
Grant Types: General Support.

Financial Summary

Total Giving: $589,000 (fiscal year ending June 30, 2001); $456,000 (fiscal 1999); $278,100 (fiscal 1996)
Giving Analysis: Giving for fiscal 2000 includes: foundation scholarships ($5,000)
Assets: $14,577,712 (fiscal 2001); $15,447,183 (fiscal 1999); $10,946,559 (fiscal 1996)

Typical Recipients

Arts & Humanities: Ballet, Libraries, Museums/Galleries, Music, Opera, Theater
Civic & Public Affairs: Clubs, Community Foundations, Economic Development, Civic & Public Affairs-General, Urban & Community Affairs, Women's Affairs, Zoos/Aquariums
Education: Afterschool/Enrichment Programs, Business Education, Colleges & Universities, Education-General, Health & Physical Education, Medical Education, Minority Education, Private Education (Precollege), Religious Education, Special Education
Health: AIDS/HIV, Cancer, Children's Health/Hospitals, Clinics/Medical Centers, Health Organizations, Hospitals, Hospitals (University Affiliated), Public Health, Single-Disease Health Associations
Religion: Religion-General, Jewish Causes, Ministries, Religious Organizations, Religious Welfare, Seminaries
Science: Science Museums
Social Services: Big Brother/Big Sister, Community Service Organizations, Counseling, Day Care, Family Services, Food/Clothing Distribution, Homes, People with Disabilities, Recreation & Athletics, Shelters/Homelessness, YMCA/YWCA/YMHA/YWHA, Youth Organizations

Application Procedures

Initial Contact: The foundation requests applications be made in writing. Include a description of organization, purpose of funds sought, amount requested, and list of directors.
Deadlines: None.

Additional Information

Trust(s): Bank One TX NA

Grants Analysis

Disclosure Period: fiscal year ending June 30, 2001
Total Grants: $589,000
Number of Grants: 31
Average Grant: $15,467*
Highest Grant: $125,000
Typical Range: $7,000 to $30,000
*Note: Average grant figure excludes highest grant.

Recent Grants

Note: Grants derived from fiscal 2000 Form 990.

General

75,000	Cook Children's Medical Center, Ft. Worth, TX
25,000	Amon Carter Museum, Ft. Worth, TX
25,000	Hill School, Ft. Worth, TX
25,000	Jewel Charity Ball, Ft. Worth, TX -- benefiting Cook Children's Medical Center
25,000	Oakridge School, Arlington, TX
25,000	Oakridge School, Arlington, TX
20,000	Fort Worth Ballet, Ft. Worth, TX
15,000	Fort Worth Museum of Science and History, Ft. Worth, TX
15,000	Harbor Club, Ft. Worth, TX
10,000	All Saints Health Care, Ft. Worth, TX

JOHN MCSHAIN CHARITIES

Giving Contact

Mary H. McShain, President
300 East Lancaster Avenue, Suite 200
Wynnewood, PA 19096-2105
Fax: (215)564-2343

Description

Founded: 1949
EIN: 236276091
Organization Type: Family Foundation
Giving Locations: PA: Philadelphia some grants nationally.
Grant Types: General Support, Project, Scholarship.

Donor Information

Founder: The foundation was established in Pennsylvania in 1949 with funds donated by John McShain of John McShain, Inc. Mr. McShain, a prominent builder, restored the White House during the Truman administration.

Financial Summary

Total Giving: $2,533,779 (fiscal year ending March 31, 1999); $2,469,718 (fiscal 1998); $2,462,629 (fiscal 1997)
Assets: $59,422,771 (fiscal 1999); $56,855,515 (fiscal 1998); $57,446,379 (fiscal 1997)

Typical Recipients

Arts & Humanities: Arts Associations & Councils, Libraries, Museums/Galleries
Civic & Public Affairs: Civic & Public Affairs-General
Education: Arts/Humanities Education, Colleges & Universities, Education Associations, Education Funds, Education-General, Private Education (Precollege), Public Education (Precollege), Religious Education, Secondary Education (Private), Special Education, Student Aid, Vocational & Technical Education

Health: AIDS/HIV, Clinics/Medical Centers, Health Organizations, Hospitals, Long-Term Care
International: Health Care/Hospitals, International Affairs, International Environmental Issues
Religion: Churches, Dioceses, Religion-General, Jewish Causes, Ministries, Religious Organizations, Religious Welfare, Social/Policy Issues
Science: Science-General
Social Services: Community Service Organizations, People with Disabilities, Social Services-General

Application Procedures

Initial Contact: The foundation has no formal grant application procedure or application form. Prospective applicants should send a letter of inquiry and state the purpose of funds sought.
Deadlines: None.

Restrictions

Applicant organizations must be IRS approved, and organized and operated exclusively for religious, charitable, scientific, or educational purposes.

Foundation Officials

Fenton J. Fitzpatrick: trustee
Sister Pauline Mary: president
Patricia J. McFillin: trustee
William L. Shinners: vice president
Mary K. Tompkins: secretary-treasurer

Grants Analysis

Disclosure Period: fiscal year ending March 31, 1999
Total Grants: $2,533,779
Number of Grants: 151
Average Grant: $16,780
Highest Grant: $300,000
Typical Range: $1,000 to $25,000

Recent Grants

Note: Grants derived from 2000 Form 990.

General

250,000	Archdiocese of Philadelphia, Philadelphia, PA
250,000	Archdiocese of Philadelphia, Philadelphia, PA
250,000	Connelly School of the Holy Child, Potomac, MD
250,000	Connelly School of the Holy Child, Potomac, MD
175,000	Rosemont College, Rosemont, PA
100,000	Roman Catholic High School, Philadelphia, PA
100,000	Roman Catholic High School, Philadelphia, PA
100,000	Rosemont College, Rosemont, PA
100,000	Rosemont College, Rosemont, PA
100,000	Society of the Holy Child Jesus, Drexel Hill, PA

MCWANE CORP.

Company Headquarters

2900 Hwy. 280, Ste. 300
Birmingham, AL 35223
Phone: (205)414-3100
Fax: (205)414-3180

Company Description

Founded: 1921
Revenue: US$1.5 billion (2002)
Employees: 5200 (2002)
SIC(s): 3321 Gray & Ductile Iron Foundries, 3491 Industrial Valves.

Operating Locations

McWane Corp. (IL--Oak Brook; IA--Oskaloosa; OH--Coshocton)

McWane Foundation

Giving Contact

Jeanette Sommers, Corporate Secretary
2900 Highway 280, Suite 300
Birmingham, AL 35223
Phone: (205)414-3100
Fax: (205)414-3180

Alternate Contact

C. Phillip McWane, Trustee
McWane Foundation
PO Box 43327
Birmingham, AL 35243

Description

Founded: 1961
EIN: 636044384
Organization Type: Corporate Foundation
Giving Locations: AL
Grant Types: Capital, General Support, Scholarship.

Financial Summary

Total Giving: $1,893,260 (2000); $2,615,900 (1999); $2,004,066 (1997)
Giving Analysis: Giving for 2000 includes: foundation scholarships ($50,000); foundation ($1,843,260); 1999: foundation scholarships ($26,800) foundation ($2,589,100)
Assets: $490,273 (2000); $561,621 (1999); $813,693 (1997)
Gifts Received: $1,780,000 (2000); $2,500,000 (1999); $1,775,000 (1997). Note: In 1996 and 1997, contributions were received from McWane, Inc.

Typical Recipients

Arts & Humanities: Arts Associations & Councils, Arts Festivals, Arts Funds, Ballet, Dance, Historic Preservation, Libraries, Museums/Galleries, Music, Performing Arts, Public Broadcasting, Theater
Civic & Public Affairs: African American Affairs, Civil Rights, Clubs, Economic Development, Civic & Public Affairs-General, Housing, Law & Justice, Municipalities/Towns, Philanthropic Organizations, Safety, Urban & Community Affairs, Zoos/Aquariums
Education: Arts/Humanities Education, Business Education, Colleges & Universities, Education Funds, Education Reform, Engineering/Technological Education, Education-General, Literacy, Private Education (Precollege), Public Education (Precollege), Student Aid
Environment: Environment-General, Resource Conservation
Health: Arthritis, Cancer, Children's Health/Hospitals, Diabetes, Emergency/Ambulance Services, Health Organizations, Heart, Hospitals, Mental Health, Multiple Sclerosis, Single-Disease Health Associations
Religion: Churches, Dioceses, Jewish Causes, Religious Welfare, Social/Policy Issues
Science: Science Museums
Social Services: Animal Protection, At-Risk Youth, Big Brother/Big Sister, Community Service Organizations, Counseling, Crime Prevention, Family Services, Recreation & Athletics, Scouts, Social Services-General, Substance Abuse, YMCA/YWCA/YMHA/YWHA, Youth Organizations

Application Procedures

Initial Contact: Send written request.
Deadlines: None.

Corporate Officials

Glenda Burson: vice president, treasurer, chief executive officer, treasurer PRIM CORP EMPL vice president, treasurer: McWane.

John J. McMahon, Jr.: chairman, president, chief executive officer, treasurer PRIM CORP EMPL chairman, president, chief executive officer, treasurer: McWane Inc. CORP AFFIL director: John H. Harland Co.; director: Protective Life Corp.; director: Birmingham Airport Authority; chief executive officer: Clow Corp.

Foundation Officials
John J. McMahon, Jr.: trustee (see above)

Grants Analysis
Disclosure Period: calendar year ending 2000
Total Grants: $1,843,260*
Number of Grants: 43
Average Grant: $20,078*
Highest Grant: $1,000,000
Lowest Grant: $160
Typical Range: $500 to $50,000
*Note: Giving excludes scholarships. Average grant figure excludes highest grant.

Recent Grants
Note: Grants derived from 2001 Form 990.

Library-Related
50,000	Emmet O'Neal Library, Mountain Brook, AL

General
151,000	Sloss Furnace Association, Birmingham, AL
100,000	Glenwood, Inc., Birmingham, AL
60,000	Alabama Ballet, Birmingham, AL
52,000	Birmingham Southern College, Birmingham, AL
50,000	Alabama Children's Hospital Foundation, Birmingham, AL
40,000	YWCA, Birmingham, AL
30,000	Alabama Symphony Orchestra, Birmingham, AL
25,000	Nature Conservancy
24,000	Auburn University Foundation, Auburn University, AL
20,000	A Education Foundation, Montgomery, AL

MDU RESOURCES GROUP, INC.

Company Headquarters
PO Box 5650
Bismarck, ND 58506-5650
Web: http://www.mdures.com

Company Description
Founded: 1924
Ticker: MDU
Exchange: NYSE
Assets: US$2.937 billion (2002)
Employees: 6983 (2002)
SIC(s): 1221 Bituminous Coal & Lignite--Surface, 1442 Construction Sand & Gravel, 4911 Electric Services.

Nonmonetary Support
Type: Loaned Employees; Loaned Executives

MDU Resources Foundation

Giving Contact
Robert E. Wood, President
PO Box 5650
Bismarck, ND 58506-5650
Phone: (701)222-7828
Fax: (701)222-7607

E-mail: robert.wood@mduresources.com
Web: http://www.mdu.com/corp-fdtn.html

Description
EIN: 450378937
Organization Type: Corporate Foundation
Giving Locations: near operating locations.
Grant Types: Award, Capital, Challenge, General Support, Multiyear/Continuing Support, Operating Expenses.

Financial Summary
Total Giving: $742,346 (2002 approx); $525,897 (2001); $427,523 (2000)
Giving Analysis: Giving for 2001 includes: foundation grants to United Way ($32,322); foundation scholarships ($52,350); foundation ($441,225); 1999: foundation scholarships ($42,340); foundation grants to United Way ($43,175) foundation ($259,200)
Assets: $2,009,633 (2001); $2,068,964 (2000); $2,061,609 (1999)
Gifts Received: $674,445 (2001); $544,868 (2000); $334,252 (1999). Note: In 2001, contributions were received from MDU Resources Group, Inc. ($139,820), Utility Services, Inc. ($47,912), Knife River Corp. ($211,588), Williston Basin Interstate Pipeline Company ($138,540), WBI Production, Inc. ($26,670), Prairielands Energy Marketing, Inc. ($2,421), and Fidelity Oil Co. ($107,404). In 1999, contributions were received from MDU Resources Group ($129,252), Utility Services Inc. ($10,018), Knife River Corp. ($104,342), WBI Energy Services Inc. ($4,863), and Fidelity Oil Co. ($85,777). In 1996, contributions were received from MDU Resources Group ($69,453), Williston Basin Interstate Pipeline Co. ($47,074), Knife River Coal Mining Co. ($60,467), KRC Holdings ($6,452), and Fidelity Oil Co. ($133,918).

Typical Recipients
Arts & Humanities: Arts Associations & Councils, Arts Centers, Ballet, Arts & Humanities-General, History & Archaeology, Libraries, Museums/Galleries, Music, Opera, Performing Arts, Public Broadcasting
Civic & Public Affairs: Botanical Gardens/Parks, Community Foundations, Civic & Public Affairs-General, Housing, Municipalities/Towns, Urban & Community Affairs, Zoos/Aquariums
Education: Business Education, Colleges & Universities, Community & Junior Colleges, Education Funds, Elementary Education (Public), Engineering/Technological Education, Education-General, Leadership Training, Medical Education, Private Education (Precollege), Public Education (Precollege), Religious Education, Science/Mathematics Education, Student Aid
Environment: Resource Conservation, Wildlife Protection, Wildlife Protection
Health: Alzheimers Disease, Children's Health/Hospitals, Clinics/Medical Centers, Emergency/Ambulance Services, Eyes/Blindness, Health-General, Health Policy/Cost Containment, Health Organizations, Hospitals, Long-Term Care, Medical Rehabilitation, Mental Health, Public Health, Research/Studies Institutes
Religion: Churches
Social Services: Animal Protection, Camps, Child Welfare, Community Centers, Community Service Organizations, Domestic Violence, Family Services, Food/Clothing Distribution, Homes, People with Disabilities, Recreation & Athletics, Scouts, Senior Services, Social Services-General, Special Olympics, United Funds/United Ways, YMCA/YWCA/YMHA/YWHA, Youth Organizations, Youth Organizations

Application Procedures
Initial Contact: Request application form.
Application Requirements: Include proof of tax-exempt status.
Deadlines: None.

Restrictions
Does not support individuals, athletics, labor, fraternal organizations, veterans, political or lobbying groups, religious organizations, economic development, or requests for loans, venture capital, or loan pool participation.

Additional Information
Provides scholarships to children and spouses of active, full-time employees of MDU Resources Group and its subsidiaries and divisions.
Publications: Application Form; Guidelines

Corporate Officials
Douglas C. Kane: executive vice president, chief operating officer, director PRIM CORP EMPL executive vice president, chief operating officer, director: MDU Resources Group.
Warren L. Robinson: exe vice president, treasurer, chief financial officer B Logan, UT 1950. ED Brigham Young University (1974); Boise State University (1976). PRIM CORP EMPL vice president, treasurer, chief financial officer: MDU Resources Group. CORP AFFIL treasurer, assistant secretary: Fidelity Oil Holdings; treasurer, assistant secretary: Centennial Energy Holdings; treasurer, assistant secretary: Fidelity Oil Co. NONPR AFFIL member: National Investor Relations Institute; secretary, treasurer: Prairielands Energy Marketing; member: Financial Executives Institute. CLUB AFFIL Elks Club; Rotary Club.

Foundation Officials
Douglas C. Kane: vice president, director (see above)
Warren L. Robinson: secretary, treasurer, director (see above)
Ronald D. Tipton: director

Grants Analysis
Disclosure Period: calendar year ending 2001
Total Grants: $441,225*
Number of Grants: 243
Average Grant: $1,816
Highest Grant: $25,000
Lowest Grant: $50
Typical Range: $250 to $10,000
*Note: Giving excludes scholarship and United Way.

Recent Grants
Note: Grants derived from 2001 Form 990.

Library-Related
5,000	Friends of Pelican Rapid Library, Pelican Rapids, MN -- capital construction

General
25,000	Bismarck State College Foundation, Bismarck, ND -- capital construction
15,000	Emanuel Medical Center Foundation, Portland, OR -- capital construction
12,500	North Dakota Lewis and Clark Bicentennial Foundation, Inc., Washburn, ND
10,000	Missouri Slope Areawide United Way, Bismarck, ND
10,000	YMCA of Billings, Billings, MT -- capital construction
7,500	Billings Deaconess Hospital Development Foundation, Billings, MT
7,000	Dakota Zoological Society, Bismarck, ND -- capital construction
7,000	United Fund of Yellowstone County, Billings, MT
6,667	City of Redwood Falls, Redwood Falls, MN -- purchase equipment
6,500	United Fund of Rapid City, Rapid City, SD

GILBERT AND JAYLEE MEAD FAMILY FOUNDATION

Giving Contact

Linda Smith, Grants Manager
2700 Virginia Ave. NW, No. 701
Washington, DC 20037
Phone: (202)338-0398
Fax: (202)338-4407
E-mail: jayleemead@aol.com

Description

Founded: 1989
EIN: 521646030
Organization Type: Private Foundation
Giving Locations: DC: Washington; MD: Montgomery County
Grant Types: General Support.

Donor Information

Founder: Established in 1989 by Gilbert D. Mead and Jaylee M. Mead.

Financial Summary

Total Giving: $891,100 (2001); $632,100 (2000); $531,580 (1999)
Giving Analysis: Giving for 1999 includes: foundation scholarships ($8,000)
Assets: $18,253,213 (2001); $19,031,026 (2000); $11,083,125 (1999)
Gifts Received: $50,014 (2001); $7,346,859 (2000); $740,000 (1999). Note: In 2001, contributions were received from Gilbert and Jaylee Mead ($20,000); Elizabeth Mead ($10,007); Diana Mead-Siohan ($10,007); and Marilyn Mead ($10,007). In 2000, contributions were received from Gilbert and Jaylee Mead ($7,314,644), Elizabeth Mead ($10,0005), Diana Mead-Siohan ($12,210) and Marilyn Mead ($10,000). In 1998 and 1999, contributions were received from Gilbert and Jaylee Mead, Elizabeth Mead ($10,000), and Diane Mead-Siohan ($10,000).

Typical Recipients

Arts & Humanities: Arts Associations & Councils, Arts Centers, Arts Funds, Arts Outreach, Dance, Libraries, Museums/Galleries, Music, Opera, Performing Arts, Theater, Visual Arts
Civic & Public Affairs: Asian American Affairs, Economic Development, Employment/Job Training, Civic & Public Affairs-General, Housing, Inner-City Development, Safety, Urban & Community Affairs
Education: Afterschool/Enrichment Programs, Arts/Humanities Education, Education Associations, Education-General, International Exchange, International Studies, Leadership Training, Literacy, Minority Education, Preschool Education, Private Education (Precollege), Science/Mathematics Education, Secondary Education (Public), Student Aid
Environment: Environment-General
Health: AIDS/HIV, Children's Health/Hospitals, Eyes/Blindness, Hospices, Mental Health, Single-Disease Health Associations
International: Foreign Arts Organizations, Foreign Educational Institutions, International-General, Health Care/Hospitals, International Organizations, International Relief Efforts
Religion: Ministries, Religious Welfare
Social Services: At-Risk Youth, Child Abuse, Child Welfare, Community Service Organizations, Crime Prevention, Day Care, Family Planning, Family Services, Food/Clothing Distribution, Homes, Recreation & Athletics, Sexual Abuse, Substance Abuse, Youth Organizations

Application Procedures

Initial Contact: New applicants should first send a brief letter of inquiry describing the organization, the intended project, anticipated costs, and proof of tax-exempt status at least four weeks before the deadlines. A board member will contact the organization regarding the inquiry.
Application Requirements: Proposals must contain a cover sheet that includes contact information, amount requested, and purpose of funds sought. Also include a detailed budget; copy of IRS determination letter; financial statements from the previous year; a full description of the purpose of funds sought and expected accomplishments and means of evaluation; a list of officers; and a list of foundations who made grants in the previous fiscal year, including amounts. Include any additional information, such as brochures, newsletters, or newspaper clippings.
Deadlines: June 15 and December 15 for proposals; May 1 and November 1 for letters of inquiry.
Evaluative Criteria: Grants manager will respond to letters of inquiry. Once a proposal is submitted (with approval), applicants will be notified of status in August (those who submit by June 15) or February (those who submit by December 15).

Restrictions

Grants are not made to individuals. Do not submit proposals or letters via fax or e-mail. First-time grants are in the $5,000 range and are restricted to Washington, DC, and Montgomery County, MD. Previous grantees may request up to $10,000.

Additional Information

Publications: Proposal Guidelines

Foundation Officials

Elizabeth Mead: president, treasurer, director
Gilbert Dunbar Mead: chairman, director B Madison, WI 1930. ED Yale University BS (1952); University of California at Berkeley PhD (1962); University of Maryland JD (1991). CORP AFFIL director, chairman audit committee: Consolidated Papers. NONPR AFFIL member: American Geophysics Union; member: Maryland State Bar Association.
Jaylee M. Mead: vice president, director
Marilyn K. Mead: director
Diana Mead-Siohan: secretary, director

Grants Analysis

Disclosure Period: calendar year ending 2001
Total Grants: $891,100
Number of Grants: 96
Average Grant: $9,282
Highest Grant: $30,000
Typical Range: $1,000 to $15,000

Recent Grants

Note: Grants derived from 2001 Form 990.

General

50,000	Food for the Hungry, Scottsdale, AZ -- school dormitory and library expansion in Bolivia
30,000	Community Development Support Collaborative, Washington, DC -- revitalization of DC neighborhoods
25,000	Hospice Caring, Gaithersburg, MD -- staff to develop and direct model hospice day program in new facility
25,000	Mercy Ships, Garden Valley, TX -- improvement of school facilities for children of crew on medical ship in Africa
12,000	Center for Artistry in Teaching, Washington, DC -- general operating expenses to support innovative teaching in public schools
12,000	For Love of Children, Washington, DC -- expansion of after-school tutoring program
12,000	Heads Up, Washington, DC -- mentoring/tutoring program partnering university students with teens living in public housing
12,000	KHI Services, Rockville, MD -- wilderness challenge program for troubled youth
12,000	Lutheran Social Services of the National Capital Area - Family Friends Program, Washington, DC -- family respite program pairing seniors and families of children with disabilities
12,000	Martha's Table, Washington, DC -- programs for low-income children and families

GILES W. AND ELISE G. MEAD FOUNDATION

Giving Contact

Ms. Parry W. Mead, Vice President
PO Box 2218
Napa, CA 94558
Phone: (707)226-2164
Web: http://www.gileswmeadfoundation.org

Description

Founded: 1961
EIN: 956040921
Organization Type: Private Foundation
Giving Locations: Western North America.
Grant Types: General Support.

Donor Information

Founder: the late Elise G. Mead

Financial Summary

Total Giving: $1,309,790 (fiscal year ending October 31, 2001); $950,450 (fiscal 2000); $746,750 (fiscal 1998)
Assets: $19,693,731 (fiscal 2001); $25,694,896 (fiscal 2000); $14,965,653 (fiscal 1997)

Typical Recipients

Arts & Humanities: Museums/Galleries
Civic & Public Affairs: Civic & Public Affairs-General, Housing, Public Policy
Education: Colleges & Universities, Environmental Education, Public Education (Precollege), Science/Mathematics Education
Environment: Air/Water Quality, Forestry, Environment-General, Research, Resource Conservation, Watershed, Wildlife Protection
International: Health Care/Hospitals, International Environmental Issues
Religion: Churches, Religious Welfare
Science: Science Museums, Scientific Centers & Institutes, Scientific Organizations
Social Services: Child Welfare, Youth Organizations

Application Procedures

Initial Contact: Send a brief letter of inquiry.
Application Requirements: Include information on a description of organization, amount requested, time frame of project, other funding sources, proof of tax-exempt status, list of staff directors associated with project (including affiliation or expertise), and recently audited financial statement.
Deadlines: The Board meets in January, June, and October to review proposals.

Restrictions

Does not support individuals, provide loans, local or regional environmental organizations outside the Western U.S., individuals or for general operating expenses.

Additional Information

Supports environmentally oriented organizations with an emphasis on problems in western North America. Funding in areas such as science, education, and the arts is limited to grants proposals initiated by individual Board members.

Publications: Application and program guidelines.

Foundation Officials

Stafford Robert Grady: vchairman B Grand Rapids, MI 1921. ED George Washington University (1943). PRIM CORP EMPL vice chairman emeritus, director: Sanwa Bank CA. CORP AFFIL member advisor committee: Coldwell Banker Fund; director: Pic N Save Corp.; director: CIGNA Corp.
Katherine Cone Keck: director
Clader M. Mackay: secretary, treasurer
Richard N. Mackay: vice president
Daniel E. McArthur: assistant treasurer
Giles W. Mead, Jr.: president
Jane W. Mead: director
Parry W. Mead: vice president

Grants Analysis

Disclosure Period: fiscal year ending October 31, 2001
Total Grants: $1,309,790
Number of Grants: 39
Average Grant: $29,994*
Highest Grant: $100,000
Lowest Grant: $1,750
Typical Range: $10,000 to $50,000
*Note: Average grant figure excludes two highest grants ($200,000).

Recent Grants

Note: Grants derived from 2000 Form 990.

General

80,000	Center for Public Integrity, Washington, DC
70,000	Round Valley Institute for Man & Nature, Weaverville, CA
50,000	Co-Op America, Washington, DC
50,000	Earthwatch Institute, Watertown, MA
50,000	Epiphany School, Seattle, WA
50,000	Idaho Rivers United, Boise, ID
50,000	Justin-Siena High School, Napa, CA
50,000	Napa Valley Museum, Yountville, CA
40,000	Institute for Sustainable Forestry, Redway, CA
40,000	International Union for Conservation of Nature and Natural Resources-US, Washington, DC

THE MEADOWS FOUNDATION

Giving Contact

Bruce H. Esterline, Vice President, Grants
3003 Swiss Avenue
Wilson Historic District
Dallas, TX 75204-6049
Phone: (214)826-9431
Fax: (214)827-7042
Web: http://www.mfi.org

Alternate Contact

Phone: 800-826-9431
Note: Toll-free number for calls from outside the Dallas, TX area.

Description

Founded: 1948
EIN: 756015322
Organization Type: Family Foundation
Giving Locations: TX: emphasis on Dallas
Grant Types: Award, Capital, Challenge, Emergency, Employee Matching Gifts, Endowment, Loan,
Matching, Multiyear/Continuing Support, Operating Expenses, Project, Research.

Donor Information

Founder: The Meadows Foundation was incorporated in 1948 by the late Algur Hurtle Meadows and his first wife, the late Virginia Meadows . Mr. Meadows helped found the General American Oil Company of Texas in 1936 and diversified its corporate empire into mortgage banking, insurance, real estate, and crude oil and gas development. Mr. Meadows was named chairman of General American Oil in 1950, and most of the foundation's original assets were securities of the company. The company was purchased by Phillips Petroleum in 1983 and dissolved as a corporate entity.

Mr. Meadows was interested in art, and over the years donated millions of dollars to Southern Methodist University for the Meadows Museum (developed as a memorial to his first wife) for art acquisitions, the museum's endowment, and for Southern Methodist University's School of Arts. Until his death in 1978, Mr. Meadows was the foundation's president.

Financial Summary

Total Giving: $32,600,000 (2002 approx); $35,298,406 (2001); $31,933,622 (2000)
Giving Analysis: Giving for 2000 includes: foundation matching gifts ($40,670); 1998: foundation scholarships ($25,000) foundation matching gifts ($54,458)
Assets: $796,146,859 (2001); $901,640,541 (2000); $901,198,098 (1999)

Typical Recipients

Arts & Humanities: Arts Associations & Councils, Arts Centers, Arts Funds, Arts Institutes, Arts Outreach, Ballet, Community Arts, Dance, Ethnic & Folk Arts, Historic Preservation, History & Archaeology, Libraries, Museums/Galleries, Music, Opera, Performing Arts, Public Broadcasting, Theater, Visual Arts

Civic & Public Affairs: Asian American Affairs, Botanical Gardens/Parks, Business/Free Enterprise, Community Foundations, Economic Development, Employment/Job Training, Civic & Public Affairs-General, Hispanic Affairs, Housing, Law & Justice, Legal Aid, Minority Business, Municipalities/Towns, Native American Affairs, Nonprofit Management, Parades/Festivals, Public Policy, Safety, Urban & Community Affairs, Women's Affairs, Zoos/Aquariums

Education: Afterschool/Enrichment Programs, Arts/Humanities Education, Colleges & Universities, Community & Junior Colleges, Continuing Education, Education Funds, Education Reform, Elementary Education (Private), Elementary Education (Public), Engineering/Technological Education, Faculty Development, Education-General, Health & Physical Education, Literacy, Medical Education, Minority Education, Preschool Education, Private Education (Precollege), Public Education (Precollege), Science/Mathematics Education, Secondary Education (Private), Secondary Education (Public), Special Education, Student Aid, Vocational & Technical Education

Environment: Air/Water Quality, Forestry, Environment-General, Environment-General, Research, Resource Conservation, Wildlife Protection

Health: AIDS/HIV, Alzheimers Disease, Cancer, Children's Health/Hospitals, Clinics/Medical Centers, Diabetes, Emergency/Ambulance Services, Eyes/Blindness, Health-General, Geriatric Health, Health Policy/Cost Containment, Health Funds, Health Organizations, Heart, Home-Care Services, Hospices, Hospitals, Hospitals (University Affiliated), Kidney, Long-Term Care, Medical Training, Mental Health, Outpatient Health Care, Preventive Medicine/Wellness Organizations, Public Health, Single-Disease Health Associations, Speech & Hearing, Transplant Networks/Donor Banks

Religion: Churches, Dioceses, Jewish Causes, Ministries, Religious Organizations, Religious Welfare

Science: Science Museums, Scientific Centers & Institutes, Scientific Research

Social Services: Animal Protection, At-Risk Youth, Camps, Child Abuse, Child Welfare, Community Centers, Community Service Organizations, Counseling, Crime Prevention, Day Care, Delinquency & Criminal Rehabilitation, Domestic Violence, Emergency Relief, Family Planning, Family Services, Food/Clothing Distribution, Homes, People with Disabilities, Recreation & Athletics, Refugee Assistance, Scouts, Senior Services, Shelters/Homelessness, Social Services-General, Substance Abuse, United Funds/United Ways, Volunteer Services, Volunteer Services, YMCA/YWCA/YMHA/YWHA, Youth Organizations

Application Procedures

Initial Contact: Contact the foundation or its web site for application guidelines. Applicants should submit one, unbound copy of a proposal describing the project and organization for which funds are sought. The foundation accepts applications submitted over the Internet, but cannot guarantee the confidentiality of information contained in electronic submittals. Applicants for the Charitable Schools Program should contact the foundation or visit the foundation web site to obtain an application form.

Application Requirements: The proposal should include a brief history of the organization and description of existing services; a description of the proposed program, including a statement of need, program components and logistics, and population and number to be served; amount requested and date funds are needed; a list anticipated and committed sources of funding including dollar amounts; project budget listing income and expenses; plans to support the project after the grant period; methods of evaluating the project, including measurable, time-specific goals, a description of information to be collected to measure progress, how that information will be gathered, and (if available) current or baseline levels; a list of trustees or directors and officers including titles for board of directors, profession, ethnicity, and gender; names and qualifications of staff involved with project; organization's current operating budget and year-to-date financial statements; most recent certified audit; and proof of tax-exempt status.

Deadlines: None for general proposals; October 1 for Charitable Schools Program applications.

Review Process: A concise and brief proposal will speed the foundation's processing of a grant application. All requests are reviewed as soon as possible after their receipt. The foundation will acknowledge receipt of all applications within a week. The time required to process a proposal is generally three to four months.

Evaluative Criteria: The foundation finds special value in a proposal in which one or more of the following conditions are present: foundation support would be vital or catalytic to a proposed project's success; the project impact is enhanced through a collaborative network; adequate community and other support exists to ensure that the project will be implemented and continue after the grant period; the proposal makes innovative and efficient use of funds; resources are shared with other agencies or groups to reduce expenses; the project is well-planned; the project promotes better human relationships and a sense of community; and the project involves volunteers where appropriate.

Notes: Submit Internet grant applications to grants@mfi.org (no file attachments). A printed copy of the application should follow all electronic submittals.

Restrictions

The foundation's charter requires that the foundation only distribute grants to qualified public entities or 501(c)(3) charities serving the people of Texas. The foundation generally does not favor contributions for church or seminary construction projects, annual fund-raising drives or general sustentation drives, professional conferences and symposia, or out-of-state performances or competition expenses. The foundation does not make grants or loans to individuals, and reports that endowment gifts are rare.

Additional Information

The foundation maintains a twenty-two acre nonprofit agency campus with over twenty-five tenant agencies and a conference center where seminars, workshops, conferences, and proposal writing assistance are available. community; and the program would enhance the capabilities of families and/or foster traditional family values.

The foundation maintains a twenty-two acre nonprofit agency campus with over twenty-five tenant agencies and a conference center where seminars, workshops, conferences, and proposal writing assistance are available.

Publications: Annual Report; Guidelines in English and Spanish and on Audio-Cassette

Foundation Officials

Evelyn Meadows Acton: director emeritus
Martha L. Benson: vice president, treasurer, chief financial officer
John W. Broadfoot, Jr.: director
J. W. Bullion: trustee, director B 1914. CORP AFFIL secretary: Toreador Royalty Corp.
True Miller Campbell: director
Daniel H. Chapman: director, trustee
Judy B. Culbertson: director, trustee
Bruce H. Esterline: vice president grants
Linda Perryman Evans: president, chief executive officer, trustee, director B Dallas, TX 1950. ED University of Texas BS (1972); East Texas State University (1975); Southern Methodist University (1976). NONPR AFFIL director: Texas Business Hall FAME Foundation; director: YMCA Dallas; director: Dallas Citizens Council; director: Equest; member: Crystal Charity Ball Committee; member: Dallas Assembly; member: Cattle Baron's Ball.
Deborah R. Gill: director
John A. Hammack: trustee, director NONPR AFFIL vice chairman, director: Association Grads U.S. Military Academy.
Virginia Wilson Hanson: trustee, director
Emily J. Jones: assistant vice president, corporate secretary
Sally Rhodus Lancaster, PhD: director emeritus B Gladewater, TX 1938. ED Southern Methodist University BA (1960); Southern Methodist University MA (1979); East Texas State University PhD (1983). NONPR AFFIL member: Phi Beta Kappa; member: Philosophers Society Texas; member advisory board: Communication Foundation Texas; director: Institute Nautical Archaeology.
P. Michael McCullough: director, trustee
Curtis W. Meadows, Jr.: director emeritus B 1938. ED University of Texas (1962).
Eric R. Meadows: director
John M. Meadows: trustee, director
Mark L. Meadows: trustee, director
Robert A. Meadows: chairman, trustee, vice president, director
Sally C. Miller: director emeritus
William A. Nesbitt: trustee, director
Michael E. Patrick: vice president, chief investment officer CORP AFFIL director: Cooper Energy Services; director: Cooper Turbo Compressor; director: Cooper Cameron Valves; director: BJ Services Co.; director: Cooper Cameron Corp.
G. Tom Rhodus: director, trustee
Evy Kay Ritzen: director
Eloise Meadows Rouse: director emeritus B Shreveport, LA 1931.
Robert E. Weiss: vice president admin
Dorothy Cheney Wilson: director emeritus B Gardiner, ME 1904. ED Bates College AB (1925).

Grants Analysis

Disclosure Period: calendar year ending 2001
Total Grants: $34,798,406*
Number of Grants: 324*

Average Grant: $95,179*
Highest Grant: $4,000,000
Lowest Grant: $2,000
Typical Range: $25,000 to $250,000
*Note: Giving excludes United Way and matching gifts. Number of grants excludes awards for charitable schools projects. Average grant figure excludes highest grant.

Recent Grants

Note: Grants derived from 2001 Form 990.

General

4,000,000 Southeast Texas Arts Council, Beaumont, TX -- Toward constructing a new Meadows Museum, on the Southern Methodist University campus
750,000 Boys & Girls Clubs of Greater Dallas, Dallas, TX -- Toward building two new clubs and renovating seven existing clubs
626,635 Lyndon Baines Johnson Foundation, Austin, TX -- Toward endowment and start-up funds for education and research programs
543,800 Community Council of Greater Dallas, Dallas, TX -- To enroll additional uninsured children in the state's Children's Health Insurance Program
500,000 National Wildlife Federation, Austin, TX -- Toward a collaborative, multi-year project to inform and involve the public on sustainable water use plan for Texas
500,000 St Paul Medical Center Foundation, Dallas, TX -- Toward capital needs of the Center for Advanced Heart and Lung Disease
500,000 United Way Metropolitan Dallas, Dallas, TX -- Toward constructing a new headquarters building
500,000 University of Texas Medical Branch Galveston, Galveston, TX -- Toward expanding telehealth technology to maternal and child health programs
372,320 Dallas Independent School District, Dallas, TX -- Toward developing a comprehensive plan to successfully recruit, select and hire quality teachers
371,007 Los Barrios Unidos Community Clinic, Dallas, TX -- Toward constructing a community clinic

MEADWESTVACO CORP.

Company Headquarters

1 High Ridge Park
Stamford, CT 06905
Web: http://www.meadwestvaco.com

Company Description

Ticker: MWV
Exchange: NYSE
Revenue: US$3.935 billion (2001)
Employees: 32500 (2001)
SIC(s): 2411 Logging, 2421 Sawmills & Planing Mills--General, 2426 Hardwood Dimension & Flooring Mills, 2621 Paper Mills.

Operating Locations

Mead Corp. (AL--Birmingham, Cottonton, Phenix City, Stevenson; AZ--Glendale, Phoenix, Tucson; AR--Little Rock; CA--Buena Park, Eureka, Fresno, Garden Grove, National City, Sacramento, San Francisco, Santa Maria; CO--Denver; DC--Washington; FL--Fort Myers, Jacksonville, Orlando, Tampa; GA--Atlanta, Columbus, Smyrna; HI--Honolulu; ID--Boise; IL--Chicago, Godfrey, Hillside; IN--Hartford City, Indianapolis; KY--Louisville; MA--South Lee; MI--Champion, Detroit, Flint, Grand Rapids, Gulliver, Kalamazoo; MN--Minneapolis; MO--North Kansas City, St.

Joseph, St. Louis; NV--Las Vegas; NC--Charlotte, Raleigh; OH--Akron, Cincinnati, Cleveland, Columbus, Miamisburg, Washington Court House; OK--Oklahoma City, Tulsa; PA--Alexandria, Fairless Hills, Pittsburgh; SC--Spartanburg; TN--Kingsport, Knoxville, Memphis, Nashville; UT--Salt Lake City; VA--Charlottesville, Richmond; WA--Seattle, Wenatchee; WI--Menasha)
Note: Operates internationally.

Nonmonetary Support

Range: $550,000 - $750,000
Type: Donated Equipment; Donated Products; In-kind Services
Phone: (937)495-3849
Note: Nonmonetary support is provided by the company.

Meadwestvaco Corp. Foundation

Giving Contact

Ronald F. Budzik, Executive Director
Courthouse Plaza, Northeast
Dayton, OH 45463
Phone: (937)495-3428
Fax: (937)495-4103
Web: http://www.meadwestvaco.com/corporate.nsf/company/foundation
Note: Submit requests for education grants to the foundation.

Description

Founded: 1957
EIN: 316040645
Organization Type: Corporate Foundation
Giving Locations: AL: Cottonton, Lanett, Phenix City; CA: Alisa Viejo, Buena Park, Garden Grove, Huntington Beach, Irvine, Los Angeles, Pasadena, San Francisco; CO: Boulder, Denver; CT: Enfield, Norwich, Stamford; DE: Newark, Wilmington; DC: Washington; FL: Coral Gables, Tampa; GA: Atlanta, Greenville, Smyrna; IL: Chicago, Franklin Park, Jacksonville, Melrose Park, Schaumburg; KS: Overland Park; KY: Louisville, Wickliffe; LA: DeRidder; ME: Rumford; MD: Laurel, Luke; MA: Pittsfield, South Lee, Springfield; MI: Brooklyn Park, Detroit, Escanaba; MO: St. Joseph, St. Louis; NJ: East Rutherford, Pine Brook; NY: Potsdam, Sidney; NC: Garner, Grover, Mebane; OH: Chillicothe, Cincinnati, Cleveland, Dayton, Fremont; OR: Portland; PA: Alexandria, Warrington, Williamsburg; SC: North Charleston, Summerville; TX: Dallas, Evadale, Garland, Houston, Silsbee; VA: Covington, Louisa, Low Moor, Richmond; WA: Seattle; WV: Rupert; WI: Kenosha operating locations.
Grant Types: Capital, Employee Matching Gifts, General Support, Multiyear/Continuing Support, Project.
Note: Employee matching gift ratio: 1 to 1. Higher education is matched for $50 or more up to $5,000. Volunteer leader grants are matched of $25 or more up to $2,500.

Financial Summary

Total Giving: $5,492,529 (2001); $4,814,670 (2000); $5,110,494 (1999)
Giving Analysis: Giving for 2001 includes: foundation grants to United Way ($541,378); 2000: foundation scholarships ($600); foundation grants to United Way ($538,504); foundation ($4,275,566); 1999: foundation scholarships ($1,000); foundation grants to United Way ($510,466); foundation ($4,599,028).
Assets: $32,628,081 (2001); $38,432,894 (2000); $43,914,206 (1999)
Gifts Received: $2,000,000 (2001); $2,000,000 (1996); $2,000,200 (1995). Note: Contributions were received from Mead Corp.

Typical Recipients

Arts & Humanities: Arts Associations & Councils, Arts Centers, Arts Festivals, Arts Institutes, Community Arts, Dance, Historic Preservation, History & Archaeology, Libraries, Museums/Galleries, Music, Opera, Performing Arts, Public Broadcasting, Theater

Civic & Public Affairs: African American Affairs, Botanical Gardens/Parks, Business/Free Enterprise, Chambers of Commerce, Community Foundations, Economic Development, Civic & Public Affairs-General, Municipalities/Towns, Native American Affairs, Nonprofit Management, Philanthropic Organizations, Professional & Trade Associations, Safety, Urban & Community Affairs, Women's Affairs, Zoos/Aquariums

Education: Arts/Humanities Education, Colleges & Universities, Community & Junior Colleges, Community & Junior Colleges, Continuing Education, Economic Education, Education Associations, Education Funds, Education Reform, Engineering/Technological Education, Education-General, Health & Physical Education, Literacy, Minority Education, Public Education (Precollege), Science/Mathematics Education, Secondary Education (Public), Vocational & Technical Education

Environment: Environment-General, Protection, Resource Conservation, Wildlife Protection

Health: Diabetes, Emergency/Ambulance Services, Health-General, Hospices, Medical Rehabilitation, Public Health, Respiratory

International: International Development, International Organizations

Religion: Missionary Activities (Domestic), Religious Welfare

Science: Science Museums, Scientific Centers & Institutes

Social Services: Big Brother/Big Sister, Child Welfare, Community Centers, Community Service Organizations, Domestic Violence, Emergency Relief, Family Services, Food/Clothing Distribution, People with Disabilities, Recreation & Athletics, Scouts, Shelters/Homelessness, Social Services-General, Special Olympics, United Funds/United Ways, YMCA/YWCA/YMHA/YWHA, Youth Organizations

Application Procedures

Initial Contact: Request guidelines; submit a written request to local Mead unit manager. Organizations located in the Miami Valley region or outside Mead communities should direct requests to foundation.

Application Requirements: Include organization mission, vision, goals, and objectives; community needs that the organization addresses; program/services developed to meet those needs; how organization defines and measures success; list of board of directors and officers; proof of tax-exempt status; specific need for funding; specific project for which funding is requested; measures for evaluation; timeframe; and budget, including long and short-term funding plans.

Deadlines: None.

Review Process: Initial review by local Mead unit manager or foundation staff, then referred to governing committee for decision.

Evaluative Criteria: Program provides greater efficiency and coordination of services, or use an integrated problem solving approach; encourages citizen involvement and volunteerism; and deals with root problems rather than secondary ones.

Decision Notification: Within six weeks of receipt.

Notes: No telephone or mass mail solicitations will be accepted.

Restrictions

Does not support individuals; scholarships, grants, or sponsorships for individual students; national, fraternal, labor, or veterans organizations, religious or denominational organizations for religious purposes; or goodwill advertising, dinners, or tickets. Generally does not fund amateur or professional athletic events.

Funding is generally limited to tax-exempt organizations in company operating areas within the United States.

Additional Information

Mead unit managers review local requests and are encouraged to adjust charitable priorities to meet local needs.

Mead Corp. and Westvaco Corp. recently completed a merger. The new company is known as MeadWestvaco. No information is currently available about the impact of this merger on the future of the companies' separate giving programs.

Publications: Guidelines

Corporate Officials

James A. Buzzard: president ED North Carolina State University BS; University of Pennsylvania Wharton School MBA. PRIM CORP EMPL president: MeadWestvaco Corp.

Cynthia A. Niekamp: senior vice president, chief financial officer ED Harvard University MBA; Purdue University BS. PRIM CORP EMPL senior vice president, chief financial officer: MeadWestvaco Corp.

Foundation Officials

J. C. Dutton: board of directors
D. L. Meine: assistant secretary
P. C. Norris: secretary
A. R. Rosenberger: board of directors
S. R. Scherger: board of directors
L. M. Sheffield: treasurer
W. A. Wendell: board of directors

Grants Analysis

Disclosure Period: calendar year ending 2001
Total Grants: $4,951,151*
Number of Grants: 775 (approx)
Average Grant: $4,459*
Highest Grant: $1,500,000
Lowest Grant: $50
Typical Range: $1,000 to $10,000
***Note:** Giving excludes United Way. Average grant figure excludes highest grant.

Recent Grants

Note: Grants derived from 2001 Form 990.

Library-Related
105,000 Ludden Memorial Library, Dixfield, ME

General
1,500,000	Dayton Foundation, Dayton, OH
400,820	Wright State University Foundation, Fairborn, OH
309,570	American Red Cross Disaster Relief Fund
238,375	University of Dayton, Dayton, OH
103,500	Paper Technology Foundation, Kalamazoo, MI
100,000	2003 Fund Committee, Dayton, OH
100,000	Downtown Dayton Partnership, Dayton, OH
94,400	United Way Dayton Area, Dayton, OH
87,500	United Way of Ross County - Chillicothe, Chillicothe, OH
80,000	Nature Conservancy Michigan Chapter, East Lansing, MI

MORRIS A. MECHANIC FOUNDATION

Giving Contact

Clarisse B. Mechanic, President
PO Box 1623
Baltimore, MD 21203
Phone: (410)837-3913

Description

Founded: 1942
EIN: 526034753
Organization Type: Private Foundation
Giving Locations: MD: Baltimore
Grant Types: General Support.

Donor Information

Founder: the late Morris A. Mechanic

Financial Summary

Total Giving: $169,500 (2002); $176,750 (2001); $120,500 (2000)
Assets: $3,686,345 (2002); $3,812,066 (2001); $3,722,611 (2000)
Gifts Received: $103,333 (2001); $48,000 (1998); $40,000 (1996). Note: In 1998 and 2001, contributions were received from the estate of Morris A. Mechanic.

Typical Recipients

Arts & Humanities: Arts Associations & Councils, Arts Outreach, Community Arts, Ethnic & Folk Arts, History & Archaeology, Libraries, Museums/Galleries, Music, Opera, Public Broadcasting

Civic & Public Affairs: Civic & Public Affairs-General, Public Policy

Education: Arts/Humanities Education, Colleges & Universities, Economic Education, Education Funds, Education Reform, Elementary Education (Private), Elementary Education (Public), Education-General, Legal Education, Literacy, Private Education (Precollege), Special Education, Student Aid

Health: Arthritis, Cancer, Children's Health/Hospitals, Emergency/Ambulance Services, Health Organizations, Heart, Hospitals, Respiratory, Single-Disease Health Associations

International: International Organizations

Religion: Churches, Religion-General, Religious Organizations, Religious Welfare

Social Services: Child Abuse, Child Welfare, Community Service Organizations, Crime Prevention, Day Care, Domestic Violence, Family Planning, Family Services, Food/Clothing Distribution, People with Disabilities, Scouts, Shelters/Homelessness, United Funds/United Ways, Youth Organizations

Application Procedures

Initial Contact: Requests should be in narrative form explaining in detail the specific programs to which grants would apply and the nature of the organization applying for a grant.

Deadlines: None.

Restrictions

Maximum grant will not exceed $50,000.

Foundation Officials

Blue Baron: secretary
Clarisse B. Mechanic: president

Grants Analysis

Disclosure Period: calendar year ending 2002
Total Grants: $169,500
Number of Grants: 23
Average Grant: $7,370
Highest Grant: $15,000
Lowest Grant: $1,000
Typical Range: $2,000 to $15,000

Recent Grants

Note: Grants derived from 2001 Form 990.

General
21,250	Harbor Hospital, Baltimore, MD
15,000	Baltimore Child Abuse Center, Inc., Baltimore, MD
15,000	Baltimore Mentoring, Baltimore, MD
15,000	Baltimore Symphony, Baltimore, MD
15,000	Lancers Boys Club, Baltimore, MD
15,000	Maryland Public Television, Baltimore, MD

10,000	College of Notre Dame, Baltimore, MD
10,000	Florence Crittenton Services, Baltimore, MD
10,000	Florida Grand Opera, Palm Beach, FL
10,000	Signal 13 Foundation, Baltimore, MD

MEDINA FOUNDATION

Giving Contact
Patricia G. McKay, Executive Director
801 2nd Avenue, Floor 13
Seattle, WA 98104
Phone: (206)652-8783
Fax: (206)652-8791
E-mail: info@medinafoundation.org
Web: http://www.medinafoundation.org

Description
Founded: 1948
EIN: 910745225
Organization Type: Family Foundation
Giving Locations: WA: greater Puget Sound region
Grant Types: Capital, General Support, Project.

Donor Information
Founder: Norton Clapp, president of the foundation, and other members of the Clapp family incorporated the Medina Foundation in the state of Washington in 1948. Several Clapp family members serve as trustees. The Clapp family are descendants of Matthew G. Clapp, one of the founders of the Weyerhaeuser Company.

Financial Summary
Total Giving: $3,453,881 (2001); $3,211,540 (2000); $2,428,508 (1999)
Giving Analysis: Giving for 2000 includes: foundation matching gifts ($100,000); 1999: foundation scholarships ($15,000) foundation matching gifts ($30,000)
Assets: $91,034,729 (2001); $96,046,253 (2000); $95,272,345 (1999)
Gifts Received: $17,693,367 (1998)

Typical Recipients
Arts & Humanities: Libraries, Public Broadcasting
Civic & Public Affairs: Asian American Affairs, Business/Free Enterprise, Clubs, Community Foundations, Economic Development, Employment/Job Training, First Amendment Issues, Civic & Public Affairs-General, Hispanic Affairs, Housing, Legal Aid, Municipalities/Towns, Native American Affairs, Philanthropic Organizations, Professional & Trade Associations, Public Policy, Urban & Community Affairs, Women's Affairs, Zoos/Aquariums
Education: Business Education, Continuing Education, Education Associations, Education Reform, Elementary Education (Private), Education-General, Literacy, Medical Education, Preschool Education, Private Education (Precollege), Public Education (Precollege), Science/Mathematics Education, Secondary Education (Private), Secondary Education (Public), Special Education, Student Aid
Health: Cancer, Children's Health/Hospitals, Clinics/Medical Centers, Emergency/Ambulance Services, Geriatric Health, Health Organizations, Hospitals, Medical Rehabilitation, Mental Health, Preventive Medicine/Wellness Organizations, Single-Disease Health Associations
Religion: Dioceses, Ministries, Religious Organizations, Religious Welfare
Science: Scientific Centers & Institutes
Social Services: At-Risk Youth, Big Brother/Big Sister, Child Welfare, Community Centers, Community Service Organizations, Counseling, Day Care, Delinquency & Criminal Rehabilitation, Domestic Violence, Emergency Relief, Family Services, Food/Clothing Distribution, Homes, People with Disabilities, Recreation & Athletics, Refugee Assistance, Scouts, Senior Services, Shelters/Homelessness, Social Services-General, Substance Abuse, Volunteer Services, YMCA/YWCA/YMHA/YWHA, Youth Organizations

Application Procedures
Initial Contact: Submit a brief letter.
Application Requirements: The letter should include a description of the proposed project and request.
Deadlines: None.
Review Process: The foundation gives preference to direct service delivery programs over capital requests. If the program falls within the foundation's interests, an application form will be sent.

Restrictions
Grants are not made to individuals. The foundation limits its grantmaking to the greater Puget Sound region. The foundation lists the following top limits on individual grants in a single year: 10% of project operating budget, including private and government funds; 15% of start-up or program expansion budget, including private and government funds; 10% of an applicant's capital budget including private and government funds not to exceed a total of $25,000 (normally made on a contingency basis); and in no event more than 25% of total private funding.

Additional Information
Publications: Application Guidelines

Foundation Officials
Gregory P. Barlow: executive director
Samuel H. Brown: trustee
Davis O. Clapp: vice president, trustee
Jacqueline Clapp: trustee
James N. Clapp, II: trustee
K. Elizabeth Clapp: trustee
Kristina H. Clapp: vice president, trustee
Matthew N. Clapp, Jr.: assistant treasurer, trustee CORP AFFIL officer: Pioneer Broadcasting Co.
Tamsin O. Clapp: trustee
Marion Hand: president
Patricia M. Henry: trustee
Gary MacLeod: trustee PRIM CORP EMPL chairman: Norton Laird Trust Co. CORP AFFIL director: Northwest Building Corp.
Rosalyn Owen: secretary
Anne M. Simons: trustee

Grants Analysis
Disclosure Period: calendar year ending 2001
Total Grants: $3,453,881
Number of Grants: 165
Average Grant: $18,122*
Highest Grant: $250,000
Lowest Grant: $300
Typical Range: $5,000 to $30,000
*Note: Average grant figure excludes two highest grants ($500,000).

Recent Grants
Note: Grants derived from 2001 Form 990.

General
250,000	Npower, Seattle, WA -- for technology support of the faith based nonprofits
250,000	YMCA of Seattle King County and Snohomish County, Seattle, WA -- for capital campaign funds
175,000	One Childhood, Langley, WA -- for assistance to homeless children
150,000	Emerald City Outreach Ministries, Seattle, WA -- for operating funds
122,000	Northwest Center for the Retarded, Seattle, WA -- for the purchase of equipment
100,000	Housing Hope, Everett, WA -- for capital campaign
100,000	Seattle Chinatown International District PDA, Seattle, WA -- for support of Village Square Phase 2
100,000	Tacoma Rescue Mission, Tacoma, WA -- for capital campaign
75,000	Vision House, Renton, WA -- for operating expenses
75,000	Washington Partnership, Seattle, WA -- for operating expenses

MEDTRONIC, INC.

Company Headquarters
710 Medtronic Parkway NE
Minneapolis, MN 55432-5604
Web: http://www.medtronic.com

Company Description
Founded: 1949
Ticker: MDT
Exchange: NYSE
Revenue: US$6.41 billion (2002)
Employees: 28000 (2002)

Nonmonetary Support
Value: $2,357,000 (2002); $1,300,000 (1998)
Type: Donated Products
Volunteer Programs: The foundation's Medtronic Time-n-Talent Fund donates $500 to qualifying nonprofit organizations at which an employee or retiree volunteers at least 40 hours per year. If a volunteer who has donated 40 hours and also makes a financial contribution of $25 to $500 to the same organization, the foundation will match the contribution.
Note: Medtronic businesses make decisions regarding product donations.

Medtronic Foundation

Giving Contact
Penny Hunt, Foundation Executive Director & Vice President, Community Affairs
Medtronic Foundation
710 Medtronic Parkway
MS LC110
Minneapolis, MN 55432-5604
Phone: (763)505-2640
Fax: (763)505-2648
Web: http://www.medtronic.com/foundation

Description
EIN: 411306950
Organization Type: Corporate Foundation
Giving Locations: MN: Minneapolis metropolitan area, St. Paul metropolitan area internationally in Medtronic plant communities; nationally in Medtronic plant communities.
Grant Types: General Support, Multiyear/Continuing Support, Project.
Note: The foundation matches gifts to educational institutions up to $7,000 per employee annually.

Donor Information
Founder: Organized by the company in 1978.

Financial Summary
Total Giving: $25,000,000 (fiscal year ending April 30, 2002 approx.); $14,045,759 (fiscal 2001); $12,034,302 (fiscal 2000). Note: Contributes through corporate direct giving program and foundation.
Giving Analysis: Giving for fiscal 2001 includes: foundation ($14,045,759); fiscal 2000: foundation matching gifts ($639,213); foundation grants to United Way ($1,425,886); foundation ($9,969,203); fiscal 1999: foundation matching gifts ($497,425); foundation grants to United Way ($1,187,037); foundation ($7,902,377);
Assets: $58,790,098 (fiscal 2002); $21,287,883 (fiscal 2001); $15,741,331 (fiscal 2000)

Gifts Received: $47,580,000 (fiscal 2002); $20,400,000 (fiscal 2001); $68,679 (fiscal 2000). Note: Contributions are received from Medtronic, Inc.

Typical Recipients

Arts & Humanities: Arts Centers, Arts Institutes, Arts Outreach, Arts & Humanities-General, Libraries, Museums/Galleries, Music, Opera, Performing Arts, Public Broadcasting, Theater, Visual Arts

Civic & Public Affairs: African American Affairs, Botanical Gardens/Parks, Community Foundations, Economic Development, Employment/Job Training, Hispanic Affairs, Housing, Municipalities/Towns, Safety, Urban & Community Affairs, Zoos/Aquariums

Education: Arts/Humanities Education, Business Education, Colleges & Universities, Community & Junior Colleges, Education Reform, Elementary Education (Private), Engineering/Technological Education, Faculty Development, Education-General, Health & Physical Education, International Exchange, Literacy, Medical Education, Minority Education, Private Education (Precollege), Public Education (Precollege), Science/Mathematics Education, Social Sciences Education, Student Aid

Health: Adolescent Health Issues, AIDS/HIV, Cancer, Children's Health/Hospitals, Clinics/Medical Centers, Emergency/Ambulance Services, Health-General, Geriatric Health, Health Policy/Cost Containment, Health Organizations, Heart, Hospices, Hospitals, Long-Term Care, Medical Research, Multiple Sclerosis, Nursing Services, Preventive Medicine/Wellness Organizations, Public Health, Research/Studies Institutes, Single-Disease Health Associations, Trauma Treatment

International: Foreign Educational Institutions, International-General, Health Care/Hospitals, Human Rights, International Affairs, International Development, International Environmental Issues, International Relief Efforts

Religion: Religious Welfare

Science: Science Exhibits & Fairs, Science Museums, Scientific Centers & Institutes

Social Services: At-Risk Youth, Community Centers, Community Service Organizations, Family Services, Senior Services, Social Services-General, United Funds/United Ways, Volunteer Services, YMCA/YWCA/YMHA/YWHA, Youth Organizations

Application Procedures

Initial Contact: See the foundation's web site for application form and guidelines (or apply using the Minnesota Common Application Form), then send written proposal.

Application Requirements: Submit a description of organization; all previous Medtronic Foundation grants received by organization; current requested amount of funds and purpose for their use; project description, including constituents served, geographic area, use of volunteers, and major accomplishments; implementation timetable; evaluation criteria; organization's current operating budget, including income (with top five donors and amounts given), and anticipated expenses; budget for proposed project, including income, expenses and grants pending; for requests for renewal of support provide brief but specific report on results of grant; copy of IRS 501(c)(3) nonprofit determination letter; list of officers and directors and their affiliations; latest annual report; most recent audited financial statement; any other information that aids in understanding how the organization or program operates.

Deadlines: None for employee committees outside the Twin Cities; January 15, July 15, and October 15 for Twin Cities and national programs; July 18 for Community Arts Program requests; October 15 for HeartRescue requests.

Review Process: Requests are reviewed by staff, then go to appropriate committee and, if necessary, to the foundation board; the board is comprised of members of Medtronic's management; and foundation has four standing committees, comprised of company employees and the board members; employee committees in communities outside Minneapolis-St. Paul determine grants up to $20,000 in their communities.

Evaluative Criteria: Programs that receive funds usually support a Medtronic focus area of emphasis; are innovative, yet simple in design; address factors causing problems in lives of people; are developed or implemented with assistance of Medtronic employees; and serve as a model that could be replicated in other communities.

Decision Notification: Generally within 90 days of receipt.

Restrictions

The foundation does not support capital or capital projects; fiscal agents; fundraising events/activities, social events, or goodwill advertising; general operating support; general support of educational institutions; Greater Twin Cities United Way-supported programs; individuals, including scholarships for individuals; lobbying, political, or fraternal activities; long-term counseling or personal development; program endowments; purchases of automatic external defibrillators (AEDs); religious groups for religious purposes.

Additional Information

Company is committed to contributing at least 2% of pretax profits to charitable organizations.

Company sponsors employee volunteer programs and supports minority vendors whenever possible. For direct gifts, a committee--comprised of the company's president and CEO, company's vice-chairman, and the foundation's chairman--considers grant requests. Most contributions are for one-time projects or events and to organizations supported by employees in their communities. Some corporate contributions are leveraged with additional support from public relations, employee relations, or customer relations. Medtronic facilities also provide some contributions to projects and programs in their immediate vicinity and are generally less than $250.

Publications: Medtronic Community Affairs Annual Report; Application Form; Medtronic Foundation Matching Gifts to Education Programs; Foundation Guidelines; Matching Gifts to Education Form

Corporate Officials

Arthur D. Collins, Jr.: chairman, chief executive officerhuman resources B December 10, 1947. ED Miami University (1969); University of Pennsylvania Wharton School MBA (1973). PRIM CORP EMPL chairman, chief executive officer: Medtronic Inc.

Janet S. Fiola: senior vice president human resources PRIM CORP EMPL senior vice president human resources: Medtronic Inc.

Giving Program Officials

Penny Hunt: executive director staff PRIM CORP EMPL executive director community affairs: Medtronic, Inc.

Foundation Officials

Penny Hunt: executive director staff (see above)
Bob Ryan: board chairman

Grants Analysis

Disclosure Period: fiscal year ending April 30, 2002
Total Grants: $12,511,690*
Number of Grants: 493
Average Grant: $25,379
Highest Grant: $550,000
Typical Range: $2,000 to $50,000
*Note: Giving includes matching gifts; United Way.

Recent Grants

Note: Grants derived from fiscal 2001 Form 990.

General

1,214,626 Greater Twin Cities United Way, Minneapolis, MN -- Support for the 2001 employee campaign

774,816	Matching Gifts to Education, Cleveland, OH
550,000	North American Society of Pacing and Electrophysiology, Natick, MA -- Advanced Training/Clinical Fellowship Awards
500,000	NYCCPI Twin Towers Fund, New York, NY -- Twin Towers Fund
411,000	Public Radio International, Minneapolis, MN -- Underwrite Marketplace Morning reports and the World
350,000	Project Hope, Millwood, VA -- Regional Healthy Heart Program
335,535	Citizens' Scholarship Foundation of America, Minneapolis, MN -- Scholarship program
300,000	Duke University Medical Center, Durham, NC -- Patient Centered Care in Chronic Heart Failure
300,000	Harvard Medical School, Boston, MA -- Integrative care center
300,000	Scripps Foundation, La Jolla, CA -- Scripps Medtronic Integrative Life Enhancement Program

RICHARD MEIER FOUNDATION

Giving Contact

Richard Meier, Trustee
475 Tenth Avenue, Floor 6
New York, NY 10018-1120
Phone: (212)967-6060

Description

Founded: 1997
EIN: 133978415
Organization Type: Private Foundation
Giving Locations: CT; MA; NY
Grant Types: General Support.

Financial Summary

Total Giving: $56,625 (2001); $19,450 (1999); $36,495 (1998)
Assets: $1,292,540 (2001); $1,004,930 (1999); $1,074,807 (1998)
Gifts Received: $1,047,750 (1997). Note: In 1997, contributions were received from Richard Meier.

Typical Recipients

Arts & Humanities: Arts & Humanities-General, History & Archaeology, Libraries, Museums/Galleries, Public Broadcasting

Civic & Public Affairs: Civic & Public Affairs-General

Education: Arts/Humanities Education, Colleges & Universities, International Exchange

Social Services: Community Service Organizations, Social Services-General, Substance Abuse

Application Procedures

Initial Contact: Send a brief letter of inquiry.
Deadlines: None.

Restrictions

Foundation does not support organizations that are not 501(c)3 organizations.

Foundation Officials

Sanford B. Ehrenkranz: trustee
Richard Meier: trustee

Grants Analysis

Disclosure Period: calendar year ending 2001
Total Grants: $56,625
Number of Grants: 17
Average Grant: $2,412*
Highest Grant: $10,000
Lowest Grant: $125

Typical Range: $500 to $5,000
*Note: Average grant excludes two highest grants ($20,000).

Recent Grants

Note: Grants derived from 2001 Form 990.

Library-Related

2,500	Museum of Modern Art, New York, NY
500	Pencil, Inc., New York, NY

General

10,000	Cooper Hewitt national Design Museum, New York, NY
10,000	Huggy Bears, New York, NY
8,500	National Design Museum, New York, NY
5,000	American Academy in Rome, New York, NY
5,000	Cornell University, Ithaca, NY
5,000	Cornell University, Ithaca, NY
5,000	Yale University, Hartford, CT
1,000	American Academy of Arts and Science, Cambridge, MA
1,000	MUSE Film & Television, New York, NY
1,000	National Center on Addiction and Substance Abuse, New York, NY

MEINDERS FOUNDATION

Giving Contact

Mo Grotjohn, Executive Director & Treasurer
4101 Perimeter Ctr., Drive, Suite 210
Oklahoma City, OK 73112
Phone: (405)947-2422

Description

Founded: 1994
EIN: 731438459
Organization Type: Private Foundation
Giving Locations: OK
Grant Types: General Support.

Donor Information

Founder: Established in 1994 by Herman Meinders.

Financial Summary

Total Giving: $843,899 (2001); $737,612 (2000); $739,974 (1999)
Assets: $11,981,459 (2001); $14,066,313 (2000); $15,346,389 (1999)
Gifts Received: $395,800 (2000); $800,000 (1995); $7,029,550 (1994). Note: In 1995 and 2000, contributions were received from Herman Meinders.

Typical Recipients

Arts & Humanities: Arts Associations & Councils, Museums/Galleries, Music
Civic & Public Affairs: Botanical Gardens/Parks, Civic & Public Affairs-General, Housing
Education: Agricultural Education, Business Education, Faculty Development, Education-General, Science/Mathematics Education
Environment: Forestry, Environment-General
Health: Clinics/Medical Centers, Emergency/Ambulance Services
Religion: Churches, Ministries, Religious Welfare, Seminaries
Science: Science Museums
Social Services: Child Welfare, Family Services, Social Services-General

Application Procedures

Initial Contact: Send a brief letter of inquiry. Include a description of organization, amount requested, purpose of funds sought, recently audited financial statement, and proof of tax-exempt status. There are no deadlines.
Deadlines: None.

Foundation Officials

Mo Grotjohn: executive director, treasurer
Herman Meinders: president, trustee
LaDonna Meinders: vice president, trustee
Robert Meinders: secretary, trustee

Grants Analysis

Disclosure Period: calendar year ending 2001
Total Grants: $843,899
Number of Grants: 20
Average Grant: $35,772*
Highest Grant: $150,000
Lowest Grant: $10,000
Typical Range: $15,000 to $50,000
*Note: Average grant figure excludes two highest grants ($200,000).

Recent Grants

Note: Grants derived from 2000 Form 990.

General

100,000	Lutheran Church, St. Louis, MO -- to support congregational outreach project
100,000	Pipestone Jasper School District, Pipestone, MN -- for new library
72,000	City Rescue Mission, Oklahoma City, OK -- for capital campaign
50,000	Phillips Theological Seminary, Tulsa, OK -- professor chair
37,500	Oklahoma Garden Festival, Oklahoma City, OK -- seed money for first event
34,000	Oklahoma City Art Museum, Oklahoma City, OK -- school children project
30,000	Great Expectations Foundation, Tahlequah, OK -- operational support
30,000	Oklahoma City Philharmonic Orchestra, Oklahoma City, OK -- operational support
25,500	Tree Bank Foundation of Oklahoma, Oklahoma City, OK -- for projects
25,000	Canterbury Choral Society, Oklahoma City, OK -- for children's chorus

EDWARD ARTHUR MELLINGER EDUCATIONAL FOUNDATION

Giving Contact

Selection Committee
1025 E. Broadway
PO Box 770
Monmouth, IL 61462
Phone: (309)734-2419
Fax: (309)734-4435
E-mail: info@mellinger.org
Web: http://www.mellinger.org

Description

Founded: 1959
EIN: 362428421
Organization Type: Private Foundation
Giving Locations: limited to students residing in western Illinois and eastern Iowa.
Grant Types: Loan, Scholarship.

Donor Information

Founder: the late Mrs. Inez M. Hensleigh

Financial Summary

Total Giving: $1,416,838 (2000); $1,125,370 (1999); $996,764 (1998)
Giving Analysis: Giving for 2000 includes: foundation scholarships ($1,050,138) 1999: foundation scholarships ($991,945)
Assets: $26,800,017 (2000); $28,548,579 (1999); $27,254,684 (1998)

Gifts Received: $50 (2000); $493 (1999); $23,189 (1998). Note: In 1998, contributions were received from Jeffrey's Trust ($22,803).

Typical Recipients

Arts & Humanities: Libraries
Education: Colleges & Universities, Medical Education, Science/Mathematics Education

Application Procedures

Initial Contact: Request application form.
Deadlines: May 1.

Additional Information

Provides scholarships to individuals for higher education.
Publications: Application Guidelines; Program Policy Statement

Foundation Officials

David D. Fleming: president
Tom Johnson: trustee, secretary
Wyatt Thomas Johnson, Jr.: secretary, trustee B Macon, GA 1941. ED University of Georgia AB (1963); Harvard University MBA (1965). PRIM CORP EMPL president, director: Cable News Network. NONPR AFFIL director: Mayo Foundation; member: Sigma Nu; chairman: John S. & James Knight Foundation; member: Georgia Alumni Society; chairman: Lyndon B. Johnson Foundation; member: Council Foreign Relations.
Mary Frances Miller: trustee
Arthur W. Murray: trustee
Charles Slamar, Jr.: trustee
Gary Willhardt, PhD: trustee
Merle R. Yontz: vice president, trustee

Grants Analysis

Disclosure Period: calendar year ending 2000
Total Grants: $366,700*
Number of Grants: 5
Highest Grant: $360,000
Lowest Grant: $700
*Note: Giving excludes scholarships.

Recent Grants

Note: Grants derived from 2001 Form 990.

General

3,750	Illinois College of Optometry, Chicago, IL
2,500	Harvard Radcliffe, Cambridge, MA
2,500	Illinois Institute of Technology, Chicago, IL
2,500	Midwestern University, Glendale, AZ
2,500	Northern Illinois University, De Kalb, IL
2,500	Purdue University West Lafayette, West Lafayette, IN
2,500	Southern College of Optometry, Memphis, TN
2,500	Southern Illinois University School of Medicine, Carbondale, IL
2,500	University of Cincinnati, Cincinnati, OH
2,500	University of Illinois, Chicago, IL

R. K. MELLON FAMILY FOUNDATION

Giving Contact

Michael Watson, Vice President
One Mellon Center
500 Grant Street, Suite 4106
Pittsburgh, PA 15219-2502
Phone: (412)392-2800
Fax: (412)392-2849
Web: http://www.fdncenter.org/grantmaker/rkmellon

Description

Founded: 1978
EIN: 251356145
Organization Type: Family Foundation
Giving Locations: PA: Western Pennsylvania, Pittsburgh
Grant Types: Capital, Challenge, Emergency, General Support, Matching, Operating Expenses, Research, Seed Money.

Donor Information

Founder: The R.K. Mellon Family Foundation was established in 1978 after the merger of the Loyalhanna, Rachelwood, Cassandra Mellon Henderson, and Landfall Foundations. The four predecessor foundations were created, respectively, by donors Richard P. Mellon, the late Constance B. Mellon , Cassandra Mellon Milbury, and Seward Prosser Mellon, all children of Richard King Mellon. Richard King Mellon was the chairman of Mellon National Bank from 1946 to 1966 and a director of Alcoa and Gulf Oil. R.K. Mellon was also governor and president of T. Mellon and Sons. He handled his family's financial empire until his death in 1970.

Financial Summary

Total Giving: $1,944,550 (2001); $2,014,900 (2000); $1,973,260 (1998)
Giving Analysis: Giving for 2000 includes: foundation scholarships ($30,000) 1997: foundation scholarships ($20,000)
Assets: $39,571,913 (2001); $49,283,759 (2000); $46,549,414 (1998)

Typical Recipients

Arts & Humanities: Arts Associations & Councils, Arts Centers, Arts Funds, Arts Institutes, Arts Outreach, Ballet, Ethnic & Folk Arts, Film & Video, Arts & Humanities-General, Historic Preservation, History & Archaeology, Libraries, Museums/Galleries, Music, Performing Arts, Theater
Civic & Public Affairs: Botanical Gardens/Parks, Business/Free Enterprise, Community Foundations, Economic Development, Economic Policy, Employment/Job Training, Civic & Public Affairs-General, Inner-City Development, Philanthropic Organizations, Professional & Trade Associations, Rural Affairs, Safety, Urban & Community Affairs, Women's Affairs, Zoos/Aquariums
Education: Afterschool/Enrichment Programs, Business Education, Colleges & Universities, Colleges & Universities, Community & Junior Colleges, Economic Education, Education Funds, Education Reform, Engineering/Technological Education, Environmental Education, Education-General, Gifted & Talented Programs, International Studies, Medical Education, Minority Education, Preschool Education, Private Education (Precollege), Public Education (Precollege), Science/Mathematics Education, Special Education, Student Aid
Environment: Forestry, Environment-General, Resource Conservation, Watershed, Wildlife Protection
Health: AIDS/HIV, Cancer, Clinics/Medical Centers, Emergency/Ambulance Services, Health-General, Health Funds, Health Organizations, Hospitals, Hospitals (University Affiliated), Long-Term Care, Medical Rehabilitation, Medical Research, Medical Training, Mental Health, Nursing Services, Preventive Medicine/Wellness Organizations, Single-Disease Health Associations, Transplant Networks/Donor Banks
International: Foreign Arts Organizations, Health Care/Hospitals, International Environmental Issues, International Organizations, International Relief Efforts
Religion: Churches, Jewish Causes, Ministries, Religious Organizations, Religious Welfare
Science: Science Museums, Scientific Centers & Institutes, Scientific Labs, Scientific Research

Social Services: Animal Protection, Child Welfare, Community Centers, Community Service Organizations, Delinquency & Criminal Rehabilitation, Domestic Violence, Emergency Relief, Family Services, Homes, People with Disabilities, Recreation & Athletics, Sexual Abuse, Shelters/Homelessness, Substance Abuse, United Funds/United Ways, Volunteer Services, YMCA/YWCA/YMHA/YWHA, Youth Organizations

Application Procedures

Initial Contact: Contact the foundation to obtain an application form, or download the form from the foundation's web site. The foundation also accepts the Common Grant Application Format (with foundation's required attachments), available at www.cmu.edu/develop/infoserv/prop/cgaf.html.
Application Requirements: Proposals must include the completed application form, proof of tax-exempt status, an executive summary providing an overview of the organization and describing the proposed program or project, how it will benefit the community, and the organization's capacity and plan to operate the project; a description of the plan to document progress and results; project budget; organization's history, including goals, current programs and activities, and accomplishments; a list of board of directors and officers, with affiliations, addresses and telephone numbers; audited financial statements for the last two years with corresponding operating budgets; and other sources of funding and financial plan to sustain project. copy of the IRS determination letter indicating tax-exempt status under Section 509(a) and 501(c)(3), and audited financial statements for the most recent two years, must be submitted. Include any printed material on the organization, such as annual reports or catalogs, if available.
Deadlines: None.
Evaluative Criteria: The foundation prefers projects and programs that have a clearly defined evaluation component.
Decision Notification: All proposals are acknowledged in writing.

Restrictions

Proposals are not considered unless accompanied by a copy of IRS classification. The foundation does not give to individuals or to conduit organizations which pass on funds to other organizations, nor does it make grants outside of the United States.

Additional Information

Publications: Guidelines; Application Form

Foundation Officials

Robert B. Burr, Jr.: trustee
Lawrence S. Busch: assistant treasurer
Ann Marie Helms: program associate, assistant secretary
Seward Prosser Mellon: don, director, trustee B Chicago, IL 1942. ED Susquehanna University BA (1965). PRIM CORP EMPL president: Richard K. Mellon & Sons. CORP AFFIL president: Rolling Rock Farms; director: Mellon Bank NA; director: Mellon Bank Corp. NONPR AFFIL chairman real estate committee, chairman finance & executive: Valley School Ligonier; life member: W Pennsylvania Conservancy; member: Phi Mu Delta; president: LoyalHanna Association. CLUB AFFIL Vintage Club; Rolling Rock Westmoreland Hunt Club; Laurel Valley Golf Club; Rolling Rock Club; Duquesne Club.
John J. Turcik: controller
Mason Walsh, Jr.: vice chairman, trustee B Philadelphia, PA 1935. ED Pennsylvania State University BS (1957); Harvard University LLB (1960). PRIM CORP EMPL executive vice president, general counsel: Richard K. Mellon & Sons. NONPR AFFIL director: Childrens Hospital Pittsburgh.
Michael B. Watson: vice president, director

Grants Analysis

Disclosure Period: calendar year ending 2001
Total Grants: $1,944,550
Number of Grants: 71
Average Grant: $27,388
Highest Grant: $120,000
Lowest Grant: $1,000
Typical Range: $10,000 to $50,000

Recent Grants

Note: Grants derived from 2001 Form 990.

General

120,000	University of Pittsburgh, Pittsburgh, PA -- Charles Gray Watson Surgical Education Center
100,000	Latrobe Presbyterian Church, Latrobe, PA -- endowment fund for maintenance of the church
100,000	St. Michael's of the Valley Episcopal Church, Ligonier, PA -- capital improvements
100,000	Western Pennsylvania Conservancy, Pittsburgh, PA -- help reach Kresge Foundation match for Fallingwater
75,000	Humane Society of Boulder Valley, Boulder, CO -- capital campaign to build a new facility
75,000	Pigeon Key Foundation, Marathon, FL -- for marine ecology and environment education center
75,000	Yampa Valley Land Trust, Inc., Steamboat Springs, CO -- land conservation of northwest Colorado
60,000	Valley School of Ligonier, Ligonier, PA -- scholarship
50,000	Allegheny Conference on Community Development, Pittsburgh, PA -- for planning of French Indian War and other amenities projects
50,000	Brandywine Conservancy, Chadds Ford, PA

ANDREW W. MELLON FOUNDATION

Giving Contact

Michele S. Warman, General Counsel & Secretary
140 East 62nd Street
New York, NY 10021
Phone: (212)838-8400
Fax: (212)888-4172
Web: http://www.mellon.org

Description

Founded: 1969
EIN: 131879954
Organization Type: General Purpose Foundation
Giving Locations: nationally.
Grant Types: Award, Challenge, Endowment, Fellowship, Matching, Multiyear/Continuing Support, Research.

Donor Information

Founder: The Andrew W. Mellon Foundation is the product of the 1969 consolidation of two previously independent foundations: the Avalon Foundation, established by Ailsa Mellon Bruce , and the Old Dominion Foundation, established by her brother, Paul Mellon. As the children of Pittsburgh financier Andrew W. Mellon, Paul and Ailsa inherited one of the nation's largest fortunes, including substantial holdings in the Mellon National Bank and Trust Co., Gulf Oil Corp., Aluminum Co. of America, Koppers Co., and Carborundum Co. The foundation received additional funds from the estate of Mrs. Ailsa Mellon Bruce upon her death in 1969.

Financial Summary

Total Giving: $182,321,993 (2002); $205,870,148 (2001); $142,216,007 (1998)
Giving Analysis: Giving for 1998 includes: foundation matching gifts ($7,114,590); foundation scholarships ($11,848,250); foundation matching gifts ($12,385,750) international subsidiaries ($13,012,155)
Assets: $4,135,567,000 (2001 approx); $4,889,898,441 (2000); $4,615,683,000 (1999)
Gifts Received: In 1989, contributions were received from the estate of Margaret Meehan.

Typical Recipients

Arts & Humanities: Arts Associations & Councils, Arts Centers, Arts Institutes, Ballet, Dance, Historic Preservation, History & Archaeology, Libraries, Literary Arts, Museums/Galleries, Music, Opera, Performing Arts, Theater
Civic & Public Affairs: Botanical Gardens/Parks, Economic Policy, Civic & Public Affairs-General, Hispanic Affairs, Nonprofit Management, Philanthropic Organizations, Public Policy, Women's Affairs, Zoos/Aquariums
Education: Arts/Humanities Education, Business Education, Colleges & Universities, Continuing Education, Economic Education, Education Associations, Education Funds, Education Reform, Engineering/Technological Education, Environmental Education, Faculty Development, Faculty Development, Education-General, International Studies, Legal Education, Literacy, Medical Education, Minority Education, Science/Mathematics Education, Social Sciences Education, Student Aid
Environment: Environment-General, Research, Resource Conservation
Health: Medical Research, Public Health
International: Foreign Arts Organizations, Foreign Educational Institutions, International-General, Health Care/Hospitals, International Affairs, International Development, International Environmental Issues, International Organizations, International Peace & Security Issues, International Relations, Trade
Science: Scientific Centers & Institutes, Scientific Organizations, Scientific Research
Social Services: Family Planning

Application Procedures

Initial Contact: Letter of request of a page or less is sufficient.
Application Requirements: Include the need, the nature, and the amount of the request and the justification for it. Evidence of classification by the IRS should be included. Supplementary exhibits may be submitted.
Deadlines: None.

Restrictions

The foundation does not give grants to individuals or to primarily local organizations.

Additional Information

Prospective applicants are encouraged to explore their ideas informally with foundation staff (preferably in writing) before submitting formal proposal.
Publications: Annual Report

Foundation Officials

William O. Baker: chairman emeritus
Lewis W. Bernard: trustee
William G. Bowen: president, trustee
Drew G. Faust: trustee
Hanna Holborn Gray, PhD: chairman, trustee B Heidelberg, Germany 1930. ED Bryn Mawr College AB (1950); Harvard University PhD (1957); Yale University MA (1971); Yale University LLD (1978). PRIM NONPR EMPL professor of history: University of Chicago. CORP AFFIL director: JP Morgan & Co. Inc.; director: Morgan Guaranty Trust Co. New York; director: Atlantic Richfield Co.; director: Cummins Engine Co. Inc.; director: Ameritech Corp. NONPR AFFIL member: Renaissance Society America; board regents: Smithsonian Institute; member: National Academy Education; member: Phi Beta Kappa; trustee: Harvard University; trustee: Marlboro School Music; fellow: Center Advanced Study Behavioral Science; director: Council Foreign Relations; fellow: American Academy of Arts & Sciences; member: American Philosophical Society.

John Hull: vice president finance
Patricia L. Irvin: vice president, operations and planning
Paul LeClerc: trustee
Colin Lucas: trustee
Dr. Walter Eugene Massey: trustee B Hattiesburg, MS 1938. ED Morehouse College BS (1958); Washington University MA (1966); Washington University PhD (1966). PRIM NONPR EMPL president: Morehouse College. CORP AFFIL director: Motorola Inc.; director: BP Amoco Corp.; director: McDonalds Corp.; director: BankAmerica Corp. NONPR AFFIL member: American Physics Society; member: Sigma Xi; member: American Association Advancement Science.
Mary Patterson McPherson, PhD: vice president B Abington, PA 1935. ED Smith College AB (1957); University of Delaware MA (1960); Bryn Mawr College PhD (1969). NONPR AFFIL member: American Philosophical Society; director: Philadelphia Contributionship. CLUB AFFIL Cosmopolitan Club.
Timothy Mellon: trustee B Pittsburgh, PA 1942. ED Yale University BA (1964); Yale University School of Art & Architecture MCP (1966). PRIM CORP EMPL chairman, chief executive officer, director: Guilford Transportation Industries Inc.
Walter Taylor Reveley, III: trustee B Churchville, VA 1943. ED Princeton University AB (1965); University of Virginia JD (1968). PRIM NONPR EMPL dean: College of William & Mary School of Law. CORP AFFIL director: New Covenant Trust Co. NONPR AFFIL president: Virginia Museum Fine Arts; board directors: Virginia Museum Foundation; member: Virginia Bar Association; member: Virginia Bar Foundation; president symphony council: Richmond Symphony; trustee: Union Theological Seminary; member: Richmond Bar Association; trustee: Princeton University; member: Raven Society; board directors, member: Princeton Association Virginia; member: Phi Beta Kappa; president, director: Presbyterian Outlook Foundation Book Service; member: Order Coif; elder: Grace Covenent Presbyterian Church; member: Omicron Delta Kappa; member: Edn Lawyers; member: American Society International Law; member: District of Columbia Bar Association; member: American Judicature Society; member: American Bar Association; member: American Bar Foundation. CLUB AFFIL Downtown Club; Knickerbocker Club; Country Club Virginia.
Charles Andrew Ryskamp: trustee B East Grand Rapids, MI 1928. ED Calvin College AB (1950); Yale University MA (1951); Cambridge University Pembroke College (1953-1954); Yale University PhD (1956). NONPR AFFIL member, board managers: Yale University Lewis Walpole Library; member advisory board: Yale University Private Papers James Boswell; member: Wordsworth Rydel Mt Trust; professor: Princeton University Library; member advisory board: Skowhegan School Painting Sculpture; special correspondent: New York Genealogical & Biographical Society; member advisory council: Princeton University Art Museum; member: Museum Council New York City; member: Neuropathy Association; visiting committee: Metropolitan Museum Art; member, board advisors: Metropolitan Opera Association; member: Keats-Shelley Association America; president: Master Drawings Association; advisory board: Foundation French Museum; director: Frick Collection; member: Cowper Society; member national committee: Drawing Society; trustee: Amon Carter Museum Western Art; honorary trustee: Corning Museum Glass; patron: William Blake Trust; committee honoraryor, member: Association Internationale de Bibliophilie; member: Bibliographical Society America; member: American Philosophical Society; member: Association Art Museum Directors; member: American Academy of Arts & Sciences; member: American Antiquarian Society; member: Academy American Poets. CLUB AFFIL Roxburghe Club; Lotos Club; Pilgrims Club; Grolier Club; Knickerbocker Club; Century Association; Elizabethan Club.
Eileen Scott: treasurer, assistant secretary
T. Dennis Sullivan: vice president fin
Anne M. Tatlock: trustee B White Plains, NY 1939. ED Vassar College BA (1961); New York University MA Economics (1968). PRIM CORP EMPL chairman, chief executive officer: Fiduciary Trust Co. International. CORP AFFIL vice chairman, director: Franklin Resources Inc.; chairman, trustee: Cultural Institutional Retirement System; director: Fortune Brands Inc.; director: American General Corp. NONPR AFFIL trustee: Mayo Foundation; trustee: Vassar College; chairman nominating committee, trustee: American Ballet Theater.
Michele S. Warman: secretary, general counsel
John C. Whitehead: chairman emeritus
Harriet Zuckerman: senior vice president B New York, NY 1937. ED Vassar College AB (1958); Columbia University PhD (1965). CORP AFFIL director: Annual Reviews Inc. NONPR AFFIL member advisory board: Social Science Citation Index; member: Society Social Studies Science; member advisory board: Institute Scientific Information; professor emerita, sr res scholar: Columbia University; member: Council Foreign Relations; trustee: Center Advanced Study Behavioral Science; member: Century Association; member: American Philosophical Society; member: American Academy of Arts & Sciences.

Grants Analysis

Disclosure Period: calendar year ending 2001
Total Grants: $205,870,148
Number of Grants: 494
Average Grant: $416,741
Highest Grant: $4,150,000
Typical Range: $50,000 to $750,000

Recent Grants

Note: Grants derived from 2001 Form 990.

Library-Related

1,475,000 American Philosophical Society, Philadelphia, PA -- to increase number of and extend the trial period for fellowships for faculty members

900,000 Missouri Botanical Gardens, St. Louis, MO -- toward costs of a program of ecological research and training

General

3,000,000 Woodrow Wilson National Fellowship Foundation, Princeton, NJ -- in support of the Andrew W. Mellon Foundation Fellowships in Humanistic Studies

2,800,000 JSTOR, New York, NY -- toward the initial costs of adding a cluster of art history journals to its database

2,750,000 Art Institute of Chicago, Chicago, IL -- for a Conservation Scientist Position

2,600,000 Woodrow Wilson National Fellowship Foundation, Princeton, NJ -- in support of fellowships for junior faculty from underrepresented groups

2,500,000 Philadelphia Museum of Art, Philadelphia, PA -- endowment of a Senior Conservatorship

2,500,000 Wellesley College, Wellesley, MA -- toward costs of a collaborative program of faculty career enhancement

2,300,000 American Council of Learned Societies, New York, NY -- in support of a program of research leaves for junior faculty who have completed at least 2 years of teaching

2,000,000 American Council of Learned Societies, New York, NY -- permanent endowment

2,000,000 Duke University, Durham, NC -- to support a program of postdoctoral fellowships in the humanities and social sciences

2,000,000 Theater Communications Group, New York, NY -- to support costs of establishing New Generations

RICHARD KING MELLON FOUNDATION

Giving Contact

Michael Watson, Vice President and Director
One Mellon Center
500 Grant Street, Suite 4106
Pittsburgh, PA 15219-2502
Phone: (412)392-2800
Web: http://fdncenter.org/grantmaker/rkmellon/

Description

Founded: 1947
EIN: 251127705
Organization Type: General Purpose Foundation
Giving Locations: PA: Southwestern Pennsylvania, Pittsburgh nationally for conservation programs.
Grant Types: Capital, Challenge, General Support, Project, Seed Money.

Donor Information

Founder: The Richard King Mellon Foundation was established in 1947 by Richard King Mellon , son of Richard Beatty Mellon, and nephew of Andrew Mellon. Mr. Mellon, a lieutenant general in the United States Army Reserve, managed his family's many interests from the 1930s until his death on June 3, 1970. He served as president of the Mellon National Bank and chairman of the board of Mellon National Bank and Trust Company. He was also a director of many of the companies closely linked to the Mellon family, including the Aluminum Company of America and Gulf Oil Corporation. Mr. Mellon played a leading role in the movement to revitalize Pittsburgh and was active in civic and philanthropic affairs in Pittsburgh and Ligonier, PA. He married Constance Mary Prosser, who served as the foundation's chairman of the board of trustees from its inception in 1947 until her death in 1980.

Financial Summary

Total Giving: $58,608,007 (2001); $91,699,221 (2000); $87,360,739 (1999). Note: Nonmonetary support is in the form of land donations provided through the Foundation's American Land Conservation Program.
Giving Analysis: Giving for 2000 includes: foundation grants to United Way ($2,780,000); nonmonetary support ($65,690,212); 1998: foundation grants to United Way ($3,003,000); nonmonetary support ($23,649,852); 1997: foundation grants to United Way ($435,000) nonmonetary support ($23,649,852)
Assets: $1,661,153,320 (2001); $1,910,014,037 (2000); $1,972,896 (1999)

Typical Recipients

Arts & Humanities: Arts Associations & Councils, Arts Centers, Arts Institutes, Arts Outreach, Ballet, Community Arts, Dance, Ethnic & Folk Arts, Film & Video, Arts & Humanities-General, Historic Preservation, History & Archaeology, Libraries, Museums/Galleries, Music, Opera, Performing Arts, Public Broadcasting, Theater
Civic & Public Affairs: African American Affairs, Botanical Gardens/Parks, Business/Free Enterprise, Community Foundations, Economic Development, Economic Policy, Employment/Job Training, Civic & Public Affairs-General, Housing, Inner-City Development, Law & Justice, Municipalities/Towns, Nonprofit Management, Philanthropic Organizations, Professional & Trade Associations, Rural Affairs, Safety,

Urban & Community Affairs, Women's Affairs, Zoos/Aquariums
Education: Afterschool/Enrichment Programs, Agricultural Education, Arts/Humanities Education, Business Education, Colleges & Universities, Community & Junior Colleges, Economic Education, Education Associations, Education Funds, Education Reform, Elementary Education (Private), Elementary Education (Public), Environmental Education, Faculty Development, Education-General, Gifted & Talented Programs, International Studies, Leadership Training, Literacy, Medical Education, Minority Education, Preschool Education, Private Education (Precollege), Public Education (Precollege), Religious Education, Science/Mathematics Education, Special Education, Student Aid, Vocational & Technical Education
Environment: Air/Water Quality, Forestry, Environment-General, Protection, Research, Resource Conservation, Watershed, Wildlife Protection
Health: AIDS/HIV, Cancer, Children's Health/Hospitals, Clinics/Medical Centers, Emergency/Ambulance Services, Geriatric Health, Health Policy/Cost Containment, Health Organizations, Hospices, Hospitals, Long-Term Care, Medical Rehabilitation, Medical Research, Medical Training, Mental Health, Nursing Services, Prenatal Health Issues, Preventive Medicine/Wellness Organizations, Public Health, Research/Studies Institutes, Single-Disease Health Associations
International: International Environmental Issues, International Relief Efforts
Religion: Churches, Dioceses, Jewish Causes, Ministries, Religious Organizations, Religious Welfare, Seminaries, Synagogues/Temples
Science: Science Museums, Scientific Centers & Institutes, Scientific Labs
Social Services: Camps, Child Welfare, Community Centers, Community Service Organizations, Day Care, Delinquency & Criminal Rehabilitation, Domestic Violence, Emergency Relief, Family Planning, Family Services, Food/Clothing Distribution, Homes, People with Disabilities, Recreation & Athletics, Scouts, Senior Services, Sexual Abuse, Shelters/Homelessness, Social Services-General, Substance Abuse, United Funds/United Ways, Volunteer Services, YMCA/YWCA/YMHA/YWHA, Youth Organizations

Application Procedures

Initial Contact: Obtain an application form either from the foundation's web site or through a letter requesting application materials.
Application Requirements: Proposals should include an executive summary describing the sponsoring organization, proposed project, the problems it seeks to address, the population it will serve, and how it will be operated. Background information on the requesting organization should include its history, purpose, the types of programs it offers, and the names and affiliations of members of the board and Chairman and/or President. Financial information must include an operating budget and timetable for the proposed project, and audited financial statements for the most recent two years. A copy of the latest IRS determination letter of tax-exempt status under sections 501(c)(3) and 509(a) is required. Information on the proposed project should include its specific purpose and objective, budget, and timetable. Include a description of the proposed methods of operation and evaluation, and the qualifications of the individuals who will conduct the undertaking. A statement of other sources of support for the project should also be included, with an explanation of how the project will be financed at the expiration of the proposed grant. Supporting printed material, including annual reports, pamphlets, and brochures may be included.
Deadlines: None.
Review Process: The board of trustees meets twice a year, usually in June and December.
Notes: The foundation shows preference for projects and programs that have a clearly defined evaluation component.

Restrictions

Will not consider requests on behalf of individuals, and normally does not consider requests for grants to conduit organizations that pass on funds to other organizations. The foundations does not make grants outside the United States.

Additional Information

Publications: Annual Report; Fact Sheet; Grant Application; Special Program Publications

Foundation Officials

Robert B. Burr, Jr.: treasurer, trustee
Lawrence S. Busch: trustee, assistant treasurer
Ann Marie Helms: assistant secretary
Scott D. Izzo: program associate, secretary
Richard Prosser Mellon: chairman, trustee B Chicago, IL 1939. ED University of Pittsburgh (1958-1960). NONPR AFFIL member national executive committee life member: Ducks Unlimited Inc.; coordinator: Western Pennsylvania School Blind; director: Ducks Unlimited Foundation. CLUB AFFIL Rolling Rock Club; Rolling Rock Westmoreland Hunt Club; The Links New York City Club; National Steeplechase & Hunt Association; Duquesne Club; Laurel Valley Golf Club.
Seward Prosser Mellon: president, chairman executive comm, trustee B Chicago, IL 1942. ED Susquehanna University BA (1965). PRIM CORP EMPL president: Richard K. Mellon & Sons. CORP AFFIL president: Rolling Rock Farms; director: Mellon Bank NA; director: Mellon Bank Corp. NONPR AFFIL chairman real estate committee, chairman finance & executive: Valley School Ligonier; life member: W Pennsylvania Conservancy; member: Phi Mu Delta; president: LoyalHanna Association. CLUB AFFIL Vintage Club; Rolling Rock Westmoreland Hunt Club; Laurel Valley Golf Club; Rolling Rock Club; Duquesne Club.
Arthur D. Miltenberger: vice president PRIM CORP EMPL treasurer: Richard K. Mellon & Sons. CORP AFFIL director: Caterair Holdings Corp.
John J. Turcik: controller
Mason Walsh, Jr.: vice chairman, trustee B Philadelphia, PA 1935. ED Pennsylvania State University BS (1957); Harvard University LLB (1960). PRIM CORP EMPL executive vice president, general counsel: Richard K. Mellon & Sons. NONPR AFFIL director: Childrens Hospital Pittsburgh.
Michael B. Watson: vice president, trustee

Grants Analysis

Disclosure Period: calendar year ending 2001
Total Grants: $57,608,007*
Number of Grants: 142
Average Grant: $405,690
Highest Grant: $3,000,000
Lowest Grant: $2,500
Typical Range: $100,000 to $1,000,000
*Note: Giving excludes United Way.

Recent Grants

Note: Grants derived from 2001 Form 990.

General

2,000,000 Phipps Conservatory and Botanical Garden, Pittsburgh, PA -- Visitors Education Center

2,000,000 Sports and Exhibition Authority of Pittsburgh and Allegheny County, Pittsburgh, PA -- construction of Riverfront Park

1,750,000 Conservation Fund, Arlington, VA -- in-kind gift of land

1,000,000 United Way Allegheny County, Pittsburgh, PA

1,000,000 Western Pennsylvania Conservancy, Pittsburgh, PA -- capital campaign

900,000 Conservation Fund, Arlington, VA -- capital campaign

750,000   Chesapeake Bay Foundation, Annapolis, MD -- Pennsylvania Watershed Restoration Program
750,000   Foundation for California University of Pennsylvania, California, PA -- Riparian Buffer Project
750,000   Washington and Jefferson College, Washington, PA -- capital campaign
600,000   Ligonier Camp and Conference Center, Ligonier, PA -- purchase land

MEMORIAL FOUNDATION FOR THE BLIND

Giving Contact
Roger W. Greene, President
Memorial Foundation for the Blind
51 Harvard Street
Worcester, MA 01609
Phone: (508)752-3053

Description
EIN: 041611615
Organization Type: Private Foundation
Giving Locations: MA: Worcester including surrounding area
Grant Types: General Support.

Financial Summary
Total Giving: $238,306 (fiscal year ending March 31, 2002); $234,548 (fiscal 2001); $177,622 (fiscal 2000). Note: Fiscal 1997 Giving includes scholarship ($1,000).
Giving Analysis: Giving for fiscal 2002 includes: foundation gifts to individuals ($11,217); fiscal 2001: foundation gifts to individuals ($1,000); fiscal 2000: foundation gifts to individuals ($9,219)
Assets: $4,333,777 (fiscal 2002); $4,576,618 (fiscal 2001); $5,192,725 (fiscal 2000)
Gifts Received: $1,233 (fiscal 2002); $79,372 (fiscal 2001); $1,175 (fiscal 1997)

Typical Recipients
Arts & Humanities: Libraries, Public Broadcasting
Civic & Public Affairs: Municipalities/Towns, Urban & Community Affairs
Education: Colleges & Universities, Special Education
Health: Health Organizations, Hospitals, Kidney, Single-Disease Health Associations
Social Services: People with Disabilities

Application Procedures
Initial Contact: Send a brief letter of inquiry.
Application Requirements: Include a description of organization.
Deadlines: None.

Foundation Officials
Eleanor Brockway: director
Stephanie S. Burnett: treasurer
Kleber A. Campbell, III: director
Gilbert S. Davis: director
T. Ashley Edwards: assistant treasurer
Helen D. Fifield: director
Janet B. Foley: director
Roger W. Greene: director
Barbara Higgins: director
Nancy S. Hudson: director
Nancy Jeppson: director
Helen Koskinas: director
Diane MacConnell: director
Gary MacConnell: director
Larry Raymond: vice president
Janet Reidy: director
Joseph Reidy: director
Dr. C. Reid Roberts: director
Judy Savageau: director

Betty Simpson: clerk
Alice Taylor: director
Wyatt R. Wade: president

Grants Analysis
Disclosure Period: fiscal year ending March 31, 2002
Total Grants: $227,089*
Number of Grants: 7
Highest Grant: $113,856
Lowest Grant: $2,588
Typical Range: $4,000 to $30,000
*Note: Giving excludes gifts to individuals.

Recent Grants
Note: Grants derived from 2000 Form 990.

Library-Related
6,600   Talking Book Library, Worcester, MA

General
73,420   Massachusetts Association for the Blind, Worcester, MA
57,490   Audio Journal, Worcester, MA
19,530   City of Worcester, Worcester, MA
5,386   Massachusetts Association for Parents of Visually Impaired, Worcester, MA
3,000   Fidelco Guide Dog, Worcester, MA
2,910   Central Massachusetts Bay State, Worcester, MA
67   Kidney Dialysis Unit, Memorial Hospital, Worcester, MA -- transportation for the blind

MEMTON FUND

Giving Contact
Lillian I. Daniels, Secretary
515 Madison Avenue
Suite 3702
New York, NY 10022
Phone: (212)644-4915

Description
Founded: 1936
EIN: 136096608
Organization Type: Private Foundation
Giving Locations: Northeast USA.
Grant Types: Capital, Endowment, General Support, Scholarship.

Donor Information
Founder: the late Albert G. Milbank, the late Charles M. Cauldwell

Financial Summary
Total Giving: $481,100 (2001); $658,230 (2000); $392,400 (1999)
Giving Analysis: Giving for 1999 includes: foundation scholarships ($29,000)
Assets: $10,847,121 (2001); $11,654,274 (2000); $11,911,323 (1999)

Typical Recipients
Arts & Humanities: Arts Associations & Councils, Arts Funds, Ballet, Community Arts, Dance, Film & Video, Arts & Humanities-General, Historic Preservation, Libraries, Museums/Galleries, Music, Performing Arts, Public Broadcasting, Theater
Civic & Public Affairs: Botanical Gardens/Parks, Business/Free Enterprise, Community Foundations, Employment/Job Training, Civic & Public Affairs-General, Hispanic Affairs, Housing, Philanthropic Organizations, Professional & Trade Associations, Public Policy, Urban & Community Affairs, Women's Affairs, Zoos/Aquariums
Education: Afterschool/Enrichment Programs, Arts/Humanities Education, Colleges & Universities, Engineering/Technological Education, Education-General, Leadership Training, Legal Education, Literacy,

Medical Education, Private Education (Precollege), Public Education (Precollege), Science/Mathematics Education, Secondary Education (Private), Special Education, Student Aid
Environment: Environment-General, Resource Conservation, Wildlife Protection
Health: AIDS/HIV, Cancer, Children's Health/Hospitals, Clinics/Medical Centers, Hospices, Hospitals, Long-Term Care, Medical Rehabilitation, Medical Research, Mental Health, Nursing Services, Public Health, Single-Disease Health Associations
International: Foreign Arts Organizations, Health Care/Hospitals, International Relief Efforts, Missionary/Religious Activities
Religion: Churches
Science: Scientific Centers & Institutes
Social Services: Animal Protection, Community Centers, Community Service Organizations, Crime Prevention, Delinquency & Criminal Rehabilitation, Family Services, Food/Clothing Distribution, People with Disabilities, Recreation & Athletics, Scouts, Social Services-General, United Funds/United Ways, Youth Organizations

Application Procedures
Initial Contact: Send a brief letter of inquiry.
Application Requirements: Include a description of organization and its activities.
Deadlines: None, although decisions on major requests are only made at the annual board of directors meeting in May. Applications should be received at least six weeks prior to that date.

Restrictions
Does not support individuals.

Foundation Officials
Lillian I. Daniels: secretary, treasurer
Elenita M. Drumwright: president
Elizabeth Drumwright: director
Robert V. Edgar: director
Elizabeth S. Farrar: director
Marjorie M. Farrar: vice president
Olivia Farrar-Wellman: director
Alexandra Giordano: director
David L. Milbank: director
Michelle Milbank: director
Samuel L. Milbank: director
Thomas L. Milbank: director
Karen Quackenbush: director
Pamela White: director

Grants Analysis
Disclosure Period: calendar year ending 2001
Total Grants: $481,100
Number of Grants: 146
Average Grant: $3,295
Highest Grant: $15,000
Typical Range: $1,000 to $10,000

Recent Grants
Note: Grants derived from 2001 Form 990.

Library-Related
15,000   Folger Shakespeare Library, Washington, DC -- operating support
15,000   Folger Shakespeare Library, Washington, DC -- operating support

General
15,000   Foundation for Advanced Education in the Sciences, Bethesda, MD -- operating support
15,000   Suicide Prevention and Crisis, San Francisco, CA -- operating support
10,000   Horse Cave Theatre, Bowling Green, KY -- operating support
10,000   Hospice of Northern Virginia, Falls Church, VA -- operating support
10,000   International Center for Photography, New York, NY -- operating support

10,000	King Manor Museum, Jamaica, NY -- operating support
10,000	Princeton University, Princeton, NJ -- operating support
10,000	Recordings for the Blind and Dyslexic, Denver, CO -- operating support
10,000	St. Mark's Church, New Canaan, CT -- Bell Restoration Project
10,000	Tompkins County Society for the Prevention of Cruelty to Animals, Ithaca, NY -- operating support

MENDEL FOUNDATION

Giving Contact
Herbert Mendel, President
5500 Collins Ave. Tower Apt. 1101
Miami Beach, FL 33140-2501
Phone: (305)868-3600

Description
Founded: 1964
EIN: 386099787
Organization Type: Private Foundation
Giving Locations: MI
Grant Types: General Support.

Donor Information
Founder: Herbert D. Mendel

Financial Summary
Total Giving: $20,000 (fiscal year ending April 30, 2001); $109,150 (fiscal 2000); $321,500 (fiscal 1999)
Giving Analysis: Giving for fiscal 2000 includes: foundation grants to United Way ($10,000)
Assets: $31,571 (fiscal 2001); $35,897 (fiscal 2000); $115,592 (fiscal 1999)
Gifts Received: $50,000 (fiscal 1997). Note: In 1990, contributions were received from Herbert D. Mendel. Fiscal 1997, contributions were received from Herbert D. Mendel.

Typical Recipients
Arts & Humanities: Arts Associations & Councils, Arts Centers, Ballet, Community Arts, Dance, Arts & Humanities-General, History & Archaeology, Libraries, Music, Opera, Performing Arts, Public Broadcasting, Theater
Civic & Public Affairs: Community Foundations, Civic & Public Affairs-General, Urban & Community Affairs, Women's Affairs
Education: Arts/Humanities Education, Colleges & Universities, Minority Education, Private Education (Precollege)
Health: AIDS/HIV, Alzheimers Disease, Clinics/Medical Centers, Emergency/Ambulance Services, Health Organizations, Medical Research, Prenatal Health Issues, Single-Disease Health Associations
International: Foreign Educational Institutions, International Relief Efforts, Missionary/Religious Activities
Religion: Jewish Causes, Religious Organizations, Synagogues/Temples
Social Services: Child Welfare, Community Service Organizations, Family Planning, Senior Services, United Funds/United Ways, Youth Organizations

Application Procedures
Initial Contact: The foundation has no formal grant application procedure or application form.
Deadlines: None.

Foundation Officials
Audre D. Mendel: vice president
Herbert D. Mendel: president B Chicago, IL 1922. ED University of Illinois (1947). PRIM CORP EMPL chairman, president: MSA IndustriesCorp. CORP AFFIL director: Peoples State Bank.
Julie Mendel: director
Eleanor A. Simon: secretary

Grants Analysis
Disclosure Period: fiscal year ending April 30, 2001
Total Grants: $20,000
Number of Grants: 5
Highest Grant: $5,000
Lowest Grant: $2,500
Typical Range: $2,500 to $5,000

Recent Grants
Note: Grants derived from fiscal 2000 Form 990.

General
25,000	Ballet Theater Foundation, New York, NY
25,000	Cornerstone Alliance, Benton Harbor, MI
13,000	Shakespeares Globe, New York, NY
10,000	United Way South Western Michigan, Benton Harbor, MI
8,500	Mount Sinai Medical Center, Miami Beach, FL
7,500	Concert Association, Miami Beach, FL
5,000	Harid Conservatory of Music, Boca Raton, FL
5,000	Miami City Ballet, Miami, FL
3,500	National Symphony Orchestra, Washington, DC
2,500	Dance Visions

GLENN AND RUTH MENGLE FOUNDATION

Giving Contact
D. Edward Chaplin, Vice President & Trust Officer
c/o First Commonwealth Trust Co.
PO Box 1046
Du Bois, PA 15801
Phone: (814)371-0660

Description
Founded: 1956
EIN: 256067616
Organization Type: Private Foundation
Giving Locations: PA: Brockway, Dubois, Erie
Grant Types: General Support, Scholarship.

Donor Information
Founder: the late Glenn A. Mengle, the late Ruth E. Mengle Blake

Financial Summary
Total Giving: $605,094 (2000); $623,289 (1999); $648,317 (1998). Note: 1997 Giving includes United Way ($30,000).
Giving Analysis: Giving for 2000 includes: foundation scholarships ($15,000); foundation grants to United Way ($30,000); foundation matching gifts ($36,500) 1999: foundation grants to United Way ($30,000)
Assets: $14,155,592 (2000); $13,910,299 (1999); $13,858,086 (1998)
Gifts Received: $415,161 (1995)

Typical Recipients
Arts & Humanities: Arts Associations & Councils, Arts Funds, Arts & Humanities-General, Libraries, Museums/Galleries, Public Broadcasting
Civic & Public Affairs: Clubs, Civic & Public Affairs-General, Municipalities/Towns, Philanthropic Organizations, Professional & Trade Associations, Urban & Community Affairs
Education: Arts/Humanities Education, Business Education, Colleges & Universities, Education Funds, Leadership Training, Literacy, Private Education (Precollege), Science/Mathematics Education, Secondary Education (Private), Special Education, Student Aid
Environment: Air/Water Quality, Environment-General, Resource Conservation

Health: Children's Health/Hospitals, Clinics/Medical Centers, Hospitals, Long-Term Care, Nursing Services
Religion: Churches, Religion-General, Religious Organizations, Religious Welfare
Social Services: At-Risk Youth, Child Welfare, Community Centers, Community Service Organizations, Family Services, Food/Clothing Distribution, Homes, People with Disabilities, Recreation & Athletics, Scouts, United Funds/United Ways, YMCA/YWCA/YMHA/YWHA, Youth Organizations

Application Procedures
Initial Contact: Send cover letter and full proposal.
Application Requirements: Include current financial statements, financial statements for the past three years, and the budget for next operating year.
Deadlines: September 1.

Additional Information
Trust(s): First Commonwealth Trust Co

Foundation Officials
DeVere L. Sheesley: trustee

Grants Analysis
Disclosure Period: calendar year ending 2000
Total Grants: $523,594*
Number of Grants: 50
Average Grant: $10,472
Highest Grant: $50,000
Typical Range: $5,000 to $20,000
***Note:** Giving excludes United Way, scholarships, and matching gifts.

Recent Grants
Note: Grants derived from 2001 Form 990.

Library-Related
| 35,000 | Mengle Memorial Library, DuBois, PA |

General
57,000	DuBois Area YMCA, DuBois, PA
52,500	Bucktail Council B.S.A., DuBois, PA
45,000	Free Medical Clinic of DuBois, DuBois, PA
30,000	DuBois Area United Way, DuBois, PA
25,000	Alfred University, Alfred, NY -- renovation of Kanakadea Hall
25,000	Brockway Volunteer Hose Company, Brockway, PA -- purchase truck
25,000	DuBois Senior and Community Center, DuBois, PA
22,000	YMCA of Greater Erie, Erie, PA -- for capital improvements to Camp Sherwin
17,500	WPSX Public Television, University Park, PA
16,000	Christ the King Manor, DuBois, PA

MERCK FAMILY FUND

Giving Contact
Jenny Russell, Executive Director
303 Adams Street
Milton, MA 02186
Phone: (617)696-3580
Fax: (617)696-7262
E-mail: merck@merckff.org
Web: http://www.merckff.org

Description
Founded: 1954
EIN: 226063382
Organization Type: Family Foundation
Giving Locations: MA: Boston community-building program; NY: New York community-building program; RI: Providence community-building program nationally for the Sustainable Economics program; Northern forests, Southern Appalachians, and Southern Coastal Plain for the Eastern Ecosystems program.

Grant Types: General Support, Multiyear/Continuing Support, Project.

Donor Information

Founder: The fund was incorporated in 1954 by members of the Merck family.

Financial Summary

Total Giving: $3,000,000 (2003 approx); $3,000,000 (2002 approx); $3,655,712 (2001)
Assets: $55,800,000 (2002 approx); $72,000,000 (2001 approx); $83,660,460 (2000)
Gifts Received: $1,004,387 (2000); $120 (1993). Note: In 2000, contributions were received from Josephine Merck.

Typical Recipients

Arts & Humanities: Arts Associations & Councils, Arts Funds, History & Archaeology, Libraries, Museums/Galleries, Music, Public Broadcasting, Theater
Civic & Public Affairs: Asian American Affairs, Botanical Gardens/Parks, Business/Free Enterprise, Clubs, Economic Development, Economic Policy, Employment/Job Training, Gay/Lesbian Issues, Civic & Public Affairs-General, Hispanic Affairs, Housing, Minority Business, Municipalities/Towns, Nonprofit Management, Philanthropic Organizations, Public Policy, Urban & Community Affairs, Women's Affairs, Zoos/Aquariums
Education: Environmental Education, Education-General, Literacy, Public Education (Precollege), Science/Mathematics Education, Secondary Education (Public)
Environment: Air/Water Quality, Air/Water Quality, Forestry, Environment-General, Protection, Research, Resource Conservation, Watershed
Health: Home-Care Services, Hospitals, Long-Term Care, Preventive Medicine/Wellness Organizations
International: International Affairs, International Environmental Issues
Religion: Religious Welfare
Science: Scientific Centers & Institutes, Scientific Organizations
Social Services: At-Risk Youth, Child Welfare, Community Service Organizations, Day Care, Family Planning, Family Services, Food/Clothing Distribution, People with Disabilities, Recreation & Athletics, Shelters/Homelessness, Social Services-General, Youth Organizations

Application Procedures

Initial Contact: The fund requests initial contact be made through a brief letter of inquiry (not to exceed two pages) rather than by a full proposal, phone call, or meeting.
Application Requirements: Inquiries should describe the project, its purpose, and its likely impact. The letter should also briefly describe the organization and its goals and specify the amount of funds requested. A member of the foundation's staff will review the letter and decide whether to invite a full proposal.
Deadlines: Complete, invited proposals are due February 30 for the May meeting and July 30 for the October meeting.
Review Process: Letters of inquiry are acknowledged as soon as possible. Unsolicited full proposals are not acknowledged.

Restrictions

The fund awards grants only to tax-exempt organizations in the United States. It does not make grants to individuals or for-profit organizations. It does not fund governmental Organizations, endowments, debt reduction, annual fund-raising campaigns, capital construction, purchase of equipment, acquisition of land, or film or video projects. The fund does not generally support academic research or books. It does not make grants intended to support candidates for political office.

Additional Information

Publications: Annual Report; Grant Guidelines

Foundation Officials

Sharman B. Altshuler: secretary, trustee
Patience Chamberlin: trustee
Oona Coy: trustee
Francis W. Hatch, III: president, trustee
Antony M. Merck: treasurer, trustee
Josephine A. Merck: vice president, trustee
Wilhelm M. Merck: trustee
Jenny D. Russell: executive director
Serena H. Whitridge: trustee

Grants Analysis

Disclosure Period: calendar year ending 2001
Total Grants: $3,655,712
Number of Grants: 105
Average Grant: $34,816
Highest Grant: $500,000
Lowest Grant: $225
Typical Range: $15,000 to $50,000

Recent Grants

Note: Grants derived from 2000 Form 990.

General

253,893	Randolph Foundation, Hopewell, VA
251,553	Nature Conservancy Maine Chapter, New York, NY
99,901	South Carolina Coastal Conservation League, Charleston, SC
64,931	Co-Op America, Washington, DC
51,517	Center for a New American Dream, Takoma Park, MD
51,517	Northern Forest Alliance, Montpelier, VT
51,458	Forest Society of Maine, ME
51,417	Redefining Progress, San Francisco, CA
50,134	Center for a Sustainable Economy, Washington, DC
49,995	Business for Social Responsibility Education Fund, Washington, DC

MERCURY AIRCRAFT, INC.

Company Headquarters

PO Box 338
Hammondsport, NY 14840
Web: http://www.mercuryaircraft.com

Company Description

Employees: 600
SIC(s): 3444 Sheet Metal Work, 3449 Miscellaneous Metal Work, 3469 Metal Stampings Nec.

Mercury Aircraft Foundation

Giving Contact

Gregory Hintz, Manager
17 Wheeler Ave.
Hammondsport, NY 14840-9566
Phone: (607)569-4200

Description

EIN: 166028162
Organization Type: Corporate Foundation
Giving Locations: NY: Western New York
Grant Types: Capital, General Support.

Financial Summary

Total Giving: $139,500 (2001); $146,450 (2000); $134,600 (1999)
Giving Analysis: Giving for 2001 includes: foundation grants to United Way ($8,500); foundation ($131,000); 2000: foundation grants to United Way ($8,500); 1999: foundation grants to United Way ($4,750); foundation ($129,850)
Assets: $2,374,021 (2001); $2,796,492 (2000); $2,840,204 (1999)
Gifts Received: $40,000 (2001); $50,000 (2000); $58,750 (1999). Note: In 2001, contributions were received from Mercury Minnesota.

Typical Recipients

Arts & Humanities: Arts Associations & Councils, Arts & Humanities-General, Libraries, Museums/Galleries
Civic & Public Affairs: Chambers of Commerce, Clubs, Economic Development, Civic & Public Affairs-General, Housing, Safety, Urban & Community Affairs
Education: Colleges & Universities
Health: Cancer, Clinics/Medical Centers, Emergency/Ambulance Services, Health-General, Health Organizations, Heart, Hospitals, Respiratory
Religion: Churches, Religious Welfare
Science: Science-General, Science Museums, Scientific Centers & Institutes, Scientific Organizations
Social Services: Animal Protection, Emergency Relief, Family Planning, Food/Clothing Distribution, Homes, People with Disabilities, Recreation & Athletics, Scouts, United Funds/United Ways, Youth Organizations

Application Procedures

Initial Contact: The foundation has no formal grant application procedure or application form.
Deadlines: None.

Corporate Officials

Gregory J. Hintz: treasurer PRIM CORP EMPL treasurer: Mercury Aircraft.
Joseph F. Meade, Jr.: chairman, director B Freeport, NY 1921. ED Alfred University (1943). PRIM CORP EMPL chairman, director: Mercury Aircraft. CORP AFFIL director: Bath National Bank; chairman: Mercury Minnesota; president, director: Atlas Metla Industries; director: Bath & Hammondsport Railroad.
Joseph F. Meade, III: president PRIM CORP EMPL president: Mercury Aircraft.

Foundation Officials

Marcia M. Coon: trustee
Gregory J. Hintz: mgr (see above)
Joseph F. Meade, III: trustee (see above)
Joseph F. Meade, Jr.: trustee (see above)

Grants Analysis

Disclosure Period: calendar year ending 2001
Total Grants: $131,000*
Number of Grants: 45
Average Grant: $2,911
Highest Grant: $30,000
Typical Range: $1,000 to $5,000
*Note: Giving excludes United Way.

Recent Grants

Note: Grants derived from 2001 Form 990.

Library-Related

5,000	Hammondsport Public Library, Hammondsport, NY

General

30,000	Alfred University, Alfred, NY
20,500	Glenn H. Curtis Museum, Hammondsport, NY
10,000	J.E. Meade Memorial Science Fund
10,000	Keuka Health Care, Keuka Park, NY
8,500	United Way of Chemung and Steuben Counties, Corning, NY
6,000	Keuka College, Keuka Park, IN -- community association campaign
4,000	Hammondsport - Methodist Church, Hammondsport, NY
4,000	Hammondsport - Presbyterian Church, Hammondsport, NY

4,000   Hammondsport St. Gabriels Catholic Church, Hammondsport, NY

4,000   Hammondsport - St. James Episcopal Church, Hammondsport, NY

MERKLEY CHARITABLE TRUST

Giving Contact
Dawn Bentley, Trust Officer
c/o Citizens Bank, Trust Div.
328 S. Saginaw Street
Flint, MI 48502-2412
Phone: (810)342-7390

Description
Founded: 1990
EIN: 386528749
Organization Type: Private Foundation
Giving Locations: MI: Genesee County
Grant Types: General Support.

Financial Summary
Total Giving: $377,512 (fiscal year ending November 30, 2001); $234,013 (fiscal 2000); $190,491 (fiscal 1999)
Assets: $4,539,670 (fiscal 2001); $5,071,657 (fiscal 2000); $5,194,280 (fiscal 1999)
Gifts Received: $230 (fiscal 1992). Note: In fiscal 1992, contributions were received from the family of Dorothy Church.

Typical Recipients
Arts & Humanities: Arts Centers, Arts Institutes, Ballet, Arts & Humanities-General, Libraries, Museums/Galleries, Music, Theater
Civic & Public Affairs: African American Affairs, Botanical Gardens/Parks, Community Foundations, Urban & Community Affairs
Education: Education Reform, Public Education (Precollege), Vocational & Technical Education
Environment: Environment-General
Health: Alzheimers Disease, Clinics/Medical Centers, Emergency/Ambulance Services, Geriatric Health, Respiratory
Religion: Jewish Causes, Religious Welfare
Science: Science Exhibits & Fairs
Social Services: Animal Protection, Big Brother/Big Sister, Child Welfare, Food/Clothing Distribution, Recreation & Athletics, Scouts, Senior Services, YMCA/YWCA/YMHA/YWHA, Youth Organizations

Application Procedures
Initial Contact: The foundation requests applications be made in writing.
Application Requirements: Include a description of organization, amount requested, purpose of funds sought, recently audited financial statement, and proof of tax-exempt status.
Deadlines: None.

Restrictions
Provides grants to organizations providing services to youth or the elderly in Genesee County, MI.

Additional Information
Trust(s): Citizens Bank

Grants Analysis
Disclosure Period: fiscal year ending November 30, 2001
Total Grants: $377,512
Number of Grants: 16
Average Grant: $11,409*
Highest Grant: $206,380
Lowest Grant: $1,500
Typical Range: $1,000 to $20,000
*Note: Average grant figure excludes highest grant.

Recent Grants
Note: Grants derived from fiscal 2000 Form 990.

General
111,156	Genesee County Parks, Flint, MI
37,052	Genesee County Humane Society, Flint, MI
16,000	Flint Jewish Family & Children's Services, Flint, MI
10,000	American Red Cross, Flint, MI
10,000	Flint Institute of Arts, Flint, MI
10,000	Food Bank of Eastern Michigan, Flint, MI
10,000	New Direction Youth Program, Flint, MI
9,800	Genesee Chamber Foundation, Flint, MI
5,005	Flint Children's Museum, Flint, MI
5,000	Flint Institute of Music, Flint, MI

MERRICK FOUNDATION

Giving Contact
Johnnie L. Rolen, Executive Secretary
2932 NW 122nd St., Suite D
Oklahoma City, OK 73120-1955
Phone: (405)755-5571
E-mail: fwmerrick@foundationmanagementinc.com

Description
Founded: 1947
EIN: 736111622
Organization Type: Private Foundation
Giving Locations: OK: emphasis on Southern Oklahoma
Grant Types: Capital, General Support, Seed Money.

Donor Information
Founder: the late Mrs. Frank W. Merrick

Financial Summary
Total Giving: $524,400 (2001); $554,700 (2000); $517,126 (1999)
Giving Analysis: Giving for 2001 includes: foundation grants to United Way ($16,000); 2000: foundation grants to United Way ($15,000); 1999: foundation grants to United Way ($15,000); foundation scholarships ($53,598);
Assets: $12,281,623 (2001); $13,425,680 (2000); $14,004,540 (1999)

Typical Recipients
Arts & Humanities: Arts Associations & Councils, Arts Centers, Arts Funds, Arts Institutes, Historic Preservation, History & Archaeology, Libraries, Literary Arts, Museums/Galleries, Music, Performing Arts
Civic & Public Affairs: African American Affairs, Botanical Gardens/Parks, Chambers of Commerce, Clubs, Community Foundations, Economic Development, Civic & Public Affairs-General, Municipalities/Towns, Nonprofit Management, Philanthropic Organizations, Public Policy, Urban & Community Affairs
Education: Business Education, Colleges & Universities, Economic Education, Education Associations, Education Reform, Education-General, Literacy, Private Education (Precollege), Public Education (Precollege), Science/Mathematics Education, Special Education, Student Aid
Health: Children's Health/Hospitals, Clinics/Medical Centers, Diabetes, Emergency/Ambulance Services, Health Organizations, Hospitals, Medical Research, Mental Health, Transplant Networks/Donor Banks
Religion: Churches, Ministries, Religious Organizations, Religious Welfare
Science: Science Museums, Scientific Centers & Institutes
Social Services: At-Risk Youth, Child Welfare, Community Centers, Community Service Organizations, Day Care, Domestic Violence, Family Services, Food/Clothing Distribution, People with Disabilities, Recreation & Athletics, Scouts, Social Services-General, Substance Abuse, United Funds/United Ways, YMCA/YWCA/YMHA/YWHA, Youth Organizations

Application Procedures
Initial Contact: Send a brief letter of inquiry.
Application Requirements: Include documentation stating need and purpose of funds sought.
Deadlines: August 15 for letters summarizing projects; September 30 for grant applications.
Review Process: Proposals considered at trustees' November meeting.
Decision Notification: A response will be made to each request.

Restrictions
Does not support individuals, endowments, or provide operating funds. Limited to 501(c)(3) institutes.

Additional Information
Publications: Annual Report; Grant Policies and Procedures

Foundation Officials
Valda M. Buchanan: secretary
Michael A. Cawley: trustee B 1947. PRIM NONPR EMPL president, trustee: Samuel Roberts Noble Foundation Inc. CORP AFFIL director: Noble Affiliates Inc.
Laura Clay: trustee
Charles R. Coe, Jr.: trustee
Elizabeth Merrick Coe: president, trustee
Ross M. Coe: trustee
Ward I. Coe: trustee
William R. Goddard, Jr.: trustee
Frank W. Merrick: trustee
Robert B. Merrick: trustee
Ward S. Merrick, Jr.: trustee

Grants Analysis
Disclosure Period: calendar year ending 2001
Total Grants: $508,400*
Number of Grants: 51
Average Grant: $6,641*
Highest Grant: $100,000
Lowest Grant: $500
Typical Range: $1,000 to $10,000
*Note: Giving excludes United Way. Average grant figure excludes two highest grants ($183,000).

Recent Grants
Note: Grants derived from 2000 Form 990.

General
100,000	Oklahoma Medical Research Foundation, Oklahoma City, OK
51,537	Greater Ardmore Scholarship Foundation, Ardmore, OK
25,000	Ardmore Regional Park Authority, Ardmore, OK
25,000	Ardmore Tiger Quarterback Club, Ardmore, OK
25,000	City Rescue Mission, Oklahoma City, OK
25,000	National Cowboy Hall of Fame, Oklahoma City, OK
25,000	Oklahoma City Art Museum, Oklahoma City, OK
25,000	Oklahoma Garden Festival, Oklahoma City, OK
25,000	Payne Education Center, Ardmore, OK
20,000	Youth Services for Oklahoma County, Oklahoma City, OK

MERRILL LYNCH & COMPANY, INC.

Company Headquarters
New York, NY
Web: http://www.ml.com

Company Description

Founded: 1885
Ticker: MER
Exchange: NYSE
Operating Revenue: US$18.608 billion (2002)
Profit: US$2.513 billion (2002)
Employees: 50900 (2002)
Fortune Rank: 48, per FORTUNE Magazine's list of 500 Largest U.S. Corporations (2002).
SIC(s): 6211 Security Brokers & Dealers, 6719 Holding Companies Nec.

Nonmonetary Support

Type: Donated Equipment; In-kind Services
Volunteer Programs: The company sponsors an Employee Community Involvement Program, which provides grants of $100 to $1,000 to organizations where employees volunteer.
Contact: Bettina Lauf, Assistant Vice President, Corporate Responsibility
Note: Company donates equipment when available.

Merrill Lynch & Co. Foundation Inc.

Giving Contact

Eddy Bayardelle, Director, Philanthropic Programs
200 Union Ave.
Cresskill, NJ 07626
Phone: (201)871-0350
Web: http://www.ml.com

Alternate Contact

Merrill Lynch & Co. Foundation, Inc.
Phone: (212)614-4260

Description

Founded: 1950
EIN: 136139556
Organization Type: Corporate Foundation
Giving Locations: NY: New York metropolitan area national organizations; primarily in areas where Merrill Lynch & Co. maintains offices.
Grant Types: Capital, Employee Matching Gifts, General Support, Multiyear/Continuing Support.
Note: Employee matching gift ratio: 1 to 1 up to $1,500 annually to employee-chosen causes in the areas of the art/culture, environment, independent college funds, private elementary schools, secondary or private high schools, special education, universities/colleges, health care, and hospitals.

Financial Summary

Total Giving: $23,464,499 (2001); $42,608,527 (2000); $12,076,119 (1999). Note: Contributes through corporate direct giving program and foundation. The corporate direct giving amount includes giving by domestic and international subsidiaries.
Giving Analysis: Giving for 2001 includes: foundation ($13,275,361); corporate direct giving ($21,648,680); 2000: foundation grants to United Way ($760,000); foundation scholarships ($2,800,329); foundation matching gifts ($4,740,816); foundation ($6,096,096); corporate direct giving ($28,211,286); 1999: foundation scholarships ($582,980); foundation grants to United Way ($760,000); foundation matching gifts ($4,012,889); foundation ($6,720,250);
Assets: $43,989,135 (2001); $29,917,334 (2000); $41,465,189 (1999)
Gifts Received: $25,470,000 (2001); $13,411,164 (1999); $11,691,271 (1994). Note: Gifts received from Merrill Lynch and Company, Inc.

Typical Recipients

Arts & Humanities: Arts Associations & Councils, Arts Centers, Arts Outreach, Ethnic & Folk Arts, Historic Preservation, History & Archaeology, Libraries, Museums/Galleries, Music, Opera, Performing Arts, Public Broadcasting, Theater
Civic & Public Affairs: African American Affairs, Asian American Affairs, Botanical Gardens/Parks, Business/Free Enterprise, Civil Rights, Community Foundations, Economic Development, Employment/Job Training, Ethnic Organizations, Civic & Public Affairs-General, Hispanic Affairs, Housing, Municipalities/Towns, Public Policy, Urban & Community Affairs, Women's Affairs, Zoos/Aquariums
Education: Business Education, Business-School Partnerships, Colleges & Universities, Economic Education, Education Reform, Education-General, Health & Physical Education, International Studies, Journalism/Media Education, Leadership Training, Legal Education, Literacy, Medical Education, Minority Education, Private Education (Precollege), Science/Mathematics Education, Special Education, Student Aid
Environment: Environment-General, Wildlife Protection
Health: AIDS/HIV, Cancer, Children's Health/Hospitals, Clinics/Medical Centers, Emergency/Ambulance Services, Geriatric Health, Health Organizations, Heart, Hospitals, Medical Research, Research/Studies Institutes, Single-Disease Health Associations, Transplant Networks/Donor Banks
International: Foreign Educational Institutions, International-General, Health Care/Hospitals, International Affairs, International Development, International Peace & Security Issues, International Relations, International Relief Efforts
Religion: Jewish Causes, Religious Welfare
Science: Science Museums, Scientific Centers & Institutes, Scientific Labs
Social Services: At-Risk Youth, Child Welfare, Community Centers, Community Service Organizations, Crime Prevention, Day Care, Emergency Relief, Family Services, Food/Clothing Distribution, People with Disabilities, Recreation & Athletics, Scouts, Senior Services, Shelters/Homelessness, Substance Abuse, United Funds/United Ways, Veterans, YMCA/YWCA/YMHA/YWHA, Youth Organizations

Application Procedures

Initial Contact: Send a proposal in letter form (no more than two to three pages in length); if outside greater New York area, apply directly to local branch office.
Application Requirements: Include organization's mission; history and current activities of the organization; goals and timelines for implementing the program; explanation of how the program relates to the goals of the foundation; objectives for the program and how they would be measured; the specific activities to be carried out to meet the objectives; groups and neighborhoods to be served and how they will benefit from the program; how short-term and long-term program results will be measured; organization and program budgets; and how the program will be sustained. The following documents should accompany the proposal: proof of tax-exempt status; list of the board of directors, with their affiliations (schools must submit a list of members of the board of education or PTA board); annual report and/or current operating budget; recently audited financial statement; list of current corporate and foundation funding sources, including amounts contributed within the most recent 12 months or last fiscal year. See Web site at: www.ml.com/philanthropy.
Deadlines: None.
Review Process: Proposals reviewed by manager of corporate contributions and foundation president for recommendation to board of trustees; decision to decline request made immediately; trustees meet quarterly.
Evaluative Criteria: Priority given to national organizations and organizations located in the greater New York metropolitan area. Preference is given to specific programs and projects (as opposed to general operating support) that are innovative, sustainable, creating opportunities for employees to volunteer, easily expanded from a local to a global perspective, and having a measurable impact.

Decision Notification: Decisions for direct gifts are generally made within 30 days of receipt.

Restrictions

The company will not make grants to the following: private foundations; individuals; fundraising activities related to individual sponsorship, such as walk-a-thons; seed money for new organizations; political causes, candidates and campaigns, and organizations designed specifically for lobbying; religious, fraternal, social or other membership organizations that provide services mainly to their own constituencies; athletic events and tournaments; fundraising events; endowments, construction and renovation projects, special purpose campaigns, chairs, or purchase of major equipment; conferences, workshops, or seminars; research; video/film production; United Way-supported agencies, except in the case of an emergency relief effort; or for-profit entities.
The company will not make grants for the reduction of an operating deficit or to liquidate a debt.

Additional Information

The company will consider support of capital needs when the specific project submitted has distinctive importance or the promise of a unique contribution to the field.
Since the company has a predetermined limit on multiyear commitments, grants usually are of a one-year duration. Requests for continuing support are considered using the company's priorities for the proposed grant year.
Publications: Responsible Citizenship Annual Report

Corporate Officials

Paul W. Critchlow: senior vice president marketing & communications PRIM CORP EMPL senior vice president marketing & communications: Merrill Lynch & Co., Inc.
Stephen Lawrence Hammerman: vice chairman, general counsel B Brooklyn, NY 1938. ED University of Pennsylvania BS (1959); New York University LLB (1962). PRIM CORP EMPL vice chairman, general counsel: Merrill Lynch & Co., Inc. ADD CORP EMPL general counsel: Merrill Lynch Pierce Fenner & Smith. NONPR AFFIL member: New York Stock Exchange Inc.; member: Securities Industry Association; member, investment committee chairman: Association Bar New York City.
David H. Komansky: chairman, chief executive officer B Mount Vernon, NY 1939. ED University of Miami. PRIM CORP EMPL chairman, chief executive officer: Merrill Lynch & Co., Inc. ADD CORP EMPL president: Merrill Lynch, Pierce, Fenner & Smith Inc. CORP AFFIL director: New York Stock Exchange Inc.
Westina Lomax Matthews: senior director, first vice president corporate respons B Chillicothe, OH 1948. ED University of Dayton BS (1970); University of Dayton MS (1974); University of Chicago PhD (1980). PRIM CORP EMPL senior director, first vice president corporate respons: Merrill Lynch & Co., Inc.
John Laundon Steffens: executive vice president B Cleveland, OH 1941. ED Dartmouth College (1963). PRIM CORP EMPL executive vice president: Merrill Lynch & Co., Inc. CORP AFFIL executive vice president: Merrill Lynch Pierce Fenner & Smith.

Foundation Officials

Stanley Baumblatt: assistant secretary
William L. Burke: trustee
Paul W. Critchlow: president, trustee (see above)
Stephen Lawrence Hammerman: vice president, trustee (see above)
David H. Komansky: trustee, vice president (see above)
Thomas J. Lombardi: treasurer
Westina Lomax Matthews: secretary, trustee (see above)
Mary E. Taylor: vice president, trustee

Grants Analysis

Disclosure Period: calendar year ending 2001
Total Grants: $6,506,354*
Number of Grants: 99*
Average Grant: $66,000
Typical Range: $1,000 to $20,000
*Note: Giving excludes united way, matching gifts, and scholarships.

Recent Grants

Note: Grants derived from 2001 Form 990.

General

2,481,750	ML Scholarship Builder Program
513,450	McCarthy Scholarship Program

MESSING FAMILY CHARITABLE FOUNDATION

Giving Contact

Wilma E. Messing, Trustee
30 Westwood Country Club
St. Louis, MO 63131
Phone: (314)432-8898

Description

Founded: 1961
EIN: 436034863
Organization Type: Private Foundation
Giving Locations: MO: St. Louis
Grant Types: General Support, Research.

Donor Information

Founder: Roswell Messing, Jr., Mrs. Roswell Messing, Jr.

Financial Summary

Total Giving: $207,872 (2001); $196,644 (2000); $123,313 (1999)
Giving Analysis: Giving for 2001 includes: foundation grants to United Way ($2,000); 2000: foundation grants to United Way ($1,000) 1999: foundation grants to United Way ($1,000)
Assets: $4,999,066 (2001); $5,096,093 (2000); $4,574,645 (1999)
Gifts Received: $130,775 (2001); $58,670 (2000); $157,587 (1999). Note: In 2001, contributions were received from Wilma Messing ($100,593) and ($30,182). In 2000, contributions were received from Noel Hefty ($28,535), Roswell Messing III ($30,135). In 1999, contributions were received from Wilma Messing ($99,526), Noel Hefty ($28,294), Roswell Messing III ($29,767). In 1995, contributions were received from Noel and Terry Hefty.

Typical Recipients

Arts & Humanities: Arts Associations & Councils, Dance, Arts & Humanities-General, Libraries, Music, Opera, Performing Arts, Public Broadcasting, Theater
Civic & Public Affairs: Civic & Public Affairs-General, Urban & Community Affairs, Women's Affairs, Zoos/Aquariums
Education: Arts/Humanities Education, Business Education, Colleges & Universities, Education-General, International Studies, Medical Education, Private Education (Precollege), Public Education (Precollege), Student Aid
Environment: Resource Conservation
Health: AIDS/HIV, Children's Health/Hospitals, Clinics/Medical Centers, Health Organizations, Hospices, Hospitals, Medical Research, Single-Disease Health Associations
Religion: Jewish Causes, Religious Organizations, Religious Welfare, Synagogues/Temples

Social Services: Animal Protection, Camps, Community Service Organizations, Day Care, Family Planning, Substance Abuse, United Funds/United Ways, Youth Organizations

Application Procedures

Initial Contact: The foundation has no formal grant application procedure or application form.
Deadlines: None.

Foundation Officials

Harold S. Goodman: trustee B Saint Louis, MO 1937. ED University of Missouri AB (1960); Washington University LLB (1963); Washington University JD (1963). PRIM CORP EMPL partner: Gallop, Johnson & Neuman. NONPR AFFIL member: Washington University Law Alumni Association; member: Zeta Beta Tau; member: Phi Delta Phi; member: Saint Louis Bar Association; member: Laumeier Sculpture Park; member: Missouri Bar Association; member: American Bar Association; trustee: Cystic Fibrosis Foundation.
Noel M. Hefty: trustee
Terrance Hefty: trustee
Roswell Messing, III: trustee
Wilma E. Messing: trustee
Arlene M. Naschke: trustee

Grants Analysis

Disclosure Period: calendar year ending 2001
Total Grants: $205,872*
Number of Grants: 59
Average Grant: $2,408*
Highest Grant: $38,115
Lowest Grant: $250
Typical Range: $500 to $5,000
*Note: Giving excludes United Way. Average grant figure excludes two highest grants ($68,615).

Recent Grants

Note: Grants derived from 2001 Form 990.

General

38,115	Perry Mansfield Dance School, Steamboat Springs, CO
30,500	Synergy School, Memphis, TN
10,000	Family Education Center, Petaluma, CA
10,000	Nature Conservancy
10,000	St. Louis Zoo, St. Louis, MO
10,000	University of Missouri, St. Louis, MO
7,500	Colorado Dance Festival, Denver, CO
7,000	Temple Emanu EL
5,000	Dance St. Louis, St. Louis, MO
5,000	MICDS, St. Louis, MO

METAL INDUSTRIES, INC.

Company Headquarters

PO Box 4490
Clearwater, FL 33758
Web: http://www.metalaire.com

Company Description

Employees: 2,200
SIC(s): 3442 Metal Doors, Sash & Trim.

Metal Industries Foundation

Giving Contact

Sarah Walker Guthrie, Trustee
861 N. Hercules Avenue
Clearwater, FL 33765-1922
Phone: (727)461-0501
Fax: (727)442-4291

Alternate Contact

Brenda Brannon, Corporate Contributions
Phone: (813)441-2651
Note: Ms. Brannon may be reached at ext. 460.

Description

Founded: 1971
EIN: 237098483
Organization Type: Corporate Foundation
Giving Locations: FL
Grant Types: General Support.

Donor Information

Founder: Metal Industries, Inc.

Financial Summary

Total Giving: $134,195 (fiscal year ending October 31, 2001); $67,116 (fiscal 2000); $94,972 (fiscal 1997)
Assets: $3,014,017 (fiscal 2001); $2,940,970 (fiscal 2000); $2,864,646 (fiscal 1997)

Typical Recipients

Arts & Humanities: History & Archaeology, Libraries, Museums/Galleries, Public Broadcasting
Civic & Public Affairs: Business/Free Enterprise, Chambers of Commerce, Clubs, Civic & Public Affairs-General, Housing, Legal Aid, Municipalities/Towns, Philanthropic Organizations, Professional & Trade Associations, Safety, Urban & Community Affairs
Education: Business Education, Colleges & Universities, Community & Junior Colleges, Elementary Education (Private), Elementary Education (Public), Education-General, Private Education (Precollege), Secondary Education (Public)
Environment: Environment-General, Resource Conservation, Wildlife Protection
Health: Alzheimers Disease, Cancer, Children's Health/Hospitals, Health-General, Geriatric Health, Health Organizations, Heart, Hospices, Hospices, Hospitals, Medical Research, Multiple Sclerosis, Preventive Medicine/Wellness Organizations, Public Health, Research/Studies Institutes, Single-Disease Health Associations, Transplant Networks/Donor Banks
International: Health Care/Hospitals
Religion: Churches, Religion-General, Jewish Causes, Ministries, Religious Welfare, Synagogues/Temples
Science: Science Museums
Social Services: Animal Protection, At-Risk Youth, Child Welfare, Community Service Organizations, Day Care, Family Services, Food/Clothing Distribution, People with Disabilities, Recreation & Athletics, Social Services-General, United Funds/United Ways, YMCA/YWCA/YMHA/YWHA, Youth Organizations

Application Procedures

Initial Contact: Send brief letter of inquiry.
Application Requirements: Describe project or request application for student loan program.
Deadlines: None.

Restrictions

Recipients must be worthy or needy. Does not support political or lobbying groups.

Corporate Officials

Pete DeSoto: chairman, president, chief executive officer B Boston, MA 1939. ED University of Florida BSBA (1962). PRIM CORP EMPL chairman, president, chief executive officer: Metal Industries. NONPR AFFIL member: Elizabethville Rotary; member: Screen Manufacturer Association.
Janet Fasenmyer: controller PRIM CORP EMPL controller: Metal Industries.

Foundation Officials

Sarah Walker Cuthrie: trustee
Jay K. Poppleton: trustee
James T. Walker: trustee

Grants Analysis

Disclosure Period: fiscal year ending October 31, 2001
Total Grants: $134,195
Number of Grants: 22
Average Grant: $2,460*
Highest Grant: $50,000
Lowest Grant: $25
Typical Range: $500 to $5,000
*Note: Average grant figure excludes two highest grants ($85,000).

Recent Grants

Note: Grants derived from 2000 Form 990.

Library-Related

30,000	Merrill Area Public Library, Merrill, WI

General

17,500	Mount Zion United Methodist Church, Clearwater, FL
9,006	YMCA Northern Dauphin County Branch, Harrisburg, PA
2,500	Greenspring Village Benevolent Fund, Springfield, VA
1,500	Gator Boosters, Gainesville, FL
1,000	American Lung Association, Cheyenne, WY
1,000	Birchwood Glen Owners Corporation, Heltsville, NY
1,000	Florida Blood Services Foundation, Petersburg, FL
1,000	Morton Plant Mease Foundation, Clearwater, FL
940	YMCA Northern Dauphin County Branch, Harrisburg, PA
500	Brazil Police Department Emergency Response Team, Brazil, IN

METRIS COMPANIES, INC.

Company Headquarters

10900 Wayzata Blvd.
Minnetonka, MN 55305-1534
Web: http://www.metriscompanies.com

Company Description

Founded: 1996
Ticker: MXT
Exchange: NYSE
Assets: US$2.594 billion (2002)
Employees: 3700 (2002)
SIC(s): 6141 Personal Credit Institutions.

Nonmonetary Support

Volunteer Programs: The company participates in volunteer programs with charities in its operating communities.

Metris Companies Foundation

Giving Contact

Anne Morrow, Director of Community Relations
Metris Companies, Inc.
10900 Wayzata Blvd.
Minnetonka, MN 55305-1534
Phone: (652)525-5020
Web: http://www.metriscompanies.com/Community/index.html

Description

Founded: 2000
EIN: 411949946
Organization Type: Corporate Foundation
Giving Locations: AZ: Scottsdale; FL: Jacksonville, Orlando; MD: White Marsh; MN: Duluth; OK: Tulsa
Grant Types: General Support.

Financial Summary

Total Giving: $713,980 (2002); $897,644 (2001); $913,596 (2000)
Giving Analysis: Giving for 2002 includes: foundation ($713,980); 2001: foundation ($897,644) 2000: foundation ($913,596)
Assets: $1,830,117 (2002); $2,502,078 (2001); $2,316,400 (2000)
Gifts Received: $1,000,000 (2001); $1,200,000 (2000). Note: Contributions are received from Metris Companies Inc.

Typical Recipients

Arts & Humanities: Libraries, Museums/Galleries, Theater
Civic & Public Affairs: African American Affairs, Business/Free Enterprise, Civic & Public Affairs-General, Hispanic Affairs, Nonprofit Management, Urban & Community Affairs
Education: Business Education, Colleges & Universities, Education Funds, Education-General, Private Education (Precollege)
Health: Health Organizations, Public Health, Single-Disease Health Associations
Religion: Churches, Religious Welfare
Social Services: Big Brother/Big Sister, Child Welfare, Community Service Organizations, Emergency Relief, Food/Clothing Distribution, People with Disabilities, Recreation & Athletics, Social Services-General, Substance Abuse, Youth Organizations

Application Procedures

Initial Contact: Contact the foundation to obtain guidelines and an application form.
Application Requirements: Proposals should include a cover letter; completed application form; proposal narrative of no more than 5 pages describing the organization's background, need, how the program fits the foundation's areas of interest, activities to be carried out, qualifications of staff involved in the activities, and anticipated outcomes; organization budget for current year; project budget; recently audited financial statement; proof of tax-exempt status; and list of board of directors and their affiliations.
Deadlines: The first Friday in February, May, August, and November.

Restrictions

Does not support individuals; fraternal organizations; religious organizations for sectarian purposes; political parties, candidates, campaigns, or organizations where the majority of activity is lobbying; fundraising events; or requests conferring direct benefits, such as auctions, raffles, dues, reduced tuition, conference fees, etc.

Corporate Officials

Dan N. Piteleski: executive vice president, chief information officer
David D. Wesselink: chairman, chief executive officer
John A. Witham: executive vice president, chief financial officer

Foundation Officials

John D. Armbruster: treasurer
Richard G. Evans: secretary
Joseph A. Hoffman: director
Jon B. Mendel: director
David R. Reak: director
Michael S. Smith: vice president
David D. Wesselink: president, director (see above)

Grants Analysis

Disclosure Period: calendar year ending 2002
Total Grants: $897,644
Number of Grants: 70
Average Grant: $8,201*
Highest Grant: $190,000
Lowest Grant: $75
Typical Range: $1,000 to $15,000

*Note: Average grant figure excludes two highest grants ($340,000).

Recent Grants

Note: Grants derived from 2001 Form 990.

Library-Related

2,500	Friends of the Minneapolis Public Library, Minneapolis, MN

General

140,000	Cystic Fibrosis Foundation, Hunt Valley, MD
128,000	Tom Lehman Golf Charities, Inc, Minneapolis, MN
97,500	Uptown Association, Minneapolis, MN
87,000	Thunderbird American Graduate School of International Management, Glendale, AZ
70,000	Second Harvest Heartland, St. Paul, MN
45,000	Gillette Children's Foundation, St. Paul, MN
37,000	First Tee, St. Augustine, FL
30,000	University of Minnesota Foundation, Minneapolis, MN
28,000	Blake School, Hopkins, MN
25,000	AFS Consumer Credit Education Foundation, Washington, DC

METROPOLITAN LIFE INSURANCE CO.

Company Headquarters

1 Madison Avenue
New York, NY 10010-3690
Phone: (212)578-2211
Fax: (212)578-3320
Web: http://www.metlife.com

Company Description

Ticker: MET
Exchange: OTC
Also Known As: MetLife.
Revenue: US$34.055 billion (2002)
Profit: US$1.605 billion (2002)
Employees: 42,300
Fortune Rank: 38, per FORTUNE Magazine's list of 500 Largest U.S. Corporations (2002).
SIC(s): 6311 Life Insurance, 6371 Pension, Health & Welfare Funds.

Operating Locations

Metropolitan Life Insurance Co. (CA--Orange, Walnut Creek; CT--Guilford; FL--Clearwater; HI--Honolulu; IL--Lisle, Mount Prospect, Naperville, Niles, Rockford; KS--Overland Park; MI--Jackson; NJ--Cherry Hill, Iselin; NY--Brooklyn, Flushing, New Hyde Park; OK--Sallisaw; OR--Lake Oswego; PA--Wayne; TX--Round Rock; WV--Summersville)

Subsidiary Companies

MO: GenAmerica Financial Corp., St. Louis

Nonmonetary Support

Type: Donated Equipment; In-kind Services; Loaned Employees; Loaned Executives
Volunteer Programs: Recognizes company volunteers with the MetLife Volunteer ServiceAwards; also sponsors an employee volunteer program that helps employees find volunteer opportunities with nonprofits, schools, and other public agencies. There is a full-time volunteer coordinator at the headquarters location, and several branch offices have structured volunteer programs. Company makes small grants to organizations where employees actively volunteer, through the Volunteer Ventures program.
Contact: Dennis White, Vice President

Note: The company also offers select use of facilities by nonprofits.

MetLife Foundation

Giving Contact

Sibyl C. Jacobson, President & Chief Executive Officer
MetLife Foundation
1 Madison Avenue
New York, NY 10010-3690
Phone: (212)578-7049
Fax: (212)685-1435
Web: http://www.metlife.org

Alternate Contact

Dennis White
MetLife Social Investment Program
Corporate Investments Department
334 Madison Avenue
Convent Station, NJ 07961

Description

EIN: 132878224
Organization Type: Corporate Foundation
Giving Locations: nationally; special consideration to communities in which Metropolitan has a major presence.
Grant Types: Employee Matching Gifts, General Support, Loan, Multiyear/Continuing Support, Project, Research, Scholarship, Seed Money.
Note: Employee matching gift ratio: 1 to 1. Scholarships are for employees children only.

Financial Summary

Total Giving: $23,513,915 (2001); $19,614,198 (2000); $13,186,931 (1999). Note: Contributes through corporate direct giving program and foundation.
Giving Analysis: Giving for 2001 includes: foundation grants to United Way ($1,412,710); corporate direct giving ($5,285,471); foundation ($16,815,734); 2000: foundation scholarships ($234,672); foundation matching gifts ($773,569); foundation grants to United Way ($1,404,000); corporate direct giving ($5,104,457); foundation ($12,097,500); 1999: foundation scholarships ($242,254); foundation matching gifts ($769,956); foundation grants to United Way ($1,372,000); foundation ($13,802,721);
Assets: $181,570,141 (2001); $256,419,866 (2000); $205,772,717 (1999)
Gifts Received: $53,000 (1998); $144,833,024 (1996); $1,625,000 (1994)

Typical Recipients

Arts & Humanities: Arts Associations & Councils, Arts Centers, Arts Institutes, Ballet, Dance, Ethnic & Folk Arts, Film & Video, Historic Preservation, History & Archaeology, Libraries, Museums/Galleries, Music, Opera, Performing Arts, Public Broadcasting, Theater, Visual Arts
Civic & Public Affairs: African American Affairs, Botanical Gardens/Parks, Business/Free Enterprise, Civil Rights, Community Foundations, Economic Development, Economic Policy, Employment/Job Training, Civic & Public Affairs-General, Hispanic Affairs, Housing, Law & Justice, Municipalities/Towns, Professional & Trade Associations, Public Policy, Rural Affairs, Safety, Urban & Community Affairs, Women's Affairs, Zoos/Aquariums
Education: Agricultural Education, Arts/Humanities Education, Business Education, Colleges & Universities, Community & Junior Colleges, Economic Education, Education Associations, Education Funds, Education Reform, Engineering/Technological Education, Faculty Development, Education-General, Health & Physical Education, Leadership Training, Literacy, Medical Education, Minority Education, Public Education (Precollege), Science/Mathematics Education, Student Aid

Environment: Environment-General
Health: AIDS/HIV, Alzheimers Disease, Cancer, Children's Health/Hospitals, Clinics/Medical Centers, Geriatric Health, Health Policy/Cost Containment, Health Funds, Health Organizations, Heart, Hospitals, Medical Research, Medical Training, Mental Health, Nursing Services, Nutrition, Prenatal Health Issues, Public Health, Research/Studies Institutes, Respiratory, Transplant Networks/Donor Banks
International: Foreign Arts Organizations, Foreign Educational Institutions, Health Care/Hospitals, International Organizations, International Peace & Security Issues, International Relief Efforts
Religion: Religious Welfare
Science: Science Museums, Scientific Centers & Institutes
Social Services: At-Risk Youth, Child Welfare, Community Service Organizations, Counseling, Crime Prevention, Delinquency & Criminal Rehabilitation, Emergency Relief, Family Services, Food/Clothing Distribution, Homes, Scouts, Shelters/Homelessness, Substance Abuse, United Funds/United Ways, Volunteer Services, YMCA/YWCA/YMHA/YWHA, Youth Organizations

Application Procedures

Initial Contact: Send a written request.
Application Requirements: Include a description of organization (legal name, history, activities, purpose, and governing board), purpose for which grant is requested, amount requested and list of other sources of financial support, most recently audited financial statement, copy of IRS determination letter indicating 501(c)(3) tax-exempt status, and Form 990; requests for funds to support a specific project or program should include fully defined need, objective, benefits, plans (including time frame and evaluative criteria), staff, and budget (including sources of financial support committed and pending).
Deadlines: None; requests reviewed throughout year.
Evaluative Criteria: Considers organization's general structure, history, objectives, and management capability, relationship to community and population served, position and service relative to similar organizations, financial position and sources of income; projects are evaluated on goals and implementation plans, time frame, ultimate disposition of project, staff capabilities, benefits of the project, and sources of financial and other support.
Notes: If request falls under foundation guidelines and program priorities, organization may be asked to provide more complete information before a decision is made. Foundation occasionally issues requests for proposals.

Restrictions

Grants are not made to individuals; private foundations; hospitals; organizations receiving support from United Way; organizations whose activities are mainly international; local chapters of national organizations; disease-specific organizations; organizations primarily engaged in patient care or direct treatment; drug treatment centers or community health clinics; elementary or secondary schools; endowments; courtesy advertising or festival participation; labor organizations; or religious, fraternal, political, athletic, social, or veterans organizations.

Additional Information

Occasionally, foundation establishes particular areas of interest for emphasis within a program area. When this is done, foundation actively seeks opportunities for providing grants and may issue requests for proposals.
Grant renewals are not automatic and cannot be guaranteed from year to year.
In addition to Metropolitan Life's grant programs, the company and foundation sponsor the Metlife Social Investment Program. This program provides loans, guarantees, equity investments and other financial

programs to community ventures that do not meet the traditional investment criteria of private and institutional investors. The program typically underwrites projects relating to affordable housing, commercial revitalization, land preservation, health and rehab treatment centers, business development arts, and education. Although most investments are for nonprofit organizations, for-profit entities that have a clear social purpose are also considered.
Publications: Contributions Report

Corporate Officials

James M. Benson: president PRIM CORP EMPL chief executive officer: Metropolitan Life Insurance Co. ADD CORP EMPL chairman, chief executive officer: New England Life Insurance Co.
Harry Paul Kamen: chairman, president, chief executive officer B Montreal, QC Canada 1933. ED University of Pennsylvania AB (1954); Harvard University LLB (1957). PRIM CORP EMPL chairman, president, chief executive officer: Metropolitan Life Insurance Co. CORP AFFIL director: Pfizer Inc.; director: Bethlehem Steel Corp.; director: New England Investment Companies LP; director: Banco Santander. NONPR AFFIL government: National Association Securities Dealers; director: New England Financial; director: American Council Life Insurance.
Catherine Amelia Rein: vice president B Lebanon, PA 1943. ED Pennsylvania State University BA (1965); New York University JD (1968). PRIM CORP EMPL vice president: Metropolitan Life Insurance Co. ADD CORP EMPL president, chief executive officer: Metropolitan Property Casualty Insurance Co. CORP AFFIL director: Corning Inc.; director: GPU Inc.; director: Bank New York Co. Inc.; director: Broadmoor Housing Inc.

Foundation Officials

C. Robert Henrickson: director
Sibyl C. Jacobson: president, chief executive officer, director PRIM CORP EMPL senior vice president external affairs: Metropolitan Life Insurance Co.
Deborah Mandel: assistant treasurer
Joseph A. Reali: secretary, counsel
Catherine Amelia Rein: director (see above)
Vincent P. Reusing: director
Timothy Schmidt: director, treasurer
Robert C. Tarnok: controller
William J. Toppeta: director
Lisa M. Weber: director
A. Dennis White: vice president

Grants Analysis

Disclosure Period: calendar year ending 2001
Total Grants: $17,392,773*
Number of Grants: 283
Average Grant: $61,459
Highest Grant: $1,250,000
Lowest Grant: $1,000
Typical Range: $2,500 to $200,000
*Note: Giving excludes matching gifts; scholarships; United Way; fundraising events; and affiliate contributions.

Recent Grants

Note: Grants derived from 2001 Form 990.

Library-Related
150,000   Libraries for the Future, New York, NY

General
1,250,000 Lincoln Center for the Performing Arts, New York, NY
1,000,000 September 11th Fund, New York, NY -- disaster relief
1,000,000 Twins Towers Fund, New York, NY -- disaster relief
971,323   Health and Safety Education Program
675,000   Awards for Medical Research, Manchester, MA
435,000   Boys and Girls Clubs of America, Atlanta, GA

300,000	Families and Work Institute, New York, NY
300,000	University of Texas, Dallas, TX -- Community College Leadership Program
275,000	Local Initiatives Support Corporation, New York, NY
275,000	Trust for Public Land, San Francisco, CA

MEX-AM CULTURAL FOUNDATION

Giving Contact
Andrew M. Klinger, Trustee
c/o Grant, Herrmann, Schwartz and Klinger
675 Third Avenue
New York, NY 10017
Phone: (212)682-1800

Description
Founded: 1985
EIN: 133328723
Organization Type: Private Foundation
Giving Locations: NY: New York nationally.
Grant Types: General Support.

Donor Information
Founder: the Wolfgang Schoenborn Trust

Financial Summary
Total Giving: $155,000 (fiscal year ending September 30, 2001); $173,860 (fiscal 2000); $161,050 (fiscal 1998)
Giving Analysis: Giving for fiscal 2001 includes: foundation scholarships ($30,000); fiscal 2000: foundation scholarships ($30,000) fiscal 1998: foundation scholarships ($45,000)
Assets: $2,017,022 (fiscal 2001); $2,168,594 (fiscal 2000); $2,433,384 (fiscal 1998)

Typical Recipients
Arts & Humanities: Arts Festivals, Arts Funds, Arts Institutes, Dance, Ethnic & Folk Arts, Film & Video, Arts & Humanities-General, Libraries, Museums/Galleries, Music, Opera, Theater, Visual Arts
Civic & Public Affairs: Civic & Public Affairs-General, Parades/Festivals
Education: Arts/Humanities Education, International Studies, Legal Education, Medical Education, Minority Education
International: Foreign Arts Organizations, Health Care/Hospitals, Human Rights
Religion: Religious Welfare

Application Procedures
Initial Contact: Send a brief letter of inquiry.
Application Requirements: Detail specific need for which request is made.
Deadlines: None.

Foundation Officials
William J. Brown: trustee
Andrew M. Klinger: trustee
Milton Schwartz: trustee

Grants Analysis
Disclosure Period: fiscal year ending September 30, 2001
Total Grants: $125,000*
Number of Grants: 14
Average Grant: $8,929
Highest Grant: $20,000
Lowest Grant: $2,000
Typical Range: $4,000 to $15,000
***Note:** Giving excludes scholarships.

Recent Grants
Note: Grants derived from fiscal 2000 Form 990.

General
68,000	Mexican Culture Institute of New York, New York, NY -- Mexican independence celebration
27,860	Cineteca Fototeca Nuevo Leon -- support of the exhibit El Arte del Riesgo
20,000	International Arts Relations Inc., New York, NY -- to support video featuring the work of Mexican artist in New York City
15,000	Cornell University Medical College, New York, NY -- in support of Mexican related research and or scholarships
15,000	Duke University, Durham, NC -- in support of Mexican undergraduate scholarships
7,000	Federacion Mexicana De Asociaiones de Amigos de los Museos -- support of the first National Congress of the Federacion Mexicana de Asociaciones de Amigos de los Museos
5,000	Chamber Music International, New York, NY -- in support or Chamber Music International
5,000	Hamptons Shakespeare Festival, Amagansett, NY -- in support of Hampton's Shakespeare Festival
5,000	Installation, San Diego, CA -- to support publication to be prepared in conduction with InSITE2000
3,000	Mexican Culture Institute of New York, New York, NY -- to support international studio project

MEYER FAMILY FOUNDATION

Giving Contact
Cheryl McRoberts, Foundation Administrator
1 Westbrook Corporate Center
Suite 300
Westchester, IL 60154
Phone: (708)449-7755

Description
Founded: 1946
EIN: 366053404
Organization Type: Private Foundation
Giving Locations: FL: St. Augustine including metropolitan area; IL: Chicago including metropolitan area; NC: Pinehurst including metropolitan area
Grant Types: Capital, Challenge, Emergency, Endowment, General Support, Multiyear/Continuing Support, Project, Research, Scholarship.

Donor Information
Founder: the M. L. Meyer Trust

Financial Summary
Total Giving: $604,175 (2001); $420,700 (2000); $454,420 (1999)
Assets: $11,733,188 (2001); $14,062,894 (2000); $14,472,473 (1999)
Gifts Received: $50,224 (2001); $102,954 (2000); $506 (1999). Note: Contributions are received from the Mary Lumen Meyer Trust.

Typical Recipients
Arts & Humanities: Arts Appreciation, Arts Centers, Arts Festivals, Arts Institutes, Ballet, Dance, Arts & Humanities-General, Libraries, Museums/Galleries, Music, Opera, Public Broadcasting
Civic & Public Affairs: Botanical Gardens/Parks, Community Foundations, Civic & Public Affairs-General, Housing, Law & Justice, Women's Affairs

Education: Afterschool/Enrichment Programs, Agricultural Education, Arts/Humanities Education, Business Education, Colleges & Universities, Community & Junior Colleges, Education Associations, Education Funds, Elementary Education (Private), Education-General, Minority Education, Private Education (Precollege), Public Education (Precollege), Religious Education, Secondary Education (Private), Secondary Education (Public), Student Aid
Environment: Environment-General
Health: Cancer, Children's Health/Hospitals, Clinics/Medical Centers, Diabetes, Health-General, Hospitals, Hospitals (University Affiliated), Medical Rehabilitation, Medical Research, Multiple Sclerosis, Public Health, Research/Studies Institutes, Respiratory, Single-Disease Health Associations
Religion: Churches, Religion-General, Ministries
Science: Science-General, Science Museums
Social Services: Animal Protection, At-Risk Youth, Child Welfare, Community Service Organizations, Crime Prevention, Emergency Relief, Food/Clothing Distribution, People with Disabilities, Recreation & Athletics, Shelters/Homelessness, Social Services-General, Volunteer Services, Youth Organizations

Application Procedures
Initial Contact: Send a brief letter of inquiry.
Application Requirements: Provide a description of organization, its objectives, amount requested, proof of tax-exempt status, annual report, recently audited financial statement, and list of other contributors to the project.
Deadlines: October 1.

Restrictions
Does not support individuals, religious organizations for sectarian purposes, political or lobbying groups, or organizations outside operating areas.

Foundation Officials
Charles Foster Brown, III: trustee B Omaha, NE 1947. ED Union College (1969). PRIM CORP EMPL vice chairman: Robertson-Ceco Corp.
Mary Heidi Hall-Jones: trustee CORP AFFIL director: Ceco Industries.
Ned A. Ochiltree, Jr.: trustee B Omaha, NE December 23, 1919. ED Purdue University BS (1942). CORP AFFIL director: Ceco Industries; director: Ceco Corp. NONPR AFFIL member: Chicago Crime Commission.

Grants Analysis
Disclosure Period: calendar year ending 2001
Total Grants: $604,175
Number of Grants: 57
Average Grant: $10,600
Highest Grant: $150,000
Lowest Grant: $250
Typical Range: $1,000 to $50,000

Recent Grants
Note: Grants derived from 2001 Form 990.

General
150,000	Marklund Charities, Glendale Heights, IL
50,000	O'Neal School, Southern Pines, NC
50,000	Penland School of Crafts, Penland, NC
50,000	Sandhills Community College, Pinehurst, NC
25,000	American Red Cross Disaster Relief Fund
25,000	New York Police and Fire Widows and Children Benefit Fund, New York, NY
16,800	Associated Colleges of Illinois, Chicago, IL
15,000	Junior Achievement of Chicago, Chicago, IL
15,000	WTTW Channel 11, Chicago, IL
14,500	Chicago Symphony Orchestra, Chicago, IL

PAUL J. MEYER FAMILY FOUNDATION

Giving Contact
Paul J. Meyer, Sr., President & Director
PO Box 7411
Waco, TX 76714-7411
Phone: (254)776-0034

Description
Founded: 1985
EIN: 742357421
Organization Type: Private Foundation
Giving Locations: TX
Grant Types: General Support.

Donor Information
Founder: Paul J. Meyer, Alice Jane Meyer

Financial Summary
Total Giving: $850,858 (1999); $787,315 (1998); $388,538 (1996)
Giving Analysis: Giving for 1999 includes: foundation grants to United Way ($9,000) 1998: foundation grants to United Way ($9,000)
Assets: $10,909,134 (1999); $7,711,953 (1998); $4,547,161 (1996)
Gifts Received: $1,986,093 (1999); $431,426 (1998); $756,874 (1996). Note: In 1999, contributions were received from Cayhesse ($1,636,975), Paul J. Meyer ($46,545), L-K Marketing ($205,000), Rapport ($20,000), Leslie Jane Meyer Trust ($70,447), and others less than $5,000 each ($7,126). In 1998, contributions were received from Janna Trust. In 1996, contributions were received from Japale, Ltd. ($686,500), Kim Lund ($42,869), and Paul J. Meyer ($23,440); miscellaneous contributions of less than $5,000 each totaling $4,065 also were received.

Typical Recipients
Arts & Humanities: History & Archaeology, Libraries, Museums/Galleries, Theater
Civic & Public Affairs: Clubs, Community Foundations, Economic Policy, Employment/Job Training, Civic & Public Affairs-General, Hispanic Affairs, Housing, Public Policy, Urban & Community Affairs, Zoos/Aquariums
Education: Colleges & Universities, Education-General, Private Education (Precollege), Public Education (Precollege), Religious Education, Secondary Education (Private), Student Aid
Health: Arthritis, Cancer, Eyes/Blindness, Heart, Prenatal Health Issues
International: International Peace & Security Issues, Missionary/Religious Activities
Religion: Churches, Religion-General, Jewish Causes, Ministries, Missionary Activities (Domestic), Religious Organizations, Religious Welfare, Seminaries, Social/Policy Issues
Social Services: Child Welfare, Community Service Organizations, Domestic Violence, Family Services, People with Disabilities, Recreation & Athletics, Scouts, Shelters/Homelessness, Social Services-General, United Funds/United Ways, YMCA/YWCA/YMHA/YWHA, Youth Organizations

Application Procedures
Initial Contact: Send a brief letter.
Application Requirements: Include a a description of organization and purpose of funds sought.
Deadlines: None.

Foundation Officials
Joe E. Baxter: secretary, treasurer, director
Alice Jane Meyer: vice president, director
Paul J. Meyer, Sr.: president, director B San Mateo, CA 1928. PRIM CORP EMPL founder, chairman, director: SMI/USA. CORP AFFIL founder, chairman, director: Leadership Management. NONPR AFFIL member: National Republican Finance Committee; member: National Speakers Bureau; member: International Franchise Association; member: American Management Association; director: Boys Club Waco.
Dr. William A. Meyer: vice president, director

Grants Analysis
Disclosure Period: calendar year ending 1999
Total Grants: $841,858*
Number of Grants: 47
Average Grant: $3,408
Highest Grant: $23,000
Typical Range: $200 to $5,000
*Note: Giving excludes United Way.

Recent Grants
Note: Grants derived from 1999 Form 990.

Library-Related

30,000	Floyd Co. Library Friends, Floydada, TX -- build public library in Floydada

General

180,000	Haggai Institute, Atlanta, GA
120,000	Wayland Baptist University, Plainview, TX -- Harral auditorium addition and remodeling
73,305	Friends for Life, New York, NY
67,200	First Baptist Church of Woodway
43,600	Fair Theatre, Inc., The, Plainview, TX
36,000	Ron Herrod Ministries
34,000	Larue Learning Center
34,000	Waco Covenant Academy, Waco, TX
33,500	Mission Waco
33,180	Baylor University, Waco, TX -- Joe Baxter Funds

ALICE KLEBERG REYNOLDS MEYER FOUNDATION

Giving Contact
Alice K. Meyer, President & Treasurer
PO Box 6985
San Antonio, TX 78209
Phone: (210)820-0552

Description
Founded: 1978
EIN: 742020227
Organization Type: Private Foundation
Giving Locations: TX
Grant Types: Capital, General Support.

Donor Information
Founder: Alice K. Meyer

Financial Summary
Total Giving: $140,000 (1999); $142,876 (1996); $250,950 (1995)
Assets: $8,267,528 (1999); $5,217,033 (1996); $4,770,637 (1995)
Gifts Received: $28,473 (1996); $100,000 (1995); $22,389 (1994). Note: In 1996, contributions were received from Alice K. Meyer.

Typical Recipients
Arts & Humanities: Arts Centers, Arts Institutes, Arts Outreach, Community Arts, Historic Preservation, Libraries, Literary Arts, Museums/Galleries, Music, Public Broadcasting, Theater
Civic & Public Affairs: Botanical Gardens/Parks, Economic Policy, Hispanic Affairs, Nonprofit Management, Public Policy, Urban & Community Affairs, Women's Affairs, Zoos/Aquariums
Education: Colleges & Universities, Education Funds, Education Reform, Environmental Education, Minority Education, Private Education (Precollege), Science/Mathematics Education, Special Education, Student Aid, Vocational & Technical Education
Environment: Environment-General
Health: Cancer, Children's Health/Hospitals, Clinics/Medical Centers, Emergency/Ambulance Services, Health Organizations, Long-Term Care, Medical Rehabilitation, Medical Research, Nursing Services, Public Health, Respiratory
International: Foreign Arts Organizations
Religion: Ministries, Religious Organizations
Science: Science Museums, Scientific Organizations, Scientific Research
Social Services: Child Welfare, Community Service Organizations, Counseling, Food/Clothing Distribution, Homes, Scouts, Special Olympics, Substance Abuse, United Funds/United Ways, Volunteer Services, Youth Organizations

Application Procedures
Initial Contact: Send a brief letter on organization's letterhead signed by a member of the board of directors or an officer of the organization. Include specific information about the purpose of funds sought, a copy of the organization's charter and by-laws, and proof of tax-exempt status.
Deadlines: None.

Foundation Officials
Alice K. Meyer: president, treasurer B Corpus Christi, TX 1928. ED University of Texas BA (1945-1949). NONPR AFFIL treasurer: Laguna Gloria Art Museum; member: Phi Beta Kappa; treasurer, trustee, member: Antonio Museum Association; president, treasurer, member: Junior League. CLUB AFFIL Giraud Club; San Antonia Country Club; Argyle Club.
Vaughan B. Meyer: vice president, secretary
Jesse Halff Oppenheimer: assistant secretary B San Antonio, TX January 04, 1919. ED University of Arizona BA (1939); Harvard University JD (1942). PRIM CORP EMPL partner: Oppenheimer, Blend, Harrison & Tate. CORP AFFIL director: Standard Electric Co.; director, organizer: Southwest Texas National Bank. NONPR AFFIL member: University Texas Chancellors Council Centennial Comm; trustee: Woodrow Wilson International Center Scholars; director, member executive committee: Symphony Society San Antonio; member: Kenwood Neighborhood Council; trustee, president: Marion Koogler McNay Museum; member: American Bar Association. CLUB AFFIL Argyle Club; San Antonio Country Club.

Grants Analysis
Disclosure Period: calendar year ending 1999
Total Grants: $140,000
Note: No grants list available for 1999.

Recent Grants
Note: Grants derived from 1999 Form 990.

General

50,000	People's Community Clinic, Austin, TX -- full time ob/gyn physician
50,000	Saint Andrew's Episcopal School, Austin, TX
10,000	San Pedro Playhouse, San Antonio, TX -- restoration of playhouse
10,000	University of Texas Health Science Center, San Antonio, TX -- Robert B Welch Foundation chair in chemistry
5,000	Children's Hospital Foundation of Austin, Austin, TX -- child life program endowment
5,000	Driscoll Children's Hospital, Corpus Christi, TX -- ABC crisis fund
5,000	Guadalupe Cultural Arts Center, San Antonio, TX -- San Antonio Cinefestival
2,000	Any Baby Can, San Antonio, TX
2,000	College Fund/UNCF, San Antonio, TX
1,000	Special Olympics of Texas, Austin, TX

Eugene And Agnes E. Meyer Foundation

Giving Contact
Julie L. Rogers, President
1400 16th Street Northwest, Suite 360
Washington, DC 20036-2217
Phone: (202)483-8294
Fax: (202)328-6850
Web: http://www.meyerfoundation.org

Description
Founded: 1944
EIN: 530241716
Organization Type: General Purpose Foundation
Giving Locations: DC: Washington metropolitan area; MD: suburban Maryland; VA: Northern Virginia
Grant Types: General Support, Loan, Operating Expenses.

Donor Information
Founder: The Meyer Foundation was established in December 1944. The foundation's donors, Mr. and Mrs. Eugene Meyer , were active in national affairs as well as community affairs in Washington, D.C. Mr. Meyer, who died in 1959, was a Wall Street investment banker, governor of the Federal Reserve, first president of the World Bank, and chairman of the board of the Washington Post, which he purchased in 1933. Agnes E. Meyer , who died in 1970, founded the Urban Service Corps in 1961 and the National Committee for Support of Public Schools in 1962. Mrs. Meyer was a journalist and author interested in public education, urban renewal, social action, and the arts. The AEM Foundation in New York City, founded by Mrs. Meyer in 1960, supports organizations in which she was interested.

Financial Summary
Total Giving: $7,314,972 (2000); $5,929,086 (1998); $5,958,641 (1997)
Giving Analysis: Giving for 1998 includes: foundation matching gifts ($500)
Assets: $148,769,334 (2000); $146,859,147 (1998); $139,448,552 (1997)
Gifts Received: $214,943 (1998); $128,417 (1997); $462,072 (1993). Note: In 1998, contributions were received from Intergroup Fund Revenue ($205,478) and Advancement Fund contributions ($9,465).

Typical Recipients
Arts & Humanities: Arts Associations & Councils, Arts Centers, Arts Outreach, Ballet, Community Arts, Dance, Ethnic & Folk Arts, Film & Video, Arts & Humanities-General, Historic Preservation, History & Archaeology, Literary Arts, Museums/Galleries, Music, Performing Arts, Public Broadcasting, Theater
Civic & Public Affairs: Asian American Affairs, Botanical Gardens/Parks, Business/Free Enterprise, Civil Rights, Community Foundations, Economic Development, Employment/Job Training, Civic & Public Affairs-General, Hispanic Affairs, Housing, Law & Justice, Legal Aid, Nonprofit Management, Philanthropic Organizations, Public Policy, Urban & Community Affairs, Women's Affairs
Education: Afterschool/Enrichment Programs, Arts/Humanities Education, Colleges & Universities, Community & Junior Colleges, Education Funds, Elementary Education (Private), Faculty Development, Education-General, International Studies, Legal Education, Literacy, Minority Education, Preschool Education, Public Education (Precollege), Science/Mathematics Education
Environment: Protection, Resource Conservation
Health: AIDS/HIV, Children's Health/Hospitals, Clinics/Medical Centers, Health-General, Health Organizations, Hospices, Long-Term Care, Mental Health, Prenatal Health Issues, Public Health
International: International Development

Religion: Religion-General, Jewish Causes, Ministries, Religious Welfare
Social Services: At-Risk Youth, Child Welfare, Child Welfare, Community Centers, Community Service Organizations, Counseling, Crime Prevention, Delinquency & Criminal Rehabilitation, Domestic Violence, Family Planning, Family Services, Food/Clothing Distribution, Homes, People with Disabilities, Recreation & Athletics, Refugee Assistance, Senior Services, Shelters/Homelessness, Social Services-General, Substance Abuse, Volunteer Services, YMCA/YWCA/YMHA/YWHA, Youth Organizations

Application Procedures
Initial Contact: Applicants are urged to submit a preliminary letter of inquiry of no more than two pages in length to the program officer.
Application Requirements: The letter of inquiry should include: summary of proposal; primary mission and activities; amount requested, total proposed budget, and funding committed to date; annual operating budget; contact person and telephone number.
Deadlines: The letter of inquiry should be sent to the foundation at least six weeks before proposals are due. Deadlines for full proposals are March 15 for the June board meeting, July 15 for the October meeting, and November 15 for the February meeting.
Review Process: Receipt of proposals will be acknowledged in writing. The foundation staff will review the preliminary letter and contact the applicant with their best judgment whether or not the project would be of interest to the board.
Notes: The foundation does not accept faxed proposals or proposals by e-mail. If a staff member advises the applicant to send a full proposal, the foundation will provide specific details on what must be covered in the written narrative. Full proposals are reviewed upon receipt. If a proposal is considered, the project and organization are researched and an interview may be requested. All proposals are reviewed by the board, and the decision is sent in writing by the end of the month. The foundation discourages phone calls.

Restrictions
The foundation prefers not to provide continuing support to organizations. It does not contribute to programs intended to serve constituencies outside the Washington metropolitan area. The foundation does not make grants to individuals, award scholarships or financial assistance, make grants to projects which are primarily sectarian in nature, endowment drives, scientific or medical research, or special events or conferences.

Additional Information
Publications: Annual Report; Guidelines

Foundation Officials
Edward H. Bersoff, PhD: vice chair B 1942. PRIM CORP EMPL chairman: BTG Inc.
Thomas W. Chapman: section treasurer PRIM CORP EMPL vice president finance, treasurer: Qualchoice of Arkansas Inc. CORP AFFIL board member: Rooney, Ida, Nolt & Ahern.
Newman T. Halvorson, Jr.: assistant secretary/treasurer, B Detroit, MI 1936. ED Princeton University AB (1958); Harvard University LLB (1961). PRIM CORP EMPL partner: Covington & Burling. NONPR AFFIL member: District of Columbia Bar Association; board trustee, member executive committee: Greater Washington Research Center; trustee: Cleveland Park Historical Society; member: Committee 100 Federal City; member: American Bar Association. CLUB AFFIL Metro Club; Chevy Chase Country Club.
Boisfeuillet Jones, Jr.: director B Atlanta, GA 1946. ED Harvard University AB (1968); Harvard University JD (1974); Oxford University DPhil (1981). PRIM CORP EMPL president, general manager: Washington Post Co. CORP AFFIL director: Bowater Mersey Paper Co.; director: Robinson Terminal Warehouse Corp. NONPR AFFIL director: Greater Washington

Board Trade; director: Saint Albans School; director: Federal City Council.
James W. Jones: board chair B Texarkana, TX 1945. ED Trinity University BA (1967); New York University JD (1970). PRIM CORP EMPL managing partner: Arnold & Porter.
Patricia A. McGuire: director B Philadelphia, PA 1952. ED Trinity College BA (1974); Georgetown University JD (1977). PRIM NONPR EMPL president, trustee: Trinity College. NONPR AFFIL member dollar coin design advisory committee: United States Mint; director: Women's College Coalition; member advisory board: National College Access Network; member: Trinity College Alumnae Association; commissioner: Mid-State Commission Higher Education; director: National Association Independent Colleges & Universities; board visitors: Joint Military Intelligence College; member advisory board: Merion Mercy Academy & Sisters Mercy; director: Elderhostel Inc.; adj professor law: Georgetown University Law Center; director: Association Catholic Colleges & Universities; member: Council Advancement & Support Education; member commission government relations: American Council Education; member: Association American Law Schools; director: Acacia Group; member: American Bar Association.
Francey Lim Youngberg: director

Grants Analysis
Disclosure Period: calendar year ending 2000
Total Grants: $7,314,972*
Number of Grants: 284
Average Grant: $25,757
Highest Grant: $200,000
Lowest Grant: $1,000
Typical Range: $5,000 to $25,000 and $50,000 to $100,000
***Note:** Giving excludes matching gifts.

Recent Grants
Note: Grants derived from 2000 Form 990.

General
500,000	Historical Society of Washington, Washington, DC -- support for the City Museum Capital Campaign
150,000	Bread for the City, Washington, DC -- support for capital campaign
150,000	Community Foundation for the National Capital Region, Washington, DC -- support for Initiative to Strengthen Neighborhood Assets program over two years
150,000	Mary's Center for Maternal and Child Care, Washington, DC -- support for construction phase
100,000	African Continuum Theatre Company, Washington, DC -- to support the theatre's future
100,000	Covenant House, Washington, DC -- support for construction of a new Community Service Center
100,000	Martha's Table, Washington, DC -- support for capital campaign
100,000	SERVE, Inc., Manassas, VA
90,000	Technology Works for Good, Washington, DC -- support for Circuit Rider program
80,000	IISC Foundation, Washington, DC -- support for screening of low-income children for developmental disabilities and delays

Robert R. Meyer Foundation

Giving Contact
Carla B. Gail, Vice President & Trustee
AmSouth Bank of Alabama
PO Box 11426
Birmingham, AL 35202

Phone: (205)326-4696
Fax: (205)581-7433

Description
Founded: 1949
EIN: 636019645
Organization Type: General Purpose Foundation
Giving Locations: AL: Birmingham metropolitan area
Grant Types: Capital, General Support, Multiyear/Continuing Support, Research, Scholarship.

Donor Information
Founder: The Robert R. Meyer Foundation was established in 1923 by John E. Meyer and the late Robert R. Meyer (d. 1947).

Financial Summary
Total Giving: $1,822,072 (2000); $2,040,831 (1998); $1,634,645 (1997)
Giving Analysis: Giving for 2000 includes: foundation grants to United Way ($15,000)
Assets: $44,185,225 (2000); $43,992,763 (1998); $39,108,137 (1997)

Typical Recipients
Arts & Humanities: Arts Associations & Councils, Arts Festivals, Ballet, Dance, Historic Preservation, History & Archaeology, Libraries, Literary Arts, Museums/Galleries, Music, Theater
Civic & Public Affairs: Business/Free Enterprise, Civil Rights, Clubs, Employment/Job Training, Civic & Public Affairs-General, Housing, Nonprofit Management, Urban & Community Affairs, Zoos/Aquariums
Education: Arts/Humanities Education, Business Education, Colleges & Universities, Education Reform, Elementary Education (Private), Gifted & Talented Programs, Literacy, Medical Education, Minority Education, Private Education (Precollege), Public Education (Precollege), Secondary Education (Private), Special Education
Environment: Air/Water Quality, Wildlife Protection
Health: AIDS/HIV, Cancer, Clinics/Medical Centers, Eyes/Blindness, Health Organizations, Hospitals, Long-Term Care, Mental Health, Nursing Services, Public Health, Research/Studies Institutes, Speech & Hearing
International: International Organizations
Religion: Churches, Jewish Causes, Ministries, Religious Welfare
Science: Scientific Centers & Institutes
Social Services: At-Risk Youth, Big Brother/Big Sister, Camps, Child Welfare, Community Centers, Community Service Organizations, Crime Prevention, Day Care, Domestic Violence, Family Planning, Family Services, Homes, People with Disabilities, Recreation & Athletics, Scouts, Senior Services, Social Services-General, Substance Abuse, United Funds/United Ways, Volunteer Services, YMCA/YWCA/YMHA/YWHA, Youth Organizations

Application Procedures
Initial Contact: There are no specific application forms. Proposals should be sent with an original and seven copies.
Application Requirements: Include name and address of the applying organization, list of directors, position of individual signing the grant request, amount needed, statement attesting to the need for the program, proposed budget, expected goal of the program, project timetable (including desired starting date and projected date of termination), list of other sources of funding, proof of tax exemption, and statement that this status has not been revoked or modified.
Deadlines: March 1 and September 1.
Review Process: The board of trustees meets in June and December.

Restrictions
No grants are made to individuals, or organizations not classified as 501(c)(3) by the IRS. Grants are made only in the greater Birmingham, AL, area.

Additional Information
AmSouth Bank in Birmingham, AL, is listed as corporate trustee of the foundation.

Foundation Officials
Hon. Sharon L. Blackburn: member advisory committee
Elmer Beseler Harris: member advisory committee B Chilton County, AL 1939. ED Auburn University BS (1962); Auburn University MS (1968); Auburn University MBA (1970). CORP AFFIL director: Southern Energy Resources Inc.; director: Southern Co. Services Inc.; president, director: Southern Electric Generating Co.; executive vice president, director: Southern Co. Inc.; director: AmSouth Bank NA; director: SCI Holdings Inc.; director: Alabama Property Co.; director: AmSouth Bancorp. NONPR AFFIL trustee: Southern Research Institute; director: United Way America; member: Southeast Electric Exchange; trustee: Samford University; member: Society American Military Engineers; member advisory board: Saint Vincent Hospital; member: Edison Electric Institute; director: Public Affairs Research Council Alabama; director: Boy Scouts America Birmingham Area Council; director: Alabama Council Economic Education. CLUB AFFIL Summit Club; Montgomery Club; Rotary Club.
William M. Spencer, III: member advisory committee B Birmingham, AL December 10, 1920. ED University of the South (1941); Harvard University (1947). PRIM CORP EMPL chairman: Molecular Engineering Associates. CORP AFFIL director: Biocryst Pharmaceuticals Inc.; director: Porter, White & Co.

Grants Analysis
Disclosure Period: calendar year ending 2000
Total Grants: $1,807,072*
Number of Grants: 73
Average Grant: $22,320*
Highest Grant: $200,000
Typical Range: $10,000 to $40,000
*Note: Giving excludes United Way. Average grant figure excludes highest grant.

Recent Grants
Note: Grants derived from 2000 Form 990.

General
23,500	South Baldwin United Way, Foley, AL
11,000	Gulf Shores High School
6,000	Christian Service Center
6,000	Zoo Foundation, The
5,000	Mercy Medical
2,000	American Cancer Service, New York, NY
2,000	Baldwin County Sheriff, Foley, AL
1,000	Lighthouse, Lincoln, NE
1,000	St. Benedict
500	Association for Retarded Citizens

MEYER MEMORIAL TRUST

Giving Contact
Doug Stamm, Executive Director
425 NW 10th Ave., Suite 400
Portland, OR 97209
Phone: (503)228-5512
E-mail: mmt@mmt.org
Web: http://www.mmt.org

Description
Founded: 1982
EIN: 930806316
Organization Type: General Purpose Foundation
Giving Locations: OR; WA: Clark County

Grant Types: Capital, Matching, Multiyear/Continuing Support.

Donor Information
Founder: The trust is the residuary beneficiary of the estate of Fred G. Meyer , and was established in 1978. Fred Meyer, who died in 1978, bequeathed the trust approximately two million shares of stock in Fred Meyer, Inc. Mr. Meyer was born in 1886 into a family of Brooklyn grocers. After working his way through the wheat fields of the Dakotas and Montana and the gold fields of Alaska, he moved to Portland, OR, in 1909. He then became successful at peddling coffee and managing a downtown street market. Later he invested all of his assets in an "all package" grocery store, and began a chain of stores throughout the Pacific Northwest. By 1979, his stores employed more than 13,000 people and had over $1 billion in annual sales.

Fred Meyer's wife of 41 years, Eva, was an integral part of this success. She managed several store departments in the early years and became a director and the secretary-treasurer of Fred Meyer, Inc.

Fred Meyer's life and career exemplified ingenuity, hard work, and a commitment to the communities where he built his stores. He introduced innovative marketing concepts to the Northwest, including the packaging of bulk goods, one-stop shopping, cash-and-carry purchasing, self-service drug stores, and other creative and convenient services. He also supported economic development of the Northwest. He bought local products whenever possible, and he fostered the production of new crops in the region. He helped finance new business ventures as well as some in danger of failing.

Financial Summary
Total Giving: $24,735,559 (fiscal year ending March 31, 2002); $23,607,542 (fiscal 2001); $23,657,153 (fiscal 2000)
Giving Analysis: Giving for fiscal 1999 includes: foundation matching gifts ($632,237)
Assets: $475,246,555 (fiscal 2002); $495,849,256 (fiscal 2001); $536,744,752 (fiscal 2000)

Typical Recipients
Arts & Humanities: Arts Associations & Councils, Arts Centers, Arts Festivals, Arts Institutes, Arts Outreach, Ballet, Community Arts, Dance, Ethnic & Folk Arts, Arts & Humanities-General, Historic Preservation, History & Archaeology, Libraries, Museums/Galleries, Music, Opera, Performing Arts, Public Broadcasting, Theater, Visual Arts
Civic & Public Affairs: African American Affairs, Asian American Affairs, Botanical Gardens/Parks, Economic Development, Employment/Job Training, Ethnic Organizations, Civic & Public Affairs-General, Hispanic Affairs, Housing, Law & Justice, Legal Aid, Municipalities/Towns, Native American Affairs, Nonprofit Management, Philanthropic Organizations, Public Policy, Rural Affairs, Safety, Urban & Community Affairs, Zoos/Aquariums
Education: Afterschool/Enrichment Programs, Arts/Humanities Education, Business Education, Business-School Partnerships, Colleges & Universities, Community & Junior Colleges, Continuing Education, Education Associations, Education Reform, Elementary Education (Private), Elementary Education (Public), Environmental Education, Faculty Development, Education-General, International Exchange, International Studies, Leadership Training, Literacy, Medical Education, Minority Education, Preschool Education, Private Education (Precollege), Public Education (Precollege), School Volunteerism, Science/Mathematics Education, Secondary Education (Private), Special Education
Environment: Air/Water Quality, Forestry, Environment-General, Protection, Resource Conservation, Watershed, Wildlife Protection
Health: AIDS/HIV, Alzheimers Disease, Cancer, Children's Health/Hospitals, Clinics/Medical Centers,

Emergency/Ambulance Services, Geriatric Health, Health Policy/Cost Containment, Health Organizations, Heart, Hospices, Hospitals, Long-Term Care, Medical Rehabilitation, Medical Research, Medical Training, Mental Health, Nursing Services, Prenatal Health Issues, Public Health, Single-Disease Health Associations
International: International Affairs
Religion: Jewish Causes, Ministries, Religious Organizations, Religious Welfare, Seminaries
Science: Science Museums, Scientific Centers & Institutes
Social Services: At-Risk Youth, Child Abuse, Child Welfare, Community Centers, Community Service Organizations, Day Care, Delinquency & Criminal Rehabilitation, Domestic Violence, Family Planning, Family Services, Food/Clothing Distribution, Homes, People with Disabilities, Recreation & Athletics, Refugee Assistance, Senior Services, Sexual Abuse, Shelters/Homelessness, Social Services-General, Substance Abuse, YMCA/YWCA/YMHA/YWHA, Youth Organizations

Application Procedures

Initial Contact: A grant application guidelines packet should be requested before submitting a proposal.
Application Requirements: The applicant should submit a completed application cover sheet (part of the packet); the organization's legal name and address; name, title, address, and telephone number of the person in charge of the project; a description of organization, including a summary of its background and its qualifications in the area for which funds are sought; list of names and primary affiliations of the organization's board of directors; organization's most recent financial statement; and a copy of the IRS tax-exemption letter. Only one copy of these materials should be submitted. The proposal itself should contain a statement from the chief operating officer that the project has been reviewed and recommended for submission by the governing board; description of the project and why it is important to undertake; description of the people, organizations, or groups expected to benefit from the project's outcome and the ways they would benefit; substantiation of the extent of need for these benefits; explanation of why the applicant organization is the appropriate one to conduct the project; description of the plan of action and a timetable for implementation; methods and criteria for assessing the project's effectiveness; qualifications of people involved in implementing the project; detailed descriptions of previous budgets, if the project is already in operation; detailed current budget for the project; description of other possible sources of support; and an explanation of how the project could be sustained after the period for which support has been requested.
Deadlines: None, for general proposals; January 15, April 15, and October 15 for the Small Grants program; and February 1 for the Support our Teacher Initiatives program.
Review Process: If a proposal submitted under the General Purpose guidelines passes a first review by the trustees, a staff member will contact the applicant for additional information. Final action on proposals passing first review will be made three to five months after submission. If a proposal is outside the field of interest of the trust, notification is given within two months. An applicant will be notified shortly after a decision has been reached on a proposal. Under the Small Grants program, a final decision will normally be made about twelve weeks after a deadline; incomplete proposals will not be considered. Under the Support for Teacher Initiatives program guidelines, applications submitted for the February 1 deadline are reviewed, and grantss will be announced in May.

Restrictions

The trust does not favor proposals seeking funds for direct grants, scholarships, or fellowships to individuals; endowments; general fund drives or annual appeals; general ongoing operating budgets; indirect or overhead costs (except as specifically and essentially related to the grant project); debt retirement or operational deficits; projects of sectarian or religious organizations whose principal benefit is for their own members; or propagandizing or influencing elections or legislation.
The trust will not replace funding for activities or materials previously provided by federal, state, or school district funds.

Additional Information

Applications are invited only from Oregon and Clark County, WA.
Publications: Annual Report; Grant Application Guidelines; Support for Teacher Initiatives Program Guidelines; General Purpose Grants Program Guidelines; Small Grants Program Guidelines

Foundation Officials

Debbie F. Craig: trustee
Travis Cross: trustee emeritus
Marie Deatherage: special programs officer
John Emrick: trustee
Orcilia Zuniga Forbes: trustee
Alice McCartor: program officer
Charline McDonald: program officer
Victor Merced: program officer
Warne Harry Nunn: trustee
Wayne George Pierson: treasurer ED California State University BS (1973). CORP AFFIL member advisory committee: Veta Partners; member advisory committee: New Enterprise Associates; member advisory committee: Roanoke Venture. NONPR AFFIL member: Oregon Society CPAs; member: Portland Society Financial Analysts; member: Association Investment Management & Research; member: Institute Chartered Financial Analysts Federation; member: American Institute of Certified Public Accountants.
G. Gerald Pratt: trustee
Charles S. Rooks: executive director B Whiteville, NC 1937. ED Wake Forest College BA (1959); Duke University MA (1964); Duke University PhD (1968). NONPR AFFIL advisory board: Neighborhood Partnership Fund; director: Pacific Northwest Grantmakers Forum.
Doug Stamm: executive director

Grants Analysis

Disclosure Period: fiscal year ending March 31, 2002
Total Grants: $24,735,559*
Number of Grants: 323
Average Grant: $76,581
Highest Grant: $1,350,000
Lowest Grant: $600
Typical Range: $600 to $1,350,000
***Note:** Grants analysis provided by foundation.

Recent Grants

Note: Grants derived from 2000 Form 990.

Library-Related
750,000	Lewis and Clark College, Portland, OR -- to expand and modernize the Northwestern School of Law Library
300,000	Southern Oregon Library Information System, Medford, OR -- for a shared automated catalog system

General
1,000,000	Oregon Coast Aquarium, Newport, OR -- for underwater passage
1,000,000	Portland Art Museum, Portland, OR -- complete renovation of the Bellschi Building complex
900,000	I Have A Dream Foundation, Portland, OR -- for start-up costs
800,000	Portland Opera Association, Portland, OR -- operating support
800,000	St. Mary's Home for Boys, Beaverton, OR -- renovate and expand the school

on the campus of this residential treatment facility for youth with emotional disabilities
500,000	Portland State University, Portland, OR -- for the Urban Center/University Plaza development
500,000	Southern Oregon University, Ashland, OR -- for the Center for the Visual Arts
382,763	Northwest Regional Education Service District, Hillsboro, OR -- for a 14 matching grant for students to build 10,000 computers for schools throughout Oregon
300,000	Arts Council of Pendleton, Inc., Pendleton, OR -- to restore the historic Carnegie Library building in Pendleton for use as a regional arts center
300,000	Oregon Children's Foundation, Portland, OR -- for a challenge grant to raise funds to expand the SMART Book and Reading Program

MEYERS CHARITABLE FAMILY FUND

Giving Contact

David R. Meyers, President
8748 S. Kells Dr.
Hickory Hills, IL 60457
Phone: (708)598-8111

Description

Founded: 1988
EIN: 363610777
Organization Type: Private Foundation
Grant Types: General Support.

Financial Summary

Total Giving: $199,370 (2001); $200,205 (2000); $198,685 (1999)
Assets: $2,325,416 (2001); $2,596,759 (2000); $2,788,578 (1999)

Typical Recipients

Arts & Humanities: Arts Centers, Ballet, Historic Preservation, Libraries, Music, Opera, Public Broadcasting, Theater
Civic & Public Affairs: Civic & Public Affairs-General, Native American Affairs, Public Policy, Urban & Community Affairs, Zoos/Aquariums
Education: Arts/Humanities Education, Colleges & Universities, International Studies, Medical Education, Private Education (Precollege), Secondary Education (Private), Special Education, Student Aid
Environment: Environment-General, Resource Conservation, Wildlife Protection
Health: AIDS/HIV, Children's Health/Hospitals, Clinics/Medical Centers, Medical Rehabilitation, Research/Studies Institutes
International: International Environmental Issues, International Organizations, International Peace & Security Issues
Religion: Churches, Religious Welfare, Social/Policy Issues
Science: Science Museums
Social Services: Animal Protection, At-Risk Youth, Child Welfare, Community Service Organizations, Family Services, Homes, People with Disabilities, Recreation & Athletics

Application Procedures

Initial Contact: The foundation has no formal grant application procedure or application form. Send a brief letter of inquiry.
Deadlines: None.

Restrictions

Grants are not made to individuals.

Foundation Officials

Margery McGrew: director
David R. Meyers: president, director
Frederick C. Meyers: secretary, treasurer

Grants Analysis

Disclosure Period: calendar year ending 2001
Total Grants: $199,370
Number of Grants: 141
Average Grant: $1,414
Highest Grant: $9,500
Typical Range: $1,000 to $5,000

Recent Grants

Note: Grants derived from 2001 Form 990.

General

9,500	Metropolitan Opera Association, New York, NY
7,500	Presbyterian College, Clinton, SC
7,400	Chicago Zoological Society, Chicago, IL
6,900	Sun Valley Summer Symphony, Sun Valley, ID
5,700	Cook Children's Hospital, Ft. Worth, TX
5,500	San Francisco Jazz Organization, San Francisco, CA
5,350	American Ballet Theater, New York, NY
5,000	Dennis Keller Scholarship Fund, Hinsdale, IL
5,000	NPR Foundation, San Francisco, CA
5,000	Roundabout Theater, New York, NY

MGE ENERGY, INC.

Company Headquarters

133 S. Blair St.
Madison, WI 53788
Web: http://www.mge.com

Company Description

Ticker: MGEE
Exchange: AMEX
Former Name: Madison Gas & Electric Co. (2001).
Assets: US$541.5 million (2001)
Employees: 676 (2001)
SIC(s): 4939 Combination Utility Nec.

Madison Gas & Electric Foundation

Giving Contact

Bonnie Juul, Grants Coordinator
PO Box 1231
Madison, WI 53701-1231
Phone: (608)252-7279

Description

Founded: 1966
EIN: 396098118
Organization Type: Corporate Foundation
Giving Locations: WI
Grant Types: General Support.

Donor Information

Founder: Madison Gas And Electric Co.

Financial Summary

Total Giving: $654,752 (2001); $379,142 (2000); $334,700 (1999)
Giving Analysis: Giving for 2001 includes: foundation scholarships ($2,000); foundation grants to United Way ($73,625); foundation ($579,127); 2000: foundation scholarships ($2,000); foundation grants

to United Way ($84,500); foundation ($292,592); 1999: foundation ($334,700)
Assets: $6,685,757 (2001); $8,542,502 (2000); $6,473,389 (1999)
Gifts Received: $1,250,000 (2001); $140,550 (1997); $116,222 (1996). Note: In 1996 and 2001, contributions were received from Madison Gas & Electric Co.

Typical Recipients

Arts & Humanities: Arts Associations & Councils, Arts Centers, Community Arts, Arts & Humanities-General, History & Archaeology, Libraries, Museums/Galleries, Music, Public Broadcasting, Theater
Civic & Public Affairs: African American Affairs, Asian American Affairs, Botanical Gardens/Parks, Business/Free Enterprise, Chambers of Commerce, Clubs, Community Foundations, Economic Development, Civic & Public Affairs-General, Housing, Parades/Festivals, Safety, Urban & Community Affairs, Women's Affairs, Zoos/Aquariums
Education: Business-School Partnerships, Colleges & Universities, Education Funds, Elementary Education (Public), Engineering/Technological Education, Education-General, Gifted & Talented Programs, Literacy, Minority Education, Preschool Education, Private Education (Precollege), Public Education (Precollege), Secondary Education (Public), Special Education, Student Aid
Environment: Environment-General
Health: AIDS/HIV, Cancer, Children's Health/Hospitals, Health Organizations, Heart, Hospices, Hospitals, Medical Rehabilitation, Medical Research, Prenatal Health Issues, Public Health, Single-Disease Health Associations
Religion: Ministries, Religious Organizations, Religious Welfare
Science: Scientific Centers & Institutes
Social Services: At-Risk Youth, Child Welfare, Community Centers, Community Service Organizations, Day Care, Domestic Violence, Emergency Relief, Family Services, Food/Clothing Distribution, Homes, People with Disabilities, Recreation & Athletics, Scouts, Senior Services, Shelters/Homelessness, Social Services-General, Special Olympics, United Funds/United Ways, Veterans, YMCA/YWCA/YMHA/YWHA, Youth Organizations

Application Procedures

Initial Contact: Scholarship application forms and deadline information are published in company newsletter. For organization grants, send a brief letter of inquiry.
Application Requirements: Include name, address, amount requested, and purpose of funds sought.
Deadlines: None.

Restrictions

Organizations must be located within Madison Gas & Electric Co.'s service territory in order to be considered.

Corporate Officials

Mr. Terry Hanson: chief financial officer vice president administration PRIM CORP EMPL chief financial officer: Madison Gas & Electric Co.
David Cummins Mebane: chairman, president, chief executive officer, director B Toledo, OH 1933. ED Arizona State University (1957); University of Wisconsin (1960). PRIM CORP EMPL chairman, president, chief executive officer, director: Madison Gas & Electric Co. CORP AFFIL director: First Federal Savings Bank Madison/LaCrosse; director: First Capital Investment Corp. Madison; director: First Federal Capital Corp. NONPR AFFIL director: Madison Gas & Electric Foundation Madison; trustee: University Wisconsin Research Park Corp.
Carol A. Wiskowski: assistant vice president administration PRIM CORP EMPL assistant vice president administration: Madison Gas & Electric Co.

Gary J. Wolter: senior vice president administration PRIM CORP EMPL senior vice president administration: Madison Gas & Electric Co.

Foundation Officials

Mr. Terry Hanson: secretary, treasurer (see above)
David Cummins Mebane: chairman, president (see above)
Richard Henry Thies: assistant treasurer B Reedsburg, WI 1941. ED University of Wisconsin (1963). PRIM CORP EMPL vice president gas system operation: Madison Gas & Electric Co. NONPR AFFIL secretary, director: Diggers Hotline; member: Midwest Gas Association; member: American Gas Association; member: American Public Works Association.
Carol A. Wiskowski: secretary (see above)
Gary J. Wolter: vice president (see above)

Grants Analysis

Disclosure Period: calendar year ending 2001
Total Grants: $579,127*
Number of Grants: 119
Average Grant: $3,739*
Highest Grant: $137,887
Lowest Grant: $50
Typical Range: $25 to $10,000
*Note: Giving excludes United Way and scholarships.

Recent Grants

Note: Grants derived from 2001 Form 990.

Library-Related

10,000	Monona Library, Monona, WI -- building fund

General

137,887	Madison Metropolitan School District, Madison, WI -- program support
62,092	Middleton-Cross Plains Area School District, Middleton, WI -- program support
53,625	United Way Dane County, Madison, WI -- program support
40,385	Edgewood High School, Ellettsville, IN -- program support
25,000	Genesis Development Corporation -- program support
25,000	Madison Community Foundation, Madison, WI -- program support
24,558	Abundant Life Christian School -- program support
23,682	Monona Grove School District, Monona, WI -- program support
20,000	Friends of Henry Vilas Zoological Society -- program support
20,000	United Way Dane County, Madison, WI -- for building program

HERBERT I. AND ELSA B. MICHAEL FOUNDATION

Giving Contact

c/o US Bank National Association
PO Box 3058
Salt Lake City, UT 84110-3058
Phone: (801)534-6085

Description

Founded: 1950
EIN: 876122556
Organization Type: Private Foundation
Giving Locations: UT
Grant Types: General Support, Scholarship.

Donor Information

Founder: the late Elsa B. Michael

Financial Summary

Total Giving: $487,677 (fiscal year ending September 30, 2001); $346,500 (fiscal 2000); $319,256 (fiscal 1998). Note: Fiscal 1997 Giving includes matching gifts ($6,000); scholarship ($2,500).
Giving Analysis: Giving for fiscal 2001 includes: foundation scholarships ($44,500); fiscal 2000: foundation scholarships ($23,000); fiscal 1998: foundation grants to United Way ($5,000) foundation scholarships ($23,250)
Assets: $7,028,683 (fiscal 2001); $9,202,618 (fiscal 2000); $6,862,226 (fiscal 1998)

Typical Recipients

Arts & Humanities: Arts Associations & Councils, Arts Centers, Ballet, Dance, Historic Preservation, History & Archaeology, Libraries, Museums/Galleries, Music, Opera, Public Broadcasting
Civic & Public Affairs: Botanical Gardens/Parks, Civil Rights, Clubs, Law & Justice, Legal Aid, Urban & Community Affairs
Education: Arts/Humanities Education, Business Education, Colleges & Universities, Education Funds, Education-General, International Exchange, Legal Education, Literacy, Medical Education, Preschool Education, Science/Mathematics Education, Student Aid
Environment: Resource Conservation, Wildlife Protection
Health: AIDS/HIV, Alzheimers Disease, Children's Health/Hospitals, Clinics/Medical Centers, Emergency/Ambulance Services, Health Organizations, Hospices, Hospitals, Medical Training, Prenatal Health Issues, Public Health, Respiratory, Single-Disease Health Associations, Speech & Hearing, Trauma Treatment
International: Foreign Arts Organizations
Religion: Religious Organizations, Religious Welfare, Social/Policy Issues
Social Services: At-Risk Youth, Child Welfare, Community Service Organizations, Crime Prevention, Day Care, Domestic Violence, Family Planning, Family Services, Food/Clothing Distribution, People with Disabilities, YMCA/YWCA/YMHA/YWHA, Youth Organizations

Application Procedures

Initial Contact: The foundation requests applications be made in writing. Include purpose of funds sought.
Deadlines: None.

Additional Information

Trust(s): US Bank National Association

Foundation Officials

Peter Billings, Jr.: trustee
Arthur K. Smith: trustee
Tracy D. Smith: trustee
Hal Swenson: trustee
Michael David Zimmerman: trustee B Chicago, IL 1943. ED University of Utah BS (1966); University of Utah JD (1969). NONPR AFFIL fellow: UT Constitutional Revisions Comm; chairman, fellow: UT Judicial Council; fellow: UT Bar Association; chief justice: Supreme Court Utah; prof law: University Utah; fellow: Salt Lake County Bar Association; dir, fellow: Snowbird Institute Arts & Humanities; trustee: Rowland-Hall Saint Marks School; member: Phi Kappa Phi; trustee: Hubert & Eliza B. Phibard Foundation; fellow: Judical Conf; member: Order Coif; director: Conf Chief Justices; fellow: Am Law Institute; fellow: Awareness Day Foundation; fellow: Am Inns Court VII; director: Am Judicature Society; fellow: Am Bar Association; fellow: Am Bar Foundation.

Grants Analysis

Disclosure Period: fiscal year ending September 30, 2001
Total Grants: $443,177*
Number of Grants: 49
Average Grant: $3,670*
Highest Grant: $100,000
Typical Range: $1,000 to $10,000
*Note: Giving excludes scholarships. Average grant figure excludes two highest grants ($170,677).

Recent Grants

Note: Grants derived from fiscal 2000 Form 990.

General

100,000	Scottish Rite Foundation of Utah, UT -- Herbert I & Elsa Michael Diagnostic Center
20,000	Westminster College, Salt Lake City, UT -- scholarships for needy students
12,500	Guadeloupe Center, Salt Lake City, UT -- instructional costs early learning center
10,000	University of Utah, Salt Lake City, UT -- tuition wavers for entering freshman
10,000	University of Utah College of Law, Salt Lake City, UT -- needy law students
10,000	University of Utah Museum of Natural History, Salt Lake City, UT -- upgrading outreach kits program
10,000	Utah Legal Services, Salt Lake City, UT -- community involvement project
7,500	Junior Achievement of Utah, Salt Lake City, UT -- programs
7,500	University of Utah Center for Science Education and Outreach, Salt Lake City, UT -- Edison project
6,500	Utah Opera Company, Salt Lake City, UT -- community outreach program

MICROSOFT CORP.

Company Headquarters

Redmond, WA
Web: http://www.microsoft.com

Company Description

Founded: 1975
Ticker: MSFT
Exchange: NASDAQ
Operating Revenue: US$28.365 billion (2002)
Profit: US$7.829 billion (2002)
Employees: 50500 (2002)
Fortune Rank: 47, per FORTUNE Magazine's list of 500 Largest U.S. Corporations (2002).
SIC(s): 7371 Computer Programming Services, 7372 Prepackaged Software.

Operating Locations

Microsoft Corp. (CA--Foster City, Sacramento; CO--Boulder; CT--Farmington; DC--Washington; FL--Fort Lauderdale; IL--Villa Park; IN--Indianapolis; MA--Newton, Waltham; MN--Bloomington; MO--Kansas City, St. Louis; NY--New York, Rochester; NC--Charlotte; OH--Chagrin Falls, Cincinnati; TX--Dallas, Houston; WA--Bothell)
Note: Operates in 21 countries.

Nonmonetary Support

Value: $179,023,000 (2001); $199,456,000 (2000); $79,013,000 (1999)
Type: Donated Products
Note: Product donations recorded at estimated retail value.
Contact: Jane Meseck, Program Manager

Giving Contact

Bruce M. Brooks, Director, Community Affairs
One Microsoft Way
Redmond, WA 98052-6399

Phone: (425)882-8080
Fax: (425)936-7329
E-mail: giving@microsoft.com
Web: http://www.microsoft.com/Giving

Description

Organization Type: Corporate Giving Program
Giving Locations: WA: some national initiatives.
Grant Types: Capital, Emergency, Employee Matching Gifts, General Support, Matching, Scholarship.
Note: Employee matching gift ratio: 1 to 1 for contributions of cash, stock, or software up to $12,000 per employee annually.

Financial Summary

Total Giving: $246,900,000 (fiscal year ending June 31, 2002); $215,777,000 (fiscal 2001); $233,711,000 (fiscal 2000). Note: Contributes through corporate direct giving program only.
Giving Analysis: Giving for fiscal 2001 includes: foundation scholarships ($453,000); corporate direct giving ($18,722,000); corporate matching gifts ($44,707,000); nonmonetary support ($151,895,000); fiscal 2000: international subsidiaries ($8,590,000); corporate direct giving ($34,254,500); domestic subsidiaries ($196,245,500); nonmonetary support ($199,456,000); fiscal 1999: corporate direct giving ($25,646,000); nonmonetary support ($79,013,000);

Typical Recipients

Arts & Humanities: Arts Associations & Councils, Arts & Humanities-General, Historic Preservation, Libraries, Museums/Galleries
Civic & Public Affairs: African American Affairs, Business/Free Enterprise, Civic & Public Affairs-General, Hispanic Affairs, Zoos/Aquariums
Education: Colleges & Universities, Education Associations, Education Reform, Education-General, Minority Education, Private Education (Precollege)
Environment: Environment-General, Protection, Wildlife Protection
Health: AIDS/HIV, Cancer, Children's Health/Hospitals, Emergency/Ambulance Services, Kidney, Medical Rehabilitation, Single-Disease Health Associations, Transplant Networks/Donor Banks
International: Foreign Educational Institutions, International Relief Efforts, Missionary/Religious Activities
Religion: Jewish Causes, Religious Organizations, Religious Welfare
Science: Science Museums, Scientific Centers & Institutes
Social Services: Child Welfare, Community Service Organizations, Domestic Violence, Family Services, Food/Clothing Distribution, People with Disabilities, Social Services-General, YMCA/YWCA/YMHA/YWHA, Youth Organizations

Application Procedures

Initial Contact: Contact community relations to request guidelines or review them on the Microsoft giving web site. Nonprofit organizations located in Washington State may submit a full proposal for cash donations. Washington organizations wishing to apply for a software donation should request an application form. Nonprofit organizations located outside of Washington State and wishing to apply for a cash or product donation should contact its local Microsoft field office, as each office has its own set of guidelines. A list of field offices is available at the following web site: www.microsoft.com/usa/map.asp.
Application Requirements: Washington State proposals should include a description of organization, including mission, major accomplishments, governance, area and population served; amount requested and a detailed description of the project or activity for which support is being requested; operating budget for the current fiscal year, including fund sources; list of funding sources for the current fiscal year, including amounts received; project budget (if applicable); list of current board members and

key staff; recently audited financial statement; and copy of IRS tax-exempt determination letter.

Deadlines: For community support grants, tax-exempt organizations may submit requests throughout the year. However, internal grantmaking deadlines are the 15th of February, May, or October.

Decision Notification: Applicants will be notified approximately one month after the deadline.

Notes: Proposal materials cannot be returned. Company will request further information, if necessary.

Restrictions

The following are not eligible for Microsoft donations of cash or software: individuals; private foundations; nonprofit organizations without 501(c)(3) status; hospitals; conferences of symposia; sponsorship of events, tables, exhibitions, or performances; fundraising events such as luncheons, dinners, walks, runs, or sports; U.S.-based organizations serving people and communities outside the country; K-12 schools; political, labor and fraternal organizations; and religious organizations without a secular community designation.

Additional Information

Publications: Annual Report; Guidelines

Corporate Officials

Steven Anthony Ballmer: president, chief executive officer, director administration, chief financial officer B Detroit, MI March 24, 1956. ED Harvard University Graduate School of Business Administration; Stanford University Graduate School of Business Administration. PRIM CORP EMPL president, chief executive officer, director: Microsoft Corp.

Bruce M. Brooks: director community affairs PRIM CORP EMPL director community affairs: Microsoft Corp. ADD CORP EMPL senior vice president: MMW/Savit.

John Connors: senior vice president finance & administration, chief financial officer PRIM CORP EMPL senior vice president finance & administration, chief financial officer: Microsoft Corp.

William Henry Gates, III: co-founder, chairman, chief software architect B Seattle, WA October 28, 1955. ED Harvard University (1975). PRIM CORP EMPL co-founder, chairman, chief software architect: Microsoft Corp. ADD CORP EMPL chairman: Corbis Corp. CORP AFFIL director: ICOS; director: Teledesic Corp.

Robert J. Herbold: executive vice president ED Case Western Reserve University MS; Case Western Reserve University PhD. PRIM CORP EMPL executive vice president: Microsoft Corp.

Giving Program Officials

Rodney Hines: program manager

Christopher Jones: senior program officer (see above)

Cathleen MacCaul: communications manager

Sarah Meyer: senior program officer (see above)

Heidi Salstrom: program manager

Linda Testa: program manager

Jane Meseck Yeager: program manager (see above)

Grants Analysis

Disclosure Period: fiscal year ending June 31, 2001

Total Grants: $170,617,000*

Number of Grants: 5,000 (approx)

Average Grant: $34,123 (approx)

Typical Range: $5,000 to $25,000

*Note: Giving excludes matching gifts. Giving includes nonmonetary support.

Recent Grants

Note: Grants derived from 2001 Annual Report.

Library-Related

Milwaukee Public Library, Milwaukee, WI
Albany Public Library, Albany, NY

General

AIDS Project Los Angeles, Los Angeles, CA
Alder Planetarium, Chicago, IL
American Council on Education, Washington, DC
Arizona Center for the Blind and Visually Impaired, Phoenix, AZ
Association for Cultural Exchange, New York, NY
Battered Women's Alternatives, San Francisco, CA
Boys and Girls Clubs of Greater Dallas, Inc., Dallas, TX
California Health Collaborative Foundation, Fresno, CA
Catholic Charities, Syracuse, NY
Catholic Community Services of Western Washington, Bremerton, WA

MID-IOWA HEALTH FOUNDATION

Giving Contact

Kathryn Bradley, Principal Manager
550 39th St., Suite 104
Des Moines, IA 50312
Phone: (515)277-6411
Fax: (515)274-4188

Description

Founded: 1984
EIN: 421235348
Organization Type: Private Foundation
Giving Locations: IA: Polk County and the eight surrounding counties
Grant Types: Capital, General Support, Operating Expenses, Scholarship.

Financial Summary

Total Giving: $599,725 (2002); $772,166 (1999); $745,754 (1998)
Giving Analysis: Giving for 1999 includes: foundation scholarships ($24,000) 1998: foundation scholarships ($24,000)
Assets: $14,479,291 (2002); $17,575,699 (1999); $17,960,117 (1998)

Typical Recipients

Arts & Humanities: Arts & Humanities-General, Libraries, Public Broadcasting

Civic & Public Affairs: Business/Free Enterprise, Community Foundations, Employment/Job Training, Civic & Public Affairs-General, Housing, Women's Affairs

Education: Afterschool/Enrichment Programs, Agricultural Education, Colleges & Universities, Community & Junior Colleges, Health & Physical Education, Medical Education, Preschool Education, Public Education (Precollege), Student Aid

Health: AIDS/HIV, Alzheimers Disease, Arthritis, Cancer, Children's Health/Hospitals, Clinics/Medical Centers, Diabetes, Emergency/Ambulance Services, Health-General, Geriatric Health, Health Organizations, Home-Care Services, Hospices, Hospitals, Medical Rehabilitation, Mental Health, Mental Health, Nursing Services, Nutrition, Prenatal Health Issues, Public Health, Respiratory, Trauma Treatment

Religion: Churches, Ministries, Religious Welfare

Social Services: At-Risk Youth, Big Brother/Big Sister, Child Abuse, Child Welfare, Community Service Organizations, Counseling, Day Care, Family Planning, Family Services, Food/Clothing Distribution, People with Disabilities, Recreation & Athletics, Scouts, Senior Services, Shelters/Homelessness, Special Olympics, Substance Abuse, United Funds/United Ways, YMCA/YWCA/YMHA/YWHA, Youth Organizations

Application Procedures

Initial Contact: Send a brief letter of inquiry.

Application Requirements: Request application form.

Deadlines: None. Applications are reviewed quarterly.

Restrictions

Grants are awarded for health service programs.

Additional Information

Publications: Application Guidelines

Foundation Officials

Rex Burns: vice chairman
Terry Caldwell-Johnson: director
Simon Casady: director
Nolden Gentry: director
Don C. Green: secretary, treasurer
Rob Hayes: director
Thomas Jeschke: director
Ivan Johnson: chairman
Sally Pederson: director
T. Ward Phillips: director
Judith Vogel: director

Grants Analysis

Disclosure Period: calendar year ending 2002
Total Grants: $599,725
Number of Grants: 47
Average Grant: $12,760
Highest Grant: $50,000
Lowest Grant: $1,000
Typical Range: $5,000 to $25,000

Recent Grants

Note: Grants derived from 2002 Form 990.

General

50,000	Center for Healthy Communities, Des Moines, IA -- Robert Wood Johnson Neighborhood Health Access Initiative
45,000	Des Moines Health Center, Des Moines, IA -- Dental Sealant and Education Program
35,000	Heart and Hands Inc. -- expansion of clinic services
30,000	La Clinica de la Esperanza -- Centering Pregnancy Program
25,000	Convalescent Home for Children, Ames, IA -- Child Serve campaign
25,000	Des Moines Health Center, Des Moines, IA -- oral health mobile van
25,000	Greater Des Moines Community Foundation, Des Moines, IA -- Number One Quest campaign
25,000	Primary Health Care, Inc. -- emergency funding
16,500	Young Women's Resource Center, Des Moines, IA -- health programs
15,000	Creative Visions, Des Moines, IA -- support for outreach liaison

MIDCONTINENT MEDIA, INC.

Company Headquarters

7900 Xerxes Avenue S., Suite 1100
Minneapolis, MN 55431
Web: http://www.midcocomm.com

Company Description

Employees: 1,100
SIC(s): 4800 Communications, 4832 Radio Broadcasting Stations, 4833 Television Broadcasting Stations, 4841 Cable & Other Pay Television Services.

Operating Locations

Midcontinent Media Inc. (SD--Aberdeen, Sioux Falls; WI--Madison)

Nonmonetary Support

Type: Donated Equipment; In-kind Services

Midcontinent Media Foundation

Giving Contact

Steven E. Grosser, Vice President & Director
Midcontinent Media Foundation
3600 Minnesota Dr., Suite 700
Minneapolis, MN 55435
Phone: (952)844-2600
Fax: (952)844-2660
Web: http://www.midcocomm.com/foundation.php

Description

Founded: 1987
EIN: 363556764
Organization Type: Corporate Foundation
Giving Locations: operating locations.
Grant Types: Employee Matching Gifts, General Support, Operating Expenses, Project.

Donor Information

Founder: Midcontinent Media

Financial Summary

Total Giving: $135,446 (fiscal year ending August 31, 2001); $164,787 (fiscal 1999); $103,362 (fiscal 1998)
Giving Analysis: Giving for fiscal 2001 includes: foundation grants to United Way ($4,702); fiscal 1999: foundation grants to United Way ($8,500) foundation ($156,287)
Assets: $103,262 (fiscal 2001); $382,202 (fiscal 1999); $229,312 (fiscal 1998)
Gifts Received: $100,000 (fiscal 1999); $105,000 (fiscal 1998); $100,000 (fiscal 1997). Note: In fiscal 1999, contributions were received from Midcontinent Media Inc. In fiscal 1994, contributions were received from Midcontinent Media.

Typical Recipients

Arts & Humanities: Ethnic & Folk Arts, Arts & Humanities-General, Historic Preservation, History & Archaeology, Libraries, Museums/Galleries, Music, Performing Arts, Public Broadcasting, Theater
Civic & Public Affairs: Botanical Gardens/Parks, Clubs, Community Foundations, Economic Development, Employment/Job Training, Civic & Public Affairs-General, Housing, Legal Aid, Municipalities/Towns, Philanthropic Organizations, Professional & Trade Associations, Public Policy, Safety, Urban & Community Affairs, Women's Affairs, Zoos/Aquariums
Education: Afterschool/Enrichment Programs, Agricultural Education, Business Education, Colleges & Universities, Elementary Education (Public), Education-General, Literacy, Private Education (Precollege), Public Education (Precollege)
Environment: Resource Conservation
Health: Children's Health/Hospitals, Emergency/Ambulance Services, Hospitals, Medical Rehabilitation, Multiple Sclerosis, Prenatal Health Issues
Religion: Ministries, Religious Organizations, Religious Welfare
Social Services: At-Risk Youth, Camps, Child Welfare, Community Service Organizations, Day Care, Domestic Violence, Family Services, Food/Clothing Distribution, People with Disabilities, Recreation & Athletics, Scouts, Senior Services, Social Services-General, Special Olympics, United Funds/United Ways, Volunteer Services, YMCA/YWCA/YMHA/YWHA, Youth Organizations

Application Procedures

Initial Contact: Obtain and complete a "Requestor Form" from a company employee. Attach additional literature that will assist the board in its consideration of the request.
Deadlines: August 1 and February 1.

Restrictions

Only requests submitted and sponsored by an employee of a Midcontinent Media operating company are considered. Preference is given to special projects rather than general operating funds.

Additional Information

The guidelines brochure includes the foundation's evaluative criteria and a list of operating companies.
Publications: Guidelines; Requestor Form

Corporate Officials

Nathan L. Bentson: chairman, chief executive officer, director PRIM CORP EMPL chairman, chief executive officer, director: Midcontinent Media.
Joseph H. Floyd: president, director PRIM CORP EMPL president, director: Midcontinent Media.

Foundation Officials

Nathan L. Bentson: chairman, president (see above)
Henry Clark: vice president, director
David Fetters: vice president, director
Joseph H. Floyd: vice president, director (see above)
Vickie Geier: secretary
Steven E. Grosser: executive director, treasurer
Tom Simmons: assistant secretary, director PRIM CORP EMPL vice president: Midcontinent Media Inc.
Jerry Steever: vice president, director

Grants Analysis

Disclosure Period: fiscal year ending August 31, 2001
Total Grants: $130,744*
Number of Grants: 100
Average Grant: $1,307
Highest Grant: $10,000
Lowest Grant: $25
Typical Range: $500 to $2,500
*Note: Giving excludes United Way.

Recent Grants

Note: Grants derived from 2000 Form 990.

General

9,036	United Way
8,250	Madison Community Foundation, Madison, WI
7,000	American Red Cross Sioux Falls, Sioux Falls, SD
6,456	United Way
6,000	South Dakota Discovery Center and Aquarium, Pierre, SD
5,000	Habitat for Humanity
4,760	Variety 99 Carousel Gala
4,000	Resource Center for Women and Their Families, Somerville, NJ
3,000	Mayport Hockey Association
3,000	Sioux Falls Sound and Light Show, Sioux Falls, SD

MIDDENDORF FOUNDATION

Giving Contact

E. Phillips Hathaway, President & Trustee
2 East Read Street
Baltimore, MD 21202
Phone: (410)752-7088
Fax: (410)625-5728

Description

Founded: 1953
EIN: 526048944
Organization Type: General Purpose Foundation
Giving Locations: MD

Grant Types: Endowment, General Support, Matching, Professorship.

Donor Information

Founder: Incorporated in 1953 by the late J. William Middendorf Jr. and the late Alice C. Middendorf .

Financial Summary

Total Giving: $1,000,000 (fiscal year ending March 31, 2002 approx); $1,675,500 (fiscal 2001); $1,086,200 (fiscal 1999)
Giving Analysis: Giving for fiscal 2001 includes: foundation grants to United Way ($15,000) fiscal 1997: foundation scholarships ($190,000)
Assets: $27,000,000 (fiscal 2002 approx); $32,100,226 (fiscal 2001); $30,048,059 (fiscal 1999)

Typical Recipients

Arts & Humanities: Arts Centers, Arts Institutes, Arts Outreach, Dance, Historic Preservation, History & Archaeology, Libraries, Museums/Galleries, Music, Opera, Public Broadcasting, Theater
Civic & Public Affairs: Botanical Gardens/Parks, Community Foundations, Economic Development, Employment/Job Training, Civic & Public Affairs-General, Legal Aid, Philanthropic Organizations, Professional & Trade Associations, Zoos/Aquariums
Education: Agricultural Education, Arts/Humanities Education, Colleges & Universities, Education Funds, Education Reform, Education-General, Medical Education, Private Education (Precollege), Science/Mathematics Education, Special Education, Student Aid
Environment: Air/Water Quality, Environment-General, Wildlife Protection
Health: Cancer, Clinics/Medical Centers, Emergency/Ambulance Services, Eyes/Blindness, Health-General, Geriatric Health, Health Organizations, Hospices, Hospitals, Mental Health, Prenatal Health Issues, Preventive Medicine/Wellness Organizations, Public Health, Respiratory, Single-Disease Health Associations, Trauma Treatment
International: Health Care/Hospitals, International Organizations, International Relief Efforts
Religion: Churches, Dioceses, Religion-General, Ministries, Religious Organizations, Religious Welfare
Science: Scientific Centers & Institutes
Social Services: Child Abuse, Child Welfare, Community Service Organizations, Crime Prevention, Emergency Relief, Family Planning, Family Services, Family Services, Food/Clothing Distribution, People with Disabilities, Recreation & Athletics, Scouts, Shelters/Homelessness, Special Olympics, Substance Abuse, United Funds/United Ways, YMCA/YWCA/YMHA/YWHA, Youth Organizations

Application Procedures

Initial Contact: The foundation requests applications be made in writing.
Application Requirements: The foundation requests that applicants include all supporting documentation in the initial proposal.
Deadlines: None.

Restrictions

Grants are not made to individuals.

Foundation Officials

Forrest F. Bramble, Jr.: vice president, trustee PRIM CORP EMPL partner: Barton & Wilmer Niles. CORP AFFIL director: C R Daniels Inc.; secretary: Crosby Marketing Communications.
E. Phillips Hathaway: president, trustee ED University of Virginia (1942).
Sealy H. Hopkinson: trustee
Theresa N. Knell: secretary, trustee
Craig Lewis: treasurer, trustee B 1930. PRIM NONPR EMPL principal, director: Investment Counsel Maryland.

Grants Analysis

Disclosure Period: fiscal year ending March 31, 2001
Total Grants: $1,660,500*
Number of Grants: 41
Average Grant: $20,554*
Highest Grant: $250,000
Typical Range: $10,000 to $40,000
*Note: Giving excludes United Way. Average grant excludes four highest grants ($900,000).

Recent Grants

Note: Grants derived from 2000 Form 990.

General

250,000	Faison Presbyterian Church, Faison, NC -- to aid survivors of Hurricane Floyd
75,000	Goodwill Industries of the Chesapeake, Inc, Baltimore, MD -- capital campaign
50,000	Boys Latin School of Maryland, Baltimore, MD -- computer technology and endowment fund
50,000	Ladew Topiary Gardens, Monkton, MD -- endowment for nature walk
50,000	Living Classrooms Foundation, Baltimore, MD -- toward Project SERVE
50,000	University of Virginia Alumni Association, Charlottesville, VA -- Jefferson Scholarship Program
35,000	Baltimore Association for Retarded Citizens, Baltimore, MD -- capital campaign
30,000	Family and Children Services of Central Maryland, Baltimore, MD -- support funding of marketing campaign
30,000	National Council on Alcoholism Maryland Chapter, Baltimore, MD -- expand program
25,000	Episcopal Ministries to the Aging, Inc., Sykesville, MD -- endowment fund

GEORGE H. AND JANE A. MIFFLIN MEMORIAL FUND

Giving Contact

Peter B. Loring, Trustee
c/o Loring, Wolcott & Coolidge
230 Congress St.
Boston, MA 02110
Phone: (617)523-6531

Description

EIN: 046384983
Organization Type: Private Foundation
Giving Locations: MA
Grant Types: Project, Scholarship.

Donor Information

Founder: George H. Mifflin, Jane A. Mifflin

Financial Summary

Total Giving: $1,850,700 (fiscal year ending September 30, 2000); $1,245,500 (fiscal 1998); $999,500 (fiscal 1997)
Giving Analysis: Giving for fiscal 1998 includes: foundation scholarships ($36,000); fiscal 1997: foundation scholarships ($62,000) foundation ($937,500)
Assets: $46,934,738 (fiscal 2000); $30,931,417 (fiscal 1998); $28,455,734 (fiscal 1997)
Gifts Received: $22,639 (fiscal 1997); $1,563,602 (fiscal 1996); $78,741 (fiscal 1992)

Typical Recipients

Arts & Humanities: Historic Preservation, Libraries, Literary Arts, Museums/Galleries, Music, Theater
Civic & Public Affairs: Botanical Gardens/Parks, Economic Development, Employment/Job Training, Civic & Public Affairs-General, Hispanic Affairs, Housing, Law & Justice, Legal Aid, Municipalities/Towns, Public Policy, Urban & Community Affairs, Women's Affairs, Zoos/Aquariums
Education: Colleges & Universities, Continuing Education, Education Reform, Education-General, Leadership Training, Minority Education, Preschool Education, Private Education (Precollege), Public Education (Precollege), Secondary Education (Private), Student Aid, Vocational & Technical Education
Environment: Forestry, Environment-General, Resource Conservation, Wildlife Protection
Health: AIDS/HIV, Clinics/Medical Centers, Health Organizations, Mental Health, Public Health, Single-Disease Health Associations
International: International Affairs, International Environmental Issues
Religion: Ministries, Religious Organizations, Social/Policy Issues
Social Services: Animal Protection, Community Service Organizations, Counseling, Crime Prevention, Domestic Violence, Family Services, Food/Clothing Distribution, Recreation & Athletics, Senior Services, Shelters/Homelessness, Volunteer Services, Youth Organizations

Application Procedures

Initial Contact: Contact foundation by phone or in writing.
Deadlines: None.

Restrictions

Does not support individuals.

Foundation Officials

John G. Brooks, Esq.: trustee
Lawrence Coolidge: trustee B Boston, MA 1936. ED Harvard University Graduate School of Business Administration (1962). PRIM CORP EMPL chairman: Seven Islands Land Co. CORP AFFIL director: Hollingsworth & Vose Co.; trustee: Loring Wolcott & Co.olidge Office; director: Big Sandy Co.
Peter B. Loring: trustee

Grants Analysis

Disclosure Period: fiscal year ending September 30, 2000
Total Grants: $1,850,700
Number of Grants: 79
Average Grant: $23,427
Highest Grant: $100,000
Typical Range: $5,000 to $50,000

Recent Grants

Note: Grants derived from fiscal 2000 Form 990.

General

100,000	New England Forestry Foundation, Groton, MA -- for the purchase of a conservation easement on Pingree forestland
80,000	Boston Athenaeum, Boston, MA -- for a renovation project
80,000	Peabody Essex Museum, Essex, MA -- for the third century campaign
75,000	Foundation of Success, Bellevue, WA -- for operating support
60,000	Greater Boston Legal Services, Boston, MA -- for the window replacement project
57,000	South Boston Harbor Academy Charter School, South Boston, MA -- for the development director
55,000	Conservatory Lab Charter School, Boston, MA -- for the development director
55,000	Roxbury College Preparatory Charter School, Roxbury, MA -- for the development director
53,000	Academy of the Pacific Rim, Hyde Park, MA -- for the development director
51,000	Lowell Middlesex Academy Charter School, Lowell, MA -- for the development director

MILLBROOK TRIBUTE GARDEN

Giving Contact

Kathy Shanks, Secretary
PO Box AC
Millbrook, NY 12545
Phone: (845)677-6823

Description

Founded: 1943
EIN: 141340079
Organization Type: General Purpose Foundation
Giving Locations: NY: Millbrook and vicinity
Grant Types: Capital, General Support, Project, Scholarship.

Financial Summary

Total Giving: $1,437,809 (fiscal year ending September 30, 2001); $1,349,500 (fiscal 1998); $1,243,300 (fiscal 1997)
Assets: $36,760,397 (fiscal 2001); $33,222,051 (fiscal 1998); $32,733,085 (fiscal 1997)

Typical Recipients

Arts & Humanities: Art History, Arts Associations & Councils, Arts Festivals, Arts Institutes, Ballet, Film & Video, History & Archaeology, Libraries, Music, Public Broadcasting, Theater
Civic & Public Affairs: Botanical Gardens/Parks, Clubs, Community Foundations, Civic & Public Affairs-General, Municipalities/Towns, Zoos/Aquariums
Education: Colleges & Universities, Environmental Education, Literacy, Minority Education, Private Education (Precollege), Secondary Education (Private), Secondary Education (Public), Student Aid
Environment: Environment-General, Protection, Research, Resource Conservation, Wildlife Protection
Health: AIDS/HIV, Hospices, Hospitals, Medical Rehabilitation
International: International Environmental Issues
Religion: Churches, Religious Organizations, Religious Welfare
Social Services: Animal Protection, Big Brother/Big Sister, Child Welfare, Community Service Organizations, Family Planning, Family Services, Homes, Recreation & Athletics, Scouts, Senior Services, Social Services-General, Volunteer Services, Youth Organizations

Application Procedures

Initial Contact: The foundation requests applications be made in writing.
Application Requirements: Written proposals should include supporting materials explaining the purpose of the request and a financial statement.
Deadlines: None.

Restrictions

The foundation makes grants only to public charities under section 501(c)(3) of the IRS code, in the immediate vicinity of Millbrook, NY. Grants are not made to individuals.

Foundation Officials

Felicitas Selter Thorne: vice president
Oakleigh Thorne: trustee B 1957. ED Boston University BS (1980); Columbia University MBA (1986). PRIM CORP EMPL president, chief executive officer: CCH Inc. CORP AFFIL director: Connecticut Corp. System.
Oakleigh Blakeman Thorne: president, trustee B Santa Barbara, CA 1932. ED Harvard University BA (1954). PRIM NONPR EMPL chairman, president legal info: Commerce Clearing House. CORP AFFIL director: Bank Millbrook; chairman, director: Connecticut Corp. System.
Vincent N. Turletes: trustee CORP AFFIL director: Bank Millbrook.

George T. Whalen, Jr.: trustee PRIM CORP EMPL president, director: Bank Millbrook.
Robert W. Whalen: trustee

Grants Analysis

Disclosure Period: fiscal year ending September 30, 2001
Total Grants: $1,437,809
Number of Grants: 74
Average Grant: $14,733*
Highest Grant: $200,000
Typical Range: $5,000 to $25,000
*Note: Averge grant figure excludes two highest grants ($377,000).

Recent Grants

Note: Grants derived from fiscal 2000 Form 990.

Library-Related

120,000	Millbrook Free Library, Millbrook, NY

General

200,000	Dutchess Day School, Millbrook, NY
115,000	St. Francis Hospital, Poughkeepsie, NY
110,000	Cardinal Hayes Home, Millbrook, NY
100,000	Millbrook School, Millbrook, NY
78,500	Village of Millbrook, Millbrook, NY
70,000	Lyall Memorial Federated Church, Millbrook, NY
50,000	Bard College, Annandale-on-Hudson, NY
50,000	Institute of Ecosystems, Millbrook, NY
35,000	Dutchess Land Conservancy, Bangall, NY
35,000	Millbrook Central School, Millbrook, NY

MILLER BREWING CO. (EDEN, NC)

Company Headquarters

863 E. Meadow Rd.
Eden, NC 27288
Web: http://www.millerbrewingcompany.com

Company Description

Employees: 900
SIC(s): 2000 Food & Kindred Products.
Parent Company: Altria Group, Inc., 120 Park Ave., New York, NY, United States

Nonmonetary Support

Type: Donated Equipment; Donated Products; Loaned Employees

Giving Contact

Brenda Williams, Community Relations
PO Box 3327
Eden, NC 27289
Phone: (336)627-2100

Description

Organization Type: Corporate Giving Program
Giving Locations: principally near operating locations and to national organizations.
Grant Types: Emergency, General Support, Multiyear/Continuing Support.

Typical Recipients

Arts & Humanities: Arts Appreciation, Arts Associations & Councils, Arts Festivals, Arts Funds, Arts Outreach, Community Arts, Dance, Ethnic & Folk Arts, Arts & Humanities-General, Historic Preservation, Libraries, Museums/Galleries, Music, Performing Arts, Theater, Visual Arts
Civic & Public Affairs: African American Affairs, Business/Free Enterprise, Chambers of Commerce, Civil Rights, Clubs, Economic Development, Employment/Job Training, Ethnic Organizations, Gay/Lesbian Issues, Civic & Public Affairs-General, Hispanic Affairs, Municipalities/Towns, Parades/Festivals, Philanthropic Organizations, Rural Affairs, Safety, Women's Affairs
Education: Afterschool/Enrichment Programs, Agricultural Education, Arts/Humanities Education, Business-School Partnerships, Colleges & Universities, Community & Junior Colleges, Elementary Education (Private), Engineering/Technological Education, Education-General, Literacy
Environment: Environment-General, Resource Conservation, Wildlife Protection
Health: AIDS/HIV, Emergency/Ambulance Services, Health-General, Health Policy/Cost Containment, Hospices, Nutrition
International: Health Care/Hospitals
Science: Science-General
Social Services: Animal Protection, At-Risk Youth, Camps, Community Centers, Community Service Organizations, Counseling, Delinquency & Criminal Rehabilitation, Food/Clothing Distribution, Homes, Shelters/Homelessness, Social Services-General, Substance Abuse, United Funds/United Ways

Application Procedures

Initial Contact: Send a brief letter of inquiry.
Application Requirements: a description of organization, amount requested, purpose of funds sought, and proof of tax-exempt status.

Restrictions

Does not support religious organizations for sectarian purposes or political or lobbying groups.

Additional Information

Profile reflects the charitable priorities of the Eden, NC, plant location. Contributions are limited to organizations within a 150-mile radius of the plant. National organizations should contact corporate headquarters (see separate entry).

Corporate Officials

Patricia Henry: plant manager PRIM CORP EMPL plant manager: Miller Brewing Co./Eden North Carolina.

Grants Analysis

Typical Range: $1,000 to $2,500

HOWARD E. AND NELL E. MILLER CHARITABLE FOUNDATION

Giving Contact

Bruce Bickel, Senior Vice President
2 PNC Plaza, 25th Floor
620 Liberty Avenue
Pittsburgh, PA 15222-2719
Phone: (412)762-3502

Description

Founded: 1988
EIN: 256305933
Organization Type: Private Foundation
Giving Locations: PA: Pittsburgh
Grant Types: General Support.

Donor Information

Founder: the late Nellie E. Miller

Financial Summary

Total Giving: $291,000 (fiscal year ending May 31, 1999); $284,418 (fiscal 1997); $221,002 (fiscal 1996)
Assets: $8,557,007 (fiscal 1999); $6,978,010 (fiscal 1997); $6,313,841 (fiscal 1996)
Gifts Received: $131,620 (fiscal 1993); $12,481 (fiscal 1992). Note: In fiscal 1993, contributions were received from the estate of Nellie E. Miller.

Typical Recipients

Arts & Humanities: Arts Associations & Councils, Arts Festivals, Community Arts, Ethnic & Folk Arts, Arts & Humanities-General, Libraries, Music, Opera, Theater
Civic & Public Affairs: Civic & Public Affairs-General, Housing, Legal Aid, Urban & Community Affairs
Education: Afterschool/Enrichment Programs, Arts/Humanities Education, Colleges & Universities, Education Funds, Literacy, Preschool Education, Private Education (Precollege)
Health: Children's Health/Hospitals, Clinics/Medical Centers, Emergency/Ambulance Services, Hospices, Hospitals, Mental Health, Single-Disease Health Associations
Religion: Churches, Religion-General, Ministries, Religious Organizations, Religious Welfare
Social Services: Community Centers, Community Service Organizations, Community Service Organizations, Family Services, Food/Clothing Distribution, Homes, People with Disabilities, Recreation & Athletics, Scouts, Senior Services, Shelters/Homelessness, YMCA/YWCA/YMHA/YWHA, Youth Organizations

Application Procedures

Initial Contact: Send a brief letter of inquiry and a full proposal.
Application Requirements: Include a description of organization, amount requested, purpose of funds sought, recently audited financial statement, proof of tax-exempt status, and history of previous miller support.
Deadlines: None.

Restrictions

Does not support individuals, political or lobbying groups, and organizations outside operating areas.

Additional Information

Request application form before submitting proposal.
Trust(s): PNC Bank

Foundation Officials

Thomas M. Mulroy, Esq.: trustee

Grants Analysis

Disclosure Period: fiscal year ending May 31, 1999
Total Grants: $291,000
Number of Grants: 32
Average Grant: $9,094
Highest Grant: $22,000
Typical Range: $2,500 to $20,000

Recent Grants

Note: Grants derived from 2000 Form 990.

General

25,000	Pittsburgh Opera, Pittsburgh, PA
25,000	Pittsburgh Opera, Pittsburgh, PA
15,000	Greater Pittsburgh Food Bank, Pittsburgh, PA
15,000	Manchester Youth Development, Pittsburgh, PA
15,000	Mars Home for Youth, Mars, PA
15,000	Opera Theater of Pittsburgh, Pittsburgh, PA
10,000	Bridge to Independence, Pittsburgh, PA
10,000	Children's Hospital, Mars, PA
10,000	Coalition for Christian Outreach, Mars, PA
10,000	Moms House, Mars, PA

MILLER FOUNDATION

Giving Contact

Rebecca A. Engelhardt, Secretary, Treasurer & Trustee
Miller Foundation
310 WahWahTaySee Way
Battle Creek, MI 49015

Phone: (616)964-3542
Fax: (616)964-8455
Web: http://www.willard.lib.mi.us/npa/miller/

Description
Founded: 1963
EIN: 386064925
Organization Type: Private Foundation
Giving Locations: MI: Battle Creek and surrounding area
Grant Types: Capital, Emergency, Endowment, General Support, Loan, Scholarship, Seed Money.

Donor Information
Founder: the late Louise B. Miller, Robert B. Miller

Financial Summary
Total Giving: $976,875 (2001); $1,038,785 (2000); $628,985 (1998)
Giving Analysis: Giving for 2001 includes: foundation grants to United Way ($121,825); 2000: foundation grants to United Way ($84,260); 1998: foundation grants to United Way ($1,500)
Assets: $33,246,004 (2001); $35,546,373 (2000); $15,887,775 (1998)
Gifts Received: $115,000 (1997); $5,162 (1995); $76,836 (1994). Note: In 1995, contributions were received from an anonymous donor.

Typical Recipients
Arts & Humanities: Arts Associations & Councils, Arts Centers, History & Archaeology, Libraries, Music
Civic & Public Affairs: Botanical Gardens/Parks, Community Foundations, Economic Development, Civic & Public Affairs-General, Housing, Municipalities/Towns, Nonprofit Management, Parades/Festivals, Philanthropic Organizations, Professional & Trade Associations, Urban & Community Affairs, Zoos/Aquariums
Education: Arts/Humanities Education, Business Education, Colleges & Universities, Community & Junior Colleges, Education Funds, International Exchange, Preschool Education, Public Education (Precollege), Science/Mathematics Education, Special Education, Student Aid
Environment: Resource Conservation
Health: Clinics/Medical Centers, Emergency/Ambulance Services, Hospices, Nursing Services, Public Health
Religion: Ministries, Religious Organizations, Religious Welfare
Social Services: Big Brother/Big Sister, Community Centers, Community Service Organizations, Counseling, Crime Prevention, Day Care, Domestic Violence, Family Planning, Family Services, Food/Clothing Distribution, People with Disabilities, Scouts, Senior Services, Social Services-General, Substance Abuse, United Funds/United Ways, YMCA/YWCA/YMHA/YWHA, Youth Organizations

Application Procedures
Initial Contact: Request application guidelines and form.
Application Requirements: Include a description of organization, including history, mission, goals, current activities, and current collaborations; purpose of funds sought, including name of program, amount requested, specific purpose of funds, how program will be staffed, who will benefit, and involvement in program planning of persons benefiting from said program; description of any coordination or collaboration of organization, including similar or complimentary organizations and programs, and future plans for coordination; a one page logic model for programs over $100,000, including inputs, activities, outputs, and outcomes; detailed budget, including expenses, revenue sources, current status of other proposals, and in-kind items; annual operating statements; and explanation of future need after Miller Foundation grant is expended.
Deadlines: January 1, April 1, July 1, or October 1.

Additional Information
Publications: Annual Report; Application Form; Guidelines

Foundation Officials
Arthur W. Angood: president, chief executive officer, trustee
Barbara L. Comai: trustee
Gary Edward Costley: trustee B Caldwell, ID 1943. ED Oregon State University MS; Oregon State University BS (1966); Oregon State University PhD (1970). PRIM CORP EMPL executive vice president: Kellogg Co. CORP AFFIL president: Kellogg U.S.A. Inc. NONPR AFFIL trustee: Duke University Medicine School- Sarah W Stedman Center; trustee: Youth Understanding International Exchange; member: American Institute Nutrition; trustee: American Health Foundation.
Rebecca A. Engelhardt: secretary, treasurer, trustee
Rance Leaders: secretary, treasurer, trustee
W. James McQuiston: chairman, trustee
Allen L. Miller: trustee
Robert Branson Miller, Jr.: trustee B Battle Creek, MI 1935. ED Michigan State University BA (1959). PRIM CORP EMPL publisher: Battle Creek Enquirer. NONPR AFFIL director Battle Creek MI chapter: American Red Cross.
Robert Branson Miller, Sr.: trustee emeritus B Ottawa, KS June 25, 1906. ED Williams College BA (1929).
Paul Ohm: trustee
Gloria J. Robertson: trustee
Fred M. Woodruff, Jr.: trustee

Grants Analysis
Disclosure Period: calendar year ending 2001
Total Grants: $855,050*
Highest Grant: $100,000
*Note: Giving excludes United Way.

Recent Grants
Note: Grants derived from 2001 Form 990.

General
100,000	Kellogg Community College, Battle Creek, MI -- for Capstone Project
100,000	Leila Arboretum Society, Battle Creek, MI -- for BC Green Project
100,000	Neighborhoods, Inc., Battle Creek, MI -- for ongoing operational cost
100,000	United Way of Greater Battle Creek, Battle Creek, MI -- for 2001 capital campaign
100,000	Y Family Center, Battle Creek, MI -- for Health Enhancement Center
55,578	Neighborhoods, Inc., Battle Creek, MI -- for development director
42,847	Calhoun Area Millennium Partnership, LLC, Battle Creek, MI -- to put operational structure in place
25,000	Girl Scouts, Kalamazoo, MI -- capital campaign
21,825	United Way of Greater Battle Creek, Battle Creek, MI -- for matching grant
20,000	Calhoun Intermediate School District, Marshall, MI -- network for young children

EARL B. AND LORAINE H. MILLER FOUNDATION

Giving Contact
Walter M. Florie, Jr., President & Chief Executive Officer
111 W. Ocean Boulevard, 22nd Floor
Long Beach, CA 90802
Phone: (562)491-3187

Description
Founded: 1967
EIN: 952500545
Organization Type: Private Foundation
Giving Locations: CA: Long Beach
Grant Types: General Support, Project.

Financial Summary
Total Giving: $1,832,909 (fiscal year ending June 30, 2002); $1,485,346 (fiscal 2001); $1,564,204 (fiscal 2000)
Giving Analysis: Giving for fiscal 1999 includes: foundation scholarships ($35,000)
Assets: $34,425,850 (fiscal 2002); $35,191,515 (fiscal 2001); $36,318,803 (fiscal 2000)

Typical Recipients
Arts & Humanities: Arts Centers, Libraries, Museums/Galleries, Music
Civic & Public Affairs: African American Affairs, Urban & Community Affairs
Education: Education-General, Preschool Education
Health: Children's Health/Hospitals, Clinics/Medical Centers, Eyes/Blindness, Respiratory
Social Services: Child Welfare, Community Service Organizations, Day Care, Delinquency & Criminal Rehabilitation, Scouts, YMCA/YWCA/YMHA/YWHA, Youth Organizations

Application Procedures
Initial Contact: Send a brief letter of inquiry, not exceeding 3 pages, succinctly describing project and amount needed.
Application Requirements: Include a description of organization, amount requested, and purpose of funds sought. Also indicate how the request relates to foundation's areas of giving.
Deadlines: June 30.

Restrictions
Special consideration is given to children's education, family and development, moral citizenship, and the arts. Does not support individuals, political initiatives, or activities outside of Long Beach, CA.

Additional Information
Publications: Application Form

Foundation Officials
Ron R. Arias: trustee
Kent C. Browning: trustee
Lawrence A. Collins, Jr.: trustee
Walter M. Florie, Jr.: president
Jeanne Karatsu: trustee
William H. Marmion: trustee
Harlan Miller: treasurer, trustee
Marilyn L. Reilly: secretary, mgr
Warren R. Schulten: vice president

Grants Analysis
Disclosure Period: fiscal year ending June 30, 2002
Total Grants: $1,832,909
Number of Grants: 46
Average Grant: $26,884*
Highest Grant: $350,000
Typical Range: $10,000 to $50,000
*Note: Average grant figure excludes two highest grants ($650,000).

Recent Grants
Note: Grants derived from fiscal 2000 Form 990.

Library-Related
50,000	Long Beach Public Library Foundation, Long Beach, CA -- family learning center

General
139,000	Long Beach Symphony Association, Long Beach, CA -- music programs for elementary children

130,000	Children's Clinic, Long Beach, CA -- asthma
129,000	YMCA of Greater Long Beach, Long Beach, CA -- operations
120,000	American Lung Association of Los Angeles County, Los Angeles, CA -- outpatient facility
114,710	Long Beach Museum of Art, Long Beach, CA -- collaborative pilot program
100,000	Memorial Medical Center Foundation, Long Beach, CA -- marketing/outreach
100,000	Memorial Medical Center Foundation, Long Beach, CA -- signage
64,732	Long Beach Education Foundation, Long Beach, CA -- mentoring/tutoring programs
60,000	Children's Clinic, Long Beach, CA -- eye clinic
60,000	Children's Clinic, Long Beach, CA -- adolescent program

STEVE J. MILLER FOUNDATION

Giving Contact
Thomas N. Tuttle, Jr., Secretary, Treasurer
1000 N. Water St., 13th Floor
Milwaukee, WI 53202
Phone: (414)287-7184

Description
Founded: 1946
EIN: 396051879
Organization Type: Private Foundation
Giving Locations: AZ: Tucson; WI
Grant Types: General Support.

Donor Information
Founder: Central Cheese Co., Inc., the late Steve Miller

Financial Summary
Total Giving: $344,500 (2000); $258,800 (1999); $207,000 (1998)
Giving Analysis: Giving for 1999 includes: foundation grants to United Way ($1,000)
Assets: $4,725,327 (2000); $5,034,017 (1999); $4,044,262 (1996)

Typical Recipients
Arts & Humanities: Community Arts, Dance, History & Archaeology, Libraries, Museums/Galleries, Music, Opera, Performing Arts, Theater
Civic & Public Affairs: Clubs, Employment/Job Training, Civic & Public Affairs-General, Women's Affairs
Education: Agricultural Education, Arts/Humanities Education, Colleges & Universities, Environmental Education, Education-General, Literacy, Medical Education, Minority Education, Private Education (Precollege), Public Education (Precollege), Science/Mathematics Education, Student Aid
Environment: Environment-General
Health: Children's Health/Hospitals, Clinics/Medical Centers, Health Organizations, Hospitals, Medical Research, Mental Health, Multiple Sclerosis, Nursing Services, Prenatal Health Issues
Religion: Churches, Religious Organizations, Religious Welfare
Social Services: Child Abuse, Child Welfare, Community Service Organizations, Food/Clothing Distribution, People with Disabilities, Scouts, Social Services-General, United Funds/United Ways, YMCA/YWCA/YMHA/YWHA, Youth Organizations

Application Procedures
Initial Contact: Send a brief letter of inquiry and a full proposal.
Deadlines: None.

Restrictions
Does not support individuals.

Foundation Officials
Isabelle E. Black: vice president
William Thomas Gaus: treasurer B Berlin, Germany 1928. ED Marquette University (1951); Marquette University JD (1954). PRIM CORP EMPL senior vice president, chief trustee officer: Marshall & Ilsley Trust Co.
Norman C. Miller: president
Theodore W. Miller: trustee
Kurt Spreyer: trustee
Harvey D. TeStrake: mgr, secretary
Thomas N. Tuttle, Jr.: treasurer, secretary

Grants Analysis
Disclosure Period: calendar year ending 2000
Total Grants: $344,500*
Number of Grants: 42
Average Grant: $6,207*
Highest Grant: $90,000
Typical Range: $1,000 to $15,000
*Note: Average grant figure excludes highest grant.

Recent Grants
Note: Grants derived from 2001 Form 990.

General
40,000	St. Andrew's Crippled Children's Clinic, Nogales, AZ
25,000	Lura Turner Homes, Inc., Phoenix, AZ
20,000	Milwaukee Center for Independence, Milwaukee, WI
20,000	Thomas Jefferson School, St. Louis, MO
15,000	Opportunity Development Center, Marshfield, WI
10,000	Sacred Heart Catholic Church, Shawano, WI
10,000	SOS Children's Village of Wisconsin, Milwaukee, WI
10,000	United Performing Arts, Milwaukee, WI
10,000	University of Wisconsin, Madison, WI -- agriculture and life sciences
8,000	Richmond Educational Learning Center, Richmond, CA

MILLER-MELLOR ASSOCIATION

Giving Contact
James Ludlow Miller, Secretary & Treasurer
708 E. 47th St.
Kansas City, MO 64110
Phone: (816)561-4307

Description
Founded: 1950
EIN: 446011906
Organization Type: Private Foundation
Giving Locations: MO: Kansas City
Grant Types: General Support.

Financial Summary
Total Giving: $157,015 (fiscal year ending June 30, 2001); $500,465 (fiscal 2000); $107,820 (fiscal 1999)
Giving Analysis: Giving for fiscal 2001 includes: foundation grants to United Way ($5,200); fiscal 1999: foundation grants to United Way ($2,200) foundation ($105,620)
Assets: $4,232,391 (fiscal 2001); $3,810,189 (fiscal 2000); $4,456,779 (fiscal 1999)

Typical Recipients
Arts & Humanities: Arts Associations & Councils, Arts Institutes, Community Arts, Arts & Humanities-General, History & Archaeology, Libraries, Literary Arts, Museums/Galleries, Music, Performing Arts, Public Broadcasting, Theater
Civic & Public Affairs: Community Foundations, Civic & Public Affairs-General, Law & Justice, Municipalities/Towns, Safety, Urban & Community Affairs
Education: Colleges & Universities, Private Education (Precollege), Secondary Education (Private), Secondary Education (Public)
Environment: Environment-General, Wildlife Protection
Health: Children's Health/Hospitals, Emergency/Ambulance Services, Health Policy/Cost Containment, Health Organizations, Heart, Hospitals, Nursing Services, Prenatal Health Issues, Preventive Medicine/Wellness Organizations, Public Health
Religion: Churches, Dioceses, Religious Organizations, Religious Welfare
Science: Scientific Labs
Social Services: Animal Protection, Child Welfare, Community Service Organizations, Crime Prevention, Delinquency & Criminal Rehabilitation, Family Planning, Food/Clothing Distribution, People with Disabilities, Recreation & Athletics, Scouts, Senior Services, Shelters/Homelessness, Social Services-General, United Funds/United Ways, Youth Organizations

Application Procedures
Initial Contact: The foundation has no formal grant application procedure or application form. Send a brief letter of inquiry.
Deadlines: None.

Foundation Officials
James Ludlow Miller: secretary, treasurer
JoZach Miller, IV: vice president
Helena Miller Norquist: president

Grants Analysis
Disclosure Period: fiscal year ending June 30, 2001
Total Grants: $151,815*
Number of Grants: 43
Average Grant: $3,531
Highest Grant: $20,000
Typical Range: $1,000 to $5,000
*Note: Giving excludes United Way.

Recent Grants
Note: Grants derived from fiscal 2000 Form 990.

General
121,700	Mary Atkins Trust, Kansas City, MO
20,000	Children's Mercy Hospital, Kansas City, MO
19,200	Rockhurst University, Kansas City, MO
19,000	St. Martha Catholic Church, Sarasota, FL
17,000	Little Sisters of the Poor, Kansas City, MO
15,000	Benedictine College, Kansas City, MO
15,000	Notre Dame de Sion, Kansas City, MO
12,000	St. Dominic's Catholic Church, Oyster Bay, NY
10,000	Avila College, Kansas City, MO
10,000	Barstow School, Kansas City, MO

MILLIPORE CORP.

Company Headquarters
Bedford, MA
Web: http://www.millipore.com

Company Description
Founded: 1954
Ticker: MIL
Exchange: NYSE
Revenue: US$704.2 million (2002)
Employees: 4310 (2002)
SIC(s): 3081 Unsupported Plastics Film & Sheet, 3089 Plastics Products Nec, 3826 Analytical Instruments.

Operating Locations

Millipore Corp. (MA--Marlboro, Milford; NH--Jaffrey; PA--Pittsburgh; PR--Cidra)

Nonmonetary Support

Type: Donated Equipment; Donated Products
Volunteer Programs: Under the Voluntary Service Grant Program, employees who are currently doing volunteer work in their communities can petition the foundation for funds to support a special need or program of the organization where they volunteer. The program now provides a grant of up to $5,000 to support specific projects of eligible community organizations in which the Millipore employee is actively involved. The SkillsBank program is open to current employees, retirees, and family members who want to get involved in volunteer work. SkillsBank is a computerized program linked to the United Way's Voluntary Action Center, The Massachusetts Volunteer Network, and local charitable organizations. It acts as a clearinghouse between 500 agencies and the volunteers. Employees and others are matched with nonprofit agencies and organizations that can benefit from their specific skills, talent and knowledge.
Note: Nonmonetary support is provided by both the company and the foundation.

The Millipore Foundation

Giving Contact

Charleen Johnson, Executive Director
80 Ashby Road
Bedford, MA 01730-2271
Phone: (781)533-2210
Fax: (781)533-3301
E-mail: Charleen_Johnson@millipore.com
Web: http://www.millipore.com/foundation

Description

EIN: 222583952
Organization Type: Corporate Foundation
Giving Locations: MA: cash grants made primarily in Massachusetts matching gifts awarded nationally.
Grant Types: Capital, Employee Matching Gifts, General Support, Matching, Multiyear/Continuing Support.
Note: Employee matching gift ratio: 2 to 1 up to $5,000 annually per employee.

Financial Summary

Total Giving: $1,414,387 (fiscal year ending September 30, 2001); $1,204,440 (fiscal 2000); $1,338,402 (fiscal 1999). Note: Contributes through foundation only.
Giving Analysis: Giving for fiscal 2001 includes: foundation matching gifts ($520,874); foundation ($893,513); fiscal 2000: foundation scholarships ($53,500); foundation matching gifts ($424,490); foundation ($726,450); fiscal 1999: foundation matching gifts ($448,372); foundation ($890,029);
Assets: $133,766 (fiscal 2001); $144,119 (fiscal 2000); $180,372 (fiscal 1999)
Gifts Received: $1,418,364 (fiscal 2001); $1,176,998 (fiscal 2000); $300,000 (fiscal 1999). Note: Contributions are received from Millipore Corp.

Typical Recipients

Arts & Humanities: Arts Associations & Councils, Arts Centers, Arts Funds, Arts Outreach, Ballet, Libraries, Museums/Galleries, Music, Performing Arts, Public Broadcasting
Civic & Public Affairs: African American Affairs, Clubs, Employment/Job Training, Civic & Public Affairs-General, Hispanic Affairs, Legal Aid, Municipalities/Towns, Native American Affairs, Nonprofit Management, Philanthropic Organizations, Professional & Trade Associations, Public Policy, Urban & Community Affairs, Zoos/Aquariums

Education: Afterschool/Enrichment Programs, Business Education, Business-School Partnerships, Colleges & Universities, Community & Junior Colleges, Education Reform, Elementary Education (Public), Engineering/Technological Education, Education-General, Leadership Training, Literacy, Medical Education, Minority Education, Preschool Education, Private Education (Precollege), Public Education (Precollege), Religious Education, Science/Mathematics Education, Secondary Education (Private), Secondary Education (Public), Student Aid, Vocational & Technical Education
Environment: Forestry, Environment-General, Wildlife Protection
Health: AIDS/HIV, Cancer, Children's Health/Hospitals, Clinics/Medical Centers, Diabetes, Emergency/Ambulance Services, Health Organizations, Home-Care Services, Hospitals, Medical Research, Medical Training, Mental Health, Public Health, Respiratory, Single-Disease Health Associations
International: Foreign Educational Institutions, International Relief Efforts
Religion: Jewish Causes
Science: Science Exhibits & Fairs, Science Museums, Scientific Centers & Institutes, Scientific Organizations, Scientific Research
Social Services: At-Risk Youth, Child Welfare, Community Service Organizations, Delinquency & Criminal Rehabilitation, Family Services, Food/Clothing Distribution, Homes, People with Disabilities, Recreation & Athletics, Substance Abuse, United Funds/United Ways, Youth Organizations

Application Procedures

Initial Contact: Send written inquiries and proposals.
Application Requirements: Application should include summary of proposed program or project, including specific goals and objectives; dollar amount or nature of request; purpose of requested funds; background; itemized budget for project; financial statements for most recently completed fiscal year; proof of tax-exempt status; history and accomplishments of requesting organization; list of staff and board of directors; other sources of support; and current contact name, address, and phone number.
Deadlines: None.
Decision Notification: The board meets quarterly to evaluate proposals.
Notes: Foundation accepts the Associated Grantmakers of Massachusetts Common Proposal format.

Restrictions

The foundation does not support religious or political programs.

Additional Information

The foundation will support new projects or new nonprofit organizations in certain cases.
The foundation conducts periodic evaluations and does not guarantee continuing support for a project or program.
Publications: Foundation Annual Report

Corporate Officials

Francis Lunger: chief financial officer, corporate vice president B Erie, PA 1945. ED Gannon University BS (1968). PRIM CORP EMPL chief financial officer, corporate vice president: Millipore Corp. CORP AFFIL director: Stormedia Inc.
Jeffrey Rudin: vice president, general counsel PRIM CORP EMPL vice president, general counsel: Millipore Corp.

Foundation Officials

Charleen Johnson: executive director
Jeffrey Rudin: trustee (see above)

Grants Analysis

Disclosure Period: fiscal year ending September 30, 2001
Total Grants: $893,513*

Number of Grants: 106
Average Grant: $8,429
Highest Grant: $70,800
Lowest Grant: $300
Typical Range: $1,000 to $10,000
***Note:** Giving excludes matching gifts.

Recent Grants

Note: Grants derived from fiscal 2001 Form 990.

Library-Related
10,000   New York Public Library, New York, NY

General
70,800   City Year, Inc., Boston, MA -- social services
40,000   Citizens Scholarship Foundation, St. Peter, MN -- education
37,500   Lahey Clinic, Burlington, MA -- health care
30,000   Museum of Science, Boston, MA
25,480   Jaffrey-Rindge Cooperative School District, Jaffrey, NH
25,000   Boston Partners in Education, Inc., Boston, MA -- education
25,000   Boston Renaissance Charter School, Boston, MA -- education
23,416   Fondos Unidos de Puerto Rico, San Juan, PR
19,246   Northfield Mount Hermon School, Northfield, MA
16,600   One With One, Brighton, MA -- social services

FRANCES GOLL MILLS FUND

Giving Contact

Helen James
c/o Citizens Bank Saginaw
101 N. Washington Ave.
Saginaw, MI 48607
Phone: (517)776-7368

Description

Founded: 1982
EIN: 382434002
Organization Type: Private Foundation
Giving Locations: MI: Saginaw County
Grant Types: Capital, General Support, Multiyear/Continuing Support, Operating Expenses, Seed Money.

Donor Information

Founder: the late Frances Goll Mills

Financial Summary

Total Giving: $272,570 (fiscal year ending September 30, 2001); $380,850 (fiscal 1999); $135,755 (fiscal 1998). Note: 1997 Giving includes United Way ($19,500).
Giving Analysis: Giving for fiscal 2001 includes: foundation grants to United Way ($11,000); fiscal 1999: foundation grants to United Way ($11,000) fiscal 1998: foundation grants to United Way ($17,000)
Assets: $4,699,924 (fiscal 2001); $5,761,590 (fiscal 1999); $4,984,064 (fiscal 1998)

Typical Recipients

Arts & Humanities: History & Archaeology, Libraries, Museums/Galleries, Music
Civic & Public Affairs: African American Affairs, Community Foundations, Economic Development, Civic & Public Affairs-General, Housing, Legal Aid, Municipalities/Towns, Parades/Festivals, Urban & Community Affairs, Zoos/Aquariums

Education: Agricultural Education, Business Education, Colleges & Universities, Engineering/Technological Education, Public Education (Precollege), Science/Mathematics Education, Student Aid

Health: Children's Health/Hospitals, Clinics/Medical Centers, Emergency/Ambulance Services, Health-General

International: International Relations

Religion: Churches, Religious Organizations, Religious Welfare

Social Services: At-Risk Youth, Community Centers, Community Service Organizations, Emergency Relief, Family Services, People with Disabilities, Scouts, Special Olympics, United Funds/United Ways, YMCA/YWCA/YMHA/YWHA, Youth Organizations

Application Procedures

Initial Contact: Request application guidelines.
Deadlines: None.

Additional Information

Publications: Application Guidelines
Trust(s): Citizens Bank NA

Grants Analysis

Disclosure Period: fiscal year ending September 30, 2001
Total Grants: $261,570*
Number of Grants: 18
Average Grant: $7,438*
Highest Grant: $50,000
Typical Range: $1,000 to $15,000
*Note: Giving excludes United Way. Average grant figure excludes three highest grants ($150,000).

Recent Grants

Note: Grants derived from fiscal 2000 Form 990.

General

50,000	Saginaw Valley State University, University Center, MI
49,350	Saginaw Zoological Society, Saginaw, MI
45,000	First Congregation Church, Saginaw, MI
28,000	Covenant Health Care, Saginaw, MI
25,000	YMCA, Saginaw, MI
25,000	YMCA of Saginaw, Saginaw, MI -- health enhancement program
20,000	Boysville/St. Vincent Home, Saginaw, MI
20,000	Lutheran Child and Family Services, Bay City, MI
15,000	Boys and Girls Clubs of Bay County, Bay City, MI
15,000	City Rescue Mission, Saginaw, MI

MINE SAFETY APPLIANCES CO.

Company Headquarters

Pittsburgh, PA
Web: http://www.msanet.com

Company Description

Founded: 1914
Ticker: MSA
Exchange: AMEX
Revenue: US$564.4 million (2002)
Employees: 0 (2002)
SIC(s): 3823 Process Control Instruments, 3842 Surgical Appliances & Supplies.

Operating Locations

Mine Safety Appliances Co. (RI--Esmond)
Note: Operates internationally.

Mine Safety Appliances Co. Charitable Foundation

Giving Contact

Dennis L. Zeitler, Vice President
PO Box 426
Pittsburgh, PA 15230
Phone: (412)967-3000
Fax: (412)967-3367
Web: http://www.msanet.com

Description

EIN: 256023104
Organization Type: Corporate Foundation
Giving Locations: PA: Pittsburgh operating location communities.
Grant Types: Capital, Conference/Seminar, General Support, Project.

Financial Summary

Total Giving: $950,850 (2001); $719,000 (2000); $771,062 (1999)
Giving Analysis: Giving for 2001 includes: foundation grants to United Way ($326,000); foundation ($624,850); 2000: foundation grants to United Way ($305,000); foundation ($414,850); 1999: foundation grants to United Way ($255,000); foundation ($516,062).
Assets: $2,496,598 (2001); $2,844,350 (2000); $3,186,716 (1999)
Gifts Received: $500,000 (2001); $1,706 (2000); $7,807 (1999)

Typical Recipients

Arts & Humanities: Arts Centers, Arts Festivals, Arts Outreach, Ballet, Dance, Libraries, Museums/Galleries, Music, Opera, Performing Arts, Public Broadcasting, Theater

Civic & Public Affairs: Botanical Gardens/Parks, Clubs, Community Foundations, Economic Development, Economic Policy, Civic & Public Affairs-General, Professional & Trade Associations, Public Policy, Safety, Urban & Community Affairs, Zoos/Aquariums

Education: Business Education, Colleges & Universities, Community & Junior Colleges, Economic Education, Education Associations, Education Funds, Engineering/Technological Education, Education-General, Minority Education, Preschool Education, Private Education (Precollege), Private Education (Precollege), Science/Mathematics Education, Special Education, Student Aid

Environment: Environment-General

Health: AIDS/HIV, Alzheimers Disease, Children's Health/Hospitals, Diabetes, Emergency/Ambulance Services, Health Funds, Health Organizations, Hospitals, Kidney, Long-Term Care, Medical Rehabilitation, Mental Health, Multiple Sclerosis, Respiratory, Single-Disease Health Associations

International: International Affairs, International Peace & Security Issues, International Relations, International Relief Efforts

Religion: Dioceses, Ministries, Religious Organizations, Religious Welfare, Seminaries

Science: Observatories & Planetariums, Scientific Centers & Institutes

Social Services: Child Welfare, Community Service Organizations, Emergency Relief, Family Services, Food/Clothing Distribution, People with Disabilities, Recreation & Athletics, Scouts, Social Services-General, Special Olympics, United Funds/United Ways, Youth Organizations

Application Procedures

Initial Contact: Send brief letter of introduction.
Application Requirements: Include a description of organization, amount requested, purpose of funds

sought, recently audited financial statement, proof of tax-exempt status.
Deadlines: None.

Restrictions

Foundation does not award scholarships or provide grants to individuals.

Additional Information

Trust(s): PNC Bank

Corporate Officials

James E. Herald: vice president financeo PRIM CORP EMPL vice president finance: Mine Safety Appliances Co.

John Thomas Ryan, III: chairman, chief executive officer B Pittsburgh, PA 1943. ED University of Notre Dame AB (1965); Harvard University MBA (1969). PRIM CORP EMPL chairman, chief executive officer: Mine Safety Appliances Co. CORP AFFIL director: Penns Southwest; director: Auergesellschaft GmbH; chairman: Federal Reserve Bank Cleveland. NONPR AFFIL member: Council Foreign Relations; vice chairman, director: Industrial Safety Equipment Association.

Foundation Officials

James E. Herald: secretary (see above)

Grants Analysis

Disclosure Period: calendar year ending 2001
Total Grants: $624,850*
Number of Grants: 103
Average Grant: $4,553*
Highest Grant: $100,000
Lowest Grant: $50
Typical Range: $1,000 to $5,000
*Note: Giving excludes United Way. Average grant figure excludes two highest grants ($165,000).

Recent Grants

Note: Grants derived from 2001 Form 990.

General

240,000	United Way of Southwestern Pennsylvania, Pittsburgh, PA
100,000	New York Firefighters 9-11 Disaster Relief Fund, New York, NY
65,000	Uniformed Firefighters Association Widows and Children's Fund, New York, NY
45,000	United Way of Butler County, Butler, PA
35,000	Patrolmen's Benevolent Association of the City of New York, New York, NY -- Widows and Children's Fund
35,000	United Way of Westmoreland County, Greensburg, PA
21,000	Pittsburgh Regional Alliance, Pittsburgh, PA
20,000	City of Hope, Los Angeles, CA
16,800	Pennsylvania Economy League, Western Division, Pittsburgh, PA
16,500	Pittsburgh Symphony Orchestra, Pittsburgh, PA

JULIA J. MINGENBACK FOUNDATION

Giving Contact

Don C. Steffes, President
1008 Turkey Creek Drive
McPherson, KS 67460
Phone: (620)241-0700

Description

Founded: 1959
EIN: 486109567
Organization Type: Private Foundation
Giving Locations: KS: McPherson County
Grant Types: Capital, Operating Expenses.

Donor Information
Founder: the late E. C. Mingenback

Financial Summary
Total Giving: $221,500 (2001); $186,000 (2000); $259,638 (1999)
Assets: $4,651,137 (2001); $5,831,553 (2000); $5,624,411 (1999)

Typical Recipients
Arts & Humanities: Arts Associations & Councils, Community Arts, Libraries, Museums/Galleries, Opera
Civic & Public Affairs: Municipalities/Towns
Education: Colleges & Universities, Private Education (Precollege), Religious Education
Health: Hospitals
Social Services: Community Centers, Family Services, Food/Clothing Distribution, Homes, Senior Services, Social Services-General, YMCA/YWCA/YMHA/YWHA, Youth Organizations

Application Procedures
Initial Contact: Send a brief letter of inquiry.
Application Requirements: Include specific needs.
Deadlines: None.

Restrictions
Generally limited to educational and cultural activities of organizations in McPherson County, KS.

Additional Information
Trust(s): Peoples Bank and Trust IV KS NA

Foundation Officials
Bev Hess: secretary, treasurer
James Lee Ketcherside: director B Topeka, KS 1935. PRIM CORP EMPL chairman, president: Farmers Alliance Mutual Insurance Co.
Edwin T. Pyle: director
Brett Reber: director
Don C. Steffes: president
B. Carver Swindoll: director

Grants Analysis
Disclosure Period: calendar year ending 2001
Total Grants: $221,500
Number of Grants: 7
Average Grant: $31,643
Highest Grant: $50,000
Lowest Grant: $1,500
Typical Range: $25,000 to $50,000

Recent Grants
Note: Grants derived from 2001 Form 990.

General

50,000	Central Christian College, McPherson, KS -- capital improvements
50,000	McPherson College, McPherson, KS -- capital improvements
40,000	Memorial Hospital, McPherson, KS -- capital improvements
30,000	City of McPherson, McPherson, KS -- capital improvements
25,000	Elyria Christian School, McPherson, KS -- capital improvements
25,000	McPherson Opera House, McPherson, KS -- capital improvements
1,500	McPherson Family Life, McPherson, KS -- for operations and programs

MINNESOTA MINING & MANUFACTURING CO.

Company Headquarters
St. Paul, MN
Web: http://www.mmm.com

Company Description
Founded: 1902
Ticker: MMM
Exchange: NYSE
Also Known As: 3M.
Revenue: US$16.332 billion (2002)
Employees: 71669 (2002)
Fortune Rank: 110, per FORTUNE Magazine's list of 500 Largest U.S. Corporations (2002).
SIC(s): 2672 Coated & Laminated Paper Nec, 2834 Pharmaceutical Preparations, 2891 Adhesives & Sealants, 2899 Chemical Preparations Nec.

Operating Locations
Minnesota Mining & Manufacturing Co. (AL--Birmingham, Decatur, Guin; AK--Anchorage; AZ--Phoenix, Tucson; CA--Camarillo, Chico, Costa Mesa, Fresno, Irvine, Los Angeles, Northridge, Ontario, Petaluma, San Francisco, Tustin, Unitek; CO--Denver; CT--Wallingford; DC; FL--Pompano Beach, Sanford; GA--Atlanta; HI--Honolulu; IL--Chicago, Cordova, DeKalb, Hinsdale; IN--Indianapolis; IA--Ames, Forest City, Knoxville; KY--Cynthiana; MD--Westminster; MA, Cambridge, Chelmsford; MI, Detroit, Midland; MN, Cottage Grove, Eagan, Fairmont, Hutchinson, Park Rapids, Pine City, St. Paul, Staples; MO--Nevada, Springfield, St. Louis; NE--Valley; NJ--Belle Mead, Eatontown, Freehold, West Deptford; NY--Honeoye, Lennox Hill, Rochester; NC--Charlotte, High Point; OH--Baltimore, Cincinnati, Cleveland, Columbus, Mentor; OK--Weatherford; OR--Eugene, White City; PA--Philadelphia; SC--Greenville, North Charleston; SD--Aberdeen; TN--Nashville; TX--Austin, Brownwood, El Paso, Fort Worth, Houston, Rio Grande; UT--Salt Lake City; WA--Seattle; WV--Middleway; WI--Cumberland, Menomonee, Nekoosa, Wausau, Wisconsin Rapids)

Nonmonetary Support
Value: $18,100,000 (2000); $16,608,454 (1998)
Type: Donated Products; In-kind Services
Volunteer Programs: The 3M GIVES (Grants Initiated by Volunteer Service) program matches 25 hours of employee/retiree volunteer service with $200 to the volunteer's designated nonprofit organization. The company also supports a Community Volunteer Award program through which it selects 25 exceptional employee/retiree volunteers annually and awards $1,000 to a nonprofit organization selected by each winner. Volunteer programs contact is Anne E. Mazurowski.
Contact: Richard E. Hanson, Director Community Affairs; Vice President
3M Foundation
Note: Donated equipment at fair market value.

3M Foundation

Giving Contact
Cynthia F. Kleven, Manager Contributions
3M Community Affairs
Contributions Program
3M Center, Bldg. 225-01-S-23
St. Paul, MN 55144-1000
Phone: (651)733-0144
Fax: (651)737-3061
E-mail: cfkleven@mmm.com
Web: http://www.3M.com/about3m/community

Alternate Contact
Richard E. Hanson, Contact
3M Foundation
St. Paul, MN 55144
Phone: (651)733-8335

Description
Founded: 1953
EIN: 416038262
Organization Type: Corporate Foundation

Giving Locations: headquarters and operating communities.
Grant Types: General Support, Operating Expenses, Project.
Note: Employee matching gift ratio: 1 to 1.

Financial Summary
Total Giving: $16,553,268 (2001); $34,400,000 (2000 approx); $29,618,000 (1999 approx). Note: Contributes through corporate direct giving program and foundation.
Giving Analysis: Giving for 2001 includes: foundation matching gifts ($1,674,331); corporate direct giving (approx $3,625,669); foundation (approx $16,500,000); nonmonetary support (approx $25,300,000); 2000: corporate direct giving ($5,700,000); foundation ($10,600,000); nonmonetary support ($18,100,000); 1999: corporate direct giving ($6,756,000); foundation ($8,513,000); nonmonetary support ($14,349,000);
Assets: $54,259,082 (2001); $74,028,370 (2000); $73,701,844 (1999)
Gifts Received: $3,232,020 (1996)

Typical Recipients
Arts & Humanities: Arts Associations & Councils, Arts Centers, Arts Institutes, Arts Outreach, Ethnic & Folk Arts, Historic Preservation, History & Archaeology, Libraries, Museums/Galleries, Music, Opera, Performing Arts, Public Broadcasting, Theater
Civic & Public Affairs: African American Affairs, Business/Free Enterprise, Chambers of Commerce, Community Foundations, Economic Development, Employment/Job Training, Civic & Public Affairs-General, Hispanic Affairs, Legal Aid, Municipalities/Towns, Native American Affairs, Nonprofit Management, Parades/Festivals, Professional & Trade Associations, Safety, Urban & Community Affairs
Education: Business Education, Colleges & Universities, Economic Education, Education Associations, Education Funds, Engineering/Technological Education, Faculty Development, Education-General, International Exchange, Journalism/Media Education, Medical Education, Minority Education, Private Education (Precollege), Public Education (Precollege), Science/Mathematics Education, Social Sciences Education, Student Aid, Vocational & Technical Education
Environment: Environment-General, Protection, Resource Conservation
Health: Clinics/Medical Centers, Emergency/Ambulance Services, Geriatric Health, Health Policy/Cost Containment, Health Organizations, Hospices, Hospitals, Medical Rehabilitation, Mental Health, Public Health, Transplant Networks/Donor Banks
International: Foreign Educational Institutions
Religion: Religious Welfare, Social/Policy Issues
Science: Science Museums, Scientific Centers & Institutes, Scientific Research
Social Services: Child Welfare, Community Centers, Community Service Organizations, Counseling, Crime Prevention, Day Care, Delinquency & Criminal Rehabilitation, Domestic Violence, Emergency Relief, Family Services, Food/Clothing Distribution, Homes, People with Disabilities, Recreation & Athletics, Scouts, Senior Services, Shelters/Homelessness, Social Services-General, Substance Abuse, United Funds/United Ways, Volunteer Services, YMCA/YWCA/YMHA/YWHA, Youth Organizations

Application Procedures
Initial Contact: Submit a brief letter of inquiry. Telephone requests are not accepted, but requests may be submitted by mail, fax, or e-mailed using the link at www.3m.com/about3m/contact.
Application Requirements: Include brief organizational history, project description, evaluation and impact, targeted group of people who will be benefit, specific amount requested, and proof of tax-exempt status.

Deadlines: September 30 and January 31 for formal requests.

Review Process: If letter of inquiry demonstrates your organization meet 3M criteria, and geographic restrictions and funding priorities are met, you may be invited to submit a formal grant application.

Evaluative Criteria: Preference is given to proposals and programs that have broad-based community support, a reputation for high-quality service delivery, and measurable results.

Restrictions

Grants are not considered for advocacy and lobbying efforts to influence legislation; individuals; religious, fraternal, social, veterans, or military organizations; travel for individuals or groups; purchase of equipment not manufactured by 3M; for-profit organizations; endowment funds; disease-specific organizations; film/video productions; or scholarship funds. Generally, grants are not made to organizations outside of 3M communities; conferences, seminars, symposiums or workshops or publications of their proceedings; fund-raising, testimonial, athletic, or special events; emergency operating support; funding for more than 10 percent of an organization's annual budget or campaign goal; funding programs beyond three years; individual K-12 schools; or hospitals. Letters of inquiry are accepted only from 501(c)(3) organizations located in 3M communities.

Additional Information

In countries where 3M has subsidiary operations, requests should be directed to that location. For more information regarding international giving, contact Richard Hanson, director, Community Affairs, and vice president, 3M Foundation.

Inquiries from the Minneapolis/St. Paul, MN area should be addressed to the designated staff person at the above address or may directed at one of the following program-specific contact people: Cynthia F. Kleven, Health & Human Services/Arts and Culture/Environment at (651) 733-1721, cfkleven@mmm.com; Anne E. Mazurowski, Volunteer Programs at (651) 733-1421, aemazurowski1@mmm.com; and Barbara W. Kaufmann, Education at (651) 733-1241, bkaufmann@mmm.com. For locations outside of St. Paul where 3M has an operation, contact Cynthia Kleven at 613-733-1721 or your local 3M facility.

Publications: Giving Guidelines

Corporate Officials

J. Marc Adam: vice president marketingo, director B Montreal, ON Canada 1938. ED University of Ottawa. PRIM CORP EMPL vice president marketing: Minnesota Mining & Manufacturing Co. CORP AFFIL directory: Clarcor Inc.

Harry C. Andrews: executive vice president B Glendale, CA 1943. ED Stanford University (1964); University of Southern California (1968). PRIM CORP EMPL executive vice president: Minnesota Mining & Manufacturing Co. NONPR AFFIL member: Institute Electrical Electronic Engineers.

Ronald Oliver Baukol: director, executive vice president B Chicago, IL 1937. ED Iowa State University BSChemE (1959); Massachusetts Institute of Technology MSChemE (1960). PRIM CORP EMPL director, executive vice president: Minnesota Mining & Manufacturing Co. CORP AFFIL director: Toro Co.; director: Graco Inc. NONPR AFFIL trustee: U.S. Council International Business.

John W. Benson: executive vice president health care B Saint James, MN 1944. ED University of Minnesota (1966); University of Washington (1968). PRIM CORP EMPL executive vice president health care: Minnesota Mining & Manufacturing Co.

M. Kay Grenz: vice president human resources B Owatonna, MN 1946. ED University of North Dakota (1969). PRIM CORP EMPL vice president human resources: Minnesota Mining & Manufacturing Co. CORP AFFIL director: Eastern Heights Bank. NONPR AFFIL member: Human Resources Roundtable Group; director: INROADS; member: Human Resources Planning Society; director: Gillette Children's Specialty Healthcare.

Cynthia F. Kleven: director community affairs PRIM CORP EMPL director community affairs: Minnesota Mining & Manufacturing Co.

W. James McNerney, Jr.: chairman, chief executive officer, director B August 22, 1949. ED Yale University BA (1971); Harvard University MBA (1975). PRIM CORP EMPL chairman, chief executive officer, director: Minnesota Mining & Manufacturing Co.

Mohamed S. Nozari: executive vice president PRIM CORP EMPL executive vice president: Minnesota Mining & Manufacturing Co.

Charles Reich: executive vice president PRIM CORP EMPL executive vice president: Minnesota Mining & Manufacturing Co.

John Joseph Ursu: general counsel, senior vice president legal affairs B Detroit, MI 1939. ED University of Michigan AB (1962); University of Michigan JD (1965). PRIM CORP EMPL general counsel, senior vice president legal affairs: Minnesota Mining & Manufacturing Co. NONPR AFFIL member: Association General Counsel; member: CLO Roundtable; member: American Bar Association.

Ronald A. Weber: executive vice president PRIM CORP EMPL executive vice president: Minnesota Mining & Manufacturing Co.

Harold J. Wiens: executive vice president PRIM CORP EMPL executive vice president: Minnesota Mining & Manufacturing Co.

Janet L. Yeomans: vice president, treasurer B Washington, DC 1948. ED Connecticut College (1970); University of Chicago MBA (1979). PRIM CORP EMPL vice president, treasurer: Minnesota Mining & Manufacturing Co.

Giving Program Officials

J. Marc Adam: president, director B Montreal, ON Canada 1938. ED University of Ottawa. PRIM CORP EMPL vice president marketing: Minnesota Mining & Manufacturing Co. CORP AFFIL directory: Clarcor Inc.

John W. Benson: director B Saint James, MN 1944. ED University of Minnesota (1966); University of Washington (1968). PRIM CORP EMPL executive vice president health care: Minnesota Mining & Manufacturing Co.

Richard E. Hanson: vice president, director PRIM CORP EMPL director community affairs: Minnesota Mining & Manufacturing Co.

Barbara W. Kaufmann: director PRIM CORP EMPL supervisor corporate contributions art & education: Minnesota Mining & Manufacturing Co.

John Joseph Ursu: director (see above)

Janet L. Yeomans: treasurer, director (see above)

Foundation Officials

J. Marc Adam: president, director (see above)

M. Kay Grenz: director (see above)

Richard E. Hanson: vice president, director (see above)

Cynthia F. Kleven: secretary, director (see above)

John Joseph Ursu: director (see above)

Janet L. Yeomans: treasurer, director (see above)

Grants Analysis

Disclosure Period: calendar year ending 2001
Total Grants: $20,125,669 (approx)*
Number of Grants: 471
Average Grant: $31,052*
Highest Grant: $2,942,387
Typical Range: $2,000 to $50,000

*Note: Giving excludes matching gifts and nonmonetary support contributions. Average grant figure excludes two highest grants.

Recent Grants

Note: Grants derived from 2001 Form 990.

General

2,718,333	University of Minnesota Foundation, Minneapolis, MN
1,800,000	Nature Conservancy, Minneapolis, MN
790,497	Greater Twin Cities United Way, Minneapolis, MN
735,000	United Way St. Paul Area, St. Paul, MN
500,000	United Hospital Foundation, St. Paul, MN
435,941	American Red Cross St. Paul Area Chapter, St. Paul, MN
327,568	SSGA
235,000	Guthrie Theater Foundation, Minneapolis, MN
200,000	Dakota County Technical College Foundation, Rosemount, MN
155,000	Minnesota State Opportunities Industrialization Council, St. Paul, MN

MINNESOTA MUTUAL LIFE INSURANCE CO.

Company Headquarters

Saint Paul, MN
Web: http://www.minnesotamutual.com

Company Description

Employees: 4,000
SIC(s): 6311 Life Insurance, 6321 Accident & Health Insurance.

Nonmonetary Support

Value: $1,068,000 (2001 approx); $500,000 (2000)
Type: Donated Equipment; In-kind Services; Loaned Employees; Loaned Executives; Workplace Solicitation
Note: Company also allows organizations the use of buildings and facilities.
Volunteer Programs: Company conducts a special program that recognizes employee volunteerism with $100 donations to organizations where employees volunteer their time.

Minnesota Mutual Foundation

Giving Contact

Lori J. Koutsky, Manager
Minnesota Mutual Foundation
400 Robert St. North
St. Paul, MN 55101-2098
Phone: (651)665-3501
Fax: (651)665-3551
E-mail: lori.koutsky@minnesotamutual.com
Web: http://www.minnesotamutual.com/about/community.asp

Description

EIN: 363608619
Organization Type: Corporate Foundation
Giving Locations: MN: Minneapolis metropolitan area, St. Paul metropolitan area
Grant Types: Capital, Employee Matching Gifts, General Support, Multiyear/Continuing Support.
Note: Employee matching gift ratio: 1 to 1 for gifts to higher education, arts and cultural organizations, and hospitals.

Financial Summary

Total Giving: $3,000,000 (2002 approx); $2,930,523 (2001 approx); $1,354,096 (2000 approx). Note: Contributes through corporate direct giving program and foundation.

Giving Analysis: Giving for 2001 includes: corporate direct giving ($422,615); nonmonetary support ($1,068,000); foundation ($1,439,908); 2000: foundation scholarships ($2,000); foundation matching gifts ($108,571); foundation grants to United Way ($320,000); foundation ($923,525); 1999: foundation scholarships ($2,000); foundation matching gifts ($107,754); foundation grants to United Way ($302,000); foundation ($1,164,375);

Assets: $30,321,833 (2001); $28,568,254 (2000); $26,596,197 (1999)

Gifts Received: $1,800,014 (2001); $1,642,875 (2000); $1,537,500 (1999). Note: In 2001, contributions were received from Securian Holding Company. In 2000, contributions were received from Cisco Systems, Inc. In 1999, contributions were received from Ciena Corp.

Typical Recipients

Arts & Humanities: Arts Centers, Arts Funds, Arts Institutes, Arts & Humanities-General, Historic Preservation, History & Archaeology, Libraries, Museums/Galleries, Music, Opera, Public Broadcasting, Theater

Civic & Public Affairs: Asian American Affairs, Business/Free Enterprise, Clubs, Economic Development, Employment/Job Training, Civic & Public Affairs-General, Housing, Law & Justice, Legal Aid, Minority Business, Nonprofit Management, Parades/Festivals, Professional & Trade Associations, Public Policy, Urban & Community Affairs, Women's Affairs, Zoos/Aquariums

Education: Arts/Humanities Education, Business Education, Business-School Partnerships, Colleges & Universities, Economic Development, Economic Education, Education Reform, Elementary Education (Private), Education-General, Leadership Training, Literacy, Minority Education, Private Education (Precollege), Science/Mathematics Education

Health: AIDS/HIV, Children's Health/Hospitals, Emergency/Ambulance Services, Health-General, Health Funds, Hospices, Hospitals, Long-Term Care, Medical Rehabilitation, Medical Research, Nursing Services, Prenatal Health Issues, Public Health, Research/Studies Institutes

International: Human Rights, International Organizations

Religion: Religion-General, Jewish Causes, Religious Organizations, Religious Welfare

Science: Science Museums

Social Services: Child Abuse, Community Service Organizations, Crime Prevention, Day Care, Domestic Violence, Emergency Relief, Family Services, Food/Clothing Distribution, People with Disabilities, Refugee Assistance, Scouts, Shelters/Homelessness, Social Services-General, Substance Abuse, United Funds/United Ways, YMCA/YWCA/YMHA/YWHA, Youth Organizations

Application Procedures

Initial Contact: Call or write for guidelines and applications, then send a written proposal.

Application Requirements: A cover letter, a completed Minnesota Common Grant Application, and the following attachments: financial statements from most recent fiscal year, organization and project budgets, list of funding sources with dollar amounts, a copy of the applicant's most recent IRS Form 990, list of board members with affiliations, and proof of tax-exempt status.

Deadlines: February 15, May 15, August 15, and November 15.

Evaluative Criteria: Supports direct gifts rather than benefit activities; organizations must meet either requirements of Minnesota Charitable Solicitation Act of the National Information Bureau, meet guidelines of foundation, or meet an important need not otherwise met; program has reasonable chance of success; program is not a duplication of effort; substantial support from other sources.

Restrictions

Does not support political, lobbying or fraternal activities; start-up funding for new organizations; religious organizations for sectarian purposes; organizations that do not possess 501(c)(3) tax-exempt status; fundraising events, benefits, sponsorships or advertising support; individuals or individual scholarships; endowment campaigns; athletic, recreation or sports-related organizations; services traditionally supported by government agencies; international organizations; veteran and fraternal organizations; trips or tours; hospitals or health care services that are generally supported by third party mechanisms (hospitals are eligible for matching gifts); conferences, seminars, workshops or symposiums; and public and private K-12 schools (schools are eligible for matching gifts).

Additional Information

Publications: Corporate Contributions Policy

Corporate Officials

Dennis E. Prohofsky: senior vice president, general counsel, secretary B Saint Paul, MN 1940. ED University of Minnesota (1965); William Mitchell College of Law (1972). PRIM CORP EMPL senior vice president, general counsel, secretary: Minnesota Mutual Life Insurance Co. ADD CORP EMPL secretary: Mimlic Sales Corp. CORP AFFIL director: Sargasso Mutual.

Robert L. Senkler: chairman, president, chief executive officer B Saint Paul, MN 1952. ED University of Minnesota, Duluth College BA (1979). PRIM CORP EMPL chairman, president, chief executive officer: Minnesota Mutual Life Insurance Co. NONPR AFFIL member, fellow: Society Actuaries.

Gregory S. Strong: vice president actuary B 1944. PRIM CORP EMPL vice president actuary: Minnesota Mutual Life Insurance Co.

Foundation Officials

Keith M. Campbell: vice president, director B 1945. PRIM CORP EMPL vice president: Minnesota Mutual Life Insurance Co.

Lori J. Koutsky: foundation manager

Dennis E. Prohofsky: secretary (see above)

Robert L. Senkler: president, director (see above)

Gregory S. Strong: treasurer (see above)

Grants Analysis

Disclosure Period: calendar year ending 2001
Total Grants: $962,575*
Number of Grants: 111
Average Grant: $7,614*
Highest Grant: $125,000
Lowest Grant: $300
Typical Range: $1,000 to $15,000
*Note: Giving excludes matching gifts; United Way. Average grant figure excludes highest grant.

Recent Grants

Note: Grants derived from 2001 Form 990.

General

335,000	United Way Campaign, St. Paul, MN -- annual support for 75 agencies
125,000	University of Minnesota, Minneapolis, MN -- leadership course and speaker series
75,000	St. Paul Chamber Orchestra, St. Paul, MN -- annual support
60,000	Minnesota Business Academy, Minneapolis, MN -- annual support
51,000	Minnesota Children's Museum, St. Paul, MN -- annual support
50,000	Friends of the St. Paul Farmers' Market, Shoreview, MN -- capital improvements
44,000	YMCA, St. Paul, MN -- programs for disadvantaged families
32,000	Ordway Music Theater, St. Paul, MN -- annual support and building campaign
30,000	Girl Scout Council of St. Croix Valley, St. Croix, MN -- capital campaign f
30,000	KTCA, St. Paul, MN -- support of educational television

MINSTER MACHINE CO.

Company Headquarters
PO Box 120
Minster, OH 45865
Web: http://www.minster.com

Company Description
Employees: 775
SIC(s): 3542 Machine Tools--Metal Forming Types, 3714 Motor Vehicle Parts & Accessories.

Minster Machine Co. Foundation

Giving Contact
Robert Sudhoff, Vice President, Finance & Chief Financial Officer
240 W. 5th St.
Minster, OH 45865-1027
Phone: (419)628-2331

Description
EIN: 346559271
Organization Type: Corporate Foundation
Giving Locations: OH
Grant Types: General Support.

Financial Summary
Total Giving: $60,800 (fiscal year ending November 30, 2001); $63,183 (fiscal 2000); $44,881 (fiscal 1999)
Giving Analysis: Giving for fiscal 1999 includes: foundation ($44,881)
Assets: $854,991 (fiscal 2001); $868,396 (fiscal 2000); $726,299 (fiscal 1999)
Gifts Received: $16,100 (fiscal 2001); $160,000 (fiscal 2000); $250,000 (fiscal 1994). Note: Contributions were received from the Minster Machine Co.

Typical Recipients

Arts & Humanities: Arts Associations & Councils, Arts Institutes, Community Arts, History & Archaeology, Libraries, Museums/Galleries, Opera, Public Broadcasting

Civic & Public Affairs: Clubs, Community Foundations, Civic & Public Affairs-General, Professional & Trade Associations, Public Policy, Safety, Urban & Community Affairs

Education: Agricultural Education, Arts/Humanities Education, Colleges & Universities, Education Associations, Education Funds, Engineering/Technological Education, Education-General, Special Education, Student Aid

Health: Alzheimers Disease, Cancer, Children's Health/Hospitals, Clinics/Medical Centers, Emergency/Ambulance Services, Heart, Hospices, Hospitals, Medical Research, Nursing Services, Prenatal Health Issues, Single-Disease Health Associations

Religion: Religious Organizations, Religious Welfare

Science: Scientific Organizations

Social Services: Big Brother/Big Sister, Child Welfare, Community Service Organizations, Counseling, Crime Prevention, Domestic Violence, People with Disabilities, Recreation & Athletics, Scouts, Social Services-General, Special Olympics, Substance Abuse, YMCA/YWCA/YMHA/YWHA, Youth Organizations

Application Procedures

Initial Contact: Send brief letter explaining need and wants. There are no deadlines.
Deadlines: None.

Corporate Officials

Robert J. Sudhoff: vice president financial, chief financial officerc B Coldwater, OH 1955. ED Wright State University (1977). PRIM CORP EMPL vice president financial, chief financial officer: Minister Machine Co.

John Winch: president, chief operating officer, director B Lima, OH 1962. ED Southern Methodist University (1984); Ohio State University (1988). PRIM CORP EMPL president, chief operating officer, director: Minster Machine Co. CLUB AFFIL Rotary Club.

Foundation Officials

Robert J. Sudhoff: vice president, secretary (see above)
David C. Winch: treasurer
Harold S. Winch: president
Heather E. Winch: secretary
John Winch: vice president (see above)
Nancy E. Winch: president

Grants Analysis

Disclosure Period: fiscal year ending November 30, 2001
Total Grants: $60,800
Number of Grants: 32
Average Grant: $1,062*
Highest Grant: $10,000
Lowest Grant: $50
Typical Range: $250 to $2,000
*Note: Average grant figure excludes three highest grants ($30,000).

Recent Grants

Note: Grants derived from fiscal 2001 Form 990.

General

10,000	BMH Foundation, Muncie, IN
10,000	Boonshoft Museum of Discovery, Dayton, OH
10,000	PMA Educational Foundation, Independence, OH
5,000	Dayton Art Institute, Dayton, OH
5,000	Hospice of Darke and Mercer Counties, Greenville, OH
5,000	JTD Hospital Foundation, St. Marys, OH
2,000	Minster High School Scholarship Fund, Minster, OH
2,000	Village of Minster Fire Department, Minster, OH
1,500	National Child Safety Council, Minster, OH
1,000	Knights of Columbus 2158, Minster, OH

MITSUBISHI MOTOR SALES OF AMERICA, INC.

Company Headquarters

6400 Katella Avenue
Cypress, CA 90630-5208
Web: http://www.mitsubishicars.com

Company Description

Revenue: US$25.939 billion (2001)
Employees: 1100 (2001)
SIC(s): 5012 Automobiles & Other Motor Vehicles.
Parent Company: Mitsubishi Corp., 6-3, Marunouchi 2-chome, Chiyoda-ku, Tokyo, Japan
Parent Revenue: US$32,689,000,000 (2001)

Operating Locations

Mitsubishi Fuso Truck of America (NJ--Bridgeport); Mitsubishi Motor Sales of America, Inc. (CA--Orange; FL--Orlando; IL--Itasca; TX--Irving); Mitsubishi Motors America (MI--Southfield); Mitsubishi Motors Credit of America (CA--Cypress; NY--Purchase)

Nonmonetary Support

Type: Cause-related Marketing & Promotion; Donated Equipment; Donated Products; In-kind Services; Workplace Solicitation
Note: Cause-related marketing and promotion is handled by the marketing services department. Company also sponsors an employee volunteer program.

Giving Contact

Stephanie Martin, Corp. Relations
6400 Katella Ave.
Cypress, CA 90630
Phone: (714)372-6454
Fax: (714)934-7656

Description

Organization Type: Corporate Giving Program
Giving Locations: Communities where company has a major presence.
Grant Types: General Support, Multiyear/Continuing Support, Operating Expenses, Scholarship, Seed Money.

Financial Summary

Total Giving: Company does not disclose contributions figures.

Typical Recipients

Arts & Humanities: Libraries, Performing Arts, Theater
Civic & Public Affairs: African American Affairs, Asian American Affairs, Chambers of Commerce, Civil Rights, Employment/Job Training, Ethnic Organizations, Civic & Public Affairs-General, Hispanic Affairs, Safety, Women's Affairs
Environment: Environment-General

Application Procedures

Initial Contact: Send a full proposals.
Application Requirements: Inlcude a brief overview of the organization, including the specific project for which funding is requested; the exact amount requested; a short background of the organization, including the number of paid and volunteer employees; specific project information, including the purpose for desired funds, time period of proposed program, goals and how they will be attained, projected results and how they will be assessed, how the organization will report and evaluate results, geographical area served and number of people who will benefit; financial disclosure including full budget for current year, current sources of funding, ratio of administrative costs to total budget, and proportion of funding to be derived from contributions. Additional information required is a copy of IRS tax-exempt document per Section 501(c)(3); copy of current Form 990; audited financial statements from the previous two years; list of present board of directors; and support documents such as an annual report, catalogs, brochures, news clippings, and any other pertinent information.

Restrictions

Does not support political parties, candidates, or lobbying organizations; organizations that are not tax-exempt; individuals; or organizations whose major area of influence is outside the United States.

Additional Information

Company has formulated a series of guidelines by which it reviews all requests. To be considered, applicant organizations must promote safe driving or fall within other areas of support; be focused within communities where company has a major presence; allow company to review its list of contributors; show a specific use for contributions of $10,000 or less; and be able to exist independently of company's contribution. Additionally, the organization should enjoy the support of its local constituency, including community leaders. Financial support is granted on a one-time basis, and further support or renewal is not implied.

However, additional orfuture funding may be available pending submission of a new request.
Publications: Guidelines for Corporate Giving

Corporate Officials

Pierre Gagnon: chief operating officer, president PRIM CORP EMPL chief operating officer, president: Mitsubishi Motor Sales America.
Hirao Iijima: chairman PRIM CORP EMPL chairman: Mitsubishi Motor Sales of America, Inc.
Takashi Sanobe: senior chief executive officer, chairman PRIM CORP EMPL senior chief executive officer, chairman: Mitsubishi Motor Sales of America.

Grants Analysis

Typical Range: $2,500 to $5,000

MITSUBISHI SEMICONDUCTOR AMERICA

Company Headquarters

3 Diamond Lane
Durham, NC 27704
Web: http://www.msai.com

Company Description

Employees: 500
SIC(s): 3674 Semiconductors & Related Devices.
Parent Company: Mitsubishi Corp., 6-3, Marunouchi 2-chome, Chiyoda-ku, Tokyo, Japan
Parent Revenue: US$32,689,000,000 (2001)

Nonmonetary Support

Type: Donated Equipment
Volunteer Programs: The company has an active volunteer committee that donates time and services to local communities. It is a member of the Durham Business Volunteer Council.

Mitsubishi Semiconductor America, Inc. Funds

Giving Contact

Gary Edge, President
Mitsubishi Semiconductor America, Inc. Funds
2635 Meridian Parkway
Durham, NC 27713
Phone: (919)767-7779

Description

Founded: 1989
EIN: 561637250
Organization Type: Corporate Foundation
Giving Locations: NC
Grant Types: Employee Matching Gifts, General Support, Multiyear/Continuing Support.

Financial Summary

Total Giving: $113,000 (2001); $51,500 (2000); $206,050 (1998)
Giving Analysis: Giving for 2000 includes: foundation ($51,500); 1998: foundation grants to United Way ($2,500) foundation grants ($203,550).
Assets: $1,568,981 (2001); $1,621,597 (2000); $1,587,880 (1998)

Typical Recipients

Arts & Humanities: Arts Associations & Councils, Arts Centers, Community Arts, Arts & Humanities-General, Libraries, Museums/Galleries, Music

Civic & Public Affairs: Asian American Affairs, Business/Free Enterprise, Clubs, Community Foundations, Civic & Public Affairs-General, Housing, Philanthropic Organizations, Safety, Urban & Community Affairs
Education: Agricultural Education, Business-School Partnerships, Colleges & Universities, Community & Junior Colleges, Engineering/Technological Education, Education-General, International Exchange, International Studies, Private Education (Precollege), Public Education (Precollege), Science/Mathematics Education, Vocational & Technical Education
Health: Cancer, Children's Health/Hospitals, Heart, Hospitals, Prenatal Health Issues, Respiratory, Single-Disease Health Associations
International: Foreign Arts Organizations, International-General, International Organizations, International Relations
Religion: Religious Welfare
Science: Science Museums
Social Services: At-Risk Youth, Child Welfare, Community Service Organizations, Domestic Violence, Food/Clothing Distribution, Homes, People with Disabilities, Shelters/Homelessness, Social Services-General, United Funds/United Ways, Volunteer Services, YMCA/YWCA/YMHA/YWHA

Application Procedures

Initial Contact: Return a completed application form.
Application Requirements: Include a copy of the most recent balance sheet, income tax statements, and audit report; current operating budget; line-item budget for the project for which funding is requested; annual report; list of board members and their affiliations; and proof of tax-exempt status.
Deadlines: None.
Notes: Recipients must also submit a written agreement to repay the foundation any funds not expended for the original purpose described.

Restrictions

Does not support individuals, religious organizations for sectarian purposes, political or lobbying groups, or organizations outside operating areas.

Corporate Officials

Kathy H. Cayton: treasurer, chief financial officer, chief executive officer PRIM CORP EMPL treasurer, chief financial officer: Mitsubishi Semiconductor of America.
Masataka Takehara: chairman, president, chief executive officer PRIM CORP EMPL chairman, president, chief executive officer: Mitsubishi Semiconductor of America.

Giving Program Officials

Jim Bowen: PRIM CORP EMPL section manager administration: Mitsubishi Semiconductor of America.

Foundation Officials

Kathy H. Cayton: treasurer (see above)
Gary Edge: president
Kim Evans: treasurer
Pat Hefferan: vice president
Leah Shaw: secretary
Masataka Takehara: president, director (see above)

Grants Analysis

Disclosure Period: calendar year ending 2001
Total Grants: $113,000
Number of Grants: 5
Highest Grant: $80,000
Lowest Grant: $5,000
Typical Range: $5,000 to $15,000

Recent Grants

Note: Grants derived from 2000 Form 990.

General
35,000   North Carolina State University, Raleigh, NC

6,000   Duke University, Durham, NC
6,000   North Carolina State University, Raleigh, NC
5,000   Education Foundation, Chapel Hill, NC
500   North Carolina State University, Raleigh, NC

MITSUBISHI SILICON AMERICA

Company Headquarters
1351 Tandem Ave., NE
Salem, OR 97303
Web: http://www.mitsubishisilicon.com

Company Description
Revenue: US$196.8 million (2001)
Employees: 200
SIC(s): 3674 Semiconductors & Related Devices.
Parent Company: Mitsubishi Materials Corp., 1-5-1 Otemachi, Chiyoda-ku, Tokyo, Japan

Operating Locations
Mitsubishi Materials (NY--New York); Mitsubishi Silicon America (CA--Palo Alto; OR--Salem); Mitsubishi Silicon America - Eastern Regional Sales Office (CT--Westport); Mitsubishi Silicon America - Southwest Regional Sales Office (TX--Dallas); MMC Electronics America (IL--Rolling Meadows); Salem Manufacturing Facility (OR--Salem)

Nonmonetary Support
Type: Donated Equipment; Loaned Executives

Giving Contact
Judy Nix, Vice President, Human Resources
PO Box 7748
Salem, OR 97303-4199
Phone: (503)371-0041
Fax: (503)361-3539
E-mail: judy.nix@mitsubishisilicon.com
Web: http://www.mitsubishisilicon.com

Alternate Contact
1351 Tandem Avenue NE
Salem, OR 97303

Description
Organization Type: Corporate Giving Program
Giving Locations: operating locations.
Grant Types: Multiyear/Continuing Support, Operating Expenses, Project, Scholarship.

Typical Recipients
Arts & Humanities: Arts Festivals, Arts & Humanities-General, Historic Preservation, Libraries, Museums/Galleries, Music
Civic & Public Affairs: Community Foundations, Economic Development, Civic & Public Affairs-General, Women's Affairs
Education: Afterschool/Enrichment Programs, Education Funds, Elementary Education (Public), Education-General, Public Education (Precollege), Special Education
Health: Hospices
Social Services: Child Welfare, Community Centers, Domestic Violence, People with Disabilities, Recreation & Athletics, Shelters/Homelessness, Social Services-General, Substance Abuse, United Funds/United Ways, Volunteer Services

Application Procedures
Initial Contact: Submit a brief letter of inquiry.
Application Requirements: Include a description of the organization and purpose of funds sought.

Restrictions
Does not support organizations outside operating area

Corporate Officials
Shigeru Masuda: chairman, directorvice president administration PRIM CORP EMPL chairman, director: Mitsubishi Silicon of America.
Stanley Thomas Myers: president, chief executive officer, director B McPherson, KS 1936. ED University of Kansas (1960). PRIM CORP EMPL president, chief executive officer, director: Mitsubishi Silicon of America. CORP AFFIL director: Semiconductor Equip & Materials International; president: Siltec Expitaxial Corp.; director: CYBEQ System.
Hisashi Uchida: senior executive vice president administration PRIM CORP EMPL senior executive vice president administration: Mitsubishi Silicon of America.

Grants Analysis
Typical Range: $1,000 to $2,500

MOLDAW FAMILY FOUNDATION

Giving Contact
Stuart G. Moldaw, President
1550 El Camino Real, Suite 290
Menlo Park, CA 94025
Phone: (650)696-7489
Fax: (650)696-7585

Description
Founded: 1977
EIN: 942450734
Organization Type: Private Foundation
Giving Locations: CA: gives nationally
Grant Types: General Support.

Donor Information
Founder: members of the Moldaw Family

Financial Summary
Total Giving: $231,150 (fiscal year ending November 30, 2001); $230,000 (fiscal 2000); $118,895 (fiscal 1998). Note: $101,514 (fiscal year ending November 30, 1996); $1,049,845 (fiscal 1995); $141,787 (fiscal 1994).
Giving Analysis: Giving for fiscal 2001 includes: foundation grants to United Way ($10,000); fiscal 2000: foundation scholarships ($6,000); nonmonetary support ($115,000); fiscal 1998: foundation scholarships ($6,000) foundation ($112,895).
Assets: $2,828,419 (fiscal 2001); $3,119,464 (fiscal 2000); $2,921,736 (fiscal 1998)

Typical Recipients
Arts & Humanities: Arts Associations & Councils, Arts Festivals, Arts Institutes, Arts Outreach, Ballet, Ethnic & Folk Arts, Historic Preservation, History & Archaeology, Libraries, Museums/Galleries, Music, Opera, Public Broadcasting, Theater
Civic & Public Affairs: Civic & Public Affairs-General, Municipalities/Towns, Women's Affairs
Education: Colleges & Universities, Education Reform, Education-General, Private Education (Precollege), Public Education (Precollege), Student Aid
Health: Cancer, Children's Health/Hospitals, Heart, Hospitals, Hospitals (University Affiliated), Long-Term Care, Medical Research, Single-Disease Health Associations, Speech & Hearing
International: Human Rights, International Affairs, International Affairs, International Relations, Missionary/Religious Activities
Religion: Churches, Jewish Causes, Religious Organizations
Science: Science Museums

Social Services: Community Service Organizations, Crime Prevention, Domestic Violence, Food/Clothing Distribution, People with Disabilities, Recreation & Athletics, United Funds/United Ways, Youth Organizations

Application Procedures
Initial Contact: The foundation has no formal grant application procedure or application form.
Deadlines: April 15.

Additional Information
Publications: Application Form

Foundation Officials
Carol A. Moldaw: director
Phyllis Moldaw: vice president, treasurer
Stuart G. Moldaw: president
Susan J. Moldaw: director

Grants Analysis
Disclosure Period: fiscal year ending November 30, 2001
Total Grants: $221,150*
Number of Grants: 53
Average Grant: $4,173
Highest Grant: $40,000
Lowest Grant: $50
Typical Range: $1,000 to $10,000
***Note:** Giving excludes United Way.

Recent Grants
Note: Grants derived from fiscal 2000 Form 990.

Library-Related
10,000	School of the Sacred Heart, San Francisco, CA

General
10,000	Athenian School, The, Danville, CA
10,000	Athenian School, The, Danville, CA
10,000	Synergy School, Memphis, TN
10,000	Town School for Boys, San Francisco, CA
10,000	White House Endowment Fund, Washington, DC
6,000	ARCS Foundation, San Francisco, CA
5,000	Boys and Girls Club of the Peninsula, Menlo Park, CA
5,000	Boys and Girls Club of the Peninsula, Menlo Park, CA
5,000	Jewish Community Fund, San Francisco, CA -- JDC Hunger Relief
3,750	San Francisco Museum of Modern Art, San Francisco, CA -- collectors forum

MONADNOCK PAPER MILLS, INC.

Company Headquarters
117 Antrim Road
Bennington, NH 03442
Web: http://www.monadnockpaper.com

Company Description
Revenue: US$77.5 million (2001)
Employees: 232 (2001)
SIC(s): 2621 Paper Mills, 2672 Coated & Laminated Paper Nec, 2676 Sanitary Paper Products, 2678 Stationery Products.

Gilbert Verney Foundation

Giving Contact
Richard G. Verney, Chairman & Chief Executive Officer
117 Antrim Rd.
Bennington, NH 03442-4205

Phone: (603)588-3311
Fax: (603)588-3561

Description
EIN: 026007363
Organization Type: Corporate Foundation
Giving Locations: MA; NH
Grant Types: Capital, Endowment, General Support, Operating Expenses, Project, Research.

Donor Information
Founder: Monadnock Paper Mills

Financial Summary
Total Giving: $175,579 (2000); $107,765 (1999); $117,854 (1998)
Giving Analysis: Giving for 1999 includes: foundation scholarships ($500); foundation ($107,265); 1998: foundation scholarships ($5,000) foundation ($112,854)
Assets: $4,170,464 (2000); $4,368,126 (1999); $3,627,439 (1998)
Gifts Received: $125,000 (2000); $125,000 (1999); $100,000 (1998). Note: In 1998 and 2000, contributions were received from Monadnock Paper Mills.

Typical Recipients
Arts & Humanities: Arts Associations & Councils, Arts Centers, Arts Funds, Arts Institutes, Arts Outreach, Dance, Arts & Humanities-General, Historic Preservation, History & Archaeology, Libraries, Literary Arts, Museums/Galleries, Music, Opera, Performing Arts, Public Broadcasting, Theater, Visual Arts
Civic & Public Affairs: Civic & Public Affairs-General, Native American Affairs, Public Policy, Urban & Community Affairs, Women's Affairs
Education: Agricultural Education, Business Education, Colleges & Universities, Economic Education, Environmental Education, Education-General, Leadership Training, Private Education (Precollege), Science/Mathematics Education, Secondary Education (Private), Special Education
Environment: Forestry, Environment-General, Resource Conservation
Health: Health-General, Home-Care Services, Hospices, Hospitals, Medical Rehabilitation, Public Health
International: Health Care/Hospitals
Religion: Churches, Religion-General, Religious Organizations, Religious Welfare
Science: Scientific Centers & Institutes
Social Services: Animal Protection, Child Welfare, Day Care, Domestic Violence, Family Services, Recreation & Athletics, Social Services-General, YMCA/YWCA/YMHA/YWHA, Youth Organizations

Application Procedures
Initial Contact: Send a brief letter of inquiry, including a description of organization, amount requested, purpose of funds sought, recently audited financial statement, and proof of tax-exempt status.
Deadlines: None.

Restrictions
Does not make contributions to individuals or to organizations carrying on propoganda or otherwise attempting to influence legislation.

Corporate Officials
Andrew Manns: vice president financial, treasurerc PRIM CORP EMPL vice president financial, treasurer: Manadnock Paper Mills.
Richard Greville Verney: chairman, chief executive officer, director B Providence, RI 1946. ED Brown University AB (1968). PRIM CORP EMPL chairman, chief executive officer, director: Monadnock Paper Mills. CORP AFFIL director: Sales Association Paper Industry; director: Business Indiana Association New Hampshire; director: American Forest & Paper Association; director: Boston Paper Trade Association.

NONPR AFFIL vice president trustee: Nantucket Consult Foundation; hon trustee: Saint Georges School; trustee: Monadnock County Hosp; trustee: Crotched Mt Foundation. CLUB AFFIL New York Yacht Club; Algonquin Club; Nantucket Yacht Club.

Foundation Officials
Lumina V. Greenway: trustee
E. Geoffrey Verney: trustee PRIM CORP EMPL vice president business development & corporate communications: Monadnock Paper Mills.
Richard Greville Verney: president (see above)

Grants Analysis
Disclosure Period: calendar year ending 2000
Total Grants: $175,579
Number of Grants: 77
Average Grant: $2,280
Highest Grant: $15,000
Typical Range: $1,000 to $5,000

Recent Grants
Note: Grants derived from 2001 Form 990.

Library-Related
5,000	Stephenson Memorial Library, Greenfield, NH

General
125,000	Nantucket Conservation Foundation, Inc., Nantucket, MA
15,000	All Saints Parish, Brookline, MA
15,000	Monadnock Community Hospital, Peterborough, NH
12,500	Nantucket Historical Association, Nantucket, MA
12,500	Society for the Protection of New Hampshire Forests, Concord, NH
10,000	Institute of American Indian Arts Foundation, Santa Fe, NM
10,000	Nantucket Conservation Foundation, Inc., Nantucket, MA
9,025	St. George's School
8,500	Sharon Arts Center, Sharon, NH
8,225	Crotched Mountain Foundation, Greenfield, NH

MONFORT FAMILY FOUNDATION

Giving Contact
Dave Evans, Administrator
PO Box 337300
Greeley, CO 80633
Phone: (970)454-1357
Fax: (970)454-2535

Description
Founded: 1970
EIN: 237068253
Organization Type: Family Foundation
Giving Locations: CO: Northern Colorado
Grant Types: General Support, Scholarship.

Donor Information
Founder: Established in 1970 by Margery Monfort Wilson and Richard L. Monfort.

Financial Summary
Total Giving: $7,021,869 (2000); $2,500,000 (1999 approx); $2,723,338 (1998)
Giving Analysis: Giving for 2000 includes: foundation scholarships ($1,000)
Assets: $33,338,426 (2000); $42,310,118 (1998); $39,812,405 (1997)
Gifts Received: $54,963 (1992). Note: In 1991, contributions were received from the estate of Margery Monfort Wilson ($1,680,000) and Richard L. Monfort

($11,360). In 1992, contributions were received from the estate of Margery Monfort Wilson.

Typical Recipients

Arts & Humanities: Ballet, History & Archaeology, Libraries, Museums/Galleries, Music, Performing Arts, Public Broadcasting, Theater

Civic & Public Affairs: African American Affairs, Botanical Gardens/Parks, Business/Free Enterprise, Clubs, Community Foundations, Economic Development, Civic & Public Affairs-General, Hispanic Affairs, Housing, Municipalities/Towns, Parades/Festivals, Professional & Trade Associations, Rural Affairs, Women's Affairs, Zoos/Aquariums

Education: Agricultural Education, Arts/Humanities Education, Business Education, Colleges & Universities, Community & Junior Colleges, Economic Education, Education Funds, Education Reform, Elementary Education (Public), Education-General, Literacy, Minority Education, Private Education (Precollege), Public Education (Precollege), School Volunteerism, Student Aid, Vocational & Technical Education

Environment: Environment-General

Health: AIDS/HIV, Arthritis, Cancer, Children's Health/Hospitals, Clinics/Medical Centers, Hospitals, Medical Rehabilitation, Multiple Sclerosis, Prenatal Health Issues, Public Health, Respiratory, Single-Disease Health Associations, Speech & Hearing, Trauma Treatment

Religion: Churches, Religious Welfare

Social Services: Animal Protection, At-Risk Youth, Child Welfare, Community Centers, Community Service Organizations, Crime Prevention, Family Services, Food/Clothing Distribution, People with Disabilities, Recreation & Athletics, Scouts, Scouts, Senior Services, Shelters/Homelessness, Social Services-General, Special Olympics, Substance Abuse, United Funds/United Ways, Veterans, Volunteer Services, Youth Organizations

Application Procedures

Initial Contact: Contact the foundation for application guidelines.

Application Requirements: Applications should include the organization's name, total budget of the organization, total project budget, amount requested, summary of proposal, other sources of funding, future funding, and list of board members.

Deadlines: Deadlines for applications are May 1 and October 1.

Foundation Officials

Kyle Monfort Futo: vice president
Myra Monfort: secretary
Kaye C. Monfort Montera: president PRIM CORP EMPL president, director: High County Investor Inc.

Grants Analysis

Disclosure Period: calendar year ending 2000
Total Grants: $7,020,869*
Number of Grants: 39
Average Grant: $33,657*
Highest Grant: $5,250,433
Typical Range: $15,000 to $50,000
*Note: Giving excludes scholarships. Average grant figure excludes two highest grants ($5,775,563).

Recent Grants

Note: Grants derived from 2000 Form 990.

Library-Related
10,000	Grover Regional Library Association, Grover, CO

General
5,250,433	University of Colorado, Boulder, CO
525,120	Colorado State University Foundation, Ft. Collins, CO -- student programs
300,000	Colorado Farm Show, Denver, CO -- capital expenditures
201,607	University of Northern Colorado Foundation, Greeley, CO
200,000	Community Foundation, Greeley, CO
200,000	Mountain View Academy, Greeley, CO -- student programs
60,000	World War II Memorial, Washington, DC
50,000	ARC of Colorado, Denver, CO
32,500	Denver Broncos Charities, Denver, CO
27,000	Channel Six, Denver, CO

MONSANTO CO.

Company Headquarters

800 N. Lindbergh Blvd.
St. Louis, MO 63167
Web: http://www.monsanto.com

Company Description

Founded: 1933
Ticker: MON
Exchange: NYSE
Acquired: Dekalb Genetics Corp. (1998).
Revenue: US$4.673 billion (2002)
Employees: 13700 (2002)
SIC(s): 2821 Plastics Materials & Resins, 2834 Pharmaceutical Preparations.

Nonmonetary Support

Type: Donated Equipment

Monsanto Fund

Giving Contact

Deborah J. Patterson, President
Monsanto Fund
800 N. Lindbergh Boulevard
St. Louis, MO 63167
Phone: (314)694-1000
Fax: (314)694-7658
E-mail: monsanto.fund@monsanto.com
Web: http://www.monsantofund.org

Description

EIN: 436044736
Organization Type: Corporate Foundation
Giving Locations: operating facilities.
Grant Types: Employee Matching Gifts, Project.
Note: Employee matching gift ratio: 1 to 1, up to $5,000 per employee per year.

Financial Summary

Total Giving: $17,300,000 (2002 approx); $18,631,009 (2001 approx); $13,741,661 (2000). Note: Contributes through corporate direct giving program and foundation.

Giving Analysis: Giving for 2001 includes: foundation matching gifts ($875,016); foundation grants to United Way ($1,769,020); corporate direct giving (approx $2,400,000); foundation ($13,586,973); 2000: foundation matching gifts ($1,208,929); foundation grants to United Way ($1,479,970); foundation ($11,052,762); 1999: foundation matching gifts ($1,317,327); foundation grants to United Way ($1,567,635); foundation ($13,259,251);

Assets: $22,643,547 (2001); $37,847,443 (2000); $2,591,000 (1999)

Gifts Received: $127,526 (2001); $47,552,201 (2000); $2,075,387 (1999). Note: In 2001, contributions were received from Monsanto Co. In 2000 and 1999, contributions were received from Monsanto Co. and the Searle Patients in Need Foundation.

Typical Recipients

Arts & Humanities: Arts Associations & Councils, Arts Centers, Dance, Ethnic & Folk Arts, Arts & Humanities-General, Historic Preservation, History & Archaeology, Libraries, Museums/Galleries, Music, Opera, Performing Arts, Public Broadcasting, Theater

Civic & Public Affairs: African American Affairs, Botanical Gardens/Parks, Business/Free Enterprise, Clubs, Community Foundations, Economic Development, Employment/Job Training, Civic & Public Affairs-General, Housing, Municipalities/Towns, Nonprofit Management, Professional & Trade Associations, Public Policy, Safety, Urban & Community Affairs, Zoos/Aquariums

Education: Afterschool/Enrichment Programs, Arts/Humanities Education, Business Education, Colleges & Universities, Colleges & Universities, Community & Junior Colleges, Education Funds, Education Reform, Engineering/Technological Education, Education-General, Journalism/Media Education, Minority Education, Private Education (Precollege), Public Education (Precollege), Science/Mathematics Education, Secondary Education (Private), Secondary Education (Public), Student Aid, Vocational & Technical Education

Environment: Resource Conservation

Health: AIDS/HIV, Alzheimers Disease, Cancer, Children's Health/Hospitals, Clinics/Medical Centers, Diabetes, Emergency/Ambulance Services, Health Policy/Cost Containment, Health Organizations, Hospitals, Medical Research, Research/Studies Institutes

International: Foreign Educational Institutions, International-General, International Environmental Issues, International Organizations

Religion: Dioceses, Jewish Causes, Religious Welfare, Social/Policy Issues

Science: Observatories & Planetariums, Science Museums, Scientific Centers & Institutes, Scientific Organizations

Social Services: Child Welfare, Community Service Organizations, Crime Prevention, Day Care, Domestic Violence, Family Services, Food/Clothing Distribution, Scouts, Shelters/Homelessness, Social Services-General, Substance Abuse, United Funds/United Ways, YMCA/YWCA/YMHA/YWHA, Youth Organizations

Application Procedures

Initial Contact: Organizations near a Monsanto manufacturing facility should contact local manager. Other organizations should contact the fund or see website for application information, then submit a Preliminary Funding Request (PFR).

Application Requirements: PFR may not exceed three pages, and should include: name and mission of the organization; description of the project and how it relates to one of the priority giving areas (Agricultural Abundance, the Environment, Science Education, and Our Communities); estimated budget; amount requested; methods for evaluating project's results; contact name, phone, mailing address and email; names of any Monsanto employees associated with the organization; attach proof of 501(c)(3) tax-exempt status. PFR should not include any extraneous materials, should be on standard-sized white paper with a font no smaller than 12 points, should not be in a folder or binder, and should be mailed (faxed or emailed PFR's are not accepted).

Deadlines: PFR's are due January 1 and July 1.

Evaluative Criteria: Applicants must be tax-exempt charities; project must fit within one of the priority giving areas; nonprofit must be experienced, established, and reputable (foundation does not work with start-ups); nonprofit must be financially sound, have a diverse funding base, and be audited annually.

Decision Notification: Fund attempts to respond to written requests within three months; proposals that do not meet guidelines are turned down immediately.

Restrictions

Unsolicited proposals are rarely considered.

Long-term commitments are rarely made. Fund occasionally makes grants for two years at most. Organizations repeating a request in the same year are not considered for additional funding.

Fund does not support individuals; religious, politically partisan, or similar organizations; fraternal, labor, or veterans groups, unless project benefits the general public; benefits, dinners, or goodwill advertising; underwriting of deficits; endowments; activities that directly support marketing programs; projects in which Monsanto Company has a financial interest or could derive a financial benefit through cash or rights to intellectual property; organizations that discriminate based on race, creed, ethnicity, religion, sex, age, or national origin.

Additional Information

Decisions concerning organizations near a Monsanto facility are made by that particular facility; plant locations establish giving priorities autonomously.

Grant requests must be resubmitted on an annual basis unless otherwise stipulated.

In the 1990s, the fund continued to sharpen its focus on supporting programs with measurable results. It funded more "catalyst" projects and fewer "maintenance" programs; it looked for creative partnerships with nonprofit organizations; and awarded fewer but more sizable grants. In future years, the fund will play a greater role in supporting communities outside the United States, a reflection of the company's growing international identity.

Monsanto Co. merged with Pharmacia & Upjohn in January 2000.$13,586,973

Corporate Officials

Hugh Grant: president, chief executive officer ED University of Edinburgh MS; University of Glasgow BS. PRIM CORP EMPL president, chief executive officer: Monsanto Co.

Grants Analysis

Disclosure Period: calendar year ending 2001
Total Grants: $13,586,973*
Number of Grants: 226
Average Grant: $27,275*
Highest Grant: $7,450,000
Typical Range: $500 to $100,000
*Note: Giving excludes matching gifts; United Way; and corporate direct giving. Average grant figure excludes highest grant.

Recent Grants

Note: Grants derived from 2001 Form 990.

General

7,450,000	Donald Danforth Plant Science Center, St. Louis, MO
600,000	St. Louis Zoo Association Insectarium 2004, St. Louis, MO
550,000	United Way of Greater St. Louis, St. Louis, MO
550,000	United Way of Greater St. Louis, St. Louis, MO
500,000	Greater Kalamazoo United Way, Kalamazoo, MI
500,000	Liberty Science Center, Jersey City, NJ
250,000	American Red Cross, St. Louis, MO
250,000	CAB International United Kingdom
250,000	Citizen Scholarship Foundation of America, St. Peter, MN
250,000	Missouri Historical Society, St. Louis, MO

MONY GROUP, INC.

Company Headquarters

New York, NY
Web: http://www.mony.com

Company Description

Founded: 1843
Ticker: MNY
Exchange: NYSE
Former Name: The Mutual Life Insurance Co. of New York.
Assets: US$19.925 billion (2002)
Employees: 4014 (2002)

SIC(s): 6311 Life Insurance, 6321 Accident & Health Insurance.

Operating Locations

MONY Group (NJ--Teaneck; NY--Syracuse)

Nonmonetary Support

Value: $280,000 (1999)
Type: Donated Equipment; In-kind Services; Workplace Solicitation
Volunteer Programs: The company sponsors the Volunteer Incentive at MONY (VIM) program, which encourages employee volunteerism at nonprofit organizations by providing semi-annual grants to those served by MONY Group volunteers. Another program, the Volunteer Incentive Award Program (VIP), makes an annual monetary award to a nonprofit social service agency in the community of each of its two major sites to encourage volunteer programs that effectively maximize their recourses by creatively utilizing employed volunteers.

MONY Foundation

Giving Contact

Lynn Stekas, President
MONY Foundation
1740 Broadway
New York, NY 10019
Phone: (212)708-2377
Fax: (212)708-2001
Web: http://www.mony.com/AboutMONY/InsideMONY/Foundation

Alternate Contact

Phone: (212)708-2473
Note: Contact number for information on Volunteer Incentive at MONY (VIM), Volunteer Incentive Award Program (VIP), and Matching Gifts program.

Description

EIN: 133398852
Organization Type: Corporate Foundation
Former Name: MONY Life Insurance of New York.
Giving Locations: NY: New York, Syracuse headquarters and operating communities.
Grant Types: Award, Employee Matching Gifts, Project.
Note: Employee matching gift ratio: 1 to 1. Company matches gifts up to $1,000 in contributions made by eligible employees, financial professionals, and retirees throughout the U.S. Matching gifts are open to nonprofit, tax-exempt organizations and post-secondary educational institutions. Political, sectarian, religious, or United Way organization are not eligible for matching gifts.

Financial Summary

Total Giving: $1,006,977 (2001); $875,590 (2000); $1,141,530 (1999). Note: Contributes through corporate direct giving program and foundation.
Giving Analysis: Giving for 2001 includes: foundation grants to United Way ($190,750); foundation matching gifts ($276,270); foundation ($539,957); 1999: foundation grants to United Way ($130,750); foundation matching gifts ($310,752); corporate direct giving (approx $321,751); foundation ($378,277); 1997: corporate grants to United Way ($130,256); corporate matching gifts ($290,950) foundation ($942,186)
Assets: $272,407 (2001); $386,798 (2000); $285,239 (1999)
Gifts Received: $1,032,500 (2001); $904,150 (2000); $943,736 (1997). Note: In 2001, contributions were received from The MONY Life Insurance Co.

Typical Recipients

Arts & Humanities: Arts Centers, Dance, Libraries, Literary Arts, Museums/Galleries, Opera, Performing Arts, Public Broadcasting, Theater

Civic & Public Affairs: African American Affairs, Asian American Affairs, Business/Free Enterprise, Community Foundations, Economic Development, Employment/Job Training, Ethnic Organizations, Gay/Lesbian Issues, Civic & Public Affairs-General, Hispanic Affairs, Housing, Inner-City Development, Law & Justice, Legal Aid, Nonprofit Management, Philanthropic Organizations, Public Policy, Urban & Community Affairs, Women's Affairs

Education: Business Education, Colleges & Universities, Economic Education, Education-General, Leadership Training, Literacy, Minority Education, Preschool Education, Private Education (Precollege), Public Education (Precollege), Social Sciences Education

Environment: Environment-General

Health: AIDS/HIV, Cancer, Clinics/Medical Centers, Emergency/Ambulance Services, Health-General, Health Organizations, Hospices, Medical Research, Mental Health, Prenatal Health Issues, Public Health, Research/Studies Institutes, Single-Disease Health Associations

International: International Development

Religion: Churches, Religious Organizations, Religious Welfare

Science: Science Museums

Social Services: Big Brother/Big Sister, Child Welfare, Community Centers, Community Service Organizations, Counseling, Day Care, Family Planning, Family Services, Food/Clothing Distribution, People with Disabilities, Refugee Assistance, Scouts, Senior Services, Shelters/Homelessness, Social Services-General, Substance Abuse, United Funds/United Ways, Volunteer Services, YMCA/YWCA/YMHA/YWHA, Youth Organizations

Application Procedures

Initial Contact: Submit a brief written proposal.
Application Requirements: Proposals must include organizational, and grant information, and attached documentation. Organization information should include name and address of the organization; contact person, title, a phone number; history and background of organization; and geographic area and target population served by the organization. Grant information should include amount requested, specifics on how funds will be used; project description, including target population, needs addressed, planned activities; objectives, staff, qualifications, and proposed timetable; and a proposed line-item budget. Required documentation includes proof of tax-exempt status; recently audited financial statement; IRS 990 tax form; current list of board of directors; current list of project funders, including grant amounts; and, if available, the organization's most recent annual report, brochure, and newsletter.
Deadlines: None.
Evaluative Criteria: Funding goes to well-defined programs that conform to the company's giving priorities; well-managed organizations, with ability to achieve specific objectives; organizations within company operating areas requesting reasonable amounts.
Decision Notification: Please call each site for timelines.
Notes: After reviewing the material, the foundation requests additional information if necessary. Contributions guidelines should be reviewed before submitting request.

Restrictions

The MONY Foundation makes grants only to organizations that are classified as tax exempt under 501(c)(3). In general, MONY will not consider requests for the following: capital fund drives; private foundations; research activities; fully participating members of the United Way; religious, fraternal, political, athletic, social, or veterans organizations; endowments, memorials, or contingency funds; individuals; fundraising activities such as benefits, charitable dinners, or sporting events; legislative or lobbying efforts;

books, magazines, articles, film/video productions or advertising; or organizations with a financial deficit. Foundation gives to colleges and universities in the form of matching funds only.

Additional Information

In addition to direct grants given through the Corporate Social Policy Division in New York, NY, a portion of the contributions budget is disbursed through the Syracuse Operations Center, Syracuse, NY; and Glenpointe Marketing Center, Teaneck, NJ.

Corporate Officials

Samuel J. Foti: president, chief operating officer, director B 1952. ED University of Pennsylvania Wharton School MA; University of Pennsylvania Wharton School BS. PRIM CORP EMPL president, chief operating officer, director: The Mutual Life Insurance Co. of New York Inc. CORP AFFIL president, director: Mony Life Insurance of America Arizona Corp.

Kenneth M. Levine: executive vice president, chief investment officer, director B Bronx, NY 1946. ED City University of New York (1968). PRIM CORP EMPL executive vice president, chief investment officer, director: The Mutual Life Insurance Co. of New York ADD CORP EMPL director: 1740 Advisors Inc.; president: 1740 Ventures Inc.; executive vice president: MONY Group Inc.; executive vice president: MONY Life Insurance Co.; executive vice president: MONY Life Insurance of American Arizona Corp.; president: MONY Realty Partners Inc. NONPR AFFIL member: Society Actuaries.

Michael I. Roth: chairman, chief executive officer, director B Brooklyn, NY 1945. ED City College of New York BS (1967); Boston University JD (1971); New York University LLM (1973). PRIM CORP EMPL chairman, chief executive officer, director: The Mutual Life Insurance Co. of New York. CORP AFFIL director: Promus Hotel Corp.; chairman: Mony Life Insurance of America Arizona Corp.; director: Pitney Bowes Inc. NONPR AFFIL director: Life Insurance Council; director: Metropolitan Development Association; director: Insurance Marketplace Standards Association; director: Enterprise Foundation; director: Enterprise Group; director: Committee for Economic Development; member: American Council Life Insurance; member: American Institute CPAs.

Foundation Officials

Samuel J. Foti: president, chief executive officer (see above)
Kenneth M. Levine: director (see above)
Michael I. Roth: director (see above)

Grants Analysis

Disclosure Period: calendar year ending 2001
Total Grants: $528,957*
Number of Grants: 62
Average Grant: $8,532
Highest Grant: $45,000
Lowest Grant: $3,000
Typical Range: $1,000 to $10,000
*Note: Giving excludes corporate direct giving; matching gifts; United Way; and funds distributed through the volunteer incentive program.

Recent Grants

Note: Grants derived from 2001 Form 990.

General

104,500	United Way Tri-State, New York, NY
86,250	United Way Central New York, New York, NY
45,000	Bank Street College, New York, NY
25,000	Florida A&M University School of Business and Industry, Tallahassee, FL
17,500	Lincoln Center Consolidated Corporate Fund, New York, NY
15,000	Enterprise Foundation, New York, NY
15,000	Fresh Youth Initiatives, New York, NY
15,000	Literacy, Inc., New York, NY
15,000	New York AIDS Coalition, New York, NY
12,000	After School Corporation, New York, NY

MOODY FOUNDATION

Giving Contact

Peter M. Moore, Grants Director
2302 Postoffice Street, Suite 704
Galveston, TX 77550
Phone: (409)763-5333
Fax: (409)763-5564
E-mail: pmoore@moodyf.org
Web: http://www.moodyf.org

Alternate Contact

Sandy Griffin, Scholarship Administrator
704 Moody National Bank Building
Galveston, TX 77550
Note: Contact to request information on the Moody Scholars program.

Description

Founded: 1942
EIN: 741403105
Organization Type: Family Foundation
Giving Locations: TX, Dallas, Galveston
Grant Types: Capital, Department, Endowment, Fellowship, General Support, Research, Scholarship.

Donor Information

Founder: In 1942, William Lewis Moody Jr. (1865-1954), and his wife, Libbie Rice Shearn Moody (1869-1943), established the Moody Foundation "for the perpetual benefit of present and future generations of Texans." Their financial interests included banks, newspapers, ranches, hotels, and the American National Insurance Company. William Moody was involved in cotton, railroad, and banking enterprises. Today, their daughter-in-law, Mrs. Frances Moody Newman, chairs the board of trustees; their grandson, Robert L. Moody, and great-grandson, Ross R. Moody, are trustees of the foundation.

Financial Summary

Total Giving: $600,000 (2001); $6,034,961 (2000); $40,167,123 (1999)
Giving Analysis: Giving for 2000 includes: foundation scholarships ($160,390) 1999: foundation scholarships ($189,575)
Assets: $428,000,000 (2001); $815,100,261 (2000); $697,913,391 (1999)
Gifts Received: $18,363,736 (2000); $18,181,360 (1999); $17,791,049 (1998). Note: Contributions were received from The Libby Shearn Moody Trust.

Typical Recipients

Arts & Humanities: Arts Centers, Ballet, Film & Video, Historic Preservation, History & Archaeology, Libraries, Museums/Galleries, Music, Opera, Performing Arts, Public Broadcasting, Theater
Civic & Public Affairs: Botanical Gardens/Parks, Economic Development, Employment/Job Training, Civic & Public Affairs-General, Housing, Municipalities/Towns, Nonprofit Management, Parades/Festivals, Safety, Urban & Community Affairs, Zoos/Aquariums
Education: Arts/Humanities Education, Colleges & Universities, Continuing Education, Elementary Education (Private), Engineering/Technological Education, Faculty Development, Education-General, International Exchange, Leadership Training, Medical Education, Minority Education, Private Education

(Precollege), Public Education (Precollege), Science/Mathematics Education, Social Sciences Education, Student Aid
Environment: Environment-General, Resource Conservation, Wildlife Protection
Health: AIDS/HIV, Cancer, Children's Health/Hospitals, Emergency/Ambulance Services, Eyes/Blindness, Geriatric Health, Health Policy/Cost Containment, Health Organizations, Heart, Hospices, Hospitals (University Affiliated), Kidney, Long-Term Care, Medical Rehabilitation, Medical Research, Mental Health, Nursing Services, Prenatal Health Issues, Respiratory, Single-Disease Health Associations, Speech & Hearing, Transplant Networks/Donor Banks
International: Foreign Arts Organizations, International Environmental Issues, International Relief Efforts
Religion: Churches, Ministries, Religious Welfare, Seminaries
Science: Science Museums, Scientific Research
Social Services: Animal Protection, Big Brother/Big Sister, Camps, Child Welfare, Community Service Organizations, Crime Prevention, Day Care, Domestic Violence, Family Planning, People with Disabilities, Recreation & Athletics, Senior Services, Shelters/Homelessness, Special Olympics, Substance Abuse, United Funds/United Ways, Youth Organizations

Application Procedures

Initial Contact: Submit a one-page letter of inquiry or call the foundation to request the foundation's guidelines.
Application Requirements: Inquiries should describe the project and its intended purpose. If the project falls within the scope of the foundation, a detailed and complete application may be presented when the foundation sends a written guideline.
Deadlines: Six weeks prior to quarterly meetings.
Review Process: After the application has been received and studied by the foundation's staff, who may request further information either written or by interview, the board will review the application at a formal meeting, and a decision will be conveyed to the applicant. Applicants should allow two to three months for the application to be processed.
Notes: Direct or personal presentations to the board are not the practice.

Restrictions

Applicants must be tax-exempt nonprofit organizations located in Texas. No grants are given to individuals (except students covered by a scholarship program in Galveston County); the foundation generally does not give funds toward operating budgets, continuing support, annual campaigns, debt financing, or loans.

Additional Information

Currently, the foundation is concentrating its resources on projects in Galveston and Dallas, TX. Also provides advice to grant seekers.
Publications: Annual Report; Guidelines; Format for Grant Application

Foundation Officials

Sandy Griffin: scholarship administration
Harold C. MacDonald: comptroller B 1933. ED University of Houston BBA (1960). CORP AFFIL director: Seal Fleet Inc.; director: American National Insurance Co.; director: American National Property & Casualty Co. NONPR AFFIL vice president, director: Transitional Learning Center.
Wayne E. Magee: grants analyst
Allan Matthews: program officer
E. Douglas McLeod: director/development B Galveston, TX 1941. ED North Texas State University

BBA (1965); Southern Methodist University (1965-1966); South Texas College of Law JD (1990); University of Houston LLM (1993). PRIM CORP EMPL president, owner: McLeod Properties & Co. CORP AFFIL director: National Western Life Insurance Co.; board director: Anrem Corp.; vice president, board director: Colonel Inc.; board director: American National Insurance Co. NONPR AFFIL chairman, director: Palm Beach at Moody Gardens; director: Saint Stephen's School; chairman, board director: Moody Gardens Inc.; chairman, director: Hope Therapy Program; member: Marine Corps League; member: Granaderos De Galvez; board director: Center Transportation & Commerce; board member: Chamber of Commerce.

Frances A. Moody: executive director CORP AFFIL director: American National Insurance Co.; director: National Western Life Insurance Co.

Ross R. Moody: trustee B 1962. ED Harvard University MBA (1986). PRIM CORP EMPL president, chief operating officer, director: National Western Life Insurance Co. CORP AFFIL director: American National Property & Casualty Co.

Peter M. Moore: grants director B Kansas City, MO 1939. ED University of the South BA (1963). NONPR AFFIL member advisory board: Galveston Historical Foundation; member advisory board: Grand 1894 Opera House; committee chairman, management consult: Conference Southwest Foundations; speaker: Funding Information Center.

Frances Moody Newman: chairman, trustee B 1912.

Gerald J. Smith: program officer CORP AFFIL director: Seal Fleet Inc.

Bernice C. Torregrossa: grants analyst

Jean Wylie: regional grants director

Grants Analysis

Disclosure Period: calendar year ending 2000
Total Grants: $5,874,571*
Number of Grants: 39
Average Grant: $61,857*
Highest Grant: $3,523,996
Typical Range: $2,000 to $50,000
*Note: Giving excludes scholarships. Average grant figure excludes highest grant.

Recent Grants

Note: Grants derived from 2000 Form 990.

Library-Related

3,450	Rosenberg Library, Galveston, TX

General

3,523,996	Transitional Learning Community, Galveston, TX -- support over a two year period, of ongoing expanded programs
468,490	Moody Gardens, Galveston, TX -- funding of Phase IV development
421,872	Moody Gardens, Galveston, TX -- for operating expenses
325,686	Moody Gardens, Galveston, TX -- for operations and hotel preopening expenses
123,196	Moody Hospitality Institute, Galveston, TX -- first-year funding for Institute and the Center for Professional Development
122,510	Moody Hospitality Institute, Galveston, TX -- first-year funding for Institute and the Center for Professional Development
100,000	St. Andrew's Episcopal School, Austin, TX -- assistance in expanding the capacity of the Lower School
100,000	SPCA of Texas, Dallas, TX -- medical annex for the care of animals
99,426	Moody Gardens, Galveston, TX -- funding for the acquisition of animal specimens for the planned Aquarium at Moody Gardens
81,111	Moody Gardens, Galveston, TX

KENNETH S. MOORE AND ARLETTA E. MOORE FOUNDATION

Giving Contact

A. Dean Decker, Advisory Committee Member & Trustee
101 N. State St.
PO Box 89
Geneseo, IL 61254-0089
Phone: (309)944-5601

Description

Founded: 1993
EIN: 366914860
Organization Type: Private Foundation
Grant Types: General Support.

Financial Summary

Total Giving: $137,917 (fiscal year ending June 30, 2001); $280,301 (fiscal 2000); $38,732 (fiscal 1998)
Assets: $2,191,079 (fiscal 2001); $2,522,976 (fiscal 2000); $2,392,572 (fiscal 1998)

Typical Recipients

Arts & Humanities: History & Archaeology, Libraries
Civic & Public Affairs: Botanical Gardens/Parks, Municipalities/Towns, Safety, Urban & Community Affairs
Education: Arts/Humanities Education, Public Education (Precollege)
Health: Emergency/Ambulance Services
Religion: Churches
Social Services: Animal Protection, Scouts, Social Services-General, Youth Organizations

Application Procedures

Initial Contact: The foundation has no formal grant application procedure or application form. Send a brief letter of inquiry.
Deadlines: None.

Foundation Officials

Paul Bliss: adv comm mem
Neil Castelyn: adv comm mem
A. Dean Decker: adv comm mem, trustee
Darryl R. Gibson: adv comm mem
David Matthews: adv comm mem
Anita Oetzel: adv comm mem
Glenda Sampson: adv comm mem

Grants Analysis

Disclosure Period: fiscal year ending June 30, 2001
Total Grants: $137,917
Number of Grants: 8
Highest Grant: $50,000
Lowest Grant: $2,087
Typical Range: $2,000 to $8,000

Recent Grants

Note: Grants derived from fiscal 2000 Form 990.

Library-Related

7,500	Henry C. Adams Library -- equipment - reader/printer

General

200,000	Prophetstown Community Park District -- building addition
15,000	City of Prophetstown -- equipment
10,000	Whinning Wheels -- building addition
7,500	Prophetstown Historical Society -- building improvements
7,500	Prophetstown Main Street -- annual budget
6,300	Whiteside County Sheriff's Department -- equipment - car video
5,000	Prophetstown Community Park District -- grounds improvement
3,000	Prophetstown Community Park District -- grounds improvement
2,500	Village of Lyndon -- equipment - siren
2,000	Advent Christian Church, Morrisville, VT -- grant

MARJORIE MOORE CHARITABLE FOUNDATION

Giving Contact

Marjorie Alexander Davis
777 Main St.
Hartford, CT 06115
Phone: (860)986-7696

Description

Founded: 1958
EIN: 066050196
Organization Type: Private Foundation
Giving Locations: CT: Kensington
Grant Types: Capital, Endowment, General Support, Multiyear/Continuing Support, Operating Expenses, Project, Scholarship, Seed Money.

Donor Information

Founder: the late Marjorie Moore

Financial Summary

Total Giving: $307,457 (fiscal year ending July 31, 2002); $197,078 (fiscal 2001); $130,178 (fiscal 2000)
Giving Analysis: Giving for fiscal 2002 includes: foundation scholarships ($25,000)
Assets: $3,207,245 (fiscal 2002); $3,873,112 (fiscal 2001); $4,140,405 (fiscal 2000)

Typical Recipients

Arts & Humanities: Arts Associations & Councils, History & Archaeology, Libraries, Museums/Galleries, Music
Civic & Public Affairs: Chambers of Commerce, Clubs, Civic & Public Affairs-General, Law & Justice, Municipalities/Towns, Safety, Urban & Community Affairs
Education: Elementary Education (Public), Literacy, Preschool Education, Private Education (Precollege), Public Education (Precollege), Science/Mathematics Education, Secondary Education (Public), Special Education, Student Aid
Health: AIDS/HIV, Emergency/Ambulance Services, Health Organizations, Hospices, Hospitals, Medical Research, Mental Health, Nursing Services, Public Health, Single-Disease Health Associations
Religion: Churches
Social Services: Camps, Child Welfare, Community Centers, Community Service Organizations, Crime Prevention, Delinquency & Criminal Rehabilitation, Family Services, People with Disabilities, Recreation & Athletics, Scouts, Senior Services, United Funds/United Ways, YMCA/YWCA/YMHA/YWHA, Youth Organizations

Application Procedures

Initial Contact: The foundation requests applications be made in writing.
Deadlines: None.

Restrictions

The foundation limits grants to charities that will benefit Kensington, CT area residents.

Additional Information

Trust(s): Fleet National Bank

Grants Analysis

Disclosure Period: fiscal year ending July 31, 2002
Total Grants: $282,457*
Number of Grants: 20

Average Grant: $11,248*
Highest Grant: $40,000
Typical Range: $1,000 to $20,000
*Note: Giving excludes scholarships. Average grant figure excludes two highest grants ($80,000).

Recent Grants

Note: Grants derived from 2000 Form 990.

Library-Related

27,500	Berlin-Peck Memorial Library, Kensington, CT -- support salary for library science staff

General

50,000	Town of Berlin, Kensington, CT -- beautify parking area on paper goods pond
23,000	Kensington Nursery School, Kensington, CA -- purchase new playground equipment
11,510	Berlin-Kensington YMCA -- purchase equipment for childcare program
8,168	Berlin High School, Berlin, WI -- upbeat program - provide summer activities to students
5,000	Berlin Childrens Fund -- provide campership to Berlin kids for camp
3,000	Connecticut Rivers Council Boy Scouts of America, East Hampton, CT -- purchase equipment for camping
2,000	Emma Hart Willard School -- purchase material for literacy program

B.C. MOORE & SONS

Company Headquarters

101 S. Green St.
Wadesboro, NC 28170

Company Description

Employees: 1,300
SIC(s): 5300 General Merchandise Stores.

B.C. Moore & Sons Foundation

Giving Contact

Carl E. Bennett, Secretary
PO Drawer 72
Wadesboro, NC 28170
Phone: (704)694-2171
Fax: (704)694-6748

Description

EIN: 566062082
Organization Type: Corporate Foundation
Giving Locations: Southeast USA.
Grant Types: General Support.

Financial Summary

Total Giving: $135,500 (fiscal year ending January 31, 2002); $126,060 (fiscal 2001); $113,100 (fiscal 2000)
Giving Analysis: Giving for fiscal 2000 includes: foundation ($113,000).
Assets: $2,228,103 (fiscal 2002); $2,864,617 (fiscal 2001); $2,803,600 (fiscal 2000)
Gifts Received: $100,000 (fiscal 1993); $100,000 (fiscal 1992)

Typical Recipients

Arts & Humanities: Arts Associations & Councils, Arts Centers, History & Archaeology, Libraries, Opera, Performing Arts, Theater
Civic & Public Affairs: Botanical Gardens/Parks, Civic & Public Affairs-General, Municipalities/Towns, Safety, Urban & Community Affairs

Education: Colleges & Universities, Community & Junior Colleges, Education Funds, Minority Education, Religious Education, Secondary Education (Public), Student Aid, Vocational & Technical Education
Environment: Resource Conservation
Health: Alzheimers Disease, Emergency/Ambulance Services, Hospices, Hospitals, Long-Term Care, Research/Studies Institutes
Religion: Churches, Ministries, Missionary Activities (Domestic), Religious Organizations, Religious Welfare
Social Services: Community Centers, People with Disabilities, Recreation & Athletics, Scouts, Special Olympics, YMCA/YWCA/YMHA/YWHA

Application Procedures

Initial Contact: Send brief letter describing program.
Deadlines: None.

Additional Information

Trust(s): Compass Bank

Corporate Officials

James C. Crawford, Jr.: chairman, president, chief executive officer, director PRIM CORP EMPL chairman, president, chief executive officer, director: B.C. Moore & Sons.
Kirk Crawford: chief financial officer PRIM CORP EMPL chief financial officer: B.C. Moore & Sons.

Grants Analysis

Disclosure Period: fiscal year ending January 31, 2002
Total Grants: $135,500
Number of Grants: 53
Average Grant: $2,557
Highest Grant: $15,000
Lowest Grant: $500
Typical Range: $500 to $5,000

Recent Grants

Note: Grants derived from 2000 Form 990.

General

8,000	Newberry Opera House Foundation, Newberry, SC
5,000	Alabama Independent Colleges, Birmingham, AL
5,000	Anson Athletic Association
5,000	Brevard College, Brevard, NC
5,000	Georgia Foundation for Independent Colleges, Atlanta, GA
5,000	Independent College Fund
5,000	Independent Colleges and Universities, Columbia, SC
5,000	McCallie School's Honors Scholarship Program, Chattanooga, TN
5,000	United Negro College Fund
5,000	Wofford College, Spartanburg, SC

MARIETTA MCNEILL MORGAN AND SAMUEL TATE MORGAN, JR. FOUNDATION

Giving Contact

Elizabeth D. Seaman, Advisor
Bank of America
10 Light St.
Baltimore, MD 21202
Phone: (410)605-1105

Description

Founded: 1967
EIN: 546069447
Organization Type: Private Foundation

Giving Locations: VA
Grant Types: Capital, General Support.

Donor Information

Founder: the late Marietta McNeill Morgan and the late Samuel T. Morgan, Jr.

Financial Summary

Total Giving: $815,000 (fiscal year ending June 30, 2002); $1,639,200 (fiscal 2001); $1,739,250 (fiscal 2000)
Assets: $17,929,859 (fiscal 2002); $21,719,740 (fiscal 2001); $27,057,482 (fiscal 2000)
Gifts Received: $8,666 (fiscal 1996); $10,000 (fiscal 1995); $1,389 (fiscal 1994). Note: In fiscal 1994, contributions were received from S.T. Morgan Trust.

Typical Recipients

Arts & Humanities: Arts Centers, Ballet, Community Arts, Dance, Historic Preservation, History & Archaeology, Libraries, Literary Arts, Museums/Galleries, Music
Civic & Public Affairs: Botanical Gardens/Parks, Economic Development, Civic & Public Affairs-General, Housing, Nonprofit Management, Urban & Community Affairs, Women's Affairs, Zoos/Aquariums
Education: Arts/Humanities Education, Colleges & Universities, Education Funds, Medical Education, Private Education (Precollege), Public Education (Precollege), Secondary Education (Private), Secondary Education (Public), Special Education
Environment: Forestry, Wildlife Protection
Health: AIDS/HIV, Children's Health/Hospitals, Clinics/Medical Centers, Emergency/Ambulance Services, Health Organizations, Heart, Hospitals, Long-Term Care, Medical Research, Research/Studies Institutes
Religion: Ministries, Religious Organizations, Religious Welfare, Seminaries
Science: Observatories & Planetariums, Science Museums
Social Services: Animal Protection, Camps, Child Welfare, Community Service Organizations, Day Care, Domestic Violence, Family Services, Food/Clothing Distribution, Homes, People with Disabilities, Recreation & Athletics, Scouts, Senior Services, United Funds/United Ways, YMCA/YWCA/YMHA/YWHA, Youth Organizations

Application Procedures

Initial Contact: Submit a full proposal.
Application Requirements: Include a concise description of the project, detailed project budget and schedule, a description of organization, current balance sheet and operating statement, list of qualifications of project personnel, names and affiliations of organization's trustees or directors, and proof of tax-exempt status.
Deadlines: Applications may be submitted any time; however, proposals must be received by May 1 for the June meeting of the allocations committee, and by November 1 for the February meeting. The foundation strongly encourages matching or challenge grants.

Restrictions

Does not support individuals.

Additional Information

Publications: Informational Brochure (including Application Guidelines)
Trust(s): Bank of America

Foundation Officials

Elizabeth D. Seaman: consult

Grants Analysis

Disclosure Period: fiscal year ending June 30, 2002
Total Grants: $815,000
Number of Grants: 25
Average Grant: $32,600

Highest Grant: $60,000
Typical Range: $15,000 to $50,000

Recent Grants

Note: Grants derived from fiscal 2000 Form 990.

Library-Related

75,000	Thomas Jefferson Memorial Foundation Inc, Charlottesville, VA -- construction of Jefferson Research Library

General

75,000	Boys and Girls Clubs of Metro Richmond, Richmond, VA -- repairs at Camp Little Hawk
75,000	Corporation for Jefferson's Poplar Forest, Forest, VA -- restoration of east wing
75,000	Historic Richmond Foundation, Richmond, VA -- repair work on monumental church building
75,000	Richmond Society for Prevention of Cruelty to Animals, Richmond, VA -- building renovation to create new humane care and education center
60,000	Virginia Home, Richmond, VA -- building renovation
50,000	Foundation for the Preservation of Virginia's Executive Mansion, Richmond, VA -- building repairs and renovation
50,000	Friends Association for Children, Richmond, VA -- renovation of Gilpin and Flarfield Day Care Center
50,000	Little Sisters of the Poor St. Joseph's Home for the Elderly, Richmond, VA -- construction of independent living facilities
50,000	MCV Foundation for MCV Heart Center, Richmond, VA -- development of research lab
50,000	New Community School, Richmond, VA -- outdoor campus improvements

W. AND E. MORGAN CHARITABLE RESIDUAL TRUST

Giving Contact

Jerry Moore, President & Trust Officer
c/o Citizens Bank and Trust
PO Box 70
Rock Port, MO 64482
Phone: (660)744-5333
Fax: (660)744-2565

Description

Founded: 1989
EIN: 436347180
Organization Type: Private Foundation
Giving Locations: MO
Grant Types: Department, General Support.

Financial Summary

Total Giving: $190,675 (2000); $180,700 (1999); $161,768 (1998)
Assets: $4,795,408 (2000); $3,997,601 (1999); $3,927,524 (1998)

Typical Recipients

Arts & Humanities: Arts Institutes, History & Archaeology, Libraries, Public Broadcasting
Civic & Public Affairs: Botanical Gardens/Parks, Clubs, Civic & Public Affairs-General, Municipalities/Towns, Parades/Festivals, Safety, Urban & Community Affairs
Education: Colleges & Universities, Faculty Development, Education-General, Minority Education, Preschool Education, Private Education (Precollege), Public Education (Precollege), Religious Education,

Science/Mathematics Education, Special Education, Student Aid
Environment: Environment-General
Health: Children's Health/Hospitals, Emergency/Ambulance Services, Eyes/Blindness, Hospitals, Nutrition
International: Missionary/Religious Activities
Religion: Churches, Ministries, Missionary Activities (Domestic), Religious Organizations, Religious Welfare, Religious Welfare
Social Services: Camps, Community Centers, Community Service Organizations, Crime Prevention, Emergency Relief, Recreation & Athletics, Scouts, Social Services-General, Substance Abuse, YMCA/YWCA/YMHA/YWHA, Youth Organizations

Application Procedures

Initial Contact: The foundation has no formal grant application procedure or application form.
Deadlines: None.

Additional Information

Trust(s): Citizens Bank & Trust

Foundation Officials

Jody Ellison: trustee
Sharon Gaines: trust
Kay Gibson: trustee
Tim Whelan: trustee

Grants Analysis

Disclosure Period: calendar year ending 2000
Total Grants: $190,675
Number of Grants: 72
Average Grant: $2,648
Highest Grant: $20,000
Typical Range: $1,000 to $5,000

Recent Grants

Note: Grants derived from 1999 Form 990.

Library-Related

3,500	Atchison County Library, Atchison, KS -- audio books

General

10,000	Atchison County Sheriff's Department, Atchison, KS -- equipment
10,000	Rockport Christian Church, Rockport, ME -- building project
10,000	Rockport Park Board, Rockport, ME -- fencing and helmets
7,700	Rockport School, Rockport, ME -- playground equipment, drama club, teacher of year award, etc.
7,500	Fairfax R-II Schools -- for 25 teachers
7,500	NWMO Learning Center -- lawnmower
5,000	Atchison County Salvation Army, Atchison, KS
5,000	NoWeMo -- land
5,000	Rockport School, Rockport, ME -- track project
4,000	Atchison Holt Ambulance, Atchison, KS

BURTON D. MORGAN FOUNDATION

Giving Contact

John V. Frank, President
PO Box 1500
Akron, OH 44309-1500
Phone: (330)258-6512
Fax: (330)258-6559
Web: http://www.bdmorganfdn.org

Description

Founded: 1967
EIN: 346598971
Organization Type: General Purpose Foundation

Giving Locations: OH: Summit County
Grant Types: Capital, General Support, Scholarship, Seed Money.

Donor Information

Founder: Established in 1967 by Burton D. Morgan.

Financial Summary

Total Giving: $3,338,900 (2000); $2,248,400 (1998); $1,887,100 (1997)
Giving Analysis: Giving for 2000 includes: foundation fellowships ($54,000); foundation scholarships ($252,000); 1998: foundation scholarships ($115,000); 1997: foundation matching gifts ($20,000) foundation scholarships ($38,000)
Assets: $84,011,248 (2000); $58,464,326 (1998); $48,544,969 (1997)
Gifts Received: $350,000 (1998); $3,333,000 (1997); $350,000 (1996). Note: Contributions were received from Burton D. Morgan.

Typical Recipients

Arts & Humanities: Arts Outreach, Ballet, Dance, Historic Preservation, History & Archaeology, Libraries, Museums/Galleries, Music, Performing Arts, Public Broadcasting
Civic & Public Affairs: Botanical Gardens/Parks, Business/Free Enterprise, Clubs, Economic Development, Civic & Public Affairs-General, Legal Aid, Municipalities/Towns, Nonprofit Management, Parades/Festivals, Philanthropic Organizations, Professional & Trade Associations, Safety, Women's Affairs, Zoos/Aquariums
Education: Arts/Humanities Education, Business Education, Colleges & Universities, Economic Education, Elementary Education (Public), Engineering/Technological Education, Education-General, Health & Physical Education, Medical Education, Private Education (Precollege), Private Education (Precollege), Public Education (Precollege), Religious Education, Science/Mathematics Education, Secondary Education (Private), Secondary Education (Public), Social Sciences Education, Student Aid
Environment: Environment-General
Health: Children's Health/Hospitals, Emergency/Ambulance Services, Health Organizations, Heart, Hospices, Hospitals, Mental Health, Nursing Services, Public Health, Research/Studies Institutes
International: Missionary/Religious Activities
Religion: Churches, Religious Organizations, Religious Welfare
Science: Science Museums, Scientific Centers & Institutes
Social Services: Child Welfare, Community Centers, Community Service Organizations, Delinquency & Criminal Rehabilitation, Domestic Violence, Family Planning, Family Services, People with Disabilities, Recreation & Athletics, Scouts, Senior Services, Shelters/Homelessness, Substance Abuse, United Funds/United Ways, YMCA/YWCA/YMHA/YWHA, Youth Organizations

Application Procedures

Initial Contact: Before making a formal request, contact the foundation regarding your proposal.
Application Requirements: The foundation requests proposals be made in writing, not to exceed three pages. The letter must give a clear and concise description of the purpose for the request. Attachments to the letter must include a copy of the IRS tax-determination letter, a separate nonprofit determination letter, a list of the current board of trustees, and a copy of the organization's most recent financial statement or audited report. Additional material may be submitted to supplement the application.
Deadlines: May 1 and October 1. Requests for health and mental health grants are considered once a year at the January meeting and must be submitted by September 1.
Review Process: The board meets two times per year during July and January. Requests that do not

fall within the trustees' interests are declined within 30 days. Requests from the same organization can only be considered once every 12 months.

Restrictions

The foundation primarily makes grants to educational, research, mental health, and charitable organizations. Grants are not made to individuals., annual fund drives, units of government, and tax-supported organizations.

Additional Information

Publications: Application Guidelines; ANN Report

Foundation Officials

Keith A. Brown: trustee B 1951. ED Purdue University (1974). PRIM CORP EMPL president: Chimera Corp. CORP AFFIL president: PolyShades Corp.; director: USG Corp.; president: Global Film & Packaging Corp.

Weldon Wood Case: trustee B Hudson, OH 1921. ED Case Western Reserve University (1939-1940); Ohio Wesleyan University (1940-1941). NONPR AFFIL member: U.S. Independent Telephone Association. CLUB AFFIL Royal Palm Club.

Richard A. Chenoweth: trustee PRIM CORP EMPL principal: Buckingham, Doolittle & Burroughs. CORP AFFIL director: Caliber System Inc.; director: Roadway Services.

J. Martin Erbaugh: trustee B 1948. ED Case Western Reserve University Law School (1973); Denison University (1969-1973); Kent State University MBA (1978). PRIM CORP EMPL chairman board, president, director: Erbaugh Corp. CORP AFFIL director: Lesco Inc.

John V. Frank: president, trustee B Cleveland, OH 1936. ED Babson College (1956-1957); University of Miami BBA (1960). PRIM CORP EMPL president: Summit Capital Management Co. NONPR AFFIL trustee: Rectory School; member finance committee: University Akron; member: Cleveland Society Security Analysts; board overseers: Blossom Music Center; councilman: City Akron; member: Akron Emergency Medical Advisory Board; trustee: Akron Rural Cemetery; president, trustee: Akron Civil War Memorial Society. CLUB AFFIL Hillsboro Club; Portage Country Club.

Stanley Carleton Gault: trustee B Wooster, OH 1926. ED College of Wooster BA (1948). PRIM CORP EMPL chairman, chief executive officer: Goodyear Tire & Rubber Co. CORP AFFIL director: Rubbermaid; director: Timken Co.; director: PPG Industries; director: Little Tikes Co.; director: New York Stock Exchange Inc.; director: Kelly-Springfield Tire Co.; director: Avon Products Inc.; director: International Paper Co. NONPR AFFIL director: National Association Manufacturers; member executive board: National Business Council Consumer Affairs; chairman board: College Wooster.

Grants Analysis

Disclosure Period: calendar year ending 2000
Total Grants: $3,032,900*
Number of Grants: 32
Average Grant: $49,448*
Highest Grant: $1,500,000
Typical Range: $5,000 to $15,000 and $100,000 to $500,000
***Note:** Giving excludes scholarships; fellowships. Average grant excludes highest grant.

Recent Grants

Note: Grants derived from 2000 Form 990.

Library-Related

100,000	Old Trail School, Bath, OH -- construct a new admissions building
1,000	Foundation Center, The, Cleveland, OH -- library services expenses

General

1,500,000	Stark Community Foundation, Canton, OH -- donor-advised fund
500,000	First Congregational Church of Hudson, Hudson, OH
250,000	Lynn University, Boca Raton, FL -- establish and endow the Weldon W. Case Aviation Scholarship
200,000	Kent State University Foundation, Kent, OH -- for the Shannon Rogers and Jerry Silverman School of Fashion Design and Merchandising
100,000	Ashland University, Ashland, OH -- special capital projects
100,000	Purdue University, West Lafayette, IN -- special capital projects
95,900	College of Wooster, Wooster, OH -- special capital projects
60,000	Denison University, Granville, OH -- special capital projects
56,000	Foundation for Teaching Economics, Davis, CA -- for the Economics for Leaders Program
54,000	Family Institute at Northwestern University, Evanston, IL -- to establish the Dr. John J. B. Morgan Fellowship

LOUIE R. AND GERTRUDE MORGAN FOUNDATION

Giving Contact

Robert Summerall, Jr., Vice President & Treasurer
PO Box 550
Arcadia, FL 34265
Phone: (941)494-1551

Description

Founded: 1960
EIN: 596142359
Organization Type: Private Foundation
Giving Locations: FL
Grant Types: General Support.

Donor Information

Founder: the late Louie R. Morgan, the late Mildred Morgan, Gertrude Morgan, Eleanor Morgan

Financial Summary

Total Giving: $110,000 (2000); $180,000 (1999); $80,000 (1994)
Assets: $2,770,482 (2000); $2,796,555 (1999); $2,538,172 (1994)

Typical Recipients

Arts & Humanities: Libraries
Civic & Public Affairs: Hispanic Affairs, Municipalities/Towns
Education: Secondary Education (Public)
Health: Hospitals
Religion: Churches, Religion-General, Religious Organizations, Religious Welfare
Social Services: Community Service Organizations, People with Disabilities, Senior Services

Application Procedures

Initial Contact: Send a written description of the project and purpose of funds sought.
Deadlines: None.

Foundation Officials

George E. Bellamy: director
Bobby C. Mixon: president
Lewis W. Smith: director
Robert Summerall, Jr.: director
Richard Wertich: secretary
James R. Wierichs: secretary

Grants Analysis

Disclosure Period: calendar year ending 2000
Total Grants: $110,000
Number of Grants: 21
Highest Grant: $5,000
Lowest Grant: $5,000

Recent Grants

Note: Grants derived from 2001 Form 990.

General

5,000	Arcadia Church of God, Arcadia, FL
5,000	Arcadia Spanish Church of God, Arcadia, FL
5,000	Assembly of Praise, Arcadia, FL
5,000	Elizabeth Baptist Church, Arcadia, FL
5,000	First Presbyterian Church, Arcadia, FL
5,000	Fort Ogden Church of God, Ft. Ogden, FL
5,000	Friendship Missionary Baptist, Arcadia, FL
5,000	Heritage Baptist Church, Arcadia, FL
5,000	House of God, Arcadia, FL
5,000	Ivey Chapel Afro Methodist, Arcadia, FL

MORIAH FUND, INC.

Giving Contact

Janice Edwards, Grants Manager
1 Farragut Square South
1634 I Street Northwest, Suite 1000
Washington, DC 20006
Phone: (202)783-8488
Fax: (202)783-8499
E-mail: jedwards@moriahfund.org

Alternate Contact

Susan Feit
PO Box 2788
60190 Neve Monosson, Israel
Note: For projects in Israel.

Description

Founded: 1985
EIN: 311129589
Organization Type: General Purpose Foundation
Giving Locations: DC: Washington; MD; NY internationally; emphasis on Latin America, particularly Guatemala.
Grant Types: General Support, Matching, Multiyear/Continuing Support.
Note: Also provides grants for technical assistance.

Donor Information

Founder: The Moriah Fund was established in 1985 by the late Clarence W. Efroymson and the late Robert A. Efroymson , both lifelong philanthropic contributors, who held the Jewish values and concern for the disadvantaged that the fund emulates today. The Gershon Ben-Ephraim Fund and the Gustave Aaron Efroymson Fund were also donors.

Financial Summary

Total Giving: $8,600,000 (2003 approx); $9,757,500 (2002 approx); $10,271,000 (2001)
Giving Analysis: Giving for 1998 includes: foundation grants to United Way ($24,000)
Assets: $131,000,000 (2002 approx); $170,111,239 (2001); $218,722,431 (2000)
Gifts Received: $7,421,286 (2000); $5,582 (1998); $5,174 (1997). Note: In 2000, contributions were received from Debra Efroymson and the trust of Clarence Efroymson.

Typical Recipients

Arts & Humanities: Libraries

Civic & Public Affairs: Asian American Affairs, Civil Rights, Economic Development, Civic & Public Affairs-General, Hispanic Affairs, Housing, Law & Justice, Legal Aid, Native American Affairs, Public Policy, Urban & Community Affairs, Women's Affairs

Education: Colleges & Universities, Education Funds, Education-General, International Studies, Leadership Training, Preschool Education, Private Education (Precollege), Public Education (Precollege), Social Sciences Education, Vocational & Technical Education

Environment: Air/Water Quality, Energy, Forestry, Environment-General, Research, Resource Conservation, Wildlife Protection

Health: Adolescent Health Issues, Children's Health/Hospitals, Clinics/Medical Centers, Health Policy/Cost Containment, Health Organizations, Long-Term Care, Medical Training, Mental Health, Prenatal Health Issues, Public Health

International: Foreign Educational Institutions, Health Care/Hospitals, Human Rights, International Affairs, International Development, International Environmental Issues, International Organizations, International Peace & Security Issues, International Relations, International Relief Efforts, Missionary/Religious Activities

Religion: Jewish Causes, Religious Organizations, Religious Welfare, Seminaries, Social/Policy Issues

Social Services: Child Welfare, Community Centers, Community Service Organizations, Crime Prevention, Day Care, Delinquency & Criminal Rehabilitation, Family Planning, Family Services, Food/Clothing Distribution, People with Disabilities, Recreation & Athletics, Shelters/Homelessness, Social Services-General, United Funds/United Ways, Youth Organizations

Application Procedures

Initial Contact: A first-time applicant must send a short two- to three-page letter of inquiry at least one month prior to proposal deadlines. Based on the letter, the fund will decide whether or not to invite a full proposal.

Application Requirements: The letter of inquiry should include an outline of the organization's history, purpose, and goals; amount of funding requested; purpose and activities of specific project; and the total budgets for the project and the organization.

A full proposal should include the following: a cover sheet including the name, address, and phone/fax number(s) of the organization; the contact person's and Chief Executive Officer's names; the purpose of the organization; organization and total project budgets for the past, current, and projected years; dates of fiscal year; purpose, amount and period of time for which grant is requested; and other sources of income committed and pending for the period in which support is requested. The narrative for general support (ten pages maximum), should include details the history, purpose, goals, major programs and accomplishments of the organization; plans and priorities; qualifications to complete project; and methods of evaluation. If requesting a project grant, narrative should include history of organization; major programs and accomplishments; description of activities to be supported with specific goals and measurable objectives; recent and anticipated accomplishments; project goals and plan of action with timeline; qualifications of organization to accomplish project; method of evaluation; and long-term project plans including future financing. All proposals should include the following financial information: revenue and expense statements for the past, current and future years; list of organization's major institutional funders with amounts; and an audit if available. Other information that should be included: proof of IRS tax-exemption 501c(3) and non-private foundation 509(a) status; list of the board of directors and their affiliations; and an annual report if available.

Deadlines: For letters of inquiry, are February 1 and July 1. Proposals must be received by March 1 and August 1.

Review Process: Letters of inquiry are reviewed throughout the year. Proposals are reviewed by the board of directors for spring or fall grant cycle depending on the date they are received.

Restrictions

The Moriah Fund does not consider grants for individuals, arts organizations, private foundations, medical research, lobbying, non-U.S. organizations or political campaigns.

Additional Information

Publications: Annual Report; Guidelines; Proposal Checklist

Foundation Officials

Geeta Rao Gupta: director

Judith Lichtman: 1st vice president, treasurer B 1940. ED Hofstra University (1963); University of Wisconsin Law School (1965). PRIM NONPR EMPL president: Women's Legal Defense Fund.

Karl Mathiasen: secretary

Norman Rosenburg: director

Mary Ann Efroymson Stein: president

Grants Analysis

Disclosure Period: calendar year ending 2000
Total Grants: $9,255,500
Number of Grants: 170
Average Grant: $38,352*
Highest Grant: $2,774,000
Lowest Grant: $5,000
Typical Range: $15,000 to $75,000
*Note: Average grant figure excludes highest grant.

Recent Grants

Note: Grants derived from 2000 Form 990.

General

2,774,000	New Israel Fund, Washington, DC -- support of programs it funds
245,000	American Jewish World Service, New York, NY -- to support the Jewish Community Development Fund
230,000	Reproductive Health Technologies Project, Washington, DC -- for the Microbicide Development Fund
195,000	Center on Budget and Policy Priorities, Washington, DC -- for the establishment of the DC Fiscal Policy Institute
175,000	Natural Resources Defense Council, New York, NY -- to direct a grassroots and media campaign for the Grand Canyon Parachant National Monument Designation Project
150,000	Tides Center, San Francisco, CA -- support of the Center for Health and Gender Equity
100,000	North American Conference on Ethiopian Jewry, New York, NY -- support to provide children's lunches and educational programs for Ethiopian Jews in Addis Abada and Gondar
90,000	EcoLogic Development Fund, Cambridge, MA -- for support of its work in Guatemala
90,000	Rights Action, Washington, DC -- to provide education, training and financial support to human rights organizations working at the community level
80,000	Center for Community Change, Washington, DC -- to support the Organizing Committee for a National Campaign on Jobs and Income

MORLEY FOUNDATION

Giving Contact

Robert S. Morley, President
PO Box 2485
Saginaw, MI 48605-2485
Phone: (989)753-3438

Description

Founded: 1948
EIN: 386055569
Organization Type: Private Foundation
Giving Locations: MI: Saginaw greater Saginaw area
Grant Types: General Support, Multiyear/Continuing Support, Operating Expenses, Project, Research, Seed Money.

Donor Information

Founder: the late Ralph Chase Morley, the late Mrs. Ralph Chase Morley, Sr.

Financial Summary

Total Giving: $342,288 (2001); $383,520 (2000); $321,705 (1999)

Giving Analysis: Giving for 2001 includes: foundation grants to United Way ($9,200); foundation scholarships ($37,500); 2000: foundation matching gifts ($3,270); foundation grants to United Way ($9,100); foundation scholarships ($14,500); 1999: foundation matching gifts ($2,775); foundation grants to United Way ($8,800) foundation scholarships ($9,500)

Assets: $6,162,422 (2001); $6,579,325 (2000); $6,474,103 (1999)

Gifts Received: $2,018 (2001); $1,242 (2000); $68,391 (1999). Note: In 1992, contributions were received from Charles W. Morley Trust.

Typical Recipients

Arts & Humanities: Arts Centers, Arts Festivals, Dance, Arts & Humanities-General, Historic Preservation, History & Archaeology, Libraries, Literary Arts, Museums/Galleries, Music, Performing Arts, Public Broadcasting, Theater

Civic & Public Affairs: Botanical Gardens/Parks, Business/Free Enterprise, Chambers of Commerce, Community Foundations, Economic Development, Employment/Job Training, Civic & Public Affairs-General, Housing, Law & Justice, Parades/Festivals, Professional & Trade Associations, Public Policy, Safety, Urban & Community Affairs, Zoos/Aquariums

Education: Arts/Humanities Education, Business Education, Colleges & Universities, Education Funds, Environmental Education, Education-General, Education-General, Minority Education, Private Education (Precollege), Public Education (Precollege), Science/Mathematics Education, Secondary Education (Private), Student Aid

Environment: Forestry, Resource Conservation

Health: AIDS/HIV, Emergency/Ambulance Services, Eyes/Blindness, Health-General, Hospitals, Long-Term Care, Medical Research, Nursing Services, Single-Disease Health Associations

Religion: Churches, Religious Welfare

Science: Science Exhibits & Fairs

Social Services: At-Risk Youth, Big Brother/Big Sister, Camps, Child Abuse, Child Welfare, Community Centers, Community Service Organizations, Crime Prevention, Day Care, Delinquency & Criminal Rehabilitation, Domestic Violence, Emergency Relief, Family Services, Food/Clothing Distribution, Recreation & Athletics, Scouts, Senior Services, Shelters/Homelessness, Substance Abuse, United Funds/United Ways, YMCA/YWCA/YMHA/YWHA, Youth Organizations

Application Procedures

Initial Contact: Send a brief letter of inquiry and a full proposal.
Application Requirements: Include an outline of the program, amount requested, description of organization, and proof of tax-exempt status, lists of board members, and other organizations contacted for funding.
Deadlines: None.

Restrictions

Does not support individuals or provide funds for deficit financing, land acquisition, or renovation projects.

Foundation Officials

Michael M. Brand: trustee
Lois K. Guttowsky: secretary
Burrows Morley, Jr.: trustee
Christopher Morley: trustee
David H. Morley: trustee
Edward B. Morley, Jr.: past president, trustee
George B. Morley, Jr.: trustee
Katharyn M. Morley: trustee
Mark B. Morley: treasurer
Peter B. Morley, Jr.: trustee
Robert S. Morley: president
Carol Morley Beck: trustee
Lucy M. Thomson: vice president, trustee
Richard B. Thomson, Jr.: trustee

Grants Analysis

Disclosure Period: calendar year ending 2001
Total Grants: $295,588*
Number of Grants: 56
Average Grant: $5,278
Highest Grant: $25,000
Lowest Grant: $500
Typical Range: $1,000 to $10,000
*****Note:** Giving excludes United Way and scholarship.

Recent Grants

Note: Grants derived from 2001 Form 990.

General

25,000	Saginaw Art Museum, Saginaw, MI -- capital campaign
25,000	Saginaw County Historical Society, Saginaw, MI -- Morley Room
25,000	Saginaw Valley State University, University Center, MI -- scholarships
21,108	Saginaw Children's Zoo, Saginaw, MI -- expansion
15,000	Saginaw Art Museum, Saginaw, MI
15,000	Saginaw Art Museum, Saginaw, MI -- salary support
14,000	Michigan Colleges Foundation, Inc., Southfield, MI -- endowment fund
13,750	WUCM - TV Delta College, University Center, MI -- weekly program
10,000	Interlochen Center for the Arts, Interlochen, RI -- building improvements
10,000	Saginaw City Rescue Mission, Saginaw, MI -- building expansion

MORRILL CHARITABLE FOUNDATION

Giving Contact

Tom James
Northern Trust Co.
50 S. LaSalle, L-5
Chicago, IL 60675
Phone: (312)630-6000

Description

Founded: 1983
EIN: 351584396
Organization Type: Private Foundation

Giving Locations: IN: Ft. Worth
Grant Types: Capital, General Support.

Financial Summary

Total Giving: $427,902 (fiscal year ending November 30, 2001); $475,087 (fiscal 2000); $307,133 (fiscal 1999)
Assets: $6,029,239 (fiscal 2001); $6,623,213 (fiscal 2000); $6,984,352 (fiscal 1999)
Gifts Received: $72,918 (fiscal 2001); $72,918 (fiscal 2000); $72,918 (fiscal 1999). Note: CRF the Morrill Charitable Annuity Trust.

Typical Recipients

Arts & Humanities: Arts Associations & Councils, Community Arts, History & Archaeology, Libraries, Museums/Galleries, Music, Performing Arts, Public Broadcasting, Theater
Civic & Public Affairs: Botanical Gardens/Parks, Chambers of Commerce, Community Foundations, Civic & Public Affairs-General, Urban & Community Affairs
Education: Business Education, Colleges & Universities, Engineering/Technological Education, Gifted & Talented Programs, Private Education (Precollege), Religious Education
Health: Cancer, Clinics/Medical Centers, Health Organizations, Public Health
Religion: Churches, Ministries, Religious Organizations, Religious Welfare
Science: Scientific Centers & Institutes
Social Services: Child Welfare, Community Service Organizations, Crime Prevention, Homes, People with Disabilities, Recreation & Athletics, Scouts, United Funds/United Ways, YMCA/YWCA/YMHA/YWHA, Youth Organizations

Application Procedures

Initial Contact: Send brief letter describing program.
Application Requirements: Include purpose of funds sought and proof of tax-exempt status.
Deadlines: None.

Foundation Officials

Amy B. Morrill: trustee

Grants Analysis

Disclosure Period: fiscal year ending November 30, 2001
Total Grants: $427,902*
Typical Range: $1,500 to $20,000
*****Note:** Complete grants list unavailable for 2001.

Recent Grants

Note: Grants derived from fiscal 2000 Form 990.

Library-Related

5,000	Stephenson Memorial Library, Greenfield, NH
5,000	Stephenson Memorial Library, Greenfield, NH

General

10,000	Fellowship of Christians in Universities and Schools
6,000	Matthew 25 Clinic, Ft. Wayne, IN
5,000	Congregational Church of Salisbury
5,000	Gordon Conwell Theological Seminary, South Hamilton, MA
5,000	Johns Hopkins University Center for Talented Youth, Baltimore, MD
2,714	Junior Achievement, Ft. Wayne, IN

CHARLES M. MORRIS CHARITABLE TRUST

Giving Contact

Joanna M. Mayo, Vice President
c/o National City Bank
20 Stanwix St., 16th Floor
Loc 25-162
Pittsburgh, PA 15222-4802

Phone: (412)644-8002
E-mail: joanna.mayo@nationalcity.com
Web: http://www.morrisfoundation.org

Description

Founded: 1988
EIN: 256312920
Organization Type: Private Foundation
Giving Locations: PA
Grant Types: General Support.

Donor Information

Founder: the late Charles M. Morris

Financial Summary

Total Giving: $1,746,960 (2002); $1,412,854 (2001); $1,773,200 (2000)
Giving Analysis: Giving for 2002 includes: foundation grants to United Way ($25,000); 1997: foundation grants to United Way ($22,000) foundation ($1,126,218)
Assets: $26,979,308 (2002); $33,935,480 (2001); $38,066,320 (2000)
Gifts Received: $135,000 (1993); $5,079,245 (1992). Note: In 1993, contributions were received from the estate of Charles M. Morris.

Typical Recipients

Arts & Humanities: Ballet, Arts & Humanities-General, Libraries, Museums/Galleries, Music, Theater
Civic & Public Affairs: African American Affairs, Employment/Job Training, Housing
Education: Colleges & Universities, Community & Junior Colleges, Education Funds, Education-General, Preschool Education, Private Education (Precollege), Religious Education
Health: Children's Health/Hospitals, Clinics/Medical Centers, Health Organizations, Medical Rehabilitation, Single-Disease Health Associations
Religion: Churches, Religion-General, Jewish Causes, Ministries, Religious Organizations, Religious Welfare, Synagogues/Temples
Social Services: Child Welfare, Community Service Organizations, Crime Prevention, Day Care, Delinquency & Criminal Rehabilitation, Family Planning, Family Planning, Family Services, Food/Clothing Distribution, Senior Services, Social Services-General, Substance Abuse, United Funds/United Ways, YMCA/YWCA/YMHA/YWHA, Youth Organizations

Application Procedures

Initial Contact: Send a brief letter of inquiry requesting application form.
Deadlines: None.

Restrictions

Grants are not made to support individuals, political or lobbying groups, or multiple year request.

Additional Information

Publications: Application form.
Trust(s): Natl City Bank PA

Foundation Officials

Arthur Fidel: dist committee member
Arthur Fiedl: dist committee member
Charles Perlow: dist committee member

Grants Analysis

Disclosure Period: calendar year ending 2002
Total Grants: $1,721,960
Number of Grants: 49
Average Grant: $21,291*
Highest Grant: $700,000
Typical Range: $10,000 to $40,000
*****Note:** Average grant figure excludes highest grant.

Recent Grants

Note: Grants derived from 2002 Form 990.

General

700,000	United Jewish Federation, Pittsburgh, PA -- annual appeal
50,000	City Theatre Company, Inc., Pittsburgh, PA -- for renovations
50,000	Jewish University of Pittsburgh, Pittsburgh, PA -- capital campaign
50,000	Kollel Jewish Learning Center, Pittsburgh, PA -- capital campaign
50,000	North Tahoe Hebrew Congregation, Incline Village, NV -- capital campaign
50,000	Pittsburgh Children's Museum, Pittsburgh, PA -- capital campaign
50,000	United Jewish Federation, Pittsburgh, PA -- for Squirrel Hill Revitalization Committee
50,000	United Jewish Federation, Pittsburgh, PA -- for Israel emergency appeal
30,000	Hillel Academy, Pittsburgh, PA -- for computers and printers
30,000	Jewish Education Institute, Pittsburgh, PA -- for holocaust memorial

MORRIS
COMMUNICATIONS CORP.

Company Headquarters

825 Broad Street
Augusta, GA 30903
Phone: (706)724-0851
Web: http://www.morriscomm.com

Company Description

Former Name: Stauffer Communications.
Revenue: US$578 million (2001)
Employees: 6000 (2001)
SIC(s): 2711 Newspapers, 2721 Periodicals.

Operating Locations

Morris Communications Corp. (FL--Winter Haven; KS--Topeka; MN--Brainerd; MO--Independence; SD--Brookings)

Stauffer Communications Foundation

Giving Contact

William S. Morris, IV, Trustee
PO Box 936
Augusta, GA 30903-0936
Phone: (706)823-3462
Fax: (785)295-1144
Note: Mr. Stauffer's direct line is: (785)295-1118.

Description

EIN: 486212412
Organization Type: Corporate Foundation
Giving Locations: KS; OK
Grant Types: Employee Matching Gifts, General Support.

Financial Summary

Total Giving: $118,057 (2001); $150,000 (1999 approx); $230,836 (1998). Note: Contributes through foundation only.
Giving Analysis: Giving for 1998 includes: foundation matching gifts ($2,250) foundation ($228,586).
Assets: $1,160,241 (2001); $1,157,206 (1998); $1,167,972 (1996)
Gifts Received: $99,250 (2001); $106,000 (1998); $100,000 (1995). Note: Contributions are received from Morris Communications Corp.

Typical Recipients

Arts & Humanities: Community Arts, Arts & Humanities-General, Historic Preservation, History & Archaeology, Libraries, Literary Arts, Museums/Galleries, Public Broadcasting, Theater
Civic & Public Affairs: Botanical Gardens/Parks, Chambers of Commerce, Civil Rights, Clubs, Community Foundations, Economic Development, Employment/Job Training, Civic & Public Affairs-General, Law & Justice, Legal Aid, Municipalities/Towns, Philanthropic Organizations, Professional & Trade Associations, Public Policy, Rural Affairs, Urban & Community Affairs
Education: Arts/Humanities Education, Business Education, Colleges & Universities, Community & Junior Colleges, Education Associations, Education Funds, Engineering/Technological Education, Education-General, Journalism/Media Education, Legal Education, Medical Education, Private Education (Precollege), Religious Education, Science/Mathematics Education, Secondary Education (Public), Student Aid, Vocational & Technical Education
Environment: Resource Conservation
Health: Alzheimers Disease, Cancer, Children's Health/Hospitals, Clinics/Medical Centers, Emergency/Ambulance Services, Health Organizations, Hospitals, Public Health
International: Foreign Arts Organizations, Human Rights
Religion: Religious Organizations, Religious Welfare
Science: Scientific Research
Social Services: Animal Protection, Child Abuse, Child Welfare, Community Centers, Community Service Organizations, People with Disabilities, Recreation & Athletics, Scouts, Shelters/Homelessness, United Funds/United Ways, YMCA/YWCA/YMHA/YWHA, Youth Organizations

Application Procedures

Initial Contact: There is no specific application form.
Deadlines: None.

Corporate Officials

William A. Herman, III: secretary, treasurer, director B Augusta, GA 1938. ED University of Georgia (1963). PRIM CORP EMPL secretary, treasurer, director: Morris Communications Corp. CORP AFFIL secretary, treasurer, director: Southeastern Newspaper Corp.; secretary, treasurer, director: Stauffer Communications Inc.; secretary, treasurer, director: Mill Haven Co. Inc.; secretary, treasurer, director: Shivers Trading & Operating Co.; secretary, treasurer, director: Azalea Development Co.; treasurer: Broadcaster Press Inc.; secretary, treasurer, director: Athens Newspapers Inc. CLUB AFFIL Knights of Columbus.
William Shivers Morris, III: founder, chairman, chief executive officer, director B Augusta, GA 1934. ED University of Georgia AB (1956). PRIM CORP EMPL founder, chairman, chief executive officer, director: Morris Communications Corp. CORP AFFIL chairman, chief executive officer: Southwest Newspapers Corp.; chairman: Stauffer Communications Inc.; director: Southern Co. Inc.; chief executive officer: Shivers Trading & Operating Co.; chairman, chief executive officer: Southeastern Newspaper Corp.; director: Georgia Power Co.; chairman, chief executive officer: North America Publs Inc.; chairman, chief executive officer: Florida Publishing Co.; publ, chairman, chief executive officer: Augusta Chronicle; chairman: Broadcaster Press Inc.; chairman, chief executive officer: Athens Newspapers Inc. NONPR AFFIL member: Southeastern Newspaper Publisher's Association; member: Southern Newspaper Publishers Association; member: International Press Institute; member: American Newspaper Publishers Association; trustee: Augusta College Foundation. CLUB AFFIL University Club; Pinnacle Club; Commerce Club; Oglethorpe Club.
William Shivers Morris, IV: president, director B 1938. PRIM CORP EMPL president, director: Morris Communications Corp. CORP AFFIL president:

Southeastern Newspaper Corp.; president: Stauffer Communications Inc.; president: Shivers Trading & Operating Co.; president: Athens Newspapers Inc.; president: Broadcaster Press Inc.

Foundation Officials

John Fish: trustee
Gregg A. Ireland: trustee
William Shivers Morris, III: trustee (see above)
William Shivers Morris, IV: trustee (see above)
John H. Stauffer: trustee B Arkansas City, KS 1928. ED University of Kansas BS (1949). PRIM CORP EMPL director: Morris Communications Corp. CORP AFFIL chairman: Topeka-Capital Journal; director: Mercantile Bank Topeka. NONPR AFFIL member: Top Tower; member: Topeka Chamber of Commerce; member: Phi Delta Theta; member: Kansas City Chamber of Commerce; member: Kansas Press Association; member: Inland Press Association. CLUB AFFIL Topeka Country Club.

Grants Analysis

Disclosure Period: calendar year ending 2001
Total Grants: $116,357*
Number of Grants: 33
Average Grant: $3,526
Highest Grant: $20,000
Lowest Grant: $100
Typical Range: $100 to $6,000
*Note: Giving excludes matching gifts.

Recent Grants

Note: Grants derived from 2001 Form 990.

General

20,000	Topeka Civic Theater, Topeka, KS
11,667	Conway Area Chamber of Commerce
11,667	Topeka YWCA, Topeka, KS
10,000	Washburn Living Learning Center
6,000	Harry S. Truman Library and Museum, Kansas City, MO
5,000	Salvation Army of Topeka, Topeka, KS
5,000	Topeka Peaceful Schools Project, Topeka, KS
4,000	New Century Alliance
3,500	Santa Fe Trail Boys Scouts, Santa Fe, NM
3,333	Salvation Army of Pittsburgh, Pittsburgh, PA

MORRIS FAMILY FOUNDATION

Giving Contact

William C. Morris, Treasurer
c/o J&W Seligman & Co., Inc
100 Park Avenue, 8th Fl.
New York, NY 10017-5516
Phone: (212)850-1888

Description

Founded: 1996
EIN: 133862049
Organization Type: Private Foundation
Grant Types: General Support.

Donor Information

Founder: Established in 1996 by William C. Morris.

Financial Summary

Total Giving: $373,700 (1999); $40,000 (1998); $325,000 (1997)
Assets: $8,412,888 (1999); $7,159,307 (1998); $7,222,033 (1997)
Gifts Received: $75,000 (1997); $3,000,000 (1995). Note: In 1995 and 1997, contributions were received from William C. Morris.

Typical Recipients

Arts & Humanities: Libraries, Public Broadcasting
Civic & Public Affairs: Botanical Gardens/Parks, Zoos/Aquariums
Education: Colleges & Universities, Elementary Education (Private), Health & Physical Education, Leadership Training, Medical Education, Private Education (Precollege), Science/Mathematics Education, Student Aid
Environment: Environment-General, Protection, Resource Conservation, Wildlife Protection
Health: Cancer, Children's Health/Hospitals, Hospitals
Religion: Churches
Science: Scientific Centers & Institutes, Scientific Labs
Social Services: Animal Protection, YMCA/YWCA/YMHA/YWHA

Application Procedures

Initial Contact: Submit request.
Application Requirements: Include a description of organization, goals of the project, key personnel to be involved, amount of funding sought, history and mission of applicant organization, listing of officers and board of directors, current operating budget including financial statement and list of other funding sources, and evidence of tax-exempt status
Deadlines: October 31.
Review Process: In November.
Notes: If foundation is interested, additional information will be requested from organization or individual; at least one on-site visit might be required and a written report containing a narrative account of a will be requested of all grantees by June following receipt of a grant.

Restrictions

Does not support individuals. Grants are not given when they would be only a small fraction of a large organization's budget. Grants are not made to capital or annual campaigns and are not given to large umbrella nonprofit institutions. Individual grants are not made under $5,000 nor, at present, for more than $100,000.

Additional Information

Foundation makes most of its grants in two areas: 1. projects or programs in the environment (marine ecosystems concentrating on the Rhode Island shore and the Florida Keys); concern for water quality in these waters; and preservation of the biodiverse life of these bodies of water. 2. projects or programs involving the development of children into productive, responsible adults. Support is given to both education-related and health-related issues.

Foundation Officials

David Lockhart Morris: trustee
Edward Follett Morris: trustee
Kenneth Van Avery Morris: trustee
Susan F. Morris: chairman, secretary, trustee
William C. Morris: treasurer, assistant secretary, trustee

Grants Analysis

Disclosure Period: calendar year ending 1999
Total Grants: $373,700
Number of Grants: 34
Average Grant: $10,991
Highest Grant: $60,000
Typical Range: $1,000 to $3,000 and $10,000 to $50,000

Recent Grants

Note: Grants derived from 1999 Form 990.

Library-Related

3,000	Columbia University ALS Gift Fund
2,000	Memorial and Library Association Westerly, Westerly, RI

General

60,000	University of Miami Rosenstiel School of Marine and Atmospheric Science, Miami, FL
50,000	Wildlife Conservation Fund, Columbus, OH
50,000	Zoological Society of Houston, Houston, TX
40,700	University of Virginia Fund, Charlottesville, VA
35,000	Riverdale Country School, New York, NY
30,000	Woods Hole Oceanographic Institute, Woods Hole, MA
20,000	Audubon Society of Rhode Island, Providence, RI
20,000	Nature Conservancy Florida Chapter, Ft. Pierce, FL
15,000	St. Philips Academy
10,000	Brooklyn Botanic Garden, Brooklyn, NY

MARGARET T. MORRIS FOUNDATION

Giving Contact

Eugene P. Polk, Trustee
PO Box 592
Prescott, AZ 86302
Phone: (928)445-4010

Description

Founded: 1967
EIN: 866057798
Organization Type: General Purpose Foundation
Giving Locations: nationally.
Grant Types: Capital, General Support, Matching, Operating Expenses, Project, Scholarship.

Donor Information

Founder: The foundation was established in 1967 by the late Margaret T. Morris .

Financial Summary

Total Giving: $3,609,964 (2001); $2,179,976 (2000); $1,900,475 (1998)
Giving Analysis: Giving for 2000 includes: foundation matching gifts ($15,000); foundation scholarships ($160,000); 1998: foundation matching gifts ($51,000) 1997: foundation matching gifts ($160,308)
Assets: $16,073,717 (2001); $89,847,049 (2000); $45,271,218 (1998)
Gifts Received: $4,050 (1994)

Typical Recipients

Arts & Humanities: Art History, Arts Associations & Councils, Arts Centers, Arts Festivals, Arts Funds, Arts Institutes, Arts Outreach, Ballet, Dance, Film & Video, Historic Preservation, History & Archaeology, Libraries, Museums/Galleries, Music, Opera, Performing Arts, Public Broadcasting, Theater, Visual Arts
Civic & Public Affairs: Botanical Gardens/Parks, Business/Free Enterprise, Community Foundations, Economic Development, Economic Policy, Employment/Job Training, Civic & Public Affairs-General, Hispanic Affairs, Housing, Law & Justice, Legal Aid, Municipalities/Towns, Native American Affairs, Public Policy, Public Policy, Urban & Community Affairs, Women's Affairs, Zoos/Aquariums
Education: Arts/Humanities Education, Colleges & Universities, Continuing Education, Education Associations, Education-General, Health & Physical Education, Medical Education, Private Education (Precollege), Public Education (Precollege), Science/Mathematics Education, Student Aid
Environment: Environment-General, Resource Conservation, Wildlife Protection
Health: AIDS/HIV, Alzheimers Disease, Cancer, Children's Health/Hospitals, Clinics/Medical Centers, Emergency/Ambulance Services, Health-General, Geriatric Health, Health Policy/Cost Containment, Health Organizations, Home-Care Services, Hospices, Hospitals, Long-Term Care, Medical Research, Mental Health, Prenatal Health Issues, Preventive Medicine/Wellness Organizations, Public Health, Research/Studies Institutes, Single-Disease Health Associations
International: Foreign Arts Organizations, Health Care/Hospitals, International Development, International Environmental Issues, International Organizations, International Peace & Security Issues, International Relief Efforts
Religion: Jewish Causes, Religious Organizations, Religious Welfare, Social/Policy Issues
Science: Science Museums, Scientific Centers & Institutes, Scientific Organizations
Social Services: At-Risk Youth, Child Welfare, Community Service Organizations, Counseling, Crime Prevention, Day Care, Emergency Relief, Family Planning, Family Services, Food/Clothing Distribution, Homes, People with Disabilities, Recreation & Athletics, Scouts, Senior Services, Shelters/Homelessness, Social Services-General, Special Olympics, Volunteer Services, YMCA/YWCA/YMHA/YWHA, Youth Organizations

Application Procedures

Initial Contact: Submit a brief letter of inquiry.
Application Requirements: Letter should include a description of the problem to be addressed, the nature of the project, and the objectives of the program. A copy of the IRS tax-exempt ruling and appropriate documentation should also be included.
Deadlines: Foundation prefers to receive applications between May and November.
Notes: The foundation reports that nearly all grants are internally initiated. Information letters of inquiry will be accepted, but may not receive a response.

Restrictions

The foundation does not make grants to individuals or sectarian religious organizations.

Foundation Officials

Eugene P. Polk: trustee

Grants Analysis

Disclosure Period: calendar year ending 2001
Total Grants: $3,602,464*
Number of Grants: 104
Average Grant: $34,639
Highest Grant: $275,000
Lowest Grant: $1,000
Typical Range: $10,000 to $50,000
*Note: Giving excludes matching gifts.

Recent Grants

Note: Grants derived from 2001 Form 990.

Library-Related

100,000	Pierpont Morgan Library, New York, NY -- towards the building fund

General

275,000	Hospital for Special Surgery, New York, NY -- research endowment
210,000	Adult Care Services, Inc., Prescott, AZ -- towards salary of administrative assistant
200,000	Arizona Community Foundation, Phoenix, AZ -- towards the Prescott Arizona Charitable Fund
150,000	Scottsdale Healthcare Foundation, Scottsdale, AZ -- towards construction of the Virginia G. Piper Cancer Center
100,000	Arizona Friends of Foster Children Foundation, Phoenix, AZ -- towards endowment
100,000	Arizona Science Center, Phoenix, AZ
100,000	Connecticut College, New London,

100,000	CT -- endowment, operations, athletic program
100,000	Cornell University, Ithaca, NY -- towards scholarship endowment for students from Arizona
100,000	Foundation for Blind Children, Phoenix, AZ -- towards a new facility
100,000	Museum of the City of New York, New York, NY -- towards capital fund for new construction

NORMAN M. MORRIS FOUNDATION

Giving Contact

106 Corporate Park Dr.
White Plains, NY 10604
Phone: (914)694-2000

Description

Founded: 1947
EIN: 136119134
Organization Type: Private Foundation
Giving Locations: NY
Grant Types: General Support.

Donor Information

Founder: Norman M. Morris

Financial Summary

Total Giving: $334,826 (2001); $489,695 (2000); $540,135 (1999)
Giving Analysis: Giving for 2001 includes: foundation grants to United Way ($300); 2000: foundation grants to United Way ($300) 1999: foundation grants to United Way ($300)
Assets: $9,746,229 (2001); $10,095,345 (2000); $10,467,156 (1999)
Gifts Received: $442,502 (2001); $442,502 (2000); $442,502 (1999). Note: In 2001, contributions were received from Norman M. Morris Trust. In 1999 and 2000, contributions were received from Norman M. Morris.

Typical Recipients

Arts & Humanities: Community Arts, Historic Preservation, Libraries, Museums/Galleries, Public Broadcasting
Civic & Public Affairs: Botanical Gardens/Parks, Clubs, Civic & Public Affairs-General, Legal Aid, Municipalities/Towns, Public Policy
Education: Arts/Humanities Education, Colleges & Universities, Medical Education, Preschool Education, Private Education (Precollege), Religious Education, Student Aid
Health: Alzheimers Disease, Cancer, Clinics/Medical Centers, Geriatric Health, Health Organizations, Home-Care Services, Hospitals, Hospitals (University Affiliated), Long-Term Care, Medical Research, Mental Health, Nursing Services, Prenatal Health Issues, Respiratory, Single-Disease Health Associations, Transplant Networks/Donor Banks
International: International Peace & Security Issues, Missionary/Religious Activities
Religion: Jewish Causes, Religious Organizations, Religious Welfare, Seminaries, Social/Policy Issues, Synagogues/Temples
Science: Scientific Centers & Institutes
Social Services: Animal Protection, Community Service Organizations, Delinquency & Criminal Rehabilitation, People with Disabilities, Recreation & Athletics, Senior Services, United Funds/United Ways, Youth Organizations

Application Procedures

Initial Contact: Send a brief letter of inquiry. Include a description of organization and amount requested and purpose of funds sought.
Deadlines: None.

Foundation Officials

Arline J. Lubin: trustee
Kenneth A. Lubin: trustee
Marvin Lubin: vice president
Leland M. Morris: trustee
Norman M. Morris: president
Robert E. Morris: secretary, treasurer

Grants Analysis

Disclosure Period: calendar year ending 2001
Total Grants: $334,526*
Number of Grants: 52
Average Grant: $1,777*
Highest Grant: $50,100
Typical Range: $500 to $2,500
*Note: Giving excludes United Way. Average grant figure excludes five highest grants ($251,000).

Recent Grants

Note: Grants derived from 2000 Form 990.

Library-Related

50,000	Greenwich Library Development Foundation, Greenwich, CT

General

100,000	Hebrew Home for the Aged at Riverdale, New York, NY
100,000	Hospital for Joint Diseases, New York, NY
100,000	Memorial Sloan Kettering Cancer Center, New York, NY
50,000	Greenwich United Jewish Appeal Federation, Greenwich, CT
25,000	St. Andrews School, Boca Raton, FL
9,000	Oakwood School, North Hollywood, CA
5,000	Jewish Council of Yonkers, Yonkers, NY
5,000	Steadman Hawkins Foundation, Vail, CO
5,000	Stepping Stone Day School, Inc, Garden Hills, NY
5,000	Weill Medical College of Cornell, New York, NY

WILLIAM T. MORRIS FOUNDATION

Giving Contact

Edward A. Antonelli, President, Chief Executive Officer & Director
230 Park Avenue, Suite 622
New York, NY 10169-0622
Phone: (212)986-8036
Fax: (212)370-1962

Description

Founded: 1937
EIN: 131600908
Organization Type: General Purpose Foundation
Giving Locations: CT; NY; PA
Grant Types: Department, Fellowship, General Support, Project, Research, Scholarship.

Donor Information

Founder: The William T. Morris Foundation was established in 1937, with the late William T. Morris as donor.

Financial Summary

Total Giving: $1,855,000 (fiscal year ending June 30, 2002); $2,060,000 (fiscal 1999); $1,727,500 (fiscal 1998)
Assets: $57,885,978 (fiscal 1999); $55,272,364 (fiscal 1998); $51,278,277 (fiscal 1997)

Typical Recipients

Arts & Humanities: Arts Centers, Ballet, Dance, Historic Preservation, History & Archaeology, Libraries, Literary Arts, Museums/Galleries, Music, Opera, Performing Arts, Theater
Civic & Public Affairs: Botanical Gardens/Parks, Clubs, Civic & Public Affairs-General, Inner-City Development, Public Policy, Urban & Community Affairs, Zoos/Aquariums
Education: Arts/Humanities Education, Colleges & Universities, Education Funds, Education-General, Health & Physical Education, Medical Education, Minority Education, Private Education (Precollege), Student Aid
Environment: Air/Water Quality, Environment-General, Resource Conservation, Wildlife Protection
Health: Alzheimers Disease, Arthritis, Arthritis, Cancer, Clinics/Medical Centers, Emergency/Ambulance Services, Eyes/Blindness, Health Funds, Heart, Hospitals, Medical Rehabilitation, Medical Research, Multiple Sclerosis, Respiratory, Single-Disease Health Associations, Speech & Hearing
Religion: Religious Welfare
Science: Science Museums
Social Services: People with Disabilities, Recreation & Athletics, Scouts, United Funds/United Ways, YMCA/YWCA/YMHA/YWHA, Youth Organizations

Application Procedures

Initial Contact: Are not accepting new applications for funding.
Application Requirements: There is no prescribed form of application.
Deadlines: None. Scholarship applications must be submitted by April 1.

Foundation Officials

Edward A. Antonelli: president, chief executive officer, director
Bruce A. August: secretary, director
Edward W. Burns: assistant treasurer
Arthur Charles Laske, Jr.: treasurer, director
David S. MacAllaster: assistant secretary
Wilmot Fitch Wheeler, Jr.: vice president, director B Southport, CT 1923. ED Yale University BA (1945); New York University postgrad (1947-1948). PRIM CORP EMPL chairman, director: Jelliff Corp. CORP AFFIL trustee: Peoples Mutual Holdings; director: Sormir Petroleum Inc.; director: Peoples Bank Connecticut. CLUB AFFIL Sky Club; Yale Club; Fairfield Country Club.

Grants Analysis

Disclosure Period: fiscal year ending June 30, 2001
Total Grants: $2,060,000
Number of Grants: 45
Average Grant: $40,568*
Highest Grant: $275,000
Lowest Grant: $5,000
Typical Range: $10,000 to $75,000
*Note: Average grant figure excludes highest grant.

Recent Grants

Note: Grants derived from fiscal 2000 Form 990.

General

250,000	Metropolitan Opera Association, Inc., New York, NY
100,000	Memorial Sloan-Kettering Cancer Center, New York, NY
75,000	Assumption College, Worcester, MA
75,000	Boston College, New York, NY
75,000	Bowdoin College, Brunswick, ME
75,000	Dartmouth College, Hanover, NH
75,000	Fairfield University, Fairfield, CT
75,000	Hartwick College, Oneonta, NY
75,000	Hospital for Special Surgery, New York, NY
75,000	Marymount Manhattan College, New York, NY

PAULINE A. AND GEORGE R. MORRISON CHARITABLE TRUST

Giving Contact
L. Douglas Hoyt, Trustee
825 E. Speer Blvd., Suite 100A
Denver, CO 80218
Phone: (303)333-2194

Description
Founded: 1980
EIN: 846166335
Organization Type: Private Foundation
Giving Locations: CO
Grant Types: Capital.

Donor Information
Founder: George R. Morrison

Financial Summary
Total Giving: $55,000 (fiscal year ending November 30, 2001); $150,000 (fiscal 2000); $135,000 (fiscal 1999)
Assets: $4,873,768 (fiscal 2001); $4,716,736 (fiscal 2000); $4,672,383 (fiscal 1999)

Typical Recipients
Arts & Humanities: Historic Preservation, Libraries, Museums/Galleries, Public Broadcasting, Visual Arts
Civic & Public Affairs: Botanical Gardens/Parks, Zoos/Aquariums
Environment: Environment-General, Wildlife Protection
Science: Science Museums

Application Procedures
Initial Contact: Send a brief letter of inquiry.
Application Requirements: Include a description of organization, name, address, and proof of tax-exempt status; title of the person signing the application; a list of officers and directors; recently audited financial statement, a description of the project detailing the need; a statement of how the organization will obtain complete funding for the project; qualifications of personnel involved; and how progress will be reported to the foundation.
Deadlines: None.

Restrictions
Requests for grants to defray general operating costs will not be considered.

Additional Information
Publications: Application Guidelines

Foundation Officials
Robert W. Findlay: trustee
L. Douglas Hoyt: trustee
Robert D. Ibbotson: trustee
Jerry I. Maine: trustee

Grants Analysis
Disclosure Period: fiscal year ending November 30, 2001
Total Grants: $55,000
Number of Grants: 2
Highest Grant: $50,000
Lowest Grant: $5,000

Recent Grants
Note: Grants derived from fiscal 2000 Form 990.

General
150,000   Denver Zoological Foundation, Denver, CO -- primate panorama phase II

HARRY W. MORRISON FOUNDATION

Giving Contact
Velma V. Morrison, President
3505 Crescent Rim Dr.
Boise, ID 83706
Phone: (208)345-5225

Description
Founded: 1952
EIN: 826008111
Organization Type: Private Foundation
Giving Locations: ID: Boise
Grant Types: Capital, General Support.

Donor Information
Founder: the late Harry W. Morrison

Financial Summary
Total Giving: $522,839 (2000); $568,602 (1999); $185,658 (1997)
Giving Analysis: Giving for 2000 includes: foundation scholarships ($2,000); 1999: foundation scholarships ($300); foundation grants to United Way ($5,000); 1997: foundation scholarships ($275); foundation grants to United Way ($5,000) foundation ($180,383)
Assets: $12,607,934 (2000); $12,285,488 (1999); $14,188,365 (1997)
Gifts Received: $29,000 (1999). Note: In 1999, contributions were received from Estate of Edith Miller Klein.

Typical Recipients
Arts & Humanities: Arts Associations & Councils, Ballet, Historic Preservation, History & Archaeology, Libraries, Museums/Galleries, Music, Opera, Performing Arts, Public Broadcasting, Theater
Civic & Public Affairs: Botanical Gardens/Parks, Civil Rights, Housing, Municipalities/Towns, Parades/Festivals, Zoos/Aquariums
Education: Arts/Humanities Education, Business Education, Colleges & Universities, Elementary Education (Public), Engineering/Technological Education, Literacy, Medical Education, Secondary Education (Public), Student Aid
Environment: Resource Conservation, Wildlife Protection
Health: Arthritis, Cancer, Children's Health/Hospitals, Clinics/Medical Centers, Diabetes, Emergency/Ambulance Services, Health-General, Health Organizations, Heart, Hospices, Hospitals, Kidney, Long-Term Care, Medical Research, Nursing Services, Single-Disease Health Associations
International: Health Care/Hospitals, International Affairs, International Environmental Issues, International Relief Efforts, Missionary/Religious Activities
Religion: Churches, Religion-General, Missionary Activities (Domestic), Religious Organizations, Religious Welfare
Social Services: Animal Protection, At-Risk Youth, Child Welfare, Community Centers, Community Service Organizations, Family Services, Food/Clothing Distribution, People with Disabilities, Recreation & Athletics, Scouts, Senior Services, Shelters/Homelessness, Social Services-General, Special Olympics, United Funds/United Ways, YMCA/YWCA/YMHA/YWHA, Youth Organizations

Application Procedures
Initial Contact: Send a brief letter of inquiry.
Application Requirements: Applications should include a statement of the organization's background and its purposes, objectives, and past activities; explanation of current financial status, latest balance sheet showing assets and liabilities, and a list of officers and directors and their affiliations; statement of major sources of financial support including any form

of federal or state aid and if support has been received from this foundation in past years; explanation of current financial needs and any special projects or programs requiring aid; proof of tax-exempt status; and employer identification number.
Deadlines: Feb. 28.

Restrictions
Does not support individuals.

Additional Information
Publications: Application Guidelines

Foundation Officials
John J. Hockberger: director
Edith Miller Klein: director
Linda Klingner: secretary, treasurer
Velma V. Morrison: president B Woodville, CA 1920. PRIM CORP EMPL director: Morrison-Knudsen Corp. NONPR AFFIL director: Saint Lukes Hospital; trustee: Sansum Medicine Clinic; director: Pepperdine University; director: College ID; president: Morrison Center Performing Arts. CLUB AFFIL Hillcrest Country Club.
Judith V. Roberts: vice president
Michael E. Thomas: director
Frank Winsor: director

Grants Analysis
Disclosure Period: calendar year ending 2000
Total Grants: $520,839*
Number of Grants: 33
Average Grant: $6,995*
Highest Grant: $210,982
Typical Range: $1,000 to $12,500
*Note: Giving excludes scholarships. Average grant figure excludes three highest grants ($310,982).

Recent Grants
Note: Grants derived from 2001 Form 990.

General

200,000	Boise State University Foundation, Boise, ID -- Harry W. Morrison Scholl of Civil Engineering
50,000	Fred Hutchinson Cancer Research, Seattle, WA -- for patient care research fund
37,500	Idaho Anne Frank Human Rights Education Center, Boise, ID -- for reflective chasm
33,333	Bogus Basin Lifetime Sports, Boise, ID -- for Frontier Point Lodge Project
25,000	Council Community Hospital, Council, ID -- for Save the Hospital fund
25,000	First United Methodist Church, Boise, ID -- capital building fund
25,000	University of Idaho Foundation, Moscow, ID -- for the Albertson building fund
15,000	World Center for Birds of Prey, Boise, ID -- for renovations
10,000	Velma V. Morrison Center for Performing Arts, Boise, ID -- for Music Week
7,720	Minnidoka County Senior Center, Rupert, ID -- for repairs to Senior Center facility

EMIL MOSBACHER, JR. FOUNDATION

Giving Contact
R. Bruce Mosbacher, President
2200 Sand Hill Road, Suite 150
Menlo Park, CA 94025-6936
Phone: (650)854-1818

Description

Founded: 1974
EIN: 237454106
Organization Type: Private Foundation
Giving Locations: CT; NY
Grant Types: General Support.

Donor Information

Founder: Emil Mosbacher, Jr., Emil Mosbacher III, John D. Mosbacher, R. Bruce Mosbacher

Financial Summary

Total Giving: $672,500 (fiscal year ending November 30, 2001); $535,000 (fiscal 2000); $268,400 (fiscal 1998)
Giving Analysis: Giving for fiscal 2001 includes: foundation grants to United Way ($1,000) fiscal 1997: foundation grants to United Way ($36,430)
Assets: $14,324,527 (fiscal 2001); $12,562,433 (fiscal 2000); $7,100,382 (fiscal 1998)
Gifts Received: $1,794,000 (fiscal 2001); $114,037 (fiscal 1995). Note: In fiscal 2001, contributions were received from The Emil Mosbacker Jr. Charitable Annuity Trust. In fiscal 1995, contributions were received from Emil Mosbacher, Jr.

Typical Recipients

Arts & Humanities: Arts & Humanities-General, History & Archaeology, Libraries, Museums/Galleries, Opera, Public Broadcasting, Theater
Civic & Public Affairs: Botanical Gardens/Parks, Civil Rights, Community Foundations, Civic & Public Affairs-General, Hispanic Affairs, Philanthropic Organizations, Public Policy
Education: Colleges & Universities, Faculty Development, International Exchange, Legal Education, Medical Education, Private Education (Precollege), Public Education (Precollege), Science/Mathematics Education
Health: AIDS/HIV, Cancer, Children's Health/Hospitals, Clinics/Medical Centers, Health Funds, Health Organizations, Heart, Hospices, Hospitals, Medical Rehabilitation, Medical Research, Single-Disease Health Associations
International: Foreign Educational Institutions, Health Care/Hospitals, Human Rights, International Organizations, International Peace & Security Issues
Religion: Churches, Religious Welfare
Science: Science Museums
Social Services: Animal Protection, Community Service Organizations, Family Services, People with Disabilities, Recreation & Athletics, Scouts, Substance Abuse, United Funds/United Ways, YMCA/YWCA/YMHA/YWHA, Youth Organizations

Application Procedures

Initial Contact: Send brief letter.
Application Requirements: Describe program and include any pertinent information.
Deadlines: None.

Restrictions

Does not support individuals.

Foundation Officials

Emil Mosbacher, Jr.: president B White Plains, NY 1922. ED Dartmouth College BA (1943). CORP AFFIL director: Federal Insurance Co.; director: Vigilant Insurance Co.; director: Chubb Corp.; director: Avon Products Inc.; director: Chemical Bank; director: Amax Gold Inc. NONPR AFFIL member: U.S. Seniors Golf Association; member: U.S. Yacht Racing Association; member: Pilgrims U.S.; member: Independent Petroleum Association America; trustee: Lenox Hill Hospital; member, board overseers: Hoover Institute.
Nancy Ditz Mosbacher: secretary, treasurer
Patricia R. Mosbacher: vice president
R. Bruce Mosbacher: vice president, secretary, treasurer

Grants Analysis

Disclosure Period: fiscal year ending November 30, 2001
Total Grants: $671,500*
Number of Grants: 59
Average Grant: $6,865*
Highest Grant: $180,200
Lowest Grant: $50
Typical Range: $1,000 to $10,000
*Note: Giving excludes United Way. Average grant figure excludes two highest grants ($280,200).

Recent Grants

Note: Grants derived from fiscal 2000 Form 990.

General

100,000	Stanford University, Stanford, CA
88,070	Fidelity Charitable Gift Fund, Boston, MA
50,000	Hospital for Special Surgery, New York, NY
50,000	Regents of the University of California San Francisco, San Francisco, CA
25,000	Lucille Packard Foundation
25,000	Ragazzi
20,000	Memorial Sloan Kettering Cancer Center, New York, NY
20,000	Phillips Brooks School, Menlo Park, CA
20,000	Stanford Law School, Stanford, CA
10,000	Castilleja School, Palo Alto, CA

HENRY AND LUCY MOSES FUND, INC.

Giving Contact

Irving Sitnick, President & Director
Moses and Singer
1301 Avenue of the Americas, 40th Fl.
New York, NY 10019-6076
Phone: (212)554-7800
Fax: (212)554-7700

Description

Founded: 1942
EIN: 136092967
Organization Type: General Purpose Foundation
Giving Locations: NY: New York metropolitan area some funding nationally.
Grant Types: Capital, Endowment, General Support, Operating Expenses.

Donor Information

Founder: Established in New York in 1942 by Mr. Henry L. Moses and his wife, Lucy Moses . Mr. Moses, an attorney and banker, was a partner in the law firm of Moses and Singer. He also was chairman of the Public National Bank and Trust Company and, upon its merger with Bankers Trust Company, a director of that bank. Mr. Moses was a noted philanthropist, with a special interest in hospitals. He served as president and chairman of the board of Montefiore Hospital and as director of the planning commission of the Hospital Council of Greater New York and the United Hospital Fund.

Financial Summary

Total Giving: $1,277,838 (2000); $1,248,500 (1998); $3,700,500 (1995)
Assets: $2,040,374 (2000); $1,984,313 (1998); $1,883,073 (1995)
Gifts Received: $1,165,000 (2000); $1,155,000 (1998); $3,605,000 (1995). Note: The foundation receives contributions from the Henry and Lucy Moses Foundation Trust, and the Lucy G. Moses Trust.

Typical Recipients

Arts & Humanities: Ballet, Dance, Arts & Humanities-General, Libraries, Museums/Galleries, Music, Opera, Performing Arts, Public Broadcasting, Theater

Civic & Public Affairs: African American Affairs, Botanical Gardens/Parks, Civil Rights, Economic Development, Civic & Public Affairs-General, Housing, Legal Aid, Philanthropic Organizations, Urban & Community Affairs, Zoos/Aquariums
Education: Arts/Humanities Education, Colleges & Universities, Education Associations, Education Reform, Legal Education, Literacy, Medical Education, Minority Education, School Volunteerism, Special Education, Student Aid
Environment: Environment-General, Resource Conservation, Wildlife Protection, Wildlife Protection
Health: Cancer, Clinics/Medical Centers, Health Organizations, Hospitals, Long-Term Care, Medical Research, Nursing Services, Single-Disease Health Associations
International: Foreign Educational Institutions
Religion: Jewish Causes, Religious Organizations, Religious Welfare
Social Services: Child Welfare, Community Centers, Community Service Organizations, Family Planning, Family Services, Food/Clothing Distribution, People with Disabilities, Recreation & Athletics, Senior Services, Shelters/Homelessness, Social Services-General, Volunteer Services, YMCA/YWCA/YMHA/YWHA

Application Procedures

Initial Contact: Send a brief letter of inquiry.
Application Requirements: Include a description of organization, and project, and proof of tax-exempt status.

Restrictions

The foundation does not make grants to individuals, or for loans, film production, or travel.

Additional Information

The foundation reported that it is closely affiliated with the Henry and Lucy Moses Foundation Trust, the Henry L. Moses Trust, and the Lucy G. Moses Trust. All are located in the state of New York.
The foundation states that "the annual amount available for grants generally is committed to the activities supported in previous years by the foundation."

Foundation Officials

Joseph L. Fishman: vice president, director, treasurer, secretary PRIM CORP EMPL partner: Moses & Singer.
Jacqueline Schneider: vice president, director
Irving Sitnick: president, director PRIM CORP EMPL partner: Moses & Singer.

Grants Analysis

Disclosure Period: calendar year ending 2000
Total Grants: $1,277,838
Number of Grants: 84
Average Grant: $13,144*
Highest Grant: $100,000
Typical Range: $5,000 to $25,000
*Note: Average grant excludes 2 highest grants ($200,000).

Recent Grants

Note: Grants derived from 2001 Form 990.

Library-Related

15,000	Brooklyn Public Library, Brooklyn, NY

General

100,000	Montefiore Medical Center, New York, NY
100,000	United Jewish Appeal - Federation of Jewish Philanthropies of New York, New York, NY
50,000	Central Park Conservancy, New York, NY

50,000	Columbia Law School, New York, NY
50,000	Legal Aid Society, New York, NY
25,000	Brooklyn Museum of Art, Brooklyn, NY
25,000	City College Fund, New York, NY
25,000	Educational Alliance, New York, NY
25,000	Jewish Association for Services of the Aged, New York, NY
25,000	Lucy Moses School for Music and Dance, New York, NY

SAMUEL B. MOSHER FOUNDATION

Giving Contact
Robert R. Fredrickson, Secretary & Treasurer
3278 Loma Riviera Dr.
San Diego, CA 92110-5513
Phone: (619)226-6122

Description
Founded: 1951
EIN: 956037266
Organization Type: Private Foundation
Giving Locations: AZ; CA
Grant Types: Capital, General Support, Operating Expenses, Scholarship.

Donor Information
Founder: the late Samuel B. Mosher, Goodwin I. Pelissero, Deborah S. Pelissero

Financial Summary
Total Giving: $253,300 (fiscal year ending August 31, 2001); $386,250 (fiscal 2000); $259,500 (fiscal 1998)
Assets: $8,966,594 (fiscal 2001); $7,142,048 (fiscal 2000); $6,424,232 (fiscal 1998)
Gifts Received: $1,280,000 (fiscal 2001)

Typical Recipients
Arts & Humanities: Arts Festivals, Libraries, Museums/Galleries, Music, Opera
Civic & Public Affairs: Botanical Gardens/Parks, Civic & Public Affairs-General, Public Policy, Zoos/Aquariums
Education: Arts/Humanities Education, Colleges & Universities, Education Associations, Education-General, Private Education (Precollege), Religious Education, Student Aid
Health: Clinics/Medical Centers, Hospitals, Medical Research, Research/Studies Institutes, Single-Disease Health Associations
Religion: Churches, Religion-General, Religious Welfare, Seminaries
Social Services: Child Welfare, Community Service Organizations, Family Services, Social Services-General, Youth Organizations

Application Procedures
Initial Contact: Send a brief letter of inquiry.
Application Requirements: Include a description of organization, amount requested, and purpose of funds sought.
Deadlines: None.
Notes: Submissions are retained for one year.

Restrictions
Most grants are made for educational purposes. Does not support individuals or provide scholarships.

Foundation Officials
Edward Birch: trustee
Celeste Botania: trustee
Marjorie Chelini: trustee
Robert R. Fredrickson: secretary, treasurer, trustee
James McCann: trustee
R. Bruce McFadden: trustee
Margaret C. Mosher: president, trustee
Michelle Paulaula: vice president, trustee

Grants Analysis
Disclosure Period: fiscal year ending August 31, 2001
Total Grants: $253,300
Number of Grants: 14
Average Grant: $18,093
Highest Grant: $50,000
Lowest Grant: $3,300
Typical Range: $5,000 to $25,000

Recent Grants
Note: Grants derived from 2000 Form 990.

General
82,450	Holy Family School, Pasadena, CA
55,000	Orme School, Phoenix, AZ
50,000	Fredrick N. Griffith Foundation, Santa Barbara, CA
45,000	University of California Foundation, Santa Barbara, CA
25,000	Goleta Boys and Girls Club, Goleta, CA
15,000	Santa Barbara Symphony, Santa Barbara, CA
13,300	Los Angeles Orphanage Guild, Los Angeles, CA
10,500	St. Vincents, Los Angeles, CA
10,000	John Tracy Clinic, Los Angeles, CA
10,000	Nuclear Age Peace Foundation, Santa Barbara, CA

MOSINEE PAPER CORP.

Company Headquarters
100 Main St.
Mosinee, WI 54455
Web: http://www.wausaupaper.com

Company Description
Employees: 1,303
SIC(s): 2621 Paper Mills, 2672 Coated & Laminated Paper Nec, 2676 Sanitary Paper Products.

Operating Locations
Mosinee Paper Corp. (KY--Harrodsburg; MS--Jackson; OH--Middletown; WI--Columbus)

Nonmonetary Support
Type: Donated Products

Mosinee Paper Corp. Foundation

Giving Contact
Foundation Officer
1244 Kronenwetter Dr.
Mosinee, WI 54455-9099
Phone: (715)693-4470

Description
EIN: 396074298
Organization Type: Corporate Foundation
Giving Locations: headquarters and operating communities.
Grant Types: Capital, General Support, Scholarship.

Financial Summary
Total Giving: $191,837 (1997); $133,620 (1996); $127,417 (1994). Note: Fiscal 1997 Giving includes United Way ($49,400).
Assets: $604,476 (1996); $3,247 (1993); $11,469 (1992)
Gifts Received: $770,000 (1996); $123,000 (1993); $45,000 (1992). Note: In 1996, contributions were received from the Mosinee Paper Corp.

Typical Recipients
Arts & Humanities: Arts Associations & Councils, Arts Festivals, Community Arts, Arts & Humanities-General, Historic Preservation, History & Archaeology, Libraries, Museums/Galleries, Performing Arts, Theater, Visual Arts
Civic & Public Affairs: Botanical Gardens/Parks, Business/Free Enterprise, Chambers of Commerce, Community Foundations, Economic Development, Civic & Public Affairs-General, Municipalities/Towns, Philanthropic Organizations, Professional & Trade Associations, Public Policy, Safety, Women's Affairs
Education: Business Education, Colleges & Universities, Education Funds, Education-General, Public Education (Precollege), Science/Mathematics Education, Secondary Education (Public), Student Aid, Vocational & Technical Education
Environment: Environment-General, Resource Conservation, Wildlife Protection
Health: AIDS/HIV, Cancer, Children's Health/Hospitals, Emergency/Ambulance Services, Health-General, Hospitals, Single-Disease Health Associations
Social Services: Camps, Community Service Organizations, Family Services, People with Disabilities, Recreation & Athletics, Scouts, Senior Services, Social Services-General, Special Olympics, United Funds/United Ways, Volunteer Services, YMCA/YWCA/YMHA/YWHA, Youth Organizations

Application Procedures
Initial Contact: Company provides scholarships to graduating seniors of the local high school. In addition, it sponsors the Norman S. Stone Memorial Scholarship, which is limited to the study of pulp and paper technology, and paper science. Applications should be addressed to the principal of the Mosinee High School, 1000 High St., Mosinee, WI 54455, (715) 693-3200. For general requests, send a brief letter of inquiry and a full proposal. Include a description of organization, amount requested, purpose of funds sought, and proof of tax-exempt status.
Deadlines: None.

Restrictions
Does not support individuals, religious organizations for sectarian purposes, political or lobbying groups, or organizations outside operating areas.

Corporate Officials
Stuart R. Carlson: executive vice president administration PRIM CORP EMPL executive vice president administration: Wausau-Mosinee Paper Corp.
Scott P. Doescher: senior vice president, secretary, treasurer PRIM CORP EMPL senior vice president, secretary, treasurer: Wausau-Mosinee Paper Corp.
Thomas J. Howatt: president, chief executive officer, director PRIM CORP EMPL president, chief executive officer, director: Wausau-Mosinee Paper Corp.
San Watterson Orr, Jr.: chairman, director B Madison, WI 1941. ED University of Wisconsin BBA (1963); University of Wisconsin JD (1966). PRIM CORP EMPL chairman, director: Wausau-Mosinee Paper Corp. CORP AFFIL president, director: Woodson Fudiciary Corp.; secretary, treasurer, director: Yawkey Lumber Co.; chairman, director: Mosinee Paper Corp.; director: Marshall & Ilsley Corp.; director: MDU Resources Group; director: M & I First America Bank; chairman, director: Marathon Electric Manufacturing Corp.; president, director: Forewood. NONPR AFFIL director: Leigh Yawkey Woodson Art Museum; vice president, director: YMCA Foundation Wausau; director: WI Taxpayers Alliance; member: WI Bar Association; director: WI Policy Research Institute; director: University Wisconsin Hospital & Clinic; member, board regents: University Wisconsin Systems; director: University Wisconsin Foundation; member: American Law Institute; director: Competitive Wisconsin. CLUB AFFIL Wausau Club.
Richard Louis Radt: vice chairman B Chicago, IL 1932. ED University of Illinois (1956). PRIM CORP EMPL vice chairman: Wausau-Mosinee Paper Corp.

NONPR AFFIL director: Leigh Yawkey Woodson Art Museum.

Foundation Officials

Theresa M. Legner: assistant secretary PRIM CORP EMPL manager pension & savings: Mosinee Paper Corp.
San Watterson Orr, Jr.: vice president, director (see above)
Richard Louis Radt: treasurer, director (see above)

Grants Analysis

Disclosure Period: calendar year ending 1997
Total Grants: $142,437*
Number of Grants: 47
Average Grant: $3,030
Highest Grant: $15,000
Typical Range: $50 to $2,500
*Note: Giving excludes United Way. A more recent grants list was unavailable.

Recent Grants

Note: Grants derived from 1997 Form 990.

General

24,200	United Way Marathon County, Wausau, WI
16,000	United Way, Middletown, OH
15,000	YMCA, Wausau, WI
11,000	University of Wisconsin Foundation, Madison, WI
10,000	North Central Technical College Foundation, Mansfield, OH
10,000	Wausau Area Community Foundation, Wausau, WI
9,000	Mercer County Senior Citizens, Harrodsburg, KY
8,000	University of Wisconsin Stevens Point Paper Science Foundation, Stevens Point, WI
7,000	Mosinee Fire Department, Mosinee, WI
7,000	United Way Mercer County, Harrodsburg, KY

FINIS M. MOSS CHARITABLE TRUST

Giving Contact

Donald B. Russell, Co-Trustee
108 W. Walnut
Nevada, MO 64772
Phone: (417)667-6616
Fax: (417)667-3013

Description

Founded: 1975
EIN: 237451729
Organization Type: Private Foundation
Giving Locations: MO; NV
Grant Types: Capital, Operating Expenses.

Donor Information

Founder: the late Finis M. Moss

Financial Summary

Total Giving: $367,196 (fiscal year ending March 31, 2000); $370,251 (fiscal 1999); $66,990 (fiscal 1998)
Giving Analysis: Giving for fiscal 1999 includes: foundation grants to United Way ($7,500); fiscal 1998: foundation grants to United Way ($5,000) foundation ($61,990)
Assets: $7,536,565 (fiscal 2000); $7,573,664 (fiscal 1999); $7,417,790 (fiscal 1998)
Gifts Received: $64,116 (fiscal 1997)

Typical Recipients

Arts & Humanities: Historic Preservation, History & Archaeology, Libraries
Civic & Public Affairs: Clubs, Economic Development, Civic & Public Affairs-General, Municipalities/Towns, Safety, Urban & Community Affairs
Education: Arts/Humanities Education, Colleges & Universities, Education-General, Literacy, Preschool Education, Private Education (Precollege), Public Education (Precollege), Science/Mathematics Education, Student Aid
Environment: Environment-General, Resource Conservation, Wildlife Protection
Health: Children's Health/Hospitals, Clinics/Medical Centers, Emergency/Ambulance Services, Health Organizations, Hospitals
Religion: Religious Welfare
Social Services: Animal Protection, Child Welfare, Community Service Organizations, Crime Prevention, Day Care, Delinquency & Criminal Rehabilitation, Family Services, Family Services, Food/Clothing Distribution, People with Disabilities, Recreation & Athletics, Scouts, United Funds/United Ways, YMCA/YWCA/YMHA/YWHA

Application Procedures

Initial Contact: Application form required.
Deadlines: January 31.

Foundation Officials

Lee Gilbert: co-trustee
Robert Lasley: co-trustee
Donald B. Russell: co-trustee PRIM CORP EMPL chairman, director: Farm & Home Savings Association.

Grants Analysis

Disclosure Period: fiscal year ending March 31, 2000
Total Grants: $367,196*
Number of Grants: 30
Average Grant: $5,971*
Highest Grant: $100,000
Typical Range: $1,000 to $10,000
*Note: Giving excludes United Way. Average grant excludes 2 highest grants ($200,000).

Recent Grants

Note: Grants derived from 1999 Form 990.

General

100,000	Cottey College, Nevada, MO
100,000	YMCA, Nevada, MO
41,221	Council on Families in Crisis, Nevada, MO
39,744	University of Missouri, Nevada, MO
24,000	Community Outreach, Nevada, MO
15,000	Pittsburgh State University Center for Reading Difficulty, Pittsburg, KS
14,000	Cottey College, Nevada, MO
7,500	United Community Funds, Nevada, MO
7,064	Nevada Boxing Club, Nevada, MO
5,000	NAEDC, Nevada, MO

MOTOROLA, INC.

Company Headquarters

1303 E. Algonquin Rd.
Schaumburg, IL 60196
Web: http://www.mot.com

Company Description

Founded: 1928
Ticker: MOT
Exchange: NYSE
Revenue: US$26.679 billion (2002)
Employees: 137000 (2002)

Nonmonetary Support

Type: Donated Equipment; Donated Products
Note: NOT Nonmonetary support is provided by the company.
Volunteer Programs: The company sponsors volunteer programs that enable employees to support local organizations and schools in their communities. The foundation sponsors a volunteer grants program.

Motorola Foundation

Giving Contact

Judy Adkins, Program Administrator
1303 E Algonquin Rd.
Schaumburg, IL 60196
Phone: (847)576-6200
Fax: (847)576-3997
Web: http://fdncenter.org

Description

EIN: 366109323
Organization Type: Corporate Foundation
Giving Locations: headquarters community, plant locations, and to select national organizations.
Grant Types: Capital, Employee Matching Gifts, General Support, Multiyear/Continuing Support, Project, Scholarship.
Note: The foundation offers employee matching gift programs.

Financial Summary

Total Giving: $3,123,200 (2002 approx); $11,014,049 (2001); $9,712,915 (2000). Note: Contributes through corporate direct giving program and foundation.
Giving Analysis: Giving for 2000 includes: foundation grants to United Way ($1,074,400); foundation matching gifts ($1,854,294); foundation ($6,784,221); 1998: foundation grants to United Way ($1,090,500); foundation matching gifts ($1,574,639); foundation ($4,264,816); 1997: foundation grants to United Way ($1,059,900); foundation matching gifts ($1,340,267) foundation ($4,212,776)
Assets: $92,648,562 (2001); $110,460,710 (2000); $14,293,590 (1998)
Gifts Received: $10,293,125 (1993); $5,107,670 (1992). Note: Contributions are received from Motorola, Inc.

Typical Recipients

Arts & Humanities: Arts Associations & Councils, Arts Funds, Arts Institutes, Dance, Ethnic & Folk Arts, Museums/Galleries, Music, Opera, Performing Arts, Public Broadcasting, Theater
Civic & Public Affairs: African American Affairs, Business/Free Enterprise, Civil Rights, Clubs, Economic Development, Economic Policy, Employment/Job Training, Civic & Public Affairs-General, Housing, Law & Justice, Legal Aid, Nonprofit Management, Philanthropic Organizations, Professional & Trade Associations, Public Policy, Safety, Urban & Community Affairs, Women's Affairs, Zoos/Aquariums
Education: Agricultural Education, Business Education, Colleges & Universities, Community & Junior Colleges, Community & Junior Colleges, Continuing Education, Economic Education, Education Associations, Education Funds, Engineering/Technological Education, Education-General, Gifted & Talented Programs, Literacy, Minority Education, Private Education (Precollege), Public Education (Precollege), Science/Mathematics Education, Student Aid
Environment: Environment-General
Health: Emergency/Ambulance Services, Hospices, Hospitals, Single-Disease Health Associations
International: Foreign Educational Institutions, International-General, Health Care/Hospitals, International Affairs, International Organizations, International Relief Efforts
Religion: Ministries, Religious Welfare

Science: Observatories & Planetariums, Science Exhibits & Fairs, Science Museums, Scientific Centers & Institutes

Social Services: Child Welfare, Community Service Organizations, Counseling, Crime Prevention, Family Services, Food/Clothing Distribution, People with Disabilities, Recreation & Athletics, Senior Services, Shelters/Homelessness, Substance Abuse, United Funds/United Ways, Volunteer Services, YMCA/YWCA/YMHA/YWHA, Youth Organizations

Application Procedures

Initial Contact: Submit a query letter of no more than two pages.

Application Requirements: Query letters should provide a description of goals and objectives of the organization or program; geographic and demographics served by the organization; name, address, and telephone number of the chief executive officer; amount requested; and proof of tax-exempt status.

Deadlines: June 30 for Illinois and national programs; local operating locations have various deadlines.

Notes: Specific deadlines for local requests can be obtained by contacting the Community Relations Representative at the following operating locations:

1303 E. Algonquin Road, Schaumburg, IL 60196; (847) 576-6200 (National headquarters).

1301 N. Algonquin Road, Schaumburg, IL 60196; (847) 538-4041 (Northwest suburbs).

1475 W. Shure Drive, Arlington Heights, IL 60004; (847) 632-6021.

3102 N. 56th Street, Phoenix, AZ 85018; (602) 952-4022.

1500 Gateway Blvd., Boynton Beach, FL 33426; (561) 739-8658.

8000 W. Sunrise Blvd., Plantation, FL 33322; (954) 739-2238.

6501 Wm. Gannon Drive, Austin, TX 78735; (512) 895-8866.

5555 N. Beach Street, Ft. Worth, TX 76137; (817) 245-2102.

National requests should be sent to the foundation; regional requests should be sent to operating facility in area.

International requests are accepted. However, the Motorola Foundation only accepts international grant requests from the Motorola facility within that country. A global giving priority is to fund in those areas where Motorola has a significant presence. If a Community Relations Representative from an area is not listed above, contact Schaumburg National Headquarters at the above phone number for more information.

Restrictions

Foundation does not fund individuals, including scholarships or other forms of financial assistance; political or lobbying groups, candidates or campaigns; endowment funds; sports sponsorships; fund-raising events, conferences or benefits, including sponsorships, dinners, tickets, or courtesy advertising; national health organizations or their local chapters; single-disease health organizations; capital fund drives; trade schools; or private foundations described under IRS Code Section 509(a).

The foundation does not lease or donate Motorola products or equipment.

Additional Information

Grants are made on an annual basis only with no renewals implied.

Publications: Guidelines

Corporate Officials

Albert R. Brashear: senior vice president, director corporate communications PRIM CORP EMPL senior vice president, director corporate communications: Motorola Inc.

Christopher B. Galvin: president, chief executive officer, director B 1951. ED Northwestern University BA; Northwestern University Kellogg Graduate School of Management MBA (1977). PRIM CORP

EMPL president, chief executive officer, director: Motorola Inc. CORP AFFIL chief executive officer: Indala Corp.; president: Motorola de Puerto Rico Inc.

Carl F. Koenemann: chief financial officer, executive vice president ED DePaul University BS (1964); Loyola University Chicago MBA (1969). PRIM CORP EMPL chief financial officer, executive vice president: Motorola Inc. CORP AFFIL vice president: Motorola Cellular Service Inc.; chief financial officer, director: Motorola Communication & Electricity; chief financial officer: Indala Corp.

Garth Leroy Milne: senior vice president, treasurer B Saint George, UT 1942. ED University of Utah BS (1966); Harvard University MBA (1968).

John Francis Mitchell: vice chairman, director B Chicago, IL 1928. ED Illinois Institute of Technology BS (1950). PRIM CORP EMPL vice chairman, director: Motorola Inc.

Foundation Officials

Albert R. Brashear: director public affairs (see above)

Steve Earhart: vice president

Carol Forsyte: assistant secretary

Christopher B. Galvin: director (see above)

Roberta W. Gutman: program administrator

Anthony Knapp: vice president

A. Peter Lawson: vice president

Dennis Roberson: vice president, director

Caroline T. Swinney: assistant secretary

Grants Analysis

Disclosure Period: calendar year ending 2001

Total Grants: $3,832,335*

Number of Grants: 302

Average Grant: $12,700*

Highest Grant: $1,033,962

Lowest Grant: $350

Typical Range: $1,000 to $22,000

*Note: Giving excludes matching gifts and United Way. Average grant excludes highest grant.

Recent Grants

Note: Grants derived from 2001 Form 990.

General

1,033,962	Twin Towers Fund, New York, NY
750,000	Live Brave Coalition, Schaumburg, IL
500,000	United Way Crusade of Mercy, Chicago, IL
315,933	Federal Employee Education and Assistance Fund, Littleton, CO
300,000	Abraham Lincoln Presidential Library and Museum Foundation, Springfield, IL
300,000	Georgia Tech Foundation, Atlanta, GA
250,000	Live Brave Coalition, Schaumburg, IL
200,000	Arizona State University Foundation, Tempe, AZ
200,000	China Youth Development Foundation, Beijing People's Republic of China
192,025	National Merit Scholarship Corporation, Evanston, IL

CHARLES STEWART MOTT FOUNDATION

Giving Contact

Office of Proposal Entry
Mott Foundation Building
503 S. Saginaw Street, Suite 1200
Flint, MI 48502-1851
Phone: (810) 238-5651
Fax: (810) 766-1753
E-mail: info@mott.org
Web: http://www.mott.org

Alternate Contact

Charles Stewart Mott Foundation
Zitna 8
120 00
Prague, Czech Republic

Description

Founded: 1926

EIN: 381211227

Organization Type: General Purpose Foundation

Giving Locations: MI: Flint internationally; nationally.

Grant Types: Conference/Seminar, General Support, Matching, Multiyear/Continuing Support, Operating Expenses, Seed Money.

Note: Also provides technical assistance.

Donor Information

Founder: Charles Stewart Mott , an industrialist, established the foundation in Flint, MI, in 1926. From his earliest years in his adopted community, Mr. Mott was concerned with the city's welfare, and served two years as mayor. He also served as chairman of U.S. Sugar Corporation, president of the Northern Illinois Water Company, director of and one of the largest individual stockholders in General Motors, a principal stockholder in the Continental Water Company, and a trustee of Stevens Institute of Technology. Mr. Mott also started a medical and dental clinic for children and helped establish the YMCA and the Boy Scouts in Flint, as well as the Whaley Children's Center. Mr. Mott died in 1973. His son, Charles Stewart Harding Mott, guided the foundation from its earliest days until his death in 1989.

Financial Summary

Total Giving: $129,745,474 (2001); $152,970,798 (2000); $113,901,901 (1999)

Giving Analysis: Giving for 1999 includes: foundation grants to United Way ($315,000); foundation matching gifts ($857,499); 1998: foundation grants to United Way ($122,500) foundation matching gifts ($330,000)

Assets: $2,470,000,000 (2001 approx); $2,880,296,978 (2000); $3,227,653,816 (1999)

Gifts Received: $6,714 (1998). Note: In 1998, contributions were received from Herold W. Parker.

Typical Recipients

Arts & Humanities: Arts Centers, Arts & Humanities-General, Libraries, Public Broadcasting

Civic & Public Affairs: African American Affairs, Business/Free Enterprise, Civil Rights, Community Foundations, Economic Development, Economic Policy, Employment/Job Training, Civic & Public Affairs-General, Hispanic Affairs, Housing, Legal Aid, Native American Affairs, Nonprofit Management, Philanthropic Organizations, Professional & Trade Associations, Public Policy, Rural Affairs, Safety, Urban & Community Affairs, Women's Affairs

Education: Business Education, Colleges & Universities, Education Associations, Education Funds, Education Reform, Engineering/Technological Education, Faculty Development, Education-General, International Exchange, International Studies, International Studies, Leadership Training, Minority Education, Public Education (Precollege), Science/Mathematics Education, Social Sciences Education, Vocational & Technical Education

Environment: Energy, Environment-General, Protection, Resource Conservation

Health: AIDS/HIV, Health Policy/Cost Containment, Home-Care Services, Public Health, Research/Studies Institutes

International: Foreign Educational Institutions, International-General, Human Rights, International Affairs, International Development, International Environmental Issues, International Organizations,

International Peace & Security Issues, International Relations, International Relief Efforts

Religion: Religious Welfare

Social Services: At-Risk Youth, Child Welfare, Community Service Organizations, Crime Prevention, Day Care, Family Planning, Family Services, People with Disabilities, Scouts, Substance Abuse, United Funds/United Ways, Volunteer Services, Youth Organizations

Application Procedures

Initial Contact: The foundation has no formal grant application procedure or application form. Letters of inquiry, including a brief description of the project and the range of the needed funding, are acceptable for initial contact.

Application Requirements: Formal proposals should contain the following: a cover letter detailing the amount of money requested for a specified grant period that is signed by the person ultimately responsible for signing grant contracts on behalf of grant applicant; the project description, including an explanation of why the project is needed, who will be served, and what will be accomplished during a specific period; information on the feasibility and sustainability of the proposed grant activity; information on lasting benefits to the organization, program participants, the community, or other organizations working in the field; an appropriate plan for evaluation, reporting, and dissemination; a documented line-item budget and projected sources of funds for the proposed grant period; information about the organization seeking funds, including its staff, board of directors, legal classification, and history and accomplishments. Applicants will also be required to submit copies of their annual report and audited financial statements or IRS Form 990.

Deadlines: None. The foundation strongly encourages applicants to submit proposals during the first quarter of the year for which funding is requested. Grant funds for any year are committed by September 1 of that year.

The entire review process takes up to four months from proposal receipt; therefore, proposals should be submitted at least four months prior to the start of the proposed grant period.

Review Process: Proposals are reviewed by program staff for initial recommendation of denial or approval. The proposal review committee, composed of senior management, makes the final recommendation. The proposal may then be approved by the president under delegated authority or referred to the board of trustees, which meets quarterly, for further action.

Notes: To prevent conflict-of-interest problems, grant applicants should not route proposals through trustees or solicit their assistance. Trustees are prohibited from voting on grant proposals where they have a conflict of interest. Because of the large number of requests, foundation visits, unless by invitation, are discouraged. Requests for meetings with foundation trustees and staff will be initiated only by the foundation.

Video tapes are discouraged and will not be returned.

Restrictions

The foundation does not make grants or loans to individuals or for religious activities or programs that serve a specific religious group. Outside the Flint, MI, area, the foundation makes capital and endowment grants only when necessary to carry out other foundation objectives, and grants are not made for local projects unless the projects are part of a national demonstration or foundation-planned network of grants and have clear and significant implications for replication in other communities. The foundation does not support research except when it is instrumental for other grant-making purposes or for strengthening relevant public policy. It does not provide ongoing support for projects normally supported or which should be supported by taxpayers. The foundation also does not grant scholarships.

Additional Information

The foundation occasionally considers activities of a non-grant nature that help to achieve program objectives. These may include program-related investments, direct technical or fund-raising assistance, research, and the dissemination of findings. Most foundation grants are for up to one year, although applicants may submit multi-year proposals.

To receive publications without charge, call the hotline at (800) 645-1766 (US/Canada) or (414) 273-6943 (elsewhere).

Publications: Annual Report; Facts on Grants; Guidelines; Quarterly Newsletter; Grant Listings by Program

Foundation Officials

A. Marshall Acuff, Jr.: trustee

Karen B. Aldridge: program officer

Jon R. Blyth: program director

Gavin Clabaugh: vice president information services

Alonzo A. Crim: trustee B Chicago, IL 1928. ED Roosevelt University BA (1950); Chicago Teachers College (1953-1954); University of Chicago MA (1958); Harvard University EdD (1969). PRIM NONPR EMPL professor education administration: Georgia State University. CORP AFFIL director: Scholastic Inc.

Donald F. Dahlstrom: communications officer

Lois R. DeBacker: program officer

Katherine Woodruff Fanning: trustee B Chicago, IL 1927. ED Smith College BA (1949). CORP AFFIL director: Boston Globe Publishing. NONPR AFFIL trustee: Kettering Foundation; member: Society Professional Journalists; director: International Center Journalists; member: Council Foreign Relations; sr advisory board: Harvard University Joan Shorenstein Barone Center; director: Boston Public Library Foundation; member: American Academy of Arts & Sciences; member, director: American Society Newspaper Editors. CLUB AFFIL Badminton & Tennis Club; Saint Botolph Club.

Suzanne L. Feurt: program officer

Neal R. Hegarty: program officer

Rushworth Moulton Kidder: trustee B Providence, RI 1944. ED Amherst College BA (1965); Columbia University MA (1966); Columbia University PhD (1969). NONPR AFFIL member values & ethics committee: Independent Sector; member board director: Principia College; member advisory council: Friends of the University of Natal; member: Center Strategic & Information Studies International; advisor counselor: Character Education Partnership.

Jim L. Krause: director grants administration, assistant treasurer

Marianne Kugler: program officer

Christa Kuljian: program officer

Marilyn Stein LeFeber: vice president communications

Jack A. Litzenberg: program officer

Tiffany W. Lovett: trustee

Webb Franklin Martin: trustee B Flint, MI 1944. ED Michigan State University (1966); Wayne State University JD (1969). PRIM CORP EMPL senior vice president: Bank One Corp.

Olivia P. Maynard: trustee

Edmund J. Miller: program officer

John Morning: trustee B Cleveland, OH 1932. ED Pratt Institute BFA (1955). PRIM CORP EMPL president: John Morning Design. CORP AFFIL director: Dime Savings Bank. NONPR AFFIL member, board director: New York Landmarks Conservancy; chairman: Vivian Beaumont Theater; member education committee: Museum Modern Art; vice chairman: New York City Cultural Affairs Advisory Committee; director: Association Government Boards, Colleges & Universities; trustee: City University New York; member: American Academy Dramatic Arts.

Maryanne T. Mott: trustee

Ruth Rawlings Mott: trustee emeritus B El Paso, TX 1901.

Douglas Xavier Patino: trustee B Calexico, CA 1939. ED Imperial Valley College AA (1960); California State University BA (1962); California State University MA (1966); United States International University PhD (1972). PRIM CORP EMPL president: The Patino Group PRIM NONPR EMPL vice chancellor emeritus: California State University ADD NONPR EMPL professor: California State University Los Angeles. NONPR AFFIL member, chairman: Hispanics Philanthropy; member: Staff Advisor Committee Human Resources Committee; commr: Enterprise Americans; member, board directors: American Public Welfare Association; department director: California Employment Development Department.

Phillip Peters: vice president administration, secretary-treasurer

William H. Piper: vice chairman, trustee B Flint, MI 1933. ED Yale University BA (1955). CORP AFFIL director: US Sugar Corp. NONPR AFFIL vice chairman, trustee emeritus: McLaren General Hospital; member advisory board professional corporate: University Michigan Flint; member executive committee: General Motors Institute Business Industry Center; section, treasurer: Genesee Area Focus Council. CLUB AFFIL University Club; Flint Golf Club.

Willa B. Player: trustee emeritus

John W. Porter: trustee B Fort Wayne, IN 1931. ED Albion College BA (1953); Michigan State University MA (1957); Michigan State University PhD (1962). PRIM NONPR EMPL chief executive officer: Urban Education Alliance Inc. CORP AFFIL director: Comerica Bank. NONPR AFFIL member: Sigma Pi Phi; member: Tuskeegee Airmen; member: Phi Delta Kappa; life member: NAACP; member: National Measurement Council; member: Michigan State Chamber of Commerce; member: Michigan Martin Luther King Junior Holiday Commission; honorary life member: Michigan Parent Teachers Association; director: Michigan International Council; director: Michigan Congress Parents & Teachers; member: Michigan Governments Blue Ribbon Commission Welfare Reform; member: Greater Detroit Chamber of Commerce; member: Catherine McAuley Health Systems Board; president: Eastern Michigan University Alumni Association; trustee: East Lansing Edgewood United Church; member: East Lansing Human Relations Commission; member: American Association School Administrations; chairman: American Association State Colleges & Universities Task Force Excellence Education; trustee: Albion College. CLUB AFFIL Economic Club.

Richard Kent Rappleye: vice president field services B Oswego, NY 1940. ED Miami University AB (1962); Boston University (1962-1963); University of Pennsylvania Wharton School MBA (1964); DePaul University (1965-1966). NONPR AFFIL member: Michigan Association CPAs; lecturer: University Michigan; member: American Institute of Certified Public Accountants. CLUB AFFIL Masons Club; Rotary International Club.

Judy Y. Samelson: vice president communications NONPR AFFIL director: Hurley Medical Center Inc.

Tamas A. Scsaurszki: program officer

Jean Simi: executive assistant, corporate assistant secretary

Michael J. Smith: assistant vice president investments

Maureen H. Smyth: vice president programs

Marise M.M. Stewart: trustee

Christine Sturgis: program officer

Robert E. Swaney, Jr.: vice president, chief investment officer

George A. Trone: program officer

Claire Mott White: trustee

Ronald M. White: program officer

William Samuel White: chairman, president, chief executive officer, trustee, chairman several com B Cincinnati, OH 1937. ED Dartmouth College BA (1959); Dartmouth College MBA (1960). CORP AFFIL director: US Sugar Corp.; director: Continental Water Corp. NONPR AFFIL chairman: Flint Area Focus Council; director: Independent Sector; director: European Foundation Center; director: Civicus.

George S. Whyel: trustee emeritus

Grants Analysis

Disclosure Period: calendar year ending 2001

Total Grants: $129,745,474*

Number of Grants: 647

Average Grant: $200,534

Highest Grant: $3,975,000

Lowest Grant: $5,000

Typical Range: $20,000 to $250,000

*Note: Grants analysis provided by foundation.

Recent Grants

Note: Grants derived from 2000 Form 990.

General

8,500,000 Foundation for the Flint Cultural Center, Flint, MI -- endowment fund

7,100,000 Flint Cultural Center Foundation, Flint, MI -- building repairs and improvement

7,000,000 Kettering University, Flint, MI -- Mechanical Engineering and Chemistry Center

4,000,000 German Marshall Fund of the United States, Washington, DC -- trust for civil society in central and eastern Europe

3,142,314 National Center for Community Education, Flint, MI -- training for the 21st Center for Community Learning Centers

2,000,000 Corporation for Enterprise Development, Washington, DC -- investment in innovations fund

2,000,000 Nelson Mandela Children's Fund Republic of South Africa -- endowment fund

1,500,000 Center for Community Change, Washington, DC -- national campaign for jobs and income support

1,375,000 University of Michigan, Flint, MI -- digital conservation of WFUM/TV28

1,260,000 Advertising Council, Inc., New York, NY -- after-school PSA campaign

MUCHNIC FOUNDATION

Giving Contact

David C. Mize, Secretary
104 S. Cascade Ave., Suite 202
Colorado Springs, CO 80903-5102
Phone: (913)367-4164

Alternate Contact

704 North 4th Street
PO Box 329
Atchison, KS 66002

Description

Founded: 1946

EIN: 486102818

Organization Type: Private Foundation

Giving Locations: CO

Grant Types: General Support.

Donor Information

Founder: Valley Co., the late Helen Q. Muchnic, the late H. E. Muchnic

Financial Summary

Total Giving: $407,700 (fiscal year ending November 30, 2001); $334,000 (fiscal 2000); $325,600 (fiscal 1999). Note: 1997 Giving includes United Way ($10,000).

Giving Analysis: Giving for fiscal 2001 includes: foundation grants to United Way ($10,000); fiscal 2000: foundation grants to United Way ($10,000); fiscal 1998: foundation grants to United Way ($10,000); foundation scholarships ($10,000) foundation ($371,415)

Assets: $9,221,320 (fiscal 2001); $10,382,432 (fiscal 2000); $8,709,677 (fiscal 1999).

Typical Recipients

Arts & Humanities: Arts Associations & Councils, Arts Funds, History & Archaeology, Libraries, Museums/Galleries, Performing Arts

Civic & Public Affairs: Clubs, Municipalities/Towns, Urban & Community Affairs

Education: Agricultural Education, Arts/Humanities Education, Colleges & Universities, Education Reform, Engineering/Technological Education, Environmental Education, International Studies, Literacy, Preschool Education, Private Education (Precollege), Public Education (Precollege), Religious Education, Student Aid

Environment: Environment-General, Resource Conservation, Wildlife Protection

Health: Alzheimers Disease, Arthritis, Cancer, Children's Health/Hospitals, Hospitals, Prenatal Health Issues, Research/Studies Institutes, Single-Disease Health Associations

International: Health Care/Hospitals, International Environmental Issues, International Organizations, International Relief Efforts

Religion: Churches, Ministries, Religious Welfare

Science: Science Museums

Social Services: Animal Protection, Child Welfare, Community Centers, Community Service Organizations, Scouts, Substance Abuse, United Funds/United Ways, YMCA/YWCA/YMHA/YWHA, Youth Organizations

Application Procedures

Initial Contact: The foundation has no formal grant application procedure or application form. Send a brief letter of inquiry.

Deadlines: October 31.

Foundation Officials

Elizabeth M. Elicker: trustee

Ann Mize: director

David C. Mize: secretary

Daphne Nan Muchnic: director

Grants Analysis

Disclosure Period: fiscal year ending November 30, 2001

Total Grants: $397,700*

Number of Grants: 61

Average Grant: $5,795*

Highest Grant: $50,000

Lowest Grant: $500

Typical Range: $1,000 to $10,000

*Note: Giving excludes United Way. Average grant figure excludes highest grant.

Recent Grants

Note: Grants derived from fiscal 2000 Form 990.

Library-Related

8,000 Atchison Library, Atchison, KS

General

50,000 Saint Francis Academy, Salina, KS

25,000 Kansas University Endowment, Lawrence, KS

20,000 Atchison Art Association, Atchison, KS

13,000 Kansas State Engineering, Manhattan, KS

13,000 Saint Francis Academy, Atchison, KS

10,000 Atchison United Way, Atchison, KS

10,000 Benedictine College, Atchison, KS

10,000 City of Atchison, Atchison, KS

10,000 FINCA International, Washington, DC

10,000 Kansas University Endowment, Lawrence, KS

JANE T. MUHLETHALER FOUNDATION, INC.

Giving Contact

James D. Funnell, Jr., Secretary
Care of Hermenze & Marcantonio
19 Ludlow Road, Suite 101
Westport, CT 06880
Phone: (203)226-6552

Description

Founded: 1997

EIN: 061481432

Organization Type: Private Foundation

Giving Locations: CT: Lower Fairfield County, Norwalk, Wilton

Grant Types: Operating Expenses.

Financial Summary

Total Giving: $120,269 (2001); $115,353 (2000); $98,753 (1999)

Assets: $1,952,787 (2001); $1,918,002 (2000); $1,867,874 (1999)

Gifts Received: $1,924,401 (1997)

Typical Recipients

Arts & Humanities: Libraries

Civic & Public Affairs: Civic & Public Affairs-General

Education: Colleges & Universities

Health: Cancer, Emergency/Ambulance Services, Hospitals, Long-Term Care

Social Services: People with Disabilities, Social Services-General, YMCA/YWCA/YMHA/YWHA

Application Procedures

Initial Contact: Send a brief letter of inquiry and a full proposal

Application Requirements: Include a description of organization, amount requested, and purpose of funds sought.

Deadlines: November 1; preference for October submissions.

Restrictions

The foundation restricts its giving to nonprofit organizations located in lower Fairfield County, CT, with preference given to organizations serving Wilton and Norwalk, CT.

Foundation Officials

James D. Funnell, Jr.: secretary

William P. Middeleer: vice president

Jane T. Muhlethaler: president

Edward S. Rimer: treasurer

Grants Analysis

Disclosure Period: calendar year ending 2001

Total Grants: $120,269

Number of Grants: 9

Average Grant: $9,409*

Highest Grant: $45,000

Lowest Grant: $5,000

Typical Range: $5,000 to $15,000

*Note: Average grant figure excludes highest grant.

Recent Grants

Note: Grants derived from 2000 Form 990.

General

36,000	Nursing Home & Care, Inc., Wilton, CT
28,000	Center for Hope, Darien, CT
13,500	Wilton Ambulance Corps., Wilton, CT
10,000	Fidelco
10,000	University of Connecticut Foundation, Storrs, CT
5,000	Norwalk Hospital Foundation - Cancer Center, Norwalk, CT
5,000	Norwalk Hospital Foundation - Emergency Department, Norwalk, CT
4,000	Wilton Salvation Army, Wilton, CT
3,853	Plan of Connecticut, Inc.

MULCAHY FOUNDATION

Giving Contact

Robert D. Lohse, President
2440 E. Broadway
Tucson, AZ 85719
Phone: (520)791-3939

Description

Founded: 1957
EIN: 866053461
Organization Type: Private Foundation
Giving Locations: AZ: emphasis on the Tucson area
Grant Types: Capital, Emergency, Endowment, General Support, Multiyear/Continuing Support, Operating Expenses, Project, Research.

Donor Information

Founder: the late John A. Mulcahy, Mulcahy Lumber Co.

Financial Summary

Total Giving: $120,940 (fiscal year ending June 30, 2002); $131,300 (fiscal 2001); $131,300 (fiscal 2000)
Assets: $2,193,579 (fiscal 2002); $2,138,335 (fiscal 2001); $2,138,335 (fiscal 2000)
Gifts Received: $125,000 (fiscal 1999); $25,000 (fiscal 1992). Note: In fiscal 1999, contributions were received from Calistri Foundation.

Typical Recipients

Arts & Humanities: Community Arts, History & Archaeology, Libraries, Museums/Galleries, Opera, Performing Arts, Theater
Civic & Public Affairs: Clubs, Civic & Public Affairs-General, Hispanic Affairs
Education: Arts/Humanities Education, Colleges & Universities, Community & Junior Colleges, Economic Education, Education Reform, Environmental Education, Education-General, Medical Education, Public Education (Precollege), Religious Education, Science/Mathematics Education, Student Aid
Health: Cancer
Religion: Churches, Religious Welfare
Social Services: Community Service Organizations, Crime Prevention, Food/Clothing Distribution, United Funds/United Ways, YMCA/YWCA/YMHA/YWHA, Youth Organizations

Application Procedures

Initial Contact: Requests should be brief and informal with a proposed budget and a copy of the organization's IRS determination letter attached.
Deadlines: None.

Restrictions

Most grants are for educational purposes. Does not support individuals.

Foundation Officials

Ashby I. Lohse: secretary
Florence Lohse: vice president
Kathy Lohse: treasurer
Linda Lohse: secretary, treasurer
Robert D. Lohse: president
Carmen Moline: treasurer

Grants Analysis

Disclosure Period: fiscal year ending June 30, 2002
Total Grants: $120,940
Number of Grants: 11
Average Grant: $4,721*
Highest Grant: $73,735
Lowest Grant: $1,000
Typical Range: $1,000 to $10,000
*Note: Average grant figure excludes highest grant.

Recent Grants

Note: Grants derived from fiscal 2002 Form 990.

General

73,735	University of Arizona, Tucson, AZ -- education
14,125	Pima Community College Foundation, Tucson, AZ -- education
10,000	Fox Tucson Theatre Foundation, Tucson, AZ -- for community historic preservation
6,380	Northern Arizona University, Flagstaff, AZ -- education
4,200	Pima Community College, Tucson, AZ -- education
2,500	Afro-American Historical and Genealogical Society, Green Valley, AZ -- education
2,500	Arizona State University, Tempe, AZ -- education
2,500	Barbea Williams Performing Company, Tucson, AZ -- education
2,000	Educational Enrichment Foundation, Tucson, AZ -- education
2,000	Life Long Learning, Inc., Phoenix, AZ -- education

CLARENCE E. MULFORD TRUST

Giving Contact

David R. Hastings, Jr., Trustee
PO Box 290
Fryeburg, ME 04037
Phone: (207)935-2061
Fax: (207)935-3939
E-mail: hlo@landmarknet.net

Description

Founded: 1950
EIN: 010247548
Organization Type: Private Foundation
Giving Locations: ME: Fryeburg and neighboring towns
Grant Types: General Support.

Donor Information

Founder: the late Clarence E. Mulford

Financial Summary

Total Giving: $441,360 (2000); $453,154 (1999); $426,630 (1998)
Assets: $10,425,722 (2000); $9,836,777 (1999); $10,349,245 (1998)

Typical Recipients

Arts & Humanities: Arts Institutes, Historic Preservation, History & Archaeology, Libraries, Music
Civic & Public Affairs: Clubs, Civic & Public Affairs-General, Municipalities/Towns, Urban & Community Affairs, Women's Affairs
Education: Business Education, Colleges & Universities, Education-General, Literacy, Private Education (Precollege), Public Education (Precollege)
Environment: Resource Conservation

Health: Health Organizations, Hospices, Hospitals
Religion: Churches, Religious Organizations
Social Services: Animal Protection, Community Service Organizations, Recreation & Athletics, Scouts, Senior Services, Youth Organizations

Application Procedures

Initial Contact: Send a brief letter of inquiry. Include a description of organization, amount requested, purpose of funds sought, recently audited financial statement, and proof of tax-exempt status.
Deadlines: January 10 and July 10.

Restrictions

Does not support individuals or provide loans, matching gifts, or scholarships.

Foundation Officials

David R. Hastings, II: trustee
Peter G. Hastings: trustee

Grants Analysis

Disclosure Period: calendar year ending 2000
Total Grants: $441,360
Number of Grants: 30
Average Grant: $5,616*
Highest Grant: $278,510
Typical Range: $1,000 to $10,000
*Note: Average grant figure excludes highest grant.

Recent Grants

Note: Grants derived from 2001 Form 990.

Library-Related

3,300	Library Club of Lovell, Lovell, ME -- for public library purposes

General

289,311	Fryeburg Academy, Fryeburg, ME -- for educational purposes
97,650	Town of Fryeburg, Fryeburg, ME -- municipal purposes
12,500	Fryeburg Rescue Association, Inc., Fryeburg, ME -- for charitable purposes
5,000	Paugus Grange 540, Fryeburg, ME -- for charitable purposes
5,000	First Congregational Church of Fryeburg, Fryeburg, ME -- for religious purposes
5,000	St. Elizabeth Ann Seton Church, Fryeburg, ME -- for religious purposes
4,500	Frank W. Shaw Post 137 American Legion, Fryeburg, ME -- for charitable purposes
3,000	Brownfield Community Church, Brownfield, ME -- for religious purposes
3,000	Gibson Center for Senior Services, Inc., North Conway, NH -- for charitable purposes
2,500	Church of the New Jerusalem, Fryeburg, ME -- for religious purposes

J. K. MULLEN FOUNDATION

Giving Contact

John F. Malo, President & Director
333 Logan St., Suite 100
Denver, CO 80203
Phone: (303)722-3557

Description

Founded: 1924
EIN: 846002475
Organization Type: Private Foundation
Giving Locations: CO: Denver
Grant Types: General Support.

Donor Information

Founder: the late John K. Mullen, the late Catherine S. Mullen, the J. K. Mullen Co.

Financial Summary

Total Giving: $303,075 (fiscal year ending July 31, 2002); $296,550 (fiscal 2000); $225,000 (fiscal 1999 approx)
Assets: $4,523,200 (fiscal 2002); $5,252,432 (fiscal 2001); $5,285,002 (fiscal 2000)

Typical Recipients

Arts & Humanities: Arts Associations & Councils, Libraries, Museums/Galleries, Music, Opera, Public Broadcasting
Civic & Public Affairs: Botanical Gardens/Parks, Employment/Job Training, Civic & Public Affairs-General, Native American Affairs, Public Policy, Women's Affairs, Zoos/Aquariums
Education: Business Education, Colleges & Universities, Economic Education, Education-General, Health & Physical Education, Leadership Training, Private Education (Precollege), Public Education (Precollege), Religious Education, Secondary Education (Public)
Environment: Environment-General
Health: AIDS/HIV, Children's Health/Hospitals, Health Organizations, Hospices, Hospitals, Hospitals (University Affiliated), Medical Rehabilitation, Mental Health, Multiple Sclerosis, Preventive Medicine/Wellness Organizations, Public Health, Single-Disease Health Associations
Religion: Churches, Religious Organizations, Religious Welfare, Seminaries, Social/Policy Issues
Science: Science Museums
Social Services: Animal Protection, Big Brother/Big Sister, Child Welfare, Community Service Organizations, Domestic Violence, Food/Clothing Distribution, Homes, People with Disabilities, Senior Services, Substance Abuse, Volunteer Services, Youth Organizations

Application Procedures

Initial Contact: Send a letter of application.
Application Requirements: Include a description of organization, amount requested, purpose of funds sought, current financial statements, and proof of tax-exempt status.
Deadlines: June 1.

Restrictions

Does not support individuals or organizations that do not have federally approved tax-exempt status.

Foundation Officials

J. Kenneth Malo, Jr.: director
John F. Malo: president, director
Kathleen Malo: director
Timothy M. O'Connor: secretary, director
Sheila Sevier: director
Heather Weckbaugh: director
John K. Weckbaugh: vice president, director
Walter S. Weckbaugh: treasurer, director

Grants Analysis

Disclosure Period: fiscal year ending July 31, 2002
Total Grants: $303,075
Number of Grants: 60
Average Grant: $5,051
Highest Grant: $30,000
Lowest Grant: $1,000
Typical Range: $1,000 to $10,000

Recent Grants

Note: Grants derived from 2002 Form 990.

General

30,000	Regis High School, Aurora, CO
25,000	Denver Academy, Denver, CO
20,000	J.K. Mullen High School, Denver, CO
15,000	St. Mary's Academy, Denver, CO
10,000	Bayaud Industries, Denver, CO
10,000	Colorado Academy, Denver, CO
10,000	Graland Country Day School, Denver, CO
10,000	Havern Center, Lakewood, CO
10,000	Kent Denver School, Cherry Hills Village, CO
10,000	Little Sisters of the Poor, Denver, CO

W. B. MUNSON FOUNDATION TRUST

Giving Contact

Norma Farrer
c/o Bank One, Texas, NA
200 N. Travis
Sherman, TX 75090-5961
Phone: (903)868-0701

Description

Founded: 1943
EIN: 756015068
Organization Type: Private Foundation
Giving Locations: TX: Grayson County with focus on Denison
Grant Types: Capital, Endowment, Operating Expenses, Scholarship.

Financial Summary

Total Giving: $263,265 (2000); $335,389 (1999); $310,930 (1996)
Giving Analysis: Giving for 2000 includes: foundation scholarships ($3,000); 1999: foundation scholarships ($21,500); 1996: foundation scholarships ($13,000) foundation ($297,930).
Assets: $8,334,870 (2000); $8,314,874 (1999); $6,979,508 (1996)

Typical Recipients

Arts & Humanities: Arts Outreach, Community Arts, Film & Video, Historic Preservation, History & Archaeology, Libraries, Museums/Galleries, Music, Performing Arts
Civic & Public Affairs: Clubs, Community Foundations, Civic & Public Affairs-General, Housing, Municipalities/Towns, Urban & Community Affairs
Education: Arts/Humanities Education, Business Education, Colleges & Universities, Engineering/Technological Education, Education-General, Literacy, Public Education (Precollege), Science/Mathematics Education, Student Aid
Health: Cancer, Clinics/Medical Centers, Diabetes, Emergency/Ambulance Services, Geriatric Health, Health Organizations, Heart, Hospitals, Medical Rehabilitation, Medical Research
International: International Development, International Organizations
Religion: Churches, Religious Welfare
Social Services: At-Risk Youth, Big Brother/Big Sister, Camps, Community Centers, Community Service Organizations, Day Care, Delinquency & Criminal Rehabilitation, Emergency Relief, Family Planning, Food/Clothing Distribution, Homes, Recreation & Athletics, Scouts, Shelters/Homelessness, United Funds/United Ways, Volunteer Services, Youth Organizations

Application Procedures

Initial Contact: Send a brief letter of inquiry describing program or project.
Application Requirements: Include amount requested and purpose of funds sought.
Deadlines: None.

Restrictions

Grants are limited to educational, medical, and cultural organizations.

Additional Information

Trust(s): Bank One

Foundation Officials

Margaret Bishop: gov
Steve Jones: gov
Ben Munson, IV: gov
David Munson, Jr.: gov
David M. Munson, Sr.: gov
John K. Munson: gov
Peter Munson: gov

Grants Analysis

Disclosure Period: calendar year ending 2000
Total Grants: $263,265
Typical Range: $1,000 to $20,000
Note: Complete grant list not available for 2000.

Recent Grants

Note: Grants derived from 2001 Form 990.

General

38,318	Denison Community Foundation, Denison, TX -- for Ballpark Field improvement
36,500	Denison Public Library, Denison, TX -- for Read to Win Program
32,500	Denison Sister Cities, Denison, TX
26,073	Denison Community Foundation, Denison, TX -- for Ballpark Field improvement
24,500	Grayson County College, Denison, TX -- for capital improvements to TV Munson Memorial
17,000	American Red Cross, Denison, TX -- for full size van
15,000	Austin College, Sherman, TX -- to sponsor Pat Mitchell as keynote speaker
10,000	American Heart Association, Dallas, TX -- for CPR training
10,000	Grayson County Shelter, Denison, TX -- for operating expenses
10,000	Locust Volunteer Fire Department, Pottsboro, TX -- for equipment purchase

M. J. MURDOCK CHARITABLE TRUST

Giving Contact

John Van Zytveld, Senior Program Director
PO Box 1618
Vancouver, WA 98668
Phone: (360)694-8415
Fax: (360)694-1819
Web: http://www.murdock-trust.org

Description

Founded: 1975
EIN: 237456468
Organization Type: General Purpose Foundation
Giving Locations: AK; ID; MT; OR; WA: Pacific Northwest USA.
Grant Types: Capital, Matching.

Donor Information

Founder: M. J. (Jack) Murdock was born in Portland, OR, in 1917. Upon completion of high school, he opened a shop for the sale and service of radio and electrical appliances. In 1937, he began an association with Howard Vollum which culminated in the founding of Tektronix. He served as secretary-treasurer until 1960 when he was elected chairman of the board. Mr. Murdock died in 1971. The trust was established in 1975 by the terms of his will.

Financial Summary

Total Giving: $34,450,640 (2002); $33,509,080 (2001); $34,611,574 (2000)
Assets: $619,066,798 (2001); $717,470,921 (2000); $548,000,000 (1999 approx)

Typical Recipients

Arts & Humanities: Arts Centers, Arts Festivals, Arts Outreach, Ballet, Historic Preservation, History & Archaeology, Libraries, Museums/Galleries, Music, Opera, Performing Arts, Public Broadcasting, Theater
Civic & Public Affairs: Botanical Gardens/Parks, Business/Free Enterprise, Clubs, Economic Development, Economic Policy, Employment/Job Training, Housing, Legal Aid, Native American Affairs, Philanthropic Organizations, Professional & Trade Associations, Public Policy, Rural Affairs, Urban & Community Affairs, Zoos/Aquariums
Education: Afterschool/Enrichment Programs, Arts/Humanities Education, Business Education, Colleges & Universities, Community & Junior Colleges, Education Reform, Education Reform, Engineering/Technological Education, Environmental Education, Faculty Development, Education-General, Health & Physical Education, International Exchange, Leadership Training, Medical Education, Private Education (Precollege), Public Education (Precollege), Religious Education, Science/Mathematics Education, Special Education, Student Aid
Environment: Environment-General, Research, Resource Conservation, Wildlife Protection
Health: Alzheimers Disease, Cancer, Children's Health/Hospitals, Clinics/Medical Centers, Emergency/Ambulance Services, Eyes/Blindness, Health Policy/Cost Containment, Hospitals, Hospitals (University Affiliated), Medical Rehabilitation, Medical Research, Mental Health, Preventive Medicine/Wellness Organizations, Public Health
International: Health Care/Hospitals, International Environmental Issues, International Peace & Security Issues, International Relief Efforts
Religion: Bible Study/Translation, Ministries, Religious Organizations, Religious Welfare, Seminaries
Science: Science-General, Science Museums, Scientific Centers & Institutes, Scientific Research
Social Services: Camps, Child Welfare, Community Centers, Community Service Organizations, Family Services, People with Disabilities, Recreation & Athletics, Scouts, Shelters/Homelessness, Social Services-General, United Funds/United Ways, YMCA/YWCA/YMHA/YWHA, Youth Organizations

Application Procedures

Initial Contact: If the proposal represents a major priority of the trust, an applicant should send an initial letter of inquiry summarizing the main elements of the proposal in order to determine whether a formal application would be within the trust's interests.
Application Requirements: Letters of inquiry should provide a brief background on the organization, a description of the project for which funds are sought, a proposed budget for the total cost of the project, and reasons for approaching the trust for this project. If the proposed project appears eligible for consideration, a grant application packet containing an application form will be sent. Proposals should be written and presented in a concise manner. Tables, charts, and appendices may be used. Elaborate and bulky bindings should be avoided.
Deadlines: None.
Review Process: The full proposal, including staff summary and analysis, is submitted to the trustees for their consideration and review. Review of proposals may take six to nine months.

Restrictions

The foundation does not consider grants to individuals; for loans; for conduit organizations, for political purposes; to institutions that discriminate on the basis of race, ethnic origin, sex, creed, or religion; to sectarian or religious organizations whose principal activity is for the benefit of their own members; or for projects requiring a financial obligation over a period of several years. Organizations outside the United States also are excluded from consideration.
In addition, the foundation will not consider funding requests for endowment; grant making organizations; debt retirement; continuation of programs previously financed by external sources; general fund drives or annual charitable appeals; emergency funding; and requests from organizations whose priorities do not match the foundation's major priorities. Requests from organizations and projects normally financed by tax funds are not favored.

Additional Information

Publications: Grant Application Packet; Annual Report; Guidelines

Foundation Officials

John W. Castles: trustee B Portland, OR 1947. ED University of Washington (1966-1967); Linfield College (1968); Portland State University (1969-1972). PRIM CORP EMPL chairman: Oregon Resource & Technology Development Account. CORP AFFIL director: ASN Ventures Inc. CLUB AFFIL West Hills Racquet Club; Multnomah Athletic Club.
Christopher Gillem: program director
Janice Kennedy: program director
Terry Stokesbary: program director
Lynwood W. Swanson: trustee B 1934. ED University of California, Davis PhD; University of the Pacific BS. PRIM CORP EMPL FEI Co.
Neal O. Thorpe: executive director, trustee
John Van Zytveld: senior program director

Grants Analysis

Disclosure Period: calendar year ending 2002
Total Grants: $34,450,640
Number of Grants: 188
Average Grant: $162,232*
Highest Grant: $1,600,000
Lowest Grant: $10,000
Typical Range: $50,000 to $300,000
*Note: Average grant figure excludes four highest grants ($4,600,000).

Recent Grants

Note: Grants derived from 2000 Form 990.

General

1,600,000	Reed Institute, Portland, OR -- for building expansion and renovation
1,000,000	KOTS Television, Seattle, WA -- acquisition of digital television equipment
1,000,000	Lewis and Clark College, Portland, OR -- for library expansion and renovation
900,000	Oregon Coast Aquarium, Newport, OR -- for new exhibits and renovation
700,000	Alaska Bible College, Glennallen, AK -- for construction of student center
675,000	Whitman College Trustees, Walla Walla, WA -- for expansion and renovation
500,000	Oregon Zoo Foundation, Portland, OR -- for new exhibit construction
499,000	University of Washington, Seattle, WA -- for acquisition of equipment
450,000	Nature Conservancy of Washington, Seattle, WA -- for land acquisition, research and management
400,000	Providence Alaska Foundation, Anchorage, AK -- for children's hospital renovation

LLUELLA MOREY MURPHEY FOUNDATION

Giving Contact

Alfred B. Hastings, Jr., Trustee
PO Box 1419
La Quinta, CA 92253
Phone: (760)564-3488

Description

Founded: 1967
EIN: 956152669
Organization Type: Private Foundation
Giving Locations: CA: southern
Grant Types: Capital, General Support, Matching, Research, Scholarship.

Donor Information

Founder: the late Lluella Morey Murphey

Financial Summary

Total Giving: $92,290 (2001); $142,355 (2000); $146,140 (1999)
Giving Analysis: Giving for 2001 includes: foundation scholarships ($9,500); 2000: foundation scholarships ($7,000) 1999: foundation scholarships ($10,500)
Assets: $5,682,795 (2001); $6,199,494 (2000); $6,603,400 (1999)

Typical Recipients

Arts & Humanities: Arts Associations & Councils, Arts Funds, Arts & Humanities-General, Historic Preservation, History & Archaeology, Libraries, Museums/Galleries, Music
Civic & Public Affairs: Botanical Gardens/Parks, Community Foundations, Employment/Job Training, Civic & Public Affairs-General, Hispanic Affairs, Housing, Law & Justice, Urban & Community Affairs, Women's Affairs
Education: Arts/Humanities Education, Colleges & Universities, Education Reform, Engineering/Technological Education, Education-General, Leadership Training, Legal Education, Literacy, Minority Education, Preschool Education, Private Education (Precollege), Public Education (Precollege), Religious Education, Science/Mathematics Education, Special Education, Student Aid, Vocational & Technical Education
Environment: Forestry
Health: Cancer, Children's Health/Hospitals, Clinics/Medical Centers, Emergency/Ambulance Services, Eyes/Blindness, Health-General, Health Organizations, Heart, Hospitals, Kidney, Long-Term Care, Medical Research, Mental Health, Multiple Sclerosis, Prenatal Health Issues, Preventive Medicine/Wellness Organizations, Public Health, Research/Studies Institutes, Respiratory, Speech & Hearing
International: Health Care/Hospitals, International Environmental Issues, Missionary/Religious Activities
Religion: Churches, Religious Organizations, Religious Welfare
Social Services: Animal Protection, At-Risk Youth, Child Welfare, Community Service Organizations, Counseling, Crime Prevention, Domestic Violence, Emergency Relief, Family Planning, Family Services, Food/Clothing Distribution, People with Disabilities, Recreation & Athletics, Scouts, Senior Services, Shelters/Homelessness, Social Services-General, Special Olympics, Substance Abuse, United Funds/United Ways, YMCA/YWCA/YMHA/YWHA, Youth Organizations

Application Procedures

Initial Contact: Send a brief letter of inquiry.
Application Requirements: Include a a description of organization, amount requested, and purpose of funds sought.
Deadlines: None.

Restrictions

Does not support individuals, political or lobbying groups, or organizations outside operating areas.

Foundation Officials

Alfred B. Hastings, Jr.: trustee
Leonard M. Marangi: trustee
Corene L. Pindroh: trustee
James A. Schlinger: trustee

Grants Analysis

Disclosure Period: calendar year ending 2001
Total Grants: $82,790*
Number of Grants: 29
Average Grant: $2,855
Highest Grant: $5,000
Lowest Grant: $500
Typical Range: $1,000 to $5,000
*Note: Giving excludes scholarships.

Recent Grants

Note: Grants derived from 2000 Form 990.

General

5,000	Betty Ford Center at Eisenhower, Rancho Mirage, CA -- provide scholarship funding for twenty five children to "California Children's Program"
5,000	Children's Hospital Los Angeles, Los Angeles, CA -- fund a portion of LIFE for cancer and blood disease
5,000	FACT Foundation, Burbank, CA -- purchase furniture and equipment for resident computer lab at Villa Gardens
5,000	Los Angeles Regional Food Bank, Los Angeles, CA -- operating support to aid in obtaining, storing and distributing thirty four million pounds of food
5,000	Mourning Star Center, Inc, Palm Desert, CA -- provide free support group services to grieving children and their adult caregivers
5,000	Union Station Foundation, Pasadena, CA -- help homeless rebuild their lives
5,000	University of California Los Angeles Jonsson Cancer Center, Los Angeles, CA -- to provide tow hand held computers for genetic fingerprinting project'
5,000	Women at Work, Pasadena, CA -- toward job information services
5,000	Young & Healthy, Pasadena, CA -- help with Mobile Dental Clinic in Fall 2000
3,500	Desert Samaritans for the Elderly, Palm Desert, CA -- to be used for the "Buddy Program"

G.C. MURPHY CO. FOUNDATION

Giving Contact

Edwin W. Davis, Secretary, Administrator & Director
211 Oberdick Dr.
Mc Keesport, PA 15135
Phone: (412)751-6649

Description

Founded: 1952
EIN: 256028651
Organization Type: Private Foundation
Giving Locations: PA: Southeastern Allegheny County, McKeesport
Grant Types: General Support.

Financial Summary

Total Giving: $233,000 (2001); $266,000 (2000); $253,700 (1999)
Assets: $4,325,107 (2001); $4,977,973 (2000); $5,135,622 (1999)

Typical Recipients

Arts & Humanities: Arts Centers, History & Archaeology, Libraries, Music, Theater
Civic & Public Affairs: Chambers of Commerce, Clubs, Community Foundations, Economic Development, Employment/Job Training, Civic & Public Affairs-General, Housing, Municipalities/Towns, Safety, Urban & Community Affairs, Women's Affairs

Education: Business Education, Colleges & Universities, Engineering/Technological Education, Education-General, Preschool Education, Special Education, Student Aid
Environment: Environment-General
Health: Cancer, Clinics/Medical Centers, Geriatric Health, Health Organizations, Hospices, Hospitals, Medical Rehabilitation, Mental Health, Multiple Sclerosis, Public Health, Single-Disease Health Associations
Religion: Churches, Ministries, Religious Organizations, Religious Welfare
Social Services: Child Welfare, Community Service Organizations, Counseling, Emergency Relief, Family Services, Food/Clothing Distribution, Homes, People with Disabilities, Scouts, Senior Services, Social Services-General, Special Olympics, Volunteer Services, YMCA/YWCA/YMHA/YWHA, Youth Organizations

Application Procedures

Initial Contact: The foundation requests applications be made in writing.
Application Requirements: Include a description of organization with some background information as to the organization's charitable purpose and the purpose of funds sought.
Deadlines: None.

Additional Information

The G.C. Murphy Co. Foundation is independently administered and is not affiliated with G.C. Murphy Co. or McCrory Corp.

Foundation Officials

Charles Breckenridge: vice president, director
Edwin W. Davis: secretary, administrator, director
Alice J. Hajduk: vice president, director
Thomas F. Hudak: president, treasurer, director B Dunora, PA 1942. ED Saint Vincent College BS (1963); Ohio State University MBA (1968). PRIM CORP EMPL treasurer: Mack Realty Co. CORP AFFIL president, director: Terry Farris Stores; director: RXI Corp.; treasurer: Spotsylvania Realty Co.; member advisory board: Liberty Mutual Insurance; treasurer: Murphy Development Corp.; chairman, president: Continental Plastics; treasurer: Court House Village Co. NONPR AFFIL member: Spice Traders Association; member: U.S. Chamber of Commerce; member: Risk & Insurance Management Society; member: National Retail Merchants Association; member: Peanut Butter & National Processors Association; fin council, member: Machinery & Allied Products Institute; member: National Association Corp. Divs; member: Financial Executives Institute; president, director: GC Murphy Co. Foundation; member: American Institute of CPA's; member: Dressing & Sauces.
C.A. McElhinny: vice president, director
Robert T. Messner: vice president, director B McKeesport, PA 1938. ED Dartmouth College BA (1960); University of Pennsylvania LLB (1963). PRIM CORP EMPL vice president, secretary, general counsel: Dollar Bank. CORP AFFIL secretary: G C Murphy Co. NONPR AFFIL member: Theta Delta Chi; director: YMCA McKeesport; chairman corporate law department committee, member: Pennsylvania Bar Association; fin advisor: Pennsylvania Legis; member: American Society of Corporate Secretaries; director: Braddocks Field Historical Society; member: American Corporate Counsel Association; member: Allegheny Bar Association; member: American Bar Association. CLUB AFFIL Gateway Center Pittsburgh Club; Rivers Club; Dartmouth Western Pennsylvania Club.

Grants Analysis

Disclosure Period: calendar year ending 2001
Total Grants: $233,000
Number of Grants: 37
Average Grant: $6,297

Highest Grant: $20,000
Typical Range: $1,000 to $15,000

Recent Grants

Note: Grants derived from 2001 Form 990.

General

20,000	South Hills Interfaith Ministries, Pittsburgh, PA -- program support
15,000	McKeesport Heritage Center, McKeesport, PA -- for building fund
15,000	Outreach Teen and Family Service, Pittsburgh, PA -- program support
10,000	Braddock's Field Historical Society, Braddock, PA -- program support
10,000	Central Food Pantry of Elizabeth Township, Buena Vista, PA -- building fund
10,000	Greater Pittsburgh Community Food Bank, McKeesport, PA -- operations
10,000	LaRosa Boys and Girls Club of McKeesport, McKeesport, PA -- for program support
10,000	Penn State McKeesport, McKeesport, PA -- student union building fund
10,000	Ventures in People, Mckeesport, IA -- program support
6,000	Otterbein College, Westerville, OH -- for scholarship fund

MURPHY FOUNDATION

Giving Contact

Edward W. Marsh, Secretary & Treasurer
200 N. Jefferson St., Suite 400
Union Bldg.
El Dorado, AR 71730
Phone: (870)862-4961

Description

Founded: 1958
EIN: 716049826
Organization Type: General Purpose Foundation
Giving Locations: AR: Southern Arkansas
Grant Types: Capital, Endowment, General Support, Scholarship.

Donor Information

Founder: The foundation was established in Arkansas in 1958 by Charles Haywood Murphy, Jr., and other members of the Murphy family. Mr. Murphy is chairman of Murphy Oil Corporation.

Financial Summary

Total Giving: $1,138,991 (fiscal year ending April 30, 2002); $1,006,534 (fiscal 2001); $829,847 (fiscal 2000). Note: Fiscal 1997 Giving includes scholarship ($109,836), United Way ($65,250).
Giving Analysis: Giving for fiscal 2002 includes: foundation grants to United Way ($40,222); foundation scholarships ($133,142); fiscal 2001: foundation grants to United Way ($40,196) foundation scholarships ($133,553).
Assets: $33,278,772 (fiscal 2002); $29,443,785 (fiscal 2001); $21,910,370 (fiscal 2000)
Gifts Received: $3,000 (fiscal 2002); $6,000 (fiscal 2001); $424,096 (fiscal 1997). Note: In fiscal 1997 and 2000, contributions were received from C.N. Murphy, Jr.

Typical Recipients

Arts & Humanities: Arts Centers, Historic Preservation, History & Archaeology, Libraries, Museums/Galleries, Music, Performing Arts, Public Broadcasting
Civic & Public Affairs: Economic Development, Civic & Public Affairs-General, Public Policy
Education: Arts/Humanities Education, Colleges & Universities, Elementary Education (Private), Education-General, Literacy, Medical Education, Public Education (Precollege), Secondary Education (Public), Student Aid

Health: Respiratory
International: International Development
Religion: Churches, Religious Welfare
Social Services: Animal Protection, Crime Prevention, Recreation & Athletics, Scouts, United Funds/United Ways, YMCA/YWCA/YMHA/YWHA, Youth Organizations

Application Procedures

Initial Contact: For general giving program, send a brief letter of inquiry describing the program, individual student aid, request for foundation's standard application form.
Application Requirements: For student aid program, include a copy of the applicant's scholastic record.
Deadlines: August 1.
Notes: Educational grants are restricted to students from the southern Arkansas area.

Restrictions

Educational grants are restricted to students from the southern Arkansas area.

Foundation Officials

Edward W. Marsh: secretary, treasurer
Charles H. Murphy, Jr.: director
Johnie W. Murphy: president, director
R. Madison Murphy: president, director
Lucy A. Ring: director
Perry Silliman: secretary-treasurer

Grants Analysis

Disclosure Period: fiscal year ending April 30, 2002
Total Grants: $965,627*
Number of Grants: 46
Average Grant: $17,115*
Highest Grant: $112,445
Lowest Grant: $80
Typical Range: $5,000 to $30,000
*Note: Giving excludes scholarship and United Way. Average grant figure excludes two highest grants ($212,551).

Recent Grants

Note: Grants derived from fiscal 2000 Form 990.

Library-Related
17,400   Barton Library, El Dorado, AR

General
300,003   Hendrix College, Conway, AR
35,200   American Lung Association, Little Rock, AR
35,000   American Lung Association, El Dorado, AR
34,800   Arkansas Policy Foundation, Little Rock, AR
30,961   Arkansas Policy Foundation, Little Rock, AR
29,000   Boy Scouts of America, Desota Area Council
29,000   United Way of Union County, Elizabeth, NJ -- endowment fund
26,100   Boys and Girls Club of El Dorado, El Dorado, AR
26,100   South Arkansas Arts Center, El Dorado, AR
25,000   Arkansas Policy Foundation, Little Rock, AR

R. C. AND KATHARINE M. MUSSON CHARITABLE FOUNDATION

Giving Contact

Ben D. Segars, Jr., Trustee
PO Box 7038
Akron, OH 44306
Phone: (330)773-7651

Description

Founded: 1984
EIN: 341549070
Organization Type: Private Foundation
Giving Locations: OH: Summit County
Grant Types: General Support.

Donor Information

Founder: the late R. C. Musson

Financial Summary

Total Giving: $313,690 (fiscal year ending June 30, 2002); $259,813 (fiscal 2001); $281,800 (fiscal 2000). Note: Fiscal 1997 Giving includes contribution returned by Summa ($10,000).
Giving Analysis: Giving for fiscal 2001 includes: foundation grants to United Way ($40,000)
Assets: $4,447,345 (fiscal 2002); $4,672,273 (fiscal 2001); $4,741,001 (fiscal 2000)

Typical Recipients

Arts & Humanities: Arts Institutes, Ballet, Historic Preservation, History & Archaeology, Libraries, Music, Performing Arts, Theater
Civic & Public Affairs: Botanical Gardens/Parks, Community Foundations, Economic Development, Employment/Job Training, Civic & Public Affairs-General, Housing, Municipalities/Towns, Urban & Community Affairs, Zoos/Aquariums
Education: Arts/Humanities Education, Colleges & Universities, Education Funds, Education Reform, Education-General, Private Education (Precollege), Religious Education, Secondary Education (Public), Special Education, Student Aid
Health: Cancer, Children's Health/Hospitals, Clinics/Medical Centers, Diabetes, Geriatric Health, Health Funds, Health Organizations, Heart, Hospices, Hospitals, Long-Term Care, Medical Rehabilitation, Multiple Sclerosis, Nursing Services, Prenatal Health Issues, Public Health
Religion: Churches, Ministries, Religious Welfare
Science: Science Museums
Social Services: At-Risk Youth, Big Brother/Big Sister, Child Welfare, Community Service Organizations, Counseling, Crime Prevention, Delinquency & Criminal Rehabilitation, Domestic Violence, Family Planning, Family Services, Food/Clothing Distribution, Homes, People with Disabilities, Scouts, Senior Services, Shelters/Homelessness, Substance Abuse, United Funds/United Ways, Volunteer Services, YMCA/YWCA/YMHA/YWHA, Youth Organizations

Application Procedures

Initial Contact: Submit a narrative, a brief letter of inquiry, and a full proposal.
Application Requirements: Include a description of organization, amount requested, purpose of funds sought, recently audited financial statement, and proof of tax-exempt status.
Deadlines: None.

Restrictions

Does not support individuals, religious organizations for sectarian purposes, political or lobbying groups, or organizations outside operating areas.

Foundation Officials

Irvin J. Musson, III: trustee
Irvin J. Musson, Jr.: trustee
Ben Segers: trustee
Robert S. Segers: trustee B Akron, OH 1960. ED University of Akron (1984). PRIM CORP EMPL vice president: RC Musson Rubber Co.

Grants Analysis

Disclosure Period: fiscal year ending June 30, 2002
Total Grants: $313,690
Number of Grants: 63
Average Grant: $4,979
Highest Grant: $40,000

Lowest Grant: $500
Typical Range: $1,000 to $5,000

Recent Grants

Note: Grants derived from fiscal 2000 Form 990.

General
35,000   United Way, Akron, OH
27,500   Akron University Keyboard Campaign, Akron, OH
12,000   Summit Academy, Akron, OH
11,250   Catholic Social Services, Akron, OH
10,000   Civil War Chapel, Akron, OH
10,000   Community Drug Board, Inc., Akron, OH
10,000   Stan Hywet Hall and Gardens, Akron, OH
10,000   Victim Assistance Program, Akron, OH
7,500   Haven of Rest Ministries, Akron, OH
7,500   Sumner Home Endowment, Akron, OH

MYERS CHARITABLE TRUST

Giving Contact

Judy Konecki, Trust Officer
Wells Fargo Bank Illinois NA
121 West First Street
Geneseo, IL 61254-1341
Phone: (309)944-5361

Description

Founded: 1997
EIN: 367233377
Organization Type: Private Foundation
Giving Locations: IL: Geneseo area of Henry County
Grant Types: General Support, Scholarship.

Financial Summary

Total Giving: $57,178 (2001); $63,927 (2000); $64,324 (1999)
Giving Analysis: Giving for 2001 includes: foundation scholarships ($28,684); 2000: foundation scholarships ($22,656) 1999: foundation scholarships ($17,215)
Assets: $1,337,606 (2001); $1,366,041 (2000); $1,324,841 (1999)

Typical Recipients

Arts & Humanities: Libraries
Civic & Public Affairs: African American Affairs
Education: Arts/Humanities Education, Faculty Development, Medical Education, Student Aid
Health: Hospitals

Application Procedures

Initial Contact: For scholarships, request application form.
Deadlines: None.

Additional Information

Provides scholarships only to students who attend or have attended the Geneseo schools and are attending or have been accepted by an accredited college or university in medical, dentistry, law or registered nurse programs.
Trust(s): Wells Fargo Bank IL NA

Foundation Officials

Paul F. Lindsey: vice president, trust officer

Grants Analysis

Disclosure Period: calendar year ending 2001
Total Grants: $28,494*
Number of Grants: 2
Highest Grant: $14,247
Lowest Grant: $14,247
*Note: Giving excludes scholarship.

Recent Grants

Note: Grants derived from 2000 Form 990.

Library-Related

20,655	Geneseo Public Library District, Geneseo, IL -- for equipment	

General

20,656	Hammond-Henry District Hospital, Geneseo, IL -- equipment
6,000	Harvard School of Dental Medicine, Cambridge, MA -- scholarship
6,000	University of Chicago, Chicago, IL -- scholarship
6,000	University of Illinois, Chicago, IL -- scholarship
2,000	University of Iowa, Iowa City, IA -- scholarship
750	Trinity College of Nursing, Moline, IL -- scholarship
700	Black Hawk College, Moline, IL -- scholarship
630	Trinity College of Nursing, Moline, IL -- scholarship
536	University of Iowa, Iowa City, IA -- scholarship

E. NAKAMICHI FOUNDATION

Giving Contact

Ray Privette, Secretary/Treasurer
E. Nakamichi Foundation
446 S. Anaheim Hills Road, Suite 221
Anaheim Hills, CA 92807
Phone: (714)771-9677
Fax: (714)282-8179
E-mail: admin@enfoundation.com
Web: http://www.enfoundation.com

Description

Founded: 1985
EIN: 953870341
Organization Type: Specialized/Single Purpose Foundation
Giving Locations: no geographic restrictions.
Grant Types: Award, Project.

Donor Information

Founder: The foundation was endowed in 1985 by the founder of Nakamichi Corporation of Japan, the manufacturer of high-quality stereo equipment used by professional musicians and audiophiles. Mr. E. Nakamichi developed a love for music while designing his first equipment in his garage. He found Baroque music to have the most precise rhythm and tone to test the quality of his products. As his company grew, so did his love for Baroque music. Toward the end of his life, Mr. Nakamichi held weekly concerts in his home. He maintained his Japanese citizenship, but kept a home in Southern California, near the headquarters of Nakamichi, U.S.A. and Nakamichi America.

Financial Summary

Total Giving: $6,562 (2001); $178,223 (2000); $92,515 (1999)
Assets: $7,665,584 (2001); $8,789,873 (2000); $9,998,000 (1999)

Typical Recipients

Arts & Humanities: Arts Festivals, Arts & Humanities-General, Libraries, Music, Opera, Performing Arts, Public Broadcasting
Civic & Public Affairs: Nonprofit Management, Professional & Trade Associations
Education: Arts/Humanities Education, Colleges & Universities, Private Education (Precollege)
International: Foreign Arts Organizations

Application Procedures

Initial Contact: Applicants should submit initial proposal via website.
Application Requirements: a description of organization, summary of proposed grant, and amount requested. If asked to submit a full proposal, include IRS tax-exempt letter and a copy of the most recent annual financial statement.
Deadlines: February 1 and September 15.
Review Process: Board of Directors meet in the spring and in the autumn to decide on grants. Applicants who appear to match the foundation's interests may be asked to submit a full proposal.
Notes: The foundation commits its grant dollars approximately twelve to eighteen months in advance, so applicants are encouraged to apply well in advance of the date funding is needed.

Restrictions

Grants are not made to individuals for independent study, research, travel, or participation in a musical event. The Foundation does not award grants toward capital campaigns, endowments, or deficit operations, nor does it make grants for the construction or maintenance of buildings, or for the purchase of equipment. Furthermore, public broadcasting grants are awarded only to the broadcaster. Consequently, inquiries and applications must come directly from the television/radio station. The foundation does not administer activities for which it awards grants, nor does it administer its own programs. The foundation does not make multi-year grants.

Additional Information

The foundation only considers requests from 501(c)(3) organizations. The Nakamichi Foundation has no special grant application forms or guidelines.
Publications: Information Package Containing Grants List; Program Statement; List of Officers and Directors

Foundation Officials

Edward Y. Kakita: director PRIM NONPR EMPL superior court judge: Los Angeles County.
Les Mitchnick: vice president, secretary, executive director
Ray Privette: treasurer, director PRIM CORP EMPL director human resources: Shimano American Corp.
Shunji Shinoda: director PRIM CORP EMPL president: Shinoda Construction Management.
Ted Tanaka: director PRIM CORP EMPL president: Tanaka International.
Ken Yamasaki: director
Koichi Yamasaki: director PRIM CORP EMPL president: Yamasaki Financial Planning.
Yashiro Yamazaki: president, director PRIM CORP EMPL president: CEM Inc.

Grants Analysis

Disclosure Period: calendar year ending 2001
Total Grants: $6,562
Number of Grants: 2
Average Grant: $5,412
Highest Grant: $1,150

Recent Grants

Note: Grants derived from 2000 Form 990.

General

50,000	Aspen Music Festival, Aspen, CO -- promotion of Baroque and Classical music
50,000	Lincoln Center for Performing Arts, New York, NY -- promotion of Baroque and Classical music
30,000	Da Camera Society, Houston, TX -- promotion of Baroque and Classical music
25,000	Brooklyn Academy of Music, Brooklyn, NY -- promotion of Baroque and Classical music
15,000	Los Angeles Chamber Orchestra, Los Angeles, CA -- promotion of Baroque and Classical music
5,823	Mainichi Shimbun Sha -- promotion of Baroque and Classical music
1,370	SCAP, Los Angeles, CA -- promotion of Baroque and Classical music
1,030	Council on Foundations, Washington, DC -- promotion of Baroque and Classical music

NATIONAL CITY BANK OF INDIANA

Company Headquarters

101 W. Washington St., A400E
Indianapolis, IN 46255

Company Description

Former Name: Merchants National Corp.
SIC(s): 6021 National Commercial Banks.
Parent Company: National City Corp., 1900 E. 9th Street, Cleveland, OH, United States

National City Bank Foundation

Giving Contact

Michele Delaney
PO Box 110
Ft. Wayne, IN 46801
Phone: (219)461-6199
Fax: (219)461-6238

Description

Founded: 1984
EIN: 356020622
Organization Type: Corporate Foundation
Giving Locations: IN
Grant Types: General Support.

Financial Summary

Total Giving: $3,762 (fiscal year ending February 28, 2000); $372,752 (fiscal 1999); $400,000 (fiscal 1997 approx). Note: Contributes through foundation only. 1996 Giving includes United Way ($156,120).
Giving Analysis: Giving for fiscal 2000 includes: foundation ($3,762); fiscal 1999: foundation grants to United Way ($132,314) foundation ($240,438).
Assets: $3,733 (fiscal 1999); $409,053 (fiscal 1996); $472,141 (fiscal 1995)
Gifts Received: $300,000 (fiscal 1996); $200,000 (fiscal 1995); $400,000 (fiscal 1993). Note: In fiscal 1996, contributions were received from Fort Wayne National Bank.

Typical Recipients

Arts & Humanities: Arts Associations & Councils, Libraries, Museums/Galleries, Public Broadcasting, Theater
Civic & Public Affairs: Botanical Gardens/Parks, Civic & Public Affairs-General, Housing, Parades/Festivals, Zoos/Aquariums
Education: Business Education, Colleges & Universities, Education Funds, Engineering/Technological Education, Education-General, Minority Education, Secondary Education (Public), Student Aid, Vocational & Technical Education
Environment: Resource Conservation
Health: Hospitals, Public Health
Religion: Churches, Religious Welfare
Science: Scientific Centers & Institutes
Social Services: Big Brother/Big Sister, Community Service Organizations, Food/Clothing Distribution, People with Disabilities, Recreation & Athletics, Scouts, Social Services-General, United Funds/

United Ways, Volunteer Services, YMCA/YWCA/YMHA/YWHA, Youth Organizations

Application Procedures

Initial Contact: Send a brief letter of inquiry.
Application Requirements: Include purpose of funds sought and proof of tax-exempt status.
Deadlines: None.

Additional Information

Trust(s): National City Bank of Indiana

Grants Analysis

Disclosure Period: fiscal year ending February 28, 2000
Total Grants: $3,762
Number of Grants: 1

Recent Grants

Note: Grants derived from fiscal 1999 Form 990.

General

132,314	United Way Allen County, Inc., Ft. Wayne, IN
59,000	Arts United of Greater Fort Wayne, Ft. Wayne, IN
50,000	YMCA, Ft. Wayne, IN -- family activity center
25,000	Headwaters State Park Commission, Ft. Wayne, IN
25,000	YWCA, Ft. Wayne, IN
15,000	Science Central, Ft. Wayne, IN -- corporate connection
10,000	Anthony Wayne Area Council Boy Scouts of America, Ft. Wayne, IN
10,000	Fort Wayne Children's Zoo, Ft. Wayne, IN
10,000	Junior Achievement, Ft. Wayne, IN
10,000	Lincoln Museum, Ft. Wayne, IN -- "Coast to Coast on the Lincoln Highway"

NATIONAL CITY CORP.

Company Headquarters

1900 E. 9th Street
Cleveland, OH 44114-3404
Web: http://www.nationalcity.com

Company Description

Founded: 1845
Ticker: NCC
Exchange: NYSE
Holding Company for: National City Bank.
Assets: US$118.258 billion (2002)
Profit: US$1.593 billion (2002)
Employees: 32731 (2002)
Fortune Rank: 215, per FORTUNE Magazine's list of 500 Largest U.S. Corporations (2002).
SIC(s): 6021 National Commercial Banks, 6712 Bank Holding Companies.

Operating Locations

National City Corp. (KY--Ashland, Louisville; OH--Akron, Ashland, Norwalk, Sandusky, Toledo, Youngstown)

National City Corp. Charitable Foundation II

Giving Contact

Bruce McCrodden
Care of National City Bank Cleveland
PO Box 5756
Cleveland, OH 44101
Phone: (216)575-2994

Alternate Contact

NCC Charitable Foundation
PO Box 94651
Cleveland, OH 44101-4651
Phone: (216)222-2934

Description

Founded: 1996
EIN: 347050989
Organization Type: Corporate Foundation
Grant Types: General Support.

Financial Summary

Total Giving: $17,707,736 (fiscal year ending June 30, 2002); $17,127,194 (fiscal 2000); $14,393,379 (fiscal 1999)
Giving Analysis: Giving for fiscal 2002 includes: foundation grants to United Way ($2,391,538) fiscal 1998: foundation grants to United Way ($3,872,806)
Assets: $70,984,878 (fiscal 2002); $44,080,889 (fiscal 2000); $61,235,248 (fiscal 1999)
Gifts Received: $52,736,492 (fiscal 2002); $15,368,720 (fiscal 1998). Note: In fiscal 2002, contributions were received from National City Corp. In fiscal 1998, contributions were received from National City Bank NY.

Typical Recipients

Arts & Humanities: Arts Associations & Councils, Arts Funds, Arts Institutes, Arts Outreach, Arts & Humanities-General, History & Archaeology, Libraries, Museums/Galleries, Music, Performing Arts, Public Broadcasting
Civic & Public Affairs: African American Affairs, Botanical Gardens/Parks, Community Foundations, Economic Development, Economic Policy, Employment/Job Training, Civic & Public Affairs-General, Housing, Municipalities/Towns, Urban & Community Affairs, Zoos/Aquariums
Education: Arts/Humanities Education, Colleges & Universities, Community & Junior Colleges, Education Associations, Education Funds, Education-General, Medical Education, Private Education (Pre-college)
Health: Cancer, Emergency/Ambulance Services, Health Organizations, Hospitals
Religion: Dioceses, Ministries
Social Services: Counseling, Food/Clothing Distribution, Recreation & Athletics, Senior Services, United Funds/United Ways

Application Procedures

Deadlines: None.

Restrictions

Emphasis is on prevention of child abuse in the U.S. and its possessions.

Additional Information

Trust(s): National City Bank

Corporate Officials

Bruce McCrodden: senior vice president, corp. public affairs

Foundation Officials

David A. Daberko: officer B Hudson, OH 1945. ED Denison University BA (1967); Case Western Reserve University MBA (1970). PRIM CORP EMPL chairman, chief executive officer: National City Corp. CORP AFFIL director: National City Bank Pennsylvania; director: National City Bank, Pittsburgh; director: National City Bank Kalamazoo; director: National City Bank Kentucky; director: National City Bank Fort Wayne; director: National City Bank Indiana; director: Federal Reserve Bank Cleveland; chairman, chief operating officer: National City Bank Cleveland. NONPR AFFIL trustee: University Hospital Cleveland; trustee: University Hospital Health System; trustee: University

Circle Inc.; trustee: Hawken School; trustee: Neighborhood Progress; trustee: Cleveland Tomorrow; trustee: Greater Cleveland Growth Association; member: Bankers Roundtable; trustee: Case Western Reserve University.

Grants Analysis

Disclosure Period: fiscal year ending June 30, 2002
Total Grants: $13,746,844*
Number of Grants: 1,573
Average Grant: $8,739
Highest Grant: $392,700
Lowest Grant: $25
Typical Range: $1,000 to $15,000
*Note: Giving excludes matching gifts and United Way.

Recent Grants

Note: Grants derived from fiscal 2002 Form 990.

General

392,700	United Way Greater Kalamazoo, Kalamazoo, MI
342,700	United Way Greater Kalamazoo, Kalamazoo, MI
340,000	American Red Cross, Cleveland, OH
300,000	Economic Development Fund, Portage, MI
290,000	Metro United Way, Louisville, KY
276,702	United Way Detroit, Detroit, MI
212,500	United Way Services, Cleveland, OH
212,500	United Way Services, Cleveland, OH
200,000	Cuyahoga Community College, Cleveland, OH
200,000	United Way of Allegheny County, Pittsburgh, PA

NATIONAL GRANGE MUTUAL INSURANCE CO.

Company Headquarters

55 West Street
Keene, NH 03431-3348
Web: http://www.msagroup.com

Company Description

Assets: US$442.4 million (2001)
Employees: 900 (2001)
SIC(s): 6331 Fire, Marine & Casualty Insurance, 6351 Surety Insurance.

National Grange Mutual Charitable Trust

Giving Contact

Richard Hyatt, Principal Administrator & Trustee
55 West St.
Keene, NH 03431
Phone: (603)352-4000
Fax: (603)358-1173

Alternate Contact

Phone: 800-225-5646

Description

Founded: 1972
EIN: 237228264
Organization Type: Corporate Foundation
Giving Locations: CA; MD; NH: emphasis on Keene; VA
Grant Types: Award, Capital, Challenge, Employee Matching Gifts, Endowment, General Support, Matching, Project, Research.

Donor Information

Founder: National Grange Mutual Insurance Co.

Financial Summary

Total Giving: $128,973 (2001); $119,461 (2000); $79,527 (1999)

Giving Analysis: Giving for 2001 includes: foundation matching gifts ($6,100); foundation grants to United Way ($69,253); 2000: foundation grants to United Way ($57,837); 1999: foundation ($29,527); foundation grants to United Way ($50,000)

Assets: $2,355,179 (2001); $2,534,054 (2000); $2,640,936 (1999)

Typical Recipients

Arts & Humanities: Arts Associations & Councils, Arts Festivals, Arts & Humanities-General, History & Archaeology, Libraries, Museums/Galleries, Public Broadcasting, Theater

Civic & Public Affairs: Botanical Gardens/Parks, Chambers of Commerce, Clubs, Economic Development, Civic & Public Affairs-General, Housing, Professional & Trade Associations, Public Policy, Safety, Women's Affairs

Education: Arts/Humanities Education, Business Education, Colleges & Universities, Education Funds, Engineering/Technological Education, Education-General, Private Education (Precollege), Secondary Education (Public), Student Aid, Vocational & Technical Education

Environment: Environment-General, Resource Conservation

Health: Arthritis, Cancer, Children's Health/Hospitals, Clinics/Medical Centers, Emergency/Ambulance Services, Health-General, Health Organizations, Heart, Home-Care Services, Hospices, Kidney, Medical Research, Multiple Sclerosis, Nursing Services, Prenatal Health Issues

International: International Development

Religion: Churches, Religious Welfare

Social Services: Animal Protection, Community Service Organizations, Crime Prevention, Domestic Violence, Emergency Relief, Food/Clothing Distribution, Homes, Recreation & Athletics, Scouts, Social Services-General, Special Olympics, Substance Abuse, United Funds/United Ways, YMCA/YWCA/YMHA/YWHA

Application Procedures

Initial Contact: The foundation requests applications be made in writing.

Application Requirements: a description of organization, amount requested, and purpose of funds sought.

Deadlines: None.

Restrictions

No support for educational endeavors. Grants are not made to individuals.

Corporate Officials

Philip D. Koerner: chairman, president, chief executive officer, director B Bridgeport, CT 1946. ED University of New Hampshire (1969). PRIM CORP EMPL chairman, president, chief executive officer: National Grange Mutual Insurance Co. CORP AFFIL chairman, president, chief executive officer: Main Saint America Financial Corp.; director: Guilderland Reins Co. NONPR AFFIL director: Alliance American Insurers.

David L. Royer: vice president, treasurer, chief financial officer, director PRIM CORP EMPL vice president, treasurer, chief financial officer, director: National Grange Mutual Insurance Co.

Foundation Officials

Norman E. Brackett: trustee B 1929. ED Bates College AB (1952). PRIM CORP EMPL senior vice president, chief financial officer: Hannaford Brothers Co.

Cotton Mather Cleveland: trustee PRIM CORP EMPL president: Mather Associates.

Jeanne Eddy: trustee

Charles Albert Farmer: trustee B South Newbury, NH 1930. ED Boston University (1952). PRIM CORP EMPL director: National Grange Mutual Insurance Co.

Susan Hay: manager

Raymond Huizenga: trustee

Richard Hyatt: trustee

Terry S. Jacobs: trustee

Philip D. Koerner: trustee (see above)

Thomas M. Van Berkel: trustee

Grants Analysis

Disclosure Period: calendar year ending 2001

Total Grants: $53,620*

Number of Grants: 29

Average Grant: $1,159*

Highest Grant: $20,000

Typical Range: $100 to $7,000

*Note: Giving excludes United Way, matching gifts. Average grant figure excludes highest grant.

Recent Grants

Note: Grants derived from 2001 Form 990.

General

62,000	Monadnock United Way, Keene, NH
20,000	Keene State College, Keene, NH
7,000	Center Stage, Baltimore, MD
5,320	Greater Keene Chamber of Commerce, Keene, NH
5,000	American Red Cross National Disaster Relief Fund
4,000	United Way of Northeast Florida, Jacksonville, FL
2,753	United Way Services
2,500	American Cancer Society, Baltimore, MD -- for Relay for Life
2,500	InVEST, Alexandria, VA
2,000	Grand Monadnock Arts Council, Monadnock, NH

NATIONAL MACHINERY CO.

Company Headquarters

Tiffin, OH

Web: http://www.nationalmachinery.com

Company Description

Revenue: US$8.7 million (2001)

Employees: 55 (2001)

SIC(s): 3452 Bolts, Nuts, Rivets & Washers.

National Machinery Foundation, Inc.

Giving Contact

Don B. Bero, Assistant Secretary

161 Greenfield Street

Tiffin, OH 44883

Phone: (419)447-5211

Fax: (419)443-2380

Description

EIN: 346520191

Organization Type: Corporate Foundation

Giving Locations: OH: Seneca County

Grant Types: General Support.

Financial Summary

Total Giving: $915,581 (2001); $1,871,700 (2000); $878,844 (1998). Note: Contributes through foundation only.

Giving Analysis: Giving for 1999 includes: foundation grants to United Way ($35,000); foundation gifts to individuals ($109,706); foundation ($884,145); 1998: foundation grants to United Way ($35,000); foundation gifts to individuals ($39,848); foundation scholarships ($65,465); foundation ($738,531); 1996: foundation grants to United Way ($35,000); foundation gifts to individuals ($45,280); foundation scholarships ($61,350); foundation ($519,986);

Assets: $12,989,122 (2001); $15,114,580 (2000); $16,513,477 (1998)

Typical Recipients

Arts & Humanities: Arts Festivals, Arts & Humanities-General, History & Archaeology, Libraries, Performing Arts, Public Broadcasting, Theater

Civic & Public Affairs: Botanical Gardens/Parks, Economic Development, Employment/Job Training, Civic & Public Affairs-General, Housing, Law & Justice, Legal Aid, Municipalities/Towns, Parades/Festivals, Safety, Urban & Community Affairs

Education: Afterschool/Enrichment Programs, Agricultural Education, Business Education, Colleges & Universities, Community & Junior Colleges, Education Funds, Elementary Education (Public), Education-General, Literacy, Minority Education, Preschool Education, Private Education (Precollege), Public Education (Precollege), Religious Education, School Volunteerism, Science/Mathematics Education, Secondary Education (Public), Student Aid, Vocational & Technical Education

Health: AIDS/HIV, Cancer, Children's Health/Hospitals, Clinics/Medical Centers, Emergency/Ambulance Services, Health-General, Geriatric Health, Health Organizations, Heart, Hospices, Hospitals, Medical Rehabilitation, Nursing Services, Single-Disease Health Associations

Religion: Religious Welfare

Social Services: At-Risk Youth, Big Brother/Big Sister, Camps, Child Welfare, Community Centers, Community Service Organizations, Crime Prevention, Day Care, Domestic Violence, Emergency Relief, Family Services, Homes, Recreation & Athletics, Refugee Assistance, Scouts, Senior Services, Substance Abuse, United Funds/United Ways, YMCA/YWCA/YMHA/YWHA, Youth Organizations

Application Procedures

Initial Contact: Send a letter of request.

Application Requirements: Specify financial need and purpose.

Deadlines: None.

Restrictions

Distributions are limited to organizations and individuals in the general Seneca County area.

Additional Information

In addition to grant making, the foundation assists needy individuals, operates a scholarship program, and awards citizenship gifts.

Corporate Officials

Larry Baker: vice president employee relations PRIM CORP EMPL vice president employee relations: National Machinery Co.

Foundation Officials

Larry Baker: secretary, treasurer, trustee (see above)

Patricia Hillmer: trustee

Donna J. Kin: executive secretary

N. E. Martin: trustee

Grants Analysis

Disclosure Period: calendar year ending 2001

Total Grants: $815,885*

Number of Grants: 91

Average Grant: $4,621*

Highest Grant: $400,000

Lowest Grant: $100

Typical Range: $1,000 to $10,000

*Note: Giving excludes gifts to individuals, scholarship, and United Way. Average grant figure excludes highest grant.

Recent Grants

Note: Grants derived from 2001 Form 990.

Library-Related
8,655	Tiffin-Seneca Public Library, Tiffin, OH

General
400,000	Tiffin Theatre Inc., Tiffin, OH
50,000	Betty Jane Memorial Rehabilitation Center, Tiffin, OH
50,000	Heidelberg College, Tiffin, OH
40,250	United Way, Tiffin, OH
30,806	Tiffin Theatre Inc., Tiffin, OH
30,000	Betty Jane Memorial Rehabilitation Center, Tiffin, OH
20,000	St. Francis Home, Tiffin, OH
20,000	St. Mary's Catholic School, Tiffin, OH
10,000	Patchworks House, Tiffin, OH
10,000	Teen Center of Tiffin, Tiffin, OH

NATIONAL MANUFACTURING CO.

Company Headquarters

7 W. Madison St.
Chicago, IL 60602

Company Description

Employees: 1,000
SIC(s): 2400 Lumber & Wood Products, 3400 Fabricated Metal Products.

NMC Foundation

Giving Contact

Joseph L. Bittorf, Chairperson
NMC Foundation
1 1st Avenue
Sterling, IL 61081
Phone: (815)625-1320
Fax: (815)625-1333
E-mail: jlbittorf@natman.com

Description

EIN: 363802369
Organization Type: Corporate Foundation
Giving Locations: headquarters area only.

Financial Summary

Total Giving: $289,860 (2000); $197,114 (1999); $168,375 (1998)
Giving Analysis: Giving for 1999 includes: foundation matching gifts ($5,025); foundation grants to United Way ($47,500); foundation ($144,589); 1998: foundation matching gifts ($3,125) foundation grants to United Way ($45,900)
Assets: $695,262 (2000); $898,077 (1999); $450,328 (1998)
Gifts Received: $70,000 (2000); $605,000 (1999); $190,000 (1998). Note: In 1998, 1999, and 2000, contributions were received from National Manufacturing Co.

Typical Recipients

Arts & Humanities: Music, Visual Arts
Civic & Public Affairs: Botanical Gardens/Parks, Chambers of Commerce, Clubs, Municipalities/Towns
Education: Arts/Humanities Education, Colleges & Universities, Community & Junior Colleges, Elementary Education (Public), International Studies, Private Education (Precollege), Public Education (Precollege), Science/Mathematics Education, Secondary Education (Private), Secondary Education (Public), Student Aid, Vocational & Technical Education
Health: Cancer, Emergency/Ambulance Services, Heart, Hospices, Public Health
Religion: Religious Welfare
Social Services: Animal Protection, Camps, Food/Clothing Distribution, Scouts, Substance Abuse, United Funds/United Ways, YMCA/YWCA/YMHA/YWHA

Application Procedures

Initial Contact: Send an application in writing.
Application Requirements: Include a description of organization, purpose of funds sought, and proof of tax-exempt status.
Deadlines: None.

Restrictions

Foundation does not provide grants for religious, political, fraternal, or labor organizations; organizations which discriminate on any basis other than need; sponsorship of teams or others whose purpose is to in turn raise money for another cause; sponsorship of athletic teams; solicitation in the form of mass mailings; or goodwill advertising or sponsorship of publications.

Corporate Officials

Keith W. Benson, III: president, chief executive officer PRIM CORP EMPL president, chief executive officer: National Manufacturing Co.
Keith W. Benson, Jr.: chairman, director PRIM CORP EMPL chairman, director: National Manufacturing Co. CORP AFFIL chairman: National Manufacturing Co.
Charles R. Phillips: vice president finance PRIM CORP EMPL vice president finance: National Manufacturing Co.

Foundation Officials

Peter M. Benson: director CORP AFFIL director: National Manufacturing Co.
Joseph L. Bittorf: chairperson PRIM CORP EMPL vice president engineering: National Manufacturing Co.
John M. Gvozdjak: secretary, treasurer
Timothy B. Sullivan: vice chairperson CORP AFFIL director: National Manufacturing Co.

Grants Analysis

Disclosure Period: calendar year ending 1999
Total Grants: $144,589*
Number of Grants: 44
Average Grant: $3,286
Highest Grant: $20,000
Typical Range: $500 to $5,000
*Note: Giving excludes matching gifts totaling $3,125 and United Way.

Recent Grants

Note: Grants derived from 2000 Form 990.

General
145,025	City of Sterling, Sterling, IL
74,200	Whiteside County Secondary Schools, IL
27,500	Whiteside County Elementary Schools, IL
12,300	Whiteside County, IL -- civic organizations
11,700	Public, Private, and Technical Colleges of Illinois, IL
6,850	Whiteside County, IL
3,000	Associated Colleges of Illinois, Chicago, IL -- educational aid
2,550	Whiteside County Secondary Schools, IL
1,150	City of Sterling, Sterling, IL -- private charities
350	Whiteside County Elementary Schools, IL

NATIONAL SERVICE INDUSTRIES, INC.

Company Headquarters

Atlanta, GA
Web: http://www.nationalservice.com

Company Description

Founded: 1928
Ticker: NSI
Exchange: NYSE
Revenue: US$532.4 million (2002)
Employees: 7100 (2002)
SIC(s): 2677 Envelopes, 2782 Blankbooks & Loose-leaf Binders, 3646 Commercial Lighting Fixtures, 7213 Linen Supply.

Operating Locations

National Service Industries, Inc. (GA--Conyers, Dalton; NC--Wilmington)

National Service Foundation

Giving Contact

Carol Morgan
1420 Peachtree Street, N.E.
Atlanta, GA 30309-3002
Phone: (404)853-1000
Fax: (404)858-1015

Description

Founded: 1969
EIN: 586051102
Organization Type: Corporate Foundation
Giving Locations: GA: Eastern US.
Grant Types: General Support.

Financial Summary

Total Giving: $713,025 (fiscal year ending August 31, 2001); $647,284 (fiscal 2000); $514,595 (fiscal 1999). Note: Contributes through foundation only.
Giving Analysis: Giving for fiscal 2001 includes: foundation grants to United Way ($105,000); foundation ($608,025); fiscal 2000: foundation grants to United Way ($95,000); foundation ($552,284); fiscal 1999: foundation grants to United Way ($85,500) foundation ($429,095)
Assets: $525,720 (fiscal 2001); $498,571 (fiscal 1999); $472,613 (fiscal 1998)
Gifts Received: $700,108 (fiscal 2001); $525,000 (fiscal 1999); $447,298 (fiscal 1998). Note: Contributions are received from National Service Industries, Inc.

Typical Recipients

Arts & Humanities: Arts Associations & Councils, Arts Centers, Arts Festivals, Arts Outreach, Historic Preservation, History & Archaeology, Libraries, Museums/Galleries, Music, Opera, Theater
Civic & Public Affairs: Botanical Gardens/Parks, Business/Free Enterprise, Chambers of Commerce, Clubs, Community Foundations, Economic Development, Economic Policy, Civic & Public Affairs-General, Municipalities/Towns, Philanthropic Organizations, Public Policy, Safety, Urban & Community Affairs, Women's Affairs, Zoos/Aquariums
Education: Afterschool/Enrichment Programs, Arts/Humanities Education, Business Education, Colleges & Universities, Economic Education, Education Funds, Engineering/Technological Education, Education-General, Education-General, Leadership Training, Legal Education, Literacy, Medical Education, Minority Education, Private Education (Precollege), Public Education (Precollege), Vocational & Technical Education

Environment: Air/Water Quality, Environment-General, Resource Conservation
Health: Arthritis, Cancer, Clinics/Medical Centers, Diabetes, Heart, Hospitals, Medical Rehabilitation, Medical Research, Multiple Sclerosis, Prenatal Health Issues
International: Health Care/Hospitals, International Affairs, International Organizations
Religion: Jewish Causes, Religious Organizations, Religious Welfare, Social/Policy Issues
Social Services: Animal Protection, Camps, Child Abuse, Child Welfare, Community Centers, Community Service Organizations, Domestic Violence, Emergency Relief, Food/Clothing Distribution, Homes, People with Disabilities, Recreation & Athletics, Scouts, Social Services-General, United Funds/United Ways, Volunteer Services, YMCA/YWCA/YMHA/YWHA, Youth Organizations

Application Procedures

Initial Contact: Submit a written request.
Deadlines: None.

Corporate Officials

James S. Balloun: chairman, chief executive officer, president B Sibley, IA 1938. ED Iowa State University of Science & Technology BS (1960); Harvard University MBA (1965). PRIM CORP EMPL chairman, chief executive officer, president: National Service Industries, Inc. ADD CORP EMPL chairman: Holophane Corp. CORP AFFIL director: Radiant System Inc.; director: Wachovia Corp.; director: Georgia-Pacific Corp.
Brock Alan Hattox: executive vice president, chief financial officer B Ecru, MS 1948. ED University of Mississippi BCE (1969); Harvard University Graduate School of Business Administration MBA (1971). PRIM CORP EMPL executive vice president, chief financial officer: National Service Industries Inc.

Foundation Officials

Mark Bachman: director
Brock Alan Hattox: director (see above)
David Levy: trustee B Atlanta, GA 1937. ED Emory University BA (1959); Emory University School of Law LLB (1961); Georgetown University Law Center LLM (1964). PRIM CORP EMPL executive vice president administration, counsel, director: National Service Industries, Inc. NONPR AFFIL member: American Bar Association; member: American Society of Corporate Secretaries.
Carol Morgan: chairperson

Grants Analysis

Disclosure Period: fiscal year ending August 31, 2001
Total Grants: $608,025*
Number of Grants: 198
Average Grant: $3,071
Highest Grant: $50,200
Lowest Grant: $50
Typical Range: $50 to $25,000
*Note: Giving excludes United Way.

Recent Grants

Note: Grants derived from 2001 Form 990.

General
105,000	United Way, Atlanta, GA
50,200	Atlanta Jewish Federation, Atlanta, GA
50,000	East Lake Community Foundation, Atlanta, GA
45,000	Atlanta Symphony Endowment Campaign, Atlanta, GA
25,000	Christian City, Atlanta, GA
25,000	Ranch of Excellence
20,500	Shepherd Spinal Center, Atlanta, GA
20,100	Camp Twin Lakes, Atlanta, GA
17,050	American Heart Association, Atlanta, GA
15,500	Midtown Alliance, Atlanta, GA

NATIONAL STANDARD CO.

Company Headquarters

1618 Terminal Rd.
Niles, MI 49120
Web: http://www.nationalstandard.com

Company Description

Employees: 1,495
SIC(s): 3300 Primary Metal Industries, 3400 Fabricated Metal Products.

Nonmonetary Support

Type: Workplace Solicitation

National Standard Foundation

Giving Contact

R. D. McMillion, Vice President & Secretary
1618 Terminal Rd.
Niles, MI 49120
Phone: (616)683-8100
Fax: (616)683-2803

Description

EIN: 386089682
Organization Type: Corporate Foundation
Giving Locations: headquarters community.
Grant Types: General Support, Scholarship.

Financial Summary

Total Giving: $32,140 (fiscal year ending January 31, 2001); $40,000 (fiscal 2000); $39,048 (fiscal 1997). Note: Fiscal 1997 Giving includes scholarship ($22,000), United Way ($6,500).
Giving Analysis: Giving for fiscal 2001 includes: foundation grants to United Way ($9,940); foundation scholarships ($15,000); fiscal 2000: foundation grants to United Way ($9,000); foundation ($12,000) foundation scholarships ($19,000)
Assets: $2,093 (fiscal 2001); $13,779 (fiscal 2000); $40,604 (fiscal 1997)
Gifts Received: $26,700 (fiscal 2001); $35,000 (fiscal 2000); $40,000 (fiscal 1997). Note: Contributions were received from National-Standard Co.

Typical Recipients

Arts & Humanities: Arts Centers, Libraries, Public Broadcasting
Civic & Public Affairs: Clubs, Community Foundations, Civic & Public Affairs-General, Public Policy, Safety, Urban & Community Affairs
Education: Agricultural Education, Business Education, Colleges & Universities, Education-General, Secondary Education (Public)
Health: Cancer, Health-General, Health Organizations, Public Health, Single-Disease Health Associations
Religion: Religious Welfare
Social Services: Community Service Organizations, Crime Prevention, Food/Clothing Distribution, Recreation & Athletics, Shelters/Homelessness, Social Services-General, United Funds/United Ways, Veterans, Volunteer Services, YMCA/YWCA/YMHA/YWHA

Application Procedures

Initial Contact: Send a brief letter of inquiry. with detailed description of how the contribution will be used.
Deadlines: None.

Additional Information

Foundation also provides scholarships for children of employees.

Corporate Officials

W. D. Grafer: vice president financeo, director PRIM CORP EMPL vice president finance: National Standard Co.
John E. Guth, Jr.: chairman, director PRIM CORP EMPL chairman, director: National Standard Co.
Michael B. Savitske: president, chief executive officer, director B Allentown, PA 1941. ED University of Notre Dame BS (1964); University of Notre Dame (1964). PRIM CORP EMPL president, chief executive officer, director: National Standard Co. CORP AFFIL director: Factory Mutual Insurance Co.

Foundation Officials

Michael K. Conn: vice president, secretary PRIM CORP EMPL manager human resources: National Standard Co.
W. D. Grafer: treasurer (see above)
R.D. McMillion: vice president, secretary
G.R. Northcutt: president
Michael B. Savitske: president (see above)
F.K. Welling: treasurer

Grants Analysis

Disclosure Period: fiscal year ending January 31, 2001
Total Grants: $7,200*
Number of Grants: 4
Highest Grant: $4,000
Lowest Grant: $100
*Note: Giving excludes scholarships and United Way.

Recent Grants

Note: Grants derived from 2000 Form 990.

General
5,500	United Way of Greater Niles, Niles, MI
4,440	Stillwater Area United Way, Stillwater, OK
4,000	Lake Michigan College Educational Fund, Benton Harbor, MI
2,000	Greater Niles Community Development Corp., Niles, MI
100	Niles Service League, Niles, MI
100	South Bend Youth Hockey, Inc., South Bend, IN

NEBCO EVANS

Company Headquarters

Greenwich, CT

Company Description

Employees: 400
SIC(s): 3273 Ready-Mixed Concrete.

Abel Foundation

Giving Contact

J. Ross McCown, Vice President
PO Box 80268
Lincoln, NE 68501
Phone: (402)434-1212
Fax: (402)434-1799
Web: http://www.abelfoundation.org

Description

Founded: 1951
EIN: 476041771
Organization Type: Corporate Foundation
Giving Locations: NE
Grant Types: General Support, Matching, Multiyear/Continuing Support.

Donor Information

Founder: Abel Construction Co.

Financial Summary

Total Giving: $493,790 (2001); $484,493 (2000); $514,863 (1999). Note: Contributes through foundation only.

Giving Analysis: Giving for 2001 includes: foundation grants to United Way ($45,640); foundation ($448,150); 1999: foundation grants to United Way ($38,053); foundation ($277,000); foundation ($476,810) 1997: foundation grants to United Way ($35,055)

Assets: $3,470,601 (2001); $4,203,657 (2000); $4,341,564 (1999)

Gifts Received: $1,191,288 (1999); $170,000 (1997); $169,000 (1996). Note: In 1996, contributions were received from NEBCO ($150,000); and Constructors, Inc. ($19,000). In 1994, contributions were received from NEBCO ($830,921); and Constructors, Inc. ($14,500).

Typical Recipients

Arts & Humanities: Arts Associations & Councils, Arts Centers, Arts Festivals, Ballet, Arts & Humanities-General, History & Archaeology, Libraries, Literary Arts, Museums/Galleries, Music, Performing Arts, Public Broadcasting, Theater

Civic & Public Affairs: Botanical Gardens/Parks, Community Foundations, Economic Development, Economic Policy, Employment/Job Training, Civic & Public Affairs-General, Housing, Professional & Trade Associations, Urban & Community Affairs, Zoos/Aquariums

Education: Agricultural Education, Arts/Humanities Education, Business Education, Colleges & Universities, Economic Education, Education Funds, Elementary Education (Public), Education-General, Health & Physical Education, Leadership Training, Literacy, Preschool Education, Private Education (Precollege), Public Education (Precollege), Science/Mathematics Education, Secondary Education (Public), Student Aid

Environment: Environment-General, Resource Conservation

Health: Children's Health/Hospitals, Emergency/Ambulance Services, Health-General, Health Organizations, Heart, Hospitals, Mental Health, Research/Studies Institutes, Transplant Networks/Donor Banks

Religion: Churches, Religion-General, Religious Organizations, Religious Welfare

Social Services: Animal Protection, At-Risk Youth, Child Welfare, Community Centers, Community Service Organizations, Counseling, Domestic Violence, Family Planning, Family Services, Food/Clothing Distribution, Homes, People with Disabilities, Recreation & Athletics, Recreation & Athletics, Scouts, Senior Services, Social Services-General, United Funds/United Ways, YMCA/YWCA/YMHA/YWHA, Youth Organizations

Application Procedures

Initial Contact: Send a brief letter of inquiry.

Application Requirements: Include a description of organization, amount requested, purpose of funds sought, recently audited financial statement, and proof of tax-exempt status.

Deadlines: None.

Corporate Officials

James P. Abel: president, director B 1950. PRIM CORP EMPL president, director: NEBCO. CORP AFFIL vice president: Concrete Industries Inc.; director: Constructors Inc.; director: Ameritas Life Insurance Corp.

Foundation Officials

Alice Abel: director

James P. Abel: president (see above)

John C. Abel: director CORP AFFIL officer: Constructors Inc.; officer: Kerford Limestone Inc.

J. Ross McCown: vice president, secretary B 1946. ED University of Nebraska. PRIM CORP EMPL vice president: NEBCO.

Grants Analysis

Disclosure Period: calendar year ending 2001

Total Grants: $448,150*

Number of Grants: 87

Average Grant: $5,151

Highest Grant: $60,000

Typical Range: $100 to $20,000

*Note: Giving excludes United Way.

Recent Grants

Note: Grants derived from 2001 Form 990.

Library-Related

1,500	Friends of Libraries, Lincoln, NE

General

60,000	Lincoln Children's Museum, Lincoln, NE
50,000	Audubon Nebraska, Lincoln, NE
50,000	Lincoln Parks & Recreation Foundation, Lincoln, NE
40,000	YMCA Lincoln, Lincoln, NE
27,420	United Way, Lincoln, NE
25,000	Capital Sports Foundation, Inc., Lincoln, NE
24,000	First Plymouth Church, Plymouth, NE -- annual fund
23,000	Nebraska Wesleyan University, Lincoln, NE
20,000	Boy Scouts Cornhusker Council, Lincoln, NE
20,000	Girl Scouts of America Homestead Council, Lincoln, NE

GEORGE W. NEILSON FOUNDATION

Giving Contact

c/o Lowry Hill
733 Marquette Avenue S N93306-044
Minneapolis, MN 55479
Phone: (612)667-6362
Fax: (612)667-2013

Description

Founded: 1962

EIN: 416022186

Organization Type: Private Foundation

Giving Locations: MN: Bemidgi including surrounding area

Grant Types: General Support.

Donor Information

Founder: the late George W. Neilson

Financial Summary

Total Giving: $621,200 (2000); $400,250 (1999); $352,900 (1998)

Giving Analysis: Giving for 2000 includes: foundation grants to United Way ($10,000); 1999: foundation grants to United Way ($10,000); 1998: foundation grants to United Way ($10,000); foundation scholarships ($20,000)

Assets: $28,842,940 (2000); $13,880,693 (1999); $10,747,119 (1998)

Gifts Received: $8,695,378 (2000); $15,009 (1999); $240,513 (1998). Note: In 2000, contributions were received from G.W. Nielson Trust for Katherine Cram and Katherine Cram Rev Trust. In 1998 and 1999, contributions were received from Katherine N. Cram. In 1996, contributions were received from Katherine N. Cram.

Typical Recipients

Arts & Humanities: Community Arts, History & Archaeology, Libraries, Literary Arts, Museums/Galleries, Music, Theater

Civic & Public Affairs: Community Foundations, Economic Development, Employment/Job Training, Civic & Public Affairs-General, Nonprofit Management, Safety, Urban & Community Affairs, Zoos/Aquariums

Education: Agricultural Education, Arts/Humanities Education, Business Education, Colleges & Universities, Education Funds, Gifted & Talented Programs, Minority Education, Public Education (Precollege), Science/Mathematics Education, Secondary Education (Public)

Environment: Environment-General

Health: Children's Health/Hospitals, Emergency/Ambulance Services, Hospices, Hospitals, Medical Rehabilitation, Nursing Services, Public Health

International: International Environmental Issues

Religion: Religious Organizations, Religious Welfare

Science: Scientific Centers & Institutes

Social Services: Animal Protection, Child Welfare, Community Service Organizations, Family Planning, Recreation & Athletics, Scouts, Senior Services, United Funds/United Ways, Youth Organizations

Application Procedures

Notes: Foundation is not accepting applications at this time.

Restrictions

Does not support individuals or provide funds for endowments or fellowship.

Foundation Officials

Edward M. Arundel: off

Ann B. Burns: officer

Katharine Neilson Cram: off

Henry Doerr: off

Larry R. Henneman: officer

Grants Analysis

Disclosure Period: calendar year ending 2000

Total Grants: $611,200*

Number of Grants: 26

Average Grant: $18,448*

Highest Grant: $150,000

Typical Range: $10,000 to $40,000

*Note: Giving excludes United Way. Average grant figure excludes highest grant.

Recent Grants

Note: Grants derived from 1999 Form 990.

General

50,000	Beltrami County Historical Society, Bemidji, MN
50,000	Beltrami Humane Society, Bemidji, MN
50,000	Minnesota Historical Society, St. Paul, MN
50,000	Opportunities in Science, Bemidji, MN
25,000	Headwaters School of Music & Arts, Bemidji, MN
25,000	Northwest Minnesota Foundation, Bemidji, MN
20,000	Minnesota Transportation Museum, St. Paul, MN
15,500	St. Mary's Mission - Red Lake, Red Lake, MN
10,000	Concordia College, Moorhead, MN
10,000	Minnesota Institute for Talented Youth, St. Paul, MN

NESHOLM FAMILY FOUNDATION

Giving Contact

140 Lakeside Avenue., Suite 230
Seattle, WA 98122
Phone: (206)324-3339

Description
Founded: 1987
EIN: 943055422
Organization Type: Private Foundation
Giving Locations: WA: Seattle
Grant Types: Project.

Donor Information
Founder: the late Elmer J. Nesholm

Financial Summary
Total Giving: $1,789,680 (2000); $1,159,007 (1999); $947,845 (1998)
Assets: $67,357,029 (2000); $78,802,649 (1999); $29,986,496 (1998)

Typical Recipients
Arts & Humanities: Arts Centers, Arts Funds, Arts Outreach, Ballet, Community Arts, Dance, Ethnic & Folk Arts, Historic Preservation, History & Archaeology, Libraries, Museums/Galleries, Music, Opera, Performing Arts, Public Broadcasting, Theater
Civic & Public Affairs: Botanical Gardens/Parks, Civil Rights, Economic Development, Employment/Job Training, Housing, Municipalities/Towns, Native American Affairs, Public Policy, Urban & Community Affairs, Women's Affairs, Zoos/Aquariums
Education: Afterschool/Enrichment Programs, Arts/Humanities Education, Colleges & Universities, Education Reform, Environmental Education, Education-General, Leadership Training, Legal Education, Literacy, Private Education (Precollege), Public Education (Precollege), Science/Mathematics Education, Special Education
Health: Adolescent Health Issues, AIDS/HIV, Alzheimers Disease, Cancer, Children's Health/Hospitals, Clinics/Medical Centers, Emergency/Ambulance Services, Geriatric Health, Health Organizations, Home-Care Services, Hospices, Hospitals, Long-Term Care, Mental Health, Nursing Services, Prenatal Health Issues, Preventive Medicine/Wellness Organizations, Public Health, Respiratory
International: Foreign Arts Organizations, International Affairs, International Organizations
Religion: Religious Organizations, Religious Welfare
Science: Scientific Centers & Institutes
Social Services: At-Risk Youth, Child Welfare, Community Centers, Community Service Organizations, Day Care, Delinquency & Criminal Rehabilitation, Domestic Violence, Emergency Relief, Family Planning, Family Services, Food/Clothing Distribution, Homes, Recreation & Athletics, Refugee Assistance, Senior Services, Sexual Abuse, Shelters/Homelessness, Substance Abuse, Volunteer Services, YMCA/YWCA/YMHA/YWHA, Youth Organizations

Application Procedures
Initial Contact: Request application guidelines. Foundation accepts the Pacific Northwest Grantmakers Common Application.
Review Process: Foundation meets monthly, excluding July and August, to consider requests.

Additional Information
Publications: Application Guidelines
Trust(s): Bank of Aemrica NT & SA (SeaFirst) WA

Foundation Officials
Joseph M. Gaffney: director
Edgar K. Marcuse, MD: director
John F. Nesholm: director
Laurel Nesholm: executive director

Grants Analysis
Disclosure Period: calendar year ending 2000
Total Grants: $1,789,680
Number of Grants: 81
Average Grant: $16,100*
Highest Grant: $250,000
Typical Range: $5,000 to $35,000

*Note: Average grant figure excludes four highest grants ($550,000).

Recent Grants
Note: Grants derived from 1999 Form 990.

General
75,000	Seattle Opera, Seattle, WA -- production of Die Fledermaus
50,000	Alliance for Education, Seattle, WA -- Tom B. Foster Award for Excellence
50,000	Alliance for Education, Seattle, WA -- Galef Institute's different ways of knowing curriculum
50,000	Seattle Opera, Seattle, WA -- The Ring Cycle
50,000	Seattle Symphony, Seattle, WA -- capital campaign
40,000	Seattle Art Museum, Seattle, WA -- sculpture garden
37,400	Technology Access Foundation, Seattle, WA -- technical teens internship program
35,000	KCTS Television Local and National Broadcast, Seattle, WA -- Seattle Symphony's Home at Last program
30,000	Planned Parenthood -- capital campaign
25,000	Children's Hospital -- touch therapies program

NESTLE PURINA PETCARE CO.

Company Headquarters
Checkerboard Sq.
St. Louis, MO 63164-0001
Web: http://www.purina.com

Company Description
Employees: 22,435
SIC(s): 2047 Dog & Cat Food, 3692 Primary Batteries--Dry & Wet.
Parent Company: Nestle S.A., Avenue Nestle 55, Vevey, Switzerland

Operating Locations
Ralston Purina Co. (CA--Los Angeles, San Diego; CO--Denver; CT; KY--Louisville; MN--Minneapolis; MO--St. Louis; NY; OH--Zanesville; TN--Memphis)

Nonmonetary Support
Type: Cause-related Marketing & Promotion; Donated Equipment; Donated Products; In-kind Services; Loaned Employees; Loaned Executives; Workplace Solicitation

Ralston Purina Trust Fund

Giving Contact
Fred H. Perabo, Secretary
Ralston Purina Co.
Checkerboard Square
St. Louis, MO 63164-0001
Phone: (314)982-3234
Fax: (314)982-2752
Web: http://Purina.com/company/profile/profile_articles.asp?article=367

Description
EIN: 431209652
Organization Type: Corporate Foundation
Giving Locations: MO: St. Louis headquarters and operating communities.
Grant Types: Capital, Employee Matching Gifts, Endowment, General Support, Project.

Note: Employee matching gift ratio: 1 to 1, up to $1,000 annually.

Financial Summary
Total Giving: $1,780,702 (fiscal year ending August 31, 2001); $2,239,816 (fiscal 2000); $2,054,917 (fiscal 1998). Note: Contributes through corporate direct giving program and foundation.
Giving Analysis: Giving for fiscal 2000 includes: foundation scholarships ($3,500); foundation matching gifts ($151,816); foundation ($594,684); foundation grants to United Way ($750,000); fiscal 1998: foundation grants to United Way ($753,000) foundation ($1,301,917).
Assets: $18,968,516 (fiscal 2001); $34,484,159 (fiscal 2000); $28,342,439 (fiscal 1998)
Gifts Received: $3,750,000 (fiscal 1996); $1,000,000 (fiscal 1994); $1,000,000 (fiscal 1993). Note: Contributions are received from the Ralston Purina Company.

Typical Recipients
Arts & Humanities: Arts Associations & Councils, Arts Centers, Historic Preservation, History & Archaeology, Libraries, Museums/Galleries, Music, Performing Arts, Public Broadcasting, Theater
Civic & Public Affairs: African American Affairs, Botanical Gardens/Parks, Business/Free Enterprise, Chambers of Commerce, Civil Rights, Clubs, Community Foundations, Economic Development, Employment/Job Training, Civic & Public Affairs-General, Housing, Municipalities/Towns, Nonprofit Management, Parades/Festivals, Professional & Trade Associations, Public Policy, Urban & Community Affairs, Women's Affairs, Zoos/Aquariums
Education: Arts/Humanities Education, Business Education, Colleges & Universities, Community & Junior Colleges, Education Funds, Education-General, Literacy, Medical Education, Minority Education, Preschool Education, Private Education (Precollege), Public Education (Precollege), Science/Mathematics Education, Secondary Education (Private), Secondary Education (Public), Special Education, Student Aid, Vocational & Technical Education
Environment: Environment-General
Health: Alzheimers Disease, Children's Health/Hospitals, Health Policy/Cost Containment, Health Organizations, Hospices, Hospitals, Medical Research, Nursing Services, Single-Disease Health Associations
International: International Relations
Religion: Jewish Causes, Religious Organizations, Religious Welfare, Social/Policy Issues
Science: Scientific Centers & Institutes
Social Services: Animal Protection, At-Risk Youth, Child Welfare, Community Centers, Community Service Organizations, Community Service Organizations, Crime Prevention, Delinquency & Criminal Rehabilitation, Domestic Violence, Family Planning, Family Services, Food/Clothing Distribution, Homes, People with Disabilities, Recreation & Athletics, Scouts, Senior Services, Shelters/Homelessness, Substance Abuse, United Funds/United Ways, Volunteer Services, YMCA/YWCA/YMHA/YWHA, Youth Organizations

Application Procedures
Initial Contact: Request guidelines, then send a written proposal.
Application Requirements: Complete applications will include: clear statement of need, timetable of accomplishment, background on organization and staff who would administer grant, plan for post-grant evaluation, proof of 501(c)(3) status, amount requested, detailed program budget, and copy of most recent financial statement.
Deadlines: None.
Evaluative Criteria: Project can be duplicated and has a prevention component.
Decision Notification: Proposals are reviewed quarterly.

Restrictions

The fund does not support individuals; religious or politically partisan causes; projects that require funding outside the United States or its possessions; loans or investment funds; veterans or fraternal organizations, unless they furnish services to the general public; tickets for dinners, benefits, exhibits, conferences, sports events, or other short-term activities; advertisements; or underwriting of deficits or post-event funding.

Additional Information

Publications: Contribution Guidelines

Corporate Officials

W. Patrick McGinnis: chief executive officer B 1947. PRIM CORP EMPL chief executive officer: Ralston Purina Co.

Foundation Officials

Fred H. Perabo: secretary board control PRIM CORP EMPL director community affairs: Ralston Purina Co.

Grants Analysis

Disclosure Period: fiscal year ending August 31, 2001
Total Grants: $1,044,900*
Number of Grants: 57
Average Grant: $13,407*
Highest Grant: $200,000
Lowest Grant: $1,000
Typical Range: $5,000 to $30,000
***Note:** Giving excludes United Way and matching gifts. Average grant figure excludes two highest grants totaling $307,500.

Recent Grants

Note: Grants derived from 2001 Form 990.

General

200,000	Washington University, St. Louis, MO
187,500	United Way Greater St. Louis, St. Louis, MO
150,000	United Way Greater St. Louis, St. Louis, MO
150,000	United Way Greater St. Louis, St. Louis, MO
150,000	United Way Greater St. Louis, St. Louis, MO
107,500	Animal Protective Association of Missouri, Brentwood, MO
52,000	Jewish Community Centers Association of St. Louis, St. Louis, MO
50,000	Cardinal Ritter College Prep, St. Louis, MO
50,000	Missouri Historical Society, St. Louis, MO
33,000	Papal Visit 1999, St. Louis, MO

Roy R. And Marie S. Neuberger Foundation

Giving Contact

Gloria Silverman
Roy R. and Marie S. Neuberger Foundation
605 3rd Avenue, 41st Floor
New York, NY 10158
Phone: (212)476-5866

Description

Founded: 1954
EIN: 136066102
Organization Type: Private Foundation
Giving Locations: NY
Grant Types: General Support.

Donor Information

Founder: Roy R. Neuberger, Marie S. Neuberger

Financial Summary

Total Giving: $782,069 (2001); $1,078,070 (2000); $1,749,870 (1999)
Assets: $15,571,656 (2001); $16,404,513 (2000); $15,332,950 (1999)
Gifts Received: $88,575 (1994). Note: In 1991, contributions were received from Roy R. Neuberger.

Typical Recipients

Arts & Humanities: Arts Associations & Councils, Arts Centers, Arts Institutes, Arts Outreach, Dance, Ethnic & Folk Arts, Arts & Humanities-General, Historic Preservation, History & Archaeology, Libraries, Museums/Galleries, Music, Performing Arts, Public Broadcasting
Civic & Public Affairs: African American Affairs, Botanical Gardens/Parks, Civic & Public Affairs-General, Urban & Community Affairs, Women's Affairs, Zoos/Aquariums
Education: Arts/Humanities Education, Business Education, Colleges & Universities, Education-General, Legal Education, Private Education (Precollege), Science/Mathematics Education, Social Sciences Education
Environment: Resource Conservation, Wildlife Protection
Health: Emergency/Ambulance Services, Health Organizations, Hospitals, Medical Research, Mental Health, Nursing Services, Research/Studies Institutes, Single-Disease Health Associations
Religion: Jewish Causes, Religious Organizations, Synagogues/Temples
Social Services: Community Service Organizations, People with Disabilities, United Funds/United Ways, Youth Organizations

Application Procedures

Initial Contact: Send a brief letter of inquiry describing program or project.
Application Requirements: Include proof of tax-exempt status.
Deadlines: None.

Restrictions

Provides grants for higher education, cultural programs, and fine arts. Does not support individuals.

Foundation Officials

Ann N. Aceves: vice president
James Kaufman: secretary
James A. Neuberger: vice president
Marie S. Neuberger: vice president
Roy R. Neuberger: president, treasurer, director B Bridgeport, CT July 21, 1903. ED New York University. PRIM CORP EMPL senior partner: Neuberger & Berman. CORP AFFIL chairman: Guardian Mutual Fund. NONPR AFFIL member: Society Securities Analysts; trustee emeritus: Whitney Museum American Art; member: New York Society Security Analysts Institute; member: Society Ethical Culture; member president council: Museum City New York; member collector's committee: National Gallery Art; council friends: Institute Fine Arts; trustee: Metropolitan Museum Art; director coll ctr: Bard College; director: City Center Music Drama New York; member: American Federation Arts. CLUB AFFIL City Athletic Club; Harmonie Club; Century Association.
Roy S. Neuberger: vice president

Grants Analysis

Disclosure Period: calendar year ending 2001
Total Grants: $782,069
Number of Grants: 121
Average Grant: $5,684*
Highest Grant: $100,000
Lowest Grant: $175
Typical Range: $1,000 to $10,000
***Note:** Average grant figure excludes highest grant.

Recent Grants

Note: Grants derived from 2000 Form 990.

General

400,000	Bryn Mawr College, Bryn Mawr, PA
125,000	Central Park Conservancy, New York, NY
50,000	Metropolitan Museum of Art, New York, NY
50,000	Straus Conservation Center, Cambridge, MA
50,000	United Jewish Appeal Federation of Jewish Philanthropies, New York, NY
35,000	Hineni, New York, NY
25,000	Adam Smith Educational Productions, Inc., New York, NY
25,000	Mount Holyoke College, South Hadley, MA
25,000	Thirteen - WNET, New York, NY
25,000	Washington Chamber Symphony, Washington, DC

New England Business Service

Company Headquarters

500 Main St.
Groton, MA 01471
Web: http://www.nebs.com

Company Description

Founded: 1952
Ticker: NEB
Exchange: NYSE
Revenue: US$557.5 million (2002)
Employees: 3611 (2002)
SIC(s): 2700 Printing & Publishing.

Operating Locations

New England Business Service (MO--Maryville; NH--Peterborough)

NEBS Foundation

Giving Contact

Robert H. Glaudel, Investor Relations Analyst
NEBS Foundation
500 Main Street
Groton, MA 01471
Phone: (508)448-6111

Alternate Contact

Kim Roy, Executive Secretary

Description

EIN: 042772172
Organization Type: Corporate Foundation
Giving Locations: headquarters and operating communities.
Grant Types: Capital, Employee Matching Gifts, General Support, Operating Expenses.

Financial Summary

Total Giving: $123,950 (fiscal year ending August 31, 2001); $126,120 (fiscal 1999); $425,226 (fiscal 1998). Note: Contributes through corporate direct giving program and foundation.
Giving Analysis: Giving for fiscal 1999 includes: foundation grants to United Way ($24,000); foundation ($102,120) fiscal 1997: foundation ($96,718)
Assets: $2,509 (fiscal 2001); $6,576 (fiscal 1997); $6,124 (fiscal 1996)
Gifts Received: $123,950 (fiscal 2001); $100,000 (fiscal 1997); $75,000 (fiscal 1996). Note: In fiscal 1996 and 2001, contributions were received from New England Business Service.

Typical Recipients

Arts & Humanities: Arts Associations & Councils, Community Arts, Libraries, Museums/Galleries, Music, Performing Arts
Civic & Public Affairs: Employment/Job Training, Philanthropic Organizations, Safety, Zoos/Aquariums
Education: Colleges & Universities, Community & Junior Colleges, Education Funds, Private Education (Precollege), Public Education (Precollege)
Environment: Air/Water Quality, Watershed
Health: Hospitals
Religion: Religious Welfare
Science: Observatories & Planetariums, Science Museums
Social Services: Community Centers, Community Service Organizations, Food/Clothing Distribution, Scouts, Senior Services, Sexual Abuse, United Funds/United Ways

Application Procedures

Initial Contact: Send a full proposal.
Application Requirements: Include a description of organization, services offered and community served, amount requested, purpose of funds sought, research, budgeted financial requirements for proposed project, summary biographies of key personnel/volunteers.
Deadlines: None.

Restrictions

Does not support individuals, religious organizations for sectarian purposes, political or lobbying groups, or organizations outside operating areas.

Corporate Officials

George P. Allman: senior vice president business management development B Naussau, NY 1942. ED Boston College (1963); Boston College (1972). PRIM CORP EMPL senior vice president: New England Business Service Inc.
Timothy D. Althof: vice president investor relations B Russell, MS 1948. PRIM CORP EMPL vice president investor relations: New England Business Service. NONPR AFFIL member: Financial Executives Institute; member: National Investor Relations Institute.
Jeffrey W. Angus: senior vice president information system PRIM CORP EMPL senior vice president information system: New England Business Service.
J. Craig Barrows: general counsel, secretary PRIM CORP EMPL general counsel, secretary: New England Business Service.
Edward M. Bolesky: senior vice president PRIM CORP EMPL senior vice president: New England Business Service.
John Fairbanks: senior vice president PRIM CORP EMPL senior vice president: New England Business Service.
David G. Foster: vice president, corporate controller PRIM CORP EMPL vice president, corporate controller: New England Business Service.
Robert H. Glaudel: senior vice president human resources PRIM CORP EMPL senior vice president human resources: New England Business Service.
Daniel M. Junius: senior vice president, chief financial officer, treasurer PRIM CORP EMPL senior vice president, chief financial officer, treasurer: New England Business Service.
Robert J. Murray: chairman, president, chief executive officer PRIM CORP EMPL chairman, president, chief executive officer: New England Business Service.
John J. Paukstis: vice president PRIM CORP EMPL vice president: New England Business Service. CORP AFFIL president: McBee.
Richard T. Riley: senior vice president PRIM CORP EMPL senior vice president: New England Business Service. CORP AFFIL president: Rapidforms.
Steven G. Schlerf: senior vice president manufacturing technical operations PRIM CORP EMPL senior vice president manufacturing technical operations: New England Business Service.

Robert D. Warren: senior vice president business management development PRIM CORP EMPL senior vice president business management development: New England Business Service.

Foundation Officials

Robert L. Gable: director B Baltimore, MD 1930. ED University of Maryland (1952); University of Maryland School of Business Administration (1953). PRIM CORP EMPL chairman, director: Unitrode Corp. CORP AFFIL director: Symbolics Inc.; chairman: New Hampshire Savings Bank Corp.; chairman: Rockingham County Trust Co.; director: Financial Concepts; director: H K Webster Co.; director: Apollo Computer. NONPR AFFIL vice chairman: Outward Bound.
Benjamin H. Lacy: treasurer, clerk, director CORP AFFIL director: New England Business Service.
Richard H. Rhoads: director B Philadelphia, PA 1930. ED University of Virginia (1952); Columbia University (1962).

Grants Analysis

Disclosure Period: fiscal year ending August 31, 1999
Total Grants: $102,120*
Number of Grants: 18
Average Grant: $5,673
Highest Grant: $12,000
Typical Range: $2,500 to $10,000
*Note: Giving excludes United Way. A more recent grants list was unavailable.

Recent Grants

Note: Grants derived from 1997 Form 990.

General

17,500	United Way North Central Massachusetts, Fitchburg, MA
13,500	Associated Grantmakers of Massachusetts, Boston, MA
10,000	Indian Hill Arts, Littleton, MA
10,000	Lawrence Academy, Groton, MA
7,000	Boston Symphony Orchestra, Boston, MA
5,000	Cooperative Elder Services, Arlington, MA
5,000	Nashua River Watershed Association, NH
5,000	United Way Nordway Council
2,718	Discovery Museums
2,500	Children's Hands On Museum

NEW HAVEN SAVINGS BANK

Company Headquarters

195 Church St.
New Haven, CT 06510
Web: http://www.nhsb.com

Company Description

Founded: 1838
Assets: US$373 million (2002)
Employees: 600 (2002)
SIC(s): 6036 Savings Institutions Except Federal.

New Haven Savings Bank Foundation, Inc.

Giving Contact

Kim A. Healey, Vice President
195 Church St.
New Haven, CT 06510-2009
Phone: (203)784-5057
Web: http://www.nhsb.com/foundation/default.asp

Description

Founded: 1998
EIN: 061506887
Organization Type: Corporate Foundation
Grant Types: General Support.

Financial Summary

Total Giving: $426,317 (fiscal year ending March 31, 2002); $379,880 (fiscal 2001); $205,500 (fiscal 1999)
Giving Analysis: Giving for fiscal 2002 includes: foundation grants to United Way ($93,700) fiscal 2001: foundation grants to United Way ($84,000)
Assets: $10,039,467 (fiscal 2002); $8,671,739 (fiscal 2001); $4,210,493 (fiscal 1999)
Gifts Received: $1,464,439 (fiscal 2002); $2,700,000 (fiscal 2001); $2,200,137 (fiscal 1999).
Note: Contributions were received from New Haven Savings Bank.

Typical Recipients

Arts & Humanities: Arts Associations & Councils, Ballet, Community Arts, Arts & Humanities-General, Historic Preservation, Libraries, Museums/Galleries, Music, Theater
Civic & Public Affairs: Community Foundations, Economic Development, Civic & Public Affairs-General, Housing, Municipalities/Towns, Philanthropic Organizations, Urban & Community Affairs
Education: Arts/Humanities Education, Business Education, Colleges & Universities, Education-General, Literacy, Private Education (Precollege), School Volunteerism
Health: Hospitals, Nursing Services, Single-Disease Health Associations
Social Services: Animal Protection, Big Brother/Big Sister, Child Welfare, Community Centers, Community Service Organizations, Counseling, Family Services, Social Services-General, United Funds/United Ways, YMCA/YWCA/YMHA/YWHA, Youth Organizations

Application Procedures

Initial Contact: No specific form required at this time.
Application Requirements: Include certification of nonprofit status, audited financial statements, a description of need and authorization by board of requesting charity.
Deadlines: None.

Foundation Officials

Paul McCraven: vice president, secretary, trustee
Julia McNamara: vice chairman, trustee
Cornell Scott: chairman, trustee

Grants Analysis

Disclosure Period: fiscal year ending March 31, 2002
Total Grants: $332,617*
Number of Grants: 115
Average Grant: $2,892
Highest Grant: $25,000
Lowest Grant: $40
Typical Range: $1,000 to $5,000
*Note: Giving excludes United Way.

Recent Grants

Note: Grants derived from 2001 Form 990.

Library-Related

2,500	Southern Connecticut Library Council, CT

General

88,200	United Way Greater New Haven, New Haven, CT
25,000	Central Connecticut Coast YMCA, Bridgeport, CT
22,500	Neighborhood Housing Services of New Haven, New Haven, CT
20,000	National Arts Stabilization, New York, NY

20,000	St. Raphael Foundation, New Haven, CT
15,000	Yale New Haven Hospital, New Haven, CT
10,000	Amistad Academy, New Haven, CT
10,000	Summerbridge New Haven, New Haven, CT
7,500	Learning for Life Connecticut Yankee Council, CT
7,500	Southern Connecticut Conference, CT

NEW JERSEY NATURAL GAS CO.

Company Headquarters
1415 Wyckoff Rd.
Wall, NJ 07719
Web: http://www.njliving.com

Company Description
Employees: 832
SIC(s): 4924 Natural Gas Distribution.
Parent Company: New Jersey Resources Corp., 1415 Wyckoff Rd., Wall, NJ, United States

Nonmonetary Support
Type: Donated Equipment; Loaned Employees

New Jersey Natural Gas Foundation

Giving Contact
Tom Kononowitz, Vice President
PO Box 1464
Wall, NJ 07719
Phone: (732)938-1134
Fax: (732)938-7183
Web: http://www2.njng.com/community/

Alternate Contact
Jim O'Keefe, Community Relations

Description
EIN: 222835065
Organization Type: Corporate Foundation
Former Name: New Jersey Resources Foundation, Inc. (1998).
Giving Locations: NJ: Monmouth County, Ocean County, portions of Morris County company's service area.
Grant Types: General Support, Matching.

Financial Summary
Total Giving: $244,885 (fiscal year ending September 30, 2000); $264,639 (fiscal 1999); $250,000 (fiscal 1998 approx). Note: Contributes through foundation only.
Giving Analysis: Giving for fiscal 2000 includes: foundation matching gifts ($7,575); foundation grants to United Way ($25,739); foundation ($211,571); fiscal 1999: foundation scholarships ($1,000); foundation matching gifts ($7,500); foundation grants to United Way ($25,582) foundation ($229,337)
Assets: $72,516 (fiscal 2000); $35,901 (fiscal 1999); $37,007 (fiscal 1997)
Gifts Received: $262,395 (fiscal 2000); $253,319 (fiscal 1999); $229,751 (fiscal 1997). Note: Contributions are received from New Jersey Natural Gas Co.

Typical Recipients
Arts & Humanities: Arts Centers, Arts & Humanities-General, Libraries
Civic & Public Affairs: African American Affairs, Botanical Gardens/Parks, Community Foundations, Economic Development, Civic & Public Affairs-General, Philanthropic Organizations, Public Policy, Safety, Urban & Community Affairs, Women's Affairs
Education: Colleges & Universities, Community & Junior Colleges, Education Funds, Education Reform, Education-General, Minority Education, Public Education (Precollege), Secondary Education (Public), Student Aid
Environment: Environment-General
Health: Cancer, Children's Health/Hospitals, Clinics/Medical Centers, Diabetes, Emergency/Ambulance Services, Health-General, Health Organizations, Hospitals, Prenatal Health Issues, Public Health, Single-Disease Health Associations, Single-Disease Health Associations
Religion: Jewish Causes, Religious Welfare, Social/Policy Issues
Social Services: Big Brother/Big Sister, Child Welfare, Community Centers, Community Service Organizations, Day Care, Family Services, Food/Clothing Distribution, People with Disabilities, Recreation & Athletics, Scouts, Social Services-General, Substance Abuse, United Funds/United Ways, YMCA/YWCA/YMHA/YWHA, Youth Organizations

Application Procedures
Initial Contact: Send a typewritten letter of inquiry.
Application Requirements: Provide a statement of purpose, amount requested, description of constituency served, and proof of tax-exempt status.
Deadlines: None.
Review Process: Inquiries are reviewed and evaluated weekly; foundation requests additional information as necessary.
Decision Notification: The foundation board meets quarterly to review larger requests; small requests are decided upon within a shorter time frame.

Additional Information
In 1998, Co. changed foundation name because New Jersey Natural Gas is a more recognized name. Foundation priorities did not change.

Corporate Officials
Laurence M. Downes: president, chief executive officer, director, chairman B Hackensack, NJ 1957. ED Iona College BA (1979); Iona College MBA (1981). PRIM CORP EMPL president, chief executive officer, director, chairman: New Jersey Resources Corp. CORP AFFIL president: New Jersey Natural Energy Co.; president, chief executive officer, chairman: New Jersey Natural Gas Co.; president: New Jersey Energy Co. NONPR AFFIL member: Financial Executives Institute; member: National Investor Relations Institute; chairman: American Gas Association.
Glenn C. Lockwood: senior vice president, chief financial officer B 1961. ED Saint Peter's College BS (1983). PRIM CORP EMPL senior vice president, chief financial officer: New Jersey Resources Corp. ADD CORP EMPL chief financial officer, treasurer: New Jersey Energy Co.

Foundation Officials
Laurence M. Downes: trustee (see above)
Oleta J. Harden: secretary ED University of California, Los Angeles JD (1979). PRIM CORP EMPL senior vice president, secretary, general counsel: New Jersey Resources Corp. CORP AFFIL secretary: New Jersey Natural Energy Co.; secretary: NJR Energy Corp.; secretary: Commercial Realty Resources Corp.
Thomas J. Kononowitz: vice president B 1942. PRIM CORP EMPL senior vice president marketing & consumer service: New Jersey Natural Gas Co. CORP AFFIL senior vice president: New Jersey Resources Corp.
Glenn C. Lockwood: treasurer (see above)
Mary Ann Martin: trustee PRIM CORP EMPL vice president consumer & community relations: New Jersey Natural Gas Co.

Grants Analysis
Disclosure Period: fiscal year ending September 30, 2000
Total Grants: $211,571*
Number of Grants: 239
Average Grant: $885
Highest Grant: $14,237
Lowest Grant: $40
Typical Range: $100 to $5,000
*Note: Giving excludes scholarships, United Way, and matching gifts.

Recent Grants
Note: Grants derived from fiscal 2001 Form 990.

General
| 6,650 | March of Dimes, Lakewood, NJ -- sponsor |

NEW-LAND FOUNDATION

Giving Contact
Renee Schwartz, Secretary
1114 Avenue of the Americas, 46th Floor
New York, NY 10036-7798
Phone: (212)479-6162
Fax: (212)841-6275

Description
Founded: 1941
EIN: 136086562
Organization Type: General Purpose Foundation
Giving Locations: nationally.
Grant Types: General Support, Operating Expenses, Project, Research.

Donor Information
Founder: The New-Land Foundation was incorporated in 1941 in New York by Joseph Buttinger and Muriel Buttinger.

Financial Summary
Total Giving: $1,602,804 (2000); $1,810,698 (1999); $1,414,594 (1998). Note: Amount given figures for 1995-1997 were provided by the foundation.
Giving Analysis: Giving for 1999 includes: foundation scholarships ($7,500)
Assets: $35,017,263 (2000); $38,502,796 (1999); $36,320,323 (1998)
Gifts Received: $290,824 (1994); $162,008 (1993); $2,899,992 (1992). Note: Contributions were received from the estate of Joseph Buttinger.

Typical Recipients
Arts & Humanities: Arts Institutes, Arts Outreach, Historic Preservation, Libraries, Museums/Galleries, Music
Civic & Public Affairs: African American Affairs, Botanical Gardens/Parks, Civil Rights, Economic Development, Economic Policy, Civic & Public Affairs-General, Hispanic Affairs, Law & Justice, Legal Aid, Native American Affairs, Professional & Trade Associations, Public Policy, Urban & Community Affairs, Women's Affairs
Education: Colleges & Universities, Education Associations, Education Funds, Education Reform, Engineering/Technological Education, Education-General, Legal Education, Literacy, Medical Education, Minority Education, Science/Mathematics Education, Special Education, Student Aid
Environment: Air/Water Quality, Air/Water Quality, Energy, Environment-General, Resource Conservation, Watershed, Wildlife Protection
Health: Clinics/Medical Centers, Hospitals, Medical Research, Mental Health, Research/Studies Institutes

International: Health Care/Hospitals, Human Rights, International Development, International Environmental Issues, International Organizations, International Peace & Security Issues, International Relations
Religion: Jewish Causes
Science: Scientific Centers & Institutes
Social Services: Child Welfare, Community Service Organizations, Family Planning, Family Services, Homes, Senior Services, Volunteer Services, Youth Organizations

Application Procedures

Initial Contact: Initial contact should be in writing to request guidelines, application form, and proposal format.
Application Requirements: Organizations requesting support from the foundation will need to submit an application form, a proposal abstract, the budget of the orgainzation or project which includes sources and amounts of additional support, a list of the board and executive staff members, a copy of the applicant's tax exempt ruling, a copy of the organization's annual report and/or last audited financial statement, and a one-page letter summarizing the proposal. The letter should state the purpose of the project and anticipated results, the nature and number of clients t he project will serve, and the method of follow-up the applicant will employ to authenticate results.
Deadlines: Deadlines for receipt of proposals are February 1 and August 1.
Review Process: Only notification of the board's positive decisions are sent, approximately two weeks after the semi-annual board meetings.

Restrictions

Grants are not made to individuals. Grants are made to foreign charities only if the charity has a fiscal agent in the United States with tax-exempt status. The foundation does not typically fund programs in the following areas: educational institutions, medicine, religion, and general social programs including homelessness, poverty, domestic violence, drug addiction, or crime rehabilitation. The foundation does not typically award grants for capital campaigns, publications, films, endowment campaigns, building campaigns, or conferences.

Additional Information

Publications: Application Guidelines; Application Form

Foundation Officials

Ann Harvey: director
Joan Harvey: director
Joseph Harvey: director
Thomas Hal Harvey: president B Aspen, CO 1960. ED Stanford University BSE (1982); Stanford University MS (1984). PRIM NONPR EMPL executive director: The Energy Foundation. NONPR AFFIL chairman board: Institute Global Communications.
Renee Gerstler Schwartz: secretary-treasurer, director B Brooklyn, NY 1933. ED Brooklyn College AB (1953); Columbia University LLB (1955). PRIM CORP EMPL attorney, partner: Kronish, Lieb, Weiner & Hellman LLP. NONPR AFFIL member: Association Bar New York City.
Dr. Albert Jay Solnit: director B Los Angeles, CA August 26, 1919. ED University of California BA (1940); University of California MA (1942); University of California MD (1943). PRIM NONPR EMPL professor: Yale University. NONPR AFFIL Sterling professor: Yale University; member committee publics: Yale University Press; train supervising analyst: W New England Institute Psychoanalysis; member: New York Psychoanalytic Society; member: Society Professionals Child Psychiatry; train supervising analyst: New York Psychoanalytic Institute; member: National Academy Sciences Institute Medicine; consult: National Institute Mental Health Division Mental Health

Service Program; member: International Psychoanalytic Association; member advisory council: Erikson Institute Early Childhood Education; member: International Pediatric Society; consult: Childrens Bureau Health Education & Welfare; commissioner: Connecticut State Department Mental Health; member division medical sciences: Assembly Life Sciences; member: American Orthopsychiatric Association; member: American Psychoanalytic Association; member: American Association Advancement Science; member: American Association Child Psychoanalysis; member: American Academy Pediatrics; member advisory board: Action Childrens Television; member: American Academy Child & Adolescent Psychiatry.

Grants Analysis

Disclosure Period: calendar year ending 2000
Total Grants: $1,602,804
Number of Grants: 106
Average Grant: $15,121
Highest Grant: $140,000
Typical Range: $5,000 to $30,000

Recent Grants

Note: Grants derived from 1999 Form 990.

General
130,000	Ms. Foundation, New York, NY
90,000	Ploughshares Fund, San Francisco, CA
90,000	Ploughshares Fund, San Francisco, CA
30,000	Anna Freud Foundation, New York, NY
30,000	Center for Reproductive Law and Policy, New York, NY
30,000	Earth Day Network, Inc., Seattle, WA
30,000	Institute for Policy Studies, Washington, DC
25,000	Alaska Conservation Foundation, Anchorage, AK
25,000	American Rivers, Inc., Washington, DC
25,000	Jackson Hole Land Trust, Jackson, WY

NEW YORK FOUNDATION

Giving Contact

Madeline Lee, Executive Director
350 Fifth Avenue, Suite 2901
New York, NY 10118-2996
Phone: (212)594-8009
Web: http://www.nyf.org

Description

Founded: 1909
EIN: 135626345
Organization Type: General Purpose Foundation
Giving Locations: NY: New York metropolitan area
Grant Types: General Support, Project, Seed Money.

Donor Information

Founder: "The New York Foundation was established in 1909 by a gift of $1 million from the late Alfred A. Heinsheimer , bequeathed to him by his brother, Louis A. Heinsheimer." In 1925, the foundation received a $2.4 million bequest from the estate of Lionel J. Salomon , specifically designated for programs for needy youth and the elderly. In 1929, the foundation received an additional $6 million bequest upon the death of Alfred M. Heinsheimer , then the president of the foundation.

Financial Summary

Total Giving: $5,108,265 (2001); $4,378,315 (2000); $4,428,000 (1999)
Assets: $78,268,578 (2001); $82,028,705 (2000); $81,850,000 (1999)

Typical Recipients

Arts & Humanities: Film & Video, Libraries, Theater
Civic & Public Affairs: African American Affairs, Asian American Affairs, Botanical Gardens/Parks,

Business/Free Enterprise, Civil Rights, Clubs, Community Foundations, Economic Development, Employment/Job Training, Ethnic Organizations, Gay/Lesbian Issues, Civic & Public Affairs-General, Hispanic Affairs, Housing, Law & Justice, Legal Aid, Minority Business, Nonprofit Management, Philanthropic Organizations, Public Policy, Urban & Community Affairs, Women's Affairs, Zoos/Aquariums
Education: Colleges & Universities, Community & Junior Colleges, Education Funds, Education Reform, Education-General, International Studies, Leadership Training, Minority Education, Public Education (Precollege), Social Sciences Education, Student Aid
Environment: Environment-General
Health: Adolescent Health Issues, AIDS/HIV, Cancer, Geriatric Health, Health Policy/Cost Containment, Health Organizations, Heart, Hospitals, Hospitals (University Affiliated), Mental Health, Nutrition, Outpatient Health Care, Prenatal Health Issues, Preventive Medicine/Wellness Organizations, Public Health, Single-Disease Health Associations
International: Foreign Educational Institutions, Human Rights, International Affairs, International Environmental Issues, International Peace & Security Issues, International Relief Efforts
Religion: Churches, Jewish Causes, Religious Organizations, Religious Welfare
Social Services: Animal Protection, Child Welfare, Community Centers, Community Service Organizations, Community Service Organizations, Counseling, Crime Prevention, Delinquency & Criminal Rehabilitation, Domestic Violence, Emergency Relief, Family Services, Food/Clothing Distribution, Homes, People with Disabilities, Recreation & Athletics, Refugee Assistance, Senior Services, Shelters/Homelessness, Social Services-General, Substance Abuse, Volunteer Services, Youth Organizations

Application Procedures

Initial Contact: The foundation cannot review suggested projects by telephone and requests that inquiries be made in writing. Send a letter of inquiry.
Application Requirements: The initial letter should include information outlining the project, the organization's budget needs, and the amount requested. If interested, the foundation will request a full proposal following the New York-New Jersey Common Application Form.
Deadlines: Proposals must be received by November 1 for the February trustees' meeting, March 1 for the June meeting, and July 1 for the October meeting. Applicants are advised not to wait until application deadlines to submit a letter of request or to receive help in meeting emergency needs.
Review Process: Applicants generally will receive a response to the initial letter within ten days. All grants are made by the board of trustees, which meets three times a year. Foundation officers generally meet with applicants to evaluate the proposed project.

Restrictions

The foundation does not make grants to individuals and does not support capital campaigns, research studies, films, conferences, international organizations, or publications other than those initiated by the foundation. Grant requests for programs outside New York City will be considered only if they focus on youth, the elderly, or the poor.

Additional Information

After the foundation has dispensed a grant, they offer support to the grant recipient. Services include: training sessions; informal meetings with the foundation staff and board; and opportunities to meet with other organizations being funded.
Publications: Annual Report

Foundation Officials

Thomas I. Acosta: vice chairman
Alan Altschuler: trustee
Nancy Ashen: fiscal officer

Grants Analysis

Disclosure Period: calendar year ending 2001
Total Grants: $5,108,265
Number of Grants: 309
Average Grant: $16,532
Highest Grant: $40,000
Lowest Grant: $82
Typical Range: $10,000 to $30,000

Recent Grants

Note: Grants derived from 2001 Form 990.

General

150,000	New York Immigration Coalition, New York, NY -- for Immigrant Access Project
40,000	Community Resource Exchange, New York, NY -- to provide individual technical assistance
40,000	Community Resource Exchange, New York, NY -- to provide individual technical assistance
33,900	Community Resource Exchange, New York, NY -- for technical assistance
30,500	National Mobilization Against Sweatshops, New York, NY -- for Disaster Assistance Project
28,500	Latin American Workers Project, Brooklyn, NY -- to help relatives and dislocated workers gain access to relief funds
26,500	New York City Coalition Against Hunger, New York, NY -- for food stamps, WIC, school meals, and earned income
25,000	National Campaign for Jobs and Income Support, Manhasset, NY -- to link New York City and state organizing efforts
25,000	National Campaign for Jobs and Income Support, Manhasset, NY -- to link New York City and state organizing efforts
25,000	Puerto Rican Legal Defense and Education Fund, New York, NY -- for legal services to immigrants

NEW YORK LIFE INSURANCE CO.

Company Headquarters

New York, NY
Web: http://www.newyorklife.com

Company Description

Assets: US$129.34 billion (2002)
Profit: US$423.5 million (2002)
Employees: 12200 (2002)
Fortune Rank: 65, per FORTUNE Magazine's list of 500 Largest U.S. Corporations (2002).
SIC(s): 6311 Life Insurance.

Operating Locations

New York Life Insurance Co. (CT--Greenwich; DE--Wilmington; GA--Marietta; NJ--Fort Lee; TX--Austin, Dallas)

Nonmonetary Support

Volunteer Programs: Provides grants to local grassroots organizations where employees volunteer.

New York Life Foundation

Giving Contact

Peter J. Bushyeager, President
51 Madison Avenue, Room 604
New York, NY 10010-1655
Phone: (212)576-6902
E-mail: NYLFoundation@newyorklife.com
Web: http://www.newyorklife.com/foundation

Alternate Contact

Phone: (212)576-3865

Description

EIN: 132989476
Organization Type: Corporate Foundation
Giving Locations: CA: San Francisco/San Ramon; FL: Tampa; GA: Atlanta; MN: Minneapolis; NY: New York; OH: Cleveland; TX: Dallas nationally.
Grant Types: Capital, Employee Matching Gifts, General Support, Project, Scholarship.
Note: Employee matching gift ratio: 1 to 1 for higher education.

Financial Summary

Total Giving: $9,663,615 (2001); $4,570,509 (2000); $3,826,688 (1999). Note: Contributes through foundation only.
Giving Analysis: Giving for 2000 includes: foundation matching gifts ($465,673); foundation grants to United Way ($1,062,550); foundation ($3,042,286); 1999: foundation grants to United Way ($418,550); foundation matching gifts ($420,643); foundation ($2,987,495); 1998: foundation matching gifts ($616,601); foundation grants to United Way ($1,025,150); foundation ($2,208,357);
Assets: $72,615,739 (2001); $69,783,373 (2000); $69,684,155 (1999)
Gifts Received: $8,655,780 (2001); $4,563,327 (2000); $4,540,561 (1999). Note: Contributions are received from the New York Life Insurance Company.

Typical Recipients

Arts & Humanities: Arts Associations & Councils, Arts Centers, Ballet, Community Arts, Historic Preservation, Libraries, Museums/Galleries, Music, Performing Arts, Public Broadcasting, Theater
Civic & Public Affairs: African American Affairs, Asian American Affairs, Botanical Gardens/Parks, Business/Free Enterprise, Civil Rights, Community Foundations, Economic Development, Economic Policy, Employment/Job Training, Civic & Public Affairs-General, Housing, Law & Justice, Legal Aid, Municipalities/Towns, Nonprofit Management, Philanthropic Organizations, Professional & Trade Associations, Public Policy, Urban & Community Affairs, Women's Affairs, Zoos/Aquariums
Education: Arts/Humanities Education, Business Education, Business Education, Colleges & Universities, Community & Junior Colleges, Education Associations, Education Funds, Education-General, Health & Physical Education, International Studies, Legal Education, Literacy, Medical Education, Minority Education, Religious Education, Science/Mathematics Education, Special Education, Student Aid
Environment: Environment-General
Health: AIDS/HIV, Clinics/Medical Centers, Emergency/Ambulance Services, Eyes/Blindness, Geriatric Health, Health Organizations, Hospitals, Medical Rehabilitation, Medical Research, Medical Training, Mental Health, Nursing Services, Single-Disease Health Associations
Science: Science Museums, Scientific Organizations
Social Services: Big Brother/Big Sister, Camps, Child Welfare, Community Centers, Community Service Organizations, Counseling, Crime Prevention, Day Care, Domestic Violence, Emergency Relief, Family Services, Food/Clothing Distribution, People with Disabilities, Recreation & Athletics, Scouts, Senior Services, Shelters/Homelessness, Substance Abuse, United Funds/United Ways, Volunteer Services, YMCA/YWCA/YMHA/YWHA, Youth Organizations

Application Procedures

Initial Contact: Send a written proposal, no longer than two pages in length, on the applicant organization's letterhead.
Application Requirements: Include a brief description of the specific program for which support is sought, including objectives, timetable for implementation, population and geographic area served, budget, how the project will be sustained, methods for evaluation and utilization results; proof of tax-exempt status; list of officers and board members; brief a description of organization; latest annual report; recently audited financial statement; current IRS Form 990; current itemized budget and funding sources; and a list of corporate and foundation contributors during the prior 12 months. Supportive material and documentation may be attached.
Deadlines: None.
Review Process: Foundation staff review and research each proposal to determine its eligibility for foundation funding. If the foundation is interested in a particular proposal, the foundation will request interviews with the applicant organization's staff and conduct site visits.
Evaluative Criteria: The foundation gives preference to proposals that include opportunities for New York Life employee volunteer involvement.
Decision Notification: Board meets in March, June, September, and December.

Restrictions

In general, the foundation does not make grants to individuals; government agencies; sectarian or religious organizations; social, professional, athletic, or veterans' organizations; seminars, conferences or trips; endowments, memorials, or capital campaigns; organizations that are members of United Ways already supported by the foundation; fundraising events, telethons, races, or similar activities; goodwill advertising; basic or applied research; or organizations that discriminate on the basis of race, color, creed, gender, or national origin.

Additional Information

The foundation requires periodic reports from all organizations that it supports.
Publications: Foundation Annual Report; Application Guidelines

Corporate Officials

Michael John McLaughlin: senior vice president, deputy general counsel B Cambridge, MA 1944. ED Boston College AB (1965); New York University School of Law JD (1968). PRIM CORP EMPL senior vice president, deputy general counsel: New York Life Insurance Co. NONPR AFFIL member: American Bar Association; member: New York State Bar Association.
Carol Joan Reuter: vice president B Brooklyn, NY 1941. ED Saint John's University BA (1962). PRIM CORP EMPL vice president: New York Life Insurance Co. NONPR AFFIL member corporate associates: United Way America.

Foundation Officials

George August William Bundschuh: trustee B Yonkers, NY 1933. ED Pace University BBA (1955); Columbia University School of Business Administration MS (1959). NONPR AFFIL trustee: Pace University.
Carolyn M. Buscarino: director
Peter J. Bushyeager: president, director
Michael T. Delahaye: director
Celia Holtzberg: treasurer
Theodore J. Kohnen: treasurer
Michael John McLaughlin: secretary (see above)
Carol Joan Reuter: chief executive officer, director (see above)
Sy Stemberg: chairman, director
George J. Trapp: secretary, director
Richard W. Zuccaro: vice president

Grants Analysis

Disclosure Period: calendar year ending 2001
Total Grants: $7,889,348*
Number of Grants: 202
Average Grant: $19,447*
Highest Grant: $3,000,000
Lowest Grant: $500
Typical Range: $500 to $50,000 and $130,000 to $500,000
*Note: Giving excludes matching gifts and United Way.

Recent Grants

Note: Grants derived from 2001 Form 990.

Library-Related
223,000	The New York Public Library, New York, NY
15,000	New York Public Library, New York, NY

General
3,000,000	Community Funds, Inc., New York, NY
1,000,000	American Red Cross - National, Washington, DC
650,000	United Way Tri-State, New York, NY
577,500	New Visions for Public Schools, New York, NY
500,000	City University of New York, New York, NY
354,000	Boys and Girls Clubs of America, New York, NY
250,000	Girl Scout Council of Greater New York, New York, NY
250,000	YWCA of Greater New York, New York, NY
229,000	ASPIRA Association, Washington, DC
130,000	Police Athletic League, New York, NY

NEW YORK MERCANTILE EXCHANGE

Company Headquarters

1 NOR End Ave.
New York, NY 10282
Web: http://www.nymex.com

Company Description

Employees: 375
SIC(s): 6231 Security & Commodity Exchanges.

Nonmonetary Support

Type: Donated Equipment

New York Mercantile Exchange Charitable Foundation

Giving Contact

Madeline Boyd, Chairman Executive Committee
New York Mercantile Exchange Charitable Foundation
Executive Committee
1 North End Avenue
World Financial Center, Room 1440
New York, NY 10282-1101
Phone: (212)299-2517
E-mail: charitablefoundation@nymex.com
Web: http://www.nymex.com/jsp/about/cs_relief_fund.jsp

Description

Founded: 1989
EIN: 133586378
Organization Type: Corporate Foundation
Giving Locations: principally near operating locations and to national organizations.
Grant Types: Emergency, General Support, Project, Research, Scholarship, Seed Money.

Donor Information

Founder: Established in 1989 by the New York Mercantile Exchange.

Financial Summary

Total Giving: $1,287,536 (2001); $1,308,274 (2000); $1,203,293 (1999)
Giving Analysis: Giving for 2000 includes: foundation ($1,308,274) 1999: foundation ($1,203,293)
Assets: $2,249,701 (2001); $1,435,000 (2000); $1,311,605 (1999)
Gifts Received: $1,776,956 (2001); $1,313,583 (2000); $1,289,904 (1999). Note: In 2000 and 2001, substantial contributions were received from the New York Mercantile Exchange Corp. In 1995, contributions were received from the New York Mercantile Exchange Corp. ($500,000), MBF Clearing Corp. ($11,440), Pioneer Futures ($15,270), Tudor Investment Corp. ($10,000), Richard Schaeffer ($7,000), and Philbro Energy ($5,000); miscellaneous contributions of less than $5,000 each also were received.

Typical Recipients

Arts & Humanities: Arts Associations & Councils, Arts Outreach, Community Arts, Arts & Humanities-General, Libraries, Museums/Galleries, Music, Performing Arts, Public Broadcasting

Civic & Public Affairs: Asian American Affairs, Botanical Gardens/Parks, Business/Free Enterprise, Community Foundations, Employment/Job Training, Ethnic Organizations, Civic & Public Affairs-General, Hispanic Affairs, Housing, Inner-City Development, Professional & Trade Associations, Public Policy, Urban & Community Affairs, Women's Affairs
Education: Afterschool/Enrichment Programs, Colleges & Universities, Education Reform, Elementary Education (Public), Environmental Education, Faculty Development, Education-General, Gifted & Talented Programs, Medical Education, Private Education (Precollege), Public Education (Precollege), Public Education (Precollege), Special Education, Student Aid
Environment: Air/Water Quality, Environment-General, Resource Conservation
Health: AIDS/HIV, Cancer, Children's Health/Hospitals, Clinics/Medical Centers, Diabetes, Emergency/Ambulance Services, Health-General, Hospitals, Medical Rehabilitation, Multiple Sclerosis, Public Health, Research/Studies Institutes, Single-Disease Health Associations, Trauma Treatment
Religion: Churches, Dioceses, Religion-General, Jewish Causes, Religious Welfare, Synagogues/Temples
Social Services: Big Brother/Big Sister, Camps, Child Welfare, Community Centers, Community Service Organizations, Counseling, Crime Prevention, Day Care, Delinquency & Criminal Rehabilitation, Domestic Violence, Emergency Relief, Family Services, Food/Clothing Distribution, People with Disabilities, Recreation & Athletics, Senior Services, Shelters/Homelessness, Social Services-General, Substance Abuse, YMCA/YWCA/YMHA/YWHA, Youth Organizations

Application Procedures

Initial Contact: Send a brief letter of inquiry.
Deadlines: None.

Restrictions

Does not support individuals.

Corporate Officials

Patrick F. Conroy: vice president, director PRIM CORP EMPL vice president: New York Mercantile Exchange.
Daniel Rappaport: chairman, director PRIM CORP EMPL chairman, director: New York Mercantile Exchange.
R. Patrick Thomson: president, director PRIM CORP EMPL president, director: New York Mercantile Exchange.

Foundation Officials

Neil Citrone: director
Albert Helmig: director
Steven Karvellas: director
Daniel Rappaport: president, director (see above)
Gary Rizzi: secretary, director
Richard Schaeffer: director
Mitchell Steinhause: vice president, director
Vincent Viola: chairman, director

Grants Analysis

Disclosure Period: calendar year ending 2001
Total Grants: $1,287,536
Number of Grants: 191
Average Grant: $6,741
Highest Grant: $100,000
Lowest Grant: $1,000
Typical Range: $2,000 to $10,000

Recent Grants

Note: Grants derived from 2001 Form 990.

General
100,000	American Camping Association, New York, NY
41,630	UFA Widow's and Children's Fund, New York, NY

25,000	Manhattan Youth Recreation and Resources, New York, NY
22,000	Carl McCain Memorial Foundation, Houston, TX
15,122	Happiness is Camping, Bronx, NY
15,000	Swim Across America, Darien, CT
11,500	PS 89 Parents and Teachers Association, Inc., New York, NY
11,500	PS 89 Parents and Teachers Association, Inc., New York, NY
11,250	Chai Lifeline Camp Simcha, New York, NY
10,000	Big Apple Circus, New York, NY

NEW YORK STATE ELECTRIC & GAS CORP.(NYSEG)

Company Headquarters
Binghamton, NY
Web: http://www.nyseg.com

Company Description
Employees: 4,117
SIC(s): 4911 Electric Services, 4924 Natural Gas Distribution, 4931 Electric & Other Services Combined.
Parent Company: Energy East Corp., PO Box 12904, Albany, NY, United States

NYSEG Foundation, Inc.

Giving Contact
Paul Karakantas, Treasurer/Secretary
c/o NYSEG Foundation, Inc.
PO Box 3287
Ithaca, NY 14852
Phone: (607)347-2530
Fax: (607)347-2417
E-mail: ptkarakantas@energyeast.com
Web: http://www.nyseg.com/nysegweb/ComCalendar.nsf/events?OpenView

Description
EIN: 161559224
Organization Type: Corporate Foundation
Giving Locations: NY: Binghamton, Ithaca headquarters and operating communities.
Grant Types: Award, Capital, Employee Matching Gifts, General Support, Matching, Multiyear/Continuing Support.

Financial Summary
Total Giving: $730,000 (2002 approx); $775,904 (2001); $756,615 (2000). Note: Contributes through foundation only.
Giving Analysis: Giving for 2000 includes: foundation grants to United Way ($109,950) foundation ($646,665)
Assets: $113,187 (2000); $721,036 (1999)
Gifts Received: $757,783 (2001); $126,576 (2000); $1,199,631 (1999). Note: Contributions are received from New York State Electric & Gas Corp.

Typical Recipients
Arts & Humanities: Arts & Humanities-General
Civic & Public Affairs: Civic & Public Affairs-General, Public Policy
Education: Colleges & Universities, Community & Junior Colleges, Education Funds, Education-General
Health: Emergency/Ambulance Services, Health-General
Science: Scientific Centers & Institutes

Social Services: Family Services, Social Services-General, United Funds/United Ways, YMCA/YWCA/YMHA/YWHA

Application Procedures
Initial Contact: Send a brief letter of inquiry.
Application Requirements: Include a description of organization, amount requested, purpose of funds sought, recently audited financial statement, and proof of tax-exempt status.
Deadlines: None.

Restrictions
Corporation only supports organizations within its service area.

Foundation Officials
Ralph Tedesco: member

Grants Analysis
Disclosure Period: calendar year ending 2001
Total Grants: $665,504*
Number of Grants: 147
Average Grant: $4,527*
Highest Grant: $265,283
Lowest Grant: $25
Typical Range: $1,000 to $10,000
*Note: Giving excludes United Way. Average grant figure excludes highest grant. Grants analysis provided by foundation.

Recent Grants
Note: Grants derived from 2000 Form 990.

General

289,076	American Red Cross American Red Cross, Binghamton, NY -- for Project Share
33,000	United Way of Broome County, Binghamton, NY
25,000	Paleontological Research Institute, Ithaca, NY -- for capital expenses
20,000	Empire State Games, Albany, NY -- for capital expenses
20,000	Science Center, Ithaca, NY -- for capital expenses
18,180	Binghamton University Foundation, Binghamton, NY -- capital expenses
17,300	United Way of Buffalo and Erie, Buffalo, NY
17,000	United Way of Tompkins County, Ithaca, NY
15,000	BC Open Charities, Endicott, NY -- for capital expenses
15,000	Hospicare of Tompkins County, Ithaca, NY -- for health and welfare

NEW YORK STOCK EXCHANGE, INC.

Company Headquarters
New York, NY
Web: http://www.nyse.com

Company Description
Employees: 1,440
SIC(s): 6231 Security & Commodity Exchanges.

New York Stock Exchange Foundation, Inc.

Giving Contact
Robert T. Zito
11 Wall Street, 6th Floor
New York, NY 10005

Phone: (212)656-5057
Fax: (212)656-5629

Alternate Contact
Phone: (212)656-5290

Description
EIN: 133203195
Organization Type: Corporate Foundation
Giving Locations: DC: Washington; NY: New York
Grant Types: Employee Matching Gifts, General Support.

Financial Summary
Total Giving: $2,370,963 (2001); $2,547,851 (2000); $1,727,450 (1999). Note: Contributes through foundation only.
Giving Analysis: Giving for 2000 includes: foundation matching gifts ($117,851); foundation grants to United Way ($120,000); foundation ($2,310,000); 1999: foundation grants to United Way ($95,500); foundation matching gifts ($121,950); foundation ($1,510,000); 1998: foundation grants to United Way ($98,000); foundation matching gifts ($106,860); foundation ($678,500);
Assets: $23,219,248 (2001); $28,186,655 (2000); $33,228,852 (1999)
Gifts Received: $1,500,000 (2001); $1,500,000 (2000); $6,850,289 (1999). Note: Contributions are received from New York Stock Exchange, Inc.

Typical Recipients
Arts & Humanities: Arts Associations & Councils, Arts Centers, Ballet, Community Arts, History & Archaeology, Libraries, Museums/Galleries, Music, Opera, Performing Arts, Public Broadcasting, Theater
Civic & Public Affairs: African American Affairs, Botanical Gardens/Parks, Economic Development, Economic Policy, Ethnic Organizations, Civic & Public Affairs-General, Law & Justice, Municipalities/Towns, Philanthropic Organizations, Public Policy, Safety, Urban & Community Affairs, Women's Affairs
Education: Business Education, Business-School Partnerships, Colleges & Universities, Economic Education, Education-General, Health & Physical Education, Legal Education, Medical Education, Minority Education, Private Education (Precollege), Student Aid
Environment: Environment-General
Health: Adolescent Health Issues, Cancer, Hospitals
Religion: Religious Organizations, Religious Welfare
Social Services: At-Risk Youth, Camps, Child Welfare, Community Service Organizations, Crime Prevention, Day Care, Food/Clothing Distribution, People with Disabilities, Recreation & Athletics, Scouts, Shelters/Homelessness, Social Services-General, United Funds/United Ways, Volunteer Services, YMCA/YWCA/YMHA/YWHA, Youth Organizations

Application Procedures
Initial Contact: Send a brief letter.
Application Requirements: Include a description of the program.
Deadlines: None.

Corporate Officials
James E. Buck: senior vice president, secretary PRIM CORP EMPL senior vice president, secretary: New York Stock Exchange, Inc.
Richard A. Grasso: chairman, chief executive officer B 1946. ED Pace University BS; Harvard University Advanced Management Program (1985). PRIM CORP EMPL chairman, chief executive officer: New York Stock Exchange, Inc. CORP AFFIL director: Computer Associates International Inc. NONPR AFFIL advisory board: Yale University School Management; trustee: YMCA Greater New York; co-chairman: Project Smart School; director: New York City Police Foundation; director: New York City Public Private Initiatives; member: International Cap Markets Advisory Committee; director: National Italian American

Foundation; honorary chairman: Friends of Statue of Liberty National Monument/Ellis Island; director: Centurion Foundation.

Foundation Officials

James E. Buck: secretary (see above)
William B. Harrison, Jr.: director
Keith R. Helsby: treasurer B Scranton, PA 1944. ED Gettysburg College (1966). PRIM NONPR EMPL senior vice president, chief financial officer: New York Stock Exchange, Inc.
Alan Holzer: controller
William R. Johnston: director PRIM CORP EMPL senior managing director: La Branche & Co. ADD CORP EMPL president: New York Stock Exchange Inc.
Joseph A. Mahoney: director
Deryck C. Maughan: director B Consett, United Kingdom 1947. ED University of London Kings College BA (1969); Stanford University MBA (1978). PRIM CORP EMPL vice chairman: Citigroup Inc. CORP AFFIL officer: New York Stock Exchange Inc.; director: Salomon Brothers Inc.; vice chairman: Citigroup Inc.
George C. McNamee: chairman, director

Grants Analysis

Disclosure Period: calendar year ending 2001
Total Grants: $2,110,000*
Number of Grants: 57
Average Grant: $27,857*
Highest Grant: $550,000
Lowest Grant: $5,000
Typical Range: $5,000 to $50,000
*Note: Giving excludes matching gifts and United Way. Average grant figure excludes highest grant.

Recent Grants

Note: Grants derived from 2001 Form 990.

Library-Related
15,000   New York Public Library, New York, NY

General
25,000   Trooper Foundation, New York, NY
25,000   United Negro College Fund, New York, NY
20,000   Centurion Foundation, New York, NY
20,000   WNET/Channel 13, New York, NY
15,000   Brooklyn Museum of Art, Brooklyn, NY
15,000   Change for Kids, New York, NY
15,000   City Harvest, New York, NY
15,000   Clear Pool Camp, New York, NY
15,000   CSC Foundation, Seaside, CA
15,000   South Street Seaport Museum, New York, NY

NEW YORK TIMES CO.

Company Headquarters

229 W. 43rd Street
New York, NY 10036
Phone: (212)556-1234
Web: http://www.nytco.com

Company Description

Founded: 1896
Ticker: NYT
Exchange: NYSE
Revenue: US$3.079 billion (2002)
Profit: US$299.7 million (2002)
Employees: 12050 (2001)
Fortune Rank: 486, per FORTUNE Magazine's list of 500 Largest U.S. Corporations (2002).
SIC(s): 2711 Newspapers, 2721 Periodicals, 4832 Radio Broadcasting Stations, 4833 Television Broadcasting Stations.

Operating Locations

New York Times Co. (AL--Florence, Gadsden, Huntsville, Tuscaloosa; CA--Santa Barbara, Santa Rosa; CT--Trumbull; FL--Avon Park, Gainesville, Lake City, Lakeland, Leesburg, Ocala, Palatka, Sarasota, Sebring; IL--Moline; KY--Harlan, Madisonville, Middlesboro; LA--Opelousas, Thibodaux; ME--Madison; MA--Billerica, Boston; MS--Booneville, Corinth; NJ--Carlstadt, Cherry Hill; NC--Hendersonville, Lexington, Wilmington; PA--Avoca; RI--Newport; SC--Spartanburg; TN--Memphis, Tazewell)

New York Times Co. Foundation

Giving Contact

Jack Rosenthal, President
229 W. 43rd Street
New York, NY 10036-3959
Phone: (212)556-1091
Fax: (212)556-4450
Web: http://nytco.com/company/foundation/index.html

Description

EIN: 136066955
Organization Type: Corporate Foundation
Giving Locations: NY: New York metropolitan area communities served by company affiliates; some internationally; some nationally.
Grant Types: Employee Matching Gifts, General Support, Multiyear/Continuing Support, Scholarship.
Note: Employee matching gift ratio: 1.5 to 1 up to $3,000 annually.

Financial Summary

Total Giving: $5,859,668 (2001); $4,617,105 (2000); $4,813,993 (1999). Note: Contributes through corporate direct giving program and foundation.
Giving Analysis: Giving for 2000 includes: foundation matching gifts ($1,149,475); foundation ($3,467,630); 1999: foundation matching gifts ($945,613); foundation ($3,868,380); 1997: foundation matching gifts ($1,057,693);
Assets: $2,110,418 (2001); $1,840,732 (2000); $2,408,476 (1999)
Gifts Received: $5,700,000 (2001); $5,500,000 (1999); $5,000,000 (1997). Note: Contributions are received from The New York Times Company.

Typical Recipients

Arts & Humanities: Arts Centers, Arts Festivals, Arts Institutes, Arts Outreach, Ballet, Community Arts, Dance, Ethnic & Folk Arts, Film & Video, Historic Preservation, History & Archaeology, Libraries, Literary Arts, Museums/Galleries, Music, Opera, Performing Arts, Public Broadcasting, Theater
Civic & Public Affairs: Botanical Gardens/Parks, Clubs, Economic Development, Employment/Job Training, First Amendment Issues, Civic & Public Affairs-General, Housing, Law & Justice, Municipalities/Towns, Professional & Trade Associations, Safety, Urban & Community Affairs, Women's Affairs
Education: Arts/Humanities Education, Business Education, Colleges & Universities, Community & Junior Colleges, Engineering/Technological Education, Faculty Development, Journalism/Media Education, Leadership Training, Legal Education, Literacy, Minority Education, Private Education (Precollege), Public Education (Precollege), School Volunteerism, Science/Mathematics Education, Special Education, Student Aid
Environment: Air/Water Quality, Environment-General, Wildlife Protection
Health: Children's Health/Hospitals
International: Foreign Arts Organizations, Foreign Educational Institutions
Religion: Jewish Causes

Science: Science Exhibits & Fairs, Science Museums, Scientific Centers & Institutes
Social Services: Community Service Organizations, Crime Prevention, Delinquency & Criminal Rehabilitation, Food/Clothing Distribution, Homes, Recreation & Athletics, Senior Services, Shelters/Homelessness, Social Services-General, Social Services-General, Substance Abuse, United Funds/United Ways, Volunteer Services, YMCA/YWCA/YMHA/YWHA, Youth Organizations

Application Procedures

Initial Contact: Submit a brief letter. Letters from organizations in New York should be addressed to the foundation president; letters from organizations located outside New York should be addressed to the nearest Times Company business unit.
Application Requirements: Include a description of organization, amount requested, purpose of funds sought, recently audited financial statement, proof of tax-exempt status, list of the board of directors, and other potential sources of support.
Deadlines: December 1 and June 1.
Decision Notification: The board of directors meets at least twice annually, within the first and third quarter of each calendar year, to review the president's recommendations and authorize grants to be disbursed.
Notes: An optional application form is available on the foundation's web site. The foundation discourages elaborate/lengthy proposals.

Restrictions

Does not support individuals; sectarian religious institutions and causes; capital improvements; or health, drug, or alcohol therapy.

Additional Information

The company also administers the New York Times Neediest Cases Fund, which raises about $5 million annually for organizations that respond to urban needs such as hunger and homelessness.
Grantees must submit a post-grant report accounting for expenditures.
Publications: Foundation Annual Report

Corporate Officials

John Fellows Akers: member, director, publisher B Boston, MA 1934. ED Yale University BS (1956). PRIM CORP EMPL consultant: New York Times Co. CORP AFFIL director: Springs Industries Inc.; director: W.R. Grace & Co.; director: PepsiCo. NONPR AFFIL trustee: California Institute Technology; trustee: Metropolitan Museum Art.
Russell T. Lewis: president, chief executive officer B 1947. PRIM CORP EMPL president, chief operating officer: New York Times Co. CORP AFFIL vice chairman: Affiliated Publications Inc.
Arthur Ochs Sulzberger, Junior: director, chairman, publisher B Mount Kisco, NY 1951. ED Tufts University BA (1974); Harvard University Graduate School of Business Administration (1985). PRIM CORP EMPL director, chairman emeritus: New York Times Co. NONPR AFFIL member: Newspaper Association America; director: Times Square Business Improvement District.

Foundation Officials

R. Anthony Benten: assistant treasurer
Rhonda L. Brauer: secretary
Laura J. Corwin: secretary B Cambridge, MA 1945. ED Brown University AB (1966); University of Pennsylvania MA (1967); University of Pennsylvania PhD (1970); Yale University JD (1975). PRIM CORP EMPL vice president, secretary: New York Times Co. ADD CORP EMPL secretary: Golf Digest/Tennis Inc.; secretary: Sarasota Herald-Tribune Co.
Jacqueline H. Dryfoos: chairman, director
Michael Golden: senior vice president, director
James C. Lessersohn: vice president, treasurer
Ellen R. Marram: director
John M. O'Brien: senior vice president

Randall K. Short: assistant treasurer

Donald M. Stewart: director PRIM NONPR EMPL president, chief executive officer: College Board. CORP AFFIL director: Campbell Soup Co. NONPR AFFIL advisor: Grinnell College; adj lect: John F. Kennedy School Government; president, chief executive officer: Chicago Community Trust.

Solomon Brown Watson, IV: senior vice president, general counsel B Salem, NJ 1944. ED Howard University BA (1966); Harvard University JD (1971). PRIM CORP EMPL senior vice president, general counsel: New York Times Co. ADD CORP EMPL secretary, director: Cruising World Publishings. CORP AFFIL director: Affiliated Publications Inc. NONPR AFFIL member legal aff committee: Newspaper Association America; director: Veterans Advisor Board; member: Massachusetts Bar Association; member: Association Bar New York City; director: Legal Aid Society; member: American Bar Association; director: American Corporate Counsel Association; director: American Arbitration Association; director: Agent Orange Asst Fund.

Grants Analysis

Disclosure Period: calendar year ending 2000
Total Grants: $3,467,630*
Number of Grants: 351
Average Grant: $9,879
Highest Grant: $175,000
Typical Range: $4,000 to $50,000
*Note: Giving includes matching gifts.

Recent Grants

Note: Grants derived from 2001 Form 990.

General

100,000	American Museum of Natural History, New York, NY -- for biobulletin in hall of biodiversity
50,000	Roundabout Theater, New York, NY -- for arts in education for public schools
50,000	Studio in a School, New York, NY -- for Child Care Centers
45,000	Foreign Policy Association, New York, NY -- for production of world maps and web post for publication
40,000	Argus Community, Bronx, NY -- for recovering substance abuse
40,000	City Parks Foundation, New York, NY -- for Nature Programs
30,000	Brooklyn Botanic Garden, Brooklyn, NY -- for environment and sciences programs for teachers and children
30,000	Center for Court Innovation, New York, NY -- for operating expenses
30,000	Chamber Music Society of Lincoln Center, New York, NY -- for career development for young musicians
30,000	Columbia Business School, New York, NY -- for MBSA Real Estate Program

THE NEW YORKER MAGAZINE

Company Headquarters

4 Broadway
New York, NY 10004
Web: http://www.newyorker.com

Company Description

Employees: 400
SIC(s): 2700 Printing & Publishing.
Parent Company: Advance Magazine Publishers

Nonmonetary Support

Type: Donated Equipment

Giving Contact

David Carey, Publisher
4 Times Square 42nd St. 7th Ave.
New York, NY 10036
Phone: (212)286-5900

Description

Organization Type: Corporate Giving Program
Giving Locations: headquarters area only.
Grant Types: Award, Employee Matching Gifts, General Support, Multiyear/Continuing Support, Scholarship.

Financial Summary

Total Giving: Company does not disclose contributions figures.

Typical Recipients

Arts & Humanities: Arts Appreciation, Arts Associations & Councils, Arts Centers, Arts Festivals, Arts Funds, Arts Institutes, Community Arts, Dance, Ethnic & Folk Arts, Arts & Humanities-General, Historic Preservation, Libraries, Literary Arts, Museums/Galleries, Music, Opera, Performing Arts, Public Broadcasting, Theater, Visual Arts
Civic & Public Affairs: Civil Rights, First Amendment Issues, Civic & Public Affairs-General, Law & Justice, Legal Aid, Women's Affairs, Zoos/Aquariums
Education: Arts/Humanities Education, Colleges & Universities, Education Associations, Education Funds, Elementary Education (Private), Education-General, Journalism/Media Education, Literacy, Medical Education, Minority Education, Preschool Education, Public Education (Precollege), Science/Mathematics Education, Special Education
Health: Emergency/Ambulance Services, Health-General, Geriatric Health, Health Policy/Cost Containment, Health Funds, Health Organizations, Hospices, Hospitals, Medical Rehabilitation, Medical Research, Medical Training, Mental Health, Nursing Services, Nutrition, Public Health, Single-Disease Health Associations
International: Health Care/Hospitals
Science: Observatories & Planetariums, Scientific Centers & Institutes, Scientific Organizations
Social Services: Child Welfare, Community Service Organizations, Domestic Violence, Family Planning, Family Services, Food/Clothing Distribution, People with Disabilities, Refugee Assistance, Senior Services, Shelters/Homelessness, Social Services-General, Substance Abuse, United Funds/United Ways, Volunteer Services, Youth Organizations

Application Procedures

Initial Contact: Send a brief letter of inquiry and a full proposal.
Application Requirements: Include a description of organization, amount requested, purpose of funds sought, and proof of tax-exempt status.
Deadlines: None.

Restrictions

Does not support individuals, religious organizations for sectarian purposes, or political or lobbying groups.

Corporate Officials

Thomas Florio: chairman, president, chief executive officer, director PRIM CORP EMPL chairman, president, chief executive officer, director: New Yorker Magazine.

Grants Analysis

Typical Range: $50 to $1,000

CHARLOTTE W. NEWCOMBE FOUNDATION

Giving Contact

Janet A. Fearon, Executive Director
35 Park Place
Princeton, NJ 08542-6918
Phone: (609)924-7022

Description

Founded: 1979
EIN: 232120614
Organization Type: Specialized/Single Purpose Foundation
Giving Locations: nationally.
Grant Types: Endowment, Fellowship, Matching, Scholarship.

Donor Information

Founder: The Charlotte W. Newcombe Foundation is a private foundation created under the will of Mrs. Newcombe, who died in 1979, and left a fortune in excess of $34 million. In her will, Mrs. Newcombe nominated five trustees, charged them with the creation of a scholarship foundation to bear her name, and funded the foundation with half of her residual estate.
The Charlotte W. Newcombe Foundation was chartered in Pennsylvania in November 1979, and opened its administrative offices in Princeton, NJ, in January 1980.

Financial Summary

Total Giving: $1,928,950 (2001); $2,243,315 (2000); $2,130,070 (1999)
Assets: $45,295,265 (2001); $47,391,525 (2000); $50,805,850 (1999)

Typical Recipients

Arts & Humanities: Libraries
Civic & Public Affairs: Community Foundations, Nonprofit Management
Education: Colleges & Universities, Community & Junior Colleges, Continuing Education, Education Funds, Religious Education, Student Aid
Religion: Seminaries

Application Procedures

Initial Contact: Prospective applicant institutions should send a letter or telephone the foundation. For fellowships, applicants should request applications by mid-November from the Woodrow Wilson National Fellowship Foundation, CN 5281, Princeton, NJ 08543-5281, (609)452-7007. Information on the scholarships will be sent to qualifying schools who call or write the foundation. Colleges and universities applying for scholarships for students with disabilities and scholarships for mature women can obtain application materials from June through October.
Deadlines: Deadlines for returning completed applications are November 1 for applying organizations for students with disabilities and mature women scholarships and mid-December for fellowships. No deadlines are listed for the scholarships at Presbyterian colleges.
Review Process: For colleges and universities in the Foundation's Programs, trustees' decisions are announced in May for funding beginning in July. Applicants for fellowships will be notified in April for fellowships that begin in June or September.

Restrictions

The foundation only supports colleges and universities through scholarships and fellowships for undergraduate and graduate students; no aid is available for post-doctoral fellowships. Funding goes to programs that have been developed and continued by the Foundation's trustees. Scholarships are not granted for publicly supported two-year colleges. In

the program for mature women, no grants are made to professional schools. A college or university may apply for funding in only one of these two scholarship programs. No grants are given to individuals, community organizations, or for staffing, program development, or building funds. No loans are made.
The foundation does not make grants to individual students. grants to individual students. The foundation primarily supports preselected organizations.

Additional Information

The Foundation funds selected colleges and universities. These institutions handle all administrative details, including selection of recipients and the awarding of fellowships and scholarships. Individuals may not apply directly to the foundation for grants.
The foundation asks applicant colleges/universities to call to determine eligibility.
Publications: Annual Report

Foundation Officials

Robert Merrihew Adams: trustee B Philadelphia, PA 1937. ED Princeton University AB (1959); Oxford University BA (1961); Princeton Theological Seminary BD (1962); Oxford University MA (1965); Cornell University MA (1967); Cornell University PhD (1969). PRIM NONPR EMPL professor philosophy: University of California, Los Angeles. NONPR AFFIL member: Society Christian Ethics; member: Society Christian Philosophers; member: American Philosophical Association; member: American Academy Religion; member: American Association University Professors; member: American Academy of Arts & Sciences.
K. Roald Bergethon: trustee B Tromso, Norway June 08, 1918. ED DePauw University AB (1938); Cornell University MA (1940); Cornell University PhD (1945). NONPR AFFIL member: Phi Theta Pi; member: Sigma Delta Chi; member: Phi Eta Sigma; member: Phi Kappa Phi; president emeritus: Lafayette College; member: Phi Beta Kappa. CLUB AFFIL Cornell Club; Northampton Country Club.
Sallie G. Campbell: associate director
Janet A. Fearon: executive director, trustee
Aaron E. Gast: trustee ED Wheaton College BA (1950); Princeton Theological Seminary MDiv (1953); Edinburgh University PhD (1956). PRIM NONPR EMPL executive director: Philadelphia Presbytery Homes Inc. CORP AFFIL director: Premier Life Insurance Co.; director: Covenant Life Insurance Co. NONPR AFFIL member: Presbytery Philadelphia; member: Union League Philadelphia; vice president: Philadelphia Presbytery Apartments; director: Presbyterian/University Pennsylvania Medical School; member: American Management Association.
Thomas P. Glassmoyer: trustee B Reading, PA September 04, 1915. ED Ursinus College AB (1936); University of Pennsylvania LLB (1939). PRIM CORP EMPL retired partner: Schnader Harrison Segal & Lewis. CORP AFFIL secretary, director: Lawrence McFadden Co. NONPR AFFIL trustee: Bernard G Segal Foundation; chairman executive committee: Ursinus College; member: Philadelphia Bar Association; fellow: Pennsylvania Bar Foundation; member: Pennsylvania Folklife Society; member: Order Coif; member: Pennsylvania Bar Association; lecturer: New York University Institute Federal Taxation; member: Order Arrow; member: Lawyers Club; member: National Association College & University Attorneys; member: Judge Advocates Association; member: American Bar Association; member: Federation Bar Association. CLUB AFFIL Union League Club; Manorlu Club; Manufacturers Golf Club & Country Club.

Grants Analysis

Disclosure Period: calendar year ending 2001
Total Grants: $1,928,950*
Number of Grants: 53
Average Grant: $36,395
Highest Grant: $759,500

Typical Range: $15,000 to $50,000
*Note: Grants analysis provided by foundation.

Recent Grants

Note: Grants derived from 2001 Form 990.

General

50,000	Columbia University School of General Studies, New York, NY
45,000	University of Maryland, Adelphi, MD
40,000	Fordham University, Bronx, NY
38,000	Rider University, Lawrenceville, NJ
34,000	Rutgers University Foundation, New Brunswick, NJ
34,000	Towson State University, Towson, MD
34,000	Widener University, Chester, PA
32,000	Hunter College, New York, NY
32,000	LaSalle University, Philadelphia, PA
30,000	Beaver College, Glenside, PA

HENRY MAYO NEWHALL FOUNDATION

Giving Contact

Prudence J. Noon, President
96 Fountainhead Ct.
Martinez, CA 94553
Phone: (925)228-9821
E-mail: info@newhallfoundation.org
Web: http://www.newhallfoundation.org/

Description

Founded: 1963
EIN: 946073084
Organization Type: Private Foundation
Giving Locations: CA
Grant Types: General Support.

Donor Information

Founder: the late Alice O'Meara, Newhall Land and Farming Co.

Financial Summary

Total Giving: $546,391 (2000); $345,276 (1996); $361,434 (1995)
Assets: $10,458,337 (2000); $8,567,638 (1996); $8,387,884 (1995)

Typical Recipients

Arts & Humanities: Arts Institutes, Historic Preservation, Libraries, Music, Theater
Civic & Public Affairs: Economic Development, Civic & Public Affairs-General, Hispanic Affairs, Rural Affairs, Urban & Community Affairs
Education: Agricultural Education, Arts/Humanities Education, Colleges & Universities, Elementary Education (Private), Elementary Education (Public), Private Education (Precollege), Public Education (Precollege), Secondary Education (Public), Student Aid
Environment: Environment-General
Health: Children's Health/Hospitals, Clinics/Medical Centers, Emergency/Ambulance Services, Hospitals, Research/Studies Institutes
Religion: Churches, Religious Welfare
Science: Science Museums
Social Services: Child Welfare, Community Service Organizations, Domestic Violence, Family Services, Food/Clothing Distribution, Recreation & Athletics, Shelters/Homelessness, United Funds/United Ways, YMCA/YWCA/YMHA/YWHA, Youth Organizations

Application Procedures

Initial Contact: Send a brief letter of inquiry describing program or project.
Deadlines: None.

Foundation Officials

Mrs. Robert Chesebrough, Jr.: director
Judith McBean Cosper: director
Mary V. Gorman: chief financial officer
David N. Hill: president
Marion Hill: vice president
Anthony Newhall: secretary
David S. Newhall: president
George A. Newhall: director
Jane Newhall: director B 1914. CORP AFFIL director: Newhall Land & Farming Co.
Jon Newhall: director
Roger Newhall: director
Edwin Newhall Woods: director PRIM CORP EMPL director: Newhall Land and Farming.
Prudence J. Noon: president

Grants Analysis

Disclosure Period: calendar year ending 2000
Total Grants: $546,391
Number of Grants: 61
Average Grant: $8,957
Highest Grant: $40,000
Typical Range: $1,000 to $15,000

Recent Grants

Note: Grants derived from 1999 Form 990.

General

40,000	Hart High School
16,500	Fillmore Piru Schools -- art teacher
16,000	Santa Maria High School
15,000	Boys and Girls Club of Santa Clarita
15,000	Santa Clarita YMCA
13,000	Saugus School District
10,000	College of the Canyons
10,000	Santa Clarita Food Pantry
8,000	Fillmore High School -- scholarship fund
8,000	Firebaugh High School

JEROME A. AND ESTELLE R. NEWMAN ASSISTANCE FUND

Giving Contact

Howard A. Newman, Chairman & Director
925 Westchester Ave., Suite 308
White Plains, NY 10604
Phone: (914)993-0777

Description

Founded: 1954
EIN: 136096241
Organization Type: Private Foundation
Giving Locations: NY
Grant Types: General Support.

Donor Information

Founder: Howard A. Newman and the late Jerome A. Newman

Financial Summary

Total Giving: $428,500 (fiscal year ending June 30, 2002); $377,000 (fiscal 2001); $325,500 (fiscal 2000). Note: Fiscal 1997 Giving includes scholarship ($20,000).
Giving Analysis: Giving for fiscal 2000 includes: foundation scholarships ($60,000) fiscal 1999: foundation scholarships ($50,000)
Assets: $8,824,706 (fiscal 2002); $8,845,545 (fiscal 2001); $8,704,516 (fiscal 1999)

Typical Recipients

Arts & Humanities: Arts Festivals, Ballet, Community Arts, Libraries, Museums/Galleries, Music, Opera, Performing Arts, Public Broadcasting, Theater

Civic & Public Affairs: Civil Rights, Civic & Public Affairs-General, Housing, Law & Justice, Municipalities/Towns, Philanthropic Organizations, Public Policy, Women's Affairs
Education: Business Education, Colleges & Universities, Legal Education, Private Education (Precollege), Student Aid
Health: Clinics/Medical Centers, Heart, Hospitals, Medical Research, Multiple Sclerosis, Nursing Services, Research/Studies Institutes
International: International Development, Missionary/Religious Activities
Religion: Jewish Causes, Religious Organizations
Science: Scientific Centers & Institutes
Social Services: Animal Protection, Child Welfare, Community Service Organizations, People with Disabilities, Recreation & Athletics, United Funds/United Ways, Youth Organizations

Application Procedures

Initial Contact: The foundation requests applications be made in writing.
Application Requirements: a description of organization and activities.
Deadlines: None.

Foundation Officials

Michael Greenberg: treasurer, director
Robert H. Haines: secretary, director
Andrew H. Levy: director
Patricia Nanon: vice president, director
Howard A. Newman: chairman, director
William C. Newman: president, director B New York, NY 1926. ED City College of New York BBA (1947). PRIM CORP EMPL chairman, chief executive officer: New Plan Realty Trust. NONPR AFFIL trustee: Baruch College Fund; member: National Association Real Estate Investment Trusts. CLUB AFFIL Princeton Club; Boca Rio Country Club; Braeburn Country Club; Aspinal Curzon Club.
Victoria Woolner Samuels: director
William C. Scott: director
Jerry I. Speyer: director

Grants Analysis

Disclosure Period: fiscal year ending June 30, 2002
Total Grants: $428,500
Number of Grants: 20
Average Grant: $11,156*
Highest Grant: $100,000
Lowest Grant: $2,000
Typical Range: $2,000 to $20,000
***Note:** Average grant figure excludes four highest grants ($250,000).

Recent Grants

Note: Grants derived from fiscal 2000 Form 990.

Library-Related

2,000 Jewish Braille Institute, New York, NY -- for library

General

65,000 Jewish Guild for the Blind, New York, NY -- for facility renovations
50,000 Columbia College, New York, NY -- for J.A. Newman scholarship fund
50,000 Trickle Up Program, New York, NY -- for training and equipment purchase
50,000 United Jewish Appeal Federation of Jewish Philanthropies, New York, NY -- for services to the poor aged
50,000 Yard, Inc. The, New York, NY -- for community workshops, classes, and facility renovations
15,000 New York Shakespeare Festival, New York, NY -- for theatre renovations
10,000 American Civil Liberties Union of Massachusetts Foundation, Boston, MA -- for computer equipment
10,000 American Jewish Committee, New York, NY -- for library materials

10,000 Bennington College, Bennington, VT -- for scholarship
5,000 Learning Tree, Springfield, MA -- for the purchase of equipment

NEWMAN FAMILY FOUNDATION

Giving Contact

Craig S. Skulsky, Treasurer
5455 Corporate Dr., Suite 300
Troy, MI 48098-2620
Phone: (248)641-8400

Description

Founded: 1992
EIN: 382986180
Organization Type: Private Foundation
Grant Types: General Support.

Financial Summary

Total Giving: $96,433 (2001); $183,384 (2000); $96,158 (1999)
Assets: $1,822,410 (2001); $1,806,843 (2000); $1,583,760 (1999)

Typical Recipients

Arts & Humanities: Libraries, Museums/Galleries, Public Broadcasting
Civic & Public Affairs: African American Affairs, Gay/Lesbian Issues, Civic & Public Affairs-General, Law & Justice
Education: Colleges & Universities, Medical Education, Social Sciences Education, Student Aid
Health: Alzheimers Disease, Cancer, Emergency/Ambulance Services, Health-General, Health Organizations, Hospitals, Medical Research, Research/Studies Institutes
Religion: Jewish Causes, Religious Welfare, Synagogues/Temples
Social Services: Community Centers

Application Procedures

Initial Contact: The foundation requests applications be made in writing.
Deadlines: None.

Foundation Officials

Donald L. Newman: vice president
Max K. Newman: president
Steven E. Newman: secretary
Craig S. Skulsky: treasurer

Grants Analysis

Disclosure Period: calendar year ending 2001
Total Grants: $96,433
Number of Grants: 62
Average Grant: $761*
Highest Grant: $50,000
Lowest Grant: $10
Typical Range: $100 to $1,000
***Note:** Average grant figure excludes highest grant.

Recent Grants

Note: Grants derived from 2000 Form 990.

General

100,000 University of Michigan, Ann Arbor, MI
50,000 University of Michigan, Ann Arbor, MI
10,000 Lubavitch Foundation, Bloomfield, MI
5,000 North Carolina State University, Raleigh, NC
3,500 Beaumont Hospital Neurological Research, Troy, MI
1,100 United States Holocaust Memorial, Washington, DC
1,000 Albion College, Albion, MI
1,000 American Civil Liberties Union, Raleigh, NC

1,000 American Medical Association, Chicago, IL
1,000 Detroit Public Television WTVS, Detroit, MI

NEWMAN'S OWN, INC.

Company Headquarters

Westport, CT
Web: http://www.newmansown.com

Company Description

Revenue: US$100 million (2001)
Employees: 20 (2001)
SIC(s): 5149 Groceries & Related Products Nec.

Newman's Own Foundation

Giving Contact

Joan Williams
Newman's Own Foundation
246 Post Road East
Westport, CT 06880-3615
Phone: (203)222-0136
Fax: (203)227-5630
Web: http://www.newmansown.com/5_good.html

Description

Founded: 1989
EIN: 061247230
Organization Type: Corporate Foundation
Giving Locations: internationally, where Newman's Own is sold; Australia; New Zealand
Grant Types: General Support.

Financial Summary

Total Giving: $220,785 (fiscal year ending August 31, 2001); $370,965 (fiscal 2000); $10,625 (fiscal 1999). Note: Contributes through corporate direct giving program and foundation.
Giving Analysis: Giving for fiscal 2001 includes: foundation ($220,785); fiscal 2000: foundation ($370,965) fiscal 1999: foundation ($10,625)
Assets: $718,535 (fiscal 2001); $619,241 (fiscal 2000); $619,693 (fiscal 1999)
Gifts Received: $299,954 (fiscal 2001); $358,566 (fiscal 2000); $424,990 (fiscal 1999). Note: The foundation receives contributions from Meadowlea Foods.

Typical Recipients

Arts & Humanities: Community Arts, Libraries, Museums/Galleries, Public Broadcasting, Theater
Civic & Public Affairs: Housing, Public Policy
Education: Literacy, Public Education (Precollege)
Environment: Environment-General
Health: Arthritis, Children's Health/Hospitals, Health Funds, Hospices, Hospitals, Medical Rehabilitation, Single-Disease Health Associations
International: Foreign Arts Organizations, Foreign Educational Institutions, International-General, Health Care/Hospitals, International Development, International Environmental Issues, International Organizations, International Peace & Security Issues, International Relations, International Relief Efforts, Missionary/Religious Activities
Religion: Religious Welfare
Social Services: Camps, Child Abuse, Child Welfare, Community Centers, Community Service Organizations, Delinquency & Criminal Rehabilitation, Domestic Violence, Family Services, Food/Clothing Distribution, Homes, People with Disabilities, Senior Services, Shelters/Homelessness, Youth Organizations

Application Procedures

Initial Contact: Send a detailed written proposal after reviewing guidelines. Grant guidelines are posted on the company's web site in March.
Deadlines: Proposals are accepted between April 1 and July 1.
Review Process: Proposals are acknowledged within 6-8 weeks of receipt.
Notes: Only award recipients are notified.
Faxed proposals are not accepted. Any materials submitted are nonreturnable.

Restrictions

Funds may not be used for propaganda purposes or to attempt to influence legislation.

Additional Information

Foundation requires regular reports of the progress of the project for which funds are granted. In addition to application information listed above, grant seekers must furnish specific certificates or other adequate proof that the organization is recognized as a bona fide charity under the laws of the country in which it operates.
Publications: Guidelines Sheet

Corporate Officials

Aaron Edward Hotchner: vice president, treasurer B Saint Louis, MO June 28, 1920. ED Washington University AB (1941). PRIM CORP EMPL vice president, treasurer: Newman's Own Inc. NONPR AFFIL member: PEN; member: Writers Guild America; vice president: Hole in the Wall Gang Camp; member: Missouri Bar Association; member: Authors Guild Foundation; member: Dramatists Guild; member: Authors Guild. CLUB AFFIL Century Club.
Paul L. Newman: president B Cleveland, OH 1925. ED Kenyon College BA (1949); Yale University School of Drama (1951).

Foundation Officials

Jamie K. Gerard: attorney CORP AFFIL secretary: Newmans Own Inc.
Aaron Edward Hotchner: vice president, director, executive (see above)
Paul L. Newman: president (see above)
Joanne Gignilliat Woodward: director B Thomasville, GA 1930. ED Neighborhood Playhouse Dramatic School; Louisiana State University (1947-1949).

Grants Analysis

Disclosure Period: fiscal year ending August 31, 2001
Total Grants: $220,785
Number of Grants: 52
Average Grant: $4,246
Highest Grant: $15,000
Lowest Grant: $780
Typical Range: $2,500 to $15,000

Recent Grants

Note: Grants derived from 2001 Form 990.

General

16,640	Motor Neurone Disease Association Australia -- information and services for people with MND
13,000	Camp Quality, QL Australia -- camp for children with cancer
13,000	Canteen Australia -- programs for teens with cancer
12,480	DEBRAA, NW Australia -- support for people with epidermolysis bullosa
10,400	Lifeline Central Australia -- anonymous crisis telephone counseling
10,400	Microsearch Foundation of Australia Australia -- for surgical research
7,800	Child Abuse Prevention Service, NW Australia -- programs to prevent child abuse
7,800	Kambalda Individual Disability Australia -- programs for disabled children
7,800	Technical Aid to the Disabled Australia -- technology to help people with disabilities
6,240	Ardoch Youth Foundation Australia -- program for homeless and disadvantaged youth

NEWMIL BANCORP

Company Headquarters

New Milford, CT
Web: http://www.newmil.com

Company Description

Founded: 1987
Ticker: NMIL
Exchange: NASDAQ
Assets: US$661.6 million (2002)
Employees: 183 (2002)
SIC(s): 6036 Savings Institutions Except Federal, 6712 Bank Holding Companies.

New Milford Savings Bank Foundation

Giving Contact

Francis J. Wiatr, President & Chief Executive Officer
19 Main St.
PO Box 600
New Milford, CT 06776-0600
Phone: (860)355-7600

Description

Founded: 1985
EIN: 061140115
Organization Type: Corporate Foundation
Giving Locations: CT: Northwest Connecticut
Grant Types: General Support.

Financial Summary

Total Giving: $83,407 (2001); $66,046 (1999); $242,901 (1998)
Giving Analysis: Giving for 1999 includes: foundation scholarships ($500); foundation grants to United Way ($3,700); foundation ($61,846) 1998: foundation grants to United Way ($32,000)
Assets: $531,630 (2001); $606,970 (1999); $667,724 (1998)

Typical Recipients

Arts & Humanities: Arts Associations & Councils, Arts Centers, Historic Preservation, History & Archaeology, Libraries, Music, Performing Arts, Theater
Civic & Public Affairs: Chambers of Commerce, Clubs, Community Foundations, Economic Development, Employment/Job Training, Civic & Public Affairs-General, Housing, Parades/Festivals, Safety, Urban & Community Affairs, Women's Affairs
Education: Arts/Humanities Education, Private Education (Precollege), Public Education (Precollege), Secondary Education (Public), Student Aid
Environment: Environment-General
Health: Emergency/Ambulance Services, Health Funds, Health Organizations, Home-Care Services, Hospices, Hospitals, Mental Health, Prenatal Health Issues
International: Health Care/Hospitals
Religion: Churches, Jewish Causes, Religious Welfare, Synagogues/Temples
Social Services: Child Welfare, Community Centers, Community Service Organizations, Day Care, Family Services, Food/Clothing Distribution, Homes, Recreation & Athletics, Scouts, Senior Services, Sexual Abuse, Shelters/Homelessness, Social Services-General, United Funds/United Ways, YMCA/YWCA/YMHA/YWHA, Youth Organizations

Application Procedures

Initial Contact: The foundation has no formal grant application procedure or application form.
Deadlines: None.

Corporate Officials

Ian McMahon: chief financial officer, treasurer, director B Limerick, Ireland 1959. ED University of Dublin (1980); University of Dublin (1981). PRIM CORP EMPL chief financial officer, treasurer: NewMil Bancorp. CORP AFFIL treasurer, chief financial officer: Nowalk Bank.
Francis J. Wiatr: president, chief executive officer, director PRIM CORP EMPL president, chief executive officer, director: NewMil Bancorp.

Foundation Officials

Willis H. Barton, Jr.: vice president, director
Herbert E. Bullock: director
Joseph Carlson, II: director
Kevin L. Dumas: director
Laurie G. Gonthier: director
John V. Haxo, MD: director
Paul N. Jaber: director
Robert J. McCarthy: director
Ian McMahon: treasurer (see above)
Betty F. Pacocha: secretary
Suzanne L. Powers: director
Anthony M. Rizzo: director
Francis J. Wiatr: director (see above)
Mary C. Williams: vice president, director

Grants Analysis

Disclosure Period: calendar year ending 2001
Total Grants: $83,407
Number of Grants: 203
Average Grant: $309*
Highest Grant: $20,950
Lowest Grant: $10
Typical Range: $25 to $500
*Note: Average grant figure excludes highest grant.

Recent Grants

Note: Grants derived from 2000 Form 990.

General

20,000	New Milford Hospital Foundation, New Milford, CT
3,500	Housatonic-Shepaug United Way, New Milford, CT
3,000	Waterbury Symphony Orchestra, Waterbury, CT
2,500	Children's Center of New Milford, New Milford, CT
1,500	Habitat for Humanity, New Milford, CT
1,000	Connecticut Junior Republic, Litchfield, CT
1,000	Keggi Orthopedic Foundation, Waterbury, CT
1,000	Kent Children's Center, Kent, CT
1,000	Moonlight Run 5K, New Milford, CT
1,000	St. Vincent de Paul Society, New Milford, CT

NIAGARA MOHAWK HOLDINGS, INC.

Company Headquarters

300 Erie Boulevard West
Syracuse, NY 13202
Phone: (315)474-1511
Fax: (315)460-1429
Web: http://www.niagramohawk.com

Company Description

Founded: 1998
Ticker: NMK
Exchange: NYSE
Employees: 8,400
SIC(s): 4911 Electric Services, 4925 Gas Production & Distribution Nec, 4931 Electric & Other Services Combined.

Operating Locations

Niagara Mohawk Power Corp. (DC--Washington; NY--Buffalo, Camillus, Cortland, Fulton, Hudson, Manlius, New Hartford, Niagara Falls, Oswego, Pulaski, Syracuse)

Nonmonetary Support

Type: Donated Equipment
Volunteer Programs: Sponsors a volunteer grant program and a community action team.

Niagara Mohawk Foundation

Giving Contact

Carolyn A. May
Niagara Mohawk Foundation
300 Erie Boulevard
Syracuse, NY 13202
Phone: (315)428-5691

Description

EIN: 223132237
Organization Type: Corporate Foundation
Giving Locations: NY: Upstate New York service areas.
Grant Types: Capital, Employee Matching Gifts, Matching, Multiyear/Continuing Support.
Note: Employee matching gift ratio: 1 to 1.

Financial Summary

Total Giving: $1,938,438 (2001); $1,787,205 (2000); $1,728,391 (1999)
Giving Analysis: Giving for 2000 includes: foundation scholarships ($96,948); foundation grants to United Way ($584,862); foundation ($1,105,395); 1999: foundation ($1,728,391); 1998: corporate direct giving ($295,391) foundation ($1,573,057)
Assets: $2,915,556 (2001); $2,996,775 (2000); $3,085,319 (1999)
Gifts Received: $1,843,037 (2001); $1,517,477 (2000); $1,738,000 (1999). Note: Grants are received from Niagara Mohawk Foundation Checking.

Typical Recipients

Arts & Humanities: Arts Associations & Councils, Ethnic & Folk Arts, Arts & Humanities-General, Historic Preservation, History & Archaeology, Libraries, Literary Arts, Museums/Galleries, Music, Performing Arts, Public Broadcasting, Theater
Civic & Public Affairs: Botanical Gardens/Parks, Economic Development, Employment/Job Training, Civic & Public Affairs-General, Housing, Municipalities/Towns, Native American Affairs, Parades/Festivals, Professional & Trade Associations, Rural Affairs, Safety, Urban & Community Affairs, Zoos/Aquariums
Education: Agricultural Education, Business Education, Colleges & Universities, Community & Junior Colleges, Education-General, Legal Education, Minority Education, Preschool Education, Science/Mathematics Education, Social Sciences Education
Environment: Environment-General, Resource Conservation, Wildlife Protection
Health: Cancer, Children's Health/Hospitals, Clinics/Medical Centers, Emergency/Ambulance Services, Health-General, Heart, Hospices, Hospitals, Prenatal Health Issues, Trauma Treatment
Religion: Religious Welfare, Social/Policy Issues
Science: Science Museums
Social Services: Child Welfare, Community Service Organizations, Delinquency & Criminal Rehabilitation, Food/Clothing Distribution, People with Disabilities, Recreation & Athletics, Scouts, Shelters/Homelessness, Social Services-General, Special Olympics, United Funds/United Ways, YMCA/YWCA/YMHA/YWHA, Youth Organizations

Application Procedures

Initial Contact: Send a brief letter of inquiry.
Application Requirements: Include a description of organization, amount requested, purpose of funds sought, recently audited financial statements, and proof of tax-exempt status.
Deadlines: None.
Decision Notification: Requests are reviewed quarterly on a case-by-case basis.

Restrictions

The foundation does not support organizations outside of company service area, individuals, or religious organizations for sectarian purposes. Grants are restricted to the area serviced by Niagara Mohawk.

Corporate Officials

Albert J. Budney, Jr.: president, director B 1948. ED Princeton University BS (1968); Harvard University MBA (1974). PRIM CORP EMPL president: Niagara Mohawk Holdings Inc. CORP AFFIL director: Telergy Inc.; director: Telergy Operating Inc.
William E. Davis: chairman, chief executive officer B Schenevus, NY 1942. ED United States Naval Academy (1964); George Washington University (1971). PRIM CORP EMPL chairman, chief executive officer: Niagara Mohawk Power Corp. CORP AFFIL director: Utilities Mutual Insurance Co.; director: Canadian Niagara Power; director: Opinac Energy. NONPR AFFIL director: Edison Electric Institute; director: Nuclear Energy Institute; director: Center for Clean Air Policy; director: Crouse-Irving Memorial Hospital; director: Association of Edison Illuminating Companies.

Foundation Officials

David J. Arrington: trustee
Thomas H. Baron: trustee
Albert J. Budney, Jr.: trustee (see above)
William E. Davis: trustee (see above)
Edward J. Dienst: trustee
Jacqueline DiMaggio: treasurer
William F. Edwards: trustee
J. Phillip Frazier: trustee
Darlene D. Kerr: trustee
Gary J. Lavine: trustee
Carolyn A. May: director
Tina Moran: secretary
John H. Mueller: trustee

Grants Analysis

Disclosure Period: calendar year ending 2001
Total Grants: $693,062*
Number of Grants: 173
Average Grant: $4,006
Highest Grant: $131,803
Lowest Grant: $100
Typical Range: $500 to $20,000
*Note: Giving excludes matching gifts, United Way, and volunteer grants.

Recent Grants

Note: Grants derived from 2001 Form 990.

General

161,743	United Way Central New York, Syracuse, NY
131,803	American Red Cross, Syracuse, NY
100,010	United Way Buffalo and Erie County, Buffalo, NY
70,350	Syracuse University, Syracuse, NY
54,583	Syracuse Symphony Orchestra, Syracuse, NY
50,000	National Audubon Society, Ithaca, NY
50,000	United Way September 11th Fund, New York, NY
40,000	Ringgold Fire Department, Ringgold, NY
31,830	United Way Greater Utica and Kirkland, Utica, NY
30,234	Museum of Science and Technology, Syracuse, NY

NLI INTERNATIONAL, INC.

Company Headquarters

1251 Ave. Of The America
New York, NY 10020

Company Description

SIC(s): 6311 Life Insurance.
Parent Company: Nippon Life Insurance Co., 5-12 Imabashi 3-chome, Chuo-ku, Osaka, Japan

Operating Locations

Nippon Life Insurance Co. of America (NY--New York); NLI Asset Management Corp. (NY--New York); NLI Properties (NY--New York); NLI Properties Central (IL--Chicago); NLI Properties West (CA--Los Angeles); NLI Research Institute (NY--New York); PanAgora Asset Management (MA--Boston)

Giving Contact

Kyoko Yamaguchi, Administrative Coordinator
1251 Avenue of the Americas, Suite 5210
New York, NY 10020
Phone: (212)403-3400
Fax: (212)764-9773

Description

Organization Type: Corporate Giving Program
Giving Locations: headquarters community.
Grant Types: Seed Money.

Financial Summary

Total Giving: $5,000 (1994)

Typical Recipients

Arts & Humanities: Ethnic & Folk Arts, Arts & Humanities-General, Libraries
Civic & Public Affairs: Asian American Affairs, Botanical Gardens/Parks, Inner-City Development, Public Policy, Urban & Community Affairs
Education: Education Associations, Elementary Education (Public), Education-General, Private Education (Precollege), Special Education
Environment: Environment-General, Resource Conservation
Health: Children's Health/Hospitals, Hospitals
International: International-General, International Relations
Social Services: Community Centers, Community Service Organizations, Social Services-General, United Funds/United Ways

Application Procedures

Initial Contact: Unsolicited requests are not encouraged.

Restrictions

Does not support individuals, religious organizations for sectarian purposes, or political or lobbying groups.

Corporate Officials

Mr. Takeshi Furichi: president, chief executive officer PRIM CORP EMPL president, chief executive officer: NLI International.

EDWARD JOHN NOBLE FOUNDATION, INC.

Giving Contact

E.J. Noble Smith, President
PO Box 954
383 Main Street, Unit 2
Ridgefield, CT 06877
Phone: (203)438-5690

Description

Founded: 1940
EIN: 061055586
Organization Type: General Purpose Foundation
Giving Locations: GA: Georgia coast; NY: New York metropolitan area
Grant Types: Capital, Challenge, Endowment, General Support, Multiyear/Continuing Support, Operating Expenses, Project, Research.

Donor Information

Founder: The foundation was established in Connecticut in 1940 by the late Edward John Noble . Successful in confectionery manufacturing and commercial broadcasting, Mr. Noble was chairman of the board of Beechnut Lifesavers, and chairman of the finance committee of American Broadcasting Company and Paramount Theaters. He created the American Broadcasting Company from National Broadcasting Company's Blue Network, which he had purchased.

A pilot, Mr. Noble spoke out on the need for federal regulations for private and commercial aviation, and in 1938 President Franklin D. Roosevelt appointed him chairman of the newly created Civil Aeronautics Authority. Following this assignment, he became the first Under Secretary of Commerce. In addition, Mr. Noble's commitment to preserving the St. Lawrence River Valley's natural beauty while increasing commerce led President Dwight D. Eisenhower to appoint him to the board of the St. Lawrence Seaway Commission in 1954.

Financial Summary

Total Giving: $6,638,855 (2001); $8,560,892 (2000); $6,018,240 (1998)
Giving Analysis: Giving for 1998 includes: foundation scholarships ($25,000) 1997: foundation fellowships ($65,000)
Assets: $140,885,073 (2001); $155,935,485 (2000); $158,109,154 (1998)

Typical Recipients

Arts & Humanities: Arts Associations & Councils, Arts Centers, Arts Festivals, Arts Funds, Arts Outreach, Dance, Film & Video, Arts & Humanities-General, Historic Preservation, History & Archaeology, Libraries, Museums/Galleries, Music, Opera, Performing Arts, Public Broadcasting, Theater, Visual Arts
Civic & Public Affairs: Botanical Gardens/Parks, Economic Development, Civic & Public Affairs-General, Law & Justice, Legal Aid, Nonprofit Management, Philanthropic Organizations, Urban & Community Affairs, Zoos/Aquariums
Education: Arts/Humanities Education, Colleges & Universities, Education Associations, Education Reform, Environmental Education, Faculty Development, Health & Physical Education, Medical Education, Minority Education, Private Education (Precollege), School Volunteerism, Science/Mathematics Education, Secondary Education (Public), Special Education
Environment: Forestry, Environment-General, Protection, Resource Conservation, Wildlife Protection
Health: Cancer, Clinics/Medical Centers, Health-General, Health Organizations, Hospitals, Medical Research, Medical Training, Trauma Treatment

International: Foreign Educational Institutions, Health Care/Hospitals, International Affairs, International Environmental Issues, International Relations
Religion: Religion-General
Science: Science Museums, Scientific Labs, Scientific Organizations
Social Services: At-Risk Youth, Child Welfare, Community Centers, Community Service Organizations, Counseling, Counseling, Family Planning, Family Services, Senior Services, Volunteer Services, YMCA/YWCA/YMHA/YWHA, Youth Organizations

Application Procedures

Initial Contact: Applicants should send a brief letter to the foundation describing the project.
Application Requirements: A brief description and purpose of the organization; a statement of need, project objectives, and duration; qualifications of personnel; program budget; other sources of income, and those being sought; a copy of the most recent 501(c)(3) and 509(a) rulings from the IRS; a recent financial statement; and a list of officers and directors or trustees. If there is a sufficient interest, a formal grant application will be sent.
Deadlines: None, for letter requests. Grant applications must be received the first day of the month preceding the month of a Trustee meeting. The Trustees meet quarterly in January, April, July, and October.
Review Process: All requests are reviewed and answered as soon as possible. If interested, the foundation will request further information as needed and a meeting, if appropriate. Notification of Trustee's decision on grant applications is usually made within 2 weeks.
Notes: The foundation only reviews requests from organizations that are tax-exempt under the 501(c)(3) IRS code.

Restrictions

Grants are not made to individuals, publications, performances, films, or television projects. The foundation does not consider support for buildings or equipment. In medical education and health care, the directors have generally limited grants to hospitals with which the foundation has had long association.

Additional Information

Publications: Annual Report

Foundation Officials

Dr. William G. Conway: director
Ellen Victoria Futter: director B New York, NY 1949. ED University of Wisconsin (1967-1969); Barnard College AB (1971); Columbia University JD (1974). PRIM NONPR EMPL president: American Museum Natural History. CORP AFFIL director: Morgan Guaranty Trust Co. New York; director: Consolidated Edison Co. New York Inc.; director: JP Morgan & Co. Inc.; director: Bristol-Myers Squibb Corp.; director: CB South Inc. NONPR AFFIL member: New York State Bar Association; member: Phi Beta Kappa; partner: New York City Partnership; president: Hayden Planetarium; member: National Institute Social Sciences; member: Association Bar New York City; member: Council Foreign Relations; president: American Museum Natural History Hayden Planetarium; member: American Bar Association; trustee: American Museum Natural History; member: American Academy of Arts & Sciences; director: American Assembly. CLUB AFFIL Century Club; Cosmopolitan Club.
E. Mary Heffernan: treasurer
Harold B. Johnson: director
Frank Y. Larkin: vice chairman, director B 1917. ED Princeton University (1937). NONPR AFFIL treasurer: Saint Catherine Island Foundation.
June Noble Larkin: chairwoman, director B New York, NY 1922. ED Sarah Lawrence College BA (1944). CORP AFFIL board directors: US Trust Co. Connecticut. NONPR AFFIL committee member: New York Public Library, Library Performing Arts;

president: Saint Catherine Island Foundation; member: New York International Festival Arts; trustee: Museum Modern Art; member: National Society Colonial Dames State New York; chairman, trustee: Juilliard School Music; member, board directors: Lincoln Center Performing Arts. CLUB AFFIL Colony Club; Sulgrave Club.
Deborah A. Menton: executive director, secretary
Howard Phipps, Jr.: director B 1934. ED Harvard University AB (1955). CORP AFFIL director: Bessemer Trust Co. NA.
Dr. Joseph W. Polisi: director B New York, NY 1947. ED University of Connecticut BA (1969); Tufts University MA (1970); Tufts University MusM (1973); Tufts University MMusArts (1975); Yale University DMA (1980). PRIM NONPR EMPL president: Juilliard School.
Bradford K. Smith: director
David S. Smith, Jr.: director
E.J. Noble Smith: president, director
Jeremy T. Smith: director
Carroll Livingston Wainwright, Jr.: director B New York, NY 1925. ED Yale University AB (1949); Harvard University LLB (1952). PRIM CORP EMPL partner: Milbank, Tweed, Hadley & McCloy. CORP AFFIL trustee: US Trust Co. New York; director: US Trust Co. NONPR AFFIL member government board: New York Community Trust; member: New York State Bar Association; honorary trustee: Cooper Union Advancement Science Art; member: Association Bar New York City; trustee: Boys Club New York; honorary trustee: American Museum Natural History; member: American Bar Association. CLUB AFFIL Maidstone Club; Union Club; Downtown Club.

Grants Analysis

Disclosure Period: calendar year ending 2001
Total Grants: $6,638,855
Number of Grants: 59
Average Grant: $79,980*
Highest Grant: $2,000,000
Lowest Grant: $5,000
Typical Range: $25,000 to $150,000
***Note:** Average grant figure excludes highest grant.

Recent Grants

Note: Grants derived from 2001 Form 990.

General

2,000,000	Museum of Modern Art, New York, NY -- support of education center
610,000	Wildlife Conservation Society, Bronx, NY -- Wildlife Survival Center
500,000	American Museum of Natural History, New York, NY -- discovery room
400,000	Juilliard School, New York, NY -- endowment fund for Distinguished Scholars and Honors Program
400,000	St. Catherine's Island Foundation, Midway, GA
300,000	Greenwich Academy, Greenwich, CT -- campaign support
250,000	Brooklyn Museum of Art, Brooklyn, NY -- audience development initiative
150,000	Jazz at Lincoln Center, New York, NY
150,000	Juilliard School, New York, NY -- Jazz Program
130,000	American Museum of Natural History, New York, NY -- for curator and conservation of archeological materials

SAMUEL ROBERTS NOBLE FOUNDATION

Giving Contact

Michael A. Cawley, President & Trustee
PO Box 2180
2510 Sam Noble Parkway
Ardmore, OK 73402

Phone: (580)223-5810
Fax: (580)221-6212
E-mail: macawley@noble.org
Web: http://www.noble.org

Description

Founded: 1945
EIN: 730606209
Organization Type: General Purpose Foundation
Giving Locations: OK: Southwestern USA.
Grant Types: Capital, Employee Matching Gifts, Endowment, General Support, Matching, Multiyear/Continuing Support, Operating Expenses, Project, Research.

Donor Information

Founder: Lloyd Noble, an Oklahoma oilman who developed the Noble Drilling and Samedan Oil corporations, provided the funding to create the Samuel Roberts Noble Foundation in 1945. The foundation was named for Lloyd Noble's father. Six family members sit on the current board of trustees.

Financial Summary

Total Giving: $9,576,032 (fiscal year ending October 31, 2001 approx); $17,554,773 (fiscal 2000); $20,361,620 (fiscal 1999)
Giving Analysis: Giving for fiscal 2000 includes: foundation matching gifts ($109,767); fiscal 1998: foundation grants to United Way ($12,113); foundation matching gifts ($80,719); foundation fellowships ($217,315) foundation scholarships ($439,938)
Assets: $971,672,376 (fiscal 2000); $870,443,404 (fiscal 1999); $863,347,245 (fiscal 1998)
Gifts Received: $25,000 (fiscal 2000); $728,991 (fiscal 1996); $100,010 (fiscal 1995). Note: In fiscal 1996, the foundation received a gift from Sam Noble. A gift was received in fiscal 1995 from Ray London.

Typical Recipients

Arts & Humanities: Arts Centers, Arts Institutes, Ethnic & Folk Arts, Historic Preservation, History & Archaeology, Libraries, Museums/Galleries, Music, Performing Arts, Public Broadcasting
Civic & Public Affairs: Botanical Gardens/Parks, Business/Free Enterprise, Chambers of Commerce, Community Foundations, Economic Development, Economic Policy, Civic & Public Affairs-General, Housing, Law & Justice, Legal Aid, Municipalities/Towns, Nonprofit Management, Parades/Festivals, Professional & Trade Associations, Public Policy, Rural Affairs, Safety, Urban & Community Affairs, Zoos/Aquariums
Education: Afterschool/Enrichment Programs, Agricultural Education, Business Education, Colleges & Universities, Continuing Education, Economic Education, Education Associations, Education Funds, Education Reform, Faculty Development, Education-General, Health & Physical Education, Journalism/Media Education, Literacy, Medical Education, Private Education (Precollege), Public Education (Precollege), Science/Mathematics Education, Secondary Education (Public), Social Sciences Education, Special Education, Student Aid
Environment: Environment-General, Wildlife Protection
Health: Cancer, Children's Health/Hospitals, Clinics/Medical Centers, Diabetes, Emergency/Ambulance Services, Eyes/Blindness, Health Policy/Cost Containment, Health Organizations, Heart, Hospices, Hospitals, Medical Rehabilitation, Medical Research, Mental Health, Nursing Services, Preventive Medicine/Wellness Organizations, Public Health, Research/Studies Institutes, Single-Disease Health Associations, Transplant Networks/Donor Banks
International: International Affairs, International Organizations, International Peace & Security Issues, Missionary/Religious Activities
Religion: Churches, Religion-General, Ministries, Religious Organizations, Religious Welfare

Science: Science Museums, Scientific Centers & Institutes, Scientific Organizations
Social Services: Animal Protection, At-Risk Youth, Child Abuse, Child Welfare, Community Service Organizations, Day Care, Domestic Violence, Family Planning, Family Services, Food/Clothing Distribution, Homes, People with Disabilities, Recreation & Athletics, Scouts, Senior Services, Shelters/Homelessness, Social Services-General, Substance Abuse, United Funds/United Ways, Volunteer Services, YMCA/YWCA/YMHA/YWHA, Youth Organizations

Application Procedures

Initial Contact: Applicants should send a preliminary letter addressed to Mr. Michael A. Cawley, President, summarizing the project for which a grant is requested.
Application Requirements: The proposal summary for public affairs should not exceed two pages and should contain information about the organization, the project for which the organization is seeking funds, and the specific request. If there is sufficient interest, the foundation will send the applicant a formal grant application. For primary areas of giving, the letter should contain background information about the requesting organization, specific details about the proposed project, and the amount needed. The foundation will then send application forms as needed.
Deadlines: March 1, June 1, September 1, and December 1.
Review Process: Notification of the trustees' decision is usually made within two weeks following the meeting.
Notes: Formal proposals received prior to review of the summary will not be considered.

Restrictions

Grants are not made to individuals. The foundation does not make loans.

Additional Information

Publications: Annual Report; Guidelines; Application Form

Foundation Officials

Elizabeth A. Aldridge: secretary
Ann Noble Brown: trustee
David R. Brown, MD: trustee
Michael A. Cawley: president B 1947. PRIM NONPR EMPL president, trustee: Samuel Roberts Noble Foundation Inc. CORP AFFIL director: Noble Affiliates Inc.
Vivian Noble DuBose: trustee
Patrick Jones: chief financial officer
Edward E. Noble: trustee B Ardmore, OK 1928. ED University of Oklahoma BS Geology (1951).
Maria Noble: trustee
Mary Jane Noble: trustee
Larry Pulliam: executive vice president B 1948.

Grants Analysis

Disclosure Period: fiscal year ending October 31, 2000
Total Grants: $17,554,773*
Number of Grants: 132
Average Grant: $76,564*
Highest Grant: $4,448,333
Lowest Grant: $1,800
Typical Range: $5,000 to $50,000 and $100,000 to $500,000
*Note: Average grant excludes three highest grants($1,000,000, $2,000,000, and $4,448,333).

Recent Grants

Note: Grants derived from 2000 Form 990.

General

4,448,333 University of Oklahoma Foundation, Inc., Norman, OK -- for Lloyd Noble Center renovation and expansion

2,100,000 Mercy Memorial Health Center, Ardmore, OK -- for diagnostic imaging equipment and lab improvements
1,000,000 Oklahoma Medical Research Foundation, Oklahoma City, OK -- for capital campaign
975,566 Oak Hall Episcopal School, Ardmore, OK -- for gymnasium construction and capital improvements
845,000 Oklahoma State University Foundation, Stillwater, OK -- for Bovine Respiratory Disease research
720,000 Heritage Foundation, Washington, DC -- operating support
510,495 Hardy Murphy Coliseum Authority, Ardmore, OK -- capital improvements
500,000 Whitefield Academy, Atlanta, GA -- for campus renovation
400,000 Central Oklahoma United Methodist Retirement Facility, Oklahoma City, OK -- for construction of an Alzheimer's Unit
400,000 University of Oklahoma Foundation, Inc., Norman, OK -- support President's Professors of Excellence Program

JAMES AND ELISE NOLAN CHARITABLE TRUST

Giving Contact

Judith A. Baker
PO Box 927
Wrangell, AK 99929
Phone: (907)874-2323
Fax: (907)874-7595

Description

Founded: 1992
EIN: 926021559
Organization Type: Private Foundation
Giving Locations: AK: Southeastern Alaska
Grant Types: General Support.

Financial Summary

Total Giving: $426,725 (2001); $307,297 (1999); $265,963 (1998)
Assets: $5,544,574 (2001); $6,138,161 (1999); $6,063,659 (1998)

Typical Recipients

Arts & Humanities: Arts Associations & Councils, Ethnic & Folk Arts, Arts & Humanities-General, Historic Preservation, History & Archaeology, Libraries, Museums/Galleries, Music, Public Broadcasting, Theater
Civic & Public Affairs: Chambers of Commerce, Clubs, Civic & Public Affairs-General, Native American Affairs, Parades/Festivals, Urban & Community Affairs
Education: Arts/Humanities Education, Business Education, Colleges & Universities, Literacy, Public Education (Precollege), Student Aid
Environment: Environment-General
Health: Children's Health/Hospitals, Clinics/Medical Centers, Emergency/Ambulance Services, Hospitals, Medical Research, Public Health, Transplant Networks/Donor Banks
Religion: Churches, Ministries, Religious Organizations, Religious Welfare
Social Services: Camps, Community Service Organizations, Recreation & Athletics, Scouts, Social Services-General, Substance Abuse, Veterans, Youth Organizations

Application Procedures

Initial Contact: Send a brief letter of inquiry.
Application Requirements: Include purpose of funds sought and proof of tax-exempt status.
Deadlines: None. Committee meets to award funds in early October.

Restrictions

Grants are not made to individuals.

Foundation Officials

Maribeth Conway: vice president, trustee
David L. Dobbs: trustee

Grants Analysis

Disclosure Period: calendar year ending 2001
Total Grants: $426,725
Number of Grants: 17
Average Grant: $7,643*
Highest Grant: $304,432
Lowest Grant: $300
Typical Range: $5,000 to $10,000
***Note:** Average grant figure excludes highest grant.

Recent Grants

Note: Grants derived from 2001 Form 990.

Library-Related

22,264	Friends of the Library, Wrangelle, AK -- for landscaping and exterior modifications
5,600	Irene Ingle Public Library, Wrangell, AK -- for computer purchases

General

20,000	Seventh Day Adventist Church, Wrangell, AK -- for camp renovation
18,000	St. Philip's Episcopal Church, Wrangell, AK -- for roof repairs
15,000	Wrangell Public Schools, Wrangell, AK -- for Scholarship Program
7,500	Wrangell Public Schools, Wrangell, AK -- for Southeast Alaska Art Festival
1,600	4-H Youth Shooting Program, Wrangell, AK
1,065	Wrangell Little League, Wrangell, AK -- for backstops
1,000	Discovery Southeast, Juneau, AK -- for Nature Studies Program
1,000	Wrangell Public Schools, Wrangell, AK -- for school libraries
500	KSTK Wrangell Radio Group, Wrangell, AK -- for performing arts promotion

NORCLIFFE FOUNDATION

Giving Contact

Dana Pigott, President
999 3rd Ave., Suite 1006
Seattle, WA 98104
Phone: (206)682-4820
E-mail: arline@thenorcliffefoundation.com
Web: http://www.thenorcliffefoundation.com

Description

Founded: 1952
EIN: 916029352
Organization Type: Private Foundation
Giving Locations: Pacific Northwest USA.
Grant Types: Capital, Conference/Seminar, Emergency, Endowment, General Support, Operating Expenses, Project, Seed Money.

Donor Information

Founder: the late Theiline M. McCone

Financial Summary

Total Giving: $4,622,820 (fiscal year ending November 30, 2002); $4,059,275 (fiscal 2000); $5,389,052 (fiscal 1999)
Giving Analysis: Giving for fiscal 2002 includes: foundation grants to United Way ($85,000); fiscal 2000: foundation grants to United Way ($85,000) fiscal 1999: foundation grants to United Way ($75,000)
Assets: $116,059,823 (fiscal 2002); $77,202,077 (fiscal 2000); $66,056,205 (fiscal 1999)

Gifts Received: $1,639,394 (fiscal 2002); $447,974 (fiscal 2000); $1,949,553 (fiscal 1999). Note: In fiscal 2002, contributions were received from Lee W. Rolfe ($26,000), Ann Wyckoff ($152,964), Mary Pigott ($65,480), Charles Pigott ($1,295,100), and Martha Wyckoff ($99,850). In fiscal 2000, contributions were received from Lee W. Rolfe ($45,000), Judy Pigott Swenson ($24,973), Mary Pigott ($65,250), Theiline P. Scheumann ($312,750). In fiscal 1999, contributions were received from James C. Pigott ($156,157), Ann P. Wyckoff ($1,699,563), and Lee W. Rolfe ($93,833). In fiscal 1999 contributions were received from James C. Pigott ($156,157), Ann P. Wyckoff ($1,699,563) and Lee W. Rlofe ($93.833). In fiscal 1996, contributions were received from James C. Pigott ($125,775), Ann P. Wyckoff ($290,875), T. Evans Wyckoff ($145,973), Lee W. Rolfe ($35,700), Susan Wyckoff Pohl ($7,073), Theiline P. Scheumann ($35,000), Martha W. Byrne ($144,300), Glen and Alison Milliman ($45,380), Charles M. Pigott ($581,714), and Wyco LP ($25,500).

Typical Recipients

Arts & Humanities: Ballet, Historic Preservation, History & Archaeology, Libraries, Museums/Galleries, Music, Opera, Performing Arts, Public Broadcasting, Theater
Civic & Public Affairs: Clubs, Community Foundations, Community Development, Economic Policy, Civic & Public Affairs-General, Housing, Rural Affairs, Urban & Community Affairs, Women's Affairs, Zoos/Aquariums
Education: Business Education, Colleges & Universities, Legal Education, Private Education (Precollege), Public Education (Precollege), Religious Education, Science/Mathematics Education, Secondary Education (Private), Special Education
Environment: Environment-General, Resource Conservation
Health: AIDS/HIV, Cancer, Children's Health/Hospitals, Clinics/Medical Centers, Emergency/Ambulance Services, Geriatric Health, Health Funds, Hospices, Hospitals, Medical Research, Mental Health, Nursing Services, Research/Studies Institutes, Single-Disease Health Associations
International: Health Care/Hospitals
Religion: Churches, Dioceses, Religion-General, Ministries, Religious Organizations, Religious Welfare
Science: Science Museums, Scientific Centers & Institutes
Social Services: Animal Protection, Child Welfare, Community Centers, Community Service Organizations, Family Services, Food/Clothing Distribution, Refugee Assistance, Senior Services, United Funds/United Ways, YMCA/YWCA/YMHA/YWHA, Youth Organizations

Application Procedures

Initial Contact: Send one copy of a letter proposal.
Application Requirements: Include a list of board members and proof of tax-exempt status.
Deadlines: None.

Restrictions

Areas of funding include capital campaigns, operating budgets, and special projects. Does not support individuals or deficit financing.

Additional Information

Publications: Program Policy Statement; Application Guidelines

Foundation Officials

Lisa Anderson: trustee
Theiline Cramer: trustee
Arline Hefferline: secretary
Mary Ellen Hughes: trustee
Dana Pigott: trustee
James C. Pigott: trustee B Seattle, WA 1936. ED Stanford University BCE (1959); Harvard University

Graduate School of Business Administration MBA (1963). PRIM CORP EMPL president: Pigott Enterprises. CORP AFFIL vice chairman: EK Williams & Co.; director: PACCAR; president, director: Norcliffe Co.; director: Northern Life Insurance Co.; director: Americold Corp.; president: Management Reports & Services. NONPR AFFIL chairman, trustee: Seattle University. CLUB AFFIL Bohemian Club; Rainier Club.
Mary P. Pigott: trust
Susan Wyckoff Pohl: trustee
Lee W. Rolfe: trustee
Theiline P. Scheumann: treasurer
Ann Pigott Wyckoff: president

Grants Analysis

Disclosure Period: fiscal year ending November 30, 2002
Total Grants: $4,537,820*
Number of Grants: 183
Average Grant: $20,893*
Highest Grant: $735,359
Lowest Grant: $100
Typical Range: $10,000 to $50,000
***Note:** Giving excludes United Way. Average grant figure excludes highest grant.

Recent Grants

Note: Grants derived from fiscal 2002 Form 990.

Library-Related

335,179	Seattle Public Library Foundation, Seattle, WA

General

735,359	Seattle University, Seattle, WA
366,510	Young Men's Christian Association of Seattle, Seattle, WA
335,179	Young Men's Christian Association of Seattle, Seattle, WA
306,400	University Preparatory Academy, Seattle, WA
166,666	Puget Sound Environmental Learning Center, Seattle, WA
151,545	Seattle Center Foundation, Seattle, WA
125,000	Fred Hutchinson Cancer Research Center, Seattle, WA
125,000	Overlake School, Seattle, WA
125,000	St. Luke Parish
113,236	Kindering Center, Belleevue, WA

NORCROSS WILDLIFE FOUNDATION

Giving Contact

Grants Administrator
PO Box 269
Wales, MA 01081-0269
Phone: (212)362-4831
Fax: (212)362-4783
Web: http://www.norcrossws.org
Note: Application address.

Alternate Contact

250 West 88th St.
Suite 806
New York, NY 10024
Phone: (212)362-4831
Fax: (212)362-4783
Note: Foundation headquarters.

Description

Founded: 1964
EIN: 132041622
Organization Type: Specialized/Single Purpose Foundation
Giving Locations: nationally.
Grant Types: General Support, Project.

Donor Information

Founder: The foundation was established in 1964 by Arthur D. Norcross and June Norcross Webster , both deceased.

Financial Summary

Total Giving: $1,869,461 (2001); $2,588,472 (2000); $1,724,098 (1999)
Assets: $67,553,653 (2001); $75,306,253 (2000); $80,643,346 (1999)
Gifts Received: $102,000 (2001); $28,534 (2000); $419,937 (1997). Note: In 2001, contributions were received from James & Diana Young. In 2000, contributions were received from the estate of A. Norcross. In 1997, contributions were received from the estate of A. Norcross and the New England Salmon Association.

Typical Recipients

Arts & Humanities: History & Archaeology, Museums/Galleries
Civic & Public Affairs: Botanical Gardens/Parks, Clubs, Community Foundations, Employment/Job Training, Gay/Lesbian Issues, Civic & Public Affairs-General, Hispanic Affairs, Municipalities/Towns, Native American Affairs, Nonprofit Management, Public Policy, Rural Affairs, Safety, Urban & Community Affairs, Zoos/Aquariums
Education: Agricultural Education, Arts/Humanities Education, Colleges & Universities, Environmental Education, Medical Education, Private Education (Precollege), School Volunteerism, Special Education
Environment: Air/Water Quality, Forestry, Environment-General, Resource Conservation, Watershed, Wildlife Protection
Health: AIDS/HIV, Children's Health/Hospitals, Clinics/Medical Centers, Emergency/Ambulance Services, Hospitals
International: International Development, International Environmental Issues, International Organizations
Religion: Religion-General, Jewish Causes, Religious Welfare
Science: Science Museums, Scientific Centers & Institutes, Scientific Labs, Scientific Organizations, Scientific Research
Social Services: Camps, Child Welfare, Community Service Organizations, Counseling, Crime Prevention, Family Services, Food/Clothing Distribution, Homes, People with Disabilities, Recreation & Athletics, Youth Organizations

Application Procedures

Initial Contact: Applicants should send a letter requesting application guidelines to Richard Reagan, PO Box 269, Wales, MA 01081.
Application Requirements: Grant proposals should be on the organization's letterhead, in letter form no longer than two pages (with an optional one-page budget breakdown), describing the organization's work/objectives and containing the request itself, with a specific funding amount. Fourteen copies must be submitted and one copy of the IRS tax determination letter.
Deadlines: None.
Review Process: Only those requests conforming to the foundation's guidelines will be accepted; others will be returned. Decisions are made approximately quarterly. Final notification will be made quarterly.
Notes: Applications will not be accepted without guidelines.

Restrictions

The foundation does not renew earlier grants, match other grantmakers' gifts, or fund research. It does not contribute to general operating budgets, cover salaries, personnel or other overhead items; nor does it make multiyear commitments of funds or contribute to endowments.

Applying organizations should not send annual reports, fancy brochures, abstracts, press releases, newspaper articles, or glowing testimonials. The foundation does not want proposals in impressive but useless binders. It requires that proposals are sent via regular First Class or Priority Mail only. Requests sent by certified or overnight express mail are a waste of money and will be refused/returned automatically. Requests sent via FAX will not be accepted.

Additional Information

The foundation offers programs in environmental education at the 5,000-acre Norcross Wildlife Sanctuary in Monson, MA. Call (413) 267-9654 for more information.
Publications: Application Guidelines

Foundation Officials

Fred C. Anderson: director
Warren Balgooyen: director
Joseph A. Catalano: secretary, director
Albia Dugger: director
Edward Gallagher: director
Arthur D. Norcross, Jr.: director
Karen Outlaw: director NONPR AFFIL controller: Robin Hood Foundation.
Michael Patrick: director
Richard Reagan: president, treasurer, director B 1940.
Chris Stresser: director
Ted Wilson: director

Grants Analysis

Disclosure Period: calendar year ending 2001
Total Grants: $1,869,461
Number of Grants: 272 (approx)
Average Grant: $6,873
Highest Grant: $55,000
Typical Range: $5,000 to $20,000

Recent Grants

Note: Grants derived from 2001 Form 990.

General

55,000	Town of Wales, Wales, MA -- unrestricted grant
25,000	Town of Monson, Monson, MA -- unrestricted grant
20,000	Berkshire Natural Resource Council, Stockbridge, MA -- help purchase 632-acre tract
20,000	Greater Worcester Community Foundation, Worcester, MA -- help purchase 300-acre tract
20,000	Green Mountain Club, Waterbury Center, VT -- purchase of Black Falls tract
20,000	Massachusetts Audubon Society, Lincoln, MA -- help to purchase the 86-acre Burt Farm
20,000	Natural Resources Defense Council, New York, NY -- upgrade communications network
20,000	Natural Resources Protective Association, Staten Island, NY -- purchase of underwater remote video equipment
20,000	Randolph Foundation, Hopewell, VA -- purchase and protect open land
20,000	Trust for Public Land, New York, NY -- for publishing a scientific resource about Western Staten Island

NORD FAMILY FOUNDATION

Giving Contact

Sharon White, Controller
347 Midway Boulevard, Suite 210
Elyria, OH 44035
Phone: (440)324-2822
Fax: (440)324-6427
E-mail: exedir@nordff.org
Web: http://www.nordff.org
Note: toll free (800)745-8946

Description

Founded: 1988
EIN: 341595929
Organization Type: General Purpose Foundation
Giving Locations: CO: Denver; OH: Cuyahoga County area, Lorain County area; SC: Columbia
Grant Types: Challenge, Endowment, General Support, Operating Expenses, Project.

Donor Information

Founder: The Nord Family Foundation, established in late 1988, is the successor to the Nordson Foundation, which was created as a trust by the late Walter G. Nord in 1952, and dissolved in October 1988. Mr. Nord believed that business has a social responsibility to the community from which it draws its human resources. To that end, the Nordson Corporation eventually began to designate five percent of its pre-tax domestic profits as its philanthropic commitment to the communities where it operated. Much of this commitment was fulfilled through annual contributions to the Nordson Foundation. Because of this relationship, the foundation often awarded grants with the corporation's interests in mind and adopted the corporation's geographic giving preferences as its own.

By the late 1980s, certain factors had emerged which resulted in a decision to dissolve the Nordson Foundation. IRS divestiture rules required the foundation, by the end of 1989, to phase out its ownership of a substantial number of Nordson Corporation shares bequeathed by Virginia Nord, the widow of Walter Nord. The divestiture resulted in large increases in assets and grant making, and by 1988 the foundation had become one of the ten largest private foundations in Ohio.

However, financial matters were not the only factors that influenced the decision to create a new foundation. If the foundation were to continue on the mission begun by Walter and Virginia Nord, it was felt that the foundation needed to begin nurturing a new generation of trustees. In addition, since the corporation had acquired new leadership, the time had come for it to establish its own direct grant-making program.

The result of these considerations was the creation of the Nord Family Foundation and Nordson Corporation Foundation, two new and separate entities to carry on the philanthropic traditions of Walter and Virginia Nord and the Nordson Corporation.

Financial Summary

Total Giving: $4,615,035 (2000); $4,512,505 (1999); $3,902,066 (1998)
Giving Analysis: Giving for 2000 includes: foundation matching gifts ($11,930); foundation scholarships ($27,500); 1999: foundation matching gifts ($17,574); foundation scholarships ($128,250); 1998: foundation grants to United Way ($37,232); foundation matching gifts ($50,000) foundation scholarships ($114,750)
Assets: $83,133,887 (2000); $89,861,567 (1999); $90,352,197 (1998)

Typical Recipients

Arts & Humanities: Arts Centers, Arts Outreach, Dance, History & Archaeology, Libraries, Museums/Galleries, Music, Opera, Performing Arts, Public Broadcasting, Theater, Visual Arts
Civic & Public Affairs: Botanical Gardens/Parks, Business/Free Enterprise, Civil Rights, Community Foundations, Economic Development, Economic Policy, Employment/Job Training, Civic & Public Affairs-General, Hispanic Affairs, Housing, Legal Aid, Minority Business, Municipalities/Towns, Native American Affairs, Philanthropic Organizations, Professional & Trade Associations, Public Policy, Urban & Community Affairs, Women's Affairs
Education: Afterschool/Enrichment Programs, Arts/Humanities Education, Colleges & Universities, Colleges & Universities, Community & Junior Colleges,

Education Associations, Education Funds, Education Reform, Education-General, Leadership Training, Minority Education, Private Education (Precollege), Public Education (Precollege), Social Sciences Education, Special Education, Student Aid

Environment: Air/Water Quality, Environment-General, Resource Conservation

Health: Adolescent Health Issues, Alzheimers Disease, Cancer, Children's Health/Hospitals, Clinics/Medical Centers, Emergency/Ambulance Services, Eyes/Blindness, Health-General, Health Organizations, Mental Health, Nursing Services, Public Health

Religion: Religion-General, Ministries, Religious Welfare

Science: Scientific Centers & Institutes

Social Services: At-Risk Youth, Big Brother/Big Sister, Big Brother/Big Sister, Child Abuse, Child Welfare, Community Centers, Community Service Organizations, Crime Prevention, Day Care, Domestic Violence, Family Planning, Family Services, Food/Clothing Distribution, Homes, People with Disabilities, Recreation & Athletics, Senior Services, Sexual Abuse, Social Services-General, United Funds/United Ways, Volunteer Services, YMHA/YWCA/YMHA/YWHA, Youth Organizations

Application Procedures

Initial Contact: The foundation does not currently use an application form. Only one copy of a proposal is required.

Application Requirements: Proposals should include a cover letter from the organization's chief executive director; one-page abstract of the proposal; detailed description of the project, including background information, statement of objectives, project budget, and plan for evaluating results; and a copy of the organization's IRS tax-exempt status letter. The application should also include a statement of the organization's purpose; list of current board members; and a copy of the organization's most recent financial statements.

Deadlines: Applications are due April 1 for a June decision, August 1 for an October decision, and December 1 for a February decision.

Review Process: Foundation trustees meet at least three times a year to review grant requests. These meetings are usually held in October, February, and June.

Restrictions

Endowment funds, debt reduction, and research projects are not within the foundation's areas of interest. In general, the foundation does not support capital campaigns unless the projects meet specific criteria. General support requests will be considered under certain conditions. The foundation does not fund advertising, tickets for fundraising activities, or individuals.

Additional Information

The staff of the Nord Family Foundation is available to answer questions or discuss problems concerning grant applications. The foundation maintains a library of reference materials and grant-writing tools and will assist potential applicants in the process of applying for a grant.

Publications: Annual Report; Guidelines

Foundation Officials

Randall Barbato: treasurer
Elizabeth Bausch: trustee
Sam Berk: secretary, trustee
John Clark: trustee
Brenda Grier-Miller: trustee
Joseph N. Ignat: president, trustee PRIM CORP EMPL vice president: Jergens Inc. CORP AFFIL vice president: Jergens Industries Supply; vice president: Tooling Components Division; vice president: ASG Division.
Pam Ignat: trustee

Emma Newby Mason: trustee B Bowling Green, OH 1937. ED Mercyhurst College BA (1959); Case Western Reserve University JD (1978). PRIM CORP EMPL senior vice president: Lorain National Bank. NONPR AFFIL member: Rotary International.
Cynthia W. Nord: vice president, trustee
Eric Thomas Nord: trustee B Amherst, OH November 08, 1917. ED Case Institute of Technology BS (1939). PRIM CORP EMPL chairman: Nordson Corp. NONPR AFFIL board trustee: Oberlin College.
Richard Nord: trustee
Shannon Nord: trustee

Grants Analysis

Disclosure Period: calendar year ending 2000
Total Grants: $4,603,105*
Number of Grants: 265
Average Grant: $17,370
Highest Grant: $125,000
Typical Range: $100 to $1,000 and $10,000 to $50,000
*Note: Giving excludes matching gifts.

Recent Grants

Note: Grants derived from 2000 Form 990.

Library-Related

33,750	Oberlin Public Library, Oberlin, OH

General

125,000	Center for Leadership in Education, Amherst, OH -- to create and articulate a vision for educational restructuring on a school-by-school basis in Lorain County
125,000	Center for Leadership in Education, Amherst, OH -- to create and articulate a vision for educational restructuring on a school-by-school basis in Lorain County
115,000	Center for Leadership in Education, Amherst, OH -- to create and articulate a vision for educational restructuring on a school-by-school basis in Lorain County
100,000	Lorain County Metro Parks, La Grange, OH -- support for construction of a regional aquatic center in Oberlin, Ohio
83,000	Linden School, Elyria, OH -- to purchase equipment and materials for use in new facility
71,797	South Carolina Campaign to Prevent Teen Pregnancy, Columbia, SC
70,000	Oberlin Early Childhood Center, Oberlin, OH -- in continued support of KIDSsmART, art program for young children
63,395	Oberlin Early Childhood Center, Oberlin, OH -- in continued support of KIDSsmART, art program for young children
60,000	Elyria United Methodist Village, Elyria, OH -- to support the construction of an intergenerational child daycare/community meeting facility in partnership with Linden School
55,000	Lorain Civic Center Committee, Inc, Lorain, OH -- for capital improvements

NORDSON CORP.

Company Headquarters

28601 Clements Rd.
Westlake, OH 44145
Web: http://www.nordson.com

Company Description

Founded: 1909
Ticker: NDSN
Exchange: NASDAQ
Revenue: US$647.8 million (2002)
Employees: 3572 (2002)
SIC(s): 3569 General Industrial Machinery Nec, 5084 Industrial Machinery & Equipment.

Operating Locations

Nordson Corp. (CA--Sand City; GA--Atlanta, Norcross; OH--Amherst, Elyria; WI--Menomonee, New Richmond)

Nonmonetary Support

Type: Donated Equipment; Donated Products; Loaned Employees
Volunteer Programs: Company operates the Time'n Talent (T'nT) program, which links employees with volunteer opportunities in the community and generates new community service projects.

Nordson Corp. Foundation

Giving Contact

Constance Haqq, Executive Director
28601 Clemens Road
Westlake, OH 44145-1148
Phone: (440)892-1580
Fax: (440)892-9507
E-mail: kladiner@nordson.com
Web: http://www.nordson.com/corporate/grants.html
Note: Contact for Northeastern Ohio requests.

Alternate Contact

Symone McClain, Community Relations Manager/Atlanta
Nordon Corp.
11475 Lakefield Drive
Duluth, GA 30097
Phone: (770)497-3661
E-mail: smcclain@nordson.com
Note: Contact for Greater Atlanta requests.

Description

EIN: 341596194
Organization Type: Corporate Foundation
Giving Locations: CA: San Diego County; GA: Atlanta; MA: Southeastern Massachusetts; OH; RI headquarters and operating communities.
Grant Types: Capital, Employee Matching Gifts, General Support, Project, Research.
Note: Employee matching gift ratio: 1 to 1 up to $5,000 annually per employee or retiree.

Financial Summary

Total Giving: $1,862,460 (fiscal year ending October 31, 2000); $2,000,000 (fiscal 1999 approx); $1,948,411 (fiscal 1998 approx). Note: Contributes through corporate direct giving program and foundation.
Giving Analysis: Giving for fiscal 2000 includes: foundation ($1,862,460)
Assets: $4,776,224 (fiscal 2000); $6,188,844 (fiscal 1997); $5,848,651 (fiscal 1996)
Gifts Received: $800,000 (fiscal 2000); $1,000,000 (fiscal 1997); $1,500,000 (fiscal 1995). Note: Contributions are received from Nordson Corp.

Typical Recipients

Arts & Humanities: Arts Centers, Arts Festivals, Arts Institutes, Arts Outreach, Community Arts, Ethnic & Folk Arts, Arts & Humanities-General, Historic Preservation, History & Archaeology, Libraries, Museums/Galleries, Music, Opera, Performing Arts, Public Broadcasting, Theater

Civic & Public Affairs: African American Affairs, Botanical Gardens/Parks, Business/Free Enterprise, Civil Rights, Community Foundations, Economic Development, Employment/Job Training, Civic & Public Affairs-General, Hispanic Affairs, Housing, Legal Aid, Municipalities/Towns, Native American Affairs, Nonprofit Management, Professional & Trade Associations, Public Policy, Urban & Community Affairs, Zoos/Aquariums

Education: Arts/Humanities Education, Business Education, Colleges & Universities, Community & Junior

Colleges, Education Associations, Education Funds, Education Reform, Elementary Education (Public), Engineering/Technological Education, Education-General, International Studies, Leadership Training, Literacy, Medical Education, Minority Education, Preschool Education, Private Education (Precollege), Public Education (Precollege), Science/Mathematics Education, Secondary Education (Public), Social Sciences Education, Student Aid, Vocational & Technical Education

Environment: Environment-General

Health: Clinics/Medical Centers, Emergency/Ambulance Services, Hospices, Medical Research, Mental Health, Nursing Services, Single-Disease Health Associations, Speech & Hearing

International: International Relations

Religion: Churches, Religion-General, Ministries, Religious Welfare

Science: Science Exhibits & Fairs, Science Museums, Scientific Centers & Institutes

Social Services: At-Risk Youth, Big Brother/Big Sister, Child Welfare, Community Centers, Community Service Organizations, Counseling, Crime Prevention, Day Care, Delinquency & Criminal Rehabilitation, Domestic Violence, Family Services, Food/Clothing Distribution, Homes, People with Disabilities, Recreation & Athletics, Scouts, Senior Services, Substance Abuse, United Funds/United Ways, Volunteer Services, YMCA/YWCA/YMHA/YWHA, Youth Organizations

Application Procedures

Initial Contact: Write to request application from foundation staff in Westlake, OH, Atlanta, GA, or Monterey, CA, or obtain the application from the foundation's web site.

Application Requirements: Send an original and one copy of the completed application form, a copy of current 501(c)(3) form and a list of organization's officers and trustees, with affiliations.

Deadlines: November 15 for review in January, February 15 for review in April, May 15 for July and August 15 for review in October.

Review Process: The foundation board of trustees reviews written applications at quarterly meetings in January, April, July, and October.

Evaluative Criteria: Geographic location and constituency served; special interest in disadvantaged persons, minorities, the handicapped, and projects which attack root causes of problems.

Decision Notification: Applicants are notified of the trustees' funding decisions in writing.

Notes: The foundation encourages potential applicants to contact a foundation staff member prior to submitting an application to ensure that a grant request falls within the foundation's priorities.

Additional Information

Approximately 5% of pretax profit is budgeted for charitable contributions.

On October 31, 1988, approximately $51 million in foundation assets were transferred to the Nord Family Foundation. The Nordson Foundation (EIN: 34-6539234) was liquidated and transferred $1.5 million to a newly established Nordson Corporation Foundation (EIN: 34-1596194) that continues to support charitable causes located in Nordson Corp. manufacturing cities. manufacturing cities. manufacturing cities. manufacturing cities.

Publications: Contributions Report to the Community

Corporate Officials

Christian C. Bernadotte: vice president B 1949. PRIM CORP EMPL vice president: Nordson Corp.

Foundation Officials

Christian C. Bernadotte: vice president (see above)
Constance T. Haqq: executive director
John E. Jackson: trustee B Eagle Pass, TX 1945. ED United States Air Force Academy BS (1967); Harvard

University Graduate School of Business Administration MBA (1973). PRIM CORP EMPL senior vice president: Nordson Corp.

Grants Analysis

Disclosure Period: fiscal year ending October 31, 2000
Total Grants: $1,862,460*
Number of Grants: 170
Average Grant: $10,956
Highest Grant: $250,000
Lowest Grant: $750
Typical Range: $1,000 to $25,000
*Note: Giving excludes corporate direct giving. Grants analysis provided by foundation.

Recent Grants

Note: Grants derived from 2000 Form 990.

Library-Related
15,000   Oberlin Public Library, Oberlin, OH

General
250,000   Center for Leadership in Education, Amherst, OH
125,000   Cleveland Opera, Cleveland, OH
121,000   Playhouse Square Foundation, Cleveland, OH
60,000   Lorain County Community College, Elyria, OH
50,000   Cleveland Clinic Foundation, Cleveland, OH
50,000   Lorain Palace Civic Center, Lorain, OH
39,000   Ohio Foundation of Independent Colleges, Columbus, OH
37,500   Cleveland Advanced Manufacturing Program (CAMP), Cleveland, OH
30,000   El Centro de Servicios Sociales, Lorain, OH
30,000   Lorain County Urban League, Elyria, OH

NORFOLK SHIPBUILDING & DRYDOCK CORP.

Company Headquarters

750 W. Berkley Ave.
Norfolk, VA 23523

Company Description

Employees: 2,000
SIC(s): 3731 Ship Building & Repairing.

Norfolk Shipbuilding and Drydock Corp. Charitable Trust

Giving Contact

Norfolk Shipbuilding and Drydock Corp. Charitable Trust
Bank of America
PO Box 2100
Norfolk, VA 23501
Phone: (804)788-2067

Description

EIN: 546036745
Organization Type: Corporate Foundation
Giving Locations: headquarters and operating communities.
Grant Types: Capital, General Support, Multiyear/Continuing Support.

Financial Summary

Total Giving: $32,000 (2000); $23,000 (1999); $44,550 (1998)
Giving Analysis: Giving for 1999 includes: foundation ($23,000)
Assets: $526,828 (2000); $539,741 (1999); $527,173 (1998)
Gifts Received: $58 (1999); $1,453 (1995); $200,144 (1992). Note: In 1992, major contributions were received from Norfolk Shipbuilding & Drydock Corp. ($200,000).

Typical Recipients

Arts & Humanities: Arts Associations & Councils, Arts Centers, Arts Funds, Arts & Humanities-General, Historic Preservation, History & Archaeology, Libraries, Museums/Galleries, Music, Opera, Public Broadcasting

Civic & Public Affairs: African American Affairs, Business/Free Enterprise, Civic & Public Affairs-General, Professional & Trade Associations, Urban & Community Affairs, Zoos/Aquariums

Education: Business Education, Colleges & Universities, Community & Junior Colleges, Economic Education, Education Associations, Education Funds, Medical Education, Minority Education, Private Education (Precollege), Student Aid

Environment: Air/Water Quality, Resource Conservation

Health: Children's Health/Hospitals, Emergency/Ambulance Services, Health-General, Health Organizations, Hospitals

Science: Science Exhibits & Fairs, Scientific Centers & Institutes, Scientific Organizations

Social Services: Child Welfare, Community Service Organizations, Emergency Relief, Social Services-General, United Funds/United Ways

Application Procedures

Initial Contact: Send a brief letter of inquiry.
Deadlines: None.

Additional Information

Trust(s): Bank of America

Corporate Officials

Thomas J. Bradburn: chief executive officer, president chief operating officer, secretary, director PRIM CORP EMPL chief executive officer, president: Norfolk Shipbuilding & Drydock Corp.

William Peavy Fricks: chairman, chief executive officer B Byron, GA 1944. ED Auburn University BS (1966); College of William & Mary MBA (1970). PRIM CORP EMPL chairman, chief executive officer: Newport News Shipbuilding, Inc.

John L. Roper, IV: executive vice president, chief operating officer, secretary, director B Norfolk, VA 1953. ED Hampden-Sydney College (1975). PRIM CORP EMPL executive vice president, chief operating officer, secretary, director: Norfolk Shipbuilding & Drydock Corp. CORP AFFIL secretary, treasurer, director: Marepcon Corp. International; director: John L. Roper Corp.; director: Lonsdale Corp.

John Lonsdale Roper, III: president, chief executive officer, director B Norfolk, VA 1927. ED University of Virginia BSME (1949); Massachusetts Institute of Technology BS (1951). PRIM CORP EMPL president, chief executive officer, director: Norfolk Shipbuilding & Drydock Corp. NONPR AFFIL director, member executive committee: Shipbuilders Council America; member: Society Naval Architects & Marine Engineers; president, director: Marepcon Corp. International; president, director: John L Roper Corp.; director: Flagship Group Ltd; president, director: Lonsdale Corp.; director: American Bureau Shipping; director: Cruise International.

Grants Analysis

Disclosure Period: calendar year ending 2000
Total Grants: $32,000
Number of Grants: 5
Highest Grant: $10,000
Lowest Grant: $1,000

Recent Grants

Note: Grants derived from 2001 Form 990.

General

10,000	Mariner's Museum, Newport News, VA
10,000	Virginia Opera Association, Norfolk, VA
6,800	Wisconsin Foundation, Madison, WI
2,000	Chrysler Museum, Norfolk, VA
2,000	Virginia Foundation for Independent Colleges, Richmond, VA
1,000	Coastal Conservation Association, Houston, TX
1,000	Virginia College Fund, Richmond, VA

CARL A. NORGREN FOUNDATION

Giving Contact

Leigh H. Norgren, President, Treasurer & Trustee
2696 S. Colorado Blvd., No. 585-4
Denver, CO 80222
Phone: (303)758-8393

Description

Founded: 1951
EIN: 846034195
Organization Type: Private Foundation
Giving Locations: CO: Denver
Grant Types: Capital, General Support.

Donor Information

Founder: the late Carl A. Norgren, Juliet E. Norgren, C.A. Norgren Co.

Financial Summary

Total Giving: $32,202 (1998); $132,115 (1996); $135,600 (1995)
Assets: $3,318,370 (1996); $3,191,847 (1995); $2,731,599 (1994)

Typical Recipients

Arts & Humanities: Historic Preservation, Libraries, Museums/Galleries, Music, Opera, Public Broadcasting
Civic & Public Affairs: Civic & Public Affairs-General, Philanthropic Organizations, Professional & Trade Associations, Rural Affairs, Zoos/Aquariums
Education: Agricultural Education, Colleges & Universities, Environmental Education, Education-General, Minority Education, Private Education (Precollege)
Environment: Environment-General
Health: Cancer, Children's Health/Hospitals, Clinics/Medical Centers, Health Organizations, Hospitals, Medical Rehabilitation, Medical Research, Public Health, Research/Studies Institutes, Single-Disease Health Associations
Religion: Churches, Ministries, Missionary Activities (Domestic)
Science: Science Museums
Social Services: Child Welfare, Community Service Organizations, Family Planning, Family Services, Food/Clothing Distribution, People with Disabilities, Recreation & Athletics, Scouts, Shelters/Homelessness, United Funds/United Ways, Volunteer Services, Youth Organizations

Application Procedures

Initial Contact: Send a brief outline of the program or project with sufficient detail to evaluate the proposal. Include the name, address, and phone number of the organization, proof of tax-exempt status, date of establishment and a brief history, purpose of funds sought, amount requested, and recently audited financial statement.
Deadlines: None.

Additional Information

The foundation reported it dissolved in 1998. All assets were distributed between the Denver Zoological Foundation ($10,000) and the Sewall Rehabilitation Center Foundation ($22,202). The Sewall Rehabilitation Center Foundation received the majority of all assets.
Publications: Annual Report (including Application Guidelines)

Foundation Officials

Gene N. Koelbel: vice president, trustee
Donald K. Norgren: trustee
Leigh H. Norgren: president, treasurer, trustee
Vanda N. Werner: secretary, trustee

Grants Analysis

Disclosure Period: calendar year ending 1998
Total Grants: $32,202
Number of Grants: 2
Highest Grant: $22,202
Typical Range: $500 to $5,000

Recent Grants

Note: Grants derived from 1998 Form 990.

General

22,202	Sewall Rehabilitation Center Foundation, Englewood, CO
10,000	Denver Zoological Foundation City Park, Denver, CO

NORMAN FOUNDATION

Giving Contact

June Makela, Program Director
147 East 48th Street
New York, NY 10017
Phone: (212)230-9830
Fax: (212)230-9849
E-mail: info@normanfdn.org
Web: http://www.normanfdn.org

Description

Founded: 1938
EIN: 131862694
Organization Type: General Purpose Foundation
Giving Locations: nationally.
Grant Types: General Support.

Donor Information

Founder: The Norman Foundation was created in 1935 by the late Aaron E. Norman , and has since been augmented by his children and grandchildren. The original name of the foundation was the Assistance Fund, which in 1943 was changed to the Aaron E. Norman Fund, and then to the current name in 1970. Today, its members and directors include the descendants of Aaron E. Norman and their spouses.

Financial Summary

Total Giving: $1,065,050 (2002); $1,115,311 (2001); $1,965,500 (1999)
Assets: $22,484,170 (2002); $23,016,587 (2001); $33,377,779 (1998)
Gifts Received: $5,000 (1995). Note: Contributions were received from Dorothy Norman.

Typical Recipients

Arts & Humanities: Arts Associations & Councils, Arts Centers, Arts & Humanities-General, Museums/Galleries, Public Broadcasting
Civic & Public Affairs: African American Affairs, Asian American Affairs, Botanical Gardens/Parks, Business/Free Enterprise, Civil Rights, Community Foundations, Economic Development, Economic Policy, Employment/Job Training, First Amendment Issues, Gay/Lesbian Issues, Civic & Public Affairs-General, Hispanic Affairs, Housing, Law & Justice, Legal Aid, Minority Business, Native American Affairs, Nonprofit Management, Philanthropic Organizations, Professional & Trade Associations, Public Policy, Rural Affairs, Safety, Urban & Community Affairs, Women's Affairs
Education: Colleges & Universities, Education Funds, Education Reform, Education-General, International Studies, Leadership Training, Private Education (Precollege)
Environment: Air/Water Quality, Environment-General, Protection, Resource Conservation
Health: AIDS/HIV, Children's Health/Hospitals, Health Policy/Cost Containment, Hospices, Medical Research, Mental Health, Public Health
International: Health Care/Hospitals, Human Rights, International Affairs, International Development, International Environmental Issues
Religion: Churches, Religious Welfare, Social/Policy Issues
Social Services: Animal Protection, Child Welfare, Community Service Organizations, Counseling, Crime Prevention, Day Care, Domestic Violence, Family Planning, Family Services, Food/Clothing Distribution, People with Disabilities, Recreation & Athletics, Refugee Assistance, Shelters/Homelessness, Special Olympics, Youth Organizations

Application Procedures

Initial Contact: The foundation has no standard application form. Prospective grantees are encouraged to initiate the process by sending a brief letter of inquiry to the Program Director. The foundation does accept the New York Area Common Application Form. The foundation actively seeks letters of inquiry from new organizations that may lack previous fundraising experience.
Application Requirements: An initial inquiry should explain the scope and significance of the problem to be addressed; the organization's proposed response and (if appropriate) how this strategy builds upon the organization's past work; the specific, demonstrable effects the project would have if successful; and how the project promotes systemic change and otherwise relates to the foundation's philosophy. If the proposal is deemed promising, the organization would be encouraged to submit a full proposal which should include detailed organization and project budgets, including a breakdown of cur rent and prospective income from foundations and other sources; background on project staff; a descriptive list of board members; a letter of support; and documentation of tax-exempt status.
Deadlines: Applications may be submitted any time.
Review Process: The foundation acknowledges receipt of proposals by postcard or letter. The committee meets at least three times a year.

Restrictions

The foundation only makes grants to tax-exempt organizations that focus on domestic issues. Grants are never made to individuals, universities or to support conferences, scholarships, research, cultural films, media and arts projects, direct social service delivery programs, capital funding projects, fund-raising drives or other grant-making organizations.

Additional Information

Publications: Annual Report; Grant Guidelines

Foundation Officials

Melissa Bunnen: director, treasurer
Robert L. Bunnen, Jr.: director
Alice Franklin: director, vice president
Andrew D. Franklin: director

Grants Analysis

Disclosure Period: calendar year ending 2002
Total Grants: $1,065,050
Number of Grants: 48
Average Grant: $22,189
Highest Grant: $25,000
Lowest Grant: $15,000
Typical Range: $15,000 to $25,000

Recent Grants

Note: Grants derived from 2000 Form 990.

General

25,000	Hobart College, Geneva, NY -- educational college
15,000	Kentucky Horse Park Foundation, Lexington, KY -- community service
11,000	Los Angeles Alliance for a New Economy, Los Angeles, CA -- public education
10,000	Milton Academy, Milton, MA -- capital campaign
6,500	Lovett School, Atlanta, GA -- educational activities
5,000	Creative Time, New York, NY -- arts education
5,000	Maret School, Washington, DC -- educational activities
5,000	Washington Tennis and Education Foundation, Washington, DC -- community service
3,000	Hurricane Island Outward Bound School, Rockland, ME -- educational activities
2,500	Atlanta Women's Foundation, Atlanta, GA -- community service

SUMMERS A. NORMAN FOUNDATION

Giving Contact

Gordon Thrall, Trustee
Summers A. Norman Foundation
215 E. Commerce
Jacksonville, TX 75766
Phone: (903)586-3641

Description

Founded: 1989
EIN: 752249004
Organization Type: Private Foundation
Giving Locations: TX
Grant Types: General Support.

Donor Information

Founder: Established in 1989 by the late Mary Nell Norman.

Financial Summary

Total Giving: $602,025 (1998); $146,968 (1996); $231,031 (1995)
Assets: $671,840 (1998); $1,396,137 (1996); $1,436,896 (1995)

Typical Recipients

Arts & Humanities: Libraries, Museums/Galleries, Music, Public Broadcasting, Theater
Civic & Public Affairs: Botanical Gardens/Parks, Chambers of Commerce, Clubs, Economic Development, Civic & Public Affairs-General, Municipalities/Towns, Native American Affairs, Safety
Education: Arts/Humanities Education, Colleges & Universities, Education-General, Literacy, Private Education (Precollege), Public Education (Precollege), Science/Mathematics Education, Student Aid
Health: Emergency/Ambulance Services, Hospitals, Medical Research, Single-Disease Health Associations
Religion: Churches, Dioceses, Religion-General, Religious Welfare, Seminaries
Science: Science-General
Social Services: Animal Protection, Community Service Organizations, Counseling, Crime Prevention, Food/Clothing Distribution, Homes, Recreation & Athletics, Scouts, United Funds/United Ways, Youth Organizations

Application Procedures

Initial Contact: Applications must be in writing stating clearly the purpose of funds sought.
Deadlines: None.

Foundation Officials

Crawford Godfrey: trustee
Jimmy Staton: trustee
Gordon Thrall: trustee
Evelyn Underhill: trustee

Grants Analysis

Disclosure Period: calendar year ending 1998
Total Grants: $602,025
Number of Grants: 25
Average Grant: $12,584*
Highest Grant: $300,000
Typical Range: $100 to $25,000
*Note: Average grant figure excludes highest grant.

Recent Grants

Note: Grants derived from 1998 Form 990.

Library-Related

170,000	Jacksonville College, Jacksonville, TX -- library

General

300,000	Nan Travis Foundation, Jacksonville, TX -- ICU unit
48,000	Baptist Theological Seminary, Jacksonville, TX -- endowment fund
23,000	Lon Morris College, Jacksonville, TX -- Alumni Center
10,000	Brookdale Hill School, Bullard, TX -- classroom
5,000	Bullard Fire Department, Bullard, TX
5,000	Cherokee County, Jacksonville, TX -- Lake Palestine VFD
5,000	Jacksonville Independent School District, Jacksonville, TX -- Athletic Booster Club
5,000	Jacksonville Independent School District, Jacksonville, TX -- Adopt-A-School Program
5,000	Jacksonville Independent School District, Jacksonville, TX -- middle school tennis court
5,000	Jacksonville Literacy Council, Jacksonville, TX

NORMANDIE FOUNDATION

Giving Contact

Andrew E. Norman, President & Treasurer
147 E. 48th St.
New York, NY 10017
Phone: (212)230-9800

Description

Founded: 1966
EIN: 136213564
Organization Type: Private Foundation
Giving Locations: MA: Barnstable County; NY: Rockland County, New York
Grant Types: General Support.

Donor Information

Founder: Andrew E. Norman, the Aaron E. Norman Fund

Financial Summary

Total Giving: $293,583 (2001); $190,317 (1999); $51,285 (1996)
Giving Analysis: Giving for 2001 includes: foundation grants to United Way ($2,500) 1999: foundation grants to United Way ($1,500)
Assets: $6,294,456 (2001); $4,937,423 (1999); $3,053,831 (1996)
Gifts Received: $30,102 (2001); $309,068 (1999); $298,500 (1994). Note: In 2001, contributions were received from Margaret Norman ($21,634) and Abigail Norman ($8,468). In 1999, contributions were received from Andrew E. Norman and Margaret Norman.

Typical Recipients

Arts & Humanities: Arts Centers, Community Arts, History & Archaeology, Libraries, Museums/Galleries, Performing Arts, Public Broadcasting
Civic & Public Affairs: African American Affairs, Civil Rights, Civic & Public Affairs-General, Legal Aid, Parades/Festivals, Philanthropic Organizations, Public Policy, Urban & Community Affairs
Education: Arts/Humanities Education, Colleges & Universities, Education Funds, Legal Education, Medical Education, Minority Education
Environment: Air/Water Quality, Environment-General, Resource Conservation
Health: AIDS/HIV, Hospices, Hospitals
International: Foreign Educational Institutions, Human Rights, International Affairs, International Development, International Environmental Issues, International Organizations, International Peace & Security Issues, International Relations, International Relief Efforts
Religion: Religion-General, Religious Welfare, Seminaries
Science: Science Museums, Scientific Centers & Institutes, Scientific Labs, Scientific Research
Social Services: At-Risk Youth, Child Welfare, Community Service Organizations, Emergency Relief, Family Planning, Food/Clothing Distribution, Recreation & Athletics, Social Services-General, Substance Abuse, United Funds/United Ways, Volunteer Services, Youth Organizations

Application Procedures

Initial Contact: Send a brief letter of inquiry.
Application Requirements: Include description of proposals and proof of tax-exempt status.
Deadlines: None.

Foundation Officials

Nancy Norman Lassalle: vice president, secretary
Andrew E. Norman: president, treasurer B New York, NY 1930. ED Harvard University BA (1951); Harvard University JD (1954).

Grants Analysis

Disclosure Period: calendar year ending 2001
Total Grants: $291,083*
Number of Grants: 62
Average Grant: $2,768*
Highest Grant: $75,000
Lowest Grant: $65
Typical Range: $1,000 to $5,000
*Note: Giving excludes United Way. Average grant figure excludes two highest grants ($125,000).

Recent Grants

Note: Grants derived from 2001 Form 990.

General

75,000	International Rescue Committee, New York, NY
50,000	Africa Action, Washington, DC
25,250	ACLU Foundation, New York, NY
25,000	Africa Fund, New York, NY
20,000	Vanguard Foundation, San Francisco, CA
16,600	Somerville Haitian Coalition, Somerville, MA
15,000	Vanguard Foundation, San Francisco, CA
10,000	Government Accountability Project, Washington, DC
10,000	International Society for Ecology and Culture, Berkeley, CA
10,000	Neighbor to Neighbor Education Fund, CA

DELLORA A. AND LESTER J. NORRIS FOUNDATION

Giving Contact

Eugene W. Butler, Treasurer
303 E. Main Street
PO Box 4325
St. Charles, IL 60174
Phone: (630)584-2500
Fax: (630)584-1020

Description

Founded: 1979
EIN: 363054939
Organization Type: Family Foundation
Giving Locations: CO; FL; IL: nationally.
Grant Types: General Support.

Donor Information

Founder: The foundation was established in 1979 in Illinois by the late Dellora A. Norris and Lester J. Norris.

Financial Summary

Total Giving: $2,000,000 (2002 approx); $2,448,000 (2001); $2,498,250 (2000)
Giving Analysis: Giving for 2000 includes: foundation grants to United Way ($5,000) 1997: foundation grants to United Way ($5,000)
Assets: $37,464,674 (2001); $43,482,962 (2000); $43,332,236 (1998)
Gifts Received: $967,549 (1997); $1,290,066 (1993); $645,033 (1992). Note: Contributions were received from the estate of Lester J. Norris.

Typical Recipients

Arts & Humanities: Arts Centers, Arts Festivals, Ethnic & Folk Arts, History & Archaeology, Libraries, Museums/Galleries, Music, Opera

Civic & Public Affairs: Botanical Gardens/Parks, Clubs, Community Foundations, Economic Development, Civic & Public Affairs-General, Municipalities/ Towns, Parades/Festivals, Philanthropic Organizations, Professional & Trade Associations, Urban & Community Affairs, Women's Affairs, Zoos/ Aquariums

Education: Business Education, Colleges & Universities, Private Education (Precollege), Public Education (Precollege), Science/Mathematics Education, Secondary Education (Private), Secondary Education (Public), Special Education, Student Aid

Health: AIDS/HIV, Cancer, Children's Health/Hospitals, Clinics/Medical Centers, Diabetes, Health Funds, Health Organizations, Heart, Hospices, Hospitals, Medical Rehabilitation, Medical Research, Mental Health, Public Health, Respiratory, Single-Disease Health Associations

International: International-General

Religion: Churches, Religion-General, Religious Organizations, Religious Welfare

Social Services: Child Welfare, Community Centers, Crime Prevention, Day Care, Emergency Relief, Family Services, Food/Clothing Distribution, People with Disabilities, Recreation & Athletics, Scouts, Senior Services, Substance Abuse, United Funds/United Ways, YMCA/YWCA/YMHA/YWHA, Youth Organizations

Application Procedures

Initial Contact: Submit a preliminary letter to the foundation.
Deadlines: None. Applications are accepted throughout the year.

Foundation Officials

Eugene W. Butler: treasurer B 1932. PRIM CORP EMPL chairman: Harris Bank Batavia National Association. CORP AFFIL chairman, president: Harris Bank Saint Charles; director: Cedric Spring Associates.
George N. Gaynor: vice president
John D. Norris: director
Robert C. Norris: chairman
Joann N. Pace: president
Howard S. Tuthill, III: secretary B Mount Vernon, NY 1947. PRIM CORP EMPL partner: Kelley, Drye & Warren.

Grants Analysis

Disclosure Period: calendar year ending 2001
Total Grants: $2,443,000*
Number of Grants: 105
Average Grant: $23,267
Highest Grant: $250,000
Lowest Grant: $1,000
Typical Range: $10,000 to $40,000
*Note: Giving excludes United Way.

Recent Grants

Note: Grants derived from 2001 Form 990.

General

250,000	Seacrest Country Day School
100,000	International College, Naples, FL
100,000	Northwestern University, Evanston, IL
100,000	YMCA of Collier County, Naples, FL
75,000	Denver Zoological Society, Denver, CO
75,000	Kent Denver School, Englewood, CO
75,000	St. Anne's Episcopal School, Denver, CO
75,000	St. Ignatius College Preparatory, Chicago, IL
75,000	St. Matthew's House
55,000	Naples Botanical Garden, Naples, FL

KENNETH T. AND EILEEN L. NORRIS FOUNDATION

Giving Contact

Ronald R. Barnes, Executive Director & Trustee
11 Golden Shore, Suite 450
Long Beach, CA 90802
Phone: (562)435-8444
Fax: (562)436-0584
E-mail: gerringer@ktn.org
Web: http://www.norrisfoundation.org

Description

Founded: 1963
EIN: 956080374
Organization Type: General Purpose Foundation
Giving Locations: CA: Los Angeles County area
Grant Types: Capital, Endowment, General Support, Matching, Multiyear/Continuing Support, Operating Expenses, Professorship, Project, Research, Scholarship.

Donor Information

Founder: The late Kenneth T. Norris and his late wife, Eileen Norris , established the foundation in 1963. Mr. Norris was the founder, chairman of the board, and president of Norris Industries in Los Angeles. He had a great interest in supporting the Los Angeles area community. His special focus was in academic achievement and research.

Financial Summary

Total Giving: $9,121,291 (fiscal year ending November 30, 2001); $8,682,688 (fiscal 2000); $7,380,690 (fiscal 1999)
Assets: $198,488,135 (fiscal 2000); $213,169,771 (fiscal 1999); $213,169,771 (fiscal 1998)
Gifts Received: $139,378 (fiscal 1993); $190,000 (fiscal 1992 approx)

Typical Recipients

Arts & Humanities: Arts Associations & Councils, Arts Centers, Arts Institutes, Community Arts, Film & Video, Libraries, Museums/Galleries, Music, Performing Arts, Public Broadcasting, Theater

Civic & Public Affairs: African American Affairs, Botanical Gardens/Parks, Employment/Job Training, Civic & Public Affairs-General, Hispanic Affairs, Public Policy

Education: Arts/Humanities Education, Colleges & Universities, Engineering/Technological Education, Education-General, Health & Physical Education, Medical Education, Private Education (Precollege), Public Education (Precollege), Science/Mathematics Education, Secondary Education (Private), Special Education, Vocational & Technical Education

Health: AIDS/HIV, Alzheimers Disease, Cancer, Children's Health/Hospitals, Clinics/Medical Centers, Diabetes, Emergency/Ambulance Services, Eyes/Blindness, Health Organizations, Heart, Hospices, Hospitals, Kidney, Medical Rehabilitation, Medical Research, Research/Studies Institutes, Respiratory, Single-Disease Health Associations, Speech & Hearing, Trauma Treatment

International: Health Care/Hospitals, International Relief Efforts

Religion: Religious Welfare

Science: Science Museums, Scientific Centers & Institutes, Scientific Organizations

Social Services: At-Risk Youth, Child Welfare, Community Service Organizations, Crime Prevention, Day Care, Emergency Relief, Family Planning, Family Services, Food/Clothing Distribution, People with Disabilities, Recreation & Athletics, Shelters/Homelessness, Social Services-General, Substance Abuse, Volunteer Services, YMCA/YWCA/YMHA/ YWHA, Youth Organizations

Application Procedures

Initial Contact: Organizations should request the application guidelines.

Application Requirements: A full proposal must include the history and goals of the organization, a project description, the action plan and expected outcomes of the project, a list of other contributors to the project, most recent audited financial statements, proof of 501(c)(3) tax-exempt status, the percentage of revenues coming from federal, state, and local governments, a list of current directors, the foundation's Grant Application form, and any additional information about the project.

Deadlines: Applications accepted from November 1 through February 15 for Medicine grants; February 15 through May 31 for Education/Science and Youth grants; and from April 1 though June 30 for Community and Cultural grants.

Decision Notification: The foundation responds within four months of the application deadline.

Restrictions

The foundation does not fund political organizations/campaigns, foreign organizations, or individuals.

Additional Information

Due to funding limitations, the trustees prefer to initiate the grants given.

The Norris Foundation provides continuous funding for many organizations, and because of this, few new programs are added to the budget each year.

The foundation provides accounting services and investment advice to nonprofits.

Publications: Annual Report; Grant Qualifications; Guidelines; Application Form

Foundation Officials

William G. Corey, MD: medical advisor, trustee
Lisa D. Hansen: trustee
Bradley K. Norris: trustee
Harlyne J. Norris: medical advisory, trustee
Walter J. Zanino: controller, trustee

Grants Analysis

Disclosure Period: fiscal year ending November 30, 2001
Total Grants: $9,121,291*
Number of Grants: 249
Average Grant: $36,632
Highest Grant: $500,000
Lowest Grant: $2,000
Typical Range: $2,000 to $500,000
*Note: Grants analysis provided by foundation.

Recent Grants

Note: Grants derived from fiscal 2001 Form 990.

General

2,145,000	Norris Cancer Center, Los Angeles, CA
500,000	California Institute of Technology, Pasadena, CA
400,000	Huntington, San Marino, CA
400,000	Keck Graduate Institute of Applied Life Sciences, Claremont, CA
205,000	September 11th Fund, New York, NY
200,000	Accelerated School, Los Angeles, CA
174,000	Children's Hospital of Los Angeles, Los Angeles, CA
174,000	Children's Hospital of Los Angeles, Los Angeles, CA
150,000	Las Floristas, San Marino, CA
150,000	Norris Center for the Performing Arts, Rolling Hills Estates, CA

NORTH AMERICAN ROYALTIES

Company Headquarters

2800 Broad St.
Chattanooga, TN 37408

Company Description

Chap. 11 Reorg. Bankruptcy (2001).
Employees: 1,760
SIC(s): 1311 Crude Petroleum & Natural Gas.

North American Royalties Foundation

Giving Contact

Directory Human Resources
1418 Winding Way
Chattanooga, TN 37405
Phone: (423)265-0295

Description

EIN: 626052490
Organization Type: Corporate Foundation
Giving Locations: TN: Chattanooga
Grant Types: General Support, Scholarship.

Financial Summary

Total Giving: $91,633 (2001); $164,000 (2000); $166,785 (1999)
Giving Analysis: Giving for 2000 includes: foundation grants to United Way ($40,000); foundation scholarships ($44,000); foundation ($80,000); 1998: foundation grants to United Way ($50,500); foundation scholarships ($58,000) foundation ($184,000)
Assets: $1,028,649 (2001); $1,117,167 (2000); $1,173,484 (1999)
Gifts Received: $500 (2001); $58,377 (2000); $122,146 (1999). Note: Contributions are received from North American Royalties.

Typical Recipients

Arts & Humanities: Arts Funds, Arts & Humanities-General, Historic Preservation, History & Archaeology, Libraries, Museums/Galleries, Public Broadcasting
Civic & Public Affairs: Business/Free Enterprise, Chambers of Commerce, Economic Development, Civic & Public Affairs-General, Municipalities/Towns, Parades/Festivals, Urban & Community Affairs, Zoos/Aquariums
Education: Colleges & Universities, Education Funds, Elementary Education (Public), Engineering/Technological Education, Education-General, Literacy, Private Education (Precollege), Public Education (Precollege), Science/Mathematics Education, Student Aid, Vocational & Technical Education
Environment: Air/Water Quality, Environment-General, Wildlife Protection
Health: Cancer, Clinics/Medical Centers, Health-General, Respiratory
Religion: Religious Welfare, Religious Welfare
Social Services: Food/Clothing Distribution, Homes, People with Disabilities, United Funds/United Ways, YMCA/YWCA/YMHA/YWHA, Youth Organizations

Application Procedures

Initial Contact: Send a brief letter of inquiry. Scholarship application forms are available for employees.
Application Requirements: Scholarship applications must include College Board or ACT test scores and high school transcripts; letter of recommendation; and letter from applicant covering aims of college and why that particular college was chosen.
Deadlines: March 1 for scholarship applications.

Restrictions

Does not support individuals except for scholarships for dependents of employees.

Corporate Officials

Gordon P. Street, Jr.: chairman, president, chief executive officer, director B Chattanooga, TN 1938. ED University of North Carolina (1960). PRIM CORP EMPL chairman, president, chief executive officer, director: North American Royalties. CORP AFFIL director: First Tennessee National Corp.; director: Provident Life & Accident Insurance Co.; director: Cincinnati, New Orleans, & Texas Railway; director: First Tennessee Bank NA Corp.
David Williams: chief financial officer PRIM CORP EMPL chief financial officer: North American Royalties.

Foundation Officials

Francis Street Smith: secretary, treasurer
Gordon L. Smith, Jr.: trustee PRIM CORP EMPL vice president planning: North American Royalties.
Gordon P. Street, Jr.: trustee (see above)
Ruth L. Street: vice president

Grants Analysis

Disclosure Period: calendar year ending 2001
Total Grants: $40,133*
Number of Grants: 8
Average Grant: $2,876*
Highest Grant: $20,000
Lowest Grant: $300
Typical Range: $500 to $6,333
*Note: Giving excludes scholarship, United Way. Average grant figure excludes highest grant.

Recent Grants

Note: Grants derived from 2001 Form 990.

General

20,000	Creative Discovery Museum, Chattanooga, TN
7,500	United Way, Chattanooga, TN
6,333	Westside Community Development Corp., Chattanooga, TN
6,000	Washington University, St. Louis, MO -- for scholarship
5,000	Allied Arts of Greater Chattanooga, Chattanooga, TN -- for arts in education
5,000	Salvation Army, Chattanooga, TN
4,000	Marymount University, Manhattan, NY -- for scholarship
4,000	Mercer University, Atlanta, GA -- for scholarship
4,000	Tennessee State University, Nashville, TN -- for scholarship
4,000	University of Georgia, Athens, GA -- scholarship

NORTH FAMILY TRUST

Giving Contact

Edward T. Hogan, Trustee
North Family Trust
212 Main Street, Suite 4
Wakefield, RI 02879
Phone: (401)782-4488

Description

Founded: 1992
EIN: 056091467
Organization Type: Private Foundation
Giving Locations: RI: Newport County
Grant Types: General Support.

Financial Summary

Total Giving: $142,500 (fiscal year ending June 30, 2001); $135,255 (fiscal 1999); $70,700 (fiscal 1997)
Assets: $2,987,589 (fiscal 2001); $2,870,656 (fiscal 1999); $2,098,878 (fiscal 1997)
Gifts Received: $410,260 (fiscal 1997); $632 (fiscal 1995); $519 (fiscal 1994). Note: In fiscal 1997, contributions were received from the Charles Stuart North Trust (EIN 056076208) which was merged into the North Family Trust on June 28, 1996.

Typical Recipients

Arts & Humanities: Arts & Humanities-General, Libraries, Museums/Galleries, Music
Civic & Public Affairs: Urban & Community Affairs
Education: Colleges & Universities, Elementary Education (Public), Private Education (Precollege), Science/Mathematics Education, Special Education
Health: Cancer, Hospices, Hospitals, Mental Health, Nursing Services
Religion: Religious Welfare
Social Services: Big Brother/Big Sister, Community Centers, Community Service Organizations, Domestic Violence, Family Services, Food/Clothing Distribution, Recreation & Athletics, Youth Organizations

Application Procedures

Initial Contact: Send a brief letter of inquiry.
Application Requirements: Include proof of tax-exempt status and specific purpose of funds sought.
Deadlines: Within 30 days from date of advertisement.

Restrictions

Restricted to Newport County, RI.

Foundation Officials

Robert Cummings: trustee
Edward T. Hogan: trustee

Grants Analysis

Disclosure Period: fiscal year ending June 30, 2001
Total Grants: $142,500
Number of Grants: 50
Average Grant: $2,850
Highest Grant: $10,000
Typical Range: $1,000 to $5,000

Recent Grants

Note: Grants derived from fiscal 2001 Form 990.

General

10,000	Rogers High School Science Department, Newport, RI -- science computer facility for high tech
8,000	Visiting Nurse Health Services, Portsmouth, RI -- provide hospice service
5,000	Hospice Care of Rhode Island, Providence, RI -- care for terminally ill
5,000	Lucy's Hearth, Newport, RI -- programs for homeless mothers
5,000	Newport Art Museum, Newport, RI -- funding for program with Boys and Girls Clubs
5,000	Newport Hospital Foundation, Newport, RI -- stress/EKG room in cardiopulmonary department
5,000	Rhode Island Meals on Wheels, Providence, RI -- meals to homebound elderly
5,000	Swanhurst Chorus, Newport, RI -- support performances
5,000	University of Rhode Island, Kingston, RI -- for graduate and undergraduate programs
3,500	Elmhurst Elementary School, Portsmouth, RI -- funding for Marine Programs

NORTH SHORE FOUNDATION

Giving Contact

Toy D. Savage, Jr., Secretary, Treasurer & Director
Bank of America Center, Suite 1420
Norfolk, VA 23510
Phone: (757)640-1414

Description

Founded: 1982
EIN: 521296293
Organization Type: Private Foundation
Giving Locations: VA
Grant Types: General Support.

Donor Information

Founder: Constance S. duPont Darden

Financial Summary

Total Giving: $157,000 (fiscal year ending April 30, 2002); $408,500 (fiscal 2001); $863,500 (fiscal 2000)
Giving Analysis: Giving for fiscal 2001 includes: foundation grants to United Way ($33,500)
Assets: $1,164,019 (fiscal 2002); $830 (fiscal 2001); $237,663 (fiscal 2000)
Gifts Received: $1,320,589 (fiscal 2002); $173,561 (fiscal 2001); $273,222 (fiscal 2000). Note: In fiscal 2000 and 2002, contributions were received from Constance S. duPont Darden.

Typical Recipients

Arts & Humanities: Arts Associations & Councils, Arts Centers, Arts Funds, Arts & Humanities-General, History & Archaeology, Libraries, Museums/Galleries, Music, Opera, Performing Arts, Public Broadcasting
Civic & Public Affairs: Civil Rights, Economic Development, Employment/Job Training, Civic & Public Affairs-General, Housing, Urban & Community Affairs, Zoos/Aquariums
Education: Business Education, Colleges & Universities, Community & Junior Colleges, Education Funds, International Studies, Minority Education, Private Education (Precollege), Student Aid
Environment: Air/Water Quality, Environment-General, Resource Conservation, Wildlife Protection
Health: Children's Health/Hospitals, Emergency/Ambulance Services, Health Funds, Medical Research, Mental Health
International: Health Care/Hospitals, Human Rights, International Affairs, International Development, International Organizations, International Relations, International Relief Efforts, Missionary/Religious Activities
Religion: Churches, Dioceses, Ministries, Missionary Activities (Domestic), Religious Organizations, Religious Welfare
Social Services: Animal Protection, Big Brother/Big Sister, Child Welfare, Community Centers, Community Service Organizations, Day Care, Family Planning, Family Services, Homes, Senior Services, United Funds/United Ways, Youth Organizations

Application Procedures

Initial Contact: Send a brief letter of inquiry describing program or project.
Deadlines: None.

Foundation Officials

Constance S. duPont Darden: director B 1904.
Joshua P. Darden, Jr.: president, director
Toy D. Savage, Jr.: secretary, treasurer, director B Norfolk, VA 1921. ED University of Virginia BA (1943); University of Virginia LLB (1948). chairman distribution committee: Norfolk Foundation; trustee: Virginia Foundation for Independent Colleges; trustee: East Virginia Medicine School Foundation CORP AFFIL trustee: Chrysler Museum; director: Sentara Health System. NONPR AFFIL trustee deacon: Freemason St Baptist Church; trustee: Virginia Historical Society.

Grants Analysis

Disclosure Period: fiscal year ending April 30, 2002
Total Grants: $157,000
Number of Grants: 7
Average Grant: $13,667*
Highest Grant: $75,000
Lowest Grant: $2,000
Typical Range: $5,000 to $20,000
*Note: Average grant figure excludes highest grant.

Recent Grants

Note: Grants derived from fiscal 2000 Form 990.

General

296,000	Norfolk Foundation, Norfolk, VA
100,000	American Red Cross, Norfolk, VA
100,000	North Country Animal League, Morrisville, VT
70,000	Alfred I. duPont Hospital for Children, Richmond, VA
70,000	Virginia Foundation of Independent Colleges, Richmond, VA
30,000	Church of the Good Shepherd, Norfolk, VA
30,000	Church of the Good Shepherd, Norfolk, VA
25,000	Virginia Opera, Norfolk, VA
20,000	Amnesty International, U.S.A., New York, NY
15,000	American Society of Ancient Instruments, Elkins Park, PA

NORTHERN TRUST CORP.

Company Headquarters

50 S. LaSalle Street
Chicago, IL 60675
Web: http://www.ntrs.com

Company Description

Founded: 1889
Ticker: NTRS
Exchange: NASDAQ
Assets: US$39.664 billion (2001)
Employees: 9453 (2001)
SIC(s): 6022 State Commercial Banks.

Operating Locations

Northern Trust Co. (AZ--Phoenix, Scottsdale, Sun City, Tucson; CA--Los Angeles, Newport Beach, Pasadena, San Diego, San Jose, Santa Barbara; FL--Aventura, Coral Gables, Fort Lauderdale, Fort Myers, Miami, Naples, North Palm Beach, Palm Beach, Venice; IL--Bensenville, Lake Bluff, Naperville, Oak Brook, Schaumburg, Winnetka; TX--Dallas, Houston); Northrn Trust Co. (FL--Boca Raton, Key Biscayne)

Nonmonetary Support

Type: Cause-related Marketing & Promotion; Donated Equipment; In-kind Services; Loaned Executives
Volunteer Programs: Company supports a volunteer grants program which makes grants to organizations where employees volunteer.

Northern Trust Co. Charitable Trust

Giving Contact

Eleanor Alcantara
The Northern Trust Co.
Community Affairs Division
50 S. LaSalle Street, M-5
Chicago, IL 60675
Phone: (312)444-4059
E-mail: eta1@ntrs.com
Web: http://www.ntrs.com/aboutus/community/index.html

Alternate Contact

Larry Wisniewski
Phone: (312)444-3533
Note: For information on the matching gift program.

Description

EIN: 366147253
Organization Type: Corporate Foundation
Giving Locations: IL: Chicago metropolitan area, with priority given to Cook County
Grant Types: Capital, Endowment, General Support, Project.

Financial Summary

Total Giving: $3,775,854 (2001); $3,701,098 (2000); $3,425,352 (1999). Note: Contributes through corporate direct giving program and foundation.
Giving Analysis: Giving for 2000 includes: foundation scholarships ($88,750); foundation grants to United Way ($562,500); foundation matching gifts ($889,831); foundation ($2,160,017); 1999: foundation ($3,425,352); 1998: corporate scholarships ($24,625); corporate matching gifts ($647,407); corporate grants to United Way ($650,000) foundation ($1,566,805)
Assets: $60,731 (2000); $150,172 (1999); $117,251 (1998)
Gifts Received: $3,673,612 (2001); $3,570,600 (2000); $3,448,000 (1999). Note: Contributions received from Northern Trust Company.

Typical Recipients

Arts & Humanities: Arts Funds, Arts Institutes, Dance, Libraries, Museums/Galleries, Music, Opera, Performing Arts, Public Broadcasting, Theater
Civic & Public Affairs: African American Affairs, Asian American Affairs, Botanical Gardens/Parks, Business/Free Enterprise, Civil Rights, Clubs, Economic Development, Employment/Job Training, Hispanic Affairs, Housing, Inner-City Development, Law & Justice, Municipalities/Towns, Public Policy, Urban & Community Affairs, Women's Affairs, Zoos/Aquariums
Education: Arts/Humanities Education, Business Education, Colleges & Universities, Education Funds, Education Reform, Education-General, Literacy, Minority Education, Preschool Education, Private Education (Precollege), Public Education (Precollege), Special Education, Student Aid
Environment: Environment-General, Resource Conservation
Health: Adolescent Health Issues, AIDS/HIV, Children's Health/Hospitals, Clinics/Medical Centers, Emergency/Ambulance Services, Health Funds, Health Organizations, Hospices, Hospitals, Medical Rehabilitation, Medical Training, Mental Health, Multiple Sclerosis, Nutrition, Public Health, Research/Studies Institutes
Religion: Jewish Causes, Religious Welfare
Science: Observatories & Planetariums, Science Museums, Scientific Centers & Institutes
Social Services: At-Risk Youth, Child Welfare, Community Centers, Community Service Organizations, Day Care, Domestic Violence, Family Planning, Family Services, Food/Clothing Distribution, People with Disabilities, Recreation & Athletics, Scouts, Sexual Abuse, Shelters/Homelessness, Substance Abuse, United Funds/United Ways, Volunteer Services, YMCA/YWCA/YMHA/YWHA, Youth Organizations

Application Procedures

Initial Contact: New applicants must submit a formal two- to five-page letter of inquiry at least six weeks before the appropriate application deadline. Current grant recipients seeking renewed support do not need to submit a letter of inquiry.
Application Requirements: If invited to apply for a grant, submit a completed application form, including information about the purpose, timeline, expected outcomes of the project, and the applicant's capacity to manage it. Also include the agency's operating budget for the current year and most recent monthly year-to-date report on the status of the budget; the agency's financial statements for the previous two years and an audited financial statement, if available; a list of Chicago-area corporate and foundation contributors

and the amounts they've contributed in the last and current years; any funding received from the United Way; proof of tax-exempt status; a list of board members and their affiliations; and a list of the organization's management staff and their qualifications. If program support is sought, include a project or program budget.
Deadlines: January 15 and August 15 for Social Welfare Programs; May 15 for Education and Arts & Culture Programs.
Review Process: Applications are reviewed in late March, July and October.

Restrictions

The Trust does not support individuals; fraternal groups; individual churches or sectarian organizations; scholarships for individual students; research; political activity; special event fundraising; or general operations of agencies receiving more than 5% of their funding from the United Way.

Corporate Officials

Perry R. Pero: senior executive vice president, chief financial officer B 1939. ED Clark University BA (1961); Harvard University MBA (1963). PRIM CORP EMPL senior executive vice president, chief financial officer: Northern Trust Co. ADD CORP EMPL officer: North Trust Global Advs.

Foundation Officials

Janet Gray: member
John Iwanicki: member
Steve Krause: member
Marjorie W. Lundy: secretary contributions committee PRIM CORP EMPL vice president: Northern Trust Co.
Loren Miller: member
William N. Setterstrom: vice chairman B Brooklyn, NY 1942. ED Hobart College (1964). PRIM CORP EMPL senior vice president human resources: Northern Trust Co.

Grants Analysis

Disclosure Period: calendar year ending 2001
Total Grants: $2,116,101*
Number of Grants: 282
Average Grant: $7,504
Highest Grant: $50,000
Typical Range: $1,000 to $10,000
***Note:** Giving excludes matching gifts; United Way.

Recent Grants

Note: Grants derived from 2001 Form 990.

Library-Related

25,000	Newberry Library, Chicago, IL -- capital support

General

200,000	United Way Crusade of Mercy, Chicago, IL -- support of member agencies
200,000	United Way Crusade of Mercy, Chicago, IL -- support of member agencies
200,000	United Way Crusade of Mercy, Chicago, IL -- support of member agencies
200,000	United Way Crusade of Mercy, Chicago, IL -- support of member agencies
50,000	Northwestern University, Evanston, IL -- fund to endow the Freshman Urban Program
40,000	YMCA Metropolitan Chicago, Chicago, IL -- for construction of the new Logan Square facility
35,000	Big Shoulders Fund, Chicago, IL -- support for inner city schools
33,000	Chicago Public Education Fund, Chicago, IL -- operating support
30,000	Chicago Zoological Society, Brookfield, IL -- capital support
30,000	Local Initiatives Support Corporation, Highland Park, IL -- campaign for communities

NORTHWEST NATURAL GAS CO.

Company Headquarters

Portland, OR
Web: http://www.nwnatural.com

Company Description

Founded: 1859
Ticker: NWN
Exchange: NYSE
Assets: US$1.342 billion (2002)
Employees: 1261 (2002)
SIC(s): 4924 Natural Gas Distribution.

Operating Locations

Northwest Natural Gas Co. (OR--Newport)

Nonmonetary Support

Type: Donated Equipment; Donated Products; In-kind Services; Loaned Employees; Loaned Executives

Giving Contact

Marie Krasnow, Administrative Assistant
220 Northwest 2nd Avenue
Portland, OR 97209
Phone: (503)226-4211
Fax: (503)220-2584
E-mail: george.richardson@nwnatural.com
Note: Extension 3346

Description

Organization Type: Corporate Giving Program
Giving Locations: headquarters and operating communities.
Grant Types: Capital, Employee Matching Gifts, General Support, Multiyear/Continuing Support, Operating Expenses, Project, Research, Scholarship, Seed Money.
Note: Employee matching gifts support the United Way.

Financial Summary

Total Giving: $825,000 (2003 approx); $725,000 (2002); $686,600 (2001). Note: Contributes through corporate direct giving program only.

Typical Recipients

Arts & Humanities: Arts Appreciation, Arts Associations & Councils, Arts Centers, Arts Festivals, Arts Funds, Arts Institutes, Community Arts, Dance, Ethnic & Folk Arts, Arts & Humanities-General, Historic Preservation, Libraries, Museums/Galleries, Music, Opera, Performing Arts, Public Broadcasting, Theater, Visual Arts
Civic & Public Affairs: Economic Development, Civic & Public Affairs-General, Housing, Professional & Trade Associations, Urban & Community Affairs, Women's Affairs, Zoos/Aquariums
Education: Business Education, Colleges & Universities, Elementary Education (Private), Education-General, Minority Education
Health: Health-General, Health Organizations, Hospices, Hospitals, Medical Rehabilitation, Mental Health, Single-Disease Health Associations
Science: Science Exhibits & Fairs
Social Services: Animal Protection, Child Welfare, Community Centers, Counseling, Day Care, Delinquency & Criminal Rehabilitation, Food/Clothing Distribution, Homes, People with Disabilities, Senior Services, Shelters/Homelessness, Social Services-General, Substance Abuse, United Funds/United Ways, Volunteer Services, Youth Organizations

Application Procedures

Initial Contact: A brief letter of inquiry and a full proposal.
Application Requirements: Description of organization, amount requested, purpose of funds sought, and proof of tax-exempt status.
Deadlines: None.

Restrictions

Does not support individuals, religious organizations for sectarian purposes, or political or lobbying groups. Company will not accept proposals from organizations outside of company service areas.

Additional Information

The company gives to the Oregon Community Foundation, who in turn re-grants to nonprofit organizations.

Corporate Officials

Gregg Kantor: vice president, chief executive officer, chairman PRIM CORP EMPL vice president: Northwest Natural Gas Co.
Richard G. Reiten: president, chief executive officer, chairman PRIM CORP EMPL president, chief executive officer, chairman: Northwest Natural Gas Co.
George E. Richardson, Jr.: chairman contributions PRIM CORP EMPL chairman contributions: Northwest Natural Gas Co.

Grants Analysis

Disclosure Period: calendar year ending 2000
Total Grants: $619,900
Typical Range: $500 to $5,000

PETER NORTON FAMILY FOUNDATION

Giving Contact

Anne Etheridge, Executive Director
225 Arizona Ave., Suite 350
Santa Monica, CA 90401
Phone: (310)576-7700
Fax: (310)576-7701

Description

Founded: 1988
EIN: 954195347
Organization Type: Private Foundation
Giving Locations: CA
Grant Types: General Support.

Donor Information

Founder: Peter Norton, Eileen Norton

Financial Summary

Total Giving: $3,203,064 (2000); $2,488,250 (1999); $5,500,695 (1997)
Assets: $44,047,649 (2000); $50,280,846 (1999); $38,426,443 (1997)
Gifts Received: $13,294,044 (1997). Note: In 1997, contributions were received from Peter Norton.

Typical Recipients

Arts & Humanities: Arts Associations & Councils, Arts Centers, Arts Funds, Arts Institutes, Dance, Ethnic & Folk Arts, Film & Video, Arts & Humanities-General, Historic Preservation, Libraries, Museums/Galleries, Music, Public Broadcasting, Visual Arts
Civic & Public Affairs: African American Affairs, Civil Rights, Gay/Lesbian Issues, Women's Affairs
Education: Arts/Humanities Education, Colleges & Universities, Education-General, Minority Education, Private Education (Precollege)
Environment: Air/Water Quality
Health: AIDS/HIV, Cancer, Clinics/Medical Centers
International: Foreign Arts Organizations

Social Services: Child Welfare, Community Centers, Community Service Organizations, Domestic Violence, Family Planning, Family Services, People with Disabilities, Youth Organizations

Application Procedures

Initial Contact: Submit a brief letter of inquiry.
Application Requirements: Include a description of organization, amount requested, and purpose of funds sought.
Deadlines: None.

Restrictions

Foundation does not accept support individuals or religious organizations for sectarian purposes.

Foundation Officials

Anne Etheridge: secretary, treasurer
Eileen Norton: vice president
Peter Norton: president B 1943. CORP AFFIL director: Symantec Corp.

Grants Analysis

Disclosure Period: calendar year ending 2000
Total Grants: $3,203,064
Number of Grants: 154
Average Grant: $18,974*
Highest Grant: $300,000
Typical Range: $10,000 to $40,000
*Note: Average grant figure excludes highest grant.

Recent Grants

Note: Grants derived from 1999 Form 990.

General

425,000	Signature Theatre Company, New York, NY
279,500	Museum of Modern Art, New York, NY
250,000	California Institute of the Arts, Santa Clarita, CA
125,700	New Museum of Contemporary Art, New York, NY
100,000	ACLU Foundation, New York, NY
100,000	American Friends of Turkey, Washington, DC
100,000	Creative Capital Foundation, New York, NY
100,000	Harvard Business School, Boston, MA
100,000	Los Angeles Women's Foundation, Los Angeles, CA
65,938	UCLA at the Armand Hammer Museum of Art, Los Angeles, CA

NORTON FOUNDATION

Giving Contact

Lucy Crawford, Executive Director
Norton Foundation
4350 Brownsboro Rd., Suite 133
Louisville, KY 40207
Phone: (502)893-9549
Fax: (502)896-9378
E-mail: nortfound@aol.com
Web: http://www.nortonfoundation.com

Description

Founded: 1958
EIN: 616024040
Organization Type: Private Foundation
Giving Locations: KY
Grant Types: General Support, Operating Expenses.

Donor Information

Founder: Mrs. George W. Norton

Financial Summary

Total Giving: $997,400 (2001); $955,447 (2000); $912,434 (1998)
Giving Analysis: Giving for 2001 includes: foundation grants to United Way ($31,250); 2000: foundation

grants to United Way ($25,000); 1998: foundation grants to United Way ($25,000) foundation ($887,434).
Assets: $20,233,473 (2001); $23,207,243 (2000); $21,622,716 (1998)

Typical Recipients

Arts & Humanities: Arts Centers, Arts Festivals, Arts Funds, Ballet, Community Arts, Ethnic & Folk Arts, Libraries, Museums/Galleries, Music, Opera, Performing Arts, Public Broadcasting, Theater, Visual Arts
Civic & Public Affairs: African American Affairs, Botanical Gardens/Parks, Community Foundations, Economic Development, Civic & Public Affairs-General, Housing, Law & Justice, Legal Aid, Philanthropic Organizations, Urban & Community Affairs, Women's Affairs, Zoos/Aquariums
Education: Colleges & Universities, Economic Education, Education Associations, Education Funds, Education Reform, Education-General, Private Education (Precollege), Public Education (Precollege), Special Education
Environment: Environment-General, Resource Conservation, Wildlife Protection
Health: Preventive Medicine/Wellness Organizations, Public Health
International: International Peace & Security Issues, Missionary/Religious Activities
Religion: Churches, Religion-General, Ministries, Religious Organizations, Religious Welfare
Science: Scientific Centers & Institutes
Social Services: At-Risk Youth, Child Welfare, Community Centers, Community Service Organizations, Domestic Violence, Family Planning, Family Services, Food/Clothing Distribution, Homes, People with Disabilities, Shelters/Homelessness, Substance Abuse, United Funds/United Ways, Volunteer Services, Youth Organizations

Application Procedures

Initial Contact: Send a cover letter and full proposal.
Application Requirements: Include a description of organization, amount requested, recently audited financial statement, proof of tax-exempt status (three copies of each).
Deadlines: Quarterly; contact foundation.

Restrictions

Does not support individuals or private foundations. Local charitable needs are given priority.

Foundation Officials

Mr. Richard H. C. Clay: director
Lucy Crawford: executive director
Jane Norton Dulaney: president
Robert W. Dulaney: vice president
Jane Norton Newton: vice president

Grants Analysis

Disclosure Period: calendar year ending 2001
Total Grants: $966,150*
Number of Grants: 28
Average Grant: $28,831*
Highest Grant: $116,540
Typical Range: $10,000 to $50,000
*Note: Giving excludes United Way. Average grant figure excludes two highest grants ($216,540).

Recent Grants

Note: Grants derived from 2000 Form 990.

General

100,000	Home of the Innocence, Louisville, KY
65,000	Cabbage Patch Settlement House, Louisville, KY
60,000	Association of Walden Schools of North America, Inc., Fair Oaks, CA
50,000	Legal Aid Society, Louisville, KY
47,500	National Institute on Children and Youth, Louisville, KY

43,468	Jefferson County Public Schools, Louisville, KY
40,000	Kentucky Arts & Crafts Foundation, Louisville, KY
38,484	Family Place, Louisville, KY
35,000	Meredith Dunn Learning Center, Louisville, KY
30,000	Family and Children's Counseling Center, Louisville, KY

GERALDI NORTON MEMORIAL CORP.

Giving Contact
Christopher S. Eklund, Treasurer
c/o Hackbarth and Hudson, P.C.
20 N. Wacker Dr., Suite 1520
Chicago, IL 60606

Description
Founded: 1952
EIN: 366069997
Organization Type: Private Foundation
Giving Locations: IL: Chicago metropolitan area
Grant Types: General Support.

Donor Information
Founder: the late Grace Geraldi Norton

Financial Summary
Total Giving: $141,800 (2000); $154,500 (1999); $206,750 (1998)
Assets: $4,071,872 (2000); $4,205,956 (1999); $1,646,879 (1997)

Typical Recipients
Arts & Humanities: Arts Centers, Arts Festivals, Arts Institutes, Historic Preservation, History & Archaeology, Libraries, Museums/Galleries, Music, Opera, Performing Arts, Public Broadcasting, Theater
Civic & Public Affairs: Clubs, Community Foundations, Law & Justice, Legal Aid, Nonprofit Management, Zoos/Aquariums
Education: Colleges & Universities, Education Funds, Legal Education, Medical Education, Minority Education, Private Education (Precollege), Science/Mathematics Education, Secondary Education (Private), Student Aid
Environment: Forestry, Environment-General, Resource Conservation, Watershed
Health: Alzheimers Disease, Cancer, Children's Health/Hospitals, Clinics/Medical Centers, Diabetes, Health Organizations, Hospices, Hospitals, Medical Rehabilitation, Medical Research, Mental Health, Prenatal Health Issues, Research/Studies Institutes, Single-Disease Health Associations, Speech & Hearing
International: Health Care/Hospitals
Religion: Religious Welfare
Science: Science Museums
Social Services: Child Welfare, Community Service Organizations, Family Services, Recreation & Athletics, Shelters/Homelessness, United Funds/United Ways, Volunteer Services, Youth Organizations

Application Procedures
Initial Contact: Send a brief letter of inquiry describing program.
Application Requirements: purpose of funds sought.
Deadlines: None. Grants usually are awarded in December.

Restrictions
Does not support individuals.

Foundation Officials
Christopher S. Eklund: treasurer
Dariel Ann Eklund: vice president
Peter H. Eklund: member

Sally S. Eklund: secretary
Kathryn E. Wise: secretary

Grants Analysis
Disclosure Period: calendar year ending 2000
Total Grants: $141,800
Number of Grants: 43
Average Grant: $2,424*
Highest Grant: $40,000
Typical Range: $1,000 to $5,000
*Note: Average grant figure excludes highest grant.

Recent Grants
Note: Grants derived from 1999 Form 990.

General
40,000	University of Chicago Arthur L. Herbst Professorship, Chicago, IL
15,000	Harvard College Fund, The, Cambridge, MA
10,000	Juvenile Diabetes Association, New York, NY
10,000	University of Chicago Department of Radiation and Cellular Oncology, Chicago, IL
6,000	Music Institute of Chicago, Chicago, IL
5,000	Children's Memorial Medical Center, Chicago, IL
5,000	Narsad Research Institute, Great Neck, NY
5,000	Women's Board of Northwestern Memorial Hospital, Chicago, IL
2,500	Art Institute of Chicago, Chicago, IL
2,500	Chicago Historical Society, Chicago, IL

NOVELL

Company Headquarters
Orem, UT
Web: http://www.novell.com

Company Description
Employees: 5,800
SIC(s): 3500 Industrial Machinery & Equipment, 7300 Business Services.

Operating Locations
Novell (UT--Salem)

Nonmonetary Support
Type: Donated Products

Giving Contact
Corporate Giving Program
PO Box 1156
Salem, UT 84653
Phone: (801)861-7000

Alternate Contact
Linda Linfield
1555 North Technology Way
Orem, UT 84097-2399

Description
Organization Type: Corporate Giving Program
Giving Locations: CA: Santa Clara County; UT: Wasatch Front
Grant Types: Award, Multiyear/Continuing Support, Project.

Typical Recipients
Arts & Humanities: Arts Associations & Councils, Arts Centers, Arts Festivals, Arts Outreach, Ballet, Community Arts, Dance, Ethnic & Folk Arts, Arts & Humanities-General, Libraries, Museums/Galleries, Music, Opera, Performing Arts, Theater

Civic & Public Affairs: Business/Free Enterprise, Community Foundations, Civic & Public Affairs-General, Philanthropic Organizations, Professional & Trade Associations
Education: Business Education, Faculty Development, Education-General, Science/Mathematics Education, Vocational & Technical Education
Environment: Wildlife Protection
Health: Arthritis, Cancer, Diabetes, Health-General, Home-Care Services, Nursing Services
Science: Science-General, Observatories & Planetariums, Science Museums, Scientific Centers & Institutes, Scientific Organizations
Social Services: Community Centers, Community Service Organizations, Food/Clothing Distribution, Homes, People with Disabilities, Shelters/Homelessness, Social Services-General, United Funds/United Ways, Volunteer Services

Application Procedures
Initial Contact: Send letter requesting corporate giving guidelines. Deadline for cash grants is July 31. Requests for software donations may be submitted throughout the year.

Restrictions
Does not support individuals, religious organizations for sectarian purposes, political or lobbying groups, organizations that discriminate, conferences, national health organizations, sports or entertainment marketing, fraternal organizations, or organizations outside operating areas.

Additional Information
Publications: Corporate Giving Guidelines

Corporate Officials
Jack L. Messman: president, chief executive officer ED Harvard University MBA; University of Delaware BS. PRIM CORP EMPL president, chief executive officer: Novell.
Dr. Eric Schmidt: chairman ED Princeton University BSEE; University of California at Berkeley PhD; University of California at Berkeley MSEE. PRIM CORP EMPL chairman: Novell.

Grants Analysis
Typical Range: $1,000 to $2,500

NICHOLAS H. NOYES, JR. MEMORIAL FOUNDATION

Giving Contact
Nancy Ayres, President
1950 E. Greyhound Pass, 18-356
Carmel, IN 46033-7730
Phone: (317)844-8009
Fax: (317)844-8099
E-mail: admin@noyesfoundation.org
Web: http://www.noyesfoundation.org

Description
Founded: 1951
EIN: 351003699
Organization Type: Family Foundation
Giving Locations: IN: Indianapolis
Grant Types: Capital, Endowment, General Support, Multiyear/Continuing Support, Project, Scholarship.

Donor Information
Founder: Incorporated in 1951 by the late Nicholas H. Noyes and the late Marguerite Lilly Noyes .

Financial Summary
Total Giving: $3,000,000 (2003 approx); $3,700,000 (2002 approx); $3,700,000 (2001 approx)
Giving Analysis: Giving for 2000 includes: foundation grants to United Way ($100,000); foundation

scholarships ($415,000); 1999: foundation grants to United Way ($140,000) 1998: foundation grants to United Way ($110,000)

Assets: $58,000,000 (2002 approx); $84,000,000 (2000 approx); $70,222,731 (1999)

Gifts Received: $6,640 (1996). Note: In 1998, the foundation received gifts from the Nicholas H. Noyes Employees Trust.

Typical Recipients

Arts & Humanities: Arts Associations & Councils, Arts Centers, Ballet, Dance, Historic Preservation, Libraries, Museums/Galleries, Music, Opera, Performing Arts, Public Broadcasting, Theater

Civic & Public Affairs: Botanical Gardens/Parks, Community Foundations, Employment/Job Training, Civic & Public Affairs-General, Housing, Urban & Community Affairs, Zoos/Aquariums

Education: Agricultural Education, Arts/Humanities Education, Business Education, Colleges & Universities, Education Associations, Education Funds, Elementary Education (Private), Engineering/Technological Education, International Studies, Literacy, Minority Education, Private Education (Precollege), Public Education (Precollege), Science/Mathematics Education, Secondary Education (Private), Student Aid, Vocational & Technical Education

Environment: Environment-General, Resource Conservation

Health: Cancer, Children's Health/Hospitals, Clinics/Medical Centers, Diabetes, Emergency/Ambulance Services, Hospitals, Medical Rehabilitation, Medical Research, Nursing Services, Single-Disease Health Associations

International: Foreign Arts Organizations

Religion: Churches, Ministries, Religious Welfare, Seminaries

Social Services: Animal Protection, Big Brother/Big Sister, Camps, Child Welfare, Community Centers, Community Service Organizations, Counseling, Day Care, Family Planning, Family Services, Food/Clothing Distribution, Homes, People with Disabilities, Refugee Assistance, Scouts, Scouts, Shelters/Homelessness, Social Services-General, Special Olympics, Substance Abuse, United Funds/United Ways, YMCA/YWCA/YMHA/YWHA, Youth Organizations

Application Procedures

Initial Contact: The foundation requests applications be made in writing.

Application Requirements: Potential applicants are encouraged to check the foundation's website or call the foundation for current deadlines and guidelines.

Review Process: Board meets twice a year; proposals received by the deadlines will normally be reviewed in the two months following.

Restrictions

Grants are not made to individuals or for loans. Grants are usually awarded to organizations within Indiana.

Foundation Officials

Mrs. Avery Augustine: director
Nancy Ayres: president, director
Lisa Carrington: director
Kelly L. Mills: assistant secretary
Elizabeth H. Noyes: director
Evan L. Noyes, Jr.: director
Henry S. Noyes: director
Nicholas S. Noyes: director
Robert Hugh Reynolds: vice president, secretary B Saint Louis, MO 1937. ED Yale University BA (1958); Harvard University JD (1964). PRIM CORP EMPL partner: Barnes & Thornburg. CORP AFFIL vice chairman: Terralex. NONPR AFFIL director: Japan American Society Indiana; board governors: Legacy Fund; member: International Bar Association; board director: Indianapolis Convention & Visitors Association; board director: Indianapolis Economic Development Corp.; member: Indianapolis Bar Association; fellow: Indianapolis Bar Foundation; member: Indiana Bar

Association; fellow: Indiana Bar Foundation; board director: Greater Indianapolis Foreign Trade Zone; board director: Greater Indianapolis Progress Committee; member: Greater Indianapolis Chamber of Commerce; member: American Bar Association; board director: Boy Scouts America Crossroads Council. CLUB AFFIL University Club; Economic Club Indianapolis; Skyline Club.

L. Gene Tanner: treasurer B Indianapolis, IN 1932. ED Indiana University BA (1955). PRIM CORP EMPL vice chairman: NatCity Investments. CORP AFFIL director: Biomet Inc.; director: Circle Ventures Inc.

Grants Analysis

Disclosure Period: calendar year ending 2000
Total Grants: $3,166,675*
Number of Grants: 131
Average Grant: $21,667*
Highest Grant: $350,000
Lowest Grant: $1,000
Typical Range: $1,000 to $25,000
*Note: Giving excludes United Way and scholarships. Average grant figure excludes highest grant.

Recent Grants

Note: Grants derived from 2000 Form 990.

General

350,000	United Way Central Indiana, Indianapolis, IN -- promote Community Service Programs
150,000	Crossroads of America Boys Scouts of America, Indianapolis, IN -- promote community service programs
150,000	Sarah Lawrence College, Bronxville, NY -- higher education fund for student and campus life
125,000	Children's Museum of Indianapolis, Indianapolis, IN -- promote Cultural Programs
125,000	Herron School of Art, Indianapolis, IN -- promote Cultural Programs
100,000	Ballet Internationale, Indianapolis, IN -- promote Cultural Programs
100,000	Park Tudor School, Indianapolis, IN -- new auditorium
100,000	United Way Central Indiana, Indianapolis, IN -- promote Community Service Programs
75,000	Independent Colleges of Indiana Foundation, Indianapolis, IN -- scholarship
75,000	Indiana State Museum, Indianapolis, IN -- promote Cultural Programs

NSTAR

Company Headquarters

800 Boylston St.
Boston, MA 02199
Phone: (617)424-2000
Fax: (617)424-2904
Web: http://www.nstaronline.com

Company Description

Founded: 1999
Ticker: NST
Exchange: NYSE
Formed by Merger of: BEC Energy and Commonwealth Energy System (1999).
Assets: US$5.328 billion (2001)
Employees: 3400 (2001)
SIC(s): 4900 Electric, Gas & Sanitary Services, 6500 Real Estate, 6700 Holding & Other Investment Offices.

Operating Locations

Commonwealth Energy Systems (MA--Cambridge); NSTAR Electric (MA--Wareham)

Nonmonetary Support

Type: Donated Equipment; Workplace Solicitation
Note: Co. donates used furniture. Co. donated approximately $20,000 in equipment in 1998.

NSTAR Foundation

Giving Contact

Foundation Administrator
NSTAR Foundation
800 Boylston St.
Boston, MA 02199
Phone: (781)441-8853
Web: http://www.nstaronline.com/index2.asp?lk=comm

Description

EIN: 042754285
Organization Type: Corporate Foundation
Giving Locations: MA: Eastern Massachusetts, Boston
Grant Types: Capital, Challenge, Employee Matching Gifts, General Support, Matching, Project, Seed Money.
Note: Employee matching gift ratio: 1 to 1 to education.

Financial Summary

Total Giving: $1,300,000 (1999 approx); $1,085,000 (1998 approx); $1,099,000 (1997). Note: Contributes through corporate direct giving program and foundation.

Assets: $18,594 (2000); $1,800,000 (1999 approx); $1,700,000 (1998 approx)

Gifts Received: $1,100,000 (1994); $1,100,000 (1993); $700,000 (1992). Note: Contributions were received from the Boston Edison Co.

Typical Recipients

Arts & Humanities: Arts Institutes, Arts Outreach, Ballet, Dance, Historic Preservation, Libraries, Museums/Galleries, Music, Performing Arts

Civic & Public Affairs: Economic Development, Employment/Job Training, Housing, Law & Justice, Municipalities/Towns, Philanthropic Organizations, Professional & Trade Associations, Safety, Urban & Community Affairs, Zoos/Aquariums

Education: Afterschool/Enrichment Programs, Business-School Partnerships, Colleges & Universities, Education Reform, Elementary Education (Public), Engineering/Technological Education, Leadership Training, Minority Education, Preschool Education, Private Education (Precollege), Religious Education, Science/Mathematics Education, Student Aid

Health: AIDS/HIV, Alzheimers Disease, Cancer, Clinics/Medical Centers, Emergency/Ambulance Services, Health Organizations, Hospices, Hospitals, Long-Term Care, Nursing Services, Single-Disease Health Associations

Religion: Religious Welfare, Social/Policy Issues

Science: Science Museums

Social Services: Community Centers, Community Service Organizations, Counseling, Emergency Relief, Family Services, Food/Clothing Distribution, People with Disabilities, Recreation & Athletics, Senior Services, Shelters/Homelessness, United Funds/United Ways, Youth Organizations

Application Procedures

Initial Contact: All proposals must be submitted using an Associated Grantmakers of Massachusetts Common Proposal Format; guidelines revised in 1998.

Application Requirements: Include recent annual report, budget for organization and specific project requiring funding, specific amount of funding requested, other funding sources either at hand or anticipated, provision for accountability to project sponsors, and proof of tax-exempt status.

Deadlines: February 15 (for April assessment), July 15 (for September), and October 1 (for December).
Review Process: Company volunteers serve on the Foundation Task Force and review requests, make site visits, and conduct interviews; Task Force makes recommendations to foundation trustees.
Evaluative Criteria: Organization is tax-exempt and serves an Edison community; program has measurable goals and objectives that relate to a foundation concern; realistic strategy for achieving goals; provide company with appropriate recognition; employee volunteer involvement; funding is for a specific project, not general support; positive impact on the community; demonstrated need; non-duplication of services; plans for continued operation; long-term solutions.
Decision Notification: Trustees assess proposals in April, September, and December.

Restrictions

Proposals for same project will not be considered more than once within a one-year period. The foundation does not usually support capital campaigns (building as well as renovation); commitments beyond one year; events such as dinners, conferences, workshops, symposiums, etc.; and programs receiving substantial support from others. The foundation also limits its consideration of contributions to third party organizations, preferring to support direct program grants.

Additional Information

In 1999, Boston Edison's holding company, BEC Energy, and Commonwealth Energy System merged to form NSTAR. Boston Edison is a subsidiary of NSTAR.
Publications: Foundation Annual Report; Guidelines

Corporate Officials

Alison Alden: senior vice president sales, service, human resources PRIM CORP EMPL senior vice president sales, service, human resources: Boston Edison Co. CORP AFFIL senior vice president sales, services, human resources: BEC Energy.
John J. Connolly: director corporate relations PRIM CORP EMPL director corporate relations: Boston Edison Co.
Douglas S. Horan: senior vice president, general counsel, secretary ED Case Western Reserve University BS; Johns Hopkins University MA; Northeastern University JD. PRIM CORP EMPL senior vice president, general counsel, secretary: NSTAR ADD CORP EMPL senior vice president, general counsel: BEC Energy.
James J. Judge: senior vice president corporate service business unit, treasurer ED Babson College. PRIM CORP EMPL senior vice president corporate service business unit, treasurer: Boston Edison Co. ADD CORP EMPL vice president, treasurer: BEC Energy Inc.; treasurer: Boston Energy Technology Group Inc.; treasurer: Harbor Electric Energy Co.; senior vice president, chief financial officer: NSTAR.
Ronald A. Ledgett: senior vice president B 1938. ED Stanford University. PRIM CORP EMPL senior vice president: Boston Edison Co.

Foundation Officials

Alison Alden: trustee (see above)
John J. Connolly: director (see above)
Douglas S. Horan: trustee (see above)
James J. Judge: trustee (see above)
Catherine J. Keuthen: legal adv
Ronald A. Ledgett: trustee (see above)

Grants Analysis

Disclosure Period: calendar year ending 1998
Total Grants: $1,085,000*
Number of Grants: 115

Average Grant: $9,435
Typical Range: $1000 to $10,000
*Note: Grant analysis provided by foundation. A more recent grants list was unavailable.

Recent Grants

Note: Grants derived from 1996 Form 990.

General
1,743   Associate Grant Making Baystate, Boston, MA -- operating support

THE JOHN NUVEEN CO.

Company Headquarters

Chicago, IL
Web: http://www.nuveen.com

Company Description

Founded: 1992
Ticker: JNC
Exchange: NYSE
Former Name: Nuveen & Co., Inc.
Operating Revenue: US$396.4 million (2002)
Employees: 597 (2002)
SIC(s): 6200 Security & Commodity Brokers.
Parent Company: St. Paul Companies, Inc., 385 Washington Street, St. Paul, MN, United States

Nonmonetary Support

Type: Donated Equipment; Donated Products; In-kind Services

Giving Contact

Janice Thea
333 W. Wacker Dr.
Chicago, IL 60606
Phone: (312)917-7700

Description

Organization Type: Corporate Giving Program
Giving Locations: headquarters and operating communities.
Grant Types: Capital, Employee Matching Gifts, General Support, Matching, Multiyear/Continuing Support, Operating Expenses.

Typical Recipients

Arts & Humanities: Arts Associations & Councils, Arts Centers, Arts Festivals, Arts Institutes, Arts Outreach, Community Arts, Arts & Humanities-General, Libraries, Museums/Galleries, Music, Opera, Public Broadcasting
Civic & Public Affairs: Clubs, Economic Development, Economic Policy, Employment/Job Training, Ethnic Organizations, Housing, Inner-City Development, Minority Business, Philanthropic Organizations, Public Policy, Urban & Community Affairs, Women's Affairs, Zoos/Aquariums
Education: Afterschool/Enrichment Programs, Arts/Humanities Education, Business Education, Colleges & Universities, Community & Junior Colleges, Economic Education, Education Associations, Education Funds, Elementary Education (Private), Faculty Development, Education-General, International Exchange, Journalism/Media Education, Legal Education, Literacy, Preschool Education, Private Education (Precollege), Secondary Education (Private), Secondary Education (Public)
Health: Cancer, Children's Health/Hospitals, Clinics/Medical Centers, Health Policy/Cost Containment, Health Funds, Hospices, Hospitals (University Affiliated), Long-Term Care, Medical Research, Multiple Sclerosis
International: International Affairs
Science: Science Museums
Social Services: At-Risk Youth, Child Welfare, Community Centers, Community Service Organizations, Counseling, Day Care, Delinquency & Criminal Rehabilitation, Domestic Violence, Family Planning, Family

Services, Food/Clothing Distribution, Homes, People with Disabilities, Senior Services, Shelters/Homelessness, Social Services-General, Substance Abuse, United Funds/United Ways, Youth Organizations

Application Procedures

Initial Contact: a full proposal
Application Requirements: a description of organization, amount requested, purpose of funds sought, recently audited financial statement, and proof of tax-exempt status

Restrictions

Does not support individuals, religious organizations for sectarian purposes, political or lobbying groups, or organizations outside operating areas.

Additional Information

Publications: Corporate Contributions Guidelines; Application Form

Corporate Officials

John P. Amboian: executive vice president, chief financial officer PRIM CORP EMPL president: John Nuveen Co.
Anthony Taylor Dean: president, chief operating officer B McPherson, KS 1945. ED University of Chicago; Yale University (1967). PRIM CORP EMPL president, chief operating officer: John Nuveen Co.
Timothy R. Schwertfeger: chairman, chief executive officer B Chicago, IL 1949. ED Northwestern University (1971); Georgetown University (1974). PRIM CORP EMPL chairman, chief executive officer: John Nuveen Co.

Grants Analysis

Typical Range: $2,500 to $5,000

OAK GROVE SCHOOL

Giving Contact

Joann Clark-Austin, President
PO Box 150
South China, ME 04358
Phone: (207)622-6339

Alternate Contact

Lucia Whittelsey
163 Silver Street
Waterville, ME 04901
Note: For scholarship requests.

Description

Founded: 1993
EIN: 010211537
Organization Type: Private Foundation
Grant Types: General Support, Scholarship.

Financial Summary

Total Giving: $107,073 (fiscal year ending June 30, 2001); $111,258 (fiscal 1998); $95,541 (fiscal 1997)
Giving Analysis: Giving for fiscal 2001 includes: foundation scholarships ($10,000); fiscal 1998: foundation scholarships ($38,625) foundation ($72,633)
Assets: $1,892,997 (fiscal 2001); $1,984,440 (fiscal 1998); $1,911,580 (fiscal 1997)
Gifts Received: $6,073 (fiscal 2001); $25,028 (fiscal 1998); $5,236 (fiscal 1997). Note: Note: In fiscal 1998, contributions were received from Archie W. Berry Jr. ($20,000).

Typical Recipients

Arts & Humanities: Arts Centers, Film & Video, Libraries, Opera
Education: Arts/Humanities Education, Colleges & Universities, Faculty Development, Education-General, International Studies, Medical Education, Minority Education, Private Education (Precollege), Public

Education (Precollege), Science/Mathematics Education, Secondary Education (Private), Secondary Education (Public), Student Aid
Health: Adolescent Health Issues, Hospices, Nursing Services
Religion: Religious Organizations, Religious Welfare
Social Services: Community Service Organizations, Family Planning, Youth Organizations

Application Procedures
Initial Contact: Request application form and guidelines.
Deadlines: January 15.

Additional Information
Publications: Oak Grove Application Form and financial aid forms.

Foundation Officials
Leroy Austin: corporator
Archie Berry: corporator
Margaret Cates: corporator
Paul Cates: corporator
Joann Clark Austin, Esq.: president
Elizabeth Cole: corporator
David Duplessie: corporator
Elizabeth Eldridge: corporator
Richard Guttmacher: vice president
Bernard Huebner: corporator
Gerald Robbins: corporator
Nathaniel Shed: treasurer
Lucia Whittelsey: clerk

Grants Analysis
Disclosure Period: fiscal year ending June 30, 2001
Total Grants: $97,073*
Number of Grants: 31*
Average Grant: $2,894*
Highest Grant: $10,268
Lowest Grant: $500
Typical Range: $1,000 to $7,000
*Note: Giving excludes scholarships. Average grant figure excludes highest grant.

Recent Grants
Note: Grants derived from fiscal 2001 Form 990.

General
10,268	Madison High School, Madison, ME -- TV and video production class
10,000	Meeting School, Rindge, NH -- scholarships
5,240	Lawrence High school, Fairfield, ME
5,171	Mt. View High School, Thorndike, ME
5,000	Community School, Camden, ME -- Passages Program
5,000	Family Planning Association of Maine, Augusta, ME -- teen outreach program
5,000	Friends of Art and Film, Waterville, ME -- Maine International Film Festival
4,387	Erskine Academy, China, ME -- Eleanor Woodman Fund-Nursing Services
4,000	Maine Youth Alliance, Waterville, ME -- cultural arts
3,800	Hospice Volunteers, Waterville, ME -- art therapy in youth grieving

OAK TREE CHARITABLE FOUNDATION

Giving Contact
Sherwood C. Chillingworth, Executive Vice President
285 W. Huntington Dr.
Arcadia, CA 91007
Phone: (626)574-6346

Description
Founded: 1995
EIN: 954506950
Organization Type: Private Foundation
Giving Locations: CA: San Gabriel Valley, Southern California, Los Angeles metropolitan area
Grant Types: General Support.

Donor Information
Founder: Established in 1995 by the Oak Tree Racing Assn.

Financial Summary
Total Giving: $359,842 (fiscal year ending May 31, 2001); $245,733 (fiscal 1999); $193,600 (fiscal 1998)
Giving Analysis: Giving for fiscal 1999 includes: foundation grants to United Way ($1,000)
Assets: $5,564,328 (fiscal 2001); $5,271,944 (fiscal 1999); $4,307,751 (fiscal 1996)
Gifts Received: $4,000,000 (fiscal 1995). Note: In fiscal 1995, contributions were received from the Oak Tree Racing Assn.

Typical Recipients
Arts & Humanities: History & Archaeology, Museums/Galleries, Music
Civic & Public Affairs: Civic & Public Affairs-General, Professional & Trade Associations, Women's Affairs
Education: Agricultural Education, Colleges & Universities, Education-General, School Volunteerism, Student Aid, Vocational & Technical Education
Health: Cancer, Hospitals, Medical Rehabilitation, Medical Research, Single-Disease Health Associations
Religion: Churches, Religious Welfare
Science: Scientific Labs
Social Services: Animal Protection, Big Brother/Big Sister, Camps, Child Welfare, Community Service Organizations, Crime Prevention, Recreation & Athletics, Scouts, Substance Abuse

Application Procedures
Initial Contact: Contact foundation for its grant application.
Application Requirements: Include a description of organization, amount requested, purpose of funds sought, recently audited financial statement, and proof of tax-exempt status.
Deadlines: March 31 of each year

Restrictions
Does not support individuals, religious organizations for sectarian purposes, political or lobbying groups, or organizations outside operating areas.

Additional Information
Foundation will support organizations outside its operating area that benefit the thoroughbred horse racing industry.
Publications: Application Form

Foundation Officials
John H. Barr: vice president
Thomas R. Capehart: vice president
Sherwood C. Chillingworth: executive vice president
Clement L. Hirsch: president
William T. Pascoe, III: vice president, treasurer
Mrs. Bernard J. Ridder: vice president
Jack K. Robbins: vice president, secretary

Grants Analysis
Disclosure Period: fiscal year ending May 31, 2001
Total Grants: $359,842*
Number of Grants: 84
Average Grant: $3,372*
Highest Grant: $80,000
Lowest Grant: $100

Typical Range: $200 to $5,000
*Note: Average grant figure excludes highest grant.

Recent Grants
Note: Grants derived from 2001 Form 990.

General
80,000	California Thoroughbred Trainers, Arcadia, CA
68,000	California Thoroughbred Horsemen's Foundation, Arcadia, CA -- health and recreation programs for low-income families
60,000	Edwin J. Gregson Foundation, Arcadia, CA -- stable recreation and staff support
25,000	Grayson-Jockey Club Research Foundation, New York, NY
20,000	Race Track Chaplaincy of America, Belmont, CA -- spiritual and social welfare programs
17,500	California Philharmonic Foundation, Pasadena, CA -- community symphony orchestra
10,500	Race Track Chaplaincy of America, Belmont, CA -- spiritual and social welfare programs
10,000	Church of Our Saviour, El Monte, CA -- food pantry and job training for low income families, capital campaign
10,000	Don MacBeth Memorial Jockey Fund, Beverly Hills, CA -- thoroughbred riders
10,000	Edwin J. Gregson Foundation, Arcadia, CA -- assistance to backstretch employees and families

CHARLES O'BLENESS FOUNDATION

Giving Contact
c/o Huntington National Bank NA
41 S. High St.
Columbus, OH 43215
Phone: (614)480-5453

Description
Founded: 1963
EIN: 316042978
Organization Type: Private Foundation
Giving Locations: OH: Athens County
Grant Types: General Support.

Donor Information
Founder: the late Charles O'Bleness, Charles O'Bleness Foundation No. 1

Financial Summary
Total Giving: $170,402 (fiscal year ending June 30, 2002); $163,652 (fiscal 2001); $137,075 (fiscal 2000)
Giving Analysis: Giving for fiscal 2000 includes: foundation scholarships ($2,100); fiscal 1999: foundation scholarships ($2,500) foundation ($104,615)
Assets: $3,240,781 (fiscal 2002); $3,566,394 (fiscal 2001); $3,664,171 (fiscal 2000)

Typical Recipients
Arts & Humanities: Arts Associations & Councils, Arts Centers, Arts Festivals, Historic Preservation, History & Archaeology, Libraries, Museums/Galleries, Performing Arts, Theater
Civic & Public Affairs: Botanical Gardens/Parks, Chambers of Commerce, Economic Development, Civic & Public Affairs-General, Nonprofit Management, Parades/Festivals, Rural Affairs
Education: Colleges & Universities, International Studies, Medical Education, Secondary Education (Public), Student Aid
Environment: Environment-General
Health: Emergency/Ambulance Services, Hospices, Hospitals, Nursing Services, Prenatal Health Issues

Religion: Churches, Religious Welfare
Social Services: Animal Protection, Child Welfare, Community Service Organizations, Crime Prevention, Recreation & Athletics, Recreation & Athletics, Scouts, Social Services-General, United Funds/United Ways, Youth Organizations

Application Procedures

Initial Contact: The foundation has no formal grant application procedure or application form.
Deadlines: October 15.

Additional Information

Trust(s): Huntington National Bank NA

Foundation Officials

John M. Jones: adv
David Vogt: adv
Theodore Vogt: adv

Grants Analysis

Disclosure Period: fiscal year ending June 30, 2002
Total Grants: $170,402
Number of Grants: 10
Average Grant: $7,822*
Highest Grant: $100,000
Lowest Grant: $75
Typical Range: $5,000 to $15,000
*Note:** Average grant figure excludes highest grant.

Recent Grants

Note: Grants derived from fiscal 2000 Form 990.

Library-Related

9,000	Coonskin Library Association, Amesville, OH

General

71,429	Athens High School, Athens, TX -- for century club for tennis association courts
35,715	O'Blesness Memorial Hospital -- for pledge payment
21,000	O'Blesness Memorial Hospital -- for Betty Anastas nursing scholarship
10,000	Ohio University, Athens, OH -- for kids on campus for endowment/education
5,000	Ferndale Park Association -- for gazebo and landscaping
2,500	Reuse Industries -- for "recovering over roots" pledge
1,000	United Appeal of Athens County, Athens, GA
200	Donors Forum of Ohio, Columbus, OH -- for conference in Athens
75	Athens Marching Bank Festival -- for grand champion sponsor fee
56	National Child Safety Council, Greenwood, SC -- for safety pup program

A. LINDSAY AND OLIVE B. O'CONNOR FOUNDATION

Giving Contact

Donald F. Bishop, Jr., President & Executive Director
PO Box D
Hobart, NY 13788
Phone: (607)538-9248
Fax: (607)538-1650

Description

Founded: 1965
EIN: 166063485
Organization Type: General Purpose Foundation
Giving Locations: NY: Delaware County and contiguous rural counties in upstate New York
Grant Types: Capital, Endowment, General Support, Project, Scholarship.

Donor Information

Founder: The foundation was established in 1965 by the late Olive B. O'Connor .

Financial Summary

Total Giving: $2,981,839 (2001); $2,515,845 (1999); $3,132,543 (1998)
Giving Analysis: Giving for 1999 includes: foundation matching gifts ($30,000) foundation scholarships ($273,000)
Assets: $72,766,636 (2001); $74,707,970 (1999); $70,851,690 (1998)
Gifts Received: $2,894,720 (1998)

Typical Recipients

Arts & Humanities: Arts Associations & Councils, Arts Centers, Arts Institutes, Historic Preservation, History & Archaeology, Libraries, Museums/Galleries, Music, Theater
Civic & Public Affairs: Botanical Gardens/Parks, Community Foundations, Economic Development, Employment/Job Training, Civic & Public Affairs-General, Housing, Law & Justice, Municipalities/Towns, Philanthropic Organizations, Professional & Trade Associations, Safety, Urban & Community Affairs, Zoos/Aquariums
Education: Agricultural Education, Colleges & Universities, Community & Junior Colleges, Education Funds, Education Reform, Elementary Education (Private), Engineering/Technological Education, Education-General, Health & Physical Education, Legal Education, Medical Education, Private Education (Precollege), Public Education (Precollege), School Volunteerism, Student Aid
Environment: Forestry, Environment-General, Resource Conservation, Watershed
Health: Emergency/Ambulance Services, Heart, Hospices, Hospitals, Single-Disease Health Associations
Religion: Churches, Ministries, Religious Organizations, Religious Welfare
Science: Science Museums
Social Services: Community Centers, Community Service Organizations, Day Care, People with Disabilities, Scouts, Senior Services, Social Services-General, United Funds/United Ways, Youth Organizations

Application Procedures

Initial Contact: Applicants should contact the foundation for an application form. Foundation accepts phone calls Monday through Friday from 9 a.m. to 3 p.m. only.
Application Requirements: In addition to the information required on the application, the foundation requires applicants to provide proof of tax-exempt status under IRS section 501(c)(3) or proof that the applicant is a unit of the government. It is preferred, but not required, to have sketches or drawings submitted on legal size or smaller paper. In almost all cases, a site visit will be arranged after the full application has been filed. Proposals of $5,000 or less are considered on a monthly basis if the proposal meets the following conditions: the organization is located in or directly benefits Delaware County, NY; applicant has not received a grant from the foundation for the same project in the last three years; and applicant is prepared to match funds dollar for dollar.
Deadlines: None, for grant requests of $5,000 or less.

Restrictions

As a general rule, the foundation will not make grants to individuals; for meeting annual operating expenditures or retiring existing debts, and prefers to make grants of a non-recurring nature. Grants are generally restricted to programs that have a direct impact on the quality of life in Delaware County and the seven contiguously surrounding counties in upstate New York (Broome, Chenango, Greene, Otsego, Schoharie, Sullivan, and Ulster).

Additional Information

Publications: Program Policy Statement; Grant Application

Foundation Officials

Donald F. Bishop, II: president, executive director
Robert L. Bishop, II: chairman, member advisory committee
Charlotte Bishop Hill: vchairwoman, mem adv comm
Pamela Hill: executive secretary
William J. Murphy: director, mem adv comm
Eugene E. Peckham: director, mem adv comm B Stamford, CT 1940. ED Wesleyan University BA (1962); Harvard University JD (1965). PRIM CORP EMPL partner: Hinman, Howard & Kattell. NONPR AFFIL member: New York State Bar Association; adj professor acctg: State University New York Binghamton; member: House of Delaware; treasurer: Joint Legislative Advisory Committee Estates Powers & Trusts Law & Surrogates Court Procedure Act; member: Broome County Bar Association; member: Federal Bar Associations 6th Judicial District; fellow: American College Trust & Estate Counsel; trustee: Binghampton Boys Girls Club.

Grants Analysis

Disclosure Period: calendar year ending 2001
Total Grants: $2,646,339*
Number of Grants: 272
Average Grant: $9,729
Highest Grant: $200,000
Lowest Grant: $27
Typical Range: $5,000 to $20,000
*Note:** Giving excludes scholarships.

Recent Grants

Note: Grants derived from 2001 Form 990.

Library-Related

200,000	Olive Free Library, West Shokan, NY -- permanent endowment
100,000	Broome Library Foundation, Binghamton, NY
20,000	Catskill Mountain Crafts Collective, Stamford, NY -- color and crafts festival

General

100,000	Delhi Fire Department, Delhi, NY -- new pumper truck
100,000	Roberson Museum and Science Center, Binghamton, NY -- operations
88,330	Delaware County Office of Employment and Training, Delhi, NY -- special education skills training and work experience for youth
75,000	Assembly of God, Delhi, NY -- cost of performances and cultural center
65,000	O'Connor Hospital, Delhi, NY -- costs of expanding the surgical services at the hospital
63,200	Bassett Hospital, Delhi, NY -- facility master plan
58,900	Catskill Revitalization Center, Stamford, NY -- 2001 operating budget
58,900	Catskill Revitalization Corporation, Stamford, NY -- 2001 operating budget
58,900	Catskill Revitalization Corporation, Stamford, NY -- 2001 operating budget
50,000	Delaware City Office for the Aging, Delhi, NY -- replace outdated lifeline emergency units

KATHRYN O'CONNOR FOUNDATION

Giving Contact

D. H. Braman, Jr., President
1 O'Connor Plz., Suite 1100
Victoria, TX 77901
Phone: (361)578-6271

Description

Founded: 1951
EIN: 746039415
Organization Type: Private Foundation
Giving Locations: TX: Southern Texas, especially Victoria and Refugio counties and the surrounding area
Grant Types: Capital, Emergency, Endowment, General Support, Multiyear/Continuing Support, Operating Expenses, Professorship, Seed Money.

Donor Information

Founder: the late Kathryn S. O'Connor, Tom O'Connor, Jr., Dennis O'Connor

Financial Summary

Total Giving: $394,424 (2000); $376,138 (1999); $360,367 (1998)
Assets: $6,588,093 (2000); $6,393,143 (1999); $6,400,049 (1998)
Gifts Received: $16,429 (2000); $87 (1995); $55 (1994). Note: In 2000, contributions were received from Louise S. O'Connor. In 1995, contributions were received from the Texas Sanitation Co. ($65) and Alice Wilson ($22).

Typical Recipients

Arts & Humanities: Arts Associations & Councils, Ethnic & Folk Arts, History & Archaeology, Libraries, Museums/Galleries, Music, Theater
Civic & Public Affairs: Municipalities/Towns, Parades/Festivals
Education: Continuing Education, Literacy, Medical Education, Private Education (Precollege), Public Education (Precollege), Religious Education, Science/Mathematics Education, Secondary Education (Private), Student Aid
Health: Arthritis, Health Organizations, Hospices, Hospitals, Kidney, Prenatal Health Issues
Religion: Churches, Dioceses, Ministries, Religious Organizations, Religious Welfare
Science: Science Museums
Social Services: Child Abuse, Community Service Organizations, Domestic Violence, Food/Clothing Distribution, Homes, People with Disabilities, Senior Services, Social Services-General, Substance Abuse, Youth Organizations

Application Procedures

Initial Contact: Send a brief letter of inquiry describing program or project. Include a resume of activities and amount requested.
Deadlines: None.

Restrictions

Generally limited to religious and educational organizations. Does not support individuals.

Foundation Officials

Robert L. Coffey: treasurer
Dennis O'Connor: president B Victoria, TX 1907. ED University of Texas BA (1928). PRIM CORP EMPL senior director emeritus: Victoria Bankshares.
Thomas O'Connor, Jr.: vice president B Victoria, TX 1915. ED Victoria Junior College. PRIM CORP EMPL senior chairman, director: Victoria Bankshares.
Venable B. Proctor: secretary

Grants Analysis

Disclosure Period: calendar year ending 2000
Total Grants: $394,424
Number of Grants: 22
Average Grant: $9,579*
Highest Grant: $135,000
Typical Range: $1,000 to $20,000
*Note: Average grant figure excludes two highest grants ($202,835).

Recent Grants

Note: Grants derived from 1999 Form 990.

General

135,000	St. Joseph High School, Victoria, TX
85,638	St. Dennis Church, Victoria, TX
22,500	Nazareth Academy, Victoria, TX
22,500	Our Lady of Victory School, Victoria, TX
22,500	Trinity Episcopal School, Victoria, TX
20,000	Friends of Texas Historical Commission, Austin, TX
12,500	Refugio County Memorial Hospital District, Refugio, TX
10,000	Perpetual Help Home, Victoria, TX
10,000	Youth Home of Victoria, Victoria, TX
6,000	Our Lady of Guadalupe Church, Tivoli, TX

ROBERT STEWART AND HELEN PFEIFFER ODELL FUND

Giving Contact

Gene Ranghiasci, Vice President
Wells Fargo Bank
420 Montgomery St., 7th Fl.
San Francisco, CA 94104
Phone: (415)396-3215
Fax: (415)834-0604

Description

Founded: 1967
EIN: 946132116
Organization Type: General Purpose Foundation
Giving Locations: CA: Northern California, with emphasis on San Francisco
Grant Types: General Support.

Donor Information

Founder: Established in 1967 by the late Robert Stewart Odell and the late Helen Pfeiffer Odell .

Financial Summary

Total Giving: $2,300,000 (2001); $2,192,635 (2000); $2,345,000 (1999)
Giving Analysis: Giving for 1999 includes: foundation scholarships ($57,828) 1997: foundation scholarships ($25,000)
Assets: $40,000,000 (2001); $53,070,862 (2000); $57,915,030 (1999)

Typical Recipients

Arts & Humanities: Arts Festivals, Ethnic & Folk Arts, History & Archaeology, Libraries, Museums/Galleries, Music, Opera, Performing Arts, Theater
Civic & Public Affairs: Community Foundations, Economic Development, Housing, Law & Justice, Legal Aid, Parades/Festivals, Public Policy, Safety, Urban & Community Affairs, Zoos/Aquariums
Education: Afterschool/Enrichment Programs, Business Education, Colleges & Universities, Economic Education, Education Funds, Elementary Education (Private), International Studies, Preschool Education, Private Education (Precollege), Religious Education, School Volunteerism, Science/Mathematics Education, Secondary Education (Private), Secondary Education (Public), Student Aid
Environment: Environment-General, Resource Conservation
Health: Children's Health/Hospitals, Clinics/Medical Centers, Eyes/Blindness, Health Organizations, Hospitals, Medical Rehabilitation, Medical Research, Mental Health, Public Health
International: Foreign Educational Institutions, Human Rights, International Affairs, International Environmental Issues, International Organizations, Missionary/Religious Activities

Religion: Churches, Religious Organizations, Religious Welfare, Seminaries
Science: Science Museums, Scientific Centers & Institutes
Social Services: At-Risk Youth, Child Welfare, Community Service Organizations, Day Care, Family Services, Homes, People with Disabilities, Recreation & Athletics, Scouts, Shelters/Homelessness, United Funds/United Ways, Youth Organizations

Application Procedures

Initial Contact: Organizations should send a letter to the Fund.
Application Requirements: Letters should detail the project for which the grant is sought and a copy of the Federal tax exemption letter showing that the applicant is a public charity.
Deadlines: None. The board meets four or five times per year. The foundation requests that applications be sent early in the calendar year to assure consideration.
Review Process: The trustees make payments between October 15 and December 31 of each year.

Restrictions

The fund only makes grants to public charities. Grants are not made to individuals.

Additional Information

Wells Fargo Bank serves as a corporate trustee to the Fund.
Publications: Guidelines

Foundation Officials

James P. Conn: trustee B 1938. PRIM CORP EMPL president, director: Bay Meadows Catering Inc. CORP AFFIL president: The Tipsters.
Paul B. Fay, Jr.: trustee B 1918. PRIM CORP EMPL president: Fay Improvement Co. CORP AFFIL director: First America Title Insurance Co.; director: Vestaur Securities Inc.; director: First America Finance Corp.

Grants Analysis

Disclosure Period: calendar year ending 2000
Total Grants: $2,192,635
Number of Grants: 86
Average Grant: $25,496
Highest Grant: $60,000
Typical Range: $10,000 to $50,000

Recent Grants

Note: Grants derived from 1999 Form 990.

General

62,672	Archbishop Alemany Scholarship Fund, San Francisco, CA
60,000	Bellarmine College Preparatory, Louisville, KY
60,000	Blind Babies Foundation, San Francisco, CA
60,000	Dominican Sisters of Mission San Jose, San Jose, CA
60,000	Thomas Aquinas College, Santa Paula, CA
60,000	Youth Tennis Foundation
55,000	Community Foundation Silicon Valley, San Jose, CA
50,000	Bay Area Scholarships for Inner City Children, San Francisco, CA
50,000	Mount St. Joseph - St. Elizabeth, San Francisco, CA
50,000	Saint Elizabeth High School

O'DONNELL FOUNDATION

Giving Contact

Carolyn R. Bacon, Executive Director
100 Crescent Court, Suite 1660
Dallas, TX 75201

Phone: (214)871-5800
Fax: (214)855-8988
Web: http://www.odf.org

Description

Founded: 1957
EIN: 756023326
Organization Type: General Purpose Foundation
Giving Locations: TX
Grant Types: Capital, Endowment, General Support, Research.

Donor Information

Founder: The O'Donnell Foundation was established in Texas in 1957 by Peter O'Donnell Jr., and Mrs. Peter O'Donnell Jr.

Financial Summary

Total Giving: $4,163,489 (fiscal year ending November 30, 2001); $19,908,458 (fiscal 2000); $14,236,600 (fiscal 1999). Note: Fiscal 1997 Giving includes stock donation ($5,415,206).
Assets: $147,567,013 (fiscal 2001); $138,435,724 (fiscal 2000); $140,668,448 (fiscal 1999)
Gifts Received: $650,000 (fiscal 2001); $3,282,875 (fiscal 1999); $1,537,500 (fiscal 1998). Note: In fiscal 2001, contributions were received from Edith Jones O'Donnell and Peter O'Donnell, Jr. In fiscal 2000, contributions were received from Edith Jones O'Donnell ($3,376,875) and Peter O'Donnell, Jr. ($435,238).

Typical Recipients

Arts & Humanities: Arts Centers, Arts Outreach, Community Arts, Ethnic & Folk Arts, Arts & Humanities-General, History & Archaeology, Libraries, Literary Arts, Museums/Galleries, Music, Opera, Public Broadcasting
Civic & Public Affairs: Botanical Gardens/Parks, Business/Free Enterprise, Community Foundations, Economic Development, Economic Policy, Civic & Public Affairs-General, Municipalities/Towns, Philanthropic Organizations, Public Policy, Urban & Community Affairs
Education: Business Education, Colleges & Universities, Education Associations, Education Reform, Elementary Education (Private), Elementary Education (Public), Engineering/Technological Education, Faculty Development, Education-General, Literacy, Medical Education, Minority Education, Minority Education, Private Education (Precollege), Public Education (Precollege), Science/Mathematics Education, Secondary Education (Private), Secondary Education (Public), Student Aid
Environment: Forestry
Health: Clinics/Medical Centers, Hospitals (University Affiliated), Respiratory
International: Foreign Arts Organizations
Religion: Churches
Science: Scientific Centers & Institutes, Scientific Organizations, Scientific Research
Social Services: Child Welfare, Counseling, Scouts

Application Procedures

Initial Contact: Requests for grants should be made by letter.
Application Requirements: Applicants should submit a brief letter outlining the project and including a timetable, budget, list of funds already pledged to the project, and the specific contribution requested. A list of the organization's governing board and a copy of the IRS determination letter of tax-exempt status for the organization should be attached to the application.
Deadlines: None.
Review Process: The board of directors meets as required.

Restrictions

The foundation prefers to give charitable and educational grants to local institutions. No grants are made to individuals, and the foundation does not award scholarships, fellowships, loans, or prizes.

Foundation Officials

Carolyn R. Bacon: chief executive director PRIM CORP EMPL secretary, treasurer, director: Baker Brokerage.
Duncan Eugene Boeckman: director
Rita C. Clements: vice president NONPR AFFIL vice chairman: University Texas System.
Dr. Philip O'Bryan Montgomery, Jr.: director B Montgomery, AL 1921. ED Southern Methodist University BS (1942); Columbia University MD (1945). PRIM NONPR EMPL professor: Southwestern Medical School. NONPR AFFIL member: Texas Medical Association; member: Tissue Culture Association; member: Society Experimental Biology & Medicine; member: Professional Group Medical Electronic Institute Radio Engineers; trustee: Saint Marks School Texas; member: Pan-American Medical Association; member: International Society Cell Biology; founder: Optical Society Texas; member: International Federation Medical Electronic; member: Biophysics Society; member: International Academy Pathology; fellow: American Society Clinical Pathologists; member: American Society Experimental Pathology; member: American Society Cell Biology; member: American Association University Professors; member: American Medical Association; member: American Association Cancer Research; member: American Association Pathologists & Bacteriologists; member: American Academy Forensic Sciences; member: American Academy of Arts & Sciences. CLUB AFFIL president, director: Damon Runyon Club.
Edith Jones O'Donnell: secretary, treasurer
Peter O'Donnell, Jr.: president

Grants Analysis

Disclosure Period: fiscal year ending November 30, 2000
Total Grants: $19,908,458
Number of Grants: 47
Average Grant: $15,968*
Highest Grant: $18,321,207
Lowest Grant: $385
Typical Range: $1,000 to $5,000
***Note:** Average grant excludes three highest grants ($18,321,207, $2,211,840, and $125,900).

Recent Grants

Note: Grants derived from fiscal 2000 Form 990.

General

18,321,207	University of Texas at Austin, Austin, TX -- building
1,211,840	Dallas Public Schools, Dallas, TX
125,900	College Entrance Examination Board, New York, NY
23,122	Plano Senior High School, Plano, TX
20,000	Garland Independent School District, Garland, TX
19,225	Dallas Museum of Art, Dallas, TX
19,129	Duncanville High School, Duncanville, TX
17,550	Booker T. Washington High School, Dallas, TX -- AP
13,910	Plano East High School, Plano, TX -- AP
11,291	Texas Christian University, Ft. Worth, TX

SYLVAN AND ANN OESTREICHER FOUNDATION

Giving Contact

Robert F. Welch, Secretary
156 Pine St.
Garden City, NY 11530
Phone: (516)741-0917

Description

Founded: 1948
EIN: 136085974
Organization Type: Private Foundation
Grant Types: General Support.

Donor Information

Founder: the late Sylvan Oestreicher

Financial Summary

Total Giving: $392,950 (fiscal year ending April 30, 2002); $480,970 (fiscal 2000); $236,650 (fiscal 1999)
Assets: $12,244,009 (fiscal 2002); $14,060,735 (fiscal 2000); $13,313,843 (fiscal 1998)

Typical Recipients

Arts & Humanities: Arts Centers, Ethnic & Folk Arts, Libraries, Literary Arts, Museums/Galleries, Music, Opera, Public Broadcasting
Civic & Public Affairs: Community Foundations, Ethnic Organizations, Civic & Public Affairs-General, Parades/Festivals, Philanthropic Organizations
Education: Arts/Humanities Education, Colleges & Universities, Community & Junior Colleges, Education Associations, Education-General, International Studies, Medical Education, Private Education (Precollege), Student Aid
Environment: Resource Conservation
Health: Cancer, Children's Health/Hospitals, Clinics/Medical Centers, Emergency/Ambulance Services, Geriatric Health, Hospices, Hospitals, Long-Term Care, Medical Research, Mental Health, Research/Studies Institutes, Research/Studies Institutes, Single-Disease Health Associations
International: Foreign Arts Organizations, Health Care/Hospitals, International Organizations, International Relief Efforts, Missionary/Religious Activities
Religion: Churches, Jewish Causes, Missionary Activities (Domestic), Religious Organizations, Religious Welfare
Social Services: Animal Protection, Child Welfare, Community Service Organizations, Homes, People with Disabilities, Shelters/Homelessness, United Funds/United Ways, Youth Organizations

Application Procedures

Initial Contact: Send a brief letter of inquiry.
Deadlines: None.

Foundation Officials

Merwin Lewis: vice president
Ann Oestreicher: president
Robert F. Welch: secretary

Grants Analysis

Disclosure Period: fiscal year ending April 30, 2002
Total Grants: $392,950
Number of Grants: 156
Average Grant: $2,206*
Highest Grant: $51,000
Lowest Grant: $200
Typical Range: $1,000 to $5,000
***Note:** Average grant figure excludes highest grant.

Recent Grants

Note: Grants derived from fiscal 2000 Form 990.

Library-Related

50,000	Richard Nixon Library and Birthplace Foundation, Washington, DC
5,300	New York Public Library, New York, NY

General

55,300	Memorial Sloan-Kettering, New York, NY
25,000	International Music Foundation, Chicago, IL
15,000	Northwestern Memorial Hospital Foundation, Chicago, IL
11,500	Metropolitan Opera Association, New York, NY

10,000	Alfred E. Smith Memorial Foundation, New York, NY
10,000	Emory University School of Medicine, Atlanta, GA
10,000	F.I.T. Alumni Association
10,000	Washington University in St. Louis, St. Louis, MO
9,900	Menninger Foundation, Topeka, KS
8,000	Irvington Institute, New York, NY

THE OFFIELD FAMILY FOUNDATION

Giving Contact
Marie Larson, Secretary
400 North Michigan Avenue, Room 407
Chicago, IL 60611
Phone: (312)467-5480
Fax: (312)467-0473

Description
Founded: 1953
EIN: 366066240
Organization Type: Family Foundation
Giving Locations: nationally.
Grant Types: General Support.

Donor Information
Founder: Incorporated in 1940 by Dorothy Wrigley Offield.

Financial Summary
Total Giving: $6,471,822 (fiscal year ending June 30, 1999); $4,904,000 (fiscal 1998); $4,135,100 (fiscal 1997)
Assets: $112,808,917 (fiscal 1999); $111,401,234 (fiscal 1998); $90,625,914 (fiscal 1997)
Gifts Received: $1,623,211 (fiscal 2000); $633,661 (fiscal 1998); $10,252,548 (fiscal 1997)

Typical Recipients
Arts & Humanities: Arts Associations & Councils, Arts Centers, Film & Video, Arts & Humanities-General, History & Archaeology, Libraries, Museums/Galleries, Music, Performing Arts, Public Broadcasting
Civic & Public Affairs: Botanical Gardens/Parks, Clubs, Community Foundations, Civic & Public Affairs-General, Public Policy, Urban & Community Affairs, Women's Affairs, Zoos/Aquariums
Education: Arts/Humanities Education, Colleges & Universities, Education Funds, Environmental Education, Education-General, Medical Education, Private Education (Precollege), Public Education (Precollege), Student Aid
Environment: Air/Water Quality, Environment-General, Protection, Resource Conservation, Watershed, Wildlife Protection
Health: Cancer, Children's Health/Hospitals, Clinics/Medical Centers, Emergency/Ambulance Services, Health Funds, Health Organizations, Hospices, Hospitals, Hospitals (University Affiliated), Medical Research, Public Health, Transplant Networks/Donor Banks, Trauma Treatment
International: International Environmental Issues
Religion: Churches, Religious Welfare
Science: Science Museums, Scientific Centers & Institutes
Social Services: Animal Protection, At-Risk Youth, Camps, Child Welfare, Community Service Organizations, Day Care, Family Planning, Family Services, Food/Clothing Distribution, Homes, People with Disabilities, Recreation & Athletics, Scouts, Substance Abuse, United Funds/United Ways, Youth Organizations

Application Procedures
Initial Contact: Applicants should mail a letter of inquiry describing the proposed project, information about the organization, and its future goals.

Deadlines: None.
Review Process: The board makes final decisions on grants at its meeting in June.

Additional Information
Although the Santa Catalina Island Conservancy is a private foundation, the Offield Family Foundation maintains expenditures responsibility.

Foundation Officials
Raymond Hibner Drymalski: assistant treasurer, assistant secretary B Chicago, IL 1936. ED Georgetown University BA (1958); University of Michigan JD (1961). PRIM CORP EMPL partner: Bell Boyd & Lloyd. CORP AFFIL director: Northwestern Memorial Corp. NONPR AFFIL member: American Bar Association; director: Northwestern Memorial Hospital. CLUB AFFIL Economic Club.
Marie Larson: secretary
Edna Jean Offield: chairman, director
James S. Offield: vice president, treasurer, director PRIM CORP EMPL president: El Rojo Grande Ranch.
Paxson H. Offield: president, director B 1951. ED University of Denver (1975). PRIM CORP EMPL president: Santa Catalina Island Co. ADD CORP EMPL president: SCI.

Grants Analysis
Disclosure Period: fiscal year ending June 30, 2000
Total Grants: $4,904,000
Number of Grants: 103
Average Grant: $35,710*
Highest Grant: $500,000
Lowest Grant: $500
Typical Range: $1,000 to $25,000 and $50,000 to $200,000
*Note: Average grant figure excludes three highest grants ($500,000, $390,821, and $335,000).

Recent Grants
Note: Grants derived from fiscal 2000 Form 990.

Library-Related
50,000	Sedona Public Library, Sedona, AZ

General
500,000	Sedona Cultural Park, Sedona, AZ
390,821	Verde Valley Medical Center, Cottonwood, AZ
335,000	Catalina Seabass Fund, Avalon, CA
300,000	Greater Sedona Community Foundation, Sedona, AZ
250,000	Catalina Island Conservancy, Avalon, CA
250,000	Planned Parenthood Association, Chicago, IL
250,000	Sedona Medical Center, Sedona, AZ
200,000	Peregrine Fund, Boise, ID
200,000	Peregrine Fund, Boise, ID
200,000	Sedona Cultural Park, Sedona, AZ

OG&E ELECTRIC SERVICES

Company Headquarters
Oklahoma City, OK
Web: http://www.oge.com

Company Description
Former Name: Oklahoma Gas & Electric Co.
Employees: 2,765
SIC(s): 1311 Crude Petroleum & Natural Gas, 4911 Electric Services, 4922 Natural Gas Transmission.

Nonmonetary Support
Type: Loaned Employees; Loaned Executives
Note: Nonmonetary support is provided by the company.

Oklahoma Gas & Electric Co. Foundation

Giving Contact
Erma Elliot, Secretary & Treasurer
Box 321
Oklahoma City, OK 73101
Phone: (405)553-3196
Fax: (405)553-3567

Alternate Contact
321 North Harvey
Oklahoma City, OK 73102

Description
Founded: 1957
EIN: 736093572
Organization Type: Corporate Foundation
Giving Locations: OK: headquarters and operating communities.
Grant Types: Capital, Employee Matching Gifts, General Support, Scholarship.

Donor Information
Founder: Oklahoma Gas and Electric Co.

Financial Summary
Total Giving: $926,521 (2001); $892,669 (2000); $919,318 (1999). Note: Contributes through foundation only.
Giving Analysis: Giving for 2000 includes: foundation grants to United Way ($25,000); foundation matching gifts ($52,703); foundation ($814,966); 1999: foundation matching gifts (approx $55,000); foundation matching gifts ($68,569); foundation (approx $627,416); foundation ($850,749); 1998: foundation matching gifts ($55,647); foundation ($840,167);
Assets: $1,310,413 (2001); $790,243 (2000); $1,044,264 (1999)
Gifts Received: $1,400,000 (2001); $600,000 (2000); $800,000 (1999). Note: Contributions are received from Oklahoma Gas and Electric Co.

Typical Recipients
Arts & Humanities: Arts Associations & Councils, Arts Funds, Arts Institutes, Ballet, Ethnic & Folk Arts, Arts & Humanities-General, Historic Preservation, History & Archaeology, Libraries, Museums/Galleries, Music, Theater
Civic & Public Affairs: Botanical Gardens/Parks, Business/Free Enterprise, Community Foundations, Economic Development, Civic & Public Affairs-General, Municipalities/Towns, Professional & Trade Associations, Urban & Community Affairs, Zoos/Aquariums
Education: Business Education, Colleges & Universities, Community & Junior Colleges, Economic Education, Education-General, Medical Education, Private Education (Precollege), Public Education (Precollege), Science/Mathematics Education, Secondary Education (Public), Special Education
Environment: Resource Conservation
Health: Children's Health/Hospitals, Clinics/Medical Centers, Emergency/Ambulance Services, Health-General, Health Organizations, Heart, Hospitals, Medical Research, Public Health
International: International Affairs
Religion: Religious Welfare
Science: Science Museums
Social Services: Camps, Community Service Organizations, Counseling, Emergency Relief, Family Planning, Family Services, Food/Clothing Distribution, People with Disabilities, Recreation & Athletics, Scouts, Senior Services, Special Olympics, United Funds/United Ways, YMCA/YWCA/YMHA/YWHA, Youth Organizations

Application Procedures

Initial Contact: Send a brief letter.
Application Requirements: Include an outline of the proposed project, amount requested, and proof of 501(c)(3) status.
Deadlines: None.

Restrictions

Does not support fraternal organizations, individuals, political or lobbying groups, or religious organizations for sectarian purposes. Preference given to organizations in service areas.

Foundation Officials

Steven Moore: president B Sayre, OK 1946. ED University of Oklahoma BBA (1968); University of Oklahoma JD (1971). PRIM CORP EMPL chairman, president, chief executive officer, director: OGE Energy Corp.
A. M. Strecker: executive vice president, chief operating officer B Seiling, OK 1943. ED Oklahoma State University BSEE (1971). PRIM CORP EMPL executive vice president, chief operating officer: OG&E Electric Services. CORP AFFIL senior vice president: Oklahoma Gas & Electric Co.

Grants Analysis

Disclosure Period: calendar year ending 2001
Total Grants: $854,999*
Number of Grants: 73
Average Grant: $11,712
Highest Grant: $60,000
Lowest Grant: $500
Typical Range: $1,000 to $10,000 and $25,000 to $60,000
*Note: Giving excludes matching gifts.

Recent Grants

Note: Grants derived from 2001 Form 990.

General

80,000	Oklahoma Christian University of Science and Arts, Oklahoma City, OK
60,000	Allied Arts Foundation, Oklahoma City, OK
60,000	National Cowboy and Western Heritage Museum, Oklahoma City, OK
60,000	Oklahoma State University Foundation, Stillwater, OK
50,000	Cultural Development Corporation, Oklahoma City, OK
50,000	Oklahoma City Memorial Foundation, Oklahoma City, OK
50,000	Oklahoma City University, Oklahoma City, OK
50,000	Oklahoma City University, Oklahoma City, OK
35,000	Downtown Oklahoma City, Inc., Oklahoma City, OK
35,000	Special Care, Inc., Oklahoma City, OK

OHIO NATIONAL LIFE INSURANCE CO.

Company Headquarters

2720 S. River Rd.
Des Plaines, IL 60018

Company Description

Employees: 600
SIC(s): 6311 Life Insurance, 6321 Accident & Health Insurance.

Nonmonetary Support

Type: Donated Equipment; Workplace Solicitation

Ohio National Foundation

Giving Contact

Anthony G. Esposito, Vice President, Human Resources & Corporate Services
Ohio National Life Insurance Co.
PO Box 237
Cincinnati, OH 45201
Phone: (513)794-6594

Description

Founded: 1987
EIN: 311230164
Organization Type: Corporate Foundation
Giving Locations: OH: Cincinnati
Grant Types: Capital, Employee Matching Gifts, General Support, Multiyear/Continuing Support, Research, Scholarship.

Donor Information

Founder: Ohio National Life Insurance Co.

Financial Summary

Total Giving: $592,871 (2001); $600,000 (2000 approx); $500,000 (1999 approx)
Giving Analysis: Giving for 2001 includes: foundation matching gifts ($20,205); foundation grants to United Way ($142,330) foundation ($430,336)
Assets: $2,009,598 (2001); $1,925,055 (1996); $1,563,712 (1995)
Gifts Received: $1,002,675 (2001); $143,374 (1996); $500,000 (1995)

Typical Recipients

Arts & Humanities: Arts Centers, Arts Festivals, Arts Funds, Arts Institutes, Ballet, Film & Video, Arts & Humanities-General, Libraries, Museums/Galleries, Music, Opera, Performing Arts, Public Broadcasting, Theater
Civic & Public Affairs: African American Affairs, Botanical Gardens/Parks, Chambers of Commerce, Clubs, Community Foundations, Economic Policy, Employment/Job Training, Civic & Public Affairs-General, Housing, Inner-City Development, Law & Justice, Municipalities/Towns, Public Policy, Safety, Urban & Community Affairs, Women's Affairs, Zoos/Aquariums
Education: Arts/Humanities Education, Business Education, Colleges & Universities, Colleges & Universities, Continuing Education, Economic Education, Education Associations, Education Funds, Education-General, Legal Education, Literacy, Minority Education, Private Education (Precollege), Religious Education, Student Aid
Environment: Environment-General
Health: AIDS/HIV, Alzheimers Disease, Cancer, Children's Health/Hospitals, Clinics/Medical Centers, Diabetes, Eyes/Blindness, Health-General, Health Policy/Cost Containment, Heart, Home-Care Services, Hospices, Hospitals, Medical Rehabilitation, Medical Research, Multiple Sclerosis, Public Health
Religion: Dioceses, Religion-General, Jewish Causes, Ministries, Religious Welfare, Social/Policy Issues
Science: Scientific Research
Social Services: Child Welfare, Community Centers, Family Services, Food/Clothing Distribution, People with Disabilities, Recreation & Athletics, Scouts, Senior Services, Shelters/Homelessness, Special Olympics, Substance Abuse, United Funds/United Ways, YMCA/YWCA/YMHA/YWHA, Youth Organizations

Application Procedures

Initial Contact: Send a brief letter of inquiry.
Application Requirements: Include a description of organization and proof of tax-exempt status.
Deadlines: None.

Restrictions

Does not support individuals, religious organizations for sectarian purposes, or political or lobbying groups.

Corporate Officials

Howard C. Becker: vice president, president, chief executive officer, director PRIM CORP EMPL vice president: Ohio National Life Insurance Co.
Ronald J. Dolan: senior vice president, chief financial officer, director B Cincinnati, OH 1947. ED University of Cincinnati (1969); University of Michigan (1970). PRIM CORP EMPL executive vice president, chief financial officer, director: Ohio National Life Insurance Co.
David B. O'Maley: chairman, president, chief executive officer, director PRIM CORP EMPL chairman, president, chief executive officer, director: Ohio National Life Insurance Co.

Foundation Officials

Howard C. Becker: trustee (see above)
Joseph P. Brom: vice president, trustee PRIM CORP EMPL executive vice president: Ohio National Financial Service.
Ronald J. Dolan: trustee (see above)
Anthony G. Esposito: secretary, trustee PRIM CORP EMPL senior vice president human resources: Ohio National Life Insurance Co.
David B. O'Maley: president, trustee (see above)
Stuart G. Summers: senior vice president, general counsel

Grants Analysis

Disclosure Period: calendar year ending 2001
Total Grants: $430,336*
Number of Grants: 73
Average Grant: $5,895
Highest Grant: $38,500
Lowest Grant: $145
Typical Range: $250 to $5,000
*Note: Giving excludes matching gifts and United Way.

Recent Grants

Note: Grants derived from 2001 Form 990.

General

142,330	United Way, Cincinnati, OH -- annual campaign
38,500	University of Cincinnati Foundation, Cincinnati, OH -- operating fund
35,000	Fine Arts Fund, Cincinnati, OH -- annual campaign
30,000	Greater Cincinnati Foundation, Cincinnati, OH -- operating fund
25,000	Cincinnati 2012, Inc., Cincinnati, OH -- capital fund
25,000	Million Dollar Round Table, Park Ridge, IL
22,500	Children's Hospital, Cincinnati, OH -- family/professional resources center
21,500	Cincinnati Parks Foundation, Cincinnati, OH -- capital fund
20,000	Cincinnati Institute of Fine Arts, Cincinnati, OH -- operating support
16,000	Southwestern Ohio Seniors Services, Cincinnati, OH -- capital fund

GEORGE A. OHL, JR. TRUST

Giving Contact

George A. Ohl, Jr. Trust
Care of First Union National Bank
401 S. Tryon Street
Charlotte, NC 28288
Phone: (704)383-2882

Description

Founded: 1947
EIN: 226024900
Organization Type: Private Foundation
Giving Locations: NJ
Grant Types: Capital, Project, Research, Scholarship, Seed Money.

Donor Information

Founder: the late George A. Ohl, Jr.

Financial Summary

Total Giving: $304,738 (2000); $274,903 (1999); $371,458 (1998)
Assets: $5,653,617 (2000); $5,771,271 (1999); $5,797,858 (1998)
Gifts Received: $2,893 (1994)

Typical Recipients

Arts & Humanities: Arts Associations & Councils, Arts Festivals, Arts Funds, Arts Outreach, History & Archaeology, Libraries, Museums/Galleries, Performing Arts, Theater
Civic & Public Affairs: Employment/Job Training, Civic & Public Affairs-General, Housing, Philanthropic Organizations, Urban & Community Affairs, Zoos/Aquariums
Education: Arts/Humanities Education, Colleges & Universities, Education Associations, Education Funds, Education Reform, Engineering/Technological Education, Education-General, Medical Education, Minority Education, Private Education (Precollege), Public Education (Precollege), Science/Mathematics Education, Secondary Education (Private), Secondary Education (Public), Student Aid, Vocational & Technical Education
Environment: Environment-General
Health: AIDS/HIV, Arthritis, Cancer, Children's Health/Hospitals, Clinics/Medical Centers, Geriatric Health, Health Organizations, Heart, Hospitals, Long-Term Care, Medical Rehabilitation, Mental Health, Outpatient Health Care, Prenatal Health Issues, Public Health, Single-Disease Health Associations
International: Health Care/Hospitals
Religion: Jewish Causes, Ministries, Religious Welfare, Social/Policy Issues
Science: Scientific Centers & Institutes
Social Services: At-Risk Youth, Child Abuse, Child Welfare, Community Centers, Community Service Organizations, Crime Prevention, Day Care, Delinquency & Criminal Rehabilitation, Domestic Violence, Family Planning, Family Services, Food/Clothing Distribution, People with Disabilities, Recreation & Athletics, Scouts, Senior Services, Substance Abuse, Veterans, YMCA/YWCA/YMHA/YWHA, Youth Organizations

Application Procedures

Initial Contact: Send a brief letter of inquiry.
Deadlines: October 31.

Additional Information

Publications: Application Guidelines
Trust(s): First Union Bank NA NJ

Grants Analysis

Disclosure Period: calendar year ending 2000
Total Grants: $304,738
Number of Grants: 60
Average Grant: $5,079
Highest Grant: $7,500
Typical Range: $2,500 to $7,500

Recent Grants

Note: Grants derived from 2000 Form 990.

General

7,500	Crisis Ministry, Trenton, NJ
7,500	Cystic Fibrosis Foundation of New Jersey, NJ
7,500	Easter Seal Society, East Brunswick,

	NJ -- for program expansion for the elderly in Huntersdon County
7,500	New Jersey AIDS Partnership, Morristown, NJ
7,500	UJA Federation of Bergen County, River Edge, NJ
7,200	CPC Behavioral Health Care, Trenton, NJ
6,500	Farleigh Dickinson University, Teaneck, NJ
6,500	Lifetime Support, Inc., NJ
6,500	Saint Clare's Foundation, Denville, NJ
6,500	St. Paul's Community Development Corporation, Paterson, NJ

THE JOHN R. OISHEI FOUNDATION

Giving Contact

Thomas E. Baker, Executive Director
One HSBC Center, Suite 3650
Buffalo, NY 14203-2805
Phone: (716)856-9490
Fax: (716)856-9493
Web: http://www.oisheifdt.org

Description

Founded: 1941
EIN: 160874319
Organization Type: General Purpose Foundation
Former Name: Julia R. and Estelle L. Foundation (1997).
Giving Locations: NY: Greater Western New York area, Buffalo
Grant Types: Challenge, Multiyear/Continuing Support, Professorship, Research, Seed Money.

Financial Summary

Total Giving: $13,000,000 (2002 approx); $13,706,439 (2000); $11,270,364 (1999)
Giving Analysis: Giving for 2000 includes: foundation grants to United Way ($25,000); foundation scholarships ($202,022); 1999: foundation scholarships ($36,618); 1998: foundation scholarships ($180,000) foundation grants to United Way ($522,000)
Assets: $226,000,000 (2002 approx); $236,343,606 (2000); $250,000,000 (1999 approx)
Gifts Received: $640,020 (2000); $3,105,671 (1996); $37,884,369 (1995). Note: In 2000, contributions were received from the John R. Oishei Consolidated Trust. In 1996, gifts were received from the John R. Oishei trusts and the Jean R. Oshei Estate.

Typical Recipients

Arts & Humanities: Arts Institutes, Historic Preservation, History & Archaeology, Libraries, Literary Arts, Museums/Galleries, Music, Performing Arts, Public Broadcasting, Theater, Visual Arts
Civic & Public Affairs: Community Foundations, Civic & Public Affairs-General, Legal Aid, Public Policy, Safety, Zoos/Aquariums
Education: Afterschool/Enrichment Programs, Colleges & Universities, Education Associations, Education-General, Medical Education, Private Education (Precollege), Secondary Education (Private), Secondary Education (Public), Special Education, Student Aid
Health: AIDS/HIV, Alzheimers Disease, Children's Health/Hospitals, Emergency/Ambulance Services, Geriatric Health, Health Organizations, Hospices, Hospitals, Long-Term Care, Medical Research
International: Foreign Educational Institutions, Health Care/Hospitals, Human Rights, International Affairs
Religion: Churches, Dioceses, Religious Welfare, Seminaries
Social Services: Animal Protection, Camps, Child Welfare, Community Service Organizations, Family

Services, Food/Clothing Distribution, People with Disabilities, Scouts, Senior Services, Shelters/Homelessness, Substance Abuse, United Funds/United Ways, YMCA/YWCA/YMHA/YWHA, Youth Organizations

Application Procedures

Initial Contact: Prospective applicants should send a preliminary letter of inquiry to the foundation. There are no formal application procedures.
Application Requirements: A proposal should contain the following information: a concise statement of the program or project, the amount of funding requested, a brief description of the nature and activities of the applicant, proof of tax-exempt status, and a list of officers and directors of the organization.
Deadlines: None.
Review Process: In most instances, applicants will receive a written response within two months; distributions are made throughout the year.

Restrictions

The foundation reports that its support is limited to the Buffalo, NY, metropolitan area. Additionally, the foundation does not make grants for operating expenses, endowment funds, capital campaigns or collegiate scholarships. Private foundations and individuals are also not eligible for funding.

Additional Information

The foundation has undergone a process of review and change, which has resulted in a major change in giving focus.
Publications: Guidelines

Corporate Officials

Erland E. Kailbourne: director B Whitesville, NY 1941. ED State University of New York Alfred AAS (1961). CORP AFFIL director: Chautauqua Airlines. NONPR AFFIL director, member: Rochester Chamber of Commerce; trustee: State University New York; senior chapter president: Robert Morris Associates. CLUB AFFIL Wellsville Country Club; Rochester Country Club; Shriners Club; Masons Club; Elks Club; Genesee Valley Club.

Foundation Officials

Thomas E. Baker: executive director, secretary
Robert J. Donough: member
Christopher T. Dunstan: member, director
Richard D. Fors: director
Erland E. Kailbourne: director, board chairman (see above)
Albert R. Mugel: director B 1917. ED State University of New York Buffalo Law School LLB (1941). PRIM CORP EMPL partner: Jaeckle, Fleischmann & Mugel PRIM NONPR EMPL professor: State University of New York, Buffalo Law School. NONPR AFFIL member: Erie County Bar Association; member: New York State Bar Association; member: American Bar Association.
Allan R. Wiegley: treasurer, director

Grants Analysis

Disclosure Period: calendar year ending 2000
Total Grants: $13,681,439*
Number of Grants: 70
Average Grant: $143,845*
Highest Grant: $2,900,000
Typical Range: $3,000 to $35,000 and $100,000 to $350,000
*Note: Giving excludes scholarships and United Way. Average grant figure excludes two highest grants ($3,900,000).

Recent Grants

Note: Grants derived from 2000 Form 990.

Library-Related

200,000	Library Foundation of Buffalo and Erie

County, Buffalo, NY -- support rare book expansion project

200,000   Library Foundation of Buffalo and Erie County, Buffalo, NY -- support the Western New York rare book consortium

General

2,900,000   Buffalo Independent Secondary School Network (BISSNET), Buffalo, NY -- support the development of state-of-art telecommunications technologies

1,000,000   Martin House Restoration Corporation, Buffalo, NY -- support the welcoming the world to Buffalo

600,000   Kaleida Health System Foundations, Buffalo, NY -- for the Toshiba Stroke Research Center

500,000   Hauptman-Woodward Medical Research Institute, Buffalo, NY -- support to establish and fund a structural biology center

500,000   Niagara University, Niagara University, NY -- support to establish of center of excellence in hospitality and tourism management

490,000   Canisius College, Buffalo, NY -- support the Oishei Professorship Program

400,000   Buffalo General Foundation, Buffalo, NY

350,000   Fredonia College Foundation, Fredonia, NY -- support Educational Enrichment in the Arts Program

300,000   American Red Cross Greater Buffalo Chapter, Buffalo, NY -- support LIFE Program

250,000   Buffalo Niagara Partnership Foundation, Buffalo, NY -- funding of Buffalo Niagara Enterprise activities

OKI AMERICA, INC.

Company Headquarters

Hackensack, NJ
Web: http://oki.co.jp

Company Description

Employees: 1,700
SIC(s): 3661 Telephone & Telegraph Apparatus, 3663 Radio & T.V. Communications Equipment, 3674 Semiconductors & Related Devices.
Parent Company: Oki Electric Industry Company, Ltd., 7-12 Toranomon 1-chome, Minato-ku, Tokyo, Japan

Operating Locations

Cascade Design Automation (CA--Santa Clara; WA--Bellevue); Oki (CA--Costa Mesa); Oki Advanced Technology (CA--San Jose); Oki America Inc. (CA--San Francisco, Sunnyvale; GA--Atlanta; NJ--Camden, Mount Laurel; NY--New York; OR--Tualatin); OKI Semiconductor Group (CA--Sunnyvale); OKI Telecom Group (GA--Swanee); Okidata Group (NJ--Mount Laurel)

Nonmonetary Support

Type: Donated Products; Workplace Solicitation

Giving Contact

Elva Peelo, HR Asst.
785 North Mary Ave.
Sunnyvale, CA 94085
Phone: (408)720-1900
Fax: (408)720-1918

Description

Organization Type: Corporate Giving Program
Giving Locations: NJ: Bergen County operating locations.
Grant Types: Multiyear/Continuing Support, Scholarship.

Financial Summary

Total Giving: Company does not disclose contributions figures.

Typical Recipients

Arts & Humanities: Community Arts
Civic & Public Affairs: Professional & Trade Associations
Education: Education-General, International Exchange
Social Services: Emergency Relief

Application Procedures

Notes: Oki America is currently not accepting proposals at this time. The Co. is currently in the process of corporate-wide reorganization efforts and their definition of local communities, corporate giving policies, and procedure will be significantly altered in the future.

Corporate Officials

Tetsuji Banno: president PRIM CORP EMPL president: Oki America Inc. ADD CORP EMPL chief executive officer: Oki Telecom Inc.

Grants Analysis

Note: A more recent grants list was unavailable.

Recent Grants

Note: Grants derived from 1996 grants list.

Library-Related
Fort Lee Public Library, Ft. Lee, NJ

General
Japan Society, New York, NY
Japanese Chamber of Commerce, New York, NY
Music from Japan, New York, NY
Palisade Chamber Orchestra, Palisade, NJ

OLD DOMINION BOX CO.

Company Headquarters

120 Dillard Rd.
Madison Heights, VA 24572

Company Description

Employees: 600
SIC(s): 2600 Paper & Allied Products, 3500 Industrial Machinery & Equipment.

Operating Locations

Old Dominion Box Co. (VA--Lynchburg)

Old Dominion Box Co. Foundation

Giving Contact

Wayne Lankford, Chairman
PO Box 680
Lynchburg, VA 24505
Phone: (434)929-6701

Description

EIN: 546036792
Organization Type: Corporate Foundation
Giving Locations: VA
Grant Types: General Support.

Financial Summary

Total Giving: $29,300 (fiscal year ending November 30, 2001); $32,000 (fiscal 2000); $11,375 (fiscal 1999)
Giving Analysis: Giving for fiscal 1999 includes: foundation ($11,375); fiscal 1998: foundation grants to United Way ($2,000) foundation ($9,900)
Assets: $565,798 (fiscal 2001); $759,628 (fiscal 2000); $766,087 (fiscal 1999)

Gifts Received: $50,000 (fiscal 1996); $250 (fiscal 1994); $100 (fiscal 1992). Note: In fiscal 1994, contributions were received from Old Dominion Box Co. In fiscal 1996, contributions were received from Dillard Investment Corp.

Typical Recipients

Arts & Humanities: Arts Centers, Historic Preservation, Libraries, Music
Civic & Public Affairs: African American Affairs, Clubs, Economic Development, Employment/Job Training, Civic & Public Affairs-General, Legal Aid, Professional & Trade Associations, Safety, Urban & Community Affairs, Women's Affairs
Education: Arts/Humanities Education, Business Education, Colleges & Universities, Community & Junior Colleges, Education Associations, Education Funds, Engineering/Technological Education, Education-General, Private Education (Precollege)
Environment: Forestry
Health: Emergency/Ambulance Services, Health Organizations, Heart, Single-Disease Health Associations
Religion: Churches, Jewish Causes, Religious Welfare, Social/Policy Issues
Social Services: Animal Protection, Community Service Organizations, Counseling, Crime Prevention, Food/Clothing Distribution, Recreation & Athletics, Special Olympics, United Funds/United Ways, YMCA/YWCA/YMHA/YWHA, Youth Organizations

Application Procedures

Initial Contact: Send brief letter describing program.
Deadlines: None.

Corporate Officials

Frank H. Buhler: chairman, chief financial officer B Arlington, VA 1926. ED Miami University (1950). PRIM CORP EMPL chairman: Old Dominion Box Co. CORP AFFIL director: Smithfield Co.; chairman, president: Palmetto Box; director: Piedmont Label Co.; chairman: Halltown Paperboard Co.; president: Little Rock Packaging Co.; chairman: Dacam Corp.; president, director: Dillard Investment Corp. NONPR AFFIL president, director: Old Dominion Box Co. Foundation.
Michael O. Buhler: president, director PRIM CORP EMPL president, director: Old Dominion Box Co.
R. Lewis Francis: vice president, chief financial officer PRIM CORP EMPL vice president, chief financial officer: Old Dominion Box Co.

Foundation Officials

Amy Buhler: secretary, treasurer
Frank H. Buhler: president (see above)
Michael O. Buhler: vice president (see above)
R. Lewis Francis: secretary, treasurer (see above)

Grants Analysis

Disclosure Period: fiscal year ending November 30, 2001
Total Grants: $29,300
Number of Grants: 9
Highest Grant: $20,000
Lowest Grant: $200

Recent Grants

Note: Grants derived from fiscal 2001 Form 990.

General

20,000   Lynchburg College, Lynchburg, VA

5,000   Academy of Music, Lynchburg, VA

1,000   Colonial Williamsburg Foundation, Williamsburg, VA

1,000   New Land Jobs, Lynchburg, VA

1,000   Virginia Foundation for Independent Colleges, Richmond, VA

300   Moneli Volunteer Rescue Squad, Madison Heights, VA

250   Crisis Line of Central Virginia, Lynchburg, VA

250   James River Day School, Lynchburg, VA
200   New Vistas School, Lynchburg, VA
200   Virginia College Fund, Richmond, VA

OLESON FOUNDATION

Giving Contact
Dr. John R. Spencer, Director
6645 N. Long Lake Rd.
Traverse City, MI 49684
Phone: (616)946-9349

Description
Founded: 1959
EIN: 386083080
Organization Type: Private Foundation
Giving Locations: MI: northwestern area of Michigan
Grant Types: General Support.

Donor Information
Founder: Gerald W. Oleson, Frances M. Oleson Foundation

Financial Summary
Total Giving: $737,810 (2001); $412,477 (2000); $440,341 (1999)
Giving Analysis: Giving for 2001 includes: foundation grants to United Way ($5,000); 1999: foundation grants to United Way ($17,500) 1997: foundation grants to United Way ($1,000)
Assets: $16,397,882 (2001); $10,945,116 (2000); $8,497,472 (1999)
Gifts Received: $1,650,100 (1997); $2,385,928 (1994). Note: In 1994, contributions were received from the estate of Frances M. Oleson.

Typical Recipients
Arts & Humanities: Arts Institutes, Historic Preservation, History & Archaeology, Libraries, Museums/Galleries, Opera, Performing Arts
Civic & Public Affairs: Botanical Gardens/Parks, Clubs, Community Foundations, Civic & Public Affairs-General, Housing, Parades/Festivals, Urban & Community Affairs
Education: Agricultural Education, Colleges & Universities, Elementary Education (Public), Education-General, Private Education (Precollege), Public Education (Precollege), School Volunteerism, Special Education
Environment: Environment-General, Resource Conservation, Watershed, Wildlife Protection
Health: Children's Health/Hospitals, Clinics/Medical Centers, Health Organizations, Hospitals, Prenatal Health Issues, Public Health, Transplant Networks/Donor Banks
Religion: Churches, Ministries, Religious Organizations, Religious Welfare
Science: Scientific Centers & Institutes
Social Services: Animal Protection, At-Risk Youth, Big Brother/Big Sister, Camps, Child Welfare, Community Service Organizations, Counseling, Crime Prevention, Family Services, Recreation & Athletics, Scouts, Senior Services, Social Services-General, Special Olympics, United Funds/United Ways, Volunteer Services, Youth Organizations

Application Procedures
Initial Contact: Send a brief letter of inquiry.
Application Requirements: Include a description of organization, amount requested, purpose of funds sought, and proof of tax-exempt status.
Deadlines: None.

Foundation Officials
Julius H. Beers: treasurer
Richard Ford: secretary
Donald W. Oleson: vice president

Gerald W. Oleson: president
John R. Spencer, MD: director

Grants Analysis
Disclosure Period: calendar year ending 2001
Total Grants: $732,810*
Number of Grants: 67
Average Grant: $9,952*
Highest Grant: $76,000
Lowest Grant: $100
Typical Range: $2,500 to $20,000
*Note: Giving excludes United Way. Average grant figure excludes highest grant.

Recent Grants
Note: Grants derived from 2001 Form 990.

General
76,000   Traverse City Area Public Schools, Traverse City, MI
45,000   Grand Traverse Regional Land Conservancy, Traverse City, MI
33,600   Cherryland Humane Society, Traverse City, MI
30,000   Great Lakes Children's Museum, Traverse City, MI
25,000   Charlevoix Area Hospital, Charlevoix, MI
25,000   Grand Traverse County Parks and Recreation Department, Traverse City, MI
25,000   Grand Traverse Heritage Center, Traverse City, MI
25,000   Music House Museum, Acme, MI
25,000   St. Mary's School, Lake Leelanau, MI
20,000   Conversation Resource Alliance, Traverse City, MI

OLIN CORP.

Company Headquarters
Norwalk, CT
Web: http://www.olin.com

Company Description
Founded: 1892
Ticker: OLN
Exchange: NYSE
Revenue: US$1.301 billion (2002)
Employees: 6200 (2002)
SIC(s): 2812 Alkalies & Chlorine, 2819 Industrial Inorganic Chemicals Nec, 2821 Plastics Materials & Resins, 2865 Cyclic Crudes & Intermediates.

Operating Locations
Olin Corp. (AL--McIntosh; AZ--Chandler; CA--San Leandro, Santa Clara; CT--New Haven, Stamford, Stratford, Waterbury; FL--St. Marks, St. Petersburg; GA--Augusta; IL--Marion; LA--Lake Charles; MO--Independence; NJ--West Paterson; NY--Niagara Falls; TN--Charleston; WA--Redmond; WV--South Charleston; WI--Baraboo)

Nonmonetary Support
Volunteer Programs: Supports programs which include employee volunteers. Also awards Volunteer Recognition grants; organizations where employees volunteer receive grants of $500 to $3,000.
Contact: Carmella Piacentini, Manager Corporate Contributions
Note: Annual competitive award program for long-term significant employee, retiree or family member volunteer affiliation.

Olin Corp. Charitable Trust

Giving Contact
Carmella V. Piacenini, Administrator
501 Merritt 7
PO Box 4500
Norwalk, CT 06856-4500
Phone: (203)750-3301
Fax: (203)750-3065
E-mail: cpiacentini@corp.olin.com
Web: http://www.olin.com/about/charitable.asp

Alternate Contact
Care of Wachovia Bank N.A.
PO Box 3099, NC6732
Winston-Salem, NC 27150-6732
Phone: (336)732-5252

Description
EIN: 436022750
Organization Type: Corporate Foundation
Giving Locations: communities where employees work and live; some support for national organizations.
Grant Types: Award, Capital, Challenge, Conference/Seminar, Department, Emergency, Employee Matching Gifts, Fellowship, General Support, Multiyear/Continuing Support, Project, Research, Scholarship, Seed Money.
Note: Employee matching gift ratio: 1 to 1 for active employees; 0.5 to 1 for retirees.

Financial Summary
Total Giving: $1,086,558 (2001); $1,281,699 (2000); $1,500,000 (1999). Note: Contributes through corporate direct giving program and foundation. Giving includes trust.
Giving Analysis: Giving for 2000 includes: foundation matching gifts ($179,313); foundation grants to United Way ($196,300) foundation ($906,086)
Assets: $515,761 (2001); $687,022 (2000); $6,975,079 (1997)
Gifts Received: $1,200,000 (2001). Note: In 2001, contributions were received from Orlin Corp.

Typical Recipients
Arts & Humanities: Arts Associations & Councils, Arts Centers, Arts Institutes, Community Arts, Dance, Historic Preservation, Libraries, Museums/Galleries, Music, Opera, Performing Arts, Public Broadcasting, Theater, Visual Arts
Civic & Public Affairs: African American Affairs, Business/Free Enterprise, Chambers of Commerce, Civil Rights, Economic Development, Economic Policy, Employment/Job Training, Civic & Public Affairs-General, Minority Business, Municipalities/Towns, Professional & Trade Associations, Public Policy, Urban & Community Affairs, Zoos/Aquariums
Education: Business Education, Business-School Partnerships, Colleges & Universities, Community & Junior Colleges, Education Associations, Elementary Education (Public), Elementary Education (Public), Engineering/Technological Education, Education-General, Literacy, Medical Education, Minority Education, Private Education (Precollege), Public Education (Precollege), Science/Mathematics Education, Secondary Education (Public), Student Aid, Vocational & Technical Education
Environment: Air/Water Quality, Environment-General, Protection, Resource Conservation, Wildlife Protection
Health: Cancer, Children's Health/Hospitals, Clinics/Medical Centers, Emergency/Ambulance Services, Geriatric Health, Health Organizations, Hospices, Hospitals, Medical Rehabilitation, Mental Health, Nursing Services, Public Health, Single-Disease Health Associations

International: Foreign Educational Institutions, International Affairs, International Development, International Environmental Issues
Religion: Religious Organizations
Science: Science Museums, Scientific Centers & Institutes
Social Services: At-Risk Youth, Community Centers, Community Service Organizations, Family Services, Food/Clothing Distribution, Scouts, Senior Services, Shelters/Homelessness, Substance Abuse, United Funds/United Ways, Volunteer Services, YMCA/YWCA/YMHA/YWHA, Youth Organizations

Application Procedures

Initial Contact: Submit a one- or two-page letter.
Application Requirements: Provide a description of organization, amount requested, purpose of funds sought, recently audited financial statement, and proof of tax-exempt status.
Deadlines: None.
Review Process: The foundation conducts an initial review to determine relation to priorities, areas of interest, and geographic proximity
Decision Notification: Ongoing.

Restrictions

Foundation does not support loans, dinners or special events, fraternal organizations, goodwill advertising, individuals, political or lobbying groups, or religious organizations for sectarian purposes.
Does not provide general support to member agencies of united funds. May consider capital campaign support.

Corporate Officials

Peter C. Kosche: senior vice president corporate affairs PRIM CORP EMPL senior vice president corporate affairs: Olin Corp.
Anthony W. Ruggiero: executive vice president, chief financial officer ED Fordham University BS (1963); Columbia University MBA (1964). PRIM CORP EMPL executive vice president, chief financial officer: Olin Corp.

Foundation Officials

Peter C. Kosche: trustee (see above)
Carmella V. Piacentini: administrator

Grants Analysis

Disclosure Period: calendar year ending 2001
Total Grants: $791,306*
Number of Grants: 248
Average Grant: $3,191
Highest Grant: $75,000
Lowest Grant: $150
Typical Range: $500 to $15,000
*Note: Giving excludes matching gifts, scholarship, and United Way.

Recent Grants

Note: Grants derived from 2001 Form 990.

General

85,000	United Way Partnership, Alton, IL
75,000	University of Evansville, Evansville, IN
50,000	Buffalo Bill Memorial Association, Cody, WY
42,514	Alabama Association of Rescue Squads, Inc., Birmingham, AL
40,000	INROADS, St. Louis, MO
40,000	Norwalk Community Technical College Foundation, Norwalk, CT
25,000	St. Louis Regional Educational and Public Television Commission, St. Louis, MO
25,000	University of Connecticut Foundation, Farmington, CT
20,000	Global Environmental Management Initiative, Washington, DC
20,000	United Way of Niagara Falls, Niagara Falls, NY

JOHN M. OLIN FOUNDATION

Giving Contact

James Piereson, Executive Director
330 Madison Avenue, 22nd Floor
New York, NY 10017
Phone: (212)661-2670
Fax: (212)661-5917
Web: http://www.jmof.org

Description

Founded: 1953
EIN: 376031033
Organization Type: General Purpose Foundation
Giving Locations: internationally; nationally.
Grant Types: Conference/Seminar, Fellowship, Professorship, Project, Research.

Donor Information

Founder: The John M. Olin Foundation was established in 1953 by the late John Merrill Olin (1892-1982), an inventor, industrialist, conservationist, and philanthropist. "Mr. Olin was committed to the preservation of the principles of political and economic liberty as they have been expressed in American thought, institutions and practice."
In 1994, the foundation received a gift of $94 million from a trust created for John M. Olin's wife, Evelyn. Mrs. Olin died in 1993.

Financial Summary

Total Giving: $17,000,000 (2002 approx); $20,486,946 (2001); $20,850,430 (2000). Note: 1997 Giving includes matching gifts ($7,411).
Giving Analysis: Giving for 1998 includes: foundation matching gifts ($10,048); 1997: foundation scholarships ($81,640) foundation program-related investments ($400,511)
Assets: $60,000,000 (2002 approx); $71,196,916 (2001); $91,730,109 (2000)
Gifts Received: $50,000 (1996); $94,305,566 (1994); $120,000 (1993). Note: In 1990, the foundation's gift came from the Killgore Trusts. In January 1994, the foundation received $94 million from a trust created for John M. Olin's wife, Evelyn; Mrs. Olin died in 1993.

Typical Recipients

Arts & Humanities: Arts Associations & Councils, Film & Video, History & Archaeology, Libraries, Literary Arts, Museums/Galleries, Public Broadcasting
Civic & Public Affairs: Business/Free Enterprise, Civil Rights, Economic Policy, Civic & Public Affairs-General, Law & Justice, Legal Aid, Professional & Trade Associations, Public Policy, Women's Affairs
Education: Arts/Humanities Education, Business Education, Colleges & Universities, Continuing Education, Economic Education, Education Associations, Education Funds, Education Reform, Faculty Development, Education-General, International Exchange, International Studies, Journalism/Media Education, Legal Education, Social Sciences Education
Environment: Environment-General
Health: Health Policy/Cost Containment, Health Organizations, Single-Disease Health Associations
International: Foreign Educational Institutions, International Affairs, International Peace & Security Issues, International Relations
Religion: Jewish Causes, Social/Policy Issues
Science: Scientific Centers & Institutes
Social Services: Crime Prevention

Application Procedures

Initial Contact: The foundation does not have a formal grant application form. Applicants should submit a letter of inquiry.
Application Requirements: The letter of inquiry should state briefly and concisely the objectives and

significance of the proposed project, provide background information on the organization and its current sources of funding, and indicate the amount sought. Included with the letter should be a project budget, biographical information on key personnel, an audited financial statement, and a copy of the IRS tax-exempt status letter.
Deadlines: None.
Review Process: The board of trustees meets quarterly. All proposals are reviewed and acknowledged promptly, usually within 90 days. After a review of the request, the foundation staff will communicate with the individual in charge of the proposed project to indicate whether the project meets eligibility requirements, and to request any additional information. Trustees act on grant requests only after a full investigation by the foundation staff.

Restrictions

The foundation normally does not fund administrative overhead costs. In addition, grants will not be considered for endowment or building programs, annual giving programs, direct support for individuals, or programs without significant import for national affairs. Grants will be made only to institutions that provide a responsible fiscal agent and are tax-exempt under section 501(c)(3) of the Internal Revenue Code.

Additional Information

Grantees must be able to demonstrate the capacity to administer grants from the foundation and are expected to provide financial accounts of expenditures to make certain that funds are used for their intended purposes. The foundation conducts an annual evaluation of grants, and grantees are asked to provide periodic reports on the progress of work.
Publications: Annual Report

Foundation Officials

Peter Magnus Flanigan: trustee B New York, NY 1923. ED Princeton University BA (1947). CORP AFFIL director: Per Scholas Inc.; advisor: Warburg Dillon Read LLC.
Richard Mortimer Furlaud: trustee B New York, NY 1923. ED Princeton University AB (1944); Harvard University LLB (1947). CORP AFFIL director: International Flavors & Fragrances Inc.; director: Shearson Lehman Brothers Holdings Inc.; director, honorary chairman: American Express Co. NONPR AFFIL chairman: Rockefeller Archives Center; chairman board trustees: Rockefeller University; chairman: Millbrook Research Field Center; member: Association Bar New York City; member: Council Foreign Relations. CLUB AFFIL The Links Club; River Club.
George Joseph Gillespie, III: president, treasurer B New York, NY 1930. ED Georgetown University AB (1952); Harvard University LLB (1955). PRIM CORP EMPL partner: Cravath, Swaine & Moore. CORP AFFIL director: Washington Post Co. NONPR AFFIL director, chairman emeritus: National Multiple Sclerosis Society; trustee: New York University Medical Center; director: Madison Square Boys Club; secretary, director: Museum Television & Radio; member: Century Association; trustee, treasurer: Cooper-Hewitt National Design Museum. CLUB AFFIL Prouts Neck Country Club; Winged Foot Golf Club; member: Portland Country Club; Double Eagle Club; Falmouth Country Club; American Yacht Club.
Caroline M. Hemphill: director special programs, assistant secretary-treasurer
Charles Field Knight: trustee B Lake Forest, IL January 20, 1936. ED Cornell University BS (1958); Cornell University MBA (1959). CORP AFFIL director: Southwest Bell Corp.; director: Morgan Stanley Dean Witter Co.; director: SBC Communications Inc.; director: Caterpillar Inc.; director: IBM Corp.; director: Anheuser-Busch Companies Inc.; director: Baxter International Inc. NONPR AFFIL member: Sigma Phi Epsilon; director, trustee: Washington University; director: Arts & Education Council. CLUB AFFIL Log Cabin

Club; Saint Louis Country Club; Crystal Downs Club; Glen View Golf Club; Chicago Club.

James Piereson, PhD: section, trustee B Grand Rapids, MI 1946. ED Michigan State University BA (1968); Michigan State University PhD (1973). NONPR AFFIL member: Philadelphia Society; member advisory committee: University Rochester Simon Graduate School Business Administration; director: DonorsTrust; member: American Historical Association. CLUB AFFIL Union League Club.

Janice B. Riddell: program officer

Damon A. Vangelis: program associate

William Voegeli: program officer

Eugene Flewellyn Williams, Jr.: chairman, trustee B Saint Louis, MO 1923. ED Yale University BA (1945). CORP AFFIL director: Pitchfork Land & Cattle Co.; director: Saint Louis Refrigerator Car Co.; director: Manufacturers Railway Co.; director: American Airlines Inc.; director: Emerson Electric Co.

Grants Analysis

Disclosure Period: calendar year ending 2000
Total Grants: $20,850,430*
Number of Grants: 221
Average Grant: $87,559*
Highest Grant: $1,500,000
Lowest Grant: $5,000
Typical Range: $5,000 to $75,000 and $100,000 to $200,000
***Note:** Giving excludes matching gifts. Average grant figure excludes highest grants ($1,500,000).

Recent Grants

Note: Grants derived from 2000 Form 990.

General

1,500,000	Harvard Law School, Cambridge, MA -- John M. Olin Program in Law and Economics
640,000	University of Rochester William E. Simon Graduate School of Business Administration, Rochester, NY
627,500	Harvard University Center for International Affairs, Cambridge, MA -- the programs of the John M. Olin Institute of Strategic Studies under the direction of Samuel P. Huntington
456,812	University of Chicago John M. Olin Center for Inquiry Into the Theory and Practice of Democracy, Chicago, IL
429,000	University of Chicago Law School, Chicago, IL -- for John M. Olin Program in Law and Economics
400,000	Manhattan Institute for Policy Research, New York, NY -- for the Center for Educational Innovation
373,899	Stanford University Law School, Stanford, CA -- for John M. Olin Program in Law and Economics under the direction of A. Mitchell Polinsky
343,034	Yale Law School, Center for Study in Law, Economics, and Public Policy, New Haven, CT -- the John M. Olin Program in Law and Economics under the direction of George L. Priest
308,850	Harvard University Department of Government, Cambridge, MA -- program on Constitutional Government under the direction of Harvey C. Mansfield, Jr. and R. Shep Melnick
250,000	Heritage Foundation, Washington, DC -- for the Domestic Policy Studies Program

SPENCER T. AND ANN W. OLIN FOUNDATION

Giving Contact

Warren M. Shapleigh, President
7701 Forsyth Boulevard, Suite 1040
St. Louis, MO 63105

Phone: (314)727-6202
Fax: (314)727-6157

Description

Founded: 1957
EIN: 376044148
Organization Type: General Purpose Foundation
Giving Locations: nationally.
Grant Types: Fellowship, General Support, Project, Research.

Donor Information

Founder: The foundation was established in 1957 by the late Ann W. Olin and Spencer T. Olin, and receives distributions from the S. Truman Olin Jr., Charitable Lead Trust and the Spencer T. Olin Charitable Lead Trust.

Financial Summary

Total Giving: $8,241,972 (2001); $14,538,525 (2000); $15,518,527 (1998)
Giving Analysis: Giving for 2001 includes: foundation grants to United Way ($25,000); 2000: foundation grants to United Way ($25,000) 1998: foundation grants to United Way ($25,000)
Assets: $32,562,550 (2001); $40,232,549 (2000); $65,662,839 (1998)
Gifts Received: $607,503 (2000); $2,276,490 (1998); $12,482,240 (1995). Note: contributions were received from the Spencer T. Olin Charitable Lead Trust and the S. Truman Olin, Jr., Charitable Lead Trust.

Typical Recipients

Arts & Humanities: Arts Associations & Councils, Arts Centers, Arts Festivals, Arts Funds, Arts & Humanities-General, Historic Preservation, History & Archaeology, Libraries, Museums/Galleries, Music, Opera, Public Broadcasting, Theater

Civic & Public Affairs: African American Affairs, Botanical Gardens/Parks, Business/Free Enterprise, Community Foundations, Employment/Job Training, Civic & Public Affairs-General, Nonprofit Management, Philanthropic Organizations, Professional & Trade Associations, Public Policy, Urban & Community Affairs, Women's Affairs, Zoos/Aquariums

Education: Afterschool/Enrichment Programs, Arts/Humanities Education, Business Education, Colleges & Universities, Community & Junior Colleges, Continuing Education, Economic Education, Education Associations, Education Funds, Education Reform, Engineering/Technological Education, Education-General, Leadership Training, Medical Education, Minority Education, Private Education (Precollege), Public Education (Precollege), Science/Mathematics Education, Secondary Education (Private), Special Education, Student Aid, Vocational & Technical Education

Environment: Energy, Environment-General, Protection, Resource Conservation, Wildlife Protection

Health: Alzheimers Disease, Arthritis, Cancer, Clinics/Medical Centers, Emergency/Ambulance Services, Geriatric Health, Hospices, Hospitals, Nursing Services, Preventive Medicine/Wellness Organizations

International: Foreign Educational Institutions, International Environmental Issues

Religion: Churches, Dioceses, Religious Organizations, Religious Welfare

Science: Science Museums, Scientific Centers & Institutes

Social Services: Animal Protection, Community Service Organizations, Day Care, Family Planning, Family Services, People with Disabilities, Recreation & Athletics, Social Services-General, United Funds/United Ways, YMCA/YWCA/YMHA/YWHA, Youth Organizations

Application Procedures

Initial Contact: Applicants should send a brief letter to the foundation's president.

Application Requirements: The letter should include a brief description of the program or project for which funding is requested and the need for it; information about the total cost of the program or project; specific amount requested; list of other sources of funding and amount raised or expected to be secured; time frame in which the funds are to be expended; copy of the most recent financial statement with balance sheet and income and expense statement; and a copy of the IRS letter determining tax-exempt status.

Restrictions

The foundation reports that it is only considering proposals from those organizations where there is a history of past support; no new proposals are being accepted because of long term commitments, to which the foundation is attending in stages.

It is the general policy of the foundation not to make grants for endowment funds, deficit financing, or ordinary annual operating expenses; for secondary education, except in special cases and for projects where there is a history of past support; to provide funding for more than three consecutive years; to support projects which are substantially financed by public tax funds; to make grants to individuals or for individual scholarships; to fund conferences, seminars, workshops, travel, or exhibits; or to make grants to national health or welfare organizations, to churches for religious purposes, or to other private foundations or projects requiring expenditure responsibility.

Foundation Officials

Eunice O. Higgins: secretary, trustee
Marquita L. Kunce: assistant treasurer
John Peters McCarthy: trustee B Saint Louis, MO 1933. ED Princeton University BA (1954); Harvard University LLB (1959). CORP AFFIL director: Ocean Drilling & Exploration Co.; director: Union Electric Co.; chairman, chief executive officer: Boatmens Trust Co.
Rolla Mottaz: board member, trustee
John C. Pritzlaff, Jr.: board member, trustee
Warren M. Shapleigh: president, trustee CORP AFFIL director: Barry-Wehmiller Group Inc.; director: Midland Container Corp.
Barbara Olin Taylor: board member, trustee
F. Morgan Taylor, Jr.: board member, trustee

Grants Analysis

Disclosure Period: calendar year ending 2001
Total Grants: $8,216,972*
Number of Grants: 41
Average Grant: $90,553*
Highest Grant: $2,000,047
Typical Range: $50,000 to $200,000
***Note:** Giving excludes United Way. Average grant excludes four highest grants ($4,775,952).

Recent Grants

Note: Grants derived from 2001 Form 990.

General

2,000,047	Institute of Living
1,000,048	All Kinds of Minds, Chapel Hill, NC
992,523	Washington University School of Medicine, St. Louis, MO
783,334	World Resource Institute, Washington, DC
500,000	Arizona Orthopedic Education Foundation, AZ
500,000	Lakes Region Conservation Trust, Meredith, NH
375,000	Central Institute for the Deaf, St. Louis, MO
327,684	Kent State University, Kent, OH
229,494	Solana Incorporated
223,477	CERES, Boston, MA

OLIVER MEMORIAL TRUST FOUNDATION

Giving Contact

Charles F. Nelson, Trust Officer and Vice President
c/o Wells Fargo Bank Indiana
112 W. 49th St., 14th Fl.
South Bend, IN 46601
Phone: (219)237-3475
Fax: (219)237-3317

Description

Founded: 1959
EIN: 356013076
Organization Type: Private Foundation
Giving Locations: IN: South Bend
Grant Types: Capital, Endowment, Multiyear/Continuing Support, Project, Seed Money.

Donor Information

Founder: the late C. Frederick Cunningham, Gertrude Oliver Cunningham, the late Walter C. Steenburg, Jane Cunningham Wanner, J. Oliver Cunningham

Financial Summary

Total Giving: $591,835 (2001); $582,601 (2000); $507,963 (1999)
Giving Analysis: Giving for 2001 includes: foundation grants to United Way ($11,000); 2000: foundation grants to United Way ($21,000) 1999: foundation grants to United Way ($10,500)
Assets: $11,518,224 (2001); $13,042,466 (2000); $11,955,458 (1999)
Gifts Received: $20,000 (2001); $20,017 (2000); $20,000 (1999). Note: In 2000, contributions were received from Jane Warriner. In 1999, contributions were received from Mr. and Mrs. J. Oliver Cunningham. In 1993, contributions were received from Jane C. Warriner ($25,000) and J. Oliver Cunningham ($25,000).

Typical Recipients

Arts & Humanities: Arts Associations & Councils, Arts Festivals, Community Arts, Dance, Historic Preservation, History & Archaeology, Libraries, Museums/Galleries, Music, Performing Arts
Civic & Public Affairs: Botanical Gardens/Parks, Civic & Public Affairs-General, Parades/Festivals, Zoos/Aquariums
Education: Business Education, Colleges & Universities, Education Associations, Education Funds, Journalism/Media Education, Medical Education, Minority Education, Religious Education, Student Aid
Health: Children's Health/Hospitals, Hospices, Hospitals, Medical Research
Religion: Churches, Ministries, Religious Organizations, Religious Welfare, Seminaries
Social Services: At-Risk Youth, Big Brother/Big Sister, Camps, Child Welfare, Community Service Organizations, People with Disabilities, Shelters/Homelessness, Social Services-General, United Funds/United Ways, YMCA/YWCA/YMHA/YWHA, Youth Organizations

Application Procedures

Initial Contact: Send a brief letter of inquiry.
Application Requirements: Include proof of tax-exempt status, purpose of funds sought, amount requested, what percent of the total cost the request is, and a breakdown of how the money will be spent.
Deadlines: None.

Restrictions

Does not support individuals or organizations outside operating areas.

Additional Information

Trust(s): Wells Fargo Bank NA

Grants Analysis

Disclosure Period: calendar year ending 2001
Total Grants: $580,835*
Number of Grants: 30
Average Grant: $17,595*
Highest Grant: $53,000
Typical Range: $5,000 to $30,000
*Note: Giving excludes United Way. Average grant figure excludes highest grant.

Recent Grants

Note: Grants derived from 2001 Form 990.

General

53,000	Camp Millhouse, South Bend, IN
50,000	Northern Indiana Historical Society, South Bend, IN
50,000	Notre Dame University, Notre Dame, IN
40,634	Northern Indiana Historical Society, South Bend, IN
40,634	Northern Indiana Historical Society, South Bend, IN
40,634	Northern Indiana Historical Society, South Bend, IN
40,634	Northern Indiana Historical Society, South Bend, IN
30,000	Potawatomi Zoological Society, South Bend, IN
25,000	Bethel College, South Bend, IN
25,000	Homeless Center, Notre Dame, IN

GEORGE AND CAROL OLMSTED FOUNDATION

Giving Contact

103 West Broad Street, Suite 330
Falls Church, VA 22046-4237
Phone: (703)536-3500
Web: http://www.olmstedfoundation.org

Description

Founded: 1960
EIN: 546049005
Organization Type: Private Foundation
Giving Locations: DC: Washington metropolitan area
Grant Types: General Support, Scholarship.

Donor Information

Founder: George Olmsted

Financial Summary

Total Giving: $639,453 (2000); $267,805 (1999); $645,188 (1998)
Giving Analysis: Giving for 2000 includes: foundation scholarships ($1,500); 1999: foundation scholarships ($160,805) 1998: foundation gifts to individuals ($544,088)
Assets: $19,110,242 (2000); $12,926,001 (1999); $12,762,513 (1998)
Gifts Received: $7,000,000 (2000); $1,556,222 (1996); $153,067 (1995). Note: In 1996, contributions were received from the estate of Carol Olmsted.

Typical Recipients

Arts & Humanities: Historic Preservation, History & Archaeology, Libraries, Museums/Galleries
Education: Colleges & Universities, International Studies, Student Aid
Social Services: Community Service Organizations, Scouts, Veterans, Youth Organizations

Application Procedures

Initial Contact: Grant requests must be initiated by a member of the board of director and approved by a majority of the members of the board.
Review Process: Board meets in January, April, July, and October.

Restrictions

Does not support individuals (except for Olmsted Scholars).

Additional Information

Provides educational grants for two years of graduate study and other educational experiences in a foreign country to three competitively selected career officers per year.
Publications: Annual Report

Foundation Officials

Col. Daniel J. Bohlin: director
Emerson N. Gardner: director
Mjr. Gen. Stanley G. Genega: director ED Massachusetts Institute of Technology MS; United States Military Academy (1965). PRIM CORP EMPL director: U.S. Army Corp.s Engrs Civil Works Headquarters.
Adm. James Lemuel Holloway, III: director B Charleston, SC 1922. ED United States Naval Academy BSEE (1942). CORP AFFIL director: UNC; director: Statia Terminals; director: U South Life Inst Co. NONPR AFFIL director: Olmstead Foundation; president, trustee: Saint James School; president: Naval History Foundation; trustee: George C. Marshall Foundation; chairman: Naval Academy Foundation; chairman: Historic Annapolis Foundation; director: Mariners Museum; director: Atlantic Council; member: Association Naval Aviation. CLUB AFFIL Society Cincinnati; Metro Club; New York Yacht Club; Brook Club; Maryland Club; Alfalfa Club; Annapolis Yacht Club.
Howard Hussing: president, chief executive officer, director
Rear Adm. Larry R. Marsh: director
Joseph McManus, Esq.: secretary, treasurer
Bernard Francis Saul, II: mem B Washington, DC 1932. ED Villanova University BS (1954); University of Virginia LLB (1957). PRIM CORP EMPL chairman, president: BF Saul Co. CORP AFFIL trustee: BF Saul Real Estate Investment Trust Co.; director: Colonial Williamsburg Hotel Properties Inc.; chief executive officer, trustee: Saul Centers; chairman, chief executive officer: Chevy Chase Bank FSB. NONPR AFFIL director: Wadsworth Preservation Trust; director bd visitors & govs: Washington College; member trustee counc: Natl Gallery Arts; member visiting committee: University Virginia School Architecture; member: National Association Real Estate Investment Trusts; trustee: National Geographic Society; member honors comm: John F. Kennedy Ctr Performing Arts; trustee: Federation City Council; member: Folger Shakespeare Library; life trustee: Corcoran Gallery Art; hon trustee: Brookings Institute; member bd adv: CLW Life & Annuity Acquisition Corp. CLUB AFFIL Wianno Club; Knights of Malta; Metro Club; Friendly Sons Saint Patrick; Chevy Chase Country Club; Farmington Country Club; Burning Tree Club; Alibi Club; Brook Club; Alfalfa Club.
Barbara S. Schimpff: executive vice president, registered agt
Brig. Gen. Bruce K. Scott: director
Adm. David Shiverick Smith: chairman, director B Omaha, NE 1918. ED Sorbonne University (1938); Dartmouth College BA (1939); Columbia University JD (1942). PRIM CORP EMPL director: Un Services Life InsuranceCorp. CORP AFFIL director: Liberian Services; director: USLICO Corp.; director: International Bank; member advisor counc: Johns Hopkins University School Advanced International Studies. NONPR AFFIL member: Society Mayflower Descendants; member: Washington Institute Foreign Affairs; member: Phi Beta Kappa; member: Pilgrims U.S.; member: Hudson Institute; member: New York State

Bar Association; member: Fed Bar Association; member: France-American Society; secretary, director, member: Council American Ambassadors; member: English Speaking Union; member: Asia Society; member: Connecticut Bar Association; member: American Foreign Law Association; member: American Society International Law; member: American Bar Association. CLUB AFFIL Old Guard Society; Palm Beach Golfers Club; Metropolitan Club; Everglades Club; Meadow Club; Chevy Chase Club; Crocodiles Club; Bathing Corp. Southampton Club; Brook Club; Bath & Tennis Club.

Col. Robert A. Stratton: director

Adm. Carlisle Albert H. Trost: director B Valmeyer, IL 1930. ED Washington University (1948-1949); United States Naval Academy BS (1953); University of Freiberg (1960-1962). CORP AFFIL director: Louisiana Land & Exploration Co.; director: Precision Components Corp.; director: GPU Nuclear Corp.; director: Lockheed Martin Corp.; director: General Public Utility Corp.; director: Bird-Johnson Co.; director: General Dynamics Corp. NONPR AFFIL trustee, member: U.S. Naval Alumni Association; member: U.S. Naval Institute; trustee: U.S. Naval Academy Foundation.

Grants Analysis

Disclosure Period: calendar year ending 2000
Total Grants: $637,953*
Number of Grants: 6
Highest Grant: $400,000
Lowest Grant: $3,750
*Note: Giving excludes scholarship.

Recent Grants

Note: Grants derived from 1999 Form 990.

General

50,000	Society of the Cincinnati, Washington, DC -- educational support of museum functions
25,000	National Capital Area Council Boy Scouts of America, Bethesda, MD -- operation and maintenance of Camp Olmsted
15,000	Saint James School, St. James, MD -- educational scholarship assistance
15,000	United States Naval Academy, Annapolis, MD -- educational
8,500	United States Air Force Academy, Colorado Springs, CO -- education and military history symposium
7,500	Arlington Historical Society, Arlington, VA -- Arlington Historical Magazine
1,500	Coe College, Cedar Rapids, IA -- educational support of work scholarship endowment
1,000	National WWII Memorial, Arlington, VA -- assistance in building the memorial

ELIS OLSSON MEMORIAL FOUNDATION

Giving Contact

Thelma Downey, Executive Director
PO Box 151
West Point, VA 23181
Phone: (804)843-9066
Fax: (804)843-9068

Description

Founded: 1966
EIN: 546062436
Organization Type: Family Foundation
Giving Locations: VA
Grant Types: Fellowship, General Support, Professorship.

Donor Information

Founder: Established in 1966 by the late Inga Olsson Nylander and the late Signe Maria Olsson .

Financial Summary

Total Giving: $1,220,989 (2001); $1,291,623 (2000); $1,040,675 (1998)
Assets: $25,752,783 (2001); $26,651,154 (2000); $27,534,026 (1998)
Gifts Received: $20,330 (2001); $28,885 (2000); $32,529 (1998). Note: In 1998 and 2001, contributions were received from The Sture Gordon Olsson Charitable Lead Unitrust.

Typical Recipients

Arts & Humanities: Arts Appreciation, Arts Associations & Councils, Arts Centers, Arts Festivals, Arts Institutes, Historic Preservation, History & Archaeology, Libraries, Literary Arts, Museums/Galleries, Performing Arts, Theater

Civic & Public Affairs: African American Affairs, Employment/Job Training, Civic & Public Affairs-General, Municipalities/Towns, Nonprofit Management, Philanthropic Organizations, Public Policy, Safety, Urban & Community Affairs, Zoos/Aquariums

Education: Agricultural Education, Arts/Humanities Education, Business Education, Colleges & Universities, Community & Junior Colleges, Education Funds, Elementary Education (Private), Engineering/Technological Education, Faculty Development, Education-General, Legal Education, Literacy, Medical Education, Minority Education, Private Education (Precollege), Religious Education, School Volunteerism, Science/Mathematics Education, Secondary Education (Private), Secondary Education (Public), Student Aid, Vocational & Technical Education

Environment: Air/Water Quality, Forestry, Environment-General, Resource Conservation, Wildlife Protection

Health: Alzheimers Disease, Cancer, Children's Health/Hospitals, Clinics/Medical Centers, Emergency/Ambulance Services, Health-General, Health Funds, Health Organizations, Heart, Hospices, Hospitals, Hospitals (University Affiliated), Long-Term Care, Medical Rehabilitation, Medical Research, Public Health, Research/Studies Institutes, Respiratory, Single-Disease Health Associations

International: Missionary/Religious Activities

Religion: Churches, Dioceses, Ministries, Religious Organizations, Religious Welfare, Seminaries

Science: Science Museums, Scientific Centers & Institutes

Social Services: Animal Protection, Camps, Child Welfare, Community Service Organizations, Counseling, Day Care, Emergency Relief, Family Services, Food/Clothing Distribution, Homes, People with Disabilities, Scouts, Senior Services, Shelters/Homelessness, Social Services-General, Volunteer Services, Youth Organizations

Application Procedures

Initial Contact: The foundation requests applications be made in writing.
Application Requirements: Applications should be in written form and a copy of the organization's tax determination letter should be attached to the proposal. The foundation notes that the applicant's charitable purpose should be clearly stated.
Deadlines: None.

Restrictions

Grants are not made on individuals or political groups.

Foundation Officials

Dennis Irl Belcher: treasurer, trustee B Wheeling, WV 1951. ED College of William & Mary BA (1973); University of Richmond JD (1976). PRIM CORP EMPL partner, member executive committee: McGuire, Woods, Battle & Boothe. NONPR AFFIL fellow: American College Trust & Estate Counsel; member:

Virginia Bar Association; member: American Bar Association. CLUB AFFIL Bull & Bear Club; Country Club Virginia.

Thelma L. Downey: assistant secretary, assistant treasurer

Shirley Olsson: vice president, trustee

Sture Gordon Olsson: president, trustee B Richmond, VA July 01, 1920. ED University of Virginia BS (1942). PRIM CORP EMPL chairman emeritus: Chesapeake Corp. CORP AFFIL director: Citizens & Farmers Bank. CLUB AFFIL West Point Country Club.

Grants Analysis

Disclosure Period: calendar year ending 2001
Total Grants: $1,220,989
Number of Grants: 87
Average Grant: $9,659*
Highest Grant: $200,000
Lowest Grant: $1,000
Typical Range: $1,000 to $15,000
*Note: Average grant figure excludes two highest grants ($400,000).

Recent Grants

Note: Grants derived from 2001 Form 990.

General

200,000	Town of West Point Public Schools, West Point, VA
200,000	University of Virginia School of Engineering and Applied Science, Charlottesville, VA
100,000	Diocese of Virginia, Richmond, VA
100,000	National D-Day Memorial Foundation, Bedford, VA
50,000	Christchurch School, Christchurch, VA
50,000	Virginia Historical Society, Richmond, VA
50,000	Virginia Institute of Marine Science, Gloucester Point, VA
25,000	Children's Hospital, Richmond, VA
25,000	Delta Waterfowl Foundation, Bismarck, ND
25,000	St. Catherine's School, Lawrenceville, VA

ONDEO NALCO CO.

Company Headquarters

ONDEO Nalco Center
1601 W. Diehl Road
Naperville, IL 60563-1198
Phone: (630)305-1000
Fax: (630)305-2900
Web: http://www.nalco.com

Company Description

Former Name: Nalco Chemical Co. (2001).
Employees: 7,000
SIC(s): 2819 Industrial Inorganic Chemicals Nec, 2843 Surface Active Agents, 2869 Industrial Organic Chemicals Nec, 2899 Chemical Preparations Nec.

Operating Locations

Nalco Chemical Co. (AK--Anchorage, Kenai; CA--Bakersfield, Concord, Long Beach, Modesto; FL--Miami, Orlando, Pensacola; GA--Atlanta; HI--Honolulu; IL--Chicago, Mount Carmel, Naperville, Peoria; IN--Indianapolis; IA--Windsor Heights; KS--Shawnee Mission; LA--Garyville, Jena, Kenner; ME--South Portland; MA--Braintree; MI--Farmington Hills, Kalamazoo, Kingsley; MN--Duluth, Plymouth; MS--Natchez; MO--Maryland Heights; NJ--Paulsboro; NY--New York, Saratoga Springs, Skaneateles; OH--Cleveland, Miamisburg, Youngstown; OK--Oklahoma City; PA--Blue Bell, Pittsburgh; SC--North Charleston; SD--Sioux Falls; TN--Knoxville, Memphis; TX--Beaumont, Beeville, El Paso, Freeport, Kilgore, Odessa,

Sugar Land; UT--Salt Lake City; VA--Marion; WA--Vancouver; WV--Dunbar, Hepzibah; WI--Stevens Point, Waukesha; WY--Gillette)

Nonmonetary Support

Type: Donated Equipment
Note: Support is provided by the company.

ONDEO Nalco Foundation

Giving Contact

Ellen B. DeLordo, President
1 ONDEO Nalco Center
Naperville, IL 60563-1198
Phone: (630)305-1566
Fax: (630)305-2896
E-mail: foundation@ondeo-nalco.com
Web: http://www.ondeo-nalco.com

Description

EIN: 366065864
Organization Type: Corporate Foundation
Giving Locations: CA: Carson; IL: DuPage County, Chicago metropolitan area; LA: Garyville; TX: Freeport, Sugarland
Grant Types: Capital, General Support, Project.
Note: Employee matching gift ratio: 1 to 1 for contributions over $25 to colleges and universities, up to $2,000 annually; 1 to 1 for gifts to hospitals and cultural institutions, up to $500 annually.

Financial Summary

Total Giving: $677,434 (2001); $1,171,459 (2000); $1,364,992 (1999). Note: Contributes through corporate direct giving program and foundation.
Giving Analysis: Giving for 2000 includes: foundation ($1,171,459); 1999: foundation ($1,364,992); 1998: corporate grants to United Way ($232,639); corporate direct giving ($324,352); corporate matching gifts ($338,211); foundation ($1,646,220);
Assets: $2,430,251 (2001); $4,614,226 (1998); $5,239,257 (1997)
Gifts Received: $7,000,073 (1994). Note: Gifts were received from Nalco Chemical Company.

Typical Recipients

Arts & Humanities: Arts Associations & Councils, Arts Funds, Arts Institutes, Community Arts, Dance, Historic Preservation, History & Archaeology, Libraries, Museums/Galleries, Music, Opera, Performing Arts, Public Broadcasting, Theater
Civic & Public Affairs: Business/Free Enterprise, Employment/Job Training, Civic & Public Affairs-General, Housing, Law & Justice, Legal Aid, Nonprofit Management, Professional & Trade Associations, Safety, Urban & Community Affairs, Women's Affairs, Zoos/Aquariums
Education: Business Education, Colleges & Universities, Economic Education, Education Associations, Engineering/Technological Education, Faculty Development, Education-General, Literacy, Medical Education, Minority Education, Preschool Education, Public Education (Precollege), Science/Mathematics Education, Social Sciences Education, Special Education, Student Aid
Environment: Environment-General
Health: AIDS/HIV, Alzheimers Disease, Cancer, Children's Health/Hospitals, Clinics/Medical Centers, Emergency/Ambulance Services, Geriatric Health, Health Policy/Cost Containment, Health Organizations, Heart, Home-Care Services, Hospices, Hospitals, Hospitals (University Affiliated), Medical Rehabilitation, Medical Research, Mental Health, Prenatal Health Issues, Preventive Medicine/Wellness Organizations, Public Health, Single-Disease Health Associations, Trauma Treatment

International: Foreign Educational Institutions, International Development, International Environmental Issues
Religion: Ministries, Religious Organizations, Religious Welfare
Science: Observatories & Planetariums, Science Museums, Scientific Centers & Institutes
Social Services: At-Risk Youth, Child Welfare, Community Centers, Community Service Organizations, Counseling, Delinquency & Criminal Rehabilitation, Domestic Violence, Emergency Relief, Family Services, Food/Clothing Distribution, People with Disabilities, Scouts, Shelters/Homelessness, Social Services-General, Special Olympics, Substance Abuse, YMCA/YWCA/YMHA/YWHA, Youth Organizations

Application Procedures

Initial Contact: Request guidelines or submit proposal in writing.
Application Requirements: Provide legal name and history of organization, summary of specified project or need, intended use of funds, program evaluation (for program-specific requests only), latest financial statement or budget, list of board of directors and their affiliations and addresses, list of corporate and foundation contributions, proof of tax-exempt status, copy of annual report (if available), breakdown of expenses (if not already included in other material) and IRS Form 990.
Deadlines: None.
Review Process: Proposals are acknowledged and are reviewed at next scheduled board meeting.
Decision Notification: Board meetings are held on a quarterly basis, generally in March, June, September, and December; applicant notified as soon as possible after meeting.

Restrictions

The foundation generally does not support individuals, political activities or lobbying groups, churches or religious education, secondary or elementary schools, state-supported colleges or universities, endowment funds, advertising in charitable publications, or purchase of tickets for fund-raising activities.

Additional Information

The foundation limits its giving to nonprofit organizations that provide services in the areas of education, community & civic affairs, health, and culture & art. The company sponsors a "Community Involvement" program, which is defined as the "giving of time and effort by individuals to special causes, with the company participating as originator or organizer." In addition, the program also includes the establishment of Community Advisory Groups at facilities around the country, facility tours for students, teachers and neighbors, and the hiring of college students in the Cooperative Education program. the Cooperative Education program. the Cooperative Education program.
Publications: Contributions Report

Corporate Officials

David R. Bertran: senior vice president manufacturing & logistics ED University of Waterloo BS; University of Waterloo MS (1967). PRIM CORP EMPL senior vice president manufacturing & logistics: Nalco Chemical Co. NONPR AFFIL trustee: Elmhurst College; member: Ontario Association Professional Engineering.
William E. Buchholz: senior vice president, chief financial officer B 1942. ED Michigan State University MBA (1965); Michigan State University BS (1966). PRIM CORP EMPL senior vice president, chief financial officer: Nalco Chemical Co. ADD CORP EMPL chairman: Nalco Leasing Corp. NONPR AFFIL director: Financial Executives Institute.
James F. Lambe: senior vice president human resources B 1945. ED University of Illinois BScE (1969); DePaul University JD (1972). PRIM CORP EMPL senior vice president human resources: Nalco Chemical

Co. NONPR AFFIL member: American Bar Association; trustee: North Central College.
Christian Maurin: chairman, chief executive officer PRIM CORP EMPL chairman, chief executive officer: Nalco Chemical Co.
William E. Parry: vice president, general counsel B Massena, NY 1951. ED University of Notre Dame BA (1973); Duquesne University JD (1978). PRIM CORP EMPL vice president, general counsel: Nalco Chemical Co. NONPR AFFIL member: American Corporate Counsel Association.

Foundation Officials

David R. Bertran: director (see above)
Charles F. Canfield: director
Ellen B. DeLordo: president
Joanne C. Ford: president, director
Craig J. Holderness: assistant treasurer PRIM CORP EMPL assistant treasurer: Nalco Chemical Co.
Michael E. Kahler: director, chairman
Gerald LaMarche: director
James F. Lambe: director (see above)
J. Michael Newton: director
Terrence J. Taylor: treasurer
Katie A. Townsend: treasurer
Mary Jane Wilson: secretary

Grants Analysis

Disclosure Period: calendar year ending 2001
Total Grants: $677,434
Number of Grants: 94
Average Grant: $7,207
Highest Grant: $34,000
Lowest Grant: $1,000
Typical Range: $2,500 to $30,000

Recent Grants

Note: Grants derived from 2001 Form 990.

Library-Related
5,000   Newberry Library, Chicago, IL

General
34,000   YMCA Metropolitan Chicago, Chicago, IL -- for Be a Neighborhood Hero' Capital Campaign
30,000   East Fort Bend Human Needs Ministry, Inc., Stafford, TX -- for new facility in East Fort Bend County
30,000   Rehabilitation Institute of Chicago, Chicago, IL -- for the Best Gets Even Better Capital Campaign
25,000   Benedictine University, Lisle, IL -- capital campaign for Hall of Science
20,000   Giant Steps Illinois, Inc., Westmont, IL -- for capital campaign for new school
19,496   Associated Colleges, Chicago, IL -- for science equipment grants for member colleges
15,000   John G. Shedd Aquarium, Chicago, IL -- for River Journey Gallery
15,000   Window to the World Communications/WTTW, Chicago, IL -- underwrite "Nature" series
15,000   Window to the World Communications/WTTW, Chicago, IL -- underwrite "Nature" series
12,000   Marianjoy Rehabilitation Center, Wheaton, IL -- for Mananjoy Rehablink

ONE VALLEY BANK NA

Company Headquarters

7th St. & Avery St.
Parkersburg, WV 26101

Company Description

Employees: 1,600
SIC(s): 6022 State Commercial Banks.
Parent Company: One Valley Bancorp, Inc.

One Valley Bank Foundation

Giving Contact

Michael W. Stajduhar, Senior Vice President
BB & T
PO Box 1793
Charleston, WV 25326
Phone: (304)348-7000

Description

EIN: 556017269
Organization Type: Corporate Foundation
Giving Locations: WV
Grant Types: General Support.

Financial Summary

Total Giving: $581,600 (2001); $199,200 (2000); $182,126 (1999)
Giving Analysis: Giving for 2001 includes: foundation grants to United Way ($68,500); 2000: foundation grants to United Way ($66,000); foundation ($133,200); 1999: foundation grants to United Way ($64,000); foundation ($118,126)
Assets: $10,728,155 (2001); $1,271,796 (2000); $1,499,822 (1999)
Gifts Received: $10,083,253 (2001); $112,631 (2000); $139,130 (1999). Note: In 1994, contributions were received from Bank of West Virginia Charitable Trust ($3,125), Atlantic Financial Charitable Foundation ($33,154), and One Valley Bank ($34,359).

Typical Recipients

Arts & Humanities: Arts Associations & Councils, Arts Funds, Arts & Humanities-General, History & Archaeology, Libraries, Museums/Galleries, Music, Public Broadcasting
Civic & Public Affairs: Chambers of Commerce, Economic Development, Employment/Job Training, Civic & Public Affairs-General, Housing, Parades/Festivals, Public Policy, Urban & Community Affairs, Women's Affairs
Education: Business Education, Colleges & Universities, Education Funds, Education Reform, Education-General, Legal Education, Literacy, Public Education (Precollege), Science/Mathematics Education, Special Education
Health: Children's Health/Hospitals, Clinics/Medical Centers, Health-General, Health Policy/Cost Containment, Health Organizations, Hospices, Hospitals, Single-Disease Health Associations
Religion: Religious Welfare
Social Services: At-Risk Youth, Camps, Child Welfare, Community Centers, Community Service Organizations, Food/Clothing Distribution, Homes, People with Disabilities, Recreation & Athletics, Scouts, Senior Services, Social Services-General, United Funds/United Ways, Volunteer Services, YMCA/YWCA/YMHA/YWHA, Youth Organizations

Application Procedures

Initial Contact: The foundation has no formal grant application procedure or application form.
Deadlines: None.

Restrictions

Does not support individuals. Foundation supports organizations in the state of West Virginia only.

Corporate Officials

Phyllis H. Arnold: president, chief executive officer, director B Parkersburg, WV 1948. ED West Virginia State University (1970); Marshall University (1976). PRIM CORP EMPL president, chief executive officer, director: One Valley Bank NA. NONPR AFFIL trustee: CAMCARE.
Frederick H. Belden, Jr.: executive vice president PRIM CORP EMPL executive vice president: One Valley Bancorp Inc.

J. Holmes Morrison: chairman, director PRIM CORP EMPL chairman, director: One Valley Bancorp of West Virginia.

Foundation Officials

Phyllis H. Arnold: mem, trustee (see above)
Robert Francis Baronner: director B Hollidaysburg, PA 1926. ED Saint Francis College BS (1950); University of Wisconsin (1958). PRIM CORP EMPL chairman: One Valley Bancorp Inc. ADD CORP EMPL director: One Valley Bnk NA. CLUB AFFIL Rotary Club.
Frederick H. Belden, Jr.: mem, trustee (see above)
Lloyd P. Calvert: mem, trustee B Charleston, WV 1936. ED Marshall University (1958); Rutgers University (1972). PRIM CORP EMPL senior vice president corporate committee: One Valley Bank NA.
Nelle Ratrie Chilton: member, trustee
J. Holmes Morrison: mem, trustee (see above)
John L. D. Payne: mem, trustee
Brent Robinson: member, trustee
Steven M. Rubin: member, trustee
K. Richard C. Sinclair: mem, trustee
Michael W. Stajduhar: mem PRIM CORP EMPL senior vice president: One Valley Bank NA.
Edwin H. Welch: member, trustee
Thomas D. Wilkerson: mem, trustee
John Williams: member, trustee

Grants Analysis

Disclosure Period: calendar year ending 2001
Total Grants: $513,100*
Number of Grants: 102
Average Grant: $4,101*
Highest Grant: $53,000
Lowest Grant: $300
Typical Range: $1,000 to $10,000
*Note: Giving excludes United Way. Average grant figure excludes highest grants ($103,000).

Recent Grants

Note: Grants derived from 2000 Form 990.

Library-Related

2,500	Kanawha County Library Foundation, Charleston, WV

General

66,000	United Way, Charleston, WV
63,000	West Virginia Foundation for Independent Colleges, Charleston, WV
10,000	Sojourners, Charleston, WV
10,000	West Virginia University Foundation, Morgantown, WV
8,000	Religious Coalition for Community Renewal, Charleston, WV
5,000	Mason County Action Group, Pt. Pleasant, WV
5,000	West Virginia Health Right, Inc., Charleston, WV
3,500	Covenant House, Charleston, WV
3,000	Daymark, Charleston, WV
3,000	Ohio Valley College, Parkersburg, WV

ONEIDA SAVINGS BANK

Company Headquarters

182 Main Street
Oneida, NY 13421-0240
Web: http://www.oneidabank.com

Company Description

Founded: 1866
SIC(s): 6036 Savings Institutions Except Federal.
Parent Company: Oneida Financial Corp., 182 Main St., Oneida, NY, United States

Oneida Savings Bank Charitable Foundation

Giving Contact

Eric Stickels
PO Box 240
182 Main Street
Oneida, NY 13421-0240
Phone: (315)363-2000

Description

Founded: 1999
EIN: 161561680
Organization Type: Corporate Foundation
Giving Locations: principally near operating locations and to national organizations.
Grant Types: General Support.

Financial Summary

Total Giving: $53,635 (2001); $36,000 (2000)
Assets: $1,583,190 (2001); $838,186 (2000); $880,522 (1998)
Gifts Received: $801,620 (1998). Note: In 1998, contributions were received from Oneida Financial Corp.

Typical Recipients

Arts & Humanities: Libraries
Civic & Public Affairs: Clubs, Civic & Public Affairs-General, Safety
Education: Student Aid
Social Services: Camps, Family Services, Recreation & Athletics, Senior Services

Application Procedures

Initial Contact: Submit a letter of request.
Deadlines: None.

Foundation Officials

Thomas H. Dixon: director
Michael R. Kallet: president
William Matthews: director
Ann K. Pierz: director
Eric E. Stickels: treasurer, secretary

Grants Analysis

Disclosure Period: calendar year ending 2001
Total Grants: $53,635
Number of Grants: 13
Average Grant: $2,683*
Highest Grant: $21,435
Lowest Grant: $500
Typical Range: $1,000 to $10,000
*Note: Average grant figure excludes highest grant.

Recent Grants

Note: Grants derived from 2001 Form 990.

Library-Related

10,000	Hamilton Public Library, Hamilton, NY -- building fund

General

21,435	Madison County Chapter of NYSARC
4,000	CAP
4,000	Orchard Hill Club of the Oneida Healthcare Center, Oneida, NY
3,000	Camden Soccer Club
2,500	Madison County Children's Camp
2,200	Oneida Fireman's Benevolent Association Grant, Oneida, NY
2,000	Camden Rotary Club Grant
1,000	Canastota Dollars for Scholars
1,000	Madison Family Outreach
1,000	Mid-York Senior Homes, Inc., Utica, NY

ONTARIO CORP.

Company Headquarters
123 E. Adams St.
Muncie, IN 47305
Web: http://www.muncieontheweb.com

Company Description
Employees: 612
SIC(s): 3700 Transportation Equipment, 3800 Instruments & Related Products.

Nonmonetary Support
Type: Donated Equipment; In-kind Services; Loaned Employees; Loaned Executives; Workplace Solicitation

Ontario Corp. Foundation

Giving Contact
Mark C. Smith, President
Ontario Corp. Foundation
123 East Adams Street
Muncie, IN 47305
Phone: (765)747-9001
Fax: (765)747-0331

Description
EIN: 310991589
Organization Type: Corporate Foundation
Giving Locations: IN
Grant Types: Award, Capital, Challenge, Employee Matching Gifts, Endowment, General Support, Multiyear/Continuing Support, Operating Expenses, Project, Scholarship, Seed Money.

Financial Summary
Total Giving: $142,550 (fiscal year ending June 30, 2001); $224,813 (fiscal 2000); $69,940 (fiscal 1999)
Giving Analysis: Giving for fiscal 2001 includes: foundation grants to United Way ($9,500); fiscal 2000: foundation grants to United Way ($6,000); fiscal 1999: foundation grants to United Way ($9,000); foundation ($60,940);
Assets: $1,138,318 (fiscal 2001); $1,295,621 (fiscal 2000); $1,443,755 (fiscal 1999)
Gifts Received: $85,000 (fiscal 2001); $199,298 (fiscal 1998); $15,000 (fiscal 1997)

Typical Recipients
Arts & Humanities: Arts Associations & Councils, Arts Centers, Arts Festivals, Community Arts, Arts & Humanities-General, History & Archaeology, Libraries, Museums/Galleries, Music, Performing Arts, Public Broadcasting, Theater
Civic & Public Affairs: Business/Free Enterprise, Chambers of Commerce, Community Foundations, Economic Development, Economic Policy, Civic & Public Affairs-General, Professional & Trade Associations, Public Policy, Zoos/Aquariums
Education: Arts/Humanities Education, Business Education, Business-School Partnerships, Colleges & Universities, Community & Junior Colleges, Economic Education, Education Associations, Engineering/Technological Education, Education-General, Minority Education, Private Education (Precollege), Science/Mathematics Education, Secondary Education (Public), Vocational & Technical Education
Environment: Environment-General, Resource Conservation
Health: Health-General, Health Organizations, Heart, Hospitals
Religion: Ministries, Religious Organizations, Religious Welfare, Seminaries
Science: Science Exhibits & Fairs

Social Services: At-Risk Youth, Big Brother/Big Sister, Family Services, Recreation & Athletics, Scouts, Social Services-General, Special Olympics, United Funds/United Ways, Volunteer Services, Youth Organizations

Application Procedures
Initial Contact: The foundation has no formal grant application procedure or application form.
Deadlines: None.

Restrictions
Does not support individuals or political or lobbying groups.

Corporate Officials
John W. Martin: chief financial officer PRIM CORP EMPL chief financial officer: Ontario Corp.
Van P. Smith: chairman B Oneida, NY 1928. ED Colgate University (1950); Georgetown University Law Center (1955). PRIM CORP EMPL chairman: Ontario Corp. CORP AFFIL partner: Village Developers; director: Standard Locknut & Lockwasher; director: Summit Bank Muncie; partner: Smitties Mens Store; chairman: Pyromet Industries; chairman: Sherry Laboratories; chairman: Pyromet Corp.; chairman: Pyromet Enterprises; director: PSI Resources; chairman: Pyromet; director: Ontario Tech; director: PSI Energy; chairman: Ontario Forge Corp.; chairman: Ontario System Corp.; chairman: Ontario Development Corp.; chairman: Ontario Environmental; director: Meridian Mutual Insurance Co.; chairman: Metlab Testing Services; director: Maxon Corp.; chairman: James Laboratories; director: Lilly Industries; director: Duland Toll & Engineering; director: NG Gilbert Corp.; director: Dalton Foundries Inc.; partner: DE Aviation; vice chairman, director: AAA Hoosier Motor Club & Affiliated Companies; chairman: CDS Engineering. NONPR AFFIL member: Theta Chi; director: U.S. Chamber of Commerce; director: Newman Foundation Indiana; member: W. W. Rich Foundation; director: Muncie Symphony Association; director: National Advisory Council Small Business Administration; trustee: Interlochen Center Arts; trustee: La Lumiere School; director: Indiana Labor & Management Council; director: Indiana Manufacturers Association; director: Indiana Commission Higher Education; director: Indiana Economic Develop Council; member: Indiana Bar Association; director: Indiana Chamber of Commerce; director: Governments Fiscal Policy Advisory Council; member: Delta Theta Phi; member: Forging Industry Association; trustee: Colgate University; director: Delta Sigma Pi; director: Business-Industry Political Action Committee; trustee: Catholic University America; member: American Bar Association; member: Beta Gamma Sigma; director: Alliance Metalworking Industry; director: American Automobile Association; trustee: Academy Community Leadership. CLUB AFFIL Rotary International Club; Skyline Club; Knights of Columbus; Meridian Hills Country Club; Elks Club; In Society Chicago Club; Columbia Club.
Mr. Kelly N. Stanley: president, chief executive officer PRIM CORP EMPL president, chief executive officer: Ontario Corp.

Foundation Officials
Jan P. Abbs: secretary
John W. Martin: treasurer (see above)
Mark C. Smith: president
Van P. Smith: chairman (see above)
Mr. Kelly N. Stanley: vice president (see above)

Grants Analysis
Disclosure Period: fiscal year ending June 30, 2001
Total Grants: $128,075*
Number of Grants: 58
Average Grant: $1,979*
Highest Grant: $15,300
Lowest Grant: $250
Typical Range: $1,000 to $5,000

*Note: Giving excludes United Way and miscellaneous grants totaling ($4,975). Average grant figure excludes highest grant.

Recent Grants
Note: Grants derived from fiscal 2000 Form 990.

Library-Related
5,000	Muncie Public Library, Muncie, IN

General
58,250	Muncie Children's Museum, Muncie, IN
20,000	Cardinal Greenway, Muncie, IN
15,000	Delaware County Chamber of Commerce, Muncie, IN
15,000	Hoosier Heritage Foundation, Indianapolis, IN
10,000	Delaware Advancement Corp, Muncie, IN
9,250	Community Foundation of Del County, Muncie, IN
9,000	Muncie Symphony Orchestra, Muncie, IN
7,932	Ball State Foundation, Muncie, IN
6,000	United Way of Delaware County, Muncie, IN
5,500	Ivy Tech, Muncie, IN

OPPENSTEIN BROTHERS FOUNDATION

Giving Contact
Sheila K. Rice, Program Officer
PO Box 13095
Kansas City, MO 64199-3095
Phone: (816)234-8671
Fax: (816)234-8690

Description
Founded: 1975
EIN: 436203035
Organization Type: General Purpose Foundation
Giving Locations: MO: Kansas City metropolitan area
Grant Types: Capital, Challenge, Conference/Seminar, Department, Emergency, General Support, Operating Expenses, Project, Seed Money.
Note: Metropolitan Kansas City area only.

Donor Information
Founder: Established in 1975 by the late Michael Oppenstein .
The Oppenstein brothers --Louis, Sam, Harry, and Michael-- moved from Denver, CO, to Kansas City, MO, in 1902. In Kansas City, they opened a jewelry store, which they eventually sold to begin business activities directed toward investments in downtown real estate.
All four brothers were active in community affairs.

Financial Summary
Total Giving: $1,532,700 (fiscal year ending March 31, 2002); $32,109,166 (fiscal 2001); $1,974,396 (fiscal 2000)
Assets: $31,353,648 (fiscal 2002); $33,760,956 (fiscal 2000); $33,825,719 (fiscal 1999)

Typical Recipients
Arts & Humanities: Arts Associations & Councils, Arts Funds, Arts Outreach, Ballet, Dance, Libraries, Museums/Galleries, Music, Opera, Performing Arts, Theater
Civic & Public Affairs: Clubs, Community Foundations, Civic & Public Affairs-General, Hispanic Affairs, Housing, Philanthropic Organizations, Professional & Trade Associations, Safety, Urban & Community Affairs, Women's Affairs, Zoos/Aquariums
Education: Colleges & Universities, Community & Junior Colleges, Economic Education, Education

Funds, Education-General, Gifted & Talented Programs, Private Education (Precollege), Public Education (Precollege), Science/Mathematics Education, Special Education, Vocational & Technical Education

Environment: Environment-General, Environment-General

Health: AIDS/HIV, Alzheimers Disease, Cancer, Children's Health/Hospitals, Clinics/Medical Centers, Emergency/Ambulance Services, Eyes/Blindness, Health Organizations, Heart, Hospices, Hospitals, Medical Rehabilitation, Mental Health, Prenatal Health Issues, Public Health, Single-Disease Health Associations

International: International Relations

Religion: Jewish Causes, Ministries, Religious Organizations, Religious Welfare

Social Services: Camps, Child Abuse, Child Welfare, Community Centers, Community Service Organizations, Counseling, Day Care, Domestic Violence, Family Planning, Family Services, Food/Clothing Distribution, Homes, People with Disabilities, Recreation & Athletics, Scouts, Senior Services, Sexual Abuse, Shelters/Homelessness, Social Services-General, Substance Abuse, United Funds/United Ways, Volunteer Services, YMCA/YWCA/YMHA/YWHA, Youth Organizations

Application Procedures

Initial Contact: The foundation requests applications be made in writing. Guidelines are available upon request.

Application Requirements: Before submitting a proposal to the disbursement committee, current background information must be submitted including: agency name, address, phone number and contact person; agency mission statement and brief history; list of board of directors, the number giving financial support and their aggregate support; number of full and part time staff and volunteers, and the hours they serve; most recent audited financial statement and current statement of income and expenses; budget for the coming year; and a copy of the IRS tax determination letter and agency's EIN. Additional information is needed when submitting a full proposal; refer to guidelines pamphlet for specifics.

Deadlines: Proposals must be submitted three weeks prior to a board meeting.

Review Process: The board generally meets every other month. Decisions are made within two to four months.

Restrictions

The foundation does not give to individuals, medical research, annual campaigns, building funds, scholarships, fellowships, medical equipment, endowment funds, or loans. Grants will be made only to agencies that provide direct services in the Kansas City metropolitan area for religious, charitable, scientific, and educational purposes.

Additional Information

Grants for significant improvements in quality or quantity of services will be favored over grants for deficit financing.

Publications: Informational Brochure (including Application Guidelines)

Foundation Officials

Mary Bloch: member disbursement committee
Laura Kemper Fields: mem disbursement comm
Roger T. Hurwitz: mem disbursement comm
John A. Morgan: chairman disbursement comm
Sheila K. Rice: program officer NONPR AFFIL finance director: YMCA Springfield Missouri.
Estelle G. Sosland: mem disbursement comm

Grants Analysis

Disclosure Period: fiscal year ending March 31, 2002
Total Grants: $1,532,700*
Number of Grants: 87

Average Grant: $17,617
Typical Range: $1,000 to $400,000
***Note:** Grants analysis provided by foundation.

Recent Grants

Note: Grants derived from 2000 Form 990.

General

200,000	Nelson Gallery Foundation, Kansas City, MO -- for support of the arts
200,000	Nelson Gallery Foundation, Kansas City, MO -- for support of the arts
166,667	Kansas City Museum Association, Kansas City, MO -- for educational purposes
60,000	Children's Mercy Hospital, Kansas City, MO -- for medical purposes
50,000	Guadeloupe Center, Inc., Kansas City, MO
50,000	Jewish Federation of Greater Kansas City, Overland Park, KS
50,000	Jewish Federation of Greater Kansas City, Overland Park, KS
50,000	Village Shalom, Overland Park, KS
50,000	Village Shalom, Overland Park, KS
45,000	Swope Parkway Health Center, Kansas City, MO

JOHN M. O'QUINN FOUNDATION

Giving Contact

John M. O'Quinn, President
440 Louisiana
Houston, TX 77002
Phone: (713)236-2659

Description

Founded: 1986
EIN: 760206844
Organization Type: Private Foundation
Giving Locations: TX
Grant Types: General Support.

Donor Information

Founder: John M. O'Quinn

Financial Summary

Total Giving: $3,249,663 (2000); $2,230,158 (1999); $7,108,754 (1998)
Assets: $38,006,844 (2000); $51,549,713 (1999); $25,350,399 (1998)
Gifts Received: $15,000,000 (1995); $8,429,788 (1994). Note: In 1995, contributions were received from John M. O'Quinn.

Typical Recipients

Arts & Humanities: Ballet, Libraries, Museums/Galleries, Opera, Public Broadcasting, Theater
Civic & Public Affairs: African American Affairs, Botanical Gardens/Parks, Civil Rights, Clubs, Civic & Public Affairs-General, Housing, Law & Justice, Legal Aid, Municipalities/Towns, Public Policy, Safety, Urban & Community Affairs, Women's Affairs
Education: Agricultural Education, Arts/Humanities Education, Colleges & Universities, Continuing Education, Education Funds, Elementary Education (Public), Engineering/Technological Education, Education-General, International Studies, Legal Education, Medical Education, Minority Education, Private Education (Precollege), Public Education (Precollege), School Volunteerism, Secondary Education (Private), Student Aid
Environment: Environment-General, Resource Conservation

Health: AIDS/HIV, Cancer, Children's Health/Hospitals, Clinics/Medical Centers, Diabetes, Health Organizations, Heart, Hospitals, Kidney, Multiple Sclerosis, Prenatal Health Issues, Public Health, Respiratory, Single-Disease Health Associations
International: International Relief Efforts
Religion: Churches, Jewish Causes, Ministries, Religious Welfare
Science: Science Museums
Social Services: Animal Protection, Child Welfare, Community Centers, Community Service Organizations, Crime Prevention, Family Planning, Food/Clothing Distribution, People with Disabilities, Recreation & Athletics, Scouts, Senior Services, Social Services-General, Substance Abuse, Youth Organizations

Application Procedures

Initial Contact: The foundation has no formal grant application procedure or application form.
Deadlines: None.

Foundation Officials

Robert A. Higley: secretary, treasurer
John M. O'Quinn: president B 1941. ED Rice University; University of Houston BS (1965); University of Houston JD (1967). PRIM CORP EMPL partner: O'Quinn, Kerensky & McAninch. NONPR AFFIL director: University Houston Law Alumni Association; trustee: University Houston Law Foundation; member: Texas Bar Association; director: Texas Trial Lawyers Association; director: Houston Trial Lawyers Association; trustee: Regent University; director: American Trial Lawyers Association.

Grants Analysis

Disclosure Period: calendar year ending 2000
Total Grants: $3,249,663
Number of Grants: 32
Average Grant: $43,092*
Highest Grant: $1,000,000
Typical Range: $20,000 to $100,000
***Note:** Average grant figure excludes three highest grants ($2,000,000).

Recent Grants

Note: Grants derived from 1999 Form 990.

General

1,000,000	Neighborhood Center, Houston, TX
500,000	Foundation for the Council on Alcohol and Drug Abuse, Houston, TX
150,000	South Texas College of Law, Houston, TX
100,000	Maryland Anderson Cancer, Houston, TX
68,000	Houston Athletic Committee, Houston, TX
66,133	End Hunger Network, Houston, TX
50,000	Greater Houston Community Foundation, Houston, TX
50,000	Houston International Sports Committee, Houston, TX
50,000	Texas Aviation Hall of Fame, Galveston, TX
50,000	Texas Heart Institute, Houston, TX

ORCHARD FOUNDATION

Giving Contact

M. Gordon Erlich, Trustee
Bingham McCutchen, LLP
PO Box 2587
South Portland, ME 04116
Phone: (207)799-0686
E-mail: orchard@maine.rr.com
Web: http://www.orchardfoundation.org

Description

Founded: 1991
EIN: 046660214
Organization Type: Private Foundation
Giving Locations: NY: New England area.
Grant Types: Award, Capital, General Support, Multiyear/Continuing Support, Operating Expenses, Project, Seed Money.

Financial Summary

Total Giving: $924,202 (2002); $939,027 (2001); $1,029,777 (2000). Note: Contributes through foundation only.
Giving Analysis: Giving for 2000 includes: foundation ($1,029,777); 1999: foundation scholarships ($10,000) foundation ($1,004,385)
Assets: $11,366,770 (2002); $13,647,021 (2001); $12,320,294 (2000)
Gifts Received: $2,981,162 (2001); $1,049,573 (2000); $1,026,449 (1999). Note: Contributions were received from Leigh Fibers.

Typical Recipients

Arts & Humanities: Arts Associations & Councils, Arts Centers, Arts Festivals, Film & Video, Arts & Humanities-General, Historic Preservation, History & Archaeology, Libraries, Museums/Galleries, Music, Public Broadcasting
Civic & Public Affairs: Community Foundations, Economic Development, Economic Policy, Employment/Job Training, Civic & Public Affairs-General, Hispanic Affairs, Native American Affairs, Philanthropic Organizations, Public Policy, Women's Affairs
Education: Arts/Humanities Education, Business Education, Colleges & Universities, Community & Junior Colleges, Education Funds, Engineering/Technological Education, Environmental Education, Education-General, International Studies, Literacy, Medical Education, Minority Education, Private Education (Precollege), Private Education (Precollege), Public Education (Precollege), Science/Mathematics Education, Secondary Education (Private), Vocational & Technical Education
Environment: Air/Water Quality, Forestry, Environment-General, Protection, Resource Conservation, Watershed, Wildlife Protection
Health: AIDS/HIV, Alzheimers Disease, Arthritis, Children's Health/Hospitals, Clinics/Medical Centers, Health Funds, Hospices, Hospitals, Medical Research, Multiple Sclerosis, Nursing Services, Outpatient Health Care
International: Health Care/Hospitals, International Development, International Environmental Issues, International Organizations, International Relief Efforts
Religion: Churches, Dioceses, Religious Organizations, Religious Welfare
Science: Scientific Centers & Institutes, Scientific Research
Social Services: Camps, Child Abuse, Child Welfare, Community Centers, Community Service Organizations, Counseling, Crime Prevention, Delinquency & Criminal Rehabilitation, Domestic Violence, Family Planning, Family Services, People with Disabilities, Senior Services, Shelters/Homelessness, Youth Organizations

Application Procedures

Initial Contact: See foundation website for application procedures, then send a one-page concept letter via fax or e-mail.
Application Requirements: Concept letters should include a description of organization and its history, project title, goal, means for accomplishing goal, and anticipated result. Include the total organization budget, total project budget, and amount requested. Ensure that the letter includes a contact name, address, phone number, e-mail address, and organizational website address (if applicable). Do not send material in plastic covers or binders. Videos and cassettes will not be accepted.

Deadlines: Applications must be postmarked by March 1 and September 1.
Notes: If the foundation is interested in a project described in the concept letter, it will request a four-page proposal. Grantees must file progress reports with the foundation.

Restrictions

Grants are not made to individuals, endowments, annual or capital campaigns, museums, religious programs or religion-affiliated organizations, conference participation/travel unrelated to current foundation grant, scholarships, fellowships, equipment needs, film and video projects, building projects, or loans.

Additional Information

The foundation office is staffed by a part-time executive director and is closed for most of June, July and August. The foundation encourages potential applicants to leave messages and reports that all phone or e-mail messages will be answered in time.
Publications: Proposal Guidelines

Corporate Officials

Carl P. Lehner: president, chief executive officer ED Amherst College. PRIM CORP EMPL president, chief executive officer: Leigh Fibers, Inc.
Philip Lehner: chairman B 1924. ED Harvard College. PRIM CORP EMPL chairman: Leigh Fibers, Inc.

Foundation Officials

Carl P. Lehner: trustee (see above)
Philip Lehner: trustee (see above)

Grants Analysis

Disclosure Period: calendar year ending 2002
Total Grants: $924,202
Number of Grants: 103
Average Grant: $8,160*
Highest Grant: $50,000
Lowest Grant: $100
Typical Range: $3,000 to $15,000
*Note: Average grant does not include two highest grants of $50,000 each.

Recent Grants

Note: Grants derived from 2000 Form 990.

Library-Related
10,000	Hingham Public Library, Hingham, MA

General
100,000	Massachusetts Institute of Technology, Cambridge, MA -- Mechanical Engineering Department
33,000	Nature Conservancy - Maine Chapter, Brunswick, ME -- St. John River project
30,000	Middlebury College, Middlebury, VT
25,000	Christ Church Episcopal School, Greenville, SC
25,000	Christ Church Episcopal School, Greenville, SC
25,000	M.I.S.S. Incorporated of the Treasure Coast, Stuart, FL
25,000	Trustees of Amherst College, Amherst, MA
25,000	Trustees of Hampshire College, Amherst, MA -- Endowed writing program
20,000	Lahey Clinic Foundation, Burlington, MA -- Institute of Urology
20,000	Scenic Hudson, Poughkeepsie, NY

ORE-IDA FOODS

Company Headquarters

345 Bobwhite Ct.
Boise, ID 83706

Company Description

Employees: 5,600
SIC(s): 2037 Frozen Fruits & Vegetables, 2038 Frozen Specialties Nec.
Parent Company: H.J. Heinz Co., 600 Grant Street, Pittsburgh, PA, United States

Operating Locations

Ore-Ida Foods (OR; WI)

Nonmonetary Support

Type: Donated Equipment; Donated Products; In-kind Services

Heinz Foundation

Giving Contact

Tammy Aupperle, Program Directory
PO Box 185
Pittsburgh, PA 15230-9897
Phone: (412)234-5255
E-mail: heinz.foundation@hjheinz.com
Web: http://www.heinz.com/jsp/foundation.jsp

Description

EIN: 256018924
Organization Type: Corporate Foundation
Giving Locations: headquarters and operating communities.
Grant Types: Capital, Conference/Seminar, Employee Matching Gifts, Endowment, General Support, Scholarship.

Financial Summary

Total Giving: $5,699,101 (2001); $6,690,018 (1998)
Giving Analysis: Giving for 2001 includes: foundation grants to United Way ($818,500); foundation matching gifts ($1,164,766); 1998: foundation grants to United Way ($565,000) foundation ($6,125,018)
Assets: $1,153,903 (2001); $1,236,850 (1998)
Gifts Received: $6,000,000 (2001); $6,000,000 (1998). Note: In 2001, contributions were received from H.J. Heinz Co.

Typical Recipients

Arts & Humanities: Arts Funds, Dance, Arts & Humanities-General, Libraries, Museums/Galleries, Music, Opera, Performing Arts, Public Broadcasting, Theater
Civic & Public Affairs: African American Affairs, Economic Development, Civic & Public Affairs-General, Philanthropic Organizations
Education: Agricultural Education, Arts/Humanities Education, Business Education, Colleges & Universities, Elementary Education (Private), Environmental Education, Education-General, Literacy, Medical Education, Minority Education, Preschool Education, Private Education (Precollege), Public Education (Precollege), Student Aid
Health: Children's Health/Hospitals, Hospitals, Nutrition
International: Foreign Educational Institutions, International Environmental Issues
Science: Science-General
Social Services: Animal Protection, Child Welfare, Day Care, Family Services, Food/Clothing Distribution, Shelters/Homelessness, United Funds/United Ways, Volunteer Services, Youth Organizations

Application Procedures

Initial Contact: Send a brief letter of inquiry.
Application Requirements: Include program information that describes purposes/goals of the organization, plans for current year, and summary of previous year's programs/projects; the specific purpose for funds being requested; how program/project objectives will be accomplished; two whom and where the program will be offered, including populations and/or geographic areas; how the project will be sustained

after the grant ends. Policy decisions should include the type of governing structure, including the names of those on the governing board; a brief description of the major decisions over the last year affecting policy, goals, finances, etc. by the governing body. Provide the following financial and tax information: copy of current sources of income and expense (annual budget), copy of project budget related to proposed grant, copy of 501(c)(3) letter; the impact of the proposed program; indicate the extent to which Heinz employees, retirees, or directors are involved with the organization and any volunteer opportunities available within the organization.

Restrictions

Does not support individuals, religious organizations for sectarian purposes, or political or lobbying groups.

Additional Information

Company gives through its parent company's foundation, the Heinz Foundation. Profile reflects Ore-Ida's priorities.
Trust(s): Mellon Bank

Corporate Officials

Richard M. Wamhoff: president, chief executive officer, director PRIM CORP EMPL president, chief executive officer, director: Ore-Ida Foods.

Grants Analysis

Disclosure Period: calendar year ending 2001
Total Grants: $5,699,101*
Number of Grants: 1,111
***Note:** Giving excludes United Way.

Recent Grants

Note: Grants derived from 2001 Form 990.

General

485,000	United Way of Allegheny County, Pittsburgh, PA -- for operating support
250,000	Hospital for Sick Children, Washington, DC -- in support of the Sprinkles research in Toronto
100,000	American Ireland Fund -- in support of chair in the Institute for Neuroscience at Trinity College
100,000	Carnegie Mellon University, Pittsburgh, PA -- for endowment
100,000	Center for Environmental Science and Economics, Washington, DC -- for endowment support
100,000	Extra Mile Education Foundation, Pittsburgh, PA -- for inner-city parochial schools
100,000	Irish Educational Foundation, Cambridge, MA -- for endowed research fellowship
100,000	National Underground Railroad Freedom Center, Cincinnati, OH -- to endow the Teacher Candidate's Summer Institute on Freedom
100,000	Robert Morris College, Pittsburgh, PA -- for college's Communications Skills Program
100,000	United Way of Allegheny County, Pittsburgh, PA -- for parochial schools

EDWARD B. OSBORN CHARITABLE TRUST

Giving Contact

Gloria M. Osborn, Trustee
c/o US Trust Co. of New York
114 W. 47th St.
New York, NY 10036
Phone: (212)852-1000

Description

Founded: 1961
EIN: 136071296
Organization Type: Private Foundation
Giving Locations: FL; NY
Grant Types: General Support.

Donor Information

Founder: Edward B. Osborn

Financial Summary

Total Giving: $415,600 (fiscal year ending October 31, 2001); $774,300 (fiscal 2000); $305,750 (fiscal 1999)
Giving Analysis: Giving for fiscal 2001 includes: foundation grants to United Way ($1,000) fiscal 2000: foundation grants to United Way ($10,000)
Assets: $7,303,416 (fiscal 2001); $9,136,506 (fiscal 2000); $8,747,678 (fiscal 1999)
Gifts Received: $1,474 (fiscal 1994)

Typical Recipients

Arts & Humanities: Arts Associations & Councils, Arts Centers, Ballet, Dance, Historic Preservation, Libraries, Museums/Galleries, Music, Opera, Performing Arts, Public Broadcasting, Theater
Civic & Public Affairs: Botanical Gardens/Parks, Civic & Public Affairs-General, Urban & Community Affairs, Women's Affairs, Zoos/Aquariums
Education: Colleges & Universities, Education-General, Private Education (Precollege)
Environment: Air/Water Quality, Environment-General, Resource Conservation
Health: Alzheimers Disease, Cancer, Clinics/Medical Centers, Diabetes, Heart, Hospices, Hospitals, Medical Research, Nursing Services, Single-Disease Health Associations
International: International Relations
Religion: Churches
Social Services: Community Service Organizations, Family Planning, Food/Clothing Distribution, People with Disabilities, Recreation & Athletics, Substance Abuse, Veterans, Youth Organizations

Application Procedures

Initial Contact: Send a brief letter of inquiry.
Application Requirements: Include a description of organization.
Deadlines: None.

Additional Information

Trust(s): US Trust Co NY

Grants Analysis

Disclosure Period: fiscal year ending October 31, 2001
Total Grants: $411,600*
Number of Grants: 49
Average Grant: $5,904*
Highest Grant: $50,000
Lowest Grant: $300
Typical Range: $1,000 to $10,000
***Note:** Giving excludes United Way. Average grant excludes three highest grants ($140,000).

Recent Grants

Note: Grants derived from 2000 Form 990.

Library-Related

10,000	Frick Collection, New York, NY

General

100,000	Boys Club of New York, New York, NY
100,000	Central Park Conservancy, New York, NY
100,000	Minnesota Landscape Arboretum, Chanhassen, MN
100,000	Purnell School, Pottersville, NJ
82,500	Minnetonka Center for the Arts, Minneapolis, MN
50,000	Center of the American Experiment, Minneapolis, MN

50,000	High Peaks Foundation
50,000	University of Minnesota Men's Athletic Department, MN
10,000	Alzheimer's Association
10,000	Chrysalis Center for Women

I. A. O'SHAUGHNESSY FOUNDATION

Giving Contact

W-1271 First Bank Bldg.
332 Minnesota Street
St. Paul, MN 55101
Phone: (651)222-2323
Fax: (651)222-6368
E-mail: iaoshaughnessyfd@qwest.net
Note: Alternate Phone (651)222-2323

Description

Founded: 1941
EIN: 416011524
Organization Type: Family Foundation
Giving Locations: IL; KS; MN; TX
Grant Types: Capital, Endowment, General Support, Matching, Multiyear/Continuing Support, Project, Seed Money.

Donor Information

Founder: Mrs. I. A. O'Shaughnessy established the O'Shaughnessy Foundation in 1941. In 1960, a bequest of $5 million from the estate of Mrs. I. A. O'Shaughnessy went to the foundation. The Globe Oil and Refining Companies and Lario Oil and Gas were also donors.

Financial Summary

Total Giving: $2,725,000 (2001); $4,300,298 (2000); $4,619,680 (1999)
Giving Analysis: Giving for 1998 includes: foundation grants to United Way ($15,000)
Assets: $83,573,060 (2001); $95,537,410 (2000); $100,014,883 (1999)

Typical Recipients

Arts & Humanities: Arts Associations & Councils, Arts Festivals, Arts Funds, Arts Institutes, Arts Outreach, Historic Preservation, History & Archaeology, Libraries, Literary Arts, Museums/Galleries, Music, Performing Arts, Public Broadcasting, Theater
Civic & Public Affairs: Chambers of Commerce, Clubs, Community Foundations, Employment/Job Training, Civic & Public Affairs-General, Hispanic Affairs, Housing, Philanthropic Organizations, Urban & Community Affairs
Education: Business Education, Colleges & Universities, Economic Education, Education Funds, Elementary Education (Private), Elementary Education (Public), Engineering/Technological Education, Faculty Development, Education-General, International Exchange, Literacy, Literacy, Medical Education, Minority Education, Preschool Education, Private Education (Precollege), Public Education (Precollege), Religious Education, Science/Mathematics Education, Secondary Education (Private), Secondary Education (Public), Social Sciences Education, Student Aid
Environment: Environment-General
Health: Alzheimers Disease, Cancer, Children's Health/Hospitals, Clinics/Medical Centers, Heart, Hospices, Hospitals, Medical Rehabilitation, Prenatal Health Issues
International: International-General, International Development, International Organizations, Missionary/Religious Activities
Religion: Churches, Religion-General, Jewish Causes, Ministries, Religious Organizations, Religious Welfare, Social/Policy Issues
Science: Science Museums

Social Services: Animal Protection, Child Welfare, Community Centers, Community Service Organizations, Domestic Violence, Family Services, Food/Clothing Distribution, People with Disabilities, Recreation & Athletics, Shelters/Homelessness, United Funds/United Ways, YMCA/YWCA/YMHA/YWHA, Youth Organizations

Application Procedures

Initial Contact: Applicants should send a brief letter of inquiry requesting a grant application form. All grant actions are initiated by the directors or their representatives for the geographical regions in which they reside. Application information received at the foundation office is forwarded to the directors for their review.
Application Requirements: If, after reviewing the grant application form, the directors determine that the application falls within the foundation's areas of interest, they will request additional information and/or a full proposal.
Deadlines: None.
Review Process: The board meets several times each year.
Decision Notification: No notification is sent if a grant request is denied.

Restrictions

The foundation does not make grants to individuals or organizations in foreign countries.

Additional Information

Normally grant actions are initiated by the directors or their representatives and for the areas in which they reside.
Publications: Application Form; Guidelines

Foundation Officials

John Bultena: secretary, treasurer
Carol Lyman: director
Barbara O'Shaughnessy: director
Daniel J. O'Shaughnessy: director
Eileen O'Shaughnessy: director
J. Michael O'Shaughnessy: director
John F. O'Shaughnessy, Jr.: director B 1939. PRIM CORP EMPL president, treasurer, director: General Parts & Supply Co.
Lawrence M. O'Shaughnessy: president, director
Mary Kay O'Shaughnessy: director
Michelle O'Shaughnessy Traeger: director
Kathryn Wysong: director

Grants Analysis

Disclosure Period: calendar year ending 2001
Total Grants: $2,275,000*
Number of Grants: 59
Average Grant: $50,000
Highest Grant: $330,000
Lowest Grant: $5,000
Typical Range: $5,000 to $75,000
*Note: Grants analysis provided by foundation.

Recent Grants

Note: Grants derived from 2000 Form 990.

General
582,500	University of Notre Dame, Notre Dame, IN
416,250	University of St. Thomas, St. Paul, MN
335,000	Midland College, Midland, TX
217,000	Newman University, Wichita, KS
200,000	Oblate School of Theology, San Antonio, TX
166,250	Catholic Community Foundation, St. Paul, MN
166,250	Marian Center Foundation, St. Paul, MN
166,250	St. Thomas Academy, Mendota Heights, MN
100,000	Charter Fund, Denver, CO
100,000	Lake Country Montessori School, Minneapolis, MN

BERNARD OSHER FOUNDATION

Giving Contact

Patricia Tracy-Nagle, Executive Administrator & Secretary
909 Montgomery, No. 300
San Francisco, CA 94133
Phone: (415)861-5587
Fax: (415)677-5868
E-mail: nagle@osherfoundation.com

Description

Founded: 1977
EIN: 942506257
Organization Type: General Purpose Foundation
Giving Locations: CA: Alameda County, San Francisco County
Grant Types: Fellowship, Project, Research, Scholarship, Seed Money.

Donor Information

Founder: The foundation was established in 1977 by Bernard Osher. Mr. Osher is a prominent businessman and community leader in the San Francisco Bay Area.

Financial Summary

Total Giving: $9,634,848 (2000); $14,176,765 (1999); $15,218,265 (1998)
Giving Analysis: Giving for 1998 includes: foundation grants to United Way ($25,000) 1997: foundation scholarships ($1,016,500)
Assets: $36,297,798 (1998); $48,357,029 (1997); $49,130,307 (1996)
Gifts Received: $19,687,500 (1996). Note: In 1996, contributions were received from Benard Osher.

Typical Recipients

Arts & Humanities: Arts Associations & Councils, Arts Centers, Arts Festivals, Arts Funds, Arts Institutes, Arts Outreach, Ballet, Dance, Ethnic & Folk Arts, Film & Video, Arts & Humanities-General, History & Archaeology, Libraries, Literary Arts, Museums/Galleries, Music, Opera, Performing Arts, Public Broadcasting, Theater
Civic & Public Affairs: Botanical Gardens/Parks, Civic & Public Affairs-General, Hispanic Affairs, Legal Aid, Parades/Festivals, Public Policy, Urban & Community Affairs, Zoos/Aquariums
Education: Afterschool/Enrichment Programs, Arts/Humanities Education, Colleges & Universities, Continuing Education, Education-General, International Studies, International Studies, Journalism/Media Education, Leadership Training, Medical Education, Private Education (Precollege), Science/Mathematics Education, Student Aid, Vocational & Technical Education
Environment: Environment-General, Resource Conservation, Wildlife Protection
Health: AIDS/HIV, Cancer, Diabetes, Health Organizations, Hospitals, Medical Research, Mental Health
International: Foreign Arts Organizations, International Affairs, International Organizations, International Peace & Security Issues, International Relations, Missionary/Religious Activities
Religion: Churches, Religious Organizations, Religious Welfare
Science: Science Museums, Scientific Centers & Institutes
Social Services: At-Risk Youth, Community Centers, Community Service Organizations, Family Planning, Family Services, Family Services, Food/Clothing Distribution, People with Disabilities, Shelters/Homelessness, Social Services-General, Substance Abuse, United Funds/United Ways, Youth Organizations

Application Procedures

Initial Contact: Applicants should submit a letter of inquiry.
Application Requirements: Initial letters should include a background of the organization, including qualifications of people involved; a description of the nature and scope of proposed project or program and anticipated results; a preliminary timetable and budget outline; financial statement for most recent completed year of operation; evidence of tax-exempt status; names of appropriate governing authority; and evidence of request approval.
Deadlines: None.
Review Process: If the letter of inquiry falls within the foundation's areas of interest, the board will request a more detailed proposal. All applications will receive a prompt response from the foundation.

Restrictions

Generally, the foundation does not fund requests for capital improvements, normal operating expenses, deficits, or fundraising campaigns. The foundation may not make direct grants to individuals.

Additional Information

Publications: Application Guidelines

Foundation Officials

David Agger: director
Dr. Frederick Emery Balderston: director B 1923. PRIM CORP EMPL associate dean: University California Graduate School Business Administration. NONPR AFFIL board trustees: American Field Service International Scholarships Inc.
Judith Ciani: director B Medford, MA 1943. ED Thayer Academy (1961); Mount Holyoke College MA (1965); Boston College JD (1970). PRIM CORP EMPL partner: Pillsbury Madison Sutro. CORP AFFIL president: Common Fund Legal Services. NONPR AFFIL fellow: American Bar Foundation; member, director: Bar Association San Francisco.
Phyllis Cook: director NONPR AFFIL director: Jewish Community Federation San Francisco.
Robert Friend: director PRIM CORP EMPL president, chief executive officer, director: Kutler Clothiers Inc.
Ron Kaufman: director
Barbro Osher: president
Bernard A. Osher: treasurer B 1928. PRIM CORP EMPL director: Golden West Financial Corp. ADD CORP EMPL vice president, director: I R C O; vice president, director: Irving Rabin Co. CORP AFFIL director: West Golden Financial Corp.; director: World Savings & Loan Association; director: Ryko Corp.; vice president, director: Six Sixty Graphics.
Patricia Tracy-Nagle: senior vice president

Grants Analysis

Disclosure Period: calendar year ending 2000
Total Grants: $9,634,848*
Number of Grants: 143
Average Grant: $85,752*
Highest Grant: $2,000,000
Typical Range: $3,000 to $50,000
*Note: Giving excludes scholarships, United Way. Average grant figure excludes highest grant.

Recent Grants

Note: Grants derived from 2000 Form 990.

Library-Related
100,000	Berkeley Public Library, Berkeley, CA
25,000	San Francisco Public Library, San Francisco, CA
25,000	San Francisco Public Library, San Francisco, CA

General
1,075,000	KQED, San Francisco, CA
1,025,000	Asian Art Museum, San Francisco, CA
1,000,000	Golden Gate National Parks Association, San Francisco, CA

1,000,000	Maine Technical College, Portland, ME
1,000,000	University of Maine, Orono, ME -- endowment
900,000	California College of Arts and Crafts, Oakland, CA
875,000	Exploratorium, San Francisco, CA
120,000	American Himalayan Foundation, San Francisco, CA
100,000	California Academy of Sciences, San Francisco, CA
100,000	Maine College of Art, Portland, ME

OSHKOSH B'GOSH, INC.

Company Headquarters

Oshkosh, WI
Web: http://www.oshkoshbgosh.com

Company Description

Founded: 1895
Ticker: GOSHA
Exchange: NASDAQ
Revenue: US$437 million (2002)
Employees: 4650 (2002)
SIC(s): 2325 Men's/Boys' Trousers & Slacks, 2326 Men's/Boys' Work Clothing, 2369 Girls'/Children's Outerwear Nec.

Operating Locations

Oshkosh B'Gosh, Inc. (CA--Los Angeles; KY--Albany, Columbia, Liberty; NY--New York; TN--Byrdstown, Celina, Gainesboro, Jamestown, McEwen, White House; TX--Dallas)

Nonmonetary Support

Type: Donated Products
Note: Nonmonetary support is provided in the form of gift certificates.
Contact: Anne Spangler

Oshkosh B'Gosh Foundation Inc.

Giving Contact

Michael D. Wachtel, Executive Vice President
112 Otter Ave.
Oshkosh, WI 54901
Phone: (920)231-8800
Fax: (920)231-8621
Web: http://www.oshkoshbgosh.com

Description

EIN: 391525020
Organization Type: Corporate Foundation
Giving Locations: operating locations.
Grant Types: Award, Capital, Emergency, General Support, Scholarship.
Note: Scholarships are available for high school graduates in the communities in which Oshkosh B'Gosh, Inc. plants or facilities are located.

Financial Summary

Total Giving: $415,745 (2001); $425,000 (2000); $419,217 (1999). Note: Contributes through foundation only.
Giving Analysis: Giving for 2001 includes: foundation scholarships ($78,750); foundation grants to United Way ($83,777); foundation ($253,218); 1999: foundation grants to United Way ($43,504); foundation scholarships ($90,875); foundation ($284,837); 1998: foundation grants to United Way ($36,500); foundation scholarships ($98,875); foundation ($195,934);
Assets: $1,159,821 (2001); $926,886 (1999); $722,380 (1998)

Gifts Received: $450,000 (2001); $600,000 (1999); $400,000 (1997). Note: Contributions are received from Oshkosh B'Gosh, Inc.

Typical Recipients

Arts & Humanities: Arts Associations & Councils, Arts Centers, Arts Festivals, Community Arts, Dance, Libraries, Museums/Galleries, Music, Opera, Performing Arts, Public Broadcasting
Civic & Public Affairs: Botanical Gardens/Parks, Business/Free Enterprise, Chambers of Commerce, Community Foundations, Civic & Public Affairs-General, Housing, Parades/Festivals, Philanthropic Organizations, Professional & Trade Associations, Public Policy, Urban & Community Affairs, Zoos/Aquariums
Education: Agricultural Education, Arts/Humanities Education, Business Education, Colleges & Universities, Community & Junior Colleges, Education Funds, Elementary Education (Private), Education-General, Literacy, Medical Education, Minority Education, Private Education (Precollege), Public Education (Precollege), Science/Mathematics Education, Student Aid, Vocational & Technical Education
Environment: Environment-General, Watershed
Health: Cancer, Children's Health/Hospitals, Clinics/Medical Centers, Diabetes, Emergency/Ambulance Services, Eyes/Blindness, Health Organizations, Heart, Medical Rehabilitation, Mental Health, Respiratory, Single-Disease Health Associations, Speech & Hearing
International: International-General, International Environmental Issues, International Organizations, International Relief Efforts
Religion: Jewish Causes
Science: Science Museums
Social Services: At-Risk Youth, Big Brother/Big Sister, Camps, Child Abuse, Child Welfare, Community Service Organizations, Day Care, Domestic Violence, Family Services, People with Disabilities, Recreation & Athletics, Scouts, Senior Services, Sexual Abuse, Special Olympics, United Funds/United Ways, YMCA/YWCA/YMHA/YWHA, Youth Organizations

Application Procedures

Initial Contact: Send brief letter.
Application Requirements: Include a description of organization; amount requested and purpose of funds sought; audited financial statement; and proof of tax-exempt status.
Deadlines: None.
Notes: The foundation reports there are no standard application procedures for grants. Scholarship applicants located in Oshkosh B'Gosh operating communities should contact their high school guidance counselor to obtain a formal application and deadline date.

Restrictions

The foundation only supports organizations and provides scholarships to individuals where a corporate office or sewing facility is located.

Corporate Officials

Douglas W. Hyde: chairman, president, chief executive officer B 1950. PRIM CORP EMPL chairman, president, chief executive officer: Oshkosh B'Gosh, Inc.
David L. Omachinski: chief financial officer, treasurer, vice president B Appleton, WI 1952. ED University of Wisconsin BA (1974). PRIM CORP EMPL chief financial officer, treasurer, vice president: Oshkosh B'Gosh Inc. CORP AFFIL director: White Clover Dairy; director: Archorbank SSB; director: Fox Cities Bank. NONPR AFFIL member: Knights of Columbus; member: Rotary International; treasurer: Art Paine Center & Arboretum; member: Financial Executives Institute; member: American Institute CPAs.
Michael D. Wachtel: chief operating officer B 1954. ED University of Wisconsin Pharmacy (1977). PRIM CORP EMPL chief operating officer: Oshkosh B'Gosh, Inc.

Foundation Officials

Michael D. Wachtel: president (see above)

Grants Analysis

Disclosure Period: calendar year ending 2001
Total Grants: $253,218*
Number of Grants: 43
Average Grant: $3,688*
Highest Grant: $51,000
Lowest Grant: $250
Typical Range: $500 to $5,000
*Note: Giving excludes scholarships; United Way. Average grant figure excludes two highest grants totaling $102,000.

Recent Grants

Note: Grants derived from 2001 Form 990.

General

59,516	United Way, Oshkosh, WI
51,000	Mercy Medical Center Foundation, Oshkosh, WI
51,000	Oshkosh YMCA, Oshkosh, WI
40,000	Paine Art Center and Arboretum, Oshkosh, WI
24,261	United Way of Sumner County, Gallatin, TN
10,000	Boys & Girls Club of Oshkosh, Oshkosh, WI
10,000	Grand Opera House Fund, Oshkosh, WI
7,500	Oshkosh Symphony, Oshkosh, WI
6,700	Junior Achievement of Oshkosh, Oshkosh, WI
6,500	University of Wisconsin Oshkosh Foundation, Oshkosh, WI -- scholarship

OTTENHEIMER BROTHERS FOUNDATION

Giving Contact

Grainger Williams, Board Member
425 West Capital, Suite 1516
Little Rock, AR 72201
Phone: (501)372-6167

Description

Founded: 1965
EIN: 716059988
Organization Type: Private Foundation
Giving Locations: AR: Pulaski County, Little Rock, North Little Rock
Grant Types: General Support.

Financial Summary

Total Giving: $263,698 (fiscal year ending April 30, 2002); $241,180 (fiscal 2001); $238,594 (fiscal 2000)
Assets: $5,829,137 (fiscal 2002); $5,834,108 (fiscal 2001); $5,273,356 (fiscal 2000)

Typical Recipients

Arts & Humanities: Arts Centers, Historic Preservation, Libraries
Civic & Public Affairs: Botanical Gardens/Parks, Business/Free Enterprise, Chambers of Commerce, Clubs, Economic Development, Civic & Public Affairs-General, Housing, Public Policy, Urban & Community Affairs
Education: Afterschool/Enrichment Programs, Business Education, Colleges & Universities, Literacy, Science/Mathematics Education
Environment: Environment-General
Health: AIDS/HIV, Children's Health/Hospitals, Health Organizations
Religion: Religion-General, Jewish Causes, Religious Organizations, Synagogues/Temples
Science: Science Museums
Social Services: Animal Protection, Camps, Child Welfare, Community Centers, Community Service Organizations, Family Planning, Family Services, Food/

Clothing Distribution, Food/Clothing Distribution, People with Disabilities, Recreation & Athletics, Sexual Abuse, Youth Organizations

Application Procedures

Initial Contact: Send a brief letter of inquiry. and a full proposal.
Application Requirements: Include a description of organization, amount requested, purpose of funds sought, recently audited financial statement, and proof of tax-exempt status.
Deadlines: None.

Restrictions

Foundation does not support individuals, religious organizations for sectarian purposes, political or lobbying groups, organizations outside operating areas, or scholarships.

Foundation Officials

Larry Alman: board of directors
Steve Bauman: secretary
Gus Blass, III: board of directors
Noland Blass, Jr.: board director
E. C. Eichenbaum: chairman
Judy Grundfest: board director
Julianne D. Grundfest: board of directors
Edward M. Penick: board director
Louis Rosen: board director
Fred Selz: board director
Sam C. Sowell: board of directors
Sam B. Strauss, Jr.: board director
E. Grainger Williams: board director

Grants Analysis

Disclosure Period: fiscal year ending April 30, 2002
Total Grants: $263,698
Number of Grants: 20
Average Grant: $8,616*
Highest Grant: $100,000
Lowest Grant: $100
Typical Range: $500 to $31,250
*Note: Average grant figure excludes highest grant.

Recent Grants

Note: Grants derived from fiscal 2002 Form 990.

Library-Related

31,250	Central Arkansas Library, Little Rock, AR

General

100,000	University of Arkansas Medical Sciences, Little Rock, AR
31,250	Arkansas Territorial Restoration, Little Rock, AR
25,000	Arkansas Arts Center, Little Rock, AR
25,000	Greater Little Rock Chamber of Commerce, Little Rock, AR
15,000	Park Positive Atmosphere Reaches Kids
12,500	Little Rock Boys and Girls Club, Little Rock, AR
5,268	B'nai Israel Temple, Evansville, IN
5,000	B'nai Israel Cemetery Foundation
5,000	Planned Parenthood of Arkansas and East Oklahoma, OK
3,000	Rotary Club of Little Rock International Youth Project, Little Rock, AR

OVERLAKE FOUNDATION

Giving Contact

Thomas L. Keller, Vice President & Treasurer
PO Box 2549
Victoria, TX 77902
Phone: (361)573-4383

Description

Founded: 1981
EIN: 751793068
Organization Type: Private Foundation
Giving Locations: TX
Grant Types: General Support.

Donor Information

Founder: Mary Alice Fitzpatrick

Financial Summary

Total Giving: $514,981 (fiscal year ending November 30, 2001); $500,735 (fiscal 2000); $395,350 (fiscal 1999)
Giving Analysis: Giving for fiscal 1998 includes: foundation scholarships ($1,000)
Assets: $7,793,452 (fiscal 2001); $10,030,802 (fiscal 2000); $9,850,763 (fiscal 1999)

Typical Recipients

Arts & Humanities: Arts Associations & Councils, Arts & Humanities-General, Historic Preservation, History & Archaeology, Libraries, Literary Arts, Museums/Galleries, Music, Public Broadcasting, Theater
Civic & Public Affairs: Clubs, Community Foundations, Civic & Public Affairs-General, Nonprofit Management, Parades/Festivals, Professional & Trade Associations, Rural Affairs, Safety, Urban & Community Affairs, Women's Affairs, Zoos/Aquariums
Education: Agricultural Education, Arts/Humanities Education, Colleges & Universities, Education Funds, Elementary Education (Public), Engineering/Technological Education, Education-General, Literacy, Medical Education, Private Education (Precollege), Science/Mathematics Education, Secondary Education (Private), Student Aid
Health: Cancer, Children's Health/Hospitals, Emergency/Ambulance Services, Health Funds, Health Organizations, Hospices, Hospitals, Medical Rehabilitation, Medical Research, Nursing Services, Public Health, Research/Studies Institutes, Single-Disease Health Associations
Religion: Bible Study/Translation, Churches, Religious Organizations, Religious Welfare
Science: Scientific Labs
Social Services: Animal Protection, At-Risk Youth, Camps, Child Welfare, Community Service Organizations, Counseling, Day Care, Domestic Violence, Family Services, Homes, Recreation & Athletics, Sexual Abuse, Shelters/Homelessness, Social Services-General, Substance Abuse, YMCA/YWCA/YMHA/YWHA, YMCA/YWCA/YMHA/YWHA, Youth Organizations

Application Procedures

Initial Contact: The foundation has no formal grant application procedure or application form.

Foundation Officials

Michael Scott Anderson: director
Steven Craig Anderson: director
Rayford L. Keller: president, assistant treasurer
Thomas L. Keller: vice president, treasurer, assistant secretary
Donald J. Malouf: vice president, secretary

Grants Analysis

Disclosure Period: fiscal year ending November 30, 2001
Total Grants: $514,981
Number of Grants: 56
Average Grant: $5,833*
Highest Grant: $100,000
Lowest Grant: $1,000
Typical Range: $1,000 to $10,000
*Note: Average grants figure excludes highest two highest grants ($200,000).

Recent Grants

Note: Grants derived from fiscal 2000 Form 990.

General

100,000	Hockaday School, Dallas, TX
100,000	St. Mark's School of Texas, Dallas, TX
40,000	Barrow Neurological Foundation, Phoenix, AZ
20,000	Our Lady of Victory Cathedral, Victoria, TX
20,000	Texas Scottish Rite Hospital for Crippled Children, Dallas, TX
18,656	Peaster Elementary School, Peaster, TX
15,000	Elf Louise, San Antonio, TX
15,000	Texas Zoo, Victoria, TX
10,000	American Social Health Association, Research Triangle Park, NC
10,000	Golden Crescent Casa, Inc., Victoria, TX

OWEN INDUSTRIES

Company Headquarters

501 Ave. H
Carter Lake, IA 51510

Company Description

Employees: 480
SIC(s): 3441 Fabricated Structural Metal, 6719 Holding Companies Nec.

Operating Locations

Owen Industries (IA--Carter Lake)

Owen Foundation

Giving Contact

Robert E. Owen, President, Trustee
2200 Abbott Dr.
Carter Lake, IA 51510
Phone: (712)347-5500

Description

Founded: 1959
EIN: 476025298
Organization Type: Corporate Foundation
Giving Locations: NE
Grant Types: General Support.

Donor Information

Founder: Paxton & Vierling Steel Co., Missouri Valley Steel Co., Northern Plains Steel Co.

Financial Summary

Total Giving: $73,600 (fiscal year ending November 30, 2001); $233,333 (fiscal 2000); $217,900 (fiscal 1998)
Assets: $20,260 (fiscal 2001); $39,480 (fiscal 2000); $177,912 (fiscal 1998)
Gifts Received: $54,000 (fiscal 2001); $200,000 (fiscal 2000); $180,000 (fiscal 1998). Note: Contributions were received from Owen Industries, Inc.

Typical Recipients

Arts & Humanities: Arts Appreciation, Arts Associations & Councils, Community Arts, Historic Preservation, History & Archaeology, Libraries, Museums/Galleries, Music, Opera, Performing Arts, Theater
Civic & Public Affairs: Botanical Gardens/Parks, Civic & Public Affairs-General, Women's Affairs, Zoos/Aquariums
Education: Agricultural Education, Colleges & Universities, Private Education (Precollege)
Environment: Resource Conservation
Health: Children's Health/Hospitals, Diabetes, Emergency/Ambulance Services, Health Organizations, Hospitals, Transplant Networks/Donor Banks

Religion: Churches, Ministries, Religious Welfare
Social Services: Animal Protection, Child Welfare, Community Service Organizations, People with Disabilities, Recreation & Athletics, Scouts, United Funds/United Ways, YMCA/YWCA/YMHA/YWHA, Youth Organizations

Application Procedures

Initial Contact: The foundation has no formal grant application procedure or application form.
Deadlines: None.

Corporate Officials

Carl Harrison: vice president finance, chief financial officero B Lawton, IA 1936. ED Morningside College (1961). PRIM CORP EMPL vice president finance, chief financial officer: Owens Industries. CORP AFFIL vice president fin: Northern Plains Steel Co.; vice president fin: Paxton & Vierling Steel Co.; vice president fin: Missouri Valley Steel Co.; vice president fin: Central Plains Steel Co.; vice president fin: Lincoln Steel Co.
Robert E. Owen: chairman, president, chief executive officer B Omaha, NE 1943. ED Iowa State University of Science & Technology (1966). PRIM CORP EMPL chairman, president, chief executive officer: Owen Industries. CORP AFFIL vice president, director: Northern Plains Steel Co.; president: Paxton & Vierling Steel Co.; president, director: Missouri Valley Steel Co.; president, director: Central Plains Steel Co.; president, director: Lincoln Steel Co.

Foundation Officials

Sam R. Brower: secretary, treasurer
Dolores C. Owen: trustee
Richard F. Owen: vice president, trustee
Robert E. Owen: president, trustee (see above)

Grants Analysis

Disclosure Period: fiscal year ending November 30, 2001
Total Grants: $73,600
Number of Grants: 7
Average Grant: $8,100*
Highest Grant: $25,000
Lowest Grant: $500
Typical Range: $1,000 to $15,000
*Note: Average grant figure excludes highest grant.

Recent Grants

Note: Grants derived from fiscal 2001 Form 990.

General
25,000	Boys and Girls Club of Omaha, Omaha, NE
22,600	Knights of AkSarBen Foundation, Omaha, NE
20,000	Bellevue University Foundation, Bellevue, NE
2,500	Boy Scouts of America, Evansville, IN
2,000	Child Saving Institute, Omaha, NE
1,000	University of Nebraska Foundation, Lincoln, NE
500	Council Bluffs YMCA, Council Bluffs, IA

ALVIN AND LUCY OWSLEY FOUNDATION

Giving Contact
Alvin M. Owsley, Jr., Trustee
65 Briar Hollow Ln.
Houston, TX 77027
Phone: (713)622-1352

Description
Founded: 1950
EIN: 756047221
Organization Type: Private Foundation
Giving Locations: TX

Grant Types: Capital, Emergency, General Support, Multiyear/Continuing Support, Operating Expenses, Research, Scholarship, Seed Money.

Donor Information
Founder: the late Alvin M. Owsley, Lucy B. Owsley

Financial Summary
Total Giving: $465,655 (2001); $382,605 (2000); $491,755 (1999)
Giving Analysis: Giving for 2001 includes: foundation scholarships ($500); 2000: foundation grants to United Way ($500); 1999: foundation grants to United Way ($1,000);
Assets: $7,894,548 (2001); $7,958,068 (2000); $8,524,514 (1999)
Gifts Received: $500 (2000). Note: In fiscal 2001, contributions were received from Alvin Owsley ($500).

Typical Recipients
Arts & Humanities: Arts Centers, Arts Festivals, Ballet, Community Arts, Dance, Historic Preservation, History & Archaeology, Libraries, Museums/Galleries, Music, Opera, Theater
Civic & Public Affairs: Botanical Gardens/Parks, Clubs, Civic & Public Affairs-General, Municipalities/Towns, Rural Affairs, Urban & Community Affairs
Education: Arts/Humanities Education, Colleges & Universities, Education-General, Health & Physical Education, Legal Education, Medical Education, Private Education (Precollege), Public Education (Precollege), Secondary Education (Public), Student Aid
Environment: Environment-General, Wildlife Protection
Health: Adolescent Health Issues, AIDS/HIV, Cancer, Children's Health/Hospitals, Clinics/Medical Centers, Diabetes, Eyes/Blindness, Health Policy/Cost Containment, Heart, Hospitals, Medical Research, Mental Health, Multiple Sclerosis, Prenatal Health Issues, Public Health, Single-Disease Health Associations
International: International Environmental Issues
Religion: Churches, Missionary Activities (Domestic), Religious Welfare
Science: Science Museums, Scientific Centers & Institutes, Scientific Research
Social Services: Animal Protection, At-Risk Youth, Child Abuse, Child Welfare, Community Centers, Community Service Organizations, Crime Prevention, Domestic Violence, Family Planning, Family Services, People with Disabilities, Recreation & Athletics, Scouts, Shelters/Homelessness, United Funds/United Ways, Volunteer Services, YMCA/YWCA/YMHA/YWHA, Youth Organizations

Application Procedures
Initial Contact: Send a letter of not more than two pages.
Deadlines: None.
Notes: Enclosures not accepted with initial contact.

Restrictions
Does not support individuals or provide loans. Awards restricted to Texas only.

Foundation Officials
Wendy Garrett: trustee
Alvin Mansfield Owsley, Jr.: trustee B Dallas, TX 1926. ED Princeton University AB (1949); University of Texas JD, LLB (1952). PRIM CORP EMPL chairman, director: Ball Corp. NONPR AFFIL member: Society Mayflower Descendants; member: Texas Bar Association; member: Phi Delta Phi; fellow: Houston Bar Association Foundation; member, board visitors: M D Anderson Cancer Center; member: Houston Bar Association; member: American Bar Association; fellow: American College Trial Lawyers. CLUB AFFIL Tejas Club; Houston Country Club; Leland Country Club.

David Thomas Owsley: trustee B Dallas, TX 1929. ED Harvard University AB (1951); New York University MFA (1964). NONPR AFFIL member acquisition committee: Dallas Mas Art; member advisory council: Institute Asia Studies. CLUB AFFIL Leland Country Club; Ducks Unlimited Club; Knickerbocker Club.

Grants Analysis
Disclosure Period: calendar year ending 2001
Total Grants: $464,155*
Number of Grants: 50
Average Grant: $6,483*
Highest Grant: $100,000
Typical Range: $1,000 to $10,000
*Note: Giving excludes United Way; Scholarship. Average grant figure excludes two highest grants ($140,000).

Recent Grants
Note: Grants derived from 2001 Form 990.

General
100,000	Dallas Museum of Art, Dallas, TX
40,000	Botanical Research Institute of Texas, Ft. Worth, TX
35,500	Baylor College of Medicine, Houston, TX
35,000	Houston Ballet Foundation, Houston, TX
25,000	Boy Scouts of America Sam Houston Area, Houston, TX
10,000	Boys and Girls Country, Hockley, TX
10,000	Boys and Girls Harbor, Inc., Houston, TX
10,000	First Presbyterian Church, Dallas
10,000	Houston Arboretum and Nature Center, Houston, TX
10,000	National Center Policy Analysis, Dallas, TX

OXFORD FOUNDATION

Giving Contact
Philip L. Calhoun, Executive Director
125D Lancaster Avenue
Strasburg, PA 17579
Phone: (717)687-9335
Fax: (717)687-9336
E-mail: pcalhoun@oxfordfoundation.org
Web: http://www.oxfordfoundation.org

Description
Founded: 1947
EIN: 236278067
Organization Type: Family Foundation
Giving Locations: PA
Grant Types: Capital, Endowment, Fellowship, General Support, Multiyear/Continuing Support, Research, Scholarship.

Donor Information
Founder: Established in 1947 by John H. Ware III and Marian S. Ware.

Financial Summary
Total Giving: $3,250,000 (2003 approx); $3,250,000 (2002 approx); $3,010,843 (2001)
Giving Analysis: Giving for 2000 includes: foundation scholarships ($6,500); foundation grants to United Way ($12,000); 1999: foundation grants to United Way ($2,000); foundation matching gifts ($15,000); foundation scholarships ($71,000) nonmonetary support ($1,006,992)
Assets: $65,000,000 (2002 approx); $62,681,937 (2001); $56,276,486 (2000)
Gifts Received: $122,498 (2000). Note: In 2000, contributions were received from the Charitable Lead Annuity Trust.

Typical Recipients

Arts & Humanities: Dance, Historic Preservation, History & Archaeology, Libraries, Museums/Galleries, Music, Opera, Performing Arts, Public Broadcasting, Theater

Civic & Public Affairs: Botanical Gardens/Parks, Community Foundations, Economic Policy, Ethnic Organizations, Civic & Public Affairs-General, Municipalities/Towns, Philanthropic Organizations, Professional & Trade Associations, Public Policy, Safety, Urban & Community Affairs, Zoos/Aquariums

Education: Agricultural Education, Arts/Humanities Education, Colleges & Universities, Economic Education, Education-General, International Exchange, Medical Education, Minority Education, Private Education (Precollege), Public Education (Precollege), Special Education

Environment: Environment-General, Resource Conservation, Wildlife Protection

Health: Alzheimers Disease, Arthritis, Cancer, Children's Health/Hospitals, Clinics/Medical Centers, Diabetes, Emergency/Ambulance Services, Hospices, Hospitals, Hospitals (University Affiliated), Medical Research, Mental Health, Nursing Services, Prenatal Health Issues, Public Health, Single-Disease Health Associations

International: Health Care/Hospitals, International Environmental Issues

Religion: Churches, Religious Organizations, Religious Welfare, Seminaries

Science: Scientific Centers & Institutes

Social Services: Animal Protection, Big Brother/Big Sister, Child Welfare, Community Centers, Community Service Organizations, Crime Prevention, Day Care, Domestic Violence, Family Planning, People with Disabilities, Recreation & Athletics, Scouts, Senior Services, Sexual Abuse, Social Services-General, Substance Abuse, YMCA/YWCA/YMHA/YWHA, Youth Organizations

Application Procedures

Initial Contact: See foundation website for application procedures.
Deadlines: None.

Restrictions

The foundation does not make grants to individuals, for scholarships, or loans.

Foundation Officials

Carol W. Gates: vice president, treasurer
Marilyn Ware Lewis: vice president, secretary B Philadelphia, PA 1944. ED American University; University of Pennsylvania. PRIM CORP EMPL chairman, director: American Water Works Co. Inc. CORP AFFIL director: Penn Fuel Gas Inc.; PP&L Resources Inc.; director: CIGNA Corp.
Eleanor Ross: assistant secretary, assistant treasurer
John H. Ware, IV: vice president
Marian S. Ware: chairman, president
Paul W. Ware: vice president B Philadelphia, PA 1946. ED Franklin and Marshall College (1972). CORP AFFIL retired chairman: Penn Fuel Gas Inc.; director: York Water Co.; director: America Water Works Co. Inc.; director: Emerald Asset Management Inc.

Grants Analysis

Disclosure Period: calendar year ending 2001
Total Grants: $3,010,843*
Number of Grants: 220
Average Grant: $13,686
Highest Grant: $485,517
Typical Range: $1,000 to $25,000
*Note: Grants analysis provided by foundation.

Recent Grants

Note: Grants derived from 2000 Form 990.

General

509,819	University of Pennsylvania Medical Center, Philadelphia, PA -- Alzheimer's research
100,000	Conservation Fund, Arlington, VA -- for Lancaster County Office
100,000	Southern Chester County YMCA, West Grove, PA -- Reaching Out to the Future Capital Campaign
100,000	University of Pennsylvania School of Nursing, Philadelphia, PA -- discretionary
100,000	YWCA of Chester, Chester, PA
75,000	American Enterprise Institute, Washington, DC -- capital fund
60,000	Upland Country Day School, Kennett Square, PA -- campaign fund
50,000	Canine Partners for Life, Cochranville, PA -- for 4-year building project
50,000	Lancaster Country Day School, Lancaster, PA -- endowment and capital grant
50,000	Regional Performing Arts Center, Philadelphia, PA -- endowment pledge

PACIFIC LIFE INSURANCE CO.

Company Headquarters

Newport Beach, CA
Web: http://www.pacificlife.com

Company Description

Revenue: US$3.816 billion (2002)
Profit: US$49.8 million (2002)
Employees: 2500 (2001)
Fortune Rank: 419, per FORTUNE Magazine's list of 500 Largest U.S. Corporations (2002).
SIC(s): 6311 Life Insurance, 6321 Accident & Health Insurance, 6371 Pension, Health & Welfare Funds, 6799 Investors Nec.

Operating Locations

Pacific Mutual Life Insurance Co. (CA--Covina, Fountain Valley, Los Angeles, Newport Beach, Walnut Creek; CT--Farmington; FL--Tampa, West Palm Beach; MA--Framingham; NC--Greensboro; OH--Dayton; OR--Portland; TN--Nashville; TX--Dallas, Houston; UT--Ogden; WA--Kirkland)

Nonmonetary Support

Value: $503,182 (2001)
Type: Donated Equipment; In-kind Services
Volunteer Programs: Company supports employee volunteerism through the Good Guys program, steering volunteers to local community projects.
Note: Nonmonetary support is provided by the company.

Pacific Life Foundation

Giving Contact

Robert G. Haskell, President
700 Newport Center Drive
Newport Beach, CA 92660-6397
Phone: (949)219-3787
Web: http://www.pacificlife.com/AboutPacificLife/FoundationorCommunity/index.htm

Description

EIN: 953433806
Organization Type: Corporate Foundation
Giving Locations: AZ: Phoenix; CA: Orange County, and some statewide organizations primarily to organizations in areas with large concentrations of company employees; some funding nationally.

Grant Types: Award, Capital, Employee Matching Gifts, General Support, Multiyear/Continuing Support.
Note: Employee matching gift ratio: 1 to 1 for higher education.

Financial Summary

Total Giving: $3,220,297 (2000); $2,400,000 (1999 approx); $2,000,000 (1998 approx). Note: Contributes through corporate direct giving program and foundation. 2000 total giving does not include Pacific Life in-kind support; corporate direct giving figure includes Pacific Life direct grants ($200,000) and event support ($132,300).
Giving Analysis: Giving for 2001 includes: foundation grants to United Way ($308,127); foundation matching gifts ($397,213); nonmonetary support ($503,182); foundation ($2,644,833); 2000: foundation grants to United Way ($315,242); corporate direct giving ($332,300) foundation ($2,572,737)
Assets: $41,876,034 (2000); $39,600,000 (1999 approx); $33,000,000 (1998 approx)
Gifts Received: $7,022,104 (2000); $6,372,707 (1997); $30,281 (1996). Note: Contributions were received from Pacific Life Insurance Company.

Typical Recipients

Arts & Humanities: Arts Associations & Councils, Arts Centers, Arts Festivals, Arts Funds, Arts Institutes, Ballet, Dance, Ethnic & Folk Arts, Film & Video, Arts & Humanities-General, Historic Preservation, Libraries, Museums/Galleries, Music, Opera, Performing Arts, Public Broadcasting, Theater

Civic & Public Affairs: Asian American Affairs, Botanical Gardens/Parks, Civil Rights, Clubs, Community Foundations, Economic Development, Economic Policy, Employment/Job Training, Civic & Public Affairs-General, Hispanic Affairs, Housing, Law & Justice, Legal Aid, Municipalities/Towns, Nonprofit Management, Professional & Trade Associations, Public Policy, Safety, Urban & Community Affairs, Women's Affairs, Zoos/Aquariums

Education: Business Education, Business-School Partnerships, Colleges & Universities, Continuing Education, Economic Education, Education Funds, Education Reform, Education-General, Health & Physical Education, Leadership Training, Medical Education, Minority Education, Private Education (Precollege), Public Education (Precollege), School Volunteerism, Science/Mathematics Education, Secondary Education (Public), Special Education, Student Aid

Environment: Air/Water Quality, Environment-General, Wildlife Protection

Health: AIDS/HIV, Alzheimers Disease, Cancer, Children's Health/Hospitals, Emergency/Ambulance Services, Eyes/Blindness, Geriatric Health, Health Policy/Cost Containment, Health Organizations, Heart, Hospices, Hospitals, Medical Research, Medical Training, Mental Health, Multiple Sclerosis, Nutrition, Public Health, Single-Disease Health Associations, Speech & Hearing, Trauma Treatment

International: Health Care/Hospitals, International Environmental Issues, Missionary/Religious Activities

Religion: Jewish Causes, Religious Welfare

Science: Science Museums, Scientific Centers & Institutes

Social Services: At-Risk Youth, Child Abuse, Child Welfare, Community Service Organizations, Counseling, Day Care, Delinquency & Criminal Rehabilitation, Domestic Violence, Emergency Relief, Family Planning, Family Services, Food/Clothing Distribution, Homes, People with Disabilities, Recreation & Athletics, Senior Services, Shelters/Homelessness, Social Services-General, Substance Abuse, United Funds/United Ways, Veterans, Volunteer Services, YMCA/YWCA/YMHA/YWHA, Youth Organizations

Application Procedures

Initial Contact: Request grant application form and guidelines, then submit a full proposal.

Application Requirements: Proposals should include a completed Pacific Life Foundation Grant Application Form (available from the foundation's website); a description of organization (1-2 pages); description of the program/project to be funded, including a needs statement and objectives (1-2 pages); organization's current annual budget (revenues and expenditures) and most recent audited financial statement; budget for project to be funded; list of other agency contributors and levels of support; a list of the agency's board of directors, advisory board members, and staff; proof of tax-exempt status; and a copy of the agency's information brochure, if available.

Deadlines: August 31 (postmark date), for consideration for the following calendar year's budget.

Evaluative Criteria: Applications are evaluated on the type of activity being promoted; population affected; how regional issues are confronted; how progress can be documented; supportiveness of public welfare; need served by proposed activity and duplication of function; and the benefit to or involvement of employees.

Decision Notification: Applicants are notified of funding decisions in mid-December, with payment made before the end of January.

Notes: The foundation does not accept faxed or e-mailed applications, nor does it accept videos.

Restrictions

Foundation does not support individuals; political parties, candidates, or partisan political organizations; veterans and labor organizations, fraternal organizations, athletic clubs, or social clubs; religious organizations for sectarian or denominational purposes, except for programs that are available to anyone; fundraising events; or advertising sponsorship.

Additional Information

Generally prefers to make annual grants. Organizations may reapply annually, but grants typically are made to one organization for no more than three consecutive years.

The foundation reports that each year it selects five to seven areas of special focus (e.g. AIDS, homelessness, Hispanic needs) and makes major grants in that focus area. These grants are usually made later in the calendar year after the foundation has done considerable research. research. research.

Publications: Community Involvement Report

Corporate Officials

Marianne Beaz: vice president client service & pension investments PRIM CORP EMPL vice president client service & pension investments: Pacific Mutual Life Insurance Co.

Anthony J. Bonno: senior vice president human resources PRIM CORP EMPL senior vice president human resources: Pacific Mutual Life Insurance Co.

David R. Carmichael: senior vice president, general counsel, director PRIM CORP EMPL senior vice president, general counsel, director: Pacific Mutual Life Insurance Co. CORP AFFIL senior vice president: Pacific Life Insurance Co.; director: PM Group Life Insurance Co.

Marc Scott Franklin: senior vice president strategic planning B Norwalk, CT 1959. ED Claremont McKenna College (1982); University of Chicago (1982). PRIM CORP EMPL senior vice president strategic planning: Pacific Mutual Life Insurance Co.

Robert G. Haskell: senior vice president public affairs B Orange, CA 1952. ED University of Southern California (1974); University of Southern California (1979). PRIM CORP EMPL senior vice president public affairs: Pacific Mutual Life Insurance Co.

Audrey L. Milfs: vice president, corporate secretary, director B 1945. PRIM CORP EMPL vice president, corporate secretary, director: Pacific Mutual Life Insurance Co. CORP AFFIL secretary: Pacific Mutual Distributors.

Michele Myszka: community relations director, public affairs

Glenn Stanley Schafer: president, director B Saint Johns, MI 1949. ED Michigan State University (1971); University of Detroit (1975). PRIM CORP EMPL president, director: Pacific Mutual Life Insurance Co. ADD CORP EMPL chief financial officer: Pacific Financial Asset Management Corp.; director: Pacific Life & Annuity Co.; president: Pacific Mutual Holding Co. CORP AFFIL director: Pimco Advisor LP. NONPR AFFIL member: Financial Executives Institute; fellow: Life Management Institute; director: Court Appointed Special Advocates; member: American Institute CPAs.

Thomas C. Sutton: chairman, chief executive officer, director B Atlanta, GA 1942. ED University of Toronto BS (1965); Harvard University (1982). PRIM CORP EMPL chairman, chief executive officer, director: Pacific Mutual Life Insurance Co. CORP AFFIL chairman: PM Group Life Insurance Co.; director: Pimco Advisor LP; chairman: Pacific Life Corp.; director: Pacific Mutual Distributors; director: Pacific Finance Asset Management Corp.; director: Edison International; director: Newhall Land & Farming Co. NONPR AFFIL fellow: Society Actuaries; member affiliates advisory board: University California Irvine School Management; member: Pacific Studies Actuarial Club; member: American Academy of Actuaries.

Khanh T. Tran: executive vice president, chief financial officer, director B Saigon, Vietnam 1956. ED Whittier College (1977); University of California (1980). PRIM CORP EMPL senior vice president, chief financial officer, director: Pacific Mutual Life Insurance Co. NONPR AFFIL member: Life Office Management Association; member: Treasury Management Association; member: Finance Executive Institute; member: Finance Officer Group.

Raymond L. Watson: vice chairman PRIM CORP EMPL vice chairman: Irvine Co. CORP AFFIL director: Walt Disney Co.

Foundation Officials

Edward R. Byrd: chief financial officer PRIM CORP EMPL chief financial officer: Pacific Mutual Distributor.

Robert G. Haskell: president, director (see above)

Michael T. McLaughlin: general counsel

Audrey L. Milfs: secretary (see above)

Donn Biddle Miller: president, trustee B Gallipolis, OH 1929. ED Ohio Wesleyan University BA (1951); University of Michigan JD (1954); Harvard University (1974). PRIM CORP EMPL president, chief executive officer: Pearson-Sibert Oil Co. of Texas. CORP AFFIL director: Pacific Life Insurance Co. NONPR AFFIL vice chairman, director: Automobile Club Southern California.

Michele Myszka: vice president, director (see above)

Thomas C. Sutton: chairman, director (see above)

Grants Analysis

Disclosure Period: calendar year ending 2001

Total Grants: $2,644,833*

Number of Grants: 173

Average Grant: $15,288

Highest Grant: $145,405

Typical Range: $2,500 to $10,000 and $10,000 to $100,000

*Note: Giving excludes United Way, matching gifts, and nonmonetary support.

Recent Grants

Note: Grants derived from 2000 Form 990.

Library-Related

15,000	Sherman Library and Gardens, Newport Beach, CA -- capital campaign

General

285,242	United Way Orange County, Garden Grove, CA
110,000	South Coast Repertory, Costa Mesa, CA
79,087	Whale Conservation Institute, Lincoln, MA

74,000	Serving People in Need, Newport Beach, CA
65,000	Ballet Pacifica, Laguna Beach, CA
62,500	John Henry Foundation, Orange, CA
57,500	Working Wardrobes for a New Start, Garden Grove, CA
56,600	Food Finders, Inc., Seal Beach, CA
55,500	Arts Orange County, Irvine, CA
55,000	Friends of the Sea Lions Marine Mammal Center, Los Angeles, CA

PACIFICORP

Company Headquarters

Portland, OR

Web: http://www.pacificorp.com

Company Description

Founded: 1910

Ticker: SPI

Exchange: NYSE

Assets: US$10.671 billion (2001)

Employees: 6300 (2001)

SIC(s): 1041 Gold Ores, 1044 Silver Ores, 1094 Uranium, Radium & Vanadium Ores, 4911 Electric Services.

Operating Locations

PacifiCorp (AK--Anchorage, Bethel, Fairbanks; MT--Billings; OR--Hillsboro, Salem, Wilsonville; WA--Vancouver; WV)

Nonmonetary Support

Type: Donated Equipment; Workplace Solicitation

Note: Nonmonetary support is provided by the company.

PacifiCorp Foundation

Giving Contact

Ernest Bloch, Jr., Executive Director

825 NE Multnomah, Suite 2000

Portland, OR 97232-4116

Phone: (503)813-7257

Fax: (503)813-7249

Web: http://www.pacificorpfoundation.org/

Description

Founded: 1988

EIN: 943089826

Organization Type: Corporate Foundation

Giving Locations: CA: Northern California; ID; NV; OR; UT; WA; WY

Grant Types: Capital, Emergency, General Support, Multiyear/Continuing Support, Project, Research, Scholarship

Donor Information

Founder: Pacific Power & Light Co., Utah Power & Light Co., Pacific Telecom, Inc., Pacificorp Financial Services

Financial Summary

Total Giving: $2,750,000 (fiscal year ending March 31, 2002 approx); $2,538,471 (fiscal 2001); $949,499 (fiscal 2000). Note: In 2000, the foundation changed from a calendar year to a fiscal year. Giving for 1999 reflects grants made from 01/01/1999 to 12/31/1999; giving for fiscal 2000 includes grants made from 01/01/2000 to 03/31/2000; giving for fiscal 2001 reflects grants made from 04/01/2000 to 03/31/2001.

Giving Analysis: Giving for fiscal 2001 includes: foundation scholarships ($58,750); foundation matching gifts ($142,274); foundation grants to United Way ($354,536); foundation ($1,982,911); fiscal 1999: corporate grants to United Way ($557,255); foundation ($2,225,533); fiscal 1998: corporate direct giving

($342,862); foundation grants to United Way ($583,431); foundation ($2,508,446);

Assets: $37,361,708 (fiscal 2001) $43,720,995 (fiscal 2000); $38,181,882 (fiscal 1999)

Gifts Received: $5,000,000 (fiscal 2000); $3,303,081 (fiscal 1998); $3,784,220 (fiscal 1996). Note: Contributions are received from Pacific Power & Light Co., Pacific Telecom, Inc. and PacifiCorp Holdings, Inc.

Typical Recipients

Arts & Humanities: Arts Associations & Councils, Arts Festivals, Ballet, Historic Preservation, Libraries, Museums/Galleries, Music, Opera, Performing Arts, Public Broadcasting, Theater

Civic & Public Affairs: African American Affairs, Botanical Gardens/Parks, Community Foundations, Economic Development, Employment/Job Training, Civic & Public Affairs-General, Housing, Rural Affairs, Urban & Community Affairs, Zoos/Aquariums

Education: Afterschool/Enrichment Programs, Arts/Humanities Education, Business Education, Colleges & Universities, Education Funds, Elementary Education (Public), Education-General, Private Education (Precollege), Public Education (Precollege), Science/Mathematics Education, Student Aid

Environment: Energy, Environment-General, Resource Conservation, Wildlife Protection

Health: Children's Health/Hospitals, Emergency/Ambulance Services, Health Organizations, Hospitals, Public Health

International: International Organizations

Science: Science Museums

Social Services: At-Risk Youth, Child Welfare, Community Centers, Community Service Organizations, Family Planning, Food/Clothing Distribution, People with Disabilities, Recreation & Athletics, Scouts, Shelters/Homelessness, United Funds/United Ways, YMCA/YWCA/YMHA/YWHA, Youth Organizations

Application Procedures

Initial Contact: Send a one-page summary and a proposal of no more than 20 pages (including attachments and application form) to foundation; contact appropriate subsidiary or local manager.

Application Requirements: Complete, submit, and print a copy of application form, which includes contact information and TIN for applicant; information concerning previously received support from the Foundation or Pacificorp subsidiaries; signed acknowledgement by organization's CEO of proposal approval; a description of organization and its particular qualifications for funding activity; and an estimate of people served and their locations. Include a letter of request, no more than one page requesting Foundation assistance. On the one page summary, include project seeking support; importance of project; total project budget; percentage of total operating budget that project budget represents; amount requested; itemized amounts of financial support requested by other donors, or already pledged or contributed by other donors, and indication if it is a matched grant; and the way in which funds would be applied and the resulting benefits. Other information on the project should include, project description and who will benefit; statement of project status (new or continuing) and whether it is demonstration, pilot, or replication; explanation of needs that the project addresses and indication of community support; overall project goals, impact, and specific and measurable objectives; description of how project will be evaluated; description of project staff and qualifications; and indication of collaboration with other organizations doing similar work. Budget information should include, breakdown of items in each category; purpose of funds sought and the application of funds; itemized description of other financial support received or pledged; explanation of project sustainability after funding period is over; and recently audited financial statement. Proof of tax-exempt status is also required.

Deadlines: March 15 for education and research organizations; June 15 for civic and community grants

and others not covered in other categories; September 15 for arts and cultural organizations; December 15 for health, welfare, and social service organizations.

Review Process: Requests up to $5,000 are reviewed quarterly by the Foundation Contributions Committee. Largest grants are considered at quarterly foundation board meetings.

Restrictions

Foundation grants are not made to any non-charitable purpose; establishment or support of endowments; operating deficits; individuals; to religious organizations for religious purposes; political organizations, campaigns, or candidates for political office; organizations that discriminate against individuals on the basis of creed, color, sex, age, national origin or veteran status; veterans or fraternal organizations; sponsorship or advertising that directly benefits marketing or sales programs of PacifiCorp or its operating companies; memberships in chambers of commerce, taxpayer associations, and other bodies; capital campaigns; conferences, conventions, and events; and projects outside the six-state region served by PacifiCorp subsidiaries. benefit PacifiCorp or its operating companies.

Additional Information

Direct giving by the company will go only to organizations that are ineligible for grants under foundation guidelines. Subsidiaries and divisions of PacifiCorp that contribute to the PacifiCorp Foundation include Pacific Power, Pacific Telecom, and PacifiCorp Holdings, Inc.

Subsidiaries: Pacific Power, 920 SW 6th Ave., Portland, OR 97204 (503) 464-5000; Pacific Telecom, 805 Broadway, Box 9901, Vancouver, WA 98669, (360) 905-5800; PacifiCorp Holdings, Inc., 825 NE Multnomah, Suite 775, Portland, OR 97232.

PacifiCorp merged with Scottish Power in November 1999. 825 NE Multnomah, Suite 775, Portland, OR 97232.

PacifiCorp merged with Scottish Power in November 1999.

Corporate Officials

John A. Bohling: senior vice president, chief operating officer B Salt Lake City, UT 1943. ED University of Utah BSEE (1968); University of Delaware MBA (1972). PRIM CORP EMPL senior vice president: PacifiCorp.

Richard T. O'Brien: executive vice president, chief operating officer ED Chicago State University BA (1976); Portland State University JD (1985). PRIM CORP EMPL senior executive vice president, chief financial officer: PacifiCorp.

Foundation Officials

John A. Bohling: board member (see above)
Pamela Bradford: executive director
Tom Imeson: chairman, director PRIM CORP EMPL vice president public affairs & communications: Public Affairs & Communications.
Richard T. O'Brien: member (see above)
Alan Richardson: executive director

Grants Analysis

Disclosure Period: fiscal year ending March 31, 2001

Total Grants: $1,982,911*
Number of Grants: 305
Average Grant: $6,501
Highest Grant: $100,000
Typical Range: $1,000 to $10,000
*Note: Giving excludes matching gifts, scholarship, United Way.

Recent Grants

Note: Grants derived from 2001 Form 990.

General

110,000   United Way Great Salt Lake Area, Salt

	Lake City, UT -- general program support
100,000	Governor's Music & Education Program, Salt Lake City, UT
55,000	United Way Columbia-Willamette, Portland, OR -- health and welfare
55,000	United Way Columbia-Willamette, Portland, OR -- health and welfare
50,000	Oregon Food Bank, Portland, OR
50,000	Oregon Independent College Foundation, Portland, OR -- annual support
50,000	Portland State University Foundation, Portland, OR -- school and business and school of engineering
50,000	Utah Field House of Natural History, Vernal, UT
50,000	Utah State University, Logan, UT
41,660	United Way of Sweetwater County, Rock Springs, WY -- program support

DAVID AND LUCILE PACKARD FOUNDATION

Giving Contact

Richard T. Schlosberg, III, President & Trustee
300 Second Street, Suite 200
Los Altos, CA 94022
Phone: (650)948-7658
Fax: (650)948-5793
Web: http://www.packard.org

Description

Founded: 1964
EIN: 942278431
Organization Type: Family Foundation
Giving Locations: CA: Monterey County, San Mateo County, Santa Clara County, Santa Cruz County internationally; nationally.
Grant Types: Award, Capital, Challenge, Conference/Seminar, Emergency, Employee Matching Gifts, Fellowship, General Support, Loan, Matching, Multiyear/Continuing Support, Operating Expenses, Project, Seed Money.

Donor Information

Founder: The David and Lucile Packard Foundation was established in 1964. The foundation's donors are David Packard, the foundation's president, and his late wife, Lucile Salter Packard . The couple's four children, David Woodley Packard, Nancy Ann Packard Burnett, Susan Packard Orr, and Julie Elizabeth Packard, have all served on their parents' foundation. David Packard and William Hewlett founded Hewlett-Packard Company in 1938. The company became a major manufacturer of test and measurement instruments and microcomputers. Mr. Packard also served as United States Secretary of Defense between 1969 and 1971.

Financial Summary

Total Giving: $200,000,000 (2003 approx); $198,858,516 (2002); $428,897,276 (2001)
Giving Analysis: Giving for 2000 includes: foundation matching gifts ($396,246); foundation grants to United Way ($1,033,333); 1998: foundation grants to United Way ($135,000); 1997: foundation scholarships ($200,000) foundation fellowships ($10,000,000)
Assets: $4,800,000,000 (2002 approx); $6,196,520,868 (2001); $9,793,212,529 (2000)
Gifts Received: $1,323,421 (2000); $1,744,006 (1998); $1,744,006 (1997). Note: In 2000, contributions were received from the Estate of David Packard ($807,611) and the David and Lucile S. Packard Trust II ($515,810). In 1997 and 1998, contributions were received from the David and Lucile S. Packard Trust II. The foundation received annual contributions from Hewlett-Packard common stock through 2003.

Typical Recipients

Arts & Humanities: Arts Associations & Councils, Arts Centers, Arts Funds, Ballet, Community Arts, Dance, Ethnic & Folk Arts, Film & Video, Arts & Humanities-General, Historic Preservation, History & Archaeology, Libraries, Literary Arts, Museums/Galleries, Music, Opera, Performing Arts, Public Broadcasting, Theater

Civic & Public Affairs: Botanical Gardens/Parks, Business/Free Enterprise, Civil Rights, Community Foundations, Economic Development, Employment/ Job Training, Civic & Public Affairs-General, Housing, Municipalities/Towns, Native American Affairs, Nonprofit Management, Philanthropic Organizations, Professional & Trade Associations, Public Policy, Rural Affairs, Urban & Community Affairs, Women's Affairs, Zoos/Aquariums

Education: Afterschool/Enrichment Programs, Arts/ Humanities Education, Business Education, Colleges & Universities, Education Associations, Education Reform, Elementary Education (Private), Engineering/Technological Education, Environmental Education, Faculty Development, Education-General, International Exchange, International Studies, Literacy, Medical Education, Minority Education, Private Education (Precollege), Public Education (Precollege), School Volunteerism, Science/Mathematics Education, Secondary Education (Public), Student Aid, Vocational & Technical Education

Environment: Air/Water Quality, Energy, Forestry, Environment-General, Protection, Resource Conservation, Watershed, Wildlife Protection

Health: Children's Health/Hospitals, Clinics/Medical Centers, Emergency/Ambulance Services, Health-General, Health Policy/Cost Containment, Health Organizations, Heart, Hospitals, Long-Term Care, Medical Research, Nursing Services, Nutrition, Prenatal Health Issues, Preventive Medicine/Wellness Organizations, Public Health, Research/Studies Institutes

International: Foreign Educational Institutions, Health Care/Hospitals, International Environmental Issues, International Organizations, International Peace & Security Issues, International Relations, International Relief Efforts

Religion: Churches, Religion-General, Jewish Causes, Religious Welfare

Science: Science Museums, Scientific Centers & Institutes, Scientific Organizations, Scientific Research

Social Services: At-Risk Youth, Child Welfare, Community Centers, Community Service Organizations, Counseling, Day Care, Family Planning, Family Services, Food/Clothing Distribution, Homes, People with Disabilities, Shelters/Homelessness, United Funds/ United Ways, YMCA/YWCA/YMHA/YWHA, Youth Organizations

Application Procedures

Initial Contact: See foundation website for program and application information, then submit a brief letter of inquiry in area of interest.

Application Requirements: Letter of inquiry should provide descriptive title for the project and should explain the project's objectives, significance, funding needs, and relationship to the specific grantmaking priorities of the foundation. Proposals should include a cover letter with a description of organization; amount requested; organization's legal name, address and telephone number; and name of contact person. Background information should include history and purpose of organization, as well as the people and groups served. Also include a description of the program and its objectives; evidence of program's need; geographic area to be served; outline of program; and anticipated methods of evaluation. Personnel information should include who will implement the program and their qualifications, as well as names and affiliations of the directors, senior staff and trustees. Financial information should include sources of the organization's funds (both public and private); organization's budget for the years in which the program will take place; detailed project budget showing other sources

of support, and the amount requested from the foundation; and the most recent audited financial statement. Attach to proposal a copy of the IRS exemption letter; documentation that the proposal is supported by organization's board of directors; attach other supporting material if necessary.

Deadlines: December 15, March 15, June 15, and September 15 for proposals.

Review Process: The foundation's board meets in March, June, September, and December.

Restrictions

Foundation does not make grants to individuals or to support religious purposes.

Additional Information

The foundation is affiliated with the Monterey Bay Aquarium Research Institute, the Stanford Theater Foundation, and the Packard Humanities Institute. The foundation provides other services such as management assistance and loans for land purchase and low-income housing.

Request a copy of guidelines and a faculty directory for contacts in the specific program areas.

Publications: Annual Report; Program Guidelines; The Future of Children (Quarterly Journal)

Foundation Officials

Nancy Ann Packard Burnett: trustee, vice chairman NONPR AFFIL director: Monterey Bay Aquarium Foundation.

Hugh Burroughs: director philanthropy program

Sarah Clark: director population program

Jaleh Daie: director science program

Robin Chandler Tippett Duke: trustee B Baltimore, MD 1923. CORP AFFIL director: River Bank America; director: American Home Products Corp.; director: International Flavors & Fragrances Inc. NONPR AFFIL director: East River Bank; member: World Affairs Council; member: Council Foreign Relations; member: American Academy of Arts & Sciences. CLUB AFFIL River Club; Colony Club; Metropolitan Washington Club.

Robert Joy Glaser, MD: honorary emeritus trustee B Saint Louis, MO September 11, 1918. ED Harvard University SB (1940); Harvard University MD (1943); Rush University Medical College LHO (1973); City University of New York Mount Sinai Medical School DS (1984). CORP AFFIL director: Hanger Orthopedic Group Inc.; director: Nellcor; director: Alza Corp.; director: California Water Service Co.; director: Affymax. NONPR AFFIL trustee: Washington University; member: Western Association Physicians; member: Sigma Xi; consulting professor: Stanford University; editor: Pharos; trustee: Saint Louis University; director: Packard Humanities; director: Pharmagenesis; member: National Academy Sciences; member: National Institute Allergy Infectious Disease; member: Harvard University Medical School Alumni; member: Institute Medicine; member: Central Society Clinical Research; director: DCI; member: Association American Physicians; member: American Society Experimental Pathology; member: Association American Medical Colleges; member: American Federation Clinical Research; member: American Society Clinical Investigation; fellow: American Association Advancement Science; member: American Clinical & Climatological Association; member: Alpha Omega Alpha; fellow: American Academy of Arts & Sciences. CLUB AFFIL Harvard Club; Century Club.

Nancy Glaze: director arts program

Mary Gunn: director Pueblo, CO program

Barbara Kibbe: director organizational effectiveness program

Pam King: director Pueblo, CO program

Carol S. Larson: vice president, director programs

Jim Leape: director, conservation and science program

Jane Lubchenco: trustee

Stephanie McAuliffe: director organizational effectiveness

Dean O. Morton: trustee, treasurer B 1932. ED Kansas State University BE (1954); Harvard University MBA (1960). CORP AFFIL director: Raychem Corp.; director: Kaiser Foundation Health Plan; director: KLA Tencor Corp.; director: Centigram Communications Corp.; director: Clorox Co.; director: Alza Corp. NONPR AFFIL director: Kaiser Foundation Hospitals.

Franklin M. Orr, Jr.: trustee

Susan Packard Orr: chairman, trustee ED Stanford University BA (1968); Stanford University MBA (1970); New Mexico Institute Mining and Technology MS (1984). PRIM CORP EMPL chief executive officer president, owner: Technology Resource Assistance Center. CORP AFFIL director: Hewlett-Packard Co. NONPR AFFIL director: Childrens Health Counsel; trustee: Stanford University.

Julie Elizabeth Packard: vice chairman, trustee B 1954. ED University of California, Santa Cruz (1978). NONPR AFFIL chairman: Monterey Bay Aquarium Research Institute.

Lewis Emmett Platt: trustee B Johnson City, NY 1941. ED Cornell University BSME (1964); University of Pennsylvania MBA (1966). CORP AFFIL director: Boeing Co. NONPR AFFIL chairman: World Trade Organization Task Force Member; board counsel: YMCA United States of America; member: Science Apparatus Manufacturing Association; member: Mid-Peninsula Young Men's Christian Association; vice chairman: Morehouse School of Medicine; co-chairman: Joint Venture Silicon Valley Network Board; director: Cornell University; member: Institute Electrical & Electronics Engineers; member: Computer Systems Policy Project; member: Business Roundtable.

William Kane Reilly: trustee B Decatur, IL 1940. ED Yale University BA (1962); Harvard University JD (1965); Columbia University MS (1971). PRIM CORP EMPL president, chief executive officer: Aqua International Partners LP. CORP AFFIL director: E.I. du Pont de Nemours & Co.

Frank H. Roberts: honorary emeritus trustee

Allan Rosenfield, MD: trustee

Lois Salisbury: director children & families program ED Reed College BA; University of California at Berkeley JD.

Richard T. Schlosberg, III: president, chief executive officer B 1943. ED United States Air Force Academy BS (1965); Harvard University Graduate School of Business Administration MBA (1972).

Jeanne Sedgwick: director conservation program

Robert Stephens: trustee

Edwin E. Van Bronkhorst: honorary emeritus trustee CORP AFFIL director: Luxcom Inc.

George Vera: director finance and administration

Colburn S. Wilbur: trustee B Palo Alto, CA 1935. ED Stanford University BA (1956); Stanford University MBA (1960).

Barbara Wright: secretary PRIM CORP EMPL partner: Finch, Montgomery & Wright. CORP AFFIL director: Albany International Corp.

Lorraine Zippiroli: director children families communities program

Grants Analysis

Disclosure Period: calendar year ending 2002
Total Grants: $198,858,516*
Number of Grants: 836
Average Grant: $237,869
Typical Range: $5,000 to $800,000
*Note: Giving includes fellowships.

Recent Grants

Note: Grants derived from 2000 Form 990.

General

31,353,087 Monterey Bay Aquarium Research Institute, Moss Landing, CA -- operating support
30,000,000 Lucile Packard Foundation for Children's Health, Palo Alto, CA -- support for Children's Health Initiative

25,000,000 Peninsula Open Space Trust, Menlo Park, CA

10,000,000 Lucile Packard Foundation for Children's Health, Palo Alto, CA -- support for expansion of community grantmaking program

9,000,000 DDB, Seattle, WA -- for increasing public awareness of family planning needs

8,164,962 Energy Foundation, San Francisco, CA -- support for the Climate Change and the China Sustainable Energy Program

8,000,000 National Abortion and Reproductive Rights Action League Foundation, Washington, DC -- support for the implementation of a national integrated advertising and constituency outreach campaign

7,000,000 DDB, Seattle, WA -- for increasing public awareness of family planning needs

7,000,000 Monterey Bay Aquarium Research Institute, Moss Landing, CA -- operating support

5,750,000 Great Valley Center, Modesto, CA -- support for a conservation re-granting program

WILLIAM S. PALEY FOUNDATION, INC.

Giving Contact

Patrick S. Gallagher, Executive Director
1 East 53rd Street
New York, NY 10022
Phone: (212)888-2520
Fax: (212)308-7845
E-mail: wspf@asan.com

Description

Founded: 1936
EIN: 136085929
Organization Type: General Purpose Foundation
Giving Locations: NY: New York
Grant Types: Capital, General Support, Multiyear/Continuing Support.

Donor Information

Founder: The foundation was established in 1936 by the late William S. Paley (1901-1990), the founder and former chairman of CBS. He bequeathed more than $40 million to the foundation from his estimated personal fortune of $460 million.

Mr. Paley, a native of Chicago, began his college education at the University of Chicago but earned his bachelors of science degree from the University of Pennsylvania in 1922. He also received honorary PhDs from Ithaca College, University of Southern California, Adelphi University, Bates College, University of Pennsylvania, Brown University, Pratt Institute, Dartmouth College, and Columbia University, where he served as a trustee from 1950 to 1973.

Mr. Paley lived in New York City, home to two of his favorite charities, the Museum of Broadcasting, which he founded in 1976, and the Museum of Modern Art, where he served as chairman from 1972 to 1985. In his will, he left his valuable private art collection to the museum.

Mr. Paley, divorced from his first wife, married Barbara (Babe) Cushing in 1947. Barbara Paley died in 1978. Jeffrey Hearst and Hillary Hearst Byers are his two children from his first marriage to the former Dorothy Hart Hearst. He has two stepchildren by his second marriage, Amanda Ross and Stanley Mortimer, III, and two children, Kate C. Paley and William C. Paley, who currently serve as officers of the foundation.

Financial Summary

Total Giving: $3,900,000 (2003 approx); $3,900,000 (2002 approx); $9,037,939 (2000)
Assets: $95,000,000 (2002 approx); $123,168,908 (2000); $125,284,905 (1998)
Gifts Received: $84,276 (1995); $108,691 (1992).
Note: Gifts were received from the estate of William Paley and from the Employees Trust Under Will of Samuel Paley in 1995.

Typical Recipients

Arts & Humanities: Arts Associations & Councils, Arts Centers, Arts Funds, Arts Outreach, Dance, Historic Preservation, History & Archaeology, Libraries, Museums/Galleries, Performing Arts, Public Broadcasting, Theater, Visual Arts
Civic & Public Affairs: Botanical Gardens/Parks, Civic & Public Affairs-General, Legal Aid, Municipalities/Towns, Professional & Trade Associations, Public Policy, Safety, Urban & Community Affairs, Zoos/Aquariums
Education: Arts/Humanities Education, Colleges & Universities, Elementary Education (Public), Education-General, International Studies, Legal Education, Literacy, Medical Education, Private Education (Precollege), Public Education (Precollege), Religious Education, Secondary Education (Private), Secondary Education (Public), Social Sciences Education, Special Education
Environment: Resource Conservation
Health: Alzheimers Disease, Cancer, Children's Health/Hospitals, Clinics/Medical Centers, Health Organizations, Hospices, Hospitals, Hospitals (University Affiliated), Single-Disease Health Associations
International: Foreign Arts Organizations, Foreign Educational Institutions, International Organizations, International Relations, International Relief Efforts, Missionary/Religious Activities
Religion: Religion-General, Jewish Causes, Religious Organizations, Religious Welfare, Seminaries
Social Services: Animal Protection, At-Risk Youth, Child Welfare, Community Service Organizations, Counseling, Delinquency & Criminal Rehabilitation, Emergency Relief, Family Planning, Family Services, Food/Clothing Distribution, Food/Clothing Distribution, Scouts, Social Services-General, Substance Abuse, YMCA/YWCA/YMHA/YWHA, Youth Organizations

Application Procedures

Initial Contact: Proposals should be made in writing.
Application Requirements: The foundation reports that no particular application form is required, but full financial information should be disclosed.
Deadlines: None.

Restrictions

The foundation does not make grants to individuals.

Foundation Officials

George Joseph Gillespie, III: director B New York, NY 1930. ED Georgetown University AB (1952); Harvard University LLB (1955). PRIM CORP EMPL partner: Cravath, Swaine & Moore. CORP AFFIL director: Washington Post Co. NONPR AFFIL director, chairman emeritus: National Multiple Sclerosis Society; trustee: New York University Medical Center; director: Madison Square Boys Club; secretary, director: Museum Television & Radio; member: Century Association; trustee, treasurer: Cooper-Hewitt National Design Museum. CLUB AFFIL Prouts Neck Country Club; Winged Foot Golf Club; member: Portland Country Club; Double Eagle Club; Falmouth Country Club; American Yacht Club.
Sidney W. Harl: director
Daniel L. Mosley: director, secretary, treasurer
William Cushing Paley: director B 1948. PRIM CORP EMPL president, vice president, director: VM Development. CORP AFFIL executive vice president, director: Texwipe Co.
Phillip A. Raspe, Jr.: assistant treasurer

Grants Analysis

Disclosure Period: calendar year ending 2000
Total Grants: $9,148,750
Number of Grants: 42
Average Grant: $29,186*
Highest Grant: $3,636,582
Lowest Grant: $1,000
Typical Range: $1,000 to $25,000
*Note: Average grant excludes three highest grants ($3,636,582, $2,529,939, and $1,756,418).

Recent Grants

Note: Grants derived from 2000 Form 990.

Library-Related
2,500 Katonah Village Library, Katonah, NY
2,500 Katonah Village Library, Katonah, NY
1,000 Greenwich Library, Greenwich, CT

General
3,636,582 Museum of Television and Radio, New York, NY -- capital campaigns
2,529,939 Museum of Modern Art, New York, NY
1,756,418 Museum of Television and Radio, New York, NY -- endowment
500,000 Museum of Television and Radio, New York, NY -- Paley Television Festival
225,000 Greenpark Foundation, New York, NY -- Paley Park
100,000 Museum of Modern Art, New York, NY
75,000 Jerusalem Foundation, Inc., New York, NY -- Paley Art Center
25,000 Auburn Theological Seminary, New York, NY
25,000 Mount Sinai Medical Center, New York, NY -- Dickinson Multiple Sclerosis Center
25,000 National Center on Addiction and Substance Abuse, New York, NY

PALISADES EDUCATIONAL FOUNDATION

Giving Contact

Gerald J. Dunworth, Treasurer
665 5th Ave., 11th Fl.
New York, NY 10022
Phone: (212)688-5151

Description

Founded: 1949
EIN: 516015053
Organization Type: Private Foundation
Giving Locations: CT: Southern Connecticut; NJ: Northern New Jersey; NY headquarters and operating communities.
Grant Types: Multiyear/Continuing Support, Operating Expenses, Scholarship.

Donor Information

Founder: Prentice-Hall

Financial Summary

Total Giving: $300,000 (2001); $304,000 (2000); $268,000 (1999)
Giving Analysis: Giving for 2001 includes: foundation scholarships ($12,500); 2000: foundation scholarships ($13,000); 1999: foundation scholarships ($13,000)
Assets: $5,698,314 (2001); $6,350,433 (2000); $6,577,116 (1999)

Typical Recipients

Arts & Humanities: Arts Associations & Councils, Arts Centers, Arts & Humanities-General, Libraries, Music
Civic & Public Affairs: Employment/Job Training, Civic & Public Affairs-General, Native American Affairs

Education: Arts/Humanities Education, Business Education, Colleges & Universities, Community & Junior Colleges, Education Associations, Education Funds, International Studies, Legal Education, Medical Education, Minority Education, Private Education (Precollege), Science/Mathematics Education, Special Education, Student Aid

Health: Cancer, Children's Health/Hospitals, Clinics/ Medical Centers, Emergency/Ambulance Services, Hospitals, Medical Research, Prenatal Health Issues, Single-Disease Health Associations

International: Foreign Educational Institutions

Religion: Religious Welfare

Science: Science Museums

Social Services: At-Risk Youth, Camps, Child Welfare, Community Service Organizations, Crime Prevention, Family Services, Homes, People with Disabilities, Recreation & Athletics, Scouts, Senior Services, Shelters/Homelessness, Substance Abuse, Volunteer Services, YMCA/YWCA/YMHA/YWHA, Youth Organizations

Application Procedures

Initial Contact: Send a brief letter of inquiry describing program and projected budget.
Deadlines: None.

Foundation Officials

Frederick W. Anthony: secretary
Ralph F. Anthony: president, director
Gerald J. Dunworth: treasurer, director
Colin Gunn: director
Donald A. Schaefer: vice president, director

Grants Analysis

Disclosure Period: calendar year ending 2001
Total Grants: $287,500*
Number of Grants: 36
Average Grant: $8,455
Highest Grant: $35,000
Typical Range: $1,000 to $20,000
*Note: Giving excludes scholarships.

Recent Grants

Note: Grants derived from 2001 Form 990.

General

35,000	Colgate University, Hamilton, NY -- for educational fund
35,000	Marist Brothers Cancer Camp, South Orange, NJ
27,000	Englewood Hospital, Englewood, NJ
20,000	University of Bridgeport, Bridgeport, CT -- for annual fund
15,000	Contact We Care, Inc., Westfield, NJ
15,000	Volunteer Center of Bergen County, Hackensack, NJ
12,000	Coalition for the Homeless, Summit, NJ -- for operating expenses
7,500	Gettysburg College, Gettysburg, PA -- for Bob Smith scholarship fund
7,500	Medical Missions for Children, Jersey City, NJ
7,500	National Center for Adoption, Washington, DC

FRANK LOOMIS PALMER FUND

Giving Contact

Marjorie Davis, Vice President
Fleet Bank
777 Main St., CTEH 40222B
Hartford, CT 06115
Phone: (860)952-7405
Fax: (860)952-7395
E-mail: marjorie_alexandre_davis@fleet.com

Description

Founded: 1936
EIN: 066026043
Organization Type: General Purpose Foundation
Giving Locations: CT: New London
Grant Types: Award, Capital, Conference/Seminar, Matching, Multiyear/Continuing Support, Project, Research, Scholarship, Seed Money.

Donor Information

Founder: Established in 1936 by the late Virginia Palmer in memory of her father, Frank Loomis Palmer.

Financial Summary

Total Giving: $1,109,736 (fiscal year ending July 31, 2001); $387,408 (fiscal 1996); $725,270 (fiscal 1995)
Assets: $40,779,915 (fiscal 1999); $33,709,757 (fiscal 1998); $28,389,800 (fiscal 1997)
Gifts Received: $20,000 (fiscal 1995). Note: In 1995, the foundation received a contribution from the Bodenwein Foundation.

Typical Recipients

Arts & Humanities: Arts Centers, Arts Festivals, Arts Outreach, Historic Preservation, History & Archaeology, Libraries, Museums/Galleries, Music, Opera, Theater

Civic & Public Affairs: Community Foundations, Economic Development, Employment/Job Training, Civic & Public Affairs-General, Hispanic Affairs, Housing, Municipalities/Towns, Parades/Festivals, Professional & Trade Associations, Public Policy, Safety, Urban & Community Affairs, Women's Affairs, Zoos/ Aquariums

Education: Afterschool/Enrichment Programs, Arts/ Humanities Education, Colleges & Universities, Education Reform, Elementary Education (Public), Engineering/Technological Education, Education-General, International Studies, Leadership Training, Literacy, Minority Education, Private Education (Precollege), Public Education (Precollege), School Volunteerism, Secondary Education (Private), Social Sciences Education, Student Aid, Vocational & Technical Education

Environment: Environment-General

Health: AIDS/HIV, Children's Health/Hospitals, Emergency/Ambulance Services, Health Organizations, Hospices, Hospitals, Medical Rehabilitation, Mental Health, Nursing Services, Public Health, Single-Disease Health Associations

Religion: Churches, Jewish Causes, Missionary Activities (Domestic), Religious Welfare

Science: Science Museums, Scientific Centers & Institutes, Scientific Organizations

Social Services: At-Risk Youth, Big Brother/Big Sister, Child Welfare, Community Centers, Community Service Organizations, Counseling, Domestic Violence, Emergency Relief, Family Planning, Family Services, Food/Clothing Distribution, People with Disabilities, Recreation & Athletics, Scouts, Shelters/ Homelessness, Social Services-General, Substance Abuse, United Funds/United Ways, Volunteer Services, YMCA/YWCA/YMHA/YWHA, Youth Organizations

Application Procedures

Initial Contact: Initial contact should be by telephone to request an application and guidelines.
Application Requirements: Proposal should include a completed application form, an audited financial statement for the most recent year or a treasurer's report, and a project budget (for organizations in the formative stages), an IRS tax-exempt letter dated after 1969, and a proposed operating budget for the period of time in which the desired grant will be used.

For organizations that are new or unfamiliar to the foundation, a brief organizational background is required. Please see guidelines for additional requirements for churches and municipalities.

Deadlines: Completed applications including all required supporting data for grants must be submitted by May 15 and November 15 of each year. If these dates fall on a Saturday or Sunday, the deadline is not extended. Applications postmarked on the day of the deadline are accepted. Complete applications received after the deadline will be held for the next review period.

Review Process: Grant awards are announced on February 1 and August 1 in "The Day" newspaper. Following the announcement, a letter will be sent to all applicants confirming the approval or denial of their request.

Notes: If awarded, a post grant evaluation is due one year from the date of the grant.

Restrictions

Grants will be limited to activities conducted or organizations located in New London. Special consideration may be given to grantees whose programs offer the possibility of matching grants. Grants are not made to individuals, for endowments, for deficit financing, or for reimbursement for items purchased prior to grant request.

Additional Information

The foundation lists the Fleet Bank as a corporate trustee.
Publications: Informational Brochure (including Application Guidelines)

Foundation Officials

Sheilah B. Rostow: vice president

Grants Analysis

Disclosure Period: fiscal year ending July 31, 2001
Total Grants: $1,109,736
Number of Grants: 65
Average Grant: $17,073
Highest Grant: $90,500
Typical Range: $5,000 to $35,000

Recent Grants

Note: Grants derived from 2000 Form 990.

General

100,000	Coast Guard Foundation, Stonington, CT -- raise funds for National Coast Guard Museum
100,000	Garde Arts Center, New Haven, CT -- improvements to theater
65,000	Save Ocean Beach, New London, CT -- purchase and install playscape
60,000	Opportunities Industrialization Center, New London, CT -- support comprehensive training and job
40,800	New London Main Street, New London, CT
40,000	Leadership, Education, and Athletics in Partnership, New Haven, CT -- support Youth Development Program
38,000	New London Maritime Society, New London, CT -- restore waterfront entry, landscaping and paving
35,670	First Step, New London, CT -- develop and evaluate employment service
33,500	Chemical Abuse Prevention Institute, Sherman Oaks, CA -- support Challenges and Choice Program
33,170	Science Center of Eastern Connecticut, New London, CT -- produce small-scale at the Science Center

PAMIDA, INC.

Company Headquarters
Omaha, NE
Web: http://www.pamida.com

Company Description
Revenue: US$300 million (2001)
Employees: 2500 (2001)
SIC(s): 5300 General Merchandise Stores.

Operating Locations
Pamida, Inc. (IL; IA; KS; MI; MO; MT; NE; ND; WI; WY)

Giving Contact
Mary Linley, Secr.
PO Box 3856
Omaha, NE 68103
Phone: (402)339-2400
Fax: (402)596-7330

Description
Organization Type: Corporate Giving Program
Giving Locations: headquarters and operating communities.
Grant Types: Challenge, Conference/Seminar, Emergency, Endowment, General Support.

Typical Recipients
Arts & Humanities: Arts Funds, Arts & Humanities-General, Libraries, Museums/Galleries
Civic & Public Affairs: Botanical Gardens/Parks, Clubs, Community Foundations, Civic & Public Affairs-General, Parades/Festivals, Safety, Urban & Community Affairs
Education: Agricultural Education, Colleges & Universities, Elementary Education (Public), Education-General, Private Education (Precollege), School Volunteerism, Student Aid
Health: Children's Health/Hospitals, Emergency/Ambulance Services, Health-General, Geriatric Health, Health Funds, Hospitals
Social Services: Community Centers, Community Service Organizations, Crime Prevention, Food/Clothing Distribution, People with Disabilities, Recreation & Athletics, Senior Services, Social Services-General, Substance Abuse, Veterans, Youth Organizations

Application Procedures
Initial Contact: Send a brief letter of inquiry.
Application Requirements: Include a description of organization, amount requested, purpose of funds sought, and proof of tax-exempt status.
Deadlines: None.

Restrictions
Does not support individuals, religious organizations for sectarian purposes, political or lobbying groups, or organizations outside operating areas.

Additional Information
The Pamida Foundation was dissolved in 1995. The company continues to support local organizations through a decentralized corporate giving program with individual stores handling requests and administering independent budgets. The focus is on addressing needs at the local level. Pamida's stores in its 15-state operating region handle requests from local organizations. Contact the stores directly. Organizations in Omaha may contact corporate headquarters.

Corporate Officials
Steven S. Fishman: chairman, president, chief executive officer PRIM CORP EMPL chairman, president, chief executive officer: Pamida.

Grants Analysis
Typical Range: $100 to $1,000

THOMAS ANTHONY PAPPAS CHARITABLE FOUNDATION

Giving Contact
John C. Pappas, Executive Director
PO Box 463
Belmont, MA 02478-0004
Phone: (781)862-2802

Description
Founded: 1975
EIN: 510153284
Organization Type: Family Foundation
Giving Locations: MA
Grant Types: Capital, Endowment, Fellowship, Research, Scholarship.

Donor Information
Founder: Incorporated in 1975 by the late Thomas Anthony Pappas .

Financial Summary
Total Giving: $826,670 (2001); $575,000 (2000); $583,000 (1999)
Giving Analysis: Giving for 1999 includes: foundation scholarships ($10,000); foundation fellowships ($25,000) 1998: foundation scholarships ($180,000)
Assets: $20,321,536 (2001); $19,942,418 (2000); $19,489,985 (1999)

Typical Recipients
Arts & Humanities: Arts Centers, Ballet, Dance, Arts & Humanities-General, Historic Preservation, History & Archaeology, Literary Arts, Museums/Galleries, Music, Performing Arts, Public Broadcasting, Theater
Civic & Public Affairs: Clubs, Community Foundations, Economic Development, Ethnic Organizations, Civic & Public Affairs-General, Law & Justice, Municipalities/Towns, Parades/Festivals, Philanthropic Organizations, Professional & Trade Associations, Public Policy, Urban & Community Affairs, Women's Affairs, Zoos/Aquariums
Education: Arts/Humanities Education, Colleges & Universities, Community & Junior Colleges, Education-General, International Studies, Leadership Training, Legal Education, Medical Education, Minority Education, Private Education (Precollege), Science/Mathematics Education, Secondary Education (Private), Special Education, Student Aid
Health: Alzheimers Disease, Arthritis, Cancer, Children's Health/Hospitals, Clinics/Medical Centers, Eyes/Blindness, Health-General, Health Organizations, Heart, Hospices, Hospitals, Kidney, Long-Term Care, Medical Rehabilitation, Medical Research, Nursing Services, Research/Studies Institutes, Respiratory, Single-Disease Health Associations
International: Foreign Educational Institutions, Health Care/Hospitals, Missionary/Religious Activities
Religion: Churches, Dioceses, Religion-General, Jewish Causes, Religious Organizations, Religious Welfare
Science: Science-General, Scientific Research
Social Services: Animal Protection, Big Brother/Big Sister, Camps, Child Welfare, Community Service Organizations, Counseling, Delinquency & Criminal Rehabilitation, Emergency Relief, Family Services, Food/Clothing Distribution, Homes, People with Disabilities, Recreation & Athletics, Scouts, Senior Services, Shelters/Homelessness, Special Olympics, Substance Abuse, YMCA/YWCA/YMHA/YWHA, Youth Organizations

Application Procedures
Initial Contact: The foundation requests applications be made in writing.
Application Requirements: Applications should include the name and address of the organization, telephone number, fax number, e-mail address, and individual to contact; the purpose of the organization; amount requested; the organization's other sources of support; a detailed description of the project and the use of the funds requested; and an IRS current exemption status and a copy of the latest determination letter.
Deadlines: September 30.

Restrictions
The foundation reports no private foundations will be considered without complete expenditure control. Grants are not made to individuals.

Additional Information
Publications: Program Policy Statement; Application Guidelines

Foundation Officials
Helen K. Pappas: director PRIM CORP EMPL clerk, director: Dudley Supermarket Inc.
John C. Pappas: director
Sophia H. Pappas: director
Donald J. Young: director

Grants Analysis
Disclosure Period: calendar year ending 2001
Total Grants: $826,670
Number of Grants: 43
Average Grant: $19,225
Highest Grant: $200,000
Lowest Grant: $1,000
Typical Range: $1,000 to $10,000 and $100,000 to $200,000

Recent Grants
Note: Grants derived from 2001 Form 990.

General

200,000	Perkins School for the Blind, Watertown, MA
100,000	Bentley College, Waltham, MA -- CAP lecture series
100,000	Perkins School for the Blind, Watertown, MA
100,000	Town of Belmont, Belmont, MA -- fitness center at BPD
25,000	Greek Orthodox Taxiarche, Watertown, MA -- books/bible for Sunday School
25,000	Isabella Steward Gardner Museum, Boston, MA -- artist in residence
25,000	St. Nicholas Lexington, Lexington, MA -- repairs/renovations
25,000	Tabor Academy, Marion, MA -- scholarship change name to CAP
25,000	Wheaton College, Chicago, IL -- TAP scholarship
22,420	Outward Bound, Boston, MA -- Wilauer School

PARAMETRIC TECHNOLOGY CORP.

Company Headquarters
140 Kendrick St.
Needham, MA 02494
Web: http://www.ptc.com

Company Description
Founded: 1985
Ticker: PMTC
Exchange: NASDAQ
Operating Revenue: US$742 million (2002)

Employees: 3803 (2002)
SIC(s): 7372 Prepackaged Software.

Nonmonetary Support
Type: Donated Equipment

Giving Contact
Susan Carens-Peterson, Treasury Analyst
100 Crosby Dr.
Bedford, MA 01730
Phone: (617)275-1800
Note: Ext. 2901

Description
Organization Type: Corporate Giving Program
Grant Types: General Support.

Typical Recipients
Arts & Humanities: Arts & Humanities-General, Libraries, Public Broadcasting
Civic & Public Affairs: Employment/Job Training, Civic & Public Affairs-General, Urban & Community Affairs
Education: Education-General, Preschool Education, Private Education (Precollege), Public Education (Precollege)
Health: Health-General, Hospitals
Social Services: Child Welfare

Corporate Officials
Eugene Bullis: chief financial officer PRIM CORP EMPL chief financial officer: Computervision Corp.
Kathleen Cole: president, chief executive officer PRIM CORP EMPL president, chief executive officer: Computervision Corp.
Russell E. Planitzer: chairman B South Orange, NJ 1944. ED United States Naval Academy (1966); Harvard University Graduate School of Business Administration (1974). PRIM CORP EMPL chairman: Computervision Corp. CORP AFFIL director: Voyager Software Corp.; director: Wellfleet Communication; director: Stardent Computer; director: Easel Corp.; director: Intersolv.

SAMUEL P. PARDOE FOUNDATION

Giving Contact
Mary Phillips, Administrator
c/o Grants Management Associates
77 Summer St. 8th Floor
Boston, MA 02110
Phone: (617)426-7172
Fax: (617)426-5441
Web: http://www.grantsmanagement.com

Description
Founded: 1989
EIN: 521660757
Organization Type: Private Foundation
Giving Locations: NH
Grant Types: Capital, General Support, Project.

Donor Information
Founder: Helen P. Pardoe Trust, the late Samuel P. Pardoe

Financial Summary
Total Giving: $594,739 (fiscal year ending June 30, 2002); $580,099 (fiscal 2000); $368,172 (fiscal 1999)
Assets: $10,349,633 (fiscal 2002); $10,971,269 (fiscal 2000); $10,871,312 (fiscal 1999)
Gifts Received: $7,892 (fiscal 1994). Note: In fiscal 1994, contributions were received from Tiffey and Pardoe ($2,566) and Pardoe and Hansen ($5,326).

Typical Recipients
Arts & Humanities: History & Archaeology, Libraries, Museums/Galleries, Music
Civic & Public Affairs: Economic Development, Civic & Public Affairs-General, Housing, Philanthropic Organizations, Women's Affairs
Education: Colleges & Universities, Education Reform, Education-General, Minority Education, Preschool Education, Private Education (Precollege), Secondary Education (Private), Secondary Education (Public), Special Education
Environment: Air/Water Quality, Forestry, Environment-General, Resource Conservation, Wildlife Protection
Health: AIDS/HIV, Cancer, Children's Health/Hospitals, Clinics/Medical Centers, Prenatal Health Issues, Public Health
Religion: Churches, Jewish Causes, Religious Welfare
Science: Scientific Centers & Institutes
Social Services: Child Welfare, Community Service Organizations, Counseling, Family Services, Food/Clothing Distribution, People with Disabilities, Recreation & Athletics, Shelters/Homelessness, Social Services-General, Youth Organizations

Application Procedures
Initial Contact: Request application form and guidelines.
Deadlines: Prior to January 15.

Restrictions
Does not support religious organizations for sectarian purposes, individuals, political or lobbying groups, operating expenses, endowments, scholarships, loans, deficits, special events, fundraising activities, or advertising.

Additional Information
Publications: Application Form; Guidelines

Foundation Officials
Charles E. Pardoe: treasurer
Charles H. Pardoe, II: president
Prescott Bruce Pardoe: vice president
E. Spencer Pardoe Ballou: secretary
Elizabeth E. Pardoe Gray: assistant treasurer

Grants Analysis
Disclosure Period: fiscal year ending June 30, 2002
Total Grants: $594,739
Number of Grants: 53
Average Grant: $9,202*
Highest Grant: $116,250
Lowest Grant: $200
Typical Range: $5,000 to $20,000
*Note: Average grant figure excludes highest grant.

Recent Grants
Note: Grants derived from fiscal 2000 Form 990.

General

50,000	Prescott Conservancy, Inc., Boston, MA
20,000	Appalachian Mountain Club, Boston, MA
20,000	Child and Family Services, Manchester, NH
20,000	Society for the Protection of New Hampshire Forests, Concord, NH
18,000	Lakes Region Habitat for Humanity, Laconia, NH
16,800	Kidworks Learning Center, Meredith, NH
16,000	Belknap County Conservation District, Laconia, NH
15,500	Antioch New England Graduate School, Keene, NH
15,500	University of New Hampshire Cooperative Extension, Durham, NH
15,000	Coral Reef Alliance, Berkeley, CA

PARK BANK

Company Headquarters
1700 W. Bender Rd.
Milwaukee, WI 53209

Company Description
Employees: 164

Park Bank Foundation

Giving Contact
Carolyn Torcivia, Secretary
Park Bank Foundation
330 E. Kilbourn Ave.
Milwaukee, WI 53202
Phone: (414)270-3209

Description
Founded: 1980
EIN: 391365837
Organization Type: Corporate Foundation
Giving Locations: WI: Milwaukee metropolitan area
Grant Types: General Support.

Financial Summary
Total Giving: $163,570 (2001); $152,125 (2000); $163,240 (1999)
Giving Analysis: Giving for 2000 includes: foundation grants to United Way ($22,000); 1999: foundation grants to United Way ($21,000); foundation ($142,240); 1998: foundation grants to United Way ($21,000); foundation ($122,190);
Assets: $899,012 (2001); $890,726 (2000); $853,061 (1999)
Gifts Received: $150,000 (2001); $149,000 (2000); $150,000 (1999). Note: contributions were received from Park Bank.

Typical Recipients
Arts & Humanities: Arts Centers, Arts Funds, Arts Institutes, Dance, Historic Preservation, Libraries, Museums/Galleries, Performing Arts, Public Broadcasting, Theater
Civic & Public Affairs: Botanical Gardens/Parks, Clubs, Economic Development, Employment/Job Training, Civic & Public Affairs-General, Hispanic Affairs, Housing, Municipalities/Towns, Parades/Festivals, Public Policy, Safety, Urban & Community Affairs, Women's Affairs
Education: Business Education, Colleges & Universities, Education Funds, Engineering/Technological Education, Medical Education, Private Education (Precollege), Public Education (Precollege), Religious Education, Secondary Education (Private), Student Aid
Environment: Environment-General, Environment-General
Health: Arthritis, Cancer, Children's Health/Hospitals, Clinics/Medical Centers, Emergency/Ambulance Services, Health Organizations, Heart, Hospitals, Long-Term Care, Medical Training, Nursing Services, Public Health, Single-Disease Health Associations, Transplant Networks/Donor Banks
International: Foreign Arts Organizations
Religion: Churches, Jewish Causes, Ministries, Religious Welfare
Social Services: Child Abuse, Child Welfare, Community Centers, Community Service Organizations, Counseling, Family Services, Food/Clothing Distribution, People with Disabilities, Recreation & Athletics, Scouts, Social Services-General, United Funds/United Ways, YMCA/YWCA/YMHA/YWHA, Youth Organizations

Application Procedures
Initial Contact: Send letter of inquiry describing the requesting organization; include financials and tax-exempt status.

Application Requirements: a description of organization, amount requested, purpose of funds sought, recently audited financial statement, and proof of tax-exempt status

Deadlines: None. Board meets quarterly, and proposals are only reviewed during those meetings.

Restrictions

Gives only in the greater Milwaukee area.

Additional Information

Company reports that about 30% of contributions support social services; 30%, civic affairs and community development; 20%, health organizations; 12%, arts and humanities; 7%, education; and 1%, conservation and historic preservation.

Corporate Officials

P. Michael Mahoney: chairman, president, chief executive officer, director PRIM CORP EMPL chairman, president, chief executive officer, director: Park Bank. CORP AFFIL president: Bank Managers Corp.
Bob Makowski: chief financial officer PRIM CORP EMPL chief financial officer: Park Bank.

Foundation Officials

Lorraine A. Kelly: vice president, director
Michael J. Kelly: vice president, director
P. Michael Mahoney: president, director (see above)
Carolyn Torcivia: secretary
James W. Wright: treasurer, director

Grants Analysis

Disclosure Period: calendar year ending 2002
Total Grants: $141,070*
Number of Grants: 110
Average Grant: $1,294
Highest Grant: $22,500
Typical Range: $500 to $3,000
*Note: Giving excludes United Way.

Recent Grants

Note: Grants derived from 2001 Form 990.

Library-Related
5,000	Friends of the Butler Library, Inc., Butler, WI

General
22,500	United Way of Greater Milwaukee, Milwaukee, WI
6,000	Rogers Memorial Hospital Foundation, Oconomowoc, WI
5,000	Jewish Community Center, Milwaukee, WI
5,000	Medical College of Wisconsin, Milwaukee, WI
5,000	Milwaukee Redevelopment Corporation, Milwaukee, WI
5,000	United Performing Arts Fund, Milwaukee, WI
5,000	Wisconsin Lutheran College, Milwaukee, WI
3,000	MACC Fund, Brookfield, WI
3,000	Milwaukee Repertory Theater, Milwaukee, WI
2,500	Friends of Schlitz Audubon Center, Milwaukee, WI

PARK FOUNDATION

Giving Contact

Leslie . Myers, Executive Director
PO Box 550
Ithaca, NY 14851
Phone: (607)272-9124
Fax: (607)272-6057

Description

Founded: 1966
EIN: 166071043
Organization Type: Private Foundation
Giving Locations: NY: Central New York
Grant Types: Award, Emergency, Fellowship, General Support, Matching, Multiyear/Continuing Support.

Donor Information

Founder: RHP, Inc.

Financial Summary

Total Giving: $29,473,930 (2001); $28,377,147 (2000); $22,369,904 (1999)
Giving Analysis: Giving for 2000 includes: foundation grants to United Way ($250,000)
Assets: $546,921,909 (2001); $600,084,849 (2000); $650,000,000 (1999 approx)
Gifts Received: $2,852,613 (1999); $1,004,674 (1994). Note: In 1994, contributions were received from Dorothy D. Park.

Typical Recipients

Arts & Humanities: Art History, Arts & Humanities-General, Historic Preservation, Libraries, Museums/Galleries, Music, Public Broadcasting
Civic & Public Affairs: Economic Development, Civic & Public Affairs-General, Safety, Urban & Community Affairs, Zoos/Aquariums
Education: Arts/Humanities Education, Business Education, Colleges & Universities, Community & Junior Colleges, Economic Education, Education Funds, Environmental Education, Faculty Development, Education-General, Journalism/Media Education, Leadership Training, Legal Education, Private Education (Precollege), Religious Education, Science/Mathematics Education, Secondary Education (Public), Special Education, Student Aid
Environment: Air/Water Quality, Forestry, Environment-General, Protection, Research
Health: Cancer, Diabetes, Eyes/Blindness, Heart, Hospices, Hospitals, Medical Rehabilitation, Prenatal Health Issues
International: Foreign Arts Organizations, Missionary/Religious Activities
Religion: Churches, Missionary Activities (Domestic), Religious Welfare, Synagogues/Temples
Science: Science Museums, Scientific Labs, Scientific Research
Social Services: Animal Protection, Big Brother/Big Sister, Community Service Organizations, Homes, United Funds/United Ways, YMCA/YWCA/YMHA/YWHA

Application Procedures

Initial Contact: Request grant inquiry form.
Application Requirements: Letters of request should include a description of organization and purpose of funds sought.
Deadlines: None.

Restrictions

Does not support: individuals, religious organizations for sectarian purposes, political or lobbying groups, or for-profit organizations.

Additional Information

Publications: Brochure; Grant Inquiry Form

Foundation Officials

Joanne V. Florino: executive director
Elizabeth P. Fowler: treasurer
Adelaide P. Gomer: second vice president, secretary
Alicia P. Gomer: jr. advisory
Jerome B. Libin: director
Dorothy D. Park: president
Roy H. Park, III: jr. advisory
Roy H. Park, Jr.: first vice president
Richard G. Robb: director

Grants Analysis

Disclosure Period: calendar year ending 2001
Total Grants: $29,247,930*
Number of Grants: 455
Average Grant: $59,301*
Highest Grant: $1,192,263
Lowest Grant: $30
Typical Range: $10,000 to $100,000
*Note: Giving excludes United Way. Average grant figure excludes two highest grants ($2,384,526).

Recent Grants

Note: Grants derived from 2001 Form 990.

General
1,192,263	Cornell University Johnson Graduate School of Management, Ithaca, NY -- Park Leadership Fellows Program
1,192,263	Cornell University Johnson Graduate School of Management, Ithaca, NY -- Park Leadership Fellows Program
750,000	Educational Broadcasting Corporation, New York, NY -- Underwriting for Nature and American Masters
750,000	Educational Broadcasting Corporation, New York, NY -- Underwriting for Nature and American Masters
750,000	WGBH Educational Foundation, Springfield, MA -- Underwrite the series NOVA
750,000	WGBH Educational Foundation, Springfield, MA -- Underwrite the series NOVA
662,393	North Carolina State University, Raleigh, NC -- (Class of 2005) Park Scholarships
563,920	University of North Carolina at Chapel Hill, Chapel Hill, NC -- Park Fellowships in the master's and doctoral program
563,915	University of North Carolina at Chapel Hill, Chapel Hill, NC -- Park Fellowships in the master's and doctoral program
500,000	Educational Broadcasting Corporation, New York, NY -- Support production of three specials

MOSES L. PARSHELSKY FOUNDATION

Giving Contact

Tony B. Berk, Trustee
26 Court St.
Brooklyn, NY 11242
Phone: (718)875-8883

Description

Founded: 1949
EIN: 111848260
Organization Type: Private Foundation
Giving Locations: NY: Brooklyn, Queens
Grant Types: General Support.

Donor Information

Founder: Moses L. Parshelsky

Financial Summary

Total Giving: $268,600 (2001); $258,950 (2000); $235,450 (1999)
Assets: $7,785,198 (2001); $8,060,731 (2000); $7,974,874 (1999)

Typical Recipients

Arts & Humanities: Arts Associations & Councils, Arts Institutes, Dance, Libraries, Literary Arts, Museums/Galleries, Music, Performing Arts
Civic & Public Affairs: Botanical Gardens/Parks, Civic & Public Affairs-General, Philanthropic Organizations, Zoos/Aquariums
Education: Colleges & Universities, Faculty Development, Religious Education, Special Education

Health: Cancer, Children's Health/Hospitals, Clinics/Medical Centers, Eyes/Blindness, Geriatric Health, Health Funds, Hospitals, Medical Research, Mental Health, Prenatal Health Issues, Respiratory, Single-Disease Health Associations
Religion: Jewish Causes, Religious Organizations
Social Services: Camps, Community Centers, Community Service Organizations, Family Planning, Family Services, Food/Clothing Distribution, People with Disabilities, Recreation & Athletics, Senior Services, YMCA/YWCA/YMHA/YWHA, Youth Organizations

Application Procedures

Initial Contact: Send a brief letter of inquiry.
Application Requirements: Include a description of organization, amount requested, purpose of funds sought, and proof of tax-exempt status. No phone inquiries.
Deadlines: May 31.

Restrictions

Emphasis is on medical, rehabilitation, and geriatric treatment facilities, and religious, educational, and youth services organizations.

Foundation Officials

Tony B. Berk: trustee
Josephine B. Krinsky: trustee
Robert Daniel Krinsky: trustee B Brooklyn, NY 1937. ED Antioch College BA (1957). PRIM CORP EMPL chairman: Segal (Martin E) Co. NONPR AFFIL member working committee: National Coordinating Comm Multi-employer Pension Plans; chairman, member, director: National Dance Institute; fellow: Conference Actuaries Public Practice; director: Harbor Festival Foundation; member, director: Association Private Pension and Welfare Plans; member: Century Association; member: American Academy of Actuaries; chairman, trustee: Antioch University.

Grants Analysis

Disclosure Period: calendar year ending 2001
Total Grants: $268,600
Number of Grants: 32
Average Grant: $7,051*
Highest Grant: $50,000
Typical Range: $1,000 to $10,000
*Note: Average grant excludes highest grant.

Recent Grants

Note: Grants derived from 2001 Form 990.

Library-Related
4,000	New York Public Library, New York, NY -- to support the Jewish Division of the library
2,500	Brooklyn Public Library, Brooklyn, NY -- for the Ready to Read Educational Program for children

General
50,000	Brookdale Hospital & Medical Center, Brooklyn, NY -- for hospital services
30,000	Metropolitan Jewish Geriatric Foundation, Brooklyn, NY -- for repairs, renovations and capital improvements
20,000	Vacamas Programs for Youth, New York, NY -- to support and maintain Camp Vacuums
16,500	National Jewish Center for Immunology and Respiratory Medicine, Denver, CO -- for young patients with asthma and rheumatism
16,000	Jewish Braille Institute of America, New York, NY -- on behalf of Talking Book Library
9,999	DOROT, Inc., New York, NY -- to feed and befriend the needy elderly
7,500	Lexington School and Center for the Deaf, Jackson Heights, NY -- hearing support for the Elderly
6,500	Helen Keller Services for the Blind,

	Brooklyn, NY -- for ongoing programs for blind and visually impaired senior citizens
6,000	North Shore Long Island Jewish Health System Foundation, Great Neck, NY -- for Schneider Children's Hospital
5,500	92nd Street YM & YMHA, New York, NY -- for year-end purposes

RALPH M. PARSONS FOUNDATION

Giving Contact

Wendy Hoppe, Executive Director & Secretary
1055 Wilshire Boulevard, Suite 1701
Los Angeles, CA 90017
Phone: (213)482-3185
Fax: (213)482-8878
E-mail: hoppe@rmpf.org
Web: http://www.rmpf.org

Alternate Contact

Wendy Hoppe, Program Director

Description

Founded: 1961
EIN: 956085895
Organization Type: General Purpose Foundation
Giving Locations: CA: Los Angeles County
Grant Types: Capital, Challenge, General Support, Project, Seed Money.
Note: The foundation also considers requests for unrestricted funds.

Donor Information

Founder: The foundation was established in 1961 by Ralph M. Parsons (1896-1974). Despite his modest beginnings as the son of a Long Island fisherman, Mr. Parsons established and led one of the world's largest engineering and construction firms, Parsons Corporation. He was a pioneer in missile and space launch facilities and nuclear plants.
In 1961, Mr. Parsons established a modest foundation. Upon his death in 1974, the grant-making organization received a bequest from his estate valued at approximately $154 million. This foundation is managed independently of the Parsons Corporation.

Financial Summary

Total Giving: $13,000,000 (2003 approx); $15,000,000 (2002); $17,322,318 (1998)
Assets: $265,000,000 (2003 approx); $298,000,000 (2002); $323,000,000 (2001)

Typical Recipients

Arts & Humanities: Arts Centers, Arts Institutes, Arts Outreach, Ballet, Ethnic & Folk Arts, Historic Preservation, History & Archaeology, Libraries, Museums/Galleries, Music, Performing Arts, Public Broadcasting, Theater
Civic & Public Affairs: Botanical Gardens/Parks, Civil Rights, Employment/Job Training, Hispanic Affairs, Housing, Law & Justice, Nonprofit Management, Philanthropic Organizations, Professional & Trade Associations, Public Policy, Safety, Urban & Community Affairs, Zoos/Aquariums
Education: Arts/Humanities Education, Colleges & Universities, Economic Education, Education Associations, Education Funds, Education Reform, Elementary Education (Private), Engineering/Technological Education, Engineering/Technological Education, Faculty Development, Education-General, Health & Physical Education, Legal Education, Literacy, Minority Education, Preschool Education, Private Education (Precollege), Public Education (Precollege), Science/Mathematics Education, Secondary Education (Public), Special Education, Student Aid, Vocational & Technical Education

Environment: Environment-General
Health: Adolescent Health Issues, AIDS/HIV, Alzheimers Disease, Cancer, Children's Health/Hospitals, Clinics/Medical Centers, Eyes/Blindness, Geriatric Health, Health Organizations, Heart, Hospitals, Hospitals (University Affiliated), Long-Term Care, Medical Research, Mental Health, Prenatal Health Issues, Preventive Medicine/Wellness Organizations, Speech & Hearing, Trauma Treatment
International: Health Care/Hospitals
Religion: Churches, Jewish Causes, Religious Welfare
Science: Science Museums, Scientific Centers & Institutes, Scientific Research
Social Services: At-Risk Youth, Child Abuse, Child Welfare, Community Centers, Community Service Organizations, Counseling, Crime Prevention, Day Care, Delinquency & Criminal Rehabilitation, Domestic Violence, Emergency Relief, Family Planning, Family Services, Food/Clothing Distribution, People with Disabilities, Recreation & Athletics, Refugee Assistance, Scouts, Senior Services, Shelters/Homelessness, Substance Abuse, Volunteer Services, YMCA/YWCA/YMHA/YWHA, Youth Organizations

Application Procedures

Initial Contact: Submit a preliminary letter to the executive director, outlining the nature of the project for which funding is sought, the amount requested, and justification for such a request.
Application Requirements: The preliminary letter should include brief information on the applying organization and proof of tax-exempt status.
Deadlines: None. The staff submits applications to the board of directors five times each year, in alternate months beginning in February. For the sake of fairness, applications are considered in chronological order. Due to the large number of proposals that the foundation receives, applicants should be prepared for a period of delay leading up to a final decision.
Review Process: The foundation's staff makes an initial screening of the application and a decision is made within three months on whether the applicant is qualified. The foundation does not encourage communications with its directors. If the decision is affirmative, more detailed information may be requested and a date set for a meeting or on-site visit.

Restrictions

The foundation only contributes to tax-exempt, 501(c)(3) organizations that are not classified as private foundations.
The foundation generally does not support fund-raising events, dinners, or mass mailings; individuals; conferences, seminars, or workshops; religious or fraternal purposes; tax-supported organizations; endowments; federated fundraising appeals; programs for which substantial support from government or other sources is readily available; or to support candidates for political office, or to influence legislation.

Additional Information

Publications: Annual Report

Foundation Officials

Albert A. Dorskind: vice president, chief financial officer, director B New York, NY 1922. ED Cornell University (1943); Cornell University LLB (1948). PRIM CORP EMPL chairman: MCA Development Co. CORP AFFIL director: Environmental Industries Inc.
Robert F. Erburu: director B Ventura, CA 1930. ED University of Southern California BA (1952); Harvard University JD (1955). PRIM CORP EMPL director: The Times Mirror Co. CORP AFFIL director: Marsh & McLennan Companies Inc.; director: Tejon Ranch Co.; director: Cox Communications Inc. NONPR AFFIL chairman board trustee: H.E. Huntington Library Art Gallery; life director: Independent Colleges Southern California; member: American Bar Association.
Joseph G. Hurley: president, director PRIM CORP EMPL president: Hurley Grassini & Wrinkle.

Edgar R. Jackson: vice president, director
Everett Broadstone Laybourne: vice president, director B Springfield, OH October 26, 1911. ED Ohio State University BA (1932); Harvard University JD (1935). CORP AFFIL director: Viking Industries; director: McBain Instruments; director: Pacific Energy Corp.; director: CalEnergy Co. Inc.; director: Coldwater Investment Co.; director: Brouse-Whited Packaging Co. NONPR AFFIL chairman: WAIF Inc.; member: World Affairs Council; member: Roscomare Valley Association; member: Selden Society; member: Los Angeles County Bar Association; member: Phi Beta Kappa; member: Big Ten Universities Club Southern California. CLUB AFFIL California Club; Bel-Air Country Club.
Elizabeth H. Lowe: director
James A. Thomas: director B 1935. PRIM CORP EMPL managing partner: Maguire Partners.
Franklin E. Ulf: director B Pittsburgh, PA 1932. ED Pomona College BA (1953); University of Southern California MBA (1960). CORP AFFIL chairman: Pacific Homes Corp.; chairman: US Trust Co.
Gayle Wilson: director ED Stanford University BS. PRIM NONPR EMPL first lady: State of California. NONPR AFFIL trustee: California Institute Technology; trustee: Center Excellence in Education.

Grants Analysis

Disclosure Period: calendar year ending 2001
Total Grants: $16,769,818*
Number of Grants: 202
Average Grant: $73,482*
Highest Grant: $2,000,000
Typical Range: $10,000 to $60,000
*Note: Giving excludes scholarships. Average grant excludes highest grant.

Recent Grants

Note: Grants derived from 2000 Form 990.

General

1,000,000	Huntington Memorial Hospital, Pasadena, CA
1,000,000	Performing Arts Center of Los Angeles County, Los Angeles, CA
750,000	California Institute for Technology, Pasadena, CA
537,771	Keck Graduate Institute of Applied Life Sciences, Claremont, CA
500,000	Harvey Mudd College, Claremont, CA
500,000	Hospitaller Foundation of California, Los Angeles, CA
500,000	Keck Graduate Institute of Applied Life Sciences, Claremont, CA
500,000	Skirball Cultural Center, Los Angeles, CA
350,000	Performing Arts Center of Los Angeles County, Los Angeles, CA
250,000	California Polytechnic State University, San Luis Obispo, CA

ALBERT PARVIN FOUNDATION

Giving Contact

Harvey G. Joffe, Chief Financial Officer & Director
c/o Lewis, Joffee & Co.
10880 Wilshire Boulevard, Suite 520
Los Angeles, CA 90024
Phone: (310)475-5676
Fax: (310)475-5268

Description

Founded: 1960
EIN: 952158989
Organization Type: Private Foundation
Giving Locations: CA
Grant Types: Endowment, General Support.

Donor Information

Founder: Albert O. Parvin

Financial Summary

Total Giving: $381,156 (2001); $298,015 (2000); $323,620 (1999)
Assets: $8,420,821 (2001); $8,243,773 (2000); $7,920,587 (1999)
Gifts Received: $50,000 (1997)

Typical Recipients

Arts & Humanities: Film & Video, Arts & Humanities-General, Libraries, Museums/Galleries, Music, Public Broadcasting, Theater
Civic & Public Affairs: Botanical Gardens/Parks, Clubs, Civic & Public Affairs-General, Housing, Law & Justice, Legal Aid, Parades/Festivals, Philanthropic Organizations, Public Policy, Safety, Urban & Community Affairs, Women's Affairs
Education: Arts/Humanities Education, Colleges & Universities, Education Funds, Minority Education, Science/Mathematics Education, Special Education
Health: AIDS/HIV, Alzheimers Disease, Cancer, Children's Health/Hospitals, Emergency/Ambulance Services, Eyes/Blindness, Geriatric Health, Health Organizations, Heart, Hospices, Hospitals, Long-Term Care, Medical Research, Mental Health, Prenatal Health Issues, Preventive Medicine/Wellness Organizations, Public Health, Research/Studies Institutes
International: Foreign Arts Organizations, Foreign Educational Institutions, International-General, Health Care/Hospitals, International Affairs, International Relief Efforts
Religion: Jewish Causes, Religious Organizations, Religious Welfare, Social/Policy Issues
Science: Science Museums
Social Services: Camps, Child Welfare, Community Service Organizations, Domestic Violence, Family Planning, People with Disabilities, Senior Services, Social Services-General, YMCA/YWCA/YMHA/YWHA, Youth Organizations

Application Procedures

Initial Contact: Send a brief letter of inquiry.
Application Requirements: Include a description of organization and purpose of funds sought.
Deadlines: None.

Foundation Officials

Harvey G. Joffe: cfo, director
Phyllis Parvin: president
Stanley Parvin: director
Mary C. Rudin: director
Bernard Silbert: director
Steven Silbert: director

Grants Analysis

Disclosure Period: calendar year ending 2001
Total Grants: $381,156
Number of Grants: 52
Average Grant: $3,697*
Highest Grant: $90,000
Lowest Grant: $125
Typical Range: $500 to $5,000
*Note: Average grant figure excludes three highest grants ($200,071).

Recent Grants

Note: Grants derived from 2000 Form 990.

Library-Related

1,500	Library Foundation of Los Angeles, Los Angeles, CA

General

90,000	UCLA Kennamer Fund, Los Angeles, CA
50,000	University of Hawaii, Honolulu, HI
40,000	Fund for the Performing Arts, Los Angeles, CA

25,000	University of South Carolina Neighborhood, Columbia, SC
15,375	Haven House
15,300	Jewish Free Loan Association, Los Angeles, CA
15,000	One Voice, Charlotte, NC
6,000	Save a Heart Foundation, Los Angeles, CA
5,000	Berkshire Theater, Stockbridge, MA
5,000	Wellness Community, New York, NY

PATRON SAINTS FOUNDATION

Giving Contact

Jacquie Fennessy, Executive Director
Patron Saints Foundation
PO Box 40706
Pasadena, CA 91104-7706
Phone: (626)797-2303

Description

Founded: 1986
EIN: 953484257
Organization Type: Private Foundation
Giving Locations: CA: West San Gabriel Valley area
Grant Types: Capital, General Support.

Financial Summary

Total Giving: $515,342 (fiscal year ending June 30, 2001); $500,000 (fiscal 2000 approx); $379,396 (fiscal 1999)
Assets: $10,636,378 (fiscal 2001); $11,217,334 (fiscal 1999); $5,072,925 (fiscal 1997)
Gifts Received: $875,000 (fiscal 1998). Note: In fiscal 1998, contributions were received from the Rose Trust.

Typical Recipients

Civic & Public Affairs: Hispanic Affairs
Education: Education Associations, Medical Education, Preschool Education, Special Education
Environment: Resource Conservation
Health: AIDS/HIV, Cancer, Children's Health/Hospitals, Clinics/Medical Centers, Emergency/Ambulance Services, Health Organizations, Heart, Hospitals, Medical Research, Mental Health, Nursing Services, Prenatal Health Issues, Preventive Medicine/Wellness Organizations, Public Health, Trauma Treatment
Religion: Religious Organizations, Religious Welfare, Social/Policy Issues
Social Services: Community Service Organizations, Counseling, Day Care, Domestic Violence, Family Services, Homes, People with Disabilities, Recreation & Athletics, Senior Services, Substance Abuse, YMCA/YWCA/YMHA/YWHA

Application Procedures

Initial Contact: Submit grant application form.
Application Requirements: Include completed application form, proof of tax-exempt status, a recent annual report, a recent audited statement, a list of board members including affiliations, a budget for the current year, a current financial statement, and a list of major sources of support.
Deadlines: March 1 and October 1.

Restrictions

Supports health care programs/projects which are not inconsistent with the moral and religious principles of the Patron Saints Foundation.

Additional Information

Publications: Application Guidelines; Application Form

Foundation Officials

Gretchen Berger: director
Michael J. Costello: director PRIM CORP EMPL executive administration: Santa Teresita Hospital.
J. Benjamin Earl: director
Dr. W. Allan Edmiston: president, director PRIM CORP EMPL physician: Pasadena Cardiovasular Consultants.
Jacquie Fennessy: executive director
Lydia Fernandez-Palmer: director
James W. Graunke: secretary, director PRIM CORP EMPL executive director: Scripps Home.
Margaret Landry: adv PRIM CORP EMPL clinical resource specialist: HF System.
James R. Lee: director
Albert Lowe: director
Dr. Robert Nesbitt: director
Victor Petrone: director
Dorothy B. Shea: president, director
Sally Sims: director PRIM CORP EMPL educator: Covina Valley Unified School District.
Debra J. Spiegel: adv PRIM CORP EMPL financial consultant: Kemper Securities Group.
Melinda Thompson: treasurer, director PRIM CORP EMPL enrolled agent: Melinda Thompson & Associates.
Sharon Thralls: director
Melinda Winston: hon director

Grants Analysis

Disclosure Period: fiscal year ending June 30, 2001
Total Grants: $515,342
Number of Grants: 40
Average Grant: $12,884
Highest Grant: $34,000
Typical Range: $5,000 to $15,000

Recent Grants

Note: Grants derived from fiscal 2001 Form 990.

General

34,000	Santa Teresita Hospital Foundation, Pasadena, CA -- medical equipment
26,000	Scripps Home, Altadena, CA -- hospital beds
25,000	Villa Esperanza, Pasadena, CA -- speech therapy
19,320	Community Health Alliance, Pasadena, CA -- clinic services
18,000	Pasadena Unified School District, Pasadena, CA -- Early Childhood Program
17,455	LaVie Counseling Center, Pasadena, CA -- pregnancy prevention
16,500	Sisters of Social Service, Los Angeles, CA -- psychological counseling
15,000	AIDS Service Center, Pasadena, CA -- Family and Pediatrics Program
15,000	American Cancer Society, Pasadena, CA -- patient transportation
15,000	Descanso Gardens, La Canada, CA -- Horticultural Therapist

PATTEE FOUNDATION

Giving Contact

Gordon B. Patee, President & Director
c/o Dennis Mc Curry
State 700 Krystal Building
Chattanooga, TN 37402-2581
Phone: (423)756-6585

Description

Founded: 1989
EIN: 621376116
Organization Type: Private Foundation

Giving Locations: nationally.
Grant Types: General Support.

Financial Summary

Total Giving: $420,000 (fiscal year ending June 30, 2002); $396,500 (fiscal 2001); $351,500 (fiscal 2000)
Giving Analysis: Giving for fiscal 2002 includes: foundation grants to United Way ($20,000)
Assets: $5,600,487 (fiscal 2002); $7,375,848 (fiscal 2001); $10,742,113 (fiscal 2000)
Gifts Received: $2,252,734 (fiscal 1997); $1,360,625 (fiscal 1995)

Typical Recipients

Arts & Humanities: Ballet, History & Archaeology, Libraries, Museums/Galleries, Music
Civic & Public Affairs: Civic & Public Affairs-General, Professional & Trade Associations
Education: Colleges & Universities, Private Education (Precollege), Science/Mathematics Education, Student Aid
Environment: Wildlife Protection
Health: Clinics/Medical Centers, Medical Research
International: International Environmental Issues
Religion: Churches
Science: Science Museums

Application Procedures

Initial Contact: Send a brief letter of inquiry.
Deadlines: None.

Foundation Officials

Anne L. Pattee: secretary, director
Dorothy E. Pattee: director
Gordon B. Pattee: president, director

Grants Analysis

Disclosure Period: fiscal year ending June 30, 2002
Total Grants: $400,000*
Number of Grants: 16
Average Grant: $10,667*
Highest Grant: $140,000
Lowest Grant: $500
Typical Range: $5,000 to $20,000
***Note:** Giving excludes United Way. Average grant figure excludes two highest grants ($240,000).

Recent Grants

Note: Grants derived from fiscal 2000 Form 990.

Library-Related

10,000	St. Andrew's School, Middletown, DE

General

117,000	World Wildlife Fund, Washington, DC
50,000	Creative Discovery Museum, Chattanooga, TN
40,000	Church of the Good Shepherd, Lookout Mountain, TN
25,000	National Horse Sports Foundation, New York, NY
15,000	New York City Ballet, New York, NY
10,000	Cate School, Carpinteria, CA
10,000	Cate School, Carpinteria, CA
10,000	Creative Discovery Museum, Chattanooga, TN
10,000	Stanford University, Stanford, CA
10,000	Windward School, White Plains, NY

W. I. PATTERSON CHARITABLE FUND

Giving Contact

Robert B. Shust, Trustee
407 Oliver Bldg.
Pittsburgh, PA 15222
Phone: (412)281-5580

Description

Founded: 1955
EIN: 256028639
Organization Type: Private Foundation
Giving Locations: PA: Allegheny County
Grant Types: Capital, Emergency, General Support, Operating Expenses, Research.

Donor Information

Founder: the late W. I. Patterson

Financial Summary

Total Giving: $259,675 (fiscal year ending July 31, 2000); $228,840 (fiscal 1999); $186,944 (fiscal 1998)
Giving Analysis: Giving for fiscal 2000 includes: foundation scholarships ($2,000)
Assets: $4,989,029 (fiscal 2000); $5,116,738 (fiscal 1998); $4,694,647 (fiscal 1997)

Typical Recipients

Arts & Humanities: Arts Associations & Councils, Historic Preservation, Libraries, Music, Opera, Public Broadcasting
Civic & Public Affairs: Economic Policy, Employment/Job Training, Urban & Community Affairs, Zoos/Aquariums
Education: Colleges & Universities, Education Funds, Legal Education, Minority Education, Special Education
Health: Arthritis, Cancer, Children's Health/Hospitals, Diabetes, Emergency/Ambulance Services, Eyes/Blindness, Health Funds, Heart, Hospitals, Kidney, Medical Rehabilitation, Medical Research, Nursing Services, Public Health, Single-Disease Health Associations
International: Health Care/Hospitals
Religion: Ministries, Religious Welfare
Science: Scientific Centers & Institutes
Social Services: Big Brother/Big Sister, Child Abuse, Child Welfare, Community Service Organizations, Emergency Relief, Family Planning, Family Services, Food/Clothing Distribution, Homes, People with Disabilities, Senior Services, Sexual Abuse, Shelters/Homelessness, Special Olympics, Youth Organizations

Application Procedures

Initial Contact: Send brief letter describing program and full proposal.
Application Requirements: Description of organization, purpose of funds sought, proof of tax-exempt status, and list of officers and directors.
Deadlines: June 30.

Restrictions

Does not support individuals.

Foundation Officials

Martin L. Moore, Jr.: trustee
Cynthia K. Rarig: trustee
Robert B. Shust: trustee
Robert B. Wolf: trustee

Grants Analysis

Disclosure Period: fiscal year ending July 31, 2000
Total Grants: $257,675*
Number of Grants: 67
Average Grant: $3,117*
Highest Grant: $51,935
Typical Range: $1,000 to $5,000
***Note:** Giving excludes scholarships. Average grant figure excludes highest grant.

Recent Grants

Note: Grants derived from 2000 Form 990.

Library-Related

51,935	Carnegie Library of Pittsburgh, Pittsburgh, PA -- for public library system

General

7,000	Pittsburgh Symphony Orchestra, Pittsburgh, PA -- for musical support
6,240	Society of the Preservation of the Duquesne Heights Incline, Pittsburgh, PA -- for civic and historical programs
6,000	Goodwill Industries of Pittsburgh, Pittsburgh, PA -- for the humanitarian support
6,000	Pace School, Pittsburgh, PA -- for emotionally and behaviorally disturbed children
5,000	Alzheimer Association, Pittsburgh, PA -- Alzheimer's programs and services for patients and families
5,000	Bradley Center, Pittsburgh, PA -- for children with mental, emotional and developmental disabilities and their families
5,000	Bridge to Independence, Braddock, PA -- for homeless women and their children
5,000	Children's Home of Pittsburgh, Pittsburgh, PA -- for residential and adoption services for children
5,000	Family Resources, Pittsburgh, PA -- to prevent child abuse and for family therapy
5,000	Genesis of Pittsburgh, Inc., Pittsburgh, PA -- for pregnant women, children and adoptive families

HAZEL PATTERSON MEMORIAL TRUST

Giving Contact

William D. Omohundro, Trustee
130 S. Main St.
Buffalo, WY 82834-1846
Phone: (307)684-2207

Description

Founded: 1990
EIN: 742557301
Organization Type: Private Foundation
Giving Locations: WY: Johnson County
Grant Types: General Support.

Donor Information

Founder: Established in 1990 by the late Hazel Patterson.

Financial Summary

Total Giving: $61,501 (fiscal year ending September 30, 2001); $55,009 (fiscal 2000); $59,252 (fiscal 1998)
Assets: $1,244,974 (fiscal 2001); $1,432,667 (fiscal 2000); $1,299,323 (fiscal 1998)

Typical Recipients

Arts & Humanities: Arts & Humanities-General, History & Archaeology, Libraries, Museums/Galleries
Civic & Public Affairs: Clubs, Civic & Public Affairs-General, Public Policy
Education: Agricultural Education, Preschool Education
Environment: Resource Conservation
Health: Emergency/Ambulance Services, Hospitals, Prenatal Health Issues, Preventive Medicine/Wellness Organizations, Research/Studies Institutes
Social Services: Animal Protection, Child Welfare, Community Service Organizations, Domestic Violence, Emergency Relief, Food/Clothing Distribution, Recreation & Athletics, Senior Services, Social Services-General, YMCA/YWCA/YMHA/YWHA, Youth Organizations

Application Procedures

Initial Contact: Request an application from the trust and send a brief letter of inquiry.
Deadlines: Variable deadlines.

Additional Information

Limited to Johnson County, WY.

Foundation Officials

Donald P. Kraen: trustee
William D. Omohundro: trustee
Sandra Todd: trustee

Grants Analysis

Disclosure Period: fiscal year ending September 30, 2001
Total Grants: $61,501
Number of Grants: 20
Average Grant: $3,075
Highest Grant: $9,345
Lowest Grant: $500
Typical Range: $500 to $5,000

Recent Grants

Note: Grants derived from fiscal 2000 Form 990.

General

9,640	Buffalo Children's Center, Buffalo, WY -- for scholarships and equipment
8,430	Johnson County YMCA, Buffalo, WY -- for pool and exercise equipment
8,000	Buffalo Senior Center, Buffalo, WY -- for adult day care meals on wheels
3,500	Hoofprints in the Past, Kaycee, WY -- for blacksmith shop
3,500	Johnson Sheridan Youth Home, Buffalo, WY -- for a copier
3,449	Jim Gatchell Museum, Buffalo, WY -- for security cameras
3,000	Buffalo Skating Association, Buffalo, WY -- for construction
3,000	Northern Wyoming Mental Health, Buffalo, WY -- for shelving and resource materials
2,750	Buffalo Swim Club, Buffalo, WY -- for equipment
2,000	Buffalo Headstart, Buffalo, WY -- for equipment purchases

JOSEPHINE BAY PAUL AND C. MICHAEL PAUL FOUNDATION

Giving Contact

Frederick Bay, Chairman
PO Box 20218
New York, NY 10025
Phone: (212)932-0408

Description

Founded: 1962
EIN: 131991717
Organization Type: Private Foundation
Giving Locations: NY: New York City Nationally, with focus on Northeastern states.
Grant Types: General Support, Multiyear/Continuing Support, Operating Expenses, Project, Seed Money.

Donor Information

Founder: Josephine Bay Paul

Financial Summary

Total Giving: $1,923,078 (2001); $2,966,465 (2000); $1,866,610 (1999)
Giving Analysis: Giving for 2000 includes: foundation grants to United Way ($1,000); foundation gifts to individuals ($150,000) 1999: foundation gifts to individuals ($180,000)
Assets: $50,418,380 (2001); $52,833,438 (2000); $51,645,950 (1999)

Typical Recipients

Arts & Humanities: Arts Associations & Councils, Arts Outreach, Libraries, Music, Performing Arts, Theater
Civic & Public Affairs: Botanical Gardens/Parks, Civic & Public Affairs-General, Public Policy, Rural Affairs
Education: Arts/Humanities Education, Colleges & Universities, Education Reform, Environmental Education, Education-General, Leadership Training, Medical Education, Private Education (Precollege), Public Education (Precollege), School Volunteerism, Secondary Education (Public)
Environment: Research
Science: Science Museums
Social Services: Community Service Organizations, Family Planning

Application Procedures

Initial Contact: Send a brief letter of inquiry requesting guidelines.
Application Requirements: Include a description of organization, proof of tax-exempt status, purpose of funds sought, amount requested, and recently audited financial statement.
Deadlines: March 1, September 1, and December 1.

Restrictions

Grants restricted primarily to arts in education, educational restructuring., environmental education, service learning and united support for chamber music ensembles.

Foundation Officials

Frederick Bay: chairman
Daniel Anthony Demarest: secretary, treasurer B Plainfield, NJ 1924. ED Harvard University BA (1948); Harvard University LLB (1951). NONPR AFFIL member: City Bar Association; member: Phi Beta Kappa. CLUB AFFIL Knickerbocker New York Club.
Hans A. Ege: vice president
Synnova Bay Hayes: president
Corrine Steel: director

Grants Analysis

Disclosure Period: calendar year ending 2001
Total Grants: $1,889,850*
Number of Grants: 141
Average Grant: $11,035*
Highest Grant: $400,000
Typical Range: $5,000 to $30,000
*Note: Giving excludes awards to individuals. Average grant figure excludes largest grant.

Recent Grants

Note: Grants derived from 2001 Form 990.

General

400,000	Marine Biological Laboratory, Woods Hole, MA
132,500	Harmony School Education Center, Bloomington, IN
125,000	Lake Champlain Maritime Museum at Basin Harbor, Inc., Vergennes, VT
100,000	Snelling Center for Government, Burlington, VT
100,000	University of Vermont, Burlington, VT -- John Dewey Project
75,000	Lake Champlain Maritime Museum at Basin Harbor, Inc., Vergennes, VT
50,000	Center for Peace Education, Carrboro, NC
50,000	Community School, S. Tamworth, NH
50,000	Education Commission of the States, Denver, CO
35,000	Citizens' Committee for Children of New York, New York, NY

FRANK E. AND SEBA B. PAYNE FOUNDATION

Giving Contact

M. Catherine Ryan, Vice President, Bank of America
Bank of America
231 South LaSalle Street
Chicago, IL 60697
Phone: (312)828-1785
Fax: (312)828-0806

Description

Founded: 1962
EIN: 237435471
Organization Type: Family Foundation
Giving Locations: IL: Chicago; PA: Bethlehem
Grant Types: Capital, General Support, Operating Expenses, Project.

Donor Information

Founder: The Frank E. and Seba B. Payne Foundation was established in 1962 by Seba B. Payne, the widow of Frank E. Payne.

Financial Summary

Total Giving: $7,000,000 (fiscal year ending June 30, 2003 approx); $7,000,000 (fiscal 2002 approx); $7,576,380 (fiscal 2000)
Giving Analysis: Giving for fiscal 1999 includes: foundation scholarships ($107,020)
Assets: $143,608,102 (fiscal 2000); $159,769,844 (fiscal 1999); $150,000,000 (fiscal 1998 approx)

Typical Recipients

Arts & Humanities: Arts Festivals, Historic Preservation, History & Archaeology, Libraries, Literary Arts, Museums/Galleries, Music, Public Broadcasting, Theater
Civic & Public Affairs: Community Foundations, Economic Development, Civic & Public Affairs-General, Law & Justice, Municipalities/Towns, Urban & Community Affairs
Education: Arts/Humanities Education, Colleges & Universities, Education Associations, Education Funds, Education-General, Literacy, Minority Education, Preschool Education, Private Education (Precollege), Public Education (Precollege), Religious Education, Science/Mathematics Education, Special Education, Student Aid
Environment: Wildlife Protection
Health: AIDS/HIV, Children's Health/Hospitals, Clinics/Medical Centers, Emergency/Ambulance Services, Emergency/Ambulance Services, Eyes/Blindness, Hospitals, Nursing Services, Public Health, Single-Disease Health Associations, Speech & Hearing, Transplant Networks/Donor Banks
Religion: Churches, Dioceses, Ministries, Religious Organizations, Religious Welfare
Social Services: Animal Protection, Big Brother/Big Sister, Child Welfare, Community Service Organizations, Crime Prevention, Day Care, Delinquency & Criminal Rehabilitation, Domestic Violence, Family Planning, Food/Clothing Distribution, Homes, People with Disabilities, Scouts, Senior Services, Shelters/Homelessness, Social Services-General, Substance Abuse, United Funds/United Ways, Volunteer Services, YMCA/YWCA/YMHA/YWHA, Youth Organizations, Youth Organizations

Application Procedures

Initial Contact: Requests should be submitted in writing.
Application Requirements: Requests should include the name, address, and a brief history of the organization; a list of its officers and directors; purpose for which funds are requested; evidence of need for the proposed project; most recent financial statements, including sources of funds and information on fund-raising activities and costs; estimate of time and funds required to complete project; and proof of tax-exempt status.
Deadlines: None.
Review Process: The foundation's board generally meets in the spring and fall.

Restrictions

Grants are not made to individuals. Giving is generally limited to the Bethlehem, PA area.

Additional Information

Bank of America serves as a corporate trustee for the foundation.
Publications: Instructions to Applicants

Foundation Officials

Susan Hurd Cummings: trustee

Grants Analysis

Disclosure Period: fiscal year ending June 30, 2000
Total Grants: $7,576,380*
Number of Grants: 44
Average Grant: $38,486*
Highest Grant: $3,183,000
Lowest Grant: $5,000
Typical Range: $10,000 to $50,000
*Note: Giving excludes scholarships. Average grant figure excludes three highest grants ($3,183,000, $2,200,000, and $500,000).

Recent Grants

Note: Grants derived from fiscal 2001 Form 990.

Library-Related
92,000	Bethlehem Area Public Library, Bethlehem, PA
50,000	Southern Lehigh Public Library, Coopersburg, PA
5,000	Hellertown Area Library, Hellertown, PA

General
3,183,000	Morvian College, Bethlehem, PA
2,200,000	St. Luke's Hospital, Bethlehem, PA
500,000	DeSales University, Center Valley, PA
250,000	Lehigh Valley Public Broadcasting System, Bethlehem, PA
120,000	Riegelsville-Palisades Emergency Medical, Riegelsville, PA
100,000	Associated Colleges of Illinois, Chicago, IL
76,000	Visiting Nurse Association of Eastern Pennsylvania, Bethlehem, PA
75,000	New Bethany Ministries, Bethlehem, PA
50,000	Allentown Art Museum of Lehigh Valley, Bethlehem, PA
50,000	American Red Cross Lehigh Valley Chapter, Bethlehem, PA

AMELIA PEABODY CHARITABLE FUND

Giving Contact

Margaret N. St. Clair, Trustee
1 Hollis Street
Wellesley, MA 02482-4631
Phone: (781)237-6468
Web: http://www.ameliapeabody.org

Description

Founded: 1942
EIN: 237364949
Organization Type: General Purpose Foundation
Giving Locations: MA: Boston metropolitan area New England.
Grant Types: Capital, Challenge, Endowment, Matching, Project, Research, Scholarship.

Donor Information

Founder: The Amelia Peabody Charitable Fund was established in Massachusetts. In 1985, the fund absorbed a share of the assets of the Eaton Foundation, also based in Massachusetts.

Financial Summary

Total Giving: $7,000,000 (2003 approx); $7,000,000 (2002 approx); $9,504,600 (2001)
Assets: $176,000,000 (2002 approx); $183,155,805 (2000); $199,135,760 (1998)
Gifts Received: $80,000 (2002 approx); $155,000 (1998); $560,000 (1995)

Typical Recipients

Arts & Humanities: Art History, Arts Centers, Ballet, Arts & Humanities-General, Historic Preservation, History & Archaeology, Libraries, Museums/Galleries, Music, Opera, Performing Arts, Public Broadcasting, Theater
Civic & Public Affairs: Asian American Affairs, Botanical Gardens/Parks, Clubs, Economic Development, Employment/Job Training, Civic & Public Affairs-General, Hispanic Affairs, Housing, Philanthropic Organizations, Professional & Trade Associations, Public Policy, Urban & Community Affairs, Women's Affairs, Zoos/Aquariums
Education: Afterschool/Enrichment Programs, Arts/Humanities Education, Colleges & Universities, Education Associations, Education Reform, Engineering/Technological Education, Faculty Development, Education-General, International Studies, Leadership Training, Legal Education, Medical Education, Minority Education, Private Education (Precollege), Public Education (Precollege), Religious Education, Science/Mathematics Education, Secondary Education (Private), Special Education, Student Aid, Vocational & Technical Education
Environment: Environment-General, Resource Conservation, Wildlife Protection
Health: Alzheimers Disease, Arthritis, Cancer, Children's Health/Hospitals, Clinics/Medical Centers, Diabetes, Emergency/Ambulance Services, Eyes/Blindness, Health-General, Geriatric Health, Health Organizations, Heart, Home-Care Services, Hospitals, Long-Term Care, Medical Research, Medical Training, Nursing Services, Prenatal Health Issues, Public Health, Single-Disease Health Associations, Speech & Hearing
International: Health Care/Hospitals
Religion: Churches, Jewish Causes, Religious Welfare, Social/Policy Issues
Science: Science Museums, Scientific Centers & Institutes, Scientific Labs
Social Services: Animal Protection, At-Risk Youth, Camps, Child Welfare, Community Centers, Community Service Organizations, Day Care, Family Planning, Family Services, Homes, People with Disabilities, Recreation & Athletics, Scouts, Senior Services, Shelters/Homelessness, Substance Abuse, Volunteer Services, YMCA/YWCA/YMHA/YWHA, Youth Organizations

Application Procedures

Initial Contact: Applicants should request guidelines from the foundation.
Application Requirements: Proposals should be made by letter. The letter should explain the nature of the nonprofit operation, and must include a copy of the IRS exemption letter. Include figures indicating the amount of the budget spent on overhead and the amount for programs, financial statements for the last fiscal year, a copy of the applicant's most recent 990, and a list of directors/trustees. Also, proposals should identify applications pending with other foundations and any commitments confirmed.
Deadlines: None. Proposals for summer program funding must be submitted by the February deadline.

Restrictions

Grants are not made to organizations funded principally with tax dollars. Further, the trustees do not fund operating budgets or start-up funds, and funds for salaries are never considered. No funds are granted to religious organizations, nonprofits outside the United States, political action groups, to other grant-making organizations, or to any annual appeal. Grants are not made to individuals. The fund does not give to any state or municipal agency (including any public school, university, or public property) or for the purpose of producing any type of film, theatrical production, publication, exhibit, or conference. The fund does not make loans or give multiyear commitments.

Additional Information

The foundation reports that most of its grants are for capital expenses. The foundation does not fund specific areas of interest; rather, decisions are based primarily on the quality and need of a proposal.
Publications: Guidelines

Foundation Officials

JoAnne Borek: executive director, trustee
Richard Leahy: trustee
William A. Lowell: trustee PRIM CORP EMPL vice president: Bath Iron Works Corp. CORP AFFIL vice president: Portland Ship Repair.
J. Elisabeth Rice: trustee
Patricia E. Rice: trustee

Grants Analysis

Disclosure Period: calendar year ending 2000
Total Grants: $8,675,001
Number of Grants: 94
Average Grant: $92,287
Highest Grant: $668,000
Typical Range: $5,000 to $25,000 and $100,000 to $500,000

Recent Grants

Note: Grants derived from 2000 Form 990.

General

500,000	Massachusetts General Hospital, Charlestown, MA -- robotic drug screening facility
327,000	Massachusetts Eye and Ear Infirmary, Boston, MA -- equipment for molecular biology unit
325,000	Morgan Memorial Goodwill Industries, Boston, MA -- technology
250,000	Appalachian Mountain Club, Boston, MA -- construction environmental center
250,000	Boston College, Chestnut Hill, MA -- renovations and reconstruction
250,000	Boston Medical Center, Boston, MA -- renovations
250,000	Schepens Eye Research Institute, Boston, MA -- construction new laboratories
245,000	Jackson Laboratory, Rockland, ME -- monitoring equipment
200,000	American International College, Springfield, MA -- construction project
200,000	Wellesley College, Wellesley, MA -- renovations construction

AMELIA PEABODY FOUNDATION

Giving Contact

Margaret N. St. Clair, Co-Managing Trustee
One Hollis Street, Suite 215
Wellesley, MA 02482
Phone: (781)237-6468
Fax: (781)237-5014
E-mail: jsmith@ameliapeabody.org
Web: http://www.ameliapeabody.org

Description

Founded: 1985
EIN: 046036558
Organization Type: General Purpose Foundation
Giving Locations: MA
Grant Types: Capital, Challenge, General Support, Matching, Multiyear/Continuing Support, Operating Expenses, Seed Money.

Donor Information

Founder: Established in 1985 by the late Amelia Peabody .

Financial Summary

Total Giving: $7,847,790 (2001); $8,675,001 (2000); $8,134,500 (1999)
Assets: $173,027,835 (2001); $183,155,805 (2000); $193,505,590 (1999)
Gifts Received: $9,776 (1992)

Typical Recipients

Arts & Humanities: Ethnic & Folk Arts, Film & Video, Libraries, Museums/Galleries, Opera, Performing Arts
Civic & Public Affairs: African American Affairs, Botanical Gardens/Parks, Clubs, Community Foundations, Economic Development, Employment/Job Training, Civic & Public Affairs-General, Hispanic Affairs, Housing, Law & Justice, Legal Aid, Municipalities/Towns, Public Policy, Urban & Community Affairs, Women's Affairs
Education: Afterschool/Enrichment Programs, Agricultural Education, Colleges & Universities, Continuing Education, Education Associations, Education Reform, Elementary Education (Private), Education-General, Leadership Training, Medical Education, Preschool Education, Private Education (Precollege), Public Education (Precollege), Public Education (Precollege), Secondary Education (Private), Special Education, Student Aid
Environment: Environment-General
Health: Clinics/Medical Centers, Diabetes, Emergency/Ambulance Services, Health Organizations, Hospitals, Medical Research, Public Health, Single-Disease Health Associations
International: Health Care/Hospitals
Religion: Ministries, Religious Organizations, Religious Welfare
Science: Science Museums
Social Services: At-Risk Youth, Big Brother/Big Sister, Camps, Child Welfare, Community Centers, Community Service Organizations, Day Care, Family Services, Food/Clothing Distribution, Homes, People with Disabilities, Recreation & Athletics, Shelters/Homelessness, Social Services-General, Substance Abuse, United Funds/United Ways, YMCA/YWCA/YMHA/YWHA, Youth Organizations

Application Procedures

Initial Contact: The foundation requests that an applicant's first contact with the foundation be a completed Grant Proposal Form, available on the foundation's web site. Calls may be made to the foundation's office with procedural questions about the application process itself, but foundation staff does not provide preliminary advice on the appropriateness of proposals.
Application Requirements: Proposals must include seven copies of the completed Grant Proposal Form, a cover summary, organization profile, proposal narrative, board-approved organization budget, project budget, and a listing of funding sources. One copy of the following attachments is also required: proof of tax-exempt status (or, if a fiscal agent is used, a copy of their 501(c)(3) along with a statement from them accepting fiscal responsibility); a current listing of board members including town residences, positions held, and other affiliations; a listing of key staff people, including relevant background information; year-to-date financial statement; and recently audited financial statement, or if none is available, most recent tax

filing. These materials should be submitted in hard copy to the foundation's office, and a single e-mail copy of the following components should be sent to jsmith@ameliapeabody.org: cover summary, organization profile, proposal narrative, organization budget, and project budget.
Deadlines: January 30; May 1; August 14; and November 6. Verify current deadlines, as they may vary slightly from year to year.

Restrictions

The foundation does not make grants to support projects outside the state of Massachusetts. Grants are generally not made to individuals or for endowment funds, scholarships, fellowships, loans, performances, film making, conferences, professorships, research, or program-related investments.

Additional Information

Publications: Guidelines Letter

Foundation Officials

Margaret N. St. Clair: co-managing trustee
Bayard D. Waring: co-managing trustee
Philip B. Waring: vice president grant making

Grants Analysis

Disclosure Period: calendar year ending 2001
Total Grants: $7,847,790
Number of Grants: 116
Average Grant: $67,654
Highest Grant: $750,000
Typical Range: $10,000 to $200,000

Recent Grants

Note: Grants derived from 2001 Form 990.

General

750,000	Metro Lacrosse, Boston, MA -- new initiative
750,000	YMCA, Boston, MA -- building new Malden YMCA
600,000	Boston Bar Foundation, Boston, MA -- James D. St. Clair Court Education Project
400,000	Paige Company, Inc/Paige Academy, Roxbury, MA -- renovations at Paige Academy
203,000	Project Adventure, Inc., Atlanta, GA -- Lawrence Youth Program
200,000	Friends of Lynn Community Charter Schools, Inc. -- expansion of school facility and program
170,000	Adelante, Inc, Lawrence, MA -- School Success Program
150,000	Boys and Girls Club of Boston, Boston, MA -- capital campaign
150,000	Citizens School, Boston, MA -- technology initiative
150,000	Old Colony Y, Brockton, MA -- capital campaign

PELL FAMILY FOUNDATION

Giving Contact

Eda Pell, President
100 Smith Ranch Rd., No. 325
San Rafael, CA 94903-1900
Phone: (415)491-0901
Fax: (415)491-1431

Description

Founded: 1991
EIN: 680262734
Organization Type: Private Foundation
Giving Locations: CA
Grant Types: General Support.

Donor Information

Founder: Established in 1991 by Joseph and Eda Pell.

Financial Summary

Total Giving: $489,785 (fiscal year ending September 30, 2001); $331,615 (fiscal 2000); $276,050 (fiscal 1999)

Giving Analysis: Giving for fiscal 2000 includes: foundation grants to United Way ($1,500); fiscal 1999: foundation grants to United Way ($1,000); fiscal 1998: foundation grants to United Way ($1,000) foundation ($327,392)

Assets: $5,466,414 (fiscal 2001); $5,591,063 (fiscal 2000); $4,296,549 (fiscal 1999)

Gifts Received: $1,000,600 (fiscal 2001); $1,000,000 (fiscal 2000); $1,000,000 (fiscal 1999). Note: Contributions were received from Joseph and Eda Pell.

Typical Recipients

Arts & Humanities: Ballet, Film & Video, Libraries, Museums/Galleries, Music

Civic & Public Affairs: Women's Affairs

Education: Arts/Humanities Education, Colleges & Universities, Community & Junior Colleges, Education Associations, Preschool Education, Private Education (Precollege), Religious Education, School Volunteerism

Health: Cancer, Emergency/Ambulance Services, Hospitals, Medical Research

International: Foreign Educational Institutions, Missionary/Religious Activities

Religion: Jewish Causes, Missionary Activities (Domestic), Synagogues/Temples

Social Services: Child Welfare, Community Centers, Community Service Organizations, Emergency Relief, Family Services, Food/Clothing Distribution, Senior Services, Social Services-General, Substance Abuse, United Funds/United Ways

Application Procedures

Initial Contact: Send a brief letter of inquiry on organization's letterhead.

Deadlines: None.

Foundation Officials

Eda Pell: president

Joseph Pell: chief executive officer

Grants Analysis

Disclosure Period: fiscal year ending September 30, 2001

Total Grants: $489,785

Number of Grants: 46

Average Grant: $3,177*

Highest Grant: $250,000

Lowest Grant: $140

Typical Range: $1,000 to $5,000

***Note:** Average grant figure excludes two highest grants ($350,000).

Recent Grants

Note: Grants derived from fiscal 2000 Form 990.

General

150,000	University of California Berkeley Foundation, Berkeley, CA -- educational needs
50,000	Jewish Community Federation -- community needs
27,500	Lehrhaus Judaica, Berkeley, CA -- community needs
25,000	Jewish Community Center -- community needs
11,000	Marin General Hospital, Marin City, CA -- community/medical needs
8,500	Jewish Scott Senior Housing -- community needs
5,000	Hebrew Union College -- educational needs
5,000	Integrated Community Services, San Rafael, CA -- community needs
5,000	Israel Policy Forum, New York, NY -- community needs
5,000	Jewish Home for the Aged -- community needs

PELLA CORP.

Company Headquarters

Pella, IA

Web: http://www.pella.com

Company Description

Revenue: US$922 million (2002)

Employees: 6945 (2002)

SIC(s): 2431 Millwork, 3231 Products of Purchased Glass.

Operating Locations

Pella Corp. (IA--Pella)

Pella Rolscreen Foundation

Giving Contact

Mary Van Zante, Secretary
Pella Rolscreen Foundation
102 Main Street
Pella, IA 50219
Phone: (641)621-6224
E-mail: mavzante@pella.com

Description

EIN: 237043881

Organization Type: Corporate Foundation

Giving Locations: IA: central and western Iowa

Grant Types: Capital, Conference/Seminar, Employee Matching Gifts, Endowment, General Support.

Note: Employee matching gift ratio: 1 to 1.

Financial Summary

Total Giving: $1,978,350 (2001); $3,258,639 (2000); $2,128,061 (1999). Note: Contributes through corporate direct giving program and foundation.

Giving Analysis: Giving for 2001 includes: foundation scholarships (approx $47,000); foundation ($3,286,129); 2000: foundation grants to United Way ($24,000); foundation matching gifts ($442,769); foundation ($2,744,870); 1999: foundation scholarships ($135,868); foundation matching gifts ($467,674); foundation ($1,524,519).

Assets: $14,067,517 (2001); $15,147,044 (2000); $16,094,665 (1999)

Gifts Received: $1,046,104 (2001); $1,200,000 (2000); $1,702,475 (1999). Note: Contributions received from Pella Corp.

Typical Recipients

Arts & Humanities: Arts Associations & Councils, Arts Centers, Historic Preservation, History & Archaeology, Libraries, Literary Arts, Museums/Galleries, Music, Opera, Performing Arts, Public Broadcasting, Theater, Visual Arts

Civic & Public Affairs: Botanical Gardens/Parks, Business/Free Enterprise, Chambers of Commerce, Clubs, Economic Development, Civic & Public Affairs-General, Housing, Municipalities/Towns, Parades/Festivals, Philanthropic Organizations, Professional & Trade Associations, Safety, Urban & Community Affairs, Zoos/Aquariums

Education: Arts/Humanities Education, Business Education, Colleges & Universities, Community & Junior Colleges, Education Funds, Education Reform, Elementary Education (Private), Engineering/Technological Education, Faculty Development, Education-General, Preschool Education, Private Education (Precollege), Public Education (Precollege), Science/Mathematics Education, Secondary Education (Private), Secondary Education (Public), Special Education, Student Aid, Vocational & Technical Education

Environment: Forestry, Environment-General

Health: AIDS/HIV, Cancer, Clinics/Medical Centers, Emergency/Ambulance Services, Health Policy/Cost Containment, Hospices, Hospitals, Outpatient Health Care, Transplant Networks/Donor Banks

Religion: Churches, Ministries, Religious Organizations, Religious Welfare

Science: Scientific Centers & Institutes

Social Services: Camps, Child Abuse, Child Welfare, Community Centers, Community Service Organizations, Crime Prevention, Day Care, Family Services, Food/Clothing Distribution, People with Disabilities, Recreation & Athletics, Scouts, Senior Services, Social Services-General, Substance Abuse, United Funds/United Ways, Volunteer Services, YMCA/YWCA/YMHA/YWHA, Youth Organizations

Application Procedures

Initial Contact: Submit a full proposal.

Application Requirements: Include a description of organization, statement of need, amount requested, purpose of funds sought, project budget, recently audited financial statement, and proof of tax-exempt status.

Deadlines: None; board meets quarterly.

Restrictions

Grants are not made to individuals, except to children of employees under scholarship program. Product donations are not made.

Corporate Officials

Gary M. Christensen: president, chief executive officer B 1943. PRIM CORP EMPL president, chief executive officer: Pella Corp. CORP AFFIL director: Butler Manufacturing Co.

Charles Farver: chairman PRIM CORP EMPL chairman: Pella Corp.

Joan Kuyper Farver: chairman emeritus, director B 1919. ED Grinnell College BA (1941). PRIM CORP EMPL chairman emeritus, director: Pella Corp.

Foundation Officials

Gary M. Christensen: president, director (see above)

Charles Farver: treasurer, director (see above)

Joan Kuyper Farver: director (see above)

Mary Van Zante: secretary

Grants Analysis

Disclosure Period: calendar year ending 2001

Total Grants: $1,416,269*

Number of Grants: 279

Average Grant: $3,656*

Highest Grant: $400,000

Lowest Grant: $100

Typical Range: $500 to $20,000

***Note:** Giving excludes matching gifts; scholarship; gifts to individuals; United Way. Average grant figure excludes highest grant.

Recent Grants

Note: Grants derived from 2001 Form 990.

General

400,000	Community Betterment Foundation, Asheville, NC
217,088	Central College, Pella, IA
125,565	Third Reformed Church, Pella, IA
82,120	Pella Historical Society, Pella, IA
33,619	Covenant Reformed Church, Pella, IA
30,000	Opera House, San Francisco, CA
22,372	Jubilee Family Church, Oskaloosa, IA
21,925	Northwestern College, Orange City, IA
20,500	Iowa College Foundation, Des Moines, IA
20,344	American Fund for Afghan Children, Washington, DC

H.E. AND RUBY PELZ TRUST

Giving Contact
William A. Abney, Co-Trustee
PO Box 1386
Marshall, TX 75671-1386
Phone: (903)938-6611

Description
Founded: 1992
EIN: 746392477
Organization Type: Private Foundation
Former Name: Ruby Pelz Foundation (2002).
Giving Locations: TX
Grant Types: General Support, Operating Expenses.

Financial Summary
Total Giving: $54,378 (2001); $52,295 (2000); $46,463 (1999)
Giving Analysis: Giving for 2001 includes: foundation gifts to individuals ($518); 2000: foundation gifts to individuals ($6,495) 1999: foundation gifts to individuals ($4,393)
Assets: $1,197,379 (2001); $1,177,087 (2000); $1,154,859 (1999)

Typical Recipients
Arts & Humanities: Arts Associations & Councils, Historic Preservation, Libraries, Museums/Galleries, Music
Civic & Public Affairs: African American Affairs, Civic & Public Affairs-General
Education: Colleges & Universities, Literacy, Private Education (Precollege), Secondary Education (Public), Student Aid
Health: Clinics/Medical Centers, Emergency/Ambulance Services, Health-General, Health Organizations, Hospices
International: International Organizations
Religion: Religion-General, Religious Welfare
Social Services: Child Welfare, Community Service Organizations, Crime Prevention, Scouts, Youth Organizations

Application Procedures
Initial Contact: Send a brief letter of inquiry.
Deadlines: None.

Additional Information
Trust(s): Bank One NA

Foundation Officials
Cary M. Abney: secretary
Ruben K. Abney: co-trustee
William A. Abney: co-trustee
Martha Key: co-trustee

Grants Analysis
Disclosure Period: calendar year ending 2001
Total Grants: $53,860*
Number of Grants: 26
Average Grant: $2,071
Highest Grant: $5,000
Typical Range: $500 to $5,000
*Note: Giving excludes grants to individuals.

Recent Grants
Note: Grants derived from 2001 Form 990.

Library-Related
500	Marshall Public Library, Marshall, TX -- operations

General
7,270	Drug Shop, The, Marshall, TX -- medical
5,000	Hospice of East Texas, Tyler, TX -- operations
5,000	Michelson Museum of Art, Marshall, TX -- operations
5,000	Society of St. Stephen, Marshall, TX -- operations
5,000	Trinity Day School, Marshall, TX -- operations
3,000	Marshall Symphony Society, Marshall, TX -- operations
2,500	Boys and Girls Club of Harrison County, Marshall, TX -- operations
2,500	Courthouse Centennial Campaign, Marshall, TX -- operations
2,500	Empty Stocking Fund, Marshall, TX -- operations
2,500	Harrison County Foster Children, Marshall, TX -- operations

WILLIAM PENN FOUNDATION

Giving Contact
Kathryn J. Engebretson, President
2 Logan Sq., 11th Fl.
100 N 18th St.
Philadelphia, PA 19103-2757
Phone: (215)988-1830
Fax: (215)988-1823
E-mail: moreinfo@williampennfoundation.org
Web: http://www.wpennfdn.org/

Alternate Contact
Barbara Scace, Manager, Grants Management

Description
Founded: 1945
EIN: 231503488
Organization Type: General Purpose Foundation
Giving Locations: PA: Philadelphia including Bucks, Camden, Chester, Delaware, Montgomery, and Philadelphia counties
Grant Types: Capital, Challenge, General Support, Loan, Matching, Multiyear/Continuing Support, Operating Expenses, Project.

Donor Information
Founder: The William Penn Foundation was established in 1945 by Otto Haas (1872-1960) and his wife, Phoebe. Mr. Haas immigrated to the United States from Germany at the turn of the century. He helped develop and market an innovative leather tanning process which proved to be highly popular in the United States and later in South America. He built a career based on his expertise in industrial chemicals. His wife, Phoebe Waterman Haas , was born in North Dakota, educated at Vassar, and was an astronomer. In 1945, Otto and Phoebe Haas established the Phoebe Waterman Foundation. Reflecting the founders' postwar concerns, grants were used to fund European relief, provide scholarships for fatherless children, and support medical and educational institutions. When Otto Haas died in 1960, the foundation received the bulk of his estate. Mrs. Haas continued adding funds to the foundation until her death in 1967. In 1970, the name of the foundation was changed to the Haas Community Foundation. In 1974, it was renamed the William Penn Foundation, reflecting its close ties to Philadelphia.

Financial Summary
Total Giving: $63,726,388 (2002 approx); $65,181,777 (2001); $1,106,800 (1998). Note: 1998 Giving includes two special Fiftieth Anniversary Grants totaling $7,639,747.
Giving Analysis: Giving for 2001 includes: foundation matching gifts ($988,745); foundation grants to United Way ($4,692,454); 1998: foundation matching gifts ($959,934) foundation grants to United Way ($3,604,109)
Assets: $904,488,083 (2002); $1,047,720,982 (2001); $1,170,193,129 (2000)
Gifts Received: $19,147,000 (1998); $17,517,315 (1997); $16,341,893 (1996). Note: In 1998, contributions were received from Otto Haas Charitable Trusts.

Typical Recipients
Arts & Humanities: Arts Associations & Councils, Arts Centers, Arts Festivals, Arts Funds, Arts Institutes, Arts Outreach, Ballet, Community Arts, Dance, Ethnic & Folk Arts, Historic Preservation, History & Archaeology, Libraries, Literary Arts, Museums/Galleries, Music, Opera, Performing Arts, Public Broadcasting, Theater, Visual Arts
Civic & Public Affairs: Botanical Gardens/Parks, Civil Rights, Clubs, Community Foundations, Economic Development, Economic Policy, Employment/Job Training, First Amendment Issues, Civic & Public Affairs-General, Hispanic Affairs, Housing, Professional & Trade Associations, Public Policy, Urban & Community Affairs, Women's Affairs, Zoos/Aquariums
Education: Afterschool/Enrichment Programs, Arts/Humanities Education, Business-School Partnerships, Colleges & Universities, Community & Junior Colleges, Economic Education, Education Funds, Elementary Education (Private), Engineering/Technological Education, Environmental Education, Faculty Development, Legal Education, Literacy, Medical Education, Minority Education, Preschool Education, Public Education (Precollege), School Volunteerism, Science/Mathematics Education, Secondary Education (Public), Social Sciences Education
Environment: Air/Water Quality, Environment-General, Resource Conservation, Watershed, Wildlife Protection
Health: Children's Health/Hospitals, Clinics/Medical Centers, Emergency/Ambulance Services, Geriatric Health, Health Organizations, Nursing Services, Prenatal Health Issues, Public Health
Religion: Religious Organizations, Religious Welfare
Science: Science Museums, Scientific Labs
Social Services: At-Risk Youth, Child Abuse, Child Welfare, Community Centers, Community Service Organizations, Counseling, Crime Prevention, Day Care, Delinquency & Criminal Rehabilitation, Domestic Violence, Family Planning, Family Services, Homes, Recreation & Athletics, Senior Services, Shelters/Homelessness, Social Services-General, United Funds/United Ways, Volunteer Services, YMCA/YWCA/YMHA/YWHA, Youth Organizations

Application Procedures
Initial Contact: Visit foundation website, email moreinfo@wpennfoundation.org, or call to request application guidelines or register for an Information Session (held every few weeks for grantseekers).
Deadlines: None.
Review Process: All proposals are initially reviewed to determine whether they fall within the foundation's geographic areas of interest and current funding priorities. Those meeting these criteria are then subject to further study and investigation. Those not meeting the criteria receive prompt notification. If additional information is required during the further review, which may take several months, applicants will be contacted by a staff member. Applicants receive written notice of a decision within a week after it is made.
Notes: The foundation prefers that proposals not be elaborate or expensively packaged.

Restrictions
Only written requests are accepted. Grants are made only to IRS 501(c)(3) organizations located in the five-county southeast Pennsylvania area and Camden County, New Jersey. Grants are not made to institutions that discriminate on the basis of race, creed, gender, or sexual orientation; scholarships, fellowships, or grants to individuals; debt reduction; sectarian religious activities, political lobbying, or legislative

activities; hospital capital projects; profit-making enterprises; non-public schools or charter schools; programs to treat or rehabilitate those with specific physical, medical, or psychological conditions or diagnoses; programs targeted for the elderly; medical research; direct replacement of discontinued government support; private foundations; or national or international programs.

Additional Information

Foundation holds regular information sessions at its offices.

Publications: Annual Report; Grantmaking Priorities and Guidelines

Foundation Officials

Carolyn T. Adams: director
Carol R. Collier: director
C. Richard Cox: vice president programs
Joanne R. Denworth: director
Joseph A. Dworetzky: director
Kathryn J. Engebretson: director
Louise M. Foster: chief financial officer ED Saint Joseph's University BA.
David W. Haas: vice chairman, secretary CORP AFFIL director: Rohm and Haas Co.
Duncan Haas: director
Frederick R. Haas: director
Janet F. Haas: president, director B 1952. PRIM NONPR EMPL physician: Moss Rehabilitation Hospital. NONPR AFFIL assistant clinical professor: Temple University School Medicine.
John O. Haas: director
Leonard C. Haas: director
Nancy B. Haas: director
Thomas W. Haas: director
William D. Haas: director
Robert E. Hanrahan, Jr.: director
Ernest E. Jones: director
Thomas M. McKenna: director
John P. Mulroney: director
Robert E. Naylor: director B Nashville, AR 1932. ED University of North Carolina (1951); Harvard University (1956). PRIM CORP EMPL group vice president, director: Rohm & Haas Co. CORP AFFIL director: Airgas Inc.
John Nyheim: director NONPR AFFIL vice chairman, director: Philadelphia Museum Art; vice chairman, director: Rodin Museum; vice chairman, director: Museum Shop.
Rush L. Russell: vice president programs
Judge Anthony J. Scirica: director
Gary Walker: director
James S. White: director
Lise Yasui: director

Grants Analysis

Disclosure Period: calendar year ending 2002
Total Grants: $63,726,388*
Number of Grants: 223
Average Grant: $285,769
Highest Grant: $4,000,000
Lowest Grant: $3,000
Typical Range: $50,000 to $500,000
*Note: Giving excludes matching gifts.

Recent Grants

Note: Grants derived from 2001 Form 990.

Library-Related
329,950   Athenaeum of Philadelphia, Philadelphia, PA -- toward the Philadelphia architects and buildings project

General
4,090,000   Fairmont Park Commission, Philadelphia, PA -- toward the restoration of seven watershed parks
2,428,851   United Way Southeastern Pennsylvania, Philadelphia, PA -- extension of foundation's Child Care Matters Initiative
1,295,603   United Way Southeastern Pennsylvania,

Philadelphia, PA -- Center for Youth Development
1,100,000   Eastern National Park and Monument Association -- development and construction of Independence Park Institute
1,100,000   Nature Conservancy, Inc. (New Jersey Field Office), Chester, NJ -- acquisition and management of threatened natural areas
1,015,000   Pennsylvania Economy League, Pittsburgh, PA -- toward a joint effort with the Reinvesting Fund
962,500   Pennsylvania Horticultural Society, Philadelphia, PA -- Philadelphia Green Program
850,000   Philadelphia Foundation, Philadelphia, PA -- enrich Summer Camp Programs
660,000   United Way Southeastern Pennsylvania, Philadelphia, PA -- toward Philadelphia neighborhood development collaborative
605,000   United Way Southeastern Pennsylvania, Philadelphia, PA -- operating support

WILLIAM N. AND MYRIAM PENNINGTON FOUNDATION

Giving Contact

Kent Green, Controller
William N. and Myriam Pennington Foundation
441 W. Plumb Lane
Reno, NV 89509
Phone: (775)333-9100

Description

Founded: 1989
EIN: 943096845
Organization Type: Private Foundation
Giving Locations: NV
Grant Types: Capital, General Support, Scholarship.

Donor Information

Founder: William N. Pennington

Financial Summary

Total Giving: $583,850 (2001); $575,035 (2000); $509,800 (1999)
Giving Analysis: Giving for 2001 includes: foundation scholarships ($43,000); 1999: foundation scholarships ($20,000) 1998: foundation scholarships ($15,000)
Assets: $11,382,755 (2001); $12,152,844 (2000); $11,474,113 (1999)
Gifts Received: $631,250 (2000); $2,000,000 (1998); $3,475,000 (1996). Note: In 1998 and 2000, contributions were received from William N. Pennington.

Typical Recipients

Arts & Humanities: Public Broadcasting
Civic & Public Affairs: Civic & Public Affairs-General, Parades/Festivals
Education: Colleges & Universities, Education-General, Medical Education, Public Education (Precollege), Special Education, Student Aid
Health: Cancer, Emergency/Ambulance Services, Health-General, Health Organizations, Respiratory, Speech & Hearing
Social Services: Community Service Organizations, Family Services, People with Disabilities, Recreation & Athletics, Scouts, Senior Services, YMCA/YWCA/YMHA/YWHA

Application Procedures

Initial Contact: Send a narrative of the project or program.
Application Requirements: Include a description of organization, purpose of funds sought, recently

audited financial statement, proof of tax-exempt status, and most recent Form 990.
Deadlines: None.
Review Process: Applications are reviewed only twice each year.

Restrictions

Grants are restricted to education, health, and medical research.

Foundation Officials

Richard P. Banis: treasurer
Donald L. Carano: trustee
John Mackell: trustee
Myriam Pennington: trustee
William N. Pennington: chairman B 1923. CORP AFFIL director: Circus Circus Enterprises.

Grants Analysis

Disclosure Period: calendar year ending 2001
Total Grants: $540,850*
Number of Grants: 25
Average Grant: $12,341*
Highest Grant: $200,000
Lowest Grant: $1,000
Typical Range: $3,000 to $40,000
*Note: Giving excludes scholarships. Average grant figure excludes two highest grants ($300,000).

Recent Grants

Note: Grants derived from 2001 Form 990.

General
200,000   University of Nevada Reno School of Medicine, Reno, NV -- for medical library and educational building
100,000   Rochester General Hospital Foundation, Rochester, NY -- for neurosurgical center
40,000   University of Nevada Reno Foundation, Reno, NV -- for scholarships
30,000   CAP, Reno, NV -- for New York Disaster Relief
25,000   American Academy of Achievement, Malibu, CA
25,000   Assistance League of Reno-Sparks, Reno, NV -- for operation school bell and senior food pantry
20,000   Boys and Girls Club of the Truckee, Reno, NV -- for After School Food Program
20,000   St. Mary's Health Network, Reno, NV -- for Youth Dental Sealant Program
19,300   University of Nevada Reno Department of Speech Pathology and Audiology, Reno, NV -- for equipment purchases
15,000   YMCA of the Sierra, Reno, NV -- for Before and After School Childcare Programs

PEOPLES ENERGY CORP.

Company Headquarters

Chicago, IL
Web: http://www.pecorp.com

Company Description

Founded: 1855
Ticker: PGL
Exchange: NYSE
Assets: US$2.727 billion (2002)
Employees: 2479 (2002)
SIC(s): 4924 Natural Gas Distribution, 6719 Holding Companies Nec.

Operating Locations

Peoples Energy Corp. (IL--Chicago, Waukegan)

Nonmonetary Support

Type: Donated Equipment; In-kind Services; Loaned Employees; Loaned Executives
Volunteer Programs: Company sponsors an employee volunteer program at a local childcare agency and in annual community service projects.

Giving Contact

Richard Turner, Manager, Corporate Contributions
Peoples Energy Corp.
130 E. Randolph Dr.
Chicago, IL 60601
Phone: (312)240-7516
Fax: (312)240-4389

Alternate Contact

Marilyn Randell-Ellis, Corporate Contributions Representative

Description

Organization Type: Corporate Giving Program
Giving Locations: company service area.
Grant Types: Employee Matching Gifts, General Support, Operating Expenses, Project.
Note: Employee matching gift ratio: 2 to 1 for gifts to primary and secondary schools and hospitals; 1 to 1 for gifts to other eligible institutions.

Financial Summary

Total Giving: $1,750,000 (fiscal year ending , 2003 approx); $1,750,000 (fiscal 2002); $900,000 (fiscal 2001 approx). Note: Contributes through corporate direct giving program only.
Giving Analysis: Giving for fiscal 2002 includes: corporate direct giving (approx $978,000) fiscal 2001: corporate direct giving (approx $900,000)

Typical Recipients

Arts & Humanities: Arts Associations & Councils, Arts Institutes, Dance, Ethnic & Folk Arts, Historic Preservation, Libraries, Museums/Galleries, Opera, Performing Arts, Public Broadcasting, Theater
Civic & Public Affairs: Civil Rights, Economic Development, Economic Policy, Employment/Job Training, Housing, Law & Justice, Professional & Trade Associations, Urban & Community Affairs, Women's Affairs, Zoos/Aquariums
Education: Colleges & Universities, Community & Junior Colleges, Elementary Education (Private), Literacy, Private Education (Precollege), Public Education (Precollege)
Health: Health Organizations, Hospitals
Science: Observatories & Planetariums
Social Services: Child Welfare, Community Centers, Community Service Organizations, Family Services, Homes, Senior Services, Shelters/Homelessness, United Funds/United Ways, Volunteer Services, Youth Organizations

Application Procedures

Initial Contact: Send letter requesting guidelines and application form, then send written proposal. Company accepts, but does not require, the Chicago Area Grant Application Form.
Application Requirements: Application packet should include: one-page cover letter with organization name, full mailing address, and telephone number of contact person, statement of purpose of the request, and amount requested; brief narrative summary (one to three pages) describing background and objectives of the program, concise history of organization, description of program, anticipated timelines, expected outcomes, evaluation methodology, the applicant's capacity to manage the planned activity, and discussion of how program fits company's funding interests; operating budget with planned expenses and income sources; project budget with funds raised and sources; recently audited financial statement; list

of Chicago-area contributors and amounts given; proof of tax-exempt status; and list of governing board members with affiliations.
Deadlines: None.
Review Process: All requests are reviewed by the contributions staff; this review process sometimes includes a visit to the soliciting agency and an evaluation of audited financial statements; gathered information then is evaluated against the company's overall contribution policies and grants are disbursed to those who qualify.
Evaluative Criteria: Clearly-stated objectives, long-range planning, active participation of board members, and description of funding sources that will help expand agency's support.

Restrictions

Contributions will not be made to individuals; organizations not eligible for tax-deductible support; organizations that discriminate by race, color, creed, or national origin; political organizations or campaigns; organizations whose prime purpose is to influence legislation; religious organizations for purely sectarian purposes; agencies or institutions owned and operated by local, state, or federal governments; trips or tours; or special occasion or goodwill advertising. Services greater Chicago area only.

Additional Information

Requests for specific capital or endowment purposes are generally limited to 0.5% of total amount sought.
Publications: Contribution Guidelines; Application Form

Corporate Officials

Desiree Glapion Rogers: senior vice president B New Orleans, LA 1959. ED Wellesley College BS (1981); Harvard University MBA (1985). PRIM CORP EMPL senior vice president: People's Energy Corp. CORP AFFIL vice president corporate communications: Peoples Gas, Light & Coke Co. NONPR AFFIL director: Smithsonian Institute; director: WTTW Channel 11; director: National Museum Natural History; trustee: Museum Contemporary Art; director: Museum Science & Industry; chairman: Chicago Children's Museum; trustee: Harvard Business School Club Chicago. CLUB AFFIL Economic Club; Wellesley Club.

Giving Program Officials

Richard Turner: manager corporate contributions

PEPCO HOLDINGS, INC.

Company Headquarters

701 9th St. NW
Washington, DC 20068
Web: http://www.pepcoholdings.com

Company Description

Founded: 2002
Ticker: POM
Exchange: NYSE
Former Name: Potomac Electric Power Co. (2001);
Acquired: Conectiv (2002).
Operating Revenue: US$4.324 billion (2002)
Profit: US$231.1 million (2002)
Employees: 6078 (2002)
Fortune Rank: 377, per FORTUNE Magazine's list of 500 Largest U.S. Corporations (2002).
SIC(s): 4911 Electric Services.

Operating Locations

Potomac Electric Power Co. (DC; MD; PA; TX)

Giving Contact

Pamela Holman, Contributions Coordinator
701 9th NW, Suite 1003
Washington, DC 20068

Phone: (202)872-3488
Fax: (202)872-2472
Web: http://www.pepco.com

Description

Organization Type: Corporate Giving Program
Giving Locations: DC: Washington company service area of greater Washington DC
Grant Types: Capital, Project.

Financial Summary

Total Giving: Contributes through corporate direct giving program only.

Typical Recipients

Arts & Humanities: Arts Associations & Councils, Arts Centers, Dance, Historic Preservation, Libraries, Museums/Galleries, Music, Opera, Performing Arts, Public Broadcasting, Theater
Civic & Public Affairs: Business/Free Enterprise, Civil Rights, Employment/Job Training, Municipalities/Towns, Urban & Community Affairs, Women's Affairs
Education: Colleges & Universities, Education Associations, Education Funds, Literacy, Minority Education, Public Education (Precollege), Science/Mathematics Education, Student Aid
Environment: Environment-General
Health: Health Organizations, Hospices, Hospitals, Medical Research, Single-Disease Health Associations
International: International Peace & Security Issues
Religion: Churches, Religious Organizations
Social Services: Animal Protection, Child Welfare, Community Service Organizations, Family Services, Food/Clothing Distribution, People with Disabilities, Recreation & Athletics, Senior Services, Shelters/Homelessness, Substance Abuse, United Funds/United Ways, Youth Organizations

Application Procedures

Initial Contact: Submit a written proposal.
Application Requirements: Include a description of organization, including goals, structure, and sources of funding; amount requested, purpose of funds sought; proof of tax-exempt status.
Deadlines: None, but proposal should be submitted well in advance of need.
Review Process: Contributions Committee reviews requests on a case-by-case basis.

Restrictions

Funds only organizations in company's service territory; does not provide operating funds.

Corporate Officials

Dennis Wraase: president, chief executive officer ED George Washington University MS; University of Maryland BS. PRIM CORP EMPL president, chief executive officer: Pepco Holdings Inc. CORP AFFIL director: Southeastern Electric Exchange; director: Association of Edison Illuminating Companies. NONPR AFFIL director: Washington Hospital Center; director: Washington Performing Arts Society; executive board member: National Capital Area Council Boy Scouts of America; member: Federation City Council.

Giving Program Officials

William T. Torgerson: vice president, cfo B Annapolis, MD 1944. ED Princeton University BA (1966); University of Maryland JD (1973). PRIM CORP EMPL senior vice president external affairs, general counsel: Potomac Electric Power Co. CORP AFFIL senior vice president: Constellation Energy Corp.

ANN PEPPERS FOUNDATION

Giving Contact

Jack H. Alexander, Secretary
PO Box 50146
Pasadena, CA 91115-0146
Phone: (626)449-0793

Description

Founded: 1959
EIN: 952114455
Organization Type: Private Foundation
Giving Locations: CA: Los Angeles metropolitan area
Grant Types: General Support, Scholarship.

Donor Information

Founder: the late Ann Peppers

Financial Summary

Total Giving: $500,253 (2001); $601,060 (2000); $599,750 (1999)
Giving Analysis: Giving for 2001 includes: foundation scholarships ($135,000); 2000: foundation scholarships ($183,500); 1999: foundation scholarships ($207,500)
Assets: $10,452,956 (2001); $11,592,118 (2000); $11,689,725 (1999)

Typical Recipients

Arts & Humanities: Arts Centers, History & Archaeology, Libraries, Museums/Galleries, Music, Public Broadcasting
Civic & Public Affairs: Employment/Job Training, Housing, Law & Justice, Public Policy, Women's Affairs
Education: Afterschool/Enrichment Programs, Arts/Humanities Education, Colleges & Universities, Education Funds, Education Reform, Engineering/Technological Education, Faculty Development, Education-General, Leadership Training, Literacy, Medical Education, Minority Education, Preschool Education, Private Education (Precollege), Public Education (Precollege), Science/Mathematics Education, Social Sciences Education, Special Education, Student Aid, Vocational & Technical Education
Environment: Environment-General
Health: Cancer, Children's Health/Hospitals, Clinics/Medical Centers, Emergency/Ambulance Services, Eyes/Blindness, Health-General, Geriatric Health, Health Organizations, Hospitals, Kidney, Medical Research, Mental Health, Prenatal Health Issues, Public Health, Research/Studies Institutes, Speech & Hearing
International: Health Care/Hospitals
Religion: Churches, Religion-General, Religious Organizations, Religious Welfare, Seminaries, Social/Policy Issues
Social Services: Animal Protection, At-Risk Youth, Child Welfare, Community Centers, Community Service Organizations, Crime Prevention, Domestic Violence, Family Services, Food/Clothing Distribution, Homes, People with Disabilities, Recreation & Athletics, Scouts, Scouts, Senior Services, Shelters/Homelessness, Social Services-General, Volunteer Services, Youth Organizations

Application Procedures

Initial Contact: Send a full proposal.
Application Requirements: Include a description of organization, amount requested, purpose of funds sought, recently audited financial statement, and proof of tax-exempt status.
Deadlines: None.
Notes: Grants are usually made quarterly.

Restrictions

Does not support individuals or government entities.

Foundation Officials

Jack H. Alexander: secretary
Philip V. Swan: vice president, treasurer
Howard O. Wilson: treasurer

Grants Analysis

Disclosure Period: calendar year ending 2001
Total Grants: $365,253*
Number of Grants: 73
Average Grant: $5,003
Highest Grant: $25,000
Lowest Grant: $1,000
Typical Range: $1,000 to $10,000
*Note: Giving excludes scholarship.

Recent Grants

Note: Grants derived from 2001 Form 990.

Library-Related

5,000	Huntington Library, San Marino, CA -- school tours

General

15,000	California Institute of Technology, Pasadena, CA -- scholarship
10,000	Polytechnic School, Pasadena, CA -- Skills Enrichment Program
8,000	Historical Society of Southern California, Los Angeles, CA -- Pasadena Sketch Book
5,000	Florence Crittenton Center, Los Angeles, CA -- fund residential treatment
5,000	House Ear Institute, Los Angeles, CA -- help family camp
5,000	Los Angeles Area Council Boy Scouts of America, Los Angeles, CA -- teach good character and citizenship
5,000	Mount St. Mary's College, Los Angeles, CA -- scholarship
5,000	Volunteers of America of Los Angeles, Los Angeles, CA -- expansion of drop-in center
4,353	Young and Healthy, Pasadena, CA -- computer work stations
3,500	Pasadena Senior Center, Pasadena, CA -- program endowment fund

PEPSICO INC.

Company Headquarters

Purchase, NY
Web: http://www.pepsico.com

Company Description

Founded: 1965
Ticker: PEP
Exchange: NYSE
Acquired: Quaker Oats Co. (2001).
Revenue: US$25.112 billion (2002)
Profit: US$3.313 billion (2002)
Employees: 135000 (2002)
Fortune Rank: 62, per FORTUNE Magazine's list of 500 Largest U.S. Corporations (2002).
SIC(s): 2052 Cookies & Crackers, 2086 Bottled & Canned Soft Drinks, 2087 Flavoring Extracts & Syrups Nec, 2096 Potato Chips & Similar Snacks.

Operating Locations

PepsiCo, Inc. (CA--Irvine; KS--Wichita; KY--Louisville; NY--Purchase, Valhalla; TX--Dallas, Plano)

Nonmonetary Support

Type: Donated Products
Volunteer Programs: Contributions are matched dollar for dollar to institutions and organizations that are determined tax-exempt by the I.R.S. When an employee volunteers in addition to a financial contribution, the foundation will double the match. Employee Community Involvement Grants are made to non-profit organizations where employees volunteer.

PepsiCo Foundation, Inc.

Giving Contact

Jacqueline R. Millan, Vice President, Contributions
700 Anderson Hill Road
Purchase, NY 10577
Phone: (914)253-3153
Fax: (914)253-3553

Description

Founded: 1962
EIN: 136163174
Organization Type: Corporate Foundation
Giving Locations: headquarters and operating communities.
Grant Types: Employee Matching Gifts, General Support, Project, Scholarship.
Note: Employee matching gift ratio: 1 to 1; 2 to 1 if employee volunteers in the organization. Majority of grants are initiated by employees volunteering in non-profit organisation.

Financial Summary

Total Giving: $15,785,407 (2002); $10,541,880 (2000); $9,212,361 (1999). Note: Contributes through foundation only.
Giving Analysis: Giving for 1999 includes: foundation grants to United Way ($1,951,244); foundation matching gifts ($2,019,003); foundation scholarships ($2,170,224); foundation ($3,071,890); 1998: foundation scholarships ($1,842,120); foundation matching gifts ($1,850,445); foundation grants to United Way ($1,860,820); foundation ($2,781,420); 1997: foundation scholarships ($1,493,514); foundation grants to United Way ($2,172,054); foundation matching gifts ($2,861,034);
Assets: $84,145,015 (2002); $36,909,223 (2000); $34,236,614 (1999)
Gifts Received: $46,000,000 (2002); $11,000,000 (2000); $8,214,000 (1999). Note: Contributions are received from PepsiCo, Inc.

Typical Recipients

Arts & Humanities: Arts Associations & Councils, Arts Centers, Arts Festivals, Dance, Film & Video, Historic Preservation, History & Archaeology, Libraries, Museums/Galleries, Music, Opera, Performing Arts, Public Broadcasting, Theater
Civic & Public Affairs: African American Affairs, Botanical Gardens/Parks, Business/Free Enterprise, Economic Development, Employment/Job Training, Ethnic Organizations, Civic & Public Affairs-General, Hispanic Affairs, Housing, Minority Business, Municipalities/Towns, Professional & Trade Associations, Public Policy, Urban & Community Affairs, Zoos/Aquariums
Education: Business Education, Business-School Partnerships, Colleges & Universities, Community & Junior Colleges, Continuing Education, Economic Education, Education Associations, Education Funds, Education Reform, Engineering/Technological Education, Education-General, International Exchange, International Studies, Medical Education, Minority Education, Private Education (Precollege), Science/Mathematics Education, Secondary Education (Public), Student Aid
Environment: Forestry, Resource Conservation
Health: Cancer, Children's Health/Hospitals, Clinics/Medical Centers, Emergency/Ambulance Services, Health Organizations, Hospitals, Multiple Sclerosis
International: Foreign Educational Institutions, International-General, Health Care/Hospitals, Human

Rights, International Affairs, International Development, International Organizations, International Peace & Security Issues, International Relations, International Relief Efforts, Trade
Religion: Churches, Religious Welfare
Science: Science Museums, Scientific Organizations
Social Services: Child Welfare, Community Service Organizations, Family Planning, Food/Clothing Distribution, People with Disabilities, Scouts, Social Services-General, Substance Abuse, United Funds/United Ways, YMCA/YWCA/YMHA/YWHA, Youth Organizations

Application Procedures
Initial Contact: Send a written request.
Application Requirements: Include a statement of organization's objectives, proposed use and primary objective of grant, history of organization's achievements, list of officers and directors, copy of IRS 501(c)(3) letter, and financial statements.
Deadlines: None.
Evaluative Criteria: The foundation focuses on projects where Pepsico employees are actively involved as volunteers.

Restrictions
The foundation does not provide grants to individuals.

Additional Information
PepsiCo is the parent company of a number of operating divisions, at the following addresses: Frito-Lay, Inc., 7701 Legacy Dr., Plano, TX 75024, phone: (214) 334-7000; Pizza Hut, Inc., 17841 Dallas Parkway, Dallas, TX 75240; Taco Bell Corp., 17901 Von Karman, Irvine, CA 92714, phone: (714) 863-4500; Pepsi-Cola Co., Somers, NY 10589, phone: (914) 767-6000; and KFC, 1441 Gardiner Ln., Louisville, KY 40213. phone: (502)456-8300. Contributions activity is handled at each division based on Community needs.
Organizations recommended by PepsiCo employees are also eligible for grants and will be considered.
Publications: Foundation Guidelines

Corporate Officials
David R. Andrews: senior vice president and general counsel
David L. Gonzales: vice president community affairs
Ronald E. Harrison: senior vice president global diversity, community affairs
Donald M. Kendall: co-founder
Tod J. MacKenzie: senior vice president, corporate communications
Matthew M. McKenna: senior vice president of finance B Washington, DC 1950. ED Hamilton College (1972); Georgetown University (1978). PRIM CORP EMPL senior vice president finance: PepsiCo, Inc.
Jacqueline R. Millan: director PRIM CORP EMPL manager corporate contributions: PepsiCo, Inc.
Margaret D. Moore: senior vice president, human resources
Ms. Indra K. Nooyi: president, chief financial officer, director PRIM CORP EMPL president, chief financial officer, director: PepsiCo Inc.
Steve S. Reinemund: chairman, chief executive officer, director B Queens, NY April 06, 1948. ED United States Naval Academy BS (1970); University of Virginia MBA (1978). PRIM CORP EMPL chairman, chief executive officer, director: PepsiCo Inc. CORP AFFIL director: ServiceMaster Co.; director: PepsiCo; director: Provident Life Insurance. NONPR AFFIL chairman: National Council of Laraza.

Foundation Officials
David R. Andrews: president (see above)
Kathleen Allen Luke: vice president PRIM CORP EMPL vice president: PepsiCo Inc.
Matthew M. McKenna: secretary (see above)
Jacqueline R. Millan: vice president, manager corporate contributions (see above)
Lionel L. Nowell, III: treasurer

Grants Analysis
Disclosure Period: calendar year ending 1999
Total Grants: $3,071,890*
Number of Grants: 109
Average Grant: $28,182
Highest Grant: $400,000
Typical Range: $1,000 to $50,000
*Note: Giving excludes matching gifts; scholarships; United Way.

Recent Grants
Note: Grants derived from 2002 Form 990.

General
2,152,319   National Merit Scholarship Corporation, Evanston, IL
1,713,149   Citizens Scholarship Foundation, Minneapolis, MN
1,500,000   SEEDCO, Winston-Salem, NC
1,000,000   National Council of La Raza, Washington, DC
766,877   United Way of Metropolitan Dallas, Dallas, TX
582,221   United Way of Chicago, Chicago, IL
383,177   United Way Westchester, White Plains, NY
336,852   United Way of Manatee County, Bradenton, FL
334,000   Duke University Library, Durham, NC
250,000   Miami University, Miami, OH

PERDUE FARMS

Company Headquarters
517 W. Main St.
Salisbury, MD 21801
Web: http://www.perdue.com

Company Description
Revenue: US$2.7 billion (2001)
Employees: 18,500
SIC(s): 0251 Broiler, Fryer & Roaster Chickens, 2015 Poultry Slaughtering & Processing.

Operating Locations
Perdue Farms (MD--Salisbury)

Arthur W. Perdue Foundation

Giving Contact
Howard L. Millard
Arthur W. Perdue Foundation
PO Box 1537
Salisbury, MD 21802-1537
Phone: (410)543-3217
Fax: (410)543-3908

Description
EIN: 526054332
Organization Type: Corporate Foundation
Giving Locations: AL; CT; DE; IN; KY; MD; NC; SC; TN; VA; WV
Grant Types: General Support.

Financial Summary
Total Giving: $2,410,000 (2001); $10,000 (1999); $10,000 (1998)
Giving Analysis: Giving for 2001 includes: foundation ($2,410,000) 1999: foundation ($10,000)
Assets: $4,327,871 (2001); $6,983,429 (2000); $199,380 (1999)
Gifts Received: $6,598,429 (2000). Note: In 2000, contributions were received from Franklin P. Perdue.

Typical Recipients
Arts & Humanities: Libraries
Civic & Public Affairs: Community Foundations, Municipalities/Towns
Education: Elementary Education (Public), Literacy, Public Education (Precollege)
Health: Hospices
Religion: Churches
Social Services: Social Services-General

Application Procedures
Initial Contact: Send a brief letter of inquiry.
Application Requirements: Include a description of organization, amount requested, and purpose of funds sought.
Deadlines: None.

Corporate Officials
James Arthur Perdue: chairman, chief executive officer, director B 1949. ED Wake Forest University BS (1973); Southeastern Massachusetts University MS (1976); University of Washington PhD (1983). PRIM CORP EMPL chairman, chief executive officer: Perdue Farms. CORP AFFIL chairman: Perdue Transportation.
Bob Turley: president, chief operating officer, director PRIM CORP EMPL president, chief operating officer, director: Perdue Farms.

Foundation Officials
Francis H. Connolly: secretary, treasurer PRIM CORP EMPL director taxes: Perdue Farms.
Franklin P. Perdue: president B 1920. ED Salisbury State University. PRIM CORP EMPL chairman executive committee: Perdue Farms.
James Arthur Perdue: vice president (see above)

Grants Analysis
Disclosure Period: calendar year ending 2001
Total Grants: $2,410,000
Number of Grants: 4
Average Grant: $136,667*
Highest Grant: $2,000,000
Typical Range: $10,000 to $200,000
*Note: Average grant figure excludes highest grant.

Recent Grants
Note: Grants derived from 2001 Form 990.

General
2,000,000   Community Foundation of the Eastern Shore, Salisbury, MD -- support phase II of Kresge challenge grant
200,000   City of Salisbury, Salisbury, NC -- for community playground
200,000   Community Foundation of the Eastern Shore, Salisbury, MD -- support phase I of Kresge challenge grant
10,000   Ridge Campaign of North Carolina, Charlotte, NC -- for YMCA support

PERRY FOUNDATION

Giving Contact
Frances H. Fife, President & Trustee
PO Box 558
Charlottesville, VA 22902
Phone: (434)977-5679

Description
Founded: 1946
EIN: 546036446
Organization Type: Private Foundation
Giving Locations: VA: Charlottesville
Grant Types: General Support.

Donor Information

Founder: the late Hunter Perry, the late Lillian Perry Edwards

Financial Summary

Total Giving: $1,161,674 (2002); $1,197,900 (2001); $1,400,315 (2000)

Giving Analysis: Giving for 2002 includes: foundation grants to United Way ($55,000); 2000: foundation grants to United Way ($55,000) 1999: foundation grants to United Way ($50,000)

Assets: $21,336,906 (2002); $25,450,454 (2001); $28,002,300 (2000)

Typical Recipients

Arts & Humanities: Historic Preservation, History & Archaeology, Libraries, Museums/Galleries, Music, Performing Arts, Public Broadcasting, Theater

Civic & Public Affairs: Botanical Gardens/Parks, Clubs, Employment/Job Training, Civic & Public Affairs-General, Housing, Municipalities/Towns, Public Policy, Urban & Community Affairs

Education: Colleges & Universities, Community & Junior Colleges, Education Funds, Education Reform, Faculty Development, Education-General, Minority Education, Private Education (Precollege), Public Education (Precollege), Science/Mathematics Education, Special Education, Student Aid

Environment: Air/Water Quality, Environment-General, Resource Conservation, Wildlife Protection

Health: Children's Health/Hospitals, Clinics/Medical Centers, Emergency/Ambulance Services, Health Organizations, Heart, Hospices, Hospitals, Mental Health, Prenatal Health Issues

Religion: Churches, Ministries, Religious Welfare

Science: Science Museums

Social Services: Animal Protection, At-Risk Youth, Camps, Community Service Organizations, Emergency Relief, Family Services, Food/Clothing Distribution, People with Disabilities, Recreation & Athletics, Senior Services, Shelters/Homelessness, United Funds/United Ways

Application Procedures

Initial Contact: Send a brief letter of inquiry. or a full proposal.

Application Requirements: Include a description of organization, purpose of funds sought, amount requested, and proof of tax-exempt status.

Deadlines: None.

Restrictions

Grants are not made to individuals.

Foundation Officials

Roberta F. Brownfield: trustee
Susan M. Cabell: trustee
Francis Fife: vice president, trustee
Gary C. McGee: secretary, trustee B Washington, DC 1940. ED College of William & Mary BS (1962); University of Virginia LLB (1965). PRIM CORP EMPL partner: MacQuire, Woods, Battle & Boothe. NONPR AFFIL member: Virginia State Bar; member: Virginia State Bar Association; member: Charlottesville Bar Association; member: Omicron Delta Kappa.
George C. Palmer, II: president, trustee B Columbus, GA 1922. ED University of Virginia (1942). PRIM CORP EMPL chairman: Piedmont Tractor Co. CORP AFFIL director: Dominion Resources Inc.; director: Sovran Financial Corp. NONPR AFFIL director: Atlantic Rural Exposition; trustee: Thomas Jefferson Memorial Foundation.
Suzanne J. Straton: trustee
Wade Tremblay: trustee

Grants Analysis

Disclosure Period: calendar year ending 2002
Total Grants: $1,106,674*
Number of Grants: 32
Average Grant: $28,127*
Highest Grant: $100,000

Lowest Grant: $3,789
Typical Range: $10,000 to $50,000
***Note:** Giving excludes United Way. Average grant figure excludes three highest grants ($291,000).

Recent Grants

Note: Grants derived from 2001 Form 990.

General

155,000	United Way, Charlottesville, VA
100,000	Blue Ridge School, Dyke, VA -- wastewater treatment plant
100,000	Charlottesville Albemarle Rescue Squad, Charlottesville, VA
100,000	Paramount Theater, Charlottesville, VA
88,000	Jefferson Area Board for Aging, Charlottesville, VA
75,000	Charlottesville Albemarle SPCA, Charlottesville, VA
67,000	Piedmont Housing Alliance, Charlottesville, VA
54,150	Bridge Ministry, Charlottesville, VA
50,000	Shenandoah Shakespeare, Staunton, VA
45,000	Village School, Charlottesville, VA

PETER KIEWIT SONS' INC.

Company Headquarters

1000 Kiewit Plaza
Omaha, NE 68131-3374
E-mail: miscellaneous@kiewit.com
Web: http://www.kiewit.com

Company Description

Revenue: US$3.699 billion (2002)
Profit: US$193 million (2002)
Employees: 14500 (2001)
Fortune Rank: 432, per FORTUNE Magazine's list of 500 Largest U.S. Corporations (2002).
SIC(s): 6719 Holding Companies Nec.

Operating Locations

Peter Kiewit Sons' Inc. (MD--Aberdeen)

Nonmonetary Support

Type: Loaned Employees; Loaned Executives; Workplace Solicitation
Note: Co. provides nonmonetary support.

Kiewit Companies Foundation

Giving Contact

Michael L. Faust, Foundation Administrator
1000 Kiewit Plaza
Omaha, NE 68131-3374
Phone: (402)271-2950
Fax: (402)943-1302
E-mail: mike.faust@kiewit.com
Web: http://www.kiewit.com

Description

Founded: 1963
EIN: 476098282
Organization Type: Corporate Foundation
Giving Locations: NE: Omaha operating locations.
Grant Types: Capital, General Support, Multiyear/Continuing Support, Operating Expenses, Project, Scholarship.

Financial Summary

Total Giving: $5,400,000 (2000); $3,240,301 (1999); $4,937,159 (1998). Note: Contributes through foundation only.

Giving Analysis: Giving for 1999 includes: corporate scholarships ($10,000); corporate grants to United Way ($144,482) corporate direct giving ($2,695,000)

Assets: $10,600,000 (2000); $15,300,000 (1999); $15,900,000 (1998)

Gifts Received: $2,500,000 (2000); $2,000,000 (1999). Note: In 1999 and 2000, contributions were received from Peter Kiewit Sons', Inc.

Typical Recipients

Arts & Humanities: Arts Associations & Councils, Arts Centers, Dance, Historic Preservation, Libraries, Museums/Galleries, Music, Opera, Theater

Civic & Public Affairs: Botanical Gardens/Parks, Business/Free Enterprise, Economic Development, Safety, Urban & Community Affairs, Zoos/Aquariums

Education: Colleges & Universities, Community & Junior Colleges, Economic Education, Engineering/Technological Education, Legal Education, Minority Education, Science/Mathematics Education

Environment: Environment-General

Health: Arthritis, Clinics/Medical Centers, Health Organizations

Social Services: Animal Protection, Child Welfare, Community Centers, Community Service Organizations, Food/Clothing Distribution, Homes, People with Disabilities, Recreation & Athletics, Scouts, United Funds/United Ways, YMCA/YWCA/YMHA/YWHA, Youth Organizations

Application Procedures

Initial Contact: Send brief letter or proposal.

Application Requirements: Include a description of organization, mission statement explaining how it makes a positive impact on the quality of life in a Kiewit community, amount requested, purpose of funds sought, recently audited financial statement, proof of tax-exempt status.

Deadlines: None.

Review Process: Decisions are made approximately every eight weeks.

Restrictions

The foundation generally does not support endowment funds, grant-making organizations, social or fraternal organizations, conferences or seminars, study or travel, academic or medical research, advocacy organizations or controversial causes, churches or religious organizations, production of films or sponsorship of television programming, elementary schools, or sponsorship of athletic teams or athletic events.

Additional Information

The majority of funding is repeat grants to local organizations in Omaha, NE. Limited funding is available to new grant seekers.

Corporate Officials

Kenneth E. Stinson: chairman, chief executive officer, director B 1942. ED University of Notre Dame BS (1964); Stanford University MS (1970). PRIM CORP EMPL chairman, chief executive officer, director: Peter Kiewit Sons' Inc. CORP AFFIL director: MFS Communications Co.; director: United Metro Materials Inc.; director: Kiewit Western Co.; director: Kiewit Industrial Co.; executive vice president: Peter Kiewit Sons Inc.; chairman, chief executive officer, director: Kiewit Construction Group Inc.; director: Kiewit Diversified Group Inc.; director: Kiewit Construction Co.; director: ConAgra Inc.; director: Global Surety & Insurance Co.

Foundation Officials

Michael L. Faust: administrator PRIM CORP EMPL assistant to chairman: Peter Kiewit Sons' Inc.
Walter Scott, Jr.: chairman emeritus B Omaha, NE 1931. ED Colorado State University BS (1953). PRIM CORP EMPL chairman: Peter Kiewit Sons' Inc. CORP AFFIL director: MidAmerica Holdings Inc.; director: Level 3 Telecommunications Holdings Inc.; director: MidAmerica Energy Holdings Co.; chairman: Level 3 Communications Inc.; president: Kiewit Coal Properties Inc.; director: Kiewit Mining Group Inc.; director:

ConAgra Inc.; director: Burlington Resources Inc.; director: CalEnergy Co. Inc.; director: Berkshire Hathaway Inc. NONPR AFFIL director: Hastings College Foundation; president: Joslyn Art Museum; chairman: Creighton University.

Kenneth E. Stinson: member contributions committee (see above)

Grants Analysis

Disclosure Period: calendar year ending 2000
Total Grants: $5,400,000*
Number of Grants: 255
Average Grant: $9,486*
Highest Grant: $2,000,000
Typical Range: $1,000 to $10,000
*Note: Giving includes matching gifts to United Way by employees and scholarships. Average grant figure excludes two highest grants totaling $3,000,000.

Recent Grants

Note: Grants derived from 2000 Form 990.

Library-Related

103,000	Bloomfield Library Foundation, Bloomfield, NE
100,000	City of Ralston, Ralston, NE

General

2,400,000	Omaha Botanical Center, Omaha, NE
1,500,000	University of Nebraska Foundation, Lincoln, NE -- for the Institute of Information, Science, Technology and Engineering
955,242	City of Omaha, Omaha, NE -- for OK Electric Company, Inc.
500,000	Bellevue University, Bellevue, NE
500,000	Boys and Girls Club of Omaha, Omaha, NE
500,000	Fontenelle Forest Association, Omaha, NE
500,000	Iowa Western Community College Foundation, Council Bluffs, IA
472,372	City of Omaha, Omaha, NE -- for D.F. Lanoha Landscape Nursery
471,710	City of Omaha, Omaha, NE -- for Edlaw, Inc.
450,000	Fontenelle Forest Association, Omaha, NE

PETERLOON FOUNDATION

Giving Contact

Paul George Sittenfeld, Secretary & Trustee
201 E. 5th St.
Cincinnati, OH 45202
Phone: (513)421-5886

Description

Founded: 1958
EIN: 316037801
Organization Type: Private Foundation
Giving Locations: KY: Northern part of state; OH: Cincinnati metropolitan area
Grant Types: Capital, Emergency, General Support, Multiyear/Continuing Support.

Donor Information

Founder: the late John J. Emery

Financial Summary

Total Giving: $75,836 (fiscal year ending December 30, 2001); $128,450 (fiscal 2000); $157,702 (fiscal 1999)
Giving Analysis: Giving for fiscal 2001 includes: foundation grants to United Way ($10,000); fiscal 2000: foundation grants to United Way ($10,000) fiscal 1999: foundation grants to United Way ($10,000)
Assets: $6,397,070 (fiscal 2001); $6,676,610 (fiscal 2000); $6,730,474 (fiscal 1999)

Typical Recipients

Arts & Humanities: Arts Associations & Councils, Arts Centers, Arts Funds, Arts Institutes, Community Arts, Ethnic & Folk Arts, Historic Preservation, History & Archaeology, Libraries, Museums/Galleries, Music, Performing Arts, Public Broadcasting, Theater, Visual Arts
Civic & Public Affairs: Botanical Gardens/Parks, Community Foundations, Economic Development, Civic & Public Affairs-General, Housing, Legal Aid, Safety, Urban & Community Affairs, Zoos/Aquariums
Education: Arts/Humanities Education, Colleges & Universities, Continuing Education, Engineering/Technological Education, Environmental Education, Faculty Development, Education-General, Literacy, Private Education (Precollege), Science/Mathematics Education, Secondary Education (Public), Vocational & Technical Education
Environment: Environment-General
Health: Cancer, Clinics/Medical Centers, Eyes/Blindness, Health Organizations, Heart, Hospices, Long-Term Care, Multiple Sclerosis, Preventive Medicine/Wellness Organizations, Single-Disease Health Associations
International: International Environmental Issues
Religion: Religious Welfare
Science: Science Museums
Social Services: At-Risk Youth, Child Welfare, Community Centers, Community Service Organizations, Day Care, Delinquency & Criminal Rehabilitation, Family Planning, Food/Clothing Distribution, Homes, People with Disabilities, Recreation & Athletics, Scouts, Senior Services, Shelters/Homelessness, Social Services-General, United Funds/United Ways, YMCA/YWCA/YMHA/YWHA, Youth Organizations

Application Procedures

Initial Contact: The foundation has no formal grant application procedure or application form.
Deadlines: None.

Foundation Officials

John L. Campbell: trustee
Ethan Emery: trustee
Irene E. Goodale: trustee
John E. Lanier: trustee
Melissa Emery Lanier: vice president, trustee
Judith M. Mitchell: trustee
Paul George Sittenfeld: secretary, trustee
Lela Emery Steele: president, treasurer, trustee
Elizabeth Steele Hoyt: trustee

Grants Analysis

Disclosure Period: fiscal year ending December 30, 2001
Total Grants: $65,836*
Number of Grants: 24
Average Grant: $2,243*
Highest Grant: $12,000
Typical Range: $1,000 to $5,000
*Note: Giving excludes United Way. Average grant figure excludes highest grant.

Recent Grants

Note: Grants derived from 2001 Form 990.

General

12,000	Fine Arts Fund, Cincinnati, OH -- annual fund
10,000	United Way, Cincinnati, OH -- annual fund
8,000	Salvation Army, Cincinnati, OH -- for emergency fund
5,000	Cincinnati Institute of Fine Arts, Cincinnati, OH -- memorial grant for community art programs
5,000	Drop Inn Center Shelterhouse, Cincinnati, OH -- for Chemical Dependency and Education Programs
5,000	St. Paul Lutheran Village, Cincinnati,

5,000	OH -- assist with purchasing a bus for physically impaired residents
5,000	Taft Museum, Cincinnati, OH -- for capital campaign
5,000	Wellness Community, Cincinnati, OH -- for Hope Campaign
3,000	Summer Bridge of Cincinnati, Cincinnati, OH -- for special programs for elementary and middle school children
2,500	Children's International Summer Villages, Cincinnati, OH -- support for children's summer programs

EDWARD V. AND JESSIE L. PETERS CHARITABLE TRUST

Giving Contact

Susan K. Betz, Trust Officer
Care of National City Bank
PO Box 318
Oil City, PA 16301
Phone: (814)678-3625

Description

Founded: 1991
EIN: 256358729
Organization Type: Private Foundation
Giving Locations: PA
Grant Types: General Support.

Financial Summary

Total Giving: $42,000 (2001); $42,300 (2000); $33,550 (1999)
Assets: $6,346,665 (2001); $1,011,392 (2000); $1,013,011 (1999)
Gifts Received: $2,754,182 (2001). Note: In 2001, contributions were received from Jessie L. Peters Trusts.

Typical Recipients

Arts & Humanities: Historic Preservation, History & Archaeology, Libraries, Museums/Galleries
Health: Cancer, Children's Health/Hospitals, Clinics/Medical Centers, Emergency/Ambulance Services, Hospitals, Nursing Services
Social Services: Community Service Organizations, Emergency Relief, Family Services, People with Disabilities, Scouts

Application Procedures

Initial Contact: Send letter stating purpose of funds sought. Enclose proof of tax-exempt status.
Application Requirements: Provide proof of tax-exempt status and purpose of funds sought.
Deadlines: November 1.

Additional Information

Trust(s): Natl City Bank PA

Foundation Officials

Joyce I. Hughes: trustee
Michael F. Hughes: trustee
Bruce T. Rosen: trustee

Grants Analysis

Disclosure Period: calendar year ending 2001
Total Grants: $42,000
Number of Grants: 5
Highest Grant: $20,000
Lowest Grant: $3,500
Typical Range: $5,000 to $10,000

Recent Grants

Note: Grants derived from 2000 Form 990.

Library-Related

3,000	Franklin Library Association, Franklin, PA

General

3,000	American Cancer Society, Oil City, PA
3,000	Boy Scouts of America French Creek, Erie, PA
3,000	Children's Hospital, Pittsburgh, PA
3,000	Community Ambulance Service, Inc., Franklin, PA
3,000	Community Services of Venango County, Oil City, PA
3,000	Keystone Tall Tree Girl Scout Council, Kittanning, PA
3,000	Northwest Medical Center, Oil City, PA
3,000	Pennsylvania Association for Blind, Harrisburg, PA
3,000	Shriners Hospital for Children, Tampa, FL
3,000	Venango County Association for Blind, Oil City, PA

CHARLES F. PETERS FOUNDATION

Giving Contact

Joanna M. Mayo, Vice President
c/o National City Bank of PA
20 Stanwix Street
Pittsburgh, PA 15222-4802
Phone: (412)644-8002

Description

Founded: 1965
EIN: 256070765
Organization Type: Private Foundation
Giving Locations: PA: McKeesport
Grant Types: General Support.

Donor Information

Founder: Charles F. Peters

Financial Summary

Total Giving: $138,500 (2000); $133,500 (1999); $105,750 (1998)
Assets: $3,746,420 (2000); $3,892,247 (1999); $3,487,572 (1998)

Typical Recipients

Arts & Humanities: Arts Associations & Councils, History & Archaeology, Libraries, Literary Arts, Music
Civic & Public Affairs: Clubs, Urban & Community Affairs
Education: Colleges & Universities, Private Education (Precollege)
Health: Hospitals
Religion: Churches, Religious Organizations, Religious Welfare, Synagogues/Temples
Social Services: Community Service Organizations, Food/Clothing Distribution, Homes, United Funds/United Ways, YMCA/YWCA/YMHA/YWHA, Youth Organizations

Application Procedures

Initial Contact: a brief letter of inquiry and full proposal
Application Requirements: a description of organization, amount requested, purpose of funds sought, proof of tax-exempt status, and geographic area served
Deadlines: None.

Restrictions

Grants may not exceed $5,000.

Additional Information

Preference is given to churches and public civic causes, and other charitable organizations in and near McKeesport, PA
Trust(s): National City Bank of PA

Foundation Officials

Herman A. Haase: admin
Joanna M. Mayo: director
Robert A. Stone: admin

Grants Analysis

Disclosure Period: calendar year ending 2000
Total Grants: $138,500
Number of Grants: 82
Average Grant: $1,689
Highest Grant: $5,000
Typical Range: $300 to $3,000

Recent Grants

Note: Grants derived from 1999 Form 990.

Library-Related

5,000	Carnegie Free Library of McKeesport, McKeesport, PA

General

5,000	Concordia Evangelical Lutheran Church and Sonshine Kitchen, McKeesport, PA
5,000	Greater Pittsburgh Community Food Bank, McKeesport, PA
5,000	McKeesport Hospital Foundation, McKeesport, PA
5,000	McKeesport Symphony Orchestra, McKeesport, PA
5,000	McKeesport YMCA, McKeesport, PA
5,000	Pauline Auberle Foundation, McKeesport, PA
5,000	Salvation Army, McKeesport, PA
5,000	YWCA of McKeesport, McKeesport, PA
3,000	Evangelical Congregational Church, McKeesport, PA
3,000	McKeesport Heritage Center, McKeesport, PA

LEON S. PETERS FOUNDATION

Giving Contact

Alice Peters, President & Chief Financial Officer
4170 S. Fowler
Fresno, CA 93725
Phone: (559)442-3437

Description

Founded: 1959
EIN: 946064669
Organization Type: Private Foundation
Giving Locations: CA: Fresno
Grant Types: Capital, General Support, Operating Expenses, Scholarship.

Donor Information

Founder: the late Leon S. Peters

Financial Summary

Total Giving: $1,361,624 (fiscal year ending November 30, 2001); $843,000 (fiscal 2000); $1,266,890 (fiscal 1999). Note: Fiscal 1997 Giving includes United Way ($10,000).
Giving Analysis: Giving for fiscal 2000 includes: foundation grants to United Way ($5,000); fiscal 1999: foundation grants to United Way ($5,000) fiscal 1998: foundation grants to United Way ($5,000)
Assets: $15,128,822 (fiscal 2001); $16,549,081 (fiscal 2000); $16,148,451 (fiscal 1999)

Typical Recipients

Arts & Humanities: Dance, History & Archaeology, Libraries, Museums/Galleries, Music, Public Broadcasting, Theater
Civic & Public Affairs: Botanical Gardens/Parks, Ethnic Organizations, Civic & Public Affairs-General, Parades/Festivals, Zoos/Aquariums
Education: Colleges & Universities, Community & Junior Colleges, Education Funds, Faculty Development, Legal Education, Literacy, Minority Education, Private Education (Precollege), Public Education (Precollege), Secondary Education (Public), Student Aid
Environment: Forestry, Environment-General, Resource Conservation
Health: Cancer, Children's Health/Hospitals, Clinics/Medical Centers, Emergency/Ambulance Services, Heart, Hospices, Hospitals, Mental Health, Public Health, Single-Disease Health Associations
International: International Organizations, International Relief Efforts, Missionary/Religious Activities
Religion: Bible Study/Translation, Churches, Missionary Activities (Domestic), Religious Organizations, Religious Welfare, Seminaries
Science: Science Museums
Social Services: At-Risk Youth, Big Brother/Big Sister, Child Welfare, Community Service Organizations, Emergency Relief, Family Services, Food/Clothing Distribution, Homes, People with Disabilities, Scouts, Shelters/Homelessness, Social Services-General, United Funds/United Ways, YMCA/YWCA/YMHA/YWHA, Youth Organizations

Application Procedures

Initial Contact: Send a brief letter of inquiry.
Deadlines: None.

Restrictions

Does not support individuals.

Foundation Officials

Craig Apregan: director
Alice A. Peters: president, chief financial officer
Darrell Peters: director
Kenneth Peters: director
Peter P. Peters: vice president, secretary
Ronald Peters: director

Grants Analysis

Disclosure Period: fiscal year ending November 30, 2001
Total Grants: $1,361,624
Number of Grants: 54
Average Grant: $9,126*
Highest Grant: $150,000
Lowest Grant: $1,000
Typical Range: $5,000 to $20,000
*****Note:** Average grant figure excludes five highest grants ($914,440).

Recent Grants

Note: Grants derived from fiscal 2000 Form 990.

Library-Related

2,000	Fresno County Library, Fresno, CA -- funds for operation and administration

General

225,000	Fresno Community Hospital, Fresno, CA -- funds for operation and administration
51,000	Fresno Metropolitan Museum, Fresno, CA
50,000	California State University Fresno, Fresno, CA -- funds for operation and scholarships
50,000	Channel 18, Fresno, CA
30,000	Boy Scouts, Fresno, CA
25,000	Boys and Girls Club, Fresno, CA
25,000	Fresno City College Fund, Fresno, CA -- funds for endowment and scholarships

25,000	Poverello House, Fresno, CA -- funds for operation and administration
20,000	Salvation Army, Fresno, CA
15,000	Fresno Philharmonic, Fresno, CA -- funds for operation and administration

R. D. AND LINDA PETERS FOUNDATION

Giving Contact

Richard Hugo, Director
c/o Bank One Wisconsin Trust Co. NA
PO Box 1308
Milwaukee, WI 53201
Phone: (414)765-2800

Description

Founded: 1965
EIN: 396097994
Organization Type: Private Foundation
Giving Locations: WI: Brillion
Grant Types: General Support, Research, Scholarship.

Donor Information

Founder: the late R. D. Peters

Financial Summary

Total Giving: $331,694 (2001); $367,725 (2000); $320,941 (1999)
Giving Analysis: Giving for 2001 includes: foundation ($331,694); 1999: foundation scholarships ($83,000); 1998: foundation scholarships ($78,500) foundation ($241,203)
Assets: $6,346,995 (2001); $6,882,968 (2000); $7,332,556 (1999)

Typical Recipients

Arts & Humanities: History & Archaeology, Libraries, Museums/Galleries, Theater
Civic & Public Affairs: Botanical Gardens/Parks, Municipalities/Towns, Zoos/Aquariums
Education: Agricultural Education, Colleges & Universities, Environmental Education, Education-General, Medical Education, Public Education (Precollege), Science/Mathematics Education, Secondary Education (Public), Student Aid
Environment: Forestry, Environment-General, Resource Conservation, Wildlife Protection
Health: Children's Health/Hospitals, Health Organizations
International: International Environmental Issues
Religion: Churches, Religion-General, Religious Organizations, Religious Welfare
Science: Observatories & Planetariums
Social Services: Child Welfare, Community Service Organizations, Homes, People with Disabilities, Senior Services, Social Services-General, YMCA/YWCA/YMHA/YWHA, Youth Organizations

Application Procedures

Initial Contact: Send a brief letter of inquiry.
Application Requirements: Include a description of organization, purpose of funds sought, and amount requested.
Deadlines: None.
Review Process: Board meets quarterly.

Restrictions

Grants are normally restricted to the Brillion area, conservation endeavors, metallurgical research, and projects for youth.

Additional Information

Trust(s): Bank One WI Trust Co NA

Foundation Officials

Richard Hugo: assistant secretary, assistant treasurer
Lowell O. Reese: director
Harold Wolf: director

Grants Analysis

Disclosure Period: calendar year ending 2001
Total Grants: $331,694
Number of Grants: 30
Average Grant: $8,496*
Highest Grant: $85,300
Typical Range: $1,000 to $15,000
***Note:** Average grant figure exludes highest grant.

Recent Grants

Note: Grants derived from 2001 Form 990.

Library-Related

5,000	Brillion Public Library, Brillion, WI

General

85,300	Brillion High School, Brillion, WI
55,200	New Hope Center, Chilton, WI
50,000	Medical College of Wisconsin, Milwaukee, WI
25,000	Children's Hospital of Wisconsin, Milwaukee, WI
15,000	Holy Family Catholic Church, South Pasadena, CA
11,000	Trinity Evangelical Lutheran Church, Brillion, WI
10,044	Brillion Public Schools, Brillion, WI
10,000	International Crane Foundation, Baraboo, WI
8,000	Brillion Nature Center, Brillion, WI
6,300	Center for Deaf and Blind Persons, Milwaukee, WI

ELLSWORTH AND CARLA PETERSON CHARITABLE FOUNDATION

Giving Contact

Carla J. Peterson, Trustee
Ellsworth and Carla Peterson Charitable Foundation
55 Utopia Circle
Sturgeon Bay, WI 54235-1542
Phone: (920)743-4093

Description

Founded: 1992
EIN: 396566719
Organization Type: Private Foundation
Giving Locations: WI
Grant Types: General Support.

Donor Information

Founder: the late Ellsworth L. Peterson

Financial Summary

Total Giving: $556,490 (fiscal year ending October 31, 2001); $173,000 (fiscal 1998); $324,580 (fiscal 1997)
Giving Analysis: Giving for fiscal 2001 includes: foundation scholarships ($1,000); foundation grants to United Way ($10,000) fiscal 1997: foundation scholarships ($2,500)
Assets: $3,188,441 (fiscal 2001); $5,461,976 (fiscal 1998); $3,821,002 (fiscal 1997)
Gifts Received: $335,962 (fiscal 1998); $500,360 (fiscal 1997); $1,107,279 (fiscal 1994). Note: Contributions were received from Ellsworth L. Peterson Revocable Trust.

Typical Recipients

Arts & Humanities: Arts Centers, Arts Festivals, Ethnic & Folk Arts, Historic Preservation, History & Archaeology, Libraries, Museums/Galleries, Music, Performing Arts, Public Broadcasting, Theater
Civic & Public Affairs: Economic Development, Civic & Public Affairs-General, Housing, Urban & Community Affairs
Education: Arts/Humanities Education, Colleges & Universities, Education-General, Medical Education, Preschool Education
Environment: Environment-General
Health: Cancer, Health Organizations, Hospitals
Religion: Churches, Religious Welfare
Science: Science Museums
Social Services: Animal Protection, Community Centers, Community Service Organizations, Day Care, Family Services, Recreation & Athletics, Scouts, United Funds/United Ways, Veterans, YMCA/YWCA/YMHA/YWHA

Application Procedures

Initial Contact: Send an outline of the purpose of funds sought.
Deadlines: None.

Restrictions

The foundation does not support religious organizations for sectarian purposes, political or lobbying groups, or organizations outside operating areas.

Foundation Officials

Carla J. Peterson: trustee
Ellsworth Lorin Peterson: trustee B Sturgeon Bay, WI 1924. ED United States Merchant Marine Academy (1946). PRIM CORP EMPL chief executive officer, director: Peterson Builders. CORP AFFIL chairman: Bank Sturgeon Bay. NONPR AFFIL director: Shipbuilders Council America; member: Society Naval Architects & Marine Engineers; member: National Security Industry Association; member: American Society Naval Engineers. CLUB AFFIL Rotary Club.

Grants Analysis

Disclosure Period: fiscal year ending October 31, 2001
Total Grants: $545,490*
Number of Grants: 90
Average Grant: $1,702*
Highest Grant: $394,035
Typical Range: $250 to $5,000
***Note:** Giving excludes scholarships and United Way. Average grant figure excludes highest grant.

Recent Grants

Note: Grants derived from 2001 Form 990.

Library-Related

8,333	New Northern Door Library Fund, The

General

394,034	YMCA, Lima, OH
25,000	Fairfield Public Gallery
25,000	United States Merchant Marine Academy Foundation, Inc., Kings Point, NY
10,000	Crossroad at Big Creek
10,000	Retreat at Upland Farm, St. Bonifacius, MN
10,000	United Way Door County, Sturgeon Bay, WI
8,000	American Folklore Theater, Fish Creek, WI
5,250	Door Community Auditorium, Fish Creek, WI
5,000	Door County Humane Society, Sturgeon Bay, WI
5,000	Door County Land Trust Inc., Ephraim, WI

FOLKE H. PETERSON CHARITABLE FOUNDATION

Giving Contact
Howard L. Usher, Trust Officer
c/o SunBank South FL
PO Box 14728
Ft. Lauderdale, FL 33302
Phone: (305)765-7477

Description
Founded: 1988
EIN: 656040055
Organization Type: Private Foundation
Grant Types: General Support.

Donor Information
Founder: the late Folke H. Peterson

Financial Summary
Total Giving: $1,363,593 (fiscal year ending November 30, 2000); $1,181,500 (fiscal 1998); $1,181,500 (fiscal 1997)
Assets: $21,363,161 (fiscal 2000); $24,975,493 (fiscal 1998); $24,975,493 (fiscal 1997)
Gifts Received: $7,300,451 (fiscal 1994); $1,126,200 (fiscal 1992). Note: In fiscal 1992, contributions were received from the estate of Folke H. Peterson.

Typical Recipients
Arts & Humanities: Libraries, Public Broadcasting
Civic & Public Affairs: Botanical Gardens/Parks, Civic & Public Affairs-General, Zoos/Aquariums
Education: Colleges & Universities
Environment: Environment-General, Resource Conservation, Wildlife Protection
International: International Environmental Issues
Science: Science Museums
Social Services: Animal Protection, Community Service Organizations

Application Procedures
Initial Contact: Send a brief letter of inquiry.
Deadlines: None.

Restrictions
Emphasis is on organizations that provide care and prevent cruelty to animals.

Additional Information
Trust(s): Suntrust Bank South FL

Foundation Officials
Don E. Champion: trustee
Richard K. Kornmeier: trustee
Emily Van Vliet: trustee
Frank Van Vliet: trustee

Grants Analysis
Disclosure Period: fiscal year ending November 30, 2000
Total Grants: $1,363,593
Number of Grants: 60
Average Grant: $5,502*
Highest Grant: $350,000
Typical Range: $1,000 to $10,000
*Note: Average grant figure excludes three highest grants ($1,050,000).

Recent Grants
Note: Grants derived from fiscal 1999 Form 990.

Library-Related
13,000 Broward Public Library Foundation, Ft. Lauderdale, FL

General
400,000 University of Florida, Gainesville, FL
400,000 University of Miami, Miami, FL
400,000 Wildlife Care Center SPCA, Ft. Lauderdale, FL
12,000 Ocean Impact, West Palm Beach, FL
11,500 Beaks
11,000 National Greyhound Adoption, Philadelphia, PA
8,000 Florida Wildlife Care, Inc., FL
8,000 H.A.W.K.E. Inc
7,800 Zoological Society, FL
7,500 WJCT TV Inc., FL

HAL AND CHARLIE PETERSON FOUNDATION

Giving Contact
John Mosty, Secretary-Treasurer
PO Box 293870
Kerrville, TX 78029-3870
Phone: (830)896-2262
Fax: (830)896-2283
E-mail: hcpfn@ktc.com

Description
Founded: 1990
EIN: 741109626
Organization Type: Private Foundation
Giving Locations: TX: Kerr and adjacent counties
Grant Types: General Support.

Donor Information
Founder: Established in 1990 by James Avery Craftsman.

Financial Summary
Total Giving: $2,639,893 (2000); $1,569,128 (1998); $1,736,365 (1997)
Giving Analysis: Giving for 2000 includes: foundation grants to United Way ($22,300) 1997: foundation grants to United Way ($21,000)
Assets: $53,482,048 (2000); $53,375,346 (1998); $47,704,591 (1997)
Gifts Received: $60,940 (2000); $116,991 (1998); $1,680,827 (1997). Note: In 1998, a substantial contributor was the F. Galbraith Trust ($104,309).

Typical Recipients
Arts & Humanities: Arts Associations & Councils, Arts Centers, Ballet, Ethnic & Folk Arts, Arts & Humanities-General, Historic Preservation, History & Archaeology, Libraries, Museums/Galleries, Music, Performing Arts
Civic & Public Affairs: Botanical Gardens/Parks, Clubs, Civic & Public Affairs-General, Housing, Inner-City Development, Safety
Education: Agricultural Education, Arts/Humanities Education, Colleges & Universities, Community & Junior Colleges, Education Funds, Education-General, Literacy, Medical Education, Preschool Education, Private Education (Precollege), Public Education (Precollege), Science/Mathematics Education, Student Aid, Vocational & Technical Education
Environment: Environment-General, Resource Conservation
Health: Alzheimers Disease, Cancer, Clinics/Medical Centers, Emergency/Ambulance Services, Health-General, Hospices, Hospitals, Medical Rehabilitation, Nursing Services, Preventive Medicine/Wellness Organizations
Religion: Churches, Religion-General, Religious Organizations, Religious Welfare
Social Services: Animal Protection, At-Risk Youth, Big Brother/Big Sister, Camps, Child Welfare, Community Service Organizations, Counseling, Crime Prevention, Day Care, People with Disabilities, Recreation & Athletics, Scouts, Senior Services, Shelters/Homelessness, Social Services-General, Special

Olympics, Substance Abuse, United Funds/United Ways, Volunteer Services, YMCA/YWCA/YMHA/YWHA, Youth Organizations

Application Procedures
Initial Contact: Request application form and guidelines.
Deadlines: None.

Restrictions
Organization must be 501 c(3) to be considered for grants.

Additional Information
Publications: Application Form; Guidelines

Foundation Officials
W. H. Cowden, Jr.: vice president
Charles H. Johnston: director
Nowlin McBryde: director
John Mosty: secretary, treasurer
Scott Parker: president
C. D. Peterson: director
James Stehling: director

Grants Analysis
Disclosure Period: calendar year ending 2000
Total Grants: $2,617,593*
Number of Grants: 48
Average Grant: $54,533
Highest Grant: $250,000
Typical Range: $5,000 to $100,000
*Note: Giving excludes United Way.

Recent Grants
Note: Grants derived from 2001 Form 990.

Library-Related
45,000 Medina Community Library, Medina, TX -- to assist with renovations of building for new library

General
250,000 Playhouse 2000, Inc., Kerrville, TX -- assist with renovations and improvements to the Kathleen C. Caillouix City Center
199,600 Schreiner University, Kerrville, TX -- fund various programs
183,800 Notre Dame School, Kerrville, TX -- fund purchase of various gymnasium equipment
135,504 Kerrville Playscape, Inc., Kerrville, TX -- fund installation of playground equipment in the Singing Wind Park
120,000 Schreiner College, Kerrville, TX -- fund street repairs on the college campus
96,708 Ingram Independent School District, Ingram, TX -- fund the purchase and installation of new computer lab equipment
92,925 Kerr County Sheriff's Department, Kerrville, TX -- fund video equipment for the Sheriff's Department
89,038 Holy Cross Lutheran School, Kerrville, TX -- fund playground equipment, copier and van
83,200 Hill Country Community MHMR Center, Kerrville, TX -- fund purchase of vehicles for agency use
80,400 Star Programs, Inc., Ingram, TX -- assist with construction of new Gym Activity Center

LORENE M. PETRIE TRUST

Giving Contact
Aaron Jackson, Assistant Vice President
c/o Bank of America
PO Box 34474
Seattle, WA 98124
Phone: (206)358-7977

Description

Founded: 1983
EIN: 916256555
Organization Type: Private Foundation
Giving Locations: WA: Kittatas County, Yakima County
Grant Types: General Support.

Donor Information

Founder: the late Lorene Petrie

Financial Summary

Total Giving: $50,000 (fiscal year ending July 31, 2001); $279,564 (fiscal 2000); $513,451 (fiscal 1999). Note: Fiscal 1997 Giving includes United Way ($26,000).
Assets: $866,854 (fiscal 2002); $978,940 (fiscal 2001); $1,115,366 (fiscal 2000)

Typical Recipients

Arts & Humanities: Arts Associations & Councils, Community Arts, History & Archaeology, Libraries, Museums/Galleries, Music, Public Broadcasting, Theater
Civic & Public Affairs: Botanical Gardens/Parks, Community Foundations, Municipalities/Towns, Rural Affairs, Urban & Community Affairs, Women's Affairs
Education: Colleges & Universities, Community & Junior Colleges, Education-General, Student Aid, Vocational & Technical Education
Environment: Environment-General
Health: Clinics/Medical Centers, Emergency/Ambulance Services, Health Organizations, Hospitals, Public Health
Social Services: Child Welfare, Food/Clothing Distribution, Recreation & Athletics, YMCA/YWCA/YMHA/YWHA, Youth Organizations

Application Procedures

Initial Contact: Send brief letter describing program.
Deadlines: None.

Additional Information

Trust(s): Bank of America
Trust(s): Bank of America

Grants Analysis

Disclosure Period: fiscal year ending July 31, 2002
Note: No grants awarded in fiscal 2002.

Recent Grants

Note: Grants derived from 2000 Form 990.

General

65,500	YMCA, Tacoma, WA
50,000	Perry Technical Foundation, Yakima, WA
50,000	Providence Health System
50,000	Sunnyside Community Hospital, Sunnyside, WA
40,000	Heritage College, Toppenish, WA
13,400	Upper Valley Sports and Recreation Association
4,800	Yakima Symphony, Yakima, WA
2,500	Yakima Neighborhood Health Services, Yakima, WA
1,688	Yakima Schools Foundation, Yakima, WA
1,676	Yakima Food Bank, Yakima, WA

JACK PETTEYS MEMORIAL FOUNDATION

Giving Contact

Judy Gunnon
PO Box 324
Brush, CO 80723

Phone: (970)842-5101
Fax: (970)842-5105

Description

Founded: 1943
EIN: 846036239
Organization Type: Private Foundation
Giving Locations: AL; CO: Northeastern Colorado
Grant Types: General Support, Scholarship.

Financial Summary

Total Giving: $407,465 (2001); $361,150 (2000); $421,005 (1999)
Giving Analysis: Giving for 2001 includes: foundation grants to United Way ($1,350); foundation scholarships ($94,100); 2000: foundation scholarships ($1,350); foundation scholarships ($97,569); 1999: foundation scholarships ($90,080);
Assets: $7,688,720 (2001); $9,007,177 (2000); $7,505,365 (1999)

Typical Recipients

Arts & Humanities: Arts Associations & Councils, History & Archaeology, Libraries, Museums/Galleries, Performing Arts, Public Broadcasting
Civic & Public Affairs: Civic & Public Affairs-General, Municipalities/Towns, Parades/Festivals, Safety, Urban & Community Affairs
Education: Agricultural Education, Arts/Humanities Education, Colleges & Universities, Community & Junior Colleges, Public Education (Precollege), Science/Mathematics Education, Student Aid
Health: Children's Health/Hospitals, Clinics/Medical Centers, Emergency/Ambulance Services, Geriatric Health, Health Organizations, Hospitals, Long-Term Care, Medical Rehabilitation, Mental Health
International: Health Care/Hospitals
Religion: Ministries
Social Services: Community Service Organizations, Day Care, Family Services, Food/Clothing Distribution, People with Disabilities, People with Disabilities, Recreation & Athletics, Scouts, Senior Services, United Funds/United Ways, Youth Organizations

Application Procedures

Initial Contact: Send a brief letter of inquiry.
Deadlines: December 1.

Restrictions

Northeastern Colorado area.

Additional Information

Trust(s): Farmers State Bank

Foundation Officials

Robert Hansen: director
Robert A. Petteys: director
Helen C. Watrous: director

Grants Analysis

Disclosure Period: calendar year ending 2001
Total Grants: $312,015*
Number of Grants: 10
Average Grant: $6,037*
Highest Grant: $131,650
*Note: Giving excludes scholarships, United Way. Average grant figure excludes two highest grants ($251,650).

Recent Grants

Note: Grants derived from 2001 Form 990.

General

131,650	East Morgan County Hospital, Brush, CO -- equipment
120,000	East Morgan County Hospital Foundation, Brush, CO -- new century challenge
15,000	Eastern County Services for the Developmentally Disabled, Sterling, CO -- materials
12,500	City of Brush, Brush, CO -- boys and girls baseball
10,435	Brush Volunteer Fire Department, Brush, CO -- equipment
7,500	Fort Morgan Heritage Foundation, Ft. Morgan, CO -- remodel and expansion project
7,200	Colorado School of Mines, Golden, CO -- scholarships
4,000	Rocky Mountain Public Broadcasting Services, Denver, CO
2,260	Northeastern Colorado Transportation Authority, Denver, CO -- van
750	United Way of Morgan County, Decatur, AL -- 2001 campaign

PEW CHARITABLE TRUSTS

Giving Contact

Rebecca W. Rimel, President & CEO
One Commerce Sq.
2005 Market St., Suite 1700
Philadelphia, PA 19103
Phone: (215)575-9050
Fax: (215)575-4939
E-mail: info@pewtrusts.com
Web: http://www.pewtrusts.com

Alternate Contact

Phone: (215)419-6000

Description

Founded: 1948
EIN: 236299309
Organization Type: General Purpose Foundation
Giving Locations: PA: Philadelphia internationally; nationally.
Grant Types: Conference/Seminar, Fellowship, General Support, Project, Research.

Donor Information

Founder: The Pew Charitable Trusts is the collective name for the seven individual charitable trusts established by the two sons and two daughters of Joseph N. Pew, the founder of the Sun Oil Company. The first of the trusts, the Pew Memorial Trust, was founded in 1948. Smaller trusts were subsequently established to fund the Pews' personal philanthropic interests. Those included within the Pew Charitable Trusts are the Pew Memorial Trust; J. Howard Pew Freedom Trust; Mabel Pew Myrin Trust; J. N. Pew, Jr., Charitable Trust; Medical Trust; Mary Anderson Trust; and Knollbrook Trust. Because there is overlap in the areas that the seven trusts support, they share a single set of guidelines to establish eligibility for funding. Grant funds are allocated from the individual trusts based on their funding priorities.

John Howard Pew, the second son of Joseph N. Pew, was born in 1882 in Bradford, PA. Following graduation from Grove City College in 1900, and after taking several advanced courses at the Massachusetts Institute of Technology, he joined the Sun Oil Company. He and his brother, Joseph N. Pew Jr., assumed control of the company in 1912 after their father's death. His personal trust, established in 1957, supports organizations and institutions embodying the values of hard work, Christian values, free enterprise, and access to opportunity for all individuals. He also assisted numerous organizations dedicated to improving the quality of life in Philadelphia. J. Howard Pew died in 1971.

Mary Ethel Pew, the third child of Joseph N. Pew, was born in 1884 in Pittsburgh, PA. After graduating from Bryn Mawr College in 1906, she remained in Philadelphia where the Pew family relocated from Pittsburgh. Following her mother's death from cancer, Mary Ethel Pew devoted her resources to the support of cancer research and health care both as a volunteer and a board member for various institutions. She became particularly interested in Philadelphia's Lankenau Hospital and Institute for Cancer Research. She also funded various Philadelphia cultural, educational, and social service organizations. The Medical Trust was established in 1979 through her will.

Joseph N. Pew Jr., the youngest son of Joseph N. Pew, was born in 1886 in Pittsburgh, PA. After graduating with a degree in mechanical engineering from Cornell University in 1908, he worked briefly in the administrative offices of Sun Oil before leaving to learn the business from the ground up as an oilman in Illinois and as a roadlayer in South America. In 1912, upon his father's death, he became a vice president of the company. During his years at Sun, Mr. Pew focused his energies on designing new methods and products for the company. His contributions to educational and charitable institutions reflected his belief in free political expression, equal opportunity, and the free market system. The J. N. Pew, Jr., Charitable Trust was established from his estate following his death in 1963.

Mabel Pew Myrin, the youngest daughter of Joseph N. Pew, was born in 1889 in Pittsburgh, PA. Married in 1919, she and her husband, H. Alarik W. Myrin, moved to Argentina where they managed ranch property and developed mineral resources. After returning to the United States in the 1930s, they dedicated themselves to improving educational methods, aiding the handicapped, and preserving soil fertility. Mrs. Myrin strongly supported both the Waldorf educational method which takes a holistic approach to teaching, and the Camphill movement which applies Waldorf methods to the care and education of the handicapped. She also served as a trustee or board member for many institutions. The Mabel Pew Myrin Trust was established in 1957 to improve the human condition through support to the arts, education, health, and human services. She died in 1972.

Financial Summary

Total Giving: $166,330,000 (2002); $230,135,400 (2001); $235,605,000 (2000)

Assets: $3,800,000,000 (2002 approx); $4,682,000,000 (2001 approx); $4,800,000,000 (2000 approx)

Typical Recipients

Arts & Humanities: Arts Festivals, Arts Funds, Arts Outreach, Dance, Ethnic & Folk Arts, Film & Video, Historic Preservation, History & Archaeology, Libraries, Museums/Galleries, Music, Opera, Performing Arts, Public Broadcasting, Theater, Visual Arts

Civic & Public Affairs: Botanical Gardens/Parks, Business/Free Enterprise, Clubs, Economic Development, Economic Policy, Employment/Job Training, First Amendment Issues, Civic & Public Affairs-General, Housing, Philanthropic Organizations, Professional & Trade Associations, Public Policy, Rural Affairs, Urban & Community Affairs, Women's Affairs, Zoos/Aquariums

Education: Afterschool/Enrichment Programs, Arts/Humanities Education, Arts/Humanities Education, Colleges & Universities, Continuing Education, Education Associations, Education Reform, Elementary Education (Private), Environmental Education, Faculty Development, Education-General, International Exchange, International Studies, Journalism/Media Education, Leadership Training, Literacy, Medical Education, Minority Education, Private Education (Precollege), Public Education (Precollege), Religious Education, Science/Mathematics Education, Social Sciences Education, Student Aid, Vocational & Technical Education

Environment: Air/Water Quality, Energy, Forestry, Environment-General, Protection, Resource Conservation, Watershed, Wildlife Protection

Health: Adolescent Health Issues, AIDS/HIV, Cancer, Children's Health/Hospitals, Emergency/Ambulance Services, Geriatric Health, Health Policy/Cost Containment, Health Organizations, Home-Care Services, Nutrition, Prenatal Health Issues, Public Health

International: Foreign Arts Organizations, Foreign Educational Institutions, Health Care/Hospitals, Human Rights, International Affairs, International Development, International Environmental Issues, International Organizations, International Peace & Security Issues, International Relations, International Relief Efforts, Missionary/Religious Activities, Trade

Religion: Churches, Religion-General, Jewish Causes, Ministries, Religious Organizations, Religious Welfare, Seminaries, Social/Policy Issues

Science: Science Museums, Scientific Centers & Institutes, Scientific Organizations, Scientific Research

Social Services: Child Welfare, Community Service Organizations, Crime Prevention, Domestic Violence, Family Planning, Family Services, Refugee Assistance, Senior Services, Substance Abuse, United Funds/United Ways, Volunteer Services, Youth Organizations

Application Procedures

Initial Contact: Contact the Trusts for application guidelines, which include a list of program staff members. Send a brief letter of inquiry (preferably fewer than three pages), summarizing the proposal, to the appropriate program staff member.

Application Requirements: The inquiry should summarize the project for which support is sought. This should fit within guidelines for funding. Letters should include a description of the organization, nature of work and a brief history of achievements, especially as they relate to the issue to be addressed; a statement of the problem to be addressed and an explanation of how it will be addressed; brief description of anticipated achievements or outcomes; description of time frame of proposed activities; estimated costs for the project or activity; and what is being requested from the Trusts. Full proposals are not encouraged without an initial contact with the staff.

Deadlines: None.

Review Process: Letters of inquiry are reviewed by the appropriate program staff and grant seekers will be notified within four to six weeks either by telephone or letter whether a request meets the funding criteria and guidelines of the program. If the request is of interest to the Trusts, the applicant will be asked to submit a full proposal, and an application package will be forwarded for completion. If the proposal is approved for funding, the applicant will be notified by letter within four to six weeks of a board meeting. The board of trustees meets in March, June, September, and December.

Notes: Prospective applicants are encouraged to request a copy of the Trusts' annual program guidelines and procedures pamphlet that provides detailed information on areas of interest to the Trusts, as well as funding restrictions. Examples of work, articles, reports, videos or other material should not be submitted with a letter of inquiry.

Restrictions

In general, the Trusts do not provide funding for capital funds, endowments, debt reduction, general operations, library acquisitions, or individuals.

Additional Information

The Glenmede Trust Company manages the funds and serves as trustee. In 1986, it reorganized the seven Trusts into one division for purposes of grantmaking and administration.

Although the Trusts have an interdisciplinary grants fund for proposals that fit within the guidelines of two or more programs, this status is determined by program officers at the Trusts. Applicants should apply to the program that suits their proposal.

The Trusts report that they offer occasional seminars and workshops on how to apply for grants to special programs, as well as communications and strategic planning assistance to selected grantees.

Publications: Annual Report; Application Form; Guidelines

Foundation Officials

Henry B. Bernstein: director finance
Maureen K. Byrnes: director health human services program NONPR AFFIL vice president: Association American Universities.
Robert Henderson Campbell: director B Pittsburgh, PA 1937. ED Princeton University BS (1959); Carnegie Mellon University MS (1961); Massachusetts Institute of Technology MA (1978). CORP AFFIL director: Philadelphia National Bank; director: Hershey Foods Corp.; director: CIGNA Corp.; director: Elwyn Institute. NONPR AFFIL member: American Petroleum Institute.
Susan Williams Catherwood: director CORP AFFIL director: PECO Energy Co. NONPR AFFIL chairman: University Pennsylvania Health System.
Bruce C. Compton: grants information manager
Michael X. Delli Carpini: director public policy program
Eugenia Dobron: proposal coord
Marian A. Godfrey: director culture program
Joy A. Horwitz: director legal affairs
Donald Kimelman: director venture fund
Thomas W. Langfitt, MD: director B Clarksburg, WV 1927. ED Princeton University AB (1949); Johns Hopkins University MD (1953). PRIM CORP EMPL chairman, president, chief executive officer, director: Glenmede Trust Co. NONPR AFFIL fellow: Royal College Surgeons; member: Society Neural Surgeons; member: National Academy Sciences; member: American Philosophical Society; member: Institute Medicine. CLUB AFFIL Union League Club.
Luis E. Lugo: director religion program
David J. Morse: director public affairs
Arthur E. Pew, III: director
J. Howard Pew, II: director
J. N. Pew, III: director
Joseph N. Pew, IV, MD: director
Mary Catharine Pew, MD: director
Robert Anderson Pew: director B Philadelphia, PA 1936. ED Princeton University (1954-1956); Temple University BS (1959); Massachusetts Institute of Technology MS (1970). CORP AFFIL director: Sunoco Inc.; operations assistant prod, division: Sun Oil Co.; director: Glenmede Trust Co.; director: Sun Co. Inc.; director: Glenmede Corp. NONPR AFFIL trustee, chairman: Childrens Hospital Philadelphia; trustee: Curtis Institute Music; honorary member: American Hospital Association; trustee, vice chairman: Bryn Mawr College; member: Aircraft Owners & Pilots Association. CLUB AFFIL Union League Club; Northeast Harbor Fleet Club; Seal Harbor Club; Merion Cricket Club.
Sandy Pew: director
Joshua S. Reichert: director environment program
Rebecca Webster Rimel: president, chief executive officer, director ED University of Virginia BS (1973); James Madison University MBA (1983). CORP AFFIL director: Alex Brown Flag Investors Funds; executive vice president, director: Glenmede Trust Co. NONPR AFFIL director: Thomas Jefferson Memorial Foundation; member: Virginia State Nurses Association; member: Emergency Department Nurses Association; member: American Public Health Association; member: Council Foundations; member: American Association Neurosurgical Nurses; member: American Nurses Association; member: American Academy Nursing.
Susan Urahn: director education
Elizabeth A. W. Williams: director administration
Robert G. Williams: director

Grants Analysis

Disclosure Period: calendar year ending 2002
Total Grants: $166,330,000*
Number of Grants: 287
Average Grant: $579,547
Highest Grant: $9,920,000
Lowest Grant: $15,000
Typical Range: $250,000 to $1,000,000
***Note:** Grants alalysis provided by foundation.

Recent Grants

Note: Grants derived from 2001 Form 990.

General

1,000,000	Energy Foundation, San Francisco, CA
1,000,000	Union of Concerned Scientists, Inc., Washington, DC -- support efforts to increase the nation's commitment to energy efficiency and renewable energy
975,000	Pennsylvania Conservation Center, Harrisburg, PA -- for a statewide environmental organization for Pennsylvania
766,000	Strategies for the Global Environment, Inc., Arlington, VA -- support of the Pew Center
734,000	U.S. Working Group, Washington, DC -- to establish a certification infrastructure in Canada
666,000	Children's Hospital Foundation, Philadelphia, PA -- to support an information system for primary care delivery and outcomes research
633,000	Border WaterWorks, Santa Fe, NM -- help communities along the United State-Mexico border
600,000	Environmental Defense Fund, New York, NY -- for continuation of the Alliance for Environmental Innovation
571,000	Earthjustice Legal Defense Fund, Washington, DC -- continued support of the Ocean Law Project
566,000	Center for Agricultural Partnerships, Inc., Asheville, NC -- help implement practices resulting measurable and long-term benefits for farmers and the environment

PFIZER INC.

Company Headquarters

235 E. 42nd St.
New York, NY 10017-5755
Web: http://www.pfizer.com

Company Description

Founded: 1910
Ticker: PFE
Exchange: NYSE
Acquired: Warner-Lambert (2000); Pharmacia Corp. (2003).
Revenue: US$32.373 billion (2002)
Profit: US$9.126 billion (2002)
Employees: 90000 (2002)
Fortune Rank: 37, per FORTUNE Magazine's list of 500 Largest U.S. Corporations (2002).
SIC(s): 2833 Medicinals & Botanicals, 2834 Pharmaceutical Preparations, 3841 Surgical & Medical Instruments, 3842 Surgical Appliances & Supplies.

Operating Locations

Pfizer Inc. (CA--Irvine; CO--Denver; CT--Groton; DC--Washington; GA--Atlanta; IL--Schaumburg; IN--Terre Haute; MA--Boston; MI--Lansing, Linden; MN--St. Paul; NE--Lincoln; NY--Albany, Brooklyn, New York; PA--Slatington)

Nonmonetary Support

Value: $376,686,715 (2001); $283,300,000 (2000); $119,200,000 (1999)
Type: Donated Products
Volunteer Programs: The company sponsors the Pfizer Volunteer Program (PVP) which provides grants of $1,000 to nonprofit organizations with which the company's employees and retirees are regularly involved.
Contact: Kim Frawley, Manager Product Donations
Note: Nonmonetary contributions include donations of medicine and equipment to emergency relief and disaster aid. Product donations at fair market value.

Pfizer Foundation

Giving Contact

Rick Luftglass, Grants Coordinator
Pfizer Inc.
235 East 42nd Street
New York, NY 10017-5755
Phone: 800-733-4717
E-mail: Grant.Info@Pfizer.com
Web: http://www.pfizer.com/pfizerinc/philanthropy

Alternate Contact

Phone: (212)573-4477

Description

EIN: 136083839
Organization Type: Corporate Foundation
Giving Locations: NY: New York principally near operating locations and to national organizations.
Grant Types: Award, Conference/Seminar, Department, Emergency, Employee Matching Gifts, General Support, Matching.
Note: Employee matching gift ratio: 1 to 1.

Financial Summary

Total Giving: $446,968,724 (2001); $341,313,646 (2000); $154,800,000 (1999 approx). Note: Contributes through corporate direct giving program and foundation.
Giving Analysis: Giving for 2001 includes: foundation ($26,145,976); corporate direct giving ($44,136,033); nonmonetary support ($376,686,715); 2000: foundation ($20,486,436); corporate direct giving ($37,527,210); nonmonetary support ($283,300,000); 1999: foundation (approx $11,700,000); corporate direct giving ($23,900,000); nonmonetary support ($119,200,000);
Assets: $397,739,075 (2001); $352,434,496 (2000); $299,363,201 (1998)
Gifts Received: $300,000,000 (1998)

Typical Recipients

Arts & Humanities: Arts Associations & Councils, Arts Centers, Arts Funds, Dance, Arts & Humanities-General, Historic Preservation, History & Archaeology, Libraries, Museums/Galleries, Music, Opera, Performing Arts, Public Broadcasting, Theater
Civic & Public Affairs: African American Affairs, Asian American Affairs, Botanical Gardens/Parks, Business/Free Enterprise, Civil Rights, Economic Development, Economic Policy, Employment/Job Training, Civic & Public Affairs-General, Hispanic Affairs, Housing, Law & Justice, Legal Aid, Municipalities/Towns, Philanthropic Organizations, Professional & Trade Associations, Public Policy, Safety, Urban & Community Affairs, Women's Affairs, Zoos/Aquariums
Education: Agricultural Education, Arts/Humanities Education, Business Education, Business-School Partnerships, Colleges & Universities, Community & Junior Colleges, Economic Education, Education Associations, Education Funds, Education Reform, Elementary Education (Private), Elementary Education (Public), Engineering/Technological Education, Faculty Development, Education-General, International Exchange, International Studies, Leadership Training, Legal Education, Literacy, Medical Education, Minority Education, Private Education (Precollege), Public Education (Precollege), Science/Mathematics Education, Secondary Education (Public), Student Aid
Environment: Environment-General, Resource Conservation
Health: Adolescent Health Issues, AIDS/HIV, Alzheimers Disease, Arthritis, Cancer, Children's Health/Hospitals, Clinics/Medical Centers, Diabetes, Emergency/Ambulance Services, Eyes/Blindness, Health-General, Geriatric Health, Health Policy/Cost Containment, Health Funds, Health Organizations, Home-Care Services, Hospices, Hospitals, Medical Rehabilitation, Medical Research, Mental Health, Preventive Medicine/Wellness Organizations, Public Health, Single-Disease Health Associations, Transplant Networks/Donor Banks
International: Foreign Arts Organizations, Foreign Educational Institutions, International-General, Health Care/Hospitals, International Development, International Peace & Security Issues, International Relations
Science: Science-General, Science Exhibits & Fairs, Science Museums, Scientific Centers & Institutes, Scientific Labs, Scientific Labs, Scientific Research
Social Services: Child Abuse, Child Welfare, Community Centers, Community Service Organizations, Counseling, Day Care, Delinquency & Criminal Rehabilitation, Emergency Relief, Family Services, Food/Clothing Distribution, People with Disabilities, Recreation & Athletics, Senior Services, Shelters/Homelessness, Substance Abuse, United Funds/United Ways, Volunteer Services, YMCA/YWCA/YMHA/YWHA, Youth Organizations

Application Procedures

Initial Contact: Organizations in communities where Pfizer is located are advised to contact the community relations representative at the site.
Application Requirements: Include background on the organization and a statement of history and accomplishments to date; a brief description of the program for which funding is requested, including rationale, amount requested, specific objectives, and timetable.
Deadlines: None.
Notes: Pfizer generally solicits proposals from organizations and is unlikely to fund unsolicited requests.

Restrictions

Does not support individuals; political causes or candidates; anti-business organizations; or organizations that practice discrimination or limit membership on the basis of race, creed, gender, age, sexual orientation, or national origin. Pfizer does not support fundraising events or activities such as telethons, walk-athons, and races; specific performances or concerts; sporting events; endowment campaigns; building fund drives and capital campaigns (except science lab renovations in partner schools and universities); film, video, television, or radio projects; request for loans or debt retirement; trips, tours, or cultural exchange programs; conferences, seminars, briefing programs and similar activities (except in instances where the event evolves from company programs in health care and science education); organizations already supported through United Way contributions; or operating expenses of United Way local agencies (except through annual United Way campaigns).
Both the company and the foundation only consider applicants meeting requirements of Internal Revenue Code Section 501(c)(3); foundation requires that applicants also meet requirements of Section 509(a)(1), (2), or (3).

Additional Information

Generally, the company sponsors local organizations in company operating communities.
Gives special consideration to programs at which employees volunteer.
Disaster aid generally dispensed through established international relief organizations. Contact operating divisions for information on nonmonetary support, and contact the corporate office for product donations.
In February 2000, Pfizer Inc. announced plans to merge with Warner-Lambert Co.

Corporate Officials

C. Lou Clemente: executive vice president corporate affairs, secretary, corporate counsel B New York, NY 1937. ED College of the Holy Cross AB (1958); Columbia University LLB (1961). PRIM CORP EMPL executive vice president corporate affairs, secretary, corporate counsel: Pfizer Inc. NONPR AFFIL director:

Project Hope; member executive committee: U.S. Council International Business; chairman: International Trachoma Initiative Inc.; director: American Women's Economic Development Corp.; director: Fisk University.

Jeffrey B. Kindler: senior vice president, general counsel ED Tufts University BA (1977); Harvard Law School JD (1980). PRIM CORP EMPL senior vice president, general counsel: Pfizer Inc. NONPR AFFIL member: Citizens Crime Commission; member: City Bar Fund; member: Atlantic Legal Foundation; board member: Jane Addams Juvenile Court Foundation; member: American Arbitration Association.

Henry A. McKinnell, PhD: chairman, chief executive officer, director B February 23, 1943. ED Stanford University PhD; Stanford University MBA; University of British Columbia BA. PRIM CORP EMPL chairman, chief executive officer, director: Pfizer Inc. CORP AFFIL director: Aviall Inc.; director: Dun & Bradstreet Corp.

John F. Niblack, PhD: vice chairman, president global research & development, director ED Oklahoma State University BS; University of Illinois PhD; University of Illinois MS. PRIM CORP EMPL vice chairman, president global research & development, director: Pfizer Inc.

David L. Shedlarz: executive vice president, chief financial officer ED Michigan State University BS (1970); New York University Leonard N. Stern School of Business MBA (1975). PRIM CORP EMPL executive vice president, chief financial officer: Pfizer Inc. CORP AFFIL director: Pitney Bowes Inc.; advisory board member: J.P. Morgan Chase & Co. NONPR AFFIL board member: National Multiple Sclerosis Society.

Giving Program Officials

Paula Luff: senior program officer PRIM CORP EMPL manager corporate philanthropy programs: Pfizer Inc.

Sarah Williams: assistant director

Foundation Officials

C. Lou Clemente: chairman (see above)

Terence Joseph Gallagher: secretary, director B New York, NY 1934. ED Manhattan College BA (1955); Harvard University JD (1958); New York University LLM (1966). PRIM CORP EMPL vice president, assistant secretary, attorney: Pfizer Inc. CORP AFFIL secretary, director: Adforce Inc. NONPR AFFIL member: Independent Order Sons Malta; member: New York State Bar Association; trustee: Business Advisory Council Federal Reports; director: Calvary Hospital Fund; member: American Bar Association; director: American Society of Corporate Secretaries.

James Richard Gardner: vice president B Wellsville, NY 1944. ED United States Military Academy BS (1966); Princeton University MA (1968); Long Island University MBA (1977); Princeton University PhD (1977); United States Army War College (1989). NONPR AFFIL member: USMA Association Graduates; member: West Point Society New York; member advisory committee: Princeton University Department Astrophysical Science; member: Planning Forum; member advisory council: Princeton University Center International Studies; member: North American Society Corporate Planning; member: Phi Kappa Phi; director: Boy Scouts America New York Council; member: National Investor Relations Institute.

Charles Hardwick: executive director foundation

Kevin Keating: treasurer PRIM CORP EMPL assistant treasurer: Pfizer Overseas Inc.

Jay P. Kosminsky: president PRIM CORP EMPL executive director communications philanthropy: Pfizer Inc.

Paula Luff: senior program officer (see above)

Rick Luftglass: associate director corporate philanthropy

B. J. Robison: vice president

Grants Analysis

Disclosure Period: calendar year ending 2001
Total Grants: $44,136,033*
Number of Grants: 433
Average Grant: $86,668
Highest Grant: $5,000,000
Typical Range: $5,000 to $150,000
*Note: Giving excludes foundation giving and nonmonetary support. Grants analysis provided by the corporation.

Recent Grants

Note: Grants derived from 2001 Form 990.

General

5,000,000	Twin Towers Fund, New York, NY	
500,000	Louisiana State University Health Sciences Center, Shreveport, LA	
500,000	MCV Foundation, Richmond, VA	
500,000	Project Hope, Douglasville, GA	
500,000	San Francisco AIDS Foundation, San Francisco, CA	
462,930	President and Fellows of Harvard, Cambridge, MA	
315,000	San Francisco AIDS Foundation, San Francisco, CA	
300,000	Asian Foundation	
300,000	Duke University, Durham, NC	
300,000	United States Fund for UNICEF, New York, NY	

The Carl And Lily Pforzheimer Foundation, Inc.

Giving Contact

Mary Kitabjian, III, Executive Secretary
650 Madison Avenue, 23rd Floor
New York, NY 10022
Phone: (212)223-6500
Fax: (212)223-2693

Description

Founded: 1942
EIN: 135624374
Organization Type: General Purpose Foundation
Giving Locations: NY: New York nationally.
Grant Types: General Support.

Donor Information

Founder: The foundation was established in 1942 by Carl H. Pforzheimer. Many members of the family serve as officers or directors of the foundation.

Financial Summary

Total Giving: $5,712,000 (2002 approx); $5,465,334 (2000); $4,644,750 (1998)
Assets: $29,000,000 (2002 approx); $53,261,923 (2000); $60,030,413 (1998)

Typical Recipients

Arts & Humanities: Arts Associations & Councils, Arts Centers, Arts Institutes, Community Arts, Dance, Film & Video, Historic Preservation, History & Archaeology, Libraries, Literary Arts, Museums/Galleries, Music, Opera, Performing Arts, Public Broadcasting, Theater, Visual Arts
Civic & Public Affairs: Botanical Gardens/Parks, Clubs, Community Foundations, Economic Development, Employment/Job Training, Civic & Public Affairs-General, Law & Justice, Municipalities/Towns, Nonprofit Management, Professional & Trade Associations, Public Policy, Urban & Community Affairs, Zoos/Aquariums
Education: Arts/Humanities Education, Colleges & Universities, Community & Junior Colleges, Education Associations, Education Reform, Environmental Education, Education-General, Literacy, Minority Education, Private Education (Precollege), Public Education (Precollege), Secondary Education (Public), Student Aid
Environment: Environment-General
Health: AIDS/HIV, Clinics/Medical Centers, Emergency/Ambulance Services, Eyes/Blindness, Hospitals, Nursing Services
International: Foreign Arts Organizations, International Affairs, International Development
Religion: Synagogues/Temples
Science: Science Museums, Scientific Centers & Institutes, Scientific Organizations
Social Services: At-Risk Youth, Child Welfare, Community Centers, Community Service Organizations, Emergency Relief, Family Services, People with Disabilities, Substance Abuse

Application Procedures

Initial Contact: Send full outline of the project.
Application Requirements: There is no formal application form, but proposals should include financial information.
Deadlines: None.
Review Process: The board meets quarterly in April, June, October, and December. Notification usually occurs following the meeting.

Restrictions

The foundation does not make grants to individuals or for bricks and mortar projects.

Foundation Officials

Edgar D. Aronson: director B New York, NY 1934. ED Harvard University AB (1956); Harvard University MBA (1962). PRIM CORP EMPL president: EDACO Inc. CORP AFFIL director: Petrogas Ltd.; director: HL Oakes Co. Inc.; director: MidAmerican Energy Holdings Co.; director: CalEnergy Co. Inc.; director: Hertford Inc. NV; director: APL NV. NONPR AFFIL member: Marine Corps Res Officers Association; trustee: South Street Seaport Museum; member: Cruising Association; member: 1st Marine Division Association. CLUB AFFIL Royal York YS; Mensa; New York Yacht Club; Eire Club; Harvard Club; Annabels Club; Bass Harbor Yacht Club.

Nancy P. Aronson: vice president, director

Anthony L. Ferranti: comptroller

George L. K. Frelinghuysen: assistant treasurer, director ED Princeton University (1973); Columbia University (1975).

Mary Kitabjian: assistant secretary

Carl A. Pforzheimer: director

Carl Howard Pforzheimer, III: president, treasurer, director B 1936. ED Harvard University MBA (1963). PRIM CORP EMPL Carl H Pforzheimer & Co. NONPR AFFIL chairman board, director: Visiting Nurse Service New York.

Carol K. Pforzheimer: director

Elizabeth S. Pforzheimer: director

Martin Franklin Richman: secretary B Newark, NJ 1930. ED Saint Lawrence University BA (1950); Harvard University LLB (1953). PRIM CORP EMPL counsel: Kirkpatrick & Lockhart LLP. NONPR AFFIL fellow: New York State Bar Foundation; vice chairman, trustee: Saint Lawrence University; member: New York State Bar Association; director: Friends Law Library Congress; member: New York County Lawyers Association; member: Association Bar New York City; member: Federal Bar Association; member: American Law Institute; member: American Bar Association; fellow: American Bar Foundation.

Alison A. Sherman: director

Thomas Sobol: director

Grants Analysis

Disclosure Period: calendar year ending 2000
Total Grants: $5,465,334
Number of Grants: 51
Average Grant: $66,215*
Highest Grant: $1,088,361

Lowest Grant: $2,125
Typical Range: $15,000 to $100,000
*Note: Average grants figure excludes two highest grants ($1,088,361 and $1,000,000).

Recent Grants

Note: Grants derived from 2000 Form 990.

Library-Related

1,088,361	New York Public Library, New York, NY
2,125	Fremont County Library Foundation

General

1,000,000	Pace University, White Plains, NY
500,000	Bank Street College of Education, New York, NY
500,000	Horace Mann School, Bronx, NY
275,000	Mount Sinai Medical Center, New York, NY -- EAP
250,000	National Humanities Center, Research Triangle Park, NC
200,000	Radcliffe College, Cambridge, MA
150,000	Dance Theater of Harlem, New York, NY
100,000	Lincoln Center Institute, New York, NY
100,000	National Civic League, Denver, CO
100,000	University of Texas at Austin, Austin, TX

PHELPS DODGE CORP.

Company Headquarters

Phoenix, AZ
Web: http://www.phelpsdodge.com

Company Description

Founded: 1834
Ticker: PD
Exchange: NYSE
Acquired: Cyprus Amax (1999).
Revenue: US$3.722 billion (2002).
Employees: 11000 (2001)
Fortune Rank: 428, per FORTUNE Magazine's list of 500 Largest U.S. Corporations (2002).
SIC(s): 1021 Copper Ores, 2819 Industrial Inorganic Chemicals Nec, 2895 Carbon Black, 3331 Primary Copper.

Operating Locations

Phelps Dodge Corp. (AZ--Morenci, Phoenix; AR--El Dorado; CA--Irvine; FL--Coral Gables; GA--Atlanta, Trenton; IN--Fort Wayne; KY--Edmonton, Henderson, Hopkinsville; LA--Franklin; NJ--Bayway, Elizabeth; NM--Hurley, Santa Rita, Tyrone; NY--Ossining; NC--Laurinburg; OH--Springfield; TX--El Paso; WV--Moundsville)

Nonmonetary Support

Type: Donated Products; In-kind Services

Phelps Dodge Foundation

Giving Contact

Ann Gibson, Community Affairs
2600 N. Central Avenue
Phoenix, AZ 85004-3014
Phone: (602)366-8100
Fax: (602)234-8082
E-mail: phx-communityaffairs@phelpsdodge.com
Web: http://www.phelpsdodge.com/index-community.html

Alternate Contact

Grants Administrator
Phelps Dodge Corp.
One N. Central Avenue
Phoenix, AZ 85004-4416
Phone: 800-528-1182

Note: Contact for proposal submission and general questions. Inquiries to the 800 number should be directed to extension 6050.

Description

EIN: 136077350
Organization Type: Corporate Foundation
Giving Locations: communities where company maintains major operating facilities.
Grant Types: Employee Matching Gifts, General Support, Multiyear/Continuing Support, Scholarship.
Note: Matching gifts, equal to 25% to 30% of annual grants, are made to educational, non-profit voluntary hospitals, family issues, cultural organizations and institutions.

Financial Summary

Total Giving: $2,101,793 (2001); $2,173,688 (2000); $2,000,000 (1999 approx). Note: Contributes through corporate direct giving program and foundation.
Giving Analysis: Giving for 2000 includes: foundation scholarships ($21,210); foundation grants to United Way ($178,451); foundation matching gifts ($408,537); foundation ($1,565,490); 1998: foundation matching gifts ($350,000); foundation scholarship ($379,150); foundation ($824,247); 1997: foundation matching gifts ($363,688); foundation scholarships ($393,227) foundation ($848,710)
Assets: $18,470,532 (2001); $21,418,319 (2000); $18,407,619 (1998)
Gifts Received: $500,000 (1995)

Typical Recipients

Arts & Humanities: Arts Associations & Councils, Arts Centers, Arts Funds, Ballet, Community Arts, History & Archaeology, Libraries, Museums/Galleries, Music, Opera, Performing Arts, Public Broadcasting, Theater
Civic & Public Affairs: Botanical Gardens/Parks, Business/Free Enterprise, Civil Rights, Economic Development, Economic Policy, Employment/Job Training, Civic & Public Affairs-General, Housing, Law & Justice, Public Policy, Safety, Urban & Community Affairs, Women's Affairs, Zoos/Aquariums
Education: Arts/Humanities Education, Business Education, Colleges & Universities, Community & Junior Colleges, Economic Education, Education Associations, Education Funds, Engineering/Technological Education, Environmental Education, Education-General, Health & Physical Education, International Exchange, International Studies, Medical Education, Minority Education, Private Education (Precollege), Science/Mathematics Education, Student Aid
Environment: Environment-General
Health: Cancer, Children's Health/Hospitals, Clinics/Medical Centers, Emergency/Ambulance Services, Geriatric Health, Health Funds, Health Organizations, Hospitals, Kidney, Medical Research, Medical Training
International: Foreign Educational Institutions, International-General, Health Care/Hospitals, International Peace & Security Issues, International Relations, International Relief Efforts
Religion: Religious Organizations, Religious Welfare
Science: Science Museums, Scientific Centers & Institutes
Social Services: Child Abuse, Child Welfare, Community Service Organizations, Counseling, Day Care, Domestic Violence, Family Planning, Family Services, Recreation & Athletics, Scouts, Senior Services, Shelters/Homelessness, Social Services-General, United Funds/United Ways, YMCA/YWCA/YMHA/YWHA, Youth Organizations

Application Procedures

Initial Contact: Send a brief letter on the organization's letterhead and a proposal.
Application Requirements: Include a two-page summary statement of the organization's project or program and current needs, including amount requested, purpose of funds sought, funding period, and key program or deadline dates; program budget outlining all sources of financial support, including amounts committed or pending that may leverage a contributions by Phelps Dodge; audited financial statement for the most recent fiscal year; and proof of tax-exempt status. Requests for more than $5,000 must also include a brief description of how the proposal meets community needs that are not currently being met by other organizations; an explanation of how the organization is qualified to carry out the proposal; an evaluation plan; a project timetable for implementation, communication and evaluation; the organization's operating budget for the past two years, indicating the percentages allocated for program/services; administration; fundraising and general expenses.
Deadlines: None.
Decision Notification: The budget is determined at the annual meeting held in September.

Restrictions

Does not support discriminatory organizations; programs in communities where Phelps Dodge does not operate; individuals; advertising; fraternal, veterans or labor organizations; religious activities, churches, or church sponsored programs limited to church members; political or lobbying groups; foundations that are grant-making entities; auxiliary organizations (unless the auxiliary is the sole fundraising arm of the parent organization); debt-reduction or operation deficit funding; capital campaigns or equipment; or organizations that pose a conflict with the goals, programs, products or employees of Phelps Dodge.

Additional Information

Company matches employee contributions to accredited colleges and universities, including junior colleges; privately financed, nonprofit accredited secondary schools; voluntary hospitals; museums; performing arts organizations; botanical gardens; public broadcasting services; or zoological societies.
Publications: A Tradition of Giving

Corporate Officials

S. David Colton: vice president, general counsel ED Brigham Young University BA; Brigham Young University J. Reuben Clark College of Law JD. PRIM CORP EMPL senior vice president, general counsel: Phelps Dodge Corp. NONPR AFFIL member: American Bar Association; member: Utah State Bar Association.
Ramiro G. Peru: senior vice president, chief financial officer B Morenci, AZ 1956. ED University of Arizona BS (1978). PRIM CORP EMPL senior vice president, chief financial officer: Phelps Dodge Corp.
David L. Pulatie: senior vice president human resources ED Arizona State College BS; Northern Arizona University MA.
Timothy R. Snider: senior vice president ED Northern Arizona University BS. PRIM CORP EMPL senior vice president: Phelps Dodge Corp. ADD CORP EMPL president: Phelps Dodge Mining Co.
Gregory W. Stevens: vice president, treasurer ED Yale University BA. PRIM CORP EMPL vice president, treasurer: Phelps Dodge Corp.
Robert C. Swan: vice president, secretary PRIM CORP EMPL vice president, secretary: Phelps Dodge Corp.
J. Steven Whisler: chairman, president, chief executive officer B 1954. ED Colorado School of Mines MS; University of Colorado BS; University of Denver College of Law JD. PRIM CORP EMPL chairman, president, chief executive officer: Phelps Dodge Corp. CORP AFFIL director: Burlington Northern Santa Fe Corp.; director: Southern Peru Copper Corp. NONPR AFFIL chairman: Copper Development Association; member: Mining Metallurgical Society America; member: American Institute Mining Engineers.

Foundation Officials

Kalidas Madhavpeddi: vice president
Robert C. Swan: president (see above)

Grants Analysis

Disclosure Period: calendar year ending 2001
Total Grants: $1,524,968*
Number of Grants: 106
Average Grant: $14,386
Highest Grant: $140,000
Lowest Grant: $1,000
Typical Range: $2,500 to $30,000
*Note: Giving excludes matching gifts; scholarship; United Way.

Recent Grants

Note: Grants derived from 2001 Form 990.

Library-Related

18,000	Town of Jerome Library, Jerome, AZ

General

140,000	Colorado School of Mines, Golden, CO
92,000	American Red Cross, Phoenix, AZ
75,000	Habitat for Humanity, Phoenix, AZ
55,000	Phoenix Zoo, Phoenix, AZ
50,000	Challenger Learning Center of Arizona, Phoenix, AZ
49,960	National Merit Scholarship Corporation, Evanston, IL
37,500	University of Arizona, Tucson, AZ
31,000	Arizona State University, Tempe, AZ
30,000	Colorado School of Mines, Golden, CO
27,000	Women's Center for Southeastern Connecticut, Norwich, CT

DR. AND MRS. ARTHUR WILLIAM PHILLIPS CHARITABLE TRUST

Giving Contact

William J. McFate, Trustee
229 Elm St.
PO Box 316
Oil City, PA 16301-0316
Phone: (814)676-2736

Description

Founded: 1978
EIN: 256201015
Organization Type: Private Foundation
Giving Locations: PA: Northwestern Pennsylvania
Grant Types: General Support, Project, Scholarship.

Donor Information

Founder: the late Arthur William Phillips

Financial Summary

Total Giving: $586,375 (fiscal year ending September 30, 2002); $695,623 (fiscal 2000); $857,916 (fiscal 1997)
Giving Analysis: Giving for fiscal 2001 includes: foundation scholarships ($150,000)
Assets: $11,857,963 (fiscal 2002); $16,551,801 (fiscal 2000); $14,755,614 (fiscal 1997)

Typical Recipients

Arts & Humanities: Arts Centers, Historic Preservation, History & Archaeology, Libraries, Museums/Galleries, Music, Theater
Civic & Public Affairs: Botanical Gardens/Parks, Civic & Public Affairs-General, Safety, Urban & Community Affairs
Education: Colleges & Universities, Education Associations, Education Funds, Minority Education, Science/Mathematics Education, Secondary Education (Private), Student Aid

Health: Cancer, Children's Health/Hospitals, Emergency/Ambulance Services, Health Organizations, Heart, Hospitals, Nursing Services, Prenatal Health Issues, Single-Disease Health Associations
Religion: Churches, Religious Welfare
Science: Scientific Organizations
Social Services: Camps, Child Welfare, Community Service Organizations, Domestic Violence, Family Services, People with Disabilities, Recreation & Athletics, Scouts, Senior Services, YMCA/YWCA/YMHA/YWHA, Youth Organizations

Application Procedures

Initial Contact: Requests must be submitted in triplicate. Include a description of organization, annual budget, and proof of tax-exempt status.
Deadlines: None.

Restrictions

Preference is given to organizations having medical or educational purposes.

Foundation Officials

Judge William E. Breene: trustee
Edith Gilmore Letcher: director
Edith Gilmore Letcher: trustee
William J. McFate: trustee

Grants Analysis

Disclosure Period: fiscal year ending September 30, 2002
Total Grants: $436,375*
Number of Grants: 28
Average Grant: $10,053*
Highest Grant: $100,000
Lowest Grant: $1,500
Typical Range: $5,000 to $20,000
*Note: Giving excludes scholarships. Average grant figure excludes two highest grants ($175,000).

Recent Grants

Note: Grants derived from fiscal 2000 Form 990.

Library-Related

7,870	Clarion Free Library, Clarion, PA -- purchase new copier

General

100,000	Grove City College, Grove City, PA -- assist with construction of new academic classroom building
100,000	Westminster College, New Wilmington, PA -- assist with the renovation of Thompson-Clark Hall
76,148	Sugar Valley Lodge, Franklin, PA -- food costs for residents with inadequate income
50,000	Emlenton Presbyterian Church, Emlenton, PA -- upgrade bell tower and steeples, install chair lift
50,000	Pennsylvania State Erie, The Behrend College, Erie, PA -- matching addition to both existing scholarship fund
50,000	Salvation Army, Oil City, PA -- capital improvement project
50,000	Slippery Rock University, Slippery Rock, PA -- matching addition to existing scholarship fund
25,000	Clarion University, Clarion, PA -- assist with renovation of Harvey Hall at Venago Campus
25,000	Thiel College, Greenville, PA -- assist with installation of multimedia projection system and to purchase language lab equipment
20,000	Oil City YMCA, Oil City, PA -- renovation of fitness center

L. E. PHILLIPS FAMILY FOUNDATION

Giving Contact

Mary Jo Cohen, President and Director
National Presto Industries
3925 N. Hastings Way
Eau Claire, WI 54703
Phone: (715)839-2139
Fax: (715)839-2148
Web: http://www.goPresto.com

Description

Founded: 1943
EIN: 396046126
Organization Type: Family Foundation
Giving Locations: WI: Chippewa County, Eau Claire County, Northwestern Wisconsin
Grant Types: Capital, General Support, Operating Expenses, Professorship, Project, Research, Scholarship.

Donor Information

Founder: Lewis E. Phillips established the L. E. Phillips Charities in Wisconsin in 1943. The foundation's name recently was changed to the L. E. Phillips Family Foundation. Mr. Phillips was president and director of the manufacturing business of Ed Phillips and Sons Company. He was head of National Presto Industries, formerly named the National Pressure Cooker Company, for over 25 years. The foundation is administered primarily by members of the Phillips family, including Lewis E. Phillip's son-in-law, Melvin Samuel Cohen, who is the current chairman of National Presto Industries.

Financial Summary

Total Giving: $2,707,000 (fiscal year ending February 28, 2003 approx); $2,707,000 (fiscal 2002 approx); $2,815,010 (fiscal 2001)
Giving Analysis: Giving for fiscal 2001 includes: foundation scholarships ($4,200); foundation grants to United Way ($15,000); fiscal 1999: foundation scholarships ($51,500); foundation ($1,315,000) fiscal 1997: foundation scholarships ($52,556)
Assets: $63,000,000 (fiscal 2002 approx); $60,613,751 (fiscal 2001); $58,685,770 (fiscal 1999)
Gifts Received: $127,201 (fiscal 1997); $127,201 (fiscal 1996); $599,849 (fiscal 1995). Note: In fiscal 1993-1997, contributions were received from Edith Phillips 1983 Charitable Trust. In fiscal 1995, contributions were also received from Boy Scout Camp Trust u/w L. E. Phillips.

Typical Recipients

Arts & Humanities: Arts Associations & Councils, Arts Centers, Arts Institutes, Ballet, Dance, Libraries, Museums/Galleries, Music, Opera, Public Broadcasting, Theater
Civic & Public Affairs: Business/Free Enterprise, Clubs, Community Foundations, Employment/Job Training, Ethnic Organizations, Civic & Public Affairs-General, Law & Justice, Legal Aid, Parades/Festivals, Philanthropic Organizations, Professional & Trade Associations, Public Policy, Safety, Urban & Community Affairs
Education: Arts/Humanities Education, Business Education, Colleges & Universities, Faculty Development, Education-General, Gifted & Talented Programs, Leadership Training, Legal Education, Medical Education, Medical Education, Minority Education, Private Education (Precollege), Public Education (Precollege), Religious Education, Secondary Education (Private), Secondary Education (Public), Student Aid, Vocational & Technical Education
Environment: Resource Conservation, Wildlife Protection
Health: AIDS/HIV, Children's Health/Hospitals, Health-General, Geriatric Health, Health Policy/Cost

Containment, Health Organizations, Heart, Hospitals, Hospitals (University Affiliated), Medical Rehabilitation, Medical Research, Public Health, Single-Disease Health Associations

International: Foreign Arts Organizations, International Environmental Issues, International Peace & Security Issues, Missionary/Religious Activities

Religion: Churches, Dioceses, Jewish Causes, Religious Welfare, Social/Policy Issues, Synagogues/ Temples, Synagogues/Temples

Social Services: Animal Protection, Big Brother/Big Sister, Community Centers, Community Service Organizations, Crime Prevention, Day Care, People with Disabilities, Recreation & Athletics, Scouts, Senior Services, Special Olympics, Substance Abuse, United Funds/United Ways, YMCA/YWCA/YMHA/ YWHA, Youth Organizations

Application Procedures

Initial Contact: The foundation has no formal application requirements or procedures. Applicants should send a letter of inquiry.

Application Requirements: The letter should describe the organization and project for which funds are sought and include a budget.

Deadlines: The foundation prefers to receive inquiries before the end of the fiscal year in February.

Restrictions

Grants are not made to individuals.

Foundation Officials

James F. Bartl: secretary, director B Saint Paul, MN 1940. ED Saint Thomas University (1962); Marquette University JD (1965). PRIM CORP EMPL secretary: National Presto Industries, Inc. CORP AFFIL assistant secretary: Presto Manufacturing Co. NONPR AFFIL member: American Society of Corporate Secretaries.

Eileen Phillips Cohen: director

Maryjo Rose Cohen: vice president, treasurer, director B Eau Claire, WI 1952. ED University of Michigan (1973); University of Michigan JD (1976). PRIM CORP EMPL president, chief executive officer, director: National Presto Industries, Inc. CORP AFFIL secretary, treasurer, director: Presto Export Ltd.; secretary, treasurer, director: Presto Manufacturing Co.; vice president, director: National Pipeline Co.; secretary, treasurer, director: National Defense Corp.; secretary, assistant treasurer, director: National Holding Investment Co.; vice president, secretary, treasurer, director: Jackson Sales & Storage Co.; vice president, director: National Automatic Pipeline Oper Inc.; secretary, treasurer, director: Canton Sales & Storage Co.; secretary, treasurer, director: Century Leasing & Liquidating Inc.

Melvin Samuel Cohen: president, director B Minneapolis, MN January 16, 1918. ED University of Minnesota BS (1939); University of Minnesota JD (1941). PRIM CORP EMPL chairman: National Presto Industries, Inc. ADD CORP EMPL vice president, director: National Automatic Pipeline Oper Inc.; president: National Defense Corp.; president: National Holding International Co.; vice president, director: National Pipeline Co.; president: Canton Sales & Storage Co.; president, director: Jackson Sales & Storage Co.; chairman, president, director: Presto International Ltd.; president, director: Presto Manufacturing Co.; president: Presto Export Ltd. CORP AFFIL president: Presto Export Ltd.; chairman, president: Presto Manufacturing Co.; president: Canton Sales & Storage Co.; president: Century Leasing & Liquidating Inc.

Patricia Ellenson: assistant secretary-treasurer

Edith Phillips: vice president, director

Grants Analysis

Disclosure Period: fiscal year ending February 28, 2001

Total Grants: $2,795,810*

Number of Grants: 65

Average Grant: $8,138*

Highest Grant: $2,275,000

Typical Range: $1,000 to $15,000

*Note: Giving excludes scholarships and United Way. Average grant figure excludes highest grant.

THE JAY AND ROSE PHILLIPS FAMILY FOUNDATION

Giving Contact

Patricia A. Cummings, Executive Director & Secretary
10 Second Street NE, Suite 200
Minneapolis, MN 55413
Phone: (612)623-1654
Fax: (612)623-1653
E-mail: phillipsfnd@phillipsfnd.org
Web: http://www.phillipsfnd.org

Description

Founded: 1944

EIN: 416019578

Organization Type: Family Foundation

Giving Locations: MN: seven-county metropolitan area of Minneapolis/St. Paul, MN

Grant Types: Capital, Project, Research, Scholarship, Seed Money.

Donor Information

Founder: The Jay and Rose Phillips Family Foundation was incorporated in 1944, with funds donated by Jay Phillips and members of the Phillips family.

Financial Summary

Total Giving: $9,529,712 (2001); $8,952,776 (2000); $7,764,095 (1999)

Giving Analysis: Giving for 1999 includes: foundation grants to United Way ($20,000) foundation scholarships ($86,000)

Assets: $194,210,759 (2001); $214,666,565 (2000); $211,059,726 (1999)

Gifts Received: $243,024 (1994); $13,208,515 (1993); $1,360,157 (1992)

Typical Recipients

Arts & Humanities: Arts Associations & Councils, Arts Centers, Historic Preservation, Libraries, Museums/Galleries, Music, Public Broadcasting, Theater

Civic & Public Affairs: African American Affairs, Civil Rights, Community Foundations, Economic Development, Ethnic Organizations, Civic & Public Affairs-General, Hispanic Affairs, Housing, Native American Affairs, Philanthropic Organizations, Professional & Trade Associations, Public Policy, Urban & Community Affairs, Women's Affairs, Zoos/Aquariums

Education: Colleges & Universities, Education Associations, Education Funds, Elementary Education (Private), Education-General, International Studies, Legal Education, Medical Education, Minority Education, Private Education (Precollege), Public Education (Precollege), Public Education (Precollege), Religious Education, Secondary Education (Private), Social Sciences Education, Student Aid

Environment: Environment-General

Health: AIDS/HIV, Cancer, Children's Health/Hospitals, Clinics/Medical Centers, Health-General, Health Organizations, Heart, Hospices, Hospitals, Long-Term Care, Medical Rehabilitation, Medical Research, Multiple Sclerosis, Prenatal Health Issues, Public Health, Research/Studies Institutes, Single-Disease Health Associations

International: Health Care/Hospitals

Religion: Religion-General, Jewish Causes, Ministries, Religious Organizations, Religious Welfare, Social/Policy Issues, Synagogues/Temples

Science: Science Museums

Social Services: At-Risk Youth, Camps, Child Welfare, Community Centers, Community Service Organizations, Counseling, Crime Prevention, Day Care, Emergency Relief, Family Planning, Family Services, Food/Clothing Distribution, Homes, People with Disabilities, Recreation & Athletics, Senior Services, Sexual Abuse, Shelters/Homelessness, United Funds/ United Ways, Volunteer Services, YMCA/YWCA/ YMHA/YWHA, Youth Organizations

Application Procedures

Initial Contact: Applicants who are unsure about whether they meet the foundation's funding criteria are encouraged to submit a one-page letter of interest to the foundation. The foundation staff reviews all letters of interest, and the applicant will be notified regarding whether the foundation would like the organization to submit a full proposal.

Application Requirements: Send one unbound copy including information on purpose of funds sought and amount requested; type of request (special program or project, capital, technical assistance, general operating support, etc.); a description of organization including date founded, history, mission, and current and planned programs; objectives and activities for funds sought; evidence of need; how the request addresses the foundation's guidelines and special concerns; population to be served, including geographical area, number of persons to be served, ages income levels, and special needs of individuals served. Provide evidence of the organization's ability to manage the program/project, including qualifications and experience of the administrative staff responsible for management of your organization and project. Describe the expected outcomes of your program or project in terms of real changes in the lives of your constituents. Describe methods used to measure outcomes. Include description of short and longer-range fundraising costs, and statement of the percentage of annual operating budget expended on direct fundraising costs and lobbying activities, if applicable. Your application must be signed by your executive director and your board chair or his/her designee before it can be considered. All applications must include proof of tax-exempt status, copy of most recent annual report, recently audited financial statement; current year-to-date operating budget; percentage of budget used for fundraising; current donors and list of proposals pending with other funding sources.

If you are requesting funding for a special or capital project, you must submit the following: board approved project budget including projected income and expenses, total amount requested and sources of funds received or committed, list of proposals pending with other funding sources, organizational chart, a list of current board members and officers, and final report or progress report on last grant, if applicable.

Deadlines: None.

Review Process: The foundation will send confirmation of application receipt. The trustees meet approximately every four months and completed applications are reviewed in the order in which they are received. The foundation reports that the review process usually takes about four-to-six months.

Evaluative Criteria: The foundation gives special attention to proposals that reflect the following values: self-sufficiency should be a goal of all efforts to assist people; families should be strengthened as nurturing and financially stable environments for children; the quality of health care should be continually improved for the benefit of all people; quality education is the key to individual success; people with disabilities and the elderly should be able to live as independently as possible; good relations among people of all races and religions should be fostered and discrimination should be actively opposed; and the arts should be supported primarily as a vehicle to address social issues.

Restrictions

The foundation will not make grants to organizations operating for profit, political campaigns or lobbying efforts to influence legislation, endowment campaigns, or individuals. The foundation requests that all initial inquiries from prospective applicants be by mail, not by telephone or by personal visits to the foundation office.

Funding is restricted to the state of Minnesota. Previously funded organizations will be reviewed only after a full report on the previous grant has been received. Grants are awarded only to 501(c)(3) organizations.

Additional Information

The foundation was formerly called Phillips Foundation. be fostered and discrimination should be actively opposed; and the arts should be supported primarily as a vehicle to address social issues. Grants are awarded only to 501(c)(3) organizations.
Publications: Annual Report; Guidelines

Foundation Officials

Erik P. Bernstein: trustee
Paula P. Bernstein: trustee
William E. Bernstein: trustee PRIM CORP EMPL chief executive officer: Lockheed Information Technology Co.
Patricia A. Cummings: executive director
Jack I. Levin: trustee
John P. Levin: trustee
Suzan Levin: trustee
Edward Jay Phillips: trustee
Jeanne Phillips: trustee
Morton B. Phillips: trustee
Pauline Phillips: trustee emeritus
Rose Phillips: trustee

Grants Analysis

Disclosure Period: calendar year ending 2001
Total Grants: $9,509,612*
Number of Grants: 390
Average Grant: $24,384
Highest Grant: $650,000
Typical Range: $15,000 to $100,000
*Note: Giving excludes United Way.

Recent Grants

Note: Grants derived from 2001 Form 990.

General

650,000	Minneapolis Jewish Federation, Minneapolis, MN -- Rottenberg Family Assisted Living Residence
350,000	Minneapolis Jewish Federation, Minneapolis, MN
249,000	Jewish Family Service of Colorado, Denver, CO
200,000	Stanford University, Palo Alto, CA -- campaign for undergraduate education
183,345	Temple Israel, Minneapolis, MN
180,000	Jewish Family & Children's Services of San Francisco, San Francisco, CA -- disability project
130,000	Jay Phillips Center for Jewish-Christian Learning, St. Paul, MN -- Seminary education fund
100,000	Anti-Defamation League of B'nai B'rith, Los Angeles, CA
100,000	Emergency Foodshelf Network, Minneapolis, MN
100,000	Goodwill Industries, St. Paul, MN -- Creating Solutions capital campaign

ELLIS L. PHILLIPS FOUNDATION

Giving Contact

Ellis L. Phillips, III, President
Ellis L. Phillips Foundation
233 Commonwealth Avenue, Suite 2
Boston, MA 02116

Phone: (617)424-7607
Fax: (617)424-6391
E-mail: elpfndtn@gis.net
Web: http://www.ellislphillipsfndn.org

Description

Founded: 1930
EIN: 135677691
Organization Type: Private Foundation
Giving Locations: MA: Boston and surrounding areas Northern New England.
Grant Types: General Support, Seed Money.

Donor Information

Founder: the late Ellis L. Phillips

Financial Summary

Total Giving: $530,640 (fiscal year ending June 30, 2002); $528,195 (fiscal 2001); $505,115 (fiscal 1999);
Assets: $4,681,344 (fiscal 2002); $6,009,230 (fiscal 2001); $7,350,550 (fiscal 1999)
Gifts Received: $50,000 (fiscal 2002)

Typical Recipients

Arts & Humanities: Arts Associations & Councils, Community Arts, Historic Preservation, History & Archaeology, Libraries, Museums/Galleries, Music, Theater, Visual Arts
Civic & Public Affairs: Nonprofit Management, Philanthropic Organizations, Women's Affairs
Education: Arts/Humanities Education, Education Funds, Environmental Education, Education-General, Private Education (Precollege), Science/Mathematics Education
Environment: Forestry, Environment-General, Wildlife Protection
Health: Clinics/Medical Centers
Religion: Churches
Social Services: Camps, Child Welfare, Community Centers, Community Service Organizations, Family Services

Application Procedures

Initial Contact: Send a brief letter of inquiry requesting application guidelines.
Application Requirements: 2-4 page letter describing the organization, history, mission, major accomplishments, problem to be addressed, proposed solution, planned activities, and anticipated outcomes. Also include an abstract summarizing above information, proof of tax-exempt status, itemized project budget, and organization budget. For grants of $7,500 or more, include recently audited financial statement, listing of board of directors with affiliations and titles, and three independent references (optional).
Deadlines: January 1, April 1, and September 1.
Review Process: The board meets in February, May, and October.
Evaluative Criteria: Evaluated on the priority of the project within the Foundation's program interests, the anticipated impact of the project on the public and the organization, the organizational capacity, and the resources requested and current funds available.

Restrictions

Does not support individuals or provide funds for scholarships.

Additional Information

Publications: Annual Report (including Application Guidelines)

Foundation Officials

David Lloyd Brown: director
Cornelia Grumman: director
David L. Grumman: director, mem
Dr. George E. McCully: director
Walter C. Paine: director
Ellis Laurimore Phillips, III: president, director, mem

Ellis Laurimore Phillips, Jr.: vice president, director, mem B New York, NY 1921. ED Princeton University AB (1942); Columbia University LLB (1948); Keuka College LLD (1956).
Cynthia Phillips Prosser: secretary, director
E. Clinton Swift: director
K. Noel P. Zimmermann: secretary, director

Grants Analysis

Disclosure Period: fiscal year ending June 30, 2002
Total Grants: $530,640
Number of Grants: 5
Highest Grant: $467,500
Lowest Grant: $640

Recent Grants

Note: Grants derived from fiscal 2002 Form 990.

General

467,500	Catalog for Philanthropy, Boston, MA -- support experimental project
25,000	Boston Modern Orchestra Project, Boston, MA -- transfer of foundation
25,000	New England Conservatory, Boston, MA -- capital campaign
12,500	Barton Center for Diabetes Education, Oxford, MA -- capital campaign
640	Council on Foundations, Washington, DC -- portion of annual dues

COLUMBUS PHIPPS FOUNDATION

Giving Contact

Paul D. Buchanan, Trustee
PO Box 113
Clintwood, VA 24228
Phone: (540)926-8152

Description

Founded: 1994
EIN: 546338751
Organization Type: Private Foundation
Giving Locations: VA: Dickenson County
Grant Types: General Support.

Donor Information

Founder: Established in 1994 by Beulah G. Phipps.

Financial Summary

Total Giving: $192,045 (fiscal year ending March 31, 2001); $173,994 (fiscal 2000); $172,370 (fiscal 1999). Note: Fiscal 1997 Giving includes scholarship ($92,070).
Giving Analysis: Giving for fiscal 2001 includes: foundation scholarships ($130,350); fiscal 2000: foundation scholarships ($121,000) fiscal 1998: foundation scholarships ($96,600)
Assets: $3,869,886 (fiscal 2001); $4,943,430 (fiscal 2000); $4,150,351 (fiscal 1999)
Gifts Received: $2,166 (fiscal 2001); $270,589 (fiscal 1999); $242,650 (fiscal 1997). Note: In fiscal 1997 and fiscal 1999, contributions were received from the estate Beulah G. Phipps.

Typical Recipients

Arts & Humanities: Arts Associations & Councils, Arts Centers, Libraries, Music, Opera, Theater
Civic & Public Affairs: Botanical Gardens/Parks, Municipalities/Towns
Education: Arts/Humanities Education, Colleges & Universities, Community & Junior Colleges, Education-General, Legal Education, Medical Education, Public Education (Precollege), Student Aid
Science: Science Exhibits & Fairs

Application Procedures
Initial Contact: Request application form.
Deadlines: May 15.

Restrictions
Grants are restricted to cultural activities for residents of Dickenson County, VA and scholarships for graduates of Dickenson County.

Additional Information
Publications: Application Form

Foundation Officials
Carol P. Buchanan: trustee
Phyllis Davidson: mem
Betty Jo Dodson: mem
Rita F. Justice: mem
William R. McFall: trustee
Kenneth M. Smith: director

Grants Analysis
Disclosure Period: fiscal year ending March 31, 2001
Total Grants: $61,695*
Number of Grants: 10
Highest Grant: $10,000
Typical Range: $1,000 to $5,000
*Note: Giving excludes scholarships. Average grant excludes highest grant.

Recent Grants
Note: Grants derived from 2000 Form 990.

Library-Related
3,000	Jonnie B. Deel Memorial Library, Wise, VA
2,600	Haysi Public Library, Haysi, VA

General
38,750	University of Virginia College at Wise, Wise, VA
25,000	Town of Clintwood, Clintwood, VA
19,250	Mountain Empire Community College, Big Stone Gap, VA
7,000	Appalachian School of Law, Clinchco, VA
6,500	East Carolina University, Greenville, NC
5,341	Clintwood High School, Clintwood, VA
4,551	Haysi High School ', Haysi, VA
4,000	Mercer University School of Pharmacy, Atlanta, GA
3,500	Virginia Intermont College, Bristol, VA
3,064	Ervinton High School, Nora, VA

PHOENIX HOME LIFE MUTUAL INSURANCE CO.

Company Headquarters
Hartford, CT
Web: http://www.phl.com

Company Description
Employees: 3,800
SIC(s): 6311 Life Insurance.

Operating Locations
Phoenix Home Life Mutual Insurance Co. (CT--Enfield, Hartford; MA--Greenfield; NY--Albany)

Nonmonetary Support
Type: Cause-related Marketing & Promotion

Phoenix Foundation

Giving Contact
Jane L. Driscoll, Vice President
Phoenix Foundation
1 American Row
Hartford, CT 06102-5056

Phone: (860)403-5863
Fax: (860)403-5755
E-mail: Tina.Muzzy@phoenixwm.com
Web: http://www.phoenixwm.com

Alternate Contact
Phone: (860)403-7831
Web: http://www.ctphilanthropy.org
Note: Alternate contact information is for grant application requests.

Description
EIN: 061493188
Organization Type: Corporate Foundation
Giving Locations: nationally.
Grant Types: Employee Matching Gifts, General Support.
Note: Employee matching gift ratio: 1 to 1.

Financial Summary
Total Giving: $2,366,361 (2001); $1,340,842 (2000); $1,100,000 (1999 approx). Note: Contributes through corporate direct giving program and foundation. Giving includes matching gifts. 1998 Giving includes corporate direct giving ($300,000); foundation ($800,000).
Giving Analysis: Giving for 2000 includes: foundation grants to United Way ($43,730).
Assets: $8,911,779 (2001); $20,460,615 (2000)
Gifts Received: $98,866 (2001); $15,725,734 (2000)

Typical Recipients
Arts & Humanities: Arts Associations & Councils, Arts Centers, Arts Funds, History & Archaeology, Libraries, Music, Public Broadcasting
Civic & Public Affairs: African American Affairs, Civil Rights, Community Foundations, Economic Development, Employment/Job Training, Civic & Public Affairs-General, Housing, Public Policy
Education: Business Education, Colleges & Universities, Education Associations, Education-General, Public Education (Precollege), Student Aid
Health: AIDS/HIV, Cancer, Children's Health/Hospitals, Emergency/Ambulance Services, Health-General, Hospices, Hospitals, Prenatal Health Issues, Single-Disease Health Associations
Religion: Churches, Dioceses, Ministries, Religious Welfare
Social Services: Camps, Child Welfare, Community Service Organizations, Counseling, Family Services, Recreation & Athletics, United Funds/United Ways, YMCA/YWCA/YMHA/YWHA, Youth Organizations

Application Procedures
Initial Contact: Send written request for application.
Application Requirements: Include description of agency and its objectives; amount requested and how it will be used; organization budget for upcoming year; description of other support received, including support received from the United Way or any government entities; account of staff size, including qualifications; statement of organization's board's composition and affiliations; copy of most recent annual report; demonstration that organization serves one of the giving areas; description of how organization measures progress towards its goals; and proof of tax-exempt status. Also include a narrative of no more than five pages providing organization information, grant purpose, evaluation process, financial information, and other supporting materials.
Deadlines: September 15.
Decision Notification: Requests are considered during the fourth quarter of each calendar year; company will notify agencies of outcome during early January of the following year. first quarter

Additional Information
Publications: Guidelines; Application form

Grants Analysis
Disclosure Period: calendar year ending 2001
Total Grants: $1,650,756*
Number of Grants: 442
Average Grant: $3,735
Highest Grant: $125,000
Lowest Grant: $25
Typical Range: $100 to $15,000
*Note: Giving excludes scholarship; United Way.

Recent Grants
Note: Grants derived from 2001 Form 990.

General
300,000	Doc Hurley Scholarship Foundation, Hartford, CT
250,000	Bushnell Memorial Hall, Hartford, CT
175,000	United Way September 11th Fund, New York, NY
145,000	United Way of Capital Area, Hartford, CT
130,500	University of Connecticut, Storrs, CT
125,000	Bushnell Memorial Hall, Hartford, CT
100,000	Commission on Economic Opportunity, Troy, NY
100,000	Trinity College, Hartford, CT
90,000	Hartford Hospital, Hartford, CT
80,000	Sea Research Foundation, Mystic, CT

PHYSICIANS MUTUAL INSURANCE CO.

Company Headquarters
Omaha, NE
Web: http://www.pmic.com/

Company Description
Assets: US$3.411 billion (2001)
Employees: 1300 (2001)
SIC(s): 6321 Accident & Health Insurance.

Operating Locations
Physicians Mutual Insurance Co. (NE--Omaha)

Nonmonetary Support
Type: Donated Equipment; In-kind Services; Loaned Executives; Workplace Solicitation

Physicians Mutual Insurance Co. Foundation

Giving Contact
Jerome Coon, Secretary/Treasurer
2600 Dodge Street
Omaha, NE 68131
Phone: (402)633-1000
Fax: (402)633-1096

Description
EIN: 363424068
Organization Type: Corporate Foundation
Giving Locations: NE; VA: Alexandria
Grant Types: Capital, Emergency, Endowment, General Support, Operating Expenses, Scholarship.

Financial Summary
Total Giving: $186,667 (fiscal year ending November 30, 2001); $217,859 (fiscal 2000); $221,109 (fiscal 1999). Note: Contributes through corporate direct giving program and foundation.

Giving Analysis: Giving for fiscal 2001 includes: foundation grants to United Way ($66,300); foundation ($120,367); fiscal 2000: foundation grants to United Way ($59,300); foundation ($158,559); fiscal 1999: foundation grants to United Way ($56,350); foundation ($164,759);
Assets: $670,026 (fiscal 2001); $822,300 (fiscal 2000); $972,958 (fiscal 1999)

Typical Recipients

Arts & Humanities: Arts Associations & Councils, Arts Festivals, Arts Funds, Ballet, History & Archaeology, Libraries, Museums/Galleries, Music, Opera, Performing Arts, Public Broadcasting, Theater
Civic & Public Affairs: African American Affairs, Chambers of Commerce, Clubs, Community Foundations, Ethnic Organizations, Civic & Public Affairs-General, Hispanic Affairs, Housing, Law & Justice, Native American Affairs, Parades/Festivals, Philanthropic Organizations, Professional & Trade Associations, Public Policy, Safety, Urban & Community Affairs, Women's Affairs, Zoos/Aquariums
Education: Agricultural Education, Business Education, Business-School Partnerships, Colleges & Universities, Colleges & Universities, Community & Junior Colleges, Continuing Education, Economic Education, Education Funds, Elementary Education (Private), Elementary Education (Public), Faculty Development, Education-General, Literacy, Minority Education, Private Education (Precollege), Religious Education, Secondary Education (Private), Special Education
Environment: Environment-General
Health: Alzheimers Disease, Arthritis, Cancer, Children's Health/Hospitals, Diabetes, Emergency/Ambulance Services, Health-General, Health Policy/Cost Containment, Health Organizations, Heart, Hospices, Hospitals, Long-Term Care, Medical Research, Multiple Sclerosis, Nursing Services, Public Health, Respiratory, Single-Disease Health Associations
International: International Relations, International Relief Efforts
Religion: Churches, Dioceses, Jewish Causes, Religious Organizations, Religious Welfare
Social Services: At-Risk Youth, Big Brother/Big Sister, Camps, Child Welfare, Community Centers, Community Service Organizations, Counseling, Crime Prevention, Delinquency & Criminal Rehabilitation, Emergency Relief, Family Services, Food/Clothing Distribution, Homes, People with Disabilities, Recreation & Athletics, Refugee Assistance, Scouts, Senior Services, Shelters/Homelessness, Social Services-General, Special Olympics, Substance Abuse, United Funds/United Ways, Veterans, Volunteer Services, YMCA/YWCA/YMHA/YWHA, YMCA/YWCA/YMHA/YWHA, Youth Organizations

Application Procedures

Initial Contact: Send a written request.
Application Requirements: Include a description of organization, amount requested, purpose of funds sought, and proof of tax-exempt status.
Deadlines: None.

Restrictions

Does not support individuals or political or lobbying groups.

Corporate Officials

Bill R. Benson: executive vice president, chief financial officer PRIM CORP EMPL executive vice president, chief financial officer: Physicians Mutual Insurance Co.
Robert A. Reed: president, chief executive officer B 1939. ED Creighton University BA (1961). PRIM CORP EMPL president, chief executive officer: Physicians Mutual Insurance Co.

Foundation Officials

Bill R. Benson: vice president (see above)
Jerome J. Coon: treasurer PRIM CORP EMPL treasurer: Physicians Mutual Insurance Co.

Stewart Crosbie: secretary
John B. Davis, MD: director B Omaha, NE 1922. ED Yale University (1941-1943); Yale University (1946-1947); University of Nebraska MD (1951). PRIM NONPR EMPL associate professor surgery: University Northeast Medical College. CORP AFFIL co-owner, president: Miracle Hill Golf & Tennis Center; director: Physicians Mutual Insurance Co.
William R. Hamsa, MD: director, assistant secretary PRIM CORP EMPL partner: Hamsa, O'Neil & Ferlic. CORP AFFIL director: Physicians Mutual Insurance Co.
Harry W. McFadden, Jr. MD: assistant treasurer, director CORP AFFIL director: Physicians Mutual Insurance Co.
Robert A. Reed: president, director (see above)
John D. Woodbury, MD: director CORP AFFIL director: Physicians Mutual Insurance Canada.

Grants Analysis

Disclosure Period: fiscal year ending November 30, 2001
Total Grants: $120,367*
Number of Grants: 48
Average Grant: $1,228*
Highest Grant: $62,652
Lowest Grant: $55
Typical Range: $100 to $3,000
*Note: Giving excludes United Way. Average grant figure excludes highest grant.

Recent Grants

Note: Grants derived from fiscal 2001 Form 990.

General

66,300	United Way of the Midlands, Omaha, NE
62,652	Creighton University, Omaha, NE
10,000	Donors Trust, Alexandria, VA
5,650	Omaha Chamber Foundation, Omaha, NE
3,000	Direct Marketing Education Foundation, New York, NY
3,000	Joslyn Art Museum, Omaha, NE
2,500	Nebraska Independent College Foundation, Omaha, NE
2,500	Omaha Community Foundation, Omaha, NE
2,500	Omaha Symphony, Omaha, NE
2,000	Boys and Girls Club of Omaha, Omaha, NE

TATIANA PIANKOVA FOUNDATION

Giving Contact

Mildred C. Brinn, President, Treasurer & Director
570 Park Avenue
New York, NY 10021
Phone: (212)758-7764

Description

Founded: 1983
EIN: 133142090
Organization Type: Private Foundation
Grant Types: General Support.

Donor Information

Founder: Susan Polachek

Financial Summary

Total Giving: $325,850 (fiscal year ending July 31, 2001); $327,900 (fiscal 2000); $106,250 (fiscal 1998)
Assets: $5,220,391 (fiscal 2001); $7,418,037 (fiscal 2000); $6,339,367 (fiscal 1998)

Typical Recipients

Arts & Humanities: Arts Associations & Councils, Arts Centers, Arts Institutes, Ballet, Community Arts, Dance, Arts & Humanities-General, Historic Preservation, History & Archaeology, Libraries, Literary Arts, Museums/Galleries, Music, Opera, Performing Arts, Theater, Visual Arts
Civic & Public Affairs: Botanical Gardens/Parks, Civic & Public Affairs-General, Urban & Community Affairs, Women's Affairs
Education: Arts/Humanities Education, Colleges & Universities, Education-General, Medical Education, Preschool Education, Private Education (Precollege), Religious Education
Environment: Resource Conservation
Health: Cancer, Health Organizations, Hospices, Hospitals, Long-Term Care, Medical Research
International: Foreign Arts Organizations, Foreign Educational Institutions, International Affairs, International Organizations, International Relations
Religion: Churches
Science: Science Museums
Social Services: Child Welfare, Community Service Organizations, Counseling, Family Services, Homes, People with Disabilities, Recreation & Athletics, Senior Services, Social Services-General, Veterans, Youth Organizations

Application Procedures

Initial Contact: Send a brief letter of inquiry.
Application Requirements: Include an outline of purpose and requirements of the organization.
Deadlines: None.

Restrictions

Primarily supports preselected organizations.

Foundation Officials

Mildred Cunningham Brinn: president, treasurer, director
Peter F. De Gaetano: secretary, director

Grants Analysis

Disclosure Period: fiscal year ending July 31, 2001
Total Grants: $325,850
Number of Grants: 51
Average Grant: $3,257*
Highest Grant: $163,000
Lowest Grant: $100
Typical Range: $1,000 to $5,000
*Note: Average grant figure excludes highest grant.

Recent Grants

Note: Grants derived from 2000 Form 990.

Library-Related

3,000	Rogers Memorial Library, Southampton, NY

General

140,000	Parish Art Museum, Southampton, NY
54,000	Ballet Theatre Foundation, New York, NY
25,000	Snowhegan School of Painting and Sculpture
10,000	Metropolitan Opera, New York, NY
10,000	Southampton Hospital, Southampton, NY
7,000	St. Bartholomew's Church, New York, NY
6,000	Southampton Fresh Air Home, Southampton, NY
5,000	American Federation of Arts, New York, NY
5,000	Mount Vernon Nazarene College, Mt. Vernon, OH
5,000	Museum of Modern Art, New York, NY

ALBERT PICK, JR. FUND

Giving Contact
Cleopatra B. Alexander, Executive Director
30 North Michigan Avenue, Suite 1002
Chicago, IL 60602
Phone: (312)236-1192
E-mail: info@albertpickjrfund.org
Web: http://www.albertpickjrfund.org

Description
Founded: 1947
EIN: 366071402
Organization Type: General Purpose Foundation
Giving Locations: IL: Chicago
Grant Types: Capital, General Support, Multiyear/Continuing Support, Project.

Donor Information
Founder: Incorporated in 1947 by the late Albert Pick Jr.

Financial Summary
Total Giving: $1,608,000 (2000); $1,300,000 (1999 approx); $1,042,058 (1998)
Assets: $24,357,503 (2000); $25,695,586 (1998); $21,007,128 (1996)
Gifts Received: $92,364 (2000); $12,976 (1998); $12,200 (1996). Note: In 2000, contributions were received from Corinne F. Pick Trust. In 1996, contributions were received from Harris Associates.

Typical Recipients
Arts & Humanities: Arts Associations & Councils, Arts Festivals, Arts Institutes, Arts Outreach, Dance, History & Archaeology, Libraries, Museums/Galleries, Music, Opera, Public Broadcasting, Theater
Civic & Public Affairs: Asian American Affairs, Botanical Gardens/Parks, Economic Development, Employment/Job Training, Civic & Public Affairs-General, Hispanic Affairs, Housing, Municipalities/Towns, Nonprofit Management, Philanthropic Organizations, Public Policy, Urban & Community Affairs, Zoos/Aquariums
Education: Afterschool/Enrichment Programs, Agricultural Education, Arts/Humanities Education, Colleges & Universities, Continuing Education, Education Associations, Education Reform, Education-General, International Studies, Literacy, Minority Education, Preschool Education, Public Education (Precollege), Science/Mathematics Education, Special Education, Student Aid
Environment: Air/Water Quality, Environment-General, Resource Conservation
Health: AIDS/HIV, Children's Health/Hospitals, Clinics/Medical Centers, Emergency/Ambulance Services, Health Organizations, Hospices, Hospitals, Long-Term Care, Medical Training, Prenatal Health Issues, Preventive Medicine/Wellness Organizations, Public Health, Single-Disease Health Associations
International: Foreign Arts Organizations, Human Rights
Religion: Jewish Causes, Religious Organizations, Religious Welfare
Science: Observatories & Planetariums, Science Museums, Scientific Organizations
Social Services: Child Welfare, Community Service Organizations, Day Care, Domestic Violence, Family Planning, Family Services, Food/Clothing Distribution, Homes, People with Disabilities, Scouts, Senior Services, Sexual Abuse, Shelters/Homelessness, Substance Abuse, United Funds/United Ways, YMCA/YWCA/YMHA/YWHA, Youth Organizations

Application Procedures
Initial Contact: Call or write the fund for application form.
Application Requirements: Proposals should be as brief as possible and include the following: a history of the organization, a description of current programs, a description of the proposed project, and the intended use of the funds requested; proof of tax-exempt status from the IRS and a ruling that the organization is publicly supported under section 509(a) of the IRS code; the names, affiliations, and addresses of governing board members, officers, and staff; a current financial statement, preferably audited; the projected annual budgets for the organization and the project; a list of principal sources of income; and a description of the geographic area served.
Deadlines: January 21, April 1, July 1, and October 1. Proposals from cultural organizations should be submitted by the July 1 deadline.
Review Process: The board meets in March or April, June, September, and December.

Restrictions
The fund will not consider proposals from organizations whose fiscal year ends on the same month as the board meeting's review of that request. Grants are not made to religious organizations or for political purposes. The fund does not support individuals, hospitals, local chapters of single-disease associations, umbrella organizations, building or endowment funds, deficit financing, long-term projects, advertising, scholarships, fundraising, or fraternal, veterans, labor, or athletic groups. Additionally, the fund does not support student aid, scholarship programs, or campaigns for reduction of debts.

Additional Information
Publications: Program Policy Statement; Application Guidelines

Foundation Officials
Cleopatra B. Alexander: executive director
Gregory M. Darnieder: secretary
Berton B. Kaplan: vice president
Ralph I. Lewy: treasurer B Leiwen, Germany 1931. ED Roosevelt University BS (1953). PRIM CORP EMPL president: Ralph Lewy Ltd. NONPR AFFIL member: American Institute of Certified Public Accountants.
Robert Lifton: director, chairman
Albert Pick, III: vice president, director
Nadine Van Sant: president

Grants Analysis
Disclosure Period: calendar year ending 2000
Total Grants: $1,608,000
Number of Grants: 153
Average Grant: $8,605*
Highest Grant: $300,000
Typical Range: $1,500 to $15,000
*Note: Average grant figure excludes highest grant.

Recent Grants
Note: Grants derived from 1999 Form 990.

Library-Related
100,000	Chicago Public Library Foundation, Chicago, IL -- Tyrannosaurus Reads

General
266,666	Chicago Academy of Sciences, Chicago, IL
100,000	Chicago Shakespeare Theater, Chicago, IL -- teacher resource center
75,000	Carole Robertson Center for Learning, Chicago, IL
75,000	Citizens' Scholarship Foundation of America, Minneapolis, MN
50,000	Deborah's Place, Chicago, IL -- education and employment services
50,000	Heartland Alliance for Human Needs and Human Rights, Chicago, IL -- operating support for Neon Street
50,000	Ravinia Festival Association, Chicago, IL -- Rising Stars series
50,000	Robert Crown Center for Health Education, Hinsdale, IL -- H Lawndale/Homan Square Outreach Program
35,000	Metropolitan Family Services, Chicago, IL -- Childhood Socialization Program
25,000	Chicago Children's Museum, Chicago, IL

MARY PICKFORD FOUNDATION

Giving Contact
Henry Stotsenberg, President
43460 Ridge Park Dr.
Temecula, CA 92590
Phone: 800-333-8128
Web: http://www.marypickford.com/found.html

Description
Founded: 1968
EIN: 956093487
Organization Type: Private Foundation
Giving Locations: CA
Grant Types: Endowment, General Support, Scholarship.

Donor Information
Founder: the late Mary Pickford Rogers

Financial Summary
Total Giving: $831,950 (fiscal year ending May 31, 2001); $786,200 (fiscal 2000); $779,300 (fiscal 1999). Note: Fiscal 1997 Giving includes scholarship ($170,000), United Way ($1,000).
Giving Analysis: Giving for fiscal 2001 includes: foundation scholarships ($9,000); fiscal 2000: foundation scholarships ($36,500); fiscal 1999: foundation scholarships ($376,000);
Assets: $14,181,524 (fiscal 2001); $15,632,422 (fiscal 2000); $12,545,427 (fiscal 1999)
Gifts Received: $1,289,454 (fiscal 2000)

Typical Recipients
Arts & Humanities: Arts Funds, Arts Outreach, Film & Video, Historic Preservation, Libraries, Museums/Galleries, Music, Public Broadcasting, Theater, Visual Arts
Civic & Public Affairs: Clubs, Civic & Public Affairs-General, Philanthropic Organizations, Professional & Trade Associations, Urban & Community Affairs
Education: Arts/Humanities Education, Colleges & Universities, Education-General, Legal Education, Science/Mathematics Education, Student Aid
Health: Children's Health/Hospitals, Clinics/Medical Centers, Emergency/Ambulance Services, Geriatric Health, Health Organizations, Hospitals, Long-Term Care, Medical Research, Prenatal Health Issues, Single-Disease Health Associations
International: Health Care/Hospitals, International Affairs, Missionary/Religious Activities
Religion: Jewish Causes, Religious Welfare
Science: Science Museums
Social Services: Child Welfare, Community Service Organizations, Domestic Violence, Homes, People with Disabilities, Scouts, Senior Services, Shelters/Homelessness, Youth Organizations

Application Procedures
Initial Contact: Send a brief letter of inquiry.
Application Requirements: Include amount requested and purpose of funds sought.
Deadlines: None.

Restrictions
Provides grants to worthy and needy students and charities.

Foundation Officials
Keith Lawrence: secretary
Sull Lawrence: secretary
Charles B. Rogers: treasurer

Gary E. Shoffner: director
Edward Stotsenberg: president, chief financial officer
Henry Stotsenberg: president

Grants Analysis

Disclosure Period: fiscal year ending May 31, 2001
Total Grants: $822,950*
Number of Grants: 71
Average Grant: $10,742*
Highest Grant: $71,000
Lowest Grant: $450
Typical Range: $1,000 to $20,000
*Note: Giving excludes scholarships. Average grant figure excludes highest grant.

Recent Grants

Note: Grants derived from 2000 Form 990.

Library-Related
30,000	Academy Foundation, Los Angeles, CA

General
50,000	Santa Monica College, Santa Monica, CA
50,000	USC School of Gerontology, Los Angeles, CA
40,000	American Film Institute, Los Angeles, CA
40,000	Pepperdine University, Malibu, CA
40,000	UCLA Film and Television, Los Angeles, CA
40,000	USC Cinema - Television, Los Angeles, CA
35,000	Jewish Home for the Aging, Reseda, CA
25,000	Art Center College of Design, Pasadena, CA
25,000	Brigham Young University, Provo, UT
25,000	Crossroads School for Arts and Sciences, Santa Monica, CA

HAROLD WHITWORTH PIERCE CHARITABLE TRUST

Giving Contact

Elizabeth D. Nichols, Grant Administrator
c/o Nichols and Pratt
50 Congress St., Suite 832
Boston, MA 02109
Phone: (617)523-8368
Fax: (617)523-8949
E-mail: piercetrust@nichols-pratt.com

Description

Founded: 1960
EIN: 046019896
Organization Type: Private Foundation
Giving Locations: MA: Boston area
Grant Types: Capital, General Support, Project, Seed Money.

Donor Information

Founder: the late Harold Whitworth Pierce

Financial Summary

Total Giving: $1,376,400 (2002); $1,242,685 (2001); $510,000 (2000)
Giving Analysis: Giving for 2002 includes: foundation grants to United Way ($5,000); 2000: foundation fellowships ($30,000) foundation scholarships ($50,000)
Assets: $23,122,298 (2002); $26,345,200 (2001); $26,983,285 (1999)

Typical Recipients

Arts & Humanities: Arts Centers, Ballet, Historic Preservation, History & Archaeology, Libraries, Museums/Galleries, Music, Public Broadcasting, Theater
Civic & Public Affairs: Asian American Affairs, Botanical Gardens/Parks, Clubs, Economic Development, Employment/Job Training, Civic & Public Affairs-General, Hispanic Affairs, Municipalities/Towns, Native American Affairs, Nonprofit Management, Urban & Community Affairs, Women's Affairs, Zoos/Aquariums
Education: Arts/Humanities Education, Business-School Partnerships, Colleges & Universities, Education Associations, Education Funds, Education Reform, Engineering/Technological Education, Faculty Development, Education-General, International Studies, Leadership Training, Literacy, Medical Education, Minority Education, Preschool Education, Private Education (Precollege), Science/Mathematics Education, Student Aid, Vocational & Technical Education
Environment: Air/Water Quality, Forestry, Environment-General, Research, Wildlife Protection
Health: Emergency/Ambulance Services, Health Organizations, Hospitals, Medical Research
International: Human Rights, International Environmental Issues
Religion: Churches, Religious Organizations, Religious Welfare, Social/Policy Issues
Science: Science Museums, Scientific Centers & Institutes
Social Services: At-Risk Youth, Camps, Child Welfare, Community Centers, Community Service Organizations, Day Care, Family Planning, Family Services, Food/Clothing Distribution, People with Disabilities, Recreation & Athletics, YMCA/YWCA/YMHA/YWHA, Youth Organizations

Application Procedures

Initial Contact: Send a brief letter of inquiry.
Application Requirements: Include brochure, financial statement, proof of tax-exempt status, how goals will be met, amount requested, and how additional needed money will be raised.
Deadlines: Concept letters due March 1 and September 15. Invited proposals due mid April and mid October.

Restrictions

Trustees are required to give 25% of the trust's yearly net income to Milton Hospital and $5,000 to St. Michael's Church. Remaining funds are awarded to other charities at the discretion of the trustees. Unsolicited medical research proposals are not accepted.

Foundation Officials

James R. Nichols: trustee
Harold I. Pratt: trustee

Grants Analysis

Disclosure Period: calendar year ending 2002
Total Grants: $1,371,400*
Number of Grants: 53
Average Grant: $21,565*
Highest Grant: $250,000
Lowest Grant: $5,000
Typical Range: $10,000 to $50,000
*Note: Giving excludes United Way. Average grant figure excludes highest grant.

Recent Grants

Note: Grants derived from 2001 Form 990.

General
100,000	Massachusetts Audubon Society, Lincoln, MA
75,000	Milton Hospital, Milton, MA
75,000	Milton Medical Center, Milton, MA
75,000	Unitarian Universalist Association, Boston, MA
50,000	Boys and Girls Club for Chelsea, Chelsea, OK

43,665	Woods Hole Research Center, Woods Hole, MA
30,000	Boston Center for the Arts, Boston, MA
30,000	Boston Plan for Excellence, Boston, MA
30,000	Boston Plan for Excellence - Annenberg, Boston, MA
30,000	Medical Foundation, Boston, MA

PINE TREE FOUNDATION

Giving Contact

A. Morris Williams, Jr., Chairman, Treasurer, & Director
120 Righters Mill Rd.
Gladwyne, PA 19035
Phone: (610)649-4601

Description

Founded: 1986
EIN: 222751187
Organization Type: Private Foundation
Giving Locations: PA
Grant Types: General Support.

Donor Information

Founder: A. Morris Williams, Jr., Ruth W. Williams

Financial Summary

Total Giving: $1,445,000 (fiscal year ending July 31, 2002); $1,070,000 (fiscal 2000); $750,000 (fiscal 1997)
Assets: $23,012,047 (fiscal 2002); $20,928,359 (fiscal 2001); $21,464,246 (fiscal 2000)
Gifts Received: $648,350 (fiscal 2002); $4,539,755 (fiscal 1997); $750,000 (fiscal 1996). Note: In fiscal 2002, contributions were received from A. Morris & Ruth W. Williams Jr.

Typical Recipients

Arts & Humanities: Ballet, Arts & Humanities-General, Libraries, Music, Performing Arts
Civic & Public Affairs: Economic Development, Civic & Public Affairs-General, Housing, Zoos/Aquariums
Education: Colleges & Universities, Education Funds, Education-General, Literacy, Private Education (Precollege), Religious Education
Environment: Environment-General
Health: Clinics/Medical Centers, Mental Health
International: Foreign Arts Organizations, Health Care/Hospitals, International Relief Efforts
Religion: Religious Welfare
Social Services: Community Service Organizations, Food/Clothing Distribution, Recreation & Athletics, Shelters/Homelessness, Social Services-General

Application Procedures

Initial Contact: Send brief letter describing program. Include a description of organization, amount requested, purpose of funds sought, recently audited financial statement, and proof of tax-exempt status.
Deadlines: None.

Foundation Officials

Susan W. Beltz: director
Joanne W. Markman: director
A. Morris Williams, Jr.: president, director
Ruth W. Williams: secretary, treasurer, director

Grants Analysis

Disclosure Period: fiscal year ending July 31, 2002
Total Grants: $1,445,000
Number of Grants: 22
Average Grant: $65,682
Highest Grant: $300,000
Lowest Grant: $5,000
Typical Range: $20,000 to $100,000

Recent Grants

Note: Grants derived from 2002 Form 990.

Library-Related

50,000	Free Library of Philadelphia, Philadelphia, PA

General

300,000	CARE, Atlanta, GA
200,000	Duke University, Durham, NC
200,000	Habitat for Humanity, Americus, GA
200,000	Philadelphia Orchestra, Philadelphia, PA
100,000	College of Wooster, Wooster, OH
100,000	Philadelphia Scholars Fund, Philadelphia, PA
100,000	Salvation Army, Philadelphia, PA
50,000	Project Forward Leap, Lancaster, PA
25,000	Pennsylvania Ballet, Philadelphia, PA
20,000	Stop ALD Foundation, Houston, TX

PINEYWOODS FOUNDATION

Giving Contact

Bob Bowman, Secretary
515 S. 1st St.
Lufkin, TX 75901
Phone: (936)634-7444

Alternate Contact

PO Box 3659
Lufkin, TX 75903
Phone: (936)634-4415

Description

Founded: 1984
EIN: 751922533
Organization Type: Private Foundation
Giving Locations: TX
Grant Types: Capital, General Support, Project, Seed Money.

Donor Information

Founder: the Southland Foundation

Financial Summary

Total Giving: $162,113 (2001); $147,911 (2000); $140,757 (1999)
Assets: $2,923,838 (2001); $3,304,333 (2000); $3,525,473 (1999)
Gifts Received: $10,000 (2000); $10,000 (1997); $89,944 (1992). Note: In 1997, contributions were received from Brookshire Brothers. In 2000, contributions were received from from Angelina & Neches River Railroad.

Typical Recipients

Arts & Humanities: Arts Associations & Councils, Community Arts, History & Archaeology, Libraries, Museums/Galleries, Theater, Visual Arts
Civic & Public Affairs: African American Affairs, Botanical Gardens/Parks, Chambers of Commerce, Community Foundations, Economic Development, Employment/Job Training, Civic & Public Affairs-General, Housing, Law & Justice, Municipalities/Towns, Safety, Urban & Community Affairs, Women's Affairs, Zoos/Aquariums
Education: Colleges & Universities, Education Associations, Education-General, Minority Education, Public Education (Precollege), Student Aid
Environment: Air/Water Quality, Environment-General, Resource Conservation
Health: Cancer, Clinics/Medical Centers, Emergency/Ambulance Services, Health Organizations, Home-Care Services, Hospices, Hospitals, Long-Term Care, Public Health
Religion: Religious Welfare

Social Services: Animal Protection, Big Brother/Big Sister, Community Centers, Community Service Organizations, Domestic Violence, Family Services, People with Disabilities, Recreation & Athletics, Senior Services, Substance Abuse, United Funds/United Ways, Youth Organizations

Application Procedures

Initial Contact: Send correct name, address, and phone number of applicant. Also provide a brief resume of the operations of the applicant, an explanation of the request evidencing the need, service to be rendered, and how, when, and where members of the public will be benefited.
Deadlines: None.

Restrictions

Preference is for funding purchases or supplies, aiding construction projects, and administrative expenses. Grants are not made to governmental units, state colleges, universities, churches, religious organizations, and general fund drives.

Foundation Officials

John Firth Anderson: chairman B Saginaw, MI 1928. ED Michigan State University BA (1949); University of Illinois MS (1950). PRIM CORP EMPL Presbytery de Cristo. NONPR AFFIL member: Southwest Library Association; member: World Alliance Reformed Churches; member: Arizona Library Association; member: California Library Association; member: Arizona AssociationCounty Librarians; member: Arizona China Council; member: American Library Association. CLUB AFFIL member: Beta Phi Mu.
Bob Bowman: secretary
George Henderson: treasurer B Hurtsboro, AL 1932. ED Wayne State University BA (1957); Wayne State University MA (1959); Wayne State University PhD (1965). NONPR AFFIL member: Phi Kappa Phi; professor sociology: University Oklahoma; member: National Association Human Rights Workers; member: Omicron Delta Kappa; member: International Society Law Enforcement Criminal Justice Instituteructors; member: Kappa Alpha Psi; member: Inter-University Seminar Armed Forces Society; member: Delta Tau Kappa; member: Golden Key; member: Association Black Sociologists; member: Association Supervision Curriculum Development; member: American Association University Professors; member: American Sociological Association; member: American Association Higher Education.

Grants Analysis

Disclosure Period: calendar year ending 2001
Total Grants: $162,113
Number of Grants: 22
Average Grant: $6,327*
Highest Grant: $29,250
Lowest Grant: $1,500
Typical Range: $2,500 to $10,000
*Note: Average grant figure excludes highest grant.

Recent Grants

Note: Grants derived from 2000 Form 990.

Library-Related

6,825	Kurth Memorial Library, Lufkin, TX -- for operations
5,025	Rube Sessions Memorial Library, Wells, TX -- for operations
5,000	Cold Spring Area Public Library, Coldspring, TX -- for operations

General

22,247	City of Lufkin, Lufkin, TX -- for A&NRR mural
15,000	Memorial Medical Center, Lufkin, TX -- for public sleep diagnosis machine
15,000	Polk County Emergency Management, Livingston, TX -- for operations
10,958	Angelina County Exposition Center, Lufkin, TX -- for new sound system

10,000	City of Lufkin, Lufkin, TX -- for playground equipment
6,000	Love, Inc. of Lufkin, Lufkin, TX -- for operations
5,000	Consumer Credit Counseling, Lufkin, TX -- for money management by mail
5,000	Friends of Ellen Trout Zoo, Lufkin, TX -- for hippo fund
5,000	Generation Builders, Lufkin, TX -- for operations
5,000	Kountze Economic Development, Kountze, TX -- for operations

PINKERTON FOUNDATION

Giving Contact

Joan Colello, Executive Director & Secretary
630 Fifth Ave., Ste. 1755
New York, NY 10111
Phone: (212)332-3385
Fax: (212)332-3399
Web: http://www.fdncenter.org/grantmaker/pinkerton

Description

Founded: 1966
EIN: 136206624
Organization Type: General Purpose Foundation
Giving Locations: NY: New York City
Grant Types: Project, Seed Money.

Donor Information

Founder: The Pinkerton Foundation was established in 1966 by the late Robert Allan Pinkerton (1904-1967). Mr. Pinkerton served as the chairman and chief executive officer of Pinkerton's Inc. for more than 35 years. He was the great-grandson of Allan Pinkerton, a Scottish immigrant, who had founded in 1850 what would become the oldest and largest security company in the world. The company was sold in 1983, and today there is no connection between the foundation and Pinkerton's Inc.

Financial Summary

Total Giving: $6,630,610 (2001); $6,237,689 (2000); $5,054,634 (1998). Note: 1998 Giving includes Trustee-Designated grants ($175,000).
Giving Analysis: Giving for 2000 includes: foundation matching gifts ($1,718) 1998: foundation matching gifts ($325)
Assets: $139,240,102 (2002); $141,531,849 (2001); $138,912,814 (2000)
Gifts Received: $26,000 (2000); $17,100 (1998); $14,145 (1997). Note: In 1998 and 2000, contributions were received from Berkshire Hathaway.

Typical Recipients

Arts & Humanities: Arts Centers, Ballet, Dance, Ethnic & Folk Arts, History & Archaeology, Literary Arts, Museums/Galleries, Music, Public Broadcasting, Theater
Civic & Public Affairs: Botanical Gardens/Parks, Clubs, Community Foundations, Economic Development, Employment/Job Training, Civic & Public Affairs-General, Hispanic Affairs, Housing, Law & Justice, Municipalities/Towns, Nonprofit Management, Professional & Trade Associations, Public Policy, Urban & Community Affairs, Women's Affairs, Zoos/Aquariums
Education: Afterschool/Enrichment Programs, Arts/Humanities Education, Business Education, Colleges & Universities, Education Associations, Education Funds, Education Reform, Elementary Education (Private), Elementary Education (Public), Education-General, Leadership Training, Literacy, Minority Education, Preschool Education, Private Education (Precollege), Public Education (Precollege), School Volunteerism, Science/Mathematics Education, Special Education, Student Aid

Environment: Environment-General
Health: AIDS/HIV, Clinics/Medical Centers, Hospitals, Hospitals (University Affiliated), Nursing Services, Outpatient Health Care, Public Health, Research/Studies Institutes
Religion: Religious Organizations, Religious Welfare
Science: Scientific Centers & Institutes
Social Services: At-Risk Youth, Big Brother/Big Sister, Child Welfare, Community Centers, Community Service Organizations, Counseling, Crime Prevention, Day Care, Delinquency & Criminal Rehabilitation, Domestic Violence, Family Planning, Family Services, Food/Clothing Distribution, People with Disabilities, Recreation & Athletics, Social Services-General, Volunteer Services, YMCA/YWCA/YMHA/YWHA, Youth Organizations

Application Procedures

Initial Contact: Applicants should write a brief letter of inquiry, not to exceed two pages, prior to a formal proposal or application for a grant.
Application Requirements: The letter should describe the grantee organization, the proposed project and its goals, an estimated budget, IRS 501(c)(3) status, list of other agencies solicited, and the name and qualifications of the person directing the project. For other than direct service projects, the program description should also include the possibilities for practical application of the project's efforts and findings.
Deadlines: None. Letters of inquiry are welcome throughout the year.
Review Process: The board meets in May and December.

Restrictions

Grants are awarded only to nonprofit, public organizations that are tax-exempt under IRS 501(c)(3). The foundation does not make grants to individuals, provide emergency assistance, nor does it support medical research or the direct provision of health care or religious education. It generally does not make grants to support conferences, publications, or media. Proposals for building renovations or other capital projects are not considered unless they are integrally related to the foundation's program objectives or are an outgrowth of one of its grantee's programs.

Additional Information

Publications: Guidelines for Grant Seekers; Biennial Report

Foundation Officials

Joan Colello: secretary, executive director, trustee
Eugene E. Fey: treasurer, trustee
George Joseph Gillespie, III: president, trustee B New York, NY 1930. ED Georgetown University AB (1952); Harvard University LLB (1955). PRIM CORP EMPL partner: Cravath, Swaine & Moore. CORP AFFIL director: Washington Post Co. NONPR AFFIL director, chairman emeritus: National Multiple Sclerosis Society; trustee: New York University Medical Center; director: Madison Square Boys Club; secretary, director: Museum Television & Radio; member: Century Association; trustee, treasurer: Cooper-Hewitt National Design Museum. CLUB AFFIL Prouts Neck Country Club; Winged Foot Golf Club; member: Portland Country Club; Double Eagle Club; Falmouth Country Club; American Yacht Club.
Michael Stewart Joyce: trustee B Cleveland, OH 1942. ED Cleveland State University BA (1967); Walden University PhD (1974). CORP AFFIL director: Blue Cross Blue Shield United Wisconsin. NONPR AFFIL director: United Wisconsin Services Inc.; member: White House Fellowships Eastern Regional Selection Panel; director: United Way Wisconsin; member: Sovereign Military Order Malta; member advisory board: U.S. Information Agency International Cultural & Education Exchange; chairman: Philanthropy Roundtable; member executive committee: President

Private Sector Study Cost Control Grace Commission; member: Mont Pelerin Society; member: National Committee Civic Renewal; trustee: Foundation Cultural Review; secretary: Institute Education Affairs; member: Cardinal's Committee Laity Archdiocese New York; member selection committee: Clare Booth Luce Fund. CLUB AFFIL University Milwaukee Club; Milwaukee Club; Union League New York City Club.
Daniel L. Mosley: trustee
Richard M. Smith: trustee B Detroit, MI 1946. ED Albion College BA (1968); Columbia University MS (1970); Albion College LLD (1993). PRIM CORP EMPL president, editor-in-chief, director: Newsweek Inc. NONPR AFFIL director: Magazine Publishers Association; member: Phi Beta Kappa; trustee: Cooper-Hewitt National Design Museum; council: Foreign Relations; member: American Society Magazine Editors; council: Century Association; trustee: Albion College.
Thomas Joseph Sweeney, Jr.: trustee B New York, NY 1923. ED New York University BA (1947); Columbia University JD (1949). PRIM CORP EMPL partner: Decker, Hubbard, Welden & Sweeney. CORP AFFIL chairman inst trustee & investment committee: Morgan Guaranty Trust Co. New York. NONPR AFFIL director: WR Kenan Fund; member: New York State Bar Association.

Grants Analysis

Disclosure Period: calendar year ending 2001
Total Grants: $6,630,610*
Number of Grants: 123
Highest Grant: $450,000
Typical Range: $25,000 to $50,000
*Note: Giving excludes matching gifts. Average grant figure excludes two highest grants ($916,760).

Recent Grants

Note: Grants derived from 2000 Form 990.

General

466,760	Fund for the City of New York, New York, NY
450,000	Public/Private Ventures, Philadelphia, PA
172,240	United Neighborhood Houses of New York, Inc., New York, NY
150,000	Vera Institute of Justice, New York, NY
111,652	Goddard Riverside Community Center, New York, NY
100,000	Good Shepherd Services, New York, NY
100,000	St. Nicholas Neighborhood Preservation Corporation, Brooklyn, NY
100,000	Vocational Foundation, Inc., New York, NY
94,000	Center for Arts Education, New York, NY
76,750	Edwin Gould Academy, New York, NY

PIONEER TRUST BANK, NA

Company Headquarters

1190 Oak St., SE
Salem, OR 97301

Company Description

Employees: 50
SIC(s): 6000 Depository Institutions.

Operating Locations

Pioneer Trust Bank, NA (OR--Salem)

Pioneer Trust Bank, NA, Foundation

Giving Contact

Pioneer Trust Bank, NA Foundation
PO Box 2305
Salem, OR 97308
Phone: (503)363-3136

Description

EIN: 930881673
Organization Type: Corporate Foundation
Giving Locations: OR: Salem
Grant Types: Challenge, Emergency, General Support, Operating Expenses, Project, Research, Seed Money.

Financial Summary

Total Giving: $53,500 (2001); $53,500 (2000); $49,600 (1999)
Giving Analysis: Giving for 2001 includes: foundation grants to United Way ($3,500); 2000: foundation grants to United Way ($3,500); 1999: foundation grants to United Way ($3,500); foundation ($46,100)
Assets: $942,762 (2001); $991,404 (2000); $1,063,662 (1999)
Gifts Received: $91,650 (1992). Note: In 1992, contributions were received from Pioneer Trust Bank Corp.

Typical Recipients

Arts & Humanities: Arts Associations & Councils, Arts Festivals, Arts Outreach, Arts & Humanities-General, Historic Preservation, History & Archaeology, Libraries, Museums/Galleries, Music, Performing Arts, Public Broadcasting, Theater, Visual Arts
Civic & Public Affairs: Clubs, Community Foundations, Civic & Public Affairs-General, Housing, Municipalities/Towns, Urban & Community Affairs, Women's Affairs
Education: Elementary Education (Public), Education-General, Literacy, Private Education (Precollege), Secondary Education (Public), Student Aid
Environment: Environment-General, Resource Conservation
Health: Emergency/Ambulance Services, Eyes/Blindness, Health-General, Health Organizations, Hospices, Hospitals, Medical Research
Religion: Missionary Activities (Domestic), Religious Welfare
Social Services: Animal Protection, Child Welfare, Community Service Organizations, Domestic Violence, Family Services, Food/Clothing Distribution, People with Disabilities, Scouts, Social Services-General, Special Olympics, United Funds/United Ways, YMCA/YWCA/YMHA/YWHA, Youth Organizations

Application Procedures

Initial Contact: Send a brief letter of inquiry.
Application Requirements: Include a description of organization, amount requested, purpose of funds sought, recently audited financial statement, and proof of tax-exempt status.
Deadlines: October 31.

Restrictions

Does not support individuals, political or lobbying groups, or organizations outside operating areas. Generally does not support organizations located outside of Salem, OR and the surrounding area.

Additional Information

Trust(s): Pioneer Trust Bank NA

Corporate Officials

Michael S. Compton: president PRIM CORP EMPL president: Pioneer Trust Bank NA.

Grants Analysis

Disclosure Period: calendar year ending 2001
Total Grants: $50,000*
Number of Grants: 38
Average Grant: $1,316
Highest Grant: $12,500
Typical Range: $500 to $2,000
*Note: Giving excludes United Way.

Recent Grants

Note: Grants derived from 2001 Form 990.

Library-Related

1,150	Salem Public Library Foundation, Salem, OR

General

12,500	Salem Area Habitat for Humanity, Salem, OR
5,000	Salem Riverfront Carousel, Salem, OR
3,500	United Way, Salem, OR
2,000	American Red Cross, Salem, OR
1,100	Assistance League of Salem, Salem, OR
1,100	Young Women's Christian Association, Salem, OR
1,000	Boys and Girls Club of Salem, Salem, OR
1,000	Cascade Area Council for Boy Scouts, Salem, OR
1,000	Family Building Blocks, Salem, OR
1,000	Friends of Deepwood, Salem, OR

MINNIE STEVENS PIPER FOUNDATION

Giving Contact

Carlos Otero, Executive Director & Secretary
GPM South Tower, Suite 200
800 NW Loop 410
San Antonio, TX 78216-5699
Phone: (210)525-8494
Fax: (210)341-6627
E-mail: cotero@mspf.org
Web: http://www.mspf.org

Description

Founded: 1950
EIN: 741292695
Organization Type: General Purpose Foundation
Giving Locations: TX
Grant Types: Loan, Scholarship.

Donor Information

Founder: Incorporated in 1950 by the late Randall G. Piper and the late Minnie Stevens Piper.

Financial Summary

Total Giving: $1,500,000 (2002 approx); $567,640 (2001); $391,125 (2000)
Giving Analysis: Giving for 2000 includes: foundation grants to United Way ($2,500); foundation scholarships ($272,625); 1997: foundation scholarships ($216,400); 1996: foundation scholarships ($232,600)
Assets: $25,497,565 (2001); $26,408,248 (2000); $26,744,071 (1999)
Gifts Received: $343 (2001); $55,886 (2000); $37,993 (1999). Note: In 2000, contributions were received from William C. & Alta Foster. In 1999, substantial contributions were received from William C. & Alta Foster ($25,632 non-cash) and Denton Engineering Co. ($11,000).

Typical Recipients

Arts & Humanities: Arts Centers, Arts Festivals, Arts Funds, Arts Institutes, Ballet, Community Arts, Ethnic & Folk Arts, Historic Preservation, History & Archaeology, Libraries, Museums/Galleries, Music, Opera, Performing Arts, Public Broadcasting, Theater
Civic & Public Affairs: Hispanic Affairs, Law & Justice, Nonprofit Management, Philanthropic Organizations, Professional & Trade Associations
Education: Arts/Humanities Education, Colleges & Universities, Community & Junior Colleges, Education Funds, Education Reform, Engineering/Technological Education, Faculty Development, Education-General, International Studies, Legal Education, Literacy, Medical Education, Minority Education, Minority Education, Private Education (Precollege), Public Education (Precollege), Religious Education, Science/Mathematics Education, Secondary Education (Private), Secondary Education (Public), Social Sciences Education, Student Aid
Health: Cancer, Eyes/Blindness, Health Organizations, Hospitals, Medical Research, Mental Health, Public Health
International: Health Care/Hospitals
Religion: Churches
Science: Science Exhibits & Fairs, Scientific Centers & Institutes
Social Services: Child Welfare, Community Centers, Community Service Organizations, Crime Prevention, Domestic Violence, Food/Clothing Distribution, People with Disabilities, Substance Abuse, United Funds/United Ways, YMCA/YWCA/YMHA/YWHA, Youth Organizations

Application Procedures

Initial Contact: The foundation has no formal grant application procedure or application form. for grants. Student loan inquiries should contact the foundation for a loan application.
Application Requirements: Written grant proposals should be accompanied by proof of tax-exempt status.
Deadlines: Grant applications should be submitted by February 1 and July 1. Deadlines for scholarships, student loan requests, fellowships and professor awards vary by program.
Review Process: The board meets twice annually.

Restrictions

The Bexar County Scholarship Clearing House program is restricted to students in Bexar County, Texas. The Pipers Scholars Program is restricted to certain counties in Texas. Scholarships awarded by invitation only by nomination process from high school counselor. No grants are made to institutions outside the State of Texas, or to organizations which discriminate on the grounds of race, color, creed, or sex. Grant requests will be considered only from organizations which have qualified for non-profit status by the Internal Revenue Service under the IRS code and applicable regulations. The foundation will not consider grant requests for building fund campaigns or endowments, unless under exceptional circumstances.

Additional Information

The foundation provides grants from income only. Though continuing programs of the foundation require the greater portion of annual distributable income, the remainder is granted in minimal amounts by the board of directors for a variety of purposes, with a focus on projects in the field of higher education, especially those that are student oriented.
Publications: Purpose; Policy; Programs Brochure; Application Guidelines

Foundation Officials

Paul T. Curl: director
Lewis M. Fox: director
Martin R. Harris: treasurer
Carlos Otero: executive director, assistant secretary-treasurer
J. Burleson Smith: director
John H. Wilson, II: president B 1927. ED Colorado School of Mines (1944-1949). PRIM CORP EMPL president, director: Piper Petroleum Co. CORP AFFIL principal: Wilson Exploration Co.

Grants Analysis

Disclosure Period: calendar year ending 2001
Total Grants: $167,500*
Number of Grants: 34
Average Grant: $3,047*
Highest Grant: $35,000
Lowest Grant: $50
Typical Range: $1,000 to $5,000
*Note: Giving excludes scholarships and United Way. Average grant figure excludes two highest grants ($70,000).

Recent Grants

Note: Grants derived from 2001 Form 990.

Library-Related

5,000	San Antonio Public Library Foundation, San Antonio, TX

General

322,640	Piper Professors Program, San Antonio, TX
75,000	Piper Professors Program, San Antonio, TX -- for Superior Teaching Awards
35,000	Cancer Therapy and Research Center, San Antonio, TX
35,000	Southwest Foundation for Biomedical Research, San Antonio, TX
5,000	Baptist Memorial Hospital, San Antonio, TX
5,000	Cancer Therapy and Research Center, San Antonio, TX
5,000	College of St. Thomas More in Texas, Ft. Worth, TX
5,000	James Dick Foundation for Performing Arts Festival, Institute at Round Top, Round Top, TX
5,000	Our Lady of the Lake University, San Antonio, TX
5,000	St. Edward's University, Austin, TX

PITT-DES MOINES, INC.

Company Headquarters

Pittsburgh, PA

Company Description

Employees: 2,082
SIC(s): 1500 General Building Contractors, 3400 Fabricated Metal Products, 5000 Wholesale Trade--Durable Goods.

Operating Locations

Pitt-Des Moines Inc. (CA; IA; PA--Pittsburgh; WI)

Pitt-Des Moines Inc. Charitable Trust

Giving Contact

William R. Jackson, Trustee
Pitt-Des Moines Inc. Charitable Trust
3400 Grand Ave.
Pittsburgh, PA 15225-1582
Phone: (412)331-3000

Description

EIN: 256032139
Organization Type: Corporate Foundation
Giving Locations: CA; IA; PA: PA, IA, CA, WI; WI
Grant Types: General Support.

Financial Summary

Total Giving: $131,260 (2000); $88,515 (1999); $88,060 (1998)
Giving Analysis: Giving for 2000 includes: foundation grants to United Way ($22,730); 1999: foundation grants to United Way ($22,590); foundation ($65,925) 1998: foundation grants to United Way ($19,410)

Assets: $1,702,763 (2000); $1,677,743 (1999); $1,798,086 (1998)

Gifts Received: $100,000 (1996). Note: In 1996, contributions were received from Pitt-Des Moines.

Typical Recipients

Arts & Humanities: Arts Associations & Councils, Arts Centers, Community Arts, Arts & Humanities-General, Historic Preservation, History & Archaeology, Libraries, Museums/Galleries, Opera, Public Broadcasting

Civic & Public Affairs: African American Affairs, Botanical Gardens/Parks, Business/Free Enterprise, Civil Rights, Economic Development, Economic Policy, Employment/Job Training, Civic & Public Affairs-General, Housing, Legal Aid, Philanthropic Organizations, Public Policy, Urban & Community Affairs, Zoos/Aquariums

Education: Colleges & Universities, Education Associations, Education Funds, Education-General, Minority Education

Environment: Environment-General, Resource Conservation

Health: Children's Health/Hospitals, Emergency/Ambulance Services, Health-General, Health Organizations, Hospitals, Medical Rehabilitation

International: International-General, International Peace & Security Issues, Missionary/Religious Activities

Religion: Religion-General, Ministries, Missionary Activities (Domestic), Religious Organizations, Religious Welfare

Science: Science-General

Social Services: Camps, Community Service Organizations, Emergency Relief, Scouts, Social Services-General, United Funds/United Ways, Youth Organizations

Application Procedures

Initial Contact: Send a brief letter of inquiry.

Application Requirements: a description of organization, amount requested, purpose of funds sought, and a copy of IRS-approved letter confirming 501(c)(3) status and issuance date.

Deadlines: None.

Restrictions

Does not support individuals.

Corporate Officials

R. A. Byers: vice president finance, treasurerc PRIM CORP EMPL vice president finance, treasurer: Pitt-Des Moines.

P. O. Elbert: chairman, director PRIM CORP EMPL chairman, director: Pitt-Des Moines.

W. W. McKee: president, chief executive officer, director PRIM CORP EMPL president, chief executive officer, director: Pitt-Des Moines.

Foundation Officials

R. A. Byers: trustee (see above)

P. O. Elbert: trustee (see above)

William R. Jackson: trustee B Des Moines, IA May 25, 1908. ED Massachusetts Institute of Technology (1930). CORP AFFIL chairman emeritus, director: Pitt-Des Moines. CLUB AFFIL mem: Shriners Club.

Grants Analysis

Disclosure Period: calendar year ending 2000

Total Grants: $108,530*

Number of Grants: 67

Average Grant: $1,208*

Highest Grant: $20,000

Typical Range: $500 to $2,500

*Note: Giving excludes United Way. Average grant figure excludes two highest grants ($30,000).

Recent Grants

Note: Grants derived from 1999 Form 990.

General

6,000	National Right to Work Legal Defense, Springfield, VA
4,000	National Right to Work Legal Defense, Springfield, VA
4,000	Pennsylvania Right to Work Defense and Education Foundation, Harrisburg, PA
3,750	United Way - Greater Eau Claire
3,000	National Right to Work Legal Defense, Springfield, VA
3,000	Young America's Foundation, Herndon, VA
2,500	Association of Independent Colleges and Universities, Harrisburg, PA
2,500	Montgomery County United Way, Crawfordsville, IN
2,500	United Way - Central Iowa, IA
2,000	United Way of Southwestern Pennsylvania, Pittsburgh, PA

PITTSBURG & MIDWAY COAL MINING CO.

Company Headquarters

Englewood, CO

Web: http://www.chevron.com

Company Description

Employees: 1,325

SIC(s): 1200 Coal Mining, 1221 Bituminous Coal & Lignite--Surface, 1222 Bituminous Coal--Underground.

Operating Locations

Pittsburg & Midway Coal Mining Co. (AL--Tuscaloosa; NM--Gallup, Raton; WY--Kemmerer)

Giving Contact

Robert Johnson, Manager, Public Affairs
PO Box 6518
Englewood, CO 80155-6518
Phone: (303)930-3600
Fax: (303)930-4189

Description

Organization Type: Corporate Giving Program

Giving Locations: principally near operating locations and to national organizations.

Grant Types: Award, Emergency, General Support, Multiyear/Continuing Support, Scholarship.

Typical Recipients

Arts & Humanities: Arts Appreciation, Arts Associations & Councils, Arts Centers, Arts Festivals, Community Arts, Arts & Humanities-General, Libraries, Museums/Galleries, Music, Public Broadcasting

Civic & Public Affairs: Botanical Gardens/Parks, Chambers of Commerce, Clubs, Civic & Public Affairs-General, Native American Affairs, Parades/Festivals, Professional & Trade Associations, Public Policy, Urban & Community Affairs

Education: Agricultural Education, Colleges & Universities, Community & Junior Colleges, Education Funds, Education Reform, Elementary Education (Public), Engineering/Technological Education, Education-General, Public Education (Precollege), Science/Mathematics Education

Environment: Air/Water Quality, Energy, Environment-General, Resource Conservation, Wildlife Protection

Health: Children's Health/Hospitals, Clinics/Medical Centers, Emergency/Ambulance Services, Eyes/Blindness, Health-General, Hospitals, Medical Rehabilitation, Prenatal Health Issues, Research/Studies Institutes

Science: Science-General, Science Exhibits & Fairs, Scientific Organizations

Social Services: Child Welfare, Community Centers, Community Service Organizations, Crime Prevention, Day Care, Delinquency & Criminal Rehabilitation, Domestic Violence, Emergency Relief, Family Services, Recreation & Athletics, Senior Services, Social Services-General, United Funds/United Ways, Volunteer Services, Youth Organizations

Application Procedures

Initial Contact: Generally, charitable contributions are made upon request/recommendation of mine managers. The company is not soliciting additional requests for contributions.

Restrictions

Does not support group or individual travel expenses.

Additional Information

Contributions typically are aligned with company business interests. As a Chevron subsidiary, all contributions are part of Chervon's total (see separate entry).

Corporate Officials

Barry G. McGrath: chairman, president PRIM CORP EMPL chairman, president: Pittsburg & Midway Coal Mining Co.

Grants Analysis

Typical Range: $10 to $1,000*

*Note: Typical grant size is less than $1,000.

Recent Grants

Note: Grants derived from 1998 Form 990.

General

4-H Clubs, Remmener, NY
Child Development Center, Remmener, NY
Ducks Unlimited, Ft. Collins, CO
Four Corners Science Fair, Gallup, MN
Gallup Lions Club Rodeo, Gallup, NM
Navajo Way, Window Rock, AZ
Rocky Mount Elic Foundation, Remmener, NY
Rocky Mountain Coal Mining Institute, Lakewood, CO
United Way, Gallup, NM

PITTSBURGH CHILD GUIDANCE FOUNDATION

Giving Contact

Dr. Claire A. Walker, Executive Director
425 Sixth Ave., Suite 2460
Pittsburgh, PA 15219
Phone: (412)434-1665
Fax: (412)434-0406
E-mail: pcgf@smartbuilding.org
Web: http://trfn.clpgh.org/pcgf/index.shtml

Description

Founded: 1982

EIN: 250965465

Organization Type: Private Foundation

Giving Locations: PA: Allegheny County

Grant Types: Project, Research.

Financial Summary

Total Giving: $218,864 (2001); $275,545 (2000); $131,025 (1999)

Assets: $5,851,065 (2001); $6,360,153 (2000); $7,067,061 (1999)

Gifts Received: $100 (1999); $100 (1997)

Typical Recipients

Arts & Humanities: Arts Centers, Arts Outreach

Civic & Public Affairs: Community Foundations, Nonprofit Management, Philanthropic Organizations, Urban & Community Affairs

Education: Afterschool/Enrichment Programs, Arts/Humanities Education, Education-General, Literacy, Preschool Education, Special Education
Health: Children's Health/Hospitals, Mental Health, Prenatal Health Issues
Religion: Churches, Ministries, Religious Organizations, Social/Policy Issues
Social Services: At-Risk Youth, Big Brother/Big Sister, Camps, Child Abuse, Child Welfare, Community Centers, Community Service Organizations, Crime Prevention, Day Care, Family Services, Food/Clothing Distribution, Recreation & Athletics, Sexual Abuse, Shelters/Homelessness, Social Services-General, Substance Abuse, YMCA/YWCA/YMHA/YWHA, Youth Organizations

Application Procedures

Initial Contact: Submit a one- to two-page letter of intent.
Application Requirements: Include the project's purpose, beneficiaries, activities, total costs, amount requested, and amounts and sources of other revenue (actual and potential).
Deadlines: Discretionary grants are typically due the first Wednesday in March and September.
Review Process: Foundation staff and trustees will review letters of intent; if a proposal is of interest to the foundation, the applicant will be invited to submit a formal application using the foundation's application form.

Restrictions

The foundation does not fund operating or capital expenses.

Additional Information

In 2003, the Foundation announced its 2003-2008 Area of Emphasis: Helping the community address the losses experienced by children whose parents are incarcerated. All Area of Emphasis Program Grants will focus on this issue. In addition to the Area of Emphasis Program, the foundation also makes Discretionary Grants, which are made to various organizations for projects that support children's development. As of press time, unsolicited requests were not being accepted for Area of Emphasis grants, and grantmaking was temporarily suspended within the Discretionary Grants program. Contact the foundation or check the foundation's web site for updates on these programs.
Publications: Informational Brochure (including Application Guidelines); Grants List

Foundation Officials

Carmen Anderson: trustee PRIM CORP EMPL executive director: Healthy Start Inc.
Duane T. Ashley: trustee
Randolph W. Brockington: trustee
Jane C. Burger: trustee
Eileen H. Christman: president
Nancy E. Curry: trustee B Brockway, PA 1931. ED Grove City College BA (1952); University of Pittsburgh MEd (1956); University of Pittsburgh PhD (1972). NONPR AFFIL member: National Association Education Young Children; professor emeritus: University Pittsburgh School Social Work; member: American Psychological Association; member: American Associate University Professors; member: American Psychoanalytic Association.
Judith M. Davenport: trustee
Carolyn D. Duronio: secretary
Jesse Fife, Junior: trustee
David B. Hartmann: trustee
John D. Houston, II: trustee
Claudia L. Hussein: trustee
Kelly J. Keckher: trustee
John G. Lovelace: trustee
W. Thomas McGough, Jr.: secretary
Thelma Lovette Morris: trustee
Evelyn L. Murrin: trustee
Ronald Edward Peters: trustee

Lloyd F. Stamy, Jr.: treasurer
Mary Margaret Stamy: trustee
Claire Walker: executive director
Nancy D. Washington: president
Jeffrey A. Wlahofsky: trustee

Grants Analysis

Disclosure Period: calendar year ending 2001
Total Grants: $218,864
Number of Grants: 11
Average Grant: $19,897
Highest Grant: $40,633
Lowest Grant: $11,500
Typical Range: $10,000 to $25,000

Recent Grants

Note: Grants derived from 2001 Form 990.

General

40,633	Schenley Heights Community Development Program, Pittsburgh, PA -- After-School Program
25,000	Young Men and Women's African Heritage Association, Pittsburgh, PA -- support for adopted and foster children
23,205	YMCA of Pittsburgh Centre Avenue Program Center, Pittsburgh, PA -- After-School Program and summer day camp
22,500	Hosanna House, Wilkinsburg, PA -- children with academic and behavior difficulties
21,000	East Side Community Collaborative, Pittsburgh, PA -- help for young children of substance abusers
19,825	Hazelwood Youth Football and Cheerleading Association, Pittsburgh, PA -- support for athletic teams and mentoring
17,501	North Hills Youth Ministry, Pittsburgh, PA -- academic assistance for children
12,926	Zion Christian Church, Pittsburgh, PA -- After-School and Summer Programs
12,500	East End Cooperative Ministry, Pittsburgh, PA -- children with academic and behavioral difficulty
12,274	Greater Pittsburgh Community Food Bank, Duquesne, PA -- foodbank services, After-School Programs

HARRY PLANKENHORN FOUNDATION

Giving Contact

Fred A. Foulkrod, Treasurer
Harry Plankenhorn Foundation
Care of Covenant United Church of Christ
202 E. Third Street
Williamsport, PA 17701
Phone: (570)326-3308

Description

Founded: 1959
EIN: 246023579
Organization Type: Private Foundation
Giving Locations: PA: Lycoming County
Grant Types: General Support.

Donor Information

Founder: the late Harry Plankenhorn

Financial Summary

Total Giving: $411,426 (2001); $467,308 (2000); $505,786 (1999)
Giving Analysis: Giving for 1999 includes: foundation scholarships ($2,500)
Assets: $8,464,548 (2001); $9,387,213 (2000); $9,427,013 (1999)

Gifts Received: $100 (2001); $50,100 (2000); $199 (1999). Note: In 1996, contributions were received from Ruth Askey.

Typical Recipients

Arts & Humanities: Libraries
Civic & Public Affairs: Civic & Public Affairs-General, Housing, Law & Justice, Safety, Urban & Community Affairs
Education: Agricultural Education, Preschool Education, Special Education, Student Aid
Health: Cancer, Clinics/Medical Centers, Emergency/Ambulance Services, Heart, Hospitals, Long-Term Care, Mental Health, Multiple Sclerosis, Preventive Medicine/Wellness Organizations, Respiratory, Single-Disease Health Associations
Religion: Churches, Religious Welfare
Social Services: Animal Protection, Camps, Child Welfare, Community Centers, Community Service Organizations, Counseling, Emergency Relief, Family Services, People with Disabilities, Recreation & Athletics, Scouts, Shelters/Homelessness, United Funds/United Ways, YMCA/YWCA/YMHA/YWHA, Youth Organizations

Application Procedures

Initial Contact: Requests may be made orally; however, any request for $5,000 or more must be made in writing and presented to the board of directors at a designated meeting.
Deadlines: None.

Foundation Officials

Rev. Bruce Druckenmiller: trustee
Barbara Ertel: trustee
Phillis Feese Guyette: trustee
Fred A. Foulkrod: vice president, treasurer
Charles F. Greevy, III: president
Carl O. Hieber: trustee
Bob Hivley: trustee
W. Herbert Poff, III: secretary
Robert M. Reeder: trustee
Carolyn Seifert: trustee
Abram M. Snyder: vice president
Nancy Stearns: trustee
Lucinda A. Wagner: trustee
Eleanor W. Whiting: assistant treasurer

Grants Analysis

Disclosure Period: calendar year ending 2001
Total Grants: $411,426
Number of Grants: 28
Average Grant: $11,719*
Highest Grant: $95,000
Lowest Grant: $120
Typical Range: $5,000 to $20,000
*Note: Average grant figure excludes highest grant.

Recent Grants

Note: Grants derived from 2000 Form 990.

Library-Related

20,000	James V. Brown Library, Williamsport, PA -- for bookmobile and operations
5,000	James V. Brown Library, Williamsport, PA -- for large print books

General

65,000	American Rescue Workers, Williamsport, PA -- for disasters, workshops and relief
52,000	YWCA, Williamsport, PA -- for cost of remodeling swimming pool and making it accessible for the handicapped
50,000	Habitat for Humanity, Williamsport, PA -- annual contribution to other operations
50,000	YMCA, Williamsport, PA -- for memberships for underprivileged
40,000	Salvation Army, Williamsport, PA -- for emergency aid and other operations

33,000	North Central Sight Services, Williamsport, PA -- annual contribution for operations
25,000	Volunteer Fire Department, Williamsport, PA -- for Parents Network Program
20,000	St. Anthony's Center, Williamsport, PA -- for medical clinic
15,000	Shepherd of the Streets, Williamsport, PA -- annual contribution
15,000	YMCA, Williamsport, PA -- contribution to Building Remodeling Program

PLOUGH FOUNDATION

Giving Contact
Rick Masson, Jr., Executive Director & Trustee
6410 Poplar Ave., Ste. 710
Memphis, TN 38119
Phone: (901)761-9180
Fax: (901)761-6186
E-mail: mail@plough.org

Description
Founded: 1960
EIN: 237175983
Organization Type: General Purpose Foundation
Giving Locations: TN: primarily in Shelby County and Memphis
Grant Types: Capital, Challenge, Emergency, Endowment, Fellowship, General Support, Multiyear/Continuing Support, Professorship, Project, Research, Scholarship, Seed Money.

Donor Information
Founder: The Plough Foundation was established in 1960, with funds donated by the late Abe Plough . In 1920, Abe Plough bought the St. Joseph Company of Chattanooga, TN, best known as the manufacturer of children's aspirin. He eventually bought twenty-seven companies. A 1971 merger with the Schering pharmaceutical company resulted in the formation of the Schering-Plough Corporation.

Financial Summary
Total Giving: $13,263,000 (2002 approx); $10,250,000 (2001); $12,000,000 (2000 approx)
Assets: $186,537,000 (2001); $216,855,000 (2000); $212,746,328 (1999)
Gifts Received: $800,000 (2000 approx); $860,000 (1999 approx); $850,000 (1998 approx). Note: Contributions have been made by Plough family members Patricia R. Burnham, Jocelyn P. Rudner, DD R. Eisenberg, and Diane R. Goldstein.

Typical Recipients
Arts & Humanities: Arts Associations & Councils, Arts Outreach, Ballet, Arts & Humanities-General, History & Archaeology, Libraries, Museums/Galleries, Music, Opera, Performing Arts, Public Broadcasting
Civic & Public Affairs: African American Affairs, Business/Free Enterprise, Chambers of Commerce, Clubs, Economic Development, Civic & Public Affairs-General, Housing, Municipalities/Towns, Nonprofit Management, Parades/Festivals, Urban & Community Affairs, Zoos/Aquariums
Education: Agricultural Education, Arts/Humanities Education, Business Education, Colleges & Universities, Education Reform, Elementary Education (Private), Engineering/Technological Education, Education-General, Medical Education, Preschool Education, Public Education (Precollege), Public Education (Precollege)
Environment: Wildlife Protection
Health: Cancer, Clinics/Medical Centers, Emergency/Ambulance Services, Hospitals, Mental Health, Outpatient Health Care, Single-Disease Health Associations
International: Missionary/Religious Activities

Religion: Jewish Causes, Ministries, Religious Organizations, Religious Welfare, Synagogues/Temples
Social Services: Big Brother/Big Sister, Child Welfare, Community Service Organizations, Family Services, Food/Clothing Distribution, People with Disabilities, Recreation & Athletics, Scouts, Senior Services, Shelters/Homelessness, Social Services-General, Special Olympics, Substance Abuse, United Funds/United Ways, YMCA/YWCA/YMHA/YWHA, Youth Organizations

Application Procedures
Initial Contact: A brief concept letter (not exceeding three pages) should be sent to the executive director. After review of the concept letter, a full application may be invited.
Application Requirements: Concept letters should include information about the purpose of the request and planned use of funds. Applications should contain a sound and efficient business plan, including such considerations as control of overhead, mergers with similar groups, and other cost-containment activities, realistic budgets, formal long and short term plans and the presence of endowment or reserve funds, evidence of strong leadership capabilities in the board and administrative staff, and evidence of the organization's tax-exempt status from the Internal Revenue Service.
Deadlines: January 10, April 10, July 10, October 10. Concept letters should be sent at least 10 days prior to the deadlines.
Review Process: Upon receipt of the application, some or all of the following steps must be completed by our office: staff review, executive committee review, application review, interview, site visit, and reference check. The process can be expected to take as much as six weeks. Approved applications will be forwarded to the board of trustees for study prior to the quarterly board meeting. The full board must approve any grants to be funded by the foundation.
Notes: Grant applications are considered on a first-come/first-served basis. It is advantageous to submit requests early to allow time for review. Every effort will be made to process all concept letters within two weeks of receipt.

Restrictions
The foundation rarely provides grants outside the Memphis and Shelby County area. The foundation will not consider requests for assistance to address a "crisis management" situation caused by poor initial planning or poor execution of the program. The foundation does not make grants to individuals or fund annual operating budgets.

Additional Information
National Bank of Commerce is listed as the corporate trustee for the foundation. Many grants carry a stipulation that other contributed amounts must be obtained by the organization as matching funds.
Publications: Brochure

Foundation Officials
Hallam Boyd, Jr.: trustee ED Yale University (1956).
Patricia R. Burnham: trustee
Eugene J. Callahan, Esq.: trustee PRIM CORP EMPL partner: Wormser Kiely Gale & Jacobs.
Robert Compton: trustee
DD Eisenberg: trustee
Diane R. Goldstein: trustee
Noris R. Haynes, Jr.: executive director, trustee
Larry Papasan: trustee B Etta, MS 1940. ED Northwest Mississippi Junior College (1959-1960); Mississippi State University BScE (1963). CORP AFFIL president, director: Smith & Nephew Richards Inc.; director: First America National Bank Memphis. NONPR AFFIL member: Tennessee Municipal Electric Power Association; member: Tennessee Valley Public Power Association; director: Memphis Boys Club; member advisory board: Memphis State University Fogelman College Business; director: Junior

Achievement Memphis; director: LeMoyne-Owen College; director: Goals Memphis; membership chairman: Boy Scouts America; director: Electric Power Research Institute; member: American Management Association; member: American Public Power Association; member: American Gas Association.
Jocelyn P. Rudner: trustee
James Francis Springfield: trustee B Memphis, TN 1929. ED Rhodes College BA (1951); Memphis State University LLB (1960). NONPR AFFIL member: Tennessee Bankers Association; member: Tennessee Bar Association; member: Sigma Nu; member board visitors: Memphis State University Cecil C Humphreys School Law; member: Omicron Delta Kappa; member advisory board: Memphis Alzheimers Association; member: Memphis and Shelby County Bar Association; member: Bank Administration Institute; member: Estate Planning Council Memphis.
Steven Wishnia: trustee

Grants Analysis
Disclosure Period: calendar year ending 2001
Total Grants: $10,250,015*
Number of Grants: 52
Average Grant: $197,116*
Highest Grant: $1,000,000
Lowest Grant: $1,000
Typical Range: $50,000 to $250,000
***Note:** Grants analysis provided by foundation. Average grant figure excludes highest grant.

Recent Grants
Note: Grants derived from 2000 Form 990.

Library-Related

385,000	Foundation for the Memphis-Shelby County Public Library, Memphis, TN -- for building and renovation
325,000	Foundation for The Memphis/Shelby County Public Library, Memphis, TN -- building
150,000	Foundation for The Memphis/Shelby County Public Library, Memphis, TN -- building

General

2,000,000	Memphis Zoological Society, Memphis, TN -- for capital campaign
1,000,000	Metropolitan Interfaith Association, Memphis, TN -- for building and renovation
1,000,000	Soulsville, Memphis, TN -- for building and renovation
1,000,000	Wonders: The International Cultural Series, Memphis, TN -- for operating support
1,000,000	Youth Villages, Memphis, TN -- for building and renovation
666,712	Memphis Redbirds Baseball Foundation, Memphis, TN -- for building/renovation
625,000	University of Memphis, Memphis, TN -- for professorships
500,000	Serenity Recovery Centers, Memphis, TN -- for building and renovation
450,000	Church Health Center, Memphis, TN -- for program development
448,236	Memphis City Schools, Memphis, TN -- for building and renovation

PLYM FOUNDATION

Giving Contact
Donald F. Walter, Vice President & Treasurer
423 Sycamore St., Suite 101
Niles, MI 49120
Phone: (616)684-3248

Description
Founded: 1952
EIN: 386069680
Organization Type: Private Foundation

Giving Locations: MI
Grant Types: Capital, General Support, Research.

Donor Information

Founder: Mrs. Francis J. Plym

Financial Summary

Total Giving: $262,500 (fiscal year ending September 30, 2001); $353,465 (fiscal 2000); $350,000 (fiscal 1999 approx)
Giving Analysis: Giving for fiscal 2001 includes: foundation grants to United Way ($2,500); fiscal 2000: foundation grants to United Way ($16,000); fiscal 1998: foundation grants to United Way ($10,000); foundation ($397,500)
Assets: $6,606,885 (fiscal 2001); $7,352,845 (fiscal 2000); $6,893,728 (fiscal 1998)
Gifts Received: $2,130,323 (fiscal 1995); $207,774 (fiscal 1994). Note: In fiscal 1995, contributions were received from the estate of Lawrence J. Plym.

Typical Recipients

Arts & Humanities: Libraries, Music, Theater
Civic & Public Affairs: Economic Development, Employment/Job Training, Civic & Public Affairs-General, Urban & Community Affairs
Education: Business Education, Colleges & Universities, Education Funds, Private Education (Precollege), Public Education (Precollege), Science/Mathematics Education, Student Aid
Environment: Environment-General, Resource Conservation
Health: Clinics/Medical Centers, Health-General, Hospices, Hospitals, Medical Research, Nursing Services, Prenatal Health Issues
Religion: Churches
Social Services: Community Service Organizations, Emergency Relief, Family Services, Senior Services, Shelters/Homelessness, Social Services-General, United Funds/United Ways, YMCA/YWCA/YMHA/YWHA, Youth Organizations

Application Procedures

Initial Contact: Send a written request.
Application Requirements: Include a description of organization, amount requested, purpose of funds sought, proof of tax-exempt status.
Deadlines: None.

Restrictions

The foundation does not support individuals, political or lobbying groups, or organizations outside operating areas.

Foundation Officials

Sarah P. Campbell: director
James F. Keenan: secretary
Andrew J. Plym: director
J. Eric Plym: president
Donald F. Walter: vice president, treasurer

Grants Analysis

Disclosure Period: fiscal year ending September 30, 2001
Total Grants: $260,000*
Number of Grants: 21
Average Grant: $8,421*
Highest Grant: $50,000
Typical Range: $1,000 to $15,000
***Note:** Giving excludes United Way. Average grant figure excludes two highest grants ($100,000).

Recent Grants

Note: Grants derived from fiscal 2000 Form 990.

Library-Related

25,000	Notre Dame Library Architecture Endowment, Notre Dame, IN -- college library

General

50,000	Cradle, Evanston, IL
50,000	Lake Michigan College Bertrand Crossings, Niles, MI -- capital fund
50,000	Niles Buchana YMCA, Niles, MI -- camp
50,000	St. Edwards School, Vero Beach, FL -- capital fund
16,000	Reef Light Preservation Society
15,000	Fernwood, Inc, Niles, MI -- nature center
15,000	Memorial Health Care, South Bend, IN
14,000	Greater Niles United Way, Niles, MI
10,000	Community Development Corporation, Niles, MI
10,000	Drummond Island Clinic

PNC FINANCIAL SERVICES GROUP, INC.

Company Headquarters

1 PNC Plaza
249 5th Ave.
Pittsburgh, PA 15222-2707
Web: http://www.pnc.com

Company Description

Ticker: PNC
Exchange: NYSE
Assets: US$66.4 billion (2002)
Profit: US$1.184 billion (2002)
Employees: 24200 (2002)
Fortune Rank: 277, per FORTUNE Magazine's list of 500 Largest U.S. Corporations (2002).

PNC Foundation

Giving Contact

Mia Hallett, Vice President and Manager
PNC Foundation
One PNC Plaza, 29th Floor
249 Fifth Avenue
Pittsburgh, PA 15222
Phone: (412)762-7076
Fax: (412)705-1062
E-mail: foundations@pncbank.com
Web: http://www.pnc.com/aboutus/pncfoundation.html

Alternate Contact

PNC Bank, NA P2-PTPP-10-3
Pittsburgh, PA 15222-2705
Phone: (412)762-2000

Description

Founded: 1970
EIN: 251202255
Organization Type: Corporate Foundation
Former Name: PNC Bank Foundation (2000).
Giving Locations: areas served by PNC Bank Corp. and affiliates.
Grant Types: Capital, Employee Matching Gifts, General Support, Multiyear/Continuing Support.
Note: Employee matching gift ratio: 1 to 1 up to $2,500.

Financial Summary

Total Giving: $11,579,055 (2001); $10,440,079 (2000); $10,600,000 (1999 approx). Note: Contributes through foundation only.
Giving Analysis: Giving for 2001 includes: foundation matching gifts ($902,000); foundation program-related investments ($1,991,000); foundation ($10,515,000); 2000: foundation ($10,440,079); 1997: foundation matching gifts ($305,950) foundation grants to United Way ($1,779,583)
Assets: $745,925 (2001); $32,129,985 (2000); $36,688,673 (1999)

Gifts Received: $8,559,680 (1995); $4,896,626 (1994); $25,000,000 (1993). Note: Foundation receives contributions from PNC Bank Corp.

Typical Recipients

Arts & Humanities: Arts Associations & Councils, Arts Centers, Arts Festivals, Arts Funds, Ballet, Community Arts, Arts & Humanities-General, Historic Preservation, History & Archaeology, Libraries, Literary Arts, Museums/Galleries, Music, Opera, Performing Arts, Public Broadcasting, Theater
Civic & Public Affairs: African American Affairs, Business/Free Enterprise, Clubs, Community Foundations, Economic Development, Economic Policy, Employment/Job Training, Civic & Public Affairs-General, Housing, Legal Aid, Municipalities/Towns, Parades/Festivals, Philanthropic Organizations, Professional & Trade Associations, Public Policy, Safety, Urban & Community Affairs, Urban & Community Affairs, Zoos/Aquariums
Education: Afterschool/Enrichment Programs, Arts/Humanities Education, Business Education, Colleges & Universities, Community & Junior Colleges, Education Associations, Education Funds, Faculty Development, Education-General, International Studies, Literacy, Preschool Education, Private Education (Precollege), Student Aid
Environment: Environment-General, Resource Conservation
Health: Cancer, Children's Health/Hospitals, Clinics/Medical Centers, Health Organizations, Heart, Home-Care Services, Hospices, Hospitals, Long-Term Care, Medical Rehabilitation, Single-Disease Health Associations
International: International Development
Religion: Churches, Jewish Causes, Ministries, Religious Welfare
Science: Science Museums, Scientific Centers & Institutes
Social Services: Child Welfare, Community Centers, Community Service Organizations, Delinquency & Criminal Rehabilitation, Domestic Violence, Emergency Relief, Family Services, Food/Clothing Distribution, People with Disabilities, Recreation & Athletics, Scouts, Senior Services, Shelters/Homelessness, United Funds/United Ways, YMCA/YWCA/YMHA/YWHA, Youth Organizations

Application Procedures

Initial Contact: Send a brief letter or proposal.
Application Requirements: Include organization name, address, e-mail address, and contact; one-page proposal summary with amount requested requested and total cost of project or program; full proposal with, brief description of the organization and its purpose; statement of problem or need to be addressed; geographic area served and population served; recruitment outreach/management structure; statement of expected accomplishments and method of evaluation; project schedule and board-approved budget; track record of working with community organizations and civic leadership; list of staff members and board members; proof of tax-exempt status; list of recent contributions and amounts; fundraising plan for the project; board-approved organization budget; audited financial statements for the previous year; resumes of key staff members; strategic or long-range plan for the organization; and brochures, pamphlets, or other descriptive material, if available.
Deadlines: None.

Restrictions

Does not support organizations that discriminate by race, color, creed, gender, or national origin; religious organizations, except for non-sectarian activities; loans or grants to individuals; conferences and seminars; or tickets and goodwill ads.

Additional Information

The company changed its name from Pittsburgh National Bank to PNC Bank Corp. and the foundation from Pittsburgh National Bank Foundation to PNC Bank Foundation.

Corporate Officials

Randall C. King: treasurer PRIM CORP EMPL senior vice president, treasurer: PNC Financial Services Group.

James Edward Rohr: chairman, chief executive officer, president, director B Cleveland, OH 1948. ED University of Notre Dame BA (1970); Ohio State University MBA (1972). PRIM CORP EMPL chief executive officer, president, director, chief operating officer: PNC Financial Services Group ADD CORP EMPL director: Blackrock Inc.; director: Midland Loan Service Inc.; president: PNC Bank National Association. CORP AFFIL director: Private Export Funding Corp.; director: Allegheny Teledyne Inc.; director: Equitable Resources Inc.; director: Allegheny Ludlum Corp. NONPR AFFIL director: United Way; member: Young President Organization; director: Shadyside Hospital; vice chairman: Pennsylvania Business Roundtable; member advisory board: Salvation Army; director: Greater Pittsburgh Council Boy Scouts America; chairman: National Flag Foundation; chairman: Civic Light Opera; director: Cultural Trust; member: Bankers Roundtable; director: Carnegie Mellon University; member: American Bankers Association; member: Allegheny Conference. CLUB AFFIL director: Duquesne Club.

Foundation Officials

Mia Hallett: vice president, manager
Thomas R. Moore: secretary, counsel
Samuel R. Peterson: controller
Thomas K. Whitford: executive director

Grants Analysis

Disclosure Period: calendar year ending 2001
Total Grants: $9,243,941*
Number of Grants: 884
Average Grant: $10,457
Highest Grant: $300,000
Lowest Grant: $250
Typical Range: $1,000 to $25,000
***Note:** Giving excludes matching gifts; United Way.

Recent Grants

Note: Grants derived from 2001 Form 990.

General

340,362	September 11th Fund, PA
300,000	Metro United Way, Louisville, KY
300,000	University of Pittsburgh, Pittsburgh, PA
287,500	United Way of Southwestern Pennsylvania, Pittsburgh, PA
287,500	United Way of Southwestern Pennsylvania, Pittsburgh, PA
262,245	United Way of Southeastern Pennsylvania, Philadelphia, PA
250,000	Cincinnati Art Museum, Cincinnati, OH
200,000	University of Pittsburgh, Pittsburgh, PA
183,000	United Way of Delaware, Wilmington, DE
150,000	Fund for the Arts, Louisville, KY

PNM RESOURCES, INC.

Company Headquarters

Alvarado Sq.
Albuquerque, NM 87158-0001
Web: http://www.pnm.com

Company Description

Founded: 1917
Ticker: PNM
Exchange: NYSE

Assets: US$3.027 billion (2002)
Employees: 2656 (2002)
SIC(s): 4900 Electric, Gas & Sanitary Services, 4923 Gas Transmission & Distribution, 4931 Electric & Other Services Combined, 4941 Water Supply.

Operating Locations

Public Service Co. of New Mexico (NM--Albuquerque)

Nonmonetary Support

Type: Donated Equipment; In-kind Services; Loaned Employees; Loaned Executives

PNM Foundation

Giving Contact

Chandra Manning, Senior Community Relations Representative
Alvarado Sq., MS 2708
Albuquerque, NM 87158-2708
Phone: (505)241-2237

Description

Founded: 1983
EIN: 850309005
Organization Type: Corporate Foundation
Giving Locations: NM
Grant Types: Award, Employee Matching Gifts, Endowment, General Support, Matching, Multiyear/Continuing Support, Seed Money.

Donor Information

Founder: Public Service Co. of New Mexico

Financial Summary

Total Giving: $486,341 (2001); $361,809 (2000); $280,841 (1999)
Giving Analysis: Giving for 2000 includes: foundation grants to United Way ($2,575); foundation matching gifts ($37,864); 1999: foundation matching gifts ($35,522) foundation ($245,319)
Assets: $11,344,461 (2001); $7,042,027 (2000); $7,810,753 (1999)
Gifts Received: $5,000,000 (2001); $30,000 (2000).
Note: In 2000, contributions were received from Public Service Co. of New Mexico.

Typical Recipients

Arts & Humanities: Arts Associations & Councils, Arts Centers, Dance, Ethnic & Folk Arts, History & Archaeology, Libraries, Literary Arts, Museums/Galleries, Music, Public Broadcasting
Civic & Public Affairs: African American Affairs, Business/Free Enterprise, Community Foundations, Employment/Job Training, Civic & Public Affairs-General, Hispanic Affairs, Housing, Law & Justice, Native American Affairs, Urban & Community Affairs, Women's Affairs, Zoos/Aquariums
Education: Agricultural Education, Arts/Humanities Education, Business Education, Business-School Partnerships, Colleges & Universities, Education Funds, Education Reform, Engineering/Technological Education, Faculty Development, Education-General, Literacy, Minority Education, Private Education (Precollege), Public Education (Precollege), Secondary Education (Public), Social Sciences Education, Student Aid
Environment: Environment-General
Health: Cancer, Diabetes, Health Organizations, Hospices, Hospitals, Prenatal Health Issues, Preventive Medicine/Wellness Organizations, Respiratory, Speech & Hearing, Transplant Networks/Donor Banks
Religion: Religion-General, Religious Organizations
Social Services: Animal Protection, Camps, Community Service Organizations, Day Care, Emergency Relief, Food/Clothing Distribution, Recreation & Athletics, Scouts, Shelters/Homelessness, Social Services-General, United Funds/United Ways, YMCA/YWCA/YMHA/YWHA, Youth Organizations

Application Procedures

Initial Contact: Send letter requesting application guidelines and form. The direct giving program has three focus areas: diversity advocacy, education, and public safety. Requests for direct contributions are reviewed the first of each month. The foundations priorities are higher education, K-12 education, and health and human services. The minimum grant is $5,000. While there are no deadlines, the foundation board of directors meets quarterly to review and approve proposals for funding.

Restrictions

Grants are not given to or for sectarian or religious organizations, programs, or activities; testimonial dinners, fund-raising events or advertising; payments of loans, interest, taxes, or debt retirement; individuals; endowments; programs or projects that duplicate existing services and/or programs; operational and maintenance expenses (except for seed money or pilot projects); or United Way agencies except for comptroller projects not normally funded by United Way gifts.

Additional Information

Publications: Grant Policies; Application Guidelines (including Application Form)

Corporate Officials

Barbara Barsky: vice president, president, chief executive officer PRIM CORP EMPL senior vice president, secretary: Public Service Co. of New Mexico.
Max H. Maerki: senior vice president B Aarau, Switzerland 1940. PRIM CORP EMPL senior vice president, chief financial officer: Public Service Co. of New Mexico. CORP AFFIL director: Sunterra Gas Processing Co.; director: ACE Insurance Co. Bermuda Ltd.; director: Sunterra Gas Gathering Co. NONPR AFFIL member: American Management Association; member: Financial Executives Institute.
Jeffry Sterba: chairman, president, chief executive officer PRIM CORP EMPL chairman, president, chief executive officer: Public Service Co. of New Mexico.

Foundation Officials

Barbara Barsky: vice president (see above)
Sarita Loehr: vice president
Pat Ortiz: senior vice president, general counsel, secretary
Eddie Padilla: senior vice president, treasurer
Carol Radosevich: president, director

Grants Analysis

Disclosure Period: calendar year ending 2000
Total Grants: $321,370*
Number of Grants: 142
Average Grant: $2,263
Highest Grant: $38,603
Typical Range: $1,000 to $5,000
***Note:** Giving excludes matching gifts and United Way.

Recent Grants

Note: Grants derived from 2000 Form 990.

General

38,603	Albuquerque Community Foundation, Albuquerque, NM
25,000	New Mexico State University Foundation, Las Cruces, NM
25,000	New Mexico State University Foundation, Las Cruces, NM
17,500	Golden Apple Foundation, Albuquerque, NM
15,000	Center for Civic Values, Albuquerque, NM
14,000	Keshet Dance Company, Albuquerque, NM
13,500	Tree New Mexico Inc., Albuquerque, NM

11,000	University of New Mexico Department of Mathematics, Albuquerque, NM
10,775	Mimbres Region Arts Council, Silver City, NM
10,000	New Mexico Jazz Workshop, Albuquerque, NM

DOROTHY W. POITRAS CHARITABLE TRUST

Giving Contact

James Poitras, Trustee
198 Highland St.
Holliston, MA 01746
Phone: (508)429-6281

Description

Founded: 1992
EIN: 046638933
Organization Type: Private Foundation
Grant Types: General Support.

Financial Summary

Total Giving: $63,500 (fiscal year ending June 30, 2000); $63,500 (fiscal 1999); $336,245 (fiscal 1998)
Giving Analysis: Giving for fiscal 2000 includes: foundation scholarships ($6,000) fiscal 1999: foundation scholarships ($6,000)
Assets: $274,719 (fiscal 2000); $274,719 (fiscal 1999); $297,089 (fiscal 1998)
Gifts Received: $35 (fiscal 1998); $16,636 (fiscal 1992). Note: In fiscal 1992, contributions were received from James W. and Patricia T. Poitras ($76) and the estate of Dorothy W. Poitras ($16,500).

Typical Recipients

Arts & Humanities: Arts Centers, Libraries
Civic & Public Affairs: Botanical Gardens/Parks, Civic & Public Affairs-General, Native American Affairs
Education: Engineering/Technological Education, Student Aid
Environment: Forestry, Environment-General, Research
Health: AIDS/HIV, Cancer, Hospices, Hospitals, Medical Research, Single-Disease Health Associations
Religion: Churches, Ministries, Religious Organizations
Social Services: Child Welfare, Community Service Organizations, Family Services, YMCA/YWCA/YMHA/YWHA, Youth Organizations

Application Procedures

Initial Contact: Send a full proposal.
Application Requirements: Include proof of tax-exempt status.
Deadlines: April 1.

Foundation Officials

Edward Poitras: trustee
James Poitras: trustee
Kay Poitras: trustee
Patricia Poitras: trustee

Grants Analysis

Disclosure Period: fiscal year ending June 30, 2000
Total Grants: $57,500*
Number of Grants: 10
Average Grant: $3,438*
Highest Grant: $20,000
Typical Range: $1,000 to $5,000
*Note: Giving excludes scholarship. Average grant figure excludes two highest grants ($30,000).

Recent Grants

Note: Grants derived from fiscal 1999 Form 990.

Library-Related
4,500	Friends of the Winter Haven Public Library, Winter Haven, FL -- for library support

General
20,000	Crossroads Community Foundation, Natick, MA
10,000	Mass Audubon Society -- for wildlife preservation
6,500	Ember Ranch, Polk City, FL
6,000	Dickinson College, Carlisle, PA -- for scholarships
4,500	St. Alban's Episcopal Church, Cape Elizabeth, ME -- for spiritual guidance
4,000	Christian Healing Ministries, Jacksonville, FL
4,000	Search Ministries, Minneapolis, MN
3,500	Running Strong for American Indian Youth -- for American Indian youth guidance
500	African Wildlife Foundation, Washington, DC -- for wildlife preservation

POLAROID CORP.

Company Headquarters

784 Memorial Dr.
Cambridge, MA 02139
Web: http://www.polaroid.com

Company Description

Ticker: PRDQE
Exchange: OTC
Chap. 11 Reorg. Bankruptcy Polaroid Corp. (2002).
Employees: 10,046
SIC(s): 3861 Photographic Equipment & Supplies.
Parent Company: Bank One Corp., 1 Bank One Plaza, Chicago, IL, United States

Operating Locations

Polaroid Corp. (CA--Santa Ana; GA--Atlanta; IL--Chicago; MA--Bedford, Cambridge, Freetown, Needham, New Bedford, Norwood, Waltham; NJ--Paramus; PR)

Nonmonetary Support

Type: Donated Products
Volunteer Programs: Polaroid employees who volunteer 50 hours of personal time per calendar year at a nonprofit organization can apply to the Polaroid Foundation for a $1,000 grant for that organization. Information on Polaroid's Volunteer Action Program is available from (800)480-4438. Polaroid employees also have the opportunity to volunteer on grantmaking committees; on company time, employee volunteers review grant proposals, visit agencies, and make funding recommendations under the direction of foundation staff members.
Note: Foundation provides photographic equipment for projects which help the disadvantaged or where immediate access to images is vital, i.e. disaster relief; animal rese

Polaroid Foundation

Giving Contact

Donna F. Eidson, Executive Director
Polaroid Foundation
784 Memorial Drive
Cambridge, MA 02139
Phone: (781)386-9400
Fax: (781)386-9818
E-mail: polaroid.foundation@polaroid.com
Web: http://www.polaroid.com/polinfo/foundation

Description

EIN: 237152261
Organization Type: Corporate Foundation
Giving Locations: MA: Boston metropolitan area, Cambridge, New Bedford including surrounding area, Waltham internationally for product donations; nationally for product donations; nationally: considers funding outside of Massachusetts to historically black educational institutions.
Grant Types: Employee Matching Gifts, General Support, Matching, Multiyear/Continuing Support, Operating Expenses, Project, Seed Money.
Note: The company matches employees' and retirees' personal financial contributions to a variety of nonprofit organizations. Additional information is available by calling (800)480-4438. In addition, special $50 grants are available to employees who raise funds for charitable organizations through participation in pledge-a-thon events.

Financial Summary

Total Giving: $68,400 (2001); $1,600,000 (2000 approx); $1,500,000 (1999 approx). Note: Contributes through corporate direct giving program and foundation.
Giving Analysis: Giving for 2001 includes: nonmonetary support ($40,000); corporate direct giving ($1,385,000); foundation ($1,400,000); 2000: foundation ($30,622) 1998: corporate direct giving (approx $1,570,000)
Assets: $1,812,876 (2001); $1,993,186 (2000); $1,957,284 (1998)
Gifts Received: $36,500 (1998); $1,747,390 (1996); $2,240,468 (1995). Note: Gifts are received from Polaroid Corporation.

Typical Recipients

Arts & Humanities: Arts Associations & Councils, Arts Centers, Arts Funds, Arts Institutes, Arts Outreach, Ballet, Community Arts, Dance, Ethnic & Folk Arts, Historic Preservation, History & Archaeology, Libraries, Museums/Galleries, Music, Opera, Performing Arts, Public Broadcasting, Theater, Visual Arts
Civic & Public Affairs: African American Affairs, Asian American Affairs, Civil Rights, Community Foundations, Economic Development, Employment/Job Training, Ethnic Organizations, Civic & Public Affairs-General, Housing, Law & Justice, Minority Business, Municipalities/Towns, Nonprofit Management, Philanthropic Organizations, Public Policy, Safety, Urban & Community Affairs, Women's Affairs, Zoos/Aquariums
Education: Arts/Humanities Education, Business Education, Business-School Partnerships, Colleges & Universities, Community & Junior Colleges, Continuing Education, Education Reform, Elementary Education (Private), Engineering/Technological Education, Faculty Development, Education-General, Health & Physical Education, Leadership Training, Literacy, Medical Education, Minority Education, Preschool Education, Private Education (Precollege), Public Education (Precollege), Science/Mathematics Education, Secondary Education (Public), Special Education, Student Aid, Vocational & Technical Education
Environment: Environment-General
Health: AIDS/HIV, Clinics/Medical Centers, Diabetes, Eyes/Blindness, Heart, Hospices, Hospitals, Medical Research, Mental Health, Nursing Services, Public Health, Speech & Hearing
International: Foreign Educational Institutions, Human Rights
Religion: Religious Welfare, Social/Policy Issues
Science: Science Exhibits & Fairs, Scientific Centers & Institutes, Scientific Labs, Scientific Organizations
Social Services: At-Risk Youth, Camps, Child Welfare, Community Service Organizations, Counseling, Crime Prevention, Day Care, Domestic Violence, Family Services, Food/Clothing Distribution, People with Disabilities, Recreation & Athletics, Shelters/

Homelessness, Social Services-General, United Funds/United Ways, YMCA/YWCA/YMHA/YWHA, Youth Organizations

Application Procedures

Initial Contact: Send a brief letter of inquiry, then a full proposal.

Application Requirements: Requests must be submitted on the organizations letterhead with a complete proposal which must include a brief history of the program, description of the population served, outline of the program or project, the annual budget for specific project or for the overall program if general support is requested, copy of the organization's 501(c)(3) tax exempt letter from the IRS (note that no proposal will be reviewed without receipt of the tax exempt letter). Al proposals should be submitted in duplicate. required, solicited and received to date. Applicants must also include a Grant Application available at the foundation's web site. The Polaroid Foundation does not accept the Associated Grantmakers of Massachusetts Common Proposal Format.

Deadlines: None; full proposals are reviewed from January through October each year. Letters of inquiry are reviewed at any time.

Review Process: Requests go through a preliminary screening by employee volunteers and then to a subcommittee for a full review; site visits are included.

Evaluative Criteria: Preference is given to programs that help participants gain measurable skills through hands-on practice, training, and experience.

Decision Notification: Letters of inquiry are generally answered within two weeks. Review of full proposals takes three to four months.

Notes: Do not call regarding status of proposal; applicants will be notified in writing of the decision.

Restrictions

The foundation does not make more than one grant to a recipient in any calendar year or make contributions commitments beyond the current funding year. The foundation does not support advertisements; individuals; political or lobbying groups; religious organizations for sectarian purposes; dinners; special events; research; or sponsor events. Foundation rarely makes grants to national organizations. The foundation's work is primarily done within Massachusetts and specifically within the Greater Boston and Cambridge area, but will consider funding elsewhere in the area of higher education benefiting minorities and in support of photographic acquisition, exhibition, and filmmaking.

Additional Information

Every month, Polaroid Foundation staff meets informally with nonprofits to answer questions before proposals are submitted. Potential applicants may register to attend by calling (781) 386-8361.

Publications: Guidelines; Application Form

Foundation Officials

William Flaherty: president

Neal Goldman: secretary-treasurer

Ralph M. Norwood: president, treasurer B Rochester, NH 1943. ED University of New Hampshire (1965); University of Virginia (1967). PRIM CORP EMPL vice president, treasurer: Polaroid Corp. NONPR AFFIL member: American Institute CPAs.

Grants Analysis

Disclosure Period: calendar year ending 2001
Total Grants: $68,400
Number of Grants: 3
Average Grant: $22,800
Highest Grant: $50,000
Lowest Grant: $8,400

Recent Grants

Note: Grants derived from 2001 Form 990.

General

50,000	Agassiz Neighborhood Council, Cambridge, MA
10,000	Optical Society of America, Washington, DC
8,400	DeCordova Museum, Boston, MA

POLK BROTHERS FOUNDATION, INC.

Giving Contact

Nikki Will Stein, Executive Director
20 West Kinzie Avenue
Suite 1110
Chicago, IL 60610
Phone: (312)527-4684
Fax: (312)527-4681
E-mail: info@polkbrosfdn.org
Web: http://www.polkbrosfdn.org

Description

Founded: 1957
EIN: 366108293
Organization Type: Family Foundation
Giving Locations: IL: Chicago
Grant Types: Capital, Employee Matching Gifts, General Support, Matching, Multiyear/Continuing Support, Operating Expenses, Project, Research.

Donor Information

Founder: The foundation was established in 1957 by the members of the Polk family, who owned and operated the Polk Bros. chain of retail stores.

Financial Summary

Total Giving: $13,500,000 (fiscal year ending August 31, 2003 approx); $14,000,000 (fiscal 2002 approx); $14,004,290 (fiscal 2000)
Giving Analysis: Giving for fiscal 1999 includes: foundation grants to United Way ($75,000) foundation matching gifts ($599,679)
Assets: $312,000,000 (fiscal 2003 approx); $317,000,000 (fiscal 2002 approx); $342,782,705 (fiscal 2000)
Gifts Received: $1,000 (fiscal 1997); $1,040,260 (fiscal 1995); $1,648,899 (fiscal 1994). Note: In fiscal 1994, contributions were received from Sol Polk Trust.

Typical Recipients

Arts & Humanities: Arts Associations & Councils, Arts Centers, Arts Festivals, Arts Funds, Arts Institutes, Arts Outreach, Dance, Ethnic & Folk Arts, History & Archaeology, Libraries, Museums/Galleries, Music, Opera, Performing Arts, Public Broadcasting, Theater, Visual Arts

Civic & Public Affairs: African American Affairs, Asian American Affairs, Botanical Gardens/Parks, Clubs, Economic Development, Economic Policy, Employment/Job Training, Civic & Public Affairs-General, Housing, Law & Justice, Legal Aid, Municipalities/Towns, Public Policy, Urban & Community Affairs, Women's Affairs, Zoos/Aquariums

Education: Afterschool/Enrichment Programs, Arts/Humanities Education, Business Education, Colleges & Universities, Education Associations, Education Funds, Education Reform, Faculty Development, Education-General, International Studies, Leadership Training, Minority Education, Preschool Education, Private Education (Precollege), Public Education (Precollege), Science/Mathematics Education, Secondary Education (Private), Student Aid

Health: AIDS/HIV, Clinics/Medical Centers, Health Organizations, Hospitals, Medical Rehabilitation, Mental Health, Nursing Services, Prenatal Health Issues, Public Health

International: Missionary/Religious Activities

Religion: Jewish Causes, Ministries, Religious Welfare

Science: Observatories & Planetariums, Science Museums, Scientific Centers & Institutes

Social Services: At-Risk Youth, Child Abuse, Child Welfare, Community Centers, Community Service Organizations, Day Care, Delinquency & Criminal Rehabilitation, Family Services, Food/Clothing Distribution, Homes, People with Disabilities, Refugee Assistance, Shelters/Homelessness, Substance Abuse, United Funds/United Ways, YMCA/YWCA/YMHA/YWHA, Youth Organizations

Application Procedures

Initial Contact: Request an application form.
Deadlines: None.
Review Process: Proposals are scheduled for review in the order in which they are received; decisions are made at quarterly board meetings in February, May, August and November. Health proposals are reviewed in the spring and fall only.
Notes: Applicants must have 501(c)(3) status. The Foundation will only award a grant once every twelve months to an organization and will not review more than three consecutive requests from an organization through the Small Grants program. A site visit or interview may be scheduled by a program officer as part of the review process.

Restrictions

Grants are not made to individuals. In addition, funds are not awarded to organizations that devote a substantial portion of their activities to attempting to influence legislation or to participating in campaigns on behalf of candidates for public office; religious institutions seeking support for programs whose participants are restricted by religious affiliation or whose services promote a particular creed; purchase dinner or raffle tickets or advertising in dinner programs; medical, scientific, or academic research; or tax-generating entities (municipalities, school districts, etc.) for services within their normal responsibilities. The foundation will generally not fund more than five percent of an organization's operating budget.

Additional Information

Publications: Application Form; Annual Report

Foundation Officials

Bruce R. Bachmann: director

Sidney Epstein: treasurer B Chicago, IL 1923. ED University of Illinois BS (1943). PRIM CORP EMPL chairman: A. Epstein & Sons International. CORP AFFIL director: Amalgamated Trust & Savings Bank; trustee: Northwestern Mutual Life Insurance Co. NONPR AFFIL member: Tau Beta Pi; life member: University Chicago Hospitals & Clinics; member: Sigma Tau; member: Sigma Xi; member: Phi Kappa Phi; member: Polish-U.S. Economic Council; life trustee: Orchestral Association Chicago; member: Phi Eta Sigma; member, board directors: Lyric Opera Chicago; director: Michael Reese Foundation; member: Chi Epsilon; founder, director: Chicago Youth Center. CLUB AFFIL Standard Club.

Sandra P. Guthman: president, chief executive officer

J. Ira Harris: vice president PRIM CORP EMPL chairman: J. I. Harris & Associates. CORP AFFIL director: Manpower Inc.; vice chairman: Pritzker Organization LLC.

Howard Polk: director

Gordon S. Prussian: secretary

Raymond F. Simon: vice president

Grants Analysis

Disclosure Period: fiscal year ending August 31, 2000
Total Grants: $14,004,290*
Number of Grants: 474
Average Grant: $29,545*
Highest Grant: $200,000

Typical Range: $1,000 to $50,000
***Note:** Giving excludes matching gifts and United Way.

Recent Grants

Note: Grants derived from 2001 Form 990.

General

400,000	Music and Dance Theater, Chicago, IL
200,000	Big Shoulders Fund, Chicago, IL
200,000	DePaul University, Chicago, IL
200,000	Millennium Park, Chicago, IL
160,000	Jewish United Fund of Metropolitan Chicago, Chicago, IL
150,000	Ezra Multiservice Center
150,000	Gads Hill Center, Chicago, IL
125,000	Chicago Accreditation Project, Chicago, IL
125,000	WTTW Channel 11, Chicago, IL
120,000	DePaul University, Chicago, IL

WILLIAM B. POLLOCK CO. FOUNDATION

Giving Contact

Jeanette McElheney, Trust Officer
c/o Bank One Trust Co.
106 East Market Street
Warren, OH 44481
Phone: (330)742-6822

Description

Founded: 1952
EIN: 346514078
Organization Type: Private Foundation
Giving Locations: OH: Youngstown
Grant Types: General Support.

Financial Summary

Total Giving: $100,000 (2000); $55,000 (1999); $71,000 (1998)
Giving Analysis: Giving for 2000 includes: foundation grants to United Way ($45,000); 1999: foundation grants to United Way ($20,000) 1998: foundation grants to United Way ($45,000)
Assets: $3,168,946 (2000); $3,156,811 (1999); $2,853,664 (1998)

Typical Recipients

Arts & Humanities: Arts Institutes, Community Arts, Historic Preservation, History & Archaeology, Libraries, Music
Civic & Public Affairs: Business/Free Enterprise, Chambers of Commerce, Clubs, Community Foundations, Economic Development, Civic & Public Affairs-General, Public Policy, Urban & Community Affairs
Education: Business Education, Colleges & Universities, Education Associations, Education Funds, Education-General, Private Education (Precollege)
Health: Children's Health/Hospitals, Clinics/Medical Centers, Emergency/Ambulance Services, Health Organizations, Home-Care Services, Hospices, Hospitals, Nutrition
Religion: Jewish Causes, Religious Organizations, Religious Welfare
Science: Scientific Centers & Institutes
Social Services: At-Risk Youth, Child Welfare, Community Service Organizations, Family Planning, Food/Clothing Distribution, People with Disabilities, Recreation & Athletics, Senior Services, Substance Abuse, United Funds/United Ways, YMCA/YWCA/YMHA/YWHA, Youth Organizations

Application Procedures

Initial Contact: The foundation has no formal grant application procedure or application form.
Deadlines: None.

Additional Information

Trust(s): Bank One Trust Co.

Foundation Officials

Franklin Bennett: trustee

Grants Analysis

Disclosure Period: calendar year ending 2000
Total Grants: $55,000*
Number of Grants: 6
Highest Grant: $20,000
Lowest Grant: $5,000
***Note:** Giving excludes United Way.

Recent Grants

Note: Grants derived from 1999 Form 990.

General

20,000	Youngstown and Mahoning Valley United Way, Youngstown, OH
10,000	Planned Parenthood, Youngstown, OH
10,000	Youngstown State University Scholarships, Youngstown, OH
10,000	Youngstown Symphony Society, Youngstown, OH
5,000	Ohio Foundation of Independent Colleges Inc., Columbus, OH

C. NORTHROP POND AND ALETHEA MARDER POND FOUNDATION

Giving Contact

Grace Pond Fisher, Trustee
c/o United Trust Bank
1130 RT 22 East
Bridgewater, NJ 08807
Phone: (908)429-2328

Description

Founded: 1999
EIN: 226727894
Organization Type: Private Foundation
Grant Types: General Support.

Financial Summary

Total Giving: $151,000 (fiscal year ending April 30, 2001); $144,000 (fiscal 2000); $129,558 (fiscal 1999)
Giving Analysis: Giving for fiscal 2001 includes: foundation grants to United Way ($4,000); fiscal 2000: foundation grants to United Way ($8,000) fiscal 1999: foundation grants to United Way ($2,800)
Assets: $2,534,043 (fiscal 2001); $2,873,277 (fiscal 2000); $2,890,855 (fiscal 1999)

Typical Recipients

Arts & Humanities: Historic Preservation, Libraries, Public Broadcasting
Civic & Public Affairs: Civic & Public Affairs-General
Education: Colleges & Universities, Private Education (Precollege), Public Education (Precollege)
Environment: Environment-General, Resource Conservation
Health: Clinics/Medical Centers, Emergency/Ambulance Services, Hospitals
Religion: Churches
Social Services: Animal Protection, United Funds/United Ways

Additional Information

Trust(s): United Trust Bank, NJ

Foundation Officials

Grace Pond Fisher: trustee
Alethea Marder Pond: trustee
Charles N. Pond, Jr.: trustee

Grants Analysis

Disclosure Period: fiscal year ending April 30, 2001
Total Grants: $147,000*
Number of Grants: 22
Average Grant: $6,682*
Highest Grant: $15,000
Typical Range: $2,000 to $10,000
***Note:** Giving excludes United Way.

Recent Grants

Note: Grants derived from fiscal 2001 Form 990.

Library-Related

4,000	South Dennis Library Fund, South Dennis, MA

General

15,000	Crescent Avenue Presbyterian Church, Plainfield, NJ
10,000	Muhlenberg Hospital Foundation, Plainfield, NJ
10,000	New Jersey Conservation Foundation, Far Hills, NJ
10,000	Plainfield Foundation, Bridgewater, NJ
10,000	Princeton University, Princeton, NJ
10,000	Salisbury School, Salisbury, CT
10,000	Wardlaw Hartidge School, Edison, NJ
8,000	Orenda Wildlife Trust, West Barnstable, MA
8,000	Plainfield Health Center, Plainfield, NJ
6,000	Liberty Hall, South Dennis, MA

WILLIAM J. AND LIA G. POORVU FOUNDATION

Giving Contact

William J. Poorvu, Trustee
PO Box 380828
Cambridge, MA 02238
Phone: (617)576-1010
Fax: (617)576-1030

Description

Founded: 1978
EIN: 042651199
Organization Type: Private Foundation
Giving Locations: MA
Grant Types: General Support.

Donor Information

Founder: William J. Poorvu

Financial Summary

Total Giving: $659,165 (2001); $1,230,250 (2000); $523,500 (1999)
Assets: $13,474,456 (2001); $11,831,175 (2000); $10,441,916 (1999)
Gifts Received: $1,025,000 (2001); $840,000 (2000); $912,438 (1999). Note: In 2001, contributions were received from William J. Poorvu ($800,000); Lia G. Poorvu ($200,000); and May C. Poorvu ($25,000). In 2000, contributions were received from Lia G. Poorvu ($200,000), May C. Poorvu ($25,000) and William J. Poorvu ($615,000). In 1999, contributions were received from Lia G. Poorvu ($100,000) and William J. Poorvu ($9,500).

Typical Recipients

Arts & Humanities: Arts Outreach, Community Arts, Film & Video, Historic Preservation, History & Archaeology, Libraries, Museums/Galleries, Music, Public Broadcasting, Theater, Visual Arts
Civic & Public Affairs: Business/Free Enterprise, Economic Development, Civic & Public Affairs-General, Law & Justice, Public Policy
Education: Arts/Humanities Education, Business Education, Colleges & Universities, Education-General, Minority Education, Private Education (Precollege), Secondary Education (Public), Student Aid

Health: AIDS/HIV, Health-General, Health Organizations, Hospitals, Medical Research, Mental Health, Public Health, Single-Disease Health Associations
International: Foreign Educational Institutions
Religion: Jewish Causes
Science: Science Museums
Social Services: At-Risk Youth, Child Welfare, Community Service Organizations, Family Planning, Recreation & Athletics, Shelters/Homelessness

Application Procedures

Initial Contact: The foundation has no formal grant application procedure or application form.
Application Requirements: Complete information on the charitable purpose of the request is required.
Deadlines: None.

Restrictions

Does not support individuals.

Foundation Officials

Lia G. Poorvu: trustee
William J. Poorvu: trustee

Grants Analysis

Disclosure Period: calendar year ending 2001
Total Grants: $659,165
Number of Grants: 31
Average Grant: $12,385*
Highest Grant: $200,000
Lowest Grant: $500
Typical Range: $5,000 to $25,000
*Note: Average grant figure excludes two highest grants ($300,000).

Recent Grants

Note: Grants derived from 2001 Form 990.

Library-Related

5,000	Boston Public Library Foundation, Boston, MA

General

200,000	Wellesley College, Wellesley, MA
100,000	Gardner Museum, Boston, MA
90,000	Yale University, New Haven, CT
75,000	National Public Radio Foundation, Boston, MA
50,000	Harvard Business School, Boston, MA
25,000	Boston Foundation, Boston, MA
25,000	Longy School of Music, Boston, MA
15,000	WGBH, Boston, MA
10,000	American Red Cross, Washington, DC
10,000	Boston Baroque, Boston, MA

JAMES HYDE PORTER TESTAMENTARY TRUST

Giving Contact

c/o SunTrust Bank
PO Box 4248
Macon, GA 31208
Phone: (478)741-2265
Fax: (478)755-5190

Description

Founded: 1949
EIN: 586034882
Organization Type: Private Foundation
Giving Locations: GA: Bibb County, Newton County
Grant Types: Capital, General Support.

Donor Information

Founder: the late James Hyde Porter

Financial Summary

Total Giving: $617,029 (2002); $425,125 (2001); $419,910 (2000)
Assets: $10,450,699 (2002); $12,569,855 (2001); $7,436,813 (2000)

Typical Recipients

Arts & Humanities: Arts Associations & Councils, Arts Festivals, Arts Institutes, Arts Outreach, Community Arts, Ethnic & Folk Arts, Historic Preservation, History & Archaeology, Libraries, Museums/Galleries, Music, Opera, Theater
Civic & Public Affairs: Clubs, Community Foundations, Civic & Public Affairs-General, Housing
Education: Arts/Humanities Education, Colleges & Universities, Engineering/Technological Education, Education-General, Literacy, Medical Education, Private Education (Precollege), Public Education (Precollege), Secondary Education (Public), Student Aid
Health: AIDS/HIV, Children's Health/Hospitals, Emergency/Ambulance Services, Health-General, Health Organizations, Hospices, Long-Term Care, Medical Research, Public Health, Speech & Hearing
Religion: Churches, Ministries, Religious Welfare
Science: Science Museums
Social Services: Child Welfare, Community Centers, Community Service Organizations, Counseling, Family Services, Food/Clothing Distribution, Homes, People with Disabilities, Recreation & Athletics, Scouts, Shelters/Homelessness, Social Services-General, United Funds/United Ways, YMCA/YWCA/YMHA/YWHA, Youth Organizations

Application Procedures

Initial Contact: Send seven copies of the proposal form, IRS and foundation documentation, and supplemental information.
Deadlines: April 20.

Additional Information

Publications: Application Guidelines
Trust(s): SunTrust Bank Middle GA NA

Foundation Officials

Rev. Lester Ariail: manager
Dr. Rodney M. Browne: mgr
Leland Collins: manager
Dr. W. L. Dobbs: mgr
Jack Ellis: manager
Ben F. Hendricks: mgr
Larry Justice: mgr
Katherine M. Kalish: mgr
Jim Marshall: manager
Don Martin: manager
Davis Morgan: mgr
Tommy Olmstead: manager
Dr. Henry Patton: mgr
Sam Ramsey: manager
Ed S. Sell, Jr.: mgr B Athens, GA 1917. ED University of Georgia BA (1937); University of Georgia JD (1939). PRIM CORP EMPL partner: Sell & Melton PRIM NONPR EMPL county atty: Bibb County. CORP AFFIL county attorney: Bibb County Georgia. NONPR AFFIL member: Shriners; trustee: Wesleyan College; member: Phi Delta Phi; member: Phi Kappa Phi; Masons: member: Phi Beta Kappa; member: Macon Bar Association; member: Macon Circuit Bar Association; member: City Lions; member: Georgia Bar Association; member: American Bar Foundation. CLUB AFFIL City Club; River North Club; 191 Club.
Rev. William Wade: manager

Grants Analysis

Disclosure Period: calendar year ending 2002
Total Grants: $617,029
Number of Grants: 40
Average Grant: $13,659*
Highest Grant: $49,000
Lowest Grant: $500
Typical Range: $5,000 to $30,000
*Note: Average grant figure excludes two highest grants ($98,000).

Recent Grants

Note: Grants derived from 2001 Form 990.

Library-Related

64,379	Newton County Library, Covington, GA

General

70,000	Concert Association Newton County, Covington, GA
25,000	Macon Rescue Mission, Macon, GA
25,000	Mercer University, Atlanta, GA
25,000	Museum of Arts and Sciences, Macon, GA
25,000	Newton Macon Inc., Macon, GA
25,000	Ronald McDonald House, Macon, GA
25,000	Tubman African American Museum, Macon, GA
25,000	Wesleyan College, Wellesley, MA
20,000	Georgia Trust for Historic Preservation, Atlanta, GA
20,000	Macon Outreach, Macon, GA

PORTSMOUTH GENERAL HOSPITAL FOUNDATION

Giving Contact

Alan Gollihue, Executive Director
360 Crawford Street
Portsmouth, VA 23704
Phone: (757)391-0000
E-mail: office@pghfoundation.org
Web: http://www.pghfoundation.org

Description

Founded: 1987
EIN: 541463392
Organization Type: Private Foundation
Giving Locations: VA
Grant Types: General Support.

Financial Summary

Total Giving: $934,226 (fiscal year ending June 30, 2002); $985,834 (fiscal 2001); $900,393 (fiscal 2000). Note: Fiscal 1997 Giving includes United Way ($360).
Giving Analysis: Giving for fiscal 1999 includes: foundation grants to United Way ($500)
Assets: $14,560,791 (fiscal 2002); $17,365,029 (fiscal 2001); $20,674,126 (fiscal 2000)
Gifts Received: $3,893 (fiscal 2002); $6,950 (fiscal 2001); $520 (fiscal 1999)

Typical Recipients

Arts & Humanities: Arts Festivals, Dance, History & Archaeology, Libraries, Museums/Galleries, Music, Theater, Visual Arts
Civic & Public Affairs: Economic Development, Civic & Public Affairs-General, Urban & Community Affairs
Education: Arts/Humanities Education, Colleges & Universities, Community & Junior Colleges, Education-General, Medical Education, Preschool Education, Private Education (Precollege), Public Education (Precollege)
Environment: Environment-General
Health: AIDS/HIV, Cancer, Children's Health/Hospitals, Clinics/Medical Centers, Diabetes, Emergency/Ambulance Services, Geriatric Health, Health Funds, Health Organizations, Heart, Hospices, Hospitals, Medical Research, Nursing Services, Public Health, Single-Disease Health Associations
International: Foreign Arts Organizations
Religion: Churches, Jewish Causes, Religious Welfare
Social Services: At-Risk Youth, Camps, Child Abuse, Child Welfare, Community Service Organizations, Crime Prevention, Day Care, Domestic Violence, Family Planning, Family Services, Food/Clothing Distribution, People with Disabilities, Scouts, Special Olympics, Substance Abuse, Volunteer Services, YMCA/YWCA/YMHA/YWHA, Youth Organizations

Application Procedures

Initial Contact: Send full proposal. Include amount requested and purpose of funds sought.
Deadlines: None.

Foundation Officials

Phyllis F. Bricker: secretary
Patrick A. Clifford: program assistant PRIM CORP EMPL chairman, director: Richard D. Irwin.
R. Faith Dajao, MD: director
Alan E. Gollihue: executive director
Leslie Harding: director
Lee E. King: director
Ann Kirk: director
H. Timothy Little: director
Carl F. Medley, Jr.: director
R. Scott Morgan: director
Karl S. Morrisette: director
Brennan J. O'Connor: treasurer
Roger C. Reinhold: president
C. Edward Russell, Jr.: secretary
Gordon E. Saffold, Jr.: past president
Theresa J. Saunders: treasurer
Horace S. Savage, Jr.: director
Harry Short: director
Burle U. Stromberg: director
Susan Taylor Hansen: director
Dr. Kevin Wilson: director
Nancy G. Wren: vice chairman
Dorothy F. Wyron: vice president

Grants Analysis

Disclosure Period: fiscal year ending June 30, 2002
Total Grants: $934,226
Number of Grants: 73
Average Grant: $12,798
Highest Grant: $63,173
Lowest Grant: $50
Typical Range: $5,000 to $20,000

Recent Grants

Note: Grants derived from fiscal 2000 Form 990.

General

63,500	Ports Community Health, Portsmouth, VA -- primary medical care
52,750	TCC -- nursing
45,637	Ports Community Corr, Portsmouth, VA -- domestic violence
40,000	Jewish Family -- personal affairs
39,000	Children and Family Service, Elizabeth, NJ -- healthy families
37,678	Academy of Music -- string program
35,000	Virginia Coalition Child, VA
30,000	Ports Schools Foundation, Portsmouth, VA -- access program
28,250	Foodbank -- look who's cooking
27,610	Jamestown Yorktown Educational Foundation, Jamestown, VA -- family education

HERMAN T. AND PHENIE R. POTT FOUNDATION

Giving Contact

James L. Collins, Executive Director
PO Box 387
St. Louis, MO 63166
Phone: (314)418-2643
Fax: (314)418-2349

Description

Founded: 1963
EIN: 436041541
Organization Type: General Purpose Foundation
Giving Locations: MO: St. Louis
Grant Types: Multiyear/Continuing Support, Operating Expenses, Project.

Donor Information

Founder: Established in 1963.

Financial Summary

Total Giving: $1,249,200 (2001); $1,230,000 (2000); $1,291,759 (1999)
Giving Analysis: Giving for 2000 includes: foundation scholarships ($4,000); foundation grants to United Way ($35,000); 1999: foundation grants to United Way ($35,000); foundation scholarships ($79,000); 1998: foundation scholarships ($3,000) foundation grants to United Way ($35,000)
Assets: $29,767,444 (2001); $29,460,384 (2000); $29,079,524 (1999)
Gifts Received: $596,361 (2000); $397,211 (1999); $578,291 (1998). Note: The foundation received a contribution in 1997 and 2000 from the Phenie R. Pott Charitable Lead Unitrust.

Typical Recipients

Arts & Humanities: Arts Associations & Councils, Historic Preservation, Libraries, Museums/Galleries, Music, Opera
Civic & Public Affairs: Botanical Gardens/Parks, Economic Development, Employment/Job Training, Civic & Public Affairs-General, Housing, Philanthropic Organizations, Public Policy, Urban & Community Affairs, Zoos/Aquariums
Education: Business Education, Colleges & Universities, Education Funds, Engineering/Technological Education, Education-General, Minority Education, Science/Mathematics Education, Special Education, Student Aid, Vocational & Technical Education
Environment: Environment-General
Health: Alzheimers Disease, Children's Health/Hospitals, Diabetes, Emergency/Ambulance Services, Eyes/Blindness, Health Organizations, Heart, Hospitals, Medical Rehabilitation, Medical Research, Mental Health, Multiple Sclerosis, Preventive Medicine/Wellness Organizations, Respiratory, Single-Disease Health Associations
Religion: Churches, Ministries, Religious Organizations, Religious Welfare
Social Services: At-Risk Youth, Big Brother/Big Sister, Camps, Child Abuse, Child Welfare, Community Service Organizations, Counseling, Day Care, Domestic Violence, Emergency Relief, Family Planning, Family Services, Food/Clothing Distribution, Homes, People with Disabilities, Scouts, Senior Services, Shelters/Homelessness, Special Olympics, United Funds/United Ways, YMCA/YWCA/YMHA/YWHA, Youth Organizations

Application Procedures

Initial Contact: Submit a brief letter of inquiry. The foundation requests applications be made in writing.
Application Requirements: proof of tax-exempt status
Deadlines: March 1.

Restrictions

Grants are made only to organizations exempt under section 501(c)(3) of the IRS code. Grants are not made to individuals. Grants are made primarily to organizations in the St. Louis area. Grants are not given to churches, but may be awarded to church special outreach programs. Grants for programs are favored over capital campaigns; no grants are made to endowments.

Foundation Officials

James Collins: executive director, member advisory committee

Grants Analysis

Disclosure Period: calendar year ending 2000
Total Grants: $1,191,000*
Number of Grants: 125
Average Grant: $8,395*
Highest Grant: $150,000
Typical Range: $2,000 to $20,000

*Note: Giving excludes scholarships and United Way. Average grant figure excludes highest grant.

Recent Grants

Note: Grants derived from 2000 Form 990.

Library-Related

80,000	St. Louis Mercantile Library Association, St. Louis, MO

General

150,000	Salvation Army, St. Louis, MO
50,000	Grace Hill Settlement House, St. Louis, MO
50,000	Washington University, St. Louis, MO
35,000	United Way, St. Louis, MO
30,000	Family Resource Center, St. Louis, MO
30,000	Missouri Colleges Fund, St. Louis, MO
30,000	Ranken Jordan Home for Convalescent Crippled Children, St. Louis, MO
25,000	Missouri Girls Town Foundation, Kingdom City, MO
25,000	St. Louis University, St. Louis, MO
22,500	Alliance for the Mentally Ill, St. Louis, MO

POTTS AND SIBLEY FOUNDATION

Giving Contact

Robert W. Bechtel, Co-Trustee, Manager & Director
PO Box 8907
Midland, TX 79708
Phone: (915)686-7051

Description

Founded: 1967
EIN: 756081070
Organization Type: Private Foundation
Giving Locations: TX
Grant Types: General Support.

Donor Information

Founder: Effie Potts Sibley Irrevocable Trust

Financial Summary

Total Giving: $204,900 (fiscal year ending July 31, 2002); $141,500 (fiscal 2001); $152,356 (fiscal 2000)
Assets: $4,432,793 (fiscal 2002); $4,154,399 (fiscal 2001); $4,045,902 (fiscal 2000)

Typical Recipients

Arts & Humanities: Arts Institutes, Community Arts, History & Archaeology, Libraries, Museums/Galleries, Music
Civic & Public Affairs: Housing, Municipalities/Towns, Zoos/Aquariums
Education: Arts/Humanities Education, Colleges & Universities, Community & Junior Colleges, Education Funds, Engineering/Technological Education, Education-General, Private Education (Precollege), Science/Mathematics Education, Social Sciences Education, Vocational & Technical Education
Environment: Environment-General, Research, Resource Conservation, Wildlife Protection
Health: Children's Health/Hospitals, Eyes/Blindness, Hospices, Hospitals, Medical Research, Mental Health, Research/Studies Institutes
International: International Environmental Issues
Religion: Churches, Religious Welfare
Science: Science Museums, Scientific Research
Social Services: People with Disabilities, Scouts

Application Procedures

Initial Contact: Application form required.
Deadlines: None.

Foundation Officials

Robert W. Bechtel: co-trustee, mgr, director
Maurice Randolph Bullock: co-trustee, director B Colorado City, TX August 20, 1913. ED University of Texas LLB (1936). OCCUPATION attorney. NONPR AFFIL member: Texas Trial Lawyers Association; member: West Texas Chamber of Commerce; fellow: Texas Bar Foundation; member executive committee: Texas Law Enforcement Foundation; member: Southwest Legal Foundation; member: Texas Bar Association; member: Permian Basin Petroleum Association; member: Order Coif; member: Pecos County Chamber of Commerce; member: Midland County Bar Association; fellow: American College Trust & Estate Counsel; member: American Judicature Society; member: American Bar Association.
Allen G. McGuire: director, co-trustee
Tom Scott: director
D. J. Sibley: director
Hiram Sibley: chairman

Grants Analysis

Disclosure Period: fiscal year ending July 31, 2002
Total Grants: $204,900
Number of Grants: 28
Average Grant: $6,478*
Highest Grant: $30,000
Lowest Grant: $2,000
Typical Range: $2,000 to $10,000
*Note: Average grant figure excludes highest grant.

Recent Grants

Note: Grants derived from 2002 Form 990.

Library-Related

6,000	Recording Library for the Blind, Midland, TX

General

30,000	Siblley Environmental Learning Center, Midland, TX
25,000	Sibley Environmental Learning Center, Midland, TX
10,000	Big Bend Educational Corporation, Alpine, TX
10,000	Community Children's Clinic, Midland, TX
10,000	Midland Memorial Hospital Foundation, Midland, TX
8,000	Herman Hospital Hyberbaric Studies, Houston, TX
7,500	Permian Basin Petroleum Museum, Midland, TX
7,500	Salvation Army, Midland, TX
7,000	Austin Symphony, Austin, TX
7,000	Chihuahuan Desert Research, Austin, TX

POWELL FAMILY FOUNDATION

Giving Contact

Carrie Hoelscher, Secretary
4350 Shawnee Mission Parkway, Suite 280
Fairway, KS 66205
Phone: (913)236-0003
Fax: (913)262-0058

Description

Founded: 1969
EIN: 237023968
Organization Type: Family Foundation
Giving Locations: MO: Kansas City metropolitan area

Grant Types: Capital, General Support, Operating Expenses, Scholarship.

Donor Information

Founder: The Powell Family Foundation was established in 1969 by George E. Powell, former chairman of the Yellow Freight System of Delaware. The foundation gives preference to projects in the the Kansas City area where Mr. Powell lived. In keeping with Mr. Powell's beliefs, the foundation continues to support organizations that enrich the family, religious values, community involvement, and youth organizations. The foundation gives priority to the funding of Christian Science programs and to activities and programs for youth. The foundation's trustees are members of the Powell family.

Financial Summary

Total Giving: $1,351,000 (2002 approx); $1,532,000 (2001); $1,859,500 (2000)
Giving Analysis: Giving for 1998 includes: foundation program-related investments ($1,000,000)
Assets: $21,918,928 (2001); $24,410,407 (1998); $24,295,667 (1997)

Typical Recipients

Arts & Humanities: Libraries, Literary Arts, Museums/Galleries, Public Broadcasting
Civic & Public Affairs: Botanical Gardens/Parks, Community Foundations, Civic & Public Affairs-General, Law & Justice, Nonprofit Management, Philanthropic Organizations, Public Policy, Safety, Urban & Community Affairs, Women's Affairs, Zoos/Aquariums
Education: Agricultural Education, Business Education, Colleges & Universities, Education Associations, Education Funds, Faculty Development, Education-General, Minority Education, Private Education (Precollege), Public Education (Precollege), Science/Mathematics Education, Special Education, Student Aid, Vocational & Technical Education
Environment: Environment-General, Resource Conservation
Health: Cancer
International: International Peace & Security Issues
Religion: Churches, Religious Organizations, Religious Welfare
Social Services: Camps, Child Welfare, Community Centers, Community Service Organizations, Family Planning, Family Services, Food/Clothing Distribution, Recreation & Athletics, Scouts, United Funds/United Ways, YMCA/YWCA/YMHA/YWHA, Youth Organizations

Application Procedures

Initial Contact: Contact the foundation to obtain guidelines.
Review Process: The trustees meet in November of each year.

Restrictions

Building programs and grants for endowment purposes are rarely considered. The foundation does not fund individuals, organizations involved in the arts, the medical field, or social welfare. No grants are made for projects outside the continental United States.
Organizations must be tax-exempt under section 501(c)(3).

Additional Information

Publications: Guidelines

Foundation Officials

Barbara Powell Allen: secretary
Nicholas K. Powell: vice president PRIM CORP EMPL president: Colt Energy Inc.

Grants Analysis

Disclosure Period: calendar year ending 2001
Total Grants: $137,500*
Number of Grants: 10
Average Grant: $13,750
Highest Grant: $25,000
Lowest Grant: $1,000
Typical Range: $1,000 to $10,000 and $15,000 to $25,000
*Note: Giving excludes grants to the Powell Gardens.

Recent Grants

Note: Grants derived from 2001 Form 990.

General

1,394,500	Powell Gardens, Kingsville, MO -- operating support
25,000	Kansas City Museum, Kansas City, MO
25,000	Pembroke Hill School, Kansas City, MO -- capital campaign
20,000	Kansas City Public Television, Kansas City, MO -- capital campaign
20,000	Wildwood Outdoor Education Center, La Cynge, KS -- capital campaign
16,000	Missouri Conservation Heritage Foundation, Jefferson City, MO -- for Discovery Center
15,000	Women's Employment Network, Kansas City, MO -- operating support
10,000	Greater Kansas City Community Foundation, Kansas City, MI -- capital campaign
3,000	Kansas City Community Gardens, Kansas City, MO -- operating
2,500	Planned Parenthood, Kansas City, MO -- for operating

POWELL FOUNDATION

Giving Contact

Nancy Powell Moore, Foundation Manager
2121 San Felipe, Suite 110
Houston, TX 77019
Phone: (713)523-7557
Fax: (713)523-7553
E-mail: info@powellfoundation.org
Web: http://www.powellfoundation.org

Description

Founded: 1967
EIN: 746104592
Organization Type: Private Foundation
Giving Locations: TX: Harris County, Travis County, Walker County
Grant Types: General Support, Project.

Donor Information

Founder: the late Ben H. Powell, Kitty King Powell

Financial Summary

Total Giving: $694,655 (2001); $748,415 (2000); $773,915 (1999)
Assets: $15,763,614 (2001); $17,337,048 (2000); $16,995,543 (1999)

Typical Recipients

Arts & Humanities: Arts Associations & Councils, Arts Festivals, Arts Outreach, Ballet, Arts & Humanities-General, Historic Preservation, History & Archaeology, Libraries, Literary Arts, Museums/Galleries, Music, Opera, Public Broadcasting, Theater, Visual Arts
Civic & Public Affairs: Botanical Gardens/Parks, Community Foundations, Economic Development, Employment/Job Training, Civic & Public Affairs-General, Hispanic Affairs, Housing, Municipalities/Towns, Professional & Trade Associations, Urban & Community Affairs, Women's Affairs, Zoos/Aquariums

Education: Afterschool/Enrichment Programs, Arts/Humanities Education, Business Education, Business-School Partnerships, Colleges & Universities, Education Associations, Education Reform, Education Reform, Elementary Education (Public), Faculty Development, Education-General, International Studies, Legal Education, Literacy, Minority Education, Private Education (Precollege), Public Education (Precollege), Science/Mathematics Education, Secondary Education (Private), Social Sciences Education, Special Education

Environment: Environment-General, Protection, Resource Conservation

Health: Adolescent Health Issues, AIDS/HIV, Clinics/Medical Centers, Emergency/Ambulance Services, Eyes/Blindness, Hospitals (University Affiliated), Mental Health, Public Health, Research/Studies Institutes, Single-Disease Health Associations, Speech & Hearing

Religion: Churches, Ministries, Religious Welfare, Seminaries

Science: Science Museums

Social Services: Child Abuse, Child Welfare, Community Centers, Community Service Organizations, Emergency Relief, Family Planning, Family Services, Homes, Scouts, Shelters/Homelessness, Substance Abuse, Volunteer Services, Youth Organizations

Application Procedures

Initial Contact: The foundation requests applications be made in writing.

Application Requirements: Include organization's purpose and a summary of its activities; its budget; a copy of the organization's IRS tax-exempt letter, evidence of its IRS status as a public entity, and a statement that the letter is current and has not been revoked; a list of board members; and a list of past and present funders, including project, date, and amount.

Deadlines: None.

Restrictions

Grants are not made to religious organizations for sectarian purposes, testimonial dinners, fund raising events, advertising, other private foundations, or individuals, or to cover past operating deficits or debt retirement, grants for building requests, or multi-year commitments.

Foundation Officials

Antonia Scott Day: vice president, director, secretary

Marian P. Harrison: director, assistant treasurer

Harvin Moore, IV: director

Nancy Powell Moore: foundation manager, director, president, treasurer

Katherine Osborne: director

Ben H. Powell, V: director, vice president

Kitty King Powell: director

Grants Analysis

Disclosure Period: calendar year ending 2001

Total Grants: $694,655

Number of Grants: 77

Average Grant: $9,021

Highest Grant: $55,000

Lowest Grant: $250

Typical Range: $300 to $25,000

Recent Grants

Note: Grants derived from 2001 Form 990.

Library-Related

10,000	Harris County Public Library, Houston, TX

General

55,000	Child-Centered School Initiative of Greater Houston Area, Houston, TX
55,000	Greater Houston Community Foundation, Houston, TX
30,000	American National Red Cross, Houston, TX
25,000	Communities in Schools Houston, Inc., Houston, TX
25,000	Teach for America, Houston, TX
22,500	KIPP, Inc, Houston, TX
15,000	Gulf Coast Trades Center, New Waverly, TX
15,000	Huntsville Independent School District, Huntsville, TX
14,400	Fifth Ward Enrichment Program, Houston, TX
12,895	Aspiring Youth Foundation, Houston, TX

POWERS FOUNDATION

Giving Contact

C. Cody White, Jr., President & Treasurer
Powers Foundation
PO Box 1607
Shreveport, LA 71165
Phone: (318)429-1525
Fax: (318)429-2070

Description

Founded: 1967

EIN: 756080974

Organization Type: Private Foundation

Giving Locations: LA: Bossier City, Shreveport

Grant Types: General Support.

Donor Information

Founder: the late Gussie N. Power

Financial Summary

Total Giving: $224,500 (fiscal year ending July 31, 2002); $217,000 (fiscal 2001); $185,200 (fiscal 2000)

Giving Analysis: Giving for fiscal 1999 includes: foundation grants to United Way ($20,000)

Assets: $4,949,005 (fiscal 2002); $4,982,784 (fiscal 2001); $4,582,008 (fiscal 2000)

Gifts Received: $50,000 (fiscal 1998)

Typical Recipients

Arts & Humanities: Ballet, History & Archaeology, Libraries, Museums/Galleries, Music

Civic & Public Affairs: Chambers of Commerce, Clubs, Community Foundations, Civic & Public Affairs-General, Urban & Community Affairs

Education: Business Education, Colleges & Universities, Education Funds, Education Reform, Literacy, Private Education (Precollege), Public Education (Precollege), Secondary Education (Public)

Health: Arthritis, Emergency/Ambulance Services, Hospitals (University Affiliated), Medical Research

Religion: Churches, Religious Organizations, Religious Welfare

Science: Science Museums

Social Services: Child Abuse, Child Welfare, Community Service Organizations, Counseling, Food/Clothing Distribution, Homes, People with Disabilities, Scouts, Scouts, Senior Services, Substance Abuse, Volunteer Services, YMCA/YWCA/YMHA/YWHA, Youth Organizations

Application Procedures

Initial Contact: Send a brief letter of inquiry.

Application Requirements: Include a description of organization and proof of tax-exempt status.

Deadlines: None.

Foundation Officials

C. Cody White, Jr.: president, treasurer

Sara Margaret White: vice president, secretary

Stephen C. White: vice president

Grants Analysis

Disclosure Period: fiscal year ending July 31, 2002

Total Grants: $224,500

Number of Grants: 27

Average Grant: $4,761*

Highest Grant: $35,000

Lowest Grant: $1,000

Typical Range: $1,000 to $10,000

***Note:** Average grant figure excludes four highest grants ($115,000).

Recent Grants

Note: Grants derived from 2002 Form 990.

General

35,000	Volunteers of America, Shreveport, LA
30,000	SCI Port Discovery Center, Shreveport, LA
25,000	Highland Center Foundation, Shreveport, LA
25,000	Youth Choirs, Inc., Shreveport, LA -- civic
15,000	Shreveport Community Renewal, Shreveport, LA -- civic
10,000	Christian Service Program, Shreveport, LA
10,000	Graland Country Day School, Denver, CO
10,000	Louisiana State University Health Sciences Center, Shreveport, LA -- for medical research
10,000	Red Cross, New York, NY
10,000	Shreveport Garden Study Club, Shreveport, LA -- civic

PPG INDUSTRIES, INC.

Company Headquarters

One PPG Place
Pittsburgh, PA 15272
Phone: (412)434-3131
Web: http://www.ppg.com

Company Description

Founded: 1883

Ticker: PPG

Exchange: NYSE

Acquired: Porter Paint Co..

Revenue: US$8.067 billion (2002)

Employees: 34100 (2002)

Fortune Rank: 233, per FORTUNE Magazine's list of 500 Largest U.S. Corporations (2002).

SIC(s): 2812 Alkalies & Chlorine, 2851 Paints & Allied Products, 2869 Industrial Organic Chemicals Nec, 2891 Adhesives & Sealants.

Parent Company: Courtaulds Coatings, Inc., 91-291 Kalaeloa Boulevard, Kapolei, HI, United States

Parent Revenue: US$15,207,700,000 (2001)

Operating Locations

PPG Industries, Inc. (AR--El Dorado; KS--Lenexa; LA--Lake Charles; OH--Cleveland; PA--Pittsburgh; WV--Natrium; WI--Oak Creek)

Porter Paint Foundation, Inc.

Giving Contact

W.R. Niblock, President
Porter Paint Foundation, Inc
419 Village Lake Drive
Louisville, KY 40245
Phone: (502)244-2205

Description

Founded: 1985

EIN: 611094575

Organization Type: Corporate Foundation

Giving Locations: KY

Grant Types: General Support.

Note: Also supports special programs.

Financial Summary

Total Giving: $11,600 (2000); $10,300 (1999); $9,900 (1998)

Giving Analysis: Giving for 1999 includes: foundation ($10,300)

Assets: $182,855 (2000); $215,631 (1999); $182,338 (1998)

Typical Recipients

Arts & Humanities: Ethnic & Folk Arts, Libraries

Civic & Public Affairs: Business/Free Enterprise, Municipalities/Towns, Professional & Trade Associations

Education: Business Education, Colleges & Universities, Economic Education, Education Associations, Education Funds, Education-General, Private Education (Precollege), Public Education (Precollege)

Science: Scientific Centers & Institutes

Social Services: Camps, People with Disabilities, Scouts, Shelters/Homelessness

Application Procedures

Initial Contact: The foundation requests applications be made in writing.

Application Requirements: Include need and purpose of funds sought.

Deadlines: None.

Restrictions

Does not support individuals, political or lobbying groups, or organizations outside operating areas.

Foundation Officials

Robert E. Champagne: director

W. Robert Niblock: president, director B Philadelphia, PA 1928. ED Drexel University BS (1951); University of Chicago Graduate School of Business Administration MBA (1956). CORP AFFIL vice president corporate devel, secretary, director: Courtaulds Coatings. NONPR AFFIL director: Junior Achievement Kentuckiana; director: Kentucky Education Foundation. CLUB AFFIL Jefferson Club; Wynn Stay Club.

Grants Analysis

Disclosure Period: calendar year ending 2000

Total Grants: $11,600

Number of Grants: 10

Average Grant: $1,160

Highest Grant: $3,000

Typical Range: $750 to $2,000

Recent Grants

Note: Grants derived from 1999 Form 990.

Library-Related

1,000	Library Foundation, Louisville, KY

General

3,000	Kentucky Council on Economic Education, Louisville, KY
2,000	Boy Scouts of America Lincoln Heritage Council, Louisville, KY
2,000	Louisville Science Center, Louisville, KY
1,000	Junior Achievement, Louisville, KY
400	Camp Piomingo YMCA of Greater Louisville, Louisville, KY
400	DePaul School, Louisville, KY
300	Kentucky Engineering Foundation, Inc., Frankfort, KY
200	Boulware Center, The, Owensboro, KY

PPG INDUSTRIES, INC.

Company Headquarters

One PPG Place
Pittsburgh, PA 15272
Phone: (412)434-3131
Web: http://www.ppg.com

Company Description

Founded: 1883

Ticker: PPG

Exchange: NYSE

Acquired: Porter Paint Co..

Revenue: US$8.067 billion (2002)

Employees: 34100 (2002)

Fortune Rank: 233, per FORTUNE Magazine's list of 500 Largest U.S. Corporations (2002).

SIC(s): 2812 Alkalies & Chlorine, 2851 Paints & Allied Products, 2869 Industrial Organic Chemicals Nec, 2891 Adhesives & Sealants.

Operating Locations

PPG Industries, Inc. (AR--El Dorado; KS--Lenexa; LA--Lake Charles; OH--Cleveland; PA--Pittsburgh; WV--Natrium; WI--Oak Creek)

Nonmonetary Support

Type: In-kind Services

Volunteer Programs: Sponsors the GIVE Program to recognize employee involvement in volunteerism. Employees may apply for one grant of $250 annually to benefit an eligible non-profit organization for whom they volunteer.

Note: PPG does not coordinate or track its in-kind giving.

PPG Industries Foundation

Giving Contact

Jeffrey R. Gilbert, Executive Director
PPG Industries Foundation
One PPG Pl.
Pittsburgh, PA 15272
Phone: (412)434-2788
Web: http://corporate.ppg.com/PPG/corporate/AboutUs/PPGIndustriesFoundation/default.htm

Description

EIN: 256037790

Organization Type: Corporate Foundation

Giving Locations: PA: Pittsburgh headquarters and operating communities; nationally.

Grant Types: Capital, Department, Emergency, Employee Matching Gifts, General Support, Matching, Multiyear/Continuing Support, Operating Expenses, Project.

Note: Employee matching gift ratio: 1 to 1 up to $10,000 per eligible donor per organization. Minimum for matching is $25 and the maximum is $10,000 for an organization. Limit is $20,000 per year per donor.

Financial Summary

Total Giving: $4,958,246 (2001); $4,896,746 (2000); $4,880,265 (1999). Note: Contributes through corporate direct giving program and foundation.

Giving Analysis: Giving for 2001 includes: foundation matching gifts ($1,390,000); foundation ($3,568,246); 2000: foundation ($4,896,746); 1999: foundation ($4,880,265);

Assets: $5,500,000 (2002 approx); $22,975,397 (2001); $24,919,605 (2000)

Gifts Received: $5,186,912 (2001); $5,000,000 (2000); $5,000,000 (1999). Note: Foundation receives contributions from PPG Industries.

Typical Recipients

Arts & Humanities: Arts Associations & Councils, Arts Festivals, Arts Outreach, Ballet, Community Arts, Dance, Historic Preservation, History & Archaeology, Libraries, Literary Arts, Museums/Galleries, Music, Opera, Performing Arts, Public Broadcasting, Theater

Civic & Public Affairs: Botanical Gardens/Parks, Business/Free Enterprise, Civil Rights, Economic Development, Economic Policy, Employment/Job Training, Civic & Public Affairs-General, Housing, Law & Justice, Municipalities/Towns, Professional & Trade Associations, Public Policy, Safety, Urban & Community Affairs, Women's Affairs, Zoos/Aquariums

Education: Business Education, Business-School Partnerships, Colleges & Universities, Community & Junior Colleges, Economic Education, Education Associations, Education Funds, Education Reform, Engineering/Technological Education, Environmental Education, Faculty Development, Education-General, International Studies, Minority Education, Private Education (Precollege), Public Education (Precollege), Science/Mathematics Education, Secondary Education (Private), Secondary Education (Public), Student Aid

Environment: Environment-General

Health: Clinics/Medical Centers, Emergency/Ambulance Services, Eyes/Blindness, Health Policy/Cost Containment, Health Organizations, Hospitals, Long-Term Care, Medical Rehabilitation, Mental Health, Nursing Services, Public Health, Single-Disease Health Associations

International: International Relations

Religion: Churches, Jewish Causes, Religious Welfare, Seminaries

Science: Observatories & Planetariums, Science Exhibits & Fairs, Scientific Centers & Institutes, Scientific Organizations

Social Services: Child Welfare, Community Centers, Community Service Organizations, Day Care, Family Services, Food/Clothing Distribution, Homes, People with Disabilities, Scouts, Senior Services, Shelters/Homelessness, Social Services-General, United Funds/United Ways, Volunteer Services, YMCA/YWCA/YMHA/YWHA, Youth Organizations

Application Procedures

Initial Contact: Send a one- to two-page letter to foundation if organizations are located in Pittsburgh area or are national in scope; organizations serving communities where PPG facilities are located should direct inquiries to local PPG agent.

Application Requirements: Include proof of tax-exempt status; organization's mission statement; grant's purpose and objectives; summary of the project; amount requested and rationale; schedule of implementation; description of benefits to be achieved and population served; plans for evaluating and reporting results; recently audited financial statement; financial analysis for the project; person in charge of the project and his or her qualifications; and list of board members and their affiliations.

Deadlines: By September for grants in the following year, though grant requests are accepted year-round.

Review Process: Screening committee reviews appeals quarterly; committee decides on grants of less than $10,000; board reviews grants of more than $10,000.

Evaluative Criteria: Correspondence of applicant's goal to foundation's priorities; available resources; financial need of organization; foundation's past experience with organization; applicant's capability and reputation; funds available from other funders; duplication of work; population served; proposal's clarity and breadth; and practices of other corporate funders. Priority is given to local organizations dedicated to enhancing the welfare of PPG communities.

Restrictions

No grant application for less than $100 will be considered. Foundation does not support operating funds of United Way agencies; political activities or organizations; individuals; endowments; organizations outside the United States or its territories; projects which would directly benefit PPG Industries, Inc.; advertising in benefit publications; sectarian groups for religious purposes; special events; or telephone solicitations.

Additional Information

To ensure sensitivity to local needs in PPG plant communities, the foundation has developed a local agent system. Approximately 40 company managers, most of whom live in PPG plant communities, have been

designated as local agents for the foundation. Once a year agents recommend a budget for contributions in their communities to a screening committee for presentation to the foundation board.
Publications: Foundation Annual Report

Corporate Officials

Raymond W. LeBoeuf: director, chairman, chief executive officer B Chicago, IL 1946. ED Northwestern University BA (1967); University of Illinois MBA (1970). PRIM CORP EMPL director, chairman, chief executive officer: PPG Industries, Inc. CORP AFFIL chairman: Keeler & Long Inc.; director: Praxair Inc. NONPR AFFIL director: Magee-Women's Hospital; trustee: Robert Morris College; member: Financial Executives Institute.

Foundation Officials

Charles E. Bunch: director
Fred Denk: secretary
James C. Diggs: vice president
Jeffrey R. Gilbert: executive director
Raymond W. LeBoeuf: director (see above)
Mary Ann Mackey: foundation accountant
David H. McClain: assistant secretary
Maurice V. Peconi: vice president B New Kensington, PA. ED Duquesne University MBA; Duquesne University BS. PRIM CORP EMPL vice president: PPG Industries Inc. NONPR AFFIL director: Pittsburgh Childrens Museum.
Sue Sloan: senior program officer
Kevin F. Sullivan: vice president B Baltimore, MD. ED Case Western Reserve University; Franklin and Marshall College. PRIM CORP EMPL vice president: PPG Industries Inc. NONPR AFFIL director: Society Plastics Industry.
Donna Lee Walker: vice president

Grants Analysis

Disclosure Period: calendar year ending 2001
Total Grants: $3,568,246*
Number of Grants: 833
Average Grant: $4,284
Highest Grant: $525,000
Typical Range: $1,000 to $20,000
*Note: Giving excludes matching gifts.

Recent Grants

Note: Grants derived from 2001 Form 990.

General

525,000	United Way Southwestern Pennsylvania, Pittsburgh, PA
398,215	National Merit Scholarship Corporation, Evanston, IL
101,890	American Red Cross, Washington, DC
100,000	Carnegie Mellon University, Pittsburgh, PA
100,000	University of Pittsburgh, Pittsburgh, PA
87,000	American Chemical Society, Detroit, MI -- minority scholarship
75,000	United Way, Southwest, LA
55,000	Pittsburgh Public Theater, Pittsburgh, PA
50,000	United Way, Huntsville, AL
45,000	Greater Pittsburgh Community Foodbank, McKeesport, PA

THE PRAIRIE FOUNDATION

Giving Contact

Benjamin L. Blake, Director
303 W. Wall Avenue, Suite 1901
Midland, TX 79701
Phone: (432)683-1777

Description

Founded: 1957
EIN: 756012458
Organization Type: Private Foundation
Giving Locations: CA: San Francisco metropolitan area; TX: Laredo, Midland, Odessa
Grant Types: General Support.

Donor Information

Founder: David Fasken Special Trust

Financial Summary

Total Giving: $374,000 (2002); $386,000 (2001); $466,100 (2000)
Giving Analysis: Giving for 2002 includes: foundation grants to United Way ($25,000); 2000: foundation grants to United Way ($25,000) 1999: foundation grants to United Way ($25,000)
Assets: $8,795,331 (2002); $8,429,353 (2001); $8,215,282 (2000)
Gifts Received: $500,000 (1995); $810,612 (1994).
Note: In 1995, contributions were received from Barbara Fasken.

Typical Recipients

Arts & Humanities: Ballet, Community Arts, Libraries, Music, Opera, Theater
Civic & Public Affairs: Botanical Gardens/Parks, Clubs, Civic & Public Affairs-General, Hispanic Affairs, Housing, Municipalities/Towns, Public Policy, Safety, Urban & Community Affairs, Zoos/Aquariums
Education: Business Education, Colleges & Universities, Education-General, Literacy, Private Education (Precollege)
Environment: Air/Water Quality, Environment-General
Health: AIDS/HIV, Cancer, Children's Health/Hospitals, Emergency/Ambulance Services, Eyes/Blindness, Health Organizations, Hospices, Hospitals, Medical Rehabilitation
Religion: Churches, Religion-General, Religious Organizations, Religious Welfare
Science: Scientific Labs
Social Services: At-Risk Youth, Big Brother/Big Sister, Camps, Child Abuse, Child Welfare, Community Service Organizations, Crime Prevention, Domestic Violence, Family Services, Food/Clothing Distribution, Homes, People with Disabilities, Recreation & Athletics, Scouts, Senior Services, Sexual Abuse, Social Services-General, Substance Abuse, United Funds/United Ways, Veterans, Youth Organizations

Application Procedures

Initial Contact: Request proposal summary form and guidelines.
Deadlines: None.

Restrictions

Does not support individuals, religious organizations for sectarian purposes, political or lobbying groups, or organizations outside operating areas.

Additional Information

Publications: Proposal Summary Form; Guidelines

Foundation Officials

Louis A. Bartha: secretary, director
Benjamin L. Blake: director
Norbert J. Dickman: vice president, director
Robert T. Dickson: president, director
Lynda James: secretary

Grants Analysis

Disclosure Period: calendar year ending 2002
Total Grants: $349,000*
Number of Grants: 39
Average Grant: $7,868*
Highest Grant: $50,000
Lowest Grant: $2,500
Typical Range: $2,500 to $15,000

*Note: Giving excludes United Way. Average grant figure excludes highest grant.

Recent Grants

Note: Grants derived from 2001 Form 990.

General

60,000	Boy Scouts of America, Midland, TX
25,000	Thacher School, Ojai, CA
25,000	United Way of Midland, Midland, TX
20,000	Four Winds Westward Ho Camp, Deer Harbor, WA
17,500	Friends of The Veterans, Monterey, CA
15,000	Casa de Amigos, Midland, TX
15,000	Safe Place, Austin, TX
12,500	LULAC Council 12, Laredo, TX
12,500	Congregation of St. John, Laredo, TX
12,500	Laredo Philharmonic Chorale, Laredo, TX

ABRA PRENTICE FOUNDATION

Giving Contact

Harris Trust & Savings Bank
Attn: T-PLIS-111/7W
PO Box 755
Chicago, IL 60690-0755
Phone: (312)461-7551

Description

Founded: 1980
EIN: 363092281
Organization Type: Private Foundation
Giving Locations: IL
Grant Types: Endowment, General Support, Multiyear/Continuing Support, Professorship.

Donor Information

Founder: Abra Prentice Wilkin

Financial Summary

Total Giving: $100,000 (2001); $360,000 (2000); $345,000 (1999)
Assets: $12,885,517 (2001); $12,025,591 (2000); $13,954,382 (1999)
Gifts Received: $600,864 (2001); $500,000 (1992).
Note: In 2001, contributions were received from Mrs. Abra P. Wilkin. In 1992, contributions were received from Abra Prentice Wilkin ($500,000).

Typical Recipients

Arts & Humanities: Historic Preservation, Libraries, Public Broadcasting
Education: Colleges & Universities, Medical Education, Private Education (Precollege), Science/Mathematics Education
Environment: Air/Water Quality
Health: Hospitals
Religion: Churches

Application Procedures

Initial Contact: The foundation has no formal grant application procedure or application form.
Deadlines: None.

Restrictions

Grants limited to organizations with 501 (c)(3) exempt status.

Foundation Officials

Robert F. Carr, III: director
Don Harold Reuben: secretary B Chicago, IL 1928. ED Northwestern University BS (1949); Northwestern University JD (1952). PRIM CORP EMPL counsel: Altheimer & Gray. CORP AFFIL director: Heitman Financial. NONPR AFFIL trustee: Northwestern University; member: Phi Eta Sigma; fellow: International Academy Trial Lawyers; member supervisory panel:

Fed Defender Program; member: Illinois Bar Association; member: Chicago Bar Association; member: Beta Alpha Psi; member: Beta Gamma Sigma; member: American Law Institute; fellow: American College Trial Lawyers; member: American Judicature Society; fellow: American Bar Foundation; fellow: American Arbitration Association; member: American Bar Association. CLUB AFFIL Tavern Club; Union League Club; Spring Club; Mid-America Club; Order of Coif; Law Club; Chicago Club; Desert Riders Palm Springs Club; Casino Club.

Jere Scott Senko: director
Abra Prentice Wilkin: president B 1942. ED Northwestern University. CORP AFFIL trustee: Northwestern Memorial Hosp.

Grants Analysis

Disclosure Period: calendar year ending 2001
Total Grants: $100,000
Number of Grants: 4
Highest Grant: $50,000
Lowest Grant: $10,000
Typical Range: $10,000 to $50,000

Recent Grants

Note: Grants derived from 2001 Form 990.

Library-Related
10,000   Newberry Library, Chicago, IL

General
50,000   St. Chrysostom's Church, Chicago, IL
25,000   WTTW Channel 11, Chicago, IL
15,000   Geneva Lake Water Safety Committee, Lake Geneva, WI

T. ROWE PRICE ASSOCIATES

Company Headquarters

PO Box 17630
Baltimore, MD 21297-1302
Phone: 800-225-5132
E-mail: info@troweprice.com
Web: http://www.troweprice.com

Company Description

Founded: 1937
Ticker: TROW
Exchange: NASDAQ
Employees: 2,587
SIC(s): 6282 Investment Advice.

Operating Locations

T. Rowe Price Associates (MD--Baltimore)

Nonmonetary Support

Type: In-kind Services
Note: Value of in-kind giving activities and gifts is not tracked.
Volunteer Programs: The foundation sponsors several volunteer events per year, including: New Song Investment Academy Program, in partnership with a local inner-city school; Habitat for Humanity, employees volunteer on a weekly basis throughout the year to build or renovate a sponsored house; United Way Day of Caring, in conjunction with the corporate United Way campaign; Dollars for Doers, matches employee's volunteer hours with a financial donation; Susan G. Komen Race for the Cure, with over 350 employee participants; Dragon Boat Race, employees practice more than 800 hours to race for a local charity; Holiday Giving Program, with employee donations for the needy; and Red Cross Blood Drive, to encourage participation in blood donation.

T. Rowe Price Associates Foundation

Giving Contact

A. C. Hubbard, Jr., President
100 E. Pratt St., 8th Fl.
Baltimore, MD 21202
Phone: (410)345-3603
Fax: (410)345-2848

Description

EIN: 521231953
Organization Type: Corporate Foundation
Giving Locations: headquarters and operating communities.
Grant Types: Capital, Employee Matching Gifts, General Support, Multiyear/Continuing Support, Project.
Note: Employee matching gift ratio: 1:1.

Financial Summary

Total Giving: $3,170,000 (2002); $3,742,327 (2001); $3,059,033 (2000). Note: Contributes through corporate direct giving program and foundation.
Giving Analysis: Giving for 2000 includes: foundation grants to United Way ($281,000); foundation ($2,778,033); 1997: foundation grants to United Way ($123,000) 1996: foundation grants to United Way ($110,800)
Assets: $17,724,000 (2002); $25,226,034 (2001); $29,925,686 (2000)
Gifts Received: $30,000 (2001); $6,045,925 (2000); $6,040,249 (1999). Note: Contributions are received from T. Rowe Price Group Inc.

Typical Recipients

Arts & Humanities: Arts Festivals, Arts Funds, Arts Institutes, Arts Outreach, Community Arts, Arts & Humanities-General, Historic Preservation, History & Archaeology, Libraries, Museums/Galleries, Music, Opera, Public Broadcasting, Theater
Civic & Public Affairs: African American Affairs, Botanical Gardens/Parks, Community Foundations, Economic Development, Employment/Job Training, Civic & Public Affairs-General, Housing, Professional & Trade Associations, Public Policy, Urban & Community Affairs, Zoos/Aquariums
Education: Arts/Humanities Education, Business Education, Colleges & Universities, Continuing Education, Education Funds, Elementary Education (Private), Education-General, Literacy, Medical Education, Minority Education, Private Education (Precollege), Public Education (Precollege), Religious Education, Secondary Education (Private), Student Aid
Environment: Environment-General, Resource Conservation
Health: Emergency/Ambulance Services, Health Organizations, Heart, Hospitals, Mental Health, Single-Disease Health Associations
Religion: Jewish Causes, Religious Welfare
Science: Science Museums
Social Services: Child Abuse, Child Welfare, Community Service Organizations, Family Services, Food/Clothing Distribution, People with Disabilities, Recreation & Athletics, Scouts, Shelters/Homelessness, Social Services-General, United Funds/United Ways, Youth Organizations

Application Procedures

Initial Contact: Send a brief letter or proposal.
Application Requirements: Include a description of the organization, with a brief history; copy of IRS determination letter; latest audited financial report; current operating budget and sources of income; list of organization's board members; annual report; and number of paid and volunteer employees. Information

regarding the particular program should include purpose and objectives; needs to be addressed; population served; plan of action and timeframe; qualifications of administrators; total funding required and projected sources; method of evaluation (measurement of success) and amount requested.
Deadlines: None.
Notes: All requests should be in writing.

Restrictions

Company does not support individuals, hospitals, healthcare providers, religious organizations for sectarian purposes, or political or lobbying groups. No support is given to organizations which are not 501(c)(3) public charities, or to United Way/Combined Health Agency organizations (although capital campaigns will be considered).

Foundation Officials

Stephen W. Boesel: vice president, secretary, treasurer, trustee B Niles, OH 1944. ED Baldwin-Wallace College (1968); University of Denver (1969). PRIM CORP EMPL managing director: T.Rowe Price Associates Inc. ADD CORP EMPL vice president: T.Rowe Price New Era Fund Inc.
Ann Allston Boyce: vice president, trustee
Albert C. Hubbard, Jr.: president
Mary J. Miller: vice president, trustee PRIM CORP EMPL vice president: T. Rowe Price. CORP AFFIL managing director: T. Rowe Price Associates Inc.
Christine D. Stein: program director
William F. Wendler, II: vice president, trustee

Grants Analysis

Disclosure Period: calendar year ending 2002
Total Grants: $2,755,000*
Number of Grants: 217*
Average Grant: $12,500
Highest Grant: $100,000
Lowest Grant: $500
Typical Range: $500 to $100,000
*Note: Giving excludes United Way. Number of grants excludes matching gifts. Grants analysis provided by foundation.

Recent Grants

Note: Grants derived from 2001 Form 990.

Library-Related
20,000   Enoch Pratt Free Library, Baltimore, MD

General
270,000   United Way of Central Maryland, Baltimore, MD
130,225   Baltimore Museum of Art, Baltimore, MD
125,834   Baltimore Symphony Orchestra, Baltimore, MD
125,000   Walters Art Museum, Baltimore, MD
100,000   PBA Widows and Children's Fund, New York, NY
100,000   UFA Widow's and Children's Fund, New York, NY
95,750   Center Stage, Baltimore, MD
90,000   Baltimore Zoo, Baltimore, MD
63,955   Loyola College, Baltimore, MD
57,500   Maryland Institute College of Art, Baltimore, MD

LOUIS AND HAROLD PRICE FOUNDATION

Giving Contact

Rosemary L. Guidone, President
450 Park Avenue, Suite 1102
New York, NY 10022-2605
Phone: (212)753-0240
Fax: (212)752-9338
E-mail: grantinquiry@pricefoundation.org
Web: http://www.pricefoundation.org

Description

Founded: 1951
EIN: 136121358
Organization Type: General Purpose Foundation
Giving Locations: CA: Los Angeles including the metropolitan area; NY: New York including the metropolitan area; Israel
Grant Types: Department, General Support, Matching, Multiyear/Continuing Support.

Donor Information

Founder: Established in 1951 by the late Louis Price and Harold Price.

Financial Summary

Total Giving: $3,359,743 (2001); $4,145,764 (2000); $4,736,772 (1999)
Assets: $82,700,172 (2001); $92,592,173 (2000); $88,886,224 (1999)

Typical Recipients

Arts & Humanities: Arts Associations & Councils, Libraries, Museums/Galleries, Music, Performing Arts, Public Broadcasting, Theater
Civic & Public Affairs: Botanical Gardens/Parks, Civil Rights, First Amendment Issues, Civic & Public Affairs-General, Housing, Law & Justice, Legal Aid, Municipalities/Towns, Philanthropic Organizations, Public Policy, Urban & Community Affairs, Women's Affairs
Education: Arts/Humanities Education, Business Education, Colleges & Universities, Education Funds, Education-General, Gifted & Talented Programs, Preschool Education, Private Education (Precollege), Public Education (Precollege), Religious Education, Student Aid
Environment: Environment-General, Protection
Health: AIDS/HIV, Alzheimers Disease, Alzheimers Disease, Arthritis, Cancer, Children's Health/Hospitals, Clinics/Medical Centers, Emergency/Ambulance Services, Eyes/Blindness, Health-General, Health Funds, Health Organizations, Heart, Hospitals, Kidney, Long-Term Care, Medical Rehabilitation, Medical Research, Mental Health, Multiple Sclerosis, Outpatient Health Care, Public Health, Research/Studies Institutes, Single-Disease Health Associations
International: Foreign Educational Institutions, International-General, Health Care/Hospitals, International Development, International Peace & Security Issues, International Relief Efforts, Missionary/Religious Activities
Religion: Churches, Jewish Causes, Religious Organizations, Religious Welfare, Synagogues/Temples, Synagogues/Temples
Social Services: Animal Protection, At-Risk Youth, Child Welfare, Community Centers, Community Service Organizations, Counseling, Crime Prevention, Delinquency & Criminal Rehabilitation, Emergency Relief, Family Services, Food/Clothing Distribution, People with Disabilities, Recreation & Athletics, Senior Services, Shelters/Homelessness, Social Services-General, United Funds/United Ways, Youth Organizations

Application Procedures

Initial Contact: Send a brief letter of inquiry. limited to two pages.
Deadlines: None.

Restrictions

The foundation does not give support for building funds, capital campaigns, or endowments; or to large, public charities.

Foundation Officials

Gloria W. Appel: president, trustee
George Asch: trustee B 1937. ED Columbia University BA (1959). PRIM CORP EMPL president: Ashton Group Inc. ADD CORP EMPL vice president: Seifert Gray & Co. Inc.
David Gerstein: trustee

Rosemary Guidone: executive vice president, trustee
Linda Vitti Herbst: trustee
Harold Price: chairman, treasurer, trustee
Pauline Price: vice president, secretary, trustee

Grants Analysis

Disclosure Period: calendar year ending 2001
Total Grants: $3,334,743*
Number of Grants: 212
Average Grant: $13,618*
Highest Grant: $250,000
Lowest Grant: $200
Typical Range: $1,000 to $25,000
*Note: Giving excludes United Way. Average grant figure excludes two highest grants ($475,000).

Recent Grants

Note: Grants derived from 2001 Form 990.

General

250,000	Jules Stein Eye Institute, Los Angeles, CA -- Harold and Pauline Price Term Endowed Chair and Retina Research Fund
225,000	United Jewish Fund, Los Angeles, CA
152,000	International Planned Parenthood Federation, London United Kingdom -- support projects in Lebanon, Malaysia and Pakistan
150,000	Children's Learning Center, Boulder, CO
115,000	Entrepreneurship Center for Music, Boulder, CO
100,000	Babson College, Babson Park, MA -- Gloria Appel Memorial Scholarship Fund
100,000	Children's Learning Center, Boulder, CO
100,000	Herbst Program of Humanities, Boulder, CO
100,000	Stern School of Business, New York, NY -- Gloria Appel Program for the Advancement of Entrepreneurship
100,000	University of California Berkeley, Berkeley, CA -- Gloria Appel Award for Outstanding Leadership in Entrepeneurship

LUCIEN B. AND KATHERINE E. PRICE FOUNDATION

Giving Contact

Dr. Edward P. Flanagan, Secretary
PO Box 790
Manchester, CT 06040
Phone: (203)627-2335

Description

Founded: 1922
EIN: 066068868
Organization Type: Private Foundation
Giving Locations: CT; VT
Grant Types: General Support.

Financial Summary

Total Giving: $202,000 (2001); $235,500 (2000); $219,500 (1999)
Giving Analysis: Giving for 1998 includes: foundation scholarships ($500)
Assets: $4,787,246 (2001); $5,111,812 (2000); $5,222,548 (1999)

Typical Recipients

Arts & Humanities: Libraries
Civic & Public Affairs: Civic & Public Affairs-General, Professional & Trade Associations, Urban & Community Affairs

Education: Colleges & Universities, Education-General, Legal Education, Preschool Education, Private Education (Precollege), Public Education (Precollege), Religious Education, Science/Mathematics Education, Secondary Education (Private), Secondary Education (Public), Student Aid
Environment: Wildlife Protection
Health: Cancer, Children's Health/Hospitals, Hospitals, Medical Rehabilitation, Nursing Services
International: Health Care/Hospitals, International Affairs, International Relief Efforts
Religion: Churches, Dioceses, Religion-General, Missionary Activities (Domestic), Religious Organizations, Religious Welfare, Seminaries
Social Services: At-Risk Youth, Camps, Community Service Organizations, Food/Clothing Distribution, Scouts, Social Services-General, Youth Organizations

Application Procedures

Initial Contact: The foundation requests applications be made in writing.
Application Requirements: Include purpose of funds sought.
Deadlines: None.

Foundation Officials

Morgan P. Ames: treasurer
Rev. Colin Bircumshaw: vice president
Rev. Colin Bircumshow: director
Rev. Joseph L. Federal: director
Rev. J. T. Fitzgerald: vice president
Dr. Edward P. Flanagan: secretary
Sheila Flanagan: treasurer
Rev. Francis V. Krukowski: president

Grants Analysis

Disclosure Period: calendar year ending 2001
Total Grants: $202,000
Number of Grants: 32
Average Grant: $3,935*
Highest Grant: $80,000
Lowest Grant: $500
Typical Range: $1,000 to $5,000
*Note: Average grant figure excludes highest grant.

Recent Grants

Note: Grants derived from 2001 Form 990.

Library-Related

8,000	St. James School Library Fund, Baltimore, MD

General

80,000	Diocese of Salt Lake City, Salt Lake City, UT
24,000	St. Francis Hospital and Medical Center, Hartford, CT
12,000	St. James School, Baltimore, MD
10,000	Hesburg CCFM
10,000	Holy Cross Brothers
10,000	St. Joseph Catholic, Macon, GA
4,000	Holy Apostle Seminary
4,000	Holy Family Retreat House
4,000	Mercyknoll, West Hartford, CT
4,000	St. James School, Baltimore, MD

PRIDDY FOUNDATION

Giving Contact

David Wolverton, President
807 8th Street
City National Building, Suite 1010
Wichita Falls, TX 76301
Phone: (940)723-8720
Fax: (940)723-8656
E-mail: info@priddyfdn.org
Web: http://www.priddyfdn.org

Description

Founded: 1963
EIN: 756029882
Organization Type: Private Foundation
Giving Locations: OK: Southern OK; TX: Northern Texas, Wichita Falls
Grant Types: Capital, Emergency, General Support, Matching, Multiyear/Continuing Support, Project.

Donor Information

Founder: Established in 1963 by the late Ashley H. Priddy , Robert T. Priddy, the late Swannanoa H. Priddy , and the late Walter M. Priddy .

Financial Summary

Total Giving: $3,600,000 (2002); $3,300,000 (2001 approx); $3,100,000 (2000)
Assets: $80,000,000 (2002); $75,000,000 (2001); $60,000,000 (2000 approx)
Gifts Received: $9,000,000 (2001); $10,478,443 (1999); $18,741,041 (1997). Note: In fiscal 1997 and 1999, contributions were received from Mr. and Mrs. Robert Priddy.

Typical Recipients

Arts & Humanities: Arts Centers, Ballet, Community Arts, Film & Video, Historic Preservation, Libraries, Museums/Galleries, Music, Performing Arts, Public Broadcasting
Civic & Public Affairs: Community Foundations, Economic Development, Employment/Job Training, Housing, Urban & Community Affairs
Education: Education Reform, Leadership Training, Medical Education, Private Education (Precollege), Student Aid
Environment: Environment-General
Health: Alzheimers Disease, Clinics/Medical Centers, Emergency/Ambulance Services, Health Organizations, Hospices, Hospitals, Medical Rehabilitation, Mental Health, Prenatal Health Issues
International: International Relations
Religion: Churches, Ministries, Religious Welfare, Religious Welfare
Social Services: At-Risk Youth, Big Brother/Big Sister, Child Welfare, Community Centers, Community Service Organizations, Counseling, Crime Prevention, Emergency Relief, Family Services, Food/Clothing Distribution, People with Disabilities, Scouts, Senior Services, Shelters/Homelessness, United Funds/United Ways, Volunteer Services, YMCA/YWCA/YMHA/YWHA, Youth Organizations

Application Procedures

Initial Contact: Request application from foundation.
Application Requirements: If a project is approved for consideration, a more detailed application is required. Include proof of tax-exempt status as defined under 501 (c)(3) of the IRS code. The applicant must be considered "not a private foundation" within the meaning of Section 509 (a) of the code. In most cases a site visit and application review session will be scheduled.
Deadlines: February 15 and August 15, for preliminary applications and March 15 and September 15 for grant applications.
Review Process: The board of the foundation meets in May and November, applicants will be notified by mail immediately following the board meeting.

Restrictions

Does not support individuals. The foundation does not normally fund annual operating budget on an ongoing basis, research, endowments, lobbying activities, individual scholarship, or specific church denominations or their projects (with exception of the first Presbyterian Church of Wichita Falls and other Presbyterian sponsored organizations).

Additional Information

Publications: Program Policy Statement; Application Form; Guidelines; annual report

Foundation Officials

Rick Boone: trustee
John Celoni: trustee
Bill Daniels: trustee
Phyllis Hiraki: trustee
Berneice R. Leath: secretary, treasurer
Nancy Marks: trustee
Jimmy Oakley: trustee
Betsy Priddy: adv director
Randy Priddy: adv director
Robert T. Priddy: trustee emeritus
Ruby N. Priddy: advisory trustee
Gale Richardson: trustee
Jesse Rogers: trustee
Beverly Williamson: trustee
David Wolverton: president PRIM NONPR EMPL United Regional Health Care System.

Grants Analysis

Disclosure Period: calendar year ending 2001
Total Grants: $3,321,000*
Number of Grants: 89
Average Grant: $32,312*
Highest Grant: $500,000
Lowest Grant: $3,000
Typical Range: $10,000 to $50,000
*Note: Grants analysis provided by foundation. Average grant figure exludes highest grant.

Recent Grants

Note: Grants derived from 2000 Form 990.

General

1,700,000	Communities Foundation of Texas, Dallas, TX -- for operating budget
50,000	Midwestern State University, Wichita Falls, TX -- for high school center scholarships
50,000	North Central Texas Community Health Care Center, Inc., Wichita Falls, TX -- for community clinic
35,000	Schreiner College, Kerrville, TX -- for learning support program
35,000	Wichita Falls Faith Mission, Inc., Wichita Falls, TX -- for operating budget
30,000	Trinity Works, Dallas, TX -- for family stabilization program
29,600	Wichita Falls Faith Mission, Inc., Wichita Falls, TX -- to refurbish building
25,000	Family Place, The, Dallas, TX -- for safe place
25,000	Foundation for Community Empowerment Vision Regeneration, Inc., Dallas, TX -- to renovate 275 units
20,500	Habitat for Humanity, Wichita Falls, TX -- to purchase pickup, trailer and tools

PRINCIPAL FINANCIAL GROUP

Company Headquarters

Des Moines, IA
Web: http://www.principal.com

Company Description

Founded: 1879
Ticker: PFG
Exchange: NYSE
Assets: US$89.9 billion (2002)
Profit: US$142.3 million (2002)
Employees: 17138 (2002)
Fortune Rank: 210, per FORTUNE Magazine's list of 500 Largest U.S. Corporations (2002).

SIC(s): 6159 Miscellaneous Business Credit Institutions, 6282 Investment Advice, 6311 Life Insurance, 6321 Accident & Health Insurance.

Operating Locations

Principal Financial Group (IA--Des Moines, Mason City, Waterloo; NE--Grand Island)
Note: Principal Financial Group and subsidiaries operate throughout the USA.

Nonmonetary Support

Type: Donated Equipment
Contact: Steve Thilges, Community Relations Associate
Note: Nonmonetary support is provided by the company to local OrganizationS only. Support in 1997 was valued at $710,145.

Principal Financial Group Foundation, Inc.

Giving Contact

Michele Walstrom, Contributions Consultant
711 High Street
Des Moines, IA 50392-0001
Phone: (515)247-5091
Fax: (515)246-5475
Web: http://www.principal.com/about/giving/index.htm

Alternate Contact

Lori Hess

Description

Founded: 1987
EIN: 421312301
Organization Type: Corporate Foundation
Giving Locations: IA: Des Moines occasional nationally and internationally; operating locations.
Grant Types: Capital, Employee Matching Gifts, General Support, Project.
Note: Employee matching gift ratio: 1 to 1 to higher education and United Way.

Financial Summary

Total Giving: $4,419,654 (2000); $4,350,045 (1999); $3,910,946 (1998). Note: Contributes through corporate direct giving program and foundation.
Giving Analysis: Giving for 2000 includes: foundation matching gifts ($155,254); foundation ($4,264,400); 1999: foundation matching gifts ($607,107); foundation grants to United Way ($968,197); foundation ($2,774,741); 1998: foundation matching gifts ($612,909); foundation grants to United Way ($894,396) foundation ($3,910,946)
Assets: $80,292,635 (2000); $83,101,216 (1999); $92,061,555 (1998)
Gifts Received: $70,000,030 (1998); $9,999,963 (1997)

Typical Recipients

Arts & Humanities: Arts Centers, Ballet, Community Arts, Dance, Arts & Humanities-General, History & Archaeology, Libraries, Museums/Galleries, Music, Opera, Performing Arts, Public Broadcasting, Theater
Civic & Public Affairs: Botanical Gardens/Parks, Business/Free Enterprise, Civil Rights, Community Foundations, Economic Development, Employment/Job Training, Housing, Parades/Festivals, Urban & Community Affairs, Women's Affairs, Zoos/Aquariums
Education: Agricultural Education, Business Education, Business-School Partnerships, Colleges & Universities, Community & Junior Colleges, Education Funds, Elementary Education (Public), Faculty Development, Education-General, International Studies, International Studies, Literacy, Minority Education, Preschool Education, Private Education (Precollege),

Public Education (Precollege), Science/Mathematics Education, Student Aid

Environment: Environment-General, Wildlife Protection

Health: AIDS/HIV, Alzheimers Disease, Cancer, Children's Health/Hospitals, Emergency/Ambulance Services, Health-General, Health Policy/Cost Containment, Health Organizations, Hospices, Medical Research, Mental Health, Respiratory, Single-Disease Health Associations

International: International Affairs, International Peace & Security Issues, International Relations

Religion: Religious Welfare

Science: Scientific Centers & Institutes

Social Services: Animal Protection, At-Risk Youth, Big Brother/Big Sister, Child Welfare, Community Service Organizations, Day Care, Day Care, Family Planning, Family Services, Food/Clothing Distribution, People with Disabilities, Recreation & Athletics, Scouts, Senior Services, Shelters/Homelessness, Social Services-General, Substance Abuse, United Funds/United Ways, Veterans, Volunteer Services, YMCA/YWCA/YMHA/YWHA, Youth Organizations

Application Procedures

Initial Contact: Contact the foundation to receive a form to return with the proposal (or obtain from the foundation's web site), then submit proposal (include ten copies with the original).

Application Requirements: Cover letter outlining amount requested, purpose of funds sought, and anticipated budget; an itemized budget including current and anticipated funds, sources of income, contributions received to date, fundraising expenses, other expected expenses, most recently audited financial statement, and current IRS tax filing; background information on the organization including goals, geographic scope, number of paid employees and total salary expense, and amount of volunteer involvement; other corporations, government agencies or foundations being approached for funding; names and business affiliations of organization's officers and board of directors (including advisory boards or committees relevant to proposal) and frequency of scheduled board meetings; need for the funding and method of program/project evaluation; proof of tax-exempt status; and evaluation of any previous years' funding that has been received from the Foundation.

Deadlines: March 1 for Health & Human Services, June 1 for Education, September 1 for Arts and Culture, and December 1 for Recreation and Tourism.

Decision Notification: Review process generally takes six to ten weeks.

Notes: Original application must be sent along with nine copies for review. One copy of the audited financial statements and annual report need to be submitted with grant proposal.

Restrictions

Does not support athletic, fraternal, social or veterans' organizations; conference, seminar, or festival participation; individuals; endowments or memorials; political or lobbying groups; trade, industry, or professional organizations; sectarian, religious and denominational organizations; fellowships; individual K-12 schools; libraries; goodwill advertising; capital fund drives for hospitals or health care facilities; grantmaking bodies (except for United Way and independent college funds); private foundations; organizations whose activities are mostly international; tax-supported organizations; scholarships, fellowships, or internships through school; or operating expenses of programs receiving United Way support. whose activities are mostly international; social organizations tax-supported organizations; or operating expenses of programs receiving United Way support.

Additional Information

Grant renewals are not automatic, and the foundation expects an annual report from all grant recipients. The foundation was formerly known as the Principal Foundation.

Publications: Guidelines; Social Responsibility Report

Grants Analysis

Disclosure Period: calendar year ending 2000
Total Grants: $4,419,654*
Number of Grants: 675 (approx)
Average Grant: $6,548
Highest Grant: $300,000
Typical Range: $5,000 to $25,000
*Note: Giving includes matching gifts; United Way.

Recent Grants

Note: Grants derived from 2000 Form 990.

General

300,000	Hoyt Sherman Place Foundation, Des Moines, IA -- for Hoyt Sherman Place preservation and theater improvement project
287,500	National Museum of American Art, Washington, DC -- for Treasures to Go
283,580	United Way Central Iowa, Des Moines, IA
244,048	United Way Central Iowa, Des Moines, IA
211,826	United Way of Central Iowa, Des Moines, IA
200,000	Drake University, Des Moines, IA -- for new campaign
200,000	Ft. Des Moines Black Officers Memorial, Inc., Des Moines, IA
186,564	United Way of Central Iowa, Des Moines, IA
83,333	Polk County Housing Trust Fund, Des Moines, IA -- for operating support
80,000	Iowa College Foundation, Des Moines, IA -- for scholarship support

PROCTER & GAMBLE COMPANY, COSMETICS DIVISION

Company Headquarters

Hunt Valley, MD
Web: http://www.pg.com

Company Description

Former Name: Noxell Corp.
SIC(s): 2844 Toilet Preparations.
Parent Company: Procter & Gamble Co., Cincinnati, OH, United States

Operating Locations

Procter & Gamble Co. Cosmetics Division (MD--Baltimore, Cockeysville)

Nonmonetary Support

Note: Employee matching gift ratio: 2 to 1.

Procter & Gamble Cosmetics Foundation

Giving Contact

Marian Lubbert, Administrator
11050 York Rd.
Hunt Valley, MD 21030
Phone: (410)785-7300
Fax: (410)316-8025

Description

Founded: 1951
EIN: 526041435
Organization Type: Corporate Foundation

Giving Locations: MD: Baltimore metropolitan area some support to nationally organizations with local chapters; NY: New York City.

Grant Types: Capital, Challenge, Employee Matching Gifts, Endowment, General Support, Research, Scholarship.

Donor Information

Founder: Noxell Corp.

Financial Summary

Total Giving: $284,279 (fiscal year ending June 30, 2001); $365,919 (fiscal 2000); $287,106 (fiscal 1999). Note: Contributes through foundation only.

Giving Analysis: Giving for fiscal 2001 includes: foundation grants to United Way ($8,500); foundation ($275,779); fiscal 2000: foundation ($365,919); fiscal 1999: foundation ($287,106);

Assets: $1,732,760 (fiscal 2001); $1,890,425 (fiscal 2000); $743,879 (fiscal 1999)

Gifts Received: $210,000 (fiscal 2000); $220,000 (fiscal 1999); $210,000 (fiscal 1998). Note: Contributions are received from Noxell Corp.

Typical Recipients

Arts & Humanities: Arts Centers, Arts Festivals, Arts Institutes, Dance, Historic Preservation, Libraries, Museums/Galleries, Music, Opera, Performing Arts, Public Broadcasting, Theater, Visual Arts

Civic & Public Affairs: African American Affairs, Business/Free Enterprise, Chambers of Commerce, Civil Rights, Clubs, Community Foundations, Economic Development, Economic Policy, Employment/Job Training, Civic & Public Affairs-General, Housing, Law & Justice, Municipalities/Towns, Nonprofit Management, Philanthropic Organizations, Professional & Trade Associations, Safety, Urban & Community Affairs, Women's Affairs, Zoos/Aquariums

Education: Arts/Humanities Education, Arts/Humanities Education, Business Education, Business-School Partnerships, Colleges & Universities, Community & Junior Colleges, Economic Education, Education Associations, Education Funds, Elementary Education (Public), Engineering/Technological Education, Education-General, Health & Physical Education, Literacy, Medical Education, Minority Education, Private Education (Precollege), Religious Education, Science/Mathematics Education, Secondary Education (Private), Secondary Education (Public), Student Aid

Environment: Environment-General

Health: AIDS/HIV, Cancer, Children's Health/Hospitals, Clinics/Medical Centers, Diabetes, Emergency/Ambulance Services, Health Organizations, Hospitals, Medical Rehabilitation, Mental Health, Nursing Services, Public Health, Respiratory, Single-Disease Health Associations

International: International Affairs, International Relations

Religion: Jewish Causes

Science: Science Museums, Scientific Centers & Institutes, Scientific Research

Social Services: At-Risk Youth, Child Welfare, Community Service Organizations, Crime Prevention, Domestic Violence, Family Services, Food/Clothing Distribution, People with Disabilities, Recreation & Athletics, Scouts, Senior Services, Shelters/Homelessness, Social Services-General, Substance Abuse, United Funds/United Ways, Volunteer Services, YMCA/YWCA/YMHA/YWHA, Youth Organizations

Application Procedures

Initial Contact: Send a brief letter of inquiry and a proposal.

Application Requirements: Include a description of organization, amount requested, purpose of funds sought, other contributors, two most recently audited financial statement, current budget, list of officers and directors, and proof of tax-exempt status.

Deadlines: None.

Review Process: The board meets semiannually, in May and November.

Restrictions

Does not support individuals or political or lobbying groups.

Foundation Officials

Marc S. Pritchard: president PRIM CORP EMPL general manager: Proctor & Gamble Co. Cosmetics & Fragrance Division. CORP AFFIL vice president: Procter & Gamble Co.

Grants Analysis

Disclosure Period: fiscal year ending June 30, 2001
Total Grants: $275,779*
Number of Grants: 83
Average Grant: $3,326
Highest Grant: $25,000
Lowest Grant: $25
Typical Range: $1,000 to $5,000
*Note: Giving excludes United Way.

Recent Grants

Note: Grants derived from fiscal 2001 Form 990.

General

25,000	Independent College Fund of Maryland, Baltimore, MD
23,500	Baltimore School for the Arts, Baltimore, MD
20,525	Center Stage, Baltimore, MD
15,333	Ruxton County School, Ruxton, MD
15,000	Baltimore Symphony Orchestra, Baltimore, MD
11,900	Junior Achievement of Central Maryland, Baltimore, MD
10,000	House of Ruth, Baltimore, MD
10,000	Kennedy Krieger Institute, Baltimore, MD
9,500	Lyric Foundation, Baltimore, MD
9,070	Maryland Public Television, Owings Mills, MD

MATTINA R. PROCTOR FOUNDATION

Giving Contact

Alvin S. Hochberg, Trustee
c/o Broude & Hochberg
75 Federal Street, Suite 1310
Boston, MA 02110-1904
Phone: (617)748-5100
Fax: (617)748-5100
E-mail: law@broude.com

Description

Founded: 1991
EIN: 111067014
Organization Type: Private Foundation
Giving Locations: ME; MA
Grant Types: General Support, Research.

Donor Information

Founder: Established in 1991 by Mattina R. Proctor.

Financial Summary

Total Giving: $331,000 (2002); $383,500 (2001); $364,500 (2000)
Assets: $4,946,537 (2002); $6,468,211 (2001); $7,956,471 (2000)
Gifts Received: $510,670 (2000); $1,514,792 (1998); $500,000 (1996). Note: In 1998, contributions were received from Mattina R. Proctor Revocable Trust.

Typical Recipients

Arts & Humanities: Arts & Humanities-General, Libraries, Music, Opera
Education: Colleges & Universities, Education-General, Health & Physical Education, Private Education (Precollege)
Health: AIDS/HIV, Cancer, Children's Health/Hospitals, Clinics/Medical Centers, Diabetes, Emergency/Ambulance Services, Eyes/Blindness, Health-General, Health Organizations, Heart, Hospitals, Medical Research, Nursing Services
International: International Affairs
Religion: Churches
Science: Science Museums
Social Services: Emergency Relief, Food/Clothing Distribution, Recreation & Athletics, Senior Services, Social Services-General

Application Procedures

Initial Contact: Send a brief letter of inquiry.
Application Requirements: Include a description of organization, purpose of funds sought, and proof of tax-exempt status.
Deadlines: None.

Foundation Officials

Alvin S. Hochberg: trustee
Mattina R. Proctor: trustee

Grants Analysis

Disclosure Period: calendar year ending 2002
Total Grants: $331,000
Number of Grants: 20
Average Grant: $7,579*
Highest Grant: $187,000
Lowest Grant: $1,500
Typical Range: $2,500 to $15,000
*Note: Average grant figure excludes highest grant.

Recent Grants

Note: Grants derived from 2001 Form 990.

General

60,000	Barbara Bush Children's Hospital Pediatric Lead Poison Screening Project, ME
50,000	Maine Health, ME -- telemedicine
50,000	MGH Pediatric Hematology/Oncology, Boston, MA
30,000	MGH Cancer Center, Boston, MA -- DNA sequencer
25,000	Boston Lyric Opera, Boston, MA
25,000	Joslin Diabetes Center, Boston, MA
25,000	MGH Cancer Center, Boston, MA
25,000	MGH Cancer Center, Boston, MA -- TB Project
20,000	University of New England, Biddeford, ME
17,000	Tatra Foundation -- recording of Shakespeare songs

MORTIMER R. PROCTOR TRUST

Giving Contact

c/o Chittenden Bank
PO Box 820
2 Burlington Sq.
Burlington, VT 05402
Phone: (802)658-4000

Description

Founded: 1978
EIN: 036020099
Organization Type: Private Foundation
Giving Locations: VT: Proctor
Grant Types: Emergency, Operating Expenses, Project.

Financial Summary

Total Giving: $210,084 (2000); $182,008 (1998); $129,550 (1996)
Assets: $4,330,326 (2000); $4,435,463 (1998); $2,882,339 (1997)
Gifts Received: $29 (1995); $48,337 (1994). Note: In 1995, contributions were received from Proctor Hospital Davis Trust Fund.

Typical Recipients

Arts & Humanities: Libraries, Music
Civic & Public Affairs: Civic & Public Affairs-General, Housing, Municipalities/Towns, Safety, Urban & Community Affairs
Education: Business Education, Elementary Education (Private), Elementary Education (Public), International Studies, Private Education (Precollege), Public Education (Precollege), Religious Education, Science/Mathematics Education, Secondary Education (Public)
Religion: Churches, Religious Organizations
Social Services: Child Welfare, Community Service Organizations, Crime Prevention, Emergency Relief, Food/Clothing Distribution, People with Disabilities, Recreation & Athletics, Scouts, Youth Organizations

Application Procedures

Initial Contact: The foundation requests applications be made in writing.
Deadlines: None.

Additional Information

Publications: Annual Report
Trust(s): Chittenden Bank

Grants Analysis

Disclosure Period: calendar year ending 2000
Total Grants: $210,084
Number of Grants: 12
Average Grant: $9,211*
Highest Grant: $108,758
Typical Range: $5,000 to $20,000
*Note: Average grant figure excludes highest grant.

Recent Grants

Note: Grants derived from 1999 Form 990.

General

127,201	Proctor School District -- purchases to cover various specific request
39,428	Town of Proctor, Proctor, VT -- support mapping, pool, skate rink
36,934	Proctor Free Library, Proctor, VT -- purchase books
11,500	St. Dominic Cemetery, Proctor, VT -- renovation of marble wall
11,000	Proctor High School Activity, Proctor, VT -- booster club specific request
10,130	Union Church of Proctor, Proctor, VT -- replace carillon bells
7,410	Proctor Volunteer Fire Department, Proctor, VT -- purchase fire fighter helmets and pagers
4,500	St. Paul Lutheran Church, Proctor, VT -- purchase new organ
2,500	Proctor High School Activity, Proctor, VT -- to cover project graduation
1,829	Proctor Boy Scout Troop, Proctor, VT -- purchase of tents and flag poles

PROGRESS ENERGY INC.

Company Headquarters

410 S. Wilmington St.
Raleigh, NC 27601-1748
Web: http://www.progress-energy.com

Company Description

Founded: 2000
Ticker: PGN
Exchange: NYSE
Former Name: Carolina Power & Light Co.;
Acquired: Florida Progress (2000); Florida Power Corp.;
Also Known As: Progress Energy Carolinas, Inc..
Assets: US$21.352 billion (2002)
Profit: US$528.4 million (2002)
Employees: 15300 (2002)
Fortune Rank: 228, per FORTUNE Magazine's list of 500 Largest U.S. Corporations (2002).
SIC(s): 4911 Electric Services.

Operating Locations

Carolina Power & Light Co. (DC--Washington); Carolina Power & Light Co. (SC; TN--Newport)

Nonmonetary Support

Value: $1,010,000 (2000 approx)
Type: Donated Equipment; In-kind Services

Progress Energy Foundation

Giving Contact

Tammy S. Brown, Manager, Corporate Community Relations
Progress Energy
Posee Statement 2
Raleigh, NC 27602-1551
Phone: (919)546-4112
Fax: (919)546-4338
Web: http://www.progress-energy.com/community/

Description

EIN: 561720636
Organization Type: Corporate Foundation
Former Name: CP&L Foundation.
Giving Locations: principally near operating locations and to national organizations.
Grant Types: Capital, Conference/Seminar, Department, Employee Matching Gifts, General Support, Matching, Project.

Financial Summary

Total Giving: $7,340,106 (2001); $9,396,015 (2000); $7,500,000 (1999). Note: Contributes through corporate direct giving program and foundation.
Giving Analysis: Giving for 1999 includes: domestic subsidiaries (approx $1,000,000); corporate direct giving (approx $1,500,000); foundation (approx $5,000,000); 1998: nonmonetary support ($1,000,000); foundation ($3,043,860) corporate direct giving (approx $3,956,140)
Assets: $8,593,262 (2001); $897,787 (2000); $4,895,503 (1998)
Gifts Received: $14,559,252 (2001); $4,500,000 (2000); $3,000,000 (1998). Note: In 2001, contributions were received from Progress Energy Co. ($9,900,000) and Florida Progress Foundation ($4,659,252).

Typical Recipients

Arts & Humanities: Arts Associations & Councils, Arts Centers, Ballet, Arts & Humanities-General, Historic Preservation, History & Archaeology, Libraries, Museums/Galleries, Music, Performing Arts, Public Broadcasting, Theater
Civic & Public Affairs: African American Affairs, Botanical Gardens/Parks, Business/Free Enterprise, Chambers of Commerce, Community Foundations, Economic Development, Civic & Public Affairs-General, Housing, Law & Justice, Municipalities/Towns, Nonprofit Management, Professional & Trade Associations, Urban & Community Affairs, Zoos/Aquariums

Education: Afterschool/Enrichment Programs, Agricultural Education, Business Education, Business-School Partnerships, Colleges & Universities, Community & Junior Colleges, Education Funds, Engineering/Technological Education, Faculty Development, Education-General, Minority Education, Private Education (Precollege), Public Education (Precollege), School Volunteerism, Science/Mathematics Education, Student Aid
Environment: Air/Water Quality, Environment-General
Health: Emergency/Ambulance Services, Health Organizations, Hospitals, Single-Disease Health Associations
Science: Science Museums
Social Services: At-Risk Youth, Child Abuse, Child Welfare, Community Service Organizations, Emergency Relief, Food/Clothing Distribution, Recreation & Athletics, United Funds/United Ways, YMCA/YWCA/YMHA/YWHA, Youth Organizations

Application Procedures

Initial Contact: Call or write for brochure.
Application Requirements: Complete applications will include a cover letter signed by the president, director, or equivalent official of the institution; proof of tax-exempt status; executive summary of planned activities; narrative section with clear a description of organization and overall strategy of proposed activities; budget for the proposed project; and additional institutional information and financial data.
Deadlines: February 1, May 1, August 1, and November 1.
Review Process: Foundation's board of directors meets in March, June, September, and December to consider and award grants. All applicants will be notified of decisions within 15 days of board meeting.
Notes: Grantees must submit written progress reports.

Restrictions

Does not support individuals, religious organizations for sectarian purposes, or goodwill advertising.

Additional Information

Progress Energy was formed in 2000 when CP&L Energy expanded into Florida and acquired Florida Progress.

Corporate Officials

William Cavanaugh, III: chairman, president, chief executive officer supply B New Orleans, LA 1939. ED Tulane University BSME (1961). PRIM CORP EMPL chairman, president, chief executive officer: Carolina Power & Light Co.
Glen Harden: executive vice president, chief financial officer B Falfurrias, TX 1951. ED Tulane University (1973); Tulane University (1975). PRIM CORP EMPL executive vice president, chief financial officer: Carolina Power & Light Co.
Robert B. McGehee: executive vice president, general counsel B Vicksburg, MS 1943. ED United States Naval Academy (1966); University of Texas JD (1973). PRIM CORP EMPL president chief operating officer: Progress Energy.
William Stanley Orser: executive vice president energy supply B New London, CT 1945. ED United States Naval Academy BS (1966); United States Naval Academy MS (1971). PRIM CORP EMPL group president: Progress Energy. NONPR AFFIL member: National Nuclear Accrediting board; member: Nuclear Energy Institute.

Giving Program Officials

Tammy Brown: manager community relations PRIM CORP EMPL manager corp. community relations: Carolina Power & Light Co.

Foundation Officials

Tammy Brown: secretary (see above)
William Cavanaugh, III: president (see above)
Fred N. Day, IV: vice president, director
Cecil L. Goodnight: vice president, director
H. William Habermeyer, Jr.: vice president, director
Glen Harden: treasurer (see above)
Robert B. McGehee: trustee (see above)
Mark Mulhern: assistant treasurer
Peter M. Scott, III: treasurer, director
Robert M. Williams: assistant secretary

Grants Analysis

Disclosure Period: calendar year ending 2001
Total Grants: $10,094,000*
Number of Grants: 1154
Average Grant: $8,747
Highest Grant: $418,000
Lowest Grant: $2,000
Typical Range: $5,000 to $25,000
*Note: Grants analysis provided by Foundation.

Recent Grants

Note: Grants derived from 2001 Form 990.

General

500,000	University of North Carolina at Chapel Hill, Chapel Hill, NC
418,040	Triangle United Way, Morrisville, NC
385,000	North Carolina Engineering Foundation, Inc., Raleigh, NC
300,000	Peace College of Raleigh, Raleigh, NC
250,000	American Red Cross
250,000	American Red Cross
250,000	Nature Conservancy, Arlington, VA
250,000	North Carolina Museum of Art, Raleigh, NC
250,000	North Carolina Museum of Art, Raleigh, NC
250,000	Performing Arts Center Foundation, Clearwater, FL

PROSPECT HILL FOUNDATION

Giving Contact

Constance Eiseman, Executive Director
99 Park Avenue, Suite 2220
New York, NY 10016-1601
Phone: (212)370-1165
Fax: (212)599-6282
E-mail: ashipley@prospecthill.org
Web: http://www.fdncenter.org/grantmaker/prospecthill

Description

Founded: 1960
EIN: 136075567
Organization Type: Family Foundation
Giving Locations: NY: nationally.
Grant Types: Capital, Challenge, Department, General Support, Matching, Project, Scholarship.
Note: The foundation operates an employee matching contributions program.

Donor Information

Founder: The Prospect Hill Foundation was established in 1960. William S. Beinecke, the foundation's donor and president, was chairman of Sperry & Hutchinson Company of New York City. In 1983, the foundation merged with the Frederick W. Beinecke Fund, which was established by his parents, Frederick and Carrie Sperry Beinecke.

Financial Summary

Total Giving: $3,549,000 (fiscal year ending June 30, 2002 approx); $4,193,283 (fiscal 2001); $2,473,242 (fiscal 1998)

Giving Analysis: Giving for fiscal 2001 includes: foundation matching gifts (approx $1,191,620) fiscal 1998: foundation matching gifts ($123,942)

Assets: $61,000,000 (fiscal 2002 approx); $72,215,204 (fiscal 2001); $67,104,930 (fiscal 1998)

Gifts Received: $6,082 (fiscal 1995). Note: Contributions are derived from trusts established by Carrie Sperry Beinecke, Frederick W. Beinecke, and William S. Beinecke. In 1989, the foundation changed its fiscal year from a calendar year to one ending June 30.

Typical Recipients

Arts & Humanities: Ballet, Dance, Historic Preservation, History & Archaeology, Libraries, Museums/Galleries, Music, Performing Arts, Theater

Civic & Public Affairs: Botanical Gardens/Parks, Clubs, Employment/Job Training, Civic & Public Affairs-General, Law & Justice, Native American Affairs, Public Policy, Urban & Community Affairs, Women's Affairs, Zoos/Aquariums

Education: Arts/Humanities Education, Colleges & Universities, Education Associations, Faculty Development, Leadership Training, Legal Education, Minority Education, Private Education (Precollege), Student Aid

Environment: Air/Water Quality, Forestry, Environment-General, Resource Conservation, Watershed, Wildlife Protection

Health: Emergency/Ambulance Services, Heart, Hospitals, Prenatal Health Issues

International: Foreign Educational Institutions, Health Care/Hospitals, International Environmental Issues, International Peace & Security Issues, International Relations, International Relief Efforts

Religion: Churches, Ministries, Religious Welfare

Science: Science Museums

Social Services: Community Service Organizations, Delinquency & Criminal Rehabilitation, Family Planning, Social Services-General, Youth Organizations

Application Procedures

Initial Contact: Thorough review of guidelines is strongly suggested prior to contacting foundation. Send two copies of a letter of application, which should be no longer than three pages.

Application Requirements: Letters should summarize the organization's history and goals; project for which funding is sought; contribution of the project to other work in the field or to the organization's own development; the organization's total budget and staff size; project budget; and a list of the organization's board of directors. If the foundation is interested in the proposal, more information will be requested.

Deadlines: None. Grant requests may be submitted anytime. The foundation's directors meet five times a year.

Review Process: All material is reviewed by the executive director and one or more board members. Response generally is provided within four weeks. Whenever possible, applicants will be visited by a representative of the foundation before it acts on a proposal.

Restrictions

Proposals from social services, arts, cultural, and educational institutions are accepted upon invitation only. The foundation does not consider grants for individuals, scholarly research, or sectarian religious activities. It favors project support over general support requests.

Additional Information

The foundation requires a final narrative and financial report from all grantees (Brochure should be requested before letter is submitted.)

Publications: Grants List; Guidelines

Foundation Officials

Robert Barletta: treasurer PRIM CORP EMPL treasurer, director: Antaeus Enterprises Inc.

Elizabeth G. Beinecke: vice president, director

Frederick William Beinecke: vice president, director B Stamford, CT 1943. ED Yale University BA (1966); University of Virginia JD (1972); Harvard University PMD (1977). PRIM CORP EMPL president, director: Antaeus Enterprises Inc.

John B. Beinecke: vice president, director PRIM CORP EMPL vice president, secretary, director: Antaeus Enterprises Inc. NONPR AFFIL director: National Audubon Society.

William Sperry Beinecke: president, director B New York, NY May 22, 1914. ED Yale University BA (1936); Columbia University LLB (1940). PRIM CORP EMPL co-founder: Casey Beinecke & Chase. CORP AFFIL director: Antaeus Enterprises Inc. NONPR AFFIL chairman emeritus: Hudson River Foundation Science & Environmental Research; honorary trustee: Pingry School; life trustee: Central Park Conservancy; member: Council Foreign Relations; honorary trustee: American Museum Natural History. CLUB AFFIL member: Yale Club; member: Ocean Club; member: Sky Club; member: Gulf Stream Golf Club; member: Little Club; member: Bohemian Club; member: Eastward Ho Country Club; member: Baltusrol Golf Club.

Constance Eiseman: executive director, secretary

Frances Beinecke Elston: director

Nettie Foskett: admin

Sarah Beinecke Richardson: director

Grants Analysis

Disclosure Period: fiscal year ending June 30, 2001

Total Grants: $4,001,663*

Number of Grants: 127

Average Grant: $27,791*

Highest Grant: $500,000

Typical Range: $10,000 to $50,000

*Note: Giving excludes matching gifts. Average grant figure excludes highest grant.

Recent Grants

Note: Grants derived from fiscal 1999 Form 990.

Library-Related

50,000	New Jersey Historical Society, Newark, NJ -- toward construction of a new library
25,000	New York Public Library, New York, NY -- toward the conservation treatment laboratory

General

1,000,000	Yale University, New Haven, CT -- to establish a professorship at the Yale School of Management
250,000	Phillips Academy, Andover, MA -- to endow a Frederick W. Beinecke Teaching Foundation
125,000	Columbia University in the City of New York, New York, NY -- for the observatory on Kitt Peak
100,000	Columbia University School of Law, New York, NY -- for the law school capital campaign
100,000	Columbia University School of Law, New York, NY -- for the law school capital campaign
100,000	Wildlife Conservation Society, Bronx, NY -- to support the Society's Geographic Information and Analysis Program
75,000	Save the Bay, Providence, RI -- for capital campaign
50,000	Adirondack Historical Association, New York, NY -- capital campaign
50,000	American Museum of Natural History, New York, NY -- last of five payments, for capital campaign
50,000	Aspetuck Land Trust, Westport, CT -- toward acquisition of Trout Brook Valley

OLIVE HIGGINS PROUTY FOUNDATION

Giving Contact

Stephen A. Bergquist, Vice President
c/o State Street Bank & Trust Co.
PO Box 351, MA-010
Boston, MA 02101
Phone: (617)664-4172

Description

Founded: 1952

EIN: 046046475

Organization Type: Private Foundation

Giving Locations: MA: Worcester Eastern part of the state, Worcester

Grant Types: General Support, Operating Expenses.

Donor Information

Founder: Olive Higgins Prouty

Financial Summary

Total Giving: $273,000 (2001); $243,000 (2000); $180,000 (1999 approx)

Assets: $4,627,119 (2001); $5,205,753 (2000); $5,488,853 (1999)

Typical Recipients

Arts & Humanities: Arts Centers, History & Archaeology, Libraries, Museums/Galleries, Music, Performing Arts, Public Broadcasting

Civic & Public Affairs: Community Foundations, Civic & Public Affairs-General, Legal Aid, Philanthropic Organizations, Public Policy, Safety, Urban & Community Affairs, Women's Affairs

Education: Agricultural Education, Colleges & Universities, Continuing Education, Education Associations, Engineering/Technological Education, Leadership Training, Minority Education, Private Education (Precollege), Secondary Education (Private)

Environment: Environment-General, Resource Conservation, Watershed

Health: Alzheimers Disease, Children's Health/Hospitals, Clinics/Medical Centers, Diabetes, Health Organizations, Hospices, Hospitals, Hospitals, Medical Research, Public Health, Single-Disease Health Associations

International: International Peace & Security Issues, International Relief Efforts

Science: Scientific Research

Social Services: Community Service Organizations, Domestic Violence, Family Planning, Family Services, Sexual Abuse, Youth Organizations

Application Procedures

Initial Contact: Send a brief letter of inquiry.

Deadlines: September 30.

Additional Information

Publications: Application Guidelines

Foundation Officials

Thomas P. Jalkut: trustee

Hillary Prouty: trustee

Lewis I. Prouty: president

Richard Prouty: trustee

William Mason Smith, III: treasurer

Grants Analysis

Disclosure Period: calendar year ending 2001

Total Grants: $273,000

Number of Grants: 43

Average Grant: $5,167*

Highest Grant: $56,000

Lowest Grant: $1,000

Typical Range: $2,000 to $7,000

*Note: Average grant figure excludes highest grant.

Recent Grants

Note: Grants derived from 2000 Form 990.

General

50,000	Children's Medical Center, Boston, MA
13,000	Austen Riggs Center, Stockbridge, MA
10,000	Southern Poverty Law Center, Montgomery, AL
8,000	Cambridge Center for Adult Education, Cambridge, MA
8,000	Morristown Memorial Hospital, Morristown, NJ
7,000	Mattapoisett Land Trust, Inc., Mattapoisett, MA
7,000	National Audubon Society, New York, NY
7,000	Tewksbury Land Trust, Chester, NJ
7,000	Upper Raritan Watershed Association, Gladstone, NJ
7,000	World Wildlife Fund, Washington, DC

PROVIDENCE GAS CO.

Company Headquarters

Providence, RI

Company Description

Employees: 539
SIC(s): 4900 Electric, Gas & Sanitary Services.
Parent Company: Providence Energy Corp., 14860 Montfort Dr., Dallas, TX, United States

Operating Locations

Providence Gas Co. (MA--North Attleboro; RI--Providence)

Nonmonetary Support

Type: Donated Equipment; In-kind Services; Loaned Executives; Workplace Solicitation

Giving Contact

Helen Toohey, Director, Community Relations
100 Weybosset St.
Providence, RI 02903
Phone: (401)272-5040
Fax: (401)273-4243

Description

Organization Type: Corporate Giving Program
Grant Types: Capital, Employee Matching Gifts, General Support, Operating Expenses.

Typical Recipients

Arts & Humanities: Arts Appreciation, Arts Associations & Councils, Arts Festivals, Arts & Humanities-General, Libraries, Museums/Galleries, Music, Opera, Performing Arts, Visual Arts
Civic & Public Affairs: Civil Rights, Economic Development, Civic & Public Affairs-General, Housing, Urban & Community Affairs
Education: Colleges & Universities, Community & Junior Colleges, Economic Education, Education-General, Health & Physical Education, Private Education (Precollege), Public Education (Precollege), Science/Mathematics Education
Environment: Environment-General
Health: Health-General
Social Services: Community Service Organizations, Food/Clothing Distribution, Shelters/Homelessness, Social Services-General, Substance Abuse, United Funds/United Ways, Youth Organizations

Application Procedures

Initial Contact: Send letter of inquiry including a description of organization, amount requested, purpose of funds sought, and proof of tax-exempt status.

Corporate Officials

James H. Dodge: chairman, chief executive officer, president, director B Toledo, OH 1940. ED University of Michigan (1962); University of Michigan (1963). PRIM CORP EMPL chairman, chief executive officer, president, director: Providence Energy Corp.
Gary S. Gillheeney: chief financial officer B Providence, RI 1955. ED American International College (1978); Bryant College (1983). PRIM CORP EMPL chief financial officer: Providence Gas Co. CORP AFFIL treasurer: North Attelboro Gas Co.; treasurer: Providence Energy Corp.; treasurer: Newport America.

PROVIDENCE JOURNAL-BULLETIN CO.

Company Headquarters

75 Fountain St.
Providence, RI 02902
Web: http://www.projo.com

Company Description

SIC(s): 2711 Newspapers, 4833 Television Broadcasting Stations, 4841 Cable & Other Pay Television Services.
Parent Company: Belo Corp., 400 S. Record Street, Dallas, TX, United States

Operating Locations

Providence Journal-Bulletin Co. (MA; RI--Providence)

Nonmonetary Support

Type: Cause-related Marketing & Promotion; Donated Equipment; Donated Products; In-kind Services; Loaned Employees; Loaned Executives; Workplace Solicitation
Note: Annual nonmonetary support is approximately $10,000.

Providence Journal Charitable Foundation

Giving Contact

Mary Ellen Ahern, Community Services and Gift Committee Director
75 Fountain Street
Providence, RI 02902-9985
Phone: (401)277-7597
Fax: (401)277-7529
E-mail: mary_ellen_ahern@projo.com

Alternate Contact

Sandra Radcliffe, Trustee
Providence Journal Charitable Foundation
Phone: (401)277-7291

Description

EIN: 056015372
Organization Type: Corporate Foundation
Giving Locations: RI
Grant Types: Capital, Endowment, General Support, Matching, Multiyear/Continuing Support, Operating Expenses, Project, Research, Scholarship, Seed Money.

Financial Summary

Total Giving: $1,452,067 (2001); $1,515,567 (2000); $1,000,000 (1999 approx). Note: Contributes through foundation only.
Giving Analysis: Giving for 2000 includes: foundation grants to United Way ($70,000) foundation ($1,320,567)
Assets: $15,413,724 (2001); $17,296,020 (2000); $17,627,204 (1998)
Gifts Received: $350,123 (1994); $3,515,353 (1992)

Typical Recipients

Arts & Humanities: Arts Appreciation, Arts Associations & Councils, Arts Centers, Ballet, Arts & Humanities-General, Historic Preservation, History & Archaeology, Libraries, Museums/Galleries, Music, Performing Arts, Public Broadcasting, Theater
Civic & Public Affairs: African American Affairs, Business/Free Enterprise, Chambers of Commerce, Community Foundations, Economic Development, Civic & Public Affairs-General, Hispanic Affairs, Housing, Legal Aid, Minority Business, Municipalities/Towns, Parades/Festivals, Professional & Trade Associations, Urban & Community Affairs, Women's Affairs, Zoos/Aquariums
Education: Arts/Humanities Education, Business Education, Colleges & Universities, Education Funds, Education-General, Literacy, Private Education (Precollege), Public Education (Precollege), Secondary Education (Private), Secondary Education (Public), Special Education, Student Aid
Environment: Environment-General, Resource Conservation, Watershed
Health: Adolescent Health Issues, AIDS/HIV, Cancer, Emergency/Ambulance Services, Geriatric Health, Health Organizations, Hospices, Hospitals, Long-Term Care, Medical Rehabilitation, Mental Health, Nursing Services, Research/Studies Institutes, Single-Disease Health Associations
International: Health Care/Hospitals, International Affairs
Religion: Churches, Religious Welfare
Social Services: Child Welfare, Community Centers, Community Service Organizations, Family Planning, Food/Clothing Distribution, People with Disabilities, Recreation & Athletics, Scouts, Senior Services, Sexual Abuse, Shelters/Homelessness, Social Services-General, Substance Abuse, United Funds/United Ways, Volunteer Services, Youth Organizations

Application Procedures

Initial Contact: Submit a written proposal.
Application Requirements: Include a description of organization; project description; amount requested; purpose of funds sought; other sources of funding, and other companies approached; a copy of IRS 501 (c)(3); recent financial statements; list of board of directors.
Deadlines: None; requests are accepted on a monthly basis.

Foundation Officials

Sandra Radcliffe: trustee
Mark Ryan: trustee
Henry D. Sharpe, Jr.: trustee
Howard Sutton: president, chief executive officer B Irvington, NJ 1950. ED University of Notre Dame (1972); Providence College (1978). PRIM CORP EMPL president, general manager, assistant publisher: The Providence Journal. CORP AFFIL president: Rhode Island Monthly Communication.
John W. Wall: trustee

Grants Analysis

Disclosure Period: calendar year ending 2001
Total Grants: $1,382,067*
Number of Grants: 72
Average Grant: $16,172*
Highest Grant: $125,000
Lowest Grant: $1,500
Typical Range: $5,000 to $25,000
*Note: Giving excludes United Way. Average grant figure excludes two highest grants totaling $250,000.

Recent Grants

Note: Grants derived from 2001 Form 990.

Library-Related

6,667	Providence Athenaeum, Providence, RI

General

125,000	Traveler's Aid Society of Rhode Island, Providence, RI

125,000	WRNI Foundation, Providence, RI
60,000	Nature Conservancy
55,000	Greater Providence Chamber Foundation, Providence, RI -- Commerce Center
50,000	Lifespan, Rochester, NY
50,000	Rhode Island Historical Society, Providence, RI
50,000	Save the Bay, Providence, RI
50,000	Trinity Repertory Company, Providence, RI
50,000	United Way of Southeastern New England, Providence, RI
50,000	University of Rhode Island Foundation, Providence, RI

PROVIDENT COMMUNITY FOUNDATION

Giving Contact

Julie Ganong, The Provident Bank
5 Market Street
Amesbury, MA 01913-2408
Phone: (978)388-0050
E-mail: jganong@theprovidentbank.com
Web: http://www.theprovidentbank.com/commfound.cfm

Description

Founded: 1997
EIN: 043397455
Organization Type: Private Foundation
Grant Types: General Support.

Financial Summary

Total Giving: $355,961 (2001); $94,268 (2000); $102,499 (1999)
Assets: $3,037,429 (2001); $2,141,835 (2000); $2,044,230 (1999)
Gifts Received: $2,151,118 (1997)

Typical Recipients

Arts & Humanities: Libraries, Museums/Galleries
Civic & Public Affairs: Ethnic Organizations, Civic & Public Affairs-General, Safety
Education: Education-General, Public Education (Precollege)
Environment: Watershed
Social Services: Community Service Organizations, Counseling, Social Services-General, YMCA/YWCA/YMHA/YWHA, Youth Organizations

Application Procedures

Initial Contact: Send a brief letter of inquiry.
Deadlines: First Tuesday in March, June, September and December.

Foundation Officials

Robert A. Becker: president
Francis J. Blood: director
John J. Cameron: director
Joseph E. Deschenes: treasurer
Robert W. Fraser: director
Robert A. Gonthier, Jr.: director
Jay E. Gould: director
Lawrence C. Hoyt, Jr.: director
Donald E. Lawliss: director
Laurie Napp: director
Richard L. Peeke: director
Raymond E. Pouliot: director
Lorraine Sanborn: director
Wayne S. Tatro: director

Grants Analysis

Disclosure Period: calendar year ending 2001
Total Grants: $355,961
Number of Grants: 36
Average Grant: $3,985*

Highest Grant: $216,487
Lowest Grant: $268
Typical Range: $1,000 to $5,000
***Note:** Average grant figure excludes highest grant.

Recent Grants

Note: Grants derived from 2000 Form 990.

Library-Related

2,248	Friends of the Amesbury Library

General

15,000	Alliance Charitable Foundation
10,000	Amesbury Carrigae Museum
10,000	Amesbury Summer Youth Program
5,000	Women's Crisis Center, New York, NY
4,000	Imagine Studios
4,000	Northeast Family YMCA, Haverhill, MA
4,000	Our Neighbor's Table
3,900	Coastal 1st Time Homebuyer Program
3,389	Our Neighbor's Table
3,333	Harbor Schools, Newbury, MA

PRUDENTIAL INSURANCE CO. OF AMERICA

Company Headquarters

751 Broad Street
Newark, NJ 07102-3777
Phone: (973)802-6000
Fax: (973)367-6476
Web: http://www.prudential.com

Company Description

Ticker: PRU
Exchange: OTC
Employees: 92,966
SIC(s): 6311 Life Insurance, 6321 Accident & Health Insurance, 6331 Fire, Marine & Casualty Insurance.

Operating Locations

Prudential Insurance Co. of America (AZ--Phoenix, Scottsdale; AR--Little Rock; CA--Fresno, Los Angeles, Pleasanton, Sacramento, Sunnyvale, Westlake Village, Woodland Hills; DC; FL--Deerfield Beach, Fort Lauderdale, Jacksonville, Maitland, Orlando; GA--Atlanta; IL--Chicago, Des Plaines, Downers Grove; LA--Monroe, New Orleans; MA--Boston; MI--Southfield; MS--Greenville; MO--Creve Coeur; NE--Kearney; NJ--Chatham, Holmdel, Iselin, Newark, Pleasantville; NY--New York; NC--Charlotte; OH--Cincinnati, Columbus; OK--Oklahoma City, Tulsa; PA--Fort Washington, Horsham; TN--Memphis, Nashville; TX--Austin, Bellaire, Houston, San Antonio; VA--Richmond; WA--Tri-Cities)

Nonmonetary Support

Type: Donated Equipment; In-kind Services; Loaned Employees; Loaned Executives
Volunteer Programs: Company supports Prudential CARES (Community, Action Renewal Efforts) which provides individual and team building volunteer programs for Prudential employees and retirees at local nonprofits. Also supports Global Volunteer Day.
Contact: Emma Perry, Community Relations Consultant
Note: 1997 employee volunteer hours totaled 76,011. 1997 nonmonetary support: $250,000.

Prudential Foundation

Giving Contact

Lata Reddy, Secretary
213 Washington Street
Newark, NJ 07102
Phone: (973)802-3780
Fax: (973)802-3345

E-mail: community.resources@prudential.com
Web: http://www.prudential.com/community

Description

EIN: 222175290
Organization Type: Corporate Foundation
Giving Locations: AZ: Phoenix; CA: Los Angeles; FL: Jacksonville; GA: Atlanta; MN: Minneapolis; NJ: particularly Newark; PA: Philadelphia; TX: Houston headquarters and operating communities; nationally.
Grant Types: Employee Matching Gifts, Fellowship, General Support, Multiyear/Continuing Support, Scholarship.
Note: Employee matching gift ratio: 2 to 1 for the first $100 donated; 1 to 1 for donations of $101 to $5,000. Contact for matching gift information: (800) 554-5846.

Financial Summary

Total Giving: $37,518,379 (2001); $25,045,110 (1999); $21,770,100 (1998 approx). Note: Contributes through corporate direct giving program and foundation.
Giving Analysis: Giving for 1997 includes: foundation matching gifts ($2,089,072); foundation grants to United Way ($3,372,368); corporate direct giving ($6,512,646) foundation ($13,000,446)
Assets: $101,178,198 (2001); $141,243,734 (1999); $129,631,000 (1996)
Gifts Received: $2,474 (2001)

Typical Recipients

Arts & Humanities: Arts Associations & Councils, Arts Centers, Arts Funds, Arts Institutes, Community Arts, Historic Preservation, History & Archaeology, Libraries, Museums/Galleries, Music, Opera, Performing Arts, Public Broadcasting
Civic & Public Affairs: African American Affairs, Botanical Gardens/Parks, Business/Free Enterprise, Civil Rights, Community Foundations, Economic Development, Economic Policy, Employment/Job Training, Civic & Public Affairs-General, Hispanic Affairs, Housing, Law & Justice, Legal Aid, Municipalities/Towns, Nonprofit Management, Professional & Trade Associations, Public Policy, Safety, Urban & Community Affairs, Women's Affairs
Education: Afterschool/Enrichment Programs, Arts/Humanities Education, Business Education, Colleges & Universities, Community & Junior Colleges, Continuing Education, Economic Education, Education Associations, Education Funds, Education Reform, Elementary Education (Private), Elementary Education (Public), Engineering/Technological Education, Faculty Development, Education-General, Health & Physical Education, Journalism/Media Education, Leadership Training, Legal Education, Literacy, Medical Education, Minority Education, Preschool Education, Private Education (Precollege), Public Education (Precollege), Religious Education, School Volunteerism, Science/Mathematics Education, Secondary Education (Private), Social Sciences Education, Special Education, Student Aid, Vocational & Technical Education
Environment: Environment-General
Health: AIDS/HIV, Children's Health/Hospitals, Clinics/Medical Centers, Emergency/Ambulance Services, Geriatric Health, Health Policy/Cost Containment, Health Organizations, Hospitals, Medical Rehabilitation, Medical Training, Mental Health, Public Health, Research/Studies Institutes
International: Human Rights, International Relations
Religion: Religious Welfare
Social Services: At-Risk Youth, Child Abuse, Child Welfare, Community Centers, Community Service Organizations, Counseling, Crime Prevention, Day Care, Delinquency & Criminal Rehabilitation, Emergency Relief, Family Planning, Family Services, Food/Clothing Distribution, Homes, People with Disabilities, Recreation & Athletics, Scouts, Senior Services, Shelters/Homelessness, Substance Abuse, United Funds/United Ways, Veterans, Volunteer Services, Youth Organizations

Application Procedures

Initial Contact: Download an application form from foundation website, or use the New York Area Common Application Form.

Application Requirements: Include 3-page concept paper (optional); completed application form; proof of tax-exempt status; latest audited financial statement; itemized budget of project; breakdown of current funding sources, including the amount received from each source; and names and qualifications of those conducting the project.

Deadlines: None.

Review Process: Proposals reviewed continuously.

Evaluative Criteria: Emphasizes direct-service, rather than policy-oriented grants. Evaluates organization's ability to direct project; identify specific and measurable short- and long-term objectives; demonstrate that approach is the most effective; develop a complete and realistic budget; ability to continue program after funding ceases; and evaluate outcome of project.

Decision Notification: For grants up to $200,000: decisions made within 30 days of receipt of application; for grants over $200,000: decisions made by Board of Trustees in April, August, and December.

Notes: Foundation requests that no faxed applications or videotapes be sent. Do not phone for application status.

Restrictions

Grants are not made to veterans, labor, religious, political, fraternal, or athletic groups, except when program benefits or provides services to the community at large; individuals; organizations that do not have 501(c)(3) status; general operating support for single-disease health organizations, except local AIDS groups; goodwill advertising; or fundraising events.

Foundation generally does not fund capital campaigns, annual fund drives, or endowments.

Additional Information

Every three years foundation staff examines public and nonprofit environments, in order to direct foundation grant-making procedures, and reviews and revises foundation's strategic plan accordingly.

Publications: Prudential Community Resources; Application Form; Guidelines

Corporate Officials

Arthur Frederick Ryan: chairman, chief executive officer B Brooklyn, NY 1942. ED Providence College BA (1963). PRIM CORP EMPL chairman, chief executive officer, president: The Prudential Insurance Co. of America. CORP AFFIL director, member policy & planning committee, chairman: Depository Trust Co. NONPR AFFIL vice chairman operations division, vice chairman government relations council: American Bankers Association; program manager: CHIPS Same Day Settlement New York Clearing House.

Giving Program Officials

Pindaros Roy Vagelos: trustee B Westfield, NJ 1929. ED University of Pennsylvania AB (1950); Columbia University MD (1954). CORP AFFIL director: Prudential Insurance Co. America; chairman, director: Regeneron Pharmaceuticals Inc.; director: Estee Lauder Companies Inc.; director: PepsiCo; director: Boeing Co. NONPR AFFIL director: New Jersey Center Performing Arts; trustee, chairman board: University Pennsylvania; member: Institute Medicine; member: National Academy Sciences; member: Business Roundtable; trustee: Danforth Foundation; member: American Philosophical Society; member: American Society Biological Chemists; member: American Academy of Arts & Sciences; member: American Chemical Society.

Foundation Officials

Martin A. Berkowitz: comptroller
C. Edward Chaplin: treasurer
Brian Cloonan: assistant comptroller
Robert C. Golden: trustee
Jean D. Hamilton: trustee
Jon F. Hanson: trustee PRIM CORP EMPL chairman: Hampshire Management Co. chairman: CORP AFFIL director: United Water New Jersey; director: United Water Resources Inc.; director: Orange & Rockland Utilities Inc.; director: Prudential Insurance Co. America; director: Consolidated Delivery Logistics; director: Neuman Health Services.
Constance J. Homer: trustee
John Kinghorn: assistant treasurer
Gabriella Morris: president
Anthony Piszel: comptroller
Mary Puryear: program officer culture & arts
Lata N. Reddy: vice president
Arthur Frederick Ryan: trustee (see above)
Dennis Sullivan: assistant comptroller
Stanley C. Van Ness: trustee

Grants Analysis

Disclosure Period: calendar year ending 2002
Total Grants: $24,991,501*
Number of Grants: 1323
Average Grant: $14,019*
Highest Grant: $3,000,000
Lowest Grant: $250
Typical Range: $250 to $50,000 and $100,000 to $350,000
*Note: Giving excludes matching gifts, scholarship, United Way and fellowships. Average grant figure excludes four highest grants ($6,500,000).

Recent Grants

Note: Grants derived from 2001 Form 990.

General

3,000,000	American National Red Cross, Washington, DC -- for disaster fund
1,500,000	Boys and Girls Clubs of Newark, Newark, NJ -- for capital and endowment support
1,000,000	Liberty State Park Development Corporation, Roseland, NJ -- for capital campaign
1,000,000	New Community Corporation, Newark, NJ -- for capital support
666,000	Association for Enterprise Opportunity, Arlington, VA -- for the Prudential Young Entrepreneur Program
600,000	Newark Performing Arts Corporation, Newark, NJ -- for capital support
500,000	National Urban League, New York, NY -- for development of Opportunity Works
500,000	New Jersey Performing Arts Center, Newark, NJ -- for the Arts Education Program
500,000	North Ward Center, Newark, NJ -- for capital support
500,000	Sesame Workshop, New York, NY -- to develop Phase II of Sesame Street Beginnings Language to Literacy

PRUDENTIAL SECURITIES, INC.

Company Headquarters

199 Water Street
New York, NY 10292
Web: http://www.prufn.com

Company Description

Former Name: Prudential-Bache Securities.
Employees: 17,000
SIC(s): 6211 Security Brokers & Dealers.

Parent Company: Prudential Insurance Co. of America, 751 Broad Street, Newark, NJ, United States

Operating Locations

Prudential Securities Inc. (IL--Chicago; MA--Boston; NJ--Newark; NY--New York)

Nonmonetary Support

Type: In-kind Services

Prudential Securities Foundation

Giving Contact

Elizabeth A. Longley, Vice President
One New York Plaza
New York, NY 10292
Phone: (212)214-4884
Fax: (212)214-5541
E-mail: liz_longley@prusec.com

Description

EIN: 136193023
Organization Type: Corporate Foundation
Giving Locations: NY
Grant Types: Award, General Support.

Financial Summary

Total Giving: $950,000 (fiscal year ending January 31, 2003 approx); $883,325 (fiscal 2001); $882,175 (fiscal 2000). Note: Contributes through foundation only.

Giving Analysis: Giving for fiscal 2001 includes: foundation ($883,325); fiscal 2000: foundation scholarships ($39,255) foundation ($842,920)

Assets: $11,465 (fiscal 2001); $91,021 (fiscal 2000); $57,191 (fiscal 1996).

Gifts Received: $803,819 (fiscal 2001); $902,895 (fiscal 2000); $730,307 (fiscal 1996). Note: In fiscal 2001, contributions were received from Prudential Securities ($800,000) and other donors.

Typical Recipients

Arts & Humanities: Arts Associations & Councils, Ballet, Ethnic & Folk Arts, History & Archaeology, Libraries, Museums/Galleries, Music, Opera, Performing Arts, Public Broadcasting, Theater

Civic & Public Affairs: African American Affairs, Botanical Gardens/Parks, Business/Free Enterprise, Civil Rights, Economic Development, Employment/Job Training, Civic & Public Affairs-General, Housing, Law & Justice, Municipalities/Towns, Public Policy, Safety, Urban & Community Affairs, Women's Affairs, Zoos/Aquariums

Education: Arts/Humanities Education, Business Education, Colleges & Universities, Economic Education, Education Associations, Education Funds, Education-General, Literacy, Minority Education, Public Education (Precollege), School Volunteerism, Student Aid

Environment: Environment-General

Health: Arthritis, Children's Health/Hospitals, Emergency/Ambulance Services, Health Organizations, Heart, Hospitals, Medical Research, Mental Health, Outpatient Health Care, Single-Disease Health Associations, Transplant Networks/Donor Banks

International: International Peace & Security Issues, Missionary/Religious Activities

Religion: Churches, Jewish Causes, Religious Organizations, Religious Welfare, Synagogues/Temples

Social Services: Big Brother/Big Sister, Community Service Organizations, Crime Prevention, Food/Clothing Distribution, People with Disabilities, Scouts, Senior Services, Shelters/Homelessness, Substance Abuse, United Funds/United Ways, YMCA/YWCA/YMHA/YWHA, Youth Organizations

Application Procedures

Initial Contact: Send a written proposal.
Deadlines: None.

Restrictions

Limited to New York, with a focus on education.

Corporate Officials

Elizabeth A. Longley: 1st vice presidenteo PRIM CORP EMPL 1st vice president: Prudential Securities Inc.

Leland B. Paton: president capital marketings, director, member executive committee B Worcester, MA 1943. PRIM CORP EMPL president capital marketings, director, member executive committee: Prudential Securities Inc. CORP AFFIL director: Prudential Securities Group Inc. NONPR AFFIL member: Securities Industry Association; member: Securities Industry Institute; member: New York Stock Exchange Inc.; director: Riverdale Country School; member: American Marketing Association; director: Chicago Board Options Exchange; exchange officer: America Stock Exchange Inc. CLUB AFFIL Mid-Ocean Club; Long Cove Club; Bond Club; Harvard Club; Apawanis Club.

Hardwick Simmons: chairman, chief executive officer B Baltimore, MD 1940. ED Harvard University BA (1962); Harvard University MBA (1966). PRIM CORP EMPL chairman, chief executive officer: Prudential Securities Inc. CORP AFFIL president, chief executive officer, director: Prudential Securities Group Inc.; chief executive officer, director: Prudential Capital & Investment Services; president: First Financial Fund Inc. NONPR AFFIL director: Chicago Board Options Exchange. CLUB AFFIL Bond Club.

Foundation Officials

Elizabeth A. Longley: vice president corporate affairs (see above)

Grants Analysis

Disclosure Period: fiscal year ending January 31, 2001
Total Grants: $883,325*
Number of Grants: 51
Average Grant: $16,000*
Highest Grant: $100,000
Lowest Grant: $500
Typical Range: $1,000 to $15,000
***Note:** Grants analysis provided by foundation. Average grant figure excludes highest and lowest grants.

Recent Grants

Note: Grants derived from 2001 Form 990.

Library-Related
15,000   New York Public Library, New York, NY

General
100,000   New York City Ballet, New York, NY
50,000   National Academy Foundation, New York, NY
45,000   South Street Seaport Museum, New York, NY
40,000   American Museum of Natural History, New York, NY
35,000   New York City Partnership Foundation/Breakthrough for Learning, New York, NY -- dues
30,000   New Jersey Performing Arts Center, Newark, NJ
25,000   Lincoln Center Theater, New York, NY
25,000   National Council on Economic Education, New York, NY
25,000   New York City 2012, New York, NY
25,000   New York City Outward Bound Center, New York, NY

PUBLIC SERVICE ELECTRIC & GAS CO.

Company Headquarters
80 Park Plaza
Newark, NJ 07102
Web: http://www.pseg.com

Company Description
SIC(s): 4931 Electric & Other Services Combined.
Parent Company: Public Service Enterprise Group Inc., 80 Park Plaza, Newark, NJ, United States

Operating Locations
Public Service Electric & Gas Co. (NJ--Camden, Elizabeth, Jersey City, New Brunswick, Paramus, Paterson, Ridgewood, Trenton)

Nonmonetary Support
Type: Donated Equipment; In-kind Services
Volunteer Programs: Company supports Dollars for Doers and Recognizing Excellence programs.
Contact: Marion C. O'Neill, Manager, Corp. Contributions

Public Service Electric & Gas Foundation

Giving Contact
William J. Walsh, President
PSEG Foundation
80 Park Plaza, Mail Code T-10
Newark, NJ 07101
Phone: (973)430-5763
Fax: (973)297-1480
E-mail: william.walsh3@pseg.com
Web: http://www.pseg.com/community

Description
EIN: 223125880
Organization Type: Corporate Foundation
Former Name: Public Service Electric & Gas Foundation.
Giving Locations: nationally for education grants; primarily in service area.
Grant Types: Challenge, Employee Matching Gifts, General Support, Multiyear/Continuing Support, Project, Scholarship, Seed Money.

Financial Summary
Total Giving: $3,600,000 (2003 approx); $3,600,000 (2002); $1,333,700 (2001). Note: Contributes through corporate direct giving program and foundation.
Giving Analysis: Giving for 2001 includes: foundation ($1,333,700); corporate direct giving ($2,045,176); 1999: foundation scholarships ($500); foundation grants to United Way ($43,500); foundation ($606,200); 1998: corporate direct giving ($1,500,000) foundation ($1,500,000).
Assets: $6,400,000 (2002); $9,603,814 (2001); $10,798,139 (1999)
Gifts Received: $10,000,000 (1999)

Typical Recipients
Arts & Humanities: Arts Centers, Arts Funds, Historic Preservation, Libraries, Museums/Galleries, Performing Arts, Public Broadcasting, Theater
Civic & Public Affairs: African American Affairs, Community Foundations, Economic Development, Employment/Job Training, Housing, Law & Justice, Professional & Trade Associations, Public Policy, Safety, Urban & Community Affairs, Women's Affairs
Education: Business Education, Colleges & Universities, Community & Junior Colleges, Elementary Education (Private), Engineering/Technological Education, Minority Education, Private Education

(Precollege), Public Education (Precollege), Science/Mathematics Education
Environment: Environment-General
Health: Cancer, Emergency/Ambulance Services, Hospitals
Science: Science Exhibits & Fairs, Scientific Centers & Institutes, Scientific Centers & Institutes
Social Services: Child Welfare, Community Service Organizations, Counseling, Delinquency & Criminal Rehabilitation, Emergency Relief, Food/Clothing Distribution, People with Disabilities, Recreation & Athletics, Senior Services, Substance Abuse, United Funds/United Ways, Veterans, YMCA/YWCA/YMHA/YWHA, Youth Organizations

Application Procedures
Initial Contact: Send a full proposal.
Application Requirements: Include general statement indicating purpose or mission of organization; names and affiliations of officers and board members; purpose and objectives of program; total cost of program; proof of tax-exempt status; audited financial statements for the last fiscal year; other support sources that have been approached, and level of support; indication as to whether organization receives United Way funds.
Deadlines: None.
Notes: Requests for funding of local initiatives should be sent to the local PSE&G office. Organization with statewide or Newark-based programs should direct application to the foundation.

Restrictions
Does not support individuals; organizations that are not tax-exempt; organizations outside company's service territory; religious organizations; political causes, candidates, organizations, or campaigns; organizations which discriminate on the basis of race, sex, or religion; lobbying organizations; athletic, labor, or fraternal groups; organizations that address single health issues; or endowments.

Additional Information
Publications: Corporate Responsibility Report

Corporate Officials
E. James Ferland: chairman, president, chief executive officersibility B Boston, MA March 19, 1942. ED Harvard University; University of Maine BSME (1964); University of New Haven MBA (1979). PRIM CORP EMPL chairman, president, chief executive officer, director: Public Service Enterprise Group Inc. CORP AFFIL director: Public Service Resources Corp.; chairman, chief executive officer, director: Public Service Electric & Gas Co.; chairman, chief executive officer, director: PSEG Energy Technologies Inc.; director: PSEG Global Inc.; director: Hartford Steam Boiler Inspection & Insurance Co.; director: HSB Group Inc.; director: First Fidelity Bancorp; director: Foster Wheeler Corp.; chairman, chief executive officer: Enterprise Diversified Holdings Inc. NONPR AFFIL member: Edison Electric Institute; director: Nuclear Energy Institute; director: Association of Edison Illuminating Companies; director: Committee for Economic Development; member: American Gas Association.

Thomas M. O'Flynn: executive vice president, chief financial officer ED Northwestern University BA (1982); University of Chicago MBA (1986). PRIM CORP EMPL executive vice president, chief financial officer: Public Service Enterprise Group Inc.

William J. Walsh: director corporate responsibility PRIM CORP EMPL director corporate responsibility: Public Service Enterprise Group Inc.

Foundation Officials
Alfred C. Koeppe: senior vice president corporate services & external affairs ED Rutgers University BA; Seton Hall University JD. PRIM CORP EMPL president, chief executive officer: Bell Atlantic New Jersey. CORP AFFIL director: Digital Solutions Inc.

Eileen Leahy: manager corporate contributions
William J. Walsh: president (see above)

Grants Analysis

Disclosure Period: calendar year ending 2001
Total Grants: $1,333,700*
Number of Grants: 500 (approx)
Average Grant: $2,667
Highest Grant: $500,000
Typical Range: $1,000 to $5,000
*Note: Grants analysis provided by foundation. Giving excludes United Way and scholarships.

Recent Grants

Note: Grants derived from 2001 Form 990.

General

500,000	Liberty Science Center, Jersey City, NJ
310,000	United Way of Essex and West Hudson, Newark, NJ
80,000	Robert Wood Johnson University, New Brunswick, NJ
40,000	New Jersey Institute of Technology, Newark, NJ
40,000	United Way of Passaic County, Paterson, NJ
38,000	United Way of Camden County, Camden, NJ
35,000	United Way of Union County, Elizabeth, NJ
30,000	Saint Vincent Academy, Newark, NJ
30,000	United Way of Greater Mercer County Inc., Lawrenceville, NJ
25,000	Garden State Cancer Center, Belleville, NJ

PUBLIC WELFARE FOUNDATION

Giving Contact

Larry Kressley, Executive Director
1200 U Street NW
Washington, DC 20009
Phone: (202)965-1800
Fax: (202)265-8852
Web: http://www.publicwelfare.org

Description

Founded: 1947
EIN: 540597601
Organization Type: General Purpose Foundation
Giving Locations: nationally.
Grant Types: General Support, Matching, Operating Expenses, Project, Seed Money.

Donor Information

Founder: The Public Welfare Foundation was founded in 1947 by Charles Edward Marsh, an Ohio newspaperman. Mr. Marsh believed that newspapers were semi-public utilities which contributed to the improvement of society. This philosophy, coupled with a strong humanitarian instinct, inspired him to use the income from some of the newspapers he owned to establish a foundation.

Financial Summary

Total Giving: $18,897,950 (fiscal year ending October 31, 2002); $19,840,600 (fiscal 2001); $18,150,000 (fiscal 2000 approx)
Giving Analysis: Giving for fiscal 1999 includes: foundation grants to United Way ($2,000) foundation scholarships ($42,000)
Assets: $370,135,448 (fiscal 2002); $410,715,283 (fiscal 2001); $446,359,535 (fiscal 2000)

Typical Recipients

Arts & Humanities: Arts Institutes, Ballet, Historic Preservation, History & Archaeology, Libraries, Music, Theater

Civic & Public Affairs: African American Affairs, Asian American Affairs, Botanical Gardens/Parks, Business/Free Enterprise, Civil Rights, Economic Development, Economic Policy, Employment/Job Training, Civic & Public Affairs-General, Hispanic Affairs, Housing, Law & Justice, Legal Aid, Native American Affairs, Nonprofit Management, Philanthropic Organizations, Public Policy, Rural Affairs, Safety, Urban & Community Affairs, Women's Affairs, Zoos/Aquariums

Education: Afterschool/Enrichment Programs, Colleges & Universities, Education Funds, Education Reform, Environmental Education, Faculty Development, Education-General, Legal Education, Private Education (Precollege), Student Aid

Environment: Air/Water Quality, Environment-General, Protection, Resource Conservation, Wildlife Protection

Health: Adolescent Health Issues, AIDS/HIV, Children's Health/Hospitals, Clinics/Medical Centers, Emergency/Ambulance Services, Health-General, Geriatric Health, Health Policy/Cost Containment, Health Organizations, Hospitals, Hospitals (University Affiliated), Medical Research, Mental Health, Nutrition, Prenatal Health Issues, Public Health

International: Health Care/Hospitals, Human Rights, International Development, International Environmental Issues, International Organizations, International Peace & Security Issues, International Relief Efforts

Religion: Churches, Ministries, Religious Welfare
Science: Science Museums
Social Services: Child Welfare, Community Service Organizations, Counseling, Crime Prevention, Delinquency & Criminal Rehabilitation, Domestic Violence, Family Planning, Family Services, Food/Clothing Distribution, Homes, People with Disabilities, Refugee Assistance, Senior Services, Shelters/Homelessness, Social Services-General, Veterans, Youth Organizations

Application Procedures

Initial Contact: Applicants should call for application guidelines and then send a letter of inquiry, including a cover letter, to the foundation. If the foundation is interested, a proposal will be requested.
Application Requirements: A two page letter of inquiry should describe the work to be conducted. The letter should be accompanied by a cover sheet, which includes: the name and address of the organization, contact person, telephone and fax numbers, one paragraph summarizing the organization's purpose and activities, one paragraph summarizing the proposal, the relationship of the proposal to the organization's mission statement, total annual organizational budget and fiscal year, total project budget, dollar amount requested, and time period the grant will cover (with beginning and ending dates), tax exempt status and amount committed from other funding sources. The narrative should include the purpose of the request, problem being addressed, demographics served, and how you will address the need or concern, and how your work promotes systemic change. Also include a one-page budget showing all funding and expenses for organization or project to be funded. See submission guidelines for funding renewal guidelines.
Deadlines: None. The screening committee reviews applications on a daily basis.
Review Process: The foundation requests that all materials be written in English and addressed to the Review Committee. Applicants should not request preliminary meetings until a letter of inquiry has been submitted. Within one month of receiving the request, the foundation will notify the applicant whether the request has been accepted for consideration. If accepted, a proposal will be requested at that time. It generally takes an additional two to three months for the foundation to notify the applicant if it has approved the proposal. Funds should be sought for the following operating year in most cases. Decisions are made by the board of directors which meets regularly during the year.

Notes: Applicants should review the foundation's annual report and guidelines before applying to increase their chances of receiving support.

Restrictions

The foundation generally does not fund conferences, endowments, foreign study, graduate work, individuals, publications, research projects, scholarships, seminars, government projects, and workshops.

Additional Information

Each year a good portion of the grantees are first-time recipients.
Publications: Annual Report; Application Guidelines (Spanish Translation Available)

Foundation Officials

Peter Benjamin Edelman: director B Minneapolis, MN 1938. ED Harvard University AB (1958); Harvard University LLB (1961). NONPR AFFIL director: New Israel Fund; member: Washington lawyers Committee Civil Rights Under Law; director: National Youth Law Center; professor law: Georgetown University; director: Juvenile Law Center; director: Center Law Social Policy; Chapin Hall Center Children; director: Americans for Peace Now; director: Center Community Change.
Antoinette M. Haskell: treasurer B 1918. CORP AFFIL president: Martinsville Bulletin Inc.
Robert H. Haskell: vice chairman, director B 1940. PRIM CORP EMPL executive vice president, director: Martinsville Bulletin Inc.
Brent Henry: director B Philadelphia, PA 1947. ED Princeton University BA (1969); Yale University MS (1973); Yale University JD (1973). PRIM CORP EMPL vice president: Green Door Inc. ADD CORP EMPL adj professor: Howard University School Business Administration; secretary: Medlantic Enterprise Inc.; vice president, general counsel: Medlantic Healthcare Group. CORP AFFIL director: Gerard Minnesota Inc.; director: Gerard Treatment Programs Inc. NONPR AFFIL member: National Bar Association; director: National Health Lawyers Association; member: District of Columbia Bar Association; director: Mental Health Law Project; member: American Bar Association; director: Combined Health Appeal National Capital Area.
Larry Kressley: executive director B Allentown, PA 1949. ED Goddard College; Antioch College MD (1976). NONPR AFFIL project director: Rural America; member; director: Washington Regional Association Grantmakers; member: National Network Grantmakers; member committee inclusiveness: Council Foundations; trustee: Goddard College.
Myrtis H. Powell: director PRIM NONPR EMPL vice president: Miami University.
Thomas J. Scanlon: chairman, director
Thomas W. Scoville: director
Jerome W. D. Stokes: director

Grants Analysis

Disclosure Period: fiscal year ending October 31, 2001
Total Grants: $19,840,600*
Number of Grants: 438
Average Grant: $45,298
Highest Grant: $200,000
Lowest Grant: $1,000
Typical Range: $10,000 to $50,000 and $100,000 to $250,000
*Note: Grants analysis provided by foundation.

Recent Grants

Note: Grants derived from 2001 Form 990.

General

200,000	National Resources Defense Council, New York, NY -- atmosphere protection initiative
170,000	Center to Prevent Handgun Violence, Washington, DC -- support legal action project

150,000	Community Catalyst, Boston, MA	
150,000	Washington Regional Association of Grantmakers Fund, Washington, DC	
100,000	Bread for the City, Washington, DC -- capital campaign	
100,000	Center for Community Change, Washington, DC	
100,000	Environmental Defense Fund, New York, NY -- support for the Global Atmosphere and International Programs	
100,000	Friends of the Earth, Washington, DC	
100,000	Mexfam Fundacion Mexicana Para La Planeacion Familiar, Tlalpan, DF Mexico -- support reproductive health education and services	
100,000	New Columbia Community Land Trust, Washington, DC	

PUBLIX SUPERMARKETS

Company Headquarters

1936 George Jenkins Boulevard
Lakeland, FL 33815
Web: http://www.publix.com

Company Description

Founded: 1921
Ticker: PUSH
Exchange: OTC
Revenue: US$15.93 billion (2002)
Profit: US$632.4 million (2002)
Employees: 123000 (2002)
Fortune Rank: 112, per FORTUNE Magazine's list of 500 Largest U.S. Corporations (2002).
SIC(s): 5411 Grocery Stores.

Operating Locations

Publix Supermarkets (FL--Lakeland)

Publix Supermarkets Charities

Giving Contact

Carol Barnett, Chairperson
PO Box 407
Lakeland, FL 33802
Phone: (863)686-8754
Web: http://www.publix.com/servlet/MainController?-action=prepareCommunityInvolvement

Description

Founded: 1967
EIN: 596194119
Organization Type: Corporate Foundation
Giving Locations: AL; FL; GA; SC
Grant Types: Capital, Challenge, Employee Matching Gifts, General Support, Multiyear/Continuing Support, Operating Expenses, Project, Scholarship.

Donor Information

Founder: The foundation was established in 1967 by George W. Jenkins.

Financial Summary

Total Giving: $24,002,437 (2001); $23,956,325 (2000); $17,241,129 (1999)
Giving Analysis: Giving for 2000 includes: foundation grants to United Way ($11,245,152); foundation ($12,711,173); 1999: foundation grants to United Way ($6,919,985) foundation ($10,321,144)
Assets: $460,932,750 (2001); $507,489,259 (2000); $506,191,824 (1999)
Gifts Received: $43,660 (1999); $2,850,350 (1997); $50,257,597 (1996). Note: In 1996, contributions were received from Florida Combined Life Insurance Co., the estate of Mr. George Jenkins, and various donors.

Typical Recipients

Arts & Humanities: Arts Associations & Councils, Arts Centers, Arts Festivals, Community Arts, Libraries, Museums/Galleries, Performing Arts, Public Broadcasting, Theater
Civic & Public Affairs: African American Affairs, Chambers of Commerce, Community Foundations, Economic Policy, Gay/Lesbian Issues, Civic & Public Affairs-General, Housing, Municipalities/Towns, Public Policy, Rural Affairs, Zoos/Aquariums
Education: Colleges & Universities, Community & Junior Colleges, Economic Education, Education Reform, Education-General, Minority Education, Private Education (Precollege), Public Education (Precollege), Secondary Education (Private), Student Aid
Environment: Environment-General
Health: Cancer, Clinics/Medical Centers, Emergency/Ambulance Services, Geriatric Health, Hospices, Hospitals, Single-Disease Health Associations, Transplant Networks/Donor Banks
International: Foreign Arts Organizations, International Affairs
Religion: Churches, Ministries, Religious Organizations, Religious Welfare
Science: Observatories & Planetariums, Science Museums, Scientific Centers & Institutes
Social Services: At-Risk Youth, Child Welfare, Community Service Organizations, Emergency Relief, Family Planning, Family Services, Food/Clothing Distribution, Homes, People with Disabilities, Scouts, Shelters/Homelessness, Substance Abuse, United Funds/United Ways, YMCA/YWCA/YMHA/YWHA, Youth Organizations

Application Procedures

Initial Contact: The foundation requests applications be made in writing.
Application Requirements: Applicants should include the purpose of the request, a copy of 501(c)(3) determination letter from IRS, and the latest financial statement of the organization.
Deadlines: None.

Restrictions

Grants are not made to individuals.

Corporate Officials

Tina Johnson: treasurer, director B 1959. PRIM CORP EMPL treasurer, director: Publix Super Markets Inc.

Foundation Officials

John Attaway: secretary
Carol Barnett: chairman, chief executive officer
Barbara Hart: director
Suzanne ReDavid: administration

Grants Analysis

Disclosure Period: calendar year ending 2001
Total Grants: $12,959,083*
Number of Grants: 3,178 (approx)
Average Grant: $4,078
Highest Grant: $400,000
Lowest Grant: $50
Typical Range: $100 to $25,000 and $100,000 to $400,000
*Note: Giving excludes scholarship and United Way.

Recent Grants

Note: Grants derived from 2001 Form 990.

General

1,415,600	United Way Central Florida, Orlando, FL	
1,130,900	United Way Atlanta Metro, Atlanta, GA	
752,000	United Way Broward County, Ft. Lauderdale, FL	
572,300	United Way Heart of Florida, Orlando, FL	
547,100	United Way Dade County, Miami, FL	
527,800	United Way Palm Beach County, Palm Beach, FL	
430,800	United Way Pinellas County, St. Petersburg, FL	
413,200	United Way Hillsborough County, Tampa, FL	
400,000	Florida Southern College, FL	
329,800	United Way Northeast Florida, Jacksonville, FL	

PULITZER, INC.

Company Headquarters

900 N. Tucker Blvd.
St. Louis, MO 63101
Web: http://www.pulitzer.net

Company Description

Founded: 1878
Ticker: PTZ
Exchange: NYSE
Former Name: Pulitzer Publishing Co..
Revenue: US$416 million (2002)
Employees: 4000 (2002)
SIC(s): 2711 Newspapers.

Operating Locations

Pulitzer, Inc. (AZ--Phoenix, Tucson; IN--Fort Wayne; KY--Louisville; MO--St. Louis; NE--Omaha; NM--Albuquerque; NC--Winston-Salem; SC--Greenville)

Nonmonetary Support

Type: Cause-related Marketing & Promotion; Donated Products; In-kind Services
Contact: Tracy Rouch, Promotions Mgr.

Pulitzer Foundation

Giving Contact

Alan G. Silverglat, Secretary & Treasurer
Pulitzer Foundation
900 North Tucker Boulevard
St. Louis, MO 63101
Phone: (314)340-8440
Fax: (314)340-3133

Description

EIN: 436052854
Organization Type: Corporate Foundation
Giving Locations: MO: St. Louis metropolitan area
Grant Types: Capital, Endowment, General Support, Project, Scholarship.

Financial Summary

Total Giving: $506,850 (2001); $473,350 (2000); $476,029 (1999). Note: Contributes through foundation only.
Giving Analysis: Giving for 2001 includes: foundation grants to United Way ($220,000); foundation ($286,850); 2000: foundation scholarships ($13,000); foundation grants to United Way ($115,000); foundation ($345,350); 1999: foundation grants to United Way ($105,000) foundation ($371,029)
Assets: $705,784 (2001); $867,038 (2000); $982,833 (1999)
Gifts Received: $375,850 (2001); $397,350 (2000); $539,329 (1999). Note: In 2001, contributions were received from St. Louis Post-Dispatch LLC ($345,850) and Pulitzer Inc. ($30,000). In 1999, contributions were received from Pulitzer Broadcasting Co.($92,000); WESH Television, Inc. ($34,000); KCCI Television Inc ($10,000); Pulitzer Inc ($261,029); WDSU Television ($16,000) and Star Publishing ($12,000).

Typical Recipients

Arts & Humanities: Arts Appreciation, Arts Associations & Councils, Arts Centers, Arts Festivals, Arts Funds, Arts Institutes, Dance, Ethnic & Folk Arts, Arts & Humanities-General, Historic Preservation,

History & Archaeology, Libraries, Museums/Galleries, Music, Opera, Performing Arts, Public Broadcasting, Theater, Visual Arts

Civic & Public Affairs: African American Affairs, Asian American Affairs, Botanical Gardens/Parks, Business/Free Enterprise, Civil Rights, Clubs, Community Foundations, Economic Development, Employment/Job Training, First Amendment Issues, Civic & Public Affairs-General, Professional & Trade Associations, Public Policy, Urban & Community Affairs, Women's Affairs, Zoos/Aquariums

Education: Arts/Humanities Education, Business Education, Colleges & Universities, Education Funds, Education-General, International Exchange, Journalism/Media Education, Legal Education, Medical Education, Minority Education, Private Education (Precollege), Public Education (Precollege), Science/Mathematics Education, Secondary Education (Private), Special Education, Student Aid, Vocational & Technical Education

Environment: Environment-General

Health: AIDS/HIV, Cancer, Children's Health/Hospitals, Emergency/Ambulance Services, Home-Care Services, Hospices, Hospitals, Long-Term Care, Mental Health, Multiple Sclerosis, Respiratory, Single-Disease Health Associations

International: International-General, Human Rights, International Organizations, International Relations

Religion: Churches, Dioceses, Jewish Causes, Religious Organizations, Religious Welfare

Science: Scientific Centers & Institutes

Social Services: Child Welfare, Community Service Organizations, Emergency Relief, Family Planning, Family Services, Food/Clothing Distribution, Homes, Recreation & Athletics, Scouts, Senior Services, United Funds/United Ways, YMCA/YWCA/YMHA/YWHA, Youth Organizations

Application Procedures

Initial Contact: Send a brief letter or proposal.
Application Requirements: Include a description of organization, amount requested, purpose of funds sought, recently audited financial statement, proof of tax-exempt status.
Deadlines: None.
Review Process: Foundation board meets every other month.

Restrictions

Applications from individuals are not accepted.

Corporate Officials

Cole C. Campbell: editorvpr B Roanoke, VA. ED University of North Carolina BA. PRIM CORP EMPL editor: Saint Louis Post Dispatch. NONPR AFFIL journalism advisory board: Norfolk State University.
Ronald H. Ridgway: senior vice president B 1938. ED Ohio State University. PRIM CORP EMPL senior vice president: Pulitzer Publishing Co. CORP AFFIL vice president: Star Publishing Co.; treasurer: WESH Television Inc.; vice president finance: KETV Television Inc.; senior vice president fin, director: Saint Louis Post Dispatch.

Foundation Officials

Cole C. Campbell: director (see above)
Terrance C.Z. Egger: director ED Augustana College. PRIM CORP EMPL vice president: Pulitzer Publishing Co.
Ronald H. Ridgway: secretary, treasurer, director (see above)

Grants Analysis

Disclosure Period: calendar year ending 2001
Total Grants: $286,850*
Number of Grants: 26
Average Grant: $11,033
Highest Grant: $50,000
Lowest Grant: $350
Typical Range: $250 to $25,000
*Note: Giving excludes United Way.

Recent Grants

Note: Grants derived from 2001 Form 990.

General

120,000	United Way, St. Louis, MO
100,000	September 11th Fund, New York, NY
50,000	Columbia University Graduate School of Journalism, New York, NY -- Pulitzer New World Room
40,000	St. Louis Symphony Orchestra, St. Louis, MO
25,000	Cardinal Ritter College Prep, St. Louis, MO
25,000	Forum for Contemporary Arts, St. Louis, MO
25,000	Grand Center, St. Louis, MO
15,000	Boy Scouts of America Friends of Scouting, St. Louis, MO
15,000	St. Louis Zoo Foundation, St. Louis, MO -- support six-year pledge
12,000	Arts and Education Fund, St. Louis, MO

NINA MASON PULLIAM CHARITABLE TRUST

Giving Contact

Mary Price
135 N. Pennsylvania Street, Suite 1200
Indianapolis, IN 46204-1956
Phone: (317)231-6075
E-mail: hivey@nmpct.org
Web: http://www.ninapulliamtrust.org/html

Alternate Contact

200 E. Van Buren
Phoenix, AZ 85004
Note: Alternate address is for Arizona organizations.

Description

Founded: 1997
EIN: 356644088
Organization Type: Private Foundation
Giving Locations: AZ; IN
Grant Types: General Support.

Financial Summary

Total Giving: $17,372,003 (2001); $16,730,932 (2000); $11,650,954 (1999)
Giving Analysis: Giving for 2001 includes: foundation grants to United Way ($145,000); 2000: foundation grants to United Way ($50,000); 1999: foundation grants to United Way ($105,000)
Assets: $367,393,493 (2001); $398,000,103 (2000); $411,145,069 (1999)
Gifts Received: $109,401 (1999); $38,128,196 (1998); $363,806,664 (1997). Note: In 1998 and 1999, contributions were received from Nina Mason Pulliam estate.

Typical Recipients

Arts & Humanities: Libraries, Museums/Galleries, Theater
Civic & Public Affairs: Botanical Gardens/Parks, Civic & Public Affairs-General, Housing, Women's Affairs, Zoos/Aquariums
Education: Colleges & Universities, Engineering/Technological Education
Environment: Wildlife Protection
Science: Scientific Centers & Institutes
Social Services: Community Centers, Community Service Organizations, People with Disabilities, YMCA/YWCA/YMHA/YWHA

Application Procedures

Initial Contact: Send a brief letter of inquiry.
Application Requirements: Preliminary proposal letter should include a description of organization, description of need, time frame, budget, and description of target population. Submit six copies of preliminary letter, preliminary application form, and board of directors listing. Submit one copy of proof of tax-exempt status and annual report.
Deadlines: January 12, May 15, and September 14 for preliminary applications.
Decision Notification: Preliminary application notification is in 3 months and final funding notification is in 6 months after preliminary deadline.

Foundation Officials

Harriet M. Ivey: president, chief executive officer
Robert L. Lowry: chief financial officer
Frank Eli Russell: trustee B Kokomo, IN December 06, 1920. ED Evansville College AB (1942); Indiana University JD (1951). PRIM CORP EMPL chairman: Central Newspapers, Inc. CORP AFFIL director: Muncie Newspapers Inc.; director: Phoenix Newspapers Inc.; chairman retirement committee: Hoosier State Press; director: Indianapolis Newspapers Inc.; president, director: Bradley Paper Co.; president, director: Central Newsprint. NONPR AFFIL member: Sigma Alpha Epsilon; member: Tax Executives Institute; member: Salvation Army; member: Shriners; member: Order Coif; member: Phi Delta Phi; member, director: Newspaper Advertising Bureau; director: Nina Mason Pulliam Charitable Trust; member: Masons; member: Midwest Pension Conference; member: Indianapolis Bar Association; member, director: Institute Newspaper Contrs & Financial Offs; director, vice president: Indiana Association Credit Management; member: Indiana Bar Association; member: Indiana Association Colleges; member: Indiana Association CPA's; director: Eiteljorg Museum; member: Free Accepted Masons; member: Ancient Accepted Scottish Rite; director: Central Newspapers Foundation; member: American Bar Association; member: American Institute CPAs. CLUB AFFIL Meridian Hills Country Club; Skyline Club; Columbia Club; Indianapolis Athletic Club.
Nancy M. Russell: trustee
Carol P. Schatt: trustee

Grants Analysis

Disclosure Period: calendar year ending 2001
Total Grants: $17,227,003*
Number of Grants: 234
Average Grant: $64,381*
Highest Grant: $1,000,000
Typical Range: $5,000 to $250,000
*Note: Giving excludes United Way. Average grant figure excludes three highest grants ($2,500,000).

Recent Grants

Note: Grants derived from 2001 Form 990.

Library-Related

750,000	Indianapolis Marion County Public Library Foundation, Indianapolis, IN -- for support toward creating the Indianapolis Special Collections Room

General

1,000,000	Eagle Creek Park Foundation, Inc., Indianapolis, IN -- to support the design engineering construction and equipment for the Peace Learning Center
750,000	Arizona Zoological Society, Phoenix, AZ -- for the creation of the Children's Education and Conservation Center
750,000	Indianapolis Zoological Society Inc., Indianapolis, IN -- for a new elephant exhibit area
500,000	Grand Canyon National Park Foundation, Grand Canyon, AZ -- for the construction of phases I and II of the Greenway Trail System
375,000	Julian Center, Julian, CA -- for renovation
300,000	Indiana Repertory Theater, Indianapolis, IN -- to expand statewide curriculum to

	children through an education endowment
250,000	Arizona Science Center, Phoenix, AZ -- to establish a cash operating reserve fund
250,000	Community Alliance of the Far Eastside, Inc., Indianapolis, IN -- to support Phase II renovation of CAFE
250,000	Habitat for Humanity Valley of the Sun, Phoenix, AZ -- to support pre development costs of the Villas Esperanza housing project
250,000	Indiana State Museum Foundation, Indianapolis, IN -- to underwrite the Ice Age Tunnel

PUTERBAUGH FOUNDATION

Giving Contact

Norris J. Welker, Managing Trustee
PO Box 1206
McAlester, OK 74502-1206
Phone: (918)426-1591

Description

Founded: 1949
EIN: 736092193
Organization Type: Private Foundation
Giving Locations: OK
Grant Types: Capital, Endowment, General Support, Matching, Professorship, Project, Research, Scholarship.

Donor Information

Founder: the late Jay Garfield Puterbaugh, the late Leela Oliver Puterbaugh

Financial Summary

Total Giving: $394,914 (2001); $299,360 (2000); $198,630 (1999). Note: 1997 Giving includes United Way ($35,200).
Giving Analysis: Giving for 2001 includes: foundation scholarships ($11,000); foundation grants to United Way ($50,000); 2000: foundation scholarships ($11,000); foundation grants to United Way ($45,000); 1999: foundation scholarships ($11,000); foundation grants to United Way ($45,000)
Assets: $8,866,936 (2001); $9,190,042 (2000); $9,026,777 (1999)

Typical Recipients

Arts & Humanities: Arts Associations & Councils, Arts Institutes, History & Archaeology, Libraries, Literary Arts, Public Broadcasting
Civic & Public Affairs: Botanical Gardens/Parks, Chambers of Commerce, Clubs, Economic Development, Civic & Public Affairs-General, Inner-City Development, Law & Justice, Legal Aid, Municipalities/Towns, Safety, Urban & Community Affairs
Education: Colleges & Universities, Economic Education, Elementary Education (Public), Education-General, Literacy, Medical Education, Preschool Education, Public Education (Precollege), Student Aid, Vocational & Technical Education
Environment: Environment-General
Health: Cancer, Children's Health/Hospitals, Clinics/Medical Centers, Emergency/Ambulance Services, Health Organizations, Hospices, Hospitals, Medical Research, Nursing Services, Speech & Hearing
Religion: Religious Welfare
Science: Scientific Centers & Institutes, Scientific Organizations
Social Services: At-Risk Youth, Child Welfare, Community Service Organizations, Crime Prevention, Family Planning, Family Services, Homes, People with Disabilities, Shelters/Homelessness, Substance Abuse, United Funds/United Ways, Youth Organizations

Application Procedures

Initial Contact: Send a full proposal.
Application Requirements: Describe the organization and program or project; include specific purpose of funds sought, other sources of support, and proof of tax-exempt status.
Decision Notification: Budget commitments are completed approximately one year in advance.

Restrictions

Does not support individuals.

Additional Information

Preference is given to local charities which provide broad public benefit.
Publications: Financial Statement

Foundation Officials

Frank G. Edwards: trustee
Don C. Phelps: mng trustee
Steven W. Taylor: trustee
Norris J. Welker: trustee

Grants Analysis

Disclosure Period: calendar year ending 2001
Total Grants: $333,914*
Number of Grants: 22
Average Grant: $9,496*
Highest Grant: $125,000
Typical Range: $1,000 to $50,000
*Note: Giving excludes United Way and scholarship. Average grant figure excludes highest grant.

Recent Grants

Note: Grants derived from 2001 Form 990.

General

125,000	Boys and Girls Club of McAlester, McAlester, OK -- program support, building project
50,928	McAlester Public Schools, McAlester, OK -- television program and program support
50,000	McAlester United Way, Inc., McAlester, OK -- program support
50,000	Oklahoma Medical Research Foundation, Oklahoma City, OK -- medical research funding
23,500	Eastern Oklahoma State College, Wilburton, OK -- Nursing Program support
15,000	American Red Cross, Pittsburg County Chapter, McAlester, OK -- program support
15,000	McAlester Chamber Foundation, McAlester, OK -- Industrial Development Program support
13,970	Youth Emergency Shelter, Inc., McAlester, OK -- facility upgrading project
8,500	McAlester Rotary Foundation, McAlester, OK -- Rotary Park
5,250	CASA of Pittsburg County, McAlester, OK -- program support

PUTNAM FOUNDATION

Giving Contact

David F. Putnam, Trustee
150 Congress St.
Keene, NH 03431-0323
Phone: (603)352-2448
Fax: (603)355-1185

Description

Founded: 1952
EIN: 026011388
Organization Type: Private Foundation
Giving Locations: NH
Grant Types: Capital, General Support.

Donor Information

Founder: David F. Putnam

Financial Summary

Total Giving: $531,178 (fiscal year ending October 31, 2001); $508,730 (fiscal 2000); $627,244 (fiscal 1999)
Giving Analysis: Giving for fiscal 2001 includes: foundation scholarships ($1,000); fiscal 2000: foundation scholarships ($24,250) fiscal 1998: foundation scholarships ($900)
Assets: $8,107,228 (fiscal 2001); $9,237,051 (fiscal 2000); $8,716,827 (fiscal 1999)
Gifts Received: $9,987 (fiscal 2001); $59,925 (fiscal 2000); $59,928 (fiscal 1998). Note: In 1998, contributions received were in the form of Markem Class C stock.

Typical Recipients

Arts & Humanities: Arts Associations & Councils, Arts Institutes, Community Arts, Dance, Ethnic & Folk Arts, Historic Preservation, History & Archaeology, Libraries, Museums/Galleries, Music, Opera, Public Broadcasting, Theater
Civic & Public Affairs: Botanical Gardens/Parks, Business/Free Enterprise, Community Foundations, Civic & Public Affairs-General, Hispanic Affairs, Housing, Municipalities/Towns, Parades/Festivals, Philanthropic Organizations, Professional & Trade Associations, Urban & Community Affairs, Women's Affairs
Education: Arts/Humanities Education, Colleges & Universities, Education Funds, Engineering/Technological Education, Education-General, International Studies, Leadership Training, Minority Education, Private Education (Precollege), Private Education (Precollege), Science/Mathematics Education, Secondary Education (Public), Social Sciences Education, Student Aid
Environment: Air/Water Quality, Forestry, Environment-General, Resource Conservation
Health: Clinics/Medical Centers, Emergency/Ambulance Services, Health Organizations, Hospitals
International: International Relations, Missionary/Religious Activities
Religion: Churches
Social Services: Community Service Organizations, Food/Clothing Distribution, Recreation & Athletics, Scouts, Social Services-General, United Funds/United Ways, YMCA/YWCA/YMHA/YWHA, Youth Organizations

Application Procedures

Initial Contact: Send a brief letter of inquiry.
Application Requirements: Include purpose of funds sought and provide relevant facts and information.
Deadlines: None.

Restrictions

Awards are limited to historical preservation, cultural enhancement, and ecological maintenance.

Foundation Officials

Rosamond P. Delori: trustee, secretary
David F. Putnam: trustee
James A. Putnam: trustee PRIM CORP EMPL president: Markem Corp.
Rosamond Putnam: trustee

Grants Analysis

Disclosure Period: fiscal year ending October 31, 2001
Total Grants: $530,178*
Number of Grants: 74
Average Grant: $7,165
Highest Grant: $33,333
Lowest Grant: $250
Typical Range: $1,000 to $10,000
*Note: Giving excludes scholarships.

Recent Grants

Note: Grants derived from 2000 Form 990.

General

25,000	Canterbury Shaker Village, Canterbury, NH -- to support the Millennium Campaign
25,000	Colonial Theater Group, Keene, NH -- to support operations
25,000	Franklin Pierce College, Rindge, NH -- to support lectureship in religion and society
25,000	Keene State College, Keene, NH -- for enrichment of film program
25,000	New Hampshire Center for Public Policy Studies, NH -- to hire deputy to assist the director
25,000	New Hampshire Center Public Policy Study, Durham, NH -- to hire deputy to assist the director
25,000	New Hampshire Public Television, Durham, NH -- to support new current affairs program
20,000	YMCA of Cheshire County, Keene, NH -- to build new program center and dining hall
12,000	New England College, Henniker, NH -- to support the Putnam International scholarship
12,000	New England College, Henniker, NH -- to support the Putnam International scholarship

QUAKER CHEMICAL CORP.

Company Headquarters

1 Quaker Park
901 Hector St.
Conshohocken, PA 19428-0809
Web: http://www.quakerchem.com

Company Description

Founded: 1918
Ticker: KWR
Exchange: NYSE
Revenue: US$274.5 million (2002)
Employees: 1038 (2002)
SIC(s): 2821 Plastics Materials & Resins, 2841 Soap & Other Detergents, 2842 Polishes & Sanitation Goods, 2899 Chemical Preparations Nec.

Operating Locations

Quaker Chemical Corp. (CA--Fontana, Placentia, Pomona, South El Monte; GA--Savannah; MI--Detroit; OK--Sapulpa; PA--Conshohocken, Philadelphia; TX--Conroe, Fort Worth)

Nonmonetary Support

Type: Loaned Employees; Loaned Executives

Quaker Chemical Foundation

Giving Contact

Kathleen Lasota, Secretary
Elm and Lee Streets
Conshohocken, PA 19428
Phone: (610)832-4127
Fax: (610)832-4282

Description

EIN: 236245803
Organization Type: Corporate Foundation
Giving Locations: headquarters and operating communities.

Grant Types: Employee Matching Gifts, General Support, Scholarship.
Note: Employee matching gift ratio: 1 to 1 for education, health and welfare, cultural organisation, and civic and community affairs, up to $1,000 annually.

Financial Summary

Total Giving: $274,977 (fiscal year ending June 31, 2001); $300,558 (fiscal 2000); $273,727 (fiscal 1999). Note: Contributes through foundation only.
Giving Analysis: Giving for fiscal 2001 includes: foundation scholarships ($39,771); foundation matching gifts ($60,403); foundation ($174,803); fiscal 2000: foundation scholarships ($59,000); foundation matching gifts ($67,491); foundation ($174,067); fiscal 1999: corporate scholarships ($44,000); corporate matching gifts ($67,833); foundation ($161,894);
Assets: $477,145 (fiscal 2001); $610,241 (fiscal 2000); $535,895 (fiscal 1998)
Gifts Received: $83,000 (fiscal 2001); $307,000 (fiscal 2000); $147,000 (fiscal 1998). Note: Contributions were received from the Quaker Chemical Corporation.

Typical Recipients

Arts & Humanities: Arts Associations & Councils, Arts Centers, Arts Funds, Arts Outreach, Ballet, Community Arts, Historic Preservation, History & Archaeology, Libraries, Museums/Galleries, Music, Opera, Performing Arts
Civic & Public Affairs: Botanical Gardens/Parks, Economic Development, Employment/Job Training, Civic & Public Affairs-General, Housing, Urban & Community Affairs, Women's Affairs, Zoos/Aquariums
Education: Arts/Humanities Education, Colleges & Universities, Community & Junior Colleges, Engineering/Technological Education, Environmental Education, Literacy, Private Education (Precollege), Special Education, Student Aid, Vocational & Technical Education
Environment: Environment-General
Health: Eyes/Blindness, Health Organizations, Heart, Home-Care Services, Hospices, Hospitals, Medical Research, Nursing Services, Nutrition, Single-Disease Health Associations
International: Health Care/Hospitals, International Affairs, International Organizations, International Relations
Religion: Religious Welfare
Science: Science Exhibits & Fairs, Science Museums, Scientific Centers & Institutes
Social Services: At-Risk Youth, Child Welfare, Community Service Organizations, Counseling, Food/Clothing Distribution, Homes, People with Disabilities, Recreation & Athletics, Scouts, Senior Services, Sexual Abuse, Social Services-General, United Funds/United Ways, Volunteer Services, Youth Organizations

Application Procedures

Initial Contact: Request guidelines, then send written grant application.
Application Requirements: Grant applications must include: project description with a pro-forma budget; annual operating budget and audited financial statements; list of funding sources, including past major contributors with amounts, recent applications with results, and anticipated future funding sources; list of board members and officers.
Deadlines: April 30.

Restrictions

Distributions limited to tax-exempt organizations in geographic locations where the corporation has operations in the United States.
Generally does not support brick and mortar projects.

Additional Information

Publications: Guidelines

Corporate Officials

Ronald James Naples: president, chief executive officer, director B Passaic, NJ 1945. ED United States Military Academy BS (1967); Tufts University Fletcher School of Law & Diplomacy MA (1972); Harvard University MBA (1974). PRIM CORP EMPL president, chief executive officer, director: Quaker Chemical Corp. CORP AFFIL director: Advanta Corp. NONPR AFFIL member: President Commission White House Fellows; director: University Arts; member: Harvard Business School Alumni Association; director: Philadelphia Museum Art; vice chairman, director: Free Library Philadelphia Federation; vice chairman: Greater Philadelphia First Corp.; director: Foreign Policy Research Institute; director: Childrens Hospital Philadelphia; member advisory board: Fletcher School Law & Diplomacy; member: Association Grads U.S. Military Academy. CLUB AFFIL Pyramid Club; Racquet Club; Harvard Business School Philadelphia Club.

Foundation Officials

Katherine N. Coughenour: trustee
Edwin J. Delattre: trustee CORP AFFIL director: Quaker Chemical Corp.
Alan J. Keyser: trustee
Kathleen Lasota: secretary
Karl Henry Spaeth: chairman, trustee B Philadelphia, PA 1929. ED Haverford College AB (1951); Oxford University (1955); Harvard University JD (1958). PRIM CORP EMPL vice president, secretary: Quaker Chemical Corp. CORP AFFIL secretary: SB Decking Inc. CLUB AFFIL Philadelphia Cricket Club; Philadelphia Club.
Jane Williams: trustee

Grants Analysis

Disclosure Period: fiscal year ending June 31, 2001
Total Grants: $174,803*
Number of Grants: 120
Average Grant: $1,457
Highest Grant: $5,000
Typical Range: $500 to $3,500
*Note: Giving excludes matching gifts and scholarship.

Recent Grants

Note: Grants derived from 2001 Form 990.

Library-Related

2,000	William Jeanes Memorial Library, Lafayette Hill, PA
1,500	Library Company, Philadelphia, PA

General

5,000	Clemson University, Clemson, SC
5,000	University of Richmond, Richmond, VA
4,000	Butler University, Indianapolis, IN
4,000	Grinnell College, Grinnell, IA
4,000	University at Buffalo, Buffalo, NY
4,000	University of Notre Dame, Notre Dame, IN
3,500	Young Audiences of Eastern Pennsylvania, Philadelphia, PA
3,000	LaSalle University, Philadelphia, PA
3,000	Opera Company of Philadelphia, Philadelphia, PA
3,000	Philadelphia Orchestra Association, Philadelphia, PA

QUANEX CORP.

Company Headquarters

1900 W. Loop S, Ste. 1500
Houston, TX 77027
Web: http://www.quanex.com

Company Description

Founded: 1927
Ticker: NX
Exchange: NYSE
Revenue: US$994.4 million (2002)
Employees: 3476 (2002)
SIC(s): 3312 Blast Furnaces & Steel Mills, 3317 Steel Pipe & Tubes, 3341 Secondary Nonferrous Metals, 3365 Aluminum Foundries.

Operating Locations

Quanex Corp. (AR--Fort Smith; IL--Chatsworth, Lincolnshire; IA--Davenport; MI--Jackson; MS--New Albany; TX--Houston; UT--Park City; WI--Rice Lake)

Nonmonetary Support

Type: Donated Equipment; Donated Products

Quanex Foundation

Giving Contact

Sandy Hatcher, Director Corporate
Communications
1900 West Loop S., Suite 1500
Houston, TX 77027
Phone: (713)961-4600

Description

Founded: 1951
EIN: 366065490
Organization Type: Corporate Foundation
Giving Locations: TX
Grant Types: General Support, Scholarship.

Donor Information

Founder: La Salle Steel Co.

Financial Summary

Total Giving: $240,483 (2001); $191,509 (2000); $192,438 (1999)
Giving Analysis: Giving for 2001 includes: foundation scholarships ($22,410); foundation grants to United Way ($49,073); foundation ($169,000); 2000: foundation scholarships ($23,835); foundation grants to United Way ($55,174); foundation ($112,500); 1999: foundation scholarships ($5,000); foundation grants to United Way ($53,668) foundation ($135,470)
Assets: $6,276,162 (2001); $6,903,170 (2000); $6,828,365 (1999)
Gifts Received: $500,000 (1999); $500,000 (1996); $200,000 (1995)

Typical Recipients

Arts & Humanities: Arts Funds, Arts Institutes, Arts Outreach, Libraries, Museums/Galleries, Music, Performing Arts, Public Broadcasting, Theater
Civic & Public Affairs: Chambers of Commerce, Clubs, Community Foundations, Economic Development, Civic & Public Affairs-General, Housing, Law & Justice, Municipalities/Towns, Parades/Festivals, Professional & Trade Associations, Rural Affairs, Safety, Urban & Community Affairs
Education: Agricultural Education, Business Education, Colleges & Universities, Community & Junior Colleges, Education Funds, Elementary Education (Private), Engineering/Technological Education, Education-General, Literacy, Minority Education, Preschool Education, Private Education (Precollege), Public Education (Precollege), Secondary Education (Private), Secondary Education (Public), Student Aid
Health: AIDS/HIV, Cancer, Children's Health/Hospitals, Clinics/Medical Centers, Diabetes, Emergency/Ambulance Services, Eyes/Blindness, Health Organizations, Heart, Hospices, Hospitals, Kidney, Medical Research, Nutrition, Public Health, Research/Studies Institutes, Single-Disease Health Associations
Religion: Ministries, Religious Welfare, Social/Policy Issues

Science: Science Museums
Social Services: Animal Protection, Big Brother/Big Sister, Community Service Organizations, Crime Prevention, Emergency Relief, People with Disabilities, Recreation & Athletics, Scouts, Senior Services, Shelters/Homelessness, Special Olympics, United Funds/United Ways, YMCA/YWCA/YMHA/YWHA, Youth Organizations

Application Procedures

Initial Contact: The foundation has no formal grant application procedure or application form. Submit a full proposal.
Deadlines: October 31.

Restrictions

Does not support individuals, religious organizations for sectarian purposes, political or lobbying groups, or organizations outside operating areas.

Corporate Officials

Paul J. Giddens: vice president human resources PRIM CORP EMPL vice president human resources: Quanex Corp.
Raymond A. Jean: chairman, president, chief executive officer, director ED University of Chicago MBA; University of Maine BS. PRIM CORP EMPL president, chief executive officer, director: Quanex Corp.
Terry M. Murphy: vice president finance, chief financial officer B Syracuse, NY 1948. ED University of Wisconsin BS (1970); Marquette University MBA (1974); Seton Hall University JD (1980). PRIM CORP EMPL vice president finance, chief financial officer: Quanex Corp. NONPR AFFIL member: American Bar Association; member: American Institute of CPA's.
Vernon E. Oechsle: chairman, director PRIM CORP EMPL chairman, director: Quanex Corp.

Foundation Officials

Paul J. Giddens: director, president (see above)
Terry M. Murphy: vice president, director (see above)
Vernon E. Oechsle: vice president, director (see above)

Grants Analysis

Disclosure Period: calendar year ending 2001
Total Grants: $169,000*
Number of Grants: 130
Average Grant: $1,300
Highest Grant: $16,910
Typical Range: $200 to $5,500
*Note: Giving excludes scholarships and United Way.

Recent Grants

Note: Grants derived from 2001 Form 990.

Library-Related

2,500	Forrest Library, Forrest, IL

General

20,000	Museum of Art Foundation, Davenport, IA
16,910	National Merit Scholarship Corporation, Evanston, IL
12,373	United Way of Texas, Houston, TX
12,000	United Way, Ft. Smith, AR
10,000	Houston Livestock Show and Rodeo, Houston, TX
10,000	India Earthquake Relief Fund, Houston, TX
7,500	Juvenile Diabetes Foundation, Houston, TX
6,800	United Way, Jackson, MI
5,500	United Way Rice Lake, Rice Lake, WI
5,500	United Way Rice Lake, Rice Lake, WI

QUINCY NEWSPAPERS

Company Headquarters

Quincy, IL
Web: http://www.whig.com

Company Description

Employees: 400
SIC(s): 2700 Printing & Publishing, 4800 Communications.

Operating Locations

Quincy Newspapers (IL--Quincy)

Oakley-Lindsay Foundation of Quincy Newspapers and Its Subsidiaries

Giving Contact

Thomas A. Oakley, Community Relations Director
1130 S. 5th St.
Quincy, IL 62301
Phone: (217)223-5100

Description

EIN: 237025198
Organization Type: Corporate Foundation
Giving Locations: IL
Grant Types: General Support, Scholarship.

Financial Summary

Total Giving: $243,966 (2000); $260,918 (1999); $234,665 (1998)
Giving Analysis: Giving for 2000 includes: foundation scholarships ($2,000) 1999: foundation ($260,918)
Assets: $849,938 (2000); $827,111 (1999); $812,353 (1998)
Gifts Received: $213,334 (2000); $178,508 (1998); $155,283 (1996). Note: In 2000, contributions were received from Quincy Broadcasting Co. ($92,582), Quincy Newspapers, Inc. ($51,606), WSJV Television, Inc. ($11,239), KTTC Television ($11,200), WVVA Television, Inc. ($11,620), KTIV Television ($16,347), WREX Television, Inc. ($9,503), and the New Jersey Herald ($9,237). In 1998, contributions were received from Quincy Broadcasting Co. ($67,351), Quincy Newspapers, INC. ($6,124), WSJV Television, INC. ($9,001), KTTC Television ($10,247), WVVA Television, INC. ($13,222), KTIV Television ($8,265), and the New Jersey Herald ($8,265).

Typical Recipients

Arts & Humanities: Arts Associations & Councils, Arts Centers, Arts Funds, Community Arts, Arts & Humanities-General, Historic Preservation, History & Archaeology, Libraries, Literary Arts, Museums/Galleries, Music, Opera, Public Broadcasting
Civic & Public Affairs: Chambers of Commerce, Community Foundations, Economic Development, Civic & Public Affairs-General, Native American Affairs, Philanthropic Organizations, Urban & Community Affairs
Education: Afterschool/Enrichment Programs, Arts/Humanities Education, Colleges & Universities, Education Funds, Education-General, Journalism/Media Education, Literacy, Private Education (Precollege), Secondary Education (Private), Student Aid, Vocational & Technical Education
Health: Alzheimers Disease, Cancer, Children's Health/Hospitals, Emergency/Ambulance Services, Hospitals, Research/Studies Institutes
Religion: Churches, Religious Welfare
Science: Science Museums
Social Services: Community Service Organizations, Day Care, Family Services, Homes, Recreation & Athletics, Senior Services, Social Services-General, Special Olympics, United Funds/United Ways, YMCA/YWCA/YMHA/YWHA, Youth Organizations

Application Procedures

Initial Contact: The foundation has no formal grant application procedure or application form.
Deadlines: None.

Corporate Officials

David Graff: chief financial officer, controller, publisher, editor PRIM CORP EMPL chief financial officer, controller: Quincy Newspapers.

Thomas A. Oakley: president, chief executive officer, publisher, editor PRIM CORP EMPL president, chief executive officer, publisher, editor: Quincy Newspapers.

Foundation Officials

Joseph Bonansinga: director
John Chadwick: director
James W. Collins: director
Joseph I. Conover: director
James L. Deschepper: director
Leo T. Henning: director
F. M. Lindsay, Jr.: director
Larry R. Manne: director
Allen M. Oakley: director
David R. Oakley: director
Donald M. Oakley: director
Peter Anthony Oakley: secretary PRIM CORP EMPL committee relations director: Quincy Newspapers.
Ralph M. Oakley: director
Thomas A. Oakley: president, treasurer (see above)
Larry C. Roe: director
R. Kent Roeder: director
Scott T. Ruff: director
Kevin J. Sargent: director
Jerome P. Watson: director
Charles E. Webb: director

Grants Analysis

Disclosure Period: calendar year ending 2000
Total Grants: $241,966*
Number of Grants: 35
Average Grant: $2,383*
Highest Grant: $83,332
Typical Range: $1,000 to $5,000
***Note:** Giving excludes scholarships. Average grant figure excludes two highest grants ($163,332).

Recent Grants

Note: Grants derived from 1999 Form 990.

General

83,332	YMCA In Quincy, Quincy, IL
80,000	Quincy University, Quincy, IL -- goal 2000 capital campaign
15,000	Catholic Social Services, Quincy, IL
10,000	Transitions of Western Illinois, Quincy, IL -- new building
7,500	John Wood Community College, Quincy, IL -- science and technology center
6,900	Good News of Christmas, Quincy, IL -- support for indigent families
5,000	Family Service Agency, Quincy, IL
4,000	Project Future Charitable Fund, South Bend, IN
3,300	Siouxland Initiative III, Sioux City, IA
3,100	Quincy Area Community Foundation, Quincy, IL

QUIVEY-BAY STATE FOUNDATION

Giving Contact

Ted Cannon, Secretary & Treasurer
1515 E. 20th St.
Scottsbluff, NE 69361
Phone: (308)635-1135
Fax: (308)635-3701

Description

Founded: 1948
EIN: 476024159
Organization Type: Private Foundation
Giving Locations: NE: Western Nebraska
Grant Types: General Support, Scholarship.

Donor Information

Founder: M. S. Oulvey, Mrs. M. S. Quivey

Financial Summary

Total Giving: $250,850 (fiscal year ending January 31, 2002); $252,040 (fiscal 2001); $172,800 (fiscal 2000)
Assets: $4,925,010 (fiscal 2002); $5,407,759 (fiscal 2001); $5,555,124 (fiscal 2000)
Gifts Received: $100 (fiscal 1999)

Typical Recipients

Arts & Humanities: Arts Centers, Historic Preservation, History & Archaeology, Libraries, Music
Civic & Public Affairs: Clubs, Economic Development, Civic & Public Affairs-General, Professional & Trade Associations, Rural Affairs, Urban & Community Affairs, Zoos/Aquariums
Education: Colleges & Universities, Community & Junior Colleges, Education Funds, Engineering/Technological Education, Education-General, Public Education (Precollege), Religious Education, Student Aid
Environment: Environment-General
Health: Cancer, Children's Health/Hospitals, Clinics/Medical Centers, Emergency/Ambulance Services, Health Organizations, Kidney, Long-Term Care, Outpatient Health Care, Prenatal Health Issues, Respiratory
International: Health Care/Hospitals
Religion: Churches, Jewish Causes, Jewish Causes, Ministries, Religious Organizations, Religious Welfare
Science: Science Museums
Social Services: Animal Protection, Camps, Child Welfare, Community Centers, Community Service Organizations, Day Care, Delinquency & Criminal Rehabilitation, Homes, People with Disabilities, Recreation & Athletics, Scouts, Social Services-General, United Funds/United Ways, Volunteer Services, YMCA/YWCA/YMHA/YWHA, Youth Organizations

Application Procedures

Initial Contact: Send a brief letter of inquiry.
Application Requirements: Include a description of organization and purpose of funds sought.
Deadlines: None.

Restrictions

Does not support individuals or provide funds for endowments.

Foundation Officials

Ted Cannon: secretary, treasurer

Grants Analysis

Disclosure Period: fiscal year ending January 31, 2002
Total Grants: $250,850
Number of Grants: 49
Average Grant: $4,617*
Highest Grant: $29,250
Lowest Grant: $150
Typical Range: $1,000 to $10,000
***Note:** Average grant figure excludes highest grant.

Recent Grants

Note: Grants derived from 2000 Form 990.

Library-Related

4,500	Friends of the Mitchell Library

General

15,000	Chadron State Foundation, Chadron, NE
15,000	Western Nevada Community College, Carson City, NV
15,000	YMCA, Omaha, NE
11,000	Nebraska Independent College Foundation, Omaha, NE
10,000	Boys Scouts of America
10,000	Camp Fire Inc., Omaha, NE
10,000	Regional West Medical Center, Scottsbluff, NE
7,500	Campus House, Inc.
7,500	Panhandle Humane Society, Omaha, NE
7,000	Guilding Star Girl Scout Council

R&B MACHINE TOOL CO.

Company Headquarters

118 E. Michigan Ave.
Saline, MI 48176
Web: http://www.rbmachine.com

Company Description

Employees: 275
SIC(s): 3500 Industrial Machinery & Equipment.

Operating Locations

R&B Machine Tool Co. (MI--Saline)

Edward F. Redies Foundation

Giving Contact

118 E. Michigan Ave.
Saline, MI 48176
Phone: (734)429-0154

Description

Founded: 1981
EIN: 382391326
Organization Type: Corporate Foundation
Giving Locations: MI
Grant Types: General Support.

Donor Information

Founder: R & B Machine Tool Co.

Financial Summary

Total Giving: $305,039 (2000); $256,000 (1999); $234,908 (1998). Note: In 1996 Giving includes scholarship ($5,000), United Way (8,000).
Assets: $6,804,713 (2000); $6,899,266 (1999); $6,301,810 (1998)
Gifts Received: $50,000 (1998); $100,000 (1995); $200,000 (1994). Note: In 1995 and 1998, contributions were received from the R & B Machine Tool Co.

Typical Recipients

Arts & Humanities: Libraries, Museums/Galleries, Theater
Civic & Public Affairs: Botanical Gardens/Parks, Chambers of Commerce, Civic & Public Affairs-General, Municipalities/Towns, Safety
Education: Business Education, Colleges & Universities, Community & Junior Colleges, Engineering/Technological Education, Education-General, Private Education (Precollege), Public Education (Precollege), Science/Mathematics Education, Secondary Education (Private), Secondary Education (Public), Special Education, Student Aid
Environment: Environment-General
Health: Children's Health/Hospitals, Clinics/Medical Centers, Emergency/Ambulance Services, Health Organizations, Hospitals, Kidney, Long-Term Care, Medical Rehabilitation, Nursing Services, Public Health
Religion: Churches, Religious Organizations, Religious Welfare

Social Services: At-Risk Youth, Camps, Community Service Organizations, Emergency Relief, Food/Clothing Distribution, Homes, People with Disabilities, Recreation & Athletics, Senior Services, Social Services-General, Special Olympics, United Funds/United Ways, Youth Organizations

Application Procedures

Initial Contact: Send a brief cover letter, signed by an authorized individual of the organization.
Application Requirements: Clearly state the purpose of funds sought, amount requested, and the time period in which funds will be used. Also include proof of tax-exempt status and detailed financial data.
Deadlines: March 31.

Restrictions

The foundation considers applications for grants from well-established, tax exempt organizations seeking funds for capital improvements, equipment purchases, or other special needs of a tangible asset nature.

Foundation Officials

Dennis M. Redies: president
Erik H. Serr: secretary

Grants Analysis

Disclosure Period: calendar year ending 2000
Total Grants: $305,039
Number of Grants: 30
Average Grant: $7,323*
Highest Grant: $60,000
Typical Range: $1,000 to $15,000
*Note: Average grant figure excludes two highest grants ($100,000).

Recent Grants

Note: Grants derived from 2001 Form 990.

Library-Related

5,000	Saline Public Library, Saline, MI

General

50,000	City of Saline Recreational Park Fund, Saline, MI
50,000	Father Gabriel Richard High School, Ann Arbor, MI -- building fund
20,000	Washtenaw Christian Academy, Saline, MI
17,000	Saline Community Hospital, Saline, MI
15,000	Father Gabriel Richard High School, Ann Arbor, MI -- scholarship fund
15,000	Houghton Memorial Scholarship-Saline Area Schools, Saline, MI
11,110	City of Saline Police Department, Saline, MI
10,000	Boysville of Michigan, Clinton, MI
10,000	Eastern Michigan University, Ypsilanti, MI
10,000	St. Louis Center for the Retarded, Chelsea, MI

R.J. REYNOLDS TOBACCO

Company Headquarters

401 N. Main Street
Winston-Salem, NC 27101
Phone: (336)741-5000
Fax: (336)741-4238
Web: http://www.rjrt.com

Company Description

Ticker: RJR
Exchange: OTC
Acquired: Nabisco Group Holdings (2000).
Revenue: US$6.211 billion (2002)
Employees: 7,900
Fortune Rank: 281, per FORTUNE Magazine's list of 500 Largest U.S. Corporations (2002).

SIC(s): 2024 Ice Cream & Frozen Desserts, 2035 Pickles, Sauces & Salad Dressings, 2038 Frozen Specialties Nec, 2043 Cereal Breakfast Foods.

Operating Locations

RJR Nabisco Inc. (CA--San Leandro; NJ--East Hanover; NY--Bronx, New York; NC--Winston-Salem; PR--Guaynabo; WI--Wrightstown)
Note: Operates throughout the USA.

R. J. Reynolds Tobacco Company Foundation

Giving Contact

Vivian L. Turner
Donald G Haver
PO Box Box 2959
Winston-Salem, NC 27102-2959
Phone: (336)741-0049

Description

Founded: 1996
EIN: 561950120
Organization Type: Corporate Foundation
Giving Locations: NC
Grant Types: General Support.

Financial Summary

Total Giving: $3,249,191 (2000)
Assets: $1,606,495 (1996)

Typical Recipients

Arts & Humanities: Arts Associations & Councils, Arts Centers, Libraries, Music
Civic & Public Affairs: Civic & Public Affairs-General, Hispanic Affairs, Housing, Professional & Trade Associations, Safety
Education: Agricultural Education, Arts/Humanities Education, Business Education, Colleges & Universities, Education-General, Private Education (Precollege), Public Education (Precollege), Secondary Education (Public), Student Aid
Health: Hospices
International: Foreign Educational Institutions
Religion: Religious Welfare
Science: Science-General
Social Services: Child Welfare, Community Service Organizations, Day Care, Family Services, People with Disabilities, Substance Abuse, United Funds/United Ways, Volunteer Services, YMCA/YWCA/YMHA/YWHA, Youth Organizations

Foundation Officials

Dan Fawley: assistant treasurer
Jackson W. Henson: director, secretary
Michael O. Johnson: director, assistant secretary
Lynn L. Lane: director, treasurer
Tommy J. Payne: director, vice president
Janet Quintal: assistant treasurer
Andrew J. Schindler: director, chairman
Frank Skinner: director, vice president
Vivian L. Turner: president

Recent Grants

Note: Grants derived from 2000 Form 990.

Library-Related

5,000	Forsyth County Public Library, Winston-Salem, NC -- establish bilingual mini-libraries

General

625,000	United Way of Forsyth County, Winston-Salem, NC -- annual campaign
125,000	Arts Council, Inc., Winston-Salem, NC -- annual campaign
100,000	North Carolina Partnership for Children, Raleigh, NC -- smart start projects
100,000	Reynolda House, Inc., Winston-Salem, NC -- capital campaign

94,000	Winston Salem Forsyth County Schools, Winston-Salem, NC -- expand AVID Program
90,000	Yadkin County School System, Yadkinville, NC -- support After-School Program
62,000	North Carolina Tobacco Foundation, Raleigh, NC -- operating expenses
43,000	University of Kentucky, Lexington, KY -- operating expense
41,667	YMCA of Greater Winston-Salem, Winston-Salem, NC -- capital campaign
40,500	National Merit Scholarship Corporation, Evanston, IL -- four year scholarships

R.R. DONNELLEY & SONS CO.

Company Headquarters

Chicago, IL
Web: http://www.rrdonnelley.com

Company Description

Ticker: DNY
Exchange: OTC
Revenue: US$4.754 billion (2002)
Profit: US$142.2 million (2002)
Employees: 33000 (2002)
Fortune Rank: 348, per FORTUNE Magazine's list of 500 Largest U.S. Corporations (2002).
SIC(s): 2732 Book Printing, 2752 Commercial Printing--Lithographic, 2754 Commercial Printing--Gravure, 2759 Commercial Printing Nec.

Operating Locations

R.R. Donnelley & Sons Co. (AR--Fayetteville; CA--Emeryville, Irvine, Los Angeles, San Francisco, Santa Clara, Sherman Oaks, Torrance; CO--Denver; CT--Hartford, Old Saybrook, Stamford; FL--Eatonville, Tampa; GA--Atlanta; IL--Burbank, Dwight, Elgin, Hinsdale, Lisle, Mendota, Warsaw; KY--Danville; ME--Portland; MA--Boston, Waltham, Wrentham; MN--Minneapolis; MS--Senatobia; NV--Reno; NC--Charlotte; OH--Willard; OR--Beaverton, Portland; PA--Lancaster, Pittsburgh; SC--Spartanburg; TN--Brentwood, Gallatin; TX--Dallas, Fort Worth, Houston, McAllen; VA--Falls Church, Harrisonburg, Richmond; WA--Bellevue)

Nonmonetary Support

Type: Donated Equipment; Loaned Executives
Volunteer Programs: The company sponsors the Donnelley Dollars for Doers program, which provides grants to organizations for which Donnelley employees or retirees volunteer. Grant amounts are based on the number of hours donated by the employee or retiree, to a maximum of $500 per employee and $5,000 to any one organization.
Note: Company donates only used equipment. Company loans executives to the United Way only.

Giving Contact

Susan M. Levy, Vice President
R.R. Donnelley Foundation
77 West Wacker Drive
Chicago, IL 60601-1696
Phone: (312)326-8102
Fax: (312)326-8262
E-mail: susan.levy@rrd.com
Web: http://www.rrdonnelley.com/cportal/public/home/publicaffairs/index.jsp

Alternate Contact

Phone: (312)326-8175

Description

Organization Type: Corporate Giving Program
Giving Locations: principally near operating locations and to national organizations.

Grant Types: Capital, Emergency, Employee Matching Gifts, General Support, Multiyear/Continuing Support, Scholarship, Seed Money.
Note: Employee matching gift ratio: 1 to 1 for educational and cultural gifts.

Financial Summary

Total Giving: $2,406,000 (2002); $2,737,000 (2001); $3,407,111 (2000). Note: Contributes through corporate direct giving program and foundation. 2000 giving excludes corporate scholarships of an undisclosed amount; matching gifts includes corporate matching gifts to educational institutions, arts organizations, and to match employee volunteer efforts. 1998 and 1999 giving includes nonmonetary support.
Giving Analysis: Giving for 2000 includes: corporate matching gifts ($465,900); corporate grants to United Way ($788,211); domestic and international subsidiaries ($953,000) corporate direct giving ($1,200,000)

Typical Recipients

Arts & Humanities: Arts Institutes, Historic Preservation, Libraries, Literary Arts, Museums/Galleries, Performing Arts, Theater
Civic & Public Affairs: Employment/Job Training, Public Policy, Urban & Community Affairs, Zoos/Aquariums
Education: Colleges & Universities, Education Associations, Literacy
Health: Hospitals, Mental Health
Social Services: Domestic Violence, Family Services, People with Disabilities, Shelters/Homelessness, United Funds/United Ways, Youth Organizations

Application Procedures

Initial Contact: Submit a short written proposal.
Application Requirements: Include a description of organization, its activities and clients; a clear statement of what is being requested; an explanation of what will be accomplished; proof of tax-exempt status; a list of board members; and an audited financial statement.
Deadlines: Proposals are accepted between January 1 and November 1.
Review Process: Requests are reviewed by the foundation's board of directors, which meets on a quarterly basis.
Notes: Organizations located in operating communities should contact local manufacturing division; requests from the Chicago area should be directed to the foundation's headquarters.

Restrictions

Neither the foundation nor the company contribute printing; award scholarships, except through the company's established programs for children of employees; or make grants for individuals, religious organizations, hospitals, disease specific organizations, clinical care, medical research or equipment, television, radio, film or video.

Additional Information

Part of Donnelley's annual giving is administered by manufacturing divisions, although division grants tend to be smaller than those awarded by the corporate office. In general, manufacturing divisions award grants ranging from $25 to $15,000 each, while the corporate office awards grants ranging from $1,000 to $125,000 each.
Publications: Corporate Contributions Annual Report

Corporate Officials

Haven E. Cockerham: senior vice president human resources PRIM CORP EMPL senior vice president human resources: R.R. Donnelly & Sons Co.
William L. Davis: chairman, president, chief executive officer B 1943. ED Princeton University BA (1965). PRIM CORP EMPL chairman, president, chief executive officer: R.R. Donnelley & Sons Co. CORP AFFIL director: Mallinckrodt Inc.
James R. Donnelley: director B Chicago, IL 1935. ED Dartmouth College BA (1957); University of Chicago MBA (1962). PRIM CORP EMPL vice chairman: R.R. Donnelley & Sons Co. CORP AFFIL director: Sierra Pacific Power Co.; director: Sierra Pacific Resources; director: Pacific Magazines & Printing Ltd.
Cheryl A. Francis: executive vice president, chief financial officer B Toledo, OH 1954. ED Cornell University BS (1976); University of Chicago MBA (1978). PRIM CORP EMPL executive vice president, chief financial officer: R.R. Donnelley & Sons Co. ADD CORP EMPL director investor relations: FMC Corp. NONPR AFFIL member: Financial Executives Institute; member: International Womens Forum.
Susan M. Levy: director community relations PRIM CORP EMPL community relations manager, director: R.R. Donnelley & Sons Co.
Cheryl Malmloff: community relations administrator PRIM CORP EMPL community relations administrator: R.R. Donnelley & Sons Co.

Giving Program Officials

Cheryl A. Francis: member (see above)

Foundation Officials

William L. Davis: chief financial officer, director (see above)
James R. Donnelley: director (see above)
Susan M. Levy: vice president (see above)

Grants Analysis

Typical Range: $1,000 to $10,000

SIDNEY AND ESTHER RABB CHARITABLE FOUNDATION

Giving Contact

Carol R. Goldberg, Trustee
c/o Avcar Group Ltd.
225 Franklin St., Suite 2700
Boston, MA 02110-2804
Phone: (617)695-1946

Description

Founded: 1952
EIN: 046039595
Organization Type: Private Foundation
Giving Locations: FL; MA: emphasis on Boston Northeast.
Grant Types: General Support.

Donor Information

Founder: the late Sidney R. Rabb

Financial Summary

Total Giving: $394,550 (2001); $362,100 (2000); $308,050 (1999)
Assets: $7,642,249 (2001); $8,292,358 (2000); $8,578,988 (1999)

Typical Recipients

Arts & Humanities: History & Archaeology, Libraries, Museums/Galleries, Music, Public Broadcasting
Civic & Public Affairs: Parades/Festivals, Women's Affairs
Education: Arts/Humanities Education, Colleges & Universities, Environmental Education, Faculty Development, Education-General, Public Education (Precollege), Science/Mathematics Education, Social Sciences Education
Health: Children's Health/Hospitals, Health Organizations, Hospices, Hospitals, Medical Rehabilitation, Medical Research
Religion: Jewish Causes, Synagogues/Temples

Science: Science Museums
Social Services: Day Care, Family Planning, Food/Clothing Distribution, Scouts, Senior Services, Sexual Abuse

Application Procedures

Initial Contact: Send a brief letter of inquiry describing program or project.
Deadlines: None.

Foundation Officials

Helene R. Cahners-Kaplan: trustee
Avram J. Goldberg: trustee
Carol Rabb Goldberg: trustee B Newton, MA 1931. ED Tufts University BA (1955); Harvard University Graduate School of Business Administration (1969). PRIM CORP EMPL president: AVCAR Group. CLUB AFFIL Commercial Merchants Boston Club.
Deborah B. Goldberg: trustee
Joshua R. Goldberg: trustee

Grants Analysis

Disclosure Period: calendar year ending 2001
Total Grants: $394,550
Number of Grants: 27
Average Grant: $8,040*
Highest Grant: $185,500
Lowest Grant: $1,000
Typical Range: $1,000 to $20,000
*Note: Average grant figure excludes highest grant.

Recent Grants

Note: Grants derived from 2001 Form 990.

Library-Related

8,000	Boston Public Library Foundation, Boston, MA

General

185,500	Combined Jewish Philanthropies, Boston, MA
25,000	Planned Parenthood League of Massachusetts, Boston, MA
20,000	Boston Latin School Foundation, Boston, MA
20,000	WGBH Education Foundation, Boston, MA
17,500	Make A Wish Foundation of Metro New York, Inc., New York, NY
15,500	University of Massachusetts Center Foundation, Amherst, MA
15,000	Boston Symphony Orchestra, Boston, MA
11,250	Putney School, Putney, VT
8,000	Brookline Senior Center, Brookline, MA
7,500	Park School

SIDNEY R. RABB CHARITABLE TRUST

Giving Contact

Carol R. Goldbert, Trustee
225 Franklin Street, Suite 2700
Boston, MA 02110-2804
Phone: (617)695-1946

Description

Founded: 1952
EIN: 222754563
Organization Type: Private Foundation
Giving Locations: MA
Grant Types: Capital.

Donor Information
Founder: Esther V. Rabb

Financial Summary
Total Giving: $734,025 (fiscal year ending August 31, 2001); $739,000 (fiscal 2000); $469,800 (fiscal 1998)
Assets: $16,637,916 (fiscal 2001); $17,359,300 (fiscal 2000); $15,227,680 (fiscal 1998)

Typical Recipients
Arts & Humanities: Community Arts, Libraries, Museums/Galleries, Music, Public Broadcasting, Theater
Civic & Public Affairs: Botanical Gardens/Parks, Community Foundations, Civic & Public Affairs-General, Nonprofit Management, Philanthropic Organizations
Education: Arts/Humanities Education, Colleges & Universities, Elementary Education (Public), Education-General, Leadership Training, Legal Education, Medical Education, Private Education (Precollege), Public Education (Precollege), Secondary Education (Private), Social Sciences Education
Health: Children's Health/Hospitals, Clinics/Medical Centers, Hospices, Hospitals, Medical Rehabilitation, Medical Research, Mental Health
Religion: Jewish Causes, Religious Organizations, Synagogues/Temples
Social Services: Big Brother/Big Sister, Child Welfare, Family Planning, Senior Services, Sexual Abuse, United Funds/United Ways, Youth Organizations

Application Procedures
Initial Contact: There is no set form for application.
Application Requirements: At a minimum, proposals should include a concise statement of the purpose of funds sought, current year's operating budget, recently audited financial statement, a list of board members, proof of tax-exempt status, and resumes of all key staff personnel. If the grant is sought for a specific program, the staff and budget for that program must be described.
Deadlines: None.

Restrictions
Does not support individuals.

Additional Information
Trust(s): Bingham Dana LLP Palmer and Dodge LLP

Foundation Officials
Nancy L. Cahners: trustee
Helene R. Cahners-Kaplan: trustee
M. Gordon Ehrlich, Esq.: trustee B Springfield, MA 1930. ED Yale University BS (1951); Harvard University LLB (1954). PRIM CORP EMPL partner: Bingham, Dana & Gould. NONPR AFFIL chairman, member: Boston Tax Forum; member: Massachusetts Bar Association; chairman, member: Boston Estate Planning & Business Council; member: American Law Institute; trustee: Beth Israel Hospital; member: American Bar Association.
Carol Rabb Goldberg: trustee B Newton, MA 1931. ED Tufts University BA (1955); Harvard University Graduate School of Business Administration (1969). PRIM CORP EMPL president: AVCAR Group. CLUB AFFIL Commercial Merchants Boston Club.
Arthur B. Page: trustee

Grants Analysis
Disclosure Period: fiscal year ending August 31, 2001
Total Grants: $734,025
Number of Grants: 27
Average Grant: $15,232*
Highest Grant: $338,000
Lowest Grant: $2,000
Typical Range: $5,000 to $30,000
*Note: Average grant figure excludes highest grant.

Recent Grants
Note: Grants derived from 2001 Form 990.

Library-Related
17,000	Boston Public Library Foundation, Boston, MA

General
338,000	Combined Jewish Philanthropies, Boston, MA
43,000	Avalon Elementary School
37,500	Boston Jewish Community Women's Fund, Boston, MA
35,000	Boston Symphony Orchestra, Boston, MA
35,000	Landmark School, Boston, MA
26,500	Beth Israel Deaconess Medical Center, Boston, MA
25,000	Brandeis University, Waltham, MA -- Women's Studies Program
25,000	Hebrew College, Brookline, MA
25,000	Naples Botanical Garden, Naples, FL
18,000	Berkshire Hills Music Academy, Inc., South Hadley, MA

ED RACHAL FOUNDATION

Giving Contact
Paul D. Altheide, Chief Executive Officer and Secretary
500 N. Shoreline, Suite 1002
Corpus Christi, TX 78471
Phone: (361)881-9040
E-mail: edrachal@edrachal.org
Web: http://www.edrachal.org/index.htm

Description
Founded: 1965
EIN: 741116595
Organization Type: Private Foundation
Giving Locations: TX
Grant Types: General Support, Scholarship.

Financial Summary
Total Giving: $501,633 (fiscal year ending August 31, 2001); $129,955 (fiscal 2000); $206,641 (fiscal 1998)
Giving Analysis: Giving for fiscal 2000 includes: foundation scholarships ($5,000)
Assets: $41,022,239 (fiscal 2001); $40,020,790 (fiscal 2000); $20,925,242 (fiscal 1998)

Typical Recipients
Arts & Humanities: Historic Preservation, Libraries, Museums/Galleries, Music, Public Broadcasting
Civic & Public Affairs: Community Foundations, Civic & Public Affairs-General, Law & Justice, Parades/Festivals, Safety
Education: Agricultural Education, Colleges & Universities, Education Funds, Engineering/Technological Education, Environmental Education, International Studies, Preschool Education, Private Education (Precollege), Public Education (Precollege), Science/Mathematics Education, Secondary Education (Public), Student Aid
Environment: Air/Water Quality, Environment-General, Resource Conservation, Wildlife Protection
Health: Cancer, Emergency/Ambulance Services, Hospitals, Medical Research, Public Health, Single-Disease Health Associations, Trauma Treatment
Religion: Churches, Religious Welfare
Social Services: Animal Protection, Big Brother/Big Sister, Camps, Child Welfare, Community Service Organizations, Crime Prevention, Delinquency & Criminal Rehabilitation, Emergency Relief, Family Planning, Family Services, Recreation & Athletics, Scouts, Shelters/Homelessness, Substance Abuse, Volunteer Services, YMCA/YWCA/YMHA/YWHA, Youth Organizations

Application Procedures
Initial Contact: Send a brief letter of inquiry describing program or project.
Deadlines: None.

Foundation Officials
Paul D. Altheide: secretary, treasurer
Claude D'Unger: vice president
Richard Schendel: treasurer
Robert L. Walker: vice president
Marianne R. Warner: president
John White: director

Grants Analysis
Disclosure Period: fiscal year ending August 31, 2001
Total Grants: $501,633
Number of Grants: 28
Average Grant: $16,542*
Highest Grant: $55,000
Lowest Grant: $500
Typical Range: $5,000 to $30,000
*Note: Average grant figure excludes highest grant.

Recent Grants
Note: Grants derived from 2000 Form 990.

General
24,000	Palmer Drug Abuse Program, Corpus Christi, TX -- salary for senior staff member
22,795	Texas A & M University, College Station, TX -- funding for three year deer survey
15,000	Brazos Valley Camp, Snook, TX -- repair and renovations
10,000	Bay Area Citizens Against Lawsuit Abuse, Corpus Christi, TX -- educational campaign
10,000	Brazos Valley Camp, Snook, TX -- repairs to building
10,000	Texas A & M University, College Station, TX -- "Field Guide to Plants" publication
5,000	Corpus Christi Area Heritage Society, Corpus Christi, TX -- Centennial House preservation
5,000	Depelchin Children Center, Houston, TX -- capital campaign
5,000	Marine Military Academy, Harlingen, TX -- purchase a bus
5,000	Sea City Work Camp, Corpus Christi, TX -- materials for building

RAHR MALTING CO.

Company Headquarters
301 4th Ave. S, Ste. 567
Minneapolis, MN 55415
Web: http://www.rahr.com

Company Description
Employees: 100
SIC(s): 2000 Food & Kindred Products, 2083 Malt.

Operating Locations
Rahr Malting Co. (MN--Shakopee)

Rahr Foundation

Giving Contact
Frederick W. Rahr, President & Director
Rahr Foundation
567 Grain Exchange
PO Box 15186
Minneapolis, MN 55415-0186
Phone: (612)332-5161
Fax: (612)332-6841

Description
Founded: 1942
EIN: 396046046
Organization Type: Corporate Foundation
Giving Locations: MN: Minneapolis metropolitan area; WI: Manitowoc
Grant Types: General Support.

Donor Information
Founder: Rahr Malting Co.

Financial Summary
Total Giving: $283,540 (2000); $239,199 (1999); $210,241 (1998)
Giving Analysis: Giving for 2000 includes: foundation scholarships ($24,000); 1999: foundation scholarships ($63,694); foundation ($175,505); 1998: foundation scholarships ($71,441) foundation ($138,800)
Assets: $7,240,637 (2000); $8,381,375 (1999); $7,450,571 (1998)

Typical Recipients
Arts & Humanities: Arts Centers, Arts Institutes, Arts Outreach, Community Arts, Ethnic & Folk Arts, Historic Preservation, History & Archaeology, Libraries, Music, Opera, Public Broadcasting, Theater
Civic & Public Affairs: Botanical Gardens/Parks, Clubs, Community Foundations, Civic & Public Affairs-General, Municipalities/Towns, Public Policy, Urban & Community Affairs, Zoos/Aquariums
Education: Agricultural Education, Arts/Humanities Education, Business Education, Colleges & Universities, Education Funds, Engineering/Technological Education, Education-General, Medical Education, Minority Education, Private Education (Precollege), Student Aid, Vocational & Technical Education
Environment: Air/Water Quality, Environment-General, Resource Conservation, Wildlife Protection
Health: Children's Health/Hospitals, Clinics/Medical Centers, Emergency/Ambulance Services, Health Organizations, Hospitals, Medical Rehabilitation, Medical Research
International: International Environmental Issues
Religion: Religious Welfare
Social Services: Animal Protection, Community Service Organizations, Domestic Violence, Family Planning, Family Services, People with Disabilities, Recreation & Athletics, Scouts, Special Olympics, United Funds/United Ways, YMCA/YWCA/YMHA/YWHA, Youth Organizations

Application Procedures
Initial Contact: Request application form.
Deadlines: March 15.

Restrictions
Does not support individuals, religious organizations for sectarian purposes, political or lobbying groups, or organizations outside operating areas.

Additional Information
Provides scholarships to children of employees of Rahr Malting Co. and its affiliates.

Corporate Officials
John F. Alsip, III: president, chief executive officer, director B 1937. PRIM CORP EMPL president, chief executive officer, director: Rahr Malting Co.
T. C. Haffenreffer, Jr.: vice chairman, director PRIM CORP EMPL vice chairman, director: Rahr Malting Co.
Jim Olson: chief financial officer, controller, vice president financial PRIM CORP EMPL chief financial officer, controller, vice president financial: Rahr Malting Co.
Guido R. Rahr, Jr.: chairman, director B Milwaukee, WI 1928. ED Dartmouth College (1951). PRIM CORP EMPL chairman, director: Rahr Malting Co. CORP AFFIL director: Manitowoc Co.

Foundation Officials
George D. Gackle: treasurer, director B Kulm, ND 1925. ED University of North Dakota (1949). PRIM CORP EMPL director: Rahr Malting Co. CORP AFFIL vice president, director: Lakeside Machine Shop.
Jack D. Gage: director
Mary Gresham: secretary, director
Frederick W. Rahr: president, director
Guido R. Rahr, Jr.: vice president, director (see above)

Grants Analysis
Disclosure Period: calendar year ending 2000
Total Grants: $259,540*
Number of Grants: 71
Average Grant: $3,655
Highest Grant: $38,500
Typical Range: $1,000 to $5,000
*Note: Giving excludes scholarships.

Recent Grants
Note: Grants derived from 1999 Form 990.

General

63,694	Rahr Foundation Scholarship Fund, Minneapolis, MN
25,000	University of Minnesota School of Nursing, Minneapolis, MN
22,500	Minnesota Private College Fund, St. Paul, MN
10,000	Open Book, Minneapolis, MN
5,000	Coalition for a Clean Minnesota River, New Ulm, MN
5,000	Guthrie Theater Foundation, The, Minneapolis, MN
5,000	Hospitality House, Minneapolis, MN
5,000	Manitowoc County Historical Society, Manitowoc, WI
5,000	Minneapolis Institute of Arts, Minneapolis, MN
5,000	Minnesota Opera, St. Paul, MN

M. E. RAKER FOUNDATION

Giving Contact
John E. Hogan, President
6207 Constitution Drive.
Ft. Wayne, IN 46804
Phone: (219)436-2182
Fax: (219)432-3146

Description
Founded: 1984
EIN: 311040474
Organization Type: Private Foundation
Giving Locations: IN
Grant Types: General Support, Scholarship.

Donor Information
Founder: the late M. E. Raker

Financial Summary
Total Giving: $540,445 (fiscal year ending June 30, 2002); $510,670 (fiscal 2001); $539,826 (fiscal 2000)
Giving Analysis: Giving for fiscal 2001 includes: foundation scholarships ($31,500); fiscal 2000: foundation scholarships ($36,500) foundation scholarships ($51,500)
Assets: $9,703,243 (fiscal 2002); $11,513,080 (fiscal 2001); $13,174,759 (fiscal 2000)

Typical Recipients
Arts & Humanities: Arts Appreciation, Arts & Humanities-General, History & Archaeology, Libraries, Museums/Galleries, Public Broadcasting, Theater
Civic & Public Affairs: Botanical Gardens/Parks, Chambers of Commerce, Employment/Job Training, Civic & Public Affairs-General, Housing, Rural Affairs, Urban & Community Affairs, Zoos/Aquariums
Education: Agricultural Education, Business Education, Colleges & Universities, Elementary Education (Private), Elementary Education (Public), Education-General, Health & Physical Education, Private Education (Precollege), Religious Education, Science/Mathematics Education, Secondary Education (Private), Special Education, Student Aid
Environment: Environment-General, Resource Conservation
Health: AIDS/HIV, Cancer, Children's Health/Hospitals, Clinics/Medical Centers, Emergency/Ambulance Services, Health Organizations, Hospitals, Mental Health
Religion: Churches, Religious Organizations, Religious Welfare
Science: Scientific Centers & Institutes
Social Services: Big Brother/Big Sister, Child Welfare, Community Service Organizations, Day Care, Food/Clothing Distribution, People with Disabilities, Recreation & Athletics, Scouts, Senior Services, Shelters/Homelessness, Substance Abuse, YMCA/YWCA/YMHA/YWHA, Youth Organizations

Application Procedures
Initial Contact: Grant application form.s will be furnished upon request.
Deadlines: None.

Restrictions
Does not support individuals or make grants in furtherance of the arts.

Additional Information
Publications: Application Form; Guidelines

Foundation Officials
John E. Hogan: president
John N. Pichon: director
Stephen J. Williams: director

Grants Analysis
Disclosure Period: fiscal year ending June 30, 2002
Total Grants: $508,945*
Number of Grants: 60
Average Grant: $8,482
Highest Grant: $25,000
Lowest Grant: $1,000
Typical Range: $1,000 to $20,000
*Note: Giving excludes scholarships.

Recent Grants
Note: Grants derived from fiscal 2000 Form 990.

General

50,000	University of Saint Francis, Ft. Wayne, IN -- Rolland Art and Visual Communication Center
25,000	Ashland University, Ashland, OH -- basic grant and capital campaign
25,000	Caylor-Nickel Foundation, Bluffton, IN -- endowment program
25,000	ELOC, Inc., Ft. Wayne, IN -- plastics technology center
25,000	Indiana Purdue University at Fort Wayne, Ft. Wayne, IN -- scholarship funding/NCAA division I proposal
25,000	Nature Conservancy, Indianapolis, IN -- geography of hope: a living legacy for Indiana
25,000	Science Central, Ft. Wayne, IN -- youth volunteer program
25,000	YWCA, Ft. Wayne, IN -- capital campaign
20,000	Fort Wayne Children's Zoo, Ft. Wayne, IN -- heart of the zoo campaign
20,000	Monroeville Community Park, Monroeville, IN -- new roof - pavilion

RALPH'S GROCERY CO.

Company Headquarters
Compton, CA
Web: http://www.ralphs.com

Company Description
Employees: 15,000
SIC(s): 5411 Grocery Stores.

Operating Locations
Ralph's Grocery Co. (CA--Compton)

Nonmonetary Support
Type: Donated Equipment; In-kind Services

Ralph's-Food 4 Less Foundation

Giving Contact
Jan Golleher, Executive Director
PO Box 54143
Los Angeles, CA 90054
Phone: (310)884-6250
Fax: (310)884-2590
Web: http://ralphs.com/
corpnewsinfo_charitablegiving_art5.htm

Alternate Contact
1100 West Artesia Boulevard
Compton, CA 90220
Note: Alternate address is for grant application pick-up.

Description
Founded: 1992
EIN: 330492352
Organization Type: Corporate Foundation
Giving Locations: CA: southern California
Grant Types: General Support, Project, Scholarship.

Donor Information
Founder: Food 4 Less Supermarkets, Ron Burkle, Ralph Grocery Co.

Financial Summary
Total Giving: $1,784,751 (2001); $1,045,555 (2000); $6,720,000 (1999 approx)
Giving Analysis: Giving for 2000 includes: foundation scholarships ($23,000); foundation ($1,022,555) 1998: foundation ($2,896,800)
Assets: $2,988,650 (2001); $3,207,400 (2000); $339,086 (1998)
Gifts Received: $1,530,344 (2001); $3,691,534 (2000); $3,613,729 (1998). Note: In 1998, contributions were received from Western Union Financial Services ($200,000); Anheuser-Busch, Inc. ($124,293); Ralphs Grocery Co. ($40,000); and numerous other donors who contributed less than $40,000 each. In 1995, contributions were received from Anheuser-Busch ($154,000), Ralphs Grocery Co. ($855,000), Western Union ($400,000), Miller Brewing Co. ($63,335), and Coors Brewing ($95,500); numerous other donors contributed less than $50,000 each.

Typical Recipients
Arts & Humanities: Arts Centers, Arts Festivals, Arts Institutes, Ethnic & Folk Arts, Film & Video, Historic Preservation, History & Archaeology, Libraries, Museums/Galleries, Music, Performing Arts, Theater
Civic & Public Affairs: African American Affairs, Asian American Affairs, Economic Development, Employment/Job Training, Ethnic Organizations, Civic & Public Affairs-General, Hispanic Affairs, Housing, Legal Aid, Public Policy, Safety, Urban & Community Affairs

Education: Afterschool/Enrichment Programs, Business Education, Colleges & Universities, Education Reform, Education-General, International Studies, Literacy, Medical Education, Minority Education, Private Education (Precollege), Public Education (Precollege), Religious Education, Science/Mathematics Education, Secondary Education (Public), Special Education, Student Aid
Environment: Environment-General, Protection
Health: AIDS/HIV, Cancer, Children's Health/Hospitals, Clinics/Medical Centers, Diabetes, Emergency/Ambulance Services, Eyes/Blindness, Health Organizations, Heart, Hospitals, Mental Health, Multiple Sclerosis, Prenatal Health Issues, Single-Disease Health Associations
International: Foreign Educational Institutions, Human Rights
Religion: Churches, Religion-General, Jewish Causes, Missionary Activities (Domestic), Religious Organizations, Religious Welfare
Science: Science Museums
Social Services: Animal Protection, At-Risk Youth, Big Brother/Big Sister, Big Brother/Big Sister, Camps, Child Abuse, Child Welfare, Community Service Organizations, Crime Prevention, Domestic Violence, Emergency Relief, Family Planning, Food/Clothing Distribution, Homes, People with Disabilities, Recreation & Athletics, Scouts, Senior Services, Social Services-General, Substance Abuse, United Funds/United Ways, YMCA/YWCA/YMHA/YWHA, Youth Organizations

Application Procedures
Initial Contact: Send letter of request.
Application Requirements: Include a thorough outline of the program, including the amount requested, how funds will be used and whom they will serve, budget, funding sources, proof of tax-exempt status, and supporting materials.
Deadlines: None.
Review Process: Foundation is administered by the community religious department of the Ralphs Grocery Company under the direction of a Board of Trustees and an executive director. Proposals are reviewed by the executive director; a grants committee appointed by the board gives final approval of allocations.

Restrictions
Grants are not made to individuals, memorial campaigns, political activities, endowment campaigns, or to fund programs that are discriminatory.

Corporate Officials
Ron Burkle: chairman, chief executive officer PRIM CORP EMPL chairman: Ralph's Grocery Co.
Sam Duncan: president, chief executive officer PRIM CORP EMPL president: Ralph's Grocery Co.

Foundation Officials
Ron Burkle: chairman (see above)
Sam Duncan: president (see above)

Grants Analysis
Disclosure Period: calendar year ending 2001
Total Grants: $1,726,201*
Number of Grants: 332
Average Grant: $5,199
Highest Grant: $235,432
Lowest Grant: $500
Typical Range: $500 to $25,000
*Note: Giving excludes scholarship.

Recent Grants
Note: Grants derived from 2002 Form 990.

Library-Related
10,000	California State Library Foundation, Sacramento, CA -- for school Library Enrichment Program

General
235,432	American Red Cross, Los Angeles, CA -- to support rescue and disaster relief
107,500	March of Dimes Southern California Chapter, Los Angeles, CA -- for Walk America 2001
100,000	Habitat for Humanity South Bay Long Beach, Long Beach, CA -- to sponsor and build a home
60,000	Tiger Woods Foundation, Los Alamitos, CA -- to support the Tiger Woods golf clinic and exhibition
33,250	Los Angeles Urban League, Los Angeles, CA -- to support the 28th Annual Whitney M. Young, Jr. Award Dinner
25,000	Catholic Charities of Orange County, Santa Ana, CA -- to sponsor the 14th annual Bishop McFarland Open Golf Tournament
25,000	Catholic Charities of Orange County, Santa Ana, CA -- to sponsor the 14th annual Bishop McFarland Open Golf Tournament
25,000	Jewish Federation Council of Greater Los Angeles, Los Angeles, CA -- to support the Federation's efforts to provide meals to seniors
25,000	Mexican American Grocers Association Foundation, Los Angeles, CA -- to assist with scholarships for students
25,000	Theatre Foundation, Temecula, CA -- to build a new theatre and arts center

RASKOB FOUNDATION FOR CATHOLIC ACTIVITIES, INC.

Giving Contact
Frederick J. Perella, Jr., Executive Vice President
PO Box 4019
Wilmington, DE 19807
Phone: (302)655-4440
Fax: (302)655-3223
Web: http://www.rfca.org

Description
Founded: 1945
EIN: 510070060
Organization Type: Family Foundation
Giving Locations: internationally; nationally.
Grant Types: Challenge, Conference/Seminar, Emergency, General Support, Loan, Matching, Multiyear/Continuing Support, Operating Expenses, Project, Seed Money.

Donor Information
Founder: The Raskob Foundation for Catholic Activities was established in 1945 by John J. Raskob and his wife, Helena S. Raskob. Mr. Raskob (d. 1950) was vice president of DuPont, chairman of the board of General Motors, and one of the builders of the Empire State Building. The foundation that he established is unusual in that it is a membership corporation, with the membership made up primarily of Raskob family members. There are over 90 members.

Financial Summary
Total Giving: $6,721,439 (2000); $5,633,000 (1999); $6,309,493 (1998)
Assets: $158,185,873 (2000); $156,669,000 (1999); $145,528,416 (1998)
Gifts Received: $20,000 (1997)

Typical Recipients

Arts & Humanities: Historic Preservation

Civic & Public Affairs: Community Foundations, Employment/Job Training, Civic & Public Affairs-General, Hispanic Affairs, Housing, Legal Aid, Native American Affairs, Safety, Urban & Community Affairs

Education: Colleges & Universities, Community & Junior Colleges, Elementary Education (Private), Faculty Development, Education-General, Medical Education, Minority Education, Private Education (Precollege), Religious Education, Secondary Education (Private), Secondary Education (Public), Special Education, Student Aid

Health: Adolescent Health Issues, AIDS/HIV, Children's Health/Hospitals, Clinics/Medical Centers, Health Organizations, Hospices, Hospitals, Medical Rehabilitation, Mental Health, Nursing Services, Preventive Medicine/Wellness Organizations, Public Health

International: Foreign Educational Institutions, International-General, Health Care/Hospitals, International Development, International Environmental Issues, International Organizations, International Peace & Security Issues, International Relief Efforts, Missionary/Religious Activities

Religion: Bible Study/Translation, Churches, Dioceses, Religion-General, Ministries, Missionary Activities (Domestic), Religious Organizations, Religious Welfare, Social/Policy Issues

Science: Science-General

Social Services: Child Welfare, Community Centers, Community Service Organizations, Counseling, Day Care, Delinquency & Criminal Rehabilitation, Domestic Violence, Emergency Relief, Family Planning, Family Services, Food/Clothing Distribution, Homes, People with Disabilities, Recreation & Athletics, Refugee Assistance, Senior Services, Shelters/Homelessness, Social Services-General, Substance Abuse, Volunteer Services, Youth Organizations

Application Procedures

Initial Contact: The foundation should be contacted by letter or fax to determine eligibility and to obtain an application form and guidelines.

Application Requirements: A full application requires a completed original application form; narrative summary of the proposal (not to exceed five pages); detailed budget of the proposed project; copy of the latest annual auditor's report or financial statement, listing actual income, assets, and expenditures; and a letter from the Ordinary of the Diocese (where the project will take place) commenting on the proposed project. Religious orders not under the jurisdiction of an Ordinary must send a letter to the local Ordinary from the Provincial, Abbot, Mother Superior, etc., informing him about the application. A copy of the letter must be submitted to the foundation.

Deadlines: Applications for the springboard of trustees meeting must be received between December 8 and February 8. Applications for the fall meeting must be received between June 8 and August 8. Applicants are urged to submit applications as early as possible during these time periods.

Review Process: The board of trustees meets twice a year, in the spring and fall. Applications are considered on their merits. Need and the good to be accomplished are prime considerations. It is the board's policy to stretch its funds to help as many different Catholic activities as it can. Most grants are, therefore, under $15,000.

Restrictions

The foundation only accepts applications from Roman Catholic tax-exempt organizations listed in the *Official Catholic Directory* published by P.J. Kenedy & Sons, New York. The foundation does not accept applications for debt reduction, scholarly research leading to a degree, continuing subsidies, or for after-the-fact funding. It makes no grants to individuals or for tuition. It does not consider applications for scholarships, fellowships, or endowments. As a general rule, capital campaigns and construction projects have a low priority. The Foundation does not generally make contributions to the same organization on a continuing or regular basis.

Additional Information

The foundation has a particular interest in projects in which self-help and local support are demonstrated. **Publications:** Biennial Report; Application Form; Guidelines

Foundation Officials

Theodore H. Bremekamp, III: trustee
Helen R. Doordan: first vice president
Michael G. Duffy: trustee at large
Gerard S. Garey: president, ex-officio trustee B 1932.
John J. Harmon: chairperson
Kathryn F. Lyon: secretary
Frederick J. Perella, Jr.: executive vice president, ex-officio trustee
Anthony W. Raskob, Jr.: trustee
B. Russell Raskob: treasurer
Jakob T. Raskob: trustee
Peter A. Robinson: trustee at large
Kathleen D. Smith: trustee
Katherine R. Van Loan: trustee at large

Grants Analysis

Disclosure Period: calendar year ending 2000
Total Grants: $6,721,439*
Number of Grants: 642
Average Grant: $10,470
Highest Grant: $348,200
Lowest Grant: $100
Typical Range: $10,000 to $160,000
*Note: Grants analysis provided by foundation.

Recent Grants

Note: Grants derived from 2000 Form 990.

General

348,200   Pacific Institute for Community Organization, Oakland, CA -- implement the Skipper Initiative by four congregation-based community organizations

320,000   National Catholic Community Foundation, Annapolis, MD -- for operational costs of NCCF during five-year start-up period

100,000   Catholic Relief Services, Baltimore, MD -- toward costs of a water and sanitation development project in Marale and Orica, Honduras

75,000   Pontifical Ratisbonne Institute, Jerusalem Israel -- supplement for annual operating expenses of Centre specializing in in-depth study of Judaism

70,000   Southern African Catholic Bishops' Conference, Pretoria Republic of South Africa -- salaries, supplies, workshop expenses, rent, and similar items for hospice centers, orphan placement, and similar services

50,000   Archdiocese of Washington, Washington, DC -- to hire a team of related service practitioners to provide occupational and physical therapy

50,000   Catholic High School of Baltimore, Baltimore, MD -- toward construction and for salaries

50,000   Center of Concern, Washington, DC -- to train local community leaders in social analysis, faith reflection and media outreach

50,000   Ministry of Caring, Wilmington, DE -- operating expenses of Il Bambino, an infant-care center for the children of low-income parents

50,000   National Center for the Laity, Chicago, IL -- salaries and benefits for executive director and support staff

MILTON M. RATNER FOUNDATION

Giving Contact

Charles R. McDonald, Vice President, Secretary & Trustee
6336 Aspen Ridge
West Bloomfield, MI 48322
Phone: (414)765-2017

Description

Founded: 1968
EIN: 386160330
Organization Type: Private Foundation
Giving Locations: GA; MI
Grant Types: Capital, Endowment, General Support, Project, Research, Scholarship.

Donor Information

Founder: Milton M. Ratner Trust

Financial Summary

Total Giving: $569,700 (fiscal year ending August 31, 2001); $517,000 (fiscal 2000); $397,965 (fiscal 1998)
Giving Analysis: Giving for fiscal 2001 includes: foundation grants to United Way ($50,000); fiscal 2000: foundation grants to United Way ($40,000) fiscal 1998: foundation grants to United Way ($30,000)
Assets: $9,450,329 (fiscal 2001); $11,250,578 (fiscal 2000); $9,054,578 (fiscal 1998)

Typical Recipients

Arts & Humanities: Arts Associations & Councils, History & Archaeology, Libraries, Music

Civic & Public Affairs: Civic & Public Affairs-General, Municipalities/Towns, Urban & Community Affairs

Education: Colleges & Universities, Continuing Education, Education Funds, Engineering/Technological Education, Education-General, Legal Education, Literacy, Medical Education, Private Education (Precollege), Public Education (Precollege), Religious Education, Science/Mathematics Education, Secondary Education (Public), Student Aid, Vocational & Technical Education

Health: Alzheimers Disease, Children's Health/Hospitals, Clinics/Medical Centers, Diabetes, Emergency/Ambulance Services, Health Organizations, Heart, Hospices, Hospitals, Medical Research, Single-Disease Health Associations

Religion: Churches, Jewish Causes, Ministries, Religious Organizations, Religious Welfare, Synagogues/Temples

Social Services: Animal Protection, At-Risk Youth, Child Welfare, Community Service Organizations, Delinquency & Criminal Rehabilitation, Family Services, People with Disabilities, Recreation & Athletics, Scouts, United Funds/United Ways, Volunteer Services, Youth Organizations

Application Procedures

Initial Contact: Send a brief letter of inquiry.
Application Requirements: Include proof of tax-exempt status, an outline of the proposed budget, and program objectives.
Deadlines: September 15.

Restrictions

Does not support individuals.

Foundation Officials

Mary Jo Ratner Corley: president, trustee
J. Beverly Langford: treasurer, trustee
Charles R. McDonald: vice president, secretary, trustee
Therese M. Thorn: trustee

Grants Analysis

Disclosure Period: fiscal year ending August 31, 2001
Total Grants: $519,700*
Number of Grants: 59
Average Grant: $8,808
Highest Grant: $25,000
Lowest Grant: $1,000
Typical Range: $5,000 to $15,000
***Note:** Giving excludes United Way.

Recent Grants

Note: Grants derived from 2000 Form 990.

General

25,000	Gordon Hospital Foundation, Calhoun, GA
20,000	United Way of Gordon County, Calhoun, GA
20,000	United Way of Southeastern Michigan, Detroit, MI
15,000	Alzheimer's Association, Sacramento, CA
15,000	Berry College, Mt. Berry, GA
15,000	Jewish Welfare Foundation, Detroit, MI
15,000	United Jewish Appeal, New York, NY
13,500	Gordon County Schools, Calhoun, GA
10,000	Boysville of Michigan, MI
10,000	Brewton Parker College, Mt. Vernon, GA

A. C. RATSHESKY FOUNDATION

Giving Contact

Michealle Larkins, Program Officer
c/o GMA
77 Summer Street, 8th Fl.
Boston, MA 02110-1006
Phone: (617)426-7080
Fax: (617)426-7087
E-mail:
ratsheskyfoundation@grantsmanagement.com
Web: http://www.grantsmanagement.com/ratshesky.html
Note: Ms. Larkins' telephone extension is 302.

Description

Founded: 1916
EIN: 046017426
Organization Type: Private Foundation
Giving Locations: MA: Boston and contiguous communities
Grant Types: Capital, Emergency, General Support, Operating Expenses, Project.

Donor Information

Founder: the late A. C. Ratshesky and family

Financial Summary

Total Giving: $233,600 (2001); $504,490 (2000); $443,340 (1999)
Giving Analysis: Giving for 1998 includes: foundation scholarships ($24,500) foundation ($371,100)
Assets: $8,077,012 (2001); $8,793,940 (2000); $9,196,363 (1999)
Gifts Received: $34,794 (1995); $7,000 (1994); $87,410 (1992). Note: In 1995, contributions were received from the estate of Hetty Kaffenburgh.

Typical Recipients

Arts & Humanities: Arts Associations & Councils, Arts Centers, Arts Outreach, Community Arts, Dance, Ethnic & Folk Arts, History & Archaeology, Libraries, Museums/Galleries, Music, Opera, Performing Arts, Theater
Civic & Public Affairs: Asian American Affairs, Civil Rights, Economic Development, Employment/Job Training, Ethnic Organizations, Civic & Public Affairs-General, Hispanic Affairs, Housing, Law & Justice, Municipalities/Towns, Parades/Festivals, Philanthropic Organizations, Public Policy, Safety, Urban & Community Affairs, Women's Affairs
Education: Afterschool/Enrichment Programs, Arts/Humanities Education, Business Education, Education Reform, Elementary Education (Private), Education-General, Literacy, Minority Education, Preschool Education, Private Education (Precollege), School Volunteerism, Science/Mathematics Education, Secondary Education (Private), Secondary Education (Public)
Health: Clinics/Medical Centers, Public Health
Religion: Religion-General, Jewish Causes, Religious Welfare
Science: Science Museums
Social Services: Big Brother/Big Sister, Camps, Child Welfare, Community Service Organizations, Counseling, Day Care, Domestic Violence, Family Planning, Family Services, Refugee Assistance, Senior Services, Shelters/Homelessness, Social Services-General, Substance Abuse, Volunteer Services, Youth Organizations

Application Procedures

Initial Contact: Submit a full proposal.
Application Requirements: The foundation accepts the Common Proposal Format available at http://www.agmconnect.org.
Deadlines: March 1, for evaluation at a May/June board meeting; September 1, for a November meeting; and December 1, for a February/March meeting. All applications for summer programs are due in March.
Notes: The foundation does not accept proposals submitted in folders, binders, or report covers.

Restrictions

Does not support individuals; national organizations; capital campaigns, endowments, or fundraising activities; conferences; web sites; research; municipal, state, or federal agencies; religious instruction or worship services; health programs; or public schools, including pilot and charter schools.

Additional Information

Publications: Annual Report; Application Guidelines

Foundation Officials

Michealle Larkins: program officer
Roberta Morse Levy: secretary
Edith Morse Millender: assistant secretary
Alan Morse: vice president
Alan R. Morse, Jr.: trustee
Cecily Morse: director
Eric Robert Morse: president
John Morse, Jr.: treasurer
Timothy Morse: assistant treasurer
Rebecca Morse Steinfield: trustee
Linda G. Ortwein: trustee
Laurie Morse Sprague: assistant treasurer

Grants Analysis

Disclosure Period: calendar year ending 2001
Total Grants: $233,600
Number of Grants: 51
Average Grant: $4,580
Highest Grant: $15,000
Typical Range: $3,000 to $10,000

Recent Grants

Note: Grants derived from 2001 Form 990.

General

15,000	Management Consulting Services Management Consulting Services, Boston, MA
8,000	Summerbridge Cambridge, Cambridge, MA

7,500	Casa Myrna Vasquez, Boston, MA
7,000	Casa Esperanza, Roxbury, MA
6,000	Cambodian Community of Massachusetts, Chelsea, MA
6,000	Greater Boston Youth Symphony Orchestras (GBYSO), Boston, MA
5,000	Algebra Project, Boston, MA
5,000	Arts in Progress, Boston, MA
5,000	Associated Grantmakers, Boston, MA
5,000	Brookline Library Foundation, Brookline, MA

RAY FOUNDATION

Giving Contact

James C. Ray, President & Director
2241 Park Place Suite A-1
Minden, NV 89423
Phone: (775)782-8337

Description

Founded: 1962
EIN: 810288819
Organization Type: Private Foundation
Giving Locations: NV; NM; ND; WA
Grant Types: Capital, Emergency, General Support, Multiyear/Continuing Support, Operating Expenses, Project, Research, Scholarship, Seed Money.

Donor Information

Founder: James C. Ray, the late Joan L. Ray

Financial Summary

Total Giving: $200,000 (fiscal year ending June 30, 2002 approx); $3,892,859 (fiscal 2001); $2,487,117 (fiscal 2000)
Giving Analysis: Giving for fiscal 2001 includes: foundation scholarships ($50,000)
Assets: $13,718,219 (fiscal 2001); $23,857,208 (fiscal 2000); $21,607,552 (fiscal 1997)
Gifts Received: $1,770,000 (fiscal 1995). Note: In fiscal 1995, contributions were received from James C. Ray.

Typical Recipients

Arts & Humanities: Arts Centers, Historic Preservation, History & Archaeology, Libraries, Museums/Galleries, Music, Performing Arts, Theater
Civic & Public Affairs: Housing, Philanthropic Organizations, Professional & Trade Associations, Safety, Urban & Community Affairs
Education: Colleges & Universities, Community & Junior Colleges, Journalism/Media Education, Leadership Training, Private Education (Precollege), Public Education (Precollege), Science/Mathematics Education, Special Education, Student Aid
Environment: Air/Water Quality, Resource Conservation
Health: Clinics/Medical Centers, Hospices, Long-Term Care, Medical Rehabilitation, Mental Health
Religion: Religious Welfare
Science: Science Museums, Scientific Centers & Institutes
Social Services: At-Risk Youth, Child Welfare, Community Service Organizations, Family Services, Recreation & Athletics, Substance Abuse, Youth Organizations

Application Procedures

Initial Contact: Send brief letter of inquiry, not exceeding two pages, summarizing the grant request. Include the exact name of applicant, address, telephone number, date of application, a description of organization, proof of tax-exempt status, purpose of funds sought, budget for the project, amount requested and sources of other funding, plans for cooperation with other institutions or organizations, if any, and signatures and titles of project director and chief administrative officer.

Deadlines: None.
Review Process: Applications are considered as they are received.

Restrictions

Emphasis is on programs that address the problem of substance abuse and preventative projects involving children. Does not support individuals.

Additional Information

Publications: Application Guidelines

Foundation Officials

Mary Cornwall: secretary, treasurer
John S. Darrell: director
Jeffrey L. Hesson: director
Carrie Landvater: secretary, treasurer
James C. Ray: president
June M. Ray: director
Jeffrey J. Tempas: director

Grants Analysis

Disclosure Period: fiscal year ending June 30, 2001
Total Grants: $3,842,859*
Number of Grants: 6
Average Grant: $69,818*
Highest Grant: $3,073,950
Typical Range: $20,000 to $100,000
*Note: Giving excludes scholarship. Average grant figure excludes two highest grants ($3,423,950).

Recent Grants

Note: Grants derived from fiscal 2002 Form 990.

General

3,073,950	University of North Dakota Center of Innovation, Grand Forks, ND -- for UN-DCOIF endowment
350,000	University of North Dakota Center of Innovation, Grand Forks, ND -- for entrepreneurship chair and School of Business
250,000	Museum of Flight, Seattle, WA -- NASA Aeronautics Education Lab
60,625	EAA Aviation Foundation, Oshkosh, WI -- for lodge on lower level
50,000	Bosque School, Albuquerque, NM -- for the Center for Performing Arts
50,000	University of North Dakota Aerospace Foundation, Grand Forks, ND -- for Graduate Capstone Project
50,000	University of North Dakota Foundation, Grand Forks, ND -- for Donald Smith Aerospace Scholarship
5,000	Family Support Council, Minden, NV -- for Safe House Project
3,284	Albuquerque Little Theatre, Albuquerque, NM -- for eclipse night

RAYMOND CORP.

Company Headquarters

South Canal St.
PO Box 130
Greene, NY 13778-0130
Phone: (607)656-2311
Web: http://www.raymondcorp.com

Company Description

Founded: 1928
Revenue: US$430 million (2001)
Employees: 2,900
SIC(s): 3500 Industrial Machinery & Equipment.

Operating Locations

Raymond Corp. (NY--Binghamton; VI--St. Thomas)

Raymond Foundation

Giving Contact

Theresa Brant, Assistant Executive Secretary
Raymond Foundation
PO Box 1273E
Greene, NY 13778
Phone: (607)656-8897

Description

Founded: 1964
EIN: 166047847
Organization Type: Corporate Foundation
Giving Locations: CA: limited to areas of company operations; NY: limited to areas of company operations
Grant Types: Capital, Matching, Project.

Donor Information

Founder: the late George G. Raymond

Financial Summary

Total Giving: $306,132 (2000); $268,574 (1999); $220,169 (1997)
Giving Analysis: Giving for 2000 includes: foundation grants to United Way ($500); foundation matching gifts ($11,900); foundation scholarships ($16,813) 1999: foundation ($268,574)
Assets: $6,301,729 (2000); $6,621,615 (1999); $5,640,057 (1997)
Gifts Received: $130,000 (1999); $166,515 (1997); $180,980 (1996)

Typical Recipients

Arts & Humanities: Art History, Arts Associations & Councils, Historic Preservation, History & Archaeology, Libraries, Music, Performing Arts, Public Broadcasting
Civic & Public Affairs: Business/Free Enterprise, Chambers of Commerce, Clubs, Employment/Job Training, Civic & Public Affairs-General, Housing, Municipalities/Towns, Parades/Festivals, Public Policy, Rural Affairs, Safety, Urban & Community Affairs, Zoos/Aquariums
Education: Business Education, Colleges & Universities, Community & Junior Colleges, Education Associations, Education Funds, Engineering/Technological Education, Education-General, Literacy, Private Education (Precollege), Public Education (Precollege), Secondary Education (Private), Student Aid
Health: Cancer, Cancer, Children's Health/Hospitals, Clinics/Medical Centers, Emergency/Ambulance Services, Eyes/Blindness, Health Organizations, Heart, Hospices, Hospitals, Kidney, Respiratory, Single-Disease Health Associations
International: Missionary/Religious Activities
Religion: Religious Welfare
Science: Science Museums, Scientific Centers & Institutes
Social Services: Animal Protection, Big Brother/Big Sister, Child Welfare, Community Service Organizations, Day Care, Recreation & Athletics, Scouts, Senior Services, Special Olympics, United Funds/United Ways, Veterans, Volunteer Services, YMCA/YWCA/YMHA/YWHA, Youth Organizations

Application Procedures

Initial Contact: Send a brief letter of inquiry.
Application Requirements: detailed request, other sources of funding, proof of tax-exempt status, annual budget, annual report, and projet budget.
Deadlines: None.

Additional Information

Publications: Application Guidelines

Corporate Officials

James J. Malvaso: president, chief executive officer, director PRIM CORP EMPL president, chief executive officer, director: Raymond Corp.

Foundation Officials

Theresa Brant: assistant executive secretary
Patrick J. McManus: treasurer
Richard Najarian: trustee
George G. Raymond, III: executive secretary
John Riley: trustee

Grants Analysis

Disclosure Period: calendar year ending 2000
Total Grants: $279,919*
Number of Grants: 85
Average Grant: $3,293
Highest Grant: $40,000
Typical Range: $1,000 to $5,000
*Note: Giving excludes United Way, scholarships, and matching gifts.

Recent Grants

Note: Grants derived from 2001 Form 990.

General

50,000	Discovery Center -- capital fund drive for building
35,000	Greene Central School Marching Band -- purchase new uniforms for marching band
25,000	Genegantslet Fire Company -- purchase of new fire truck
25,000	Norwich YMCA, Norwich, NY
25,000	RKC - Scholarship Fund -- scholarships on material handling
25,000	Triangle Fire Company, Lexington, KY -- funding toward purchase of new fire truck
20,000	Lourdes Cancer Center Foundation -- pledge to build local Cancer Center
15,000	Genegantslet Fire Company -- project to replace Scott air packs
10,000	New York State Special Olympics, Brooklyn, NY
5,500	American Heart Association, Panama City, FL -- annual heart ball

RAYONIER, INC.

Company Headquarters

Jacksonville, FL
Web: http://www.rayonier.com

Company Description

Founded: 1926
Ticker: RYN
Exchange: NYSE
Former Name: ITT Rayonier.
Revenue: US$1.117 billion (2002)
Employees: 2200 (2002)
SIC(s): 2411 Logging, 2421 Sawmills & Planing Mills--General, 2611 Pulp Mills, 3087 Custom Compound of Purchased Resins.

Operating Locations

Rayonier Inc. (CT--Hartford, Stamford, Trumbull; MA--Boston; NJ--Midland Park, Paramus, Secaucus; WA--Hoquiam)

Nonmonetary Support
Type: In-kind Services

Rayonier Foundation

Giving Contact
Jay A. Fredericksen, Vice President
50 North Laura Street, Suite 1900
Jacksonville, FL 32202
Phone: (904)357-9100

Description
Founded: 1952
EIN: 136064462
Organization Type: Corporate Foundation
Giving Locations: headquarters area only.
Grant Types: Employee Matching Gifts, General Support, Scholarship.

Donor Information
Founder: ITT Rayonier, Inc.

Financial Summary
Total Giving: $576,308 (2000); $641,677 (1999); $701,016 (1998)
Giving Analysis: Giving for 2000 includes: foundation scholarships ($85,495); foundation grants to United Way ($132,410); foundation ($358,403); 1999: foundation scholarships ($79,450); foundation grants to United Way ($116,081) foundation ($446,146)
Assets: $5,139,806 (2000); $5,072,433 (1999); $5,210,255 (1998)
Gifts Received: $1,040,700 (2000); $220,000 (1999); $239,000 (1998). Note: Contributions received from Rayonier, Inc.

Typical Recipients
Arts & Humanities: Arts Associations & Councils, Arts Centers, Historic Preservation, History & Archaeology, Libraries, Museums/Galleries, Music, Performing Arts, Public Broadcasting
Civic & Public Affairs: Business/Free Enterprise, Chambers of Commerce, Clubs, Economic Development, Economic Policy, Employment/Job Training, Civic & Public Affairs-General, Municipalities/Towns, Philanthropic Organizations, Professional & Trade Associations, Safety, Urban & Community Affairs, Zoos/Aquariums
Education: Agricultural Education, Arts/Humanities Education, Business Education, Colleges & Universities, Community & Junior Colleges, Economic Education, Education Associations, Education Funds, Elementary Education (Public), Engineering/Technological Education, Environmental Education, Education-General, International Studies, Legal Education, Literacy, Minority Education, Preschool Education, Private Education (Precollege), Public Education (Precollege), Science/Mathematics Education, Secondary Education (Public), Special Education, Student Aid, Vocational & Technical Education
Environment: Forestry, Environment-General
Health: Children's Health/Hospitals, Hospices, Hospitals, Mental Health
Religion: Religious Welfare
Science: Science Museums
Social Services: Camps, Child Abuse, Child Welfare, Community Centers, Community Service Organizations, Counseling, Day Care, Delinquency & Criminal Rehabilitation, Domestic Violence, Emergency Relief, Food/Clothing Distribution, People with Disabilities, Recreation & Athletics, Scouts, Senior Services, Shelters/Homelessness, Substance Abuse, United Funds/United Ways, Volunteer Services, YMCA/YWCA/YMHA/YWHA, Youth Organizations

Application Procedures
Initial Contact: Send a a brief letter of inquiry.
Application Requirements: Include a description of organization and program, amount requested, and proof of tax-exempt status.

Deadlines: November 15 for scholarships.
Decision Notification: Board meets in February; notification one month after meeting.
Notes: Application forms are available for scholarship programs from the foundation.

Additional Information
Foundation awards scholarships to outstanding black students residing within and graduating from a high school within Wayne County, GA, or Nassau County, FL. Also awards scholarships to outstanding students (without regard to race) residing within and graduating from a high school within Wayne, GA, Nassau, FL, and Mason, Clallam, and Grays Harbor, WA. Scholarship decisions are made locally. Contact foundation for more information and applications.
Company reports that it is no longer affiliated with ITT Corp.

Corporate Officials
William S. Berry: executive vice president forest resources & wood products B Placerville, CA 1941. ED University of California at Berkeley BS (1964); University of Michigan MS (1965). PRIM CORP EMPL executive vice president forest resources & wood products: Rayonier Inc. CORP AFFIL president, director: Rayonier New Zealand.
Wallace L. Nutter: president, chief executive officer, director B Astoria, OR 1944. ED University of Washington BA (1967); Harvard University Graduate School of Business Administration (1987). PRIM CORP EMPL president, chief executive officer, director: Rayonier Inc. CORP AFFIL director: Rayonier Forest Resources Co. NONPR AFFIL member board governments: National Council Paper Industry Air & Stream Improvement.

Foundation Officials
MacDonald Auguste: treasurer B 1948. ED City University of New York BA (1969-1976); Pace University MBA (1979). CORP AFFIL treasurer: Rayonier Timberlands LP.
William S. Berry: director (see above)
John Beckman Canning: secretary B Chicago, IL 1943. ED Princeton University AB (1965); Columbia University LLB (1968). PRIM CORP EMPL corporate secretary, associate general counsel: Rayonier Inc. CORP AFFIL vice president, director: Beckman Bros. NONPR AFFIL member: Columbia University Law School Alumni Association; director: Stamford Symphony Orchestra; member: American Society of Corporate Secretaries; member: American Bar Association.
Jay A. Fredericksen: vice president, director CORP AFFIL vice president corp. relations: Rayonier Inc.
Wallace L. Nutter: director (see above)
Wendy Pugnetti: assistant secretary

Grants Analysis
Disclosure Period: calendar year ending 2000
Total Grants: $358,403*
Number of Grants: 280
Average Grant: $1,280
Highest Grant: $100,000
Typical Range: $100 to $5,000
*Note: Giving excludes scholarship and United Way.

Recent Grants
Note: Grants derived from 2000 Form 990.

General

100,000	University of Oklahoma, Norman, OK
42,600	United Way of South Georgia, Waycross, GA
40,820	United Way, Waycross, GA
25,000	United Way Northeast Florida, Jacksonville, FL
13,600	University of Georgia, Jesup, GA
12,590	United Way King County, Seattle, WA
11,250	Altamaha Technical Institute Foundation, Jesup, GA
8,165	Georgia Southern University, Jesup, GA
8,000	Jacksonville Symphony, Jacksonville, FL
8,000	University of Miami, Coral Gables, FL

RBC CENTURA

Company Headquarters
1910 Wesleyan Blvd.
Rocky Mount, NC 27804
Web: http://www.centura.com

Company Description
Employees: 2,100
SIC(s): 6700 Holding & Other Investment Offices.
Parent Company: RBC Financial Group, 200 Bay St., Toronto, ON, Canada

Centura First Savings Foundation of Rutherford County

Giving Contact
David Whilden, Assistant to the Chairman
PO Box 388
Forest City, NC 28043
Phone: (828)236-8814

Description
Founded: 1993
EIN: 561832201
Organization Type: Corporate Foundation
Giving Locations: NC: Rutherford County
Grant Types: General Support.

Financial Summary
Total Giving: $75,000 (2000); $75,000 (1999); $75,000 (1998). Note: 1997 Giving includes United Way ($6,000).
Giving Analysis: Giving for 2000 includes: foundation grants to United Way ($6,000); 1999: foundation grants to United Way ($5,000); foundation ($70,000); 1998: foundation grants to United Way ($5,000); foundation ($70,000);
Assets: $1,857,837 (2000); $1,897,506 (1999); $1,817,532 (1998)

Typical Recipients
Arts & Humanities: History & Archaeology, Libraries, Museums/Galleries, Music
Civic & Public Affairs: Business/Free Enterprise, Employment/Job Training, Civic & Public Affairs-General, Housing
Health: Cancer, Emergency/Ambulance Services, Hospices, Mental Health
Religion: Ministries, Religious Organizations, Religious Welfare
Social Services: Animal Protection, At-Risk Youth, Community Service Organizations, Crime Prevention, Emergency Relief, Family Planning, Family Services, Recreation & Athletics, Scouts, Special Olympics, United Funds/United Ways, Youth Organizations

Application Procedures
Initial Contact: Request application form.
Deadlines: None.

Restrictions
Preference is made to organizations and individuals in Rutherford County.

Additional Information
Trust(s): Centura Bank

Corporate Officials
Steven Goldstein: chief financial officer, president PRIM CORP EMPL chief financial officer: Centura Bank.

Frank Pattillo: vice chairman PRIM CORP EMPL vice chairman: Centura Bank.
Cecil W. Sewell, Jr.: chairman, president B Morehead City, NC 1946. ED University of North Carolina (1969); Rollins College (1971). PRIM CORP EMPL chairman, president: Centura Bank.

Grants Analysis

Disclosure Period: calendar year ending 2000
Total Grants: $69,000*
Number of Grants: 26
Average Grant: $2,654
Highest Grant: $6,000
Lowest Grant: $250
Typical Range: $1,000 to $5,000
*Note: Giving excludes United Way.

Recent Grants

Note: Grants derived from 1999 Form 990.

General
6,000	Little Symphony
5,000	Consumer Credit Counseling, Houston, TX
5,000	Family Resources, Pittsburgh, PA
3,000	Community Concert Association, Auburn, IN
2,500	Rutherford Vocational Workshop
2,000	Boy Scouts of America, Toledo, OH
2,000	Grace of God Rescue Missions
2,000	Rutherford County Youth Services
1,500	Humane Society
1,000	Academic Boosters Club

CHARLES L. READ FOUNDATION

Giving Contact

Rodger K. Herrigel, Secretary
374 Millburn Ave.
Millburn, NJ 07041
Phone: (201)379-5850

Description

Founded: 1954
EIN: 226053510
Organization Type: Private Foundation
Giving Locations: CO; MA; NJ; NY; VA
Grant Types: General Support.

Donor Information

Founder: Charles L. Read

Financial Summary

Total Giving: $170,750 (2001); $174,000 (2000); $175,000 (1999)
Assets: $3,681,615 (2001); $3,784,517 (2000); $3,917,653 (1999)

Typical Recipients

Arts & Humanities: Dance, Ethnic & Folk Arts, Historic Preservation, History & Archaeology, Libraries, Museums/Galleries, Music, Performing Arts, Theater
Civic & Public Affairs: Clubs, Employment/Job Training, Civic & Public Affairs-General, Housing, Professional & Trade Associations, Rural Affairs, Safety, Women's Affairs
Education: Colleges & Universities, Continuing Education, Education Funds, Education-General, Legal Education, Private Education (Precollege), Public Education (Precollege), Religious Education, School Volunteerism, Student Aid
Environment: Environment-General, Protection, Resource Conservation, Watershed
Health: Arthritis, Cancer, Children's Health/Hospitals, Emergency/Ambulance Services, Eyes/Blindness, Geriatric Health, Health Organizations, Hospices,

Hospitals, Long-Term Care, Medical Research, Mental Health, Public Health, Respiratory, Speech & Hearing
International: Foreign Educational Institutions, Missionary/Religious Activities
Religion: Churches, Jewish Causes, Religious Organizations, Religious Welfare
Science: Scientific Centers & Institutes
Social Services: Camps, Child Welfare, Community Centers, Community Service Organizations, Counseling, Day Care, Homes, People with Disabilities, Recreation & Athletics, Shelters/Homelessness, United Funds/United Ways, Veterans, YMCA/YWCA/YMHA/YWHA, Youth Organizations

Application Procedures

Initial Contact: Send a brief letter of inquiry.
Application Requirements: purpose of funds sought, recently audited financial statement, and proof of tax-exempt status.
Deadlines: None.

Foundation Officials

Richard Eisenberg: vice president
Saul Eisenberg: treasurer
Fred Herrigel, III: president
Rodger K. Herrigel: secretary

Grants Analysis

Disclosure Period: calendar year ending 2001
Total Grants: $170,750
Number of Grants: 76
Average Grant: $1,905*
Highest Grant: $26,000
Lowest Grant: $500
Typical Range: $1,000 to $5,000
*Note: Average grant figure excludes highest grant.

Recent Grants

Note: Grants derived from 2001 Form 990.

Library-Related
10,000	Louise Adelia Read Memorial Library, Hancock, NY

General
26,000	Trust & Agency Fund Hancock Central School, Hancock, NY
8,000	Tanglewood, Lenox, MA
5,000	Drew University, Madison, NJ
5,000	Fairview Lake and Watershed Conservation Foundation, Stillwater, NJ
5,000	Southside Hospital, Bayshore, NY
5,000	Summit Foundation, Breckenridge, CO
4,000	Morristown Memorial Hospital, Morristown, NJ
4,000	Overlook Hospital Foundation, Summit, NJ
3,000	Barrington Stage Company, Great Barrington, MA
3,000	Carriage House, Breckenridge, CO

READER'S DIGEST ASSOCIATION, INC.

Company Headquarters

Pleasantville, NY
Web: http://www.readersdigest.com

Company Description

Ticker: RDA
Exchange: OTC
Revenue: US$2.368 billion (2002)
Employees: 5000 (2002)
SIC(s): 2721 Periodicals.

Operating Locations

Reader's Digest Association, Inc. (CT--Ridgefield; GA--Pinola, Stone Mountain; NY--Brewster)

Nonmonetary Support

Volunteer Programs: Reader's Digest employees, employee spouses, and retirees can receive grants for nonprofit groups where they actively volunteer. The company operates a Double-Match Gift Program where employees and retirees may give up to $10,000 per year to charities of their choice.

Reader's Digest Foundation

Giving Contact

Claudia L. Edwards, Executive Director
1 Reader's Digest Rd.
Pleasantville, NY 10570
Phone: (914)244-5370
Fax: (914)244-7642
E-mail: carolyn.malile@readersdigest.com
Web: http://www.rd.com/corporate/

Description

EIN: 136120380
Organization Type: Corporate Foundation
Giving Locations: nationally.
Grant Types: Employee Matching Gifts, Multiyear/Continuing Support, Scholarship.

Financial Summary

Total Giving: $3,221,938 (fiscal year ending June 30, 2001); $3,500,000 (fiscal 2000 approx); $3,500,000 (fiscal 1999 approx). Note: Contributes through corporate direct giving program and foundation.
Giving Analysis: Giving for fiscal 1998 includes: foundation program-related investments ($101,500); foundation scholarships ($144,800); foundation ($1,651,236) foundation matching gifts ($1,962,646)
Assets: $21,098,720 (fiscal 2001); $30,255,653 (fiscal 1998); $29,363,304 (fiscal 1997)
Gifts Received: $23,346 (fiscal 2001); $17,254 (fiscal 1997); $13,334 (fiscal 1996). Note: In fiscal 2001, contributions were received from DeWitt Wallace-Lila Wallace Preferred Stock Trust. 1997 contribution received from DeWitt Wallace-Lila Acheson Wallace.

Typical Recipients

Arts & Humanities: Arts Centers, Libraries, Museums/Galleries, Performing Arts, Theater
Civic & Public Affairs: Civic & Public Affairs-General, Hispanic Affairs, Municipalities/Towns, Professional & Trade Associations
Education: Afterschool/Enrichment Programs, Colleges & Universities, Education Associations, Education Reform, Engineering/Technological Education, Education-General, Journalism/Media Education, Literacy, Minority Education, Private Education (Precollege), Public Education (Precollege), Science/Mathematics Education, Special Education, Student Aid
Health: Cancer, Children's Health/Hospitals, Clinics/Medical Centers, Single-Disease Health Associations
Religion: Religion-General, Jewish Causes
Social Services: Animal Protection, Child Welfare, Community Service Organizations, Scouts, Senior Services

Application Procedures

Initial Contact: Send a brief letter.
Application Requirements: Include a description of project and the sponsoring organization; description of need, target group, and timetable; explanation of why funding would solve a problem and meet a need; the degree to which the program can generate long-term funding; a demonstration of how funding would have a direct impact on a social need; a description of community, public and private sector involvement (if applicable); a description of measurable outcomes

and timetables; audited financial statements for the current year; current itemized budget for project and organization; total project cost, other funding sources, and total requested from foundation; and evidence of tax-exempt status and latest IRS Form 990. Form 990, **Deadlines:** April 1, August 1, and December 1, to be considered in the following month.
Review Process: If initial letter meets foundation guidelines, full proposals (due by the dates listed above) will be requested.

Restrictions

The foundation does not support individuals or religious, veterans', fraternal, political, environmental, or cultural organizations. Grants are not made for dinners, audiovisual productions, legislative or lobbying purposes, or to organizations that are not tax-exempt. The foundation generally does not support capital or endowment campaigns, medical research, health-related activities, international charities, local chapters of national organizations, conferences, publications, or annual operating costs. Funding is generally for the company's immediate geographical area. Some programs give nationally.

Additional Information

The foundation prefers to support direct service projects rather than grants for general support or to intermediary funding agencies.
Funding is usually made on a one-time basis, and exceptions are generally limited to a maximum of three consecutive years.
The foundation seeks to support those organizations that demonstrate responsible management and that provide timely reports to the directors of the foundation on the disposition of funds and program results. results. results.
Publications: Reader's Digest Foundation Annual Report

Corporate Officials

Jack A. Smith: senior vice president PRIM CORP EMPL senior vice president: The Reader's Digest Association, Inc.

Foundation Officials

Jan Braun: program manager
Claudia L. Edwards: executive director
Mary Terry: assistant secretary

Grants Analysis

Disclosure Period: fiscal year ending June 30, 2001
Total Grants: $1,659,028*
Number of Grants: 46
Average Grant: $10,180*
Highest Grant: $1,100,000
Lowest Grant: $1,468
Typical Range: $3,000 to $20,000
*Note: Giving excludes matching gifts; scholarships; volunteer program-related investments. Average grant figure excludes two highest grants ($1,211,111).

Recent Grants

Note: Grants derived from fiscal 2001 Form 990.

Library-Related
25,000	Western Connecticut Library Council, Middlebury, CT
10,500	Ossining Public Library, Ossining, NY
10,500	White Plains Public Library Foundation, White Plains, NY
8,449	Field Library, Peekskill, NY

General
1,100,000	Imus Ranch, Inc., New York, NY
111,111	Laird Center, Marshfield Clinic, Marshfield, WI
35,000	United Negro College Fund, Fairfax, VA
30,000	City School District of Peekskill, Peekskill, NY
25,000	Institute for Student Achievement, Mt. Vernon, NY
25,000	Mid-Hudson Library, Poughkeepsie, NY
20,000	City of Peekskill, Peekskill, NY
20,000	Learning Foundation, Mahopac, NY
20,000	Westchester Hispanic Coalition, Yonkers, NY
19,960	Maharishi Spiritual Center of America, Boone, NC

RED DEVIL

Company Headquarters
2400 Vauxhall Rd.
Union, NJ 07083
Web: http://www.reddevil.com

Company Description
Employees: 350
SIC(s): 2800 Chemicals & Allied Products, 3400 Fabricated Metal Products.

Red Devil Foundation

Giving Contact
Jane T. Lee, Chairman & Director
Red Devil Foundation
2400 Vauxhall Road
Union, NJ 07083-5035
Phone: (908)688-6900
Note: Contact for information on grant program.

Alternate Contact
Human Resources Department
Red Devil Inc.
Note: Contact for information on scholarship program.

Description
EIN: 226063889
Organization Type: Corporate Foundation
Giving Locations: NJ
Grant Types: General Support, Scholarship.

Financial Summary
Total Giving: $17,137 (fiscal year ending November 30, 2001); $22,331 (fiscal 2000); $21,670 (fiscal 1999)
Giving Analysis: Giving for fiscal 2001 includes: foundation scholarships ($3,050); fiscal 2000: foundation scholarships ($2,425) fiscal 1999: foundation scholarships ($3,925)
Assets: $43,579 (fiscal 2001); $73,761 (fiscal 2000); $91,891 (fiscal 1999)
Gifts Received: $18,750 (fiscal 2000); $36,250 (fiscal 1999); $18,750 (fiscal 1998). Note: Contributions were received from Red Devil Inc.

Typical Recipients
Arts & Humanities: Arts Associations & Councils, Arts & Humanities-General, Historic Preservation, History & Archaeology, Museums/Galleries, Music, Opera, Performing Arts, Theater
Civic & Public Affairs: Clubs, Civic & Public Affairs-General, Parades/Festivals, Professional & Trade Associations, Public Policy, Urban & Community Affairs, Zoos/Aquariums
Education: Arts/Humanities Education, Business Education, Colleges & Universities, Medical Education, Private Education (Precollege), School Volunteerism, Student Aid
Environment: Environment-General, Resource Conservation
Health: Cancer, Children's Health/Hospitals, Clinics/Medical Centers, Emergency/Ambulance Services, Health Organizations, Hospitals, Hospitals (University Affiliated), Medical Rehabilitation, Medical Research, Single-Disease Health Associations
International: International Environmental Issues
Religion: Churches, Dioceses

Social Services: Animal Protection, Child Welfare, Community Service Organizations, Crime Prevention, People with Disabilities, Recreation & Athletics, Scouts, Social Services-General, Youth Organizations

Application Procedures
Initial Contact: Request application form for scholarships; for grants, send a brief letter of inquiry detailing request.
Deadlines: For scholarships; April 1, for grants None.

Restrictions
Does not support individuals, political or lobbying groups, or organizations outside operating areas.

Additional Information
Provides scholarships to children of employees.
Publications: Scholarship Application

Corporate Officials
Jane T. Lee: chairman, director, director B Morristown, NJ 1954. ED Fairleigh Dickinson University; Randolph-Macon College (1976). PRIM CORP EMPL chairman, director: Red Devil. NONPR AFFIL chairman: Hunterdon Hall Farm; member: National Association Manufacturer; director: Hand Tools Institute; member: American Cutlery Mfr Association; member: American Hardware Manufacturer Association.
D. R. MacPherson: president, chief executive officer, director PRIM CORP EMPL president, chief executive officer, director: Red Devil.

Foundation Officials
George Ludlow Lee, Jr.: trustee B Newark, NJ 1926. ED Rutgers University; Cornell University (1948). PRIM CORP EMPL chairman, chief executive officer: Red Devil.
Jane T. Lee: trustee (see above)
Mary Lee: trustee
Mary Lee Subourne: trustee

Grants Analysis
Disclosure Period: fiscal year ending November 30, 2001
Total Grants: $14,087*
Number of Grants: 68
Average Grant: $243
Highest Grant: $1,750
Lowest Grant: $15
Typical Range: $100 to $500
*Note: Giving excludes scholarships.

Recent Grants
Note: Grants derived from fiscal 2000 Form 990.

General
2,700	New Jersey Performing Arts Center, Newark, NJ -- membership and support
1,200	Paper Mill Playhouse, Millburn, NJ -- fundraiser support
1,000	Somerset Medical Center, Somerset, NJ -- fundraiser
600	Drew University, Madison, NJ -- scholarship
600	Drew University, Madison, NJ -- scholarship
600	Louisiana State University, Baton Rouge, LA -- scholarship
600	Louisiana State University, Baton Rouge, LA -- scholarship
600	Northeastern State University, Tahlequah, OK -- scholarship
600	Northeastern State University, Tahlequah, OK -- scholarship
600	Northeastern State University, Tahlequah, OK -- scholarship

RED WING SHOE COMPANY, INC.

Company Headquarters
314 Main St., Ste. 2
Red Wing, MN 55066
Web: http://www.redwingshoe.com

Company Description
Employees: 1,300
SIC(s): 3143 Men's Footwear Except Athletic.

Red Wing Shoe Co. Foundation

Giving Contact
Stacy Crownhart, Secretary
Red Wing Shoe Co. Foundation
314 Main Street
Red Wing, MN 55066-2300
Phone: (651)388-8211
Fax: (651)385-1760

Description
EIN: 416020177
Organization Type: Corporate Foundation
Giving Locations: KY: Danville; MN: Minneapolis, Red Wing, St. Paul; MO: Potosi
Grant Types: Award, Capital, General Support.

Financial Summary
Total Giving: $799,803 (2001); $864,255 (2000); $623,685 (1999). Note: Contributes through foundation only.
Giving Analysis: Giving for 2000 includes: foundation grants to United Way ($40,000); foundation ($824,255); 1999: foundation grants to United Way ($43,000); 1998: foundation grants to United Way ($32,500); foundation ($548,795).
Assets: $815,950 (2001); $910,100 (2000); $1,475,587 (1999)
Gifts Received: $700,000 (2001); $215,000 (2000); $910,000 (1999). Note: Contributions are received from the Red Wing Shoe Co.

Typical Recipients
Arts & Humanities: Arts Associations & Councils, Arts Centers, Arts Institutes, Film & Video, Arts & Humanities-General, Historic Preservation, History & Archaeology, Libraries, Museums/Galleries, Music, Performing Arts, Public Broadcasting, Theater
Civic & Public Affairs: Botanical Gardens/Parks, Business/Free Enterprise, Chambers of Commerce, Clubs, Community Foundations, Economic Development, Civic & Public Affairs-General, Housing, Law & Justice, Municipalities/Towns, Nonprofit Management, Philanthropic Organizations, Public Policy, Safety, Urban & Community Affairs, Women's Affairs, Zoos/Aquariums
Education: Arts/Humanities Education, Business Education, Colleges & Universities, Economic Education, Education Associations, Education Funds, Education Reform, Environmental Education, Faculty Development, Education-General, Public Education (Precollege), Science/Mathematics Education, Secondary Education (Public), Social Sciences Education, Special Education
Environment: Air/Water Quality, Environment-General, Resource Conservation, Wildlife Protection
Health: Cancer, Children's Health/Hospitals, Clinics/Medical Centers, Emergency/Ambulance Services, Health Organizations, Hospices, Medical Rehabilitation, Preventive Medicine/Wellness Organizations, Single-Disease Health Associations
International: International Development, International Environmental Issues, International Organizations

Religion: Churches, Religion-General, Religious Welfare
Science: Science Museums, Scientific Centers & Institutes
Social Services: Child Welfare, Community Centers, Community Service Organizations, Crime Prevention, Emergency Relief, Family Services, Food/Clothing Distribution, People with Disabilities, Recreation & Athletics, Scouts, Social Services-General, Special Olympics, Substance Abuse, United Funds/United Ways, YMCA/YWCA/YMHA/YWHA, Youth Organizations

Application Procedures
Initial Contact: Send a brief letter.
Application Requirements: Include description of activities or projects, and a copy of tax exemption certificate.
Deadlines: None.

Restrictions
Grants are not made to individuals.

Foundation Officials
Rick Bawek: chief executive officer
Shirley L. Perkins: secretary
William J. Sweasy: president B 1953. PRIM CORP EMPL chairman: Red Wing Hotel Co.

Grants Analysis
Disclosure Period: calendar year ending 2001
Total Grants: $774,803*
Number of Grants: 30
Average Grant: $5,053*
Highest Grant: $333,333
Lowest Grant: $400
Typical Range: $1,000 to $15,000
*Note: Giving excludes United Way. Average grant figure excludes two highest grants totaling $633,333.

Recent Grants
Note: Grants derived from 2001 Form 990.

General
333,333	Red Wing Family YMCA, Red Wing, MN -- for capital fund
300,000	Independent School District 256, Red Wing, MN -- environmental education
40,000	Sheldon Theatre, Red Wing, MN
25,000	Charity Ride Across America, Harrisburg, NC
25,000	United Way, Red Wing, MN
20,000	American Wind Symphony Orchestra, Pittsburgh, PA -- community concert
10,500	Red Wing Family YMCA, Red Wing, MN
5,000	Lake City Environmental Learning Center, Lake City, MN -- environmental education
5,000	Science Museum of Minnesota, St. Paul, MN
3,000	American Red Cross Goodhue County Chapter, Red Wing, MN -- capital fund

NELL J. REDFIELD FOUNDATION

Giving Contact
Gerald C. Smith, Director
PO Box 61
Reno, NV 89501
Phone: (702)323-1373
Fax: (702)323-4476

Description
Founded: 1982
EIN: 237399910
Organization Type: Private Foundation
Giving Locations: NV: Reno
Grant Types: Capital, General Support, Scholarship.

Donor Information
Founder: the late Nell J. Redfield

Financial Summary
Total Giving: $1,305,946 (2001); $2,248,747 (1999); $1,403,292 (1998)
Assets: $30,365,747 (2001); $28,693,866 (1999); $25,883,735 (1998)
Gifts Received: $3,174,519 (2001); $3,280,000 (1999); $5,914,633 (1998). Note: In 1998, 1999, and 2001, contributions were received from the Nell J. Redfield Trust.

Typical Recipients
Arts & Humanities: Arts Outreach, Libraries, Music, Public Broadcasting, Theater
Education: Afterschool/Enrichment Programs, Arts/Humanities Education, Business Education, Colleges & Universities, Community & Junior Colleges, Elementary Education (Public), Education-General, Literacy, Private Education (Precollege), Public Education (Precollege), Science/Mathematics Education, Student Aid
Health: Adolescent Health Issues, Children's Health/Hospitals, Diabetes, Health-General, Hospices, Hospitals, Medical Research, Public Health, Single-Disease Health Associations, Speech & Hearing
Religion: Religious Organizations, Religious Welfare
Social Services: Animal Protection, At-Risk Youth, Child Welfare, Community Service Organizations, Crime Prevention, Domestic Violence, Family Planning, Family Services, Food/Clothing Distribution, Homes, People with Disabilities, Recreation & Athletics, Scouts, Senior Services, Shelters/Homelessness, Substance Abuse, United Funds/United Ways, YMCA/YWCA/YMHA/YWHA, Youth Organizations

Application Procedures
Initial Contact: Send letter requesting application form.
Deadlines: June 1. Applications accepted beginning January 15.

Restrictions
Grants are limited to advancement of healthcare, medical research, care of handicapped children and the aged, education, and religion.

Additional Information
Trust(s): Farmers & Merchants Trust Co

Foundation Officials
Helen Jeane Jones: director
Gerald C. Smith: manager, director
Kenneth G. Walker: director

Grants Analysis
Disclosure Period: calendar year ending 2001
Total Grants: $1,305,946
Number of Grants: 54
Average Grant: $15,476*
Highest Grant: $250,000
Lowest Grant: $2,386
Typical Range: $5,000 to $25,000
*Note: Average grant figure excludes three highest grants ($516,667).

Recent Grants
Note: Grants derived from 2000 Form 990.

General
927,000	Excellence in Education, Reno, NV -- construction of middle school
250,000	University of Nevada Reno Foundation, Reno, NV -- fund the Nell J. Redfield Campus building
150,000	University of Nevada, Reno, NV -- fund for the Neil J. Redfield Campus building

107,285	Oneida County Hospital -- equipment
100,000	University of Nevada, Reno, NV -- new medical library and education
100,000	University of Nevada Reno Foundation, Reno, NV -- new medical library and education building
58,500	Health Access Washoe County, Reno, NV -- dental care to children in need
50,000	Saint Mary's Midwife and Well Child Program -- operating expenses
50,000	Saint Mary's Sun Valley -- assist with operating expenses of program
25,000	Stadium 2000, Reno, NV -- assist with track and field portion of Stadium 2000

REED FOUNDATION (NY)

Giving Contact

Jane Gregory Rubin, Secretary & Director
444 Madison Ave., Suite 2901
New York, NY 10022-6903
Phone: (212)688-2170

Description

Founded: 1949
EIN: 131990017
Organization Type: General Purpose Foundation
Giving Locations: NY: emphasis on New York broad geographic distribution.
Grant Types: General Support, Project.

Donor Information

Founder: the late Samuel Rubin

Financial Summary

Total Giving: $1,241,456 (2001); $1,146,110 (2000); $1,150,765 (1998)
Assets: $14,676,266 (2001); $15,494,296 (2000); $14,103,164 (1998)

Typical Recipients

Arts & Humanities: Arts Associations & Councils, Arts Centers, Arts Festivals, Arts Funds, Arts Outreach, Community Arts, Ethnic & Folk Arts, Film & Video, Arts & Humanities-General, Historic Preservation, History & Archaeology, Libraries, Literary Arts, Museums/Galleries, Music, Opera, Performing Arts, Public Broadcasting, Theater
Civic & Public Affairs: Asian American Affairs, Civil Rights, Community Foundations, Employment/Job Training, Civic & Public Affairs-General, Legal Aid, Nonprofit Management, Philanthropic Organizations, Professional & Trade Associations, Public Policy, Urban & Community Affairs
Education: Arts/Humanities Education, Colleges & Universities, International Exchange, International Studies, Legal Education, Medical Education, Private Education (Precollege)
Health: Heart, Medical Research, Research/Studies Institutes
International: Foreign Arts Organizations, Foreign Educational Institutions, Human Rights, International Relations
Science: Scientific Centers & Institutes
Social Services: Community Service Organizations, Recreation & Athletics

Application Procedures

Initial Contact: Send a brief letter of inquiry.
Deadlines: None.

Restrictions

Grants are not made to individuals.

Foundation Officials

David Latham: admin assistant
Jane Lockhart Gregory Rubin: treasurer B Richmond, VA 1944. ED Vassar College BA (1965); Columbia University JD (1975); New York University

LLM (1984). PRIM CORP EMPL director: InterAmericas. NONPR AFFIL advisory board: Vermont Studio Center; vice chairman, director: Volunteer Lawyers Arts; member: Union Internationale des Avocats; member: Copyright Society USA; member professional advisory council: Lincoln Center Performing Arts; member: Association Bar New York City; board governors: John Carter Brown Library; member: American Arbitration Association; member: American Bar Association.
Lara R. Rubin: director
Maia A. Rubin: treasurer
Peter L. Rubin: director
Reed Rubin: president

Grants Analysis

Disclosure Period: calendar year ending 2001
Total Grants: $1,241,456
Number of Grants: 61
Average Grant: $13,030*
Highest Grant: $306,000
Lowest Grant: $250
Typical Range: $5,000 to $25,000
***Note:** Average grant figure excludes two highest grants ($472,666).

Recent Grants

Note: Grants derived from 2000 Form 990.

Library-Related

40,000	John Carter Brown Library, Providence, RI
15,000	American Trust for the British Library, New York, NY
10,000	Library of Congress, Washington, DC

General

318,500	New York Foundation for The Arts, New York, NY
120,000	Research Institute for The Study of Man, New York, NY
83,333	Minetta Brook, New York, NY
72,590	Caribbean Contemporary Arts Trinidad and Tobago
50,620	New York City Opera, New York, NY
45,000	Smithsonian Institution, Washington, DC
40,000	Columbia University, New York, NY
35,000	Museum of Modern Art, New York, NY
25,000	El Museo del Barrio, New York, NY
25,000	English-Speaking Union of the United States, New York, NY

REEVES FOUNDATION (OH)

Giving Contact

Don A. Ulrich, Executive Director
PO Box 441
Dover, OH 44622-0441
Phone: (330)364-4660

Description

Founded: 1966
EIN: 346575477
Organization Type: General Purpose Foundation
Giving Locations: OH: Tuscarawas County
Grant Types: Capital, Project, Scholarship.

Donor Information

Founder: Established in 1966 by the late Margaret J. Reeves, the late Helen F. Reeves, and the late Samuel J. Reeves.

Financial Summary

Total Giving: $742,745 (2001); $1,148,864 (2000); $1,100,000 (1999 approx)
Giving Analysis: Giving for 2000 includes: foundation scholarships ($15,000) 1998: foundation scholarships ($15,000)

Assets: $23,622,428 (2001); $24,936,118 (2000); $24,446,490 (1998)

Typical Recipients

Arts & Humanities: Historic Preservation, History & Archaeology, Libraries, Museums/Galleries, Music, Public Broadcasting, Theater
Civic & Public Affairs: Botanical Gardens/Parks, Civic & Public Affairs-General, Municipalities/Towns, Safety, Urban & Community Affairs
Education: Agricultural Education, Arts/Humanities Education, Colleges & Universities, Education Funds, Elementary Education (Private), Elementary Education (Public), Education-General, Private Education (Precollege), Public Education (Precollege), Science/Mathematics Education, Secondary Education (Private), Secondary Education (Public), Student Aid
Environment: Environment-General, Resource Conservation
Health: Alzheimers Disease, Cancer, Children's Health/Hospitals, Clinics/Medical Centers, Emergency/Ambulance Services, Hospices, Hospitals, Hospitals, Public Health
Religion: Churches, Religious Welfare
Social Services: Animal Protection, Big Brother/Big Sister, Community Centers, Counseling, Crime Prevention, Emergency Relief, People with Disabilities, Recreation & Athletics, Scouts, Senior Services, United Funds/United Ways, Volunteer Services, YMCA/YWCA/YMHA/YWHA, Youth Organizations

Application Procedures

Initial Contact: Applications should be in writing.
Application Requirements: Include a concise outline of the amount requested and purpose of funds sought.
Deadlines: None.
Review Process: The board meets bimonthly.

Restrictions

The foundation reports grants are made for charitable and educational purposes, with emphasis on capital expenditures rather than operating budgets. No grants are made to individuals, or for annual campaigns, seed money, emergency funds, deficit financing, land acquisition, renovation projects, endowment funds, fellowships, special projects, publications, conferences, or loans.

Foundation Officials

W. E. Lieser: secretary, treasurer, trustee
Thomas V. Patton: trustee
Ronald L. Pissocra: trustee
Margaret H. Reeves: president, trustee
Thomas R. Scheffer: vice president, trustee
Don A. Ulrich: executive director
Jeffrey T. Wagner: trustee
W. E. Zimmerman: executive vice president, trustee

Grants Analysis

Disclosure Period: calendar year ending 2001
Total Grants: $742,745
Number of Grants: 28
Average Grant: $26,527
Highest Grant: $151,465
Lowest Grant: $1,259
Typical Range: $10,000 to $40,000

Recent Grants

Note: Grants derived from 2001 Form 990.

General

151,465	Claymont Community Center, Uhrichsville, OH -- building renovation project
100,000	Warwick Township, New Philadelphia, OH -- towards new fire station
86,227	Moravian College, Bethlehem, PA -- shelving and chairs
62,354	Village of Strasburg, Strasburg, OH -- lights for football field
45,000	Dover Historical Society, Dover, OH -- operation fund

40,000	Immaculate Conception School, Dennison, OH -- window replacement
33,334	Tuscarawas County YMCA, Dover, OH -- Fitness Center project
30,000	Tuscarawas County Council for Churches, New Philadelphia, OH -- 2002 campaign
25,000	New Philadelphia Schools, New Philadelphia, OH -- playground equipment
25,000	Northeastern Educational Television of Ohio, Kent, OH -- program and television broadcasting

REGENSTEIN FOUNDATION

Giving Contact
Thomas Staszak, Acting Vice President
8600 West Bryn Mawr Avenue, Suite 705N
Chicago, IL 60631
Phone: (773)693-6464
Fax: (773)693-2480

Alternate Contact
Robert H. Mecca

Description
Founded: 1950
EIN: 363152531
Organization Type: General Purpose Foundation
Giving Locations: IL: Chicago metropolitan area
Grant Types: Capital, Endowment, General Support, Loan, Multiyear/Continuing Support, Operating Expenses, Project.

Donor Information
Founder: The foundation was established in 1950, with the late Joseph Regenstein and Helen Regenstein as donors.

Financial Summary
Total Giving: $2,500,000 (2002 approx); $52,500,000 (2001); $3,709,175 (2000)
Giving Analysis: Giving for 2000 includes: foundation grants to United Way ($10,000) 1998: foundation grants to United Way ($10,000)
Assets: $68,000,000 (2002 approx); $72,000,000 (2001); $124,614,962 (2000)

Typical Recipients
Arts & Humanities: Arts Institutes, Historic Preservation, History & Archaeology, Libraries, Museums/Galleries, Music, Opera, Public Broadcasting
Civic & Public Affairs: Clubs, Law & Justice, Nonprofit Management, Philanthropic Organizations, Professional & Trade Associations, Public Policy, Zoos/Aquariums
Education: Colleges & Universities, Education-General, Medical Education, Preschool Education, Private Education (Precollege)
Health: Clinics/Medical Centers, Health Organizations, Heart, Hospitals, Medical Rehabilitation, Mental Health, Nursing Services, Prenatal Health Issues, Transplant Networks/Donor Banks
Religion: Jewish Causes, Religious Organizations, Religious Welfare, Synagogues/Temples
Science: Science Museums
Social Services: Animal Protection, Child Welfare, Community Service Organizations, Crime Prevention, Delinquency & Criminal Rehabilitation, Family Planning, Family Services, Food/Clothing Distribution, Homes, People with Disabilities, Scouts, Senior Services, Sexual Abuse, United Funds/United Ways, Volunteer Services, Youth Organizations

Application Procedures
Initial Contact: Proposals should be made in writing.
Application Requirements: Applicants should send a cover letter summarizing request, one copy of full proposal, and supplementary materials including total need for project and source of other funding (if any), copy of IRS tax-exempt letter, and a copy of the most recent audited annual report.
Deadlines: None.
Notes: Applications should be signed by the Chief Executive Officer of organization.

Restrictions
The foundation reports that most grants are made on the initiative of the foundation's trustees; only a very small percentage of applicants can expect to obtain funds. Because long-range pledges often make income unavailable for substantial periods of time, it is suggested that applicants needing immediate help apply to individuals or businesses in a position to make immediate grants. The foundation does not make grants to individuals. The foundation does not conduct personal interviews with an applicant except upon the foundation's initiative.

Additional Information
Publications: General Information Letter

Foundation Officials
Anita Bury: assistant secretary
Joan Gorsuch: secretary
Betty Regenstein Hartman: vice president, director
Robert A. Mecca: vice president, director, treasurer B 1951.
Joseph Regenstein, Jr.: president, director B Chicago, IL 1923. ED Brown University (1945). PRIM CORP EMPL chairman: Arvey Corp.
Thomas A. Staszak: contr, assistant treasurer

Grants Analysis
Disclosure Period: calendar year ending 2000
Total Grants: $3,699,175*
Number of Grants: 20
Average Grant: $73,641*
Highest Grant: $2,300,000
Lowest Grant: $500
Typical Range: $1,000 to $10,000 and $50,000 to $300,000
*Note: Giving excludes United Way. Average grant figure excludes highest grant.

Recent Grants
Note: Grants derived from 2000 Form 990.

Library-Related

2,000	Newberry Library, Chicago, IL

General

2,300,000	Lincoln Park Zoological Society, Chicago, IL -- Research & modify large mammal exhibit
500,000	Northwestern Memorial Hospital, Chicago, IL -- purchase of advanced diagnostic/treatment equipment for Gastrointestinal Laboratory
300,000	Ravinia Festival, Highland Park, IL
300,000	Shore Community Services, Evanston, IL -- support of operation
76,675	Art Institute of Chicago, Chicago, IL -- Renovation of Departments
75,000	Orchestral Association, Chicago, IL -- support of operation
50,000	Lyric Opera of Chicago, Chicago, IL -- support of operation
50,000	WTTW Chicago, Chicago, IL -- operation support
20,000	Metropolitan Family Services, Chicago, IL -- support of operation
10,000	Boys and Girls Clubs, Chicago, IL -- operation support

REGIS CORP.

Company Headquarters
7201 Metro Blvd.
Edina, MN 55439

Company Description
Ticker: RGIS
Exchange: AMEX
Employees: 31,000 (1999)
SIC(s): 7231 Beauty Shops.

Operating Locations
Regis Corp. (MN--Eden Prairie, Minneapolis)

Regis Foundation

Giving Contact
Myron Kunin, President
7201 Metro Boulevard
Minneapolis, MN 55439-2103
Phone: (952)947-7777
Fax: (952)947-7900
Web: http://www.regiscorp.com/corporate/communityInvolve.html

Description
Founded: 1981
EIN: 411410790
Organization Type: Corporate Foundation
Giving Locations: MN: Minneapolis and surrounding area
Grant Types: General Support, Scholarship.
Note: Scholarship program is administered by the Minneapolis Board of Education.

Financial Summary
Total Giving: $1,330,615 (fiscal year ending June 31, 2001); $1,309,446 (fiscal 2000); $852,201 (fiscal 1998). Note: Contributes through foundation only.
Giving Analysis: Giving for fiscal 1998 includes: foundation grants to United Way ($10,000); foundation ($842,201); fiscal 1997: foundation grants to United Way ($15,000) foundation ($582,002)
Assets: $150,055 (fiscal 2001); $4,843 (fiscal 2000); $316 (fiscal 1998)
Gifts Received: $1,334,327 (fiscal 2001); $1,309,066 (fiscal 2000); $852,517 (fiscal 1998). Note: Foundation receives contributions from Regis Corp.

Typical Recipients
Arts & Humanities: Arts Associations & Councils, Arts Centers, Arts Institutes, Arts & Humanities-General, Museums/Galleries, Music, Opera, Public Broadcasting, Theater
Civic & Public Affairs: Community Foundations, Civic & Public Affairs-General, Housing, Law & Justice, Urban & Community Affairs
Education: Business Education, Colleges & Universities, Education Associations, Education-General, Public Education (Precollege), Social Sciences Education, Student Aid
Health: Cancer
Religion: Jewish Causes, Religious Organizations, Synagogues/Temples
Social Services: Child Welfare, Community Service Organizations, People with Disabilities, United Funds/United Ways, YMCA/YWCA/YMHA/YWHA, Youth Organizations

Application Procedures
Initial Contact: Submit a brief letter of inquiry.
Application Requirements: Include a description of organization, amount requested, and purpose of funds sought.
Deadlines: None.

Notes: Applications for scholarships are available at Minneapolis public high schools.

Corporate Officials

Myron Kunin: chairman, director B Minneapolis, MN 1928. ED University of Minnesota BA (1949). PRIM CORP EMPL chairman, director: Regis Corp. CORP AFFIL ltd. partner: Rosepointe Housing; director: Supercuts Inc.; president: Regis Collection Inc.; chairman, principal stockholder: Curtis Squire Inc.; president: Red River Broadcasting Corp.

Foundation Officials

Frank E. Evangelist: secretary B 1936. PRIM CORP EMPL senior vice president finance, secretary, director: Regis Corp.

Bert M. Gross: senior vice president, general council, secretary B 1929. PRIM CORP EMPL senior vice president, general council, secretary: Regis Corporation. CORP AFFIL legal counsel: Phillips Gross & Aaron Pennsylvania.

Myron Kunin: president (see above)

Grants Analysis

Disclosure Period: fiscal year ending June 31, 2001
Total Grants: $1,154,615*
Number of Grants: 16
Average Grant: $17,893*
Highest Grant: $475,000
Lowest Grant: $1,000
Typical Range: $1,500 to $50,000
***Note:** Giving excludes scholarship; United Way. Average grant figure excludes three highest grants ($922,003).

Recent Grants

Note: Grants derived from 2001 Form 990.

General

475,000	Minneapolis Jewish Federation, Minneapolis, MN
290,000	Minneapolis Institute of Arts, Minneapolis, MN -- for art collection
157,003	University of Minnesota Foundation, St. Paul, MN -- contribution for Holocaust studies
130,000	Minneapolis Public Schools, Minneapolis, MN -- scholarship fund
56,000	St. Cloud State University, St. Cloud, MN -- for holocaust education incentive
46,000	United Way, Minneapolis, MN
43,397	Witness and Legacy Costs -- for traveling art exhibit costs
42,000	Walker Art Center, Minneapolis, MN -- for Regis Dialogues
25,000	Student in Free Enterprise, Springfield, MO
20,000	Sholom Foundation, St. Louis Park, MN -- growth fund

REICHHOLD CHEMICALS, INC.

Company Headquarters

PO Box 13582
Research Triangle Park, NC 27709
Phone: (919)990-7500
Fax: (919)990-7711
Web: http://www.reichhold.com

Company Description

Founded: 1929
Employees: 3,500
SIC(s): 2821 Plastics Materials & Resins.

Operating Locations

DIC Americas (NJ--Fort Lee); DIC Digital Supply Corp. (NJ--Teaneck); DIC Trading (U.S.A.) (NJ--Fort Lee); Dynaric (NJ--Teaneck); Earthrise Farms (CA--Glendale); Earthrise Trading Co. (CA--Petaluma); Film Division (NJ--Clark); General Printing Ink (IL--Northlake); Kohl & Madden Printing Ink Corp. Division (NJ--Fort Lee); KVK (U.S.A.) (NJ--New Brunswick); Polychrome Corp. Division (NJ--Fort Lee); Premier Polymers (TX--Alvin); Product Design Center (OH--Westerville); RBH Dispersions (NJ--Bound Brook); Reichhold Chemicals (NY--Buffalo; NC--Durham); Spencer Kellogg (NY--Buffalo); Sun Chemical Corp. (NJ--Fort Lee); Sun Chemical Corp. of Michigan (MI--Muskegon); Sun Chemical General Printing (IL--Northlake); Sun Chemical Pigments Division (OH--Cincinnati); Surface Technologies (NC--Durham); US Ink Corp. (NJ--Carlstadt)

Giving Contact

PO Box 13582
Research Triangle Park, NC 27709
Phone: (919)990-7500

Description

Organization Type: Corporate Giving Program
Giving Locations: headquarters area only.
Grant Types: Capital, Employee Matching Gifts.

Typical Recipients

Arts & Humanities: Arts Funds, Libraries, Museums/Galleries, Music, Performing Arts
Education: Business Education, Colleges & Universities, Economic Education, Public Education (Precollege)
Health: Health Organizations, Hospitals, Single-Disease Health Associations
Social Services: Community Service Organizations, United Funds/United Ways, Youth Organizations

Application Procedures

Initial Contact: Send letter of inquiry including a description of organization, need addressed, and amount requested. Plants can be contacted directly. Other subsidiaries of Dai Nippon administer independent programs.

Corporate Officials

Phillip D. Ashkettle: president, chief executive officer, director PRIM CORP EMPL president, chief executive officer, director: Reichhold Chemicals.
William Eberle: controller PRIM CORP EMPL controller: Reichhold Chemicals.

REIDLER FOUNDATION

Giving Contact

Diana L. James, Secretary & Treasurer
c/o Fleet Bank, Trust Dept.
101 W. Broad St., Box 518
Hazleton, PA 18201
Phone: (570)454-7654

Description

Founded: 1944
EIN: 246022888
Organization Type: Private Foundation
Giving Locations: PA: Ashland, Hazleton
Grant Types: General Support.

Donor Information

Founder: John W. Reidler

Financial Summary

Total Giving: $485,000 (fiscal year ending October 31, 2001); $465,000 (fiscal 2000); $420,000 (fiscal 1999). Note: Fiscal 1997 Giving includes scholarship ($26,500); United Way ($5,000).

Giving Analysis: Giving for fiscal 2001 includes: foundation grants to United Way ($5,000); foundation scholarships ($14,500); fiscal 2000: foundation grants to United Way ($5,000); foundation scholarships ($11,750); fiscal 1998: foundation grants to United Way ($5,000); foundation scholarships ($24,000) foundation ($291,000)

Assets: $9,119,636 (fiscal 2001); $10,288,676 (fiscal 2000); $10,092,740 (fiscal 1999)

Gifts Received: $31,458 (fiscal 2001); $30,984 (fiscal 2000); $35,950 (fiscal 1998). Note: In fiscal 1998, 2000, and 2001, contributions were received from Dr. Howard D. and Mrs. Ann B. Fegan.

Typical Recipients

Arts & Humanities: Arts Associations & Councils, Arts & Humanities-General, History & Archaeology, Libraries, Music, Public Broadcasting
Civic & Public Affairs: Community Foundations, Economic Development, Employment/Job Training, Civic & Public Affairs-General, Native American Affairs, Zoos/Aquariums
Education: Arts/Humanities Education, Colleges & Universities, Education Funds, Medical Education, Private Education (Precollege), Science/Mathematics Education, Secondary Education (Private), Student Aid
Environment: Environment-General, Resource Conservation, Wildlife Protection
Health: Cancer, Children's Health/Hospitals, Clinics/Medical Centers, Emergency/Ambulance Services, Health-General, Hospices, Hospitals, Multiple Sclerosis, Nursing Services
International: International Development, International Peace & Security Issues
Religion: Churches, Dioceses, Ministries, Religious Welfare
Social Services: Animal Protection, Child Welfare, Community Centers, Community Service Organizations, Delinquency & Criminal Rehabilitation, Family Planning, Family Services, Food/Clothing Distribution, Homes, People with Disabilities, Senior Services, United Funds/United Ways, YMCA/YWCA/YMHA/YWHA, Youth Organizations

Application Procedures

Initial Contact: Send a brief letter of inquiry describing program or project, and letter from supervising provincial.
Deadlines: None.

Restrictions

Does not support individuals.

Foundation Officials

Ann B. Fegan: president
Howard D. Fegan: trustee
John H. Fegan: trustee
Eugene C. Fish, Esq.: trustee B 1910. ED University of Pennsylvania Wharton School (1931); University of Pennsylvania School of Law (1934). PRIM CORP EMPL chairman, secretary, director: Eastern Foundry Co. CORP AFFIL chairman: Peerless Industries Inc.
Robert K. Gicking: vice president B Hazleton, PA 1931. ED Lafayette College (1952). PRIM CORP EMPL president, director: Hazleton National Bank. CORP AFFIL president: First Valley Corp.
Diana L. James: secretary, treasurer
Carl J. Reidler: trustee
Paul G. Reidler: president emeritus

Grants Analysis

Disclosure Period: fiscal year ending October 31, 2001
Total Grants: $465,500*
Number of Grants: 69
Average Grant: $6,206*
Highest Grant: $43,500
Lowest Grant: $500
Typical Range: $1,000 to $10,000

*Note: Giving excludes scholarships; United Way. Average grant figure excludes highest grant.

Recent Grants

Note: Grants derived from 2000 Form 990.

Library-Related

59,500	Bethlehem Area Public Library, Bethlehem, PA -- reference and audio visual renovation

General

41,500	Schuykill Area Community Foundation, Ashland, PA -- charitable trust and Schreck Memorial fund
40,000	Grace Episcopal Church, Allentown, PA -- endowment fund
40,000	Midlands Conservancy, Emmaus, PA -- Monocacy Creek restoration
34,000	Hazleton Area Public Library, Hazleton, PA -- endowment fund
21,000	WVIA Public Television and Radio, Pittston, PA -- capital campaign and endowment fund
19,000	Lebanon Valley College, Annville, PA
18,000	YMCA, Hazleton, PA -- capital development project
18,000	YWCA, Hazleton, PA -- capital development project
13,000	Lehigh University Mathematics Department, Bethlehem, PA -- mathematics department and E. Assmus Memorial fund
10,000	Planned Parenthood of Northeast Pennsylvania, Prexlertown, PA -- Hazleton health center

REINBERGER FOUNDATION

Giving Contact

Robert N. Reinberger, Co-Director
27600 Chagrin Boulevard
Cleveland, OH 44122
Phone: (216)292-2790
Fax: (216)292-4466

Description

Founded: 1968
EIN: 346574879
Organization Type: Family Foundation
Giving Locations: OH: Cleveland, Columbus
Grant Types: Capital, Challenge, Endowment, General Support.

Donor Information

Founder: The Reinberger Foundation was established in 1968 by Clarence T. Reinberger , a Cleveland businessman who developed the Automotive Parts Company and later became the chairman of Genuine Parts. Following Mr. Reinberger's death in 1968, the foundation received half of its current assets. The remainder of its assets were acquired following the death of Mr. Reinberger's wife, Louise Reinberger . The Reinbergers had no children; the foundation is directed by two of Mr. Reinberger's nephews.

Financial Summary

Total Giving: $3,679,056 (2002); $5,201,505 (2000); $4,348,459 (1998)
Assets: $94,823,407 (2000); $95,976,802 (1998); $84,730,791 (1997)

Typical Recipients

Arts & Humanities: Arts Associations & Councils, Arts Centers, Arts Festivals, Arts Institutes, Ballet, Historic Preservation, History & Archaeology, Libraries, Literary Arts, Museums/Galleries, Music, Opera, Performing Arts, Public Broadcasting, Theater, Visual Arts

Civic & Public Affairs: Botanical Gardens/Parks, Clubs, Community Foundations, Economic Development, Employment/Job Training, Civic & Public Affairs-General, Housing, Law & Justice, Nonprofit Management, Philanthropic Organizations, Professional & Trade Associations, Urban & Community Affairs, Zoos/Aquariums

Education: Arts/Humanities Education, Colleges & Universities, Education Funds, Engineering/Technological Education, Education-General, Legal Education, Literacy, Medical Education, Private Education (Precollege), Public Education (Precollege), Science/Mathematics Education

Health: Alzheimers Disease, Cancer, Children's Health/Hospitals, Clinics/Medical Centers, Health-General, Health Organizations, Hospitals, Hospitals (University Affiliated), Long-Term Care, Medical Rehabilitation, Medical Research, Public Health, Speech & Hearing

Religion: Churches, Jewish Causes, Religious Welfare

Science: Science Museums, Scientific Centers & Institutes

Social Services: Animal Protection, At-Risk Youth, Big Brother/Big Sister, Camps, Child Welfare, Community Centers, Community Service Organizations, Family Planning, Family Services, Food/Clothing Distribution, People with Disabilities, Recreation & Athletics, Senior Services, Social Services-General, YMCA/YWCA/YMHA/YWHA, Youth Organizations

Application Procedures

Initial Contact: There are no application forms or guidelines. Applicants should submit one copy of a full proposal.
Application Requirements: Written applications should include a clear statement of purpose and a copy of the organization's exemption letter from the IRS. The foundation will request further information on proposals of interest.
Deadlines: None.
Review Process: The board of directors meets in November, February, May and August. The review process takes about six months. The board acknowledges the receipt of an application and may require an interview.

Restrictions

Grants are not made to individuals.

Foundation Officials

Sara R. Dyer: trustee
Karen R. Hooser: trustee
Richard Heer Oman: trustee B Columbus, OH 1926. ED Ohio State University BA (1948); Ohio State University JD (1951). PRIM CORP EMPL counsel: Vorys, Sater, Seymour & Pease. NONPR AFFIL member: Ohio State Bar Association; fellow: Ohio State Bar Foundation; member: Columbus Bar Association; member: American Bar Association; member: American College Trust & Estate Counsel. CLUB AFFIL Nantucket Yacht Club; Rocky Fort Hunt & Country Club; Columbus Club; Kit Kat Club.
Robert N. Reinberger: co-director, trustee
William C. Reinberger: co-director, trustee

Grants Analysis

Disclosure Period: calendar year ending 2000
Total Grants: $5,201,505
Number of Grants: 90
Average Grant: $57,795
Highest Grant: $250,000
Typical Range: $5,000 to $30,000 and $50,000 to $100,000

Recent Grants

Note: Grants derived from 2000 Form 990.

General

250,000	Cleveland Orchestra, Cleveland, OH
250,000	Western Reserve Historical Society, Cleveland, OH
208,333	Great Lakes Science Center, Cleveland, OH
200,000	Case Western Reserve University School of Medicine, Cleveland, OH
200,000	Cleveland Botanical Garden, Cleveland, OH
180,000	Playhouse Square Center, Cleveland, OH
166,667	Cleveland Clinic Foundation, Cleveland, OH
166,667	Health Museum of Cleveland, Cleveland, OH
153,680	Judson Retirement Community, Cleveland, OH
110,000	Berea Children's Home and Family Services, Berea, OH

RELIABLE LIFE INSURANCE CO.

Company Headquarters

231 W. Lockwood Ave.
Webster Groves, MO 63119
Web: http://www.unitrin.com/lhi.htm

Company Description

Employees: 1,250
SIC(s): 6311 Life Insurance, 6321 Accident & Health Insurance.

Operating Locations

Reliable Life Insurance Co. (AR--El Dorado, Jonesboro, Little Rock, Texarkana; TX--Austin, Beaumont, Corpus Christi, Dallas, Fort Worth, Harlingen, Houston, Lubbock, McAllen, Midland, San Antonio, Tyler, Waco)

Nonmonetary Support

Type: Loaned Employees; Workplace Solicitation

Reliable Life Insurance Co. Foundation

Giving Contact

Anne Skelton, Trustee
231 W. Lockwood Ave.
St. Louis, MO 63119-2327
Phone: (314)968-6743

Description

EIN: 431735442
Organization Type: Corporate Foundation
Giving Locations: MO; WI: states where company does business.
Grant Types: Emergency, General Support, Multiyear/Continuing Support, Scholarship.

Financial Summary

Total Giving: $14,066 (2001); $100,000 (2000); $14,875 (1999)
Giving Analysis: Giving for 1999 includes: foundation ($14,875)
Assets: $13,666 (2000); $46 (1999); $14,951 (1998)
Gifts Received: $250 (1998). Note: In 1998, contributions were received from A. Riley, Virginia Broleman, Garden Club, and The Reliance Life Insurance Company.

Typical Recipients

Arts & Humanities: Arts Appreciation, Arts Centers, Arts & Humanities-General, Libraries, Museums/Galleries, Music, Theater

Civic & Public Affairs: African American Affairs, Botanical Gardens/Parks, Community Foundations, Employment/Job Training, Civic & Public Affairs-General, Housing, Inner-City Development, Philanthropic Organizations, Zoos/Aquariums

Education: Afterschool/Enrichment Programs, Arts/Humanities Education, Business Education, Colleges & Universities, Education Funds, Education-General, Special Education

Health: Adolescent Health Issues, Alzheimers Disease, Arthritis, Cancer, Children's Health/Hospitals, Health-General, Heart, Speech & Hearing

Religion: Religion-General, Missionary Activities (Domestic), Religious Welfare

Science: Science Museums

Social Services: At-Risk Youth, Child Welfare, Community Centers, Community Service Organizations, Day Care, Emergency Relief, Family Services, Food/Clothing Distribution, Homes, People with Disabilities, Scouts, Social Services-General, Special Olympics, United Funds/United Ways, YMCA/YWCA/YMHA/YWHA, Youth Organizations

Application Procedures

Initial Contact: Send a brief letter of inquiry and a full proposal. Include a description of organization, amount requested, purpose of funds sought, recently audited financial statement, and proof of tax-exempt status.

Deadlines: None.

Restrictions

Does not support individuals, religious organizations for sectarian purposes, political or lobbying groups, or organizations outside operating areas.

Corporate Officials

David Chomeau: chairman, president, chief operating officer, director B Saint Louis, MO 1937. ED Carleton College (1958). PRIM CORP EMPL chairman, president, chief operating officer, director: Reliable Life Insurance Co.

Stuart Chomeau: vice chairman, director PRIM CORP EMPL vice chairman, director: Reliable Life Insurance Co.

Lewis Baker Shepley: executive vice president, chief financial officer, director B Saint Louis, MO 1939. ED Yale University (1962); Yale University (1965). PRIM CORP EMPL executive vice president, chief financial officer, director: Reliable Life Insurance Co.

Foundation Officials

David D. Chomeau: trustee
Gregory P. LaVigne: trustee
James F. Seidler: trustee
Anne Skelton: trustee

Grants Analysis

Disclosure Period: calendar year ending 2000
Total Grants: $100,000
Number of Grants: 1

Recent Grants

Note: Grants derived from 2001 Form 990.

General

9,000	Missouri College Fund, Jefferson City, MO
3,000	Hope Center Salvation Army, St. Louis, MO
1,000	Friends of Father Dickson Cemetery, St. Louis, MO
500	Children's Home Society, St. Louis, MO
500	KidzLink, St. Louis, MO
66	Tatman Foundation, Ephraim, WI -- for University of California Marine Science Department

RESCO, INC.

Company Headquarters

Honolulu, HI

Company Description

Employees: 300
SIC(s): 5000 Wholesale Trade--Durable Goods.

Locations Foundation

Giving Contact

Board of Directors
Locations Foundation
3465 Waialae Avenue, 4th Floor
Honolulu, HI 96816-2660
Phone: (808)735-4200

Description

Founded: 1988
EIN: 990267351
Organization Type: Corporate Foundation
Giving Locations: HI: Honolulu
Grant Types: General Support.

Donor Information

Founder: Resco, Inc.

Financial Summary

Total Giving: $19,634 (2000); $11,005 (1999); $6,675 (1998). Note: 1997 Giving includes United Way ($2,500).
Giving Analysis: Giving for 2000 includes: foundation grants to United Way ($3,000); 1999: foundation grants to United Way ($3,000) foundation ($8,005).
Assets: $203,492 (2000); $196,903 (1999); $191,301 (1998)
Gifts Received: $18,760 (2000); $14,074 (1999); $16,426 (1998)

Typical Recipients

Arts & Humanities: Arts & Humanities-General, Libraries, Music, Performing Arts, Public Broadcasting, Theater

Civic & Public Affairs: Asian American Affairs, Botanical Gardens/Parks, Clubs, Civic & Public Affairs-General, Public Policy, Urban & Community Affairs, Women's Affairs

Education: Colleges & Universities, Preschool Education, Private Education (Precollege), School Volunteerism, Science/Mathematics Education, Secondary Education (Private), Secondary Education (Public)

Health: Arthritis, Cancer, Children's Health/Hospitals, Diabetes, Health Organizations, Heart, Hospices, Hospitals, Medical Rehabilitation, Mental Health, Prenatal Health Issues, Public Health, Respiratory, Single-Disease Health Associations

Religion: Religious Organizations, Religious Welfare

Social Services: Big Brother/Big Sister, Child Welfare, Community Centers, Community Service Organizations, Crime Prevention, Emergency Relief, Family Services, Food/Clothing Distribution, Recreation & Athletics, Scouts, Special Olympics, Substance Abuse, United Funds/United Ways, YMCA/YWCA/YMHA/YWHA, Youth Organizations

Application Procedures

Initial Contact: The foundation has no formal grant application procedure or application form.
Deadlines: None.

Restrictions

Grants are not made to individuals.

Corporate Officials

William Chee: chairman, president, director PRIM CORP EMPL chairman, president, director: Resco Products.

Foundation Officials

Delores Bediones: trustee
William Chee: trustee (see above)
Brenda Ching: secretary
John Hayama: vice president
Robert Isonaga: treasurer
Karen Robertshaw: trustee

Grants Analysis

Disclosure Period: calendar year ending 2000
Total Grants: $16,634*
Number of Grants: 39
Average Grant: $359*
Highest Grant: $3,100
Typical Range: $100 to $1,000
***Note:** Giving excludes United Way. Average grant figure excludes highest grant.

Recent Grants

Note: Grants derived from 1999 Form 990.

General

3,000	Aloha United Way, Honolulu, HI
2,200	American Cancer Society, Honolulu, HI
1,750	Christmas Families
1,025	YWCA of Oahu, Oahu, HI
1,000	Adult Friends for Youth, Honolulu, HI
675	Ronald McDonald House
500	Juvenile Diabetes Foundation
325	Women In Need
200	Mental Help Hawaii, Honolulu, HI
100	MDA

RESEARCH CORP.

Giving Contact

Dr. Raymond Kellman, Vice President
Science Advancement Program
101 North Wilmot Road, Suite 250
Tucson, AZ 85711-3335
Phone: (520)571-1111
Fax: (520)571-1119
E-mail: awards@rescorp.org
Web: http://www.rescorp.org

Description

Founded: 1912
EIN: 131963407
Organization Type: Specialized/Single Purpose Foundation
Giving Locations: nationally; Canada
Grant Types: Award.

Donor Information

Founder: The Research Corporation was founded in 1912, with the late Frederick Gardner Cottrell as a donor. Dr. Cottrell, a noted scientist, inventor, and philanthropist, established the foundation for the advancement of science and technology with the assistance of the Secretary of the Smithsonian Institution, Charles Doolittle Walcott. The Research Corporation, which was one of the first U.S. foundations, was the only one wholly devoted to science.

Dr. Cottrell, born in Oakland, CA, in 1877, received a bachelor's degree from the University of California in 1896. He taught high school chemistry, before pursuing advanced degrees from the University of Berlin in 1901 and the University of Leipzig in 1902. Dr. Cottrell then returned to America to teach at the University of California.

While an instructor at the University of California, he invented the Cottrell Electrical Precipitator. The device, which is still in use today, became the primary means for controlling industrial air pollution and the basis for his fortune.

In 1912, after taking a job with the U.S. Bureau of Mines, he established the Research Corporation with the patent rights from his invention. Dr. Cottrell believed that science should be the principal beneficiary for his invention and wanted the foundation to develop it and use any monies from it to provide means for scientific investigation and research by contributing funds to the Smithsonian Insitution and other institutions. For the foundation's board, he recruited men prominent in academe and industry, including Dr. Walcott, as the foundation's co-founder.

Over the past eighty years, the Research Corporation has contributed well over $125 million to research projects proposed by young academic scientists, twenty-three of whom have won Nobel Prizes. A number of other prominent academic inventors have followed Dr. Cottrell's example and have contributed inventions to the corporation for the furthering of academic science.

Dr. Cottrell married Jessie Mae Fulton in 1904. Dr. Cottrell died in 1948, leaving no immediate survivors.

Financial Summary

Total Giving: $6,067,278 (2000); $6,232,985 (1999); $4,116,453 (1998)

Assets: $158,416,094 (2000); $166,157,034 (1999); $137,199,083 (1998)

Gifts Received: $198,053 (2000); $438,138 (1998); $444,697 (1997). Note: In 2000, contributions were received from the MJ Murdock Charitable Trust ($170,553) and the Camille and Henry Dreyfus Foundation ($27,500).

Typical Recipients

Arts & Humanities: Ballet, Arts & Humanities-General, Libraries, Museums/Galleries, Music, Public Broadcasting, Theater

Civic & Public Affairs: Business/Free Enterprise, Hispanic Affairs, Nonprofit Management, Public Policy

Education: Afterschool/Enrichment Programs, Agricultural Education, Arts/Humanities Education, Business Education, Colleges & Universities, Economic Education, Faculty Development, Education-General, Journalism/Media Education, Medical Education, Science/Mathematics Education, Secondary Education (Public)

Health: Diabetes, Health-General

International: Foreign Educational Institutions

Religion: Religious Welfare

Science: Scientific Organizations, Scientific Research

Social Services: Child Welfare, Recreation & Athletics, Senior Services, Special Olympics, Substance Abuse, YMCA/YWCA/YMHA/YWHA, Youth Organizations

Application Procedures

Initial Contact: See foundation website for application guidelines.

Application Requirements: Applicants should read the complete guidelines at the foundation website, then submit the electronic application request form found at the end of the guidelines.

Deadlines: There are target dates for specific programs at the foundation, such as the Cottrell College Science Awards and Cottrell Scholars Awards. Contact the foundation for specific deadlines.

Review Process: After internal evaluation, formal applications will be invited from those inquiries that are of further interest.

Restrictions

The foundation does not make awards to individuals or businesses. Cottrell College Science Awards encourage research with undergraduates and are open to faculty in non-PhD granting departments of astronomy, chemistry, and physics. Cottrell Scholars Awards are for young university faculty members in their third year of a tenure track position who wish to excel at both research and teaching.

Research Innovation Awards are for research university faculty in chemistry, physics, and astronomy who propose original, innovative research and teaching program; they are open to faculty whose first tenure-track position began in the current or preceding calendar year. Research Opportunity Awards target tenured science faculty at graduate institutions aimed at re-establishing research programs. It is restricted to PhD granting departments of astronomy, chemistry, and physics, and the first step is a nomination by the department chair. Guidelines for specific programs are available from the foundation website.

Occasionally, proposals may be considered for novel research projects that are unlikely to receive support from more traditional sources. Requests for funding that might be obtained from other more appropriate sources, to supplement already substantial funding or to simply extend mature projects, are not encouraged.

Additional Information

Publications: Annual Report (including Applicaiton Guidelines); Application Form; Program Brochures; Occasional Reports on Research and Education in the Physical Sciences; Newsletter

Foundation Officials

Herbert S. Adler: director ED University of Pennsylvania. PRIM CORP EMPL principal: Halcyon/Slifka Management Co. NONPR AFFIL member: American Friends English Heritage; member: American Friends Winchester Cathedral.

Stuart Jessup Bigelow Crampton: director B New York, NY 1936. ED Williams College BA (1958); Oxford University Worcester College BA (1960); Harvard University PhD (1964); Oxford University Worcester College MA (1965). PRIM NONPR EMPL professor: Williams College. CORP AFFIL consult: Sherman Fairchild Scientific Equipment Program Westat Inc. NONPR AFFIL member: Sigma Phi; member: Sigma Xi; member board assessment physics labs: National Institute Standards & Technology; member: American Association Physics Teachers; fellow: American Physics Society.

Michael P. Doyle, PhD: vice president, secretary ED Iowa State University PhD; University of Saint Thomas.

Robert Michael Gavin, Jr.: director B Coatesville, PA 1940. ED Saint John's University BA (1962); Iowa State University PhD (1966). ADD CORP EMPL president: Cranbrook Educational Community. CORP AFFIL director: Fortis Money Fund Inc.; director: Research Corp.; director: Fortis Income Portfolios Inc.; director: Fortis Funds Research Corp.; director: Fortis Growth Fund Inc.; director: Fortis Financial Group Inc.

Robert Holland, Jr.: director B 1940. ED City University of New York Bernard M. Baruch College MBA; Union College BSME. CORP AFFIL director: UNC Ventures Inc.; director: TruMark Manufacturing Co.; director: AC Nielsen Corp.; director: Olin Corp.; director: Mutual Life Insurance Co. New York; director: Frontier Corp.; director: Middlesex Mutual Insurance Co. NONPR AFFIL director: Lincoln Center Theater; chairman, trustee: Spelman College; director: Harlem Junior Tennis Program; trustee: Atlanta University Center.

Suzanne Denbo Jaffe: treasurer B Washington, DC 1943. PRIM CORP EMPL managing director: Hamilton Co. CORP AFFIL director: Olin Corp.; director: Creative Biomolecules Axel Johnson Inc.; director: Crossroads Capital LP. NONPR AFFIL trustee: University Pennsylvania; member: Women's Forum; trustee: Pennsylvania Women; director: National Postal Forum; member New York women business committee: Oversees Education Fund International; member: International Womens Forum; board governors, vice president: Jewish Community Relations Council; member: Finance Womens Association; director: Fordham University; member advisory committee: Childrens Aid Society; business advisory board: Columbia University Graduate School Business; president: American Jewish Committee. CLUB AFFIL Economic Club; Harmonie Club.

John Paul Schaefer, PhD: president, chief executive officer B New York, NY 1934. ED Polytechnic Institute Brooklyn BS (1955); University of Illinois PhD (1958).

PRIM NONPR EMPL chairman, director: Research Corp. Techs Inc. CORP AFFIL chairman, director: Research Corp. Techs Inc.; director: Tucson Airport Authority; director: Olin Corp. NONPR AFFIL member: Tucson Audubon Society; member faculty: University Arizona; member: Phi Lambda Upsilon; member: Sigma Xi; member: Newcomen Society; member: Phi Kappa Phi; member: Nature Conservancy; member: Arizona Academy; member: National Audubon Society; member: American Association Advancement Science; member: American Chemical Society.

Joan Selverstone Valentine: director

Geoffrey King Walters: director B Baton Rouge, LA 1931. ED Rice University BA (1953); Duke University PhD (1956). PRIM NONPR EMPL professor: Rice University. NONPR AFFIL fellow: American Physics Society.

Laurel Lynn Wilkening: director B Richland, WA 1944. ED Reed College BA (1966); University of California, San Diego PhD (1970). PRIM NONPR EMPL chancellor: University of California, Irvine. CORP AFFIL director: Research Corp.; director: Seagate Technology Inc. NONPR AFFIL trustee: Reed College; trustee: UCAR; member: Phi Beta Kappa; director: Planetary Society; member: American Association Advancement Science; member: American Geophysical Union.

Grants Analysis

Disclosure Period: calendar year ending 2000

Total Grants: $6,067,278

Number of Grants: 352

Average Grant: $17,237

Highest Grant: $75,000

Typical Range: $19,000 to $46,000

Recent Grants

Note: Grants derived from 2000 Form 990.

Library-Related

160	Friends of the Library, Tucson, AZ
120	Friends of the Library, Tucson, AZ

General

5,000	Arizona Friends of Chamber Music, Tucson, AZ
3,000	IUPAC Company Associates, Tucson, AZ
2,770	University of Arizona, Phoenix, AZ -- Priority Seating
2,500	Angel Charity For Children, Tucson, AZ
2,500	Ott Family YMCA 2000 Support Campaign, Tucson, AZ
2,500	Tucson Museum of Art, Tucson, AZ
2,340	Tucson Urban League, Tucson, AZ
2,320	University of Arizona, Phoenix, AZ -- Priority Seating
2,180	YWCA Women on the Move, Tucson, AZ
1,900	Pima Council on Aging, Tucson, AZ

RETIREMENT RESEARCH FOUNDATION

Giving Contact

Marilyn Hennessy, President
8765 West Higgins Road, Suite 430
Chicago, IL 60631-4170
Phone: (773)714-8080
Fax: (773)714-8089
E-mail: info@rrf.org
Web: http://www.rrf.org

Description

Founded: 1950

EIN: 362429540

Organization Type: General Purpose Foundation

Giving Locations: FL: direct service projects; IL: Chicago metropolitan area nationally; Midwest: direct service projects.

Grant Types: Matching, Multiyear/Continuing Support, Project, Research, Seed Money.

Donor Information

Founder: "The Retirement Research Foundation was established by John D. MacArthur , a Chicago resident and businessman, in 1950. Upon Mr. MacArthur's death in 1978, the foundation was the recipient of major assets and began active grant making in 1979. MacArthur also established the John D. and Catherine T. MacArthur Foundation. However, each foundation is separate and totally independent of the other."

Financial Summary

Total Giving: $11,175,090 (2000); $14,770,701 (1999); $9,552,045 (1998)
Giving Analysis: Giving for 2000 includes: foundation grants to United Way ($221,051); foundation ($10,954,039); 1998: foundation scholarships ($39,000) foundation matching gifts ($170,170).
Assets: $190,666,818 (2000); $197,737,780 (1999); $202,201,408 (1998)

Typical Recipients

Arts & Humanities: Film & Video, Libraries
Civic & Public Affairs: Asian American Affairs, Community Foundations, Economic Development, Employment/Job Training, Civic & Public Affairs-General, Hispanic Affairs, Housing, Law & Justice, Legal Aid, Nonprofit Management, Professional & Trade Associations, Public Policy, Rural Affairs, Safety, Urban & Community Affairs, Women's Affairs
Education: Arts/Humanities Education, Colleges & Universities, Community & Junior Colleges, Continuing Education, Economic Education, Education Associations, Education-General, Health & Physical Education, Literacy, Medical Education, Private Education (Precollege), School Volunteerism, Secondary Education (Private), Social Sciences Education
Environment: Resource Conservation
Health: Alzheimers Disease, Alzheimers Disease, Cancer, Children's Health/Hospitals, Clinics/Medical Centers, Diabetes, Emergency/Ambulance Services, Geriatric Health, Health Policy/Cost Containment, Health Organizations, Heart, Home-Care Services, Hospices, Hospitals, Long-Term Care, Medical Research, Mental Health, Nursing Services, Preventive Medicine/Wellness Organizations, Public Health, Single-Disease Health Associations, Speech & Hearing, Transplant Networks/Donor Banks
Religion: Churches, Jewish Causes, Religious Organizations, Religious Welfare, Seminaries
Social Services: Big Brother/Big Sister, Community Centers, Community Service Organizations, Counseling, Crime Prevention, Day Care, Family Planning, Family Services, Food/Clothing Distribution, Homes, People with Disabilities, Senior Services, Shelters/Homelessness, Volunteer Services, YMCA/YWCA/YMHA/YWHA

Application Procedures

Initial Contact: The foundation does not have a standard application form. Applications must be submitted in writing. Contact the foundation for guidelines.
Application Requirements: Applications should include a two- to three-page summary of the project, its significance, and its cost. In addition, proposals should address specific project objectives and give a description of the methods. A timetable and line item budget, including other sources of funds and a budget justification, should be included. If relevant, plans for continued support should be described. Curricula vitae, not to exceed eight pages, should be included for project directors and key staff. Information on the applicant organization should include its history, accomplishments, audited financial reports, annual reports, and specific qualifications for the proposed project. Include a plan for the dissemination of project results, as appropriate. A copy of the applicant's tax-exempt status under Section 501(c)(3), and of classification as "not a private foundation" under Section 509(a) of the Internal Revenue Code, must be included. All applications must be signed by the chief executive officer of the applicant organization and submitted in triplicate.
Research proposals should describe the experimental design, procedures to be used to accomplish the objectives, sequence of the investigation, kinds of data to be obtained, and the means by which data will be analyzed and interpreted.
Model projects and service proposals should describe the project design, target group, change to be effected, resources and method of delivery, sequence of activities planned to meet project objectives, and methods and criteria to be used to evaluate the outcome of the project.
Education and training proposals should describe the target group; educational needs to be met; content, methods, sequence, and location of educational experiences; and the methods and criteria which will be used to evaluate the educational program.
Deadlines: Deadlines for receipt of applications are February 1, May 1, and August 1.
Review Process: Decisions are usually made four months after the deadline dates.

Restrictions

The foundation does not provide support for construction or renovation of facilities; general operating expenses of established organizations; endowment or developmental campaigns; scholarships; loans; grants to individuals; projects outside the United States; dissertation research; production of films or videos; computer equipment; or conferences, publications, and travel, unless they are components of foundation-funded projects. Generally, support of projects beyond a three-year period will not be provided.

Additional Information

The foundation is particularly interested in innovative projects that develop and/or demonstrate new approaches to the problems of older adults and have the potential for regional or national impact. Consideration of service or service development projects that do not have this potential are limited geographically to Illinois, Indiana, Iowa, Kentucky, Michigan, Missouri, Wisconsin, and Florida.
Publications: Program Guidelines; Application Procedures; Two-Year Report; 10-Year Retrospective Report

Foundation Officials

William J. Gentle: trustee, treasurer
Marilyn Hennessy: president B 1936.
Brian F. Hofland, PhD: senior vice president
Webster H. Hurley: trustee
Sister Stella Louise: trustee B November 13, 1920. NONPR AFFIL president, director: Saint Mary Nazareth Hospital.
Sharon F. Markham: vice president
Nathaniel P. McParland, MD: trustee
Marvin Meyerson: trustee CORP AFFIL director: Bankers Life Insurance Co. New York.
Bart Murphy: trustee
John F. Santos, PhD: trustee
Ruth Ann Watkins: secretary, trustee
Nancy Zweibel, PhD: program officer

Grants Analysis

Disclosure Period: calendar year ending 2000
Total Grants: $10,954,039*
Number of Grants: 312
Average Grant: $35,109
Highest Grant: $105,356
Lowest Grant: $1,100
Typical Range: $31,000 to $35,000 and $50,000 to $100,000
*Note: Giving excludes matching gifts.

Recent Grants

Note: Grants derived from 2000 Form 990.

General

198,399	Heather Hill Hospital, Health and Care Center, Chardon, OH -- dementia care mapping
175,000	Brothers of Holy Cross, Notre Dame, IN -- Holy Cross Village at Notre Dame
140,532	National Chronic Care Consortium, Bloomington, MN -- Evaluation of the Chronic Care Network for Alzheimer's Disease
125,557	Alzheimer's Disease & Related Disorders, Chicago, IL -- evaluation of the chronic care networks for Alzheimer's Disease
116,000	St. Teresa of Avila Parish, Chicago, IL -- renovation project
105,356	Loretto Foundation, Jamesville, NY -- for frail low-income elderly safety aging in place
100,000	Archbishop Thomas J. Murphy High School, Everett, WA
100,000	Evergreen Institute on Elder Environments, Bloomington, IN -- Evergreen Place - Challenge grant
100,000	Illinois Retired Teachers Association Foundation, Springfield, IL -- Illinois Community Advocates NOW (ICAN)
97,775	California State University, Los Angeles, CA -- for short and long term effectiveness of a multidimensional fall risk reduction

ALLENE REUSS MEMORIAL TRUST

Giving Contact

LeBoeuf, Lamb, Greene & Mac Rae, LLP
Attn: Mr. Richard Pershan, Esq. Trustee
125 West 55th Street
New York, NY 10019-5389
Phone: (212)635-1518

Description

Founded: 1996
EIN: 137086745
Organization Type: Private Foundation
Giving Locations: NY: New York and surrounding area
Grant Types: General Support.

Financial Summary

Total Giving: $652,003 (2001); $709,170 (2000); $517,543 (1999)
Assets: $13,907,326 (2001); $15,732,709 (2000); $17,172,999 (1999)
Gifts Received: $46,691 (2001); $5,138,913 (1996).
Note: In 2001, contributions were received from the Estate of Henry Reuss.

Typical Recipients

Arts & Humanities: Libraries
Civic & Public Affairs: Civic & Public Affairs-General
Education: Colleges & Universities, Preschool Education
Health: Clinics/Medical Centers, Eyes/Blindness
Religion: Jewish Causes
Social Services: Community Service Organizations, Day Care, People with Disabilities

Application Procedures

Application Requirements: Send a brief letter of inquiry.
Deadlines: None.

Additional Information
Trust(s): Bank of NY

Foundation Officials
Richard Pershan, Esq.: trustee
Richard Pershan, Esq.: co trustee

Grants Analysis
Disclosure Period: calendar year ending 2001
Total Grants: $652,003
Number of Grants: 14
Average Grant: $38,084*
Highest Grant: $105,000
Lowest Grant: $5,000
Typical Range: $25,000 to $60,000
*Note: Average grant excludes two highest grants ($195,000).

Recent Grants
Note: Grants derived from 2001 Form 990.

Library-Related
90,000	New York Public Library, New York, NY

General
105,000	Hunter College, New York, NY
60,000	Yale University, New Haven, CT
51,142	Baruch College, New York, NY -- for computer center
50,861	Recording for the Blind and Dyslexic, Princeton, NJ
50,000	Lighthouse, Philadelphia, PA
50,000	Orbis, New York, NY
50,000	Saint Vincent's Catholic Medical Center
40,000	Visions, New York, NY
37,000	Joan and Sanford Weill Medical College, New York, NY
25,000	New York Community Trust, New York, NY

CHARLES H. REVSON FOUNDATION

Giving Contact
Eli N. Evans, President
55 East 59th Street
New York, NY 10022
Phone: (212)935-3340
Fax: (212)688-0633
E-mail: info@revsonfoundation.org
Web: http://www.revsonfoundation.org

Description
Founded: 1956
EIN: 136126105
Organization Type: General Purpose Foundation
Giving Locations: NY: New York internationally; nationally.
Grant Types: Fellowship, General Support, Project, Research, Scholarship, Seed Money.

Donor Information
Founder: Charles H. Revson was born in Boston in 1906, was brought up in Manchester, NH, and went to New York City as a young man. In 1932, he founded Revlon, Inc., which he subsequently built into a major international corporation. In 1956, he established the Charles H. Revson Foundation, through which he donated more than $10 million during his lifetime. The majority of these gifts went to organizations serving the Jewish community, medical institutions, and schools and universities, particularly in New York, his adopted city. On his death in 1975, Charles Revson endowed the foundation from his estate. He gave the board of directors unusual freedom to innovate, leaving them the discretion to chart the foundation's course. In 1978, with its first full-time staff and formal grantmaking procedures, the foundation began to make special project grants.

Financial Summary
Total Giving: $10,500,000 (2000 approx); $7,847,441 (1999); $5,164,652 (1998)
Giving Analysis: Giving for 1999 includes: foundation fellowships ($597,975)
Assets: $199,488,289 (2000); $227,910,326 (1999); $196,925,895 (1998)

Typical Recipients
Arts & Humanities: Arts Funds, Arts Institutes, Arts Outreach, Ballet, Dance, Ethnic & Folk Arts, Libraries, Literary Arts, Museums/Galleries, Public Broadcasting, Theater
Civic & Public Affairs: African American Affairs, Community Foundations, Economic Development, Economic Policy, Employment/Job Training, Ethnic Organizations, Housing, Law & Justice, Legal Aid, Nonprofit Management, Philanthropic Organizations, Professional & Trade Associations, Public Policy, Urban & Community Affairs, Women's Affairs
Education: Arts/Humanities Education, Colleges & Universities, Education Reform, Elementary Education (Private), Education-General, Legal Education, Medical Education, Preschool Education, Public Education (Precollege), Science/Mathematics Education, Social Sciences Education, Student Aid
Environment: Environment-General
Health: AIDS/HIV, Cancer, Clinics/Medical Centers, Medical Research
International: Foreign Arts Organizations, Foreign Educational Institutions, Human Rights, International Affairs, International Development, International Organizations, International Peace & Security Issues, Missionary/Religious Activities
Religion: Jewish Causes, Religious Welfare, Seminaries, Social/Policy Issues
Social Services: Child Welfare, Community Service Organizations, Food/Clothing Distribution, Refugee Assistance, Shelters/Homelessness, Youth Organizations

Application Procedures
Initial Contact: Applicants should send a letter to the foundation.
Application Requirements: The letter should include a description of the proposed project and the purpose and activities of the applicant organization. It also should include background information on the project, objectives of the project, and methods to be used in accomplishing them; qualifications and responsibilities of the principal staff members; current and projected budgets; latest audited financial statement; amount, duration, and specific purposes of requested grant; plans for evaluation and future funding; other sources of support; tax-exempt status and classification; financial statements; and a list of the board of directors with their affiliations.
Deadlines: None.
Review Process: Proposals are reviewed by the foundation staff and acted on by the board of directors at regular meetings. The evaluation of grant applications is ongoing throughout the year.

Restrictions
Support is not given for local health appeals, individuals, building or endowment campaigns, matching gifts, grass-roots organizations, direct service, or routine budgetary support. No loans are made.

Additional Information
Publications: Report (biennially); Guidelines

Foundation Officials
Eli N. Evans: president B 1936.
Philip Leder: director, chairman B Washington, DC 1934. ED Harvard University AB (1956); Harvard University MD (1960). PRIM NONPR EMPL professor genetics: Harvard University, School of Medicine.
CORP AFFIL director: Monsanto Co.; director: Genome Therapeutic Corp. NONPR AFFIL member: Institute Medicine; member: National Academy Sciences; senior investigator: Howard Hughes Medical Institute; professor genetics: Harvard University Medical School.
Dr. Ruth Mandel: director PRIM CORP EMPL president: Boca Beauty Franchise Inc.
Martha Louise Minow: director ED University of Michigan AB (1975); Harvard University EdM (1976); Yale University JD (1979). PRIM NONPR EMPL professor: Harvard University. NONPR AFFIL trustee emeritus: Judge Baker Children's Center; member: Law Society Association; executive co-director: Harvard Children's Studies; director: Judge David L. Bazelon Center Mental Health Law; director: Covenant Foundation.
Charles H. Revson, Jr.: secretary, treasurer
Robert Singer Rifkind: chairman B New York, NY 1936. ED Yale University BA (1958); Harvard University JD (1961). PRIM CORP EMPL partner: Cravath, Swaine & Moore. NONPR AFFIL fellow: New York State Bar Foundation; member: Phi Beta Kappa; board governors, chairman: Jewish Theological Seminary; member: Association Bar New York City; member: Council Foreign Relations; president, director: American Jewish Committee; member: American Law Institute; fellow: American College Trial Lawyers; member: American Bar Association; member: American Bar Foundation.
Harold Tanner: president B New York, NY 1932. ED Cornell University BS (1952); Harvard University MBA (1956). PRIM CORP EMPL president: Tanner & Co. CORP AFFIL director: TIG Holdings Inc. NONPR AFFIL member: Council Foreign Relations; co-founder: Volunteer Urban Consult Group; chairman: Classroom Inc.; chairman board trustee: Cornell University; chairman: American Jewish Committee. CLUB AFFIL Century Country Club; Harmonie Club.

Grants Analysis
Disclosure Period: calendar year ending 1999
Total Grants: $7,249,466*
Number of Grants: 60
Average Grant: $120,824
Highest Grant: $600,000
Lowest Grant: $1,000
Typical Range: $20,000 to $350,000
*Note: Giving excludes fellowships.

Recent Grants
Note: Grants derived from 1999 Form 990.

General
600,000	Educational Netcasting Foundation, Cambridge, MA -- to enable the WEB DuBois Institute to develop and disseminate educational and curricular materials to a company the Encarta African
400,000	Jerusalem Institute for Israel Studies, Jerusalem Israel -- for continued support of the Jerusalem Institute for Israel Studies
322,556	Columbia University in the City of New York, New York, NY -- for continued support of the Charles H. Revson Fellows Program on the Future of the City of New York
317,975	New York University School of Law, New York, NY -- for continued support of the Charles H. Revson Law Students Public Interest Fellowship Program for New York area law students
275,000	New York Times Company Foundation, Inc., New York, NY -- to create and evaluate the Teachers Who Make a Difference Awards Program, which operates in conjunction w/New York Times college scholarships
250,000	Center on Budget and Policy Priorities,

Washington, DC -- for continued support of its monitoring and public education activities

250,000   Israel Academy of Sciences and Humanities, Jerusalem Israel -- support the local initiatives for Research in Science & Technology Program

250,000   Jewish Media Fund, New York, NY -- for continued support of the Jewish Heritage Video Collection

250,000   Tides Foundation, New York, NY -- to join w/other foundations to support a 5th national nonpartisan media campaign for television, radio, and print outlets, urging to vote in 2000

237,600   Jewish Theological Seminary of America, New York, NY -- continued support of the Charles H. Revson Scholars in Advanced Jewish Studies as well as for support of a 25th anniversary conference

Rexam, Inc.

Company Headquarters

4201 Congress St., Ste. 340
Charlotte, NC 28209
Web: http://www.rexam.com

Company Description

Employees: 3,200
SIC(s): 3081 Unsupported Plastics Film & Sheet, 6719 Holding Companies Nec.
Parent Company: Rexam Plc, 4 Millbank, London, United Kingdom

Operating Locations

McCorquodale ColorCard (MD--Whiteford); MiTek Industries (MO--Chesterfield); Mitek Industries (MO--St. Louis); Otis Specialty Papers (ME--Jay); Rexam Cartons (NC--Pineville); Rexam Closures (IN--Evansville, Princeton); Rexam Containers-US (IL--Flora; MO--Union); Rexam Custom (NC--Matthews; SC--Spartanburg); Rexam DSI (MA--South Hadley); Rexam Extrusions (WI--Oshkosh); Rexam Flexible Packaging (NC--Greensboro); Rexam Graphics (MA--South Hadley; OR--Portland); Rexam Medical Packaging (IL--Mundelein; MA--Ashland; MN--Lakeville; NJ--Mount Holly); Rexam Mulox U.S.A. (GA--Baxley, Macon); Rexam Performance Products (SC--Lancaster); Rexam Plastics Group (NC--Charlotte); Rexam Print Packaging Group (NC--Charlotte); Rexam Release (IL--Bedford Park, Chicago, Oak Brook)

Rexam Foundation

Giving Contact

Frank Brown, President
4201 Congress St., Ste. 340
Charlotte, NC 28209
Phone: (704)551-1500
Fax: (704)551-1572

Description

EIN: 136165669
Organization Type: Corporate Foundation
Giving Locations: operating communities.
Grant Types: Capital, Challenge, Employee Matching Gifts, Endowment, General Support, Scholarship.

Financial Summary

Total Giving: $61,551 (1999); $68,923 (1997); $86,687 (1996). Note: 1997 Giving includes matching gifts ($18,510), scholarship ($14,500).
Assets: $6,263 (1999); $284 (1997); $284 (1996)
Gifts Received: $67,787 (1999); $69,464 (1997); $86,620 (1996)

Typical Recipients

Arts & Humanities: Arts Associations & Councils, Libraries, Music, Performing Arts
Civic & Public Affairs: Chambers of Commerce
Education: Business-School Partnerships, Colleges & Universities, Community & Junior Colleges, Private Education (Precollege), Student Aid
Health: Health Organizations, Hospices, Single-Disease Health Associations
International: International Environmental Issues
Science: Science Museums
Social Services: Child Welfare, United Funds/United Ways, YMCA/YWCA/YMHA/YWHA, Youth Organizations

Application Procedures

Initial Contact: The foundation requests applications be made in writing.
Deadlines: None.

Corporate Officials

Frank C. Brown: president PRIM CORP EMPL president: Rexam.

Foundation Officials

Frank C. Brown: president (see above)
Joseph P. Keniry: vice president

Grants Analysis

Disclosure Period: calendar year ending 1999
Total Grants: $61,551*
*Note: Giving excludes matching gifts, scholarships. A more recent grants list was unavailable.

Recent Grants

Note: Grants derived from 1997 Form 990.

General

10,000	Johnson C. Smith University, Charlotte, NC
5,500	YMCA
5,000	Arts and Science Council
5,000	Discovery Place, Charlotte, NC
5,000	Queens College, Charlotte, NC
4,913	United Way Central Carolinas, Charlotte, NC
500	World Wildlife Fund, Washington, DC

Christopher Reynolds Foundation

Giving Contact

Andrea Panaritis, Executive Director, Secretary, & Treasurer
267 5th Avenue, Suite 1001
New York, NY 10016
Phone: (212)532-1606
Fax: (212)532-1403
E-mail: crfny@aol.com
Web: http://www.creynolds.org

Description

Founded: 1952
EIN: 136129401
Organization Type: General Purpose Foundation
Giving Locations: MI; NY; OH; U.S. organizations working in Indochina; Cambodia; Lao People's Democratic Republic; Vietnam
Grant Types: Conference/Seminar, General Support, Multiyear/Continuing Support, Project, Research.

Donor Information

Founder: Incorporated in 1952 by the late Libby Holman Reynolds .

Financial Summary

Total Giving: $2,233,012 (fiscal year ending January 31, 2001); $1,713,307 (fiscal 1999); $1,500,000 (fiscal 1998 approx)
Assets: $35,680,927 (fiscal 2001); $37,000,275 (fiscal 1999); $33,000,000 (fiscal 1998 approx)
Gifts Received: $3,084 (fiscal 1997); $331,944 (fiscal 1996)

Typical Recipients

Arts & Humanities: Arts & Humanities-General, Libraries, Literary Arts
Civic & Public Affairs: African American Affairs, Asian American Affairs, Civil Rights, Community Foundations, Economic Development, Economic Policy, Employment/Job Training, Ethnic Organizations, Civic & Public Affairs-General, Hispanic Affairs, Law & Justice, Native American Affairs, Nonprofit Management, Public Policy, Urban & Community Affairs
Education: Afterschool/Enrichment Programs, Colleges & Universities, Education Reform, Education-General, Health & Physical Education, International Exchange, International Studies, Medical Education, Minority Education, Private Education (Precollege), Student Aid
Environment: Environment-General, Protection
Health: Clinics/Medical Centers, Mental Health, Public Health, Public Health, Speech & Hearing
International: Foreign Arts Organizations, Foreign Educational Institutions, International-General, Health Care/Hospitals, Human Rights, International Affairs, International Development, International Environmental Issues, International Organizations, International Peace & Security Issues, International Relations, International Relief Efforts, Missionary/Religious Activities
Religion: Churches, Religion-General, Religious Organizations, Religious Welfare
Science: Science-General
Social Services: Community Service Organizations, Refugee Assistance, Social Services-General, Veterans, Youth Organizations

Application Procedures

Initial Contact: The foundation does not use a formal grant application form.
Application Requirements: Proposals should include specific objectives, detailed estimated budgets, qualifications of the organizations and individuals involved, and proof of tax-exempt status from the IRS. Six copies of the proposal are required.
Deadlines: Contact the foundation by phone, fax, or e-mail for dates.
Review Process: Meetings are generally held in January, May, and September.

Restrictions

The foundation does not make grants for building funds, medical research, educational or religious institutions (except in relation to research on subjects that fall within the scope of the foundation's current interests), or general operating or overhead expenses (except for newly organized entities whose objectives fall within the areas of the foundation's current interests).

Additional Information

Publications: Multi-Year Report (including Application Guidelines)

Foundation Officials

Dr. John R. Boettiger: director
Jack Clareman: treasurer
Suzanne Derrer: director
Dr. Michael Kahn: president, director
Andrea Panaritis: executive director, secretary
Robert Vitarelli: program officer

Grants Analysis

Disclosure Period: fiscal year ending January 31, 2001
Total Grants: $2,233,012
Number of Grants: 96
Average Grant: $20,347*
Highest Grant: $300,000
Lowest Grant: $500
Typical Range: $10,000 to $40,000
*Note: Average grant figure excludes highest grant.

Recent Grants

Note: Grants derived from 2001 Form 990.

General

300,000	New World Foundation, Washington, DC -- Joint California Initiative
100,000	American Council of Learned Societies, New York, NY -- Cuba working group
100,000	Aspen Institute, Inc. -- Cuba
100,000	Center for Labor Research and Studies -- Cuba
70,000	World Policy Institute New School for Social Research, New York, NY -- Cuba program
60,000	MEDICC -- Cuba
60,000	National Security Archive, Washington, DC -- conference
60,000	Washington Office on Latin America, Washington, DC
55,000	Latin American Working Group -- Cuba United States policy
54,050	Fund for Reconciliation and Development -- Cuba

DONALD W. REYNOLDS FOUNDATION

Giving Contact

Karina K. Mayer, Administrative Officer
1701 Village Center Circle
Las Vegas, NV 89134
Phone: (702)804-6000
Fax: (702)804-6099
E-mail: generalquestions@dwrf.org
Web: http://www.dwreynolds.org

Description

Founded: 1954
EIN: 716053383
Organization Type: General Purpose Foundation
Giving Locations: AR; NV; OK: nationally for aging and cardiovascular research programs.
Grant Types: Capital, Challenge, Employee Matching Gifts, General Support.

Donor Information

Founder: Established in 1954 by Donald W. Reynolds , who signed over all his stock and assets to the foundation in 1977 and who generously endowed it through his estate upon his death in 1993. Mr. Reynolds owned Donrey Media Group which includes more than 50 daily newspapers, radio and television stations, and billboard and cable operations.
Mr. Reynolds graduated from the University of Missouri School of Journalism in 1927. He purchased his first newspaper in 1940 in Oklahoma. He lived in Las Vegas, NV. Mr. Reynolds is survived by three children and was married three times. His children are not involved with the foundation.
The original incorporators and members of the first governing board are Clifford A. Jones; Carol Delander; Louis Wiener, Jr.; and Herbert M. Jones, all from Las Vegas, NV.

Financial Summary

Total Giving: $105,189,603 (2001); $69,342,821 (2000); $60,088,117 (1999)
Giving Analysis: Giving for 2001 includes: foundation matching gifts ($209,124); foundation grants to United Way ($513,895); 1999: foundation grants to United Way ($105,500) foundation scholarships ($115,000)
Assets: $1,177,625,162 (2001); $1,269,083,024 (2000); $1,359,723,466 (1999)
Gifts Received: $803,824,000 (1994); $802,000,000 (1993)

Typical Recipients

Arts & Humanities: Arts Associations & Councils, Arts Centers, Community Arts, Dance, Arts & Humanities-General, Historic Preservation, Libraries, Museums/Galleries, Music, Performing Arts, Public Broadcasting, Theater
Civic & Public Affairs: Business/Free Enterprise, Clubs, Economic Development, First Amendment Issues, Civic & Public Affairs-General, Hispanic Affairs, Housing, Legal Aid, Municipalities/Towns, Professional & Trade Associations, Urban & Community Affairs, Women's Affairs
Education: Business Education, Colleges & Universities, Community & Junior Colleges, Education Associations, Education Funds, Elementary Education (Public), Engineering/Technological Education, Education-General, Journalism/Media Education, Legal Education, Literacy, Medical Education, Preschool Education, Private Education (Precollege), Public Education (Precollege), Secondary Education (Private), Social Sciences Education, Student Aid
Environment: Environment-General, Wildlife Protection
Health: AIDS/HIV, Cancer, Clinics/Medical Centers, Emergency/Ambulance Services, Geriatric Health, Health Funds, Health Organizations, Heart, Hospices, Hospitals, Single-Disease Health Associations
Religion: Churches, Religion-General, Religious Welfare
Social Services: Big Brother/Big Sister, Child Welfare, Community Centers, Community Service Organizations, Counseling, Family Services, Food/Clothing Distribution, Homes, People with Disabilities, Recreation & Athletics, Scouts, Senior Services, Shelters/Homelessness, Substance Abuse, United Funds/United Ways, Volunteer Services, YMCA/YWCA/YMHA/YWHA, Youth Organizations

Application Procedures

Initial Contact: A thorough review of the foundation's guidelines is strongly recommended to determine eligibility.
Grants provided through the Aging & Quality of Life and Cardiovascular Clinical Research programs are available through a request for proposals process initiated by the foundation.
The Capital Grants program is extremely competitive and applicants must adhere to a strict set of guidelines, which may be obtained by contacting the foundation or consulting the foundation's web page.
The Community Services Centers grant program also has a very specific set of guidelines, which can be obtained from the foundation or its web site.
Planning and Technical Assistance grants are restricted to organizations that meet the eligibility standards of the Capital Grants program. If eligibility requirements are met, a prospective applicant may obtain a Planning Grant application form and guidelines by contacting the foundation or consulting its web site.
Notes: The grant program is extremely competitive. A successful application must demonstrate that the project is responsive to a well-documented need; is provided in an efficient manner that minimizes administrative costs; is thoroughly planned; will benefit the applicant organization and its clients and community; is driven by effective volunteer and staff leadership; is financially viable and, once the project is complete, is

financially secure for the foreseeable future; is appropriate for the program(s) to be housed in the proposed facility; is cost-effective; and increases the capacity, effectiveness, efficiency, quality and/or success of the applicant and program. Proposals submitted via fax or electronic mail will not be accepted. An applicant wishing to know when their proposal arrived should send it "return receipt requested" or contact their carrier to confirm delivery; the foundation's small staff cannot track the numerous applications.

Restrictions

Refer to foundation guidelines for complete eligibility requirements. eligible if the program is governed by an independent board, is separately incorporated and tax-exempt in its own right, and provides services to a diverse population without regard to religious preference. The foundation will not serve as a substitute funding source for civic or governmental projects normally provided by local, state, or federal tax dollars, bonds, or user fees.
The foundation will not consider the following: grants to individuals; proposals for site acquisition, endowments, or debt retirement; proposals for program support or annual fund-raising appeals; and renovation and capital equipment projects with total costs of less than $500,000.

Additional Information

The trustees reserve the right to amend the program at any time.
Publications: Annual Report; Guidelines

Foundation Officials

Steven L. Anderson: president
Dr. Keith G. Boman: trustee PRIM CORP EMPL partner: Cardiovascular Consultants NV.
John L. Goolsby: trustee B 1941. PRIM CORP EMPL chief executive officer, president: Howard Hughes Corp. CORP AFFIL chief executive officer, president: Howard Hughes Properties Ltd. Partner; director: Nevada Power Co.; director: America West Holdings Corp.
Barbara H. Hanna: trustee
Linda P. Lambert: trustee
Courtney E. Latta: senior program officer
Neal R. Pendergraft: trustee
Donald E. Pray: trustee B Tulsa, OK 1932. ED University of Tulsa BS (1955); University of Oklahoma LLB (1963). PRIM CORP EMPL counsel: Jackman, Pray, Walker. NONPR AFFIL president: Tulsa Estate Planning Forum; president: Tulsa Mineral Lawyers Sect; director: Saint Johns Medical Center; director: Tulsa Ballet Theater; fellow: American Bar Foundation; director: Philbrook Art Museum; member: American Bar Association. CLUB AFFIL president: Summit Club.
John V. Schlereth: trustee PRIM CORP EMPL owner: Four Points Hotel ITT Sheridan.
Fred W. Smith: chairman B Arkoma, OK 1934. ED Arizona Polytechnic College. PRIM CORP EMPL president, chief executive officer: Donrey Media Group ADD CORP EMPL vice president: Scores Inc.
Jonathan Smith, OD: trustee
Wes Smith: trustee
Barbara Smith Campbell: trustee
Debby Smith Magness: trustee
Joel R. Stubblefield: trustee PRIM NONPR EMPL president: Westark Community College.
Debra L. Tunney: program associate

Grants Analysis

Disclosure Period: calendar year ending 2001
Total Grants: $104,466,584*
Number of Grants: 186 (approx)
Highest Grant: $27,584,459
Typical Range: $50,000 to $2,000,000
*Note: Giving excludes matching gifts; United Way.

Recent Grants

Note: Grants derived from 2001 Form 990.

General

27,584,459	Smithsonian Institution, Washington, DC -- lansdowne portrait of George Washington national tour exhibit space
7,795,006	University of Texas Southwestern Medical Center at Dallas, Dallas, TX -- Cardiovascular Clinical Research Center
3,271,900	University of Oklahoma Health Sciences Center, Oklahoma City, OK -- Department of Geriatrics Program support
2,110,115	Search Institute, Minneapolis, MN -- Project "Building Community Capacity to Raise Healthy Children"
2,000,000	America's Second Harvest, Chicago, IL -- Enterprise Project
1,278,645	University of Arkansas for Medical Sciences, Little Rock, AR -- Geriatric Program support
1,000,000	Razorback Foundation, Fayetteville, AR -- supplemental funds for Razorback Stadium
810,235	University of Arkansas for Medical Sciences, Little Rock, AR -- supplemental grant for Center on Aging
500,000	University of Hawaii, Honolulu, HI -- program to strengthen physicians in geriatric
500,000	University of Iowa College of Medicine, Iowa City, IA -- program to strengthen physicians training in geriatrics

EDGAR & FRANCIS REYNOLDS FOUNDATION

Giving Contact

Fred Glade, Trustee
PO Box 1492
Grand Island, NE 68802
Phone: (308)384-0957
E-mail: lbbst@kdsi.net

Description

Founded: 1977
EIN: 470589941
Organization Type: Private Foundation
Giving Locations: NE: Central Nebraska, Grand Island
Grant Types: Capital, Research, Scholarship.

Donor Information

Founder: the late Edgar Reynolds

Financial Summary

Total Giving: $376,857 (2001); $382,900 (2000); $253,620 (1999)
Giving Analysis: Giving for 2001 includes: foundation grants to United Way ($1,000); 2000: foundation grants to United Way ($1,000) 1999: foundation grants to United Way ($1,520)
Assets: $8,723,640 (2001); $9,917,145 (2000); $9,742,344 (1999)
Gifts Received: $1,910,989 (1998)

Typical Recipients

Arts & Humanities: Arts Associations & Councils, History & Archaeology, Libraries, Museums/Galleries
Civic & Public Affairs: Botanical Gardens/Parks, Chambers of Commerce, Community Foundations, Housing, Municipalities/Towns, Philanthropic Organizations, Safety, Zoos/Aquariums
Education: Agricultural Education, Business Education, Colleges & Universities, Community & Junior Colleges, Education Funds, Education-General, Public Education (Precollege)
Environment: Air/Water Quality, Environment-General, Wildlife Protection

Health: Clinics/Medical Centers, Hospitals
Religion: Religious Welfare
Social Services: Animal Protection, At-Risk Youth, Big Brother/Big Sister, Child Welfare, Crime Prevention, Emergency Relief, Food/Clothing Distribution, People with Disabilities, Recreation & Athletics, Recreation & Athletics, United Funds/United Ways, Veterans, YMCA/YWCA/YMHA/YWHA, Youth Organizations

Application Procedures

Initial Contact: Request an application form.
Application Requirements: Provide full details on proposed project and need.
Deadlines: None.

Restrictions

Does not support religious organizations for sectarian purposes, political or lobbying groups, or organizations outside operating areas.

Additional Information

Publications: Application Guidelines

Foundation Officials

John R. Brownell: secretary PRIM CORP EMPL attorney: Lauritsen, Brownell, Brostrom, Stehlik & Thayer.
Kent Coen: trustee
Fred M. Glade, Jr.: trustee
Don Jelinek: trustee
Clarence Walters: trustee

Grants Analysis

Disclosure Period: calendar year ending 2001
Total Grants: $375,857*
Number of Grants: 17
Average Grant: $9,500*
Highest Grant: $142,857
Lowest Grant: $900
Typical Range: $1,000 to $25,000
*Note: Giving excludes United Way. Average grant excludes three highest grants ($242,857).

Recent Grants

Note: Grants derived from 2001 Form 990.

General

142,857	Fonner Park Event Center, Grand Island, NE -- program support
50,000	Central Community College, Grand Island, NE -- program support
50,000	YMCA, Grand Island, NE -- program support
25,000	Crane Meadows Nature Center, Grand Island, NE -- program support
25,000	Hall County Historical Society, Grand Island, NE -- program support
25,000	YWCA, Grand Island, NE
20,000	Crisis Center, Grand Island, NE -- program support
12,500	Nebraska Independent College Foundation, Omaha, NE -- program support
7,500	Grand Island Youth Baseball, Inc., Grand Island, NE -- program support
6,100	American Red Cross, Grand Island, NE -- program support

RICHARD S. REYNOLDS FOUNDATION

Giving Contact

Victoria Pitrelli, Executive Director
1403 Pemberton Road, Suite 102
Richmond, VA 23233
Phone: (804)740-7350
Fax: (804)740-7807

Description

Founded: 1965
EIN: 546037003
Organization Type: General Purpose Foundation
Giving Locations: VA: Central Virginia, particularly Richmond
Grant Types: Capital, Challenge, Emergency, Endowment, General Support, Matching, Multiyear/Continuing Support, Operating Expenses, Professorship, Project, Research, Scholarship.

Donor Information

Founder: The foundation was established in 1965 by the late Julia L. Reynolds .

Financial Summary

Total Giving: $1,600,000 (fiscal year ending June 30, 2003 approx); $1,600,000 (fiscal 2002 approx); $1,456,780 (fiscal 2001)
Giving Analysis: Giving for fiscal 2001 includes: foundation fellowships ($45,000) foundation scholarships ($126,070)
Assets: $34,000,000 (fiscal 2002 approx); $39,562,412 (fiscal 2001); $39,000,000 (fiscal 2000 approx)
Gifts Received: $38,526 (fiscal 2001); $47,800 (fiscal 2000 approx); $47,843 (fiscal 1999). Note: Contributions were received from the trust of David P. Reynolds.

Typical Recipients

Arts & Humanities: Arts Associations & Councils, Arts Outreach, Ballet, Dance, Historic Preservation, History & Archaeology, Libraries, Museums/Galleries, Music, Opera, Performing Arts, Theater
Civic & Public Affairs: Botanical Gardens/Parks, Business/Free Enterprise, Community Foundations, Economic Policy, Employment/Job Training, Civic & Public Affairs-General, Housing, Nonprofit Management, Professional & Trade Associations, Urban & Community Affairs, Zoos/Aquariums
Education: Afterschool/Enrichment Programs, Business Education, Colleges & Universities, Education Associations, Education Funds, Engineering/Technological Education, Environmental Education, Faculty Development, Education-General, Literacy, Medical Education, Private Education (Precollege), Public Education (Precollege), Science/Mathematics Education, Secondary Education (Private), Special Education, Student Aid
Environment: Environment-General
Health: Cancer, Children's Health/Hospitals, Clinics/Medical Centers, Emergency/Ambulance Services, Health Funds, Heart, Hospitals, Medical Rehabilitation, Medical Research, Mental Health, Multiple Sclerosis, Respiratory
International: Human Rights, International Organizations
Religion: Churches, Religious Organizations, Religious Welfare, Seminaries
Science: Science Museums
Social Services: Animal Protection, At-Risk Youth, Child Welfare, Community Service Organizations, Emergency Relief, Family Services, Food/Clothing Distribution, Homes, People with Disabilities, Recreation & Athletics, Scouts, Senior Services, Shelters/Homelessness, YMCA/YWCA/YMHA/YWHA, Youth Organizations

Application Procedures

Initial Contact: Applicants should send a brief letter with a description of the organization's primary focus and an outline of the proposal.
Application Requirements: Proposals should include verification of applicant's tax-exempt status by the IRS and a current budget or recent set of financial statements.
Deadlines: October 31 and April 30.
Review Process: The board meets in November and May each year.

Notes: Grants are typically made prior to the fiscal year end in June.

Foundation Officials

Glenn R. Martin: vice president, director

David Parham Reynolds: president, director B Bristol, TN June 16, 1915. ED Princeton University. PRIM CORP EMPL chairman emeritus, director: Reynolds Metals Co. NONPR AFFIL member: Primary Aluminum Institute; trustee emeritus: University Richmond; trustee emeritus: Lawrenceville School; member: Aluminum Association; honorary member: American Institute Architects.

Richard Samuel Reynolds, III: secretary, director B New York, NY 1934. ED Princeton University BA (1956). PRIM CORP EMPL managing director: Reynolds Trusts. NONPR AFFIL vice president: Missionary Emergency Fund.

William Gray Reynolds, Jr.: treasurer, director B New York, NY 1939. ED University of Pennsylvania BA (1962); University of Virginia JD (1965). PRIM CORP EMPL vice president government relations & public affairs: Reynolds Metals Co. CORP AFFIL director: Wachovia Corp.

Grants Analysis

Disclosure Period: fiscal year ending June 30, 2001
Total Grants: $1,285,710*
Number of Grants: 45
Average Grant: $28,571
Highest Grant: $125,821
Lowest Grant: $1,000
Typical Range: $15,000 to $50,000
*Note: Giving excludes scholarships and fellowship.

Recent Grants

Note: Grants derived from fiscal 2000 Form 990.

Library-Related

50,000	Randolph-Macon College, Lynchburg, VA -- audio-visual classroom

General

124,910	Yad Yisroel
100,344	Yad Yisroel
99,917	Yad Yisroel
87,800	Union Theological Seminary, Richmond, VA -- final payment/rare books room
84,936	Thomas Jefferson Memorial -- second of three payments
52,139	Appomattox Regional Governor's School, Petersburg, VA -- capital campaign
51,070	Riverside School, Bon Air, VA -- second of three payments/Margaret Harris
50,792	Richmond Ballet, Richmond, VA -- final payment/raising the roof campaign
50,534	Virginia Historical Society, Richmond, VA -- second of five payments/story of Virginia
50,170	Foxcroft School, Waynesboro, VA -- science department endowment

RGK FOUNDATION

Giving Contact

Gregory A. Kozmetsky, President, Chairman
1301 West 25th Street
Suite 300
Austin, TX 78705-4236
Phone: (512)474-9298
Fax: (512)474-7281
E-mail: jhampton@rgkfoundation.org
Web: http://www.rgkfoundation.org

Description

Founded: 1966
EIN: 746077587
Organization Type: Family Foundation
Giving Locations: nationally.

Grant Types: Challenge, Conference/Seminar, Multiyear/Continuing Support, Project, Research.

Donor Information

Founder: The RGK Foundation was established in 1966 by Dr. George Kozmetsky and his wife, Ronya Kozmetsky. Dr. Kozmetsky currently sits on the board of several corporations including Teledyne, Inc., which he co-founded in 1960.

Dr. Kozmetsky, a son of Russian immigrants, was born in Seattle, WA, in 1917. He taught at Harvard University and Carnegie-Mellon University before he started his business career in Los Angeles with Hughes Aircraft Company (1952-54), then Litton Company (1954-59). He left Teledyne in 1966 when he took the position of dean of the college and graduate school of business at the University of Texas at Austin. He stayed there for sixteen years until 1982 when he went on to head the school's Institute for Constructive Capitalism.

Currently, Dr. Kozmetsky serves on the RGK Foundation as its donor and trustee. His wife, Ronya, and his two children, Gregory Allen Kozmetsky and Nadya Anne Kozmetsky Scott, also serve on the foundation.

Financial Summary

Total Giving: $3,693,276 (2002); $5,962,637 (2001); $10,140,537 (2000)
Giving Analysis: Giving for 1999 includes: foundation grants to United Way ($25,000) 1998: foundation scholarships ($58,478)
Assets: $103,516,130 (2001); $108,483,771 (2000); $115,836,936 (1999)
Gifts Received: $8,002,313 (2000); $1,000 (1998); $16,500,000 (1997). Note: The majority of yearly donations come in the form of stock from George and Ronya Kozmetsky.

Typical Recipients

Arts & Humanities: Arts Outreach, Film & Video, Libraries, Museums/Galleries, Music, Opera, Public Broadcasting

Civic & Public Affairs: Business/Free Enterprise, Clubs, Economic Development, Employment/Job Training, Civic & Public Affairs-General, Hispanic Affairs, Housing, Legal Aid, Public Policy, Urban & Community Affairs, Women's Affairs

Education: Afterschool/Enrichment Programs, Arts/Humanities Education, Business Education, Colleges & Universities, Continuing Education, Education Reform, Elementary Education (Public), Engineering/Technological Education, Environmental Education, Faculty Development, Education-General, International Studies, Leadership Training, Legal Education, Literacy, Medical Education, Medical Education, Minority Education, Preschool Education, Private Education (Precollege), Public Education (Precollege), Science/Mathematics Education, Secondary Education (Public), Social Sciences Education, Special Education, Student Aid, Vocational & Technical Education

Environment: Environment-General, Resource Conservation

Health: Arthritis, Cancer, Children's Health/Hospitals, Clinics/Medical Centers, Diabetes, Eyes/Blindness, Geriatric Health, Health Policy/Cost Containment, Health Organizations, Heart, Hospices, Hospitals, Hospitals (University Affiliated), Kidney, Medical Research, Mental Health, Nursing Services, Prenatal Health Issues, Public Health, Research/Studies Institutes, Respiratory, Single-Disease Health Associations, Speech & Hearing, Transplant Networks/Donor Banks

International: Foreign Educational Institutions, Health Care/Hospitals, International Development

Religion: Religion-General, Jewish Causes, Religious Welfare

Science: Science-General, Scientific Centers & Institutes

Social Services: At-Risk Youth, Child Abuse, Child Welfare, Community Centers, Community Service Organizations, Crime Prevention, Day Care, Domestic Violence, Family Services, People with Disabilities, Scouts, Senior Services, Shelters/Homelessness, Social Services-General, Substance Abuse, Youth Organizations

Application Procedures

Initial Contact: Applicants should call or write the foundation to request an application form.

Application Requirements: The following information must accompany one unbound copy of the grant proposal: completed RGK application form; current annual report, if applicable; a brief background of the organization; a description of the proposed project; a concise statement of the necessity for the project; an explanation of the use of the funds; the amount requested; a detailed project budget; other potential sources of funding; current financial statements, including current annual operating budget; most recently filed IRS Form 990; list of board of directors; and proof of charitable status.

Deadlines: None.

Review Process: Grant proposals are reviewed on an ongoing basis. Upon receipt of a completed application, applicants are asked to allow three months for proposal review.

Restrictions

The foundation does not fund individuals, organizations limited by race or religion, organizations that are not tax-exempt, facilities or equipment, or for indirect costs.

Additional Information

Medical grant requests should follow NIH guidelines, but only one copy of proposal is required.

The foundation requires grantees to provide interim and final grant reports.

Publications: Informational Brochure (including Application Guidelines); Application Form

Foundation Officials

Patricia Ann Hayes: trustee B Binghamton, NY 1944. ED College of Saint Rose BA (1968); Georgetown University PhD (1974). PRIM NONPR EMPL president: Saint Edwards University. NONPR AFFIL president: Saint Edward's University Inc.; executive vice president, chief operating officer: Seton Healthcare Network; director: KLRU-Public Television.

Charles Edwin Hurwitz: trustee B Kilgore, TX 1940. ED University of Oklahoma BA (1962). PRIM CORP EMPL chairman, chief executive officer, president: MAXXAM Group Inc. ADD CORP EMPL chairman, chief executive officer, president: MAXXAM Group Holdings Inc. CORP AFFIL director: Kaiser Aluminum Corp.; director: KLU; vice chairman, director: Kaiser Aluminum & Chemical Corp.

Cynthia Kozmetsky: trustee, treasurer, vice president, secretary

Gregory Allen Kozmetsky: president, chairman, trustee B 1946. ED University of Texas, Austin (1968-1972). PRIM CORP EMPL president: KMS Ventures Inc.

Ronya Kozmetsky: don, trustee B 1927. PRIM CORP EMPL vice president: KMS Ventures Inc.

Nadya Ann Kozmetsky Scott: vice president, trustee

Grants Analysis

Disclosure Period: calendar year ending 2002
Total Grants: $3,693,276
Number of Grants: 115
Average Grant: $28,011*
Highest Grant: $500,000
Lowest Grant: $2,400
Typical Range: $10,000 to $50,000
*Note: Average grant figure excludes highest grant.

Recent Grants

Note: Grants derived from 2001 Form 990.

General

1,000,000	University of Texas at Austin, Austin, TX -- support the establishment of the RGK Center for Philanthropy and Community Service
304,390	SafePlace, Austin, TX -- support to construct an on-site school for children
254,000	University of Texas Medical Branch at Galveston, Galveston, TX -- for Web-Based Nursing Distance Education Program
200,000	Children's Hospital Foundation of Austin, Austin, TX -- to establish permanent endowment fund for Child Life Program
165,000	Health Sciences Foundation of the Medical University of South Carolina, Charleston, SC -- support Scleroderma research
163,437	Detroit Public Schools, Detroit, MI -- support for "Project Read"
150,000	Project Grad, Los Angeles, CA -- for residential math institute
145,000	James Dick Foundation, Round Top, TX -- for Festival Institute
142,372	Texas Fragile Families Initiative, Austin, TX -- for Tandem Prenatal and Parenting Program
125,000	Austin Public Education Foundation, Austin, TX -- for Principles of Learning Initiative

RHEINSTROM HILL COMMUNITY FOUNDATION

Giving Contact

Richard Koskey, President
502 Union St.
Hudson, NY 12534
Phone: (518)828-1565

Description

Founded: 1987
EIN: 141683989
Organization Type: Private Foundation
Giving Locations: NY: Columbia County
Grant Types: Project.

Financial Summary

Total Giving: $278,510 (fiscal year ending 1, 2002); $319,750 (fiscal 2001); $93,423 (fiscal 1999)
Giving Analysis: Giving for fiscal 2002 includes: foundation grants to United Way ($2,500)
Assets: $1,411,327 (fiscal 2002); $1,739,503 (fiscal 2001); $1,805,440 (fiscal 1999)
Gifts Received: $141,500 (fiscal 2002). Note: In fiscal 2002, contributions were received from Irene and Carroll Rheinstrom Trust.

Typical Recipients

Arts & Humanities: Historic Preservation, Libraries, Music
Civic & Public Affairs: Clubs, Civic & Public Affairs-General, Housing, Safety
Education: Community & Junior Colleges, Elementary Education (Private), Literacy, Private Education (Precollege), Student Aid
Health: Emergency/Ambulance Services, Hospitals
Religion: Churches
Social Services: People with Disabilities, United Funds/United Ways

Application Procedures

Initial Contact: The foundation reports no specific application guidelines. Send a brief letter of inquiry, including statement of purpose, amount requested, and proof of tax-exempt status.
Deadlines: None.

Restrictions

Grants are generally limited to applicants in Columbia County, NY.

Foundation Officials

Ed Herrington: vice president
Jean Howe Lossi: secretary
Richard P. Koskey: secretary
Carmi Rapport: vice president
Carrol Rheinstrom: president
Majorie Rheinstrom: vice president

Grants Analysis

Total Grants: $276,010*
Number of Grants: 28
Average Grant: $4,847*
Highest Grant: $100,000
Lowest Grant: $250
Typical Range: $2,000 to $25,000
*Note: Giving excludes United Way. Average grant figure excludes two highest grants ($150,000).

Recent Grants

Note: Grants derived from fiscal 2002 Form 990.

Library-Related

2,500	Hillsdale Public Library, Hillsdale, NY

General

100,000	Taconic Hills Central Schools, Taconic, NY -- aquatic center funding
50,000	Hawthorne Valley School, Ghent, NY -- campus construction
25,000	Town of Ancram, Ancram, NY
23,000	Community Rescue Squad, Hudson, NY -- squad upgrades
10,000	Columbia Green Community College, Columbia Green, NY
10,000	Hudson Boys and Girls Club, Hudson, NY
10,000	Town of Copake, Copake, NY
6,000	Northeast Millerton Library, Millerton, NY
5,000	Camphill Village USA, Copake, NY
5,000	Irondale Cemetery Association, Irondale, NY -- operational repairs and losses

ALBERT W. RICE CHARITABLE FOUNDATION

Giving Contact

Stephen Fritch
Albert W. Rice Charitable Foundation
c/o Fleet Asset Management Grantmaking
PO Box 6767
Providence, RI 02940
Phone: (401)276-7248
Web: http://www.fleet.com

Description

Founded: 1959
EIN: 046028085
Organization Type: Private Foundation
Giving Locations: MA: Worcester
Grant Types: Capital, General Support, Project.

Donor Information

Founder: the late Albert W. Rice

Financial Summary

Total Giving: $100,500 (2000); $174,001 (1999); $213,000 (1998)
Giving Analysis: Giving for 1999 includes: foundation grants to United Way ($5,000); foundation grants to United Way ($10,000); 1998: foundation grants to United Way ($15,000) foundation ($198,000)
Assets: $6,467,416 (2000); $5,855,406 (1999); $5,977,108 (1998)

Typical Recipients

Arts & Humanities: Arts Associations & Councils, Arts Centers, Arts Festivals, Arts Funds, Community Arts, Ethnic & Folk Arts, Historic Preservation, History & Archaeology, Libraries, Museums/Galleries, Music, Performing Arts, Public Broadcasting, Theater
Civic & Public Affairs: Clubs, Community Foundations, Economic Development, Civic & Public Affairs-General, Hispanic Affairs, Municipalities/Towns, Rural Affairs, Urban & Community Affairs
Education: Arts/Humanities Education, Business Education, Colleges & Universities, Community & Junior Colleges, Education Associations, Education Reform, Engineering/Technological Education, Faculty Development, Preschool Education, Private Education (Precollege), Secondary Education (Private)
Environment: Environment-General, Resource Conservation, Wildlife Protection
Health: Cancer, Clinics/Medical Centers, Emergency/Ambulance Services, Health Funds, Health Organizations, Home-Care Services, Hospices, Medical Research, Public Health
International: Foreign Arts Organizations
Religion: Churches
Science: Scientific Centers & Institutes, Scientific Labs, Scientific Research
Social Services: Child Welfare, Community Service Organizations, Family Services, Food/Clothing Distribution, Substance Abuse, United Funds/United Ways, YMCA/YWCA/YMHA/YWHA, Youth Organizations

Application Procedures

Initial Contact: Send a brief letter of inquiry, or call to request guidelines.
Application Requirements: Include a description of program or project.
Deadlines: April and October of each year.

Restrictions

Does not support individuals, religious organizations for sectarian purposes, political or lobbying groups, or organizations outside operating areas.

Additional Information

Supports local education, family service, and preventive health care.
Trust(s): Fleet Natl Bank MA

Foundation Officials

Christine Feeney: grantmaking associate
Kerry H. Sullivan: director grant making PRIM CORP EMPL vice president: Fleet Investment Services.

Grants Analysis

Disclosure Period: calendar year ending 2000
Total Grants: $95,500*
Number of Grants: 12
Average Grant: $6,409*
Highest Grant: $25,000
Typical Range: $5,000 to $10,000
*Note: Giving excludes United Way. Average grant figure excludes highest grant.

Recent Grants

Note: Grants derived from 2000 Form 990.

General

25,000	EcoTarium, Worcester, MA
15,000	Children's Friend Society, Worcester, MA
7,500	American Cancer Society, Worcester, MA
7,500	Great Brook Valley Health Center, Worcester, MA
7,500	Worcester Dynamy, Worcester, MA
5,000	Family Services of Central Massachusetts, Worcester, MA
5,000	Junior Achievement of Central Massachusetts, Worcester, MA
5,000	United Way of Central Massachusetts, Worcester, MA
5,000	VNA of Worcester Home Health Systems, Inc., Worcester, MA
5,000	Worcester Academy, Worcester, MA

RICE FOUNDATION

Giving Contact

Peter Nolan, President
8600 Gross Point Road
Skokie, IL 60077-2151
Phone: (847)581-9999

Description

Founded: 1947
EIN: 366043160
Organization Type: General Purpose Foundation
Giving Locations: IL: Chicago
Grant Types: General Support.

Donor Information

Founder: The Rice Foundation was established in 1947 by the late Daniel F. Rice .

Financial Summary

Total Giving: $3,885,342 (2000); $4,403,600 (1998); $1,992,469 (1997)
Giving Analysis: Giving for 1998 includes: foundation grants to United Way ($500)
Assets: $85,715,183 (2000); $88,443,154 (1998); $89,475,863 (1997)
Gifts Received: $4,800 (1993); $300 (1992)

Typical Recipients

Arts & Humanities: Arts Associations & Councils, Arts Festivals, Arts Funds, Arts Institutes, Ballet, Historic Preservation, History & Archaeology, Libraries, Literary Arts, Museums/Galleries, Music, Opera, Performing Arts, Public Broadcasting, Theater
Civic & Public Affairs: Botanical Gardens/Parks, Community Foundations, Economic Development, Employment/Job Training, Ethnic Organizations, Civic & Public Affairs-General, Law & Justice, Legal Aid, Philanthropic Organizations, Public Policy, Safety, Urban & Community Affairs, Women's Affairs, Zoos/Aquariums
Education: Arts/Humanities Education, Colleges & Universities, Community & Junior Colleges, Education Associations, Education Funds, Elementary Education (Public), Environmental Education, Education-General, International Studies, Medical Education, Private Education (Precollege), Public Education (Precollege), School Volunteerism, Science/Mathematics Education, Secondary Education (Private), Special Education
Environment: Environment-General, Resource Conservation, Wildlife Protection
Health: Arthritis, Cancer, Children's Health/Hospitals, Clinics/Medical Centers, Health-General, Geriatric Health, Health Organizations, Home-Care Services, Hospitals, Hospitals (University Affiliated), Long-Term Care, Medical Rehabilitation, Mental Health, Prenatal Health Issues, Single-Disease Health Associations
International: Foreign Educational Institutions
Religion: Religion-General, Religious Organizations, Religious Welfare
Science: Observatories & Planetariums, Science Museums
Social Services: Big Brother/Big Sister, Child Welfare, Community Centers, Community Service Organizations, Crime Prevention, Family Services, Homes, People with Disabilities, Recreation & Athletics, Senior Services, Shelters/Homelessness, Social Services-General, United Funds/United Ways, Volunteer Services, Youth Organizations

Application Procedures

Initial Contact: Applications should be submitted in writing.
Application Requirements: Applications should include a statement describing the applicant organization and its activities, the amount and purpose of the grant requested, and proof of IRS tax-exempt status.
Deadlines: None.

Restrictions

Grants are not made to individuals.

Foundation Officials

Marilynn Bruder Alsdorf: director ED Northwestern University (1946).
John Grey: director
Arthur A. Nolan, Jr.: chairman, director
Patricia Nolan: vice president, treasurer, director
Peter G. Nolan: president, director, secretary
David P. Winchester: director
Barbara M. J. Wood: director

Grants Analysis

Disclosure Period: calendar year ending 2000
Total Grants: $3,885,342
Number of Grants: 91
Average Grant: $36,504*
Highest Grant: $1,500,000
Typical Range: $100 to $20,000 and $50,000 to $500,000
*Note: Average grant figure excludes highest grant.

Recent Grants

Note: Grants derived from 2000 Form 990.

General

1,500,000	Rush Presbyterian St. Luke's Medical Center, Chicago, IL
973,000	Mercy Home for Boys and Girls, Chicago, IL
500,000	Maryville Academy, Des Plaines, IL
150,000	Saint Mary of the Angels, Chicago, IL
50,000	Art Institute of Chicago, Chicago, IL
50,000	Mobile C.A.R.E. Foundation, Evanston, IL
50,000	Ravenswood Hospital Medical Center, Chicago, IL
40,000	Chicago Botanical Garden, Chicago, IL
36,100	Brookfield Zoo, Brookfield, IL
30,000	Lutheran General Children's Hospital, Chicago, IL

RICH FOUNDATION

Giving Contact

Anne Berg, Grant Consultant
11 Piedmont Center, Suite 204
Atlanta, GA 30305
Phone: (404)262-2266
Fax: (404)266-2123

Description

Founded: 1942
EIN: 586038037
Organization Type: General Purpose Foundation

Giving Locations: GA: Atlanta metropolitan area
Grant Types: Capital, Endowment, General Support.

Donor Information

Founder: The foundation was established in 1942 in Georgia by the officers of Rich's, Inc., a chain of department stores based in Atlanta, and was funded by profits of Rich's, Inc. until 1976.

Financial Summary

Total Giving: $2,103,000 (fiscal year ending January 31, 1999); $1,697,000 (fiscal 1997); $1,600,000 (fiscal 1996 approx)
Assets: $55,423,123 (fiscal 1999); $40,592,834 (fiscal 1997); $35,000,000 (fiscal 1996 approx)

Typical Recipients

Arts & Humanities: Arts Centers, Arts Outreach, Ballet, Dance, History & Archaeology, Libraries, Museums/Galleries, Music, Opera, Performing Arts, Public Broadcasting, Theater
Civic & Public Affairs: Botanical Gardens/Parks, Clubs, Community Foundations, Employment/Job Training, Civic & Public Affairs-General, Housing, Law & Justice, Legal Aid, Philanthropic Organizations, Women's Affairs, Zoos/Aquariums
Education: Colleges & Universities, Economic Education, Education Associations, Education Funds, Education-General, International Studies, Literacy, Medical Education, Minority Education, Preschool Education, Private Education (Precollege), Private Education (Precollege), Science/Mathematics Education, Special Education
Environment: Environment-General, Resource Conservation
Health: Cancer, Children's Health/Hospitals, Emergency/Ambulance Services, Eyes/Blindness, Health Organizations, Heart, Hospitals, Medical Research, Mental Health, Nursing Services, Prenatal Health Issues, Single-Disease Health Associations
International: Health Care/Hospitals
Religion: Jewish Causes, Ministries, Religious Organizations, Religious Welfare
Social Services: Animal Protection, Big Brother/Big Sister, Camps, Child Abuse, Child Welfare, Community Centers, Community Service Organizations, Counseling, Family Services, Food/Clothing Distribution, Homes, People with Disabilities, Scouts, Senior Services, Shelters/Homelessness, Social Services-General, United Funds/United Ways, Volunteer Services, YMCA/YWCA/YMHA/YWHA, Youth Organizations

Application Procedures

Initial Contact: Applicants should submit a preliminary letter to the foundation requesting an official grant application.
Application Requirements: The letter should include an autobiographical sketch of the organization, estimate of project expenses, and lists of other sources of funding.
Deadlines: The quarterly deadlines for submitting proposals are December 15, March 15, June 15, and September 15.
Review Process: Trustees meet quarterly to review grant proposals.
Notes: Application must include a completed official application form for proposal to be considered.

Restrictions

The foundation does not support individuals, conferences and seminars, accumulated debt or loans, religious purposes, special events such as fundraising dinners and sporting events, legislative or lobbying efforts, political or fraternal organizations. Organizations must be non-sectarian in services to be eligible.

Additional Information

Publications: Application Form; Application Guidelines

Foundation Officials

Thomas J. Asher: vice president, secretary
David S. Baker: trustee B Jacksonville, FL 1937. ED University of Pennsylvania BS (1958); Harvard University LLB (1961). NONPR AFFIL member: Georgia Bar Association; trustee, chairman: Howard School; fellow: American Bar Foundation; member: American Law Institute; member: American Bar Association. CLUB AFFIL Standard Club; Ashford Club.
Anne P. Berg: grant consultant
Joel Goldberg: president
Margaret S. Weiller: treasurer, trustee

Grants Analysis

Disclosure Period: fiscal year ending January 31, 1999
Total Grants: $2,103,000
Number of Grants: 76
Average Grant: $27,671
Highest Grant: $250,000
Typical Range: $5,500 to $30,000

Recent Grants

Note: Grants derived from 2000 Form 990.

Library-Related
5,000   Project Read, San Francisco, CA

General
200,000   United Way of Atlanta, Atlanta, GA
100,000   Oglethorpe University, Atlanta, GA
100,000   Trust for Public Land
100,000   Woodruff Arts Center, Atlanta, GA
100,000   Zoo Atlanta, Atlanta, GA
50,000   Piedmont Park Conservancy, Atlanta, GA
50,000   Senior Connections, Decatur, GA
50,000   William Bremen Jewish Heritage Museum
30,000   Women's Resource Center
25,000   Morehouse College, Atlanta, GA

RICH FOUNDATION INC.

Giving Contact

Robert N. Rich, President
1 Landmark Sq.
Stamford, CT 06901
Phone: (203)359-2900

Description

Founded: 1984
EIN: 222544173
Organization Type: Private Foundation
Giving Locations: CT: Stamford primarily in lower Stamford
Grant Types: General Support.

Donor Information

Founder: F.D. Rich Co., Inc., members of the Rich family

Financial Summary

Total Giving: $52,600 (fiscal year ending June 30, 2001); $78,600 (fiscal 1999); $57,200 (fiscal 1998)
Giving Analysis: Giving for fiscal 2001 includes: foundation grants to United Way ($10,000); fiscal 1999: foundation grants to United Way ($10,000) fiscal 1998: foundation grants to United Way ($5,000)
Assets: $844,876 (fiscal 2001); $591,130 (fiscal 1998); $575,766 (fiscal 1997)
Gifts Received: $39,000 (fiscal 2001); $30,000 (fiscal 1998); $15,000 (fiscal 1996). Note: In fiscal 19986, contributions were received from F. D. Rich Company.

Typical Recipients

Arts & Humanities: Arts Centers, Arts Festivals, Libraries, Museums/Galleries, Music, Opera, Public Broadcasting
Civic & Public Affairs: Economic Development, Civic & Public Affairs-General, Housing, Urban & Community Affairs
Education: Colleges & Universities, Education-General
Environment: Environment-General
Health: Hospitals, Medical Research
Religion: Religion-General, Jewish Causes, Religious Welfare
Social Services: Child Welfare, Community Service Organizations, People with Disabilities, United Funds/United Ways, YMCA/YWCA/YMHA/YWHA, Youth Organizations

Application Procedures

Initial Contact: Contact the foundation by phone to request an application form. Applicants are urged to consult with the foundation staff in the development of their proposals.
Decision Notification: Board meets in September for budgets commencing October 1 and ending September 30 of the following calendar year and in March for supplementary budget requests.

Restrictions

Grants are made only to selected, qualified non-profit organizations. Foundation does not make contributions to organizations whose purpose involves the solicitation of propaganda or to organizations that attempt to influence legislation, the outcome of public elections, or voter registration drives.

Foundation Officials

Colleen Graham: secretary
Frank D. Rich, Jr.: president PRIM CORP EMPL chairman, director: F.D. Rich Co.
Robert N. Rich: vice president PRIM CORP EMPL president, director: F.D. Rich Co.
Thomas L. Rich: vice president

Grants Analysis

Disclosure Period: fiscal year ending June 30, 2001
Total Grants: $42,600*
Number of Grants: 26
Average Grant: $1,638
Highest Grant: $5,000
Lowest Grant: $200
Typical Range: $1,000 to $5,000
*Note: Giving excludes United Way.

Recent Grants

Note: Grants derived from fiscal 2001 Form 990.

Library-Related
1,000   Ferguson Library Foundation, Stamford, CT

General
10,000   United Way, Stamford, CT
5,500   Stamford Symphony, Stamford, CT
5,000   St. Luke's Life Works, Stamford, CT
5,000   Stamford Center for Arts, Stamford, CT
5,000   Stamford Center for Arts, Stamford, CT
3,250   Stamford Downtown Special Services, Stamford, CT
3,000   Kids in Crisis, Cos Cob, CT
1,800   Boys and Girls Club of Stamford, Stamford, CT
1,400   Stamford Education, Stamford, CT
1,000   Castle Cares Inc., Stamford, CT

RICH PRODUCTS CORP.

Company Headquarters

1150 Niagara St.
Buffalo, NY 14213
Web: http://www.richs.com

Company Description

Revenue: US$1.58 billion (2002)
Employees: 6500 (2002)
SIC(s): 2037 Frozen Fruits & Vegetables, 2038 Frozen Specialties Nec, 2053 Frozen Bakery Products Except Bread.

Operating Locations

Rich Products Corp. (CA--Escalon; GA--St. Simons Island; NJ--Vineland; OH--Dayton, Hilliard; TN--Gallatin)

Rich Family Foundation

Giving Contact

David A. Rich, Executive Director
Rich Family Foundation
PO Box 245
Buffalo, NY 14240-0245
Phone: (716)878-8363
Fax: (716)878-8775

Description

Founded: 1961
EIN: 166026199
Organization Type: Corporate Foundation
Giving Locations: NY: Buffalo
Grant Types: General Support.

Donor Information

Founder: Rich Products Corporation

Financial Summary

Total Giving: $737,478 (2000); $499,610 (1997); $582,524 (1996). Note: Contributes through foundation only.
Giving Analysis: Giving for 2000 includes: foundation scholarships ($5,000); foundation grants to United Way ($44,302); foundation ($688,176); 1997: foundation grants to United Way ($46,715); foundation ($452,895); 1996: foundation grants to United Way ($28,950); foundation ($553,574);
Assets: $3,604,975 (2000); $2,695,630 (1997); $1,791,557 (1996)
Gifts Received: $660,000 (2000); $970,000 (1997); $420,000 (1996). Note: In 2000, contributions were received from Rich Products Corporation. In 1997, contributions were received from Rich Products Corporation and Robert E. Rich.

Typical Recipients

Arts & Humanities: Arts Associations & Councils, Arts Centers, Arts Institutes, Historic Preservation, History & Archaeology, Libraries, Museums/Galleries, Music, Performing Arts, Public Broadcasting, Theater
Civic & Public Affairs: Botanical Gardens/Parks, Business/Free Enterprise, Clubs, Community Foundations, Economic Development, Civic & Public Affairs-General, Professional & Trade Associations, Safety, Urban & Community Affairs, Zoos/Aquariums
Education: Arts/Humanities Education, Business Education, Colleges & Universities, Continuing Education, Education-General, Leadership Training, Legal Education, Literacy, Private Education (Precollege), Religious Education, Special Education, Student Aid
Environment: Wildlife Protection
Health: Alzheimers Disease, Cancer, Children's Health/Hospitals, Clinics/Medical Centers, Diabetes, Emergency/Ambulance Services, Health-General, Health Organizations, Heart, Hospitals, Medical Rehabilitation, Medical Research, Multiple Sclerosis, Prenatal Health Issues, Public Health, Single-Disease Health Associations
International: Missionary/Religious Activities
Religion: Churches, Dioceses, Religion-General, Jewish Causes, Ministries, Religious Organizations, Religious Welfare, Social/Policy Issues
Science: Science Museums

Social Services: Animal Protection, Child Welfare, Community Centers, Community Service Organizations, Family Services, Food/Clothing Distribution, Recreation & Athletics, Substance Abuse, Substance Abuse, United Funds/United Ways, Youth Organizations

Application Procedures

Initial Contact: Send formal letter of request.
Deadlines: None.

Corporate Officials

Robert E. Rich, Jr.: president, director B Buffalo, NY 1941. ED University of Rochester MBA; Williams College (1963). PRIM CORP EMPL president, director: Rich Products Corp. ADD CORP EMPL president: BR Guest Ltd.; president: Bison Baseball Inc.; president: Palm Beach National Golf Country Club; president: Wichita Baseball Inc. CORP AFFIL vice chairman: Casa Di Bertacchi Corp. NONPR AFFIL vice chairman, director: Buffalo Sabres Hockey Club.

Foundation Officials

Robert E. Rich, Jr.: secretary (see above)

Grants Analysis

Disclosure Period: calendar year ending 2000
Total Grants: $688,176*
Number of Grants: 145
Average Grant: $3,390*
Highest Grant: $200,000
Typical Range: $100 to $5,000
*Note: Giving excludes United Way and scholarships. Average grant figure excludes highest grant.

Recent Grants

Note: Grants derived from 2000 Form 990.

General

200,000	University of Buffalo Foundation, Buffalo, NY
50,000	School Food Service Foundation, Alexandria, VA
50,000	University at Buffalo Foundation, Buffalo, NY
25,000	Buffalo Fine Arts Academy, Buffalo, NY
25,000	Hospitality Industry Alliance, Chicago, IL
25,000	Johnson and Wales University, Providence, RI
25,000	Shea's Performing Arts Center, Buffalo, NY
25,000	Students in Free Enterprise, Springfield, MO
20,000	Buffalo Philharmonic Orchestra Society, Buffalo, NY
10,000	Children's Hospital of Buffalo Foundation, Buffalo, NY

C. E. RICHARDSON BENEVOLENT FOUNDATION

Giving Contact

Betty S. King, Secretary
PO Box 1120
Pulaski, VA 24301
Phone: (540)980-6628

Description

Founded: 1979
EIN: 510227549
Organization Type: Private Foundation
Giving Locations: VA: limited to 30 miles north and south of Interstate 81 from Lexington to Abingdon, VA
Grant Types: General Support.

Financial Summary

Total Giving: $200,000 (fiscal year ending May 31, 2001); $252,428 (fiscal 2000); $209,250 (fiscal 1999)
Assets: $4,634,867 (fiscal 2001); $4,511,144 (fiscal 2000); $4,808,801 (fiscal 1999)

Typical Recipients

Arts & Humanities: Arts Centers, History & Archaeology, Libraries, Museums/Galleries, Theater
Civic & Public Affairs: Civic & Public Affairs-General, Municipalities/Towns, Safety, Women's Affairs
Education: Agricultural Education, Arts/Humanities Education, Colleges & Universities, Community & Junior Colleges, Education Funds, Education-General, Medical Education, Private Education (Precollege), Religious Education, Science/Mathematics Education, Secondary Education (Public), Student Aid
Health: Cancer, Children's Health/Hospitals, Clinics/Medical Centers, Emergency/Ambulance Services, Health Funds, Hospices, Preventive Medicine/Wellness Organizations
Religion: Churches, Religious Welfare
Social Services: Animal Protection, Big Brother/Big Sister, Community Service Organizations, Emergency Relief, Emergency Relief, Family Services, Food/Clothing Distribution, People with Disabilities, Recreation & Athletics, Scouts, Senior Services, Special Olympics, United Funds/United Ways, YMCA/YWCA/YMHA/YWHA, Youth Organizations

Application Procedures

Initial Contact: Application form required.
Deadlines: September 15.

Restrictions

Does not support individuals.

Additional Information

Publications: Application Guidelines

Foundation Officials

Betty S. King: secretary
James D. Miller: trustee
Annie S. Muire: trustee
James C. Turk: trustee B Roanoke, VA 1923. ED Roanoke College AB (1949); Washington & Lee University LLB (1952). PRIM CORP EMPL chief judge: U.S. District Court. CORP AFFIL director: 1st & Merchants National Bank Rafford. NONPR AFFIL trustee: Rafford Community Hospital; member: Virginia Senate; member: Phi Beta Kappa; member: Omnicron Delta Kappa; member: Order Coif.

Grants Analysis

Disclosure Period: fiscal year ending May 31, 2001
Total Grants: $179,650*
Number of Grants: 43
Average Grant: $4,178
Highest Grant: $30,000
Typical Range: $1,000 to $10,000
*Note: Giving excludes scholarships.

Recent Grants

Note: Grants derived from 2000 Form 990.

General

30,000	Roanoke College, Roanoke, VA -- for partial financing of renovation and enhancement of the Donald M. Sutton Campus Center
25,000	Radford University Foundation, Radford, VA -- in support of Living History Farm Museum
15,000	Friends of the Pulaski Theatre, Pulaski, VA -- toward restoration of the theatre
10,000	Town of Pulaski, Pulaski, VA -- for the purchase of a new passenger bus/van
10,000	Warm Hearth Foundation, Blacksburg, VA -- toward the cost of furnishing and decorating 18 standard semi-private rooms
9,100	New River Community College Educational Foundation, Dublin, VA -- to establish a reference library at the Christiansburg Site
8,664	Radford University Foundation, Radford, VA -- for student scholarship assistance
7,500	Fine Arts Center for the New River Valley, Inc., Pulaski, VA -- for partial financing of right-of-way signage on interstate 81 to fine arts center
7,500	Hensel Eckman YMCA, Pulaski, VA -- to support the subsidized programs and for a computer lab for all ages
7,500	Virginia Foundation of Independent Colleges, Richmond, VA -- to strengthening library services

SID W. RICHARDSON FOUNDATION

Giving Contact

Valleau Wilkie, Jr., Executive Vice President & Executive Director
309 Main Street
Ft. Worth, TX 76102
Phone: (817)336-0494
Fax: (817)332-2176
E-mail: cjohns@sidrichardson.org
Web: http://www.sidrichardson.org

Description

Founded: 1947
EIN: 756015828
Organization Type: General Purpose Foundation
Giving Locations: TX: Ft. Worth some giving in other areas of Texas
Grant Types: Capital, Challenge, General Support, Operating Expenses, Project, Research.

Donor Information

Founder: The foundation was established in 1947 by the late Sid W. Richardson (d. 1959) to support organizations and programs serving the people of Texas. The purpose of the foundation, as stated in the charter, is "to support any benevolent, charitable, educational, or missionary undertaking."
In 1962, the foundation acquired substantial assets from the late Mr. Richardson's estate. In 1965, income from the assets became available, and the foundation began its major grant-making program. Sid Richardson was a life-long resident of Texas, with interests in oil, cattle, and land. He also collected western art, which is on permanent exhibit in the foundation-supported Sid Richardson Collection of Western Art. "Although his interests reached beyond Texas and his personal contacts were world-wide, he retained his immediate concern for the people of his home state. For this reason, he provided in the Foundation's charter that all grants be awarded to recipients within the state of Texas."

Financial Summary

Total Giving: $11,000,000 (2003 approx); $11,000,000 (2002 approx); $34,798,143 (2001)
Giving Analysis: Giving for 2000 includes: foundation grants to United Way ($75,000).
Assets: $230,000,000 (2002 approx); $257,816,716 (2001); $295,296,884 (2000)

Typical Recipients

Arts & Humanities: Arts Associations & Councils, Arts Centers, Ballet, Ethnic & Folk Arts, Libraries, Literary Arts, Museums/Galleries, Music, Opera, Performing Arts, Public Broadcasting, Theater
Civic & Public Affairs: Botanical Gardens/Parks, Chambers of Commerce, Community Foundations, Economic Development, Employment/Job Training,

Civic & Public Affairs-General, Housing, Law & Justice, Public Policy, Rural Affairs, Urban & Community Affairs, Women's Affairs

Education: Afterschool/Enrichment Programs, Arts/Humanities Education, Business Education, Colleges & Universities, Education Associations, Education Funds, Elementary Education (Private), Engineering/Technological Education, Environmental Education, Faculty Development, Education-General, Health & Physical Education, Leadership Training, Literacy, Medical Education, Preschool Education, Private Education (Precollege), Public Education (Precollege), School Volunteerism, Science/Mathematics Education, Secondary Education (Public), Social Sciences Education, Student Aid

Environment: Environment-General, Research, Wildlife Protection

Health: Cancer, Children's Health/Hospitals, Clinics/Medical Centers, Diabetes, Emergency/Ambulance Services, Eyes/Blindness, Health-General, Health Policy/Cost Containment, Health Organizations, Heart, Hospitals, Hospitals (University Affiliated), Medical Research, Nursing Services, Outpatient Health Care, Prenatal Health Issues, Public Health, Research/Studies Institutes, Research/Studies Institutes

Religion: Churches, Ministries, Religious Organizations, Religious Welfare

Science: Science Museums, Scientific Centers & Institutes, Scientific Research

Social Services: At-Risk Youth, Child Welfare, Community Centers, Community Service Organizations, Crime Prevention, Day Care, Family Planning, Family Services, Food/Clothing Distribution, Homes, People with Disabilities, Recreation & Athletics, Scouts, Senior Services, Social Services-General, Substance Abuse, United Funds/United Ways, Volunteer Services, YMCA/YWCA/YMHA/YWHA, Youth Organizations

Application Procedures

Initial Contact: Applicants should send a preliminary letter briefly describing the project or program prior to filing a formal application. If the project falls within foundation guidelines, a formal proposal will be accepted.

Application Requirements: The foundation will supply a grant application form requesting information regarding the nature of the organization, objectives, activities, personnel, need to be met, and the project that meets this need. Applicants may submit any additional information and a supplementary proposal in narrative form, to clarify and explain the application. A copy of the organization's 501(c)(3) letter should also be included, where applicable.

Deadlines: Applications must be received by March 1 or September 1 for consideration at directors meetings in the spring or fall, respectively.

Review Process: Foundation staff may conduct a site visit after a formal application has been accepted. Board decisions on all requests are reported by mail.

Restrictions

Grants are not made to individuals. Grants are limited to programs and projects in Texas. Organizations must be classified as tax-exempt under Section 501(c)(3) of the Internal Revenue Code, and as other than a private foundation, Section 509(a). Alternatively, an organization may qualify if it is classified under Section 170(c)(1) and the contribution is to be used exclusively for public purposes.

Additional Information

Grantees receive a letter of agreement outlining the terms and conditions of the grant. The Sid Richardson Foundation is related to the Bass Foundation (Ft. Worth).

Publications: Annual Report (including Guidelines)

Foundation Officials

Edward Perry Bass: vice president, director B Fort Worth, TX 1945. ED Yale University (1968). PRIM CORP EMPL owner: Fine Line Inc.

Lee M. Bass: vice president, director

Nancy Lee Bass: vice president, director

Perry Richardson Bass: president, director B Wichita Falls, TX November 11, 1914. ED Yale University BS (1937). PRIM CORP EMPL president, director: Perry R. Bass Inc. CORP AFFIL chairman, chief executive officer, director: Sid Richardson Carbon & Gas Co.; chairman: Bass Enterprises Production Co. NONPR AFFIL member ad hoc committee: Texas Energy Natural Resources Advisory Committee; member executive committee: Texas Mid-Continent Oil & Gas Association; member advisory committee board visitors: Maryland Anderson Hospital & Tumor Institute; member: Independent Petroleum Association America; member: American Association Petroleum Geologists; member executive committee: American Petroleum Institute; member: All-American Wildcatters. CLUB AFFIL Royal Ocean Racing Club; Petroleum Club; River Crest Country Club; Fort Worth Club; New York Yacht Club; president: City Club Fort Worth Inc.; Fort Worth Boat Club.

Sid Richardson Bass: vice president, director B Fort Worth, TX 1943. ED Yale University (1965); Stanford University MBA (1968). PRIM CORP EMPL Sid R. Bass Inc. CORP AFFIL president: Bass Enterprises Production Co.; vice president: Sid Richardson Carbon & Gas Co.

M. E. Chappell: treasurer, director B 1916. PRIM CORP EMPL vice president, director: Mel Wheeler Inc.

Jo Helen Rosacker: secretary, associate director

Grants Analysis

Disclosure Period: calendar year ending 2001
Total Grants: $34,723,143*
Number of Grants: 133
Average Grant: $81,236*
Highest Grant: $24,000,000
Lowest Grant: $3,000
Typical Range: $25,000 to $150,000
*Note: Giving excludes United Way. Average grant figure excludes highest grant.

Recent Grants

Note: Grants derived from 2001 Form 990.

Library-Related

175,000   Fort Worth Public Library Foundation, Ft. Worth, TX -- Provide office space for Library Foundation in new facility

General

24,000,000 MPA Foundation, Ft. Worth, TX -- Support construction of the new Modern Art Museum

500,000   Amon Carter Museum of Western Art, Ft Worth, TX -- Support Amon Carter Museum in the expansion of the facility

500,000   Fort Worth Symphony Orchestra Association, Ft. Worth, TX -- Support for the last half of the 00-01 season and the first half of the 01-02 season

400,000   Harris Hospital - Methodist, Ft Worth, TX -- Assist in the construction of the Neurointernventional Radiology Suite

360,000   Performing Arts Fort Worth, Inc., Ft. Worth, TX -- Support completion of the rehearsal facilities

300,000   Fort Worth Country Day School Faculty Bonus Trust, Ft. Worth, TX -- General support for 5/01 through 4/02

259,200   Fort Worth Education and Research Foundation for Pain Management, Ft. Worth, TX -- Assist in expenses relating to the closing of the institute

250,000   Boys and Girls Club of Greater Ft

Worth, Ft Worth, TX -- Support establishment of the new Polytechnic Heights Club

250,000   Van Cliburn Foundation, Ft. Worth, TX -- Support the Eleventh Piano Competition

210,000   University of Texas at Austin Marine Science Institute, Austin, TX -- Support Marine Fisheries Research project

ANN S. RICHARDSON FUND

Giving Contact

Stephen Bois, Trust Officer
c/o Chase Manhattan Bank
1211 Avenue of the Americas, 34th Fl.
New York, NY 10036
Phone: (212)789-4073

Description

Founded: 1965
EIN: 136192516
Organization Type: Private Foundation
Giving Locations: CT; NY
Grant Types: General Support.

Donor Information

Founder: the late Anne S. Richardson

Financial Summary

Total Giving: $1,086,498 (fiscal year ending July 31, 2001); $290,500 (fiscal 2000); $290,500 (fiscal 1999)
Assets: $13,734,294 (fiscal 2001); $15,608,200 (fiscal 2000); $14,008,627 (fiscal 1998)
Gifts Received: $20,000 (fiscal 1998)

Typical Recipients

Arts & Humanities: Arts Associations & Councils, Historic Preservation, History & Archaeology, Libraries, Museums/Galleries, Music, Opera, Performing Arts, Public Broadcasting

Civic & Public Affairs: Botanical Gardens/Parks, Clubs, Economic Development, Housing, Public Policy, Women's Affairs

Education: Arts/Humanities Education, Colleges & Universities, Education-General, Literacy, Minority Education, Private Education (Precollege), Student Aid

Environment: Environment-General, Resource Conservation

Health: Cancer, Children's Health/Hospitals, Clinics/Medical Centers, Health Organizations, Heart, Hospices, Hospitals, Long-Term Care, Medical Research, Single-Disease Health Associations

International: International Affairs, International Organizations

Religion: Churches, Religious Organizations, Religious Welfare

Science: Science Museums, Scientific Centers & Institutes

Social Services: Child Welfare, Community Centers, Community Service Organizations, Counseling, Domestic Violence, Family Planning, Family Services, Food/Clothing Distribution, Scouts, Senior Services, Substance Abuse, United Funds/United Ways, Volunteer Services, Youth Organizations

Application Procedures

Initial Contact: Send a brief letter of inquiry.
Deadlines: None.

Restrictions

Does not support individuals or provide endowment funds, scholarships, or loans.

Additional Information

Trust(s): Chase Manhattan Bank

Grants Analysis

Disclosure Period: fiscal year ending July 31, 2001
Total Grants: $1,086,498
Number of Grants: 130
Average Grant: $8,358
Highest Grant: $25,000
Typical Range: $3,500 to $15,000

Recent Grants

Note: Grants derived from 2000 Form 990.

General

10,000	American Heart Association
10,000	Boys Club of New York, New York, NY
10,000	Boys Scouts, Westchester, NY
10,000	Garden and Conservation Trust, New York, NY
10,000	Memorial Sloan-Kettering, New York, NY
10,000	Morningside House Nursing, Bronx, NY
10,000	New York Hospital, New York, NY
10,000	New York Landmarks Conservancy, New York, NY
10,000	Norwalk Hospital Development Fund, Norwalk, CT
10,000	Prep for Prep, New York, NY

RIDER-POOL FOUNDATION

Giving Contact

c/o PNC Bank NA
1600 Market Street, 4th Floor
Philadelphia, PA 19103
Phone: (215)585-3997

Description

Founded: 1957
EIN: 236207356
Organization Type: Private Foundation
Giving Locations: PA: Allentown
Grant Types: Capital, Emergency, Endowment, Fellowship, General Support, Project, Research.

Donor Information

Founder: Dorothy Rider-Pool

Financial Summary

Total Giving: $503,400 (2000); $503,497 (1999); $535,208 (1998)
Giving Analysis: Giving for 1998 includes: foundation grants to United Way ($15,000)
Assets: $11,496,418 (2000); $12,175,853 (1999); $10,864,648 (1998)
Gifts Received: $20,000 (2000)

Typical Recipients

Arts & Humanities: Arts Centers, Ballet, History & Archaeology, Libraries, Museums/Galleries, Music, Performing Arts, Theater
Civic & Public Affairs: Community Foundations, Economic Development, Civic & Public Affairs-General, Hispanic Affairs, Municipalities/Towns, Professional & Trade Associations, Urban & Community Affairs
Education: Arts/Humanities Education, Business Education, Business-School Partnerships, Colleges & Universities, Community & Junior Colleges, Education Funds, Faculty Development, Education-General, Private Education (Precollege), Public Education (Precollege), Secondary Education (Private), Special Education, Student Aid
Environment: Environment-General, Resource Conservation, Wildlife Protection
Health: Health Organizations, Public Health
Religion: Churches, Religious Welfare
Science: Scientific Centers & Institutes
Social Services: Animal Protection, Child Welfare, Community Service Organizations, Crime Prevention, Food/Clothing Distribution, People with Disabilities, Recreation & Athletics, Scouts, Senior Services, United Funds/United Ways, YMCA/YWCA/YMHA/YWHA, Youth Organizations

Application Procedures

Initial Contact: The foundation requests applications be made in writing.
Deadlines: None.

Additional Information

Trust(s): PNC Bank NA

Foundation Officials

Edward J. Donley: trustee
Leon Conrad Holt, Jr.: treasurer B Reading, PA 1925. ED Lehigh University BS (1948); University of Pennsylvania JD (1951). CORP AFFIL director: VF Corp.; director: Air Products & Chemicals. NONPR AFFIL member: Tunkhannock Creek Association; member advisory board: University Pennsylvania Institute Law & Economics; trustee: Pool (Dorothy Rider) Health Care Trust; director: Pennsylvanians Modern Courts; director: Pocono Lake Preserve; member: New York City Bar Association; member: Pennsylvania Society; member executive committee: Machinery & Allied Products Institute; director: Nature Conservancy Pennsylvania Chapter; trustee: Committee for Economic Development; director: Lehigh County United Fund; member: American Bar Association; member: Allentown Chamber of Commerce; member: Alpha Tau Omega; trustee: Allentown Art Museum. CLUB AFFIL Lehigh Country Club.
John P. Jones, III: trustee

Grants Analysis

Disclosure Period: calendar year ending 2000
Total Grants: $503,400
Number of Grants: 61
Average Grant: $7,160*
Highest Grant: $73,780
Typical Range: $1,000 to $15,000
*Note: Average grant figure excludes highest grant.

Recent Grants

Note: Grants derived from 1999 Form 990.

General

51,766	Dorothy Rider Pool Health Care Charitable, The
41,500	Alliance for Building Communities, Allentown, PA
25,000	Central Catholic High School, Lawrence, MA
25,000	Community Action of Development, Allentown, PA
20,000	Civic Theater of Allentown, Allentown, PA
20,000	Girls Club of Allentown, Allentown, PA
17,500	Congregations United for Neighborhood Action, Allentown, PA
16,667	Bach Choir, Bethlehem, PA
16,000	Allentown College of St. Francis de Sales, Allentown, PA
15,000	Allentown Art Museum, Allentown, PA

RIEDMAN FOUNDATION

Giving Contact

John R. Riedman, Principal Manager
45 East Avenue
Rochester, NY 14604
Phone: (716)232-4424

Description

Founded: 1980
EIN: 222279168
Organization Type: Private Foundation
Giving Locations: NH; NY; ND
Grant Types: General Support, Research.

Donor Information

Founder: Frank J. Riedman, Jr., John R. Riedman, Riedman Corp.

Financial Summary

Total Giving: $634,400 (2001); $450,100 (2000); $389,475 (1999)
Giving Analysis: Giving for 2001 includes: foundation grants to United Way ($6,000); 2000: foundation grants to United Way ($15,550) 1999: foundation grants to United Way ($22,200)
Assets: $11,068,106 (2001); $13,681,496 (2000); $9,627,982 (1999)
Gifts Received: $370,000 (2000); $300,251 (1999); $225,623 (1996). Note: In 2000, contributions were received from John R. Riedman ($220,000) and the Riedman Corp. ($211,623).In 1996, contributions were received from John R. Riedman ($14,000) and the Riedman Corp. ($150,000).

Typical Recipients

Arts & Humanities: Arts Associations & Councils, Libraries, Museums/Galleries, Music, Public Broadcasting
Civic & Public Affairs: Chambers of Commerce, Economic Development, Civic & Public Affairs-General, Housing, Municipalities/Towns, Zoos/Aquariums
Education: Colleges & Universities, Community & Junior Colleges, Private Education (Precollege), Science/Mathematics Education
Health: Cancer, Children's Health/Hospitals, Clinics/Medical Centers, Emergency/Ambulance Services, Health Organizations, Hospitals, Medical Rehabilitation, Single-Disease Health Associations
International: Foreign Arts Organizations
Science: Science Museums, Scientific Centers & Institutes
Social Services: Child Welfare, Community Service Organizations, Emergency Relief, Homes, Scouts, United Funds/United Ways, YMCA/YWCA/YMHA/YWHA

Application Procedures

Initial Contact: The foundation has no formal grant application procedure or application form.
Deadlines: None.

Foundation Officials

John R. Riedman: manager

Grants Analysis

Disclosure Period: calendar year ending 2001
Total Grants: $628,400*
Number of Grants: 46
Average Grant: $6,270*
Highest Grant: $250,000
Typical Range: $500 to $10,000
*Note: Giving excludes United Way. Average grant figure excludes two highest grants ($340,000).

Recent Grants

Note: Grants derived from 2001 Form 990.

Library-Related

25,000	Rundel Library Foundation, Rochester, NY

General

250,000	Rochester Museum and Science Center, Rochester, NY
90,000	County of Monroe, Rochester, NY
50,000	Trinity Medical Center Foundation, Minot, ND
25,000	St. John Fisher College, Rochester, NY
25,000	WXXI, Rochester, NY
10,000	Alfred University, Alfred, NY
10,000	Chamber of Commerce, Rochester, NY
10,000	Housing Opportunities, Rochester, NY
10,000	Rochester Museum and Science Center, Rochester, NY
10,000	Society for the Protection of Children, Concord, NH

RIEKE CORP.

Company Headquarters
Auburn, IN
Web: http://www.riekepackaging.com

Company Description
Revenue: US$62.1 million (2001)
Employees: 350
SIC(s): 3000 Rubber & Miscellaneous Plastics Products, 3053 Gaskets, Packing & Sealing Devices, 3400 Fabricated Metal Products, 3412 Metal Barrels, Drums & Pails.
Parent Company: TriMas Corp.

Rieke Corp. Foundation

Giving Contact
Donald E. Kelley, Trustee
500 W. 7th St.
Auburn, IN 46706
Phone: (260)461-6470
Fax: (260)925-0023

Description
EIN: 510158651
Organization Type: Corporate Foundation
Giving Locations: IN; NY; TX
Grant Types: Emergency, General Support.

Financial Summary
Total Giving: $68,500 (fiscal year ending September 30, 2001); $47,300 (fiscal 2000); $47,200 (fiscal 1999)
Giving Analysis: Giving for fiscal 1999 includes: foundation ($47,200) fiscal 1998: foundation grants to United Way ($6,000)
Assets: $1,162,806 (fiscal 2001); $1,371,650 (fiscal 2000); $1,420,411 (fiscal 1999)
Gifts Received: $20,000 (fiscal 2001); $20,000 (fiscal 2000); $20,000 (fiscal 1999)

Typical Recipients
Arts & Humanities: Arts Associations & Councils, Historic Preservation, History & Archaeology, Libraries, Museums/Galleries, Music
Civic & Public Affairs: Chambers of Commerce, Community Foundations, Economic Development, Housing, Municipalities/Towns, Urban & Community Affairs
Education: Business Education, Colleges & Universities, Public Education (Precollege), Special Education
Health: Cancer, Geriatric Health, Health Organizations, Hospitals
Religion: Ministries
Science: Science Exhibits & Fairs
Social Services: Animal Protection, Big Brother/Big Sister, Child Welfare, Community Service Organizations, Food/Clothing Distribution, People with Disabilities, Recreation & Athletics, Senior Services, Shelters/Homelessness, Substance Abuse, United Funds/United Ways, YMCA/YWCA/YMHA/YWHA, YMCA/YWCA/YMHA/YWHA, Youth Organizations

Application Procedures
Initial Contact: Submit either a written or personal request.
Deadlines: August 31.

Additional Information
Trust(s): Wells Fargo Bank IN NA

Corporate Officials
Lynn A. Brooks: president, chief executive officer PRIM CORP EMPL president, chief executive officer: Rieke Corp.
Phillip Keating: chairman PRIM CORP EMPL chairman: Rieke Corp.

Dave Worthington: chief financial officer PRIM CORP EMPL chief financial officer: Rieke Corp.

Foundation Officials
Donald E. Kelley: trustee
Glenn T. Rieke: trustee
Mahlon E. Rieke: trustee

Grants Analysis
Disclosure Period: fiscal year ending September 30, 2001
Total Grants: $68,500
Number of Grants: 14
Average Grant: $2,607*
Highest Grant: $20,000
Typical Range: $1,000 to $5,000
*Note: Average grant figure excludes two highest grants ($32,000).

Recent Grants
Note: Grants derived from fiscal 2001 Form 990.

Library-Related
7,000	Eckhart Public Library, Eckhart, IN

General
20,000	City of Auburn, Auburn, NY
12,000	DeKalb Council On Aging, IN
12,000	DeKalb Council On Aging, IN
5,000	Auburn Cord Duesenberg Museum, Auburn, IN
5,000	DeKalb County YMCA, IN
3,000	Children First Center, IN
3,000	DeKalb Central School, IN
3,000	Filling Station Youth Center
2,500	DeKalb County Habitat for Humanity, Auburn, IN
2,500	DeKalb Humane Society, DeKalb, IN

MABEL LOUISE RILEY FOUNDATION

Giving Contact
Nancy Saunders, Administrative Manager
Kirkpatrick & Lockhart, LLP
77 Summer Street, 8th Floor
Boston, MA 02110
Phone: (617)399-1850
Fax: (617)399-1851
E-mail: rileyfoundation@kl.com
Web: http://www.agmconnect.org/riley1.html

Description
Founded: 1972
EIN: 046278857
Organization Type: General Purpose Foundation
Giving Locations: MA: Boston
Grant Types: Capital, Challenge, Endowment, General Support, Multiyear/Continuing Support, Project, Seed Money.

Donor Information
Founder: Mabel Louise Riley , the only child of Agnes Winslow Riley and Charles E. Riley, was born in Boston in 1883. Her father was president of H & B American Machine Company in Pawtucket, RI. Described as "generous and concerned for the needs of others," she supported numerous charities throughout her lifetime. Miss Riley died in 1971, and with her death provided for the charitable organizations she had supported. A portion of her wealth went to friends, families, and charities. The remainder was used to establish the Mabel Louise Riley Charitable Trust, now known as the Mabel Louise Riley Foundation, which became active in May 1972.

Financial Summary
Total Giving: $2,000,000 (2003 approx); $1,900,000 (2002 approx); $3,776,182 (2000)
Assets: $65,628,564 (2000); $64,470,045 (1999); $53,920,617 (1997)

Typical Recipients
Arts & Humanities: Arts Associations & Councils, Arts Centers, Arts Funds, Ballet, Community Arts, Dance, Ethnic & Folk Arts, Film & Video, Historic Preservation, History & Archaeology, Libraries, Museums/Galleries, Music, Performing Arts, Theater, Visual Arts
Civic & Public Affairs: African American Affairs, Asian American Affairs, Botanical Gardens/Parks, Business/Free Enterprise, Civil Rights, Clubs, Community Foundations, Economic Development, Employment/Job Training, Civic & Public Affairs-General, Hispanic Affairs, Housing, Municipalities/Towns, Nonprofit Management, Philanthropic Organizations, Professional & Trade Associations, Public Policy, Safety, Urban & Community Affairs, Women's Affairs, Zoos/Aquariums
Education: Agricultural Education, Arts/Humanities Education, Business Education, Colleges & Universities, Elementary Education (Private), Environmental Education, Faculty Development, Education-General, Leadership Training, Legal Education, Literacy, Medical Education, Minority Education, Preschool Education, Private Education (Precollege), Public Education (Precollege), Religious Education, Science/Mathematics Education, Social Sciences Education, Special Education
Environment: Environment-General, Resource Conservation, Wildlife Protection
Health: Clinics/Medical Centers, Diabetes, Emergency/Ambulance Services, Health Policy/Cost Containment, Long-Term Care, Mental Health, Prenatal Health Issues
International: Human Rights
Religion: Churches, Religious Organizations, Religious Welfare, Seminaries
Social Services: At-Risk Youth, Big Brother/Big Sister, Camps, Child Welfare, Community Centers, Community Service Organizations, Counseling, Crime Prevention, Day Care, Family Planning, Family Services, Food/Clothing Distribution, People with Disabilities, Recreation & Athletics, Refugee Assistance, Scouts, Shelters/Homelessness, Social Services-General, Substance Abuse, United Funds/United Ways, Veterans, Volunteer Services, YMCA/YWCA/YMHA/YWHA, Youth Organizations

Application Procedures
Initial Contact: Applicants are required to submit a brief summary of their proposal (not more than 2 pages) before submitting a formal grant request. The Foundation will notify the applicant if a grant request will be reviewed by the foundation. If the filing of a grant request is authorized, it must be made using the Common Proposal Format of Associated Grantmakers in Boston, Massachusetts.
Application Requirements: All proposals must include a brief history of the organization, its goals, achievements, indication of whom it serves, and what services it performs; list of board members and resumes and qualifications of involved staff; organization's current and anticipated operating budgets, recent audited financial statement, and complete copy of the most recent IRS 990 form; and a current copy of the IRS tax exemption letter that additionally indicates the organization's status as a public charity. The proposal should also provide a brief description of the reason for which the grant is required, including goals, specific objectives, explanation of the project's compatibility with other programs implemented by the organization, description of special events or approaches planned, and a timetable of these activities. Also required are the project's budget, indication of other potential sources of support, future means of support, summary of expected benefits of the project,

and the proposed method of evaluation of these benefits.

Deadlines: Grant meetings of the foundation are scheduled for March, June, September, and December. A formal grant request will not be acted upon unless filed at least 30 days before the first day of the month in which the grant meeting occurs.

Review Process: Applicants are welcome to contact the program staff before submitting proposals. The trustees may make field visits to interesting programs and will hold meetings with those organizations selected for funding.

Restrictions

Grants generally are not made to charitable organizations outside Massachusetts, toward deficits or regular operating budgets, as the sole source of support, for activities supported by the general public, to units of government, or to individuals or organizations on behalf of individuals. Grants are not made to support personal needs, travel, research, publications, loans, scholarships, national organizations, campaigns, or sectarian religious purposes.

Additional Information

Applicants who have been invited to submit a formal proposal and whose request was subsequently turned down, must wait a full year prior to reapplication. Organizations that have received grants should wait two full years before reapplication.

Publications: Annual Report; Guidelines; Application Form

Foundation Officials

Andrew C. Bailey, Esq.: trustee B Waltham, MA 1921. ED Amherst College AB (1944); Cornell University LLB (1948). PRIM CORP EMPL attorney: Powers & Hall. CORP AFFIL clerk, director: Warwick Mills Holding Co. Inc.

Douglas Danner: trustee B Philadelphia, PA 1924. ED Harvard University AB (1946); Boston University JD (1949). PRIM CORP EMPL attorney: Powers & Hall.

Robert W. Holmes, Jr.: trustee B Fall River, MA 1944. ED Harvard University BA (1967); Boston University JD (1970). PRIM CORP EMPL attorney: Powers & Hall. CORP AFFIL clerk, director: MacDonald Mott Inc.; vice president, clerk, director: Powers & Hall Prof Corp.

Grants Analysis

Disclosure Period: calendar year ending 2000
Total Grants: $3,776,182
Number of Grants: 44
Average Grant: $85,822
Highest Grant: $265,000
Typical Range: $50,000 to $100,000

Recent Grants

Note: Grants derived from 2000 Form 990.

Library-Related
165,000   Boston Public Library Foundation, Boston, MA

General
265,000   Family Nurturing Center -- Reach Out and Read Home Visitation Program
200,000   Dudley Street Neighborhood Initiative, Roxbury, MA
200,000   Generations Inc.
200,000   Tent City Corporation, Boston, MA
110,000   Associated Grantmakers, Boston, MA
100,000   Asian Community Development Corp, Boston, MA
100,000   Bay Cove Human Services, Bay Cove, MA
100,000   Community Day Charter School, Lawrence, MA
100,000   Epiphany Middle School, Dorchester, MA

100,000   Executive Services Corps, Indianapolis, IN

GEORGE AND MARY RITTER CHARITABLE TRUST

Giving Contact

Imogene S. Meyer, Trust Officer
c/o Key Trust Co. Ohio NA
PO Box 10099
Toledo, OH 43699-0099
Phone: (419)259-4968

Description

Founded: 1982
EIN: 346781636
Organization Type: Private Foundation
Giving Locations: OH: Toledo
Grant Types: General Support, Operating Expenses, Scholarship.

Donor Information

Founder: the late George W. Ritter

Financial Summary

Total Giving: $578,245 (fiscal year ending November 30, 2000); $534,630 (fiscal 1999); $239,816 (fiscal 1998)
Giving Analysis: Giving for fiscal 1999 includes: foundation scholarships ($13,940) fiscal 1998: foundation scholarships ($31,640)
Assets: $13,618,915 (fiscal 2000); $12,613,537 (fiscal 1999); $11,187,839 (fiscal 1998)
Gifts Received: $885,858 (fiscal 2000). Note: In 2000, contributions were received from George W. Ritter Trusts.

Typical Recipients

Arts & Humanities: Libraries, Museums/Galleries
Civic & Public Affairs: Clubs, Civic & Public Affairs-General, Law & Justice
Education: Colleges & Universities, Student Aid
Health: Children's Health/Hospitals, Hospitals, Hospitals (University Affiliated)
Religion: Churches, Religious Organizations, Religious Welfare, Synagogues/Temples
Social Services: Community Service Organizations, Scouts, YMCA/YWCA/YMHA/YWHA, Youth Organizations

Application Procedures

Initial Contact: Request application form.
Deadlines: None.

Additional Information

Publications: Application Form
Trust(s): Key Trust Company

Foundation Officials

Larry Firestine: adv
Edgar A. Gibson: adv
James D. Harvey: adv

Grants Analysis

Disclosure Period: fiscal year ending November 30, 2000
Total Grants: $533,645*
Number of Grants: 25
Average Grant: $21,345
Highest Grant: $80,044
Typical Range: $10,000 to $40,000
*Note: Giving excludes Scholarships.

Recent Grants

Note: Grants derived from fiscal 1999 Form 990.

Library-Related
52,073   Ritter Library, Vermilion, OH

General
78,110   Toledo Hospital, Toledo, OH
52,073   Baldwin Wallace College, Berea, OH
52,073   Toledo Museum of Art, Toledo, OH
38,505   Shriner's Hospital, Atlanta, GA
21,656   St. Vincent Hospital, Toledo, OH
20,829   Flower Hospital, Sylvania, OH
20,829   Ohio State Bar Foundation, Columbus, OH
20,829   Riverside Foundation for Riverside Hospital, Toledo, OH
20,829   St. Luke's Hospital, Maumee, OH
20,829   Toledo Rotary Club Foundation, Toledo, OH

JOHN A. AND DELIA T. ROBERT CHARITABLE TRUST 2

Giving Contact

S. Collins Compere, Trust Officer
Regions Bank
PO Box 10247
Birmingham, AL 35202

Description

Founded: 1995
EIN: 636193757
Organization Type: Private Foundation
Giving Locations: AL: Birmingham

Financial Summary

Total Giving: $63,315 (fiscal year ending March 31, 2001); $48,000 (fiscal 1999); $60,633 (fiscal 1997)
Giving Analysis: Giving for fiscal 1999 includes: foundation scholarships ($13,500) foundation ($34,500)
Assets: $1,188,064 (fiscal 2001); $1,394,585 (fiscal 1999); $1,273,444 (fiscal 1997)

Typical Recipients

Arts & Humanities: Libraries
Civic & Public Affairs: Civic & Public Affairs-General
Education: Public Education (Precollege), Student Aid
Health: Health Organizations, Hospitals, Public Health
Religion: Churches, Religious Welfare
Social Services: Child Abuse, Community Service Organizations, People with Disabilities

Application Procedures

Initial Contact: Send a letter describing project. Include a list of other sources of funding, proof of tax-exempt status, current financial data, and amount requested.
Application Requirements: Include a list of other sources of funding, proof of tax-exempt status, current financial data, and amount requested.
Deadlines: None.

Restrictions

Political gifts are excluded per REGS IRC SEC 501 (c)(3) and 170(c)(2).

Additional Information

Grants are awared for religious, science, literary, as education purposes.
Trust(s): Regions Bank

Foundation Officials
Arlene S. Henley: co-trustee

Grants Analysis
Disclosure Period: fiscal year ending March 31, 2001
Total Grants: $63,315
Number of Grants: 12
Average Grant: $4,483*
Highest Grant: $14,000
Lowest Grant: $2,000
Typical Range: $2,500 to $7,500
*Note: Average grant figure excludes highest grant.

Recent Grants
Note: Grants derived from 2000 Form 990.

Library-Related
5,000	Birmingham Public Library, Birmingham, AL

General
15,000	Leeds Historical Society
14,942	University of Alabama Birmingham School of Nursing, Birmingham, AL
8,000	First Light, Inc., Birmingham, AL
7,671	Lakeshore Foundation, Birmingham, AL
5,000	East Lake United Methodist Church
3,000	Cornerstone Schools, Birmingham, AL
3,000	Jimmy Hale Mission
2,000	Assistance League, Birmingham, AL
1,000	Clowns Care, Birmingham, AL

DORA ROBERTS FOUNDATION

Giving Contact
Rick Piersall, Senior Vice President, Bank One
PO Box 2050
Ft. Worth, TX 76113
Phone: (817)884-4442
Fax: (817)884-4294

Description
Founded: 1948
EIN: 756013899
Organization Type: General Purpose Foundation
Giving Locations: TX: Big Spring
Grant Types: Capital, General Support, Project.

Donor Information
Founder: Established in 1948 by the late Dora Roberts.

Financial Summary
Total Giving: $2,522,454 (fiscal year ending June 30, 2001); $1,534,100 (fiscal 1999); $1,948,400 (fiscal 1998)
Assets: $40,798,084 (fiscal 2001); $43,064,161 (fiscal 1999); $41,700,515 (fiscal 1998)
Gifts Received: $5,000 (fiscal 1994); $5,000 (fiscal 1993)

Typical Recipients
Arts & Humanities: Historic Preservation, History & Archaeology, Libraries, Museums/Galleries, Music
Civic & Public Affairs: Chambers of Commerce, Clubs, Employment/Job Training, Civic & Public Affairs-General, Hispanic Affairs, Housing, Municipalities/Towns, Safety, Urban & Community Affairs
Education: Business Education, Colleges & Universities, Community & Junior Colleges, Education Funds, Engineering/Technological Education, Medical Education, Private Education (Precollege), Public Education (Precollege), Secondary Education (Public), Student Aid
Health: Cancer, Heart, Hospices, Hospitals, Medical Rehabilitation
Religion: Churches, Religious Welfare

Social Services: Animal Protection, At-Risk Youth, Child Welfare, Community Centers, Community Service Organizations, Crime Prevention, Food/Clothing Distribution, Homes, Recreation & Athletics, Scouts, Senior Services, Sexual Abuse, YMCA/YWCA/YMHA/YWHA, Youth Organizations

Application Procedures
Initial Contact: The foundation requests applications be made in writing.
Application Requirements: Proposals should include the purpose and amount of the request, a brief narrative history of the organization's purpose and work, budgetary information pertaining to the requested grant, a list of trustees or directors and principal staff, and a copy of an IRS exemption letter.
Deadlines: Proposals must be received by September 30.
Review Process: The board meets annually in November or December. Decisions are generally made by the end of December.

Restrictions
Grants are not made to individuals or outside the state of Texas.

Additional Information
Bank One, Texas, N.A. serves as a corporate trustee for the foundation.

Foundation Officials
Lisa Canter: board member
Roger Canter: board member
Hon. Judge Bob Moore: board mem
Sue Garrett Partee: board mem
Rick Piersall: sr vice president
J. P. Taylor: board mem PRIM CORP EMPL president, director: First National Bank.
R. H. Weaver: board mem CORP AFFIL director: First National Bank.

Grants Analysis
Disclosure Period: fiscal year ending June 30, 2001
Total Grants: $2,522,454*
Number of Grants: 48
Average Grant: $40,592
Highest Grant: $270,000
Typical Range: $1,000 to $100,000
*Note: No grants list available for 2001.

Recent Grants
Note: Grants derived from fiscal 2000 Form 990.

General
289000	Howard College
230000	First United Meth Church Big Spring
200000	Big Spring Salvation Army
150000	Big Spring Humane Society
100000	Big Spring YMCA
95,000	Heritage Museum
65,000	Howard County Fair Association
52,000	City of Big Spring
50,000	Big Spring Symphony Association
50,000	Big Spring Tennis Boosters

ROBERTSHAW CHARITABLE FOUNDATION

Giving Contact
Deborah L. Bridge, Manager
116 N. Main Street
Greensburg, PA 15601
Phone: (724)832-7576

Description
Founded: 1990
EIN: 251622184
Organization Type: Private Foundation
Giving Locations: PA: Western Pennsylvania with emphasis on Westmoreland County
Grant Types: General Support.

Donor Information
Founder: Established in 1990 by John A. Robertshaw, Jr.

Financial Summary
Total Giving: $101,146 (fiscal year ending June 30, 2001); $103,200 (fiscal 2000); $85,843 (fiscal 1997)
Assets: $1,506,276 (fiscal 2001); $1,809,690 (fiscal 2000); $1,531,350 (fiscal 1997)
Gifts Received: $82,600 (fiscal 1997); $30,000 (fiscal 1995); $10,000 (fiscal 1994). Note: In fiscal 1997, contributions were received from John A. Robertshaw, Jr.

Typical Recipients
Arts & Humanities: Arts Festivals, Historic Preservation, Libraries, Museums/Galleries, Music, Public Broadcasting, Theater
Civic & Public Affairs: Botanical Gardens/Parks, Community Foundations, Economic Development, Municipalities/Towns
Education: Arts/Humanities Education, Colleges & Universities, Education-General, Gifted & Talented Programs, International Studies, Private Education (Precollege), Science/Mathematics Education, Secondary Education (Private), Student Aid
Environment: Environment-General, Resource Conservation
Health: Children's Health/Hospitals, Emergency/Ambulance Services, Hospitals
Religion: Religion-General, Religious Organizations, Religious Welfare
Social Services: Animal Protection, At-Risk Youth, Community Service Organizations, Food/Clothing Distribution, Homes, People with Disabilities, People with Disabilities, Recreation & Athletics, Scouts, Social Services-General, Special Olympics, Youth Organizations

Application Procedures
Initial Contact: Send a brief letter of inquiry.
Application Requirements: Include a description of organization.
Deadlines: Semi-annually.

Foundation Officials
Natalie R. Kelley: director
Lisa Robertshaw Moeller: director
Anne B. Robertshaw: director
John A. Robertshaw, III: director
John A. Robertshaw, Jr.: chairman
Marc B. Robertshaw: director

Grants Analysis
Disclosure Period: fiscal year ending June 30, 2001
Total Grants: $101,146
Number of Grants: 40
Average Grant: $2,529
Highest Grant: $6,000
Typical Range: $1,000 to $5,000

Recent Grants
Note: Grants derived from fiscal 2000 Form 990.

Library-Related
5,000	Greensburg Hempfield Area Library, Greensburg, PA -- toward library technology upgrades

General
6,000	Seton Hill College, Greensburg, PA -- toward hardware and software for academic computing laboratory
5,000	Action for Animals Humane Society,

	Inc., Latrobe, PA -- toward facility expansion	
5,000	Greensburg Community Development Corporation, Greensburg, PA -- toward the St. Clair Park project	
5,000	Westmoreland Trust, Greensburg, PA -- toward computer equipment	
4,165	St. Emma Monastery and Retreat House, Greensburg, PA -- toward repairs to pipe organ	
4,000	Ligonier Volunteer Hose Co. 1, Ligonier, PA -- toward a new pumper/rescue truck	
4,000	American Red Cross Westmoreland County, Greensburg, PA -- toward supplies and equipment	
4,000	Aquinas Academy, Greensburg, PA -- toward gymnasium repairs and upgrades	
4,000	Big Brothers Big Sisters of Westmoreland County, Inc., Greensburg, PA -- towards the "COUL Kids" program	
4,000	Economic Growth Connection of Westmoreland, Greensburg, PA -- toward new hardware/software for merger	

ROBINSON-BROADHURST FOUNDATION

Giving Contact

Charles K. McKenzie, Executive Director & President
101 Main St.
PO Box 160
Stamford, NY 12167-0160
Phone: (607)652-2508

Description

Founded: 1984
EIN: 222558699
Organization Type: Private Foundation
Giving Locations: CT: Stamford; MA: Winchendon; NY: Worcester
Grant Types: Capital, General Support, Project, Scholarship.

Donor Information

Founder: the late Anna Broadhurst, the late R. Avery Robinsn

Financial Summary

Total Giving: $1,805,751 (fiscal year ending April 30, 2001); $2,347,534 (fiscal 2000); $1,021,008 (fiscal 1997)
Giving Analysis: Giving for fiscal 2001 includes: foundation scholarships ($28,000) fiscal 2000: foundation scholarships ($25,000)
Assets: $48,692,761 (fiscal 2001); $47,413,548 (fiscal 2000); $28,085,605 (fiscal 1997)
Gifts Received: $7,319,909 (fiscal 2000); $742,692 (fiscal 1997); $484 (fiscal 1996). Note: In fiscal 2000, contributions were received from Estate of Winnie M. Robinson.

Typical Recipients

Arts & Humanities: Arts Associations & Councils, Arts Centers, History & Archaeology, Libraries, Museums/Galleries, Music, Public Broadcasting
Civic & Public Affairs: Botanical Gardens/Parks, Community Foundations, Economic Development, Civic & Public Affairs-General, Housing, Municipalities/Towns, Public Policy, Safety, Urban & Community Affairs
Education: Arts/Humanities Education, Community & Junior Colleges, Education-General, Private Education (Precollege), Public Education (Precollege), Science/Mathematics Education, Secondary Education (Public), Student Aid

Health: Clinics/Medical Centers, Emergency/Ambulance Services, Health Funds, Health Organizations, Hospices, Public Health
Religion: Churches, Ministries, Religious Organizations, Religious Welfare
Social Services: Camps, Child Welfare, Community Centers, Day Care, Family Planning, Recreation & Athletics, Scouts, Senior Services, Social Services-General, Youth Organizations

Application Procedures

Initial Contact: Request application form.
Deadlines: December 31.

Foundation Officials

Ralph Beisler: secretary, trustee
Earnest P. Fletcher, Jr.: treasurer, trustee
David R. Hillson: executive director, secretary
William H. Lister: trustee
Charles McKenzie: trustee
Martin A. Parks: trustee
Winnie M. Robinson: president, trustee

Grants Analysis

Disclosure Period: fiscal year ending April 30, 2001
Total Grants: $1,777,751*
Number of Grants: 83
Average Grant: $19,546*
Highest Grant: $175,000
Typical Range: $10,000 to $40,000
***Note:** Giving excludes scholarship. Average grant figure excludes highest grant.

Recent Grants

Note: Grants derived from fiscal 2000 Form 990.

General

219,415	Stamford Health Care, Inc., Stamford, NY -- medical equipment	
217,500	Stamford Central School, Stamford, NY -- building renovations	
200,000	United Parish of Winchendon, Winchendon, MA -- capital improvement	
175,000	Wendell P. Clark Memorial, Winchendon, MA	
100,000	Immaculate Heart of Mary Church, Winchendon, MA -- capital improvements	
92,400	Town of Harpersfield, Harpersfield, NY -- equipment	
80,034	Stamford Central School, Stamford, NY -- equipment for computer lab	
80,000	Village of Stamford, Stamford, NY -- playground athletic equipment	
72,500	First Presbyterian Church of Stamford, Stamford, NY -- capital improvements	
72,200	Society and Church of the Unity, Winchendon, MA -- capital improvements	

DONALD AND SYLVIA ROBINSON FAMILY FOUNDATION

Giving Contact

Donald Robinson, President
Donald and Sylvia Robinson Family Foundation
6507 Wilkins Ave.
Pittsburgh, PA 15217
Phone: (412)661-1200

Description

EIN: 237062017
Organization Type: Private Foundation
Giving Locations: PA: Pittsburgh including metropolitan area
Grant Types: Emergency, General Support.

Donor Information

Founder: Donald and Sylvia Robinson

Financial Summary

Total Giving: $267,885 (fiscal year ending October 31, 2001); $235,771 (fiscal 2000); $181,703 (fiscal 1999)
Assets: $3,464,316 (fiscal 2001); $5,327,096 (fiscal 2000); $5,235,185 (fiscal 1999)
Gifts Received: $198,096 (fiscal 2000); $303,775 (fiscal 1999); $349,863 (fiscal 1998). Note: In fiscal 1998 and 2000, contributions were received from Donald and Sylvia Robinson.

Typical Recipients

Arts & Humanities: Arts Associations & Councils, Arts Centers, Arts Funds, Film & Video, Arts & Humanities-General, Historic Preservation, History & Archaeology, Libraries, Museums/Galleries, Music, Performing Arts, Public Broadcasting, Theater, Visual Arts
Civic & Public Affairs: Botanical Gardens/Parks, Economic Development, Civic & Public Affairs-General, Urban & Community Affairs, Women's Affairs
Education: Colleges & Universities, Education-General, Minority Education, Private Education (Precollege), Student Aid
Environment: Environment-General, Research, Resource Conservation, Watershed
Health: AIDS/HIV, Children's Health/Hospitals, Eyes/Blindness, Hospices, Hospitals, Preventive Medicine/Wellness Organizations
International: International Peace & Security Issues, Missionary/Religious Activities
Religion: Churches, Jewish Causes, Religious Organizations, Religious Welfare, Synagogues/Temples
Science: Science Museums, Scientific Centers & Institutes
Social Services: Community Service Organizations, Delinquency & Criminal Rehabilitation, Family Services, Sexual Abuse, Shelters/Homelessness, United Funds/United Ways

Application Procedures

Initial Contact: Send a brief letter of inquiry. Include a description of organization, amount requested, purpose of funds sought, recently audited financial statement, and proof of tax-exempt status.
Application Requirements: Include a description of organization, amount requested, purpose of funds sought, and proof of tax-exempt status.
Deadlines: None.

Restrictions

Grants are not made to individuals.

Foundation Officials

Carol Robinson: trustee
Donald Robinson: trustee
Stephen Robinson: trustee
Sylvia Robinson: trustee

Grants Analysis

Disclosure Period: fiscal year ending October 31, 2001
Total Grants: $267,885
Number of Grants: 196
Average Grant: $1,194*
Highest Grant: $35,000
Lowest Grant: $18
Typical Range: $100 to $3,000
***Note:** Average grant figure excludes highest grant.

Recent Grants

Note: Grants derived from 2000 Form 990.

General

25,000	United Jewish Federation, Pittsburgh, PA	
15,000	Southern Alleghenies Museum of Art, Loretto, PA	

10,000	Southern Alleghenies Museum of Art, Loretto, PA
10,000	Southern Alleghenies Museum of Art, Loretto, PA
7,500	Carnegie Institute, Pittsburgh, PA
5,000	Hillel Academy, Pittsburgh, PA
5,000	Hillel Academy, Pittsburgh, PA
5,000	Southern Alleghenies Museum of Art, Loretto, PA
4,000	Phipps Conservatory and Botanical Garden, Pittsburgh, PA
3,000	Family House, Pittsburgh, PA

MAURICE R. ROBINSON FUND

Giving Contact
Marian I. Steffens, Secretary
c/o Chase Bank
1211 Sixth Ave., 34th Fl.
New York, NY 10036
Phone: (212)789-4073

Description
Founded: 1960
EIN: 136161094
Organization Type: Private Foundation
Giving Locations: NY: nationally.
Grant Types: General Support.

Donor Information
Founder: Maurice R. Robinson, Florence L. Robinson

Financial Summary
Total Giving: $529,900 (fiscal year ending June 30, 2000); $420,500 (fiscal 1999); $496,250 (fiscal 1998)
Giving Analysis: Giving for fiscal 1998 includes: foundation ($496,250)
Assets: $12,614,065 (fiscal 2000); $12,000,000 (fiscal 1999); $9,549,246 (fiscal 1998)
Gifts Received: $49,980 (fiscal 1993); $40,000 (fiscal 1992). Note: In fiscal 1993, contributions were received from Scholastic, Inc. ($48,980) and Scott Newman Foundation ($1,000).

Typical Recipients
Arts & Humanities: Arts Associations & Councils, Arts Centers, Arts Festivals, Arts Funds, Arts Institutes, Arts Outreach, Community Arts, Dance, Arts & Humanities-General, History & Archaeology, Libraries, Literary Arts, Museums/Galleries, Music
Civic & Public Affairs: Civil Rights, Economic Development, Employment/Job Training, Civic & Public Affairs-General, Professional & Trade Associations, Public Policy
Education: Arts/Humanities Education, Colleges & Universities, Education Funds, Education Reform, Elementary Education (Public), Faculty Development, Journalism/Media Education, Leadership Training, Private Education (Precollege), Public Education (Precollege), Secondary Education (Private), Social Sciences Education, Special Education, Student Aid
Environment: Environment-General
Health: Hospitals
International: International Affairs
Religion: Churches, Ministries, Religious Organizations
Science: Observatories & Planetariums
Social Services: Child Welfare, Community Service Organizations, Delinquency & Criminal Rehabilitation, Family Services, Social Services-General

Application Procedures
Initial Contact: Send a brief letter of inquiry.
Application Requirements: a description of organization, purpose of funds sought, and proof of tax-exempt status.
Deadlines: None.

Restrictions
Preference is given to educational institutions for youth and colleges offering majors in communications, broadcasting, and journalism.

Foundation Officials
Katherine Carsky: vice president
Claudia Cohl: vice president B Detroit, MI 1939. ED Wayne State University BA (1961). PRIM CORP EMPL vice president, founding editor: Home Office Co. CORP AFFIL vice president, pub director: Professional Publishing Group.
Ernest B. Fleishman: first vice president PRIM CORP EMPL senior vice president ed & corporate relations: Scholastic.
John Quinn: treasurer
Marian I. Steffens: secretary
Barbara D. Sullivan, Esq: president

Grants Analysis
Disclosure Period: fiscal year ending June 30, 2000
Typical Range: $5,000 to $25,000
Note: No grants list available for 2000.

Recent Grants
Note: Grants derived from fiscal 2001 Form 990.

General

450,000	Alliance for Young Arts, New York, NY
20,000	Constitutional Rights Foundation, Los Angeles, CA
20,000	Seton Hall Prep, New York, NY
10,000	Harlem RBI, New York, NY
10,000	NCTE
10,000	See Forever, Washington, DC
10,000	Trinity College, Washington, DC
10,000	Very Special Arts
5,000	Alaska Sea Life Project
5,000	Catamount Arts, St. Johnsbury, VT

ROCKEFELLER BROTHERS FUND, INC.

Giving Contact
Benjamin R. Shute, Jr., Secretary
437 Madison Avenue, 37th Floor
New York, NY 10022-7001
Phone: (212)812-4200
Fax: (212)812-4299
E-mail: rock@rbf.org
Web: http://www.rbf.org
Note: The Fund also has an office in Pocantico Hills, NY.

Description
Founded: 1940
EIN: 131760106
Organization Type: Family Foundation
Formed by Merger of: Rockefeller Brothers Fund and Charles E. Culpeper Foundation (1999).
Giving Locations: NY: New York internationally; nationally.
Grant Types: Capital, Challenge, Conference/Seminar, Fellowship, General Support, Matching, Multiyear/Continuing Support, Operating Expenses, Project, Seed Money.

Donor Information
Founder: The Rockefeller family's fortune stems from John Davison Rockefeller (1839-1937), founder of the Standard Oil Trust and the first billionaire in history. His five grandsons, Nelson Rockefeller, John Rockefeller, Laurance S. Rockefeller, Winthrop Rockefeller, and David Rockefeller, and his granddaughter, Abby Rockefeller Mauze, established the Rockefeller Brothers Fund in 1940. A substantial gift from their father, John D. Rockefeller Jr., in 1951, and a bequest from his estate in 1960, constitute the fund's basic

endowment. The fund is also affiliated with the Asian Cultural Council in New York.

Financial Summary
Total Giving: $20,288,000 (2003 approx); $25,657,906 (2001); $32,113,573 (2000)
Giving Analysis: Giving for 2000 includes: foundation matching gifts ($19,544); foundation scholarships ($1,296,000); 1999: foundation matching gifts ($50,000); foundation fellowships ($64,000); foundation gifts to individuals ($133,089); foundation scholarships ($1,778,000); 1997: foundation matching gifts ($21,155) foundation gifts to individuals ($140,000)
Assets: $586,754,000 (2002 approx); $684,464,383 (2001); $797,789,300 (2000)
Gifts Received: $282,934 (2001); $654,901 (2000); $5,000 (1998). Note: The fund occasionally receives gifts from various Rockefeller family members.

Typical Recipients
Arts & Humanities: Arts Associations & Councils, Arts Institutes, Dance, Arts & Humanities-General, Historic Preservation, Libraries, Museums/Galleries, Music, Opera, Public Broadcasting, Theater
Civic & Public Affairs: Asian American Affairs, Botanical Gardens/Parks, Clubs, Community Foundations, Economic Development, Civic & Public Affairs-General, Housing, Law & Justice, Nonprofit Management, Philanthropic Organizations, Professional & Trade Associations, Public Policy, Rural Affairs, Urban & Community Affairs
Education: Arts/Humanities Education, Colleges & Universities, Education Associations, Education Reform, Elementary Education (Public), Environmental Education, Faculty Development, Education-General, International Exchange, International Studies, Literacy, Minority Education, Preschool Education, Public Education (Precollege), Science/Mathematics Education, Social Sciences Education, Vocational & Technical Education
Environment: Air/Water Quality, Energy, Forestry, Environment-General, Protection, Research, Resource Conservation, Watershed, Wildlife Protection
Health: Speech & Hearing
International: Foreign Arts Organizations, Foreign Educational Institutions, International-General, Health Care/Hospitals, International Affairs, International Development, International Environmental Issues, International Organizations, International Peace & Security Issues, International Relations, International Relief Efforts, Trade
Social Services: Child Welfare, Community Service Organizations, Day Care, Family Services, Social Services-General, Volunteer Services

Application Procedures
Initial Contact: Letters of inquiry (no more than two to three pages in length) should be addressed to the fund's secretary.
Application Requirements: Letters of inquiry should include a description of organization and project for which funding is sought, how it relates to the fund's program, information on principal staff members involved with the proposal, synopsis of the budget, and the amount requested.

Full proposals, when requested, should include a complete a description of organization or project, background and research leading to the development of the proposal, methods by which the project will be carried out, qualifications and experience of the project's or organization's principal staff members, list of board members and advisors, detailed budget, copy of the organization's IRS determination letter of tax-exempt status, and a copy of the organization's most recent financial statement (preferably audited).
Deadlines: None, except for the Charles E. Culpeper Scholarships in Medical Science, for which deadlines are posted on the foundation's web site.

Review Process: If a project is taken up for grant consideration, the staff will ask for additional information, including a full proposal, and, usually, an interview. Proposals from former grantees will be considered only after earlier grants have been evaluated and the grantees have submitted the necessary reports of expenditures of those grants. Grants are awarded by the trustees, who meet regularly throughout the year.

Restrictions

The fund does not support building projects or land acquisition. Neither, as a general rule, does the fund make grants to individuals nor does it support research, graduate study, or the writing of books or dissertations by individuals. There are three exceptions. The Rockefeller Brothers Fund Fellowships, under the education program, are awarded to individuals selected from colleges that, because of their particular support of minority students, have been invited by the fund to participate in the fellowship program. Second, through the Program for Asian Projects, the fund supports projects that exemplify both the spirit of the Ramon Magsaysay Awards and the program concerns of the fund; these grants are available only to Ramon Magsaysay Awardees, including individuals, and to the Ramon Magsaysay Award Foundation. Third, the Charles E. Culpeper Scholarships in Medical Science are designed to support the career development of academic physicians.

The Fund has certain geographic restrictions based on program area. The Sustainable Resource Use and Global Security programs focus on North America and East and Southeast Asia; the Sustainable Resource Use program also includes the Russian Far East and the Global Security program also includes Central and Eastern Europe and Southern Africa. The Nonprofit Sector program places an emphasis on the United States, as well as East and Southeast Asia. The Arts and Culture, Health, and Education programs provide grants only in the United States.

Additional Information

The Fund for Asian Projects supports projects in Asia related to the interests of the Ramon Magsaysay Award Foundation and of the Magsaysay awardees. Grants from this fund are made by the trustees of the Rockefeller Brothers Fund with recommendations from a board of advisors made up of Magsaysay Awardees and officers of the Ramon Magsaysay Award Foundation.

The Fund's Pocantico Conference Center provides a setting where nonprofit organizations and public-sector institutions can bring together people of diverse backgrounds and perspectives to engage critical issues related to the fund's philanthropic program, leading to new levels of understanding and creative resolution of problems.

In July 1999, the Charles E. Culpeper Foundation of Stamford, Connecticut, merged with the Rockefeller Brothers Fund to form the Rockefeller Brothers Fund, Inc.

Publications: Annual Report; Guidelines; Grants Listing; Occasional Papers; Press Releases

Foundation Officials

Catharine O. Broderick: trustee
David Jacobus Callard: trustee B Boston, MA 1938. ED Princeton University AB (1959); Union Theological Seminary (1964-1965); New York University JD (1969). PRIM CORP EMPL president: Wand Partners Inc. NONPR AFFIL trustee: Panorana Trust; board directors: Union Theological Seminary; director: Episcopal Charities Diocese New York. CLUB AFFIL Elkridge Club; Knickerbocker Club.
Richard M. Chasin: trustee B Brooklyn, NY 1936. ED Yale University BA (1956); Harvard University MD (1960). NONPR AFFIL del: International Physicians Prevention Nuclear War; member: Phi Beta Kappa; co-director: Family (Therapy) Institute Cambridge; associate professor clin psychiatry: Harvard University Medical School; member: American Family Therapy

Academy; member: American Psychiatric Association; member: American Academy Child & Adolescent Psychiatry.
Jessica P. Einhorn: trustee
Jonathan Foster Fanton: trustee B Mobile, AL 1943. ED Yale University BA (1965); Yale University MA (1977); Yale University PhD (1978). CORP AFFIL co-chair: 14th Street Union Square Local Development Corp. NONPR AFFIL trustee: New York Commission Inc. Colleges & Universities; co-chairman: Taynbee Foundation; co-chairman: International Committee Academic Freedom; board directors: Foundation Civil Society; chairman: Helsinki Watch Committee; member: American Historical Association; member: Council Foreign Relations; board directors: American Ditchley Foundation. CLUB AFFIL Economic Club.
Neva R. Goodwin: vice chairman, trustee B New York, NY 1944. ED Harvard College BA (1962); Harvard University Kennedy School of Government MPA (1982); Boston University PhD (1987). NONPR AFFIL trustee: Winrock International Institute Agricultural Development; founding trustee: World Game Institute; director: College Atlantic; co-director: Tufts University Global Development & Environment Institute.
Stephen B. Heintz: president
Linda E. Jacobs: vice president
Hunter Lewis: trustee
Priscilla Lewis: director communications, special assistant to the president
William Henry Luers: advisory trustee B Springfield, IL 1929. ED Hamilton College AB (1951); Northwestern University (1951-1952); Columbia University MA (1957). PRIM NONPR EMPL president: Metropolitan Museum of Art. CORP AFFIL director: Wickes Lumber Co.; director: Wickes Inc.; director: Scudder New Europe Fund; director: Story First Corp.; director: Scudder Equities & Security Funds; director: Scudder Global/International Funds; director: Brazil Fund; director: IDEX Corp. NONPR AFFIL director: Institute East-West Studies; advisory council: Trust Mutual Understanding; trustee, advisory council: Appeal Conscience Foundation; member: Council Foreign Relations; fellow: American Academy of Arts & Sciences. CLUB AFFIL board directors: Economic Club New York.
William F. McCalpin: executive vice president, chief operating officer
James E. Moltz: trustee B Williamsport, PA 1932. ED Williams College BS (1954); University of Pennsylvania Wharton School MBA (1956). PRIM CORP EMPL chief investment officer: Deutsche Bank Securities Inc. NONPR AFFIL member financial committee: Williams College; chairman: Woods Hole Oceanographic Institute; trustee: Sterling Francine Clark Art Institute; member: Financial Analysts Federation; member: Society Security Analysts; trustee: Darien Library. CLUB AFFIL Windsor Club; director: Wee Burn Country Club; Rockefeller Center Club; Union League Club.
John Morning: trustee B Cleveland, OH 1932. ED Pratt Institute BFA (1955). PRIM CORP EMPL president: John Morning Design. CORP AFFIL director: Dime Savings Bank. NONPR AFFIL member, board director: New York Landmarks Conservancy; chairman: Vivian Beaumont Theater; member education committee: Museum Modern Art; vice chairman: New York City Cultural Affairs Advisory Committee; director: Association Government Boards, Colleges & Universities; trustee: City University New York; member: American Academy Dramatic Arts.
Abby Milton Rockefeller O'Neill: advisory trustee B Oyster Bay, NY 1928.
Robert B. Oxnam: trustee
Richard D. Parsons: advisory trustee
Joseph A. Pierson: trustee
David Rockefeller, Sr.: advisory trustee B New York, NY June 12, 1915. ED Harvard University BS (1936); University of Chicago PhD (1940). CORP AFFIL chairman: Rockefeller Center Properties Trust Inc.; director: Chase International Advisory Committee;

stockholder: Greenrock Corp. NONPR AFFIL honorary trustee: Rockefeller Family Fund; life trustee: University Chicago; member: International Executive Service Corps; honorary chairman: International House; director, honorary chairman: Center Inter-American Relations; director: Council Foreign Relations; honorary chairman: American Society. CLUB AFFIL River Club; University Club; The Links Club; New York Yacht Club; Century Club; Harvard Club.
David Rockefeller, Jr.: trustee B New York, NY 1941. ED Harvard University AB (1963); Harvard University JD (1966). PRIM CORP EMPL vice chairman: Rockefeller Family & Associates. CORP AFFIL officer: Metromedia Fiber Network Inc. NONPR AFFIL director: Asian Cultural Council.
Laurance Spelman Rockefeller: advisory trustee B New York, NY 1910. ED Princeton University BA (1932). CORP AFFIL chairman: Woodstock Resort Corp.; director: SKI Realty Inc. NONPR AFFIL life trustee: Wildlife Conservation Society; honorary director: Woodstock Foundation; trustee emeritus: Princeton University; honorary director: National Wildflower Center; commissioner emeritus: Palisades Interstate Park Comm; honorary trustee: National Geographic Society; life member: Massachusetts Institute Technology; honorary chairman: Memorial Sloan-Kettering Cancer Center; trustee, chairman emeritus: Jackson Hole Preserve Inc.; honorary chairman: American Conservation Association; chairman: Historic Hudson Valley. CLUB AFFIL University Club; Sleepy Hollow Country Club; Princeton Club; River Club; Lotos Club; Knickerbocker Club; The Links Club; Capitol Hill Club; Boone & Crockett Club; Brook Club.
Richard Gilder Rockefeller: trustee B 1949. ED Harvard University (1971); Harvard University EdM (1973); Harvard University MD (1979). PRIM CORP EMPL physician: Clinical Faculty.
Steven Clark Rockefeller: chairman, trustee B 1936. ED Princeton University AB (1958); Union Theological Seminary MDiv (1963); Columbia University PhD (1973). NONPR AFFIL director: Asian Cultural Council.
Benjamin R. Shute, Jr.: secretary ED Harvard University (1959). CLUB AFFIL Cosmopolitan Club.
Russell E. Train: advisory trustee
Edmond D. Villani: trustee B 1947. ED Georgetown University BA (1968); University of Pennsylvania PhD (1973). PRIM CORP EMPL president: Scudder Kemper Investments.
Boris Wessely: treasurer
Frank Wisner: trustee
Tadataka Yamada, MD: trustee B Tokyo, Japan 1945. ED Stanford University BA; New York University School Medicine MD (1971). PRIM NONPR EMPL councillor: Association American Physicians. CORP AFFIL director: Healtheon Corp.; director: diaDexus Inc.; director: GlaxoSmithKline. NONPR AFFIL member: American Society Clinical Investigation; member: IOM; member: American Academy of Arts & Sciences; member: American College Physicians; member: AGA.

Grants Analysis

Disclosure Period: calendar year ending 2001
Total Grants: $25,657,906*
Number of Grants: 550 (approx)
Average Grant: $46,651
Highest Grant: $500,000
Typical Range: $25,000 to $100,000
*Note: Giving includes scholarships.

Recent Grants

Note: Grants derived from 2001 Form 990.

Library-Related
250,000   Pierpont Morgan Library, New York,
          NY -- for endowment

General
500,000   Demos-A Network for Ideas and Actions, LTD, New York, NY -- for operating support

500,000	Museum of Modern Art, New York, NY -- for an endowment in the name of Charles E. Culpeper
400,000	Solar Development Foundation, Arlington, VA
300,000	Colonial Williamsburg Foundation, Williamsburg, VA -- for an endowment
300,000	Demos-A Network for Ideas and Actions, LTD, New York, NY
250,000	Forest Stewardship Council, Oaxaca, OX Mexico
250,000	Philanthropic Research, Inc., Williamsburg, VA -- to support its GuideStar web site
225,000	Cornerstone Theater Company, Los Angeles, CA -- for endowment
200,000	Asian Cultural Council, New York, NY -- to the organization's unrestricted grants program in 2001
200,000	Ecotrust Canada, Vancouver, BC Canada -- to its efforts to create a conservation economy along the British Columbia coast

DAVID ROCKEFELLER FUND

Giving Contact

Marnie Pillsbury, Executive Director
30 Rockefeller Plz., Rm. 5600
New York, NY 10112
Phone: (212)649-5600

Description

Founded: 1989
EIN: 133533359
Organization Type: Private Foundation
Giving Locations: ME: Seal Harbor; NY: Pocantico
Grant Types: General Support.

Donor Information

Founder: Established in 1989 by David Rockefeller, Jr.

Financial Summary

Total Giving: $2,931,457 (2001); $464,850 (2000); $214,850 (1998)
Giving Analysis: Giving for 2000 includes: foundation grants to United Way ($21,000)
Assets: $7,980,949 (2001); $10,844,921 (2000); $5,742,078 (1998)
Gifts Received: $1,215,000 (2000); $742,786 (1998); $260,000 (1994). Note: In 1998 and 2000, contributions were received from David Rockefeller.

Typical Recipients

Arts & Humanities: Arts Associations & Councils, Ethnic & Folk Arts, Arts & Humanities-General, Historic Preservation, History & Archaeology, Libraries, Museums/Galleries, Music, Public Broadcasting, Theater
Civic & Public Affairs: Botanical Gardens/Parks, Economic Development, Civic & Public Affairs-General, Housing, Law & Justice, Municipalities/Towns, Parades/Festivals, Philanthropic Organizations, Safety, Urban & Community Affairs, Women's Affairs
Education: Arts/Humanities Education, Colleges & Universities, Education-General, Leadership Training, Private Education (Precollege), Public Education (Precollege), Science/Mathematics Education
Environment: Air/Water Quality, Environment-General, Resource Conservation
Health: Children's Health/Hospitals, Clinics/Medical Centers, Hospitals, Hospitals, Nursing Services, Prenatal Health Issues, Public Health
Religion: Churches, Missionary Activities (Domestic), Religious Welfare
Science: Science Museums, Scientific Labs

Social Services: Child Welfare, Community Service Organizations, Counseling, Day Care, Delinquency & Criminal Rehabilitation, Family Planning, Family Services, Food/Clothing Distribution, Homes, Recreation & Athletics, Scouts, United Funds/United Ways, YMCA/YWCA/YMHA/YWHA, Youth Organizations

Application Procedures

Initial Contact: The foundation has no formal grant application procedure or application form.
Deadlines: None.
Decision Notification: The Fund does not notify organizations requesting grants of its decision unless a grant is awarded.

Restrictions

Does not support individuals or organizations outside operating areas. Foundation only supports tax-exempt organizations which are located in and contribute to Seal Harbor, Maine, and the Counties of Westchester and Columbia in New York.

Foundation Officials

Colin G. Cambell: director
Christopher J. Kennan: director
Marnie S. Pillsbury: executive director
Richard E. Salomon: secretary, treasurer, director

Grants Analysis

Disclosure Period: calendar year ending 2001
Total Grants: $2,905,507*
Number of Grants: 119
Average Grant: $5,872*
Highest Grant: $2,212,657
Typical Range: $500 to $15,000
*Note: Giving excludes Matching Gifts. Average grant excludes highest grant.

Recent Grants

Note: Grants derived from 2001 Form 990.

General

2,212,657	Stone Barns Restoration Corporation, New York, NY
50,000	College of the Atlantic, Bar Harbor, ME
25,000	Cases, New York, NY
25,000	Historic Hudson Valley, Tarrytown, NY
25,000	Lower Manhattan Cultural Council, Manhattan, NY
25,000	Northwest Atlantic Marine Alliance, Saco, ME
25,000	Osborne Association, New York, NY
25,000	Women's Prison Association and Home, Inc., New York, NY
20,000	Conservation International, Washington, DC
20,000	Correctional Association of New York, New York, NY

ROCKWELL AUTOMATION INC.

Company Headquarters

777 E. Wisconsin Avenue, Suite 1400
Milwaukee, WI 53202
Web: http://www.rockwellautomation.com

Company Description

Ticker: ROK
Exchange: NYSE
Former Name: Rockwell International Corp..
Revenue: US$3.909 billion (2002)
Profit: US$121 million (2002)
Employees: 22000 (2002)
Fortune Rank: 409, per FORTUNE Magazine's list of 500 Largest U.S. Corporations (2002).

SIC(s): 3465 Automotive Stampings, 3493 Steel Springs Except Wire, 3555 Printing Trades Machinery, 3679 Electronic Components Nec.

Operating Locations

Rockwell International Corp. (CA--Costa Mesa, Downey, Hayward, Newbury Park, Pleasanton, Seal Beach; CO--Fort Carson; FL--Melbourne; GA--Tucker; IL--Decorra; IA--Cedar Rapids, Fairfield; KY--Florence, Frankfort, Hopkinsville; LA--Shreveport; MA--Westford; MI--Brighton, Southfield; MO--St. Ann; NE--Bellevue; NJ--Lebanon; NC--Maxton; OH--Heath; OK--McAlester, Oklahoma City; PA--Pittsburgh; SC--York; TN--Gordonsville, Morristown; TX--El Paso, Houston; VA--Arlington, Vienna; WA--Kirkland, Renton; WI--Oshkosh)

Nonmonetary Support

Type: Cause-related Marketing & Promotion; Donated Equipment; Donated Products; In-kind Services; Loaned Employees
Note: Company provides nonmonetary support.

Rockwell International Corp. Trust

Giving Contact

Christine G. Rodriguez
777 E. Wisconsin Avenue, Suite 1400
Milwaukee, WI 53202
Phone: (414)212-5258
Web: http://rockwellautomation.com/about_us/citizenship.html

Description

EIN: 251072431
Organization Type: Corporate Foundation
Giving Locations: headquarters and operating communities; nationally to education.
Grant Types: Capital, Employee Matching Gifts, General Support, Multiyear/Continuing Support, Scholarship.
Note: Employee matching gift ratio: 1 to 1 to accredited colleges and accredited public and private elementary and high schools. Company will match gifts of more than $25 to a maximum of $10,000 per employee annually.

Financial Summary

Total Giving: $5,560,644 (fiscal year ending September 30, 2001); $5,429,554 (fiscal 2000); $4,976,583 (fiscal 1999). Note: Contributes through corporate direct giving program and foundation.
Giving Analysis: Giving for fiscal 2001 includes: foundation scholarships ($78,774); foundation matching gifts ($602,220); foundation grants to United Way ($1,178,500); foundation ($4,382,144); fiscal 2000: foundation scholarships ($71,213); foundation matching gifts ($651,541); foundation grants to United Way ($1,055,500); foundation ($3,651,280); fiscal 1999: foundation scholarships ($104,870); foundation matching gifts ($615,362); foundation grants to United Way ($962,200) foundation ($3,294,151)
Assets: $15,386,346 (fiscal 2001); $20,105,587 (fiscal 2000); $14,265,947 (fiscal 1999)
Gifts Received: $10,000,000 (fiscal 2000); $10,000,000 (fiscal 1999); $8,500,000 (fiscal 1994). Note: Contributions received from Rockwell International Corporation.

Typical Recipients

Arts & Humanities: Arts Associations & Councils, Arts Centers, Arts Festivals, Arts Funds, Arts Institutes, Community Arts, Dance, Arts & Humanities-General, Historic Preservation, History & Archaeology, Libraries, Museums/Galleries, Music, Opera, Performing Arts, Public Broadcasting, Theater

Civic & Public Affairs: African American Affairs, Asian American Affairs, Business/Free Enterprise, Chambers of Commerce, Civil Rights, Economic Development, Economic Policy, Employment/Job Training, Civic & Public Affairs-General, Hispanic Affairs, Housing, Law & Justice, Legal Aid, Municipalities/Towns, Nonprofit Management, Professional & Trade Associations, Public Policy, Safety, Urban & Community Affairs, Women's Affairs, Zoos/Aquariums

Education: Business Education, Colleges & Universities, Community & Junior Colleges, Continuing Education, Economic Education, Education Associations, Education Funds, Education Reform, Engineering/Technological Education, Faculty Development, Education-General, Gifted & Talented Programs, International Studies, Literacy, Minority Education, Private Education (Precollege), Public Education (Precollege), Science/Mathematics Education, Special Education, Student Aid, Vocational & Technical Education

Environment: Environment-General, Resource Conservation

Health: Cancer, Children's Health/Hospitals, Emergency/Ambulance Services, Health Policy/Cost Containment, Health Organizations, Hospices, Hospitals, Medical Rehabilitation, Mental Health, Public Health, Single-Disease Health Associations

International: International Affairs, International Peace & Security Issues, International Relations

Religion: Bible Study/Translation, Churches, Religious Welfare

Science: Science-General, Science Exhibits & Fairs, Science Museums, Scientific Centers & Institutes, Scientific Organizations

Social Services: Big Brother/Big Sister, Child Welfare, Community Centers, Community Service Organizations, Counseling, Delinquency & Criminal Rehabilitation, Domestic Violence, Emergency Relief, Family Services, People with Disabilities, Recreation & Athletics, Scouts, Shelters/Homelessness, Substance Abuse, United Funds/United Ways, Volunteer Services, YMCA/YWCA/YMHA/YWHA, Youth Organizations

Application Procedures

Initial Contact: Send a brief letter or proposal.

Application Requirements: Information should include a description of organization, amount requested, purpose of funds sought, recently audited financial statement, proof of tax-exempt status, list of other funding sources, and any other pertinent information.

Deadlines: None.

Decision Notification: Within 90 days of receipt of proposal.

Notes: Organizations providing services in communities with Rockwell facilities should contact the local Community Affairs administrator to start a grant request. "The Rockwell International Corporation Trust has identified two distinct funding priorities, and special consideration will be given to proposals that integrate these issues: 1) Education and youth development, with emphasis in math, science, and engineering; and 2) Culture and the arts, with emphasis on youth educational programs." Rockwell International Corporation Trust Guidelines. Trust also gives to health, social services, and civic organizations and gives special consideration to organizations where employees volunteer. The majority of giving to these organizations is through United Way.

Restrictions

Does not support individuals, fraternal organizations, religious organizations for sectarian purposes, general endowments, deficit reduction, federated campaigns, organizations or projects outside the US, non tax-exempt organizations or projects, or private foundations.

Corporate Officials

W. Michael Barnes: senior vice president finance & planning, chief financial officer B 1938. ED Texas A&M University MA; Texas A&M University BA; Texas

A&M University PhD (1968). PRIM CORP EMPL senior vice president finance & planning, chief financial officer: Rockwell International Corp. NONPR AFFIL member: Council Financial Executives.

Donald Ray Beall: director, executive committee B Beaumont, CA 1938. ED University of California, Los Angeles; San Jose State University BS (1960); University of Pittsburgh MBA (1961). PRIM CORP EMPL chairman, executive committee: Rockwell Collins, Inc. ADD CORP EMPL president: Collins International Service Corp. CORP AFFIL chairman: Procter & Gamble Co.; chairman: Times Mirror Co.; director: Conexant Systems Inc.; director: Meritor Automotive Inc.; director: BP Amoco Corp. NONPR AFFIL fellow: American Institute Aeronautics & Astronautics; fellow: Society Manufacturing Engineers.

William Joseph Calise, Junior: senior vice president, secretary, general counsel B New York, NY 1938. ED Bucknell University BA (1960); Columbia University JD (1963); Columbia University MBA (1963). PRIM CORP EMPL senior vice president, secretary, general counsel: Rockwell Automation, Inc.. NONPR AFFIL member: Association Bar New York City. CLUB AFFIL Rockefeller Center Club; Duquesne Club.

Donald H. Davis, Jr.: president, chief executive officer, chairman B 1939. ED Texas A&M University BSME (1962); Texas A&M University MBA (1963). PRIM CORP EMPL president, chief executive officer, chairman: Rockwell International Corp. CORP AFFIL director: Ingram Micro Inc.

Joseph H. Garrett, Junior: vice president government & international operations PRIM CORP EMPL vice president government & international operations: Rockwell International Corp.

Foundation Officials

W. Michael Barnes: member trust committee (see above)

John A. Coleman: assistant secretary

Donald H. Davis, Jr.: chairman trust committee (see above)

Grants Analysis

Disclosure Period: fiscal year ending September 30, 2001

Total Grants: $4,382,144*

Number of Grants: 230

Average Grant: $19,053

Highest Grant: $300,000

Lowest Grant: $1,000

Typical Range: $1,000 to $25,000 and $50,000 to $300,000

*Note: Giving excludes matching gifts, scholarships, and United Way.

Recent Grants

Note: Grants derived from fiscal 2001 Form 990.

General

300,000	United Way of Greater Milwaukee, Milwaukee, WI -- health and human services
300,000	University of California UCI Foundation, Irvine, CA -- education
230,000	United Way Services, Cleveland, OH -- health and human services
211,700	United Way East Central Iowa, Cedar Rapids, IA -- health and human services
200,000	Clemson University Foundation, Clemson, SC -- education
200,000	Museum of Science and Industry, Chicago, IL -- arts and culture
125,000	United Performing Arts Fund, Milwaukee, WI -- arts and culture
115,000	Cedar Rapids-Marion Area Chamber of Commerce Foundation, Cedar Rapids, IA -- civic and community
100,000	Greater Milwaukee Committee, Milwaukee, WI -- civic and community
100,000	Iowa State University Foundation, Ames, IA -- education

ROCKWELL FUND, INC.

Giving Contact

Martha Vogt, Senior Program Officer
1330 Post Oak Boulevard, Suite 1825
Houston, TX 77056
Phone: (713)629-9022
Fax: (713)629-7702
E-mail: mvogt@rockfund.org
Web: http://www.rockfund.org

Description

Founded: 1931

EIN: 746040258

Organization Type: General Purpose Foundation

Giving Locations: TX: Houston limited giving outside of the Houston area

Grant Types: Capital, Endowment, Fellowship, General Support, Matching, Scholarship.

Note: The fund also provides equipment and technical support.

Donor Information

Founder: Established in 1931 by members of the James M. Rockwell family, Rockwell Brothers & Company, and the Rockwell Lumber Company.

Financial Summary

Total Giving: $5,019,675 (2002); $5,755,860 (2001); $5,019,675 (2000)

Giving Analysis: Giving for 2001 includes: foundation scholarships ($87,500)

Assets: $126,037,839 (2002); $117,251,750 (2001); $126,268,836 (2000)

Typical Recipients

Arts & Humanities: Arts Associations & Councils, Arts Institutes, Arts Outreach, Ballet, Dance, Historic Preservation, History & Archaeology, Libraries, Museums/Galleries, Music, Opera, Performing Arts, Public Broadcasting, Theater

Civic & Public Affairs: African American Affairs, Botanical Gardens/Parks, Community Foundations, Economic Development, Employment/Job Training, Hispanic Affairs, Housing, Legal Aid, Urban & Community Affairs, Women's Affairs, Zoos/Aquariums

Education: Agricultural Education, Arts/Humanities Education, Business Education, Colleges & Universities, Community & Junior Colleges, Education Associations, Education Reform, Elementary Education (Private), Engineering/Technological Education, Environmental Education, Faculty Development, Education-General, Health & Physical Education, Legal Education, Literacy, Preschool Education, Private Education (Precollege), Religious Education, School Volunteerism, Science/Mathematics Education, Secondary Education (Private), Special Education, Student Aid

Environment: Environment-General, Resource Conservation

Health: Adolescent Health Issues, AIDS/HIV, Cancer, Children's Health/Hospitals, Clinics/Medical Centers, Emergency/Ambulance Services, Eyes/Blindness, Health Organizations, Heart, Hospices, Hospitals, Medical Rehabilitation, Medical Research, Mental Health, Nursing Services, Prenatal Health Issues, Public Health, Single-Disease Health Associations, Single-Disease Health Associations, Speech & Hearing, Transplant Networks/Donor Banks

Religion: Churches, Ministries, Religious Organizations, Religious Welfare

Science: Science Exhibits & Fairs, Science Museums

Social Services: Animal Protection, At-Risk Youth, Child Abuse, Child Welfare, Community Centers, Community Service Organizations, Counseling, Day Care, Delinquency & Criminal Rehabilitation, Emergency Relief, Family Planning, Family Services, Food/Clothing Distribution, Homes, People with Disabilities, Recreation & Athletics, Scouts, Senior Services, Shelters/Homelessness, Substance Abuse, United Funds/

United Ways, Volunteer Services, YMCA/YWCA/YMHA/YWHA, Youth Organizations

Application Procedures

Initial Contact: Applicants should contact the fund to request a copy of its application form and guidelines.

Application Requirements: One unbound copy of the proposal should be submitted and should include the following: a one page cover letter written on the organization's letterhead, and signed by the president or chairman of the board; grant application form; copy of IRS determination letter; financial statement of past fiscal year, audited, if available; complete copy of IRS 990 tax return most recently submitted; list of current officers and board members; copies of either a small general information brochure or a one-page general information fact sheet--not to be substituted with an annual report; and a proposal narrative limited to no more than five pages. This needs to be concise and to the point, and should consist of the following: the organization's mission statement and a brief history; a discussion on the use of the proposed grant; specific amount requested; and the projected timetable for the use of the grant. If the funds are for a project, the total cost of the project should be given as well as the total raised and pledged so far, and the project budget including income and expenses. Graphs, floor plans, photographs, maps or diagrams are included in the five page limit. After reviewing the proposal, if additional materials are needed, the staff will then make a request.

Deadlines: February 1, May 1, August 1, and November 1.

Review Process: The staff reviews proposals to determine whether they fall within the Fund's current areas of interest and funding priorities. Written notification is sent within three weeks after a quarterly meeting (generally held in January, April, July, and October) to advise applicants of the decisions of the trustees.

Notes: Omission of any required information, as outlined in the guideline and application form, or receipt after deadline date, will result in delay of consideration or rejection of the application.

Restrictions

The Fund does not make grants or loans to individuals, for trips, dinners, or special events, or for medical research. The Fund does not participate in feasibility studies or fundraising benefits, nor does it respond to mass appeal solicitations.

Additional Information

In 2002, the foundation reported that grantmaking guidelines were under review. Changes will be posted on the foundation website.

Publications: Application Form; Guidelines

Foundation Officials

R. Terry Bell: president, trustee B 1945. PRIM CORP EMPL partner: Caolo & Bell.
Bennie Green: treasurer, trustee
Mary Jo Loyd: corp secretary, trustee
Helen N. Sterling: trustee emerita B 1906.
Martha Vogt: senior program officer

Grants Analysis

Disclosure Period: calendar year ending 2001
Total Grants: $5,668,360*
Number of Grants: 215
Average Grant: $26,364
Highest Grant: $126,000
Lowest Grant: $3,000
Typical Range: $10,000 to $30,000
*Note: Giving excludes scholarships.

Recent Grants

Note: Grants derived from 2000 Form 990.

Library-Related
25,000   Goliad County Library, Houston, TX -- capital campaign for building renovation

General
125,000   KIPP, Inc, Houston, TX -- operating support and moving/transitional expenses to permanent location
100,000   Association for Community Television, Houston, TX -- contribution to Capital Campaign, purchase of digital equipment
100,000   Briarwood-Brockwood, Brookshire, TX -- program support to continue and expand the horticulture therapy/enterprise program at Brookwood community
100,000   Crohn's & Colitis Foundation of America, Inc., Houston, TX -- contribution to Capital Campaign for education, support and research
100,000   Galveston Historical Foundation, Galveston, TX -- support of educational programs and Dickens on the Strand "Rainy Day Fund"
100,000   Healthy Families Initiatives, Houston, TX -- program support to expand services to high risk children and families in Harris County
100,000   Rice University, William Marsh, Houston, TX -- two postdoctoral fellowship endowments
100,000   Texas Tech University Foundation, Lubbock, TX -- Rockwell professorships in the College of Human Science and the College of Agriculture and Natural Resources
100,000   University of Texas Health Science Center Houston, Houston, TX -- establishment of endowed chair in Society and Health at the School of Public Health
75,000   Houston Read Commission, Houston, TX -- ten-yr. literacy campaign & general operating support to continue expansion & development of literacy centers & programs

FRED M. RODDY FOUNDATION

Giving Contact

Augusta Haydock
c/o Fleet National Bank
100 Federal St.
Boston, MA 02110
Phone: (617)434-4644

Alternate Contact

Phone: (401)278-8700

Description

Founded: 1969
EIN: 056037528
Organization Type: Private Foundation
Giving Locations: RI: nationally.
Grant Types: General Support.

Donor Information

Founder: the late Fred M. Roddy

Financial Summary

Total Giving: $585,052 (2000); $657,243 (1999); $726,484 (1998)
Giving Analysis: Giving for 2000 includes: foundation scholarships ($70,000)
Assets: $17,247,045 (2000); $17,353,289 (1999); $16,993,986 (1998)

Typical Recipients

Arts & Humanities: Libraries
Civic & Public Affairs: Civic & Public Affairs-General, Hispanic Affairs, Housing, Urban & Community Affairs

Education: Afterschool/Enrichment Programs, Colleges & Universities, Elementary Education (Private), Education-General, Medical Education, Minority Education, Private Education (Precollege), Secondary Education (Private), Student Aid
Health: AIDS/HIV, Cancer, Children's Health/Hospitals, Clinics/Medical Centers, Emergency/Ambulance Services, Health Organizations, Heart, Hospitals, Long-Term Care, Medical Research, Nursing Services, Prenatal Health Issues
Religion: Religious Organizations, Religious Welfare
Social Services: At-Risk Youth, Big Brother/Big Sister, Camps, Family Services, Food/Clothing Distribution, People with Disabilities, Senior Services, YMCA/YWCA/YMHA/YWHA, Youth Organizations

Application Procedures

Initial Contact: Send a written proposal and an annual report.
Deadlines: None.

Additional Information

Trust(s): Fleet National Bank NA

Foundation Officials

Peter Arnold: director
Shawn P. Buckless: clerk
Mrs. Lee Kintzel: co-trustee
Richard B. Lafleur: treasurer
David I. McIntyre: clerk
John W. McIntyre, Esq.: co-trustee

Grants Analysis

Disclosure Period: calendar year ending 2000
Total Grants: $515,052*
Number of Grants: 26
Average Grant: $19,810
Highest Grant: $50,000
Typical Range: $10,000 to $40,000
*Note: Giving excludes scholarships.

Recent Grants

Note: Grants derived from 2000 Form 990.

General
50,000   Lifespan, Rochester, NY
50,000   Progreso Latino, Central Falls, RI
50,000   University of Tennessee, Knoxville, TN
50,000   University of Tennessee, Knoxville, TN
40,000   Brown University, Providence, RI
40,000   Providence College, Providence, RI
32,243   Bradley Hospital Foundation, Providence, RI
30,200   Camp Twin Lakes, Atlanta, GA
29,000   Family Service, Providence, RI
25,000   University of Tennessee, Knoxville, TN

ROGERS FAMILY FOUNDATION

Giving Contact

Irving E. Rogers, III, Trustee
PO Box 100
Lawrence, MA 01842
Phone: (978)946-2000

Description

Founded: 1957
EIN: 046063152
Organization Type: Private Foundation
Giving Locations: MA: the greater Merrimack Valley, MA area
Grant Types: General Support.

Donor Information

Founder: Irving E. Rogers, Eagle-Tribune Publishing Co., Martha B. Rogers

Financial Summary

Total Giving: $955,887 (2000); $751,620 (1998); $645,700 (1997)
Giving Analysis: Giving for 2000 includes: foundation grants to United Way ($50,000)
Assets: $20,760,713 (2000); $14,189,709 (1996); $12,976,864 (1995)
Gifts Received: $665,354 (2000); $250,705 (1996); $238,632 (1995). Note: In 2000, contributions were received from Andover Publishing Co. ($38,000), Eagle-Tribune Publishing Co. ($500,000), Eagle-Tribune Realty Trust ($100,000), Rogers Investment Corp ($9,000), Consolidated Press Inc. ($15,000) and Derry Publishing Co. ($3,354). In 1996, contributions were received from Andover Publishing Co. ($23,000), Eagle-Tribune Publishing Co. ($197,250), Eagle-Tribune Realty Trust ($10,000), Rogers Investment Corp ($3,400), and Derry Publishing Co. ($17,055).

Typical Recipients

Arts & Humanities: Arts Festivals, Community Arts, Ethnic & Folk Arts, Historic Preservation, History & Archaeology, Libraries, Museums/Galleries, Music, Theater
Civic & Public Affairs: Community Foundations, Civic & Public Affairs-General, Housing, Parades/Festivals, Urban & Community Affairs
Education: Business Education, Colleges & Universities, Community & Junior Colleges, Education-General, Legal Education, Minority Education, Private Education (Precollege), Secondary Education (Private), Student Aid
Environment: Watershed
Health: Clinics/Medical Centers, Emergency/Ambulance Services, Home-Care Services, Hospitals, Medical Rehabilitation, Medical Research, Respiratory
Religion: Churches, Religion-General, Ministries, Religious Organizations, Religious Welfare, Synagogues/Temples
Science: Science Museums
Social Services: Big Brother/Big Sister, Child Welfare, Community Centers, Community Service Organizations, Day Care, Family Services, Homes, People with Disabilities, Recreation & Athletics, Senior Services, Shelters/Homelessness, United Funds/United Ways, YMCA/YWCA/YMHA/YWHA, Youth Organizations

Application Procedures

Initial Contact: The foundation has no formal grant application procedure or application form. Submit a brief outline of the proposed project and budget.
Deadlines: None.

Restrictions

Does not support individuals.

Foundation Officials

Irving E. Rogers, III: trustee
Irving E. Rogers, Jr.: trustee PRIM CORP EMPL president, publisher, treasurer, general manager: Eagle-Tribune Publishing Co.
Jacqueline H. Rogers: trustee
Stephen Hitchcock Rogers: trustee B Flushing, NY 1930. ED Princeton University BA (1952); Columbia University MA (1956); Harvard University MDA (1962).

Grants Analysis

Disclosure Period: calendar year ending 2000
Total Grants: $905,887*
Number of Grants: 72
Average Grant: $6,421*
Highest Grant: $450,000
Typical Range: $1,000 to $10,000

*Note: Giving excludes United Way. Average grant amount excludes highest grant.

Recent Grants

Note: Grants derived from 1999 Form 990.

General

340,000	Merrimack College, North Andover, MA
50,000	Free Christian Church, Andover, MA
50,000	Free Christian Church, Andover, MA
38,000	Merrimack Valley United Way, Lawrence, MA
25,000	Free Christian Church, Andover, MA
25,000	Holy Family Hospital, Methuen, MA
25,000	Joseph N. Hermann Youth Center, Inc., North Andover, MA
25,000	Lawrence Boys and Girls Club, Lawrence, MA
25,000	St. Augustine's Parish, Andover, MA
25,000	St. Michael's Rectory, North Andover, MA

RUSSELL HILL ROGERS FUND FOR THE ARTS

Giving Contact

Jean Winchell, Managing Trustee
4040 Broadway, Suite 605
San Antonio, TX 78209
Phone: (210)826-8781

Description

Founded: 1986
EIN: 742403914
Organization Type: Private Foundation
Giving Locations: TX: Bexar County
Grant Types: General Support.

Financial Summary

Total Giving: $836,860 (2001); $762,835 (2000); $806,104 (1999)
Assets: $14,672,580 (2001); $16,576,203 (2000); $17,352,568 (1999)

Typical Recipients

Arts & Humanities: Arts Centers, Ballet, Community Arts, Dance, Ethnic & Folk Arts, Arts & Humanities-General, Libraries, Museums/Galleries, Music, Opera, Performing Arts, Public Broadcasting, Theater
Education: Arts/Humanities Education
International: Foreign Arts Organizations
Religion: Jewish Causes
Social Services: Community Centers

Application Procedures

Initial Contact: The foundation has no formal grant application procedure or application form.
Deadlines: None.

Restrictions

Grants are not made to individuals.

Additional Information

Supports creative and performing arts in the San Antonio metropolitan area.
Trust(s): Bank of America, N.A.

Foundation Officials

Frank P. Christian: mng trustee
Barbara S. Condos: mng trustee
Robert R. Linde: mng trustee
Allan G. Paterson, Jr.: mng trustee
Jean Rogers Winchell: mng trustee

Grants Analysis

Disclosure Period: calendar year ending 2001
Total Grants: $836,860
Number of Grants: 24

Average Grant: $23,619*
Highest Grant: $170,000
Typical Range: $15,000 to $50,000
*Note: Average grant figure excludes two highest grants ($270,000).

Recent Grants

Note: Grants derived from 2001 Form 990.

Library-Related

170,000	San Antonio Public Library Foundation, San Antonio, TX -- promotion of the arts

General

100,000	McNay Art Museum, San Antonio, TX -- promotion of the arts
85,000	Arts San Antonio, San Antonio, TX -- promotion of the arts
85,000	Lyric Opera of San Antonio, San Antonio, TX -- promotion of the arts
83,500	San Antonio Symphony, San Antonio, TX -- promotion of the arts
81,235	San Pedro Playhouse, San Antonio, TX -- promotion of the arts
45,000	KLRN - Public Television, San Antonio, TX -- promotion of the arts
25,000	San Antonio Chamber Music Society, San Antonio, TX -- promotion of the arts
20,000	Firelight Players, San Antonio, TX -- promotion of the arts
20,000	Tuesday Musical Club - Artist Series, San Antonio, TX -- promotion of the arts
15,000	Cactus Pear Music Festival, San Antonio, TX -- promotion of the arts

ROGOW BIRKEN FOUNDATION

Giving Contact

Gary Greenberg, President
c/o Birken Mfg.
3 Old Windsor Rd.
Bloomfield, CT 06002
Phone: (860)242-2211
Fax: (860)242-2749

Description

Founded: 1981
EIN: 061051591
Organization Type: Private Foundation
Giving Locations: NY: New York
Grant Types: General Support.

Donor Information

Founder: Louis B. Rogow

Financial Summary

Total Giving: $436,009 (2000); $373,480 (1999); $369,723 (1998)
Giving Analysis: Giving for 2000 includes: foundation scholarships ($78,009); 1999: foundation scholarships ($55,223) 1998: foundation scholarships ($76,503)
Assets: $3,700,136 (2000); $4,056,652 (1999); $3,807,998 (1998)
Gifts Received: $1,540,554 (1994); $8,807,407 (1993). Note: In fiscal 1994, contributions were received from the estate of Louis B. Rogow.

Typical Recipients

Arts & Humanities: Libraries, Opera
Civic & Public Affairs: Civic & Public Affairs-General
Education: Colleges & Universities, Education-General, Private Education (Precollege), Student Aid
Health: Arthritis, Cancer, Clinics/Medical Centers, Medical Research
International: Health Care/Hospitals, Missionary/Religious Activities

Religion: Jewish Causes, Religious Welfare
Social Services: Youth Organizations

Application Procedures

Initial Contact: The foundation requests applications be made in writing.
Deadlines: None.

Foundation Officials

Paul Bourdeau: secretary
Gary Greenberg: vice president
Sidney Greenberg: president
Bruce Rogow: executive vice president
Helen Rogow: vice president

Grants Analysis

Disclosure Period: calendar year ending 2000
Total Grants: $358,000*
Number of Grants: 30
Average Grant: $5,872*
Highest Grant: $187,700
Typical Range: $1,000 to $10,000
*Note: Giving excludes scholarships. Average grant figure excludes highest grant.

Recent Grants

Note: Grants derived from 1999 Form 990.

Library-Related
25,000	Broward Public Library Foundation, Ft. Lauderdale, FL

General
187,000	American Society for Technion
36,000	Jewish Federation
20,000	Renbrook School, West Hartford, CT
19,500	Boys Town Jerusalem, Washington, DC
8,700	Packer Collegiate Institution, Brooklyn, NY
5,141	Bryant College, Smithfield, RI
4,000	Carnegie Mellon University, Pittsburgh, PA
3,000	Eckerd College, St. Petersburg, FL
3,000	University of Connecticut, Storrs, CT
3,000	University of Connecticut, Storrs, CT

FELIX AND ELIZABETH ROHATYN FOUNDATION

Giving Contact

Felix G. Rohatyn, President & Director
c/o Lazard, Freres & Co.
30 Rockefeller Plaza
New York, NY 10020
Phone: (212)750-0666

Description

Founded: 1968
EIN: 237015644
Organization Type: Private Foundation
Giving Locations: DC; NY: New York metropolitan area; TX; WY
Grant Types: Emergency, General Support, Multiyear/Continuing Support.

Donor Information

Founder: Felix G. Rohatyn

Financial Summary

Total Giving: $2,447,221 (2001); $2,189,339 (2000); $2,091,434 (1999)
Assets: $8,403,323 (2001); $9,873,601 (2000); $8,859,619 (1999)
Gifts Received: $1,000,000 (2001); $2,000,000 (2000); $2,000,000 (1999). Note: In 2001, contributions were received from Felix G. Rohatyn ($1,000,000). In 2000, contributions were received from Elizabeth F. Rohatyn. In 1999, contributions were received from Felix G. Rohatyn ($700,000) and

Elizabeth F. Rohatyn ($1,300,000). In 1998, contributions were received from Felix G. Rohatyn ($967,112) and Elizabeth F. Rohatyn ($510,000).

Typical Recipients

Arts & Humanities: Arts Associations & Councils, Arts Centers, Arts Funds, Arts Outreach, Ballet, Community Arts, Dance, Historic Preservation, History & Archaeology, Libraries, Literary Arts, Museums/Galleries, Music, Opera, Public Broadcasting, Theater, Visual Arts
Civic & Public Affairs: Botanical Gardens/Parks, Civic & Public Affairs-General, Municipalities/Towns, Public Policy, Urban & Community Affairs, Women's Affairs
Education: Colleges & Universities, Continuing Education, Education Funds, Education Reform, Elementary Education (Private), Faculty Development, Education-General, International Exchange, Literacy, Medical Education, Minority Education, Private Education (Precollege), Public Education (Precollege), Secondary Education (Private), Special Education, Student Aid
Environment: Environment-General, Resource Conservation
Health: Cancer, Emergency/Ambulance Services, Eyes/Blindness, Hospitals, Medical Research, Single-Disease Health Associations, Transplant Networks/Donor Banks
International: Foreign Arts Organizations, Health Care/Hospitals, Human Rights, International Organizations, International Relations, International Relief Efforts, Missionary/Religious Activities
Religion: Churches, Jewish Causes, Religious Organizations, Religious Welfare
Science: Scientific Centers & Institutes
Social Services: Big Brother/Big Sister, Child Welfare, Community Centers, Community Service Organizations, Family Services, People with Disabilities, Senior Services, Shelters/Homelessness, Youth Organizations

Application Procedures

Initial Contact: Send a brief letter of inquiry.
Application Requirements: a description of organization.
Deadlines: None.

Foundation Officials

Vivien Stiles Duffy: executive director
Melvin L. Heinemen: secretary, treasurer, director
Elizabeth Rohatyn: vice president, director
Felix George Rohatyn: president, director B Vienna, Austria 1928. ED Middlebury College BS (1948). PRIM CORP EMPL partner: Lazard Freres & Co. CORP AFFIL director: General Instrument; director: Pfizer Co.
Nicholas Rohatyn: secretary, treasurer, director

Grants Analysis

Disclosure Period: calendar year ending 2001
Total Grants: $2,447,221
Number of Grants: 132
Average Grant: $7,033*
Highest Grant: $700,000
Typical Range: $1,000 to $10,000
*Note: Average grant figure excludes five highest grants ($1,518,884).

Recent Grants

Note: Grants derived from 2001 Form 990.

Library-Related
100,000	New York Public Library, New York, NY
75,000	New York Public Library, New York, NY

General
700,000	Carnegie Hall Society, New York, NY
443,884	Teaching Matters, New York, NY
200,000	Memorial Sloan-Kettering Cancer Center, New York, NY

85,834	Lenox Hill Neighborhood House, New York, NY
50,000	Center for Strategic and International Studies, Washington, DC
50,000	Drawing Center, New York, NY
50,000	Nature Conservancy of Wyoming, Lander, WY
50,000	Progressive Policy Institute, Washington, DC
50,000	University of Texas at Dallas, Dallas, TX
40,000	American Jewish Historical Society, New York, NY

ROLLINS-LUETKEMEYER FOUNDATION

Giving Contact

Robert F. Wilson, Treasurer & Foundation Manager
105 W. Chesapeake Avenue
Suite 109
Towson, MD 21204-4710
Phone: (410)296-2948
Fax: (410)337-2682

Description

Founded: 1961
EIN: 526041536
Organization Type: Private Foundation
Giving Locations: MD: Baltimore metropolitan area
Grant Types: General Support.

Donor Information

Founder: the late Mary S. Rollins

Financial Summary

Total Giving: $3,098,182 (2001); $3,061,600 (2000); $2,303,833 (1998)
Assets: $62,125,046 (2001); $61,693,992 (2000); $57,207,672 (1998)
Gifts Received: $65,381 (2001); $180,097 (2000); $12,577,633 (1998). Note: In 2001 and 2000, contributions were received fromv John A. Luetkemeyer, Jr. In 1998, contributions were received from John A. Luetremeyer, Sr.($5,287,225); John A. Luetkemeyer, Jr. Charitable remainder trust ($4,284,440); estate of Anne A. Luetkemeyer ($3,005,968).

Typical Recipients

Arts & Humanities: Arts Centers, Arts Institutes, Community Arts, Arts & Humanities-General, History & Archaeology, Libraries, Museums/Galleries, Music, Theater
Civic & Public Affairs: Botanical Gardens/Parks, Community Foundations, Civic & Public Affairs-General, Housing, Law & Justice, Parades/Festivals, Safety, Urban & Community Affairs
Education: Colleges & Universities, Education Funds, Environmental Education, Education-General, Private Education (Precollege), Public Education (Precollege), Religious Education, Student Aid
Environment: Environment-General, Resource Conservation
Health: Clinics/Medical Centers, Emergency/Ambulance Services, Hospitals, Medical Research, Mental Health, Multiple Sclerosis, Preventive Medicine/Wellness Organizations, Preventive Medicine/Wellness Organizations
Religion: Churches, Jewish Causes, Seminaries
Science: Scientific Centers & Institutes
Social Services: Child Abuse, Community Service Organizations, Family Services, Food/Clothing Distribution, Homes, People with Disabilities, Recreation & Athletics, Scouts, Special Olympics, United Funds/United Ways

Application Procedures

Initial Contact: Send a brief letter of inquiry.
Application Requirements: Include a description of organization, amount requested, purpose of funds sought, and proof of tax-exempt status.
Deadlines: None.

Restrictions

Does not support individuals.

Foundation Officials

Richard E. Levine: secretary
Anne A. Luetkemeyer: secretary, director
John A. Luetkemeyer, Jr.: president
Anne L. Stone: vice president
James D. Stone: director
Robert F. Wilson: treasurer

Grants Analysis

Disclosure Period: calendar year ending 2001
Total Grants: $3,098,182
Number of Grants: 35
Average Grant: $56,912*
Highest Grant: $1,163,182
Lowest Grant: $3,500
Typical Range: $10,000 to $100,000
*Note: Average grant figure excludes highest grant.

Recent Grants

Note: Grants derived from 2001 Form 990.

General

1,163,182	McDonogh School, Owings Mills, MD
550,000	Lawrenceville School, Lawrenceville, NJ
260,000	Williams College, Hanover, NH
100,000	Garrison Forest School, Owings Mills, MD
75,000	Ladew Topiary Gardens, Monkton, MD
60,000	Maryland Historical Society, Baltimore, MD
51,000	Irvine Nature Center, Baltimore, MD
50,000	Baltimore Chesapeake Bay Outward Bound Program, Baltimore, MD
50,000	Baltimore Museum of Art, Baltimore, MD
50,000	Brown Memorial Woodbrook Presbyterian Church, Baltimore, MD

ROSAMARY FOUNDATION

Giving Contact

Richard W. Freeman, Jr., Chairman
PO Box 13218
New Orleans, LA 70185-3218
Phone: (504)895-1984
Fax: (504)895-1988
Web: http://www.rosamary.org

Description

Founded: 1939
EIN: 726024696
Organization Type: Family Foundation
Giving Locations: LA: New Orleans
Grant Types: Capital, Challenge, Endowment, General Support, Matching, Multiyear/Continuing Support, Operating Expenses, Project, Seed Money.

Donor Information

Founder: The RosaMary Foundation was established in 1939, with funds donated by members of the Alfred Bird Freeman family. Alfred Bird Freeman (1881-1957) was chairman of the Louisiana Coca-Cola Bottling Company. The foundation was named after Mr. Freeman's daughters, Mrs. Rosa Keller and Mrs. Mary Ella Wisdom.

Financial Summary

Total Giving: $2,519,800 (2002 approx); $2,486,092 (2001); $2,526,414 (2000)
Giving Analysis: Giving for 2000 includes: foundation grants to United Way ($250,000)
Assets: $39,289,100 (2002 approx); $54,860,341 (2001); $54,860,341 (2000)
Gifts Received: $37,719 (1998)

Typical Recipients

Arts & Humanities: Arts Associations & Councils, Arts Centers, Arts Festivals, Arts Outreach, Ballet, Arts & Humanities-General, Historic Preservation, Libraries, Museums/Galleries, Music, Opera, Performing Arts, Public Broadcasting, Theater
Civic & Public Affairs: African American Affairs, Botanical Gardens/Parks, Community Foundations, Economic Development, Civic & Public Affairs-General, Housing, Philanthropic Organizations, Professional & Trade Associations, Public Policy, Safety, Urban & Community Affairs, Zoos/Aquariums
Education: Afterschool/Enrichment Programs, Arts/Humanities Education, Business Education, Colleges & Universities, Economic Education, Education Reform, Education-General, International Studies, Literacy, Minority Education, Private Education (Precollege), Public Education (Precollege), Science/Mathematics Education, Secondary Education (Private), Student Aid
Environment: Air/Water Quality, Environment-General
Health: AIDS/HIV, Clinics/Medical Centers, Eyes/Blindness, Health Organizations, Hospitals, Medical Research, Research/Studies Institutes, Transplant Networks/Donor Banks
International: Foreign Educational Institutions
Religion: Churches, Dioceses, Religion-General, Religious Organizations, Religious Welfare, Social/Policy Issues
Social Services: Animal Protection, At-Risk Youth, Big Brother/Big Sister, Camps, Child Welfare, Community Service Organizations, Crime Prevention, Day Care, Emergency Relief, Family Planning, Homes, People with Disabilities, Recreation & Athletics, Scouts, Shelters/Homelessness, Social Services-General, Special Olympics, United Funds/United Ways, YMCA/YWCA/YMHA/YWHA, Youth Organizations

Application Procedures

Initial Contact: Applicants should request an application form and guidelines, or download the necessary documents from the foundation's web site.
Application Requirements: Proposals should include a proposal narrative, including background on the organization, a description of the program for which funding is sought, and plans for program evaluation; completed Proposal Summary Sheet and a Status Certification Form (available from the foundation). The following attachments are required: financial information for the overall organization, including the organization's current and prior year operating budget and recently audited financial statement; financial information for the project/program (if applicable), including a project/program budget, list of staff members involved with their percentage of time to be spent on project, list of names and amounts requested of other funding sources, specific uses of the requested grant, and in-kind support; list of the organization's board of directors and their principal affiliations; criteria for board selection; one-paragraph resumes of key organizational staff including key project/program staff; name, address and telephone number of a person familiar with the organization, excluding a board member or employee; IRS determination letter indicating 501(c)(3) and 509(a) tax exempt status; most recent annual report, if available; and agency affiliation with federated funds or public agencies.

Deadlines: Deadlines for submitting proposals are February 1 and September 1. Applicants are encouraged to submit proposals early to receive appropriate consideration.
Review Process: The trustees meet twice a year, in the spring and in the fall to make funding decisions.
Notes: Interviews are conducted only at the initiation of the foundation. Videotapes are not accepted.

Restrictions

Organizations must be tax-exempt under IRS Code Section 501(c)(3) or be a governmental agency. Grants are not made to individuals. The foundation does not purchase tickets or participate in fund-raising events such as galas.

Additional Information

Publications: Guidelines

Foundation Officials

Adelaide Wisdom Benjamin: trustee B New Orleans, LA 1932. ED Hollins College (1950-1952); Newcomb College BA (1954); Tulane University JD (1956). NONPR AFFIL advisory board: Tulane Summer Lyric Theatre; instructor: Tulane University extension; trustee: Southeast Louisiana Girl Scouts Council; trustee: Newcomb Childrens Center; director: Public Radio WWNO; trustee: New Orleans Museum Art Fellows Forum; director: National Symphony Orchestra Washington; member: New Orleans Bar Association; trustee: Loyola University; member: Louisiana Bar Association; trustee: Louisiana Museum Foundation Board; member: American Bar Association; member: League Women Voters. CLUB AFFIL life member: Thomas Wolfe Society; member: Quarante Club; member: Sybarites Club; member: Le Debut des Jeunes Filles; member: New Orleans Town Gardeners Club; member: Junior League New Orleans; member: American Symphony Orchestra League; member: Debutante Club.
Andrew Benjamin: trustee
Richard W. Freeman, Jr.: chairman, trustee ED Tulane University (1960).
Tina Freeman: trustee B New Orleans, LA 1951. ED Art Center College BFA (1972). PRIM CORP EMPL president: Decatur Studio. NONPR AFFIL member: International Womens Forum; member: Society Photography Education; member: American Society Media Professionals; member: American Society Magazine Photographers; member: American Society Media Photographers.
Caroline Loughlin: trustee
Toni Myers: admin
Betty Wisdom: trustee
Carlos Zervigon: trustee
Mary K. Zervigon: trustee

Grants Analysis

Disclosure Period: calendar year ending 2001
Total Grants: $2,236,092*
Number of Grants: 56
Average Grant: $39,930
Highest Grant: $350,000
Lowest Grant: $500
Typical Range: $15,000 to $75,000
*Note: Giving excludes United Way.

Recent Grants

Note: Grants derived from 2002 Form 990.

General

500,000	New Orleans Museum of Art, New Orleans, LA -- for the Sydney and Walda Besthoff Sculpture Garden
400,000	Greater New Orleans Educational Television Foundation, New Orleans, LA -- for New Orleans Teleplex
50,000	Greater New Orleans Foundation, New Orleans, LA -- operating support
50,000	Louisiana Children's Museum, New Orleans, LA -- for Zoom Zone Exhibit
45,000	Neighborhood Housing Services, New

Orleans, LA -- for children's arts and cultural center

35,000	Louisiana Philharmonic Orchestra, New Orleans, LA -- support for 2002 season
30,000	Resources for Human Development, Philadelphia, PA -- for New Orleans Womanspace
26,000	New Orleans Museum of Art, New Orleans, LA -- for Educational Program for 2002-2003
25,000	Archbishop's Community Appeal, New Orleans, LA -- annual support
25,000	Greater New Orleans Foundation, New Orleans, LA -- for operating support

BILLY ROSE FOUNDATION

Giving Contact

Terri C. Mangino, Executive Director
805 Third Ave., 23rd Floor
New York, NY 10022
Phone: (212)407-7745
Fax: (212)407-7799

Description

Founded: 1958
EIN: 136165466
Organization Type: General Purpose Foundation
Giving Locations: NY: New York
Grant Types: General Support, Project.

Donor Information

Founder: Incorporated in 1958 by Billy Rose (d. 1966), whose interests included theatrical production, songwriting, the stock market, real estate investments, and art collecting. His activities in the stock market accounted for much of the fortune. His will provided for a bequest of more than $10 million to the foundation.

Financial Summary

Total Giving: $1,000,000 (2002 approx); $1,014,000 (2001); $1,022,000 (1998)
Assets: $13,231,942 (2001); $15,844,974 (1998); $13,323,340 (1997)
Gifts Received: $5,000 (1993)

Typical Recipients

Arts & Humanities: Arts Associations & Councils, Arts Centers, Arts Festivals, Arts Funds, Arts Institutes, Arts Outreach, Ballet, Dance, Ethnic & Folk Arts, Film & Video, Arts & Humanities-General, Historic Preservation, Libraries, Literary Arts, Museums/Galleries, Music, Opera, Performing Arts, Public Broadcasting, Theater, Visual Arts
Civic & Public Affairs: Botanical Gardens/Parks, Civic & Public Affairs-General, Philanthropic Organizations, Public Policy
Education: Arts/Humanities Education, Business Education, Colleges & Universities, Education Associations, Education Reform, Education-General, Legal Education, Student Aid
Environment: Environment-General
Health: Cancer, Clinics/Medical Centers, Health Organizations, Hospitals, Medical Rehabilitation, Medical Research, Nursing Services, Single-Disease Health Associations, Transplant Networks/Donor Banks
International: Foreign Arts Organizations, Missionary/Religious Activities
Religion: Churches, Religion-General, Jewish Causes, Religious Organizations, Religious Welfare
Social Services: Community Centers, Community Service Organizations, Family Planning, Family Services, People with Disabilities, YMCA/YWCA/YMHA/YWHA, Youth Organizations

Application Procedures

Initial Contact: Applications should be submitted in letter form.
Application Requirements: The letter should summarize the need for support and include the amount of the request. A copy of the IRS determination letter of tax-exempt status and any recent publicity articles also should be included.
Deadlines: None.

Restrictions

Grants are made only to organizations described in section 170(c) of the IRS code of 1954/1986: (501(c)3 designations only), and not to individuals.

Foundation Officials

James R. Cherry: chairman, treasurer, director
James R. Cherry, Jr.: vice president, assistant treasurer, director B New York, NY 1938. ED Harvard University (1959); New York University School of Law JD (1962). PRIM CORP EMPL associate general counsel: Philip Morris Management Corp. NONPR AFFIL member: American Bar Association.
Terri C. Mangino: executive director, assistant secretary
Edward J. Walsh, Jr.: secretary
John Wohlstetter: vice president, director

Grants Analysis

Disclosure Period: calendar year ending 2001
Total Grants: $1,014,000
Number of Grants: 74
Average Grant: $9,438*
Highest Grant: $325,000
Lowest Grant: $1,000
Typical Range: $2,500 to $25,000
*Note: Average grant figure excludes highest grant.

Recent Grants

Note: Grants derived from 2001 Form 990.

Library-Related

| 10,000 | Queens Borough Public Library, Queens, NY |

General

325,000	American Friends of Israel Museum, New York, NY
50,000	UFA Widow's and Children's Fund
35,000	National Symphony Orchestra, Washington, DC
25,000	American Theater Wing, New York, NY
25,000	Clarisse B. Kampel Foundation
25,000	Museum of Modern Art, New York, NY
25,000	National Foundation for Facial Reconstruction, New York, NY
25,000	Skin Cancer Foundation, New York, NY
20,000	Convent of the Sacred Heart, New York, NY
20,000	Fordham University, Tivoli, NY

ROSENBERG FOUNDATION

Giving Contact

Kirke P. Wilson, President, Secretary
47 Kearny Street, Suite 804
San Francisco, CA 94108
Phone: (415)421-6105
Fax: (415)421-0141
E-mail: rosenfdn@rosenbergfdn.org
Web: http://www.rosenbergfdn.org

Description

Founded: 1935
EIN: 941186182
Organization Type: General Purpose Foundation
Giving Locations: CA: grantss are made outside California to operate productions in California and to national organizations benefiting Californians
Grant Types: Project.

Donor Information

Founder: Established in 1936 with a bequest from Max L. Rosenberg , a native Californian and head of Rosenberg Brothers and Co., a San Francisco dried fruit firm. In 1969, the foundation received an additional bequest from the estate of Mrs. Charlotte S. Mack , one of the foundation's early directors.

Financial Summary

Total Giving: $2,876,411 (2000); $3,300,000 (1999 approx); $2,171,977 (1998)
Assets: $72,640,276 (2000); $64,000,000 (1999 approx); $65,212,139 (1998)
Gifts Received: $4,898 (1998); $44,000 (1997); $50,106 (1996). Note: In 1997 and 1998, contributions were received from the Ben Goldberger Trust.

Typical Recipients

Arts & Humanities: Libraries, Music
Civic & Public Affairs: African American Affairs, Asian American Affairs, Business/Free Enterprise, Civil Rights, Community Foundations, Economic Development, Economic Policy, Employment/Job Training, First Amendment Issues, Civic & Public Affairs-General, Hispanic Affairs, Housing, Law & Justice, Legal Aid, Nonprofit Management, Philanthropic Organizations, Professional & Trade Associations, Public Policy, Rural Affairs, Urban & Community Affairs, Women's Affairs
Education: Education-General, International Studies, Minority Education, Social Sciences Education
Environment: Environment-General
Health: Health Policy/Cost Containment
International: Human Rights, International Development, International Relief Efforts
Religion: Religious Welfare
Social Services: Child Welfare, Child Welfare, Community Service Organizations, Day Care, Emergency Relief, Family Services, Refugee Assistance, Senior Services, Social Services-General, United Funds/United Ways, Youth Organizations

Application Procedures

Initial Contact: Letters of inquiry describing the proposed project, the applying organization, and anticipated budget should be sent to the foundation. If the proposed project falls within the foundation's program priorities, a formal application will be requested.
Application Requirements: A formal application should include a narrative proposal indicating the problem to be addressed; the plan of the project and its activities and goals; names and qualifications of the staff; the lasting significance of the project; anticipated goals and proposed evaluation of the project; plan for disseminating results of the project; future plans for the project; an itemized budget indicating project cost; grant amount requested; other sources of support; length of time for which support is requested and estimated future budgets; and materials describing the organization such as history, experience, a copy o f IRS form indicating tax-exempt status, list of board members, and indication of the organization's status on affirmative action in reference to gender and minority groups.
Deadlines: None.
Review Process: After a formal application has been received by the foundation, a visit and interview will be arranged. There is generally a two or three month waiting period before the foundation reviews an application.

Restrictions

The Foundation's policies preclude grants to continue or expand projects started with funds from other sources. Grants are not given for scholarships, endowments, capital purposes, operating purposes, or matching gifts. Grants are not made to individuals, for fund-raising events, for construction or acquisition of property, for direct service programs, or for the operating expenses of ongoing programs. The Foundation makes grants to purchase equipment, produce films, or publish materials only when such grants are a necessary part of a larger project supported by the Foundation. The Foundation recommends applicants review grants listed on the website to get a sense of projects that receive funding.

Additional Information

Approved grants are paid in installments. Organizations receiving support are required to provide the foundation with periodic progress reports and itemized expenditure lists. The foundation expects unexpended funds to be returned.

Publications: Guidelines; Annual Report

Foundation Officials

Phyllis Cook: director NONPR AFFIL director: Jewish Community Federation San Francisco.

James M. Edgar: treasurer B New York, NY 1936. ED Cornell University BA (1959); Cornell University MBA (1960). PRIM CORP EMPL senior partner: Edgar, Dunn & Co. CORP AFFIL director: Associated Oregon Industries Service Corp. NONPR AFFIL member: San Francisco Planning and Urban Research Board; director: Tau Beta Pi; director: San Francisco Chamber of Commerce; director: California Society Certified Public Accountants; director: Harding Lawson Association Group; director: American Institute of Certified Public Accountants; member: Bay Area Council; director: Active San Francisco Mayor's Financial Advisory Committee. CLUB AFFIL Pacific-Union Club.

Robert F. Friedman: director

Charlene Harvey: director, vice chair

Shauna I. Henry: director

Bill Ong Hing: chair

Herma Hill Kay: director B Orangeburg, SC 1934. ED Southern Methodist University BA (1956); University of Chicago JD (1959). PRIM NONPR EMPL dean, professor: University of California, Berkeley. NONPR AFFIL director: Equal Rights Advocates California; member: Order Coif; member: California Bar Association; member: California Women Lawyers; member: Association American Law Schools; member: Bar U.S. Supreme Court; member: American Academy of Arts & Sciences; member council: American Law Institute.

Leslie L. Luttgens: director

Albert F. Moreno: director ED University of San Diego BA (1966); University of California at Berkeley JD (1970). PRIM CORP EMPL senior vice president, general counsel, secretary: Levi Strauss & Co. CORP AFFIL director: New Century Energies Inc.

S(amuel) Donley Ritchey, Jr.: director B Derry Township, PA 1933. ED San Diego State University BS (1955); San Diego State University MS (1963); Stanford University (1964). CORP AFFIL director: SBC Communications Inc.; director: Pacific Telesis Group; director: Sacramento Bee; director: Modesto Bee; director: Pacific Bell; director: McClatchy Co. Inc.; director: McClatchy Newspapers Inc.; partner: Alpine Partners; director: Fresno Bee. NONPR AFFIL advisory council: Stanford University Graduate School Business; director: Western Association Food Chains; member: Mexican-American Legal Defense & Education Fund; director: Sloan Alumni Advisor Board; director: De La Salle Institute; director, vice chairman industrial relations: Food Marketing Institute; chairman governing board: California Power Exchange.

Kirke P. Wilson: president, secretary

Grants Analysis

Disclosure Period: calendar year ending 2000

Total Grants: $2,876,411

Number of Grants: 70

Average Grant: $41,092

Highest Grant: $150,000

Typical Range: $10,000 to $60,000

Recent Grants

Note: Grants derived from 2000 Form 990.

General

150,000	National Immigration Law Center of the Legal Aid Foundation of Los Angeles, Los Angeles, CA -- for Immigration and Employment Rights Projects
150,000	Western Center on Law and Poverty, Los Angeles, CA -- for Monitoring and Analyzing California's Welfare-to-Work Polices
132,500	Employment Law Center of Legal Aid Society of San Francisco, San Francisco, CA -- Welfare Advocacy Project
127,500	National Center for Youth Law, San Francisco, CA -- Child Support Enforcement Project
125,000	National Women's Law Center, Washington, DC -- Child Support Enforcement Project
110,000	Farmworker Justice Fund, Washington, DC -- for Guestworker Project
100,000	Center for Law and Social Policy, Washington, DC -- Child Support Assurance Project
92,500	Public Counsel Center, Los Angeles, CA -- welfare reform/job training and vocational school monitoring project
90,000	Association for Children for Enforcement of Support, Toledo, OH -- California Child Support Enforcement Project
85,000	Mexican American Legal Defense and Educational Fund, Los Angeles, CA -- California Language Rights Program

LOUISE AND CLAUDE ROSENBERG, JR. FAMILY FOUNDATION

Giving Contact

Claude N. Rosenberg, Jr., Secretary
c/o Hughes Bookkeeping Service
1459 18th St., Suite 167
San Francisco, CA 94107
Phone: (415)824-1288

Description

Founded: 1986

EIN: 943031132

Organization Type: Private Foundation

Giving Locations: CA: San Francisco

Grant Types: General Support, Research.

Donor Information

Founder: Claude N. Rosenberg, Jr., Louise J. Rosenberg

Financial Summary

Total Giving: $1,729,800 (fiscal year ending October 31, 2000); $3,018,555 (fiscal 1999); $976,715 (fiscal 1996)

Assets: $36,206,968 (fiscal 2000); $36,651,031 (fiscal 1999); $23,880,619 (fiscal 1996)

Gifts Received: $1,352,260 (fiscal 1995); $1,780,227 (fiscal 1994); $1,200,050 (fiscal 1993). Note: In fiscal 1994, contributions were received from Claude and Louise Rosenberg, Jr. ($1,548,408) and the estate of Claude Rosenberg, Sr. ($231,819).

Typical Recipients

Arts & Humanities: Arts Appreciation, Arts Centers, Arts Festivals, Arts Outreach, Ballet, Dance, Ethnic & Folk Arts, Arts & Humanities-General, Libraries, Literary Arts, Museums/Galleries, Music, Opera, Performing Arts, Public Broadcasting, Theater, Visual Arts

Civic & Public Affairs: Botanical Gardens/Parks, Community Foundations, Economic Development, Civic & Public Affairs-General, Municipalities/Towns, Parades/Festivals, Philanthropic Organizations, Public Policy, Urban & Community Affairs, Women's Affairs, Zoos/Aquariums

Education: Afterschool/Enrichment Programs, Arts/Humanities Education, Business Education, Colleges & Universities, Continuing Education, Education Funds, Education Reform, Elementary Education (Public), Education-General, Literacy, Private Education (Precollege), Public Education (Precollege), Religious Education, School Volunteerism, Science/Mathematics Education, Secondary Education (Private), Secondary Education (Public), Student Aid

Environment: Air/Water Quality, Environment-General, Resource Conservation, Wildlife Protection

Health: Cancer, Clinics/Medical Centers, Diabetes, Eyes/Blindness, Geriatric Health, Health Organizations, Hospitals, Medical Rehabilitation, Medical Research, Multiple Sclerosis, Research/Studies Institutes, Single-Disease Health Associations

International: Foreign Educational Institutions, Human Rights, International Affairs, International Environmental Issues, International Peace & Security Issues, International Relations, Missionary/Religious Activities

Religion: Churches, Jewish Causes, Synagogues/Temples

Social Services: Camps, Child Welfare, Community Centers, Community Service Organizations, Crime Prevention, Family Services, Food/Clothing Distribution, People with Disabilities, Recreation & Athletics, United Funds/United Ways, Volunteer Services, Youth Organizations

Application Procedures

Initial Contact: The foundation has no formal grant application procedure or application form.

Deadlines: None.

Foundation Officials

John P. Levin, Jr.: director

Claude Newman Rosenberg, Jr.: secretary B San Francisco, CA 1928. ED Stanford University BA (1950); Stanford University MBA (1952). CORP AFFIL lecturer, member advisor counc: Grad Sch Business. NONPR AFFIL chairman advisory council: Stanford University School Business; trustee: University High School San Francisco; director: San Francisco Ballet Association; president: Stanford University Graduate School Business Alumni Association; director: Jewish Welfare Federation; director: Presbyterian Childrens Cancer Research Center; director: Jewish Community Center; member: Financial Analysts San Francisco; director: International Hospitality Center. CLUB AFFIL Concordia-Argonaut Club; Family Club; California Tennis Club.

Louise J. Rosenberg: president

Grants Analysis

Disclosure Period: fiscal year ending October 31, 2000

Total Grants: $1,729,800

Number of Grants: 54

Average Grant: $8,954*

Highest Grant: $500,000

Typical Range: $1,000 to $15,000

*Note: Average grant figure excludes six highest grants ($1,300,000).

Recent Grants

Note: Grants derived from 2000 Form 990.

General

500,000	Institute For Neurodegenerative Diseases, San Francisco, CA -- renovation and construction of laboratory
300,000	Partners for Democratic Change, San Francisco, CA
200,000	University of California San Francisco,

100,000	San Francisco, CA -- nonprofit endowed named scholarship
100,000	Conservation International, Washington, DC
100,000	Harvard Graduate School of Education, Cambridge, MA -- origins of human creativity project
100,000	United Way, San Francisco, CA -- San Francisco promise
50,000	Cazadero Performing Arts Camp, San Francisco, CA
50,000	The Hausen Center, Cambridge, MA
50,000	San Francisco Conservatory of Music, San Francisco, CA -- conservatory preparatory program
35,000	Columbia Park Boys and Girls Club, San Francisco, CA

HAROLD C. AND MARJORIE Q. ROSENBERRY TUSCARAWAS COUNTY FOUNDATION

Giving Contact

Larry Gibbs, Trust Officer
c/o Belmont National Bank
PO Box 249
St. Clairsville, OH 43950
Phone: (740)695-3323

Description

Founded: 1994
EIN: 341772635
Organization Type: Private Foundation
Giving Locations: OH: Tuscarawas County
Grant Types: General Support.

Financial Summary

Total Giving: $362,647 (2001); $353,949 (2000); $341,575 (1999)
Giving Analysis: Giving for 1998 includes: foundation grants to United Way ($12,500)
Assets: $7,371,757 (2001); $7,312,676 (2000); $7,307,997 (1999)
Gifts Received: $6,026,133 (1994)

Typical Recipients

Arts & Humanities: Community Arts, Historic Preservation, History & Archaeology, Libraries, Museums/Galleries, Music, Theater
Civic & Public Affairs: Botanical Gardens/Parks, Clubs, Civic & Public Affairs-General, Parades/Festivals, Rural Affairs, Safety, Urban & Community Affairs
Education: Arts/Humanities Education, Public Education (Precollege), School Volunteerism, Science/Mathematics Education, Secondary Education (Private), Secondary Education (Public)
Environment: Resource Conservation
Health: Children's Health/Hospitals, Emergency/Ambulance Services, Hospitals
Religion: Religious Welfare
Science: Observatories & Planetariums
Social Services: Big Brother/Big Sister, Community Centers, Community Service Organizations, People with Disabilities, Recreation & Athletics, Senior Services, Substance Abuse, United Funds/United Ways, YMCA/YWCA/YMHA/YWHA, Youth Organizations

Application Procedures

Initial Contact: Request application from the selection committee.
Deadlines: None.

Additional Information

Trust(s): Belmont National Bank

Foundation Officials

Larry Gibbs: trustee

Grants Analysis

Disclosure Period: calendar year ending 2001
Total Grants: $362,647
Number of Grants: 32
Average Grant: $11,333
Highest Grant: $35,255
Lowest Grant: $999
Typical Range: $5,000 to $20,000

Recent Grants

Note: Grants derived from 2000 Form 990.

Library-Related

35,000	Newcomerstown Public Library, Newcomerstown, OH -- elevator for new public library

General

35,000	Dover City Schools, Dover, OH -- improving athletic complexes at the middle school and Crater Stadium
26,120	Twin City Hospital, Dennison, OH -- materials to build phase one of the pediatric wellness center
25,000	Tuscarawas County YMCA, Dover, OH -- building expansion
20,000	City of New Philadelphia New Philadelphia Fire Department, New Philadelphia, OH -- equipping dive rescue and trench rescue team
15,000	Tuscarawas County Agricultural Society, Dover, OH -- construction of new restroom facility at the county fairgrounds
14,000	Harbor House, New Philadelphia, OH -- renovation of garage area to group counseling room
10,750	City of Dover, Dover, OH -- Dover Fire Department retrofitting engine one
10,000	Dennison Railroad Festival, Inc., Dennison, OH -- gazebo-amphitheater for downtown Dennison
10,000	Union Hospital, Dover, OH -- G.E. senographe DMR mammography X-ray system
10,000	Village of Baltic, Baltic, OH -- purchase Howell rescue system for fire department

IDA AND WILLIAM ROSENTHAL FOUNDATION

Giving Contact

Catherine C. Brawer, President & Director
67A E. 77th St.
New York, NY 10021-4335
Phone: (212)737-1011

Description

Founded: 1953
EIN: 136141274
Organization Type: Private Foundation
Giving Locations: NY: New York metropolitan area; Dominican Republic: ; support for projects in the Dominican Republic through national organizations.
Grant Types: Project, Scholarship, Seed Money.

Donor Information

Founder: the late Ida Rosenthal, the late William Rosenthal

Financial Summary

Total Giving: $119,405 (fiscal year ending August 31, 2000); $115,558 (fiscal 1999); $171,232 (fiscal 1998)
Giving Analysis: Giving for fiscal 1999 includes: foundation scholarships ($47,200); foundation ($68,358); fiscal 1998: foundation scholarships ($52,800) foundation ($118,432)
Assets: $4,306,964 (fiscal 2000); $4,152,646 (fiscal 1999); $3,674,776 (fiscal 1998)

Typical Recipients

Arts & Humanities: Arts Associations & Councils, Arts Centers, Arts Institutes, Dance, Historic Preservation, History & Archaeology, Libraries, Museums/Galleries, Music, Public Broadcasting, Theater
Civic & Public Affairs: Botanical Gardens/Parks, Civil Rights, Ethnic Organizations, Hispanic Affairs, Legal Aid, Public Policy, Women's Affairs
Education: Afterschool/Enrichment Programs, Arts/Humanities Education, Colleges & Universities, Education Funds, Minority Education, Preschool Education, Private Education (Precollege), Secondary Education (Public), Student Aid
Social Services: Day Care, Scouts

Application Procedures

Initial Contact: Send a brief letter of proposal with an a full proposal.
Application Requirements: Include a brief narrative history of the organization, including the scope of its current activities and the kind and size of the audience served; and explanation of how the proposed project meets the objectives of the organization; a list of board members; a list of government, corporate, and foundation support received over the past five years; recently audited financial statement; proof of tax-exempt status; the name, title, and resume of the person who will direct the project; and itemized budget showing how the rest of the project will be funded; and an agreement to provide the foundation with a self-evaluation of the project within three months of completion. completion.
Deadlines: None.

Restrictions

Does not support individuals or provide loans. The foundation no longer accepts applications from social service agencies.

Additional Information

Publications: Application Procedures

Foundation Officials

Catherine Coleman Brawer: president, director B New York, NY 1943. ED Sarah Lawrence College (1964); New York University (1966). CORP AFFIL director: Maidenform Inc.
Robert A. Brawer: vice president, director
Abraham Pascal Kanner: vice president B New York, NY 1911. ED New York University (1931); Harvard University (1933). PRIM CORP EMPL vice president, treasurer: Maidenform.
Steven N. Masket: assistant secretary
Ann Brownell Sloane: assistant treasurer

Grants Analysis

Disclosure Period: fiscal year ending August 31, 1999
Total Grants: $68,358*
Number of Grants: 15
Average Grant: $4,557
Highest Grant: $11,550
Typical Range: $1,000 to $10,000
***Note:** Giving excludes scholarships.

Recent Grants

Note: Grants derived from 2000 Form 990.

General

20,000	Katonah Museum of Art, Katonah, NY -- toward catalogues for exhibitions, including the catalogue for the exhibition Britain's Portable Empire
15,000	Independent Curators International, New York, NY -- in support of the catalogue for the exhibition Lee Krasner Palingenesis
15,000	Institute of Find Arts, New York University, New York, NY -- for the Ida and William Rosenthal Foundation Fellowship for one or more outstanding first-year students
15,000	University of Chicago, Chicago, IL -- for the Rosenthal Scholarship Fund in a support of a graduate student completing a dissertation in the Department of English
14,800	Music Conservatory of West Chester, White Plains, NY -- for the Instrumental and Choral Music Program at Community School 211 during the 2000-2001 school year
6,000	Boy Scouts of America - Northern New Jersey Chapter, Verona, NJ -- Restricted operating funds for Camp Lewis in Marcella, New Jersey
5,000	Plymoth Plantation, Plymouth, MA -- for the publication of the proceedings of the 1999 Annual Conference on Native American History
3,500	Sarah Lawrence College, Bronxville, NY -- toward the Theater Outreach Program, including the Oral History Video Project at Community School 211
3,200	Music Conservatory of West Chester, White Plains, NY -- partial scholarships for four female minority students with need
2,500	Ensemble Studio Theater, New York, NY -- toward audience development in connection with the production of the Shaneaqua Chronicles

LOIS AND RICHARD ROSENTHAL FOUNDATION

Giving Contact

Richard Rosenthal, Officer
1507 Dana Ave.
Cincinnati, OH 45207
Phone: (513)531-2222

Description

Founded: 1987
EIN: 311203666
Organization Type: Private Foundation
Giving Locations: OH: Cincinnati
Grant Types: General Support.

Financial Summary

Total Giving: $153,150 (2001); $2,043,833 (2000); $180,430 (1999)
Assets: $5,536,204 (2001); $5,671,338 (2000); $3,620,378 (1999)
Gifts Received: $4,097,898 (2000). Note: In 2000, contributions were received from Richard Rosenthal.

Typical Recipients

Arts & Humanities: Arts Centers, Arts Funds, Ballet, Libraries, Museums/Galleries, Performing Arts, Theater
Civic & Public Affairs: Botanical Gardens/Parks
International: International Relations
Religion: Religious Organizations

Social Services: Family Planning, Food/Clothing Distribution

Application Procedures

Initial Contact: Send a brief letter of inquiry.
Application Requirements: Include purpose of funds sought, budget, and date funds are needed.
Deadlines: None.

Foundation Officials

Jennie D. Berliant: trustee
Mark H. Berliantt: trustee
Toni Birckhead: trustee
David S. Rosenthal: trustee
Lois R. Rosenthal: trustee
Richard H. Rosenthal: trustee

Grants Analysis

Disclosure Period: calendar year ending 2001
Total Grants: $153,150
Number of Grants: 12
Average Grant: $12,763
Highest Grant: $50,000
Lowest Grant: $350
Typical Range: $1,000 to $30,000

Recent Grants

Note: Grants derived from 2001 Form 990.

Library-Related

15,000	Mercantile Library, Cincinnati, OH

General

50,000	Freestore and Food Bank, Cincinnati, OH
30,000	Cincinnati Playhouse in the Park, Cincinnati, OH
30,000	Cincinnati Playhouse in the Park, Cincinnati, OH
12,500	Contemporary Arts Center, Cincinnati, OH
10,000	Cincinnati Ballet, Cincinnati, OH
2,000	Contemporary Arts Center, Cincinnati, OH
2,000	Contemporary Arts Center, Cincinnati, OH
1,000	Cincinnati Parks Foundation, Cincinnati, OH
350	Cincinnati Ballet, Cincinnati, OH
250	PPSONK, Cincinnati, OH

ROSS FOUNDATION

Giving Contact

Hal Ross, Vice President
105 S. Broadway, Suite 740
Wichita, KS 67202-2009
Phone: (316)264-4981
Fax: (316)264-4981

Description

Founded: 1961
EIN: 486125814
Organization Type: Private Foundation
Giving Locations: CA; CT; FL; KS; NE; OH
Grant Types: Emergency, Endowment, General Support, Research, Scholarship.

Donor Information

Founder: the late G. Murray Ross

Financial Summary

Total Giving: $264,960 (2001); $234,865 (2000); $253,763 (1999)
Giving Analysis: Giving for 2001 includes: foundation scholarships ($100,000)
Assets: $5,915,076 (2001); $5,543,725 (2000); $5,431,086 (1999)
Gifts Received: $1,168,584 (1997)

Typical Recipients

Arts & Humanities: Arts Associations & Councils, Arts Centers, Ballet, Community Arts, Arts & Humanities-General, Historic Preservation, History & Archaeology, Libraries, Museums/Galleries, Music
Civic & Public Affairs: Civic & Public Affairs-General, Law & Justice, Parades/Festivals, Zoos/Aquariums
Education: Colleges & Universities, Education Associations, Education-General, Public Education (Precollege), Religious Education
Environment: Environment-General
Health: Cancer, Clinics/Medical Centers
Religion: Churches, Religion-General, Religious Organizations, Religious Welfare
Social Services: Animal Protection, Big Brother/Big Sister, Child Welfare, Community Service Organizations, People with Disabilities, Youth Organizations

Application Procedures

Initial Contact: send a brief letter of inquiry
Application Requirements: a description of organization, amount requested, purpose of funds sought, proof of tax-exempt status
Deadlines: None.

Restrictions

Does not support individuals, political or lobbying groups, organizations outside operating areas

Additional Information

The foundation has no formal grant application procedure or application form.

Foundation Officials

Norman W. Jeter: president
Hal Ross: vice president
Susan Ross Sheets: secretary, treasurer

Grants Analysis

Disclosure Period: calendar year ending 2001
Total Grants: $164,960*
Number of Grants: 30
Average Grant: $2,999*
Highest Grant: $75,000
Typical Range: $1,000 to $5,000
*Note: Giving excludes scholarships. Average grant excludes highest grant.

Recent Grants

Note: Grants derived from 2001 Form 990.

Library-Related

5,000	Hays Public Library Trust, Hays, KS

General

100,000	Ottawa University, Ottawa, KS
75,000	Kansas State University Endowment Association, Manhattan, KS
10,000	Communities in School, Fernandina, FL
10,000	New Leash on Life, A, Bethel, CT
8,955	Oxford-Sumner County Historical Museum
5,000	Big Brothers and Big Sisters, LaGrange, KY
5,000	Chase County Courthouse, Imperial, NE
5,000	First Presbyterian Church, Hays, KS
5,000	Kansas State Historical Society, Topeka, KS
5,000	Victory in the Valley, Wichita, KS

WILL ROSS MEMORIAL FOUNDATION

Giving Contact

Mary Ann W. LaBahn, Vice President & Treasurer
PO Box 17814
Milwaukee, WI 53217
Phone: (414)765-2800

Description

Founded: 1963
EIN: 396044673
Organization Type: Private Foundation
Giving Locations: WI: Milwaukee metropolitan area
Grant Types: Capital, General Support, Project.

Financial Summary

Total Giving: $320,500 (2000); $351,500 (1999); $339,500 (1998). Note: 1997 Giving includes United Way ($75,000).
Giving Analysis: Giving for 2000 includes: foundation grants to United Way ($75,000); 1999: foundation grants to United Way ($75,000); 1998: foundation grants to United Way ($75,000) foundation grants to United Way ($264,500)
Assets: $3,215,191 (2000); $3,641,162 (1999); $3,691,524 (1998).
Gifts Received: $42,588 (1997). Note: In 1997, contributions were received from the estate of Pearl L. Baldwin.

Typical Recipients

Arts & Humanities: Arts Centers, Arts Funds, Arts Institutes, Community Arts, Dance, Libraries, Literary Arts, Museums/Galleries, Music, Opera, Performing Arts, Theater
Civic & Public Affairs: Botanical Gardens/Parks, Economic Development, Employment/Job Training, Civic & Public Affairs-General, Hispanic Affairs, Housing, Municipalities/Towns, Urban & Community Affairs, Zoos/Aquariums
Education: Arts/Humanities Education, Colleges & Universities, Continuing Education, Health & Physical Education, Literacy, Medical Education, Minority Education, Private Education (Precollege), Public Education (Precollege), Student Aid
Environment: Environment-General, Resource Conservation
Health: AIDS/HIV, Alzheimers Disease, Cancer, Children's Health/Hospitals, Clinics/Medical Centers, Eyes/Blindness, Geriatric Health, Health Organizations, Hospitals, Medical Rehabilitation, Mental Health, Nursing Services, Public Health, Respiratory, Transplant Networks/Donor Banks
Science: Scientific Centers & Institutes
Social Services: At-Risk Youth, Child Welfare, Community Centers, Community Service Organizations, Family Planning, Food/Clothing Distribution, Homes, People with Disabilities, Shelters/Homelessness, United Funds/United Ways, Veterans, Youth Organizations

Application Procedures

Initial Contact: The foundation has no formal grant application procedure or application form. Send Send a brief letter of inquiry and a full proposal. include amount requested, purpose of funds sought, a description of organization, recently audited financial statement, and pts.
Deadlines: December.
Notes: Applications are considered at quarterly meetings.

Restrictions

Does not support individuals, religious organizations for sectarian purposes, political or lobbying groups, or organizations outside operating areas.

Foundation Officials

John D. Bryson, Jr.: president
David Lucas Kinnamon: secretary, director B Madison, WI 1941. ED University of Wisconsin BA (1963); University of Wisconsin JD (1966). PRIM CORP EMPL partner: Quarles & Brady. CORP AFFIL member: Wisconsin Acad Scis Arts & Letters; member: Phi Beta Kappa; member: Phi Beta Phi; member: Estate Counsel Forum; member: Order Coif. NONPR AFFIL director: Riveredge Nature Center; member: WI Bar Association; trustee: Nature Conservancy Wisconsin Chapter; director: Park People Milwaukee

County; director: Ice Park & Trail Foundation; member: Milwaukee Bar Association; fellow: American College Trust & Estate Counsel; member: American Bar Association. CLUB AFFIL University Club.
Mary Ann LaBahn: vice president, treasurer

Grants Analysis

Disclosure Period: calendar year ending 2000
Total Grants: $245,500*
Number of Grants: 42
Average Grant: $5,845
Highest Grant: $28,000
Typical Range: $1,000 to $10,000
*Note: Giving excludes United Way.

Recent Grants

Note: Grants derived from 2001 Form 990.

General

75,000	United Way of Greater Milwaukee, Milwaukee, WI
70,000	UPAF, Milwaukee, WI
34,000	Milwaukee Art Museum, Milwaukee, WI
25,000	Medical College of Wisconsin Cancer Center, Milwaukee, WI
15,000	Planned Parenthood, Milwaukee, WI
10,000	Blood Center Research Foundation, Milwaukee, WI
9,000	Milwaukee Public Museum, Milwaukee, WI
6,000	Harambee Community School, Milwaukee, WI
6,000	Milwaukee Institute of Art and Design, Milwaukee, WI
5,500	Riveredge Nature Center, Newburg, WI

ROSS PRODUCTS DIVISION, ABBOTT LABORATORIES

Company Headquarters

625 Cleveland Ave.
Columbus, OH 43215

Company Description

Former Name: Ross Laboratories.
Employees: 500
SIC(s): 2000 Food & Kindred Products, 2023 Dry, Condensed & Evaporated Dairy Products.

Nonmonetary Support

Type: Donated Equipment; Donated Products

Giving Contact

Contributions Committee
625 Cleveland Ave.
Columbus, OH 43215
Phone: (614)624-7677
Note: ALT: (800)986-8510

Description

Organization Type: Corporate Giving Program
Giving Locations: headquarters and operating communities.
Grant Types: General Support, Multiyear/Continuing Support, Operating Expenses, Project, Research, Scholarship.

Financial Summary

Total Giving: Company does not disclose contributions figures.

Typical Recipients

Arts & Humanities: Arts Associations & Councils, Ballet, Community Arts, Arts & Humanities-General, Libraries, Museums/Galleries, Opera, Theater
Civic & Public Affairs: Chambers of Commerce, Civil Rights, Civic & Public Affairs-General, Inner-City

Development, Philanthropic Organizations, Urban & Community Affairs, Zoos/Aquariums
Education: Colleges & Universities, Education Associations, Education Funds, Education-General
Health: AIDS/HIV, Alzheimers Disease, Cancer, Children's Health/Hospitals, Health-General, Health Organizations, Hospitals, Hospitals (University Affiliated), Medical Research, Nutrition, Prenatal Health Issues
Science: Science-General
Social Services: Camps, Child Welfare, Community Centers, Community Service Organizations, Domestic Violence, Emergency Relief, Family Services, Food/Clothing Distribution, Homes, Senior Services, Shelters/Homelessness, Social Services-General, United Funds/United Ways, Youth Organizations

Application Procedures

Initial Contact: Send a brief letter of inquiry.
Application Requirements: a description of organization, amount requested, purpose of funds sought, and proof of tax-exempt status.

Restrictions

Does not support individuals and religious organizations for sectarian purposes.

Corporate Officials

Joyce Amundson: president, chief executive officer Ross Products Division PRIM CORP EMPL president, chief executive officer Ross Products Division: Abbott Laboratories.

Grants Analysis

Typical Range: $50 to $1,000

WILLIAM AND ALICE ROSSI FOUNDATION

Giving Contact

William Rossi, President, Treasurer
26 Gaynor Avenue
Nesconset, NY 11767
Phone: (631)361-7433

Description

Founded: 1999
EIN: 113416821
Organization Type: Private Foundation
Grant Types: General Support.

Financial Summary

Total Giving: $11,650 (fiscal year ending September 30, 2001); $11,250 (fiscal 2000); $51,050 (fiscal 1999)
Giving Analysis: Giving for fiscal 2001 includes: foundation grants to United Way ($2,500)
Assets: $291,075 (fiscal 2001); $511,693 (fiscal 2000); $646,119 (fiscal 1999)
Gifts Received: $364,108 (fiscal 1999). Note: In fiscal 1999, contributions were received from William Rossi.

Typical Recipients

Arts & Humanities: Libraries, Music
Civic & Public Affairs: Philanthropic Organizations
Education: Colleges & Universities
Health: Cancer, Children's Health/Hospitals, Emergency/Ambulance Services
Religion: Churches
Social Services: Youth Organizations

Foundation Officials

William Gardner: vice president
Alice Rossi: vice president, secretary
William Rossi: president, treasurer

Grants Analysis

Disclosure Period: fiscal year ending September 30, 2001
Total Grants: $9,150*
Number of Grants: 8
Average Grant: $593*
Highest Grant: $5,000
Lowest Grant: $200
Typical Range: $250 to $1,000
***Note:** Giving excludes United Way. Average grant figure excludes highest grant.

Recent Grants

Note: Grants derived from fiscal 2000 Form 990.

Library-Related

2,500 Smithtown Elementary Library Fund

General

2,500	St. Patrick Church, Terre Haute, IN
2,000	St. Patrick Church, Terre Haute, IN
1,000	Buttonwood Foundation, New York, NY
1,000	North Shore University Foundation, Manhasset, NY
1,000	Philharmonic Center for the Arts, Naples, FL
500	Make A Wish Foundation of Metro New York, New York, NY
250	American Cancer Society
250	Suffolk County Chapter American Red Cross
250	Youth Haven, Inc., Naples, FL

JUDITH ROTHSCHILD FOUNDATION

Giving Contact

Elizabeth Slater, Vice President, Grant Program
1110 Park Ave.
New York, NY 10128
Phone: (212)831-4114
Fax: (212)831-6222
Web: http://fdncenter.org/grantmaker/rothschild

Description

Founded: 1993
EIN: 133736320
Organization Type: Private Foundation
Giving Locations: NY: New York
Grant Types: General Support.

Donor Information

Founder: Established in 1993 by the late Judith Rothschild.

Financial Summary

Total Giving: $270,000 (2003); $250,000 (2002 approx); $8,027,058 (2001)
Assets: $28,099,647 (2001); $35,508,736 (1999); $36,156,173 (1998)
Gifts Received: $248,200 (2001); $345,400 (1999); $40,456,223 (1994). Note: In 2001, contributions were received from Boris Kerdimun ($107,700), Elaine Lustig Cohen ($6,900) and Varvara Rodchenko ($133,600). In 1994, contributions were received from the estate of Judith Rothschild.

Typical Recipients

Arts & Humanities: Arts Associations & Councils, Arts Centers, Arts Funds, Arts Outreach, Ethnic & Folk Arts, Arts & Humanities-General, Historic Preservation, Literary Arts, Museums/Galleries, Visual Arts
Civic & Public Affairs: Civic & Public Affairs-General
Education: Arts/Humanities Education, Colleges & Universities
Health: Cancer
International: Foreign Arts Organizations, Foreign Educational Institutions
Social Services: Community Service Organizations

Application Procedures

Initial Contact: Request application guidelines.
Deadlines: Applications are accepted between April 15 and September 15.

Additional Information

Publications: Application Guidelines

Foundation Officials

Harvey S. Shipley Miller: trustee

Grants Analysis

Disclosure Period: calendar year ending 2003
Total Grants: $270,000
Number of Grants: 22
Average Grant: $12,272
Highest Grant: $30,000
Lowest Grant: $5,000
Typical Range: $5,000 to $20,000

Recent Grants

Note: Grants derived from 2001 Form 990.

General

6,500,000	American Swedish Heritage Museum
1,056,000	Philadelphia Museum of Art, Philadelphia, PA -- artwork
75,775	Philadelphia Museum of Art, Philadelphia, PA -- Women's Committee
25,000	Addison Gallery of American Art, Andover, MA
25,000	Albright Knox Art Gallery, Buffalo, NY
20,000	El Paso Museum of Art, El Paso, TX
17,950	Museum of Modern Art, New York, NY
16,100	Museum of American Folk Art, New York, NY
15,912	American Museum in Britain United Kingdom
15,400	Phillips Collection, Washington, DC

ROUSE CO.

Company Headquarters

10400 Little Patuxent Parkway
Columbia, MD 21044
Web: http://www.therousecompany.com

Company Description

Founded: 1939
Ticker: RSE
Exchange: NYSE
Operating Revenue: US$1.221 billion (2002)
Employees: 3396 (2002)
SIC(s): 1531 Operative Builders, 6512 Nonresidential Building Operators.

Operating Locations

Rouse Co. (AR--Fayetteville; CA--Santa Monica; CO--Colorado Springs, Denver; DC--Washington; FL--Jacksonville, Miami, Tallahassee; GA--Atlanta, Augusta, Decatur; IA--Ames, Keokuk, Marshalltown, Muscatine, West Burlington; KY--Louisville; LA--Gretna, New Orleans, Shreveport; MD--Baltimore, Easton, Glen Burnie, Parkville; MA--Springfield; MI--Taylor; MN--Minnetonka; MO--St. Louis; NJ--Burlington, Cherry Hill, Paramus, Voorhees, Woodbridge; NY--New York, Staten Island; OH--Dayton; PA--Exton, Greensburg, Philadelphia, Plymouth Meeting; TX--Austin, Galveston, Houston, San Antonio; WA--Seattle; WI--Milwaukee)

Nonmonetary Support

Value: $50,000 (1999); $50,000 (1998)
Type: Donated Equipment; In-kind Services; Loaned Employees
Volunteer Programs: The company encourages its employees to volunteer time to nonprofit groups and organizations through its Volunteer Contributions Program. Through this program, the company provides

grants of up to $1,000 to nonprofit organizations at which the Rouse employees volunteer. Volunteer grants are awarded in the fields of health, education, human services, arts and humanities, community affairs, museums, conservation and preservation.

Rouse Co. Foundation

Giving Contact

Margaret P. Mauro, Executive Director
Rouse Co. Foundation
10275 Little Patuxent Pkwy.
Columbia, MD 21044
Phone: (410)992-6000
Fax: (410)992-6363
Web: http://therousecompany.com/whoweare/community/index.html

Description

Founded: 1967
EIN: 526056273
Organization Type: Corporate Foundation
Giving Locations: MD: Central Maryland
Grant Types: Capital, Challenge, Department, Employee Matching Gifts, Endowment, General Support, Matching, Multiyear/Continuing Support, Operating Expenses, Project, Scholarship, Seed Money.
Note: The company matches employee gifts to accredited colleges and universities, elementary, middle and high schools, both public and private.

Donor Information

Founder: Rouse Co.

Financial Summary

Total Giving: $1,312,756 (2001); $1,374,576 (2000); $2,552,368 (1999 approx). Note: Contributes through corporate direct giving program and foundation.
Giving Analysis: Giving for 2000 includes: foundation grants to United Way ($160,000); foundation ($1,214,576); 1999: nonmonetary support ($50,000); foundation grants to United Way ($125,000); foundation ($877,368); corporate direct giving (approx $1,500,000); 1998: foundation scholarships ($30,000); foundation grants to United Way ($120,000); foundation ($819,202).
Assets: $4,031,326 (2001); $4,394,502 (2000); $4,862,722 (1999)
Gifts Received: $1,000,000 (2001); $925,000 (2000); $350,000 (1999). Note: Contributions were received from The Hughes Corp.

Typical Recipients

Arts & Humanities: Arts Associations & Councils, Arts Centers, Arts Festivals, Arts Funds, Arts Institutes, Arts Outreach, Community Arts, Dance, Ethnic & Folk Arts, Film & Video, Arts & Humanities-General, Historic Preservation, History & Archaeology, Libraries, Literary Arts, Museums/Galleries, Music, Opera, Performing Arts, Public Broadcasting, Theater, Visual Arts
Civic & Public Affairs: Botanical Gardens/Parks, Community Foundations, Economic Development, Employment/Job Training, Civic & Public Affairs-General, Housing, Public Policy, Urban & Community Affairs, Zoos/Aquariums
Education: Arts/Humanities Education, Business Education, Colleges & Universities, Colleges & Universities, Community & Junior Colleges, Education Funds, Education Reform, Education-General, Legal Education, Minority Education, Public Education (Precollege), Social Sciences Education, Student Aid
Environment: Environment-General, Research, Resource Conservation
Health: Cancer, Clinics/Medical Centers, Hospices, Hospitals, Hospitals (University Affiliated), Prenatal Health Issues, Preventive Medicine/Wellness Organizations, Single-Disease Health Associations
International: International Relations
Religion: Ministries, Religious Welfare

Science: Scientific Centers & Institutes
Social Services: Big Brother/Big Sister, Camps, Child Welfare, Community Centers, Community Service Organizations, Crime Prevention, Domestic Violence, Family Services, Food/Clothing Distribution, Food/Clothing Distribution, Homes, People with Disabilities, Recreation & Athletics, Scouts, Senior Services, Sexual Abuse, Shelters/Homelessness, Substance Abuse, United Funds/United Ways, Volunteer Services, YMCA/YWCA/YMHA/YWHA, Youth Organizations

Application Procedures

Initial Contact: Make a preliminary inquiry by telephone or in writing.
Application Requirements: If foundation feels that the request for funding falls within foundation guidelines, a written request may be submitted. Include amount requested and intended use; a description of organization, its history and activities; the name(s) and qualifications of the person(s) who will administer the grant; a copy of the most recent tax-exemption ruling statement from the IRS. If the request is for a specific project or program, provide goals and objectives for project or program; population to be served; schedule for implementation; and method of evaluating its effectiveness. Requests for $2,500 or more should also include a list of the organization's board of directors and officers, a copy of the most recent audited financial statement, and an organizational or project budget for the current year showing expenses and income by source.
Deadlines: None.

Restrictions

Does not support religious programs, endowments, individuals, or political advocacy. Organizations must be tax-exempt under 501(c)(3) or 509(a). Grants are primarily provided to organizations located in the Central Maryland area.

Additional Information

Publications: Informational Brochure (including Application Guidelines)

Corporate Officials

Anthony W. Deering: chairman, chief executive officer chief financial officer B 1945. ED Drexel University BS (1969); University of Pennsylvania MBA (1971). PRIM CORP EMPL chairman, chief executive officer: Rouse Co. CORP AFFIL president: Village Cross Keys Inc.; president: White Marsh Mall Inc.; president: Rouse-Tampa Inc.; treasurer: Salem Mall Inc.; president: Rouse-Oakwood Shopping Center; chief financial officer: Rouse Philadelphia Inc.; president: Rouse-Milwaukee Inc.; president: Rouse Missouri Holding Inc.; chief financial officer: Rouse Management Service Corp.; chairman: Rouse Marshalltown Center; senior vice president: Rouse Co. Saint Louis Inc.; senior vice president: Rouse Co. Texas Inc.; president: Rouse Co. Oregon Inc.; officer: Rouse Co. Owings Mills Inc.; chief financial officer: Rouse Co. Ohio Inc.; treasurer: Rouse Co. Massachusetts Inc.; president: Rouse Co. Michigan Inc.; president: Rouse Co. Florida Inc.; president: Rouse Co. Illinois Inc.; director: Plymouth Meeting Mall Inc.; president: Rouse Co. Colorado Inc.; senior vice president: North Star Mall Inc.; president: Paramus Park Inc.; senior vice president: Hanendale Mall Inc.; president: Louisville Shopping Center; chairman: Exton Square Inc.; treasurer: Governor's Square Inc.; president: Columbia Mall Inc.; chief financial officer: Columbia Management Inc.; chief financial officer: Charlottetown Inc.
Jeffrey H. Donahue: senior vice president, chief financial officer ED University of Pennsylvania MBA; Cornell University (1966). PRIM CORP EMPL senior vice president, chief financial officer: Rouse Co. CORP AFFIL vice president: Village Cross Keys Inc.; chief financial officer: Woodbridge Center Inc.; chief financial officer: Rouse-Tampa Inc.; treasurer: Salem

Mall Inc.; chairman: Rouse Marshalltown Center; treasurer: Rouse Philadelphia Inc.; chief financial officer: Rouse Hotel Management Inc.; chief financial officer: Rouse Management Service Corp.; chief financial officer: Rouse Co. New Jersey Inc.; trustee: Rouse Co. Owings Mills Inc.; trustee: North Star Mall Inc.; vice president: Rouse Co. Massachusetts Inc.; chief financial officer: Exton Square Inc.; vice president: Governor's Square Inc.; vice president: Charlottetown Inc.

Foundation Officials

Anthony W. Deering: chairman, president, trustee (see above)
Margaret Mauro: executive director, secretary, trustee
Douglas A. McGregor: trustee B 1942. ED Rutgers University BA (1963); Case Western Reserve University JD (1967). PRIM CORP EMPL executive vice president development & Cope: The Rouse Co. CORP AFFIL president: Rouse-Teachers Properties Inc.; executive vice president: Woodbridge Center Inc.; executive vice president: North Star Mall Inc.; executive vice president: Rouse Co. Owings Mills Inc.

Grants Analysis

Disclosure Period: calendar year ending 2001
Total Grants: $1,202,756*
Number of Grants: 292
Average Grant: $4,119
Highest Grant: $100,000
Typical Range: $250 to $10,000
*Note: Giving excludes United Way.

Recent Grants

Note: Grants derived from 2001 Form 990.

General

135,000	United Way of Central Maryland, Baltimore, MD
100,000	Enterprise Foundation, New York, NY
80,000	Peabody Institute, Baltimore, MD
40,000	Center Stage, Baltimore, MD
40,000	Columbia Foundation, Columbia, MD
30,000	Port Discover, The Children's Museum, Baltimore, MD
30,000	Walker Art Museum, Baltimore, MD
25,000	New Song Community Learning Center, Baltimore, MD
25,000	New Song Community Learning Center, Baltimore, MD
25,000	Uniformed Firefighters Association Widows and Children's Fund, New York, NY

MAY MITCHELL ROYAL FOUNDATION

Giving Contact

Richard O. Hartley, Chairman, Grants Committee
11735 Quail Village Way
Naples, FL 34119-8802
Phone: (941)598-4148
Fax: (941)514-1834

Alternate Contact

PO Box 75000, MC 3302
Detroit, MI 48275-3302
Phone: (517)839-2285

Description

Founded: 1981
EIN: 382387140
Organization Type: Private Foundation
Giving Locations: FL; HI; MI
Grant Types: General Support, Research, Scholarship.

Donor Information

Founder: May Mitchell Royal Trust Foundation

Financial Summary

Total Giving: $149,179 (fiscal year ending September 30, 2001); $141,547 (fiscal 2000); $144,100 (fiscal 1999)
Giving Analysis: Giving for fiscal 2001 includes: foundation scholarships ($10,000); fiscal 2000: foundation scholarships ($10,000) fiscal 1998: foundation scholarships ($8,000)
Assets: $2,797,842 (fiscal 2001); $3,021,702 (fiscal 2000); $2,966,971 (fiscal 1999)

Typical Recipients

Arts & Humanities: Libraries, Public Broadcasting
Civic & Public Affairs: Clubs
Education: Colleges & Universities, Medical Education, Student Aid
Health: Cancer, Children's Health/Hospitals, Clinics/Medical Centers, Diabetes, Emergency/Ambulance Services, Eyes/Blindness, Health Organizations, Heart, Hospices, Hospitals, Medical Research, Mental Health, Public Health, Single-Disease Health Associations, Transplant Networks/Donor Banks
Religion: Churches
Social Services: Child Welfare, Community Service Organizations, Domestic Violence, Family Services, People with Disabilities, Substance Abuse, Veterans, Youth Organizations

Application Procedures

Initial Contact: Send a brief letter of inquiry.
Application Requirements: Include proof of tax-exempt status, financial information, and a list of officers and trustees.
Deadlines: May 30.

Restrictions

Preference is given to research and treatment of cancer, vision and heart diseases, hospital equipment, and nurse training.

Additional Information

Trust(s): Comerica Bank

Foundation Officials

Tyrone W. Gillespie: grant comm
Richard O. Hartley: chairman grant comm
Susan J. Hartley: grant committee
Michael Kennerly: grant committee
Ruth C. Lishman: grant comm

Grants Analysis

Disclosure Period: fiscal year ending September 30, 2001
Total Grants: $139,179*
Number of Grants: 14
Average Grant: $7,363*
Highest Grant: $25,823
Lowest Grant: $2,000
Typical Range: $2,500 to $15,000
*Note: Giving excludes scholarships. Average grant figure excludes two highest grants ($50,823).

Recent Grants

Note: Grants derived from fiscal 2000 Form 990.

General

23,578	St. Joseph Mercy Hospital, Pontiac, MI -- cardiac monitoring equipment
19,816	Shriners Hospital for Crippled, Honolulu, HI -- purchase surgical equipment's
16,000	American Red Cross Indian River, Vero Beach, FL -- for new Ford Van
15,000	Kresge Eye Institute, Detroit, MI -- eye diseases research
10,000	Hawaii Lions Foundation, Honolulu, HI -- support corneal transplant program
10,000	Mid-Michigan Medical Center, Midland,

	MI -- for Michigan breast cancer program
10,000	Saginaw Valley State University, University Center, MI -- college of nursing scholarships
8,500	American Red Cross, Midland, MI -- purchase 6 computers and monitors
8,500	Leader Dogs for the Blind, Rochester, MI -- purchase autoclaves for sterilizing equipment
5,000	DARE, Midland, MI -- support drug awareness

ROYAL & SUNALLIANCE USA, INC.

Company Headquarters
PO Box 1000
Charlotte, NC 28201
Web: http://www.royalsunalliance-usa.com

Company Description
Founded: 1978
Former Name: Royal Insurance Co. of America;
Acquired: Orion Capital Companies (1999).
Revenue: US$3.051 billion (2002)
Employees: 5,700 (2002)
SIC(s): 6331 Fire, Marine & Casualty Insurance, 6719 Holding Companies Nec.
Parent Company: Royal & SunAlliance Insurance Group Plc, 30 Berkeley Sq., London, United Kingdom

Operating Locations
American & Foreign Insurance Co. (NC--Charlotte); Commericial Marketing Systems (NC--Charlotte); Globe Indemnity Co. (NC--Charlotte); Milbank Insurance Co. (SD--Milbank); Newark Insurance Co. (NC--Charlotte); Phoenix Assurance of New York (NY--New York); Royal Indemnity Co. (NC--Charlotte); Royal Life Insurance Co. of America (NY--New York; NC--Charlotte); Royal & SunAlliance U.S.A., Inc. (KS; ME; MD; MA; NH; NJ; NY; NC--Charlotte; PA; TX; UT; VA); Safeguard Insurance Co. (NC--Charlotte); Sun Alliance U.S.A. (NY--New York); Sun Insurance Co. of New York (NY--New York)

Nonmonetary Support
Type: Cause-related Marketing & Promotion; Donated Equipment; In-kind Services
Volunteer Programs: Company actively encourages employee volunteerism, including an Education Week. Special consideration is given to requests for funding if an employee is involved in the organization in a meaningful voluntary capacity.

Royal & SunAlliance Insurance Foundation, Inc.

Giving Contact
Fred E. Dabney, Executive Director
Royal & SunAlliance Insurance Foundation
9300 Arrowpoint Blvd.
Charlotte, NC 28201-1000
Phone: (704)522-2056
Fax: (704)522-2055

Description
Founded: 1989
EIN: 561658178
Organization Type: Corporate Foundation
Giving Locations: areas where producers, employees, and customers reside.
Grant Types: Employee Matching Gifts, General Support, Multiyear/Continuing Support.

Note: Employee matching gift ratio: 1 to 1 up to $1,000 for gifts to higher education only.

Donor Information
Founder: Established in 1989 by Royal Insurance.

Financial Summary
Total Giving: $1,039,630 (2001); $847,955 (2000); $693,745 (1999). Note: Contributes through corporate direct giving program and foundation.
Giving Analysis: Giving for 2001 includes: foundation matching gifts ($32,287); foundation grants to United Way ($174,560); foundation ($832,783); 2000: foundation matching gifts ($44,232); foundation grants to United Way ($146,025); foundation ($657,698); 1999: foundation matching gifts ($43,519); foundation grants to United Way ($168,492); foundation ($481,734);
Assets: $896,543 (2001); $647,556 (2000); $466,593 (1999)
Gifts Received: $1,365,000 (2001); $1,000,000 (2000); $844,670 (1999). Note: In 2001, contributions were received from Royal Group Inc., Security Insurance Co. of Hartford, and Royal Indemnity Co.

Typical Recipients
Arts & Humanities: Arts Appreciation, Arts Associations & Councils, Arts Centers, Community Arts, Dance, Ethnic & Folk Arts, Arts & Humanities-General, Historic Preservation, Libraries, Museums/Galleries, Music, Opera, Performing Arts, Public Broadcasting, Theater, Visual Arts
Civic & Public Affairs: African American Affairs, Business/Free Enterprise, Civil Rights, Economic Development, Civic & Public Affairs-General, Housing, Philanthropic Organizations, Public Policy, Safety
Education: Business Education, Colleges & Universities, Community & Junior Colleges, Continuing Education, Education Funds, Education Reform, Elementary Education (Private), Education-General, Literacy, Minority Education, Preschool Education, Private Education (Precollege), Public Education (Precollege), Science/Mathematics Education, Special Education, Student Aid
Environment: Environment-General
Health: Adolescent Health Issues, AIDS/HIV, Cancer, Children's Health/Hospitals, Emergency/Ambulance Services, Health-General, Geriatric Health, Health Funds, Health Organizations, Heart, Home-Care Services, Hospices, Hospitals, Mental Health, Public Health, Single-Disease Health Associations
Religion: Ministries, Religious Welfare
Science: Science Museums
Social Services: Child Abuse, Child Welfare, Community Centers, Community Service Organizations, Counseling, Crime Prevention, Emergency Relief, Family Services, Homes, People with Disabilities, Recreation & Athletics, Refugee Assistance, Senior Services, Shelters/Homelessness, Social Services-General, Special Olympics, Substance Abuse, United Funds/United Ways, Volunteer Services, YMCA/YWCA/YMHA/YWHA, Youth Organizations

Application Procedures
Initial Contact: Write for application form, then submit written proposal.
Application Requirements: Include completed application; what makes Royal & SunAlliance an appropriate donor; list of current board of directors; schedule of board meetings; budgetary information; sources of income, with amounts; proof of IRS tax-exemption; and current financial statement.
Deadlines: None.
Evaluative Criteria: Priority is given to education, health, and human service organizations, and to geographic areas where the largest numbers of the company's producers, customers, and employees reside; also favors requests from organizations when an employee is involved in a meaningful voluntary capacity.

Restrictions
Does not support individuals, religious organizations for sectarian purposes, political or lobbying groups, organizations outside operating areas, fraternal organizations, medical research, veterans' organizations, broadcast fundraising, or endowments. With few exceptions, does not support operating funds of United Way member agencies nor other Foundations which support various organizations.
No funding may be secured through telephone solicitation or direct mail marketing. Contributions also will not be made to an organization solely because a company officer or employee is involved in fundraising efforts. fundraising efforts.

Additional Information
Royal & Sun Alliance was created in 1996 with the merger of two of Britain's biggest insurance companies, Royal Insurance and Sun Alliance.
The majority of contributions stay within the state of North Carolina and are decided upon at corporate headquarters. Field offices across the United States have autonomy to make smaller discretionary donations. At the headquarters, the board of directors meets quarterly to vote on all expenditures of over $2,500.
Capital funding requests are presented for consideration once per year at the annual meeting of the board of directors. Priority is given to industry-related projects.
Publications: Application Guidelines; Brochure

Grants Analysis
Disclosure Period: calendar year ending 2001
Total Grants: $832,783*
Number of Grants: 94
Average Grant: $8,859
Highest Grant: $125,000
Lowest Grant: $100
Typical Range: $1,000 to $25,000
*Note: Giving excludes matching gifts; United Way.

Recent Grants
Note: Grants derived from 2001 Form 990.

General

125,000	American Red Cross, Charlotte, NC -- Budget-Convention
100,000	Spencer Education Foundation, Inc. -- Broderick/Tighe
50,000	American Red Cross, Charlotte, NC -- Unbudgeted-9-11 Disaster Relief Fund
50,000	Charlotte Symphony Orchestra, Charlotte, NC -- Budget Pops in Park-McLaughlin
50,000	New York Fire 9-11 Disaster Relief Fund, Washington, DC -- Unbudgeted-9-11 Disaster Relief Fund
42,600	United Way Central Carolinas, Charlotte, NC -- Budget
42,500	United Way Central Carolinas, Charlotte, NC -- Budget
42,500	United Way Central Carolinas, Charlotte, NC -- Budget
42,500	United Way Central Carolinas, Charlotte, NC -- Budget
40,000	Arts and Science Council, Charlotte, NC -- Budget-Dabney

CELE H. AND WILLIAM B. RUBIN FAMILY FUND

Giving Contact
Ellen R. Gordon, President
32 Monadnock Road
Wellesley Hills, MA 02481-1338
Phone: (781)235-4751
Fax: (781)235-4692

Description

Founded: 1943
EIN: 116026235
Organization Type: Family Foundation
Giving Locations: nationally.
Grant Types: General Support.

Donor Information

Founder: Incorporated in 1943 by members of the Joseph Rubin family, the Sweets Co. of America, Inc., Joseph Rubin and Sons, Inc., Tootsie Roll Industries, Inc., and others.

Financial Summary

Total Giving: $2,709,536 (2000); $1,887,350 (1998); $1,314,365 (1997)
Giving Analysis: Giving for 2000 includes: foundation grants to United Way ($6,000); 1998: foundation grants to United Way ($6,000) 1997: foundation grants to United Way ($6,000)
Assets: $64,266,926 (2000); $54,530,079 (1998); $46,537,887 (1997)
Gifts Received: $1,100,000 (2000); $1,000,000 (1998); $900,000 (1997). Note: Contributions were received from Tootsie Roll Industries, Inc.

Typical Recipients

Arts & Humanities: Arts Funds, Ballet, Historic Preservation, History & Archaeology, Libraries, Museums/Galleries, Music, Performing Arts
Civic & Public Affairs: Botanical Gardens/Parks, Economic Development, Civic & Public Affairs-General, Hispanic Affairs, Housing, Law & Justice, Municipalities/Towns, Philanthropic Organizations, Public Policy, Urban & Community Affairs, Women's Affairs, Zoos/Aquariums
Education: Business Education, Colleges & Universities, Community & Junior Colleges, Continuing Education, Education Funds, Engineering/Technological Education, Education-General, Legal Education, Medical Education, Preschool Education, Private Education (Precollege), Public Education (Precollege), Secondary Education (Private)
Environment: Air/Water Quality, Environment-General, Research, Resource Conservation, Wildlife Protection
Health: Alzheimers Disease, Arthritis, Cancer, Clinics/Medical Centers, Diabetes, Health Organizations, Heart, Hospices, Hospitals, Kidney, Medical Rehabilitation, Medical Research, Multiple Sclerosis, Prenatal Health Issues, Public Health, Research/Studies Institutes, Single-Disease Health Associations
International: Health Care/Hospitals, Human Rights, International Affairs, International Relief Efforts, Missionary/Religious Activities
Religion: Jewish Causes, Religious Organizations, Religious Welfare
Science: Observatories & Planetariums, Science Museums, Scientific Centers & Institutes
Social Services: Child Welfare, Community Service Organizations, Community Service Organizations, Delinquency & Criminal Rehabilitation, Family Services, Food/Clothing Distribution, Homes, People with Disabilities, Recreation & Athletics, Refugee Assistance, Shelters/Homelessness, United Funds/United Ways, YMCA/YWCA/YMHA/YWHA, Youth Organizations

Application Procedures

Initial Contact: The foundation has no formal grant application procedure or application form.
Deadlines: None.

Foundation Officials

Ellen Rubin Gordon: president, director B New York, NY 1931. ED Vassar College (1948-1950); Brandeis University BA (1965); Harvard University (1968). PRIM CORP EMPL president, chief operating officer, director: Tootsie Roll Industries. CORP AFFIL director: Bestfoods; vice president, director: HDI Investment Corp. NONPR AFFIL member advisory council:

Stanford University Graduate School Business; member council division biological science: University Chicago Pritzker School Medicine; member: Radcliffe College Partner; member advisory council: Northwestern University Kellogg Graduate School Management; active: Presidents Export Council; trustee, member: Northwestern University Associates; member, board fellows: Harvard University Medical School; member, director: National Confectioners Association; member university resources & overseers committee: Harvard University.
Melvin Jay Gordon: vice president, director B Boston, MA November 26, 1919. ED Harvard University BA (1941); Harvard University MBA (1943). PRIM CORP EMPL chairman, chief executive officer, director: Tootsie Roll Industries. CORP AFFIL president, director: HDI Investment Corp.

Grants Analysis

Disclosure Period: calendar year ending 2000
Total Grants: $2,703,536*
Number of Grants: 76
Average Grant: $12,180*
Highest Grant: $1,790,000
Lowest Grant: $100
Typical Range: $100 to $5,000 and $10,000 to $80,000
*Note: Giving excludes United Way. Average grant figure excludes highest grant.

Recent Grants

Note: Grants derived from 2000 Form 990.

Library-Related
5,000	Loyola Academy, Wilmette, IL
1,000	Wellesley Free Library, Wellesley, MA

General
1,790,000	Old Colony Charitable Fund, Boston, MA
500,000	Harvard University Medical School, Boston, MA
100,000	Harvard College Fund, The, Cambridge, MA
68,000	Combined Jewish Philanthropies of Greater Boston, Boston, MA
50,000	Brigham and Women's Hospital, Boston, MA
30,000	Kellogg Graduate School of Management, Evanston, IL
25,000	Juvenile Diabetes Foundation, Chicago, IL
15,000	Food Allergy Institute, New York, NY
10,000	Brigham Medical Center, Boston, MA
10,000	Greater Chicago Food Depository, Chicago, IL

SAMUEL RUBIN FOUNDATION

Giving Contact

Cora Weiss, President
777 United Nations Plaza, Suite 10D
New York, NY 10017
Phone: (212)697-8945
Fax: (212)682-0886
Web: http://www.samuelrubinfoundation.org

Description

Founded: 1949
EIN: 136164671
Organization Type: General Purpose Foundation
Giving Locations: internationally; nationally.
Grant Types: General Support, Project.

Donor Information

Founder: Incorporated in New York in 1949 from funds donated by the late Samuel Rubin , the founder of Faberge. He was also a founder of the New York

University Bellevue Medical Center and the American Symphony Orchestra.

Financial Summary

Total Giving: $1,253,935 (fiscal year ending June 30, 2000); $1,276,699 (fiscal 1999); $1,169,806 (fiscal 1998)
Assets: $15,680,280 (fiscal 2000); $16,455,186 (fiscal 1999); $15,628,511 (fiscal 1998)
Gifts Received: $660 (fiscal 1994); $30,000 (fiscal 1993)

Typical Recipients

Arts & Humanities: Arts Associations & Councils, Arts Centers, Arts Funds, Community Arts, Film & Video, Arts & Humanities-General, History & Archaeology, Libraries, Literary Arts, Museums/Galleries, Music, Performing Arts, Public Broadcasting, Theater
Civic & Public Affairs: Asian American Affairs, Botanical Gardens/Parks, Business/Free Enterprise, Civil Rights, Community Foundations, Economic Development, Economic Policy, Employment/Job Training, Civic & Public Affairs-General, Housing, Law & Justice, Nonprofit Management, Parades/Festivals, Philanthropic Organizations, Public Policy, Safety, Urban & Community Affairs, Women's Affairs
Education: Arts/Humanities Education, Colleges & Universities, Colleges & Universities, Community & Junior Colleges, Education Associations, Education Funds, Education Reform, Education-General, Health & Physical Education, International Studies, Legal Education, Public Education (Precollege), Science/Mathematics Education, Social Sciences Education
Environment: Air/Water Quality, Environment-General
Health: Health-General, Hospitals, Medical Research
International: Foreign Educational Institutions, International-General, Health Care/Hospitals, Human Rights, International Affairs, International Development, International Environmental Issues, International Organizations, International Peace & Security Issues, International Relations, International Relief Efforts, Missionary/Religious Activities
Religion: Churches, Jewish Causes, Religious Welfare
Science: Scientific Centers & Institutes
Social Services: Child Welfare, Community Service Organizations, Crime Prevention, Domestic Violence, Food/Clothing Distribution, Homes, Shelters/Homelessness, Veterans, YMCA/YWCA/YMHA/YWHA, Youth Organizations

Application Procedures

Initial Contact: The foundation has no formal application procedures. Applicants should submit a proposal in writing.
Application Requirements: A proposal must describe in detail the organization and the project. Include a budget and tax-exempt status letter.
Deadlines: January 7, May 1, and September 1.
Review Process: The board of directors meets three times a year. However, limited funds and recurring commitments restrict the board's grantmaking ability.

Restrictions

The foundation does not award grants for building funds, scholarships, endowments, or to individuals.

Additional Information

Applications sent by facsimile transmission or e-mail will not be given consideration.
Publications: Program Policy Statement

Foundation Officials

Charles L. Mandelstam: secretary B Brookline, MA 1927. ED Harvard College BA (1949); Yale College LLB (1952). PRIM CORP EMPL partner: Dornbush, Mensch, Mandelstam & Silverman New York City. NONPR AFFIL member: Phi Beta Kappa; member, director: Societe d'Exploitation Agricole Rhodienne;

member: Association Bar New York City; counselor: North Salem New York Open Land Foundation.

Cora Weiss: president B New York, NY 1934. ED University of Wisconsin BA (1956); Hunter College (1956-1958). NONPR AFFIL director: Peace Action; director: US-NIS Women's Consortium; vice president: International Peace Bureau; director: Downtown Community TV; director: Interlegal USA.

Daniel Weiss: director

Judy Weiss: vice president

Peter Weiss: treasurer B Vienna, Austria 1925. ED Saint John's College AB (1949); Yale University JD (1952). CORP AFFIL counsel: The Chanel Co. Ltd. NONPR AFFIL co-president: International Association Lawyers Against Nuclear Arms; chairman: Lawyers Committee Nuclear Policy; vice president: Center Constitutional Rights.

Tamara Weiss: director

Grants Analysis

Disclosure Period: fiscal year ending June 30, 2000
Total Grants: $1,238,943
Number of Grants: 108
Average Grant: $9,985*
Highest Grant: $170,543
Typical Range: $1,000 to $10,000
*Note: Average grant figure excludes highest grant.

Recent Grants

Note: Grants derived from fiscal 2000 Form 990.

General

170,543	Transitional Institute
75,000	Public Media, New York, NY
51,500	Institute for Policy Studies, Washington, DC
50,000	Center for Constitutional Rights, New York, NY
50,000	Hague Appeal for Peace
40,000	Lawyers Committee on Nuclear Policy, New York, NY
35,000	Africa Fund, New York, NY
30,000	Americans for Peace Now, Washington, DC
25,000	A.J. Muste Memorial Institute, New York, NY -- for International Peace Bureau
25,000	Downtown Community Television Center, New York, NY

HELENA RUBINSTEIN FOUNDATION

Giving Contact

Diane Moss, President & Chief Executive Officer
477 Madison Avenue, 7th Floor
New York, NY 10022-5802
Phone: (212)750-7310
Fax: (212)750-9798
Web: http://www.fdncenter.org/grantmaker/rubinstein

Description

Founded: 1953
EIN: 136102666
Organization Type: General Purpose Foundation
Giving Locations: NY: New York
Grant Types: Fellowship, General Support, Operating Expenses, Project, Research, Scholarship.

Donor Information

Founder: Established in 1953 by businesswoman Helena Rubinstein, who was born in Poland in 1871. At the age of twenty she began her cosmetics business with one product, a face cream. Her cosmetics empire expanded to London in 1902, to Paris in 1906, and to New York in 1912. During her lifetime she accumulated significant collections of African sculptures, modern paintings and sculptures, Oriental and

Oceanic art, and Egyptian antiques. The foundation was a major beneficiary of her legacy when she died in 1965.

Financial Summary

Total Giving: $2,598,150 (fiscal year ending May 31, 2001); $2,530,023 (fiscal 2000); $2,062,742 (fiscal 1999)
Assets: $40,474,526 (fiscal 2001); $41,794,981 (fiscal 2000); $39,513,686 (fiscal 1999)

Typical Recipients

Arts & Humanities: Arts Associations & Councils, Arts Centers, Arts Festivals, Arts Funds, Arts Outreach, Ballet, Dance, Libraries, Museums/Galleries, Music, Opera, Performing Arts, Public Broadcasting, Theater, Visual Arts

Civic & Public Affairs: Economic Development, Employment/Job Training, Housing, Municipalities/Towns, Public Policy, Urban & Community Affairs, Women's Affairs

Education: Arts/Humanities Education, Colleges & Universities, Education Reform, Faculty Development, Health & Physical Education, Legal Education, Literacy, Medical Education, Minority Education, Preschool Education, Science/Mathematics Education, Social Sciences Education, Special Education, Student Aid, Vocational & Technical Education

Environment: Air/Water Quality, Resource Conservation

Health: AIDS/HIV, Alzheimers Disease, Cancer, Children's Health/Hospitals, Clinics/Medical Centers, Eyes/Blindness, Geriatric Health, Health Organizations, Hospitals, Medical Rehabilitation, Medical Research, Medical Training, Nursing Services, Prenatal Health Issues, Preventive Medicine/Wellness Organizations, Public Health, Single-Disease Health Associations

International: Foreign Arts Organizations, Health Care/Hospitals, Human Rights, International Affairs, International Peace & Security Issues, International Relief Efforts

Religion: Jewish Causes

Science: Science Museums, Scientific Centers & Institutes

Social Services: At-Risk Youth, Child Welfare, Community Centers, Community Service Organizations, Counseling, Day Care, Family Planning, Family Services, Recreation & Athletics, Senior Services, Shelters/Homelessness, Substance Abuse, United Funds/United Ways, YMCA/YWCA/YMHA/YWHA, Youth Organizations

Application Procedures

Initial Contact: The foundation does not publish an application form, but the New York Common Application Form may be used. Organizations seeking funding should submit a brief letter rather than make telephone inquiries.

Application Requirements: Letters of inquiry should include an outline of project; goals; budget; amount requested; other funding sources; a description of the organization and its current budget.

Deadlines: None.

Review Process: Every proposal and inquiry is acknowledged by letter. Additional information may be requested if the proposal is of interest to the foundation. A meeting or site visit may be arranged by the foundation. Proposals are acted upon by the board of directors, which meets semi-annually, in May and November. Grants are not renewed automatically, but are considered on the basis of evaluation of reports, site visits, priorities, and the availability of funds.

Restrictions

Grants are made only to tax-exempt non-profit organizations. Generally, they are for a one-year period. Scholarship and fellowship grants are made directly to institutions. General operating grants are made, but the foundation prefers to support specific projects

or programs. The foundation does not support individuals or film or video projects. Grants are rarely made to support endowments or capital campaigns. The foundation does not make loans, or provide emergency funds. Grants are typically restricted to organizations in New York City.

Additional Information

Grantees are expected to submit interim reports within six to eight months after receipt of a grant award. A final report is also recommended at the end of the grant period.

Publications: Biennial report

Foundation Officials

Deborah DeCotis: director

Robert S. Friedman: secretary, treasurer

Gertrude Geraldine Michelson: chairman B Jamestown, NY 1925. ED Pennsylvania State University BA (1945); Columbia University LLB (1947). CORP AFFIL director, member executive committee: RH Macy & Co. Inc.; director: National Broadcasting Co. Inc.; director: Goodyear Tire & Rubber Co.; director: Federal Insurance Co.; director: General Electric Co. NONPR AFFIL board overseers: Teachers Insurance Annuity Association American College Ret Equities Fund; member: Women's Forum; vice chairman, member: New York City Partnership; life trustee: Spelman College; chairman emeritus board trustee: Columbia University; member, executive committee, vice chairman, board director: New York City Chamber of Commerce; governor: American Stock Exchange Inc. CLUB AFFIL Economic Club.

Diane Moss: president, chief executive officer

Louis E. Slesin: director

Suzanne Slesin: director

Grants Analysis

Disclosure Period: fiscal year ending May 31, 2001
Total Grants: $2,598,150
Number of Grants: 169
Average Grant: $15,374
Highest Grant: $150,000
Lowest Grant: $1,000
Typical Range: $10,000 to $25,000
Note: Grants analysis provided by foundation.

Recent Grants

Note: Grants derived from 2000 Form 990.

Library-Related

200,000	New York Public Library, New York, NY

General

150,000	Thirteen/WNET, New York, NY
150,000	United Jewish Appeal Federation of Jewish Philanthropies of New York, Inc., New York, NY
100,000	Whitney Museum of American Art, New York, NY
50,000	Museum of Modern Art, New York, NY
50,000	New York Foundation of the Arts, New York, NY
50,000	Police Athletic League, New York, NY
35,000	Columbia University School of General Studies, New York, NY
30,000	Caramoor Center for Music and the Arts, Katonah, NY
30,000	Caramoor Center for Music and the Arts, Katonah, NY
30,000	Children's Blood Foundation, New York, NY

RUDIN FOUNDATION

Giving Contact

Susan H. Rapaport, Administrator
345 Park Ave.
New York, NY 10154
Phone: (212)407-2400

Description

Founded: 1960
EIN: 136113064
Organization Type: Private Foundation
Giving Locations: NY: New York
Grant Types: General Support.

Donor Information

Founder: Jack Rudin, Lewis Rudin

Financial Summary

Total Giving: $1,264,416 (2000); $1,324,719 (1999); $873,303 (1996)
Giving Analysis: Giving for 1999 includes: foundation scholarships ($2,000)
Assets: $580,339 (2000); $523,298 (1999); $10,982 (1996)
Gifts Received: $1,425,900 (2000); $1,970,300 (1999); $916,200 (1996). Note: In 2000, major contributions were received from 945 Fifth Ave. ($102,000), Rudin Estates Co. ($115,600) and 415 Madison ($1,180,400); 12 other donors made contributions of $34,800 or less each. In 1994, major contributions were received from 945 Fifth Ave. ($102,000), 80 Pine ($341,600), 415 Madison ($62,800), Rudin Estates Co. ($54,000), and Rudin Management Co. ($46,000); 16 other donors made contributions of $33,700 or less each.

Typical Recipients

Arts & Humanities: Arts Associations & Councils, Arts Funds, Dance, Film & Video, Libraries, Museums/Galleries, Music, Performing Arts, Theater
Civic & Public Affairs: African American Affairs, Botanical Gardens/Parks, Business/Free Enterprise, Economic Development, Civic & Public Affairs-General, Law & Justice, Municipalities/Towns, Parades/Festivals, Philanthropic Organizations, Public Policy, Safety, Urban & Community Affairs, Women's Affairs, Zoos/Aquariums
Education: Arts/Humanities Education, Business Education, Colleges & Universities, Elementary Education (Private), Faculty Development, Education-General, Literacy, Minority Education, Private Education (Precollege), Public Education (Precollege), Science/Mathematics Education, Secondary Education (Public), Social Sciences Education
Health: Clinics/Medical Centers, Geriatric Health, Health Organizations, Hospitals, Long-Term Care, Medical Research, Respiratory, Single-Disease Health Associations, Speech & Hearing
International: International Environmental Issues, International Organizations
Religion: Churches, Dioceses, Jewish Causes, Religious Organizations, Religious Welfare, Seminaries, Synagogues/Temples
Social Services: Big Brother/Big Sister, Child Welfare, Community Centers, Community Service Organizations, Crime Prevention, Delinquency & Criminal Rehabilitation, Family Services, Food/Clothing Distribution, Recreation & Athletics, Senior Services, Shelters/Homelessness, Substance Abuse, United Funds/United Ways, Volunteer Services, Youth Organizations

Application Procedures

Initial Contact: Send a brief letter of inquiry.
Application Requirements: Include a description of organization and proof of tax-exempt status.
Deadlines: None.

Foundation Officials

Beth Rudin DeWoody: president, director
David B. Levy: treasurer, director
John Lewin: vice president, director
Jack Rudin: chairman, director B 1924. PRIM CORP EMPL chairman, director: Rudin Management Co. Inc. CORP AFFIL partner: 345 Park Co.; partner: Whitehall Co.

Lewis Rudin: vchairman, director B 1927. PRIM CORP EMPL vice chairman, director: Rudin Management Co. Inc. CORP AFFIL partner: Whitehall Co.; partner: 345 Park Co.; trustee: New York Racing Association Inc.; partner: 41 Madison Co. NONPR AFFIL trustee: Lenox Hill Hospital; director: New York Blood Center.
John Leland Sills: director B New York, NY 1942. ED Rensselaer Polytechnic Institute BS (1964); Rensselaer Polytechnic Institute MS (1965); Fordham University JD (1969); New York University LLM (1974). CORP AFFIL director: Park Place Productions Inc. NONPR AFFIL member: New York State Bar Association; director: Westchester Lyric Festival; member: Association Bar of City of New York; member: American Bar Association. CLUB AFFIL member: New York Road Runners Club.
Richard C. Snider: secretary, director
Jeffrey Steinman: executive vice president, director

Grants Analysis

Disclosure Period: calendar year ending 2000
Total Grants: $1,264,416
Number of Grants: 186
Average Grant: $5,754*
Highest Grant: $200,000
Typical Range: $1,000 to $10,000
*Note: Average grant figure excludes highest grant.

Recent Grants

Note: Grants derived from 1999 Form 990.

Library-Related
25,000	New York Public Library, New York, NY

General
204,000	United Jewish Appeal and Federation of Jewish Philanthropies, New York, NY
50,000	Columbia University, New York, NY
42,000	Central Synagogue, New York, NY
40,000	Jewish Theological Seminary of America, New York, NY
25,900	Police Athletic League, New York, NY
25,000	Congregation Rodeph Shalom, New York, NY
25,000	Cool Schools Corporation of New York City, Inc, New York, NY
25,000	Museum of Jewish Heritage, New York, NY
25,000	NAACP, New York, NY
23,600	United Hospital Fund, New York, NY

SAMUEL AND MAY RUDIN FOUNDATION

Giving Contact

Susan H. Rapaport, Administrator
c/o Rudin
345 Park Avenue
New York, NY 10154
Phone: (212)407-2400

Description

Founded: 1976
EIN: 132906946
Organization Type: Private Foundation
Giving Locations: NY: New York
Grant Types: General Support.

Donor Information

Founder: the late Samuel Rudin

Financial Summary

Total Giving: $4,252,985 (fiscal year ending June 30, 1999); $3,830,985 (fiscal 1997); $3,330,790 (fiscal 1996)
Assets: $49,340 (fiscal 1999); $569 (fiscal 1998); $485,732 (fiscal 1997)

Gifts Received: $4,000,000 (fiscal 1997); $3,188,199 (fiscal 1996); $5,940,608 (fiscal 1995). Note: In fiscal 1996, contributions were received from the trust of Samuel Rudin.

Typical Recipients

Arts & Humanities: Arts Associations & Councils, Arts Centers, Arts Festivals, Dance, Historic Preservation, History & Archaeology, Libraries, Museums/Galleries, Music, Public Broadcasting, Theater, Visual Arts
Civic & Public Affairs: Botanical Gardens/Parks, Employment/Job Training
Education: Arts/Humanities Education, Colleges & Universities, Legal Education, Medical Education, Minority Education, Religious Education, Social Sciences Education, Student Aid
Environment: Environment-General, Resource Conservation
Health: AIDS/HIV, Cancer, Children's Health/Hospitals, Emergency/Ambulance Services, Eyes/Blindness, Health Organizations, Heart, Hospitals, Long-Term Care, Mental Health, Transplant Networks/Donor Banks
International: Health Care/Hospitals, Missionary/Religious Activities
Religion: Jewish Causes
Science: Science Exhibits & Fairs, Science Museums
Social Services: At-Risk Youth, Child Welfare, Community Service Organizations, People with Disabilities, Recreation & Athletics, Scouts, Substance Abuse

Application Procedures

Initial Contact: Send a brief letter of inquiry.
Application Requirements: brochure describing organization's purpose and activities and proof of tax-exempt status.
Deadlines: None.

Restrictions

Preference is given to museums and educational institutions.

Additional Information

The foundation's 2001 990 indicates that it is liquidating its assets and giving away its funds.

Foundation Officials

Beth Rudin DeWoody: president, director
Madeleine Rudin Johnson: vice president, director
Eric C. Rudin: secretary, treasurer, director
Jack Rudin: chairman, director B 1924. PRIM CORP EMPL chairman, director: Rudin Management Co. Inc. CORP AFFIL partner: 345 Park Co.; partner: Whitehall Co.
Katherine L. Rudin: vice president, director
Lewis Rudin: vice president, director B 1927. PRIM CORP EMPL vice chairman, director: Rudin Management Co. Inc. CORP AFFIL partner: Whitehall Co.; partner: 345 Park Co.; trustee: New York Racing Association Inc.; partner: 41 Madison Co. NONPR AFFIL trustee: Lenox Hill Hospital; director: New York Blood Center.
William Rudin: vice president, director

Grants Analysis

Disclosure Period: fiscal year ending June 30, 1998
Total Grants: $0
Note: A more recent grants list was unavailable.

Recent Grants

Note: Grants derived from fiscal 1996 Form 990.

General
500,000	United Jewish Appeal, New York, NY -- Operation Exodus
215,000	Memorial Sloan-Kettering Cancer Center, New York, NY -- Roberta C. Rudin Leukemia Research Fund
150,000	Columbia University Harlem Hospital

Center, New York, NY -- Incarnation Children's Center Medical Staff

75,000	New York University, New York, NY -- Rudin Merit Scholarship Program
60,000	St. Vincent's Hospital and Medical Center, New York, NY -- supportive care program for AIDS patients
50,000	Children's Storefront, New York, NY
50,000	Conservancy for Historic Battery Park, New York, NY -- summer concert series
50,000	Cornell University Medical College New York Hospital, New York, NY -- optic nerve regeneration for glaucoma
50,000	Margaret M. Dyson Vision Research Institute, Cornell University Medical College, New York, NY -- research on optic nerve and glaucoma
50,000	Medical Development for Israel, Children's Medical Center, New York, NY

FRAN AND WARREN RUPP FOUNDATION

Giving Contact
David R. Irvin
Fran and Warren Rupp Foundation
Care of Key Bank NA
42 North Main Street
Mansfield, OH 44902
Phone: (419)525-7665

Description
Founded: 1977
EIN: 341230690
Organization Type: Private Foundation
Giving Locations: OH: Mansfield
Grant Types: General Support.

Donor Information
Founder: Fran Rupp, Warren Rupp

Financial Summary
Total Giving: $1,514,669 (2000); $1,201,684 (1999); $891,505 (1998). Note: In 1996 Giving includes scholarship ($78,500).
Giving Analysis: Giving for 1998 includes: foundation scholarships ($7,500)
Assets: $20,334,719 (2000); $22,283,547 (1999); $21,014,466 (1998)
Gifts Received: $36,000 (2000); $36,000 (1999); $36,000 (1998). Note: In 2000, contributions were received from John W. Rupp Charitable Lead Trust ($12,000), Sheron A. Rupp Charitable Lead Trust ($12,000) and Suzanne R. Hartung Charitable Lead Trust ($12,000). In 1998, contributions were received from John W. Rupp Charitable Lead Trust ($12,000), Sheron A. Rupp Charitable Lead Trust ($12,000) and Suzanne R. Hartung Charitable Lead Trust ($12,000).

Typical Recipients
Arts & Humanities: Arts Associations & Councils, Arts Funds, Community Arts, Film & Video, History & Archaeology, Libraries, Museums/Galleries, Music, Public Broadcasting, Theater
Civic & Public Affairs: Civic & Public Affairs-General, Housing, Safety, Urban & Community Affairs
Education: Arts/Humanities Education, Colleges & Universities, Environmental Education, Education-General, Minority Education, Private Education (Precollege), Science/Mathematics Education, Student Aid, Vocational & Technical Education
Environment: Environment-General, Resource Conservation, Sanitary Systems, Wildlife Protection
Health: Children's Health/Hospitals, Clinics/Medical Centers, Eyes/Blindness, Hospitals, Kidney, Medical Rehabilitation, Medical Research, Nursing Services, Public Health, Research/Studies Institutes
Religion: Religious Organizations

Science: Science-General, Scientific Centers & Institutes
Social Services: Animal Protection, Camps, Child Welfare, Community Service Organizations, Crime Prevention, Domestic Violence, Family Planning, Family Services, People with Disabilities, Scouts, Shelters/Homelessness, Volunteer Services, YMCA/YWCA/YMHA/YWHA, Youth Organizations

Application Procedures
Initial Contact: Send a brief letter of inquiry. Applicants will be provided with appropriate forms for submitting proposals.
Deadlines: None.

Additional Information
Publications: Application Form

Foundation Officials
Frances R. Christian: chairman
Miles W. Christian: trustee
Suzanne R. Hartung: vice president
Sheron Adeline Rupp: vice president B Mansfield, OH 1943. ED Denison University BA (1965); University of Massachusetts MFA (1982). NONPR AFFIL guest artist, lecturer: Springfield Museum Fine Arts; guest artist, lecturer: University Massachusetts; guest artist, lecturer: Portland School Art; guest artist, lecturer: Massachusetts College Art; guest artist, lecturer: New York University; guest artist, lecturer: Deerfield Academy; guest artist, lecturer: Hartford School Art; guest artist, lecturer: Bard College; guest artist, lecturer: Boston Musical School.
Donald E. Smith: president
Timothy S. Smith: secretary, treasurer

Grants Analysis
Disclosure Period: calendar year ending 2000
Total Grants: $1,514,669
Number of Grants: 47
Average Grant: $22,215*
Highest Grant: $265,000
Typical Range: $5,000 to $50,000
*Note: Average grant figure excludes two highest grants ($515,000).

Recent Grants
Note: Grants derived from 2000 Form 990.

Library-Related
50,000	Richmond Academy of the Arts, Mansfield, OH -- capital campaign
35,000	Main Street Mansfield, Mansfield, OH -- Richland County Rail-Trail Commission
25,000	Loudonville Public Library, Loudonville, OH -- capital campaign

General
265,000	Richland Performing Arts Association, Mansfield, OH -- parking lot gift
250,000	Mansfield Area Community Y, Mansfield, OH -- construction project
125,000	Malabar Farm Foundation, Inc., Lucas, OH -- support Louis Bromfield Center
100,000	Community Health Access Project, Mansfield, OH -- assist in Chap Program
60,000	Third Street Community Clinic, Mansfield, OH -- financial support
50,000	Third Street Community Clinic, Mansfield, OH -- dental health care
50,000	Volunteers of America Central Office, Inc., Mansfield, OH -- men's homeless shelter
47,900	Wyoming Nature Conservancy, Lander, WY -- building project
45,000	Community Action for Capable Youth, Mansfield, OH -- Informed Teens funding
33,334	Michigan School in The Out-of-Doors, Inc., Butler, OH -- phase two construction adult facility

TOM RUSSELL CHARITABLE FOUNDATION

Giving Contact
Thomas A. Hearn, Vice President & Director
2 Transam Plaza, Suite 200
Oakbrook Terrace, IL 60181
Phone: (630)916-0123
Fax: (630)916-0567

Description
Founded: 1960
EIN: 366082517
Organization Type: Private Foundation
Giving Locations: IL: Chicago metropolitan area
Grant Types: General Support.

Donor Information
Founder: the late Thomas C. Russell, Wrap-On Co., Inc., Huron and Orleans Building Corp.

Financial Summary
Total Giving: $676,140 (fiscal year ending August 31, 2000); $600,900 (fiscal 1998); $450,000 (fiscal 1996). Note: Fiscal 1996 Giving includes United Way ($4,000).
Giving Analysis: Giving for fiscal 2000 includes: foundation grants to United Way ($5,000); foundation scholarships ($25,000) fiscal 1998: foundation grants to United Way ($5,000)
Assets: $20,503,587 (fiscal 2000); $13,269,844 (fiscal 1998); $11,267,986 (fiscal 1996)

Typical Recipients
Arts & Humanities: Historic Preservation, Libraries, Public Broadcasting
Civic & Public Affairs: Employment/Job Training, Civic & Public Affairs-General, Housing, Legal Aid, Parades/Festivals, Philanthropic Organizations, Zoos/Aquariums
Education: Arts/Humanities Education, Colleges & Universities, Education Reform, Education-General, Private Education (Precollege), Secondary Education (Private), Student Aid
Environment: Environment-General
Health: Cancer, Hospitals, Hospitals (University Affiliated), Medical Rehabilitation, Medical Research, Single-Disease Health Associations
International: International Organizations, International Relief Efforts
Religion: Churches, Religious Organizations, Religious Welfare
Science: Scientific Centers & Institutes, Scientific Organizations
Social Services: At-Risk Youth, Child Welfare, Community Centers, Community Service Organizations, Food/Clothing Distribution, People with Disabilities, Scouts, Senior Services, Shelters/Homelessness, YMCA/YWCA/YMHA/YWHA, Youth Organizations

Application Procedures
Initial Contact: The foundation has no formal grant application procedure or application form.
Application Requirements: Request should include descriptive material about the organization and the most current financial data.
Deadlines: None.

Additional Information
Publications: Application Guidelines

Foundation Officials
J. Kirby Aiken: auxiliary director
John L. Bishop: auxiliary director
Leslie R. Bishop: assistant secretary/treasurer, director
Thomas A. Hearn: vice president, treasurer, director

David S. Lindquist: auxiliary director
John N. Lindquist, MD: president, director
J. Tod Meserow: secretary, director
Frank S. Scarlati, Jr.: auxiliary director

Grants Analysis

Disclosure Period: fiscal year ending August 31, 2000
Total Grants: $646,140*
Number of Grants: 84
Average Grant: $7,692
Highest Grant: $35,000
Typical Range: $2,000 to $35,000
*Note: Giving excludes scholarships and United Way.

Recent Grants

Note: Grants derived from 2000 Form 990.

General

35,000	Montessori School of Raleigh, Raleigh, NC
30,000	Foodbank of North Carolina, NC
25,000	Donka, Inc, Wheaton, IL
25,000	Duke University Medical Center, Duke Comprehensive Cancer Center, Durham, NC
20,000	Building Together, Raleigh, NC
20,000	Cumberland College, Williamsburg, KY
20,000	Raleigh Mennonite Church, Raleigh, NC
20,000	Sigma Alpha Epsilon Foundation, Cincinnati, OH
15,000	Kiwanis International Foundation, Indianapolis, IN
15,000	Ten Thousand Villages, Raleigh, NC

JOSEPHINE S. RUSSELL CHARITABLE TRUST

Giving Contact

Lee Crooks, Trust Officer
c/o PNC Bank NA
PO Box 1198
Cincinnati, OH 45201
Phone: (513)651-8377

Description

Founded: 1976
EIN: 316195446
Organization Type: Private Foundation
Giving Locations: OH: Cincinnati metropolitan area
Grant Types: Capital, Project, Seed Money.

Donor Information

Founder: the late Josephine Schell Russell

Financial Summary

Total Giving: $820,050 (fiscal year ending June 30, 2001); $698,850 (fiscal 2000); $433,833 (fiscal 1997)
Giving Analysis: Giving for fiscal 2001 includes: foundation grants to United Way ($7,500); foundation scholarships ($10,000); fiscal 2000: foundation grants to United Way ($10,000); foundation scholarships ($10,000) fiscal 1997: foundation grants to United Way ($5,000)
Assets: $13,240,951 (fiscal 2001); $15,909,061 (fiscal 2000); $11,543,747 (fiscal 1997)

Typical Recipients

Arts & Humanities: Arts Centers, Arts Institutes, Ballet, Community Arts, Arts & Humanities-General, Historic Preservation, Libraries, Literary Arts, Museums/Galleries, Music, Opera, Performing Arts, Public Broadcasting, Theater
Civic & Public Affairs: African American Affairs, Botanical Gardens/Parks, Clubs, Community Foundations, Economic Development, Employment/Job Training, Civic & Public Affairs-General, Housing, Legal Aid, Native American Affairs, Parades/Festivals,

Urban & Community Affairs, Women's Affairs, Zoos/Aquariums
Education: Afterschool/Enrichment Programs, Arts/Humanities Education, Colleges & Universities, Continuing Education, Elementary Education (Private), Education-General, Literacy, Private Education (Precollege), Public Education (Precollege), Science/Mathematics Education, Secondary Education (Private), Special Education, Student Aid
Environment: Environment-General, Resource Conservation
Health: Adolescent Health Issues, Cancer, Children's Health/Hospitals, Health Organizations, Home-Care Services, Hospices, Long-Term Care, Mental Health, Prenatal Health Issues, Public Health, Respiratory, Single-Disease Health Associations, Speech & Hearing
Religion: Churches, Jewish Causes, Ministries, Religious Welfare, Social/Policy Issues
Social Services: Big Brother/Big Sister, Child Welfare, Community Centers, Community Service Organizations, Day Care, Delinquency & Criminal Rehabilitation, Domestic Violence, Domestic Violence, Family Services, Food/Clothing Distribution, People with Disabilities, Scouts, Senior Services, Shelters/Homelessness, Substance Abuse, United Funds/United Ways, Volunteer Services, YMCA/YWCA/YMHA/YWHA, Youth Organizations

Application Procedures

Initial Contact: Submit seven copies of proposal.
Application Requirements: Include name, address, telephone number, and founding date of organization; names and titles of trustees, officers, and key executives or employees; a description of organization and its current activities; geographic area and population served; purpose of funds sought and community benefits expected; amount requested and expected budget; plan for permanent financial support of project, if applicable; listing of any other area organizations with similar purpose or services; listing of other sources solicited for funding; budget and most recent financial information; and proof of tax-exempt status.
Deadlines: One month prior to scheduled meeting on third Friday of January and July.

Additional Information

Publications: Informational Brochure (including Application Guidelines)
Trust(s): PNC Bank OH NA

Grants Analysis

Disclosure Period: fiscal year ending June 30, 2001
Total Grants: $802,550*
Number of Grants: 56
Average Grant: $14,331
Highest Grant: $50,000
Typical Range: $5,000 to $25,000
*Note: Giving excludes United Way and scholarships.

Recent Grants

Note: Grants derived from fiscal 2000 Form 990.

General

50,000	Local Initiatives Support, New York, NY -- to capitalize a community development program
50,000	National Underground Railroad, Cincinnati, OH -- for capital campaign
40,000	United Home Care, Cincinnati, OH -- laptop computer and software
30,000	Boys/Girls Clubs of Cincinnati, Cincinnati, OH -- new Avondale club and repairs
30,000	Cincinnati Association for Blind, Cincinnati, OH -- renovations
25,000	Bayley Place, Cincinnati, OH -- construction of Village Center
25,000	Boy Scouts of America, Cincinnati, OH -- capital campaign
25,000	Contemporary Arts Center, Cincinnati, OH -- capital campaign

25,000	Friars Club, Inc, Cincinnati, OH -- repair of facilities
25,000	Legal Aid Society of Cincinnati, Cincinnati, OH -- capital campaign

JOSEPHINE G. RUSSELL TRUST

Giving Contact

Clifford E. Elias, Managing Trustee
70 East St.
Methuen, MA 01844
Phone: (978)687-0501

Description

Founded: 1934
EIN: 042136910
Organization Type: Private Foundation
Giving Locations: MA: Lawrence including surrounding communities
Grant Types: Capital, Emergency, General Support, Project, Scholarship.

Donor Information

Founder: the late Josephine G. Russell

Financial Summary

Total Giving: $357,235 (2000); $335,940 (1999); $373,637 (1998). Note: 1997 Giving includes United Way ($5,000).
Assets: $10,346,590 (2000); $11,029,484 (1999); $10,563,924 (1998)

Typical Recipients

Arts & Humanities: Arts Centers, History & Archaeology, Libraries, Museums/Galleries
Civic & Public Affairs: Asian American Affairs, Chambers of Commerce, Community Foundations, Civic & Public Affairs-General, Hispanic Affairs, Housing, Legal Aid, Municipalities/Towns, Urban & Community Affairs
Education: Business Education, Colleges & Universities, Community & Junior Colleges, Education-General, Private Education (Precollege), Public Education (Precollege), School Volunteerism, Secondary Education (Private)
Health: Children's Health/Hospitals, Clinics/Medical Centers, Home-Care Services, Hospitals, Medical Research, Nursing Services, Trauma Treatment
International: International Organizations
Religion: Churches, Jewish Causes, Religious Welfare
Social Services: At-Risk Youth, Big Brother/Big Sister, Big Brother/Big Sister, Child Welfare, Community Centers, Community Service Organizations, Family Services, Food/Clothing Distribution, People with Disabilities, Recreation & Athletics, Scouts, Shelters/Homelessness, United Funds/United Ways, YMCA/YWCA/YMHA/YWHA, Youth Organizations

Application Procedures

Initial Contact: Request application guidelines.
Deadlines: January 31.

Restrictions

Grants are awarded for the care, healing, and nursing of the sick and injured, the relief and aid of the poor, the training and education of the young, and for social services in the city of Lawrence. Does not support individuals.

Additional Information

Publications: Application Guidelines

Foundation Officials

Archer L. Bolton, Jr.: trustee
Clifford E. Elias, Esq.: managing trustee
Eileen M. Khoury: trustee

Rev. Joachim Lally: trustee
Marsha E. Rich: trustee

Grants Analysis

Disclosure Period: calendar year ending 2000
Total Grants: $357,235
Number of Grants: 38
Average Grant: $9,400
Highest Grant: $40,000
Typical Range: $5,000 to $20,000

Recent Grants

Note: Grants derived from 2001 Form 990.

General

50,000	Lawrence General Hospital, Lawrence, MA
40,000	Holy Family Hospital
25,000	Central Catholic High School
20,000	Merrimack College, North Andover, MA
15,000	Lawrence Youth Center, Lawrence, MA
14,500	Lazarus House, Lawrence, MA
14,175	Lawrence Boys & Girls Club, Lawrence, MA
12,000	Seton Asian Community Center
10,000	Lawrence Public Schools, Lawrence, MA
10,000	Neighbors In Need, Seattle, WA

RUSSER FOODS

Company Headquarters

665 Perry St.
Buffalo, NY 14210
Web: http://www.foodbrands.com/divrusser.htm

Company Description

Revenue: US$181 million (2001)
Employees: 230 (2001)
SIC(s): 2013 Sausages & Other Prepared Meats, 5147 Meats & Meat Products.

Operating Locations

Russer Foods (NY--Buffalo)

Russer Foods/Zemsky Family Trust

Giving Contact

Sam Zemsky, Manager
6420 SE Harbor Circle
Stuart, FL 34996-1958
Phone: (407)225-1602

Alternate Contact

Shirley Zemsky
Phone: (716)566-2990
Fax: (786)826-5138

Description

Founded: 1987
EIN: 112867625
Organization Type: Corporate Foundation
Giving Locations: NY: Buffalo
Grant Types: General Support.

Donor Information

Founder: Zemco Industries

Financial Summary

Total Giving: $372,170 (2001); $197,339 (2000); $251,483 (1999). Note: Contributes through foundation only.
Giving Analysis: Giving for 2000 includes: foundation grants to United Way ($8,900); foundation ($188,439); 1999: foundation grants to United Way ($1,000); foundation ($250,483); 1998: foundation

grants to United Way ($1,000); foundation ($179,125);
Assets: $3,150,851 (2001); $2,433,929 (2000); $287,496 (1999)
Gifts Received: $1,000,000 (2001); $2,013,000 (2000); $150,000 (1998). Note: In 2001, contributions were received from Sam Zemsky. In 2000, contributions were received from Zemco Industries and Sam Zemsky.

Typical Recipients

Arts & Humanities: Arts Associations & Councils, Arts Centers, Arts Festivals, Arts Institutes, Ballet, Dance, Arts & Humanities-General, Historic Preservation, History & Archaeology, Libraries, Museums/Galleries, Music, Performing Arts, Public Broadcasting, Theater
Civic & Public Affairs: Botanical Gardens/Parks, Civil Rights, Community Foundations, Employment/Job Training, Civic & Public Affairs-General, Law & Justice, Municipalities/Towns, Parades/Festivals, Philanthropic Organizations, Urban & Community Affairs, Zoos/Aquariums
Education: Arts/Humanities Education, Business Education, Colleges & Universities, Education-General, Private Education (Precollege), Religious Education, Secondary Education (Private), Student Aid
Environment: Air/Water Quality, Wildlife Protection
Health: Alzheimers Disease, Arthritis, Cancer, Children's Health/Hospitals, Diabetes, Geriatric Health, Health Organizations, Heart, Hospices, Hospitals, Medical Research, Mental Health, Multiple Sclerosis, Prenatal Health Issues, Public Health, Research/Studies Institutes, Respiratory, Single-Disease Health Associations
International: Foreign Arts Organizations, Missionary/Religious Activities
Religion: Jewish Causes, Religious Welfare, Synagogues/Temples
Science: Science Museums
Social Services: Animal Protection, Camps, Child Welfare, Community Centers, Community Service Organizations, Domestic Violence, Family Planning, Family Services, Food/Clothing Distribution, People with Disabilities, Recreation & Athletics, Scouts, Senior Services, Social Services-General, Special Olympics, Substance Abuse, United Funds/United Ways, YMCA/YWCA/YMHA/YWHA

Application Procedures

Initial Contact: An application form is not required. Send a brief letter of inquiry.
Application Requirements: Include purpose of funds sought and proof of tax-exempt status.
Deadlines: None.
Notes: Foundation does not have a formal application form.

Corporate Officials

Howard Zemsky: president B 1959. ED Michigan State University (1981). PRIM CORP EMPL president: Zemco Industries Inc. Delaware.
Sam Zemsky: chairman, director B 1926. PRIM CORP EMPL chairman, director: Zemco Industries Inc. Delaware.

Foundation Officials

Howard Zemsky: trustee (see above)
Sam Zemsky: trustee (see above)
Shirley Zemsky: trustee

Grants Analysis

Disclosure Period: calendar year ending 2001
Total Grants: $372,170
Number of Grants: 39
Average Grant: $6,478*
Highest Grant: $126,000
Lowest Grant: $200
Typical Range: $500 to $7,500
*Note: Average grant figure excludes highest grant.

Recent Grants

Note: Grants derived from 2002 Form 990.

General

126,000	Temple Beth Zion, Philadelphia, PA
75,000	Martin House Restoration Corp, Buffalo, NY
40,000	Chautauqua Fund, Chautauqua, NY
25,000	New Jewish High School, Newton Center, MA
25,000	Tourette Syndrome Association, New York, NY
12,500	Lyric Theater
10,000	Atlantic Classical Orchestra, Vero Beach, FL
5,000	Bestar Soc Chautaugus Institute
5,000	New York Foundation for The Arts, New York, NY -- common ground world project
5,000	Shea's Performing Arts Center Endowments, Buffalo, NY

DAVID CLAUDE RYAN FOUNDATION

Giving Contact

Jerome D. Ryan, President
PO Box 6409
San Diego, CA 92166
Phone: (619)497-1171

Description

Founded: 1959
EIN: 956051140
Organization Type: Private Foundation
Giving Locations: CA: statewide, San Diego
Grant Types: Multiyear/Continuing Support.

Donor Information

Founder: Jerome D. Ryan, Gladys B. Ryan

Financial Summary

Total Giving: $42,050 (2001); $148,730 (2000); $41,650 (1999)
Assets: $2,818,542 (2001); $3,051,046 (2000); $2,383,968 (1999)
Gifts Received: $20,000 (2001); $30,000 (2000); $50,568 (1999). Note: In 2001, contributions were received from Jerome D. Ryan ($10,000) and Anne E. Ryan ($10,000). In 2000, contributions were received from Jerome D. Ryan. In 1999, contributions were received from Anne E. Ryan ($40,600) and Jerome D. Ryan ($9,968).

Typical Recipients

Arts & Humanities: Libraries, Museums/Galleries, Public Broadcasting
Civic & Public Affairs: Civic & Public Affairs-General, Legal Aid, Zoos/Aquariums
Education: Colleges & Universities, Education-General, Medical Education, Minority Education, Private Education (Precollege), Special Education
Health: Children's Health/Hospitals, Emergency/Ambulance Services, Eyes/Blindness, Hospices, Single-Disease Health Associations
International: Health Care/Hospitals, International Organizations, International Relief Efforts, Missionary/Religious Activities
Religion: Bible Study/Translation, Churches, Religion-General, Ministries, Missionary Activities (Domestic), Religious Organizations, Religious Welfare
Science: Science-General, Science Museums
Social Services: At-Risk Youth, Camps, Child Welfare, Community Service Organizations, Community Service Organizations, Domestic Violence, Family Services, Food/Clothing Distribution, People with Disabilities, Recreation & Athletics, Scouts, Special Olympics, United Funds/United Ways, YMCA/YWCA/YMHA/YWHA, Youth Organizations

Application Procedures

Initial Contact: Send a brief letter of inquiry.
Application Requirements: Include the organization's charitable activities and proof of tax-exempt status.
Deadlines: None.

Restrictions

Does not support individuals.

Foundation Officials

Gladys B. Ryan: vice president, secretary, treasurer
Jerome D. Ryan: president
Stephen M. Ryan: vice president, secretary, treasurer

Grants Analysis

Disclosure Period: calendar year ending 2001
Total Grants: $42,050
Number of Grants: 33
Average Grant: $1,274
Highest Grant: $4,000
Lowest Grant: $100
Typical Range: $1,000 to $5,000

Recent Grants

Note: Grants derived from 2001 Form 990.

General

4,000	San Diego Aerospace Museum, San Diego, CA
3,500	World Vision International, Monrovia, CA
3,300	Pacific Legal Foundation, Sacramento, CA
3,000	Peninsula YMCA, San Mateo, CA
2,800	San Diego Rescue Mission, San Diego, CA
2,100	Capital Ministries, Santa Ana, CA
2,000	Children's Hospital
2,000	Community Campership Council, San Diego, CA
2,000	Coral Ridge Ministries, Ft. Lauderdale, FL
2,000	Salvation Army, Port Huron, MI

S.G. FOUNDATION

Giving Contact

Richard Kieding, Director & President
PO Box 444
Buellton, CA 93427
Phone: (805)688-0088
Fax: (805)686-1250
E-mail: sgfound@utech.net

Description

Founded: 1984
EIN: 330048410
Organization Type: Private Foundation
Giving Locations: CA; CO; CT; HI; IL; OR; WA; WI
Grant Types: Endowment, Fellowship.

Donor Information

Founder: F. Javier Alverdo

Financial Summary

Total Giving: $875,421 (2001); $806,092 (2000); $579,099 (1999)
Giving Analysis: Giving for 2001 includes: foundation fellowships ($60,000)
Assets: $10,386,999 (2001); $11,048,084 (2000); $11,147,563 (1999)

Typical Recipients

Arts & Humanities: Libraries
Civic & Public Affairs: Community Foundations, Economic Development, Employment/Job Training,
Civic & Public Affairs-General, Legal Aid, Public Policy
Education: Agricultural Education, Colleges & Universities, International Exchange, Leadership Training, Literacy, Medical Education, Minority Education, Private Education (Precollege), Science/Mathematics Education
Health: Health-General
International: Health Care/Hospitals, International Affairs, International Development, International Relief Efforts
Religion: Churches, Ministries, Missionary Activities (Domestic), Religious Organizations, Religious Welfare
Social Services: Animal Protection, Camps, Community Service Organizations, Crime Prevention, Day Care, Domestic Violence, Family Services, Food/Clothing Distribution, People with Disabilities, Sexual Abuse, Shelters/Homelessness, Substance Abuse, YMCA/YWCA/YMHA/YWHA, Youth Organizations

Application Procedures

Initial Contact: Send a brief letter of inquiry.
Application Requirements: Include a description of organization and program or project.
Deadlines: None.

Foundation Officials

Jeffrey L. Cotter: secretary, treasurer
John Donati: director
Russell Fraser: director
Lynn R. Gildred: secretary
Stuart C. Gildred: president, director
Richard Kieding: president
Joseph Lambert: treasurer
William Sauer: vice president
Dessie Schmidt: assistant secretary

Grants Analysis

Disclosure Period: calendar year ending 2001
Total Grants: $875,421*
Number of Grants: 22
Average Grant: $21,806*
Highest Grant: $250,700
Typical Range: $5,000 to $30,000
***Note:** Giving excludes fellowships. Average grant figure excludes two highest grants ($355,700).

Recent Grants

Note: Grants derived from 2001 Form 990.

Library-Related

16,000	Friends of the Guadalupe Public Library, Guadalupe, CA -- library expansion

General

250,700	Mercy Corp, Portland, OR -- food and housing in Korea and Honduras
105,000	Focus on the Family, Colorado Springs, CO -- drop camera television studio
64,400	Ashoka, Arlington, VA -- Central American Projects
60,000	Intervarsity Christian Fellowship, Madison, WI -- training and expansion
56,204	Santa Ynez Valley Foundation, Santa Ynez, CA
36,862	Central Coast Literacy Council, Santa Maria, CA -- Volunteer Recruitment Program
36,862	Christian Brother's Foundation, Santa Barbara, CA -- education program Peru
36,100	Power of God Christian Center, Santa Maria, CA -- youth gang prevention
30,000	Haitian Health Foundation, Norwich, CT -- hospital expansion Haiti
30,000	Latin American Assistance, Inc., Solvang, CA -- Christian Camp Costa Rica

S&T BANCORP, INC.

Company Headquarters

43 S. 9th St.
Indiana, PA 15701
Web: http://www.stbank.com/

Company Description

Founded: 1902
Ticker: STBA
Exchange: NASDAQ
Assets: US$2.332 billion (2001)
Employees: 688 (2001)
SIC(s): 6022 State Commercial Banks, 6712 Bank Holding Companies.

Operating Locations

S&T Bancorp (PA--Indiana)

S&T Bancorp Charitable Foundation

Giving Contact

James C. Miller, President
Main Office
PO Box 190
Indiana, PA 15701-0190
Phone: (724)465-1443

Description

Founded: 1993
EIN: 251716950
Organization Type: Corporate Foundation
Giving Locations: headquarters and operating communities.
Grant Types: Capital, General Support, Scholarship.

Financial Summary

Total Giving: $346,275 (2001); $246,250 (2000); $261,800 (1999)
Giving Analysis: Giving for 2001 includes: foundation grants to United Way ($41,000); foundation ($305,275); 2000: foundation grants to United Way ($43,000); foundation ($203,293); 1999: foundation ($261,800);
Assets: $180,099 (2001); $552,080 (2000); $813,246 (1999)
Gifts Received: $60,350 (2001); $72,900 (2000); $64,800 (1999). Note: Contributions are received from S&T Bank.

Typical Recipients

Arts & Humanities: Arts Associations & Councils, Arts Festivals, Ballet, Community Arts, History & Archaeology, Libraries, Museums/Galleries, Music
Civic & Public Affairs: Botanical Gardens/Parks, Business/Free Enterprise, Clubs, Community Foundations, Economic Development, Employment/Job Training, Civic & Public Affairs-General, Municipalities/Towns, Parades/Festivals, Professional & Trade Associations, Safety, Urban & Community Affairs
Education: Agricultural Education, Business Education, Colleges & Universities, Community & Junior Colleges, Education Reform, Education-General, Preschool Education, Public Education (Precollege), Student Aid, Vocational & Technical Education
Health: Cancer, Children's Health/Hospitals, Clinics/Medical Centers, Diabetes, Emergency/Ambulance Services, Heart, Hospitals, Nursing Services, Public Health, Single-Disease Health Associations
Religion: Religious Welfare
Social Services: Big Brother/Big Sister, Child Welfare, Community Centers, Community Service Organizations, Emergency Relief, Family Services, People with Disabilities, Recreation & Athletics, Scouts, Senior Services, Special Olympics, United Funds/United Ways, Veterans, YMCA/YWCA/YMHA/YWHA, Youth Organizations

Application Procedures

Initial Contact: Submit a written application.
Application Requirements: Include amount requested and purpose of funds sought.
Deadlines: None.
Review Process: The contributions committee meets monthly.

Restrictions

Does not support organizations outside bank's marketing area.

Additional Information

Trust(s): S&T Bank

Corporate Officials

Robert D. Duggan: chairman, chief executive officer chief financial officer PRIM CORP EMPL chairman, chief executive officer: S&T Bancorp.
James C. Miller: president, director PRIM CORP EMPL president, director: S&T Bancorp.
Robert E. Rout: senior vice president, chief financial officer PRIM CORP EMPL senior vice president, chief financial officer: S&T Bancorp.

Foundation Officials

Robert D. Duggan: chairman (see above)
James C. Miller: president (see above)

Grants Analysis

Disclosure Period: calendar year ending 2001
Total Grants: $305,275*
Number of Grants: 93
Average Grant: $3,036*
Highest Grant: $26,000
Lowest Grant: $500
Typical Range: $1,000 to $5,000
***Note:** Giving excludes United Way. Average grant figure excludes highest grant.

Recent Grants

Note: Grants derived from 2001 Form 990.

Library-Related

1,200	Rebecca M. Arthurs Memorial Library, Brookville, PA

General

100,000	Indiana Healthcare Foundation, Indiana, PA
26,000	United Way Indiana County, Indiana, PA
25,000	Punxsutawney Area Hospital, Punxsutawney, PA
12,000	Du Bois Area United Way, Du Bois, PA
10,000	Du Bois Area Schools and Community Building Fund (DASC), Du Bois, PA
10,000	Jefferson County Fair Association, Brookville, PA
6,000	Jefferson County Area Agency on Aging, Brookville, PA
5,750	United Fund, Brookville, PA
5,000	Big Brothers and Big Sisters, Indiana, PA
5,000	Citizens Ambulance, Indiana, PA

FRANKLIN I. SAEMANN FOUNDATION

Giving Contact

Amy C. Kilgus-Chamley
PO Box 105
Morrison, IL 61270
Phone: (219)267-8141

Description

Founded: 1983
EIN: 626171002
Organization Type: Private Foundation

Giving Locations: IA
Grant Types: General Support.

Donor Information

Founder: Franklin I. Saemann

Financial Summary

Total Giving: $557,500 (fiscal year ending June 30, 2002); $586,475 (fiscal 2000); $527,000 (fiscal 1999)
Giving Analysis: Giving for fiscal 2000 includes: foundation grants to United Way ($10,000) fiscal 1999: foundation grants to United Way ($12,500)
Assets: $9,649,232 (fiscal 2002); $10,691,497 (fiscal 2000); $13,105,169 (fiscal 1999)
Gifts Received: $1,494,527 (fiscal 1999); $1,249,837 (fiscal 1997); $6,443,962 (fiscal 1996).
Note: In fiscal 1999, contributions were received from Irene Saemann Estate.

Typical Recipients

Arts & Humanities: Community Arts, Arts & Humanities-General, History & Archaeology, Libraries, Literary Arts, Public Broadcasting
Civic & Public Affairs: Botanical Gardens/Parks, Community Foundations, Municipalities/Towns, Urban & Community Affairs
Education: Colleges & Universities, Education-General, Literacy, Minority Education
Health: Cancer, Hospices, Hospitals, Prenatal Health Issues, Single-Disease Health Associations
Religion: Bible Study/Translation, Churches, Religious Welfare
Social Services: Big Brother/Big Sister, Child Welfare, Community Service Organizations, Domestic Violence, Family Planning, People with Disabilities, Senior Services, Shelters/Homelessness, United Funds/United Ways, YMCA/YWCA/YMHA/YWHA, Youth Organizations

Application Procedures

Initial Contact: Send a brief letter of inquiry.
Application Requirements: Include brief description, current budget, amount requeted, financial statement from previous year, IRS determination letter, and current list of board of directors.
Deadlines: April 1

Foundation Officials

Amy C. Kilgus: trustee
Joann A. Kilgus: trustee
Thomas E. List: trustee
June Waller: trustee
Katherine A. Waller: trustee

Grants Analysis

Disclosure Period: fiscal year ending June 30, 2002
Total Grants: $557,500
Number of Grants: 33
Average Grant: $5,241*
Highest Grant: $295,000
Typical Range: $1,000 to $10,000
***Note:** Average grant figure excludes two highest grants.

Recent Grants

Note: Grants derived from fiscal 2002 Form 990.

General

295,000	Wartburg College, Waverly, IA -- further education
100,000	Carthage College, Kenosha, WI -- further higher education
22,500	Cardinal Center, Warsaw, IN -- for services for disabled persons
15,000	Wartburg Seminary, Waverly, IA -- to further education
10,500	Charleston Public Library, Charleston, WV -- further education
10,000	Arts and Cultural Alliance, Newport, RI -- to promote art and culture
10,000	Heartline Pregnancy Center, Warsaw, IN -- services for pregnant women
10,000	Kosciusko Community Senior Service, Warsaw, IN -- to promote senior services
10,000	Kosciusko Community YMCA, Warsaw, IN -- youth activities
10,000	United Way Kosciusko County, Warsaw, IN -- community services

SAFECO CORP.

Company Headquarters

Seattle, WA
Web: http://www.safeco.com

Company Description

Founded: 1923
Ticker: SAFC
Exchange: NASDAQ
Revenue: US$7.065 billion (2002)
Profit: US$301.1 million (2002)
Employees: 12000 (2001)
Fortune Rank: 260, per FORTUNE Magazine's list of 500 Largest U.S. Corporations (2002).
SIC(s): 6159 Miscellaneous Business Credit Institutions, 6211 Security Brokers & Dealers, 6311 Life Insurance, 6719 Holding Companies Nec.

Operating Locations

SAFECO Corp. (CA--Fountain Valley, Glendale, San Ramon; CO--Denver; GA--Stone Mountain; IL--Hoffman Estates; MO--St. Louis; OH--Cincinnati; TN--Nashville; TX--Plano; VA--Midlothian)

Nonmonetary Support

Volunteer Programs: Company has a Volunteer Awards Program through which over 11,000 employees nationwide can participate.

Giving Contact

Rose Lincoln, Assistant Vice President & Director, Community Relations
SAFECO Corp.
SAFECO Plaza
Seattle, WA 98185
Phone: (206)545-6279
Fax: (206)545-5730
E-mail: roslin@safeco.com
Web: http://www.safeco.com/safeco/about/giving/giving.asp

Alternate Contact

Phone: (206)545-5299
E-mail: hocr@safeco.com
Note: For Seattle-area grant seekers.

Description

Organization Type: Corporate Giving Program
Giving Locations: headquarters and operating communities in the United States.
Grant Types: Conference/Seminar, Employee Matching Gifts, General Support.
Note: Company matches employee gifts to local organisation and the United Way.

Financial Summary

Total Giving: $4,000,000 (2002 approx); $4,100,000 (2001 approx); $4,800,000 (2000 approx). Note: Contributes through corporate direct giving program only.

Typical Recipients

Arts & Humanities: Arts Funds, Community Arts, Dance, Historic Preservation, Libraries, Museums/Galleries, Opera, Performing Arts, Public Broadcasting, Visual Arts

Civic & Public Affairs: Economic Development, Employment/Job Training, Housing, Nonprofit Management, Public Policy, Safety, Urban & Community Affairs, Zoos/Aquariums

Education: Arts/Humanities Education, Business Education, Colleges & Universities, Continuing Education, Economic Education, Education Associations, Elementary Education (Private), Literacy, Minority Education, Private Education (Precollege), Public Education (Precollege)

Environment: Environment-General

Health: Health Policy/Cost Containment, Health Organizations, Mental Health, Nutrition, Public Health, Single-Disease Health Associations

Social Services: Community Service Organizations, Day Care, Delinquency & Criminal Rehabilitation, Emergency Relief, People with Disabilities, Senior Services, Shelters/Homelessness, Substance Abuse, United Funds/United Ways, Volunteer Services, Youth Organizations

Application Procedures

Initial Contact: Call or write for application and guidelines, then call before submitting a formal proposal.

Application Requirements: A formal proposal should be four pages of less, plus attachments. Include cover letter; completed application form; how project meets guidelines and criteria; organization's mission statement and purpose, history of accomplishments, governance, area and population served, and role of volunteers (if a collaboration, describe lead agency and relation to others); needs statement, acknowledging existing similar projects, and how proposed project differs, and any efforts to work cooperatively; proposal, including how needs will be addressed, projected goals, objectives, timeline, anticipated impact, population to benefit, how work will be monitored and success evaluated, potential and actual sources of current support, and plan for future support; the following attachments: proof of tax-exempt status, list of board members with affiliations, key organizational staff with titles and functions, IRS Form 990, most recent audited financial statement, one-page summary of actual income and expenses for the past two years, listing of funding sources and amounts for those years, organization's operating budget, detailed project budget, letters from collaborating agencies (if appropriate).

Deadlines: None.

Review Process: All requests are evaluated, either at home office or branch office.

Evaluative Criteria: Program's capability and soundness of financial management and fiscal policies; competency and policy-making authority of board of directors; demonstration that program does not represent unnecessary duplication of services; program is designed to promote self-sufficiency, focuses on prevention rather treatment of problems; can sustain itself beyond company funding; and the organization promotes collaboration between other organizations and individuals.

Decision Notification: Grant requests are reviewed on a quarterly basis.

Notes: Application should be sent to nearest company office.

Restrictions

As a general rule, SAFECO does not make contributions to individuals; projects or programs operating outside the United States; national programs; endowment funds; religious, fraternal, or political groups or projects; general fundraising events; goodwill advertising; loans or investments; film or video production; operating deficits or debt retirement; health education, research, or prevention; amateur arts; amateur sports teams or athletic scholarships; conferences; research; or fraternal, professional, or membership organizations.

Additional Information

Company was founded in 1923 as a property and casualty insurance company. Today, they've added life and health insurance; real estate management and investments and commercial credit and asset management to their list of operations.

Company sets aside approximately two percent of pre-tax income annually for contributions programs. Company will consider requests from communities where significant numbers of SAFECO employees live and work.

Contributions are given for one year with no implied renewals.

Company may require recipients to provide an audited financial statement at year's end and periodic reports on the project.

Publications: Boomerang Giving: Flight Instruction Manual (guidelines); Application Form

Grants Analysis

Disclosure Period: calendar year ending 2001
Total Grants: $4,100,000
Number of Grants: 600 (approx)
Average Grant: $6,833 (approx)
Highest Grant: $500,000
Lowest Grant: $25
Typical Range: $10,000 to $15,000* and $1,000 to $2,000*

***Note:** First grant range represents grants made by the home office; second grant range represents grants made by field offices.

SAGE FOUNDATION

Giving Contact

Melissa Sage Fadim, Chairman, President & Treasurer
PO Box 1919
Brighton, MI 48116
Phone: (810)227-7660

Description

Founded: 1954
EIN: 386041518
Organization Type: Family Foundation
Giving Locations: nationally.
Grant Types: Capital, Endowment, General Support, Matching, Multiyear/Continuing Support.

Donor Information

Founder: Established in 1954 by the late Charles F. Sage (d. 1961) and his wife, the late Effa L. Sage . After Mr. Sage's death, the foundation received stock in Tecumseh Products Company, valued at more than $7 million.

Financial Summary

Total Giving: $2,636,467 (2001); $2,686,220 (2000); $2,540,000 (1999 approx)
Giving Analysis: Giving for 1997 includes: foundation scholarships ($57,160)
Assets: $57,127,616 (2001); $59,572,565 (2000); $60,599,000 (1999 approx)

Typical Recipients

Arts & Humanities: Arts Associations & Councils, Arts Centers, Arts Festivals, Arts Funds, Arts Institutes, Film & Video, Arts & Humanities-General, Libraries, Museums/Galleries, Music, Opera, Performing Arts, Public Broadcasting, Theater

Civic & Public Affairs: Botanical Gardens/Parks, Clubs, Community Foundations, Economic Development, Civic & Public Affairs-General, Hispanic Affairs, Municipalities/Towns, Nonprofit Management, Parades/Festivals, Philanthropic Organizations, Public Policy, Safety, Urban & Community Affairs, Zoos/Aquariums

Education: Agricultural Education, Arts/Humanities Education, Colleges & Universities, Education-General, International Studies, Legal Education, Legal Education, Minority Education, Preschool Education, Private Education (Precollege), Public Education (Precollege), Science/Mathematics Education, Secondary Education (Private), Secondary Education (Public), Special Education, Student Aid

Health: AIDS/HIV, Alzheimers Disease, Arthritis, Cancer, Children's Health/Hospitals, Clinics/Medical Centers, Emergency/Ambulance Services, Geriatric Health, Health Funds, Health Organizations, Heart, Hospices, Hospitals, Hospitals (University Affiliated), Long-Term Care, Medical Research, Mental Health, Public Health, Single-Disease Health Associations

International: Foreign Arts Organizations, Health Care/Hospitals, Human Rights, Missionary/Religious Activities

Religion: Churches, Churches, Religion-General, Religious Organizations, Religious Welfare

Science: Science-General, Science Museums

Social Services: Child Welfare, Community Service Organizations, Counseling, Crime Prevention, Domestic Violence, Family Services, Homes, People with Disabilities, Recreation & Athletics, Shelters/Homelessness, Substance Abuse, Youth Organizations

Application Procedures

Initial Contact: Initial contact should be in writing.

Application Requirements: Applicants should include the amount of funds needed, intended outcome of the project or program, plans to reach the objective, plans to evaluate the results, photocopy of the organization's tax-exempt determination letter, and the name of the individual responsible for administering the program. General information that would aid the board of trustees in making a decision should be included.

Deadlines: None.

Restrictions

The foundation has no grant-making restrictions as to geographic area, charitable fields, or types of institutions.

Foundation Officials

John J. Ayaub: vice president, secretary, trustee
Melissa Sage Booth Fadim: chairwoman, president, treasurer, trustee
Ann Sage Price: trustee
James E. Van Doren: trustee

Grants Analysis

Disclosure Period: calendar year ending 2001
Total Grants: $2,636,467
Number of Grants: 152
Average Grant: $17,345
Highest Grant: $330,000
Lowest Grant: $1,000
Typical Range: $1,000 to $50,000

Recent Grants

Note: Grants derived from 2001 Form 990.

Library-Related

10,000	Frick Collection, New York, NY -- charitable and educational purposes	

General

330,000	Orchestral Association of Chicago, Chicago, IL -- Carnegie Hall three year residency	
115,000	Public Broadcasting Service, Alexandria, VA -- fund the production of the documentary "Over&Over&Over&Over"	
100,000	Immaculate Heart High School, Tucson, AZ -- air conditioning system	
100,000	Purple Rose Theatre Company, Chelsea, MI	

100,000	University of Chicago Hospitals, Chicago, IL -- used by University of Chicago Children's Hospital
75,000	Orchestral Association of Chicago, Chicago, IL
60,000	Loyola University School of Law, Chicago, IL
60,000	St. John's Jesuit High School, Toledo, OH -- Appalachian Christian Service Program
50,067	Rush Presbyterian St. Luke's Medical Center, Chicago, IL -- to be used by the organization to fund the pancreatic cancer research program developed by Jules E. Hams and Dr. Janet Plate
50,000	Bixby Community Health Foundation, Adrian, MI -- expansion and renovation of the Hickman Cancer Center

LOUIS P. SAIA FOUNDATION

Giving Contact
Louis P. Saia, Trustee
Louis P. Saia Foundation
1405 Bayou Black Drive
Houma, LA 70360-7453
Phone: (985)876-0660

Description
Founded: 1987
EIN: 721086475
Organization Type: Private Foundation
Giving Locations: LA: Harahan, Houma, Lockport, New Orleans, Schriever; OH: Steubenville; TN: Memphis
Grant Types: General Support, Research.

Financial Summary
Total Giving: $71,550 (2000)
Assets: $1,260,951 (2000)

Typical Recipients
Arts & Humanities: Arts & Humanities-General
Education: Arts/Humanities Education, Private Education (Precollege), Student Aid
Health: Children's Health/Hospitals, Hospitals
Religion: Churches, Dioceses, Religion-General, Religious Organizations, Religious Welfare
Social Services: Child Welfare, Food/Clothing Distribution, People with Disabilities, Substance Abuse

Application Procedures
Initial Contact: Apply verbally or in writing.
Deadlines: None.

Foundation Officials
Ann M. Saia, Jr.: trustee
Louis P. Saia, Jr.: trustee
Lyndon Saia, Jr.: trustee

Grants Analysis
Disclosure Period: calendar year ending 2000
Total Grants: $71,550
Number of Grants: 27
Average Grant: $2,650
Highest Grant: $22,500
Lowest Grant: $200
Typical Range: $500 to $5,000

Recent Grants
Note: Grants derived from 2000 Form 990.

General
22,500	St. Francis de Sales Cathedral, Houma, LA -- operations
5,200	Bayou Area Children's Foundation, Houma, LA -- operations

5,000	Children's Hospital, New Orleans, LA -- medical research
5,000	St. Jude Children's Research Hospital, Memphis, TN -- endowment fund
4,200	Vanderbilt Catholic High School, Houma, LA -- operations
3,600	St. Francis De Sales School, Houma, LA -- operations
2,000	Annual Bishop's Appeal Dioceses of Houma, Schriever, LA -- bishop's appeal fund
2,000	Sisters of Reparation to the Most Sacred Heart, Steubenville, OH -- operations
1,800	American-Italian Renaissance Foundation, New Orleans, LA -- museum, library and scholarship fund
1,800	Cabrini High School, New Orleans, LA

SAINT CROIX FOUNDATION

Giving Contact
Jeffrey T. Peterson, Assistant Secretary
c/o US Bank NA
332 Minnesota St.
PO Box 64704
St. Paul, MN 55164
Phone: (651)244-0942

Description
Founded: 1950
EIN: 416011826
Organization Type: Private Foundation
Giving Locations: MN; WI
Grant Types: Capital, Emergency, General Support, Operating Expenses.

Donor Information
Founder: Ianthe B. Hardenbergh, I. Hardenbergh Charitable Annuity Trust, Gabrielle Hardenbergh

Financial Summary
Total Giving: $596,200 (2001); $532,700 (2000); $489,200 (1999)
Giving Analysis: Giving for 2001 includes: foundation grants to United Way ($37,000); 2000: foundation grants to United Way ($34,500); 1999: foundation grants to United Way ($34,500)
Assets: $10,762,101 (2001); $11,131,098 (2000); $11,851,552 (1999)
Gifts Received: $421,526 (2001); $472,500 (2000); $324,089 (1999). Note: In 2001, contributions were received from Hardenbergh Charitable Annuity Trust ($249,000), and Gabrielle Hardenbergh ($2,775,000). In 2000, contributions were received from I. Hardenbergh Charitable Annuity Trust ($170,000) and Cabrielle Hardenbergh ($302,500). In 1999, contributions were received from I. Hardenbergh Charitable Annuity Trust ($320,000) and Cabrielle Hardenbergh ($4,089). In 1998, contributions were received from Hardenbergh Charitable Annunity Trust ($170,000) and Cabrielle Hardenbergh ($149,926).

Typical Recipients
Arts & Humanities: Arts Centers, Arts Funds, Community Arts, Historic Preservation, History & Archaeology, Museums/Galleries, Music, Opera, Performing Arts, Theater
Civic & Public Affairs: Economic Development, Civic & Public Affairs-General, Housing, Urban & Community Affairs
Education: Colleges & Universities, Education Funds, Private Education (Precollege), Public Education (Precollege)
Health: Cancer, Children's Health/Hospitals, Clinics/Medical Centers, Emergency/Ambulance Services,

Health-General, Health Organizations, Heart, Hospitals, Medical Rehabilitation, Prenatal Health Issues, Public Health
International: Health Care/Hospitals
Religion: Churches, Religious Organizations, Religious Welfare
Science: Science Museums
Social Services: Camps, Child Welfare, Community Service Organizations, Day Care, Family Services, People with Disabilities, Scouts, United Funds/United Ways, Volunteer Services, YMCA/YWCA/YMHA/YWHA, Youth Organizations

Application Procedures
Initial Contact: The foundation requests applications be made in writing. Provide complete information so that request may be evaluated.
Deadlines: None.

Restrictions
Grants are made only to organizations located in the Stillwater/St. Paul area in Minnesota. Grants are made to charitable institutions of learning, hospitals, sanitariums, and churches and religious organizations to aid and assist needy and oppressed persons.

Foundation Officials
Edgerton Bronson: treasurer
Robert S. Davis: president, director B Stillwater, MN 1914. ED University of Minnesota (1934). PRIM CORP EMPL director: H M Smyth Co. CORP AFFIL director: Heartland Technology. CLUB AFFIL Elks Club.
Gabrielle Hardenbergh: secretary
Quentin O. Heimerman: vice president
Jeffrey T. Peterson: secretary, director
Raymond A. Reister: director B Sioux City, IA 1929. ED Harvard University AB (1952); Harvard University LLB (1955). NONPR AFFIL member: Minneapolis Bar Association; vice president: Minneapolis Historical Society; member: American College Trust & Estate Counsel; member: Hennipin County Bar Association; member: American Bar Association. CLUB AFFIL Minneapolis Club; Harvard Club.

Grants Analysis
Disclosure Period: calendar year ending 2001
Total Grants: $559,200*
Number of Grants: 85
Average Grant: $5,402*
Highest Grant: $100,000
Typical Range: $1,000 to $10,000
*Note: Giving excludes United Way. Average grant figure excludes highest grant.

Recent Grants
Note: Grants derived from 2001 Form 990.

General
100,000	Croixdale Residence and Apartments, Bayport, MN -- capital campaign
32,000	United Way of St. Paul Area, St. Paul, MN
30,000	Children's Home Society of Minnesota, St. Paul, MN -- capital campaign
30,000	Presbyterian Homes, St. Paul, MN -- Arden Hills Apartments
21,000	Indianhead Council BSA, St. Paul, MN
20,000	Children's Health Care Foundation, Roseville, MN -- Midwest Children's Resource Center
20,000	Family Means of St. Croix, St. Paul, MN
19,000	HOPE Adoption and Family Services, St. Paul, MN -- capital campaign
16,000	Girl Scout Council of St. Croix Valley, St. Croix, MN
16,000	Minnesota Private College Fund, Minneapolis, MN

SAINT FRANCIS BANK

Company Headquarters
Milwaukee, WI

Company Description
Employees: 247
SIC(s): 6035 Federal Savings Institutions.
Parent Company: St. Francis Capital Corp., 13400
Bishops Lane, Ste. 350, Brookfield, WI, United States

Operating Locations
Saint Francis Bank (WI--Brookfield)

St. Francis Bank Foundation

Giving Contact
Maryann Zapall, Secretary
13400 Bishops Ln., Suite 350
Brookfield, WI 53005-6203
Phone: (262)787-8722

Description
Founded: 1984
EIN: 391535393
Organization Type: Corporate Foundation
Giving Locations: WI: Milwaukee
Grant Types: General Support.

Financial Summary
Total Giving: $227,439 (fiscal year ending September 30, 2000); $136,773 (fiscal 1999); $99,917 (fiscal 1998)
Giving Analysis: Giving for fiscal 2000 includes: foundation matching gifts ($11,239); foundation grants to United Way ($15,000); foundation ($201,200); fiscal 1999: foundation grants to United Way ($8,100); foundation matching gifts ($14,523); foundation ($114,150); fiscal 1998: foundation grants to United Way ($5,250) foundation matching gifts ($14,297)
Assets: $722,174 (fiscal 2000); $1,099,475 (fiscal 1999); $1,102,610 (fiscal 1998)
Gifts Received: In fiscal 1991, contributions were received from St. Francis Bank, F.S.B. ($30,300) and others ($2,500).

Typical Recipients
Arts & Humanities: Arts Centers, Arts Festivals, Ballet, Historic Preservation, History & Archaeology, Libraries, Museums/Galleries, Music, Performing Arts
Civic & Public Affairs: Botanical Gardens/Parks, Economic Development, Civic & Public Affairs-General, Hispanic Affairs, Housing, Municipalities/Towns, Urban & Community Affairs
Education: Business-School Partnerships, Colleges & Universities, Education-General, Private Education (Precollege), Vocational & Technical Education
Health: AIDS/HIV, Alzheimers Disease, Clinics/Medical Centers, Health Organizations, Heart, Public Health
Religion: Jewish Causes, Religious Welfare
Science: Science Museums
Social Services: Big Brother/Big Sister, Community Centers, Community Service Organizations, Food/Clothing Distribution, Social Services-General, United Funds/United Ways, YMCA/YWCA/YMHA/YWHA, Youth Organizations

Application Procedures
Initial Contact: Send a brief letter of inquiry.
Application Requirements: Include amount requested and purpose of funds sought.
Deadlines: None.

Corporate Officials
Thomas R. Perz: president, chief executive officer PRIM CORP EMPL president, chief executive officer: St Francis Bank.
John C. Schlosser: chairman, director B Englewood, NJ 1928. ED Pace University (1953). PRIM CORP EMPL chairman, director: St Francis Bank ADD CORP EMPL chairman: Saint Francis Capital Corp.
John Sorenson: chief financial officer PRIM CORP EMPL chief financial officer: St Francis Bank.

Foundation Officials
William F. Double: director
Rudolph T. Hoppe: director
Brian T. Kaye: secretary PRIM CORP EMPL executive vice president: St Francis Bank.
Edward W. Mentzer: director
Thomas R. Perz: vice president, director (see above)
Robert V. Rice: director
John C. Schlosser: president, director (see above)
Bruce R. Sherman: treasurer
Edward O. Templeton: director CORP AFFIL director: Saint Francis Capital Corp.

Grants Analysis
Disclosure Period: fiscal year ending September 30, 1999
Total Grants: $201,200*
Number of Grants: 24
Average Grant: $6,574*
Highest Grant: $50,000
Lowest Grant: $100
Typical Range: $100 to $15,000
*Note: Giving excludes United Way and matching gifts. Average grant excludes highest grant.

Recent Grants
Note: Grants derived from fiscal 2000 Form 990.

Library-Related
26,000	St. Francis Public Library Foundation, St. Francis, WI

General
50,000	IMAX Theater, Memphis, TN
33,000	YWCA
25,000	Sharon Lynne Wilson Center for The Arts, Milwaukee, WI
15,000	10/36 Friends, Inc.
15,000	United Way
10,000	Centers Campaign
10,000	Marian Center, St. Paul, MN
10,000	Milwaukee Mentors Program, Milwaukee, WI
5,000	Milwaukee Ballet, Milwaukee, WI
5,000	St. Ann Adult Day Care, Inc., Milwaukee, WI

ST. GILES FOUNDATION

Giving Contact
Richard T. Arkwright, President
420 Lexington Avenue, Suite 2329
New York, NY 10170
Phone: (212)338-9001

Description
Founded: 1979
EIN: 111630806
Organization Type: General Purpose Foundation
Giving Locations: NY
Grant Types: General Support, Research, Scholarship.

Donor Information
Founder: Established by the James Tisdale Trust, Jesse Ridley, the late Louis W. Arnold , and the late Marvin Leavens .

Financial Summary
Total Giving: $842,837 (fiscal year ending March 31, 2002); $648,677 (fiscal 2001); $842,500 (fiscal 1999)
Giving Analysis: Giving for fiscal 2001 includes: foundation scholarships ($50,000)
Assets: $26,660,901 (fiscal 2002); $27,995,630 (fiscal 2001); $36,091,329 (fiscal 1999)
Gifts Received: $27,236 (fiscal 2001); $10,180 (fiscal 2000); $55,701 (fiscal 1999). Note: In fiscal 2002, contributions were received from the estate of Daisy Oliver Berry. Contributions were received from the Estate of Ann B. Hallet.

Typical Recipients
Arts & Humanities: Historic Preservation
Education: Colleges & Universities, Faculty Development, Medical Education, Special Education, Student Aid
Health: AIDS/HIV, Cancer, Children's Health/Hospitals, Clinics/Medical Centers, Health-General, Hospitals, Medical Rehabilitation, Medical Research, Mental Health, Prenatal Health Issues
Religion: Religious Organizations, Religious Welfare
Science: Scientific Labs
Social Services: Community Service Organizations, Day Care, Emergency Relief, Family Services, People with Disabilities

Application Procedures
Initial Contact: The foundation requests applicants submit a detailed written request for funding.
Deadlines: None.

Restrictions
The foundation reports that although it does not impose restrictions on giving, it does have a primary interest in children's orthopedics.

Foundation Officials
Richard T. Arkwright: president PRIM CORP EMPL executive vice president: Seifert Gray & Co. Inc. NONPR AFFIL president, director: Brooklyn Society for Prevention.
John J. Bennett, Jr.: secretary
Edward Ridley Finch, Jr.: general counsel, trustee B Westhampton Beach, NY August 31, 1919. ED Princeton University AB (1941); New York University JD (1947). NONPR AFFIL president, director: Saint Nicholas Society New York; trustee: Whittell Trust College; treasurer: Jessie Ridley Foundation; member: Pennsylvania Bar Association; member faculty advisory committee department politics: Princeton University; president, director: New York Institute Special Education; member: New York State Bar Association; life trustee: Metropolitan Museum Art; director: National Space Society; member: International Institute Space Law; member: Judge Advocates Association; member: International Astronautical Academy; member: International Bar Association; member: Florida Bar Association; member: Inter-American Bar Association; member: Federal Bar Association; president: Finch Trusts; member: American Law Institute; member: Association Bar New York City; sr member: American Institute Aeronautics & Astronautics; member: American Judicature Society; member: American Bar Association; fellow: American Bar Foundation; treasurer: Adams Memorial Fund; panelist: American Arbitration Association. CLUB AFFIL University Washington Club; Westhampton Country Club; Union League Club; University New York Club; Princeton Club; Union Club; Bathing Corp. Southampton Club; Long Island Club.
John H. Livingston: vice president
Robert Battin Mackay: trustee B Brooklyn, NY 1945. ED Boston University BS (1968); Harvard University MEd (1972); Boston University PhD (1980). PRIM NONPR EMPL director: Society for the Preservation of Long Island Antiquities. NONPR AFFIL member advisory committee: New York State Historic Maritime Areas; trustee: Theodore Roosevelt Association; member: New York State County Parks; member:

New York State Heritage Areas; trustee: Homsland Foundation; chairman: New York State Board Historical Preservation. CLUB AFFIL New York Yacht Club.
Samuel H. Owens: treasurer

Grants Analysis

Disclosure Period: fiscal year ending March 31, 2002
Total Grants: $792,837*
Number of Grants: 9
Highest Grant: $400,000
Lowest Grant: $15,000
*****Note:** Giving excludes scholarships.

Recent Grants

Note: Grants derived from 2002 Form 990.

General

400,000	Hospital for Special Surgery, New York, NY -- St. Giles Chair in Pediatric Genetic Research
265,000	Rockefeller University, New York, NY -- research for childhood leukemia
182,837	Cold Spring Harbor Laboratory Association, Cold Spring Harbor, NY -- for research study
135,000	Brigham and Women's Hospital, Harvard Medical School, Boston, MA -- for research extension study of the Role of Ca2 Sensing Receptor in Bone Disease
125,000	New York Presbyterian Hospital, New York, NY -- reconstruction program
50,000	September 11th Fund, New York, NY -- help needy families and children
35,000	Pediatric Orthopedic Society of North America, Rosemont, IL -- for the Memorial Award
25,000	Cumberland College, Williamsburg, KY -- Scholarship Assistance Program
25,000	St. Hilda's and St. Hugh's School, New York, NY -- for scholarship assistance program to aid disabled and financially needy students
17,500	Interfaith Neighbors, Inc., New York, NY -- Peace of Mind Project

ST. PAUL COMPANIES, INC.

Company Headquarters

385 Washington Street
St. Paul, MN 55102
Phone: (651)310-7911
Fax: (651)310-8294
Web: http://www.stpaul.com

Company Description

Ticker: SPC
Exchange: OTC
Assets: US$39.879 billion (2002)
Profit: US$217.8 million (2002)
Employees: 9700 (2002)
Fortune Rank: 207, per FORTUNE Magazine's list of 500 Largest U.S. Corporations (2002).
SIC(s): 6331 Fire, Marine & Casualty Insurance.

Operating Locations

Saint Paul Companies Inc. (CO; CT; DE; FL; ID; IL; IN; KS; MA; MN; MT; NJ; NY; ND; OH; OR; TX; WA; WI)

Subsidiary Companies

IL: The John Nuveen Co., Chicago

Nonmonetary Support

Type: Donated Equipment; Loaned Employees; Workplace Solicitation
Volunteer Programs: Company-sponsored volunteer projects have included: Junior Achievement, Metro Paint-A-Thon, Voluntary Action Center, Wilson

Hi-Rise, Retiree Volunteer Program, Special Olympics, Habitat for Humanity, and school pairing projects.
Contact: Ron McKinley, Vice President
Phone: (651)310-2623
Note: The company also provides printing services to nonprofits.

St. Paul Companies Inc. Foundation

Giving Contact

Mary Pickard, President & Executive Director
St. Paul Companies, Inc. Foundation
385 Washington Street
St. Paul, MN 55102-1396
Phone: (651)310-7911
Fax: (651)310-2327
Web: http://www.stpaul.com

Description

EIN: 411924256
Organization Type: Corporate Foundation
Giving Locations: MD: Baltimore area; MN: Minneapolis, St. Paul; select areas where company has large business presence; United Kingdom
Grant Types: Capital, Employee Matching Gifts, Endowment, Fellowship, General Support, Matching, Multiyear/Continuing Support, Project, Scholarship.
Note: Employee matching gift ratio: 1 to 1; 2 to 1 for organisation with 50 hours of employee volunteer time.

Financial Summary

Total Giving: $8,356,419 (2002); $12,000,348 (2001); $9,672,621 (2000). Note: Contributes through corporate direct giving program and foundation.
Giving Analysis: Giving for 2000 includes: foundation matching gifts ($884,578); foundation ($8,788,043); 1999: corporate fellowships ($30,000); corporate scholarships ($594,000); corporate grants to United Way ($1,177,081); corporate direct giving ($5,442,868); foundation ($7,393,754); 1997: domestic and international subsidiaries ($57,415); corporate grants to United Way ($610,351); corporate matching gifts ($920,221); corporate direct giving ($9,375,625);
Assets: $231,540 (2002); $28,620 (2000); $323,518 (1999)
Gifts Received: $8,625,605 (2002); $9,503,359 (2000); $7,786,709 (1999). Note: Contributions are received from The St. Paul Companies, Inc.

Typical Recipients

Arts & Humanities: Arts Associations & Councils, Arts Centers, Arts Funds, Arts Institutes, Arts Outreach, Community Arts, Dance, Ethnic & Folk Arts, Arts & Humanities-General, History & Archaeology, Libraries, Literary Arts, Museums/Galleries, Music, Performing Arts, Public Broadcasting, Theater
Civic & Public Affairs: African American Affairs, Asian American Affairs, Business/Free Enterprise, Chambers of Commerce, Clubs, Economic Development, Employment/Job Training, Civic & Public Affairs-General, Hispanic Affairs, Housing, Municipalities/Towns, Native American Affairs, Nonprofit Management, Philanthropic Organizations, Professional & Trade Associations, Urban & Community Affairs, Women's Affairs, Zoos/Aquariums
Education: Arts/Humanities Education, Business Education, Colleges & Universities, Community & Junior Colleges, Education Reform, Faculty Development, Education-General, International Studies, Leadership Training, Literacy, Minority Education, Private Education (Precollege), Public Education (Precollege), Social Sciences Education, Student Aid
Environment: Environment-General
Health: Adolescent Health Issues, AIDS/HIV, Cancer, Clinics/Medical Centers

International: International-General, International Affairs
Religion: Religious Welfare
Science: Science Museums, Scientific Centers & Institutes
Social Services: At-Risk Youth, Child Welfare, Community Centers, Community Service Organizations, Day Care, Emergency Relief, Family Services, Recreation & Athletics, Scouts, Senior Services, United Funds/United Ways, Volunteer Services, YMCA/YWCA/YMHA/YWHA, Youth Organizations

Application Procedures

Initial Contact: Submit a one- to two-page letter to the foundation describing the request.
Application Requirements: Include the organization's mission; purpose of funds sought; amount requested; and time span for funding.
Deadlines: None.
Review Process: Staff committee conducts initial review and prepares research report for executive management.
Evaluative Criteria: Preference is given organizations that demonstrate a commitment to their communities by ensuring that their governing bodies include representatives from the community and collaborative efforts and initiatives that fit more than one of the Foundation's priority funding areas. National organizations may be considered for specific initiatives that fall within the Foundation's focus areas; such requests are more likely to receive funding if they support or leverage the potential of other Foundation grantees.
Decision Notification: Foundation staff responds by phone within two weeks of receiving letter of inquiry to indicate whether or not a full proposal is advised.
Notes: If you have received Foundation funding in the past, you may contact the foundation directly to obtain application materials without going through the letter of inquiry phase.

Restrictions

Does not fund sectarian religious organizations unless the funds will be used in the direct interest of the entire community; veterans' or fraternal organizations; political or lobbying organizations; benefits, fundraisers, walk-a-thons, telethons, galas, or other revenue-generating events; advertising; scholarships to individuals; health or disease-specific organizations; health care or other emergency assistance to individuals; hospitals or other health services generally supported by third-party reimbursement mechanisms; replacement of government funding; start-up, capital, or operations of public or charter schools; human services such as counseling, chemical abuse, or family programs; environmental programs; special events, except when the event is a key strategy in a continuum of efforts to achieve community goals in the foundation's priority areas; organizations that discriminate on the basis of race, gender, religion, culture, age, physical disability, sexual orientation, or veteran status; or nonacademic job placement programs.

Additional Information

The company also provides some grants through The St. Paul Companies Maryland Foundation.
Corporate contributions currently average about 2% of pretax operating earnings averaged over a three-year period.
Regional offices have separate giving programs.
St. Paul Companies completed its merger with USF& G Corp. in April 1998. USF&G and St. Paul had combined revenues of $9.6 billion in 1997.
Publications: Community Affairs Distribution Report; Grant Application; Partners in Giving - St. Paul's Matching Gift Program Brochure; Guidelines; Application Information

Corporate Officials

James E. Gustafson: president, chief operating officeraffairs B 1946. ED University of South Dakota BA (1965-1969). PRIM CORP EMPL president, chief operating officer: Saint Paul Companies Inc. CORP AFFIL president: General Reinsurance Service Corp.; chairman: National Reinsurance Corp.

Karen Himle: vice president corporate committee PRIM CORP EMPL vice president corporate committee: St. Paul Companies Inc.

Paul J. Liska: executive vice president, chief financial officer B 1956. ED University of Notre Dame BBA (1977); Northwestern University MM (1983). PRIM CORP EMPL executive vice president, chief financial officer: Saint Paul Companies Inc. ADD CORP EMPL executive vice president: Saint Paul Insurance Co. Inc.; executive vice president: Saint Paul Fire & Mar Insurance Co.; chief financial officer: Saint Paul Mercury Insurance Co.; chief financial officer: Fidelty & Guaranty Insurance; director: John Nuveen Corp.; chief financial officer: Seaboard Surety Co. CORP AFFIL director: Renaissance Reinsurance. NONPR AFFIL director: Walker Art Center.

Mary Pickard: vice president committee affairs PRIM CORP EMPL vice president committee affairs: St. Paul Companies Inc.

Giving Program Officials

Deb Anderson: manager

Foundation Officials

Andy Bessette: director, vice chairman
Thomas Bradley: director, treasurer
Jay Fishman: director, chairman
Christopher Gerst: assistant corporate secretary
John MacColl: director
Michael Newman: vice president
Kurt Schwarzkopf: corporate secretary

Grants Analysis

Disclosure Period: calendar year ending 2002
Total Grants: $6,066,180*
Number of Grants: 168
Average Grant: $26,529
Highest Grant: $200,000
Lowest Grant: $50
Typical Range: $50 to $1,500 and $5,000 to $100,000
*Note: Giving excludes matching gifts; scholarship; United Way.

Recent Grants

Note: Grants derived from 2002 Form 990.

General

450,000	Greater Twin Cities United Way, Minneapolis, MN -- operating support
250,000	Manhattan College, Riverdale, NY -- scholarships
200,000	Children's Theater Company, Minneapolis, MN -- capital support
200,000	Hamline University, St. Paul, MN -- support for the Center for Excellence in Urban Teaching
200,000	Minnesota Private College Fund, St. Paul, MN -- Urban Education Scholarship Program
200,000	Project for Pride in Living, Inc., Minneapolis, MN -- capital support
150,000	Family Housing Fund, Minneapolis, MN -- Public Education initiative
140,000	Local Initiatives Support Corporation, New York, NY -- operating support
100,000	Hmong American Partnership, St. Paul, MN -- capital support
100,000	Minnesota Minority Education Partnership, Minneapolis, MN -- operating support

SALOMON SMITH BARNEY HOLDINGS, INC.

Company Headquarters

388 Greenwich St.
New York, NY 10013
Web: http://www.salomonsmithbarney.com

Company Description

Ticker: ASB
Exchange: AMEX
Formed by Merger of: Salomon Brothers and Smith Barney (1997).
Operating Revenue: US$27.374 billion (2001)
Employees: 42,360 (2001)
SIC(s): 2911 Petroleum Refining, 6211 Security Brokers & Dealers, 6221 Commodity Contracts Brokers & Dealers, 6719 Holding Companies Nec.
Parent Company: Citigroup Inc., 399 Park Ave., New York, NY, United States

Operating Locations

Salomon Smith Barney (CA--Los Angeles, San Francisco; CT--Westport; GA--Atlanta; MA--Boston; TX--Dallas)

Giving Contact

Jane E. Heffner, Vice President, Corporate Contributions
Salomon Smith Barney Community Investment Program
New York, NY 10048
Phone: (718)248-1656
Fax: (212)783-4262

Alternate Contact

Patricia Byrne
Phone: (212)793-8885

Description

Organization Type: Corporate Giving Program
Former Name: Salomon Foundation.
Former Name: Traveler's Group Foundation.
Former Name: Traveler's Foundation.
Giving Locations: headquarters and operating communities; nationally.
Grant Types: Employee Matching Gifts, General Support, Scholarship.
Note: Employee matching gift ratio: 1 to 1.

Financial Summary

Total Giving: $11,336,073 (1997); $4,300,000 (1996 approx); $4,200,000 (1995 approx). Note: Contributes through corporate direct giving program only.
Giving Analysis: Giving for 1998 includes: foundation ($11,336,073)
Assets: $7,835,584 (1997); $23,639,516 (1995); $17,539,615 (1994)
Gifts Received: $4,500,000 (1997); $638,445 (1995); $17,332,588 (1994). Note: Contributions are received from Salomon Brothers, Inc., and Salomon Brothers Holding Corp.

Typical Recipients

Arts & Humanities: Ballet, Historic Preservation, Libraries, Museums/Galleries, Music, Opera, Performing Arts, Public Broadcasting, Theater, Visual Arts
Civic & Public Affairs: Economic Development, Employment/Job Training, Law & Justice, Legal Aid, Women's Affairs, Zoos/Aquariums
Education: Arts/Humanities Education, Business Education, Economic Education, Elementary Education (Private), Literacy, Minority Education, Public Education (Precollege)
Health: Hospitals, Medical Research, Single-Disease Health Associations
Science: Scientific Centers & Institutes

Social Services: Delinquency & Criminal Rehabilitation, Emergency Relief, Family Planning, Food/Clothing Distribution, Recreation & Athletics, Substance Abuse, Youth Organizations

Application Procedures

Initial Contact: Contact the company for specific guidelines.
Deadlines: None.

Restrictions

Fraternal organizations, political or lobbying groups, or religious groups for sectarian purposes are not considered for contributions.

Additional Information

Travelers Foundation and Citicorp Foundation merged to form Citigroup Foundation in 1999. Salomon Smith Barney now gives directly through its Community Investment Program.

Giving Program Officials

Jane E. Heffner: vice president PRIM CORP EMPL vice president corporate contributions: Salomon Brothers Inc.

Grants Analysis

Disclosure Period: calendar year ending 1997
Total Grants: $942,917
Number of Grants: 9
Average Grant: $32,153*
Highest Grant: $250,000
Typical Range: $10,000 to $50,000
*Note: Average grant excludes three highest grants totaling $750,000.

RICHARD SALTONSTALL CHARITABLE FOUNDATION

Giving Contact

Dudley Willis, Trustee
50 Congress Street, Rm. 800
Boston, MA 02109
Phone: (617)227-8660
Fax: (617)227-4470

Description

Founded: 1964
EIN: 046078934
Organization Type: Private Foundation
Giving Locations: MA
Grant Types: General Support, Research.

Financial Summary

Total Giving: $1,200,000 (2000); $900,000 (1998); $550,000 (1995)
Giving Analysis: Giving for 2000 includes: foundation grants to United Way ($205,000) 1998: foundation grants to United Way ($151,666)
Assets: $25,661,767 (2000); $22,699,622 (1998); $14,444,347 (1995)

Typical Recipients

Arts & Humanities: Dance, Libraries, Museums/Galleries, Music, Public Broadcasting
Civic & Public Affairs: Botanical Gardens/Parks, Clubs, Civic & Public Affairs-General, Native American Affairs, Rural Affairs, Women's Affairs, Zoos/Aquariums
Education: Agricultural Education, Health & Physical Education, Leadership Training, Medical Education, Minority Education, Private Education (Precollege), Special Education
Environment: Air/Water Quality, Environment-General, Protection, Resource Conservation, Watershed

Health: Alzheimers Disease, Children's Health/Hospitals, Clinics/Medical Centers, Eyes/Blindness, Hospices, Hospitals
Science: Science Museums
Social Services: Counseling, Day Care, Family Services, People with Disabilities, Substance Abuse, United Funds/United Ways, Youth Organizations

Application Procedures

Initial Contact: The foundation has no formal grant application procedure or application form.
Deadlines: None.

Foundation Officials

Robert Ashton Lawrence: trustee B Boston, MA 1926. ED Yale University (1947). PRIM CORP EMPL partner: Saltonstall Co. CORP AFFIL director: State Street Growth Fund Inc.; director: State Street Investment Trust; director: State Street Exchange Fund; director: Metropolitan Series Fund; director: New York Times Co.; director: Metropolitan Life Portfolios; director: Metropolitan Life State Street Mutual Funds; director: Fifty Associates; executive vice president: FMR Corp.
Emily S. Lewis: trustee
Dudley H. Willis: trustee
Sally S. Willis: trustee

Grants Analysis

Disclosure Period: calendar year ending 2000
Total Grants: $995,000*
Number of Grants: 35
Average Grant: $28,429
Highest Grant: $150,000
Lowest Grant: $2,500
Typical Range: $2,500 to $50,000
*Note: Giving excludes United Way.

Recent Grants

Note: Grants derived from 2000 Form 990.

General

150,000	United Way of Massachusetts Bay, Boston, MA
100,000	Boston Symphony Orchestra, Boston, MA
100,000	Brigham and Women's Hospital, Boston, MA
100,000	New England Aquarium, Boston, MA
100,000	New England Medical Center, Boston, MA
100,000	Peabody Essex Museum, Salem, MA
75,000	Charles River School, Dover, MA
70,000	WGBH Educational Foundation, Boston, MA
60,000	Harvard University School of Public Health, Cambridge, MA
55,000	United Way of Massachusetts Bay, Boston, MA -- special fund

EARL C. SAMS FOUNDATION

Giving Contact

Bruce Sams Hawn, President
101 N. Shoreline Blvd., Suite 602
Corpus Christi, TX 78401
Phone: (361)888-6485
Fax: (361)884-4241

Description

Founded: 1946
EIN: 741463151
Organization Type: General Purpose Foundation
Giving Locations: TX: Southern Texas
Grant Types: General Support, Matching, Project.

Donor Information

Founder: Incorporated in 1946 by the late Earl C. Sams .

Financial Summary

Total Giving: $1,194,700 (2001); $1,169,462 (2000); $1,298,514 (1999 approx)
Giving Analysis: Giving for 1998 includes: foundation matching gifts ($150,000)
Assets: $28,260,350 (2001); $29,928,434 (2000); $28,346,532 (1999 approx)

Typical Recipients

Arts & Humanities: Arts Centers, Ballet, Museums/Galleries, Music, Performing Arts, Public Broadcasting, Theater
Civic & Public Affairs: Asian American Affairs, Botanical Gardens/Parks, Community Foundations, Employment/Job Training, Civic & Public Affairs-General, Housing, Municipalities/Towns, Philanthropic Organizations, Public Policy, Rural Affairs, Women's Affairs, Zoos/Aquariums
Education: Colleges & Universities, Elementary Education (Public), Engineering/Technological Education, Environmental Education, Faculty Development, Education-General, Literacy, Medical Education, Private Education (Precollege), Public Education (Precollege), School Volunteerism, Science/Mathematics Education, Student Aid
Environment: Air/Water Quality, Environment-General, Environment-General, Protection, Resource Conservation, Wildlife Protection
Health: AIDS/HIV, Alzheimers Disease, Arthritis, Cancer, Children's Health/Hospitals, Diabetes, Emergency/Ambulance Services, Health-General, Heart, Kidney, Medical Rehabilitation, Medical Research, Mental Health
International: International Relations
Religion: Churches, Ministries, Religious Welfare, Social/Policy Issues
Science: Science Museums, Scientific Research
Social Services: Animal Protection, At-Risk Youth, Child Abuse, Child Welfare, Community Service Organizations, Counseling, Crime Prevention, Emergency Relief, Family Planning, Family Services, Family Services, Food/Clothing Distribution, People with Disabilities, Recreation & Athletics, Scouts, Shelters/Homelessness, Social Services-General, Substance Abuse, United Funds/United Ways, Volunteer Services, YMCA/YWCA/YMHA/YWHA, Youth Organizations

Application Procedures

Initial Contact: The foundation requests written proposals with documentation to support request and adequate information for the board of directors to evaluate the proposal.
Deadlines: None. The foundation requests that proposals are submitted one month prior to board meetings to be considered at that meeting.
Review Process: The board meets quarterly.

Restrictions

Grants are made solely to tax-exempt 501(c)(3) organizations. The foundation does not make grants to individuals.

Foundation Officials

Bruce Sams Hawn: president, chief executive officer, director
Nancy Hawn: director
Ed Jensen: assistant treasurer
Susan Ohnmacht: secretary
Susan Hawn Yuras: chairman, vice president, director

Grants Analysis

Disclosure Period: calendar year ending 2001
Total Grants: $1,194,700
Number of Grants: 60
Average Grant: $19,912

Highest Grant: $155,000
Lowest Grant: $1,000
Typical Range: $1,000 to $25,000

Recent Grants

Note: Grants derived from 2001 Form 990.

General

155,000	Texas State Aquarium, Corpus Christi, TX -- toward the construction of Dolphin Bay Exhibit
100,000	Making Main Street Happen, Inc., Houston, TX -- redevelopment of Main Street Houston
100,000	St. James Episcopal School, Houston, TX -- toward capital campaign
100,000	South Texas Public Broadcasting, Corpus Christi, TX -- toward the cost for conversion to DTV
77,500	Valley Zoological Society, Brownsville, TX -- White Rhino Moat Project
50,000	Palmer Drug Abuse Program, Corpus Christi, TX -- operating budget
40,000	Corpus Christi Metro Ministries, Corpus Christi, TX -- toward the support of the Rainbow House and Rustic House
30,000	Charity League, Corpus Christi, TX -- toward Charity League's 2000 Charity
30,000	Del Mar College Foundation, Corpus Christi, TX -- toward the construction of the Center for Early Learning
25,000	Art Center of Corpus Christi, Corpus Christi, TX -- toward renovation and expansion of existing facility

FAN FOX AND LESLIE R. SAMUELS FOUNDATION

Giving Contact

Joseph Mitchell, President, Treasurer, and Director
350 Fifth Avenue, Suite 4301
New York, NY 10118
Phone: (212)239-3030
Fax: (212)239-3039
E-mail: info@samuels.org
Web: http://www.samuels.org

Description

Founded: 1981
EIN: 133124818
Organization Type: General Purpose Foundation
Giving Locations: NY: New York metropolitan area
Grant Types: Multiyear/Continuing Support, Project, Seed Money.

Donor Information

Founder: Established in Utah in 1959 by the late Mr. Leslie R. Samuels and Mrs. Leslie R. Samuels. The Foundation was originally called the Samuels-Auerbach Foundation and was reincorporated in New York in 1981.

Financial Summary

Total Giving: $10,046,033 (fiscal year ending July 31, 2001); $8,651,384 (fiscal 2000); $7,990,196 (fiscal 1998)
Giving Analysis: Giving for fiscal 2001 includes: foundation scholarships ($202,750); fiscal 1998: foundation scholarships ($40,000) foundation matching gifts ($215,000)
Assets: $222,235,661 (fiscal 2001); $240,422,454 (fiscal 2000); $211,895,561 (fiscal 1998)
Gifts Received: $180,934 (fiscal 2000); $711,701 (fiscal 1998); $29,771 (fiscal 1993). Note: In fiscal 1998 and 2000, contributions were received from the trusts of Fannie Fox Samuels and Leslie R. Samuels.

Typical Recipients

Arts & Humanities: Arts Centers, Arts Funds, Arts Outreach, Ballet, Dance, Libraries, Music, Opera, Performing Arts, Theater
Civic & Public Affairs: Public Policy
Education: Arts/Humanities Education, Colleges & Universities, Education-General, Medical Education
Health: Adolescent Health Issues, AIDS/HIV, Alzheimers Disease, Cancer, Children's Health/Hospitals, Clinics/Medical Centers, Diabetes, Geriatric Health, Health Policy/Cost Containment, Health Organizations, Heart, Home-Care Services, Hospices, Hospitals, Long-Term Care, Medical Rehabilitation, Medical Research, Mental Health, Nursing Services, Prenatal Health Issues, Public Health, Research/Studies Institutes, Respiratory
Religion: Jewish Causes
Social Services: Community Service Organizations, Delinquency & Criminal Rehabilitation, Family Services, People with Disabilities, Substance Abuse

Application Procedures

Initial Contact: Letters of inquiry should be directed to the foundation's program officer. There are no application forms.
Application Requirements: Include a copy of 501(c)(3) letter, board of directors list, project budget, most recent financial statement, and current contributors list. Letters should briefly summarize the proposal and state the amount requested. Costly presentations are discouraged.
Deadlines: None.
Review Process: All letters are acknowledged within two months. If a proposal is of interest, an appointment will be arranged to discuss details before it is presented to the board, which meets in January, April, July, and October.

Restrictions

All funding is restricted to the five boroughs of New York City. The foundation reports that it no longer supports community service organizations, education, or media. It also does not support individuals. The foundation has a small budget for arts-in-education programming. No grants are made for operating expenses, building funds, or fund-raising campaigns.

Additional Information

Publications: Biennial Report

Foundation Officials

Morton J. Bernstein: director B 1917.
Marvin A. Kaufman: chairman, director B 1932.
Robert Marx: director, vice president
Joseph C. Mitchell: president, director
Carlos Dupre Moseley: director B Laurens, SC September 21, 1914. ED Duke University BA (1935); Philadelphia Conservatory of Music (1941-1944). NONPR AFFIL member: Phi Eta Sigma; member: Pi Kappa Lambda; member: Mu Phi Epsilon; member: Phi Beta Kappa; life trustee: Converse College; member: Metropolitan Opera Association; member: Century Association. CLUB AFFIL Piedmont Club.

Grants Analysis

Disclosure Period: fiscal year ending July 31, 2001
Total Grants: $9,843,283*
Number of Grants: 298
Average Grant: $31,459*
Highest Grant: $500,000
Typical Range: $15,000 to $50,000
*Note: Giving excludes scholarships. Average grant figure excludes highest grant.

Recent Grants

Note: Grants derived from 2001 Form 990.

General

1,000,000	Metropolitan Opera Association, Inc., New York, NY -- renovation of the Carlos Moseley Pavilion
500,000	Lincoln Center for the Performing Arts, New York, NY -- phase one of redevelopment project
500,000	Lincoln Center for the Performing Arts, New York, NY -- support for Lincoln Center Redevelopment Project
300,000	Metropolitan Opera Association, Inc., New York, NY -- support for next season's production of Sergei Prokofiev's The Gambler
300,000	Philharmonic Symphony Society of New York, New York, NY -- support for the 2000-2001 rush hour and Saturday matinee concert series
250,000	Carnegie Hall Society, New York, NY -- concert programming, artistic planning
250,000	New York City Ballet, New York, NY -- continued support for the Robert Irving Guest Conductor's Chair
200,000	Lincoln Center for the Performing Arts, New York, NY -- support for Live from Lincoln Center
200,000	Partnership for Caring, Washington, DC -- strengthening health care agency leadership summit conference
160,500	Partnership for Caring, Washington, DC -- grand coordination center

GEORGE H. SANDY FOUNDATION

Giving Contact

Chester R. MacPhee, Jr., Trustee
PO Box 591717
San Francisco, CA 94159-1717
Phone: (415)765-2122

Description

Founded: 1960
EIN: 946054473
Organization Type: Private Foundation
Giving Locations: CA: San Francisco Bay area
Grant Types: Capital, Emergency, Multiyear/Continuing Support, Operating Expenses, Project, Scholarship.

Donor Information

Founder: the late George H. Sandy

Financial Summary

Total Giving: $1,222,000 (2001); $1,126,000 (2000); $1,165,000 (1999)
Giving Analysis: Giving for 2001 includes: foundation scholarships ($110,000); 2000: foundation scholarships ($105,000) 1999: foundation scholarships ($90,000)
Assets: $20,121,630 (2001); $21,352,605 (2000); $21,658,840 (1999)

Typical Recipients

Arts & Humanities: Libraries, Museums/Galleries
Civic & Public Affairs: Employment/Job Training, Civic & Public Affairs-General, Hispanic Affairs, Philanthropic Organizations, Urban & Community Affairs, Women's Affairs
Education: Afterschool/Enrichment Programs, Business-School Partnerships, Colleges & Universities, Elementary Education (Private), Elementary Education (Public), Education-General, Leadership Training, Legal Education, Literacy, Medical Education, Preschool Education, Private Education (Precollege), School Volunteerism, Science/Mathematics Education, Secondary Education (Public), Special Education, Student Aid
Environment: Wildlife Protection
Health: AIDS/HIV, Cancer, Children's Health/Hospitals, Emergency/Ambulance Services, Health Organizations, Heart, Home-Care Services, Hospitals, Hospitals, Long-Term Care, Medical Research, Mental

Health, Prenatal Health Issues, Single-Disease Health Associations, Speech & Hearing, Trauma Treatment
International: Health Care/Hospitals, International Organizations, Missionary/Religious Activities
Religion: Churches, Jewish Causes, Religious Organizations, Religious Welfare
Social Services: Animal Protection, Big Brother/Big Sister, Camps, Child Abuse, Child Welfare, Community Service Organizations, Counseling, Day Care, Domestic Violence, Family Services, Food/Clothing Distribution, Homes, People with Disabilities, Recreation & Athletics, Shelters/Homelessness, Substance Abuse, Veterans, Volunteer Services, Youth Organizations, Youth Organizations

Application Procedures

Initial Contact: Send a brief letter of inquiry describing program or project.
Deadlines: None.

Restrictions

Contributions are made primarily to support local activities benefiting the handicapped and infirm.

Additional Information

Trust(s): Union Bank CA

Foundation Officials

Thomas J. Feeney, Esq.: trustee
Chester R. MacPhee, Jr.: trustee

Grants Analysis

Disclosure Period: calendar year ending 2001
Total Grants: $1,012,000*
Number of Grants: 75
Average Grant: $13,493
Highest Grant: $35,000
Typical Range: $10,000 to $20,000
*Note: Giving excludes scholarships.

Recent Grants

Note: Grants derived from 2001 Form 990.

General

35,000	San Francisco Society for the Prevention of Cruelty to Animals, San Francisco, CA -- Hearing Dog Program
30,000	Books Aloud, San Jose, CA -- to support their Books Aloud Program
30,000	Eastside College Preparatory School, East Palo Alto, CA -- for the Shoot for the Starts and tuition free co-educational private school education
30,000	Environmental Travel Companions, San Francisco, CA -- provides first hand environmental education and wilderness experiences to handicapped, disabled and needy persons
30,000	RCH, Inc., San Francisco, CA -- for After School and Day Camp Program
30,000	Volunteer Auxiliary of the Youth Guidance Center, San Francisco, CA -- for assistance for abandoned, neglected, abused and troubled children
25,000	Halleck Creek Riding Club for the Handicapped Children, Inverness, CA -- recreational and therapeutic activities for handicapped and disabled children
25,000	Jean Weingarten Peninsula Oral School for the Deaf, San Francisco, CA -- to support the expansion of their Parent and Infant Toddler Program
25,000	Laguna Honda Hospital Volunteers, San Francisco, CA -- to support volunteer efforts
25,000	Larkin Street Youth Center, San Francisco, CA -- for the Lark Inn Program

SANDY HILL FOUNDATION

Giving Contact
Frank E. Walsh, Jr., Chairman
330 South St.
PO Box 1975
Morristown, NJ 07962-1975
Phone: (973)540-9020

Description
Founded: 1987
EIN: 222668774
Organization Type: Private Foundation
Giving Locations: NJ
Grant Types: Capital, General Support, Multiyear/Continuing Support, Operating Expenses, Scholarship.

Donor Information
Founder: Frank E. Walsh, Jr.

Financial Summary
Total Giving: $1,842,352 (2001); $3,374,120 (2000); $2,314,140 (1999)
Giving Analysis: Giving for 2001 includes: foundation grants to United Way ($50,000); 2000: foundation grants to United Way ($35,000); 1999: foundation grants to United Way ($35,000); foundation scholarships ($50,000);
Assets: $35,711,035 (2001); $41,496,689 (2000); $43,790,380 (1999)
Gifts Received: $2,089,644 (2000); $88,750 (1999); $6,651,784 (1996). Note: In 2000, contributions were received from Frank E. Walsh.

Typical Recipients
Arts & Humanities: Arts Funds, History & Archaeology, Libraries, Performing Arts
Civic & Public Affairs: Community Foundations, Employment/Job Training, Civic & Public Affairs-General, Parades/Festivals, Philanthropic Organizations, Public Policy, Safety, Urban & Community Affairs
Education: Arts/Humanities Education, Colleges & Universities, Education Associations, Education Funds, Education Reform, Legal Education, Private Education (Precollege), Secondary Education (Private), Student Aid
Health: AIDS/HIV, Alzheimers Disease, Cancer, Clinics/Medical Centers, Health Organizations, Hospices, Hospitals, Medical Research, Single-Disease Health Associations
International: International Relief Efforts
Religion: Churches, Dioceses, Religious Organizations, Religious Welfare, Seminaries, Social/Policy Issues
Social Services: At-Risk Youth, Child Welfare, Community Service Organizations, Domestic Violence, Emergency Relief, Food/Clothing Distribution, Homes, People with Disabilities, Recreation & Athletics, Senior Services, Shelters/Homelessness, United Funds/United Ways, Youth Organizations

Application Procedures
Initial Contact: The foundation has no formal grant application procedure or application form.
Deadlines: None.

Foundation Officials
Meghan Walsh Cioffi: vice president
Robert F. Cioffi: vice president
Frank E. Walsh, III: vice president
Frank E. Walsh, Jr.: chairman B 1941. PRIM CORP EMPL executive vice president: Wesray Capital Corp. CORP AFFIL director: WJAR TV.
Jeffrey R. Walsh: secretary, treasurer
Joseph Walsh: president
Karen R. Walsh: vice president
Mary D. Walsh: vice president

Grants Analysis
Disclosure Period: calendar year ending 2001
Total Grants: $1,792,353*
Number of Grants: 136
Average Grant: $11,972*
Highest Grant: $200,000
Typical Range: $5,000 to $20,000
***Note:** Giving excludes United Way. Average grant figure excludes highest grant. .

Recent Grants
Note: Grants derived from 2001 Form 990.

General
200,000	Diocese of Paterson, Clifton, NJ
100,000	Catholic Charities USA, Washington, DC
100,000	Covenant House, Newark, NJ
100,000	Seton Hall Preparatory School, West Orange, NJ
100,000	Seton Hall University, South Orange, NJ
90,000	University of Vermont, Burlington, VT
30,000	Children's Center, Cedar Knolls, NJ
25,000	Boys and Girls Club of Newark, Newark, NJ
25,000	Community Foodbank of New Jersey, Hillside, NJ
25,000	Corpus Christi Church, Chatham, NJ

ELSIE O. AND PHILIP D. SANG FOUNDATION

Giving Contact
Elsie O. Sang, President
180 E. Pearson St., Apt. 5805
Chicago, IL 60611

Description
Founded: 1954
EIN: 366214200
Organization Type: Private Foundation
Giving Locations: IL: Chicago
Grant Types: General Support.

Financial Summary
Total Giving: $2,146,532 (fiscal year ending October 31, 1997); $42,350 (fiscal 1996); $337,550 (fiscal 1994)
Assets: $2,078,044 (fiscal 1996); $1,895,704 (fiscal 1994); $2,238,558 (fiscal 1993)

Typical Recipients
Arts & Humanities: Arts Funds, Arts Institutes, Historic Preservation, Libraries, Music, Opera, Public Broadcasting
Civic & Public Affairs: Civic & Public Affairs-General
Education: Arts/Humanities Education, Colleges & Universities, Religious Education, Student Aid
Health: Cancer, Clinics/Medical Centers, Hospitals, Long-Term Care, Medical Research, Research/Studies Institutes, Single-Disease Health Associations
International: International Peace & Security Issues, Missionary/Religious Activities
Religion: Jewish Causes, Religious Organizations, Religious Welfare, Synagogues/Temples
Social Services: Child Welfare, Community Service Organizations, People with Disabilities, Senior Services, Shelters/Homelessness, United Funds/United Ways

Application Procedures
Initial Contact: The foundation has no formal grant application procedure or application form. Send a brief letter of inquiry.
Deadlines: None.

Restrictions
Does not support individuals.

Foundation Officials
Bernard Sang: secretary
Donald Sang: assistant secretary
Elsie O. Sang: president

Grants Analysis
Disclosure Period: fiscal year ending October 31, 1997
Total Grants: $2,146,532
Highest Grant: $1,839,182
Lowest Grant: $100
Typical Range: $100 to $1,000
Note: A more recent grants list was unavailable.

Recent Grants
Note: Grants derived from 1997 Form 990.

General
1,839,182	Olin-Sang-Ruby Union Institute, Chicago, IL
103,000	Oak Park Temple, Oak Park, IL
103,000	Rosary College, River Forest, IL
100,000	Lincoln College, Lincoln, IL
1,000	Pacific Clinic, Pasadena, CA
250	La Ciza Contra El Cancer, Chicago, IL
100	Pasadena Rosary Foundation, Pasadena, CA

SARA LEE CORP.

Company Headquarters
Chicago, IL
Web: http://www.saralee.com

Company Description
Founded: 1939
Ticker: SLE
Exchange: NYSE
Revenue: US$17.628 billion (2002)
Profit: US$1.01 billion (2002)
Employees: 154900 (2002)
Fortune Rank: 101, per FORTUNE Magazine's list of 500 Largest U.S. Corporations (2002).
SIC(s): 2011 Meat Packing Plants, 2013 Sausages & Other Prepared Meats, 2032 Canned Specialties, 2038 Frozen Specialties Nec.

Operating Locations
Sara Lee Corp. (AL--Athens, Florence, Montgomery, Scottsboro; AZ--Glendale; AR--Clarksville, Little Rock; CA--Hayward, Los Angeles, Modesto, San Diego, San Francisco; CT--Stamford; DE--Dover; FL--Miami, Pinellas Park; GA--Atlanta, Calhoun, Cartersville, Eastman, Fitzgerald, Midway, Milledgeville, Newnan, Wrightsville; IL--Bensenville, Champaign, Chicago, Elk Grove Village; IN--Dubois, Indianapolis; IA--Des Moines, New Hampton, Storm Lake; KS--Lenexa; KY--Alexandria; MI--Detroit, Grand Rapids, Livonia, Traverse City; MN--Minneapolis; MS--Jackson, Olive Branch, West Point; MO--Kansas City, St. Joseph, St. Louis; NV--Henderson; NJ--Secaucus; NM--Las Cruces; NY--New York, Rochester; NC--Asheboro, Asheville, Cary, Charlotte, Dunn, Eden, Forest City, High Point, Kernersville, Laurel Hill, Lumberton, Maxton, Morganton, Mount Airy, Rockingham, Rural Hill, Sanford, Tarboro, Weaverville, Winston-Salem, Yadkinville; OH--Cincinnati, Columbus, Valley View; PA--Douglassville, Philadelphia, Pittsburgh; SC--Barnwell, Charleston, Columbia, Conway, Florence, Greenville, Hartsville, Marion; TN--LaVergne, Martin, Memphis, Mountain City, Nashville; TX--Dallas; VA--Galax, Gretna, Hillsville, Rocky Mount, Salem; WA--Algona, Tacoma; WI--Milwaukee, New London)

Subsidiary Companies

NC: Sara Lee Hosiery, Inc., Winston-Salem

Nonmonetary Support

Value: $19,000,000 (2000 approx); $23,420,000 (1999)

Type: Donated Products

Note: NOT The estimated value for fiscal 1999 is at cost.

Volunteer Programs: Company maintains a 15 to 20 person "Employee Volunteerism Committee," which is responsible for organizing approximately eight programs per year. Also sponsors a "Board Placement Program," through which company executives in the Chicago area are recruited to serve on nonprofit boards. These organizations also may be eligible for a $1,000 grant.

Contact: Robin Tryloff, Executive Director

Note: Various division-level personnel are responsible for nonmonetary distributions.

Sara Lee Foundation

Giving Contact

Robin Tryloff, President, Executive Director
3 First National Plaza
49th Floor
Chicago, IL 60602-4260
Phone: (312)558-8426
Fax: (312)419-3192
Web: http://www.saraleefoundation.org

Description

EIN: 363150460

Organization Type: Corporate Foundation

Giving Locations: IL: Chicago metropolitan area principally near operating locations and to national organizations.

Grant Types: Award, Capital, Employee Matching Gifts, General Support, Operating Expenses, Project.

Note: Employee matching gift ratio: 2 to 1 up to $1,000 per employee annually. Employee matching gift ratio: 1 to 1 up to $10,000.

Financial Summary

Total Giving: $6,939,421 (fiscal year ending June 30, 2001); $38,782,000 (fiscal 2000 approx); $43,813,258 (fiscal 1999)

Giving Analysis: Giving for fiscal 1999 includes: international subsidiaries ($1,663,000); domestic subsidiaries ($3,700,000); corporate direct giving ($6,291,258); foundation ($8,739,000); nonmonetary support ($23,420,000); fiscal 1997: international subsidiaries ($1,136,000); corporate direct giving ($2,704,000); domestic subsidiaries ($2,986,000); foundation ($5,980,735); nonmonetary support ($20,834,000); fiscal 1996: international subsidiaries ($834,000); nonmonetary support ($2,644,678); corporate direct giving ($2,760,000); domestic subsidiaries ($4,445,000) foundation ($5,400,322)

Assets: $10,800,325 (fiscal 2001); $19,156,061 (fiscal 2000); $26,865,020 (fiscal 1999)

Gifts Received: $568,842 (fiscal 2001); $501,854 (fiscal 2000); $468,373 (fiscal 1999). Note: Contributions are received from Sara Lee Corp.

Typical Recipients

Arts & Humanities: Arts Associations & Councils, Arts Centers, Arts Festivals, Arts Funds, Arts Institutes, Community Arts, Dance, Ethnic & Folk Arts, Film & Video, Historic Preservation, History & Archaeology, Libraries, Museums/Galleries, Music, Opera, Performing Arts, Public Broadcasting, Theater, Visual Arts

Civic & Public Affairs: African American Affairs, Asian American Affairs, Business/Free Enterprise, Civil Rights, Economic Development, Employment/Job Training, Civic & Public Affairs-General, Hispanic Affairs, Housing, Law & Justice, Legal Aid, Nonprofit Management, Philanthropic Organizations, Professional & Trade Associations, Public Policy, Urban & Community Affairs, Women's Affairs, Zoos/Aquariums

Education: Arts/Humanities Education, Business Education, Colleges & Universities, Education Associations, International Exchange, International Studies, Legal Education, Literacy, Minority Education, Private Education (Precollege), Student Aid

Health: AIDS/HIV, Cancer, Health Organizations, Hospitals, Nutrition, Prenatal Health Issues, Public Health, Research/Studies Institutes

International: Foreign Educational Institutions, Human Rights, International Peace & Security Issues, International Relations, International Relief Efforts

Religion: Jewish Causes, Religious Organizations, Religious Welfare

Science: Observatories & Planetariums, Science Museums

Social Services: Child Welfare, Community Centers, Community Centers, Community Service Organizations, Counseling, Day Care, Domestic Violence, Family Planning, Family Services, Food/Clothing Distribution, Homes, People with Disabilities, Refugee Assistance, Scouts, Senior Services, Shelters/Homelessness, Social Services-General, Substance Abuse, United Funds/United Ways, Volunteer Services, YMCA/YWCA/YMHA/YWHA, Youth Organizations

Application Procedures

Initial Contact: Send a brief letter, or call requesting annual contributions report and application; to apply to divisions, call local division for information.

Application Requirements: Along with your completed application form, submit audit for most recently completed fiscal year (or an IRS Form 990 with a financial statement, for organizations with expenses of less than $150,000 that have not had an audit); current fiscal year operating budget, including anticipated revenues and expenses; list of current members of the board of directors with their titles and affiliations; list of key administrative and program/artistic staff, including a one-paragraph biography for each key staff member; proof of tax-exempt status; list of confirmed grants of $1,000 or more from private and public sources for the most recent fiscal year, including donor name and specific amounts; most recent annual report, or other descriptive information if an annual report is not produced; if project support is requested, submit a current and projected budget for the year for which funds are being requested with anticipated income and expenses; for cultural requests, attach reviews and/or samples of artistic work from the previous 18 months (include no more than six reviews/samples). Include two complete sets of all requested materials.

Deadlines: No later than first working day of March or September for consideration at quarterly meetings held after those months.

Review Process: Acknowledgment of receipt is sent to applicant. If proposal meets guidelines, it is placed on foundation agenda. If proposal does not meet guidelines, it is declined. Foundation staff reviews approved proposals and schedules meetings and site visits, if needed. Foundation discusses applicants at quarterly board meetings and approves or rejects requests.

Evaluative Criteria: Proposals are evaluated based on relevance to the foundation's priorities; unique contribution of the applicant; the ability of the project to reach underserved communities, populations, or audiences; innovation; leadership; effectiveness; feasibility and perceived need for services or the project; community support and involvement; sound management; and employee involvement.

Decision Notification: Applications are acknowledged upon receipt and organizations are notified by letter of the foundation's decision after quarterly meetings.

Notes: Proposals must be submitted on the foundation's application form.

Restrictions

The following are not eligible for grants: capital and endowment campaigns; individuals; organizations with a limited constituency, such as fraternal or veterans groups; organizations that limit services to members of one religious group or seek to propagate a particular belief or creed; governmental or quasi-governmental organizations; political organizations or groups promoting one ideological view; elementary or secondary schools, either public or private; single-disease health organizations or hospitals concentrating their research or treatment in one area of human disease; tickets to dinners and other events; goodwill advertising in yearbooks or dinner or event programs; or national or international organizations with limited relationship to local Sara Lee operations.

Additional Information

Company has operating locations in nearly all 50 states. Sara Lee's contributions program is decentralized. About two-fifths of total contributions are made by the foundation, which is the main philanthropic vehicle for the Chicago corporate office. The remainder is distributed by divisions, which administer their own programs including nonmonetary giving and volunteer services.

Organizations should not submit a contribution application more than once in any 12-month period. Grants are not automatically renewed, and recipients desiring renewed support should submit a request approximately two months prior to the anniversary of their grant(s). A renewal request should include the organization's most recent audited financial statement, current year's operating budget, updated board of directors list, and summary of how the previous year's grant was used. An application form is not necessary for grant renewal requests.

Sara Lee maintains a policy that annual cash and product contributions shall represent at least 2% of domestic pretax income.

At the corporate and division levels, company forms active partnerships with particularly effective local organizations and encourages employee involvement.

Corporate Officials

Paul A. Allaire: director
Frans H.J.J. Andriessen: director
Duane L. Burnham: director
Charles W. Coker: director
James S. Crown: director
Willie D. Davis: director
Vernon E. Jordan, Jr.: director
James L. Ketelsen: director
Joan D. Manley: director
C. Steven McMillan: president, chief executive officer PRIM CORP EMPL president, chief executive officer: Sara Lee Corp.
Cary D. McMillan: executive vice president, chief financial officer, chief administrative officer PRIM CORP EMPL executive vice president, chief financial officer, chief administrative officer: Sara Lee Corp.
Frank L. Meysman: director
Rozanne L. Ridgway: director
Richard L. Thomas: director
Robin Tryloff: executive director community relations PRIM CORP EMPL director community relations: Sara Lee Corp.
Hans B. Van Liemt: director
John D. Zeglis: director

Foundation Officials

Julie B. A. Brooks: grants coordinator
James K. Hahn: assistant secretary
R. Henry Kleeman: assistant secretary
Mary T. Malloy: secretary
C. Steven McMillan: director (see above)
Ho Yan J. Ng: supervisor administration and budget
Roderick A. Palmore: vice president, secretary
Cassandra M. Pulley: director
Robert J. Rizzo: senior coordinator

Timothy M. Russell: manager community initiatives program
Judy E. Schaefer: assistant vice president
Patrick M. Sheahan: deputy director, assistant vice president
Robin Tryloff: president, executive director, director (see above)
James A. Wabich: assistant secretary
J. Randall White: director
Elynor Alberta Williams: director B Baton Rouge, LA 1946. ED Spelman College BS (1966); Cornell University Graduate School of Business Administration MS (1973). PRIM CORP EMPL president, managing director: Chestnut, Pearson & Assoc.. NONPR AFFIL member: National Association Female Executives; member: Public Relations Society America; member: International Association of Business Communications.
Cheryl L. Yuen: consultant - cultural program

Grants Analysis
Disclosure Period: fiscal year ending June 30, 2001
Total Grants: $6,071,765*
Number of Grants: 411 (approx)
Average Grant: $14,773*
Highest Grant: $63,910
Lowest Grant: $68
Typical Range: $2,500 to $25,000
*Note: Giving excludes matching gifts and United Way.

Recent Grants
Note: Grants derived from fiscal 2001 Form 990.

General
474,576	United Way Crusade of Mercy, Chicago, IL
100,000	America's Second Harvest, Chicago, IL
63,911	Arts Council, Winston-Salem, NC
60,000	Mujeres Latinas En Accion, Chicago, IL
57,890	Youth for Understanding, Washington, DC
56,000	Metropolitan Chicago Information Center, Chicago, IL
50,273	National Merit Scholarship Corporation, Chicago, IL
50,000	Homan Square Community Center Foundation, Chicago, IL
42,429	Arts Council, Winston-Salem, NC
40,000	Art Institute of Chicago, Chicago, IL

NEWELL B. SARGENT FOUNDATION

Giving Contact
Newell B. Sargent, Trustee
PO Box 18
Worland, WY 82401
Phone: (307)577-0724

Description
Founded: 1984
EIN: 830271536
Organization Type: Private Foundation
Giving Locations: WY: emphasis on Worland
Grant Types: General Support, Scholarship.

Donor Information
Founder: Newell B. Sargent

Financial Summary
Total Giving: $607,894 (fiscal year ending October 31, 2000); $897,744 (fiscal 1999); $372,788 (fiscal 1998)
Giving Analysis: Giving for fiscal 2000 includes: foundation matching gifts ($5,000); foundation scholarships ($101,000); fiscal 1998: foundation scholarships ($29,000) foundation ($343,788)

Assets: $12,494,584 (fiscal 2000); $12,279,391 (fiscal 1999); $12,413,526 (fiscal 1998)
Gifts Received: $200,000 (fiscal 2000); $200,000 (fiscal 1999); $805,406 (fiscal 1997). Note: In fiscal 1998 and 2000, contributions were received from Newell B. Sargent.

Typical Recipients
Arts & Humanities: Arts Festivals, Community Arts, Dance, History & Archaeology, Libraries, Museums/Galleries, Music, Theater
Civic & Public Affairs: Business/Free Enterprise, Chambers of Commerce, Clubs, Community Foundations, Economic Development, Employment/Job Training, Civic & Public Affairs-General, Law & Justice, Municipalities/Towns, Parades/Festivals, Public Policy, Safety, Urban & Community Affairs, Women's Affairs
Education: Colleges & Universities, Community & Junior Colleges, Education-General, Literacy, Medical Education, Minority Education, Public Education (Precollege), Secondary Education (Public), Student Aid
Environment: Environment-General, Resource Conservation
Health: Alzheimers Disease, Cancer, Children's Health/Hospitals, Emergency/Ambulance Services, Eyes/Blindness, Health Organizations, Heart, Hospitals, Respiratory, Speech & Hearing
International: International-General
Religion: Churches, Religious Organizations, Religious Welfare
Social Services: Animal Protection, Child Welfare, Community Service Organizations, Counseling, Crime Prevention, Emergency Relief, Food/Clothing Distribution, Homes, People with Disabilities, Scouts, Senior Services, Shelters/Homelessness, Veterans, Youth Organizations

Application Procedures
Initial Contact: The foundation has no formal grant application procedure or application form. Send a brief letter of inquiry.
Deadlines: None.

Foundation Officials
Douglas W. Morrison: trustee
Newell B. Sargent: trustee
Charles W. Smith: trustee

Grants Analysis
Disclosure Period: fiscal year ending October 31, 2000
Total Grants: $501,894*
Number of Grants: 41
Average Grant: $2,443*
Highest Grant: $306,618
Typical Range: $1,000 to $5,000
*Note: Giving excludes scholarships and matching gifts. Average grant figure excludes two highest grants ($406,618).

Recent Grants
Note: Grants derived from 2000 Form 990.

Library-Related
2,500	Washakie County Library, Worland, WY

General
306,618	NOWCAP, Thermopolis, WY -- Christmas baskets
100,000	New Hope Humane Endowment, Laramie, WY
100,000	Wyoming Community Foundation, Laramie, WY
40,000	Wyoming Community Foundation - Washakie County Museum, Laramie, WY
9,950	Washakie County Museum, Worland, WY
9,215	New Hope Humane Society, Worland, WY -- cemetery fund and general

5,000	Boys & Girls Club of Central Wyoming, Casper, WY
5,000	Boys & Girls Club of Northwest Wyoming, Worland, WY
5,000	Victims Of Foreign Wars, Worland, WY
5,000	Wyoming Girl Scout Council, Casper, WY

SARKEYS FOUNDATION

Giving Contact
Susan Frantz
530 East Main Street
Norman, OK 73071
Phone: (405)364-3703
Fax: (405)364-8191
Web: http://www.sarkeys.org

Description
Founded: 1962
EIN: 730736496
Organization Type: Private Foundation
Giving Locations: OK
Grant Types: Capital, Endowment, Matching, Multiyear/Continuing Support, Project.

Donor Information
Founder: Established in 1962 by S. J. Sarkeys .

Financial Summary
Total Giving: $2,876,899 (fiscal year ending November 30, 2001); $4,262,318 (fiscal 2000); $3,884,296 (fiscal 1999)
Giving Analysis: Giving for fiscal 1999 includes: foundation scholarships ($290,000)
Assets: $93,131,312 (fiscal 2001); $90,648,087 (fiscal 2000); $93,775,099 (fiscal 1999)

Typical Recipients
Arts & Humanities: Art History, Arts Associations & Councils, Arts Centers, Arts Funds, Arts Institutes, Ballet, Dance, Historic Preservation, History & Archaeology, Libraries, Museums/Galleries, Music, Opera, Performing Arts, Theater
Civic & Public Affairs: Asian American Affairs, Botanical Gardens/Parks, Community Foundations, Economic Development, Employment/Job Training, Civic & Public Affairs-General, Hispanic Affairs, Housing, Municipalities/Towns, Native American Affairs, Nonprofit Management, Urban & Community Affairs, Zoos/Aquariums
Education: Afterschool/Enrichment Programs, Agricultural Education, Arts/Humanities Education, Colleges & Universities, Community & Junior Colleges, Education Reform, Engineering/Technological Education, Education-General, Leadership Training, Legal Education, Literacy, Medical Education, Private Education (Precollege), Public Health, Public Health, Single-Disease Health Associations, Speech & Hearing
Environment: Environment-General, Research, Resource Conservation
Health: AIDS/HIV, Alzheimers Disease, Cancer, Children's Health/Hospitals, Clinics/Medical Centers, Diabetes, Emergency/Ambulance Services, Eyes/Blindness, Health Organizations, Hospices, Hospitals, Medical Rehabilitation, Medical Research, Mental Health, Prenatal Health Issues, Public Health, Single-Disease Health Associations, Speech & Hearing
International: International Relations
Religion: Churches, Ministries, Religious Organizations, Religious Welfare
Science: Science Museums, Scientific Centers & Institutes, Scientific Labs, Scientific Research
Social Services: Animal Protection, Big Brother/Big Sister, Camps, Child Abuse, Child Welfare, Community Centers, Community Service Organizations, Counseling, Domestic Violence, Family Planning, Family Services, Food/Clothing Distribution, Homes,

People with Disabilities, Scouts, Senior Services, Sexual Abuse, Shelters/Homelessness, Social Services-General, Special Olympics, Substance Abuse, YMCA/YWCA/YMHA/YWHA, Youth Organizations

Application Procedures

Initial Contact: Contact the foundation for an application form or obtain the form from the foundation's web site.

Application Requirements: The application form should be single-spaced, unbound, stapled, and printed on only one side of white, 8 1/2- by 11-inch paper. Along with the completed application form, the foundation requires the following attachments: a cover letter; a description of organization (one- to two-pages in length); a three- to four-page description of the project that describes the problem or need, how the project will solve or alleviate the problem, how the project relates to or helps fulfill the organization's mission, the organization's qualifications to address the problem or need (if the problem or need is external), anticipated outcomes of the project, the mechanisms in place to evaluate the success or failure of the project, project time frame, and how ongoing or future needs will be funded after the grant ends; a line-item budget for each year of the project; a list of secured funds and pledges for this project; a list of all outstanding requests and their amounts for this project; a list of other potential sources of funding, if any, for this project; a list of current board members which includes their names and professions; a list of current staff members and their position titles; a complete copy of the IRS tax-exempt determination letter stating that the organization is not a private foundation and that it has IRS Code section 501(c)(3) status; and a copy of the organization's most recent audit.

Deadlines: Proposals are accepted from December 15 through February 1 for inclusion on the foundation's April agenda, and from June 1 through August 1 for inclusion on the October agenda.

Review Process: The trustees meet in April, and October to consider proposals. Organizations whose applications are accepted for inclusion on the agenda for the April or October meetings will be notified.

Notes: The foundation does not accept faxed or e-mailed proposals. Organizations are limited to one application per calendar year or twelve-month period.

Restrictions

The foundation normally does not fund local programs appropriately financed within the community, direct mail solicitations and annual campaigns, out-of-state institutions, hospitals, operating expenses, purchase of vehicles, grants to individuals, responsibility for permanent financing of a program, for-profit organizations or programs, start-up funding for new organizations, feasibility studies, grants which trigger expenditure responsibility by the Sarkeys Foundation, direct support to government agencies, individual public or private elementary or secondary schools (unless they are serving the needs of a special population which are not being met elsewhere), or religious institutions and their subsidiaries. E-mailed proposals.

Additional Information

Close adherence to the guidelines will maximize the opportunity for a successful proposal.

Publications: Guidelines Brochure

Foundation Officials

Richard A. Bell: trustee, vice president PRIM CORP EMPL attorney: Richardd A. Bell.

Cheri D. Cartwright: executive director, assistant secretary-treasurer

Susan C. Frantz: program officer

Fred Gipson: trustee

Dan Little: trustee PRIM CORP EMPL president: Fayette Enterprises Inc.

Joseph W. Morris: trustee, secretary-treasurer PRIM CORP EMPL partner: Gable & Gotwals.

Robert S. Rizley: trustee

Dr. Paul F. Sharp: president, trustee B Kirksville, MO January 19, 1918. ED Phillips University AB (1939); University of Minnesota PhD (1947). NONPR AFFIL president emeritus: University Oklahoma; distinguished professor history: University Science and Arts Oklahoma; member: Phi Kappa Phi; member: Pi Gamma Nu; member: Phi Beta Kappa; member: Phi Delta Kappa; member: Phi Alpha Theta.

Ann M. Way: program officer

Terry W. West: trustee

Lee Anne Wilson: trustee

Grants Analysis

Disclosure Period: fiscal year ending November 30, 2001

Total Grants: $2,876,899

Number of Grants: 65

Average Grant: $44,260

Highest Grant: $534,000

Lowest Grant: $1,939

Typical Range: $10,000 to $50,000

Recent Grants

Note: Grants derived from fiscal 2001 Form 990.

Library-Related

50,000	Cartwright Memorial Library, Clayton, OK -- for the construction of a new facility

General

534,000	University of Oklahoma Foundation, Norman, OK -- for the Law Library
200,000	Oklahoma Arts Institute, Oklahoma City, OK -- for endowment
200,000	Oklahoma School of Science and Mathematics Foundation, Oklahoma City, OK -- for construction and naming of the dormitory addition
150,000	Assistance League of Norman, Norman, OK -- for capital campaign
120,000	Oklahoma State University Foundation, Stillwater, OK -- for Veterinary Medical Surgical Laser Lab and OSU/OKC Project Second Chance
100,000	Special Care, Inc., Oklahoma City, OK -- construction of a new facility
75,000	Norman Community Foundation, Norman, OK -- for staff and office expenses
67,000	Tulsa Historical Society, Tulsa, OK -- for the renovation and expansion of the Samuel Travis Mansion
50,000	Calm Waters Center for Children and Families, Inc., Oklahoma City, OK -- establishing a Development Program
50,000	Cameron College Foundation, Lawton, OK -- for renovating a building to house the Advanced Technology and Research Center

SASCO FOUNDATION

Giving Contact

Uwe Linder, Vice President & Trust Officer
JP Morgan Chase Bank
1211 Avenue of the Americas, 34th Fl.
New York, NY 10036-8890
Phone: (212)789-4159

Description

Founded: 1951

EIN: 136046567

Organization Type: Private Foundation

Giving Locations: CT; ME; NY

Grant Types: General Support.

Donor Information

Founder: the late Leila E. Riegel, Katherine R. Emory

Financial Summary

Total Giving: $273,500 (2001); $381,000 (1999); $330,000 (1998)

Assets: $6,482,312 (2001); $8,547,248 (1999); $7,886,892 (1998)

Typical Recipients

Arts & Humanities: Historic Preservation, History & Archaeology, Libraries, Music, Public Broadcasting

Civic & Public Affairs: Botanical Gardens/Parks, Community Foundations, Civic & Public Affairs-General, Native American Affairs, Nonprofit Management, Philanthropic Organizations, Public Policy, Urban & Community Affairs, Women's Affairs, Zoos/Aquariums

Education: Afterschool/Enrichment Programs, Colleges & Universities, Private Education (Precollege), Secondary Education (Private)

Environment: Air/Water Quality, Forestry, Environment-General, Resource Conservation, Wildlife Protection

Health: Alzheimers Disease, Cancer, Clinics/Medical Centers, Emergency/Ambulance Services, Hospitals, Medical Research, Nursing Services, Transplant Networks/Donor Banks

International: Health Care/Hospitals, International Relief Efforts

Religion: Churches, Religious Organizations, Religious Welfare

Science: Science Museums

Social Services: Animal Protection, Child Welfare, Community Service Organizations, Delinquency & Criminal Rehabilitation, Family Planning, Family Services, Food/Clothing Distribution, Scouts, Shelters/Homelessness, United Funds/United Ways, Volunteer Services, YMCA/YWCA/YMHA/YWHA, Youth Organizations

Application Procedures

Initial Contact: Send cover letter and full proposal.

Application Requirements: Include goals and purpose of funds sought.

Deadlines: November 30.

Additional Information

Trust(s): JPMorgan Chase Bank

Foundation Officials

Lucy E. Ambach: trustee

Benjamin Emory: trustee

Katherine Emory Stookey: trustee

Grants Analysis

Disclosure Period: calendar year ending 2001

Total Grants: $273,500

Number of Grants: 40

Average Grant: $6,838

Highest Grant: $25,000

Lowest Grant: $1,000

Typical Range: $1,000 to $15,000

Recent Grants

Note: Grants derived from 2001 Form 990.

General

25,000	Children's Aid Society, New York, NY
15,000	Family Care International, New York, NY
15,000	Landmark Volunteers, Sheffield, MA
12,500	Central Park Conservancy, New York, NY
12,500	Land Trust Alliance, Washington, DC
10,000	Blue Hill Heritage Trust, Blue Hill, ME
10,000	Chapin School, New York, NY
10,000	Connecticut Fund for the Environment, New Haven, CT
10,000	Maine Coast Heritage Trust, Brunswick, ME

10,000   Maine Coast Heritage Trust, Brunswick, ME

HELEN M. SAUNDERS CHARITABLE FOUNDATION TRUST

Giving Contact
Coleman H. Casey, Attorney
c/o Shipman and Goodwin LLP
1 American Row
Hartford, CT 06103-2819
Phone: (860)251-5000

Description
Founded: 1985
EIN: 066284362
Organization Type: Private Foundation
Giving Locations: CA: emphasis on Hartford
Grant Types: Endowment, General Support.

Financial Summary
Total Giving: $265,625 (fiscal year ending June 30, 2001); $203,029 (fiscal 2000); $166,950 (fiscal 1999).
Note: Fiscal 1997 Giving includes United Way ($1,250).
Giving Analysis: Giving for fiscal 2001 includes: foundation grants to United Way ($3,000) fiscal 1999: foundation grants to United Way ($1,750)
Assets: $5,864,667 (fiscal 2001); $7,104,424 (fiscal 2000); $6,111,322 (fiscal 1999)

Typical Recipients
Arts & Humanities: Arts Associations & Councils, Arts Centers, Arts & Humanities-General, Libraries, Literary Arts, Music, Opera, Performing Arts, Public Broadcasting
Civic & Public Affairs: Botanical Gardens/Parks, Employment/Job Training, Civic & Public Affairs-General
Education: Arts/Humanities Education, Colleges & Universities, Education Associations, Education Funds, Faculty Development, Literacy, Private Education (Precollege), Public Education (Precollege), Student Aid
Health: Hospitals, Nursing Services
International: Foreign Arts Organizations
Religion: Churches, Ministries, Religious Organizations, Religious Welfare
Social Services: Camps, Child Welfare, People with Disabilities, United Funds/United Ways, YMCA/YWCA/YMHA/YWHA

Application Procedures
Initial Contact: Request guidelines.
Deadlines: None.

Restrictions
Does not support individuals. Supports only organizations with tax-exempt documentation.

Additional Information
Publications: Grant Request Guidelines

Foundation Officials
Coleman H. Casey: trustee

Grants Analysis
Disclosure Period: fiscal year ending June 30, 2001
Total Grants: $262,625*
Number of Grants: 41
Average Grant: $6,405*
Highest Grant: $30,000
Lowest Grant: $150
Typical Range: $100 to $10,000
*Note: Giving excludes UNW.

Recent Grants
Note: Grants derived from fiscal 2001 Form 990.

Library-Related
30,000   Wadsworth Athenaeum, Hartford, CT -- Michael Sweerts exhibition
20,000   Wadsworth Athenaeum, Hartford, CT -- Sol LeWitt Cube Show
15,000   Wadsworth Athenaeum, Hartford, CT -- Gauguin exhibit

General
20,000   Hartford Symphony Orchestra, Hartford, CT
20,000   Lasell College, Hartford, CT
17,500   Lasell College, Hartford, CT
15,000   Greater Hartford Arts Council, Hartford, CT -- United Arts campaign
14,000   Hartford Symphony Orchestra, Hartford, CT -- Capriccio
13,500   Loomis Chaffee School, Hartford, CT
10,000   Asylum Hill Congregational Church, Hartford, CT -- music series
10,000   Cedar Hill Cemetery Association, Hartford, CT
10,000   CONCORA, New Britain, CT -- support Great Sacred Music of the Mystics
10,000   Connecticut Public Television and Radio, Hartford, CT -- Partners for a Digital Connecticut

SAWYER CHARITABLE FOUNDATION

Giving Contact
Carol S. Parks, Manager & Trustee
200 Newbury Street, 4th Fl.
Boston, MA 02116-2504
Phone: (617)262-6920

Description
Founded: 1957
EIN: 046088774
Organization Type: Private Foundation
Giving Locations: greater New England area.
Grant Types: Endowment, General Support.

Donor Information
Founder: Frank Sawyer, William Sawyer, The Brattle Co. Corp., St. Botolph Holding Co., First Franklin Parking Corp.

Financial Summary
Total Giving: $379,900 (2000); $349,000 (1999); $345,125 (1998). Note: 1997 Giving includes United Way ($5,000).
Giving Analysis: Giving for 2000 includes: foundation grants to United Way ($2,500); 1998: foundation grants to United Way ($5,000) foundation ($340,125)
Assets: $7,256,616 (2000); $7,455,288 (1999); $6,799,843 (1998)
Gifts Received: $36,827 (1998); $341,000 (1997); $1,000 (1995). Note: In 1998, contributions were received from the Estate of Beryl Mills.

Typical Recipients
Arts & Humanities: Arts Centers, Historic Preservation, Libraries, Museums/Galleries, Performing Arts
Civic & Public Affairs: African American Affairs, Clubs, Employment/Job Training, Civic & Public Affairs-General, Public Policy, Urban & Community Affairs, Women's Affairs
Education: Colleges & Universities, Community & Junior Colleges, Education-General, Legal Education, Private Education (Precollege), Secondary Education (Public), Special Education
Environment: Air/Water Quality
Health: AIDS/HIV, Cancer, Children's Health/Hospitals, Clinics/Medical Centers, Emergency/Ambulance

Services, Health Organizations, Hospices, Hospitals, Medical Research, Respiratory, Single-Disease Health Associations, Transplant Networks/Donor Banks, Trauma Treatment
International: Health Care/Hospitals, International Relief Efforts
Religion: Churches, Dioceses, Jewish Causes, Religious Organizations, Religious Welfare, Synagogues/Temples
Science: Science Museums
Social Services: Animal Protection, Camps, Child Welfare, Community Service Organizations, Family Services, Homes, People with Disabilities, Scouts, Shelters/Homelessness, Social Services-General, Substance Abuse, United Funds/United Ways, Veterans, Youth Organizations

Application Procedures
Initial Contact: Send cover letter and full proposal.
Application Requirements: Includes purpose of funds sought and proof of tax-exempt status.
Deadlines: October 15.

Restrictions
Does not support individuals or provide funds for administrative expenses, payroll, or building projects.

Foundation Officials
Carol S. Parks: mgr, trustee
Mary S. Quinn: mgr
John R. Sawyer: mgr
Mildred F. Sawyer: mgr, trustee

Grants Analysis
Disclosure Period: calendar year ending 2000
Total Grants: $377,400*
Number of Grants: 88
Average Grant: $4,289
Highest Grant: $50,000
Typical Range: $1,000 to $10,000
*Note: Giving excludes United Way.

Recent Grants
Note: Grants derived from 2000 Form 990.

Library-Related
2,000   Boston Public Library Foundation, Boston, MA

General
50,000   Suffolk University, Boston, MA
25,000   Carroll Center for the Blind, Newton, MA
20,000   American Cancer Society, Worcester, MA
15,000   Archdiocese of Boston, Boston, MA
15,000   Salvation Army, Fresno, CA
11,000   Shriner's Burns Institute
10,000   Cardinal's Residence
10,000   Dana Farber, Inc., Boston, MA
10,000   Fidelco Guide Dog Foundation, Bloomfield, CT
5,000   Boston Living Center, Boston, MA

SBC COMMUNICATIONS INC.

Company Headquarters
175 E. Houston
San Antonio, TX 78205-2233
Web: http://www.sbc.com

Company Description
Founded: 1983
Ticker: SBC
Exchange: NYSE
Former Name: Ameritech.
Revenue: US$51.755 billion (2002)
Profit: US$5.653 billion (2002)
Employees: 192550 (2002)

Fortune Rank: 27, per FORTUNE Magazine's list of 500 Largest U.S. Corporations (2002).

SBC Foundation

Giving Contact
Laura P. Sanford, President
130 Travis Street, Suite 350
San Antonio, TX 78205
Phone: 800-591-9663
Fax: (210)351-2259
Web: http://www.sbc.com/Community/
SBC_Foundation

Alternate Contact
Ben Voris, Corporate Manager
Phone: (210)351-5154

Description
EIN: 431353948
Organization Type: Corporate Foundation
Former Name: Southwestern Bell Foundation.
Formed by Merger of: PacTel Foundation (1998).
Giving Locations: AR; CA; CT; DC: Washington; IL; IN; KS; MI; MO; NV; NY; OH; OK; TX; VA; WI nationally.
Grant Types: Capital, Challenge, Employee Matching Gifts, Endowment, General Support, Matching, Multiyear/Continuing Support, Project.
Note: Employee matching gift ratio: 1 to 1 to higher education and cultural institutions.

Financial Summary
Total Giving: $95,800,000 (2002 approx); $69,111,239 (2001); $100,300,000 (2000 approx). Note: Contributes through corporate direct giving program and foundation.
Giving Analysis: Giving for 2001 includes: corporate direct giving (approx $30,300,000); foundation (approx $68,900,000); 2000: foundation ($45,820,742); corporate direct giving (approx $55,500,000); 1998: foundation matching gifts ($1,500,000); corporate matching gifts ($1,549,595); foundation scholarships ($2,700,000); corporate scholarships ($2,753,239); corporate grants to United Way ($3,810,405); foundation grants to United Way ($6,200,000); foundation ($23,277,045); corporate direct giving ($23,600,000); **Assets:** $703,000,000 (2002 approx); $536,184,004 (2001); $113,680,164 (2000)
Gifts Received: $209,112,587 (2001); $29,915,650 (2000); $33,100,000 (1999). Note: Contributions are received from SBC Communications Inc. and its subsidiaries.

Typical Recipients
Arts & Humanities: Arts Appreciation, Arts Associations & Councils, Arts Centers, Arts Festivals, Arts Funds, Arts Institutes, Arts Outreach, Community Arts, Dance, Ethnic & Folk Arts, Historic Preservation, History & Archaeology, Libraries, Museums/Galleries, Music, Opera, Performing Arts, Public Broadcasting, Theater
Civic & Public Affairs: African American Affairs, Botanical Gardens/Parks, Business/Free Enterprise, Clubs, Community Foundations, Economic Development, Employment/Job Training, Ethnic Organizations, Civic & Public Affairs-General, Hispanic Affairs, Minority Business, Municipalities/Towns, Parades/Festivals, Public Policy, Urban & Community Affairs, Women's Affairs, Zoos/Aquariums
Education: Arts/Humanities Education, Business Education, Colleges & Universities, Community & Junior Colleges, Education Associations, Education Funds, Education Reform, Engineering/Technological Education, Faculty Development, Education-General, Leadership Training, Literacy, Medical Education, Minority Education, Public Education (Precollege), School Volunteerism, Science/Mathematics Education, Special Education, Student Aid, Vocational & Technical Education

Environment: Research
Health: AIDS/HIV, Alzheimers Disease, Cancer, Children's Health/Hospitals, Emergency/Ambulance Services, Health-General, Health Organizations, Hospitals, Medical Research, Mental Health, Public Health
International: Foreign Arts Organizations, Foreign Educational Institutions
Religion: Churches, Dioceses, Jewish Causes, Ministries, Religious Welfare
Science: Science Museums, Scientific Centers & Institutes
Social Services: Child Welfare, Community Centers, Community Service Organizations, Emergency Relief, Family Services, People with Disabilities, Scouts, Senior Services, Shelters/Homelessness, Social Services-General, Special Olympics, United Funds/United Ways, Volunteer Services, YMCA/YWCA/YMHA/YWHA, Youth Organizations

Application Procedures
Initial Contact: Obtain a grant application from the foundation. Completed applications should be prefaced with a brief cover letter; grant requests of a local or statewide nature should be sent to local subsidiary or division; requests of a regional or national nature should be addressed directly to the Foundation.
Application Requirements: Include proof of tax-exempt status; description of how project fits with foundation's priorities; total project budget and amount requested; brief statement of history and accomplishments; statement of current objectives, including problem being addressed, program budget and amount sought; linkage of project's goals to the foundation's priorities; timetable for implementation and description of expected results; details of fund-raising plans, including sources, amounts, and commitments; plans for sustaining activities after conclusion of foundation support; annual report or budget for organization, showing all income sources and expenditures; list of board members; list of accrediting agencies; one-page evaluation component detailing how project success will be measured; line-item budget for project.
Deadlines: None.
Review Process: All requests will be evaluated within four to six weeks after receipt; requesting organization may be contacted for additional information.
Evaluative Criteria: The foundation prefers to fund organizations in operating areas, project-specific proposals within areas of interest, projects that directly impact human needs and have the potential to be self-sustaining and adaptable to other settings, projects that stimulate partnerships among community organizations, and projects with well-defined goals, a clear picture of the need addressed, and specific tracking and evaluation procedures. Organizations seeking support should demonstrate clearly stated objectives, long-range planning, active participation of the governing board, strategies and plans to move from dependency on any one source of support, sound financial principles and practices, and close monitoring of programs.
Notes: Organizations are asked not to submit a proposal more than once in a 12-month period.

Restrictions
Foundation does not support private foundations or organizations without tax-exempt status; organizations that practice discrimination by race, color, creed, gender, sexual orientation, age, or national origin; hospital operating funds or capital funds; operating expenses for organizations supported by the United Way; individuals; political activities or organizations; religious organizations for sectarian purposes; fraternal, veteran, or labor groups when serving only their memberships; disease specific organizations; individual K-12 schools or districts, local school systems or school-system foundations; sports programs or events; cause-related marketing; donation of products or services; or special occasion goodwill advertising and ticket or dinner purchases.

Additional Information
Foundation states a preference for organizations that operate in corporate operating locations and in communities where a significant number of employees live; project-oriented proposals rather than requests for grants to underwrite operating or capital budgets; projects that promote citizen participation and volunteerism; projects that generate public awareness and offer opportunities to leverage contributions; projects that address human needs and whose services are provided directly rather than through intermediary organizations; and projects that develop leadership skills.
SBC Communications is in the process of purchasing Ameritech Corp.
In 1998, the company acquired Pacific Telesis (PacTel) and that company's foundation. The PacTel Foundation was merged into the SBC Foundation.
Publications: Contributions Guidelines

Corporate Officials
Janet Kendall: associate vice presidentc, chief executive officer PRIM CORP EMPL associate vice president: SBC Communications Inc.
Donald E. Kiernan, Sr.: senior vice president, chief financial officer, treasurer B Trumbull, CT 1940. ED Boston College BS (1962); Florida State University MBA (1970). PRIM CORP EMPL senior vice president, chief financial officer, treasurer: SBC Communications Inc. CORP AFFIL director: Southwest Bell Mobile Systems; director: Southwest Bell Telephone Co.
Edward E. Whitacre, Jr.: chairman, director, chief executive officer B Ennis, TX 1941. ED Texas Technology University BS (1964). PRIM CORP EMPL chairman, director, chief executive officer: SBC Communications Inc. CORP AFFIL president: Southwest Bell Telephone Co.; director: Emerson Electric Co.; director: May Department Stores Co.; director: Anheuser-Busch Companies Inc.; director: Burlington Northern Santa Fe Corp. NONPR AFFIL trustee: Southwest Research Institute; board regents: Texas Technology University & Health Science; member: Learning National Advisory Board; member executive board national council & southern reg: Boy Scouts America.

Foundation Officials
Royce S. Caldwell: director B 1939. ED Abilene Christian University BBA (1961). PRIM CORP EMPL president, chief executive officer, director: Southwest Bell Operations. CORP AFFIL president: SBC Communications Inc.; president, ceo: Southwest Bell Telephone Co.
Cassandra Colvin Carr: director B Champaign, IL 1944. ED Vanderbilt University BA (1966); University of Texas MA (1973). PRIM CORP EMPL senior vice president human resources, director: SBC Communications Inc. ADD CORP EMPL officer: Southwestern Bell Telephone Co. CORP AFFIL director: Yellow Corp.; director: Destec Energy Inc. NONPR AFFIL member: National Association Corporate Treasurers; commissioner: Saint Louis Regional Conv Sports Complex Authority; trustee: Foundation Womens Resources; director: Conference Board; member: Financial Executives Institute; director: Arch Funds Inc. CLUB AFFIL Forest Hills Country Club; Saint Louis Club.
Gloria Delgado: president
James D. Ellis: director B 1943. ED University of Iowa BBA (1965); University of Missouri JD (1968). PRIM CORP EMPL senior executive vice president, general counsel: SBC Communications Inc. ADD CORP EMPL secretary: Southwestern Bell Telephone Co. CORP AFFIL director: Southwest Bell Mobile Systems.
Charles E. Foster: director B 1936. ED University of Oklahoma BSME (1961); Washington University (1967). PRIM CORP EMPL directory: McNay Art Museum. CORP AFFIL director: Southwest Bell Mobile Systems; director: Southwest Bell Telephone Co.

Karen E. Jennings: director
Janet Kendall: chairman (see above)
Donald E. Kiernan, Sr.: director (see above)
Linda S. Mills: director
Harold E. Rainbolt: vice president, secretary B Norman, OK 1929. ED University of Oklahoma (1951); University of Oklahoma (1957). PRIM CORP EMPL chairman: BancFirst Corp. CORP AFFIL director: Sonic Corp.; director: Trend Venture Corp.
Laura Sanford: president
Stan Sigman: director
Larry Walther: chairman
Roger W. Wohlert: vice president, treasurer PRIM CORP EMPL treasurer: SBC Asset Management Inc.

Grants Analysis

Disclosure Period: calendar year ending 2001
Total Grants: $49,200,000*
Number of Grants: 1,344*
Average Grant: $22,500
Highest Grant: $2,000,000
Lowest Grant: $1,000
Typical Range: $1,000 to $50,000
*Note: Grants analysis provided by foundation and represents foundation giving only. Giving excludes matching gifts; United Way; scholarships.

Recent Grants

Note: Grants derived from 2001 Form 990.

Library-Related

1,000,000	Performing Arts Center of Los Angeles County, Los Angeles, CA -- construction of the Walt Disney Concert Hall

General

2,111,463	Citizen's Scholarship Foundation of America, St. Peter, MN -- new recipient and renewal scholarship awards
2,000,000	Women's Museum, An Institute for the Future, Austin, TX -- challenge grant
1,527,000	United Way Crusade of Mercy, Chicago, IL -- annual support
1,068,400	United Way Bay Area, San Francisco, CA -- annual support
1,000,000	Cancer Therapy and Research Center, San Antonio, TX -- to help create six endowed chairs in order to carry out research for new drugs
1,000,000	Historical Centre Foundation, San Antonio, TX -- expansion and restoration campaign
1,000,000	New York Times Neediest Cases Fund, New York, NY -- disaster relief aid
1,000,000	Texas Tech University Foundation, Lubbock, TX -- Texas Tech Horizon campaign
760,000	United Way Greater St. Louis, St. Louis, MO -- annual support
700,000	Abraham Lincoln Presidential Library and Museum Foundation, Springfield, IL -- Holavision Theater

SCAIFE FAMILY FOUNDATION

Giving Contact

Joanne B. Beyer, Vice President, Secretary & Treasurer
One Oxford Centre
301 Grant St., Suite 3900
Pittsburgh, PA 15219-6401
Phone: (412)392-2900
Fax: (412)392-2922
Web: http://www.scaifefamily.org

Description

Founded: 1983
EIN: 251427015
Organization Type: Family Foundation

Giving Locations: PA: Western Pennsylvania, Pittsburgh nationally.
Grant Types: Capital, Conference/Seminar, Department, General Support, Operating Expenses, Project, Scholarship.

Donor Information

Founder: Established in 1983 by the late Sarah Mellon Scaife (d. 1965) by the conditions of a trust she provided for her grandchildren. She was the sister of Richard King Mellon, daughter of Richard B. Mellon, and granddaughter of Judge Thomas Mellon, who founded the family's banking and investment fortune.

Financial Summary

Total Giving: $7,710,135 (2000); $9,206,190 (1999); $7,344,900 (1998)
Giving Analysis: Giving for 2000 includes: foundation grants to United Way ($175,000) 1999: foundation grants to United Way ($50,000)
Assets: $108,063,816 (2000); $240,099,702 (1999); $195,650,470 (1998)
Gifts Received: The foundation receives gifts from the trust for the grandchildren of Sarah Mellon Scaife.

Typical Recipients

Arts & Humanities: Film & Video, Historic Preservation, Libraries, Museums/Galleries, Opera, Public Broadcasting
Civic & Public Affairs: Botanical Gardens/Parks, Business/Free Enterprise, Civil Rights, Economic Development, Economic Policy, Employment/Job Training, Civic & Public Affairs-General, Housing, Law & Justice, Legal Aid, Municipalities/Towns, Parades/Festivals, Philanthropic Organizations, Public Policy, Safety, Urban & Community Affairs, Women's Affairs
Education: Arts/Humanities Education, Business Education, Colleges & Universities, Community & Junior Colleges, Economic Education, Education Associations, Education Funds, Education Reform, Elementary Education (Public), Environmental Education, Education-General, Education-General, Leadership Training, Literacy, Medical Education, Minority Education, Private Education (Precollege), Public Education (Precollege), Science/Mathematics Education, Social Sciences Education, Special Education, Student Aid
Environment: Environment-General, Resource Conservation
Health: Cancer, Children's Health/Hospitals, Clinics/Medical Centers, Eyes/Blindness, Health Funds, Health Organizations, Hospices, Hospitals, Kidney, Medical Rehabilitation, Medical Research, Mental Health, Nursing Services, Prenatal Health Issues, Public Health, Single-Disease Health Associations, Speech & Hearing
International: Health Care/Hospitals, International Affairs
Religion: Churches, Ministries, Missionary Activities (Domestic), Religious Organizations, Religious Welfare, Social/Policy Issues
Social Services: Animal Protection, Big Brother/Big Sister, Child Abuse, Child Welfare, Community Centers, Community Service Organizations, Counseling, Day Care, Delinquency & Criminal Rehabilitation, Family Planning, Family Services, Food/Clothing Distribution, People with Disabilities, Recreation & Athletics, Senior Services, Shelters/Homelessness, Social Services-General, Substance Abuse, United Funds/United Ways, Volunteer Services, Youth Organizations

Application Procedures

Initial Contact: Initial inquiries to the foundation should be in letter form signed by the organization's president, or authorized representative, and have the approval of the organization's board of directors.
Application Requirements: The letter should include a concise description of the specific program for which funds are requested. Additional information must include a budget for the program and for the

organization, the latest audited financial statement, annual report, list of the board of directors, and a copy of the organization's current IRS tax exemption ruling under section 501(c)(3). Additional information may be requested if needed for further evaluation.
Deadlines: None. The foundation normally considers grants at quarterly meetings.
Review Process: The foundation indicates that requests will be acted upon as expeditiously as possible.

Restrictions

The foundation does not make loans and will not consider grants to individuals.

Additional Information

Publications: Annual Report

Foundation Officials

J. Nicholas Beldecos: trustee
Joanne B. Beyer: vice president, secretary, treasurer
Donald A. Collins: trustee
Sanford Barnett Ferguson: president, trustee B Boston, MA 1947. ED Dartmouth College BA (1970); Oxford University MA (1972); Yale University JD (1975). PRIM CORP EMPL partner, chairman: Kirkpatrick & Lockhart LLP. CORP AFFIL director: Innovation Works Inc.; director: Solutions Cons Inc.; director: Avalon Holdings Inc. NONPR AFFIL member: Pennsylvania Bar Association; director, vice chairman: United Way Allegheny County; member: American Law Institute; member: Allegheny County Bar Association; member: American Bar Association. CLUB AFFIL Duquesne Club; Fox Chapel Golf Club.
David N. Scaife: co-chairman, trustee
Jennie K. Scaife: co-chairman, trustee
James Mellon Walton: trustee B Pittsburgh, PA 1930. ED Yale University BA (1953); Harvard University MBA (1958). PRIM CORP EMPL vice chairman, director: MMC Group Inc. NONPR AFFIL member sponsoring comm: Pennsylvania Southwest Association; director: World Affairs Council Pittsburgh; director: Irish Investment Fund Inc.; director: One Hundred Friends Pittsburgh Art; life trustee: Carnegie-Mellon University; member: Cultural District Development Committee; treasurer: Carnegie Hero Fund Commission.
Joseph Carroll Walton: trustee B Frankfurt, Germany 1955. ED Williams College BA (1979); University of Texas MBA (1983). PRIM CORP EMPL vice president: Tiber Investment Corp. NONPR AFFIL member: Governments Task Force Business Development & Job Creation. CLUB AFFIL Rolling Rock Club; bd directors: Beaumaris Yacht Club.

Grants Analysis

Disclosure Period: calendar year ending 1999
Total Grants: $9,156,190*
Number of Grants: 114
Average Grant: $80,317*
Highest Grant: $300,000
Typical Range: $20,000 to $100,000
*Note: Giving excludes United Way.

Recent Grants

Note: Grants derived from 2000 Form 990.

General

1,000,000	Magee Women's Health Foundation, Pittsburgh, PA
288,235	Susan G. Komen Foundation, Dallas, TX
250,000	Animal Rescue League of West Pennsylvania, Pittsburgh, PA
250,000	Children of Alcoholics Foundation, New York, NY -- project support
250,000	Johns Hopkins University, Baltimore, MD
250,000	Mercy Hospital Foundation, Pittsburgh, PA

225,000 Beginning with Books, Inc., Pittsburgh, PA
225,000 Bethlehem Haven of Pittsburgh, Pittsburgh, PA
200,000 Civic Light Opera, Pittsburgh, PA -- Creative Vision Program
200,000 Extra-Mile Education Foundation, Inc., Pittsburgh, PA

L. P. SCHENCK CHARITABLE FOUNDATION

Giving Contact
Claudia Latorre, Vice President & Trust Officer
L. P. Schenck Charitable Foundation
c/o PNC Bank NA
41 Oak St.
Ridgewood, NJ 07450
Phone: (201)493-2152

Description
Founded: 1960
EIN: 226040581
Organization Type: Private Foundation
Giving Locations: NJ
Grant Types: General Support, Project.

Donor Information
Founder: the late Lillian Pitkin Schenck

Financial Summary
Total Giving: $544,400 (fiscal year ending August 31, 2001); $410,700 (fiscal 1999); $453,000 (fiscal 1998 approx)
Assets: $11,061,676 (fiscal 2001); $12,077,500 (fiscal 1999); $10,815,370 (fiscal 1998)
Gifts Received: $850 (fiscal 1996)

Typical Recipients
Arts & Humanities: Arts Associations & Councils, Arts Centers, Arts Outreach, Community Arts, Libraries, Museums/Galleries, Music, Performing Arts, Theater
Civic & Public Affairs: Ethnic Organizations, Civic & Public Affairs-General, Urban & Community Affairs
Education: Public Education (Precollege), Science/Mathematics Education
Environment: Environment-General
Health: Cancer, Emergency/Ambulance Services, Health Organizations, Hospitals, Mental Health, Single-Disease Health Associations
Religion: Churches, Religious Organizations, Religious Welfare
Social Services: At-Risk Youth, Child Welfare, Community Centers, Community Service Organizations, Day Care, Family Planning, Family Services, Food/Clothing Distribution, Homes, People with Disabilities, Scouts, Senior Services, Shelters/Homelessness, Substance Abuse, Volunteer Services, YMCA/YWCA/YMHA/YWHA, Youth Organizations

Application Procedures
Initial Contact: Send a brief letter of inquiry. and a full proposal.
Application Requirements: Include a description of organization, amount requested, purpose of funds sought, recently audited financial statement, and proof of tax-exempt status. Also include previous year's annual report.
Deadlines: August 1.

Restrictions
Does not support individuals, religious organizations for sectarian purposes, political or lobbying groups, or organizations outside operating areas.

Additional Information
Trust(s): PNC Bank NA

Grants Analysis
Disclosure Period: fiscal year ending August 31, 2001
Total Grants: $544,400
Number of Grants: 60
Average Grant: $8,041*
Highest Grant: $70,000
Typical Range: $1,000 to $15,000
***Note:** Average grant figure excludes highest grant.

Recent Grants
Note: Grants derived from 1999 Form 990.

General
59,000 Family and Social Services Federation, Englewood, NJ
40,000 Community Centers for Mental Health, Dumont, NJ
30,000 Englewood Hospital and Medical Center, Englewood, NJ
20,000 Van Ost Institute for Family Living, Inc., Englewood, NJ
18,000 American Stage Company, Teaneck, NJ
18,000 Friendship House, Hackensack, NJ
18,000 Volunteer Center of Bergen County, Hackensack, NJ
15,000 John Harms Center for the Arts, Englewood, NJ
15,000 Senior Service Director for Independent Living, Englewood, NJ
15,000 YWCA of Bergen County, Ridgewood, NJ

KARLA SCHERER FOUNDATION

Giving Contact
Karla Scherer, Chairman, Chief Executive Officer, & Trustee
737 North Michigan Ave.
Suite 2330
Chicago, IL 60611
Phone: (312)943-9191
Fax: (312)943-9271
Web: http://comnet.org/kschererf

Description
Founded: 1990
EIN: 382877392
Organization Type: Private Foundation
Giving Locations: internationally.
Grant Types: General Support, Scholarship.

Donor Information
Founder: Established in 1990 by Karla Scherer.

Financial Summary
Total Giving: $182,155 (2001); $184,965 (2000); $127,755 (1999)
Giving Analysis: Giving for 2001 includes: foundation scholarships ($122,000); 2000: foundation scholarships ($118,000) 1999: foundation scholarships ($76,000)
Assets: $5,710,738 (2001); $6,048,083 (2000); $5,947,712 (1999)
Gifts Received: $1,000 (2000); $5,000 (1992). Note: In fiscal 1992, contributions were received from the Leon and Toby Cooperman Foundation.

Typical Recipients
Arts & Humanities: Arts Centers, Arts Institutes, History & Archaeology, Libraries, Museums/Galleries, Music, Public Broadcasting, Theater

Civic & Public Affairs: Business/Free Enterprise, Civil Rights, Economic Policy, Civic & Public Affairs-General, Urban & Community Affairs, Women's Affairs
Education: Arts/Humanities Education, Business Education, Colleges & Universities, Economic Education, Education Associations, Engineering/Technological Education, Education-General, International Studies, Legal Education, Preschool Education, Private Education (Precollege), Student Aid, Vocational & Technical Education
Environment: Environment-General, Resource Conservation
Health: Cancer, Children's Health/Hospitals, Clinics/Medical Centers, Health Organizations, Hospitals, Medical Research, Mental Health, Prenatal Health Issues
International: Foreign Arts Organizations, Foreign Educational Institutions, Health Care/Hospitals
Religion: Churches, Religious Welfare
Social Services: Animal Protection, Camps, Child Welfare, Community Centers, Family Planning, People with Disabilities, Social Services-General, Veterans, Youth Organizations

Application Procedures
Initial Contact: Write to request a scholarship application form.
Application Requirements: Describe the particular area(s) of academic interest and a detailed description of career plans. Include a self-addressed, stamped envelope.
Deadlines: March 1 is the deadline for written requests for application forms.
Review Process: If the application form request letter meets the foundation's requirements, an application package will be sent to the applicant.

Restrictions
Scholarship applicants must be women accepted to the Master of Arts program at the University of Chicago.

Additional Information
Beginning in the 2004-2005 school year, scholarships will only be provided to women participating in the Master of Arts program at the University of Chicago.

Foundation Officials
Katherine Ross: executive director
John S. Scherer: trustee
Karla Scherer: chairman, chief executive officer B Detroit, MI 1937. ED University of Michigan BA (1957). NONPR AFFIL member: Women's Economic Club Detroit; member: Women's Forum Michigan; member visitors committee: Fordham University Graduate School Business Administration; director: Economic Club Detroit; trustee: Eton Academy. CLUB AFFIL Grosse Pointe Club; Renaissance Club; Detroit Country Club; Detroit Athletic Club; Detroit Club.
Theodore Souris: assistant secretary, trustee

Grants Analysis
Disclosure Period: calendar year ending 2001
Total Grants: $60,155*
Number of Grants: 30
Average Grant: $2,005
Highest Grant: $20,000
Typical Range: $500 to $3,000
***Note:** Giving excludes scholarships.

Recent Grants
Note: Grants derived from 2001 Form 990.

General
20,000 The Cradle, Evanston, IL
10,000 Planned Parenthood Chicago, Chicago, IL
7,500 Cornell University, Ithaca, NY -- scholarship
7,500 New York University, New York, NY -- scholarship

7,500	University of Pennsylvania, Philadelphia, PA -- individual scholarship
7,500	University of Texas, Austin, TX -- scholarship
7,500	University of Virginia, Charlottesville, VA -- scholarship
7,000	American University, Washington, DC -- scholarship
7,000	Carnegie Mellon University, Pittsburgh, PA -- scholarship
6,670	Chicago Symphony Orchestra, Chicago, IL

SCHERING-PLOUGH CORP.

Company Headquarters
2000 Galloping Hill Rd.
Kenilworth, NJ 07033-0530
Web: http://www.sch-plough.com

Company Description
Ticker: SGP
Exchange: OTC
Formed by Merger of: Plough Inc. (1971).
Revenue: US$10.18 billion (2002)
Profit: US$1.974 billion (2002)
Employees: 29800 (2001)
Fortune Rank: 187, per FORTUNE Magazine's list of 500 Largest U.S. Corporations (2002).
SIC(s): 2833 Medicinals & Botanicals, 2834 Pharmaceutical Preparations, 2836 Biological Products Except Diagnostic, 2844 Toilet Preparations, 3842 Surgical Appliances & Supplies, 3851 Ophthalmic Goods, 6719 Holding Companies Nec.
Parent Company: Schering AG, Mullerstr. 178, Berlin, Germany

Operating Locations
Schering-Plough Corp. (AR--Little Rock; CA--La Mirada, Palo Alto, San Leandro; DE--Millsboro; FL--Pembroke Pines; GA--Chamblee, Chatsworth; IL--Alsip, Chicago, Des Plaines, Niles; IN--Terre Haute; LA--Baton Rouge; MO--Kansas City; NE--Elkhorn, Omaha; NJ--Bloomfield, Carteret, Creamridge, Kenilworth, Liberty Corner, Madison, Maplewood, Union; PR--Hato Rey, Las Piedras, Manati; TN--Cleveland; TX--Irving)

Nonmonetary Support
Type: Donated Equipment; Donated Products; In-kind Services
Volunteer Programs: Provides small grants through its Dollar for Volunteer program most used by employees and their families, American Red Cross, healthcare services to low-income working people, and university schools of pharmacy.
Contact: Joseph Starkey, Director, Community Affairs

Schering-Plough Foundation

Giving Contact
Christine Fahey, Assistant Secretary
Schering-Plough Foundation
2000 Galloping Hill Road
Kenilworth, NJ 07033-1310
Phone: (908)298-7232
Fax: (908)298-7349
Web: http://www.sch-plough.com/cr/philanthropy.html

Alternate Contact
Andrew Hageman, Secretary
Schering-Plough Foundation
Phone: (973)822-7000
Note: For direct contributions.

Description
EIN: 221711047
Organization Type: Corporate Foundation
Giving Locations: principally near operating locations and to national organizations.
Grant Types: Capital, Employee Matching Gifts, Endowment, Fellowship, General Support, Multiyear/Continuing Support, Professorship, Research, Scholarship, Seed Money.
Note: Employee matching gift ratio: 1 to 1 for secondary and higher education, hospitals and hospices.

Financial Summary
Total Giving: $8,500,000 (2003 approx); $8,500,000 (2002 approx); $2,451,174 (2001). Note: Contributes through corporate direct giving program and foundation.
Giving Analysis: Giving for 2001 includes: foundation matching gifts ($234,404); foundation ($2,216,770); 2000: foundation matching gifts ($591,659); foundation ($2,166,040); 1999: foundation (approx $2,300,000);
Assets: $15,000,000 (2003 approx); $15,000,000 (2002); $15,859,026 (2001)
Gifts Received: $1,500,000 (2000); $1,500,000 (1997); $1,500,000 (1996). Note: The foundation receives gifts from the Schering-Plough Corp.

Typical Recipients
Arts & Humanities: Arts Associations & Councils, Arts Centers, Arts Festivals, Arts Funds, Community Arts, Dance, Ethnic & Folk Arts, Arts & Humanities-General, Historic Preservation, History & Archaeology, Libraries, Museums/Galleries, Music, Performing Arts, Theater
Civic & Public Affairs: Civil Rights, Community Foundations, Economic Development, Economic Policy, Ethnic Organizations, Civic & Public Affairs-General, Hispanic Affairs, Housing, Legal Aid, Nonprofit Management, Philanthropic Organizations, Professional & Trade Associations, Public Policy, Urban & Community Affairs, Zoos/Aquariums
Education: Afterschool/Enrichment Programs, Arts/Humanities Education, Business Education, Colleges & Universities, Colleges & Universities, Education Associations, Education Funds, Engineering/Technological Education, Faculty Development, Education-General, Health & Physical Education, Literacy, Medical Education, Minority Education, Preschool Education, Private Education (Precollege), Science/Mathematics Education, Student Aid
Health: Alzheimers Disease, Cancer, Children's Health/Hospitals, Clinics/Medical Centers, Emergency/Ambulance Services, Health-General, Geriatric Health, Health Policy/Cost Containment, Health Organizations, Hospices, Hospitals, Hospitals (University Affiliated), Long-Term Care, Medical Rehabilitation, Medical Research, Medical Training, Mental Health, Public Health, Research/Studies Institutes, Single-Disease Health Associations, Single-Disease Health Associations, Transplant Networks/Donor Banks
International: Health Care/Hospitals, International Affairs, International Peace & Security Issues, International Relations
Religion: Churches, Religious Welfare
Science: Scientific Centers & Institutes, Scientific Labs, Scientific Research
Social Services: Child Welfare, Community Service Organizations, Domestic Violence, Family Services, Food/Clothing Distribution, People with Disabilities, Shelters/Homelessness, Substance Abuse, United Funds/United Ways, YMCA/YWCA/YMHA/YWHA, Youth Organizations

Application Procedures
Initial Contact: Submit a written proposal. Application forms are available by request and from the foundation's web site.

Application Requirements: Include specific purpose of funds sought, background information on requesting organization, major programs and services rendered, proof of tax-exempt status, latest audited financial statements, program budget (if application relates to specific activity); supporting material (including annual report) is desirable.
Deadlines: July 1 for foundation only.
Decision Notification: Requests are reviewed continually; board meets annually in the fall.
Notes: Requests that do not include the information above will be returned to applicants.

Restrictions
Grants are not made to individuals.

Additional Information
Occasionally makes product donations, primarily to assist efforts of U.S. organizations working in developing countries. Surplus equipment is made available to organizations in operating communities.
Foundation historically pays grants for annual support in the fourth quarter of the year.

Corporate Officials
Fred Hassan: chairman, chief executive officer B 1945. ED Harvard University MBA; University of London BS. PRIM CORP EMPL chairman, chief executive officer: Schering-Plough Corp. CORP AFFIL director: EDS Corp.; director: Avon Products Inc. NONPR AFFIL chairman: HealthCare Institute New Jersey.
Jack L. Wyszomierski: executive vice president, chief financial officer B 1955. ED Carnegie Mellon University BS (1977); Carnegie Mellon University MS (1978). PRIM CORP EMPL executive vice president, chief financial officer: Schering-Plough Corp. CORP AFFIL chief financial officer: Canji Inc.

Foundation Officials
Hugh Alfred D'Andrade: trustee, member B Metuchen, NJ 1938. ED Rutgers University BA (1961); Columbia University LLB (1964). PRIM CORP EMPL vice chairman, chief administrative officer: Schering-Plough Corp. CORP AFFIL director: Autoimmune Inc. NONPR AFFIL member: American Bar Association.
Christine Fahey: assistant secretary
Andrew F. Hageman: secretary PRIM CORP EMPL manager corporate philanthropy: Schering-Plough Corp.
Richard J. Kinney: president PRIM CORP EMPL staff vice president public affairs: Schering-Plough Corp.
E. Kevin Moore: treasurer PRIM CORP EMPL vice president, treasurer: Schering-Plough Corp.
Jack L. Wyszomierski: trustee, member (see above)

Grants Analysis
Disclosure Period: calendar year ending 2001
Total Grants: $2,216,770*
Number of Grants: 66
Average Grant: $33,587
Highest Grant: $200,000
Lowest Grant: $5,000
Typical Range: $10,000 to $50,000
*Note: Giving excludes matching gifts.

Recent Grants
Note: Grants derived from 2001 Form 990.

General

200,000	St. Barnabas Health Care System
100,000	Drew University, Madison, NJ
100,000	New Jersey Performing Arts Center, Newark, NJ
100,000	Tufts University, Boston, MA
86,000	North Carolina Central University, Durham, NC
76,700	National Merit Scholarship Corporation, Evanston, IL
75,000	People-to-People Health Foundation, Millwood, VA -- Project Hope

60,000	Pharmaceutical Research and Manufactures of America Foundation, Washington, DC
50,000	American Liver Foundation Greater New York Chapter, New York, NY
50,000	Cerebral Palsy League, Cranford, NJ

SCHERMAN FOUNDATION

Giving Contact
Sandra Silverman, President & Executive Director
16 East 52nd Street, Suite 601
New York, NY 10022-5306
Phone: (212)832-3086
Fax: (212)838-0154
Web: http://www.scherman.org

Description
Founded: 1943
EIN: 136098464
Organization Type: General Purpose Foundation
Giving Locations: NY: New York emphasis on metropolitan New York City for the arts and social welfare
Grant Types: General Support, Multiyear/Continuing Support.

Donor Information
Founder: Established in 1941 by members of the Scherman family, including the late Harry Scherman (d. 1969), one of the founders of the Book-of-the-Month Club. During his lifetime, Mr. Scherman served as a director of the National Bureau of Economic Research and as a trustee of the Mannes College of Music.

Financial Summary
Total Giving: $6,110,200 (2001); $6,838,980 (2000); $6,416,680 (1999)
Giving Analysis: Giving for 1999 includes: foundation matching gifts ($45,200)
Assets: $87,473,557 (2001); $110,088,080 (2000); $119,515,813 (1999)

Typical Recipients
Arts & Humanities: Arts Centers, Arts Funds, Ballet, Dance, Libraries, Literary Arts, Museums/Galleries, Music, Opera, Performing Arts, Public Broadcasting, Theater, Visual Arts
Civic & Public Affairs: African American Affairs, Botanical Gardens/Parks, Civil Rights, Economic Development, Economic Policy, Employment/Job Training, Hispanic Affairs, Housing, Law & Justice, Legal Aid, Municipalities/Towns, Professional & Trade Associations, Public Policy, Safety, Urban & Community Affairs, Women's Affairs, Zoos/Aquariums
Education: Arts/Humanities Education, Colleges & Universities, Education Associations, Education Reform, Education-General, International Studies, Minority Education, School Volunteerism, Special Education
Environment: Air/Water Quality, Environment-General, Protection, Resource Conservation
Health: AIDS/HIV, Health Organizations, Outpatient Health Care
International: Health Care/Hospitals, Human Rights, International Development, International Environmental Issues, International Organizations, International Peace & Security Issues, International Relations, International Relief Efforts, Missionary/Religious Activities
Religion: Jewish Causes, Religious Welfare, Social/Policy Issues
Science: Science Museums, Scientific Centers & Institutes, Scientific Organizations
Social Services: At-Risk Youth, Child Welfare, Community Service Organizations, Counseling, Crime Prevention, Domestic Violence, Family Planning, Family Planning, Family Services, Food/Clothing Distribution, Senior Services, Shelters/Homelessness, Social Services-General, Volunteer Services, Youth Organizations

Application Procedures
Initial Contact: Applicants should submit a brief letter to the president outlining the purpose for which funds are sought.
Application Requirements: Include a budget; program description; recent audited financial statement; present sources of support; evidence of tax-exempt status; and list of the board of directors and key personnel.
Deadlines: None.
Review Process: Applications that fall within the scope of interests of the foundation will be asked to provide additional information. The board meets four times a year; dates of the meetings are not fixed.
Decision Notification: Applicants are notified within six weeks if a proposal has been declined or is under consideration.
Notes: The foundation does not accept proposals via fax or over the Internet.

Restrictions
The foundation generally does not fund individuals, colleges, universities, or professional schools; conferences, symposia, capital campaigns, specific film, video or art productions; or medical, science or engineering research. In the fields of arts and social welfare, priorities are in New York City only. No grants are made for medical, science, or engineering research.

Additional Information
Grants are made only to 501 (c) (3) organizations.
Publications: Annual Report; Statement of Policy and Procedures

Foundation Officials
Susanna Bergtold: director
Hillary Brown: director
David Forgan Freeman: special advisor B Chicago, IL June 28, 1918. ED Princeton University AB (1940); Yale University LLB (1947). CLUB AFFIL Seabright Tennis Club.
Gordon Litwin: director
Archibald R. Murray: director B 1933. ED Howard University BA (1954); Fordham University LLB (1960). NONPR AFFIL member: Association Bar New York City; member: New York State Bar Association; member: American Bar Association.
John J. O'Neil, Esq.: director
Mitchell C. Pratt: treasurer, program officer
Axel G. Rosin: director, chairman emeritus
Katharine S. Rosin: secretary, director
Anthony M. Schulte: director
Sandra Silverman: president, executive director, assistant secretary
Karen R. Sollins: chairman, director
Marcia T. Thompson: director

Grants Analysis
Disclosure Period: calendar year ending 2001
Total Grants: $6,110,200
Number of Grants: 158
Average Grant: $38,672
Highest Grant: $300,000
Lowest Grant: $500
Typical Range: $10,000 to $50,000

Recent Grants
Note: Grants derived from 2000 Form 990.

Library-Related
325,000	New York Public Library, New York, NY

General
100,000	Center for Reproductive Law and Policy, New York, NY
100,000	Partnership Project, Washington, DC -- "Protect the Environment"
100,000	United Neighborhood Houses of New York, Inc., New York, NY
90,000	Conservation Law Foundation, Boston, MA
90,000	New York Foundation of the Arts, New York, NY
75,000	Alvin Ailey Dance Foundation, New York, NY
75,000	Center for Community Change, Washington, DC
75,000	Earth Justice Legal Defense Fund, Malibu, CA
75,000	International Rescue Commission, New York, NY
75,000	Natural Resources Defense Council, New York, NY

FRANCES SCHERMER CHARITABLE TRUST

Giving Contact
Steve Volk, Vice President & Trust Officer
Frances Schermer Charitable Trust
Care of City National Bank
PO Box 1141
Beverly Hills, CA 90210
Phone: (310)888-6324
Fax: (310)888-6288

Description
Founded: 1980
EIN: 956685749
Organization Type: Private Foundation
Giving Locations: CA; OH; PA
Grant Types: General Support.

Donor Information
Founder: the late Charles I. Schermer, Frances Schermer

Financial Summary
Total Giving: $110,752 (fiscal year ending June 30, 2002); $106,554 (fiscal 2001); $103,094 (fiscal 2000)
Giving Analysis: Giving for fiscal 2002 includes: foundation grants to United Way ($2,500) fiscal 2001: foundation grants to United Way ($2,500)
Assets: $2,114,984 (fiscal 2002); $2,308,382 (fiscal 2001); $2,486,260 (fiscal 2000)

Typical Recipients
Arts & Humanities: Arts Associations & Councils, Arts Institutes, Libraries, Music, Public Broadcasting, Theater
Civic & Public Affairs: Business/Free Enterprise, Clubs, Community Foundations, Ethnic Organizations, Civic & Public Affairs-General, Urban & Community Affairs
Education: Colleges & Universities, Education-General, Minority Education, Private Education (Precollege), Religious Education, Secondary Education (Private)
Health: AIDS/HIV, Cancer, Children's Health/Hospitals, Clinics/Medical Centers, Emergency/Ambulance Services, Eyes/Blindness, Health Organizations, Hospices, Kidney, Long-Term Care, Multiple Sclerosis
International: International-General, Missionary/Religious Activities
Religion: Churches, Jewish Causes, Ministries, Religious Organizations, Religious Welfare, Synagogues/Temples
Social Services: Camps, Child Welfare, Community Centers, Community Service Organizations, Counseling, Domestic Violence, Food/Clothing Distribution, People with Disabilities, Scouts, Senior Services, Shelters/Homelessness, United Funds/United Ways, YMCA/YWCA/YMHA/YWHA, Youth Organizations

Application Procedures

Initial Contact: Send a brief letter of inquiry.
Deadlines: None.

Additional Information

Trust(s): City National Bank

Foundation Officials

Saul Friedman: co-trustee
James L. Pazol: co-trustee
Bruce Sherman: co-trustee

Grants Analysis

Disclosure Period: fiscal year ending June 30, 2002
Total Grants: $108,252*
Number of Grants: 45
Average Grant: $2,406
Highest Grant: $10,000
Lowest Grant: $250
Typical Range: $500 to $10,000
*****Note:** Giving excludes United Way.

Recent Grants

Note: Grants derived from fiscal 2002 Form 990.

General

10,000	Mahoning Lodge 339, Youngstown, OH
10,000	Youngstown Area Jewish Federation, Youngstown, OH
10,000	Youngstown State University, Youngstown, OH
10,000	Zionist Organization of America, Southfield, MI
6,250	Los Angeles Jewish Federation Foundation, Los Angeles, CA
5,000	HELP Hotline Crisis Center, Youngstown, OH
5,000	United Jewish Communities, Youngstown, OH
5,000	Youngstown Area Jewish Federation, Youngstown, OH
5,000	Youngstown Foundation, Boardman, OH
5,000	Youngstown Foundation for Jewish Federation, Youngstown, OH

S. H. AND HELEN R. SCHEUER FAMILY FOUNDATION INC.

Giving Contact

Linda Ehrlich, Administrative Director
350 Fifth Avenue, Suite 1413
New York, NY 10118
Phone: (212)947-9009
Fax: (212)947-9770
E-mail: linda@61associates.com

Description

Founded: 1943
EIN: 136062661
Organization Type: Family Foundation
Giving Locations: NY: New York metropolitan area; Israel
Grant Types: General Support, Scholarship.

Donor Information

Founder: Established in New York in 1943 by the late S. H. Scheuer , a New York investor and philanthropist, and his late wife, Helen R. Scheuer , with other family members. Mr. Scheuer was interested in subsidized housing for the elderly.

Financial Summary

Total Giving: $1,616,995 (fiscal year ending November 30, 2001); $1,603,241 (fiscal 2000); $1,500,000 (fiscal 1999 approx)

Giving Analysis: Giving for fiscal 2000 includes: foundation scholarships ($85,000)
Assets: $12,886,102 (fiscal 2001); $13,781,585 (fiscal 2000); $14,871,967 (fiscal 1998)
Gifts Received: $452,000 (fiscal 2001); $452,000 (fiscal 2000); $2,523,402 (fiscal 1998). Note: In fiscal 2001, contributions were received from the Helen R. Scheuer Trust 3. In fiscal 2000, contributions were received from the trusts of Helen R. and S. H. Scheuer.

Typical Recipients

Arts & Humanities: Arts Associations & Councils, Arts Centers, Dance, History & Archaeology, Museums/Galleries, Music, Opera, Performing Arts, Theater
Civic & Public Affairs: Botanical Gardens/Parks, Business/Free Enterprise, Chambers of Commerce, Economic Development, Law & Justice, Philanthropic Organizations, Public Policy, Urban & Community Affairs, Women's Affairs
Education: Arts/Humanities Education, Colleges & Universities, Education Associations, Education Reform, Engineering/Technological Education, Environmental Education, Faculty Development, Education-General, Gifted & Talented Programs, International Studies, Legal Education, Literacy, Medical Education, Preschool Education, Private Education (Precollege), Religious Education, Social Sciences Education, Special Education, Student Aid
Environment: Air/Water Quality, Environment-General
Health: Clinics/Medical Centers, Geriatric Health, Hospitals, Mental Health, Nursing Services
International: Foreign Arts Organizations, Foreign Educational Institutions, Health Care/Hospitals, International Environmental Issues, International Peace & Security Issues, International Relations, International Relief Efforts, Missionary/Religious Activities
Religion: Jewish Causes, Missionary Activities (Domestic), Religious Organizations, Religious Welfare, Seminaries, Synagogues/Temples
Science: Scientific Centers & Institutes
Social Services: Child Welfare, Community Service Organizations, Counseling, Day Care, Domestic Violence, Family Planning, Family Services, People with Disabilities, Recreation & Athletics, Senior Services, United Funds/United Ways, YMCA/YWCA/YMHA/YWHA, Youth Organizations

Application Procedures

Initial Contact: Applicants should send a brief letter proposal of one to three pages.
Application Requirements: The proposal should contain the following: proof of IRS tax-exempt status; a short history of the organization and its purpose; a description of the project goal and qualifications of the staff involved; the amount of funding requested; and anticipated long- and short-term advantages of the project affecting the foundation, as well as all others who stand to benefit.
Deadlines: None.

Restrictions

Foundation primarily supports preselected organizations, but does review unsolicited requests as well.

Foundation Officials

Linda Ehrlich: administrative director
Elizabeth H. Scheuer: secretary
Laura L. Scheuer: vice president
Richard Jonas Scheuer: president B Long Lake, NY 1917. ED Harvard University (1939); New York University MA (1971). NONPR AFFIL chairman board governors: Hebrew Union College.
Sidney J. Silberman, Esq.: treasurer

Grants Analysis

Disclosure Period: fiscal year ending November 30, 2001
Total Grants: $1,615,995*

Number of Grants: 174
Average Grant: $9,287
Highest Grant: $122,828
Lowest Grant: $1,000
Typical Range: $5,000 to $20,000
*****Note:** Giving excludes United Way.

Recent Grants

Note: Grants derived from fiscal 2001 Form 990.

General

1,611,168	Jewish Communal Fund, New York, NY
122,828	Jewish Board of Family and Children's Services, New York, NY -- capital campaign
90,018	Center for Preventive Psychiatry, White Plains, NY
50,000	Jewish Board of Family and Children's Services, New York, NY
50,000	Sarah Lawrence College, Bronxville, NY
50,000	Scenic Hudson, Poughkeepsie, NY
46,616	Steven and Alida Brill Scheuer Foundation
45,000	Swarthmore College, Swarthmore, PA
40,000	New Israel Fund, Washington, DC
37,000	Shakespeare Theater, Washington, DC

SARAH I. SCHIEFFELIN RESIDUARY TRUST

Giving Contact

Grace Allen, Trust Officer
c/o The Bank of New York
1290 6th Avenue
New York, NY 10020
Phone: (212)635-1520

Description

Founded: 1976
EIN: 136724459
Organization Type: Private Foundation
Giving Locations: NY: New York
Grant Types: Multiyear/Continuing Support.

Donor Information

Founder: the late Sarah I. Schieffelin

Financial Summary

Total Giving: $683,711 (fiscal year ending March 31, 2001); $649,912 (fiscal 2000); $500,433 (fiscal 1999)
Assets: $14,692,378 (fiscal 2001); $14,740,588 (fiscal 2000); $14,827,453 (fiscal 1999)

Typical Recipients

Arts & Humanities: Arts Centers, Historic Preservation, History & Archaeology, Libraries, Museums/Galleries, Music, Opera, Performing Arts
Civic & Public Affairs: Botanical Gardens/Parks, Civic & Public Affairs-General, Zoos/Aquariums
Education: Colleges & Universities, Education Reform, Private Education (Precollege)
Environment: Environment-General, Resource Conservation, Wildlife Protection
Health: Cancer, Children's Health/Hospitals, Emergency/Ambulance Services, Heart, Hospitals
Religion: Churches
Science: Science Museums
Social Services: Animal Protection, At-Risk Youth, Child Welfare, Community Service Organizations, People with Disabilities, Shelters/Homelessness

Application Procedures

Initial Contact: Send a brief letter of inquiry.
Deadlines: March 31.

Additional Information

Trust(s): Bank of NY

Foundation Officials

Thomas B. Fenlon, Esq.: trustee B Long Branch, NJ November 12, 1904. ED Georgetown University AB (1925); Columbia University LLB (1928). PRIM CORP EMPL partner: Emmet, Marvin & Martin. NONPR AFFIL trustee: Saint Catherines Church; director: Traphagen School Fashion; member: New York State Bar Association; member: American Bar Association; member: New York City Bar Association.

Grants Analysis

Disclosure Period: fiscal year ending March 31, 2001
Total Grants: $683,711
Number of Grants: 41
Average Grant: $16,676
Highest Grant: $100,000
Lowest Grant: $1,000
Typical Range: $1,000 to $30,000

Recent Grants

Note: Grants derived from 2001 Form 990.

Library-Related
25,000	New York Public Library, New York, NY

General
38,500	National Audubon Society, New York, NY
38,500	National Wildlife Federation, New York, NY
38,500	St. Mary's Church, Manhasset, MA
38,500	St. Thomas Church, New York, NY
30,000	American Red Cross, New York, NY
25,000	Covenant House, New York, NY
15,000	Community Service Society, New York, NY
10,000	Calvary Fund
10,000	Central Park Conservancy, New York, NY
10,000	Lincoln Center for the Performing Arts, New York, NY

DOROTHY SCHIFF FOUNDATION

Giving Contact

Adele Hall-Sweet, President
53 E. 66th St.
New York, NY 10021
Phone: (212)789-5042

Description

Founded: 1951
EIN: 136018311
Organization Type: Private Foundation
Giving Locations: MA; NY
Grant Types: Emergency, General Support, Research, Scholarship.

Donor Information

Founder: the late Dorothy Schiff, New York Post Corp.

Financial Summary

Total Giving: $840,000 (2001); $769,000 (2000); $742,000 (1999)
Giving Analysis: Giving for 2001 includes: foundation scholarships ($25,000) 1999: foundation scholarships ($25,000)

Assets: $12,304,777 (2001); $13,755,874 (2000); $13,755,305 (1999)
Gifts Received: $49,500 (1993)

Typical Recipients

Arts & Humanities: Arts Associations & Councils, History & Archaeology, Libraries, Museums/Galleries, Public Broadcasting
Civic & Public Affairs: Clubs, Economic Development, Employment/Job Training, Civic & Public Affairs-General, Law & Justice, Municipalities/Towns, Professional & Trade Associations, Public Policy, Urban & Community Affairs
Education: Arts/Humanities Education, Colleges & Universities, Education Reform, Engineering/Technological Education, Medical Education, Minority Education, Private Education (Precollege), Public Education (Precollege), School Volunteerism, Science/Mathematics Education, Secondary Education (Private), Social Sciences Education, Special Education, Student Aid
Environment: Environment-General, Resource Conservation
Health: AIDS/HIV, Cancer, Hospitals, Medical Research, Medical Research, Prenatal Health Issues, Single-Disease Health Associations
International: Health Care/Hospitals, Human Rights
Religion: Jewish Causes
Science: Scientific Centers & Institutes, Scientific Labs
Social Services: At-Risk Youth, Child Welfare, Community Centers, Community Service Organizations, Crime Prevention, Family Planning, Family Services, People with Disabilities, Refugee Assistance, Shelters/Homelessness, Youth Organizations

Application Procedures

Initial Contact: Send a brief letter of inquiry describing program or project.
Deadlines: None.

Additional Information

Trust(s): JPMorgan Bank

Foundation Officials

Mortimer W. Hall: treasurer
Sara Ann Kramarsky: secretary
Adele Hall Sweet: president

Grants Analysis

Disclosure Period: calendar year ending 2001
Total Grants: $815,000*
Number of Grants: 44
Average Grant: $18,523
Highest Grant: $40,000
Typical Range: $15,000 to $25,000
*Note: Giving excludes scholarships.

Recent Grants

Note: Grants derived from 2001 Form 990.

Library-Related
25,000	New York Public Library, New York, NY

General
40,000	Brearley School, New York, NY
40,000	Exodus House, The East Harlem School, New York, NY
40,000	Harbor Science and Arts Charter School, New York, NY
40,000	Learning Leaders, Inc., New York, NY
35,000	Lenox Hill Hospital, New York, NY -- Primary Care Center
30,000	College of Physicians and Surgeons, New York, NY
30,000	Planned Parenthood of NYC, New York, NY
25,000	Cold Spring Harbor Laboratory, Cold Spring Harbor, NY
25,000	Cornell University College of Veterinary Medicine, Ithaca, NY
25,000	Global Kids, New York, NY

EDWARD G. SCHLIEDER EDUCATIONAL FOUNDATION

Giving Contact

Pierre F. Lapeyre, Assistant Secretary
Hibernia National Bank
313 Carondelet St., 1st Fl.
New Orleans, LA 70130
Phone: (504)533-5535
Fax: (504)533-3669

Description

Founded: 1945
EIN: 720408974
Organization Type: Specialized/Single Purpose Foundation
Giving Locations: LA: limited to educational institutions in Louisiana
Grant Types: Capital, Endowment, Operating Expenses, Research.

Donor Information

Founder: Incorporated in 1945 by the late Edward G. Schlieder .

Financial Summary

Total Giving: $417,773 (2001); $2,081,939 (2000); $1,750,000 (1998)
Assets: $41,639,221 (2001); $42,424,510 (2000); $30,627,348 (1998)

Typical Recipients

Arts & Humanities: Arts & Humanities-General, Libraries
Education: Business Education, Colleges & Universities, Elementary Education (Private), Engineering/Technological Education, Environmental Education, Faculty Development, Education-General, Medical Education, Preschool Education, Private Education (Precollege), Public Education (Precollege), Religious Education, Science/Mathematics Education, Secondary Education (Private), Secondary Education (Public)
Environment: Wildlife Protection
Health: Cancer, Children's Health/Hospitals, Health Policy/Cost Containment, Health Organizations, Hospitals (University Affiliated), Medical Research, Nutrition
Religion: Religion-General, Religious Welfare, Seminaries
Social Services: Recreation & Athletics

Application Procedures

Initial Contact: The foundation requests applications be made in writing, outlining the proposal.
Deadlines: None.

Restrictions

The foundation reports grants are made only to educational institutions within the state of Louisiana.

Foundation Officials

Pierre S. Lapeyre: executive consult, assistant secretary
Donald J. Nalty: chairman, director B 1932. PRIM CORP EMPL vice president: Hibernia National Bank. CORP AFFIL vice president: Controlled Business Inc.
Elizabeth S. Nalty: president, director
Jill Nalty: treasurer, director
John M. Ward: director, secretary
Thomas D. Westfeldt: director, vice president B 1951. ED Louisiana State University (1975). PRIM CORP EMPL president: Westfeldt Brothers.

Grants Analysis

Disclosure Period: calendar year ending 2001
Total Grants: $417,773
Number of Grants: 3
Average Grant: $139,258
Highest Grant: $333,000
Lowest Grant: $25,000
Typical Range: $25,000 to $150,000

Recent Grants

Note: Grants derived from 2001 Form 990.

General

333,000	Tulane University, New Orleans, LA -- for Westfeldt Practice Competition Complex
59,773	Louisiana State University Health Science Center Foundation, New Orleans, LA -- surgical chairs and lights
25,000	Jesuit High School, New Orleans, LA -- for capital and facilities Maintenance Program

ALBERT G. AND OLIVE H. SCHLINK FOUNDATION

Giving Contact

Robert A. Wiedemann, President & Secretary
49 Benedict Ave., Suite C
Norwalk, OH 44857
Phone: (419)668-8211

Description

Founded: 1966
EIN: 346574722
Organization Type: Private Foundation
Giving Locations: AL; CA; MI; NC; OH
Grant Types: Capital, Emergency, General Support, Research, Scholarship.

Donor Information

Founder: the late Albert G. Schlink, the late Olive H. Schlink

Financial Summary

Total Giving: $618,767 (2001); $708,685 (2000); $764,733 (1999)
Assets: $14,353,030 (2001); $16,192,863 (2000); $16,377,196 (1999)

Typical Recipients

Arts & Humanities: History & Archaeology, Libraries
Civic & Public Affairs: Clubs, Community Foundations, Civic & Public Affairs-General
Education: Colleges & Universities, Medical Education, Private Education (Precollege)
Health: Cancer, Clinics/Medical Centers, Diabetes, Eyes/Blindness, Health-General, Geriatric Health, Health Organizations, Hospices, Hospitals, Long-Term Care, Medical Rehabilitation, Medical Research, Research/Studies Institutes, Respiratory, Single-Disease Health Associations
Religion: Churches, Religion-General, Religious Welfare
Science: Science Museums
Social Services: Animal Protection, Community Service Organizations, Food/Clothing Distribution, People with Disabilities, Recreation & Athletics, Scouts, Senior Services, Shelters/Homelessness

Application Procedures

Initial Contact: Send a a brief letter of inquiry.
Application Requirements: Include a description of organization, amount requested, purpose of funds sought, proof of tax-exempt status.
Deadlines: None.

Restrictions

Does not support individuals. Grants to religious organizations are favored, as are grants for the indigent aged and the handicapped, especially the visually handicapped.

Additional Information

Grants to religious organisation are favored as are grants to assist programs for the aged, especially the indigent aged and for the handicapped, especially the visually handicapped, so long as such programs to not duplicate existing or governmental programs.
Publications: Application Guidelines

Foundation Officials

John D. Allton: treasurer
Thomas Huff: trustee
Thomas D. Huff: trustee
Curtis J. Koch: vice president
Dorothy E. Wiedemann: trustee
Robert A. Wiedemann: president, secretary

Grants Analysis

Disclosure Period: calendar year ending 2001
Total Grants: $618,767
Number of Grants: 31
Average Grant: $16,734*
Highest Grant: $100,000
Typical Range: $10,000 to $50,000
*Note: Average grant figure excludes highest grant.

Recent Grants

Note: Grants derived from 2001 Form 990.

Library-Related

24,510	Norwalk Public Library, Norwalk, OH

General

100,000	Little Sisters of the Poor, Oregon, OH
65,706	Little Sisters of the Poor, Cleveland, OH
60,000	Community Foundation of the Greater Lorain County, Lorain, OH
43,188	St. Francis Health Care Centre, Green Springs, OH
35,000	Salk Institute, La Jolla, CA
30,020	Sight Center, Toledo, OH
30,000	Bowling Green State University, Bowling Green, OH
25,505	Stein Hospice Service, Sandusky, OH
18,120	Heart of Ohio Council Boy Scouts of America, Ashland, OH
15,882	Norwalk Catholic Schools, Norwalk, OH

SCHLUMBERGER LTD.

Company Headquarters

153 E. 53rd St., 57th Fl.
New York, NY 10022-4624
Web: http://www.slb.com

Company Description

Founded: 1972
Ticker: SLB
Exchange: NYSE
Revenue: US$13.612 billion (2002)
Employees: 78500 (2002)
SIC(s): 1300 Oil & Gas Extraction, 3500 Industrial Machinery & Equipment, 3600 Electronic & Other Electrical Equipment, 3800 Instruments & Related Products.

Operating Locations

Anadrill (TX--Sugar Land); Dowell Schlumber Inc. (TX--Houston); Geco Geophysical Company, Inc. (TX--Houston); Schlumberger CAD/CAM Div. (MI--Ann Arbor); Schlumberger Industries-Electricity Management (GA--Norcross); Schlumberger Ltd. (CA--Mountain View, Oxnard, San Jose; CT--Bridgeport;

GA--Norcross; MI--Ann Arbor; NY--Elmsford; OR--Medford; PA--Archbold; TX--Dallas, Houston); Schlumberger Well Services (TX--Houston)
Note: Operates internationally.

Schlumberger Foundation

Giving Contact

Arthur W. Alexander, Executive Director
Schlumberger Foundation
153 E. 53 Street, 57th Floor
New York, NY 10022
Phone: (212)350-9400
Fax: (212)350-9440
Web: http://www.slb.com/seed/

Description

EIN: 237033142
Organization Type: Corporate Foundation
Giving Locations: NY: New York nationally to education.
Grant Types: Capital, Fellowship, General Support, Professorship, Project, Research, Scholarship.

Financial Summary

Total Giving: $1,464,404 (2001); $1,602,612 (2000); $2,476,896 (1999). Note: Contributes through foundation only.
Giving Analysis: Giving for 2001 includes: foundation fellowships ($105,000); foundation scholarships ($213,267); foundation ($541,137); foundation gifts to individuals ($605,000); 2000: foundation fellowships ($120,000); foundation scholarships ($209,670); foundation ($571,300); foundation gifts to individuals ($701,642); 1999: foundation fellowships ($120,000); foundation scholarships ($192,683); foundation gifts to individuals ($615,000); foundation ($1,549,213);
Assets: $26,268,715 (2001); $29,984,897 (2000); $26,507,383 (1999)

Typical Recipients

Arts & Humanities: Arts Centers, Ballet, Dance, Ethnic & Folk Arts, Historic Preservation, Libraries, Literary Arts, Museums/Galleries, Music, Opera, Performing Arts, Public Broadcasting, Theater
Civic & Public Affairs: Botanical Gardens/Parks, Economic Development, Economic Policy, Civic & Public Affairs-General, Legal Aid, Minority Business, Nonprofit Management, Professional & Trade Associations, Women's Affairs
Education: Arts/Humanities Education, Business Education, Colleges & Universities, Economic Education, Education Associations, Education Reform, Engineering/Technological Education, Faculty Development, Education-General, International Studies, Medical Education, Minority Education, Private Education (Precollege), Public Education (Precollege), Science/Mathematics Education, Social Sciences Education, Special Education, Student Aid
Environment: Environment-General, Resource Conservation, Wildlife Protection
Health: Alzheimers Disease, Cancer, Children's Health/Hospitals, Eyes/Blindness, Hospices, Hospitals, Medical Research, Single-Disease Health Associations
International: Foreign Educational Institutions, International Relations
Religion: Churches, Religious Organizations
Science: Science Museums, Scientific Centers & Institutes
Social Services: Child Welfare, Community Service Organizations, Day Care, Family Planning, Family Services, Food/Clothing Distribution, People with Disabilities, Shelters/Homelessness, Social Services-General, Substance Abuse, Youth Organizations

Application Procedures

Initial Contact: Send a brief letter or proposal.
Application Requirements: Include a description of organization, amount requested, purpose of funds sought, recently audited financial statement, time period covered, and proof of tax-exempt status.
Deadlines: None.

Restrictions

Grants are generally limited to colleges and universities emphasizing engineering and natural sciences, and cultural institutions.

Additional Information

According to Schlumberger Ltd., it has three headquarters: Paris, France; The Hague, Netherlands; and New York, NY.

Corporate Officials

Dugald Euan Baird: chairman, president, chief executive officer B Aberdeen, United Kingdom 1937. ED Aberdeen University (1955); Cambridge University BA (1960); Trinity College (1957-1960); Aberdeen University LLD (1995); Dundee University LLD (1998). PRIM CORP EMPL chairman, president, chief executive officer: Schlumberger Ltd. CORP AFFIL director: Paribas. NONPR AFFIL trustee: Carnegie Institute of Washington; trustee: The Haven Management Trust.

Arthur Lindenauer: executive vice president, chief financial officer B New York, NY 1937. ED Dartmouth College BA (1958); Dartmouth College Amos Tuck Graduate School of Business Administration MBA (1959). PRIM CORP EMPL executive vice president, chief financial officer: Schlumberger Ltd. ADD CORP EMPL president: Schlumberger Technology Corp.; president: Schlumberger Electricities. NONPR AFFIL member: American Institute CPAs.

Grants Analysis

Disclosure Period: calendar year ending 2001
Total Grants: $541,137*
Number of Grants: 38
Average Grant: $14,240
Highest Grant: $60,000
Lowest Grant: $1,000
Typical Range: $1,000 to $10,000 and $20,000 to $50,000
*Note: Giving excludes scholarships; fellowships; and targeted technical grants to individuals.

Recent Grants

Note: Grants derived from 2001 Form 990.

General

60,000	Georgia Tech Foundation, Atlanta, GA
35,000	MIT, Cambridge, MA
30,000	California Institute of Technology, Pasadena, CA
30,000	Cornell University, Ithaca, NY
30,000	Georgia Institute of Technology, Atlanta, GA
30,000	Harvard University, Cambridge, MA
30,000	MIT, Cambridge, MA
30,000	MIT, Cambridge, MA
30,000	Princeton University, Princeton, NJ
30,000	Princeton University, Princeton, NJ

JACOB G. SCHMIDLAPP TRUST NO. 1

Giving Contact

Lawra J. Baumann, Foundation Officer
Care of Fifth Third Bank
Department 00864
Cincinnati, OH 45263
Phone: (513)579-6034
Fax: (513)744-6997

Description

Founded: 1927
EIN: 316019680
Organization Type: General Purpose Foundation
Giving Locations: OH: Cincinnati metropolitan area
Grant Types: Capital, Challenge, Seed Money.

Donor Information

Founder: Established in 1927 by Jacob Godfrey Schmidlapp (1849-1919), a successful Cincinnati banker and industrialist. Mr. Schmidlapp was also a deeply committed philanthropist. In addition to establishing the Jacob G. Schmidlapp Trust, he funded the Emma Louise Schmidlapp wing of the Cincinnati Art Museum in memory of his daughter; the Rudolph Oscar Schmidlapp Fund to maintain the Cincinnati Art Museum, in memory of an infant son; and the Emilie Balke Schmidlapp dormitory at the Cincinnati College of Music, in memory of his wife. He also created the Charlotte Schmidlapp Fund in memory of another daughter killed in an automobile accident.

Unusual for its time, this fund has been providing no-interest education loans and counseling to women from the Cincinnati area since 1908. Mr. Schmidlapp funded his charitable trusts in 1908 and played an active role in deciding what each should support. He believed that experiments in grant making should be encouraged. Even if unsuccessful, the knowledge gained from one's mistakes would ensure overall progress.

Financial Summary

Total Giving: $3,215,499 (fiscal year ending September 30, 2001); $2,217,444 (fiscal 2000); $3,228,723 (fiscal 1999)
Giving Analysis: Giving for fiscal 2001 includes: foundation grants to United Way ($25,000) fiscal 1997: foundation grants to United Way ($90,000)
Assets: $63,103,712 (fiscal 2001); $88,350,741 (fiscal 2000); $74,385,109 (fiscal 1999)

Typical Recipients

Arts & Humanities: Arts Associations & Councils, Arts Centers, Arts Funds, Arts Institutes, Historic Preservation, Libraries, Museums/Galleries, Music, Opera, Public Broadcasting

Civic & Public Affairs: African American Affairs, Botanical Gardens/Parks, Clubs, Community Foundations, Economic Development, Employment/Job Training, Civic & Public Affairs-General, Housing, Municipalities/Towns, Philanthropic Organizations, Urban & Community Affairs, Women's Affairs, Zoos/Aquariums

Education: Afterschool/Enrichment Programs, Arts/Humanities Education, Colleges & Universities, Community & Junior Colleges, Economic Education, Education Reform, Environmental Education, Faculty Development, Education-General, Medical Education, Minority Education, Preschool Education, Private Education (Precollege), Public Education (Precollege), Religious Education, Science/Mathematics Education, Secondary Education (Private), Secondary Education (Public), Special Education, Student Aid

Health: Adolescent Health Issues, Arthritis, Cancer, Children's Health/Hospitals, Clinics/Medical Centers, Diabetes, Emergency/Ambulance Services, Geriatric Health, Health Funds, Health Organizations, Heart, Hospices, Hospitals, Long-Term Care, Medical Rehabilitation, Mental Health, Nursing Services, Prenatal Health Issues, Preventive Medicine/Wellness Organizations, Public Health, Single-Disease Health Associations, Speech & Hearing, Trauma Treatment

Religion: Churches, Dioceses, Dioceses, Jewish Causes, Ministries, Missionary Activities (Domestic), Religious Organizations, Religious Welfare

Science: Science Museums, Scientific Centers & Institutes

Social Services: At-Risk Youth, Child Welfare, Community Centers, Community Service Organizations, Counseling, Day Care, Domestic Violence, Emergency Relief, Family Planning, Family Services, Food/

Clothing Distribution, Homes, People with Disabilities, Recreation & Athletics, Scouts, Senior Services, Shelters/Homelessness, Substance Abuse, United Funds/United Ways, Volunteer Services, YMCA/YWCA/YMHA/YWHA, Youth Organizations

Application Procedures

Initial Contact: A short letter should be sent to the foundation officer describing a proposal before submitting a completed application. The trust does not have an application form; it does provide detailed information on the desired format of a written application upon request.

Application Requirements: Formal applications should include name, address, and telephone number of the organization; date established; national affiliations, if any; purposes and activities of the organization and services provided; purpose and amount of requested grant; budget; list of other sources of funding; plans for permanent funding if project is a continuing one; latest balance sheet and annual operating statement, including percentages of budget received from United Way and from federal, state, or other sources; percentage of costs paid by program recipients; and date of the most recent prior application to a foundation administered by the Fifth Third Bank. A document must also be provided stating that if a grant is received, a report will be made within one month of completion of the project detailing how the funds were spent. Additional material, such as pamphlets or supporting letters, should not be included.
Deadlines: February 10, May 10, August 10, and November 10.
Review Process: The committee meets quarterly. All grants are reviewed by the Charitable Foundations Screening Committee which forwards recommendations to the trust committee of the board of directors of the Fifth Third Bank. All grants must be approved by the trust committee.

Restrictions

The trust does not make grants for operating expenses, sectarian religious or political purposes, for scholarships, or to other foundations or individuals.

Additional Information

Organizations receiving grants from any of the trusts are generally not eligible for additional grants during the following three years. Recipients must be a tax-exempt organization.
Publications: Guidelines
Trust(s): Fifth Third Bank

Foundation Officials

Lawra Baumann: foundation officer

Grants Analysis

Disclosure Period: fiscal year ending September 30, 2001
Total Grants: $3,190,499*
Number of Grants: 46
Average Grant: $69,359
Highest Grant: $250,000
Lowest Grant: $10,000
Typical Range: $10,000 to $100,000
*Note: Giving excludes United Way.

Recent Grants

Note: Grants derived from fiscal 2001 Form 990.

General

250,000	Bayley Place, Cincinnati, OH
250,000	Juvenile Arthritis Foundation, Cincinnati, OH -- for research
166,665	Dan Beard Council Boy Scouts of America, Cincinnati, OH
150,000	Archbishop Moelter High School, Cincinnati, OH -- capital campaign
137,500	Toledo Museum of Art, Toledo, OH -- for capital and endowment campaigns
100,000	Cleveland State University Foundation,

Cleveland, OH -- to establish Viking
Fund

100,000	College of Mount St. Joseph, Cincinnati, OH -- for renovations
100,000	Elder High School, Cincinnati, OH -- for capital campaign
100,000	Grand Valley State University, Allendale, MI -- for capital campaign
100,000	Medical College of Ohio, Toledo, OH -- for capital and endowment campaigns

JACOB G. SCHMIDLAPP TRUST NO. 2

Giving Contact
Lawra Baumann, Trust Officer
c/o Fifth Third Bank
38 Fountain Sq. Plz., Department 00864
Cincinnati, OH 45263
Phone: (513)579-6034

Description
Founded: 1916
EIN: 316020109
Organization Type: Private Foundation
Giving Locations: OH: Cincinnati metropolitan area
Grant Types: Capital, General Support.

Donor Information
Founder: the late Jacob G. Schmidlapp

Financial Summary
Total Giving: $270,000 (fiscal year ending September 30, 2000); $200,000 (fiscal 1998); $301,300 (fiscal 1997)
Giving Analysis: Giving for fiscal 1998 includes: foundation grants to United Way ($85,000) fiscal 1997: foundation grants to United Way ($60,000)
Assets: $5,602,357 (fiscal 2000); $5,175,315 (fiscal 1998); $4,935,326 (fiscal 1997)
Gifts Received: $474,638 (fiscal 1992)

Typical Recipients
Arts & Humanities: Ballet, Historic Preservation, History & Archaeology, Libraries, Museums/Galleries, Performing Arts, Public Broadcasting
Civic & Public Affairs: Clubs, Community Foundations, Economic Development, Employment/Job Training, Nonprofit Management, Urban & Community Affairs
Education: Colleges & Universities, Education Funds, Elementary Education (Private), Environmental Education, Education-General, Literacy, Private Education (Precollege), Science/Mathematics Education, Secondary Education (Private)
Environment: Environment-General
Health: Cancer, Clinics/Medical Centers, Hospitals
Religion: Dioceses, Religious Welfare
Science: Scientific Centers & Institutes
Social Services: Community Centers, Community Service Organizations, Counseling, Day Care, United Funds/United Ways, Youth Organizations

Application Procedures
Initial Contact: Request application guidelines.
Deadlines: February 1, May 1, August 1, and November 1.

Restrictions
Does not support individuals, religious organizations for sectarian purposes, or political or lobbying groups.

Additional Information
Publications: Annual Report; Application Guidelines
Trust(s): Fifth Third Bank

Grants Analysis
Disclosure Period: fiscal year ending September 30, 2000
Total Grants: $270,000

Number of Grants: 7
Average Grant: $38,571
Highest Grant: $50,000
Typical Range: $20,000 to $50,000

Recent Grants
Note: Grants derived from fiscal 2000 Form 990.

General
50,000	Catholic Diocese of Cleveland, Cleveland, OH -- contribution
50,000	Catholic Inner-City Schools, Cincinnati, OH -- contribution
50,000	Southwest Community Health Foundation, Cleveland, OH -- contribution
40,000	Blue Grass Community Foundation, Lexington, KY -- contribution
30,000	Historic Southwest Ohio, Cincinnati, OH -- contribution
30,000	Louisville Science Center, Louisville, KY -- contribution
20,000	Lexington Children's Museum, Lexington, KY -- contribution

KILIAN J. AND CAROLINE F. SCHMITT FOUNDATION

Giving Contact
Gary J. Lindsay, Secretary & Treasurer
care of HSBC Bank U.S.A.
One HSBC Plaza
Rochester, NY 14604-2407
Phone: (716)264-0030

Description
Founded: 1991
EIN: 223087449
Organization Type: Private Foundation
Giving Locations: NY: Rochester
Grant Types: General Support.

Donor Information
Founder: the late Killian J. Schmitt, the late Caroline F. Schmitt

Financial Summary
Total Giving: $595,818 (fiscal year ending February 28, 2000); $407,293 (fiscal 1997); $430,500 (fiscal 1996)
Assets: $13,581,464 (fiscal 2000); $10,763,785 (fiscal 1997); $9,739,512 (fiscal 1996)

Typical Recipients
Arts & Humanities: Libraries, Museums/Galleries, Public Broadcasting
Civic & Public Affairs: Clubs, Economic Development, Employment/Job Training, Civic & Public Affairs-General, Zoos/Aquariums
Education: Arts/Humanities Education, Colleges & Universities, Engineering/Technological Education, Faculty Development, Medical Education, Private Education (Precollege), Religious Education, Science/Mathematics Education, Special Education, Student Aid
Environment: Resource Conservation
Health: Alzheimers Disease, Cancer, Children's Health/Hospitals, Emergency/Ambulance Services, Health-General, Home-Care Services, Hospices, Kidney, Long-Term Care, Medical Rehabilitation, Public Health, Speech & Hearing
International: Health Care/Hospitals, International Organizations
Religion: Churches, Dioceses, Religious Welfare
Science: Scientific Centers & Institutes
Social Services: Camps, Child Welfare, Community Service Organizations, Domestic Violence, Food/Clothing Distribution, People with Disabilities, Senior Services, Shelters/Homelessness

Application Procedures
Initial Contact: Request application form.
Deadlines: None.

Restrictions
Emphasis is on higher education and medical research.

Additional Information
Publications: Application Form

Foundation Officials
James R. Dray: director
Leon Fella: director
Robert H. Fella: president
Alfred Hallenbeck: director
Roger D. Lathan: director
Gary J. Lindsay: secretary, treasurer
Michael Charles Walker, Sr: vice president B Rochester, NY 1940. ED University of Colorado BA (1962); Columbia Pacific University MBA (1982); Columbia Pacific University DBA (1984). CORP AFFIL president, chief executive officer: Presbyterian Residence Center Corp. NONPR AFFIL member professional advisory committee: Self Help Hard Hearing; member business advisory board: State University New York; member: New York Saint Board Professional Medicine Conduct; member: Rotary; member: New York Association Homes & Services Aging; member: New York Saint Bankers Association; chairman: Monroe County Bond Services Comm; chairman, director: Genesee Region Home Care Association; vice president, director: Kilian & Caroline Schmitt Foundation; member: American Marketing Association; member: American Association Homes Aging. CLUB AFFIL Ridgemont Country Club.

Grants Analysis
Disclosure Period: fiscal year ending February 28, 2000
Total Grants: $595,818
Number of Grants: 33
Average Grant: $18,055
Highest Grant: $156,240
Typical Range: $500 to $60,000

Recent Grants
Note: Grants derived from fiscal 2000 Form 990.

Library-Related
| 25,000 | Rundel Library Foundation, Rochester, NY -- computer upgrade, program and restoration of Rundel building |

General
156,240	St. John Fisher College, Rochester, NY -- nursing lab for primary care
125,000	University of Rochester, Rochester, NY -- Eastman School of Music
50,000	Roberts Wesleyan College, Rochester, NY -- capital campaign
50,000	Unity Health System, Chesterfield, MO -- establishment of wellstream for women's health
50,000	University of Rochester, Rochester, NY -- brain symposium
50,000	WXXI Public Broadcasting, Rochester, NY -- digital t.v. conversion
29,578	George Eastman House, Rochester, NY -- upgrade library's online system
10,000	David Hochstein Music School, Rochester, NY -- school renovation of recital hall
10,000	Rochester Rotary Trust, Rochester, NY -- sunshine camp improvements
5,000	Crestwood Children's Foundation, Rochester, NY -- annual support

Schmoker Family Foundation

Giving Contact

Catherine S. Schmoker, President
6616 Biscayne Blvd.
Edina, MN 55436-1704
Phone: (612)336-3126

Description

Founded: 1987
EIN: 363493282
Organization Type: Private Foundation
Giving Locations: MN
Grant Types: General Support, Operating Expenses.

Financial Summary

Total Giving: $186,500 (2001); $29,300 (1999); $29,050 (1998)
Giving Analysis: Giving for 2001 includes: foundation grants to United Way ($10,000)
Assets: $2,808,337 (2001); $908,141 (1999); $750,527 (1998)
Gifts Received: $42,626 (2001). Note: In 2001, contributions were received from NBC Foundation ($40,880) and Catherine Stuart Schmoker ($1,746).

Typical Recipients

Arts & Humanities: Libraries, Music, Performing Arts, Theater
Civic & Public Affairs: Civic & Public Affairs-General, Women's Affairs
Education: Colleges & Universities, Education-General, Public Education (Precollege)
Health: Hospices
Religion: Seminaries
Social Services: United Funds/United Ways

Application Procedures

Initial Contact: The foundation reports no specific application guidelines. Send a brief letter of inquiry, including statement of purpose, amount requested, and proof of tax-exempt status.
Application Requirements: Include a description of organization, purpose of funds sought, and amount requested. The organization should also furnish an opinion to the effect that: 1) the organization has been certified by the IRS and is in fact acting as an organization described in Section 501(c)(3) of the Internal Revenue Code to which contributions are deductible under Section 170(c)(2)(b) of the Code, and furnish the organization's tax identification number; and 2) that the organization is either a) one which comes within the definition contained in paragraphs 1, 2, or 3 of Section 509(a) of the Internal Revenue Code, or b) that if the organization is a "private foundation" as described in Section 509(a) that it is also an "operating foundation" as defined in Section 4942(j)(3) of the Internal Revenue Code.
Deadlines: None.
Decision Notification: Notice of approval, rejection, or requests for additional information are usually sent within two months of application.

Foundation Officials

Lisa S. Hesdorffer: vice president, director
Catherine S. Hunnewell: vice president, director, assistant secretary
Regina Schirmer: assistant treasurer
Catherine M. Schmoker: vice president
Lisa St. Schmoker: vice president
Richard C. Schmoker: treasurer, director
William C. Schmoker: secretary

Grants Analysis

Disclosure Period: calendar year ending 2001
Total Grants: $176,500*
Number of Grants: 13
Average Grant: $5,958*

Highest Grant: $105,000
Lowest Grant: $1,000
Typical Range: $1,000 to $20,000
***Note:** Giving excludes United Way. Average grant figure excludes highest grant.

Recent Grants

Note: Grants derived from 2001 Form 990.

Library-Related

2,500	Library Foundation of Hennepin County, Edina, MN

General

105,000	University of Nebraska Foundation, Lincoln, NE
20,000	Women's Club of Minneapolis, Minneapolis, MN
15,000	Jeremiah Program, Minneapolis, MN
10,000	Children's Theatre Company, Minneapolis, MN
10,000	Greater Twin Cities United Way, Minneapolis, MN
5,000	Blake Schools, Edina, MN
5,000	United Theological Seminary, Minneapolis, MN
3,000	North Carolina Little Memorial Hospice, Inc., NC
3,000	Voyageur Outward Bound, Edina, MN
2,500	Ordway Center for the Performing Arts, The, Minneapolis, MN

Dr. Louis A. and Anne B. Schneider Foundation

Giving Contact

Louis A. Schneider, Trustee
9512 Camberwell Dr.
Ft. Wayne, IN 46804-4762

Description

Founded: 1987
EIN: 311193706
Organization Type: Private Foundation
Giving Locations: IN: Ft. Wayne; NY: New York
Grant Types: General Support.

Financial Summary

Total Giving: $20,136 (fiscal year ending November 30, 2001); $23,275 (fiscal 2000); $16,935 (fiscal 1999)
Assets: $374,157 (fiscal 2001); $405,089 (fiscal 2000); $426,432 (fiscal 1999)

Typical Recipients

Arts & Humanities: Arts Funds, Libraries, Opera, Public Broadcasting, Theater
Education: Colleges & Universities, Education-General, Medical Education
International: Foreign Arts Organizations
Religion: Religious Welfare
Science: Scientific Centers & Institutes, Scientific Research
Social Services: Food/Clothing Distribution

Application Procedures

Initial Contact: Send a brief letter of inquiry.
Application Requirements: Include purpose of funds sought, amount requested, and proof of tax-exempt status.
Deadlines: None.

Foundation Officials

Louis A. Schneider: trustee

Grants Analysis

Disclosure Period: fiscal year ending November 30, 2001
Total Grants: $20,136

Number of Grants: 15
Average Grant: $974*
Highest Grant: $6,500
Lowest Grant: $100
Typical Range: $100 to $5,000
***Note:** Average grant figure excludes highest grant.

Recent Grants

Note: Grants derived from fiscal 2001 Form 990.

Library-Related

125	Friends of the Library, Ft. Wayne, IN

General

6,500	Fort Wayne Jewish Federation, Ft. Wayne, IN
5,200	New York University School of Medicine, New York, NY
5,100	Metropolitan Opera, New York, NY
700	Community Harvest Food Bank, Ft. Wayne, IN
700	Matthew 25, Ft. Wayne, IN
550	Stratford Shakespeare Festival, Stratford, ON Canada
300	American Friends of Hebrew University, New York, NY
300	Weizmann Institute of Science, New York, NY
150	WBNI Public Radio, Ft. Wayne, IN
111	American Society for Technion, Chicago, IL

Schoenleber Foundation

Giving Contact

Peter C. Haensel, President & Director
111 E. Wisconsin Ave., Suite 1800
Milwaukee, WI 53202
Phone: (414)276-3400

Description

Founded: 1965
EIN: 391049364
Organization Type: Private Foundation
Giving Locations: WI: Milwaukee metropolitan area
Grant Types: General Support, Scholarship.

Donor Information

Founder: the late Marie and Louise Schoenleber

Financial Summary

Total Giving: $393,500 (2000); $400,100 (1999); $328,000 (1998)
Assets: $7,513,331 (2000); $7,024,166 (1999); $6,819,240 (1998)
Gifts Received: $500 (1992). Note: In 1992, contributions were received from Arnold Investment Counsel.

Typical Recipients

Arts & Humanities: Arts Associations & Councils, Arts Institutes, Community Arts, Historic Preservation, History & Archaeology, Libraries, Museums/Galleries, Music, Theater
Civic & Public Affairs: Business/Free Enterprise, Employment/Job Training, Ethnic Organizations, Civic & Public Affairs-General, Hispanic Affairs, Housing, Law & Justice, Public Policy, Urban & Community Affairs, Zoos/Aquariums
Education: Arts/Humanities Education, Business Education, Colleges & Universities, Engineering/Technological Education, Literacy, Medical Education, Private Education (Precollege), Public Education (Precollege), Student Aid
Environment: Environment-General
Health: Children's Health/Hospitals, Hospitals, Long-Term Care, Medical Rehabilitation, Medical Research, Single-Disease Health Associations
International: International Affairs

Religion: Churches, Religious Welfare
Social Services: Community Centers, Community Service Organizations, Counseling, Family Planning, Family Services, People with Disabilities, Recreation & Athletics, Shelters/Homelessness, YMCA/YWCA/YMHA/YWHA, Youth Organizations

Application Procedures

Initial Contact: Request application form.
Deadlines: August 30.

Additional Information

Publications: Application Form

Foundation Officials

Frank W. Bastian: secretary, director
Peter C. Haensel: president, director
Walter Schorrak: director

Grants Analysis

Disclosure Period: calendar year ending 2000
Total Grants: $393,500
Number of Grants: 23
Average Grant: $13,341*
Highest Grant: $100,000
Typical Range: $5,000 to $25,000
*Note: Average grant figure excludes highest grant.

Recent Grants

Note: Grants derived from 1999 Form 990.

Library-Related

100,000	Milwaukee Public Library Foundation, Milwaukee, WI
15,000	General Library System, UW-Madison, Madison, WI

General

50,000	University of Wisconsin Foundation, Madison, WI
32,600	Milwaukee Art Museum, Milwaukee, WI
25,000	State Historical Society of Wisconsin, Madison, WI
20,000	Friends of the Pabst Theater, Milwaukee, WI
20,000	Milwaukee Symphony Orchestra, Milwaukee, WI
15,000	Center for Deaf-Blind Persons, Milwaukee, WI
15,000	Milwaukee Institute of Art and Design, Milwaukee, WI
15,000	Milwaukee School of Engineering, Milwaukee, WI
15,000	Sierra Club Foundation, The, San Francisco, CA
15,000	Wisconsin Heritages, Inc. a.k.a. Pabst Mansion, Milwaukee, WI

DR. SCHOLL FOUNDATION

Giving Contact

Pamela Scholl, President
1033 Skokie Boulevard, Suite 230
Northbrook, IL 60062
Phone: (312)782-5210
Web: http://www.drschollfoundation.com

Description

Founded: 1947
EIN: 366068724
Organization Type: General Purpose Foundation
Giving Locations: IL: nationally.
Grant Types: Project.

Donor Information

Founder: The Dr. Scholl Foundation (formerly William M. Scholl Foundation) was created in 1947 by Dr. William M. Scholl . "At 18, he enrolled in Illinois Medical College, now Loyola University, and was awarded his M.D. degree in 1904. That same year, he established Scholl, Inc., a manufacturer of orthopedic devices and footwear. He died in 1968 leaving Scholl, Inc., and the foundation in the hands of his nephews. The foundation received the bulk of his estate, and Scholl, Inc., was sold in 1979."

Financial Summary

Total Giving: $12,815,494 (2000); $11,190,728 (1998); $10,354,715 (1996)
Giving Analysis: Giving for 2000 includes: foundation fellowships ($530,000) foundation scholarships ($2,185,000)
Assets: $186,645,652 (2000); $205,598,216 (1998); $181,999,580 (1997)

Typical Recipients

Arts & Humanities: Arts Institutes, History & Archaeology, Libraries, Museums/Galleries, Music, Opera, Public Broadcasting
Civic & Public Affairs: Clubs, Employment/Job Training, Civic & Public Affairs-General, Housing, Law & Justice, Native American Affairs, Professional & Trade Associations, Public Policy, Zoos/Aquariums
Education: Arts/Humanities Education, Colleges & Universities, Education Associations, Education Reform, Elementary Education (Private), Engineering/Technological Education, Faculty Development, Education-General, Legal Education, Medical Education, Minority Education, Private Education (Precollege), Science/Mathematics Education, Secondary Education (Private), Special Education, Student Aid
Environment: Environment-General, Resource Conservation, Resource Conservation
Health: Cancer, Children's Health/Hospitals, Clinics/Medical Centers, Eyes/Blindness, Health Funds, Health Organizations, Heart, Hospices, Hospitals, Medical Research, Prenatal Health Issues, Research/Studies Institutes, Single-Disease Health Associations
International: Foreign Arts Organizations, Foreign Educational Institutions, International-General, Health Care/Hospitals, International Affairs, International Organizations, International Peace & Security Issues, International Relief Efforts
Religion: Churches, Religious Organizations, Religious Welfare
Science: Science Museums, Scientific Organizations
Social Services: Animal Protection, Child Welfare, Community Centers, Crime Prevention, Family Services, Food/Clothing Distribution, Homes, People with Disabilities, Recreation & Athletics, Scouts, Senior Services, Shelters/Homelessness, Substance Abuse, Volunteer Services, YMCA/YWCA/YMHA/YWHA, Youth Organizations

Application Procedures

Initial Contact: Applicants should obtain a copy of the foundation's standard application form and guidelines. The form is required along with one copy of a full proposal.
Deadlines: Applications must be received by March 1 to be considered for the current year program.
Review Process: Applications are acknowledged. The foundation notifies applicants of its decisions in November, and distribution of grants occurs in December.

Restrictions

"In general, the Foundation does not consider the following for funding: organizations not eligible for tax-deductible support; political organizations or campaigns, or groups whose prime purpose is to influence legislation; foundations that are themselves grant-making bodies; public education; grants to individuals; general endowment grants; unrestricted purpose grants; general support grants; grants for the reduction of an operating deficit or to liquidate a debt; testimonial dinners and similar benefit programs involving purchases of tables, tickets, or advertisements; or installment grants, but the Foundation gives consideration to subsequent applications pertaining to the same project." Written requests only.

Additional Information

Applicants must present their request in the form of a special project or program designed to achieve a desirable result. All grantees are asked to sign an agreement that requires a full report to be filed at the conclusion of the project, including a statement of the results achieved by the grant. Only one application per organization will be considered annually.
Publications: Application Form; Program Guidelines

Foundation Officials

Neil Flanagin: director B Chicago, IL 1930. ED Yale University BA (1953); University of Michigan JD (1956). PRIM CORP EMPL partner: Sidley & Austin (Chicago).
David L. Royalty: treasurer, director
Jack E. Scholl: secretary
Jeanne M. Scholl: director
Michael W. Scholl: director
Pamela Scholl: president, director
Susan Scholl: director
William H. Scholl: chairman, director
Douglas C. Witherspoon: director

Grants Analysis

Disclosure Period: calendar year ending 2000
Total Grants: $10,102,679*
Number of Grants: 418
Average Grant: $24,169
Highest Grant: $500,000
Typical Range: $5,000 to $50,000
*Note: Giving excludes scholarships and fellowships.

Recent Grants

Note: Grants derived from 2000 Form 990.

Library-Related

93,513	Northwestern University, Evanston, IL -- funding for heart research
50,000	Newberry Library, Chicago, IL -- funding for endowment

General

500,000	American Friends of Cambridge University, New York, NY -- funding for Teaching Fellowship
500,000	Big Shoulders Fund, Chicago, IL -- partial funding for scholarship assistance
300,000	Dr. William M. Scholl College, Chicago, IL -- for scholarships and museum programs
300,000	Museum of Science and Industry, Chicago, IL -- partial funding for submarine project endowment
262,584	Cambridge Foundation, Cambridge United Kingdom -- partial funding for endowed lectureship
200,000	Metropolitan Family Services, Chicago, IL -- for Jumpstart Program
150,000	Field Museum of Natural History, Chicago, IL -- funding for Jason Project
136,000	Evanston Northwestern Healthcare Corporation, Evanston, IL -- funding for research and surgical microscope system
125,000	St. Gabriel School Foundation, Berkshire United Kingdom -- funding for gymnasium furnishing and sports hall
100,000	American Battle Monuments Commission, Arlington, VA -- funding for World War II Memorial

SCHOOLER FAMILY FOUNDATION (OHIO)

Giving Contact
S. Dean Schooler, President, Treasurer
4414 Apple Way
Boulder, CO 80301-1739
Phone: (303)449-0918

Description
Founded: 1987
EIN: 311157433
Organization Type: Private Foundation
Giving Locations: OH: Coshocton County
Grant Types: Capital, Conference/Seminar, Endowment, General Support, Project, Research, Seed Money.

Donor Information
Founder: Seward D. Schooler, Edith Schooler

Financial Summary
Total Giving: $364,752 (2001); $403,868 (2000); $391,914 (1999)
Giving Analysis: Giving for 2001 includes: foundation matching gifts ($9,503); foundation scholarships ($10,000); 2000: foundation scholarships ($20,000) foundation matching gifts ($33,000)
Assets: $6,866,795 (2001); $7,944,192 (2000); $8,381,910 (1999)
Gifts Received: $693,297 (1996); $4,069,000 (1993). Note: In 1996, contributions were received from Seward D. Schooler Sr.

Typical Recipients
Arts & Humanities: Film & Video, Historic Preservation, Libraries, Museums/Galleries, Music, Performing Arts, Public Broadcasting
Civic & Public Affairs: Botanical Gardens/Parks, Community Foundations, Economic Development, Civic & Public Affairs-General, Nonprofit Management, Philanthropic Organizations, Professional & Trade Associations, Urban & Community Affairs
Education: Arts/Humanities Education, Business Education, Colleges & Universities, Education Funds, Education-General, Literacy, Preschool Education, Private Education (Precollege), Religious Education, Science/Mathematics Education, Secondary Education (Public), Special Education, Student Aid
Health: Cancer, Children's Health/Hospitals, Clinics/Medical Centers, Emergency/Ambulance Services, Health Organizations, Hospices, Hospitals, Transplant Networks/Donor Banks
International: Foreign Educational Institutions
Religion: Churches
Social Services: Big Brother/Big Sister, Community Service Organizations, Domestic Violence, People with Disabilities, Recreation & Athletics, Scouts

Application Procedures
Initial Contact: Send a brief letter of inquiry requesting guidelines.
Application Requirements: Include a description of organization, amount requested, purpose of funds sought, recently audited financial statement, and proof of tax-exempt status.
Deadlines: None.

Restrictions
Grants are not made to individuals.

Additional Information
Publications: Application Guidelines

Foundation Officials
Willard S. Breon: vice president
C. Fenning Pierce: secretary
David R. Schooler: vice president

Dean Schooler: president
Heather L. Schooler: trustee

Grants Analysis
Disclosure Period: calendar year ending 2001
Total Grants: $345,249*
Number of Grants: 12
Average Grant: $9,525*
Highest Grant: $150,000
Lowest Grant: $148
Typical Range: $5,000 to $20,000
***Note:** Giving excludes scholarships and matching gifts. Average grant figure excludes two highest grants ($250,000).

Recent Grants
Note: Grants derived from 2000 Form 990.

General
150,000	Mount Union College, Alliance, OH -- lecture series endowment fund
50,000	Muskingum Valley Council, Boy Scouts of America, Coshocton County, OH -- aquatic area and pool
33,000	Foundation for Appalachian Ohio, Appalachian, OH -- challenge grant
30,000	First Step: Family Violence Prevention Services, Coshocton, OH -- shelter improvement project
25,000	Coshocton Foundation, Coshocton, OH -- recreational trail maintenance fund
13,000	Coshocton Foundation, Coshocton, OH -- 2000 operating support/leadership Coshocton County
10,000	Coshocton Community Choir, Coshocton, OH -- development and program operating support
10,000	Fresno United Methodist Church, Coshocton, OH -- Fresno Community Park construction project
10,000	Ohio Association for Community Leadership, Youngstown, OH -- statewide office development
10,000	Ohio Foundation of Independent Colleges, Columbus, OH -- scholars program

SCHOONMAKER J-SEWKLY VALLEY HOSPITAL TRUST

Giving Contact
Laurie Moritz, Trust Officer
c/o Mellon Bank NA
PO Box 185
Pittsburgh, PA 15230
Phone: (412)234-0023

Description
EIN: 256016020
Organization Type: Private Foundation
Giving Locations: PA: Pittsburgh
Grant Types: General Support.

Financial Summary
Total Giving: $402,500 (fiscal year ending September 30, 2001); $321,875 (fiscal 2000); $374,844 (fiscal 1998)
Giving Analysis: Giving for fiscal 2001 includes: foundation grants to United Way ($57,500); fiscal 2000: foundation scholarships ($2,000); fiscal 1998: foundation scholarships ($2,500); foundation grants to United Way ($10,000); foundation ($362,344);
Assets: $7,804,093 (fiscal 2001); $8,649,295 (fiscal 2000); $7,818,616 (fiscal 1998)

Typical Recipients
Arts & Humanities: Historic Preservation, History & Archaeology, Libraries, Museums/Galleries, Music
Civic & Public Affairs: Botanical Gardens/Parks, Chambers of Commerce, Civic & Public Affairs-General, Urban & Community Affairs, Women's Affairs
Education: Colleges & Universities, Education Funds, Legal Education, Medical Education, Private Education (Precollege), Religious Education, Student Aid
Environment: Environment-General
Health: AIDS/HIV, Emergency/Ambulance Services, Health Organizations, Hospitals
Religion: Churches, Religion-General, Seminaries
Science: Scientific Centers & Institutes
Social Services: At-Risk Youth, Community Service Organizations, Family Services, Scouts, Shelters/Homelessness, United Funds/United Ways, Youth Organizations

Application Procedures
Initial Contact: Send letter requesting application form.
Deadlines: None.

Additional Information
Publications: Application Form
Trust(s): Mellon Bank NA

Grants Analysis
Disclosure Period: fiscal year ending September 30, 2001
Total Grants: $345,000*
Number of Grants: 22
Average Grant: $11,600*
Highest Grant: $57,500
Lowest Grant: $2,000
Typical Range: $5,000 to $20,000
***Note:** Giving excludes United Way. Average grant figure excludes two highest grants ($113,000).

Recent Grants
Note: Grants derived from fiscal 2000 Form 990.

General
50,000	First Lutheran Church
50,000	Kenmore Association, Fredericksburg, VA
50,000	Wooster School, Danbury, CT
40,000	All Saints' Memorial Church, Navesink, NJ
40,000	First English Evangelical Lutheran Church, Pittsburgh, PA
25,000	Fox Chapel Conservation Council
25,000	Princeton University, Princeton, NJ
10,000	Harvard University Law School Fund, Cambridge, MA
10,000	United Way Allegheny County, Pittsburgh, PA
5,000	Boys Scouts of America, Pittsburgh, PA

SCHOWALTER FOUNDATION

Giving Contact
Willis Harder, President
900 N. Poplar, Suite 200
Newton, KS 67114
Phone: (316)283-3720
Fax: (316)283-2039

Description
Founded: 1953
EIN: 480623544
Organization Type: Private Foundation
Giving Locations: Midwest.
Grant Types: Capital, General Support, Project, Scholarship.

Donor Information
Founder: the late J. A. Schowalter

Financial Summary
Total Giving: $425,456 (2001); $412,850 (2000); $419,390 (1999)
Giving Analysis: Giving for 2001 includes: foundation scholarships ($134,000) 2000: foundation scholarships ($114,500)
Assets: $10,135,659 (2001); $10,136,611 (2000); $9,638,169 (1999)

Typical Recipients
Arts & Humanities: Arts & Humanities-General, History & Archaeology, Libraries, Literary Arts, Museums/Galleries, Music
Civic & Public Affairs: Economic Development, Civic & Public Affairs-General, Housing, Urban & Community Affairs
Education: Arts/Humanities Education, Colleges & Universities, International Studies, Minority Education, Preschool Education, Private Education (Precollege), Religious Education, Student Aid
Environment: Environment-General
Health: Emergency/Ambulance Services, Health-General, Health Organizations, Hospitals
International: Foreign Educational Institutions, Health Care/Hospitals, International Organizations, International Peace & Security Issues, Missionary/Religious Activities
Religion: Bible Study/Translation, Churches, Jewish Causes, Ministries, Missionary Activities (Domestic), Religious Organizations, Religious Organizations, Religious Welfare, Seminaries, Social/Policy Issues
Social Services: At-Risk Youth, Community Service Organizations, Crime Prevention, Day Care, Emergency Relief, United Funds/United Ways

Application Procedures
Initial Contact: Submit a cover letter and full proposal. Ten copies must be submitted.
Application Requirements: Include a description of organization, amount requested, purpose of funds sought, recently audited financial statement, proof of tax-exempt status.
Deadlines: March 1 and September 1.

Restrictions
Grants are not made to individuals or foreign organizations.

Additional Information
Priority is given to Mennonite denominations and their institutions. For grants originating outside of the three denominations, geographical preference is given to projects in Kansas and nearby states.
Publications: Application Guidelines

Foundation Officials
Howard E. Baumgartner: trustee
Allen Becker: trustee
Willis Harder: president
Howard Hershberger: trustee
Sue Ann Jantz: trustee
Mitchell Kingsley: trustee
Elwood Koehn: trustee
Eugene Unruh: trustee
Diane Yoder: trustee
Elvin D. Yoder: trustee

Grants Analysis
Disclosure Period: calendar year ending 2001
Total Grants: $291,456*
Number of Grants: 47
Average Grant: $6,201
Highest Grant: $17,000
Typical Range: $1,000 to $10,000
*Note: Giving excludes scholarships.

Recent Grants
Note: Grants derived from 2000 Form 990.

General

30,000	Bethel College, North Newton, KS -- for international student aid
25,000	Bluffton College, Bluffton, OH -- for international student aid
25,000	Goshen College, Goshen, AR -- for Menno Simons scholarships
25,000	Mennonite Central Committee, Akron, PA -- for building housing in Akron
20,000	Mennonite Board of Missions, Newton, KS -- for Mongolian dairy project
12,500	Health Ministries of Harvey County, Newton, KS -- for medical supplies
12,000	Hesston College, Hesston, KS -- for international student aid
12,000	Primera Mennonite Church, San Benito, TX -- to finish church building
10,000	Arts in Prison, Inc., Kansas City, KS -- to develop rehabilitative arts program
10,000	Associated Mennonite Biblical Seminary, Elkhart, IN -- for student scholarships

WALTER SCHROEDER FOUNDATION

Giving Contact
William T. Gaus, Vice President & Director
1000 N. Water St.
Milwaukee, WI 53202
Phone: (414)287-7177

Description
Founded: 1963
EIN: 396065789
Organization Type: General Purpose Foundation
Giving Locations: WI: Milwaukee County
Grant Types: Capital, General Support, Project, Research.

Donor Information
Founder: Established in 1963 by Walter Schroeder, president of Chris Schroeder and Son Company, a general insurance, real estate, and mortgage loan company in Milwaukee. He was also president of several hotel companies, and was a member of numerous hotel and restaurant associations. The foundation is principally funded from Mr. Schroeder's trust.

Financial Summary
Total Giving: $5,472,500 (fiscal year ending June 30, 2002); $2,074,938 (fiscal 2001); $688,080 (fiscal 2000). Note: Fiscal 1997 Giving includes United Way ($20,000).
Giving Analysis: Giving for fiscal 2002 includes: foundation grants to United Way ($30,000); fiscal 2001: foundation grants to United Way ($25,000) fiscal 1999: foundation grants to United Way ($20,000)
Assets: $2,317,725 (fiscal 2002); $7,397,266 (fiscal 2001); $8,680,193 (fiscal 2000)

Typical Recipients
Arts & Humanities: Arts Centers, Arts Festivals, Arts Funds, Arts Institutes, History & Archaeology, Libraries, Museums/Galleries, Music, Opera, Performing Arts, Theater
Civic & Public Affairs: Botanical Gardens/Parks, Business/Free Enterprise, Community Foundations, Hispanic Affairs, Zoos/Aquariums
Education: Arts/Humanities Education, Business Education, Colleges & Universities, Education Funds, Education-General, Medical Education, Private Education (Precollege), Public Education (Precollege), Secondary Education (Private), Secondary Education (Public)

Environment: Environment-General, Wildlife Protection
Health: Cancer, Children's Health/Hospitals, Emergency/Ambulance Services, Eyes/Blindness, Health Organizations, Hospitals, Medical Research, Nursing Services, Single-Disease Health Associations, Transplant Networks/Donor Banks
International: International Environmental Issues
Religion: Religious Organizations, Religious Welfare
Science: Scientific Organizations
Social Services: Animal Protection, Child Welfare, Community Centers, Community Service Organizations, Counseling, Family Services, Homes, People with Disabilities, Recreation & Athletics, Scouts, Senior Services, Social Services-General, United Funds/United Ways, Volunteer Services, YMCA/YWCA/YMHA/YWHA, Youth Organizations

Application Procedures
Initial Contact: Applicants should send a letter to the foundation.
Application Requirements: There is no formal policy for applications. A letter outlining the nature of the proposed grant is recommended.
Deadlines: None.
Review Process: Final notification on decisions varies.

Restrictions
Grants are not made to individuals.

Foundation Officials
William Thomas Gaus: vice president, director B Berlin, Germany 1928. ED Marquette University (1951); Marquette University JD (1954). PRIM CORP EMPL senior vice president, chief trustee officer: Marshall & Ilsley Trust Co.
Robert Morrison Hoffer: director B Muncie, IN 1921. ED Ball State University BS (1948); University of Michigan MBA (1949). NONPR AFFIL member: Institute Gas Technology.
Ruthmarie M. Lawrenz: director
Marjorie A. Vallier: secretary, director
James B. Wigdale: president, director

Grants Analysis
Disclosure Period: fiscal year ending June 30, 2002
Total Grants: $5,442,500*
Number of Grants: 99
Average Grant: $23,568*
Highest Grant: $2,000,000
Lowest Grant: $500
Typical Range: $5,000 to $50,000
*Note: Giving excludes United Way. Average grant figure excludes three highest grants ($3,180,000).

Recent Grants
Note: Grants derived from fiscal 2000 Form 990.

Library-Related

19,680	MSOE/Walter Schroeder Library Endowment Fund, Milwaukee, WI

General

50,000	Boys and Girls Club of Greater Milwaukee, Milwaukee, WI
50,000	Milwaukee Art Museum, Milwaukee, WI
50,000	Milwaukee Public Museum, Milwaukee, WI
30,000	Blood Center and Research Fund, Milwaukee, WI
30,000	Friends of Boerner Botanical Gardens, Milwaukee, WI
25,000	Interurban Car 26 Restoration Association, Cedar Grove, WI
25,000	Scimitar Foundation, Inc., Milwaukee, WI
20,000	Boy Scouts of America - Milwaukee County, Milwaukee, MI
20,000	Heartlove Place, Milwaukee, WI
20,000	Milwaukee County War Memorial Center, Milwaukee, WI

SCHUMANN FUND FOR NEW JERSEY

Giving Contact

Barbara Reisman, Executive Director
21 Van Vleck Street
Montclair, NJ 07042
Phone: (973)509-9883
Fax: (973)509-1149
E-mail: breisman@worldnet.att.net
Web: http://fdncenter.org/grantmaker/schumann/index.html

Description

Founded: 1988
EIN: 521556076
Organization Type: General Purpose Foundation
Giving Locations: NJ: Essex County
Grant Types: Conference/Seminar, General Support, Multiyear/Continuing Support, Project, Seed Money.

Donor Information

Founder: Established in 1988 by the Florence and John Schumann Foundation.

Financial Summary

Total Giving: $2,019,615 (2001); $2,272,222 (2000); $1,885,165 (1999)
Assets: $34,671,553 (2001); $39,342,385 (2000); $41,749,225 (1999)

Typical Recipients

Arts & Humanities: Historic Preservation, Libraries, Music, Public Broadcasting
Civic & Public Affairs: Botanical Gardens/Parks, Clubs, Community Foundations, Economic Development, Civic & Public Affairs-General, Hispanic Affairs, Housing, Legal Aid, Nonprofit Management, Public Policy, Urban & Community Affairs, Women's Affairs
Education: Afterschool/Enrichment Programs, Colleges & Universities, Education Associations, Education Funds, Education Reform, Elementary Education (Private), Elementary Education (Public), Environmental Education, Faculty Development, Education-General, Leadership Training, Literacy, Minority Education, Preschool Education, Private Education (Precollege), Public Education (Precollege), School Volunteerism, Social Sciences Education, Social Sciences Education, Special Education, Student Aid
Environment: Air/Water Quality, Forestry, Environment-General, Protection, Resource Conservation, Watershed
Health: AIDS/HIV, Diabetes, Health Organizations, Mental Health, Prenatal Health Issues, Public Health, Single-Disease Health Associations
Religion: Churches, Dioceses, Religious Welfare
Social Services: At-Risk Youth, Child Abuse, Child Welfare, Community Service Organizations, Counseling, Day Care, Emergency Relief, Family Planning, Family Services, Scouts, Shelters/Homelessness, Social Services-General, Volunteer Services, YMCA/YWCA/YMHA/YWHA, Youth Organizations, Youth Organizations

Application Procedures

Initial Contact: Submit a written request. The New York/New Jersey common application form. may be used if applicants so choose.
Application Requirements: Include a description of the organization's objectives, activities, and leadership; amount requested; purpose of funds sought; and plans for its accomplishment. Proposal should be accompanied by a copy of organization's recently audited financial statement, an expense budget identifying all sources of income, project's time frame and future funding plans, list of the board of directors, and a copy of organization's IRS tax-exempt determination letter.

Deadlines: January 15, April 15, July 15, or October 15.
Review Process: The board meets four times a year in March, June, September, and December. The foundation indicates that action on proposals may be reserved for a later quarter, but it will reply promptly to requests.

Restrictions

In general, the fund does not accept applications for capital campaigns, annual giving, endowment, direct support of individuals, or local programs in counties other than Essex. Projects in the arts, healthcare, and housing development are generally beyond the foundation's scope.

Additional Information

Publications: Annual Report

Foundation Officials

Aubin Z. Ames: trustee
Leonard S. Coleman, Jr.: trustee B Montclair, NJ 1949. ED Harvard University MPA; Princeton University BA. PRIM CORP EMPL president, treasurer: National League of Professional Baseball Clubs. CORP AFFIL director: Omnicom Group Inc.; director: Owens Corning; director: H.J. Heinz Co.; director: New Jersey Resources Corp.; director: Beneficial Corp.; director: Cendant Corp.; director: Avis Group Holdings Inc.; director: Avis Rent-A-Car Inc.
Christopher J. Daggett: chairman PRIM CORP EMPL William E Simon & Sons.
Andrew Christian Halvorsen: treasurer, trustee B Englewood, NJ 1946. ED Brown University AB (1968); University of Pennsylvania MBA (1972). PRIM CORP EMPL chief financial officer, director: Beneficial Corp. CORP AFFIL chief financial officer: Beneficial Arizona Inc.
George R. Harris: trustee
John Noonan: trustee
Alan Rosenthal: trustee

Grants Analysis

Disclosure Period: calendar year ending 2001
Total Grants: $2,007,115*
Number of Grants: 96
Average Grant: $20,907
Highest Grant: $73,265
Lowest Grant: $1,500
Typical Range: $10,000 to $50,000
*Note: Giving excludes United Way.

Recent Grants

Note: Grants derived from 2000 Form 990.

General

75,000	New Jersey Community Loan Fund, Trenton, NJ -- to expand efforts on behalf of early care and education providers
50,000	Association for Children of New Jersey, Newark, NJ -- to launch a public education campaign
50,000	Center for Analysis of Public Issues, Princeton, NJ -- for operating support
50,000	Center for Early Education at Rutgers, New Brunswick, NJ -- to conduct evaluations, policy analysis and professional development activities to improve early childhood education
50,000	Chad School Foundation, Newark, NJ -- for operating support
50,000	ISLES, Trenton, NJ -- support for community based Urban Environment Initiative
50,000	Learning Project, New York, NY -- support for the launch of the Newark Charter School
50,000	New Jersey Community Loan Fund, Trenton, NJ -- implementation of the Newark Lighthouse
50,000	Tri-State Transportation Campaign, New

York, NY -- for work to reform investment policy and transportation spending in New Jersey
| 48,000 | Babyland Family Services, Inc., Newark, NJ -- for operating support |

VICTOR E. AND CAROLINE E. SCHUTTE FOUNDATION

Giving Contact

David P. Ross, Senior Vice President & Trust Officer
Bank of America, N.A.
1200 Main St., 14th Fl.
Kansas City, MO 64105
Phone: (816)979-7481

Description

Founded: 1994
EIN: 431661684
Organization Type: Private Foundation
Giving Locations: KS: Kansas City
Grant Types: General Support.

Financial Summary

Total Giving: $832,500 (2000); $835,833 (1999); $1,068,315 (1998)
Assets: $16,597,097 (2000); $17,622,861 (1999); $16,620,568 (1998)
Gifts Received: $56,721 (1998); $2,461,056 (1995); $9,253,700 (1994). Note: In 1998, contributions were received from the estate of Caroline Schutte.

Typical Recipients

Arts & Humanities: Libraries, Theater
Education: Business Education, Special Education
Health: Cancer, Children's Health/Hospitals, Clinics/Medical Centers, Home-Care Services, Hospitals, Kidney
Religion: Churches, Synagogues/Temples
Social Services: Family Services, Recreation & Athletics, Senior Services, Youth Organizations

Application Procedures

Initial Contact: Send a letter of no more than three pages.
Application Requirements: Include appropriate attachments.
Deadlines: None.

Additional Information

Trust(s): Bank of America, NA

Foundation Officials

Donald Chisholm: co-trustee
Dick H. Woods: co-trustee

Grants Analysis

Disclosure Period: calendar year ending 2000
Total Grants: $832,500
Number of Grants: 10
Average Grant: $61,944*
Highest Grant: $275,000
Lowest Grant: $10,000
Typical Range: $25,000 to $100,000
*Note: Average grant figures excludes highest grant.

Recent Grants

Note: Grants derived from 1999 Form 990.

General

275,000	St. Luke's Hospital Foundation, Kansas City, MO -- to fund the Dr. Maxwell G. Berry chair in internal medicine 3rd payment on a 4 year 1,100,000 grant
250,000	Truman Medical Center, Kansas City, MO -- for the Schutte endowment chair in Women's Health, second payment on a 5 year 1,206,013 grant

185,000	Children's Mercy Hospital, Kansas City, MO -- to fund the Joseph Boone Gregg Chair for Cardiac Surgery, Second Payment on a 3 year 550,000 grant
62,500	St. Luke's Hospital Foundation, Kansas City, MO -- for partial funding of the Paul G. Koontz, MO chair in breast disease second payment on a 4 year 250,000 grant
33,333	Genesis/Boys & Girls Clubs of Greater Kansas City, Kansas City, MO -- supports of the capital campaign final payment on a 3 year 100,000 grant
15,000	Unity Temple on the Plaza, Kansas City, MO -- supports the Skinner organ third installment on a 5 year 75,000 grant
10,000	Menorah Medical Center, Kansas City, MO -- the naming of the new main lobby of the new inpatient facility for Arthur Mag, 3rd payment on a 5 year 50,000 grant
5,000	Unicorn Theater, Kansas City, MO

SCHWAB-ROSENHOUSE MEMORIAL FOUNDATION

Giving Contact

Connie Grueter
PO Box 23470
Oakland, CA 94623
Phone: (510)873-8034

Description

Founded: 1998
EIN: 686136241
Organization Type: Private Foundation
Giving Locations: CA: Sacramento including surrounding counties
Grant Types: Scholarship.

Financial Summary

Total Giving: $871,500 (2001); $803,200 (2000); $353,200 (1998)
Giving Analysis: Giving for 2001 includes: foundation scholarships ($859,000); 2000: foundation scholarships ($803,200) 1998: foundation scholarships ($353,200)
Assets: $10,196,929 (2001); $12,289,119 (2000); $8,106,684 (1998)
Gifts Received: $750,000 (1998). Note: In 1998, contributions were received from Rosenhouse Family Trust.

Typical Recipients

Arts & Humanities: Libraries
Education: Colleges & Universities

Application Procedures

Initial Contact: Request application form.
Deadlines: February 1.

Foundation Officials

Sandra Felderstein: distribution trustee
Candice Fields: Distribution trustee
Iving Herman, Ph.D.: Distribution trustee
Dr. Marvin Kamras: distribution trustee
John Lewis: Distribution trustee
Charles Nadler, Ph.D.: Distribution trustee
Rabbi Reuvin Taff: distribution trustee
Linda Van Rees: financial trustee
Joel Zimmerman: distribution trustee

Grants Analysis

Disclosure Period: calendar year ending 2001
Total Grants: $12,500*
Number of Grants: 1
*Note: Giving excludes scholarships.

Recent Grants

Note: Grants derived from 2000 Form 990.

Library-Related
12,500	Sacto Public Library Foundation, Sacramento, CA -- for Scholarship Resource Center

General
5,000	Mills College, Oakland, CA
5,000	Mills College, Oakland, CA
5,000	Pacific Union College, Angwin, CA
5,000	Saint Mary's College of California, Moraga, CA
5,000	Saint Mary's College of California, Moraga, CA
5,000	Santa Clara University, Santa Clara, CA
5,000	Santa Clara University, Santa Clara, CA
5,000	Stanford University, Stanford, CA
5,000	Stanford University, Stanford, CA
5,000	Stanford University, Stanford, CA

ARNOLD A. SCHWARTZ FOUNDATION

Giving Contact

Steven A. Kunzman, Vice President
15 Mountain Boulevard
Warren, NJ 07059-5611
Phone: (908)757-7800

Description

Founded: 1953
EIN: 226034152
Organization Type: Private Foundation
Giving Locations: NJ: central New Jersey
Grant Types: General Support.

Donor Information

Founder: the late Arnold A. Schwartz

Financial Summary

Total Giving: $421,200 (fiscal year ending November 30, 2001); $432,600 (fiscal 2000); $331,700 (fiscal 1999)
Assets: $5,831,457 (fiscal 2001); $9,191,553 (fiscal 2000); $9,611,429 (fiscal 1999)

Typical Recipients

Arts & Humanities: History & Archaeology, Libraries
Civic & Public Affairs: Clubs, Employment/Job Training, Civic & Public Affairs-General, Housing
Education: Arts/Humanities Education, Colleges & Universities, Gifted & Talented Programs, Private Education (Precollege), Public Education (Precollege), Special Education, Student Aid
Environment: Wildlife Protection
Health: Alzheimers Disease, Cancer, Children's Health/Hospitals, Clinics/Medical Centers, Emergency/Ambulance Services, Eyes/Blindness, Health Organizations, Heart, Hospitals, Mental Health, Multiple Sclerosis, Outpatient Health Care, Prenatal Health Issues, Public Health, Single-Disease Health Associations
Religion: Jewish Causes, Religious Organizations, Religious Welfare
Social Services: At-Risk Youth, Camps, Child Welfare, Community Service Organizations, Counseling, Day Care, Family Services, Food/Clothing Distribution, People with Disabilities, Recreation & Athletics, Senior Services, Shelters/Homelessness, Substance Abuse, United Funds/United Ways, Volunteer Services, YMCA/YWCA/YMHA/YWHA, Youth Organizations

Application Procedures

Initial Contact: Send a brief letter of inquiry. stating the purpose of the contribution.
Deadlines: September 30.

Restrictions

Does not support individuals or provide funds for endowments.

Foundation Officials

Victor DiLeo: trustee
Louis Harding: vice president
Edward D. Kunzman: president
Steven Kunzman: secretary, treasurer
David Lackland: trustee
Robert Shapiro: trustee B Plainfield, NJ 1942. ED University of California, Los Angeles BS (1965); Loyola University JD (1968). NONPR AFFIL member: National Association Criminal Defense Lawyers; member: Trial Lawyers Public Justice; member: California Attys Criminal Justice; member: Century City Bar Association.
Kenneth W. Turnbull: trustee CORP AFFIL president, chief executive officer: United National Bank.

Grants Analysis

Disclosure Period: fiscal year ending November 30, 2001
Total Grants: $421,200
Number of Grants: 68
Average Grant: $6,194
Highest Grant: $30,000
Lowest Grant: $500
Typical Range: $1,000 to $10,000

Recent Grants

Note: Grants derived from fiscal 2000 Form 990.

Library-Related
20,000	Arnold Schwartz Memorial Library, Dunellen, NJ

General
20,000	Muhlenberg Foundation, Inc., Plainfield, NJ -- purchase a transesophageal echocardiography probe
15,000	Deborah Hospital Foundation, Browns Mills, NJ -- purchase two patient stretcher beds
10,000	Bonnie Brae, Liberty Corner, NJ -- construction of a new recreation activity building
10,000	Center for Great Expectations, Somerville, NJ -- purchase land for contraction of buildings
10,000	Cerebral Palsy League, Cranford, NJ -- help renovate a newly acquired building
10,000	Fish Hospitality Program, Inc., Dunellen, NJ -- program operation
10,000	Fish, Inc., Piscataway, NJ
10,000	JFK Medical Center Foundation, Edison, NJ -- provide care and supervision to financially needy clients
10,000	McAuley School, Watchung, NJ
10,000	Somerset Health Care Foundation, Somerset, NJ -- for Somerset family practice center

ARNOLD AND MARIE SCHWARTZ FUND FOR EDUCATION AND HEALTH RESEARCH

Giving Contact

Marie D. Schwartz, President
465 Park Ave.
New York, NY 10022

Description

Founded: 1971
EIN: 237115019
Organization Type: Private Foundation

Giving Locations: NY: New York
Grant Types: General Support.

Donor Information
Founder: Arnold Schwartz Charitable Trust.

Financial Summary
Total Giving: $478,492 (fiscal year ending March 31, 2002); $719,380 (fiscal 2001); $333,050 (fiscal 2000)
Assets: $5,743,214 (fiscal 2002); $2,387,442 (fiscal 2001); $5,891,179 (fiscal 2000)

Typical Recipients
Arts & Humanities: Arts Associations & Councils, Arts Festivals, Arts Institutes, Ballet, Dance, Ethnic & Folk Arts, Historic Preservation, History & Archaeology, Libraries, Museums/Galleries, Music, Opera, Performing Arts, Public Broadcasting
Civic & Public Affairs: Botanical Gardens/Parks, Clubs, Civic & Public Affairs-General, Housing, Law & Justice, Minority Business, Parades/Festivals, Professional & Trade Associations, Public Policy, Safety, Women's Affairs, Zoos/Aquariums
Education: Arts/Humanities Education, Colleges & Universities, Education Reform, Health & Physical Education, Medical Education
Environment: Air/Water Quality, Environment-General, Wildlife Protection
Health: Cancer, Emergency/Ambulance Services, Health Organizations, Hospitals, Hospitals (University Affiliated), Medical Research, Single-Disease Health Associations
International: Foreign Educational Institutions, Human Rights, Missionary/Religious Activities
Religion: Bible Study/Translation, Churches, Jewish Causes, Ministries, Religious Organizations, Religious Welfare, Synagogues/Temples
Social Services: Child Welfare, Community Service Organizations, Crime Prevention, Family Services, Recreation & Athletics, Youth Organizations

Application Procedures
Initial Contact: Send a brief letter of inquiry describing program or project.
Deadlines: None.

Foundation Officials
Sylvia Kassel: director
Ruth Kerstein: secretary, director
Nellie Jane McDonald: director
Marie D. Schwartz: president

Grants Analysis
Disclosure Period: fiscal year ending March 31, 2002
Total Grants: $478,492
Number of Grants: 52
Average Grant: $1,208*
Highest Grant: $200,000
Lowest Grant: $10
Typical Range: $100 to $5,000
*Note: Average grant figure excludes four highest grants ($420,500).

Recent Grants
Note: Grants derived from 2000 Form 990.

General
100,000	Arnold and Marie Schwartz College of Pharmacy, Brooklyn, NY
52,250	Metropolitan Opera Association, New York, NY
51,000	National Trust for Historic Preservation, Tarrytown, NY
13,370	Historical Society of Greenwich, Greenwich, CT
12,000	San Antonio Museum of Art, San Antonio, TX
11,000	Norton Museum of Art, West Palm Beach, FL
10,000	United States Department of State
10,000	University of Rochester, Rochester, NY
9,250	Lady Bird Johnson Wildflower Center, Austin, TX
6,000	Metropolitan Museum of Art, New York, NY

SCOTT FETZER CO.

Company Headquarters
865 Bassett Rd.
Westlake, OH 44145
Web: http://www.berkshirehathaway.com

Company Description
Employees: 14,000
SIC(s): 3400 Fabricated Metal Products, 3600 Electronic & Other Electrical Equipment.
Parent Company: Berkshire Hathaway Inc., 1440 Kiewit Plaza, Omaha, NE, United States

Operating Locations
Scott Fetzer Co. (OH--Westlake)

Scott & Fetzer Foundation

Giving Contact
Edie DeSantis, Executive Secretary
28800 Clemens Rd.
Westlake, OH 44145
Phone: (440)892-3000

Description
Founded: 1967
EIN: 346596076
Organization Type: Corporate Foundation
Giving Locations: OH
Grant Types: General Support.

Donor Information
Founder: the Scott Fetzer Co.

Financial Summary
Total Giving: $249,764 (2000); $227,995 (1999); $249,675 (1998)
Giving Analysis: Giving for 2000 includes: foundation grants to United Way ($63,910); 1999: foundation grants to United Way ($37,910) 1998: foundation grants to United Way ($52,660)
Assets: $385,573 (2000); $289,872 (1999); $451,974 (1998)
Gifts Received: $333,067 (2000); $52,955 (1999); $313,201 (1998). Note: In 1990, contributions were received from the Scott Fetzer Co.

Typical Recipients
Arts & Humanities: Arts Associations & Councils, Arts Centers, Community Arts, History & Archaeology, Libraries, Music, Opera, Performing Arts, Public Broadcasting, Theater
Civic & Public Affairs: Business/Free Enterprise, Clubs, First Amendment Issues, Civic & Public Affairs-General, Legal Aid, Municipalities/Towns, Parades/Festivals, Safety, Urban & Community Affairs
Education: Business Education, Colleges & Universities, Community & Junior Colleges, Economic Education, Education Associations, Education Funds, Elementary Education (Public), Education-General, Private Education (Precollege), Public Education (Precollege), Secondary Education (Private), Secondary Education (Public), Student Aid
Health: Arthritis, Cancer, Children's Health/Hospitals, Health Funds, Health Organizations, Heart, Hospices, Hospitals, Medical Research, Multiple Sclerosis, Prenatal Health Issues, Public Health, Single-Disease Health Associations

International: Foreign Educational Institutions, International Organizations
Religion: Social/Policy Issues
Science: Science Exhibits & Fairs, Science Museums
Social Services: Camps, Child Welfare, Community Service Organizations, Food/Clothing Distribution, Recreation & Athletics, Special Olympics, United Funds/United Ways, Volunteer Services, Youth Organizations

Application Procedures
Initial Contact: The foundation requests applications be made in writing. Federal identification number is required.
Deadlines: None.

Restrictions
Grants are not made to individuals.

Corporate Officials
Ralph Edward Schey: chairman, chief executive officer, director B Cleveland, OH 1924. ED Ohio University (1948); Harvard University BusAdmin (1950). PRIM CORP EMPL chairman, chief executive officer, director: Scott Fetzer Co. CORP AFFIL director: Hauserman Co.
Kenneth J. Semelsberger: president, chief executive officer, chief operating officer, director B Marsteller, PA 1936. ED Ohio State University BBA (1970); Cleveland State University MBA (1972). PRIM CORP EMPL president, chief executive officer, chief operating officer, director: Scott Fetzer Co. CORP AFFIL production manager: Holan Corp.; president: Stahl Division Scott & Fetzer Co.; Sales & Contracts manager: Barth Cleve McNeil Corp.
William W. T. Stephans: chief financial officer PRIM CORP EMPL chief financial officer: Scott Fetzer Co.

Foundation Officials
John W. Gretta: assistant treasurer
Timothy S. Guster: vice president, secretary
Patricia M. Scanlon: secretary
Ralph Edward Schey: chairman (see above)
Kenneth J. Semelsberger: president (see above)
William W. T. Stephans: vice president, treasurer (see above)

Grants Analysis
Disclosure Period: calendar year ending 2000
Total Grants: $185,864*
Number of Grants: 75
Average Grant: $1,160*
Highest Grant: $100,000
Typical Range: $500 to $2,500
*Note: Giving excludes United Way. Average grant figure excludes highest grant.

Recent Grants
Note: Grants derived from 1999 Form 990.

Library-Related
10,000	American Library Association, Chicago, IL

General
25,000	Cleveland Musical Arts Association, Cleveland, OH
25,000	Playhouse Square Foundation, Cleveland, OH
20,000	Cleveland Opera, Cleveland, OH
20,000	Cleveland Playhouse, Cleveland, OH
15,000	Direct Selling Education Foundation, Washington, DC
11,250	United Way, Cleveland, OH
11,250	United Way Services, Cleveland, OH
11,250	United Way Services, Cleveland, OH
10,000	Cleveland Orchestra, Cleveland, OH
5,000	Komen Northeast Ohio Race for the Cure, Cleveland, OH

VIRGINIA STEELE SCOTT FOUNDATION

Giving Contact
Maria O. Grant, President & Director
1151 Oxford Rd.
San Marino, CA 91108
Phone: (626)583-7847

Description
Founded: 1974
EIN: 237365076
Organization Type: Private Foundation
Giving Locations: CA: Pasadena/Los Angeles
Grant Types: General Support.

Donor Information
Founder: the late Virginia Steele Scott, Grace C. Scott

Financial Summary
Total Giving: $268,000 (fiscal year ending June 30, 2002); $275,000 (fiscal 2001); $3,817,000 (fiscal 2000)
Assets: $9,741,773 (fiscal 2002); $10,053,308 (fiscal 2001); $10,737,457 (fiscal 2000)
Gifts Received: In 1991, contributions were received from the Grace C. Scott Trust.

Typical Recipients
Arts & Humanities: Arts Associations & Councils, Arts Centers, Arts Institutes, Community Arts, Arts & Humanities-General, Libraries, Museums/Galleries, Music, Performing Arts, Theater
Civic & Public Affairs: Botanical Gardens/Parks
Education: Arts/Humanities Education
International: Foreign Arts Organizations
Social Services: Community Centers

Application Procedures
Initial Contact: Send a one-page letter of inquiry.
Application Requirements: Include five copies of the following: one-page statement of organization's mission and specific need for financial support; one-page financial summary of the most recent fiscal year; and most recent IRS letter proving non-profit status.
Deadlines: September 30.

Restrictions
Grants are limited to visual and performing arts in Pasadena and Los Angeles.

Foundation Officials
Mrs. James Galbraith: director
Maria O. Grant: director
Paul Johnson Karlstrom: director B Seattle, WA 1941. ED Stanford University BA (1964); University of California, Los Angeles MA (1969); University of California, Los Angeles PhD (1973). NONPR AFFIL member adv board: Jacob Lawrence Catalogue Raisonni Project; director: Southwest Art History Council; West coast reg director: Huntington Library; member editorial board: California Historical Society; member adv board: Humanities West; director: Bay Area Video Coalition.
Jack Pettker: member
Henry J. Tanner: director
Robert Rodgers Wark: president B Edmonton, AB Canada 1924. ED University of Alberta BA (1944); University of Alberta MA (1946); Harvard University MA (1949); Harvard University PhD (1952). NONPR AFFIL member: College Art Association America.

Grants Analysis
Disclosure Period: fiscal year ending June 30, 2002
Total Grants: $268,000
Number of Grants: 11
Average Grant: $7,800*
Highest Grant: $190,000

Lowest Grant: $4,000
Typical Range: $5,000 to $10,000
*Note: Average grant figure excludes highest grant.

Recent Grants
Note: Grants derived from fiscal 2000 Form 990.

Library-Related
3,500,000	Huntington Library, San Marino, CA
210,000	Huntington Library, San Marino, CA
40,500	Huntington Library, San Marino, CA

General
8,000	Southwest Chamber Music, Pasadena, CA
7,500	Armory Center for Arts, Pasadena, CA
7,500	Art Center College of Design, Pasadena, CA
7,500	Pacific Asia Museum, Pasadena, CA
7,000	Pasadena Symphony, Pasadena, CA
6,000	Pasadena Shakespeare, Pasadena, CA
5,000	Coleman Chamber Music Association, Pasadena, CA
5,000	Los Angeles Children's Chorus, Pasadena, CA
5,000	Pasadena Playhouse State Theatre of California, Pasadena, CA
4,000	Foothill Master Chorale, Pasadena, CA

WILLIAM E. SCOTT FOUNDATION

Giving Contact
Robert W. Decker, President, Treasurer & Director
801 Cherry Street, Suite 2000
Ft. Worth, TX 76102-3708
Phone: (817)336-2400

Description
Founded: 1960
EIN: 756024661
Organization Type: Private Foundation
Giving Locations: LA; NM; OK; TX: emphasis on the Fort Worth-Tarrant County area
Grant Types: Capital, General Support, Project.

Donor Information
Founder: the late William E. Scott

Financial Summary
Total Giving: $394,751 (fiscal year ending May 31, 2002); $857,200 (fiscal 2001); $1,098,581 (fiscal 1999)
Giving Analysis: Giving for fiscal 2001 includes: foundation grants to United Way ($25,000)
Assets: $17,053,058 (fiscal 2002); $18,563,962 (fiscal 2001); $19,763,541 (fiscal 1999)

Typical Recipients
Arts & Humanities: Arts Associations & Councils, Arts Festivals, Arts Funds, Ballet, Community Arts, Dance, Historic Preservation, History & Archaeology, Libraries, Museums/Galleries, Music, Opera, Performing Arts, Public Broadcasting, Theater
Civic & Public Affairs: Clubs, Community Foundations, Civic & Public Affairs-General, Housing, Nonprofit Management, Professional & Trade Associations, Safety, Urban & Community Affairs, Women's Affairs, Zoos/Aquariums
Education: Afterschool/Enrichment Programs, Arts/Humanities Education, Colleges & Universities, Community & Junior Colleges, Education Reform, Education-General, Medical Education, Private Education (Precollege), Public Education (Precollege), Special Education
Health: AIDS/HIV, Children's Health/Hospitals, Clinics/Medical Centers, Emergency/Ambulance Services, Health Organizations, Medical Research, Prenatal Health Issues, Research/Studies Institutes, Respiratory, Single-Disease Health Associations

International: Foreign Arts Organizations, Missionary/Religious Activities
Religion: Churches, Ministries, Religious Welfare, Social/Policy Issues
Science: Science Museums
Social Services: Big Brother/Big Sister, Child Welfare, Community Centers, Community Service Organizations, Crime Prevention, Delinquency & Criminal Rehabilitation, Domestic Violence, Family Planning, Homes, People with Disabilities, Recreation & Athletics, Scouts, Substance Abuse, United Funds/United Ways, Volunteer Services, YMCA/YWCA/YMHA/YWHA, YMCA/YWCA/YMHA/YWHA, Youth Organizations

Application Procedures
Initial Contact: The foundation requests applications be made in writing.
Deadlines: None.

Additional Information
Publications: Application Guidelines

Foundation Officials
Robert W. Decker: president, treasurer, director
Raymond B. Kelly, III: vice president, secretary, director

Grants Analysis
Disclosure Period: fiscal year ending May 31, 2002
Total Grants: $394,751
Number of Grants: 30
Average Grant: $6,955*
Highest Grant: $100,000
Lowest Grant: $50
Typical Range: $1,000 to $10,000
*Note: Average grant figure excludes two highest grants ($200,000).

Recent Grants
Note: Grants derived from 2000 Form 990.

General
130,000	All Saints Health System, Ft. Worth, TX
100,000	Fort Worth Zoological Association, Ft. Worth, TX
35,000	Art Council of Fort Worth and Tarrant County, Ft. Worth, TX
35,000	Fort Worth Academy, Ft. Worth, TX
25,000	American Red Cross, Ft. Worth, TX
25,000	Fort Worth Dallas Ballet, Ft. Worth, TX
25,000	United Way of Metropolitan Tarrant County, Ft. Worth, TX
25,000	YMCA of Metropolitan Tarrant County, Ft. Worth, TX
20,000	Adolescent Pregnancy Prevention, Ft. Worth, TX
20,000	Health Education Learning Project, Ft. Worth, TX

WILLIAM H., JOHN G., AND EMMA SCOTT FOUNDATION

Giving Contact
Hugh K. Leary, Executive Director & Treasurer
c/o Davenport & Co. LLC
PO Box 85678
Richmond, VA 23285
Phone: (804)780-2000

Description
Founded: 1956
EIN: 540648772
Organization Type: Private Foundation
Giving Locations: VA: Commonwealth
Grant Types: Capital, General Support, Scholarship.

Donor Information

Founder: the late John G. Scott, Emma Scott Taylor

Financial Summary

Total Giving: $435,000 (fiscal year ending September 30, 2001); $541,415 (fiscal 2000); $405,000 (fiscal 1999)

Giving Analysis: Giving for fiscal 2001 includes: foundation grants to United Way ($23,000); fiscal 2000: foundation grants to United Way ($20,000); foundation scholarships ($21,000) fiscal 1997: foundation scholarships ($25,000)

Assets: $10,554,105 (fiscal 2001); $12,473,445 (fiscal 2000); $10,561,974 (fiscal 1998)

Typical Recipients

Arts & Humanities: Arts Associations & Councils, Arts Centers, Ballet, History & Archaeology, Libraries, Literary Arts, Museums/Galleries, Music, Public Broadcasting

Civic & Public Affairs: Botanical Gardens/Parks, Clubs, Civic & Public Affairs-General, Housing, Rural Affairs, Urban & Community Affairs

Education: Colleges & Universities, Education Funds, Private Education (Precollege), Public Education (Precollege), Religious Education, Science/Mathematics Education, Student Aid

Environment: Environment-General

Health: Clinics/Medical Centers, Emergency/Ambulance Services

Religion: Churches, Dioceses, Ministries, Religious Organizations, Religious Welfare, Seminaries

Science: Science Museums

Social Services: At-Risk Youth, Child Abuse, Child Welfare, Community Service Organizations, Day Care, Food/Clothing Distribution, Homes, People with Disabilities, Scouts, Senior Services, Shelters/Homelessness, YMCA/YWCA/YMHA/YWHA, Youth Organizations

Application Procedures

Initial Contact: Send a letter stating financial need.
Deadlines: None.

Foundation Officials

William Hill Brown, III: director
Suzanne B. Crump: director
Charles M. Guthridge: trustee
Hugh K. Leary: executive director, treasurer
T. Justin Moore, Jr.: vice president B Richmond, VA 1925. ED Princeton University (1947); University of Virginia (1950). PRIM CORP EMPL counsel: Hunton & Williams. CORP AFFIL director: Central Fidelity Banks Inc.; director: Dominion Resources Inc.
Edwin Palmer Munson: assistant secretary B Richmond, VA 1935. ED University of Virginia (1957); University of Richmond (1980). PRIM CORP EMPL vice president, legal counsel: Computer Co.
Robert Fillmore Norfleet, Jr.: trustee B Richmond, VA 1940. ED Washington & Lee University BA (1962); Rutgers University (1972). PRIM CORP EMPL executive vice president, senior credit officer: Crestar Bank Corp.
C. Cotesworth Pinckney: secretary
E. Bryson Powell: trustee

Grants Analysis

Disclosure Period: fiscal year ending September 30, 2001
Total Grants: $412,000*
Number of Grants: 17
Average Grant: $20,800*
Highest Grant: $50,000
Lowest Grant: $10,000
Typical Range: $10,000 to $40,000
***Note:** Giving excludes scholarships. Average grant figure excludes two highest grants ($100,000).

Recent Grants

Note: Grants derived from fiscal 2000 Form 990.

Library-Related
15,000 Braille Circulating Library, Richmond, VA -- headquarter renovations

General
100,000 Grymes Memorial School, Orange, VA -- professional development
100,000 Hampden-Sydney College, Hampden-Sydney, VA -- capital campaign
52,000 St. Christopher's School, Richmond, VA -- gym renovations
32,000 New Community School, Richmond, VA -- property renovations
30,000 Interfaith Housing Corporation, Richmond, VA -- child care center
30,000 Sacred Heart Center, Richmond, VA -- capital campaign
25,000 Daily Planet, Richmond, VA -- capital acquisition
25,000 Stuart Hall School, New Orleans, LA -- activity bus
20,000 Chesapeake Academy, Irvington, VA -- capital renovations
20,000 Homeward United Way Services, Richmond, VA -- client tracking system

SCOTTSMAN INDUSTRIES

Company Headquarters

Vernon Hills, MI
Web: http://www.scotsman-ice.com

Company Description

Former Name: Kysor Industrial Corp.
Revenue: US$633 million (2001)
Employees: 4500 (2001)
SIC(s): 3500 Industrial Machinery & Equipment, 3700 Transportation Equipment.

Operating Locations

Scottsman Industries (GA--Columbus, Conyers; IL--Byron; MI--Cadillac, Walker; NC--Charlotte; OR--Portland; TX--Fort Worth)
Note: Includes division and plant locations.

Scotsman Industries Foundation

Giving Contact

Richard Holden, Vice President, Human Resources
820 Forest Edge Drive
Vernon Hills, IL 60061-3105
Phone: (847)215-4500

Description

EIN: 237199469
Organization Type: Corporate Foundation
Giving Locations: operating locations.
Grant Types: Award, Capital, Employee Matching Gifts, General Support, Operating Expenses.

Financial Summary

Total Giving: $119,561 (fiscal year ending May 31, 1999); $120,080 (fiscal 1997); $113,290 (fiscal 1996). Note: Fiscal 1997 Giving includes United Way ($34,399).
Giving Analysis: Giving for fiscal 1999 includes: foundation grants to United Way ($40,750) foundation ($78,811)
Assets: $2,864,263 (fiscal 1999); $2,666,638 (fiscal 1998); $2,386,499 (fiscal 1997)
Gifts Received: $100,000 (fiscal 1996); $100,000 (fiscal 1995); $100,000 (fiscal 1994). Note: In fiscal 1995, contributions were received from Kysor Industrial Corp.

Typical Recipients

Arts & Humanities: Arts Appreciation, Arts Associations & Councils, Arts Centers, Arts Institutes, Community Arts, Arts & Humanities-General, Historic Preservation, History & Archaeology, Libraries, Museums/Galleries, Music, Opera, Public Broadcasting

Civic & Public Affairs: Business/Free Enterprise, Clubs, Economic Development, Economic Policy, Employment/Job Training, Civic & Public Affairs-General, Housing, Law & Justice, Urban & Community Affairs

Education: Arts/Humanities Education, Business Education, Colleges & Universities, Community & Junior Colleges, Economic Education, Engineering/Technological Education, Education-General, International Studies, Private Education (Precollege), Secondary Education (Public), Student Aid

Environment: Environment-General, Resource Conservation, Wildlife Protection

Health: AIDS/HIV, Cancer, Children's Health/Hospitals, Health-General, Geriatric Health, Health Organizations, Hospices, Medical Rehabilitation, Medical Research, Multiple Sclerosis, Prenatal Health Issues, Public Health, Single-Disease Health Associations

International: International Relief Efforts

Religion: Religious Welfare

Science: Science-General, Science Exhibits & Fairs

Social Services: Animal Protection, At-Risk Youth, Big Brother/Big Sister, Camps, Child Welfare, Community Centers, Community Service Organizations, Counseling, Day Care, Delinquency & Criminal Rehabilitation, Domestic Violence, Family Services, Food/Clothing Distribution, Homes, Recreation & Athletics, Senior Services, Shelters/Homelessness, Social Services-General, Substance Abuse, United Funds/United Ways, Volunteer Services, Youth Organizations

Application Procedures

Initial Contact: Send brief letter of inquiry.
Application Requirements: Include a description of organization, amount requested, purpose of funds sought, other funding sources, list of board of trustees, recently audited financial statements, and proof of tax-exempt status.
Deadlines: None.

Restrictions

Does not support individuals, religious organizations for sectarian purposes, or political or lobbying groups.

Additional Information

Publications: Foundation Contribution Guidelines

Corporate Officials

Peter W. Gravelle: president, chief operating officer, director B Fitchburg, MA 1938. ED Clark University BA (1966); Suffolk University JD (1970); Dartmouth College (1986). PRIM CORP EMPL president, chief operating officer, director: Kysor Industries Corp.
George Roger Kempton: chairman, chief executive officer, director B New York, NY 1934. ED Andrews University BA (1955). PRIM CORP EMPL chairman, chief executive officer, director: Kysor Industries Corp. CORP AFFIL director: Simpson Industries; director: Guardsman Products; member: Interlochen Corp. Council. NONPR AFFIL member, director: Michigan Mfr Association; member: Society Automotive Engineers.

Foundation Officials

David W. Crooks: assistant secretary
Richard G. De Boer: treasurer
Peter W. Gravelle: president, chief operating officer (see above)
Mary C. Janik: mgr PRIM CORP EMPL assistant secretary: Kysor Industries Corp.
Robert L. Joseph: comptroller
George Roger Kempton: chief executive officer (see above)

Grants Analysis

Disclosure Period: fiscal year ending May 31, 1999
Total Grants: $78,811*
Number of Grants: 161
Average Grant: $490
Highest Grant: $5,000
Typical Range: $100 to $2,000
*Note: Giving excludes United Way.

Recent Grants

Note: Grants derived from 1999 Form 990.

Library-Related

3,000	Nancy Quinn Memorial Library, Conyers, GA

General

8,000	United Way - Atlanta, Atlanta, GA
8,000	United Way - Columbus, Columbus, GA
6,500	United Way of Lake County, Libertyville, IL
6,000	United Way of Allendale County, Allendale, SC
5,000	Mt. Pleasant Community Fund, Mt. Pleasant, MI
5,000	United Way - Isabella County, Mt. Pleasant, MI
4,000	March of Dimes, Atlanta, GA
4,000	United Way - Des Moines, Des Moines, IA
3,000	Conyers Rockdale Boys and Girls, Conyers, GA
2,000	Conyers Rockdale Community Food Bank, Conyers, GA

SCOULAR CO.

Company Headquarters

2027 Dodge St.
Omaha, NE 68102

Company Description

Employees: 240
SIC(s): 4200 Trucking & Warehousing, 4221 Farm Product Warehousing & Storage, 5100 Wholesale Trade--Nondurable Goods.

Operating Locations

Scoular Co. (AZ; CA; CO; FL; IL; KS; MN; MO; NE--Omaha; NY; OH; SC)

Scoular Foundation

Giving Contact

Marshall E. Faith, Chairman
2027 Dodge St., Suite 300
Omaha, NE 68102
Phone: (402)342-3500
Fax: (402)342-4493

Description

EIN: 363323189
Organization Type: Corporate Foundation
Giving Locations: headquarters and operating communities.
Grant Types: General Support.

Financial Summary

Total Giving: $110,665 (2000); $99,047 (1999); $110,400 (1998)
Giving Analysis: Giving for 2000 includes: foundation grants to United Way ($3,100); 1999: foundation grants to United Way ($3,050); foundation ($95,997); 1998: foundation grants to United Way ($3,000); foundation ($107,400);
Assets: $96 (2000); $461 (1999); $458 (1998)
Gifts Received: $110,300 (2000); $99,050 (1999); $110,050 (1998)

Typical Recipients

Arts & Humanities: Arts Associations & Councils, Arts Funds, Arts Outreach, Arts & Humanities-General, History & Archaeology, Libraries, Museums/Galleries, Music, Opera, Performing Arts, Theater
Civic & Public Affairs: Chambers of Commerce, Employment/Job Training, Civic & Public Affairs-General, Housing, Rural Affairs, Urban & Community Affairs, Zoos/Aquariums
Education: Business Education, Colleges & Universities, Education Funds, Faculty Development, Education-General, Minority Education, Student Aid
Health: Alzheimers Disease, Cancer, Children's Health/Hospitals, Diabetes, Emergency/Ambulance Services, Heart, Hospices, Hospitals, Respiratory
Religion: Churches, Ministries, Missionary Activities (Domestic), Religious Organizations, Religious Welfare, Social/Policy Issues
Social Services: At-Risk Youth, Big Brother/Big Sister, Camps, Child Welfare, Community Service Organizations, Day Care, Family Services, Food/Clothing Distribution, Homes, People with Disabilities, Recreation & Athletics, Scouts, United Funds/United Ways, Veterans, YMCA/YWCA/YMHA/YWHA, Youth Organizations

Application Procedures

Initial Contact: Submit a brief letter of inquiry.
Application Requirements: Include a description of organization, amount requested, purpose of funds sought, and proof of tax-exempt status.
Deadlines: None.

Restrictions

Does not support individuals, political or lobbying groups, or organizations outside operating areas.

Corporate Officials

Marshall E. Faith: chairman, director PRIM CORP EMPL chairman, director: Scoular Co.
Duane A. Fischer: president, chief executive officer, director PRIM CORP EMPL president, chief executive officer, director: Scoular Co.
Timothy J. Regan: chief financial officer B Atchison, KS 1956. ED Kansas State University BS (1978). PRIM CORP EMPL chief financial officer: Scoular Co. NONPR AFFIL member: Elks; member: Knights of Columbus; director: Catholic Charities.

Foundation Officials

Marshall E. Faith: trustee (see above)
Duane A. Fischer: trustee (see above)
Timothy J. Regan: trustee (see above)

Grants Analysis

Disclosure Period: calendar year ending 2000
Total Grants: $107,565*
Number of Grants: 33
Average Grant: $3,260
Highest Grant: $25,000
Typical Range: $1,000 to $5,000
*Note: Giving excludes United Way.

Recent Grants

Note: Grants derived from 2001 Form 990.

General

10,000	Creighton University, Omaha, NE
10,000	Kansas State University Foundation, Manhattan, KS
10,000	Quality Living, Omaha, NE
7,000	Salvation Army, Omaha, NE
6,000	American Red Cross, Omaha, NE
5,000	Durham Center for Western Studies, Omaha, NE
5,000	Fox Theatre, Salina, KS
3,100	United Way of the Midlands, Omaha, NE
2,500	Omaha Community Playhouse Foundation, Omaha, NE
2,500	Omaha Symphony, Omaha, NE

E.W. SCRIPPS CO.

Company Headquarters

Cincinnati, OH
Web: http://www.scripps.com

Company Description

Founded: 1878
Ticker: SSP
Exchange: NYSE
Revenue: US$1.535 billion (2002)
Employees: 7700 (2002)
SIC(s): 2711 Newspapers.

Operating Locations

E.W. Scripps Co. (AL--Birmingham; AZ--Phoenix; CA--Los Angeles, Redding, San Luis Obispo, South Gate, Thousand Oaks, Tulare, Watsonville; CO--Denver, Longmont; DC; FL--Destin, Jupiter, Naples, Palm Beach, Stuart, Tampa; GA--Rome; IN--Evansville; MD--Baltimore; MI--Detroit; MO--Kansas City; NM--Albuquerque; OH--Cincinnati, Cleveland; OK--Tulsa; SC; TN--Knoxville, Memphis; TX--El Paso; VA; WV)

Nonmonetary Support

Type: Donated Equipment; Donated Products; In-kind Services; Loaned Employees; Loaned Executives
Note: NOT Scripps newspapers and broadcast stations across the United States determine their level of involvement in the community. Contact local Scripps executive.

Scripps Howard Foundation

Giving Contact

Judith G Clabes, President & CEO
Scripps Howard Foundation
312 Walnut Street
PO Box 5380
Cincinnati, OH 45201-5380
Phone: (513)977-3035
Fax: (513)977-3800
E-mail: cottingham@scripps.com
Web: http://www.scripps.com/foundation

Alternate Contact

Judith G. Clabes, President & Chief Executive Officer
Scripps Howard Foundation
Phone: (513)977-3048
E-mail: clabes@scripps.com
Note: Receives Greater Cincinnati Fund, Community Fund, and Journalism Fund proposals.

Description

EIN: 316025114
Organization Type: Corporate Foundation
Giving Locations: OH: operating locations, Cincinnati metropolitan area nationally, with emphasis on operating locations; particularly Greater Cincinnati, OH.
Grant Types: Award, Capital, Conference/Seminar, Employee Matching Gifts, Endowment, Fellowship, General Support, Operating Expenses, Project, Research, Scholarship, Seed Money.
Note: Scholarships are awarded to students preparing for careers in print and electronic journalism. Matches gifts to educational institutions.

Financial Summary

Total Giving: $6,817,871 (2001); $6,676,715 (2000); $4,770,472 (1999)
Giving Analysis: Giving for 2001 includes: foundation matching gifts ($165,000); foundation scholarships ($984,342); foundation ($5,565,185); 2000: foundation matching gifts ($527,310); foundation

scholarships ($936,402); foundation ($5,192,324); 1999: foundation ($4,770,472);

Assets: $79,188,870 (2001); $85,838,950 (2000); $92,511,831 (1999)

Gifts Received: $4,811,161 (2002 approx); $5,353,518 (2001); $4,566,622 (2000). Note: In 2001, contributions were received from E.W. Scripps Co. ($96,619); Edward W. Scripps, Jr. ($85,000); Robert P. Scripps ($1,508,400); William H. Scripps ($50,000); Mary Kay Blake ($5,000); Annie Lou Hanna ($19,204); Jack R. Howard Trust ($3,355,711); Cindy S. Leising ($125,000); Lawrence A. Leser ($13,240); Ruth A. May ($25,000); and miscellaneous contributions of less than $5,000 per person ($70,345).

Typical Recipients

Arts & Humanities: Arts Centers, Arts Festivals, Arts Funds, Community Arts, History & Archaeology, Libraries, Literary Arts, Museums/Galleries, Music, Performing Arts, Public Broadcasting, Theater

Civic & Public Affairs: African American Affairs, Botanical Gardens/Parks, Business/Free Enterprise, Chambers of Commerce, Clubs, Community Foundations, Economic Development, Employment/Job Training, First Amendment Issues, Civic & Public Affairs-General, Housing, Law & Justice, Minority Business, Municipalities/Towns, Nonprofit Management, Professional & Trade Associations, Public Policy, Urban & Community Affairs, Women's Affairs, Zoos/Aquariums

Education: Arts/Humanities Education, Business Education, Colleges & Universities, Economic Education, Education Funds, Elementary Education (Public), Engineering/Technological Education, Environmental Education, Faculty Development, Journalism/Media Education, Legal Education, Literacy, Minority Education, Preschool Education, Private Education (Precollege), Religious Education, Science/Mathematics Education, Secondary Education (Public), Special Education, Student Aid, Vocational & Technical Education

Environment: Environment-General

Health: Children's Health/Hospitals, Emergency/Ambulance Services, Geriatric Health, Prenatal Health Issues, Preventive Medicine/Wellness Organizations

International: Foreign Arts Organizations, International-General, Human Rights, International Affairs, International Relations

Religion: Dioceses, Religion-General, Religious Welfare

Science: Science Museums

Social Services: Big Brother/Big Sister, Child Welfare, Community Centers, Community Service Organizations, Food/Clothing Distribution, People with Disabilities, Recreation & Athletics, Scouts, Substance Abuse, United Funds/United Ways, YMCA/YWCA/YMHA/YWHA, Youth Organizations

Application Procedures

Initial Contact: Send a full written proposal.

Application Requirements: For Greater Cincinnati Fund or Community Fund requests, include a description of organization, recently audited financial statement, a description of the program for which support is requested including rationale, a detailed projected budget, schedule of implementation, methods of evaluating and reporting results, and qualification of program manager; description of other sources of funding; a copy of the IRC Section 501(c)(3) determination letter; recent financial statement; and names and affiliations of members of the organization's Board of Directors or other governing body.

For Journalism Fund requests, submit an appropriate request in writing.

Deadlines: None.

Review Process: Decisions are based on written proposals; personal interviews are discouraged.

Evaluative Criteria: For scholarships: good scholastic standing, interest in journalism and evidence of work in this field, letters of recommendation from faculty or employer, financial need, willingness of student

to pay part of educational expenses, U.S. citizenship. For Greater Cincinnati Fund and Community Fund grants: programs which impact communities where company operates, are measurable with stated goals and objectives, demonstrate effectiveness and innovation, can serve as models, and can be eventually self-supporting.

Decision Notification: Proposals will be reviewed and applicants notified within 90 days after receipt of all required information.

Restrictions

Contributions for capital needs, including renovation, equipment and construction, are not encouraged except in special circumstances; specific projects and programs are preferred over general operating funds. In general, only one contribution per year will be made to any single organization, including support for fundraising events. Multi-year contributions are discouraged. The foundation normally does not provide support to organizations that receive United Way or Fine Arts or other general campaign funds that are already supported by the foundation.

The foundation does not make contributions to individuals; religious organizations unless they are engaged in a significant program benefiting the entire community; political causes or candidates; anti-business organizations; courtesy advertising; organizations that discriminate on the basis of race, creed, religion, gender or national origin; private foundations; organizations not qualifying as IRS Section 501(c)(3) organizations; or veterans', fraternal, or labor groups. Fundraising events such as walks, runs, golf outings, or neighborhood-special events, except for those in which an employee is personally participating. The foundation does not support disease-related events or events strictly related to research, nor does it purchase tables for public or private K-12 schools, school districts, or their foundations.

Additional Information

Capital requests are not encouraged; specific programs or projects are favored over operating support. The Scripps Howard Foundation was incorporated in 1962, as a charitable nonprofit organization.

Publications: Scripps Howard Foundation Progress Report; Guidelines for Scholarships; Special Journalism Grants and Awards

Corporate Officials

William Robert Burleigh: chairman, chief executive officer, director B Evansville, IN 1935. ED Marquette University BA (1957). PRIM CORP EMPL chairman: E.W. Scripps Co. CORP AFFIL director: Ohio National Financial Services; director: Xtek Inc.; director: Evansville Courier Co. Inc.

Colleen Christner Conant: branch manager B Oklahoma City, OK 1947. ED Oklahoma City University MusB (1970). PRIM CORP EMPL branch manager: EW Scripps Co. CORP AFFIL chief executive officer: Boulder Publishing Inc.

Alan M. Horton: senior vice president newspapers ED Yale University (1965). PRIM CORP EMPL senior vice president newspapers: E.W. Scripps Co.

Kenneth W. Lowe: president, chief executive officer, director B April 07, 1950. PRIM CORP EMPL president, chief executive officer, director: E.W. Scripps Co.

J. Robert Routt: vice president, controller B 1954. ED University of Kentucky BS. PRIM CORP EMPL vice president, controller: E.W. Scripps Co.

Charles Edward Scripps: chairman executive committee, director B San Diego, CA January 27, 1920. ED College of William & Mary (1938-1940); Pomona College (1940-1941). PRIM CORP EMPL chairman executive committee, director: E.W. Scripps Co. CORP AFFIL director: Scripps Howard Broadcasting Co.; director: Evansville Courier Co. Inc. NONPR AFFIL trustee: Edward W. Scripps Trust; member: Theta Delta Chi; trustee: Freedoms Foundation; member

national board advisors: Salvation Army; member: CAP.

Paul K. Scripps: vice president, director PRIM CORP EMPL vice president, director: E W Scripps Co.

Foundation Officials

William Robert Burleigh: member (see above)

Judy G. Clabes: president, chief executive officer, member B Henderson, KY 1945. ED University of Kentucky BA (1967); Indiana State University MPA (1984).

Deborah Cooper: administrator assistant

Patty Cottingham: executive director, secretary

Pamela (Howard) Gumprecht: trustee ED Sarah Lawrence College (1963). CLUB AFFIL Cosmopolitan Club.

Julia Scripps Heidt: trustee

J. Robert Routt: trustee (see above)

Charles Edward Scripps: member (see above)

Edward Wyllis Scripps, II: member B San Diego, CA 1929. ED Pomona College.

Maggie Scripps: trustee

Paul K. Scripps: trustee (see above)

Grants Analysis

Disclosure Period: calendar year ending 2001

Total Grants: $6,817,871*

Number of Grants: 347

Average Grant: $19,648

Typical Range: $1,000 to $10,000

*Note: Giving excludes matching gifts; scholarships.

Recent Grants

Note: Grants derived from 2001 Form 990.

General

1,000,000	Hampton University, Hampton, VT -- journalism building
250,000	Hampton University, Hampton, VT -- professorship of journalism endowment
250,000	Marquette University, Milwaukee, WI
225,270	University of Colorado Foundation, Boulder, CO -- environmental fellowship
212,849	Columbia University, New York, NY -- for international fellowships
120,000	Hampton University, Hampton, VT -- Endowed Journalism Scholarship Fund
102,500	United Way, Cincinnati, OH -- for annual fund drive
100,000	Foundation for American Communications, Pasadena, CA -- for science institute
100,000	Hampton University, Hampton, VT -- Endowed Journalism Scholarship Fund
100,000	National Underground Railroad Freedom Center, Cincinnati, OH -- capital campaign

SCURLOCK FOUNDATION

Giving Contact

Elizabeth Blanton Wareing, President
700 Louisiana, Suite 3920
Houston, TX 77002
Phone: (713)236-0550
Fax: (713)222-2419

Description

Founded: 1954

EIN: 741488953

Organization Type: Private Foundation

Giving Locations: TX

Grant Types: Award, Emergency, General Support, Multiyear/Continuing Support.

Donor Information

Founder: Established in 1954 by the late E. C. Scurlock , the late D. E. Farnsworth , the late W. C. Scurlock , I. S. Blanton, and Scurlock Oil Co.

Financial Summary

Total Giving: $1,049,052 (2000); $814,741 (1999); $874,031 (1998)
Giving Analysis: Giving for 2000 includes: foundation grants to United Way ($10,000) 1999: foundation grants to United Way ($10,000)
Assets: $20,634,065 (2000); $20,893,304 (1999); $19,191,978 (1998)
Gifts Received: $6,327 (2000); $6,500 (1999); $6,040 (1998). Note: In 2000, contributions were received from Scurlock Oil Company.

Typical Recipients

Arts & Humanities: Arts Associations & Councils, Arts Festivals, Arts Outreach, Ballet, Dance, Arts & Humanities-General, Historic Preservation, History & Archaeology, Libraries, Literary Arts, Museums/Galleries, Music, Opera, Performing Arts, Theater, Visual Arts
Civic & Public Affairs: Botanical Gardens/Parks, Clubs, Community Foundations, Professional & Trade Associations, Urban & Community Affairs, Women's Affairs, Zoos/Aquariums
Education: Afterschool/Enrichment Programs, Arts/Humanities Education, Business Education, Business-School Partnerships, Colleges & Universities, Continuing Education, Education Associations, Education Reform, Engineering/Technological Education, Education-General, Health & Physical Education, Medical Education, Private Education (Precollege), Secondary Education (Private), Secondary Education (Public), Social Sciences Education, Special Education, Student Aid
Environment: Environment-General, Research, Resource Conservation, Wildlife Protection
Health: Cancer, Children's Health/Hospitals, Clinics/Medical Centers, Diabetes, Eyes/Blindness, Geriatric Health, Hospices, Hospitals, Hospitals (University Affiliated), Medical Research, Mental Health, Multiple Sclerosis, Public Health, Single-Disease Health Associations, Speech & Hearing
International: Foreign Arts Organizations, International Affairs
Religion: Bible Study/Translation, Churches, Religion-General, Jewish Causes, Ministries, Religious Organizations, Religious Organizations, Religious Welfare
Science: Science Museums
Social Services: Animal Protection, Camps, Child Welfare, Community Centers, Community Service Organizations, Crime Prevention, Day Care, Delinquency & Criminal Rehabilitation, Emergency Relief, Family Services, Homes, People with Disabilities, Recreation & Athletics, Scouts, Senior Services, United Funds/United Ways, Volunteer Services, YMCA/YWCA/YMHA/YWHA, Youth Organizations

Application Procedures

Initial Contact: Send a request on the organization's letterhead.
Application Requirements: Provide a description of organization, purpose of funds sought, and proof of tax-exempt status.
Deadlines: None.

Restrictions

The foundation does not support individuals or provide loans.

Foundation Officials

Eddy S. Blanton: vice president, director
Jack S. Blanton, Jr.: vice president, director B Houston, TX 1953. ED University of Texas (1975). PRIM CORP EMPL chairman: Nicklos Drilling Co.
Laura L. Blanton: president, director
Kenneth Fisher: secretary, treasurer, director B Tacoma, WA 1944. ED University of Oregon BS (1968); University of Oregon BFA (1969); University of Oregon MFA (1971). OCCUPATION sculptor. NONPR AFFIL member: Portland Art Association.
Elizabeth B. Wareing: president

Grants Analysis

Disclosure Period: calendar year ending 2000
Total Grants: $1,039,052*
Number of Grants: 147
Average Grant: $7,136
Highest Grant: $135,000
Lowest Grant: $100
Typical Range: $500 to $25,000
*Note: Giving excludes United Way.

Recent Grants

Note: Grants derived from 2000 Form 990.

Library-Related
5,000	Houston Public Library, Houston, TX

General
135,000	Lon Morris College, Jacksonville, TX
111,500	Lady Bird Johnson Wildflower Center, Austin, TX
76,500	Museum of Fine Arts - Houston, Houston, TX
75,000	Brookwood Community Volunteers
50,000	Episcopal High School, Houston, TX
50,000	Texas Southern University School of Business, TX
31,050	St. John the Divine Church, Houston, TX
25,000	Baylor College of Medicine, Dallas, TX
20,000	American Council for Arts, New York, NY
20,000	University of Texas - Ex Students Association, Austin, TX

SEABURY FOUNDATION

Giving Contact

Tom Iskalis
c/o Northern Trust Co.
50 S. LaSalle Street
Chicago, IL 60675
Phone: (312)630-6000

Description

Founded: 1947
EIN: 366027398
Organization Type: Family Foundation
Giving Locations: IL: Chicago metropolitan area
Grant Types: General Support, Project, Scholarship.

Donor Information

Founder: Established in 1947 by the late Charles Ward Seabury and the late Louise Lovett Seabury .

Financial Summary

Total Giving: $2,438,490 (2001); $2,618,919 (2000); $1,697,348 (1998)
Assets: $27,928,499 (2001); $36,494,356 (2000); $35,471,944 (1998)

Typical Recipients

Arts & Humanities: Arts Associations & Councils, Arts Centers, Arts Outreach, Dance, Ethnic & Folk Arts, History & Archaeology, Libraries, Museums/Galleries, Music, Opera, Performing Arts, Public Broadcasting, Theater
Civic & Public Affairs: Asian American Affairs, Botanical Gardens/Parks, Clubs, Community Foundations, Employment/Job Training, Civic & Public Affairs-General, Hispanic Affairs, Housing, Native American Affairs, Public Policy, Safety, Urban & Community Affairs, Women's Affairs, Zoos/Aquariums
Education: Afterschool/Enrichment Programs, Arts/Humanities Education, Colleges & Universities, Education Reform, Education-General, Health & Physical Education, International Studies, Literacy, Minority Education, Preschool Education, Private Education

(Precollege), Public Education (Precollege), Religious Education, Secondary Education, Secondary Education (Public), Social Sciences Education, Special Education, Student Aid
Environment: Forestry, Environment-General, Resource Conservation, Watershed, Wildlife Protection
Health: Adolescent Health Issues, Cancer, Children's Health/Hospitals, Clinics/Medical Centers, Emergency/Ambulance Services, Hospices, Hospitals, Medical Rehabilitation, Medical Research, Mental Health, Nursing Services, Prenatal Health Issues, Public Health, Single-Disease Health Associations
International: Foreign Arts Organizations, Foreign Educational Institutions, International Development, Missionary/Religious Activities
Religion: Religion-General, Ministries, Religious Welfare, Seminaries
Science: Science Museums, Scientific Research
Social Services: Child Welfare, Community Centers, Community Service Organizations, Day Care, Delinquency & Criminal Rehabilitation, Domestic Violence, Emergency Relief, Family Planning, Family Services, Food/Clothing Distribution, Homes, People with Disabilities, Scouts, United Funds/United Ways, Volunteer Services, YMCA/YWCA/YMHA/YWHA, Youth Organizations

Application Procedures

Initial Contact: The foundation has no formal policy for accepting applications.
Deadlines: None..
Notes: The foundation prefers first-time requests for special projects funds, though requests for operating funds will occasionally be considered.
The foundation has developed a schedule of qualified charitable organizations in various fields generally restricted to greater the Chicago area to which contributions are made on a somewhat annual basis, based upon need.

Restrictions

Unsolicited applications are accepted from the Chicago metropolitan area only. The foundation does not make loans, nor does it fund benefits, capital campaigns, or individuals.

Additional Information

Trust(s): Northern Trust Co.

Foundation Officials

D. William Boone: trustee
Robert S. Boone: trustee
Robert D. Fisk: trustee
Seabury J. Hibben: trustee
Louise Fisk Morris: trustee B 1942. PRIM CORP EMPL chairman: Pinnacle Oil Co.
Charlene Brown Seabury: executive secretary, trustee
David D. Seabury: trustee

Grants Analysis

Disclosure Period: calendar year ending 2001
Total Grants: $2,438,490
Number of Grants: 162
Average Grant: $15,052
Highest Grant: $135,000
Lowest Grant: $250
Typical Range: $5,000 to $30,000

Recent Grants

Note: Grants derived from 2001 Form 990.

General
135,000	Children's Memorial Medical Center, Chicago, IL
60,000	Good News Partners, Chicago, IL
53,500	Pima College Center, Tucson, AZ
51,000	Family Matters, Chicago, IL
50,000	Faith, Inc., Chicago, IL
50,000	Life Leadership Development, Indianapolis, IN

50,000	Potter's Clay Ministries
50,000	Starfish Learning Center, Chicago, IL
46,000	Institute of Cultural Affairs, Chicago, IL
40,000	Imagine Chicago, Chicago, IL

GEORGE AND EFFIE SEAY MEMORIAL TRUST

Giving Contact

Elizabeth D. Seaman, Consultant
c/o Bank of America
PO Box 26903
Richmond, VA 23261
Phone: (804)788-2963

Description

Founded: 1957
EIN: 546030604
Organization Type: Private Foundation
Giving Locations: VA
Grant Types: Capital, General Support, Operating Expenses, Project.

Donor Information

Founder: the late George J. Seay, the late Effie L. Seay

Financial Summary

Total Giving: $386,505 (fiscal year ending June 30, 2001); $335,050 (fiscal 2000); $139,200 (fiscal 1997)
Assets: $3,516,512 (fiscal 2001); $5,477,368 (fiscal 2000); $4,258,600 (fiscal 1997)
Gifts Received: $4,298 (fiscal 1997)

Typical Recipients

Arts & Humanities: Arts Associations & Councils, Arts Outreach, History & Archaeology, Libraries, Museums/Galleries, Music, Opera, Performing Arts, Theater
Civic & Public Affairs: Employment/Job Training, Civic & Public Affairs-General, Housing
Education: Afterschool/Enrichment Programs, Agricultural Education, Colleges & Universities, Education-General, Literacy, Medical Education, Private Education (Precollege), Special Education, Vocational & Technical Education
Environment: Environment-General, Resource Conservation
Health: Cancer, Children's Health/Hospitals, Clinics/Medical Centers, Health Organizations, Heart, Hospices
Religion: Churches, Ministries, Religious Organizations, Religious Welfare
Social Services: Animal Protection, Camps, Child Welfare, Community Centers, Community Service Organizations, Day Care, Emergency Relief, Family Planning, Family Services, Food/Clothing Distribution, People with Disabilities, Scouts, Senior Services, Shelters/Homelessness, United Funds/United Ways, Volunteer Services, Youth Organizations

Application Procedures

Initial Contact: Request application guidelines.
Application Requirements: Include a description of project; budget; amount of matching funds, plans for procurement of additional funds; recently audited financial statement; qualifications of project personnel; list of trustees and directors; proof of tax-exempt status.
Deadlines: May 1 and November 1.

Restrictions

The foundation does not support individuals, religious organizations for sectarian purposes, annual fund appeals, or scholarship.

Additional Information

Publications: Informational Brochure (including Application Guidelines)
Trust(s): Bank of America NA

Foundation Officials

Elizabeth D. Seaman: consult

Grants Analysis

Disclosure Period: fiscal year ending June 30, 2001
Total Grants: $386,505
Number of Grants: 29
Average Grant: $13,328
Highest Grant: $50,000
Typical Range: $5,000 to $25,000

Recent Grants

Note: Grants derived from fiscal 2001 Form 990.

General

50,000	Downtown Presents, Richmond, VA -- phase one development of Brown's Island
26,000	South Richmond Adult Day Care Center, Richmond, VA -- building improvements and hiring of staff
25,000	South Hampton Roads Habitat for Humanity, Norfolk, VA -- house construction
20,000	Chaplain Service of The Churches of Virginia, Inc, Norfolk, VA -- Operation Turnaround
20,000	Virginia Department of Historic Resources, Richmond, VA -- Solving History's Mysteries exhibit
16,000	Recording for the Blind and Dyslexic, Charlottesville, VA -- current technology conversion of a recording booth
15,000	Alexandria Neighborhood Health Services, Inc, Alexandria, VA -- family education and support program
15,000	Art Museum of Western Virginia, Roanoke, VA -- art venture project
15,000	Child Health Investment Partnership, Roanoke, VA -- Family Strengthening and Support Program
15,000	Christian Children's Fund, Richmond, VA -- earthquake disaster relief

SEBASTIAN FOUNDATION

Giving Contact

David S. Sebastian, Trustee
3333 Evergreen Dr. NE, Suite 110
Grand Rapids, MI 49525
Phone: (616)361-1996

Description

Founded: 1980
EIN: 382340219
Organization Type: Private Foundation
Giving Locations: MI: Kent County, Grand Rapids
Grant Types: General Support.

Donor Information

Founder: Audrey M. Sebastian, James R. Sebastian

Financial Summary

Total Giving: $1,348,800 (fiscal year ending August 31, 2001); $1,263,000 (fiscal 2000); $969,550 (fiscal 1998)
Giving Analysis: Giving for fiscal 2001 includes: foundation grants to United Way ($180,000); fiscal 2000: foundation grants to United Way ($180,000) fiscal 1998: foundation grants to United Way ($75,000)
Assets: $23,366,398 (fiscal 2001); $28,935,812 (fiscal 2000); $16,425,276 (fiscal 1998)

Gifts Received: $4,000,000 (fiscal 1995). Note: In fiscal 1995, contributions were received from James R. Sebastian.

Typical Recipients

Arts & Humanities: Arts Associations & Councils, Arts Institutes, Community Arts, History & Archaeology, Libraries, Museums/Galleries, Music, Opera
Civic & Public Affairs: African American Affairs, Botanical Gardens/Parks, Clubs, Economic Development, Civic & Public Affairs-General, Housing, Legal Aid, Native American Affairs, Nonprofit Management, Philanthropic Organizations, Women's Affairs, Zoos/Aquariums
Education: Afterschool/Enrichment Programs, Arts/Humanities Education, Business Education, Colleges & Universities, Education Funds, Medical Education, Minority Education, Private Education (Precollege), Public Education (Precollege), Secondary Education (Private), Secondary Education (Public)
Environment: Resource Conservation
Health: Emergency/Ambulance Services, Health-General, Geriatric Health, Health Organizations, Home-Care Services, Hospices, Nursing Services, Public Health, Single-Disease Health Associations
International: International Affairs, International Relations
Religion: Churches, Ministries, Religious Organizations, Religious Welfare
Social Services: At-Risk Youth, Camps, Child Welfare, Community Centers, Community Service Organizations, Family Planning, Family Services, Homes, People with Disabilities, Scouts, Senior Services, United Funds/United Ways, Volunteer Services, YMCA/YWCA/YMHA/YWHA, Youth Organizations

Application Procedures

Initial Contact: Send a brief letter of inquiry.
Application Requirements: Include purpose of funds sought, budget, balance sheet, officers and directors, other contributors, and proof of tax-exempt status.
Deadlines: None.

Restrictions

Does not support individuals.

Foundation Officials

Audrey M. Sebastian: trustee
David S. Sebastian: trustee
John O. Sebastian: trustee

Grants Analysis

Disclosure Period: fiscal year ending August 31, 2001
Total Grants: $1,168,800*
Number of Grants: 52
Average Grant: $19,486*
Highest Grant: $175,000
Lowest Grant: $500
Typical Range: $10,000 to $30,000
*Note: Giving excludes United Way. Average grant figure excludes highest grant.

Recent Grants

Note: Grants derived from 2000 Form 990.

Library-Related

25,000	Ryerson Library Foundation, Grand Rapids, MI -- support annual fund

General

200,000	Grand Valley State University, Allendale, MI -- support annual fund
180,000	Heart of West Michigan United Way, Grand Rapids, MI -- support annual fund
85,000	St. Mary's Health Services, Grand Rapids, MI -- support annual fund
80,000	Albion College, Albion, MI -- support annual fund

60,000	Porter Hills Presbyterian Village, Grand Rapids, MI -- support annual fund
50,000	Camp Blodgett, Grand Rapids, MI -- support annual fund
35,000	Local Initiatives Support Corporation (LISC), Grand Rapids, MI -- support annual fund
33,000	Home Repair Services, Grand Rapids, MI -- support annual fund
25,000	Aquinas College, Grand Rapids, MI -- support annual fund
25,000	Faith, Inc., Grand Rapids, MI -- support annual fund

SECOND FOUNDATION

Giving Contact
Phillip A. Ranney, Secretary
1111 Superior Ave. Suite 1000
Cleveland, OH 44114-2507
Phone: (216)696-4200
Fax: (216)696-7303
E-mail: pranney@ssrl.com

Description
Founded: 1984
EIN: 341436198
Organization Type: General Purpose Foundation
Giving Locations: OH: Cuyahoga County
Grant Types: Capital, Endowment, General Support, Matching, Multiyear/Continuing Support, Operating Expenses, Seed Money.

Donor Information
Founder: Established in 1984 by the 1525 Foundation.

Financial Summary
Total Giving: $3,398,380 (2000); $3,872,500 (1999); $1,258,337 (1998)
Giving Analysis: Giving for 2000 includes: foundation grants to United Way ($20,000) foundation scholarships ($125,000)
Assets: $12,244,241 (2000); $15,753,840 (1999); $18,244,086 (1998)

Typical Recipients
Arts & Humanities: Libraries, Museums/Galleries, Music
Civic & Public Affairs: Botanical Gardens/Parks, Community Foundations, Economic Development, Civic & Public Affairs-General, Hispanic Affairs, Municipalities/Towns, Nonprofit Management, Philanthropic Organizations, Urban & Community Affairs, Women's Affairs
Education: Colleges & Universities, Education-General, Private Education (Precollege), Student Aid
Environment: Environment-General, Resource Conservation
Health: Clinics/Medical Centers, Health Funds, Hospitals, Hospitals (University Affiliated), Research/Studies Institutes
Religion: Churches, Religious Organizations, Religious Welfare
Science: Science Museums, Scientific Centers & Institutes
Social Services: Child Abuse, Child Welfare, Community Centers, Community Service Organizations, Domestic Violence, Emergency Relief, Food/Clothing Distribution, Recreation & Athletics, Senior Services, Social Services-General, United Funds/United Ways, YMCA/YWCA/YMHA/YWHA, Youth Organizations

Application Procedures
Initial Contact: There are no formal grant application forms. Written applications should be sent to the foundation.
Application Requirements: Written proposals should not exceed five pages but should include a brief description of organization, the purpose of the grant request, any applicable financial data, the names of other contributors to the project, and a copy of the organization's IRS tax-exempt letter.
Deadlines: None.
Review Process: The foundation's trustees meet frequently and will usually notify the organization one month after receipt of the proposal.

Restrictions
The foundation does not make grants to individuals.

Foundation Officials
Elmer G. Demer: trustee
William B. LaPlace: vice president, trustee
Phillip A. Ranney: secretary, treasurer, director
CORP AFFIL director: General Housewares Corp.
Thelma G. Smith: president, director

Grants Analysis
Disclosure Period: calendar year ending 2000
Total Grants: $3,253,380*
Number of Grants: 28
Average Grant: $42,438*
Highest Grant: $1,650,000
Typical Range: $20,000 to $75,000
***Note:** Giving excludes scholarships, United Way. Average grant excludes two highest grants ($2,150,000).

Recent Grants
Note: Grants derived from 2000 Form 990.

Library-Related

1,740,000	Case Western Reserve University Library, Cleveland, OH
3,000	Foundation Center Library, Cleveland, OH
1,000	Friends of Cleveland Public Library, Cleveland, OH

General

750,000	Great Lakes Science Center, Cleveland, OH
500,000	Cleveland Scholarship Programs, Cleveland, OH
150,000	Cleveland Botanical Garden, Cleveland, OH
150,000	Judson Retirement Community, Cleveland, OH
100,000	City Year Cleveland, Cleveland, OH
90,000	Lake Erie College, Cleveland, OH
90,000	Senior Citizens Resources, Cleveland, OH
50,000	Lake Erie Nature and Science Center, Bay Village, OH
50,000	Mohican School in the Out-of-Doors, Cleveland, OH
50,000	Parkworks, Cleveland, OH

SECURITY BENEFIT LIFE INSURANCE CO.

Company Headquarters
Topeka, KS
Web: http://www.securitybenefit.com

Company Description
Employees: 600
SIC(s): 6153 Short-Term Business Credit, 6311 Life Insurance, 6321 Accident & Health Insurance.

Operating Locations
Security Benefit Life Insurance Co. (KS--Topeka)

Nonmonetary Support
Type: Donated Equipment; In-kind Services

Security Benefit Life Insurance Co. Charitable Trust

Giving Contact
Howard Fricke, Contact
700 Southwest Harrison Street
Topeka, KS 66636-0001
Phone: (785)431-3215

Description
Founded: 1976
EIN: 486211612
Organization Type: Corporate Foundation
Giving Locations: KS: Topeka some giving in other areas of Kansas
Grant Types: General Support, Matching.

Financial Summary
Total Giving: $564,378 (2001); $459,066 (1999); $300,435 (1998). Note: Contributes through foundation only.
Giving Analysis: Giving for 2001 includes: foundation scholarships ($100); foundation grants to United Way ($73,020); foundation ($491,258); 1999: corporate grants to United Way ($58,000); foundation ($401,066); 1998: foundation grants to United Way ($30,244); foundation ($270,191);
Assets: $1,562,483 (2001); $2,926,156 (1999); $1,794,880 (1998)
Gifts Received: $1,500,000 (1999); $333,840 (1998); $367,500 (1996). Note: Contributions were received from Security Benefit Life Industry Co.

Typical Recipients
Arts & Humanities: Arts Associations & Councils, Arts Centers, Ballet, Dance, Historic Preservation, History & Archaeology, Libraries, Museums/Galleries, Music, Performing Arts, Public Broadcasting, Theater
Civic & Public Affairs: African American Affairs, Clubs, Employment/Job Training, Civic & Public Affairs-General, Hispanic Affairs, Housing, Municipalities/Towns, Parades/Festivals, Professional & Trade Associations, Public Policy, Urban & Community Affairs, Women's Affairs, Zoos/Aquariums
Education: Business Education, Colleges & Universities, Economic Education, Education Associations, Education Funds, Education Reform, Environmental Education, Faculty Development, Education-General, Education-General, Medical Education, Minority Education, Private Education (Precollege), Public Education (Precollege), Secondary Education (Private), Secondary Education (Public)
Environment: Resource Conservation
Health: Cancer, Children's Health/Hospitals, Diabetes, Emergency/Ambulance Services, Health Organizations, Hospices, Mental Health, Prenatal Health Issues, Single-Disease Health Associations
Religion: Churches, Religious Organizations, Religious Welfare
Science: Scientific Research
Social Services: Animal Protection, Big Brother/Big Sister, Child Welfare, Community Service Organizations, Family Planning, Family Services, Food/Clothing Distribution, People with Disabilities, Scouts, Senior Services, Shelters/Homelessness, Social Services-General, United Funds/United Ways, United Funds/United Ways, Volunteer Services, YMCA/YWCA/YMHA/YWHA, Youth Organizations

Application Procedures
Initial Contact: Send a brief letter.
Deadlines: None.

Additional Information
The trust lists Security Benefit Trust Company as a corporate trustee.

Corporate Officials

Howard R. Fricke: chairman B 1936. PRIM CORP EMPL chairman: Security Benefit Life Insurance Co. CORP AFFIL president: Security Distributor Inc. Co. LLC; president: Security Management; president, director: Security Benefit Group Inc.; director: Oneok Inc.; director: Payless Shoe Source Inc.

Foundation Officials

Howard R. Fricke: trustee (see above)

Grants Analysis

Disclosure Period: calendar year ending 2001
Total Grants: $491,258*
Number of Grants: 318
Average Grant: $1,323*
Highest Grant: $72,000
Lowest Grant: $25
Typical Range: $300 to $4,500
***Note:** Giving excludes scholarship, and United Way. Average grant figure excludes highest grant.

Recent Grants

Note: Grants derived from 2001 Form 990.

Library-Related
10,000 Library Foundation, Topeka, KS

General
72,000 United Way of Greater Topeka, Topeka, KS
28,000 Kansas Foundation for Excellence in Education, Topeka, KS
25,000 Brown Foundation, Topeka, KS
25,000 Midland Hospice, Topeka, KS
25,000 Salvation Army, Topeka, KS
25,000 Washburn University, Topeka, KS
20,000 Capper Foundation, Topeka, KS
20,000 Topeka Performing Arts Center, Topeka, KS
20,000 YWCA, Topeka, KS
15,000 Topeka Performing Arts Center, Topeka, KS

SECURITY LIFE OF DENVER INSURANCE CO.

Company Headquarters

1331 17th St., Ste. 808
Denver, CO 80202
Web: http://www.ing-securitylife.com

Company Description

Employees: 650
SIC(s): 6311 Life Insurance.

Operating Locations

Security Life of Denver Insurance Co. (CA; CO--Denver; FL; GA; KS; MA; TX)

Nonmonetary Support

Type: Donated Equipment; Workplace Solicitation

Giving Contact

Nancy Montgomery
Security Life of Denver
Security Life Center
1290 Broadway
Denver, CO 80203
Phone: (303)860-1290
Web: http://www.ing-securitylife.com

Description

Organization Type: Corporate Giving Program
Giving Locations: CO: emphasis on Denver states where there is an agent.
Grant Types: Capital, Employee Matching Gifts, General Support, Multiyear/Continuing Support, Operating Expenses, Project.

Financial Summary

Total Giving: $260,000 (2001); $250,000 (2000); $255,000 (1999 approx). Note: Contributes through corporate direct giving program only.

Typical Recipients

Arts & Humanities: Arts Associations & Councils, Arts Outreach, Ballet, Arts & Humanities-General, Historic Preservation, History & Archaeology, Libraries, Museums/Galleries, Music, Opera, Public Broadcasting
Civic & Public Affairs: Botanical Gardens/Parks, Chambers of Commerce, Urban & Community Affairs, Zoos/Aquariums
Education: Afterschool/Enrichment Programs, Arts/Humanities Education, Business Education, Elementary Education (Private), Elementary Education (Public), Education-General, Literacy
Health: AIDS/HIV, Cancer, Eyes/Blindness, Health-General, Single-Disease Health Associations
Religion: Jewish Causes
Social Services: At-Risk Youth, Domestic Violence, Emergency Relief, Food/Clothing Distribution, People with Disabilities, Recreation & Athletics, Senior Services, Social Services-General, United Funds/United Ways, Youth Organizations

Application Procedures

Initial Contact: Send a brief letter of inquiry.
Application Requirements: Include a description of organization, amount requested, purpose of funds sought, and time frame within which contribution is needed.

Restrictions

Does not support political or lobbying groups or religious organizations for sectarian purposes.

Corporate Officials

Stephen Christopher: president, chief operating officer, chief executive officer PRIM CORP EMPL president, chief operating officer: Security Life Denver Insurance Co. CORP AFFIL director: First Ing Life Insurance of New York. NONPR AFFIL director: Professional Examination Service.

Grants Analysis

Total Grants: $325,000
Typical Range: $1,000 to $5,000
Note: A more recent grants list was unavailable.

Recent Grants

Note: Grants derived from 1996 grants list.

Library-Related
Denver Public Library, Denver, CO

General
Bayaud Industries, Denver, CO
Community Resources, Denver, CO
Denver Public Schools, Denver, CO
Food Bank of the Rockies, Denver, CO
Metro State College, Denver, CO
Oneday Foundation, Denver, CO
Safe House of Denver, Denver, CO
Volunteers for Outdoor Colorado, Denver, CO
Colorado Symphony Orchestra, Denver, CO

SEDGWICK, INC.

Company Headquarters

Memphis, TN
Web: http://www.sedgwick.com

Company Description

Former Name: Sedgwick James Inc.
Employees: 360
SIC(s): 6411 Insurance Agents, Brokers & Service.
Parent Company: Sedgwick Group, Inc., 153 N. Saluda Dr., No. H, Marietta, SC, United States

Operating Locations

Sedgwick, Inc. (TN--Memphis); Sedgwick Noble Lowndes (TN--Memphis)

Giving Contact

Jean Swolenski, Matching Gifts Program
1000 Ridgeway Loop Rd.
Memphis, TN 38120
Phone: (901)684-3797

Description

Organization Type: Corporate Giving Program
Giving Locations: TN: principally near operating locations and to national organizations.
Grant Types: Employee Matching Gifts.

Typical Recipients

Arts & Humanities: Arts Appreciation, Arts Associations & Councils, Arts Centers, Arts Festivals, Arts Funds, Arts Institutes, Community Arts, Dance, Ethnic & Folk Arts, Historic Preservation, Libraries, Literary Arts, Museums/Galleries, Music, Opera, Performing Arts, Public Broadcasting, Theater, Visual Arts
Civic & Public Affairs: Safety, Zoos/Aquariums
Education: Agricultural Education, Arts/Humanities Education, Business Education, Colleges & Universities, Community & Junior Colleges, Continuing Education, Economic Education, Education Associations, Education Funds, Elementary Education (Private), Engineering/Technological Education, Faculty Development, Health & Physical Education, International Exchange, International Studies, Journalism/Media Education, Legal Education, Literacy, Medical Education, Minority Education, Preschool Education, Private Education (Precollege), Public Education (Precollege), Science/Mathematics Education, Social Sciences Education, Special Education, Student Aid
Environment: Environment-General
Science: Observatories & Planetariums, Scientific Organizations
Social Services: Social Services-General

Application Procedures

Initial Contact: Send brief letter of inquiry.
Application Requirements: Include a description of organization, amount requested, purpose of funds sought, recently audited financial statements, and proof of tax-exempt status.
Deadlines: December 15, all requests after the deadline will be considered the following year.

Restrictions

Does not support individuals, religious organizations for sectarian purposes (however programs sponsored by a religious organization may be eligible), fraternal organizations, veteran's organizations, unions, or political or lobbying groups.

Additional Information

As a member of the Per Cent Club in the U.K., Sedgwick contributes a minimum of 0.5% of its U.K. pretax profit to community initiatives through single donations or contributions phased over several years.

Corporate Officials

Ronald J. Kutella: president vice president, chief financial officer, director PRIM CORP EMPL president: Sedgwick.
Quill O'Healy: chairman, chief executive officer, director PRIM CORP EMPL chairman, chief executive officer, director: Sedgwick.
James B. Wiertelak: senior vice president, chief financial officer, director PRIM CORP EMPL senior vice president, chief financial officer, director: Sedgwick.

SEHERR-THOSS FOUNDATION

Giving Contact

Mark Karlin, Trust Officer
c/o Bessemer Trust Co. NA
630 5th Ave.
New York, NY 10111
Phone: (212)708-9309

Description

Founded: 1990
EIN: 136959146
Organization Type: Private Foundation
Grant Types: General Support.

Donor Information

Founder: Sonia Seherr-Thoss

Financial Summary

Total Giving: $229,060 (2000); $203,465 (1999); $185,838 (1998)
Assets: $4,746,351 (2000); $4,984,962 (1999); $4,460,728 (1998)
Gifts Received: $1,000,000 (1992)

Typical Recipients

Arts & Humanities: History & Archaeology, Libraries
Civic & Public Affairs: Civic & Public Affairs-General
Education: Education Associations, Secondary Education (Public)
Religion: Churches, Religious Organizations, Religious Welfare
Science: Scientific Centers & Institutes

Application Procedures

Initial Contact: Send a written request.
Deadlines: None.

Restrictions

Grants are not made to individuals.

Additional Information

Trust(s): Bessemer Trust Co NA

Foundation Officials

Bruce C. Farrell: off
Deborah C. Foord: officer
Perley H. Grimes, Jr.: officer
Susan B. Magary, Esq.: officer
Roderic M. Oneglia: officer
Henry W. Seherr-Thoss: officer
Sonia P. Seherr-Thoss: officer
Clayton B. Spencer: officer

Grants Analysis

Disclosure Period: calendar year ending 2000
Total Grants: $229,060
Number of Grants: 8
Highest Grant: $100,000
Lowest Grant: $5,920

Recent Grants

Note: Grants derived from 1999 Form 990.

Library-Related
5,715   Oliver Walcott Library, Litchfield, CT

General
98,000   Meeting House, Inc, Litchfield, CT
38,089   First Congregational Church, Litchfield, CT
15,000   United Methodist Church of Litchfield, Litchfield, CT
11,900   Litchfield Historical Society, Litchfield, CT
10,330   St. Michael's Parish, Litchfield, CT
9,970   Milton Congregation Church, Litchfield, CT

6,280   Tyler-Seward-Kubish Post American Legion, Bantam, CT
6,000   Litchfield Board of Education, Litchfield, CT
2,357   Borough of Litchfield, Litchfield, CT

SEIDMAN FAMILY FOUNDATION

Giving Contact

Robin Volock
Seidman Family Foundation
8316 Calle Petirrojo NW
Albuquerque, NM 87120
Phone: (505)898-4977

Description

Founded: 1950
EIN: 136098204
Organization Type: Private Foundation
Giving Locations: nationally.
Grant Types: Capital, Endowment, General Support, Multiyear/Continuing Support, Research.

Donor Information

Founder: the late Frank E. Seidman, the late Esther I. Seidman

Financial Summary

Total Giving: $227,725 (2001); $187,350 (1999); $195,650 (1998)
Giving Analysis: Giving for 2001 includes: foundation grants to United Way ($4,000) 1999: foundation grants to United Way ($1,000)
Assets: $4,196,289 (2001); $4,887,175 (1999); $4,732,453 (1998)
Gifts Received: $5,000 (1992). Note: In fiscal 1992, contributions were received from American Institute of Certified Public Accountants.

Typical Recipients

Arts & Humanities: Arts Associations & Councils, Arts Outreach, Ballet, Community Arts, Dance, Arts & Humanities-General, Historic Preservation, History & Archaeology, Libraries, Museums/Galleries, Performing Arts, Public Broadcasting, Theater
Civic & Public Affairs: Botanical Gardens/Parks, Community Foundations, Gay/Lesbian Issues, Civic & Public Affairs-General, Housing, Native American Affairs, Urban & Community Affairs, Women's Affairs, Zoos/Aquariums
Education: Agricultural Education, Arts/Humanities Education, Business Education, Colleges & Universities, Elementary Education (Public), Education-General, Journalism/Media Education, Leadership Training, Legal Education, Literacy, Preschool Education, Private Education (Precollege), Public Education (Precollege), School Volunteerism, Science/Mathematics Education, Secondary Education (Private), Special Education, Student Aid
Environment: Air/Water Quality, Environment-General, Resource Conservation
Health: AIDS/HIV, Emergency/Ambulance Services, Heart, Hospitals, Medical Rehabilitation, Nursing Services
International: Health Care/Hospitals, International Relief Efforts
Religion: Churches, Religious Welfare
Science: Scientific Centers & Institutes
Social Services: Big Brother/Big Sister, Child Welfare, Community Service Organizations, Counseling, Domestic Violence, Family Planning, Family Services, Food/Clothing Distribution, People with Disabilities, Recreation & Athletics, Substance Abuse, United Funds/United Ways, Youth Organizations

Application Procedures

Initial Contact: The foundation has no formal grant application procedure or application form.
Deadlines: None.

Foundation Officials

Margaret Ann Cole: trustee
B. Thomas Seidman: trustee
Jane R. Seidman: trustee
Lewis William Seidman: trustee B Grand Rapids, MI 1921. ED Dartmouth College AB (1943); Harvard University LLB (1948); University of Michigan MBA (1949). NONPR AFFIL member: DC Bar Association. CLUB AFFIL University Club; Nantucket Yacht Club; Chevy Chase Club; Crystal Downs Club.
Nancy Caroline Seidman: trustee
Sarah B. Seidman: trustee
Sarah L. Seidman: trustee
Tracy H. Seidman: trustee
Henry Van Ee: admin

Grants Analysis

Disclosure Period: calendar year ending 2001
Total Grants: $223,725*
Number of Grants: 85
Average Grant: $2,632
Highest Grant: $50,000
Lowest Grant: $110
Typical Range: $500 to $5,000
*Note: Giving excludes United Way.

Recent Grants

Note: Grants derived from 2001 Form 990.

Library-Related
2,000   Kellogg-Hubbard Library, Montpelier, VT

General
50,000   Grand Rapids Youth Commonwealth, Grand Rapids, MI
25,000   Grand Valley State University, Grand Rapids, MI
15,000   Keshet Dance Co., Albuquerque, NM
12,000   Nantucket Conservation Foundation, Nantucket, MA
10,000   Nantucket College Hospital, Nantucket, MA
10,000   National Stroke Association, Englewood, CO
6,000   Cibola High School
5,000   American Theater of Actors, New York, NY
5,000   National Dance Institute of New Mexico, Tesuque, NM
5,000   New Mexico Water Dialogue, Santa Fe, NM

WILLIAM G. SELBY AND MARIE SELBY FOUNDATION

Giving Contact

Debra M. Jacobs, President
1800 Second Street, Suite 750
Sarasota, FL 34236
Phone: (941)957-0442
Fax: (941)957-3135
Web: http://www.selbyfdn.org

Alternate Contact

Debra Jacobs
PO Box 267
Sarasota, FL 34230

Description

Founded: 1955
EIN: 596121242
Organization Type: General Purpose Foundation

Giving Locations: FL: Sarasota Manatee, Charlotte, DeSoto Florida counties
Grant Types: Capital, Challenge.

Donor Information

Founder: Established in 1955 by the late William G. Selby (d. 1956) and his wife, Marie Selby . Mr. Selby, who was a co-founder of the Selby Oil Company in Ohio. In addition, he was a large stockholder in Texaco, and owned extensive mineral interests in the Colorado Rocky Mountain region. The foundation is affiliated with the Beattie, Sarasota County, Paddock, and Posey Foundations, all of First Union Bank.

Financial Summary

Total Giving: $3,706,228 (fiscal year ending May 31, 2001); $3,500,000 (fiscal 2000 approx); $3,229,390 (fiscal 1999)
Giving Analysis: Giving for fiscal 1999 includes: foundation grants to United Way ($100,000) fiscal 1998: foundation scholarships ($540,600)
Assets: $78,520,483 (fiscal 2001); $87,000,000 (fiscal 2000 approx); $82,736,760 (fiscal 1999)
Gifts Received: $2,245,267 (fiscal 1993)

Typical Recipients

Arts & Humanities: Arts Associations & Councils, Ballet, Film & Video, History & Archaeology, Libraries, Museums/Galleries, Music, Performing Arts, Public Broadcasting, Theater, Visual Arts
Civic & Public Affairs: Botanical Gardens/Parks, Business/Free Enterprise, Community Foundations, Economic Policy, Employment/Job Training, Civic & Public Affairs-General, Hispanic Affairs, Housing, Law & Justice, Municipalities/Towns, Urban & Community Affairs, Women's Affairs, Zoos/Aquariums
Education: Afterschool/Enrichment Programs, Agricultural Education, Arts/Humanities Education, Business Education, Colleges & Universities, Community & Junior Colleges, Economic Education, Education Associations, Engineering/Technological Education, Education-General, Literacy, Minority Education, Preschool Education, Public Education (Precollege), School Volunteerism, Science/Mathematics Education, Secondary Education (Private), Secondary Education (Public), Student Aid, Vocational & Technical Education
Environment: Air/Water Quality, Resource Conservation
Health: AIDS/HIV, Cancer, Children's Health/Hospitals, Emergency/Ambulance Services, Hospices, Medical Research, Mental Health, Prenatal Health Issues, Research/Studies Institutes, Single-Disease Health Associations
Religion: Dioceses, Ministries, Religious Welfare
Science: Science Museums, Scientific Labs
Social Services: Animal Protection, At-Risk Youth, Child Welfare, Community Centers, Community Service Organizations, Day Care, Domestic Violence, Family Planning, Family Services, Food/Clothing Distribution, People with Disabilities, Recreation & Athletics, Senior Services, Substance Abuse, United Funds/United Ways, YMCA/YWCA/YMHA/YWHA, Youth Organizations

Application Procedures

Initial Contact: Applicants should contact the administrative agent for a copy of their application procedures.
Application Requirements: Along with the completed application, supporting information may be submitted to describe the organization and the project.
Deadlines: February 1 and August 1.
Review Process: The grants committee reviews proposals and notifies applicants of their decisions within five months of the deadline. The trustees evaluate applications on the basis of the proposed project's value to society, soundness of sponsoring organization, sources of other financial support, and assurance

of future maintenance of the project without an undesirable financial burden to the sponsoring organization or taxpayer.
Decision Notification: Applicants will be notified in writing of the acceptance or rejection of their request within the time frame outlined on the Foundation Matrix.

Restrictions

No grants are given to individuals, or for endowment funds, operating budgets, continuing support, annual campaigns, deficit financing, seed money, or emergency funds. It also does not support special projects, research, graduate study, publications, travel, surveys, seminars, workshops, conferences, loans, fund raising, or program advertising. The foundation does not give to organizations outside of Sarasota and adjoining counties, to other foundations, or to the United Way. It prefers not to support projects that are normally financed by public tax funds. The foundation usually does not make grants payable in installments in future years.

Additional Information

First Union Bank serves as corporate trustee for the foundation.
In order to be eligible for a Selby scholarship, a student must be a bona fide resident of Sarasota or Manatee counties before attending college, and must attend a participating Florida college or university. A minimum grade point average of 3.0 is required. Students seeking a scholarship should write to the Florida college or university in which he or she has an interest. The foundation reports that scholarships are also available for Sarasota County residents who choose to attend colleges outside the State of Florida. These students should apply directly to the Foundation office by March 1 for the upcoming academic year.
Publications: Guidelines; Application Form

Foundation Officials

Dan Bailey: president
John Davidson: member admin committee B 1931. ED Duke University; University of Colorado. PRIM CORP EMPL president: Davidson Drugs Inc.
Debra M. Jacobs: president, member administration committee NONPR AFFIL vice president: Ringling School Art & Design.
Charles E. Stottlemyer: chairman, mem admin comm CORP AFFIL director: FCCI Mutual Insurance Co.; director: Florida Employers Insurance Service Corp.

Grants Analysis

Disclosure Period: fiscal year ending May 31, 2001
Total Grants: $3,706,228*
Number of Grants: 63
Average Grant: $58,829
Highest Grant: $305,000
Lowest Grant: $5,000
Typical Range: $10,000 to $100,000
*Note: Grants analysis provided by foundation.

Recent Grants

Note: Grants derived from 2001 Form 990.

General

305,000	Community Foundation for Sarasota County, Sarasota, FL
300,000	John and Mable Ringling Museum of Art Foundation, Sarasota, FL
241,480	Florida College General Scholarship Program, Temple Terrace, FL
200,000	Sarasota Family YMCA, Sarasota, FL
150,000	Mote Marine Laboratory, Orlando, FL
150,000	Senior Friendship Centers Foundation, Sarasota, FL
125,000	Charlotte County Family YMCA, Charlotte, NC
100,500	Education Foundation of Sarasota County, Sarasota, FL
100,000	Children First, Inc, Sarasota, FL
100,000	Community AIDS Network, Sarasota, FL

SELF FAMILY FOUNDATION

Giving Contact

Mamie W. Nicholson, Program Officer
PO Box 1017
Greenwood, SC 29648-1017
Phone: (864)941-4011
Fax: (864)941-4091
E-mail: application@selffoundation.org
Web: http://www.selffoundation.org

Description

Founded: 1942
EIN: 570400594
Organization Type: Family Foundation
Giving Locations: SC: emphasis on Greenwood area
Grant Types: Capital, Challenge, Conference/Seminar, Endowment, Project, Research, Scholarship.

Donor Information

Founder: Founded in 1942 by the late James C. Self . Mr. Self was the founder of Greenwood Mills in Greenwood, SC. The original purpose of the foundation was to construct a hospital for Greenwood County. This mission was realized on November 1, 1951. At the time of the hospital's dedication, Mr. Self remarked that it was "a debt of gratitude to the community that has been good to me."

Financial Summary

Total Giving: $11,498,322 (2001); $2,049,578 (2000); $1,859,391 (1999)
Giving Analysis: Giving for 2000 includes: foundation grants to United Way ($15,000); foundation scholarships ($82,750); 1999: foundation scholarships ($79,500); foundation grants to United Way ($117,000); 1998: foundation grants to United Way ($72,742); foundation matching gifts ($139,700) foundation scholarships ($174,500)
Assets: $38,883,095 (2001); $53,204,629 (2000); $52,983,753 (1999)

Typical Recipients

Arts & Humanities: Arts Associations & Councils, Historic Preservation, History & Archaeology, Libraries, Museums/Galleries, Opera, Performing Arts, Public Broadcasting, Theater
Civic & Public Affairs: Clubs, Community Foundations, Economic Development, Civic & Public Affairs-General, Housing, Municipalities/Towns, Nonprofit Management, Philanthropic Organizations, Professional & Trade Associations, Safety, Zoos/Aquariums
Education: Afterschool/Enrichment Programs, Arts/Humanities Education, Business Education, Business-School Partnerships, Colleges & Universities, Continuing Education, Education Funds, Education Reform, Elementary Education (Private), Elementary Education (Public), Faculty Development, Education-General, Leadership Training, Literacy, Medical Education, Preschool Education, Private Education (Precollege), Public Education (Precollege), Science/Mathematics Education, Social Sciences Education, Special Education, Student Aid, Vocational & Technical Education
Environment: Environment-General
Health: Adolescent Health Issues, Alzheimers Disease, Cancer, Children's Health/Hospitals, Clinics/Medical Centers, Eyes/Blindness, Heart, Home-Care Services, Hospices, Hospitals, Medical Research, Research/Studies Institutes
Religion: Ministries, Religious Welfare
Science: Scientific Centers & Institutes

Social Services: At-Risk Youth, Child Abuse, Child Welfare, Community Centers, Community Service Organizations, Day Care, Domestic Violence, Family Planning, Family Services, Food/Clothing Distribution, People with Disabilities, Recreation & Athletics, Senior Services, Sexual Abuse, Special Olympics, United Funds/United Ways, YMCA/YWCA/YMHA/YWHA, Youth Organizations

Application Procedures

Initial Contact: Contact the foundation program officer by phone or submit a letter of inquiry prior to submitting a full proposal.

Application Requirements: If a proposal is requested by the foundation, it should include description of objectives and activities, organization leadership, purpose of funds sought, an implementation plan (using existing community assets, both human and financial), and how results will be measured. Applicants also must include a copy of IRS tax-exempt determination letter and recently audited financial statement, including a budget identifying income sources and expenses.

Deadlines: Proposals must be received by February 15, May 15, August 15, or November 15.

Review Process: Trustees meet the third week of March, June, September, and December. Late applications are held for consideration at the next meeting.

Restrictions

Grants are made from income only and for periods not to exceed three years. Grants are not made to individuals. The foundation does not provide loans, recurring grants, or operational support. Applicants must have the financial potential to sustain the project on a continuing basis after foundation funding.

Additional Information

Publications: Annual Report

Foundation Officials

William B. Allin: treasurer
George W. Ballentine, Jr.: trustee B 1954. ED Clemson University (1975). PRIM CORP EMPL vice president: George Ballentine Ford Inc.
David L. Bell: trustee
Virginia S. Brennan: trustee, chairman CORP AFFIL director: Greenwood Mills Inc.
R. Boykin Curry, Jr.: trustee emeritus CORP AFFIL director: United Savings Bank.
Gwen Dickenson: administrative assistant
John Murphy: trustee
Mamie W. Nicholson: program officer
James Cuthbert Self, III: trustee PRIM CORP EMPL vice president: Greenwood Mills Inc.
Dr. Sally E. Self: secretary, trustee
William Matthews Self: vice chairman, trustee B 1948. PRIM CORP EMPL president, chief executive officer, director: Greenwood Mills Inc. ADD CORP EMPL director: Greenwood Development Corp.; chairman: Greenwood Holding Corp.; president, chief executive officer, director: Lindale Manufacturing Co.
Paul E. Welder: trustee B Kansas City, MO 1943. ED University of Virginia (1965). PRIM CORP EMPL executive vice president financial, director: Greenwood Mills Inc. CORP AFFIL director: Jeantex SACA; director: Tejidos Argentinos SA; director: Crescent-Greenwood.
Frank J. Wideman, III: president

Grants Analysis

Disclosure Period: calendar year ending 2001
Total Grants: $11,465,322*
Number of Grants: 48
Average Grant: $31,177*
Highest Grant: $10,000,000
Lowest Grant: $1,000
Typical Range: $10,000 to $75,000
*Note: Giving excludes United Way. Average grant figure excludes highest grant.

Recent Grants

Note: Grants derived from 2001 Form 990.

General

10,000,000	Upper Savannah Council of Governments, Greenwood, SC -- establish the Upper Savannah Sudden and Severe Economic Dislocation Loan Fund
325,000	Greenwood Genetic Center, Greenwood, SC -- unrestricted grant in memory of Jim Sell
90,000	Arts Council of Greenwood, Greenwood, SC -- Cultural Center Feasibility Study
85,000	American Legion Post 20, Greenwood, SC -- Restoration of American Legion Building
75,000	Partnership for a Greenwood County, Greenwood, SC -- support of workforce development in Greenwood County
64,450	South Carolina Aquarium, Charleston, SC -- support the education leadership program for South Carolina Teachers
63,322	Greenwood Community Children's Center, Greenwood, SC -- Healthy Beginnings Programs
56,000	Lander Foundation, Greenwood, SC -- additional funding for Montessori Education program
51,200	Greenwood Genetic Center, Greenwood, SC -- configuring additional research and diagnostic laboratories and acquiring gene and chromosome analytic instruments
50,200	Lander Foundation, Greenwood, SC -- pre-kindergarten through graduate studies professional education at Lander University

SEMMES FOUNDATION

Giving Contact

Thomas R. Semmes, President & Director
800 Navarro, Suite 210
San Antonio, TX 78205
Phone: (210)225-0887

Description

Founded: 1952
EIN: 746062264
Organization Type: Private Foundation
Giving Locations: TX: San Antonio
Grant Types: Capital, Conference/Seminar, Emergency, General Support, Multiyear/Continuing Support, Operating Expenses, Professorship, Project, Research, Seed Money.

Donor Information

Founder: the late Douglas R. Semmes

Financial Summary

Total Giving: $1,022,410 (2000); $777,230 (1999); $436,900 (1998)
Giving Analysis: Giving for 2000 includes: foundation grants to United Way ($15,000); foundation scholarships ($202,000); 1999: foundation grants to United Way ($15,000) foundation scholarships ($56,000)
Assets: $20,469,407 (2000); $19,983,125 (1999); $18,322,949 (1998)
Gifts Received: $45,738 (2000); $45,738 (1999); $32,330 (1998). Note: In 1999 and 2000, contributions were received from the Julia Yates Semmes.

Typical Recipients

Arts & Humanities: Arts Centers, Arts Festivals, Ethnic & Folk Arts, Libraries, Museums/Galleries, Music, Public Broadcasting

Civic & Public Affairs: Community Foundations, Employment/Job Training, Nonprofit Management, Philanthropic Organizations
Education: Colleges & Universities, Literacy, Private Education (Precollege), Public Education (Precollege), Science/Mathematics Education, Student Aid
Health: Cancer, Children's Health/Hospitals, Heart, Hospices, Nutrition
International: International Affairs
Religion: Churches, Religious Welfare, Social/Policy Issues
Science: Science Museums, Scientific Centers & Institutes
Social Services: Animal Protection, Child Abuse, Child Welfare, Community Service Organizations, Day Care, Family Planning, Family Planning, Family Services, People with Disabilities, United Funds/United Ways, YMCA/YWCA/YMHA/YWHA, Youth Organizations

Application Procedures

Initial Contact: Send a concise written proposal with proof of tax-exempt status.
Deadlines: None.

Restrictions

Does not support individuals or provide loans.

Foundation Officials

Carol Duffell: secretary, treasurer
John R. Hannah: cpa, director
Lucian L. Morrison, Jr.: director CORP AFFIL director: Group Maintenance America.
D. R. Semmes, Jr.: director
Julia Yates Semmes: director
Patricia A. Semmes: director
Thomas R. Semmes: president, director

Grants Analysis

Disclosure Period: calendar year ending 2000
Total Grants: $805,410*
Number of Grants: 11
Average Grant: $30,541*
Highest Grant: $500,000
Lowest Grant: $500
*Note: Giving excludes United Way, scholarships. Average grant figure excludes highest grant.

Recent Grants

Note: Grants derived from 1999 Form 990.

Library-Related

350,000	San Antonio Public Library Foundation, San Antonio, TX -- endowment for visual impairment

General

90,000	Texas Military Institute, San Antonio, TX -- toward property purchase
70,000	YMCA of San Antonio, San Antonio, TX -- toward downtown YMCA renovations
60,000	Judson Montessori School, San Antonio, TX -- school construction
60,000	Santa Rosa Children's Hospital Foundation, San Antonio, TX -- miracle 2000 campaign
56,000	Trinity University, San Antonio, TX -- various scholarship funds
25,000	McNay Art Museum, San Antonio, TX -- internship program
16,000	Mind Science Foundation, San Antonio, TX -- imagineers program
15,000	United Way of San Antonio and Bexar County, San Antonio, TX
14,230	McNay Art Museum, San Antonio, TX -- museum library
10,000	McNay Art Museum, San Antonio, TX

LOUISE TAFT SEMPLE FOUNDATION

Giving Contact
Penny Freedman
425 Walnut Street
Cincinnati, OH 45202
Phone: (513)381-2838
Fax: (513)381-0205

Alternate Contact
Phone: (513)357-9489

Description
Founded: 1941
EIN: 310653526
Organization Type: Family Foundation
Giving Locations: OH: Hamilton County, Cincinnati
Grant Types: Capital, Challenge, Endowment, Project.

Donor Information
Founder: Incorporated in 1941 by the late Louise Taft Semple .

Financial Summary
Total Giving: $1,223,125 (2000); $1,172,000 (1998); $992,700 (1997)
Giving Analysis: Giving for 2000 includes: foundation scholarships ($25,000); foundation grants to United Way ($72,000) 1998: foundation grants to United Way ($69,000)
Assets: $25,490,577 (2000); $25,967,219 (1998); $18,973,099 (1996)

Typical Recipients
Arts & Humanities: Arts Associations & Councils, Arts Centers, Arts Funds, Arts Outreach, Ballet, Ethnic & Folk Arts, Arts & Humanities-General, Historic Preservation, History & Archaeology, Libraries, Museums/Galleries, Music, Opera, Performing Arts, Public Broadcasting, Theater
Civic & Public Affairs: African American Affairs, Botanical Gardens/Parks, Clubs, Economic Development, Employment/Job Training, Civic & Public Affairs-General, Housing, Inner-City Development, Legal Aid, Municipalities/Towns, Parades/Festivals, Public Policy, Urban & Community Affairs, Women's Affairs, Zoos/Aquariums
Education: Afterschool/Enrichment Programs, Arts/Humanities Education, Colleges & Universities, Colleges & Universities, Education Funds, Engineering/Technological Education, Faculty Development, Education-General, Legal Education, Private Education (Precollege), Public Education (Precollege), Science/Mathematics Education, Secondary Education (Private), Secondary Education (Public), Special Education, Student Aid
Environment: Environment-General, Resource Conservation
Health: Children's Health/Hospitals, Medical Rehabilitation, Preventive Medicine/Wellness Organizations, Speech & Hearing
International: International Affairs, International Relations
Religion: Religion-General, Religious Organizations, Religious Welfare
Social Services: Camps, Child Welfare, Community Centers, Community Service Organizations, Family Services, Homes, People with Disabilities, Recreation & Athletics, Scouts, Substance Abuse, Substance Abuse, United Funds/United Ways, YMCA/YWCA/YMHA/YWHA, Youth Organizations

Application Procedures
Initial Contact: Initial contact may be a letter outlining purpose of proposal, other financial support, and amount requested. The foundation does not have a specific application form.

Application Requirements: Full proposals should include the name, address, and telephone number of the applying organization, as shown on the IRS tax-exempt letter; the purpose and activities of the organization; the geographic areas served by the organization; the names of the officers, board of directors or trustees, executive director, and secretary; the amount of the grant requested with a budget for the project and the purpose for which it will be used; any other sources contacted for support, with the amounts requested from each; and the organization's latest balance sheet and annual opera ting statement.
Deadlines: The foundation's board of trustees meets the first Mondays of April, July, October, and December. Applications should be submitted accordingly.
Review Process: The foundation's board of trustees considers grant proposals and makes funding decisions.

Restrictions
The foundation does not support individuals, general purposes, research, or loans.

Foundation Officials
James Ralph Bridgeland, Jr.: secretary, trustee B Cleveland, OH 1929. ED University of Akron BA (1951); Harvard University MA (1955); Harvard University JD (1957). CORP AFFIL director: SHV North America Inc.; director, member executive committee: Star Banc Cincinnati; director: Seinau-Fisher Studios Inc.; director, member executive committee: Firstar Bank NA; director: David J. Joseph Co.; director: Robert A. Cline Co.; director: Art Stamping Inc. NONPR AFFIL member: Ohio Bar Association; instructor: University Cincinnati; trustee: Jobs Cincinnati Graduates; member: Harvard University Alumni Association; trustee: Hillside Trust; president, trustee: Cincinnati Symphony Orchestra; trustee: Cincinnati Institute Fine Arts; trustee: Cincinnati Opera; member: Cincinnati Bar Association; member: American Bar Association; member: Association Library Scholars Critics; member: American Arbitration Association. CLUB AFFIL mem: Queen City Club; mem: Harvard Club; mem: Cincinnati Literacy Club; mem: Commonwealth Club.
William De Witt: trustee
Anne T. Lawrence: trustee
John T. Lawrence, Jr.: treasurer, trustee CORP AFFIL director: America Annuity Group Inc.
Dudley S. Taft: chairman, trustee PRIM CORP EMPL president, chief executive officer: Taft Broadcasting Co. CORP AFFIL director: Tribune Co.; director: Union Central Life Insurance Co.; director: Fifth Third Bank; director: CINergy Corp.; director: Fifth Third Bancorp. CLUB AFFIL treasurer, director: Queen City Club.
Mrs. Robert A. Taft, II: trustee
John Tytus: trustee

Grants Analysis
Disclosure Period: calendar year ending 2000
Total Grants: $1,126,125*
Number of Grants: 38
Average Grant: $29,635
Highest Grant: $75,000
Lowest Grant: $5,000
Typical Range: $5,000 to $50,000
*Note: Giving excludes United Way; scholarships.

Recent Grants
Note: Grants derived from 2000 Form 990.

General
75,000	Xavier University, Cincinnati, OH
71,429	Cincinnati Country Day School, Cincinnati, OH
71,429	Seven Hills School, Cincinnati, OH
50,000	Boy Scouts of America, Cincinnati, OH
50,000	Children's Home, Cincinnati, OH
50,000	Children's Hospital Medical Center, Cincinnati, OH
50,000	Children's Museum
50,000	Cincinnati Ballet, Cincinnati, OH
50,000	Cincinnati Opera, Cincinnati, OH
50,000	Cincinnati Youth Artworks, Cincinnati, OH

SEMPRA ENERGY

Company Headquarters
101 Ash Street
San Diego, CA 92101-3017
Phone: (619)696-2000
Fax: (619)696-4463
Web: http://www.sempra.com

Company Description
Ticker: SRE
Exchange: NYSE
Former Name: San Diego Gas & Electric;
Formed by Merger of: Pacific Enterprises and Enova (2001);
Former Name: Southern California Gas Co. (2001).
Assets: US$17.757 billion (2002)
Profit: US$591 million (2002)
Employees: 12197 (2002)
Fortune Rank: 291, per FORTUNE Magazine's list of 500 Largest U.S. Corporations (2002).
SIC(s): 1521 Single-Family Housing Construction, 4923 Gas Transmission & Distribution, 4931 Electric & Other Services Combined, 6552 Subdividers & Developers Nec, 6719 Holding Companies Nec.

Operating Locations
Sempra Energy (CA--Carlsbad, Chula Vista, Coronado, Encino, Irvine, San Diego, San Onofre, Santa Ana)

Nonmonetary Support
Type: Cause-related Marketing & Promotion; Donated Equipment; In-kind Services; Workplace Solicitation
Volunteer Programs: The company promotes employee volunteerism through Team San Diego Gas & Electric, a group of nearly 1,200 employees and family members who volunteer in hands-on community service projects.

Giving Contact
Molly Cartmill, Director Corporate Community Relations
Sempra Energy
101 Ash St.
San Diego, CA 92101-3017
Phone: (619)696-4297
Fax: (619)696-1868
E-mail: community@sempra.com
Web: http://sempra.com/community/

Alternate Contact
Phone: 877-SEMPRA-9
Note: Toll free number.

Description
Organization Type: Corporate Giving Program
Giving Locations: CA: Southern California
Grant Types: Conference/Seminar, Emergency, Employee Matching Gifts, Project.

Financial Summary
Total Giving: $7,980,000 (2002 approx); $8,590,000 (2001); $4,000,000 (1997 approx). Note: Contributes through corporate direct giving program only. Giving includes corporate direct giving; memberships; local economic development. 1996 Giving includes nonmonetary support.
Giving Analysis: Giving for 1997 includes: corporate direct giving ($2,250,000)
Assets: $15,156,000,000 (2001)

Typical Recipients

Arts & Humanities: Arts Centers, Arts Festivals, Arts Funds, Arts Institutes, Community Arts, Dance, Ethnic & Folk Arts, Historic Preservation, Libraries, Museums/Galleries, Music, Opera, Performing Arts, Theater, Visual Arts

Civic & Public Affairs: Economic Development, Employment/Job Training, Legal Aid, Professional & Trade Associations, Safety, Zoos/Aquariums

Education: Arts/Humanities Education, Business Education, Colleges & Universities, Economic Education, Education Funds, Elementary Education (Private), Engineering/Technological Education, Health & Physical Education, Literacy, Medical Education, Minority Education, Preschool Education, Science/Mathematics Education

Environment: Environment-General

Health: Geriatric Health, Health Organizations, Hospices, Hospitals, Medical Research, Mental Health, Single-Disease Health Associations

Science: Observatories & Planetariums, Science Exhibits & Fairs, Scientific Organizations

Social Services: Child Welfare, Community Centers, Community Service Organizations, Counseling, Day Care, Delinquency & Criminal Rehabilitation, Emergency Relief, Family Services, Food/Clothing Distribution, People with Disabilities, Recreation & Athletics, Senior Services, Shelters/Homelessness, Substance Abuse, United Funds/United Ways, Volunteer Services, Youth Organizations

Application Procedures

Initial Contact: See website for Community Partnership Request Form, then submit a written request.

Application Requirements: Include name of organization, contact person and title, address, phone and fax number; a description of organization, including purpose, size and audience served; description of program or project, with target audience: ethnicity, number of people, age, etc.; amount requested; geographic area served; description of need, including relevant research; budget for the project, including personnel, operating and direct costs; list of other contributors and funding levels; method of evaluation; current budget for organization, including revenue sources and reserve or contingency funds; description of volunteer support; list of board members, advisory board, and staff; proof of tax-exempt status; description of how SDG&E's participation will be highlighted; and tax I.D. number.

Deadlines: None.

Evaluative Criteria: Project is in one of company's focus areas; builds alliances between businesses, nonprofits, schools and media; delivers specific benefits or services to community; provides company with leadership opportunity; demonstrates commitment to measuring results; use financial, labor, and volunteer resources wisely; reach ethnically diverse communities. The company prefers to make direct contributions, rather than to other grant-making organizations; to fund programs that reach consumers or businesses with direct benefits; and to fund single-year efforts as opposed to multi-year commitments.

Decision Notification: Applicants are notified on a monthly basis.

Restrictions

The company generally does not provide funds for general operating expenses; travel expenses; loans or loan guarantees; debt reduction or past operating deficits; liquidating an organization; reducing or donating the cost of any gas or electric service that other customers must pay for (except for customers who are helped through our winter assistance program); building funds or capital campaigns.

No grants are made to individuals; private foundations or endowment funds; grantmaking organizations; discriminatory organizations; sectarian religious activities or political activities.

No grants are made to individuals; private foundations or endowment funds; grantmaking organizations; discriminatory organizations; sectarian religious activities or political activities.

Additional Information

The company provides for corporate and regional contributions. Corporate contributions dollars exist to support community-wide organizations and activities that benefit citizens throughout the markets where they do business. Regional contributions dollars exist to support organizations and activities that benefit citizens living within certain geographic areas of the community.

The company supports the Employee Contributions Club, which funds local community projects, and a holiday food drive.

Publications: Community Partnership Request Form; Annual Review

Corporate Officials

Donald E. Felsinger: president, chief executive officer B Safford, AZ 1947. ED University of Arizona (1972). PRIM CORP EMPL president: Sempra Energy. CORP AFFIL member: Pacific Coast Gas Association; director: Institute Medical Quality; director: Calstart; director: Institute America. NONPR AFFIL director: Edison Electric Institute.

Giving Program Officials

Molly Cartmill: director corporate contributions PRIM CORP EMPL chairman president: Sempra Energy.

Grants Analysis

Typical Range: $1,000 to $50,000

SENECA FOODS CORP.

Company Headquarters

1162 Pittsford Victor Rd.
Pittsford, NY 14534

Company Description

Employees: 1,336

SIC(s): 2000 Food & Kindred Products, 2300 Apparel & Other Textile Products, 4500 Transportation by Air.

Operating Locations

Seneca Foods Corp. (MN--Rochester; NY--Marion, Pittsford)

Seneca Foods Foundation

Giving Contact

Kraig H. Kayser, President, Chief Executive Officer, Director
3736 S. Main St.
Marion, NY 14505
Phone: (315)926-8100

Description

Founded: 1989

EIN: 222996324

Organization Type: Corporate Foundation

Giving Locations: headquarters and operating communities.

Grant Types: General Support.

Financial Summary

Total Giving: $177,953 (fiscal year ending March 31, 2001); $263,371 (fiscal 2000); $80,213 (fiscal 1997). Note: Fiscal 1997 Giving includes United Way ($8,825).

Giving Analysis: Giving for fiscal 2001 includes foundation grants to United Way ($11,500); fiscal

2000: foundation grants to United Way ($10,500) foundation ($252,871)

Assets: $3,132,580 (fiscal 2001); $2,161,996 (fiscal 2000); $3,478,281 (fiscal 1997)

Gifts Received: $24,699 (fiscal 2001); $13,500 (fiscal 1997); $52,000 (fiscal 1996). Note: Contributions were received from Seneca Foods Corp.

Typical Recipients

Arts & Humanities: Arts Associations & Councils, Arts & Humanities-General, Libraries, Museums/Galleries, Music, Performing Arts, Public Broadcasting

Civic & Public Affairs: Botanical Gardens/Parks, Chambers of Commerce, Clubs, Economic Policy, Civic & Public Affairs-General, Housing, Minority Business, Parades/Festivals, Professional & Trade Associations, Safety, Urban & Community Affairs, Zoos/Aquariums

Education: Agricultural Education, Business Education, Colleges & Universities, Community & Junior Colleges, Environmental Education, Education-General, Private Education (Precollege), Public Education (Precollege), Science/Mathematics Education, Secondary Education (Private), Student Aid, Vocational & Technical Education

Environment: Research, Wildlife Protection

Health: Alzheimers Disease, Cancer, Children's Health/Hospitals, Diabetes, Emergency/Ambulance Services, Health-General, Health Organizations, Heart, Hospices, Hospitals, Medical Rehabilitation, Multiple Sclerosis, Prenatal Health Issues

International: International Environmental Issues

Religion: Churches, Jewish Causes, Religious Welfare

Science: Science-General

Social Services: Big Brother/Big Sister, Camps, Child Welfare, Community Service Organizations, Delinquency & Criminal Rehabilitation, Emergency Relief, Family Services, People with Disabilities, Recreation & Athletics, Scouts, Social Services-General, Special Olympics, Substance Abuse, United Funds/United Ways, Veterans, YMCA/YWCA/YMHA/YWHA, Youth Organizations

Application Procedures

Initial Contact: The foundation has no formal grant application procedure or application form.

Deadlines: None.

Corporate Officials

Kraig H. Kayser: president, chief executive officer, director PRIM CORP EMPL president, chief executive officer, director: Seneca Foods Corp.

Arthur S. Wolcott: chairman, director B Corning, NY 1926. ED Cornell University (1949). PRIM CORP EMPL chairman, director: Seneca Foods Corp. CORP AFFIL director: Moog.

Foundation Officials

Devra A. Bevona: assistant secretary, treasurer

Kraig H. Kayser: president, chief executive officer, director (see above)

Philip G. Paras: treasurer, assistant secretary

Susan W. Stuart: director

Jeffrey L. Van Riper: secretary B Ithaca, NY 1956. ED Morrisville College (1976); Clarkson University (1978). PRIM CORP EMPL secretary, controller: Seneca Foods Corp. NONPR AFFIL member: Institute of Management Accountants.

Arthur S. Wolcott: chairman, director (see above)

Grants Analysis

Disclosure Period: fiscal year ending March 31, 2001

Total Grants: $166,453*

Number of Grants: 124

Average Grant: $948*

Highest Grant: $49,788

Typical Range: $100 to $2,000

*Note: Giving excludes United Way. Average grant figure excludes highest grant.

Recent Grants

Note: Grants derived from 2000 Form 990.

General

33,916	NY Agriculture Research, NY
33,500	Rochester Institute of Technology, Rochester, NY
25,000	Cornell University, Ithaca, NY
20,000	City of Glencoe Parks
20,000	University of Wisconsin, Madison, WI
16,000	Midwest Food Processing Association
15,000	Harley School, Rochester, NY
12,400	FFA
10,900	United Way Funds
10,000	Clasp Homes, Westport, CT

SENTRY INSURANCE, A MUTUAL CO.

Company Headquarters

Stevens Point, WI
Web: http://www.sentry-insurance.com

Company Description

Employees: 4,314
SIC(s): 6311 Life Insurance.

Operating Locations

Sentry Insurance, A Mutual Co. (WI--Stevens Point)

Nonmonetary Support

Note: Undisclosed amounts of nonmonetary support are given by the company.

Sentry Insurance Foundation Inc.

Giving Contact

Margie Coker-Nelson, Executive Director, Vice President
1800 N Point Drive
Stevens Point, WI 54481
Phone: (715)346-6000
Fax: (715)346-6405

Description

EIN: 391037370
Organization Type: Corporate Foundation
Giving Locations: nationally; areas with large employee populations.
Grant Types: Employee Matching Gifts, General Support, Scholarship.

Financial Summary

Total Giving: $957,244 (2001); $640,397 (1999); $639,549 (1998). Note: Contributes through foundation only.
Giving Analysis: Giving for 2001 includes: foundation scholarships ($124,767); foundation grants to United Way ($129,250); foundation matching gifts ($281,156); foundation ($422,071); 1999: foundation grants to United Way ($118,550); foundation scholarships ($138,400); foundation ($169,780); foundation matching gifts ($213,667) 1997: foundation grants to United Way ($112,800)
Assets: $379,221 (2001); $1,963,680 (1999); $2,016,989 (1998)
Gifts Received: $499,875 (1999); $670,750 (1998); $2,510,155 (1997). Note: Contributions are received from Sentry Insurance, A Mutual Co.

Typical Recipients

Arts & Humanities: Arts Associations & Councils, Arts Festivals, Community Arts, History & Archaeology, Libraries, Music, Public Broadcasting, Theater

Civic & Public Affairs: Business/Free Enterprise, Chambers of Commerce, Clubs, Community Foundations, Employment/Job Training, Civic & Public Affairs-General, Housing, Public Policy, Urban & Community Affairs
Education: Business Education, Colleges & Universities, Community & Junior Colleges, Economic Education, Education Funds, Engineering/Technological Education, Education-General, Gifted & Talented Programs, Minority Education, Private Education (Precollege), Public Education (Precollege), Religious Education, Science/Mathematics Education, Secondary Education (Private), Secondary Education (Public), Student Aid, Vocational & Technical Education
Environment: Environment-General, Wildlife Protection
Health: Cancer, Health Organizations, Heart, Hospitals, Medical Research, Public Health
International: Health Care/Hospitals
Religion: Religion-General, Religious Organizations, Religious Welfare, Seminaries
Social Services: Animal Protection, At-Risk Youth, Camps, Community Service Organizations, Delinquency & Criminal Rehabilitation, Domestic Violence, Emergency Relief, People with Disabilities, Recreation & Athletics, Scouts, Social Services-General, Special Olympics, Substance Abuse, United Funds/ United Ways, Veterans, YMCA/YWCA/YMHA/ YWHA, Youth Organizations

Application Procedures

Initial Contact: Send letter of request.
Application Requirements: Include description of program and amount of contribution sought.
Deadlines: None.

Corporate Officials

Gregory C. Mox: vice president human resources PRIM CORP EMPL vice president human resources: Sentry Insurance, A Mutual Co.
Dale R. Schuh: president, chief executive officer, chairman ED Lawrence University. PRIM CORP EMPL president, chief executive officer, chairman: Sentry Insurance, A Mutual Co. CORP AFFIL chairman: Sentry Life Insurance Co.

Foundation Officials

Gregory C. Mox: president, chairman, director (see above)
William M. O'Reilly: secretary

Grants Analysis

Disclosure Period: calendar year ending 2001
Total Grants: $422,071*
Number of Grants: 41
Average Grant: $6,786*
Highest Grant: $150,626
Typical Range: $100 to $15,000
*Note: Giving excludes matching gifts, scholarships, and United Way. Average grant figure excludes highest grant.

Recent Grants

Note: Grants derived from 2001 Form 990.

General

150,626	Portage County Business Council Foundation, Inc., Stevens Point, WI
121,000	United Way Portage County, Ravenna, OH
60,000	St. Paul Lutheran School Foundation, St. Paul, MN
60,000	Stevens Point Area Catholic School, Stevens Point, WI
60,000	YMCA, Lima, OH
56,000	University of Wisconsin Stevens Point Foundation, Stevens Point, WI -- for scholarship program
41,613	September 11th Fund, New York, NY
40,000	Community Industries, Stevens Point, WI

25,000	Wisconsin Foundation of Independent Colleges, Milwaukee, WI
15,000	University of Wisconsin Whitewater Foundation, Whitewater, WI

SETON CO.

Company Headquarters

Morristown, PA

Company Description

Former Name: Seton Leather Co.
Employees: 1,400
SIC(s): 3111 Leather Tanning & Finishing.

Seton Co. Foundation

Giving Contact

Gail Kurz
Seton Co. Foundation
c/o Seton Co.
101 Eisenhower Parkway
Roseland, NJ 07068
Phone: (973)226-4551

Description

EIN: 226029254
Organization Type: Corporate Foundation
Giving Locations: FL; MA; MI; NJ; NY; PA
Grant Types: General Support.

Financial Summary

Total Giving: $80,085 (2001); $124,667 (2000); $77,744 (1999)
Giving Analysis: Giving for 2001 includes: foundation grants to United Way ($2,250); 2000: foundation grants to United Way ($400); 1999: foundation grants to United Way ($500);
Assets: $1,276,913 (2001); $1,344,776 (2000); $1,460,740 (1999)
Gifts Received: $112,165 (2001); $250,000 (1997); $250,000 (1996). Note: In 2001, contributions were received from Seton Co. ($100,000); Sadelco USA Corp. ($11,275); and anonymous donors. In 1997, contributions were received from Seton Co.

Typical Recipients

Arts & Humanities: Ballet, Libraries, Music, Opera, Performing Arts, Public Broadcasting, Theater
Civic & Public Affairs: Chambers of Commerce, Clubs, Economic Development, Civic & Public Affairs-General, Housing, Parades/Festivals, Safety, Women's Affairs
Education: Colleges & Universities, Community & Junior Colleges, Education Funds, Education Reform, Engineering/Technological Education, Education-General, Legal Education, Literacy, Medical Education, Private Education (Precollege), Science/Mathematics Education, Secondary Education (Private), Student Aid
Environment: Air/Water Quality, Resource Conservation
Health: AIDS/HIV, Cancer, Clinics/Medical Centers, Health Organizations, Hospices, Hospitals, Medical Rehabilitation, Mental Health, Multiple Sclerosis, Prenatal Health Issues, Preventive Medicine/Wellness Organizations
International: Health Care/Hospitals, International Peace & Security Issues
Religion: Churches, Jewish Causes, Ministries, Religious Welfare, Social/Policy Issues
Science: Scientific Labs
Social Services: Animal Protection, At-Risk Youth, Child Welfare, Community Centers, Community Service Organizations, Family Planning, Recreation & Athletics, Scouts, Special Olympics, United Funds/ United Ways, YMCA/YWCA/YMHA/YWHA, Youth Organizations

Application Procedures

Initial Contact: Send a brief letter of inquiry.
Application Requirements: Include a description of organization, amount requested, and statement of program.
Deadlines: None.

Corporate Officials

Philip David Kaltenbacher: chairman, president, chief executive officer, director B Orange, NJ 1937. ED Yale University (1959); Yale University (1963). PRIM CORP EMPL chairman, president, chief executive officer, director: Seton Co. CORP AFFIL chairman, chief executive officer: Selco Trucking Co.; chairman, chief executive officer: Wilmington Leather Coatings; chairman, chief executive officer: Norwood Industries.

Foundation Officials

Robert DeMajistre: trustee
Philip David Kaltenbacher: trustee (see above)

Grants Analysis

Disclosure Period: calendar year ending 2001
Total Grants: $77,835*
Number of Grants: 62
Average Grant: $1,255
Highest Grant: $15,000
Typical Range: $500 to $3,000
*Note: Giving excludes United Way.

Recent Grants

Note: Grants derived from 2001 Form 990.

General

15,000	Sarasota Memorial Healthcare Foundation, Sarasota, FL
12,000	American Jewish Committee, Sarasota, FL
5,000	Animal Rescue Coalition, Sarasota, FL
5,000	Focus HOPE, Detroit, MI
5,000	Goucher College, Baltimore, MD
5,000	Jewish Federation of Palm Beach, Palm Beach, FL
2,400	Boy Scouts of America, Sarasota, FL
2,370	Congregation B'nai Jeshurun, Short Hills, NJ
2,000	United Way Community Services, Detroit, MI
1,500	Dartmouth College, Hanover, NH

SETZER FOUNDATION

Giving Contact

Hardie C. Setzer, Trustee
2555 3rd St., Suite 200
Sacramento, CA 95818
Phone: (916)422-2555

Description

Founded: 1965
EIN: 946115578
Organization Type: Private Foundation
Giving Locations: CA
Grant Types: General Support.

Donor Information

Founder: members of the Setzer family

Financial Summary

Total Giving: $904,496 (fiscal year ending March 31, 2001); $446,335 (fiscal 2000); $355,550 (fiscal 1997). Note: Fiscal 1997 Giving includes scholarship ($400), United Way ($3,200).

Giving Analysis: Giving for fiscal 2000 includes: foundation scholarships ($1,000) foundation grants to United Way ($2,200)
Assets: $10,135,778 (fiscal 2001); $11,837,658 (fiscal 2000); $10,053,737 (fiscal 1997)
Gifts Received: $1,814 (fiscal 1997)

Typical Recipients

Arts & Humanities: Ballet, Community Arts, Arts & Humanities-General, History & Archaeology, Libraries, Museums/Galleries, Music, Opera, Public Broadcasting, Theater
Civic & Public Affairs: Community Foundations, Economic Development, Civic & Public Affairs-General, Legal Aid, Nonprofit Management, Public Policy, Safety, Urban & Community Affairs, Zoos/Aquariums
Education: Business Education, Colleges & Universities, Environmental Education, Education-General, Legal Education, Private Education (Precollege), Secondary Education (Private)
Environment: Forestry, Environment-General, Wildlife Protection
Health: Arthritis, Cancer, Children's Health/Hospitals, Clinics/Medical Centers, Diabetes, Emergency/Ambulance Services, Health Organizations, Heart, Hospitals, Kidney, Medical Research, Multiple Sclerosis, Prenatal Health Issues, Single-Disease Health Associations, Speech & Hearing, Transplant Networks/Donor Banks
International: International Environmental Issues
Religion: Religious Welfare
Science: Scientific Centers & Institutes
Social Services: Animal Protection, At-Risk Youth, Child Welfare, Community Service Organizations, Emergency Relief, Family Services, Food/Clothing Distribution, People with Disabilities, Recreation & Athletics, Scouts, Senior Services, United Funds/United Ways, YMCA/YWCA/YMHA/YWHA, Youth Organizations

Application Procedures

Initial Contact: The foundation has no formal grant application procedure or application form.
Deadlines: None.

Foundation Officials

G. Cal Setzer: trustee
Hardie C. Setzer: trustee
Mark Setzer: trustee

Grants Analysis

Disclosure Period: fiscal year ending March 31, 2001
Total Grants: $904,496*
Number of Grants: 384
Average Grant: $1,056*
Highest Grant: $500,000
Typical Range: $500 to $3,000
*Note: Average grant figure excludes highest grant.

Recent Grants

Note: Grants derived from 2000 Form 990.

General

25,000	Crocker Art Museum Association, Sacramento, CA
15,000	Sacramento Blood Center, Sacramento, CA
15,000	Sacramento Opera Association, Sacramento, CA
15,000	Sacramento S P C A, Sacramento, CA
15,000	Valley Vision, Sacramento, CA -- second of three
15,000	Yuba County 4-H Club Council, Yuba City, CA
10,000	Boys Scouts of America, Sacramento, CA
10,000	California State University, Sacramento, CA
10,000	Jean Runyan Little Theatre Restoration Fund, Sacramento, CA
10,000	McGeorge School of Law, Sacramento, CA

SEVEN SPRINGS FOUNDATION

Giving Contact

Martha D. Lyddon, President
PO Box 697
Cupertino, CA 95015
Phone: (408)252-2728

Description

Founded: 1979
EIN: 942570260
Organization Type: Private Foundation
Giving Locations: CA
Grant Types: Project.

Financial Summary

Total Giving: $240,106 (2001); $269,800 (2000); $232,250 (1999)
Assets: $4,813,971 (2001); $5,145,957 (2000); $5,899,703 (1999)
Gifts Received: $1,803 (1995); $262,291 (1994); $4,137 (1993). Note: In 1995, contributions were received from Dorothy S. Lyddon.

Typical Recipients

Arts & Humanities: Arts Associations & Councils, Ethnic & Folk Arts, Film & Video, History & Archaeology, Libraries, Literary Arts, Museums/Galleries, Public Broadcasting
Civic & Public Affairs: Botanical Gardens/Parks, Economic Policy, Employment/Job Training, Civic & Public Affairs-General, Public Policy, Urban & Community Affairs, Women's Affairs, Zoos/Aquariums
Education: Colleges & Universities, Faculty Development, Medical Education, Private Education (Precollege), Religious Education, Social Sciences Education
Environment: Air/Water Quality, Environment-General, Protection, Resource Conservation, Wildlife Protection
Health: Mental Health, Nursing Services, Public Health
International: Human Rights, International Affairs, International Development, International Environmental Issues, International Environmental Issues, International Organizations, International Peace & Security Issues, International Relations
Religion: Religion-General, Religious Organizations, Religious Welfare
Science: Scientific Centers & Institutes, Scientific Research
Social Services: At-Risk Youth, Child Welfare, Community Service Organizations, Counseling, Domestic Violence, Family Planning, Food/Clothing Distribution, United Funds/United Ways, YMCA/YWCA/YMHA/YWHA, Youth Organizations

Application Procedures

Initial Contact: The foundation has no formal grant application procedure or application form.
Deadlines: None.

Foundation Officials

Alvin T. Levitt, Esq.: secretary, treasurer
Grant Lyddon: vice president
John Knight Lyddon: trustee
Martha D. Lyddon: president
Dorothy Stauffer Lyddon: chairman

Grants Analysis

Disclosure Period: calendar year ending 2001
Total Grants: $240,106
Number of Grants: 60
Average Grant: $4,002
Highest Grant: $20,000
Typical Range: $1,000 to $10,000

Recent Grants

Note: Grants derived from 2001 Form 990.

General

20,000	Institute of Noetic Sciences, Sausalito, CA
20,000	Resource Renewal Institute, San Francisco, CA
15,000	Institute of Noetic Sciences, Sausalito, CA
10,000	International Forum on Globalization, San Francisco, CA
10,000	Planetary Coral Reef Foundation, Santa Fe, NM
10,000	Resource Center for Teachers, San Jose, CA
7,500	Earth Island Institute, San Francisco, CA
6,000	Waterkeeper, San Francisco, CA
5,000	Commonwealth, Bolinas, CA
5,000	Environmental Research Foundation, Annapolis, MD

ADAM AND MARIA SARAH SEYBERT INSTITUTION FOR POOR BOYS AND GIRLS

Giving Contact

Judith L. Bardes, Executive Directory
PO Box 8228
Philadelphia, PA 19101-8228
Phone: (215)828-8145

Description

Founded: 1914
EIN: 236260105
Organization Type: Private Foundation
Giving Locations: PA: Philadelphia
Grant Types: Emergency, Research, Scholarship, Seed Money.

Donor Information

Founder: the late Henry Seybert

Financial Summary

Total Giving: $279,500 (2000); $245,532 (1999); $277,560 (1998). Note: In 1996 Giving includes scholarship ($2,500).
Assets: $8,202,452 (2000); $8,776,520 (1999); $7,495,029 (1998)

Typical Recipients

Arts & Humanities: Arts & Humanities-General, Libraries, Theater
Civic & Public Affairs: Botanical Gardens/Parks, Economic Development, Employment/Job Training, Hispanic Affairs, Housing, Urban & Community Affairs, Women's Affairs
Education: Afterschool/Enrichment Programs, Arts/Humanities Education, Colleges & Universities, Education Funds, Education Reform, Elementary Education (Private), Elementary Education (Public), Engineering/Technological Education, Literacy, Preschool Education, Private Education (Precollege), School Volunteerism, Science/Mathematics Education, Secondary Education (Public), Student Aid

Health: AIDS/HIV, Children's Health/Hospitals, Clinics/Medical Centers, Health Funds, Health Organizations, Hospitals, Prenatal Health Issues, Public Health
Religion: Churches, Dioceses, Religious Organizations, Religious Welfare
Science: Scientific Centers & Institutes
Social Services: Camps, Child Abuse, Child Welfare, Community Service Organizations, Counseling, Day Care, Domestic Violence, Family Planning, Family Services, Food/Clothing Distribution, Homes, Sexual Abuse, YMCA/YWCA/YMHA/YWHA, Youth Organizations

Application Procedures

Initial Contact: Request application guidelines.
Deadlines: January 2, April 1, and October 1.

Restrictions

Does not support individuals.

Additional Information

Publications: Application Guidelines; Annual Report

Foundation Officials

Judith L. Bardes: mgr
William C. Bullitt: president, trustee
Susan C. Day, MD: vice president, trustee
Graham Stanley Finney: trustee B Greenwich, CT 1930. ED Washington & Lee University (1948-1949); Yale University BA (1952); Harvard University MPA (1954). PRIM CORP EMPL senior partner: Conservation Co. NONPR AFFIL director: Replication & Program Systems; member: Union Benevolent Association; member: 21st Century League. CLUB AFFIL mem: Yale Club.
Hon. Lois G. Forer: vice president, trustee
Steven R. Garfinkel: secretary, treasurer, trustee B Philadelphia, PA 1943. ED Temple University (1966). PRIM CORP EMPL senior vice president, com partner: CoreStates Finance Corp.
Rev. David I. Hagan: trustee
Lallie L. O'Brien: trustee
Carver A. Portlock: trustee

Grants Analysis

Disclosure Period: calendar year ending 2000
Total Grants: $279,500
Number of Grants: 48
Average Grant: $4,883*
Highest Grant: $50,000
Typical Range: $1,000 to $10,000
*Note: Average grant figure excludes highest grant.

Recent Grants

Note: Grants derived from 1999 Form 990.

General

13,000	Greater Philadelphia Urban Affairs Coalition, Philadelphia, PA -- for 1999 Summer Career Exploration Program
10,000	Douglas Elementary School, Philadelphia, PA -- for North Star Outreach
5,000	Academy of Community Music, Ft. Washington, PA -- for the Crescendo program at Walnut Head Start in West Philadelphia
5,000	Asian Arts Initiative, Philadelphia, PA -- for youth arts workshop
5,000	Centro Pedro Claver, Philadelphia, PA -- for after-school and summer activities for young people
5,000	Children's Seashore House, Philadelphia, PA -- for health promotion program for deaf girls and women
5,000	CHOICE, Philadelphia, PA -- for teen pregnancy prevention program
5,000	Congreso de Latino Unidos, Philadelphia, PA -- for START program
5,000	Foundation for Architecture, Philadelphia, PA -- for architecture in education program in 4 Philadelphia schools
5,000	Freedom Theater, Philadelphia, PA --

for bridge to the Repertory Internship Program

CHARLES MORTON SHARE TRUST

Giving Contact

c/o Heritage Trust Co.
1900 N.W. Expressway
50 Penn Place, Suite R225
Oklahoma City, OK 73118
Phone: (405)848-8899

Description

Founded: 1959
EIN: 736090984
Organization Type: Private Foundation
Giving Locations: OK
Grant Types: Scholarship.

Donor Information

Founder: the late Charles Morton Share

Financial Summary

Total Giving: $102,174 (fiscal year ending June 30, 2001); $368,863 (fiscal 2000); $856,738 (fiscal 1998)
Assets: $10,145,493 (fiscal 2001); $9,384,653 (fiscal 2000); $9,231,607 (fiscal 1998)

Typical Recipients

Arts & Humanities: Arts Associations & Councils, Arts Institutes, History & Archaeology, Libraries, Museums/Galleries, Music, Performing Arts, Theater
Civic & Public Affairs: Clubs, Community Foundations, Civic & Public Affairs-General, Municipalities/Towns, Parades/Festivals, Professional & Trade Associations, Safety, Urban & Community Affairs
Education: Colleges & Universities, Education Funds, Education Reform, Literacy, Medical Education, Public Education (Precollege), Secondary Education (Public)
Environment: Air/Water Quality
Health: Clinics/Medical Centers, Diabetes, Eyes/Blindness, Hospitals, Medical Research
Religion: Religious Welfare
Science: Science Museums
Social Services: Community Service Organizations, Crime Prevention, Delinquency & Criminal Rehabilitation, Delinquency & Criminal Rehabilitation, Family Services, People with Disabilities, Recreation & Athletics, Scouts, Veterans, Youth Organizations

Application Procedures

Initial Contact: The foundation has no formal grant application procedure or application form. Send enough information to identify the organization and the nature of the request.
Deadlines: None.

Restrictions

Does not support individuals.

Additional Information

Trust(s): Heritage Trust Company

Foundation Officials

Donald Benson: trustee
J. R. Holder: trustee
Johnny C. Jones: trustee
Darrell Kline: trustee
Gertrude Myers: trustee
B. H. Thornton: trustee

Grants Analysis

Disclosure Period: fiscal year ending June 30, 2001
Total Grants: $102,174
Number of Grants: 9
Average Grant: $5,786*

Highest Grant: $31,195
Lowest Grant: $2,500
Typical Range: $2,500 to $10,000
*Note: Average grant figure excludes two highest grants ($61,674).

Recent Grants

Note: Grants derived from fiscal 2000 Form 990.

General

178,762	Department of Corrections, Alva, OK
60,000	Woods County Commissioners, Oklahoma City, OK
36,026	Alva Independent School District, Alva, OK
25,000	Freedom Museum, Oklahoma City, OK
25,000	Northwest Family Service Inc, Oklahoma City, OK
15,000	NWOSU Foundation, Alva, OK
12,170	Pioneer Spirit Foundation, Oklahoma City, OK
5,000	Oklahoma Arts Institute, Oklahoma City, OK
5,000	Town of Freedom, Oklahoma City, OK
4,000	American Legion Baseball, Hopeton, OK

SHARON STEEL CORP.

Company Headquarters

Farrell, PA

Company Description

Employees: 3,000
SIC(s): 1200 Coal Mining, 3300 Primary Metal Industries, 3400 Fabricated Metal Products, 5000 Wholesale Trade--Durable Goods.
Parent Company: Sharon Specialty Steel, Inc.

Operating Locations

Sharon Steel Corp. (PA--Farrell)

Sharon Steel Foundation

Giving Contact

Hume R. Steyer, Esq.
c/o Seward and Kissel
1 Battery Park Plaza
New York, NY 10004

Description

Founded: 1953
EIN: 256063133
Organization Type: Corporate Foundation
Giving Locations: PA
Grant Types: General Support.

Donor Information

Founder: Sharon Steel Corp.

Financial Summary

Total Giving: $278,272 (2000); $232,179 (1999); $149,034 (1997)
Giving Analysis: Giving for 2000 includes: foundation grants to United Way ($20,000); foundation scholarships ($99,536); 1999: foundation grants to United Way ($20,000); foundation scholarships ($84,227); foundation ($127,952); 1997: foundation grants to United Way ($30,000) foundation scholarships ($39,034)
Assets: $5,672,228 (2000); $5,216,381 (1999); $4,448,214 (1997)

Typical Recipients

Arts & Humanities: Arts Institutes, Community Arts, Libraries, Music, Opera, Performing Arts, Public Broadcasting, Theater

Civic & Public Affairs: Botanical Gardens/Parks, Business/Free Enterprise, Chambers of Commerce, Clubs, Economic Development, Civic & Public Affairs-General, Housing, Municipalities/Towns, Professional & Trade Associations
Education: Business Education, Colleges & Universities, Continuing Education, Education-General, Minority Education, Private Education (Precollege), Science/Mathematics Education, Student Aid
Environment: Air/Water Quality
Health: Children's Health/Hospitals, Health Funds, Hospitals, Medical Research, Prenatal Health Issues, Single-Disease Health Associations
Religion: Churches, Religious Organizations, Religious Welfare
Social Services: Camps, Child Welfare, Community Service Organizations, Counseling, Family Services, People with Disabilities, Recreation & Athletics, Scouts, United Funds/United Ways, YMCA/YWCA/YMHA/YWHA, Youth Organizations

Application Procedures

Initial Contact: Send a brief letter of inquiry. Include a description of organization, amount requested, purpose of funds sought, recently audited financial statement, and proof of tax-exempt status.
Deadlines: None.

Additional Information

The company remained in Chapter 11 bankruptcy as of July 1995. Charitable contributions were severely curtailed.

Foundation Officials

Christian L. Oberbeck: trustee
Malvin Gustav Sandler: trustee B Pittsburgh, PA 1946. ED Bucknell University BS (1967); Duquesne University JD (1972). PRIM CORP EMPL senior vice president, general counsel, secretary: Sharon Steel Corp. CORP AFFIL member: Pennsylvania Bar Association; member: Coalition Empl through Exports; member: America Bar Association; member: America Trial Lawyers Association. NONPR AFFIL member: Delta Theta Phi.
Hume R. Steyer: trustee

Grants Analysis

Disclosure Period: calendar year ending 2000
Total Grants: $158,736*
Number of Grants: 15
Average Grant: $9,064*
Highest Grant: $31,836
Typical Range: $1,000 to $20,000
*Note: Giving excludes scholarships and United Way. Average grant figure excludes highest grant.

Recent Grants

Note: Grants derived from 1999 Form 990.

General

24,884	Pennsylvania State University, Sharon, PA -- spring tuition
24,452	St. Michael School, Greenville, PA -- grant to upgrade computer technology
20,000	Phillips Exeter Academy, Exeter, NH -- renaissance scholarship fund
20,000	United Way of Mercer County, Sharon, PA -- contribution campaign
15,000	Prince of Peace Center, Youngstown, OH -- grant to purchase a mini van
15,000	Westminster College, New Wilmington, PA -- grants for scholars
14,000	Keystone Blind Association, Sharon, PA -- development of an adaptive technology center
10,000	Greenwich Country Day School, Greenwich, CT -- trustee initiated grant
10,000	Mercer County Family Center, Farrell, PA -- grant for fun with nature summer camp
10,000	MSGR Geno Monti School, Farrell, PA -- scholarship assistance

EVELYN SHARP FOUNDATION

Giving Contact

Paul Cronson, Secretary & Trustee
c/o Peter Sharp & Co.
545 Madison Ave.
New York, NY 10022
Phone: (212)977-1300

Description

Founded: 1952
EIN: 136119532
Organization Type: Private Foundation
Giving Locations: NY
Grant Types: General Support.

Donor Information

Founder: Evelyn Sharp

Financial Summary

Total Giving: $493,844 (fiscal year ending June 30, 2000); $480,328 (fiscal 1999); $496,856 (fiscal 1998)
Assets: $15,492,320 (fiscal 2000); $16,774,227 (fiscal 1999); $12,585,114 (fiscal 1998)

Typical Recipients

Arts & Humanities: Arts Associations & Councils, Arts Centers, Arts Funds, Arts Outreach, Ballet, Dance, Ethnic & Folk Arts, Arts & Humanities-General, Libraries, Museums/Galleries, Music, Opera, Performing Arts, Public Broadcasting, Theater
Civic & Public Affairs: Botanical Gardens/Parks, Employment/Job Training, Civic & Public Affairs-General, Parades/Festivals, Public Policy, Urban & Community Affairs, Women's Affairs
Education: Arts/Humanities Education, Colleges & Universities, Education-General, Private Education (Precollege)
Health: Heart, Hospitals, Medical Research, Prenatal Health Issues
International: Foreign Arts Organizations, International Organizations, International Relations
Religion: Jewish Causes, Religious Organizations, Religious Welfare
Science: Science Museums
Social Services: Child Welfare, Community Service Organizations, Family Planning, Family Services, People with Disabilities, Youth Organizations

Application Procedures

Initial Contact: Send a brief letter of inquiry.
Deadlines: None.

Foundation Officials

Mary Cronson: president, trustee
Paul Cronson: secretary, trustee
Barry Tobias: treasurer, trustee
Claus Virch: trustee

Grants Analysis

Disclosure Period: fiscal year ending June 30, 2000
Total Grants: $493,844
Number of Grants: 144
Average Grant: $2,579*
Highest Grant: $125,000
Typical Range: $1,000 to $5,000
*Note: Average grant figure excludes highest grant.

Recent Grants

Note: Grants derived from fiscal 1999 Form 990.

General

50,000	Julliard School, New York, NY
50,000	Solomon Guggenheim Museum, New York, NY

40,000	New York City Opera, New York, NY
30,000	New York City Ballet, New York, NY
20,000	Planned Parenthood of New York City, New York, NY
10,000	Brooklyn Academy of Music, Brooklyn, NY
10,000	Donald Byrd Dance Foundation, New York, NY
10,000	La Maison Francaise, New York, NY
10,000	Mount Sinai Hospital, New York, NY
10,000	New York City Opera, New York, NY

SHATZ, SCHWARTZ & FENTIN PC

Company Headquarters
1441 Main St., No. 1100
Springfield, MA 01103

Company Description
SIC(s): 8100 Legal Services.

Shatz, Schwartz & Fentin Charitable Foundation

Giving Contact
Steven J. Schwartz, Trustee
1441 Main St., Suite 1100
Springfield, MA 01103
Phone: (413)737-1131
Fax: (413)736-0375

Description
EIN: 042712836
Organization Type: Corporate Foundation
Giving Locations: headquarters area only.
Grant Types: General Support.

Donor Information
Founder: Gary S. Fentin, Timothy P. Mulhern, Steven J. Schwartz, Stephen A. Shatz, James B. Sheils

Financial Summary
Total Giving: $52,492 (fiscal year ending August 31, 2002); $82,642 (fiscal 2001); $16,340 (fiscal 2000)
Giving Analysis: Giving for fiscal 2002 includes: foundation grants to United Way ($5,000); fiscal 2001: foundation grants to United Way ($5,000) fiscal 2000: foundation grants to United Way ($5,000)
Assets: $7,497 (fiscal 2002); $38,892 (fiscal 2001); $457 (fiscal 2000)
Gifts Received: $21,383 (fiscal 2002); $120,994 (fiscal 2001); $16,408 (fiscal 2000). Note: In fiscal 2001, contributions were received from Ellen W. Freyman and Steven Weiss. In fiscal 1995, contributions were received from Stephen A. Shatz ($3,250), Steven J. Schwartz ($3,250), Gary S. Fentin ($3,000), Timothy P. Mulhern ($1,750), James B. Sheils ($1,100), and Ann I. Weber ($1,000).

Typical Recipients
Arts & Humanities: Arts Associations & Councils, Libraries, Public Broadcasting
Civic & Public Affairs: Clubs, Civic & Public Affairs-General, Housing, Law & Justice, Legal Aid, Parades/Festivals, Urban & Community Affairs
Education: Afterschool/Enrichment Programs, Arts/Humanities Education, Business Education, Community & Junior Colleges, Education-General, Private Education (Precollege), Public Education (Precollege), School Volunteerism, Secondary Education (Public), Student Aid
Environment: Environment-General
Health: AIDS/HIV, Alzheimers Disease, Cancer, Children's Health/Hospitals, Clinics/Medical Centers, Emergency/Ambulance Services, Heart, Hospices, Research/Studies Institutes, Respiratory, Single-Disease Health Associations
Religion: Jewish Causes, Synagogues/Temples
Social Services: Child Welfare, Community Service Organizations, Day Care, Family Services, Food/Clothing Distribution, People with Disabilities, Recreation & Athletics, Scouts, Senior Services, United Funds/United Ways, YMCA/YWCA/YMHA/YWHA, Youth Organizations

Application Procedures
Initial Contact: The foundation has no formal grant application procedure or application form.
Deadlines: None.

Corporate Officials
Gary S. Fentin: senior partner PRIM CORP EMPL senior partner: Shatz Schwartz & Fentin PC.
Timothy P. Mulhern: partner PRIM CORP EMPL partner: Shatz Schwartz & Fentin PC.
Steven J. Schwartz: senior partner PRIM CORP EMPL senior partner: Shatz Schwartz & Fentin PC.
Stephen A. Shatz: counsel PRIM CORP EMPL counsel: Shatz Schwartz & Fentin PC.
James Bernard Sheils: partner, vice president B New Rochelle, NY 1950. ED Holy Cross College AB (1972); Boston College JD (1975). PRIM CORP EMPL partner, vice president: Shatz Schwartz & Fentin PC. NONPR AFFIL member: Massachusetts Bar Association; member: Smaller Business Association; member: Hampden County Bar Association; member: American Bar Association; member: Association Commercial Financial Attorney.
A. I. Weber: partner PRIM CORP EMPL partner: Shatz Schwartz & Fentin PC.

Foundation Officials
Gary S. Fentin: trustee (see above)
Timothy P. Mulhern: trustee (see above)
Steven J. Schwartz: trustee (see above)
Stephen A. Shatz: trustee (see above)
James Bernard Sheils: trustee (see above)

Grants Analysis
Disclosure Period: fiscal year ending August 31, 2002
Total Grants: $47,492*
Number of Grants: 30
Average Grant: $431*
Highest Grant: $35,000
Lowest Grant: $25
Typical Range: $100 to $1,000
*****Note:** Giving excludes United Way. Average grant figure excludes highest grant.

Recent Grants
Note: Grants derived from 2000 Form 990.

Library-Related

2,050	Springfield Library and Museums Association, Springfield, MA -- support for public libraries and museums

General

5,000	United Way, Springfield, MA
1,700	Business Friends of the Arts, Springfield, MA -- promote appreciation for the arts
1,000	Community Music School, Springfield, MA -- provide support for education in music
1,000	Ludlow Boys and Girls Club, Ludlow, MA -- provide support for childcare and social program
1,000	Western Massachusetts Legal Services, Springfield, MA -- provide legal representation to low income
600	Community Music School of Springfield, Springfield, MA -- to provide education in music
500	Center for Human Development, Springfield, MA -- provide support for anti-truancy program
500	Open Pantry Community Services, Springfield, MA -- to feed homeless and indigent persons
500	Pioneer Valley Girl Scout Council, Inc., East Longmeadow, MA -- support programs to enrich the lives of girls
400	Goodwill Industries of Springfield-Hartford, Springfield, MA -- provide support and training for people in need

ARCH W. SHAW FOUNDATION

Giving Contact
William W. Shaw, Trustee
HC 3 Box 60B
Birch Tree, MO 65438
Phone: (417)764-3701
Fax: (417)764-3706

Description
Founded: 1949
EIN: 366055262
Organization Type: Private Foundation
Giving Locations: IL; MA; MO
Grant Types: General Support.

Donor Information
Founder: the late Arch W. Shaw

Financial Summary
Total Giving: $525,000 (2001); $550,000 (2000); $650,000 (1999)
Giving Analysis: Giving for 1999 includes: foundation scholarships ($30,000)
Assets: $11,458,670 (2001); $10,114,672 (2000); $12,065,236 (1999)

Typical Recipients
Arts & Humanities: Historic Preservation, History & Archaeology, Libraries, Museums/Galleries, Music, Theater
Civic & Public Affairs: Botanical Gardens/Parks, Clubs, Law & Justice, Women's Affairs, Zoos/Aquariums
Education: Arts/Humanities Education, Colleges & Universities, Environmental Education, Medical Education, Private Education (Precollege), Science/Mathematics Education, Secondary Education (Private), Student Aid
Environment: Environment-General, Resource Conservation
Health: Alzheimers Disease, Cancer, Children's Health/Hospitals, Clinics/Medical Centers, Diabetes, Emergency/Ambulance Services, Eyes/Blindness, Health Funds, Hospices, Hospitals, Medical Rehabilitation, Medical Research, Outpatient Health Care, Prenatal Health Issues
International: International Relief Efforts
Religion: Religious Organizations, Religious Welfare
Social Services: Child Welfare, Community Centers, Community Service Organizations, Emergency Relief, Family Services, Food/Clothing Distribution, People with Disabilities, Substance Abuse, United Funds/United Ways, Youth Organizations

Application Procedures
Initial Contact: Send a brief letter of inquiry.
Application Requirements: Describe purpose of funds sought.
Deadlines: None.

Restrictions
Does not support individuals or private foundations.

Foundation Officials
Arch W. Shaw, II: trustee
Bruce P. Shaw: trustee
Roger D. Shaw, Jr.: trustee
William J. Shaw: trustee PRIM CORP EMPL president, chief operating officer: Marriott International Inc.
William W. Shaw: trustee

Grants Analysis
Disclosure Period: calendar year ending 2001
Total Grants: $525,000
Number of Grants: 79
Average Grant: $6,646
Highest Grant: $30,000
Typical Range: $2,500 to $15,000

Recent Grants
Note: Grants derived from 2001 Form 990.

General

30,000	Good Shepherd Hospital, Barrington, IL -- outpatient center
25,000	Ozarks Medical Center Foundation, West Plains, MO -- endowment
23,000	Children's Service Society, Racine, WI
20,000	Good Shepherd Hospital, Barrington, IL -- outpatient center
20,000	Theater Workshop of Nantucket, Nantucket, MA
15,000	Fessenden School, West Newton, MA -- endowment
15,000	Yale University, New Haven, CT
10,000	American Red Cross-Kansas City, Kansas City, MO
10,000	Bowdoin College, Bowdoin, ME
10,000	Christos House, West Plains, MO

SHAW'S SUPERMARKETS, INC.

Company Headquarters
East Bridgewater, MA
Web: http://www.shaws.com

Company Description
Revenue: US$4.4 billion (2001)
Employees: 29765 (2001)
SIC(s): 5411 Grocery Stores.
Parent Company: J. Sainsbury Plc, 33 Holborn, London, United Kingdom

Operating Locations
Shaw's Supermarkets, Inc. (CT; ME--Portland; MA; NH; NJ--East Bridgewater)

Nonmonetary Support
Type: Donated Products

Shaw's Supermarkets Charitable Foundation

Giving Contact
Bernard J. Rogan, Corporate Communications Director
Shaw's Supermarkets, Inc.
140 Laurel Street
PO Box 600
East Bridgewater, MA 02333
Phone: (508)350-3316
Fax: (508)350-3112
Web: http://www.shaws.com/Public/about_us/community_commitment.cfm

Alternate Contact
Shaw's Supermarkets Charitable Foundation
Fleet National Bank, Trustee
Two Portland Square
Portland, ME 04104

Description
Founded: 1959
EIN: 016008389
Organization Type: Corporate Foundation
Giving Locations: CT; ME; MA; NH; RI; VT: headquarters and operating communities.
Grant Types: Capital, Challenge, General Support.

Donor Information
Founder: Brockton Public Market, Inc. & George C. Shaw Co., & Subsidiaries

Financial Summary
Total Giving: $508,500 (fiscal year ending July 31, 2001); $190,200 (fiscal 2000); $447,000 (fiscal 1998). Note: Contributes through corporate direct giving program and foundation.
Giving Analysis: Giving for fiscal 2001 includes: foundation ($208,500); foundation grants to United Way ($300,000); fiscal 2000: foundation grants to United Way ($23,700); foundation ($166,500); fiscal 1998: foundation grants to United Way ($288,000)
Assets: $1,414,044 (fiscal 2001); $975,173 (fiscal 2000); $1,531,686 (fiscal 1998)
Gifts Received: $940,000 (fiscal 2001); $300,000 (fiscal 1998); $250,000 (fiscal 1997). Note: Contributions are received from Shaw's Supermarkets.

Typical Recipients
Arts & Humanities: Arts Appreciation, Arts Associations & Councils, Arts Funds, Arts Outreach, Historic Preservation, History & Archaeology, Libraries, Museums/Galleries, Music, Public Broadcasting, Theater
Civic & Public Affairs: Business/Free Enterprise, Community Foundations, Economic Development, Civic & Public Affairs-General, Safety, Urban & Community Affairs, Zoos/Aquariums
Education: Colleges & Universities, Education Funds, Environmental Education, Secondary Education (Public)
Environment: Environment-General
Health: Children's Health/Hospitals, Clinics/Medical Centers, Emergency/Ambulance Services, Eyes/Blindness, Geriatric Health, Health Funds, Health Organizations, Hospitals, Nursing Services, Public Health, Single-Disease Health Associations
Science: Science Museums
Social Services: Child Welfare, Community Service Organizations, Day Care, Food/Clothing Distribution, Recreation & Athletics, Senior Services, Shelters/Homelessness, United Funds/United Ways, YMCA/YWCA/YMHA/YWHA, Youth Organizations

Application Procedures
Initial Contact: For regional requests in Maine, New Hampshire, Vermont and the Greater Boston area of Massachusetts, contact: Regional Vice President, Northern Region Office, Shaw's Supermarkets, Inc., P.O. Box 3566 Portland, ME 04104 For requests in Connecticut, Rhode Island and all other parts of Massachusetts, contact: Regional Vice President, Southern Region Office, Shaw's Supermarkets, Inc., P.O. Box 300 South Easton, MA 02375. For corporate funding, contact: Senior Vice President, Operations Shaw's Supermarkets, Inc., 140 Laurel St., East Bridgewater, MA 02333.
Application Requirements: Include proof of 501(c)(3) status and full description of event or cause with request.

Additional Information
Trust(s): Fleet National Bank

Corporate Officials
David Brimner: chairman vice president administration, treasurer, director PRIM CORP EMPL chairman: Shaw's Supermarkets, Inc.
Ross McLaren: chief executive officer PRIM CORP EMPL chief executive officer: Shaw's Supermarkets, Inc.
Scott W. Ramsay: executive vice president administration, treasurer, director PRIM CORP EMPL executive vice president administration, treasurer, director: Shaw's Supermarkets, Inc. ADD CORP EMPL treasurer: Shaw Equipment Corp.

Foundation Officials
Scott W. Ramsay: trustee (see above)

Grants Analysis
Disclosure Period: fiscal year ending July 31, 2001
Total Grants: $208,500*
Number of Grants: 28
Average Grant: $4,769*
Highest Grant: $80,000
Lowest Grant: $1,000
Typical Range: $1,000 to $10,000
Note: Giving excludes corporate direct giving; United Way. Average grant figure excludes highest grant.

Recent Grants
Note: Grants derived from 2001 Form 990.

General

300,000	United Ways of New England, Boston, MA
80,000	Old Colony Y, Brockton, MA
10,000	Fuller Museum of Art, Brockton, MA
10,000	Good Shepherd Food Bank, Auburn, ME
10,000	Maine Discovery Museum, Portland, ME
10,000	South Shore Health and Education Foundation, South Weymouth, MA
6,000	Boys and Girls Club of Taunton, Taunton, MA
6,000	Young Audiences of Massachusetts, Boston, MA
5,000	Boston Medical Center, Boston, MA
5,000	Boys and Girls Club of Brockton, Brockton, MA

SHEAFFER PEN CORP.

Company Headquarters
Fort Madison, IA
Web: http://www.bicpen.com

Company Description
Former Name: Sheaffer Inc.
Revenue: US$69.5 million (2001)
Employees: 450 (2001)
SIC(s): 3951 Pens & Mechanical Pencils.

Operating Locations
Gefinor U.S.A. (NY--New York); Sheaffer Pen Corp. (IA--Fort Madison); Sheaffer Pen Crownmark (RI--Lincoln)

Nonmonetary Support
Type: Donated Products; Workplace Solicitation

Giving Contact
Michele Beach, Admin. Asst.
301 Ave. H
Ft. Madison, IA 52627
Phone: (319)372-3300
Fax: (319)376-3148
E-mail: michele.beach@brcworld.com

Description

Organization Type: Corporate Giving Program
Grant Types: Capital, General Support.

Typical Recipients

Arts & Humanities: Arts Associations & Councils, Arts Centers, Community Arts, Dance, Historic Preservation, Libraries, Museums/Galleries, Music, Performing Arts, Theater
Civic & Public Affairs: Employment/Job Training
Education: Colleges & Universities
Health: Health Policy/Cost Containment, Health Organizations, Hospitals, Mental Health, Single-Disease Health Associations
Social Services: Child Welfare, Community Centers, Community Service Organizations, Family Services, People with Disabilities, Substance Abuse, United Funds/United Ways, Youth Organizations

Application Procedures

Initial Contact: For large grants, write letter one year in advance. For smaller contributions, send a letter any time and include the same information.
Application Requirements: Include a description of organization, amount and purpose of funds sought, a recently audited financial statement, and proof of tax-exempt status.

Corporate Officials

Keith Bloomquist: controller, chief operating officer, director PRIM CORP EMPL controller: Sheaffer Pen Corp.
Owen Jones: chief executive officer, chief operating officer, director PRIM CORP EMPL chief executive officer, chief operating officer, director: Sheaffer Pen Corp.

EDNA M. SHEARY TRUST FOR CHARITY

Giving Contact

Martha M. Heil, Senior Trust Specialist
c/o Mellon Bank NA
PO Box 346
Lewisburg, PA 17837
Phone: (717)523-1230

Description

Founded: 1991
EIN: 251695940
Organization Type: Private Foundation
Giving Locations: PA
Grant Types: General Support.

Donor Information

Founder: Established in 1991 by the late Edna M. Sheary.

Financial Summary

Total Giving: $397,983 (fiscal year ending May 31, 2001); $506,930 (fiscal 2000); $768,424 (fiscal 1999)
Assets: $1,672,338 (fiscal 2001); $2,034,828 (fiscal 2000); $2,360,791 (fiscal 1999)

Typical Recipients

Arts & Humanities: History & Archaeology, Libraries, Museums/Galleries, Music, Public Broadcasting
Civic & Public Affairs: Business/Free Enterprise, Civic & Public Affairs-General, Legal Aid, Public Policy, Safety, Urban & Community Affairs, Women's Affairs
Education: Colleges & Universities, Education-General, Private Education (Precollege), Public Education (Precollege), School Volunteerism, Secondary Education (Public)
Environment: Resource Conservation

Health: Cancer, Emergency/Ambulance Services, Health Organizations, Home-Care Services, Hospitals, Long-Term Care, Research/Studies Institutes
Religion: Churches, Religion-General, Ministries, Religious Organizations, Religious Welfare, Seminaries
Social Services: Camps, Community Centers, Community Service Organizations, Day Care, Family Services, People with Disabilities, Recreation & Athletics, Scouts, Youth Organizations

Application Procedures

Initial Contact: Request application form.
Deadlines: April 1.

Additional Information

Publications: Application Form
Trust(s): Mellon Bank NA NA

Grants Analysis

Disclosure Period: fiscal year ending May 31, 2001
Total Grants: $397,983
Number of Grants: 14
Average Grant: $8,908*
Highest Grant: $200,000
Typical Range: $5,000 to $20,000
***Note:** Average grant excludes three highest grants ($300,000).

Recent Grants

Note: Grants derived from 2000 Form 990.

Library-Related
50,000	Public Library Union County	
40,000	Kaufman County Library, Kaufman, TX	

General
200,000	Christ Lutheran Church, Abbotsford, WI	
50,000	Hemlock Girl Scout Council, Harrisburg, PA	
50,000	Susquehanna University, Selinsgrove, PA	
30,000	Mifflinburg Buggy Museum	
22,250	Albright Life Learning, Reading, PA	
20,000	Evangelical Community Hospital, Lewisburg, PA	
12,716	Slifer House Museum	
9,088	Messiah Evangelical Lutheran Church, Fairview Park, OH	
8,947	Noah's Ark Day Care Center	
6,525	Concern, Bartlesville, OK	

RALPH C. SHELDON FOUNDATION INC.

Giving Contact

Miles L. Lasser, Executive Director, Secretary & Assistant Treasurer
7 E. 3rd St.
Jamestown, NY 14701
Phone: (716)664-9890
Fax: (716)483-6116

Description

Founded: 1948
EIN: 166030502
Organization Type: Private Foundation
Giving Locations: NY: Southern Chautauqua County
Grant Types: Capital, Emergency, General Support.

Donor Information

Founder: Julia S. Livengood, Isabel M. Sheldon

Financial Summary

Total Giving: $1,680,312 (fiscal year ending May 31, 2002); $1,477,190 (fiscal 2001); $1,400,000 (fiscal 2000 approx)

Giving Analysis: Giving for fiscal 2002 includes: foundation grants to United Way ($88,500); fiscal 2001: foundation grants to United Way ($83,000); fiscal 1999: foundation grants to United Way ($67,000); foundation grants to United Way ($68,300); foundation ($1,035,117).
Assets: $9,441,899 (fiscal 2002); $10,152,667 (fiscal 2001); $10,431,982 (fiscal 1999)
Gifts Received: $1,737,326 (fiscal 2002); $1,380,143 (fiscal 2001); $1,086,042 (fiscal 1997). Note: Contributions were received from the Ralph C. Sheldon Trust.

Typical Recipients

Arts & Humanities: Arts Associations & Councils, Arts Centers, Arts Funds, Community Arts, Arts & Humanities-General, History & Archaeology, Libraries, Museums/Galleries, Music, Performing Arts, Theater
Civic & Public Affairs: Community Foundations, Economic Development, Employment/Job Training, Hispanic Affairs, Housing, Urban & Community Affairs, Zoos/Aquariums
Education: Colleges & Universities, Community & Junior Colleges, Continuing Education, Education-General, Literacy, Private Education (Precollege), Public Education (Precollege), Special Education, Student Aid
Environment: Environment-General, Resource Conservation, Wildlife Protection
Health: Cancer, Heart, Hospices, Hospitals, Medical Training, Nursing Services
Social Services: Big Brother/Big Sister, Camps, Child Welfare, Community Service Organizations, Crime Prevention, Day Care, Family Services, Food/Clothing Distribution, People with Disabilities, Recreation & Athletics, Scouts, Senior Services, United Funds/United Ways, YMCA/YWCA/YMHA/YWHA, Youth Organizations

Application Procedures

Initial Contact: Send a brief letter of inquiry.
Application Requirements: Include a description of organization, amount requested, purpose of funds sought, how project benefits Southern Chantauqua County, recently audited financial statement, and proof of tax-exempt status.
Deadlines: None.

Restrictions

Does not support individuals, religious organizations for sectarian purposes, political or lobbying groups, or organizations outside operating areas. Only supports organizations in Southern Chautauqua County.

Additional Information

Publications: Application Form

Foundation Officials

Mark I. Hampton: vice president
Miles L. Lasser: executive director
J. Elizabeth Sheldon: president
Peter B. Sullivan: treasurer, assistant secretary
Barclay O. Wellman: vice president

Grants Analysis

Disclosure Period: fiscal year ending May 31, 2002
Total Grants: $1,591,812*
Number of Grants: 64
Average Grant: $11,341*
Highest Grant: $600,000
Lowest Grant: $100
Typical Range: $1,000 to $20,000
***Note:** Giving excludes United Way. Average grant figure excludes three highest grants ($900,000).

Recent Grants

Note: Grants derived from 2000 Form 990.

Library-Related
100,000	James Prendergast Library Association, Jamestown, PA -- air conditioner system	

70,000	Chautauqua Catteraugus Library System, Jamestown, NY -- new bookmobile
65,000	James Prendergast Library Association, Jamestown, PA -- books and tapes
57,500	Sinclairville Free Library, Sinclairville, NY

General

340,000	Lutheran Social Services of Upstate New York, Inc., Jamestown, NY -- retirement
25,0000	Fund for the Arts of Chautauqua County, Jamestown, NY -- annual fund drive
115,000	YMCA, Jamestown, NY -- Camp Onyasha
100,000	Jamestown Community College, Jamestown, NY -- Sheldon House
75,000	United Way of Southern Chautauqua County, Chautauqua, NY -- 1999 fund drive
55,172	Chautauqua Lake Association, Chautauqua, NY -- equipment
50,000	YMCA/Chautauqua Striders, Jamestown, NY -- joint outreach program
50,000	YWCA, Jamestown, NY -- capital campaign
45,000	Chautauqua Institution, Jamestown, NY -- annual fund drive
45,000	Chautauqua Striders, Chautauqua, NY -- lighted school house program

SHELL OIL CO.

Company Headquarters

One Shell Plaza
Houston, TX 77002
Web: http://www.shellus.com

Company Description

Acquired: Pennzoil-Quaker State Co. (2002).
Revenue: US$26.943 billion (2001)
Employees: 0 (2001)
SIC(s): 1311 Crude Petroleum & Natural Gas, 2819 Industrial Inorganic Chemicals Nec, 2822 Synthetic Rubber, 2879 Agricultural Chemicals Nec.
Parent Company: Royal Dutch/Shell Group of Companies, Carel Van Bylandtlaan 16, The Hague, Netherlands

Operating Locations

Billiton Metals, Inc. (NY--New York); Criterion Catalyst Co. L.P. (TX--Houston); LL&E Petroleum Marketing (LA--New Orleans); Shell Chemical Co. (TX--Houston); Shell Development Co. (TX--Houston); Shell Oil Co. (CA--Bishop, Concord, Elk Grove, Livermore, Los Angeles, Madera, Martinez, Moreno Valley, Riverside, San Bruno, San Jose, Van Nuys, Willows; CT--Bridgeport; DC--Washington; FL--Bradenton, Fort Lauderdale, Holly Hill, Melbourne, Miami, New Port Richey, North Port, Ocala, Tampa; GA--Atlanta, Nashville; HI--Honolulu, Kahului; IL--Arlington Heights, Berwyn, Chatham, Effingham, Harristown, Mount Auburn, Sibley, Skokie; IN--Hammond; KY--Louisville; LA--Gibson, Golden Meadow, Kenner, Metairie, Norco, Plaquemine; MD--Rockville; MA--Fall River, West Boylston, Westwood, Worcester; MI--Farmington Hills, Grand Haven, Jackson, South Boardman, Spring Lake; MN--Minneapolis; MS--Collins, Columbus, Jackson, Pelahatchie; MO--St. Louis; NV--Reno; NJ--Swearen; NY--Jamaica, New York; OH--Cincinnati, Columbus, Dayton, Lima, Sunbury, Tipp City, Westerville, Willoughby; PA--Pittsburgh; SC--Spartanburg; TN--Knoxville; TX--Baytown, Deer Park, Douglassville, Houston, Mount Pleasant, Pharr, Seminole, Sugar Land; VA--Reston); Shell Pipe Line Corp. (TX--Houston); Tejas Gas Corp. (TX--Houston)
Note: Operates internationally.

Nonmonetary Support

Type: Loaned Employees; Loaned Executives
Volunteer Programs: Company sponsors "Shell Employees and Retirees Volunteerism Effort" (SERVE), through which company employees and retirees have participated in housing rehabilitation projects, educational television solicitations, school clothing drives, and picnics for mentally handicapped children. Employees also serve on the boards of various organizations and loaned executives work with United Way campaigns.
Note: Contact the Manager of Corporate Relations for nonmonetary support information.

Shell Oil Co. Foundation

Giving Contact

Betty Lynn McHam, vice president
Shell Oil Co. Foundation
One Shell Plaza
PO Box 2099
Houston, TX 77252
Phone: (713)241-4480
Fax: (713)241-3329
E-mail: SOCFoundation@shellus.com
Web: http://www.countonshell.com/community/involvement/shell_foundation.html

Description

Founded: 1953
EIN: 136066583
Organization Type: Corporate Foundation
Giving Locations: nationally, with emphasis on communities where Shell employees are located.
Grant Types: Capital, Department, Emergency, Employee Matching Gifts, Fellowship, General Support, Operating Expenses, Project, Research.
Note: Employee matching gift ratio: 2 to 1 up to $500; 1 to 1 up to $5,000 per employee annually, for higher education only.

Donor Information

Founder: Shell Oil Co. & other participating companies.

Financial Summary

Total Giving: $23,000,000 (2002 approx); $24,039,664 (2001); $20,882,470 (2000). Note: Contributes through corporate direct giving program and foundation.
Giving Analysis: Giving for 2000 includes: foundation fellowships ($360,820); foundation scholarships ($599,498); foundation matching gifts ($2,735,905); foundation grants to United Way ($4,530,775); foundation ($12,655,472); 1999: foundation fellowships ($406,876); foundation scholarships ($615,000); foundation matching gifts ($2,584,240); foundation grants to United Way ($3,839,499); foundation ($12,905,273); 1997: foundation matching gifts ($2,373,833); foundation scholarships ($3,052,445); foundation ($15,306,671);
Assets: $66,393,687 (2001); $84,615,447 (2000); $60,752,688 (1999)
Gifts Received: $11,028,000 (2001); $1,290,897 (2000); $987,900 (1999). Note: In 2001, Shell Co. Foundation received contributionss from miscellaneous Shell Companies ($11,003,000); Ron Leftwich ($25,000).

Typical Recipients

Arts & Humanities: Arts Centers, Arts Festivals, Arts Outreach, Ballet, Dance, Historic Preservation, History & Archaeology, Libraries, Museums/Galleries, Music, Opera, Performing Arts, Theater
Civic & Public Affairs: African American Affairs, Botanical Gardens/Parks, Business/Free Enterprise, Civil Rights, Clubs, Community Foundations, Economic Development, Economic Policy, Employment/ Job Training, Civic & Public Affairs-General, Hispanic Affairs, Housing, Law & Justice, Parades/Festivals, Philanthropic Organizations, Public Policy, Rural Affairs, Safety, Urban & Community Affairs, Women's Affairs, Zoos/Aquariums, Zoos/Aquariums
Education: Business Education, Colleges & Universities, Economic Education, Education Associations, Education Funds, Education Reform, Elementary Education (Private), Engineering/Technological Education, Faculty Development, Education-General, Health & Physical Education, International Studies, Journalism/Media Education, Legal Education, Medical Education, Minority Education, Private Education (Precollege), Public Education (Precollege), Science/ Mathematics Education, Secondary Education (Private), Secondary Education (Public), Student Aid
Environment: Environment-General, Resource Conservation, Wildlife Protection
Health: Children's Health/Hospitals, Clinics/Medical Centers, Eyes/Blindness, Health Funds, Health Organizations, Heart, Hospices, Hospitals, Hospitals, Hospitals (University Affiliated), Medical Rehabilitation, Medical Research, Mental Health, Single-Disease Health Associations
International: International Organizations, International Peace & Security Issues, International Relations
Religion: Ministries, Religious Welfare
Science: Science Exhibits & Fairs, Science Museums, Scientific Centers & Institutes, Scientific Organizations
Social Services: Child Welfare, Community Centers, Community Service Organizations, Delinquency & Criminal Rehabilitation, Emergency Relief, Family Services, Food/Clothing Distribution, People with Disabilities, Recreation & Athletics, Scouts, Senior Services, Shelters/Homelessness, Substance Abuse, United Funds/United Ways, Volunteer Services, Youth Organizations

Application Procedures

Initial Contact: Send a brief letter and full proposal to the National Merit Scholarship Corporation.
Application Requirements: Include a description of structure, purpose, history, and programs of organization; summary of need for support and proposed use; detailed financial data on organization (independent audit, budget, sources of income, breakdown of expenditures by program, administration, and fund raising); copies of forms 501(c)(3), 509(a), and Form 990; list of donors, and their level of support.
Deadlines: August 15 before the year the organization or project needs funding.

Restrictions

Foundation does not fund organizations outside the United States; educational capital campaigns; endowments; endowed chairs at colleges and universities; or hospital operating expenses; fundraising events; or individuals. The foundation does not provide in-kind donations or product contributions.

Additional Information

Companies participating in the Shell Oil Co. Foundation include Shell Oil Co.; Shell Offshore, Inc.; Shell Pipe Line Corp.; Shell Western E&P, Inc.; Pecten Chemicals, Inc.; Pecten International Co.; and Pecten Middle East Services Co.
Shell Oil also contributes internationally through the Shell Foundation; see www.shellfoundation.org for details.
Publications: Foundation Annual Report

Corporate Officials

Michael Howard Grasley: senior vice president B Barberton, OH 1937. ED University of Kentucky MS; Ohio University (1958); University of Florida PhD (1963). PRIM CORP EMPL senior vice president: Shell Oil Co. NONPR AFFIL director: Chemical Manufacturers Association; member: Society Chemical Industry.

Foundation Officials

S. Allen Lackey: director B Jackson, MS 1942. ED University of Mississippi BBA (1963); University of Mississippi JD (1968). PRIM CORP EMPL vice president, general counsel: Shell Oil Co.

B. W. Levan: vice president, director B Saint Louis, IL 1941. ED Southern Illinois University (1964); University of Illinois MS (1966). PRIM CORP EMPL vice president human resources: Shell Oil Co.

Grants Analysis

Disclosure Period: calendar year ending 2001
Total Grants: $24,039,664*
Number of Grants: 751
Average Grant: $24,020
Highest Grant: $1,000,000
Lowest Grant: $825
Typical Range: $1,000 to $35,000
*Note: Giving excludes matching gifts, fellowships, scholarships, and United Way.

Recent Grants

Note: Grants derived from 2001 Form 990.

Library-Related
100,000	Library of Congress, Washington, DC

General
3,806,000	United Way of Texas Gulf Coast, Houston, TX
3,000,000	United Way of New York City, New York, NY
1,000,000	Cantor Fitzgerald Relief Fund, New York, NY
1,000,000	Community Foundation for the National Capital Region, Washington, DC
1,000,000	National Fish and Wildlife Foundation, Washington, DC
677,000	United Way Greater New Orleans Area, New Orleans, LA
500,000	Greater New Orleans Foundation, New Orleans, LA
250,000	Awty International School, Houston, TX
250,000	National Wildlife Federation, Vienna, VA
250,000	Nature Conservancy, Arlington, VA

SHELTER MUTUAL INSURANCE CO.

Company Headquarters

1817 W. Broadway
Columbia, MO 65203
Web: http://www.shelterinsurance.com

Company Description

Assets: US$752 million (2001)
Employees: 1600 (2001)
SIC(s): 6311 Life Insurance, 6321 Accident & Health Insurance.

Operating Locations

Shelter Mutual Insurance Co. (MO--Columbia)

Shelter Insurance Foundation

Giving Contact

Raymond E. Jones, Secretary & Director
1817 West Broadway
Columbia, MO 65218
Phone: (573)214-4290
Fax: (573)446-5727

Description

Founded: 1981
EIN: 431224155
Organization Type: Corporate Foundation

Giving Locations: AK; CO; IL; IN; IA; KS; KY; LA; MS; MO, Columbia; NE; OK; TN
Grant Types: General Support, Research, Scholarship.

Financial Summary

Total Giving: $623,787 (fiscal year ending June 30, 2001); $400,000 (fiscal 2000 approx); $469,540 (fiscal 1999). Note: Contributes through corporate direct giving program and foundation.
Giving Analysis: Giving for fiscal 2001 includes: foundation ($168,087); foundation scholarships ($455,000); fiscal 1999: foundation ($99,540); foundation scholarships ($370,000) fiscal 1997: foundation scholarships ($295,250).
Assets: $6,447,804 (fiscal 2001); $6,837,580 (fiscal 1999); $4,373,607 (fiscal 1997)
Gifts Received: $134,803 (fiscal 2001); $1,928,642 (fiscal 1999); $485,725 (fiscal 1997). Note: Contributions are received from Shelter Life Insurance Co., Shelter Mutual Insurance Co., the Buffalo News, and Sidlee W. Leeper.

Typical Recipients

Arts & Humanities: History & Archaeology, Libraries, Music
Civic & Public Affairs: Clubs, Civic & Public Affairs-General, Housing, Parades/Festivals, Public Policy, Safety, Urban & Community Affairs
Education: Arts/Humanities Education, Business Education, Colleges & Universities, Education Associations, Education-General, Legal Education, Medical Education, Private Education (Precollege), Public Education (Precollege), Religious Education, Secondary Education (Public), Special Education, Student Aid
Health: AIDS/HIV, Alzheimers Disease, Cancer, Children's Health/Hospitals, Heart, Medical Research, Single-Disease Health Associations
Religion: Churches, Religious Welfare
Social Services: Child Welfare, Community Service Organizations, Crime Prevention, People with Disabilities, Recreation & Athletics, Scouts, Senior Services, Youth Organizations

Application Procedures

Initial Contact: Send a preliminary letter to the foundation.
Application Requirements: Include a brief description of the request.
Deadlines: None.
Notes: Corporate grants are made only through scholarships by a local Shelter Insurance agent for local high schools in that area.

Corporate Officials

Max J. Dills: director PRIM CORP EMPL director: Shelter Mutual Insurance Co.
Robert J. Feller: vice president B Cairo, IL 1941. ED Western Illinois University (1964). PRIM CORP EMPL vice president: Shelter Mutual Insurance Co.
Raymond E. Jones: executive vice president, secretary B Chillocothe, MO 1941. ED Missouri State University (1962). PRIM CORP EMPL executive vice president, secretary: Shelter Mutual Insurance Co. CORP AFFIL secretary: Daniel Boone Underwriters LLC.
Gustav J. Lehr: chairman, director B 1930. PRIM CORP EMPL chairman, director: Shelter Mutual Insurance Co. CORP AFFIL chairman: Daniel Boone Underwriters LLC; chairman, director: Shelter General Insurance Co.
David C. Mattson: director PRIM CORP EMPL director: Shelter Mutual Insurance Co.

Foundation Officials

Robert T. Cox: director PRIM CORP EMPL executive: Ace Manufacturing & Parts Co. CORP AFFIL director: Shelter Financial Services.
J. Donald Duello: president, treasurer, director B 1943. ED University of Missouri, Columbia (1961-1965). PRIM CORP EMPL vice president finance:

Shelter Financial Services. CORP AFFIL vice president: Shelter General Insurance Co.
Jerry French: director
Raymond E. Jones: secretary, director (see above)
Gustav J. Lehr: vice president, director (see above)
John W. Lenox: director CORP AFFIL president: Shelter Financial Services; president: Shelter General Insurance Co.
Joe Moseley: director
James A. Offutt: director B Mexico, MO 1934. ED University of Missouri. PRIM CORP EMPL executive vice president, director, chairman: Shelter Mutual Insurance Co. CORP AFFIL director: Shelter Financial Services; vice president: Shelter General Insurance Co.

Grants Analysis

Disclosure Period: fiscal year ending June 30, 2001
Total Grants: $168,087*
Number of Grants: 76
Average Grant: $2,221
Highest Grant: $30,000
Lowest Grant: $100
Typical Range: $1,000 to $5,000
*Note: Giving excludes scholarships.

Recent Grants

Note: Grants derived from fiscal 2001 Form 990.

Library-Related
2,000	Daniel Boone Regional Library Foundation, Columbia, MO

General
30,000	University of Missouri Columbia, Columbia, MO
15,430	Fayette R-III Public Schools, Fayette, MO
11,800	University of Missouri Columbia, Columbia, MO
10,000	University of Missouri Columbia, Columbia, MO
5,000	Central Missouri State University, Warrensburg, MO
5,000	Central Missouri State University, Warrensburg, MO
5,000	Ellis Fischel Cancer Center, Columbia, MO
5,000	Missouri United Methodist Church Windows Capital Fund, Columbia, MO
5,000	Salvation Army, Columbia, MO -- for Tools for Schools
5,000	Show Me Central Habitat for Humanity, Columbia, MO

SHENANDOAH LIFE INSURANCE CO.

Company Headquarters

2301 Brambleton Ave., SW
Roanoke, VA 24015
Web: http://www.shenlife.com

Company Description

Assets: US$1.951 billion (2002)
Employees: 300 (2002)
SIC(s): 6311 Life Insurance.

Operating Locations

Shenandoah Life Insurance Co. (VA--Roanoke)

Nonmonetary Support

Type: Donated Equipment; In-kind Services; Loaned Employees; Loaned Executives; Workplace Solicitation

Giving Contact

Betty Lafon, Administrative Assistant to the
President
PO Box 12847
2301 Bramboeton Ave.
Roanoke, VA 24029
Phone: (540)985-4400
Fax: (540)857-5914

Description

Organization Type: Corporate Giving Program
Giving Locations: VA
Grant Types: Capital, Emergency, Employee Matching Gifts, General Support, Operating Expenses, Project, Scholarship.

Financial Summary

Total Giving: Figures do not include public relations
donations.

Typical Recipients

Arts & Humanities: Arts Appreciation, Arts Associa-
tions & Councils, Arts Centers, Dance, Ethnic & Folk
Arts, Historic Preservation, Libraries, Literary Arts,
Museums/Galleries, Music, Opera, Performing Arts,
Public Broadcasting, Theater, Visual Arts
Civic & Public Affairs: Civil Rights, Economic Devel-
opment, Economic Policy, Employment/Job Training,
Professional & Trade Associations, Safety, Urban &
Community Affairs, Zoos/Aquariums
Education: Business Education, Colleges & Univer-
sities, Community & Junior Colleges, Economic Edu-
cation, Education Associations, Education Funds,
Faculty Development, Health & Physical Education,
Medical Education, Minority Education, Special Edu-
cation, Student Aid
Environment: Environment-General
Health: Emergency/Ambulance Services, Health Pol-
icy/Cost Containment, Health Funds, Health Organi-
zations, Medical Research, Medical Training, Mental
Health, Single-Disease Health Associations
Science: Observatories & Planetariums, Science Exhibits & Fairs
Social Services: Community Service Organizations,
Counseling, Emergency Relief, Food/Clothing Distribution, Recreation & Athletics, Shelters/Home-
lessness, United Funds/United Ways, Youth Organizations

Application Procedures

Initial Contact: Send full proposal.
Application Requirements: Include a description of
organization, amount requested, the purpose of funds
sought, and proof of tax-exempt status. All requests
must be in writing.
Deadlines: None.

Restrictions

Does not support individuals, religious organizations
for sectarian purposes, entertainment groups, war
veterans organizations, advertising, athletic events
such as golf or tennis tournaments, fund-raising endeavors of United Way agencies, or political or lobbying groups.

Additional Information

Publications: Contributions Policy

Corporate Officials

Robert W. Clark: president, chief executive officer,
director B Brattleboro, VT 1946. ED University of Con-
necticut (1968); University of Hartford (1973). PRIM
CORP EMPL president, chief executive officer, direc-
tor: Shenandoah Life Insurance Co.
Warner Norris Dalhouse: director B Roanoke, VA
1934. ED University of Virginia BS (1956). PRIM
CORP EMPL director: Shenandoah Life Insurance
Co. CORP AFFIL chairman, chief executive officer:
First United Nations National Bank Virginia; director:
Carilion Health Systems. NONPR AFFIL member:

University Virginia; member: Virginia Governor Economic Advisory Council; president: Roanoke Public
Library Foundation; member: Partnership for Urban
Virginia.
Edward J. Machado: senior vice president, chief financial officer PRIM CORP EMPL senior vice president, chief financial officer: Shenandoah Life Insurance Co.

Grants Analysis

Note: Company reports that grant size varies.

SHENANDOAH TELECOMMUNICATIONS CO.

Company Headquarters

124 S. Main St.
Edinburg, VA 22824
Web: http://www.shentel.com

Company Description

Founded: 1902
Ticker: SHEN
Exchange: NASDAQ
Revenue: US$93 million (2002)
Employees: 268 (2002)
SIC(s): 4813 Telephone Communications Except Ra-
diotelephone, 4841 Cable & Other Pay Television
Services.

ShenTel Foundation

Giving Contact

Christopher E. French, President
ShenTel Foundation
PO Box 459
Edinburg, VA 22824
Phone: (540)984-4141

Description

Founded: 1990
EIN: 541549765
Organization Type: Corporate Foundation
Grant Types: General Support.

Donor Information

Founder: Shenandoah Telecommunications Co.

Financial Summary

Total Giving: $174,820 (2000); $68,636 (1996);
$78,459 (1995)
Assets: $2,849,556 (2000); $1,866,595 (1996);
$1,591,987 (1995)

Typical Recipients

Arts & Humanities: Libraries, Music, Public Broad-
casting
Civic & Public Affairs: Community Foundations,
Employment/Job Training, Civic & Public Affairs-Gen-
eral, Parades/Festivals, Safety
Education: Agricultural Education, Community & Ju-
nior Colleges, Education-General, Literacy, Private
Education (Precollege), Public Education (Precol-
lege), Student Aid
Health: Cancer, Emergency/Ambulance Services,
Heart, Hospitals, Prenatal Health Issues
Religion: Religious Welfare
Social Services: Community Service Organizations,
Counseling, Food/Clothing Distribution, Scouts, Shel-
ters/Homelessness

Application Procedures

Initial Contact: Request application form.
Application Requirements: With completed application, include the latest annual report, a list of board
members, and a current detailed budget.
Deadlines: None.

Restrictions

Limited to organizations within the service area of
Shenandoah Telecommunications Company and its
subsidiaries.

Corporate Officials

Noel M. Borden: vice chairman, director PRIM CORP
EMPL vice chairman, director: Shenandoah Telecom-
munications Co.
Christopher E. French: president, director PRIM
CORP EMPL president, director: Shenandoah Tele-
communications Co.
Warren B. French, Jr.: chairman, director PRIM
CORP EMPL chairman, director: Shenandoah Tele-
communications Co.
Lawrence Paxton: vice president financial PRIM
CORP EMPL vice president financial: Shenandoah
Telecommunications Co.

Foundation Officials

Noel M. Borden: secretary (see above)
Dick D. Bowman: treasurer
Ken L. Burch: director
Christopher E. French: president (see above)
Warren B. French, Jr.: director (see above)
Grover M. Holler, Jr.: director
I. Clinton Miller: director CORP AFFIL director:
Shenandoah Telecommunications Co.
Harold Morrison, Jr.: director CORP AFFIL director:
Shenandoah Telecommunications Co.
Zane Neff: director CORP AFFIL director: Shenan-
doah Telecommunications Co.
Lawrence Paxton: vice president fin (see above)
James E. Zerkel, II: director CORP AFFIL director:
Shenandoah Telecommunications Co.

Grants Analysis

Disclosure Period: calendar year ending 2000
Total Grants: $174,820
Number of Grants: 136*
Average Grant: $1,286
Highest Grant: $40,000
Typical Range: $100 to $5,000
*Note: Number of grants is approximate.

Recent Grants

Note: Grants derived from 2000 Form 990.

Library-Related

40,000	Shenandoah County Central Library, Edinburg, VA
500	Fort Valley Community Library, Ft. Val-ley, VA
500	Mount Jackson Community Library, Mt. Jackson, VA
500	New Market Area Library, New Market, VA
500	Strasburg Community Library, Stras-burg, VA
500	Woodstock Community Library

General

30,000	Lord Fairfax Community College, Middle-town, VA
15,000	Massanutten Military Academy, Wood-stock, VA
10,000	Shenandoah Valley Academy
6,750	WVPT, Harrisonburg, VA
2,500	American Cancer Society, Woodstock, VA
2,500	Boy Scouts of America Shenandoah Area, Winchester, VA
1,500	Shenandoah Valley Music Festival, Woodstock, VA

1,250	Shenandoah Area Girls Scouts
1,000	Citizens Scholarship Foundation of Shenandoah County, Woodstock, VA
1,000	Shenandoah Community Foundation, Waynesboro, VA

HAROLD AND HELEN SHEPHERD FOUNDATION

Giving Contact

H. H. Hayner, Trustee
PO Box 1757
Walla Walla, WA 99362-0348
Phone: (509)527-3500

Description

Founded: 1996
EIN: 911708510
Organization Type: Private Foundation
Grant Types: General Support, Scholarship.

Financial Summary

Total Giving: $293,100 (2001); $197,520 (2000); $430,562 (1999)
Giving Analysis: Giving for 2001 includes: foundation scholarships ($71,000)
Assets: $5,626,259 (2001); $6,647,998 (2000); $8,077,897 (1999)
Gifts Received: $92,278 (1998); $4,913,983 (1996).
Note: In 1998, contributions were received from the Helen Shepherd Foundation ($80,682), Charles Schwab & Co. ($11,500), and Baker Boyer National Bank ($96).

Typical Recipients

Arts & Humanities: History & Archaeology, Libraries, Music
Civic & Public Affairs: Botanical Gardens/Parks, Chambers of Commerce, Municipalities/Towns, Professional & Trade Associations
Education: Colleges & Universities, Medical Education, Public Education (Precollege)
Health: Hospices, Public Health
Religion: Churches, Ministries
Social Services: Recreation & Athletics, Senior Services

Application Procedures

Initial Contact: Send a brief letter of inquiry.
Deadlines: November 1.

Foundation Officials

Herman Henry Hayner: trustee B Fairfield, WA September 25, 1916. ED Washington State University BA (1938); University of Oregon JD (1946). NONPR AFFIL member: Walla Walla County Bar Association; member: Washington State Bar Association; fellow: American College Trust & Estate Counsel; member: Walla Walla Chamber of Commerce; fellow: American Bar Association. CLUB AFFIL Walla Walla Country Club; Rotary Club.
Gary Houser: trustee

Grants Analysis

Disclosure Period: calendar year ending 2001
Total Grants: $222,100*
Number of Grants: 17
Average Grant: $10,719*
Highest Grant: $50,600
Lowest Grant: $500
Typical Range: $5,000 to $20,000
***Note:** Giving excludes scholarship. Average grant figure excludes highest grant.

Recent Grants

Note: Grants derived from 2000 Form 990.

Library-Related
20,000	Garfield County, Pomeroy, WA -- memorial library and fairgrounds

General
35,000	Crown of Thorns Church, Pomeroy, WA
33,000	Pomeroy School District, Pomeroy, WA -- operations
25,000	Washington State University, Pullman, WA -- Cougar Athletic Foundation
20,000	City of Pomeroy, Pomeroy, WA -- swimming pool maintenance
15,000	Garfield County Port District, Pomeroy, WA -- Road and Bridge Project
10,800	Pomeroy Youth Baseball, Pomeroy, WA -- baseball field upgrades
10,000	Walla Walla Symphony, Walla Walla, WA
10,000	Washington State University, Pullman, WA
7,000	City of Pomeroy, Pomeroy, WA -- Chamber of Commerce
5,000	Washington State University, Pullman, WA -- Veterinary Teaching Hospital

MARGARET E. SHERMAN TRUST

Giving Contact

Linwood M. Erskine, Jr., Trustee
Margaret E. Sherman Trust
30 Highland Street
Worcester, MA 01609-2704
Phone: (508)753-7100

Description

Founded: 1987
EIN: 046047750
Organization Type: Private Foundation
Giving Locations: MA: primarily Worcester County
Grant Types: General Support.

Financial Summary

Total Giving: $91,000 (2001); $93,000 (2000)
Assets: $1,956,103 (2001); $2,233,234 (2000)

Typical Recipients

Arts & Humanities: Historic Preservation, History & Archaeology, Libraries, Museums/Galleries, Music
Civic & Public Affairs: Botanical Gardens/Parks
Education: Colleges & Universities, Medical Education
Environment: Watershed
Health: Medical Research
Religion: Churches
Science: Scientific Centers & Institutes

Application Procedures

Initial Contact: The foundation reports no specific application guidelines. Send a brief letter of inquiry, including statement of purpose, amount requested, and proof of tax-exempt status.
Deadlines: None.

Restrictions

The foundation restricts its funding to historical, educational, and medical organizations in Massachusetts.

Foundation Officials

Linwood M. Erskine, Jr.: trustee

Grants Analysis

Disclosure Period: calendar year ending 2001
Total Grants: $91,000
Number of Grants: 20

Average Grant: $4,550
Highest Grant: $12,000
Lowest Grant: $2,000
Typical Range: $2,000 to $10,000

Recent Grants

Note: Grants derived from 2000 Form 990.

Library-Related
9,000	American Antiquarian Society, Worcester, MA -- research library
3,000	Beaman Memorial Public Library, West Boylston, MA
3,000	Northboro Public Library, Northboro, MA

General
9,000	Northboro Historical Society, Northboro, MA
9,000	Worcester County Horticultural Society, Boylston, MA
9,000	Worcester Historical Museum, Worcester, MA
6,000	Higgins Armory Museum, Worcester, MA
6,000	Worcester County Mechanics Association, Worcester, MA -- historic preservation
5,000	Gardner Museum, Gardner, MA
5,000	George Marston Whitin Community Association, Whitinsville, MA -- historic preservation
5,000	Worcester Foundation for Biomedical Research, Worcester, MA
3,000	EcoTarium, Worcester, MA
3,000	Friends of Wachusett Watershed, Sterling, MA

SHERWIN-WILLIAMS CO.

Company Headquarters

Cleveland, OH
Web: http://www.sherwinwilliams.com

Company Description

Founded: 1866
Ticker: SHW
Exchange: NYSE
Revenue: US$5.184 billion (2002)
Profit: US$127.6 million (2002)
Employees: 25789 (2002)
Fortune Rank: 321, per FORTUNE Magazine's list of 500 Largest U.S. Corporations (2002).
SIC(s): 2816 Inorganic Pigments, 2819 Industrial Inorganic Chemicals Nec, 2851 Paints & Allied Products, 2869 Industrial Organic Chemicals Nec.

Operating Locations

Sherwin-Williams Co. (CA--Anaheim, Emeryville, Hayward, Oakland; FL--Winter Haven; GA--Buford, La Grange, Morrow; IL--Effingham, Elk Grove Village; IN--Greencastle; KS--Coffeyville; MD--Baltimore, Crisfield, Hunt Valley; MI--Holland; NV--Reno, Sparks; NJ--Newark; OH--Bedford Heights, Columbus, Deshler; PA--York; PR--San Juan; TX--Garland, Waco)

Sherwin-Williams Foundation

Giving Contact

Barbara Gadosik, Director, Corporate Contributions
Sherwin-Williams Co.
101 Prospect Avenue NW
Cleveland, OH 44115
Phone: (216)566-2000
Fax: (216)566-3266

Description

EIN: 346555476
Organization Type: Corporate Foundation
Giving Locations: headquarters and operating communities, primarily Cleveland.
Grant Types: Capital, Employee Matching Gifts, General Support.

Financial Summary

Total Giving: $1,015,720 (2001); $998,657 (2000); $990,359 (1999). Note: Contributes through foundation only.
Giving Analysis: Giving for 2001 includes: foundation matching gifts ($177,476); 2000: foundation matching gifts ($184,172); foundation grants to United Way ($205,440); foundation ($609,045); 1999: foundation scholarships ($21,000); foundation matching gifts ($185,260); foundation grants to United Way ($207,250); foundation ($576,849);
Assets: $14,727,501 (2001); $15,055,692 (2000); $13,952,939 (1999)
Gifts Received: $1,000,000 (2000); $12,000 (1999); $660,000 (1996). Note: Foundation receives contributions from Sherwin-Williams Co.

Typical Recipients

Arts & Humanities: Arts Centers, Ballet, Arts & Humanities-General, Historic Preservation, History & Archaeology, Libraries, Museums/Galleries, Music, Opera, Performing Arts, Theater
Civic & Public Affairs: Business/Free Enterprise, Community Foundations, Economic Development, Economic Policy, Employment/Job Training, Civic & Public Affairs-General, Housing, Municipalities/Towns, Parades/Festivals, Philanthropic Organizations, Professional & Trade Associations, Public Policy, Safety, Urban & Community Affairs
Education: Agricultural Education, Business Education, Business-School Partnerships, Colleges & Universities, Economic Education, Education Funds, Engineering/Technological Education, Education-General, Medical Education, Medical Education, Minority Education, Preschool Education, Private Education (Precollege), Science/Mathematics Education, Secondary Education (Private), Student Aid, Vocational & Technical Education
Health: Cancer, Diabetes, Emergency/Ambulance Services, Hospices, Hospitals, Hospitals (University Affiliated), Long-Term Care, Medical Rehabilitation, Preventive Medicine/Wellness Organizations, Public Health, Single-Disease Health Associations
International: Health Care/Hospitals
Religion: Churches, Dioceses, Religion-General, Jewish Causes, Ministries, Religious Organizations, Religious Welfare
Science: Science Museums, Scientific Centers & Institutes
Social Services: Big Brother/Big Sister, Camps, Community Centers, Community Service Organizations, Crime Prevention, Family Services, People with Disabilities, Recreation & Athletics, Scouts, Senior Services, Shelters/Homelessness, Social Services-General, United Funds/United Ways, Volunteer Services, YMCA/YWCA/YMHA/YWHA, Youth Organizations

Application Procedures

Initial Contact: Send a written proposal.
Application Requirements: Include a description of organization, including its structure, purpose, and history; list of officers and directors; detailed description of current programs and activities; amount requested; purpose of funds sought; description of project, including community needs to be addressed, program objectives, activities to be undertaken, timetable, fully defined project budget, and sources of committed and pending support; current operating budget with income and expenditures; current list of donors and amounts received; recent annual report; most recently

audited financial statement; annual report; and proof of tax-exempt status.
Deadlines: None.

Restrictions

Foundation does not support endowments, individuals, research, religious or political organizations, dinners or special events, fraternal organizations, goodwill advertising, member agencies of united funds, sports programs, or elementary and secondary education. Only organizations serving company operating areas receive support.

Corporate Officials

Thomas Allen Commes: president, chief operating officer, director B Aurora, IL 1942. ED Saint Thomas College BA (1964). PRIM CORP EMPL president, chief operating officer, director: Sherwin-Williams Co. CORP AFFIL director: Centerior Energy Corp.; officer: KeyCorp.
Thomas E. Hopkins: vice president human resources ED Malone College (1978); Cleveland State University (1982). PRIM CORP EMPL vice president human resources: Sherwin-Williams Co. NONPR AFFIL member: Students Free Enterprise.

Foundation Officials

Barbara Gadosik: director corporate contributions PRIM CORP EMPL director corporate contributions: Sherwin-Williams Co.
Thomas E. Hopkins: assistant secretary, trustee (see above)

Grants Analysis

Disclosure Period: calendar year ending 2001
Total Grants: $622,974*
Number of Grants: 106
Average Grant: $5,877
Highest Grant: $140,000
Lowest Grant: $10
Typical Range: $1,000 to $15,000
*Note: Giving excludes matching gifts; scholarships; and United Way.

Recent Grants

Note: Grants derived from 2001 Form 990.

General

177,476	Matching Gift Plan
177,000	United Way Services, Inc., Cleveland, OH
40,000	City Mission, Cleveland, OH
37,500	Cleveland Tomorrow, Cleveland, OH
28,000	Musical Arts Association, Cleveland, OH
25,000	Students in Free Enterprise, Springfield, MO
20,000	Catholic Diocese of Cleveland Foundation, Cleveland, OH
20,000	Cleveland Advanced Manufacturing Program (CAMP), Cleveland, OH
20,000	Cleveland Scholarship Programs, Inc., Cleveland, OH
20,000	Great Lakes Museum, Cleveland, OH

BARBARA INGALLS SHOOK FOUNDATION

Giving Contact

Barbara Ingalls Shook, Chairman & Treasurer
206 Hart Fell Crescent
Birmingham, AL 35223-2905
Phone: (205)970-0060

Description

Founded: 1980
EIN: 630792812
Organization Type: Private Foundation
Giving Locations: AL; CO
Grant Types: General Support, Research.

Donor Information

Founder: Robert I. Ingalls Testamentary Trust II

Financial Summary

Total Giving: $320,255 (fiscal year ending August 31, 2001); $323,450 (fiscal 2000); $371,572 (fiscal 1999)
Assets: $7,068,820 (fiscal 2001); $8,417,913 (fiscal 2000); $8,071,687 (fiscal 1999)
Gifts Received: In 1990, contributions were received from Robert Ingalls Testamentary Trust.

Typical Recipients

Arts & Humanities: Arts Centers, Arts Festivals, Ballet, Dance, Film & Video, History & Archaeology, Libraries, Museums/Galleries, Music, Theater
Civic & Public Affairs: Botanical Gardens/Parks, Clubs, Community Foundations, Civic & Public Affairs-General, Native American Affairs, Philanthropic Organizations, Public Policy, Urban & Community Affairs, Zoos/Aquariums
Education: Arts/Humanities Education, Colleges & Universities, Education Reform, Medical Education, Private Education (Precollege), Special Education
Environment: Environment-General, Wildlife Protection
Health: Alzheimers Disease, Cancer, Children's Health/Hospitals, Clinics/Medical Centers, Eyes/Blindness, Health Funds, Heart, Hospitals, Medical Rehabilitation, Medical Research, Mental Health, Public Health, Research/Studies Institutes
International: Health Care/Hospitals, International Environmental Issues, International Organizations, International Peace & Security Issues
Religion: Churches, Ministries, Missionary Activities (Domestic), Religious Organizations, Religious Welfare
Science: Science Museums, Scientific Centers & Institutes
Social Services: Animal Protection, At-Risk Youth, Child Welfare, Community Service Organizations, Counseling, People with Disabilities, Scouts, Senior Services, Shelters/Homelessness, Substance Abuse, United Funds/United Ways, YMCA/YWCA/YMHA/YWHA, Youth Organizations

Application Procedures

Initial Contact: Send a brief letter of inquiry including proof of tax-exempt status.
Deadlines: None.
Review Process: Decisions usually are made within six months.

Restrictions

The majority of grants are made for medical purposes.

Additional Information

Publications: Application Form

Foundation Officials

Joseph E. Gibbs: trustee
Adele Shook Merck: trustee
Barbara Ingalls Shook: chairman, treasurer
Elesabeth Ridgely Shook: trustee
Robert P. Shook: president, secretary
Lem C. Stabler, Jr.: trustee
William Bew White, Jr.: trustee

Grants Analysis

Disclosure Period: fiscal year ending August 31, 2001
Total Grants: $320,255
Number of Grants: 59
Average Grant: $3,042*
Highest Grant: $143,800
Lowest Grant: $100
Typical Range: $1,000 to $5,000
*Note: Average grant figure excludes highest grant.

Recent Grants

Note: Grants derived from 2000 Form 990.

Library-Related

5,000	Mountain Brook Library Foundation, Mountain Brook, AL

General

108,000	UAB Medical and Educational Foundation for the Psychiatric Department
75,600	St. Vincent's Foundation Centennial Lodge Fund
37,000	Aspen Valley Community Foundation
20,200	University of Alabama Birmingham School of Nursing, Birmingham, AL
10,000	Aspen Music Festival and School, Aspen, CO
8,500	Aspen Valley Medical Foundation Limited, Aspen, CO
7,000	Better Basics, Birmingham, AL
6,500	Birmingham Museum of Art, Birmingham, AL
5,000	Virginia Episcopal School, Lynchburg, VA
4,500	Independent Presbyterian Church

SHORE FUND

Giving Contact

Laurie Moritz, Trust Officer
c/o Mellon Bank
PO Box 185
Pittsburgh, PA 15230-0185
Phone: (412)234-0023

Description

Founded: 1982
EIN: 256220659
Organization Type: Private Foundation
Giving Locations: FL; MD; MO; PA
Grant Types: General Support, Operating Expenses, Research.

Donor Information

Founder: Benjamin R. Fisher, Fisher Charitable Trusts I and II

Financial Summary

Total Giving: $83,500 (2001); $207,000 (2000); $256,500 (1999)
Giving Analysis: Giving for 1998 includes: foundation grants to United Way ($2,000) foundation ($498,000)
Assets: $4,569,472 (2000); $4,740,883 (1999); $4,393,612 (1998)
Gifts Received: $1,750 (2001); $25,000 (1998); $192,982 (1996). Note: In fiscal 1996, contributions were received from the Benjamin Fisher and Lillian Shore Fund.

Typical Recipients

Arts & Humanities: History & Archaeology, Libraries, Literary Arts, Museums/Galleries, Music, Theater
Civic & Public Affairs: Botanical Gardens/Parks, Business/Free Enterprise, Community Foundations, Economic Development, Civic & Public Affairs-General, Housing, Legal Aid, Parades/Festivals, Philanthropic Organizations, Urban & Community Affairs
Education: Arts/Humanities Education, Colleges & Universities, Education Funds, Education-General, International Studies, Literacy, Private Education (Precollege), Public Education (Precollege), Religious Education, Science/Mathematics Education, Secondary Education (Private), Secondary Education (Public), Student Aid
Environment: Environment-General, Resource Conservation
Health: Cancer, Children's Health/Hospitals, Clinics/Medical Centers, Emergency/Ambulance Services, Health Organizations, Hospices, Hospitals, Kidney,

Medical Rehabilitation, Medical Research, Mental Health, Nursing Services, Public Health, Trauma Treatment
International: Foreign Arts Organizations, Health Care/Hospitals, International Affairs
Religion: Churches, Jewish Causes, Ministries, Religious Welfare, Seminaries
Science: Scientific Centers & Institutes, Scientific Labs
Social Services: Animal Protection, Big Brother/Big Sister, Child Welfare, Community Service Organizations, Counseling, Delinquency & Criminal Rehabilitation, Emergency Relief, Family Planning, Family Services, Food/Clothing Distribution, People with Disabilities, Senior Services, Shelters/Homelessness, Special Olympics, Substance Abuse, United Funds/United Ways, Volunteer Services, YMCA/YWCA/YMHA/YWHA, Youth Organizations

Application Procedures

Initial Contact: Request application guidelines and deadline information.

Additional Information

Trust(s): Mellon Bank

Grants Analysis

Disclosure Period: calendar year ending 2001
Total Grants: $83,500
Number of Grants: 12
Average Grant: $6,958
Highest Grant: $25,000
Typical Range: $1,000 to $15,000

Recent Grants

Note: Grants derived from 2001 Form 990.

General

25,000	Hammond-Harwood House Association, Annapolis, MD
15,000	Western Pennsylvania Humane Society, Pittsburgh, PA
10,000	University of Pittsburgh, Pittsburgh, PA
5,000	Carriage House Children's Center, Pittsburgh, PA
5,000	Mary Institute and St. Louis Country Day School, St. Louis, MO
5,000	Race for the Cure, Pittsburgh, PA
5,000	Trinity By-The-Cove Episcopal Church, Naples, FL
3,500	Conservancy of Southwest Florida, Naples, FL
2,500	Calvary Fund of the Women Center and Shelter, Pittsburgh, PA
2,500	Carol R. Brown Fund, Pittsburgh, PA

HUGH I. SHOTT, JR. FOUNDATION

Giving Contact

Richard W. Wilkinson, President
c/o First Century Bank of Bluefield
500 Federal Street
PO Box 1559
Bluefield, WV 24701
Phone: (304)325-8181
Fax: (304)325-3727

Description

Founded: 1985
EIN: 550650833
Organization Type: General Purpose Foundation
Giving Locations: VA: Southwest Virginia; WV: Southern West Virginia
Grant Types: Capital, Challenge, General Support, Professorship.

Donor Information

Founder: Established in 1985 by the late Hugh I. Shott Jr. .

Financial Summary

Total Giving: $1,840,830 (2001); $2,025,549 (2000); $800,484 (1998)
Giving Analysis: Giving for 1998 includes: foundation grants to United Way ($7,500)
Assets: $37,309,229 (2001); $40,264,988 (2000); $37,402,469 (1998)

Typical Recipients

Arts & Humanities: Arts Appreciation, Arts Associations & Councils, Arts Funds, Community Arts, Film & Video, Arts & Humanities-General, Historic Preservation, History & Archaeology, Libraries, Museums/Galleries, Performing Arts
Civic & Public Affairs: Botanical Gardens/Parks, Business/Free Enterprise, Clubs, Community Foundations, Economic Development, Civic & Public Affairs-General, Housing, Municipalities/Towns, Philanthropic Organizations, Safety, Urban & Community Affairs, Women's Affairs
Education: Business Education, Colleges & Universities, Community & Junior Colleges, Continuing Education, Education Associations, Faculty Development, Journalism/Media Education, Private Education (Precollege), Public Education (Precollege), Religious Education, Science/Mathematics Education, Secondary Education (Public)
Environment: Environment-General, Sanitary Systems
Health: Clinics/Medical Centers, Emergency/Ambulance Services, Hospices, Hospitals, Public Health
Religion: Ministries, Religious Organizations, Religious Welfare
Science: Scientific Centers & Institutes
Social Services: Community Centers, Community Service Organizations, Crime Prevention, Emergency Relief, Family Planning, Food/Clothing Distribution, Homes, People with Disabilities, Recreation & Athletics, Scouts, Senior Services, Shelters/Homelessness, United Funds/United Ways, Volunteer Services, Youth Organizations

Application Procedures

Initial Contact: Write foundation for application form, then submit full proposal.
Application Requirements: Completed application form must be accompanied by a grant proposal briefly describing project, detailed project budget, qualifications of personnel, financial statements for latest fiscal year, list of principal officers and directors, and a copy of IRS tax-exempt letter.
Deadlines: None.
Review Process: The board meets bimonthly.

Restrictions

The foundation's grantmaking is restricted to southwest Virginia and southern West Virginia.

Additional Information

Publications: Application Form

Foundation Officials

Byron K. Satterfield: treasurer PRIM CORP EMPL executive vice president, trust officer, director: First Century Bank NA.
Scott Shott: vice president B Bluefield, WV 1926. ED West Virginia University (1950); Washington & Lee University JD (1951). PRIM CORP EMPL secretary, director: Paper Supply Co. CORP AFFIL director: First Century Bank NA; director: Mountaineer Resources Inc.; director: Cumberland Care Center Inc.
Richard W. Wilkinson: president B Welch, WV 1932. ED University of Virginia (1955-1962); University of Virginia JD (1962). PRIM CORP EMPL president,

chief executive officer, director: First Century Bank NA. CORP AFFIL president, director: Pocahontas Bankshares.

Grants Analysis

Disclosure Period: calendar year ending 2001
Total Grants: $1,840,830
Number of Grants: 30
Average Grant: $61,361
Highest Grant: $250,000
Lowest Grant: $3,750
Typical Range: $15,000 to $100,000

Recent Grants

Note: Grants derived from 2001 Form 990.

Library-Related

50,000	Craft Memorial Library, Bluefield, WV

General

250,000	City of Bluefield, Bluefield, WV
225,000	Boy Scouts of America- Buckskin Council, Bluefield, WV
170,000	McDowell County Economic Development Authority, McDowell, WV
111,000	East River Soccer Association, Bluefield, WV
105,370	City of Bluefield, Bluefield, WV
100,000	McDowell County Board of Education, McDowell, WV
100,000	Mercer County Board of Education, Princeton, WV
100,000	Tazewell County Board of Education, Bluefield, VA
68,210	Lecture Series, Bluefield, WV
50,000	American Red Cross, Bluefield, WV

SHUBERT FOUNDATION

Giving Contact

Vicki Reiss, Executive Director
234 W 44th St.
New York, NY 10036
Phone: (212)944-3777
Fax: (212)944-3767
Web: http://www.shubertfoundation.org

Description

Founded: 1945
EIN: 136106961
Organization Type: Specialized/Single Purpose Foundation
Giving Locations: nationally.
Grant Types: Operating Expenses.

Donor Information

Founder: Established in 1945 as the Sam S. Shubert Foundation by Lee Shubert and Jacob J. Shubert , in memory of their brother. The name was changed to the Shubert Foundation in 1971. The brothers contributed annually to the foundation. The foundation's funds were increased significantly by funds received from the estate of Lee Shubert in 1970 and from the estate of Jacob J. Shubert in 1972. The foundation is the sole shareholder of the Shubert Organization, which owns and operates the Shubert theaters.

Financial Summary

Total Giving: $12,562,000 (fiscal year ending May 31, 2001); $11,131,000 (fiscal 2000); $10,119,000 (fiscal 1999)
Assets: $251,889,489 (fiscal 2001); $249,612,295 (fiscal 2000); $220,117,201 (fiscal 1999)

Gifts Received: $188,797 (fiscal 2001); $291,499 (fiscal 2000); $140,502 (fiscal 1999). Note: In 1999, 2000 and 2001, contributions were received from the trust of Lee Shubert. In 1995, contributions were received from the trust of Lee Shubert and the estate of Karina Adair.

Typical Recipients

Arts & Humanities: Arts Associations & Councils, Arts Festivals, Ballet, Dance, Arts & Humanities-General, Libraries, Music, Opera, Performing Arts, Theater, Visual Arts
Civic & Public Affairs: Municipalities/Towns
Education: Afterschool/Enrichment Programs, Arts/Humanities Education, Colleges & Universities
Health: Clinics/Medical Centers, Hospitals (University Affiliated)
International: Foreign Arts Organizations
Religion: Jewish Causes

Application Procedures

Initial Contact: All requests must be submitted on the foundation's application form.
Application Requirements: Include a copy of letter of tax-exempt determination, and audited financial statements for the most recent fiscal year. The audited financial statement should include a comparative statement to the prior year.
Deadlines: Applications must be received no later than December 1 to qualify for a grant.
Review Process: All grants are announced and disbursed in late May.

Restrictions

The foundation does not provide funds for audience development, direct subsidies to reduced-price admissions, or performing groups whose principal purpose is to bring theatrical productions to specialized audiences. Support is generally not provided for "bricks and mortar" projects.

Additional Information

The foundation maintains an archive for the preservation of performing arts history.
Publications: Annual Report; Guidelines; Application Form

Foundation Officials

Constance Harvey: program director
John Werner Kluge: director B Chemnitz, Germany 1914. ED Columbia University BA (1937). PRIM CORP EMPL president, chairman board, executive vice president: Benale Holdings Corp. ADD CORP EMPL chairman board, president: Metromedia Co.; chairman, director: Metromedia International Group Inc.; chairman, president, director: Metromedia Hotels New York Inc.; chairman, director: Morven Farms; chairman, treasurer, president: Silver City Sales Co.; chairman, treasurer: Tri-Suburban Broadcasting Corp. CORP AFFIL chairman, treasurer: Tri-Suburban Broadcasting Corp.; director: Waldorf Astoria Corp.; chairman, president, director: Radisson Empire Hotel; chairman, treasurer, president: Silver City Sales Co.; director: Occidental Petroleum Corp.; shareholder: Muze Inc.; director: National Bank Maryland; member advisory council: Manufacturers Hanover Trust Co.; director: Marriott-Hot Shoppes Inc.; director: Kluge Finkelstein & Co.; chairman, director: JWK Properties Inc.; chairman, treasurer: Kluge & Co.; general partner: Jost Hotels LLC; director: Just One Break Inc.; director: Jimbo's Jumbos Inc.; director: Chock Full O Nuts Corp.; director: Conair Inc.; director: Belding Hemingway Co. Inc. NONPR AFFIL member: Washington Board Trade; member: Washington Food Brokers Association; vice president, board directors: United Cerebal Palsy Research & Education Foundation Inc.; member: National Sugar

Brokers Association; board governors: New York College Osteopathic Medicine; member: National Association Radio & Television Broadcasters; member: National Food Brokers Association; trustee: Miliken University Strang Clinic; member: Grocery Manufacturer Reps Washington; member: Grocery Wheels Washington; member: Advertising Council New York City; director: Brand Names Foundation; member: Advertising Club Washington. CLUB AFFIL University New York Club; University District of Columbia Club; Metropolitan New York Club; Olympic Club; Figure Skating Club; Marco Polo Club; Columbia Associates; Army-Navy Country Club; Broadcasters Club.
Vicki Reiss: executive director
Gerald Schoenfeld: chairman, director B 1924. ED University of Illinois BS (1947); New York University LLB (1949). PRIM CORP EMPL chairman, director: Shubert Organization Inc. ADD CORP EMPL chairman, director: Shubert Ticketing Services Division. NONPR AFFIL first vice president, director: League American Theatres.
Lee J. Seidler: treasurer, director B Newark, NJ 1935. ED Columbia College BA (1956); Columbia University MS (1957); Columbia University PhD (1965). PRIM CORP EMPL manager director emeritus: Bear Stearns & Co. Inc. CORP AFFIL director: Shubert Organization; director: Synthetic Indiana Inc.; director: Players International.
Philip J. Smith: director
Michael Ira Sovern: director, president B New York, NY 1931. ED Columbia University AB (1953); Columbia University LLB (1955). PRIM NONPR EMPL chancellor Kent professor: Columbia University School Law. CORP AFFIL director: Warner-Lambert Co.; director: Sequa Corp.; director: Shubert Organization; director: Kollsman Systems Management Division; director: Parke-Davis Division; director: Kollsman Military Systems Division; director: Kollsman Avionics Division; director: Kollsman Instrument Division; director: Consumer Health Products Division; director: Greater New York Insurance Group; director: AT&T Corp.; director: Chase Manhattan Bank NA; director: America Chicle Division. NONPR AFFIL member: New Jersey Board Mediation Panel Arbitration; director: WNET-TV/Channel 13; trustee: Kaiser Family Foundation; member: National Academy Arbitrators; member: Freedom Forum Newseum Inc.; chairman: Japan Society; chairman national advisory council: Freedom Forum Media Studies Center; member: Association Bar New York City; member: Council Foreign Relations; member: American Law Institute; director: Asian Cultural Council; member: American Arbitration Association; member: American Bar Association; chairman: American Academy Rome; fellow: American Academy of Arts & Sciences.
Irving M. Wall: director

Grants Analysis

Disclosure Period: fiscal year ending May 31, 2001
Total Grants: $12,562,000
Number of Grants: 334
Average Grant: $37,611
Highest Grant: $275,000
Typical Range: $15,000 to $75,000

Recent Grants

Note: Grants derived from 2000 Form 990.

General

275,000	Vivian Beaumont Theater, New York, NY
220,000	Chicago Theatre Group, Chicago, IL
220,000	South Coast Repertory, Costa Mesa, CA
220,000	Washington Drama Society, Washington, DC
210,000	New York Shakespeare Festival Public Theater, New York, NY
210,000	Roundabout Theater Company, New York, NY

190,000	Manhattan Theater Club, New York, NY
175,000	Ballet Theatre Foundation, New York, NY
165,000	Connecticut Players Foundation, Inc., New Haven, CT
160,000	New York City Ballet, New York, NY

SIERRA HEALTH FOUNDATION

Giving Contact
Len McCandliss, President & Chief Executive Officer
1321 Garden Highway
Sacramento, CA 95833
Phone: (916)922-4755
Fax: (916)922-4024
E-mail: info@sierrahealth.org
Web: http://www.sierrahealth.org/

Description
Founded: 1984
EIN: 680050036
Organization Type: Specialized/Single Purpose Foundation
Giving Locations: CA: 26 counties in Northern California
Grant Types: Capital, Challenge, Conference/Seminar, Employee Matching Gifts, General Support, Matching, Multiyear/Continuing Support, Seed Money.

Donor Information
Founder: The perpetual funding base for Sierra Health Foundation's philanthropic efforts was provided by Foundation Health Plan and Foundation Health Corporation, formerly known as Americare Health Corporation. Sierra Health Foundation was incorporated in 1984, in conjunction with the conversion of Foundation Health Plan (FHP) from nonprofit to for-profit status.

Financial Summary
Total Giving: $2,066,392 (2001); $2,649,098 (2000); $7,500,000 (1999 approx)
Giving Analysis: Giving for 1998 includes: foundation grants to United Way ($49,000)
Assets: $156,278,280 (2001); $168,643,990 (2000); $148,000,000 (1999 approx)

Typical Recipients
Arts & Humanities: Community Arts, Libraries, Music, Public Broadcasting
Civic & Public Affairs: Asian American Affairs, Clubs, Community Foundations, Economic Policy, Municipalities/Towns, Nonprofit Management, Public Policy, Rural Affairs, Urban & Community Affairs, Women's Affairs
Education: Elementary Education (Public), Education-General, Health & Physical Education, Legal Education, Medical Education, Public Education (Precollege), School Volunteerism
Environment: Air/Water Quality
Health: Adolescent Health Issues, AIDS/HIV, Cancer, Children's Health/Hospitals, Clinics/Medical Centers, Emergency/Ambulance Services, Eyes/Blindness, Geriatric Health, Health Policy/Cost Containment, Health Organizations, Heart, Hospices, Hospitals, Long-Term Care, Medical Research, Mental Health, Nursing Services, Outpatient Health Care, Prenatal Health Issues, Public Health, Research/Studies Institutes, Respiratory, Single-Disease Health Associations, Trauma Treatment
International: Health Care/Hospitals
Religion: Religion-General, Religious Welfare
Social Services: At-Risk Youth, Child Abuse, Child Welfare, Community Service Organizations, Crime Prevention, Domestic Violence, Emergency Relief,

Family Planning, Family Services, People with Disabilities, Scouts, Senior Services, Shelters/Homelessness, Youth Organizations

Application Procedures
Initial Contact: Unsolicited grants are suspended temporarily.
Notes: Contact for mini-grants is Ms. Dorothy Meehan, Vice President.

Restrictions
The foundation does not support individuals, endowments, lobbying efforts, or projects that benefit only the members of a private or religious group. General fund drives and annual appeals are not supported. The foundation will not generally support recreation programs, operating budgets, deficits, clinical research, major equipment purchases, or conferences.

Additional Information
Besides making grants, the foundation also provides program development and technical assistance.
Publications: Grants List; Newsletter; Application Guidelines Application Form; Informational Brochure; Fact Sheet; occasional report

Foundation Officials
Steve Barrow: program officer
Byron Demorest, MD: director
George Deubel: director
J. Rodney Eason: chairman, director
Manuel A. Esteban, PhD: director B Barcelona, Spain 1940. ED University of Calgary BA (1969); University of Calgary MA (1970); University of California, Santa Barbara PhD (1976). PRIM CORP EMPL president, professor: California State University, Chico.
Wendy Everett: director
Albert R. Jonsen: director B San Francisco, CA 1931. ED Gonzaga University BA (1955); Gonzaga University MA (1956); University of Santa Clara (1963); Yale University PhD (1967). PRIM NONPR EMPL professor of medical ethics: University of Washington, School of Medicine. NONPR AFFIL member: Society Health & Human Values; chairman department medical history & ethics: University Washington Medicine School; member: National Rifle Association; member: Society Christian Ethics; member: Institute Medicine NAS; fellow: Institute Social Ethics & Life Science; member: American Society Law & Medicine; member: Commission AIDS Research.
Father Leo McAllister: secretary, director
Len McCandliss: president, director
Dorothy A. Meehan: vice president B 1953. ED University of Washington (1975); University of Cincinnati (1978-1981).
Leah Morris, RN: program officer managed care and health grants
Robert E. Petersen: director B Los Angeles, CA 1926. PRIM CORP EMPL founder, chairman board emeritus: Petersen Publishing Co. ADD CORP EMPL owner: Petersen Aviation Inc.; owner, chairman board: Petersen Properties. NONPR AFFIL founder: Petersen Automotive Museum; director: Thalians; director: Boys Club America. CLUB AFFIL Southern California Safari Club; Chevaliers du Tastevin Club; Conferie de la Chaine des Rotisseurs Club; Balboa Bay Yacht Club; Catalina Island Yacht Club.
James Schubert, MD: director
Sandra R. Smoley, RN: director PRIM NONPR EMPL secretary: California Department Health & Welfare.
Steve Vorous: chief financial officer

Grants Analysis
Disclosure Period: calendar year ending 2001
Total Grants: $2,066,392*
Number of Grants: 83
Average Grant: $25,000*
Highest Grant: $306,000
Lowest Grant: $1,000

Typical Range: $10,000 to $75,000
*Note: Giving excludes United Way. Grants analysis provided by foundation.

Recent Grants
Note: Grants derived from 2000 Form 990.

General
390,000	Public Health Institute, Berkeley, CA -- to provide grant administration, monitoring and technical assistance to the community partnerships for health children initiative
260,000	SRI International, Menlo Park, CA -- for evaluation of CPHC
235,000	Public Health Institute, Berkeley, CA -- to provide grant administration, monitoring and technical assistance to the community partnerships for health children initiative
100,000	Center for Health Care Rights, Los Angeles, CA -- to develop a consumer education and ombuds program for managed care health insurance purchasers and enrollees
87,500	Children's Home, Stockton, CA -- to support major expansion and renovation of The Children's Receiving Home facilities
87,500	Children's Receiving Home, Sacramento, CA -- to support major expansion and renovation
85,000	Boys and Girls Club of Chino, California, Chino, CA
75,740	St. Mary's Interfaith Dining Room, Stockton, CA -- to provide increased dental services to the poor and homeless
75,000	Center for Health Care Rights, Los Angeles, CA -- to develop a consumer education and ombuds program for managed care health insurance purchasers and enrollees
75,000	Shasta Community Health Center, Redding, CA -- to increase access to primary and specialty health care services through the purchase and renovation of a new clinic facility

SIERRA PACIFIC INDUSTRIES

Company Headquarters
Redding, CA
Web: http://www.sierrapacificind.com

Company Description
Revenue: US$1.425 billion (2002)
Employees: 3900 (2002)
SIC(s): 2421 Sawmills & Planing Mills--General, 2431 Millwork.

Sierra Pacific Foundation

Giving Contact
Stephanie Donham
PO Box 496028
Redding, CA 96049-6028
Phone: (530)378-8000
Fax: (530)378-8109
E-mail: foundation@spi-ind.com
Web: http://www.sierrapacificind.com/Company/SPFoundation.htm

Description
Founded: 1978
EIN: 942574178
Organization Type: Corporate Foundation

Giving Locations: headquarters and operating communities.
Grant Types: General Support, Scholarship.

Donor Information

Founder: Established and funded in 1979 by R. H. "Curly" Emmerson and Sierra Pacific Industries.

Financial Summary

Total Giving: $496,729 (fiscal year ending June 30, 2002); $325,375 (fiscal 2001); $498,797 (fiscal 2000). Note: Contributes through foundation only.
Giving Analysis: Giving for fiscal 2003 includes: foundation scholarships ($367,125); fiscal 2002: foundation scholarships ($260,507); fiscal 2001: foundation scholarships ($325,375);
Assets: $345,795 (fiscal 2002); $648,112 (fiscal 2000); $1,001,522 (fiscal 1998)
Gifts Received: $375,250 (fiscal 2002); $550,250 (fiscal 2000); $200 (fiscal 1998). Note: In fiscal 2002, contributions were received from Sierra Pacific Industries. In fiscal 1996, contributions were received from Sierra Pacific Industries ($500,000) and the Memorial for Ida. C. Emmerson ($22,812). In fiscal 2000, contributions Sierra Pacific Industries.

Typical Recipients

Arts & Humanities: Arts Associations & Councils, Arts Centers, Arts Festivals, Arts & Humanities-General, Libraries, Museums/Galleries, Music, Opera, Public Broadcasting
Civic & Public Affairs: Botanical Gardens/Parks, Business/Free Enterprise, Chambers of Commerce, Clubs, Civic & Public Affairs-General, Housing, Parades/Festivals, Rural Affairs, Safety, Urban & Community Affairs, Women's Affairs
Education: Agricultural Education, Business Education, Colleges & Universities, Elementary Education (Public), Engineering/Technological Education, Education-General, Minority Education, Private Education (Precollege), Public Education (Precollege), Secondary Education (Public), Student Aid, Vocational & Technical Education
Environment: Environment-General, Resource Conservation, Wildlife Protection
Health: Cancer, Emergency/Ambulance Services, Health Organizations, Heart, Hospices, Hospitals, Medical Research, Nutrition, Single-Disease Health Associations, Transplant Networks/Donor Banks
International: International Relief Efforts
Religion: Churches, Religious Welfare
Science: Observatories & Planetariums, Science Museums
Social Services: Child Welfare, Community Centers, Community Service Organizations, Crime Prevention, Food/Clothing Distribution, Recreation & Athletics, Scouts, Senior Services, Shelters/Homelessness, Social Services-General, Volunteer Services, YMCA/YWCA/YMHA/YWHA, Youth Organizations

Application Procedures

Initial Contact: Obtain a contribution request form from nearest Sierra Pacific office or by calling (530) 378-8000.
Deadlines: March 31.

Restrictions

Scholarships are restricted to dependent children of Sierra Pacific employees. Foundation primarily funds preselected organizations.

Corporate Officials

A. A. Emmerson: president B 1929. PRIM CORP EMPL president: Sierra Pacific Industries.
George Emmerson: vice president B 1956. ED Oregon State University (1978). PRIM CORP EMPL vice president: Sierra Pacific Industries.

Foundation Officials

Carolyn Emmerson Dietz: chairman, president B 1959.
George Emmerson: director (see above)

Grants Analysis

Disclosure Period: fiscal year ending June 30, 2002
Total Grants: $236,222*
Number of Grants: 266
Average Grant: $888
Highest Grant: $25,000
Lowest Grant: $25
Typical Range: $100 to $2,000
*Note: Giving excludes scholarships.

Recent Grants

Note: Grants derived from fiscal 2002 Form 990.

General

3,500	Universal Technical Institute
3,000	University of California Davis, Davis, CA
2,000	Humboldt State University, Arcata, CA
1,750	Brigham Young University, Provo, UT
1,750	Brigham Young University, Provo, UT
1,750	Brigham Young University, Provo, UT
1,750	Brigham Young University, Provo, UT
1,750	Brigham Young University, Provo, UT
1,750	Florida Institute of Technology, Melbourne, FL
1,750	LeTourneau University, Longview, TX

SIERRA PACIFIC RESOURCES

Company Headquarters

Reno, NV
Web: http://www.sierrapacificresources.com

Company Description

Founded: 1984
Ticker: SRP
Exchange: NYSE
Revenue: US$2.991 billion (2002)
Employees: 3333 (2001)
Fortune Rank: 494, per FORTUNE Magazine's list of 500 Largest U.S. Corporations (2002).
SIC(s): 4924 Natural Gas Distribution, 4931 Electric & Other Services Combined, 6719 Holding Companies Nec.

Operating Locations

Sierra Pacific Resources (NV--Reno)

Nonmonetary Support

Type: In-kind Services
Volunteer Programs: Company employees are active in the community, participating in the Day of Caring, blood drives, and events such as the Special Olympics and the March of Dimes WalkAmerica.

Sierra Pacific Resources Charitable Foundation

Giving Contact

Karen Foster, Secretary, Treasurer
PO Box 30150
Reno, NV 89520
Phone: (702)579-1589
E-mail: kfoster@sppc.com
Web: http://www.sierrapacific.com/comenv/comrel/foundation/

Description

Founded: 1988
EIN: 880244735
Organization Type: Corporate Foundation

Giving Locations: CA: Northeastern California; NV: Northern Nevada headquarters and operating communities.
Grant Types: Employee Matching Gifts, General Support, Project.
Note: Employee matching gift ratio: 1 to 1 for donations to Special Assistance Fund for Energy (SAFE).

Donor Information

Founder: Sierra Pacific Resources

Financial Summary

Total Giving: $327,750 (2001); $481,235 (2000); $352,835 (1999). Note: Contributes through corporate direct giving program and foundation.
Giving Analysis: Giving for 2000 includes: foundation scholarships ($1,200); foundation grants to United Way ($88,000); foundation ($392,035); 1999: foundation grants to United Way ($48,000); foundation ($352,835); 1998: foundation scholarships ($100); foundation grants to United Way ($47,000); foundation ($330,416);
Assets: $265,939 (2001); $261,799 (2000); $259,943 (1999)
Gifts Received: $320,000 (2001); $469,300 (2000); $386,605 (1999). Note: Contributions received from Sierra Pacific Resources.

Typical Recipients

Arts & Humanities: Arts Associations & Councils, Arts Centers, Arts Funds, Community Arts, Ethnic & Folk Arts, Arts & Humanities-General, Libraries, Museums/Galleries, Music, Opera, Performing Arts, Public Broadcasting, Theater
Civic & Public Affairs: African American Affairs, Botanical Gardens/Parks, Business/Free Enterprise, Clubs, Community Foundations, Economic Development, Employment/Job Training, Civic & Public Affairs-General, Hispanic Affairs, Housing, Municipalities/Towns, Native American Affairs, Parades/Festivals, Professional & Trade Associations, Rural Affairs, Safety, Urban & Community Affairs, Women's Affairs
Education: Agricultural Education, Business Education, Colleges & Universities, Colleges & Universities, Community & Junior Colleges, Education Reform, Elementary Education (Public), Engineering/Technological Education, Education-General, Legal Education, Literacy, Preschool Education, Public Education (Precollege), Religious Education, Science/Mathematics Education
Environment: Forestry, Environment-General, Resource Conservation, Wildlife Protection
Health: Alzheimers Disease, Cancer, Children's Health/Hospitals, Diabetes, Emergency/Ambulance Services, Heart, Hospitals, Mental Health, Public Health, Respiratory, Single-Disease Health Associations
Religion: Religion-General, Religious Welfare, Social/Policy Issues
Science: Scientific Research
Social Services: Animal Protection, Camps, Child Welfare, Child Welfare, Community Centers, Community Service Organizations, Crime Prevention, Delinquency & Criminal Rehabilitation, Family Planning, Family Services, Food/Clothing Distribution, People with Disabilities, Recreation & Athletics, Scouts, Senior Services, Social Services-General, United Funds/United Ways, YMCA/YWCA/YMHA/YWHA, Youth Organizations

Application Procedures

Initial Contact: Submit a brief letter of inquiry.
Deadlines: None.

Restrictions

The foundation does not make grants to individuals, athletic or sporting events/teams, and does not fund religious organizations. Grants are limited to areas of service. The organization will provide limited employee time to nonprofit organizations if the circumstances require.

Additional Information
Publications: Annual Report

Corporate Officials
Walter M. Higgins: chairman, president, chief executive officer treasurer B Washington, DC August 18, 1944. ED United States Naval Academy BS (1966); George Washington University (1975-1977); Stanford University (1989). PRIM CORP EMPL chairman, president, chief executive officer: Sierra Pacific Resources.

William E. Peterson: general counsel B 1943. ED College of the Holy Cross; North Carolina State University BA; University of South Carolina. PRIM CORP EMPL secretary: Sierra Energy Co. ADD CORP EMPL general counsel: Sierra Pacific Power Co. CORP AFFIL senior vice president, general counsel, corp. secretary: Sierra Pacific Resources.

Mark A. Ruelle: senior vice president, chief financial officer, treasurer ED University of North Dakota BA; University of North Dakota MBA. PRIM CORP EMPL senior vice president, chief financial officer, treasurer: Sierra Pacific Resources. CORP AFFIL chief financial officer: Sierra Pacific Power Co. NONPR AFFIL member: National Association Business Economists; member: Planning Forum; member strategic planning committee: Edison Electric Institute; member: American Gas Association.

Foundation Officials
Gary Aldax: director
Jeff Ceccarelli: chairman
Karen C. Foster: secretary, treasurer
Lisa Harris: administrator
Greg Lambert: director
Don Sims: director
Sandy Walsh: director

Grants Analysis
Disclosure Period: calendar year ending 2001
Total Grants: $290,250*
Number of Grants: 156
Average Grant: $1,144*
Highest Grant: $89,000
Lowest Grant: $50
Typical Range: $500 to $5,000
***Note:** Giving excludes United Way. Average grant figure excludes two highest grants ($114,000).

Recent Grants
Note: Grants derived from 2001 Form 990.

General
89,000	University of Nevada Reno Foundation, Reno, NV
25,000	Nevada Museum of Art, Reno, NV
15,000	American Red Cross, Reno, NV
12,500	United Way Northern Nevada, Reno, NV
12,500	United Way Northern Nevada, Reno, NV
12,500	United Way Northern Nevada, Reno, NV
6,669	Girl Scouts of the Sierra Nevada, Reno, NV
5,217	Boy Scouts of America, Melbourne, FL
5,000	Care Chest of Sierra Nevada, Reno, NV
5,000	Food Bank of Northern Nevada, Reno, NV

SILVER LINING FOUNDATION

Giving Contact
Philip W. Halperin, President
Pier 1, Bay 2
San Francisco, CA 94111

Phone: (415)398-0770
E-mail: info@silverliningfoundation.org
Web: http://www.silverliningfoundation.org/welcome.htm

Description
Founded: 1997
EIN: 943285094
Organization Type: Private Foundation
Grant Types: General Support.

Financial Summary
Total Giving: $4,346,068 (2000); $3,065,233 (1999); $70,000 (1997)
Assets: $70,261,972 (2000); $100,163,346 (1999); $46,042,456 (1997)
Gifts Received: $46,456,297 (1997). Note: In 1997, contributions were received from Mark R. Halperin.

Typical Recipients
Arts & Humanities: Libraries, Museums/Galleries
Civic & Public Affairs: Civic & Public Affairs-General, Urban & Community Affairs
Education: Afterschool/Enrichment Programs, Colleges & Universities, Education-General, Literacy, Public Education (Precollege), Special Education
Health: Cancer, Research/Studies Institutes
Social Services: Community Centers, Community Service Organizations, Family Services, Social Services-General, Youth Organizations

Application Procedures
Initial Contact: Send written request.
Deadlines: None.

Foundation Officials
Peggy Anne Dow: secretary, chief financial officer, director
Philip W. Halperin: president
Julie Shafer: manager

Grants Analysis
Disclosure Period: calendar year ending 2000
Total Grants: $4,346,068
Number of Grants: 68
Average Grant: $59,901*
Highest Grant: $332,733
Typical Range: $25,000 to $100,000
***Note:** Average grant figure excludes highest grant.

Recent Grants
Note: Grants derived from 1999 Form 990.

Library-Related
200,000	Take Home Library, Menlo Park, CA
100,000	Take Home Library, San Francisco, CA

General
332,733	Developmental Studies Center, Oakland, CA
100,000	Columbia Park Boys and Girls Club, San Francisco, CA
100,000	Edgewood, San Francisco, CA -- Wraparound
100,000	Edgewood, San Francisco, CA -- Project Success
100,000	Friends Foundation, San Francisco, CA
100,000	Stanford University, Stanford, CA
95,000	California Tomorrow, Oakland, CA
85,000	San Francisco Educational Services, San Francisco, CA
80,000	Aim High, San Francisco, CA
80,000	Summerbridge, San Francisco, CA

MELVIN AND BREN SIMON CHARITABLE FOUNDATION NUMBER ONE

Giving Contact
Deborah Simon
PO Box 7033
Indianapolis, IN 46207-7033
Phone: (317)636-1600

Description
Founded: 1998
EIN: 352049367
Organization Type: Private Foundation
Grant Types: General Support.

Financial Summary
Total Giving: $1,439,007 (fiscal year ending June 30, 2001); $297,148 (fiscal 1999)
Giving Analysis: Giving for fiscal 2001 includes: foundation grants to United Way ($5,000)
Assets: $3,917,281 (fiscal 2001); $3,002,771 (fiscal 1999); $3,601,562 (fiscal 1998)
Gifts Received: $3,062,875 (fiscal 2001); $3,609,375 (fiscal 1998). Note: In fiscal 2001, contributions were received from Melvin Simon & Associates, Inc. In fiscal 1998, contributions were received from Melvin and Bren Simon.

Typical Recipients
Arts & Humanities: Museums/Galleries, Music
Civic & Public Affairs: Civic & Public Affairs-General
Education: Arts/Humanities Education, Education-General, Private Education (Precollege)
Health: Children's Health/Hospitals
Religion: Jewish Causes
Social Services: Animal Protection, Community Service Organizations, Shelters/Homelessness

Application Procedures
Initial Contact: The foundation requests applications be made in writing.
Application Requirements: Include a description of organization, amount requested, and purpose of funds sought.

Foundation Officials
Bren Simons: trustee
Melvin J. Simons: trustee

Grants Analysis
Disclosure Period: fiscal year ending June 30, 2001
Total Grants: $1,434,007*
Number of Grants: 42
Average Grant: $34,143
Highest Grant: $221,000
Typical Range: $15,000 to $50,000
***Note:** Giving excludes United Way.

Recent Grants
Note: Grants derived from fiscal 2001 Form 990.

General
221,000	Jewish Welfare Federation, Indianapolis, IN
201,908	New Hope Charities, Miami Beach, FL -- MIR Foundation
118,189	New Hope Charities, Miami Beach, FL -- vocational school
100,000	Jewish Welfare Federation, Indianapolis, IN
100,000	Please Touch Museum, Philadelphia, PA -- first installment of pledge
100,000	William J. Clinton Presidential Foundation, Little Rock, AR -- Clinton Library
81,491	New Hope Charities, Miami Beach, FL -- The Vocational school

55,000	Indianapolis Children's Choir, Indianapolis, IN -- "A Child's Opera"
53,849	New Hope Charities, Miami Beach, FL -- Campo Esperanza
50,000	Congregation Beth-El Zedek, Indianapolis, IN -- roots and wings pledge

SIDNEY, MILTON, AND LEOMA SIMON FOUNDATION

Giving Contact
Joseph C. Warner, Trustee
Sidney, Milton, and Leoma Simon Foundation
4259 NW 64th Lane
Boca Raton, FL 33496
Phone: (561)241-9298

Description
Founded: 1964
EIN: 656282105
Organization Type: Private Foundation
Grant Types: General Support, Research.

Donor Information
Founder: the late Milton Simon

Financial Summary
Total Giving: $648,000 (fiscal year ending May 31, 2001); $629,000 (fiscal 2000); $627,000 (fiscal 1999)
Assets: $16,328,864 (fiscal 2001); $15,180,045 (fiscal 2000); $14,604,738 (fiscal 1999)

Typical Recipients
Arts & Humanities: Libraries, Performing Arts, Public Broadcasting, Theater
Civic & Public Affairs: Civic & Public Affairs-General, Zoos/Aquariums
Education: Arts/Humanities Education, Business Education, Legal Education, Private Education (Precollege), Public Education (Precollege)
Environment: Environment-General, Wildlife Protection
Health: Arthritis, Cancer, Clinics/Medical Centers, Diabetes, Eyes/Blindness, Geriatric Health, Health Organizations, Hospitals, Medical Research, Prenatal Health Issues, Respiratory, Single-Disease Health Associations, Speech & Hearing
International: Health Care/Hospitals, International Peace & Security Issues, International Relations
Religion: Jewish Causes, Synagogues/Temples
Social Services: Camps, Child Welfare, Crime Prevention, People with Disabilities, Recreation & Athletics, Special Olympics, Youth Organizations

Application Procedures
Initial Contact: Send a brief letter of inquiry.
Application Requirements: Describe program or project.
Deadlines: None.

Foundation Officials
Burt Bergenfield: trustee
Joseph C. Warner: trustee
Meryll Warner: trustee
Allan B. Wechsler: trustee PRIM CORP EMPL manager human resources: Brown Brothers Harriman & Co.

Grants Analysis
Disclosure Period: fiscal year ending May 31, 2001
Total Grants: $648,000
Number of Grants: 68
Average Grant: $9,529
Highest Grant: $14,000
Lowest Grant: $3,000
Typical Range: $5,000 to $14,000

Recent Grants
Note: Grants derived from 2000 Form 990.

General
13,000	American Foundation for the Blind, New York, NY
13,000	Beth Israel Hospital
13,000	National Jewish Medical and Research Center
12,000	American Jewish Committee, Chicago, IL
12,000	American Jewish Joint Distribution Committee, New York, NY
12,000	United Jewish Appeal Federation, New York, NY
11,000	Columbia Presbyterian Medical Center, New York, NY
11,000	Defense Research Foundation
11,000	Hadassah Hospital Medical Organization, Jerusalem Israel
11,000	Leukemia Society of America, New York, NY

WILLIAM E. SIMON FOUNDATION

Giving Contact
William E. Simon, Jr., Co-Chairman
310 South Street, PO Box 1913
Morristown, NJ 07962-1913
Phone: (973)898-0290
Fax: (973)898-4733
Web: http://www.wesimonfoundation.org

Alternate Contact
J. Peter Simon, Co-Chairman

Description
Founded: 1967
EIN: 136217788
Organization Type: Family Foundation
Former Name: William E. and Carol G. Simon Foundation.
Giving Locations: nationally, with emphasis in New York Metro, Los Angeles, and the San Francio Bar metropolitan areas.
Grant Types: Employee Matching Gifts, Endowment, General Support, Matching, Multiyear/Continuing Support.

Donor Information
Founder: Established in the mid 1980s by William E. Simon, former secretary of the treasury under former Presidents Richard Nixon and Gerald Ford.
Mr. Simon was born in 1927 in Paterson, NJ, went to Newark Academy, then Lafayette College where he graduated in 1951 with a bachelor's degree in government and law. He went right to work on Wall Street, specializing in government securities and municipal bonds. He rose to become a senior partner in Salomon Brothers, a large investment firm where his annual salary is estimated to have been between $2 million and $3 million in 1971 and 1972.
He left Wall Street in 1972 when he was appointed as the deputy secretary of the treasury under George Schultz. One year later, Mr. Simon was named the administrator of the Federal Energy Office where, as the "energy czar," he coordinated the country's energy policy during the energy crisis. He left that post to become the secretary of the treasury in 1974 where he served until 1977, when he left government service.
Before he began his government service, Mr. Simon had placed in a blind trust his assets which had declined about 60% in value. Once back in private life, Mr. Simon began to rebuild his personal wealth by establishing his own network of consultancies and corporate relationships. He combined his economic expertise with his recent government service to negotiate financial opportunities with the largest companies in the country. He joined a dozen or so blue-chip corporate and philanthropic boards including Xerox Corporation and the John M. Olin Foundation.
In 1981, Mr. Simon and Ray Chambers founded Wesray Corporation, an investment and banking firm that specialized in leveraged buyouts. The company became one of the largest private companies in the country with sales of $1.8 billion in 1983. Today, Mr. Simon directs his own company, William E. Simon and Sons, located in Morristown, NJ. His personal fortune was estimated to be approximately $300 million in 1991.
Mr. Simon's accomplishments reflect a personal philosophy of hard work and a belief in the free enterprise system. His associates have described him as a nonstop worker who can regularly put in 18-hour days. He authored two books, including "A Time for Truth," an account of his Washington, DC, experiences and conservative economics, which was a bestseller for 30 weeks. He donated the proceeds to his alma mater, Lafayette College in Easton, PA. He has served on or is currently serving on the boards of more than 60 charitable organizations. He has received more than 50 awards, and he is a member of more than 20 clubs across the country.
He married Carol Girard in 1950. The couple had seven children: William E. Simon, Jr., John P. Simon, Mary Beth Simon Streep, Carol Leigh Simon Porges, Aimee Simon Bloom, Julie Ann Simon, and Johanna Katrina Simon. The eight members of the family serve as officers or directors of the William E. Simon Foundation.

Financial Summary
Total Giving: $7,568,382 (2000); $7,695,238 (1999); $3,560,951 (1998)
Giving Analysis: Giving for 1998 includes: foundation grants to United Way ($785) foundation scholarships ($16,600)
Assets: $7,888,608 (2000); $12,724,417 (1999); $18,736,823 (1998)
Gifts Received: $2,957,015 (2000); $199 (1999); $10,384 (1998). Note: In 2000, contributions were received from William E. Simon.

Typical Recipients
Arts & Humanities: Arts Associations & Councils, Arts Centers, Arts Funds, Dance, Arts & Humanities-General, Historic Preservation, History & Archaeology, Libraries, Museums/Galleries, Music, Performing Arts
Civic & Public Affairs: Botanical Gardens/Parks, Business/Free Enterprise, Civil Rights, Clubs, Community Foundations, First Amendment Issues, Civic & Public Affairs-General, Housing, Municipalities/Towns, Nonprofit Management, Philanthropic Organizations, Professional & Trade Associations, Public Policy, Safety, Urban & Community Affairs, Women's Affairs, Zoos/Aquariums
Education: Arts/Humanities Education, Business Education, Colleges & Universities, Community & Junior Colleges, Education Associations, Education Funds, Education Reform, Education-General, Gifted & Talented Programs, Leadership Training, Legal Education, Minority Education, Private Education (Precollege), Religious Education, Science/Mathematics Education, Secondary Education (Private), Special Education, Student Aid
Environment: Air/Water Quality, Environment-General, Resource Conservation
Health: Cancer, Clinics/Medical Centers, Health Funds, Health Organizations, Hospices, Hospitals, Medical Rehabilitation, Medical Research, Multiple Sclerosis, Nursing Services, Public Health, Research/Studies Institutes, Single-Disease Health Associations, Transplant Networks/Donor Banks

International: Foreign Arts Organizations, International Affairs, International Organizations, International Peace & Security Issues, International Relations, International Relief Efforts, Missionary/Religious Activities
Religion: Bible Study/Translation, Churches, Dioceses, Religion-General, Ministries, Missionary Activities (Domestic), Religious Organizations, Religious Welfare, Seminaries, Social/Policy Issues
Science: Scientific Research
Social Services: Animal Protection, At-Risk Youth, Child Welfare, Community Centers, Community Service Organizations, Day Care, Family Planning, Family Services, Food/Clothing Distribution, Homes, People with Disabilities, Recreation & Athletics, Shelters/Homelessness, Social Services-General, Substance Abuse, United Funds/United Ways, Veterans, Youth Organizations

Application Procedures
Initial Contact: Request copy of guidelines and application procedures in writing or by telephone, or download them from the foundation's web site.
Deadlines: None.

Restrictions
The foundation does not make grants to individuals or for programs outside the US.

Additional Information
Publications: Guidelines; application form.

Foundation Officials
Daniel Mosley: director
James Piereson, PhD: director B Grand Rapids, MI 1946. ED Michigan State University BA (1968); Michigan State University PhD (1973). NONPR AFFIL member: Philadelphia Society; member advisory committee: University Rochester Simon Graduate School Business Administration; director: DonorsTrust; member: American Historical Association. CLUB AFFIL Union League Club.
J. Peter Simon: vice president, treasurer, director B 1927. PRIM CORP EMPL executive director, director: William E. Simon & Sons.
William Edward Simon, Jr.: president, director B 1951. PRIM CORP EMPL executive director: William E Simon & Sons.
Mary B. Simon Streep: director
William Wachenfeld: director B Orange, NJ 1926. ED Tufts University AB (1947); Duke University LLB (1950). PRIM CORP EMPL counsel: Tompkins McGuire & Wachenfeld. NONPR AFFIL member: Essex County Bar Association; member: New Jersey Bar Association; fellow: American Bar Foundation; member: American Bar Association. CLUB AFFIL HC Yacht Club; Eastward Ho Country Club.

Grants Analysis
Disclosure Period: calendar year ending 2000
Total Grants: $7,568,382
Number of Grants: 327
Average Grant: $15,930*
Highest Grant: $1,000,000
Typical Range: $50 to $25,000
*Note: Average grant figure excludes four highest grants ($2,423,151).

Recent Grants
Note: Grants derived from 2001 Form 990.

General
1,000,000	West Point Fund, West Point, NY -- operating expenses
500,000	Gregorian University Foundation, New York, NY -- scholarship
500,000	Newark Academy, Livingston, NJ
300,000	Heritage Foundation, Washington, DC -- operating expenses
268,885	Gladney Center, Ft. Worth, TX -- social welfare
250,000	Hillsdale College, Hillsdale, MI -- scholarship
250,000	Morristown Memorial Health Foundation, Inc., Morristown, NJ -- social welfare/healthcare
250,000	Newark Academy, Livingston, NJ
195,050	Thomas Aquinas College, Santa Paula, CA -- operating expenses
166,667	Angelicum University Fund, New York, NY

SIMPSON INVESTMENT CO.

Company Headquarters
1301 5th Ave., Ste. 2800
Seattle, WA 98101
Web: http://www.simpson.com

Company Description
Employees: 83
SIC(s): 6719 Holding Companies Nec.

Operating Locations
Simpson Investment Co. (MI--Plainwell, Vicksburg; OR--Eugene, Portland, West Linn; WA--Shelton, Tacoma)
Note: Operates in various cities and towns in the above states.

Nonmonetary Support
Value: $20,707 (1998)
Volunteer Programs: The company sponsors a United Way "Day of Caring" program where employees volunteer their time to help a designated United Way organization.
Note: Donated products include paper.

Simpson Fund

Giving Contact
Colleen Musgrave, Administrator
1301 5th Ave., No. 2800
Seattle, WA 98101
Phone: (206)224-5198
Fax: (206)436-1852
E-mail: cmusgra@simpson.com
Web: http://www.simpson.com

Description
EIN: 916029303
Organization Type: Corporate Foundation
Giving Locations: CA: Del Norte County, Humboldt County; OR: Lincoln County, Tillamook County; WA: Grays Harbor County, King County, Mason County, Pierce County, Thurston County
Grant Types: Capital, Employee Matching Gifts, General Support.
Note: Employee matching gift ratio: 1 to 1.

Financial Summary
Total Giving: $900,000 (2002 approx); $818,354 (2001); $633,109 (2000). Note: Contributes through corporate direct giving program and foundation.
Giving Analysis: Giving for 2002 includes: corporate direct giving (approx $285,000); foundation (approx $615,000); 2001: foundation grants to United Way ($79,497); corporate direct giving ($95,768); foundation ($643,089); 2000: foundation grants to United Way ($132,708); foundation ($500,401).
Assets: $1,320 (1993); $13,642 (1992)
Gifts Received: $633,179 (2000); $595,056 (1998); $574,975 (1997). Note: Contributions were received from Simpson Investment Company, Simpson Paper Company, Simpson Timber Company, and Pacific Western Extruded Plastics Company.

Typical Recipients
Arts & Humanities: Arts Associations & Councils, Arts Institutes, Arts & Humanities-General, Historic Preservation, History & Archaeology, Libraries, Museums/Galleries, Music, Opera, Performing Arts, Theater
Civic & Public Affairs: African American Affairs, Botanical Gardens/Parks, Community Foundations, Economic Development, Economic Policy, Civic & Public Affairs-General, Municipalities/Towns, Professional & Trade Associations, Safety, Urban & Community Affairs, Zoos/Aquariums
Education: Agricultural Education, Business Education, Colleges & Universities, Community & Junior Colleges, Continuing Education, Economic Education, Education Funds, Education Reform, Elementary Education (Private), Engineering/Technological Education, Environmental Education, Education-General, Private Education (Precollege), Public Education (Precollege), School Volunteerism, Science/Mathematics Education, Student Aid
Environment: Forestry, Environment-General, Resource Conservation, Watershed, Wildlife Protection
Health: Arthritis, Children's Health/Hospitals, Clinics/Medical Centers, Emergency/Ambulance Services, Geriatric Health, Health Organizations, Hospices, Hospitals, Nursing Services, Transplant Networks/Donor Banks, Trauma Treatment
International: International Relief Efforts
Religion: Churches, Dioceses, Religion-General, Ministries, Religious Welfare
Science: Science Exhibits & Fairs, Science Museums, Scientific Centers & Institutes
Social Services: At-Risk Youth, Big Brother/Big Sister, Child Abuse, Child Welfare, Community Centers, Community Service Organizations, Family Services, Food/Clothing Distribution, Recreation & Athletics, Scouts, Senior Services, Sexual Abuse, Shelters/Homelessness, Social Services-General, Substance Abuse, United Funds/United Ways, Volunteer Services, YMCA/YWCA/YMHA/YWHA, Youth Organizations

Application Procedures
Initial Contact: Letter or telephone call requesting grant application.
Application Requirements: Completed application form; list of other donors, including names and amounts; list of board of directors; operating budget of organization for previous year and current year-to-date; and project/program budget.
Deadlines: Annual grant-making cycle begins in January.
Evaluative Criteria: The degree of support from Simpson employees; amount of enthusiasm in the community for the organization or drive; relative size and importance of company operations in the community and balance among Simpson communities; total amount being raised in the overall campaign, compared with the request being made of Simpson; needs of organization or program for which funding is requested; amount of previous Simpson contributions to the organization; amount committed by other companies, foundations, and/or governments (projects should demonstrate broad-based community support); and proximity of the requesting organization to the company operations or headquarters. When possible, contributions will support organizations of interest to or recommended by Simpson employees. The Fund prefers to make capital contributions or provide one-time "seed money" for programs.
Decision Notification: Grant applications are reviewed throughout the year.

Restrictions
Does not support individuals or provide funds for endowments or loans.

Additional Information
Foundation is sponsored by Simpson Investment Company and its subsidiaries, which include Simpson

Paper Company, Simpson Timber Company, and Pacific Western Extruded Plastics Company. Matlock Foundation does not make grants, but allocates money to the Simpson Fund for giving. The Matlock Foundation filed its final tax return as of January 1, 2001, with a corporate giving program managed by the Simpson Fund taking its place.
Publications: Application Form

Corporate Officials

Maureen Frisch: vice president public affairs PRIM CORP EMPL vice president public affairs: Simpson Investment Co.
Colin Moseley: chairman, chief executive officer B 1960. ED Northwestern University MBA (1988). PRIM CORP EMPL chairman, chief executive officer: Simpson Investment Co.
William Garrard Reed, Jr.: director B 1939. ED Duke University; Harvard University Graduate School of Business Administration MBA (1969). PRIM CORP EMPL director: Simpson Investment Co. CORP AFFIL director: PACCAR Inc.; director: SAFECO Corp.; director: Microsoft Corp.

Foundation Officials

Kim Bishop: director
Maureen Frisch: president, director (see above)
Colin Moseley: director (see above)
Colleen Musgrave: administrator
William Garrard Reed, Jr.: director (see above)
Raymond P. Tennison: director PRIM CORP EMPL president, chief executive officer: Simpson Paper Co.

Grants Analysis

Disclosure Period: calendar year ending 2001
Total Grants: $818,354*
Number of Grants: 294
Average Grant: $2,500
Highest Grant: $50,000
Lowest Grant: $125
Typical Range: $500 to $5,000
*Note: Grants analysis provided by the company.

Recent Grants

Note: Grants derived from 2000 Form 990.

General

52,500	YMCA Seattle, Seattle, WA
36,478	United Way Mason County, Shelton, WA
35,000	Redwood Discovery Museum, Arcata, CA
34,464	United Way King County, Seattle, WA
22,000	Forest Foundation, Auburn, CA
21,500	United Funds of Humboldt County, Eureka, CA
20,000	Senior Services for South Sound, Olympia, WA
18,808	United Way of Pierce County, Tacoma, WA
15,000	Safeplace Rape Relief, Olympia, WA
14,468	Humboldt Senior Citizens Council, Eureka, CA

ALBERT E. AND NAOMI B. SINNISEN FOUNDATION

Giving Contact

Howard S. Kaylor
Albert E. and Naomi B. Sinnisen Foundation
c/o Ferris Baker Watts
113 South Potomac Street
Hagerstown, MD 21740
Phone: (301)733-7111

Description

Founded: 1987
EIN: 526321486
Organization Type: Private Foundation

Giving Locations: MD
Grant Types: General Support.

Financial Summary

Total Giving: $76,100 (2001); $38,304 (2000)
Assets: $1,405,788 (2001); $1,389,761 (2000)

Typical Recipients

Arts & Humanities: Libraries
Civic & Public Affairs: Civic & Public Affairs-General, Safety, Urban & Community Affairs
Health: Clinics/Medical Centers, Hospices
Social Services: Child Welfare, Shelters/Homelessness, Youth Organizations

Application Procedures

Initial Contact: Contact foundation to request guidelines and the Request for Funding form.
Application Requirements: Submit completed Request for Funding form, including a description of organization, proof of tax-exempt status, amount requested, project or program budget, and contact person.
Deadlines: March 31.

Foundation Officials

Howard S. Kaylor: trustee
Omer T. Kaylor: contact person
Horace D. Kefauver: trustee
Stuart L. Mullendore: trustee

Grants Analysis

Disclosure Period: calendar year ending 2001
Total Grants: $76,100
Number of Grants: 5
Highest Grant: $22,700
Lowest Grant: $9,500
Typical Range: $12,500 to $18,900

Recent Grants

Note: Grants derived from 2000 Form 990.

Library-Related

9,700	Boonsboro Ambulance and Rescue Service, Inc., Boonsboro, MD -- for external defribilation
5,000	Washington County Free Library, Baltimore, MD -- construction funding
2,354	Reach, Inc, Hagerstown, MD -- for office equipment

General

6,250	Cedar Ridge Children's Home, Williamsport, MD -- for waste water facility
5,000	Community Free Clinic, Hagerstown, MD -- for clinical office and equipment
5,000	First Hose Company of Boonsboro, Boonsboro, MD -- sets breathing apparatus
2,354	St. Johns Shelter for the Homeless -- for flooring

L. J. SKAGGS AND MARY C. SKAGGS FOUNDATION

Giving Contact

Philip M. Jelley, Secretary & Director
1221 Broadway, 21st Floor
Oakland, CA 94612-1837
Phone: (510)451-3300
Fax: (510)451-1527

Description

Founded: 1967
EIN: 946174113
Organization Type: General Purpose Foundation
Giving Locations: CA: theater grants limited to Northern California nationally.
Grant Types: General Support, Project, Research.

Donor Information

Founder: the late L. J. Skaggs, Mary C. Skaggs

Financial Summary

Total Giving: $985,000 (2001); $723,270 (2000); $495,190 (1998)
Assets: $3,664,791 (2001); $5,245,854 (2000); $856,861 (1998)
Gifts Received: $387,000 (1998); $483,000 (1997); $1,455,000 (1996). Note: In 1998, contributions were received from L. J. Skaggs Foundation Trust ($370,000), and M. C. Skaggs ($17,000). In 1997, contributions were received from the L. J. Skaggs Fdn. Trust ($450,000) and M. C. Skaggs ($33,000).

Typical Recipients

Arts & Humanities: Arts Associations & Councils, Arts Centers, Arts Festivals, Dance, Ethnic & Folk Arts, Historic Preservation, History & Archaeology, Libraries, Museums/Galleries, Music, Opera, Performing Arts, Theater
Civic & Public Affairs: Botanical Gardens/Parks, Public Policy, Rural Affairs, Zoos/Aquariums
Education: Arts/Humanities Education, Colleges & Universities, Environmental Education, Education-General, International Studies, Private Education (Precollege), Religious Education
Environment: Environment-General, Resource Conservation, Wildlife Protection
Health: AIDS/HIV, Diabetes
International: Foreign Arts Organizations, Foreign Educational Institutions, International-General, Health Care/Hospitals, International Development, International Environmental Issues, International Organizations, Missionary/Religious Activities
Religion: Religious Welfare

Application Procedures

Initial Contact: Applicants should submit a brief letter of inquiry.
Application Requirements: a description of organization, amount requested, purpose of funds sought income and expenses information, and the expertise of key personnel.
Deadlines: June 1.

Restrictions

The foundation will not fund individuals, capital or annual fund drives, residence home programs, halfway houses, sectarian religious organizations, or budget deficits.

Additional Information

Publications: Annual Report

Foundation Officials

Donald D. Crawford, Jr.: treasurer, director B Long Beach, CA 1936.
Jane C. Davis: vice president, director
Georgia Fulstone: vice president, director
Philip M. Jelley: secretary, director
Joseph W. Martin, Jr.: treasurer, director
Michael M.K. Sebree: assistant secretary, director
Mary C. Skaggs: president, director

Grants Analysis

Disclosure Period: calendar year ending 2001
Total Grants: $985,000
Number of Grants: 64
Average Grant: $11,855*
Highest Grant: $125,000
Lowest Grant: $1,000
Typical Range: $5,000 to $20,000
*Note: Average grant figure excludes two highest grants ($250,000).

Recent Grants

Note: Grants derived from 2000 Form 990.

Library-Related

10,000	Huntington Library, San Marino, CA

General

125,000	Historic Mount Vernon, VA
125,000	National Trust, London United Kingdom
100,000	San Francisco Opera, San Francisco, CA
50,000	Colonial Williamsburg Foundation, Williamsburg, VA
50,000	Santa Fe Opera, Santa Fe, NM
40,000	National Trust for Historic Preservation, Washington, DC
35,000	Oregon Shakespeare Festival, Ashland, OR
30,000	Merola Opera Program, San Francisco, CA
30,000	Painshill Park Trust, Surrey United Kingdom
25,000	California Historical Society, San Francisco, CA

SKILLMAN FOUNDATION

Giving Contact

Kari Schlachtenhaufen, President
600 Renaissance Center, Suite 1700
Detroit, MI 48243
Phone: (313)393-1185
Fax: (313)393-1187
E-mail: mailbox@skillman.org
Web: http://www.skillman.org

Description

Founded: 1960
EIN: 381675780
Organization Type: Specialized/Single Purpose Foundation
Giving Locations: MI: Wayne, Oakland, and Macomb Counties, Detroit
Grant Types: Capital, Conference/Seminar, Employee Matching Gifts, General Support, Multiyear/Continuing Support, Operating Expenses, Project, Scholarship, Seed Money.

Donor Information

Founder: The Skillman Foundation is a private foundation incorporated in Detroit, MI, in 1960 by Rose P. Skillman , who was the widow of Robert Skillman (d. 1945), an early and longtime officer and director of 3M Corporation. During their lifetimes, the Skillmans' philanthropic interests focused on providing assistance and care for children and young people, especially the disadvantaged living in Southeastern Michigan.

The foundation operated as a conduit for Rose Skillman's philanthropic giving until her death in 1983, at which time her assets were distributed to the foundation.

Financial Summary

Total Giving: $24,494,656 (fiscal year ending November 30, 2001); $25,684,918 (fiscal 2000); $25,323,298 (fiscal 1999)
Giving Analysis: Giving for fiscal 2000 includes: foundation grants to United Way ($25,000); foundation scholarships ($73,640); foundation matching gifts ($376,178) fiscal 1999: foundation matching gifts ($139,837)
Assets: $503,499,412 (fiscal 2001); $563,302,206 (fiscal 2000); $609,572,126 (fiscal 1999)

Typical Recipients

Arts & Humanities: Arts Associations & Councils, Arts Centers, Arts Funds, Arts Institutes, Ethnic & Folk Arts, History & Archaeology, Libraries, Literary Arts, Museums/Galleries, Music, Opera, Performing Arts, Public Broadcasting, Theater
Civic & Public Affairs: African American Affairs, Community Foundations, Economic Development, Employment/Job Training, Civic & Public Affairs-General, Hispanic Affairs, Housing, Law & Justice, Municipalities/Towns, Native American Affairs, Nonprofit Management, Parades/Festivals, Professional & Trade Associations, Public Policy, Urban & Community Affairs, Zoos/Aquariums
Education: Afterschool/Enrichment Programs, Agricultural Education, Arts/Humanities Education, Colleges & Universities, Colleges & Universities, Education Funds, Education Reform, Elementary Education (Public), Engineering/Technological Education, Education-General, Literacy, Medical Education, Minority Education, Preschool Education, Private Education (Precollege), Public Education (Precollege), Science/Mathematics Education, Secondary Education (Public), Social Sciences Education, Student Aid, Vocational & Technical Education
Health: Adolescent Health Issues, AIDS/HIV, Children's Health/Hospitals, Health Policy/Cost Containment, Health Organizations, Hospitals, Medical Research, Mental Health, Nursing Services, Prenatal Health Issues, Preventive Medicine/Wellness Organizations, Public Health, Research/Studies Institutes, Respiratory, Trauma Treatment
International: Health Care/Hospitals, International Relief Efforts
Religion: Jewish Causes, Religious Organizations, Religious Welfare, Social/Policy Issues
Science: Scientific Centers & Institutes
Social Services: At-Risk Youth, Big Brother/Big Sister, Child Abuse, Child Welfare, Community Service Organizations, Counseling, Crime Prevention, Day Care, Delinquency & Criminal Rehabilitation, Domestic Violence, Emergency Relief, Family Planning, Family Services, Food/Clothing Distribution, Homes, People with Disabilities, Recreation & Athletics, Scouts, Senior Services, Shelters/Homelessness, Substance Abuse, United Funds/United Ways, Volunteer Services, YMCA/YWCA/YMHA/YWHA, Youth Organizations

Application Procedures

Initial Contact: Contact the foundation or check its web site to obtain guidelines and a Letter of Intent Cover Sheet. After reviewing guidelines and eligibility criteria, submit a letter of intent.
Application Requirements: Letters of intent should be accompanied by the completed cover sheet form and should provide estimated project costs and revenues; a brief description of the purpose, objectives, and general methodology of the project; proof of tax-exempt status; recently audited financial statement; a recent annual report or brochure describing the organization; and, if available, a current strategic plan. and problems it addresses; goal of the project, including measurable objectives and results to be achieved; project plan describing project history and past accomplishments, target population, number of people served, timeline, and a list of specific activities; a description of organization, including history, mission, board, staff and current clients and description of services; revenue plan, including other sources of funding; evaluation plan, including method of evaluation, any additional questions, information sources and analysis, who will conduct the evaluation; plan for continued support of the project following the conclusion of the foundation's funding; total project budget, audited financial statement; and current annual report. audited financial statement; and current annual report.
Deadlines: None.
Review Process: During the review process, a staff member will be assigned to help develop the proposal. The program staff member will prepare a recommendation to present to the foundation's program group, which will decide whether or not the project falls within the foundation's goals. If the program group invites the applicant to submit a complete grant application, the assigned staff member will continue to assist the applicant with the full grant application process. The foundation's trustees review grant applications five times each year, generally in February, April, June, September, and November. The review process takes three months and the foundation will notify the organization in writing when their application has been received and when a decision has been made.
Evaluative Criteria: The proposed program must include a method for evaluating its effectiveness, the organization must intend to continue the program after the grant period has ended; and the grant request should be for a minimum of $10,000.
Notes: The foundation asks that applications are not faxed. The foundation will usually only make grants for one year and for no more than 25 percent of an organization's general operations cost.

Restrictions

Grants are made in Wayne, Oakland, and Macomb counties, Michigan only. The foundation reports that it does not make grants that may jeopardize an organization's public charity status because the amount requested is too large in relation to the past level of public support; to new organizations or to organizations that had IRS qualifying public revenues of less than $100,000 for the preceding year; research, or deficit funding; for generic fund-raising requests; loans; individuals; or to organizations that discriminate against people because of age, race, creed, gender, religion, disability, sexual orientation, or ethnicity. Only organizations that are tax-exempt under IRC Section 501(c)(3) and can provide a copy of a financial audit conducted by an independent certified public accountant may apply for funding. Organizations classified as a private foundation under IRC Section 509(a) are not eligible.

Additional Information

The foundation asks all prospective applicants to review its Grantmaking Policies and Procedures before submitting a proposal. The foundation discourages contact with any trustee regarding specific applications.

One month after notification of grant approval, the foundation meets with nonprofits to discuss reporting requirements. The foundation requires organizations to submit period reports and information about the program, including a signed copy of award letter, six-month progress and expenditure report, final evaluation and expenditure reports, etc.

About one-half of the foundation's grants are initiated by the foundation through collaborative projects aimed at priority goals within the foundation's program areas.

Publications: Annual Report; Newsletter; Grantmaking Policies and Procedures

Foundation Officials

Dr. Lillian Bauder: chairman, trustee B 1939. ED Douglass College (1961); University of Michigan (1973). PRIM CORP EMPL vice president corporate affairs: Masco Corp. CORP AFFIL director: Comerica Bank; director: Detroit Edison Co.
William McNulty Brodhead: trustee B Cleveland, OH 1941. ED Wayne State University AB (1965); University of Michigan JD (1967). PRIM CORP EMPL partner: Plunkett & Cooney PC. NONPR AFFIL trustee: Michigan Children.
Richard Connell: vice president, treasurer, chief information officer
Walter E. Douglas: trustee B 1933. PRIM CORP EMPL president, director: Avis Ford Inc. CORP AFFIL president: DHT Transportation Inc.
Stephen E. Ewing: trustee B 1944. ED DePauw University BA (1965); Michigan State University MBA (1971); Harvard University Graduate School of Business Administration MBA (1982). PRIM CORP EMPL president, chief executive officer, director: Michigan Consolidated Gas Co. ADD CORP EMPL branch manager: Michigan Consolidated Gas Co. Grand Rapids; president: MCN Energy Group Inc.; president: Michcon Pipeline Co. CORP AFFIL chairman: Michcon Home Services; chairman: Saginaw Bay Lateral Co.; director: Michcon Gathering Co.

Edsel B. Ford, II: trustee B 1949. PRIM CORP EMPL vice president, director: Ford Motor Co. CORP AFFIL vice chairman: Detroit Lions Inc.; director: Penske Motorsports Inc. NONPR AFFIL trustee: Henry Ford Museum; trustee: Greenfield Village; trustee: Edison Institute.
William R. Halling: trustee PRIM CORP EMPL chairman: Selectcare HMO Inc. CORP AFFIL director: Compuware Corp. NONPR AFFIL director: Lutheran Brotherhood. CLUB AFFIL president: Economic Club Detroit.
Amyre Makupson: trustee B Detroit, MI September 30, 1947. ED Fisk University BA (1970); American University MA (1972).
Kari Schlachtenhaufen: president, chief executive officer, trustee ED Pacific Lutheran University BA; University of Oregon Law School JD. NONPR AFFIL board member: New Detroit Inc.; board member: Youth Sports & Recreation Commission; board member: City Connect Detroit.
Robert S. Taubman: trustee
Jane R. Thomas: trustee

Grants Analysis

Disclosure Period: fiscal year ending November 30, 2001
Total Grants: $24,016,095*
Number of Grants: 139
Average Grant: $172,778
Highest Grant: $2,500,000
Typical Range: $10,000 to $400,000
*Note: Giving excludes matching gifts; scholarships; United Way.

Recent Grants

Note: Grants derived from fiscal 2001 Form 990.

Library-Related
2,500,000   Detroit Public Library, Detroit, MI -- for operating support

General
1,351,000   School District of the City of Detroit, Detroit, MI -- Comer Schools and Families Initiative
1,137,000   Youth Sports and Recreation Commission, Detroit, MI -- for re-granting programs
950,000   Youth Sports and Recreation Commission, Detroit, MI -- for Work Alternative for Youth (WAY) Project
800,000   Schools of the 21st Century Corporation, Detroit, MI -- for operating support
500,000   Free Press Charities, Detroit, MI -- for 2001 Children's First Summer Dream Wish Book
500,000   Local Initiatives Support Corporation, New York, NY -- for Detroit Local Initiative Support Corporation Joint Fundraising Project
450,000   Eastern Michigan University, Ypsilanti, MI -- for Comer Schools and Families Initiative
450,000   Southeastern Michigan Health Association, Detroit, MI -- to integrate immunization registry
428,000   Community Health and Social Services, Inc., Detroit, MI -- for the LaVida Program
420,000   New Detroit, Detroit, MI -- for Strengthening Community Organizations to Promote Effectiveness (SCOPE)

LILLIAN M. SLATER TRUST

Giving Contact
Donald W. Krauter, Trustee
14 Birch Lane
Scotia, NY 12302
Phone: (518)399-1869

Description
Founded: 1997
EIN: 146179935
Organization Type: Private Foundation
Giving Locations: NY: Capital district area
Grant Types: General Support.

Financial Summary
Total Giving: $92,121 (2001); $138,500 (2000); $118,600 (1999)
Assets: $2,302,009 (2001); $2,447,893 (2000); $2,414,253 (1999)

Typical Recipients
Arts & Humanities: Libraries, Museums/Galleries, Music
Civic & Public Affairs: Civic & Public Affairs-General
Religion: Churches, Ministries
Social Services: Homes, Senior Services, Social Services-General, YMCA/YWCA/YMHA/YWHA

Application Procedures
Initial Contact: Submit a brief letter of inquiry.
Application Requirements: Include purpose of funds sought, amount requested, and a description of organization.
Deadlines: September 1.

Restrictions
Applicant must be a 501(c)(3) organization, preferably in the capital district area of New York.

Foundation Officials
Donald W. Krauter: trustee
William W. Price: trustee
Frances M. Summerville: trustee

Grants Analysis
Disclosure Period: calendar year ending 2001
Total Grants: $92,121
Number of Grants: 11
Average Grant: $8,375
Highest Grant: $25,000
Lowest Grant: $1,000
Typical Range: $2,500 to $20,000

Recent Grants
Note: Grants derived from 2001 Form 990.

Library-Related
25,000   Green Mountain College, Poultney, VT -- fund to establish a chaplaincy program

General
20,000   First United Methodist Church, Schenectady, NY -- for current expense budget
10,121   First United Methodist Church, Schenectady, NY -- for advertising campaign
10,000   Annie Schaffer Senior Citizens Center, Schenectady, NY -- for new air conditioning unit
10,000   Getting the Word Out, Lake Clear, NY -- towards publishing Adirondacks explorer news publication
5,000   Bethesda House, Schenectady, NY -- to fund a chief staff position
2,500   Home Furnishings Program, Schenectady, NY -- for new larger door at warehouse
2,500   Schenectady Inner City Ministry, Schenectady, NY -- for Crisis Network Program
2,500   YMCA of Parkside, NY -- for Summer Program
2,000   Schenectady Symphony Orchestra, Schenectady, NY -- for mentoring concert with students

1,000   World Awareness Children's Museum, Glens Falls, NY -- for the 2002 Genie Challenge Fund

SLEMP FOUNDATION

Giving Contact
Patricia L. Durbin, Trust Officer
Firstar Bank
PO Box 5208 M.L. CN-WN-05EB
Cincinnati, OH 45201
Phone: (513)762-8878

Description
Founded: 1943
EIN: 316025080
Organization Type: Private Foundation
Giving Locations: VA: Lee County, Wise County
Grant Types: Endowment, General Support, Multiyear/Continuing Support, Operating Expenses, Project, Scholarship.

Donor Information
Founder: Founded in 1943 under the will of the late C. Bascom Slemp , a former U.S. Congressman from Virginia.

Financial Summary
Total Giving: $1,096,665 (fiscal year ending June 30, 2001); $850,616 (fiscal 1999); $1,100,000 (fiscal 1998). Note: Giving includes scholarship ($284,000) fiscal 1998; ($277,000) fiscal 1997.
Giving Analysis: Giving for fiscal 2001 includes: foundation scholarships ($318,000) fiscal 1999: foundation scholarships ($307,000)
Assets: $22,113,065 (fiscal 2001); $23,926,018 (fiscal 1999); $17,193,712 (fiscal 1997)
Gifts Received: $1,000 (fiscal 2001); $1,300 (fiscal 1997); $2,300 (fiscal 1996). Note: In fiscal 2001, contributions were received from David & Cathy Kinsler. In fiscal 1996, contributions were received from Katherine MacMillan, $300; Tammy and Tommy Baker, $500; and $1,500 from Wolfe & Farmer. In fiscal 1997, contributions were received from David A. and Kathy G. Kinsler, $1,000; and Katherine MacMillan, $300.

Typical Recipients
Arts & Humanities: Arts Associations & Councils, Arts Centers, Arts Outreach, Community Arts, Arts & Humanities-General, History & Archaeology, Libraries, Museums/Galleries, Music, Performing Arts, Theater
Civic & Public Affairs: Botanical Gardens/Parks, Clubs, Municipalities/Towns, Safety
Education: Afterschool/Enrichment Programs, Agricultural Education, Arts/Humanities Education, Colleges & Universities, Community & Junior Colleges, Education Associations, Elementary Education (Public), Education-General, Literacy, Private Education (Precollege), Public Education (Precollege), Science/Mathematics Education, Secondary Education (Public), Special Education, Student Aid
Environment: Air/Water Quality, Environment-General
Health: Cancer, Children's Health/Hospitals, Clinics/Medical Centers, Emergency/Ambulance Services, Hospices
Religion: Churches, Religious Welfare, Seminaries
Social Services: Camps, Child Abuse, Child Welfare, Community Centers, Community Service Organizations, People with Disabilities, Recreation & Athletics, Scouts, Senior Services, Youth Organizations

Application Procedures
Initial Contact: The foundation has no formal grant application procedure or application form.

Application Requirements: The application should include name address and telephone number of organization; any national organization affiliation; date organization was established; a copy of IRS Service letter; organization's purpose and activities; services provided; target audience and how many served per year; names of officers and governing board; copy of the most recent balance sheet and annual operating statement; percentage of budget received from United Appeal, federal or state funding, and/or other sources; percentage of costs of organization paid for by recipients; purpose of grant and how it would benefit residents of Lee and Wise Counties, VA; and budget for specific project, if applicable. project, if applicable.
Deadlines: None. Student applications due before October 15.
Review Process: The trustees meet usually in April, July, and November to review grant applications.

Additional Information

The Foundation provides scholarships to individuals for higher education (for residents or descendants of Lee or Wise Counties, Virginia).
Publications: Application Form
Trust(s): Firstar Bank NA

Foundation Officials

Mary Virginia Edmonds: trustee
Pamela S. Edmonds: director
John A. Reid: trustee
Melissa Smith Sircy: trustee
James Smith: trustee
James C. Smith: director
Nancey E. Smith: trustee

Grants Analysis

Disclosure Period: fiscal year ending June 30, 2001
Total Grants: $778,665*
Number of Grants: 27
Average Grant: $8,795*
Highest Grant: $500,000
Lowest Grant: $100
Typical Range: $1,000 to $15,000
*Note: Giving excludes scholarships. Average grant figure excludes highest grant.

Recent Grants

Note: Grants derived from fiscal 2000 Form 990.

Library-Related
100,000	Lonesome Pine Regional Library, Wise, VA -- addition to library
1,000	Library Gallery, Wise, VA
1,000	Library Gallery, Wise, VA -- education art workshops

General
95,000	Trail of the Lonesome Pine, Big Stone Gap, VA -- capital improvements and land requisition
62,500	Powell Valley High School, Big Stone Gap, VA -- renovation of high school auditorium
30,000	Virginia State Parks Foundation, Richmond, VA -- artifact appraisal
25,000	Clinch Valley College, Wise, VA -- fund for student athletes
25,000	Clinch Valley College Foundation, Wise, VA -- radio station operating expenses
20,000	Appalachia Elementary School, Appalachia, VA -- replacement of computers and technology equipment
20,000	Coeburn Middle School, Coeburn, VA -- Accelerated Reader Program
20,000	Elydale Elementary School, Ewing, VA -- purchase of computers, printers and workstations
20,000	L.F. Addington Middle School, Wise, VA -- purchase TV/GA monitors, keyboards and cables
20,000	Pennington Middle School, Pennington Gap, VA -- equipment for computer lab

ROY W. SLUSHER CHARITABLE FOUNDATION

Giving Contact

Jerry Redfern, Foundation Manager
PO Box 3357
Springfield, MO 65808-3357
Phone: (417)882-9090

Description

Founded: 1988
EIN: 436339151
Organization Type: Private Foundation
Giving Locations: MO
Grant Types: General Support.

Financial Summary

Total Giving: $188,223 (fiscal year ending February 28, 2001); $168,150 (fiscal 2000); $168,150 (fiscal 1999)
Assets: $3,543,321 (fiscal 2001); $3,680,416 (fiscal 2000); $3,533,512 (fiscal 1999)

Typical Recipients

Arts & Humanities: Libraries, Performing Arts, Public Broadcasting
Education: Colleges & Universities, Community & Junior Colleges, Student Aid
Health: Cancer, Children's Health/Hospitals, Clinics/Medical Centers, Diabetes, Heart, Hospitals, Single-Disease Health Associations
International: Foreign Arts Organizations, International Relief Efforts, Missionary/Religious Activities
Religion: Churches, Religion-General, Religious Organizations, Religious Welfare
Social Services: At-Risk Youth, Camps, Community Centers, Community Service Organizations, Counseling, Domestic Violence, Family Services, People with Disabilities, Youth Organizations

Application Procedures

Initial Contact: Request a proposal summary sheet and application guidelines from the foundation.
Deadlines: None.
Decision Notification: Board meets in March and September.

Restrictions

Does not support individuals, religious organizations for sectarian purposes, political or lobbying groups, and organizations outside operating areas.

Additional Information

Publications: Application Guidelines; Proposal Summary Sheet
Trust(s): Firstar Bank

Foundation Officials

Charles A. Fuller, Jr.: fdn mgr

Grants Analysis

Disclosure Period: fiscal year ending February 28, 2001
Total Grants: $188,223
Number of Grants: 43
Average Grant: $4,377
Highest Grant: $20,000
Lowest Grant: $500
Typical Range: $1,000 to $10,000

Recent Grants

Note: Grants derived from fiscal 2001 Form 990.

Library-Related
3,500	Forsyth Library Friends, Forsyth, MO

General
20,000	Forsyth Boys and Girls Club, Forsyth,

	MO -- aid in building of new Boys and Girls Club
20,000	Springfield Victory Mission, Springfield, MO
14,000	Business Men's Fellowship USA, Costa Mesa, CA -- for Eastern European missions
10,000	Christian Athletes, Springfield, MO
10,000	Salvation Army, Branson, MO
8,500	Young Life Joplin, Joplin, MO
6,250	College of Ozarks, Pt. Lookout, MO -- scholarships
6,250	Ozark Tech Community College, Springfield, MO
6,000	American Diabetes Association, Springfield, MO -- research
6,000	Forsyth Community Presbyterian Church, Forsyth, MO -- for benevolence

SMALL BUSINESS SERVICE BUREAU

Company Headquarters

Worcester, MA

Company Description

Employees: 100
SIC(s): 8700 Engineering & Management Services.

Small Business Service Bureau Charitable Foundation

Giving Contact

Francis R. Carroll, President
554 Main Street
PO Box 15104
Worcester, MA 01615-0014
Phone: (508)756-3513
Fax: (508)770-0528
E-mail: fcarroll@sbsb.com

Description

EIN: 222546670
Organization Type: Corporate Foundation
Giving Locations: MA; NY
Grant Types: General Support.

Financial Summary

Total Giving: $55,394 (fiscal year ending June 30, 2000); $15,305 (fiscal 1998); $27,695 (fiscal 1997)
Giving Analysis: Giving for fiscal 1998 includes: foundation grants to United Way ($3,000)
Assets: $308,969 (fiscal 2000); $291,468 (fiscal 1998); $244,244 (fiscal 1997)
Gifts Received: $50,285 (fiscal 1998); $56,203 (fiscal 1997); $225 (fiscal 1996). Note: Contributions are received from Small Business Service Bureau.

Typical Recipients

Arts & Humanities: Historic Preservation, Libraries, Music, Performing Arts, Public Broadcasting
Civic & Public Affairs: Clubs, Civic & Public Affairs-General
Education: Colleges & Universities, Education-General, Medical Education, Private Education (Precollege), Student Aid, Vocational & Technical Education
Health: Cancer, Children's Health/Hospitals, Clinics/Medical Centers, Diabetes, Heart, Hospices, Single-Disease Health Associations
International: Foreign Educational Institutions, Health Care/Hospitals
Religion: Churches, Jewish Causes, Religious Organizations, Religious Welfare
Social Services: Child Welfare, Community Service Organizations, Crime Prevention, Senior Services,

Shelters/Homelessness, Special Olympics, United Funds/United Ways, Youth Organizations

Application Procedures

Initial Contact: Send a brief letter of inquiry.
Application Requirements: Include a description of organization.
Deadlines: None.

Restrictions

Scholarships are restricted to the study of small businesses.

Corporate Officials

Francis R. Carroll: president, director PRIM CORP EMPL president, director: Small Bus Service Bur.

Foundation Officials

Francis R. Carroll: trustee (see above)
Mary M. Carroll: trustee
Patricia A. Greenlaw: trustee

Grants Analysis

Disclosure Period: fiscal year ending June 30, 1998
Total Grants: $12,305*
Number of Grants: 17
Average Grant: $1,724
Highest Grant: $3,000
Typical Range: $100 to $1,500
*Note: Giving excludes United Way.

Recent Grants

Note: Grants derived from fiscal 1998 Form 990.

Library-Related

120	Truman Library Institute, Independence, MO

General

3,000	United Way, Worcester, MA
2,700	Bishop's Fund, Worcester, MA
2,000	Juvenile Diabetes Foundation -- Walk to Cure Diabetes
1,000	Adopt-A-Student Program, Worcester, MA
800	Mass Easter Seals Society, Worcester, MA
640	Gazette Santa, Worcester, MA
500	World Teach Program, Cambridge, MA
400	Jewish National Fund, Boston, MA -- Plant 40 Trees - Israel
250	Solomon Schechter Day School, Worcester, MA
200	American Heart Association, Framingham, MA

SMART FAMILY FOUNDATION

Giving Contact

Raymond L. Smart, President
74 Pin Oak Lane
Wilton, CT 06897-1329
Phone: (203)834-0400
Fax: (203)834-0412

Description

Founded: 1951
EIN: 061232323
Organization Type: Family Foundation
Giving Locations: nationally.
Grant Types: Project, Research.

Donor Information

Founder: Established in 1951 by the Smart family.

Financial Summary

Total Giving: $7,100,001 (2001); $7,700,001 (2000); $6,999,999 (1999)
Assets: $168,327,786 (2001); $164,010,570 (2000); $149,774,972 (1999)

Typical Recipients

Arts & Humanities: Arts Centers, Arts Festivals, Arts Institutes, Ballet, Film & Video, History & Archaeology, Libraries, Literary Arts, Museums/Galleries, Music, Opera, Performing Arts, Public Broadcasting, Theater, Visual Arts
Civic & Public Affairs: Botanical Gardens/Parks, Community Foundations, Civic & Public Affairs-General, Law & Justice, Municipalities/Towns, Professional & Trade Associations, Public Policy, Urban & Community Affairs
Education: Afterschool/Enrichment Programs, Arts/Humanities Education, Business Education, Colleges & Universities, Continuing Education, Education Reform, Elementary Education (Private), Environmental Education, Faculty Development, Education-General, International Studies, Leadership Training, Medical Education, Private Education (Precollege), Public Education (Precollege), Science/Mathematics Education, Social Sciences Education
Environment: Environment-General, Protection, Resource Conservation
Health: Clinics/Medical Centers, Eyes/Blindness, Geriatric Health, Health Organizations, Hospitals, Hospitals (University Affiliated), Medical Research, Mental Health, Research/Studies Institutes
International: Foreign Educational Institutions, Health Care/Hospitals, Human Rights, International Environmental Issues, International Peace & Security Issues
Religion: Religion-General, Jewish Causes
Science: Science Museums, Scientific Centers & Institutes, Scientific Organizations
Social Services: Animal Protection, At-Risk Youth, Child Welfare, Community Service Organizations, Crime Prevention, Family Planning, Family Services, People with Disabilities, Senior Services, Social Services-General, Substance Abuse, YMCA/YWCA/YMHA/YWHA, Youth Organizations

Application Procedures

Initial Contact: An informal letter outlining the project.
Application Requirements: The letter should include the purpose for which aid is sought, resources needed, personnel involved, and a description of the methods to be used in completing the project.
Deadlines: None.

Restrictions

The Foundation does not give grants to individuals or for-profit businesses.

Foundation Officials

Ellen Oswald: director, member
Mary Smart: secretary

Grants Analysis

Disclosure Period: calendar year ending 2001
Total Grants: $7,100,001
Number of Grants: 104
Average Grant: $56,300*
Highest Grant: $744,772
Lowest Grant: $3,000
Typical Range: $20,000 to $100,000
*Note: Average grant figure excludes two highest grants ($1,357,369).

Recent Grants

Note: Grants derived from 2001 Form 990.

Library-Related

100,000	Newberry Library, Chicago, IL -- fund current operating expenses

General

744,772	University of Chicago, Chicago, IL -- for operating expenses
612,597	Amistad Academy, New Haven, CT -- fund current operating expenses
500,000	Calgary Academy, Calgary, AB Canada -- for operating expenses
250,000	Peninsula Open Space Trust, Menlo Park, CA -- fund current operating expenses
247,724	New Jersey Performing Arts Center, Newark, NJ -- fund current operating expenses
240,886	Center for Jewish History, New York, NY -- fund current operating expenses
185,000	Smart Museum of Art, Chicago, IL -- for operating expenses
180,000	Foote School, New Haven, CT -- fund current operating expenses
155,000	Harvard University, Cambridge, MA -- for operating expenses
150,000	Save the Bay's Estuary Restoration Program, Providence, RI -- fund current operating expenses

CLARA BLACKFORD SMITH AND W. AUBREY SMITH CHARITABLE FOUNDATION

Giving Contact

Linda Hunt, Board Member
Bank of America
330 W. Main St.
Denison, TX 75020
Phone: (903)415-2300

Description

Founded: 1985
EIN: 756314114
Organization Type: General Purpose Foundation
Giving Locations: TX: primarily Grayson County
Grant Types: Capital, General Support, Project, Scholarship, Seed Money.

Donor Information

Founder: Established in 1985 by the late Clara Blackford Smith for religious, charitable, educational, scientific and literary purposes.

Financial Summary

Total Giving: $1,024,490 (fiscal year ending June 30, 2000); $358,697 (fiscal 1998); $834,496 (fiscal 1997)
Giving Analysis: Giving for fiscal 2000 includes: foundation grants to United Way ($10,000); foundation scholarships ($13,000); fiscal 1999: foundation grants to United Way ($10,000); foundation scholarships ($13,098) fiscal 1997: foundation scholarships ($10,908)
Assets: $21,211,363 (fiscal 2000); $22,183,256 (fiscal 1999); $20,810,240 (fiscal 1998)

Typical Recipients

Arts & Humanities: Historic Preservation, History & Archaeology, Libraries, Museums/Galleries, Performing Arts
Civic & Public Affairs: Botanical Gardens/Parks, Community Foundations, Economic Development, Civic & Public Affairs-General, Housing, Municipalities/Towns, Safety, Urban & Community Affairs
Education: Arts/Humanities Education, Colleges & Universities, Community & Junior Colleges, Elementary Education (Public), Engineering/Technological Education, Education-General, Literacy, Medical Education, Public Education (Precollege), Special Education, Student Aid
Environment: Environment-General

Health: Cancer, Clinics/Medical Centers, Diabetes, Emergency/Ambulance Services, Geriatric Health, Health Funds, Health Organizations, Hospices, Hospitals, Medical Rehabilitation, Medical Research, Nursing Services, Public Health
Religion: Churches
Social Services: At-Risk Youth, Big Brother/Big Sister, Child Welfare, Community Service Organizations, Crime Prevention, Domestic Violence, Food/Clothing Distribution, People with Disabilities, Recreation & Athletics, Shelters/Homelessness, Substance Abuse, United Funds/United Ways, Youth Organizations

Application Procedures

Initial Contact: Request application from foundation. Applicants submit eight copies of grant application.
Application Requirements: An application with a brief a description of organization; program or project to be considered, including purpose, desired impact, timetable and criteria for evaluation; amount requested; budget information, including prior, current and projected budgets; other sources of funding; copy of IRS determination letter; and a list of trustees or directors.
Deadlines: March 31, June 30, September 30 and December 31.
Review Process: The board meets quarterly to review applicants. The foundation may request a more detailed proposal, additional information or a visit from a representative from the organization, after reviewing application.
Notes: Recipients are requested to provide the foundation with a brief report concerning the results or benefits derived from the grant.

Restrictions

The foundation does not make grants to individuals, provide loans or deficit financing, or ordinarily make general support grants for ongoing operating expenses.

Additional Information

The foundation is administered by NationsBank of Texas, N.A.
Publications: Grant Application Information Sheet

Foundation Officials

King Campbell: chairman
Jerry Culpepper: advisor, director
Wayne E. Delaney: director, advisor
Linda Hunt: board member
Daniel J. Kelly: vice president
Jack Lilley: director
H. W. Totten, Jr.: director

Grants Analysis

Disclosure Period: fiscal year ending June 30, 2000
Total Grants: $1,001,490*
Number of Grants: 42
Average Grant: $23,845
Highest Grant: $150,000
Lowest Grant: $750
Typical Range: $2,500 to $50,000
*Note: Giving excludes scholarships; United Way.

Recent Grants

Note: Grants derived from fiscal 2000 Form 990.

General
150,000	Texoma Healthcare System, Denison, TX -- to help establish M.D. Anderson Cancer Center
125,000	Denison Community Foundation, Denison, TX -- to help fund a youth baseball/softball complex for Denison
90,000	Denison Fire Department, Denison, TX -- for the purchase of type III ambulance and equipment
75,000	Texoma Healthcare System, Denison, TX -- fund to bring Reba McEntire Show to Grayson County
50,000	Austin College, Sherman, TX -- for commitment to Wright Campus Center
50,000	Grayson County Shelter, Denison, TX -- to offset funding loss from Texas Department of Housing
50,000	Kid Key, Sherman, TX -- to restore 1,400 seat auditorium
41,000	Child Guidance Clinic of Texoma, Sherman, TX -- purchase of computer and furniture for patient care area
40,379	Habitat for Humanity, Sherman, TX -- help build ninth house in Grayson County
33,500	Denison Athletic Booster Club, Denison, TX -- to assist students, coaches and sponsors to the Kaylee Scholarship Game

ARLENE H. SMITH CHARITABLE FOUNDATION

Giving Contact

Timothy M. Hunter, Treasurer
441 E. Main St.
Corry, PA 16407-0901
Phone: (814)664-9664

Description

Founded: 1982
EIN: 251515142
Organization Type: Private Foundation
Giving Locations: PA: Corry
Grant Types: General Support.

Donor Information

Founder: the late Arlene H. Smith

Financial Summary

Total Giving: $260,736 (2001); $270,450 (2000); $255,971 (1999)
Assets: $4,537,087 (2001); $4,879,626 (2000); $5,061,306 (1999)

Typical Recipients

Arts & Humanities: Libraries
Civic & Public Affairs: Clubs, Community Foundations, Civic & Public Affairs-General, Safety
Education: Colleges & Universities, Education-General
Health: Cancer, Children's Health/Hospitals, Clinics/Medical Centers, Emergency/Ambulance Services, Hospices, Hospitals
Religion: Religious Welfare
Social Services: Community Service Organizations, Counseling, Crime Prevention, Food/Clothing Distribution, Recreation & Athletics, Scouts, Shelters/Homelessness, United Funds/United Ways, YMCA/YWCA/YMHA/YWHA, Youth Organizations

Application Procedures

Initial Contact: Applications should include two copies of the request for funding provided by the foundation, proof of tax-exempt status, list of board members, recently audited financial statement, program and agency budgets, and the most recent annual report.
Deadlines: None.

Restrictions

Grants are not made to individuals.

Additional Information

Publications: Request for Funding Form; Procedures

Foundation Officials

John E. Britton, Esq.: director
James D. Cullen, Esq.: secretary, director
Timothy M. Hunter: treasurer

Stephen J. Mahoney: president, director
Frank K. Smith: vice president, director
James E. Spoden: assistant secretary

Grants Analysis

Disclosure Period: calendar year ending 2001
Total Grants: $250,736*
Number of Grants: 17
Average Grant: $15,671*
Highest Grant: $92,352
Typical Range: $1,000 to $20,000
*Note: Giving excludes United Way. Average grant figure excludes highest grant.

Recent Grants

Note: Grants derived from 2001 Form 990.

Library-Related
2,350	Corry Public Library, Corry, PA

General
92,352	YMCA of Corry, Corry, PA
35,000	Penn Lakes Girl Scout Council, Edinboro, PA
28,000	American Cancer Society, Corry, PA
25,000	Union City Volunteer Fire Department, Union City, PA
12,000	Corry Higher Education Council, Corry, PA
11,000	Corry Area Food Pantry, Corry, PA
10,000	United Fund of the Corry Area, Corry, PA
8,000	LifeCare Pregnancy and Family Rescue Center, Corry, PA
5,000	Corry Community Development, Corry, PA
5,000	Corry Rotary Club, Corry, PA

A.O. SMITH CORP.

Company Headquarters

Milwaukee, WI
Web: http://www.aosmith.com

Company Description

Founded: 1889
Ticker: AOS
Exchange: NYSE
Revenue: US$1.469 billion (2002)
Employees: 16200 (2002)
SIC(s): 3089 Plastics Products Nec, 3443 Fabricated Plate Work--Boiler Shops, 3523 Farm Machinery & Equipment, 3714 Motor Vehicle Parts & Accessories.

Operating Locations

A.O. Smith Corp. (AR--Little Rock; CA--Irvine; FL--Williston; IL--Chicago, Granite City; KS--Wichita; KY--Bowling Green, Mount Sterling; MD--Belcamp; MI--Farmington Hills; NC--Mebane; OH--Bellevue, Upper Sandusky; SC--McBee; TN--Milan; TX--El Paso; WA--Seattle; WI--Milwaukee)

A.O. Smith Foundation, Inc.

Giving Contact

Edward J. O'Connor, Secretary
PO Box 245001
Milwaukee, WI 53224-9501
Phone: (414)359-4100
Fax: (414)359-4064

Description

Founded: 1955
EIN: 396076724
Organization Type: Corporate Foundation
Giving Locations: communities where company has manufacturing facilities.

Grant Types: Capital, Employee Matching Gifts, General Support, Operating Expenses, Project, Scholarship.

Financial Summary
Total Giving: $1,158,547 (2001); $1,183,027 (2000); $1,000,000 (1999 approx). Note: Contributes through corporate direct giving program and foundation.
Giving Analysis: Giving for 2001 includes: foundation matching gifts ($29,107); foundation scholarships ($84,740); foundation grants to United Way ($231,700); 2000: foundation matching gifts ($32,057); foundation scholarships ($95,570); foundation grants to United Way ($247,825) foundation ($807,575)
Assets: $7,777,565 (2001); $9,884,911 (2000)

Typical Recipients
Arts & Humanities: Arts Funds, Dance, Historic Preservation, Libraries, Museums/Galleries, Music, Performing Arts
Civic & Public Affairs: Business/Free Enterprise, Civil Rights, Economic Development, Nonprofit Management, Safety, Urban & Community Affairs
Education: Business Education, Colleges & Universities, Community & Junior Colleges, Economic Education, Education Funds, Engineering/Technological Education, Literacy, Medical Education, Minority Education, Student Aid
Environment: Environment-General
Health: Emergency/Ambulance Services, Hospitals, Medical Rehabilitation, Mental Health, Public Health
Social Services: Child Welfare, Community Centers, Community Service Organizations, Family Services, Homes, People with Disabilities, Recreation & Athletics, Senior Services, Shelters/Homelessness, Substance Abuse, United Funds/United Ways, Youth Organizations

Application Procedures
Initial Contact: Send a letter or proposal on the organization's letterhead.
Application Requirements: Include name, location, and a description of organization; proof of tax-exempt status; geographic area served; explanation of activity for which support is sought; amount requested; description of benefits to be achieved and who will receive them; budget, including other sources of income; and plans for reporting results.
Deadlines: By October 30 to be considered for following year's budget; requests are reviewed in the order that they are received.
Review Process: The foundation is governed by a four-member board, including the company's vice president of human resources & public affairs.
Decision Notification: The board meets annually in June, with special meetings held periodically when necessary.
Notes: Also forward any printed materials describing your organization that may lend support to the application.

Restrictions
The foundation does not make contributions to politically active organizations seeking to influence legislation, nor does it fund individuals.

Additional Information
A.O. Smith Corp. employees are encouraged to take an active part in civic affairs.

Corporate Officials
John J. Kita: vice president, treasurer, controller, director PRIM CORP EMPL vice president, treasurer, controller: A.O. Smith Corp.
Robert Joseph O'Toole: chairman, president, chief executive officer, director B Chicago, IL 1941. ED Loyola University BS (1961). PRIM CORP EMPL chairman, president, chief executive officer, director: A.O. Smith Corp. CORP AFFIL director: Protection Mutual Insurance Co.; director: Smith Fiberglass

Products Inc.; director: FM Global Insurance; director: Firstar Bank NA; director: Firstar Corp.; director: Briggs & Stratton Corp.

Foundation Officials
John J. Kita: treasurer (see above)
Edward J. O'Connor: secretary, director B Saint Louis, MO. ED Saint Louis University (1962). PRIM CORP EMPL vice president human resources & public affairs: A.O. Smith Corp.
Robert Joseph O'Toole: director (see above)
Arthur O. Smith: president B 1930. CORP AFFIL director: AO Smith Corp.; chairman, chief executive officer: Smith Investment Co.; director: Central Studies Distributing Service Inc.

Grants Analysis
Disclosure Period: calendar year ending 2001
Total Grants: $813,000*
Number of Grants: 152
Average Grant: $5,026*
Highest Grant: $54,000
Lowest Grant: $250
Typical Range: $1,000 to $10,000
*Note: Giving excludes United Way, matching gifts, and scholarships. Average grant figure excludes highest grant.

RICHARD AND SUSAN SMITH FAMILY FOUNDATION

Giving Contact
Susan F. Smith, Trustee
27 Boylston St.
Chestnut Hill, MA 02467-1719
Phone: (617)278-5220

Description
Founded: 1970
EIN: 237090011
Organization Type: Private Foundation
Giving Locations: MA: Boston metropolitan area
Grant Types: Capital, Fellowship, General Support, Project

Donor Information
Founder: the late Marian Smith, and Richard A. Smith

Financial Summary
Total Giving: $1,189,750 (fiscal year ending April 30, 2001); $1,611,380 (fiscal 2000); $733,800 (fiscal 1997)
Giving Analysis: Giving for fiscal 2001 includes: foundation grants to United Way ($10,000) fiscal 2000: foundation grants to United Way ($10,000)
Assets: $91,050,784 (fiscal 2001); $13,591,809 (fiscal 2000); $9,849,243 (fiscal 1997)
Gifts Received: $75,234,795 (fiscal 2001); $1,272,627 (fiscal 2000); $889,571 (fiscal 1997). Note: In fiscal 2001, contributions were received from Richard A. & Susan F. Smith ($75,205,039) and ADR Charitable Foundation and Trust ($29,756). In fiscal 2000, contributions were received from Robert A. Smith ($73,740), Brian and Debra Knez ($73,740), John and Amy Berylson ($73,740), Richard A. and Susan F. Smith ($1,027,946), and ADR Charitable Foundation and Trust ($23,461). In fiscal 1996, contributions received from Richard A. Smith 1976 Charitable Trust ($575,000), Marian Smith DRA 1976 Charitable Trust ($315,000), and ADR Charitable Foundation and Trust ($15,358).

Typical Recipients
Arts & Humanities: Arts Institutes, Arts & Humanities-General, Libraries, Museums/Galleries, Music, Performing Arts
Civic & Public Affairs: Zoos/Aquariums

Education: Arts/Humanities Education, Business Education, Colleges & Universities, Education-General, Preschool Education, Private Education (Precollege), Public Education (Precollege)
Health: Cancer, Children's Health/Hospitals, Health-General, Health Organizations, Hospices, Hospitals, Medical Rehabilitation, Medical Research, Prenatal Health Issues, Single-Disease Health Associations, Speech & Hearing
Religion: Jewish Causes, Synagogues/Temples
Social Services: Camps, Child Welfare, Community Service Organizations, Family Services, Food/Clothing Distribution, United Funds/United Ways, Youth Organizations

Application Procedures
Initial Contact: Send a brief letter of inquiry and full proposal.
Application Requirements: Include a description of organization, purpose of funds sought, amount requested, recently audited financial statement, and proof of tax-exempt status.
Deadlines: None.

Additional Information
Publications: Application Guidelines

Foundation Officials
Amy S. Berylson: trustee
John G. Berylson: trustee
Brian J. Knez: trustee B 1957. ED Arizona State University (1979); Boston College (1984). PRIM CORP EMPL president, co-chief executive officer, director: Harcourt General, Inc. ADD CORP EMPL chief executive officer: Harcourt Inc.; president, chief executive officer, director: Harcourt Brace & Co.
Debra S. Knez: trustee
Robert A. Smith: trustee B 1959. ED Harvard University AB (1981); Harvard University MBA (1987). PRIM CORP EMPL co-chief executive officer, director, president: Harcourt General, Inc. ADD CORP EMPL co-chief executive officer: Harcourt Inc. CORP AFFIL chairman, chief executive officer group vice president: Neiman Marcus Group Inc.
Susan F. Smith: trustee
Dana A. Weiss: trustee

Grants Analysis
Disclosure Period: fiscal year ending April 30, 2001
Total Grants: $1,179,750*
Number of Grants: 27
Average Grant: $20,198*
Highest Grant: $300,000
Typical Range: $10,000 to $40,000
*Note: Giving excludes United Way. Average grant figure excludes three highest grants ($695,000).

Recent Grants
Note: Grants derived from fiscal 2000 Form 990.

Library-Related
75,000	Boston Public Library, Boston, MA -- for education

General
500,000	Buckingham Brown and Nichols School, Cambridge, MA
300,000	Combined Jewish Philanthropies, Boston, MA
200,250	Facing History & Ourselves, Brookline, MA
85,000	Brigham and Woman's Hospital, Boston, MA
80,000	Children's Museum
73,075	Beth Israel Hospital, Boston, MA
52,500	Museum of Fine Arts Boston, Boston, MA
50,000	Citizen Schools, Boston, MA
50,000	Park School, Buffalo, NY
35,000	Meadowbrook School, Weston, MA

GORDON V. AND HELEN C. SMITH FOUNDATION

Giving Contact
Gordon V. Smith, President
8716 Crider Brook Way
Potomac, MD 20854
Phone: (301)469-8597

Description
Founded: 1986
EIN: 521440846
Organization Type: Private Foundation
Giving Locations: nationally.
Grant Types: General Support, Scholarship.

Donor Information
Founder: Gordon V. Smith, Helen C. Smith, Miller and Smith, Inc.

Financial Summary
Total Giving: $790,574 (2001); $198,675 (2000); $670,059 (1999)
Giving Analysis: Giving for 2001 includes: foundation scholarships ($132,871); 2000: foundation matching gifts ($25,100) foundation scholarships ($47,741)
Assets: $25,016,947 (2001); $22,570,413 (2000); $9,197,220 (1999)
Gifts Received: $320,500 (2000); $1,245,813 (1999); $15,000 (1998). Note: In 2000, contributions were received from the estate of Helen Wiese and Miller and Smith Inc. In 1998, contributions were received from R. Nihl Crider Trust. In 1996, contributions were received from Gordon V. Smith.

Typical Recipients
Arts & Humanities: Arts Centers, Arts Outreach, Libraries, Music, Opera, Performing Arts, Public Broadcasting
Civic & Public Affairs: Clubs, Community Foundations, Employment/Job Training, Civic & Public Affairs-General, Housing, Law & Justice, Public Policy, Safety, Urban & Community Affairs, Women's Affairs
Education: Business Education, Colleges & Universities, Engineering/Technological Education, Legal Education, Medical Education, Minority Education, Private Education (Precollege), Public Education (Precollege), Religious Education, Science/Mathematics Education, Student Aid
Environment: Environment-General
Health: AIDS/HIV, Cancer, Children's Health/Hospitals, Diabetes, Emergency/Ambulance Services, Health-General, Health Organizations, Heart, Hospices, Hospitals, Medical Research, Multiple Sclerosis, Prenatal Health Issues, Public Health, Respiratory
International: Health Care/Hospitals, Human Rights, International Organizations, International Relief Efforts, Missionary/Religious Activities
Religion: Churches, Religion-General, Jewish Causes, Missionary Activities (Domestic), Religious Organizations, Religious Welfare, Seminaries
Social Services: Big Brother/Big Sister, Family Planning, People with Disabilities, Recreation & Athletics, Social Services-General, YMCA/YWCA/YMHA/YWHA, Youth Organizations

Application Procedures
Initial Contact: The foundation has no formal grant application procedure or application form.
Deadlines: None.

Foundation Officials
Cynthia Skarbek: director
Bruce G. Smith: director
Douglas I. Smith: director

Gordon Victor Smith: president B 1932. ED Harvard University MBA (1959). PRIM CORP EMPL founder, chairman: Miller & Smith Companies.
Helen C. Smith: vice president

Grants Analysis
Disclosure Period: calendar year ending 2001
Total Grants: $657,703*
Number of Grants: 50*
Average Grant: $5,107*
Highest Grant: $162,687
Lowest Grant: $50
Typical Range: $1,000 to $10,000*
*Note: Giving excludes scholarship. Number of grants, average grant and typical range do not include miscellaneous contributions of less than $100 each totaling $45. Average grant figure excludes three highest grants ($417,687).

Recent Grants
Note: Grants derived from 2001 Form 990.

General
162,687	Wesley Theological Seminary, Washington, DC -- for special gift
155,000	Opportunity International, Oak Brook, IL
100,000	Wesley Theological Seminary, Washington, DC -- for capital campaign
82,223	Ohio Wesleyan University, Delaware, OH -- annual scholarship fund
55,659	Ohio Wesleyan University, Delaware, OH -- capital campaign
50,648	Ohio Wesleyan University, Delaware, OH -- women as leaders scholarship
25,000	Northern Virginia Transportation Alliance, McLean, VA
22,618	Louisville Collegiate School, Louisville, KY
20,000	Fairfax County YMCA, Oakton, VA
20,000	Wesley Theological Seminary, Washington, DC -- annual fund

KELVIN AND ELEANOR SMITH FOUNDATION

Giving Contact
Carol W. Zett, Grants Manager
26380 Curtiss Wright Parkway, Suite 105
Cleveland, OH 44143
Phone: (216)289-5789
Fax: (216)289-5948

Description
Founded: 1955
EIN: 346555349
Organization Type: General Purpose Foundation
Giving Locations: OH: Cleveland metropolitan area
Grant Types: General Support, Operating Expenses, Project.

Donor Information
Founder: Established in 1955 by the late Kelvin Smith .

Financial Summary
Total Giving: $4,361,711 (fiscal year ending October 31, 2000); $6,462,384 (fiscal 1999); $4,857,779 (fiscal 1998)
Assets: $146,873,048 (fiscal 2000); $142,007,830 (fiscal 1999); $97,671,420 (fiscal 1998)
Gifts Received: $1,774,216 (fiscal 2000); $36,917,437 (fiscal 1999); $2,098 (fiscal 1992). Note: Contributions are received from the Estate of Eleanor A. Smith.

Typical Recipients
Arts & Humanities: Arts Associations & Councils, Arts Centers, Arts Institutes, Arts Outreach, Historic Preservation, History & Archaeology, Libraries, Museums/Galleries, Music, Opera, Performing Arts, Public Broadcasting, Theater
Civic & Public Affairs: Botanical Gardens/Parks, Clubs, Employment/Job Training, Civic & Public Affairs-General, Municipalities/Towns, Nonprofit Management, Public Policy, Urban & Community Affairs, Zoos/Aquariums
Education: Arts/Humanities Education, Business Education, Colleges & Universities, Education Reform, Education-General, Literacy, Medical Education, Private Education (Precollege), Public Education (Precollege), Special Education, Student Aid
Environment: Forestry, Environment-General, Protection, Resource Conservation
Health: Cancer, Children's Health/Hospitals, Clinics/Medical Centers, Eyes/Blindness, Health Organizations, Hospices, Hospitals (University Affiliated), Medical Rehabilitation, Mental Health, Nursing Services, Prenatal Health Issues, Speech & Hearing
International: International Affairs
Religion: Ministries, Religious Welfare
Science: Science Museums, Scientific Centers & Institutes, Scientific Research
Social Services: Animal Protection, Camps, Child Welfare, Community Service Organizations, Day Care, Family Planning, Family Services, Food/Clothing Distribution, People with Disabilities, Recreation & Athletics, Senior Services, Shelters/Homelessness, Substance Abuse

Application Procedures
Initial Contact: The foundation has no formal application form. An initial written application should be submitted.
Application Requirements: Each grant request should include a two-page cover letter that outlines the reason for the request or the specific project to be funded, and the amount of funds being requested. This letter should by signed by the Executive Director and the Board President.
The proposal should also include: background information of your organization such as history, mission, types of programs offered, clients served; the number of full-time and part-time staff positions; a description of your project or needs to be addressed, including specific goals and ways to meet them, project budget and timeline, key personnel involved, anticipated outcome or impact, method of evaluation, and plans for the continuation of your project or program. Include information on how foundation funds will be used; other foundation, government, and public support; and your plan for follow-up funding; a copy of your organization's line item expense budget and most recent audited financial statement; and a list of current board members, most recent annual report, and a copy of the IRS letter confirming your Internal Revenue Code 501(c)(3) status.
Deadlines: None.
Review Process: Each request will be acknowledged upon receipt, and a written notification of the board's decision will be sent after each meeting.
Notes: A site visit may be necessary prior to consideration of proposal.

Restrictions
The foundation does not fund endowments, individuals or political subdivisions, nor do they make loans. The foundation does not respond to mass mailings for annual appeals.

Additional Information
Publications: Application Guidelines

Foundation Officials
M. Roger Clapp: trustee
John Lyell Dampeer: chairman, treasurer, trustee B Cleveland, OH June 03, 1916. ED Harvard University

SB (1938-1938); Oxford University New College (1938-1939); Harvard University LLB (1942-1942). PRIM CORP EMPL retired partner: Thompson Hine & Flory. NONPR AFFIL member: Ohio Bar Association; member: Phi Beta Kappa; member: Greater Cleveland Bar Association; member: American Bar Association. CLUB AFFIL Union Club; Kirtland Country Club.

Michael D. Eppig, MD: trustee

Andrew Lawrie Fabens, III: assistant secretary B Washington, DC 1942. ED Yale University AB (1964); University of Chicago JD (1967). PRIM CORP EMPL partner: Thompson Hine & Flory. NONPR AFFIL member: Cleveland Bar Association; member: Ohio Bar Association; trustee: Bascom Little Fund; fellow: American College Trust & Estate Counsel; trustee: American McGregor Home. CLUB AFFIL member: Rawfand Club; member: Union Club; member: Cleveland Skating Club; member: Novel Club.

Ellen S. Mavec: vchpn, trustee

Lucia S. Nash: corp chairman, trustee

Lincoln Reavis: trustee B Cleveland, OH 1933. ED Cornell University BA (1955); Harvard University JD (1959). PRIM CORP EMPL partner: Spieth Bell McCurdy & Newell. NONPR AFFIL trustee: Judson Retirement Community; trustee: University Circle; trustee: Holden Arboretum; member: Cleveland Bar Association; trustee: Hawken School; member: American Bar Association; fellow: American College Trust & Estate Counsel. CLUB AFFIL mem: Union Club; mem: Rowfant Club; mem: Tavern Club.

Cara S. Stirn: vice president, trustee

Grants Analysis

Disclosure Period: fiscal year ending October 31, 2000
Total Grants: $4,361,711
Number of Grants: 59
Average Grant: $73,927
Highest Grant: $841,734
Lowest Grant: $2,250
Typical Range: $5,000 to $10,000 and $20,000 to $100,000

Recent Grants

Note: Grants derived from 2000 Form 990.

General

841,734	Musical Arts Association, Cleveland, OH -- capital campaign
560,698	Cleveland Botanical Garden, Cleveland, OH -- capital campaign
439,302	Cleveland Botanical Garden, Cleveland, OH -- capital campaign
418,133	Cleveland Botanical Garden, Cleveland, OH -- capital campaign
400,000	Hathaway Brown School, Shaker Heights, OH -- capital campaign
200,000	Case Western Reserve University, Cleveland, OH -- for program support
150,000	Musical Arts Association, Cleveland, OH -- for blossom initiative
125,000	Cleveland Museum of Art, Cleveland, OH -- annual fund
125,000	Musical Arts Association, Cleveland, OH -- annual fund
125,000	Rainbow Babies and Children's Hospital, Cleveland, OH -- capital campaign

RALPH L. SMITH FOUNDATION

Giving Contact

David P. Ross, Trust Officer
c/o Bank of America
1200 Main Street, 14th Floor
Kansas City, MO 64105
Phone: (816)979-7481

Description

Founded: 1952
EIN: 446008508
Organization Type: Private Foundation
Giving Locations: AZ; CA; MO; OR
Grant Types: General Support.

Donor Information

Founder: the late Harriet T. Smith, the late Ralph L. Smith

Financial Summary

Total Giving: $1,133,050 (2001); $1,204,160 (2000); $1,200,920 (1999)
Assets: $22,884,609 (2001); $25,694,172 (2000); $23,587,611 (1999)

Typical Recipients

Arts & Humanities: Ethnic & Folk Arts, Libraries, Museums/Galleries, Music, Public Broadcasting, Theater
Civic & Public Affairs: Botanical Gardens/Parks, Community Foundations, Economic Development, Gay/Lesbian Issues, Civic & Public Affairs-General, Hispanic Affairs, Housing, Legal Aid, Municipalities/Towns, Native American Affairs, Nonprofit Management, Public Policy, Rural Affairs, Women's Affairs
Education: Arts/Humanities Education, Colleges & Universities, Faculty Development, Education-General, Leadership Training, Private Education (Precollege), Public Education (Precollege), Science/Mathematics Education
Environment: Resource Conservation
Health: AIDS/HIV, Cancer, Children's Health/Hospitals, Medical Rehabilitation, Medical Research, Public Health, Single-Disease Health Associations
International: Foreign Educational Institutions, Health Care/Hospitals
Religion: Churches
Science: Scientific Organizations
Social Services: Big Brother/Big Sister, Community Service Organizations, Crime Prevention, Domestic Violence, Family Planning, Family Services, Food/Clothing Distribution, Shelters/Homelessness, Social Services-General, Substance Abuse, Youth Organizations

Application Procedures

Initial Contact: Send a brief letter of no more than three pages with appropriate attatchments after initial phone call.
Deadlines: None.

Additional Information

Trust(s): Bank of America NA

Foundation Officials

Harriet S. Denison: mgr
Martha Denison: director
Anne S. Douthat: mgr
E. M. Douthat, III: director
Neil T. Douthat: trustee
Paul N. Douthat: director
Neil T. Smith: trustee
Ralph L. Smith, Jr.: mgr

Grants Analysis

Disclosure Period: calendar year ending 2001
Total Grants: $1,133,050
Number of Grants: 149
Average Grant: $7,604
Highest Grant: $50,000
Typical Range: $1,000 to $10,000

Recent Grants

Note: Grants derived from 2001 Form 990.

General

50,000	Graffiti Abatement Program, Tucson, AZ
50,000	Scott Valley Scholarships and Educational Awards, Etina, CA -- Robert McCallister Memorial Scholarship
50,000	University of Arizona, Tucson, AZ
35,000	KUAT/Public Television, Tucson, AZ
35,000	Pima Air and Space Museum, Tucson, AZ
30,000	Planned Parenthood of Greater Kansas City, Kansas City, MO
26,000	KCPT/Channel 19, Kansas City, MO
25,000	Friendship House, Kansas City, MO
25,000	University of Arizona, Tucson, AZ -- library
20,000	Western States Center, Portland, OR

WILLIAM R. AND SARA BABB SMITH FOUNDATION

Giving Contact

James T. Chafin III, III, Secretary & Treasurer
PO Box 2000
McDonough, GA 30253
Phone: (770)957-4466

Description

Founded: 1995
EIN: 586306403
Organization Type: Private Foundation
Giving Locations: GA: Henry County

Financial Summary

Total Giving: $91,142 (2000); $68,574 (1999); $3,000 (1996)
Giving Analysis: Giving for 2000 includes: foundation scholarships ($27,000)
Assets: $1,781,119 (2000); $1,524,296 (1999); $1,482,988 (1996)
Gifts Received: $2,522 (1995); $480,963 (1994).
Note: In 1994, contributions were received from William and Sara Smith.

Typical Recipients

Arts & Humanities: Libraries
Civic & Public Affairs: Civic & Public Affairs-General, Municipalities/Towns
Education: Elementary Education (Public), Education-General, Secondary Education (Private), Secondary Education (Public), Student Aid, Vocational & Technical Education
Social Services: Community Service Organizations, Family Services, Youth Organizations

Application Procedures

Initial Contact: Send a brief letter of inquiry.
Application Requirements: Include purpose of funds sought.
Deadlines: None.

Restrictions

Emphasis is on social and educational needs.

Foundation Officials

Betty Bonner: secretary
Hans Broder: president
James Chafin: trust
Robert Gardener: trust
Mary Jane Owen: trust
Nancy Smith: vice president
Sara Babb Smith: vice chairman
William R. Smith: chairman
Roy W. Swann: trustee

Grants Analysis

Disclosure Period: calendar year ending 2000
Total Grants: $64,142*
Number of Grants: 21
Average Grant: $2,307*
Highest Grant: $18,000
Lowest Grant: $500
Typical Range: $500 to $10,000

*Note: Giving excludes scholarship. Average grant excludes highest grant ($18,000).

Recent Grants

Note: Grants derived from 2000 Form 990.

Library-Related

5,500	Henry County Library

General

18,000	Joseph Sams School, Fayetteville, GA
12,000	Fortson Youth Training
12,000	Henry County Department of Family and Children Services
10,232	Henry County Council
10,000	Friend's House, A
9,000	Joseph Sams School, Fayetteville, GA
3,410	Henry County Council
2,000	Genealogical Societies of Henry and Clayton Counties
2,000	Youth Leadership
1,000	Geneological Societies of Henry and Clayton Counties

STANLEY SMITH HORTICULTURAL TRUST

Giving Contact

William L. Culberson
PO Box 51759
Durham, NC 27717
Phone: (415)391-0292

Description

Founded: 1970
EIN: 946209165
Organization Type: Private Foundation
Giving Locations: nationally.
Grant Types: Capital, General Support, Operating Expenses, Project, Research.

Donor Information

Founder: May Smith

Financial Summary

Total Giving: $796,974 (2001); $789,205 (2000); $805,218 (1999)
Assets: $17,931,211 (2001); $19,267,069 (2000); $18,950,971 (1999)

Typical Recipients

Arts & Humanities: Arts Outreach, History & Archaeology, Libraries, Museums/Galleries
Civic & Public Affairs: Botanical Gardens/Parks, Clubs, Community Foundations, Economic Development, Civic & Public Affairs-General, Women's Affairs, Zoos/Aquariums
Education: Agricultural Education, Arts/Humanities Education, Colleges & Universities, Economic Education, Environmental Education, Education-General
Environment: Environment-General, Resource Conservation
Health: Hospitals
International: Foreign Arts Organizations, Health Care/Hospitals, International Environmental Issues, International Organizations, Trade
Science: Scientific Centers & Institutes, Scientific Organizations
Social Services: Recreation & Athletics

Application Procedures

Initial Contact: Send cover letter and full proposal.
Application Requirements: Include purpose of funds sought, proof of tax-exempt status, and a copy of most recent Form 990 PF.
Deadlines: Applications are accepted from April 15 through September 1.

Restrictions

Project must be horticultural in nature with significant educational bias. Does not support individuals.

Foundation Officials

John P. Collins, Jr.: trustee
R. M. Collins: trustee
James Ronald Gibbs: trustee
N. D. Matheny: trustee
May Smith: trustee

Grants Analysis

Disclosure Period: calendar year ending 2001
Total Grants: $796,974
Number of Grants: 55
Average Grant: $14,490
Highest Grant: $45,000
Lowest Grant: $2,500
Typical Range: $5,000 to $30,000

Recent Grants

Note: Grants derived from 2000 Form 990.

Library-Related

19,200	Henry E. Huntington Library and Art Gallery, San Marino, CA -- purchase of stereo microscopes

General

55,600	Holden Arboretum, Kirtland, OH -- support of BG-BASE windows conversion project
43,460	Missouri Botanical Garden, St. Louis, MO -- post-doctoral database position, data entry clerk
25,000	Humboldt Botanical Gardens Foundation, Eureka, CA -- director's salary and newsletter publication
20,000	Botanical Garden Society of the Ozarks, Inc., Fayetteville, AR -- director's salary
20,000	Cabrillo College Foundation, Aptos, CA -- purchase of 20 dissecting microscopes
20,000	Edgerton Garden Center, Hamden, CT -- support of a horticultural educator program
20,000	Foundation de Domaine Joly - De Lotbiniere, Sainte-Croix, QC Canada -- establishment of management software
20,000	Friends of San Luis Obispo Botanical Garden, San Luis Obispo, CA -- salary of an education director
20,000	Garden Conservancy, Cold Spring, NY
20,000	Hatcher Garden and Woodland Preserve, Inc., The, Spartanburg, SC

M. W. SMITH, JR. FOUNDATION

Giving Contact

Kenneth E. Niemeyer
c/o AmSouth Bank NA
PO Drawer 1628
Mobile, AL 36633
Phone: (251)342-0402

Description

Founded: 1960
EIN: 636018078
Organization Type: Private Foundation
Giving Locations: AL: Southwest Alabama
Grant Types: Capital, Emergency, Endowment, General Support, Multiyear/Continuing Support, Operating Expenses, Project, Research, Scholarship, Seed Money.

Donor Information

Founder: the late M. W. Smith, Jr.

Financial Summary

Total Giving: $100,565 (fiscal year ending June 30, 2002); $142,754 (fiscal 2001); $62,000 (fiscal 2000)
Giving Analysis: Giving for fiscal 2000 includes: foundation grants to United Way ($2,400)
Assets: $2,430,547 (fiscal 2002); $2,644,334 (fiscal 2001); $2,629,577 (fiscal 2000)

Typical Recipients

Arts & Humanities: Arts Associations & Councils, Community Arts, Dance, Historic Preservation, History & Archaeology, Libraries, Museums/Galleries
Civic & Public Affairs: Botanical Gardens/Parks, Civic & Public Affairs-General, Municipalities/Towns, Urban & Community Affairs, Zoos/Aquariums
Education: Science/Mathematics Education
Environment: Forestry, Environment-General, Wildlife Protection
Health: Children's Health/Hospitals, Health-General, Mental Health
Religion: Churches, Religious Welfare
Science: Science Exhibits & Fairs
Social Services: Child Welfare, Community Service Organizations, People with Disabilities, United Funds/United Ways, Youth Organizations

Application Procedures

Initial Contact: Send brief letter describing program.
Deadlines: None.

Restrictions

Does not support individuals.

Additional Information

Trust(s): Am South Bank

Foundation Officials

Joeseph Baker, Jr.: committee member
Louis M. Finley, Jr.: comm mem
John Martin: comm mem
Maida S. Pearson: chairman
Mary M. Riser: secretary

Grants Analysis

Disclosure Period: fiscal year ending June 30, 2002
Total Grants: $100,565
Number of Grants: 18
Average Grant: $4,027*
Highest Grant: $18,139
Lowest Grant: $1,000
Typical Range: $2,000 to $9,000
*Note: Average grant figure excludes two highest grants ($36,139).

Recent Grants

Note: Grants derived from fiscal 2000 Form 990.

General

18,000	St. Stephens Historical Society
12,700	Ronald McDonald House
10,000	Christ Church, Greenwich, CT
5,000	Camp Seale Harris, Florence, AL
5,000	USABC
3,400	Mobile Botanical Gardens, Mobile, AL
3,000	Toxey Preservation Society, Toxey, AL
2,400	United Way of Clark County, Arkadelphia, AR
1,000	Thomasville Church of God in Christ
1,000	Wings of Life, Hardin, IL

ETHEL SERGEANT CLARK SMITH MEMORIAL FUND

Giving Contact

Diane Stables
c/o Wachovia Bank
P.O. Box 7558
Philadelphia, PA 19101
Phone: (215)985-7917
Fax: (215)985-3922

Description

Founded: 1977
EIN: 236648857
Organization Type: Private Foundation
Giving Locations: PA: Delaware County
Grant Types: Capital, Emergency, General Support, Multiyear/Continuing Support, Operating Expenses, Project, Research, Scholarship, Seed Money.

Donor Information

Founder: the late Ethel Sergeant Clark Smith

Financial Summary

Total Giving: $726,000 (fiscal year ending May 31, 2002); $938,299 (fiscal 2001); $823,443 (fiscal 2000)
Assets: $14,730,023 (fiscal 2002); $17,532,231 (fiscal 2001); $19,309,793 (fiscal 2000)

Typical Recipients

Arts & Humanities: Arts Centers, Community Arts, Dance, Historic Preservation, Libraries, Museums/Galleries, Music
Civic & Public Affairs: Botanical Gardens/Parks, Economic Development, Employment/Job Training, Civic & Public Affairs-General, Housing, Law & Justice, Legal Aid, Safety, Urban & Community Affairs, Women's Affairs, Zoos/Aquariums
Education: Colleges & Universities, Education-General, Literacy, Private Education (Precollege), Public Education (Precollege), Science/Mathematics Education, Special Education, Vocational & Technical Education
Environment: Environment-General, Protection
Health: Clinics/Medical Centers, Health Organizations, Hospitals, Prenatal Health Issues, Public Health, Speech & Hearing
Religion: Churches, Dioceses, Ministries, Religious Organizations, Religious Welfare
Social Services: At-Risk Youth, Child Welfare, Community Centers, Community Service Organizations, Crime Prevention, Domestic Violence, People with Disabilities, Recreation & Athletics, Scouts, United Funds/United Ways, Volunteer Services, YMCA/YWCA/YMHA/YWHA, Youth Organizations

Application Procedures

Initial Contact: Send cover letter and full proposal.
Application Requirements: Include a description of organization, amount requested, purpose of funds sought, recently audited financial statement, and proof of tax-exempt status.
Deadlines: March 1 and September 1 for completed proposals.

Restrictions

Does not support individuals or provide loans.

Additional Information

Publications: Multi-Year Report (including Application Guidelines)
Trust(s): Wachovia Bank NA

Grants Analysis

Disclosure Period: fiscal year ending May 31, 2002
Total Grants: $726,000
Number of Grants: 50
Average Grant: $14,520
Highest Grant: $50,000
Lowest Grant: $1,000
Typical Range: $5,000 to $25,000

Recent Grants

Note: Grants derived from 2000 Form 990.

Library-Related
25,000   Sleighton School, Media, PA -- refurbishing library and purchase appliances

General
40,000   Cheyney University, Cheyney, PA -- renovations
25,000   Chespenn Health Services -- immunization program
25,000   CityTeam Ministries, San Jose, CA -- improvements for third floor
25,000   Delaware County Legal Assistance, DE
25,000   Delaware County Legal Assistance, DE
25,000   Domestic Abuse Project of Delaware County, Media, PA
25,000   Eastern College, St. Davids, PA -- renovations to accommodate Templeton honors college
25,000   Maternity Care Coalition, Philadelphia, PA
25,000   Riddle Memorial Hospital, Media, PA -- education center
25,000   Wayne Art Center -- expand facilities and renovation of the Masonic Hall

MAY AND STANLEY SMITH TRUST

Giving Contact

N. D. Matheny, Trustee
720 Market Street, Suite 250
San Francisco, CA 94102-2500
Phone: (415)391-0292

Description

EIN: 946435244
Organization Type: Private Foundation
Giving Locations: CA
Grant Types: General Support, Scholarship.

Donor Information

Founder: May Smith

Financial Summary

Total Giving: $458,000 (2001); $497,851 (2000); $453,100 (1999)
Giving Analysis: Giving for 2001 includes: foundation scholarships ($55,000); 2000: foundation scholarships ($18,000); 1998: foundation scholarships ($20,000)
Assets: $9,497,455 (2001); $10,224,608 (2000); $10,356,798 (1999)

Typical Recipients

Arts & Humanities: Arts Outreach, Dance, Ethnic & Folk Arts, Arts & Humanities-General, Libraries, Music, Theater, Visual Arts
Civic & Public Affairs: Employment/Job Training, Housing, Law & Justice, Parades/Festivals, Urban & Community Affairs
Education: Arts/Humanities Education, Business Education, Elementary Education (Private), Education-General, Literacy, Minority Education, Preschool Education, Private Education (Precollege), Science/Mathematics Education, Special Education, Student Aid
Health: AIDS/HIV, Arthritis, Cancer, Children's Health/Hospitals, Eyes/Blindness, Health Organizations, Home-Care Services, Hospitals, Long-Term Care, Medical Research, Mental Health, Public Health, Single-Disease Health Associations, Speech & Hearing

International: Foreign Educational Institutions, Health Care/Hospitals, Human Rights, International Organizations, Missionary/Religious Activities
Religion: Jewish Causes, Missionary Activities (Domestic), Religious Organizations, Religious Welfare
Social Services: Animal Protection, Big Brother/Big Sister, Child Abuse, Child Welfare, Community Centers, Community Service Organizations, Counseling, Delinquency & Criminal Rehabilitation, Domestic Violence, Family Services, Food/Clothing Distribution, Homes, People with Disabilities, Recreation & Athletics, Senior Services, Social Services-General, YMCA/YWCA/YMHA/YWHA, Youth Organizations

Application Procedures

Initial Contact: Send a brief letter of inquiry.
Application Requirements: Describe program or project, proof of tax-exempt status and copy of Form 990 PF.
Deadlines: Applications are accepted from April 15 through September 30.

Restrictions

Awards grants to organizations that provide care and/or housing for disadvantaged children, the blind, and the aged.

Foundation Officials

John P. Collins, Jr.: trustee
James Ronald Gibbs: trustee
N. D. Matheny: trustee

Grants Analysis

Disclosure Period: calendar year ending 2001
Total Grants: $403,000*
Number of Grants: 85
Average Grant: $4,741
Highest Grant: $6,000
Lowest Grant: $1,500
Typical Range: $2,000 to $6,000
*Note: Giving excludes scholarships.

Recent Grants

Note: Grants derived from 2000 Form 990.

General
6,000   Alta Bates Foundation, Berkeley, CA -- Tele-care services for seniors
6,000   Arthritis Foundation Northern California Chapter, San Francisco, CA -- youth programs
6,000   Better Health Foundation, Oakland, CA -- Robert Louie Family cancer support program
6,000   California Contemporary Craft Association, Sausalito, CA
6,000   Child-Rite, Inc, Taos, NM -- spring 2000 family retreat weekend
6,000   Clear Water Academy Foundation, Calgary, AB Canada
6,000   Community Justice Initiatives Association, Langley, BC Canada -- for victim offender reconciliation program
6,000   Contra Costa County Food Bank, Concord, CA -- for brown bag program for seniors
6,000   Counseling Group, Abbotsford, BC Canada -- subsidized counseling services for low income clients
6,000   Dalamation Dreams, Inc., Santa Barbara, CA

SMOOT CHARITABLE FOUNDATION

Giving Contact

Thomas J. Kennedy, Vice President
PO Box 2567
Salina, KS 67402-2567

Phone: (785)825-4674
Fax: (785)825-5936

Description
Founded: 1976
EIN: 480851141
Organization Type: Private Foundation
Giving Locations: KS: Saline County
Grant Types: General Support.

Financial Summary
Total Giving: $594,771 (fiscal year ending June 30, 2002); $631,317 (fiscal 2001); $575,949 (fiscal 2000). Note: Fiscal 1997 Giving includes United Way ($31,000).
Giving Analysis: Giving for fiscal 2002 includes: foundation grants to United Way ($45,000); fiscal 2001: foundation grants to United Way ($45,000); fiscal 2000: foundation grants to United Way ($40,000)
Assets: $12,037,051 (fiscal 2002); $13,569,193 (fiscal 2001); $12,658,370 (fiscal 2000)

Typical Recipients
Arts & Humanities: Arts Centers, Arts Institutes, Community Arts, Libraries, Museums/Galleries, Music, Theater
Civic & Public Affairs: Employment/Job Training, Civic & Public Affairs-General, Housing, Municipalities/Towns
Education: Colleges & Universities, Education-General, Private Education (Precollege), Science/Mathematics Education, Secondary Education (Private)
Religion: Churches, Religious Welfare
Social Services: Big Brother/Big Sister, Child Abuse, Child Welfare, Community Centers, Community Service Organizations, Counseling, Day Care, Domestic Violence, Emergency Relief, Food/Clothing Distribution, People with Disabilities, Recreation & Athletics, Scouts, Substance Abuse, United Funds/United Ways, YMCA/YWCA/YMHA/YWHA, YMCA/YWCA/YMHA/YWHA, Youth Organizations

Application Procedures
Initial Contact: Send a brief letter of inquiry describing program or project.
Application Requirements: Include purpose of funds sought and proof of tax-exempt status.
Deadlines: None.

Foundation Officials
Janice L. Doherty: secretary
Thomas J. Kennedy: vice president
Dr. Robert W. Weber: president
George W. Yarnevich: vice president

Grants Analysis
Disclosure Period: fiscal year ending June 30, 2002
Total Grants: $549,771*
Number of Grants: 28
Average Grant: $4,692*
Highest Grant: $337,771
Lowest Grant: $1,000
Typical Range: $1,000 to $10,000
*Note: Giving excludes United Way. Average grant figure excludes two highest grants ($427,771).

Recent Grants
Note: Grants derived from fiscal 2000 Form 990.

General

311,949	Salina Family YMCA, Salina, KS
85,000	Kansas Wesleyan University, Salina, KS
50,000	YWCA, Salina, KS
40,000	United Way Salina Area, Salina, KS
25,000	Greater Salina Community Foundation, Salina, KS
10,000	St. John's Missionary Baptist Church, Salina, KS
5,000	Occupational Center of Central Kansas, Salina, KS
5,000	Salina Art Center, Salina, KS
4,000	Martin Luther King Jr. Child Care Association, Salina, KS
3,000	Counseling and Growth Center, The, Salina, KS

FRANK LITZ SMOOT CHARITABLE TRUST

Giving Contact
Diana S. Coulthard, Trustee
c/o First Community Bank
PO Box 950
Bluefield, WV 24701-0950
Phone: (304)325-7151

Description
Founded: 1992
EIN: 550717997
Organization Type: Private Foundation
Grant Types: General Support.

Financial Summary
Total Giving: $29,200 (2000); $41,913 (1999); $37,350 (1998)
Giving Analysis: Giving for 2000 includes: foundation grants to United Way ($2,000); foundation scholarships ($7,500); 1999: foundation grants to United Way ($2,000); foundation scholarships ($9,500) 1998: foundation scholarships ($16,250)
Assets: $1,149,985 (2000); $1,157,774 (1999); $1,190,428 (1998)
Gifts Received: $300 (1994); $95,721 (1993)

Typical Recipients
Arts & Humanities: Arts Festivals, Arts Outreach, Historic Preservation, History & Archaeology, Libraries, Museums/Galleries
Civic & Public Affairs: Clubs, Economic Development, Civic & Public Affairs-General, Municipalities/Towns, Safety, Urban & Community Affairs
Education: Colleges & Universities, Community & Junior Colleges, Elementary Education (Public), Engineering/Technological Education, Education-General, Gifted & Talented Programs, Secondary Education (Public), Student Aid
Religion: Bible Study/Translation, Churches, Religious Welfare
Science: Science Museums, Scientific Centers & Institutes
Social Services: Camps, United Funds/United Ways

Application Procedures
Initial Contact: Submit a written request.
Application Requirements: Outline the organization's programs and purpose of funds sought.
Deadlines: None.

Restrictions
Limited to southern WV and southwestern VA.

Additional Information
Trust(s): First Community Bank

Foundation Officials
Diana S. Coulthard: trustee
Janet A. Mitchell: trustee
Robert Schumacher: trustee

Grants Analysis
Disclosure Period: calendar year ending 2000
Total Grants: $19,700*
Number of Grants: 11
Average Grant: $1,791
Highest Grant: $5,000
Lowest Grant: $250
Typical Range: $500 to $2,000

*Note: Giving excludes individual scholarships and United Way.

Recent Grants
Note: Grants derived from 2000 Form 990.

General

5,000	Bluefield College, Bluefield, VA -- education
3,600	Historic Crab Orchard Museum & Pioneer Park, Bluefield, WV -- operating fund
3,000	Southwest Virginia Community College Education Foundation, Richlands, WV -- education
2,000	Dr. John W. Tresch, Bluefield, VA -- research grant
2,000	United Way of the Virginias, Bluefield, WV -- operating expense
1,500	AAA Safety Foundation, Bluefield, WV -- education
1,500	Graham Historical Society, Bluefield, VA -- operating expenses
1,500	Impact Bluefield, Bluefield, WV -- operating fund
1,000	Bluefield College, Bluefield, WV -- scholarship
1,000	Concord College, Athens, WV -- scholarship

MARION C. SMYTH TRUST

Giving Contact
T. William Bigelow, Jr., Trustee
1001 Elm Street
Manchester, NH 03101
Phone: (603)623-3420

Description
Founded: 1946
EIN: 026005793
Organization Type: Private Foundation
Giving Locations: NH: Greater Manchester limited statewide giving
Grant Types: Multiyear/Continuing Support, Scholarship.

Donor Information
Founder: the late Marion C. Smyth

Financial Summary
Total Giving: $205,907 (2000); $207,963 (1999); $206,450 (1998)
Giving Analysis: Giving for 2000 includes: foundation scholarships ($68,942) 1999: foundation scholarships ($78,175)
Assets: $5,955,210 (2000); $5,790,051 (1999); $4,993,893 (1996)

Typical Recipients
Arts & Humanities: Arts Institutes, Community Arts, Libraries, Museums/Galleries, Music, Opera, Public Broadcasting, Theater
Civic & Public Affairs: Civic & Public Affairs-General
Education: Arts/Humanities Education, Colleges & Universities, Private Education (Precollege), Student Aid
Religion: Churches

Application Procedures
Initial Contact: Send a brief letter of inquiry and a full proposal.
Application Requirements: Include a description of organization, amount requested, purpose of funds sought, recently audited financial statement, proof of tax-exempt status.
Deadlines: None.
Notes: Scholarship applicants should request an application form.

Restrictions

The foundation does not support political or lobbying groups or organizations outside operating areas.

Additional Information

Provides scholarships to college students who major in music. Also supports organizations for music purposes.

Foundation Officials

T. William Bigelow: trustee
John H. Giffin, Jr.: trustee

Grants Analysis

Disclosure Period: calendar year ending 2000
Total Grants: $136,965*
Number of Grants: 25
Average Grant: $5,479
Highest Grant: $29,500
Typical Range: $500 to $10,000
*Note: Giving excludes scholarships.

Recent Grants

Note: Grants derived from 2000 Form 990.

General

29,500	University of New Hampshire, Durham, NH -- music department
17,000	University of New Hampshire, Durham, NH -- scholarships
14,640	New Hampshire Public Television, Durham, NH
12,500	Derryfield School, Manchester, NH -- music department
9,075	Notre Dame College Music Department, Manchester, NH
8,500	New Hampshire Philharmonic Orchestra, Manchester, NH
7,500	New Hampshire Music Festival, Gilford, NH
7,000	Manchester Choral Society, Manchester, NH
5,000	Concord Community Music School, Concord, NH
5,000	Manchester Community Music School, Manchester, NH

HARRY E. AND FLORENCE W. SNAYBERGER MEMORIAL FOUNDATION

Giving Contact

E. Lori Smith, Relationship Banking Specialist
c/o M & T Bank
1 S. Center St.
Pottsville, PA 17901
Phone: (570)622-4200

Alternate Contact

1 M & T Plaza, 8th Fl.
Buffalo, NY 14203
Phone: (716)842-9565

Description

Founded: 1976
EIN: 232056361
Organization Type: Private Foundation
Giving Locations: PA: Schuylkill County
Grant Types: General Support, Scholarship.

Donor Information

Founder: the late Harry E. Snayberger

Financial Summary

Total Giving: $241,985 (fiscal year ending March 31, 2002); $224,148 (fiscal 2000); $191,768 (fiscal 1997)
Giving Analysis: Giving for fiscal 2002 includes: foundation scholarships ($149,310); fiscal 2000: foundation scholarships ($179,373); fiscal 1997: foundation ($27,925) foundation scholarships ($163,843)
Assets: $4,500,186 (fiscal 2002); $5,678,837 (fiscal 2000); $4,349,823 (fiscal 1997)

Typical Recipients

Arts & Humanities: Arts Associations & Councils, Arts & Humanities-General, Libraries, Music, Theater
Civic & Public Affairs: Business/Free Enterprise
Education: Agricultural Education, Colleges & Universities, Public Education (Precollege), Special Education, Vocational & Technical Education
International: Foreign Educational Institutions
Religion: Churches, Religious Welfare
Social Services: Day Care, Family Services, People with Disabilities, Recreation & Athletics, Scouts, YMCA/YWCA/YMHA/YWHA, Youth Organizations

Application Procedures

Initial Contact: Send letter requesting application form.
Deadlines: February 26.

Restrictions

Does not fund political or lobbying groups or organizations outside operating areas.

Additional Information

Provides scholarships to individuals for higher education. Trust(s): Keystone Financial Bank
Trust(s): PA National Bank & Trust Co

Grants Analysis

Disclosure Period: fiscal year ending March 31, 2002
Total Grants: $92,675*
Number of Grants: 154
Average Grant: $602
Highest Grant: $2,500
Lowest Grant: $150
Typical Range: $250 to $2,500
*Note: Giving excludes scholarships.

Recent Grants

Note: Grants derived from 2001 Form 990.

General

2,500	Acadia University, Wolfville, NS Canada
2,500	Chester University, West Chester, PA -- for education expenses
2,500	Delaware Valley College, Doylestown, PA -- scholarship
2,500	King's College, Wilkes-Barre, PA -- for education expenses
2,500	Lebanon Valley College, Annville, PA -- scholarship
2,500	Lebanon Valley College, Annville, PA -- scholarship
2,500	Lincoln Technical Institute, Mahwah, NJ -- scholarship
2,500	Moravian College, Bethlehem, PA -- education expenses
2,500	Pennsylvania College of Technology, Williamsport, PA -- scholarship
2,500	Pennsylvania State University, University Park, PA -- for education expenses

SNEE-REINHARDT CHARITABLE FOUNDATION

Giving Contact

Virginia Davis, Director
c/o PNC Bank
2 PNC Plaza, 33rd Floor
Pittsburgh, PA 15222-2705
Phone: (412)762-3748

Description

Founded: 1987
EIN: 256292908
Organization Type: Private Foundation
Giving Locations: PA
Grant Types: General Support.

Donor Information

Founder: Katherine E. Snee

Financial Summary

Total Giving: $831,298 (2001); $456,012 (2000); $436,185 (1999)
Assets: $21,761,406 (2001); $8,241,714 (2000); $8,979,313 (1999)
Gifts Received: $11,381,781 (2001); $100 (2000); $971 (1996). Note: In 2001, contributions were received from Katherine E. Snee estate and trusts ($10,506,117) and Tim Heasley Trust ($875,664). In 1995, contributions were received from D. Osiol Crut.

Typical Recipients

Arts & Humanities: Arts Centers, Community Arts, Ethnic & Folk Arts, Arts & Humanities-General, History & Archaeology, Libraries, Literary Arts, Museums/Galleries, Music, Public Broadcasting, Theater
Civic & Public Affairs: Botanical Gardens/Parks, Economic Development, Employment/Job Training, Civic & Public Affairs-General, Housing, Municipalities/Towns, Philanthropic Organizations, Safety, Urban & Community Affairs, Women's Affairs, Zoos/Aquariums
Education: Business Education, Colleges & Universities, Education Funds, Environmental Education, Education-General, Literacy, Private Education (Precollege), Public Education (Precollege), Religious Education, Science/Mathematics Education, Special Education
Environment: Environment-General, Environment-General, Resource Conservation
Health: Alzheimers Disease, Children's Health/Hospitals, Emergency/Ambulance Services, Geriatric Health, Health Organizations, Hospitals, Kidney, Medical Rehabilitation, Medical Research, Nursing Services, Prenatal Health Issues, Single-Disease Health Associations
Religion: Churches, Dioceses, Ministries, Religious Welfare
Science: Scientific Centers & Institutes
Social Services: Child Welfare, Community Service Organizations, Crime Prevention, Family Services, Homes, People with Disabilities, Scouts, Senior Services, Shelters/Homelessness, Special Olympics, United Funds/United Ways, Volunteer Services, YMCA/YWCA/YMHA/YWHA, Youth Organizations

Application Procedures

Initial Contact: Send a brief letter of inquiry.
Deadlines: None.

Additional Information

Trust(s): PNC Bank NA

Foundation Officials

Virginia Davis: director
Karen L. Heasley: director
Paul A. Heasley: off

Timothy Heasley: director

James Walter Ummer, Esq.: director B Pittsburgh, PA 1945. ED Thiel College BA (1967); Duke University JD (1972). PRIM CORP EMPL lawyer: Babst Calland Clements & Zomnir. CORP AFFIL director: Trafford; director: SPEC Consults; managing director: Golf Course Consults; managing director: Morgan Franklin Co. NONPR AFFIL trustee: Rehabilitation Institute; trustee: Thiel College; member: Estate Planning Council Western Pennsylvania; fellow: Am College Probate Counsel. CLUB AFFIL Tax Club; Oakmont Country Club; Rolling Rock Club; Duquesne Club.

Richard T. Vale: director

Grants Analysis

Disclosure Period: calendar year ending 2001
Total Grants: $831,298
Number of Grants: 58
Average Grant: $13,532*
Highest Grant: $60,000
Lowest Grant: $500
Typical Range: $5,000 to $25,000
*Note: Average grant figure excludes highest grant.

Recent Grants

Note: Grants derived from 2000 Form 990.

General

42,000	Ohio Valley General Hospital, McKees Rocks, PA
23,170	St. Anne Home, Greensburg, PA
21,811	Goodwill Industries, Pittsburgh, PA
19,980	Crossroads Scholarship Program, Pittsburgh, PA
19,000	Perry Township Volunteer Fire Department, Perryopolis, PA
18,585	Girl Scouts of America Southwestern Pennsylvania, Pittsburgh, PA
16,240	Perryopolis Area Ambulance Service, Perryopolis, PA
15,000	National Aviary in Pittsburgh, Pittsburgh, PA
13,500	Allegheny Valley School, Coraopolis, PA
12,500	Beginning with Books, Pittsburgh, PA

JOHN BEN SNOW FOUNDATION

Giving Contact

Jonathan L. Snow, Vice President & Treasurer
50 Presidential Plaza
Syracuse, NY 13202
Phone: (315)471-5256

Description

Founded: 1948
EIN: 136112704
Organization Type: Private Foundation
Giving Locations: NY: Central NY, Oswego County
Grant Types: Capital, Matching, Project, Scholarship.

Donor Information

Founder: the late John Ben Snow

Financial Summary

Total Giving: $287,550 (2001); $254,805 (2000); $336,800 (1999)
Assets: $7,006,249 (2001); $7,371,424 (2000); $6,863,557 (1999)

Typical Recipients

Arts & Humanities: Arts Associations & Councils, Arts Institutes, Historic Preservation, History & Archaeology, Libraries, Literary Arts, Museums/Galleries, Music, Opera, Performing Arts, Public Broadcasting, Theater

Civic & Public Affairs: Botanical Gardens/Parks, Community Foundations, Employment/Job Training, Civic & Public Affairs-General, Nonprofit Management, Philanthropic Organizations
Education: Arts/Humanities Education, Colleges & Universities, Engineering/Technological Education, Education-General, Journalism/Media Education, Legal Education, Literacy, Minority Education, Private Education (Precollege), Public Education (Precollege), Special Education, Student Aid
Environment: Resource Conservation
Health: Children's Health/Hospitals, Clinics/Medical Centers, Health Organizations, Hospitals, Public Health, Speech & Hearing
Religion: Churches, Religious Organizations
Social Services: Animal Protection, Child Welfare, Community Service Organizations, Day Care, People with Disabilities, YMCA/YWCA/YMHA/YWHA, Youth Organizations

Application Procedures

Initial Contact: Send a a brief letter of inquiry on organization letterhead.
Application Requirements: Include a brief background of the organization, a description of the proposed project, and amount requested.
Deadlines: April 1, for grant application forms.
Review Process: If the letter of inquiry meets the foundation's guidelines, a grant application form will be sent to the applicant.
Decision Notification: Final funding decisions are made in writing by July 1.

Restrictions

Does not support individuals, endowments, operating budgets, tax-supported or for-profit groups, contingency funding, or religious organizations.

Additional Information

Publications: Annual Report (including Application Guidelines)

Foundation Officials

Valerie A. Macfie: board member
Allen R. Malcolm: president
Bruce L. Malcolm: board member
Rollan D. Melton: vice president
Emelie Melton-Williams: assistant secretary
David H. Snow: vice president, treasurer
Jonathan L. Snow: secretary

Grants Analysis

Disclosure Period: calendar year ending 2001
Total Grants: $287,550
Number of Grants: 24
Average Grant: $11,981
Highest Grant: $30,000
Lowest Grant: $150
Typical Range: $5,000 to $15,000

Recent Grants

Note: Grants derived from 2001 Form 990.

Library-Related

7,500	Geneva Free Library, Geneva, NY -- for community preservation

General

30,000	Syracuse University, Syracuse, NY -- education
25,000	Clarkson University, Potsdam, NY -- education
20,400	Preservation and Revitalization of Pulaski, Pulaski, NY -- for community initiatives
20,000	Community School of Music & Arts, Ithaca, NY -- for arts and culture
20,000	Peace, Inc., New York, NY -- for community initiatives
20,000	Pulaski Academy and Central School, Pulaski, NY -- education

20,000	Syracuse University, Syracuse, NY -- journalism
17,500	Learning Disabilities Association, East Syracuse, NY -- for universal access
15,000	Syracuse Stage, Syracuse, NY -- for arts and culture
11,500	Foundation Historical Association, Auburn, NY -- education

JOHN BEN SNOW MEMORIAL TRUST

Giving Contact

Jonathan Snow, Trustee
Jefferson Tower
50 Presidential Plaza, Suite 106
Syracuse, NY 13202

Description

Founded: 1974
EIN: 136633814
Organization Type: General Purpose Foundation
Giving Locations: NY: Eastern USA.
Grant Types: Capital, Challenge, Matching, Seed Money.

Donor Information

Founder: Incorporated in 1948 by the late John Ben Snow , who was born and raised in Pulaski, NY, a small village north of Syracuse. He graduated from New York University in 1904 and began employment at the Woolworth organization. A man of vision, he was attracted to mass-market sales and introduced innovative retailing techniques. He rose rapidly through the ranks of Woolworth from stock boy to corporate director, initially in New York, and finally in Great Britain, where he accumulated a small fortune through hard work, saving, and wise investments. After retiring from Woolworth's in 1939, Mr. Snow devoted the remainder of his life to building the Speidel chain of newspapers and publishing the "Western Horseman." He was fond of animals, especially horses, and enjoyed racing, fox hunting, polo, and range riding. Throughout his life, John Ben Snow shared his wealth with relatives, friends, business associates, and fellow Pulaskians. He gave generously and freely to those persons and causes he cherished. He preferred to invest in people, especially the young, by making financial assistance available. He also believed in improving the quality of life in Pulaski and its environs.

Financial Summary

Total Giving: $1,401,500 (2001); $1,550,514 (2000); $1,007,300 (1999)
Assets: $27,192,340 (2001); $29,985,247 (2000); $29,932,152 (1999)

Typical Recipients

Arts & Humanities: Arts Associations & Councils, Arts Centers, Arts Outreach, Ballet, Ethnic & Folk Arts, Film & Video, Historic Preservation, History & Archaeology, Libraries, Museums/Galleries, Music, Opera, Performing Arts, Public Broadcasting, Theater
Civic & Public Affairs: Botanical Gardens/Parks, Community Foundations, Economic Development, Employment/Job Training, Civic & Public Affairs-General, Housing, Law & Justice, Municipalities/Towns, Native American Affairs, Philanthropic Organizations, Professional & Trade Associations, Safety, Urban & Community Affairs, Women's Affairs, Zoos/Aquariums
Education: Agricultural Education, Arts/Humanities Education, Business Education, Colleges & Universities, Colleges & Junior Colleges, Community & Junior Colleges, Economic Education, Education Funds, Environmental Education, Faculty Development, Education-General, Journalism/Media Education, Legal Education, Literacy, Medical Education, Minority

Education, Private Education (Precollege), Public Education (Precollege), Science/Mathematics Education, Social Sciences Education, Student Aid
Environment: Air/Water Quality, Environment-General, Resource Conservation
Health: Cancer, Clinics/Medical Centers, Geriatric Health, Health Funds, Hospices, Hospitals, Medical Research
International: Foreign Educational Institutions, Human Rights, International Environmental Issues
Religion: Churches, Ministries, Religious Welfare
Science: Science-General, Science Museums, Scientific Centers & Institutes, Scientific Organizations
Social Services: Animal Protection, At-Risk Youth, Child Welfare, Community Service Organizations, Day Care, Delinquency & Criminal Rehabilitation, Family Planning, Food/Clothing Distribution, People with Disabilities, Recreation & Athletics, Scouts, Senior Services, Shelters/Homelessness, Social Services-General, YMCA/YWCA/YMHA/YWHA, Youth Organizations

Application Procedures

Initial Contact: An initial letter of inquiry should be sent to the trust.
Application Requirements: Letters of inquiry should include the legal name and official address of the organization; a brief summary of the project; the name and address of the person responsible for the dispersal of the grant; a copy of the organization's IRS exemption letter; and a copy of the most recent audited financial statement.
Deadlines: Proposal deadline is April 15.
Review Process: The trustees will request more information and a complete application, as necessary. The trustees meet once a year, usually in June. The present trustees prefer to give challenge and matching grants, pilot programs, and seed funding.

Restrictions

The trust does not make grants to individuals, government agencies, endowment funds, religious organizations, or unspecified projects. They generally do not contribute to tax-supported institutions.

Additional Information

Publications: Annual Report; Application Form; Guidelines
Trust(s): Bank of New York

Foundation Officials

Allen R. Malcolm: trustee
Rollan D. Melton: trustee
Ann M. Scanlon: program director
Jonathan L. Snow: trustee

Grants Analysis

Disclosure Period: calendar year ending 2001
Total Grants: $1,401,500
Number of Grants: 79
Average Grant: $17,741
Highest Grant: $100,000
Typical Range: $5,000 to $40,000

Recent Grants

Note: Grants derived from 2001 Form 990.

Library-Related
15,000   Frederick County Public Libraries, Frederick, MD -- construction

General
100,000   Reno-Sparks Theater Coalition, Reno, NV -- development, modernization of Lear Performing Arts Center
50,000   Churchill Arts Council, Fallon, NV -- ongoing campaign to refurbish cultural arts center
50,000   Pulaski Academy and Central School, Pulaski, NY -- academic achievement scholarships

48,000   Open Hand Theater, Syracuse, NY -- handicap accessibility to museum
40,000   Arizona Aerospace Foundation, Tucson, AZ -- creation of air and space hangar to house amphibious aircraft
40,000   Independent College Fund, New York, NY -- partnerships between colleges and local schools
35,000   Frost Valley YMCA, Montclair, NJ -- construction of guest residence
35,000   Papermill Playhouse, Millburn, NJ -- Paciolan ticketing system
30,000   Boys and Girls Club of Syracuse, Syracuse, NY -- support OnPoint for College Program
30,000   Delaware Valley College of Science and Agriculture, Doylestown, PA -- renovation of equine facility

HARRISON C. AND MARGARET A. SNYDER CHARITABLE TRUST

Giving Contact

Marie Boyles, Trust Officer
c/o M & T Trust Co.
One M & T Plaza, 8th Fl.
Buffalo, NY 14203
Phone: (716)842-5680

Description

Founded: 1996
EIN: 256436588
Organization Type: Private Foundation
Giving Locations: PA: Blair County

Financial Summary

Total Giving: $74,999 (2001); $79,516 (1999); $72,646 (1998)
Assets: $1,418,438 (2001); $1,700,000 (1999); $1,609,011 (1998)
Gifts Received: $15,710 (1996); $1,115,547 (1995)

Typical Recipients

Arts & Humanities: Libraries
Civic & Public Affairs: African American Affairs
Education: Business Education, Public Education (Precollege)
Health: Children's Health/Hospitals, Emergency/Ambulance Services
Religion: Churches, Religious Organizations, Religious Welfare
Social Services: Animal Protection, Big Brother/Big Sister, Food/Clothing Distribution, Social Services-General, Volunteer Services, YMCA/YWCA/YMHA/YWHA

Application Procedures

Initial Contact: Send a brief letter of inquiry.
Application Requirements: purpose of funds sought and proof of tax-exempt status.
Deadlines: November 1.

Restrictions

Limited to organizations in Blair County, PA.

Additional Information

Trust(s): M & T Trust Co.

Foundation Officials

William R. Collins, Jr.: trustee
Daniel J. Ratchford: trustee

Grants Analysis

Disclosure Period: calendar year ending 2001
Total Grants: $74,999
Number of Grants: 26

Average Grant: $2,885
Highest Grant: $7,500
Lowest Grant: $500
Typical Range: $1,000 to $5,000

Recent Grants

Note: Grants derived from 2000 Form 990.

Library-Related
5,000   Altoona Area Public Library, Altoona, PA
4,639   Hollidaysburg Free Public Library, Hollidaysburg, PA
2,139   Hollidaysburg Free Public Library, Hollidaysburg, PA

General
7,532   Altoona Food Bank, Altoona, PA
5,000   Bishop Guilfoyle, Altoona, PA
5,000   Hollidaysburg Area School, Duncansville, PA
5,000   New Day, Altoona, PA
4,277   Church of the Holy Trinity, Hollidaysburg, PA
3,500   Big Brothers Big Sister, Altoona, PA
3,000   Central Pennsylvania Humane Society, Altoona, PA
3,000   NAACP, Altoona, PA
2,800   Our Lady of Lourdes Church, Altoona, PA
2,500   American Rescue Workers, Hollidaysburg, PA

FROST AND MARGARET SNYDER FOUNDATION

Giving Contact

Michael Steadman, Assistant Vice President & Trust Officer
c/o KeyBank
1101 Pacific Ave., 3rd Fl.
Tacoma, WA 98411
Phone: (253)305-7208

Description

Founded: 1957
EIN: 916030549
Organization Type: Private Foundation
Giving Locations: WA
Grant Types: General Support.

Donor Information

Founder: the late Frost Snyder and the late Margaret Snyder

Financial Summary

Total Giving: $714,354 (2000); $689,676 (1999); $642,655 (1998)
Assets: $13,946,409 (2000); $15,281,455 (1999); $13,967,370 (1998)

Typical Recipients

Arts & Humanities: Arts & Humanities-General, Public Broadcasting
Civic & Public Affairs: Civic & Public Affairs-General, Law & Justice
Education: Colleges & Universities, Medical Education, Private Education (Precollege), Public Education (Precollege), Religious Education, Secondary Education (Private), Secondary Education (Public), Student Aid
Health: Health Organizations, Hospices, Hospitals, Medical Research, Public Health
International: International Peace & Security Issues
Religion: Churches, Dioceses, Ministries, Religious Organizations, Religious Welfare
Social Services: Community Centers, Community Service Organizations

Application Procedures

Initial Contact: Send a brief letter of inquiry.
Application Requirements: Include a description of organization, amount requested, and purpose of funds.
Deadlines: September 1.

Restrictions

Limited to Catholic organizations. Does not support individuals.

Additional Information

Trust(s): KeyBank NA

Foundation Officials

C. Brockert: trustee
M. Cunningham: trustee
August Von Boecklin: trustee

Grants Analysis

Disclosure Period: calendar year ending 2000
Total Grants: $714,354
Number of Grants: 14
Average Grant: $43,419*
Highest Grant: $150,000
Typical Range: $20,000 to $80,000
*Note: Average grant figure excludes highest grant.

Recent Grants

Note: Grants derived from 1999 Form 990.

General

100,000	Newman Center -- new building for the U of W
60,000	Archdiocese of Seattle, Seattle, WA
50,000	Eastside Catholic High School, Bellevue, WA -- remodeling and furnishing of four science classrooms
50,000	Holy Cross High School, New Orleans, LA -- new building
50,000	O'Dea High School, Seattle, WA -- new library and additional classrooms
48,140	Seattle University, Seattle, WA -- multicultural leadership training program
40,000	Bellarmine High School -- Weber building
39,336	St. Martin's College
35,000	Gonzaga University, Spokane, WA -- endowment to benefit students from Pierce County
35,000	PACE

HAROLD B. AND DOROTHY A. SNYDER FOUNDATION

Giving Contact

Audrey Snyder, Executive Director & Trustee
PO Box 671
Moorestown, NJ 08057
Phone: (856)273-9745

Description

Founded: 1971
EIN: 222316043
Organization Type: Private Foundation
Giving Locations: NJ: Union County
Grant Types: General Support, Loan, Multiyear/Continuing Support, Operating Expenses, Project, Seed Money.

Donor Information

Founder: the late Harold B. Snyder, Sr.

Financial Summary

Total Giving: $417,365 (fiscal year ending September 30, 2001); $597,591 (fiscal 2000); $485,149 (fiscal 1998)

Giving Analysis: Giving for fiscal 2001 includes: foundation scholarships ($13,821); fiscal 2000: foundation scholarships ($15,750) fiscal 1998: foundation scholarships ($16,500)
Assets: $14,439,037 (fiscal 2001); $16,070,549 (fiscal 2000); $13,744,172 (fiscal 1998)
Gifts Received: $4,550 (fiscal 2001); $950 (fiscal 2000); $1,629 (fiscal 1998). Note: In fiscal 1996, contributions were received from E. Allison ($425), A. Cortese ($545), D. Demarco ($100), F. Donlon ($100), M. Flowers ($180), J. Hoell ($1,500), T. Jones ($50), G. Karch ($100), J. Leynoe ($250), R. Nalbone ($500), A. Snyder ($1,000), N. Wu ($500), and A. Sarnese ($200).

Typical Recipients

Arts & Humanities: History & Archaeology, Libraries
Civic & Public Affairs: Community Foundations, Employment/Job Training, Civic & Public Affairs-General, Housing, Nonprofit Management, Philanthropic Organizations, Professional & Trade Associations, Urban & Community Affairs, Women's Affairs
Education: Business Education, Colleges & Universities, Engineering/Technological Education, Literacy, Medical Education, Preschool Education, Private Education (Precollege), Religious Education, Science/Mathematics Education, Special Education, Student Aid
Health: Cancer, Children's Health/Hospitals, Clinics/Medical Centers, Health-General, Health Organizations, Hospitals, Long-Term Care, Nursing Services, Prenatal Health Issues, Public Health, Single-Disease Health Associations
Religion: Churches, Churches, Religious Organizations, Religious Welfare, Seminaries
Social Services: Community Service Organizations, Counseling, Crime Prevention, Day Care, Domestic Violence, Family Services, Homes, People with Disabilities, Shelters/Homelessness, YMCA/YWCA/YMHA/YWHA, Youth Organizations

Application Procedures

Initial Contact: Submit 5 copies of a proposal, not more than 4 pages long.
Application Requirements: Include a description of organization, amount requested, purpose of funds sought, recently audited financial statement, and proof of tax-exempt status.
Deadlines: None.

Additional Information

Provides scholarships to residents of New Jersey entering the Presbyterian ministry, nursing, and the building construction industry.

Foundation Officials

Ethelyn Allison: trustee
Melvin Cook: trustee
Arline Snyder Cortese: trustee
Sandy Nalbone Menagvale: trustee
Ray Nalbone: trustee
Lillian Palumbo, PhD: trustee
Audrey Snyder: executive director, trustee
Phyllis Johnson Snyder: trustee
Joseph A. Vallene, III: trustee
James V. Whittenburg: trustee

Grants Analysis

Disclosure Period: fiscal year ending September 30, 2001
Total Grants: $403,544*
Number of Grants: 25
Average Grant: $13,493*
Highest Grant: $79,723
Lowest Grant: $500
Typical Range: $2,500 to $25,000
*Note: Giving excludes scholarships. Average grant excludes highest grant.

Recent Grants

Note: Grants derived from fiscal 2000 Form 990.

General

101,659	Union Hospital Foundation, Union, NJ -- for capital campaign
100,975	Muhlenberg Foundation, Inc., Plainfield, NJ -- for equipment
75,023	Trinitas Health Foundation, Elizabeth, NJ -- for equipment
50,385	YMCA of Eastern Union County, Elizabeth, NJ -- for capital campaign
40,383	Deborah Hospital Foundation, Browns Mills, NJ -- for equipment
35,000	Cerebral Palsy of Union County, Cranford, NJ -- capital campaign
26,708	Plainfield Health Center, Plainfield, NJ -- for senior care program
25,000	Oratory Preparatory School, Summit, NJ -- for challenge grant
18,000	Raphel's Life House, Elizabeth, NJ -- for operating support
15,778	Jersey Battered Women Service, Morris Plains, NJ -- for equipment

WILLIAM I. AND PATRICIA S. SNYDER FOUNDATION

Giving Contact

K. Sidney Neuman, Secretary
Grant Bldg., 3rd Fl.
Pittsburgh, PA 15219
Phone: (412)338-1108

Description

Founded: 1996
EIN: 251773015
Organization Type: Private Foundation
Giving Locations: PA: Pittsburgh
Grant Types: General Support.

Financial Summary

Total Giving: $322,500 (fiscal year ending August 31, 2002); $427,583 (fiscal 2000); $237,037 (fiscal 1999)
Assets: $1,710,455 (fiscal 2002); $3,545,092 (fiscal 2000); $1,851,168 (fiscal 1999)
Gifts Received: $175,679 (fiscal 1996). Note: In fiscal 1996, contributions were received from W.I. Snyder Corp.

Typical Recipients

Arts & Humanities: Arts Associations & Councils
Education: Private Education (Precollege)
Health: Children's Health/Hospitals, Hospitals
Religion: Jewish Causes
Social Services: People with Disabilities, Shelters/Homelessness

Application Procedures

Initial Contact: Submit detailed proposal with budget.
Deadlines: No deadline.

Restrictions

Foundation does not support political or lobbying groups.

Foundation Officials

K. Sidney Newman: secretary
Patricia S. Snyder: vice president
William I. Snyder: president

Grants Analysis

Disclosure Period: fiscal year ending August 31, 2002
Total Grants: $322,500
Number of Grants: 5
Highest Grant: $200,000

Lowest Grant: $5,000
Typical Range: $5,000 to $12,500

Recent Grants

Note: Grants derived from 2000 Form 990.

Library-Related

41,100	Sewickley Academy, Sewickley, PA
1,000	Carnegie Institute, Pittsburgh, PA -- for museum of art

General

200,000	Sewickley Valley Hospital, Sewickley, PA -- to renovate maternity ward
102,200	Beth El Congregation of the South Hills -- for rabbi's discretionary fund
36,000	United Jewish Federation, Pittsburgh, PA
15,333	Jewish Education Institute, Pittsburgh, PA -- for special endowment, fund salary of community scholar in residence
10,000	YMCA Capital Campaign -- for capital fund
6,500	Children's Hospital -- grant
5,000	Jewish Education Institute, Pittsburgh, PA
5,000	Presbyterian Church of Coraopolis
2,500	Pittsburgh Cultural Trust, Pittsburgh, PA
2,000	Jewish Education Institute, Pittsburgh, PA

SOLOW FOUNDATION

Giving Contact

Sheldon H. Solow, President
9 W. 57th St.
New York, NY 10019-2601
Phone: (212)751-1100

Description

Founded: 1978
EIN: 132950685
Organization Type: Private Foundation
Giving Locations: NY: New York
Grant Types: General Support.

Donor Information

Founder: Sheldon H. Solow

Financial Summary

Total Giving: $294,600 (fiscal year ending October 31, 2000); $210,500 (fiscal 1999); $139,170 (fiscal 1998)
Assets: $10,509,508 (fiscal 2000); $9,592,912 (fiscal 1999); $9,090,721 (fiscal 1998)
Gifts Received: $3,000,024 (fiscal 1994). Note: In fiscal 1994, contributions were received from Sheldon Solow.

Typical Recipients

Arts & Humanities: Arts Associations & Councils, Arts Centers, Arts Funds, Community Arts, Ethnic & Folk Arts, Libraries, Museums/Galleries, Music, Performing Arts, Theater
Civic & Public Affairs: African American Affairs, Botanical Gardens/Parks, Economic Development, Civic & Public Affairs-General, Housing, Law & Justice, Municipalities/Towns, Philanthropic Organizations, Professional & Trade Associations, Public Policy, Urban & Community Affairs
Education: Arts/Humanities Education, Colleges & Universities, Education Associations, Education Reform, Elementary Education (Private), Education-General, Legal Education, Medical Education, Public Education (Precollege), Religious Education, Social Sciences Education, Special Education, Student Aid
Environment: Air/Water Quality
Health: Clinics/Medical Centers, Heart, Hospitals, Multiple Sclerosis, Nursing Services, Research/Studies Institutes, Single-Disease Health Associations

International: Foreign Arts Organizations, Human Rights, International Development, International Organizations, Missionary/Religious Activities
Religion: Churches, Jewish Causes
Social Services: Animal Protection, Child Welfare, Community Service Organizations, Recreation & Athletics, Scouts, Social Services-General, Substance Abuse, United Funds/United Ways, Youth Organizations

Application Procedures

Initial Contact: The foundation has no formal grant application procedure or application form.
Deadlines: None.

Foundation Officials

Leonard Lazarus: secretary
Sheldon Henry Solow: don, president B 1926. PRIM CORP EMPL member: Solow Building Co. LLC ADD CORP EMPL president: Solow Management Corp.; president: Solow Realty Development Co.
Rosalie S. Wolff: vice president

Grants Analysis

Disclosure Period: fiscal year ending October 31, 2000
Total Grants: $294,600
Number of Grants: 20
Average Grant: $4,979*
Highest Grant: $200,000*
Typical Range: $1,000 to $10,000
*Note: Average grant figure excludes highest grant.

Recent Grants

Note: Grants derived from 1999 Form 990.

General

500,000	Solow Art and Architecture Foundation, New York, NY
100,000	Jewish Center of the Hamptons
40,000	Metropolitan Museum of Art, New York, NY
15,000	Museum of Modern Art, New York, NY
11,000	Federal Law Enforcement Foundation, New York, NY
11,000	Solow Art and Architecture Foundation, New York, NY
10,000	Herbert H. Lehman College Foundation, Inc., Bronx, NY
7,500	Lincoln Center Real Estate and Construction Council
6,000	Solow Art and Architecture Foundation, New York, NY
5,000	Federal Law Enforcement Foundation, New York, NY

SONOCO PRODUCTS CO.

Company Headquarters

Hartsville, SC
Web: http://www.sonoco.com

Company Description

Founded: 1899
Ticker: SON
Exchange: NYSE
Revenue: US$2.812 billion (2002)
Employees: 17400 (2002)
SIC(s): 2421 Sawmills & Planing Mills--General, 2499 Wood Products Nec, 2631 Paperboard Mills, 2679 Converted Paper Products Nec.

Operating Locations

Sonoco Products Co. (GA--Marietta; NC--Statesville; PR; SC--Hartsville)
Note: Operates 165 branch or manufacturing facilities in the U.S., 25 in Canada, and 78 in other foreign countries.

Nonmonetary Support

Type: Donated Equipment; Donated Products

Sonoco Foundation

Giving Contact

Joyce Beasley, Manager, Community Affairs
One North 2nd Street, Mail Stop A09
Hartsville, SC 29550
Phone: (843)383-7000
Fax: (843)383-7008
E-mail: joyce.beasley@sonoco.com
Web: http://www.sonoco.com/ sonoco_foundation.htm

Description

EIN: 570752950
Organization Type: Corporate Foundation
Giving Locations: SC: counties in which employees reside.
Grant Types: Award, Emergency, Employee Matching Gifts, Endowment, General Support, Matching, Multiyear/Continuing Support, Project, Research, Scholarship.
Note: Employee matching gift ratio: 1 to 1 for higher education.

Financial Summary

Total Giving: $2,029,206 (2001); $1,844,154 (2000); $1,750,198 (1998). Note: Contributes through corporate direct giving program and foundation. Giving includes foundation.
Giving Analysis: Giving for 2000 includes: foundation grants to United Way ($76,600); foundation ($1,767,554); 1998: foundation grants to United Way ($83,550) foundation ($1,666,648)
Assets: $416 (2001); $378 (2000); $2,842 (1998). Note: The asset amount for 2000 is a negative number.
Gifts Received: $2,030,000 (2001); $1,835,000 (2000); $1,295,000 (1998). Note: Contributions received from Sonoco Products Co.

Typical Recipients

Arts & Humanities: Arts Associations & Councils, Arts Centers, Arts Festivals, Arts Funds, Arts Institutes, Community Arts, Dance, Arts & Humanities-General, Historic Preservation, History & Archaeology, Libraries, Museums/Galleries, Music, Opera, Performing Arts, Public Broadcasting, Theater
Civic & Public Affairs: African American Affairs, Botanical Gardens/Parks, Business/Free Enterprise, Chambers of Commerce, Clubs, Community Foundations, Economic Development, Civic & Public Affairs-General, Hispanic Affairs, Housing, Municipalities/Towns, Parades/Festivals, Professional & Trade Associations, Public Policy, Safety, Urban & Community Affairs, Women's Affairs, Zoos/Aquariums
Education: Arts/Humanities Education, Business Education, Business-School Partnerships, Colleges & Universities, Community & Junior Colleges, Economic Education, Education Associations, Education Funds, Education Reform, Elementary Education (Private), Elementary Education (Public), Engineering/Technological Education, Environmental Education, Faculty Development, Education-General, Health & Physical Education, Minority Education, Private Education (Precollege), Public Education (Precollege), Science/Mathematics Education, Secondary Education (Public), Student Aid, Vocational & Technical Education
Environment: Forestry, Environment-General, Resource Conservation
Health: Cancer, Children's Health/Hospitals, Emergency/Ambulance Services, Eyes/Blindness, Health-General, Health Organizations, Heart, Hospitals, Medical Rehabilitation, Medical Research, Mental Health, Multiple Sclerosis, Research/Studies Institutes, Single-Disease Health Associations

Science: Science Exhibits & Fairs, Scientific Centers & Institutes

Social Services: Animal Protection, Camps, Child Welfare, Community Centers, Community Service Organizations, Domestic Violence, Emergency Relief, Family Services, Homes, People with Disabilities, Recreation & Athletics, Scouts, Shelters/Homelessness, Social Services-General, Special Olympics, Substance Abuse, United Funds/United Ways, Volunteer Services, YMCA/YWCA/YMHA/YWHA, Youth Organizations

Application Procedures

Initial Contact: Request application guidelines, then send an application letter (no more than 3 pages) with explanation of charitable purposes.

Application Requirements: Include name, address, telephone number and IRS tax-exempt classification of organization; summary of the purpose of funds, and evidence of need; amount of money requested and its proposed use.

Deadlines: None.

Review Process: Foundation reviews applications quarterly.

Restrictions

Foundation supports selected activities in the form of one-time or, on occasion, multi-year grants. One time grants receive the strongest consideration.

Requests for grants for the following are ineligible: projects in areas where the company has no operations; individuals; private foundations; courtesy advertising, testimonial dinners; loans or investments; pledges longer than five years, automatic renewal of grants; lobbying for political purposes; projects which are sensitive, controversial or harmful, or which pose a potential conflict of interest to the company; organizations that discriminate in any way and are inconsistent with national equal opportunity policies.

The foundation generally does not contribute to the following: intermediary funding agencies that channel monies to donee organizations, except the United Way; projects that consist simply of fund-raising events; grants to cover operating deficits; memorials; national organizations where local or regional chapters are supported; endowments; fraternal, social, labor or veterans' organizations; memberships; conferences, workshops, or seminars; "brick and mortar" building grants.

Foundation prefers not to be the only funding source for a project. Awards will be made to qualified charities only.

Corporate Officials

Peter C. Browning: chief executive officer, president, director B Boston, MA 1941. ED Colgate University BA (1963); University of Chicago MBA (1976). PRIM CORP EMPL chief executive officer, president, director: Sonoco Products Co. CORP AFFIL director: Phoenix Home Life Mutual Insurance Co.; director: Wachovia Corp.; director: Lowe's Co. Inc.; director: Nucor Corp. NONPR AFFIL member council: Chicago Graduate School; member board visitors: McCall School Business/Queens College. CLUB AFFIL member: DeBordieu Country Club; member: Quail Hollow Country Club.

Charles Westfield Coker: vice president B Florence, SC 1933. ED Princeton University BA (1955); Harvard University MBA (1957). PRIM CORP EMPL president: Sonoco Products Co. ADD CORP EMPL president: Sonoco Puerto Rico Inc. CORP AFFIL director: Sara Lee Corp.; director: Springs Industries Inc.; director: Carolina Power & Light Co.; director: NCNB Corp.; director: BankAmerica Corp. NONPR AFFIL director: Hollings Cancer Center; member: Palmetto Business Forum. CLUB AFFIL Rotary Club.

Harris E. DeLoach, Junior: president, chief executive officer B Columbia, SC 1944. ED University of South Carolina BBA (1966); University of South Carolina JD (1969). PRIM CORP EMPL president, chief executive officer: Sonoco Products Co. CORP AFFIL

director: Sebro Plastics Inc. NONPR AFFIL member: Rotary International; member: South Carolina Bar Association; member: Darlington County Bar Association; member: Hartsville Chamber of Commerce; member: 4th Jud. Cir. Association South Carolina; member: American Bar Association.

Harry J. Moran: executive vice president B Pasadena, CA 1932. ED Loyola University (1954). PRIM CORP EMPL executive vice president: Sonoco Products Co. CORP AFFIL president, director: Sonoco Containers Canada; director: Sonoco France; director: Sonoca Latin America; director: Engraph Corp.; director: Keating Corp.; chairman: CMB-Sonoco Europe.

Foundation Officials

Charles Westfield Coker: trustee (see above)

Charles J. Hupfer: trustee B 1946. ED University of North Carolina, Charlotte MS; University of North Carolina BS (1968). PRIM CORP EMPL vice president, secretary, chief financial officer: Sonoco Products Co. ADD CORP EMPL treasurer: Speciality Packaging Group Inc.

Grants Analysis

Disclosure Period: calendar year ending 2001

Total Grants: $2,029,206*

Number of Grants: 213

Average Grant: $9,527

Highest Grant: $300,000

Lowest Grant: $25

Typical Range: $100 to $25,000

*Note: Giving excludes United Way and scholarship.

Recent Grants

Note: Grants derived from 2001 Form 990.

General

300,000	Governors School for Science and Mathematics, SC
250,000	Thomas Hart Academy, Hartsville, SC
200,000	University of South Carolina Education Foundation, Columbia, SC
125,000	Hartsville YMCA, Hartsville, SC
100,000	Coker College, Darlington, SC
100,000	Independent Colleges and Universities of South Carolina, Columbia, SC
100,000	September 11th Fund, New York, NY
66,506	Hartsville United Way, Hartsville, SC
50,000	Black Creek Arts Council, Hartsville, SC
50,000	Edventure, Columbia, SC

SORDONI FOUNDATION

Giving Contact

William B. Sordoni, President and Treasurer
45 Owen St.
Forty Fort, PA 18704-4305
Phone: (570)283-1211
Fax: (570)288-3663

Description

Founded: 1946

EIN: 246017505

Organization Type: Private Foundation

Giving Locations: PA: Northeastern Pennsylvania

Grant Types: Capital, Endowment, General Support, Multiyear/Continuing Support, Project, Seed Money.

Donor Information

Founder: the late Andrew J. Sordoni, Sr., the late Andrew J. Sordoni, Jr., Andrew J. Sordoni III, the late Mrs. Andrew J. Sordoni, Sr., the late Mrs. Andrew J. Sordoni, Jr., Mrs. Andrew J. Sordoni III

Financial Summary

Total Giving: $774,205 (2001); $941,165 (2000); $904,319 (1999)

Giving Analysis: Giving for 2001 includes: foundation grants to United Way ($16,670); 2000: foundation

grants to United Way ($133,332) 1998: foundation grants to United Way ($71,666)

Assets: $13,007,949 (2001); $14,729,203 (2000); $16,791,270 (1999)

Gifts Received: $100 (2001); $2,325 (2000); $70,063 (1998). Note: In 1996, contributions were received from Andrew J. Sordoni, III ($25,000), William B. Sordoni ($4,800), and Sordoni Construction Co. (20,000).

Typical Recipients

Arts & Humanities: Arts Associations & Councils, Arts Festivals, Community Arts, Libraries, Museums/Galleries, Music, Public Broadcasting, Theater

Civic & Public Affairs: Botanical Gardens/Parks, Economic Development, Civic & Public Affairs-General, Municipalities/Towns, Public Policy, Urban & Community Affairs

Education: Arts/Humanities Education, Colleges & Universities, Community & Junior Colleges, Education Funds, Private Education (Precollege), Vocational & Technical Education

Environment: Environment-General, Research, Resource Conservation, Wildlife Protection

Health: Emergency/Ambulance Services, Health Organizations, Hospices, Hospitals, Medical Rehabilitation, Medical Research, Nursing Services

Religion: Religion-General, Jewish Causes, Religious Organizations, Religious Welfare, Seminaries

Science: Scientific Organizations

Social Services: Camps, Child Welfare, Community Centers, Community Service Organizations, Domestic Violence, Family Services, People with Disabilities, Scouts, Senior Services, United Funds/United Ways, YMCA/YWCA/YMHA/YWHA, Youth Organizations

Application Procedures

Initial Contact: Send a brief letter of inquiry describing program or project.

Deadlines: None.

Restrictions

Does not support individuals or provide scholarships.

Foundation Officials

Richard Allen: director

Rev. Jule Ayers: director

Benjamin Badman, Jr.: assistant secretary, assistant treasurer

Ruth Hitchner: director

A. William Kelly: director

John J. Menapace: director

Dr. Roy E. Morgan: director B Nanticoke, PA December 02, 1908. ED Pennsylvania State University BA (1931); Pennsylvania State University MA (1935). PRIM CORP EMPL president: WY Valley Broadcasting Co. CORP AFFIL treasurer: Ra-Tel Realty Co. NONPR AFFIL trustee: Hospital Association Pennsylvania; member president council: Kings College; director: Economic Development Council Northeastern Pennsylvania; chairman emeritus executive committee: ABC Radio Network Affiliates Committee.

Helen Mary Sibera: director

Patrick Solano: director

Andrew John Sordoni, III: president B Pratt, KS 1943. ED University of Notre Dame (1961-1964); King's College BA (1967). PRIM CORP EMPL chairman, director: Sordoni Construction Services ADD CORP EMPL chairman executive committee: United Pennsylvania Bank. CORP AFFIL chairman: Mercom; chairman: Public Service Enterprises Pennsylvania; director: Harsco Corp. NONPR AFFIL director: Valley Medical Center Geisinger WY; director: WVIA; director: Pennsylvanians Effective Government; director: Pennsylvania Chamber Business & Industry; member: Pennsylvania Jazz Society; member: New Jersey Jazz Society. CLUB AFFIL Sons Desert New York Club; Westmoreland Country Club; Friars Club.

Margaret Sordoni: director

Stephen Sordoni: director B 1948. PRIM CORP EMPL vice president, secretary: Sordoni Enterprises ADD CORP EMPL secretary: Sordoni Construction

Services. CORP AFFIL secretary: Sordoni Construction Services.
Susan F. Sordoni: director
William B. Sordoni: secretary, treasurer B 1944. ED University of Notre Dame; Wilkes College. PRIM CORP EMPL president, treasurer: Sordoni Construction Services. CORP AFFIL president: Sordoni Enterprises; vice chairman, president: Whiteman Tower; director: Mercom; vice chairman: Commonwealth Telephone Co.; president: Evergreen Capital Corp.

Grants Analysis

Disclosure Period: calendar year ending 2001
Total Grants: $757,535*
Number of Grants: 47
Average Grant: $10,381*
Highest Grant: $280,000
Lowest Grant: $250
Typical Range: $5,000 to $20,000
*Note: Giving excludes United Way. Average grant figure excludes highest grant.

Recent Grants

Note: Grants derived from 2000 Form 990.

General

140,000	University of Scranton, Scranton, PA
102,500	Marywood College, Scranton, PA
100,000	Wyoming Valley United Way, Wilkes-Barre, PA
75,250	Catholic Youth Center, Wilkes-Barre, PA
70,000	Wilkes University, Wilkes-Barre, PA
53,688	King's College, Wilkes-Barre, PA
50,000	Committee On Economic Growth, Wilkes-Barre, PA
50,000	Mount Laurel Center, Mt. Laurel, PA
40,000	Saint Joseph Center, Scranton, PA
33,332	United Way Lackawanna County, Scranton, PA

SOUND SHORE FOUNDATION

Giving Contact

T. Gibbs Kane, Jr., Trustee
350 Stuyvesant Ave.
Rye, NY 10580
Phone: (203)629-1980

Description

Founded: 1987
EIN: 222777141
Organization Type: Private Foundation
Giving Locations: NY
Grant Types: General Support.

Financial Summary

Total Giving: $68,100 (2001); $58,200 (2000); $22,300 (1999)
Assets: $1,115,098 (2001); $1,390,089 (2000); $364,942 (1999)
Gifts Received: $1,254 (2001)

Typical Recipients

Arts & Humanities: Libraries
Education: Minority Education, Private Education (Precollege)
Health: Health Organizations, Hospitals, Multiple Sclerosis
Religion: Churches
Social Services: Animal Protection, Social Services-General

Application Procedures

Initial Contact: The foundation reports no specific application guidelines. Send a brief letter of inquiry, including statement of purpose, amount requested, and proof of tax-exempt status.
Deadlines: None.

Grants Analysis

Disclosure Period: calendar year ending 2001
Total Grants: $68,100
Number of Grants: 19
Average Grant: $1,561*
Highest Grant: $40,000
Lowest Grant: $250
Typical Range: $1,000 to $2,500
*Note: Average grant figure excludes highest grant.

Recent Grants

Note: Grants derived from 2001 Form 990.

Library-Related

2,000	Rye Free Reading Room, Rye, NY

General

4,250	National Multiple Sclerosis, New York, NY
4,000	Immaculate Conception Church, New York, NY
1,000	International Etchells Class, New York, NY
1,000	Port Chester Carver Center, Port Chester, NY
1,000	Prep for Prep, New York, NY
850	Foundation for United Hospital, Port Chester, NY
250	ASPCA, New York, NY

SOUTH BEND TRIBUNE CORP.

Company Headquarters

225 N. Colfax Ave.
South Bend, IN 46626

Company Description

Employees: 270
SIC(s): 2711 Newspapers.
Parent Company: Schurz Communications, 223 W. Colfax Ave., South Bend, IN, United States

Operating Locations

South Bend Tribune Corp. (IN--South Bend)

Schurz Communications Foundation

Giving Contact

Todd F. Schurz, President
225 West Colfax Avenue
South Bend, IN 46624
Phone: (219)287-1001
Fax: (219)236-1765

Description

Founded: 1940
EIN: 356024357
Organization Type: Corporate Foundation
Giving Locations: IN: South Bend and surrounding area
Grant Types: General Support.

Donor Information

Founder: South Bend Tribune and WSBT

Financial Summary

Total Giving: $153,700 (2001); $196,700 (2000); $201,950 (1998)
Giving Analysis: Giving for 2001 includes: foundation grants to United Way ($56,750); foundation ($96,950); 2000: foundation grants to United Way ($57,250); foundation ($139,450) 1998: foundation grants to United Way ($46,400)
Assets: $894,910 (2001); $945,491 (2000); $795,418 (1998)
Gifts Received: $153,565 (2001); $147,891 (2000); $57,588 (1998). Note: Contributions are received from the South Bend Tribune and WSBT.

Typical Recipients

Arts & Humanities: Arts Centers, Arts Festivals, Historic Preservation, History & Archaeology, Libraries, Museums/Galleries, Music, Performing Arts, Public Broadcasting
Civic & Public Affairs: Botanical Gardens/Parks, Community Foundations, Economic Development, Civic & Public Affairs-General, Municipalities/Towns, Parades/Festivals, Urban & Community Affairs, Zoos/Aquariums
Education: Business Education, Colleges & Universities, Education Funds, Private Education (Precollege)
Health: Hospices
Religion: Religious Organizations, Religious Welfare
Social Services: Child Welfare, Community Service Organizations, United Funds/United Ways, YMCA/YWCA/YMHA/YWHA, Youth Organizations

Application Procedures

Initial Contact: The foundation has no formal grant application procedure or application form.
Deadlines: None.

Restrictions

Gives only to organizations located in the South Bend, Indiana area.

Corporate Officials

Mark Hocker: controller, editor, director PRIM CORP EMPL controller: South Bend Tribune Corp.
Todd F. Schurz: president, publisher, editor, director PRIM CORP EMPL president, publisher, editor, director: South Bend Tribune Corp.

Foundation Officials

James D. Freeman: vp
James Montgomery Schurz: president B South Bend, IN 1933. ED Stanford University (1956). PRIM CORP EMPL senator vice president newspapers, director: Schurz Communs.
Todd F. Schurz: vice president (see above)
E. Berry Smith: secretary, treasurer

Grants Analysis

Disclosure Period: calendar year ending 2001
Total Grants: $96,950*
Number of Grants: 11
Average Grant: $8,814
Highest Grant: $30,000
Lowest Grant: $500
Typical Range: $500 to $30,000
*Note: Giving excludes United Way.

Recent Grants

Note: Grants derived from 2001 Form 990.

General

39,000	United Way of St. Joseph County, South Bend, IN -- (South Bend Tribune)
30,000	Morris Performing Arts
25,000	YMCA Michiana, Elkhart, IN
16,750	United Way of St. Joseph County, South Bend, IN -- (WSBT)

10,000	Community Foundation of St. Joseph County, Indianapolis, IN
7,500	Potawatomi Zoological Society, South Bend, IN
7,000	Hospice Capital Campaign, Cincinnati, OH
5,000	Congregation of Holy Cross, Notre Dame, IN
5,000	Lake Michigan College Education Fund, Benton Harbor, MI
5,000	St. Vincent de Paul Society, South Bend, IN

SOUTH PLAINS FOUNDATION

Giving Contact
Robert P. Anderson, Director
511 Avenue K
Lubbock, TX 79408
Phone: (806)792-9915

Description
Founded: 1989
EIN: 752294100
Organization Type: Private Foundation
Giving Locations: TX: West Texas
Grant Types: Fellowship, Project, Research, Scholarship, Seed Money.

Financial Summary
Total Giving: $171,618 (fiscal year ending June 30, 2001); $190,820 (fiscal 1998); $171,500 (fiscal 1997)
Giving Analysis: Giving for fiscal 2001 includes: foundation scholarships ($7,500) fiscal 1998: foundation scholarships ($73,000)
Assets: $4,651,009 (fiscal 2001); $4,538,200 (fiscal 1998); $54,997 (fiscal 1997)
Gifts Received: $19,096 (fiscal 1997). Note: In fiscal 1990, contributions were received from the estate of Mildred Jones ($4,250) and miscellaneous donors ($191).

Typical Recipients
Arts & Humanities: History & Archaeology, Libraries, Museums/Galleries, Music, Performing Arts, Public Broadcasting
Civic & Public Affairs: Chambers of Commerce, Employment/Job Training, Civic & Public Affairs-General, Nonprofit Management, Women's Affairs
Education: Arts/Humanities Education, Colleges & Universities, Engineering/Technological Education, Education-General, Health & Physical Education, Literacy, Medical Education, Preschool Education, Public Education (Precollege), Student Aid
Health: Alzheimers Disease, Emergency/Ambulance Services, Eyes/Blindness, Health-General, Health Organizations, Hospices, Hospitals, Medical Rehabilitation, Medical Research, Mental Health, Public Health
Science: Science Museums
Social Services: Animal Protection, Family Services, Food/Clothing Distribution, People with Disabilities, Scouts, Social Services-General, Special Olympics, Substance Abuse, Volunteer Services

Application Procedures
Initial Contact: The foundation has no standard application form for either the research grant program or the small grants program; however, proposals should be a maximum of five pages and include the title of the study or project; name of the sponsoring institution; principal investigator or coordinator, with curriculum vitae attached for research grants; and abstract of the proposed study or project, not to exceed 100 words. Additionally, research grant proposals should include a statement of purpose, objectives, and goals of the study; review of relevant back ground research; procedures to be followed and populations

being studied; procedures to be followed in analyzing results; expected outcomes; and an outline of the proposed budget.
Deadlines: None.

Restrictions
The specific focus of proposals must be concerned with one of the following areas; basic research in an area of health care, clinical investigations related to the rehabilitation of people with chronic illnesses, applied research problems focused on the treatment of people with behavioral, mental, or physical problems, or research problems of a generic nature which have some applicability to human services.

Additional Information
Awards research grants to individuals for medical and/or behavioral science research focused on some aspect of health care or human services.
Publications: Proposal Guidelines

Foundation Officials
Robert P. Anderson, PhD: secretary, treasurer
Bill Armstrong: director PRIM CORP EMPL vice president: McKesson Corp.
Max L. Ince: president, director
William Miller: director
Jim S. Moore, PhD: director
Sandy Ogletree: vice president, director

Grants Analysis
Disclosure Period: fiscal year ending June 30, 2001
Total Grants: $164,118*
Number of Grants: 13
Average Grant: $4,920*
Highest Grant: $60,000
Typical Range: $1,000 to $7,000
*Note: Giving excludes scholarship. Average grant figure excludes two highest grants ($110,000).

Recent Grants
Note: Grants derived from fiscal 1999 Form 990.

General
34,021	Texas Tech University, Lubbock, TX -- for scholarships
10,000	Science Spectrum, Lubbock, TX
10,000	South Plains College, Levelland, TX -- for scholarship
10,000	South Plains Food Bank, Lubbock, TX
8,000	Lubbock Independent School District, Lubbock, TX -- for scholarships
8,000	Lubbock Youth Symphony Orchestra, Lubbock, TX -- for community service
5,000	Texas Tech University Museum, Lubbock, TX
5,000	Wayland Baptist University, Plainview, TX -- for scholarships
3,000	Covenant Health Care System
3,000	South Plains Food Bank, Lubbock, TX

SOUTH WAITE FOUNDATION

Giving Contact
Richard H. Buffett, Custodian
c/o KeyBank NA
127 Public Sq., MC OH-01-27-1708
Cleveland, OH 44114-1306
Phone: (216)828-9770

Description
Founded: 1953
EIN: 346526411
Organization Type: Private Foundation
Giving Locations: OH: Cleveland
Grant Types: Capital, Multiyear/Continuing Support, Operating Expenses.

Donor Information
Founder: the late Francis M. Sherwin, Margaret H. Sherwin

Financial Summary
Total Giving: $177,000 (2000); $182,000 (1999); $154,000 (1998)
Giving Analysis: Giving for 2000 includes: foundation scholarships ($1,000); foundation grants to United Way ($17,000); 1999: foundation scholarships ($1,000); foundation grants to United Way ($16,000); 1998: foundation scholarships ($1,000); foundation matching gifts ($15,000) foundation grants to United Way ($16,000)
Assets: $3,567,607 (2000); $3,734,469 (1999); $3,771,277 (1998)

Typical Recipients
Arts & Humanities: Arts Associations & Councils, Historic Preservation, History & Archaeology, Libraries, Museums/Galleries, Music, Public Broadcasting
Civic & Public Affairs: Botanical Gardens/Parks, Civic & Public Affairs-General, Municipalities/Towns, Parades/Festivals
Education: Colleges & Universities, Community & Junior Colleges, Health & Physical Education, Minority Education, Private Education (Precollege), Student Aid
Environment: Environment-General, Resource Conservation, Watershed, Wildlife Protection
Health: Cancer, Clinics/Medical Centers, Health Organizations, Hospitals, Medical Rehabilitation, Medical Research, Public Health, Speech & Hearing
International: International-General, International Environmental Issues, International Organizations
Science: Science Museums, Scientific Centers & Institutes, Scientific Labs
Social Services: Child Welfare, Community Service Organizations, Delinquency & Criminal Rehabilitation, Family Planning, People with Disabilities, Substance Abuse, United Funds/United Ways, YMCA/YWCA/YMHA/YWHA, Youth Organizations

Application Procedures
Initial Contact: The foundation has no formal grant application procedure or application form.
Deadlines: None.

Restrictions
The trustees normally only make grants to organizations with which they are thoroughly familiar, and they maintain a close working relationship with these selected charities.

Additional Information
Trust(s): KeyBank NA

Foundation Officials
Sherman Dye: mem, trustee B Portland, OR November 18, 1915. ED Oberlin College BA (1937); Case Western Reserve University LLB (1940). PRIM CORP EMPL partner: Baker & Hostetler. NONPR AFFIL member: Phi Delta Phi; member: Society Benchers; member: Order Coif; chairman: First Baptist Church Greater Cleveland; member: Ohio Bar Association; member: Cleveland Bar Association; member: College Club Cleveland; member, trustee: Association Continuing Education; member: American Bar Association; treasurer: American Cancer Society Cleveland.
Donald W. Gruetner: secretary, treasurer
Brian Sherwin: president
Dennis Sherwin: mem
Margaret H. Sherwin: vice president
Peter Sherwin: mem

Grants Analysis
Disclosure Period: calendar year ending 2000
Total Grants: $159,000*
Number of Grants: 22
Average Grant: $5,667*

Highest Grant: $40,000
Typical Range: $1,000 to $10,000
***Note:** Giving excludes scholarships and United Way.
Average grant figure excludes highest grant.

Recent Grants

Note: Grants derived from 2001 Form 990.

General
12,000	United Way Services, Cleveland, OH -- for operations
10,000	Cleveland Clinic Foundation, Cleveland, OH -- for prostate cancer research
10,000	Jackson Laboratory, Bar Harbor, ME -- FMS endowment
10,000	Lake Metro Park Systems, Kirtland, OH -- for Wildlife Center expansion in memory of Margaret Halle Sherwin
10,000	Nature Conservancy, Dublin, OH -- Ohio chapter unrestricted
10,000	Recovery Resources, Cleveland, OH -- for operations
10,000	Willoughby Fine Arts Association, Mentor, OH -- for operations
8,000	Chagrin River Watershed Partnership, Willoughby, OH -- for computer projection equipment
8,000	William J. and Dorothy K. O'Neill Foundation, Pepper Pike, OH -- for NY Police and Fire Widow's and Children's Fund
7,000	Laurel School, Shaker Heights, OH -- for Joan Crile Foster Memorial

SOUTHWAYS FOUNDATION

Giving Contact

Jon K. Crow; Vice President & Treasurer
c/o Sargent Management Co.
901 Marquette Ave., Suite 2630
Minneapolis, MN 55402
Phone: (612)596-3260
Fax: (612)338-2084
E-mail: southways@smcinv.com
Web: http://www.southwaysfoundation.org/

Description

Founded: 1950
EIN: 416018502
Organization Type: Private Foundation
Giving Locations: CT; MN; NY; VA
Grant Types: Capital, Endowment, General Support, Matching, Multiyear/Continuing Support, Project, Research.

Donor Information

Founder: the late John S. Pillsbury and family

Financial Summary

Total Giving: $1,193,629 (2001); $1,304,818 (2000); $781,828 (1999)
Giving Analysis: Giving for 2001 includes: foundation grants to United Way ($60,000); foundation matching gifts ($89,834); 1999: foundation scholarships ($10,000); foundation grants to United Way ($52,000) foundation matching gifts ($67,700)
Assets: $11,284,604 (2001); $13,447,450 (2000); $15,327,133 (1999)
Gifts Received: $203,997 (1994); $13,360 (1993); $1,620,012 (1992). Note: In 1994, contributions were received from Stanley R. Resor ($200,000), Sarah P. Kletter ($1,000), and Marian S. Pillsbury ($1,455); six other donors made contributions of $845 or less each.

Typical Recipients

Arts & Humanities: Arts Associations & Councils, Arts Centers, Arts Institutes, Community Arts, History & Archaeology, Libraries, Music, Opera, Performing Arts, Public Broadcasting, Theater

Civic & Public Affairs: Botanical Gardens/Parks, Public Policy, Urban & Community Affairs, Zoos/Aquariums
Education: Colleges & Universities, Education Funds, Legal Education, Literacy, Private Education (Precollege), Student Aid, Vocational & Technical Education
Environment: Air/Water Quality, Environment-General
Health: Single-Disease Health Associations
Religion: Churches, Religious Organizations
Social Services: Animal Protection, Child Welfare, Community Centers, Community Service Organizations, Crime Prevention, Family Planning, Family Services, Family Services, Recreation & Athletics, United Funds/United Ways, YMCA/YWCA/YMHA/YWHA, Youth Organizations

Application Procedures

Initial Contact: The foundation has no formal grant application procedure or application form.
Deadlines: None.

Foundation Officials

Ella P. Crosby: trustee emeritus
Jon K. Crow: vice president, treasurer
Carol J. Fetzer: assistant secretary
Kathannl P. Jose: trustee
Lucy C. Mitchell: assistant treasurer, trustee
Donald K. Morrison: vice president, treasurer
George Sturgis Pillsbury, Jr.: trustee B Crystal Bay, MN 1921. ED Yale University AB (1943). PRIM CORP EMPL chairman: Sargent Manufacturing Co. CLUB AFFIL River Club; Seminole Golf Club; Minneapolis Club; Minnetonka Yacht Club; Everglades Club; Minneapolis Athletic Club; Bath & Tennis Club.
John S. Pillsbury, III: president, trustee
John S. Pillsbury, Jr.: trustee emeritus
James P. Resor: trustee
Eleanor C. Winston: secretary, trustee

Grants Analysis

Disclosure Period: calendar year ending 2001
Total Grants: $1,043,795*
Number of Grants: 206
Average Grant: $5,067
Highest Grant: $100,000
Typical Range: $5,000 to $25,000
***Note:** Giving excludes matching gifts and United Way.

Recent Grants

Note: Grants derived from 2001 Form 990.

General
100,000	Westminster Presbyterian Church, Minneapolis, MN
50,000	Blake School, Hopkins, MN
50,000	Guthrie Theater, Minneapolis, MN
50,000	Minnesota Historical Society, St. Paul, MN
50,000	Minnesota Historical Society, St. Paul, MN
40,000	Guthrie Theater, Minneapolis, MN
40,000	Rockefeller University, New York, NY
35,000	United Way of Minneapolis Area, Minneapolis, MN
25,000	Pillsbury Neighborhood Services, Minneapolis, MN
25,000	United Way of Minneapolis Area, Minneapolis, MN

SOUTHWEST NEWS HERALD

Company Headquarters

6225 S. Kedzie Ave.
Chicago, IL 60629

Operating Locations

Herald News (IL--Joliet)

Herald Newspapers Foundation, Inc.

Giving Contact

Bruce Sagan, President
Herald Newspapers Foundation, Inc.
815 W. Van Buren, Suite 550
Chicago, IL 60607
Phone: (312)666-7776

Description

EIN: 237193553
Organization Type: Corporate Foundation
Giving Locations: IL: Chicago
Grant Types: General Support.

Financial Summary

Total Giving: $65,705 (fiscal year ending August 31, 2000); $335,815 (fiscal 1999); $318,895 (fiscal 1998)
Giving Analysis: Giving for fiscal 1999 includes: foundation ($335,815)
Assets: $1,171,989 (fiscal 2000); $1,320,965 (fiscal 1999); $1,566,035 (fiscal 1998)
Gifts Received: $50,000 (fiscal 1999); $50,000 (fiscal 1998); $53,500 (fiscal 1997). Note: In fiscal 1999, contributions were received from Paul Sagan ($25,000) and Alex Sagan ($25,000). In fiscal 1998, contributions were received from Paul Sagan and Alex Sagan. In fiscal 1997, contributions were received from Bruce Sagan.

Typical Recipients

Arts & Humanities: Arts Associations & Councils, Arts Centers, Arts Institutes, Ballet, Dance, Arts & Humanities-General, Historic Preservation, History & Archaeology, Libraries, Literary Arts, Museums/Galleries, Music, Performing Arts, Public Broadcasting, Theater, Visual Arts
Civic & Public Affairs: Botanical Gardens/Parks, Business/Free Enterprise, Civil Rights, Community Foundations, Civic & Public Affairs-General, Housing, Public Policy, Urban & Community Affairs, Women's Affairs
Education: Arts/Humanities Education, Colleges & Universities, Education Reform, Education-General, Private Education (Precollege), Religious Education, Secondary Education (Private)
Environment: Resource Conservation
Health: AIDS/HIV, Cancer, Eyes/Blindness, Medical Rehabilitation, Medical Research
International: Foreign Arts Organizations, Missionary/Religious Activities
Religion: Jewish Causes
Science: Science Museums, Scientific Centers & Institutes
Social Services: Community Service Organizations, Family Planning, People with Disabilities, Youth Organizations

Application Procedures

Initial Contact: The foundation has no formal grant application procedure or application form.
Deadlines: None.

Corporate Officials

Richard Orlikoff: vice president PRIM CORP EMPL vice president: Herald News.
Bruce Sagan: president PRIM CORP EMPL president: Herald News Paper Inc.

Foundation Officials

Richard Orlikoff: secretary (see above)
Bruce Sagan: president (see above)

Grants Analysis

Disclosure Period: fiscal year ending August 31, 2000
Total Grants: $65,705
Number of Grants: 43
Average Grant: $1,267*
Highest Grant: $12,500
Typical Range: $500 to $5,000
*Note: Average grant figure excludes highest grant.

Recent Grants

Note: Grants derived from 2002 Form 990.

Library-Related

5,000	Chicago Public Library Foundation, Chicago, IL

General

5,000	Dana Farber Cancer Institute, Boston, MA
5,000	Foundation Fighting Blindness, Hunt Valley, MD
5,000	University of Chicago, Chicago, IL
4,700	Steppenwolf Theater Company, Chicago, IL
4,120	Rush Presbyterian-St. Luke's Medical Center, Chicago, IL
3,000	Joffrey Ballet Center Concert Group Inc., Chicago, IL
2,500	Columbia Land Conservancy, Chatham, NY
2,500	Koussevitsky Music Foundation, Inc., New York, NY
2,000	Planned Parenthood Chicago, Chicago, IL
1,750	Near South Planning Board, Chicago, IL

SOUTHWESTERN ELECTRIC POWER CO.

Company Headquarters

Shreveport, LA

Company Description

Employees: 1,711
SIC(s): 4900 Electric, Gas & Sanitary Services.

Operating Locations

Southwestern Electric Power Co. (AR--Fayetteville, Texarkana; LA--Shreveport; TX--Longview)

Nonmonetary Support

Type: Donated Equipment; Loaned Employees

Giving Contact

John Hubbard, Community Service Manager
428 Travis St.
Shreveport, LA 71101
Phone: (318)222-2141
Fax: (318)673-3135

Description

Organization Type: Corporate Giving Program
Giving Locations: headquarters and operating communities.
Grant Types: Capital, General Support, Seed Money.

Typical Recipients

Arts & Humanities: Arts Associations & Councils, Arts Festivals, Community Arts, Historic Preservation, Libraries, Public Broadcasting, Theater
Civic & Public Affairs: Chambers of Commerce, Clubs, Community Foundations, Economic Development, Parades/Festivals, Urban & Community Affairs

Education: Colleges & Universities, Community & Junior Colleges, Education-General, Health & Physical Education, Science/Mathematics Education
Health: Cancer, Children's Health/Hospitals, Clinics/Medical Centers, Health-General, Heart, Hospitals, Medical Research
Social Services: Community Centers, Community Service Organizations, Emergency Relief, Family Services, Recreation & Athletics, Social Services-General, United Funds/United Ways, Youth Organizations

Application Procedures

Initial Contact: Send a brief letter of inquiry.
Application Requirements: a description of organization, amount requested, and purpose of funds sought.

Restrictions

Does not support individuals, religious organizations for sectarian purposes, or political or lobbying groups.

Corporate Officials

E. R. Brooks: chairman, chief executive officer, chief financial officer PRIM CORP EMPL chairman: Southwestern Electric Power Co.
Michael H. Madison: president, chief executive officer, chief financial officer B Tulsa, OK 1948. ED University of Oklahoma (1971). PRIM CORP EMPL president, chief executive officer, chief financial officer: Southwestern Electric Power Co.

Grants Analysis

Note: Typical grant size is less than $1,000.

SOVEREIGN BANK

Company Headquarters

Wyomissing, PA
Web: http://www.sovereignbank.com

Company Description

Employees: 4,100
SIC(s): 6035 Federal Savings Institutions.
Parent Company: Sovereign Bancorp, 1500 Market St., Philadelphia, PA, United States

Operating Locations

Sovereign Bank (DE--New Castle; NJ--Bergen, Essex, Morris Plains, Somerset; PA--Berks, Bucks, Delaware, Lancaster, Lehigh Valley, Mercer, Middlesex, Montgomery, Northampton, Union City)

Nonmonetary Support

Type: Cause-related Marketing & Promotion; Donated Equipment; Donated Products; In-kind Services; Workplace Solicitation

Sovereign Bank Foundation

Giving Contact

Joseph E. Schupp, Foundation Manager
Sovereign Bank Foundation
Two Aldwyn Center
Lancaster Avenue & Route 30
Villanova, PA 19085
Phone: (610)526-6226

Alternate Contact

1130 Berkshire Boulevard
Wyomissing, PA 19610
Phone: (610)320-8400

Description

EIN: 232548113
Organization Type: Corporate Foundation
Giving Locations: NJ: Mercer County bank or service areas.
Grant Types: Capital, General Support, Multiyear/Continuing Support.

Financial Summary

Total Giving: $1,250,804 (2001); $338,740 (2000); $363,643 (1999)
Giving Analysis: Giving for 2001 includes: foundation matching gifts ($4,340); foundation ($1,246,464); 2000: foundation matching gifts ($2,800); foundation scholarships ($4,000); foundation ($329,640); 1999: foundation matching gifts ($2,140); foundation grants to United Way ($84,550); foundation ($276,953);
Gifts Received: $1,250,804 (2001); $338,778 (2000); $363,643 (1999). Note: The foundation receives contributions from Sovereign Bank.

Typical Recipients

Arts & Humanities: Arts Festivals, Arts Outreach, Community Arts, Historic Preservation, Libraries, Museums/Galleries, Music, Opera, Public Broadcasting
Civic & Public Affairs: African American Affairs, Asian American Affairs, Business/Free Enterprise, Civil Rights, Community Foundations, Economic Development, Employment/Job Training, Ethnic Organizations, Gay/Lesbian Issues, Civic & Public Affairs-General, Hispanic Affairs, Housing, Inner-City Development, Municipalities/Towns, Native American Affairs, Nonprofit Management, Parades/Festivals, Philanthropic Organizations, Public Policy, Urban & Community Affairs, Women's Affairs
Education: Afterschool/Enrichment Programs, Colleges & Universities, Community & Junior Colleges, Education-General, Education-General, Literacy, Minority Education, Student Aid
Environment: Environment-General
Health: AIDS/HIV, Clinics/Medical Centers, Health-General, Hospitals, Public Health, Single-Disease Health Associations
Religion: Churches, Religious Welfare, Social/Policy Issues
Social Services: Camps, Child Welfare, Community Centers, Community Service Organizations, Crime Prevention, Domestic Violence, Emergency Relief, Family Planning, Family Services, Food/Clothing Distribution, Homes, People with Disabilities, Senior Services, Sexual Abuse, Shelters/Homelessness, Social Services-General, United Funds/United Ways, Volunteer Services, YMCA/YWCA/YMHA/YWHA, Youth Organizations, Youth Organizations

Application Procedures

Initial Contact: Send a full proposal.
Application Requirements: Include a description of organization, needs of the project, population served, and a listing of the directors of the organization.
Deadlines: None.

Restrictions

Does not support individuals, religious organizations for sectarian purposes, political or lobbying groups, organizations outside operating areas, organizations that are not tax-exempt/nonprofit, or beauty scholarship pageants.

Additional Information

Publications: Guidelines Brochure

Corporate Officials

Richard E. Mohn: chairman, director, chairman PRIM CORP EMPL chairman, director: Sovereign Bank. CORP AFFIL chairman: Cloister Spring Water Co.
Jay S. Sidhu: president, chief executive officer, chairman PRIM CORP EMPL president, chief executive officer, chairman: Sovereign Bank.

Foundation Officials

Richard E. Mohn: director (see above)
Jay S. Sidhu: director (see above)

Grants Analysis

Disclosure Period: calendar year ending 2001
Total Grants: $1,246,464*
Number of Grants: 304
Average Grant: $4,100
Highest Grant: $48,500
Lowest Grant: $20
Typical Range: $500 to $10,000
*Note: Giving excludes matching gifts.

Recent Grants

Note: Grants derived from 2001 Form 990.

General

48,500	Genesis Housing Corporation, Norristown, PA -- Predevelopment Fund
45,000	New Jersey Citizen Action, Hackensack, NJ -- for two mortgage & credit counseling offices
30,000	Delaware Valley Habitat for Humanity, Philadelphia, PA -- pledge
25,000	Local Initiative Support Corporation, Providence, RI
25,000	Morgan Memorial Goodwill Industries, Boston, MA
25,000	Urban Edge Housing Corp, Boston, MA
25,000	Urban Financial Services Coalition, Washington, DC
20,000	ACORN
20,000	Housing and Community Development Network, Washington, DC
16,666	Reading Berks Emergency Shelter, Reading, PA -- benefit concert

SPAHR FAMILY FOUNDATION

Giving Contact

Thomas F. Allen, Treasurer, Secretary & Director
1801 E. 9th St., Suite 730
Cleveland, OH 44114-3103
Phone: (216)771-4000

Description

Founded: 1990
EIN: 341673582
Organization Type: Private Foundation
Giving Locations: OH
Grant Types: General Support.

Donor Information

Founder: Established in 1990 by Charles E. Spahr and Mary Jane Spahr.

Financial Summary

Total Giving: $345,814 (2000); $392,498 (1999); $292,000 (1998)
Assets: $8,072,587 (2000); $8,808,012 (1999); $7,289,204 (1998)
Gifts Received: $110,000 (2000); $160,000 (1999); $186,856 (1998). Note: In 2000, contributions were received from Charles E. Spahr. In 1999, contributions were received from Charles E. Spahr and Thomas A. and Susan B. Ford. In 1997, contributions were received from Charles E. Spahr and Thomas A. and Susan B. Ford.

Typical Recipients

Arts & Humanities: Arts Associations & Councils, Arts Centers, Ballet, Historic Preservation, Libraries, Museums/Galleries, Music, Performing Arts, Theater
Civic & Public Affairs: Botanical Gardens/Parks, Employment/Job Training, First Amendment Issues, Public Policy, Women's Affairs

Education: Arts/Humanities Education, Colleges & Universities, Economic Education, Faculty Development, Education-General, International Studies, Medical Education, Preschool Education, Private Education (Precollege), Religious Education, Secondary Education (Private), Student Aid
Environment: Environment-General, Resource Conservation
Health: Children's Health/Hospitals, Emergency/Ambulance Services, Hospitals, Hospitals (University Affiliated), Mental Health, Nursing Services, Single-Disease Health Associations, Speech & Hearing
International: Foreign Educational Institutions
Religion: Churches, Religious Welfare
Science: Scientific Centers & Institutes
Social Services: At-Risk Youth, Camps, Community Centers, Community Service Organizations, Domestic Violence, Emergency Relief, Family Planning, Family Services, People with Disabilities, Senior Services, Shelters/Homelessness, Substance Abuse, United Funds/United Ways, YMCA/YWCA/YMHA/YWHA, Youth Organizations

Application Procedures

Initial Contact: The foundation has no formal grant application procedure or application form.
Deadlines: None.

Foundation Officials

Thomas F. Allen: treasurer, assistant secretary
Susan B. Ford: trustee
Thomas A. Ford: trustee
Cynthia S. Moran: trustee
Stephanie J. Schulte: secretary, trustee
Charles E. Spahr: chairman, president, trustee
Mary J. Spahr: vice president, trustee
Stephen D. Spahr: trustee
Sally Whitlow: trustee

Grants Analysis

Disclosure Period: calendar year ending 2000
Total Grants: $345,814
Number of Grants: 41
Average Grant: $5,023*
Highest Grant: $144,895
Typical Range: $1,000 to $10,000
*Note: Average grant figure excludes highest grant.

Recent Grants

Note: Grants derived from 1999 Form 990.

General

139,500	Kansas University Endowment Association, Lawrence, KS
46,010	Musical Arts Association, Cleveland, OH
26,000	St. Christopher Church, Rocky River, OH
23,135	Baldwin-Wallace College, Berea, OH
23,003	Cumberland College, Williamsburg, KY
13,000	Harvard Divinity School, Cambridge, MA -- capital campaign
10,500	Kansas University Endowment Association, Lawrence, KS
10,000	City Mission, Cleveland, OH
10,000	Cleveland Mediation Center, Cleveland, OH -- homeless prevention program 2000
10,000	Hurricane Floyd Relief Fund, Raleigh, NC -- North Carolina Floyd relief fund

ELIOT SPALDING FOUNDATION

Giving Contact

Peter T. Gianas, Secretary
4400 E. Broadway, Suite 800
Tucson, AZ 85711
Phone: (520)795-6630
Fax: (520)327-1922

Description

Founded: 1954
EIN: 866050507
Organization Type: Private Foundation
Giving Locations: AZ: Tucson
Grant Types: General Support.

Financial Summary

Total Giving: $135,000 (2001); $181,033 (2000); $165,000 (1999)
Giving Analysis: Giving for 2001 includes: foundation grants to United Way ($94,000); 2000: foundation grants to United Way ($100,033); 1999: foundation grants to United Way ($100,000); foundation grants to United Way ($100,033);
Assets: $3,740,795 (2001); $3,949,580 (2000); $4,007,904 (1999)
Gifts Received: $191,118 (1995); $23,731 (1994). Note: In 1995, contributions were received from the Ponomaref estate and the Link Trust.

Typical Recipients

Arts & Humanities: Historic Preservation, Libraries, Museums/Galleries
Civic & Public Affairs: Botanical Gardens/Parks, Civic & Public Affairs-General, Housing
Education: Colleges & Universities, Community & Junior Colleges, Student Aid
Environment: Resource Conservation
Health: Alzheimers Disease, Clinics/Medical Centers, Emergency/Ambulance Services
Religion: Churches, Religious Welfare
Social Services: Animal Protection, Child Welfare, Community Service Organizations, Day Care, Food/Clothing Distribution, People with Disabilities, Recreation & Athletics, Social Services-General, United Funds/United Ways, YMCA/YWCA/YMHA/YWHA, Youth Organizations

Application Procedures

Initial Contact: Submit a typewritten request.
Application Requirements: Include purpose of funds sought and proof of tax-exempt status.
Deadlines: November 1.

Foundation Officials

Peter T. Gianas: secretary, director, trustee
Samuel P. Goddard, Jr.: vice president, director, trustee
D. M. Lovett: president, director
Clayton E. Niles: treasurer, director
Clayton N. Niles: president
James Sakrison: director

Grants Analysis

Disclosure Period: calendar year ending 2001
Total Grants: $41,000*
Number of Grants: 9
Average Grant: $3,857
Highest Grant: $7,500
Lowest Grant: $1,000
Typical Range: $1,000 to $5,000
*Note: Giving excludes United Way.

Recent Grants

Note: Grants derived from 2001 Form 990.

Library-Related

3,000	Libraries LTD, Tucson, AZ

General

74,000	United Way of Greater Tucson, Tucson, AZ
20,000	United Way of Greater Tucson, Tucson, AZ
7,500	Angel Charity For Children, Tucson, AZ
6,000	Boys/Girls Club of Tucson, Tucson, AZ
5,000	Dollars for Scholars, Tucson, AZ
5,000	Tucson Community Food Bank, Tucson, AZ

3,000	New Horizons, Goldthwaite, TX
3,000	Southern Arizona Child Advocacy Center, Tucson, AZ
3,000	Youth Own Their Own, Tucson, AZ
2,500	Children to Children, Tucson, AZ

SPANG & CO.

Company Headquarters
100 Brugh Ave.
Butler, PA 16001

Company Description
Employees: 1,200
SIC(s): 3200 Stone, Clay & Glass Products, 3600 Electronic & Other Electrical Equipment.

Operating Locations
Spang & Co. (PA--Butler)

Spang & Co. Charitable Trust

Giving Contact
K. R. McKnight, Contact
PO Box 751
Butler, PA 16003-0751
Phone: (724)287-8781

Description
EIN: 256020192
Organization Type: Corporate Foundation
Giving Locations: PA
Grant Types: General Support.

Donor Information
Founder: Spang & Co.

Financial Summary
Total Giving: $156,115 (2000); $1,843,535 (1999); $187,855 (1998)
Giving Analysis: Giving for 2000 includes: foundation grants to United Way ($20,500); foundation ($135,615); 1999: foundation grants to United Way ($20,560); foundation ($1,822,975) 1998: foundation grants to United Way ($20,500)
Assets: $10,778,129 (2000); $10,215,301 (1999); $3,807,005 (1998)
Gifts Received: $9,864 (2000); $7,879,830 (1999); $9,644 (1998). Note: In 2000, contributions were received from employees. In 1999, contributions were received from Spang employees ($9,263) and the estate of F.E. Rath, Sr. ($7,870,567). In 1998, contributions were received from Spang & Co. employees.

Typical Recipients
Arts & Humanities: Ballet, Libraries, Music, Opera, Public Broadcasting, Theater
Civic & Public Affairs: Botanical Gardens/Parks, Community Foundations, Economic Development, Economic Policy, Civic & Public Affairs-General, Parades/Festivals, Professional & Trade Associations, Safety, Zoos/Aquariums
Education: Colleges & Universities, Medical Education, Private Education (Precollege), Special Education
Health: Cancer, Children's Health/Hospitals, Clinics/Medical Centers, Eyes/Blindness, Heart, Hospitals, Hospitals (University Affiliated), Kidney, Medical Research, Nursing Services, Single-Disease Health Associations
Science: Scientific Centers & Institutes
Social Services: Animal Protection, Camps, Child Welfare, Community Service Organizations, Crime Prevention, Delinquency & Criminal Rehabilitation, Domestic Violence, Food/Clothing Distribution, People with Disabilities, Recreation & Athletics, Scouts,

United Funds/United Ways, Volunteer Services, YMCA/YWCA/YMHA/YWHA, Youth Organizations

Application Procedures
Initial Contact: Send a brief letter of inquiry.
Application Requirements: Include name, location, a description of organization, and amount requested.
Deadlines: Ninety days before the end of the calendar quarter.

Corporate Officials
Frank E. Rath, Jr.: chairman, president, chief executive officer, director B 1946. ED Carnegie Mellon University BS (1968). PRIM CORP EMPL chairman, president, chief executive officer, director: Spang & Co.

Foundation Officials
Frank E. Rath, Jr.: trustee (see above)

Grants Analysis
Disclosure Period: calendar year ending 2000
Total Grants: $135,615*
Number of Grants: 50
Average Grant: $2,712
Highest Grant: $20,000
Typical Range: $100 to $20,000
*****Note:** Giving excludes United Way.

Recent Grants
Note: Grants derived from 2000 Form 990.

Library-Related

5,000	Butler Public Library, Butler, PA
2,500	Booneville Library, Booneville, AR

General

20,000	Johns Hopkins University/Brady Institute, Baltimore, MD
20,000	United Way of Butler County, Butler, PA
13,000	Fox Chapel Country Day School, Pittsburgh, PA
10,000	Allegheny Heart Institute
10,000	Booneville Development Corp, Booneville, AR
10,000	Carnegie Mellon University, Pittsburgh, PA
7,500	National Conference of Community and Justice, Nashville, TN
5,500	Sandy Lake VFD, Sandy Lake, PA
5,000	Boy Scouts of America, Butler, PA
5,000	Carnegie Institute, Pittsburgh, PA

SPARTAN STORES, INC.

Company Headquarters
850 76th St. SW
Grand Rapids, MI 49518-8700
Web: http://www.spartanstores.com

Company Description
Founded: 1917
Ticker: SPTN
Exchange: NASDAQ
Former Name: Seaway Food Town, Inc. (2000).
Revenue: US$2.148 billion (2003)
Employees: 7,400 (2003)
Fortune Rank: 447, per FORTUNE Magazine's list of 500 Largest U.S. Corporations (2002).
SIC(s): 5141 Groceries--General Line, 5411 Grocery Stores, 5912 Drug Stores & Proprietary Stores.

Operating Locations
Food Town Supermarkets (OH--Maumee, Toledo)
Note: Company operates 24 Food Town Supermarkets, 20 Food Town Plus Supermarkets, and 22 discount drug stores under the name of "Pharm."

Nonmonetary Support
Type: Cause-related Marketing & Promotion; Donated Products; In-kind Services; Workplace Solicitation

Giving Contact
Ms., Director, Public Relations & Community Affairs
1020 Ford Street
Maumee, OH 43537
Phone: (616)878-8513
Fax: (419)891-4907
E-mail: pat_nowak@spartansstores.com

Description
Organization Type: Corporate Giving Program
Giving Locations: MI: Southeastern Michigan; OH: Northwest Ohio area only.
Grant Types: General Support, Multiyear/Continuing Support.

Financial Summary
Total Giving: Contributes through corporate direct giving program only.

Typical Recipients
Arts & Humanities: Arts Appreciation, Arts Associations & Councils, Arts Centers, Arts Festivals, Community Arts, Ethnic & Folk Arts, Libraries, Museums/Galleries, Opera, Performing Arts, Public Broadcasting, Theater, Visual Arts
Civic & Public Affairs: Philanthropic Organizations, Zoos/Aquariums
Education: Colleges & Universities, Elementary Education (Private), Literacy
Health: Geriatric Health, Health Organizations, Hospitals, Nutrition
Religion: Churches, Synagogues/Temples
Science: Science Exhibits & Fairs
Social Services: Child Welfare, Community Centers, Community Service Organizations, Domestic Violence, Food/Clothing Distribution, Recreation & Athletics, Shelters/Homelessness, Substance Abuse, Youth Organizations

Application Procedures
Initial Contact: Submit a brief letter of inquiry and full proposal.
Application Requirements: Include a description of organization, amount requested, purpose of funds sought, and proof of tax-exempt status.
Deadlines: One month in advance of date that funds are needed.

Restrictions
Does not support individuals, political or lobbying groups, or organizations outside operating areas.

Additional Information
Seaway Food Town, Inc., was acquired by Spartan Stores, Inc., in August 2000. The company, now called Food Town Supermarkets, operates as a subsidiary of Spartan Stores, Inc.

Giving Program Officials
Pat Nowak: PRIM CORP EMPL director public relations & community affairs: Food Town Supermarkets.

Grants Analysis
Typical Range: $2,500 to $5,000

VICTOR E. SPEAS FOUNDATION

Giving Contact
David P. Ross, Senior Vice President
Bank of America
PO Box 419119
Kansas City, MO 64141-6119

Phone: (816)979-7481
Fax: (816)979-7916

Alternate Contact
Phone: 800-213-0245

Description
Founded: 1947
EIN: 446008340
Organization Type: Family Foundation
Giving Locations: MO: Kansas City metropolitan area
Grant Types: Capital, Challenge, General Support, Project, Seed Money.

Donor Information
Founder: Established as a trust in 1947 by the late Victor E. Speas , chairman of Speas Company. Both Mr. Speas and the Speas Company, a vinegar and apple products manufacturing firm, contributed to the foundation.

Financial Summary
Total Giving: $1,970,135 (2001); $1,977,473 (2000); $1,809,309 (1999)
Giving Analysis: Giving for 1998 includes: foundation scholarships ($3,500); foundation grants to United Way ($141,147) 1997: foundation gifts to individuals ($5,000)
Assets: $35,009,966 (2001); $40,227,593 (2000); $43,425,956 (1999)

Typical Recipients
Arts & Humanities: Arts Centers, Historic Preservation, Libraries, Museums/Galleries, Theater
Civic & Public Affairs: Business/Free Enterprise, Community Foundations, Economic Development, Economic Policy, Employment/Job Training, Civic & Public Affairs-General, Hispanic Affairs, Housing, Municipalities/Towns, Nonprofit Management, Philanthropic Organizations, Urban & Community Affairs, Women's Affairs
Education: Afterschool/Enrichment Programs, Business Education, Colleges & Universities, Continuing Education, Education Associations, Education-General, Health & Physical Education, Medical Education, Minority Education, Preschool Education, Private Education (Precollege), Science/Mathematics Education, Secondary Education (Public)
Health: AIDS/HIV, Cancer, Children's Health/Hospitals, Children's Health/Hospitals, Clinics/Medical Centers, Emergency/Ambulance Services, Geriatric Health, Health Policy/Cost Containment, Health Funds, Health Organizations, Heart, Home-Care Services, Hospices, Hospitals, Kidney, Medical Rehabilitation, Mental Health, Nursing Services, Nutrition, Public Health, Research/Studies Institutes, Single-Disease Health Associations, Speech & Hearing, Trauma Treatment
Religion: Jewish Causes, Ministries, Religious Welfare
Social Services: Animal Protection, At-Risk Youth, Child Welfare, Community Centers, Community Service Organizations, Counseling, Family Services, Homes, People with Disabilities, Senior Services, Sexual Abuse, Shelters/Homelessness, Substance Abuse, United Funds/United Ways, Volunteer Services, Youth Organizations

Application Procedures
Initial Contact: An initial phone call is suggested. There are no formal application forms.
Application Requirements: Initial applications should be no more than three pages and should include the appropriate attachments. Eligible grantees will be asked to submit one copy of a full proposal. Interviews may be requested if the foundation is interested in a submitted proposal.
Deadlines: None.

Review Process: The board meets bimonthly. Notification, if funding will be provided, normally takes about two months.

Restrictions
Funding is restricted to improving the quality of health care in the Kansas City area. Grants are not made for endowment campaigns.

Additional Information
The Victor E. Speas Foundation and the John W. and Effie E. Speas Memorial Trust are affiliated.
Trust(s): Bank of America

Foundation Officials
David P. Ross: bank rep, contact PRIM CORP EMPL senior vice president: NationsBank Corp.

Grants Analysis
Disclosure Period: calendar year ending 2001
Total Grants: $1,970,135
Number of Grants: 43
Average Grant: $45,817
Highest Grant: $200,000
Lowest Grant: $1,500
Typical Range: $15,000 to $60,000

Recent Grants
Note: Grants derived from 2001 Form 990.

General

200,000	Community Resource Network, Kansas City, MO -- operating support
150,000	Support Kansas City, Inc., Kansas City, MO -- start-up costs
147,000	Oznam, Kansas City, MO -- support of capital project
113,540	Healthy Kansas City, Kansas City, MO -- operating expenses and E-Health Project
79,000	Campfire Boys and Girls Heartland Council, Kansas City, MO -- Project AIM
75,000	Niles Home for Children, Kansas City, MO -- software and technology upgrades
75,000	Synergy Services, Kansas City, MO -- upgrading technology
73,550	Northland Therapeutic Riding Center, Kearney, MO -- support of start-up of program and web fees and annual audit
69,292	Amethyst Place, Kansas City, MO -- housing program for drug and alcohol recovery patients
67,000	Mattie Rhodes Center, Kansas City, MO -- capital campaign

JOHN W. AND EFFIE E. SPEAS MEMORIAL TRUST

Giving Contact
David P. Ross, Senior Vice President
Bank of America
PO Box 419119
Kansas City, MO 64105
Phone: (816)979-7481
Fax: (816)979-7916

Description
Founded: 1947
EIN: 446008249
Organization Type: Family Foundation
Giving Locations: KS: Johnson County, Wyandotte County; MO: Cass County, Clay County, Jackson County, Platte County
Grant Types: Capital, Challenge, General Support, Operating Expenses, Project, Research, Seed Money.

Donor Information
Founder: Established in 1947 by the Speas family, including the late Effie E. Speas and the late Victor E. Speas .

Financial Summary
Total Giving: $2,576,368 (2001); $2,872,134 (2000); $1,934,465 (1998)
Giving Analysis: Giving for 1997 includes: foundation grants to United Way ($5,500)
Assets: $34,860,469 (2001); $40,501,993 (2000); $39,605,543 (1998)
Gifts Received: $100,000 (1998). Note: In 1998, contributions were received from Victor Speas Foundation.

Typical Recipients
Arts & Humanities: Libraries, Public Broadcasting
Civic & Public Affairs: Business/Free Enterprise, Community Foundations, Economic Development, Employment/Job Training, Civic & Public Affairs-General, Municipalities/Towns, Nonprofit Management, Urban & Community Affairs
Education: Colleges & Universities, Community & Junior Colleges, Environmental Education, Education-General, Health & Physical Education, Medical Education, Religious Education, Science/Mathematics Education
Health: Alzheimers Disease, Cancer, Children's Health/Hospitals, Clinics/Medical Centers, Emergency/Ambulance Services, Eyes/Blindness, Geriatric Health, Health Policy/Cost Containment, Health Organizations, Heart, Home-Care Services, Hospices, Hospitals, Hospitals (University Affiliated), Kidney, Long-Term Care, Medical Rehabilitation, Medical Research, Medical Training, Mental Health, Multiple Sclerosis, Nursing Services, Nutrition, Prenatal Health Issues, Preventive Medicine/Wellness Organizations, Public Health, Single-Disease Health Associations, Speech & Hearing, Transplant Networks/Donor Banks
Religion: Jewish Causes, Religious Welfare
Social Services: At-Risk Youth, Child Abuse, Child Welfare, Community Centers, Community Service Organizations, Crime Prevention, Family Services, People with Disabilities, Recreation & Athletics, Senior Services, Shelters/Homelessness, Special Olympics, Substance Abuse, United Funds/United Ways, Volunteer Services, Youth Organizations

Application Procedures
Initial Contact: A preliminary phone call is requested. If interested, the trust will request a complete project proposal.
Application Requirements: Applications should be in the form of a three-page letter with the appropriate attachments.
Deadlines: None.
Review Process: The board meets twice a month. Notification follows about two months after receipt of proposal.

Restrictions
The trust does not fund individuals or endowments. Funding is restricted to metropolitan Kansas City.

Additional Information
Bank of America serves as the corporate trustee. The John W. and Effie E. Speas Memorial Trust and the Victor E. Speas Foundation are affiliated.

Foundation Officials
David P. Ross: bank rep, contact PRIM CORP EMPL senior vice president: NationsBank Corp.

Grants Analysis
Disclosure Period: calendar year ending 2001
Total Grants: $2,576,368
Number of Grants: 45
Average Grant: $57,253
Highest Grant: $224,000

Lowest Grant: $1,500
Typical Range: $20,000 to $100,000

Recent Grants

Note: Grants derived from 2001 Form 990.

General

224,000	Community Resource Network, Kansas City, MO -- support of infrastructure requirements
165,062	Rockhurst University, Kansas City, MO -- communication sciences
155,000	Truman Medical Center Foundation, Kansas City, MO -- Kansas City Care Network
139,000	Seton Center, Inc., Kansas City, MO -- Kansas City Community Care Project
105,000	Research Health Foundation, Kansas City, MO -- software purchase
100,000	Kansas University Endowment Association, Kansas City, KS -- construction of new center
100,000	Missouri 4-H Foundation, Columbia, MO -- Aim Urban Program
100,000	Park University, Parkville, MO -- expanded health care program
100,000	Support Kansas City, Inc., Kansas City, MO -- start-up costs
100,000	Swope Parkway Health Center, Kansas City, MO -- support of continuity campaign

SPECIALTY MANUFACTURING CO.

Company Headquarters

5858 Centerville Road
St. Paul, MN 55127
Web: http://www.specialtymfgco.com

Company Description

Employees: 140

Boss Foundation

Giving Contact

Dan McKeown, Treasurer
Boss Foundation
5858 Centerville Rd.
St. Paul, MN 55127-6804
Phone: (651)653-0599

Description

EIN: 416038452
Organization Type: Corporate Foundation
Giving Locations: MN
Grant Types: General Support.

Financial Summary

Total Giving: $203,360 (fiscal year ending June 30, 2001); $182,800 (fiscal 2000); $171,500 (fiscal 1999)
Assets: $4,505,801 (fiscal 2001); $4,530,112 (fiscal 2000); $3,588,806 (fiscal 1999)
Gifts Received: $25,000 (fiscal 2001); $26,000 (fiscal 2000); $25,000 (fiscal 1999). Note: In fiscal 2001, contributions were received from Specialty Manufacturing Co. In fiscal 1999 and fiscal 2000, contributions were received from Specialty Manufacturing Co. ($25,000) and William Boss Trust A ($76,164).

Typical Recipients

Arts & Humanities: Arts Centers, Arts Funds, Arts Institutes, Community Arts, Arts & Humanities-General, History & Archaeology, Libraries, Museums/Galleries, Music, Opera, Public Broadcasting, Theater
Civic & Public Affairs: Botanical Gardens/Parks, Clubs, Community Foundations, Native American Affairs

Education: Agricultural Education, Arts/Humanities Education, Colleges & Universities, Faculty Development
Health: Emergency/Ambulance Services
Religion: Churches
Science: Science Museums
Social Services: Community Service Organizations, Special Olympics, Substance Abuse

Application Procedures

Initial Contact: Request application guidelines.
Application Requirements: Include a one-page letter stating amount requested, purpose of funds sought, proof of tax-exempt status, and any other support documents.
Deadlines: Proposals received by September 1 will be considered at the annual meeting.

Restrictions

Preference given to organizations furthering or engaged in the performing and fine arts.

Additional Information

Publications: Application Guidelines

Corporate Officials

Bruce A. Lawin: president, chief executive officer B Long Prairie, MN 1934. ED Saint Cloud State College (1958). PRIM CORP EMPL president, chief executive officer: Specialty Manufacturing Co. CORP AFFIL president, director: Sandy Manufacturing Co.; president, director: TMichigan Plastics.
Mark Nosbush: chief financial officer PRIM CORP EMPL chief financial officer: Specialty Manufacturing Co.

Foundation Officials

W. Andrew Boss: president, director
Dan McKeown: treasurer
Heidi McKeown: vice president, secretary, director
Nancy B. Sandberg: chairman, director PRIM CORP EMPL chairman: The Specialty Manufacturing Co.

Grants Analysis

Disclosure Period: fiscal year ending June 30, 2001
Total Grants: $203,360
Number of Grants: 56
Average Grant: $3,631
Highest Grant: $6,000
Typical Range: $1,000 to $5,000

Recent Grants

Note: Grants derived from fiscal 2000 Form 990.

General

8,000	St. Anthony Park Community Foundation, St. Paul, MN
7,100	Philips Center for the Arts, Minneapolis, MN
6,000	Guthrie Theater, Minneapolis, MN
6,000	Minneapolis Institute of Arts, Minneapolis, MN
6,000	Minnesota Orchestral Society Foundation, St. Paul, MN
5,500	Minnesota Humanities Commission, St. Paul, MN
5,500	Minnesota Public Radio, St. Paul, MN
5,500	Northern Clay Center, St. Paul, MN
5,500	Ordway Theater, St. Paul, MN
5,000	Children's Theater Company, Minneapolis, MN

ROY M. SPEER FOUNDATION

Giving Contact

Richard W. Baker, Trustee
2535 Success Dr.
Odessa, FL 33556
Phone: (727)372-8808

Description

Founded: 1986
EIN: 592785945
Organization Type: Private Foundation
Grant Types: Endowment, General Support, Research.

Financial Summary

Total Giving: $860,300 (fiscal year ending June 30, 2001); $858,953 (fiscal 2000); $495,453 (fiscal 1997)
Assets: $18,089,902 (fiscal 2001); $23,949,199 (fiscal 2000); $17,440,565 (fiscal 1997)

Typical Recipients

Arts & Humanities: Libraries
Civic & Public Affairs: Civic & Public Affairs-General, Zoos/Aquariums
Education: Colleges & Universities, Private Education (Precollege), Religious Education
Health: Hospitals, Single-Disease Health Associations
Religion: Churches, Religion-General, Jewish Causes, Missionary Activities (Domestic), Religious Organizations, Religious Welfare, Synagogues/Temples
Social Services: Emergency Relief, Scouts, Senior Services

Application Procedures

Initial Contact: Foundation requests a written narrative. Include purpose of funds sought.
Deadlines: None.

Foundation Officials

Richard W. Baker: trustee

Grants Analysis

Disclosure Period: fiscal year ending June 30, 2001
Total Grants: $860,300
Number of Grants: 17
Average Grant: $27,438*
Highest Grant: $321,300
Typical Range: $10,000 to $50,000
***Note:** Average grant figure excludes two highest grants ($421,300).

Recent Grants

Note: Grants derived from fiscal 2000 Form 990.

General

249,953	University of Florida Foundation, Gainesville, FL
180,000	Practical Christianity Foundation, Odessa, FL
120,000	Wake Forest University, Winston-Salem, NC
100,000	Hurricane Relief Fund, Miami, FL
50,000	Billy Graham Crusade, Tampa, FL
42,000	First Baptist Church, Elfers, FL
41,000	World Thrust USA, Stone Mountain, GA
36,000	Christian Resource Center, Tampa, FL
30,000	Faith Community Church, Lake Mary, FL
10,000	Robert Morris College, Pittsburgh, PA

SPERANDIO FAMILY FOUNDATION

Giving Contact

Jacqueline Sperandio, Vice President
18 Twin Ponds Drive
Spencerport, NY 14559-1037
Phone: (716)637-7508

Description

Founded: 1998
EIN: 161490918
Organization Type: Private Foundation
Grant Types: General Support.

Financial Summary

Total Giving: $56,868 (fiscal year ending August 31, 2001); $67,150 (fiscal 2000); $45,900 (fiscal 1999)
Giving Analysis: Giving for fiscal 2001 includes: foundation grants to United Way ($11,000); fiscal 2000: foundation grants to United Way ($10,000) fiscal 1999: foundation grants to United Way ($10,000)
Assets: $1,977,427 (fiscal 2001); $1,186,079 (fiscal 2000); $1,121,859 (fiscal 1999)
Gifts Received: $1,445,040 (fiscal 2001); $525,100 (fiscal 1996). Note: In fiscal 2001, contributions were received from Robert and Jacqueline Sperandio.

Typical Recipients

Arts & Humanities: Libraries, Museums/Galleries, Public Broadcasting
Civic & Public Affairs: Clubs, Civic & Public Affairs-General
Education: Colleges & Universities, Education-General, Religious Education
Health: Adolescent Health Issues, Alzheimers Disease, Children's Health/Hospitals, Emergency/Ambulance Services, Health-General, Nursing Services, Public Health, Respiratory
Religion: Churches
Social Services: Domestic Violence, People with Disabilities, United Funds/United Ways, Volunteer Services, YMCA/YWCA/YMHA/YWHA

Application Procedures

Initial Contact: Send a brief letter of inquiry.
Application Requirements: Include purpose of funds sought.
Deadlines: None.

Restrictions

Funds organizations benefiting children and women.

Foundation Officials

Elizabeth S. Rickert: trustee
Jacqueline Sperandio: vice president
Mark C. Sperandio: trustee
Robert B. Sperandio: president, secretary

Grants Analysis

Disclosure Period: fiscal year ending August 31, 2001
Total Grants: $45,868*
Number of Grants: 16
Average Grant: $2,391*
Highest Grant: $10,000
Lowest Grant: $250
Typical Range: $1,000 to $5,000
*Note: Giving excludes United Way. Average grant figure excludes highest grant.

Recent Grants

Note: Grants derived from 2000 Form 990.

Library-Related
10,500	Sno Isle Library Foundation

General
11,000	YWCA Womens Resource Center
10,100	Lifetime Assistance, Rochester, NY
10,000	United Way
6,000	Stratford Festival, Toronto, ON Canada
5,000	National Children's Cancer
5,000	Spencerport Rotary
4,500	Alternatives for Battered Women, Rochester, NY
3,000	Vinfen of Boston
2,000	Aquinas Institute of Theology, St. Louis, MO
1,000	Children's Museum of SNO

BELLA SPEWACK ARTICLE 5TH TRUST

Giving Contact

Arthur Elias, Contact
Bank of New York
One Wall St.
New York, NY 10286
Phone: (212)635-1520

Alternate Contact

98 Riverside Drive
New York, NY 10024

Description

Founded: 1992
EIN: 133669246
Organization Type: Private Foundation
Giving Locations: NY
Grant Types: General Support.

Financial Summary

Total Giving: $95,000 (fiscal year ending June 30, 2001); $61,600 (fiscal 1997); $55,000 (fiscal 1996)
Assets: $1,744,522 (fiscal 2001); $1,437,802 (fiscal 1997); $1,254,749 (fiscal 1996)

Typical Recipients

Arts & Humanities: Arts Funds, Libraries, Music, Performing Arts, Theater
Civic & Public Affairs: Civil Rights, Civic & Public Affairs-General
Education: Colleges & Universities, Preschool Education
Health: Emergency/Ambulance Services, Single-Disease Health Associations
International: Health Care/Hospitals, Missionary/Religious Activities
Religion: Jewish Causes, Religious Welfare
Social Services: Child Welfare, Shelters/Homelessness

Application Procedures

Initial Contact: Send a brief letter of inquiry.
Deadlines: None.

Additional Information

Trust(s): Bank NY

Foundation Officials

Arthur Elias: trustee
Lois Elias: trustee

Grants Analysis

Disclosure Period: fiscal year ending June 30, 2001
Total Grants: $95,000
Number of Grants: 16
Average Grant: $2,333*
Highest Grant: $60,000
Typical Range: $500 to $3,000
*Note: Average grant figure excludes highest grant.

Recent Grants

Note: Grants derived from fiscal 2001 Form 990.

Library-Related
2,000	Columbia University Rare Book and Manuscript Library, New York, NY
1,000	New York Public Library, New York, NY

General
60,000	Dramatists Guild Fund, New York, NY
10,000	Friends of Israel Sport Center for the Disabled, New York, NY
3,000	Actors Fund of America, New York, NY
3,000	Interfaith Assembly of Homeless and Housing, New York, NY
3,000	United Jewish Appeal Federation, New York, NY

2,500	Children's Defense Fund, Washington, DC
2,000	Salvation Army, Abilene, TX
1,500	Dorot, New York, NY
1,500	National Council of Jewish Women, New York, NY
1,500	New York Civil Liberties Union, New York, NY

ALEXANDER C. AND TILLIE S. SPEYER FOUNDATION

Giving Contact

Alexander C. Speyer, Jr., Trustee
1202 Benedum Trees Bldg.
Pittsburgh, PA 15222
Phone: (412)281-7225

Description

Founded: 1962
EIN: 256051650
Organization Type: Private Foundation
Giving Locations: DC; MD; MA; NY; PA; VA; WY
Grant Types: General Support.

Donor Information

Founder: members of the Speyer family

Financial Summary

Total Giving: $320,696 (2001); $299,356 (2000); $263,720 (1999). Note: 1997 Giving includes United Way ($10,000).
Giving Analysis: Giving for 2001 includes: foundation grants to United Way ($17,000); 2000: foundation grants to United Way ($16,000) 1999: foundation grants to United Way ($15,000)
Assets: $5,869,718 (2001); $7,097,195 (2000); $7,432,140 (1999)
Gifts Received: $124,625 (1999); $200,028 (1996). Note: In 1999, contributions were received from A.C. Speyer, Jr. ($54,000) and Darthea Speyer ($70,625). In 1996, contributions were received from Alexander C. Speyer, Jr. ($101,313) and Darthea Speyer ($98,715).

Typical Recipients

Arts & Humanities: Arts Associations & Councils, Arts Centers, Arts Festivals, Arts Institutes, Community Arts, Ethnic & Folk Arts, Arts & Humanities-General, Libraries, Literary Arts, Museums/Galleries, Music, Public Broadcasting, Visual Arts
Civic & Public Affairs: Botanical Gardens/Parks, Civil Rights, Community Foundations, Civic & Public Affairs-General, Nonprofit Management
Education: Arts/Humanities Education, Colleges & Universities, Education Funds, Education Reform, Education-General, International Exchange, Preschool Education, Private Education (Precollege), Public Education (Precollege), Science/Mathematics Education, Secondary Education (Private)
Environment: Air/Water Quality, Environment-General, Resource Conservation
Health: Cancer, Emergency/Ambulance Services, Eyes/Blindness, Hospitals, Public Health
International: Health Care/Hospitals, International Relations, Missionary/Religious Activities
Religion: Churches, Jewish Causes, Religious Organizations, Religious Welfare, Seminaries, Synagogues/Temples
Science: Scientific Centers & Institutes
Social Services: Community Service Organizations, Crime Prevention, Delinquency & Criminal Rehabilitation, Family Planning, Food/Clothing Distribution, Homes, People with Disabilities, United Funds/United Ways

Application Procedures

Initial Contact: The foundation has no formal grant application procedure or application form.
Deadlines: None.

Foundation Officials

Alexander C. Speyer, Jr.: trustee B 1916. ED Carnegie Institute of Technology. PRIM CORP EMPL president: North Star Coal Co. CORP AFFIL president, treasurer: Parsons Coal Co.
Darthea Speyer: trustee

Grants Analysis

Disclosure Period: calendar year ending 2001
Total Grants: $303,696*
Number of Grants: 87
Average Grant: $3,225*
Highest Grant: $23,125
Typical Range: $1,000 to $5,000
*Note: Giving excludes United Way. Average grant figure excludes highest grant.

Recent Grants

Note: Grants derived from 2001 Form 990.

General

23,125	Carnegie Museum of Art, Pittsburgh, PA
22,000	Carnegie Mellon University, Pittsburgh, PA
20,000	Western Pennsylvania Conservancy, Mill Run, PA
18,000	New York Studio School of Drawing and Painting, New York, NY
17,000	United Way of Southwestern Pennsylvania, Pittsburgh, PA
15,806	Rodef Shalom Congregation, Pittsburgh, PA
15,000	New York Times Neediest Cases, New York, NY
15,000	United Jewish Federation, Pittsburgh, PA
13,000	Byrd Hoffman Foundation, New York, NY
11,500	Sidwell Friends School, Washington, DC

SETH SPRAGUE EDUCATIONAL AND CHARITABLE FOUNDATION

Giving Contact

Linda R. Franciscovich, Managing Director
U.S. Trust Co.
114 W. 47th Street
New York, NY 10036
Phone: (212)852-1000
Fax: (212)852-3377

Alternate Contact

Phone: (212)852-3629

Description

Founded: 1939
EIN: 136071886
Organization Type: General Purpose Foundation
Giving Locations: MA; NY: nationally.
Grant Types: General Support, Operating Expenses, Project, Research, Seed Money.

Donor Information

Founder: Established in 1939 by Seth Sprague , the Sprague Educational and Charitable Foundation is administered by its trustees and the United States Trust Company of New York. All of the trustees were either associates of Mr. Sprague or familiar with his philanthropic pursuits.

Seth Sprague was a graduate of Norwich Academy and a lifetime employee of F. H. Foster and Company, a Boston cotton processing corporation of which he eventually became president. Mr. Sprague died in 1941.

Financial Summary

Total Giving: $3,280,000 (2001); $3,442,723 (2000); $2,807,699 (1998)
Assets: $63,403,075 (2001); $72,790,263 (2000); $71,316,902 (1998)

Typical Recipients

Arts & Humanities: Arts Associations & Councils, Arts Funds, Arts Institutes, Ballet, Dance, Ethnic & Folk Arts, Arts & Humanities-General, Historic Preservation, History & Archaeology, Libraries, Literary Arts, Museums/Galleries, Music, Opera, Performing Arts, Public Broadcasting, Theater
Civic & Public Affairs: Botanical Gardens/Parks, Business/Free Enterprise, Clubs, Community Foundations, Economic Development, Employment/Job Training, Ethnic Organizations, Civic & Public Affairs-General, Law & Justice, Parades/Festivals, Professional & Trade Associations, Public Policy, Urban & Community Affairs, Women's Affairs, Zoos/Aquariums
Education: Arts/Humanities Education, Colleges & Universities, Colleges & Universities, Community & Junior Colleges, Education Associations, Education Funds, Education-General, International Studies, Journalism/Media Education, Legal Education, Medical Education, Minority Education, Private Education (Precollege), Public Education (Precollege), Religious Education, Social Sciences Education, Special Education, Student Aid
Environment: Air/Water Quality, Environment-General, Resource Conservation
Health: AIDS/HIV, Arthritis, Cancer, Children's Health/Hospitals, Clinics/Medical Centers, Emergency/Ambulance Services, Health-General, Geriatric Health, Health Funds, Health Organizations, Hospices, Hospitals, Medical Rehabilitation, Medical Research, Medical Training, Mental Health, Nursing Services, Single-Disease Health Associations
International: International Relations
Religion: Churches, Religious Welfare, Seminaries, Social/Policy Issues
Science: Science Museums, Scientific Centers & Institutes, Scientific Labs
Social Services: Animal Protection, At-Risk Youth, Big Brother/Big Sister, Camps, Child Welfare, Community Centers, Community Service Organizations, Counseling, Crime Prevention, Delinquency & Criminal Rehabilitation, Domestic Violence, Emergency Relief, Family Planning, Family Services, People with Disabilities, Recreation & Athletics, Senior Services, Shelters/Homelessness, Substance Abuse, Volunteer Services, Youth Organizations

Application Procedures

Initial Contact: Initial contact should be a written request.
Application Requirements: Applications should include a summary (two pages), budget, audited financial statement, and an IRS determination letter.
Deadlines: April 15.
Review Process: The board of directors meets in March, June, September and November.

Restrictions

The foundation does not give grants for research or capital expenditures. In addition, the foundation does not make grants to individuals or to organizations located outside the United States.

Additional Information

Publications: Guidelines
Trust(s): US Trust Co. of New York

Foundation Officials

Patricia Dunnington: trustee
Arline Ripley Greenleaf: trustee
Jacqueline DeNeuflize Simpkins: trustee CLUB AF-FIL Chilton Club; Colony Club.

Grants Analysis

Disclosure Period: calendar year ending 2001
Total Grants: $3,280,000
Number of Grants: 412
Average Grant: $7,961
Highest Grant: $75,000
Typical Range: $1,000 to $10,000

Recent Grants

Note: Grants derived from 2001 Form 990.

General

75,000	New York Weill Cornell Medical Center, New York, NY
50,000	Center for Coastal Studies, Provincetown, MA
50,000	Montpelier Foundation, Montpelier Station, VA
50,000	New York Presbyterian Hospital, New York, NY
50,000	Woodberry Forest School, Woodberry, VA
45,000	New York Presbyterian Hospital, New York, NY
40,000	Riley School, Glen Cove, ME
40,000	Woodberry Forest School, Woodberry, VA
35,000	Big Brothers and Big Sisters of New York City, Inc., New York, NY
35,000	Carnegie Hall, New York, NY

SPRING/CLOSE FOUNDATION

Giving Contact

Angela McRae, President
1826 Second Baxter Crossing
Ft. Mill, SC 29708
Phone: (803)548-2002
Fax: (803)548-1797

Description

Founded: 1968
EIN: 237013986
Organization Type: Private Foundation
Giving Locations: NC; SC: Chester Township, Fort Mill Township, Lancaster County
Grant Types: Capital, Conference/Seminar, General Support, Loan, Professorship, Seed Money.

Donor Information

Founder: Established in 1968 by members of the Springs and Close families.

Financial Summary

Total Giving: $3,321,348 (2002 approx); $1,129,274 (2001); $981,958 (2000)
Giving Analysis: Giving for 2001 includes: foundation scholarships ($1,900); 2000: foundation scholarships ($210,000) 1998: foundation scholarships ($5,000)
Assets: $3,000,000 (2002 approx); $14,286,512 (2001); $16,114,899 (2000)
Gifts Received: $432,053 (1998); $2,126,350 (1997); $161,100 (1996). Note: In 1998, contributions were received from Patrica Close ($255,123), Leroy S. Close ($101,113), and Frances A. Close ($75,067). In 1997, the foundation received 7 donations from individuals, including a $2,025,050 gift from Anne S. Close.

Typical Recipients

Arts & Humanities: Art History, Arts Associations & Councils, Film & Video, Historic Preservation, History & Archaeology, Libraries, Museums/Galleries, Performing Arts, Public Broadcasting, Theater

Civic & Public Affairs: Economic Development, Civic & Public Affairs-General, Housing, Law & Justice, Nonprofit Management, Philanthropic Organizations, Public Policy, Safety, Urban & Community Affairs

Education: Arts/Humanities Education, Business Education, Business-School Partnerships, Colleges & Universities, Community & Junior Colleges, Elementary Education (Private), Elementary Education (Public), Environmental Education, Education-General, Legal Education, Minority Education, Preschool Education, Private Education (Precollege), Public Education (Precollege), Science/Mathematics Education, Vocational & Technical Education

Environment: Environment-General, Resource Conservation

Health: AIDS/HIV, Alzheimers Disease, Clinics/Medical Centers, Diabetes, Emergency/Ambulance Services, Health-General, Hospices, Hospitals, Mental Health, Prenatal Health Issues

Religion: Churches, Ministries

Science: Scientific Centers & Institutes, Scientific Organizations

Social Services: Animal Protection, At-Risk Youth, Child Welfare, Community Centers, Community Service Organizations, Day Care, Emergency Relief, Food/Clothing Distribution, People with Disabilities, Recreation & Athletics, Scouts, Social Services-General, Substance Abuse, United Funds/United Ways, Youth Organizations

Application Procedures

Initial Contact: Send cover letter and full proposal.

Application Requirements: Include a description of organization, amount requested, purpose of funds sought, recently audited financial statement, and proof of tax-exempt status.

Deadlines: March 15 and November 1.

Review Process: The board meets twice per year. The fall meeting is held on the Wednesday prior to Thanksgiving.

Additional Information

The foundation was formerly known as the Close Foundation.

Publications: Annual Report

Foundation Officials

James Bradley: director CORP AFFIL director: Springs Co.

Charles Alan Bundy: director, consult B Cheraw, SC 1930. ED Wofford College BA (1951). NONPR AFFIL member: Lancaster County Chamber of Commerce; director: Springs Memorial Hospital. CLUB AFFIL Rotary Club.

Anne Springs Close: chairman, director CORP AFFIL director: Springs Co. Investment Division; director: Square Records; director: Springs Co.; director: America Insurance Agency; director: Catawba Insurance Agency.

Derick Springsteen Close: director CORP AFFIL director: Springs Co. Investment Division; director, international sales: Springs Industries Inc.; director: Springs Co.; director: Catawba Insurance Agency; director: South E Huffman Corp.; director: America Insurance Agency.

Elliott Springs Close: director CORP AFFIL director: Springs Co.; director: Springs Co. Investment Division; director: Kanawha Insurance Co. Inc.; director: America Insurance Agency; director: Catawba Insurance Agency.

Frances A. Close: director

Hugh William Close, Jr.: director

Katherine Anne Close, MD: director

Leroy Springs Close: director B 1950. PRIM CORP EMPL president, chief executive officer: Sandlapper

Fabrics. CORP AFFIL director: Springs Co. Investment Division; director: Springs Industries Inc.; director: Springs Co.; director: America Insurance Agency; director: Catawba Insurance Agency.

Patricia Close: director

Grants Analysis

Disclosure Period: calendar year ending 2001

Total Grants: $1,127,374*

Number of Grants: 37

Average Grant: $25,064*

Highest Grant: $200,000

Typical Range: $5,000 to $25,000

*Note: Giving excludes scholarships. Average grant figure excludes highest grant.

Recent Grants

Note: Grants derived from 2001 Form 990.

General

200,000	Anne Springs Close Greenway
200,000	Winthrop University, Rock Hill, SC
125,000	University of South Carolina Lancaster, Lancaster, SC -- building fund
120,000	South Carolina First Steps Program, SC
50,000	North Central Family Medical Center
50,000	Safe Passages, Inc.
50,000	South Carolina Center for Grassroots and Nonprofit Leadership, SC
50,000	York Technical College, Rock Hill, SC -- for science and technology equipment
35,000	York Technical College, Rock Hill, SC -- adults in transition
25,000	Dilworth Center for Chemical Dependency, Charlotte, NC

SPRINGS FOUNDATION, INC.

Giving Contact

Angela McCrae, Jr., Executive Director
1826 Second Baxter Crossing
Ft. Mill, SC 29708
Phone: (803)548-2002
Fax: (803)548-1797

Description

Founded: 1942

EIN: 570426344

Organization Type: General Purpose Foundation

Giving Locations: SC: Chester Township, Fort Mill Township, Lancaster County

Grant Types: Capital, Challenge, General Support, Matching, Operating Expenses, Seed Money.

Donor Information

Founder: Colonel Elliott White Springs (1896-1959) was the founder of Springs Industries, one of the largest textile manufacturers in the United States. He established the foundation, formerly called the Elliott White Springs Foundation, in 1942. His wife, Frances Ley Springs, continued her husband's philanthropic interests through her work at the foundation. "Her estate provided the means for expanded philanthropic work over a wider geographic area. Those funds began what is now called the Close Foundation."

Financial Summary

Total Giving: $1,472,090 (2001); $1,326,152 (2000); $1,438,592 (1998)

Giving Analysis: Giving for 2000 includes: foundation grants to United Way ($45,000) 1997: foundation gifts to individuals ($212,188)

Assets: $35,488,538 (2001); $40,169,478 (2000); $39,140,419 (1998)

Gifts Received: $700 (2000); $750 (1998); $1,200 (1997). Note: In 1997 and 2000, contributions were received from members of the Close family and Dehler Hart.

Typical Recipients

Arts & Humanities: Arts Associations & Councils, Community Arts, Libraries, Music, Theater

Civic & Public Affairs: Botanical Gardens/Parks, Clubs, Economic Development, Employment/Job Training, Civic & Public Affairs-General, Housing, Law & Justice, Municipalities/Towns, Safety, Urban & Community Affairs

Education: Arts/Humanities Education, Business-School Partnerships, Colleges & Universities, Education Funds, Education Reform, Elementary Education (Public), Medical Education, Public Education (Precollege), Secondary Education (Public), Student Aid

Environment: Environment-General

Health: AIDS/HIV, Cancer, Clinics/Medical Centers, Emergency/Ambulance Services, Health Organizations, Hospices, Hospitals, Mental Health, Nutrition, Prenatal Health Issues

Religion: Churches, Religion-General, Ministries, Religious Organizations, Religious Welfare

Science: Science-General

Social Services: Animal Protection, Camps, Child Welfare, Community Service Organizations, Counseling, Crime Prevention, Delinquency & Criminal Rehabilitation, Emergency Relief, Family Services, Recreation & Athletics, Scouts, Senior Services, Social Services-General, Substance Abuse, United Funds/United Ways, YMCA/YWCA/YMHA/YWHA, Youth Organizations

Application Procedures

Initial Contact: Initial contact should be in the form of a brief letter.

Application Requirements: Letters should provide a brief statement of need; a copy of tax-exempt letter should accompany initial proposal.

Deadlines: Proposals are due by March 1 and November 1.

Review Process: The president researches the proposal for merit, eligibility, and priority status. Recommendations are then presented to the board for approval. The board meets in April and November.

Restrictions

Grants are not made to individuals.

Additional Information

The Spring Foundation manages an interest-free student loan program which is available to students who reside in or whose parents work in Lancaster County, Chester Township or Fort Mill Township in South Carolina and who plan to attend a four-year accredited college in South Carolina. The Springs Foundation is also affiliated with the Close Foundation located in Lancaster, SC.

Publications: Annual Report; Guidelines; Application Form

Foundation Officials

Crandall C. Bowles: director

James Bradley: director CORP AFFIL director: Springs Co.

Charles Alan Bundy: director B Cheraw, SC 1930. ED Wofford College BA (1951). NONPR AFFIL member: Lancaster County Chamber of Commerce; director: Springs Memorial Hospital. CLUB AFFIL Rotary Club.

Anne Springs Close: donor, chairwoman, director CORP AFFIL director: Springs Co. Investment Division; director: Square Records; director: Springs Co.; director: America Insurance Agency; director: Catawba Insurance Agency.

Derick Springsteen Close: director CORP AFFIL director: Springs Co. Investment Division; director, international sales: Springs Industries Inc.; director: Springs Co.; director: Catawba Insurance Agency; director: South E Huffman Corp.; director: America Insurance Agency.

Elliott Springs Close: director CORP AFFIL director: Springs Co.; director: Springs Co. Investment Division; director: Kanawha Insurance Co. Inc.; director:

America Insurance Agency; director: Catawba Insurance Agency.

Frances A. Close: director
Hugh William Close, Jr.: president, director
Katherine Anne Close, MD: director
Leroy Springs Close: director B 1950. PRIM CORP EMPL president, chief executive officer: Sandlapper Fabrics. CORP AFFIL director: Springs Co. Investment Division; director: Springs Industries Inc.; director: Springs Co.; director: America Insurance Agency; director: Catawba Insurance Agency.
Pat Close: director
Dehler Hart: director
James H. Hodges: secretary, treasurer, director PRIM CORP EMPL secretary, general counsel: Springs Co. NONPR AFFIL member: Phi Beta Kappa.
Robert L. Holcombe, Jr.: director
William G. Taylor: director B 1956. ED Washington & Lee University BA (1978); Wake Forest University MBA (1980). PRIM CORP EMPL president, treasurer, director: Springs Co. CORP AFFIL director: Kanawha Insurance Co. Inc.; chairman: Springland Inc.

Grants Analysis

Disclosure Period: calendar year ending 2001
Total Grants: $1,047,262*
Number of Grants: 60
Average Grant: $8,852*
Highest Grant: $525,000
Lowest Grant: $1,000
Typical Range: $1,000 to $25,000
*Note: Giving excludes United Way and scholarship. Average grant excludes highest grant.

Recent Grants

Note: Grants derived from 2002 Form 990.

General

525,000	Joint Recreation Commission for Lancaster County, Lancaster, SC -- for operating support
125,000	Chester County YMCA, Chester, SC -- for indoor pool
114,500	United Way Fund of Lancaster, Lancaster, SC
100,000	Joint Recreation Commission for Lancaster County, Lancaster, SC -- for swimming pool
58,900	Chester County Hospital, Chester, SC
52,000	Chester County Emergency Medical Services, Chester, SC
50,000	Tree Tops Community Camp, Lancaster, SC
45,000	King of Kings Ministries, Lancaster, SC -- for Joshua House renovations
33,000	Christian Services of Lancaster County, Lancaster, SC -- for Adopt a Child
29,752	Lancaster County School District, Lancaster, SC

SPX CORP.

Company Headquarters

13515 Ballantyne Corporate Pl.
Charlotte, NC 28277
Web: http://www.spx.com

Company Description

Ticker: SPW
Exchange: NYSE
Former Name: Sealed Power Corp.
Revenue: US$5.045 billion (2002)
Profit: US$127.5 million (2002)
Employees: 23400 (2002)
Fortune Rank: 328, per FORTUNE Magazine's list of 500 Largest U.S. Corporations (2002).
SIC(s): 3423 Hand & Edge Tools Nec, 3429 Hardware Nec, 3491 Industrial Valves, 3544 Special Dies, Tools, Jigs & Fixtures.

Operating Locations

SPX Corp. (GA; IL--Des Plaines; IN--Auburn, Rochester; MI--Alma, Dowagiac, Jackson, Muskegon, St. Johns, Warren, Whitehall, Zeeland; MS; OH--Montpelier; PA)

SPX Foundation

Giving Contact

Tina Betlejewski, President
700 Terrace Point Drive
Muskegon, MI 49443-3301
Phone: (231)724-5121
Fax: (231)724-5720

Description

Founded: 1984
EIN: 386058308
Organization Type: Corporate Foundation
Giving Locations: primarily in plant communities.
Grant Types: Capital, Employee Matching Gifts, General Support.

Donor Information

Founder: SPX Corp.

Financial Summary

Total Giving: $512,815 (2001); $402,905 (2000); $417,957 (1998)
Giving Analysis: Giving for 2001 includes: foundation grants to United Way ($32,148); foundation matching gifts ($312,783); 2000: foundation grants to United Way ($25,677); foundation ($121,896); foundation matching gifts ($255,332); 1998: foundation grants to United Way ($77,425) foundation matching gifts ($226,383)
Assets: $1,560,588 (2001); $87,841 (2000); $376,311 (1998)
Gifts Received: $2,191,250 (2001); $781,632 (1994); $392,641 (1993). Note: In 2001, contributions were received from SPX Corp. ($300,000) and EGS Electrical Group ($1,891,250). In 1994, contributions of $780,332 were received from SPX Corp., and $1,300 received from First Chicago.

Typical Recipients

Arts & Humanities: Arts Centers, Arts Festivals, Arts & Humanities-General, Libraries, Museums/Galleries, Music, Opera, Performing Arts, Public Broadcasting, Theater
Civic & Public Affairs: Botanical Gardens/Parks, Business/Free Enterprise, Chambers of Commerce, Clubs, Community Foundations, Economic Development, Economic Policy, Civic & Public Affairs-General, Housing, Municipalities/Towns, Nonprofit Management, Parades/Festivals, Professional & Trade Associations, Safety, Urban & Community Affairs, Women's Affairs
Education: Afterschool/Enrichment Programs, Arts/Humanities Education, Business Education, Colleges & Universities, Community & Junior Colleges, Education Funds, Engineering/Technological Education, Education-General, Minority Education, Private Education (Precollege), Public Education (Precollege), Science/Mathematics Education
Environment: Environment-General
Health: Cancer, Children's Health/Hospitals, Diabetes, Emergency/Ambulance Services, Health-General, Health Organizations, Hospitals, Multiple Sclerosis, Single-Disease Health Associations
Religion: Churches, Religion-General, Ministries, Religious Organizations, Religious Welfare, Seminaries
Science: Scientific Centers & Institutes, Scientific Organizations
Social Services: Animal Protection, Child Abuse, Community Service Organizations, Crime Prevention, Emergency Relief, Family Planning, Family Services, Food/Clothing Distribution, People with Disabilities,

Recreation & Athletics, Scouts, Social Services-General, Social Services-General, Special Olympics, Substance Abuse, United Funds/United Ways, Volunteer Services, YMCA/YWCA/YMHA/YWHA, Youth Organizations

Application Procedures

Initial Contact: Send a letter of inquiry.
Application Requirements: Include a description of organization, amount requested, purpose of funds sought, and proof of tax-exempt status.
Deadlines: None.

Corporate Officials

John B. Blystone: chairman, president, chief executive officer, director B Erie, PA 1953. ED University of Pittsburgh BS (1975). PRIM CORP EMPL chairman, president, chief executive officer, director: SPX Corp. CORP AFFIL director: Worthington Indiana Inc.
Patrick J. O'Leary: vice president finance, treasurer, chief financial officer PRIM CORP EMPL vice president finance, treasurer, chief financial officer: SPX Corp.

Foundation Officials

Robert B. Foreman: vice president, trustee
Christopher J. Kearney: trustee ED DePaul University; Notre Dame College. PRIM CORP EMPL vice president, secretary, general counsel: SPX Corp.
Patrick J. O'Leary: secretary, treasurer (see above)

Grants Analysis

Disclosure Period: calendar year ending 2001
Total Grants: $167,884*
Number of Grants: 14
Average Grant: $9,068*
Highest Grant: $50,000
Lowest Grant: $150
Typical Range: $5,000 to $15,000
*Note: Giving excludes matching gifts; United Way. Average grant figure excludes highest grant.

Recent Grants

Note: Grants derived from 2001 Form 990.

General

50,000	Blystone Foundation
50,000	Blystone Foundation
15,000	Community Foundation
13,000	Western Theological Seminary, Holland, MI
12,500	Muskegon County Catholic Education Foundation, Muskegon, MI
6,085	Auburn Police Department, Auburn, IN
6,000	North Park University, Chicago, IL
5,010	United Way of Santa Clara County, San Jose, CA
5,000	American Red Cross
5,000	BDSRA

SQUARE D CO.

Company Headquarters

Palatine, IL
Web: http://www.squared.com

Company Description

Revenue: US$1.2 billion (2001)
Employees: 17000 (2001)
SIC(s): 3497 Metal Foil & Leaf, 3499 Fabricated Metal Products Nec, 3612 Transformers Except Electronic, 3613 Switchgear & Switchboard Apparatus.
Parent Company: Schneider SA, 43-45 Blvd. Franklin-Roosevelt, Rueil-Malmaison, France

Operating Locations

Electrical Distribution Business (TN--Smyrna); Schneider Automation (MA--North Andover); Square D Automation Products (WI--Milwaukee); Square D

Co. (AL--Clayton, Leeds; CA--Bakersfield, Costa Mesa; FL--Clearwater; GA--Atlanta, Norcross; IL--Niles, Palatine, Schiller Park; IN--Huntington, Peru; IA--Cedar Rapids; KY--Florence, Lexington; MO--Columbia; NE--Lincoln; NJ--Secaucus; NC--Asheville, Knightdale, Monroe, Raleigh; OH--Middletown, Oxford; PA--Harrisburg; SC--Columbia, Seneca; TN--Memphis, Nashville, Smyrna; TX--Bedford, Dallas, Fort Worth, Mesquite; WA--Mercer Island; WI--Milwaukee, Oshkosh); Square D Co.-Assembly Operations (FL--Clearwater); Square D Co.-Central Distribution Center (TN--Memphis); Square D Co.-Control Products (NC--Knightdale); Square D Co.-Pacifico (CA--San Ysidro); Square D Co.-Transformer Business Division (WI--Milwaukee); Square D Middletown Plant (OH--Middletown); Square D Oxford Plant (OH--Oxford); Square D Seneca Plant (SC--Seneca)

Nonmonetary Support

Type: Donated Equipment
Contact: Tammy Sittinger, Foundation Coordinator

Square D Foundation

Giving Contact

Harry Wilson, Secretary
Square D Foundation
1415 South Roselle Road
Palatine, IL 60067
Phone: (847)397-2600
Fax: (847)397-2804

Description

EIN: 366054195
Organization Type: Corporate Foundation
Giving Locations: manufacturing facility communities.
Grant Types: Capital, Employee Matching Gifts, Operating Expenses, Project.

Financial Summary

Total Giving: $1,946,280 (2001); $1,990,201 (2000); $1,784,205 (1999). Note: Contributes through foundation only.
Giving Analysis: Giving for 2001 includes: foundation grants to United Way ($334,868); foundation matching gifts ($340,927); foundation ($1,270,485); 2000: foundation scholarships ($100,175); foundation grants to United Way ($289,052); foundation matching gifts ($556,928); foundation ($1,044,407); 1999: foundation ($1,784,205);
Assets: $122,098 (2001); $77,926 (2000); $93,074 (1999)
Gifts Received: $2,108,060 (2001); $1,962,175 (2000); $1,649,010 (1999). Note: Foundation receives contributions from the Square D Company.

Typical Recipients

Arts & Humanities: Arts Associations & Councils, Arts Centers, Arts Festivals, Arts Funds, Arts Institutes, Dance, Libraries, Museums/Galleries, Music, Opera, Public Broadcasting, Theater
Civic & Public Affairs: Botanical Gardens/Parks, Business/Free Enterprise, Civic & Public Affairs-General, Legal Aid, Minority Business, Parades/Festivals, Philanthropic Organizations, Rural Affairs, Safety, Urban & Community Affairs
Education: Agricultural Education, Arts/Humanities Education, Business Education, Colleges & Universities, Community & Junior Colleges, Economic Education, Education Funds, Elementary Education (Public), Engineering/Technological Education, Education-General, Minority Education, Public Education (Precollege), Public Education (Precollege), Student Aid, Vocational & Technical Education
Health: Cancer, Children's Health/Hospitals, Clinics/Medical Centers, Emergency/Ambulance Services,

Health Funds, Hospitals, Long-Term Care, Medical Research, Mental Health, Single-Disease Health Associations
Religion: Religion-General
Science: Science-General, Science Museums
Social Services: At-Risk Youth, Child Welfare, Community Centers, Community Service Organizations, Emergency Relief, Family Services, Food/Clothing Distribution, Homes, People with Disabilities, Recreation & Athletics, Scouts, Senior Services, Shelters/Homelessness, United Funds/United Ways, YMCA/YWCA/YMHA/YWHA, Youth Organizations

Application Procedures

Initial Contact: Submit a written request.
Application Requirements: Include a short cover letter or proposal describing the organization, the need for funds, and plans for use of the funds; amount requested and evaluation plans; an operating budget for the current year, showing breakdown of expenses and sources of income; a list of the board's members; a list of corporate and foundation contributors in the last year; proof of tax-exempt status; and any additional information pertinent to the proposal.
Deadlines: Submit proposals to local Square D facilities/plants between June and August for funding during the next calendar year.
Evaluative Criteria: The organization must provide a general public service and be supported by the public. Grant should be for non-controversial purposes. Effective management, adequate budgetary controls, and proof of an annual audit are required.
Decision Notification: Contributions budget is established in the fourth quarter for the following year.

Restrictions

Does not make contributions to religious organizations (except where support is used for nondenominational social service); political groups and organizations; labor unions and organizations; organizations making requests by telephone; organizations listed by the U.S. Attorney General as subversive or front organizations; or individuals.
Since foundation supports United Way in corporate communities, donations normally are not made to organizations receiving support through United Way.

Corporate Officials

Walter W. Kurczewski: vice president, secretary, general counsel B 1943. ED University of Illinois AB (1965); University of Michigan JD (1968). PRIM CORP EMPL vice president, secretary, general counsel: Square D Co.
Frank P. Sullivan: vice president sales & marketing B 1953. ED Harvard University BA (1974); University of Chicago MBA (1980). PRIM CORP EMPL vice president sales & marketing: Square D Co.

Foundation Officials

R. P. Fiorani: vice president, director
Walter W. Kurczewski: president, director (see above)
Dick O'Shanna: treasurer, vice president, director
Tammy Sittinger: coord
Frank P. Sullivan: vice president, director (see above)
James R. White: secretary, director
Jo Ellyn Willis: vice president, director

Grants Analysis

Disclosure Period: calendar year ending 2001
Total Grants: $1,270,485*
Number of Grants: 265 (approx)
Average Grant: $4,794
Highest Grant: $135,000
Typical Range: $1,000 to $6,000
*Note: Giving excludes matching gifts and United Way.

Recent Grants

Note: Grants derived from 2001 Form 990.

General

112,875	National Merit Scholarship Corporation, Evanston, IL
100,000	NESC
75,000	Independent Electrical Contractors Foundation (IEC), Alexandria, VA
75,000	Independent Electrical Contractors Foundation (IEC), Alexandria, VA
54,332	United Way Triangle Area, Raleigh, NC
51,649	United Way of Asheville and Buncombe County, Asheville, NC
50,000	Clemson University Foundation, Clemson, SC
40,000	Children's Harbor, Birmingham, AL
40,000	Iowa State University, Ames, IA
40,000	University of Chicago, Chicago, IL

DONALD B. AND DOROTHY L. STABLER FOUNDATION

Giving Contact

William King, Chairman
Allfirst Trust Co.
213 Market St.
Harrisburg, PA 17105
Phone: (717)255-2045

Description

Founded: 1966
EIN: 236422944
Organization Type: Private Foundation
Giving Locations: PA
Grant Types: Capital, Endowment, General Support, Multiyear/Continuing Support, Operating Expenses, Professorship, Scholarship.

Donor Information

Founder: Stabler Companies

Financial Summary

Total Giving: $673,000 (2001); $650,250 (2000); $610,750 (1999)
Giving Analysis: Giving for 2001 includes: foundation grants to United Way ($20,000); 2000: foundation grants to United Way ($30,000); 1999: foundation grants to United Way ($20,000)
Assets: $14,739,655 (2001); $14,217,135 (2000); $13,764,576 (1999)
Gifts Received: $102,085 (2001); $51,500 (2000); $1,056,000 (1999). Note: In 2001, contributions were received from Work Area Protection corp., Eastern Industries, Inc., Protection Service, Inc., Stabler Development Co. and Miscellaneous. In 2000, contributions were received from Work Area Protection Corp ($25,000) and Eastern Industries ($25,000), and miscellaneous support of $1,500. In 1999, contributions were received from Work AWork Area Protection Corprea Protection Corp ($303,000), Center Valley Club, Inc. ($21,000), Elco-Hausman Construction Corp ($3,000), Eastern Industries, Inc. ($539,000), Precision Solar Control ($65,000), Protection Services ($102,000), Stabler Development Company ($22,000), and miscellaneous support (less than $5,000).

Typical Recipients

Arts & Humanities: Libraries, Music, Performing Arts, Public Broadcasting
Civic & Public Affairs: Clubs, Civic & Public Affairs-General, Housing
Education: Colleges & Universities, Community & Junior Colleges, Education Funds, Education Reform,

Faculty Development, Legal Education, Medical Education, Private Education (Precollege), Public Education (Precollege), Student Aid
Health: Alzheimers Disease, Clinics/Medical Centers, Emergency/Ambulance Services, Heart, Hospices, Hospitals, Medical Research, Mental Health, Prenatal Health Issues, Public Health
Religion: Churches, Dioceses, Religious Organizations, Religious Welfare
Social Services: Child Welfare, Community Service Organizations, Family Services, Food/Clothing Distribution, People with Disabilities, Scouts, Senior Services, Substance Abuse, United Funds/United Ways, Volunteer Services, YMCA/YWCA/YMHA/YWHA, Youth Organizations

Application Procedures

Initial Contact: Send a brief letter of inquiry.
Application Requirements: Describe program or project, and include purpose of funds sought and recently audited financial statement.
Deadlines: None.

Foundation Officials

Cyril C. Dunmire, Jr.: director PRIM CORP EMPL chairman, president, chief executive officer, treasurer: Stabler Companies.
William Joseph King: chairman B Philadelphia, PA 1929. ED University of Pennsylvania Wharton School (1954); LaSalle University MBA (1979). PRIM CORP EMPL chairman, chief executive officer: Dauphin Deposit Bank & Trust Co. CORP AFFIL director: Hempt Brothers; director: Millers Mutual Insurance Co.
David H. Schaper: director
Frank A. Sinon, Esq.: secretary
Richard Anson Zimmerman: director B Lebanon, PA 1932. ED Pennsylvania State University BA (1952); Lebanon Valley College LLD (1992). PRIM CORP EMPL retired chairman: Hershey Foods Corp. CORP AFFIL director: Lance Inc.; director: Westvaco Corp.; director: Eastman Kodak Co.; director: Hershey Trust Co. NONPR AFFIL trustee: Pennsylvania State University; trustee: Un Theological Seminary; director: Grocery Manufacturer America. CLUB AFFIL Carlton Club; Hershey Country Club.

Grants Analysis

Disclosure Period: calendar year ending 2001
Total Grants: $653,000*
Number of Grants: 68
Average Grant: $9,746*
Highest Grant: $60,000
Typical Range: $5,000 to $10,000
*Note: Giving excludes United Way.

Recent Grants

Note: Grants derived from 2001 Form 990.

Library-Related
10,000	Frederickson Library, Camp Hill, PA

General
60,000	Catholic Diocese of Allentown, Allentown, PA
50,000	Lehigh University, Bethlehem, PA -- Stabler Foundation fund
50,000	Lehigh University, Bethlehem, PA -- renovation of Stabler Arena
50,000	Pinnacle Health Foundation, Harrisburg, PA
50,000	Wilson College, Chambersburg, PA -- Curran Scholarship Program
45,000	Catholic Diocese of Harrisburg, Harrisburg, PA
35,000	Harrisburg Area YMCA, Harrisburg, PA
35,000	Johns Hopkins University Disease Research Center, Baltimore, MD -- rheumatic disease research
25,000	Goodwill Industries of Central Pennsylvania, Harrisburg, PA
20,000	United Way of the Capital Region, Harrisburg, PA

STACKNER FAMILY FOUNDATION

Giving Contact

John Treiber, Executive Director
PO Box 597
Hartland, WI 53029
Phone: (414)277-5000

Description

Founded: 1966
EIN: 396097597
Organization Type: Private Foundation
Giving Locations: WI: greater Milwaukee area
Grant Types: Capital, General Support, Multiyear/Continuing Support, Operating Expenses, Project, Research, Seed Money.

Donor Information

Founder: the late John S. Stackner, the late Irene M. Stackner

Financial Summary

Total Giving: $797,425 (fiscal year ending August 31, 2001); $774,500 (fiscal 2000); $800,000 (fiscal 1999 approx)
Giving Analysis: Giving for fiscal 2000 includes: foundation scholarships ($2,000); foundation grants to United Way ($20,000); fiscal 1998: foundation grants to United Way ($35,000) foundation ($626,700)
Assets: $15,665,391 (fiscal 2001); $17,577,407 (fiscal 2000); $14,023,475 (fiscal 1998)

Typical Recipients

Arts & Humanities: Arts Centers, Museums/Galleries
Civic & Public Affairs: Economic Development, Civic & Public Affairs-General, Hispanic Affairs, Housing, Parades/Festivals, Women's Affairs
Education: Education Funds, Elementary Education (Private), Education-General, Health & Physical Education, Medical Education, Private Education (Precollege), Religious Education, Science/Mathematics Education, Special Education, Student Aid
Health: Cancer, Children's Health/Hospitals, Health Organizations, Heart, Hospitals, Long-Term Care, Medical Research, Public Health, Single-Disease Health Associations
Religion: Religion-General, Religious Welfare
Science: Science Museums
Social Services: Big Brother/Big Sister, Child Welfare, Community Centers, Community Service Organizations, Recreation & Athletics, Scouts, Social Services-General, United Funds/United Ways, Youth Organizations

Application Procedures

Initial Contact: Send a letter of application.
Application Requirements: Include description of program, brochures or other descriptive materials, budget information, amount requested, purpose of funds sought, and recently audited financial statement.
Deadlines: Prior to quarterly meetings in January, April, July, and October.

Restrictions

Does not support individuals or provide scholarships or loans.

Foundation Officials

Patrick William Cotter: secretary, director
David Lee MacGregor: treasurer, director B Cedar Rapids, IA 1932. ED University of Wisconsin BBA (1954); University of Wisconsin LLB (1956). PRIM CORP EMPL partner: Quarles & Brady. NONPR AFFIL member: National Association Estate Planning

Councs; member: WI Bar Association; member: Milwaukee Bar Association; member: American Bar Association; fellow: American College Trust & Estate Counsel.
Paul J. Tilleman: treasurer, director
John A. Treiber: vice president, director
Patricia S. Treiber: president, director

Grants Analysis

Disclosure Period: fiscal year ending August 31, 2001
Total Grants: $797,425
Number of Grants: 148
Average Grant: $5,388
Highest Grant: $25,000
Lowest Grant: $125
Typical Range: $1,000 to $10,000

Recent Grants

Note: Grants derived from 2000 Form 990.

General
25,000	Heartlove Place, Milwaukee, WI
25,000	Heartlove Place, Milwaukee, WI
25,000	Heartlove Place, Milwaukee, WI
25,000	Heartlove Place, Milwaukee, WI
25,000	Milwaukee Rescue Mission, Milwaukee, WI
20,000	Milwaukee Art Museum, Milwaukee, WI
20,000	Waukesha Memorial Hospital Foundation, Inc, Waukesha, WI
15,000	Children's Community Center, Menomonee Falls, WI
15,000	Country Christian School, Nashotah, WI
15,000	Great Circus Parade, Milwaukee, WI

STACKPOLE-HALL FOUNDATION

Giving Contact

William C. Conrad, Executive Secretary
44 South St. Marys Street
St. Marys, PA 15857
Phone: (814)834-1845
Fax: (814)834-1869

Description

Founded: 1951
EIN: 256006650
Organization Type: Family Foundation
Giving Locations: PA: Elk County
Grant Types: Capital, General Support, Project, Seed Money.

Donor Information

Founder: Established as a trust in Pennsylvania in 1951 by the late L. G. Hall , J. H. Stackpole, Mrs. Adelaide Stackpole, and by Harrison C. Stackpole. James Hall Stackpole (1902-1964), son of Harrison C. Stackpole and the former Sallie Hall, was chairman of Stackpole Carbon Company. A portion of the foundation's funds are restricted by the donors through specific bequests to designated religious and educational organizations.

Financial Summary

Total Giving: $850,000 (2002 approx); $980,963 (2001); $1,454,463 (2000)
Giving Analysis: Giving for 1999 includes: foundation scholarships ($2,500)
Assets: $24,595,464 (2001); $27,154,326 (2000); $29,414,537 (1999)

Typical Recipients

Arts & Humanities: Arts Associations & Councils, Ethnic & Folk Arts, Historic Preservation, History & Archaeology, Libraries, Museums/Galleries, Music
Civic & Public Affairs: Botanical Gardens/Parks, Community Foundations, Economic Development,

Employment/Job Training, Civic & Public Affairs-General, Municipalities/Towns, Nonprofit Management, Parades/Festivals, Philanthropic Organizations, Professional & Trade Associations, Safety, Urban & Community Affairs

Education: Arts/Humanities Education, Colleges & Universities, Community & Junior Colleges, Education Associations, Education-General, Medical Education, Minority Education, Preschool Education, Private Education (Precollege), Public Education (Precollege), Religious Education, Science/Mathematics Education, Secondary Education (Private), Social Sciences Education, Vocational & Technical Education

Environment: Forestry, Environment-General, Resource Conservation

Health: Children's Health/Hospitals, Clinics/Medical Centers, Emergency/Ambulance Services, Health-General, Hospices, Hospitals, Mental Health, Nursing Services, Public Health, Speech & Hearing

Religion: Churches, Dioceses, Religion-General, Jewish Causes, Religious Organizations, Religious Welfare

Social Services: At-Risk Youth, Child Abuse, Child Welfare, Community Centers, Community Service Organizations, Family Planning, People with Disabilities, Recreation & Athletics, Scouts, Senior Services, Shelters/Homelessness, Substance Abuse, United Funds/United Ways, Volunteer Services, YMCA/YWCA/YMHA/YWHA, YMCA/YWCA/YMHA/YWHA, Youth Organizations

Application Procedures

Initial Contact: Applicants should telephone the foundation before submitting a request. After initial inquiry, a brief letter may be sent. If the board is interested in a project, it will request a more complete proposal.

Application Requirements: Applicants should include a brief background of the organization; any previous support from the foundation within the last ten years; a detailed description of the project for which the grant is being sought; an explanation of who will be responsible for carrying out project goals, with a definition of their qualifications; most recent audited financial statements; project budget, including sources of support and a statement identifying the specific amount being requested; and a list of current officers, directors, and administrative staff. Applicants should also include two copies of the IRS determination letter indicating tax-exempt status.

Deadlines: None.

Review Process: The board meets in February, May, August, and November.

Restrictions

No grants are made to individuals. Requests for operating grants or endowment grants are generally accorded low priority.

Additional Information

The Foundation Trustees have established a policy designating the area of geographic priority to be Elk County, PA, and the communities in which the donors, the donors' families, and the trustees reside.

Publications: Annual Report; Guidelines

Foundation Officials

William C. Conrad: executive secretary

Douglas R. Dobson: trustee, vice chairman PRIM CORP EMPL vice chairman, director: Stackpole Corp.

Helen Hall Drew: trustee

Lyle G. Hall: chairman, trustee B 1929. ED Yale University (1948-1951); Harvard University (1969); Boston University BS (1975); Episcopal Divinity School MA (1978). PRIM CORP EMPL chairman: Stackpole Corp.

Megan Hall: trustee PRIM CORP EMPL secretary: Pittsburgh Hearing, Speech & Deafness Service.

J. M. Hamlin Johnson: trustee B Ridgway, PA 1925. ED Grove City College BS (1949); Pennsylvania State University (1969). CORP AFFIL director: Stackpole Corp.; partner: J & B Co.; director: Hamlin Bank & Trust Co. NONPR AFFIL director: Saint Marys Regional Medical Center; director: United Fund Saint Mary; member: National Association Accountants; director: ELCAM Vocational Rehabilitation Center; director: Home Health Services; director: Community Nurses Elk Cameron Counties. CLUB AFFIL Bavarian Hills Club.

Alexander Sheble-Hall: trustee

Harrison Clinton Stackpole: honorary trustee B Ridgway, PA 1914. ED Yale University.

R. Dauer Stackpole: trustee CORP AFFIL director: Stackpole Corp.

Sara-Jane Stackpole: trustee

Scott Stackpole: trustee

Grants Analysis

Disclosure Period: calendar year ending 2001
Total Grants: $980,963
Number of Grants: 92
Average Grant: $15,809
Highest Grant: $50,000
Typical Range: $5,000 to $25,000

Recent Grants

Note: Grants derived from 2001 Form 990.

General

50,000	Elk County Community Foundation, St. Mary's, PA -- Benn F. Goodrich Fund
50,000	Elk County Community Foundation, St. Mary's, PA -- Benn F. Goodrich Fund
50,000	Elk County Community Foundation, St. Mary's, PA -- operational grant
50,000	Ridgway Community Nurses, Ridgway, PA -- computer hardware and training
48,371	Grace Episcopal Church, Ridgway, PA
39,711	Grace Episcopal Church, Ridgway, PA
37,209	Episcopal Diocese of Northwest Pennsylvania, Erie, PA
30,548	Episcopal Diocese of Northwest Pennsylvania, Erie, PA
29,461	City of St. Mary's, St. Mary's, PA -- summer job program
28,400	Keystone Tall Tree Girl Scout Council, Kittanning, PA -- Camp Resting Waters

JAMES L. STAMPS FOUNDATION

Giving Contact

Delores J. Boutault, Manager
2000 E. Fourth Street, Suite 230
Santa Ana, CA 92705
Phone: (714)568-9740
Fax: (714)568-9754

Description

Founded: 1963
EIN: 956086125
Organization Type: General Purpose Foundation
Giving Locations: CA: Southern California
Grant Types: Capital, Emergency, Matching, Operating Expenses, Project.

Donor Information

Founder: Incorporated in 1963 by the late James L. Stamps .

Financial Summary

Total Giving: $1,109,996 (2001); $1,275,910 (2000); $1,311,438 (1999)
Giving Analysis: Giving for 2000 includes: foundation scholarships ($230,000); 1999: foundation scholarships ($260,000); 1998: foundation scholarships ($278,000)

Assets: $28,518,292 (2001); $25,784,501 (2000); $24,144,060 (1999)

Typical Recipients

Arts & Humanities: Film & Video, Libraries
Civic & Public Affairs: Economic Development, Employment/Job Training, Civic & Public Affairs-General, Hispanic Affairs, Housing, Municipalities/Towns, Public Policy
Education: Colleges & Universities, Education-General, Legal Education, Private Education (Precollege), Religious Education, Science/Mathematics Education, Secondary Education (Private), Student Aid
Health: Clinics/Medical Centers, Emergency/Ambulance Services, Public Health
International: Foreign Educational Institutions, International Affairs, International Development, International Organizations, Missionary/Religious Activities
Religion: Bible Study/Translation, Churches, Religion-General, Ministries, Missionary Activities (Domestic), Religious Organizations, Religious Welfare, Seminaries, Social/Policy Issues, Social/Policy Issues
Science: Scientific Labs
Social Services: Camps, Community Service Organizations, Food/Clothing Distribution, Homes, Senior Services, Shelters/Homelessness, YMCA/YWCA/YMHA/YWHA, Youth Organizations

Application Procedures

Initial Contact: The foundation requests applications be made in writing.

Application Requirements: The foundation requests a brief inquiry that includes a copy of the organization's IRS tax-exempt letter 501(c)(3), a brief summary of the project, the amount requested, and a copy of the prior fiscal year's financial statement. The organization may be asked to develop a more detailed proposal.

Although the foundation does not require a specific form for full proposals, it suggests that an organization include the following information: a clear description of the project, what it may be expected to achieve, and its importance; a detailed expense budget, showing how the requested funds would be spent during what time periods and how the major elements of expense were estimated (if applicable); information concerning the organization and its responsible officers who intend to carry out the project, including a brief a description of organization, the names and affiliations of the directors or trustees, the name(s) and qualifications of the person(s) who would administer the grant, and an audited balance sheet and income statement for the previous fiscal year; a copy of the most recent tax-exempt ruling from the IRS, along with a statement as to any revisions which may be pending or a statement that there has been no change and none is pending; an endorsement by the administrative head if the proposal is from a department or individual of the organization (if possible, it should comment upon the relative priority of the request compared with other needs which the organization may ask the foundation to support); and a letter of support from authorities and/or organizations in the applicant's field.

Deadlines: The board meets bimonthly, and proposals should be submitted to the foundation at least one month prior to the board meeting at which consideration of the proposal is desired.

Review Process: The foundation will send written notice to applicants concerning all board decisions to approve or deny grant proposals, usually within 10 working days following the board meeting involved. Each proposal will be accepted or rejected in writing only.

Notes: Organizations wishing material returned in the event of rejection should so state in the proposal. The foundation prohibits personal interviews with trustees collectively or individually, either before or after filing a proposal.

Restrictions
The foundation primarily supports Evangelical Protestant-based organizations in the Pacific Coast States. The foundation ordinarily does not make grants in installments for future years; favor projects that are normally financed by public tax funds; favor trustee membership in organizations in which grants are made; make grants for endowments, contingency, or deficit funding, conferences, seminars, workshops, travel purposes, or exhibits the publication of books or magazines, producing films, or for public or educational radio or television purposes. No grants are made to individuals, for scholarships or fellowships.

Additional Information
Publications: Application Guidelines

Foundation Officials
Delores J. Boutault: manager
E. C. Boutault: president, trustee
Richard S. Kredel: secretary, treasurer, trustee
Willis R. Leach: trustee treasurer: Leach Grain Milling Co.
Thomas P. Lynch: chairman, trustee
Richard Salyer: vice president

Grants Analysis
Disclosure Period: calendar year ending 2001
Total Grants: $867,996*
Number of Grants: 43
Average Grant: $20,186
Highest Grant: $100,000
Lowest Grant: $500
Typical Range: $10,000 to $40,000
*Note: Giving excludes scholarships.

Recent Grants
Note: Grants derived from 2000 Form 990.

General
100,000	Azusa Pacific University, Azusa, CA -- for Theology Library Project
100,000	Biola University, La Mirada, CA -- library
100,000	California Baptist University, Riverside, CA -- for University Center Program
100,000	Westmont College, Santa Barbara, CA -- for computer technology
50,000	First Baptist Church, Downey, CA -- for electrical updates
35,000	Azusa Pacific University, Azusa, CA -- scholarships
35,000	Biola University, La Mirada, CA -- scholarships
35,000	Westmont College, Santa Barbara, CA -- scholarships
34,500	Mission Aviation Fellowship, Redlands, CA -- Mozambique Airbase Project
33,645	Vanguard University, Costa Mesa, CA -- for library computer lab

STANDARD STEEL

Company Headquarters
500 North Walnut Street
Burnham, PA 17009
Web: http://www.standardsteel.com

Company Description
Former Name: Freedom Forge Corp. (2002)
Chap. 11 Reorg. Bankruptcy (2001);
Former Name: American Welding & Manufacturing Co..
SIC(s): 3300 Primary Metal Industries.

Operating Locations
Freedom Forge Corp. (PA--Latrobe)

Freedom Forge Corp. Foundation

Giving Contact
Thomas J. McGuigan, Vice President, Human Resources & Administration
500 North Walnut Street
Burnham, PA 17009
Phone: (717)248-4911

Description
EIN: 346516721
Organization Type: Corporate Foundation
Giving Locations: OH
Grant Types: General Support, Scholarship.

Financial Summary
Total Giving: $137,237 (2000); $128,522 (1999); $109,865 (1998)
Giving Analysis: Giving for 2000 includes: foundation scholarships ($12,000); foundation grants to United Way ($37,500); 1999: foundation grants to United Way ($37,767); foundation ($90,755) 1998: foundation grants to United Way ($30,000)
Assets: $1,464,289 (2000); $1,633,147 (1999); $1,575,069 (1998)

Typical Recipients
Arts & Humanities: Arts Associations & Councils, History & Archaeology, Libraries, Museums/Galleries, Music, Performing Arts, Public Broadcasting
Civic & Public Affairs: Clubs, Economic Development, Economic Policy, Civic & Public Affairs-General, Municipalities/Towns, Professional & Trade Associations, Public Policy, Urban & Community Affairs
Education: Agricultural Education, Business Education, Colleges & Universities, Education Funds, Engineering/Technological Education, Education-General, Private Education (Precollege)
Environment: Environment-General, Resource Conservation, Wildlife Protection
Health: Cancer, Children's Health/Hospitals, Hospices, Hospitals, Kidney, Medical Research, Multiple Sclerosis, Prenatal Health Issues, Single-Disease Health Associations
Religion: Religious Welfare
Science: Science Exhibits & Fairs, Scientific Organizations
Social Services: Animal Protection, Community Service Organizations, Delinquency & Criminal Rehabilitation, Food/Clothing Distribution, People with Disabilities, Recreation & Athletics, Scouts, Special Olympics, Substance Abuse, United Funds/United Ways, YMCA/YWCA/YMHA/YWHA, Youth Organizations

Application Procedures
Initial Contact: The foundation requests applications be made in writing. Include a description of organization, amount requested, purpose of funds sought, recently audited financial statement, and proof of tax-exempt status.
Deadlines: None.

Additional Information
Trust(s): Kish Bank Asset Mgmt

Corporate Officials
Herbert C. Graves: chairman, chief operating officer, director PRIM CORP EMPL chairman: Freedom Forge Corp.
Mr. Dana L. Patterson: chief financial officer PRIM CORP EMPL chief financial officer: Freedom Forge Corp.
James A. Spendiff: president, chief operating officer, director B Troy, NY 1943. ED University of Pennsylvania (1965). PRIM CORP EMPL president, chief operating officer, director: Freedom Forge Corp. ADD CORP EMPL director, president: FFC Holding Inc.; director, president: Freedom Forge Holdings Inc.

Grants Analysis
Disclosure Period: calendar year ending 2000
Total Grants: $87,737*
Number of Grants: 36
Average Grant: $1,624*
Highest Grant: $30,896
Typical Range: $100 to $5,000
*Note: Giving excludes United Way and scholarships. Average grant figure excludes highest grant.

Recent Grants
Note: Grants derived from 2001 Form 990.

Library-Related
5,000	Mifflin County Library, Lewistown, PA
1,000	Mifflin County Library, Lewistown, PA

General
30,000	Juniata Valley YMCA, Juniata Valley, PA
10,000	Lewistown Hospital, Lewistown, PA
5,000	Belleville Minnonite School, Belleville, PA
5,000	Burnham Fire Company -- for seminar
3,500	Nittany Valley Symphony, State College, PA
2,500	American Museum of Fly Fishing, Manchester, VT -- to revitalize county
2,500	Bryn Mawr College, Bryn Mawr, PA
2,500	Pennsylvania State University, Philadelphia, PA
2,500	Pennsylvania State University, Philadelphia, PA
2,500	Pennsylvania State University, Philadelphia, PA

STANDARD STEEL SPECIALITY CO.

Company Headquarters
Beaver Falls, PA
Web: http://www.stdsteel.com

Company Description
Revenue: US$67 million (2001)
Employees: 250
SIC(s): 3300 Primary Metal Industries, 3400 Fabricated Metal Products, 3500 Industrial Machinery & Equipment.

Operating Locations
Standard Steel Speciality Co. (PA--Beaver Falls)

Standard Steel Specialty Co. Foundation

Giving Contact
R. E. Conley, Chief Financial Officer, Secretary & Treasurer
PO Box 20
Beaver Falls, PA 15010
Phone: (216)222-2934

Description
EIN: 256038268
Organization Type: Corporate Foundation
Giving Locations: PA; SC: headquarters area only.
Grant Types: General Support, Scholarship.

Financial Summary
Total Giving: $11,500 (2001); $12,545 (2000); $4,535 (1999). Note: 1996 Giving includes United Way ($3,000).

Giving Analysis: Giving for 2001 includes: foundation scholarships ($1,000); foundation grants to United Way ($5,500); 2000: foundation grants to United Way ($5,545); 1999: foundation grants to United Way ($2,035)
Assets: $77,429 (2001); $85,716 (2000); $84,238 (1999)
Gifts Received: $10,000 (2000); $15,000 (1999); $15,000 (1998). Note: In 1995, contributions were received from Standard Steel Specialty Co.

Typical Recipients

Civic & Public Affairs: Civic & Public Affairs-General
Education: Colleges & Universities, Education-General, Medical Education
Social Services: Community Service Organizations, United Funds/United Ways, YMCA/YWCA/YMHA/YWHA, Youth Organizations

Application Procedures

Initial Contact: Send a brief letter of inquiry.
Application Requirements: Include purpose of funds sought and proof of tax-exempt status.
Deadlines: None.

Additional Information

Trust(s): National City, Bank PA

Corporate Officials

T. G. Armstrong: president, chief executive officer, director PRIM CORP EMPL president, chief executive officer, director: Standard Steel Speciality Co.
R. E. Conley: chief financial officer, secretary, treasurer, director PRIM CORP EMPL chief financial officer, secretary, treasurer, director: Standard Steel Speciality Co.
Robert Moore: chairman PRIM CORP EMPL chairman: Standard Steel Speciality Co.

Foundation Officials

R. E. Conley: director (see above)

Grants Analysis

Disclosure Period: calendar year ending 2001
Total Grants: $50,000*
Number of Grants: 6
Highest Grant: $3,000
Lowest Grant: $2,000
*Note: Giving excludes United Way and scholarships.

Recent Grants

Note: Grants derived from 2001 Form 990.

General

3,000	United Way of Beaver County, Monaca, PA
2,500	United Way of The Piedmont Inc, Spartanburg, SC
2,000	University of South Carolina, Spartanburg, SC
2,000	YMCA, Beaver Falls, PA
1,000	Geneva College, Beaver Falls, PA
1,000	Penn State Beaver Campus, Monaca, PA -- for scholarship

STANLEY WORKS

Company Headquarters

New Britain, CT
Web: http://www.stanleyworks.com

Company Description

Founded: 1843
Ticker: SWK
Exchange: NYSE
Revenue: US$2.624 billion (2001)
Employees: 14400 (2001)

SIC(s): 2542 Partitions & Fixtures Except Wood, 3315 Steel Wire & Related Products, 3429 Hardware Nec, 3442 Metal Doors, Sash & Trim.

Operating Locations

The Stanley Works (AZ--Phoenix; CA--Chatsworth, Costa Mesa, Monrovia, San Dimas, Visalia; CT--Clinton, Farmington; FL--Orlando; GA--Atlanta, Covington; IN--Shelbyville; KS--Lenexa; MA--Worcester; MI--Birmingham, Novi; MN--Two Harbors; MS--Tupelo; MO--St. Louis; NH--Claremont; NC--Charlotte, Sanford; OH--Cleveland, Columbus, Georgetown, Sabina, Washington Court House; OR; PA--Allentown, Royersford, York; RI--East Greenwich; TN--Pulaski, Shelbyville; TX--Carrollton, Dallas; VT--Pittsfield, Shaftsbury; VA--Richmond, Winchester)

Nonmonetary Support

Type: Donated Products; Workplace Solicitation
Note: Nonmonetary support is approximately $150,000 annually.

Giving Contact

Contributions Administrator
1000 Stanley Drive
New Britain, CT 06053
Phone: (860)827-3566
Fax: (860)827-3581

Description

Organization Type: Corporate Giving Program
Giving Locations: operating location communities.
Grant Types: Capital, Challenge, Employee Matching Gifts, General Support, Operating Expenses, Seed Money.
Note: Employee matching gift ratio: 1 to 1.

Financial Summary

Total Giving: $1,500,000 (2001 approx); $1,300,000 (2000 approx); $2,000,000 (1999 approx). Note: Contributes through corporate direct giving program only.
Giving Analysis: Giving for 1998 includes: foundation matching gifts ($439,158).
Assets: $4,523 (1993); $1,246,241 (1992)

Typical Recipients

Arts & Humanities: Arts Associations & Councils, Community Arts, Dance, Arts & Humanities-General, Libraries, Museums/Galleries, Music, Opera, Performing Arts, Public Broadcasting, Theater
Civic & Public Affairs: African American Affairs, Business/Free Enterprise, Community Foundations, Economic Policy, Employment/Job Training, Civic & Public Affairs-General, Housing, Urban & Community Affairs
Education: Business Education, Colleges & Universities, Economic Education, Elementary Education (Private), Elementary Education (Public), Engineering/Technological Education, Literacy, Minority Education, Public Education (Precollege), Science/Mathematics Education
Environment: Environment-General, Resource Conservation
Health: Cancer, Children's Health/Hospitals, Emergency/Ambulance Services, Hospitals, Medical Research
International: International Development
Religion: Churches, Religious Welfare
Science: Science Exhibits & Fairs
Social Services: Community Service Organizations, Family Services, Homes, People with Disabilities, Shelters/Homelessness, Substance Abuse, United Funds/United Ways, Youth Organizations

Application Procedures

Initial Contact: Send a brief letter or proposal.
Application Requirements: Include a description of organization and how it will affect Stanley employees, amount requested, purpose of funds sought, recently

audited financial statement, proof of 501(c)(3) tax-exempt status, identification of company employees involved with organization.
Deadlines: Contact foundation for current deadlines.
Review Process: Reviews grant request three times a year.
Evaluative Criteria: Involvement of company personnel with organization; organization's qualifications to provide services; company's feeling of responsibility to organization or community; operate in a Stanley community; endorsement of local company management; organization's service population.

Restrictions

No funds will be given outside communities where Stanley has operations.
Company does not fund national organizations, operating funds, research projects, athletic programs, health research organizations, endowment funds, organizations which are not tax-exempt, private foundations, or individuals.

Additional Information

In 1999, the company announced that new giving program guidelines were being prepared for the 2000 grant cycle.
Publications: Guidelines Sheet; Annual Report; grants List

Corporate Officials

Herschel Herndon: director, Global Communication

Grants Analysis

Typical Range: $1,000 to $5,000

STANS FOUNDATION

Giving Contact

Steven H. Stans, President
PO Box 1018
Arcadia, CA 91007
Fax: (626)446-8285

Description

Founded: 1945
EIN: 366008663
Organization Type: Private Foundation
Giving Locations: CA
Grant Types: Capital, Conference/Seminar, General Support, Multiyear/Continuing Support, Research.

Donor Information

Founder: Maurice H. Stans, the late Kathleen C. Stans

Financial Summary

Total Giving: $339,238 (2001); $390,224 (2000); $370,925 (1999)
Giving Analysis: Giving for 2000 includes: foundation grants to United Way ($2,000) 1998: foundation grants to United Way ($3,000)
Assets: $3,499,258 (2001); $5,928,691 (2000); $8,947,769 (1999)
Gifts Received: $53,000 (1995)

Typical Recipients

Arts & Humanities: Historic Preservation, History & Archaeology, Libraries, Museums/Galleries, Music, Performing Arts, Public Broadcasting
Civic & Public Affairs: Botanical Gardens/Parks, Civil Rights, Clubs, Civic & Public Affairs-General, Housing, Legal Aid, Parades/Festivals, Public Policy, Urban & Community Affairs
Education: Colleges & Universities, Education Funds, Education Reform, Engineering/Technological Education, Education-General, International Studies, Journalism/Media Education, Private Education (Precollege)
Environment: Wildlife Protection

Health: Clinics/Medical Centers, Eyes/Blindness, Hospices, Hospitals, Medical Research, Mental Health, Research/Studies Institutes, Single-Disease Health Associations
International: International Affairs, International Affairs, International Environmental Issues, International Peace & Security Issues
Religion: Churches, Jewish Causes, Ministries, Religious Organizations, Religious Welfare, Social/Policy Issues
Science: Science Museums, Scientific Centers & Institutes
Social Services: Animal Protection, Child Welfare, Community Service Organizations, Scouts, United Funds/United Ways, Youth Organizations

Application Procedures

Initial Contact: Send a brief letter of inquiry.
Deadlines: None.

Foundation Officials

Mary C. Elia: secretary
Walter E. Helmick: vice president
Terrell S. Manley: assistant treasurer
William Manley: vice president
Steven H. Stans: president
Theodore M. Stans: vice president

Grants Analysis

Disclosure Period: calendar year ending 2001
Total Grants: $339,238
Number of Grants: 54
Average Grant: $4,514*
Highest Grant: $100,000
Lowest Grant: $250
Typical Range: $1,000 to $10,000
***Note:** Average grant figure excludes highest grant.

Recent Grants

Note: Grants derived from 2000 Form 990.

Library-Related
5,000	Richard Nixon Library, Yorba Linda, CA

General
105,000	University of Florida Foundation, Gainesville, FL
40,000	Florida Gulf Coast University Foundation, Ft. Myers, FL
40,000	Scott County Historical Society, Davenport, IA
25,000	Murphy's Landing
14,425	Florida Gulf Coast University Foundation, Ft. Myers, FL
12,500	Red Rock Audubon Society
10,000	Florida Gulf Coast University Foundation, Ft. Myers, FL
10,000	St. Marks Church Restoration 2000
5,000	Eisenhower World Affairs Institute, Washington, DC
5,000	H M R I

STARDUST FOUNDATION

Giving Contact

Gerald Bisgrove, Chief Executive Officer/Chairman
6730 North Scottsdale Road, Suite 230
Scottsdale, AZ 85253
Phone: (480)607-5800
Fax: (480)607-5801
E-mail: lkilgas@stardustco.com

Description

Founded: 1993
EIN: 860735230
Organization Type: Private Foundation
Giving Locations: AZ
Grant Types: General Support.

Donor Information

Founder: The foundation was established in 1993.

Financial Summary

Total Giving: $662,561 (2001); $646,180 (2000); $636,282 (1998)
Giving Analysis: Giving for 1998 includes: foundation grants to United Way ($10,000) 1997: foundation grants to United Way ($10,000)
Assets: $25,374,894 (2001); $25,402,308 (2000); $20,942,849 (1998)
Gifts Received: $2,000,000 (2001); $1,000,000 (2000); $5,359,869 (1998). Note: In 2000 and 2001, contributions were received from Stardust Holdings, Inc. In 1998, contributions were received from Gerald Bisgrove and Bisgrove Financial Management.

Typical Recipients

Arts & Humanities: Arts & Humanities-General, Museums/Galleries, Music, Theater
Civic & Public Affairs: Clubs, Community Foundations, Employment/Job Training, Civic & Public Affairs-General, Housing, Legal Aid, Municipalities/Towns, Native American Affairs, Nonprofit Management, Safety, Urban & Community Affairs, Women's Affairs, Zoos/Aquariums
Education: Colleges & Universities, Elementary Education (Public), Education-General, Leadership Training, Private Education (Precollege), Secondary Education (Private), Student Aid
Environment: Wildlife Protection
Health: AIDS/HIV, Cancer, Health Organizations, Heart, Medical Rehabilitation, Medical Research, Public Health
International: International Relief Efforts
Religion: Churches, Religion-General, Ministries, Religious Organizations
Science: Scientific Centers & Institutes
Social Services: Animal Protection, At-Risk Youth, Child Welfare, Community Service Organizations, Domestic Violence, Family Planning, Family Services, Food/Clothing Distribution, Homes, Recreation & Athletics, Shelters/Homelessness, Special Olympics, Substance Abuse, United Funds/United Ways, Veterans, YMCA/YWCA/YMHA/YWHA, Youth Organizations

Application Procedures

Initial Contact: Applicants should send a brief letter of inquiry.
Application Requirements: Included name and address of contact person to whom any requests for further information may be directed.
Deadlines: September 30.

Restrictions

Grants are given by invitation only.

Additional Information

Publications: Application Form

Foundation Officials

Debra Bisgrove: director
Gerald Bisgrove: president
Chris R. Heeter: secretary

Grants Analysis

Disclosure Period: calendar year ending 2001
Total Grants: $619,561*
Number of Grants: 34
Average Grant: $15,744*
Highest Grant: $100,000
Lowest Grant: $1,000
Typical Range: $5,000 to $30,000
***Note:** Giving excludes United Way. Average grant figure excludes highest grant.

Recent Grants

Note: Grants derived from 2001 Form 990.

General
100,000	Club Everst/John Paul Trust, Auburn, NY
82,500	HomeBase Youth Services, Phoenix, AZ
43,000	United Way of America, Alexandria, VA
31,511	Youth Consultation Service, Newark, NJ
25,000	Aid to Adoption of Special Kids, Phoenix, AZ
25,000	American Heart Association, Tempe, AZ
25,000	Arizona Quest for Kids, Phoenix, AZ
25,000	Fight Night Foundation, Phoenix, AZ
25,000	Perimeter Bicycling Association of America, Tucson, AZ
25,000	Safe/Back-to-School Clothing Drive, Glendale, AZ

NELDA C. AND H. J. LUTCHER STARK FOUNDATION

Giving Contact

Sherrie Sheppard, Grants Administrator
601 W. Green Avenue
PO Box 909
Orange, TX 77631-0909
Phone: (409)883-3513
Fax: (409)883-3530
Web: http://www.starkfoundation.org

Description

Founded: 1961
EIN: 746047440
Organization Type: General Purpose Foundation
Giving Locations: LA: Southwest Louisiana; TX: Southeast Texas
Grant Types: General Support, Project, Scholarship.

Donor Information

Founder: Established in 1961 by H. J. Lutcher Stark and his wife, Nelda Childers Stark. Mr. Stark's business included the Lutcher & Moore Lumber Company, the First National Bank of Orange, and Vinton Petroleum. After Mr. Stark's death in 1965, the foundation received the Stark's sizeable art collection, including American Western art of the nineteenth and twentieth centuries, Native American artifacts, and a selection of decorative arts including a collection of Steuben glass. The entire collection is now housed in the Stark Museum of Art, owned and operated by the foundation. The art museum is part of a civic and cultural center in downtown Orange, TX, that also includes the W. H. Stark House, the Frances Ann Lutcher Theater for the Performing Arts, a church, and a park. The W. H. Stark House, a restored Victorian mansion built in 1894, is open to the public for tours. The foundation built the Frances Ann Lutcher Theater for the Performing Arts for the City of Orange, TX, as the major forum for the performing arts in Orange County. In 1986, the foundation assumed responsibility for the facility's operating expenses.

Financial Summary

Total Giving: $5,125,484 (2001); $1,145,345 (2000); $481,980 (1999)
Giving Analysis: Giving for 2001 includes: foundation matching gifts ($5,000); foundation grants to United Way ($100,000); foundation scholarships ($418,400) 1999: foundation scholarships ($196,200)
Assets: $179,182,452 (2001); $152,123,240 (2000); $154,239,811 (1999)
Gifts Received: $1,110,016 (1999); $1,250,000 (1998); $1,200,000 (1997). Note: The foundation receives gifts from Nelda C. Stark, chairman, donor, and trustee of the foundation.

Typical Recipients

Arts & Humanities: Arts Associations & Councils, Historic Preservation, History & Archaeology, Libraries, Museums/Galleries, Music, Opera

Civic & Public Affairs: African American Affairs, Botanical Gardens/Parks, Civic & Public Affairs-General, Municipalities/Towns, Safety, Urban & Community Affairs

Education: Arts/Humanities Education, Business Education, Colleges & Universities, Engineering/Technological Education, Environmental Education, Education-General, Literacy, Private Education (Precollege), Social Sciences Education, Student Aid

Environment: Environment-General, Wildlife Protection

Health: Cancer, Children's Health/Hospitals, Eyes/Blindness, Hospices, Single-Disease Health Associations, Transplant Networks/Donor Banks

Religion: Churches, Religious Organizations, Religious Welfare, Religious Welfare

Social Services: At-Risk Youth, Camps, Family Services, Homes, People with Disabilities, Scouts, Social Services-General, Special Olympics, United Funds/United Ways, Veterans, Youth Organizations

Application Procedures

Initial Contact: Send five copies of a letter of proposal.

Application Requirements: The letter should include a brief description of the project signed by president or chief executive officer; brief history, description, programs, and mission of the organization; timeline (beginning and ending dates); amount requested; list of other funding sources and amounts; and proof of tax-exempt status under IRS Section 501(c)(3).

Deadlines: January 1, May 1, and September 1.

Review Process: If the Grant Committee determines the project to be within the scope of Foundation interests and funding, the organization will be requested to furnish further information. The foundation board usually meets monthly.

Restrictions

No grants are made to individuals, or for endowment, continuing support, or operating budgets. Grants for scholarships are made through the Texas Interscholastic League Foundation.

Additional Information

In 2001, the foundation changed its fiscal year to end on December 31.

Publications: Annual Report

Foundation Officials

Eunice R. Benckenstein: vice chairman, trustee B 1911.

Walter G. Riedel, III: secretary, treasurer

Nelda Childers Stark: chairman B Orange, TX 1909. ED Denton College.

Grants Analysis

Disclosure Period: calendar year ending 2001

Total Grants: $4,602,084*

Number of Grants: 48

Average Grant: $76,640*

Highest Grant: $1,000,000

Lowest Grant: $500

Typical Range: $10,000 to $100,000

*Note: Giving excludes scholarships, United Way, and matching gifts. Average grant figure excludes highest grant.

Recent Grants

Note: Grants derived from 2000 Form 990.

General

1,000,000	UTMB-Galveston, Galveston, TX -- for Diabetic Center
673,000	Lamar University, Beaumont, TX -- for completion of second floor of Allied Health Building
600,000	Salvation Army, Beaumont, TX -- funds for new building in Orange, Texas
500,000	UTMB-Galveston, Galveston, TX -- to fund diabetes center
489,000	Texas Interscholastic League Foundation, Austin, TX -- Scholarship Program
195,600	Texas Interscholastic League Foundation, Austin, TX -- Scholarship Program
165,000	Lifeshare Blood Centers, Beaumont, TX -- purchase of mobile donor center
50,000	Ducks Unlimited, Inc., Madison, MS -- fore restoration of freshwater habitat
50,000	Houston Grand Opera, Houston, TX -- to underwrite the opera Florencia en el Amazonas
50,000	Orange Fire Department, Orange, TX -- training for one officer and fireman

STARR FOUNDATION

Giving Contact

Florence A. Davis, President
70 Pine Street, 14th Fl.
New York, NY 10270
Phone: (212)770-5202
Fax: (212)425-6261
E-mail: grants@starrfoundation.org
Web: http://fdncenter.org/grantmaker/starr/

Description

Founded: 1955

EIN: 136151545

Organization Type: General Purpose Foundation

Giving Locations: NY: New York, metropolitan area internationally; nationally; nationally; internationally.

Grant Types: Capital, Emergency, Endowment, General Support, Multiyear/Continuing Support, Professorship, Project, Scholarship.

Donor Information

Founder: Established in New York in 1955 by Cornelius Vander Starr (1892-1968). Mr. Starr attended the University of California, and passed the California Bar exam at age 21. After serving in World War I, he resided in China and established the Asia Life and American Asiatic Life Insurance Companies. By the 1930s, his insurance activities and investments in real estate and automobiles extended throughout the Far East. After World War II, he renamed the companies the American Life Insurance Company. At the time of his death, his operations expanded to a group of 100 insurance companies in about 130 countries. Since the 1970s, the foundation has received considerable donations of stock from the corporate directors of American International Group.

Financial Summary

Total Giving: $219,755,392 (2001); $192,502,039 (2000); $102,786,430 (1998)

Giving Analysis: Giving for 2000 includes: foundation scholarships ($5,057,997); 1998: foundation scholarships ($4,092,992) 1997: foundation scholarships ($31,637,328)

Assets: $4,813,709,640 (2001); $6,257,848,627 (2000); $3,358,848,173 (1998)

Gifts Received: $881,289 (2001); $10,785 (2000); $2,447,309 (1997). Note: In 2000 and 2001, contributions were received from the Marion Hughes Trust. In 1997, contributions were received from the Marion Hughes Trust and Kwie Ding Wang.

Typical Recipients

Arts & Humanities: Arts Associations & Councils, Arts Centers, Arts Festivals, Arts Funds, Arts Institutes, Dance, Ethnic & Folk Arts, Historic Preservation, History & Archaeology, Libraries, Museums/Galleries, Music, Opera, Performing Arts, Public Broadcasting, Theater

Civic & Public Affairs: Botanical Gardens/Parks, Chambers of Commerce, Civil Rights, Economic Development, Economic Policy, Employment/Job Training, Ethnic Organizations, Civic & Public Affairs-General, Law & Justice, Nonprofit Management, Philanthropic Organizations, Public Policy, Rural Affairs, Urban & Community Affairs, Women's Affairs, Zoos/Aquariums

Education: Afterschool/Enrichment Programs, Arts/Humanities Education, Arts/Humanities Education, Business Education, Colleges & Universities, Economic Education, Education Associations, Education Funds, Education Reform, Engineering/Technological Education, Health & Physical Education, International Exchange, International Studies, Journalism/Media Education, Legal Education, Medical Education, Minority Education, Private Education (Precollege), Public Education (Precollege), Religious Education, Science/Mathematics Education, Special Education, Student Aid

Environment: Environment-General

Health: AIDS/HIV, Cancer, Children's Health/Hospitals, Emergency/Ambulance Services, Eyes/Blindness, Health-General, Geriatric Health, Health Policy/Cost Containment, Health Organizations, Heart, Hospices, Hospitals, Kidney, Long-Term Care, Medical Research, Medical Training, Nursing Services, Public Health, Single-Disease Health Associations, Transplant Networks/Donor Banks

International: Foreign Arts Organizations, Foreign Educational Institutions, International-General, Health Care/Hospitals, International Affairs, International Development, International Environmental Issues, International Organizations, International Peace & Security Issues, International Relations, International Relief Efforts, Trade

Religion: Churches, Jewish Causes, Religious Welfare

Science: Science Museums, Scientific Centers & Institutes, Scientific Labs

Social Services: At-Risk Youth, Camps, Child Welfare, Community Centers, Community Service Organizations, Counseling, Crime Prevention, Emergency Relief, Emergency Relief, Family Planning, Family Services, Food/Clothing Distribution, People with Disabilities, Recreation & Athletics, Refugee Assistance, Senior Services, Shelters/Homelessness, Social Services-General, Substance Abuse, YMCA/YWCA/YMHA/YWHA, Youth Organizations

Application Procedures

Initial Contact: Applications should be submitted in writing. There are no formal application forms.

Application Requirements: Proposals should include a cover letter defining the organization and setting forth the terms of the proposal; project budget; recently audited financial statement; list of other major financial supporters (current and pending); list of the organization's board members and their affiliations; proof of tax-exempt status; and details of overall administrative expenses. Supplementary materials may be included, but the foundation prefers not to receive videotapes.

Deadlines: None.

Restrictions

Grants to individuals are limited to scholarships provided through the foundation's scholarship programs. The foundation will not generally fund organizations that spend more than 25% of their annual expenses on administration and fundraising. Overseas organizations without U.S. tax-exempt status are rarely supported.

Additional Information

The foundation operates four scholarship programs: the Starr Foundation Scholarship Program for "American International" Children (U.S.), the Starr Foundation Scholarship Program for "American International" Children (overseas), the Brewster Starr Scholarship

Program, and the Lower Manhattan Starr Scholarship Program.

Publications: Annual Report

Foundation Officials

Marion I. Breen: vice president, director NONPR AF-FIL director: Starr Found Inc.

F. A. Davis: president, director

Houghton Freeman: director B Peking, People's Republic of China 1921. ED Wesleyan University BA (1943). PRIM CORP EMPL director: American International Group Inc. CORP AFFIL director: Transatlantic Holdings Inc. NONPR AFFIL trustee emeritus: Wesleyan University.

Ida E. Galler: secretary

Maurice Raymond Greenberg: chairman board, director B New York, NY 1925. ED University of Miami BA (1948); New York University School of Law JD (1950). PRIM CORP EMPL chairman, chief executive officer, president: American International Group Inc. CORP AFFIL chairman, director: Transatlantic Reinsurance Co.; director: National Union Fire Insurance Co. Pittsburgh; president, chief executive officer, director: C V Starr & Co.; director: American International Reinsurance Co.; director: American Home Assurance Co. NONPR AFFIL chairman: U.S.-China Business Council; founding chairman: United States Philippine Business Committee; president advisory committee: Trade Policy & Negotiations; member: New York State Bar Association; member: Police Athletic League; chairman board governors: New York Hospital; president advisory committee: Center Strategic & International Studies; vchmn: Council Foreign Relations; member: Business Roundtable; chairman: Asia Society. CLUB AFFIL Sky Club; India House Club; Lotos Club; Harmonie Club; City Athletic Club; Georgetown Club.

Ta Chun Hsu: president, director B 1925. CORP AF-FIL director: Chinese America Bank. NONPR AFFIL director: Smith-Kettlewell Eye Research Institute.

Edwin Alfred Grenville Manton: director B Earls Colne, United Kingdom January 22, 1909. ED University of London (1925-1927); New York Institute of Sociology (1933-1935). PRIM CORP EMPL senior advisor, director: American International Group Inc. CORP AFFIL director: American International Life Assurance New York; director: Birmingham Fire & Insurance Co. Pennsylvania.

E. E. Matthews: director

John Joseph Roberts: director B Montreal, QC Canada 1922. ED Princeton University BA (1945). PRIM CORP EMPL chairman, chief executive officer, director: American International Underwriters Inc. ADD CORP EMPL vice chairman, director: American International Group Inc. CORP AFFIL senior vice president: CV Starr & Co. Inc.; director: Starr Tech Risks Agency; director: Petroleum & Resources Corp.; director: Adams Express Co.; director: American International Marine Agency New York Inc.

H. I. Smith: treasurer, director

Ernest Edward Stemple: director B New York, NY 1916. ED Manhattan College AB (1938); Fordham University LLB (1946); New York University LLM (1949); New York University DJS (1951). PRIM CORP EMPL senior, advisor: American International Group Inc. ADD CORP EMPL president, director: Starr International Co. Inc. CORP AFFIL director: Underwriters Adjustment Co.; director: CV Starr & Co. Inc.; chairman: Phillipine American Life Insurance Co.; director: Seguros Venezuela; chairman: Pacific Union Assurance Co.; chairman: Delaware America Life Insurance Co.; chairman: Mount Mansfield Co. Inc.; chairman: Australian American Assurance Co.; director: American International Underwriters Overseas Ltd.; director: American Life Insurance Co.; director: American International Underwriters Inc.; director: American International Underwriters Mediterranean Inc.; chairman, director: American International Reinsurance Co.; director: American International Group Data

Center; director: American International Life Insurance Co. Puerto Rico; director: American International Assurance Co. Ltd. Hong Kong; director: American International Co. Ltd.; chairman: American International Assurance Co. Bermuda Ltd.; chairman: AI Life Insurance Co.; chairman: AIG Life Insurance Co. NONPR AFFIL member: American Bar Association.

Frank R. Tengi: treasurer B Garfield, NJ August 11, 1920. ED Georgetown University BS (1946); Fordham University LLD (1951). CORP AFFIL manager: World-Wide; director, assistant secretary: American International Underwriters Inc.; assistant secretary: CV Starr & Co. Inc. NONPR AFFIL member: New York State Bar Association; member: Tax Executives Institute.

Gladys R. Thomas: vice president ED Bryn Mawr College BA. CLUB AFFIL member, governor: India House Club.

E. S. Tse: director

Grants Analysis

Disclosure Period: calendar year ending 2001
Total Grants: $213,756,431*
Number of Grants: 966
Average Grant: $195,603*
Highest Grant: $25,000,000
Typical Range: $50,000 to $500,000
*Note: Giving excludes scholarships and United Way. Average grant figure excludes highest grant.

Recent Grants

Note: Grants derived from 2001 Form 990.

Library-Related
500,000	George Bush Presidential Library Foundation, College Station, TX -- for endowment or program support
500,000	Manhattan College, Riverdale, NY -- for library and endowment
500,000	New York Public Library, New York, NY -- for South Court Programs

General
25,000,000	American Museum of Natural History, New York, NY -- endowment of the genomics institute
25,000,000	Rockefeller University, New York, NY -- for endowment of clinical research facilities
25,000,000	Weill Medical College of Cornell University, New York, NY -- for construction of new outpatient facility
10,000,000	Weill Medical College of Cornell University, New York, NY -- for Genetic Medicine Program
8,000,000	New York Police and Fire Widows and Children Benefit Fund, New York, NY -- response to September 11
5,000,000	International Trachoma Initiative, Inc., New York, NY
3,000,000	Metropolitan Museum of Art, New York, NY -- for Early Chinese Empire The First Millennium, Han Through Tang
2,500,000	Hospital for Special Surgery, New York, NY -- Discovery to Recovery Research Campaign
2,500,000	Museum of Modern Art, New York, NY -- for MOMA Builds
2,500,000	United Negro College Fund, Fairfax, VA -- for technology enhancement capital campaign

STATE FARM MUTUAL AUTOMOBILE INSURANCE CO.

Company Headquarters

Bloomington, IL
Web: http://www.statefarm.com

Company Description

SIC(s): 6331 Fire, Marine & Casualty Insurance.
Parent Company: State Farm Insurance Companies, 1 State Farm Plaza, Bloomington, IL, United States

Operating Locations

State Farm Mutual Automobile Insurance Co. (AL; AZ; CA; CO; GA; IL--Bloomington; IN; LA; MI; MN; MO; NE; NY; OH; OK; OR; TN; TX; VA)

Nonmonetary Support

Type: Donated Equipment; Donated Products; In-kind Services
Volunteer Programs: Company-sponsored volunteer programs include loaned executives for United Way campaigns, Junior Achievement advisors, and Red Cross Blood drives. Interested employees complete a questionnaire, then receive a newsletter of volunteer activities. Employees participate in activities on their own initiative.
Note: The company provides nonmonetary support.

State Farm Companies Foundation

Giving Contact

Lori Manning
One State Farm Plaza, SC3
Bloomington, IL 61710-0001
Phone: (309)766-9739
Fax: (309)766-2314
Web: http://www.statefarm.com/foundati/foundati.htm

Description

Founded: 1963
EIN: 366110423
Organization Type: Corporate Foundation
Giving Locations: near major offices.
Grant Types: Capital, Employee Matching Gifts, Endowment, Fellowship, Matching, Multiyear/Continuing Support, Scholarship.
Note: Employee matching gift ratio: 1 to 1 up to $1,000 per contribution. Matching and employee matching gifts are for four-year colleges and universities only.

Financial Summary

Total Giving: $16,426,820 (2002 approx); $12,878,268 (2001); $14,957,375 (2000). Note: Contributes through corporate direct giving program and foundation.
Giving Analysis: Giving for 1998 includes: foundation gifts to individuals ($80,000); foundation fellowships ($179,250); foundation grants to United Way ($1,108,198); foundation matching gifts ($2,480,576); foundation ($6,202,875); 1997: foundation grants to United Way ($986,253); foundation scholarships ($1,534,570); foundation matching gifts ($1,898,850) foundation ($2,747,871)
Assets: $52,285,140 (2001); $62,511,350 (2000); $83,174,321 (1998)
Gifts Received: $56,000,026 (1998); $4,750,000 (1993); $3,000,000 (1992). Note: Foundation received contributions from State Farm Life Insurance Co. and State Farm Mutual Automobile Insurance Co.

Typical Recipients

Arts & Humanities: Arts Associations & Councils, Ethnic & Folk Arts, History & Archaeology, Museums/Galleries, Public Broadcasting, Theater
Civic & Public Affairs: African American Affairs, Economic Policy, Employment/Job Training, Civic & Public Affairs-General, Law & Justice, Native American Affairs, Professional & Trade Associations, Public Policy, Safety, Urban & Community Affairs, Women's Affairs, Zoos/Aquariums
Education: Arts/Humanities Education, Business Education, Colleges & Universities, Community & Junior

Colleges, Economic Education, Education Associations, Education Funds, Education-General, International Studies, Medical Education, Minority Education, Private Education (Precollege), Science/Mathematics Education, Student Aid

Health: Cancer, Children's Health/Hospitals, Clinics/Medical Centers, Hospitals, Medical Rehabilitation, Public Health

Religion: Religious Welfare

Social Services: Child Welfare, Community Service Organizations, Day Care, Family Services, Substance Abuse, United Funds/United Ways, YMCA/YWCA/YMHA/YWHA

Application Procedures

Initial Contact: Send a written proposal.

Application Requirements: Include description and purpose of the project; amount requested; project action plan and time frame; expected results; total cost and budget; sources and levels of expected funding; annual report; recently audited financial statement; copies of IRS 501(c)(3) and 509(a)1, 2, or 3 rulings; and fund-raising campaign time frame.

Deadlines: Submission deadlines for Foundation Scholarship Program, December 31 each year; Fellowship Program, February 15 each year; Doctoral Program, March 31 each year; Matching Gift and Good Neighbor Programs are ongoing.

Restrictions

Does not support seminars or conferences, or individuals (other than for scholarships). To qualify for the Foundation Scholarship Program, parents and legal guardians must be a State Farm Company employee, agent or retiree; Fellowship Program, must be a majoring in a business related field and be a U.S. citizen, at time of application, must be current full-time college junior or senior, with minimum GPA of 3.6 on a 4.0 scale; Doctoral Program, must be U.S. citizen; Matching Gift Program, must be four-year or above degree, granting U.S. accredited college or university; and Good Neighbor Grant Program, must volunteer at least 40 hours a year to a qualified nonprofit organization, public or private school, or government municipality.

Additional Information

Scholarship, fellowship, doctoral program, matching gifts, and Good Neighbor Program grants have specific forms and/or applications for submission.

Publications: Foundation Contributions Report

Corporate Officials

John Coffey: senior vice president, vice chairman, chief operating officer, director B Pekin, IL. PRIM CORP EMPL senior vice president: State Farm Mutual Automobile Insurance Co. ADD CORP EMPL vice president: State Farm General Insurance Co.; vice president: State Farm Fire & Casualty Co.

Edward Barry Rust, Jr.: chairman, president, chief executive officer, director B Chicago, IL 1950. ED Lawrence University (1968-1969); Illinois Wesleyan University BS (1972); Southern Methodist University JD (1975); Southern Methodist University MBA (1975). PRIM CORP EMPL chairman, president, chief executive officer, director: State Farm Mutual Automobile Insurance Co. CORP AFFIL director, member executive committee, member investment committee: State Farm Life Insurance Co.; president, director: State Farm Investment Management Corp.; director, member executive committee, member investment committee: State Farm Life & Annuity Co.; chairman, president, chief executive officer: State Farm Insurance Companies; president, director: State Farm International Services Inc.; director, member executive committee, member investment committee: State Farm Fire & Casualty Co.; director, member executive committee, member investment committee: State Farm General Insurance Co. NONPR AFFIL member: Texas State Bar Association; member business advisory council: University Illinois College Commerce &

Business Administration; chairman: National Alliance of Business; member, trustee: Insurance Institute America; vice chairman: Insurance Institute Highway Safety; member: Illinois Business Roundtable; trustee: Illinois Wesleyan University; member: Business Roundtable; member: Illinois Bar Association; chairman: American Enterprise Institute; member: American Institute Property & Liability Underwriters.

Laura P. Sullivan: vice president, secretary, counsel B Des Moines, IA 1947. ED Cornell University BA (1971); Drake University JD (1972). PRIM CORP EMPL vice president, secretary, counsel: State Farm Mutual Automobile Insurance Co. CORP AFFIL secretary: State Farm Lloyds Inc.; vice president, secretary, counsel: State Farm Life Insurance Co.; assistant treasurer, director: State Farm Indemnity Co.; vice president, secretary, counsel, director: State Farm Life & Accident Assurance Co.; secretary, vice president, counsel, director: State Farm General Insurance Co.; vice president, secretary, counsel: State Farm Annuity & Life Insurance Co.; secretary, vice president, counsel: State Farm Fire & Casualty Co. NONPR AFFIL director: Insurance Institute Highway Safety; member: Iowa Bar Association; member: American Corporate Counsel Association; member: American Bar Association.

Vincent Joseph Trosino: executive vice president, vice chairman, chief operating officer, director B Upland, PA 1940. ED Villanova University (1962); Illinois State University (1973). PRIM CORP EMPL executive vice president, vice chairman, chief operating officer, director: State Farm Mutual Automobile Insurance Co. CORP AFFIL vice chairman, member executive committee, director: State Farm Life Insurance Co.; vice chairman, member, executive committee: State Farm Mutual Insurance Co.; director: State Farm Life & Accident Assurance Co.; director: State Farm Life & Annuity Co.; director: State Farm International Services Inc.; director: State Farm Investment Management Corp.; member executive committee director: State Farm Fire & Casualty Co.; director: State Farm General Insurance Co.

Foundation Officials

John Coffey: vice president programs (see above)

Jill Jones: assistant secretary

Roger Scott Joslin: treasurer B Bloomington, IL 1936. ED Miami University BS (1958); University of Illinois JD (1961). PRIM CORP EMPL senior vice president, treasurer: State Farm Mutual Automobile Insurance Co. ADD CORP EMPL treasurer: State Farm General Insurance Co.; vice president, treasurer, director: State Farm International Services Inc.; vice president, treasurer, director: State Farm Investment Management Corp.; treasurer: State Farm County Mutual Insurance Co. Texas; vice president, treasurer, director: State Farm Lloyds Inc.; vice president, treasurer, director: State Farm Municipal Bond Fund Inc. CORP AFFIL director: State Farm Life Insurance Co.; vice president, treasurer, director: State Farm Interim Fund Inc.; director: State Farm Life & Accident Assurance Co.; chairman: State Farm Fire & Casualty Co.; vice president, treasurer, director: State Farm Growth Fund Inc.; director: State Farm Annuity & Life Insurance Co.; vice president, treasurer, director: State Farm Balanced Fund Inc. NONPR AFFIL chairman board trustees: Natural Disaster Coalition.

Edward Barry Rust, Jr.: chairman, president, director (see above)

Laura P. Sullivan: vice president, secretary, director (see above)

Vincent Joseph Trosino: assistant secretary (see above)

Grants Analysis

Disclosure Period: calendar year ending 2001

Total Grants: $9,443,312*

Number of Grants: 77

Average Grant: $88,358*

Highest Grant: $2,000,000

Typical Range: $2,000 to $50,000

*Note: Giving excludes matching gifts; fellowships; doctoral awards; gifts to individuals; and United Way. Average grant figure excludes three highest grants, totaling $4,704,842.

Recent Grants

Note: Grants derived from 2001 Form 990.

General

2,000,000	Illinois State University College of Business, Normal, IL
1,654,842	National Merit Scholarship Corporation, Evanston, IL
1,050,000	Illinois Wesleyan University, Bloomington, IL
600,000	Smithsonian Institution, Washington, DC
477,000	Illinois State University, Normal, IL
408,000	University of Illinois, Champaign, IL
348,000	Public Agenda Foundation, New York, NY
300,000	American College, Bryn Mawr, PA
252,280	United Way McLean County, Bloomington, IL
232,100	United Way of Kern County, Bakersfield, CA

STATE STREET CORP.

Company Headquarters

225 Franklin Street
Boston, MA 02110
Web: http://www.statestreet.com

Company Description

Founded: 1792
Ticker: STT
Exchange: NYSE
Assets: US$85.794 billion (2002)
Profit: US$1.015 billion (2002)
Employees: 19753 (2002)
Fortune Rank: 340, per FORTUNE Magazine's list of 500 Largest U.S. Corporations (2002).

Nonmonetary Support

Type: Cause-related Marketing & Promotion; Donated Equipment; In-kind Services; Loaned Employees; Loaned Executives

Volunteer Programs: State Street Global Outreach is a company-wide volunteer program that encourages employee participation in company-sponsored programs, pairs employees who are interested in volunteer opportunities with non-profit organizations with missions that are of interest to the employees, and offers each employee one work day a year for volunteer efforts.

State Street Foundation

Giving Contact

George A. Bowman, Jr., Vice President, Community Affairs
State Street Bank & Trust
225 Franklin Street
Boston, MA 02110-2804
Phone: (617)664-3381
Fax: (617)451-6315
E-mail: gabowman@statestreet.com

Description

EIN: 046401847
Organization Type: Corporate Foundation
Giving Locations: MA: Boston including the metro area
Grant Types: Capital, Challenge, Employee Matching Gifts, General Support, Project.

Financial Summary

Total Giving: $7,343,852 (2001); $9,938,140 (2000); $8,000,000 (1999 approx). Note: Contributes through foundation only.

Giving Analysis: Giving for 2001 includes: foundation ($7,343,852); 2000: foundation grants to United Way ($1,385,290); foundation ($8,552,850); 1998: corporate matching gifts ($25,164); corporate fellowships ($33,500); corporate scholarships ($36,353); corporate grants to United Way ($1,192,500)

Assets: $1,045,282 (2000); $4,950,820 (1998); $3,520,416 (1995)

Gifts Received: $9,650,000 (2000); $7,437,000 (1998); $4,254,000 (1995). Note: Contributions are received from State Street Bank & Trust and Boston Financial Data Services.

Typical Recipients

Arts & Humanities: Arts Associations & Councils, Arts Centers, Arts Institutes, Arts Outreach, Ballet, Community Arts, Dance, Ethnic & Folk Arts, Historic Preservation, History & Archaeology, Libraries, Museums/Galleries, Music, Opera, Performing Arts, Theater

Civic & Public Affairs: African American Affairs, Asian American Affairs, Botanical Gardens/Parks, Business/Free Enterprise, Civil Rights, Clubs, Economic Development, Economic Policy, Employment/Job Training, Ethnic Organizations, Civic & Public Affairs-General, Hispanic Affairs, Housing, Law & Justice, Minority Business, Municipalities/Towns, Nonprofit Management, Public Policy, Public Policy, Safety, Urban & Community Affairs, Women's Affairs, Zoos/Aquariums

Education: Afterschool/Enrichment Programs, Arts/Humanities Education, Business Education, Business-School Partnerships, Colleges & Universities, Continuing Education, Economic Education, Education Associations, Education Funds, Education Reform, Elementary Education (Private), Elementary Education (Public), Engineering/Technological Education, Faculty Development, Education-General, Leadership Training, Literacy, Medical Education, Minority Education, Preschool Education, Private Education (Precollege), Public Education (Precollege), School Volunteerism, Science/Mathematics Education, Secondary Education (Public), Social Sciences Education, Student Aid, Vocational & Technical Education

Health: Adolescent Health Issues, AIDS/HIV, Cancer, Children's Health/Hospitals, Clinics/Medical Centers, Diabetes, Eyes/Blindness, Geriatric Health, Health Policy/Cost Containment, Health Funds, Health Organizations, Hospitals, Medical Rehabilitation, Mental Health, Public Health

International: Health Care/Hospitals, International Affairs, International Relief Efforts

Religion: Jewish Causes, Religious Organizations, Religious Welfare

Science: Science Museums

Social Services: Animal Protection, At-Risk Youth, Big Brother/Big Sister, Child Abuse, Child Welfare, Community Centers, Community Service Organizations, Counseling, Delinquency & Criminal Rehabilitation, Domestic Violence, Family Services, Food/Clothing Distribution, Homes, People with Disabilities, Recreation & Athletics, Refugee Assistance, Scouts, Shelters/Homelessness, Social Services-General, United Funds/United Ways, Veterans, YMCA/YWCA/YMHA/YWHA, Youth Organizations

Application Procedures

Initial Contact: Call or write for guidelines, then send full proposal.

Application Requirements: Include an executive summary (two-page maximum) on organization's letterhead, including: statement of project's principal objective; expected measurable outcome; total project budget, including dollar amount requested and any other anticipated sources of funding; description of population to be affected; project's timetable; name and telephone number of directors, and primary contact person. The proposal (six-page maximum) should include: profile of organization and mission statement; description of the project to be funded; project's purpose; project's history and measures of success; services to be provided; cost to users of the services; profile of the population to be served; primary short- and long-term objectives; description of how the stated objectives will be achieved and the results quantified; plan for sustaining project after funding has ended. The following attachments should also be included: a copy of the organization's 501(c)(3) determination letter; a detailed projected budget for the current fiscal year (including a list of courses and amounts of support--in hand and expected--and, if applicable, the fundraising strategy for obtaining additional funds); a project and operating budget, if the request is for a project; a list of the board of directors and key officers, including business affiliations; resume of the program director and any staff members that are essential to the success of the project; audited financial statements (or IRS Forms 990) for the most recent two years; sources of corporate and foundation support for the most recent two years; and any other supporting material that would help in proposal evaluation.

Deadlines: None.

Review Process: Proposals are reviewed quarterly, in March, June, September, and December.

Decision Notification: Funding decisions are communicated by letter within about 90 days of receipt.

Notes: Also accepts the Associated Grantmakers of Massachusetts grant application form. Organizations may submit a funding request during a calendar year in which they are not receiving payments from a prior grant awarded.

Restrictions

The foundation does not support scholarships or fellowships; research projects; emergency cash flow, deficit spending, debt liquidation; seed money or start-up programs; trips, tours, or transportation expenses; or films or videos.

Foundation seldom makes multiyear grants, or for general operating support.

Additional Information

Publications: Guidelines

Trust(s): State Street Bank & Trust

Corporate Officials

George A. Bowman, Jr.: vice president community affairs PRIM CORP EMPL vice president community affairs: State Street Bank & Trust Co.

David Anthony Spina: chairman, chief executive officer B New York, NY 1942. ED College of the Holy Cross BS (1964); Harvard University MBA (1972). PRIM CORP EMPL chairman, chief executive officer: State Street Bank & Trust Co. CORP AFFIL chief financial officer, treasurer, vice chairman: State Street Boston Corp.; president, chief operating officer: State Street Corp.

Foundation Officials

George A. Bowman, Jr.: foundation manager, vice president (see above)

Lilo Navales de Garne: foundation officer

Grants Analysis

Disclosure Period: calendar year ending 2000

Total Grants: $8,552,850*

Number of Grants: 1,440

Average Grant: $5,939

Highest Grant: $250,000

Typical Range: $3,000 to $25,000

*****Note:** Giving excludes United Way.

Recent Grants

Note: Grants derived from 2000 Form 990.

General

780,000	United Way of Massachusetts Bay, Boston, MA
260,000	United Way of Massachusetts Bay, Boston, MA
250,000	Habitat for Humanity, Kansas City, MO
250,000	South Shore YMCA, Quincy, MA -- Germantown neighborhood program
200,000	Community Technology Development Inc., Boston, MA
200,000	United Way Millenium Fund, Edmonton, AB Canada
150,000	Boston Medical Center, Boston, MA
150,000	Urban League of Eastern Massachusetts, Boston, MA
125,000	Boston Housing Partnership, Boston, MA
125,000	Boston Medical Center, Boston, MA

STATLER FOUNDATION

Giving Contact

Edward M. Flynn, Chairman
107 Delaware Avenue, Suite 680
Buffalo, NY 14202
Phone: (716)852-1104
Fax: (716)852-3968

Description

Founded: 1934
EIN: 131889077
Organization Type: Specialized/Single Purpose Foundation
Giving Locations: NY: internationally; nationally.
Grant Types: Capital, Professorship, Scholarship.

Donor Information

Founder: The death of Ellsworth Milton Statler in 1928 marked the end of an era in the hotel industry and the passing of one of the most creative and resourceful hoteliers to have practiced the profession. It is also significant because Statler's will provided for the creation of the Statler Foundation "(to support) research work for the benefit of the (hotel) industry... training and making more proficient the workers in the hotels, for the benefit of the industry as a whole." To fund his posthumous endeavor, Statler transferred to the newly-created Foundation 10,000 shares of Statler Company stock, then valued at some $10 a share. Since its creation in 1934, the Foundation's endowment has grown to $28.5 million dollars, while also spinning off millions of dollars in grants to numerous educational institutions in furtherance of Statler's objectives.

For nearly 40 years, Statler's widow, Alice Seidler Statler, served as chairman of the trustees of the Statler Foundation. It was appropriate that Mrs. Statler, who served for many years as Statler's personal secretary and who remained his business confidante, should oversee the early work and development of the Foundation. On Mrs. Statler's death in 1969, the chairmanship of the Foundation passed successively to Ward B. Arbury, Peter J. Crotty, Robert Koren, and Arthur Musarra.

Financial Summary

Total Giving: $2,000,000 (2002 approx); $1,632,164 (2001); $1,992,480 (2000)

Giving Analysis: Giving for 2000 includes: foundation scholarships ($642,556) 1998: foundation scholarships ($677,176)

Assets: $34,124,284 (2001); $42,216,608 (2000); $37,281,224 (1998)

Typical Recipients

Civic & Public Affairs: Civic & Public Affairs-General, Professional & Trade Associations
Education: Arts/Humanities Education, Business Education, Colleges & Universities, Community & Junior Colleges, Continuing Education, Faculty Development, Education-General, International Studies, Minority Education, Private Education (Precollege), Science/Mathematics Education, Student Aid, Vocational & Technical Education
Health: Children's Health/Hospitals, Hospitals
International: Foreign Educational Institutions, International-General, International Affairs, International Development
Religion: Churches, Religious Welfare
Social Services: Camps, Community Centers, Community Service Organizations, Food/Clothing Distribution, People with Disabilities, Social Services-General, YMCA/YWCA/YMHA/YWHA, Youth Organizations

Application Procedures

Initial Contact: A letter of inquiry requesting application form.
Application Requirements: Along with the completed application, submit 13 copies of the following information: name, address and phone number; paragraph of history; copy of IRS tax-exempt letter; other sources of funding; list of board officers; purpose of organization; number of people served; most recent financial audit; purpose of project and description of need; amount requested; other sources that have been approached for funding; total cost of project; time period; EEO policy and affirmative action statement; other organizations assisting with project; and future support. Application must be signed by the chief executive of organization.
Deadlines: None.
Review Process: The foundation reviews and processes all requests for support by August or September.

Restrictions

The foundation makes grants for education and training in the hospitality field (hotels, motels, and food service) only.

Foundation Officials

Robert B. Bennett: trustee B Fitchburg, MA 1941. ED Babson College BSBA (1963); University of Massachusetts MBA (1966); Harvard University (1980-1981). PRIM CORP EMPL chairman, president, chief executive officer: ONBAN Corp. CORP AFFIL member: Retail Finance Services Group NA; chairman: Health Care Data System Inc.; chairman: Crouse Irving Memorial Properties Inc.; director: Fays Inc.; director: Cirrus System Inc.; member: Association Bank Holding Companies; chairman: CIMH Enterprises Inc. NONPR AFFIL trustee: Syracuse Stage; trustee: Syracuse Symphony Orchestra; director: Senior Olympics; member: National Retail Banking Planners Association; director: Onondaga County Industries Development Corp.; director: Metropolitan Development Association; trustee: Illinois College; director: Crouse Irving Memorial Hospital; director: Greater Syracuse Chamber of Commerce; director: Community Bank Association New York State; member: Financial Executives Institute; executive council: Boy Scouts America Onondaga Region; trustee: Citizens Foundation; member: Bank Administration Institute; member: American Bankers Association.
Marguerite Collesano: trustee
William J. Cunningham, Jr.: trustee
Joseph DiNardo: trustee PRIM CORP EMPL president: Dinardo Dinardo & Lukasik PC.
Peter J. Fiorella, Jr.: trustee
Edward M. Flynn: trustee
Ernestine R. Green: chairwoman, trustee
Arthur F. Musarra: trustee
Carlo M. Perfetto: trustee
Arthur V. Sabia: trustee

Herbert Siegel: chairman
Peter Vinolus: vice chairman, trustee

Grants Analysis

Disclosure Period: calendar year ending 2001
Total Grants: $1,136,881*
Number of Grants: 10
Average Grant: $79,089*
Highest Grant: $254,166
Lowest Grant: $25,000
Typical Range: $50,000 to $100,000
*Note: Giving excludes scholarships. Average grant figure excludes two highest grants ($504,166).

Recent Grants

Note: Grants derived from 2001 Form 990.

General

254,166	Niagara University, Lewiston, NY -- renovation of St. Vincent's hall
250,000	Paul Smith's College, Paul Smiths, NY -- renovation at the Statler Center of Hospitality
125,000	Cornell University, Ithaca, NY -- visiting minority Professorship
100,000	Blind Association of Western New York, Buffalo, NY -- National Statler Center for Careers in Hospitality Service
100,000	Culinary Institute of America, Hyde Park, NY -- Statler Digital Video Library
100,000	D'Youville College, Buffalo, NY -- training of Allied health Professionals
69,215	Trocaire College, Buffalo, NY -- language laboratory, scholarships and library materials
62,800	Erie Community, Williamsville, NY -- renovation of Erie Room to be renamed Statler Room
50,000	Florida International University, Biscayne Bay, FL -- Ellsworth M.Statler Professorship
25,000	Boysville of Michigan, Clinton, MI -- Holland house/window replacement

JOHN STAUFFER CHARITABLE TRUST

Giving Contact

Mr. H. Jess Senecal, Trustee
301 North Lake Avenue, 10th Floor
Pasadena, CA 91101-4108
Phone: (626)793-9400
Fax: (626)793-5900

Description

Founded: 1974
EIN: 237434707
Organization Type: Specialized/Single Purpose Foundation
Giving Locations: CA
Grant Types: Endowment, Fellowship, Professorship, Project, Research, Scholarship.
Note: The foundation also provides funding for building and equipment.

Donor Information

Founder: Established in 1974 under the will of the late John Stauffer , an officer and director of the Stauffer Chemical Company who was particularly interested in educational concerns and hospitals.

Financial Summary

Total Giving: $4,000,000 (fiscal year ending May 31, 2001); $3,244,000 (fiscal 1999); $4,000,000 (fiscal 1998 approx). Note: Figure for 1997 was provided by the foundation.
Assets: $59,971,355 (fiscal 2001); $61,716,664 (fiscal 1999); $52,000,000 (fiscal 1998 approx). Note: Figures for 1997 and 1998 provided by the foundation.

Typical Recipients

Arts & Humanities: Libraries
Education: Colleges & Universities, Engineering/Technological Education, Legal Education, Science/Mathematics Education, Student Aid
Health: Cancer, Children's Health/Hospitals, Clinics/Medical Centers, Emergency/Ambulance Services, Health Organizations, Heart, Hospitals, Medical Rehabilitation, Medical Research, Mental Health, Outpatient Health Care, Public Health
International: Health Care/Hospitals
Religion: Churches, Religious Welfare
Science: Scientific Research
Social Services: Child Welfare, Community Service Organizations, Delinquency & Criminal Rehabilitation, Family Planning, Family Services, Food/Clothing Distribution, People with Disabilities, Scouts, Senior Services, Substance Abuse, YMCA/YWCA/YMHA/YWHA, Youth Organizations

Application Procedures

Initial Contact: Send a letter stating purpose of funds sought, and amount requested, and include proof of tax-exempt status. The foundation maintains precise application guidelines; organizations are encouraged to request a copy of the guidelines before submitting a proposal.
Application Requirements: Proposals should include the amount requested; an explanation of the need for the subject of the grant; the goals; the manner in which John Stauffer's name will be memorialized; full financial information, including a detailed budget for the project to be assisted by the grant; and a statement of whether other sources of funding are being sought, and if so, which other sources are providing funding.
All applications must be executed by an officer of the grantee institution. Applications signed by a division or department head must be approved and countersigned by the head of the organization or institution, or by an officer thereof. Applicants should submit the latest IRS tax-exempt determination letter, stating that the grantee is not a private foundation, as well as the latest audited balance sheet and statement of income and expenditures. In addition, the trust would like to see a tax-exempt letter from the State of California. Letters of support from authorities and/or organizations in the applicant's field are encouraged.
All proposals and letters should be submitted in three copies, one for each of the trustees.
Deadlines: None. The board meets quarterly and accepts applications any time.
Review Process: If the proposal needs amplification or clarification, the trust will request the needed information in writing. Applicants are notified in writing whether or not the grant is being given. Decisions are made within six to nine months. Proposals will not be returned, and may be peer-reviewed.
Notes: Those receiving grants are required to send a report on the use of the funds to the trust, including a certification that the funds have been used for the purpose for which the grant was made. The trust reserves the right to call for a reasonable audit of the use of grant funds conducted by its representatives at its own expense. If grants were used for purposes other than that for which the grant was made, the total amount of the grant must be returned.

Restrictions

Grants are not made to organizations which, in turn, distribute them to others at their own discretion. Grants are not made to individuals, to influence legislation or elections, to discriminatory groups, for sectarian religious activities, for loans or operating expenses, deficit financing, or general fund drives or annual appeals.

Additional Information

Those denied a grant may submit a new application in the future, but should not request reinstatement of a prior request which has been denied. The trust prefers to participate with other donors when making grants.

Recipients may be required to provide matching funds. Also, large grants may be distributed over a period of two or more years.

Publications: Policy Guidelines

Foundation Officials

Carl M. Franklin: chairman
H. Jess Senecal: co-trustee
Michael S. Whalen: co-trustee ED California State University BA (1976); University of California at Berkeley JD (1979). NONPR AFFIL member: Order Coif; fellow: Phi Beta Kappa; member: Los Angeles County Bar Association; fellow: Center Creative Photography; director: Constitutional Rights Foundation; member: Beta Gamma Sigma.

Grants Analysis

Disclosure Period: fiscal year ending May 31, 2001
Total Grants: $4,000,000
Number of Grants: 8
Highest Grant: $750,000
Lowest Grant: $300,000

Recent Grants

Note: Grants derived from 2000 Form 990.

General

500,000	Children's Hospital Los Angeles, Los Angeles, CA
500,000	Huntington Memorial Hospital, Pasadena, CA
500,000	Stanford University, Stanford, CA
500,000	University of Redlands, Redlands, CA
500,000	University of Southern California, Los Angeles, CA
500,000	University of Southern California, Los Angeles, CA
400,000	Providence St. Joseph Medical Center, Burbank, CA
200,000	Methodist Hospital Foundation, Arcadia, CA
100,000	Claremont Graduate University, Claremont, CA
100,000	Providence St. Joseph Medical Center, Burbank, CA

STAUNTON FARM FOUNDATION

Giving Contact

Joni Schwager, Program Officer, Foundation Manager
650 Smithfield St., Suite 240
Pittsburgh, PA 15219
Phone: (412)281-8020
Fax: (412)232-3115
Web: http://www.stauntonfarm.org

Description

Founded: 1937
EIN: 250965573
Organization Type: Specialized/Single Purpose Foundation
Giving Locations: PA: Southwestern Pennsylvania
Grant Types: Award, Matching, Multiyear/Continuing Support.

Donor Information

Founder: Established in Pennsylvania in 1937 with funds donated by Mrs. Matilda S. McCready (born Matilda Staunton Craig). Mrs. McCready's original wish was that funds from the foundation would be used to erect a home for the mentally ill. However,

her estate lacked the necessary funds for such an undertaking.

Mrs. McCready realized her original intentions may not always be practical and stated, "In the event that advances in medical sciences or in social conditions render carrying on of the home...impractical, the directors of Staunton Farm may, with the consent of Orphan's Court of Allegheny County, PA, change its character so as to suit the needs of the times, keeping always in view the effort to alleviate the conditions of the sick and unfortunate."

Financial Summary

Total Giving: $2,082,428 (2001); $1,171,699 (2000); $2,067,378 (1999)
Giving Analysis: Giving for 1997 includes: foundation grants to United Way ($211,000)
Assets: $46,431,965 (2001); $47,197,631 (2000); $43,000,000 (1999 approx)

Typical Recipients

Arts & Humanities: Libraries
Civic & Public Affairs: African American Affairs, Botanical Gardens/Parks, Community Foundations, Employment/Job Training, Civic & Public Affairs-General, Professional & Trade Associations, Urban & Community Affairs, Women's Affairs
Education: Afterschool/Enrichment Programs, Colleges & Universities, Education Reform, Education-General, Gifted & Talented Programs, Literacy, Medical Education, Preschool Education, Private Education (Precollege), Public Education (Precollege)
Health: AIDS/HIV, Children's Health/Hospitals, Clinics/Medical Centers, Eyes/Blindness, Health-General, Health Funds, Health Organizations, Hospices, Hospitals, Medical Rehabilitation, Mental Health, Public Health, Single-Disease Health Associations
Religion: Churches, Jewish Causes, Ministries, Religious Organizations, Religious Welfare
Social Services: Child Welfare, Community Centers, Community Service Organizations, Counseling, Crime Prevention, Day Care, Delinquency & Criminal Rehabilitation, Domestic Violence, Emergency Relief, Family Planning, Family Services, Food/Clothing Distribution, Homes, People with Disabilities, Recreation & Athletics, Senior Services, Sexual Abuse, Shelters/Homelessness, Substance Abuse, United Funds/United Ways, YMCA/YWCA/YMHA/YWHA, Youth Organizations

Application Procedures

Initial Contact: A letter of inquiry should be sent describing the organization and proposed project. After initial review, prospective grantees may be asked to make a formal application using the Grantmakers of Western Pennsylvania Common Application Form for consideration by the Foundation's Project Committee.
Deadlines: Formal applications are generally due February 11, August 4, and November 3. Prospective grantees should plan accordingly.

Restrictions

The foundation does not usually contribute to general operating support, endowment funds, building campaigns, conferences, or grants to individuals. Exceptions have been made in situations where the conduct of the project is directly dependent upon altered or new facilities.

Additional Information

The foundation reports that current selection criteria favors those requests that focus on providing direct patient care in the mental health field.
Publications: Guidelines; Application; Brochure; Grants List; History

Foundation Officials

Ann W. Austin: member
Albert H. Burchfield, III: member PRIM CORP EMPL officer: Dollar Bank Federal Savings Bank.

Bonnie B. Casper: director
Priscilla G. Clark: member
Albert Craig, III: director
Gregory L. Craig: member
Joseph D. Dury, Jr.: director
John W. Eichleay, Jr.: director PRIM CORP EMPL secretary: Eichleay Holdings Inc. ADD CORP EMPL secretary: Eichleay Corp.
Howard K. Foster, MD: member
Rev. David C. Frederick: member
Richard Frederick, III: member
Andrea Q. Griffiths: vice president
Mary Elizabeth Griffiths: member
Philip G. Gully: member
Elizabeth G. Hahl: director
Carolyn S. Hammer: secretary
Alexander Ardley Henkels, Jr.: president B Philadelphia, PA 1953. ED Syracuse University BS (1976). PRIM CORP EMPL photo editor: Philadelphia Inquirer. CLUB AFFIL Philadelphia Cricket Club.
Kathleen C. Knight: member
Lee C. Lundback: director
Andrea Torres Mahone: member
Rev. Helsel R. Marsh, Jr.: member
Carol T. McClenahan: member
Richard W. Reed, Jr.: director
Barbara Robinson: treasurer
Marcia Roque: member
Kenneth T. Segel: director
Judith K. Sherry: director
Hon. William L. Standish: member B Pittsburgh, PA 1930. PRIM CORP EMPL judge: U.S. District Court. NONPR AFFIL member: Pennsylvania Bar Association; trustee: YMCA Sewickley; member: American Judicature Society; member: Allegheny County Bar Association; member: American Bar Association; member: Academy Trial Lawyers.
Thomas L. Wentling, Jr.: member
William Whetzel: director

Grants Analysis

Disclosure Period: calendar year ending 2001
Total Grants: $2,082,428*
Number of Grants: 67
Average Grant: $31,081
Highest Grant: $51,847
Typical Range: $30,000 to $50,000
***Note:** Grants analysis provided by foundation.

Recent Grants

Note: Grants derived from 2000 Form 990.

General

75,000	Vintage, Pittsburgh, PA
62,000	Family Services of Western Pennsylvania, Pittsburgh, PA
57,200	Comprehensive Substance Abuse Services, Pittsburgh, PA
51,862	Bethlehem Haven, Pittsburgh, PA
50,000	Pennsylvania Health Law Project, Philadelphia, PA
47,000	Pittsburgh Pastoral Institute, Pittsburgh, PA
40,000	Crossroads Foundation, Pittsburgh, PA
40,000	Pittsburgh Vision Services, Pittsburgh, PA
38,350	Parent's League for Emotional Adjustment, Pittsburgh, PA
37,500	Geneva College, Geneva, PA

KENT D. AND MARY L. STEADLEY MEMORIAL TRUST

Giving Contact

Linda M. Hodge, Trust Officer
c/o Bank of America
231 S. Main
Carthage, MO 64836

Phone: (417)359-7170
Fax: (417)359-7117

Description
Founded: 1970
EIN: 436120866
Organization Type: Private Foundation
Giving Locations: MO: Carthage
Grant Types: Capital, General Support.

Financial Summary
Total Giving: $926,950 (2001); $1,351,301 (2000); $959,770 (1999)
Assets: $20,173,304 (2001); $21,984,931 (2000); $20,334,307 (1999)

Typical Recipients
Arts & Humanities: Arts Associations & Councils, Arts Centers, Historic Preservation, Libraries, Museums/Galleries
Civic & Public Affairs: Civic & Public Affairs-General, Municipalities/Towns, Urban & Community Affairs
Education: Education Funds, Elementary Education (Private), Elementary Education (Public), Private Education (Precollege), Public Education (Precollege), Science/Mathematics Education
Health: Clinics/Medical Centers, Heart, Medical Rehabilitation
Religion: Ministries, Religious Welfare
Social Services: Animal Protection, Domestic Violence, Recreation & Athletics, Scouts, Senior Services, Substance Abuse, YMCA/YWCA/YMHA/YWHA

Application Procedures
Initial Contact: Contact the trustee to request an application form.
Deadlines: None.

Restrictions
Limited to organizations in or near Carthage, Missouri that are not beneficiaries of local or national campaigns.

Additional Information
Publications: Application Form
Trust(s): Bank of America

Grants Analysis
Disclosure Period: calendar year ending 2001
Total Grants: $926,950
Number of Grants: 22
Average Grant: $30,736*
Highest Grant: $281,500
Lowest Grant: $2,100
Typical Range: $10,000 to $50,000
*Note: Average grant figure excludes highest grant.

Recent Grants
Note: Grants derived from 2001 Form 990.

General

281,500	Carthage R-9 School, Carthage, MO -- construction and educational programs
150,000	City of Carthage, Carthage, MO -- Fair Acres sports complex
100,000	McCune Brooks Hospital, Carthage, MO -- capital budget items
56,250	Magic Moments Riding Therapy -- capital improvements
56,250	Main Street Carthage, Carthage, MO -- Carthage VIP Town Days Program
50,000	Boy Scouts of America, Joplin, MI -- multipurpose building
50,000	Community Clinic Carthage, Carthage, MO -- start up expenses
50,000	Innovative Industries, Inc., Carthage, MO -- building renovation
50,000	Ozark Area Girl Scout Council, Joplin, MO -- new lodge at Camp Mintahama

30,000	Main Street Carthage, Carthage, MO -- gazebo construction

STEARNS FOUNDATION

Giving Contact
Roger R. Stearns, Secretary
PO Box 50
Hutchinson, MN 55350-0050
Phone: (320)587-2137
Fax: (320)587-7646

Description
Founded: 1989
EIN: 411609446
Organization Type: Private Foundation
Giving Locations: MN: Hutchinson
Grant Types: General Support.

Financial Summary
Total Giving: $27,761 (fiscal year ending March 31, 2001); $27,404 (fiscal 2000); $22,807 (fiscal 1999)
Giving Analysis: Giving for fiscal 1999 includes: foundation grants to United Way ($10)
Assets: $171,163 (fiscal 2001); $122,281 (fiscal 2000); $161,554 (fiscal 1999)
Gifts Received: $23,682 (fiscal 2001); $18,173 (fiscal 2000); $45,855 (fiscal 1999). Note: In fiscal 2001, contributions were received from Stearnswood, Inc. ($23,432) and Robert H. Stearns ($250). In fiscal 2000, contributions were received from Stearnswood, Inc. In fiscal 1999, contributions were received from Robert H. Stearns ($250) and Stearnswood, Inc.($45,605).

Typical Recipients
Arts & Humanities: Libraries, Music
Civic & Public Affairs: Community Foundations, Civic & Public Affairs-General, Parades/Festivals, Safety
Education: Colleges & Universities, Economic Education, Education Funds, Elementary Education (Public), Education-General, Public Education (Precollege), Student Aid
Health: Cancer, Health Organizations, Hospices, Hospitals, Long-Term Care, Medical Rehabilitation
Social Services: At-Risk Youth, Community Service Organizations, Crime Prevention, Domestic Violence, Food/Clothing Distribution, Recreation & Athletics, Youth Organizations

Application Procedures
Initial Contact: Submit a written application.
Application Requirements: Specify the purpose of funds sought and the benefit.
Deadlines: None.

Foundation Officials
Mary A. Anderson: vice president
Robert H. Stearns: president
Roger R. Stearns: secretary

Grants Analysis
Disclosure Period: fiscal year ending March 31, 2001
Total Grants: $27,761
Number of Grants: 49
Average Grant: $567
Highest Grant: $6,700
Lowest Grant: $13
Typical Range: $100 to $1,500

Recent Grants
Note: Grants derived from 2001 Form 990.

General

6,700	Hutchinson Youth Hockey Association, Hutchinson, MN -- support arena expansion
4,680	Hutchinson Area Foundation for Health Care, Hutchinson, MN -- support to purchase equipment at hospital and nursing home
2,000	McLeod County Food Shelf, Glencoe, MN -- support for area food shelf
1,500	City of Hutchinson, Hutchinson, MN -- support for fire prevention week activities
1,400	Dollars for Scholars, Hutchinson, MN -- scholarships
1,093	American Cancer Society, Minneapolis, MN -- support for research
1,000	Courage Center, Golden Valley, MN -- support for rehabilitation center
759	Hutchinson Public Schools 423, Hutchinson, MN -- support for school children
750	Hutchinson Jaycee Water Carnival, Hutchinson, MN -- support annual community celebration
520	University of Minnesota, Minneapolis, MN -- support for athletic programs

ARTEMAS W. STEARNS TRUST

Giving Contact
Clifford E. Elias, Trustee
70 East St.
Methuen, MA 01844
Phone: (978)687-0501
Fax: (978)688-7689

Description
Founded: 1896
EIN: 042137061
Organization Type: Private Foundation
Giving Locations: MA: Lawrence including surrounding area
Grant Types: Capital, Emergency, General Support, Project, Scholarship.

Donor Information
Founder: the late Artemas W. Stearns

Financial Summary
Total Giving: $233,363 (2000); $201,265 (1999); $212,585 (1998)
Assets: $5,714,069 (2000); $6,167,456 (1999); $3,317,723 (1998)

Typical Recipients
Arts & Humanities: History & Archaeology, Libraries
Civic & Public Affairs: Chambers of Commerce, Community Foundations, Civic & Public Affairs-General, Hispanic Affairs, Housing, Municipalities/Towns, Women's Affairs
Education: Colleges & Universities, Education-General, Preschool Education, Private Education (Precollege), Public Education (Precollege), Religious Education, Science/Mathematics Education, Secondary Education (Private)
Health: Children's Health/Hospitals, Clinics/Medical Centers, Health Organizations, Home-Care Services, Hospitals, Nursing Services
International: International Affairs
Religion: Churches, Jewish Causes, Religious Welfare
Social Services: Big Brother/Big Sister, Child Welfare, Community Centers, Community Service Organizations, Counseling, Crime Prevention, Family Services, Family Services, Food/Clothing Distribution, People with Disabilities, Recreation & Athletics, Scouts, Senior Services, Shelters/Homelessness, United Funds/United Ways, YMCA/YWCA/YMHA/YWHA, Youth Organizations

Application Procedures

Initial Contact: Request application guidelines.
Deadlines: January 31.

Restrictions

Grants are awarded to non-profit and charitable homes, nursing homes, convalescent homes, retirement homes, sanitaria, homes for the aged, hospitals, and other organizations that provide care for indigent aged people and for the relief of the deserving poor of the city of Lawrence. Grants are not made to individuals.

Additional Information

Publications: Application Guidelines

Foundation Officials

Clifford E. Elias, Esq.: trustee
Eileen M. Khoury: trustee
Rev. Joachim Lally: trustee
Vincent P. Morton, Jr.: trustee
Marsha E. Rich: trustee

Grants Analysis

Disclosure Period: calendar year ending 2000
Total Grants: $233,363
Number of Grants: 28
Average Grant: $8,334
Highest Grant: $30,000
Typical Range: $1,000 to $15,000

Recent Grants

Note: Grants derived from 1999 Form 990.

General

25,000	Holy Family Hospital
25,000	Lawrence General Hospital, Lawrence, MA
17,500	Lawrence Public Schools, Lawrence, MA
15,000	Phillips Academy, Andover, MA
12,000	Bread and Roses
10,000	Lawrence Boys and Girls Club, Lawrence, MA
10,000	Lawrence Youth Center, Lawrence, MA
10,000	Merrimack College, North Andover, CA
7,500	Brooks School, North Andover, MA
7,500	Catholic Charities

BERTHA STEBENS CHARITABLE FOUNDATION

Giving Contact

Bertha Stebens Charitable Foundation
119 Second Street NW
Mason City, IA 50401-3198
Phone: (641)423-1913

Description

Founded: 1987
EIN: 421280907
Organization Type: Private Foundation
Giving Locations: IA: Cerro Gordo County, Mason City
Grant Types: General Support.

Financial Summary

Total Giving: $84,731 (fiscal year ending July 31, 2001)
Assets: $1,808,501 (fiscal 2001)

Typical Recipients

Arts & Humanities: Arts Festivals, Arts Funds, Museums/Galleries, Music, Public Broadcasting, Theater
Civic & Public Affairs: Community Foundations, Municipalities/Towns, Rural Affairs

Education: Preschool Education, Private Education (Precollege), Student Aid
Health: Clinics/Medical Centers, Hospices, Hospitals
Religion: Religious Welfare
Social Services: Community Centers, Emergency Relief, People with Disabilities, Scouts, YMCA/YWCA/YMHA/YWHA

Application Procedures

Initial Contact: Submit a written request.
Application Requirements: Include name, address, and a description of organization; proof of tax-exempt status; tax ID number; current financial statements; list of officers and directors; contact person; amount requested; purpose of funds sought; and date funds are needed.
Deadlines: May 31.

Restrictions

The foundation only funds 501(c)(3) charities located in Cerro Gordo County, IA.

Foundation Officials

Spence Abrams, Sr.: director
Otto C. McDonough: director, mgr
Harold R. Winston, Sr.: director

Grants Analysis

Disclosure Period: fiscal year ending July 31, 2001
Total Grants: $84,731
Number of Grants: 32
Average Grant: $1,927*
Highest Grant: $25,000
Lowest Grant: $500
Typical Range: $500 to $5,000
*Note: Average grant figure excludes highest grant.

Recent Grants

Note: Grants derived from 2001 Form 990.

General

25,000	Mason City Foundation, Mason City, IA -- for construction of music man square
5,000	KCMR Radio, Mason City, IA -- for new copy machine
5,000	Mason City Family YMCA, Mason City, IA -- for construction of new building
4,000	North Iowa Area Community College, Mason City, IA -- for 2 art theater scholarships
3,500	Charles H. MacNider Museum -- for puppet performances/workshops
3,000	Mason City Choral Music Guild, Mason City, IA -- for robes and costumes
3,000	Stevens Children's Theater -- for building improvements
2,500	Good Shepherd Health Center, Inc. -- for Telephone Reassurance Program
2,500	Nora Springs Rock Falls Community School, Nora Springs, IA -- for scholarships
2,000	American Red Cross -- for health and safety information resources and disaster services

STEELCASE INC.

Company Headquarters

Grand Rapids, MI
Web: http://www.steelcase.com

Company Description

Founded: 1912
Ticker: SCS
Exchange: NYSE
Revenue: US$2.586 billion (2002)
Profit: US$1 million (2002)
Employees: 19300 (2002)

Fortune Rank: 485, per FORTUNE Magazine's list of 500 Largest U.S. Corporations (2002).
SIC(s): 2521 Wood Office Furniture, 2522 Office Furniture Except Wood, 2531 Public Building & Related Furniture, 3577 Computer Peripheral Equipment Nec.

Operating Locations

Steelcase Inc. (AL--Athens; CA--Tustin; MI--Grand Rapids, Kentwood; NC--Asheville, Fletcher, High Point)

Nonmonetary Support

Type: Donated Products; In-kind Services
Contact: Howard Sutton, Vice President of Corporate Relations
Note: The company provides nonmonetary support.

Steelcase Foundation

Giving Contact

Susan K. Broman, Executive Director
Steelcase Foundation
PO Box 3636
Grand Rapids, MI 49501-3636
Phone: (616)653-0364
Fax: (616)475-2200
E-mail: sbroman@steelcase.com

Alternate Contact

Phone: (616)246-9860

Description

EIN: 386050470
Organization Type: Corporate Foundation
Giving Locations: principally near operating locations and to national organizations.
Grant Types: Capital, Employee Matching Gifts, Matching, Project, Seed Money.
Note: Employee matching gift ratio: 1 to 1 for gifts to educational institutions.

Financial Summary

Total Giving: $6,697,121 (fiscal year ending November 30, 2001); $7,197,364 (fiscal 2000); $5,195,383 (fiscal 1999). Note: Contributes through corporate direct giving program and foundation.
Giving Analysis: Giving for fiscal 2000 includes: foundation grants to United Way ($903,300); foundation ($6,294,064); fiscal 1999: corporate scholarships ($91,500); corporate matching gifts ($351,847); foundation ($4,752,036); fiscal 1998: foundation scholarships ($64,500); foundation matching gifts ($316,209); foundation grants to United Way ($1,500,000);
Assets: $117,903,929 (fiscal 2001); $123,961,148 (fiscal 2000); $124,477,408 (fiscal 1999)
Gifts Received: $3,919,422 (fiscal 2002 approx); $5,305,200 (fiscal 2001); $5,321,800 (fiscal 2000). Note: Contributions are received from Steelcase, Inc.

Typical Recipients

Arts & Humanities: Arts Associations & Councils, Arts Centers, Arts Institutes, Ballet, Dance, Ethnic & Folk Arts, Historic Preservation, History & Archaeology, Libraries, Literary Arts, Museums/Galleries, Music, Opera, Performing Arts, Public Broadcasting, Theater
Civic & Public Affairs: African American Affairs, Botanical Gardens/Parks, Business/Free Enterprise, Chambers of Commerce, Clubs, Community Foundations, Economic Development, Employment/Job Training, Civic & Public Affairs-General, Hispanic Affairs, Housing, Municipalities/Towns, Native American Affairs, Public Policy, Urban & Community Affairs, Women's Affairs, Zoos/Aquariums
Education: Agricultural Education, Arts/Humanities Education, Business Education, Colleges & Universities, Community & Junior Colleges, Economic Education, Education Funds, Environmental Education, Education-General, Leadership Training, Literacy,

Preschool Education, Private Education (Precollege), Public Education (Precollege), Religious Education, Student Aid

Environment: Protection, Resource Conservation

Health: AIDS/HIV, Arthritis, Children's Health/Hospitals, Clinics/Medical Centers, Emergency/Ambulance Services, Health-General, Geriatric Health, Health Policy/Cost Containment, Health Organizations, Hospices, Medical Rehabilitation, Mental Health, Nutrition, Prenatal Health Issues, Public Health, Single-Disease Health Associations

International: International-General

Religion: Churches, Ministries, Religious Organizations, Religious Welfare

Social Services: Animal Protection, Camps, Child Abuse, Child Welfare, Community Centers, Community Service Organizations, Counseling, Delinquency & Criminal Rehabilitation, Domestic Violence, Emergency Relief, Family Planning, Family Services, Food/Clothing Distribution, Homes, People with Disabilities, Recreation & Athletics, Scouts, Senior Services, Shelters/Homelessness, Substance Abuse, United Funds/United Ways, Volunteer Services, YMCA/YWCA/YMHA/YWHA, Youth Organizations

Application Procedures

Initial Contact: Send letter requesting application.

Application Requirements: Letter should be on organizational letterhead, signed by the chief executive, and include: description of organization and project, copy of IRS 501(c)(3) nonprofit certification. Additional information required with application are: financial statements, including current budget showing expenses and revenues and principal sources and amount requested of ongoing annual support; project budget for which funds are sought, brief narrative description of project, including indication of need; descriptive literature, if available, explaining organization and its services; if program is part of a larger organization, letter of support from management must accompany application; description of how the success of this project will be determined; names, business affiliation and address of board of directors; any other helpful material; include cover letter briefly recapping the proposal; do not submit applications in binders or folders; brief narrative of the history of the organization; and must be signed by CEO or president of the Board.

Deadlines: Contact foundation for the next deadline.

Restrictions

The foundation does not make grants to individuals, organizations that have received a foundation grant in the last 12 months, fraternal organizations, political or lobbying groups, for conferences or seminars, or for dinners or special events.

Donations to religiously-affiliated programs are made only when the objectives benefit the entire community. Programs with substantial religious overtones of a sectarian nature are not considered.

Foundation does not support groups that discriminate against people because of race, sex, disability, or national origin.

Foundation does not support groups that discriminate against people because of race, sex, disability, or national origin.

Additional Information

The foundation and company endeavor to support organizations in which company employees are board members, volunteers, or clients, or where employees are part of the benefiting community.

The foundation prefers to participate with others in providing financial support for a project and occasionally will structure its grants to encourage broad support by others.

Old Kent Bank and Trust Company serves as a corporate trustee for the foundation.

Foundation requires reports from recipients detailing financial accounting of grant expenditures and accomplishments.

Publications: Annual Report

Corporate Officials

James P. Hackett: president, chief executive officer B 1955. ED University of Michigan BA (1977). PRIM CORP EMPL president, chief executive officer: Steelcase Inc. CORP AFFIL president, chief executive officer: Steelcase North American.

David Dyer Hunting, Jr.: director B Grand Rapids, MI 1926. ED University of Michigan (1948). PRIM CORP EMPL director: Steelcase Inc.

Frank Henry Merlotti: director B Herrin, IL 1926. PRIM CORP EMPL director: Steelcase Inc.

Foundation Officials

Susan Broman: executive director

James P. Hackett: trustee (see above)

David Dyer Hunting, Jr.: trustee (see above)

Frank Henry Merlotti: trustee (see above)

Robert C. Pew: trustee

Robert Cunningham Pew, II: trustee B Syracuse, NY 1923. ED Wesleyan University BA. PRIM CORP EMPL chairman emeritus: Steelcase Inc. CORP AFFIL director: Old Kent Financial Corp.; director: Foremost Corp. America. NONPR AFFIL director: Michigan Strategic Fund; director: National Organization Disability; director: Grand Rapids Employers Association; board control: Grand Valley State College; member: Governments Commission Jobs & Economic Development; director: Grand Rapids Chamber of Commerce; director: Economic Development Corp. Grand Rapids; member: Chi Psi. CLUB AFFIL University Club; Lost Tree Club; Peninsular Club; Kent Country Club.

Howard Sutton: trustee B Chicago, IL 1936. ED Michigan State University BA (1958). NONPR AFFIL member: Association National Advertisers; member: Business & Professional Advertisers Association; member: American Advertising Federation; member: American Marketing Association.

Peter M. Wege: trustee B Grand Rapids, MI 1921. ED University of Michigan.

Kate Pew Wolters: trustee

Grants Analysis

Disclosure Period: fiscal year ending November 30, 2001

Total Grants: $6,647,121*

Number of Grants: 343

Average Grant: $19,500

Highest Grant: $862,000

Lowest Grant: $25

Typical Range: $7,300 to $100,000

*Note: Giving excludes United Way.

Recent Grants

Note: Grants derived from fiscal 2001 Form 990.

General

862,000	Heart of Western Michigan United Way, Grand Rapids, MI
500,000	American Red Cross, Grand Rapids, MI
350,000	Catholic Social Services, Grand Rapids, MI
350,000	Davenport College of Business Foundation, Grand Rapids, MI
340,000	Child and Family Resource Council, Grand Rapids, MI
250,000	Grand Action Foundation, Grand Rapids, MI
175,000	Inner-City Christian Federation, Grand Rapids, MI
166,667	Grand Valley State University, Grand Rapids, MI
166,667	Grand Valley State University, Grand Rapids, MI
150,000	Calhoun Community College Foundation, Decatur, AL

HARRY AND GRACE STEELE FOUNDATION

Giving Contact

Marie F. Kowert, Assistant Secretary
441 Old Newport Boulevard, Suite 301
Newport Beach, CA 92663
Phone: (949)631-0418
Fax: (949)631-1255

Description

Founded: 1953

EIN: 956035879

Organization Type: General Purpose Foundation

Giving Locations: CA: Orange County

Grant Types: Capital, Challenge, Endowment, General Support, Multiyear/Continuing Support, Professorship, Project, Scholarship.

Donor Information

Founder: Grace C. Steele

Financial Summary

Total Giving: $1,500,000 (fiscal year ending October 31, 2001); $1,743,648 (fiscal 2000); $8,243,391 (fiscal 1998)

Assets: $20,804,277 (fiscal 2001); $24,059,795 (fiscal 2000); $25,939,367 (fiscal 1998)

Typical Recipients

Arts & Humanities: Arts Centers, Arts Institutes, History & Archaeology, Libraries, Museums/Galleries, Music, Opera, Performing Arts, Public Broadcasting, Theater

Civic & Public Affairs: Community Foundations, Housing, Nonprofit Management, Philanthropic Organizations, Public Policy, Urban & Community Affairs, Women's Affairs, Zoos/Aquariums

Education: Colleges & Universities, Faculty Development, Education-General, Gifted & Talented Programs, Minority Education, Private Education (Precollege), Special Education, Student Aid

Environment: Environment-General, Wildlife Protection

Health: Cancer, Children's Health/Hospitals, Clinics/Medical Centers, Hospitals, Outpatient Health Care

International: Health Care/Hospitals, International Peace & Security Issues

Religion: Churches, Religion-General, Religious Organizations, Religious Welfare

Science: Science Museums

Social Services: Animal Protection, Big Brother/Big Sister, Camps, Child Welfare, Community Service Organizations, Day Care, Domestic Violence, Family Planning, Food/Clothing Distribution, People with Disabilities, Recreation & Athletics, Scouts, Senior Services, Youth Organizations

Application Procedures

Initial Contact: Send a single copy of a concise letter with supporting documentation that is signed by an officer of the organization.

Application Requirements: Include a copy of IRS letter showing section 501(c)(3) status and classification of the organization as "not a private foundation"; current list of officers, directors, or trus; evidence of need for services or facilities to be funded; list of other outstanding potential source for fund raising and administrative costs against amount expended for the purposes intended; and the amount requested from the foundation.

Deadlines: None.

Review Process: The trustees meet several times a year to consider grant requests. Grantees will not be considered for grants more often than once every three or four years. Proposals are initially reviewed by staff to see if they conform to legal requirements and foundation guidelines, and contain all essential information. Based on the information in the application, the trustees may request a visit with the applicant and will on occasion request a personal interview. Applicants should allow approximately six months for decisions on proposals.

Restrictions

The foundation does not make donations to tax-supported organizations or private foundations. No grants are given to individuals or for loans. The foundation requires progress and financial reports from recipients.

Additional Information

Publications: Annual Report Program Policy Statement

Foundation Officials

Nolan H. Baird, Jr.: trustee
Alphonse A. Burnand, III: vice president, treasurer
Audrey Steele Burnand: president
Marie F. Kowert: assistant secretary
Elizabeth R. Steele: secretary

Grants Analysis

Disclosure Period: fiscal year ending October 31, 2001
Total Grants: $1,500,000
Number of Grants: 3
Highest Grant: $940,800
Lowest Grant: $59,200

Recent Grants

Note: Grants derived from 2000 Form 990.

General

979,612	Hoag Hospital Foundation, Newport Beach, CA -- capital campaign
500,000	Orange County Performing Arts Center, Costa Mesa, CA -- for programming
133,648	Orange County Foundation, Irvine, CA
60,000	Fish Harbor Area, Newport Beach, CA
50,000	St. Paul's Lutheran Church and School, Garden Grove, CA -- for tuition assistance
20,388	Hoag Hospital Foundation, Newport Beach, CA -- capital campaign

STEELE-REESE FOUNDATION

Giving Contact

William T. Buice, III, Co-Trustee
32 Washington Square West
New York, NY 10011
Phone: (212)557-7700
Fax: (212)286-8513
Web: http://www.davidsondawson.com
Note: Contact for general inquiries.

Alternate Contact

Charles U. Buice
1 Main St., Apt. 6F
Brooklyn, NY 11201
Note: Contact for Idaho and Montana.

Description

Founded: 1955
EIN: 136034763
Organization Type: General Purpose Foundation
Giving Locations: GA: Northern Georgia; ID; KY: Appalachian region of the state; MT; NC: Appalachian region of the state; TN: Appalachian region of the state; WA
Grant Types: Endowment, General Support, Scholarship.

Donor Information

Founder: Established in 1955 by Eleanor Steele Reese , whose father Charles Steele was a partner of J.P. Morgan. Eleanor Steele was born in New York City in 1893. After pursuing a career as an opera singer and recitalist in Europe and the United States for two decades, she moved to the western United States. She met and married Emmet P. Reese in 1941. At the time of their marriage, he and Eleanor bought and operated a small working ranch near Shoup, ID. In the mid-1950s, they moved to a large ranch in Salmon, ID, which they operated until a few years before her death in 1977. Emmet P. Reese died in 1982. The original trustees of the foundation were Sidney W. Davidson and J.P. Morgan & Co., Inc. Davidson and J.P. Morgan & Co., Inc.

Financial Summary

Total Giving: $2,469,000 (fiscal year ending August 31, 2001); $2,326,200 (fiscal 2000); $2,019,500 (fiscal 1999)
Giving Analysis: Giving for fiscal 1999 includes: foundation grants to United Way ($20,000)
Assets: $44,990,348 (fiscal 2001); $53,998,613 (fiscal 2000); $48,407,866 (fiscal 1999)

Typical Recipients

Arts & Humanities: Arts Associations & Councils, Arts Outreach, Community Arts, Ethnic & Folk Arts, Arts & Humanities-General, Historic Preservation, History & Archaeology, Libraries, Literary Arts, Museums/Galleries, Opera, Public Broadcasting, Theater
Civic & Public Affairs: Civil Rights, Clubs, Community Foundations, Economic Development, Employment/Job Training, Civic & Public Affairs-General, Housing, Legal Aid, Municipalities/Towns, Philanthropic Organizations, Public Policy, Rural Affairs, Safety, Urban & Community Affairs, Women's Affairs
Education: Arts/Humanities Education, Colleges & Universities, Community & Junior Colleges, Continuing Education, Education Associations, Education Reform, Education Reform, Elementary Education (Private), Education-General, Literacy, Private Education (Precollege), Public Education (Precollege), Science/Mathematics Education, Special Education, Student Aid
Environment: Environment-General, Resource Conservation, Wildlife Protection
Health: AIDS/HIV, Alzheimers Disease, Clinics/Medical Centers, Emergency/Ambulance Services, Health-General, Heart, Hospices, Hospitals, Long-Term Care, Medical Rehabilitation, Nursing Services, Public Health, Single-Disease Health Associations, Transplant Networks/Donor Banks
International: International Peace & Security Issues, Missionary/Religious Activities
Religion: Churches, Religious Welfare
Science: Science Museums, Scientific Centers & Institutes
Social Services: Animal Protection, Child Abuse, Child Welfare, Community Centers, Community Service Organizations, Counseling, Crime Prevention, Delinquency & Criminal Rehabilitation, Domestic Violence, Family Planning, Family Services, Food/Clothing Distribution, Homes, People with Disabilities, Senior Services, Shelters/Homelessness, Social Services-General, Substance Abuse, United Funds/United Ways, Volunteer Services, Youth Organizations

Application Procedures

Initial Contact: Applicants should review the foundation's policy and criteria, available upon request, in detail. If a proposal seems warranted, applicants should write a succinct factual letter of no more than a page in length. Any brief printed material that is pertinent to an application should also be included. High school seniors in Lemhi and Custer Counties, ID, may apply for undergraduate scholarships through their schools. Personal and telephone inquiries are discouraged.

Application Requirements: A copy of IRS letter of determination with application.
Deadlines: March 1.
Review Process: Decisions on grants are made once a year in June and are paid in August or September.

Restrictions

The foundation prefers not to fund emergencies; community chests or similar drives; conferences and workshops; efforts to influence school boards and other elections; planning, research, experimental or untested projects; endowments for small organizations; recreational facilities; athletic or academic competitions or related travel; computers or other technology for schools; religious or political organizations. The foundation will not make grants to individuals or to non tax-exempt organizations.

Additional Information

Morgan Guaranty Trust Company of New York serves as the corporate trustee for the foundation.
Publications: Annual Report (includes Detailed Grant Applicaiton Information)

Foundation Officials

William T. Buice, III: co-trustee ED Duke University (1964). NONPR AFFIL chairman: Asheville School.

Grants Analysis

Disclosure Period: fiscal year ending August 31, 2001
Total Grants: $2,469,000
Number of Grants: 91
Average Grant: $27,132
Highest Grant: $80,000
Typical Range: $10,000 to $50,000

Recent Grants

Note: Grants derived from 2001 Form 990.

Library-Related

28,000	Eastern Idaho Library Network Consortium, Soda Springs, ID

General

80,000	Metropolitan Opera, New York, NY
65,000	Ashton Memorial, Inc., Ashton, ID
55,000	Mountain Association for Community Economic Development, Berea, KY
50,000	Appalachia Service Project, Johnson City, TN
50,000	Appalshop, Inc., Whitesburg, KY
50,000	Community Foundation of Western North Carolina, Inc., Asheville, NC
50,000	Eagle Rock Art Guild, Idaho Falls, ID
50,000	Homemaker Services of Idaho, Inc., Idaho Falls, ID
50,000	Interfaith of Bell County, Inc., Pineville, KY
50,000	Intermountain Planned Parenthood, Billings, MT

ALBERT STEIGER MEMORIAL FUND

Giving Contact

Albert E. Steiger, Jr., President
PO Box 392
Springfield, MA 01102-0392
Phone: (413)732-8875

Description

Founded: 1953
EIN: 046051750
Organization Type: Private Foundation
Giving Locations: MA: Hampden County
Grant Types: Capital, Project.

Donor Information
Founder: Ralph A. Steiger, Chauncey A. Steiger, Albert Steiger, Inc.

Financial Summary
Total Giving: $162,000 (2001); $308,000 (2000); $340,715 (1999)
Assets: $1,088,759 (2001); $1,265,620 (2000); $1,549,519 (1999)

Typical Recipients
Arts & Humanities: Arts Associations & Councils, Arts Funds, History & Archaeology, Libraries, Museums/Galleries, Music, Performing Arts, Public Broadcasting, Theater
Civic & Public Affairs: Botanical Gardens/Parks, Business/Free Enterprise, Community Foundations, Civic & Public Affairs-General
Education: Arts/Humanities Education, Colleges & Universities, Education Funds, Public Education (Precollege), School Volunteerism, Student Aid
Health: Health Organizations, Hospitals, Nursing Services, Prenatal Health Issues
International: Foreign Arts Organizations
Social Services: Community Centers, Community Service Organizations, Homes, Scouts, Social Services-General, United Funds/United Ways, YMCA/YWCA/YMHA/YWHA, Youth Organizations

Application Procedures
Initial Contact: Send brief letter describing program.
Deadlines: None.

Restrictions
Does not support individuals. Limited to charitable purposes in or around Hampden County, MA.

Foundation Officials
Richard Sherman Milstein: clerk B Westfield, MA 1926. ED Harvard University BA (1948); Boston University JD (1952). PRIM CORP EMPL partner: Ely & King. CORP AFFIL consulting director: Massachusetts Continuing Legal Education. NONPR AFFIL vice chairman: Westfield Academy; life member, trustee: WGBY Public Television Springfield; trustee: Visting Nurses Western MA; member: Springfield Library Museum Association; trustee, general council: Springfield Symphony Orchestra; life fellow: Massachusetts Bar Foundation; trustee: Applewood at Amherst; trustee: Baystate Hospital; member: American Law Institute; life member: American Bar Foundation; fellow: American College Trust & Estate Counsel.
Albert E. Steiger, III: director
Albert E. Steiger, Jr.: president
Allen Steiger: treasurer
Philip C. Steiger, Jr.: director
Ralph A. Steiger, II: vice president, director

Grants Analysis
Disclosure Period: calendar year ending 2001
Total Grants: $162,000
Number of Grants: 7
Average Grant: $8,857*
Highest Grant: $100,000
Lowest Grant: $4,000
Typical Range: $4,000 to $24,000 and $10,000 to $30,000
*Note: Average grant figure excludes highest grant.

Recent Grants
Note: Grants derived from 2001 Form 990.

Library-Related
4,000	Springfield Libraries and Museums, Springfield, MA

General
100,000	Community Foundation of Western Massachusetts, Springfield, MA
24,000	WGBY 57
15,000	Community Music School of Springfield, Springfield, MA
10,000	Greater Springfield YMCA, Springfield, MA
5,000	Loomis House
4,000	Springfield Symphony Orchestra, Springfield, MA

BERT L. AND PATRICIA S. STEIGLEDER CHARITABLE TRUST

Giving Contact
Henry J. Loos, Trustee
c/o Quarles & Brady
411 E. Wisconsin Ave., Suite 2040
Milwaukee, WI 53202-4497
Phone: (414)765-5047

Description
Founded: 1992
EIN: 396541246
Organization Type: Private Foundation
Giving Locations: WI: Milwaukee
Grant Types: General Support.

Donor Information
Founder: the late Bert S. Steigleder

Financial Summary
Total Giving: $582,166 (fiscal year ending June 30, 2001); $552,812 (fiscal 2000); $456,466 (fiscal 1997)
Giving Analysis: Giving for fiscal 2001 includes: foundation grants to United Way ($10,000)
Assets: $11,044,879 (fiscal 2001); $11,725,847 (fiscal 2000); $11,051,306 (fiscal 1997)
Gifts Received: $131,273 (fiscal 1995); $2,109,900 (fiscal 1994). Note: In fiscal 1995, contributions were received from the estate of Bert S. Steigleder.

Typical Recipients
Arts & Humanities: Arts Institutes, Ballet, Historic Preservation, Libraries, Museums/Galleries, Music, Opera, Performing Arts, Theater
Civic & Public Affairs: Employment/Job Training, Civic & Public Affairs-General, Public Policy
Education: Business Education, Colleges & Universities, Health & Physical Education, Legal Education, Medical Education, Private Education (Precollege), Public Education (Precollege)
Environment: Environment-General, Resource Conservation
Health: Cancer, Children's Health/Hospitals, Clinics/Medical Centers, Mental Health, Transplant Networks/Donor Banks
Religion: Religious Organizations, Religious Welfare
Social Services: Community Service Organizations, Domestic Violence, Family Planning, Senior Services, YMCA/YWCA/YMHA/YWHA, Youth Organizations, Youth Organizations

Application Procedures
Initial Contact: Send a brief letter of inquiry.
Application Requirements: proof of tax-exempt status.
Deadlines: None.

Restrictions
Grants are generally made to organizations that are cultural, artistic, educational, or health care related.

Additional Information
Trust(s): Firstar Bank

Foundation Officials
Henry J. Loos: trustee B 1940. ED Colgate University BA (1962); Harvard University LLB (1965). PRIM CORP EMPL secretary: Charter Manufacturing Co. CORP AFFIL director: Wisconsin Paper Products Co.; director: Young Radiator Co.; secretary: Olsten Milwaukee Inc. NONPR AFFIL member: Milwaukee Bar Association; member: Wisconsin Bar Association; member: American Bar Association; member: Florida Bar Association.

Grants Analysis
Disclosure Period: fiscal year ending June 30, 2001
Total Grants: $572,166*
Number of Grants: 31
Average Grant: $18,457
Highest Grant: $50,000
Typical Range: $5,000 to $30,000
*Note: Giving excludes United Way.

Recent Grants
Note: Grants derived from fiscal 2000 Form 990.

General
60,000	Milwaukee Art Museum, Milwaukee, WI
33,000	Medical College of Wisconsin, Milwaukee, WI
33,000	Wisconsin Breast Cancer Golf Event, Milwaukee, WI
30,000	Milwaukee Ballet Company, Milwaukee, WI
25,000	Blood Center Research Foundation, Milwaukee, WI
25,000	Boys & Girls Club of Greater Milwaukee, Milwaukee, WI
25,000	Children's Health System, Great Barrington, MA
25,000	Friends of Schlitz Audubon Center, Milwaukee, WI
25,000	Our Next Generation Inc., Milwaukee, WI
25,000	YWCA of Greater Milwaukee, Milwaukee, WI

B. A. AND ELINOR W. STEINHAGEN BENEVOLENT TRUST

Giving Contact
Hibernia National Bank
PO Box 3928
Beaumont, TX 77704
Phone: (409)838-0234
E-mail: imoncla@hibernia.com

Description
Founded: 1939
EIN: 746039544
Organization Type: Private Foundation
Giving Locations: TX: Jefferson County
Grant Types: Capital, Endowment, General Support, Project, Research, Seed Money.

Donor Information
Founder: the late B. A. Steinhagen, the late Elinor W. Steinhagen

Financial Summary
Total Giving: $354,184 (fiscal year ending August 31, 2001); $626,301 (fiscal 2000); $412,514 (fiscal 1999). Note: Fiscal 1997 Giving includes United Way ($15,000).
Giving Analysis: Giving for fiscal 2001 includes: foundation grants to United Way ($30,000); fiscal 2000: foundation grants to United Way ($30,000); fiscal 1998: foundation grants to United Way ($20,000) foundation ($339,748)
Assets: $6,685,697 (fiscal 2001); $7,533,998 (fiscal 2000); $6,426,404 (fiscal 1998)

Typical Recipients

Arts & Humanities: Arts Associations & Councils, Arts Centers, Community Arts, Historic Preservation, History & Archaeology, Libraries, Museums/Galleries, Public Broadcasting, Theater

Civic & Public Affairs: Botanical Gardens/Parks, Community Foundations, Civic & Public Affairs-General, Hispanic Affairs, Housing, Legal Aid, Minority Business, Urban & Community Affairs

Education: Business Education, Education Reform, Elementary Education (Private), Elementary Education (Public), Education-General, Preschool Education, Private Education (Precollege), Public Education (Precollege), Science/Mathematics Education

Environment: Wildlife Protection

Health: Cancer, Clinics/Medical Centers, Geriatric Health, Health Organizations, Medical Rehabilitation, Medical Research, Mental Health, Nutrition, Single-Disease Health Associations

Religion: Churches, Ministries, Religious Welfare

Science: Science Museums

Social Services: At-Risk Youth, Child Welfare, Community Service Organizations, Day Care, Family Services, Food/Clothing Distribution, People with Disabilities, Senior Services, Sexual Abuse, Shelters/Homelessness, Social Services-General, Substance Abuse, United Funds/United Ways, YMCA/YWCA/YMHA/YWHA, Youth Organizations

Application Procedures

Initial Contact: Application form required.
Deadlines: May 31.

Restrictions

Foundation does not fund individuals, religious organizations for sectarian purposes, political or lobbying groups, or organizations outside operating areas.

Additional Information

Publications: Application Guidelines
Trust(s): Hibernia National Bank TX

Grants Analysis

Disclosure Period: fiscal year ending August 31, 2001
Total Grants: $324,184*
Number of Grants: 24
Average Grant: $13,508
Highest Grant: $35,000
Typical Range: $5,000 to $25,000
*Note: Giving excludes United Way.

Recent Grants

Note: Grants derived from 2000 Form 990.

General

66,668	Goodwill Industries of Southeast Texas, Beaumont, TX -- third and final payment of pledge for Park Street property acquisition
66,668	Jefferson Theatre Restoration, Beaumont, TX -- third and final payment of pledge for theatre restoration
50,000	Friends of Spindletop, Beaumont, TX -- service for products of Centennial Celebration and administrative costs
35,000	CASA of Southeast Texas, Inc, Beaumont, TX -- facility renovations
35,000	Salvation Army, Beaumont, TX -- emergency homeless shelter
31,500	CASA of Southeast Texas, Inc, Beaumont, TX -- professional fees for attorneys and mediators
30,000	Southeast Texas Arts Council, Beaumont, TX -- funding of subgrant program to local non-profit organizations
30,000	United Way of Beaumont, Beaumont, TX -- funding to supplement agency allocations
26,000	UBI Caritas Community Clinic and Health Center, Beaumont, TX -- funding

25,040	for additional staff person and software and hardware for billing purposes Buckner Children's Village, Beaumont, TX -- funding for van

JAMES HALE STEINMAN FOUNDATION

Giving Contact

M. Steven Weaver, Secretary Scholarship Committee
8 W. King St.
PO Box 128
Lancaster, PA 17608-0128
Phone: (717)291-8607

Description

Founded: 1952
EIN: 236266377
Organization Type: Private Foundation
Giving Locations: PA: Lancaster
Grant Types: Capital, General Support, Scholarship.

Donor Information

Founder: the late James Hale Steinman, the late Louise Steinman von Hess, Lancaster Newspapers, Inc.

Financial Summary

Total Giving: $1,455,374 (2001); $1,203,230 (2000); $1,001,440 (1999)
Giving Analysis: Giving for 2001 includes: foundation grants to United Way ($60,000); foundation scholarships ($60,000); 2000: foundation scholarships ($48,000); foundation grants to United Way ($57,500); 1999: foundation scholarships ($37,500); foundation grants to United Way ($55,000);
Assets: $27,083,446 (2001); $28,780,800 (2000); $27,213,262 (1999)
Gifts Received: $1,000,000 (2001); $1,000,000 (2000); $1,000,000 (1999). Note: In 1999 and 2000, contributions were received from Lancaster Newspapers ($680,000), Intelligencer Printing Co. ($320,000). In 1998, contributions were received from Lancaster Newspapers, Inc. ($480,000) and Intelligence Printing Co. ($320,000). In 1996, contributions were received from Lancaster Newspapers ($360,000), Intelligencer Printing Co. ($320,000), and Delmarva Broadcasting Co. ($120,000).

Typical Recipients

Arts & Humanities: Arts Associations & Councils, Arts Festivals, Community Arts, Arts & Humanities-General, Historic Preservation, History & Archaeology, Libraries, Museums/Galleries, Music, Opera, Theater

Civic & Public Affairs: Botanical Gardens/Parks, Economic Development, Ethnic Organizations, Civic & Public Affairs-General, Municipalities/Towns, Parades/Festivals, Philanthropic Organizations, Public Policy, Urban & Community Affairs

Education: Afterschool/Enrichment Programs, Arts/Humanities Education, Business Education, Colleges & Universities, Education Associations, Education-General, Private Education (Precollege), Secondary Education (Private), Student Aid

Environment: Resource Conservation

Health: Cancer, Clinics/Medical Centers, Emergency/Ambulance Services, Eyes/Blindness, Heart, Hospices, Hospitals, Medical Research, Multiple Sclerosis, Single-Disease Health Associations

Religion: Churches, Religious Organizations, Religious Welfare, Seminaries

Social Services: Community Service Organizations, Family Planning, People with Disabilities, Recreation & Athletics, Scouts, Social Services-General, United Funds/United Ways, YMCA/YWCA/YMHA/YWHA, Youth Organizations

Application Procedures

Initial Contact: Scholarship application form available for employees' children. Others seeking grants should send a letter of inquiry describing their organization.
Deadlines: February 28 for scholarships.

Additional Information

Scholarships are awarded to newspaper carriers and children of employees.
Publications: Application Form

Foundation Officials

Dennis A. Getz: secretary PRIM CORP EMPL vice president, controller: Lancaster Newspapers.

Caroline S. Nunan: chairman CORP AFFIL director: Intelligencer Printing Co.; director: Lancaster Newspapers Inc.

Willis Weidman Shenk: treasurer B Manheim, PA 1915. PRIM CORP EMPL chairman, director: Lancaster Newspapers Inc. CORP AFFIL chairman, director: Intelligencer Printing Co.; chairman: Steinman Coal Corp.; chairman: Commonwealth Mailing Service; chairman: Delmarva Broadcasting Co. Inc. NONPR AFFIL member: National Association Accts; member: Pennsylvania Institute CPA's. CLUB AFFIL Lancaster Country Club.

Beverly R. Steinman: vchairman CORP AFFIL director: Intelligencer Printing Co.; director: Lancaster Newspapers Inc.

Grants Analysis

Disclosure Period: calendar year ending 2001
Total Grants: $1,335,374*
Number of Grants: 89
Average Grant: $10,783*
Highest Grant: $408,016
Typical Range: $1,000 to $20,000
*Note: Giving excludes United Way; scholarships. Average grant figure excludes highest grant.

Recent Grants

Note: Grants derived from 2001 Form 990.

General

408,016	Conestoga House Foundation, Conestoga, PA
75,000	Boys & Girls Club of Lancaster, Inc., Lancaster, PA
75,000	Marion DuPont Scott Equine Medical Center
75,000	Pennsylvania Academy of Music, Lancaster, PA
62,107	Conestoga House Foundation, Conestoga, PA
60,000	James Hale Stein Foundation Scholarships, Lancaster, PA
60,000	United Way of Lancaster County, Lancaster, PA
50,000	Boys & Girls Club of Lancaster, Inc., Lancaster, PA
50,000	Lancaster General Hospital, Lancaster, PA
50,000	Lititz Moravian Church

JOHN FREDERICK STEINMAN FOUNDATION

Giving Contact

M. Steven Weaner, Secretary, Fellowship Program
8 W. King St.
Lancaster, PA 17608-0128
Phone: (717)291-8607

Description

Founded: 1952
EIN: 236266378
Organization Type: Private Foundation

Giving Locations: PA: emphasis on the Lancaster area
Grant Types: Capital, Fellowship, General Support.

Donor Information
Founder: the late John Frederick Steinman, the late Shirley W. Steinman, Lancaster Newspapers

Financial Summary
Total Giving: $1,514,250 (2001); $1,429,549 (2000); $1,229,054 (1999)
Giving Analysis: Giving for 2001 includes: foundation scholarships ($58,000); foundation grants to United Way ($60,000); 2000: foundation fellowships ($58,299); 1999: foundation scholarships ($1,000) foundation fellowships ($62,004)
Assets: $27,856,450 (2001); $30,949,523 (2000); $29,974,679 (1999)
Gifts Received: $160,000 (1992)

Typical Recipients
Arts & Humanities: Arts Appreciation, Arts Associations & Councils, Arts Festivals, Community Arts, Arts & Humanities-General, Historic Preservation, History & Archaeology, Libraries, Literary Arts, Museums/Galleries, Music, Opera, Theater
Civic & Public Affairs: African American Affairs, Botanical Gardens/Parks, Community Foundations, Economic Development, Employment/Job Training, Ethnic Organizations, Civic & Public Affairs-General, Housing, Legal Aid, Municipalities/Towns, Parades/Festivals, Public Policy, Urban & Community Affairs
Education: Arts/Humanities Education, Business Education, Colleges & Universities, Community & Junior Colleges, Education-General, Literacy, Private Education (Precollege), Religious Education, Secondary Education (Private), Vocational & Technical Education
Environment: Air/Water Quality, Resource Conservation
Health: Cancer, Children's Health/Hospitals, Clinics/Medical Centers, Emergency/Ambulance Services, Eyes/Blindness, Health-General, Heart, Hospices, Hospitals, Medical Research, Mental Health, Nursing Services, Public Health, Single-Disease Health Associations
Religion: Churches, Religion-General, Religious Organizations, Religious Welfare, Seminaries
Social Services: At-Risk Youth, Community Service Organizations, Day Care, Family Planning, Family Services, People with Disabilities, Recreation & Athletics, Scouts, Sexual Abuse, Shelters/Homelessness, Substance Abuse, United Funds/United Ways, YMCA/YWCA/YMHA/YWHA, Youth Organizations

Application Procedures
Initial Contact: Application for fellowship program available upon request. For other grants, send a letter of inquiry.
Deadlines: February 1.

Restrictions
Fellowships restricted to graduate programs in mental health.

Additional Information
Provides fellowships for graduate study in mental health.
Publications: Application Form

Foundation Officials
Dennis A. Getz: secretary PRIM CORP EMPL vice president, controller: Lancaster Newspapers.
Henry Pildner, Jr.: trustee CORP AFFIL director: Intelligencer Printing Co.
Willis Weidman Shenk: treasurer B Manheim, PA 1915. PRIM CORP EMPL chairman, director: Lancaster Newspapers Inc. CORP AFFIL chairman, director: Intelligencer Printing Co.; chairman: Steinman Coal Corp.; chairman: Commonwealth Mailing Service;

chairman: Delmarva Broadcasting Co. Inc. NONPR AFFIL member: National Association Accts; member: Pennsylvania Institute CPA's. CLUB AFFIL Lancaster Country Club.
Pamela M. Thye: chairman CORP AFFIL director: Intelligencer Printing Co.

Grants Analysis
Disclosure Period: calendar year ending 2001
Total Grants: $1,396,250*
Number of Grants: 132
Average Grant: $8,885*
Highest Grant: $125,000
Typical Range: $1,000 to $25,000
*Note: Giving excludes fellowships and United Way. Average grant figure excludes two highest grants.

Recent Grants
Note: Grants derived from 2001 Form 990.

General

125,000	Boys Club and Girls Club of Lancaster, Inc., Lancaster, PA
125,000	Linden Hall School for Girls, Lititz, PA
125,000	Pennsylvania Academy of Music, Lancaster, PA
100,000	Elizabethtown College, Elizabethtown, PA
100,000	Lancaster General Hospital, Lancaster, PA
60,000	United Way of Lancaster County, Lancaster, PA
58,000	JFSF Fellowships
50,000	Arbor Place, Lancaster, PA
50,000	Harrisburg Area Community College, Harrisburg, PA
50,000	Lititz Moravian Church

STEMMONS FOUNDATION

Giving Contact
Ann C. Carlisle, Secretary, Treasurer & Manager
PO Box 143127
Irving, TX 75014-3127
Phone: (972)650-9162

Description
Founded: 1963
EIN: 756039966
Organization Type: Private Foundation
Giving Locations: TX: Dallas
Grant Types: General Support, Scholarship.

Financial Summary
Total Giving: $308,500 (2000); $271,445 (1999); $293,350 (1998)
Giving Analysis: Giving for 2000 includes: foundation grants to United Way ($25,000)
Assets: $5,173,092 (2000); $4,294,888 (1999); $4,318,071 (1998)

Typical Recipients
Arts & Humanities: Arts Outreach, Community Arts, Dance, Arts & Humanities-General, Historic Preservation, Libraries, Music, Opera, Public Broadcasting, Theater
Civic & Public Affairs: Botanical Gardens/Parks, Employment/Job Training, Civic & Public Affairs-General, Public Policy, Urban & Community Affairs, Women's Affairs, Zoos/Aquariums
Education: Arts/Humanities Education, Colleges & Universities, Education Funds, Elementary Education (Public), Education-General, Medical Education, Minority Education, Private Education (Precollege), Public Education (Precollege), Religious Education
Environment: Wildlife Protection
Health: AIDS/HIV, Alzheimers Disease, Children's Health/Hospitals, Emergency/Ambulance Services, Health Organizations, Hospitals, Kidney, Long-Term

Care, Medical Research, Mental Health, Nursing Services, Prenatal Health Issues, Public Health, Single-Disease Health Associations, Speech & Hearing
International: Human Rights, International Environmental Issues
Religion: Churches, Religion-General, Ministries, Religious Welfare
Social Services: Animal Protection, Child Welfare, Community Centers, Community Service Organizations, Family Planning, Family Services, Food/Clothing Distribution, Homes, People with Disabilities, Scouts, Social Services-General, YMCA/YWCA/YMHA/YWHA, Youth Organizations

Application Procedures
Initial Contact: Send a brief letter of inquiry describing program or project.
Application Requirements: Include a description of organization and purpose of funds sought.
Deadlines: None.

Foundation Officials
Ann C. Carlisle: secretary, treasurer, manager
Allison S. Simon: president
Heinz K. Simon: vice president
Jean H. Stemmons: vice president
John M. Stemmons, Sr.: vice president
Ruth T. Stemmons: vice president

Grants Analysis
Disclosure Period: calendar year ending 2000
Total Grants: $283,500*
Number of Grants: 44
Average Grant: $6,443
Highest Grant: $20,000
Typical Range: $1,000 to $10,000
*Note: Giving excludes United Way.

Recent Grants
Note: Grants derived from 1999 Form 990.

General

20,000	Saint Michael Outreach Program, Dallas, TX
20,000	Southwest Medical Foundation, Dallas, TX
10,000	American Red Cross Dallas Area Chapter, Dallas, TX
10,000	Dallas Arboretum & Botanical Society, Dallas, TX
10,000	Dallas Opera, The, Dallas, TX
10,000	Dallas Symphony Orchestra, Dallas, TX
10,000	Goodwill Industries of Dallas, Inc., Dallas, TX
10,000	Presbyterian Health Care Foundation, Boston, MA
10,000	SPCA of Texas, Dallas, TX
10,000	Turtle Creek Manor, Dallas, TX

STERLING-TURNER FOUNDATION

Giving Contact
Eyvonne Moser, Executive Director
815 Walker Street, Suite 1543
Houston, TX 77002-5724
Phone: (713)237-1117
Fax: (713)223-4638
E-mail: eyvonne@wt.net
Web: http://www.sterlingturnerfoundation.org

Description
Founded: 1956
EIN: 741460482
Organization Type: General Purpose Foundation
Former Name: Turner Charitable Foundation (1998).
Giving Locations: TX
Grant Types: Capital, Challenge, Department, Emergency, Endowment, Fellowship, General Support,

Matching, Operating Expenses, Project, Research, Scholarship, Seed Money.

Donor Information

Founder: Incorporated in 1956 by the late Isla Carroll Turner and the late P. E. Turner .

Financial Summary

Total Giving: $2,954,250 (2000); $2,416,188 (1999); $1,993,000 (1998)
Assets: $54,868,277 (2000); $56,000,000 (1999); $51,962,920 (1998)

Typical Recipients

Arts & Humanities: Arts Associations & Councils, Ballet, Dance, Arts & Humanities-General, Historic Preservation, Libraries, Museums/Galleries, Music, Opera, Performing Arts, Public Broadcasting, Theater
Civic & Public Affairs: Botanical Gardens/Parks, Clubs, Economic Development, Civic & Public Affairs-General, Hispanic Affairs, Philanthropic Organizations, Urban & Community Affairs, Women's Affairs, Zoos/Aquariums
Education: Agricultural Education, Arts/Humanities Education, Colleges & Universities, Elementary Education (Public), Environmental Education, Faculty Development, Education-General, Literacy, Medical Education, Preschool Education, Private Education (Precollege), Public Education (Precollege), Science/Mathematics Education, Secondary Education (Private), Social Sciences Education, Special Education, Student Aid
Environment: Environment-General, Resource Conservation
Health: AIDS/HIV, Cancer, Children's Health/Hospitals, Clinics/Medical Centers, Emergency/Ambulance Services, Eyes/Blindness, Health Organizations, Heart, Hospices, Hospitals, Medical Research, Mental Health, Research/Studies Institutes, Single-Disease Health Associations, Speech & Hearing
International: Missionary/Religious Activities
Religion: Churches, Religion-General, Religious Organizations, Religious Welfare, Social/Policy Issues
Science: Science Museums, Scientific Centers & Institutes
Social Services: At-Risk Youth, Child Welfare, Community Centers, Community Service Organizations, Day Care, Family Planning, Family Services, Food/Clothing Distribution, Homes, People with Disabilities, Recreation & Athletics, Shelters/Homelessness, Social Services-General, Substance Abuse, Volunteer Services, YMCA/YWCA/YMHA/YWHA, Youth Organizations

Application Procedures

Initial Contact: The foundation requests applications be made in writing.
Application Requirements: The application must include a copy of IRS code section 501(c)(3) exemption letter.
Deadlines: March 1 by 5:00pm.
Review Process: The board meets on the first Tuesday in April.

Restrictions

The foundation makes grants only to exempt charities in the state of Texas. Grants are not made to individuals.

Additional Information

Publications: Guidelines; Application Form

Foundation Officials

Thomas Eugene Berry: assistant secretary, trustee B San Antonio, TX 1923. ED Southwestern University BBA (1944); University of Texas BBA (1949); University of Texas LLB (1951). OCCUPATION attorney. CORP AFFIL vice president: Goodrich Operating Co. Inc. NONPR AFFIL trustee: Turner Charitable Foundation; trustee: Isla Carroll Turner Friendship Trust; member: Texas Academy Probate & Trust Lawyers;

member: State Bar Texas; board director: Student Aid Foundation; member: NG Association Texas; member: Phi Delta Phi; trustee: Hope Center Youth & Family Services; member: Houston Bar Association; trustee: R.H. and E.F. Goodrich Foundation; trustee, board director: Hermann Eye Fund; member: Delta Kappa Epsilon; trustee: MB Flake Home Old Ladies; fellow: American College Tax Counsel; fellow: American College Trust & Estate Counsel; member: American Bar Association.
Blake W. Caldwell: assistant secretary, trustee
Carroll R. Goodman: assistant secretary, trustee
Chaille W. Hawkins: assistant secretary, trustee
Christiana R. McConn: secretary, trustee
Eyvonne Moser: executive director
Isla C. Reckling: treasurer, trustee
James S. Reckling: assistant secretary, trustee
John P. Reckling: assistant secretary, trustee
Stephen M. Reckling: assistant secretary, trustee
T. R. Reckling, III: president, trustee
Thomas R. Reckling, IV: assistant secretary, trustee B 1961. OCCUPATION Texas Capital Securities Inc.
Bert F. Winston, Jr.: vice president, trustee
L. David Winston: assistant secretary, trustee

Grants Analysis

Disclosure Period: calendar year ending 2000
Total Grants: $2,954,250*
Number of Grants: 137
Average Grant: $21,564
Highest Grant: $100,000
Lowest Grant: $500
Typical Range: $5,000 to $25,000
*Note: Grants analysis provided by foundation.

Recent Grants

Note: Grants derived from 2000 Form 990.

General

100,000	Arbor Preschool, Houston, TX -- building fund
100,000	Brookwood Community, Brookshire, TX -- endowment fund
100,000	Christus St. Joseph Hospital Foundation, Houston, TX -- refurbish emergency room
100,000	Episcopal High School, Bellaire, TX -- capital building campaign
100,000	Kinkaid School, Houston, TX -- capital campaign
100,000	Playhouse 2000, Inc., Kerrville, TX -- building fund
100,000	St. Thomas High School, Houston, TX -- capital campaign
55,000	Hope Center for Children, Houston, TX -- purchase new vans
50,000	Briargrove Elementary School PTO, Houston, TX -- new computers
50,000	Brookwood Community, Brookshire, TX -- endowment fund

ABBOT AND DOROTHY H. STEVENS FOUNDATION

Giving Contact

Elizabeth A. Beland, Administrator
PO Box 111
North Andover, MA 01845
Phone: (978)688-7211
Fax: (978)686-1620

Description

Founded: 1953
EIN: 046107991
Organization Type: General Purpose Foundation
Giving Locations: MA: preference given to Merrimack Valley Area and greater Lawrence Area
Grant Types: Capital, Emergency, Endowment, General Support, Matching.

Donor Information

Founder: Established in 1953 by the late Abbot Stevens .

Financial Summary

Total Giving: $1,150,950 (2001); $1,247,460 (2000); $1,085,059 (1999)
Giving Analysis: Giving for 1999 includes: foundation grants to United Way ($22,500)
Assets: $23,997,510 (2001); $24,432,872 (2000); $24,236,002 (1999)

Typical Recipients

Arts & Humanities: Arts Centers, Arts Outreach, Ballet, Dance, Ethnic & Folk Arts, Film & Video, Historic Preservation, History & Archaeology, Libraries, Museums/Galleries, Music, Opera, Performing Arts, Public Broadcasting, Theater
Civic & Public Affairs: Community Foundations, Civic & Public Affairs-General, Hispanic Affairs, Housing, Municipalities/Towns, Native American Affairs, Philanthropic Organizations, Safety, Urban & Community Affairs, Zoos/Aquariums
Education: Arts/Humanities Education, Business Education, Colleges & Universities, Community & Junior Colleges, Education Funds, Education Reform, Elementary Education (Private), Education-General, Leadership Training, Leadership Training, Minority Education, Private Education (Precollege), Public Education (Precollege), Secondary Education (Private), Social Sciences Education, Special Education
Environment: Environment-General, Resource Conservation, Watershed, Wildlife Protection
Health: Cancer, Children's Health/Hospitals, Clinics/Medical Centers, Emergency/Ambulance Services, Health-General, Home-Care Services, Hospitals, Medical Research, Mental Health, Nursing Services
International: Missionary/Religious Activities
Religion: Churches, Dioceses, Religious Organizations
Science: Science Museums
Social Services: At-Risk Youth, Community Centers, Community Service Organizations, Delinquency & Criminal Rehabilitation, Family Services, Food/Clothing Distribution, Homes, People with Disabilities, People with Disabilities, Recreation & Athletics, Senior Services, Social Services-General, Substance Abuse, United Funds/United Ways, Veterans, YMCA/YWCA/YMHA/YWHA, Youth Organizations

Application Procedures

Initial Contact: Submit a written proposal. The foundation accepts the Associated Grantmakers of Massachusetts Common Proposal Format.
Application Requirements: The body of the proposal should be no more than five pages plus appendices. Also include a one-page cover letter summarizing the proposal and with a request for a specific grant amount. A proposal must include proof of tax-exempt status; proof of incorporation in Massachusetts; names of officers, directors or trustees of the organization; recently audited financial statement; institutional income and expense budget for the current fiscal year; detailed program budget for which support is requested; starting and completion dates of proposed program and planned cash flow; and current status of fundraising, including other sources being solicited for funds. Provide name, address and telephone number of contact person. address, and telephone number of whom you wish contacted.
Deadlines: None.
Review Process: The trustees meet monthly (except for July and August) to review applications.
Notes: Applications will be considered for experimental and demonstration projects, program expansion, evaluation, renovation, new construction programs, capital funding, and to 501(c)(3) organizations for the benefit of another awaiting its own tax-exempt status.

Restrictions

No grants will be made to individuals, state or federal agencies, national organizations, or annual campaigns. The trustees will not normally consider more than one application from an agency in the same calendar year, except for summer youth programs. The foundation funds only Massachusetts charitable organizations, with preference given to Merrimack Valley area and the Greater Lawrence area.

Additional Information

The foundation reports an affiliation with the Nathaniel and Elizabeth P. Stevens Foundation, also located in Massachusetts.
Publications: Program Policy Statement; Applications Guidelines

Foundation Officials

Elizabeth A. Beland: administrator
Phoebe S. Miner: trustee CORP AFFIL officer: Ames Textile Corp.
Christopher W. Rogers: trustee
Samuel S. Rogers: mng trustee

Grants Analysis

Disclosure Period: calendar year ending 2001
Total Grants: $1,135,950*
Number of Grants: 99
Average Grant: $11,474
Highest Grant: $100,000
Lowest Grant: $100
Typical Range: $1,000 to $25,000
***Note:** Giving excludes United Way.

Recent Grants

Note: Grants derived from 2001 Form 990.

General

100,000	American Textile History Museum, Lowell, MA
100,000	Andover ABC, Andover, MA
75,000	Northern Essex Community College, North Essex, MA
70,000	Merrimack College, North Andover, MA
50,000	Appalachian Mountain Club, Boston, MA
50,000	Community Day Charter School, Lawrence, MA
50,000	Professional Center for Handicapped Children, Andover, MA
35,000	American Textile History Museum, Lowell, MA
30,000	Veterans Northeast Outreach Center, Haverhill, MA
25,000	Greater Lowell Community Foundation, Lowell, MA

NATHANIEL AND ELIZABETH P. STEVENS FOUNDATION

Giving Contact

Elizabeth A. Beland, Administrator
PO Box 111
North Andover, MA 01845
Phone: (978)688-7211

Description

Founded: 1943
EIN: 042236996
Organization Type: Private Foundation
Giving Locations: MA: emphasis on the greater Lawrence area
Grant Types: Capital, Challenge, Emergency, Endowment, General Support, Matching, Operating Expenses, Project, Seed Money.

Donor Information

Founder: the late Nathaniel Stevens

Financial Summary

Total Giving: $981,685 (2000); $974,435 (1999); $635,510 (1998). Note: 1997 Giving includes United Way ($12,800).
Giving Analysis: Giving for 2000 includes: foundation grants to United Way ($15,500); 1999: foundation grants to United Way ($12,800) 1998: foundation grants to United Way ($12,300)
Assets: $19,217,852 (2000); $19,144,069 (1999); $17,892,206 (1998)

Typical Recipients

Arts & Humanities: Arts Centers, Ethnic & Folk Arts, Historic Preservation, History & Archaeology, Libraries, Museums/Galleries, Music, Opera, Theater
Civic & Public Affairs: Asian American Affairs, Economic Development, Civic & Public Affairs-General, Hispanic Affairs, Housing, Native American Affairs, Philanthropic Organizations, Safety, Urban & Community Affairs, Women's Affairs, Zoos/Aquariums
Education: Afterschool/Enrichment Programs, Colleges & Universities, Community & Junior Colleges, Education Reform, Faculty Development, Education-General, Leadership Training, Private Education (Precollege), Public Education (Precollege), School Volunteerism, Science/Mathematics Education, Secondary Education (Private), Secondary Education (Public)
Environment: Air/Water Quality, Environment-General, Watershed
Health: Adolescent Health Issues, Cancer, Children's Health/Hospitals, Clinics/Medical Centers, Emergency/Ambulance Services, Health Organizations, Hospitals, Medical Rehabilitation, Mental Health
Religion: Churches, Jewish Causes, Religious Organizations, Religious Welfare
Science: Science Museums
Social Services: At-Risk Youth, Child Welfare, Community Centers, Community Service Organizations, Counseling, Day Care, Family Planning, Family Services, Food/Clothing Distribution, Homes, People with Disabilities, Recreation & Athletics, Senior Services, Shelters/Homelessness, United Funds/United Ways, YMCA/YWCA/YMHA/YWHA, Youth Organizations

Application Procedures

Initial Contact: Request application guidelines.
Deadlines: None.

Restrictions

Does not support individuals.

Additional Information

Publications: Application Guidelines

Foundation Officials

Joshua L. Miner, IV: trustee
Phoebe S. Miner: trustee CORP AFFIL officer: Ames Textile Corp.
Samuel S. Rogers: trustee

Grants Analysis

Disclosure Period: calendar year ending 2000
Total Grants: $966,185*
Number of Grants: 150
Average Grant: $5,701*
Highest Grant: $62,500
Typical Range: $1,000 to $10,000
***Note:** Giving excludes United Way. Average grant figure excludes two highest grants ($122,500).

Recent Grants

Note: Grants derived from 1999 Form 990.

General

150,000	Essex County Community Foundation, Peabody, MA

89,455	American Textile History Museum, Lowell, MA
50,000	American Textile History Museum, Lowell, MA
50,000	Greater Lawrence Family Health Center, Lawrence, MA
40,000	Dummer Academy Government Capital Campaign
25,000	Outward Bound - USA, Garrison, NY
20,000	Greater Lowell Community Foundation, Lowell, MA
17,000	First Baptist Church
15,000	Bread and Roses
15,000	Iglesia De Dios

STEWARDSHIP FOUNDATION

Giving Contact

Dr. Cary A. Paine, Executive Director
PO Box 1278
Tacoma, WA 98401-1278
Phone: (253)620-1340
Fax: (253)572-2721
E-mail: info@stewardshipfdn.org
Web: http://www.stewardshipfdn.org

Description

Founded: 1962
EIN: 916020515
Organization Type: General Purpose Foundation
Giving Locations: nationally.
Grant Types: General Support, Project, Research.

Donor Information

Founder: Established in 1962 by Charles Davis Weyerhaeuser, a son of the Frederick Edward Weyerhaeuser (1872-1945), former president of Weyerhaeuser Timber Company.

Financial Summary

Total Giving: $7,400,000 (2001 approx); $7,347,400 (2000); $6,608,701 (1999)
Assets: $111,000,000 (2001); $121,705,822 (2000); $111,343,846 (1999)
Gifts Received: $14,586,654 (2000); $50,000 (1995); $500 (1994)

Typical Recipients

Arts & Humanities: Public Broadcasting, Theater
Civic & Public Affairs: Civil Rights, Employment/Job Training, Civic & Public Affairs-General, Law & Justice, Legal Aid, Professional & Trade Associations, Public Policy, Urban & Community Affairs
Education: Colleges & Universities, Education-General, International Exchange, Leadership Training, Minority Education, Private Education (Precollege), Public Education (Precollege), Religious Education, Student Aid
Environment: Environment-General
Health: Emergency/Ambulance Services, Eyes/Blindness, Medical Research, Mental Health, Public Health
International: Foreign Educational Institutions, Health Care/Hospitals, Human Rights, International Affairs, International Development, International Environmental Issues, International Organizations, International Peace & Security Issues, International Relations, International Relief Efforts, Missionary/Religious Activities
Religion: Bible Study/Translation, Churches, Religion-General, Ministries, Missionary Activities (Domestic), Religious Organizations, Religious Welfare, Seminaries, Social/Policy Issues
Science: Scientific Centers & Institutes, Scientific Research
Social Services: Camps, Child Welfare, Community Centers, Crime Prevention, Delinquency & Criminal Rehabilitation, Domestic Violence, Emergency Relief,

Family Planning, Family Services, Food/Clothing Distribution, People with Disabilities, Refugee Assistance, Social Services-General, Substance Abuse, Youth Organizations

Application Procedures

Initial Contact: Potential applicants should send a brief letter to the foundation.
Application Requirements: Letters should include a description of the proposed project along with the organization's budget and sources of revenue. If a program falls within foundation interests, an application form will be sent.
Deadlines: None.
Review Process: Directors meet quarterly. An organization making a request will usually receive a response from the foundation within 30 days from the time of the request.

Restrictions

Grants are almost exclusively given to evangelical Christian institutions.
Grants are not made for the following purposes: seed funding for start-up organizations; scholarships or fellowships to individuals; endowments; debt retirement; media time and program production; or for propagandizing or influencing elections or legislation. Grants are not made to churches, but only to para-church organizations, as well as to a few local, secular, community-based organizations. Grants are primarily made in support of operating expenses rather than for capital projects. Grants are not made to agencies that serve only their own community except for those local agencies serving the citizens of the greater Tacoma/Seattle/Puget Sound area; the foundation will, however, consider local programs that have national or international significance. Grants are not made to organizations where, because of location or other reasons, the cost of evaluation is out of proportion to the size of the anticipated grant. Grants are generally limited to 10% of total operating or capital budgets and to 25% of total funding. Grants are generally for one year's duration; multiple-year requests are considered only when subject to annual review by the distribution committee.

Foundation Officials

Carl T. Fynboe: board member
Donald W. Mowat: director
Annette Thayer Black Weyerhaeuser: board member
Dr. William Toycen Weyerhaeuser: chairman B Tacoma, WA 1943. ED Stanford University (1966); Fuller Graduate School of Psychology PhD (1975). PRIM CORP EMPL owner, chairman: Yelm Telephone Co. CORP AFFIL director: Columbia Banking System Inc.; director: Potlatch Corp.

Grants Analysis

Disclosure Period: calendar year ending 2000
Total Grants: $7,397,480*
Number of Grants: 207
Average Grant: $35,737
Highest Grant: $500,000
Lowest Grant: $5,000
Typical Range: $5,000 to $25,000
*Note: Grants analysis provided by foundation.

Recent Grants

Note: Grants derived from 2000 Form 990.

General

800,000	Opportunity International, Oak Brook, IL -- for Marantha Trust Australia's Transformation Indonesia
500,000	Whitworth College, Spokane, WA -- for academic building
350,000	Mission Aviation Fellowship, Redlands, CA -- purchase of new fleet
275,000	John Stott Ministries, Wheaton, IL -- for Langham Writers Program
250,000	World Relief, Seattle, WA -- for relocation of organization
250,000	Wycliff Bible Translators, Huntington Beach, CA -- for relocation of organization
250,000	Young Life Campaign, Colorado Springs, CO -- for Wildhorse Canyon Camp
200,000	Discovery Institute for Public Policy, Seattle, WA -- Wedge Project
170,000	Whitworth College, Spokane, WA -- for the Center for Faith and Learning
160,000	World Vision International, Monrovia, CA -- for vision youth initiative

DONNELL B. AND ELIZABETH DEE SHAW STEWART EDUCATIONAL FOUNDATION

Giving Contact

Mary Barker, Trustee
c/o First Security Bank of Utah NA
PO Box 9936
Ogden, UT 84409
Phone: (801)626-9531

Description

Founded: 1977
EIN: 876179880
Organization Type: Private Foundation
Giving Locations: UT: Ogden
Grant Types: Capital, Scholarship.

Donor Information

Founder: Elizabeth D. S. Stewart

Financial Summary

Total Giving: $7,015,887 (2000); $5,353,645 (1999); $4,750,350 (1998)
Giving Analysis: Giving for 1999 includes: foundation grants to United Way ($100,000) 1998: foundation grants to United Way ($50,000)
Assets: $126,339,413 (2000); $142,303,683 (1999); $99,328,657 (1998)
Gifts Received: $11,107 (2000); $1,078,987 (1996); $300,452 (1995). Note: In 2000, contributions were received from Elizabeth Stewart Estate.

Typical Recipients

Arts & Humanities: Arts Centers, Ballet, Dance, Libraries, Museums/Galleries, Music, Opera, Performing Arts
Civic & Public Affairs: Community Foundations, Employment/Job Training, Civic & Public Affairs-General, Municipalities/Towns, Public Policy, Safety, Urban & Community Affairs
Education: Arts/Humanities Education, Colleges & Universities, Education-General, Private Education (Precollege), Public Education (Precollege), Vocational & Technical Education
Environment: Environment-General, Resource Conservation
Health: Children's Health/Hospitals, Emergency/Ambulance Services, Eyes/Blindness, Health Organizations, Heart, Hospices, Hospitals, Single-Disease Health Associations
International: International Relief Efforts
Religion: Churches, Missionary Activities (Domestic), Religious Welfare
Science: Science Museums, Scientific Centers & Institutes
Social Services: Camps, Child Welfare, Community Centers, Community Service Organizations, Crime Prevention, Emergency Relief, Family Services, People with Disabilities, Scouts, Substance Abuse, Veterans, Youth Organizations

Application Procedures

Initial Contact: Send a brief letter of inquiry.
Deadlines: September 30.

Additional Information

Trust(s): First Security Bank

Foundation Officials

Mary L. Barker: trustee
Orville Rex Child: trustee
Dean W. Hurst: off
Jack D. Lampros: off
Donnell B. Stewart: off
Elizabeth D. Stewart: off
C. W. Stromberg: off

Grants Analysis

Disclosure Period: calendar year ending 2000
Total Grants: $7,015,887*
Number of Grants: 52
Average Grant: $53,502*
Highest Grant: $3,340,775
Typical Range: $25,000 to $100,000
*Note: Giving excludes United Way. Average grant figure excludes two highest grants ($4,340,775).

Recent Grants

Note: Grants derived from 1999 Form 990.

General

3,200,026	Weber State University, Ogden, UT
252,250	Ogden Rescue Mission, Ogden, UT
250,000	Air Force Heritage Museum, Roy, UT
160,000	Utah Opera Company, Salt Lake City, UT
150,000	Corporation of the President LDS Church, Salt Lake City, UT
127,250	Trapper Trails, Boy Scouts, Ogden, UT
107,500	St. Joseph Elementary School, Ogden, UT
100,000	American Red Cross, Northern Utah, Ogden, UT
100,000	LDS Church/ Ricks College, Rexburg, ID
100,000	LDS Foundation/ University of Florida, Salt Lake City, UT

GLEN AND DOROTHY STILLWELL CHARITABLE TRUST

Giving Contact

John F. Bradley, Trustee
301 N. Lake Ave., 10th Fl.
Pasadena, CA 91101-4108
Phone: (626)793-9400

Description

Founded: 1981
EIN: 956751888
Organization Type: Private Foundation
Giving Locations: CA: Orange County; TN: Davidson, Williamson
Grant Types: General Support.

Donor Information

Founder: Glen Stillwell, Dorothy Stillwell

Financial Summary

Total Giving: $121,500 (fiscal year ending November 30, 2001); $99,000 (fiscal 2000); $102,400 (fiscal 1999)
Assets: $2,255,783 (fiscal 2001); $2,436,145 (fiscal 2000); $2,559,467 (fiscal 1999)

Typical Recipients

Arts & Humanities: Libraries, Performing Arts
Civic & Public Affairs: Employment/Job Training, Housing
Education: Afterschool/Enrichment Programs, Special Education
Health: Children's Health/Hospitals, Eyes/Blindness, Outpatient Health Care, Single-Disease Health Associations
Religion: Religious Welfare
Social Services: At-Risk Youth, Big Brother/Big Sister, Child Abuse, Child Welfare, Community Service Organizations, Day Care, Delinquency & Criminal Rehabilitation, Domestic Violence, Family Services, Food/Clothing Distribution, Homes, People with Disabilities, Senior Services, Sexual Abuse, Shelters/Homelessness, Substance Abuse, YMCA/YWCA/YMHA/YWHA, Youth Organizations

Application Procedures

Initial Contact: Submit a letter of inquiry and full proposal.
Application Requirements: Include objectives to be achieved, the manner in which the name of the trust will be recognized, detailed budget, a description of organization, amount requested, purpose of funds sought, recently audited financial statement, proof of tax-exempt status, and proof of non-private foundation status.
Deadlines: None.

Restrictions

Emphasis is on grants to organizations which provide assistance to the needy, infirm, educationally handicapped, drug and alcohol dependent, blind, hearing impaired, abused, and other disadvantaged persons.

Additional Information

The foundation reports that 95% of contributions are allocated to Health and Human Services and 5% to Education for the blind and handicapped.
Publications: Application Guidelines

Foundation Officials

John F. Bradley: trustee
Timothy J. Gosney: trustee
Stanley C. Lagerlof: trustee B Minneapolis, MN 1915. ED University of Minnesota AB (1936); University of Southern California JD (1939). PRIM CORP EMPL attorney: Lagerlof, Senecal, Drescher & Swift.
H. Jess Senecal: trustee

Grants Analysis

Disclosure Period: fiscal year ending November 30, 2001
Total Grants: $121,500
Number of Grants: 15
Average Grant: $8,100
Highest Grant: $12,000
Lowest Grant: $2,500
Typical Range: $5,000 to $12,000

Recent Grants

Note: Grants derived from fiscal 2000 Form 990.

Library-Related

10,000	Braille Institute of Orange County, Anaheim, CA -- support of orange county library services

General

12,000	Dayle McIntosh Center, Anaheim, CA -- mentoring program to be conducted by adults with disabilities for benefit of special education students
12,000	OC Rescue Mission, Santa Ana, CA -- mobile job training facility for poverty motel residence
10,000	Boys Hope/Girls Hope CA, Garden Grove, CA -- Fullerton home for at-risk boys and girls stressing academic performance

10,000	Community Day Nursery, Garden Grove, CA -- low cost child care services for parents seeking employment or completing their education
10,000	Mercy Health Services, Franklin, TN -- build out and operational expenses for children's clinic at Franklin
10,000	OC Association Retarded Citizens, Orange, CA -- toward cost of new facilities for work for persons with disabilities
10,000	Yellowstone Women's House, Costa Mesa, CA -- program for indigent substance abusing women to learn to live sober and clean for first ten days
5,000	Concept Seven Family Support, Laguna Hills, CA -- emergency clothing program
5,000	Easter Seals Society California, Santa Ana, CA -- after school program with personalized service for special needs children
5,000	Sally's Fund, Laguna Beach, CA -- senior transportation and assistance program in Laguna Beach

STOCKER FOUNDATION

Giving Contact

Patricia O'Brien, Executive Director
559 Broadway Avenue, 2nd Floor
Lorain, OH 44052-1744
Phone: (440)246-5719
E-mail: contact@stockerfoundation.org
Web: http://www.stockerfoundation.org

Description

Founded: 1979
EIN: 341293603
Organization Type: Private Foundation
Giving Locations: AZ: Southern Arizona; NM: Dona Ana County; OH: Lorain County
Grant Types: Capital, Emergency, Endowment, General Support, Multiyear/Continuing Support, Operating Expenses, Project, Research, Scholarship, Seed Money.

Donor Information

Founder: Beth K. Stocker

Financial Summary

Total Giving: $2,481,330 (fiscal year ending September 30, 2001); $2,371,639 (fiscal 2000); $1,455,921 (fiscal 1998). Note: Fiscal 1997 Giving includes scholarship ($107,275).
Giving Analysis: Giving for fiscal 2001 includes: foundation grants to United Way ($15,000)
Assets: $35,474,642 (fiscal 2001); $47,769,327 (fiscal 2000); $34,155,496 (fiscal 1998)
Gifts Received: $1,615,903 (fiscal 2001); $1,307,542 (fiscal 2000); $689,688 (fiscal 1998). Note: In fiscal 1998 and 2001, contributions were received from Beth K. Stocker. In fiscal 1996, contributions were received from Beth K. Stocker.

Typical Recipients

Arts & Humanities: Arts Associations & Councils, Arts Outreach, Dance, History & Archaeology, Libraries, Museums/Galleries, Music, Opera, Performing Arts, Public Broadcasting, Theater, Visual Arts
Civic & Public Affairs: African American Affairs, Botanical Gardens/Parks, Community Foundations, Economic Development, Employment/Job Training, Hispanic Affairs, Housing, Legal Aid, Native American Affairs, Philanthropic Organizations, Public Policy, Urban & Community Affairs, Zoos/Aquariums
Education: Afterschool/Enrichment Programs, Agricultural Education, Arts/Humanities Education, Business Education, Colleges & Universities, Community & Junior Colleges, Education Reform, Engineering/Technological Education, Environmental

Education, Education-General, Leadership Training, Legal Education, Literacy, Private Education (Precollege), Public Education (Precollege), School Volunteerism, Student Aid, Vocational & Technical Education
Environment: Environment-General, Resource Conservation
Health: AIDS/HIV, Alzheimers Disease, Arthritis, Cancer, Children's Health/Hospitals, Clinics/Medical Centers, Emergency/Ambulance Services, Health Organizations, Hospices, Long-Term Care, Medical Rehabilitation, Medical Research, Medical Training, Mental Health, Nursing Services, Prenatal Health Issues, Preventive Medicine/Wellness Organizations, Single-Disease Health Associations
Religion: Jewish Causes, Ministries, Religious Welfare
Social Services: At-Risk Youth, Big Brother/Big Sister, Child Abuse, Child Welfare, Community Centers, Community Service Organizations, Counseling, Crime Prevention, Day Care, Domestic Violence, Emergency Relief, Family Planning, Family Services, Food/Clothing Distribution, People with Disabilities, Scouts, Senior Services, Shelters/Homelessness, Substance Abuse, United Funds/United Ways, Volunteer Services, YMCA/YWCA/YMHA/YWHA, Youth Organizations

Application Procedures

Initial Contact: Call or write the foundation requesting application guidelines before submitting a proposal.
Deadlines: January 15, May 15, and September 1.

Restrictions

Emphasis is on innovative, short-term youth development, public education, aid to the handicapped and disadvantaged, cultural programs, women's issues, and programs that have the promise of a solution. Does not provide loans or support individuals, religious organizations for sectarian purposes, political or lobbying groups, public school services required by law, deficit financing, or annual campaigns.

Additional Information

Publications: Application Guidelines

Foundation Officials

Mary Ann Dobras: trustee
Wendy Dobras: trustee
Benjamin P. Norton: trustee
Sara Jane Norton: executive director
Beth K. Stocker: president
Ann Woodling: trustee
Nancy Elizabeth Woodling: trustee

Grants Analysis

Disclosure Period: fiscal year ending September 30, 2001
Total Grants: $2,466,330*
Number of Grants: 300
Average Grant: $8,221
Highest Grant: $100,000
Lowest Grant: $50
Typical Range: $1,000 to $15,000
*Note: Giving excludes United Way.

Recent Grants

Note: Grants derived from fiscal 2000 Form 990.

General

50,000	Community Foundation for Southern Arizona, Tucson, AZ -- endowment fund
50,000	Lorain County Community College Foundation, Elyria, OH -- for student award for women
50,000	Lorain County Community College Foundation, Elyria, OH -- scholarship in engineering
50,000	Lorain County Metro Parks, La Grange, OH -- for development of a regional family aquatic center

50,000 Oberlin Community Services, Oberlin, OH -- for equipment and furniture needs

40,000 Habitat for Humanity of Tucson, Tucson, AZ -- towards the women's build 2000 project

35,000 Neighborhood House Association of Lorain County, Lorain, OH -- to support 2 new staff positions

25,000 Community Foundation of Southern New Mexico, Las Cruces, NM -- endowment fund

25,000 Dona Ana Arts Council, Las Cruces, NM -- for conversion to Rio Grande Theatre to an Arts Center

25,000 Food Bank of Community Action Agency of Southern New Mexico, Inc., Las Cruces, NM -- for endowment fund

STOCKMAN FAMILY FOUNDATION TRUST

Giving Contact

Harvey S. Stockman
1041 Matador SE
Albuquerque, NM 87123
Phone: (505)881-3953

Description

Founded: 1991
EIN: 856104630
Organization Type: Private Foundation
Giving Locations: DC: Washington; NJ; NM; NY
Grant Types: General Support.

Donor Information

Founder: Established in 1991 by Hervey S. and Sarah H. Stockman.

Financial Summary

Total Giving: $844,215 (fiscal year ending November 30, 2001); $929,928 (fiscal 2000); $753,270 (fiscal 1998)
Assets: $17,393,210 (fiscal 2001); $20,829,965 (fiscal 2000); $18,749,237 (fiscal 1998)
Gifts Received: $300,000 (fiscal 2001); $290,000 (fiscal 2000); $300,000 (fiscal 1998). Note: In fiscal 2001, 2000, 1998, and 1995, contributions were received from Hervey S. and Sarah H. Stockman.

Typical Recipients

Arts & Humanities: Arts Institutes, Ethnic & Folk Arts, Arts & Humanities-General, Historic Preservation, History & Archaeology, Libraries, Museums/Galleries, Performing Arts, Visual Arts
Civic & Public Affairs: Community Foundations, Hispanic Affairs
Education: Arts/Humanities Education, Colleges & Universities, Environmental Education, Private Education (Precollege)
International: Foreign Arts Organizations, Foreign Educational Institutions
Science: Science Museums

Application Procedures

Initial Contact: Send a brief letter of inquiry.
Application Requirements: Include proof of tax-exempt status under IRS Section 501(c)(3).
Deadlines: None.

Additional Information

Trust(s): Banker's Trust Co.

Foundation Officials

Karl W. Gustafson: treasurer
Hervey S. Stockman, Jr.: vice president
Hervey S. Stockman: president
Sarah A. Stockman: chairman, secretary

Grants Analysis

Disclosure Period: fiscal year ending November 30, 2001
Total Grants: $844,215
Number of Grants: 21
Average Grant: $26,068*
Highest Grant: $150,000
Lowest Grant: $5,896
Typical Range: $10,000 to $50,000
*Note: Average grant figure excludes three highest grants ($375,000).

Recent Grants

Note: Grants derived from fiscal 2000 Form 990.

Library-Related

12,000 Canajoharie Library and Art Gallery, Canajoharie, NY -- conservation of works in the art collection of the gallery

General

150,000 Walters Art Gallery, Baltimore, MD -- support the position of senior conservator of manuscripts and rare books

125,000 Spanish Colonial Arts Society, Santa Fe, NM -- building of the collection storage, Research and Conservation Center

100,000 New Mexico State University Foundation University Art Gallery, Las Cruces, NM

80,000 University Art Museum Center of the Arts, Albuquerque, MN -- support a working conservation lab

66,030 Maryland Historical Society, Baltimore, MD -- conservation of six paintings, and the placement of backboards on paintings

59,088 Americans for Oxford, New York, NY -- conservation and storage of textiles at the Ashmolean Museum

50,000 American Fund for Southampton University, Washington, DC -- development of conservation teaching

50,000 Baltimore Museum of Art, Baltimore, MD -- funds for an endowed chair for the museum's senior conservation

50,000 Buffalo State College Foundation, Inc., Buffalo, NY -- endowment for student fellowships and curriculum development

50,000 Lensic Performing Arts Center, Santa Fe, NM -- restore and conserve the historic murals and family crests in the lobby

STODDARD CHARITABLE TRUST

Giving Contact

Warner S. Fletcher, Chairman
370 Main Street, 12th Floor
Worcester, MA 01608
Phone: (508)798-8621
Fax: (508)791-6454
E-mail: wfletcher@ftwlaw.com

Description

Founded: 1939
EIN: 046023791
Organization Type: Family Foundation
Giving Locations: MA: Worcester
Grant Types: General Support.

Donor Information

Founder: Established in 1939 by the late Harry G. Stoddard (d. 1969), chairman of Wyman Gordon Company and of the Worcester Telegram and Gazette. He was president of the Worcester Community Chest and a director of the Worcester YMCA and the Worcester Boys Club.

Financial Summary

Total Giving: $4,774,500 (2001); $5,699,162 (2000); $3,570,500 (1999)
Giving Analysis: Giving for 2000 includes: foundation grants to United Way ($120,000); 1999: foundation grants to United Way ($100,000); 1997: foundation grants to United Way ($75,000)
Assets: $75,741,687 (2001); $86,858,771 (2000); $86,891,032 (1999)
Gifts Received: $616,969 (2001); $8,040,140 (2000); $5,726,102 (1999). Note: In 2001, contributions were received from Stephen B. Loring ($615,094) and the Estate of Helen E. Stoddard ($1,875).

Typical Recipients

Arts & Humanities: Arts Appreciation, Arts Centers, Arts Funds, Ethnic & Folk Arts, Historic Preservation, History & Archaeology, Libraries, Museums/Galleries, Music, Performing Arts, Public Broadcasting, Theater
Civic & Public Affairs: Botanical Gardens/Parks, Clubs, Community Foundations, Economic Development, Employment/Job Training, Civic & Public Affairs-General, Hispanic Affairs, Housing, Legal Aid, Municipalities/Towns, Native American Affairs, Parades/Festivals, Professional & Trade Associations, Urban & Community Affairs
Education: Agricultural Education, Arts/Humanities Education, Business Education, Colleges & Universities, Community & Junior Colleges, Education Associations, Education Reform, Elementary Education (Private), Engineering/Technological Education, Education-General, Literacy, Medical Education, Private Education (Precollege), Science/Mathematics Education, Secondary Education (Private), Special Education, Student Aid
Environment: Environment-General, Resource Conservation, Wildlife Protection
Health: Cancer, Children's Health/Hospitals, Clinics/Medical Centers, Health-General, Health Funds, Health Organizations, Home-Care Services, Hospices, Medical Research, Public Health
Religion: Churches, Jewish Causes, Ministries, Religious Welfare
Science: Science Museums, Scientific Centers & Institutes, Scientific Research
Social Services: At-Risk Youth, Big Brother/Big Sister, Child Welfare, Community Centers, Community Service Organizations, Community Service Organizations, Counseling, Day Care, Emergency Relief, Family Planning, Family Services, Food/Clothing Distribution, Homes, People with Disabilities, Scouts, Senior Services, Sexual Abuse, Shelters/Homelessness, Substance Abuse, United Funds/United Ways, YMCA/YWCA/YMHA/YWHA, Youth Organizations

Application Procedures

Initial Contact: Apply in writing.
Application Requirements: Four copies of a proposal must be submitted. Proposal should include a description of organization and its total budget, amount needed, projected budget, and proof of tax-exempt status.
Deadlines: None.
Review Process: The trust acknowledges receipt of applications. An interview may be required. The decision-making process takes about three months.

Restrictions

The trust does not make grants to individuals and rarely makes grants to organizations outside Worcester, MA.

Foundation Officials

Allen W. Fletcher: trustee B 1948. PRIM CORP EMPL chairman, treasurer: Worcester Publishing Inc. CORP AFFIL chairman, treasurer: Worcester Business Journal; chairman, treasurer: Worcester Magazine; chairman, treasurer: Hartford Business Journal.
Warner S. Fletcher: chairman, trustee B Worcester, MA 1945. ED Williams College BA (1967); Boston

University JD (1973). PRIM CORP EMPL treasurer: Fletcher, Tilton & Whipple PC. CORP AFFIL director: Wyman-Gordon Co.
Judith S. King: trustee, treasurer CORP AFFIL director: Wyman-Gordon Co.
Valerie S. Loring: trustee

Grants Analysis

Disclosure Period: calendar year ending 2001
Total Grants: $4,649,500*
Number of Grants: 59
Average Grant: $54,302*
Highest Grant: $1,500,000
Typical Range: $25,000 to $100,000
***Note:** Giving excludes United Way. Average grant figure excludes highest grant.

Recent Grants

Note: Grants derived from 2001 Form 990.

Library-Related

250,000	Friends of the Worcester Public Library, Worcester, MA -- towards renovation to Worcester Public Library

General

1,500,000	Salem Community Corp, Salem, MA -- toward support for new building project
500,000	Worcester Art Museum, Worcester, MA -- for Stoddard Discovery Fund
400,000	EcoTarium, Worcester, MA -- towards $18,000 long term Capital Development Program
300,000	Worcester Polytechnic Institute, Worcester, MA -- toward endowment for Worcester Community Project Center
120,000	United Way Central Massachusetts, Worcester, MA -- for Leadership Challenge Grant
100,000	Clark University, Worcester, MA -- for Hiatt Center for Urban Education literacy and school development
100,000	College of the Holy Cross, Worcester, MA -- towards construction of College Hall
100,000	Quinsigamond Community College Foundation, Worcester, MA -- towards capital campaign
100,000	Worcester Academy, Worcester, MA -- towards current capital campaign
100,000	YMCA Greater Worcester, Worcester, MA -- for construction

STONE FOUNDATION

Giving Contact

Gerald C. Shea, Secretary & Treasurer
Stone Foundation, Inc.
c/o HHG Foundation Services
PO Box 4004
Darien, CT 06820
Phone: (203)348-1500

Description

Founded: 1964
EIN: 237148468
Organization Type: Private Foundation
Giving Locations: CT: Eastern seaboard.
Grant Types: Capital, Endowment, General Support.

Donor Information

Founder: the late Marion H. Stone, the late Charles Lynn Stone

Financial Summary

Total Giving: $766,000 (2001); $783,164 (2000); $637,000 (1999)
Assets: $15,871,396 (2001); $16,265,302 (2000); $17,670,361 (1999)

Typical Recipients

Arts & Humanities: Arts Outreach, Libraries, Museums/Galleries, Music
Civic & Public Affairs: Economic Development, Nonprofit Management, Philanthropic Organizations, Zoos/Aquariums
Education: Arts/Humanities Education, Colleges & Universities, Faculty Development, Education-General, Medical Education, Private Education (Precollege), Science/Mathematics Education, Secondary Education (Private)
Health: Cancer, Children's Health/Hospitals, Clinics/Medical Centers, Nursing Services
Religion: Religious Welfare
Science: Science Museums, Scientific Labs
Social Services: Camps, Family Planning, Family Services, Social Services-General, Substance Abuse

Application Procedures

Initial Contact: a brief letter of inquiry
Application Requirements: Outline of the proposed project, a statement of its significance, proposed budget

Restrictions

Preference is given to established educational institutions or research organizations. Does not support individuals.

Additional Information

Grants are usually considered at the fall meeting.
Publications: Application Guidelines

Foundation Officials

Mary Stone Payson: trustee
Gerald C. Shea: secretary, treasurer
Dr. Charles Lynn Stone, Jr.: president, trustee
Edward Eldredge Stone: vice president, trustee
Sara S. Stone: trustee

Grants Analysis

Disclosure Period: calendar year ending 2001
Total Grants: $766,000
Number of Grants: 14
Average Grant: $54,714
Highest Grant: $125,000
Lowest Grant: $10,000
Typical Range: $25,000 to $100,000

Recent Grants

Note: Grants derived from 2000 Form 990.

General

250,000	All Kinds of Minds, Chapel Hill, NC -- Intervenor Software Program
100,664	Fairfield Country Day School, Fairfield, CT
100,000	Columbia School of Nursing, New York, NY -- collaborative learning for nursing and medical students
100,000	New Canaan Country Day School, New Canaan, CT -- funding for Professional Development Fund
90,000	Maritime Center, Norwalk, CT -- for Global Learning Center
45,000	Alcoholism and Drug Dependency Council, Westport, CT -- school and community education programs, counseling, and referrals
25,000	Cold Spring Harbor Laboratory, Cold Spring Harbor, NY
25,000	Family & Children's Agency, Norwalk, CT
25,000	Greenwich Academy, Greenwich, CT
12,500	Hasting College, Omaha, NE -- music scholarship for students pursuing degrees in music performance education

FRANCE STONE FOUNDATION

Giving Contact

Joseph S. Heyman, President & Trustee
608 Madison Ave., Ste. 1000
Toledo, OH 43604
Phone: (419)252-6230

Description

Founded: 1952
EIN: 346523033
Organization Type: Private Foundation
Giving Locations: IN; MI; OH
Grant Types: Capital, General Support, Multiyear/Continuing Support, Research, Scholarship.

Donor Information

Founder: the late George A. France, the France Stone Co., and subsidiaries

Financial Summary

Total Giving: $536,100 (2001); $657,100 (2000); $624,000 (1999)
Giving Analysis: Giving for 2001 includes: foundation grants to United Way ($5,000); 2000: foundation grants to United Way ($25,000) 1999: foundation grants to United Way ($50,000)
Assets: $13,177,532 (2001); $14,733,964 (2000); $15,514,822 (1999)

Typical Recipients

Arts & Humanities: Ballet, Community Arts, History & Archaeology, Libraries, Museums/Galleries, Music, Opera, Public Broadcasting
Civic & Public Affairs: Botanical Gardens/Parks, Business/Free Enterprise, Clubs, Civic & Public Affairs-General
Education: Business Education, Colleges & Universities, Education Funds, Legal Education, Literacy, Medical Education, Minority Education, Private Education (Precollege)
Health: Children's Health/Hospitals, Clinics/Medical Centers, Emergency/Ambulance Services, Eyes/Blindness, Health Organizations, Heart, Hospices, Hospitals, Multiple Sclerosis, Preventive Medicine/Wellness Organizations, Respiratory, Single-Disease Health Associations
Religion: Churches, Religious Welfare, Religious Welfare
Social Services: Animal Protection, Camps, Child Welfare, Community Centers, Community Service Organizations, Food/Clothing Distribution, Homes, People with Disabilities, Scouts, United Funds/United Ways, YMCA/YWCA/YMHA/YWHA, Youth Organizations

Application Procedures

Initial Contact: Send cover letter and full proposal.
Application Requirements: Include purpose of funds sought.
Deadlines: None.

Restrictions

Generally limited to medical, educational, and religious organizations. Does not support individuals.

Foundation Officials

Andrew E. Anderson: secretary, treasurer, trustee
Joseph S. Heyman: president, trustee
Ollie J. Risner: vice president, trustee

Grants Analysis

Disclosure Period: calendar year ending 2001
Total Grants: $531,100*
Number of Grants: 36
Average Grant: $12,317*
Highest Grant: $100,000
Lowest Grant: $1,000

Typical Range: $5,000 to $20,000
***Note:** Giving excludes United Way. Average grant figure excludes highest grant.

Recent Grants

Note: Grants derived from 2000 Form 990.

Library-Related
25,000	Library Legacy Foundation, Toledo, OH

General
100,000	Toledo Museum of Art, Toledo, OH -- total payment payable over five years
50,000	Little Sisters of the Poor, Cleveland, OH
50,000	Toledo Symphony Association, Toledo, OH
25,000	Northwest Ohio Hospice Association, Toledo, OH
25,000	United Way, Toledo, OH
25,000	YMCA of Greater Toledo, Toledo, OH
25,000	YMCA of Greater Toledo, Toledo, OH -- Camp Storer
20,000	Northwest Ohio Hospice Association, Toledo, OH -- additional
20,000	Salvation Army, Toledo, OH -- additional
20,000	Salvation Army, Toledo, OH

H. CHASE STONE TRUST

Giving Contact

Janice M. Eder, Trust Officer
c/o Bank One Colorado Springs NA
30 E. Pikes Peak
Colorado Springs, CO 80942
Phone: (719)471-5074

Description

EIN: 846066113
Organization Type: Private Foundation
Giving Locations: CO: El Paso County
Grant Types: General Support.

Financial Summary

Total Giving: $103,000 (2001); $190,730 (2000); $200,130 (1999)
Giving Analysis: Giving for 2000 includes: foundation matching gifts ($7,500); 1999: foundation scholarships ($10,000) foundation matching gifts ($30,000)
Assets: $3,655,564 (2001); $3,963,401 (2000); $4,504,930 (1999)
Gifts Received: $10,000 (1996). Note: In 1996, contributions were received from the Luther McCauley Charitable Trust.

Typical Recipients

Arts & Humanities: Arts Associations & Councils, Arts Centers, Arts Outreach, Dance, History & Archaeology, Libraries, Museums/Galleries, Music, Opera, Performing Arts, Public Broadcasting, Theater
Civic & Public Affairs: Community Foundations, Economic Development, Civic & Public Affairs-General, Housing, Municipalities/Towns, Parades/Festivals, Safety, Urban & Community Affairs, Women's Affairs, Zoos/Aquariums
Education: Arts/Humanities Education, Business Education, Colleges & Universities, Faculty Development, Education-General, Literacy, Preschool Education, Private Education (Precollege), Public Education (Precollege), Science/Mathematics Education, Student Aid
Environment: Environment-General, Environment-General
Health: Alzheimers Disease, Cancer, Children's Health/Hospitals, Clinics/Medical Centers, Emergency/Ambulance Services, Health Organizations, Hospices, Medical Research, Mental Health, Preventive Medicine/Wellness Organizations, Research/Studies Institutes, Single-Disease Health Associations

Religion: Ministries, Religious Welfare
Science: Scientific Organizations
Social Services: At-Risk Youth, Child Abuse, Community Centers, Community Service Organizations, Domestic Violence, Family Planning, Family Services, Food/Clothing Distribution, People with Disabilities, Recreation & Athletics, Scouts, Senior Services, Special Olympics, Substance Abuse, United Funds/United Ways, YMCA/YWCA/YMHA/YWHA, Youth Organizations

Application Procedures

Initial Contact: Send a written narrative letter.
Application Requirements: Include amount requested, purpose of funds sought, and who will benefit from the grant.
Deadlines: April 30 and October 31.

Restrictions

Does not support individuals.

Additional Information

Trust(s): Bank One Trust Co.

Grants Analysis

Disclosure Period: calendar year ending 2001
Total Grants: $103,000
Number of Grants: 10
Average Grant: $10,300
Highest Grant: $20,000
Typical Range: $1,000 to $20,000

Recent Grants

Note: Grants derived from 2001 Form 990.

Library-Related
20,000	Pikes Peak Library, Colorado Springs, CO

General
20,000	World Arena, Colorado Springs, CO
12,000	University of Colorado, Colorado Springs, CO -- Theatreworks
10,000	Colorado Springs Fine Arts Center, Colorado Springs, CO
10,000	Pikes Peak Historical Street Railway, Colorado Springs, CO
10,000	Short Line to Cripple Creek, Colorado Springs, CO
8,000	Children's Literacy Center, Colorado Springs, CO
6,000	Rocky Mountain PBS, Pueblo, CO
5,000	Colorado Springs Children's Chorale, Colorado Springs, CO
2,000	Rock Ledge Ranch Living History, Colorado Springs, CO

STONECUTTER MILLS CORP.

Company Headquarters

300 Dallas St.
Spindale, NC 28160
Web: http://www.stonecuttermills.com

Company Description

Employees: 1,150
SIC(s): 2221 Broadwoven Fabric Mills--Manmade, 2261 Finishing Plants--Cotton, 2262 Finishing Plants--Manmade, 2269 Finishing Plants Nec.

Operating Locations

Stonecutter Mills Corp. (NC--Spindale)

Stonecutter Foundation

Giving Contact

Van H. Lonon, Staff Assistant
Dallas Street
PO Box 157
Spindale, NC 28160
Phone: (828)286-2341
Note: Van Lonon may be reached at extension 21.

Description

EIN: 566044820
Organization Type: Corporate Foundation
Giving Locations: NC
Grant Types: General Support, Scholarship.

Financial Summary

Total Giving: $503,175 (fiscal year ending March 31, 2001); $450,000 (fiscal 2000 approx); $388,000 (fiscal 1999). Note: Contributes through foundation only.
Giving Analysis: Giving for fiscal 2001 includes: foundation grants to United Way ($5,500); foundation ($497,675); fiscal 1999: corporate grants to United Way ($2,000) foundation ($386,000)
Assets: $9,448,650 (fiscal 2001); $11,012,653 (fiscal 1999)
Gifts Received: $300 (fiscal 1999); $72,420 (fiscal 1993); $39,700 (fiscal 1992). Note: In fiscal 1999, contributions were received from Peter S. Hagerman.

Typical Recipients

Arts & Humanities: Libraries, Museums/Galleries
Civic & Public Affairs: Business/Free Enterprise, Civil Rights, Employment/Job Training, Civic & Public Affairs-General, Housing, Municipalities/Towns, Public Policy, Safety
Education: Agricultural Education, Arts/Humanities Education, Colleges & Universities, Community & Junior Colleges, Education Associations, Education Funds, Education Reform, Elementary Education (Private), Elementary Education (Public), Engineering/Technological Education, Education-General, Private Education (Precollege), Public Education (Precollege), Religious Education, Science/Mathematics Education, Secondary Education (Public)
Environment: Environment-General, Resource Conservation
Health: Hospices, Hospitals, Medical Research, Preventive Medicine/Wellness Organizations
International: Missionary/Religious Activities
Religion: Churches, Churches, Dioceses, Ministries, Religious Organizations
Science: Science Museums
Social Services: Child Welfare, Community Service Organizations, Crime Prevention, Domestic Violence, Family Services, Homes, Recreation & Athletics, Scouts, Social Services-General, United Funds/United Ways, Youth Organizations

Application Procedures

Initial Contact: Request an application form.
Deadlines: None.

Restrictions

Loans are restricted to residents of local area and require proof of acceptance at an institute of higher learning, financial need, and student records.

Additional Information

Publications: Application Form

Corporate Officials

James R. Cowan: chairman, president, chief executive officer, director B 1945. ED University of North Carolina BS (1967); Indiana University MS (1973).

PRIM CORP EMPL chairman, president, chief executive officer, director: Stonecutter Mills Corp. CORP AFFIL chairman: Mitchell Co.

Foundation Officials

James R. Cowan: vice president, director (see above)

Grants Analysis

Disclosure Period: fiscal year ending March 31, 2001
Total Grants: $497,675*
Number of Grants: 52
Average Grant: $9,571
Highest Grant: $75,000
Typical Range: $500 to $25,000
***Note:** Giving excludes United Way.

Recent Grants

Note: Grants derived from 2001 Form 990.

General

75,000	Isothermal Community College Foundation, Spindale, NC -- for education
75,000	Isothermal Community College Foundation, Spindale, NC -- for education
71,000	Isothermal Community College Foundation, Spindale, NC -- for education
45,000	Isothermal Community College Foundation, Spindale, NC -- for education
20,000	Isothermal Community College Foundation, Spindale, NC -- for education
10,000	Asheville School, Asheville, NC -- for education
10,000	Brevard College, Brevard, NC -- for education
10,000	Hillsdale College, Hillsdale, MI -- for education
10,000	Isothermal Community College Foundation, Spindale, NC -- for education
10,000	Isothermal Community College Foundation, Spindale, NC -- for education

STORA ENSO

Company Headquarters

231 1st Ave. N.
Wisconsin Rapids, WI 54495-8050
Web: http://www.storaenso.com/na

Company Description

Former Name: Consolidated Papers, Inc. (2000).
Revenue: US$2.338 billion (2001)
Employees: 7,500 (2001)
SIC(s): 2611 Pulp Mills, 2621 Paper Mills, 2631 Paperboard Mills, 2653 Corrugated & Solid Fiber Boxes.
Parent Company: Stora Enso Oyj, Kanavaranta 1, Helsinki, Finland

Operating Locations

Consolidated Papers, Inc. (IL--Chicago; NY--New York; WI--Adams, Biron, Stevens Point, Whiting)

Mead Witter Foundation, Inc.

Giving Contact

Susan Feith, President
Mead Witter Foundation
PO Box 39
Wisconsin Rapids, WI 54495-0039
Phone: (715)424-3004
Fax: (715)424-1314

Description

Founded: 1951
EIN: 396040071
Organization Type: Corporate Foundation

Giving Locations: WI: headquarters and operating communities
Grant Types: Capital, Employee Matching Gifts, Endowment, General Support, Project, Scholarship.
Note: Employee matching gift ratio: 1 to 1 for gifts to higher education, social service organisation, and the arts.

Donor Information

Founder: Consolidated Papers and George W. Mead I

Financial Summary

Total Giving: $1,051,817 (2002 approx); $2,866,922 (2001); $1,469,487 (2000)
Giving Analysis: Giving for 2000 includes: foundation grants to United Way ($35,000); foundation matching gifts ($440,765); foundation ($993,722); 1999: foundation matching gifts ($220,310); foundation grants to United Way ($279,690); foundation ($1,493,505); 1998: foundation matching gifts ($192,855); foundation grants to United Way ($288,795);
Assets: $68,711,278 (2001); $71,102,433 (2000); $58,184,984 (1999)
Gifts Received: $800,100 (2001); $48,000 (2000); $525,000 (1999). Note: In 2000, contributions were received from Sally Hands. In 1998, contributions were received from Consolidated Papers, Inc. ($680,000), Ruth Barker ($25,000), and Sally Hands (24,000). In 2001, George W. Mead II.

Typical Recipients

Arts & Humanities: Arts Associations & Councils, Arts Festivals, Arts Institutes, Ballet, Community Arts, Arts & Humanities-General, Historic Preservation, History & Archaeology, Libraries, Museums/Galleries, Music, Opera, Performing Arts, Public Broadcasting, Theater, Visual Arts
Civic & Public Affairs: Botanical Gardens/Parks, Clubs, Community Foundations, Economic Development, Employment/Job Training, Civic & Public Affairs-General, Housing, Municipalities/Towns, Professional & Trade Associations, Public Policy, Safety, Zoos/Aquariums
Education: Afterschool/Enrichment Programs, Agricultural Education, Arts/Humanities Education, Business Education, Colleges & Universities, Continuing Education, Economic Education, Education Funds, Engineering/Technological Education, Education-General, Gifted & Talented Programs, Literacy, Medical Education, Minority Education, Private Education (Precollege), Science/Mathematics Education, Secondary Education (Private), Secondary Education (Public), Student Aid, Vocational & Technical Education
Environment: Air/Water Quality, Environment-General, Resource Conservation, Wildlife Protection
Health: AIDS/HIV, Emergency/Ambulance Services, Eyes/Blindness, Health Organizations, Hospices, Hospitals, Medical Rehabilitation, Preventive Medicine/Wellness Organizations, Trauma Treatment
International: International Environmental Issues, International Relations
Religion: Religious Welfare
Science: Science Museums, Scientific Centers & Institutes
Social Services: Animal Protection, Camps, Child Welfare, Community Service Organizations, Crime Prevention, Family Planning, Food/Clothing Distribution, People with Disabilities, Recreation & Athletics, Scouts, Senior Services, Shelters/Homelessness, Social Services-General, United Funds/United Ways, YMCA/YWCA/YMHA/YWHA, Youth Organizations

Application Procedures

Initial Contact: Send a brief letter of inquiry.
Application Requirements: Information should include a description of organization, amount requested, a statement of how the request will be used, budgetary and financial documentation, and a copy

of the applicant organization's IRS letter of determination indicating that the applicant is an organization to which contributions are deductible under IRS Code Section 170.
Deadlines: March 1 for consideration at June board meeting; September 1 for meeting during late November or early December.

Restrictions

There are no restrictions or limitations on grants. However, educational institutions and charities geographically close to corporate installations of Consolidated Papers, Inc. have been favored in the past. Grants are made directly to organizations furnishing the charitable service or function. Educational institutions are favored.

Corporate Officials

Gorton M. Evans, Jr.: president, chief executive officer, director B 1938. ED Michigan State University BS (1960). PRIM CORP EMPL president, chief executive officer, director: Consolidated Papers, Inc. ADD CORP EMPL president: Inter Lake Wisconsin Inc.; president: Inter Lake Papers Inc.
George Wilson Mead, II: chairman, director B Milwaukee, WI 1927. ED Yale University BS (1950); Institute of Paper Chemistry MS (1952). PRIM CORP EMPL chairman, director: Consolidated Papers, Inc. CORP AFFIL director: Newaygo Timber Co. Ltd.; director: Snap-On Tools Inc.; chairman, director: Consolidated Water Power Co. NONPR AFFIL director, president: Consolidated Civic Foundation; trustee: Institute Paper Chemistry; director: American Forest & Paper Association; member: American Paper Institute.

Foundation Officials

Helen B. Ambuel: director
Susan Feith: vice president, executive director
Carl R. Lemke: secretary ED University of Wisconsin BBA (1965). PRIM CORP EMPL assistant secretary: Consolidated Papers, Inc.
George Wilson Mead, II: president, director (see above)

Grants Analysis

Disclosure Period: calendar year ending 2001
Total Grants: $2,836,822*
Number of Grants: 69
Average Grant: $9,839*
Highest Grant: $1,800,000
Lowest Grant: $100
Typical Range: $1,000 to $15,000
***Note:** Giving excludes United Way. Average grant does not include highest grant ($1,800,000).

Recent Grants

Note: Grants derived from 2001 Form 990.

Library-Related

100,000	City of Wisconsin Rapids McMallan Memorial Library, Wisconsin Rapids, WI

General

1,800,000	Yale University, New Haven, CT
317,900	Northland College, Ashland, WI
139,325	National Merit Scholarship Corporation, Evanston, IL
84,450	Wisconsin Public Broadcasting Foundation, Madison, WI -- TV
55,000	Friends of Mead McMillan Association, Inc., Marshfield, WI
31,600	Beloit College, Beloit, WI
31,500	Lawrence University, Appleton, WI
30,000	United Way South Wood County, Wisconsin Rapids, WI
26,950	Milwaukee School of Engineering, Milwaukee, WI
25,600	Carroll College, Waukesha, WI

STORAGE TECHNOLOGY CORP.

Company Headquarters
Louisville, CO
Web: http://www.stortek.com

Company Description
Ticker: STK
Exchange: OTC
Employees: 8,300
SIC(s): 3577 Computer Peripheral Equipment Nec.

Operating Locations
Storage Technology Corp. (CO--Longmont, Louisville; FL--Palm Bay; IL--Crestwood; PR--Mayaguez, Ponce; TX--El Paso)

Nonmonetary Support
Type: Donated Equipment; In-kind Services
Volunteer Programs: Employees actively volunteer for a variety of corporate-sponsored activities, including Meals on Wheels, Boy Scouts, community hospitals, food banks, high schools and elementary schools, 4-H clubs, and wildlife and rescue groups. The company initiated the Volunteers in Partnership with the Community (VIP.COM) program in 1998. The program not only encourages employees to volunteer commitments, but also generates additional funds from the company for nonprofit organizations to which employees dedicate time.

StorageTek Foundation

Giving Contact
Arlyce K. Lewis, Manager, Community Relations
One StorageTek Drive
Louisville, CO 80028-4305
Phone: (303)673-6833
Fax: (303)673-8876
Web: http://www.storagetek.com/home/about/foundation/

Description
EIN: 841168359
Organization Type: Corporate Foundation
Giving Locations: headquarters area only.
Grant Types: Employee Matching Gifts, General Support, Scholarship.
Note: Employee matching gift ratio: .5 to 1 for gifts to higher education and the United Way.

Financial Summary
Total Giving: $1,036,747 (2000); $1,109,038 (1998); $768,728 (1997). Note: Contributes through corporate direct giving program and foundation.
Giving Analysis: Giving for 1998 includes: foundation matching gifts ($36,990); foundation grants to United Way ($116,827); foundation ($955,221); 1997: foundation grants to United Way ($5,228); foundation matching gifts ($22,852) foundation ($740,648)
Assets: $62,305 (2000); $275,933 (1998); $814,172 (1996)
Gifts Received: $590,091 (2000); $682,000 (1998); $750,000 (1996). Note: Contributions received from Storage Technology Corp.

Typical Recipients
Arts & Humanities: Arts Appreciation, Arts Centers, Dance, Arts & Humanities-General, Libraries, Museums/Galleries, Music, Performing Arts, Public Broadcasting, Theater
Civic & Public Affairs: Business/Free Enterprise, Clubs, Community Foundations, Economic Policy, Civic & Public Affairs-General, Housing, Native American Affairs, Professional & Trade Associations, Public Policy, Urban & Community Affairs, Women's Affairs

Education: Arts/Humanities Education, Business Education, Colleges & Universities, Continuing Education, Education Associations, Education Funds, Education Reform, Engineering/Technological Education, Faculty Development, Education-General, Leadership Training, Literacy, Minority Education, Preschool Education, Private Education (Precollege), Public Education (Precollege), Science/Mathematics Education, Secondary Education (Private), Special Education, Student Aid
Health: Arthritis, Cancer, Children's Health/Hospitals, Clinics/Medical Centers, Emergency/Ambulance Services, Health-General, Health Funds, Health Organizations, Heart, Hospices, Hospitals, Medical Rehabilitation, Mental Health, Multiple Sclerosis, Nutrition, Public Health, Single-Disease Health Associations, Transplant Networks/Donor Banks
Religion: Jewish Causes
Science: Science Museums
Social Services: At-Risk Youth, Big Brother/Big Sister, Child Welfare, Community Service Organizations, Domestic Violence, Emergency Relief, Family Services, Family Services, Food/Clothing Distribution, Homes, People with Disabilities, Recreation & Athletics, Scouts, Shelters/Homelessness, Social Services-General, Special Olympics, Substance Abuse, United Funds/United Ways, Volunteer Services, YMCA/YWCA/YMHA/YWHA, Youth Organizations

Application Procedures
Initial Contact: Send a written proposal.
Application Requirements: Include a description and background of organization, project description and purpose, objectives of organization and project, amount requested and purpose of funds sought, unique aspects of project, project budget, funding sources and amounts, list of board members and officers with affiliations, current and/or proposed income and expense budget, recently audited financial statement, and proof of tax-exempt status.
Deadlines: None.
Evaluative Criteria: The foundation may request additional information and a site visit.
Decision Notification: Evaluation generally takes 2 to 3 months.

Restrictions
The company does not support individuals, religious organizations for sectarian purposes, political or lobbying groups, fraternal organizations, general operating budgets receiving more than 40% of budget from United Way, or trips or tours.

Corporate Officials
Mark McGregor: vice president, treasurer, chief executive officer, director ED Texas A&M University BA (1964). PRIM CORP EMPL vice president, treasurer: Storage Technology Corp.
David E. Weiss: chairman, president, chief executive officer, director B 1944. ED University of Colorado BA (1967); University of Colorado MBA (1989); University of Colorado MA (1989). PRIM CORP EMPL chairman, president, chief executive officer, director: Storage Technology Corp.

Foundation Officials
Michael Klatman: president PRIM CORP EMPL vice president corporate communications: Storage Technology Corp.
Mark McGregor: vice president, treasurer (see above)

Grants Analysis
Disclosure Period: calendar year ending 1998
Total Grants: $955,221*
Number of Grants: 143
Average Grant: $6,680
Highest Grant: $100,000
Typical Range: $1,000 to $20,000
*Note: Giving excludes matching gifts; United Way.

Recent Grants
Note: Grants derived from 2000 Form 990.

General

175,000	Colorado State University, Ft. Collins, CO
50,000	Community Food Share, Inc., Boulder, CO
29,291	Boulder County United Way, Boulder, CO
26,642	Boulder County United Way, Boulder, CO
26,235	Boulder County United Way, Boulder, CO
25,000	Junior Achievement Rocky Mountain, Denver, CO
20,606	Boulder County United Way, Boulder, CO
13,759	Boulder County United Way, Boulder, CO
8,800	Cancer League of Colorado, Denver, CO
5,000	American Heart Association, Denver, CO

LOUIS L. STOTT FOUNDATION

Giving Contact
Kristine Stott, Co-Trustee
250 Chandler Rd.
Chadds Ford, PA 19317
Phone: (610)388-4655

Description
Founded: 1968
EIN: 237009027
Organization Type: Private Foundation
Giving Locations: PA: nationally.
Grant Types: General Support.

Donor Information
Founder: Martha Stott Diener

Financial Summary
Total Giving: $74,000 (fiscal year ending September 30, 2001); $90,000 (fiscal 2000); $150,000 (fiscal 1999)
Assets: $2,456,079 (fiscal 2001); $3,160,235 (fiscal 2000); $2,963,351 (fiscal 1999)

Typical Recipients
Arts & Humanities: Arts Centers, Arts & Humanities-General, Historic Preservation, History & Archaeology, Libraries, Museums/Galleries, Music
Civic & Public Affairs: African American Affairs, Botanical Gardens/Parks, Civic & Public Affairs-General, Housing, Municipalities/Towns, Philanthropic Organizations, Public Policy, Urban & Community Affairs, Women's Affairs
Education: Afterschool/Enrichment Programs, Colleges & Universities, Literacy, Minority Education, Private Education (Precollege), Public Education (Precollege), Special Education, Student Aid
Environment: Air/Water Quality, Environment-General, Resource Conservation
Health: Cancer, Hospices, Hospitals, Single-Disease Health Associations
International: Foreign Educational Institutions, Health Care/Hospitals, International Organizations
Religion: Churches, Religion-General, Social/Policy Issues
Social Services: Big Brother/Big Sister, Camps, Community Service Organizations, Crime Prevention, Delinquency & Criminal Rehabilitation, Family Planning, Food/Clothing Distribution, People with Disabilities, Scouts, Social Services-General, Substance Abuse, Youth Organizations

Application Procedures

Initial Contact: Send a brief letter of inquiry.
Application Requirements: Include proof of tax-exempt status.
Deadlines: None.

Foundation Officials

Benjamin W. Stott: trustee
Edward B. Stott: trustee
Kristine Stott: trustee

Grants Analysis

Disclosure Period: fiscal year ending September 30, 2001
Total Grants: $74,000
Number of Grants: 5
Highest Grant: $50,000
Lowest Grant: $5,000
Typical Range: $5,000 to $8,000

Recent Grants

Note: Grants derived from fiscal 2000 Form 990.

Library-Related

500	West Tisbury Library, West Tisbury, MN

General

45,000	Baraka Fund, San Francisco, CA
15,000	Island Montessori, West Tisbury, MN
10,000	Wood Services Foundation, Langhorne, PA
5,000	Martha's Vineyard Hospital, Oak Bluffs, MA
4,000	MB Community Service, Vineyard Haven, MA
2,000	Yale University, New Haven, CT
2,000	Z'Arts, Vineyard Haven, MA
1,000	Habitat for Humanity, Vineyard Haven, MA
1,000	Hospice of Martha's Vineyard, Oak Bluff, MN
1,000	Indiana Mount School, Lakeville, CT

CHARLES H. STOUT FOUNDATION

Giving Contact

Richard M. Stout, President
940 Matley Lane, Suite 3
Reno, NV 89502
Phone: (775)322-4200

Description

Founded: 1982
EIN: 942797249
Organization Type: Private Foundation
Giving Locations: AK: Silvan Springs; CA: Borrego Springs, DelMar; NV: Reno; NY: New York
Grant Types: Endowment, General Support, Scholarship.

Financial Summary

Total Giving: $363,000 (fiscal year ending June 30, 2002); $306,890 (fiscal 2001); $400,900 (fiscal 2000)
Giving Analysis: Giving for fiscal 2001 includes: foundation scholarships ($48,000) fiscal 2000: foundation scholarships ($30,000)
Assets: $7,256,589 (fiscal 2002); $7,878,061 (fiscal 2001); $8,101,921 (fiscal 2000)

Typical Recipients

Arts & Humanities: Arts Associations & Councils, Arts Centers, Arts Festivals, Ethnic & Folk Arts, Arts & Humanities-General, History & Archaeology, Libraries, Museums/Galleries, Music, Opera, Performing Arts, Public Broadcasting, Theater
Civic & Public Affairs: Housing, Law & Justice, Safety, Women's Affairs

Education: Business Education, Colleges & Universities, Community & Junior Colleges, Faculty Development, Education-General, Journalism/Media Education, Legal Education, Preschool Education, Private Education (Precollege), Student Aid
Environment: Research, Wildlife Protection
Health: Alzheimers Disease, Emergency/Ambulance Services, Health Organizations, Hospitals, Public Health, Public Health
International: Health Care/Hospitals
Religion: Religious Welfare, Social/Policy Issues
Science: Science Museums
Social Services: Animal Protection, At-Risk Youth, Child Welfare, Community Service Organizations, Domestic Violence, Family Services, Food/Clothing Distribution, People with Disabilities, Recreation & Athletics, Scouts, Senior Services, Social Services-General, Substance Abuse, YMCA/YWCA/YMHA/YWHA, Youth Organizations

Application Procedures

Initial Contact: Request application form and procedures.
Application Requirements: Include proof of tax-exempt status.
Deadlines: August1.
Decision Notification: All applicants will be notified by mail shortly after the annual meeting of Trustees. If an applicant has been denied, it will not be held over for future reconsideration; a new application must be submitted.

Restrictions

Grants are not made to individuals.

Additional Information

Publications: Application Form; Procedures

Foundation Officials

Anne E. McDonald: trustee
Douglas B. McDonald: vice president, treasurer
Elizabeth West Stout: president, trustee B San Francisco, CA March 04, 1917. ED University of Nevada (1934-1937); Imperial Valley College (1990). NONPR AFFIL member: Society Vertebrate Paleontology; founding trustee: Washoe Medical Center League; member: Kappa Alpha Theta; founding trustee: Saint Marys Hos Guild; member: Anza-Borrego Desert Natural History Association; founding trustee: Desert Research Institute. CLUB AFFIL DeAnza Desert Country Club.
Richard M. Stout: treasurer, trustee
Martha Stout Gilweit: trustee, secretary

Grants Analysis

Disclosure Period: fiscal year ending June 30, 2002
Total Grants: $315,000*
Number of Grants: 41
Average Grant: $7,683
Highest Grant: $20,000
Lowest Grant: $2,000
Typical Range: $2,500 to $15,000
***Note:** Giving excludes scholarships.

Recent Grants

Note: Grants derived from fiscal 2000 Form 990.

Library-Related

10,000	Museum Library & Arts Foundation, Reno, NV -- purchase of collections

General

23,000	Life Style, Inc., Fayetteville, AR -- operating fund
20,000	ArtWatch International, Inc, New York, NY -- public awareness program
20,000	Center for Integrative Learning, Escondido, CA -- operating fund
20,000	Cookson Hills Christian School, Kansas, OK -- update hardware and software
20,000	Elfin Forest/Harmony Gove Fire Department, Elfin Forest, CA -- operating funds
20,000	Nevada Women's Fund, Reno, NV -- academic and vocational training scholarships
20,000	Textile Museum, Washington, DC -- website phase IV
15,000	Borrego Community Health Foundation, Borrego Springs, CA -- development fund
15,000	C.A.R.E. Chest of Sierra Nevada, Reno, NV -- operating fund
15,000	Mama's Kitchen, San Diego, CA -- funding for 14 clients

STRAKE FOUNDATION

Giving Contact

George W. Strake, Jr., President
712 Main Street, Suite 3300
Houston, TX 77002-3291
Phone: (713)216-2400
Fax: (713)216-2401
E-mail: foundation@strake.org

Alternate Contact

Paul L. Robison, executive director

Description

Founded: 1952
EIN: 760041524
Organization Type: General Purpose Foundation
Giving Locations: TX: nationally.
Grant Types: Capital, Emergency, Endowment, General Support, Multiyear/Continuing Support, Project, Research, Scholarship.

Donor Information

Founder: Mr. Strake was an oilman and philanthropist who left the bulk of his estate to the foundation when he died in 1969. Strake Foundation is the successor to Strake Charities Foundation, created in 1952, by a trust instrument executed by its grantors, George W. Strake Sr. , and his wife, Susan K. Strake . On January 1, 1983, Strake Foundation, a charitable trust, was dissolved, and all assets of the trust were distributed to the newly-created Strake Foundation, a Texas non-profit corporation.

Mr. Strake, who discovered the Conroe Oil Field in Montgomery County, Texas, was an active civic leader and served on the boards of numerous social service, youth, and Catholic religious organizations. The foundation is supported by Mr. Strake's endowment as well as by funds from the estate of Mrs. Strake, who died in 1975, and by gifts from the founder's children, George W. Strake, Jr. and Georganna S. Parsley, who serve as officers and trustees of the foundation. Susan S. Dilworth, also a donor and daughter of the founder, died in 1988.

Financial Summary

Total Giving: $2,454,750 (2001); $3,200,000 (2000 approx); $3,153,500 (1999)
Giving Analysis: Giving for 2000 includes: foundation grants to United Way ($15,000); foundation scholarships ($66,000); 1998: foundation grants to United Way ($13,000) foundation scholarships ($17,500)
Assets: $53,121,964 (2001); $65,000,000 (2000 approx); $61,266,989 (1999)

Typical Recipients

Arts & Humanities: Ethnic & Folk Arts, Historic Preservation, History & Archaeology, Libraries, Museums/Galleries, Music, Public Broadcasting, Theater

Civic & Public Affairs: Botanical Gardens/Parks, Business/Free Enterprise, Clubs, Economic Development, Economic Policy, Civic & Public Affairs-General, Hispanic Affairs, Housing, Minority Business, Parades/Festivals, Professional & Trade Associations, Public Policy, Rural Affairs, Urban & Community Affairs, Women's Affairs, Zoos/Aquariums

Education: Arts/Humanities Education, Business Education, Colleges & Universities, Education Associations, Education Funds, Education Reform, Engineering/Technological Education, Education-General, Literacy, Medical Education, Minority Education, Preschool Education, Private Education (Precollege), Public Education (Precollege), Religious Education, Science/Mathematics Education, Secondary Education (Private), Secondary Education (Public), Special Education, Student Aid

Environment: Environment-General

Health: Cancer, Children's Health/Hospitals, Clinics/Medical Centers, Health Policy/Cost Containment, Health Organizations, Heart, Hospices, Hospitals, Medical Rehabilitation, Medical Research, Mental Health, Prenatal Health Issues, Public Health, Single-Disease Health Associations, Speech & Hearing, Transplant Networks/Donor Banks

International: International Peace & Security Issues, International Relations

Religion: Churches, Dioceses, Jewish Causes, Ministries, Religious Organizations, Religious Organizations, Religious Welfare, Social/Policy Issues

Science: Science Museums, Scientific Organizations

Social Services: At-Risk Youth, Child Welfare, Community Centers, Community Service Organizations, Family Services, Homes, People with Disabilities, Recreation & Athletics, Scouts, Shelters/Homelessness, Social Services-General, Substance Abuse, United Funds/United Ways, Volunteer Services, YMCA/YWCA/YMHA/YWHA, Youth Organizations

Application Procedures

Initial Contact: Contact foundation for formal application guidelines and form.

Application Requirements: Completed Application Cover Sheet, one-page description of need, copy of IRS tax exemption letter. If additional information is needed, the foundation will request it.

Deadlines: April 1 and October 1.

Review Process: The board meets in May and November. Final notification is given 45 days after a board meeting.

Restrictions

The foundation does not make grants to individuals, elementary schools, or international projects, for deficit financing, consulting services, technical assistance, or loans. No grants are made to federal or state-supported institutions of higher learning.

Additional Information

The foundation requests that applications not be bound and that no extraneous materials, including videos, accompany applications.

Publications: Annual Report; Guidelines; Application Form

Foundation Officials

Georganna S. Parsley: vice president, secretary

George W. Strake, Jr.: president, treasurer B Houston, TX 1935. ED University of Notre Dame AB (1957); Harvard University MBA (1961). PRIM CORP EMPL chairman, chief executive officer, founder: Strake Trading Group Inc. CORP AFFIL principal: GW Strake Co. NONPR AFFIL director: Texas Independent Producers & Royalty Board; advisory council: University Notre Dame College Arts and Sciences; director: Task Force Public Education; director: Boy Scouts America; director: Interstate Oil Compact Commission.

Grants Analysis

Disclosure Period: calendar year ending 2000

Total Grants: $3,153,500*

Number of Grants: 413

Average Grant: $7,635

Highest Grant: $50,000

Lowest Grant: $500

Typical Range: $1,000 to $10,000

*Note: Giving excludes United Way, scholarships. Grants analysis provided by foundation.

Recent Grants

Note: Grants derived from 2000 Form 990.

General

50,000	Christus St. Joseph Hospital Foundation, Houston, TX -- campaign for St. Joseph Hospital
50,000	St. Thomas High School, Houston, TX -- for operating support
50,000	Strake Jesuit College Preparatory, Houston, TX
36,000	St. Michael Catholic School, Houston, TX -- for 2001 annual fund drive
30,000	Boys Country of Houston, Hockley, TX -- to support "Scholarships of Leve" Program
27,000	Boy Scouts of America Sam Houston Area Council, Houston, TX -- for use by Special Needs Scouting Program
26,000	Briarwood-Brookwood, Brookshire, TX -- for operating costs
25,000	Admiral Nimitz Foundation, Fredericksburg, TX -- capital campaign
25,000	Boys and Girls Clubs of Greater Houston, Houston, TX -- sponsor annual Sleek and Burgar dinner
25,000	Lighthouse of Houston, Houston, TX -- construction of Center for Education and Adaptive Technology

J. WILLIAM AND MARY HELEN STRAKER CHARITABLE FOUNDATION

Giving Contact

Susan Straker-Henderson, President & Treasurer
925 Military Road
Zanesville, OH 43701-1538
Phone: (740)453-2220

Description

Founded: 1994

EIN: 311396841

Organization Type: Private Foundation

Giving Locations: OH: Muskingum County

Grant Types: Capital, General Support, Matching, Multiyear/Continuing Support.

Donor Information

Founder: Established in 1994 by J. William and Mary H. Straker.

Financial Summary

Total Giving: $27,000 (2001); $47,500 (2000); $55,952 (1999)

Assets: $2,570,670 (2001); $3,017,267 (2000); $3,366,692 (1999)

Gifts Received: $2,190,371 (1994). Note: In 1994, contributions were received from J. William and Mary H. Straker.

Typical Recipients

Arts & Humanities: History & Archaeology, Libraries, Museums/Galleries

Civic & Public Affairs: Clubs, Civic & Public Affairs-General, Housing, Urban & Community Affairs

Education: Colleges & Universities, Education-General, Literacy, Minority Education, Private Education (Precollege), Public Education (Precollege)

Environment: Environment-General, Wildlife Protection

Health: AIDS/HIV, Long-Term Care, Single-Disease Health Associations, Transplant Networks/Donor Banks

Religion: Religious Welfare

Social Services: Animal Protection, At-Risk Youth, Big Brother/Big Sister, People with Disabilities, Scouts, United Funds/United Ways

Application Procedures

Initial Contact: The foundation has no formal grant application procedure or application form. Submit a brief letter of inquiry.

Application Requirements: Include a description of organization, amount requested, purpose of funds sought, recently audited financial statement, proof of tax-exempt status.

Deadlines: None.

Restrictions

Does not fund individuals, religious organizations for sectarian purposes, political or lobbying groups, or organizations outside operating areas.

Foundation Officials

John W. Straker, Jr.: secretary

Susan Straker Henderson: president, treasurer

Grants Analysis

Disclosure Period: calendar year ending 2001

Total Grants: $27,000

Number of Grants: 7

Average Grant: $3,857

Highest Grant: $15,000

Lowest Grant: $500

Typical Range: $1,000 to $10,000

Recent Grants

Note: Grants derived from 2001 Form 990.

General

15,000	Muskingum City Board of Mental Retardation, Zanesville, OH
5,000	West Muskingum Academic Fund, Zanesville, OH
3,500	Muskingum Area Technical College, Zanesville, OH
1,000	Beningham Museum
1,000	Granville Schools Foundation, Granville, OH
1,000	Zanesville City School Foundation, Zanesville, OH
500	Mary Washington College, Fredericksburg, VA

STRANAHAN FOUNDATION

Giving Contact

Pamela G. Roberts, Program Officer
4159 Holland-Sylvania Road, Suite 206
Toledo, OH 43623
Phone: (419)882-5575
Fax: (419)882-2072
E-mail: proberts@stranahanfoundation.org
Web: http://www.stranahanfoundation.org

Description

Founded: 1944

EIN: 346514375

Organization Type: Family Foundation

Giving Locations: OH: Northwest Ohio

Grant Types: Capital, Challenge, General Support, Matching.

Donor Information

Founder: Established as a family trust in Ohio in 1944 by Robert A. Stranahan, former president and chairman of the Champion Spark Plug Company, and his brother, Frank Stranahan. Robert A. Stranahan Jr., and Duane Stranahan have since contributed substantially to the foundation. Members of the Stranahan family still serve on the board of trustees.

Financial Summary

Total Giving: $3,983,000 (2002); $5,200,000 (2001); $4,837,973 (2000)
Giving Analysis: Giving for 1999 includes: foundation matching gifts ($240,000); foundation grants to United Way ($450,000) 1998: foundation scholarships ($520,800)
Assets: $70,000,000 (2002 approx); $100,348,341 (2000); $106,511,564 (1999)

Typical Recipients

Arts & Humanities: Arts Associations & Councils, Arts Centers, Community Arts, Dance, Historic Preservation, History & Archaeology, Libraries, Museums/Galleries, Music, Opera, Performing Arts, Public Broadcasting, Theater
Civic & Public Affairs: Botanical Gardens/Parks, Civil Rights, Clubs, Community Foundations, Economic Development, Economic Policy, Civic & Public Affairs-General, Hispanic Affairs, Housing, Law & Justice, Nonprofit Management, Philanthropic Organizations, Professional & Trade Associations, Public Policy, Urban & Community Affairs, Zoos/Aquariums
Education: Arts/Humanities Education, Business Education, Colleges & Universities, Community & Junior Colleges, Economic Education, Education Associations, Education Funds, Education Reform, Education-General, Literacy, Medical Education, Private Education (Precollege), Religious Education, Secondary Education (Private), Secondary Education (Public), Student Aid
Environment: Environment-General, Resource Conservation, Wildlife Protection
Health: AIDS/HIV, Alzheimers Disease, Children's Health/Hospitals, Clinics/Medical Centers, Emergency/Ambulance Services, Eyes/Blindness, Health-General, Geriatric Health, Hospices, Hospitals, Medical Rehabilitation, Mental Health, Preventive Medicine/Wellness Organizations, Respiratory
International: International Environmental Issues
Religion: Ministries, Missionary Activities (Domestic), Religious Organizations, Religious Welfare
Science: Scientific Centers & Institutes
Social Services: Animal Protection, Camps, Child Welfare, Community Service Organizations, Crime Prevention, Day Care, Delinquency & Criminal Rehabilitation, Family Planning, Family Services, Food/Clothing Distribution, Homes, People with Disabilities, Recreation & Athletics, Scouts, Senior Services, Social Services-General, United Funds/United Ways, Volunteer Services, YMCA/YWCA/YMHA/YWHA, Youth Organizations

Application Procedures

Initial Contact: The foundation requests an initial letter of inquiry, not more than two pages in length, which summarizes the project.
Application Requirements: The summary should describe the organization and its history and the proposed project--what is planned and how it will be accomplished--with an approximate budget. Supporting documents should include the organization's mission statement, a copy of current tax exemption letter, and the name of the organization's contact person, with telephone and fax numbers. The foundation will invite applicants to submit further materials.
Deadlines: None. Applications should reach the foundation at least three months prior to the board meetings (typically in February, June, and October) in order to be considered at that meeting. Specific dates are available from the foundation office.

Review Process: Applicants will be notified of the board's decision within two weeks after meetings.

Restrictions

The foundation only funds 501(c)(3) organizations. No grants are made for religious groups; personal businesses; deficit financing; computer projects; film, television or radio productions; international projects; endowment funds; government projects; or individuals.

Additional Information

The foundations grantmaking is guided by the following values: Self-sufficiency, in which our goal is to help people become independent and responsible citizens. Respect for oneself, others, community, and for the environment. Freedom, of thought, speech, religion, and economic choices within a just and democratic society, and Courage, to embrace change and, if necessary, to take the initiative to bring about positive change. These fundamental values are best instilled at a young age within a closely-knit environment. Many of our grants, therefore, are directed towards younger age groups and to smaller, carefully monitored program efforts.
The foundation will not support organizations that discriminate in their leadership, staffing, or service provision on the basis of age, gender, race, ethnicity, sexual orientation, disabilities, national origin, political affiliation or religious beliefs.

Foundation Officials

Diana Foster: trustee
Gerald W. Miller: trustee B Columbus, OH 1941. PRIM CORP EMPL president: Typographic Printing Co.
Frances Parry: trustee
Duane Stranahan, Jr.: trustee PRIM CORP EMPL director: Champion Spark Plug Co.
Mark Stranahan: trustee
Stephen Stranahan: trustee B 1934. PRIM CORP EMPL treasurer: Home Ranch Co. Inc. CORP AFFIL Entelco Corp.
Charles G. Yeager: trustee

Grants Analysis

Disclosure Period: calendar year ending 2002
Total Grants: $2,491,463*
Number of Grants: 50
Average Grant: $42,683*
Highest Grant: $400,000
Lowest Grant: $1,000
Typical Range: $20,000 to $100,000
*Note: Giving excludes United Way matching gifts; scholarships. Average grant figure excludes highest grant.

Recent Grants

Note: Grants derived from 2001 Form 990.

Library-Related

37,000	Way Public Library Foundation, Perrysburg, OH -- operating

General

500,000	Public Broadcasting Foundation of Northwest Ohio, Toledo, OH -- operating
400,000	Toledo Museum of Art, Toledo, OH -- operating
364,196	Toledo Community Foundation, Toledo, OH -- operating
327,000	Northwest Ohio Scholarship Fund, Inc., Toledo, OH -- operating
316,000	David Lawrence Center and Foundation, Naples, FL -- operating
300,000	United Way, Toledo, OH -- operating
281,500	Toledo Metropolitan Mission, Toledo, OH -- operating
250,000	Montana Community Foundation, Helena, MT -- operating
250,000	Toledo Symphony, Toledo, OH -- operating
213,903	Hillsdale College, Hillsdale, MI -- operating

STRAUSS FOUNDATION

Giving Contact

Reginald Middleton, Vice President
First Union National Bank
123 Broad Street, 16th Floor
Philadelphia, PA 19109-1199
Phone: (215)670-4226
Fax: (215)670-4236

Description

Founded: 1951
EIN: 236219939
Organization Type: Family Foundation
Giving Locations: CA: Los Angeles; FL: Palm Beach; PA; Israel
Grant Types: General Support, Research.

Donor Information

Founder: Established in 1951 by Maurice L. Strauss.

Financial Summary

Total Giving: $1,607,325 (2000); $1,893,400 (1999); $2,613,360 (1998)
Giving Analysis: Giving for 2000 includes: foundation scholarships ($1,000)
Assets: $29,226,273 (2000); $33,874,026 (1999); $42,138,486 (1998)
Gifts Received: $902,226 (1992)

Typical Recipients

Arts & Humanities: Arts Associations & Councils, Ballet, Ethnic & Folk Arts, Film & Video, History & Archaeology, Libraries, Museums/Galleries, Music, Opera, Performing Arts, Theater
Civic & Public Affairs: Botanical Gardens/Parks, Civic & Public Affairs-General, Philanthropic Organizations, Urban & Community Affairs, Zoos/Aquariums
Education: Arts/Humanities Education, Colleges & Universities, Education-General, Leadership Training, Medical Education, Minority Education, Private Education (Precollege)
Environment: Air/Water Quality, Environment-General, Resource Conservation, Watershed, Wildlife Protection
Health: AIDS/HIV, Alzheimers Disease, Cancer, Clinics/Medical Centers, Diabetes, Health-General, Health Policy/Cost Containment, Health Organizations, Heart, Hospitals, Medical Research, Public Health, Single-Disease Health Associations, Transplant Networks/Donor Banks, Trauma Treatment
International: Health Care/Hospitals, Human Rights, International Affairs
Religion: Jewish Causes
Science: Science Museums
Social Services: At-Risk Youth, Big Brother/Big Sister, Camps, Child Welfare, Community Service Organizations, Emergency Relief, People with Disabilities, Recreation & Athletics, Shelters/Homelessness, Social Services-General, Substance Abuse, Youth Organizations

Application Procedures

Initial Contact: The foundation reports that unsolicited applications are generally not encouraged. The foundation requests applications be made in writing.
Deadlines: None.

Restrictions

The foundation reports grants are made only to public charities. Grants are not made to individuals.

Additional Information

Trust(s): First Union National Bank

Foundation Officials

Henry A. Gladstone: trustee
Scott Rosen Isdaner: trustee B 1952. PRIM CORP EMPL president: V I P Inc.
Sandra S. Krause: trustee
Reginald Middleton: vice president
Benjamin Strauss: trustee CORP AFFIL director: Pep Boys - Manny Moe & Jack.
Robert Perry Strauss: trustee B 1941. PRIM CORP EMPL president: Noven Pharmaceuticals Inc. NONPR AFFIL director: Enterprise Florida Innovation Partners.

Grants Analysis

Disclosure Period: calendar year ending 2000
Total Grants: $1,607,325
Number of Grants: 297
Average Grant: $5,409
Highest Grant: $90,000
Typical Range: $1,000 to $10,000

Recent Grants

Note: Grants derived from 2000 Form 990.

General

90,000	Federation Allied Jewish Appeal, Philadelphia, PA
50,000	Cedars-Sinai Research of Women's Cancer, Los Angeles, CA
50,000	Regional Performing Arts Center, Philadelphia, PA
40,000	Palm Beach County Jewish Federation, Palm Beach, FL
40,000	Philadelphia Zoo, Philadelphia, PA
35,000	Jewish Big Brothers, Los Angeles, CA
30,000	Duke University, Durham, NC
26,000	Leaders in Furthering Education
26,000	Palm Beach Opera, Palm Beach, FL
25,000	Ballet Florida, West Palm Beach, FL

LEON STRAUSS FOUNDATION

Giving Contact

Robert P. Vossler, Trustee
5332 Harbor St.
Commerce, CA 90040
Phone: (323)728-5440

Description

Founded: 1976
EIN: 510205308
Organization Type: Private Foundation
Grant Types: Endowment, General Support.

Donor Information

Founder: the late Leon Strauss

Financial Summary

Total Giving: $491,500 (2000); $465,000 (1999); $451,000 (1998)
Assets: $9,904,156 (2000); $10,865,898 (1999); $8,405,709 (1996)
Gifts Received: $64,741 (2000); $43,484 (1996). Note: In 1996 and 2000, contributions were received from the Leon Strauss Trust.

Typical Recipients

Arts & Humanities: Arts Associations & Councils, Arts Centers, Arts Outreach, Libraries, Music, Opera, Public Broadcasting, Theater

Civic & Public Affairs: Civic & Public Affairs-General, Municipalities/Towns, Safety
Education: Colleges & Universities, Community & Junior Colleges, Education Associations, Secondary Education (Public), Student Aid
Environment: Environment-General
Health: AIDS/HIV, Cancer, Children's Health/Hospitals, Clinics/Medical Centers, Diabetes, Eyes/Blindness, Geriatric Health, Health Organizations, Hospitals, Medical Research, Mental Health, Research/Studies Institutes, Single-Disease Health Associations, Speech & Hearing
Religion: Churches, Jewish Causes, Ministries, Ministries, Religious Welfare
Science: Scientific Centers & Institutes
Social Services: At-Risk Youth, Child Welfare, Community Service Organizations, Crime Prevention, Family Services, People with Disabilities, Scouts, Special Olympics, Youth Organizations

Application Procedures

Initial Contact: The foundation requests applications be made in writing.
Application Requirements: Include name, address, purpose of funds sought, and proof of tax-exempt status.
Deadlines: None.

Restrictions

Preference is given to non-profit children's camps and hospitals.

Foundation Officials

Charles Curley: trustee
Paul Simon: trustee B Newark, NJ 1941. ED Brooklyn Law School; Queens College BA.
Ralph Simon: trustee
William Simon: trustee PRIM CORP EMPL president, chief executive officer: North Face.
Robert P. Vossler: trustee

Grants Analysis

Disclosure Period: calendar year ending 2000
Total Grants: $491,500
Number of Grants: 72
Average Grant: $6,826
Highest Grant: $20,000
Typical Range: $1,000 to $10,000

Recent Grants

Note: Grants derived from 2001 Form 990.

General

20,000	City of Hope, Los Angeles, CA
20,000	St. Francis Foundation, San Francisco, CA
16,000	San Rafael Canal Ministry, San Rafael, CA
15,000	John Wayne Cancer Institute, Santa Monica, CA
15,000	Juvenile Diabetes Research Foundation, Pasadena, CA
10,000	ALS Association, Los Angeles, CA
10,000	Children's Hospital, San Diego, CA
10,000	Circuit Rider Productions, Windsor, CA
10,000	City of Commerce Youth Scholarship Fund, Commerce, CA
10,000	Claremont McKenna College-Bauer Center, Claremont, CA

MARGARET DORRANCE STRAWBRIDGE FOUNDATION OF PENNSYLVANIA II

Giving Contact

Diana S. Wister, President
125 Strafford Ave., Suite 108
Wayne, PA 19087
Phone: (610)688-9260

Description

Founded: 1985
EIN: 232371943
Organization Type: Private Foundation
Giving Locations: FL; PA: Eastern USA.
Grant Types: General Support, Multiyear/Continuing Support, Operating Expenses, Research.

Donor Information

Founder: Margaret Dorrance Strawbridge Foundation

Financial Summary

Total Giving: $675,850 (1998); $539,187 (1997); $435,537 (1995)
Assets: $28,747,733 (1998); $21,842,263 (1997); $4,245,694 (1995)
Gifts Received: $6,151,609 (1998); $9,000,000 (1997); $254,217 (1995). Note: In 1998, contributions were received from Diane S. Norris Trust. In 1997, contributions were received from Diana S. Wister.

Typical Recipients

Arts & Humanities: Arts Associations & Councils, Arts Centers, Community Arts, Historic Preservation, History & Archaeology, Libraries, Museums/Galleries, Music, Performing Arts, Public Broadcasting
Civic & Public Affairs: Botanical Gardens/Parks, Clubs, Community Foundations, Civic & Public Affairs-General, Public Policy, Safety, Urban & Community Affairs, Zoos/Aquariums
Education: Agricultural Education, Arts/Humanities Education, Colleges & Universities, Private Education (Precollege), Religious Education, Student Aid
Environment: Air/Water Quality, Environment-General, Resource Conservation, Wildlife Protection
Health: Cancer, Children's Health/Hospitals, Emergency/Ambulance Services, Hospices, Hospitals, Medical Rehabilitation, Medical Research, Prenatal Health Issues, Public Health, Single-Disease Health Associations
International: Foreign Educational Institutions, International Environmental Issues
Religion: Churches, Ministries, Religious Welfare
Science: Scientific Centers & Institutes, Scientific Labs, Scientific Research
Social Services: Animal Protection, Camps, Child Welfare, Community Service Organizations, Delinquency & Criminal Rehabilitation, Family Planning, People with Disabilities, Recreation & Athletics, Senior Services, Substance Abuse

Application Procedures

Initial Contact: The foundation has no formal grant application procedure or application form.
Deadlines: None.

Restrictions

Does not support individuals or provide loans.

Foundation Officials

Diana S. Wister: president B 1939.

Grants Analysis

Disclosure Period: calendar year ending 1998
Total Grants: $675,850
Number of Grants: 71
Average Grant: $8,463*
Highest Grant: $75,000
Typical Range: $100 to $50,000
*Note: Average grant excludes highest grant.

Recent Grants

Note: Grants derived from 1998 Form 990.

General

75,000	Intercoastal Health Foundation, West Palm Beach, FL

53,000	Hanley-Hazelden Center at St. Mary's, West Palm Beach, FL
50,000	South Florida Center for Theological Study, Miami, FL
30,000	Friends of Acadia, Bar Harbor, ME
30,000	Life Christian Academy
30,000	Westover School, Middlebury, CT
25,000	Two Garden Fund, Bar Harbor, ME
23,900	Foxcroft School, Middlesbury, VA
20,000	Jackson Laboratory, Bar Harbor, ME
20,000	New Hope Foundation, Palm Beach, FL

HATTIE M. STRONG FOUNDATION

Giving Contact

Judith B. Cyphers, Secretary & Director of Grants
1620 Eye Street N.W., Suite 700
Washington, DC 20006
Phone: (202)331-1619
Fax: (202)466-2894
E-mail: hmsf@hmstrongfoundation.org
Web: http://www.hmstrongfoundation.org

Description

Founded: 1928
EIN: 530237223
Organization Type: Specialized/Single Purpose Foundation
Giving Locations: DC: Washington metropolitan area for community education grant program nationally for student loan program.
Grant Types: General Support, Loan, Professorship, Project, Research.

Donor Information

Founder: Incorporated in 1928 by the late Hattie M. Strong .

Financial Summary

Total Giving: $815,800 (fiscal year ending August 31, 2001); $800,000 (fiscal 2000 approx); $734,080 (fiscal 1999)
Giving Analysis: Giving for fiscal 2001 includes: foundation gifts to individuals ($518,810); fiscal 1999: foundation gifts to individuals ($499,050) fiscal 1997: foundation gifts to individuals ($485,695)
Assets: $31,928,267 (fiscal 2001); $23,668,000 (fiscal 1997 approx); $22,230,982 (fiscal 1996)
Gifts Received: $1,880 (fiscal 2001); $1,105 (fiscal 1999); $2,125 (fiscal 1996). Note: Gifts for fiscal 1999 and 2001 were from miscellaneous donors, all under $500.

Typical Recipients

Arts & Humanities: Arts Outreach, History & Archaeology, Museums/Galleries
Civic & Public Affairs: Economic Development, Employment/Job Training, Civic & Public Affairs-General, Hispanic Affairs, Nonprofit Management, Professional & Trade Associations, Women's Affairs
Education: Afterschool/Enrichment Programs, Arts/Humanities Education, Colleges & Universities, Community & Junior Colleges, Continuing Education, Education Funds, Education Reform, Elementary Education (Public), Engineering/Technological Education, Environmental Education, Faculty Development, Education-General, Health & Physical Education, International Studies, Leadership Training, Literacy, Minority Education, Preschool Education, Public Education (Precollege), School Volunteerism, Science/Mathematics Education, Special Education, Vocational & Technical Education
Environment: Resource Conservation

Health: Medical Rehabilitation, Research/Studies Institutes
Religion: Ministries
Social Services: Child Welfare, Community Service Organizations, Day Care, Family Services, Social Services-General, YMCA/YWCA/YMHA/YWHA

Application Procedures

Initial Contact: For the loan program, students should send an initial letter to the foundation. For the grant program, organizations interested in submitting a proposal should first contact the foundation and request written materials explaining proposal procedures and requirements.
Application Requirements: For the loan program, initial letters should provide a brief personal history and identification of the educational institution attended, the subjects studied, the date studies are expected to be completed, and the amount of funds needed (maximum loan amount is $3,000). If the student qualifies for consideration, application forms are then sent out to be completed and returned to the foundation. For the grant program, organizations should follow the foundation's proposal procedures and requirements as directed.
Deadlines: Students should apply between January 1 and March 31 for loans covering the academic year beginning the following September. Deadlines for grant proposals are January 15, April 15, July 15, and October 15 to be considered for March, June, September, and December, respectively.
Review Process: Loan applicants are normally notified of the foundation's decision in early July. After a full review of grant proposals by foundation staff, including personal interviews if necessary, proposals are presented to the board for action. Applicants are notified in writing of the board's decision.

Restrictions

For the loan program, foreign students temporarily in the United States do not qualify. For the grant program, the foundation generally does not support building or endowment funds, requests for equipment, research, conferences or seminars, projects designed to educate the general public, or programs of national or international scope. The foundation does not make grants to individuals or provide scholarships.

Additional Information

Publications: Annual Report; Application Form; Application Guidelines

Foundation Officials

Judith B. Cyphers: secretary, director grants, office
Thelma L. Eichman: director
Mary D. Janney: director
John Marmaduke Lynham, Jr.: director B Washington, DC 1952. ED Trinity College BS (1975); University of Maryland MBA (1979); George Washington University JD (1983). CORP AFFIL partner: Ross Marsh & Foster; director: JMW Settlements Inc. NONPR AFFIL member: District of Columbia Estate Planning Council; Order of Barristers; member: District of Columbia Bar Association. CLUB AFFIL Metropolitan Club; Chevy Chase Club; Lawyers Club of Washington.
Richard S. T. Marsh: director
Vincent Emory Reed: director emeritus B Saint Louis, MO 1928. ED West Virginia State College BS (1952); Howard University MA (1965); University of Pennsylvania Wharton School (1969); West Virginia State College HLD (1977). PRIM NONPR EMPL assistant secretary elementary & secondary education: U.S. Department of Education. CORP AFFIL director: Home Federal Savings & Loan Association. NONPR AFFIL volunteer: Southeast Youth Football Association; director: Washington YMCA; volunteer: South-

east Boys Club; member: National Education Association; member: Phi Delta Kappa; member: National Association School Security Officers; member: National Association Secondary School Principals; member: NAACP; staff member: District of Columbia Public Schools; member: Kappa Alpha Psi; member: District of Columbia Parent Teacher Association; member: District of Columbia PTA Washington Schools; director: District of Columbia Goodwill Industries; member: American Association School Administrations; member: American Society Business Officals; director: 12 Neediest Kids. CLUB AFFIL Kiwanis Club; Pigskin Club.
Sigrid S. Reynolds: director
Carol Levitt Schwartz: director B Greenville, MS 1944. ED University of Texas BS (1965). NONPR AFFIL director: Washington Hebrew Congregation; director: Whitman Walker Clinic; trustee: John F. Kennedy Center Community Friends Board; vice president advisory board: American Automobile Association; member at large: Council District of Columbia. CLUB AFFIL Cosmos Club.
Bente Strong: director
Henry Strong: chairman, president, officer B Rochester, NY 1923. ED Williams College AB (1949). NONPR AFFIL director: National Symphony Orchestra Association; director: Pomfret School; director: National Capital Chapter ARC; director: M. M. Post Foundation District of Columbia; director: Mount Vernon College; honorary trustee: John F. Kennedy Center Performing Arts. CLUB AFFIL Metro Club; Chevy Chase Club; Gibson Island Club.
Henry L. Strong: vice president, officer
Robin C. Tanner: treasurer, director loans, office

Grants Analysis

Disclosure Period: fiscal year ending August 31, 2001
Total Grants: $296,990*
Number of Grants: 50
Average Grant: $5,940
Highest Grant: $10,000
Typical Range: $1,000 to $10,000
*Note: Giving excludes student loans to individuals.

Recent Grants

Note: Grants derived from 1999 Form 990.

General

7,000	National Building Museum, Washington, DC -- for the city-vision program
6,500	Carlos Rosario Adult and Career Center, Washington, DC -- to expand the adult education program
6,000	Campagna Center, Alexandria, VA -- for the reading specialist program for 1st and 3rd grades
6,000	DC Scores, Washington, DC -- for a new 35 hour professional development program
6,000	Gallaudet University, Washington, DC -- for the expansion of Project Achieve, a teacher training program for Master's degree candidates
6,000	Homeless Children's Tutorial Project, Inc., Washington, DC -- for Project Northstar, which provides one-on-one tutoring
6,000	Humanities Council of Washington, Washington, DC -- for urban scholars' books for kids writers corps program
6,000	New Community After-school and Advocacy Program, Washington, DC -- for the direct education program
5,000	Center for Artistry in Teaching, Washington, DC -- for seven follow-up professional teaching workshops for 50 DCPS teachers

5,000   Chesapeake Bay Foundation, Annapolis, MD -- for the participation of 200 District students and teachers in CBF's environmental field education programs

CHARLES J. STROSACKER FOUNDATION

Giving Contact
Bobbie N. Arnold, Executive Vice President
PO Box 471
Midland, MI 48640-0471
Phone: (989)832-0066

Description
Founded: 1957
EIN: 386062787
Organization Type: General Purpose Foundation
Giving Locations: MI: Midland some statewide funding
Grant Types: Endowment, General Support, Matching, Multiyear/Continuing Support.

Donor Information
Founder: Established in 1957 by the late Charles J. Strosacker (1882-1963), one of the pioneers of the Dow Chemical Company.

Financial Summary
Total Giving: $2,681,518 (2001); $2,589,991 (2000); $2,246,401 (1998)
Giving Analysis: Giving for 2001 includes: foundation grants to United Way ($131,900); 2000: foundation grants to United Way ($79,000); 1998: foundation scholarships ($500); foundation grants to United Way ($72,000) foundation grants to United Way ($75,500)
Assets: $47,897,123 (2001); $55,642,861 (2000); $49,660,107 (1998)

Typical Recipients
Arts & Humanities: Arts Centers, Arts & Humanities-General, History & Archaeology, Museums/Galleries, Music, Performing Arts, Theater, Visual Arts
Civic & Public Affairs: Botanical Gardens/Parks, Business/Free Enterprise, Chambers of Commerce, Community Foundations, Economic Development, Economic Policy, Employment/Job Training, Civic & Public Affairs-General, Housing, Municipalities/Towns, Native American Affairs, Nonprofit Management, Parades/Festivals, Philanthropic Organizations, Safety, Urban & Community Affairs, Women's Affairs, Zoos/Aquariums
Education: Agricultural Education, Business Education, Colleges & Universities, Community & Junior Colleges, Continuing Education, Engineering/Technological Education, Education-General, Legal Education, Legal Education, Literacy, Medical Education, Minority Education, Preschool Education, Private Education (Precollege), Public Education (Precollege), Science/Mathematics Education, Secondary Education (Public), Student Aid
Environment: Air/Water Quality, Environment-General, Resource Conservation
Health: AIDS/HIV, Clinics/Medical Centers, Emergency/Ambulance Services, Geriatric Health, Health Policy/Cost Containment, Health Organizations, Hospices, Hospitals, Mental Health, Nursing Services, Public Health, Transplant Networks/Donor Banks
Religion: Churches, Religious Welfare
Science: Scientific Centers & Institutes
Social Services: At-Risk Youth, Big Brother/Big Sister, Child Welfare, Community Centers, Community Service Organizations, Crime Prevention, Domestic Violence, Family Planning, Family Services, Food/Clothing Distribution, Homes, Recreation & Athletics, Substance Abuse, United Funds/United Ways, Volunteer Services, YMCA/YWCA/YMHA/YWHA, Youth Organizations

Application Procedures
Initial Contact: Applications should be made by letter. All correspondence must be in writing, unless the foundation initiates a personal interview.
Application Requirements: The proposal should describe the purpose of the project, amount requested, timetable for funding and completion of the project, a list of other major income sources, and a list of major expenditures. The proposal should also include copies of the IRS letter granting tax-exempt status to the applicant, and the organization's latest financial statements.
Deadlines: Requests should be received by September of the year preceding the time payment is desired.

Restrictions
The foundation does not make grants to individuals.

Additional Information
Publications: Annual Report (including Application Guidelines)

Foundation Officials
David J. Arnold: trustee
Martha G. Arnold: president, trustee
John Bartos: trustee
Lawrence E. Burks: treasurer, trustee B 1934. PRIM CORP EMPL president: Chemical Bank & Trust Co. NONPR AFFIL chairman board: Saginaw-Midland Municipal Water Corp.
Ralph A. Cole: vice president, trustee
John Samuel Ludington: assistant treasurer, trustee B Detroit, MI 1928. ED Albion College BS (1951); Saginaw Valley State College JD (1977). PRIM CORP EMPL chairman emeritus, director: Dow Corning Corp. CORP AFFIL director: Comerica Bank Midland. NONPR AFFIL trustee: Midland Community Center.
Patricia E. McKelvey: secretary
Hon. Donna T. Morris: assistant secretary, trustee OCCUPATION Probate Judge.
Charles J. Thrune: assistant vice president, trustee
John W. Tysse: trustee
Eugene C. Yehle: chairman, trustee

Grants Analysis
Disclosure Period: calendar year ending 2001
Total Grants: $2,549,618*
Number of Grants: 83
Average Grant: $30,718
Highest Grant: $257,105
Lowest Grant: $500
Typical Range: $5,000 to $100,000
*Note: Giving excludes United Way.

Recent Grants
Note: Grants derived from 2000 Form 990.

General
301,179	Midland Area Community Foundation, Midland, MI
175,000	Midland Center for Accessible Health Care, Midland, MI
151,500	Delta College, University Center, MI
113,000	Midland Community Center, Midland, MI
101,000	Michigan State University, East Lansing, MI
100,000	Homer Township Fire Department
100,000	Kalamazoo College, Kalamazoo, MI -- Facilities
100,000	Midland County Council on Aging, Midland, MI
100,000	Saginaw Valley State University, University Center, MI
100,000	Thomas M. Cooley Law School, Lansing, MI

G. B. STUART CHARITABLE FOUNDATION

Giving Contact
Karen E. Faircloth, Secretary & Treasurer
3 S. Hanover St.
Carlisle, PA 17013
Phone: (717)243-3737

Description
Founded: 1977
EIN: 232042245
Organization Type: Private Foundation
Giving Locations: PA: Cumberland County
Grant Types: General Support.

Donor Information
Founder: the late George B. Stuart

Financial Summary
Total Giving: $619,198 (2000); $443,107 (1999); $424,945 (1998). Note: 1997 Giving includes United Way ($1,000).
Giving Analysis: Giving for 2000 includes: foundation grants to United Way ($101,000); 1999: foundation grants to United Way ($1,000) 1998: foundation grants to United Way ($20,000)
Assets: $16,779,084 (2000); $15,546,947 (1999); $16,650,023 (1998)
Gifts Received: $137,352 (2000). Note: In 1997, contributions were received from Henry L. Stewart.

Typical Recipients
Arts & Humanities: Historic Preservation, History & Archaeology, Libraries
Civic & Public Affairs: Employment/Job Training, Housing, Law & Justice, Municipalities/Towns, Safety
Education: Colleges & Universities, Community & Junior Colleges, Legal Education, Science/Mathematics Education
Health: Arthritis, Cancer, Children's Health/Hospitals, Diabetes, Eyes/Blindness, Health Organizations, Heart, Hospitals, Multiple Sclerosis, Prenatal Health Issues, Single-Disease Health Associations
Religion: Bible Study/Translation, Churches, Religion-General, Religious Organizations, Religious Welfare
Social Services: Emergency Relief, Food/Clothing Distribution, Social Services-General, United Funds/United Ways

Application Procedures
Initial Contact: Make a telephone inquiry about the feasibility of the request. Letters of inquiry are also accepted.
Application Requirements: Include a description of organization; amount requested; purpose of funds sought; proof of tax-exempt status
Deadlines: July 1.

Restrictions
Grants are not made to individuals.

Additional Information
Trust(s): Mellon Bank NA, Financial Trust

Foundation Officials
Alison Brockmeyer: director
Karen E. Faircloth: secretary, treasurer
Barbara E. Falconer: president
Keith D. Falconer: director
Victoria J. Macauley: vice president

Grants Analysis
Disclosure Period: calendar year ending 2000
Total Grants: $518,198*
Number of Grants: 31

Average Grant: $10,748*
Highest Grant: $105,500
Typical Range: $5,000 to $20,000
***Note:** Giving excludes United Way. Average grant figure excludes two highest grants ($206,500).

Recent Grants

Note: Grants derived from 1999 Form 990.

Library-Related
15,000	Bosler Free Library, Carlisle, PA

General
100,000	Carlisle Hospital Medical Care Foundation, Carlisle, PA
100,000	Dickinson Township, Mt. Holly Springs, PA
61,200	Cumberland County Historical Society, Carlisle, PA
50,000	Cumberland Goodwill Fire and Rescue, Carlisle, PA
40,000	Carlisle Band, Carlisle, PA
15,000	Carlisle Area Opportunities Industrialization Center, Inc., Carlisle, PA
15,000	First Presbyterian Church, Carlisle, PA
10,000	Salvation Army, Carlisle, PA
6,200	Silver Spring Presbyterian Church, Mechanicsburg, PA
6,000	Carlisle Hospital Auxiliary, Inc., Carlisle, PA

ELBRIDGE AND EVELYN STUART FOUNDATION

Giving Contact

Anne Myers
c/o Bank One Trust Co. NA
1 Bank One Plaza MS IL1-0486
70 W. Madison
Chicago, IL 60670
Phone: (414)765-2017

Description

Founded: 1961
EIN: 956014019
Organization Type: Private Foundation
Giving Locations: CA
Grant Types: General Support.

Financial Summary

Total Giving: $740,000 (2001); $730,000 (2000); $550,000 (1999)
Assets: $13,636,455 (2001); $15,355,595 (2000); $16,558,428 (1999)

Typical Recipients

Arts & Humanities: Arts Associations & Councils, Historic Preservation, History & Archaeology, Libraries, Museums/Galleries, Music, Public Broadcasting
Civic & Public Affairs: Community Foundations, Civic & Public Affairs-General, Nonprofit Management, Philanthropic Organizations
Education: Agricultural Education, Arts/Humanities Education, Business Education, Colleges & Universities, Continuing Education, Elementary Education (Private), Education-General, Private Education (Precollege), Religious Education, Science/Mathematics Education, Social Sciences Education, Special Education, Student Aid
Environment: Environment-General, Resource Conservation, Wildlife Protection
Health: Hospitals
International: Foreign Arts Organizations, Health Care/Hospitals, International Environmental Issues, International Organizations
Religion: Churches, Jewish Causes, Religious Organizations, Religious Welfare
Social Services: Social Services-General, Youth Organizations

Application Procedures

Initial Contact: Send a brief letter of inquiry describing program or project.
Application Requirements: Include a description of organization, purpose of funds sought, and proof of tax-exempt status.
Deadlines: None.

Additional Information

Trust(s): Bank One Trust Co. NA

Foundation Officials

Elizabeth Nelson: co-trustee

Grants Analysis

Disclosure Period: calendar year ending 2001
Total Grants: $740,000
Number of Grants: 47
Average Grant: $10,652*
Highest Grant: $250,000
Lowest Grant: $1,000
Typical Range: $5,000 to $20,000
***Note:** Average grant figure excludes highest grant.

Recent Grants

Note: Grants derived from 2000 Form 990.

General
150,000	St. John's Hospital, Los Angeles, CA
50,000	J. Paul Getty Trust, Los Angeles, CA
50,000	Stanford University, Stanford, CA
30,000	Community Foundation of Jackson Hole, Jackson Hole, WY
25,000	All Saints Episcopal School, Phoenix, AZ
20,000	Episcopal Diocese of Los Angeles, Los Angeles, CA
20,000	National Museum of Wildlife Art, Jackson, WY
20,000	Winrock International, Morrilton, AR
17,000	St. Matthews School, Pacific Palisades, CA
10,000	Colonial Williamsburg Foundation, Williamsburg, VA

ESTATE OF JOSEPH L. STUBBLEFIELD

Giving Contact

H. H. Hayner, Trustee
249 W. Alder St.
PO Box 1757
Walla Walla, WA 99362
Phone: (509)527-3500

Description

Founded: 1902
EIN: 916031350
Organization Type: Private Foundation
Giving Locations: OR; WA
Grant Types: Scholarship.

Donor Information

Founder: the late Joseph L. Stubblefield

Financial Summary

Total Giving: $410,640 (2001); $378,005 (2000); $302,130 (1999)
Giving Analysis: Giving for 2001 includes: foundation scholarships ($525); foundation grants to United Way ($10,000); 2000: foundation gifts to individuals ($6,216); foundation scholarships ($10,350); 1999: foundation gifts to individuals ($8,230); foundation scholarships ($29,825);

Assets: $6,631,414 (2001); $8,386,189 (2000); $9,507,662 (1999)
Gifts Received: $2,400 (2001); $173,450 (1996); $10,000 (1995). Note: In 1996, contributions were received from Frank Wilson Trust and Mike Murr.

Typical Recipients

Arts & Humanities: Arts Associations & Councils, Arts Centers, Arts & Humanities-General, History & Archaeology, Libraries, Music
Civic & Public Affairs: Business/Free Enterprise, Chambers of Commerce, Civic & Public Affairs-General, Parades/Festivals, Urban & Community Affairs
Education: Afterschool/Enrichment Programs, Business Education, Colleges & Universities, Community & Junior Colleges, Education-General, Literacy, Private Education (Precollege), Public Education (Precollege), Science/Mathematics Education, Secondary Education (Private), Student Aid
Environment: Environment-General
Health: Cancer, Hospices, Multiple Sclerosis
Religion: Churches, Religious Welfare
Social Services: Child Welfare, Community Service Organizations, Counseling, Crime Prevention, Family Planning, Homes, People with Disabilities, Recreation & Athletics, Scouts, United Funds/United Ways, YMCA/YWCA/YMHA/YWHA, Youth Organizations

Application Procedures

Initial Contact: Send a brief letter of inquiry.
Application Requirements: Include recently audited financial statement and purpose of funds sought.
Deadlines: None; but reasonable time should be allowed for review.

Restrictions

Provides grants to indigent widows.

Foundation Officials

Herman Henry Hayner: trustee B Fairfield, WA September 25, 1916. ED Washington State University BA (1938); University of Oregon JD (1946). NONPR AFFIL member: Walla Walla County Bar Association; member: Washington State Bar Association; fellow: American College Trust & Estate Counsel; member: Walla Walla Chamber of Commerce; fellow: American Bar Association. CLUB AFFIL Walla Walla Country Club; Rotary Club.
James K. Hayner: trustee

Grants Analysis

Disclosure Period: calendar year ending 2001
Total Grants: $400,115*
Number of Grants: 52
Average Grant: $5,394*
Highest Grant: $125,000
Lowest Grant: $100
Typical Range: $1,000 to $10,000
***Note:** Giving excludes United Way; scholarships. Average grant figure excludes highest grant.

Recent Grants

Note: Grants derived from 2000 Form 990.

General
100,000	Walla Walla School District, Walla Walla, WA -- expendable trust
52,500	Whitman College, Walla Walla, WA
32,200	Washington State University Foundation, Pullman, WA
20,000	YWCA, Walla Walla, WA
15,000	Children's Home Society, Walla Walla, WA
15,000	Intervarsity, Walla Walla, WA
15,000	Walla Walla Community College Foundation, Walla Walla, WA
15,000	Young Life, Walla Walla, WA

13,750	Walla Walla School District, Walla Walla, WA -- music after school
11,000	Walla Walla Catholic Schools, Walla Walla, WA

MORRIS STULSAFT FOUNDATION

Giving Contact

Joseph W. Valentine, Executive Director
100 Bush Street, Suite 825
San Francisco, CA 94104-2521
Phone: (415)986-7117
Fax: (415)986-2521
E-mail: stulsaft@aol.com
Web: http://www.stulsaft.org

Description

Founded: 1953
EIN: 946064379
Organization Type: Specialized/Single Purpose Foundation
Giving Locations: CA: Alameda County, Contra Costa County, Marin County, San Francisco County, San Mateo County, Santa Clara County
Grant Types: Capital, General Support, Project.

Donor Information

Founder: Established in California in 1953 by the Morris Stulsaft Testamentary Trust to aid San Francisco organizations for needy and deserving children, without regard to race, creed, or age.

Financial Summary

Total Giving: $1,585,400 (2002); $1,200,100 (2001); $1,654,345 (2000)
Giving Analysis: Giving for 1999 includes: foundation scholarships ($70,000); 1998: foundation matching gifts ($5,000); foundation scholarships ($70,000); 1997: foundation matching gifts ($12,500) foundation scholarships ($70,000)
Assets: $117,091 (2001); $150,212 (2000); $682,322 (1999). Note: Asset figure for 1996 is for the Morris Stulsaft Testamentary Trust which periodically distributes a percentage of its net income to the foundation.
Gifts Received: $682,322 (1999); $1,089,785 (1998); $1,075,775 (1997). Note: The foundation receives contributions from the Morris Stulsaft Testamentary Trust.

Typical Recipients

Arts & Humanities: Arts Appreciation, Arts Outreach, Dance, History & Archaeology, Libraries, Museums/Galleries, Music, Opera, Performing Arts, Public Broadcasting, Visual Arts
Civic & Public Affairs: Asian American Affairs, Botanical Gardens/Parks, Community Foundations, Economic Development, Employment/Job Training, Civic & Public Affairs-General, Hispanic Affairs, Housing, Law & Justice, Nonprofit Management, Urban & Community Affairs, Women's Affairs, Zoos/Aquariums
Education: Afterschool/Enrichment Programs, Arts/Humanities Education, Business Education, Colleges & Universities, Education Associations, Education Funds, Education Reform, Elementary Education (Private), Elementary Education (Public), Faculty Development, Education-General, Gifted & Talented Programs, Journalism/Media Education, Leadership Training, Legal Education, Literacy, Medical Education, Minority Education, Preschool Education, Private Education (Precollege), Public Education (Precollege), School Volunteerism, Science/Mathematics Education, Secondary Education (Private), Special Education, Student Aid, Vocational & Technical Education

Environment: Resource Conservation, Wildlife Protection
Health: Adolescent Health Issues, AIDS/HIV, Cancer, Children's Health/Hospitals, Diabetes, Emergency/Ambulance Services, Eyes/Blindness, Heart, Hospitals, Medical Rehabilitation, Medical Research, Mental Health, Nursing Services, Prenatal Health Issues, Preventive Medicine/Wellness Organizations, Public Health, Research/Studies Institutes, Single-Disease Health Associations, Speech & Hearing, Trauma Treatment
International: Foreign Educational Institutions, International Development, International Environmental Issues, International Relief Efforts, Missionary/Religious Activities
Religion: Jewish Causes, Ministries, Religious Welfare
Science: Science Museums, Scientific Centers & Institutes
Social Services: At-Risk Youth, Big Brother/Big Sister, Camps, Child Abuse, Child Welfare, Community Centers, Community Service Organizations, Counseling, Crime Prevention, Day Care, Delinquency & Criminal Rehabilitation, Domestic Violence, Family Planning, Family Services, Food/Clothing Distribution, Homes, People with Disabilities, Recreation & Athletics, Refugee Assistance, Senior Services, Sexual Abuse, Shelters/Homelessness, Social Services-General, Substance Abuse, Volunteer Services, YMCA/YWCA/YMHA/YWHA, Youth Organizations

Application Procedures

Initial Contact: The foundation provides an application form, which must be used.
Application Requirements: Along with the "Application for Grant" form, additional narrative information may be provided, along with descriptive attachments. In addition, the following items must be provided for each grant request: revenue and expense budget for the proposed program; current agency total revenue and expense budget; evaluation report on this program, if available; most recent agency audit or financial statements; most recent IRS Form 990, with attachments; current list of officers and directors, showing occupations and affiliations. For first time applicants, the following items must also be submitted: IRS letter of tax exemption under Section 501(c)(3), IRS letter classifying the organization as "not a private foundation" under Section 509(a), California Franchise Tax Board letter of exemption under Section 23701(d), and articles of incorporation.
Deadlines: None.
Review Process: The board meets in January, March, May, July, September, and November. If interested, the board of directors may require a representative from the applying organization to provide a presentation (of not more than half an hour) to a committee of the board. All applications are acknowledged. Notice of approval or rejection, or requests for more information, are usually made within six months.

Restrictions

No grants are made to individuals or for emergency funds, endowments, deficit funding, or sectarian purposes. Only one request per organization in a twelve-month period will be reviewed.

Additional Information

Publications: Biennial Report; Application Guidelines

Foundation Officials

Roy L. Bouque: director
Adele Corvin: president
Dana Corvin: director
Dorothy S. Corvin: director
Joan Nelson Dills: administrator
Raymond Marks: secretary, treasurer B 1922.
Edward A. Miller: director PRIM CORP EMPL partner, treasurer: Flinn Gray & Herterich.

Susan Mora: assistant administration
Isadore Pivnick: vice president, director
Joseph Valentine: director

Grants Analysis

Disclosure Period: calendar year ending 2002
Total Grants: $1,585,400*
Number of Grants: 160
Average Grant: $9,908
Highest Grant: $100,000
Lowest Grant: $5,000
Typical Range: $5,000 to $10,000
*Note: Grants analysis provided by foundation.

Recent Grants

Note: Grants derived from 2001 Form 990.

General

50,000	Jewish Community Center, San Francisco, CA -- funding for scholarships
40,000	KQED, San Francisco, CA -- Family Literacy Program
25,000	Family Service Agency of Marin, San Rafael, CA -- support of the staffing direct services
25,000	Geneva Valley Development Corp, San Francisco, CA -- multi-purpose community center
25,000	Pittsburg Preschool Coordinating Council, Pittsburg, CA -- expand infant toddler care
25,000	Saint Vincent's Day Home, Oakland, CA -- expansion of additional classrooms and Family Literacy Program
25,000	Tenderloin Neighborhood Development Corp (TNDC), San Francisco, CA -- assist in providing a safe and secure drop-in activity center for young people
20,000	Bill Wilson Marriage and Family Counseling Center, Santa Clara, CA -- purchase building complex
20,000	Palcare, Burlingame, CA -- construction costs
20,000	San Francisco Court-Appointed Special Advocates, San Francisco, CA -- support of client caseload expansion project

NORMAN J. STUPP FOUNDATION

Giving Contact

Cindy Lewis, Trust Officer
c/o Commerce Bank
8000 Forsyth Blvd.
Clayton, MO 63105
Phone: (314)746-7322

Description

Founded: 1952
EIN: 436027433
Organization Type: Private Foundation
Giving Locations: MO: St. Louis
Grant Types: Capital, Endowment, General Support, Operating Expenses, Project, Research, Scholarship.

Donor Information

Founder: the late Norman J. Stupp

Financial Summary

Total Giving: $1,004,667 (fiscal year ending June 30, 2002); $1,103,917 (fiscal 2001); $990,603 (fiscal 1999)
Assets: $18,540,637 (fiscal 2002); $21,755,161 (fiscal 2001); $23,478,926 (fiscal 1999)

Typical Recipients

Arts & Humanities: Arts Centers, Arts Outreach, Historic Preservation, History & Archaeology, Libraries, Museums/Galleries, Music, Opera, Public Broadcasting, Theater

Civic & Public Affairs: African American Affairs, Botanical Gardens/Parks, Civic & Public Affairs-General, Municipalities/Towns, Public Policy, Zoos/Aquariums

Education: Colleges & Universities, Community & Junior Colleges, Education-General, Literacy, Medical Education, Private Education (Precollege), Science/Mathematics Education, Special Education, Vocational & Technical Education

Health: AIDS/HIV, Alzheimers Disease, Cancer, Children's Health/Hospitals, Emergency/Ambulance Services, Eyes/Blindness, Health Organizations, Hospitals, Hospitals (University Affiliated), Medical Research

Religion: Religious Welfare

Science: Science Museums, Scientific Centers & Institutes

Social Services: At-Risk Youth, Big Brother/Big Sister, Camps, Child Welfare, Community Service Organizations, Domestic Violence, Family Services, Food/Clothing Distribution, People with Disabilities, Substance Abuse, United Funds/United Ways, YMCA/YWCA/YMHA/YWHA, Youth Organizations

Application Procedures

Initial Contact: The foundation has no formal grant application procedure or application form.
Deadlines: March 1 and September 1.

Additional Information

Trust(s): Commerce Bank St Louis

Grants Analysis

Disclosure Period: fiscal year ending June 30, 2002
Total Grants: $1,004,667
Number of Grants: 88
Average Grant: $11,417
Highest Grant: $66,667
Lowest Grant: $1,500
Typical Range: $5,000 to $20,000

Recent Grants

Note: Grants derived from fiscal 2000 Form 990.

General

75,000	St. Louis Symphony Society, St. Louis, MO
66,666	Loretto-Hilton Center Expansion Fund Partnership, St. Louis, MO
50,000	Forest Park Forever, St. Louis, MO
50,000	St. Louis Science Center Foundation, St. Louis, MO
50,000	St. Louis University Eye Institute, St. Louis, MO
50,000	Tower Grove Park, St. Louis, MO
30,000	Central Institute for the Deaf, St. Louis, MO
25,000	Big Brothers-Sisters of Greater St. Louis Inc., St. Louis, MO
25,000	Frank Lloyd Wright Kraus House Conservancy, St. Louis, MO
25,000	Magic House, St. Louis, MO

ROY AND CHRISTINE STURGIS CHARITABLE AND EDUCATIONAL TRUST (AR)

Giving Contact

Katie Speer, Trustee
PO Box 92
Malvern, AR 72104
Phone: (501)664-8525

Description

Founded: 1979
EIN: 710495345
Organization Type: Private Foundation
Giving Locations: AR
Grant Types: General Support.

Donor Information

Founder: the late Roy Sturgis, Christine Sturgis

Financial Summary

Total Giving: $598,244 (2001); $659,292 (2000); $653,949 (1999)
Assets: $14,903,063 (2001); $15,264,988 (2000); $16,188,218 (1999)

Typical Recipients

Arts & Humanities: Arts Centers, Historic Preservation, Libraries, Museums/Galleries, Performing Arts, Public Broadcasting, Theater

Civic & Public Affairs: Safety

Education: Arts/Humanities Education, Colleges & Universities, Education-General, Preschool Education, Private Education (Precollege), Public Education (Precollege), Secondary Education (Private), Secondary Education (Public), Vocational & Technical Education

Health: Arthritis, Children's Health/Hospitals, Home-Care Services, Hospices, Hospitals

International: Missionary/Religious Activities

Religion: Churches, Dioceses, Religious Organizations, Religious Welfare

Science: Science Museums

Social Services: Animal Protection, Child Welfare, Community Service Organizations, Recreation & Athletics, Youth Organizations

Application Procedures

Initial Contact: Send a brief letter of inquiry.
Application Requirements: Include proof of tax-exempt status, most recent Form 990, and purpose of funds sought.
Deadlines: None.

Restrictions

Gives in Arkansas only.

Foundation Officials

Barry B. Findley: trustee
Katie Speer: trustee

Grants Analysis

Disclosure Period: calendar year ending 2001
Total Grants: $598,244
Number of Grants: 33
Average Grant: $17,132*
Highest Grant: $50,000
Typical Range: $5,000 to $30,000
*Note: Average grant figure excludes highest grant.

Recent Grants

Note: Grants derived from 2001 Form 990.

General

50,000	Ouachita Baptist University, Arkadelphia, AR
40,000	Francois Baptist Church
35,000	Christ the King Church, Little Rock, AR
35,000	Cornerstone Family Church
35,000	First Baptist Church, Malvern, AR
35,000	Immaculate Conception Church, Little Rock, AR
25,000	Arkansas Easter Seal Society, Little Rock, AR
25,000	Bethal AME Church
24,000	University of Arkansas Fayetteville, Fayetteville, AR
22,000	University of Arkansas Little Rock, Little Rock, AR

ROY AND CHRISTINE STURGIS CHARITABLE AND EDUCATIONAL TRUST (TX)

Giving Contact

Daniel J. Kelly, Trust Officer
Bank of America NA
PO Box 830241
Dallas, TX 75283-0241
Phone: (214)209-2422
Fax: (214)209-1997

Description

Founded: 1981
EIN: 756331832
Organization Type: General Purpose Foundation
Giving Locations: AR; TX: Dallas County
Grant Types: Capital, Challenge, Endowment, General Support, Operating Expenses, Project, Research, Scholarship.

Donor Information

Founder: Established in 1981 by the estate of Christine Sturgis . There is a Roy and Christine Sturgis Charitable and Educational Trust in Arkansas, as well as a Roy and Christine Sturgis Foundation, also in Arkansas.

Financial Summary

Total Giving: $2,735,000 (fiscal year ending September 30, 2001); $3,002,500 (fiscal 2000); $3,000,000 (fiscal 1999)
Giving Analysis: Giving for fiscal 2000 includes: foundation grants to United Way ($100,000); foundation scholarships ($795,000) fiscal 1999: foundation scholarships ($500,000)
Assets: $51,992,162 (fiscal 2001); $60,820,561 (fiscal 2000); $59,072,085 (fiscal 1999)

Typical Recipients

Arts & Humanities: Arts Associations & Councils, Arts Centers, Arts Outreach, Ballet, Dance, Ethnic & Folk Arts, Arts & Humanities-General, Historic Preservation, History & Archaeology, Libraries, Literary Arts, Museums/Galleries, Music, Opera, Performing Arts, Public Broadcasting, Theater

Civic & Public Affairs: African American Affairs, Botanical Gardens/Parks, Clubs, Economic Development, Civic & Public Affairs-General, Hispanic Affairs, Housing, Legal Aid, Municipalities/Towns, Nonprofit Management, Public Policy, Urban & Community Affairs, Women's Affairs, Zoos/Aquariums

Education: Afterschool/Enrichment Programs, Agricultural Education, Arts/Humanities Education, Business Education, Colleges & Universities, Community & Junior Colleges, Education Funds, Education Reform, Elementary Education (Public), Education-General, Gifted & Talented Programs, Legal Education, Literacy, Medical Education, Private Education (Precollege), Public Education (Precollege), Science/Mathematics Education, Secondary Education (Private), Secondary Education (Public), Special Education, Student Aid

Environment: Environment-General

Health: Adolescent Health Issues, Alzheimers Disease, Cancer, Children's Health/Hospitals, Clinics/Medical Centers, Diabetes, Eyes/Blindness, Health-General, Health Organizations, Heart, Hospices, Hospitals, Hospitals (University Affiliated), Kidney, Long-Term Care, Nursing Services, Single-Disease Health Associations, Transplant Networks/Donor Banks

International: International Development

Religion: Churches, Ministries, Missionary Activities (Domestic), Religious Organizations, Religious Welfare

Science: Science Museums

Social Services: At-Risk Youth, Camps, Child Welfare, Community Centers, Community Service Organizations, Domestic Violence, Family Services, Food/Clothing Distribution, People with Disabilities, Recreation & Athletics, Scouts, Senior Services, Shelters/Homelessness, Social Services-General, Substance Abuse, United Funds/United Ways, Volunteer Services, YMCA/YWCA/YMHA/YWHA, Youth Organizations

Application Procedures

Initial Contact: Potential applicants must request an application form by mail.

Application Requirements: Application form should be filled out completely, with attachments to answer the questions on the form. The original and one copy of the complete application should be sent. Information that should be included with application is a copy of IRS 501(c)(3) letter; brief history of organization, its purpose and the people it serves; a one page budget outline; list of board members, with addresses and phone numbers; postcard that came with application; and the previous year's audited financial statement. The trust does not accept videos, cassettes, or books.

Deadlines: Proposals must be postmarked by December 31.

Review Process: Grant decision meetings are held in late April.

Decision Notification: Applicants will be notified by mail by May 31 of acceptance or declination of the grant request.

Notes: Personal interviews are not permitted; visits to the applicant organization will be conducted at the discretion of the trustee after application is received. Grant recipients must wait one year after final grant payment to reapply for funds.

Restrictions

The trust does not fund individuals, scholarships or tuition for individuals, seminars, loans, or political organizations. Grants are only made to charitable organizations in Arkansas and Texas.

Additional Information

Trustees consider grant requests which do not exceed $200,000. Funding for amounts above $200,000 will be considered on very limited basis.

Charitable organizations which received a one payment grant must skip a year before applying for a new grant. Organizations which receive multiyear support cannot apply again while receiving payments and must skip a year from the date last payment is received.

The foundation designates 65% of funds for the state of Arkansas and 35% for the state of Texas, mostly for organizations in Dallas County.

Publications: Guidelines; Application Form

Trust(s): Bank of America NA trustee

Grants Analysis

Disclosure Period: fiscal year ending September 30, 2001

Total Grants: $2,685,000*

Number of Grants: 53

Average Grant: $42,019*

Highest Grant: $500,000

Lowest Grant: $5,000

Typical Range: $20,000 to $100,000

*Note: Giving excludes United Way. Average grant figure excludes highest grant.

Recent Grants

Note: Grants derived from fiscal 2001 Form 990.

General

500,000	University of Arkansas, Fayetteville, AR
200,000	Henderson State University, Arkadelphia, AR -- new Honors College Hall
100,000	Arkansas Cancer Research Foundation, Little Rock, AR -- Community Cancer Control Program
100,000	Arkansas Governor's Mansion Renovation, Little Rock, AR
100,000	Hendrix College, Conway, AR
100,000	Junior League of Little Rock, Inc., Little Rock, AR -- purchase and renovate historic building in downtown
100,000	Little Rock Boys & Girls Club, Little Rock, AR
100,000	Ouachita Baptist University, Arkadelphia, AR
100,000	Tomberlin Community Development Center, Little Rock, AR -- to purchase and install pre-fabricated building
75,000	Baylor University, Waco, TX -- Sturgis Endowed Scholarship Fund

SUBARU OF AMERICA, INC.

Company Headquarters

2235 Terrace 70 W.
Cherry Hill, NJ 08002
Web: http://www.subaru.com

Company Description

Employees: 668

SIC(s): 5012 Automobiles & Other Motor Vehicles.

Parent Company: Fuji Heavy Industries, Ltd., Subaru Bldg., 7-2 Nishi-Shinjuku 1-chome, Shinjuku-ku, Tokyo, Japan

Operating Locations

Fuji Heavy Industries U.S.A. (NJ--Cherry Hill); Robin America (IL--Wood Dale); Schuman Carriage Co. (HI--Honolulu); Subaru of America (IL--Des Plaines; MD--Savage; NJ--Cherry Hill, Moorestown); Subaru of America Central Region (CO--Aurora); Subaru of America Southeast Region (FL--West Palm Beach; GA--Austell); Subaru of America Western (OR--Portland); Subaru of America Western Region (CA--Irvine); Subaru Credit Corp. (NJ--Cherry Hill); Subaru Distributor Corp. (NY--Orangeburg); Subaru Financial Services (NJ--Cherry Hill); Subaru-Isuzu Automotive (IN--Lafayette); Subaru Leasing Corp. (NJ--Cherry Hill); Subaru Mid-America (IL--Addison); Subaru of New England (MA--Norwood); Subaru Northwest Region (OR--Portland); Subaru Research & Design (CA--Garden Grove); Subaru Southwest Region (TX--San Antonio)

Subaru of America Foundation

Giving Contact

Sandra Capell, Administrator
Subaru of America Foundation
PO Box 6000
Cherry Hill, NJ 08034-6000
Phone: (856)488-5099
Fax: (856)488-3274

Description

EIN: 222531774

Organization Type: Corporate Foundation

Giving Locations: CO: Aurora; GA: Austell; IL: Addison; NJ: Cherry Hill primary focus is around the company's Cherry Hill headquarters location, Moorestown; OR: Portland

Grant Types: Employee Matching Gifts, Project.

Financial Summary

Total Giving: $236,389 (2001); $155,588 (2000); $113,233 (1999). Note: Figures for foundation only and do not include company direct giving.

Giving Analysis: Giving for 2001 includes: foundation grants to United Way ($16,000); foundation matching gifts ($22,439); foundation scholarships ($30,575); 2000: foundation grants to United Way ($16,000); foundation matching gifts ($26,788); foundation scholarships ($34,300); foundation ($78,500); 1999: foundation grants to United Way ($12,160); foundation matching gifts ($20,818) foundation ($80,255)

Assets: $1,725,758 (2001); $1,782,794 (2000); $1,623,848 (1999)

Gifts Received: $300,000 (2001); $300,000 (2000); $500,000 (1999). Note: Contributions were received from Subaru of America.

Typical Recipients

Arts & Humanities: Arts Associations & Councils, Arts Centers, Arts Outreach, Ballet, Dance, History & Archaeology, Libraries, Museums/Galleries, Music, Theater

Civic & Public Affairs: Asian American Affairs, Civic & Public Affairs-General, Nonprofit Management, Safety, Urban & Community Affairs

Education: Afterschool/Enrichment Programs, Business Education, Colleges & Universities, Education Reform, Elementary Education (Public), Faculty Development, Education-General, International Exchange, Literacy, Minority Education, Preschool Education, Private Education (Precollege), Public Education (Precollege), Science/Mathematics Education, Secondary Education (Private), Special Education, Student Aid

Environment: Resource Conservation, Wildlife Protection

Health: AIDS/HIV, Alzheimers Disease, Cancer, Children's Health/Hospitals, Diabetes, Emergency/Ambulance Services, Heart, Hospices, Hospitals, Medical Rehabilitation, Multiple Sclerosis, Nursing Services, Single-Disease Health Associations, Trauma Treatment

International: Health Care/Hospitals, International Affairs

Religion: Religious Organizations, Religious Welfare

Science: Science Museums

Social Services: At-Risk Youth, Big Brother/Big Sister, Child Abuse, Child Welfare, Community Service Organizations, Counseling, Crime Prevention, Day Care, Domestic Violence, Family Planning, Family Services, Food/Clothing Distribution, Homes, People with Disabilities, Substance Abuse, United Funds/United Ways, Veterans, YMCA/YWCA/YMHA/YWHA, Youth Organizations

Application Procedures

Initial Contact: Send a brief letter of inquiry with a 10, self-addressed unstamped envelope to the foundation to receive a copy of "Policies and Guidelines."

Restrictions

Because foundation prefers to fund grass-roots organizations, it will not consider grants to organizations that have fund balances in excess of two years of current operating budget.

Grants are limited to organizations that are tax-exempt under Section 501(c)(3). Organizations that the foundation trustees prefer not to fund include, but are not limited to, the following: individuals; veterans, fraternal, and/or labor organizations; government agencies; direct support of churches, religious groups, or sectarian groups; social, membership, or other groups that serve the special interests of their constituency; advertising in charitable publications; sponsorship of special events or athletic activities; capital campaigns; political organizations, campaigns, or candidates running for public office; organizations that benefit individuals or groups outside the U.S.; and organizations which, in policy or practice, discriminate against a person or group on the basis of age, political affiliation, race, national origin, ethnicity, gender, religious belief, disability, or sexual orientation.

Foundation does not donate vehicles.

Additional Information

As a general rule, national organizations are not eligible for foundation funds. However, small grants may be considered to organizations that impact foundation or corporate goals. Decisions will be at the sole discretion of the foundation staff, contributions committee, and trustees.

Eligibility for employee matching gifts includes non-profit institutions/organizations located in the United States that are recognized by the Internal Revenue Service as tax-exempt under Section 501(c)(3), excluding religious, political, or fraternal organizations. Recipients of grants are expected to submit a written evaluation or report concerning the impact of their project in the community.

Only proposals received in response to a RFP are accepted. The foundation does not accept unsolicited funding requests. Only one proposal per organization will be considered within any 12-month period. The foundation makes no multiyear grants, although it may consider to renew support of a project. However, all funding requests must be submitted annually in response to a RFP.

Publications: Policies and; Guidelines; Requests for Proposals (Rfps)

Corporate Officials

Thomas J. Doll: vice president, chief financial officer, director PRIM CORP EMPL vice president, chief financial officer: Subaru Am.

Yasuo Fujiki: chairman, chief executive officer, director PRIM CORP EMPL chairman, chief executive officer, director: Subaru Am.

George T. Muller: president, chief operating officer, director B Philadelphia, PA 1949. ED Duke University (1971); Philadelphia College (1972). PRIM CORP EMPL president, chief operating officer, director: Subaru Am. NONPR AFFIL member: Financial Executives Institute; member: National Investor Relations Institute; member: American Institute of CPA's.

Foundation Officials

Thomas J. Doll: trustee (see above)
Yasuo Fujiki: trustee (see above)
Monica D. Haley: trustee
George T. Muller: president, trustee (see above)
Tetsuro Nishizawa: trustee
Joseph T. Scharff: secretary, treasurer, trustee B 1944. ED LaSalle College BA (1969). PRIM CORP EMPL treasurer: Subaru American Inc. ADD CORP EMPL treasurer: Subaru Acceptance Corp.; trustee: Subaru Leasing Corp.

Grants Analysis

Disclosure Period: calendar year ending 2001
Total Grants: $167,375*
Number of Grants: 20
Average Grant: $8,369
Highest Grant: $30,000
Lowest Grant: $2,000
Typical Range: $3,000 to $15,000
*Note: Giving excludes United Way, scholarships, and matching gifts.

Recent Grants

Note: Grants derived from 2000 Form 990.

Library-Related

500	Agnes Irwin School, Rosemont, PA

General

36,000	LARC School, Bellmawr, NJ -- for operations
34,300	Scholarship Foundation, Cherry Hill, NJ -- for scholarship program
30,000	Haddonfield Symphony Society, Haddonfield, NJ -- for a pilot program
16,000	United Way Camden County, Camden, NJ -- for annual contribution
11,600	University of Pennsylvania Museum, Philadelphia, PA -- for international classroom programs
10,000	Philadelphia University, Philadelphia, PA
1,200	Duke University, Durham, NC
1,000	OJR Education Foundation
1,000	Shipley School, Bryn Mawr, PA
685	Cystic Fibrosis Foundation

ALGERNON SYDNEY SULLIVAN FOUNDATION

Giving Contact

Allen E. Strand, Jr., President
520 College Hill Dr.
Oxford, MS 38655
Phone: (662)236-6335

Description

Founded: 1930
EIN: 136084596
Organization Type: Private Foundation
Giving Locations: Southeast USA.
Grant Types: General Support, Scholarship.

Donor Information

Founder: the late Mrs. Algernon Sydney Sullivan, the late George Hammond Sullivan, the late Zilph P. Devereaux

Financial Summary

Total Giving: $1,093,000 (2001); $1,197,000 (2000); $1,196,000 (1999)
Assets: $20,271,064 (2001); $22,737,623 (2000); $26,521,780 (1999)
Gifts Received: $1,466 (1994); $32,876 (1993); $25,000 (1992). Note: In 1993, contributions were received from the estate of Vera H. Armstrong.

Typical Recipients

Arts & Humanities: Libraries
Civic & Public Affairs: Urban & Community Affairs
Education: Colleges & Universities, Elementary Education (Private), Private Education (Precollege)
Environment: Air/Water Quality
Health: Cancer, Emergency/Ambulance Services, Hospitals, Nursing Services, Respiratory
Religion: Religious Welfare
Social Services: Child Welfare, Community Service Organizations, People with Disabilities

Application Procedures

Initial Contact: Send a brief letter of inquiry describing program or project.
Deadlines: None.

Restrictions

Does not support individuals.

Additional Information

Provides scholarships and student aid to colleges in the southeastern United States.

Foundation Officials

William E. Bardusch, Jr.: president, trustee
William D. Bruen, Jr.: trustee
Charles W. Cook: treasurer, assistant secretary, trustee
Nancy Cortner: trustee
Walter Grey Dunnington, Jr.: trustee B New York, NY 1927. ED University of Virginia BA (1948); University of Virginia LLB (1950). NONPR AFFIL member: Property Council Montpelier; trustee: Woodberry Forest School; member: New York State Bar Association; member: Association Bar New York City; board governors: New York Hospital; member: American Bar Association. CLUB AFFIL Racquet & Tennis Club; National Golf The Links America Club; Brook Club; Jupiter Island Club.
R. Bruce McBratney: trustee

Frederick L. Redpath: vice president, trustee
Allan E. Strand: trustee
Darla J. Wilkinson: secretary, assistant treasurer, trustee
Gray Williams, Jr.: trustee

Grants Analysis

Disclosure Period: calendar year ending 2001
Total Grants: $1,093,000
Number of Grants: 31
Average Grant: $35,258
Highest Grant: $50,000
Typical Range: $20,000 to $50,000

Recent Grants

Note: Grants derived from 2001 Form 990.

General

50,000	Warren Wilson College, Swannanoa, NC
47,000	Lincoln Memorial University, Harrogate, TN
45,000	Lees-McRae College, Banner Elk, NC
44,000	Cumberland College, Williamsburg, KY
37,000	Alice Lloyd College, Pippapasses, KY
37,000	Bluefield College, Bluefield, VA
37,000	Brenau College, Gainesville, GA
37,000	Campbell University, Buies Creek, NC
37,000	Coker College, Hartsville, SC
37,000	Converse College, Spartanburg, SC

SULZBERGER FOUNDATION

Giving Contact

Marian S. Heiskell, President
229 West 43rd Street, 11th Floor
New York, NY 10036
Phone: (212)556-1755
Fax: (212)556-1434

Description

Founded: 1956
EIN: 136083166
Organization Type: General Purpose Foundation
Giving Locations: nationally; internationally.
Grant Types: Capital, Conference/Seminar, Emergency, Endowment, Fellowship, General Support, Operating Expenses, Professorship, Project, Scholarship, Seed Money.

Donor Information

Founder: Incorporated in 1956 by the late Arthur Hays Sulzberger and the late Iphigene Ochs Sulzberger .

Financial Summary

Total Giving: $2,526,735 (2000); $2,162,515 (1999); $1,480,151 (1998). Note: 1995 Giving includes scholarship ($76,000).
Giving Analysis: Giving for 2000 includes: foundation grants to United Way ($30,000) 1999: foundation grants to United Way ($27,500)
Assets: $49,793,952 (2000); $55,386,983 (1999); $49,576,721 (1998)
Gifts Received: $37,205 (1999); $20,092 (1998); $81,796 (1997)

Typical Recipients

Arts & Humanities: Arts Associations & Councils, Arts Funds, Ethnic & Folk Arts, Arts & Humanities-General, Historic Preservation, History & Archaeology, Libraries, Literary Arts, Museums/Galleries, Music, Opera, Performing Arts, Public Broadcasting, Theater, Visual Arts

Civic & Public Affairs: Botanical Gardens/Parks, Clubs, Community Foundations, Economic Development, Civic & Public Affairs-General, Housing, Municipalities/Towns, Philanthropic Organizations, Professional & Trade Associations, Public Policy, Safety, Urban & Community Affairs, Zoos/Aquariums

Education: Afterschool/Enrichment Programs, Arts/Humanities Education, Colleges & Universities, Continuing Education, Education Funds, Education Reform, Elementary Education (Private), Faculty Development, Education-General, International Studies, Journalism/Media Education, Leadership Training, Medical Education, Minority Education, Private Education (Precollege), Public Education (Precollege), School Volunteerism, Secondary Education (Private), Student Aid

Environment: Air/Water Quality, Forestry, Environment-General, Resource Conservation, Wildlife Protection

Health: AIDS/HIV, Cancer, Clinics/Medical Centers, Health Organizations, Hospitals, Kidney, Medical Research, Mental Health, Public Health, Single-Disease Health Associations

International: Foreign Arts Organizations, Foreign Educational Institutions, Health Care/Hospitals, International Affairs, International Environmental Issues, International Organizations, International Peace & Security Issues

Religion: Jewish Causes, Religious Organizations, Religious Welfare, Synagogues/Temples

Science: Science Museums, Scientific Organizations

Social Services: Child Welfare, Community Service Organizations, Crime Prevention, Family Planning, Family Services, Food/Clothing Distribution, People with Disabilities, Recreation & Athletics, Sexual Abuse, Shelters/Homelessness, Substance Abuse, United Funds/United Ways, Volunteer Services, Youth Organizations

Application Procedures

Initial Contact: The foundation has no formal grant application procedure or application form.
Deadlines: None. Written responses to requests are usually received within six to eight weeks.

Restrictions

The foundation makes grants only to public charities described in IRS section 501(c)(3). No grants are made to individuals, or for matching gifts or loans.

Additional Information

Publications: Annual Report

Foundation Officials

Marian Sulzberger Heiskell: president, director B New York, NY 1918. ED Frobeleague Kindergarten Training School (1941). NONPR AFFIL chairman: Council Environment New York City; director: National Audubon Society.

Frederick T. Mason: assistant secretary, assistant treasurer

Arthur Ochs Sulzberger, Sr.: vice president, secretary B New York, NY 1926. ED Columbia University BA (1951); Dartmouth College LLD (1964); Bard College LLD (1967). CORP AFFIL chairman: WQXR-FM; director: Times Printing Co.; chairman: WQEW-AM; chairman: Lakeland Ledger Publishing; chairman: Ledger; president, director: Gadsden Times Inc.; chairman: Interstate Broadcasting Co.; director: Affiliated Publishers Inc.; chairman, director: Chattanooga Times Co. NONPR AFFIL chairman, trustee: Metropolitan Museum Art; member: Sons American Revolution; trustee emeritus: Columbia University. CLUB AFFIL Metro Club; Overseas Press Club; Explorers Club.

Judith P. Sulzberger, MD: vice president, director PRIM NONPR EMPL attending physician: Columbia College, Physicians & Surgeons Genome Center. CORP AFFIL director: New York Times Co.

Grants Analysis

Disclosure Period: calendar year ending 2000
Total Grants: $2,496,735*
Number of Grants: 267
Average Grant: $9,351
Highest Grant: $148,500
Typical Range: $5,000 to $20,000
*Note: Giving excludes United Way.

Recent Grants

Note: Grants derived from 2000 Form 990.

Library-Related

12,500	Brookline Public Library, Brookline, MA

General

148,500	Rainforest Alliance, New York, NY
125,500	WGBH, Boston, MA -- expanding the vision
106,000	Wildlife Conservation Society, Bronx, NY
100,000	Columbia University, New York, NY
100,000	Jewish Campus Life Fund, New York, NY
95,000	University of Chattanooga Foundation, Chattanooga, TN
75,000	American Academy in Rome, New York, NY
53,000	Metropolitan Museum of Art, New York, NY
51,500	Creative Discovery Museum, Chattanooga, TN
50,000	American Friends of National Film and Television

SUMITOMO MITSUI BANKING CORP.

Company Headquarters

3-2 Marunouchi 1-Chome
Chiyoda-ku
Tokyo 100-0005, Japan
Web: http://www.smbc.co.jp/global

Company Description

Assets: US$911.136 billion (2002)
Employees: 24650 (2002)
SIC(s): 6081 Foreign Banks--Branches & Agencies.

Operating Locations

Sumitomo Bank, New York Branch (NY--New York)

SMBC Global Foundation, Inc.

Giving Contact

Naoyuki Kawamoto, President
SMBC Global Foundation
277 Park Avenue
New York, NY 10172
Phone: (212)224-4031

Description

Founded: 1995
EIN: 133766226
Organization Type: Corporate Foundation
Giving Locations: internationally, with emphasis on Asian countries; People's Republic of China; Malaysia; Singapore; Thailand; Vietnam

Financial Summary

Total Giving: $720,154 (2000); $900,000 (1999 approx); $718,926 (1998)
Giving Analysis: Giving for 2000 includes: foundation scholarships ($179,253); foundation ($799,151); 1998: foundation scholarships ($188,926) foundation ($530,000)

Assets: $14,628,770 (2000); $15,086,212 (1998); $11,314,677 (1996)
Gifts Received: $3,125,897 (1998); $10,139,057 (1994). Note: In 1998, contributions were received from Sumitomo Bank.

Typical Recipients

Arts & Humanities: Libraries, Museums/Galleries, Theater
Civic & Public Affairs: Civic & Public Affairs-General, Public Policy
Education: Business Education, Colleges & Universities, Community & Junior Colleges, Education Associations, Education Reform, Education-General, International Studies, Minority Education, School Volunteerism, Student Aid
Health: Children's Health/Hospitals
International: Foreign Educational Institutions, Health Care/Hospitals, International Affairs, International Organizations
Social Services: At-Risk Youth, Child Welfare, Community Centers, Domestic Violence, Social Services-General, Substance Abuse, YMCA/YWCA/YMHA/YWHA

Application Procedures

Initial Contact: For direct contributions, the company has no formal application procedures and generally preselects recipients. For scholarship program, request application guidelines. Foundation may ask applicants to submit complete biographical records and supporting materials, including a report on academic and professional careers; a detailed statement of academic plans; a statement of plans and commitments after completion of academic program; letters of reference; lists of extracurricular activities; and any other information as may be requested by the selections committee. Applicant may also be required to demonstrate financial need for grant funds. grant funds.

Restrictions

Recipients must be enrolled at an educational institution approved by the foundation or at which the foundation has established a scholarship grant program. The Foundation does not make grants to individuals.

Additional Information

In 1995, scholarships were provided for attendance at Thammasat University, Bangkok, Thailand; Chulalongkorn University, Bangkok, Thailand; Indonesia University, Jakarta, Indonesia; Airlangga University, Surabaya, Indonesia; Gadjah Mada University, Yogakarta, Indonesia; Padjadjaran University, Bandung, Indonesia; Peking University, Beijing, China; Zhongshan University, Quangdong, China; Peoples University of China, Beijing, China; University of International Business and Economics, Beijing, China; Beijing Foreign Studies University, Beijing, China; and Tsinghua University, Beijing, China.

Corporate Officials

Jane Hutta: general counsel, assistant treasurer, staff attorney PRIM CORP EMPL general counsel, assistant treasurer, staff attorney: Sumitomo Bank.

Ryuzo Kodama: director, head Americas Division PRIM CORP EMPL director, head Americas Division: Sumitomo Bank.

Natsuo Okada: president PRIM CORP EMPL president: Sumitomo Bank Securities. CORP AFFIL president: Sumitomo Bank Capital Markets.

Robert A. Rabbino, Jr.: joint general manager PRIM CORP EMPL joint general manager: Sumitomo Bank.

D. Scarborough Smith, III: joint general manager PRIM CORP EMPL joint general manager: Sumitomo Bank.

Nancy Z. Smith: vice president PRIM CORP EMPL vice president: Sumitomo Bank.

Foundation Officials

Jane Hutta: secretary (see above)
Ryuzo Kodama: director (see above)
Natsuo Okada: president, director (see above)
Robert A. Rabbino, Jr.: director (see above)
D. Scarborough Smith, III: director (see above)
Nancy Z. Smith: treasurer (see above)

Grants Analysis

Disclosure Period: calendar year ending 2000
Total Grants: $799,151*
Number of Grants: 23
Average Grant: $21,388*
Highest Grant: $200,000
Lowest Grant: $1,000
Typical Range: $5,000 to $25,000
***Note:** Giving excludes scholarships. Average grant figure excludes two highest grants ($350,000).

Recent Grants

Note: Grants derived from 2001 Form 990.

General

268,000	Manhattan Theater Club, New York, NY -- support of a non-profit theatrical company
200,000	NAFSA: Association of International Educators, Baltimore, MD -- support of scholarship programs for a non-profit organization
200,000	NAFSA: Association of International Educators, Baltimore, MD -- for Grant Program
150,000	Manhattan Theater Club, New York, NY -- for New Theatre Project
50,000	Manhattan Theater Club, New York, NY -- for Spring Gala and Grant Program
50,000	Manhattan Theater Club, New York, NY -- for Grant Program
50,000	New York University School of Education, New York, NY -- for Grant Program
50,000	Steinhardt School of Education, New York, NY -- support of the tutoring program
30,000	American Enterprise Institute, Washington, DC -- support of public policy research
30,000	American Enterprise Institute, Washington, DC

SOLON E. SUMMERFIELD FOUNDATION, INC.

Giving Contact

William W. Prager, Jr., President
1270 Avenue of the Americas
New York, NY 10020-1801
Phone: (212)218-7640

Description

Founded: 1939
EIN: 131797260
Organization Type: General Purpose Foundation
Giving Locations: NY: New York nationally; Northeast USA.
Grant Types: Endowment, General Support, Scholarship.

Donor Information

Founder: Established in 1939 by the late Solon E. Summerfield (1877-1947).

Financial Summary

Total Giving: $3,106,607 (2001); $3,077,680 (2000); $2,550,456 (1998)
Giving Analysis: Giving for 1997 includes: foundation scholarships ($20,000)

Assets: $62,719,577 (2001); $68,114,969 (2000); $66,848,581 (1998)

Typical Recipients

Arts & Humanities: Libraries, Music, Public Broadcasting
Civic & Public Affairs: Ethnic Organizations, Civic & Public Affairs-General, Law & Justice, Legal Aid, Native American Affairs, Philanthropic Organizations
Education: Arts/Humanities Education, Colleges & Universities, Community & Junior Colleges, Education Funds, Engineering/Technological Education, Education-General, Legal Education, Medical Education, Minority Education, Student Aid
Health: Clinics/Medical Centers, Emergency/Ambulance Services, Eyes/Blindness, Health Organizations, Hospitals, Long-Term Care, Medical Research, Mental Health, Nursing Services, Research/Studies Institutes
Religion: Churches, Jewish Causes, Religious Welfare
Social Services: Camps, Child Abuse, Child Abuse, Child Welfare, Community Centers, Community Service Organizations, Domestic Violence, Food/Clothing Distribution, People with Disabilities, Scouts, Shelters/Homelessness, Youth Organizations

Application Procedures

Initial Contact: Send initial letter of inquiry.
Application Requirements: Provide general information about the proposed project and the applicant.
Deadlines: None.

Restrictions

The foundation only makes contributions to organized tax exempt charitable organizations.

Additional Information

Approximately 80% of the foundation's giving goes to pre-selected charities. Generally the foundation makes smaller contributions to new proposals.

Foundation Officials

William W. Prager, Jr.: vice president PRIM CORP EMPL member: Kalb, Voorhis & Co.
Clarence R. Treeger: president, trustee B 1903. ED Columbia University LLB; University of Pennsylvania Wharton School BS. PRIM CORP EMPL partner: Spiro Felstiner Prager & Fruger.
Thomas C. Treeger: treasurer, secretary

Grants Analysis

Disclosure Period: calendar year ending 2001
Total Grants: $3,106,607
Number of Grants: 142
Average Grant: $12,434*
Highest Grant: $750,000
Typical Range: $5,000 to $30,000 and $60,000 to $75,000
***Note:** Average grant figure excludes two highest grants ($1,365,803).

Recent Grants

Note: Grants derived from 2001 Form 990.

General

750,000	Kansas University, Lawrence, KS
615,803	Kansas University Endowment Association, Lawrence, KS
75,000	American Foundation for the Blind, New York, NY
75,000	Boys Scouts of America
75,000	Endowment Fund of Phi Kappa Psi, Indianapolis, IN
75,000	Father Flanagan's Boys Home, Boys Town, NE
75,000	Federation of Jewish Philanthropies, New York, NY
75,000	Hebrew Free Loan Society, New York, NY

75,000	Jewish Guild for Blind
75,000	New York Society for Prevention of Cruelty to Children, New York, NY

SUMMERLEE FOUNDATION

Giving Contact

John W. Crain, Program Director, History
5956 Sherry Lane, Suite 610
Dallas, TX 75225-8025
Phone: (214)363-9000
Fax: (214)363-1941
E-mail: info@summerlee.org
Web: http://www.summerlee.org

Alternate Contact

Melanie Lambert, Program Director, Animals
Phone: 800-256-7515
Fax: (719)266-5459

Description

Founded: 1988
EIN: 752252355
Organization Type: Private Foundation
Giving Locations: AZ; CO; LA; MS; MT; NV; NM; ND; OK; OR; SD; TX; WA; WY
Grant Types: General Support.

Donor Information

Founder: Established by the late Annie Lee Roberts.

Financial Summary

Total Giving: $1,418,338 (fiscal year ending June 30, 2002); $2,448,750 (fiscal 2000); $905,349 (fiscal 1997)
Assets: $47,832,395 (fiscal 2002); $58,510,674 (fiscal 2000); $37,866,291 (fiscal 1997)
Gifts Received: $518 (fiscal 2002); $323,923 (fiscal 1995); $19,743,354 (fiscal 1994). Note: In fiscal 1995, contributions were received from the estate of Annie Lee Roberts.

Typical Recipients

Arts & Humanities: Arts Associations & Councils, Ethnic & Folk Arts, Historic Preservation, History & Archaeology, Libraries, Literary Arts, Museums/Galleries, Performing Arts, Public Broadcasting, Visual Arts
Civic & Public Affairs: Botanical Gardens/Parks, Community Foundations, Civic & Public Affairs-General, Municipalities/Towns, Native American Affairs, Urban & Community Affairs, Zoos/Aquariums
Education: Arts/Humanities Education, Colleges & Universities, Engineering/Technological Education, Education-General, Private Education (Precollege), Social Sciences Education
Environment: Environment-General, Resource Conservation, Wildlife Protection
Health: Health Organizations
International: International Environmental Issues, International Relations
Religion: Religious Organizations
Science: Science Exhibits & Fairs, Science Museums
Social Services: Animal Protection, Community Service Organizations, Shelters/Homelessness, Veterans

Application Procedures

Initial Contact: The foundation encourages prospective applicants to contact the appropriate program officer by phone prior to submitting a written proposal.
Application Requirements: Proposals should include a brief project summary letter (no more than two pages) signed by the organization's chief executive officer describing the proposed project, the need it fulfills, and project timeline. In addition, the application must include a project budget, including specific line items (if the request is part of a larger effort involving

more than one funding source, show how the committed funds are to be applied); a brief summary of the organization, its mission, officers and board members, and any key personnel related to the project; a copy of the organization's latest annual financial statement and/or copy of the most recently filed IRS Form 990; and proof of tax-exempt status from the IRS.

Deadlines: The 1st business day of January, May, July, and September.

Restrictions

No grants are made for religious purposes or to individuals. Geographic restrictions may apply to animal program requests; applicants to this program are encouraged to contact the foundation as the geographic restrictions frequently change. Grant requests related to the preservation of historic structures must be no greater than $50,000 and may only be used to preserve a house or building on the National Register of Historic Places.

Additional Information

Publications: Application Guidelines

Foundation Officials

John W. Crain: program director, vice president B Amarillo, TX 1944. ED University of Texas BA (1966); Southwestern Texas University MA (1970); Harvard University (1975); University of California (1979). NONPR AFFIL vice president, director: History Summerlee Foundation; member: Texas State Historical Association; director: Dallas County Historical Foundation.

Lynn Cuny: director

David D. Jackson: president

Melanie Roberts-Lambert: program director, secretary

Ronnie Curtis Tyler: director B Temple, TX 1941. ED Abilene Christian College BSE (1964); Texas Christian University MA (1966); Texas Christian University PhD (1968); Austin College DHL (1986). PRIM CORP EMPL history professor: University TX. NONPR AFFIL member: Texas Institute Letters; director: Texas State History Association; secretary, member: Philosophical Society Texas; member: American Antiquarian Society; member: Phi Beta Kappa.

Grants Analysis

Disclosure Period: fiscal year ending June 30, 2002
Total Grants: $1,418,338
Number of Grants: 116
Average Grant: $12,227
Highest Grant: $150,000
Typical Range: $2,500 to $25,000

Recent Grants

Note: Grants derived from fiscal 2002 Form 990.

General
102,401	Medicine Mounds Preserve Fund Communities Foundation of Texas, Quanah, TX
65,000	San Augustine County Historical Foundation, San Augustine, TX
32,000	SNAP, Spokane, WA
30,000	St. Joseph's Indian School, Chamberlain, SD
25,000	Amarillo Museum of Art, Amarillo, TX
25,000	National Trust for Historic Preservation, Washington, DC
25,000	Panhandle-Plains Historical Museum, Canyon, TX
25,000	Sabine County Historical Foundation, Hemphill, TX
25,000	San Augustine County Historical Foundation, San Augustine, TX
20,000	City of Gainsville, Gainesville, FL

SUN HILL FOUNDATION

Giving Contact

Donald R. Milligan, Assistant Treasurer
c/o Fred F. French Investing LLC
1 Station Pl.
Stamford, CT 06902
Phone: (203)353-5320
Fax: (203)353-5329
E-mail: sunhillfdn@aol.com

Description

Founded: 1992
EIN: 061326091
Organization Type: Private Foundation
Giving Locations: NY: New York internationally.
Grant Types: General Support.

Financial Summary

Total Giving: $1,580,332 (fiscal year ending March 31, 2001); $1,285,970 (fiscal 2000); $525,093 (fiscal 1999)
Giving Analysis: Giving for fiscal 2001 includes: foundation scholarships ($25,000) fiscal 2000: foundation scholarships ($10,000)
Assets: $8,830,987 (fiscal 2001); $10,434,618 (fiscal 2000); $9,181,964 (fiscal 1999)
Gifts Received: $1,000,000 (fiscal 2001); $1,000,000 (fiscal 2000); $3,956,447 (fiscal 1999). Note: In fiscal 2001, contributions were received from the estate of Edwin A. Malloy. In fiscal 1994, contributions were received from Edwin A. Malloy ($500) and Susan R. Malloy ($15,000).

Typical Recipients

Arts & Humanities: Libraries, Museums/Galleries, Theater
Civic & Public Affairs: Civic & Public Affairs-General, Legal Aid, Native American Affairs, Public Policy
Education: Arts/Humanities Education, Colleges & Universities, Education Reform, Education-General, Legal Education, Literacy, Medical Education, Minority Education, Vocational & Technical Education
Environment: Air/Water Quality, Environment-General, Resource Conservation
Health: Health Organizations, Medical Research
International: International Environmental Issues, International Peace & Security Issues, Missionary/Religious Activities
Religion: Jewish Causes, Synagogues/Temples
Social Services: Camps, Community Service Organizations, Counseling, Day Care, Domestic Violence, Food/Clothing Distribution, People with Disabilities

Application Procedures

Initial Contact: The foundation has no formal grant application procedure or application form.
Deadlines: None.

Foundation Officials

Iva Kaufman: program director
Susan R. Malloy: president
Timon J. Malloy: secretary
Jennifer Malloy Combs: treasurer
Donald Milligan: assistant treasurer

Grants Analysis

Disclosure Period: fiscal year ending March 31, 2001
Total Grants: $1,555,332*
Number of Grants: 44
Average Grant: $20,667*
Highest Grant: $666,666
Typical Range: $10,000 to $40,000
***Note:** Giving excludes scholarships. Average grant figure excludes highest grant.

Recent Grants

Note: Grants derived from 2000 Form 990.

Library-Related
25,000	Proprietors of the Boston Athenaeum, Boston, MA

General
666,667	American Jewish Archives, Cincinnati, OH -- construction of education building
33,333	Community Legal Services, Cambridge, MA
33,333	Marine Conservation Biology Institute, Redmond, WA
33,333	Vermont Law School, South Royalton, VT
33,000	PEF Endowment Funds, New York, NY
25,000	Eldridge Street Project, New York, NY
25,000	New Israel Fund, Washington, DC
25,000	Ozone Action, Washington, DC
25,000	President & Fellows of Harvard College, Cambridge, MA
25,000	Tides Center, San Francisco, CA

SUNDERLAND FOUNDATION

Giving Contact

James P. Sunderland, President
PO Box 25900
Overland Park, KS 66225
Phone: (913)451-8900
Fax: (913)319-6191
E-mail: sunderlandfoundation@ashgrove.com
Web: http://www.sunderlandfoundation.org

Description

Founded: 1945
EIN: 446011082
Organization Type: General Purpose Foundation
Giving Locations: AR; KS; MO; NE
Grant Types: Capital, Emergency, Endowment, Operating Expenses, Scholarship, Seed Money.

Donor Information

Founder: Incorporated in 1945 by the late Lester T. Sunderland .

Financial Summary

Total Giving: $2,809,500 (2001); $1,859,519 (1999); $1,300,000 (1998 approx)
Giving Analysis: Giving for 2001 includes: foundation scholarships ($5,000)
Assets: $76,512,513 (2001); $59,068,811 (1999); $37,000,000 (1998 approx)
Gifts Received: $9,735,000 (1999); $9,360,000 (1997). Note: In 1997 and 1999, the foundation received a gift of Vinton Corp. securities from the Paul Sunderland Trust.

Typical Recipients

Arts & Humanities: Arts Associations & Councils, Arts Centers, Arts Festivals, Arts Institutes, Arts Outreach, Ballet, Community Arts, History & Archaeology, Libraries, Museums/Galleries, Music, Opera, Performing Arts, Public Broadcasting, Theater
Civic & Public Affairs: Botanical Gardens/Parks, Community Foundations, Economic Policy, Employment/Job Training, Civic & Public Affairs-General, Hispanic Affairs, Housing, Law & Justice, Municipalities/Towns, Parades/Festivals, Philanthropic Organizations, Professional & Trade Associations, Public Policy, Rural Affairs, Urban & Community Affairs, Zoos/Aquariums
Education: Agricultural Education, Arts/Humanities Education, Business Education, Business Education,

Colleges & Universities, Community & Junior Colleges, Education-General, Private Education (Precollege), Public Education (Precollege), Secondary Education (Private), Secondary Education (Public), Special Education, Student Aid

Environment: Forestry, Resource Conservation

Health: Cancer, Children's Health/Hospitals, Clinics/Medical Centers, Eyes/Blindness, Health Organizations, Hospitals, Mental Health, Nursing Services, Research/Studies Institutes

Religion: Churches, Ministries, Religious Organizations, Religious Welfare

Science: Science Museums

Social Services: Animal Protection, Big Brother/Big Sister, Camps, Child Welfare, Community Service Organizations, Counseling, Domestic Violence, Emergency Relief, Emergency Relief, Family Planning, Family Services, Food/Clothing Distribution, Homes, People with Disabilities, Recreation & Athletics, Scouts, Senior Services, Social Services-General, United Funds/United Ways, YMCA/YWCA/YMHA/YWHA, Youth Organizations

Application Procedures

Initial Contact: The foundation requests applications be made in writing. The applicant must also make an appointment with Mr. James Sunderland.
Deadlines: None.

Restrictions

The foundation does not support individuals or provide loans.

Foundation Officials

Charles T. Sunderland: vice president B 1956. ED Trinity University (1974-1978). PRIM CORP EMPL vice president corporate administration, director: Ash Grove Cement Co. ADD CORP EMPL secretary: Ash Grove Aggregates Inc. CORP AFFIL secretary: Century Ready-Mix Inc.; vice president, director: Vinton Corp.; president: Cedar Creek Properties Inc.; vice president, director: Century Concrete Inc.

James P. Sunderland: chairman, president B Springfield, MO 1928. ED Washington & Lee University BS (1950); Washington University LLB (1952). PRIM CORP EMPL chairman, director: Ash Grove Cement Co. CORP AFFIL chairman: Vinton Corp.; director: Ash Grove Aggregates Inc.; director: Boatmens First National Bank Kansas City. NONPR AFFIL director: Greater Kansas City Community Foundation.

Kenton W. Sunderland: vice president, secretary B Kansas City, MO 1958. ED Trinity University (1980). PRIM CORP EMPL secretary, vice president, director: Ash Grove Cement Co.

Robert Sunderland: vice president, treasurer, director B Omaha, NE 1921. ED Washington University BS (1947). PRIM CORP EMPL vice president, treasurer: Vinton Corp. CORP AFFIL hon chairman: Ash Grove Cement Co. CLUB AFFIL Rotary International Club.

Grants Analysis

Disclosure Period: calendar year ending 2001
Total Grants: $2,804,500*
Number of Grants: 76
Average Grant: $36,901
Highest Grant: $200,000
Typical Range: $15,000 to $50,000
*Note: Giving excludes scholarships.

Recent Grants

Note: Grants derived from 2001 Form 990.

General
200,000	Nelson Gallery Foundation, Kansas City, MO -- for capital campaign
150,000	Habitat for Humanity, Kansas City, MO -- for building project
100,000	Greater Kansas City Community Foundation, Kansas City, MO -- for library project
100,000	MD Anderson Cancer Center, Houston, TX -- for research
100,000	Universal Design Housing Network, Kansas City, MO -- for building project
100,000	University of Kansas Endowment Association, Lawrence, KS -- for building project
75,000	Union Station Kansas City, Inc., Kansas City, MO -- for Union Station Project
60,000	Kansas City Public Television, Kansas City, MO -- for capital campaign
54,500	Kansas City Art Institute, Kansas City, MO -- for new library
51,000	American Red Cross of Greater Kansas City, Kansas City, MO -- for disaster relief

SUNNEN FOUNDATION

Giving Contact

Kurt J. Kallaus, President
7910 Manchester Avenue
St. Louis, MO 63143
Phone: (314)781-2100
Fax: (314)781-1533
Web: http://www.sunnen.com

Description

Founded: 1953
EIN: 436029156
Organization Type: General Purpose Foundation
Giving Locations: MO: St. Louis metropolitan area & statewide
Grant Types: Award, Capital, Endowment, Matching.

Donor Information

Founder: Established in Missouri in 1953 by Joseph Sunnen, founder of Sunnen Products Company, a manufacturer of high precision tools and gauges. Mr. Sunnen devoted his life and resources to create a public awareness of uncontrolled population growth. He was a pioneer in advancing the proposition that birth control is one answer to the poverty which afflicts mankind.

Financial Summary

Total Giving: $560,250 (2002 approx); $814,950 (2001 approx); $940,460 (2000)
Giving Analysis: Giving for 2000 includes: foundation grants to United Way ($35,000)
Assets: $13,230,000 (2001); $15,654,722 (2000); $17,197,692 (1999)

Typical Recipients

Arts & Humanities: Arts Centers, Historic Preservation, History & Archaeology, Libraries, Museums/Galleries, Music

Civic & Public Affairs: Botanical Gardens/Parks, Clubs, Economic Policy, First Amendment Issues, Civic & Public Affairs-General, Housing, Public Policy, Safety, Urban & Community Affairs, Women's Affairs

Education: Business Education, Colleges & Universities, Continuing Education, Economic Education, Education Associations, Education-General, Medical Education, Private Education (Precollege), Special Education, Vocational & Technical Education

Environment: Wildlife Protection

Health: Cancer, Children's Health/Hospitals, Clinics/Medical Centers, Emergency/Ambulance Services, Health Policy/Cost Containment, Health Organizations, Single-Disease Health Associations, Speech & Hearing, Transplant Networks/Donor Banks

International: Health Care/Hospitals, International Environmental Issues

Religion: Ministries, Missionary Activities (Domestic), Religious Organizations, Religious Welfare, Social/Policy Issues

Social Services: Animal Protection, At-Risk Youth, Camps, Child Welfare, Community Service Organizations, Crime Prevention, Day Care, Delinquency & Criminal Rehabilitation, Domestic Violence, Emergency Relief, Family Planning, Family Services, Food/Clothing Distribution, People with Disabilities, Scouts, Senior Services, Shelters/Homelessness, Special Olympics, Substance Abuse, United Funds/United Ways, YMCA/YWCA/YMHA/YWHA, Youth Organizations

Application Procedures

Initial Contact: Applicants should contact the foundation in writing to request guidelines.
Application Requirements: Formal proposal should not exceed ten pages in length (plus addendum) and should include: project name, name of director, address and telephone number; amount requested; statement of problem or assessment of need; goals of the project and how they will be achieved; qualifications of the organization to carry out the project; how the project will be evaluated; project budget showing type and amount of expenses and revenues, including all sources; plans for future support or funding; other donors solicited for this project and status of those requests. Addendum should include: brief organizational history; IRS letter of determination indicating 501(c)(3) status; organization's most recent audited financial statement, management report and annual report, if available; list of current board of directors. Seven copies of the proposal should be submitted; the foundation does not accept proposals in notebooks, binders, or plastic folders.
Deadlines: August 1.
Review Process: The board meets twice a year, in October and December.

Restrictions

With the exception of specific projects related to its areas of main concern, grants are not made to general operating costs, scholarships, research projects, travel or personal grants, religious bodies, educational institutions, environmental organizations, hospitals or medical charities, or the arts.

Additional Information

Grantees are required to submit a complete evaluation and financial report at the conclusion of the grant period.
Publications: Guidelines

Foundation Officials

James K. Berthold: director B Saint Louis, MO 1938. ED University of Missouri, Rolla BS (1960); Washington University MBA (1962). PRIM CORP EMPL chairman, president: Sunnen Products Co. CORP AFFIL director: Commerce Bank of Saint Louis.

C. Diane Boulware: director PRIM CORP EMPL secretary, treasurer: Sunnen Products Co.

Susan S. Brasel: director

Ruth A. Cardinale: secretary B 1961. PRIM CORP EMPL secretary: Sunnen Products Co. CORP AFFIL secretary: Sunquad Corp. Inc.

Kurt J. Kallaus: director

Helen S. Sly: president, director, fdr daughter

Grants Analysis

Disclosure Period: calendar year ending 2001
Total Grants: $814,950*
Number of Grants: 30
Average Grant: $27,165
Highest Grant: $65,500
Lowest Grant: $1,000
Typical Range: $2,000 to $50,000
*Note: Grants analysis provided by foundation.

Recent Grants

Note: Grants derived from 2000 Form 990.

General

50,000	Magic House, St. Louis, MO
50,000	Missouri Historical Society, St. Louis, MO
50,000	Museum of Transportation
50,000	Planned Parenthood, St. Louis, MO
40,000	Grinnell College, Grinnell, CA
40,000	Ranken Technical College, St. Louis, MO
40,000	YMCA - of the Ozarks
35,000	Missouri Religious Coalition for Rep Choice, MO
35,000	United Way of Greater St. Louis, St. Louis, MO
33,000	Ashland Family YMCA, Ashland, OR

SUNTRUST BANK ATLANTA

Company Headquarters

Atlanta, GA
Web: http://www.suntrust.com

Company Description

Former Name: Trust Co. Bank.
Revenue: US$7.526 billion (2002)
Profit: US$1.331 billion (2002)
Employees: 2,850
Fortune Rank: 248, per FORTUNE Magazine's list of 500 Largest U.S. Corporations (2002).
SIC(s): 6022 State Commercial Banks.
Parent Company: SunTrust Banks, Inc., 303 Peachtree Street NE, Atlanta, GA, United States

Operating Locations

Operates numerous branches in Fulton and Dekalb counties.

Nonmonetary Support

Type: Donated Equipment; Loaned Employees; Loaned Executives; Workplace Solicitation
Contact: Ed Bishop, Vice President
Note: Company provides nonmonetary support.

SunTrust Bank Atlanta Foundation

Giving Contact

William R. Bowdoin, Jr., First Vice President/ Secretary
Mail Code 041
PO Box 4418, Mail Code 041
PO Box 4418, Mail Code 041
Atlanta, GA 30302
Phone: (404)588-8246
Fax: (404)230-5550

Description

EIN: 586026063
Organization Type: Corporate Foundation
Giving Locations: GA: Atlanta metropolitan area
Grant Types: Capital, Employee Matching Gifts, General Support, Operating Expenses, Project, Research, Seed Money.

Financial Summary

Total Giving: $2,544,424 (2000); $2,569,453 (1999); $1,742,718 (1998). Note: Contributes through corporate direct giving program and foundation.
Giving Analysis: Giving for 2000 includes: foundation grants to United Way ($968,323); foundation ($1,576,101); 1999: foundation fellowships ($6,000);

foundation grants to United Way ($1,231,009); foundation ($1,332,444); 1998: foundation grants to United Way ($575,450); foundation ($1,167,268);
Assets: $21,985,824 (2000); $23,685,567 (1999); $19,696,229 (1998)
Gifts Received: $220,000 (2000); $5,264,100 (1999); $2,225,000 (1997). Note: Gifts received from SunTrust Bank; cash for matching charitable donations.

Typical Recipients

Arts & Humanities: Arts Appreciation, Arts Associations & Councils, Arts Centers, Arts Festivals, Arts Funds, Ballet, Community Arts, Dance, Ethnic & Folk Arts, Historic Preservation, History & Archaeology, Libraries, Museums/Galleries, Music, Opera, Performing Arts, Public Broadcasting, Theater
Civic & Public Affairs: Botanical Gardens/Parks, Business/Free Enterprise, Chambers of Commerce, Civil Rights, Community Foundations, Economic Development, Economic Policy, Employment/Job Training, Civic & Public Affairs-General, Housing, Law & Justice, Legal Aid, Municipalities/Towns, Nonprofit Management, Philanthropic Organizations, Public Policy, Safety, Urban & Community Affairs, Women's Affairs, Zoos/Aquariums
Education: Arts/Humanities Education, Business Education, Colleges & Universities, Economic Education, Education Funds, Engineering/Technological Education, Education-General, International Exchange, International Studies, Legal Education, Medical Education, Minority Education, Private Education (Precollege), Public Education (Precollege), Religious Education, Science/Mathematics Education, Special Education, Student Aid, Vocational & Technical Education
Environment: Environment-General, Resource Conservation
Health: Alzheimers Disease, Children's Health/Hospitals, Clinics/Medical Centers, Emergency/Ambulance Services, Geriatric Health, Health Organizations, Hospitals, Medical Rehabilitation, Medical Training, Mental Health, Nursing Services, Public Health, Single-Disease Health Associations
International: International Affairs
Religion: Religion-General, Jewish Causes
Science: Scientific Centers & Institutes
Social Services: Child Welfare, Community Centers, Community Service Organizations, Counseling, Delinquency & Criminal Rehabilitation, Domestic Violence, Emergency Relief, Family Services, Food/Clothing Distribution, Homes, People with Disabilities, Recreation & Athletics, Senior Services, Shelters/Homelessness, Social Services-General, Substance Abuse, United Funds/United Ways, Youth Organizations

Application Procedures

Initial Contact: Request guidelines and Fact Sheet from the foundation.
Application Requirements: Submit the completed Fact Sheet for grant consideration. Include the following supporting materials: IRS determination letter, list of board of directors and their affiliations, relevant financial material, and case statement or other concise supporting material.
Deadlines: November 30, March 31, or August 31.
Review Process: Applications are summarized and presented quarterly to the distribution committee.
Evaluative Criteria: Emphasis on metropolitan Atlanta, community benefit, project/community coordination and support, timeliness and precedence, organization management and governance, grant multiplier effect, human value and self-help emphasis, and financial management.
Decision Notification: Notification made by letter following meetings held in January, May, and October.

Restrictions

Foundation does not make loans or grants for maintenance or debt service. Does not support political organizations, churches, or individuals.

Additional Information

Nonmatching grants may be made to national organizations, but must benefit the metropolitan Atlanta area.
The committee expects periodic program reports from recipients.
Publications: Application Guidelines

Corporate Officials

Robert R. Long: chairman B 1937. ED Auburn University (1959); Harvard University (1967). PRIM CORP EMPL chairman: SunTrust Bank Atlanta ADD CORP EMPL director: SunTrust Service Corp.; chairman: SunTrust Bank Georgia Inc.

Foundation Officials

Robert R. Long: chairman (see above)

Grants Analysis

Disclosure Period: calendar year ending 2000
Total Grants: $1,576,101*
Number of Grants: 610
Average Grant: $2,583
Highest Grant: $105,000
Typical Range: $1,000 to $20,000
***Note:** Giving excludes United Way.

Recent Grants

Note: Grants derived from 2000 Form 990.

General

895,423	United Way Metropolitan Atlanta, Atlanta, GA -- operations support
150,000	Woodruff Arts Center, Atlanta, GA -- operations support
150,000	Woodruff Arts Center, Atlanta, GA -- operations support
45,000	Community Foundation of Central Georgia, Macon, GA -- operation support
40,000	Rabun Gap Nacoochee School, Rabun Gap, GA -- operations grant
32,000	United Way Coastal Empire, Savannah, GA -- operations support
25,000	United Negro College Fund, Atlanta, GA -- operations support
22,000	Junior Achievement of Georgia, Atlanta, GA -- operations support
21,650	United Way of the C.S.R.A., Augusta, GA
21,000	Inroads Atlanta, Atlanta, GA -- operations support

SUNTRUST BANKS, INC.

Company Headquarters

303 Peachtree Street NE
Atlanta, GA 30308
Web: http://www.suntrust.com

Company Description

Founded: 1985
Ticker: STI
Exchange: NYSE
Formed by Merger of: Crestar Finance Corp. & SunTrust Banks (1998).
Assets: US$117.3 billion (2002)
Employees: 27622 (2002)

Nonmonetary Support

Contact: James Warrick, Executive Vice President
Note: Co. provides an unspecified amount of nonmonetary support in the form of donated property or land which is no longer used by banks.

Crestar Foundation

Giving Contact

Brenda L. Skidmore, President
SunTrust Mid-Atlantic Foundation
Care of Suntrust Bank
PO Box 27385
Richmond, VA 23261-7385
Phone: (804)782-7907
Fax: (804)782-5191
Web: http://iath.virginia.edu/readings/crestar.html

Description

EIN: 237336418
Organization Type: Corporate Foundation
Former Name: Crestar Foundation.
Giving Locations: DC; MD; VA: headquarters and operating communities.
Grant Types: Employee Matching Gifts, General Support.
Note: Employee matching gift ratio: 1 to 1. Company will match any employee's contributions of $25 or more up to an aggregate of $3,000 annually, for eligible educational institutions and cultural organizations.

Financial Summary

Total Giving: $4,000,000 (2002 approx); $3,901,502 (2001); $4,102,014 (2000). Note: Contributes through corporate direct giving program and foundation.
Giving Analysis: Giving for 2002 includes: foundation (approx $4,000,000); 2001: foundation grants to United Way ($524,900); foundation ($3,376,602); 2000: foundation ($3,320,393);
Assets: $6,561,137 (2001); $6,167,275 (2000); $5,015,823 (1998)
Gifts Received: $4,000,000 (2001); $8,010,000 (2000); $8,000,000 (1998). Note: Gifts received from SunTrust (formerly Crestar) Bank.

Typical Recipients

Arts & Humanities: Arts Associations & Councils, Arts Centers, Arts Festivals, Arts Funds, Arts Outreach, Ballet, Community Arts, Ethnic & Folk Arts, Historic Preservation, History & Archaeology, Libraries, Museums/Galleries, Music, Opera, Public Broadcasting, Theater
Civic & Public Affairs: Botanical Gardens/Parks, Business/Free Enterprise, Chambers of Commerce, Economic Development, Economic Policy, Employment/Job Training, Civic & Public Affairs-General, Housing, Nonprofit Management, Parades/Festivals, Philanthropic Organizations, Public Policy, Urban & Community Affairs, Women's Affairs, Zoos/Aquariums
Education: Arts/Humanities Education, Business Education, Colleges & Universities, Colleges & Universities, Community & Junior Colleges, Economic Education, Education Funds, Engineering/Technological Education, Environmental Education, Faculty Development, Literacy, Medical Education, Minority Education, Private Education (Precollege), Public Education (Precollege), Secondary Education (Public), Special Education
Environment: Air/Water Quality, Environment-General, Resource Conservation
Health: AIDS/HIV, Cancer, Children's Health/Hospitals, Clinics/Medical Centers, Emergency/Ambulance Services, Eyes/Blindness, Health Policy/Cost Containment, Health Funds, Health Organizations, Heart, Hospices, Hospitals, Mental Health, Multiple Sclerosis, Speech & Hearing
International: Health Care/Hospitals, International Peace & Security Issues, International Relations
Religion: Religious Organizations, Religious Welfare, Social/Policy Issues
Science: Science Exhibits & Fairs, Science Museums, Scientific Centers & Institutes, Scientific Research
Social Services: At-Risk Youth, Child Welfare, Community Service Organizations, Domestic Violence, Emergency Relief, Family Services, Food/Clothing Distribution, People with Disabilities, Recreation & Athletics, Scouts, Senior Services, Shelters/Homelessness, Social Services-General, United Funds/United Ways, YMCA/YWCA/YMHA/YWHA, Youth Organizations

Application Procedures

Initial Contact: Send a written application.
Application Requirements: Include support information regarding purpose of the organization and expected benefits of program.
Deadlines: Applications for large grants should be made on or before October for consideration in the following calendar year.
Review Process: President of foundation or local SunTrust facility makes recommendations to contributions committee, which meets in July and December.
Evaluative Criteria: Request conforms to priority areas, corporate presence in geographic area served by organization, program or activity improves economy and quality of life in community, evidence of good management and active involvement of community leaders, and direct or indirect benefits to corporation or its employees.
Notes: Grants are made primarily to Virginia communities.

Restrictions

No grants are made to political or religious organizations.

Foundation Officials

Brenda L. Skidmore: president

Grants Analysis

Disclosure Period: calendar year ending 2001
Total Grants: $2,856,702*
Number of Grants: 776
Average Grant: $3,700
Highest Grant: $100,000
Lowest Grant: $25
Typical Range: $1,000 to $15,000
*Note: Giving excludes United Way.

Recent Grants

Note: Grants derived from 2001 Form 990.

Library-Related
20,000	Library of Virginia Foundation, Richmond, VA

General
162,500	St. Catherine's School Foundation, Richmond, VA
100,000	American Red Cross Disaster Relief Fund
76,000	United Way - DC, Washington, DC
65,000	United Way of Central Maryland, Baltimore, MD
62,500	Sun Trust Mid-Atlantic Foundation, Richmond, VA
55,000	Virginia Foundation for Independent Colleges, Richmond, VA
50,000	Hampton University, Hampton, VA
50,000	Virginia Museum of Fine Arts Foundation, Richmond, VA
45,000	Sun Trust Mid-Atlantic Foundation, Richmond, VA
41,667	LISC, Richmond, VA

SUNTRUST BANKS OF FLORIDA

Company Headquarters

281 N. Market Blvd.
Webster, FL 33597

Company Description

Former Name: SunBank N.A..
Employees: 7,900
SIC(s): 6022 State Commercial Banks, 6712 Bank Holding Companies.
Parent Company: SunTrust Banks, Inc., 303 Peachtree Street NE, Atlanta, GA, United States

Operating Locations

SunTrust Banks of Florida (FL--Brooksville, Cape Coral, Daytona Beach, Fort Lauderdale, Jacksonville, Miami, Naples, Ocala, Panama City, Pensacola, Plant City, Port Charlotte, Sebring, Tallahassee, Tampa, Vero Beach, Zephyrhills)

SunTrust Banks Foundation

Giving Contact

David Hanson
PO Box 3838
Orlando, FL 32802

Description

EIN: 596877429
Organization Type: Corporate Foundation
Giving Locations: FL
Grant Types: Capital, Endowment, Fellowship, Loan, Multiyear/Continuing Support, Project.

Financial Summary

Total Giving: $232,167 (2001); $141,167 (2000); $250,000 (1999 approx). Note: Contributes through foundation only.
Assets: $10,878,367 (2001); $11,339,580 (2000); $9,000,000 (1999 approx)
Gifts Received: $400,000 (2001); $717,976 (2000); $1,163,080 (1998). Note: The foundation receives contributions from Suntrust Banks, Inc.

Typical Recipients

Arts & Humanities: Historic Preservation, History & Archaeology, Libraries, Museums/Galleries
Civic & Public Affairs: Chambers of Commerce, Professional & Trade Associations, Urban & Community Affairs, Zoos/Aquariums
Education: Arts/Humanities Education, Colleges & Universities, Community & Junior Colleges, Education-General, Literacy, Minority Education, Student Aid
Health: Cancer, Clinics/Medical Centers, Hospices, Hospitals, Research/Studies Institutes
International: Foreign Arts Organizations
Science: Scientific Centers & Institutes
Social Services: Child Welfare, Family Services, People with Disabilities, Substance Abuse

Application Procedures

Initial Contact: Send a brief letter.
Application Requirements: Include relevant information and proof of tax-exempt status.
Deadlines: None.

Restrictions

Foundation gives specifically to scientific, literary, and educational institutions.

Additional Information

SunBank N.A. is corporate trustee for the foundation.

Grants Analysis

Disclosure Period: calendar year ending 2001
Total Grants: $232,167
Number of Grants: 14
Average Grant: $16,583
Highest Grant: $50,000
Lowest Grant: $2,000
Typical Range: $3,000 to $25,000

Recent Grants

Note: Grants derived from 2001 Form 990.

General

50,000	Florida Hospital Foundation, Orlando, FL
50,000	Ringling School of Art and Design, Sarasota, FL
25,000	Florida Chamber of Commerce Education Foundation, Inc., Tallahassee, FL
20,000	Jackson Memorial Foundation, Jacksonville, FL
20,000	Mayo Clinic, Scottsdale, AZ
16,667	Leadership Florida Statewide Foundation, Tallahassee, FL
15,000	Central Florida Community College, Ocala, FL
12,500	Zoological Society of Florida, Miami, FL
10,000	TMH Regional Medical Center Foundation, Tallahassee, FL
3,500	Hernando Pasco County Hospice, Brooksville, FL

HARRY AND THELMA SURRENA MEMORIAL FUND

Giving Contact

Clair Robinson
PO Box 27
Buffalo, WY 82834
Phone: (307)684-5574

Description

Founded: 1973
EIN: 237435554
Organization Type: Private Foundation
Giving Locations: WY
Grant Types: General Support.

Financial Summary

Total Giving: $245,000 (fiscal year ending October 31, 2002); $202,600 (fiscal 2000); $207,972 (fiscal 1998)
Assets: $4,694,105 (fiscal 2002); $5,288,012 (fiscal 2000); $5,068,145 (fiscal 1998)

Typical Recipients

Arts & Humanities: Libraries, Museums/Galleries
Education: Colleges & Universities
Health: Hospitals
Religion: Churches, Religious Welfare
Social Services: Child Welfare, Community Service Organizations, Day Care, People with Disabilities, Senior Services, United Funds/United Ways, YMCA/YWCA/YMHA/YWHA, Youth Organizations

Application Procedures

Initial Contact: Send written application.
Deadlines: None.
Review Process: Application approvals or rejections are usually determined in October.

Foundation Officials

Stella Barker: trustee
Ralph C. Robinson: trustee

Grants Analysis

Disclosure Period: fiscal year ending October 31, 2002
Total Grants: $245,000
Number of Grants: 15
Average Grant: $16,333
Highest Grant: $30,000
Lowest Grant: $3,000
Typical Range: $5,000 to $25,000

Recent Grants

Note: Grants derived from 2000 Form 990.

Library-Related

5,000	Story Library, Story, WY

General

44,100	Children's Center, Sheridan, WY
32,500	YMCA - Johnson County, Buffalo, WY
28,000	Buffalo Children's Center, Buffalo, WY
25,000	Advocacy and Resource Center, Sheridan, WY
25,000	YMCA - Sheridan County, Sheridan, WY
20,000	Salvation Army, Sheridan, WY
10,000	Sheridan College Fund, Sheridan, WY
5,000	Buffalo Senior Center, Buffalo, WY
5,000	Methodist Church, Buffalo, WY
3,000	Regional State Museum, Buffalo, WY

SUSQUEHANNA-PFALTZGRAFF CO.

Company Headquarters

York, PA
Web: http://www.pfaltzgraff.com

Company Description

Employees: 7,000
SIC(s): 3262 Vitreous China Table & Kitchenware, 3269 Pottery Products Nec, 4832 Radio Broadcasting Stations.

Operating Locations

Susquehanna-Pfaltzgraff Co. (PA--York)

Nonmonetary Support

Type: Donated Equipment; Donated Products; In-kind Services; Loaned Employees; Loaned Executives; Workplace Solicitation
Volunteer Programs: The company provides employee volunteer opportunities with the United Way, Junior Achievement, Boy Scouts, Adopt-A-House, blood drives, walk-a-thons, and a variety of other charities and fundraising events.

Susquehanna-Pfaltzgraff Foundation

Giving Contact

John L. Finlayson, Vice President, Finance & Administration
140 East Market Street
York, PA 17401
Phone: (717)848-5500
Fax: (717)771-1440

Description

Founded: 1966
EIN: 236420008
Organization Type: Corporate Foundation
Giving Locations: headquarters and operating communities.
Grant Types: Capital, Challenge, Emergency, Endowment, General Support, Multiyear/Continuing Support, Operating Expenses, Project.

Donor Information

Founder: Susquehanna Radio Corp., the Pfaltzgraff Co.

Financial Summary

Total Giving: $535,068 (2001); $510,084 (2000); $350,000 (1999 approx). Note: Contributes through foundation only.
Giving Analysis: Giving for 2001 includes: foundation grants to United Way ($76,150); foundation

($458,918); 1998: foundation grants to United Way ($65,050) foundation ($286,747)
Assets: $1,551,138 (2001); $1,702,908 (2000); $1,325,712 (1998)
Gifts Received: $400,000 (2001); $450,000 (2000); $350,000 (1998). Note: In 2001, contributions were received from Pfaltzgraff Co.; York Cable Television, Inc.; Radio San Francisco, Inc.; KNBR, Inc.; KPLX Broadcasting LLP; KRBE Broadcasting LLP; Susquehanna Radio Corp.; Radio Indianapolis, Inc.; Indianapolis Radio License Co.; Radio Cincinnati, Inc.; and Susquehanna Kansas City Partnership. Contributions received prior to 2001 were received from Pfaltzgraff Co., Cable TV of York, Radio San Francisco, KNBR, KLIF Co., Radio Metroplex, KRBE Co., Susquehanna Radio Corp., Radio Indianapolis, and Indianapolis Radio License Co., Radio Cincinnati.

Typical Recipients

Arts & Humanities: Arts Associations & Councils, Community Arts, Dance, Arts & Humanities-General, Historic Preservation, History & Archaeology, Libraries, Music, Opera, Performing Arts, Public Broadcasting, Theater
Civic & Public Affairs: Botanical Gardens/Parks, Chambers of Commerce, Community Foundations, Civic & Public Affairs-General, Housing, Nonprofit Management, Urban & Community Affairs
Education: Agricultural Education, Arts/Humanities Education, Colleges & Universities, Education Associations, Education Funds, Education-General, Health & Physical Education, Minority Education, Preschool Education, Private Education (Precollege), Public Education (Precollege), Secondary Education (Private), Student Aid, Vocational & Technical Education
Environment: Environment-General, Environment-General, Resource Conservation, Wildlife Protection
Health: Cancer, Children's Health/Hospitals, Eyes/Blindness, Health-General, Hospitals, Public Health, Single-Disease Health Associations
International: International Organizations
Religion: Churches, Religious Welfare, Seminaries
Science: Science-General, Science Museums
Social Services: Animal Protection, Camps, Child Welfare, Community Service Organizations, Counseling, Emergency Relief, Homes, People with Disabilities, Recreation & Athletics, Scouts, Social Services-General, United Funds/United Ways, YMCA/YWCA/YMHA/YWHA, Youth Organizations

Application Procedures

Initial Contact: Send a brief letter of inquiry.
Application Requirements: Outline need for funds sought.
Deadlines: None.

Corporate Officials

Louis J. Appell, Jr.: president, chief executive officer B 1924. ED Harvard University (1947). PRIM CORP EMPL president: Susquehanna-Pfaltzgraff Co. ADD CORP EMPL treasurer, director: Casco Cabel Television Bth Maine; vice president, director: Casco Cable Televising Inc.; president: Flemington Companies Inc.; vice president, director: LAB Cincinnati Inc.; president, treasurer, director: Nassau Radio Corp.; president: Penn York Advertising Inc.; president, treasurer, director: Radio Akron Inc.; president treasurer, director: WARM Broadcasting Co. Inc. CORP AFFIL chairman: Susquehanna Radio Corp.; director: York Bank Trust Co.; chairman: Susquehanna Media Co.; chairman: SBC Cable Co.; chief executive officer: Susquehanna Broadcasting Co. Inc.; chairman: Pfaltzgraff Outlet Co.; chairman: Radio Metroplex Inc.; chairman: KRBE Co.; chairman: Pfaltzgraff Co.
John L. Finlayson: vice president finance & administration PRIM CORP EMPL vice president finance & administration: Susquehanna-Pfaltzgraff Co. CORP AFFIL vice president: Susquehanna Media Co.; vice president: Susquehanna Radio Corp.; vice president: Susquehanna Cable Co.; vice president: Pfaltzgraff

Outlet Co.; vice president: SBC Cable Co.; vice president: Pfaltzgraff Co.

Mike Sibol: director PRIM CORP EMPL director: Susquehanna-Pfaltzgraff Co.

William H. Simpson: president, chief executive officer B Ithaca, NY 1941. ED United States Air Force Academy (1963); Harvard University (1966). PRIM CORP EMPL president, chief executive officer: Pfaltzgraff Co. CORP AFFIL president: Pfaltzgraff Outlet Co.; vice president manufacturing: Susquehanna Pfalzgraff Co.

Foundation Officials

Louis J. Appell, Jr.: president (see above)
William H. Simpson: secretary (see above)

Grants Analysis

Disclosure Period: calendar year ending 2001
Total Grants: $458,918*
Number of Grants: 40
Average Grant: $6,639*
Highest Grant: $200,000
Lowest Grant: $250
Typical Range: $1,000 to $15,000
*Note:** Giving excludes United Way. Average grant figure excludes highest grant.

Recent Grants

Note: Grants derived from 2001 Form 990.

Library-Related

15,000	Southern York County Library, York, PA
10,000	Kaltreider Benfer Library, Red Lion, PA
6,000	Hanover Public Library, Hanover, PA
500	Jersey Shore Public Library, Jersey Shore, PA

General

200,000	Strand Capitol Performing Arts Center, York, PA
70,100	United Way York County, York, PA
20,000	Penn State University, University Park, PA
17,500	York Habitat for Humanity, York, PA
16,000	Penn Laurel Girl Scout Council, York, PA
15,000	Cultural Alliance of York County, York, PA
15,000	Margaret E. Moul Home, York, PA
12,000	Historic York, Inc., York, PA
12,000	York County Chapter American Red Cross, York, PA
10,000	ARC Foundation of York County, Inc., York, PA

SWALM FOUNDATION

Giving Contact

Dr. Billy C. Ward, President, CEO
11511 Katy Freeway, Suite 430
Houston, TX 77079
Phone: (281)497-5280
Fax: (281)497-7340
Web: http://www.swalm.org

Description

Founded: 1980
EIN: 742073420
Organization Type: Family Foundation
Giving Locations: TX.
Grant Types: Award, Capital, Emergency, General Support, Matching, Operating Expenses, Scholarship.

Donor Information

Founder: Established in 1980 by Dave C. Swalm, Ron Woliver, and Texas Olefins Co.

Financial Summary

Total Giving: $3,700,000 (fiscal year ending November 30, 2002 approx); $4,710,947 (fiscal 2001); $4,200,000 (fiscal 2000)
Giving Analysis: Giving for fiscal 2001 includes: foundation matching gifts ($495,000) fiscal 1998: foundation matching gifts ($265,600)
Assets: $79,695,598 (fiscal 2001); $100,273,247 (fiscal 1999); $90,687,146 (fiscal 1998)
Gifts Received: $2,880,000 (fiscal 1999); $1,900,000 (fiscal 1998); $2,000,000 (fiscal 1997). Note: Gifts are received from Dave C. Swalm.

Typical Recipients

Arts & Humanities: Libraries, Museums/Galleries, Theater
Civic & Public Affairs: Botanical Gardens/Parks, Community Foundations, Economic Development, Economic Policy, Employment/Job Training, Hispanic Affairs, Housing, Legal Aid, Municipalities/Towns, Safety, Urban & Community Affairs, Women's Affairs, Zoos/Aquariums
Education: Arts/Humanities Education, Colleges & Universities, Elementary Education (Private), Engineering/Technological Education, Education-General, Literacy, Preschool Education, Private Education (Precollege), Public Education (Precollege), Science/Mathematics Education, Special Education, Student Aid
Health: AIDS/HIV, Alzheimers Disease, Cancer, Children's Health/Hospitals, Clinics/Medical Centers, Emergency/Ambulance Services, Eyes/Blindness, Health-General, Hospices, Hospitals, Medical Rehabilitation, Mental Health, Public Health, Research/Studies Institutes, Speech & Hearing
International: Human Rights, International Development
Religion: Churches, Jewish Causes, Ministries, Religious Organizations, Religious Welfare
Science: Science Museums
Social Services: At-Risk Youth, Big Brother/Big Sister, Camps, Child Abuse, Child Welfare, Community Centers, Community Service Organizations, Crime Prevention, Day Care, Delinquency & Criminal Rehabilitation, Domestic Violence, Family Planning, Family Services, Food/Clothing Distribution, People with Disabilities, Recreation & Athletics, Scouts, Scouts, Shelters/Homelessness, Social Services-General, Substance Abuse, United Funds/United Ways, YMCA/YWCA/YMHA/YWHA, Youth Organizations

Application Procedures

Initial Contact: To facilitate the grant process, a Grant Application Summary, copy attached, should be sent initially.
Deadlines: None.
Review Process: Applicants will be informed within four weeks if the initial proposal is within the foundation's giving focus. If so, a formal application will be sent at that time.

Restrictions

The foundation only makes grants to charitable organizations, and does not fund the following: building or operations of individual churches, synagogues, or mosques; capital campaigns, operations, or ancillary programs of institutes of higher education or medical facilities; experimental programs in public education including charter schools; capital campaigns or the operations of private schools; large national or international organizations' giving campaigns; social service programs which require or include as an element of that program formal instruction in or adherence to the tenets of a particular religion; galas or other social functions; organizations whose geographic locations preclude or inhibit foundation staff monitoring or oversight; programs that have no local community support;

summer camps, retreats, or field trips, unless there is a large component of the disadvantaged who will be participating and the purposes are therapeutic or culturally and educationally enriching; or individual scholarship or fellowships.

Additional Information

Publications: Informational Brochure (including Application Guidelines)

Foundation Officials

Mark C. Mendelovitz: secretary, trustee
David C. Swalm: vice president, trustee
Jo Beth Camp Swalm: president, trustee

Grants Analysis

Disclosure Period: fiscal year ending November 30, 2001
Total Grants: $4,710,947
Number of Grants: 188
Average Grant: $25,058
Highest Grant: $140,000
Lowest Grant: $5,000
Typical Range: $5,000 to $25,000 and $50,000 to $100,000

Recent Grants

Note: Grants derived from fiscal 2001 Form 990.

General

125,000	Family Violence Prevention Services, San Antonio, TX -- capital support
125,000	Spring Branch Center Building Foundation, Houston, TX -- capital support
100,000	Boys and Girls Club of Vernon, Inc., Vernon, TX -- capital support
100,000	Center for Community Initiatives of GHCF-GHCC, Houston, TX -- program support
100,000	Child Advocates, Inc., Houston, TX -- matching support for the Hero Society campaign
100,000	Communities in Schools Houston, Houston, TX -- program support
100,000	Houston Area Women's Center, Houston, TX -- first installment of a four year pledge
100,000	Service of the Emergency Aid Resource Center for the Homeless, Houston, TX -- operating support
80,000	Boys and Girls Clubs of Deep East Texas, Nacogdoches, TX -- operating support
75,000	Health Care for the Homeless, Houston, TX -- program support

DR. W. C. SWANSON FAMILY FOUNDATION, INC.

Giving Contact

Cindy Purcell, President
2955 Harrison Boulevard, Suite 201
Ogden, UT 84403
Phone: (801)392-0360
Fax: (801)392-0429

Description

Founded: 1978
EIN: 942478549
Organization Type: Family Foundation
Giving Locations: UT: primarily Northern Utah and Weber County; grants from the rest of Utah are next in priority, then regional requests, and lastly national and international
Grant Types: General Support, Matching, Professorship, Research, Scholarship.

Donor Information

Founder: Established in 1978 by the late Dr. W. C. Swanson with the help of his family, Beryl, Annabel, and Chuck. Lew Costley was appointed trustee and is now an advisory committee member and CFO.

Financial Summary

Total Giving: $2,837,941 (2000); $2,256,620 (1999); $2,579,637 (1998)
Giving Analysis: Giving for 1998 includes: nonmonetary support ($3,646) foundation scholarships ($210,667)
Assets: $55,000,000 (2000 approx); $53,000,000 (1999 approx); $52,438,227 (1998)

Typical Recipients

Arts & Humanities: Arts Centers, Ballet, Dance, Film & Video, Historic Preservation, History & Archaeology, Libraries, Museums/Galleries, Music, Opera, Performing Arts, Public Broadcasting, Theater
Civic & Public Affairs: Clubs, Civic & Public Affairs-General, Housing, Municipalities/Towns, Philanthropic Organizations, Public Policy, Safety, Urban & Community Affairs
Education: Afterschool/Enrichment Programs, Colleges & Universities, Elementary Education (Private), Education-General, Medical Education, Private Education (Precollege), Public Education (Precollege), Secondary Education (Private), Special Education, Student Aid, Vocational & Technical Education
Environment: Environment-General
Health: Cancer, Children's Health/Hospitals, Emergency/Ambulance Services, Health-General, Health Organizations, Heart, Hospices, Hospitals, Medical Rehabilitation, Public Health, Trauma Treatment
International: Health Care/Hospitals, International Organizations, International Relief Efforts
Religion: Churches, Religious Organizations, Religious Welfare, Social/Policy Issues
Science: Science Museums, Scientific Centers & Institutes
Social Services: Animal Protection, Big Brother/Big Sister, Child Abuse, Child Welfare, Community Centers, Community Service Organizations, Crime Prevention, Domestic Violence, Emergency Relief, Family Services, People with Disabilities, Recreation & Athletics, Scouts, Senior Services, Sexual Abuse, Social Services-General, Special Olympics, Substance Abuse, United Funds/United Ways, YMCA/YWCA/YMHA/YWHA, Youth Organizations

Application Procedures

Initial Contact: Contact the foundation for application form and guidelines.
Application Requirements: A copy of requesting organization's IRS 501(c)(3) tax-exemption letter, as well as a copy of the organization's annual report and financial statement with the completed application form and proposal narrative.
Deadlines: The end of the quarter prior to the quarter grant request is considered.
Review Process: Board meetings are held quarterly.

Restrictions

Does not provide grants to individuals. No support is given for salaries and administrative costs; very limited amounts are given for bricks and mortar.

Additional Information

The foundation supports collaboration with other agencies.
Publications: Application Form (including Guidelines); Grant Agreement Newsletter

Foundation Officials

Lew Costley: trustee B 1925. PRIM CORP EMPL secretary: A/Y Car Sales Inc.
Mike Fosmark: member administrative committee
Annabel Hofer: mem admin comm
Marlin Jensen: member administrative committee

Marcy Korgenski: member administration committee
Dr. Robert Marquardt: mem admin comm B 1925. PRIM CORP EMPL chairman, chief executive officer, director: Management & Training Corp. ADD CORP EMPL chairman, chief executive officer: MTC.
Carolyn Nebeker: mem admin comm
Cindy Purcell: member admin committee, executive director operations
Julie Snowball: president
W. Charles Swanson: chairman

Grants Analysis

Disclosure Period: calendar year ending 1998
Total Grants: $1,741,212*
Number of Grants: 197
Average Grant: $7,608*
Highest Grant: $250,000
Typical Range: $1,000 to $25,000
*Note: Giving excludes scholarships, nonmonetary support, and grants carried over to 1999. Average grant figure excludes highest grant.

Recent Grants

Note: Grants derived from 2001 Form 990.

General

15,000	United Way of Northern Utah, Ogden, UT
1,000	National Cancer Center of Mongolia, Bayanzurkh Mongolia

SWIFT PRINT COMMUNICATIONS

Company Headquarters

Chicago, IL
Web: http://www.swiftprint.com

Company Description

Former Name: John S. Swift Co. Inc.
Employees: 550
SIC(s): 2700 Printing & Publishing, 2731 Book Publishing, 2741 Miscellaneous Publishing, 2752 Commercial Printing--Lithographic.
Parent Company: J.S.S. Company, Inc.

Operating Locations

Swift Print Communications (IL--Chicago; MO--St. Louis)

John S. Swift Co. Inc. Charitable Trust

Giving Contact

Bryan Swift, President
1248 Research Boulevard
St. Louis, MO 63122
Phone: (314)991-4300
Fax: (314)991-3080
E-mail: swiftinc@intec.net

Description

Founded: 1952
EIN: 436020812
Organization Type: Corporate Foundation
Giving Locations: IL; MO
Grant Types: Challenge, Endowment, General Support.

Donor Information

Founder: John S. Swift Co., Inc.

Financial Summary

Total Giving: $101,675 (2000); $81,200 (1999); $101,650 (1998)
Giving Analysis: Giving for 1999 includes: foundation ($81,200) 1998: foundation ($101,650)

Assets: $2,059,847 (2000); $1,984,634 (1999); $2,024,823 (1998)
Gifts Received: $110 (1999). Note: In 1990, contributions were received from John S. Swift Co.

Typical Recipients

Arts & Humanities: Arts Centers, Arts Institutes, History & Archaeology, Libraries, Museums/Galleries, Public Broadcasting, Visual Arts
Civic & Public Affairs: Botanical Gardens/Parks, Clubs, Urban & Community Affairs, Zoos/Aquariums
Education: Colleges & Universities, Medical Education, Private Education (Precollege), Public Education (Precollege), Science/Mathematics Education, Student Aid
Environment: Forestry, Environment-General, Resource Conservation, Wildlife Protection
Health: Arthritis, Cancer, Children's Health/Hospitals, Hospitals, Medical Research, Multiple Sclerosis
Religion: Bible Study/Translation, Churches, Religious Welfare
Social Services: Animal Protection, Community Service Organizations, People with Disabilities, Scouts, Social Services-General, Substance Abuse, United Funds/United Ways, YMCA/YWCA/YMHA/YWHA, Youth Organizations

Application Procedures

Initial Contact: Send a brief letter of inquiry.
Deadlines: None.

Additional Information

Trust(s): Firstar Bank NA

Corporate Officials

Bryan Swift: president PRIM CORP EMPL president: Swift Print Communs.

Foundation Officials

Ben Heckel: co-trustee
Hampden M. Swift: co-trustee

Grants Analysis

Disclosure Period: calendar year ending 2000
Total Grants: $101,675
Number of Grants: 98
Average Grant: $1,038
Highest Grant: $10,000
Typical Range: $500 to $5,000

Recent Grants

Note: Grants derived from 1999 Form 990.

General

10,000	Lake Forest College, Lake Forest, IL
5,000	Cardinal Glennon Children's Hospital, St. Louis, MO
5,000	St. Louis 200 Friends Association, St. Louis, MO
5,000	Shedd Aquarium, Chicago, IL
5,000	Zoo Friends, Houston, TX
3,500	Lake Forest Academy, Lake Forest, IL
3,500	Lake Forest Country Day School, Lake Forest, IL
2,500	Detroit Institute for Children, Detroit, MI
2,500	Good Shepherd School, Philadelphia, PA
2,500	Gross Pointe Academy, Grosse Pte., MI

THE SWIG FOUNDATION

Giving Contact

Kent Swig, Trustee
220 Montgomery Street
San Francisco, CA 94104
Phone: (415)291-1100
Fax: (415)291-8373

Description

Founded: 1957
EIN: 946065205
Organization Type: Family Foundation
Giving Locations: CA; NY
Grant Types: Award, Multiyear/Continuing Support.

Donor Information

Founder: Established in 1957 by the late Benjamin H. Swig and members of the Swig family.

Financial Summary

Total Giving: $1,048,722 (2001); $1,047,727 (1998); $1,245,238 (1997)
Giving Analysis: Giving for 1998 includes: foundation grants to United Way ($5,000) 1997: foundation grants to United Way ($10,000)
Assets: $20,481,159 (2001); $21,918,791 (1998); $19,449,854 (1997)

Typical Recipients

Arts & Humanities: Arts Associations & Councils, Arts Centers, Arts Institutes, Ballet, Community Arts, Dance, Historic Preservation, History & Archaeology, Libraries, Museums/Galleries, Music, Opera, Performing Arts, Public Broadcasting, Theater
Civic & Public Affairs: Botanical Gardens/Parks, Business/Free Enterprise, Clubs, Community Foundations, Ethnic Organizations, Civic & Public Affairs-General, Housing, Municipalities/Towns, Parades/Festivals, Philanthropic Organizations, Public Policy, Safety, Urban & Community Affairs, Zoos/Aquariums
Education: Arts/Humanities Education, Business Education, Colleges & Universities, Education Associations, Faculty Development, Education-General, Preschool Education, Private Education (Precollege), Public Education (Precollege), Religious Education, School Volunteerism, Science/Mathematics Education, Social Sciences Education, Student Aid
Environment: Air/Water Quality, Energy
Health: Cancer, Children's Health/Hospitals, Clinics/Medical Centers, Geriatric Health, Health Funds, Health Organizations, Hospitals, Hospitals (University Affiliated), Medical Research
International: Foreign Arts Organizations, Foreign Educational Institutions, Human Rights, International Affairs, International Environmental Issues, International Organizations, International Peace & Security Issues, Missionary/Religious Activities
Religion: Churches, Jewish Causes, Religious Organizations, Religious Welfare, Synagogues/Temples
Science: Science Museums, Scientific Organizations
Social Services: Child Abuse, Community Service Organizations, Domestic Violence, Emergency Relief, Family Services, Food/Clothing Distribution, Homes, Recreation & Athletics, United Funds/United Ways, YMCA/YWCA/YMHA/YWHA, Youth Organizations

Application Procedures

Initial Contact: Contact the foundation for application guidelines.
Deadlines: None.

Restrictions

The foundation makes grants only to organizations exempt under section 501(c)(3). The foundation does not make grants to individuals. The foundation does not support conferences, seminars, or workshops.

Additional Information

Publications: Guidelines

Foundation Officials

Richard S. Dinner: trustee B 1921. PRIM CORP EMPL vice president, director: Swig Co.
Pam L. Peterson: secretary
Kent Swig: trustee CORP AFFIL shareholder: Brown Harris Stevens Residential.

Richard L. Swig: trustee B Boston, MA 1925. ED University of San Francisco. PRIM CORP EMPL general partner: SIC Hotel Co. CORP AFFIL chairman: AIR Missouri Corporate; general partner: Fairmont Hotel San Francisco.
Robert Swig: trustee PRIM CORP EMPL vice president, director: Swig Weiler & Dinner Development Co.
Steven L. Swig: trustee PRIM CORP EMPL secretary: Swig Co.

Grants Analysis

Disclosure Period: calendar year ending 2001
Total Grants: $1,046,222*
Number of Grants: 375
Average Grant: $2,790
Highest Grant: $50,000
Typical Range: $500 to $20,000
*Note: Giving excludes United Way.

Recent Grants

Note: Grants derived from 2001 Form 990.

General

50,000	Horace Mann School, New York, NY
25,000	Heartwood Foundation, Ketchum, ID
25,000	Pundrika Foundation, San Bruno, CA
20,000	American Jewish Committee, San Francisco, CA
20,000	KQED, San Francisco, CA
20,000	University of Oregon, Portland, OR
18,750	Drew College Preparatory School, San Francisco, CA
15,000	KQED, San Francisco, CA
15,000	KQED, San Francisco, CA
15,000	KQED, San Francisco, CA

CARL S. SWISHER FOUNDATION

Giving Contact

Kenneth G. Anderson, President & Trustee
1301 Riverplace Boulevard
Suite 2640
Jacksonville, FL 32207
Phone: (904)399-8000
Fax: (904)346-3078

Description

Founded: 1949
EIN: 590998262
Organization Type: Private Foundation
Giving Locations: FL: Jacksonville
Grant Types: Capital, General Support, Project, Scholarship.

Donor Information

Founder: the late Carl S. Swisher

Financial Summary

Total Giving: $339,050 (2001); $322,000 (2000); $306,500 (1999)
Assets: $7,510,148 (2001); $7,504,190 (2000); $7,719,914 (1999)

Typical Recipients

Arts & Humanities: Arts Associations & Councils, Historic Preservation, History & Archaeology, Libraries, Museums/Galleries, Music, Public Broadcasting
Civic & Public Affairs: Civic & Public Affairs-General, Law & Justice, Legal Aid, Urban & Community Affairs, Zoos/Aquariums
Education: Arts/Humanities Education, Business Education, Colleges & Universities, Education Funds, Engineering/Technological Education, Legal Education, Literacy, Medical Education, Minority Education, Private Education (Precollege), Religious Education, Special Education, Student Aid
Health: Children's Health/Hospitals, Clinics/Medical Centers, Diabetes, Emergency/Ambulance Services,

Hospices, Hospitals, Medical Rehabilitation, Medical Research, Research/Studies Institutes, Single-Disease Health Associations
Religion: Churches, Religion-General, Jewish Causes, Missionary Activities (Domestic), Religious Organizations, Religious Welfare
Science: Science Museums
Social Services: Animal Protection, Big Brother/Big Sister, Child Welfare, Community Service Organizations, Family Services, Food/Clothing Distribution, Homes, Senior Services, Shelters/Homelessness, United Funds/United Ways, YMCA/YWCA/YMHA/YWHA, Youth Organizations

Application Procedures

Initial Contact: Send a brief letter of inquiry.
Application Requirements: Include the applicant's name, address, employer identification number, and contact person; purpose of funds sought; amount requested; how grant will advance charitable purposes; proof of tax-exempt status; confirmation of current 501(c)(3) status; and balance sheet and income statement.
Deadlines: None.
Review Process: Board meets quarterly.

Restrictions

Does not support individuals.

Foundation Officials

Kenneth G. Anderson: president, trustee
Carolyn Charbonnet: secretary, treasurer, trustee
George S. Coulter: trustee
John Lindsey: trustee
Harold W. Smith: vice president, trustee
James P. Stevens: trustee

Grants Analysis

Disclosure Period: calendar year ending 2001
Total Grants: $339,050
Number of Grants: 62
Average Grant: $3,818*
Highest Grant: $60,000
Lowest Grant: $1,000
Typical Range: $1,000 to $5,000
*Note: Average grant excludes two highest grants ($110,000).

Recent Grants

Note: Grants derived from 2001 Form 990.

Library-Related

5,000	Jacksonville Library, Jacksonville, FL

General

60,000	Jacksonville University, Jacksonville, FL
50,000	University of Florida, Gainesville, FL
10,500	Diabetes Foundation, Jacksonville, FL
10,000	Children's Home Society of Florida, Jacksonville, FL
10,000	Downtown Ecumenical Services Council, Jacksonville, FL
10,000	Hubbard House, Jacksonville, FL
10,000	IM Sulzbacher Center for the Homeless, Jacksonville, FL
10,000	Museum of Science and History, Jacksonville, FL
10,000	Taylor Residences, Jacksonville, FL
8,000	Trinity Rescue Mission, Jacksonville, FL

F. W. SYMMES FOUNDATION

Giving Contact

Sara Gerald Huggins, Trust Officer
c/o Wachovia Bank, Trust Dept.
1401 Main St.
Columbia, SC 29226-9365
Phone: (803)765-3621

Description

Founded: 1954
EIN: 576017472
Organization Type: Private Foundation
Giving Locations: SC: Greenville
Grant Types: Capital, General Support, Project.

Donor Information

Founder: the late F.W. Symmes

Financial Summary

Total Giving: $833,500 (fiscal year ending March 31, 2002); $744,000 (fiscal 2001); $696,230 (fiscal 2000)
Assets: $14,805,030 (fiscal 2002); $15,885,753 (fiscal 2001); $19,105,168 (fiscal 2000)

Typical Recipients

Arts & Humanities: Arts Associations & Councils, Arts Centers, Arts Outreach, Historic Preservation, History & Archaeology, Libraries, Museums/Galleries, Performing Arts, Theater
Civic & Public Affairs: Civic & Public Affairs-General, Housing, Municipalities/Towns, Urban & Community Affairs, Zoos/Aquariums
Education: Arts/Humanities Education, Colleges & Universities, Education Funds, Education Reform, Literacy, Religious Education, Science/Mathematics Education, Special Education, Student Aid
Environment: Environment-General
Health: Cancer, Clinics/Medical Centers, Emergency/Ambulance Services, Health Organizations, Hospitals, Medical Rehabilitation, Speech & Hearing
Religion: Churches, Ministries, Religious Welfare
Science: Scientific Centers & Institutes
Social Services: Child Welfare, Community Service Organizations, Food/Clothing Distribution, Homes, People with Disabilities, Scouts, Shelters/Homelessness, YMCA/YWCA/YMHA/YWHA

Application Procedures

Initial Contact: Send a brief letter of inquiry describing program or project. Include purpose of funds sought and proof of tax-exempt status.
Deadlines: None.

Restrictions

Does not support individuals.

Additional Information

Publications: Application Guidelines; Informational Brochure
Trust(s): Wachovia Bank NA

Foundation Officials

William H. Orders: trustee
Eleanor Welling: trustee
F. McKinnon Wilkinson: trustee

Grants Analysis

Disclosure Period: fiscal year ending March 31, 2002
Total Grants: $833,500*
Typical Range: $20,000 to $100,000
*Note: No grants list available for 2002.

Recent Grants

Note: Grants derived from 2000 Form 990.

General

100,000	Greenville County Museum of Art, Greenville, SC
100,000	Greenville Literacy Association, Greenville, SC
100,000	South Carolina Governor's School of the Arts and Humanities -- fourth installment
50,000	Center for Developmental Services
50,000	Greater Greenville YMCA, Greenville, SC -- second installment of grant
50,000	Miracle Hill Ministries, Greenville, SC
50,000	Safe Harbor, West Chester, PA
42,000	Hidden Treasures Christian School
25,000	Governor's School for Science and Math -- second of three installments
25,000	Hollings Cancer Center, Charleston, SC

TACONIC FOUNDATION

Giving Contact

Hildy Simmons, Managing Director
J.P. Morgan & Co. Inc.
60 Wall St., 46th Fl.
New York, NY 10005
Phone: (212)789-5777
Fax: (212)648-5082

Alternate Contact

Andrew Lane, Assistant Program Officer
Phone: (212)648-3246

Description

Founded: 1958
EIN: 131873668
Organization Type: Specialized/Single Purpose Foundation
Giving Locations: NY: New York nationally.
Grant Types: General Support, Operating Expenses, Project.

Donor Information

Founder: Established in 1958 by the late Mr. Stephen R. Currier and Mrs. Audrey Currier, the former Audrey Mellon Bruce. She was the daughter of Ailsa Mellon, who was the sister of Paul Mellon and the daughter of Andrew Mellon. Mr. and Mrs. Currier, who were lost in the Caribbean on an airplane flight in 1967, left a fund having a current market value of approximately $15 million to carry on their charitable activities.

Financial Summary

Total Giving: $825,000 (2000); $747,500 (1999 approx); $695,500 (1998)
Assets: $20,892,809 (2000); $18,500,000 (1999 approx); $20,327,827 (1998)

Typical Recipients

Arts & Humanities: Arts Outreach, Libraries, Literary Arts
Civic & Public Affairs: African American Affairs, Asian American Affairs, Botanical Gardens/Parks, Civil Rights, Economic Development, Employment/Job Training, Civic & Public Affairs-General, Housing, Law & Justice, Minority Business, Nonprofit Management, Philanthropic Organizations, Public Policy, Urban & Community Affairs
Education: Afterschool/Enrichment Programs, Arts/Humanities Education, Colleges & Universities, Education Associations, Education Funds, Education Reform, Education-General, Leadership Training, Literacy, Minority Education, Private Education (Precollege), School Volunteerism
Environment: Resource Conservation
Health: Children's Health/Hospitals
International: Health Care/Hospitals, Human Rights, International Relations
Religion: Churches, Religious Welfare
Social Services: Child Welfare, Community Service Organizations, Counseling, Family Planning, Family Services, Shelters/Homelessness, Youth Organizations

Application Procedures

Application Requirements: Primary goals of organization, most recent annual report, brief history of organization, list of directors or trustees, most recent financial audit, current operating budget, list of foundation and corporate support with amount for most recent and current fiscal year, copy 501(c)3 letter, latest IRS Form 990 (including salary information), description of project including primary purpose, population to be served, anticipated duration, and current budget. Indicate whether organisation has an endowment.
Review Process: Proposals are reviewed three times each year. Final notification comes within two to three months.

Restrictions

Grants are not given for higher education, the elderly, international programs, art and cultural programs, mass media, crime and justice, health, medicine, mental health, ecology and the environment, individual economic development projects, or local community programs outside New York City. The foundation does not make grants to individuals, scholarships, fellowships, or to building or endowment funds. It rarely makes grants for research or loans.

Additional Information

The foundation accepts the New York/New Jersey Common Application Form.
Publications: application guidelines

Foundation Officials

L. F. Boker Doyle: trustee B New York, NY 1931. ED Yale University BA (1953); New York University (1963). PRIM CORP EMPL consultant: Fiduciary Trust Co. International. NONPR AFFIL trustee, secretary: American Museum Natural History; treasurer: Frick Collection.
Alan J. Dworsky: trustee
Jane Lee Eddy: trustee NONPR AFFIL chairman, trustee: Corporate for Youth Energy Corps; president, trustee: Smokey House Project.
Hon. Bill Green: trustee NONPR AFFIL deputy chairman: New York City Housing Development Corp.
Melvin Mister: trustee
John Gerald Simon: trustee B New York, NY 1928. ED Harvard University AB (1950); Yale University LLB (1953). PRIM NONPR EMPL professor: Yale University, Law School. NONPR AFFIL trustee: Open Society Institute; member: Phi Beta Kappa; vice chairman: Cooperative Assistance Fund; member graduate board: Harvard Crimson.

Grants Analysis

Disclosure Period: calendar year ending 2000
Total Grants: $825,000
Number of Grants: 48
Average Grant: $17,188
Highest Grant: $30,000
Lowest Grant: $2,500
Typical Range: $10,000 to $25,000

TANNER COMPANIES (RUTHERFORDTON, NC)

Company Headquarters

Rutherfordton, NC

Company Description

Employees: 800
SIC(s): 2331 Women's/Misses' Blouses & Shirts, 2335 Women's/Misses' Dresses.

Operating Locations

Tanner Companies (NC--Rutherfordton)

Tanner Foundation

Giving Contact

George E. Clayton, III, Treasurer
PO Box 1139
Rutherfordton, NC 28139
Phone: (828)287-4205
Fax: (828)286-2072

Description

EIN: 510151695
Organization Type: Corporate Foundation
Giving Locations: NC: Rutherford County
Grant Types: Capital, General Support, Research.

Financial Summary

Total Giving: $392,202 (2001); $233,635 (2000); $154,544 (1999)
Giving Analysis: Giving for 2001 includes: foundation grants to United Way ($49,221); foundation matching gifts ($83,550); 2000: foundation matching gifts ($10,000); foundation grants to United Way ($15,577); 1999: foundation grants to United Way ($15,000); foundation matching gifts ($49,919); foundation ($89,625)
Assets: $106,394 (2001); $142,755 (2000); $80,278 (1999)
Gifts Received: $353,758 (2001); $292,935 (2000); $100,000 (1999). Note: Contributions were received from Tanner Companies Limited Partnership.

Typical Recipients

Arts & Humanities: Arts Associations & Councils, Libraries, Museums/Galleries, Music, Public Broadcasting, Theater
Civic & Public Affairs: Community Foundations, Economic Development, Employment/Job Training, Civic & Public Affairs-General, Housing, Professional & Trade Associations, Urban & Community Affairs
Education: Arts/Humanities Education, Colleges & Universities, Community & Junior Colleges, Economic Education, Education Funds, Elementary Education (Private), Elementary Education (Public), Minority Education, Public Education (Precollege), Secondary Education (Public), Special Education
Health: Emergency/Ambulance Services, Eyes/Blindness, Health-General, Health Organizations, Heart, Hospices, Hospitals, Prenatal Health Issues, Single-Disease Health Associations
International: Health Care/Hospitals
Religion: Religious Organizations, Religious Welfare
Social Services: Child Welfare, Food/Clothing Distribution, People with Disabilities, Scouts, Special Olympics, United Funds/United Ways, Youth Organizations

Application Procedures

Initial Contact: Send a full proposal.
Application Requirements: Include a description of the project and proposed budget, amount requested, federal employer identification number, and proof of tax-exempt status.
Deadlines: December 1 for consideration in the following year.

Restrictions

Preference is given to health care, education, and social services.

Corporate Officials

Trip Clayton: chief financial officer PRIM CORP EMPL chief financial officer: Tanner Companies.
Chapman Johnston: president, chief executive officer PRIM CORP EMPL president, chief executive officer: Tanner Companies.
James T. Tanner: chairman B 1929. ED University of North Carolina (1950). PRIM CORP EMPL chairman: Tanner Companies.

Foundation Officials

Trip Clayton: director (see above)
Chapman Johnston: vice president (see above)
James T. Tanner: president (see above)
Michael S. Tanner: secretary
Pell Tanner: director

Grants Analysis

Disclosure Period: calendar year ending 2001
Total Grants: $259,431*
Number of Grants: 35
Average Grant: $5,654*
Highest Grant: $67,181
Lowest Grant: $500
Typical Range: $1,000 to $10,000
***Note:** Giving excludes United Way and matching gifts. Average grant figure excludes highest grant.

Recent Grants

Note: Grants derived from 2000 Form 990.

Library-Related
2,500	UNC - Chapel Hill Friends of the Library, Chapel Hill, NC

General
28,290	Community Foundation of Western North Carolina, Asheville, NC
20,000	Lynnwood Foundation, Charlotte, NC
15,677	United Way
13,468	Kid's Senses, Inc.
13,000	Spartanburg County Foundation, Spartanburg, SC
10,000	GT Alexander Thorpe Fund, Chippewa Falls, WI
10,000	Learning Tree, Springfield, MA
7,500	North Carolina Public Television Foundation, Research Triangle Park, NC
5,000	Community Health Counsel
5,000	Cystic Fibrosis

TARGET CORP.

Company Headquarters

1000 Nicollet Mall
Minneapolis, MN 55403
Web: http://www.target.com

Company Description

Ticker: TGT
Exchange: NYSE
Former Name: Dayton Hudson.
Revenue: US$42.722 billion (2002)
Profit: US$1.654 billion (2002)
Employees: 192000 (2002)
Fortune Rank: 25, per FORTUNE Magazine's list of 500 Largest U.S. Corporations (2002).

Nonmonetary Support

Type: Cause-related Marketing & Promotion; In-kind Services
Volunteer Programs: Each division of the company has its own volunteer program. Company-wide, Target Corp. jointly sponsors "Day of Giving" in the spring/summer.
Note: Nonmonetary support is provided by local operating divisions. Nonmonetary Support Contact: General Managers at local stores. Nonmonetary support is valued at more than $5,000,000 annually.

Target Foundation

Giving Contact

Community Relations
Target Stores
1000 Nicollet Mall, TPS30
Minneapolis, MN 55403
Phone: (612)696-6098
Fax: (612)696-5088
E-mail: bridget.mcginnis@target.com
Web: http://www.target.com/target_group/community/community_main.jhtml

Alternate Contact

Target Foundation
33 South Sixth Street, CC-28Y
Minneapolis, MN 55402
E-mail: guidelines@target.com
Web: http://www.targetfoundation.org
Note: Address for application submissions.

Description

Founded: 1918
EIN: 416017088
Organization Type: Corporate Foundation
Former Name: Dayton Hudson Corporate.
Giving Locations: headquarters and operating communities.
Grant Types: Capital, General Support, Project, Scholarship.

Donor Information

Founder: Dayton Hudson Corp. and operating divisions

Financial Summary

Total Giving: $87,200,000 (fiscal year ending January 31, 2002 approx); $85,800,000 (fiscal 2001 approx); $80,800,000 (fiscal 2000 approx). Note: Contributes through corporate direct giving program and foundation.
Giving Analysis: Giving for fiscal 2001 includes: foundation (approx $9,500,000); corporate direct giving (approx $76,300,000); fiscal 2000: foundation grants to United Way ($1,075,000); foundation ($13,369,387); corporate direct giving (approx $66,000,000); fiscal 1999: foundation grants to United Way ($1,055,000); foundation ($7,900,600); corporate direct giving (approx $57,510,000);
Assets: $16,882,628 (fiscal 2002); $25,628,038 (fiscal 2001); $38,968,296 (fiscal 2000). Note: Assets exist as a reserve fund.
Gifts Received: $2,222,267 (fiscal 2002); $397,750 (fiscal 2001); $12,756,105 (fiscal 2000). Note: Contributions were received from Target Corp.

Typical Recipients

Arts & Humanities: Arts Appreciation, Arts Associations & Councils, Arts Centers, Arts Funds, Arts Institutes, Arts Outreach, Community Arts, Dance, Ethnic & Folk Arts, Film & Video, Arts & Humanities-General, History & Archaeology, Libraries, Literary Arts, Museums/Galleries, Music, Opera, Performing Arts, Public Broadcasting, Theater, Visual Arts
Civic & Public Affairs: African American Affairs, Botanical Gardens/Parks, Business/Free Enterprise, Civil Rights, Clubs, Community Foundations, Economic Development, Employment/Job Training, Civic & Public Affairs-General, Hispanic Affairs, Housing, Legal Aid, Minority Business, Native American Affairs, Nonprofit Management, Professional & Trade Associations, Public Policy, Urban & Community Affairs, Women's Affairs
Education: Arts/Humanities Education, Colleges & Universities, Education Reform, Engineering/Technological Education, International Exchange, Literacy, Private Education (Precollege), Public Education (Precollege), School Volunteerism, Special Education, Student Aid
Health: AIDS/HIV, Children's Health/Hospitals, Health Organizations, Research/Studies Institutes
International: Trade
Religion: Churches, Religious Welfare
Social Services: At-Risk Youth, Child Welfare, Community Centers, Community Service Organizations, Domestic Violence, Emergency Relief, Family Planning, Family Services, Food/Clothing Distribution, People with Disabilities, Refugee Assistance, Shelters/Homelessness, Social Services-General, United Funds/United Ways, YMCA/YWCA/YMHA/YWHA, Youth Organizations

Application Procedures

Initial Contact: Minnesota organizations that fit the foundation's guidelines should contact the foundation to obtain a copy of the foundation's application form and guidelines. Organizations located elsewhere should obtain guidelines and application from the Target, Mervyn's, or Marshall Field's store in their community. Guidelines may also be obtained on each company's web site.

Application Requirements: For proposals to the foundation: Provide a completed application form; amount requested and purpose of funds sought; organization's history and mission statement; list of the board of directors, including names, titles, and affiliations; proof of tax-exempt status; current annual operating budget, with income and expenses; project or program budget detailing expenses and anticipated sources of income; current list of business and foundation donors including amounts; a copy of the organization's most recent audited financial statement. received. received. received.

Deadlines: None for the foundation, although preferred submission times are February through November. The foundation does not typically make grants in December and January. For corporate contributions, operating divisions may have deadlines. Most stores do not review applications during the fourth quarter of the year due to the holiday shopping season and fiscal year end.

Review Process: Reviews are conducted by foundation staff or staff of operating divisions.

Evaluative Criteria: Whether group is focused within key areas of interest for foundation or operating divisions, and whether they can realistically accomplish their objective.

Decision Notification: Usually within 90 days of receipt of proposal.

Restrictions

The foundation does not make grants to individuals; religious organizations for sectarian purposes; national ceremonies, memorials, conferences, fundraising dinners, testimonials, or similar events; health, recreation, therapeutic programs, living subsidies, or care of disabled persons. Corporate contributions programs have similar restrictions.

Additional Information

Target Corporation's philanthropic contributions policy calls for the company to donate 5% of its federal taxable income annually to charitable organizations. Target operates retail stores including Marshall Field's, Mervyn's, and Target; each chain manages its own corporate contributions program in communities where they have a presence.

The Target Stores contributions program has two program areas: Arts and Family Violence Prevention. The Arts program area focuses on affordable cultural experiences for the entire family such as art exhibits, classes, performances, and programs that bring arts to schools or that take school children to the arts. Family Violence Prevention grants typically support parenting education, family counseling, support groups, and abuse shelters.

Marshall Field's focuses contributions on three areas: Child Abuse Prevention, Youth Self-Sufficiency, and Education Through the Arts. Under the Child Abuse Prevention program, the company supports prevention and intervention programs, mentoring programs for parents and caregivers, crisis nurseries, home-visit programs for at-risk families, and awareness programs. The Youth Self-Sufficiency focus area supports programs that help youth gain employment and leadership skills through job-readiness and life skills programs, mentoring programs, and organizations that education youth of career opportunities and the importance of community service. The Education Through the Arts program funds programs that improve educational outcomes for K-12 students while encouraging youth involvement in the arts.

Mervyn's concentrates its giving on the Arts and Education. The Arts program supports arts programs that give children and families affordable access to the arts, with preference given to programs that reflect community diversity. Typical recipients include school touring programs, family matinees, children's visual arts programs, theater and dance performances, programs bringing artists into the classroom, and live musical performances. Mervyn's Education program provides direct support to schools and funds community-based nonprofit organizations aimed at enhancing the educational development of children. Examples of programs in which the company is interested are school partnerships, leadership development, after-school programs, homework assistance programs, mentoring, and tutoring.

The Target Foundation manages contributions in the Minneapolis/Saint Paul metropolitan area and a small program of national giving. The foundation focuses its giving on Arts and Social Action. Arts organizations that promote visibility and accessibility at a community level are supported. The Social Action focus area funds programs that provide the basic needs of at-risk populations by providing food, shelter, and clothing.

Publications: Summary of Community Involvement; Grant Application Guidelines

Corporate Officials

Linda L. Ahlers: president, Target Stores PRIM CORP EMPL president: Marshall Field's. CORP AFFIL director: United States Bancorp.

Bart Butzer: executive president, Target Stores

Gail J. Dorn: vice president communications PRIM CORP EMPL vice president communications: Dayton Hudson Corp.

James Thomas Hale: senior vice president, general counsel, secretary B Minneapolis, MN 1940. ED Dartmouth College BA (1962); University of Minnesota LLB (1965). PRIM CORP EMPL senior vice president, general counsel, secretary: Dayton Hudson Corp. CORP AFFIL director: North Atlantic Life Insurance Co. NONPR AFFIL member: Order Coif; member: Phi Beta Kappa; director: Minnesota Continuing Legal Education; member executive committee: Fund Legal Aid Society; member: Hennepin County Bar Association.

Diane Neal: president, Mervyns

Gregg Steinhafel: president, Target Stores

Gerald L. Storch: senior vice president strategic business B 1957. ED Harvard University JD; Harvard University BA; Harvard University MBA. PRIM CORP EMPL senior vice president strategic business: Dayton Hudson Corp.

Robert J. Ulrich: chairman, chief executive officer, director B Minneapolis, MN April 24, 1943. ED University of Minnesota (1967); Stanford University Executive Management Program (1978). PRIM CORP EMPL chairman, chief executive officer, director: Dayton Hudson Corp. PRIM NONPR EMPL chairman, chief executive officer, director: Target Stores. CORP AFFIL director: Tricon Global Restaurants Inc.

Giving Program Officials

Polly M. Talen: senior program officer, social action

Geol L. Weirs: arts senior program officer

Foundation Officials

Timothy Baer: secretary

Gail J. Dorn: trustee (see above)

Larry V. Gilpin: trustee B Benton, IL 1943. ED Louisiana State University; Western Kentucky University BS (1965); University of Kentucky MBA (1971). PRIM CORP EMPL executive vice president relations: Dayton Hudson Corp.

James Thomas Hale: trustee (see above)

Dee Henry-Williams: grants program assistant

Stephen C. Kowalke: treasurer PRIM CORP EMPL vice president, treasurer: Dayton Hudson Corp.

Christine Park: director

Robert J. Ulrich: chairman, trustee (see above)

Michael J. Wahlig: assistant secretary PRIM CORP EMPL assistant secretary: Dayton's Travel Service Inc.

Laysha L. Ward: director

Grants Analysis

Disclosure Period: fiscal year ending January 31, 2001

Total Grants: $85,800,000 (approx)*

Number of Grants: 8,500

Average Grant: $10,000

Highest Grant: $1,000,000

Lowest Grant: $1,000

Typical Range: $1,000 to $5,000

***Note:** Grants analysis provided by Target Corp.

Recent Grants

Note: Grants derived from 2002 Form 990.

General

1,225,000	Greater Twin Cities United Way, Minneapolis, MN
1,000,000	Greater Twin Cities United Way, Minneapolis, MN
547,492	Guthrie Theater, Minneapolis, MN
514,217	Children's Theatre Company, Minneapolis, MN
500,000	University of St. Thomas, Minneapolis, MN
500,000	Walker Art Center, Minneapolis, MN
250,000	Minnesota Orchestral Association, Minneapolis, MN
200,000	Bridge for Runaway Youth, Minneapolis, MN
200,000	Chicanos Latinos Unidos En Servicio, St. Paul, MN
200,000	People Serving People Inc., Minneapolis, MN

TAUBE FAMILY FOUNDATION

Giving Contact

Thaddeus Taube, Chairman & President
1050 Ralston Ave.
Belmont, CA 94002
Phone: (650)592-3960

Description

Founded: 1980

EIN: 942702180

Organization Type: Private Foundation

Giving Locations: nationally.

Grant Types: General Support.

Donor Information

Founder: members of the Taube family

Financial Summary

Total Giving: $971,904 (fiscal year ending November 30, 2001); $1,190,998 (fiscal 2000); $521,540 (fiscal 1999)

Giving Analysis: Giving for fiscal 2001 includes: foundation grants to United Way ($250,000); fiscal 2000: foundation grants to United Way ($251,000); fiscal 1999: foundation grants to United Way ($250,000)

Assets: $18,562,056 (fiscal 2001); $16,631,378 (fiscal 2000); $14,226,561 (fiscal 1999)

Gifts Received: $4,170,862 (fiscal 2001); $3,139,095 (fiscal 2000); $1,694,524 (fiscal 1999). Note: In fiscal 1996, contributions were received from the Taube Family Trust.

Typical Recipients

Arts & Humanities: Ballet, Libraries, Museums/Galleries, Music, Opera, Public Broadcasting

Civic & Public Affairs: Botanical Gardens/Parks, Business/Free Enterprise, Clubs, Community Foundations, Economic Development, Civic & Public Affairs-General, Legal Aid, Minority Business, Municipalities/Towns, Public Policy, Safety, Urban & Community Affairs, Zoos/Aquariums

Education: Business-School Partnerships, Colleges & Universities, Education Associations, Private Education (Precollege), Religious Education, School Volunteerism, Secondary Education (Private), Social Sciences Education, Student Aid

Health: Arthritis, Cancer, Children's Health/Hospitals, Geriatric Health, Hospices, Hospitals (University Affiliated), Long-Term Care, Medical Research, Multiple Sclerosis, Single-Disease Health Associations

International: Foreign Educational Institutions, International Organizations, International Peace & Security Issues, Missionary/Religious Activities

Religion: Churches, Religion-General, Jewish Causes, Religious Organizations, Religious Welfare

Social Services: Community Centers, Community Service Organizations, Family Services, People with Disabilities, Recreation & Athletics, Scouts, United Funds/United Ways, Volunteer Services, YMCA/YWCA/YMHA/YWHA, Youth Organizations

Application Procedures

Initial Contact: Send a brief letter of inquiry.
Application Requirements: Include purpose of funds sought and amount requested.
Deadlines: None.

Restrictions

Grants are not made to individuals.

Foundation Officials

Beverly Hong: treasurer
Benjamin F. Johnson: secretary
Kenneth A. Moline: president
Thaddeus N. Taube: chairman B 1931. ED Stanford University BS (1954); Stanford University MS (1957). PRIM CORP EMPL chairman, director: Woodmont Companies.

Grants Analysis

Disclosure Period: fiscal year ending November 30, 2001
Total Grants: $721,904*
Number of Grants: 66
Average Grant: $3,467*
Highest Grant: $300,000
Lowest Grant: $60
Typical Range: $1,000 to $5,000
*Note: Giving excludes United Way. Average grant figure excludes two highest grants ($500,000).

Recent Grants

Note: Grants derived from fiscal 2000 Form 990.

General

500,000	Stanford University, Stanford, CA
250,000	Untied Way
200,000	Hoover Institution, Stanford, CA
50,000	San Francisco Zoological Society, San Francisco, CA
50,000	Stanford University, Stanford, CA
24,160	San Francisco Opera Guild, San Francisco, CA
20,000	Menlo School, Menlo Park, CA
20,000	Stanford University, Stanford, CA
11,940	Youth Tennis Advantage, Oakland, CA
10,000	Glide Memorial Church, San Francisco, CA

A. ALFRED TAUBMAN FOUNDATION

Giving Contact

Fred Henshaw
PO Box 200
200 E. Long Lake Rd.
Bloomfield Hills, MI 48303-0200
Phone: (248)258-6800
Fax: (248)258-7476
E-mail: fhenshaw@taubman.com
Web: http://www.taubman.com

Description

Founded: 1979
EIN: 382219625
Organization Type: Private Foundation
Giving Locations: MI: emphasis on Detroit
Grant Types: Operating Expenses, Research.

Donor Information

Founder: A. Alfred Taubman

Financial Summary

Total Giving: $6,221,505 (fiscal year ending July 31, 2000); $1,151,510 (fiscal 1999); $1,235,965 (fiscal 1998)
Giving Analysis: Giving for fiscal 2000 includes: foundation grants to United Way ($18,000) fiscal 1999: foundation grants to United Way ($17,000)
Assets: $11,784 (fiscal 2000); $11,229 (fiscal 1999); $9,756 (fiscal 1996)
Gifts Received: $6,227,688 (fiscal 2000); $1,153,705 (fiscal 1999); $1,121,105 (fiscal 1996). Note: In fiscal 1999 and 2000, contributions were received from A. Alfred Taubman Restated Revocable Trust. In fiscal 1996, contributions were received from A. Alfred Taubman.

Typical Recipients

Arts & Humanities: Arts Festivals, Ethnic & Folk Arts, Historic Preservation, History & Archaeology, Libraries, Museums/Galleries

Civic & Public Affairs: African American Affairs, Botanical Gardens/Parks, Chambers of Commerce, Economic Development, Employment/Job Training, Ethnic Organizations, Civic & Public Affairs-General, Hispanic Affairs, Law & Justice, Legal Aid, Municipalities/Towns, Nonprofit Management, Philanthropic Organizations, Professional & Trade Associations, Public Policy, Urban & Community Affairs, Women's Affairs

Education: Colleges & Universities, Education Associations, Engineering/Technological Education, Education-General, Medical Education, Minority Education, Private Education (Precollege), Public Education (Precollege), Student Aid

Environment: Environment-General, Resource Conservation, Wildlife Protection

Health: AIDS/HIV, Alzheimers Disease, Arthritis, Cancer, Clinics/Medical Centers, Diabetes, Emergency/Ambulance Services, Health Organizations, Heart, Hospices, Hospitals, Kidney, Long-Term Care, Medical Research, Public Health, Single-Disease Health Associations, Transplant Networks/Donor Banks

International: Foreign Arts Organizations, Foreign Educational Institutions, Health Care/Hospitals, International Environmental Issues, International Organizations, International Relations, Missionary/Religious Activities

Religion: Bible Study/Translation, Churches, Jewish Causes, Religious Organizations, Religious Welfare, Social/Policy Issues, Synagogues/Temples

Science: Science Exhibits & Fairs, Scientific Centers & Institutes

Social Services: At-Risk Youth, Camps, Child Welfare, Community Service Organizations, Crime Prevention, Delinquency & Criminal Rehabilitation, Domestic Violence, Family Planning, Family Services, Homes, People with Disabilities, Recreation & Athletics, Scouts, Senior Services, Substance Abuse, United Funds/United Ways, Volunteer Services, YMCA/YWCA/YMHA/YWHA, Youth Organizations

Application Procedures

Initial Contact: Send a a brief letter of inquiry describing program or project.
Application Requirements: Include a description of organization, a brief explanation of what applicant expects to receive from the foundation and why, and a list of previous contributors.
Deadlines: None.

Foundation Officials

Gayle T. Kalisman: president
Jeffrey H. Miro: secretary PRIM CORP EMPL secretary: Sothebys Holdings. CORP AFFIL director: Taubman Co.; director: Woodward & Lothrop Inc.
Gerald R. Poissant: assistant treasurer
A. Alfred Taubman: chairman, treasurer, trustee B Pontiac, MI 1925. ED Lawrence Technological University; University of Michigan (1945-1948); Lawrence Institute of Technology (1948-1949). PRIM CORP EMPL chairman: Taubman Co. CORP AFFIL chairman: Sothebys Holdings; chairman: Taubman Centers; director: Detroit Renaissance Inc.; director: Live Entertainment Canada. NONPR AFFIL chairman: University Pennsylvania Wharton Real Estate Center; trustee: Urban Land Institute; prin benefactor: A Alfred Taubman Medicine Library University Michigan; active: State Michigan Gaming Commission; prin benefactor: A Alfred Taubman Health Care Center; nat board: Smithsonian Associates; chairman emeritus: Smithsonian Institute American Art; chairman: Program American Instns University Michigan; chairman: Michigan Partnership New Education; director: National Realty Commission; director: Friends Art Preservation Embassies; trustee: Harper-Grace Hospital; trustee: Center Creative Studies; president: Arts Community Detroit; chairman: Brown Universitys Public Policy American Instns Program.
Judith M. Taubman: trustee
Robert S. Taubman: trustee B Detroit, MI 1953. PRIM CORP EMPL president, chief executive officer, director: Taubman Co. CORP AFFIL director: Woodward & Lothrop; director: Washington John Wanamaker Department Store; director: Sotheby's International Realty Corp.; director: Taubman Investment Co. Inc.; director: Mfrs National Bank Detroit; director: A& W Restaurants. NONPR AFFIL trustee: Sinai Hospital; member: Urban Land Institute; member: International Council Shopping Centers; member, board governors: Cranbrook School. CLUB AFFIL Economic Club Detroit.
William S. Taubman: trustee CORP AFFIL director: A&W Restaurants.

Grants Analysis

Disclosure Period: fiscal year ending July 31, 2000
Total Grants: $6,203,505*
Number of Grants: 92
Average Grant: $1,129*
Highest Grant: $1,100,000
Typical Range: $500 to $2,000
*Note: Giving excludes United Way. Average grant figure excludes two highest grants ($6,101,900).

Recent Grants

Note: Grants derived from 2002 Form 990.

General

1,000,000	Jewish Federation of Metropolitan Detroit, Detroit, MI
18,000	United Way, Detroit, MI
5,500	American Jewish Committee, New York, NY

3,000	Jewish Federal of Palm Beach County, West Palm Beach, FL
2,750	Friends of the Israel Defense Forces, New York, NY
2,000	Yeshiva Beth Yehudah, Brooklyn, NY
1,500	Detroit Institute for Children, Detroit, MI
1,000	American Friends of Turkey, Washington, DC
1,000	Breast Cancer Research Foundation, New York, NY
1,000	Detroit Renaissance Foundation, Detroit, MI

ARTHUR C. AND LEE ANNE TAUCK FOUNDATION

Giving Contact

Arthur C. Tauck, Trustee
276 Post Rd. W.
Westport, CT 06880
Phone: (203)226-6911
Fax: (419)715-3034
E-mail: info@tauckfoundation.org
Web: http://www.tauckfoundation.org

Description

Founded: 1994
EIN: 061396951
Organization Type: Private Foundation
Giving Locations: PA
Grant Types: General Support.

Donor Information

Founder: Established in 1994 by Arthur C. Tauck.

Financial Summary

Total Giving: $302,173 (2000); $237,688 (1996); $250,010 (1995)
Giving Analysis: Giving for 2000 includes: foundation grants to United Way ($10,000) 1998: foundation grants to United Way ($7,000)
Assets: $15,039,508 (2000); $9,385,489 (1997); $6,093,589 (1996)
Gifts Received: $3,797,128 (1994). Note: In 1994, contributions were received from Arthur C. Tauck.

Typical Recipients

Arts & Humanities: Libraries, Music, Performing Arts, Public Broadcasting
Civic & Public Affairs: Clubs, Civic & Public Affairs-General, Housing, Parades/Festivals, Professional & Trade Associations
Education: Business Education, Colleges & Universities, Education-General, Private Education (Precollege), Public Education (Precollege)
Environment: Environment-General, Resource Conservation
Health: Emergency/Ambulance Services, Health Organizations, Hospices, Hospitals
International: International Relief Efforts
Science: Scientific Centers & Institutes
Social Services: Camps, Child Welfare, Community Service Organizations, Recreation & Athletics, United Funds/United Ways, YMCA/YWCA/YMHA/YWHA

Application Procedures

Initial Contact: The foundation has no formal grant application procedure or application form.
Deadlines: None.

Foundation Officials

Arthur C. Tauck: trustee

Grants Analysis

Disclosure Period: calendar year ending 2000
Total Grants: $292,173*
Number of Grants: 80

Average Grant: $2,116*
Highest Grant: $125,000
Lowest Grant: $50
Typical Range: $500 to $5,000
*Note: Giving excludes United Way. Average grant figure excludes highest grant.

Recent Grants

Note: Grants derived from 1999 Form 990.

Library-Related
5,000	Westport Library, Westport, CT

General
300,000	Lehigh University International Marketing, Bethlehem, PA
125,000	Travelers Conservation Fund
25,000	Travelers Conservation Fund
20,000	Institute of Certified Travel Agents, Wellesley, MA
20,000	Norwalk Symphony Society, Inc., Norwalk, CT
10,000	Kosovo Relief Fund
10,000	Norwalk Hospital Foundation, Norwalk, CT
10,000	Westport YMCA, Westport, CT
5,000	First Night Westport/Weston, Inc., CT
5,000	Save the Children, Westport, CT

TCB BANK

Company Headquarters

Tell City, IN

Company Description

Former Name: Tell City National Bank.
Employees: 62
SIC(s): 6000 Depository Institutions.

TCB Bank Foundation

Giving Contact

Eric J. Kehl, President
601 Main St.
Tell City, IN 47586
Phone: (812)547-2323
Fax: (812)468-3807

Description

EIN: 237242112
Organization Type: Corporate Foundation
Giving Locations: IN
Grant Types: General Support, Scholarship.

Financial Summary

Total Giving: $19,878 (2000); $28,250 (1999); $37,315 (1998). Note: 1997 Giving includes scholarship ($6,500).
Giving Analysis: Giving for 2000 includes: foundation grants to United Way ($200); foundation scholarships ($3,750); 1999: foundation grants to United Way ($1,650); foundation scholarships ($2,250); foundation ($24,350) 1998: foundation scholarships ($6,500)
Assets: $16,558 (2000); $36,452 (1999); $64,717 (1998)
Gifts Received: $20,150 (1998); $57,000 (1997); $26,000 (1996). Note: In 1998, contributions were received from TCB Bank.

Typical Recipients

Arts & Humanities: Arts Associations & Councils, Libraries, Music
Civic & Public Affairs: Botanical Gardens/Parks, Chambers of Commerce, Community Foundations, Economic Development, Ethnic Organizations, Civic & Public Affairs-General, Housing, Public Policy, Safety, Urban & Community Affairs

Education: Agricultural Education, Business Education, Colleges & Universities, Education Funds, Elementary Education (Public), Education-General, Private Education (Precollege), Public Education (Precollege), Science/Mathematics Education, Secondary Education (Public), Student Aid
Environment: Environment-General
Health: Emergency/Ambulance Services, Medical Rehabilitation, Research/Studies Institutes
Religion: Churches, Religious Organizations
Science: Scientific Centers & Institutes
Social Services: Animal Protection, Child Welfare, Community Centers, Recreation & Athletics, Scouts, Substance Abuse, United Funds/United Ways

Application Procedures

Initial Contact: For grants, make an oral or written request. Scholarship applications can be requested from local schools.
Deadlines: None.

Corporate Officials

Thomas R. McCart: chairman, president, chief executive officer, director PRIM CORP EMPL chairman, president, chief executive officer, director: TCB Bank.
Iris Whittman: chief financial officer PRIM CORP EMPL chief financial officer: TCB Bank.

Foundation Officials

Thomas R. McCart: president (see above)
Kenneth Mulzer: secretary, treasurer
Janet Sprinkle: director

Grants Analysis

Disclosure Period: calendar year ending 2000
Total Grants: $15,928*
Number of Grants: 21
Average Grant: $758
Highest Grant: $3,000
Typical Range: $350 to $1,500
*Note: Giving excludes scholarships and United Way.

Recent Grants

Note: Grants derived from 1999 Form 990.

General
10,000	Perry County Community Foundation, Evansville, IN
2,500	Spencer County Community Foundation, Evansville, IN
2,000	Lincolnland Economic Development, Rockport, IN
2,000	Spencer County Community Foundation, Evansville, IN
2,000	William Tell Elementary School, Tell City, IN
1,500	Junior Achievement of Perry County, Tell City, IN
1,500	Perry County Arts Council, Tell City, IN
1,350	United Way of Perry County, Tell City, IN
750	Ball State University, Muncie, IN -- scholarship
750	Indiana University, Bloomington, IN -- scholarship

TCF NATIONAL BANK MINNESOTA

Company Headquarters

Minneapolis, MN
Web: http://www.tcfbank.com

Company Description

Former Name: TCF Banking & Savings FSB.
SIC(s): 6035 Federal Savings Institutions.
Parent Company: TCF Financial Corp., 200 Lake St. E., Mail Code EX0-03-A, Wayzata, MN, United States

Operating Locations
TCF National Bank Minnesota (MN, Minneapolis)

Nonmonetary Support
Value: $120,000 (2004 approx); $120,000 (2003 approx); $120,000 (2002 approx)
Type: Donated Products; Loaned Employees; Loaned Executives
Volunteer Programs: The company encourages employee volunteerism through local divisions, including programs such as March of Dimes, paint-a-thons, and home-repair days.

TCF Foundation

Giving Contact
Kelly Sack, Corporate Affairs Officer
200 Lake Street East (EXO-02-C)
Wayzata, MN 55391-1693
Phone: (952)745-2757
Fax: (952)745-2775
E-mail: ksack@tcfbank.com

Alternate Contact
Contributions Committee
Great Lakes Bancorp
401 East Liberty
Ann Arbor, MI 48104-2298

Description
EIN: 411659826
Organization Type: Corporate Foundation
Giving Locations: MN: headquarters and operating communities
Grant Types: Employee Matching Gifts, General Support, Multiyear/Continuing Support, Project.
Note: Employee matching gift ratio: 1 to 1 for most charitable 501(c)(3) organizations.

Financial Summary
Total Giving: $1,664,000 (2004 approx); $1,849,000 (2003 approx); $1,849,000 (2002 approx)
Giving Analysis: Giving for 2000 includes: foundation ($22,500); corporate direct giving (approx $1,477,500); 1999: corporate direct giving ($1,356,943); 1998: corporate scholarships ($44,097); corporate matching gifts ($99,532); corporate grants to United Way ($101,801) corporate direct giving ($1,310,875)
Assets: $3,139 (2000); $6,378 (1998); $791,907 (1996)
Gifts Received: $25 (2000); $1,002,624 (1998); $1,623,483 (1996). Note: Contributions are received from TCF Bank Minnesota.

Typical Recipients
Arts & Humanities: Arts Associations & Councils, Arts Centers, Arts Funds, Arts Institutes, Arts & Humanities-General, Libraries, Museums/Galleries, Music, Opera, Performing Arts, Public Broadcasting, Theater
Civic & Public Affairs: African American Affairs, Asian American Affairs, Business/Free Enterprise, Chambers of Commerce, Economic Development, Employment/Job Training, Civic & Public Affairs-General, Housing, Law & Justice, Municipalities/Towns, Nonprofit Management, Professional & Trade Associations, Safety, Urban & Community Affairs, Women's Affairs
Education: Business Education, Business-School Partnerships, Colleges & Universities, Community & Junior Colleges, Education Associations, Education Funds, Faculty Development, Education-General, Private Education (Precollege), Science/Mathematics Education, Secondary Education (Public), Student Aid
Health: Children's Health/Hospitals, Clinics/Medical Centers, Health-General, Health Funds, Health Organizations, Heart, Hospitals, Medical Rehabilitation, Public Health

International: International Organizations
Religion: Ministries, Religious Organizations, Religious Welfare
Science: Observatories & Planetariums, Science Museums
Social Services: Child Welfare, Community Centers, Community Service Organizations, Food/Clothing Distribution, Recreation & Athletics, Scouts, Senior Services, Shelters/Homelessness, Social Services-General, Substance Abuse, United Funds/United Ways, Volunteer Services, YMCA/YWCA/YMHA/YWHA, Youth Organizations, Youth Organizations

Application Procedures
Initial Contact: Send a written grant request in letter form.
Application Requirements: Include a description of organization; list of board members, including information on people who will manage project; audited financial statements, current budget, and next year's budget; mission statement and summary of long-range plans; purpose of contribution requested and relationship to plans; list of major contributors and amounts given; how project relates to foundation's interests and guidelines; methods of evaluating program's effectiveness; company employee involvement; sources of income, current and planned; copy of IRS 501(c)(3) tax-exemption determination letter.
Deadlines: None.
Evaluative Criteria: Charitable grants are made (with few exceptions) only to tax-exempt 501(c)(3) organizations; special consideration is given to those institutions supported by the employees of TCF Financial Corporation or its subsidiaries through their personal contributions of time and/or money.
Decision Notification: Most funding decisions will require at least sixty days for review.
Notes: In Minnesota, all requesters are required to use the Minnesota Common Grant application form. Grant requests may be directed to offices in Michigan, Illinois, Wisconsin, or Minnesota.

Restrictions
The foundation does not make grants to individuals, political parties or candidates, lobbying groups, individual churches or sectarian activities, advertising or subsidizing publications, or social events of otherwise qualified organizations.
Support will be given only to organizations that are able to provide evidence of 501(C)(3) tax-exempt status.
Foundation does not award multi-year grants.
Grants are only made to organizations located in areas where TCF has a bank office. Grants are made to United Way campaigns in communities where TCF has well-established offices.

Additional Information
TCF Bank Minnesota, FSB, was formerly named TCF Bank Savings, FSB.
Publications: Community Affairs Report; Grant Request Guidelines

Corporate Officials
William Allen Cooper: chairman, directorFinancial Corp. B Detroit, MI 1943. ED Wayne State University BS (1967). PRIM CORP EMPL chairman, director: TCF Bank Minnesota FSB. CORP AFFIL principal: TCF finance Insurance Agency; chairman, director: TCF Financial Corp. NONPR AFFIL member: American Institute CPAs.
Gregory J. Pulles: vice chairman, TCF Financial Corp. B 1948. ED University of Minnesota BS (1970); University of Minnesota JD (1973). CORP AFFIL executive vice president, secretary: TCF Bank Minnesota FSB; secretary, director: TCF Mortgage Corp.

Giving Program Officials
Kelly Sack: community affairs officer

Foundation Officials
Jason Korstange: president

Grants Analysis
Disclosure Period: calendar year ending 2002
Total Grants: $1,849,000*
Number of Grants: 179
Average Grant: $10,000
Highest Grant: $100,000
Lowest Grant: $1,000
Typical Range: $100 to $15,000
*****Note:** Grants analysis provided by the foundation.

Recent Grants
Note: Grants derived from 2000 Form 990.

General
20,000 YMCA of Greater St. Paul, St. Paul, MN
2,500 Employment Action Center, Minneapolis, MN

TEAGLE FOUNDATION

Giving Contact
John Chasltry, Chief Executive Officer & President
10 Rockefeller Plaza, Room 920
New York, NY 10020-1903
Phone: (212)373-1970
Web: http://fdncenter.org/grantmaker/teagle/index.html

Description
Founded: 1944
EIN: 131773645
Organization Type: General Purpose Foundation
Giving Locations: nationally; Canada
Grant Types: Employee Matching Gifts, General Support, Project.
Note: Foundation also makes strategic grants.

Donor Information
Founder: Established in 1944 by the late Walter C. Teagle , former president and chairman of the Standard Oil Company (New Jersey), now Exxon Corporation. The foundation's assets also come from bequests from Mr. Teagle's wife, Rowena Lee Teagle , and their son, Walter C. Teagle Jr.

Financial Summary
Total Giving: $11,076,219 (fiscal year ending May 31, 2001); $10,869,128 (fiscal 2000); $9,587,725 (fiscal 1999)
Giving Analysis: Giving for fiscal 2001 includes: foundation grants to United Way ($10,000); foundation matching gifts ($83,489); foundation scholarships ($1,143,750); fiscal 2000: foundation grants to United Way ($9,600); foundation matching gifts ($90,448); foundation scholarships ($1,056,350); fiscal 1998: foundation matching gifts ($114,845); foundation scholarships ($1,318,908);
Assets: $184,000,000 (fiscal 2001 approx); $219,000,000 (fiscal 2000 approx); $213,196,217 (fiscal 1999)

Typical Recipients
Arts & Humanities: Arts Festivals, Arts Outreach, Ballet, Dance, Arts & Humanities-General, Libraries, Music, Opera, Performing Arts, Theater
Civic & Public Affairs: Civic & Public Affairs-General
Education: Arts/Humanities Education, Business Education, Colleges & Universities, Community & Junior Colleges, Education Associations, Education Funds, Education Reform, Engineering/Technological Education, Environmental Education, Faculty Development, Leadership Training, Medical Education, Minority Education, Private Education (Precollege),

Religious Education, Science/Mathematics Education, Student Aid
Health: Emergency/Ambulance Services, Hospitals, Hospitals (University Affiliated)
International: Missionary/Religious Activities
Religion: Churches, Religion-General, Jewish Causes, Ministries, Religious Organizations, Religious Welfare, Seminaries
Social Services: Community Service Organizations, United Funds/United Ways, Youth Organizations

Application Procedures

Initial Contact: Applicants should submit a brief preliminary letter to the foundation. Applications for the Exxon scholarship program are available within Exxon.
Application Requirements: The letter should describe the grant seeker and outline the scope and purpose of the proposed grant. If a proposal is accepted for consideration, audited financial statements, course catalogues, and current enrollment data will be required.
Deadlines: None.
Review Process: If initial reaction is favorable, a more detailed proposal will be requested. The board meets in November, February, and May to review requests.
Notes: Supplemental materials for proposals should be kept to a minimum and videotapes or letters of endorsement should be avoided altogether. Grantseekers should allow ample time when requesting funds.

Restrictions

The foundation does not support unrestricted grants for scholarships, fellowships or their functional equivalent; grants for buildings, renovation or equipment; college-based programs for pre-college youth, including partnerships with public school systems; large, complex technological systems, infrastructure development or computer hardware; grants for activities which take place outside the United States; or research or doctoral universities or public institutions of any kind.

Additional Information

Publications: Annual Report; Guidelines

Foundation Officials

George Bugliarello, MD: director B Trieste, Italy 1927. ED University of Padua DEng (1951); University of Minnesota MS (1954); Massachusetts Institute of Technology DSc (1959). PRIM NONPR EMPL president: Polytech University. CORP AFFIL director: Spectrum Information Tech Inc.; trustee: ANSER; director: Comtech Telecommunications. NONPR AFFIL member: New York Partnership; member: Sigma Xi; member: New York Academy Medicine; trustee: National Association Science Technology & Society; member, board engineering education: National Research Council; member: Italian Society Advancement Science; member: National Academy Engineering; board visitors: Duke University School Engineering; member: International Association Hydraulic Research; fellow: American Society Engineering Education; trustee: Commission Independent Colleges & Universities; fellow: American Institute Medical & Biological Engineering; fellow: American Society Civil Engineers; fellow: American Association Advancement Science.
John Steele Chalsty: board of directors B Port Elizabeth, Republic of South Africa 1933. ED University of Witwatersrand BSc (1952); University of Witwatersrand MSc (1954); Harvard University MBA (1957); Harvard University Graduate School of Business Administration MSc (1957). PRIM CORP EMPL senior advisor: Credit Suisse First Boston. CORP AFFIL director: Occidental Petroleum Corp.; director: Equitable Co. Inc.; director: IBP Inc. NONPR AFFIL chairman: New York City Economic Development Corp.;

trustee: Saint Barnabas Medical Center; vice president, director: Lincoln Center Theater; director: American Ballet Theater; trustee: Columbia University. CLUB AFFIL Short Hills Club; The Links Club; New York City University Club; Harvard Club.
Kenneth P. Cohen: director
Walter Robert Connor: president, chief executive officer B Worcester, MA 1934. ED Hamilton College BA (1956); Princeton University PhD (1961). NONPR AFFIL member: Century Association; member: Phi Beta Kappa; member: American Philosophical Society; member advisory board: Athens College; fellow: American Academy of Arts & Sciences; member: American Philosophical Association. CLUB AFFIL Princeton Club.
Peter O. Crisp: director
Richard W. Kimball: director
Richard L. Morrill: director
Anne M. Tatlock: director B White Plains, NY 1939. ED Vassar College BA (1961); New York University MA Economics (1968). PRIM CORP EMPL chairman, chief executive officer: Fiduciary Trust Co. International. CORP AFFIL vice chairman, director: Franklin Resources Inc.; chairman, trustee: Cultural Institutional Retirement System; director: Fortune Brands Inc.; director: American General Corp. NONPR AFFIL trustee: Mayo Foundation; trustee: Vassar College; chairman nominating committee, trustee: American Ballet Theater.
Walter C. Teagle, III: director
Stephen H. Weiss: director

Grants Analysis

Disclosure Period: fiscal year ending May 31, 2000
Total Grants: $9,712,730*
Number of Grants: 98
Average Grant: $99,109
Highest Grant: $275,000
Typical Range: $5,000 to $200,000
*Note: Giving excludes matching gifts, scholarships, and United Way.

Recent Grants

Note: Grants derived from 2001 Form 990.

General

1,068,350	Scholarship and Recognition Programs, Princeton, NJ -- educational scholarships
275,000	Spalding University, Louisville, KY
263,000	Quincy College, Quincy, IL -- higher education
254,000	Roman Catholic Theological School -- collaborative venture
247,000	Clarkson University, Potsdam, NY -- higher education
237,500	Iowa Wesleyan College, Mt. Pleasant, IA -- higher education
235,000	Austin Theological Seminary, Austin, TX -- collaborative venture
230,000	Central Methodist College, Fayette, MO -- higher education
227,000	Kings College, Wilkes-Barre, PA -- higher education
210,000	Southern Vermont College, Bennington, VT -- higher education

A. TEICHERT & SONS

Company Headquarters

3500 American River Dr.
Sacramento, CA 95864
Web: http://www.teichert.com

Company Description

Revenue: US$2.108 billion (2002)
Employees: 2100 (2002)
SIC(s): 1771 Concrete Work, 3200 Stone, Clay & Glass Products, 3273 Ready-Mixed Concrete.

Operating Locations

A. Teichert & Sons (CA--Sacramento)

Teichert Foundation

Giving Contact

Frederick A. Teichert, Executive Director
Teichert Foundation
3500 American River Dr.
Sacramento, CA 95864-5802
Phone: (916)484-3011
E-mail: info@teichertfoundation.org
Web: http://www.teichertfoundation.org

Description

Founded: 1990
EIN: 680212355
Organization Type: Corporate Foundation
Giving Locations: headquarters and operating communities.
Grant Types: General Support.

Financial Summary

Total Giving: $457,858 (fiscal year ending March 31, 2002); $208,655 (fiscal 2000); $194,565 (fiscal 1999)
Giving Analysis: Giving for fiscal 2002 includes: foundation grants to United Way ($2,618); fiscal 2000: foundation grants to United Way ($5,000); fiscal 1997: foundation grants to United Way ($5,000) foundation ($189,359)
Assets: $5,014,416 (fiscal 2002); $3,938,657 (fiscal 2000); $2,617,206 (fiscal 1999)
Gifts Received: $1,012,068 (fiscal 2002); $1,244,353 (fiscal 2000); $1,000,047 (fiscal 1999).
Note: In fiscal 2002, contributions were received from Teichert Inc.

Typical Recipients

Arts & Humanities: Arts Associations & Councils, Ballet, Film & Video, Libraries, Museums/Galleries, Music, Opera, Public Broadcasting, Theater
Civic & Public Affairs: African American Affairs, Chambers of Commerce, Clubs, Community Foundations, Economic Development, Employment/Job Training, Civic & Public Affairs-General, Housing, Law & Justice, Nonprofit Management, Parades/Festivals, Philanthropic Organizations, Public Policy, Safety, Urban & Community Affairs, Zoos/Aquariums
Education: Business Education, Colleges & Universities, Elementary Education (Public), Education-General, Literacy, Private Education (Precollege), Science/Mathematics Education
Environment: Air/Water Quality, Environment-General, Resource Conservation
Health: Children's Health/Hospitals, Clinics/Medical Centers, Emergency/Ambulance Services, Heart, Mental Health, Multiple Sclerosis, Prenatal Health Issues, Public Health
International: International Relief Efforts, Missionary/Religious Activities
Religion: Religious Welfare
Science: Science-General, Science Museums, Scientific Centers & Institutes
Social Services: Child Welfare, Community Service Organizations, Delinquency & Criminal Rehabilitation, Family Planning, Family Services, Food/Clothing Distribution, People with Disabilities, Recreation & Athletics, Scouts, Special Olympics, United Funds/United Ways, Volunteer Services, YMCA/YWCA/YMHA/YWHA, Youth Organizations

Application Procedures

Initial Contact: Application form required.
Application Requirements: Include a description of organization, amount requested, purpose of funds sought, recently audited financial statement, proof of tax-exempt status, and roster of Board of Directors or Advisory Board.
Deadlines: February 22 and August 30.

Restrictions

The foundation does not support individuals, religious organizations for sectarian purposes, political or lobbying groups, or organizations outside operating areas.

Additional Information

Publications: Application Form

Corporate Officials

Norman E. Eilert: senior vice president, chief financial officer PRIM CORP EMPL senior vice president, chief financial officer: A Teichert & Sons.

Louis V. Riggs: chairman, president, chief executive officer PRIM CORP EMPL chairman, president, chief executive officer: A Teichert & Sons.

John B. Sandman: executive vice president, chief operating officer PRIM CORP EMPL executive vice president, chief operating officer: A Teichert & Sons.

Foundation Officials

Thomas J. Hammer: director B Birmingham, AL 1932. ED University of California at Berkeley (1955); University of California at Berkeley (1960). PRIM CORP EMPL president, chief executive officer, director: Shasta Linen Supply.

Anne S. Haslam: secretary

Judson T. Riggs: director

Bruce Stimson: chief financial officer

Frederick A. Teichert: executive director

Melita M. Teichert: director

Grants Analysis

Disclosure Period: fiscal year ending March 31, 2002

Total Grants: $455,240*

Number of Grants: 69

Average Grant: $2,945*

Highest Grant: $255,000

Lowest Grant: $25

Typical Range: $1,000 to $5,000

*Note: Giving excludes United Way. Average grant figure excludes highest grant.

Recent Grants

Note: Grants derived from 2000 Form 990.

Library-Related

10,000	Friends of the Esparto Regional Library, Esparto, CA

General

10,000	Children's Receiving Home, Sacramento, CA
10,000	Rose Foundation, CA
7,500	Boys & Girls Club of Greater Sacramento, Sacramento, CA
7,500	Boys & Girls Club of North Lake Tahoe, Crystal Bay, NV
7,500	Greater Stockton Chamber of Commerce, CA
7,500	Sacramento Philharmonic Orchestra, Sacramento, CA
7,000	Woodland Opera House, Woodland, CA
6,000	Goodwill Industries of San Joaquin Valley, Inc., Stockton, CA
6,000	World Relief, Stockton, CA
5,000	California State University Stanislaus, Turlock, CA

TELEFLEX, INC.

Company Headquarters

630 W. Germantown Pike, Ste. 450
Plymouth Meeting, PA 19462
Web: http://www.teleflex.com

Company Description

Founded: 1943
Ticker: TFX
Exchange: NYSE
Revenue: US$2.076 billion (2002)
Employees: 18100 (2002)
SIC(s): 3625 Relays & Industrial Controls, 3812 Search & Navigation Equipment, 3841 Surgical & Medical Instruments.

Operating Locations

Teleflex Inc. (CA--Compton, Oxnard; CT--Suffield, Windsor; FL--Sarasota; MI--Hillsdale; NH--Jaffrey; OH--Van Wert; PA--Limerick Township, North Wales, Plymouth Meeting; TX--Sugar Land)
Note: Sermatech International Inc. operates 4 plants in locations.

Teleflex Foundation

Giving Contact

Thelma A. Fretz, Executive Director
630 West Germantown Pike, Suite 461
Plymouth Meeting, PA 19462
Phone: (610)831-6301
E-mail: foundation@teleflex.com
Web: http://www.teleflex.com/foundation/

Description

EIN: 232104782
Organization Type: Corporate Foundation
Giving Locations: headquarters and operating communities.
Grant Types: Employee Matching Gifts.

Financial Summary

Total Giving: $185,434 (2000); $186,500 (1999); $186,790 (1998)
Giving Analysis: Giving for 2000 includes: foundation ($185,434)
Assets: $3,638,116 (2000); $1,452,731 (1996); $993,413 (1995)
Gifts Received: $772,500 (2000); $525,000 (1996); $200,000 (1995)

Typical Recipients

Arts & Humanities: Ballet, Ethnic & Folk Arts, Arts & Humanities-General, History & Archaeology, Libraries, Museums/Galleries, Music

Civic & Public Affairs: Business/Free Enterprise, Community Foundations, Employment/Job Training, Civic & Public Affairs-General, Housing, Safety, Women's Affairs, Zoos/Aquariums

Education: Arts/Humanities Education, Business Education, Colleges & Universities, Economic Education, Education-General, Private Education (Precollege), Public Education (Precollege), Secondary Education (Public)

Environment: Air/Water Quality, Protection

Health: Children's Health/Hospitals, Health-General, Hospices, Nursing Services, Public Health, Single-Disease Health Associations

Religion: Religious Welfare

Science: Scientific Centers & Institutes

Social Services: Animal Protection, Big Brother/Big Sister, Child Welfare, Community Service Organizations, Food/Clothing Distribution, People with Disabilities, Scouts, Senior Services, Social Services-General, Special Olympics, Substance Abuse, YMCA/YWCA/YMHA/YWHA, Youth Organizations

Application Procedures

Initial Contact: Send a full proposal.
Application Requirements: Include budget for program, current funding sources, current Board of Directors with affiliations, and key staff members.

Restrictions

Does not support individuals, general operating expense, endowment funds, advertising, fundraising events, subscription fees, admission tickets, religious organizations for sectarian purposes, political or lobbying groups, or organizations outside operating areas. Capital campaigns are generally not funded. Primarily supports preselected organizations.

Corporate Officials

Lennox K. Black: chairman, director B Montreal, QC Canada 1930. ED Royal Naval College (1949); McGill University (1952). PRIM CORP EMPL chairman, director: Teleflex. CORP AFFIL director: TFX Engineering; director: Westmoreland Coal Co.; director: Quaker Chemical Corp.; director: Penn Virginia Corp.; director: Pep Boys; director: Envirite Corp.

Harold L. Zuber, Jr.: vice president, chief financial officer PRIM CORP EMPL vice president, chief financial officer: Teleflex.

Foundation Officials

Lennox K. Black: president (see above)

Grants Analysis

Disclosure Period: calendar year ending 2000
Total Grants: $185,434
Number of Grants: 85
Average Grant: $2,182
Highest Grant: $25,300
Lowest Grant: $100
Typical Range: $1,000 to $5,000

Recent Grants

Note: Grants derived from 2000 Form 990.

General

25,300	Hyde School, Bath, ME
15,000	Safety Sense Institute, Philadelphia, PA
15,000	Zoological Society of Philadelphia, Philadelphia, PA
10,000	Monadnock Community Foundation, Concord, NH
6,000	Foundation For Free Enterprise Education, Erie, PA
5,500	ALS Association, San Francisco, CA
5,000	Fellowship Farms, Pottstown, PA
5,000	Junior Achievement, Moline, IL
5,000	Van Wert YMCA
5,000	Women's Way, Philadelphia, PA

T. L. L. TEMPLE FOUNDATION

Giving Contact

Millard F. Zeagler, Assistant Executive Director
109 Temple Boulevard, Suite 300
Lufkin, TX 75901
Phone: (936)639-5197
Fax: (936)639-5199

Description

Founded: 1962
EIN: 756037406
Organization Type: General Purpose Foundation
Giving Locations: TX: East Texas Pine Timber Belt area
Grant Types: Capital, General Support, Project, Scholarship.

Donor Information

Founder: In 1894, Thomas Lewis Latane Temple started a sawmill and began acquiring timberland in eastern Texas. Arthur Temple, one of his sons, eventually served as president of Temple Industries. He was later succeeded by his son, Arthur Temple, Jr.

By 1973, the Temples owned 50% of Temple Industries stock. That same year, they merged their company into Time, Inc., and in return, the Temple family received 15% of Time stock, worth over $60 million. In 1984, Time spun off Temple-Inland, a holding company of which Arthur Temple, Jr., is chairman.

The T. L. L. Temple Foundation was established in 1962 with donations from the late Georgia T. Munz and the late Katherine S. Temple .

Financial Summary

Total Giving: $15,014,915 (fiscal year ending November 30, 2001); $11,616,743 (fiscal 1999); $15,484,284 (fiscal 1998)

Giving Analysis: Giving for fiscal 2001 includes: foundation scholarships ($55,300); foundation matching gifts ($60,550); foundation grants to United Way ($65,000) fiscal 1999: foundation grants to United Way ($35,000)

Assets: $319,332,383 (fiscal 2001); $326,718,249 (fiscal 1999); $312,610,694 (fiscal 1997)

Gifts Received: $100,000 (fiscal 1994); $100,000 (fiscal 1993). Note: Contributions were received from the estate of Katherine S. Temple.

Typical Recipients

Arts & Humanities: Arts Associations & Councils, Historic Preservation, History & Archaeology, Libraries, Museums/Galleries, Music, Opera, Performing Arts, Theater

Civic & Public Affairs: Chambers of Commerce, Clubs, Employment/Job Training, Civic & Public Affairs-General, Housing, Municipalities/Towns, Native American Affairs, Parades/Festivals, Public Policy, Safety, Urban & Community Affairs, Women's Affairs, Zoos/Aquariums

Education: Agricultural Education, Arts/Humanities Education, Business Education, Colleges & Universities, Continuing Education, Elementary Education (Private), Elementary Education (Public), Engineering/Technological Education, Environmental Education, Faculty Development, Education-General, Medical Education, Minority Education, Preschool Education, Private Education (Precollege), Public Education (Precollege), Science/Mathematics Education, Special Education, Student Aid, Vocational & Technical Education

Environment: Environment-General, Resource Conservation, Wildlife Protection

Health: Alzheimers Disease, Cancer, Children's Health/Hospitals, Clinics/Medical Centers, Emergency/Ambulance Services, Eyes/Blindness, Health Organizations, Heart, Hospices, Hospitals, Hospitals (University Affiliated), Kidney, Medical Rehabilitation, Medical Research, Mental Health, Prenatal Health Issues, Research/Studies Institutes, Single-Disease Health Associations, Transplant Networks/Donor Banks

International: International Affairs, International Relief Efforts

Religion: Churches, Ministries, Religious Organizations, Religious Welfare, Synagogues/Temples

Science: Science Museums, Scientific Centers & Institutes

Social Services: Animal Protection, Camps, Community Centers, Community Service Organizations, Counseling, Crime Prevention, Day Care, Delinquency & Criminal Rehabilitation, Domestic Violence, Family Planning, Family Services, Food/Clothing Distribution, People with Disabilities, Recreation & Athletics, Scouts, Senior Services, Shelters/Homelessness, Social Services-General, Special Olympics, Substance Abuse, United Funds/United Ways, Veterans, Volunteer Services, YMCA/YWCA/YMHA/YWHA, Youth Organizations

Application Procedures

Initial Contact: Prospective applicants should send a written request to the foundation.

Application Requirements: Applicants should provide the name, address, phone number, charter, articles of incorporation; a copy of constitution and by-laws; copy of exemption letter signed by an authorized office of the organization; names and addresses of officers and directors; a copy of the latest Form 990-PF including Schedule A (if applicable); a copy of the most recent annual audit with independent auditor's report; a detailed copy of the operating budget for the current fiscal year; a brief, but factual resume of the operations of the applicant; and an explanation of the request, with evidence of need.

Deadlines: None.

Review Process: The foundation board meets as case load demands.

Restrictions

The foundation gives only to governmental units, exempt under the Internal Revenue Code, or to nonprofit, charitable organizations having exempt status under Section 501(c)(3) of the Internal Revenue Code evidencing that it is such an organization and is not classified as a "Private Foundation."

No grants are made to churches, religious organizations, or other entities for the propagation of religious faith and/or practices. Grants are also not made to individuals for scholarships, research, or other purposes.

Foundation Officials

Ward R. Burke: trustee

A. Wayne Corley: executive director

Arthur Temple, Jr.: chairman, trustee B Texarkana, AR 1920. ED Williams College; University of Texas (1937-1938). PRIM CORP EMPL director: Contractor's Supplies INC. CORP AFFIL director: Texarkana National Bankshares; director: Temple-Inland Properties Inc.; executive vice president, director: Temple-White Co.; director, chairman emeritus: Temple-Inland Inc.; director: Temple-Eastex Inc.; director: Temple-Inland Financial Services Inc.; director: Lumbermans Investment Corp.; director: Sunbelt Insurance Co.; director: Lufkin Block. NONPR AFFIL director: Saint Michael Hospital Foundation; director: Southern Forest Products Association; director: National Park Foundation; director: Lumberman Merchants Association; director: National Forest Products Association; member: Delta Kappa Epsilon; president, director: John E. Gray Institute; trustee: American Forest Products Association. CLUB AFFIL Crown Colony Country Club.

Arthur Temple, III: trustee B Texarkana, AR April 08, 1920. ED University of Texas, Austin (1937-1938). PRIM CORP EMPL chairman, chief executive officer: Exeter Investment Co. ADD CORP EMPL treasurer: Demcp Manufacturing Co. CORP AFFIL chairman, director: First Bank & Trust East Texas; director: Guaranty Federal Bank FSB; director: Contractors Supplies Inc.

W. Temple Webber, Jr.: trustee

M. F. Zeagler: assistant executive director

Grants Analysis

Disclosure Period: fiscal year ending November 30, 2001

Total Grants: $14,834,355*

Number of Grants: 91

Average Grant: $61,257*

Highest Grant: $3,337,248

Typical Range: $30,000 to $125,000

*Note: Giving excludes United Way, scholarships, and matching gifts. Average grant excludes four highest grants ($9,504,984).

Recent Grants

Note: Grants derived from fiscal 2001 Form 990.

Library-Related

464,460	Kurth Memorial Library, Lufkin, TX -- construct new library facility
154,261	Temple Memorial Library and Archives, Diboll, TX -- for archives budget
117,520	Temple Memorial Library and Archives, Diboll, TX -- for budget deficit
55,467	J.R. Huffman Public Library, Hemphill, TX -- for furnishings
25,000	Tyler County Public Library, Woodville, TX -- expansion project

General

3,337,248	Memorial Medical Center of East Texas, Lufkin, TX -- for equipment, software and therapeutic pool
2,500,000	Alzheimer's Disease and Related Disorders Association, Chicago, IL -- Temple Discovery Awards
2,244,138	Stephen F. Austin State University, Nacogdoches, TX -- for the College of Forestry and ecosystem studies
1,423,598	Methodist Retirement Communities, Lufkin, TX -- expansion of the Arbor Facility
500,000	St. Stephen's Episcopal School, Austin, TX -- for renovations, housing facilities and dorms
268,000	St. Cyprian's Episcopal School, Lufkin, TX -- scholarship assistance
250,000	Texas Children's Hospital, Houston, TX -- building for children's capital campaign
246,484	Buckner Baptist Benevolence, Beaumont, TX -- for Buckner Family Place
183,167	Memorial Medical Center of East Texas, Lufkin, TX -- to renovate the share van
150,840	Nacogdoches Treatment Center for Handicapped Children and Adults, Nacogdoches, TX -- for budget deficit

TEMPLE-INLAND, INC.

Company Headquarters

303 S. Temple Dr.
Drawer N
Diboll, TX 75941
Web: http://www.templeinland.com

Company Description

Founded: 1983
Ticker: TIN
Exchange: NYSE
Revenue: US$4.518 billion (2002)
Employees: 16500 (2002)

Temple-Inland Foundation

Giving Contact

M. Richard Warner, Vice President
Temple-Inland Foundation
303 South Temple Drive
Diboll, TX 75941
Phone: (936)829-7950
Web: http://www.templeinland.com

Alternate Contact

PO Drawer 338
Diboll, TX 75941
Note: For matching gift applications.

Description

EIN: 751977109
Organization Type: Corporate Foundation
Giving Locations: headquarters.
Grant Types: Employee Matching Gifts, General Support, Scholarship.
Note: The foundation matches contributions to charitable organizations made by employees and retirees (employees may contribute a minimum of $25 up to $3,000); Employee matching gift ratio: 3 to 1 for each

dollar on the first $1,000, Employee matching gift ratio: 2 to 1 on the second $1,000, and Employee matching gift ratio: 1 to 1 on the third $1,000.

Financial Summary

Total Giving: $4,154,852 (fiscal year ending June 31, 2001); $3,808,323 (fiscal 2000); $3,794,750 (fiscal 1999). Note: Contributes through foundation only. 1998 and 1999 giving includes matching gifts and scholarships.
Giving Analysis: Giving for fiscal 2001 includes: foundation grants to United Way ($388,841); foundation scholarships ($1,138,250); foundation ($2,627,761); fiscal 2000: foundation grants to United Way ($249,787); foundation scholarships ($1,147,000) foundation ($2,411,536)
Assets: $400,000 (fiscal 2001); $78,747 (fiscal 2000); $88,536 (fiscal 1999)
Gifts Received: $3,812,000 (fiscal 2001); $3,895,000 (fiscal 2000); $3,185,600 (fiscal 1999)

Typical Recipients

Arts & Humanities: Arts Associations & Councils, Ethnic & Folk Arts, Arts & Humanities-General, Libraries, Museums/Galleries, Theater
Civic & Public Affairs: African American Affairs, Clubs, Community Foundations, Employment/Job Training, Civic & Public Affairs-General, Housing, Law & Justice, Municipalities/Towns, Public Policy, Safety, Urban & Community Affairs, Zoos/Aquariums
Education: Business Education, Colleges & Universities, Education Associations, Education Reform, Elementary Education (Private), Engineering/Technological Education, Education-General, Preschool Education, Private Education (Precollege), Public Education (Precollege), Religious Education, Secondary Education (Private), Secondary Education (Public), Vocational & Technical Education
Environment: Forestry, Environment-General, Resource Conservation, Wildlife Protection
Health: Cancer, Children's Health/Hospitals, Clinics/Medical Centers, Health Organizations, Hospices, Hospitals, Medical Research, Prenatal Health Issues
Religion: Religious Organizations, Religious Welfare, Seminaries
Science: Science Museums
Social Services: Camps, Child Welfare, Community Service Organizations, Crime Prevention, Family Services, Food/Clothing Distribution, People with Disabilities, Recreation & Athletics, Shelters/Homelessness, Substance Abuse, United Funds/United Ways, Volunteer Services, YMCA/YWCA/YMHA/YWHA, Youth Organizations

Application Procedures

Initial Contact: Request application form, then send a written request.
Application Requirements: Submit a completed application form, a description of organization; amount requested; purpose of funds sought; recently audited financial statements; proof of tax-exempt status.
Deadlines: None.

Restrictions

Does not provide support to individuals; fraternal or veterans organizations; political or lobbying groups; or religious organizations.

Additional Information

Inland Container, a subsidiary, also maintains a foundation.
Publications: Application Form

Foundation Officials

Kenneth M. Jastrow, II: chairman, chief executive officer B 1947. ED University of Texas BA (1970); University of Texas MBA (1971). PRIM CORP EMPL president, chief operating officer: Temple-Inland Inc. ADD CORP EMPL chairman, president: Lumbermans Investment Corp. CORP AFFIL chairman, chief executive officer: Temple-Inland Financial Services Inc.;

chairman, chief executive officer group vice president financial services: Temple-Inland Mortgage Corp.; chairman: Knutson Mortgage Corp.; chairman: Guaranty Federal Bank FSB; director: Inland Paperboard Packaging; chairman: Capitol Mortgage Bankers Inc.
Arthur Temple, III: chairman, chief executive officer B Texarkana, AR April 08, 1920. ED University of Texas, Austin (1937-1938). PRIM CORP EMPL chairman, chief executive officer: Exeter Investment Co. ADD CORP EMPL treasurer: Demcp Manufacturing Co. CORP AFFIL chairman, director: First Bank & Trust East Texas; director: Guaranty Federal Bank FSB; director: Contractors Supplies Inc.

Grants Analysis

Disclosure Period: fiscal year ending June 31, 2001
Total Grants: $2,627,761*
Number of Grants: 1,188
Average Grant: $2,212
Highest Grant: $103,855
Typical Range: $500 to $4,500 and $10,000 to $100,000
*Note: Giving excludes scholarships; United Way.

Recent Grants

Note: Grants derived from 2001 Form 990.

Library-Related

40,975	T.L.L. Temple Memorial Library, Diboll, TX

General

114,265	United Way Dallas, Dallas, TX
111,749	United Way Capital Area, Austin, TX
103,855	Ronald McDonald House, Austin, TX
85,200	Lufkin Workshop and Opportunity, Lufkin, TX
72,045	Boys and Girls Clubs of Deep East Texas, Lufkin, TX
61,000	City of Diboll, Diboll, TX
55,244	University of Texas at Austin, Austin, TX
55,000	Hudson Institute, Indianapolis, IN
53,500	Texas A&M International University, College Station, TX
50,000	American Red Cross, Houston, TX

HERBERT A. TEMPLETON FOUNDATION

Giving Contact
Ruth B. Richmond, President
1717 SW Park Avenue
Portland, OR 97201
Phone: (503)223-0036

Description
Founded: 1955
EIN: 930505586
Organization Type: Private Foundation
Giving Locations: OR
Grant Types: General Support, Operating Expenses, Project, Seed Money.

Donor Information
Founder: the late Herbert A. Templeton, members of the Templeton family

Financial Summary
Total Giving: $521,350 (2001); $556,116 (2000); $802,335 (1999)
Assets: $15,469,460 (2001); $16,426,875 (2000); $18,349,100 (1999)
Gifts Received: $301,481 (1999); $36,814 (1995); $2,734,074 (1994). Note: In 1999, contributions were received from the estate of Mr. Bryson. In 1994, contributions were received from Hall R. Templeton.

Typical Recipients

Arts & Humanities: Arts Associations & Councils, Arts Centers, Arts Outreach, Ballet, Community Arts, Ethnic & Folk Arts, Arts & Humanities-General, Historic Preservation, Libraries, Museums/Galleries, Music, Opera, Performing Arts, Theater
Civic & Public Affairs: Civil Rights, Civic & Public Affairs-General, Housing, Legal Aid, Urban & Community Affairs, Women's Affairs
Education: Afterschool/Enrichment Programs, Arts/Humanities Education, Colleges & Universities, Education Funds, Education-General, Minority Education, Private Education (Precollege), Public Education (Precollege), Science/Mathematics Education, Student Aid
Environment: Environment-General, Resource Conservation
Religion: Religious Organizations, Religious Welfare, Seminaries
Science: Science Museums
Social Services: At-Risk Youth, Camps, Child Welfare, Community Centers, Community Service Organizations, Counseling, Day Care, Domestic Violence, Family Planning, Family Services, Shelters/Homelessness, Substance Abuse, United Funds/United Ways, Volunteer Services, YMCA/YWCA/YMHA/YWHA, Youth Organizations

Application Procedures

Initial Contact: The foundation has no formal grant application procedure or application form. Send a written proposal.
Application Requirements: Include a description of organization; a description of the project for which funding is requested; potential significance to the community; anticipated costs; project budget; sources of actual or potential support; amount requested; proof of tax-exempt status, financial statements, a list of board of directors; and the name, address and telephone number of a contact person. The proposal should be covered by a one-page transmittal letter which summarizes the grant request.
Deadlines: March 15 and September 15.

Restrictions

Does not support individuals, discriminatory organizations, or capital projects. The foundation does not provide loans. The foundation prefers not to fund programs for the elderly, fellowships, medical services, scientific research and technology, parochial education, program related investment, or endowment funds.

Additional Information

Publications: Program Policy Statement (including Application Guidelines)

Foundation Officials

James E. Bryson: trustee, member
Jane T. Bryson: vice president, trustee member
John E. Bryson: member B New York, NY 1943. ED Stanford University BA (1965); Freie University Berlin (1965-1966); Yale University JD (1969). PRIM CORP EMPL chairman, chief executive officer: Edison International. CORP AFFIL chairman, chief executive officer: Southern California Edison Co.; director: Times Mirror Co.; director: Mission Group Inc.; director: Pacific America Income Shares Inc.; director: Boeing Co.; chairman: Edison Mission Energy. NONPR AFFIL director: World Resources Institute; member, board editors, associate editor: Yale University Law Journal; member: Phi Beta Kappa; member: Stanford University Alumni Association; member: District of Columbia Bar Association; member: Oregon Bar Association; member: California Water Rights Law Review Committee; trustee: Claremont University Center; member: California Bar Association; member: California Pollution Control Financing Authority.
Linda M. Girard: trustee, member
Susan Bryson Nadel: mem

Terrence Russell Pancoast: secretary, treasurer, trustee, member B Everett, WA 1942. ED Whitman College AB (1965); Harvard University LLB (1968). PRIM CORP EMPL partner: Stoel Rives Boley Fraser & Wyse. NONPR AFFIL member, board overseers: Whitman College; member: World Affairs Council; director (Portland OR): Planned Parenthood Association; director: Oregon Art Institute; member: Oregon Bar Association; member: American Bar Association.

Henry R. Richmond: assistant scr, trustee, member
Ruth B. Richmond: president, trustee, member
Robert Templeton: mem
Loren L. Wyss: trustee

Grants Analysis

Disclosure Period: calendar year ending 2001
Total Grants: $521,350
Number of Grants: 82
Average Grant: $6,358
Highest Grant: $20,000
Typical Range: $1,000 to $10,000

Recent Grants

Note: Grants derived from 2001 Form 990.

General

20,000	Self-Enhancement Incorporated, Portland, OR
20,000	YMCA Mid-Willamette Valley
15,000	Children's Museum, Boston, MA
15,000	Ethos Inc.
15,000	Outside In, Portland, OR
15,000	Portland Baroque Orchestra, Portland, OR
12,000	Home Youth and Resource Center
10,000	Albina Ministerial Alliance, Portland, OR
10,000	Boys and Girls Aid Society of Oregon, Portland, OR
10,000	CASA for Children, Inc., Portland, OR

TENNESSEE VALLEY PRINTING CO.

Company Headquarters

PO Box 2213
Decatur, AL 35609
Web: http://www.decaturdaily.com

Company Description

Employees: 130 (2001)
SIC(s): 2700 Printing & Publishing.

Decatur Daily Charitable Trust

Giving Contact

Doris Drake
PO Box 2213
Decatur, AL 35609
Phone: (256)552-9320
Fax: (256)340-2411
E-mail: news@decaturdaily.com

Alternate Contact

Clint Shelton, General Manager

Description

EIN: 636131336
Organization Type: Corporate Foundation
Giving Locations: AL
Grant Types: General Support.

Financial Summary

Total Giving: $7,635 (1999); $139,192 (1998); $127,068 (1997)
Giving Analysis: Giving for 1999 includes: foundation ($7,635)
Assets: $135,665 (1999); $82,121 (1998); $175,720 (1997)
Gifts Received: $60,000 (1999); $25,000 (1998).
Note: In 1999, contributions were received from Tennessee Valley Printing Company, Inc.

Typical Recipients

Arts & Humanities: Libraries, Theater
Civic & Public Affairs: Philanthropic Organizations, Public Policy
Education: Colleges & Universities, Community & Junior Colleges, Education Funds, Education-General, Public Education (Precollege)
Health: Hospitals
International: International Organizations
Religion: Churches
Social Services: Domestic Violence, Social Services-General

Application Procedures

Initial Contact: Send a brief letter of inquiry.
Deadlines: None.

Additional Information

Trust(s): AmSouth Bank NA

Corporate Officials

Joe Perrin: controller editor PRIM CORP EMPL controller: Tennessee Valley Printing Co.
Barrett C. Shelton, Jr.: chairman, president, chief executive officer PRIM CORP EMPL chairman, president, chief executive officer: TN Valley Printing Co.
Thomas G. Wright: executive editor PRIM CORP EMPL executive editor: Tennessee Valley Printing Co.

Foundation Officials

Barrett C. Shelton, Jr.: mem adv comm (see above)
Tolly G. Shelton: mem, adv comm

Grants Analysis

Disclosure Period: calendar year ending 1999
Total Grants: $7,635
Number of Grants: 6
Average Grant: $1,273
Highest Grant: $2,635
Lowest Grant: $250
Typical Range: $1,000 to $3,000

Recent Grants

Note: Grants derived from 1999 Form 990.

Library-Related

2,635	Wheeler Basin Regional Library, Decatur, AL

General

2,000	Tennessee Valley Outreach
1,500	Alabama Independent Colleges, Birmingham, AL
1,000	Rotary International
250	Council on Child Abuse
250	S.P.U.D.S

TERUMO MEDICAL CORP.

Company Headquarters

Somerset, NJ

Company Description

Employees: 500
SIC(s): 3841 Surgical & Medical Instruments, 5122 Drugs, Proprietaries & Sundries.

Parent Company: Terumo Corp., 44-1 2-chome Hatagaya, Shibuya-ku, Tokyo, Japan

Operating Locations

Terumo Medical Corp. (NJ--Somerset); Terumo Medical Factory (MD--Elkton); Terumo Medical-Miami (FL--Miami)

Nonmonetary Support

Type: Donated Products; In-kind Services; Loaned Executives

Giving Contact

Joseph Cupini, Manager, General Affairs
950 Elkton Blvd.
Elkton, MD 21921
Phone: 800-283-7866
Fax: (410)392-7218
E-mail: joe.cupini@terumomedical.com
Web: http://www.terumomedical.com

Description

Organization Type: Corporate Giving Program
Giving Locations: headquarters area only.
Grant Types: Capital, General Support.

Typical Recipients

Arts & Humanities: Libraries, Public Broadcasting
Civic & Public Affairs: Economic Development, Civic & Public Affairs-General, Professional & Trade Associations, Urban & Community Affairs
Education: Business Education, Colleges & Universities, Community & Junior Colleges, Elementary Education (Private), Education-General
Health: Health-General, Hospitals
Social Services: Community Service Organizations, Family Planning, Substance Abuse, Youth Organizations

Corporate Officials

Ronald DeVore: chairman, president, chief executive officer PRIM CORP EMPL chairman, president, chief executive officer: Terumo Med Corp.

TETLEY U.S.A., INC.

Company Headquarters

100 Commerce Dr.
Shelton, CT 06484
Web: http://www.tetley.com

Company Description

Founded: 1995
Former Name: Tetley, Inc.
Employees: 1,000
SIC(s): 2095 Roasted Coffee, 2099 Food Preparations Nec.
Parent Company: Tetley Group Ltd., 325 Oldfield Lane North, Greenford, United Kingdom

Operating Locations

Bustelo Coffee Roasting Co. (NY--Bronx); Southern Tea Co. (GA--Marietta); Tetley U.S.A., Inc. (CT--Shelton; FL; GA; MO; NY; PA)

Nonmonetary Support

Type: Loaned Employees

Giving Contact

Contributions Coordinator
PO Box 856
Shelton, CT 06484-0856
Phone: (203)929-9200
Fax: (203)925-0512
Web: http://www.tetleyusa.com

Description

Organization Type: Corporate Giving Program
Giving Locations: primarily headquarters and operating communities; limited support nationally.
Grant Types: Employee Matching Gifts, General Support, Multiyear/Continuing Support.

Typical Recipients

Arts & Humanities: Arts Centers, Community Arts, Dance, Historic Preservation, Libraries, Museums/Galleries, Music, Performing Arts, Public Broadcasting
Civic & Public Affairs: Economic Development, Safety
Education: Colleges & Universities
Health: Hospitals, Medical Research, Mental Health, Single-Disease Health Associations
Social Services: Community Centers, Community Service Organizations, Domestic Violence, Senior Services, Substance Abuse, United Funds/United Ways, Youth Organizations

Application Procedures

Initial Contact: Send a brief letter of inquiry in spring or fall.
Application Requirements: Include a description of organization, amount and purpose of funds sought, and proof of tax-exempt status.

Restrictions

Program does not support political or religious groups; groups which receive contributions from United Way offices to which the company has made a contribution; or groups that do not qualify as exempt under section 501(c)(3) of the Internal Revenue Code, unless there is an overriding community interest involved.

Corporate Officials

Leon Allen: chairman, chief financial officer PRIM CORP EMPL chairman: Tetley USA, Inc.
Charles McCarthy: president, chief executive officer PRIM CORP EMPL president, chief executive officer: Tetley USA, Inc.
John Petrizzo: vice president, chief financial officer PRIM CORP EMPL vice president, chief financial officer: Tetley U.S.A.

Grants Analysis

Typical Range: $100 to $5,000

JAMES H. AND ALICE TEUBERT CHARITABLE TRUST

Giving Contact

Jimelle Bowen, Executive Director
PO Box 2131
Huntington, WV 25722
Phone: (304)525-6337

Description

Founded: 1987
EIN: 556101813
Organization Type: Private Foundation
Giving Locations: WV: Cabell County, Wayne County
Grant Types: General Support.

Financial Summary

Total Giving: $1,203,805 (fiscal year ending September 30, 2001); $1,160,466 (fiscal 2000); $977,555 (fiscal 1998)
Assets: $20,598,072 (fiscal 2001); $27,274,274 (fiscal 2000); $21,762,177 (fiscal 1998)
Gifts Received: $13,414,860 (fiscal 1994)

Typical Recipients

Arts & Humanities: Libraries
Education: Colleges & Universities, Public Education (Precollege), Special Education
Health: Diabetes, Eyes/Blindness, Hospitals
International: Health Care/Hospitals
Religion: Religious Welfare
Science: Scientific Research
Social Services: People with Disabilities, Recreation & Athletics, Special Olympics, YMCA/YWCA/YMHA/YWHA, Youth Organizations

Application Procedures

Initial Contact: Send letter requesting application form.
Application Requirements: Include a description of organization, amount requested, purpose of funds sought, recently audited financial statement, and proof of tax-exempt status.
Deadlines: March1 for April Awards, October1 for November Awards. Board meets in April and October.

Restrictions

Limited to organizations which provide aid to the blind.

Foundation Officials

Ed Buckman: mem
Dr. Michael A. Fiery: mem
David H. Lunsford: mem
Grant McGuire: chairman
Michael Nuce: member
Lisa O'Dell: mem
Dr. Matthew A. Rohrbach: mem
Norma G. Wright: member

Grants Analysis

Disclosure Period: fiscal year ending September 30, 2001
Total Grants: $1,203,805
Number of Grants: 14
Average Grant: $30,200*
Highest Grant: $811,211
Lowest Grant: $100
Typical Range: $10,000 to $50,000
***Note:** Average grant figure excludes highest grant.

Recent Grants

Note: Grants derived from fiscal 2000 Form 990.

General

888,830	Cabell Wayne Association of The Blind, Huntington, WV -- aid to the blind
56,000	Prevent Blindness America, Huntington, WV -- aid to the blind
42,814	West Virginia University Foundation, Morgantown, WV -- aid to the blind
42,630	Ebenezer Medical Outreach, Huntington, WV -- aid to the blind
31,852	West Virginia Lions Sight Conservation Foundation, Huntington, WV -- aid to the blind
27,657	West Virginia School for the Blind, Romney, WV -- aid to the blind
22,260	National Federation of the Blind of West Virginia, Romney, WV -- aid to the blind
21,514	AFB, New York, NY -- aid to the blind
14,078	YMCA, Huntington, WV -- aid to the blind
8,500	Interfaith Volunteer Caregivers, Huntington, WV -- aid to the blind

TEXAS INSTRUMENTS INC.

Company Headquarters

Dallas, TX
Web: http://www.ti.com

Company Description

Founded: 1938
Ticker: TXN
Exchange: NYSE
Revenue: US$8.383 billion (2002)
Employees: 34589 (2002)
Fortune Rank: 223, per FORTUNE Magazine's list of 500 Largest U.S. Corporations (2002).
SIC(s): 3399 Primary Metal Products Nec, 3571 Electronic Computers, 3575 Computer Terminals, 3674 Semiconductors & Related Devices.

Operating Locations

Texas Instruments Inc. (AL--Huntsville; AZ--Phoenix; CA--Irvine, Redwood City, San Diego, San Jose, Woodland Hills; CO--Englewood; FL--Clearwater, Maitland, Shalimar; GA--Atlanta; IL--Arlington Heights, Chicago, Schaumburg; IN--Carmel; KS--Shawnee Mission; KY--Versailles; MD--Columbia; MA--Attleboro; MI--Central Lake, Novi; MN--Eden Prairie; MO--St. Louis; NY--East Syracuse, Fishkill, Melville, New York; NC--Apex, Charlotte, Raleigh, Shelby; OH--Beavercreek, Cincinnati, Cleveland, Dayton; TN--Johnson City; TX--Austin, Houston, Lubbock, McKinney, Midland, Plano, Stafford, Temple; VA--Arlington, Falls Church; WA--Bellevue; WI--Waukesha)

Nonmonetary Support

Type: Donated Equipment; Loaned Employees; Loaned Executives
Note: Nonmonetary support is provided under company's direct giving program. The company sponsors a $1.2 million equipment cost-sharing with Texas colleges.

Texas Instruments Foundation

Giving Contact

Ann Minnis, Grants Administrator
Texas Instruments Foundation
PO Box 660199, M/S 8656
Dallas, TX 75266-0199
Phone: (214)480-3221
Fax: (214)480-6820
Web: http://www.ti.com/corp/docs/company/citizen/index.shtml

Alternate Contact

Manager Corporate University Relations
PO Box 655474
M/S 8219
Phone: (972)480-6873

Description

EIN: 756038519
Organization Type: Corporate Foundation
Giving Locations: TX: emphasis on Texas-based organizations, Dallas nationally.
Grant Types: Capital, Challenge, Conference/Seminar, Employee Matching Gifts, General Support, Operating Expenses, Research.
Note: Employee matching gift ratio: 1 to 1.

Financial Summary

Total Giving: $6,799,585 (2001); $8,568,340 (2000); $4,710,666 (1999). Note: Contributes through corporate direct giving program and foundation.
Giving Analysis: Giving for 2000 includes: foundation matching gifts ($836,518); foundation grants to United Way ($1,433,790); foundation ($6,298,032); 1999: foundation scholarships ($6,000); foundation grants to United Way ($1,138,040); foundation ($3,556,626); 1998: foundation grants to United Way ($1,188,980); foundation ($2,036,923).
Assets: $23,764,464 (2001); $29,885,765 (2000); $32,778,767 (1999)

Gifts Received: $7,500,000 (2000); $6,000,000 (1999); $4,200,000 (1998). Note: The foundation receives gifts from Texas Instruments Inc.

Typical Recipients

Arts & Humanities: Arts Centers, Arts Funds, Arts & Humanities-General, History & Archaeology, Libraries, Museums/Galleries, Music, Opera, Performing Arts, Public Broadcasting, Theater

Civic & Public Affairs: African American Affairs, Botanical Gardens/Parks, Community Foundations, Economic Development, Economic Policy, Employment/Job Training, Civic & Public Affairs-General, Hispanic Affairs, Nonprofit Management, Women's Affairs, Zoos/Aquariums

Education: Business Education, Colleges & Universities, Community & Junior Colleges, Economic Education, Education Associations, Education Funds, Education Reform, Elementary Education (Public), Engineering/Technological Education, Faculty Development, Education-General, Health & Physical Education, Literacy, Medical Education, Minority Education, Preschool Education, Private Education (Precollege), Public Education (Precollege), Science/Mathematics Education, Secondary Education (Public), Social Sciences Education, Special Education, Student Aid

Environment: Environment-General

Health: Clinics/Medical Centers, Hospitals, Hospitals (University Affiliated), Medical Research, Nursing Services, Research/Studies Institutes

International: Foreign Educational Institutions

Religion: Ministries, Religious Welfare

Science: Science Museums, Scientific Centers & Institutes

Social Services: Child Welfare, Community Centers, Community Service Organizations, Counseling, Day Care, People with Disabilities, Scouts, Shelters/Homelessness, Substance Abuse, United Funds/United Ways, Volunteer Services, YMCA/YWCA/YMHA/YWHA, Youth Organizations

Application Procedures

Initial Contact: Send a brief proposal of not more than two pages.

Application Requirements: Include a a description of organization, population served, amount requested, purpose of funds sought, how the proposal matches funding interests of the foundation, and proof of tax-exempt status.

Deadlines: None.

Decision Notification: Foundation board meets four times a year: March, June, September, December; applicants will be notified of grant decision within three weeks of meeting. The company contributions board reviews and makes decisions as requests are received.

Restrictions

Foundation does not support individuals, political activities, sectarian or denominational religious organizations, veterans organizations, fraternal or labor organizations, courtesy advertising, benefit entertainment/sponsorships, tax-supported institutions, or donation of Texas Instruments products.

Corporate Officials

Richard John Agnich: senior vice president, secretary, general counsel B Eveleth, MN 1943. ED Stanford University AB (1965); University of Texas JD (1969). PRIM CORP EMPL senior vice president, secretary, general counsel: Texas Instruments Inc. NONPR AFFIL director: United States Com Pacific Basin Economic Council; director: United States Korea Business Council; member: Southwest Legal Foundation; member: Texas Bar Association; president: Association General Counsel; member: Dallas Bar Association; member: American Bar Association; member: American Society of Corporate Secretaries.

William Andrew Aylesworth: chief financial officer, treasurer, senior vice president B Gary, IN 1942. ED

Cornell University BSEE (1965); Carnegie Mellon University MS (1967). PRIM CORP EMPL chief financial officer, treasurer, senior vice president: Texas Instruments Inc. CORP AFFIL director: MEMC Southwest; director: FM Global Insurance; director: Arkwright Mutual Insurance Co.; director: Corp. Officers & Directors Assurance Holding Ltd. NONPR AFFIL member: National Association Corporate Treasurers; member: Tau Beta Pi; member: Financial Executives Institute; director: Children's Medical Center Foundation; director: Factory Mutual Insurance; director: Childrens Medical Center Dallas; director: Children's Health Services of Texas.

Thomas James Engibous: president, chief executive officer, chairman, director B Saint Louis, MO 1953. ED Purdue University BSEE (1975); Purdue University MSEE (1976). PRIM CORP EMPL president, chief executive officer, chairman, director: Texas Instruments Inc. CORP AFFIL president: Texas Instruments Phillines. NONPR AFFIL member visitors committee: Purdue University Engineering; trustee: Southern Methodist University; member: Dallas Citizens Council; member: Institute Electrical & Electronics Engineers; member: Business Roundtable; director: Catalyst; member: Business Council.

James Mitchell: vice president for human resources

Win Skiles: senior vice president B Louisville, KY 1941. ED Baylor University (1963); University of Texas (1968). PRIM CORP EMPL senior vice president: Texas Instruments Inc.

Foundation Officials

Richard John Agnich: director (see above)
William Andrew Aylesworth: treasurer (see above)
Thomas James Engibous: director (see above)
Ann Minnis: grants administrator, director
James Mitchell: director (see above)
Liston Michael Rice, Jr.: president, director public affairs B Dallas, TX 1927. ED University of Texas (1948-1949).
Win Skiles: vice president (see above)
Cynthia Stewart: secretary

Grants Analysis

Disclosure Period: calendar year ending 2001
Total Grants: $3,741,253*
Number of Grants: 52
Average Grant: $53,750*
Highest Grant: $1,000,000
Lowest Grant: $1,000
Typical Range: $2,000 to $100,000 and $500,000 to $1,000,000
***Note:** Giving excludes matching gifts and United Way. Average grant figure excludes highest grant.

Recent Grants

Note: Grants derived from 2001 Form 990.

General

2,000,000	University of Texas at Dallas, Richardson, TX
1,500,000	Southern Methodist University, Dallas, TX -- for Department of Reading
1,447,000	Dallas Independent School District, Dallas, TX
1,300,000	United Way of Metropolitan Dallas, Dallas, TX
1,300,000	University of Dallas, Dallas, TX
1,000,000	Southern Methodist University School of Engineering, Dallas, TX
376,000	University of Texas at El Paso, El Paso, TX
372,000	University of Texas Dallas, Dallas, TX
335,000	Dallas Independent School District, Dallas, TX -- for advanced placement incentive
319,074	Head Start of Greater Dallas, Dallas, TX -- for Junkins Center

TEXTRON, INC.

Company Headquarters

40 Westminster St.
Providence, RI 02903
Web: http://www.textron.com

Company Description

Founded: 1923
Ticker: TXT
Exchange: NYSE
Revenue: US$10.658 billion (2002)
Employees: 49000 (2002)

Textron Charitable Trust

Giving Contact

Cate M. Roberts, Director, Community Affairs
Textron Inc.
40 Westmintster Street
Providence, RI 02903
Phone: (401)457-2430
Web: http://www.textron.com/profile/community.html

Description

EIN: 256115832
Organization Type: Corporate Foundation
Giving Locations: headquarters and operating communities.
Grant Types: Capital, Employee Matching Gifts, General Support, Scholarship.
Note: Employee matching gift ratio: 2 to 1, up to $7,500 annually, to eligible secondary schools, colleges and universities; arts and cultural organizations; hospital; and environmental, conservation and wildlife groups.

Financial Summary

Total Giving: $6,085,873 (2001); $3,577,311 (2000); $3,233,275 (1999). Note: Company gives through charitable trust only.

Giving Analysis: Giving for 2001 includes: foundation scholarships ($418,447); foundation matching gifts ($991,986); foundation grants to United Way ($1,009,479); foundation ($3,665,961); 2000: foundation scholarships ($184,599); foundation matching gifts ($1,136,752); foundation ($2,255,960); 1999: foundation grants to United Way ($110,000); foundation scholarships ($208,102); foundation ($1,436,141); foundation matching gifts ($1,479,032); **Assets:** $16,151,845 (2000); $8,128,796 (1999); $5,726,804 (1998)

Gifts Received: $9,130,440 (2000); $5,815,388 (1999); $2,000,000 (1997). Note: Contributions received from Textron Corporation.

Typical Recipients

Arts & Humanities: Arts Appreciation, Arts Associations & Councils, Arts Centers, Arts Funds, Arts Institutes, Arts Outreach, Ballet, Community Arts, Dance, Ethnic & Folk Arts, Historic Preservation, Libraries, Museums/Galleries, Music, Opera, Performing Arts, Public Broadcasting, Theater, Visual Arts

Civic & Public Affairs: Botanical Gardens/Parks, Business/Free Enterprise, Chambers of Commerce, Civil Rights, Economic Development, Economic Policy, Employment/Job Training, Civic & Public Affairs-General, Housing, Law & Justice, Legal Aid, Municipalities/Towns, Philanthropic Organizations, Professional & Trade Associations, Public Policy, Public Policy, Safety, Urban & Community Affairs, Women's Affairs, Zoos/Aquariums

Education: Arts/Humanities Education, Business Education, Colleges & Universities, Community & Junior

Colleges, Economic Education, Education Associations, Education Funds, Education Reform, Engineering/Technological Education, Education-General, International Studies, Legal Education, Literacy, Medical Education, Minority Education, Private Education (Precollege), Public Education (Precollege), Science/Mathematics Education, Social Sciences Education, Student Aid, Vocational & Technical Education

Environment: Air/Water Quality, Environment-General, Resource Conservation

Health: Cancer, Children's Health/Hospitals, Emergency/Ambulance Services, Health Policy/Cost Containment, Health Organizations, Hospices, Hospitals, Medical Rehabilitation, Prenatal Health Issues, Single-Disease Health Associations

International: Foreign Educational Institutions, Human Rights, International Affairs, International Organizations, International Peace & Security Issues, International Relations

Religion: Missionary Activities (Domestic), Religious Welfare

Science: Science Exhibits & Fairs, Scientific Centers & Institutes

Social Services: Child Welfare, Community Centers, Community Service Organizations, Counseling, Emergency Relief, Family Planning, Food/Clothing Distribution, People with Disabilities, Recreation & Athletics, Refugee Assistance, Scouts, Senior Services, Shelters/Homelessness, Social Services-General, Special Olympics, Substance Abuse, United Funds/United Ways, Volunteer Services, Youth Organizations

Application Procedures

Initial Contact: Request an application form or obtain one from the company's web site.
Application Requirements: Submit the completed Textron Grant Application Form with proof of tax-exempt status; list of board members, including affiliations, background, town of residence, and number of times board meets; and financial information, including total organizational budget, most recent independent audit or account review, year-to-date financial statement for current year, and other sources of funding with dollar amounts and whether each source is committed, pending, or anticipated. For capital or project support requests, include a project or capital budget for fiscal year(s).
Deadlines: None.
Evaluative Criteria: Proposals will be evaluated on consistency with focus and mission of Textron's contributions program; purpose and impact of proposed request; and involvement of Textron employees.
Decision Notification: Funding decisions are generally communicated with six to eight weeks.

Restrictions

Does not support organizations without 501(c)(3) status; individuals; political, fraternal, or veterans organizations; religious institutions for sectarian activities; or organizations that discriminate based on race, creed, gender, ethnicity, sexual orientation, disability, or age.

Additional Information

Grant recipients are required to complete a post-grant application form and adhere to terms of the grant. A fiscal and program summary must be submitted upon completion of the project.
Rhode Island Hospital Trust National Bank serves as a corporate trustee of the trust.

Corporate Officials

John D. Butler: executive vice president, chief human resources officer ED Michigan State University. PRIM CORP EMPL executive vice president, chief human resources officer: Textron Inc.

Grants Analysis

Disclosure Period: calendar year ending 2000
Total Grants: $2,255,960*
Highest Grant: $125,000

Typical Range: $100 to $500 and $1,000 to $60,000
*Note: Giving excludes matching gifts and scholarships.

Recent Grants

Note: Grants derived from 2000 Form 990.

Library-Related
15,400	Providence Public Library, Providence, RI
15,000	Springfield Library & Museums, Springfield, MA

General
125,000	Textron Chamber Commerce Academy, Providence, RI
109,533	Providence College, Providence, RI
100,000	American Academy of Diplomacy, Washington, DC
100,000	Leadership Foundation, Washington, DC
100,000	Textron Chamber Commerce Academy, Providence, RI
55,855	National Merit Scholarship Corporation, Evanston, IL
50,000	City Arts, Providence, RI
50,000	East Lake Community Foundation, Atlanta, GA
50,000	Reading is Fundamental, Washington, DC
50,000	Trinity Repertory Company, Providence, RI

THANKSGIVING FOUNDATION

Giving Contact

Marc C. Winmill, Chairman
672 Tower Hill Rd.
Millbrook, NY 12545
Phone: (212)632-3000

Alternate Contact

Thomas H. Stine
380 Claremont Rd.
Bernardsville, NJ 07924

Description

Founded: 1985
EIN: 136861874
Organization Type: Private Foundation
Giving Locations: NJ; NY
Grant Types: General Support.

Donor Information

Founder: Thomas M. Peters, Marion Post Peters

Financial Summary

Total Giving: $497,551 (fiscal year ending July 31, 2002); $360,870 (fiscal 2001); $664,551 (fiscal 2000)
Giving Analysis: Giving for fiscal 2002 includes: foundation scholarships ($37,716) fiscal 2000: foundation scholarships ($55,000)
Assets: $7,867,952 (fiscal 2002); $10,924,611 (fiscal 2001); $13,457,104 (fiscal 2000)

Typical Recipients

Arts & Humanities: Historic Preservation, History & Archaeology, Libraries, Museums/Galleries, Music, Public Broadcasting, Theater
Civic & Public Affairs: Civic & Public Affairs-General, Housing, Municipalities/Towns, Zoos/Aquariums
Education: Colleges & Universities, Education Funds, Minority Education, Private Education (Precollege), Special Education
Environment: Air/Water Quality, Environment-General, Resource Conservation, Wildlife Protection

Health: Cancer, Children's Health/Hospitals, Eyes/Blindness, Health Organizations, Hospitals, Nursing Services
International: Health Care/Hospitals, International Affairs, International Relief Efforts
Religion: Churches, Religious Organizations, Religious Welfare
Science: Science Museums
Social Services: Camps, Child Welfare, Community Service Organizations, Family Planning, Family Services, People with Disabilities, Recreation & Athletics, United Funds/United Ways, Youth Organizations

Application Procedures

Initial Contact: Send a brief letter of inquiry in writing.
Application Requirements: Include a description of the organization, mission statement, and purpose of funds sought.
Deadlines: None.

Restrictions

Does not support individuals.

Additional Information

Trust(s): Fiduciary Trust Co

Foundation Officials

Thomas Henry Stine: trustee
Mark C. Winmill: trustee

Grants Analysis

Disclosure Period: fiscal year ending July 31, 2002
Total Grants: $459,835*
Number of Grants: 236
Average Grant: $1,754*
Highest Grant: $47,653
Lowest Grant: $23
Typical Range: $500 to $5,000
*Note: Giving excludes scholarships. Average grant figure excludes highest grant.

Recent Grants

Note: Grants derived from 2000 Form 990.

General
60,000	Sheltering Arms Childrens Service, New York, NY
50,000	Sheltering Arms Children Service, New York, NY
35,000	University of Virginia Fund, Charlottesville, VA
25,000	Duke University, Durham, NC
20,000	Westmoreland Davis Memorial Foundation
19,750	St. Georges School, Spokane, WA
15,000	Eaglebrook School Scholarship Fund
10,000	Foster Pride
10,000	Mashomack Foundation
10,000	Riverview Foundation, NJ

W. B. AND CANDACE THOMAN FOUNDATION

Giving Contact

Benjamin O. Schwendener, Jr., President & Secretary
222 N. Washington Sq., Suite 400
Lansing, MI 48933-1800
Phone: (517)377-0710
Fax: (517)484-8286
E-mail: kfl@honigmam.com

Description

Founded: 1968
EIN: 237029842
Organization Type: Private Foundation
Giving Locations: MI: Clinton County, Eaton County, Ingham County
Grant Types: Project, Scholarship, Seed Money.

Donor Information

Founder: the late W. B. Thoman, the late Candace Thoman

Financial Summary

Total Giving: $151,000 (2000); $127,725 (1999); $100,300 (1998)
Assets: $2,857,228 (2000); $2,840,282 (1999); $2,917,497 (1998)
Gifts Received: $37,715 (1999); $37,715 (1996); $39,215 (1995). Note: In 1996, contributions were received from the W. B. Thoman Residuary Charitable Lead Trust.

Typical Recipients

Arts & Humanities: Community Arts, Dance, Libraries, Music, Opera, Performing Arts, Theater
Civic & Public Affairs: Legal Aid
Education: Afterschool/Enrichment Programs, Colleges & Universities, Education Funds, Education-General, Gifted & Talented Programs, International Studies, Literacy, Public Education (Precollege), Special Education
Health: Single-Disease Health Associations
International: International Relief Efforts
Social Services: Child Welfare, Community Service Organizations, Family Services, Youth Organizations

Application Procedures

Initial Contact: Send a brief letter of inquiry.
Application Requirements: Proposals should include a description of the project and its goals and purposes, the total budget for the project, sources of funding, reasons why the project needs to be undertaken, whhther professional outside consultants or fundraisers are to be hired and the fees involved, current balance sheet and income statement, a copy of most recent 990, proof of tax-exempt status, and a verification signed by the cheif executive officer that he or she has personally examined all of the information in the grant request.
Deadlines: None.

Restrictions

Contributions are made for the education and benefit of young people who are orphans or from very poor families. No support for political organizations, churches, or religious organizations or programs.

Additional Information

Awards grants to organizations that provide education and benefits to young people who are orphans or from very poor families.
Publications: Application Guidelines

Foundation Officials

Richard Earl Chapin: trustee B Danville, IL 1925. ED Wabash College AB (1948); University of Illinois MS (1949); University of Illinois PhD (1954). PRIM CORP EMPL director, libs emeritus, professor emeritus: Michigan State University. NONPR AFFIL member: Association Research Libraries; member: Michigan Library Association; member: ALA. CLUB AFFIL mem: Phi Kappa Phi; mem: Sigma Chi; mem: Blue Key Club.
Louis E. Legg: vice president
James L. Reutter: treasurer
Benjamin O. Schwendener, Jr.: president, secretary
Dorothy Silk: trustee

Grants Analysis

Disclosure Period: calendar year ending 2000
Total Grants: $151,000
Number of Grants: 9
Highest Grant: $25,000
Lowest Grant: $4,000

Recent Grants

Note: Grants derived from 1999 Form 990.

General

39,000	Literacy Volunteers of America - Capital Area Literacy Coalition, Lansing, MI -- funding for succeed program
35,000	Michigan State University Fellowship Program, East Lansing, MI -- funding for program relating to world hunger programs
28,000	Ingham Intermediate School District, Mason, MI -- funding for gifted and talented program
19,725	Ingham County Family Court, Lansing, MI -- funding for summer tutor liaison enrichment program
5,000	Boarshead Theater, The, Lansing, MI -- funding for playwriting, acting workshops for students
1,000	Michigan Historical Foundation, Lansing, MI -- funding for on the air 1920-2000 project

JOAN AND LEE THOMAS FOUNDATION

Giving Contact

Lee B. Thomas, Director
2602 Grassland Dr.
Louisville, KY 40299-2524
Phone: (502)495-1958

Description

Founded: 1990
EIN: 611166955
Organization Type: Private Foundation
Giving Locations: KY
Grant Types: General Support.

Donor Information

Founder: Established in 1990 by Lee B. Thomas, Jr.

Financial Summary

Total Giving: $959,000 (fiscal year ending June 30, 2002); $909,500 (fiscal 2001); $863,500 (fiscal 2000)
Assets: $19,815,655 (fiscal 2002); $18,842,166 (fiscal 2001); $17,754,837 (fiscal 2000)
Gifts Received: $600,000 (fiscal 2002); $600,000 (fiscal 2001); $400,000 (fiscal 2000). Note: In fiscal 1996 and 2002, contributions were received from Lee B. and Joan E. Thomas.

Typical Recipients

Arts & Humanities: Arts Centers, Libraries, Museums/Galleries, Music, Public Broadcasting
Civic & Public Affairs: African American Affairs, Community Foundations, Economic Policy, First Amendment Issues, Civic & Public Affairs-General, Housing, Law & Justice, Legal Aid, Philanthropic Organizations, Public Policy, Rural Affairs, Urban & Community Affairs, Women's Affairs
Education: Colleges & Universities, Education Funds, Elementary Education (Private), Education-General, Literacy, Preschool Education, Private Education (Precollege), Student Aid
Health: Children's Health/Hospitals, Medical Rehabilitation, Nursing Services
International: International Development, International Environmental Issues, International Peace & Security Issues, International Relations
Religion: Religious Organizations, Religious Welfare, Social/Policy Issues
Social Services: At-Risk Youth, Child Welfare, Community Centers, Community Service Organizations, Family Services, Food/Clothing Distribution, Homes, Scouts, Senior Services, United Funds/United Ways, Youth Organizations

Application Procedures

Initial Contact: The foundation has no formal grant application procedure or application form.
Deadlines: None.

Additional Information

Gifts to charitable organizations in the City of Louisville or for the betterment of the city will be given priority.

Foundation Officials

Glenn E. Thomas: director
Dr. Joan E. Thomas: director
Lee B. Thomas: director

Grants Analysis

Disclosure Period: fiscal year ending June 30, 2002
Total Grants: $959,000
Number of Grants: 24
Average Grant: $22,809*
Highest Grant: $210,000
Lowest Grant: $2,000
Typical Range: $10,000 to $30,000
*Note: Average grant excludes three highest grants ($480,000).

Recent Grants

Note: Grants derived from fiscal 2000 Form 990.

General

165,000	Home of Innocents, Louisville, KY
150,000	Center for Women and Families, Louisville, KY
125,000	Council on Economic Priorities, New York, NY
70,000	Lincoln Foundation, Louisville, KY
50,000	Bellarmine College, Louisville, KY
50,000	Girl Scouts of Kentuckiana, Inc., Louisville, KY
40,000	Plymouth Renewal Center, Louisville, KY
30,000	Neighborhood House, Louisville, KY
25,000	Chapin School, Princeton, NJ
20,000	Court Appointed Child Advocates, Inc., Louisville, KY

THOMAS INDUSTRIES

Company Headquarters

4360 Brownboro Rd., Ste. 300
Louisville, KY 40207
Web: http://www.thomasind.com

Company Description

Founded: 1928
Ticker: TII
Exchange: NYSE
Revenue: US$184.4 million (2001)
Employees: 1070 (2001)
SIC(s): 3563 Air & Gas Compressors, 3645 Residential Lighting Fixtures, 3646 Commercial Lighting Fixtures.

Operating Locations

Thomas Industries (KY--Louisville)

Thomas Foundation

Giving Contact

Phillip J. Stuecker, Vice President & Chief Financial Officer
4360 Brownsboro Rd., Suite 300
Louisville, KY 40207
Phone: (502)893-4600
Fax: (502)895-6618

Description

EIN: 396075230
Organization Type: Corporate Foundation
Giving Locations: IL; KY: Louisville; NY
Grant Types: Capital, Emergency, General Support.

Financial Summary

Total Giving: $42,673 (2001); $35,986 (2000); $31,735 (1999)
Giving Analysis: Giving for 2001 includes: foundation ($1,113); 1999: foundation ($31,735); 1998: foundation grants to United Way ($4,114) foundation ($42,145)
Assets: $11,831 (2001); $4,587 (2000); $549 (1999)
Gifts Received: $50,000 (2001); $40,000 (2000); $15,000 (1999). Note: In 2001, contributions were received from Thomas Industries, Inc. ($50,000).

Typical Recipients

Arts & Humanities: Arts Associations & Councils, Arts Funds, History & Archaeology, Libraries, Museums/Galleries, Music, Performing Arts
Civic & Public Affairs: African American Affairs, Botanical Gardens/Parks, Business/Free Enterprise, Clubs, Community Foundations, Economic Development, Civic & Public Affairs-General, Housing, Professional & Trade Associations, Urban & Community Affairs
Education: Business Education, Colleges & Universities, Community & Junior Colleges, Economic Education, Education Associations, Education Funds, Education-General, Literacy, Public Education (Precollege), Secondary Education (Private), Special Education
Health: Arthritis, Cancer, Children's Health/Hospitals, Emergency/Ambulance Services, Health Funds, Heart, Hospices, Hospitals, Medical Rehabilitation, Multiple Sclerosis, Prenatal Health Issues, Single-Disease Health Associations
Religion: Jewish Causes, Religious Organizations, Religious Welfare
Science: Scientific Centers & Institutes
Social Services: Camps, Child Welfare, Community Service Organizations, Crime Prevention, Emergency Relief, Family Services, Food/Clothing Distribution, Homes, People with Disabilities, Scouts, Senior Services, Shelters/Homelessness, Special Olympics, United Funds/United Ways, Volunteer Services, YMCA/YWCA/YMHA/YWHA, Youth Organizations

Application Procedures

Initial Contact: Submit a brief letter of inquiry.
Deadlines: October 1.

Corporate Officials

Timothy Charles Brown: chairman, president, chief executive officer, director B Louisville, KY 1950. ED Eastern Kentucky University BBA (1972); University of Louisville MBA (1985). PRIM CORP EMPL chairman, president, chief executive officer, director: Thomas Industries. NONPR AFFIL member: Kentucky Society CPA's; state director: National Association Manufacturer; member: American Institute of CPA's.
Phillip James Stuecker: vice president, chief financial officer, secretary B Louisville, KY 1951. ED University of Louisville (1974); University of Louisville (1987). PRIM CORP EMPL vice president, chief financial officer, secretary: Thomas Industries. NONPR AFFIL member: American Institute CPA's; member: Financial Executives Institute.

Foundation Officials

Timothy Charles Brown: president (see above)
Terry L. Lange: treasurer
Phillip James Stuecker: vice president, chief financial officer, secretary (see above)
David J. Stumler: assistant secretary
Roger Whitton: contr
Ronald D. Wiseman: assistant secretary

Grants Analysis

Disclosure Period: calendar year ending 2001
Total Grants: $41,560*
Average Grant: $1,662
Highest Grant: $10,000
Typical Range: $250 to $5,000
*Note: Giving excludes United Way.

Recent Grants

Note: Grants derived from 2001 Form 990.

General

10,000	American Red Cross, Denison, TX
5,000	Greater Louisville Foundation, Louisville, KY
4,250	Boy Scouts of America - Lincoln Heritage Council
4,000	Old Walnut Street Capitol Campaign
3,500	Citizens of Louisville Organized and United Together, Louisville, KY
2,500	Camp Tall Trees
2,500	University of Louisville Foundation, Louisville, KY
1,250	Kentucky Council on Economic Education, Louisville, NY
1,113	Metro United Way, Louisville, KY
1,000	Courier Journal Newspaper in Education

THOMASVILLE FURNITURE INDUSTRIES, INC.

Company Headquarters

Thomasville, NC
Web: http://www.thomasville.com

Company Description

Employees: 7,000
SIC(s): 2511 Wood Household Furniture, 2512 Upholstered Household Furniture, 2514 Metal Household Furniture.
Parent Company: Armstrong World Industries, Inc., Lancaster, PA, United States

Operating Locations

Thomasville Furniture Industries Inc. (MS--Fayette; NC--Statesville, Thomasville; TN--Johnson City; VA--Brookneal, Carysbrook)

Nonmonetary Support

Type: Donated Equipment; Donated Products; Loaned Employees; Loaned Executives
Volunteer Programs: Thomasville employees volunteer in Communities in Schools and Chamber programs and in local school systems and YMCA's.

Thomasville Furniture Industries Foundation

Giving Contact

Vickie Holder, General Manager
PO Box 339
Thomasville, NC 27360
Phone: (336)472-4000
Fax: (336)472-4085
E-mail: vholder@thomasville.com

Description

Founded: 1960
EIN: 566047870
Organization Type: Corporate Foundation
Giving Locations: NC
Grant Types: Award, Endowment, General Support.

Donor Information

Founder: Thomasville Furniture Industries, Inc.

Financial Summary

Total Giving: $367,423 (2001); $390,822 (2000); $311,354 (1999). Note: Contributes through corporate direct giving program and foundation.
Giving Analysis: Giving for 2001 includes: foundation ($51,190); foundation scholarships ($70,050); foundation grants to United Way ($246,183); 2000: foundation scholarships ($62,900); foundation ($115,439); foundation grants to United Way ($212,483); 1999: corporate scholarships ($49,720); foundation ($83,237) corporate grants to United Way ($178,397)
Assets: $4,483,081 (2001); $5,298,076 (2000); $5,586,750 (1999)
Gifts Received: $2,257 (1997). Note: Gifts received in 1997 include those from a Thomasville employee.

Typical Recipients

Arts & Humanities: Arts Associations & Councils, Arts Festivals, Community Arts, Libraries, Museums/Galleries, Music, Performing Arts, Theater
Civic & Public Affairs: Economic Development, Civic & Public Affairs-General, Housing
Education: Arts/Humanities Education, Colleges & Universities, Community & Junior Colleges, Education Funds, Elementary Education (Public), Environmental Education, Education-General, International Studies, Literacy, Minority Education, Private Education (Precollege), Public Education (Precollege), Science/Mathematics Education, Secondary Education (Public), Student Aid
Health: Emergency/Ambulance Services, Hospitals, Medical Research
Religion: Religious Welfare
Science: Scientific Centers & Institutes
Social Services: Animal Protection, Child Welfare, Community Centers, Community Service Organizations, Crime Prevention, Family Services, Recreation & Athletics, United Funds/United Ways, YMCA/YWCA/YMHA/YWHA, Youth Organizations

Application Procedures

Initial Contact: Send a letter of request.
Deadlines: None.

Restrictions

Does not support individuals, religious organizations for sectarian purposes, political or lobbying groups, or organizations outside operating areas. Scholarships are only provided to children of employees.

Additional Information

Trust(s): Wachovia Bank, NA

Corporate Officials

Ronald G. Berrier: vice president, treasurer, assistant secretary B Winston-Salem, NC 1943. ED High Point College (1965). PRIM CORP EMPL vice president, treasurer, assistant secretary: Thomasville Furniture Industries Inc.
D. Paul Dascoli: chief financial officer, vice president B Providence, RI 1960. ED Providence College (1982). PRIM CORP EMPL chief financial officer, vice president: Thomasville Furniture Industries Inc.
Christian J. Pfaff: president, chief executive officer PRIM CORP EMPL chairman, president, chief executive officer, director: Thomasville Furniture Industries Inc.

Foundation Officials

Vickie Holder: general manager, administrator operations

Grants Analysis

Disclosure Period: calendar year ending 2001
Total Grants: $51,190*
Number of Grants: 59

Average Grant: $868
Highest Grant: $25,000
Typical Range: $100 to $3,000
***Note:** Giving includes scholarships; United Way.

Recent Grants

Note: Grants derived from 2001 Form 990.

General

175,000	North Carolina State University, Raleigh, NC
175,000	North Carolina State University, Raleigh, NC
25,000	United Way of Caldwell County, Lenoir, NC
25,000	United Way of Davidson County, Thomasville, NC
22,625	United Way of Davidson County, Thomasville, NC
13,722	United Way of Davidson County, Thomasville, NC
13,000	United Way of Caldwell County, Lenoir, NC
12,677	United Way of Davidson County, Thomasville, NC
12,000	United Way of Caldwell County, Lenoir, NC
11,846	United Way of Davidson County, Thomasville, NC

THOMPSON CHARITABLE FOUNDATION

Giving Contact

Monica Luke, Foundation Manager
4823 Old Kingston Pike
PO Box 10516
Knoxville, TN 37939-0516
Phone: (865)588-0491

Description

Founded: 1987
EIN: 581754763
Organization Type: General Purpose Foundation
Giving Locations: KY: Bell County, Clay County, Laurel County, Leslie County; TN: Anderson County, Blount County, Knox County, Scott County; VA: Buchanan County, Tazewell County
Grant Types: Capital, Department, General Support, Scholarship.

Donor Information

Founder: Established in 1987 by the estate of B. Ray Thompson Sr.

Financial Summary

Total Giving: $2,029,473 (fiscal year ending June 30, 2001); $1,016,593 (fiscal 1999); $2,796,030 (fiscal 1997)
Giving Analysis: Giving for fiscal 2001 includes: foundation scholarships ($50,000)
Assets: $46,344,119 (fiscal 2001); $49,370,829 (fiscal 1999); $68,574,817 (fiscal 1997)
Gifts Received: $894,818 (fiscal 1997); $2,784,717 (fiscal 1994); $4,353,795 (fiscal 1993)

Typical Recipients

Arts & Humanities: Arts & Humanities-General, Libraries, Music, Theater
Civic & Public Affairs: Community Foundations, Civic & Public Affairs-General, Housing, Law & Justice, Philanthropic Organizations, Safety, Urban & Community Affairs
Education: Business Education, Colleges & Universities, Community & Junior Colleges, Elementary Education (Public), Education-General, Literacy, Preschool Education, Private Education (Precollege), Religious Education, Special Education
Environment: Air/Water Quality

Health: AIDS/HIV, Cancer, Children's Health/Hospitals, Clinics/Medical Centers, Health-General, Geriatric Health, Hospices, Hospitals, Medical Rehabilitation, Nursing Services, Prenatal Health Issues, Preventive Medicine/Wellness Organizations, Preventive Medicine/Wellness Organizations, Public Health
Religion: Religion-General, Ministries, Missionary Activities (Domestic), Religious Organizations, Religious Welfare
Social Services: Child Abuse, Child Welfare, Community Centers, Community Service Organizations, Day Care, Family Planning, Family Services, Food/Clothing Distribution, Homes, People with Disabilities, Scouts, Shelters/Homelessness, Social Services-General, Volunteer Services, YMCA/YWCA/YMHA/YWHA, Youth Organizations

Application Procedures

Initial Contact: There are no specific application guidelines. Send a letter no longer than two pages describing the project.
Application Requirements: Include a description of the organization, a list of the directors and staff, project's annual budget; IRS tax exemption ruling, estimated project budget, and tentative line items.
Deadlines: March 31, June 30, September 30, and December 31.

Restrictions

The foundation does not support endowments or operating deficits.

Foundation Officials

Carl Ensor, Jr.: director CORP AFFIL director: Bank East Tennessee.
Monica Luke: manager
Jesse J. Thompson: director
Sylvia M. Thompson: director
Merle D. Wolfe: president, director PRIM CORP EMPL president, director: Sun Coal Co. CORP AFFIL director: Jewell Resources Corp.; principal: Jewell Smokeless Coal Corp.
Lindsay Young: director

Grants Analysis

Disclosure Period: fiscal year ending June 30, 2001
Total Grants: $1,979,473*
Number of Grants: 42
Average Grant: $40,777*
Highest Grant: $307,630
Typical Range: $20,000 to $75,000
***Note:** Giving excludes scholarships. Average grant figure excludes highest grant.

Recent Grants

Note: Grants derived from fiscal 2000 Form 990.

Library-Related

25,000	Tazewell County Public Library, Tazewell, VA -- technical expense
1,000	Tennessee Voices for Children, Nashville, TN -- program support

General

350,000	Buchanan County PSA, Vansant, VA -- water project
150,000	Youth Haven Children's Advocacy Ct., Oak Ridge, TN -- building construction
100,000	Boys and Girls Club, Knoxville, TX -- capital expansion
100,000	Helen Ross McNabb Foundation, Knoxville, TN -- capital expenditures
100,000	Knoxville College, Knoxville, TN -- work program
100,000	Maryville College, Maryville, TN -- capital campaign
50,000	Baptist Hospital, Knoxville, TN -- new facility
50,000	Knoxville Habitat for Humanity, Knoxville, TN -- new home construction

50,000	St. Mary's Foundation, Knoxville, TN -- Hospice
50,000	University of Tennessee, Knoxville, TN -- scholarship fund

J. WALTER THOMPSON CO.

Company Headquarters

New York, NY
Web: http://www.jwtworld.com

Company Description

Assets: US$4 billion (2001)
Employees: 9200 (2001)
SIC(s): 7311 Advertising Agencies.
Parent Company: WPP Group Plc, 27 Farm St., London, United Kingdom

Operating Locations

Anspach Grossman Enterprise (NY--New York); Carl Byoir & Associates (NY--New York); CommonHealth U.S.A. (NJ--Parsippany); Einson Freeman (NJ--Paramus); Hill & Knowlton (NY--New York); HLS Corp. (NJ--Little Falls); J. Walter Thompson Co. (AZ--Scottsdale; CA--Los Angeles, San Diego, San Francisco; DC--Washington; FL--Coral Gables; GA--Atlanta; IL--Chicago; MI--Detroit; MO--St. Ann; NJ--Cherry Hill; NY--Fairport, New York; OH--Cincinnati, Columbus; TX--Dallas; UT--Salt Lake City); Mendoza, Dillon & Associates (CA--Newport Beach); MRB Group (NY--New York); Ogilvy & Mather Worldwide (NY--New York); Pace Advertising (NY--New York); RTCdirect (DC--Washington); SBG Enterprises (CA--San Francisco); Simmons (NY--New York); Thomas G. Ferguson Associates (NJ--Parsippany); Timmons & Co. (DC--Washington); Walker Group/CNI Inc. (NY--New York); Winona Research (AZ--Phoenix); WPP Group U.S.A. (NY--New York)

Nonmonetary Support

Type: In-kind Services; Loaned Employees; Loaned Executives; Workplace Solicitation
Note: The company also provides nonmonetary support in the form of creative work/services.

J. Walter Thompson Co. Fund

Giving Contact

Donald Gammon, Secretary
466 Lexington Avenue
New York, NY 10017
Phone: (212)210-7000
Fax: (212)210-6852

Description

EIN: 136020644
Organization Type: Corporate Foundation
Giving Locations: nationally.
Grant Types: Employee Matching Gifts, General Support.
Note: Employee matching gift ratio: 1 to 1 to higher education, up to $2,500 annually.

Financial Summary

Total Giving: $94,324 (fiscal year ending November 30, 2001); $65,853 (fiscal 2000); $349,206 (fiscal 1999). **Note:** Contributes through corporate direct giving program and foundation.
Giving Analysis: Giving for fiscal 2001 includes: foundation ($94,324); fiscal 2000: foundation matching gifts ($20,633); foundation ($45,220); fiscal 1999: foundation scholarships ($14,720); foundation matching gifts ($29,806); foundation ($304,680);

Assets: $636,722 (fiscal 2001); $717,568 (fiscal 2000); $855,959 (fiscal 1999)
Gifts Received: $200,000 (fiscal 1996); $200,000 (fiscal 1994). Note: Contributions received from J. Walter Thompson.

Typical Recipients

Arts & Humanities: Arts Centers, Arts Festivals, Arts Funds, Ballet, Dance, Arts & Humanities-General, Historic Preservation, Libraries, Museums/Galleries, Music, Opera, Performing Arts, Theater
Civic & Public Affairs: African American Affairs, Botanical Gardens/Parks, Business/Free Enterprise, Economic Development, Civic & Public Affairs-General, Municipalities/Towns, Professional & Trade Associations, Public Policy, Safety, Women's Affairs
Education: Arts/Humanities Education, Business Education, Colleges & Universities, Education Funds, Education Reform, Engineering/Technological Education, Faculty Development, Education-General, International Exchange, Leadership Training, Medical Education, Minority Education, Private Education (Precollege), Public Education (Precollege), Social Sciences Education, Special Education, Student Aid
Environment: Environment-General, Resource Conservation
Health: Cancer, Clinics/Medical Centers, Diabetes, Health-General, Heart, Hospitals, Medical Rehabilitation, Medical Research, Single-Disease Health Associations, Speech & Hearing
International: Foreign Arts Organizations, International Organizations, International Relations, Trade
Religion: Jewish Causes, Religious Organizations
Science: Science Museums, Scientific Research
Social Services: At-Risk Youth, Community Centers, Community Service Organizations, Crime Prevention, Family Services, Food/Clothing Distribution, Recreation & Athletics, Scouts, Social Services-General, Substance Abuse, United Funds/United Ways, Youth Organizations

Application Procedures

Initial Contact: Submit a brief letter of inquiry.
Application Requirements: Include proof of tax-exempt status.
Deadlines: None.

Restrictions

Does not support individuals, religious organizations for sectarian purposes, or political or lobbying groups.

Corporate Officials

Christopher Jones: chief executive officer, director PRIM CORP EMPL chief executive officer: J. Walter Thompson Co.
Peter A. Schweitzer: president B Chicago, IL 1939. ED University of Michigan BA (1961); Western Michigan University MBA (1967). PRIM CORP EMPL president: J. Walter Thompson Co. NONPR AFFIL member: American Association Advertising Agencies.
Lewis J. Trencher: chief operating officer, director B 1952. ED New York Law School JD; New York University BS; New York University MBA. PRIM CORP EMPL chief operating officer, director: J. Walter Thompson Co.

Foundation Officials

Lewis J. Trencher: chairman, director (see above)

Grants Analysis

Disclosure Period: fiscal year ending November 30, 2001
Total Grants: $94,324
Number of Grants: 58
Average Grant: $1,216*
Highest Grant: $25,000
Lowest Grant: $25
Typical Range: $100 to $10,000
*Note: Average grant figure excludes highest grant.

Recent Grants

Note: Grants derived from fiscal 2001 Form 990.

General

25,000	Advertising Council, New York, NY
12,500	Consolidated Corporate Fund, New York, NY
10,000	Boys and Girls Club of America, Long Beach, CA
10,000	Duke University Libraries, Durham, NC
6,720	National Merit Scholarship Corporation, Evanston, IL
5,000	AAAA Foundation, Inc, New York, NY
2,500	Johns Hopkins University, Baltimore, MD
2,500	Mount Holyoke College, South Hadley, MA
2,500	St. Ignatius High School, Cleveland, OH
2,500	University of Michigan, Ann Arbor, MI -- LS&A Honors program

THOMAS THOMPSON TRUST

Giving Contact

William B. Tyler, Trustee
1 Financial Center
Boston, MA 02111
Phone: (617)951-1145

Description

Founded: 1869
EIN: 030179429
Organization Type: Private Foundation
Giving Locations: NY: Rhinebeck including surrounding area; VT: Brattleboro including surrounding area
Grant Types: Capital, Emergency, General Support, Matching, Project.

Donor Information

Founder: the late Thomas Thompson

Financial Summary

Total Giving: $866,345 (fiscal year ending May 31, 2001); $679,773 (fiscal 1999); $705,517 (fiscal 1998)
Assets: $17,726,342 (fiscal 2001); $7,967,809 (fiscal 1998); $13,829,192 (fiscal 1997)
Gifts Received: $500 (fiscal 1999)

Typical Recipients

Arts & Humanities: Arts Centers, Community Arts, Historic Preservation, History & Archaeology, Libraries, Museums/Galleries, Music, Performing Arts, Public Broadcasting
Civic & Public Affairs: Clubs, Community Foundations, Civic & Public Affairs-General, Housing, Municipalities/Towns, Safety, Urban & Community Affairs
Education: Arts/Humanities Education, Colleges & Universities, Education-General, International Exchange, Private Education (Precollege), Secondary Education (Public), Student Aid
Environment: Environment-General, Resource Conservation
Health: AIDS/HIV, Health Funds, Health Organizations, Hospitals, Long-Term Care, Mental Health, Nursing Services, Research/Studies Institutes
International: Foreign Educational Institutions
Religion: Religious Organizations, Religious Welfare
Social Services: At-Risk Youth, Camps, Child Welfare, Community Centers, Community Service Organizations, Counseling, Day Care, Domestic Violence, Family Planning, Homes, Recreation & Athletics, Senior Services, Shelters/Homelessness, United Funds/United Ways, Youth Organizations

Application Procedures

Initial Contact: Call foundation.
Application Requirements: Include a description of organization, amount requested, purpose of funds sought, recently audited financial statement, proof of tax-exempt status.
Deadlines: None.

Restrictions

Foundation does not support organizations that have been in operation for less than three consecutive years.

Additional Information

Trust(s): Rackmann, Sawyer & Brewster

Foundation Officials

Daniel W. Fawcett: trustee
Albert M. Fortier: trustee
William B. Tyler: trustee

Grants Analysis

Disclosure Period: fiscal year ending May 31, 2001
Total Grants: $866,345
Number of Grants: 38
Average Grant: $20,712*
Highest Grant: $100,000
Lowest Grant: $1,790
Typical Range: $1,000 to $50,000
*Note: Average grant figure excludes highest grant.

Recent Grants

Note: Grants derived from 2001 Form 990.

Library-Related

14,200	Brooks Memorial Library, Brattleboro, VT -- for Collection Improvement Program

General

100,000	NOH Foundation, Inc.
75,000	South Vermont Health Services Corporation, VT -- for 2nd installment of Diabetes Education Program
50,000	Bard College, Annandale-on-Hudson, NY -- for scholarship endowment
50,000	Marlboro College, Marlboro, VT -- for construction of new lecture hall
50,000	Marlboro College, Marlboro, VT
30,000	Brattleboro Mutual Aid Association, Brattleboro, VT -- for kitchen renovations
30,000	Louis August Jonas Foundation, Inc -- for Camp Rising Sun renovations
25,000	Rhinebeck Aerodrome Museum, Rhinebeck, NY -- for renovations
24,500	Rhinebeck Performing Arts Center, Rhinebeck, NY -- for RUST Program and Daytop Volunteers
20,295	Baptist Home, Abilene, TX -- for van

ANNA W. THORNTON AND ALEXANDER P. THORNTON CHARITABLE TRUST

Giving Contact

Rick Piersall
Care of Bank One Texas NA
PO Box 2050
Ft. Worth, TX 76113-2050
Phone: (817)884-4442

Description

Founded: 1997
EIN: 756496915
Organization Type: Private Foundation
Grant Types: General Support.

Financial Summary

Total Giving: $134,000 (fiscal year ending September 30, 2001); $139,502 (fiscal 2000); $213,500 (fiscal 1999)
Assets: $2,393,233 (fiscal 2001); $2,921,696 (fiscal 2000); $2,759,877 (fiscal 1999)

Typical Recipients

Arts & Humanities: History & Archaeology, Libraries
Civic & Public Affairs: Clubs, Hispanic Affairs
Education: Education-General, Student Aid
Health: Eyes/Blindness, Research/Studies Institutes
International: International Relief Efforts
Religion: Churches, Religious Welfare
Science: Science Museums
Social Services: Family Services, Homes, People with Disabilities, Social Services-General, YMCA/YWCA/YMHA/YWHA, Youth Organizations

Restrictions

The trust gives priority to organizations providing women's and children's services in Tarrant County.

Additional Information

Trust(s): Bank One Texas NA

Grants Analysis

Disclosure Period: fiscal year ending September 30, 2001
Total Grants: $134,000
Number of Grants: 28
Average Grant: $4,786
Highest Grant: $15,000
Lowest Grant: $1,000
Typical Range: $1,000 to $10,000

Recent Grants

Note: Grants derived from fiscal 2000 Form 990.

Library-Related

5,000	Fort Worth Public Library Foundation, Ft. Worth, TX

General

25,000	Spur Your Imagination
15,000	Camp Carter YMCA, Ft. Worth, TX
10,502	Texas Wesleyan University, Ft. Worth, TX
10,000	Historic Fort Worth, Ft. Worth, TX
5,000	Boys and Girls Clubs of Fort Worth, Ft. Worth, TX
5,000	Civitan International Research Center, Tuscaloosa, AL
5,000	Hall, The, Angleton, TX
5,000	Museum of Science and History, Ft. Worth, TX
5,000	St. Andrew's Episcopal Church, Ft. Worth, TX
5,000	Star Sponsorship Program, Inc., Ft. Worth, TX

THORNTON FOUNDATION

Giving Contact

Charles B. Thornton, Jr., President
523 W. 6th St., Suite 636
Los Angeles, CA 90014
Phone: (213)629-3867
Fax: (213)629-9201

Description

Founded: 1958
EIN: 956037178
Organization Type: Private Foundation
Giving Locations: CA; MA
Grant Types: General Support, Operating Expenses, Research.

Donor Information

Founder: the late Charles B. Thornton, Flora I. Thornton

Financial Summary

Total Giving: $925,500 (2001); $915,137 (2000); $820,000 (1999)
Assets: $24,981,068 (2001); $23,392,821 (2000); $17,994,236 (1999)
Gifts Received: $29,000 (2001); $7,800 (2000); $11,000 (1999). Note: In 1996, 2000, and 2001 contributions were received from Charles B. Thornton, Jr. In 1999, contributions were received from Charles B. Thorton ($6,000), and W. Laney Thompson ($5,000).

Typical Recipients

Arts & Humanities: Arts Centers, Historic Preservation, Libraries, Museums/Galleries, Music, Public Broadcasting
Civic & Public Affairs: Economic Development, Civic & Public Affairs-General, Municipalities/Towns, Urban & Community Affairs
Education: Afterschool/Enrichment Programs, Arts/Humanities Education, Business Education, Colleges & Universities, Education Reform, Education-General, Legal Education, Minority Education, Preschool Education, Private Education (Precollege), Public Education (Precollege), Science/Mathematics Education, Secondary Education (Private)
Environment: Wildlife Protection
Health: AIDS/HIV, Cancer, Children's Health/Hospitals, Clinics/Medical Centers, Emergency/Ambulance Services, Hospitals, Hospitals (University Affiliated), Medical Research, Research/Studies Institutes, Single-Disease Health Associations, Speech & Hearing
International: International Affairs, International Environmental Issues, International Peace & Security Issues, International Relief Efforts
Religion: Churches, Religion-General, Religious Organizations, Religious Welfare
Science: Science Museums, Scientific Centers & Institutes
Social Services: Community Centers, Day Care, People with Disabilities, Recreation & Athletics, Scouts, Youth Organizations

Application Procedures

Initial Contact: Send a brief letter of inquiry.
Application Requirements: Include a description of the program or project.
Deadlines: None.

Foundation Officials

Terry D. Chapin: secretary
Charles B. Thornton, Jr.: president
William Laney Thornton: vice president

Grants Analysis

Disclosure Period: calendar year ending 2001
Total Grants: $925,500
Number of Grants: 60
Average Grant: $9,258*
Highest Grant: $170,000
Typical Range: $1,000 to $20,000
*Note: Average grant figure excludes three highest grants ($370,000).

Recent Grants

Note: Grants derived from 2001 Form 990.

General

170,000	Greenbelt Alliance, San Francisco, CA
100,000	Harvard Westlake School, North Hollywood, CA
100,000	McLean Hospital, Belmont, MA
100,000	Stanford University, Stanford, CA
50,000	Harvard Business School, Boston, MA
50,000	Johns Hopkins Brady Center
40,000	Huntington, San Marino, CA
35,000	Diversity Alliance
25,000	California Pacific Medical Center, San Francisco, CA

25,000	Cate School, Carpinteria, CA

FLORA L. THORNTON FOUNDATION

Giving Contact

Edward A. Landry, Trustee
1 Wilshire Blvd., Suite 2400
Los Angeles, CA 90017-3321
Phone: (213)629-7657
Fax: (213)624-1376

Description

Founded: 1983
EIN: 953855595
Organization Type: Private Foundation
Grant Types: General Support.

Donor Information

Founder: Flora L. Thornton

Financial Summary

Total Giving: $1,401,050 (fiscal year ending November 30, 2001); $883,450 (fiscal 2000); $2,191,137 (fiscal 1999)
Giving Analysis: Giving for fiscal 2001 includes: foundation grants to United Way ($10,000); fiscal 2000: foundation grants to United Way ($10,000); fiscal 1999: foundation grants to United Way ($10,000);
Assets: $3,986,169 (fiscal 2001); $7,208,661 (fiscal 2000); $9,359,425 (fiscal 1999)
Gifts Received: $3,426,745 (fiscal 1998); $1,206,491 (fiscal 1996); $1,975,250 (fiscal 1994). Note: In fiscal 1996, contributions were received from Flora L. Thornton.

Typical Recipients

Arts & Humanities: Arts Institutes, Ethnic & Folk Arts, Arts & Humanities-General, Historic Preservation, History & Archaeology, Libraries, Museums/Galleries, Music, Opera, Public Broadcasting, Theater
Civic & Public Affairs: Community Foundations, Employment/Job Training, Civic & Public Affairs-General, Municipalities/Towns, Parades/Festivals, Public Policy, Urban & Community Affairs, Zoos/Aquariums
Education: Arts/Humanities Education, Colleges & Universities, Education Funds, Education Reform, Literacy, Medical Education, Private Education (Precollege), Public Education (Precollege), Secondary Education (Private), Secondary Education (Public), Student Aid
Health: Arthritis, Cancer, Children's Health/Hospitals, Emergency/Ambulance Services, Hospitals, Kidney, Medical Research, Multiple Sclerosis, Outpatient Health Care, Prenatal Health Issues
International: International Affairs
Religion: Churches, Jewish Causes, Religious Organizations
Science: Science Museums
Social Services: Child Welfare, Community Service Organizations, Food/Clothing Distribution, People with Disabilities, Scouts, Shelters/Homelessness, United Funds/United Ways, Volunteer Services, YMCA/YWCA/YMHA/YWHA, Youth Organizations

Application Procedures

Initial Contact: Send a brief letter of inquiry describing program or project.
Deadlines: None.

Foundation Officials

Glen P. McDaniel: trustee
Flora L. Thornton: trustee
William Laney Thornton: trustee

Grants Analysis

Disclosure Period: fiscal year ending November 30, 2001
Total Grants: $1,391,050*

Number of Grants: 45
Average Grant: $20,722*
Highest Grant: $250,000
Lowest Grant: $1,000
Typical Range: $5,000 to $40,000
*Note: Giving excludes United Way. Average grant figure excludes two highest grants ($500,000).

Recent Grants

Note: Grants derived from fiscal 2000 Form 990.

General

500,000	Pepperdine University, Malibu, CA -- education
50,000	National Multiple Sclerosis Society -- community improvement
25,000	Greater Los Angeles Zoo Association, Los Angeles, CA -- community improvement
25,000	KCET, Los Angeles, CA -- community improvement
25,000	Library Foundation of Los Angeles, Los Angeles, CA -- community improvement
25,000	Los Angeles Philharmonic Association, Los Angeles, CA -- community improvement
25,000	National Multiple Sclerosis Society -- community improvement
20,000	Music Academy of the West, Santa Barbara, CA -- community improvement
15,000	Pepperdine University, Malibu, CA -- education
10,000	Goodwill Industries of Southern California, Los Angeles, CA -- community improvement

TIMKEN FOUNDATION OF CANTON

Giving Contact

Don D. Dickes, Secretary & Treasurer
200 Market Ave, North, Suite 210
Canton, OH 44702-1437
Phone: (330)452-1144
Fax: (330)452-2306
E-mail: dickesd@timkenfoundation.org

Description

Founded: 1934
EIN: 346520254
Organization Type: Family Foundation
Giving Locations: OH: internationally; nationally; operating locations.
Grant Types: Capital, Challenge, Operating Expenses, Scholarship.

Financial Summary

Total Giving: $8,000,000 (fiscal year ending September 30, 2000 approx); $11,370,433 (fiscal 1999); $10,392,823 (fiscal 1998)
Giving Analysis: Giving for fiscal 1999 includes: foundation grants to United Way ($280,412) fiscal 1998: foundation grants to United Way ($101,000)
Assets: $180,000,000 (fiscal 2000 approx); $152,914,132 (fiscal 1999); $146,357,742 (fiscal 1998)

Typical Recipients

Arts & Humanities: Arts Centers, Arts Institutes, Historic Preservation, History & Archaeology, Libraries, Museums/Galleries, Theater
Civic & Public Affairs: African American Affairs, Botanical Gardens/Parks, Business/Free Enterprise, Chambers of Commerce, Clubs, Community Foundations, Economic Development, Employment/Job Training, Ethnic Organizations, Civic & Public Affairs-General, Housing, Minority Business, Municipalities/Towns, Parades/Festivals, Philanthropic Organizations, Urban & Community Affairs

Education: Afterschool/Enrichment Programs, Business Education, Colleges & Universities, Community & Junior Colleges, Education Funds, Education Reform, Engineering/Technological Education, Education-General, Medical Education, Minority Education, Preschool Education, Private Education (Precollege), Public Education (Precollege), Science/Mathematics Education, Special Education, Student Aid
Environment: Air/Water Quality, Environment-General, Resource Conservation
Health: Cancer, Clinics/Medical Centers, Emergency/Ambulance Services, Geriatric Health, Heart, Hospitals
International: Foreign Arts Organizations, Foreign Educational Institutions, International-General, Health Care/Hospitals, International Development, International Organizations, International Peace & Security Issues, International Relief Efforts, Missionary/Religious Activities
Religion: Ministries, Religious Organizations, Religious Welfare
Social Services: Animal Protection, At-Risk Youth, Camps, Child Welfare, Community Centers, Community Service Organizations, Crime Prevention, Day Care, Domestic Violence, Family Services, Food/Clothing Distribution, Recreation & Athletics, Scouts, Senior Services, Shelters/Homelessness, Social Services-General, Substance Abuse, United Funds/United Ways, YMCA/YWCA/YMHA/YWHA, Youth Organizations

Application Procedures

Initial Contact: Grant requests should be in writing.
Application Requirements: No specific form of application is required; however, the application must include proof of tax-exempt status under Internal Revenue Code 501(c)(3).
Deadlines: None.
Notes: Makes only capital grants. Does not make grants for operating funds.

Restrictions

The foundation only funds organizations located in areas where the Timken Company has manufacturing facilities.

Additional Information

The foundation is funded by members of the Timken family, who also operate the Timken Co. The company is not directly connected to the foundation.

Foundation Officials

Don D. Dickes: secretary, treasurer, trustee
William Robert Timken, Jr.: vice president, trustee B Canton, OH 1938. ED Stanford University BA (1960); Harvard University MBA (1962). PRIM CORP EMPL chairman, president, chief executive officer, director: Timken Co. CORP AFFIL director: Tejas Holdings LLC; chairman: Timken Latrobe Steel; director: Aeroquip-Vickers Inc.; director: Diebold Inc.

Grants Analysis

Disclosure Period: fiscal year ending September 30, 1999
Total Grants: $11,090,020*
Number of Grants: 103
Average Grant: $89,168*
Highest Grant: $1,994,850
Typical Range: $10,000 to $100,000
*Note: Giving excludes United Way. Average grant excludes highest grant.

Recent Grants

Note: Grants derived from fiscal 2001 Form 990.

General

2,835,675	Stark Education Partnership for Canton City School, Canton, OH -- Timken Learning Center
2,005,150	Case Western Reserve University, Cleveland, OH -- fund institute for enterprise engineering
427,000	Town Council of Sosnowiec, Sosnowiec Poland -- to purchase additional equipment for stroke department
400,000	Walsh University, Canton, OH -- university capital fund drive
375,000	Stark State College Foundation, Canton, OH -- to construct an Information Technology Building
334,192	Cleveland Clinic Foundation, Cleveland, OH -- building for Cleveland Clinic Eye Institute
300,000	Friends of Crawford Park District, Bucyrus, OH -- to construct nature center, office building and maintenance
279,588	United Way of Central Stark County, Canton, OH -- community capital campaign
221,676	Stark Education Partnership for Canton City School, Canton, OH -- fund drive
200,000	Kent State Stark Foundation, Canton, OH -- to renovate field house into a Learning Center

TINKER FOUNDATION

Giving Contact

Renate Rennie, President & Director
55 East 59th Street, 21st Fl.
New York, NY 10022
Phone: (212)421-6858
Fax: (212)223-3326
E-mail: tinker@tinker.org
Web: http://fdncenter.org/grantmaker/tinker

Description

Founded: 1959
EIN: 510175449
Organization Type: Specialized/Single Purpose Foundation
Giving Locations: internationally; nationally.
Grant Types: Conference/Seminar, Matching, Multiyear/Continuing Support, Project, Research, Seed Money.

Donor Information

Founder: Established in 1959 by Edward Larocque Tinker (1881-1968), a real estate investor in New York City. After his death in 1968, his estate was bequeathed to the foundation. He originally set up the foundation in memory of his wife, father, and grandfather. "His lifelong devotion to the Iberian tradition in the Old and New Worlds gave definition to the foundation's overall purpose."

Financial Summary

Total Giving: $3,430,445 (2001); $3,000,000 (2000 approx); $3,173,325 (1999)
Giving Analysis: Giving for 1999 includes: foundation matching gifts ($227,500)
Assets: $74,589,872 (2001); $79,516,460 (2000 approx); $79,078,596 (1999)

Typical Recipients

Arts & Humanities: Libraries
Civic & Public Affairs: Botanical Gardens/Parks, Civil Rights, Economic Development, Economic Policy, Ethnic Organizations, Civic & Public Affairs-General, Law & Justice, Nonprofit Management, Philanthropic Organizations, Public Policy, Safety, Urban & Community Affairs
Education: Business Education, Colleges & Universities, Economic Education, Education Funds, Environmental Education, International Exchange, International Studies, Legal Education, Minority Education, Science/Mathematics Education, Social Sciences Education

Environment: Air/Water Quality, Forestry, Environment-General, Resource Conservation

International: Foreign Arts Organizations, Foreign Educational Institutions, International-General, Health Care/Hospitals, Human Rights, International Affairs, International Affairs, International Development, International Environmental Issues, International Organizations, International Peace & Security Issues, International Relations, Missionary/Religious Activities, Trade

Science: Scientific Centers & Institutes

Social Services: Emergency Relief, Family Planning

Application Procedures

Initial Contact: Guidelines and forms for institutional grants are also available on the foundation's web site or by contacting the foundation. Field research grant application materials are available upon request. Telephone and e-mail inquiries are welcome.

Application Requirements: The proposal for an institutional grant should include a completed Proposal Cover Sheet; single-page description of the project including objectives, target audience, methodology, and plan for dissemination of results; full proposal providing more detail on the project's objectives and theoretical, practical and/or policy-related significance; a plan of work describing the activities to be undertaken, and any factors which could delay the plan or change the amount of time required to complete the project or alter the proposed budget; anticipated results; a plan for disseminating the results; description of plan to evaluate short -term and long-term impact of project; contact information for three individuals familiar with the proposed topic, but not directly involved with the project; an itemized project budget; an itemized budget for those expenses for which Tinker Foundation funding is sought; copy of IRS tax-exempt letter; copy of the organization's latest Federal/State Form 990 (U.S. organizations only); latest financial statement; qualifications of the project director and personnel, with curricula vitae attached; list of staff and directors; and historical overview of the applying institution. Two copies of the complete proposal, without binders, should be submitted.

Deadlines: Applications are considered semi-annually; March 1 for the summer meeting, September 1 for the winter meeting, and October 1 for field research grants.

Review Process: The board meets in June and December to review grant proposals.

Restrictions

The foundation will not consider institutional grant requests for annual fund raising appeals for such organizations as the Community Chest or United Way; individual research; funding related to health or medical issues; production costs for film, television or radio projects; funding for arts and humanities projects, including art museum collections and exhibits; endowments; construction or major equipment purchases; and general operating support.

Additional Information

The Foundation also has a field research grant competition open to recognized Centers or Institutes of Latin America or Iberian Studies with graduate doctoral programs at accredited United States universities. Contact Foundation for applications instructions. All applications must be submitted in English.

Publications: Annual Report; Application Guidelines

Foundation Officials

Raymond L. Brittenham: secretary B Moscow, Russia February 08, 1916. ED Principia College AB (1936); Kaiser Wilhelm University (1937); Harvard University LLB (1940).

William R. Chaney: director B Satanta, KS 1932. ED University of Kansas BA (1953). PRIM CORP EMPL chairman, chief executive officer: Tiffany & Co. CORP AFFIL director: Fifth Avenue Association; director: FAO Schwartz; director: Bank New York Co. Inc.

NONPR AFFIL member: Lambda Chi Alpha. CLUB AFFIL Advertising Sales Executives Club.

John A. Luke, Jr.: treasurer B New York, NY 1948. ED Lawrence University BA (1971); University of Pennsylvania Wharton School MBA (1979). PRIM CORP EMPL chairman, president, chief executive officer, director: Westvaco Corp. CORP AFFIL director: FM Global Insurance; director: Timken Co.; director: Arkwright Mutual Insurance Co.; director: Bank New York Co. Inc.; director: Arkwright Insurance Co. NONPR AFFIL board governors: NCASI; director: United Negro College Fund; trustee: Lawrence University; member: Council Foreign Relations; trustee: Institute Paper Science Technology; director: American Society; director: Council Americas; chairman: American Forest Foundation; member executive committee, director: American Forest & Paper Association. CLUB AFFIL University Club; Commonwealth Club; The Links Club.

Charles McCurdy Mathias, Jr.: director B Frederick, MD 1922. ED Haverford College BA (1944); Yale University (1943-1944); University of Maryland LLB (1949). PRIM CORP EMPL chairman: First American Bankshares. NONPR AFFIL visiting professor: Johns Hopkins University.

Martha Twitchell Muse: chairman B Dallas, TX 1926. ED Barnard College BA (1948); Columbia University MA (1955); Georgetown University DHL (1981). CORP AFFIL director: Bank New York Co. Inc.; director: Bank New York Audit & Examining Center; director: Bank New York Comm Reinvestment Accounting Center; director pension committee: ASARCO Inc. NONPR AFFIL vice chairman board directors: Spanish Institute; member: Woodrow Wilson Center International Scholars; director: New York Stock Exchange Inc.; member advisory council: Lusa-American Development Foundation; member: National Society Colonial Dames; member: Huguenot Society; member: International Executive Service Corps; member, board visitors: Georgetown University Edmund A Walsh School Foreign Service; trustee emeritus: Columbia University; director: Council Americas; member, board directors: American Portuguese Society; member, board directors: American Society Inc.; member, board directors: American Foundation; member, board directors: American Council Germany. CLUB AFFIL Colony Club; Metro Club.

Renate Rennie: president

Susan L. Segal: director

Grants Analysis

Disclosure Period: calendar year ending 2001
Total Grants: $3,430,445
Number of Grants: 79*
Average Grant: $43,423*
Highest Grant: $150,000
Typical Range: $20,000 to $75,000
*Note: Number of grants and average grant exclude miscellaneous smaller grants totaling $55,695.

Recent Grants

Note: Grants derived from 2001 Form 990.

General

150,000	Centro de Estudios Publicos, Santiago Chile -- for the Laboratory of Glaciology, Environment and Climate Change Studies
132,000	Universidad de la Republica de Uruguay Zelmar Michelini Uruguay -- Mercosur and the creation of the Free Trade Area
125,000	Manhattan Institute for Policy Research, New York, NY -- support for the Inter-American Policy Exchange
107,000	Fundacion Internacional para la Promocion del Desamollo Sustentable Futuro Latinoamericano, Quito Ecuador -- fostering a proactive Agenda on Trade and Environment in South America
100,000	ACCION International, Somerville, MA --

	improvement of Regulation and Supervision of Microfinance in Latin America
80,000	Council on Foreign Relations, New York, NY -- for public programs on an agenda for the hemisphere
77,000	Instituto Mexicano de Investigacion de Familia Poblacion, Mexico City, DF Mexico -- development of policy recommendations regarding decentralization in the education, health and social development sectors in Mexico
75,000	Environmental Defense Fund, New York, NY -- advancing the Antarctic site inventory information dissemination and directed research
75,000	Harvard University, Cambridge, MA -- for project on philanthropy in Latin America
66,000	Asociacion Civil Centro de Estudios, Buenos Aires Argentina -- civilian oversight of law enforcement

TISCORNIA FOUNDATION

Giving Contact

Laurianne T. Davis, President
1010 Main St., Suite A
St. Joseph, MI 49085
Phone: (616)983-4711
Fax: (616)983-6959

Description

Founded: 1942
EIN: 381777343
Organization Type: Private Foundation
Giving Locations: MI
Grant Types: Capital, Emergency, General Support, Multiyear/Continuing Support, Scholarship, Seed Money.

Donor Information

Founder: the late James W. Tiscornia, the late Waldo V. Tiscornia, Auto Specialties Manufacturing Co., Lambert Brake Corp.

Financial Summary

Total Giving: $349,990 (2000); $311,900 (1998); $205,438 (1996). Note: In 1996, Giving includes scholarship ($46,500).
Giving Analysis: Giving for 2000 includes: foundation grants to United Way ($15,000); foundation scholarships ($70,000); 1998: foundation grants to United Way ($15,000) foundation scholarships ($56,000)
Assets: $4,691,882 (2000); $5,275,838 (1998); $4,779,619 (1996)

Typical Recipients

Arts & Humanities: Arts Associations & Councils, Arts Centers, Arts & Humanities-General, History & Archaeology, Libraries, Literary Arts, Museums/Galleries, Music

Civic & Public Affairs: Economic Policy, Civic & Public Affairs-General, Municipalities/Towns, Parades/Festivals, Urban & Community Affairs

Education: Business Education, Colleges & Universities, Education Funds, Education-General, Literacy, Minority Education, Student Aid

Environment: Environment-General

Health: AIDS/HIV, Cancer, Children's Health/Hospitals, Clinics/Medical Centers, Diabetes, Emergency/Ambulance Services, Health Funds, Health Organizations, Hospices, Prenatal Health Issues, Public Health

Religion: Churches, Ministries, Religious Welfare

Social Services: Camps, Child Welfare, Community Centers, Community Service Organizations, Counseling, Family Planning, Family Services, Food/Clothing Distribution, Recreation & Athletics, Scouts, Shelters/Homelessness, Social Services-General, United

Funds/United Ways, Veterans, Volunteer Services, YMCA/YWCA/YMHA/YWHA, Youth Organizations

Application Procedures

Initial Contact: Send a brief letter of inquiry.
Application Requirements: outline of programs and purpose of funds sought.
Deadlines: April 1 for scholarships; October 1 for general grants.

Restrictions

Does not support individuals (except for employee-related scholarships).

Additional Information

Provides scholarships to Northern Berrien County high school students.

Foundation Officials

Laurianne T. Davis: president
Albert Dexel: assistant secretary, assistant treasurer
Henry H. Tippett: secretary, treasurer
Bernice Tiscornia: first vice president
James Tiscornia: second vice president
Lester C. Tiscornia: president, trustee ED College of the Pacific AB (1932); Andrews University LLD (1971). PRIM CORP EMPL chairman, director: Auto Specialties Manufacturing Co. CORP AFFIL director: Peoples State Bank. NONPR AFFIL member advisory board Twin Cities chapter: Salvation Army; member: Society Automotive Engineers; president: Saint Joseph Community Chest.

Grants Analysis

Disclosure Period: calendar year ending 2000
Total Grants: $264,990*
Number of Grants: 21
Average Grant: $8,250*
Highest Grant: $100,000
Typical Range: $1,000 to $15,000
*Note: Giving excludes scholarships and United Way. Average grant figure excludes highest grant.

Recent Grants

Note: Grants derived from 1999 Form 990.

General

31,450	Cornerstone Alliance, Benton Harbor, MI -- community welfare
25,500	Salvation Army, Benton Harbor, MI -- community welfare
25,000	M. Preston Palenske Library, Joseph, MI -- community welfare
21,000	Southwestern Symphony, St. Joseph, MI -- community welfare
20,000	Berrien Artists Guild, St. Joseph, MI -- community welfare
20,000	YMCA, St. Joseph, MI -- community welfare
17,500	Planned Parenthood Association of Southwestern Michigan, Benton Harbor, MI -- community welfare
15,800	WCA, St. Joseph, MI -- community welfare
15,000	Michigan Colleges Foundation, Inc., Southfield, MI -- education
15,000	United Way, Benton Harbor, MI -- community welfare

C. W. TITUS FOUNDATION

Giving Contact

Timothy T. Reynolds, Trustee
1801 Philtower Bldg.
Tulsa, OK 74103
Phone: (918)582-8095

Description

Founded: 1968
EIN: 237016981
Organization Type: Private Foundation
Giving Locations: MO; OK
Grant Types: General Support, Project, Research.

Financial Summary

Total Giving: $927,937 (2000); $1,006,917 (1999); $846,467 (1998)
Assets: $24,861,104 (2000); $22,902,276 (1999); $23,116,040 (1998)

Typical Recipients

Arts & Humanities: Arts Centers, Ballet, Dance, Historic Preservation, History & Archaeology, Libraries, Museums/Galleries, Music, Opera, Performing Arts, Public Broadcasting
Civic & Public Affairs: Economic Development, Civic & Public Affairs-General, Professional & Trade Associations, Public Policy, Urban & Community Affairs, Zoos/Aquariums
Education: Arts/Humanities Education, Colleges & Universities, Education-General, International Studies, Preschool Education, Private Education (Precollege), Public Education (Precollege), Secondary Education (Public)
Health: Alzheimers Disease, Cancer, Children's Health/Hospitals, Clinics/Medical Centers, Diabetes, Emergency/Ambulance Services, Health Organizations, Heart, Hospices, Hospitals, Medical Research, Prenatal Health Issues, Respiratory, Single-Disease Health Associations, Speech & Hearing
Religion: Religious Welfare
Social Services: Animal Protection, Community Service Organizations, Crime Prevention, Domestic Violence, Family Planning, Family Services, Food/Clothing Distribution, Homes, People with Disabilities, Scouts, Senior Services, Sexual Abuse, Substance Abuse, United Funds/United Ways, Volunteer Services, YMCA/YWCA/YMHA/YWHA, Youth Organizations

Application Procedures

Initial Contact: The foundation has no formal grant application procedure or application form.
Deadlines: None.

Foundation Officials

Timothy T. Reynolds: trustee

Grants Analysis

Disclosure Period: calendar year ending 2000
Total Grants: $927,937
Number of Grants: 80
Average Grant: $7,409*
Highest Grant: $200,000
Typical Range: $1,000 to $15,000
*Note: Average grant figure excludes two highest grants ($350,000).

Recent Grants

Note: Grants derived from 2001 Form 990.

Library-Related

80,000	Webb City Library, Webb City, MO -- for children's library

General

200,000	Ozark Public Television, Springfield, MO -- for digital master control
50,000	Development Center of the Ozarks, Springfield, MO -- for budgeted operations
50,000	Kitchen, Springfield, MO -- for budgeted operations
50,000	St. John Medical Center Foundation, Tulsa, OK -- for restorative care unit
20,000	Children's Mercy Hospital, Kansas City, MO -- cancer center
15,000	University Child Care Center, Springfield, MO -- for budgeted operations
10,000	Community Clinic of Joplin, Joplin, MO -- for budgeted operations
10,000	Ronald McDonald House, Tulsa, OK -- for budgeted operations
10,000	Southwest Missouri Chapter of Alzheimer's, Springfield, MO -- for budgeted operations
10,000	Thomas Gilcrease Museum Association, Tulsa, OK -- for budgeted operations

TJX COMPANIES, INC.

Company Headquarters

Framingham, MA
Web: http://www.tjx.com

Company Description

Founded: 1962
Ticker: TJX
Exchange: NYSE
Revenue: US$11.981 billion (2002)
Profit: US$578.4 million (2002)
Employees: 77000 (2002)
Fortune Rank: 161, per FORTUNE Magazine's list of 500 Largest U.S. Corporations (2002).
SIC(s): 5699 Miscellaneous Apparel & Accessory Stores.

Operating Locations

TJX Companies, Inc. (DC; FL--Miami, Tampa; GA--Forest Park; MA--Framingham, Mansfield, Natick, Stoughton; NY--New York)

Nonmonetary Support

Range: $150,000 - $500,000
Type: Cause-related Marketing & Promotion; Donated Equipment; Donated Products; In-kind Services; Workplace Solicitation

TJX Foundation, Inc.

Giving Contact

Christine Strickland, Foundation Manager
770 Cochituate Road, Route J5S
Framingham, MA 01701
Phone: (508)390-3199
Fax: (508)390-2091
E-mail: christy_strickland@tjx.com
Web: http://www.tjmaxx.com

Alternate Contact

Phone: (508)380-2300

Description

EIN: 042399760
Organization Type: Corporate Foundation
Giving Locations: MA: Boston principally near operating locations and to national organizations.
Grant Types: Award, Capital, Challenge, Endowment, General Support, Operating Expenses, Project, Scholarship.

Financial Summary

Total Giving: $2,675,456 (fiscal year ending January 31, 2001); $2,016,177 (fiscal 2000); $1,506,005 (fiscal 1999). Note: Contributes through corporate direct giving program and foundation.
Giving Analysis: Giving for fiscal 2001 includes: foundation grants to United Way ($48,700); foundation ($2,626,756); fiscal 2000: foundation ($2,016,177); fiscal 1999: foundation grants to United Way ($7,000); foundation scholarships ($37,000) foundation ($1,462,005)
Assets: $14,450,988 (fiscal 2001); $16,187,412 (fiscal 2000); $455,912 (fiscal 1998)
Gifts Received: $17,261,354 (fiscal 1999); $17,261,354 (fiscal 1998); $1,000,000 (fiscal 1997).

Note: Contributions received from TJX Companies, Inc.

Typical Recipients

Arts & Humanities: Arts Associations & Councils, Arts Centers, Arts Funds, Arts Institutes, Community Arts, Dance, Arts & Humanities-General, Historic Preservation, History & Archaeology, Libraries, Museums/Galleries, Performing Arts, Public Broadcasting, Theater

Civic & Public Affairs: African American Affairs, Asian American Affairs, Business/Free Enterprise, Civil Rights, Community Foundations, Employment/Job Training, Civic & Public Affairs-General, Hispanic Affairs, Housing, Law & Justice, Municipalities/Towns, Philanthropic Organizations, Public Policy, Urban & Community Affairs, Women's Affairs

Education: Afterschool/Enrichment Programs, Arts/Humanities Education, Business Education, Colleges & Universities, Education Associations, Education Funds, Elementary Education (Private), Education-General, Legal Education, Medical Education, Minority Education, Private Education (Precollege), Public Education (Precollege), Religious Education, Special Education, Student Aid

Health: AIDS/HIV, Cancer, Children's Health/Hospitals, Clinics/Medical Centers, Diabetes, Emergency/Ambulance Services, Health-General, Health Organizations, Heart, Hospices, Hospitals, Medical Rehabilitation, Medical Research, Mental Health, Nursing Services, Prenatal Health Issues, Public Health, Single-Disease Health Associations

International: Human Rights, International Relief Efforts

Religion: Jewish Causes, Ministries, Religious Welfare, Religious Welfare

Science: Scientific Centers & Institutes

Social Services: Big Brother/Big Sister, Camps, Child Abuse, Child Welfare, Community Centers, Community Service Organizations, Counseling, Crime Prevention, Domestic Violence, Family Services, Food/Clothing Distribution, Homes, People with Disabilities, Recreation & Athletics, Scouts, Shelters/Homelessness, Social Services-General, Special Olympics, Substance Abuse, United Funds/United Ways, Volunteer Services, Youth Organizations

Application Procedures

Initial Contact: Submit requests in writing.

Application Requirements: In three to five pages, include a description of the organization, its purpose, and the year the organization was founded (no more than 2 paragraphs); objective of grant and its target group; a detailed description of the program's (not the organization's) target audience (including age range, number of people, ethnic backgrounds, etc.); evidence of need for such program and organization's experience with similar problems; method of evaluation; and outline of alternative plan if all necessary funds are not raised. Supporting materials that must be included with the proposal are: program budget and amount requested; proof of tax-exempt status; current audited financial report and statement of functional expenses; current operating budget; list of board of directors, and a list of contributors and amounts received in last fiscal year.

Deadlines: None. For consideration at a specific committee meeting, proposals should be submitted four weeks prior to the meeting (applicants may call to inquire about the cut-off date). Time-sensitive corporate contributions requests must be submitted at least three months prior to the date that funds are needed.

Review Process: The TJX Foundation Allocation Committee considers grant proposals and corporate contributions requests.

Evaluative Criteria: Program within targeted areas of interest.

Decision Notification: Committee meets approximate every other month to consider proposals; decisions are made within 60 to 90 days of receiving proposal.

Notes: Contributions will conform to the following guidelines: education, to programs that benefit children of preschool age through college; social services, to families and children, including the family unit, single-parent families, domestic violence, and physically impaired; health, to organizations providing health care to underserved populations, including prenatal, immunizations and health screenings, preventative care, and alternatives to hospitalization; civic, to programs that improve race relations, community development, and housing; and art/culture, to bring art to new audiences, and encourage people to express themselves through art.

Restrictions

TJX generally will not support individuals, political groups, religious organizations for sectarian purposes, public policy research projects or advocacy, conferences/seminars, publications, international organizations, travel, cash reserves, environmental issues, unrestricted grants, seed money, education loans, fellowships, endowments, capital/renovation campaigns, salary requests, programs in operation for less than 12 months, training money, films or photography, new construction, conventions, consultant fees, other giving organizations, offenders, ex-offenders, scholarly research, endowed scholarships, corrections, daycare, federated drives, legal aid, information and referral, long-term care, multi service, recreation, consumer education, family planning, health planning, occupational safety, public health education, business development, community organizing, consumer education, leadership development, tenant rights, voter education, transportation, housing expense reduction, architecture/design, arts service organization, dance, historic preservation, and visual arts. Our charitable contributions will be directed toward those priority or targeted markets in which The TJX Companies, Inc.'s stores, home office and distribution centers are located. Since the Company Headquarters is in the greater Boston area, a larger proportion of the Company's contributions will focus on organizations that favor the Greater Boston and Metro West communities.

Additional Information

TJX Foundation had been known as the Zayre Foundation until fiscal year 1989.

The TJX Companies, Inc. consists of four operating divisions: The Marmaxx Group (T.J. Maxx and Marshalls), Winners, HomeGoods and T.K. Maxx (in Europe).

Corporate Officials

Bernard Cammarata: chairman, chief executive officer B Brooklyn, NY 1940. PRIM CORP EMPL chairman: TJX Companies, Inc.

Donald G. Campbell: executive vice president, chief financial officer B 1951. PRIM CORP EMPL executive vice president, chief financial officer: TJX Companies, Inc.

Edmond J. English: president, chief executive officer PRIM CORP EMPL president, chief executive officer: TJX Companies Inc.

Sherry Lang: vice president & director investor relations PRIM CORP EMPL vice president & director investor relations: TJX Companies, Inc.

Richard G. Lesser: executive vice president, chief operating officer, director B Boston, MA 1935. ED Northeastern University BS. PRIM CORP EMPL executive vice president, chief operating officer, director: TJX Companies, Inc. CORP AFFIL president, chief executive officer: Marshall's Inc.; director: Reebok International Ltd.; president, director: Marmaxx Group.

Virginia Nelson: corporate communications manager PRIM CORP EMPL corporate communications manager: TJX Companies, Inc.

Foundation Officials

Donald G. Campbell: treasurer, director (see above)
Sherry Lang: director (see above)
Richard G. Lesser: chief operating officer, director (see above)

Grants Analysis

Disclosure Period: fiscal year ending January 31, 2001
Total Grants: $2,626,756*
Number of Grants: 425
Average Grant: $6,181
Highest Grant: $163,440
Typical Range: $1,000 to $10,000
***Note:** Giving excludes United Way; scholarships; matching gifts.

Recent Grants

Note: Grants derived from 2001 Form 990.

Library-Related
10,000	Morse Institute Library, Natick, MA

General
163,400	Save the Children Federation, Dallas, TX
100,000	Family Violence Prevention Fund, San Francisco, CA
100,000	Special Olympics, Worcester, MA
100,000	Welfare to Work Partnership, Washington, DC
40,000	Untied Way of Tri-County, Framingham, MA
30,000	American Red Cross, Boston, MA
25,000	American Red Cross, Boston, MA
25,000	Beth Israel Deaconess Medical Center, Boston, MA
25,000	Brandeis University, Waltham, MA
25,000	Combined Jewish Philanthropies, Boston, MA

TMC INVESTMENT CO.

Company Headquarters
Pittsburgh, PA
Web: http://www.tippins.com

Company Description
Parent Company: Tippins, Inc., 435 Butler St., Pittsburgh, PA, United States

Tippins Foundation

Giving Contact
George W. Tippins, Trustee
1090 Freeport Road
Pittsburgh, PA 15238
Phone: (412)784-8804
Fax: (412)782-7210

Description
EIN: 256282382
Organization Type: Corporate Foundation
Giving Locations: PA
Grant Types: General Support.

Financial Summary
Total Giving: $511,840 (2001); $484,340 (2000); $250,640 (1998). Note: Contributes through foundation only.
Giving Analysis: Giving for 2000 includes: foundation scholarships ($10,000); foundation ($474,340); 1998: foundation ($250,640); 1997: foundation grants to United Way ($15,000); foundation ($295,450);
Assets: $1,740,864 (2001); $2,186,730 (2000); $37,722 (1998)
Gifts Received: $250,000 (2001); $1,985,229 (2000); $250,000 (1998). Note: Contributions are received from TMC Investment Co.

Typical Recipients

Arts & Humanities: Arts Associations & Councils, Ballet, Film & Video, History & Archaeology, Libraries, Museums/Galleries, Music, Opera, Public Broadcasting, Theater

Civic & Public Affairs: Botanical Gardens/Parks, Community Foundations, Economic Development, Civic & Public Affairs-General, Law & Justice, Municipalities/Towns, Public Policy, Safety, Urban & Community Affairs, Women's Affairs, Zoos/Aquariums

Education: Business Education, Colleges & Universities, Economic Education, Education Funds, Engineering/Technological Education, Education-General, Minority Education, Private Education (Precollege), Special Education

Environment: Air/Water Quality, Environment-General, Watershed

Health: Alzheimers Disease, Alzheimers Disease, Arthritis, Cancer, Children's Health/Hospitals, Clinics/Medical Centers, Diabetes, Emergency/Ambulance Services, Health-General, Health Organizations, Heart, Hospitals, Kidney, Medical Rehabilitation, Public Health, Respiratory, Single-Disease Health Associations

International: International Relief Efforts

Religion: Churches, Ministries, Religious Welfare

Social Services: Animal Protection, Big Brother/Big Sister, Child Welfare, Community Service Organizations, Counseling, Delinquency & Criminal Rehabilitation, Emergency Relief, Family Services, People with Disabilities, Recreation & Athletics, Scouts, Shelters/Homelessness, Social Services-General, United Funds/United Ways, YMCA/YWCA/YMHA/YWHA

Application Procedures

Initial Contact: Send a written request.

Application Requirements: Include a description of organization, purpose of funds sought, amount requested, proof of tax-exempt status.

Deadlines: None.

Foundation Officials

Charles J. Queenan, Jr.: trustee PRIM CORP EMPL senior counsel: Kirkpatrick & Lockhart. CORP AFFIL director: Crane Co.; director: Allegheny Teledyne Inc.; director: Babcock Lumber Co. NONPR AFFIL director: Allegheny-Singer Research Institute.

Carolyn H. Tippins: trustee

George W. Tippins: trustee

Grants Analysis

Disclosure Period: calendar year ending 2001

Total Grants: $511,840

Number of Grants: 75

Average Grant: $6,825

Highest Grant: $50,000

Lowest Grant: $500

Typical Range: $500 to $20,000

Recent Grants

Note: Grants derived from 2001 Form 990.

General

50,000	Alzheimer's Association, Chicago, IL
50,000	Genetics and Aging Unit, Charlestown, MA -- Massachusetts General Hospital
50,000	University of Pittsburgh Joseph Katz School of Business, Pittsburgh, PA
25,000	Alzheimer's Disease Research Center, Philadelphia, PA
25,000	Carnegie Mellon University, Pittsburgh, PA -- entrepreneurial assistant
25,000	Salvation Army, Pittsburgh, PA
20,000	Children's Hospital of Pittsburgh, Pittsburgh, PA
15,000	American Cancer Society, Pittsburgh, PA
15,000	American Heart Association, Pittsburgh, PA
15,000	Institute for Entrepreneurial Excellence, Pittsburgh, PA

RANDALL L. TOBIAS FOUNDATION

Giving Contact

Suzanne Hazelett, Executive Director
500 E. 96th Street, Suite 110
Indianapolis, IN 46240
Phone: (317)433-5505
Fax: (317)433-5504
E-mail: snh@rltfound.org
Web: http://www.rltfound.org

Description

Founded: 1995
EIN: 351938355
Organization Type: Private Foundation
Grant Types: General Support, Scholarship.

Donor Information

Founder: Foundation was established in 1994 by Randall L. Tobias.

Financial Summary

Total Giving: $1,196,504 (2001); $1,651,679 (2000); $1,493,000 (1999)

Giving Analysis: Giving for 2001 includes: foundation gifts to individuals ($165,000); foundation grants to United Way ($250,000); 2000: foundation grants to United Way ($250,000) foundation scholarships ($250,000)

Assets: $9,138,439 (2001); $11,238,438 (2000); $13,471,600 (1999)

Gifts Received: $60,965 (2001); $1,031,754 (1999); $7,503,130 (1998). Note: In 1996, 1998, 1999, and 2001, contributions were received from Randall L. Tobias.

Typical Recipients

Arts & Humanities: Arts Outreach, Historic Preservation, History & Archaeology, Libraries, Music, Public Broadcasting

Civic & Public Affairs: Botanical Gardens/Parks, Public Policy

Education: Business Education, Colleges & Universities, Education Reform, Elementary Education (Public), Education-General, Literacy

Religion: Churches

Social Services: Day Care, Recreation & Athletics, United Funds/United Ways, Youth Organizations

Application Procedures

Initial Contact: Request application guidelines, then send full proposal.

Application Requirements: Completed applications will include a cover sheet with date of application, amount requested, name of organization, contact person and information, EIN, and signature of responsible officer of the organization. A proposal narrative of two to five pages should include purpose of funds sought; what needs will be met by the project and who it will serve; why organization is the appropriate group to meet these needs; plan for continuing project after foundation funding ceases; other funders involved; and expected outcomes. Also attach annual report, most recent financial statement, proposed budget, list of board of directors, and proof of tax-exempt status.

Deadlines: March 1 and September 1.

Decision Notification: Grant awards are announced in the second and fourth quarters. Applicants will be contacted by mail within four weeks of the grant selection process.

Restrictions

Does not support endowment campaigns; fundraising events; federal, state, or local governmental bodies, or political candidates; individuals; or other private foundations.

Additional Information

Provides scholarships to residents of IN who need financial assistance to enable them to attend undergraduate institutions in the U.S.

Publications: Application Guidelines

Foundation Officials

Susie Hazelett: executive director

Randall L. Tobias: president, treasurer B Lafayette, IN 1942. ED Indiana University BS (1964). CORP AFFIL director: Phillips Petroleum Co.; director: Knight-Ridder Inc.; director: Northwest Publications Inc.; director: Kimberly-Clark Corp. NONPR AFFIL director: Indianapolis Symphony Orchestra; member: Theta Chi; board governors: Indianapolis Museum Art; director: Indiana University Foundation; member: Indianapolis Corp. Community Council; vice chairman: Colonial Williamsburg Foundation; trustee: Duke University; member: Business Council; member: Amwell Valley Conservancy. CLUB AFFIL University Club; Woodstock Club; Economic Club Indianapolis; Meridian Hills Country Club; Athletic Club; Columbia Club.

Todd C. Tobias: vice president

Paige N. Tobias-Button: vice president, secretary

Grants Analysis

Disclosure Period: calendar year ending 2001

Total Grants: $781,504*

Number of Grants: 40

Average Grant: $6,191*

Highest Grant: $177,000

Lowest Grant: $15

Typical Range: $1,000 to $10,000

*Note: Giving excludes scholarships, grants to individuals, and United Way. Average grant figure excludes three highest grants

Recent Grants

Note: Grants derived from 2000 Form 990.

Library-Related

250,000	Indiana University Foundation, Bloomington, IN
150,000	Indiana University Foundation, Bloomington, IN

General

333,000	Indiana Sports Corporation, Indy, IN
250,000	United Way Central Indiana, Indianapolis, IN
100,000	Colonial Williamsburg Foundation, Williamsburg, VA
100,000	Educational Choice Charitable Trust, Indianapolis, IN
68,598	Oaks Academy, The, Indianapolis, IN
25,000	Child Family School Enrichment Centers, Indy, IN
25,000	Junior Achievement, Indy, IN
21,500	Indy Reads, Indy, IN
20,000	Bicycle Action, Indianapolis, IN
20,000	Nora Elementary School, Indy, IN

A.M. TODD CO.

Company Headquarters

1717 Douglas Ave.
Kalamazoo, MI 49007
Phone: (616)343-2603

Company Description

Revenue: US$ (2001)
Employees: 100 (2001)
SIC(s): 2000 Food & Kindred Products, 2800 Chemicals & Allied Products.

Operating Locations

A.M. Todd Co. (MI--Kalamazoo)

A.M. Todd Co. Foundation

Giving Contact

Nancy Grabiak, Vice President & Trust Officer
c/o Old Kent Bank & Trust Co.
136 East Michigan Avenue
PO Box 4019
Kalamazoo, MI 49007
Phone: (616)337-6768
Fax: (616)337-6651

Description

EIN: 386055829
Organization Type: Corporate Foundation
Giving Locations: MI: Kalamazoo County
Grant Types: General Support.

Financial Summary

Total Giving: $94,880 (2000); $98,515 (1999); $91,850 (1998)
Giving Analysis: Giving for 2000 includes: foundation grants to United Way ($17,500); 1999: foundation grants to United Way ($16,875) foundation ($81,640)
Assets: $427,730 (2000); $421,509 (1999); $424,377 (1998)
Gifts Received: $100,000 (2000); $100,000 (1999); $100,000 (1998)

Typical Recipients

Arts & Humanities: Arts Associations & Councils, Arts Festivals, Arts Funds, Arts Institutes, Community Arts, Arts & Humanities-General, Historic Preservation, History & Archaeology, Libraries, Museums/Galleries, Music, Performing Arts, Public Broadcasting
Civic & Public Affairs: Botanical Gardens/Parks, Business/Free Enterprise, Clubs, Economic Development, Civic & Public Affairs-General, Housing, Municipalities/Towns, Parades/Festivals, Urban & Community Affairs, Zoos/Aquariums
Education: Agricultural Education, Business Education, Colleges & Universities, Community & Junior Colleges, Education Associations, Education Reform, Education-General, Science/Mathematics Education, Special Education, Student Aid, Vocational & Technical Education
Environment: Environment-General, Resource Conservation
Health: Cancer, Clinics/Medical Centers, Diabetes, Emergency/Ambulance Services, Health Organizations, Hospices, Prenatal Health Issues, Public Health
International: Foreign Arts Organizations
Religion: Churches, Ministries, Religious Welfare
Science: Scientific Centers & Institutes
Social Services: Big Brother/Big Sister, Camps, Child Welfare, Community Service Organizations, Family Planning, Family Services, Food/Clothing Distribution, People with Disabilities, Scouts, Senior Services, Substance Abuse, United Funds/United Ways, YMCA/YWCA/YMHA/YWHA, Youth Organizations

Application Procedures

Initial Contact: Send a brief letter of inquiry. Include proof of tax-exempt status.
Deadlines: None.

Restrictions

Does not support individuals, religious organizations for sectarian purposes, political or lobbying groups, or organizations outside operating areas.

Additional Information

Education support is primarily provided directly by A.M. Todd Co., not the foundation.
Trust(s): Old Kent Bank

Corporate Officials

Thomas F. Rose: vice president, chief financial officer, chief executive officer PRIM CORP EMPL vice president, chief financial officer: AM Todd Co.
A. J. Todd, III: chairman, president, chief executive officer PRIM CORP EMPL chairman, president, chief executive officer: AM Todd Co.

Foundation Officials

Ian D. Blair: trustee PRIM CORP EMPL vice president trading: AM Todd Co.
A. J. Todd, III: trustee (see above)

Grants Analysis

Disclosure Period: calendar year ending 2000
Total Grants: $77,380*
Number of Grants: 35
Average Grant: $2,211
Highest Grant: $15,020
Typical Range: $500 to $5,000
***Note:** Giving excludes United Way.

Recent Grants

Note: Grants derived from 2001 Form 990.

General

21,500	Kalamazoo Foundation, Kalamazoo, MI
19,250	Greater Kalamazoo United Way, Kalamazoo, MI
10,000	Lakeside Treatment and Learning Center, Kalamazoo, MI
6,500	Ministry With Community, Kalamazoo, MI
5,000	Boys and Girls Clubs, Kalamazoo, MI
5,000	Kalamazoo Neighborhood Housing Services, Kalamazoo, MI
5,000	Parks Foundation of Kalamazoo County, Kalamazoo, MI
3,000	Heritage Community of Kalamazoo, Kalamazoo, MI
1,500	Junior Achievement of Kalamazoo, Kalamazoo, MI
1,250	Kalamazoo Symphony, Kalamazoo, MI

TOLEDO BLADE CO.

Company Headquarters

541 N. Superior St.
Toledo, OH 43604
Web: http://www.toledoblank.com

Company Description

Employees: 600
SIC(s): 2711 Newspapers.
Parent Company: Block Communications, Inc., 541 N. Superior St., Toledo, OH, United States

Nonmonetary Support

Volunteer Programs: Company actively promotes employee volunteerism through participation in the United Way, Read for Literacy, and in activities with the Sherman School, its adopted school.

Blade Foundation

Giving Contact

William Block, Jr., President
Blade Foundation
541 N. Superior Street
Toledo, OH 43604
Phone: (419)245-6210

Description

EIN: 346559843
Organization Type: Corporate Foundation
Giving Locations: OH: Toledo
Grant Types: General Support, Scholarship.

Financial Summary

Total Giving: $272,939 (2001); $273,129 (2000); $257,299 (1999)
Giving Analysis: Giving for 2000 includes: foundation scholarships ($9,000); foundation grants to United Way ($65,000); foundation ($199,129); 1999: foundation scholarships ($9,000); foundation grants to United Way ($60,000); foundation ($188,299); 1998: corporate scholarships ($7,500); corporate grants to United Way ($60,000) corporate direct giving ($180,009)
Assets: $256,103 (2001); $243,497 (2000); $224,691 (1999)
Gifts Received: $275,000 (2001); $275,000 (2000); $250,000 (1999). Note: In 2000 and 2001, contributions were received from Block Communications. In 1999, contributions were received from Blade Communications.

Typical Recipients

Arts & Humanities: Arts Associations & Councils, Arts Centers, Ballet, Community Arts, History & Archaeology, Libraries, Literary Arts, Museums/Galleries, Music, Opera, Performing Arts, Public Broadcasting, Theater
Civic & Public Affairs: African American Affairs, Botanical Gardens/Parks, Business/Free Enterprise, Clubs, Economic Development, Employment/Job Training, First Amendment Issues, Civic & Public Affairs-General, Housing, Law & Justice, Municipalities/Towns, Parades/Festivals, Professional & Trade Associations, Public Policy, Urban & Community Affairs, Women's Affairs, Zoos/Aquariums
Education: Business Education, Colleges & Universities, Education Funds, Education Reform, Education-General, Literacy, Medical Education, Minority Education, Private Education (Precollege), Public Education (Precollege), Student Aid
Environment: Resource Conservation
Health: Alzheimers Disease, Arthritis, Children's Health/Hospitals, Clinics/Medical Centers, Emergency/Ambulance Services, Health Organizations, Multiple Sclerosis, Preventive Medicine/Wellness Organizations, Respiratory, Single-Disease Health Associations
International: International Affairs, International Relief Efforts
Religion: Jewish Causes, Ministries, Religious Organizations, Religious Welfare
Social Services: Child Welfare, Community Centers, Community Service Organizations, Family Planning, Food/Clothing Distribution, Recreation & Athletics, Scouts, United Funds/United Ways, Volunteer Services, YMCA/YWCA/YMHA/YWHA, YMCA/YWCA/YMHA/YWHA, Youth Organizations

Application Procedures

Initial Contact: Send a proposal in letter format.
Application Requirements: Include a description of organization, amount requested, purpose of funds sought, and proof of tax-exempt status. For scholarships include employee's name and date of employment; SAT score, with date and location where taken; college or university to be attended; expected degree and graduation date.
Deadlines: None for grants; March 1 for scholarships.

Restrictions

Does not support: individuals, religious organizations for sectarian purposes, political or lobbying groups, or organizations outside operating areas. Scholarships are limited to children or legal dependents of full-time employees of the Toledo Blade with at least three years of employment. Children of officers and directors are not eligible.

Corporate Officials

Allan James Block: directorpbl, editor-in-chief, european corresp B Toledo, OH 1954. ED University of Pennsylvania (1977). PRIM CORP EMPL director:

Toledo Blade Co. CORP AFFIL director: PG Publishing Co.; president: Blade Broadcasting Co.; director: C-SPAN. NONPR AFFIL trustee: Medical College Ohio. CLUB AFFIL Pennsylvania Club; Toledo Club; Metropolitan Club.

John Robinson Block: co-publisher, editor-in-chief, european corresp B Toledo, OH 1954. ED Yale University BA (1977). PRIM CORP EMPL co-publisher, editor-in-chief, european corresp: Toledo Blade Co. CORP AFFIL vice president, director: PG Publishing Co.; co-publ: Pittsburgh Post-Gazette; executive vice president, director: Blade Communication; co-publ, director: Monterey Peninsula Herald. NONPR AFFIL member: American Society Newspaper Editors; member: Society Professional Journalists. CLUB AFFIL mem: Belmont Country Club; mem: Yale Club.

William Block: chairman, director B New York, NY September 20, 1915. ED Yale University AB (1936). PRIM CORP EMPL chairman, director: Toledo Blade Co. CORP AFFIL co-publ: Pittsburgh Post-Gazette; chairman board: PG Publishing Co. NONPR AFFIL director: Maumee Valley Historical Society; member: Society Professional Journalists; member: International Press Institute; director: Historical Society Western Pennsylvania; director: Inland Press Association; director: Gateway Music; member: American Newspaper Publishers Association; member: American Society Newspaper Editors; trustee emeritus: American Assembly; sponsor: Allegheny Conference Community Development.

William Block, Jr.: president, director B New Haven, CT 1944. ED Trinity College BA (1967); Washington & Lee University JD (1972). PRIM CORP EMPL president, director: Toledo Blade Co. CORP AFFIL president, director: Pittsburgh Post-Gazette-Sun-Telegraph. NONPR AFFIL director: Toledo Symphony; director: United Way Toledo; director: Toledo Museum Art; member: Old Newsboys Goodfellow Association; president: Read for Literacy; member, director: Ohio Newspaper Association. CLUB AFFIL Toledo Club; Toledo Press Club.

Foundation Officials

Gary J. Blair: treasurer, trustee
Allan James Block: vice president, trustee (see above)
John Robinson Block: vice president, trustee (see above)
William Block, Jr.: president, trustee (see above)
William Block: vice president, trustee (see above)
Fritz Byers: assistant secretary
Sandra J. Chavez: secretary, trustee
Lanetta Goings: vice president, trustee

Grants Analysis

Disclosure Period: calendar year ending 2001
Total Grants: $198,939*
Number of Grants: 93
Average Grant: $2,139
Highest Grant: $20,000
Lowest Grant: $250
Typical Range: $100 to $3,000
*Note: Giving excludes scholarships and United Way.

Recent Grants

Note: Grants derived from 2001 Form 990.

Library-Related

20,000	Toledo Lucas County Public Library, Toledo, OH -- community service

General

65,000	United Way Greater Toledo, Toledo, OH -- community service
17,939	Bowling Green State University Foundation, Bowling Green, OH -- community service
11,000	Toledo Symphony Association, Toledo, OH -- community service
10,000	Local Initiatives Support Corporation, New York, NY -- community service
10,000	Lourdes College, Sylvania, OH -- community service
10,000	Read for Literacy, Toledo, OH -- community service
10,000	Toledo Museum of Art, Toledo, OH -- community service
10,000	Toledo Symphony Association, Toledo, OH -- community service
10,000	Toledo Zoo, Toledo, OH -- community service
7,320	Ronald McDonald Children's Charities, Toledo, OH -- community service

THE TOMS FOUNDATION

Giving Contact

Ronald L. Grimm, Trustee
PO Box 2466
Knoxville, TN 37901
Phone: (865)544-3000

Description

Founded: 1954
EIN: 626037668
Organization Type: Private Foundation
Giving Locations: TN: Eastern Tennessee
Grant Types: Project.

Donor Information

Founder: the late W. P. Toms

Financial Summary

Total Giving: $24,000 (fiscal year ending June 30, 2001); $13,951 (fiscal 2000); $16,917 (fiscal 1999)
Assets: $4,169,082 (fiscal 2002); $4,720,225 (fiscal 2000); $5,215,267 (fiscal 1999)

Typical Recipients

Arts & Humanities: Arts Associations & Councils, Community Arts, Arts & Humanities-General, History & Archaeology, Libraries, Museums/Galleries, Opera
Civic & Public Affairs: Civic & Public Affairs-General, Housing, Zoos/Aquariums
Education: Colleges & Universities, Education-General, Legal Education, Private Education (Precollege)
Environment: Environment-General
Health: Clinics/Medical Centers, Health Organizations, Medical Research, Single-Disease Health Associations
Religion: Religious Organizations, Religious Welfare
Social Services: Community Service Organizations, Family Services, Food/Clothing Distribution, Scouts, United Funds/United Ways, Youth Organizations

Application Procedures

Initial Contact: a brief letter of inquiry followed by proposal. Submit proposal preferably in June.
Application Requirements: Include a description of organization, amount requested, purpose of funds sought, and proof of tax-exempt status.
Deadlines: June 30. Board meets in September. Decisions are made one month after annual meeting.

Restrictions

Does not support individuals or endowments.

Additional Information

Publications: Annual Report

Foundation Officials

Janet L. Grimm: trustee
R. Brett Grimm: trustee
Ronald L. Grimm: chairman
Don McLean: treasurer
Mary Mayne Perry: trustee
Thomas R. Ramsey: secretary
Dorothy B. Wilson: vice chairman

Grants Analysis

Disclosure Period: fiscal year ending June 30, 2001
Total Grants: $24,000
Number of Grants: 2
Highest Grant: $20,000
Lowest Grant: $4,000

Recent Grants

Note: Grants derived from fiscal 2000 Form 990.

General

5,000	Knoxville Zoological Society, Knoxville, TN
4,000	University of Tennessee Law School, Knoxville, TN
1,800	Tanasi Girl Scouts, Knoxville, TN
1,000	Interfaith Health Clinic, Knoxville, TN
500	East Tennessee Discovery Center, Knoxville, TN
500	Emerald Avenue Urban Youth and Leadership Foundation, Knoxville, TN
500	Florence Crittenton Agency, Knoxville, TN
500	Habitat for Humanity Lenoir City, Loudon, TN
500	Nativity Pageant, Knoxville, TN
500	Second Harvest Food Bank, Knoxville, TN

TONYA MEMORIAL FOUNDATION

Giving Contact

Maurice H. Martin, President
c/o SunTrust Bank NA
PO Box 1638
736 Market St.
Chattanooga, TN 37402
Phone: (423)756-6600
Fax: (423)757-3691

Alternate Contact

Whitney Durand
1000 Volunteer Bldg.
Chattanooga, TN 37402
Note: Contact for application information.

Description

Founded: 1949
EIN: 626042269
Organization Type: Private Foundation
Giving Locations: TN: Chattanooga
Grant Types: Capital, Multiyear/Continuing Support.

Donor Information

Founder: the late Burkett Miller

Financial Summary

Total Giving: $44,653 (2001); $52,870 (2000); $2,495,177 (1999)
Assets: $4,263,807 (2001); $4,229,252 (2000); $4,316,990 (1999)
Gifts Received: $6,972,356 (1994). Note: In 1994, contributions were received from the Willie D. Miller Annuity Trust.

Typical Recipients

Arts & Humanities: Arts Associations & Councils, Libraries, Museums/Galleries, Performing Arts, Public Broadcasting, Theater
Civic & Public Affairs: Botanical Gardens/Parks, Business/Free Enterprise, Community Foundations, Economic Development, Civic & Public Affairs-General, Municipalities/Towns, Urban & Community Affairs, Zoos/Aquariums
Education: Colleges & Universities, Private Education (Precollege), Public Education (Precollege)

Environment: Environment-General, Resource Conservation

Social Services: Community Centers, Community Service Organizations, Homes, Substance Abuse, United Funds/United Ways, Youth Organizations

Application Procedures

Initial Contact: Submit a letter of no more than three pages describing the project.

Application Requirements: Include a description of organization, most recent Form 990, list of board members, budget for current fiscal year, and proof of tax-exempt status. Send one copy to each of the trustees.

Deadlines: January 10, April 10, July 10, and October 10.

Decision Notification: Applicants will be notified of the foundation's decision following regular meetings held quarterly.

Restrictions

New doners generally restricted to capital projects in Chattanooga, TN.

Foundation Officials

H. Whitney Durand: treasurer, trustee

James R. Hedges, III: vice president, trustee

Harry James Hitching: chairman B New York, NY November 20, 1909. ED Columbia University AB (1929); Columbia University LLB (1931); Columbia University JD (1969). PRIM CORP EMPL partner: Miller & Martin. CORP AFFIL general coun: Skyland International Corp.; div couns: Vulcan Materials Co.; director: Krystal Co. NONPR AFFIL chairman advisory board: Salvation Army Chattanooga; member: TN Bar Association; member: Newcomen Society North America; member: Georgia Bar Association; member: Miller Park Board; member: Estate Planning Council Chattanooga; director: Chattanooga Community Foundation; director: Chattanooga Ophthalmological Foundation; director, treasurer, member: Chattanooga Chamber of Commerce; vice president, member: Chattanooga Bar Association; member: Chattanooga Bar Foundation; general counselor: Benwood Foundation; general counselor: Chattanooga Area Regional Transportation Authority; member: American Bar Association. CLUB AFFIL Mountain City Club; Lookout Mountain Golf Club; Geology Club; Lookout Mountain Fairyland Club.

Maurice H. Martin: president, trustee

Grants Analysis

Disclosure Period: calendar year ending 2001

Total Grants: $44,653

Number of Grants: 2

Highest Grant: $25,000

Lowest Grant: $19,653

Recent Grants

Note: Grants derived from 2000 Form 990.

General

29,870	River Valley Partners, Chattanooga, TN
20,000	Lula Lake Land Trust, Chattanooga, TN
3,000	Weldon F. Osborne Foundation, Inc., Chattanooga, TN

HARRY A. AND MARGARET D. TOWSLEY FOUNDATION

Giving Contact

Lynn T. White, President
140 Ashman Street, P.O. Box 349
Midland, MI 48640
Phone: (989)837-1100
Fax: (989)837-3240

Description

Founded: 1959

EIN: 386091798

Organization Type: General Purpose Foundation

Giving Locations: MI: especially Ann Arbor and Washtenaw County

Grant Types: Emergency, General Support, Multiyear/Continuing Support, Operating Expenses, Project, Research.

Donor Information

Founder: Established in 1959 in Michigan by Margaret Dow Towsley, who donated a gift of Dow Chemical Company common stock.

Financial Summary

Total Giving: $3,150,929 (2001); $3,319,016 (2000); $2,664,022 (1998). Note: 1996 figure includes $34,564 in matching grants.

Giving Analysis: Giving for 2000 includes: foundation grants to United Way ($2,500) 1998: foundation matching gifts ($32,500)

Assets: $61,394,334 (2001); $69,540,905 (2000); $60,947,053 (1998)

Gifts Received: $718,729 (1997); $252,457 (1994)

Typical Recipients

Arts & Humanities: Arts Associations & Councils, Arts Centers, Arts Festivals, Arts Funds, Arts Institutes, Arts & Humanities-General, History & Archaeology, Libraries, Museums/Galleries, Music, Opera, Theater

Civic & Public Affairs: Community Foundations, Economic Development, Civic & Public Affairs-General, Housing, Nonprofit Management, Parades/Festivals, Philanthropic Organizations, Public Policy, Rural Affairs

Education: Agricultural Education, Arts/Humanities Education, Colleges & Universities, Community & Junior Colleges, Education Funds, Education Reform, Faculty Development, Education-General, Medical Education, Minority Education, Preschool Education, Private Education (Precollege), Public Education (Precollege), Public Education (Precollege), Science/Mathematics Education, Social Sciences Education, Student Aid

Environment: Environment-General, Resource Conservation, Wildlife Protection

Health: AIDS/HIV, Alzheimers Disease, Cancer, Children's Health/Hospitals, Clinics/Medical Centers, Emergency/Ambulance Services, Health-General, Geriatric Health, Health Organizations, Hospices, Hospitals, Medical Rehabilitation, Medical Research, Nursing Services, Public Health, Respiratory, Single-Disease Health Associations, Transplant Networks/Donor Banks

International: Health Care/Hospitals

Religion: Churches, Religious Organizations, Religious Welfare

Science: Science Exhibits & Fairs

Social Services: Animal Protection, Big Brother/Big Sister, Child Abuse, Child Welfare, Community Centers, Community Service Organizations, Family Planning, Family Services, Food/Clothing Distribution, Recreation & Athletics, Scouts, Senior Services, Shelters/Homelessness, Substance Abuse, United Funds/United Ways, Volunteer Services, Youth Organizations

Application Procedures

Initial Contact: Prospective applicants should submit a letter and proposal to the foundation. The foundation does not provide application form. for requests. Elaborate presentations are discouraged.

Application Requirements: Applicants should submit a copy of the tax-exempt letter from the IRS; letter establishing that the applicant is not a private foundation; amount requested, need, and intended use; and organization's latest financial statements with an operating budget and other funding sources.

Deadlines: Applications should be submitted between January 1 and March 31 of each year. Send two copies of proposals.

Review Process: Final notification to applicants usually is made during the third quarter of the year.

Restrictions

The foundation does not make direct grants to individuals, provide loan funds, grants to students for scholarships, or grants for travel and conferences. The foundation does not typically provide funds for books, publications, films, tapes, audio-visual or other communication media.

Additional Information

The trustees do not conduct personal interviews with applicants except upon the foundation's initiative. Additional information is frequently requested by the foundation after the application is received.

Publications: Annual Report; Application Guidelines

Foundation Officials

C. Wendell Dunbar: treasurer, trustee

Jennifer Poteat-Flores: trustee

John E. Riecker: secretary

Margaret Ann Riecker: president, trustee

Steven Riecker: trustee

Margaret E. Thompson, MD: trustee

Lynn T. White: vice president, trustee

Grants Analysis

Disclosure Period: calendar year ending 2000

Total Grants: $3,316,516*

Number of Grants: 101*

Average Grant: $25,551*

Highest Grant: $287,046

Typical Range: $1,000 to $50,000

*Note: Giving excludes United Way. Average grant figure excludes top six grants. ($889,174)

Recent Grants

Note: Grants derived from 2000 Form 990.

General

5,000	Carleton College, Northfield, MI
5,000	Nature Conservancy, East Lansing, MI
5,000	University of Michigan School of Music, Ann Arbor, MI
5,000	University of Michigan Theater Association, Ann Arbor, MI
3,000	Westtown School, Westtown, PA
2,500	Culver Education Foundation, Culver, IN
2,500	Grand Rapids Symphony, Grand Rapids, MI
2,500	Mid Michigan Medical Center, Midland, MI
2,500	United Way Midland, Midland, MI
2,000	First United Methodist Church

TOZER FOUNDATION

Giving Contact

Robert Davis, Director
PO Box 64704
St. Paul, MN 55164
Phone: (651)244-0958

Description

Founded: 1946

EIN: 416011518

Organization Type: General Purpose Foundation

Giving Locations: MN: Kanabec County for scholarship program, Pine County for scholarship program, Washington County for scholarship program

Grant Types: General Support, Scholarship.

Financial Summary

Total Giving: $1,571,820 (fiscal year ending October 31, 2001); $1,500,000 (fiscal 2000 approx); $1,627,254 (fiscal 1999)

Giving Analysis: Giving for fiscal 2001 includes: foundation scholarships ($1,261,750); fiscal 1998: foundation scholarships ($1,224,320) fiscal 1996: foundation scholarships ($963,767)
Assets: $29,492,909 (fiscal 2001); $35,860,800 (fiscal 1999); $31,309,581 (fiscal 1998)
Gifts Received: $213 (fiscal 2001). Note: In fiscal 2001, contributions were received from the Anna Scotten Estate.

Typical Recipients

Arts & Humanities: Arts Centers, Arts Funds, History & Archaeology, Libraries, Music, Opera, Public Broadcasting
Civic & Public Affairs: Business/Free Enterprise, Municipalities/Towns, Nonprofit Management, Parades/Festivals, Professional & Trade Associations, Public Policy, Urban & Community Affairs
Education: Business Education, Business-School Partnerships, Colleges & Universities, Economic Education, Education-General, Minority Education, Public Education (Precollege), Science/Mathematics Education, Secondary Education (Public), Student Aid
Health: Clinics/Medical Centers, Hospitals, Medical Rehabilitation
International: International Relations
Religion: Religious Organizations, Religious Welfare
Science: Science Museums
Social Services: Family Services, Recreation & Athletics, Scouts, Scouts, United Funds/United Ways, Volunteer Services, YMCA/YWCA/YMHA/YWHA, Youth Organizations

Application Procedures

Initial Contact: The foundation requests applications be made in writing. Applications for scholarships may be received through high school guidance counselors.
Application Requirements: Grant applications must outline the nature of the request. Applicant must be a resident.
Deadlines: None.
Review Process: The board meets periodically throughout the year. The board considers scholarship requests at their annual meeting in May. Decisions are made immediately after the meeting.

Foundation Officials

Robert S. Davis: president, chairman B Stillwater, MN 1914. ED University of Minnesota (1934). PRIM CORP EMPL director: H M Smyth Co. CORP AFFIL director: Heartland Technology. CLUB AFFIL Elks Club.
James Richard Oppenheimer: director B Saint Paul, MN 1921. ED Dartmouth College BA (1942); Yale University JD (1948). PRIM CORP EMPL officer counsel: Oppenheimer, Wolff & Donnelly. NONPR AFFIL member: Ramsey County Bar Association; member: Saint Paul Chamber of Commerce; trustee: Charles K Blandin Residuary Trust; member: Minnesota Bar Association; member: American Bar Association. CLUB AFFIL White Bear Yacht Club; Rotary Club.
John Thomas Simonet: vice president B Stillwater, MN 1926. ED University of Minnesota BBA (1948); University of Minnesota LLB (1951). CORP AFFIL board director: Mairs & Power Growth Fund; board director: Mairs & Power Income Fund; director: Mairs & Power Funds Inc.; director: Donovan Companies; director: First Trust Co.; director: Carondelet Life Care Corp.
Jon A. Theobald: vice president B Saint Paul, MN 1945. ED Saint John's University (1967); Saint John's University (1970). PRIM CORP EMPL executive vice president: Resource Trust Co.
John F. Thoreen: director

Grants Analysis

Disclosure Period: fiscal year ending October 31, 2001
Total Grants: $310,070*
Number of Grants: 54

Average Grant: $5,742
Highest Grant: $22,000
Typical Range: $1,000 to $10,000
*Note: Giving excludes scholarships.

Recent Grants

Note: Grants derived from 2000 Form 990.

General
82,150	University of Minnesota Twin Cities, Twin Cities, MN -- scholarship
69,350	University of Minnesota Twin Cities, Twin Cities, MN -- scholarship
60,000	United Way St. Paul, St. Paul, MN
33,350	St. Thomas College -- scholarship
29,900	University of Minnesota Duluth, Duluth, MN -- scholarship
23,500	University of Wisconsin River Falls, River Falls, WI -- scholarship
22,800	University of Wisconsin-Madison, Madison, WI -- scholarship
22,000	Minnesota Orchestral Association, Minneapolis, MN -- scholarship
21,850	Bethel College, Mishawaka, IN -- scholarship
21,150	Gustavus Adolphus College, St. Peter, MN -- scholarship

TRACTOR & EQUIPMENT CO.

Company Headquarters
Birmingham, AL

Company Description
Employees: 190
SIC(s): 5000 Wholesale Trade--Durable Goods.

Tractor & Equipment Co. Foundation

Giving Contact
Lloyd Adams, Secretary & Treasurer
Tractor & Equipment Co. Foundation
5336 Airport Hwy.
Birmingham, AL 35212
Phone: (205)591-2131
Fax: (205)591-8321

Description
Founded: 1977
EIN: 630718825
Organization Type: Corporate Foundation
Giving Locations: AL
Grant Types: General Support, Scholarship.

Donor Information
Founder: Tractor & Equipment Co.

Financial Summary
Total Giving: $98,715 (2002); $90,479 (2000); $107,361 (1999)
Giving Analysis: Giving for 2002 includes: foundation grants to United Way ($10,800); foundation ($39,400); foundation scholarships ($48,515); 2000: foundation grants to United Way ($10,500); foundation scholarships ($30,859); foundation ($49,120); 1999: foundation grants to United Way ($9,800); foundation scholarships ($45,301); foundation ($52,260); **Assets:** $139,841 (2002); $124,267 (2000); $137,931 (1999)
Gifts Received: $125,000 (2002); $75,000 (2000); $101,500 (1999). Note: In 2002, contributions were received from Tractor & Equipment Co.

Typical Recipients
Arts & Humanities: History & Archaeology, Libraries
Civic & Public Affairs: Botanical Gardens/Parks, Economic Development, Civic & Public Affairs-General, Professional & Trade Associations
Education: Colleges & Universities, Community & Junior Colleges, Education Funds, Elementary Education (Public), Education-General, Legal Education, Private Education (Precollege), Public Education (Precollege), Secondary Education (Public), Student Aid
Environment: Forestry, Resource Conservation
Health: Cancer, Heart, Hospitals, Mental Health, Multiple Sclerosis, Single-Disease Health Associations
International: Foreign Arts Organizations
Religion: Churches, Ministries, Religious Organizations, Religious Welfare, Social/Policy Issues
Social Services: Animal Protection, Camps, Child Welfare, Community Service Organizations, Recreation & Athletics, Scouts, United Funds/United Ways, Youth Organizations

Application Procedures
Initial Contact: Application form required for scholarships. No application procedure has been outlined for grants to nonprofit organizations.
Deadlines: March 1.
Notes: Scholarship applications should be addressed to: Mr. J.W. Waitzman, Jr., Tractor & Equipment Company, PO Box 12326 Birmingham, AL 35202.

Restrictions
Scholarships are restricted to children whose parents are employed by Tractor & Equipment Company and who have been accepted at or made application to an accredited institution of higher learning.

Additional Information
Provides scholarships to children of employees.

Corporate Officials
James W. Waitzman, Jr.: chairman, president, chief executive officer PRIM CORP EMPL chairman, president, chief executive officer: Tractor & Equipment Co.

Foundation Officials
Lloyd Adams: secretary, treasurer
J. C. Durden: vice president, director
K. H. Horton: director
J. O. Stracener: director
James W. Waitzman, Jr.: president, director (see above)
Benny F. Winford: secretary, treasurer, director

Grants Analysis
Disclosure Period: calendar year ending 2002
Total Grants: $39,400*
Number of Grants: 15
Average Grant: $1,367*
Highest Grant: $20,266
Typical Range: $1,000 to $5,000
*Note: Giving excludes scholarships and United Way. Average grant figure excludes highest grant.

Recent Grants
Note: Grants derived from 2002 Form 990.

Library-Related
5,000	Mountain Brook Library Foundation, Mountain Brook, AL

General
20,266	Wofford College, Spartanburg, SC -- scholarship
9,000	Stamford University, Birmingham, AL -- scholarship
8,000	University of Central Alabama, Tuscaloosa, AL
5,050	Oklahoma State University, Okmulgee, OK -- scholarship

5,000	St. Francis Xavier, Birmingham, AL
5,000	Vulcan Park Foundation, Birmingham, AL
4,358	Auburn University Foundation, Auburn University, AL -- scholarship
4,000	University of Alabama, Tuscaloosa, AL -- scholarship
3,400	Greater Alabama Council of the Boy Scouts of America, Birmingham, AL
3,000	Stamford University, Birmingham, AL -- scholarship

J. Edwin Treakle Foundation

Giving Contact

John Warren Cooke, President
PO Box 1157
Gloucester, VA 23061
Phone: (804)693-0881

Description

Founded: 1963
EIN: 546051620
Organization Type: Private Foundation
Giving Locations: VA
Grant Types: Capital, General Support, Multiyear/Continuing Support, Research, Scholarship.

Donor Information

Founder: the late J. Edwin Treakle

Financial Summary

Total Giving: $365,000 (fiscal year ending April 30, 2002); $375,000 (fiscal 2001); $360,000 (fiscal 2000)
Giving Analysis: Giving for fiscal 2002 includes: foundation scholarships ($3,300) fiscal 1999: foundation scholarships ($10,000)
Assets: $7,273,959 (fiscal 2002); $8,275,790 (fiscal 2001); $9,388,800 (fiscal 2000)
Gifts Received: $100,000 (fiscal 1992). Note: In 1992, contributions were received from the estate of James B. Martin.

Typical Recipients

Arts & Humanities: Historic Preservation, History & Archaeology, Libraries, Museums/Galleries, Music
Civic & Public Affairs: Housing, Safety, Urban & Community Affairs
Education: Arts/Humanities Education, Colleges & Universities, Community & Junior Colleges, Education Funds, Faculty Development, Education-General, Gifted & Talented Programs, Literacy, Private Education (Precollege), Public Education (Precollege), Science/Mathematics Education, Secondary Education (Public), Student Aid
Environment: Environment-General, Resource Conservation, Wildlife Protection
Health: Cancer, Clinics/Medical Centers, Emergency/Ambulance Services, Medical Research, Nursing Services, Prenatal Health Issues, Single-Disease Health Associations
Religion: Churches, Religious Welfare
Science: Scientific Centers & Institutes
Social Services: Animal Protection, Community Service Organizations, Emergency Relief, Scouts, Volunteer Services, Youth Organizations

Application Procedures

Initial Contact: Request an application form from foundation.
Deadlines: Applications are accepted between January 1 and April 30.

Restrictions

Preference is given to local and educational organizations. Does not support individuals.

Additional Information

Publications: Application Form

Foundation Officials

John Warren Cooke: president, mgr
Harry E. Dunn: vice president
Cynthia B. Horsley: grants admin
Nancy Powell: administrative assistant

Grants Analysis

Disclosure Period: fiscal year ending April 30, 2002
Total Grants: $361,700*
Number of Grants: 62
Average Grant: $5,834
Highest Grant: $24,000
Lowest Grant: $300
Typical Range: $1,000 to $10,000
*****Note:** Giving excludes scholarships.

Recent Grants

Note: Grants derived from fiscal 2000 Form 990.

Library-Related

18,000	Gloucester Library Endowment Foundation, White Marsh, VA
18,000	Mathews Memorial Library, Friends of, Mathews, VA

General

36,000	Gloucester Volunteer Fire and Rescue Squad, Inc., Gloucester, VA
18,000	Abingdon Volunteer Fire Company, Inc., Bena, VA
18,000	Abingdon Volunteer Rescue Squad, Gloucester Point, VA
18,000	Mathews Volunteer Fire Department, Inc., Mathews, VA -- purchase equipment and payment on two pumpers
18,000	Mathews Volunteer Rescue Squad, Mathews, VA -- purchase ambulance and construct new squad building
14,000	Mathews High School Crew, Mathews, VA -- use for equipment, expenses, maintenance of equipment
12,000	Gloucester-Mathews Free Clinic, Hayes, VA
10,000	Animal Care Society, Mathews, VA
10,000	Chesapeake Bay Foundation, Annapolis, MD -- support field trips for students and teachers and educational activities in Virginia
10,000	Gloucester - Mathews Humane Society, Inc., Gloucester, VA

Edith L. Trees Charitable Trust

Giving Contact

James M. Ferguson, III, Trust Officer
PNC Bank NA
One PNC Plaza, 2nd Floor
249 Fifth Avenue
Pittsburgh, PA 15222
Phone: (412)762-3808

Description

Founded: 1976
EIN: 256026443
Organization Type: Specialized/Single Purpose Foundation
Giving Locations: PA: Pittsburgh
Grant Types: Capital, Department, Endowment, General Support.

Donor Information

Founder: Established in 1976 with funds from the Edith L. Trees Trust. The late Edith Lehm Trees married the late Joe Clifton Trees in January 1929. Joe Trees, an oil and gas businessman, worked for the Benedum Trees Oil Company in western Pennsylvania and served as a trustee for the University of Pittsburgh.

Financial Summary

Total Giving: $4,245,258 (2000); $3,208,163 (1998); $2,648,472 (1997)
Assets: $80,438,412 (2000); $66,940,524 (1998); $59,977,543 (1997)
Gifts Received: $1,907,255 (2000); $1,723,710 (1998); $2,873,029 (1997). Note: Contributions were received from the Edith L. Trees Trust.

Typical Recipients

Arts & Humanities: Arts Centers, Arts Outreach, Arts & Humanities-General, Libraries, Music, Performing Arts, Theater
Civic & Public Affairs: Botanical Gardens/Parks, Community Foundations, Employment/Job Training, Civic & Public Affairs-General, Housing, Municipalities/Towns, Philanthropic Organizations, Public Policy, Urban & Community Affairs
Education: Afterschool/Enrichment Programs, Colleges & Universities, Education-General, Gifted & Talented Programs, Preschool Education, Private Education (Precollege), Public Education (Precollege), Science/Mathematics Education, Special Education, Vocational & Technical Education
Environment: Environment-General
Health: Children's Health/Hospitals, Clinics/Medical Centers, Eyes/Blindness, Health-General, Health Policy/Cost Containment, Health Organizations, Hospitals (University Affiliated), Medical Rehabilitation, Mental Health, Public Health, Single-Disease Health Associations
Religion: Religion-General
Social Services: Camps, Child Welfare, Community Service Organizations, Homes, People with Disabilities, Recreation & Athletics, Scouts, Senior Services, Social Services-General, YMCA/YWCA/YMHA/YWHA, Youth Organizations

Application Procedures

Initial Contact: Organizations should submit a written application.
Application Requirements: The application should detail services provided by the organization for the care and benefit of mentally retarded persons; financial statements for the previous three years; and a copy of IRS exemption letter; and a list of trustees and officers including their connections with the community and with mentally retarded persons.
Deadlines: November 1.

Restrictions

The trust gives only to organizations "for the benefit of mentally-retarded children, or to corporations, associations or agencies organized and operated for that purpose." The trust does not provide grants to individuals.

Additional Information

Trust(s): PNC Bank

Foundation Officials

J. Murray Eagan: trustee, contact
James M. Ferguson, III: trustee

Grants Analysis

Disclosure Period: calendar year ending 2000
Total Grants: $4,245,258
Number of Grants: 66
Average Grant: $64,322
Highest Grant: $300,000
Lowest Grant: $7,500
Typical Range: $25,000 to $100,000

Recent Grants

Note: Grants derived from 2000 Form 990.

General

300,000	Children's Hospital of Pittsburgh Down Syndrome Center of Western Pennsylvania, Pittsburgh, PA -- addition to endowment fund to support patient care, educational services and research of the Down Syndrome Center
275,000	Verland Foundation, Pittsburgh, PA -- to support continuing program of debt reduction and to add to the endowment fund
260,000	ARC Allegheny Foundation, Pittsburgh, PA -- furnish temporary relief and respite care through camping programs
200,000	Allegheny Valley School, Coraopolis, PA -- special campaign for renovations and upgrades of facilities in Western Pennsylvania
140,000	McGuire Memorial Home Foundation, New Brighton, PA -- for closing costs and renovations for another community residence
136,250	Sharp Visions, Pittsburgh, PA -- support camp and extended school year program
130,000	Clelian Heights School for Exceptional Children, Greensburg, PA -- to acquire a tractor and to support an endowment fund
126,742	St. Anthony School Programs, Pittsburgh, PA -- to acquire two vans for use in inclusive education and employment programs
125,000	Early Learning Institute, Pittsburgh, PA -- for endowment fund
100,000	United Cerebral Palsy, Pittsburgh, PA -- to support capital campaign

HARRY C. TREXLER TRUST

Giving Contact

Thomas H. Christman, Executive Director
33 South 7th Street, Suite 205
Allentown, PA 18101
Phone: (610)434-9645
Fax: (610)437-5721

Description

Founded: 1934
EIN: 231162215
Organization Type: General Purpose Foundation
Giving Locations: PA: Lehigh County
Grant Types: Capital, Operating Expenses.

Donor Information

Founder: Established in 1934, with Harry C. Trexler and Mary M. Trexler as donors. Mr. Trexler was president of Trexler Lumber Company (Allentown, PA) and chairman of Lehigh Portland Cement Company and Bell Telephone Company of Pennsylvania. He was a trustee of Allentown State Hospital, Sacred Heart Hospital (Allentown), St. Luke's Hospital, Lehigh University, Franklin and Marshall College, and Muhlenberg College.
The Trexler will stipulated that one-half of the trust's income be distributed to charitable organizations that serve the benefit of humanity in Lehigh County, one-fourth be paid to the City of Allentown for parks, and one-fourth be added to the foundation's investment assets.

Financial Summary

Total Giving: $4,924,674 (fiscal year ending March 31, 2001); $4,918,506 (fiscal 2000 approx); $3,168,525 (fiscal 1999)

Giving Analysis: Giving for fiscal 2001 includes: foundation scholarships ($60,000); fiscal 1999: foundation scholarships ($35,000) foundation ($3,133,525)
Assets: $119,632,864 (fiscal 2001); $137,993,764 (fiscal 2000 approx); $126,835,238 (fiscal 1999)
Gifts Received: $5,881 (fiscal 1992)

Typical Recipients

Arts & Humanities: Arts Associations & Councils, Arts Centers, Arts Festivals, Dance, Historic Preservation, History & Archaeology, Libraries, Museums/Galleries, Music, Opera, Performing Arts, Theater
Civic & Public Affairs: Botanical Gardens/Parks, Economic Development, Civic & Public Affairs-General, Hispanic Affairs, Housing, Municipalities/Towns, Safety, Women's Affairs
Education: Arts/Humanities Education, Business Education, Colleges & Universities, Community & Junior Colleges, Economic Education, Education-General, Literacy, Minority Education, Private Education (Precollege), Science/Mathematics Education, Secondary Education (Private), Special Education, Student Aid, Vocational & Technical Education, Vocational & Technical Education
Environment: Environment-General, Resource Conservation
Health: Children's Health/Hospitals, Clinics/Medical Centers, Emergency/Ambulance Services, Eyes/Blindness, Home-Care Services, Long-Term Care, Medical Rehabilitation, Nursing Services, Transplant Networks/Donor Banks
Religion: Churches, Dioceses, Religion-General, Jewish Causes, Religious Welfare
Science: Scientific Centers & Institutes
Social Services: Child Welfare, Community Centers, Community Service Organizations, Crime Prevention, Emergency Relief, Family Services, People with Disabilities, Recreation & Athletics, Scouts, Senior Services, Shelters/Homelessness, Social Services-General, Volunteer Services, YMCA/YWCA/YMHA/YWHA, Youth Organizations

Application Procedures

Initial Contact: Grant requests should be in letter form.
Application Requirements: Letters should state the purpose of funds sought, the amount requested, and the anticipated public benefit. Proposals also should include a copy of the organization's articles of incorporation and by-laws, proof of IRS nonprofit status, most recent financial statements, an operating budget, a list of other sources of project support, current list of board of directors, federal tax return, and detailed program descriptions with current client statistics. Also answer the following questions: Is your organization registered with the Pennsylvania Bureu of Charitable Organizations? Do you pay money or receive money from any other organizations? Are you controlled by, related to, connected with, or sponsored by another organization? Do you serve clientele from counties other than Lehigh?
Deadlines: Applications must be received prior to December 1 for funding consideration.
Review Process: Trustees meet on the third Tuesday of every month. In these meetings the trustees familiarize themselves with an organization's stated purposes and structure. They also subjectively compare organizations seeking funds, preferring to fund the organization demonstrating a more compelling benefit to the local community.
Notes: Potential grantees are encouraged to meet with the foundation staff prior to submission of a request.

Restrictions

The Foundation does not support organizations outside Lehigh County, PA, individuals, nor private foundations.

Additional Information

The foundation reports that it also offers proposal writing assistance.
Publications: Guidelines

Foundation Officials

Grants Analysis

Disclosure Period: fiscal year ending March 31, 2001
Total Grants: $4,864,674*
Number of Grants: 108
Average Grant: $34,112*
Highest Grant: $1,224,688
Typical Range: $15,000 to $75,000
*Note: Giving excludes scholarships. Average grant figure excludes highest grant.

Recent Grants

Note: Grants derived from 2000 Form 990.

Library-Related

206,000	Allentown Public Library, Allentown, PA -- debt reduction

General

1,432,175	City of Allentown, Allentown, PA -- improvement, extend and maintain parks
125,000	Allentown School District, Allentown, PA -- technology labs for middle schools
123,200	Roman Catholic Diocese of Allentown, Allentown, PA -- various needs
120,000	YMCA/YWCA Capital Campaign, Allentown, PA -- building improvements

100,000	Cedar Crest College, Allentown, PA -- addition to science center
100,000	County of Lehigh, Allentown, PA -- for game preserve exhibits
100,000	Muhlenberg College, Allentown, PA -- expansion of arts center
75,000	Minsi Trails Council, Lehigh Valley, PA -- support of urban scouting
75,000	Salvation Army, Allentown, PA -- new family shelter
70,000	Allentown Art Museum, Allentown, PA -- operating support

TRI-COUNTY TELEPHONE FOUNDATION

Giving Contact
Dennis Wallace, General Manager
PO Box 91
Belhaven, NC 27810-0091
Phone: (252)964-4211

Description
Founded: 1994
EIN: 561742130
Organization Type: Private Foundation
Grant Types: General Support.

Financial Summary
Total Giving: $23,245 (fiscal year ending September 30, 2001); $75,200 (fiscal 2000); $76,003 (fiscal 1998)
Giving Analysis: Giving for fiscal 2001 includes: foundation scholarships ($5,000); fiscal 2000: foundation scholarships ($5,000) fiscal 1998: foundation scholarships ($6,000)
Assets: $1,353,543 (fiscal 2001); $1,438,984 (fiscal 2000); $1,643,876 (fiscal 1998)
Gifts Received: $100 (fiscal 2000)

Typical Recipients
Arts & Humanities: Libraries
Civic & Public Affairs: Clubs, Civic & Public Affairs-General, Rural Affairs, Safety, Urban & Community Affairs
Education: Colleges & Universities, Community & Junior Colleges
Health: Emergency/Ambulance Services, Health Organizations
Social Services: Child Welfare, People with Disabilities, Scouts, Volunteer Services, Youth Organizations

Application Procedures
Initial Contact: The foundation has no formal grant application procedure or application form.
Deadlines: None.

Restrictions
Contributions must benefit the local service area.

Foundation Officials
Edwin M. Baldree: president
Ronald F. Cooper: assistant secretary, assistant treasurer
Jack Arliss Mason: 2nd vice president
Gary Respess: director
Jodie H. Slade: director
Cecil O. Smith: director
Clarence E. Tetterton: secretary, treasurer
Charlie F. Wallace: 1st vice president
Dennis Wallace: general manager
Frank Waters: director

Grants Analysis
Disclosure Period: fiscal year ending September 30, 2001
Total Grants: $18,245*
Number of Grants: 26
Average Grant: $530*

Highest Grant: $5,000
Lowest Grant: $50
Typical Range: $250 to $1,000
***Note:** Giving excludes scholarships. Average grant figure excludes highest grant.

Recent Grants
Note: Grants derived from fiscal 2000 Form 990.

Library-Related
5,000	Belhaven Public Library, Belhaven, NC

General
25,000	Pungo River Volunteer Fire Department
15,000	Pantego Fire Department
5,000	Friends of JAW
5,000	Sidney Volunteer Fire
1,500	Chocowinity Emergency Medical Services Inc
1,489	Tri-County Communications, Pensacola, FL
1,485	Live Stock Show and Sale Fund
1,000	Beaufort County Community College, Washington, NC
1,000	Beaufort County Community College, Washington, NC
1,000	Beaufort County Community College, Washington, NC

TRIBUNE CO.

Company Headquarters
435 N. Michigan Avenue
Chicago, IL 60611
Phone: (312)222-9100
Fax: (312)222-1573
Web: http://www.tribune.com

Company Description
Founded: 1847
Ticker: TRB
Exchange: NYSE
Acquired: Times Mirror (2000).
Revenue: US$5.384 billion (2002)
Profit: US$443 million (2002)
Employees: 25600 (2002)
Fortune Rank: 312, per FORTUNE Magazine's list of 500 Largest U.S. Corporations (2002).

Nonmonetary Support
Type: Donated Equipment; Donated Products; In-kind Services

Times Mirror Foundation

Giving Contact
Kim McCleary La France, President
Times Mirror Foundation
202 W. First St.
Los Angeles, CA 90053
Phone: (213)237-3005
Fax: (213)237-2116

Description
EIN: 956079651
Organization Type: Corporate Foundation
Giving Locations: CA: nonprofits located in Southern CA headquarters and operating communities.
Grant Types: Capital, Employee Matching Gifts, General Support, Multiyear/Continuing Support, Project, Scholarship.
Note: Employee matching gift ratio: 1 to 1. Company will match gifts made by employees and retirees with a minimum contribution of $25 and a maximum of $10,000 annually. The company grants scholarships to children of Times Mirror employees.

Financial Summary
Total Giving: $7,164,630 (2000); $3,700,000 (1997 approx); $1,879,000 (1995). Note: Contributes through corporate direct giving program and foundation. 1995 Giving includes foundation.
Giving Analysis: Giving for 2000 includes: foundation matching gifts ($1,858,502)
Assets: $6,452,561 (2000); $7,358,434 (1995)
Gifts Received: $10,650,955 (2000). Note: In 2000, contributions were received from The Times Mirror Co.

Typical Recipients
Arts & Humanities: Arts Associations & Councils, Arts Centers, Arts Institutes, Ballet, Dance, Ethnic & Folk Arts, Film & Video, Arts & Humanities-General, Historic Preservation, History & Archaeology, Libraries, Literary Arts, Museums/Galleries, Music, Performing Arts, Public Broadcasting, Theater
Civic & Public Affairs: African American Affairs, Asian American Affairs, Botanical Gardens/Parks, Chambers of Commerce, Civil Rights, Community Foundations, Economic Development, Economic Policy, Employment/Job Training, First Amendment Issues, Civic & Public Affairs-General, Hispanic Affairs, Housing, Legal Aid, Minority Business, Municipalities/Towns, Native American Affairs, Nonprofit Management, Parades/Festivals, Philanthropic Organizations, Professional & Trade Associations, Public Policy, Urban & Community Affairs, Women's Affairs, Zoos/Aquariums
Education: Afterschool/Enrichment Programs, Arts/Humanities Education, Business Education, Business-School Partnerships, Colleges & Universities, Education Funds, Education Reform, Engineering/Technological Education, Environmental Education, Faculty Development, Education-General, International Studies, Journalism/Media Education, Literacy, Minority Education, Private Education (Precollege), Public Education (Precollege), Social Sciences Education, Student Aid, Vocational & Technical Education
Environment: Environment-General
Health: Cancer, Diabetes, Emergency/Ambulance Services, Eyes/Blindness, Health-General, Respiratory
International: Foreign Arts Organizations, International Affairs, International Organizations, International Relations
Religion: Dioceses
Science: Science Museums
Social Services: Camps, Child Welfare, Community Centers, Community Service Organizations, Counseling, Domestic Violence, Family Services, Food/Clothing Distribution, Homes, People with Disabilities, Recreation & Athletics, Scouts, Senior Services, Social Services-General, United Funds/United Ways, Volunteer Services, YMCA/YWCA/YMHA/YWHA, Youth Organizations

Application Procedures
Initial Contact: Call for guidelines and a grant summary form, which must accompany a full proposal.
Application Requirements: Include a description of organization, its purpose, programs, and project to be considered; statement of the problem the project will address; qualifications of personnel; program goals; methodology; evaluation procedures; proof of tax-exempt status; list of current supporting organizations and amount of support; and organizational budget for current and upcoming fiscal years.
Deadlines: by May 1 or November 1; board meets in June and December.
Notes: Organizations in areas served by Times Mirror subsidiaries with significant employee presence should submit requests to subsidiary directly.

Restrictions
Company and foundation do not provide grants for religious, political or fraternal purposes, to veteran or labor groups, for events, or to individuals.

Repeat grant requests will not be considered within a one-year time period.

Additional Information

Grant requests to the Times Mirror Co. are considered as they are received. Company's grants are generally smaller than the foundation's and may include support for fund-raising events. Application criteria and eligibility are similar to those for the foundation.

The foundation makes grants to nonprofit organizations in regions where Times Mirror operating companies are located, a listing of which is located on their website.

Times Mirror also gives through 26 operating units, including the Los Angeles Times, CA; Newsday, Long Island, NY; and The Baltimore Sun Newspaper, MD.
Publications: Contributions Annual Report

Corporate Officials

Kathryn M. Downing: executive vice presidents ED Lewis & Clark College; Stanford University. PRIM CORP EMPL executive vice president: The Times Mirror Co. PRIM NONPR EMPL president, chief executive officer: Los Angeles Times ADD CORP EMPL president: Mosby Inc.; president, chief executive officer: Mosby Matthew Bender. NONPR AFFIL member: American Association Publishers; director: Friends Law Library Congress.
Bonnie Guiton Hill: vice president B Springfield, IL 1941. ED Mills College BA (1974); California State University, Hayward MS (1975); University of California at Berkeley EdD (1985). CORP AFFIL director: NASouth Dakota Regulation Inc.; director: Niagara Mohawk Power Corp.; director: Hershey Foods Corp.; director: Louisiana-Pacific Corp.; director: AK Steel Corp.; director: Crestar Financial Corp. NONPR AFFIL director: Joint Center Political Economic Studies; director: National Urban League.
Steven J. Schoch: vice president, treasurer B Saint Louis, MO 1958. ED Tufts University (1981); Dartmouth College (1986). ADD CORP EMPL president, chief executive officer: Times Mirror Resource Management Co.

Giving Program Officials

Stephen Charles Meier: vice chairman B Los Angeles, CA 1950. ED Occidental College (1972); Harvard University MBA (1977).

Foundation Officials

Kathryn M. Downing: vice chairman (see above)
Bonnie Guiton Hill: president, chief executive officer (see above)
Steven J. Schoch: treasurer, chief financial officer (see above)
Mark Hinckley Willes: chairman B Salt Lake City, UT 1941. ED Columbia University AB (1963); Columbia University PhD (1967). CORP AFFIL director: Ryder System Inc.; director: Talbots Inc.; director: Black & Decker Corp.; publisher: Los Angeles Times.
Donald Franklin Wright: director B Saint Paul, MN 1934. ED University of Minnesota BME (1957); University of Minnesota MBA (1958). CORP AFFIL chairman: Times Mirror Magazines Inc.; president, chief executive officer: Los Angeles Times. NONPR AFFIL vice chairman: Los Angeles Area Council Boy Scouts America; University Minnesota Alumni Association; director: Associates California Institute Technology; honorary member: Claremont University Graduate School; member: American Newspaper Publishers Association. CLUB AFFIL City Bunker Hill Club.

Grants Analysis

Disclosure Period: calendar year ending 2000
Total Grants: $4,631,128*
Number of Grants: 255
Average Grant: $14,296*
Highest Grant: $1,000,000
Typical Range: $5,000 to $30,000

*****Note:** Giving excludes matching gifts and United Way. Average grant figure excludes highest grant.

Recent Grants

Note: Grants derived from 2000 Form 990.

Library-Related
344,800	Library Foundation of Los Angeles, Los Angeles, CA

General
1,000,000	Disney Hall/Music Center of Los Angeles, Los Angeles, CA
662,350	Fidelity Investments Charitable Gift Fund, Boston, MA
539,200	Friends of the School Volunteer Program of Los Angeles, Los Angeles, CA
500,000	United Way of Greater Los Angeles, Los Angeles, CA
300,000	Friends Academy
250,000	California Institute of Technology, Pasadena, CA
250,000	Camp Courant, Hartford, CT
200,000	National Aquarium in Baltimore, Baltimore, MD
140,000	United Way Orange County, Garden Grove, CA
135,000	Los Angeles County Education Foundation, Downey, CA

TRIMIX FOUNDATION

Giving Contact

Gail S. Mixer, President
c/o A. Max Kohlenberg, Edwards and Angell
2800 BankBoston Plaza
Providence, RI 02903-2499
Phone: (401)274-9200

Description

Founded: 1997
EIN: 050494244
Organization Type: Private Foundation
Giving Locations: MA: Boston, Dalton; NY: Cedarhurst, Schenectady, White Plains; RI: Greenwich, Providence, Warwick
Grant Types: General Support.

Financial Summary

Total Giving: $479,430 (2001); $175,785 (2000); $130,011 (1999)
Assets: $4,273,645 (2001); $5,130,861 (2000); $4,745,267 (1999)
Gifts Received: $400,000 (2001); $400,000 (2000); $400,000 (1999). Note: Contributions were received from David P. Mixer.

Typical Recipients

Arts & Humanities: Arts Festivals, Arts & Humanities-General, Libraries
Civic & Public Affairs: Civil Rights, Philanthropic Organizations
Education: Business Education, Colleges & Universities, Elementary Education (Private), Elementary Education (Public), Private Education (Precollege), Secondary Education (Public)
Environment: Environment-General
Health: Cancer, Health Organizations, Hospitals
Religion: Churches
Social Services: Recreation & Athletics, Scouts, Special Olympics, Youth Organizations

Application Procedures

Initial Contact: Submit a written request on your organization's letterhead.

Application Requirements: Provide information regarding charitable status and purpose of funds sought.
Deadlines: None.

Foundation Officials

Deborah Kazlauskas: secretary
David P. Mixer: treasurer
Gail S. Mixer: president

Grants Analysis

Disclosure Period: calendar year ending 2001
Total Grants: $479,430
Number of Grants: 35
Average Grant: $6,748*
Highest Grant: $250,000
Lowest Grant: $50
Typical Range: $50 to $10,000
*****Note:** Average grant figure excludes highest grant.

Recent Grants

Note: Grants derived from 2001 Form 990.

Library-Related
500	East Greenwich Free Library, East Greenwich, CT

General
250,000	Berkshire Taconic Community Foundation, Great Barrington, MA
97,000	East Greenwich Public Schools, East Greenwich, RI
70,000	Mother Caroline Academy, Dorchester, MA
10,000	Community Recreation Association, Dalton, MA
10,000	The Providence Community Health Centers, Providence, RI
10,000	Tomorrow Fund, Providence, RI
6,175	Save the Bay, Providence, RI
5,000	The Rhode Island Foundation, Providence, RI
2,871	Citizens Memorial School, Woonsocket, RI
2,500	First Baptist Church, Greenwich, RI

WILLIAM D. TRIPPE TRUST

Giving Contact

Glenn T. York, Jr., President
P.O. Box 246
Cedartown, GA 30125
Phone: (334)690-1411

Description

Founded: 1995
EIN: 586301950
Organization Type: Private Foundation
Grant Types: General Support.

Financial Summary

Total Giving: $561,493 (2001); $522,583 (2000); $455,400 (1999)
Assets: $8,990,260 (2001); $10,126,406 (2000); $11,931,156 (1999)
Gifts Received: $1,957 (2000); $16,500 (1997); $250,000 (1996). Note: In 1996 and 1997, contributions were received from the estate of William D. Trippe.

Typical Recipients

Civic & Public Affairs: Community Foundations, Public Policy, Urban & Community Affairs
Social Services: Youth Organizations

Application Procedures

Initial Contact: Send a brief letter of inquiry.
Deadlines: None.

Restrictions

Limited to Polk County, GA.

Foundation Officials

James J. Carter, Jr.: director
Lloyd H. Gray, Jr.: director
George E. Mundy: director
Pauline Pledger: secretary
Jane C. Wyatt: director
Glen T. York: president
Michael H. York, Sr.: director

Grants Analysis

Disclosure Period: calendar year ending 2001
Total Grants: $561,493
Number of Grants: 3
Highest Grant: $524,988
Lowest Grant: $6,505

Recent Grants

Note: Grants derived from 2000 Form 990.

General

487,425	Gwinnett Foundation, Inc., Duluth, GA -- designated to donor advisory fund
17,300	City of Cedartown, Cedartown, GA -- for capital improvements to the Hawkes library
10,358	Polk School District, Cedartown, GA -- for Cedartown High School field house, furish lobby of field house
7,500	City of Cedartown, Cedartown, GA -- for capital improvements to pool house and related facilities

THE TRULL FOUNDATION

Giving Contact

E. Gail Purvis, Executive Director
404 Fourth Street
Palacios, TX 77465
Phone: (361)972-5241
Fax: (361)972-1109
E-mail: info@trullfoundation.org
Web: http://www.trullfoundation.org

Description

Founded: 1948
EIN: 237423943
Organization Type: Family Foundation
Giving Locations: TX: nationally, although Texas is given preference.
Grant Types: Conference/Seminar, Emergency, General Support, Multiyear/Continuing Support, Operating Expenses, Project, Scholarship.

Donor Information

Founder: Established in 1948 by B. W. Trull and Florence M. Trull for religious, charitable, and educational purposes. Trustees were Robert B. Trull, Harry H. Sisson, and Ralph P. Newsom. By the terms of its indenture, the original foundation expired in 1973. In 1967, the Trull family (Florence M. Trull and her four children) established a new foundation to receive the assets of the old foundation and to run until its assets were expended. The Trull family's fortune stems from farming, land management, and investments.

Financial Summary

Total Giving: $1,174,630 (2001); $1,108,536 (2000); $1,089,958 (1999)

Assets: $25,111,815 (2001); $24,111,186 (2000); $26,974,451 (1999)
Gifts Received: $10,000 (1994)

Typical Recipients

Arts & Humanities: Arts Associations & Councils, Arts Festivals, Ethnic & Folk Arts, Film & Video, Historic Preservation, History & Archaeology, Libraries, Museums/Galleries, Music, Opera, Performing Arts, Public Broadcasting, Theater, Visual Arts
Civic & Public Affairs: African American Affairs, Botanical Gardens/Parks, Civil Rights, Community Foundations, Economic Development, Employment/Job Training, Civic & Public Affairs-General, Hispanic Affairs, Housing, Law & Justice, Legal Aid, Municipalities/Towns, Nonprofit Management, Rural Affairs, Safety, Urban & Community Affairs, Women's Affairs
Education: Afterschool/Enrichment Programs, Arts/Humanities Education, Colleges & Universities, Colleges & Universities, Community & Junior Colleges, Education Reform, Education-General, Leadership Training, Literacy, Medical Education, Minority Education, Preschool Education, Private Education (Precollege), Public Education (Precollege), Religious Education, Science/Mathematics Education, Secondary Education (Private), Secondary Education (Public), Special Education, Student Aid, Vocational & Technical Education
Environment: Environment-General, Resource Conservation
Health: AIDS/HIV, Cancer, Children's Health/Hospitals, Health-General, Health Organizations, Medical Rehabilitation, Medical Research, Mental Health, Nutrition, Preventive Medicine/Wellness Organizations, Public Health, Transplant Networks/Donor Banks
International: Foreign Arts Organizations, International-General, Health Care/Hospitals, International Development, International Environmental Issues, International Peace & Security Issues, International Relations, International Relief Efforts, Missionary/Religious Activities
Religion: Bible Study/Translation, Churches, Ministries, Missionary Activities (Domestic), Religious Organizations, Religious Welfare, Seminaries, Social/Policy Issues
Science: Observatories & Planetariums
Social Services: At-Risk Youth, Camps, Child Welfare, Community Centers, Community Service Organizations, Counseling, Day Care, Delinquency & Criminal Rehabilitation, Domestic Violence, Emergency Relief, Family Planning, Family Services, Food/Clothing Distribution, Homes, Refugee Assistance, Senior Services, Shelters/Homelessness, Substance Abuse, United Funds/United Ways, Youth Organizations

Application Procedures

Initial Contact: Current guidelines and grant information available at foundation website. Applicants may also contact foundation in order to receive the proposal fact sheet and grant proposal guidelines.
Application Requirements: Applicants should submit an original and three copies of a full proposal, including: cover letter (2 pages or less), the proposal fact sheet, current agency operating budget (one page), sources of income, project budget (one page), IRS information, and up to five pages of additional information.
Deadlines: None.
Review Process: The Contributions Committee meets throughout the year and will respond to proposal within three months.
Notes: The foundation does not accept faxed proposals. Unexpended funds must be returned to the foundation.

Restrictions

The foundation reports that it usually will not make long term commitments; make grants for buildings,

endowments, or research; repeat grants in the same project longer than three years; fund operational expenses except during initial years; or make grants to individuals.

Additional Information

The foundation supports established organizations to develop new programs, assists in proposal writing to work in coordination with other foundations, and conducts seminars/workshops.
The foundation expects periodic progress reports during the funding period.
Publications: Annual Report; Guidelines; Application Form; Proposal Fact Sheet

Foundation Officials

Garland M. Brooking: founder
Gladys Trull Brooking: founder
Colleen Claybourn: secretary, treasurer, trustee, member contributions committee B Gary, IN 1934. NONPR AFFIL director: Presbyterian Historical Society Southwest; member: Sigma Tau Nu; director: Palacios Area Hististorical Association; director: Matagorda County Hististorical Society; director: Matagorda County Historical Commission, Bay City Texas.
Cara Herlin: advisory trustee
Jean Trull Herlin: founder, trustee emeritus
J. Fred Huitt: vice chairman board trustees, member investment committee
Rose C. Lancaster: trustee, member contributions committee
Sarah Olfers: advisory trustee
B. B. Shiflett: founder NONPR AFFIL secretary, executive director: Ralph M Parsons Foundation.
Laura Trull Shiflett: founder
R. Scott Trull: trustee
Robert B. Trull: founder, trustee emeritus PRIM CORP EMPL officer: City State Bank of Palacios. CORP AFFIL director: Northwest Bank Texas Bay City.

Grants Analysis

Disclosure Period: calendar year ending 2001
Total Grants: $1,174,630*
Number of Grants: 255
Average Grant: $4,608
Highest Grant: $80,000
Typical Range: $2,000 to $5,000
*Note: Grants analysis provided by foundation.

Recent Grants

Note: Grants derived from 2000 Form 990.

General

80,000	Schriener College, Kerrville, TX -- capital campaign
35,000	Friends of Elder Citizens, Inc., Palacios, TX -- for nutrition operations
30,000	Palacios Area Fund, Palacios, TX -- endowment fund 6th year payment
18,000	Mission Presbytery Outdoor Ministries, Fischer, TX -- scholarships/kitchen extension for John Knox Ranch
17,500	Friends of Elder Citizens, Inc., Palacios, TX -- nutrition program and building improvements
14,000	City of Palacios, Palacios, TX -- volunteer fire dept/fire truck
13,000	City of Palacios, Palacios, TX -- city park restoration and beautification
12,000	El Buen Pastor Early Childhood Development Center, Austin, TX -- El buen Pastor ECDC expansion project
12,000	Palacios Independent School District, Palacios, TX -- scholarships
10,000	Hilliard Alumni Association, Inc -- renovation and extension

TRUMBULL COUNTY SCHOLARSHIP FOUNDATION

Giving Contact
Michael Craig, Chairman
c/o Second National Bank
260 Niles Cortland Rd. NE
Warren, OH 44484
Phone: (330)394-3773

Description
Founded: 1987
EIN: 346545694
Organization Type: Private Foundation
Giving Locations: OH; PA
Grant Types: General Support.

Financial Summary
Total Giving: $8,000 (2001); $7,333 (2000); $8,500 (1999)
Giving Analysis: Giving for 2001 includes: foundation scholarships ($8,000)
Assets: $126,270 (2001); $125,408 (2000); $120,661 (1999)

Typical Recipients
Arts & Humanities: Libraries
Education: Colleges & Universities, Education Reform, Faculty Development, Science/Mathematics Education, Student Aid

Application Procedures
Initial Contact: Contact the foundation to request an application form.
Deadlines: Application deadline is in the spring.

Restrictions
Accepts applications for educational/scholarship purposes only.

Additional Information
Trust(s): Second National Bank of Warren

Grants Analysis
Disclosure Period: calendar year ending 2001
Total Grants: $8,000*
Number of Grants: 12
Average Grant: $667
Highest Grant: $1,500
Lowest Grant: $500
Typical Range: $500 to $1,000
*Note: Giving includes scholarships.

Recent Grants
Note: Grants derived from 2001 Form 990.

Library-Related
1,000	Pittsburgh Technology Institute, Oakdale, PA

General
1,500	Kent State University, Kent, OH
1,000	Ohio State University, Columbus, OH
500	Capital University, Columbus, OH
500	Gannon University, Erie, PA
500	Grove City College, Grove City, PA
500	John Carroll University Institute for Educational Renewal, University Heights, OH
500	Messiah College, Grantham, PA
500	Mount Union College, Alliance, OH
500	Penn State University, University Park, PA
500	Walsh University, Canton, OH

TRUST FOR MUTUAL UNDERSTANDING

Giving Contact
Richard S. Lanier, Trustee
30 Rockefeller Plaza
Room 5600
New York, NY 10112
Phone: (212)632-3405
Fax: (212)632-3409
E-mail: tmu@tmuny.org
Web: http://www.tmuny.org

Description
Founded: 1984
EIN: 133212724
Organization Type: General Purpose Foundation
Giving Locations: nationally; Czech Republic; Hungary; Poland; Russia; Slovakia
Grant Types: Conference/Seminar, Project, Research.
Note: The trust also provides grants for professional exchanges and international travel.

Financial Summary
Total Giving: $3,683,829 (2000); $3,220,921 (1999); $3,069,855 (1998)
Assets: $74,237,576 (2000); $84,888,509 (1999); $70,194,294 (1998)
Gifts Received: $7,585 (1999); $100,028 (1998); $25,000,000 (1992). Note: In 1999 and 1998, contributions were received from individual donors.

Typical Recipients
Arts & Humanities: Arts Associations & Councils, Arts Funds, Dance, Film & Video, Arts & Humanities-General, Historic Preservation, History & Archaeology, Libraries, Museums/Galleries, Music, Performing Arts, Theater, Visual Arts
Civic & Public Affairs: Botanical Gardens/Parks, Civil Rights, Ethnic Organizations, Civic & Public Affairs-General, Philanthropic Organizations, Public Policy, Urban & Community Affairs
Education: Arts/Humanities Education, Colleges & Universities, Continuing Education, Faculty Development, Education-General, International Exchange, International Studies, Journalism/Media Education, Legal Education, Medical Education, Student Aid
Environment: Environment-General, Resource Conservation, Wildlife Protection, Wildlife Protection
Health: AIDS/HIV, Health-General
International: Foreign Arts Organizations, Foreign Educational Institutions, Health Care/Hospitals, Human Rights, International Affairs, International Development, International Environmental Issues, International Organizations, International Peace & Security Issues, International Relations
Religion: Jewish Causes
Science: Scientific Centers & Institutes, Scientific Research
Social Services: Food/Clothing Distribution, Social Services-General, YMCA/YWCA/YMHA/YWHA

Application Procedures
Initial Contact: Applicants are requested to submit an initial letter of inquiry, approximately three months in advance of the deadline for submitting a proposal. Letters of inquiry should include a summary of the project, list of prinicpal institutional participants, amount requested, and a project schedule. If an activity is eligible for review, more detailed information will be requested prior to the formal consideration of a final proposal.
Application Requirements: While the initial inquiry may be made by an individual or Institution in the United States, Russia, or Eastern and Central Europe, the final proposal must be submitted by an American nonprofit involved in the implementation of the project,

as the Trust does not make grants directly to organizations in the region. If an activity is eligible for Trust support, an application form requesting more detailed information will be provided to be completed and returned by the American institutional partner.
Deadlines: Proposal deadlines are February 1 for review in June and August 1 for review in December.
Review Process: Grant awards are announced immediately after each meeting.

Restrictions
Although the trust supports institutional activities which foster the exchange of individuals as participants in projects, it does not make grants directly to individuals or to organizations for activities in which only a single participant is involved. The trust does not support one-person exhibitions; solo performance tours; fellowships; retroactive funding; multiyear commitments; inter-regional exchanges; operating expenses; capital campaigns; construction costs; salaries; honoraria; youth and undergraduate exchanges; literature and publication projects; library and equipment purchases; film, media, and mass communications; activities pertaining to nuclear weapons and arms control; or programs concentrating on economic development, public health, and agriculture.

Additional Information
Publications: Application Guidelines; Grants List

Foundation Officials
Richard S. Lanier: director B 1943. ED Tulane University BA (1965); New York University MA (1967). PRIM NONPR EMPL president: Council of Asian Culture.
Elizabeth J. McCormack: trustee ED Manhattanville College BA (1944); Fordham University PhD (1966). PRIM CORP EMPL associate: Rockefeller Family & Associates. CORP AFFIL director: United HealthCare Corp.; trustee: Alliance Capital Management; supervisory director: Arrow Ventures NV. NONPR AFFIL overseer, manager: Memorial Sloan-Kettering Cancer Center; trustee emeritus: Swarthmore College; trustee: The Juilliard School; member: Century Association; member: Council Foreign Relations; member: American Academy of Arts & Sciences; trustee: American Academy Rome.
Donal Clare O'Brien, Jr.: trustee B New York, NY 1934. ED Williams College BA (1956); University of Virginia LLB (1959). PRIM CORP EMPL partner: Milbank, Tweed, Hadley & McCloy. NONPR AFFIL trustee: Wendell Gilley Museum; trustee: Winthrop Rockefeller Charitable Trust; trustee: Trust Mutual Understanding; trustee: Waterfowl Research Foundation; chairman: Quebec Labrador Foundation; member council: Rockefeller University; trustee: North American Wildlife Foundation; trustee: JDR 3rd Fund; chairman: National Audubon Society; member: Council Environmental Quality; board directors: Greenacre Foundation; trustee: American Bird Conservancy; chairman board directors: Atlantic Salmon Federation. CLUB AFFIL mem: Century Association Anglers Club.

Grants Analysis
Disclosure Period: calendar year ending 2000
Total Grants: $3,683,829
Number of Grants: 162
Average Grant: $22,740
Highest Grant: $125,000
Typical Range: $10,000 to $30,000

Recent Grants
Note: Grants derived from 2000 Form 990.

General
125,000	CEC International Partners, New York, NY -- ArtsLink
95,000	Dance Theater Workshop, New York, NY -- suitcase fund
77,094	Foundation for a Civil Society, New York, NY

75,000	American Dance Festival, Durham, NC
75,000	Lincoln Center for the Performing Arts, New York, NY
70,000	Foundation for International Arts and Education
60,000	Eisenhower Exchange Fellowships, Philadelphia, PA -- Single Nation Program for Russia
60,000	Foundation for a Civil Society, New York, NY
60,000	Pacific Environment and Resources Center, Sausalito, CA
55,440	CEC International Partners, New York, NY

TRUST FUNDS

Giving Contact

James T. Healy, President
100 Broadway, 3rd Fl.
San Francisco, CA 94111
Phone: (415)434-3323

Description

Founded: 1934
EIN: 946062952
Organization Type: Private Foundation
Giving Locations: CA: San Francisco including the Bay area
Grant Types: Emergency, General Support, Scholarship, Seed Money.

Donor Information

Founder: Bartley P. Oliver

Financial Summary

Total Giving: $243,795 (2001); $235,412 (2000); $266,506 (1999)
Giving Analysis: Giving for 2000 includes: foundation scholarships ($12,500)
Assets: $6,490,684 (2001); $6,207,377 (2000); $5,690,605 (1999)
Gifts Received: $5,000 (2001); $20 (2000); $5,179 (1999). Note: In 2001, contributions were received from Alfreda Cullinan.

Typical Recipients

Arts & Humanities: Libraries, Museums/Galleries, Music, Opera
Civic & Public Affairs: Employment/Job Training, Housing, Nonprofit Management, Public Policy, Rural Affairs, Urban & Community Affairs, Women's Affairs
Education: Afterschool/Enrichment Programs, Arts/Humanities Education, Colleges & Universities, Elementary Education (Private), Elementary Education (Public), Faculty Development, Education-General, Literacy, Minority Education, Private Education (Precollege), Religious Education, Science/Mathematics Education, Secondary Education (Private), Secondary Education (Public), Student Aid
Health: Children's Health/Hospitals, Clinics/Medical Centers, Emergency/Ambulance Services, Geriatric Health, Hospitals, Long-Term Care, Mental Health, Prenatal Health Issues, Prenatal Health Issues, Research/Studies Institutes
International: Foreign Educational Institutions, Health Care/Hospitals, International Peace & Security Issues, Missionary/Religious Activities
Religion: Churches, Dioceses, Religion-General, Ministries, Missionary Activities (Domestic), Religious Organizations, Religious Welfare, Seminaries, Social/Policy Issues
Social Services: Community Service Organizations, Day Care, Family Planning, Family Services, Food/Clothing Distribution, Scouts, Senior Services, Shelters/Homelessness, Social Services-General, Youth Organizations

Application Procedures

Initial Contact: Send a brief letter of inquiry. Application form for Catholic schools requesting equipment grants.
Deadlines: None.

Restrictions

Preference given to Catholic charities and organizations in San Francisco area, though grants having national or global significance are considered.

Additional Information

Publications: Application Guidelines

Foundation Officials

James T. Healy: president
Thomas J. Kelley: director
Thomas F. Kubasak: chief financial officer
Joan C. O'Rourke: director
David Ramsey: secretary, director

Grants Analysis

Disclosure Period: calendar year ending 2001
Total Grants: $243,795
Number of Grants: 48
Average Grant: $5,079
Highest Grant: $15,000
Lowest Grant: $50
Typical Range: $1,000 to $10,000

Recent Grants

Note: Grants derived from 2001 Form 990.

General

15,000	Juan Diego Society, San Jose, CA -- for pro-life services
10,200	Holy Spirit School, San Jose, CA -- for reading tables and chairs
10,000	Americans United for Life, Chicago, IL -- for Pro-Life Public Interest Law and Education
10,000	Boy Scouts San Francisco Bay Area Council, San Leardro, CA
10,000	Catholic Social Services, Sacramento, CA -- for Homeless Adult Education Program
10,000	First Resort, Oakland, CA -- for Pro Life Crisis Pregnancy Program
10,000	Sacred Heart Elementary School, San Francisco, CA -- for phonics books, computer hardware and software
10,000	St. Elizabeth High School, Oakland, CA -- for new lockers
8,000	St. Gabriel School, San Francisco, CA -- for renovation of front entry
7,500	CYO San Francisco Boys and Girls Home, San Rafael, CA -- for pregnancy prevention girls' home

TSUMURA INTERNATIONAL, INC.

Company Headquarters

Secaucus, NJ

Company Description

Former Name: FMG Tsumura.
Employees: 600
SIC(s): 5122 Drugs, Proprietaries & Sundries.
Parent Company: Tsumura & Co., 12-7 Nibancho, Chiyoda-ku, Tokyo, Japan

Giving Contact

Hideo Anzai, Director
910 Sylvan Ave., Ste. 100
Englewood Cliffs, NJ 07632
Phone: (201)816-6000
Fax: (201)816-8477

Description

Organization Type: Corporate Giving Program
Giving Locations: headquarters and operating communities.
Grant Types: Employee Matching Gifts, General Support, Operating Expenses, Scholarship.

Typical Recipients

Arts & Humanities: Arts Festivals, Libraries, Public Broadcasting
Civic & Public Affairs: Economic Development, Philanthropic Organizations, Zoos/Aquariums
Health: Geriatric Health, Health Organizations, Hospitals
Social Services: Child Welfare, Community Centers, People with Disabilities, Senior Services, Shelters/Homelessness, Youth Organizations

Restrictions

Does not support requests not supported by someone within the company, dinners or special events, individuals, political or lobbying groups, or religious organizations for sectarian purposes.

Corporate Officials

Dennis Newnham: president, chief executive officer PRIM CORP EMPL president, chief executive officer: Tsumura International Inc.
Monty Tsumura: chairman PRIM CORP EMPL chairman: Tsumura International Inc.

Grants Analysis

Typical Range: $10 to $250

MICHAEL TUCH FOUNDATION

Giving Contact

Martha Tuck-Rozett, President
122 E. 42nd Street
New York, NY 10168
Phone: (212)943-9082

Description

Founded: 1946
EIN: 136002848
Organization Type: Private Foundation
Giving Locations: NY: New York
Grant Types: Fellowship, Project, Scholarship.

Donor Information

Founder: the late Michael Tuch

Financial Summary

Total Giving: $458,550 (2001); $416,800 (2000); $407,050 (1999)
Assets: $8,025,386 (2001); $8,909,665 (2000); $9,687,157 (1999)
Gifts Received: $56,023 (2001); $52,726 (2000); $53,645 (1999). Note: Contributions are received from the Michael Tuch Trust.

Typical Recipients

Arts & Humanities: Arts Centers, Arts Festivals, Arts Outreach, Community Arts, Dance, Libraries, Museums/Galleries, Music, Opera, Performing Arts, Public Broadcasting, Theater
Civic & Public Affairs: Botanical Gardens/Parks, Urban & Community Affairs, Zoos/Aquariums
Education: Arts/Humanities Education, Colleges & Universities, Education Reform, Education-General, Minority Education, Religious Education, School Volunteerism, Special Education, Vocational & Technical Education
Environment: Air/Water Quality, Environment-General, Resource Conservation, Wildlife Protection
Health: AIDS/HIV, Children's Health/Hospitals, Mental Health

International: Foreign Educational Institutions, International Relief Efforts
Religion: Jewish Causes, Religious Organizations, Religious Welfare
Science: Science Museums
Social Services: Big Brother/Big Sister, Child Welfare, Community Centers, Community Service Organizations, Day Care, Food/Clothing Distribution, People with Disabilities, Recreation & Athletics, Shelters/Homelessness, Substance Abuse, United Funds/United Ways, YMCA/YWCA/YMHA/YWHA, Youth Organizations

Application Procedures

Initial Contact: Send cover letter and full proposal.
Application Requirements: Include a description of organization, amount requested, purpose of funds sought, recently audited financial statement, and proof of tax-exempt status.
Deadlines: None.

Restrictions

Does not support individuals.

Foundation Officials

Martha Rozett: vice president
J. Jacques Stone: secretary, treasurer
Daniel H. Tuck: director
Eugene Tuck, Esq.: president
Jonathan S. Tuck: director

Grants Analysis

Disclosure Period: calendar year ending 2001
Total Grants: $458,550
Number of Grants: 102
Average Grant: $3,996*
Highest Grant: $55,000
Typical Range: $1,000 to $5,000
*Note: Average grant figure excludes highest grant.

Recent Grants

Note: Grants derived from 2001 Form 990.

Library-Related
6,000	Brooklyn Public Library, Brooklyn, NY

General
55,000	Pearl Theatre Company, Inc., New York, NY
11,000	Brooklyn Academy of Music, New York, NY
10,000	Roundabout Theatre Company, New York, NY
9,000	Learning Leaders, Inc., New York, NY
8,500	Jean Cocteau Repertory Theatre, New York, NY
7,500	City Harvest, New York, NY
7,500	Irish Repertory Theatre, New York, NY
7,500	National Choral Council, New York, NY
7,500	National Dance Institute, New York, NY
7,500	Wildlife Conservation Society, Bronx, NY

ROSE E. TUCKER CHARITABLE TRUST

Giving Contact

Terrence R. Pancoast, Trustee
900 Southwest Fifth Avenue, 26th Floor
Portland, OR 97204
Phone: (503)224-3380
Fax: (503)220-2480
E-mail: tuckertrust@stoel.com

Description

Founded: 1976
EIN: 936119091
Organization Type: General Purpose Foundation

Giving Locations: OR: Portland metropolitan area; some statewide giving
Grant Types: Capital, Challenge, Conference/Seminar, Endowment, General Support, Multiyear/Continuing Support, Operating Expenses, Research.

Donor Information

Founder: Established in 1976 by the late Rose E. Tucker and the Max and Rose Tucker Foundation.

Financial Summary

Total Giving: $1,240,750 (fiscal year ending June 30, 2001); $1,542,100 (fiscal 2000); $977,810 (fiscal 1999)
Assets: $23,122,810 (fiscal 2001); $27,133,970 (fiscal 2000); $29,211,171 (fiscal 1999)

Typical Recipients

Arts & Humanities: Arts Festivals, Arts Institutes, Ballet, Dance, Film & Video, Arts & Humanities-General, Historic Preservation, History & Archaeology, Libraries, Museums/Galleries, Music, Opera, Performing Arts, Public Broadcasting, Theater
Civic & Public Affairs: Botanical Gardens/Parks, Civil Rights, Clubs, Economic Development, Civic & Public Affairs-General, Housing, Law & Justice, Legal Aid, Native American Affairs, Parades/Festivals, Public Policy, Urban & Community Affairs, Zoos/Aquariums
Education: Afterschool/Enrichment Programs, Arts/Humanities Education, Business Education, Colleges & Universities, Community & Junior Colleges, Continuing Education, Education Funds, Elementary Education (Private), Environmental Education, Faculty Development, Education-General, Health & Physical Education, Legal Education, Minority Education, Preschool Education, Private Education (Precollege), Public Education (Precollege), Science/Mathematics Education, Student Aid
Environment: Air/Water Quality, Energy, Environment-General, Protection, Resource Conservation, Watershed, Wildlife Protection
Health: Alzheimers Disease, Clinics/Medical Centers, Emergency/Ambulance Services, Health-General, Health Funds, Health Organizations, Hospitals, Medical Rehabilitation, Mental Health, Prenatal Health Issues, Public Health, Single-Disease Health Associations
International: Foreign Educational Institutions, International Affairs, International Environmental Issues
Religion: Jewish Causes, Religious Organizations, Religious Welfare
Science: Science Museums
Social Services: Animal Protection, At-Risk Youth, Camps, Child Welfare, Community Centers, Community Service Organizations, Counseling, Crime Prevention, Day Care, Family Planning, Family Services, Food/Clothing Distribution, People with Disabilities, Scouts, Senior Services, Substance Abuse, United Funds/United Ways, YMCA/YWCA/YMHA/YWHA, Youth Organizations

Application Procedures

Initial Contact: The trust has no formal grant application procedure or application form. Foundation does require that an application be in writing.
Application Requirements: Send two copies of basic information about the applicant; list of trustees or directors; description of the project for which the funding is requested, including significance to the community; budget; sources of actual or potential support; future funding; and date funds are required. Include one copy of IRS tax exempt letter under Section 501 (c)(3), verification of private foundation status, current financial statements, and a copy of a brochure or other literature describing the applicant's purpose and activities.
Deadlines: None.
Review Process: Payments are normally made within two weeks after the grants are awarded.

Restrictions

The trust does not make grants to individuals, program-related loans or investments, organizations which unfairly discriminate, organizations classified as "private foundations" under Sec. 509(a) of the Internal Revenue Code, conduit organizations, or efforts to carry on propaganda or to influence legislation. No grants are made for fellowships or debt reduction.

Additional Information

The Trust encourages the submission of progress reports indicating how the grant was used and what results were accomplished.
Publications: Application Guidelines; Annual Report

Foundation Officials

Milo E. Ormseth: trustee B Wolf Point, MT 1932. ED Saint Olaf College BA (1954); Harvard University LLB (1959). PRIM CORP EMPL partner: Stoel Rives Boley Jones & Grey. CORP AFFIL secretary, director: Allen Forest Products Co.; secretary, treasurer, director: America River Lumber Co. Inc.
Thomas B. Stoel: trustee

Grants Analysis

Disclosure Period: fiscal year ending June 30, 2001
Total Grants: $1,240,750
Number of Grants: 195
Average Grant: $6,363
Highest Grant: $45,000
Typical Range: $1,500 to $10,000

Recent Grants

Note: Grants derived from fiscal 2000 Form 990.

General
100,000	Oregon Coast Aquarium, Newport, OR -- for Passages of the Deep Exhibit
100,000	Pioneer Courthouse Square, Portland, OR
50,000	Nature Conservancy, Arlington, VA -- Forever Oregon Campaign
50,000	Reed College, Portland, OR
45,000	Lewis and Clark College, Portland, OR -- for continuing financial support
40,000	Geneforum.Org, Lake Oswego, OR -- for Genetic Privacy Program
37,500	Oregon Public Broadcasting, Portland, OR
35,000	Willamette University, Salem, OR
30,000	Campaign for Equal Justice, Portland, OR
25,000	Ecotrust, Portland, OR

TUCKER FOUNDATION

Giving Contact

M. Hayne Hamilton, President
Tucker Foundation
600 Krystal Bldg.
Chattanooga, TN 37402
Phone: (423)756-1202

Description

Founded: 1996
EIN: 621603398
Organization Type: Private Foundation
Giving Locations: GA: Atlanta; TN: Hamilton & Bradley Counties, Chattanooga
Grant Types: General Support.

Financial Summary

Total Giving: $1,297,336 (2001); $2,046,000 (2000)
Giving Analysis: Giving for 2001 includes: foundation grants to United Way ($15,000) 2000: foundation grants to United Way ($20,000)
Assets: $22,246,539 (2001); $23,409,551 (2000); $2,930,068 (1996)

Typical Recipients

Arts & Humanities: Arts & Humanities-General, History & Archaeology, Libraries, Performing Arts
Civic & Public Affairs: Community Foundations, Economic Development
Education: Colleges & Universities, Education-General, Private Education (Precollege), Secondary Education (Private)
Environment: Environment-General
Religion: Missionary Activities (Domestic)
Social Services: Scouts

Application Procedures

Initial Contact: The foundation reports that it does not have a formal application procedure. Submit a brief letter of inquiry.
Deadlines: None.

Additional Information

Although the foundation focuses its grantmaking on Atlanta, GA and Hamilton and Bradley Counties, TN, giving is not exclusive to these locations.

Foundation Officials

Lavina J. Cherry: trustee
Andrew G. Cope: trustee
Pamela K. Cuzzort: treasurer
M. Hayne Hamilton: president
S. K. Johnston, Jr.: trustee

Grants Analysis

Disclosure Period: calendar year ending 2001
Total Grants: $1,282,336*
Number of Grants: 65
Average Grant: $10,729*
Highest Grant: $317,150
Lowest Grant: $50
Typical Range: $5,000 to $20,000
*Note: Giving excludes United Way. Average grant figure excludes three highest grants ($617,150).

Recent Grants

Note: Grants derived from 2000 Form 990.

Library-Related
150,000	Cleveland Public Library, Cleveland, TN

General
821,770	Chattanooga Community Foundation, Chattanooga, TN
300,000	Wyoming Community Foundation, Sheridan, WY
100,000	Baylor School - Scholarship Endowment, Chattanooga, TN
100,000	University of Wyoming Institute for Environment, Laramie, WY
50,000	Girls Preparatory School 2/3, Chattanooga, TN
50,000	Tri-State Exhibition Center, Atlanta, GA
35,000	Archeological Conservancy - Candies Creek, Acworth, GA
33,333	River City Company 1/3, Chattanooga, TN
30,000	Bryan College 3/4, Dayton, TN
25,000	Bright School - Capital Campaign Kindergarten, Chattanooga, TN

TUPANCY-HARRIS FOUNDATION OF 1986

Giving Contact

Robert N. Karelitz, Vice President
c/o Fiduciary Trust Co.
PO Box 1647
Boston, MA 02105-1647
Phone: (617)482-5270
Fax: (617)482-2078

Description

Founded: 1986
EIN: 046547989
Organization Type: Private Foundation
Giving Locations: MA: Nantucket
Grant Types: General Support.

Donor Information

Founder: the late Oswald A. Tupancy

Financial Summary

Total Giving: $2,284,939 (2001); $1,909,117 (2000); $1,494,412 (1999)
Assets: $28,992,626 (2001); $41,089,899 (2000); $39,643,267 (1999)
Gifts Received: $1,510 (1994); $27,309 (1993); $372 (1992)

Typical Recipients

Arts & Humanities: Arts Associations & Councils, Ethnic & Folk Arts, Historic Preservation, History & Archaeology, Libraries, Museums/Galleries, Music, Public Broadcasting, Theater
Civic & Public Affairs: Civic & Public Affairs-General, Native American Affairs, Urban & Community Affairs, Zoos/Aquariums
Education: Colleges & Universities, Community & Junior Colleges, Education-General, Public Education (Precollege)
Environment: Environment-General, Resource Conservation
Health: AIDS/HIV, Clinics/Medical Centers, Hospices, Hospitals, Prenatal Health Issues, Single-Disease Health Associations, Trauma Treatment
Religion: Churches, Religion-General, Religious Organizations
Science: Scientific Centers & Institutes
Social Services: Animal Protection, Big Brother/Big Sister, Camps, Child Welfare, Community Service Organizations, Delinquency & Criminal Rehabilitation, Family Services, Recreation & Athletics, Social Services-General, Substance Abuse, Youth Organizations

Application Procedures

Initial Contact: Send a brief letter of inquiry describing program or project.
Application Requirements: Include description of organization.
Deadlines: None.

Restrictions

Does not support individuals; religious organizations for sectarian purposes; political or lobbying groups; or organizations outside operating areas.

Additional Information

Trust(s): Fiduciary Trust Co.

Grants Analysis

Disclosure Period: calendar year ending 2001
Total Grants: $2,284,939
Number of Grants: 32
Average Grant: $62,341*
Highest Grant: $352,376
Typical Range: $20,000 to $100,000
*Note: Average grant figure excludes highest grant.

Recent Grants

Note: Grants derived from 2001 Form 990.

Library-Related
150,000	Nantucket Athenaeum, Nantucket, MA

General
352,376	Nantucket Conservation Foundation, Nantucket, MA
290,583	Nantucket Historical Association, Nantucket, MA
250,000	Museum of Afro-American History, Boston, MA
250,000	Nantucket Ice Company, Inc., Nantucket, MA
155,000	Nantucket Boys and Girls Club, Nantucket, MA
150,000	Nantucket Community Service Inc., Nantucket, MA
115,331	Sherburne Commons, Nantucket, MA
105,000	Nantucket Cottage Hospital, Nantucket, MA
100,000	Nantucket Maria Mitchell Association, Nantucket, MA
65,000	Strong Wings Inc., Nantucket, MA

COURTNEY S. TURNER CHARITABLE TRUST

Giving Contact

David P. Ross, Sr., Trust Officer
Bank of America
1200 Main St., 14th Fl.
Kansas City, MO 64105
Phone: (816)979-7481
Fax: (816)691-7916

Description

Founded: 1986
EIN: 436316904
Organization Type: General Purpose Foundation
Giving Locations: MO: Atchison, Kansas City metropolitan area
Grant Types: Capital, Matching, Project, Seed Money.

Donor Information

Founder: Established in 1986 by Courtney S. Turner.

Financial Summary

Total Giving: $1,912,907 (2001); $1,827,002 (2000); $1,531,205 (1998)
Giving Analysis: Giving for 1997 includes: foundation grants to United Way ($25,000)
Assets: $34,149,209 (2001); $36,606,697 (2000); $39,075,764 (1998)

Typical Recipients

Arts & Humanities: Arts Associations & Councils, Arts Institutes, Dance, Arts & Humanities-General, History & Archaeology, Libraries, Museums/Galleries, Music, Opera, Performing Arts, Public Broadcasting, Theater
Civic & Public Affairs: Botanical Gardens/Parks, Business/Free Enterprise, Community Foundations, Employment/Job Training, Civic & Public Affairs-General, Hispanic Affairs, Housing, Law & Justice, Legal Aid, Minority Business, Parades/Festivals, Zoos/Aquariums
Education: Arts/Humanities Education, Business Education, Colleges & Universities, Elementary Education (Private), Environmental Education, Education-General, Leadership Training, Preschool Education, Private Education (Precollege), Student Aid
Environment: Resource Conservation
Health: Children's Health/Hospitals, Clinics/Medical Centers, Health-General, Heart, Hospitals, Hospitals (University Affiliated), Multiple Sclerosis, Nursing Services, Public Health
Religion: Jewish Causes, Religious Welfare
Science: Science Museums
Social Services: At-Risk Youth, Camps, Child Welfare, Community Centers, Community Service Organizations, Counseling, Day Care, Domestic Violence, Family Services, People with Disabilities, Recreation & Athletics, Scouts, Senior Services, Sexual Abuse, Social Services-General, Substance Abuse, YMCA/YWCA/YMHA/YWHA, Youth Organizations

Application Procedures

Initial Contact: Contact David Ross directly by phone before submitting applications.
Application Requirements: Submit a letter no longer than three pages with the appropriate attachments.
Deadlines: None.

Foundation Officials

David P. Ross: trust officer PRIM CORP EMPL senior vice president: NationsBank Corp.
Daniel C. Weary: trustee B Junction City, KS 1927. ED Harvard University AB (1949); Harvard University Law School LLB (1952). PRIM CORP EMPL partner: Blackwell, Sanders, Matheny, Weary & Lombardi LLP. CORP AFFIL secretary, director: Progressive Manufacturing Co.

Grants Analysis

Disclosure Period: calendar year ending 2001
Total Grants: $1,912,907
Number of Grants: 48
Average Grant: $39,852
Highest Grant: $353,000
Lowest Grant: $1,500
Typical Range: $15,000 to $60,000

Recent Grants

Note: Grants derived from 2001 Form 990.

Library-Related

20,000	Missouri Development Finance Board, Jefferson City, MO -- classroom for democracy campaign support

General

353,000	Benedictine College, Atchison, KS -- renovation projects
200,000	Nelson Atkins Museum of Art, Kansas City, MO -- capital campaign
137,845	Atchison Community Information Network, Atchison, KS -- network's startup costs
130,000	Mid-America Heart Institute, Kansas City, MO -- cardiovascular research center expansion
100,000	KCPT/Channel 19, Kansas City, MO -- campaign for digital system
57,200	De LaSalle Education Center, Kansas City, MO -- computer technology
50,000	Donnelly College, Kansas City, KS -- support "building bridges of opportunity"
50,000	Friends of the Zoo, Kansas City, MO -- consultation costs
50,000	Gardner Institute, Kansas City, KS -- technology support
50,000	Heart of America Family Services, Kansas City, KS -- secure space for Dame La Mano

TURRELL FUND

Giving Contact

Dr. E. Belvin Williams, Executive Director & Secretary
21 Van Vleck Street
Montclair, NJ 07042-2358
Phone: (973)783-9358
Fax: (973)783-9283
E-mail: turrell@bellatlantic.net
Web: http://www.fdncenter.org/grantmaker/turrell

Description

Founded: 1935
EIN: 221551936
Organization Type: Specialized/Single Purpose Foundation
Giving Locations: NJ: Essex County, Hudson County, Passaic County, Union County; VT
Grant Types: Capital, Challenge, General Support, Project, Scholarship, Seed Money.

Donor Information

Founder: Established in 1935 by Herbert Turrell and Margaret Turrell. Mr. Turrell was associated with Parke, Davis and Co. and American Home Products. The foundation has some of its assets in the latter company. Since its inception, the Turrell Fund has aided children and youth, a major interest of the Turrells during their lifetimes. Although the foundation originally was empowered to make grants to organizations in New York, New Jersey, and Vermont, the trustees have phased out giving in New York.

Financial Summary

Total Giving: $7,373,276 (2001); $7,718,673 (2000); $10,000,000 (1999 approx)
Giving Analysis: Giving for 1998 includes: foundation grants to United Way ($52,050)
Assets: $132,067,520 (2001); $139,876,990 (2000); $159,184,721 (1998)

Typical Recipients

Arts & Humanities: Arts Outreach, History & Archaeology, Libraries, Museums/Galleries, Music, Performing Arts
Civic & Public Affairs: African American Affairs, Business/Free Enterprise, Economic Development, Employment/Job Training, Civic & Public Affairs-General, Hispanic Affairs, Housing, Urban & Community Affairs
Education: Afterschool/Enrichment Programs, Arts/Humanities Education, Business Education, Colleges & Universities, Education Associations, Education Funds, Education Reform, Elementary Education (Private), Education-General, Literacy, Medical Education, Minority Education, Preschool Education, Private Education (Precollege), Public Education (Precollege), School Volunteerism, Science/Mathematics Education, Secondary Education (Private), Secondary Education (Public), Special Education, Student Aid
Environment: Resource Conservation
Health: Adolescent Health Issues, AIDS/HIV, Children's Health/Hospitals, Clinics/Medical Centers, Hospitals, Medical Rehabilitation, Preventive Medicine/Wellness Organizations, Research/Studies Institutes
International: International Organizations, International Relief Efforts
Religion: Dioceses, Religion-General, Ministries, Religious Organizations, Religious Welfare
Social Services: At-Risk Youth, Child Welfare, Community Centers, Community Service Organizations, Counseling, Day Care, Family Planning, Family Services, Food/Clothing Distribution, People with Disabilities, Recreation & Athletics, Scouts, Social Services-General, Substance Abuse, United Funds/United Ways, Volunteer Services, YMCA/YWCA/YMHA/YWHA, YMCA/YWCA/YMHA/YWHA, Youth Organizations

Application Procedures

Initial Contact: Call or write to receive fund's request form.
Application Requirements: The proposal should include the following: completed request form; one copy of the full proposal (no more than seven pages); a copy of the IRS determination letter; a statement confirming tax-exempt status on organization's letterhead and signed by an official; a recent audited financial statement or 990 Form; project or capital budget; budget for the organization; completed copy of fund's request form; and list of the organization's board of trustees.
Deadlines: Grant requests are accepted between August 1 and September 1, and between January 1 and February 1.
Review Process: Proposals are screened by the board of trustees. Notice of the board's decision is sent out in mid-December and in mid-June.
Evaluative Criteria: Evidence of the need of the services to be provided; organizational resources (staff, facilities, finances) to meet the need; evidence of local support; plans for the organization's evaluation of the project.
Notes: Progress reports and a final accounting of the use of funds is required of all grant recipients.

Restrictions

The fund does not encourage requests for support of cultural activities, and will not fund advocacy, endowment funds, grants to individuals, and most hospital and health care services.
Grants and scholarships are given to residents of New Jersey and Vermont on a priority basis by outside selection committee.
The fund will not accept proposals which are faxed or e-mailed.

Additional Information

Publications: Annual Report

Foundation Officials

Ann G. Dinse: trustee
Curtland E. Fields: trustee
Robert H. Grasmere: trustee PRIM NONPR EMPL mayor: Maplewood, New Jersey.
Frank Joseph Hoenemeyer: retired vice chairman CORP AFFIL director: American International Group.
S. Larry Prendergast: trustee, chairman
Dr. E. Belvin Williams: executive director, trustee ED Columbia University PhD; Columbia University MS; Columbia University MA; University of Denver.
Sonyia Woloshyn: treasurer

Grants Analysis

Disclosure Period: calendar year ending 2000
Total Grants: $7,718,673
Number of Grants: 271
Average Grant: $28,482
Highest Grant: $300,000
Lowest Grant: $1,000
Typical Range: $15,000 to $50,000

Recent Grants

Note: Grants derived from 2000 Form 990.

Library-Related

50,000	Kellogg-Hubbard Library, Montpelier, VT -- construction and renovations of the children's library

General

300,000	Chad School Foundation, Newark, NJ -- program support and Chad School
165,000	Saint Vincent Academy, Newark, NJ -- staff support
140,550	Children's Aid and Family Services, Paramus, NJ -- for program support
125,000	Urban League, Jersey City, NJ -- for renovation and expansion of the New Jersey Community Charter School
100,000	Boys and Girls Clubs, Newark, NJ -- for operating support and Life Camp
100,000	New Jersey Performing Arts Center, Newark, NJ -- for Summer Youth Performance Workshop
100,000	St. Benedict's Preparatory School, Newark, NJ -- operating support
100,000	YMCA, East Orange, NJ -- program support and camperships
92,860	Community Day Nursery, East Orange, NJ -- for program support and a computer program
90,000	Family Connections, Inc., Orange, NJ -- program support

TYNDALE HOUSE FOUNDATION

Giving Contact

Mary K. Yehling, Executive Director
351 Executive Drive
Wheaton, IL 60188

Phone: (630)790-9532
Fax: (630)790-2446

Description
Founded: 1964
EIN: 362555516
Organization Type: Private Foundation
Giving Locations: CO; IL; MI; PA; WA: nationally.
Grant Types: General Support.

Donor Information
Founder: Kenneth N. Taylor, Howard A. Elkind, ENB Charitable Trust

Financial Summary
Total Giving: $869,000 (2001); $885,000 (2000); $819,000 (1999)
Giving Analysis: Giving for 2001 includes: foundation ($869,000); 2000: foundation matching gifts ($2,500); foundation ($882,500); 1999: foundation fellowships ($17,000); foundation matching gifts ($52,500).
Assets: $95,675,799 (2001); $28,732 (2000); $220,851 (1999)
Gifts Received: $96,464,443 (2001); $717,808 (2000); $839,927 (1999). Note: In 2001, contributions were received from Kenneth and Margaret Taylor ($95,524,158) and the Kenneth Taylor Charitable Trust ($890,285). In 2000, contributions were received from Kenneth Taylor Charitable Trust. In 1999, contributions were received from Kenneth Taylor Charitable Trust ($711,927), Howard Eklind ($93,000), and Three Sons Acres ($35,000).

Typical Recipients
Arts & Humanities: Music, Public Broadcasting
Civic & Public Affairs: African American Affairs, Asian American Affairs, Clubs, Civic & Public Affairs-General, Inner-City Development, Legal Aid, Native American Affairs, Urban & Community Affairs, Women's Affairs
Education: Arts/Humanities Education, Colleges & Universities, Education-General, Religious Education
Health: AIDS/HIV, Transplant Networks/Donor Banks
International: Foreign Arts Organizations, Foreign Educational Institutions, Health Care/Hospitals, International Affairs, International Organizations, International Peace & Security Issues, International Relations, International Relief Efforts, Missionary/Religious Activities
Religion: Bible Study/Translation, Churches, Religion-General, Ministries, Missionary Activities (Domestic), Religious Organizations, Religious Welfare, Seminaries
Social Services: Camps, Community Centers, Family Services, Food/Clothing Distribution, Social Services-General, Youth Organizations

Application Procedures
Initial Contact: Send a brief letter or call the foundation to request a copy of its application guidelines.
Deadlines: August 15.

Restrictions
Limited to Christian literature work.

Foundation Officials
Edward Elliott: director
Edwin L. Frizen, Jr.: president B Chicago, IL 1925. PRIM NONPR EMPL executive director: Interdenominational Foreign Mission Association ADD NONPR EMPL member missions committee: World Evang Fellowship; treasurer editorial com: Evang Missions Information Service.
Wendell C. Hawley: director B Priest River, ID 1930. ED University of Oregon (1954-1959). PRIM CORP EMPL senior vice president: Tyndale House Publs.
David Howard: director
Elizabeth Knighton: director

Paul Mathews: vice president PRIM CORP EMPL vice president, assistant secretary, director: Tyndale House Publs.
Doug C. McConnell: president
Ted Noble: director
Robert Reekie: director
Kenneth Nathaniel Taylor: director B Portland, OR May 08, 1917. ED Wheaton College BA (1938); Dallas Theological Seminary (1940-1943); Northern Baptist Theological Seminary ThM (1944). PRIM CORP EMPL chairman, director: Tyndale House Publs. NONPR AFFIL director: Tyndale House Foundation; member: Wheaton College Scholastics Honor Society; trustee: Living Bible Foundation; trustee: Fuller Theological Seminary; member advisory board: International Bible Reading Association.
Margaret W. Taylor: secretary, treasurer CORP AFFIL director: Tyndale House Publs.
Mark Douglas Taylor: assistant secretary B Geneva, IL 1951. ED Duke University BA (1973). PRIM CORP EMPL president, chief executive officer, director: Tyndale House Publs. NONPR AFFIL trustee: Taylor University; member: Wheaton Liquor Control Comm; member: International Bible Society.
Peter W. Taylor: director
Mary Kleine Yehling: executive director

Grants Analysis
Disclosure Period: calendar year ending 2000
Total Grants: $869,000*
Number of Grants: 42
Average Grant: $10,475*
Highest Grant: $250,000
Typical Range: $5,000 to $20,000
*Note: Giving excludes matching gifts. Average grant figure excludes two highest grants ($450,000). ($320,000).

Recent Grants
Note: Grants derived from 2001 Form 990.

General
250,000	International Bible Society, Colorado Springs, CO -- Let There Be Light
200,000	Wycliff Bible Translators, Santa Ana, CA -- the Seed Company
36,000	Pioneers, Orlando, FL -- Bridge to the World
25,000	Western Seminary, Holland, MI -- Viva Network
20,000	Compassion International, Inc., Colorado Springs, CO -- bibles for children
19,000	SIM -- Bible Society of Nigeria
18,000	Interserve USA, Upper Darby, PA -- Bangladesh Tee Bible
17,500	Interserve USA, Upper Darby, PA -- Bangladesh Tee Bible
16,000	Map International, Brunswick, GA -- HIV/AIDS
15,000	Latin American Mission, Miami, FL -- reprint books for ministry use

UAL CORP.

Company Headquarters
1200 E. Algonquin Rd.
Elk Grove Village, IL 60007
Web: http://www.united.com

Company Description
Ticker: UAL
Exchange: NYSE
Revenue: US$14.286 billion (2002)
Employees: 10200 (2001)
Fortune Rank: 132, per FORTUNE Magazine's list of 500 Largest U.S. Corporations (2002).

Nonmonetary Support
Volunteer Programs: Co. sponsors employee volunteer programs such as: Believers Program-an educational mentoring and tutoring program; Habitat for Humanity; Take Your Community to Work Day; and AIDS walks.
Through its United We Care Program, co. also awards grants to organizations where employees volunteer.
Note: 1997 nonmonetary support valued at $2,200,000. Co. provides nonmonetary support through air transportation.

United Airlines Foundation

Giving Contact
Caryn M. Cross, Secretary
PO Box 66100
Chicago, IL 60666
Phone: (847)700-5714
Fax: (847)700-7345
E-mail: uafoundation@UAL.com

Description
EIN: 366109873
Organization Type: Corporate Foundation
Giving Locations: internationally; focusing on major cities served by the company.
Grant Types: Department, Employee Matching Gifts, General Support, Multiyear/Continuing Support, Project.

Financial Summary
Total Giving: $2,432,031 (2000); $2,854,973 (1999); $2,964,809 (1998). Note: Contributes through corporate direct giving program and foundation.
Giving Analysis: Giving for 2000 includes: foundation scholarships ($61,806); foundation grants to United Way ($1,015,000); foundation ($1,355,225); 1999: foundation scholarships ($73,806); foundation grants to United Way ($1,007,000); foundation grants to United Way ($1,774,167); 1998: foundation grants to United Way ($1,007,000); foundation ($1,957,809).
Assets: $4,748,715 (2000); $4,048,083 (1999); $3,497,777 (1998)
Gifts Received: $3,001,756 (2000); $3,386,907 (1999); $3,216,557 (1998)

Typical Recipients
Arts & Humanities: Arts Associations & Councils, Arts Funds, Arts Institutes, Ballet, Dance, Ethnic & Folk Arts, Libraries, Museums/Galleries, Music, Opera, Theater
Civic & Public Affairs: African American Affairs, Botanical Gardens/Parks, Business/Free Enterprise, Civil Rights, Clubs, Community Foundations, Economic Development, Employment/Job Training, Housing, Safety, Urban & Community Affairs, Women's Affairs, Zoos/Aquariums
Education: Afterschool/Enrichment Programs, Arts/Humanities Education, Business Education, Business-School Partnerships, Colleges & Universities, Education Funds, Education Reform, Education-General, Literacy, Minority Education, Minority Education, Private Education (Precollege), Public Education (Precollege), School Volunteerism, Science/Mathematics Education, Student Aid
Environment: Environment-General, Resource Conservation
Health: Alzheimers Disease, Cancer, Children's Health/Hospitals, Heart, Hospitals, Medical Research, Single-Disease Health Associations
International: International-General, International Development, International Environmental Issues, International Relief Efforts
Religion: Dioceses, Religious Welfare
Science: Observatories & Planetariums, Science Exhibits & Fairs, Science Museums, Scientific Centers & Institutes

Social Services: Big Brother/Big Sister, Child Welfare, Community Centers, Community Service Organizations, Crime Prevention, Delinquency & Criminal Rehabilitation, Emergency Relief, Food/Clothing Distribution, Recreation & Athletics, Scouts, Senior Services, Social Services-General, United Funds/United Ways, Volunteer Services, YMCA/YWCA/YMHA/YWHA, Youth Organizations

Application Procedures

Initial Contact: Submit a typewritten proposal on organization letterhead.
Application Requirements: Include a one-page executive summary; project summary; date and duration of project; location of activity; target beneficiaries; number of people served; financial, human, and transportation resources requested; intended use of funds, tickets or volunteers; benefits to the community; how program fits company's philanthropic strategy; ability to attract other donors due to company's participation; background and programs; copy of IRS tax-exempt letter; list of board of directors; contributors; annual report; previous and current year budget; and other supporting documents.
Deadlines: Sixty days prior to quarterly meetings in March, June, September, and December.
Review Process: Foundation and corporate contributions committee review proposals and conduct thorough evaluations of selected programs to be reviewed by the board of directors at meetings in the spring and fall.
Evaluative Criteria: Innovative or unusual approach to meeting stated objectives; ability of program to attract or stimulate the support of others; capacity to deal with fundamental issues of critical importance; potential for improvement of society through replication or institutional change.
Decision Notification: Allow at least 90 days prior to any publication and/or event deadlines for review and response; foundation will send a written response stating that the proposal has been accepted, declined, or is pending further consideration.
Notes: Do not send videotapes to the foundation. Supporting documentation will not be returned.

Restrictions

The United Airlines Foundation does not provide in-kind gifts or funding in the following areas: capital or building grants, development campaigns, individuals, political or fraternal organizations, United Way funded agencies, individual public or private schools, or churches. Grants made in funds only to qualifying non-profit tax exempt organizations and generally restricted to communities served by UAL corporation and subsidiaries.

Additional Information

United Airlines supports Habitat for Humanity and Ronald McDonald House Charities through soliciting foreign coins from international customers on their return flights.
Publications: Foundation and Corporate Giving Guidelines

Corporate Officials

John D. Kiker: vice president corporate communications PRIM CORP EMPL vice president corporate communications: United Airlines Inc.
Francesca M. Maher: senior vice president, general counsel, secretary B Chicago, IL 1957. ED Loyola University JD; Loyola University BA. PRIM CORP EMPL senior vice president, general counsel, secretary: UAL Corp. CORP AFFIL secretary: United Vacations Inc.; senior vice president, general counsel, secretary: United Airlines Inc.; secretary: United Aviation Fuels Corp. Del; secretary: Mileage Plus Inc. NONPR AFFIL director: United Center Community Economic Development Fund; director: YMCA Metropolitan Chicago; member: American Bar Association.

Eileen M. Younglove: contributions manager PRIM CORP EMPL contributions manager: United Airlines Inc.

Foundation Officials

Stuart I. Oran: president, chief executive officer B 1950. ED Cornell University BS; University of Chicago Law School JD. PRIM CORP EMPL vice president: United Vacations Inc. CORP AFFIL president: BizJet.
Eileen M. Younglove: secretary (see above)

Grants Analysis

Disclosure Period: calendar year ending 2000
Total Grants: $1,355,225*
Number of Grants: 93
Average Grant: $12,013*
Highest Grant: $250,000
Lowest Grant: $1,000
Typical Range: $1,000 to $25,000
*Note: Giving excludes scholarships and United Way. Average grant figure excludes highest grant.

Recent Grants

Note: Grants derived from 2000 Form 990.

General

300,000	United Way Community Chest, Cincinnati, OH
300,000	United Way Crusade of Mercy, Chicago, IL
225,000	United Way Bay Area, San Francisco, CA
130,000	Mile High United Way, Denver, CO
100,000	United Way, Inc., Los Angeles, CA
74,000	United Way National Capital Area, Washington, DC
50,000	United Way Tri-State, New York, NY
30,000	United Way King County, Seattle, WA
20,000	Aloha United Way, Honolulu, HI
20,000	United Way Dade County, Miami, FL

UBS PAINEWEBBER, INC.

Company Headquarters

1285 Avenue of the Americas
New York, NY 10019
Phone: (212)713-2000
Fax: (212)713-4889
Web: http://www.painewebber.com

Company Description

Formed by Merger of: UBS AG and PaineWebber (2000).

Nonmonetary Support

Volunteer Programs: The company sponsors a national volunteer initiative through which employees can access volunteer opportunities at local and national nonprofit organizations via the PaineWebber's Intranet system.

Paine Webber Foundation

Giving Contact

Paul Greene, Foundation Contact
1000 Harvard Boulevard
Weehawken, NJ 07086
Phone: (201)352-4324

Alternate Contact

Debra Lynne, Corporate Contributions
Paine Webber
1285 Avenue of the Americas, 14th Floor
New York, NY 10019

Description

Founded: 1879
EIN: 046032804
Organization Type: Corporate Foundation
Giving Locations: NY: New York
Grant Types: General Support, Research.

Donor Information

Founder: PaineWebber

Financial Summary

Total Giving: $4,150,000 (2001); $1,410,000 (1999); $902,750 (1997). Note: Contributes through corporate direct giving program and foundation.
Giving Analysis: Giving for 1999 includes: foundation ($1,410,000); 1997: foundation ($902,750) 1994: foundation ($800,208)
Assets: $41,471,867 (2001); $48,822,784 (2000); $43,225,554 (1999)
Gifts Received: $2,056,250 (1999); $8,028,750 (1997); $1,941,091 (1993)

Typical Recipients

Arts & Humanities: Arts Associations & Councils, Arts Centers, Libraries, Museums/Galleries, Music, Theater
Civic & Public Affairs: Botanical Gardens/Parks, Clubs, Community Foundations, Employment/Job Training, Civic & Public Affairs-General, Municipalities/Towns, Women's Affairs
Education: Business Education, Colleges & Universities, Education Associations, Education Reform, Education-General, Legal Education, Minority Education, Private Education (Precollege), Religious Education, Student Aid
Environment: Environment-General
Health: AIDS/HIV, Arthritis, Cancer, Children's Health/Hospitals, Diabetes, Emergency/Ambulance Services, Health Organizations, Hospices, Hospitals, Medical Research, Public Health, Single-Disease Health Associations, Transplant Networks/Donor Banks
International: Foreign Educational Institutions, International Development, International Relief Efforts
Religion: Churches, Dioceses, Jewish Causes, Ministries, Religious Organizations, Religious Welfare
Social Services: Animal Protection, At-Risk Youth, Child Welfare, Community Service Organizations, Counseling, Day Care, Family Services, Food/Clothing Distribution, People with Disabilities, Recreation & Athletics, Shelters/Homelessness, Social Services-General, Substance Abuse, YMCA/YWCA/YMHA/YWHA, Youth Organizations

Application Procedures

Initial Contact: For foundation grant requests, submit a brief typewritten letter of inquiry on organization's letterhead. For corporate contributions requests, submit a proposal.
Application Requirements: Foundation requests should include a description of organization, amount requested, and proof of tax-exempt status. Corporate contributions requests should include a description of organization, including the audience and community served by the organization; an outline of the request and a statement explaining how it accomplishes the organization's goals; a description of the organization's anticipated outcomes and benefits resulting from the grant; a certified copy of the organization's audited financial statements for the most recent fiscal year; proof of tax-exempt status; list of board of directors and affiliations; list of major contributors for most recent fiscal year; and most recent annual report.
Deadlines: December 1, for requests submitted to the foundation. None, for proposals submitted to the company.
Review Process: Corporate contributions requests take up to 90 days for review.

Restrictions

The company does not fund mass-mail appeals, political or lobbying groups, or fraternal groups. Organizations must have tax-exempt 501(c)(3) status.

Corporate Officials

Regina A. Dolan: chief financial officer, vice president B 1955. PRIM CORP EMPL chief financial officer, senior vice president: PaineWebber Group Inc. ADD CORP EMPL chief financial officer: Paine Webber Inc.

Joseph J. Grano, Jr.: chairman, chief executive officer B Hartford, CT 1948. PRIM CORP EMPL chairman, chief executive officer: PaineWebber Group Inc. CORP AFFIL president: PaineWebber Inc.

Foundation Officials

Regina A. Dolan: trustee (see above)

Grants Analysis

Disclosure Period: calendar year ending 2001
Total Grants: $4,150,000
Number of Grants: 10
Average Grant: $311,111*
Highest Grant: $1,350,000
Lowest Grant: $50,000
Typical Range: $100,000 to $1,000,000
*Note: Average grant figure excludes highest grant.

Recent Grants

Note: Grants derived from 1999 Form 990.

Library-Related

500,000	New York Public Library, New York, NY

General

250,000	New York Foundling Hospital, New York, NY
200,000	Coalition for the Homeless, New York, NY
175,000	YMCA of Greater New York, New York, NY
125,000	National Gallery of Art, Washington, DC
75,000	Sponsors for Educational Opportunity, New York, NY
50,000	Madison Square Boys & Girls Club, New York, NY
25,000	Mentoring USA, New York, NY
10,000	New York Cares, New York, NY

UEBERROTH FAMILY FOUNDATION

Giving Contact

Virginia Ueberroth, President
PO Box 100
Laguna Beach, CA 92652
Phone: (949)720-9646

Description

Founded: 1984
EIN: 330078919
Organization Type: Private Foundation
Giving Locations: CA
Grant Types: General Support.

Donor Information

Founder: Washington Speakers Bureau

Financial Summary

Total Giving: $511,911 (fiscal year ending November 30, 2000); $358,600 (fiscal 1999); $308,568 (fiscal 1998)
Giving Analysis: Giving for fiscal 2000 includes: foundation grants to United Way ($25,000); fiscal 1999: foundation grants to United Way ($11,000) fiscal 1998: foundation grants to United Way ($10,000)
Assets: $10,592,017 (fiscal 2000) $6,639,088 (fiscal 1999); $6,166,543 (fiscal 1998)

Gifts Received: $252,000 (fiscal 2000); $155,640 (fiscal 1999); $141,000 (fiscal 1998). Note: In fiscal 2000, contributions were received from Washington Speakers Bureau ($72,000), William Thompson ($125,000), Autry Foundation ($25,000), Peter and Virginia Ueberroth ($10,000), and Deutsche Bank ($20,000). In fiscal 1997, contributions were received from the Ueberroth Family Trust ($2,293,908) and Washington Speakers Bureau ($172,000). In fiscal 1998, contributions were received from the Washington Speakers Bureau ($131,000); Young Presidents Organization ($5,000); and Time, Inc. ($5,000). In fiscal 1999, contributions were received from Washington Speakers Bureau ($130,000), Bill Budge ($640), Int'l Assn of Conference Ctrs ($10,000), and Provident Mutual ($15,000).

Typical Recipients

Arts & Humanities: Arts Festivals, Arts Institutes, Ballet, Arts & Humanities-General, History & Archaeology, Libraries, Museums/Galleries, Music, Performing Arts, Public Broadcasting
Civic & Public Affairs: African American Affairs, Botanical Gardens/Parks, Chambers of Commerce, Clubs, Community Foundations, Economic Development, Employment/Job Training, Civic & Public Affairs-General, Housing, Public Policy, Rural Affairs, Urban & Community Affairs, Women's Affairs, Zoos/Aquariums
Education: Arts/Humanities Education, Business Education, Colleges & Universities, Education Associations, Education Reform, Education-General, International Exchange, Literacy, Medical Education, Minority Education, Preschool Education, Private Education (Precollege), Public Education (Precollege), School Volunteerism, Science/Mathematics Education, Student Aid
Health: AIDS/HIV, Cancer, Children's Health/Hospitals, Clinics/Medical Centers, Emergency/Ambulance Services, Hospitals, Medical Research, Single-Disease Health Associations
International: Health Care/Hospitals, International Relations, International Relief Efforts
Religion: Churches, Jewish Causes, Religious Welfare
Science: Science Museums, Scientific Centers & Institutes
Social Services: Animal Protection, At-Risk Youth, Big Brother/Big Sister, Child Abuse, Child Welfare, Community Service Organizations, Domestic Violence, Family Planning, Family Services, Food/Clothing Distribution, People with Disabilities, Recreation & Athletics, Scouts, Social Services-General, Substance Abuse, United Funds/United Ways, Volunteer Services, YMCA/YWCA/YMHA/YWHA, Youth Organizations

Application Procedures

Initial Contact: Request application form.
Deadlines: None.

Restrictions

Preference is given to CA youth charities.

Additional Information

Publications: Application Form

Foundation Officials

Joseph Ueberroth: treas
Peter Victor Ueberroth: vice president B Evanston, IL 1937. ED San Jose State University BS (1959). PRIM CORP EMPL managing director, partner: Contrarian Group. CORP AFFIL director: Coca-Cola Co.; director: TransAmerica Corp.; director: California Angels; director: Cb Commercial Real Estate Group. NONPR AFFIL chairman: First Travel Group; chairman: Intercontinental Tours Inc.; co-chairman: Doubletree Hotels Corp.; director: Amateur Athletic Association LA; chairman: Colony Hotels.
Virginia Ueberroth: president
Vicki Ueberroth Booth: secretary

Grants Analysis

Disclosure Period: fiscal year ending November 30, 2000
Total Grants: $486,911*
Number of Grants: 87
Average Grant: $4,389*
Highest Grant: $109,500
Typical Range: $1,000 to $10,000
*Note: Giving excludes United Way. Average grant figure excludes highest grant.

Recent Grants

Note: Grants derived from fiscal 2002 Form 990.

General

121,500	ARCS Foundation, Corona Del Mar, CA
42,980	Laguna Beach Boys and Girls Club, Laguna Beach, CA
40,000	Sage Hill School, Newport Beach, CA
31,000	University of Southern California, Los Angeles, CA
30,000	Ocean Institute, Dana Point, CA
30,000	Orangewood, Garden Grove, CA
22,000	Saint Joseph Ballet, Santa Ana, CA
20,000	Autry Foundation, Los Angeles, CA
19,000	Hoag Hospital Foundation, Newport Beach, CA
16,000	Alpha Chi Omega Foundation, Indianapolis, IN

ABER D. UNGER FOUNDATION

Giving Contact

John A. Feinblatt, President
22 Hunt Cup Circle
Owings Mills, MD 21117
Phone: (410)581-9575

Description

Founded: 1960
EIN: 526034758
Organization Type: Private Foundation
Giving Locations: MD
Grant Types: General Support.

Financial Summary

Total Giving: $245,250 (fiscal year ending February 28, 2001); $219,750 (fiscal 2000); $161,500 (fiscal 1999)
Assets: $4,455,529 (fiscal 2001); $4,815,800 (fiscal 2000); $4,838,882 (fiscal 1999)

Typical Recipients

Arts & Humanities: Arts Centers, Arts Institutes, Community Arts, Libraries, Museums/Galleries, Music, Theater
Civic & Public Affairs: Employment/Job Training, Civic & Public Affairs-General, Housing, Municipalities/Towns, Philanthropic Organizations, Professional & Trade Associations, Public Policy, Urban & Community Affairs, Zoos/Aquariums
Education: Arts/Humanities Education, Colleges & Universities, Education Reform, Education-General, Health & Physical Education, Literacy, Private Education (Precollege), Student Aid
Environment: Environment-General, Resource Conservation
Health: AIDS/HIV, Arthritis, Health Organizations, Hospitals, Mental Health, Preventive Medicine/Wellness Organizations, Public Health
International: Health Care/Hospitals, Human Rights, International Development
Religion: Churches, Religious Organizations, Religious Welfare
Social Services: Child Welfare, Community Centers, Community Service Organizations, Crime Prevention,

Domestic Violence, Family Planning, Family Services, Food/Clothing Distribution, People with Disabilities, Sexual Abuse, Shelters/Homelessness, United Funds/United Ways

Application Procedures

Initial Contact: The foundation requests applications be made in writing. Include a description of organization, purpose of funds sought, value of project to community, and budget.
Deadlines: None.

Restrictions

Emphasis is on music, medical research, and service and social welfare.

Foundation Officials

Eugene M. Feinblatt: president, treasurer
John Feinblatt: director
Marjorie W. Feinblatt: director
Paul C. Wolman, III: director

Grants Analysis

Disclosure Period: fiscal year ending February 28, 2001
Total Grants: $245,250
Number of Grants: 25
Average Grant: $8,135*
Highest Grant: $50,000
Typical Range: $2,000 to $15,000
*Note: Average grant figure excludes highest grant.

Recent Grants

Note: Grants derived from fiscal 2000 Form 990.

General

37,500	Fund for the City of New York, New York, NY
25,000	Baltimore Symphony Orchestra, Baltimore, MD
25,000	Greater Baltimore Committee, Baltimore, MD
23,000	Bowery Residents Committee, New York, NY
20,000	LAMBDA, New York, NY
15,000	Center Stage, Baltimore, MD
11,500	Fund for Educational Excellence, Baltimore, MD
10,000	AIDS Interfaith Residential Services, Baltimore, MD
10,000	INNterim Housing Corporation, Baltimore, MD
10,000	LINC, Belleville, IL

UNILEVER UNITED STATES, INC.

Company Headquarters

390 Park Ave.
New York, NY 10022
Web: http://www.unilever.com

Company Description

Founded: 1978
Parent Company: Unilever NV, Weena 455, Rotteroadam, Netherlands

Nonmonetary Support

Type: Cause-related Marketing & Promotion; Donated Equipment; Donated Products

Unilever United States Foundation

Giving Contact

John T. Gould, Jr., Director, Corporate Affairs
Care of UNUS Tax Department
700 Sylvan Avenue
Englewood Cliffs, NJ 07632
Phone: (201)567-8000
Web: http://www.unilever.com/so/co.html

Description

Founded: 1952
EIN: 136122117
Organization Type: Corporate Foundation
Giving Locations: headquarters and operating communities.
Grant Types: Emergency, Employee Matching Gifts, General Support.

Donor Information

Founder: Lever Brothers Co., Van Den Bergh Foods Co, Unilever United States, Inc.

Financial Summary

Total Giving: $4,894,000 (2002 approx); $5,775,994 (2001); $4,655,088 (2000 approx). Note: Contributes through foundation only. 1995 Giving includes United Way ($325,400).
Giving Analysis: Giving for 2000 includes: foundation grants to United Way ($192,500); foundation matching gifts ($510,919); foundation ($3,951,669); 1999: foundation grants to United Way ($250,150); foundation matching gifts ($330,357); foundation ($3,683,058); 1998: foundation scholarships ($72,340); foundation grants to United Way ($160,500) foundation ($1,584,290)
Assets: $12,192,310 (2001); $510,386 (2000); $61,289 (1999)
Gifts Received: $17,069,266 (2001); $4,905,900 (2000); $3,717,525 (1999). Note: In 1995, the foundation received contributions from the sale of 20,500 shares of Colgate Palmolive Co. stock. In 1999, the foundation received $3,343,576 in Colgate Stock, the Unilever Corp. contributed $368,000, and Chesebrough Pond Foundation contributed $5,949.

Typical Recipients

Arts & Humanities: Arts Associations & Councils, Arts Centers, Arts Institutes, Dance, Ethnic & Folk Arts, Historic Preservation, Libraries, Museums/Galleries, Music, Opera, Performing Arts, Public Broadcasting, Theater
Civic & Public Affairs: African American Affairs, Botanical Gardens/Parks, Business/Free Enterprise, Civil Rights, Economic Development, Economic Policy, Employment/Job Training, Civic & Public Affairs-General, Housing, Law & Justice, Municipalities/Towns, Nonprofit Management, Philanthropic Organizations, Professional & Trade Associations, Public Policy, Safety, Urban & Community Affairs, Zoos/Aquariums
Education: Agricultural Education, Business Education, Business-School Partnerships, Business-School Partnerships, Colleges & Universities, Community & Junior Colleges, Economic Education, Education Associations, Elementary Education (Private), Engineering/Technological Education, Environmental Education, Education-General, Gifted & Talented Programs, International Studies, Literacy, Medical Education, Minority Education, Private Education (Precollege), Public Education (Precollege), Science/Mathematics Education, Student Aid
Environment: Environment-General, Resource Conservation
Health: Cancer, Children's Health/Hospitals, Clinics/Medical Centers, Diabetes, Emergency/Ambulance Services, Health Organizations, Heart, Hospitals,

Medical Research, Prenatal Health Issues, Respiratory, Single-Disease Health Associations, Trauma Treatment
International: Foreign Educational Institutions, Health Care/Hospitals, Human Rights, International Affairs, International Relations, International Relief Efforts
Religion: Jewish Causes, Religious Welfare, Seminaries
Science: Science Museums, Scientific Organizations
Social Services: Community Centers, Community Service Organizations, Day Care, Family Services, Food/Clothing Distribution, People with Disabilities, Recreation & Athletics, Senior Services, Shelters/Homelessness, Social Services-General, Special Olympics, Substance Abuse, United Funds/United Ways, Volunteer Services, YMCA/YWCA/YMHA/YWHA, Youth Organizations

Application Procedures

Initial Contact: Submit a letter or proposal on organization's letterhead and signed by its chief executive officer.
Application Requirements: Include the grant's purpose, background information on the organization, the most recent annual report, a copy of the current operating budget, and proof of tax-exempt status.
Deadlines: None; budget is determined annually in February.
Evaluative Criteria: Makes contributions to organizations with clearly defined, achievable goals that have demonstrated their effectiveness and fiscal responsibility.

Restrictions

The foundation does not award grants to individuals, goodwill advertising, fundraising events and testimonial dinners, sectarian religious organizations, labor organizations, political parties or their activities, capital fund campaigns, or veterans groups for fraternal/social purposes.

Foundation Officials

Maureen A. Collins: director
A. Peter Harwich: secretary
John W. Rice: director
Ronald M. Soiefer: director
David J. Strickland: assistant secretary
Neal P. Vorchheimer: director
Paul W. Wood: president, director
C. Perry Yeatman: director

Grants Analysis

Disclosure Period: calendar year ending 2001
Total Grants: $6,370,637*
Number of Grants: 600
Average Grant: $10,600*
Highest Grant: $1,500,000
Lowest Grant: $25
Typical Range: $1,000 to $5,000
*Note: Giving excludes matching gifts and United Way. Average grant figure excludes highest grant.

Recent Grants

Note: Grants derived from 2001 Form 990.

General

1,500,000	September 11 Fund, New York, NY
1,000,000	Citizens Scholarship Foundation of America, St. Peter, MN
670,000	National Park Foundation, New York, NY
142,357	National Merit Scholarship Corporation, Evanston, IL
119,700	Jackie Robinson Foundation, New York, NY
100,000	Unilever United States, Englewood Cliffs, NJ
91,000	International Food Information Council, Washington, DC
65,000	United Way Crusade of Mercy, Chicago, IL

| 61,000 | Children's First Fund, Chicago, IL |
| 60,000 | Patterson Habitat for Humanity, Paterson, NJ |

UNION PACIFIC CORP.

Company Headquarters

1416 Dodge Street, Room 1230
Omaha, NE 68179
Phone: (402)271-5777
Fax: (402)271-6408
Web: http://www.up.com

Company Description

Founded: 1969
Ticker: UNP
Exchange: NYSE
Operating Revenue: US$12.491 billion (2002)
Profit: US$1.341 billion (2002)
Employees: 47000 (2002)
Fortune Rank: 156, per FORTUNE Magazine's list of 500 Largest U.S. Corporations (2002).
SIC(s): 1081 Metal Mining Services, 1311 Crude Petroleum & Natural Gas, 1382 Oil & Gas Exploration Services, 6719 Holding Companies Nec.

Operating Locations

Union Pacific Corp. (AR; CA; CO; ID; KS; LA; MO; NE--Omaha; OK; OR; PA--Bethlehem; TX--Fort Worth; WA)

Union Pacific Foundation

Giving Contact

Darlynn Herweg, Director
1416 Dodge Street, Room 738
Omaha, NE 68179
Phone: (402)271-5000
Fax: (402)271-5477
Web: http://www.up.com/found/

Description

EIN: 136406825
Organization Type: Corporate Foundation
Giving Locations: AR; CA; CO; DE; DC: Washington; FL; GA; ID; IL; IN; IA; KS; LA; MD; MI; MN; MS; MT; NE; NV; NJ; NM; NY; NC; OH; OK; OR; PA; TN; TX; UT; VA; WA; WI
Grant Types: Award, Capital, Challenge, Employee Matching Gifts, General Support, Multiyear/Continuing Support, Project.
Note: Employee matching gift ratio: 2 to 1 for educational institutions; 1 to 1 for cultural institutions.

Financial Summary

Total Giving: $7,431,900 (2000); $7,302,300 (1999); $8,500,000 (1998 approx). Note: Contributes through corporate direct giving program and foundation. 1996 Giving includes foundation United Way.
Giving Analysis: Giving for 2000 includes: foundation grants to United Way ($1,712,500); foundation ($5,719,400) 1999: foundation ($7,302,300)
Assets: $1,185,981 (2000); $1,909,486 (1999); $10,271,548 (1996)
Gifts Received: $6,657,190 (2000); $6,257,059 (1999); $858,095 (1996). Note: Contributions are received from Union Pacific Corporation and affiliated Companies.

Typical Recipients

Arts & Humanities: Arts Associations & Councils, Arts Funds, Arts Institutes, Arts Outreach, Ballet, Dance, Historic Preservation, History & Archaeology, Libraries, Museums/Galleries, Music, Opera, Performing Arts, Public Broadcasting, Theater

Civic & Public Affairs: Botanical Gardens/Parks, Business/Free Enterprise, Community Foundations, Economic Development, Civic & Public Affairs-General, Professional & Trade Associations, Public Policy, Safety, Urban & Community Affairs, Zoos/Aquariums
Education: Afterschool/Enrichment Programs, Agricultural Education, Arts/Humanities Education, Business Education, Colleges & Universities, Community & Junior Colleges, Economic Education, Education Funds, Engineering/Technological Education, Environmental Education, Faculty Development, Education-General, Legal Education, Literacy, Minority Education, Religious Education, Science/Mathematics Education, Secondary Education (Public), Social Sciences Education, Special Education, Student Aid
Environment: Air/Water Quality, Environment-General, Research, Resource Conservation, Wildlife Protection
Health: Alzheimers Disease, Cancer, Children's Health/Hospitals, Clinics/Medical Centers, Emergency/Ambulance Services, Health Organizations, Hospices, Hospitals, Long-Term Care, Medical Rehabilitation, Medical Research, Mental Health, Prenatal Health Issues, Public Health
Religion: Religious Organizations, Religious Welfare
Science: Science Museums, Science Museums, Scientific Centers & Institutes, Scientific Organizations
Social Services: Child Welfare, Community Centers, Community Service Organizations, Day Care, Domestic Violence, Family Services, Food/Clothing Distribution, Homes, People with Disabilities, Recreation & Athletics, Scouts, Senior Services, Shelters/Homelessness, Substance Abuse, United Funds/United Ways, YMCA/YWCA/YMHA/YWHA, Youth Organizations

Application Procedures

Initial Contact: Write to request application form.
Application Requirements: Include description of the organization and purpose of funds sought.
Deadlines: August 15 for complete proposal, for consideration in the following year.
Review Process: If initial letter indicates organization's request complies with foundation guidelines, a formal grant request form is sent to the organization to be completed and returned with supplementary data, including recently audited financial statements, 501(c)(3) determination letter, and description of financial support from other businesses.
Evaluative Criteria: Leadership such that financial support will be used to optimum effect, significant public support of activities, non-duplication of activities of other organizations supported by foundation, corporate presence in community served by organization, evidence of other corporate support.
Decision Notification: Board meets annually in January.

Restrictions

Does not support organizations not eligible for tax-exempt status under Section 501(c)(3) of the IRS Code; specialized national health or welfare organizations other than through United Way; political organizations; organizations engaged in influencing legislation; religious organizations that are sectarian or denominational in purpose; veterans organizations, labor groups, social clubs, or fraternal organizations; individuals; dinners or special events; goodwill advertising; or grant-making organizations, except allied arts funds and independent college associations. Only reviews requests for support of capital projects from organizations funded by United Way.

Additional Information

Publications: Application Form

Corporate Officials

Darlynn Herweg: director PRIM CORP EMPL director: Union Pacific Corp.

Foundation Officials

Darlynn Herweg: assistant secretary (see above)

Grants Analysis

Disclosure Period: calendar year ending 2000
Total Grants: $5,719,400*
Number of Grants: 675 (approx)
Average Grant: $8,195*
Highest Grant: $196,000
Lowest Grant: $500
Typical Range: $1,000 to $20,000
*Note: Giving excludes United Way. Average grant excludes highest grant.

Recent Grants

Note: Grants derived from 2000 Form 990.

General

250,000	United Way of the Midlands, Omaha, NE
196,000	College Fund/UNCF, Fairfax, VA
150,000	United Way Greater St. Louis, St. Louis, MO
150,000	United Way Greater St. Louis, St. Louis, MO
125,000	Durham Western Heritage Museum, Omaha, NE
125,000	University of Nebraska, Omaha, NE
65,000	Mid-Plains United Way, Inc, Dalles, OR
65,000	United Way Pulaski County, Little Rock, AR
60,000	Heart of America United Way, Kansas City, MO
60,000	United Way of Texas Gulf Coast, Houston, TX

UNITED ARMENIAN CHARITIES

Giving Contact

Haig Dadourian, President
168 Canal St.
New York, NY 10013
Phone: (212)334-0990

Description

Founded: 1951
EIN: 136125023
Organization Type: Private Foundation
Grant Types: General Support.

Donor Information

Founder: Dadour Dadourian

Financial Summary

Total Giving: $233,710 (2000); $219,245 (1999); $142,305 (1998)
Assets: $5,378,075 (2000); $5,616,126 (1999); $5,207,664 (1998)
Gifts Received: $62,000 (1996); $10,000 (1993)

Typical Recipients

Arts & Humanities: Public Broadcasting
Civic & Public Affairs: Clubs, Community Foundations, Civic & Public Affairs-General, Women's Affairs
Education: Colleges & Universities, Minority Education, Private Education (Precollege), Secondary Education (Private)
Health: Children's Health/Hospitals, Hospices, Hospitals, Hospitals (University Affiliated), Long-Term Care, Single-Disease Health Associations
International: Foreign Educational Institutions, Health Care/Hospitals, International Relief Efforts, Missionary/Religious Activities
Religion: Churches, Dioceses, Religion-General, Missionary Activities (Domestic), Religious Organizations, Religious Welfare, Seminaries
Science: Scientific Research

Social Services: Food/Clothing Distribution, People with Disabilities, Special Olympics

Application Procedures

Initial Contact: The foundation has no formal grant application procedure or application form.
Deadlines: None.

Additional Information

Foundation gives grants primarily for Armenian religious support. The organization also gives support for Armenian education and social services.

Foundation Officials

Alexander Dadourian: vice president
Haig Dadourian: president
Peter Dadourian: treasurer

Grants Analysis

Disclosure Period: calendar year ending 2000
Total Grants: $233,710
Number of Grants: 36
Average Grant: $5,535*
Highest Grant: $40,000
Typical Range: $1,000 to $10,000
*Note: Average grant figure excludes highest grant.

Recent Grants

Note: Grants derived from 1999 Form 990.

General

76,000	Diocese of the Armenian Church, New York, NY
29,650	Armenian Assembly of the Holy Martyrs, New York, NY
25,000	Columbia University, New York, NY
20,000	Armenian Relief Fund
15,250	Armenian Women's Welfare Association, Jamaica Plain, MA
15,000	Armenian Assembly of America, Washington, DC
9,000	Pyunic, New York, NY
5,000	Eurasia Foundation, Washington, DC
5,000	Mission Parish Project
5,000	St. Mary Armenian Church

UNITED PARAMOUNT NETWORK

Company Headquarters

11800 Wilshire Blvd.
Los Angeles, CA 90025
Web: http://www.upn.com

Company Description

Revenue: US$215 million (2001)
Employees: 80 (2001)
Parent Company: Viacom, Inc., 1515 Broadway, New York, NY, United States

WPWR-TV Channel 50 Foundation

Giving Contact

Laura Sampson, Program Officer
2151 N. Elston Avenue
Chicago, IL 60614-3999
Phone: (773)292-5016
Fax: (773)276-6477
E-mail: mail@wpwr50fund.org

Description

Founded: 1992
EIN: 363805338
Organization Type: Corporate Foundation

Giving Locations: IL: Chicago including metropolitan area; IN: Northwest part of the state
Grant Types: General Support, Research.

Financial Summary

Total Giving: $3,948,723 (fiscal year ending February 28, 2002); $4,073,086 (fiscal 2000); $1,259,750 (fiscal 1997)
Giving Analysis: Giving for fiscal 2000 includes: foundation grants to United Way ($50,000) foundation ($4,023,086)
Assets: $95,978,425 (fiscal 2002); $97,109,712 (fiscal 2000); $54,233,444 (fiscal 1997)
Gifts Received: $2,160,250 (fiscal 2002); $7,769,479 (fiscal 2000); $22,029,420 (fiscal 1997). Note: In fiscal 2000 and 2002, contributions were received from Fred Eychaner. In fiscal 1997, contributions were received from Newsweb Corp. ($8,503,228) and Fred Eychaner ($13,526,192).

Typical Recipients

Arts & Humanities: Arts Associations & Councils, Ballet, Dance, Arts & Humanities-General, Historic Preservation, Libraries, Museums/Galleries, Music, Public Broadcasting, Theater
Civic & Public Affairs: Botanical Gardens/Parks, Employment/Job Training, Gay/Lesbian Issues, Civic & Public Affairs-General, Housing, Law & Justice, Legal Aid, Public Policy, Safety, Urban & Community Affairs, Women's Affairs
Education: Arts/Humanities Education, Colleges & Universities, Education Funds, International Exchange, Journalism/Media Education, Public Education (Precollege), Vocational & Technical Education
Environment: Air/Water Quality, Resource Conservation
Health: AIDS/HIV, Cancer, Health Policy/Cost Containment
Social Services: Community Service Organizations, Community Service Organizations, Refugee Assistance, United Funds/United Ways, Youth Organizations

Application Procedures

Initial Contact: Submit two-page letter of intent.
Application Requirements: Include 3 to 5 page proposal describing agency and need for support, audited financial statements, current year budget, list of directors, any relevant publications, annual report, projected income and budget for timeframe of support, current fiscal statement, copy of most recently submitted Form 990, and a copy of IRS determination letter of 501(c)(3) status. Foundation accepts Chicago area grant application form.
Deadlines: April 1 for arts and arts education; August 1 for advocacy and architecture and preservation; November 15 for domestic violence intervention/prevention.
Decision Notification: Grants are made within six months of deadline.
Notes: First time grants average $2,500.

Restrictions

Limited to arts, arts education, advocacy, domestic violence organizations, and architecture and preservation. Foundation does not provide grants to individuals, scholarships, underwriting or tables for special events, public schools, special projects or productions, religious or fraternal purposes, or political campaigns.

Foundation Officials

Barbara Eychaner: director
Fred Eychaner: president
Charles Gross: assistant secretary
Don Hilliker: secretary
Marcia Lipetz: executive director

Grants Analysis

Disclosure Period: fiscal year ending February 28, 2002
Total Grants: $3,908,723*
Number of Grants: 264
Average Grant: $14,806
Highest Grant: $300,000
Lowest Grant: $2,500
Typical Range: $2,500 to $50,000
*Note: Giving excludes United Way.

Recent Grants

Note: Grants derived from fiscal 2002 Form 990.

General

300,000	Auditorium Theater Council, Chicago, IL
250,000	Steppenwolf Theater Company, Chicago, IL
200,000	Journeyman Theatre, Chicago, IL
150,000	AIDS Foundation of Chicago, Chicago, IL
116,000	WYIN/Channel 56, Merrillville, IN
100,000	Dance Africa, Chicago, IL
100,000	Medill School of Journalism, Evanston, IL
78,425	Pennsylvania State University, University Park, CA
78,175	State University of New York Research Foundation, Syracuse, NY
62,000	Give2Asia, San Francisco, CA

U.S. BANCORP PIPER JAFFRAY

Company Headquarters

222 S. Ninth Street
Minneapolis, MN 55402
Web: http://www.piperjaffray.com

Company Description

Former Name: Piper Jaffray & Hopwood; Piper Jaffray Companies, Inc. (1999).
Employees: 3,182
SIC(s): 6211 Security Brokers & Dealers, 6719 Holding Companies Nec.
Parent Company: U.S. Bancorp, 601 Second Avenue South, Minneapolis, MN, United States

Operating Locations

Piper Jaffray Companies Inc. (AZ--Green Valley, Phoenix, Scottsdale, Sun City; CA--Los Angeles, Menlo Park, Sacramento, San Francisco; CO--Boulder, Colorado Springs, Denver, Durango; ID--Idaho Falls, Pocatello, Twin Falls; IA--Ames, Davenport, Des Moines, Mason City, Sioux City, Spencer, Storm Lake, Waterloo; KS--Lawrence; ME--Omaha; MN--Albert Lea, Austin, Bloomington, Brainerd, Duluth, Grand Rapids, Mankato, New Ulm, Rochester, St. Cloud, St. Paul, Two Harbors, Wayzata; MO--Kansas City, St. Louis; MT--Billings, Bozeman, Great Falls, Missoula; NE--Lincoln; NJ--Hoboken; ND--Fargo, Grand Forks; OR--Portland; SD--Brookings, Mitchell, Pierre, Sioux Falls; UT--Provo, Salt Lake City; WA--Aberdeen, Everett, Kennewick, Seattle, Spokane, Walla Walla, Wenatchee; WI--Appleton, Eau Claire, La Crosse, Madison, Milwaukee, Wausau; WY--Gillette, Sheridan)

Nonmonetary Support

Type: Donated Equipment; In-kind Services
Contact: Brenda Cich, Administrative Assistant
E-mail: bcich@pjc.com
Note: 1997 nonmonetary support $15,000. Company provides nonmonetary support. In-kind services are in the form of printing or meeting services; support should be requested by an employee.

U.S. Bancorp Piper Jaffray Foundation

Giving Contact
Marina Lyon, Director, Public Affairs
222 S. Ninth St.
Minneapolis, MN 55402
Phone: (612)342-5501
Fax: (612)342-6085
Web: http://www.piperjaffray.com/about/
community_involve.html

Alternate Contact
Phone: (612)342-6000

Description
Founded: 1993
EIN: 411734808
Organization Type: Corporate Foundation
Former Name: Piper Jaffray Companies Inc. (2000).
Formed by Merger of: U.S. Bancorp and Firstar (2002).
Giving Locations: MN: Twin Cities area headquarters.
Grant Types: Capital, Employee Matching Gifts, Endowment, General Support, Operating Expenses.
Note: Employee matching gift ratio: 1 to 1 to accredited educational institutions and nonprofit organisation, with a minimum of $25 and maximum of $1,000 annually.

Donor Information
Founder: Established in 1993 by Piper Jaffray Companies

Financial Summary
Total Giving: $1,795,265 (2000); $2,088,034 (1999); $2,750,000 (1998 approx). Note: 1998 giving reflects four additional grants made from October 1 to December 31, 1998. Contributes through corporate direct giving program and foundation.
Giving Analysis: Giving for 2000 includes: foundation grants to United Way ($120,400); foundation ($1,674,865); 1999: foundation grants to United Way ($240,000); foundation ($1,848,034); 1998: foundation grants to United Way ($115,000); foundation ($421,946);
Assets: $1,553,881 (2000); $3,060,710 (1999); $4,107,798 (1998). Note: 1998 asset figure reflects change of accounting period from September 30 to December 31.
Gifts Received: $541,309 (2000); $641,675 (1999); $181,018 (1998). Note: Contributions are received from Piper Jaffray Cos.

Typical Recipients
Arts & Humanities: Arts Centers, Arts Festivals, Arts Institutes, Film & Video, Arts & Humanities-General, Libraries, Museums/Galleries, Music, Opera, Performing Arts, Public Broadcasting, Theater
Civic & Public Affairs: African American Affairs, Business/Free Enterprise, Chambers of Commerce, Community Foundations, Economic Development, Employment/Job Training, Civic & Public Affairs-General, Housing, Municipalities/Towns, Native American Affairs, Nonprofit Management, Public Policy, Urban & Community Affairs, Women's Affairs, Zoos/Aquariums
Education: Arts/Humanities Education, Business Education, Colleges & Universities, Community & Junior Colleges, Economic Education, Education Funds, Education Reform, Elementary Education (Private), Education-General, Gifted & Talented Programs, Leadership Training, Minority Education, Private Education (Precollege), Public Education (Precollege), Student Aid, Vocational & Technical Education
Environment: Forestry, Environment-General, Resource Conservation

Health: Cancer, Children's Health/Hospitals, Emergency/Ambulance Services, Hospitals, Long-Term Care, Medical Rehabilitation, Multiple Sclerosis, Public Health
International: Health Care/Hospitals
Religion: Churches, Dioceses, Jewish Causes, Ministries, Religious Organizations, Religious Welfare, Social/Policy Issues
Science: Science Museums
Social Services: At-Risk Youth, Big Brother/Big Sister, Child Welfare, Community Centers, Community Service Organizations, Community Service Organizations, Domestic Violence, Emergency Relief, Family Planning, Family Services, Food/Clothing Distribution, People with Disabilities, Recreation & Athletics, Scouts, Shelters/Homelessness, Social Services-General, United Funds/United Ways, Volunteer Services, YMCA/YWCA/YMHA/YWHA, Youth Organizations

Application Procedures
Initial Contact: Organizations in the Minneapolis/St. Paul metropolitan area may request general operating support by completing an application form from the Foundation; organizations in the Twin Cities area requesting capital support should submit a proposal and supporting material to the foundation; organizations outside the Twin Cities area requesting capital support should submit a proposal to the nearest branch office.
Application Requirements: Both operating and capital support requests should include a cover letter with a summary and amount requested; recent annual report; current operating budget; list of major supporters; recent audited financial statement; copy of IRS 501(c)(3) determination letter; current list of officers, board members and key staff; and a list of contributions received (for capital requests only).
Deadlines: October 31 or May 31, for general operating support; April 30 for capital requests.
Review Process: Organizations are notified within three weeks of application receipt whether or not their applications will be reviewed.
Applications scheduled for review by the Foundation board are assigned a reviewer to discuss the application with a representative from the applying organization. After information is gathered and analyzed, the Foundation board meets and makes a decision.
Evaluative Criteria: In evaluating requests, the committee considers the petitioning organization's: organizational effectiveness, including helping individuals or improving the civic or cultural life of the community; evaluating and maintaining a set value of outcomes; qualified staff members; financial stability and operating efficiency, including fund-raising ability; ongoing support; responsible governing body, including evidence of long-range plans, a good reputation, active and sensitive board members; and Piper Jaffray employee involvement; capital requests are also considered based on how important project is to community.
Decision Notification: Requests are considered during meetings held in February, May, and September.

Restrictions
Foundation will not support the following: programs expansion; specific program costs; event sponsorships; ticket purchases at fundraising events; travel; expenses associated with team competition; basic and applied research.
Also not funded are: health or disease-specific organizations; individuals; newly formed nonprofit organizations; religious organizations for religious purposes; political, veteran, service or fraternal organizations; public or private K-12 schools; public or private higher education institutions; emergency memberships, or 501(c)(4) or (6) organizations.
The Minnesota Common Grant Application Form is not accepted.
Support for higher education is provided through the U.S. Bancorp Community and Higher Education Matching Gift Program.

Additional Information
In 1999, the foundation began the Youth Employment Strategies (YES) initiative. This two-year initiative will provide for effective employment training programs for disadvantaged youth and young adults.
The foundation reports that in 2000 more than 50% of charitable giving will be distributed by the U.S. Bancorp Piper Jaffray Foundation. Remainder of funds are distributed through branch offices and through corporate giving programs.
Publications: Community Involvement Report; Community Affairs Annual Report; Application Form and; Community Support Guidelines

Corporate Officials
Marina Lyon: director public affairs PRIM CORP EMPL president: Pohlad Family Foundation.

Grants Analysis
Disclosure Period: calendar year ending 2000
Total Grants: $1,674,865*
Number of Grants: 162
Average Grant: $10,339
Highest Grant: $80,000
Typical Range: $1,000 to $15,000
*Note: Giving excludes United Way.

Recent Grants
Note: Grants derived from 2000 Form 990.

Library-Related
10,000	Friends of the St. Paul Public Library, St. Paul, MN

General
70,000	Tree Trust, St. Louis Park, MN
70,000	YouthBiz, Inc., Denver, CO
50,000	Sonoma County People for Economic Opportunity, Santa Rosa, CA
40,000	Juma Ventures, San Francisco, CA
40,000	Minnesota Conservation Corps, St. Paul, MN
40,000	People Serving People Inc., Minneapolis, MN
30,000	Milwaukee Community Service Corp, Milwaukee, WI
30,000	Montana Conservation Corps, Inc., Bozeman, MT
30,000	Operation Fresh Start, Bakersfield, CA
30,000	United Way, St. Paul, MN

UNITED STATES-JAPAN FOUNDATION

Giving Contact
George R. Packard, President
145 East 32nd Street, 12th Floor
New York, NY 10016
Phone: (212)481-8753
Fax: (212)481-8762
E-mail: info@us-jf.org
Web: http://www.us-jf.org

Alternate Contact
Reinanzaka Building 1F, 1-14-2
Akasaka
Minato-Ku
Tokyo 107-0052, Japan
E-mail: jdu05456@nifty.ne.jp
Note: Alt. Phone: 03-3586-0541; Alt. Fax: 03-3586-1128;

Description
Founded: 1980
EIN: 133054425
Organization Type: General Purpose Foundation
Giving Locations: nationally; Japan
Grant Types: Fellowship, Project.

Note: The foundation also supports policy studies and teacher training.

Donor Information

Founder: Incorporated in 1980 under the laws of New York as a private American philanthropic organization dedicated to the promotion of greater mutual knowledge between the people of Japan and the United States. It was founded with a grant from the Japan Shipbuilding Industry Foundation so that the mutual interests of the two societies would be more clearly recognized and better appreciated.

Financial Summary

Total Giving: $4,770,126 (2001); $6,000,000 (2000 approx); $4,016,224 (1999)
Assets: $86,979,675 (2001); $99,997,997 (2000); $111,799,213 (1999)

Typical Recipients

Arts & Humanities: History & Archaeology, Libraries, Museums/Galleries, Public Broadcasting
Civic & Public Affairs: Employment/Job Training, Ethnic Organizations, Civic & Public Affairs-General, Public Policy
Education: Colleges & Universities, Environmental Education, Faculty Development, Education-General, International Exchange, International Studies, Journalism/Media Education, Public Education (Precollege), Secondary Education (Public), Social Sciences Education
International: Foreign Arts Organizations, Foreign Educational Institutions, International-General, International Affairs, International Development, International Environmental Issues, International Peace & Security Issues, International Relations, Trade
Science: Scientific Centers & Institutes
Social Services: Child Welfare

Application Procedures

Initial Contact: Applicants should submit a proposal letter of 3-4 pages. Initial letter should include: brief description of proposed project and its objectives, any necessary background information on the project and applicant, and a brief budget estimate. Proposal letters will be reviewed by foundation staff and a response will be sent promptly. Full proposals will not be reviewed an will not be returned to the applicant.
Deadlines: Proposals are accepted on a rolling basis. Decisions are made in April and October.
Review Process: The foundation will notify the grant seeker if the proposed project is not of interest. If the foundation is interested, it will request a detailed proposal.
Notes: The prospective grantee should demonstrate how the project will contribute to increased knowledge and understanding of Japan in the U.S. and the U.S. in Japan, within the context of Asia. Multilateral projects will be considered. The foundation does not accept email proposals.

Restrictions

Individuals applying on their own behalf for independent study, research, travel, or participation in meetings are not eligible.

Additional Information

The foundation is governed by a board of trustees made up of representatives from the United States and Japan. The foundation's headquarters are in New York City, with a liaison office in Tokyo.
Publications: Annual Report; Guidelines; Newsletter (quarterly)

Foundation Officials

Thomas Alva Bartlett: chairman B Salem, OR 1930. ED Stanford University AB (1951); Oxford University MA (1953); Stanford University PhD (1959).
John Brademas: trustee B Mishawaka, IN 1927. ED Harvard University BA (1949); Oxford University DPhil (1954). PRIM NONPR EMPL president emeritus: New York University. CORP AFFIL director: Texaco Inc.; director: RCA/NBC; director: Scholastic Inc.; director: NYNEX Corp.; director: Oxford University Press; director: Loews Corp. NONPR AFFIL member, board advisors: Woodrow Wilson Center International Scholars; member central committee: World Council Churches; trustee: University Notre Dame; member: Study National Needs Biomedical & Behavioral Research; board advisors: Trilateral Commission; trustee: Spelman College; senator: Phi Beta Kappa; member: Smithsonian Institute National Board; director: Alexander S. Onassis Public Benefit Foundation; director: New York Stock Exchange Inc.; president emeritus: New York University; member: National Advisory Council Public Service; member: National Committee Student Financial Assistance; chairman advisory committee: National Advisory Committee Fighting Back; member board visitors department : Massachusetts Institute Technology; member: National Academy Sciences; chairman board director: Federal Reserve Bank New York; member board overseers: Harvard University; board advisors: Emory University Carter Center; director: Council Aid Education; board advisors: Dumbarton Oaks Research Library; director: Center National Policy; trustee: Committee for Economic Development; director: Carnegie Endowment National Commission American & New World; director: Berlitz International Inc.; director: Carnegie Commission Science Technology & Government; director: Aspen Institute; director: Athens College (Greece); member: American Legion; director: American Council Arts; member, board directors: American Council Education; director: Academy Educational Development; fellow: American Academy of Arts & Sciences. CLUB AFFIL Ahepa Club; Masons Club.
Gerald L. Curtis: trustee CORP AFFIL director: Bank of Tokyo-Mitsubishi.
Robin Chandler Tippett Duke: trustee B Baltimore, MD 1923. CORP AFFIL director: River Bank America; director: American Home Products Corp.; director: International Flavors & Fragrances Inc. NONPR AFFIL director: East River Bank; member: World Affairs Council; member: Council Foreign Relations; member: American Academy of Arts & Sciences. CLUB AFFIL River Club; Colony Club; Metropolitan Washington Club.
William Frenzel: trustee B 1943. ED University of Minnesota BBA (1966). PRIM CORP EMPL president, director: Rezults.
Shinji Fukukawa: trustee
Minoru Inouye: vchairman, trustee PRIM CORP EMPL president: Kanematsu U.S.A.
Thomas Stephen Johnson: trustee B Racine, WI 1940. ED Trinity College AB (1962); Harvard University MBA (1964). PRIM CORP EMPL chairman, president, chief executive officer: GP Financial Corp. ADD CORP EMPL president, director: Manufacturers Hanover Trust Co.; chairman, chief executive officer: GreenPoint Financial Corp.; chairman, chief executive officer: GreenPoint Bank. CORP AFFIL director: Allegheny Corp.; director: RR Donnelley & Sons Co. NONPR AFFIL trustee: United Way New York; director: WNET-TV/Channel 13; trustee: United States Japan Foundation; director: Online Resources & Communications; trustee: Trinity College; director: Institute International Education; treasurer, director: Cancer Research Institute; member: Council Foreign Relations; trustee: Asia Society.
Christine Manapat: assistant secretary, treasurer
Moriyuki Motono: trustee
Dr. George R. Packard: trustee B Philadelphia, PA 1932. ED Princeton University AB (1954); Tufts University Fletcher School of Law & Diplomacy PhD (1963). PRIM NONPR EMPL vice president: International University of Japan. NONPR AFFIL member: Japan Society New York; member: Phi Beta Kappa; member: Council Foreign Relations; member: Association Asian Studies; director: Atlantic Council. CLUB AFFIL Metropolitan Club.
Yusuke Saraya: trustee, board secretary
Yohei Sasakawa: trustee

Susan Shirk: trustee
Sumiko Takahara: trustee
Jiro Ushio: vchairman board trustee

Grants Analysis

Disclosure Period: calendar year ending 1999
Total Grants: $4,016,224
Number of Grants: 32
Average Grant: $121,000
Highest Grant: $270,000
Lowest Grant: $3,500
Typical Range: $75,000 to $150,000

Recent Grants

Note: Grants derived from 2001 Form 990.

Library-Related

142,500	Library of Congress, Washington, DC -- for Library's Fall 2001 Exhibition of Japanese Art and Literature

General

253,850	Japan Forum, Tokyo Japan -- to develop a multimedia curriculum based on the real lives of seven Japanese students
206,385	Columbia University East Asian Institute, New York, NY -- for a project to explore the areas of policy coordination and cooperation between the US and Japan towards Indonesia
146,250	University of Tennessee at Chattanooga, Chattanooga, TN -- for Japan Studies Project for high school teachers
143,715	University of Maryland Foundation, Inc., College Park, MD -- for the Japan and US study and exchange that links four elementary schools in the US
142,500	Laurasian Institution, Paris, KY -- for Japan Studies Program
140,838	Japan Forum, Tokyo Japan -- to develop a multimedia curriculum based on the real lives of seven Japanese students
122,016	University of Pennsylvania, Philadelphia, PA -- to support teacher-training program in Japan studies for pre-college educators
111,864	University of Oregon Department of History, Eugene, OR -- to develop a system of performance standards and assessment instruments for use in K-12 level Japanese language instruction in the US
109,924	Aichi University of Education, Kariya City Japan -- to assist Japanese teachers increase awareness about the United States in their teaching methods
109,917	Hokkaido University of Education, Sapporo Japan -- for the American Study Program

U.S. STEEL CORP.

Company Headquarters

600 Grant St.
Pittsburgh, PA 15219-2800
Web: http://www.ussteel.com

Company Description

Ticker: X
Exchange: NYSE
Spun Off From: USX Corp (2001); Marathon Oil (2001).
Revenue: US$6.949 billion (2002)
Profit: US$61 million (2002)
Employees: 21,078 (2001)
Fortune Rank: 264, per FORTUNE Magazine's list of 500 Largest U.S. Corporations (2002).

U.S. Steel Foundation

Giving Contact

Craig D. Mallick, General Manager
U.S. Steel Foundation
600 Grant Street, Rm. 685
Pittsburgh, PA 15219-2800
Phone: (412)433-5237
Fax: (412)433-6847
Web: http://www.ussteel.com/corp/ussfoundation/us-
sfound.htm

Alternate Contact

Phone: (412)433-5093

Description

EIN: 136093185
Organization Type: Corporate Foundation
Former Name: USX Foundation (2001).
Giving Locations: nationally, with emphasis on communities where U.S. Steel Corp. operates.
Grant Types: Capital, Employee Matching Gifts, Fellowship, General Support, Matching, Multiyear/Continuing Support, Operating Expenses, Scholarship.
Note: Matching grants awarded for education only.

Financial Summary

Total Giving: $5,916,734 (fiscal year ending November 30, 2001); $6,977,577 (fiscal 2000); $6,193,476 (fiscal 1999). Note: Contributes through foundation only.
Giving Analysis: Giving for fiscal 2001 includes: foundation fellowships ($16,000); foundation scholarships ($895,004); foundation matching gifts ($1,246,619); foundation grants to United Way ($1,619,500); foundation ($2,139,611); fiscal 1999: foundation fellowships ($60,000); foundation scholarships ($762,093); foundation matching gifts ($1,076,190); foundation matching gifts ($1,076,190); foundation grants to United Way ($1,532,500); foundation ($2,762,693); fiscal 1998: foundation fellowships ($31,000); foundation scholarships ($649,850); foundation matching gifts ($938,192) foundation grants to United Way ($1,538,500)
Assets: $10,511,365 (fiscal 2001); $7,060,934 (fiscal 2000); $7,401,244 (fiscal 1999)
Gifts Received: $17,443,943 (fiscal 2001); $6,612,341 (fiscal 2000); $3,513,840 (fiscal 1999). Note: Contributions were received from USX Corp. and its subsidiaries.

Typical Recipients

Arts & Humanities: Arts Associations & Councils, Arts Centers, Arts Festivals, Ballet, Dance, Historic Preservation, History & Archaeology, Libraries, Museums/Galleries, Music, Opera, Performing Arts, Public Broadcasting, Theater
Civic & Public Affairs: Asian American Affairs, Business/Free Enterprise, Community Foundations, Economic Policy, Employment/Job Training, Civic & Public Affairs-General, Law & Justice, Professional & Trade Associations, Public Policy, Urban & Community Affairs
Education: Arts/Humanities Education, Business Education, Colleges & Universities, Community & Junior Colleges, Economic Education, Education Associations, Education Reform, Elementary Education (Public), Engineering/Technological Education, Environmental Education, Legal Education, Minority Education, Public Education (Precollege), Science/Mathematics Education, Special Education, Student Aid, Vocational & Technical Education
Environment: Environment-General
Health: Health Organizations, Medical Rehabilitation, Mental Health, Single-Disease Health Associations, Trauma Treatment
Religion: Religious Organizations, Religious Welfare
Science: Science Museums, Scientific Centers & Institutes, Scientific Organizations

Social Services: At-Risk Youth, Community Centers, Community Service Organizations, Delinquency & Criminal Rehabilitation, Family Services, Homes, People with Disabilities, Scouts, Senior Services, Substance Abuse, United Funds/United Ways, YMCA/YWCA/YMHA/YWHA, Youth Organizations

Application Procedures

Initial Contact: Send a concise letter or executive summary.
Application Requirements: Include a description of project and its goals; brief history or profile of the organization; organization's mission and need, and projected outcomes; a copy of the organization's Internal Revenue Service certification of tax-exempt status under Section 501(c)(3) of Internal Revenue Code; campaign goal or total cost of specific capital need for capital requests; operating budget for the period for which funding is requested for operating requests; and its most recent audited financial report; a statement of sources of committed funds and the amount of support from each contributor; a statement of sources of anticipated support (prospective contributors that have been, or will be, approached for support and the amounts requested); a copy of the most recently audited financial statement; a list of the organization's chief executives and members of the Board of Directors/Trustees, with affiliations; the signature of an authorized executive of the tax-exempt organization; a signed statement of approval by the chief executive of the parent organization if the application originates in a subdivision of such entity; and a signed statement of approval by the corporate relations or development officer of a college or university if the request originates in a department or subdivision.
Deadlines: January 15 for public, cultural, and scientific requests; April 15 for aid to education; July 15 for health and human services requests.
Review Process: Foundation trustees meet in April, July, and October.
Notes: Organizations in the Pittsburgh area may use the Common Grant Application format of the Grantmakers of Western Pennsylvania. Requests for personal interviews and site visits are accommodated as foundation staff schedules permit. Organizations seeking ongoing support must submit a full proposal each year.

Restrictions

The foundation does not support individuals for personal needs or scholarships (aside from the scholarship program for children of employees); religious organizations for religious purposes; organizations whose programs operate outside of the United States; organizations that are not classified as 501(c)(3) tax-exempt; hospitals; nursing homes; other grantmaking foundations; preschool through 12th grade education; individual research projects; economic development; conferences, seminars, or symposia; travel expenses; sponsorship of fundraising or special events; publication of papers, books, magazines, films, videotapes, or audio-visual materials; or operating needs of organizations supported by the United Way. accordance with the above application deadlines.

Additional Information

"In October 2001, the shareholders of USX Corporation approved a restructuring plan to separate the business units into two publicly-traded companies, United States Steel Corporation and Marathon Oil Corporation, effective December 31, 2001. On that date, the USX Foundation was renamed the United States Steel Foundation to... serve the philanthropic interests of United States Steel Corporation.
"A new foundation, the Marathon Oil Company Foundation, has been formed to serve the philanthropic interests of Marathon Oil Corporation." USX Foundation 2001 Annual Report
Publications: Foundation Annual Report

Corporate Officials

Gary Allen Glynn: president, chief executive officer B Springfield, VT 1946. ED University of Vermont BS (1968); University of Pennsylvania MBA (1970). PRIM CORP EMPL president: USX and Carnegie Pension Fund. NONPR AFFIL chairman finance committee: General Services Board Alcoholic Anonymous; member: New York Society Security Analysts; member: Financial Executives Institute; member: Association Investment Management & Research. CLUB AFFIL Tuxedo Club; Metro Club; Metro Opera Association; Drones Club; Economic Club New York.
Gretchen R. Haggerty: vice president, treasurer B 1955. ED Case Western Reserve University BS; Duquesne University JD. PRIM CORP EMPL executive vice president, treasurer, chief executive officer: USX Corp. ADD CORP EMPL vice president accounting and finance: United States Steel Group.
Robert M. Hernandez: vice chairman, chief financial officer, director B Pittsburgh, PA 1944. ED University of Pittsburgh AB (1966); University of Pennsylvania Wharton School MBA (1968). PRIM CORP EMPL vice chairman, chief financial officer, director: USX Corp. ADD CORP EMPL chairman: RTI International Metals Inc. CORP AFFIL director: America Casualty Excess Ltd.
Dan D. Sandman: senior vice president human resources, secretary, general counsel B 1949. ED Ohio State University BA (1970); Ohio State University JD (1973). PRIM CORP EMPL senior vice president, chief administrative officer, secretary, general counsel: USX Corp.
Thomas J. Usher: chairman, chief executive officer B Reading, PA 1942. ED University of Pittsburgh BS (1964); University of Pittsburgh MS (1965); University of Pittsburgh PhD (1971). PRIM CORP EMPL chairman, chief executive officer: USX Corp. CORP AFFIL director: PP&G Industries Inc.; director: Transtar Inc.; director: PNC Bank Corp. NONPR AFFIL chairman: United States-Korea Business Council; trustee: University Pittsburgh; member: Dinamo Ovia; chairman: U.S.-Japan Business Council; member: America Iron Steel Engineers; member, chairman: America Iron Steel Institute. CLUB AFFIL Rolling Rock Club; Laurel Valley Golf Club; Oakmont Country Club; Double Eagle Club; Duquesne Club; Burning Tree Club.

Foundation Officials

Albert G. Adkins: assistant comptroller
M. Sharon Cassidy: assistant secretary B Latrobe, PA 1946. ED Wheeling Jesuit University BS (1968); University of Pittsburgh JD (1974). PRIM CORP EMPL general counsel: United States Steel & Carnegie Pension Fund. NONPR AFFIL member: American Bar Association; advisory: Pension Benefit Guaranty Capital.
Patricia P. Funaro: program manager
Gary Allen Glynn: vice president, investment (see above)
David C. Gremer: assistant treasurer
Edward F. Guna: vice president, treasurer
John A. Hammerschmidt: assistant secretary
Marilyn A. Harris: trustee
Robert M. Hernandez: chief financial officer (see above)
Jerry Howard: trustee
Craig D. Mallick: general manager
John T. Mills: trustee
Dan D. Sandman: trustee (see above)
Larry G. Schultz: vice president, comptroller
Thomas J. Usher: chairman board trustees (see above)
Gary W. Walsh: tax counsel

Grants Analysis

Disclosure Period: fiscal year ending November 30, 2001
Total Grants: $2,139,611*
Number of Grants: 128
Average Grant: $9,045*
Highest Grant: $500,000

Typical Range: $1,000 to $25,000
***Note:** Giving excludes matching gifts; scholarships; fellowships; United Way. Average grant figure excludes two highest grants ($1,000,000).

Recent Grants

Note: Grants derived from fiscal 2001 Form 990.

Library-Related

125,000	Braddock's Field Historical Society, Braddock, PA -- capital

General

500,000	University of Pittsburgh, Pittsburgh, PA -- capital campaign
350,000	United Way Southwestern Pennsylvania, Pittsburgh, PA
350,000	United Way Southwestern Pennsylvania, Pittsburgh, PA
250,000	Pennsylvania State University, Du Bois, PA -- capital
200,000	Carnegie Mellon University, Pittsburgh, PA -- capital
175,000	Lake Area United Way, Griffith, IN
175,000	Lake Area United Way, Griffith, IN
128,426	University of Pittsburgh, Pittsburgh, PA
100,000	Louisiana State University, Baton Rouge, LA -- for capital campaign
100,000	Texas A&M International University, College Station, TX -- capital

UNITED STATES SUGAR CORP.

Company Headquarters

111 Ponce De Leon Ave.
Clewiston, FL 33440
Web: http://www.ussugar.com

Company Description

Employees: 2,700
SIC(s): 0133 Sugarcane & Sugar Beets, 0161 Vegetables & Melons.

Operating Locations

United States Sugar Corp. (FL--Clewiston, South Bay)

United States Sugar Corp. Charitable Trust

Giving Contact

James E. Terrill, CO-Trustee
PO Box 1207
Clewiston, FL 33440
Phone: (863)983-8121
Fax: (863)983-9827
Web: http://www.ussugar.com/aboutus/aboutus_frame.html

Description

Founded: 1952
EIN: 596142825
Organization Type: Corporate Foundation
Giving Locations: headquarters and operating communities.
Grant Types: Capital, Emergency, Fellowship, General Support, Professorship, Project.

Financial Summary

Total Giving: $137,750 (fiscal year ending October 31, 2001); $219,750 (fiscal 2000); $398,000 (fiscal 1999). Note: Contributes through corporate direct giving program and foundation.
Giving Analysis: Giving for fiscal 2000 includes: foundation ($219,750); fiscal 1999: foundation grants to United Way ($5,000); foundation scholarships

($75,000); foundation ($318,000); fiscal 1998: foundation grants to United Way ($10,000); foundation ($309,314);
Assets: $1,830,175 (fiscal 2001); $1,816,975 (fiscal 2000); $1,999,717 (fiscal 1999)
Gifts Received: $500,000 (fiscal 1998); $250,000 (fiscal 1997)

Typical Recipients

Arts & Humanities: Arts Associations & Councils, Arts Outreach, History & Archaeology, Libraries, Museums/Galleries
Civic & Public Affairs: African American Affairs, Botanical Gardens/Parks, Business/Free Enterprise, Chambers of Commerce, Clubs, Community Foundations, Economic Development, Economic Policy, Civic & Public Affairs-General, Housing, Law & Justice, Legal Aid, Municipalities/Towns, Nonprofit Management, Philanthropic Organizations, Professional & Trade Associations, Public Policy, Rural Affairs, Safety, Urban & Community Affairs, Women's Affairs
Education: Afterschool/Enrichment Programs, Agricultural Education, Arts/Humanities Education, Business Education, Colleges & Universities, Community & Junior Colleges, Economic Education, Education Associations, Education Funds, Education Reform, Elementary Education (Private), Elementary Education (Public), Environmental Education, Education-General, Literacy, Preschool Education, Private Education (Precollege), Public Education (Precollege), Science/Mathematics Education, Secondary Education (Public), Special Education, Student Aid
Environment: Environment-General, Resource Conservation
Health: Alzheimers Disease, Cancer, Children's Health/Hospitals, Clinics/Medical Centers, Diabetes, Emergency/Ambulance Services, Eyes/Blindness, Health Organizations, Heart, Hospices, Hospitals, Medical Rehabilitation, Mental Health, Public Health, Single-Disease Health Associations
International: International Relations
Religion: Churches, Jewish Causes, Religious Welfare
Science: Science Exhibits & Fairs, Scientific Centers & Institutes, Scientific Organizations
Social Services: Big Brother/Big Sister, Child Welfare, Community Centers, Community Service Organizations, Day Care, Family Services, People with Disabilities, Recreation & Athletics, Scouts, Shelters/Homelessness, Social Services-General, Substance Abuse, United Funds/United Ways, YMCA/YWCA/YMHA/YWHA, Youth Organizations

Application Procedures

Initial Contact: Send a full proposal.
Application Requirements: Include a description of organization; amount requested and purpose of funds sought; recently audited financial statement; and proof of tax-exempt status.
Deadlines: None; trustees meet four times a year.

Additional Information

United States Sugar Corp. reports that its direct giving applies only to organizations located near company's headquarters.

Corporate Officials

J. Nelson Fairbanks: president, chief executive officer, director B 1936. PRIM CORP EMPL president, chief executive officer, director: United States Sugar Corp. CORP AFFIL director: Florida East Coast Industries Inc.; president, director: US Corrulite Corp.

Grants Analysis

Disclosure Period: fiscal year ending October 31, 2001
Total Grants: $137,750
Number of Grants: 37
Average Grant: $3,132*
Highest Grant: $25,000
Lowest Grant: $1,000

Typical Range: $1,000 to $25,000
***Note:** Average grant figure excludes highest grant.

Recent Grants

Note: Grants derived from 2001 Form 990.

Library-Related

1,000	Friends of the Palm Beach Count Public Library, Inc., West Palm Beach, FL

General

25,000	Glades Day School, Belle Glade, FL
10,000	Glades Day School, Belle Glade, FL -- Athletic Program
10,000	Hendry County Schools Foundation, Labelle, FL -- for Clewiston Athletic program
7,500	Congressional Black Caucus Foundation, Washington, DC
7,500	Hendry Public Schools Foundation, Inc, Labelle, FL -- mini-grants awards scholarships
6,000	Junior Achievement of the Palm Beaches, Inc., West Palm Beach, FL -- applied business and economic courses
5,000	Boy Scouts of America Gulf Stream Council, Glades District, Palm Beach Gardens, FL
5,000	Child Care of Southwest Florida, Ft. Myers, FL -- caring for children auction
5,000	City of Pahokee, Pahokee, FL
5,000	Florida House, Washington, DC

UNITED STATES TRUST CO. OF NEW YORK

Company Headquarters

New York, NY
Web: http://www.ustrust.com

Company Description

Employees: 2,250
SIC(s): 6022 State Commercial Banks, 6036 Savings Institutions Except Federal, 6282 Investment Advice, 6289 Security & Commodity Services Nec.
Parent Company: U.S. Trust Corp., 114 W. 47th Street, New York, NY, United States
Parent Revenue: US$4,480,000,000 (2002)

Operating Locations

United States Trust Co. of New York (CA--Los Angeles; FL--West Palm Beach; MA--Boston; NY--New York)

Nonmonetary Support

Type: Donated Equipment; In-kind Services
Contact: Maureen Nuget, Vice President

U.S. Trust Corp. Foundation

Giving Contact

Carol A. Strickland, Chairman, Corporate Contributions Committee
U.S. Trust Corp. Foundation
114 West 47th Street
New York, NY 10036-1532
Phone: (212)852-1400
Fax: (212)852-1341
E-mail: foundation@ustrust.com

Description

EIN: 136072081
Organization Type: Corporate Foundation
Giving Locations: CA: Costa Mesa, Larkspur, Los Angeles, Palo Alto, San Francisco; CT: Essex, Greenwich, Stamford, West Hartford; DE: Wilmington; DC:

Washington; FL: Boca Raton, Naples, Palm Beach, Vero Beach; MN: Minneapolis, St. Paul; NJ: Jersey City, Morristown, Princeton; NY: Garden City, New York; NC: Charlotte, Greensboro, Raleigh; OR: Portland; PA: Wayne; TX: Dallas, Houston; VA: McLean; WA: Tacoma.

Grant Types: Capital, General Support, Project.

Note: Employee matching gift ratio: 1 to 1 up to $2,000 annually to eligible educational institutions.

Financial Summary

Total Giving: $600,000 (2002 approx); $392,500 (2001); $593,657 (2000). Note: Contributes through foundation only.

Giving Analysis: Giving for 2001 includes: foundation ($392,500); 2000: foundation grants to United Way ($50,000); foundation matching gifts ($56,264); foundation ($487,393); 1998: foundation grants to United Way ($50,000); foundation matching gifts ($161,423).

Assets: $34,715 (2000); $17,768 (1998); $15,317 (1997)

Gifts Received: $600,000 (2000); $485,796 (1998); $447,000 (1997)

Typical Recipients

Arts & Humanities: Arts Associations & Councils, Arts Centers, Arts Funds, Ballet, Community Arts, Dance, Historic Preservation, Libraries, Museums/Galleries, Music, Opera, Performing Arts, Public Broadcasting, Theater, Visual Arts

Civic & Public Affairs: Business/Free Enterprise, Community Foundations, Economic Development, Employment/Job Training, Housing, Legal Aid, Minority Business, Nonprofit Management, Public Policy, Rural Affairs, Urban & Community Affairs, Women's Affairs, Zoos/Aquariums

Education: Arts/Humanities Education, Business Education, Colleges & Universities, Elementary Education (Public), Education-General, International Exchange, International Studies, Literacy, Minority Education, Preschool Education, Private Education (Precollege), Public Education (Precollege), Secondary Education (Private), Special Education, Student Aid, Vocational & Technical Education

Environment: Environment-General

Health: AIDS/HIV, Cancer, Children's Health/Hospitals, Geriatric Health, Health Policy/Cost Containment, Health Funds, Health Organizations, Hospitals, Long-Term Care, Medical Rehabilitation, Nursing Services, Nutrition

Religion: Jewish Causes, Religious Welfare, Seminaries

Social Services: Child Welfare, Community Centers, Community Service Organizations, Delinquency & Criminal Rehabilitation, Family Services, Food/Clothing Distribution, Homes, People with Disabilities, People with Disabilities, Senior Services, Shelters/Homelessness, Substance Abuse, United Funds/United Ways, Volunteer Services, Youth Organizations

Application Procedures

Initial Contact: Request guidelines, then send a written proposal.

Application Requirements: Include a concise description of organization including legal name, history, purpose, activities; purpose for which the grant is requested; amount requested and list of other sources of financial support, including foundations, corporations, and government grants; copy of IRS determination letter indicating 501(c)(3) tax-exempt status; copy of organization's most recently audited financial statement and Form 990; primary goals including a statement of service area and population to which the program is primarily directed; list of officers and board members and their affiliations; budget for current year including sources of projected income and breakdown of actual income versus expense year to date; and description of how the program will be evaluated, including procedures and criteria.

Deadlines: Grant requests are grouped by program area and scheduled for review by the Corporate Contributions Committee during either the first half or second half of the year; all culture and arts grant proposals received by April 1 in any calendar year will be assured consideration for Foundation funding in the first half of the year; civic and community proposals received by September 1 will be assured funding consideration in the second half of the year.

Review Process: Grant proposals are reviewed by the Corporate Contributions Committee.

Evaluative Criteria: Preference is given to organizations which demonstrate: ability to solve problems and provide direct services; innovativeness of programs; broad-based community support; involvement of U.S. Trust employees; reliance on private support, as opposed to tax-supported organizations; self-sufficiency of participants; large number of constituents served; efficiency and effective administration of funds and programs; ability to become self-sufficient rather than dependent on yearly renewals of support; long-term solutions versus short-term remedies; stimulate broader participation and multiply the impact of the funds provided by attracting other contributors; nondiscriminatory practices; support being sought by an organization throughout the community and to the prospects for obtaining this support.

Decision Notification: Organizations applying for a grant receive an acknowledgement of their proposal within two weeks of receipt; grants are disbursed before June 30 or December 31 each year.

Notes: Program will accept the New York Area Common application form. Proposals will not be considered by the Committee until all requested information is received. Proposals that remain incomplete two months after receipt has been acknowledged will be discarded.

Restrictions

The company does not make grants to individuals for educational or any other purpose; religious, veterans, fraternal or labor organizations unless engaged in a significant project benefiting the entire community; organizations, projects or programs outside the United States; political organizations, political candidates, or in support of political activity; organizations requesting support for courtesy advertising, festival participation, telethons, marathons, races, benefits or events, fund-raising dinners, sponsorship of publications or athletic teams; or national associations and member agencies of the United Way and other organizations supported by an umbrella organization.

Additional Information

The foundation selects primarily Manhattan community grants in the area of housing. For job training initiatives, candidates are chosen from the five boroughs of New York City and Nassau County, Long Island.

Corporate Officials

Martha L. Dinerstein: managing director, head marketing & corporate communications PRIM CORP EMPL managing director, head marketing & corporate communications: United States Trust Co. of New York. NONPR AFFIL member: New York Junior League; director: Women's Economic Roundtable; member: Advertising Women New York; member: Financial Women's Association.

John L. Kirby: chief administrative officer, executive vice president PRIM CORP EMPL chief administrative officer, executive vice president: U.S. Trust Corp.

Jeffrey Stuart Maurer: president, chief operating officer, director B New York, NY 1947. ED Alfred University BA (1969); New York University MBA (1975); Saint John's University JD (1976). PRIM CORP EMPL president, chief operating officer, director: United States Trust Corp. New York.

H. Marshall Schwarz: chairman, chief executive officer B New York, NY 1936. ED Harvard University BA (1958); Harvard University MBA (1961). PRIM CORP

EMPL chairman, chief executive officer: United States Trust Co. of New York. CORP AFFIL director: Bowne & Co. Inc.; director: Atlantic Mutual Companies. NONPR AFFIL trustee: Milton Academy; director: United Way New York City; trustee: Columbia University Teachers College; chairman: American Red Cross Greater New York City.

Frederick B. Taylor: vice chairman, chief investment officer B Albany, NY 1941. ED Wesleyan University BA (1963); University of Pennsylvania Wharton School MBA (1965). PRIM CORP EMPL vice chairman, chief investment officer: United States Trust Co. of New York. CORP AFFIL vice chairman, chief investment officer: US Trust Corp.

Foundation Officials

Carol A. Strickland: chairman corporate contributions committee B Cold Spring, NY 1949. ED Skidmore College BA (1972); New York University (1978). PRIM CORP EMPL corp. secretary, managing directory: United States Trust Co. of New York. CORP AFFIL corporate secretary, senior vice president: US Trust Corp. NONPR AFFIL member: American Society of Corporate Secretaries.

Grants Analysis

Disclosure Period: calendar year ending 2001
Total Grants: $392,500*
Number of Grants: 33
Average Grant: $11,894
Highest Grant: $30,000
Typical Range: $1,000 to $15,000
*Note: Grants analysis provided by foundation.

Recent Grants

Note: Grants derived from 2000 Form 990.

Library-Related

10,000	New York Public Library, New York, NY

General

50,000	United Way of New York City, New York, NY
40,000	Metropolitan Museum of Art, New York, NY
25,000	Per Scholas, New York, NY
20,000	Lincoln Center for Performing Arts, New York, NY
15,000	Roundabout Theatre Company, New York, NY
12,500	Neighborhood 2000 Fund, New York, NY
12,500	New York Landmarks Conservancy, New York, NY
10,000	Alliance of Resident Theaters, New York, NY
10,000	Ballet Tech Foundation, Inc., New York, NY
10,000	Big Apple Circus, New York, NY

UNITED WISCONSIN SERVICES

Company Headquarters

401 W. Michigan St.
Milwaukee, WI 53203-2896
Web: http://www.cobaltcorporation.com

Company Description

Ticker: CBZ
Exchange: OTC
Former Name: United Wisconsin Services (2001).
Revenue: US$1.451 billion (2001)
Employees: 3,599 (2001)
SIC(s): 6321 Accident & Health Insurance, 8099 Health & Allied Services Nec.

United Wisconsin Services Foundation

Giving Contact

Thomas R. Hefty, Chairman & President
401 West Michigan Street
Milwaukee, WI 53203
Phone: (414)226-5756

Description

Founded: 1984
EIN: 391514703
Organization Type: Corporate Foundation
Giving Locations: WI
Grant Types: General Support, Multiyear/Continuing Support, Operating Expenses, Scholarship.

Donor Information

Founder: Blue Cross and Blue Shield United of Wisconsin, United Wisconsin Services

Financial Summary

Total Giving: $650,129 (2001); $751,855 (1999); $539,804 (1997)
Giving Analysis: Giving for 2001 includes: foundation grants to United Way ($132,350); 1999: foundation scholarships ($29,500); foundation grants to United Way ($74,770) foundation ($647,585)
Assets: $4,195,740 (2001); $5,097,314 (1999); $5,768,735 (1997)
Gifts Received: $10,000 (1999); $100 (1995); $2,800,000 (1994). Note: In 1995, contributions were received from Blue Cross & Blue Shield United of Wisconsin.

Typical Recipients

Arts & Humanities: Arts Associations & Councils, Arts Centers, Arts Festivals, Community Arts, Dance, History & Archaeology, Libraries, Museums/Galleries, Music, Opera, Performing Arts, Public Broadcasting, Theater
Civic & Public Affairs: African American Affairs, Business/Free Enterprise, Chambers of Commerce, Community Foundations, Economic Development, Economic Policy, Employment/Job Training, Civic & Public Affairs-General, Housing, Municipalities/Towns, Nonprofit Management, Parades/Festivals, Professional & Trade Associations, Public Policy, Safety, Urban & Community Affairs, Women's Affairs, Zoos/Aquariums
Education: Business Education, Colleges & Universities, Continuing Education, Economic Education, Education Funds, Education Reform, Faculty Development, Education-General, Gifted & Talented Programs, Literacy, Medical Education, Minority Education, Social Sciences Education, Student Aid, Vocational & Technical Education
Environment: Environment-General, Resource Conservation
Health: Alzheimers Disease, Arthritis, Cancer, Children's Health/Hospitals, Clinics/Medical Centers, Diabetes, Eyes/Blindness, Geriatric Health, Health Policy/Cost Containment, Health Organizations, Heart, Medical Research, Mental Health, Prenatal Health Issues, Public Health, Respiratory, Single-Disease Health Associations
International: Foreign Arts Organizations, International Environmental Issues
Religion: Religious Welfare
Social Services: Child Welfare, Community Centers, Community Service Organizations, Family Services, Food/Clothing Distribution, People with Disabilities, Recreation & Athletics, Scouts, Senior Services, Social Services-General, Substance Abuse, United Funds/United Ways, Volunteer Services, YMCA/YWCA/YMHA/YWHA, Youth Organizations

Application Procedures

Initial Contact: Submit a letter requesting guidelines and application form.
Deadlines: None.

Restrictions

Does not support individuals.
Foundation considers requests from religious organizations and institutions only when the resulting impact of the project is not primarily denominational.
Foundation considers requests from provider organizations and institutions (hospitals, clinics) only when the resulting impact of the project can be proven to benefit an entire community/region, or supports an employee's involvement with that organization.
Foundation considers requests for building projects or capital campaigns only when having a special interest to the purposes of the foundation.
Foundation does not support grant requests from member agencies of the United Way or the United Performing Arts Fund.

Additional Information

Contributions support nonprofit, charitable organizations with proof of 501(c)(3) status. Emphasis is on health and wellness activities, as well as other activities that add to the quality of life.
Contributions are awarded on a one-time basis without commitment to future giving.
Affiliates of United Wisconsin Services include Blue Cross & Blue Shield United of Wisconsin, Compcare Health Services Insurance Corp., Dentacare, Take Control Inc., Meridian Resource Corp., United Government Services, United Heartland, American Medical Security, Proservices, United Wisconsin Group, United Wisconsin Insurance Co., and United Wisconsin Life Insurance Co.
Publications: Guidelines; Application Form

Corporate Officials

Thomas R. Hefty: chairman, president, chief executive officer B 1947. ED University of Wisconsin BA (1968); Johns Hopkins University MA (1969); University of Wisconsin Law School JD (1973). PRIM CORP EMPL chairman, president, chief executive officer: United Wisconsin Services Inc. CORP AFFIL chairman, president: United Wisconsin Proservices; chief executive officer: Valley Health Plan; chairman: United Wisconsin Life Insurance; president: United Heartland Inc.; chairman: United Wisconsin Insurance Co.; chief executive officer: Meridian Resources Corp.; chairman, president: Take Control; chairman: Meridian Managed Care Inc.; chairman: Blue Cross & Blue Shield United Wisconsin; chairman: Compcare Health Services.
Penny Siewert: vice president regional services PRIM CORP EMPL vice president regional services: United Wisconsin Services ADD CORP EMPL vice president: Meridian Resource Corp.; vice president: Meridian Managed Care Inc.; secretary: Unity Health Plans Insurance. CORP AFFIL officer: Blue Cross & Blue Shield United.
Essie M. Whitelaw: president, chief operating officer B 1948. ED Utica College. PRIM CORP EMPL president, chief operating officer: Blue Cross & Blue Shield United of Wisconsin. CORP AFFIL director: WICOR Inc.; director: Universal Foods Corp.; president: American Medical Security Group; vice president: Compcare Health Services. NONPR AFFIL vice chairman: Metropolitan Milwaukee Association of Commerce.

Foundation Officials

Roger Formisano: vice president PRIM CORP EMPL president, chief operating officer: Compcare Health Services Insurance Corp. CORP AFFIL executive vice president, chief operating officer: United Wisconsin Services; vice president: Valley Health Plan; vice president: United Wisconsin Insurance Co.; vice president: United Wisconsin Life Insurance; president: Meridian Resources Corp.; director: United

Heartland Inc.; president, chief operating officer: Meridian Managed Care Inc.
Mark Howard Granoff: vice president B Brooklyn, NY 1946. ED City University of New York BA (1968); City University of New York MA (1972). PRIM CORP EMPL president, chief operating officer: United Wisconsin Group. CORP AFFIL executive president: United Wisconsin Life Insurance; vice president: United Wisconsin Services; vice president: Blue Cross & Blue Shield United Wisconsin; president: United Wisconsin Insurance Co.
Thomas R. Hefty: chairman, president, chief executive officer (see above)
Tom Luljak: executive director PRIM CORP EMPL director corporate communications: United Wisconsin Services.
Penny Siewert: vice president, secretary, treasurer (see above)
Essie M. Whitelaw: vice president (see above)

Grants Analysis

Disclosure Period: calendar year ending 2001
Total Grants: $517,779*
Number of Grants: 119
Average Grant: $4,351
Highest Grant: $87,500
Lowest Grant: $50
Typical Range: $500 to $10,000
*Note: Giving excludes United Way.

Recent Grants

Note: Grants derived from 2001 Form 990.

General

87,500	United Performing Arts Fund, Milwaukee, WI
58,000	United Way of Greater Milwaukee, Milwaukee, WI
58,000	United Way of Greater Milwaukee, Milwaukee, WI
36,225	Wisconsin Foundation of Independent Colleges, Milwaukee, WI -- scholarships
30,000	We The People, Madison, WI -- 1999 sponsorship
30,000	We The People, Madison, WI -- 1999 sponsorship
28,000	Wisconsin League for Nursing, Milwaukee, WI -- nurse of year obligation
26,000	Wisconsin League for Nursing, Milwaukee, WI -- nurse of year obligation
25,000	Coalition of Wisconsin Aging Groups, Madison, WI -- convention sponsorship
14,000	University of Wisconsin Foundation, Madison, WI -- scholarships

UNITRODE CORP.

Company Headquarters

Merrimack, NH
Web: http://www.texasinstrument.com

Company Description

Employees: 500
SIC(s): 3674 Semiconductors & Related Devices.
Parent Company: Texas Instruments Inc., Dallas, TX, United States

Operating Locations

Unitrode Corp. (CA--San Jose; NH--Merrimack; NC--Cary)

Nonmonetary Support

Type: Cause-related Marketing & Promotion; Donated Equipment; In-kind Services; Loaned Employees; Loaned Executives

Giving Contact

7 Continental Blvd.
Merrimack, NH 03054
Phone: (603)429-8770

Description

Organization Type: Corporate Giving Program
Giving Locations: headquarters and operating communities.
Grant Types: Award, Capital, Challenge, Conference/Seminar, Emergency, General Support, Operating Expenses, Project, Scholarship.

Financial Summary

Total Giving: $50,000 (1999 approx); $30,000 (1998 approx); $50,000 (1997)

Typical Recipients

Arts & Humanities: Art History, Arts Associations & Councils, Arts Centers, Arts Festivals, Arts Outreach, Community Arts, Libraries, Museums/Galleries, Music, Opera, Performing Arts, Public Broadcasting, Theater, Visual Arts
Civic & Public Affairs: Business/Free Enterprise, Chambers of Commerce, Community Foundations, Economic Development, Civic & Public Affairs-General, Housing, Municipalities/Towns, Nonprofit Management, Parades/Festivals, Professional & Trade Associations
Education: Afterschool/Enrichment Programs, Arts/Humanities Education, Business Education, Business-School Partnerships, Colleges & Universities, Education Funds, Elementary Education (Private), Environmental Education, Gifted & Talented Programs, Literacy, Private Education (Precollege), Public Education (Precollege), School Volunteerism, Science/Mathematics Education, Secondary Education (Private), Secondary Education (Public), Vocational & Technical Education
Environment: Energy
Health: Adolescent Health Issues, Arthritis, Children's Health/Hospitals, Clinics/Medical Centers, Emergency/Ambulance Services, Home-Care Services, Hospices, Hospitals, Preventive Medicine/Wellness Organizations, Public Health
Religion: Religious Welfare
Science: Science-General, Science Exhibits & Fairs, Science Museums, Scientific Organizations
Social Services: At-Risk Youth, Big Brother/Big Sister, Camps, Child Abuse, Community Centers, Community Service Organizations, Crime Prevention, Domestic Violence, Emergency Relief, Food/Clothing Distribution, People with Disabilities, Recreation & Athletics, Scouts, Senior Services, Sexual Abuse, Shelters/Homelessness, Special Olympics, United Funds/United Ways, Veterans, Volunteer Services, YMCA/YWCA/YMHA/YWHA, Youth Organizations

Application Procedures

Initial Contact: Send a brief letter of inquiry.
Application Requirements: a description of organization, amount requested, purpose of funds sought, and proof of tax-exempt status.
Deadlines: None.

Restrictions

Does not support individuals, religious organizations for sectarian purposes, or political or lobbying groups.

Corporate Officials

Robert L. Gable: chairman, director chief financial officer B Baltimore, MD 1930. ED University of Maryland (1952); University of Maryland School of Business Administration (1953). PRIM CORP EMPL chairman, director: Unitrode Corp. CORP AFFIL director: Symbolics Inc.; chairman: New Hampshire Savings Bank Corp.; chairman: Rockingham County Trust Co.; director: Financial Concepts; director: H K Webster Co.; director: Apollo Computer. NONPR AFFIL vice chairman: Outward Bound.
Robert Richardson: president, chief executive officer, director PRIM CORP EMPL president, chief executive officer, director: Unitrode Corp.
Cosmo S. Trapani: executive vice president, chief financial officer ED Boston College (1961). PRIM CORP EMPL executive vice president, chief financial

officer: Unitrode Corp. NONPR AFFIL member: American Institute CPA's.

Grants Analysis

Total Grants: $30,000 (approx)
Typical Range: $50 to $1,000

Recent Grants

Note: Grants derived from 1998 Form 990.

General
Daniel Webster College, Nashua, NH
Home, Health and Hospice, Nashua, NH
Keystone Hall, Nashua, NH
Merrimack High School, Merrimack, NH
Museum of Science, Boston, MA
Salvation Army, Manchester, NH
Songahegan Health Care Foundation, Songahegan, NH
United Way, Nashua, NH
Up Reach Riding Center, Goffstown, NH
Habitat for Humanity, Durham, NC

UNIVERSAL STUDIOS

Company Headquarters

100 Universal City Plaza
Universal City, CA 91608-1002
Web: http://www.universalstudios.com

Company Description

Employees: 15,000
SIC(s): 2396 Automotive & Apparel Trimmings, 2731 Book Publishing, 2741 Miscellaneous Publishing, 7812 Motion Picture & Video Production.
Parent Company: Vivendi Universal Entertainment, 100 Universal City Plaza, Universal City, CA, United States
Parent Revenue: US$51,125,000,000 (2001)

Operating Locations

Geffen Records (CA--Los Angeles); G.P. Putnam Sons (NY--New York); GRP Records (NY--New York); MCA Records (CA--Universal City); MCA/Universal Merchandising (CA--Universal City); Merchandising Corp. of America (CA--Universal City); October Films (NY--New York); Spencer Gifts (NJ--Egg Harbor Township); UNI Distribution Corp. (CA--Universal City); Universal Amphitheatre (CA--Universal City); Universal Film Exchanges, Inc. (NY--New York); Universal Studios (CA--Anaheim, Glendale; FL--Orlando; MI--Grand Rapids; PA--Pittsburgh); Universal Studios Development Co. (CA--Universal City); Universal Studios Distributing Co. (NY--New York); Universal Studios Enterprises (CA--Universal City); Universal Studios Hollywood (CA--Universal City); Universal Studios Home Entertainment Group (CA--Universal City); Universal Studios Manufacturing (IL--Pinckneyville; NY--Gloversville); Universal Studios Music Entertainment Group (CA--Universal City); Universal Studios New Ventures (CA--Universal City); Universal Studios Publishing Group (CA--Universal City); Universal Studios Recreation Services Group (CA--Universal City); Universal Studios Television Ltd. (CA--Universal City); Universal Studios TV (CA--Universal City); Universal Studios Videodisc (CA--Universal City); Winterland Productions (CA--San Francisco); Womp's Restaurant Bar & Grill (CA--Universal City); Yosemite Concession Services Co. (CA--Yosemite National Park)

Nonmonetary Support

Type: Donated Equipment; Donated Products; In-kind Services; Loaned Employees
Volunteer Programs: The company holds a company-wide annual Volunteer Day during which employees volunteer to work in food banks, build houses with Habitat for Humanity, beautify schools and parks, and provide books to school libraries. In addition, the company sponsors Education is Universal, through

which employee volunteers tutor children in schools, provide students with job shadowing opportunities, and hold career days to introduce students to careers within the entertainment industry.
Contact: Nancy Nemecek, Manager, Public Affairs Universal Studios
Note: Company provides nonmonetary support.

Universal Studios Foundation

Giving Contact

Helene Giambone, Foundation Contact
Universal Studios Foundation
100 Universal City Plaza
Universal City, CA 91608
Phone: (818)777-1208
Web: http://www.universalstudios.com/homepage/html/about_us/

Description

Founded: 1956
EIN: 136096061
Organization Type: Corporate Foundation
Giving Locations: CA: Los Angeles
Grant Types: Capital, General Support, Multiyear/Continuing Support, Project.

Donor Information

Founder: MCA Inc.

Financial Summary

Total Giving: $875,000 (fiscal year ending June 31, 2002 approx); $877,870 (fiscal 2001); $600,000 (fiscal 2000). Note: Contributes through foundation only.
Giving Analysis: Giving for fiscal 2001 includes: foundation ($877,870); fiscal 2000: foundation ($600,000); fiscal 1999: foundation ($949,400);
Assets: $13,897,052 (fiscal 2001); $13,408,620 (fiscal 2000); $13,703,157 (fiscal 1999)
Gifts Received: $97,054 (fiscal 2000); $38,511 (fiscal 1999); $23,109 (fiscal 1998). Note: Foundation receives gifts from Universal Studios and its subsidiaries.

Typical Recipients

Arts & Humanities: Arts Associations & Councils, Arts Centers, Arts Funds, Arts Institutes, Ballet, Dance, Film & Video, Arts & Humanities-General, Historic Preservation, History & Archaeology, Libraries, Literary Arts, Museums/Galleries, Music, Performing Arts, Public Broadcasting, Theater
Civic & Public Affairs: African American Affairs, Botanical Gardens/Parks, Business/Free Enterprise, Civil Rights, Community Foundations, Economic Development, Employment/Job Training, Civic & Public Affairs-General, Housing, Law & Justice, Philanthropic Organizations, Professional & Trade Associations, Public Policy, Urban & Community Affairs, Women's Affairs, Zoos/Aquariums
Education: Arts/Humanities Education, Business Education, Colleges & Universities, Community & Junior Colleges, Education Associations, Education Funds, Education Reform, Education-General, International Studies, Legal Education, Literacy, Medical Education, Minority Education, Special Education, Student Aid
Environment: Environment-General, Resource Conservation
Health: Cancer, Children's Health/Hospitals, Clinics/Medical Centers, Diabetes, Emergency/Ambulance Services, Eyes/Blindness, Health-General, Health Organizations, Hospitals, Medical Research, Mental Health, Multiple Sclerosis, Public Health, Research/Studies Institutes, Single-Disease Health Associations
Religion: Jewish Causes
Science: Scientific Centers & Institutes

Social Services: Animal Protection, Big Brother/Big Sister, Child Welfare, Community Centers, Community Service Organizations, Counseling, Delinquency & Criminal Rehabilitation, Emergency Relief, Family Planning, Family Services, Food/Clothing Distribution, People with Disabilities, Recreation & Athletics, Scouts, Senior Services, Social Services-General, Substance Abuse, United Funds/United Ways, Veterans, Volunteer Services, YMCA/YWCA/YMHA/YWHA, Youth Organizations

Application Procedures

Initial Contact: Send a letter or preliminary proposal of not more than three pages.

Application Requirements: Include a description of organization of organization; purpose and qualification for which support is sought; attach copy of 501(c)(3) not-for-profit IRS determination letter.

Deadlines: None.

Notes: If the foundation is interested in pursuing the possibility of working with the organization, it may request the following information: a statement of objectives, activities, accomplishments, and geographic scope; a list of the names and business or professional affiliations of the organization's officers and board of directors or trustees, the number of board meetings held in the previous year, and whether or not board members are compensated; number and total compensation of paid employees and the number of volunteer workers; a current itemized budget based on total anticipated funds (fund-raising costs should be shown); a list of sources of current income, including the amount received from each source, listing the corporations, foundations, and government agencies that are current sources of major funding; current audited financial statements; a detailed description of the specific program for which support is requested, including an explanation of what the grant is expected to accomplish, how the program will be carried out, and the method or procedure that will be used to evaluate the effectiveness of the program; and a signed statement that the organization will furnish periodic reports indicating the use of any funds provided by the foundation.

Restrictions

Does not support individuals; film, television, or video projects; group trips; private foundations; political campaigns; ad journals; or fund-raising dinners or events.

Additional Information

Publications: Application Guidelines

Corporate Officials

Ronald Meyer: president, chief executive officer B 1945. PRIM CORP EMPL president, director: Universal Studios.

Grants Analysis

Disclosure Period: fiscal year ending June 31, 2001
Total Grants: $877,870
Number of Grants: 24
Average Grant: $36,571
Highest Grant: $100,000
Lowest Grant: $2,500
Typical Range: $2,000 to $100,000

Recent Grants

Note: Grants derived from 2001 Form 990.

General

100,000	Geffen Playhouse, Los Angeles, CA
100,000	Motion Picture and Television Fund Foundation, Los Angeles, CA
100,000	Providence St. Joseph Medical Center, Burbank, CA
100,000	University of Southern California, Los Angeles, CA
50,000	Fulfillment Fund, Los Angeles, CA
50,000	Greater Los Angeles Zoo Association, Los Angeles, CA
40,000	Santa Monica College, Santa Monica, CA
30,000	Facing History and Ourselves
25,000	Children's Defense Fund, Washington, DC
25,000	Economic Alliance of the San Fernando Valley, San Fernando Valley, CA

UNOCAL CORP.

Company Headquarters

El Segundo, CA
Web: http://www.unocal.com

Company Description

Founded: 1890
Ticker: UCL
Exchange: NYSE
Revenue: US$5.251 billion (2002)
Profit: US$331 million (2002)
Employees: 6980 (2002)
Fortune Rank: 316, per FORTUNE Magazine's list of 500 Largest U.S. Corporations (2002).
SIC(s): 1311 Crude Petroleum & Natural Gas, 1321 Natural Gas Liquids, 2911 Petroleum Refining, 2992 Lubricating Oils & Greases.

Operating Locations

Unocal Corp. (AL--Saraland; AK--Anchorage, Kenai, Ketchikan; CA--El Segundo; HI--Hilo, Honolulu; LA--Starks; NM--Bloomfield, Cuba; OH--Columbus, Wadsworth; OR--Myrtle Point, Port Orford, Portland; TX--Andrews, Freeport, Snyder, Sugar Land; WA--Spokane; WI--Milwaukee; WY--Lander)

Unocal Foundation

Giving Contact

Stephen L. Hayes, Vice President
Unocal Foundation
14141 Southwest Freeway
Sugar Land, TX 77478
Phone: (281)287-7917

Description

EIN: 956071812
Organization Type: Corporate Foundation
Giving Locations: nationally, with preference given to locations with Unocal corporate facilities.
Grant Types: Challenge, Department, Employee Matching Gifts, Fellowship, General Support, Professorship, Project, Research, Scholarship.
Note: Employee matching gift ratio: 1 to 1 for education, up to $5,000 per employee annually.

Financial Summary

Total Giving: $6,200,000 (fiscal year ending January 31, 2001); $5,500,000 (fiscal 2000); $4,100,000 (fiscal 1999)
Giving Analysis: Giving for fiscal 2001 includes: foundation grants to United Way ($330,810); foundation ($630,805); corporate direct giving (approx $5,240,000); fiscal 2000: foundation scholarships ($122,650); foundation matching gifts ($393,552); foundation grants to United Way ($463,622); corporate direct giving (approx $4,500,000); fiscal 1999: foundation scholarships ($111,200); foundation grants to United Way ($349,551); foundation matching gifts ($450,079); corporate direct giving (approx $3,200,000);
Assets: $2,143,443 (fiscal 2001); $2,459,536 (fiscal 2000); $2,266,049 (fiscal 1999)
Gifts Received: $636,146 (fiscal 2001); $1,000,000 (fiscal 2000); $1,000,000 (fiscal 1999). Note: Contributions are received from Unocal Corp.

Typical Recipients

Arts & Humanities: Arts Centers, Arts Funds, Arts Institutes, Community Arts, Dance, Arts & Humanities-General, Historic Preservation, Libraries, Museums/Galleries, Music, Opera, Performing Arts, Theater

Civic & Public Affairs: African American Affairs, Botanical Gardens/Parks, Business/Free Enterprise, Civil Rights, Clubs, Economic Development, Economic Policy, Employment/Job Training, Civic & Public Affairs-General, Hispanic Affairs, Housing, Law & Justice, Legal Aid, Minority Business, Nonprofit Management, Parades/Festivals, Philanthropic Organizations, Professional & Trade Associations, Public Policy, Rural Affairs, Safety, Urban & Community Affairs, Women's Affairs

Education: Agricultural Education, Arts/Humanities Education, Business Education, Colleges & Universities, Community & Junior Colleges, Continuing Education, Economic Education, Education Associations, Education Funds, Education Reform, Engineering/Technological Education, Faculty Development, Education-General, International Exchange, International Studies, Leadership Training, Legal Education, Medical Education, Minority Education, Private Education (Precollege), Public Education (Precollege), Science/Mathematics Education, Secondary Education (Private), Secondary Education (Public), Social Sciences Education, Student Aid

Environment: Energy, Environment-General, Resource Conservation, Wildlife Protection

Health: AIDS/HIV, Arthritis, Children's Health/Hospitals, Clinics/Medical Centers, Diabetes, Emergency/Ambulance Services, Health Organizations, Hospitals, Medical Rehabilitation, Medical Research, Medical Training, Mental Health, Single-Disease Health Associations

International: Foreign Educational Institutions, International-General, International Affairs, International Organizations, International Relations

Religion: Religion-General, Religious Welfare

Science: Science Exhibits & Fairs, Science Museums, Scientific Centers & Institutes, Scientific Organizations

Social Services: At-Risk Youth, Big Brother/Big Sister, Camps, Child Welfare, Community Service Organizations, Crime Prevention, Family Services, Food/Clothing Distribution, Homes, People with Disabilities, Recreation & Athletics, Scouts, Social Services-General, Special Olympics, Substance Abuse, United Funds/United Ways, Volunteer Services, YMCA/YWCA/YMHA/YWHA, Youth Organizations

Application Procedures

Initial Contact: Request guidelines, then submit a brief letter of request.

Application Requirements: Include background of organization, including its goals and objectives; necessity/purpose of grant; amount budgeted for project; most recent audited financial statement and annual report; current year's budget; evaluative criteria; other organizations solicited and amounts received, pledged, or anticipated; copy of IRS determination letter; copy of most recent IRS Form 990.

Deadlines: Contact foundation for deadlines, as they vary by program.

Restrictions

Foundation does not support grants to individuals; elementary or secondary education; political or lobbying groups; veterans, fraternal, sectarian, social, religious, athletic, choral, band, or similar groups; courtesy advertising; conferences, films, or contests; supplemental operating support for organizations eligible for united funds; governmental agencies or departments; or trade, business, or professional associations; most capital campaigns or endowments.

Grants are not renewed automatically; a request for support must be submitted each year.

Corporate Officials

Darrell D. Chessum: treasurer, chairman, director PRIM CORP EMPL treasurer: Unocal Corp. CORP AFFIL treasurer: Poco Graphite Inc.

Michael Thacher: general manager public relations & communications PRIM CORP EMPL general manager public relations & communications: Unocal Corp.

Charles R. Williamson: chief executive officer, chairman, director ED University of Texas PhD (1978). PRIM CORP EMPL chief executive officer, chairman, director: Unocal Corp.

Foundation Officials

MacDonald G. Becket: trustee

Karen Ann Sikkema: president, trustee B Kalamazoo, MI 1946. ED Kalamazoo College (1968); University of Michigan (1970). PRIM CORP EMPL external affairs: Unocal Corp. CORP AFFIL vice president: Union Oil Co. California.

Grants Analysis

Disclosure Period: fiscal year ending January 31, 2001

Total Grants: $630,805*

Number of Grants: 204

Average Grant: $3,092

Highest Grant: $63,850

Typical Range: $1,000 to $8,000 and $100,000 to $500,000

*****Note:** Giving includes corporate direct giving and United Way. Giving includes matching gifts.

Recent Grants

Note: Grants derived from 2001 Form 990.

General

220,000	South Dakota School of Mines, Rapid City, SD
144,000	United Way of Acadiana, LA
132,000	Citizens Scholarship Foundation of America, St. Peter, MN
120,000	United Way of Acadiana, LA
80,000	Child Health Foundation, Columbia, MD
50,000	American Red Cross, Washington, DC
50,000	California 4-H Foundation, Davis, CA
50,000	Carter Center, Atlanta, GA
50,000	United Way September 11th Fund, New York, NY
41,070	Colorado School of Mines, Golden, CO

HAROLD AND GRACE UPJOHN FOUNDATION

Giving Contact

Floyd L. Parks, Secretary & Treasurer
Mall Plaza, Suite 90
157 S. Kalamazoo Mall, Suite 90
Kalamazoo, MI 49007
Phone: (616)344-2818

Description

Founded: 1958
EIN: 386052963
Organization Type: Private Foundation
Giving Locations: MI
Grant Types: Capital, General Support, Project, Seed Money.

Donor Information

Founder: the late Grace G. Upjohn

Financial Summary

Total Giving: $669,000 (fiscal year ending October 31, 2001); $971,100 (fiscal 2000); $517,203 (fiscal 1998)

Giving Analysis: Giving for fiscal 2001 includes: foundation grants to United Way ($75,000); fiscal 1998: foundation grants to United Way ($45,000) foundation ($472,203)

Assets: $12,237,916 (fiscal 2001); $13,947,314 (fiscal 2000); $12,119,363 (fiscal 1998)

Gifts Received: In fiscal 1991, contributions were received from Mary U. Meader.

Typical Recipients

Arts & Humanities: Arts Associations & Councils, Arts Centers, Arts Institutes, Arts Outreach, Dance, Ethnic & Folk Arts, Historic Preservation, History & Archaeology, Libraries, Museums/Galleries, Music, Performing Arts, Theater, Visual Arts

Civic & Public Affairs: African American Affairs, Botanical Gardens/Parks, Business/Free Enterprise, Economic Development, Employment/Job Training, Civic & Public Affairs-General, Housing, Municipalities/Towns, Nonprofit Management, Parades/Festivals, Philanthropic Organizations, Public Policy, Safety, Urban & Community Affairs, Women's Affairs, Zoos/Aquariums

Education: Arts/Humanities Education, Colleges & Universities, Community & Junior Colleges, Education Associations, Education Reform, Education-General, Gifted & Talented Programs, Minority Education, Private Education (Precollege), Public Education (Precollege), Science/Mathematics Education, Secondary Education (Private)

Environment: Environment-General, Resource Conservation

Health: AIDS/HIV, Clinics/Medical Centers, Emergency/Ambulance Services, Hospitals, Nursing Services, Preventive Medicine/Wellness Organizations

International: International Development

Religion: Churches, Jewish Causes, Ministries, Religious Organizations, Religious Welfare

Social Services: At-Risk Youth, Big Brother/Big Sister, Camps, Child Welfare, Community Service Organizations, Counseling, Emergency Relief, Family Planning, Family Services, Food/Clothing Distribution, Homes, People with Disabilities, Recreation & Athletics, Scouts, Senior Services, Substance Abuse, United Funds/United Ways, YMCA/YWCA/YMHA/YWHA, Youth Organizations

Application Procedures

Initial Contact: Contact foundation for application form.

Application Requirements: Return completed application form and cover letter signed by an authorized officer of the organization. Also include a list of board members, including occupations, proof of tax-exempt status, a one page budget, and recently audited financial statement.

Deadlines: None.

Restrictions

Does not support individuals.

Additional Information

Publications: Annual Report; Application Form; Guidelines

Foundation Officials

Janet J. Deal: trustee

Christopher Upjohn Light: vice president B Kalamazoo, MI 1937. ED Carleton University BA (1958); Columbia University MS (1962); Western Michigan University MBA (1967); Washington University PhD (1971). NONPR AFFIL member voting committee: National Academy Recording Arts & Sciences; member: Society Professional Journalists; member: Financial Management Association; trustee: Kalamazoo Symphony Orchestra Association; member: Am Society Composers, Authors & Publishers; trustee: American Symphony Orchestra League. CLUB AFFIL Gull Lake Country Club; University Chicago Club.

Mary U. Meader: trustee

Florence U. Orosz: president

Jon L. Stryker: trust

Grants Analysis

Disclosure Period: fiscal year ending October 31, 2001

Total Grants: $594,000*

Number of Grants: 39

Average Grant: $13,552*

Highest Grant: $79,020

Lowest Grant: $500

Typical Range: $5,000 to $25,000

*****Note:** Giving excludes United Way. Average grant figure excludes highest grant.

Recent Grants

Note: Grants derived from 2000 Form 990.

General

100,000	Lakeside, Kalamazoo, MI
75,000	Greater Kalamazoo United Way, Kalamazoo, MI
75,000	Heritage Community of Kalamazoo, Kalamazoo, MI
55,000	Kalamazoo Arts Council, Inc., Kalamazoo, MI
50,600	Ministry with Community, Kalamazoo, MI
50,000	Boys Club of Kalamazoo, Kalamazoo, MI
50,000	Davenport College, Kalamazoo, MI
40,000	Kalamazoo Valley Habitat for Humanity, Kalamazoo, MI
35,000	Pretty Lake Vacation Camp, Kalamazoo, MI
28,000	Kalamazoo Nature Center, Kalamazoo, MI

LUCY AND ELEANOR S. UPTON CHARITABLE FOUNDATION

Giving Contact

Francis X. O'Brien, Trustee
c/o Carpenter, Bennett & Morrissey
3 Gateway Center
100 Mulberry Street
Newark, NJ 07102-4079
Phone: (973)622-7711

Description

Founded: 1965
EIN: 226074947
Organization Type: Private Foundation
Giving Locations: NJ
Grant Types: Fellowship, General Support, Research.

Donor Information

Founder: the late Eleanor S. Upton

Financial Summary

Total Giving: $179,500 (2001); $195,500 (2000); $159,000 (1999)

Assets: $7,631,648 (2001); $8,445,553 (2000); $7,804,951 (1999)

Typical Recipients

Arts & Humanities: Community Arts, History & Archaeology, Libraries, Museums/Galleries, Music

Civic & Public Affairs: Urban & Community Affairs

Education: Arts/Humanities Education, Colleges & Universities, Private Education (Precollege)

Health: Cancer, Children's Health/Hospitals, Hospitals, Medical Research

Religion: Religious Organizations, Religious Welfare

Science: Scientific Centers & Institutes

Social Services: Child Welfare, Community Service Organizations, Shelters/Homelessness, Youth Organizations

Application Procedures

Initial Contact: The foundation has no formal grant application procedure or application form.
Deadlines: None.

Foundation Officials

William B. Cater: trustee
Thomas L. Morrissey: trustee
Paul Moschetti: trustee
Francis X. O'Brien: trustee
Samuel C. Williams, Jr.: trustee

Grants Analysis

Disclosure Period: calendar year ending 2001
Total Grants: $179,500
Number of Grants: 13
Average Grant: $13,808
Highest Grant: $40,000
Lowest Grant: $5,000
Typical Range: $5,000 to $20,000

Recent Grants

Note: Grants derived from 2000 Form 990.

Library-Related
10,000   Newark Public Library, Newark, NJ

General
40,000	Rutgers University Foundation, New Brunswick, NJ -- Thomas A. Edison Papers
36,000	St. Phillip's Academy, Newark, NJ -- endowment fund and general use
35,000	New Jersey Symphony Orchestra, Newark, NJ
20,000	Isaiah House, East Orange, NJ -- operating expenses
20,000	Memorial Sloan-Kettering Cancer Center, New York, NY -- paid research fund, Department of Neurology
16,000	Newark Museum, Newark, NJ -- general use and science center
7,500	Children's Specialized Hospital Foundation, Mountainside, NJ
6,000	Newark Boys Chorus School, Newark, NJ
5,000	New Jersey Historical Society, Newark, NJ

FREDERICK S. UPTON FOUNDATION

Giving Contact

Stephen E. Upton, Trustee
100 Ridgeway
St. Joseph, MI 49085
Phone: (616)982-1905
Fax: (616)982-0323
E-mail: supton@qtm.net

Description

Founded: 1954
EIN: 366013317
Organization Type: Family Foundation
Giving Locations: IL; IN; MA; MI: Southwest Michigan; OH; PA; SC; WI
Grant Types: Challenge, Endowment, Project.
Note: The foundation also provides technical assistance and support for special events.

Donor Information

Founder: Established in 1954 by Frederick S. Upton, who, in 1911, co-founded the Upton Machine Company, the predecessor of the Whirlpool appliance company.

Financial Summary

Total Giving: $1,748,667 (2001); $1,800,000 (2000 approx); $1,775,248 (1999)
Giving Analysis: Giving for 1998 includes: foundation grants to United Way ($226,373)
Assets: $37,534,273 (2001); $40,000,000 (2000 approx); $40,051,597 (1999)
Gifts Received: $145 (2001)

Typical Recipients

Arts & Humanities: Arts Associations & Councils, Arts Centers, Arts Festivals, Arts Funds, Arts Institutes, Arts Outreach, Ballet, Dance, Arts & Humanities-General, Historic Preservation, History & Archaeology, Libraries, Literary Arts, Museums/Galleries, Music, Performing Arts, Visual Arts
Civic & Public Affairs: Civic & Public Affairs-General, Housing, Philanthropic Organizations, Safety, Urban & Community Affairs, Women's Affairs, Zoos/Aquariums
Education: Afterschool/Enrichment Programs, Agricultural Education, Arts/Humanities Education, Business Education, Colleges & Universities, Education Funds, Environmental Education, Education-General, Literacy, Minority Education, Preschool Education, Private Education (Precollege), Public Education (Precollege), Religious Education, School Volunteerism, Science/Mathematics Education, Student Aid
Environment: Environment-General, Resource Conservation
Health: AIDS/HIV, Children's Health/Hospitals, Geriatric Health, Health Organizations, Hospitals, Public Health
International: Foreign Arts Organizations, International Organizations
Religion: Churches, Ministries, Religious Organizations, Religious Welfare, Synagogues/Temples
Social Services: Animal Protection, At-Risk Youth, Child Welfare, Community Centers, Community Service Organizations, Counseling, Domestic Violence, Family Planning, Family Services, Food/Clothing Distribution, People with Disabilities, Recreation & Athletics, Senior Services, Shelters/Homelessness, United Funds/United Ways, Volunteer Services, YMCA/YWCA/YMHA/YWHA, Youth Organizations

Application Procedures

Initial Contact: Applicants should submit a letter of inquiry to the foundation and request an application form.
Deadlines: None.
Review Process: The board of trustees usually meets four times annually and applications are considered at that time.

Additional Information

Publications: Application Form

Foundation Officials

Priscilla U. Byrns: trustee
David F. Upton: trustee
Dr. Stephen E. Upton, LHD: chairman board trustees B Benton Harbor, MI 1924. ED University of Michigan (1949). PRIM CORP EMPL senior vice president: Whirlpool Corp. NONPR AFFIL director: Gilmore Music Festival; member: Rotary International.
Sylvia Upton Wood: secretary, trustee NONPR AFFIL director: Camden Military Academy.

Grants Analysis

Disclosure Period: calendar year ending 2001
Total Grants: $1,647,492*
Number of Grants: 282
Average Grant: $5,842
Highest Grant: $100,000
Lowest Grant: $95
Typical Range: $5,000 to $100000
*Note: Giving excludes United Way.

Recent Grants

Note: Grants derived from 2001 Form 990.

General
100,000	Lake Michigan Catholic Schools, MI -- faith and vision for the future campaign
55,000	Salvation Army, Benton Harbor, MI -- Turning Point Program
50,000	American Institute of Medical Preventics, Cleveland, OH -- clinical study on chelation therapy
50,000	Berrien County Intermediate School District, Berrien Springs, MI -- Arts Education Program
50,000	Cornerstone Alliance, Benton Harbor, MI -- strategic plan
50,000	Ele's Place, Lansing, MI -- marketing and promotion of new website
50,000	Lakeland Health Foundation, Benton Harbor, MI -- M. Beckley Upton Women's Center
50,000	Olivet College, Olivet, MI -- Instrumental Music Program
50,000	Olivet College, Olivet, MI -- athletic and recreational facility
45,000	Fort Miami Heritage Society, St. Joseph, MI -- employees

US BANK

Company Headquarters

1420 Fifth Ave.
Seattle, WA 98101
Web: http://www.usbank.com

Company Description

Employees: 2,300
SIC(s): 6035 Federal Savings Institutions.
Parent Company: U.S. Bancorp, 601 Second Avenue South, Minneapolis, MN, United States

Operating Locations

US Bank, Washington (WA--Seattle)

Nonmonetary Support

Type: Donated Equipment; In-kind Services; Workplace Solicitation
Note: Workplace solicitation is for United Way only.

Giving Contact

Mary Moore, Vice President & Manager, Community Relations
1420 5th Avenue, Suite 800
PO Box 720 PD-WA-T8CR
Seattle, WA 98111-0720
Phone: (206)344-2360
Fax: (206)340-8554
E-mail: mary.moore@usbank.com
Web: http://www.usbank.com/comm_relations

Description

Organization Type: Corporate Giving Program
Giving Locations: WA
Grant Types: Capital, Employee Matching Gifts, General Support, Matching, Project, Scholarship.

Financial Summary

Total Giving: $2,000,000 (2002 approx); $2,000,000 (2001); $2,400,000 (1999 approx). Note: Contributes through corporate direct giving program only.

Typical Recipients

Arts & Humanities: Arts Associations & Councils, Arts Centers, Arts Festivals, Arts Funds, Arts Outreach, Ballet, Community Arts, Dance, Ethnic & Folk Arts, Arts & Humanities-General, Historic Preservation, Libraries, Museums/Galleries, Music, Opera, Performing Arts, Theater, Visual Arts

Civic & Public Affairs: African American Affairs, Asian American Affairs, Business/Free Enterprise, Chambers of Commerce, Civil Rights, Economic Development, Employment/Job Training, Ethnic Organizations, Gay/Lesbian Issues, Civic & Public Affairs-General, Hispanic Affairs, Housing, Inner-City Development, Native American Affairs, Professional & Trade Associations, Public Policy, Urban & Community Affairs, Women's Affairs, Zoos/Aquariums
Education: Afterschool/Enrichment Programs, Business Education, Business-School Partnerships, Colleges & Universities, Economic Education, Education Reform, Education-General, Literacy, Minority Education, Preschool Education, Special Education
Health: Adolescent Health Issues, AIDS/HIV, Cancer, Children's Health/Hospitals, Health-General, Hospices, Mental Health, Prenatal Health Issues
Science: Science Museums
Social Services: At-Risk Youth, Camps, Child Welfare, Community Centers, Community Service Organizations, Counseling, Day Care, Domestic Violence, Emergency Relief, Family Services, Food/Clothing Distribution, Homes, People with Disabilities, Refugee Assistance, Senior Services, Sexual Abuse, Shelters/Homelessness, Social Services-General, Substance Abuse, United Funds/United Ways, Volunteer Services, YMCA/YWCA/YMHA/YWHA, Youth Organizations

Application Procedures

Initial Contact: Call local branch or corporate headquarters for information.

Restrictions

Company does not make grants to individuals, religious organizations for sectarian purposes, political or lobbying groups, travel expenses, or organizations outside operating areas. Grants are not made to organizations that are not tax-exempt for endowment campaigns; deficit reduction; fundraising events or sponsorships; medically oriented charities; academic medical, or scientific research; organizations receiving United Way funds; individuals K-12 schools; "pass through" organizations or other foundations; or merchant associations chamber memberships, chamber programs, or 501 (c) (4) or (6) organizations.

Additional Information

In 1997, First Bank System acquired U.S. Bancorp of Portland, OR. The merged company is called U.S. Bancorp.

Corporate Officials

Yvonne Blumenthal: vice president & manager, community investment PRIM CORP EMPL vice president & manager, community investment: US Bank, Washington.
Ken Kirkpatrick: president
Mary Moore: vice president & manager, community relations PRIM CORP EMPL vice president & manager community relations: US Bank, Washington.

Grants Analysis

Disclosure Period: calendar year ending 1999
Total Grants: $2,400,000 (approx)*
Number of Grants: 285
Average Grant: $8,421
Highest Grant: $247,000
Typical Range: $5,000 to $10,000
*Note: Grants Analysis provided by foundation.

USG CORP.

Company Headquarters

125 S. Franklin
Chicago, IL 60680-4678
Web: http://www.usg.com

Company Description

Founded: 1902
Ticker: USG
Exchange: NYSE
Revenue: US$3.468 billion (2002)
Profit: US$43 million (2002)
Employees: 14100 (2002)
Fortune Rank: 452, per FORTUNE Magazine's list of 500 Largest U.S. Corporations (2002).
SIC(s): 2621 Paper Mills, 2891 Adhesives & Sealants, 3275 Gypsum Products, 3296 Mineral Wool.

Operating Locations

USG Corp. (AL--Birmingham; CA--Fremont, La Mirada, Plaster City, South Gate, Torrance; FL--Jacksonville; GA--Atlanta; IL--Chicago; IN--East Chicago, Wabash; IA--Fort Dodge, Sperry; LA--New Orleans; MD--Baltimore; MA--Boston; MN--Cloquet, Red Wing; MS--Greenville; MO--North Kansas City; NV--Empire; NJ--Clark, Port Reading; NY--Oakfield; OH--Gypsum, Tipp City, Westlake; OK--Southard; TX--Galena Park, Sweetwater; UT--Sigurd; VA--Norfolk; WA--Tacoma; WI--Walworth)

USG Foundation

Giving Contact

Peter K. Maitland, President
USG Foundation
PO Box 6721
Chicago, IL 60680-6721
Phone: (312)606-4297
Fax: (312)606-5316
Web: http://www.usg.com/USG_Profile/6_5_2_social_respon.asp

Alternate Contact

Margaret Clark, Assistant Secretary
USG Foundation

Description

EIN: 362984045
Organization Type: Corporate Foundation
Giving Locations: IL: nationally, with emphasis on corporate operating locations
Grant Types: Capital, Employee Matching Gifts, General Support, Scholarship.
Note: Employee matching gift ratio: 0.5 to 1.

Financial Summary

Total Giving: $766,591 (2001); $904,397 (2000); $1,090,078 (1999)
Giving Analysis: Giving for 2000 includes: foundation scholarships ($19,170); foundation matching gifts ($94,422); foundation ($790,805); 1999: foundation ($1,090,078); 1998: foundation grants to United Way ($59,016); foundation matching gifts ($89,380) foundation ($521,605)
Assets: $2,065,571 (2001); $1,755,336 (2000); $1,150,073 (1999)
Gifts Received: $1,002,797 (2001); $1,288,491 (2000); $1,000,000 (1999). Note: In 2001, contributions were received from USA Corp. Prior to 2001, contributions were received from USG Corp. and the Chicago Tourism Fund.

Typical Recipients

Arts & Humanities: Arts Associations & Councils, Arts Institutes, Arts & Humanities-General, Historic Preservation, History & Archaeology, Libraries, Museums/Galleries, Music, Opera, Performing Arts, Public Broadcasting, Theater
Civic & Public Affairs: African American Affairs, Botanical Gardens/Parks, Chambers of Commerce, Civil Rights, Economic Development, Employment/Job Training, Civic & Public Affairs-General, Hispanic Affairs, Housing, Law & Justice, Legal Aid, Public Policy, Safety, Urban & Community Affairs, Women's Affairs, Zoos/Aquariums

Education: Business Education, Colleges & Universities, Economic Education, Education Associations, Education-General, International Studies, Minority Education, Public Education (Precollege), Special Education, Student Aid
Environment: Environment-General, Resource Conservation
Health: AIDS/HIV, Cancer, Children's Health/Hospitals, Clinics/Medical Centers, Diabetes, Eyes/Blindness, Health Organizations, Heart, Hospices, Hospitals, Long-Term Care, Medical Research, Medical Training, Mental Health, Public Health, Single-Disease Health Associations
International: International Organizations, International Relations, Missionary/Religious Activities
Religion: Jewish Causes, Ministries, Religious Welfare, Social/Policy Issues
Science: Science Museums
Social Services: At-Risk Youth, Camps, Child Welfare, Community Service Organizations, Community Service Organizations, Crime Prevention, Delinquency & Criminal Rehabilitation, Emergency Relief, Family Services, Food/Clothing Distribution, People with Disabilities, Recreation & Athletics, Scouts, Social Services-General, Substance Abuse, United Funds/United Ways, Volunteer Services, YMCA/YWCA/YMHA/YWHA, Youth Organizations

Application Procedures

Initial Contact: Send a full proposal.
Application Requirements: Cover letter should include statement of need or problem; summary of background of the need or problem; specific reasons why the USG Foundation would be interested in the proposal; amount requested and how it will be used. Proposal should be accompanied by a copy of IRS determination letter and most recent financial statements; list of board members; a statement of the program's purpose, and qualifications of organization to obtain objectives; a detailed description of any proposed special project; goals and an itemized plan to achieve goals; supporting literature.
Deadlines: None.
Review Process: Foundation staff reviews all written proposals.
Evaluative Criteria: Evaluation of how the proposed program can effectively respond to societal needs, relevance in daily life, impact upon business and the future, and how grant will fit into the total contributions program.
Decision Notification: Board meets quarterly; responds within two months.
Notes: The foundation gives preference to relevant programs in which employees actively participate.

Restrictions

The foundation does not contribute to organizations without IRS tax-exempt 501(c)(3) status; sectarian organizations having an exclusively religious nature; individuals; political parties, offices, or candidates; fraternal or veterans organizations; primary or secondary schools; organizations that cannot provide adequate accounting records or procedures; or courtesy advertising. In general, organizations already receiving funds through united campaigns will not be considered for additional support.

Additional Information

Publications: Giving Guidelines

Corporate Officials

Richard Harrison Fleming: executive vice president, chief financial officer B Milwaukee, WI 1947. ED University of the Pacific BA (1969); Dartmouth College MBA (1971). PRIM CORP EMPL chief financial officer, senior vice president: USG Corp. ADD CORP EMPL president, treasurer, director: USG Foreign Investments Ltd.; vice president, treasurer, director: USG Interiors Inc. CORP AFFIL director: Family Care Services Metropolitan Chicago. NONPR AFFIL director: Child Welfare League of America.

Foundation Officials

Richard Harrison Fleming: executive vice president, chief financial officer (see above)
Peter K. Maitland: president, director B Joliet, IL 1941. PRIM CORP EMPL vice president: USG Corp.

Grants Analysis

Disclosure Period: calendar year ending 2001
Total Grants: $629,871*
Number of Grants: 72
Average Grant: $8,748
Highest Grant: $100,000
Lowest Grant: $750
Typical Range: $1,000 to $10,000
***Note:** Giving excludes matching gifts; United Way.

Recent Grants

Note: Grants derived from 2001 Form 990.

General

100,000	Child Welfare League of America
45,644	United Way Crusade of Mercy, Chicago, IL
40,000	Youth Development Foundation, New York, NY
35,000	Chicago Gateway Green Committee, Chicago, IL
30,000	National Children's Alliance
26,000	American Red Cross
25,000	Elmhurst College, Elmhurst, IL
25,000	Victory Gardens Theater, Utica, MN
21,620	National Merit Scholarship Corporation, Evanston, IL
20,000	Chicago Opera Theater, Chicago, IL

USIBELLI COAL MINE, INC.

Company Headquarters

100 River Rd.
Healy, AK 99743

Company Description

Employees: 125
SIC(s): 1221 Bituminous Coal & Lignite--Surface.

Operating Locations

Usibelli Coal Mine, Inc. (AK--Fairbanks, Healy)

Usibelli Foundation

Giving Contact

Becki Phipps, Executive Director
PO Box 1000
Healy, AK 99743
Phone: (907)452-2625
E-mail: info@usibelli.com
Web: http://www.usibelli.com/foundation.html
Note: Ext. 229

Description

Founded: 1991
EIN: 943152617
Organization Type: Corporate Foundation
Giving Locations: AK: Fairbanks, Healy
Grant Types: General Support.

Donor Information

Founder: Usibelli Coal Mine

Financial Summary

Total Giving: $105,970 (2000); $94,805 (1999); $82,000 (1998 approx)
Giving Analysis: Giving for 2000 includes: foundation grants to United Way ($16,365); 1999: foundation grants to United Way ($22,230) foundation ($72,575)

Assets: $2,182,771 (2000); $1,721,967 (1999); $1,711,204 (1997)
Gifts Received: $268,347 (2000); $3,165 (1999); $5,193 (1997)

Typical Recipients

Arts & Humanities: Arts Festivals, Film & Video, Libraries, Music, Theater
Civic & Public Affairs: Clubs, Civic & Public Affairs-General, Parades/Festivals, Public Policy
Education: Business Education, Colleges & Universities, Education-General, Literacy, Private Education (Precollege), Public Education (Precollege), Science/Mathematics Education, Secondary Education (Public)
Health: Cancer, Children's Health/Hospitals, Health-General, Hospices, Prenatal Health Issues, Public Health, Respiratory
Religion: Churches, Religious Welfare
Social Services: Big Brother/Big Sister, Child Welfare, Community Service Organizations, Counseling, Family Services, Homes, People with Disabilities, Recreation & Athletics, Scouts, Senior Services, Social Services-General, United Funds/United Ways, Youth Organizations

Application Procedures

Initial Contact: Send a brief letter of inquiry.
Application Requirements: Include a description of organization, amount requested, purpose of funds sought, recently audited financial statement, and proof of tax-exempt status.
Deadlines: None.

Restrictions

The foundation does not make grants to individuals or for travel purposes.

Corporate Officials

Rick Hundrup: vice president finance, chief financial officerc PRIM CORP EMPL vice president finance, chief financial officer: Usibelli Coal Mine.
Joseph E. Usibelli, Sr.: chairman B Suntrana, AK 1938. ED Stanford University; University of Alaska. PRIM CORP EMPL chairman: Usibelli Coal Mine. NONPR AFFIL trustee: National Coal Council; trustee: University AK Foundation; trustee: Alaska Energy Task Force.
Joseph E. Usibelli, Jr.: president, chief executive officer, director B 1958. ED University of Alaska (1980). PRIM CORP EMPL president, chief executive officer, director: Usibelli Coal Mine.

Foundation Officials

Earl Hoover Beistline: director B Juneau, AK November 24, 1916. ED University of Alaska BA (1939); University of Alaska EM (1947). PRIM CORP EMPL dean emeritus, professor: Sch Mineral Industries. NONPR AFFIL member: National Society Professional Engineers; member: Northwest Mining Association; member: Mining & Metallurgical Society America; member: Arctic Institute North America; fellow: Explorers; member: American Institute Mining & Metallurgical Engineers; member: American Society Engineering Education; fellow: American Association Advancement Science; member: Alaska Mining Association. CLUB AFFIL Pioneers Club.
Becki Gray: executive director PRIM CORP EMPL director public relations: Usibelli Coal Mine.
Marc Langland: director
A. Kirk Lanterman: director PRIM CORP EMPL secretary, treasurer: Usibelli Coal Mine.
Joseph E. Usibelli, Jr.: director (see above)
Joseph E. Usibelli, Sr.: director (see above)
Rosalie A. Whyel: director

Grants Analysis

Disclosure Period: calendar year ending 2000
Total Grants: $89,605*
Number of Grants: 68
Average Grant: $1,318

Highest Grant: $10,000
Typical Range: $1,000 to $3,000
***Note:** Giving excludes United Way.

Recent Grants

Note: Grants derived from 1999 Form 990.

General

21,230	United Way, Fairbanks, AK
2,000	North Star Council on Aging, Fairbanks, AK
1,500	Hospice Tanana Valley, Fairbanks, AK
1,000	Fairbanks Resource Agency, Fairbanks, AK
1,000	Jesse Carr Charity Fund, Anchorage, AK
1,000	Love, Inc, Fairbanks, AK
1,000	United Way - Anchorage, Anchorage, AK
500	Fairbanks Crisis Clinic Foundation, Fairbanks, AK
500	Quota Club of Fairbanks, Fairbanks, AK
500	Salvation Army, Fairbanks, AK

UTICA NATIONAL INSURANCE GROUP

Company Headquarters

180 Genesee St.
New Hartford, NY 13413

Company Description

Employees: 1,450
SIC(s): 6300 Insurance Carriers, 6400 Insurance Agents, Brokers & Service.
Parent Company: Utica Mutual Insurance Co., 10237 Southard Dr., Beltsville, MD, United States

Operating Locations

Utica National Insurance Group (NY--Utica)

Utica National Foundation

Giving Contact

John R. Zapisek, Treasurer
PO Box 530
Utica, NY 13503
Phone: (315)734-2521

Description

Founded: 1987
EIN: 161313450
Organization Type: Corporate Foundation
Giving Locations: NY: Utica and surrounding area; OH
Grant Types: Emergency, Employee Matching Gifts, General Support, Multiyear/Continuing Support.

Donor Information

Founder: Utica Mutual Insurance

Financial Summary

Total Giving: $284,405 (2001); $223,175 (2000); $244,668 (1999)
Giving Analysis: Giving for 2001 includes: foundation scholarships ($6,500); foundation grants to United Way ($153,230); 2000: foundation grants to United Way ($99,000); 1999: foundation grants to United Way ($104,500); foundation ($140,168)
Assets: $4,767,563 (2001); $4,953,239 (2000); $4,964,470 (1999)
Gifts Received: $2,803 (2001); $2,911 (2000); $256,486 (1999). Note: In 1996, contributions were received from Utica Mutual Insurance Co.

Typical Recipients

Arts & Humanities: Arts Associations & Councils, Arts Festivals, Arts Funds, Historic Preservation, Libraries, Museums/Galleries, Music, Performing Arts, Public Broadcasting

Civic & Public Affairs: African American Affairs, Economic Development, Civic & Public Affairs-General, Housing, Legal Aid, Municipalities/Towns, Safety, Urban & Community Affairs

Education: Community & Junior Colleges, Education-General, Preschool Education, Science/Mathematics Education, Student Aid

Health: AIDS/HIV, Children's Health/Hospitals, Clinics/Medical Centers, Emergency/Ambulance Services, Eyes/Blindness, Health-General, Health Organizations, Heart, Home-Care Services, Hospitals, Long-Term Care, Medical Research, Mental Health, Public Health, Single-Disease Health Associations

Religion: Churches, Religious Welfare

Science: Science Museums

Social Services: At-Risk Youth, Community Centers, Community Service Organizations, Crime Prevention, Emergency Relief, Family Services, Food/Clothing Distribution, People with Disabilities, Recreation & Athletics, Scouts, Senior Services, Shelters/Homelessness, Social Services-General, Special Olympics, United Funds/United Ways, YMCA/YWCA/YMHA/YWHA, Youth Organizations

Application Procedures

Initial Contact: Request application form.
Deadlines: The first 15 days of each calendar quarter.

Restrictions

Limited to the greater Utica area.

Corporate Officials

W. Craig Heston: chairman, chief executive officer, directorchief financial officer, treasurer, director B Philadelphia, PA 1935. ED Temple University. PRIM CORP EMPL chairman, chief executive officer, director: Utica National Corp. Group. CORP AFFIL chairman, president, chief executive officer: Utica National Insurance Co. Texas; chairman, chief executive officer: Utica National Life Insurance Co.; director: Security Mutual Life Insurance Co.; chairman, president, chief executive officer: Utica National Insurance Co. DE; director: Marine Midland Bank NA; chairman, chief executive officer: Republic-Franklin Insurance Co.; chairman, chief executive officer: Graphic Arts Mutual Insurance Co.

John R. Zapisek: senior vice president financial, chief financial officer, treasurer, director B Waterville, NY 1938. ED Syracuse University Utica College (1962). PRIM CORP EMPL senior vice president financial, chief financial officer, treasurer, director: Utica Mutual Insurance Co. CORP AFFIL trustee: Savings Bank Utica; director: WEBCO; director: Graphic Arts Mutual Insurance Co.; director: Republic Franklin Insurance Co.

Foundation Officials

C. William Bachman: director
Alfred E. Calligaris: director
Edward W. Duffy: director
Jerry J. Hartman: director
W. Craig Heston: president, director (see above)
Herbert P. Ladds, Jr.: director
J. Douglas Robinson: president, director
Linda E. Romano: director
George P. Wardley: secretary
George P. Wardley, III: secretary PRIM CORP EMPL secretary: Republic Franklin Insurance Co.
John R. Zapisek: treasurer (see above)

Grants Analysis

Disclosure Period: calendar year ending 2001
Total Grants: $124,675*
Number of Grants: 20
Average Grant: $6,234
Highest Grant: $27,000

Typical Range: $500 to $10,000
*Note: Giving excludes United Way, scholarship.

Recent Grants

Note: Grants derived from 2001 Form 990.

General

98,230	United Way of Greater Utica, Utica, NY
50,000	United Way of Greater Utica, Utica, NY
27,000	NYS Trooper Foundation, Latham, NY -- Safe Schools Program
12,500	New Horizons, Utica, NY
10,000	Compassion Coalition, Inc., Utica, NY -- roof repair
10,000	Empire State Games, Oriskany, NY -- donation
10,000	Long Island United Way, Long Island, NY -- platinum sponsor for annual fund raiser
8,000	Hospice Care, Inc., New Hartford, NY -- telethon
5,000	American Red Cross - Rome Chapter, Rome, NY -- grant food pantries
5,000	American Red Cross Utica Chapter, Utica, NY -- tribute to humanity

VALE-ASCHE FOUNDATION

Giving Contact

Mrs. Vale Asche-Russell, President
2001 Kirby Dr., Suite 1010
Houston, TX 77019-6081
Phone: (713)520-7334

Description

Founded: 1956
EIN: 516015320
Organization Type: Private Foundation
Giving Locations: TX: Houston
Grant Types: General Support, Operating Expenses, Project, Research.

Donor Information

Founder: the late Ruby Vale, the late Fred B. Asche

Financial Summary

Total Giving: $437,500 (fiscal year ending November 30, 2001); $575,000 (fiscal 2000); $513,075 (fiscal 1998)
Assets: $13,378,530 (fiscal 2001); $15,875,188 (fiscal 2000); $110,027 (fiscal 1998)

Typical Recipients

Arts & Humanities: Arts Outreach, Ballet, Libraries, Museums/Galleries, Opera, Performing Arts, Theater, Visual Arts

Civic & Public Affairs: Botanical Gardens/Parks, Clubs, Employment/Job Training, Hispanic Affairs, Housing, Urban & Community Affairs, Women's Affairs, Zoos/Aquariums

Education: Colleges & Universities, Faculty Development, Education-General, Literacy, Medical Education, Private Education (Precollege), Secondary Education (Private), Social Sciences Education, Special Education

Environment: Forestry, Environment-General

Health: Adolescent Health Issues, AIDS/HIV, Alzheimers Disease, Cancer, Children's Health/Hospitals, Clinics/Medical Centers, Emergency/Ambulance Services, Eyes/Blindness, Health Organizations, Hospices, Hospitals (University Affiliated), Medical Research, Mental Health, Single-Disease Health Associations, Speech & Hearing, Transplant Networks/Donor Banks

Religion: Churches, Ministries, Religious Organizations, Religious Welfare

Social Services: Animal Protection, At-Risk Youth, Child Abuse, Child Welfare, Community Service Organizations, Counseling, Family Planning, Food/Clothing Distribution, People with Disabilities, Scouts,

Senior Services, Shelters/Homelessness, Substance Abuse, Volunteer Services, Youth Organizations

Application Procedures

Initial Contact: The foundation has no formal grant application procedure or application form.
Deadlines: August 31.

Restrictions

Does not support political or lobbying groups or individuals.

Foundation Officials

Asche Ackerman: vice president
Mrs. Vale Asche Russell: president
William E. Blummer: secretary, treasurer
Anna B. Leonard: 2nd vice president
Anna Tippitt: vice president

Grants Analysis

Disclosure Period: fiscal year ending November 30, 2001
Total Grants: $437,500
Number of Grants: 14
Average Grant: $17,042*
Highest Grant: $133,000
Lowest Grant: $5,000
Typical Range: $10,000 to $30,000
*Note: Average grant figure excludes two highest grants ($233,000).

Recent Grants

Note: Grants derived from fiscal 2000 Form 990.

General

50,000	University of Texas M.D. Anderson Cancer Center, Houston, TX -- Bettyanne Asche Murray Fund for research in gynecologic medial oncology
40,000	Northwest Assistance Ministries, Houston, TX -- purchase mini bus
40,000	Parish School, Houston, TX -- purchase field trip vehicle
35,000	Center for Hearing and Speech, Houston, TX -- underwrite salary of an audiologist
30,000	Living Bank International, Houston, TX -- registry expansion project
25,000	Baylor College of Medicine, Houston, TX -- Scott Department of Urology
25,000	Boys and Girls Harbor, Houston, TX -- remodeling children's area of boy's teen transitional living cottage
25,000	Children's Assessment Center, Houston, TX -- support purchase of a video-colposcopy
25,000	Episcopal High School, Bellaire, TX -- support workroom in the learning resource center
25,000	Houston Area Parkinson Society, Houston, TX -- support respite care program

RUBY R. VALE FOUNDATION

Giving Contact

R. Menkiewicz, Trust Officer
c/o PNC Bank
222 Delaware Ave.
Wilmington, DE 19899
Phone: (302)429-1256 or 1456
Fax: (302)429-5558

Description

Founded: 1960
EIN: 516018883
Organization Type: Private Foundation
Giving Locations: East Coast.
Grant Types: General Support.

Donor Information

Founder: the late Ruby R. Vale

Financial Summary

Total Giving: $90,000 (2000); $65,000 (1999); $100,000 (1998)
Assets: $3,155,279 (2000); $2,983,156 (1999); $2,747,703 (1998)

Typical Recipients

Arts & Humanities: Libraries, Museums/Galleries, Visual Arts
Education: Arts/Humanities Education, Colleges & Universities, Legal Education, Private Education (Precollege)
Health: Cancer, Children's Health/Hospitals, Clinics/Medical Centers, Diabetes, Multiple Sclerosis
Social Services: Child Welfare, Community Service Organizations, Day Care, Family Services, Senior Services

Application Procedures

Initial Contact: The foundation has no formal grant application procedure or application form.
Deadlines: September 1.

Additional Information

Trust(s): PNC Bank DE

Grants Analysis

Disclosure Period: calendar year ending 2000
Total Grants: $90,000
Number of Grants: 6
Highest Grant: $25,000
Lowest Grant: $2,500

Recent Grants

Note: Grants derived from 1999 Form 990.

General
65,000	Winterthur Museum, Winterthur, DE
20,000	Bay Health Medical Center, Inc., Dover, DE
20,000	Children and Families First, Wilmington, DE
10,000	Widener University School of Law, Wilmington, DE

LAWSON VALENTINE FOUNDATION

Giving Contact

Valentine Doyle, Trustee
1000 Farmington Avenue
West Hartford, CT 06107
Phone: (860)570-0728

Description

Founded: 1989
EIN: 136920044
Organization Type: Private Foundation
Giving Locations: nationally.
Grant Types: General Support.

Donor Information

Founder: Established in 1989 by Alice P. Doyle.

Financial Summary

Total Giving: $1,038,800 (2000); $1,673,568 (1999); $1,086,147 (1998)
Assets: $19,309,546 (2000); $22,345,581 (1999); $19,788,238 (1998)
Gifts Received: $3,000 (1999); $3,864,001 (1996).
Note: In 1999, contributions were received from Merlin Foundation. In 1996, contributions were received from the Alice P. Doyle Charitable Remainder Annuity Trust.

Typical Recipients

Arts & Humanities: Arts Associations & Councils, Dance, History & Archaeology, Libraries, Museums/Galleries, Music, Opera, Performing Arts, Public Broadcasting, Theater, Visual Arts
Civic & Public Affairs: Botanical Gardens/Parks, Civil Rights, Community Foundations, Civic & Public Affairs-General, Housing, Municipalities/Towns, Professional & Trade Associations, Public Policy, Rural Affairs, Urban & Community Affairs, Women's Affairs
Education: Arts/Humanities Education, Colleges & Universities, Education-General, Literacy, Minority Education, Private Education (Precollege), Secondary Education (Public), Social Sciences Education, Student Aid
Environment: Air/Water Quality, Forestry, Environment-General, Environment-General, Research, Resource Conservation, Watershed
Health: AIDS/HIV, Cancer, Health Organizations, Long-Term Care, Medical Research, Public Health
International: Health Care/Hospitals, Human Rights, International Development, International Environmental Issues, International Organizations, International Peace & Security Issues, International Relations, International Relief Efforts
Religion: Churches, Jewish Causes, Religious Organizations, Religious Welfare, Seminaries
Social Services: Child Welfare, Community Service Organizations, Delinquency & Criminal Rehabilitation, Domestic Violence, Family Services, Food/Clothing Distribution, Senior Services, Volunteer Services

Application Procedures

Initial Contact: Send a brief letter of inquiry and a full proposal.
Deadlines: None.

Foundation Officials

Allen Doyle: trustee
Valentine Doyle: trustee
Diana Miller: trustee
Lucy Miller: trustee
Paul E. Vawter: trustee
William D. Zabel: trustee B Omaha, NE 1936. ED Princeton University AB (1958); Harvard University LLB (1961). PRIM CORP EMPL partner: Schulte Roth & Zabel LLP. NONPR AFFIL member: Samuel Wazman Cancer Research Foundation; member: Winston Foundation World Peace; advisory board: Project Death America; member: Volunteer Lawyers Arts; member: Picower Medicine Institute; chairman: Princeton University Planned Giving; member: Ottinger Foundation; member: Phi Beta Kappa; member: New York City Bar Association; member: New York State Bar Association; president: Merlin Foundation; trustee: New School Social; director, member: Lawyers Committee Human Rights; member: Lymphoma Foundation; legal counselor: International Confederation Art Dealers; member: Human Rights Watch; fellow: International Academy Estate & Trust Counsel; member: Estate Planning Council; member: Florida Bar Association; member: David H Cogan Foundation; member: Doctors World; director: Brandeis University Tauber Institute; member: American Law Institute; fellow: Brandeis University; member: American Comm Weizmann Institute Science; member: American Friends Israel Museum; member: American Bar Association; fellow: American College Trust & Estate Counsel. CLUB AFFIL Harmonie Club.

Grants Analysis

Disclosure Period: calendar year ending 2000
Total Grants: $1,038,800
Number of Grants: 80
Average Grant: $12,985
Highest Grant: $96,000
Lowest Grant: $500
Typical Range: $5,000 to $25,000

Recent Grants

Note: Grants derived from 2000 Form 990.

General
96,000	Bennington College, Bennington, VT
35,000	Rights Action, Washington, DC
35,000	Tides Center/Transnational Resource and Action Center, San Francisco, CA
30,000	American Friends Service Committee, Cambridge, MA
30,000	Doctors of the World, New York, NY
30,000	Just Food, New York, NY
30,000	Military Toxics Project, Lewiston, ME
27,500	Stony Brook-Millstone Watershed Association, Pennington, NJ
25,000	Communities United for People, Portland, OR
25,000	Farmers' Market Trust/Red Tomato, Canton, MA

VALLEY FOUNDATION

Giving Contact

Ervie L. Smith, Executive Director
16450 Los Gatos Boulevard, Suite 210
Los Gatos, CA 95032-5594
Phone: (408)358-4545
Fax: (408)358-4548
Web: http://www.valley.org

Description

Founded: 1984
EIN: 941584547
Organization Type: General Purpose Foundation
Giving Locations: CA: Santa Clara County
Grant Types: Capital, General Support, Matching.

Financial Summary

Total Giving: $3,322,454 (fiscal year ending September 30, 2002 approx); $3,078,310 (fiscal 2001); $2,822,454 (fiscal 2000)
Assets: $67,598,900 (fiscal 2002 approx); $55,340,387 (fiscal 2001); $37,598,900 (fiscal 2000 approx)

Typical Recipients

Arts & Humanities: Arts Associations & Councils, Arts Centers, Arts Funds, Arts Outreach, Ballet, Dance, Historic Preservation, History & Archaeology, Libraries, Museums/Galleries, Music, Opera, Performing Arts, Public Broadcasting, Theater
Civic & Public Affairs: Botanical Gardens/Parks, Clubs, Community Foundations, Employment/Job Training, Civic & Public Affairs-General, Housing, Philanthropic Organizations, Public Policy, Urban & Community Affairs
Education: Arts/Humanities Education, Business Education, Colleges & Universities, Education Associations, Elementary Education (Public), Faculty Development, Literacy, Medical Education, Minority Education, Public Education (Precollege), School Volunteerism, Science/Mathematics Education, Secondary Education (Public), Special Education
Environment: Resource Conservation
Health: Adolescent Health Issues, AIDS/HIV, Alzheimers Disease, Cancer, Children's Health/Hospitals, Clinics/Medical Centers, Diabetes, Emergency/Ambulance Services, Health-General, Geriatric Health, Health Funds, Health Organizations, Heart, Hospices, Medical Rehabilitation, Medical Research, Mental Health, Nutrition, Prenatal Health Issues, Preventive Medicine/Wellness Organizations, Public Health, Single-Disease Health Associations
International: International Relief Efforts
Religion: Ministries, Religious Welfare
Science: Science Museums
Social Services: Animal Protection, At-Risk Youth, Big Brother/Big Sister, Child Abuse, Child Welfare, Community Centers, Community Service Organizations, Counseling, Day Care, Domestic Violence,

Family Services, Food/Clothing Distribution, Homes, People with Disabilities, Recreation & Athletics, Scouts, Senior Services, Shelters/Homelessness, Social Services-General, Substance Abuse, Volunteer Services, YMCA/YWCA/YMHA/YWHA, Youth Organizations

Application Procedures

Initial Contact: Applicants should send a preliminary letter of one or two pages in length. If the foundation is interested, it will invite a full proposal.

Application Requirements: The preliminary letter should describe the general background and purpose of the sponsoring organization; individuals to be involved in the project; the needs to be addressed; the goals and anticipated results of the project; and the amount requested from the foundation. A full proposal should include a general background and purpose of organization; constituents served; names and affiliations of directors and trustees; copy of IRS tax-exempt letter; prior year's financial statement; total budget and sources of organization's funding; project objective and description; evidence of need and value of project; geographic area to be served; outline of project; anticipated evaluation methods; personnel involved and their qualifications; and detailed project budget, other sources of funding, and amount requested.

Deadlines: Applicants should send the preliminary letter one month prior to submitting a full proposal. Proposal deadlines are November 1 for February meeting; February 1 for May meeting; June 1 for September meeting; and August 1 for December meeting.

Review Process: Staff reviews proposals before submitting them to the board. Review often includes a site visit. The Board of Trustees decides on proposals at quarterly meetings.

Restrictions

Applications for grants are accepted only from qualified tax-exempt charitable organizations. Applications will not be accepted for the benefit of individuals or religious purposes. No disbursements may be made which would fund: contractual allowances between insurance companies and health care providers; program losses which accrue to health care providers; or subsidize deductible and coinsurance arrangements under medical and hospital care policies.

Additional Information

The foundation encourages turnover in grants and, therefore, prefers not to fund multiple year requests. Organizations must wait one full year after receiving funding before submitting an another grant.

The foundation prefers to avoid grants which provide more than one-half of an organization's total budget in any twelve- month period.

Publications: Guidelines; Application Forms; Annual Report

Foundation Officials

Phillip R. Boyce: chairman B 1944. PRIM CORP EMPL chairman: Pacific Trust Co. CORP AFFIL Comerica California Inc. NONPR AFFIL director: Physicians Clinical Lab.

Herbert Kain, MD: trustee
Edgar G. LaVeque, MD: trustee
Sydney Resnick: treasurer
Ralph Ross: vchairman
Michael Rubenstein: trustee
Richard Sieve, MD: secretary
Walter Silberman, MD: trustee
Ervie L. Smith: executive director

Grants Analysis

Disclosure Period: fiscal year ending September 30, 2001
Total Grants: $3,078,310*
Number of Grants: 64
Average Grant: $40,926*
Highest Grant: $500,000

Typical Range: $20,000 to $80,000
*Note: Average grant figure excludes highest grant.

Recent Grants

Note: Grants derived from fiscal 2001 Form 990.

Library-Related

55,000	Community Health Library of Los Gatos, Los Gatos, CA -- for operating support

General

500,000	KTEH Foundation, San Jose, CA -- support of the new Outreach Center for Children and Community
125,000	Community Foundation of Silicon Valley, San Jose, CA -- for medical and health related areas
100,000	California Institute for Medical Research, San Jose, CA -- to fund research study on Microrray-based gene expression profiling in colorectal cancer
100,000	Housing Trust of Santa Clara County, Santa Clara, CA -- towards the capitalization of the Housing Trust Fund
100,000	Resource Area for Teachers, San Jose, CA -- funding for challenge grant to go toward phase II of capital campaign of new building project
100,000	Salvation Army, San Jose, CA -- to help remodel the men's shelter and Hospitality Home
100,000	San Jose State University, San Jose, CA -- funding to establish the Adaptive Technology Center
100,000	Santa Clara University, Santa Clara, CA -- funding for equipment for the Biotechnology Program
100,000	Silicon Valley Habitat for Humanity, San Jose, CA -- to partially underwrite the construction costs of two homes
100,000	Tech Museum of Innovation, San Jose, CA -- the Life Tech, Communication and Exploration and Innovation Galleries

WAYNE AND GLADYS VALLEY FOUNDATION

Giving Contact

Stephen M. Chandler, President & Director
1939 Harrison Street, Suite 510
Oakland, CA 94612-3532
Phone: (510)466-6060
Fax: (510)466-6067

Description

Founded: 1977
EIN: 953203014
Organization Type: General Purpose Foundation
Giving Locations: CA: Alameda County, Almeda and Contra Costa county, Contra Costa County, East Bay area, Santa Clara County
Grant Types: Capital, General Support, Matching, Research.

Donor Information

Founder: Established in 1977 by Mr. F. Wayne Valley and Mrs. Gladys Valley. After Mr. Valley's death in 1986, the foundation received substantial funds from his estate and will continue to receive funds over a period of years.

Mr. Valley was the founder and major owner of Citation Builders, headquartered in San Leandro, CA, which became one of the largest single-family homebuilders in California. Besides Citation, Mr. Valley's other business activities included part-ownership of the Oakland Raiders of the National Football League. Mrs. Valley continues to serve as the chairwoman of the foundation.

Financial Summary

Total Giving: $15,712,982 (fiscal year ending September 30, 2001); $10,431,253 (fiscal 1998); $13,299,568 (fiscal 1997)

Giving Analysis: Giving for fiscal 2001 includes: foundation scholarships ($630,000); fiscal 1999: foundation matching gifts (approx $65,000) foundation scholarships (approx $737,500)

Assets: $588,367,987 (fiscal 2001); $343,585,786 (fiscal 1998); $348,687,917 (fiscal 1997)

Gifts Received: $16,965,701 (fiscal 2001); $63,737,896 (fiscal 1997); $3,841,221 (fiscal 1996). Note: Contributions were received from the estate of F. Wayne Valley, one of the original donors.

Typical Recipients

Arts & Humanities: Ballet, Ethnic & Folk Arts, Libraries, Museums/Galleries, Performing Arts, Public Broadcasting, Theater

Civic & Public Affairs: Community Foundations, Economic Policy, Employment/Job Training, Parades/Festivals, Philanthropic Organizations, Professional & Trade Associations, Urban & Community Affairs, Women's Affairs, Zoos/Aquariums

Education: Afterschool/Enrichment Programs, Arts/Humanities Education, Business Education, Colleges & Universities, Community & Junior Colleges, Continuing Education, Economic Education, Education Associations, Education Reform, Elementary Education (Public), Engineering/Technological Education, Education-General, Legal Education, Literacy, Private Education (Precollege), Public Education (Precollege), Religious Education, School Volunteerism, Science/Mathematics Education, Secondary Education (Private), Special Education, Student Aid

Environment: Resource Conservation, Wildlife Protection

Health: Alzheimers Disease, Cancer, Children's Health/Hospitals, Eyes/Blindness, Health Organizations, Heart, Hospitals, Medical Research, Mental Health, Prenatal Health Issues, Research/Studies Institutes, Single-Disease Health Associations, Speech & Hearing

Religion: Churches, Dioceses, Religious Organizations, Religious Welfare, Seminaries

Science: Observatories & Planetariums, Scientific Centers & Institutes

Social Services: Animal Protection, Camps, Child Welfare, Community Service Organizations, Day Care, Domestic Violence, Food/Clothing Distribution, Homes, People with Disabilities, Recreation & Athletics, Scouts, Senior Services, Shelters/Homelessness, Special Olympics, Volunteer Services, YMCA/YWCA/YMHA/YWHA, Youth Organizations

Application Procedures

Initial Contact: Applicants should submit a two- to three-page summary letter.

Application Requirements: The letter should include the following: goal and purpose of the project; description and brief history of the sponsoring organization; research references, if any, that show the need of the project or the efficacy of the subject method; project time frame; amount requested from the foundation, total project cost, and other funding sources; brief biographies of project administrators; and milestones by which progress or success will be measured. Other materials that should be attached to the summary letter include: income and expense budget for the project and the latest annual financial statement of the sponsoring organization; list of the board of directors of the sponsoring organization; a copy of the IRS tax-exempt determination letter; and a letter from the chief officer of the sponsoring organization stating that tax-exempt status has not been revoked or modified.

Deadlines: None.

Review Process: The board of directors meets quarterly, and the foundation promises a quick preliminary response. If the board is interested, additional information or a site visit may be requested. Personal communication with foundation directors by representatives of the applicant organization is not encouraged.

Restrictions

In general, the foundation will not provide funding to any of the following: individuals; organizations for profit or profit-making enterprises of nonprofit groups; veterans, fraternal, labor, service club, military, or similar organizations whose principal activity is for the benefit of members; lobbying, propaganda, or other attempts to influence legislation or other partisan political activities; fund-raising events, dinners, or similar affairs, or for advertising; no grants are offered outside the United States; or for private operating foundations.

Additional Information

Publications: Informational Brochure; Application Guidelines

Foundation Officials

Robert C. Brown: director

Stephen M. Chandler: president, executive director

Edwin Austin Heafey, Jr.: director B Oakland, CA 1930. ED University of Santa Clara AB (1952); Stanford University LLB (1955). PRIM CORP EMPL senior partner: Crosby, Heafey, Roach & May. CORP AFFIL director: Farmers Group Inc. NONPR AFFIL member: International Society Barristers; member: San Francisco Bar Association; member: California Trial Lawyers Association; board fellows: Georgetown Law School; member: American Trial Lawyers Association; member: California Bar Association; member: American College Trial Lawyers; member: American Bar Foundation; fellow: American Board Trial Advocates; member: Alameda County Bar Association. CLUB AFFIL Pacific-Union Club; Claremont Country Club.

Richard M. Kingsland: chief financial officer, secretary

John P. Stock: director PRIM CORP EMPL chief executive officer: Saylor Hill Co.

Tamara A. Valley: chairman

Grants Analysis

Disclosure Period: fiscal year ending September 30, 2001

Total Grants: $15,082,982*

Number of Grants: 106

Average Grant: $80,218*

Highest Grant: $2,671,750

Typical Range: $40,000 to $150,000

*Note: Giving excludes scholarships. Average grant figure excludes four highest grants ($6,900,751)

Recent Grants

Note: Grants derived from fiscal 2000 Form 990.

General

1,666,667   Chabot Observatory and Science Center, Oakland, CA -- for construction of new observatory and science center

1,500,000   John Wayne Institute for Cancer Treatment and Research, Oakland, CA -- for Cancer Vaccine Program

1,428,500   Oregon State University Foundation, Corvallis, OR -- for library campaign

1,400,000   John Wayne Institute for Cancer Treatment and Research, Oakland, CA -- for Cancer Vaccine Program

1,200,000   Chabot Observatory and Science Center, Oakland, CA -- additional funds for the establishment and construction of the new observatory and science center

1,000,000   Children's Hospital Medical Center, Oakland, CA -- interior remodeling of the old University High School

1,000,000   Santa Clara University, Santa Clara, CA -- renovation of the old Alumni Science Building

500,000   John Wayne Institute for Cancer Treatment and Research, Oakland, CA -- for Cancer Vaccine Program

500,000   John Wayne Institute for Cancer Treatment and Research, Oakland, CA -- for Cancer Vaccine Program

500,000   Roman Catholic Diocese, Oakland, CA -- for the Schools in Need Program

VALMONT INDUSTRIES, INC.

Company Headquarters

Omaha, NE

Web: http://www.valmont.com

Company Description

Ticker: VALM

Exchange: AMEX

Employees: 4,868

SIC(s): 3523 Farm Machinery & Equipment, 3612 Transformers Except Electronic, 3648 Lighting Equipment Nec.

Operating Locations

Valmont Industries, Inc. (CO--Fort Collins; IL--Danville; IN--Elkhart; NE--Omaha; OK--Tulsa; TX--Brenham, El Paso; UT--Salt Lake City)

Valmont Foundation

Giving Contact

Robert B. Daugherty, Director
One Valmont Plaza
Omaha, NE 68154-5215
Phone: (402)963-1000
Fax: (402)963-1095

Alternate Contact

Terry McClain, Director
Valmont Foundation

Description

Founded: 1976

EIN: 362895245

Organization Type: Corporate Foundation

Giving Locations: NE: limited giving nationally.

Grant Types: Capital, General Support.

Donor Information

Founder: Valmont Industries, Inc.

Financial Summary

Total Giving: $737,977 (fiscal year ending February 28, 2001); $669,845 (fiscal 2000); $420,337 (fiscal 1998). Note: Contributes through foundation only.

Giving Analysis: Giving for fiscal 2000 includes: foundation grants to United Way ($181,195); foundation ($488,650); fiscal 1998: foundation grants to United Way ($100,155); foundation ($320,182); fiscal 1997: foundation grants to United Way ($85,800); foundation ($288,933);

Assets: $62,585 (fiscal 2001); $20,319 (fiscal 2000); $17,996 (fiscal 1998)

Gifts Received: $748,561 (fiscal 2001); $649,395 (fiscal 2000); $372,413 (fiscal 1998). Note: Contributions are received from Valmont Industries.

Typical Recipients

Arts & Humanities: Arts Associations & Councils, Arts Funds, Ballet, Ethnic & Folk Arts, Arts & Humanities-General, History & Archaeology, Libraries, Museums/Galleries, Music, Opera, Performing Arts, Public Broadcasting, Theater

Civic & Public Affairs: Botanical Gardens/Parks, Business/Free Enterprise, Chambers of Commerce,

Clubs, Community Foundations, Economic Development, Ethnic Organizations, Civic & Public Affairs-General, Minority Business, Parades/Festivals, Professional & Trade Associations, Rural Affairs, Urban & Community Affairs, Women's Affairs, Zoos/Aquariums

Education: Agricultural Education, Business Education, Colleges & Universities, Community & Junior Colleges, Economic Education, Education Funds, Engineering/Technological Education, Faculty Development, Education-General, Literacy, Minority Education, Private Education (Precollege), Public Education (Precollege), Religious Education, Student Aid

Environment: Forestry, Resource Conservation, Wildlife Protection

Health: AIDS/HIV, Arthritis, Children's Health/Hospitals, Diabetes, Emergency/Ambulance Services, Heart, Hospitals, Kidney, Medical Rehabilitation, Nutrition, Single-Disease Health Associations

Religion: Religious Organizations, Religious Welfare, Social/Policy Issues

Science: Science Exhibits & Fairs

Social Services: At-Risk Youth, Child Welfare, Crime Prevention, Domestic Violence, Family Services, People with Disabilities, Recreation & Athletics, Scouts, Senior Services, Social Services-General, Special Olympics, Substance Abuse, United Funds/United Ways, YMCA/YWCA/YMHA/YWHA, Youth Organizations

Application Procedures

Initial Contact: Send a written letter of solicitation.

Application Requirements: Include statement of organization's objectives; description of proposed use of contribution; Valmont employee involvement, if any; evidence of tax-exempt status defined under section 501(c)(3) of the Internal Revenue Code; list of officers and directors; and other significant donors.

Deadlines: None.

Notes: Please do not phone or fax requests.

Restrictions

The foundation does not make contributions to individuals; organizations with a limited constituency, such as clubs or fraternal and social organizations; support for any type of travel or tours for individuals or groups; or for-profit organizations.

Valmont will generally not consider contributions for organizations in communities where Valmont does not have an operational presence; multi-year funding for a program or project beyond three years; underwriting or sponsorship of specific radio or television programming; emergency operating support for an organization; or athletic events. underwriting or sponsorship of specific radio or television programming; emergency operating support for an organization; or athletic events.

Additional Information

Publications: Guidelines

Corporate Officials

Mogens C. Bay: chairman, chief executive officer chief financial officer B 1953. PRIM CORP EMPL chairman, chief executive officer: Valmont Industries, Inc. CORP AFFIL director: Peter Kiewit Sons Inc.; director: ConAgra Inc. NONPR AFFIL director: Nebraska Health Systems.

Robert B. Daugherty: director B 1922. PRIM CORP EMPL director: Valmont Industries, Inc. NONPR AFFIL trustee: Hastings College Foundation.

Terry James McClain: senior vice president, chief financial officer B Osmond, NE 1948. ED Wayne State University BS (1970); University of South Dakota MBA (1971). PRIM CORP EMPL senior vice president, chief financial officer: Valmont Industries, Inc. NONPR AFFIL member: Financial Executives Institute.

Foundation Officials

Thomas P. Egan, Jr.: officer B 1948. ED Creighton University BSBA (1971); Creighton University JD (1973). PRIM CORP EMPL vice president, corporate counsel, secretary: Valmont Industries, Inc. CORP AFFIL secretary: Microflect Co. Inc.

Terry James McClain: director (see above)

Brian C. Stanley: officer B 1942. PRIM CORP EMPL vice president, controller: Valmont Industries, Inc.

Grants Analysis

Disclosure Period: fiscal year ending February 28, 2001

Total Grants: $602,798*

Number of Grants: 55

Average Grant: $5,900*

Highest Grant: $200,000

Lowest Grant: $300

Typical Range: $1,000 to $10,000

*Note: Giving excludes United Way. Average grant figure excludes two highest grants ($300,000).

Recent Grants

Note: Grants derived from fiscal 2002 Form 990.

Library-Related

1,000	Omaha Public Library Foundation, Omaha, NE

General

200,000	University of Nebraska Foundation, Lincoln, NE
120,180	United Way of the Midlands, Omaha, NE
100,000	DonorsTrust, Omaha, NE
41,530	Omaha Symphony Association, Omaha, NE
22,000	Knights of Ak-Sar-Ben River City Roundup
20,000	Fremont Area United Way, Fremont, NE
20,000	Mid-America Council, Boy Scouts America, Omaha, NE
15,000	Fremont Area Community Foundation, Fremont, NE
15,000	Greater Omaha Chamber of Commerce Foundation, Omaha, NE
15,000	Omaha Zoo Foundation, Omaha, NE

JAY AND BETTY VAN ANDEL FOUNDATION

Giving Contact

Jay Van Andel, President
2905 Lucerne SE
Grand Rapids, MI 49546
Phone: (616)942-3267

Description

Founded: 1963

EIN: 237066716

Organization Type: General Purpose Foundation

Giving Locations: MI

Grant Types: Capital, Challenge, Endowment, General Support, Project, Scholarship.

Donor Information

Founder: Established in 1963 by Jay Van Andel and his wife, Betty (Hoekstra) Van Andel. Mr. Van Andel, the co-chairman of Amway International, founded the corporation in 1959 with his high school friend Richard DeVos. The company, which in 1960 had sales of $500,000 and started in the basement of the Van Andel's home in Ada, MI, is today one of the world's largest direct sales organizations with recent sales of $2 billion. Mr. Van Andel's fortune was estimated in 1991 at $3 billion by *Fortune* magazine.

Financial Summary

Total Giving: $15,082,631 (2001); $20,318,038 (2000); $28,545,056 (1999)

Giving Analysis: Giving for 2000 includes: foundation grants to United Way ($25,000)

Assets: $106,597,084 (2001); $103,021,064 (2000); $116,584,888 (1999)

Gifts Received: $1,226,940 (2001); $29,660,000 (1998); $10,000,000 (1996). Note: In 2001, contributions were received from Richard M. Devos ($1,200,000) and Jay Van Andel ($26,940). In 1998, contributions were received from the Jay Van Andel Trust ($25,660,000) and Amway Corp. ($4,000,000).

Typical Recipients

Arts & Humanities: Arts Centers, Ballet, Libraries, Museums/Galleries, Music, Opera

Civic & Public Affairs: Botanical Gardens/Parks, Business/Free Enterprise, Chambers of Commerce, Economic Development, Economic Policy, Civic & Public Affairs-General, Housing, Parades/Festivals, Public Policy, Urban & Community Affairs, Zoos/Aquariums

Education: Colleges & Universities, Education-General, Private Education (Precollege), Religious Education, Secondary Education (Private), Student Aid

Environment: Research

Health: Alzheimers Disease, Children's Health/Hospitals, Clinics/Medical Centers, Health-General, Health Organizations, Hospices, Hospitals, Long-Term Care, Medical Research, Public Health, Research/Studies Institutes

International: International Relief Efforts, Missionary/Religious Activities, Trade

Religion: Bible Study/Translation, Churches, Ministries, Missionary Activities (Domestic), Religious Organizations, Religious Welfare, Seminaries, Social/Policy Issues

Science: Scientific Research

Social Services: Child Welfare, Community Centers, Community Service Organizations, Family Services, People with Disabilities, Scouts, United Funds/United Ways, YMCA/YWCA/YMHA/YWHA, Youth Organizations

Application Procedures

Initial Contact: Applicants should submit a letter of request to the foundation office.

Application Requirements: The letter should contain a brief description of the purpose for which funds are requested and a letter of reference.

Deadlines: None.

Restrictions

The foundation does not give to individuals.

Foundation Officials

Allan Engle: secretary

Kim S. Mitchell: assistant secretary

James J. Rosloniec: treasurer, trustee ED Central Michigan University (1968). PRIM CORP EMPL president, treasurer, director: Amway Properties Corp. ADD CORP EMPL treasurer: Amway Management Co.; president: Amway Capital Group; president: Amway Mutual Fund Inc.; treasurer: Amway Real Estate Corp.

David Van Andel: vice president, trustee PRIM CORP EMPL senior vice president: Amway Corp.

Jay Van Andel: president, trustee B Grand Rapids, MI 1924. ED Yale University (1943-1944); Pratt Junior College (1945); Calvin College (1942-1946). PRIM CORP EMPL senior chairman, co-founder, director: Amway Corp. ADD CORP EMPL chairman, director: Amway International Inc.; chairman, director: Amway Global Inc.; chairman: Amway Properties Corp.; chairman: Merchandising Productions Inc.

Casey Wondergem: contact PRIM CORP EMPL senior public affairs counsel: Amway Corp.

Grants Analysis

Disclosure Period: calendar year ending 2000

Total Grants: $20,293,038*

Number of Grants: 95

Average Grant: $51,538*

Highest Grant: $10,500,000

Lowest Grant: $100

Typical Range: $1,000 to $10,000 and $25,000 to $100,000

*Note: Giving excludes United Way. Average grant figure excludes two highest grants ($15,500,000).

Recent Grants

Note: Grants derived from 2001 Form 990.

General

10,500,000	Van Andel Institute, Grand Rapids, MI -- for operating
1,256,181	Van Andel Institute, Grand Rapids, MI -- for debt service
900,000	Heritage Foundation, Washington, DC
315,000	Opera Grand Rapids, Grand Rapids, MI
278,000	Ada Christian School, Ada, MI
260,000	Grand Rapids Christian School Association, Grand Rapids, MI
250,000	Grand Action Foundation, Grand Rapids, MI
200,000	Grand Valley State University, Allendale, MI
150,000	Pine Rest Christian Hospital, Grand Rapids, MI
90,000	La Grave Avenue Christian Reformed Church, Grand Rapids, MI

VAN BUREN FOUNDATION

Giving Contact

John O. Manning, Treasurer
c/o Community First Bank
Keosauqua, IA 52565
Phone: (319)293-3794
Fax: (319)293-6151

Description

Founded: 1959

EIN: 426062589

Organization Type: Private Foundation

Giving Locations: IA: Van Buren County

Grant Types: Capital, General Support, Project, Scholarship.

Donor Information

Founder: the late Ralph S. Roberts

Financial Summary

Total Giving: $217,935 (2002 approx); $92,764 (2001); $193,723 (2000)

Giving Analysis: Giving for 2001 includes: foundation scholarships ($6,049); 2000: foundation scholarships ($2,744); 1999: foundation scholarships ($1,372)

Assets: $5,757,643 (2001); $6,068,002 (2000); $6,075,939 (1999)

Gifts Received: $8,106 (2000); $7,000 (1999); $300 (1995). Note: In 1995, contributions were received from Farmers State Bank.

Typical Recipients

Arts & Humanities: Historic Preservation, History & Archaeology, Libraries, Music

Civic & Public Affairs: Botanical Gardens/Parks, Clubs, Economic Development, Civic & Public Affairs-General, Inner-City Development, Minority Business, Municipalities/Towns, Parades/Festivals, Public Policy, Rural Affairs, Safety, Urban & Community Affairs

Education: Agricultural Education, Arts/Humanities Education, Elementary Education (Private), Education-General, Literacy, Preschool Education, Private

Education (Precollege), Public Education (Precollege), Science/Mathematics Education, Secondary Education (Private), Secondary Education (Public), Vocational & Technical Education
Environment: Environment-General, Resource Conservation
Health: Emergency/Ambulance Services, Health Organizations, Hospices, Hospitals
Religion: Churches, Religious Welfare
Social Services: Crime Prevention, Emergency Relief, Recreation & Athletics, Scouts, Senior Services, Shelters/Homelessness

Application Procedures

Initial Contact: Application forms for grants and scholarships available from foundation or high school counselors in Van Buren County.
Review Process: Proposals are reviewed two times per year.
Evaluative Criteria: Foundation gives preference to requests from organizations which benefit Van Buren County, IA.

Restrictions

No funds shall be awarded to any individual or organization wherein pecuniary profits may be obtained. Grant must not be the sole or complete funds vested in any project.

Additional Information

Educational loans are made to healthcare and medical students from Van Buren county, IA. Educational grants are memorials or awards given to students meeting certain requirements.

Foundation Officials

Jon Finney: vice chairmanr
Sandy McLain: 2nd vice president
Arthur P. Ovrom: chairman
Davis E. Pollock: president
Rex Strait: vice president

Grants Analysis

Disclosure Period: calendar year ending 2001
Total Grants: $86,715*
Number of Grants: 20
Average Grant: $2,836*
Highest Grant: $30,000
Typical Range: $1,000 to $5,000
*Note: Giving excludes scholarships. Average grant figure excludes highest grant.

Recent Grants

Note: Grants derived from 2001 Form 990.

Library-Related

4,125	Keosauqua Public Library, Keosauqua, IA -- computerize circulation system
1,689	Southeastern Library Services, Davenport, IA -- software upgrade for county libraries
595	Birmingham Public Library, Birmingham, IA -- Ralph Shott Memorial

General

30,000	City of Keosauqua, Keosauqua, IA -- villages of Van Buren budget
11,000	Harmony Community School, Farmington, IA -- music sound system
7,000	City of Cantril, Cantril, IA -- park improvement
5,500	City of Farmington, Farmington, IA -- radio's for EMS
5,500	Van Buren County Conservation, Keosauqua, IA -- Greef Building roof
5,000	Van Buren County Conservation, Keosauqua, IA -- Fox River Project
3,823	Oak Grove Church, Douds, IA -- church restoration
2,000	Lick Creek Township, Birmingham, IA -- roof for Country School

2,000	Milton Heritage Association, Milton, IA -- stained glass window repair
2,000	Van Buren County Red Cross, Keosauqua, IA -- swimming lessons

ELSIE PROCTER VAN BUREN FOUNDATION

Giving Contact

Colin S. Marshall, Trustee
c/o Bingham McCutchen LLC
150 Federal Street
Boston, MA 02110
Phone: (617)951-8576

Description

Founded: 1994
EIN: 043251802
Organization Type: Private Foundation
Grant Types: General Support.

Financial Summary

Total Giving: $244,900 (2001); $180,750 (1999); $106,000 (1998). Note: In 1998, contributions were received from Elsie F. Van Buren.
Assets: $3,989,287 (2001); $5,773,417 (1999); $5,044,550 (1998)
Gifts Received: $2,393,485 (1998); $1,233,414 (1994)

Typical Recipients

Arts & Humanities: Libraries, Performing Arts, Public Broadcasting, Theater
Civic & Public Affairs: Community Foundations, Civic & Public Affairs-General, Nonprofit Management, Women's Affairs
Education: Continuing Education
Environment: Resource Conservation
International: International-General, Health Care/Hospitals, Human Rights, International Development, International Peace & Security Issues, International Relief Efforts
Religion: Churches
Science: Scientific Organizations
Social Services: Family Services, Youth Organizations

Application Procedures

Initial Contact: The foundation has no formal grant application procedure or application form. Send a brief letter of inquiry.
Deadlines: None.

Foundation Officials

Collin S. Marshall, Esq.: trustee
Elsie Procter Van Buren: trustee

Grants Analysis

Disclosure Period: calendar year ending 2001
Total Grants: $244,900
Number of Grants: 63
Average Grant: $2,337*
Highest Grant: $100,000
Lowest Grant: $500
Typical Range: $1,000 to $5,000
*Note: Average grant figure excludes highest grant.

Recent Grants

Note: Grants derived from 2000 Form 990.

Library-Related

10,000	Elm Research Institute, Westmoreland, NH

General

100,000	The Peterborough Players, Peterborough, NH
20,000	American Pan African Relief, New York, NY

10,000	Conservation Law Foundation, Boston, MA
10,000	The Nature Conservancy, Boston, MA
10,000	Union of Concerned Scientists, Cambridge, MA
10,000	Women's Fund of New Hampshire, Concord, NH
8,000	International Rescue Committee, New York, NY
8,000	Oxfam America, Boston, MA
5,000	Doctors Without Borders USA, New York, NY
5,000	Harris Center for Conservation Education, Hancock, NH

DEWITT VAN EVERA FOUNDATION

Giving Contact

Margaretta Forrester, Advisor
431 D North Pole Dr.
St. Louis, MO 63105
Phone: (314)862-0067
Fax: (314)862-0649

Description

Founded: 1959
EIN: 876117907
Organization Type: Private Foundation
Giving Locations: U.S.
Grant Types: Capital, Endowment, General Support, Operating Expenses, Scholarship.

Donor Information

Founder: the late Dewitt Van Evera, the late Caroline Irene Van Evera

Financial Summary

Total Giving: $240,500 (2001); $248,000 (2000); $185,500 (1999)
Giving Analysis: Giving for 2001 includes: foundation scholarships ($5,000)
Assets: $3,515,471 (2001); $4,353,867 (2000); $4,781,578 (1999)

Typical Recipients

Arts & Humanities: Arts Centers, Libraries, Public Broadcasting, Theater
Civic & Public Affairs: Civic & Public Affairs-General, Nonprofit Management
Education: Afterschool/Enrichment Programs, Colleges & Universities, Education Associations, Engineering/Technological Education, Minority Education, Private Education (Precollege), Science/Mathematics Education, Secondary Education (Private), Secondary Education (Public), Student Aid
Health: Emergency/Ambulance Services
International: Foreign Educational Institutions
Social Services: Community Service Organizations

Application Procedures

Initial Contact: Send a brief letter of inquiry describing program.
Deadlines: None.
Review Process: Board meets in February and September.

Restrictions

Does not support individuals.

Additional Information

Trust(s): US Bank NA

Foundation Officials

Margaretta Forrester: co-trustee
Colette Lafond: advisory board
Laura J. Van Evera LaFond: co-trustee
William P. Van Evera: co-trustee

Grants Analysis

Disclosure Period: calendar year ending 2001
Total Grants: $235,500*
Number of Grants: 14
Average Grant: $13,607*
Highest Grant: $45,000
Typical Range: $5,000 to $20,000
***Note:** Giving excludes scholarship. Average grant figure excludes highest grant.

Recent Grants

Note: Grants derived from 2001 Form 990.

General

45,000	Northland College, Ashland, WI
35,000	St. Johns Preparatory School, Collegeville, NM
25,000	People Serving People Inc., Minneapolis, MN -- capital campaign
25,000	St. Louis School Choice Partnership Fund, St. Louis, MO -- Today and Tomorrow Educational Foundation
15,000	Center of Contemporary Arts, University City, MO
15,000	College of St. Benedict, St. Joseph, MN
10,000	Blackburn College, Carlinville, IL -- program campaign
10,000	College Summit, Washington, DC
10,000	Logos High School, St. Louis, MO -- capital
10,000	Logos High School, St. Louis, MO -- operating

VAN HOUTEN MEMORIAL FUND (EDWARD W. AND STELLA C.)

Giving Contact

Ta'Lisa J. Ifezue, Trust Associate
Wachovia National Bank
190 River Rd., NJ3132
Summit, NJ 07901
Phone: (908)598-3577
Fax: (908)598-3583
E-mail: talisaifezue@wachovia.com

Description

Founded: 1979
EIN: 226311438
Organization Type: General Purpose Foundation
Giving Locations: NJ: Bergen County, Passaic County; NY; PA: children's programs are funded statewide
Grant Types: Capital, Project, Seed Money.

Donor Information

Founder: Established in 1979 by the late Stella C. Van Houten .

Financial Summary

Total Giving: $600,000 (fiscal year ending November 30, 1999 approx); $650,000 (fiscal 1998 approx); $617,000 (fiscal 1997)
Assets: $22,014,350 (fiscal 1998); $21,442,788 (fiscal 1997); $14,940,000 (fiscal 1995 approx)

Typical Recipients

Arts & Humanities: Libraries
Civic & Public Affairs: Philanthropic Organizations, Urban & Community Affairs
Education: Colleges & Universities, Medical Education, Private Education (Precollege), Special Education
Health: Cancer, Children's Health/Hospitals, Clinics/Medical Centers, Geriatric Health, Hospitals, Hospitals (University Affiliated), Medical Rehabilitation, Medical Research, Mental Health, Multiple Sclerosis,

Prenatal Health Issues, Respiratory, Single-Disease Health Associations
Religion: Churches, Religious Welfare
Social Services: Camps, Child Welfare, Day Care, Family Planning, Homes, Scouts, Youth Organizations

Application Procedures

Initial Contact: The fund requests application be made in writing.
Application Requirements: Proof of 501(c)(3) status.
Deadlines: Proposals should be received 2-3 weeks prior to February 1 for review in March; May 1 for review in June; August 1 for review in September; and November 1 for review in December.
Notes: Request grant proposal format from foundation.

Restrictions

The fund does not make grants to fund-raising events including dinners, benefits, and athletic events, or for general operating needs, endowments or loans. It also does not generally make grants outside of New Jersey, although exceptions are made for applicants in New York.

Additional Information

Publications: Application Guidelines
Trust(s): First Union Bank, NA

Foundation Officials

Ta'Lisa J. Ifezue: trust associate

Grants Analysis

Disclosure Period: fiscal year ending November 30, 1997
Total Grants: $617,000*
Number of Grants: 32
Average Grant: $19,281
Typical Range: $10,000 to $50,000
***Note:** Grants analysis provided by foundation.

VAN WERT COUNTY FOUNDATION

Giving Contact

Larry L. Wendel, Executive Secretary
138 E. Main St.
Van Wert, OH 45891
Phone: (419)238-1743
Fax: (419)238-3374
E-mail: vwcf@bright.net

Description

Founded: 1925
EIN: 340907558
Organization Type: Private Foundation
Giving Locations: OH: Paulding County, Van Wert County
Grant Types: General Support, Scholarship.

Donor Information

Founder: the late Charles F. Wassenberg, Gaylord Saltzgaber, the late John D. Ault, Kernan Wright, the late Richard L. Klein, the late Hazel Gleason, the late Constance Eirich

Financial Summary

Total Giving: $1,034,937 (2001); $1,049,047 (2000); $879,968 (1999)
Giving Analysis: Giving for 2001 includes: foundation scholarships ($379,828); 1999: foundation scholarships ($303,093); foundation scholarships ($318,261) 1998: foundation scholarships ($181,825)
Assets: $29,144,954 (2001); $29,490,768 (2000); $17,912,618 (1999)

Gifts Received: $717,956 (2001); $11,185,487 (2000); $247,929 (1999). Note: In 2001, contributions were received from the Leslie Endowment Funds ($474,194), Men's Garden Club of Van Wert ($7,645), Richard & Francis Pollock Memorial Fund ($222,350), and Kerns & Margaret White Trust Fund ($3,991). In 1999, contributions were received from Gaylord & Elizabeth Saltzgaber Music FD ($189,597), Ruth E. Cottingham Trust Estate ($34,916), Ralph and Arline Wegesin Memorial FD ($10,000), Frank W. Leslie Memorial Fund ($6,415). In 1996, contributions were received from Douglas E. Koch Memorial Funds ($4,300), the Oscar J. Scaer Memorial Fund ($89,000), the Kerns & Margaret Wright Trust Fund ($3,932),the Smith Memorial Fund ($10,000), the Knittle Irrevocable Music Trust ($20,000), the Dr. Keith Gordon Memorial Scholarship Fund ($5,720), the M. Scott and I. Doepker Memorial Fund ($165,149), and the Harry W. and Viola Clay Memorial Fund ($713,642); various contributions of less than $2,000 each also were received.

Typical Recipients

Arts & Humanities: Arts Centers, Arts Institutes, Historic Preservation, History & Archaeology, Libraries, Museums/Galleries, Music, Performing Arts, Theater
Civic & Public Affairs: Botanical Gardens/Parks, Clubs, Civic & Public Affairs-General, Housing, Municipalities/Towns, Parades/Festivals, Safety
Education: Afterschool/Enrichment Programs, Agricultural Education, Arts/Humanities Education, Business Education, Education-General, Leadership Training, Private Education (Precollege), Public Education (Precollege), Vocational & Technical Education
Environment: Air/Water Quality, Environment-General, Resource Conservation
Health: Home-Care Services, Hospitals, Mental Health, Nursing Services
Religion: Churches, Religious Welfare
Social Services: Animal Protection, Child Welfare, Community Service Organizations, Crime Prevention, Day Care, Delinquency & Criminal Rehabilitation, Domestic Violence, Emergency Relief, Family Planning, People with Disabilities, Recreation & Athletics, Senior Services, Social Services-General, United Funds/United Ways, YMCA/YWCA/YMHA/YWHA, Youth Organizations

Application Procedures

Initial Contact: Request application forms and guidelines for scholarship program and grants program.
Application Requirements: Grant proposals should include a description of organization and what will be accomplished, population to be served by project, documented line item budget, proof of tax-exempt status, and other organizational information.
Deadlines: June 3 for scholarship programs; May 15 and November 15 for other grants.

Restrictions

Does not provide loans, support religious activities, or support individuals except for scholarships.

Additional Information

Provides scholarships to residents of Van Wert or Paulding County, OH.
Publications: Application Guidelines; Application Form

Foundation Officials

D. L. Brumback, Jr.: trustee
Michael T. Cross: director PRIM CORP EMPL president: First Federal Savings & Loan Association.
William S. Derry: trustee
Clair Dudgeon: trustee
Robert W. Games: executive secretary
Bruce C. Kennedy: trustee
Kenneth Koch: trustee ED University of Pennsylvania (1976); Ohio State University (1979).
Gaylord E. Leslie: trustee
Watson Ley: trustee

Francis W. Purmort, III: director
Paul W. Purmort, Jr.: trustee
C. Allan Runser: trustee
Donald C. Sutton: trustee
Gerald D. Thatcher: trustee
Roger K. Thompson: trustee ED Rensselaer Polytechnic Institute (1951). PRIM CORP EMPL president: Kennedy Manufacturing Co.
Hon. Sumner J. Walters: trustee ED Ohio Northern University JD (1940). NONPR AFFIL president: Van Wert County Humane Society; member: VFW; member: Sigma Phi Epsilon; member: Ohio Bar Association; member: Ohio Municipal Judges Association; member: American Legion. CLUB AFFIL Shriners; Knight York Cross Honor; Masons.
Larry L. Wendel: trustee
Robert C. Young: trustee
Michael R. Zedaker: trustee

Grants Analysis

Disclosure Period: calendar year ending 2001
Total Grants: $640,719*
Number of Grants: 94
Average Grant: $6,816
Highest Grant: $63,000
Lowest Grant: $100
Typical Range: $300 to $10,000 and $49,000 to $63,000
***Note:** Giving excludes scholarships to individuals or to other miscellaneous awards.

Recent Grants

Note: Grants derived from 2001 Form 990.

General

63,000	Vantage Vocational School, Van Wert, OH -- support for Electronic Department
61,630	YMCA, Van Wert, OH -- for building improvements
57,900	YWCA, Van Wert, OH -- for building improvements
55,700	Van Wert City School, Van Wert, OH -- for Music Department
49,147	Wassenburg Art Center, Van Wert, OH
34,757	Wassenburg Art Center, Van Wert, OH -- for staff salaries and payroll taxes
25,000	Marsh Foundation, Van Wert, OH -- for renovations
25,000	Van Wert Community Concerts, Van Wert, OH
15,000	Crestview Schools, Convoy, OH -- for Music Department
15,000	Lima Symphony Orchestra, Lima, OH -- for concert in City of Van Wert

ROBERT C. VANCE CHARITABLE FOUNDATION

Giving Contact

Herbert E. Carlson, Jr., Chairman & President
21 Winesap Rd.
Kensington, CT 06037
Phone: (203)828-6037

Description

Founded: 1960
EIN: 066050188
Organization Type: Private Foundation
Giving Locations: CT: New Britain
Grant Types: General Support.

Donor Information

Founder: the late Robert C. Vance

Financial Summary

Total Giving: $452,284 (fiscal year ending January 31, 2002); $460,000 (fiscal 2001); $433,925 (fiscal 2000)

Giving Analysis: Giving for fiscal 2002 includes: foundation grants to United Way ($73,000); fiscal 2000: foundation grants to United Way ($68,000) fiscal 1999: foundation grants to United Way ($65,000)
Assets: $9,092,336 (fiscal 2002); $9,857,478 (fiscal 2001); $8,939,634 (fiscal 2000)

Typical Recipients

Arts & Humanities: Community Arts, Libraries, Museums/Galleries, Music
Civic & Public Affairs: Community Foundations, Employment/Job Training, Civic & Public Affairs-General, Urban & Community Affairs
Education: Colleges & Universities, Education-General, Literacy, Private Education (Precollege), Special Education
Health: Cancer, Hospices, Hospitals, Medical Research, Mental Health
Religion: Religious Organizations, Religious Welfare
Social Services: Child Welfare, Community Centers, Community Service Organizations, Family Planning, Family Services, People with Disabilities, United Funds/United Ways, YMCA/YWCA/YMHA/YWHA, Youth Organizations

Application Procedures

Initial Contact: Send brief letter describing program. Must conform to united community service format.
Deadlines: None.

Restrictions

Does not support individuals.

Additional Information

Trust(s): Fleet National Bank
Publications: Application Guidelines
Trust(s): Shawmut Bank NA

Foundation Officials

Rita H. Beaulieu: treasurer, director
Cheryl C. Carlson: secretary, director
Herbert E. Carlson, Sr.: treasurer, trustee
Herbert E. Carlson, Jr.: chairman, president, director
Robert E. Dragon, MD: director

Grants Analysis

Disclosure Period: fiscal year ending January 31, 2002
Total Grants: $379,284*
Number of Grants: 11
Average Grant: $8,809*
Highest Grant: $200,000
Lowest Grant: $1,000
Typical Range: $2,500 to $30,000
***Note:** Giving excludes United Way. Average grant figure excludes two highest grants totaling $300,000.

Recent Grants

Note: Grants derived from 2002 Form 990.

Library-Related

1,500	Peck Memorial Library of Berlin, Berlin, CT -- purchase large print books and audio taped books

General

200,000	Central Connecticut State University Foundation, New Britain, CT -- for Vance Distinguished Professorship
100,000	Klingberg Family Centers, New Britain, CT -- capital campaign
80,000	New Britain Museum of American Art, New Britain, CT -- capital campaign
73,000	United Way of the Capital Area, Baton Rouge, LA -- annual support
30,000	Central Connecticut State University Foundation, New Britain, CT -- for Vance Distinguished Lecture
6,784	Central Connecticut State University Foundation, New Britain, CT -- for Vance Distinguished Lecture
5,000	Mooreland Hill School, New Britain, CT -- annual support
2,500	Connecticut Choral Artists, New Britain, CT -- support of 2001-2002 season
2,500	Music Series, New Britain, CT -- support of 2002 season
1,000	Literacy Volunteers of America, New Britain, CT -- program funding

R. T. VANDERBILT TRUST

Giving Contact

Hugh B. Vanderbilt, Jr., Chairman & Trustee
30 Winfield St.
Norwalk, CT 06855
Phone: (203)853-1400
Fax: (203)853-1452

Description

Founded: 1951
EIN: 066040981
Organization Type: Private Foundation
Giving Locations: CT; MA; NY; RI
Grant Types: Capital, Endowment, General Support, Operating Expenses.

Financial Summary

Total Giving: $553,145 (2001); $601,301 (2000); $561,997 (1999)
Giving Analysis: Giving for 2001 includes: foundation grants to United Way ($5,000); 2000: foundation ($601,301); 1998: foundation grants to United Way ($2,000) foundation ($518,315)
Assets: $9,727,184 (2001); $11,006,027 (2000); $12,584,047 (1999)

Typical Recipients

Arts & Humanities: Historic Preservation, History & Archaeology, Libraries, Museums/Galleries, Music, Performing Arts
Civic & Public Affairs: Community Foundations, Civic & Public Affairs-General, Housing, Zoos/Aquariums
Education: Colleges & Universities, Private Education (Precollege), Secondary Education (Private), Vocational & Technical Education
Environment: Air/Water Quality, Environment-General, Resource Conservation, Wildlife Protection
Health: AIDS/HIV, Alzheimers Disease, Cancer, Children's Health/Hospitals, Emergency/Ambulance Services, Heart, Hospices, Hospitals, Kidney, Medical Research, Single-Disease Health Associations
International: Health Care/Hospitals, International Organizations
Religion: Churches, Ministries, Religious Organizations, Seminaries
Social Services: Animal Protection, Camps, Child Welfare, Community Service Organizations, Family Planning, Substance Abuse, United Funds/United Ways, Youth Organizations

Application Procedures

Initial Contact: Send a letter of inquiry.
Deadlines: None.

Restrictions

Does not support individuals.

Foundation Officials

Hugh Bedford Vanderbilt, Jr.: trustee
Hugh Bedford Vanderbilt, Sr.: chairman, trustee B New York, NY 1921. ED Trinity College (1942). PRIM CORP EMPL chairman, chief executive officer: Vanderbilt (RT) Co. NONPR AFFIL honorary trustee: Greenwich Historical Society; trustee: Historic Deerfield; member: Chemical Manufacturers Association. CLUB AFFIL Round Hill Club; Greenwich Country Club; Lyford Country Club; Blind Brook Country Club; Everglades Club.

Grants Analysis

Disclosure Period: calendar year ending 2001
Total Grants: $548,145*
Number of Grants: 83
Average Grant: $4,602*
Highest Grant: $100,000
Lowest Grant: $100
Typical Range: $1,000 to $10,000
*Note: Giving excludes United Way. Average grant figure excludes three highest grants ($180,000).

Recent Grants

Note: Grants derived from 2000 Form 990.

General

110,000	Planned Parenthood International Assistance, New York, NY
100,000	Historical Society of the Town of Greenwich, Cos Cob, CT
50,000	Connecticut Audubon Society, Milford, CT
35,000	Historic Deerfield, Inc, Deerfield, MA
25,000	Connecticut Audubon Society, Milford, CT
25,000	Forderverein der Paul-Guenther-Schule, Geithain Germany
25,000	Greenwich Hospital Hospice, Greenwich, CT
15,000	Wildlife Conservation Society, Bronx, NY
10,000	Camping and Education Foundation, Cincinnati, OH
10,000	Greenwich Academy, Greenwich, CT -- annual giving

VANGUARD GROUP

Company Headquarters

P.O. Box 2600
Valley Forge, PA 19482
Web: http://www.vanguard.com

Company Description

Assets: US$36 billion (2002)
Employees: 1000 (2002)
SIC(s): 6726 Investment Offices Nec.

Operating Locations

Vanguard Group (PA--Valley Forge)

Vanguard Group Foundation

Giving Contact

Tami Wise, Manager
Vanguard Group Foundation
PO Box 2600 (V38)
Valley Forge, PA 19482-2600
Phone: (610)669-6331

Description

Founded: 1994
EIN: 232699769
Organization Type: Corporate Foundation
Giving Locations: PA: Delaware Valley
Grant Types: General Support, Operating Expenses, Scholarship.

Financial Summary

Total Giving: $2,994,351 (2001); $2,726,195 (2000); $2,921,883 (1999)
Giving Analysis: Giving for 2001 includes: foundation ($1,357,351); foundation grants to United Way ($1,637,000); 2000: foundation scholarships ($1,000); foundation ($1,218,195); foundation grants to United Way ($1,507,000); 1999: foundation grants to United Way ($1,350,500); foundation ($1,571,383);
Assets: $3,843,843 (2001); $3,846,048 (2000); $3,365,743 (1999)
Gifts Received: $3,005,178 (2001); $3,007,326 (2000); $2,503,676 (1999). Note: Contributions were received from various Vanguard Group companies.

Typical Recipients

Arts & Humanities: Arts Associations & Councils, Ballet, Arts & Humanities-General, Historic Preservation, History & Archaeology, Libraries, Museums/Galleries, Music, Performing Arts, Theater
Civic & Public Affairs: Economic Development, Civic & Public Affairs-General, Housing, Municipalities/Towns, Safety, Urban & Community Affairs, Women's Affairs, Zoos/Aquariums
Education: Arts/Humanities Education, Business Education, Colleges & Universities, Economic Education, Education Funds, Education-General, International Studies, Literacy, Private Education (Precollege), Science/Mathematics Education, Student Aid
Environment: Environment-General, Resource Conservation
Health: Cancer, Emergency/Ambulance Services, Health Funds, Health Funds, Heart, Hospitals, Medical Rehabilitation, Nursing Services, Public Health
International: International Affairs
Science: Science Museums, Scientific Centers & Institutes
Social Services: Big Brother/Big Sister, Child Welfare, Community Service Organizations, Emergency Relief, Homes, People with Disabilities, Senior Services, United Funds/United Ways

Application Procedures

Initial Contact: Send letter requesting guidelines and "Summary of Grant Request" form.
Application Requirements: Proposals should include the completed Summary of Grant Request form, which requests a description of organization, including goals, history, past projects, staffing, and population served; amount requested; detailed statement on how the foundation's funding will be used and how much will be used for administrative expenses; and a program timetable. Attachments that must accompany the application form are: an audited financial statement for the organization's most recently completed fiscal year and the current year's operating budget; proof of tax-exempt status and a statement from an officer of the organization confirming that the exemption letter is valid; most recent annual report or other materials describing the organization's accomplishments; list of current contributors; list of the organization's board of directors and executive staff, including affiliations; and, if possible, a list of Vanguard employees who serve the organization or its board.
Deadlines: None.
Review Process: Requests are reviewed quarterly.
Evaluative Criteria: The foundation gives preference to requests from organizations or programs that are located in the Delaware Valley; address a well-defined and important need or concern; develop and implement long-term solutions; do not duplicate existing efforts; possess 501(c)(3) status; maintain costs at minimum levels necessary to provide high quality services; and combine the support provided by Vanguard with funds received from other contributors.
Decision Notification: Applicants will be notified about the status of proposal within four to six weeks of receipt. The foundation director will notify applicants in writing regarding the board's final funding decision.

Corporate Officials

John C. Bogle: senior chairmano PRIM CORP EMPL senior chairman: Vanguard Group.
John Joseph Brennan: director, president B Boston, MA 1954. ED Dartmouth College AB (1976); Harvard University MBA (1980). PRIM CORP EMPL director, president: Vanguard Group Inc. CORP AFFIL director: ICI Mutual Insurance Co. NONPR AFFIL member: Financial Executives Institute; government, executive vice president, member: Mutual Fund Education Alliance.
Ralph K. Packard: director, chief financial officer PRIM CORP EMPL director, chief financial officer: Vanguard Group.

Foundation Officials

John C. Bogle: chairman (see above)
John Joseph Brennan: president (see above)
Ralph K. Packard: treasurer (see above)

Grants Analysis

Disclosure Period: calendar year ending 2001
Total Grants: $1,357,351*
Number of Grants: 602
Average Grant: $2,255
Highest Grant: $150,000
Typical Range: $50 to $5,000
*Note: Giving excludes United Way.

Recent Grants

Note: Grants derived from 2001 Form 990.

Library-Related

5,000	Free Library, Philadelphia, PA

General

1,551,000	United Way Southeastern Pennsylvania, Philadelphia, PA
150,000	National Constitution Center, Philadelphia, PA
125,000	Valley of the Sun United Way, Phoenix, AZ
100,000	Regional Performing Arts Center, Philadelphia, PA
86,000	United Way of Central Carolinas, Charlotte, NC
52,125	Junior Achievement of Delaware Valley, Newtown Square, PA
50,000	Franklin Institute, Philadelphia, PA
37,500	National Council on Economic Education, New York, NY
30,000	Greater Philadelphia Urban Affairs, Philadelphia, PA
28,485	Nature Conservancy - National Chapter, Arlington, VA

VANN FAMILY FOUNDATION

Giving Contact

Sherry S. Connolly, Secretary, Treasurer & Director
11008 Carnoustie Lane
Ft. Wayne, IN 46814
Phone: (219)625-6011

Description

Founded: 1997
EIN: 352008538
Organization Type: Private Foundation
Giving Locations: IN; NC; OH
Grant Types: General Support.

Financial Summary

Total Giving: $138,280 (2001); $109,853 (2000); $56,883 (1999)
Assets: $4,047,354 (2001); $3,463,341 (2000); $2,726,450 (1999)
Gifts Received: $289,557 (2001); $490,842 (2000); $973,086 (1999). Note: In 2001, 2000, and 1999, contributions were received from James M. Vann. In 1997, contributions were received from Mr. and Mrs. James M. Vann.

Typical Recipients

Arts & Humanities: Arts Associations & Councils, Libraries, Museums/Galleries, Music
Civic & Public Affairs: Civic & Public Affairs-General, Public Policy
Education: Colleges & Universities, Student Aid
Health: Hospices, Medical Rehabilitation, Public Health
Religion: Churches, Religious Welfare
Social Services: Food/Clothing Distribution, Recreation & Athletics, Scouts, YMCA/YWCA/YMHA/YWHA

Application Procedures

Initial Contact: Send written request detailing program.
Application Requirements: Include proof of tax-exempt status, list of other contributors, and program revenue and costs.
Deadlines: None.

Foundation Officials

Sherry S. Connolly: secretary, treasurer, director
Deborah Vann Gilreath: director
Stephanie S. Moen: director
James M. Vann, III: director
James M. Vann: chairman, director
Marjorie Lee Vann: president, director

Grants Analysis

Disclosure Period: calendar year ending 2001
Total Grants: $138,280
Number of Grants: 35
Average Grant: $2,155*
Highest Grant: $65,000
Lowest Grant: $80
Typical Range: $500 to $4,000
*Note: Average grant figure excludes highest grant.

Recent Grants

Note: Grants derived from 2000 Form 990.

Library-Related

1,000	Allen County Public Library, Ft. Wayne, IN

General

34,000	Interfaith Hospitality Network, Cincinnati, OH
21,000	Indiana-Purdue Foundation at Fort Wayne, Ft. Wayne, IN
10,000	Aldersgate United Methodist Church
9,400	University of St. Francis, Wayne, IN
5,000	Davidson College, Davidson, NC
3,500	Fort Wayne YWCA, Ft. Wayne, IN
3,500	Hospice of Winston-Salem Forsyth County, Winston-Salem, NC
3,000	Fort Wayne Philharmonic, Ft. Wayne, IN
3,000	Long Center, Inc.
2,500	Fort Wayne Sports Foundation, Ft. Wayne, IN

RACHAEL AND BEN VAUGHAN FOUNDATION

Giving Contact

Ben F. Vaughan, III, President & Trustee
PO Box 2233
Austin, TX 78768-2233
Phone: (512)477-4726
E-mail: RBVF@aol.com

Description

Founded: 1952
EIN: 746040479
Organization Type: Private Foundation
Giving Locations: TX: South and Central Texas

Grant Types: Capital, Endowment, General Support, Multiyear/Continuing Support, Operating Expenses, Professorship, Project, Research.

Donor Information

Founder: the late Ben F. Vaughan, Jr., the late Rachael Vaughan

Financial Summary

Total Giving: $216,734 (fiscal year ending November 30, 2002); $195,500 (fiscal 2000); $202,675 (fiscal 1999)
Assets: $4,502,547 (fiscal 2002); $4,174,089 (fiscal 2000); $4,145,297 (fiscal 1999)
Gifts Received: $5,903 (fiscal 2000); $19,306 (fiscal 1999); $36,727 (fiscal 1997). Note: In fiscal 1999 contributions were received from, Ben F. Vaughan III ($5,903), Daphne Vaughan ($5,903), and Ben F. Vaughan IV ($5,903).

Typical Recipients

Arts & Humanities: History & Archaeology, Libraries, Museums/Galleries, Performing Arts, Public Broadcasting, Theater
Civic & Public Affairs: Economic Development, Civic & Public Affairs-General, Hispanic Affairs, Housing, Law & Justice, Legal Aid, Native American Affairs, Public Policy, Safety, Urban & Community Affairs, Women's Affairs, Zoos/Aquariums
Education: Arts/Humanities Education, Colleges & Universities, Education Reform, Environmental Education, Faculty Development, Education-General, Literacy, Private Education (Precollege), Religious Education, Science/Mathematics Education, Secondary Education (Public)
Environment: Air/Water Quality, Environment-General, Resource Conservation, Wildlife Protection
Health: AIDS/HIV, Cancer, Children's Health/Hospitals, Clinics/Medical Centers, Health Organizations, Long-Term Care, Research/Studies Institutes
International: Health Care/Hospitals, Human Rights, International Affairs, International Environmental Issues, International Organizations, International Peace & Security Issues, Missionary/Religious Activities
Religion: Churches, Religion-General, Ministries, Religious Organizations, Religious Welfare
Social Services: At-Risk Youth, Child Abuse, Child Welfare, Community Service Organizations, Domestic Violence, Emergency Relief, Family Planning, Family Services, Food/Clothing Distribution, People with Disabilities, Refugee Assistance, Scouts, Senior Services, Sexual Abuse, Shelters/Homelessness, Substance Abuse, United Funds/United Ways, Veterans, Volunteer Services, YMCA/YWCA/YMHA/YWHA, Youth Organizations

Application Procedures

Initial Contact: Send a brief letter or email to request application.
Application Requirements: Application should include a cover letter, a two- to four-page proposal requesting a specific amount of money, proof of tax-exempt status, Form 990, and detailed budgetary information.
Deadlines: June 1.

Restrictions

Does not provide support to individuals, loans, or grants to non-public charitable organizations.

Additional Information

The foundation's charitable interests are educational, cultural, religious, health care, welfare, youth, women, literacy, and environment organizations.
Publications: Application Guidelines

Foundation Officials

Ben F. Vaughan, IV: vice president, trustee
Ben F. Vaughan, III: president, trustee
Daphne duPont Vaughan: secretary, treasurer, trustee
Genevieve Vaughan: vice president, trustee
William R. Ward, Jr.: assistant secretary, treasurer

Grants Analysis

Disclosure Period: fiscal year ending November 30, 2002
Total Grants: $216,734
Number of Grants: 60
Average Grant: $3,612
Highest Grant: $10,000
Lowest Grant: $500
Typical Range: $1,000 to $5,000

Recent Grants

Note: Grants derived from fiscal 2002 Form 990.

General

10,000	San Marcos River Foundation, San Marcos, TX -- funding for environmental protection
10,000	Share Foundation Building a New El Salvador Today, San Francisco, CA -- funding for agriculture and rural development
10,000	University of Texas Marine Science Institute, Austin, TX
7,500	Any Baby Can of Austin, Austin, TX
7,500	Center for the Studies of Ancient Territories -- toward publication of Metaponto Research
7,500	Girl Scout Tip of Texas Council, Amarillo, TX -- funding for development of new camp facility
7,500	Katapultz, Inc., Austin, TX -- for funding to support technology to disadvantaged
7,500	St. Edwards University, Inc., Austin, TX -- funding for camp scholarships
7,000	Oficina Legal Del Pueblo Unido, Austin, TX -- funding to create clearinghouse for human rights issues
5,334	New Radio and Performing Arts, New York, NY -- funding for radio programs for women

VAUGHAN FURNITURE CO.

Company Headquarters

100 N. Railroad Ave.
Galax, VA 24333

Company Description

Employees: 1,400
SIC(s): 2500 Furniture & Fixtures.

Operating Locations

Vaughan Furniture Co. (VA--Galax)

Vaughan Foundation

Giving Contact

John B. Vaughan, President
1 Railroad Ave.
Galax, VA 24333
Phone: (540)236-6111

Description

EIN: 541295313
Organization Type: Corporate Foundation
Giving Locations: VA
Grant Types: General Support.

Donor Information

Founder: Vaughan Furniture Co.

Financial Summary

Total Giving: $45,590 (fiscal year ending September 30, 2001); $48,050 (fiscal 2000); $45,215 (fiscal 1998)
Giving Analysis: Giving for fiscal 2001 includes: foundation grants to United Way ($15,270); fiscal 2000: foundation grants to United Way ($18,750); foundation ($29,300); fiscal 1998: foundation grants to United Way ($18,240) foundation ($26,975)
Assets: $411,968 (fiscal 2001); $361,765 (fiscal 2000); $335,620 (fiscal 1998)
Gifts Received: $50,000 (fiscal 2001); $50,000 (fiscal 2000); $50,000 (fiscal 1998). Note: In fiscal 2001, contributions were received from Vaughan Furniture Co.

Typical Recipients

Arts & Humanities: Arts Associations & Councils, Libraries
Civic & Public Affairs: Civic & Public Affairs-General, Safety
Education: Arts/Humanities Education, Colleges & Universities, Community & Junior Colleges, Education Funds, Education Reform, Elementary Education (Public), Education-General, Secondary Education (Public), Special Education
Health: Alzheimers Disease, Cancer, Emergency/Ambulance Services, Eyes/Blindness, Health-General, Heart, Multiple Sclerosis, Prenatal Health Issues, Public Health, Respiratory, Single-Disease Health Associations
Religion: Churches, Religious Welfare
Social Services: Camps, Child Welfare, Community Service Organizations, Recreation & Athletics, Scouts, Special Olympics, Substance Abuse, United Funds/United Ways, United Funds/United Ways, Volunteer Services

Application Procedures

Initial Contact: The foundation requests applications be made in writing.
Application Requirements: Include proof of tax-exempt status, purpose of funds sought, and a description of organization's charitable purpose.
Deadlines: None.

Restrictions

Grants are not made to individuals.

Corporate Officials

John B. Vaughan: chairman, chief executive officer PRIM CORP EMPL chairman, chief executive officer: Vaughan Furniture Co.
William B. Vaughan: president PRIM CORP EMPL president: Vaughan Furniture Co.

Foundation Officials

Raymond L. Hall, Jr.: secretary, director PRIM CORP EMPL treasurer: Vaughan Furniture Co.
John B. Vaughan: president, director (see above)

Grants Analysis

Disclosure Period: fiscal year ending September 30, 2001
Total Grants: $30,320*
Number of Grants: 22
Average Grant: $1,378
Highest Grant: $7,000
Typical Range: $500 to $3,000
***Note:** Giving excludes United Way.

Recent Grants

Note: Grants derived from fiscal 2000 Form 990.

General

13,000	Twin County United Way, Galax, VA
7,000	Galax Volunteer Fire Department, Galax, VA
5,000	Patrick Springs Fire Department, Patrick Springs, VA
4,000	Virginia Foundation for Independent Colleges, Richmond, VA
4,000	WCC Educational Foundation, Wytheville, VA
2,950	Johnson City Area United Way, Johnson City, TN
2,800	United Way of Patrick County, Stuart, VA
2,000	Galax Foundation for Excellence in Education, Galax, VA
1,500	Joy Ranch, Inc, Hillsville, VA
1,000	High Point University, High Point, NC

JIM M. VAUGHN FOUNDATION

Giving Contact

Dr. James M. Vaughn, Jr., Director
830 S. Beckham
Tyler, TX 75701
Phone: (903)597-7652

Description

Founded: 1952
EIN: 756008953
Organization Type: Private Foundation
Giving Locations: TX: Tyler
Grant Types: General Support, Research.

Donor Information

Founder: the late Edgar H. Vaughn, Lillie Mae Vaughn

Financial Summary

Total Giving: $313,222 (2000); $448,512 (1999); $458,648 (1998)
Giving Analysis: Giving for 2000 includes: foundation grants to United Way ($10,200); 1999: foundation grants to United Way ($10,000); 1998: foundation grants to United Way ($10,000)
Assets: $10,834,752 (2000); $9,884,392 (1999); $9,912,827 (1998)
Gifts Received: $308,473 (1994)

Typical Recipients

Arts & Humanities: History & Archaeology, Libraries, Museums/Galleries, Music, Public Broadcasting, Theater
Civic & Public Affairs: Clubs, Economic Development, Employment/Job Training, Civic & Public Affairs-General, Urban & Community Affairs, Women's Affairs
Education: Arts/Humanities Education, Business Education, Colleges & Universities, Community & Junior Colleges, Elementary Education (Private), Education-General, Legal Education, Literacy, Minority Education, Private Education (Precollege), Public Education (Precollege), Secondary Education (Private), Student Aid
Health: Alzheimers Disease, Cancer, Clinics/Medical Centers, Emergency/Ambulance Services, Eyes/Blindness, Health Organizations, Hospices, Hospitals, Hospitals (University Affiliated), Medical Research, Mental Health, Preventive Medicine/Wellness Organizations, Speech & Hearing, Transplant Networks/Donor Banks
International: Health Care/Hospitals, International Organizations, Missionary/Religious Activities
Religion: Churches, Religious Organizations, Religious Welfare, Seminaries, Synagogues/Temples
Science: Science Museums, Scientific Centers & Institutes
Social Services: Child Welfare, Community Service Organizations, Counseling, Day Care, Delinquency & Criminal Rehabilitation, Domestic Violence, Family Planning, Family Services, Food/Clothing Distribution, People with Disabilities, Recreation & Athletics,
Scouts, Senior Services, United Funds/United Ways, YMCA/YWCA/YMHA/YWHA, Youth Organizations

Application Procedures

Initial Contact: Send a brief letter of inquiry.
Application Requirements: Include a description of organization, amount requested, purpose of funds sought, proof of tax-exempt status.

Restrictions

Does not support individuals.

Additional Information

Trust(s): Chase Manhattan Bank

Foundation Officials

Dr. James M. Vaughn: director
James M. Vaughn, Jr.: director

Grants Analysis

Disclosure Period: calendar year ending 2000
Total Grants: $303,022*
Number of Grants: 100
Average Grant: $3,030
Highest Grant: $22,100
Typical Range: $1,000 to $5,000
***Note:** Giving excludes United Way.

Recent Grants

Note: Grants derived from 1999 Form 990.

General

30,000	Hospice of East Texas, Tyler, TX
25,000	Heart of Tyler, Tyler, TX -- Main Street project
25,000	Salvation Army, Tyler, TX
25,000	Smith County Juvenile Services, Tyler, TX
25,000	Stewart Regional Blood Bank, Tyler, TX
25,000	Tyler Area Senior Citizens, Tyler, TX
25,000	University of Texas at Tyler Foundation, Tyler, TX
12,000	Tyler Junior College, Tyler, TX
12,000	University of Texas M. D. Anderson Cancer Center, Houston, TX
12,000	University of Texas Tyler, Tyler, TX

JAMES M. VAUGHN, JR. FOUNDATION FUND

Giving Contact

James M. Vaughn, Jr., President
830 S. Beckham
Tyler, TX 75701
Phone: (903)597-7652

Description

Founded: 1971
EIN: 237166546
Organization Type: Private Foundation
Grant Types: Fellowship, Research.

Financial Summary

Total Giving: $448,512 (1999); $14,000 (1997); $71,620 (1996)
Assets: $1,477,076 (2000); $9,884,392 (1999); $1,646,565 (1997)
Gifts Received: $700 (1997)

Typical Recipients

Arts & Humanities: Arts Centers, Libraries, Museums/Galleries, Theater
Civic & Public Affairs: Civic & Public Affairs-General
Education: Colleges & Universities
Health: Mental Health
Religion: Churches, Synagogues/Temples

Application Procedures

Initial Contact: Send resume and cover letter.
Deadlines: None.

Restrictions

Grants are awarded for research in mathematics.

Foundation Officials

James M. Vaughn, Jr.: president
Sally Vaughn: vice president
Jan Werner: secretary, treasurer

VERIZON COMMUNICATIONS INC.

Company Headquarters

1095 Avenue of the Americas
New York, NY 10036
Web: http://www.verizon.com

Company Description

Founded: 1983
Ticker: VZ
Exchange: NYSE
Formed by Merger of: Bell Atlantic and GTE (2000).
Revenue: US$67.625 billion (2002)
Profit: US$4.079 billion (2002)
Employees: 250309 (2002)
Fortune Rank: 10, per FORTUNE Magazine's list of 500 Largest U.S. Corporations (2002).
Parent Company: Vodafone Group Plc, The Courtyard, 2-4 London Rd., Newbury, United Kingdom

Nonmonetary Support

Type: Donated Equipment
Volunteer Programs: The Verizon Incentive Program recognizes employees' contribution of time and talent to nonprofit organizations where they live and work. Under the program, employees apply for a grant for the qualified organization where they volunteered at least 50 hours in a 12 month period. The foundation rewards them with a $500 check for presentation to the designated organization. Employees may request VIP grants on behalf of two separate organizations in a 12 month period for a total of $1,000.
The Verizon Team Incentive Program rewards teams of ten or more eligible employees to collectively raise funds for nonprofit organizations across the country through organized pledge-a-thons, such as walk-a-thons or bike-a-thons. Under the program, the foundation matches funds collected by each team up to $25,000 per team to qualified nonprofit organizations.

Verizon Foundation

Giving Contact

Suzanne A. DuBose, President
1095 Avenue of the Americas
New York, NY 10036
Phone: (212)395-2295
Fax: (212)398-0951
Web: http://foundation.verizon.com
Note: The foundation only accepts grant applications online. All correspondence should be done via e-mail. Please see the foundation's web site for details.

Description

Founded: 2000
EIN: 133319048
Organization Type: Corporate Foundation
Giving Locations: operating locations.
Grant Types: Award, Capital, Emergency, Employee Matching Gifts, Fellowship, General Support, Matching, Multiyear/Continuing Support, Scholarship.

Note: Employee matching gift ratio: 1 to 1 up to $23,750 across all giving categories for current employees; up to $15,250 for eligible retirees, only to education organizations.

Donor Information

Founder: Verizon Communications Inc.

Financial Summary

Total Giving: $77,137,397 (2001); $41,205,556 (2000); $30,000,000 (1999 approx). Note: Contributes through corporate direct giving program and foundation. Giving includes foundation only. Giving figures prior to 2000 are for the GTE Foundation.
Giving Analysis: Giving for 2001 includes: foundation scholarships ($1,348,080); foundation grants to United Way ($7,403,845); 2000: foundation grants to United Way ($6,215,587); foundation ($34,989,969); 1998: foundation scholarships ($513,446); foundation grants to United Way ($2,725,543); foundation matching gifts ($3,632,655) foundation ($19,381,279)
Assets: $80,235,431 (2001); $39,514,180 (2000); $54,000,000 (1999). Note: Asset figures before 2000 are for the GTE Foundation.
Gifts Received: $53,914,344 (2001); $70,688,063 (2000); $23,890,922 (1998)

Typical Recipients

Arts & Humanities: Arts Associations & Councils, Arts Centers, Dance, History & Archaeology, Libraries, Literary Arts, Museums/Galleries, Music, Opera, Performing Arts, Public Broadcasting, Theater, Visual Arts
Civic & Public Affairs: African American Affairs, Asian American Affairs, Economic Development, Employment/Job Training, Civic & Public Affairs-General, Hispanic Affairs, Law & Justice, Nonprofit Management, Professional & Trade Associations, Public Policy, Urban & Community Affairs, Zoos/Aquariums
Education: Afterschool/Enrichment Programs, Business Education, Business-School Partnerships, Colleges & Universities, Community & Junior Colleges, Continuing Education, Economic Education, Education Associations, Education Funds, Education Reform, Engineering/Technological Education, Environmental Education, Faculty Development, Education-General, Gifted & Talented Programs, International Studies, Literacy, Minority Education, Private Education (Precollege), Science/Mathematics Education, Student Aid, Vocational & Technical Education
Environment: Air/Water Quality, Environment-General
Health: Emergency/Ambulance Services, Geriatric Health, Health Policy/Cost Containment, Hospitals
International: Foreign Educational Institutions
Religion: Seminaries
Science: Science-General, Science Museums, Scientific Centers & Institutes
Social Services: Child Welfare, Community Centers, Community Service Organizations, Counseling, Domestic Violence, Emergency Relief, Family Services, People with Disabilities, Senior Services, Shelters/Homelessness, Substance Abuse, United Funds/United Ways, Volunteer Services, YMCA/YWCA/YMHA/YWHA, Youth Organizations

Application Procedures

Initial Contact: Submit applications online. Average grant figure excludes highest grant.
Application Requirements: Include organization name and address; mission statement; detailed objectives of the project, background, and budget; additional sources of funding; evaluation process; population served; and evidence of 501(c)(3) tax-exempt status.
Deadlines: None.
Review Process: Any proposals submitted online receive a notification of receipt from your local community relations manager within 72 hours of their submission.

Evaluative Criteria: To be eligible for consideration organizations must focus on technology applications and programs in one or more of the following areas: Literacy; Digital Divide; Workforce Development; Employee Volunteerism; Community Technology Development.
Notes: The foundation only accepts electronic proposals through its Apply Online process. See the foundation's web site for details.

Restrictions

Foundation does not support individuals; religious organizations, unless the particular program will benefit a large portion of a community and does not duplicate the work of other agencies in the community; organizations whose primary purpose is to influence legislation; organizations which discriminate on the basis of race, color, sex, sexual orientation, age, religion, national or ethnic origin, pro-life or pro-choice advocacy, or physical disability; organizations which do not have a Section 501(c)(3) public charity status; endowments or capital campaigns; film, music, television, video and media production projects or broadcast program underwriting; research studies, unless related to projects already supported by Verizon; sports sponsorships; performing arts tours; association memberships; or organizations which have received a grant from the Verizon, Bell Atlantic or GTE or the NYNEX Foundations in the last three consecutive years -- you may reapply after a one year hiatus.

Additional Information

The Verizon Foundation was formed in July 2000 after the merger of GTE and Bell Atlantic formed Verizon COIs Inc.

Corporate Officials

Lawrence T. Babbio, Jr.: vice chairman, presidentpublic affairs & communications ED Stevens Institute of Technology BE (1966); New York University MBA (1970). PRIM CORP EMPL vice chairman, president: Verizon Communications Inc.
Mary Beth Bardin: executive vice president public affairs & communications ED Ohio University BA. PRIM CORP EMPL executive vice president public affairs & communications: Verizon CommunicationS Inc.
Michael Terry Masin: vice chairman, president B Montreal, QC Canada 1945. ED Dartmouth College BA (1966); University of California, Los Angeles JD (1969). PRIM CORP EMPL vice chairman, president: Verizon Communications Inc. ADD CORP EMPL managing partner: O'Melveny & Myers. CORP AFFIL director: Trust Co. West; director: Compania Anonima Nacional Telefonos de Venezuela; director: Travelers Group Inc.; director: Citigroup Inc.; director: British Columbia Telecommunications. NONPR AFFIL member deans advisory committee: Dartmouth College; member business committee, board trustee: Museum Modern Art; board member: China American Society; member: Council Foreign Relations; member: American Bar Association; trustee: Carnegie Hall. CLUB AFFIL California Club; Brook Club.
Ivan G. Seidenberg: president, chief executive officer, director B New York, NY December 12, 1946. ED City University of New York BS (1972); Pace University MBA (1980). PRIM CORP EMPL president, chief executive officer, director: Verizon Communications Inc. CORP AFFIL director: Viacom Inc.; director: Scholastic Inc.; president, director: Telesector Resources Group Inc.; director: Melville Corp.; director: Scholastic Corp.; director: CVS Corp.; director: Honeywell International Inc. NONPR AFFIL member: Rockland Business Council; director: U.S. Telephone Association.

Foundation Officials

Gale A. Cirigliano: director eSolutions & technology programs
Suzanne A. DuBose: president
Oscar C. Gomez: director

Bruce S. Gordon: executive director
Katherine J. Harless: director
T. Britton Harris, IV: chief information officer
Eileen Hazard: program officer
Michael Terry Masin: director, secretary, treasurer (see above)
Michael W. Morrell: vice president
Neil D. Olson: vice president, treasurer
Soraya Rodriguez: director foundation operations & national programs
Agnes Strait: director national programs
Susan Sullivan: program officer
Thomas J. Tauke: executive vice president

Grants Analysis

Disclosure Period: calendar year ending 2001
Total Grants: $68,385,472*
Number of Grants: 13,065 (approx)
Average Grant: $4,638*
Highest Grant: $3,900,000
Lowest Grant: $25
Typical Range: $1,000 to $10,000
Note: Giving excludes United Way and scholarship. Average grant figure excludes two highest grants ($7,800,000).

Recent Grants

Note: Grants derived from 2001 Form 990.

Library-Related

257,000	American Library Association, Chicago, IL
250,000	American Library Association, Chicago, IL
250,000	American Library Association, Chicago, IL
200,000	American Library Association, Chicago, IL

General

3,900,000	Regional Performing Arts, Philadelphia, PA
3,900,000	Regional Performing Arts, Philadelphia, PA
3,182,000	United Way, Los Angeles, CA
3,000,000	United Way, Los Angeles, CA
1,272,580	Citizens Scholarship Foundation
1,216,791	United Way Tri-State, New York, NY
1,200,000	Verizon Pioneers
1,000,000	American Red Cross, Denison, TX
1,000,000	Stevens Institute of Technology, Hoboken, NJ
751,071	Laubach Literacy International, Syracuse, NY

VERMILION HEALTHCARE FOUNDATION

Giving Contact

Valeria Saikley
702 N. Logan
Danville, IL 61832
Phone: (217)431-7021

Description

EIN: 371225688
Organization Type: Private Foundation
Giving Locations: IL: Danville
Grant Types: General Support.

Financial Summary

Total Giving: $1,006,230 (fiscal year ending September 30, 2001); $1,393,527 (fiscal 2000); $1,406,517 (fiscal 1998)
Giving Analysis: Giving for fiscal 2000 includes: foundation fellowships ($6,030); foundation scholarships ($25,000); fiscal 1998: foundation grants to United Way ($15,000); foundation ($1,391,517); fiscal 1997: foundation grants to United Way ($30,000) foundation ($899,083)

Assets: $10,691,799 (fiscal 2001); $12,897,840 (fiscal 2000); $12,594,221 (fiscal 1998)

Typical Recipients

Arts & Humanities: Libraries, Museums/Galleries, Music, Theater
Civic & Public Affairs: Legal Aid, Municipalities/Towns
Education: Arts/Humanities Education, Community & Junior Colleges, Elementary Education (Private), Education-General, Medical Education, Public Education (Precollege), Science/Mathematics Education, Student Aid
Health: Cancer, Children's Health/Hospitals, Clinics/Medical Centers, Health-General, Hospitals, Long-Term Care, Nursing Services, Transplant Networks/Donor Banks
Religion: Religious Welfare
Social Services: Big Brother/Big Sister, Child Welfare, Community Service Organizations, Family Services, Scouts, Senior Services, Sexual Abuse, Social Services-General, United Funds/United Ways, YMCA/YWCA/YMHA/YWHA, Youth Organizations, Youth Organizations

Application Procedures

Initial Contact: Organizations seeking grants should first call and discuss in general terms the proposed project.
Deadlines: March 15, June 15, September 15, and December 15.

Restrictions

Grants are not usually made for routine operating needs or annual giving.

Additional Information

Publications: Application Guidelines

Foundation Officials

James D. Anderson: director
Mary Michael Bateman: vice chairman
Thomas Bott: chairman
Thomas Crays: director
H. Michael Finkle: director
Leo Hirsch: director
Robert Hoecker: director
Robert Kesler: secretary, treasurer
Mark Layden: director
Bruce Meachum: director
Clyde Meachum: director
Robert Muirhead: director
Michael J. Mulcahy: director
Judd Peck: director
Anthony Rocco: director
Rebecca Schlecht: director
W. John Shane: vchairman
Win C. Smith: director
Carroll E. Snyder: director
Frank Young: director

Grants Analysis

Disclosure Period: fiscal year ending September 30, 2001
Total Grants: $1,006,230
Number of Grants: 19
Average Grant: $25,594*
Highest Grant: $445,537
Lowest Grant: $2,500
Typical Range: $10,000 to $50,000
Note: Average grant figure excludes two highest grants ($545,537).

Recent Grants

Note: Grants derived from fiscal 2000 Form 990.

General

550,902	Provena USMC, Danville, IL -- for quarterly distributions
223,800	Boys and Girls Club, Danville, IL -- for

	teen reach program and capital campaign
100,000	Vermilion County Museum, Danville, IL -- for museum/visitor center funding campaign
50,000	Danville Area Community College Foundation, Danville, IL -- for learning resource center renovation
42,300	YMCA, Danville, IL -- for pools accessibility and window replacement
26,888	Hoopeston Multi-Agency Service Center, Hoopeston, IL -- for heating and A/C system
25,570	Boy Scouts of America, Danville, IL -- for well project - Camp Drake
25,000	Lakeview College of Nursing, Danville, IL -- for increase LCN's scholarship fund
25,000	Provena USMC, Danville, IL -- for labor, delivery, and recovery remodeling project
25,000	Schlarman High School, Danville, IL -- for chemistry lab rebuilding

MILES HODSDON VERNON FOUNDATION

Giving Contact

Robert C. Thomson, Jr., President, Treasurer & Director
c/o Chadbourne, O'Neill, Thomson, Whalen and Fitzgerald
PO Box 701
Sleepy Hollow, NY 10591-0701
Phone: (914)923-8499

Description

Founded: 1953
EIN: 136076836
Organization Type: Private Foundation
Giving Locations: NY: nationally.
Grant Types: Research, Scholarship.

Donor Information

Founder: the late Miles Hodsdon Vernon, Martha Hodsdon Kinney, and Louise Hodsdon

Financial Summary

Total Giving: $506,100 (2000); $495,100 (1999); $402,600 (1998)
Giving Analysis: Giving for 2000 includes: foundation scholarships ($65,000) 1999: foundation scholarships ($55,000)
Assets: $10,163,429 (2000); $9,529,227 (1999); $10,852,499 (1998)
Gifts Received: $62,416 (1995); $165,000 (1992).
Note: In 1995, contributions were received from the Miles Hodsdon Vernon Trust.

Typical Recipients

Arts & Humanities: History & Archaeology, Libraries, Music, Public Broadcasting
Education: Colleges & Universities, Education Funds, Faculty Development, Education-General, Medical Education, Private Education (Precollege), Public Education (Precollege), Science/Mathematics Education, Secondary Education (Public), Student Aid
Health: Cancer, Children's Health/Hospitals, Clinics/Medical Centers, Diabetes, Emergency/Ambulance Services, Health Organizations, Hospitals, Long-Term Care, Medical Research, Mental Health, Nursing Services, Single-Disease Health Associations, Trauma Treatment
International: Health Care/Hospitals
Religion: Churches, Religious Welfare, Seminaries
Social Services: Camps, Child Welfare, Community Centers, Community Service Organizations, Day Care, Family Services, Food/Clothing Distribution, Homes, People with Disabilities, Senior Services,

Shelters/Homelessness, YMCA/YWCA/YMHA/YWHA, Youth Organizations

Application Procedures

Initial Contact: Send cover letter and full proposal. Include purpose of funds sought, amount requested, total funds needed for project, source of other funds to be used or sought, proof of tax-exempt status, and certification that such status has not been revoked. There are no deadlines.

Foundation Officials

Dennis M. Fitzgerald: vice president, secretary, director

Michael C. Fitzgerald: director

Linda T. Murray: assistant secretary, director

Eloise Schundler: assistant secretary, director

Robert C. Thomson, Jr.: president, treasurer, director

Gertrude Whalen: director

Grants Analysis

Disclosure Period: calendar year ending 2000
Total Grants: $506,100*
Number of Grants: 25
Average Grant: $16,754*
Highest Grant: $104,000
Typical Range: $5,000 to $30,000
*Note: Giving excludes scholarship. Average grant figure excludes highest grant.

Recent Grants

Note: Grants derived from 1999 Form 990.

General

110,000	Camp Speers Eljabar YMCA -- camp scholarships, aid toward building one new cabin, rehabilitation of other cabins and equipment
65,000	Acquinas High School -- scholarship aid, educational equipment and supplies
50,000	Scotch Plains - Fanwood Board of Education -- educational supplies
50,000	Wolfeboro Area Children's Center Inc. -- aid and supplies for educational programs and children activities
40,000	Presbyterian Church of Westfield, N.J., Westfield, NJ -- aid for internship programs and assistance for the needy
20,000	Family YMCA of the Tarrytowns -- building renovations
15,000	Greenville Presbyterian Theological Seminary, Greenville, SC
15,000	Warm The Children Fund, Gloversville, NY -- providing new winter clothing for needy children
15,000	Westfield Daycare Center
10,000	Brewster Academy, Chicago, IL

VESUVIUS FOUNDATION

Giving Contact

John Culbertson
c/o PNC Bank
Two PNC Plaza
620 Liberty Avenue
Pittsburgh, PA 15222-2719
Phone: (412)762-3390

Description

Founded: 1966
EIN: 256076182
Organization Type: Private Foundation
Giving Locations: PA: Allegheny County and Southwestern part of state
Grant Types: General Support.

Financial Summary

Total Giving: $207,000 (2001); $254,000 (2000); $233,200 (1999)
Assets: $3,514,670 (2001); $4,100,999 (2000); $4,705,685 (1999)

Typical Recipients

Arts & Humanities: Arts Associations & Councils, Arts Centers, Arts Festivals, Ballet, Community Arts, Dance, Arts & Humanities-General, History & Archaeology, Libraries, Museums/Galleries, Music, Opera, Performing Arts, Theater
Civic & Public Affairs: Business/Free Enterprise, Clubs, Community Foundations, Employment/Job Training, Civic & Public Affairs-General, Parades/Festivals, Urban & Community Affairs, Zoos/Aquariums
Education: Arts/Humanities Education, Colleges & Universities, Education Funds, Environmental Education, Literacy, Medical Education, Minority Education, Private Education (Precollege)
Environment: Environment-General, Resource Conservation
Health: Alzheimers Disease, Clinics/Medical Centers, Emergency/Ambulance Services, Eyes/Blindness, Health Organizations, Hospices, Hospitals, Medical Rehabilitation, Medical Research, Outpatient Health Care, Public Health, Single-Disease Health Associations
International: International Environmental Issues
Science: Scientific Centers & Institutes
Social Services: Big Brother/Big Sister, Child Welfare, Community Service Organizations, Day Care, Domestic Violence, Family Planning, Family Services, Homes, Recreation & Athletics, Senior Services, Sexual Abuse, Shelters/Homelessness, United Funds/United Ways, YMCA/YWCA/YMHA/YWHA

Application Procedures

Initial Contact: Send a brief letter of inquiry.
Application Requirements: Include a description of organization, amount requested, and purpose of funds sought.
Deadlines: None.

Restrictions

Grants are not made to individuals.

Additional Information

Trust(s): PNC Advisors

Foundation Officials

Frank L. Arensberg, II: trustee
Robert L. Mayer: trustee
Evans Rose, Jr.: trustee
Herman Campbell Stuckeman: trustee B Pittsburgh, PA August 07, 1914. ED Pennsylvania State University BS (1937). CLUB AFFIL Pittsburgh Athletic Association; Rotary Club; Duquesne Club; Longue Vue Club.
Harry A. Thompson: trustee
Jane A. Thompson: trustee

Grants Analysis

Disclosure Period: calendar year ending 2001
Total Grants: $207,000
Number of Grants: 34
Average Grant: $6,088
Highest Grant: $20,000
Lowest Grant: $1,000
Typical Range: $1,000 to $10,000

Recent Grants

Note: Grants derived from 2001 Form 990.

General

20,000	Foundation for Independent Colleges, Mechanicsburg, PA

11,500	University of Pittsburgh, Pittsburgh, PA
10,000	Brasher Association, Pittsburgh, PA
10,000	Extra-Mile Education Foundation, Inc., Pittsburgh, PA
10,000	FAME, Pittsburgh, PA
10,000	Family Resources Administration, Pittsburgh, PA
10,000	Pittsburgh Youth Symphony Orchestra Association, Pittsburgh, PA
10,000	Pittsburgh Zoo and Aquarium, Pittsburgh, PA
10,000	Planned Parenthood of Western Pennsylvania, Pittsburgh, PA
10,000	Saltworks Theater Company, Pittsburgh, PA

G. UNGER VETLESEN FOUNDATION

Giving Contact

George Rowe, Jr., President & Director
One Rockefeller Plaza
Suite 301
New York, NY 10020-2002
Phone: (212)586-0700
Fax: (212)245-1863
E-mail: info@monellvetlesen.org
Web: http://www.monellvetlesen.org

Description

Founded: 1955
EIN: 131982695
Organization Type: General Purpose Foundation
Giving Locations: MA; NY: nationally.
Grant Types: General Support.

Donor Information

Founder: Established in 1955 by the late George Unger Vetlesen .

Financial Summary

Total Giving: $4,730,000 (2001); $4,724,763 (2000); $4,427,500 (1999)
Assets: $86,579,908 (2001); $109,955,733 (2000); $92,989,287 (1999)

Typical Recipients

Arts & Humanities: Libraries, Museums/Galleries
Civic & Public Affairs: Clubs, Ethnic Organizations, Civic & Public Affairs-General, Nonprofit Management, Professional & Trade Associations, Public Policy, Zoos/Aquariums
Education: Colleges & Universities, Education Funds, Education-General, International Studies, Leadership Training, Medical Education, School Volunteerism, Science/Mathematics Education, Special Education, Student Aid
Environment: Air/Water Quality, Energy, Forestry, Environment-General, Resource Conservation, Wildlife Protection
Health: Medical Research
International: Foreign Arts Organizations, Foreign Educational Institutions, International Environmental Issues, International Organizations, International Peace & Security Issues, International Relations
Religion: Churches
Science: Observatories & Planetariums, Observatories & Planetariums, Scientific Centers & Institutes, Scientific Labs, Scientific Organizations, Scientific Research
Social Services: Recreation & Athletics, Volunteer Services

Application Procedures

Initial Contact: Applicants should submit a full proposal, including an outline of the program or project to be funded, and amount of funding requested.
Deadlines: None.

Foundation Officials

Eugene P. Grisanti: director B Buffalo, NY 1929. ED College of the Holy Cross AB (1951); Boston University LLB (1953); Harvard University LLM (1954).
Joseph T. C. Hart: secretary
Ambrose K. Monell: director
Laura Naus: secretary
George Rowe, Jr.: president, treasurer, director B Ossining, NY 1922. ED Yale University AB (1943); Columbia University LLB (1948). PRIM CORP EMPL partner: Fulton, Duncombe & Rowe. CORP AFFIL director: International Flavors & Fragrances Inc.

Grants Analysis

Disclosure Period: calendar year ending 2001
Total Grants: $4,730,000
Number of Grants: 22
Average Grant: $94,000*
Highest Grant: $1,100,000
Lowest Grant: $2,500
Typical Range: $25,000 to $150,000
***Note:** Average grant figure excludes three highest grants ($2,850,000).

Recent Grants

Note: Grants derived from 2001 Form 990.

General

1,100,000	Woods Hole Oceanographic Institute, Woods Hole, MA
900,000	Scripps Oceanographic Institute, Claremont, CA -- Global Change Program
600,000	Lamont-Doherty Earth Observatory, Columbia, NY
250,000	Lamont-Doherty Earth Observatory, Columbia, NY -- for Climate Center Programs
250,000	Marine Biological Laboratories, Woods Hole, MA -- Center for Comparative Molecular Biology
182,500	University of Rhode Island, Kingston, RI -- Graduate school of Oceanography
150,000	Oregon State University, Corvallis, OR -- for the College of Oceanic and Atmospheric Sciences
150,000	University of Miami, Miami, FL -- climate studies at the Rosenstiel School of Marine and Atmospheric Science
150,000	University of Texas Institute of Geophysics, Austin, TX -- Climate Modeling Program
150,000	University of Washington, Seattle, WA -- Center of Excellence at the College of Ocean and Fishery Sciences

VICKSBURG FOUNDATION

Giving Contact

William Oswalt, President
PO Box 177
Vicksburg, MI 49097
Phone: (616)343-2638
Fax: (616)649-0948

Description

Founded: 1943
EIN: 386065237
Organization Type: Private Foundation
Giving Locations: MI: with emphasis on Vicksburg or S.E. Kalamazoo County
Grant Types: Award, Capital, Emergency, Employee Matching Gifts, General Support, Operating Expenses, Project.

Financial Summary

Total Giving: $238,194 (2001); $335,596 (2000); $248,001 (1998)
Giving Analysis: Giving for 2000 includes: foundation grants to United Way ($10,000); foundation scholarships ($16,000); 1998: foundation grants to United Way ($10,500) foundation scholarships ($16,000)
Assets: $4,729,962 (2001); $5,294,738 (2000); $5,405,862 (1998)
Gifts Received: $36,243 (2000); $46,671 (1998); $51,477 (1996). Note: In 1995 and 2000, contributions were received from the Stanley J. Herman Charitable Unitrust.

Typical Recipients

Arts & Humanities: Arts Funds, Arts Institutes, History & Archaeology, Libraries, Museums/Galleries
Civic & Public Affairs: Community Foundations, Civic & Public Affairs-General, Law & Justice, Municipalities/Towns, Safety, Urban & Community Affairs
Education: Agricultural Education, Arts/Humanities Education, Business Education, Colleges & Universities, Education Funds, Education Reform, Education-General, Private Education (Precollege), Public Education (Precollege), Student Aid
Health: Emergency/Ambulance Services, Hospices, Nursing Services
International: Foreign Arts Organizations
Religion: Churches
Social Services: Camps, Community Centers, Community Service Organizations, Crime Prevention, Delinquency & Criminal Rehabilitation, Family Services, People with Disabilities, Scouts, Scouts, Senior Services, United Funds/United Ways, YMCA/YWCA/YMHA/YWHA, Youth Organizations

Application Procedures

Initial Contact: Send a brief letter of inquiry describing program. Include a description of organization, amount requested, and proof of tax-exempt status.
Deadlines: None.

Restrictions

Priority is given to organizations which contribute to the betterment of life in the Vicksburg or southeast Kalamazoo County areas.

Additional Information

Trust(s): National City Bank of MI/IL

Foundation Officials

Dr. Lloyd Appell: director
Dennis Boyle: director
Danna Downing: director
Barbara Hoekzema: secretary, treasurer
Warren Lawrence: director
William Oswalt: president

Grants Analysis

Disclosure Period: calendar year ending 2000
Total Grants: $309,596*
Number of Grants: 21
Average Grant: $14,743
Highest Grant: $40,750
Typical Range: $5,000 to $25,000
***Note:** Giving excludes United Way; scholarships.

Recent Grants

Note: Grants derived from 1999 Form 990.

Library-Related

4,207	Vicksburg District Library, Vicksburg, MI -- equipment

General

204,600	Kalamazoo Foundation, Kalamazoo, MI -- operations, scholarships
36,500	Vicksburg Community Schools, Vicksburg, MI -- operations, scholarships
16,148	Kalamazoo College, Kalamazoo, MI -- programs, scholarships
16,000	Village of Vicksburg, Vicksburg, MI -- operations, recreation
11,400	Vicksburg Police Department, Vicksburg, MI -- equipment
10,000	United Way, Vicksburg, MI -- operations
10,000	Waskeshma Township, Fulton, MI -- equipment
8,000	Western Michigan University, Kalamazoo, MI -- scholarships
5,000	Boy Scout Troop 235, Vicksburg, MI -- equipment
5,000	Girl Scout Council, Kalamazoo, MI -- operations

VICTORIA FOUNDATION

Giving Contact

Catherine M. McFarland, Secretary & Executive Officer
946 Bloomfield Avenue
Glen Ridge, NJ 07028
Phone: (973)748-5300
Fax: (973)748-0016
E-mail: catherinemcfarland@victoriafoundation.org
Web: http://www.victoriafoundation.org

Description

Founded: 1924
EIN: 221554541
Organization Type: General Purpose Foundation
Giving Locations: NJ: Newark
Grant Types: Capital, Challenge, Emergency, Fellowship, General Support, Loan, Matching, Multiyear/ Continuing Support, Operating Expenses, Project, Research, Seed Money.

Donor Information

Founder: Established in 1924 by Hendon Chubb.

Financial Summary

Total Giving: $9,576,200 (2001); $10,128,366 (1999); $9,812,204 (1998)
Assets: $205,149,337 (2001); $231,846,806 (1999); $225,978,744 (1998)

Typical Recipients

Arts & Humanities: History & Archaeology, Libraries, Museums/Galleries, Music, Performing Arts
Civic & Public Affairs: African American Affairs, Clubs, Economic Development, Employment/Job Training, Civic & Public Affairs-General, Hispanic Affairs, Housing, Nonprofit Management, Urban & Community Affairs, Women's Affairs
Education: Afterschool/Enrichment Programs, Arts/ Humanities Education, Colleges & Universities, Community & Junior Colleges, Education Associations, Education Reform, Elementary Education (Private), Engineering/Technological Education, Environmental Education, Education-General, Gifted & Talented Programs, Medical Education, Minority Education, Private Education (Precollege), Public Education (Precollege), Science/Mathematics Education, Secondary Education (Private), Special Education, Student Aid, Student Aid
Environment: Air/Water Quality, Environment-General, Resource Conservation
Health: Children's Health/Hospitals, Clinics/Medical Centers, Research/Studies Institutes
Religion: Religious Welfare, Seminaries
Science: Science Museums
Social Services: Child Welfare, Community Centers, Community Service Organizations, Day Care, Emergency Relief, Family Planning, Family Services, Food/ Clothing Distribution, People with Disabilities, Scouts, Shelters/Homelessness, Substance Abuse, United Funds/United Ways, YMCA/YWCA/YMHA/YWHA, Youth Organizations

Application Procedures

Initial Contact: Applicants should contact the foundation for complete guidelines before submitting a proposal. For land acquisition grants, applicants should submit a one-page letter of inquiry. Foundation staff will invite a full proposal for land acquisition grants after reviewing letters of inquiry.

Application Requirements: Letter of inquiry for land acquisition grants should include a summary of project, estimated total cost, amount requested, maps of property and of the surrounding area, with time of closing.

Proposals for other grants should include a one-page cover sheet, which includes organization information, contact person and telephone, mission, services offered, population served, summary of request (one or two sentences) and amount sought; one-page project summary; operating budget for organization, with itemized projected budget and sources of revenue for fiscal year; one-page project budget, with itemized expenses and names and sources of revenue; narrative describing project and plans for coming year (five pages or less), including purpose of organization, need or problem to be addressed, program objectives, how project will be implemented, time table, project staff and project highlights and accomplishments of the past year (if it's a continuous project); evaluation statement describing how the effectiveness of project will be assessed; report of most recent foundation grant, if applicable (if final report has already been submitted, do not resubmit); list of project staff; list of board of directors and their affiliations; recent annual report; audited financial statement; and a copy of most recent IRS tax-exempt letter.

Deadlines: February 1 for a decision in June, August 1 for a decision in December; proposals from schools are due by March 1 for funding in the beginning of September; None, for land acquisition grants.

Review Process: Proposals are reviewed by trustee committees that make recommendations to the full board for decision. If a proposal falls within foundation guidelines and foundation priorities permit consideration of the grant request, additional information about the organization or project may be requested. As part of the evaluation process, staff members may make site visits to speak directly with project staff and/or board members and to see the organization's work first-hand.

Notes: The foundation also accepts the New York/New Jersey Area Common Application Form, but applicants must use the foundation's cover sheet as described above.

Proposals that are incomplete or are received after the deadline are not considered.

Restrictions

No grants are made to individuals, either as individuals or through a sponsoring organization.

Additional Information

Organizations may submit proposals only once a year.

Foundation asks that organizations not fax proposals. Applicants are encouraged to call or write the foundation for a copy of their application package.

Grantees must submit detailed periodic reports.

Publications: Annual Report; Grant Guidelines; Application form

Foundation Officials

Charles M. Chapin, III: trustee ED Princeton University (1958).

Percy Chubb, III: president, trustee B New York, NY 1934. ED Yale University BA (1956). PRIM CORP EMPL director: Chubb Corp. CORP AFFIL director: Federal Insurance Co.; director: Chubb Colonial Life Insurance Co.; vice chairman, director: Chubb & Son Inc.; vice chairman, director: Bellemead Development Corp. NONPR AFFIL trustee: Mystic Seaport Museum; director: New Jersey Center Performing Arts.

Sally Chubb: trustee NONPR AFFIL chairwoman board: Matheny School & Hospital.

Robert Curvin, PhD: trustee

Catherine M. McFarland: executive off, secretary CORP AFFIL director: Broad National Bancorporation.

Gordon A. Millspaugh, Jr.: assistant treasurer, trustee B 1934. ED Princeton University AB (1956); Harvard University LLB (1959). PRIM CORP EMPL partner: Herold & Haines.

Franklin E. Parker, IV: trustee

John Parker: trustee

Margaret H. Parker: vice president, trustee

Sara Chubb Sauvayre: trustee

Kevin Shanley: treasurer, trustee B New York, NY 1942. ED University of Pennsylvania (1964); Harvard University Graduate School of Business Administration (1976). PRIM CORP EMPL president, chief executive officer: Alliance Companies. CORP AFFIL chief executive officer: Memorial Investment Corp.; director: Bellemead Development Corp.; chief executive officer: Integrated Health Products. NONPR AFFIL chairman, director: Newark Museum Association.

William Turnbull: trustee

Dr. A. Zachary Yamba: trustee PRIM NONPR EMPL president: Essex Community College.

Grants Analysis

Disclosure Period: calendar year ending 2001
Total Grants: $9,576,200*
Number of Grants: 132
Average Grant: $63,575*
Highest Grant: $900,000
Lowest Grant: $1,000
Typical Range: $25,000 to $100,000
*Note: Grants analysis provided by foundation.

Recent Grants

Note: Grants derived from 2000 Form 990.

General

500,406	Newark Museum Association, Newark, NJ
500,405	Newark Museum Association, Newark, NJ
500,367	Newark Museum Association, Newark, NJ
500,000	Bank Street College of Education, New York, NY
500,000	Bank Street College of Education, New York, NY
500,000	New Community Corporation, Newark, NJ
500,000	New Jersey Performing Arts Center, Newark, NJ
500,000	St. Phillip's Academy, Newark, NJ
400,000	Trust for Public Land, New York, NY -- for the New Jersey field office
250,000	Community Agencies Corp of New Jersey, Newark, NJ -- toward purchase of a headquarters building

VIRGINIA ENVIRONMENTAL ENDOWMENT

Giving Contact

Gerald P. McCarthy, Executive Director
PO Box 790
Richmond, VA 23218
Phone: (804)644-5000
Fax: (804)644-0603
E-mail: info@vee.org
Web: http://www.vee.org

Alternate Contact

Three James Center
1051 East Cary Street, Suite 1400
Richmond, VA 23219

Description

Founded: 1977
EIN: 541041973
Organization Type: Specialized/Single Purpose Foundation
Giving Locations: DC; KY; MD; OH
Grant Types: Challenge, General Support, Matching, Project, Research.

Financial Summary

Total Giving: $1,689,318 (fiscal year ending March 31, 2001); $819,317 (fiscal 2000); $1,000,735 (fiscal 1999)
Giving Analysis: Giving for fiscal 2001 includes: foundation matching gifts ($1,664,080)
Assets: $17,372,200 (fiscal 2001); $21,504,403 (fiscal 2000); $19,112,512 (fiscal 1999)
Gifts Received: $50,000 (fiscal 1992). Note: In fiscal 1992, the endowment received settlement funds from IR International, Inc., and from Hauni Richmond, Inc.

Typical Recipients

Arts & Humanities: Historic Preservation, History & Archaeology, Libraries

Civic & Public Affairs: Botanical Gardens/Parks, Economic Development, Civic & Public Affairs-General, Housing, Municipalities/Towns, Nonprofit Management, Public Policy, Rural Affairs, Urban & Community Affairs, Zoos/Aquariums

Education: Business Education, Colleges & Universities, Economic Education, Education Reform, Elementary Education (Private), Elementary Education (Public), Engineering/Technological Education, Environmental Education, Faculty Development, Science/Mathematics Education

Environment: Air/Water Quality, Energy, Environment-General, Protection, Resource Conservation, Watershed, Wildlife Protection

Religion: Religious Welfare

Science: Science Museums, Scientific Labs, Scientific Research

Social Services: Family Services

Application Procedures

Initial Contact: Applicants should request guidelines; special eligibility guidelines for the Virginia Mini-Grant Program should be noted.

Application Requirements: Two copies of a full proposal must be sent. Each proposal should include the following: a cover letter identifying the applicant, project title, grant request, matching funds in equal amounts, project schedule, and whether the proposal is being submitted to the Virginia Program, the Virginia Mini-Grant Program, or the Kanawaha and Ohio River Valleys Program. Letter should be signed by the organization's chief executive officer or board chairman. Include a project description, limited to five pages, clearly stating the need for the project, goals and objectives, and how they will be achieved, and relevance to other work being done in the field; a description of organization, names and qualifications of key project staff, a list of the members of the governing board, the current operating budget, and a copy of the current tax-exempt ruling from the Internal Revenue Service, if applicable; a line-item budget for the proposed project, showing total project cost, the amount and proposed allocation of grant funds requested from the Endowment, and all sources and amounts of matching funds (committed and anticipated); the project schedule, with specific beginning and ending dates for requested grant support; a detailed plan for evaluating and disseminating project results; and plans for continuing project activities and raising financial support beyond the grant period. Proposals should indicate a thorough assessment of related activities in the target community, identify partnerships for collaboration, and include one or two letters of support.

Deadlines: For the Virginia Program and Virginia Mini-Grant Program: March 15, August 1, and December 1; for the Kanawha and Ohio River Valleys Program: March 15 only. When the date falls on a weekend or holiday, the following business day will be the deadline. Complete proposals must be received by the deadlines; late proposals will not be accepted.

Review Process: The Endowment does not review or comment on preliminary proposals. The board of directors meets three times a year.

Notes: The Endowment has a strict policy on receipt of complete proposals by deadlines. Without exception, late proposals will not be accepted. Proposals may not be submitted by facsimile; please do not include videotapes with grant proposals.

Restrictions

Grants are made to nonprofit, tax-exempt organizations and governmental agencies. Typically, matching funds are required and challenge grants may be offered. Grant funds are not provided for overhead, indirect costs, building renovation or construction, endowments, lawsuits or individuals. Proposals outside of geographic limitations are not reviewed.

Special eligibility guidelines apply to the Virginia Mini-grant Program.

Applicants are asked not to apply to the Endowment more than once a year.

Additional Information

Grantees are required to submit periodic progress reports and lists of expenditures as well as final evaluation reports. Approved grants are paid in installments pending receipt of reports.

Local projects should demonstrate potential to serve as models for other communities and include specific plans for dissemination. Education projects must include a teacher-training element. Partnerships among nonprofits, government agencies, and the private sector are encouraged.

Publications: Annual Report

Foundation Officials

Dixon M. Butler: president, director
Paul U. Elbling: director, treasurer
Robert Freeman: director
A. Linwood Holton, Jr.: director B Big Stone Gap, VA 1923. ED Washington & Lee University BA (1944); Harvard University LLB (1949); Virginia State College LLD (1971); Virginia Union University LLD (1972); Washington & Lee University LLD (1972); College of William & Mary LLD (1973). PRIM CORP EMPL partner: Mezzulo & McCandlish. CORP AFFIL director: Interstate Railroad Co. NONPR AFFIL member: Virginia Bar Association; member: Virginia State Bar; member: Roanoke Bar Association; chairman: University Virginia Burket Miller Center Public Affairs; member: District of Columbia Bar Association; member: Omicron Delta Kappa; member: American Bar Association.
Patricia Kluge: vice president, director
Gerald Patrick McCarthy: executive director, secretary B New York, NY 1943. ED Manhattan College BEE (1965); University of Washington MS (1967). NONPR AFFIL member advisory board: Virginia Department Games Fisheries; member: Virginia Water Center Advisory Board; member: Virginia Conservation & Recreation Foundation; board directors: National Conference Christians & Jews; member: Richmond First; member: Conservation Leadership Project; visiting professor environmental studies: Duke University. CLUB AFFIL 2300 Club; Bull & Bear Club.
Alson H. Smith, Jr.: sr vice president, director PRIM CORP EMPL officer: Jefferson Bankshares Inc.

Grants Analysis

Disclosure Period: fiscal year ending March 31, 2001
Total Grants: $1,689,318*
Number of Grants: 38

Average Grant: $28,384*
Highest Grant: $639,092
Lowest Grant: $300
Typical Range: $1,000 to $5,000 and $10,000 to $30,000
***Note:** Giving includes matching gifts. Average grant excludes highest grant.

Recent Grants

Note: Grants derived from 2001 Form 990.

Library-Related

1,000	Foundation Center, New York, NY -- for the Philanthropic Center

General

105,399	University of Virginia, Charlottesville, VA -- for creating environmentally wired kids through the use of wireless technology
65,000	American Farmland Trust, Culpepper, VA -- for Virginia Rural Lands Program
61,554	Virginia Polytechnic Institute, Blacksburg, VA -- expanding the soil factors of the Virginia phosphorus index
60,000	Kentucky Waterways Alliance, Munfordville, KY -- for watershed
50,000	Department of Environmental Quality, Richmond, VA -- for Virginia Classroom Grants Program
47,650	League of Conservation Voters, Washington, DC -- testing the viability of a natural resources funding campaign
45,000	Alliance for the Chesapeake Bay, Baltimore, MD -- for builders for the bay
40,000	University of Virginia Institute for Environmental Negotiation, Charlottesville, VA -- for the Virginia Environmental Conflict Resolution Project
30,000	University of Charleston, Charleston, WV -- for Kanawha River Project
23,000	Friends of Chesterfield's Riverfront, Chesterfield, VA -- for exemplary environmental community pilot study

VIYU FOUNDATION

Giving Contact

William Dann, Trustee
591 Main Street
East Aurora, NY 14052-1753
Phone: (716)655-3830

Description

Founded: 1991
EIN: 043064835
Organization Type: Private Foundation
Giving Locations: NY: Western New York state
Grant Types: General Support.

Donor Information

Founder: Established in 1991 by Mr. and Mrs. William Dann.

Financial Summary

Total Giving: $96,000 (fiscal year ending July 31, 2001); $96,500 (fiscal 2000); $82,000 (fiscal 1999)
Giving Analysis: Giving for fiscal 2001 includes: foundation grants to United Way ($7,000); fiscal 2000: foundation grants to United Way ($7,000) fiscal 1999: foundation grants to United Way ($6,000)
Assets: $1,614,554 (fiscal 2001); $1,722,789 (fiscal 2000); $2,014,740 (fiscal 1999)
Gifts Received: $185,280 (fiscal 1999); $257,725 (fiscal 1997); $124,500 (fiscal 1995). Note: In fiscal 1995 and fiscal 1999, contributions were received from Marion Dann.

Typical Recipients

Arts & Humanities: Historic Preservation, History & Archaeology, Libraries, Music
Civic & Public Affairs: Botanical Gardens/Parks
Education: Private Education (Precollege), Special Education, Student Aid
Environment: Environment-General, Protection
Health: Hospices, Hospitals, Medical Rehabilitation, Medical Research, Public Health, Single-Disease Health Associations
Religion: Religious Welfare, Seminaries
Science: Science Museums
Social Services: Animal Protection, Camps, Family Services, Food/Clothing Distribution, People with Disabilities, United Funds/United Ways

Application Procedures

Initial Contact: Send a brief letter of inquiry.
Deadlines: None.

Foundation Officials

Jesse Dann: trustee
Marion Dann: trustee
William Dann: trustee
William R. Dann, Jr.: trustee
E. W. Dann Stevens: trustee ED Harvard College AB (1948); Cornell University JD (1951). PRIM CORP EMPL of counsel: Hiscock & Barclay.

Grants Analysis

Disclosure Period: fiscal year ending July 31, 2001
Total Grants: $89,000*
Number of Grants: 20
Average Grant: $4,450
Highest Grant: $5,000
Lowest Grant: $1,000
Typical Range: $1,000 to $5,000
***Note:** Giving excludes United Way.

Recent Grants

Note: Grants derived from 2001 Form 990.

Library-Related

1,000	Buffalo 7 Erie County Public Library, Buffalo, NY

General

10,000	Salvation Army, Buffalo, NY
7,000	United Way Buffalo and Erie County, Buffalo, NY
5,000	Beaver Meadow Audubon Society, Buffalo, NY
5,000	Blind Association of Western New York, Buffalo, NY
5,000	Buffalo Museum of Science, Buffalo, NY
5,000	Buffalo Philharmonic Orchestra Society, Buffalo, NY
5,000	Buffalo Seminary, Buffalo, NY
5,000	Effective Parenting, Buffalo, NY
5,000	Food Bank of Western New York, Buffalo, NY
5,000	Hospice of Buffalo, Buffalo, NY

VODAFONE GROUP PLC

Company Headquarters

The Courtyard
2-4 London Rd.
Newbury RG14 1JX, United Kingdom
Web: http://www.vodafone.com

Company Description

Founded: 1982
Ticker: VOD
Exchange: NYSE
Revenue: US$34.77 billion (2001)
SIC(s): 4813 Telephone Communications Except Radiotelephone, 4899 Communications Services Nec.

Nonmonetary Support

Volunteer Programs: Company actively promotes and encourages volunteerism, both through its grantmaking and internal policies.

Vodaphone-US Foundation

Giving Contact

Sam Ginn, Chairman & President
2999 Oak Rd., 9th Floor
Walnut Creek, CA 94597
Phone: (925)210-3870

Description

Founded: 1993
EIN: 680315367
Organization Type: Corporate Foundation
Formed by Merger of: Vodafone Group (1999).
Former Name: Airtouch Communications Foundation (2000).
Giving Locations: AZ; CA, San Francisco, Walnut Creek; CO; DC: Washington; GA: Atlanta; ID; IA; MI; MN; NE; NM; ND; OH; OR; TX: Dallas; UT; WA; WY areas where company provides cellular and paging operations.
Grant Types: General Support, Project.

Financial Summary

Total Giving: $1,341,500 (2001); $1,740,000 (2000); $1,637,150 (1999). Note: Fiscal 1996 Giving includes scholarship ($16,000); United Way ($255,000).
Giving Analysis: Giving for 2000 includes foundation grants to United Way ($365,000); foundation ($1,375,000); 1998: foundation grants to United Way ($330,000) foundation ($556,200)
Assets: $29,042,041 (2001); $32,361,623 (2000); $35,066,455 (1999)
Gifts Received: $19,300 (2000); $33,567 (1999); $1,181,240 (1996). Note: In 2000, contributions were received from Vodafone Group plc/Air Touch. In 1996, contributions were received from Airtouch Communications, Inc. and Airtouch Cellular.

Typical Recipients

Arts & Humanities: Arts Associations & Councils, Arts Centers, Arts Festivals, Arts Funds, Ballet, Ethnic & Folk Arts, Arts & Humanities-General, History & Archaeology, Libraries, Museums/Galleries, Music, Opera, Performing Arts, Theater
Civic & Public Affairs: Asian American Affairs, Business/Free Enterprise, Community Foundations, Economic Development, Employment/Job Training, Civic & Public Affairs-General, Housing, Legal Aid, Nonprofit Management, Professional & Trade Associations, Public Policy, Women's Affairs, Zoos/Aquariums
Education: Afterschool/Enrichment Programs, Arts/Humanities Education, Business Education, Colleges & Universities, Continuing Education, Economic Education, Education Funds, Elementary Education (Public), Education-General, International Studies, Literacy, Minority Education, Public Education (Precollege), Science/Mathematics Education, Student Aid
Environment: Environment-General, Resource Conservation
Health: AIDS/HIV, Cancer, Children's Health/Hospitals, Emergency/Ambulance Services, Eyes/Blindness, Public Health, Research/Studies Institutes
International: International Relations, International Relief Efforts
Religion: Religious Welfare
Science: Science Museums, Scientific Centers & Institutes
Social Services: Child Abuse, Child Welfare, Community Service Organizations, Emergency Relief, Family Planning, Family Services, Recreation & Athletics, Scouts, Social Services-General, United Funds/United Ways, Volunteer Services, YMCA/YWCA/YMHA/YWHA, YMCA/YWCA/YMHA/YWHA, Youth Organizations

Application Procedures

Initial Contact: Send a letter requesting detailed guidelines.
Application Requirements: The letter should include background information about the organization and its mission, population served, and its unique role in the community; a description of the program for which funding is requested, including evidence of need, project budget, and how success will be measured; how the organization/program fits the guidelines of foundation; a description of how program/project results will be reported to the foundation; list of the board of directors and their affiliations; and current operating budget, including pending and/or committed sources of income. Copies of the organization's most recent tax return, audited financial statements, and IRS 501(c)(3) determination letter should be provided. affiliations.
Deadlines: None.
Evaluative Criteria: Preference is given to organizations that: seek and achieve excellence in their leadership, client service, operations and results; have an open and cooperative relationship with other community groups in order to most effectively solve problems and avoid duplication of effort and resources; seek funding for projects that are central to their missions; can show how their programs and projects achieve their intended results; are committed to sustaining the positive results of their work.
Decision Notification: The foundation will review and respond to proposals within 4 to 6 weeks.

Restrictions

The foundation generally does not make grants to support capital or endowment campaigns, fundraising events or goodwill advertising (including benefits), sports activities, cause-related marketing, memberships, emergency appeal or re-granting organizations. The foundation does not provide any Vodafone Communications products or services, nor does it support individuals; political organizations; religious organizations seeking grants for sectarian purposes; fraternal, veteran or labor groups; individual K-12 schools or school districts; or medical clinics or medical research. In addition, the foundation will not support organizations that practice unlawful discrimination in the provision of services.

Additional Information

Priority areas are: "Safe Communities," which includes support of efforts that promote neighborhood security through citizen involvement and that enhance the personal safety of the most vulnerable members of society, and "Transitional Assistance," which includes support of programs and projects that forge connections between people and give them the tools to become contributing and productive members of society.
In 1999, Vodafone Group acquired AirTouch Communications. The company is now known as Vodafone AirTouch Plc.
In 1999, Vodaphone Group acquired AirTouch Communications. The company is now known as Vodaphone AirTouch Plc.
Publications: Guidelines; Foundation Application Procedures; Foundation Grants Report

Grants Analysis

Disclosure Period: calendar year ending 2001
Total Grants: $1,341,500
Number of Grants: 65
Average Grant: $9,944*
Highest Grant: $500,000
Lowest Grant: $200
Typical Range: $1,500 to $25,000
*Note: Average grant figure excludes three highest grants ($725,000).

Recent Grants

Note: Grants derived from 2001 Form 990.

General

500,000	American Red Cross Bay Area Chapter, San Francisco, CA -- disaster relief fund
125,000	San Francisco Symphony Association, San Francisco, CA -- youth orchestra and instrument training
100,000	Yosemite Foundation, San Francisco, CA -- for Yosemite Falls campaign
30,000	Community Foundation of the Nappa Valley, Napa Valley, CA -- Arts for Youth Project
30,000	Saint Paul Chamber Orchestra, St. Paul, MN -- Dance in Schools Program
25,000	California Voter Foundation, Sacramento, CA -- monitoring election reform legislation and voter education
25,000	San Francisco Bay Area Boy Scouts Council, San Francisco, CA -- capital campaign
25,000	San Francisco Opera, San Francisco, CA -- for Adler Residency Program
25,000	Smuin Ballet, San Francisco, CA -- for the Christmas Ballet
25,000	YMCA of San Francisco, San Francisco, CA -- community development campaign

VOGEL FOUNDATION

Giving Contact

David L. Vogel, President
PO Box 7696
Madison, WI 53707-7696
Phone: (608)241-5454

Description

Founded: 1989
EIN: 391639595
Organization Type: Private Foundation
Giving Locations: FL: Lakeland; WI: Madison
Grant Types: Capital, General Support, Scholarship.

Financial Summary

Total Giving: $35,650 (2001); $36,550 (2000); $31,739 (1999)
Assets: $604,069 (2001); $682,210 (2000); $823,113 (1999)
Gifts Received: $250 (1996); $2,663 (1994); $25,000 (1992). Note: In 1992, contributions were received from Vogel Bros. Building Co.

Typical Recipients

Arts & Humanities: Libraries, Museums/Galleries, Public Broadcasting
Civic & Public Affairs: Economic Development, Civic & Public Affairs-General, Housing, Parades/Festivals, Safety, Urban & Community Affairs, Zoos/Aquariums
Education: Business Education, Colleges & Universities, Engineering/Technological Education, Education-General, Preschool Education, Private Education (Precollege), Science/Mathematics Education, Social Sciences Education, Student Aid
Health: Clinics/Medical Centers, Hospices, Prenatal Health Issues
Religion: Churches, Ministries, Religious Welfare
Social Services: Animal Protection, Camps, Community Centers, Homes, People with Disabilities, United Funds/United Ways, YMCA/YWCA/YMHA/YWHA, Youth Organizations

Application Procedures

Initial Contact: The foundation has no formal grant application procedure or application form.
Application Requirements: Applications should include a full description of the project, proof of tax-exempt status, a project budget and a current organizational budget, and anticipated sources of support.
Deadlines: None.
Notes: The foundation generally provides grants in the areas of education, health, and human services.

Restrictions

Grants are not awarded to individuals or for operating expenses.

Foundation Officials

Daniel C. Vogel: vice president
David L. Vogel: president
Peter C. Vogel: secretary

Grants Analysis

Disclosure Period: calendar year ending 2001
Total Grants: $35,650
Number of Grants: 27
Average Grant: $1,320
Highest Grant: $13,000
Lowest Grant: $100
Typical Range: $500 to $3,000

Recent Grants

Note: Grants derived from 2000 Form 990.

General

13,000	Madison Urban Ministry, Madison, WI
4,000	Oakwood Foundation, Madison, WI
3,000	Lakeland Family YMCA, Lakeland, FL
2,000	Genesis Development, Jefferson, IA
1,500	Salvation Army of Lakeland, Lakeland, FL
1,500	Salvation Army of Madison, Madison, WI
1,000	Hospice Care, Madison, WI
1,000	University of Florida Foundation, Gainesville, FL
1,000	University of Wisconsin, Madison, WI
1,000	University of Wisconsin Foundation, Madison, WI

LAURA B. VOGLER FOUNDATION

Giving Contact

Lawrence L. D'Amato, President & Director
PO Box 610508
Bayside, NY 11361-0508
Phone: (718)423-3000

Description

Founded: 1959
EIN: 116022241
Organization Type: Private Foundation
Giving Locations: NY: New York City and Long Island
Grant Types: General Support, Scholarship.

Donor Information

Founder: the late Laura B. Vogler, the late John J. Vogler

Financial Summary

Total Giving: $213,400 (fiscal year ending October 31, 2001); $203,550 (fiscal 2000); $185,000 (fiscal 1997)
Giving Analysis: Giving for fiscal 2001 includes: foundation grants to United Way ($25,000) fiscal 2000: foundation scholarships ($2,500)
Assets: $4,655,110 (fiscal 2001); $5,227,028 (fiscal 2000); $4,804,314 (fiscal 1997)

Typical Recipients

Arts & Humanities: Arts Associations & Councils, Arts Outreach, History & Archaeology, Libraries, Museums/Galleries, Theater
Civic & Public Affairs: Business/Free Enterprise, Employment/Job Training, Housing, Legal Aid, Nonprofit Management, Urban & Community Affairs, Women's Affairs
Education: Afterschool/Enrichment Programs, Arts/Humanities Education, Business Education, Education-General, Literacy, Private Education (Precollege), Public Education (Precollege), School Volunteerism, Secondary Education (Public), Special Education, Student Aid
Environment: Resource Conservation
Health: AIDS/HIV, Alzheimers Disease, Cancer, Children's Health/Hospitals, Clinics/Medical Centers, Emergency/Ambulance Services, Eyes/Blindness, Geriatric Health, Health Policy/Cost Containment, Health Organizations, Home-Care Services, Hospitals, Long-Term Care, Mental Health, Nursing Services, Outpatient Health Care, Prenatal Health Issues, Preventive Medicine/Wellness Organizations, Public Health
International: Foreign Educational Institutions
Religion: Ministries, Religious Welfare
Science: Science Museums, Scientific Centers & Institutes
Social Services: At-Risk Youth, Big Brother/Big Sister, Camps, Child Abuse, Child Welfare, Community Centers, Community Service Organizations, Crime Prevention, Day Care, Delinquency & Criminal Rehabilitation, Domestic Violence, Family Planning, Family Services, Food/Clothing Distribution, Homes, People with Disabilities, Recreation & Athletics, Scouts, Senior Services, Senior Services, Shelters/Homelessness, Social Services-General, Substance Abuse, YMCA/YWCA/YMHA/YWHA, Youth Organizations

Application Procedures

Initial Contact: Request application, guidelines, and deadlines.
Deadlines: January1, April1, July1, and October1.

Restrictions

Limits grants to organizations concerned with health, well being, and education of children, the disadvantaged and the elderly.

Foundation Officials

Domenico Donald D'Amato: president, director B Brooklyn, NY May 25, 1911. ED New York University BA (1932); New York University JD (1934). NONPR AFFIL member: New York State Bar Association; member: Queens County Bar Association; member: Judge Advocates Association; life member: Kiwanis; member: American College Mortgage Attys; director: Bayside Federal Savings & Loan Association; member: American Bar Association.
Lawrence L. D'Amato: treasurer, director
Lorraine Diamond: secretary
Max Kupferberg: trustee PRIM CORP EMPL president, chief executive officer, treasurer: Kepco.
I. Jerry Lasurdo: director
Rev. Stephen S. Schwander: director
Robert T. Waldbauer: director
Karen M. Yost: director

Grants Analysis

Disclosure Period: fiscal year ending October 31, 2001
Total Grants: $188,400*
Number of Grants: 60
Average Grant: $3,140
Highest Grant: $5,000
Lowest Grant: $1,000
Typical Range: $1,000 to $5,000
*Note: Giving excludes United Way.

Recent Grants

Note: Grants derived from 2000 Form 990.

General

5,000	Calvary Hospital, Bronx, NY
5,000	Everybody Wins Foundation, Inc., New York, NY -- an intergenerational project of older people reading to mentor school children
5,000	Helen Keller Services for the Blind, Brooklyn, NY -- the preschool vision screening program
5,000	Neighbors Together Corp, Brooklyn, NY
4,350	Every Person Influences Children, Inc. (EPIC), New York, NY -- training adult facilitators for Bronx parenting workshops
4,200	Louise Wise Services, New York, NY
4,000	Friends of Island Academy, New York, NY -- assisting young people in making the transition out of incarceration into their home communities
4,000	Network for Women's Services, New York, NY
4,000	New York Service Program for Older People, New York, NY
4,000	New York Society for the Prevention of Cruelty to Children, New York, NY

HENRY VOGT MACHINE CO.

Company Headquarters

1000 W. Ormsby Ave.
Louisville, KY 40210

Company Description

Employees: 20
SIC(s): 3400 Fabricated Metal Products, 3500 Industrial Machinery & Equipment.

Operating Locations

Henry Vogt Machine Co. (KY--Louisville)

Henry Vogt Foundation

Giving Contact

Henry Henser, Jr.
1000 West Ormsby
Louisville, KY 40201-1918
Phone: (502)635-3232

Description

Founded: 1958
EIN: 237416717
Organization Type: Corporate Foundation
Giving Locations: KY: Louisville
Grant Types: Capital, General Support, Multiyear/Continuing Support.

Donor Information

Founder: Henry Vogt Machine Co.

Financial Summary

Total Giving: $172,600 (fiscal year ending June 30, 2001); $183,350 (fiscal 2000); $135,275 (fiscal 1996)
Giving Analysis: Giving for fiscal 2001 includes: foundation grants to United Way ($8,500); fiscal 2000: foundation grants to United Way ($8,500) foundation ($174,850)
Assets: $3,089,426 (fiscal 2001); $3,147,995 (fiscal 2000); $2,436,766 (fiscal 1996)
Gifts Received: In 1989, contributions were received from Henry Vogt Machine Co.

Typical Recipients

Arts & Humanities: Arts Funds, Public Broadcasting
Civic & Public Affairs: Employment/Job Training, Civic & Public Affairs-General
Education: Business Education, Colleges & Universities, Economic Education, Education Funds, Elementary Education (Public), Education-General, Private Education (Precollege), Public Education (Precollege), Vocational & Technical Education
Environment: Resource Conservation
Health: Hospitals, Mental Health
Science: Science Museums
Social Services: Community Centers, Community Service Organizations, Homes, People with Disabilities, Scouts, Senior Services, United Funds/United Ways, Youth Organizations

Application Procedures

Initial Contact: Send a brief letter of inquiry.
Application Requirements: Include a description of organization, amount requested, and purpose of funds sought.

Restrictions

Does not make grants to individuals.

Corporate Officials

Henry V. Heuser: chairman, director B Louisville, KY June 14, 1914. ED Purdue University (1936). PRIM CORP EMPL chairman, director: Henry Vogt Machine Co. CORP AFFIL director: Enterprises Inc.

Foundation Officials

Margaret S. Culver: secretary, treasurer
Henry V. Heuser, Jr.: president, director
Leland D. Schlegel, Jr.: vice president, director

Grants Analysis

Disclosure Period: fiscal year ending June 30, 2001
Total Grants: $164,100*
Number of Grants: 24
Average Grant: $6,838
Highest Grant: $20,000
Typical Range: $1,000 to $10,000
*Note: Giving excludes United Way.

Recent Grants

Note: Grants derived from fiscal 2000 Form 990.

General

20,000	Dare to Care!, Louisville, KY
18,000	Fund for the Arts, Louisville, KY
15,000	Bridgehaven, Louisville, KY
10,000	DePaul School, Louisville, KY
10,000	Elderserve, Louisville, KY
10,000	Home of the Innocents, Louisville, KY
10,000	Hospice of Palliative Care, Louisville, KY
10,000	Louisville Diversified, Louisville, KY
10,000	Meredith Dunn School, Louisville, KY
10,000	Nature Conservancy, Louisville, KY

FREDERICK A. VOLLBRECHT FOUNDATION

Giving Contact

Kenneth J. Klebba, President & Treasurer
31700 Telegraph Rd., Suite 220
Beverly Hills, MI 48025
Phone: (248)646-0627
Fax: (248)646-0338
E-mail: kklebba@collinsburi.com

Description

Founded: 1959
EIN: 386056173
Organization Type: Private Foundation

Giving Locations: MI
Grant Types: General Support, Research, Scholarship.

Donor Information

Founder: the late Frederick A. Vollbrecht

Financial Summary

Total Giving: $179,740 (2001); $194,400 (2000); $187,900 (1999)
Giving Analysis: Giving for 2001 includes: foundation scholarships ($8,000) 2000: foundation scholarships ($4,000)
Assets: $2,703,286 (2001); $2,912,597 (2000); $2,995,294 (1999)

Typical Recipients

Arts & Humanities: Libraries, Music
Civic & Public Affairs: Business/Free Enterprise, Clubs, Economic Development, Civic & Public Affairs-General, Public Policy, Urban & Community Affairs
Education: Agricultural Education, Business Education, Colleges & Universities, Community & Junior Colleges, Education-General, Literacy, Private Education (Precollege), Special Education, Student Aid
Health: Cancer, Children's Health/Hospitals, Diabetes, Emergency/Ambulance Services, Health Organizations, Heart, Hospices, Hospitals, Kidney, Medical Research, Respiratory, Single-Disease Health Associations, Speech & Hearing
Religion: Religious Welfare
Social Services: At-Risk Youth, Camps, Child Welfare, Child Welfare, Community Service Organizations, Family Services, Food/Clothing Distribution, People with Disabilities, Recreation & Athletics, Scouts, United Funds/United Ways, Youth Organizations

Application Procedures

Initial Contact: The foundation requests applications be made in writing.
Deadlines: None.

Additional Information

Publications: Annual Report

Foundation Officials

Kenneth J. Klebba: president, treasurer
Richard E. Mida: vice president, secretary

Grants Analysis

Disclosure Period: calendar year ending 2001
Total Grants: $171,740*
Number of Grants: 43
Average Grant: $3,613*
Highest Grant: $20,000
Lowest Grant: $2,000
Typical Range: $1,000 to $5,000
*Note: Giving excludes scholarships. Average grant figure excludes highest grant.

Recent Grants

Note: Grants derived from 2000 Form 990.

General

22,000	Walsh College of Accountancy and Business Administration, Troy, MI
20,000	Spaulding for Children, Southfield, MI -- "Partners" endowment
10,000	American Diabetes Association Michigan Affiliate, Inc, Bingham Farms, MI -- Camp Midicha
10,000	Community House Association, Birmingham, MI -- second of three
10,000	Variety, Charity for Children, Southfield, MI -- planned giving committee
5,000	American Association of Diabetes Educators, Chicago, IL -- second of three payments
5,000	American Diabetes Association Michigan Affiliate, Inc, Bingham Farms, MI

5,000	Beaumont Foundation, Troy, MI
5,000	Boysville of Michigan, Clinton, MI
5,000	Detroit Symphony Orchestra, Detroit, MI

VPI FOUNDATION INC.

Giving Contact

Richard L Blamey
3123 S Ninth St
Sheboygan, WI 53081-6911

Description

Founded: 1993
EIN: 391768404
Organization Type: Private Foundation

Financial Summary

Assets: $297,865 (fiscal year ending , 1993)

Typical Recipients

Arts & Humanities: Libraries, Theater
Civic & Public Affairs: Civic & Public Affairs-General
Education: Business Education, Colleges & Universities, Education Funds, Student Aid
Health: Emergency/Ambulance Services
Social Services: At-Risk Youth, United Funds/United Ways, YMCA/YWCA/YMHA/YWHA, Youth Organizations

Foundation Officials

Richard L. Blamey: secretary, treasurer, director
John Crawford: vice president, director
Carol Grover: president, director
R. Bruce Grover: vice president, director
Karen Grover Scott: director
Robert H. Leverenz: director
P. Gregory Mickelson: director
Deborah Wente: director

Recent Grants

Note: Grants derived from 2001 Form 990.

Library-Related

4,000	Manitowoc Public Library, Manitowoc, WI

General

10,000	Citizens Scholarship Fund, St. Peter, MN
7,500	United Way Sheboygan, Sheboygan, WI
6,000	Sheboygan Blue Line Association, Sheboygan, WI
5,000	Above and Beyond, Sheboygan, WI
5,000	Above and Beyond, Sheboygan, WI -- Hands On Children's Museum
5,000	Boys and Girls Club, Sheboygan, WI
5,000	JMKAC (John Michael Kohler Arts Center), Sheboygan, WI
5,000	Lakeland College, Sheboygan, WI
5,000	Manitowoc YMCA, Manitowoc, WI
5,000	Sheboygan Theater Company, Sheboygan, WI

JOHN T. VUCUREVICH FOUNDATION

Giving Contact

John T. Vucurevich, Advisory Board
c/o Wells Fargo Bank SD NA
PO Box 1040
Rapid City, SD 57709
Phone: (605)394-3821

Description

Founded: 1989
EIN: 460359829
Organization Type: Private Foundation

Giving Locations: IA; MT; SD: Rapid City; VA
Grant Types: General Support.

Donor Information

Founder: Established in 1989 by John T. Vucurevich.

Financial Summary

Total Giving: $351,415 (2001); $451,480 (2000); $344,865 (1999)
Giving Analysis: Giving for 2001 includes: foundation grants to United Way ($8,000); 2000: foundation grants to United Way ($15,000); 1999: foundation grants to United Way ($7,500);
Assets: $9,115,516 (2001); $9,556,852 (2000); $9,984,685 (1999)
Gifts Received: $100,000 (2000); $1,779,548 (1997); $103,750 (1995). Note: In 1995 and 2000, contributions were received from John T. Vucurevich.

Typical Recipients

Arts & Humanities: Arts Funds, History & Archaeology, Libraries, Museums/Galleries, Music, Opera, Performing Arts, Theater
Civic & Public Affairs: Clubs, Community Foundations, Civic & Public Affairs-General, Housing, Minority Business, Rural Affairs, Urban & Community Affairs, Women's Affairs
Education: Colleges & Universities, Engineering/Technological Education, Education-General, Journalism/Media Education, Medical Education, Private Education (Precollege), School Volunteerism, Secondary Education (Private)
Environment: Wildlife Protection
Health: Children's Health/Hospitals, Hospices, Hospitals
Religion: Churches, Religion-General, Religious Organizations, Religious Welfare
Social Services: At-Risk Youth, Big Brother/Big Sister, Child Welfare, Community Service Organizations, Crime Prevention, Domestic Violence, Family Services, Food/Clothing Distribution, People with Disabilities, Recreation & Athletics, Scouts, Sexual Abuse, Substance Abuse, United Funds/United Ways, YMCA/YWCA/YMHA/YWHA, Youth Organizations

Application Procedures

Initial Contact: Send a brief letter of inquiry.
Application Requirements: Include a description of organization, purpose of funds sought, and proof of tax-exempt status.
Deadlines: March1, June1, September1, and December1.
Evaluative Criteria: Priority given to organizations in the immediate area.
Decision Notification: Within three months after deadline.

Additional Information

Trust(s): Wells Fargo Bank SD NA

Foundation Officials

Dale Clement: adv board
Renee Parker: advisory board
Alex Vucurevich: adv board
Connie L. Vucurevich: adv board
Thomas Vucurevich: adv board

Grants Analysis

Disclosure Period: calendar year ending 2001
Total Grants: $343,415*
Number of Grants: 38
Average Grant: $7,590*
Highest Grant: $55,000
Typical Range: $2,000 to $15,000
*Note: Giving excludes United Way. Average grant figures excludes highest grant.

Recent Grants

Note: Grants derived from 2001 Form 990.

General

55,000	Emmanuel Episcopal Church, Rapid City, SD
22,000	Working Against Violence, Inc, Rapid City, SD
21,600	Lutheran Social Services, Rapid City, IA
20,000	CASA Program 7th Circuit Court, Rapid City, SD
20,000	Rapid City YMCA, Rapid City, SD
15,000	Historic Homestake Opera House Society, Lead, SD
15,000	Society of St. Andrew, Big Island, VA
13,200	Youth and Family Services, Rapid City, SD
12,500	Billings Depot, Inc., Billings, MT
11,500	Black Hills Regional Food Bank, Inc., Rapid City, SD

VULCAN MATERIALS CO.

Company Headquarters

2101 Pinson Valley Parkway
Birmingham, AL 35217
Web: http://www.vulcanmaterials.com

Company Description

Founded: 1956
Ticker: VMC
Exchange: NYSE
Revenue: US$2.545 billion (2002)
Employees: 9510 (2002)
SIC(s): 1422 Crushed & Broken Limestone, 1423 Crushed & Broken Granite, 2812 Alkalies & Chlorine, 2865 Cyclic Crudes & Intermediates.

Operating Locations

Vulcan Materials Co. (AL--Birmingham, Calera, Childersburg, Gadsden, Helena, Huntsville, Lacon, Madison, Russellville, Scottsboro, Trinity, Tuscumbia; GA--Columbus, Dalton, Fairmount, Grayson, La Grange, Lithia Springs, Lithonia, Newnan, Rabun Gap, Red Oak, Stockbridge, Villa Rica; IL--Crystal Lake, Decatur, Fairbury, Joliet, Lemont, McCook, Momence, Pontiac; IN--Francesville, Lafayette, Monon, South Bend; IA--Cedar Rapids, Garrison, Mentour, Robbins; KY--Brandenburg, Elizabethtown, Fort Knox, Lexington; LA--Geismar; MI; NC--Boone, Charlotte, East Forsyth, Elkin, Enka, Gold Hill, Hendersonville, Morganton, North Wilkesboro, Rockingham, Winston-Salem; SC--Blacksburg, Gray Court, Greenville, Lyman, Pacolet; TN--Athens, Bristol, Clarksville, Cleveland, Dayton, Franklin, Holladay, Kingsport, Knox County, Knoxville, Maryville, Morristown, Nashville, Parsons, Savannah, Sevierville, South Pittsburg, Tazewell; TX--Abilene, Boyd, Bridgeport, Brownwood, Knippa, San Antonio, Uvalde; VA--Danville, Manassas, Occoquan, Richmond, South Boston, Warrenton; WI--Milwaukee, Oconomowoc, Oshkosh, Racine, Sussex)

Nonmonetary Support

Type: Donated Equipment; Donated Products; In-kind Services; Loaned Employees; Loaned Executives; Workplace Solicitation
Note: Nonmonetary support is provided by the company.

Vulcan Materials Co. Foundation

Giving Contact

Mary Russom, Manager Community Programs
Vulcan Materials Co.
PO Box 385014
Birmingham, AL 35253-5014

Phone: (205)298-3229
Fax: (205)298-2960
Web: http://www.vulcanmaterials.com

Description

EIN: 630971859
Organization Type: Corporate Foundation
Giving Locations: states in which company has operations.
Grant Types: Capital, Department, Emergency, Employee Matching Gifts, Endowment, Fellowship, General Support, Multiyear/Continuing Support, Project, Research, Scholarship, Seed Money.
Note: Employee matching gift ratio: 1 to 1 for hospitals and cultural organizations; 2 to 1 to educational institutions. Annual limit of $10,000 per employee.

Financial Summary

Total Giving: $2,760,400 (fiscal year ending November 30, 2003 approx); $2,510,018 (fiscal 2002); $2,770,519 (fiscal 2001). Note: Contributes through corporate direct giving program and foundation.
Giving Analysis: Giving for fiscal 2000 includes: foundation scholarships ($293,213); foundation grants to United Way ($588,551); fiscal 1999: foundation scholarships ($204,370); foundation grants to United Way ($550,769); foundation ($1,600,780); fiscal 1998: foundation scholarships ($154,850); foundation grants to United Way ($529,956); foundation ($1,497,195);
Assets: $2,986,455 (fiscal 2002); $4,423,500 (fiscal 2001); $6,191,513 (fiscal 2000)
Gifts Received: $544,981 (fiscal 2001); $65,610 (fiscal 2000); $118,245 (fiscal 1999). Note: Contributions are received from Vulcan Materials Company.

Typical Recipients

Arts & Humanities: Arts Associations & Councils, Arts Centers, Arts Festivals, Arts Funds, Arts Institutes, Ballet, Community Arts, Dance, Ethnic & Folk Arts, Historic Preservation, History & Archaeology, Libraries, Literary Arts, Museums/Galleries, Music, Opera, Performing Arts, Public Broadcasting, Theater, Visual Arts
Civic & Public Affairs: African American Affairs, Botanical Gardens/Parks, Business/Free Enterprise, Civil Rights, Clubs, Economic Development, Economic Policy, Civic & Public Affairs-General, Municipalities/Towns, Philanthropic Organizations, Public Policy, Urban & Community Affairs, Zoos/Aquariums
Education: Arts/Humanities Education, Arts/Humanities Education, Business Education, Colleges & Universities, Economic Education, Education Funds, Education Reform, Elementary Education (Private), Engineering/Technological Education, Education-General, Literacy, Minority Education, Public Education (Precollege), Science/Mathematics Education, Secondary Education (Public), Special Education, Student Aid
Environment: Environment-General, Resource Conservation, Sanitary Systems, Wildlife Protection
Health: Cancer, Children's Health/Hospitals, Clinics/Medical Centers, Emergency/Ambulance Services, Health-General, Health Organizations, Mental Health
International: International Organizations
Religion: Jewish Causes, Ministries, Religious Welfare
Science: Science Exhibits & Fairs, Science Museums
Social Services: Animal Protection, Child Welfare, Community Centers, Community Service Organizations, Counseling, Delinquency & Criminal Rehabilitation, Emergency Relief, Family Services, Food/Clothing Distribution, People with Disabilities, Recreation & Athletics, Scouts, Senior Services, Shelters/Homelessness, Social Services-General, Substance Abuse, United Funds/United Ways, YMCA/YWCA/YMHA/YWHA, Youth Organizations

Application Procedures

Initial Contact: Send a one or two-page letter.
Application Requirements: Include a description of organization, amount requested, purpose of funds

sought, time lines for the funding and implementation of the project; and method for evaluating success of the project, including how the organization will audit its performance. Attach proof of tax-exempt status, the current year's budget, recently audited financial statement, and a list of directors and executive staff.
Deadlines: None; applications acted upon throughout the year.
Review Process: Proposals are reviewed by secretary/treasurer of foundation; if proposal meets guidelines, it is usually referred to appropriate division office for recommendation by local contributions committee; if proposal is appropriate for decision in headquarters office in Birmingham, AL, it is approved or rejected by secretary/treasurer, president, or full board of trustees, depending on amount of request.
Evaluative Criteria: Relative benefit to community; type of project; financial soundness; organizational efficiency.
Decision Notification: Varies, depending on disposition of the proposal.
Notes: Organizations serving the Birmingham, Alabama area should submit requests to the secretary of the Vulcan Materials Company Foundation. Requests from organizations located outside Birmingham should be mailed to the Division Charitable Contributions Officer in their geographical area. Prospective applicants who have questions regarding the appropriate point of contact in their area may submit questions via e-mail: giving@vmcmail.com.

Restrictions

No grants are awarded to groups with discriminatory practices. The foundation does not fund individuals; organizations outside the United states; telephone or mass-mail appeals; political organizations; testimonial dinners; sectarian religious activities; organizations which have discriminatory practices; or athletic, labor, fraternal and veterans associations. The foundation generally only considers requests from organizations located in communities where Vulcan has operations, offices, or employees.

Giving Program Officials

Mary S. Russom: secretary, treasurer PRIM CORP EMPL administrator committee affairs: Vulcan Materials Co.

Foundation Officials

John A. Heilala: trustee B Detroit, MI 1940. ED Pennsylvania State University (1962); Washington University (1965). PRIM CORP EMPL president: Vulcan Materials Co., Chloralkali Unit.
Donald M. James: chairman B 1949. ED University of Alabama BS (1971); University of Alabama MBA (1973); University of Virginia JD (1977). PRIM CORP EMPL chairman, chief executive officer, director: Vulcan Materials Co.
Mary S. Russom: secretary, treasurer (see above)

Grants Analysis

Disclosure Period: fiscal year ending November 30, 2002
Total Grants: $2,510,018
Number of Grants: 735
Average Grant: $3,314

Recent Grants

Note: Grants derived from fiscal 2002 Form 990.

Library-Related
20,000	Ascension Parish Library Board, Baton Rouge, LA

General
173,500	Metropolitan Arts Council, Birmingham, AL
142,500	United Way Central Alabama, Birmingham, AL
119,200	Samford University, Birmingham, AL -- for Vulcan Center for Environmental Education and Sustainability

100,000	Birmingham Museum of Art, Birmingham, AL
83,333	Birmingham-Southern College, Birmingham, AL -- for Blount Monaghan Vulcan Scholarship
72,675	United Way Central Alabama, Birmingham, AL
60,000	Children's Health System, Great Barrington, MA -- capital campaign
60,000	United Way of the Plains, Wichita, KS
50,000	University of Alabama Birmingham, Birmingham, AL -- for honors scholarship School of Engineering
39,900	United Way Central Alabama, Birmingham, AL

W. A. WOODARD FOUNDATION

Giving Contact

Tod Casey Woodard, Vice President
115 W. 8th Ave., Suite 200
PO Box 10666
Eugene, OR 97440
Phone: (541)343-9402

Description

Founded: 1952
EIN: 936026550
Organization Type: Private Foundation
Giving Locations: OR
Grant Types: General Support.

Financial Summary

Total Giving: $298,280 (fiscal year ending June 30, 2001); $309,588 (fiscal 1999); $274,942 (fiscal 1997)
Assets: $6,137,156 (fiscal 2001); $6,607,482 (fiscal 1999); $5,320,957 (fiscal 1997)
Gifts Received: $10,000 (fiscal 1994)

Typical Recipients

Arts & Humanities: Arts Associations & Councils, Arts Funds, Ballet, Ethnic & Folk Arts, Film & Video, Arts & Humanities-General, History & Archaeology, Libraries, Museums/Galleries, Music, Opera, Performing Arts, Public Broadcasting, Theater
Civic & Public Affairs: Clubs, Community Foundations, Economic Development, Civic & Public Affairs-General, Housing, Legal Aid, Municipalities/Towns, Public Policy, Rural Affairs, Urban & Community Affairs, Women's Affairs
Education: Business Education, Colleges & Universities, Community & Junior Colleges, Continuing Education, Education Funds, Education-General, Health & Physical Education, Minority Education, Private Education (Precollege), Public Education (Precollege), Secondary Education (Private), Secondary Education (Public), Special Education, Student Aid
Environment: Forestry, Environment-General
Health: Cancer, Children's Health/Hospitals, Diabetes, Emergency/Ambulance Services, Health Organizations, Heart, Hospitals, Multiple Sclerosis, Prenatal Health Issues, Preventive Medicine/Wellness Organizations, Research/Studies Institutes, Single-Disease Health Associations
International: International Environmental Issues, International Relief Efforts
Religion: Churches, Religious Organizations, Religious Welfare
Science: Observatories & Planetariums, Science Museums, Scientific Centers & Institutes
Social Services: Animal Protection, At-Risk Youth, Big Brother/Big Sister, Child Welfare, Community Centers, Community Service Organizations, Counseling, Day Care, Family Services, Food/Clothing Distribution, People with Disabilities, Recreation & Athletics, Scouts, Senior Services, Special Olympics, United Funds/United Ways, Youth Organizations

Application Procedures

Initial Contact: Request application form.

Foundation Officials

Dena Woodard McCoy: director
Andrew Woodard: director
Carlton Woodard: president
Joy Woodard: director
Kim C. Woodard: director
Kristen A. Woodard: director
Tod Casey Woodard: vice president

Grants Analysis

Disclosure Period: fiscal year ending June 30, 2001
Total Grants: $298,280
Number of Grants: 107
Average Grant: $2,031*
Highest Grant: $45,000
Lowest Grant: $10
Typical Range: $50 to $10,000
***Note:** Average grant figure excludes two highest grants ($85,000).

Recent Grants

Note: Grants derived from fiscal 2001 Form 990.

General
45,000	University of Oregon Foundation, Eugene, OR
25,000	Lane Community College, Eugene, OR
20,000	McKenzie Willamette Hospital Foundation, Springfield, OR
12,500	Cottage Grove Recreation Association, Cottage Grove, OR
10,000	Aprovecho Research Center, Cottage Grove, OR
10,000	Eugene-Springfield Metro Partnership, Eugene, OR
10,000	Pacific Legal Foundation, Sacramento, CA
6,000	Melting Pot Theatre Company, New York, NY
5,500	Boy Scouts of America Oregon Trail Council, Tigard, OR
5,000	Encore Theater, Denver, CO

WACHOVIA BANK OF NORTH CAROLINA NA

Company Headquarters

100 N. Main St.
Winston-Salem, NC 27101

Company Description

Employees: 8,200
SIC(s): 6021 National Commercial Banks, 6712 Bank Holding Companies.
Parent Company: Wachovia Corp., 1 Wachovia Center, 301 S. College St., Ste. 4000, Charlotte, NC, United States

Operating Locations

Wachovia Bank of North Carolina NA (NC--Ahoskie, Andrews, Asheboro, Asheville, Bayboro, Belhaven, Belmont, Bethel, Chapel Hill, Charlotte, Durham, Eden, Elizabethtown, Fayetteville, Gastonia, Goldsboro, Greenville, Hendersonville, Hickory, High Point, Kernersville, Kinston, Laurinburg, Lumberton, Morehead, Morganton, Murphy, New Bern, Reidsville, Robersonville, Rocky Mount, Salisbury, Thomasville, Wadesboro, Washington, Williamston, Winston-Salem)

Nonmonetary Support

Type: Loaned Executives
Note: Nonmonetary Support Range: $100,000. Nonmonetary Support Contact: local bank office.

The Wachovia Foundation, Inc.

Giving Contact
100 North Main Street
Winston-Salem, NC 27102-7203
Phone: (336)732-5252
E-mail: contact.community@wachovia.com
Web: http://www.wachovia.com/inside/page/0,,139,00.html

Description
EIN: 581485946
Organization Type: Corporate Foundation
Giving Locations: GA; NC; SC
Grant Types: Capital, Challenge, Conference/Seminar, Emergency, Endowment, Fellowship, General Support, Matching.

Financial Summary
Total Giving: $9,929,899 (2000); $9,247,123 (1998); $7,612,197 (1997). Note: Contributes through corporate direct giving program and foundation.
Giving Analysis: Giving for 2000 includes: foundation scholarships ($113,861); foundation grants to United Way ($2,063,340); foundation ($7,752,698); 1998: foundation matching gifts ($3,380); foundation grants to United Way ($1,152,265) foundation ($8,091,478).
Assets: $8,789,719 (1999); $25,898,581 (1998); $14,777,132 (1997)
Gifts Received: $1,000 (2000); $1,950,000 (1998); $4,911,342 (1997). Note: Contributions are received from Wachovia Corporation.

Typical Recipients
Arts & Humanities: Arts Associations & Councils, Arts Centers, Arts Festivals, Arts Funds, Community Arts, Dance, Historic Preservation, History & Archaeology, Libraries, Museums/Galleries, Music, Opera, Performing Arts, Public Broadcasting, Theater
Civic & Public Affairs: African American Affairs, Botanical Gardens/Parks, Business/Free Enterprise, Chambers of Commerce, Civil Rights, Clubs, Community Foundations, Economic Development, Civic & Public Affairs-General, Housing, Municipalities/Towns, Philanthropic Organizations, Professional & Trade Associations, Public Policy, Urban & Community Affairs, Women's Affairs, Zoos/Aquariums
Education: Agricultural Education, Arts/Humanities Education, Business Education, Business-School Partnerships, Colleges & Universities, Community & Junior Colleges, Economic Education, Education Funds, Elementary Education (Private), Engineering/Technological Education, Education-General, Medical Education, Minority Education, Preschool Education, Private Education (Precollege), Public Education (Precollege), Science/Mathematics Education, Secondary Education (Private), Student Aid
Environment: Environment-General, Resource Conservation, Wildlife Protection
Health: Emergency/Ambulance Services, Health Funds, Health Organizations, Hospices, Hospitals, Respiratory
International: Foreign Arts Organizations, International Environmental Issues, International Peace & Security Issues
Religion: Jewish Causes, Religious Organizations, Religious Welfare
Science: Science Museums, Scientific Centers & Institutes
Social Services: Child Welfare, Community Centers, Community Service Organizations, Day Care, Delinquency & Criminal Rehabilitation, Family Planning, Family Services, Food/Clothing Distribution, People with Disabilities, Recreation & Athletics, Scouts, Senior Services, Substance Abuse, United Funds/United Ways, YMCA/YWCA/YMHA/YWHA, Youth Organizations

Application Procedures
Initial Contact: Requests a grant application from the local officer in charge of nearest branch bank.
Application Requirements: Include a description of organization and its mission; the scope, budget, and leadership of fundraising project; amount requested; purpose of funds sought; leadership of organization; recently audited financial statement; proof of tax-exempt status; and list of contributors.
Deadlines: Requests must be received by February 1, May 1, August 1, and November 1.
Review Process: Branch office requests are forwarded to general offices with recommendation of officer in charge of branch. Foundation distributor committee meets quarterly.

Restrictions
Does not support individuals, political or lobbying groups, goodwill advertising, or religious organizations for sectarian purposes.

Corporate Officials
Leslie Mayo Baker, Jr.: chairman B Brunswick, MD 1942. ED University of Richmond BA (1964); University of Virginia MBA (1969). PRIM CORP EMPL chairman: Wachovia Corp. CORP AFFIL chairman: Wachovia Bank North Carolina NA; director: National Service Industries Inc.; senior associates: Robert Morris Associates; trustee: Carolina Medicorp Inc.; director: Carolina Power & Light Co. NONPR AFFIL trustee: Colgate Darden Graduate School; chairman: Elon College; member: American Bankers Council.
Clyatt E. Loflin, Jr.: trustee officer PRIM CORP EMPL trustee officer: Wachovia Corp.
Ed Loflin: assistant treasurer PRIM CORP EMPL assistant treasurer: Wachovia Bank of North Carolina NA.
J. Walter McDowell: president, chief executive officer, director B 1951. ED University of North Carolina BS (1973). PRIM CORP EMPL president, chief executive officer, director: Wachovia Bank of North Carolina NA. CORP AFFIL executive vice president: Wachovia Corp.
G. Joseph Prendergast: chairman B 1945. ED Pace University MBA; Wesleyan University BA. PRIM CORP EMPL president chief operating officer: Wachovia Bank Georgia NA ADD CORP EMPL president chief operating officer: Wachovia Corp.; senior executive vice president: Wachovia Bank North Carolina NA; president: Wachovia Bank NA. CORP AFFIL director: Georgia Power Co.; director: Willamette Industries Inc.

Foundation Officials
Leslie Mayo Baker, Jr.: chairman (see above)
J. Walter McDowell: director (see above)
G. Joseph Prendergast: director (see above)
Will B. Spence: director

Grants Analysis
Disclosure Period: calendar year ending 2000
Total Grants: $7,752,698*
Number of Grants: 840
Average Grant: $9,229
Highest Grant: $200,000 (approx)
Typical Range: $1,000 to $20,000
*Note: Giving excludes scholarships; United Way.

Recent Grants
Note: Grants derived from 2000 Form 990.

General

324,787,80	Communities in School of Charlotte Mecklenburg, Inc., Charlotte, NC
324,787,80	Communities in School of Charlotte Mecklenburg, Inc., Charlotte, NC
200,000	North Carolina Partnership for Children, Raleigh, NC -- Smart Start Program
162,500	United Way of Metropolitan Atlanta, Inc., Atlanta, GA
162,500	United Way of Metropolitan Atlanta, Inc., Atlanta, GA
162,500	United Way of Metropolitan Atlanta, Inc., Atlanta, GA
162,500	United Way of Metropolitan Atlanta, Inc., Atlanta, GA
150,000	Mercer University, Macon, GA
140,000	Woodruff Arts Center, Atlanta, GA
116,666	Roper Foundation, Inc., Charleston, SC

CRYSTELLE WAGGONER CHARITABLE TRUST

Giving Contact
Darlene Mann, Senior Vice President & Trust Officer
c/o Bank of America
PO Box 1317
Ft. Worth, TX 76101
Phone: (817)390-6954

Description
Founded: 1982
EIN: 751881219
Organization Type: Private Foundation
Giving Locations: TX: Decatur, Fort Worth some statewide giving
Grant Types: Capital, Emergency, Endowment, General Support, Multiyear/Continuing Support, Operating Expenses, Professorship, Project, Research, Scholarship, Seed Money.

Donor Information
Founder: the late Crystelle Waggoner

Financial Summary
Total Giving: $424,550 (fiscal year ending June 30, 2001); $299,583 (fiscal 2000); $361,383 (fiscal 1998)
Assets: $11,220,880 (fiscal 2001); $13,229,337 (fiscal 2000); $9,094,360 (fiscal 1998)

Typical Recipients
Arts & Humanities: Arts Associations & Councils, Arts Festivals, Arts Funds, Arts Outreach, Ballet, Film & Video, Arts & Humanities-General, Historic Preservation, History & Archaeology, Libraries, Museums/Galleries, Music, Opera, Performing Arts, Theater
Civic & Public Affairs: Clubs, Employment/Job Training, Civic & Public Affairs-General, Hispanic Affairs, Parades/Festivals, Urban & Community Affairs, Women's Affairs
Education: Afterschool/Enrichment Programs, Colleges & Universities, Community & Junior Colleges, Leadership Training, Minority Education, Preschool Education, Private Education (Precollege), Science/Mathematics Education, Special Education, Student Aid
Environment: Environment-General, Resource Conservation
Health: Alzheimers Disease, Cancer, Children's Health/Hospitals, Clinics/Medical Centers, Emergency/Ambulance Services, Eyes/Blindness, Health Organizations, Heart, Hospitals, Medical Research, Mental Health, Nursing Services, Prenatal Health Issues, Public Health, Research/Studies Institutes, Single-Disease Health Associations, Speech & Hearing
Religion: Churches, Ministries, Social/Policy Issues
Social Services: Big Brother/Big Sister, Child Welfare, Community Service Organizations, Day Care, Domestic Violence, Family Planning, Food/Clothing Distribution, Homes, People with Disabilities, Recreation & Athletics, Scouts, Senior Services, Shelters/Homelessness, Substance Abuse, United Funds/United Ways, YMCA/YWCA/YMHA/YWHA, Youth Organizations

Application Procedures

Initial Contact: Send a brief letter of inquiry.
Application Requirements: a description of organization, amount requested, and proof of tax-exempt status.
Deadlines: June 30 and December 31.

Restrictions

Restricted to TX organizations in existence before January 24, 1982.

Additional Information

Publications: Annual Report (including Application Guidelines)
Trust(s): Bank of America

Grants Analysis

Disclosure Period: fiscal year ending June 30, 2001
Total Grants: $424,550
Number of Grants: 35
Average Grant: $12,130
Highest Grant: $30,000
Typical Range: $5,000 to $20,000

Recent Grants

Note: Grants derived from fiscal 1999 Form 990.

General

35,000	National Cowgirl Museum and Hall of Fame, Ft. Worth, TX -- for capital campaign
30,000	Amon Carter Museum, Ft. Worth, TX -- for capital campaign
20,000	Van Cliburn Foundation, Ft. Worth, TX -- for operating expenses
15,000	Boys and Girls Club of Greater Fort Worth, Ft. Worth, TX -- for youth programs
15,000	Fort Worth Dallas Ballet, Ft. Worth, TX -- funding for 1998-99 season
15,000	Fort Worth Symphony Orchestra, Ft. Worth, TX -- for concerts in garden and symphony gala
10,000	Arts Council of Fort Worth, Ft. Worth, TX -- to help underwrite toast of the town benefit 1998
10,000	Goodwill Industries, Ft. Worth, TX -- for capital campaign
10,000	Historic Fort Worth, Ft. Worth, TX -- for operating funds
10,000	United Way, Ft. Worth, TX -- to help purchase network hardware

WAHLERT FOUNDATION

Giving Contact

Robert H. Wahlert, President
PO Box 61477
Ft. Myers, FL 33906-1477
Phone: (941)590-0683
E-mail: Bob16307@aol.com

Description

Founded: 1948
EIN: 426051124
Organization Type: Private Foundation
Giving Locations: IA: Dubuque and surrounding tri-state area
Grant Types: General Support, Scholarship.

Donor Information

Founder: Dubuque Packing Co., FDL Foods, Inc., the late H. W. Wahlert, and officers of the foundation

Financial Summary

Total Giving: $282,550 (fiscal year ending November 30, 2002); $290,334 (fiscal 2000); $327,000 (fiscal 1998). Note: Giving includes United Way ($500).
Assets: $5,584,081 (fiscal 2002); $6,880,021 (fiscal 2000); $7,359,720 (fiscal 1998)
Gifts Received: $8,305 (fiscal 2002); $2,250 (fiscal 2000); $2,200 (fiscal 1998). Note: In fiscal 1997 and 2002, contributions were received from Honkamp Krueger & Co.

Typical Recipients

Arts & Humanities: Historic Preservation, History & Archaeology, Libraries, Museums/Galleries, Music, Opera
Civic & Public Affairs: Community Foundations, Economic Development, Employment/Job Training, Civic & Public Affairs-General, Housing, Urban & Community Affairs
Education: Business Education, Colleges & Universities, Community & Junior Colleges, Education Funds, Public Education (Precollege), Religious Education, Secondary Education (Public), Student Aid
Health: Alzheimers Disease, Cancer, Children's Health/Hospitals, Clinics/Medical Centers, Health Funds, Health Organizations, Hospices, Hospitals, Hospitals (University Affiliated), Mental Health, Nursing Services, Research/Studies Institutes
International: Missionary/Religious Activities
Religion: Churches, Dioceses, Religion-General, Ministries, Religious Organizations, Religious Welfare, Seminaries
Social Services: Camps, Community Centers, Community Service Organizations, Family Services, Food/Clothing Distribution, Scouts, Senior Services, Shelters/Homelessness, Special Olympics, Substance Abuse, United Funds/United Ways, Youth Organizations

Application Procedures

Initial Contact: Submit 1 page letter.
Deadlines: August 15.

Foundation Officials

Kathy Chameli: director
Alfred E. Hughes: secretary
Marni Peck: director
Amy Principi: director
Donald Strausse: trustee
Alan Wahlert: director
Celeste Wahlert: trustee
David Wahlert: trustee
Donna Wahlert: trustee
James Wahlert: trustee
Mark Wahlert: director
Nancy Wahlert: director
R. C. Wahlert, II: trustee
Robert H. Wahlert: president, treasurer B Dubuque, IA 1939. ED University of Iowa BS (1963). PRIM CORP EMPL chairman, president, chief executive officer: FDL Foods/Dubuque Packing Co. CORP AFFIL director: Rigid-Pak Corp.; director: Key City Bank & Trust Co.; director: Edelcar Corp.; director: Hawkeye Banks. NONPR AFFIL president, treasurer, director: Wahlert Foundation. CLUB AFFIL Dubuque Country Club.
Susan Wahlert: director

Grants Analysis

Disclosure Period: fiscal year ending November 30, 2002
Total Grants: $282,550
Number of Grants: 35
Average Grant: $5,221*
Highest Grant: $105,000
Lowest Grant: $250
Typical Range: $1,000 to $10,000
***Note:** Average grant figure excludes highest grant.

Recent Grants

Note: Grants derived from fiscal 2000 Form 990.

General

115,000	Wahlert High School, Dubuque, IA
25,000	Mississippi River Museum
20,000	Catholic Charities
15,000	Trappistine Sisters
10,000	Archdioceses of Dubuque, Dubuque, IA
10,000	Clarke College, Dubuque, IA
10,000	Dubuque Rescue Mission, Dubuque, IA
10,000	Stonehill Care Center
6,000	Salvation Army, Fresno, CA
5,000	Alzheimer Association

WALKER FOUNDATION

Giving Contact

John S. Jenkins, Director
2829 Lakeland Dr., Suite 1600
Jackson, MS 39208
Phone: (601)939-3003
Fax: (601)939-4433

Description

Founded: 1972
EIN: 237279902
Organization Type: Private Foundation
Giving Locations: MS
Grant Types: General Support, Project, Scholarship.

Donor Information

Founder: the late W. E. Walker, Jr., W. E. Walker Stores

Financial Summary

Total Giving: $1,063,900 (2000); $991,484 (1999); $911,337 (1998)
Giving Analysis: Giving for 2000 includes: foundation matching gifts ($41,880) 1998: foundation program-related investments ($193,000)
Assets: $12,015,467 (2000); $13,092,692 (1999); $12,181,895 (1998)
Gifts Received: $393,338 (1999); $935,515 (1998); $500,313 (1996). Note: In 1994, contributions were received from Gloria M. Walker ($523,438), Alex Langford ($350), and miscellaneous ($800).

Typical Recipients

Arts & Humanities: Arts Associations & Councils, Arts Institutes, Dance, Historic Preservation, History & Archaeology, Libraries, Museums/Galleries, Music, Opera, Performing Arts, Theater
Civic & Public Affairs: African American Affairs, Economic Development, Civic & Public Affairs-General, Housing, Nonprofit Management, Urban & Community Affairs, Zoos/Aquariums
Education: Business Education, Colleges & Universities, Continuing Education, Elementary Education (Private), Engineering/Technological Education, Education-General, Private Education (Precollege), Religious Education, Secondary Education (Private), Special Education, Student Aid
Environment: Wildlife Protection
Health: AIDS/HIV, Arthritis, Cancer, Children's Health/Hospitals, Eyes/Blindness, Health Organizations, Heart, Hospices, Hospitals, Kidney, Medical Research, Research/Studies Institutes, Single-Disease Health Associations, Transplant Networks/Donor Banks
International: Foreign Arts Organizations, Health Care/Hospitals, Missionary/Religious Activities
Religion: Churches, Ministries, Religious Organizations, Religious Welfare, Seminaries
Social Services: Animal Protection, Child Welfare, Community Service Organizations, Crime Prevention, Family Services, People with Disabilities, Recreation & Athletics, Scouts, Special Olympics, United Funds/United Ways, Youth Organizations

Application Procedures

Initial Contact: The foundation has no formal grant application procedure or application form.
Deadlines: None.

Foundation Officials

Leigh B. Allen, III: secretary PRIM CORP EMPL secretary: Walker Lands, Inc.
James M. Daughdrill, III: president
John S. Jenkins: director
W. E. Walker, III: trustee
O. B. Walton, III: assistant secretary B 1954. ED Vanderbilt University BA (1976); Harvard University Graduate School of Business Administration MBA (1978). PRIM CORP EMPL chief financial officer: Walker Lands Inc.

Grants Analysis

Disclosure Period: calendar year ending 2000
Total Grants: $658,020*
Number of Grants: 64
Average Grant: $7,270*
Highest Grant: $200,000
Typical Range: $1,000 to $20,000
***Note:** Giving excludes grant to Walker Education Foundation ($364,000) and matching gifts. Average grant figure excludes highest grant.

Recent Grants

Note: Grants derived from 1999 Form 990.

General

225,000	Walker Education Foundation, Jackson, MS
200,000	McCallie School, Chattanooga, TN
100,000	Ducks Unlimited
55,000	Mississippi Museum of Art, Jackson, MS
50,000	Hospice Ministries, Inc.
30,000	Mississippi Children's Home Society, Jackson, MS
30,000	Scripps Research Institute, La Jolla, CA
30,000	Young Life Jackson, Jackson, MS
25,000	Mississippi State University, Jackson, MS
20,000	Delta Waterfowl Foundation

GEORGE R. WALLACE FOUNDATION

Giving Contact

Nancy Nearing, Clerk
George R. Wallace Foundation
Care of Goodwin, Proctor LLP
1 Exchange Pl.
Boston, MA 02109
Phone: (617)570-1735

Description

Founded: 1963
EIN: 046130518
Organization Type: Private Foundation
Giving Locations: MA
Grant Types: Capital, Endowment.

Donor Information

Founder: the late George R. Wallace

Financial Summary

Total Giving: $545,250 (2000); $531,000 (1999); $707,600 (1996)
Giving Analysis: Giving for 2000 includes: foundation grants to United Way ($37,500)
Assets: $9,563,624 (2000); $9,433,959 (1999); $7,401,085 (1996)

Typical Recipients

Arts & Humanities: Arts Associations & Councils, Dance, Historic Preservation, History & Archaeology, Libraries, Museums/Galleries, Music, Performing Arts, Public Broadcasting
Civic & Public Affairs: Clubs, Community Foundations, Civic & Public Affairs-General, Housing, Urban & Community Affairs
Education: Business Education, Colleges & Universities, Community & Junior Colleges, Engineering/ Technological Education, Environmental Education, Education-General, International Exchange, Minority Education, Private Education (Precollege), Public Education (Precollege), Religious Education, Science/ Mathematics Education, Student Aid
Environment: Environment-General, Resource Conservation
Health: Hospices, Hospitals
Religion: Churches, Religion-General, Religious Organizations, Religious Organizations
Science: Observatories & Planetariums
Social Services: Child Welfare, Community Service Organizations, Domestic Violence, Family Planning, Recreation & Athletics, Senior Services, United Funds/United Ways, YMCA/YWCA/YMHA/YWHA, Youth Organizations

Application Procedures

Initial Contact: Send a written request.
Application Requirements: Proposals should contain a concise statement of the purpose of funds sought, the current year's operating budget, recently audited financial statement, a list of board members, resumes of all key staff people, proof of tax-exempt status, and most recent Form 990.
Deadlines: None.

Restrictions

Does not support individuals.

Foundation Officials

John Grado, Jr.: trustee
Henry Bradburg Shepard, Jr.: trustee B Exeter, NH 1927. ED University of Goettingen (1951-1952); Harvard University LLB (1957); Yale University BA (1957). PRIM CORP EMPL counsel: Goodwin, Procter & Hoar. NONPR AFFIL member: Phi Beta Kappa; trustee: George R Wallace Foundation; trustee: New Hampshire Historical Society; member: Hamilton Trust; member: Massachusetts Bar Association; member: Greater Boston Chamber of Commerce; member: Boston Bar Association; honorary trustee: Deree-Pierce College; member: American Bar Association. CLUB AFFIL Harvard Travelers Club; New Bedford Yacht Club; Country Club.
George R. Wallace, III: trustee

Grants Analysis

Disclosure Period: calendar year ending 2000
Total Grants: $507,750*
Number of Grants: 44
Average Grant: $9,483*
Highest Grant: $100,000
Typical Range: $500 to $20,000
***Note:** Giving excludes United Way. Average grant figure excludes highest grant.

Recent Grants

Note: Grants derived from 2001 Form 990.

Library-Related

25,000	Tuck Library, Concord, NH

General

100,000	Chewonki Foundation, Wiscasset, ME
50,000	Applewild School, Fitchburg, MA
50,000	Babson College, Babson Park, MA
22,695	Our Lady of the Angels, Worcester, MA
20,000	Fitchburg Historical Society, Fitchburg, MA

15,000	United Negro College Fund, Fairfax, VA
10,000	Fitchburg Senior Center, Fitchburg, MA
10,000	Lunenburg United Parish, Lunenburg, MA
10,000	Mother Caroline Academy, Dorchester, MA
10,000	Mother Caroline Academy, Dorchester, MA

DEWITT WALLACE-READER'S DIGEST FUND

Giving Contact

M. Christine DeVita, President
2 Park Avenue, 23rd Floor
New York, NY 10016
Phone: (212)251-9700
Fax: (212)679-6990
E-mail: wrdf@wallacefunds.org
Web: http://www.wallacefoundation.org

Description

Founded: 1965
EIN: 136183757
Organization Type: General Purpose Foundation
Giving Locations: nationally.
Grant Types: Multiyear/Continuing Support.

Donor Information

Founder: The fund was established in 1965 by DeWitt Wallace (1889-1981). Mr. Wallace was born in St. Paul, MN. His father was president of Macalester College, where Mr. Wallace studied for two years before transferring to the University of California at Berkeley. In 1922, Mr. Wallace and his wife, Lila Acheson Wallace , founded Reader's Digest with $5,000 in borrowed money. Upon his retirement in 1972, Reader's Digest was the world's most widely read magazine. "He was particularly interested in young people and education, and that continues to be reflected in the Fund's current grant program."

Financial Summary

Total Giving: $32,339,927 (2001); $17,776,061 (2000); $35,531,971 (1998)
Giving Analysis: Giving for 1998 includes: foundation grants to United Way ($1,363,427)
Assets: $737,601,779 (2001); $918,788,107 (2000); $804,785,419 (1998)
Gifts Received: $6,038 (1996); $375,430 (1993); $7,273 (1992)

Typical Recipients

Arts & Humanities: Arts & Humanities-General, Libraries, Literary Arts, Music
Civic & Public Affairs: African American Affairs, Botanical Gardens/Parks, Business/Free Enterprise, Civil Rights, Clubs, Community Foundations, Employment/Job Training, Hispanic Affairs, Municipalities/ Towns, Nonprofit Management, Parades/Festivals, Professional & Trade Associations, Public Policy, Urban & Community Affairs, Women's Affairs
Education: Afterschool/Enrichment Programs, Agricultural Education, Arts/Humanities Education, Business Education, Colleges & Universities, Community & Junior Colleges, Continuing Education, Education Associations, Education Funds, Education Reform, Faculty Development, Education-General, International Studies, Literacy, Minority Education, Preschool Education, Private Education (Precollege), Public Education (Precollege), School Volunteerism, Science/Mathematics Education, Secondary Education (Public), Social Sciences Education, Special Education, Student Aid, Vocational & Technical Education
Environment: Resource Conservation
Health: Clinics/Medical Centers, Hospitals, Medical Research, Research/Studies Institutes
International: International Peace & Security Issues, International Relations

Religion: Jewish Causes, Religious Organizations
Science: Scientific Centers & Institutes, Scientific Organizations
Social Services: At-Risk Youth, Big Brother/Big Sister, Camps, Child Welfare, Community Service Organizations, Crime Prevention, Family Services, Homes, People with Disabilities, Recreation & Athletics, Scouts, United Funds/United Ways, YMCA/YWCA/YMHA/YWHA, YMCA/YWCA/YMHA/YWHA, Youth Organizations

Application Procedures

Initial Contact: Send a brief letter of inquiry (no more than two pages). The fund requests that video tapes not be sent. The fund does not accept email proposals.
Application Requirements: The initial letter should describe the organization, proposed project and its goal, and include an estimated budget of the project and the portion of the budget requiring funding. The Fund will acknowledge receipt of letters. If the request falls within fund interests, a formal proposal with detailed information will be requested within four weeks.
Deadlines: None.
Review Process: The board meets four times a year to consider proposals. Proposals will be reviewed for the potential contribution to the field, the organization's ability to produce and sustain the proposed projects, plans for documenting both process and results, and the financial stability of the organization.

Restrictions

Unsolicited proposals are rarely funded. Areas currently outside giving guidelines include religious and fraternal organizations; international programs; conferences; historical restoration; health, medical, or social service programs; environmental or conservation programs; capital campaigns, emergency funds, or deficit financing; private foundations; or individuals.

Additional Information

The fund has become more national and less local in its grant making. Generally, the fund does not make grants under $100,000 or grants for long-term annual support of an organization. Multiyear funding will be considered relative to specific needs and the potential of a particular project. Resources are allocated to organizations the foundation has invited to apply, and unsolicited requests are rarely funded.
In July 2003, the foundation completed a merger with the Lila Wallace-Reader's Digest Fund and is now known as the Wallace Foundation. The foundation now has a single mission: "To enable institutions to expand learning and enrichment opportunities for all people. We do this by supporting and sharing effective ideas and practices." Wallace Foundation Website.
Publications: Annual Report; Application Guidelines

Foundation Officials

Gordon M. Ambach: director
W. Don Cornwell: director
M. Christine DeVita: president, director ED Queens College BA (1977); Fordham University (1980). CORP AFFIL director: Readers Digest Association Inc.
George Vincent Grune: chairman, director B White Plains, NY 1929. ED Duke University BA (1952); University of Florida (1955-1956). CORP AFFIL director: Travel Holiday; director: Chase Manhattan Corp.; director: Federated Department Stores Inc.; director: Avon Products Inc.; director: Bestfoods. NONPR AFFIL mng director: Metropolitan Opera Association; national leaders fellow: YMCA; member: Institute France Academy des Beaux-Arts; trustee: Metropolitan Museum Art; chairman: Boys & Girls Clubs America. CLUB AFFIL Sky Club; Union League Club; Ponte Vedra Inn Club; Sawgrass Club; Augusta National Golf Club; Blind Brook Country Club.
Susan J. Kropf: director
Peter C. Marzio: director
Robert D. Nagel: director investments

Jane Bryant Quinn: program director B Niagara Falls, NY 1939. ED Middlebury College BA (1960). PRIM CORP EMPL controller editor: Newsweek Inc. CORP AFFIL syndicated financial columnist: Washington Post Writers Group; contributing financial columnist: Good Housekeeping Magazine. NONPR AFFIL member: Phi Beta Kappa.
Laraine S. Rothenberg: director B Brooklyn, NY 1947. ED University of Pennsylvania BA (1967); Columbia University JD (1971). PRIM CORP EMPL attorney: McDermott, Will & Emery. NONPR AFFIL member: Association Bar New York City; member: New York State Bar Association.
Joseph Shenker: director
Walter Vincent Shipley: mem, director B Newark, NJ 1935. ED Williams College (1954-1956); New York University BS (1961); Harvard University Graduate School of Business Administration (1976). PRIM CORP EMPL chairman, chief executive officer: Chase Manhattan Corp. ADD CORP EMPL chairman: Chase Bank of Texas; director: Chase Equity Holding Inc. CORP AFFIL director: Verizon Communications Inc.; director: ExxonMobil Corp.; director: NYNEX Corp.; director: Champion International Corp. NONPR AFFIL director: United Way; director: United Way Tri-State; director: New York Clearing House Association; president: Goodwill Industries Greater New York; director: Lincoln Center Performing Arts; director: Conference Board; member: Council Foreign Relations; member: Business Council; member: Business Roundtable; director: Alice Tully Hall; director: Avery Fisher Hall. CLUB AFFIL The Links Club; Augusta National Golf Club; Baltusrol Golf Club.
Cecil Jesse Silas: director B Miami, FL 1932. ED Georgia Institute of Technology BS (1954). CORP AFFIL director: Milliken & Co.; director: Readers Digest Association Inc.; director: Ascent Entertainment; director: Halliburton Co. NONPR AFFIL trustee: Frank Phillips Foundation; member: U.S. Chamber of Commerce; director: Oklahoma Foundation Excellence; member: Phi Delta Theta; director: Ethics Resource Center; trustee: Georgia Technology Foundation; director: Boys & Girls Clubs America; member: American Petroleum Institute; parton council: Atlantic Council U.S. CLUB AFFIL 25 Year Club.
Bruce Trachtenberg: director commun
Valleau Wilkie, Jr.: executive vice president, executive director

Grants Analysis

Disclosure Period: calendar year ending 2001
Total Grants: $32,339,927*
Number of Grants: 125
Average Grant: $204,869*
Highest Grant: $8,853,000
Lowest Grant: $5,000
Typical Range: $100,000 to $1,853,000
*Note: Average grant figure excludes two highest grants ($11,853,000).

Recent Grants

Note: Grants derived from 2001 Form 990.

Library-Related

270,100	Urban Libraries Council, Evanston, IL -- provide technical assistance and coordination for public libraries
182,200	King County Library System, Issaquah, WA -- provide educational and employment opportunities for low-income teenagers
157,000	Public Library of Charlotte and Mecklenburg County, Charlotte, NC -- create Teens Succeed
141,900	Oakland Public Library, Oakland, ME -- expand and strengthen an educational enrichment program
130,900	Enoch Pratt Free Library, Baltimore, MD -- provide opportunities for low income youth
126,600	Tucson-Pima Public Library, Inc., Tucson, AZ -- create four teen centers
124,400	Free Library of Philadelphia, Philadelphia, PA -- collaborate with key community partnership to develop young library leaders
123,500	Fort Bend County Libraries, Richmond, TX -- provide high quality after-school educational enrichment and career development programs for low income youth
106,700	Washoe County Library System, Reno, NV -- develop teen action teams
105,600	Brooklyn Public Library, Brooklyn, NY -- provide low-income teenagers after-school educational enrichment, job readiness, career planning and leadership development

General

8,853,000	Council of Chief State School Officers, Washington, DC -- national consortium

LILA WALLACE-READER'S DIGEST FUND

Giving Contact

2 Park Avenue, 23rd Floor
New York, NY 10016
Phone: (212)251-9800
Fax: (212)679-6990
E-mail: lwrd@wallacefunds.org
Web: http://www.wallacefunds.org

Description

Founded: 1960
EIN: 136086859
Organization Type: General Purpose Foundation
Giving Locations: nationally.
Grant Types: Challenge, Project.

Donor Information

Founder: The late Lila Acheson Wallace and her late husband, DeWitt Wallace , founded Reader's Digest magazine in 1922 in New York City. The company has grown to be a leading global publisher and direct-mail marketer of magazines, books, music, and video products. Lila Wallace was a social worker who established innovative programs in conjunction with the YMCA and the U.S. Department of Labor. She also was interested in the arts and supported various museums, performing arts organizations, and programs to beautify the environment.
She and her husband established four charitable foundations to support their interests. In 1987, the DeWitt Wallace Fund, L.A.W. Fund, Lakeview Fund, and High Winds Fund were merged into two funds known as the DeWitt Wallace-Reader's Digest Fund and the Lila Wallace-Reader's Digest Fund.

Financial Summary

Total Giving: $10,028,201 (2001); $22,902,257 (2000); $32,059,661 (1999)
Giving Analysis: Giving for 2000 includes: foundation gifts to individuals ($850,000)
Assets: $566,000,000 (2001); $700,556,103 (2000); $642,431,139 (1999)
Gifts Received: $158,657 (2000); $5,733 (1993); $44,805 (1992)

Typical Recipients

Arts & Humanities: Arts Appreciation, Arts Associations & Councils, Arts Centers, Arts Festivals, Arts Funds, Arts Institutes, Arts Outreach, Ballet, Community Arts, Dance, Ethnic & Folk Arts, Arts & Humanities-General, History & Archaeology, Libraries, Literary Arts, Museums/Galleries, Music, Opera, Performing Arts, Public Broadcasting, Theater, Visual Arts
Civic & Public Affairs: Asian American Affairs, Botanical Gardens/Parks, Business/Free Enterprise,

Civil Rights, Community Foundations, Employment/Job Training, Civic & Public Affairs-General, Hispanic Affairs, Professional & Trade Associations, Public Policy, Urban & Community Affairs, Women's Affairs, Zoos/Aquariums

Education: Arts/Humanities Education, Colleges & Universities, Education Reform, Education-General, Literacy

Environment: Environment-General, Resource Conservation

International: Foreign Arts Organizations

Religion: Religion-General

Social Services: Community Service Organizations, Recreation & Athletics, YMCA/YWCA/YMHA/YWHA, Youth Organizations

Application Procedures

Initial Contact: Initial approach should be a letter of no more than two pages describing the proposed project, the applicant organization, the estimated total for the project, and the portion requiring funding. A reply will be made within twelve weeks.

Application Requirements: If the request falls within fund interests, a formal proposal with detailed information will be requested.

Deadlines: None.

Review Process: The board meets three times a year to consider proposals. Proposals will be reviewed for their potential contribution to the field, the organization's ability to produce the proposed project, the financial stability of the organization, and the potential furthering of the fund's goals.

Notes: The fund strongly discourages videotapes, and does not accept proposals sent by electronic mail.

Restrictions

Grants generally are not given to religious organizations, fraternal or veterans' groups, or private foundations. The fund generally will not make grants under $100,000, or for long-term annual support of an organization.

Resources are allocated to organizations the foundation has invited to apply, and unsolicited requests are rarely funded. No grants are awarded for health care, social services, research projects, historical restoration, capital campaigns, or public education.

Additional Information

The Fund has launched is Community Arts Partnership (CAP) Initiative, which builds connections between professional schools and community-based organizations. The Fund is also making nationwide a program to help libraries plan improvements to adult literacy programs.

In January 2000, the Lila Wallace-Reader's Digest Fund and DeWitt Wallace-Reader's Digest Fund announced that they would be combining resources and staffs and operating as the Wallace-Reader's Digest Funds. The Funds have about $1.5 billion in total assets and focus on: developing effective educational leaders to improve student learning; providing high-quality informal learning opportunities for children and families in communities; and promoting new standards of practice to increase participation in the arts. In July 2003, the foundation completed a merger with the DeWitt Wallace-Reader's Digest Fund and is now known as the Wallace Foundation. The foundation now has a single mission: "To enable institutions to expand learning and enrichment opportunities for all people. We do this by supporting and sharing effective ideas and practices." Wallace Foundation Website.

Publications: Annual Report; Guidelines

Foundation Officials

Gordon M. Ambach: director

W. Don Cornwell: director

Nancy Devine: director communities programs

M. Christine DeVita: president, secretary, director ED Queens College BA (1977); Fordham University (1980). CORP AFFIL director: Readers Digest Association Inc.

George Vincent Grune: chairman, director B White Plains, NY 1929. ED Duke University BA (1952); University of Florida (1955-1956). CORP AFFIL director: Travel Holiday; director: Chase Manhattan Corp.; director: Federated Department Stores Inc.; director: Avon Products Inc.; director: Bestfoods. NONPR AFFIL mng director: Metropolitan Opera Association; national leaders fellow: YMCA; member: Institute France Academy des Beaux-Arts; trustee: Metropolitan Museum Art; chairman: Boys & Girls Clubs America. CLUB AFFIL Sky Club; Union League Club; Ponte Vedra Inn Club; Sawgrass Club; Augusta National Golf Club; Blind Brook Country Club.

Susan J. Kropf: director

Peter C. Marzio: director

Robert D. Nagel: director investments, treasurer

Laraine S. Rothenberg: director B Brooklyn, NY 1947. ED University of Pennsylvania BA (1967); Columbia University JD (1971). PRIM CORP EMPL attorney: McDermott, Will & Emery. NONPR AFFIL member: Association Bar New York City; member: New York State Bar Association.

Joseph Shenker: director

Walter Vincent Shipley: mem, director B Newark, NJ 1935. ED Williams College (1954-1956); New York University BS (1961); Harvard University Graduate School of Business Administration (1976). PRIM CORP EMPL chairman, chief executive officer: Chase Manhattan Corp. ADD CORP EMPL chairman: Chase Bank of Texas; director: Chase Equity Holding Inc. CORP AFFIL director: Verizon Communications Inc.; director: ExxonMobil Corp.; director: NYNEX Corp.; director: Champion International Corp. NONPR AFFIL director: United Way; director: United Way Tri-State; director: New York Clearing House Association; president: Goodwill Industries Greater New York; director: Lincoln Center Performing Arts; director: Conference Board; member: Council Foreign Relations; member: Business Council; member: Business Roundtable; director: Alice Tully Hall; director: Avery Fisher Hall. CLUB AFFIL The Links Club; Augusta National Golf Club; Baltusrol Golf Club.

Holly Sidford: program director

Cecil Jesse Silas: director B Miami, FL 1932. ED Georgia Institute of Technology BS (1954). CORP AFFIL director: Milliken & Co.; director: Readers Digest Association Inc.; director: Ascent Entertainment; director: Halliburton Co. NONPR AFFIL trustee: Frank Phillips Foundation; member: U.S. Chamber of Commerce; director: Oklahoma Foundation Excellence; member: Phi Delta Theta; director: Ethics Resource Center; trustee: Georgia Technology Foundation; director: Boys & Girls Clubs America; member: American Petroleum Institute; parton council: Atlantic Council U.S. CLUB AFFIL 25 Year Club.

Bruce Trachtenberg: director commun

Grants Analysis

Disclosure Period: calendar year ending 2001

Total Grants: $10,028,201*

Number of Grants: 124

Average Grant: $69,335*

Highest Grant: $1,500,000

Typical Range: $50,000 to $200,000

*Note: Giving includes gifts to individuals. Average grant figure excludes highest grant.

Recent Grants

Note: Grants derived from 2001 Form 990.

Library-Related

200,000	American Library Association, Chicago, IL -- to develop and support a national network to build capacity and sustain public libraries

General

833,333	American Ballet Theatre, New York, NY -- to increase attendance at youth and family oriented programs
833,333	Arena Stage, Washington, DC -- to collaborate with local universities, museums and other arts organizations to conduct audience research
833,333	Armory Center for the Arts, Pasadena, CA -- to develop partnerships with schools, universities, community organizations and museums
833,333	Chicago Symphony Orchestra, Chicago, IL -- to increase access to music and music education
833,333	Des Moines Art Center, Des Moines, IA -- to build on recent, dramatic increases in attendance by expanding community engagement efforts
833,333	New Jersey Performing Arts Center, Newark, NJ -- to attract and serve new and non-traditional audiences of all ages through partnerships with more than a dozen universities
833,333	Seattle Opera, Seattle, WA -- to expand its Young Artists Program
833,333	University Musical Society, Ann Arbor, MI -- to collaborate with local organizations and University of Michigan departments to conduct annual residencies by major artists
833,333	Verba Buena Center for the Arts, San Francisco, CA -- to host four extended artist residencies annually
833,333	Walker Art Center, Minneapolis, MN -- to maintain the size of its audience and deepen people's engagement with the museum

DOROTHY WAGNER WALLIS TRUST

Giving Contact

Frederick Singley Koontz, Trustee
7 St. Paul Street, Suite 1400
Baltimore, MD 21202-1626
Phone: (410)347-8770
E-mail: fkoontz@wtplaw.com

Description

Founded: 1994
EIN: 526605828
Organization Type: Private Foundation
Giving Locations: MD: Baltimore
Grant Types: General Support.

Financial Summary

Total Giving: $375,900 (2001); $402,775 (2000); $357,675 (1999)
Assets: $8,336,311 (2001); $8,715,118 (2000); $8,073,435 (1999)

Typical Recipients

Arts & Humanities: Historic Preservation, History & Archaeology, Libraries, Museums/Galleries
Civic & Public Affairs: Civic & Public Affairs-General, Housing, Law & Justice, Legal Aid
Education: Colleges & Universities, Education-General, Private Education (Precollege)
Health: Children's Health/Hospitals, Clinics/Medical Centers, Hospitals (University Affiliated), Long-Term Care
Religion: Churches, Religious Welfare
Social Services: Animal Protection, Community Service Organizations, People with Disabilities, Senior Services, Social Services-General, Substance Abuse

Application Procedures

Initial Contact: The foundation requests applications be made in writing.

Application Requirements: Include a description of organization, purpose of funds sought, charitable activities, and any other pertinent information.

Deadlines: None.

Foundation Officials
Frederick Singley Koontz: trustee

Grants Analysis
Disclosure Period: calendar year ending 2001
Total Grants: $375,900
Number of Grants: 16
Average Grant: $15,727*
Highest Grant: $140,000
Lowest Grant: $2,500
Typical Range: $5,000 to $20,000
*Note: Average grant figure excludes highest grant.

Recent Grants
Note: Grants derived from 2001 Form 990.

General

140,000	Walters Art Gallery, Baltimore, MD
50,000	Baltimore Museum of Art, Baltimore, MD
37,500	Maryland Historical Society, Baltimore, MD
30,000	Historic Hampton, Inc., Baltimore, MD
25,000	Harvard University, Cambridge, MA
25,000	Johns Hopkins University, Baltimore, MD
20,000	Woman's Industrial Exchange of Baltimore, Baltimore, MD
11,400	AIM, Baltimore, MD
10,000	Preservation Society, Baltimore, MD
5,000	Legal Aid Bureau, Baltimore, MD

BLANCHE WALSH CHARITY TRUST

Giving Contact
Robert F. Murphy, Jr., Trustee
174 Central St., Suite 329
Lowell, MA 01852
Phone: (978)454-5654

Description
Founded: 1973
EIN: 046311841
Organization Type: Private Foundation
Giving Locations: New England.
Grant Types: Capital, General Support, Operating Expenses, Scholarship, Seed Money.

Financial Summary
Total Giving: $147,800 (2002); $180,885 (2001); $177,825 (2000)
Giving Analysis: Giving for 2002 includes: foundation scholarships ($35,000); 2000: foundation scholarships ($34,500); 1999: foundation matching gifts ($2,000) foundation scholarships ($21,000)
Assets: $4,262,247 (2002); $5,274,873 (2001); $4,875,688 (2000)

Typical Recipients
Arts & Humanities: Libraries
Civic & Public Affairs: Asian American Affairs, Employment/Job Training, Civic & Public Affairs-General, Hispanic Affairs, Housing
Education: Afterschool/Enrichment Programs, Arts/Humanities Education, Colleges & Universities, Continuing Education, Elementary Education (Private), Elementary Education (Public), International Studies, Literacy, Minority Education, Preschool Education, Private Education (Precollege), School Volunteerism, Science/Mathematics Education, Secondary Education (Private), Social Sciences Education, Special Education, Student Aid, Vocational & Technical Education
Health: AIDS/HIV, Cancer, Clinics/Medical Centers, Diabetes, Geriatric Health, Health Organizations, Home-Care Services, Hospices, Hospitals, Long-Term Care, Mental Health, Nutrition, Prenatal Health Issues, Public Health
International: Missionary/Religious Activities

Religion: Churches, Religion-General, Jewish Causes, Ministries, Religious Organizations, Religious Welfare
Social Services: At-Risk Youth, Camps, Child Welfare, Community Service Organizations, Day Care, Domestic Violence, Family Services, Food/Clothing Distribution, People with Disabilities, Recreation & Athletics, Senior Services, Shelters/Homelessness, Social Services-General, Volunteer Services, Youth Organizations

Application Procedures
Initial Contact: Applicants should contact the trust, in writing, to obtain grant application forms.
Deadlines: October 1 for application form request. December 1 for completed application to the trustees.

Restrictions
Limited to Roman Catholic charities.

Additional Information
Publications: Application Guidelines

Foundation Officials
John C. Donohoe: trustee
John E. Leggat, Esq.: trustee
Robert F. Murphy, Jr.: trustee

Grants Analysis
Disclosure Period: calendar year ending 2002
Total Grants: $112,800*
Number of Grants: 50
Average Grant: $2,256
Highest Grant: $7,000
Lowest Grant: $1,000
Typical Range: $1,000 to $5,000
*Note: Giving excludes scholarships.

Recent Grants
Note: Grants derived from 2001 Form 990.

General

10,000	Academy of Notre Dame, Tyngsborough, MA -- renovate gym
5,000	Merrimack Valley Catholic Charities, Lowell, MA -- food pantry
5,000	St. Michael School, Lowell, MA -- religious books and bible
4,000	Redemptorist Center, Denver, CO -- AIDS/HIV infected children's program
4,000	St. Christopher's Inn, Garrison, NY -- expansion for homeless people
4,000	St. Francis De Sales School, Philadelphia, PA -- after-school childcare
3,500	Central Catholic, Lawrence, MA -- scholarships
3,500	Marie Esther Health Center, Marlborough, MA -- update nursing
3,500	Presentation of Mary Academy, Methuen, MA -- scholarships
3,150	Immaculate Conception School, Lowell, MA -- lab kits for science course

WALSH FOUNDATION

Giving Contact
G. Malcolm Louden, Sr., Secretary & Treasurer
500 W. 7th St., Suite 1007
Ft. Worth, TX 76102
Phone: (817)335-3741

Description
Founded: 1956
EIN: 756021726
Organization Type: Private Foundation
Giving Locations: TX: Ft. Worth
Grant Types: General Support, Multiyear/Continuing Support, Operating Expenses, Project.

Donor Information
Founder: Mary D. Walsh, F. Howard Walsh, Sr.

Financial Summary
Total Giving: $744,140 (2000); $668,563 (1999); $121,250 (1998)
Giving Analysis: Giving for 2000 includes: foundation grants to United Way ($4,000) 1999: foundation grants to United Way ($4,000)
Assets: $5,742,547 (2000); $5,352,606 (1999); $5,082,443 (1998)
Gifts Received: $505,902 (2000); $110,516 (1999); $273,158 (1996). Note: In 1998, Holland Fleming Walsh ($10,381), F. Howard Walsh, II ($36,594.17), Parker Otwel Roe ($53,359.13), Catherine Lauren Walsh ($69,176.91), Karen Lindsey Walsh ($69,176.91), George Howard Porter, William Frederic Bonnell, Jr. ($20,180), Ellen King Walsh ($20,180), Michael Clinton Porter ($20,180), Allison Karen Walsh ($10,899), Laura Elisabeth Walsh ($10,899), Jonathan Richard Bonnell ($10,626), Tara Winston Walsh ($10,626), Mary Erin Walsh Char. Trust ($9,799), and Mary Erin Walsh '83 Char. Trust ($9,082). In 1996, contributions were received from Amy S. Walsh ($21,622), George Howard Porter ($11,931), William F. Bonnell, Jr., Ellen K. Walsh, and Michael C. Porter ($11,545 each), Allison K. Walsh and Laura E. Bonnell ($10,899 each), Jonathan R. Bonnell and Tara W. Walsh ($31,481 each), Holland F. Walsh ($21,926), F. Howard Walsh III ($20,858), Parker O. Roe ($19,995), Catherine L. Walsh and Karen L. Walsh ($19,285 each), and the Mary Erin Walsh Charitable Trusts ($18,861).

Typical Recipients
Arts & Humanities: Arts Associations & Councils, Arts Centers, Arts Institutes, Ballet, Community Arts, Dance, Historic Preservation, History & Archaeology, Libraries, Museums/Galleries, Music, Opera, Performing Arts, Public Broadcasting, Theater
Civic & Public Affairs: Botanical Gardens/Parks, Clubs, Economic Development, Civic & Public Affairs-General, Housing, Parades/Festivals, Rural Affairs, Urban & Community Affairs, Women's Affairs, Zoos/Aquariums
Education: Colleges & Universities, Education Funds, Minority Education, Private Education (Precollege), Secondary Education (Public)
Health: AIDS/HIV, Alzheimers Disease, Arthritis, Cancer, Cancer, Children's Health/Hospitals, Health Organizations, Heart, Hospitals, Medical Research, Mental Health, Research/Studies Institutes
International: Foreign Arts Organizations
Religion: Churches, Religious Organizations, Religious Welfare
Science: Science Museums
Social Services: Big Brother/Big Sister, Child Welfare, Community Centers, Community Service Organizations, Counseling, Crime Prevention, Domestic Violence, Food/Clothing Distribution, People with Disabilities, Recreation & Athletics, Scouts, United Funds/United Ways, Youth Organizations

Application Procedures
Initial Contact: Send a brief letter of inquiry outlining intended use of funds.
Deadlines: None.

Restrictions
Emphasis is on education, health, performing arts, and general welfare.

Foundation Officials
F. Howard Walsh, Jr.: assistant secretary, assistant treasurer B 1941. ED Texas Christian University BA (1963). PRIM CORP EMPL president, director: F Howard Walsh Jr Oper Co. ADD CORP EMPL owner: Walsh Oil Co.
Mary D. Fleming Walsh: vice president B Whitewright, TX October 29, 1913. ED Southern

Methodist University BA (1934). CORP AFFIL partner: Walsh Co. NONPR AFFIL honorary director: Van Cliburn International Piano Competition; life member: YWCA; member: Texas League Composers; member: Texas Boys Club Auxilliary; member: Texas Christian University Fine Arts Foundation Guild; guarantor: Texas Boys Choir; charter member: Lloyd Shaw Foundation; member: Tarrant County Auxiliary Edna Gladney Home; guarantor: Scholar Cantorum; member: Rae Reimers Bible Study; member: Round Table International; member: National Association Cowbelles; member: Opera Guild; member: Jewel Charity Ball; member: Friends Texas Boys Choir; member: Goodwill Industries Auxiliary; guarantor: Fort Worth Theatre; guarantor: Fort Worth Opera Association; member: Fort Worth Pan Hellenic; member: Fort Worth Childrens Hospital; member: Fort Worth Ballet Association; member: Fort Worth Boys Club; guarantor, member: Fort Worth Art Council; guarantor, member: Fort Worth Ballet; member: Fort Worth Art Association; member: Childrens Hospital Women's Board; member: Colorado Springs Fine Arts Center; member: Child Study Center; member: Chi Omega Carousel; member: Chi Omega Mothers; member: Chi Omega; member: American Guild Organists; member: Big Brothers Tarrant County; member: American Automobile Association; co-founder: American Field Service Fort Worth; member: American Association University Women. CLUB AFFIL Women's Club; Texas Christian University Women's Club; Ridglea Country Club; Shady Oaks Country Club; Garden of Gods Club; Colonial Country Club; Colorado Springs Country Club.

Grants Analysis

Disclosure Period: calendar year ending 2000
Total Grants: $740,140*
Number of Grants: 33
Average Grant: $13,005*
Highest Grant: $237,000
Typical Range: $5,000 to $25,000
***Note:** Giving excludes United Way. Average grant excludes two highest grants ($337,000).

Recent Grants

Note: Grants derived from 1999 Form 990.

General

197,500	Texas Christian University, Ft. Worth, TX
185,000	Dorothy Shaw Bell Choir, Ft. Worth, TX
95,000	Littlest Wiseman, Ft. Worth, TX
33,000	Cook Children's Medical Center, Ft. Worth, TX
26,500	Fort Worth Country Day School, Ft. Worth, TX
23,500	Jewel Charity Ball, Ft. Worth, TX
17,000	Fort Worth Dallas Ballet, Ft. Worth, TX
15,000	Gladney Center, Ft. Worth, TX
7,500	Ronald McDonald House, Ft. Worth, TX
6,000	Child Study Center, Ft. Worth, TX

WALT DISNEY CO.

Company Headquarters

Burbank, CA
Web: http://disney.go.com

Company Description

Founded: 1938
Ticker: DIS
Exchange: NYSE
Operating Revenue: US$25.36 billion (2002)
Profit: US$1.236 billion (2002)
Employees: 114000 (2002)
Fortune Rank: 61, per FORTUNE Magazine's list of 500 Largest U.S. Corporations (2002).
SIC(s): 6531 Real Estate Agents & Managers, 7812 Motion Picture & Video Production, 7996 Amusement Parks.

Operating Locations

Walt Disney Co. (CA--Anaheim, Glendale, Hollywood; FL--Lake Buena Vista, Orlando; NJ--Edison; NY--New York)

Walt Disney Co. Foundation

Giving Contact

Tillie J. Baptie, Executive Director
The Walt Disney Co. Foundation
500 South Buena Vista Street
Burbank, CA 91521-0987
Phone: (818)560-1006

Description

EIN: 956037079
Organization Type: Corporate Foundation
Giving Locations: CA: Los Angeles County, Orange County; FL: Orange County, Osceola County headquarters and operating communities.
Grant Types: Capital, Challenge, General Support, Operating Expenses, Project, Research, Scholarship.

Financial Summary

Total Giving: $5,548,269 (fiscal year ending September 30, 2001); $5,247,749 (fiscal 2000); $5,571,800 (fiscal 1999). Note: Contributes through corporate direct giving program and foundation.
Giving Analysis: Giving for fiscal 2000 includes: foundation scholarships ($674,549); fiscal 1999: foundation grants to United Way ($33,000); foundation matching gifts ($353,795); foundation scholarships ($860,936); fiscal 1998: foundation grants to United Way ($173,000); foundation scholarships ($615,162); fiscal 2000); $3,115,486 (fiscal 1999)
Assets: $2,973,312 (fiscal 2001); $2,935,862 (fiscal 2000); $3,115,486 (fiscal 1999)
Gifts Received: $5,479,509 (fiscal 2001); $5,000,000 (fiscal 2000); $6,765,000 (fiscal 1999). Note: In fiscal 2001, contributions were received from the Walt Disney Co. ($5,000,000) and miscellaneous contributions from the employees of the Walt Disney Co. ($479,509). Contributions are received from the Walt Disney Company.

Typical Recipients

Arts & Humanities: Arts Associations & Councils, Arts Centers, Arts Festivals, Arts Funds, Arts Institutes, Arts Outreach, Ethnic & Folk Arts, Film & Video, Arts & Humanities-General, History & Archaeology, Libraries, Museums/Galleries, Music, Performing Arts, Public Broadcasting
Civic & Public Affairs: African American Affairs, Business/Free Enterprise, Community Foundations, Economic Development, Employment/Job Training, Ethnic Organizations, Civic & Public Affairs-General, Hispanic Affairs, Law & Justice, Legal Aid, Native American Affairs, Philanthropic Organizations, Public Policy, Urban & Community Affairs, Zoos/Aquariums
Education: Arts/Humanities Education, Business Education, Colleges & Universities, Education Funds, Education Reform, Engineering/Technological Education, Education-General, Health & Physical Education, Legal Education, Medical Education, Minority Education, Science/Mathematics Education, Special Education
Environment: Environment-General, Resource Conservation, Wildlife Protection
Health: Cancer, Children's Health/Hospitals, Clinics/Medical Centers, Diabetes, Emergency/Ambulance Services, Eyes/Blindness, Health-General, Health Organizations, Hospitals, Medical Rehabilitation, Mental Health, Public Health, Single-Disease Health Associations
International: International Environmental Issues, International Relations
Religion: Missionary Activities (Domestic), Religious Welfare

Science: Scientific Centers & Institutes, Scientific Labs
Social Services: Animal Protection, Camps, Child Welfare, Child Welfare, Community Centers, Community Service Organizations, Domestic Violence, Emergency Relief, Family Services, Food/Clothing Distribution, People with Disabilities, Recreation & Athletics, Scouts, Substance Abuse, United Funds/United Ways, Volunteer Services, YMCA/YWCA/YMHA/YWHA, Youth Organizations

Application Procedures

Initial Contact: Send brief letter or proposal.
Application Requirements: Include financial statements, preferably audited; list of major contributors and sources of income; list of board members, including their affiliations; history of the organization; and proof of tax exemption.
Deadlines: Proposals should be submitted by December 31 to be evaluated the following summer; scholarship applications due by October 1 to be issued the following summer.
Review Process: Applications reviewed by foundation staff as received, then passed on to the donations committee.
Evaluative Criteria: Recipients must be tax-exempt, must have been in operation for at least three years, and must make significant use of volunteers.
Decision Notification: Donations committee makes its final decision at its annual summer meeting.

Restrictions

Foundation does not support public agencies, educational institutions, or other nonprofit organizations supported predominantly by tax dollars; agencies receiving funds from United Way, Permanent Charities Committee, or other similar consolidated giving programs to which the foundation contributes; sectarian organizations; agency building campaigns; agency start-up campaigns or for seed money purposes; medical research programs; or individuals.

Additional Information

In past years, most grants have gone to repeat recipients.
Scholarship applicant qualifications include: must be a high school senior or academic equivalent with the expectation of graduating within the 12-month period following October 1 of that year; must be in upper one-third of high school graduating class; must be qualified, upon graduation, to enroll at an accredited four-year college or university; must be a child, stepchild or adopted child of a qualified employee (a full time regular employee who has completed at least one year of continuous service and is a resident or citizen of the United States); must file an official application form which must be received no later than October 1 of the year in which the candidate is eligible to apply.
Publications: Guidelines

Corporate Officials

Roy Edward Disney: vice chairman, director B Los Angeles, CA 1930. ED Pomona College BA (1951). PRIM CORP EMPL vice chairman, director: Walt Disney Co. Inc. CORP AFFIL vice chairman: Disney Enterprises Inc.; chairman, director, founder: Shamrock Holdings Inc. NONPR AFFIL fellow: University Kentucky; member: Writers Guild America; member advisory board: Saint Joseph Medical Center; member: U.S. Naval Academy Sailing Squadron; director: Big Brothers Greater Los Angeles; member: Directors Guild American West. CLUB AFFIL San Diego Yacht Club; Transpacific Yacht Club; Los Angeles Yacht Club; Saint Francis Yacht Club; California Yacht Club; Confrerie des Chevaliers du Tastevin Club; 100 Club.
Michael Dammann Eisner: chairman, chief executive officer, director B Mount Kisco, NY 1942. ED Denison University BA (1964). PRIM CORP EMPL chairman, chief executive officer, director: Walt Disney Co. Inc. ADD CORP EMPL president: Buena

Vista International; president: WCO Parent Corp. CORP AFFIL principal: Disneyland International; chairman: Hollywood Records Inc.; chairman: Anaheim Sports Inc.; chairman: Disney Enterprises Inc. NONPR AFFIL trustee: Denison University; director: University California Los Angeles Board Medicine Science; director: Conservative International; director: American Hospital of Paris Foundation; trustee: California Institute Arts.

Sanford M. Litvack: member, director B Brooklyn, NY 1936. ED University of Connecticut BA (1956); Georgetown University LLB (1959). PRIM CORP EMPL Antigenics Inc. CORP AFFIL director: Buena Vista Home Entertainment; director: Disney International.

Foundation Officials
Roy Edward Disney: trustee, vice president (see above)
Michael Dammann Eisner: president, trustee (see above)
Robert A. Iger: trustee
Paul S. Pressler: trustee
Marsha L. Reed: secretary

Grants Analysis
Disclosure Period: fiscal year ending September 30, 2001
Total Grants: $4,407,072*
Number of Grants: 148
Average Grant: $29,778
Highest Grant: $500,000
Lowest Grant: $500
Typical Range: $1,000 to $50,000
*Note: Giving excludes scholarships, matching gifts, and United Way.

Recent Grants
Note: Grants derived from fiscal 2001 Form 990.

General
500,000	California Institute of the Arts, Valencia, CA -- operations
500,000	California Institute of the Arts, Valencia, CA -- advance against monsters premier
200,000	St. Joseph Medical Center Foundation, Burbank, CA
141,850	Wildlife Conservation Society, Washington, DC
110,000	American Zoo and Aquarium Association
100,000	California Science Center, Los Angeles, CA
100,000	Children's Hospital Foundation of Orange County, Los Angeles, CA
100,000	Entertainment Industry Foundation, Studio City, CA
100,000	Hispanic Culture Foundation, Inc.
100,000	Motion Picture and Television Fund Foundation, Los Angeles, CA

MAMIE MCFADDIN WARD HERITAGE FOUNDATION

Giving Contact
c/o Hibernia National Bank
PO Box 3928
Beaumont, TX 77704-3928
Phone: (409)880-1426
Fax: (409)880-1437

Description
Founded: 1976
EIN: 746260525
Organization Type: Family Foundation
Giving Locations: TX: Jefferson County
Grant Types: Capital, Emergency, Seed Money.

Donor Information
Founder: Established in 1976 by the late Mamie McFaddin Ward .

Financial Summary
Total Giving: $1,560,634 (2001); $226,183 (2000); $1,226,691 (1999)
Assets: $33,188,671 (2001); $31,154,711 (2000); $32,513,608 (1999)

Typical Recipients
Arts & Humanities: Arts Associations & Councils, Arts Outreach, Ballet, Historic Preservation, History & Archaeology, Libraries, Museums/Galleries, Music, Theater
Civic & Public Affairs: Community Foundations, Inner-City Development, Philanthropic Organizations
Education: Colleges & Universities, Elementary Education (Private), Legal Education, Private Education (Precollege), Religious Education, Secondary Education (Private), Secondary Education (Public)
Health: Cancer, Children's Health/Hospitals, Clinics/Medical Centers, Emergency/Ambulance Services, Geriatric Health, Long-Term Care, Medical Rehabilitation, Medical Research, Mental Health, Nutrition
Religion: Bible Study/Translation, Religious Welfare
Science: Science Museums
Social Services: At-Risk Youth, Community Service Organizations, Community Service Organizations, Counseling, Family Services, Food/Clothing Distribution, Homes, Scouts, Senior Services, Social Services-General, Substance Abuse, YMCA/YWCA/YMHA/YWHA, Youth Organizations

Application Procedures
Initial Contact: Applicants should contact the foundation to request an application form.
Application Requirements: Nine copies of the form should be submitted, along with a budget for the requested project, the current year operating budget for the organization, the organization's most recent financial audit, and the IRS determination letter of tax exempt status under Section 501(c)(3).
Deadlines: August 31.
Review Process: Applicants will be notified of the decision concerning their requests, usually in November.
Notes: Recipients are required to make a report to the trustee as to the utilization or status of awarded funds immediately upon the completion of the project or purpose for which the funds are requested, or annually if not otherwise disbursed. No applications will be considered prior to receipt of reports for previously awarded grants.

Restrictions
There is a general policy against the funding of positions, salaries, or other continuing operational expenses that would subject the organization to becoming dependent upon continued foundation support. No funds are provided for student loans, scholarships or fellowships for individual students, grants for endowment funds, annual fund raisers, or annual operating budgets. Grants are not made to individuals.

Additional Information
Hibernia National Bank is the foundation's corporate trustee.

Foundation Officials
Eugene H. B. McFaddin: trustee
James L. C. McFaddin, Jr.: trustee
Jean Moncla: vice president, trust officer
Ida M. Pyle: trustee
Rosine M. Wilson: trustee

Grants Analysis
Disclosure Period: calendar year ending 2001
Total Grants: $935,747*
Number of Grants: 16
Average Grant: $18,039*

Highest Grant: $665,168
Lowest Grant: $2,300
Typical Range: $2,000 to $45,000
*Note: Giving excludes matching gifts. Average grant figure excludes highest grant.

Recent Grants
Note: Grants derived from 2001 Form 990.

General
726,826	McFaddin Ward House, Beaumont, TX -- roof project, expand visitor's center
50,000	Beaumont Community Players, Beaumont, TX -- new facility
25,000	Texas Energy Museum, Beaumont, TX
20,280	JC Council of Alcohol & Drug Abuse, Beaumont, TX -- purchase van
20,000	All Saints Episcopal School, Beaumont, TX -- funding 3 new play areas
20,000	Jefferson Theater Preservation Society, Beaumont, TX -- building renovation
20,000	UBI Caritas, Beaumont, TX -- building renovation
10,000	Boy Scouts of America, Beaumont, TX -- 250 new tents, cots and mattresses
10,000	BUILD, Inc, Beaumont, TX -- restoration of the Hotel Beaumont
10,000	National Alliance for the Mentally Ill, Beaumont, TX -- training and education of family education

ANNA EMORY WARFIELD MEMORIAL FUND

Giving Contact
Braxton Mitchell, Jr., President
P.O. Box 674
Riderwood, MD 21139
Phone: (410)494-0090
Fax: (410)822-9173

Description
Founded: 1928
EIN: 520785672
Organization Type: Private Foundation
Giving Locations: MD: Baltimore metropolitan area
Grant Types: General Support.

Donor Information
Founder: the late S. Davies Warfield

Financial Summary
Total Giving: $222,750 (1999); $498,685 (1998); $180,050 (1996)
Giving Analysis: Giving for 1999 includes: foundation gifts to individuals ($220,800) 1998: foundation gifts to individuals ($219,835)
Assets: $7,445,775 (1999); $6,832,431 (1998); $5,158,988 (1996)
Gifts Received: $1,500 (1992)

Typical Recipients
Arts & Humanities: Libraries
Civic & Public Affairs: Civic & Public Affairs-General, Nonprofit Management, Philanthropic Organizations
Health: Hospitals
Religion: Religious Welfare
Social Services: Child Welfare, Day Care, Family Services, Homes, Senior Services

Application Procedures
Initial Contact: Send brief letter.
Application Requirements: Include purpose and personal and financial data.
Deadlines: None.

Additional Information

Provides grants to individuals to alleviate poverty and human distress.

Publications: Application Guidelines

Foundation Officials

Mrs. W. Page Dame, Jr.: trustee

Edward K. Dunn, Jr.: treasurer, trustee B Baltimore, MD 1935. ED Princeton University AB (1958); Harvard University MBA (1960). PRIM CORP EMPL chief executive officer, director: Mercantile Mortgage. CORP AFFIL vice chairman, president, director: Mercantile Safe Deposit Trust Co.; director: Aegon USA Inc. NONPR AFFIL chairman, director: Baltimore Community Foundation.

Louis W. Hargrave: vice president, trustee PRIM CORP EMPL vice president: NationsBank Corp.

Mrs. John B. Howard: trustee

Mrs. Thomas H. Maddux: trustee

Braxton D. Mitchell: vice president, trustee

Thelma K. O'Neal: secretary

Charles B. Reeves, Jr.: president, trustee B Baltimore, MD 1923. ED Princeton University BA (1947); University of Virginia LLB (1951). PRIM CORP EMPL partner: Venable Baetjer & Howard. NONPR AFFIL president: J. L. Kernan Hospital; member: Maryland Bar Association; member: American Bar Association; member: American Judicature Society.

Mrs. William F. Schmick, Jr.: trustee

Mrs. Barry Strudwick: trustee

Mrs. Lewis C. Strudwick: trustee

Mrs. Guy Warfield: trustee

Grants Analysis

Disclosure Period: calendar year ending 1999
Total Grants: $1,950*
Number of Grants: 2
Highest Grant: $1,200
*Note: Giving excludes grants to individuals.

Recent Grants

Note: Grants derived from 2001 Form 990.

General

26,645	Family and Children Services
25,000	Commission on Aging, Greenwich, CT
25,000	Keswick Multi-Care Center, Baltimore, MD
25,000	St. Ann Adult Day Care, St. Francis, WI
750	Foundation Center, Washington, DC

THE ANDY WARHOL FOUNDATION FOR THE VISUAL ARTS

Giving Contact

Pamela Clapp, Program Director
65 Bleecker St., 7th Fl.
New York, NY 10012
Phone: (212)387-7555
Fax: (212)387-7560
E-mail: info@warholfoundation.org
Web: http://www.warholfoundation.org

Alternate Contact

Tim Hunt, Curator
Note: For inquiries about art works.

Description

Founded: 1987
EIN: 133410749
Organization Type: Specialized/Single Purpose Foundation
Giving Locations: nationally.
Grant Types: Project.

Donor Information

Founder: Established in 1987, shortly after the death of pop artist Andy Warhol . Warhol was the artist who immortalized Marilyn Monroe, Jackie Kennedy Onassis, Campbell's soup cans, and other pop icons with his unique style of drawing and printmaking. He is often credited with starting a unique genre of art, called pop art, in the 1960s. Warhol died on February 22, 1987 from complications of surgery. The foundation was endowed with Warhol's investments, art works, and other personal belongings, such as furniture and jewelry. Much of Warhol's personal belongings were sold at auctions to create a permanent endowment for the foundation.

Financial Summary

Total Giving: $8,972,102 (fiscal year ending April 30, 2001); $6,503,300 (fiscal 2000); $4,000,000 (fiscal 1999 approx)
Assets: $169,345,457 (fiscal 2001); $161,123,964 (fiscal 2000); $100,000,000 (fiscal 1999 approx)
Gifts Received: $513,973 (fiscal 1996); $1,524,155 (fiscal 1995); $2,701,590 (fiscal 1994). Note: Contributions were received from the estate of Andy Warhol.

Typical Recipients

Arts & Humanities: Arts Appreciation, Arts Associations & Councils, Arts Centers, Arts Funds, Arts Institutes, Arts Outreach, Community Arts, Dance, Ethnic & Folk Arts, Film & Video, Arts & Humanities-General, Historic Preservation, History & Archaeology, Libraries, Literary Arts, Museums/Galleries, Public Broadcasting, Visual Arts

Civic & Public Affairs: Employment/Job Training, First Amendment Issues, Nonprofit Management

Education: Arts/Humanities Education, Colleges & Universities, Minority Education

Environment: Protection, Resource Conservation

Health: AIDS/HIV

International: Foreign Arts Organizations

Religion: Churches, Missionary Activities (Domestic)

Application Procedures

Initial Contact: Proposals should be submitted in the form of a two- to three-page letter and include proof of tax-exempt status.

Application Requirements: Letters should a detailed proposal, including objectives, timetables and budget.

Deadlines: None

Review Process: Grant notifications are mailed on July 1 and January 1.

Notes: The foundation will contact the organization if additional information is needed.

Restrictions

The foundation generally makes grants on a one-time basis. The foundation does not support individual artists or filmmakers. Applicant organizations must be tax_exempt under section 501(c)(3) of the IRS Code.

Additional Information

Organizations that have previously received funding from the foundation should contact the foundation before applying again.

In 1996, the foundation reported that it had discontinued its educational program area.

Publications: Guidelines

Foundation Officials

Archibald L. Gillies: president, director B 1936.
John Warhola: vice president, director

Grants Analysis

Disclosure Period: fiscal year ending April 30, 2001
Total Grants: $8,972,102
Number of Grants: 94
Average Grant: $42,706*
Highest Grant: $5,000,410
Typical Range: $20,000 to $100,000
*Note: Average grant figure excludes highest grant.

Recent Grants

Note: Grants derived from fiscal 2000 Form 990.

Library-Related

35,000	New York University, New York, NY -- Grey Art Gallery

General

3,000,000	Warhol Initiative, Cleveland, OH
750,000	Andy Warhol Museum, Pittsburgh, PA -- film preservation
252,500	New York Foundation for Arts, New York, NY -- first-year of $40,000 grant
100,000	Drawing Center, The, New York, NY -- second-year of $40,000 grant for the Viewing Program and Selections exhibition series
100,000	Los Angeles Conservancy, Los Angeles, CA
100,000	National Trust for Historic Preservation, Washington, DC -- first-year of $30,000 grant for professional support for the Cultural Diversity Scholarship Program
100,000	New York Landmark Conservancy, New York, NY
60,000	Urban Institute, Washington, DC
50,000	Cunningham Dance Foundation, New York, NY
50,000	Delaware Center for Contemporary Arts, Wilmington, DE -- visual arts programming support

ALBERT AND BESSIE WARNER FUND

Giving Contact

c/o Funding Exchange
666 Broadway, Ste. 500
New York, NY 10012
Phone: (516)725-0145

Description

Founded: 1955
EIN: 136095213
Organization Type: Private Foundation
Giving Locations: NY: New York primarily in the Northeast.
Grant Types: General Support.

Financial Summary

Total Giving: $386,870 (2001); $296,000 (2000); $287,300 (1997)
Assets: $5,659,560 (2001); $4,811,941 (2000); $5,159,084 (1997)

Typical Recipients

Arts & Humanities: Arts Centers, Arts Funds, Arts Institutes, Dance, Film & Video, Libraries, Museums/Galleries, Music, Public Broadcasting, Theater

Civic & Public Affairs: Botanical Gardens/Parks, Civil Rights, Civic & Public Affairs-General, Housing, Legal Aid, Nonprofit Management, Philanthropic Organizations, Public Policy, Urban & Community Affairs

Education: Colleges & Universities, Legal Education

Environment: Air/Water Quality, Environment-General, Resource Conservation

Health: Children's Health/Hospitals, Hospices, Hospitals, Mental Health

Religion: Jewish Causes, Religious Organizations, Religious Welfare

Social Services: Child Welfare, Community Service Organizations, Crime Prevention, Delinquency & Criminal Rehabilitation, Family Planning, Homes, Recreation & Athletics, Shelters/Homelessness, Social Services-General, Youth Organizations

Application Procedures

Initial Contact: Send a brief letter of inquiry describing program or project.
Deadlines: None.

Foundation Officials

John Steel: trustee
Kitty Steel: trustee
Lewis M. Steel: trustee
Ruth M. Steel: trustee

Grants Analysis

Disclosure Period: calendar year ending 2001
Total Grants: $386,870
Number of Grants: 29
Average Grant: $5,995*
Highest Grant: $219,000
Lowest Grant: $1,000
Typical Range: $1,000 to $10,000
*Note: Average grant figure excludes highest grant.

Recent Grants

Note: Grants derived from 2000 Form 990.

Library-Related

1,000	Rogers Memorial Library, Southampton, NY

General

150,000	Joint Foundation Support
60,000	Institute for Policy Studies, Washington, DC
20,000	Institute for Public Affairs, Chicago, IL
16,000	Parrish Art Museum, New York, NY
10,000	Jewish Fund for Justice, New York, NY
7,500	Steel Foundation, New York, NY
6,000	Columbia School of Law, New York, NY
6,000	Southampton Hospital, Southampton, NY
5,000	Coalition for the Homeless
5,000	Fordham University, Bronx, NY

RILEY J. AND LILLIAN N. WARREN AND BEATRICE W. BLANDING FOUNDATION

Giving Contact

Henry L. Hulbert, Managing Trustee
6 Ford Ave.
Oneonta, NY 13820
Phone: (607)432-6720

Description

Founded: 1972
EIN: 237203341
Organization Type: Private Foundation
Giving Locations: NY: Oneonta
Grant Types: General Support.

Donor Information

Founder: Beatrice W. Blanding

Financial Summary

Total Giving: $1,092,142 (2002); $940,850 (2001); $908,295 (2000)
Giving Analysis: Giving for 2002 includes: foundation grants to United Way ($3,000); 2000: foundation grants to United Way ($3,000) 1999: foundation grants to United Way ($3,000)
Assets: $17,930,309 (2002); $21,235,732 (2000); $23,296,171 (1999)
Gifts Received: $1,289,434 (2002); $900,000 (2001); $498,259 (2000). Note: In 1995, 2001, and 2002, contributions were received from the estate of Beatrice W. Blanding.

Typical Recipients

Arts & Humanities: History & Archaeology, Libraries, Music, Opera
Civic & Public Affairs: Community Foundations, Employment/Job Training, Civic & Public Affairs-General, Housing, Municipalities/Towns, Urban & Community Affairs
Education: Colleges & Universities, Literacy, Private Education (Precollege), Religious Education
Health: Children's Health/Hospitals, Hospices, Hospitals
Religion: Churches, Religious Organizations, Religious Welfare, Synagogues/Temples
Social Services: Community Service Organizations, Emergency Relief, Family Services, People with Disabilities, Recreation & Athletics, Social Services-General, United Funds/United Ways, Volunteer Services, Youth Organizations

Application Procedures

Initial Contact: Send a brief letter of inquiry.
Application Requirements: Include a description of the program or project.
Deadlines: November 1.

Restrictions

Primary geographic area is around Oneonta, NY.

Foundation Officials

Robert A. Harlem: trustee
Henry L. Hulbert: mng trustee
Maureen Hulbert: trustee

Grants Analysis

Disclosure Period: calendar year ending 2002
Total Grants: $1,089,142*
Number of Grants: 33
Average Grant: $16,553*
Highest Grant: $300,000
Lowest Grant: $3,000
Typical Range: $5,000 to $30,000
*Note: Giving excludes United Way. Average grant figure excludes two highest grants ($576,000).

Recent Grants

Note: Grants derived from 2001 Form 990.

General

300,000	Hartwick College, Onconta, NY
125,000	St. Mary's School, Oneonta, NY -- for parochial school
81,350	A.O. Fox Memorial Hospital Foundation, Oneonta, NY
80,000	St. Mary's School, Oneonta, NY -- for annual operations
50,000	City of Oneonta, Oneonta, NY -- for parks systems
49,000	Oneonta Boys and Girls Club, Oneonta, NY -- for annual operations
40,000	Catskill Symphony Orchestra, Oneonta, NY
30,000	Temple Beth El, Oneonta, NY -- for building project
25,000	Siena College, Loudonville, NY -- for annual operations
20,000	Catskill Area Hospice, Oneonta, NY -- for operations

WARWICK FOUNDATION

Giving Contact

Mimi Stauffer
c/o Glenmede Trust Co.
1 Liberty Pl.
1650 Market St., Suite 1200
Philadelphia, PA 19103-7391
Phone: (215)419-6000

Description

Founded: 1961
EIN: 236230662
Organization Type: Private Foundation
Giving Locations: PA: Bucks County, Philadelphia
Grant Types: Operating Expenses, Scholarship.

Donor Information

Founder: Helen H. Gemmill, Kenneth Gemmill

Financial Summary

Total Giving: $1,220,000 (2000); $562,500 (1999); $261,149 (1997)
Giving Analysis: Giving for 2000 includes: foundation scholarships ($14,000); foundation scholarships ($79,000); 1999: foundation grants to United Way ($20,000) foundation scholarships ($138,000)
Assets: $22,929,184 (2000); $18,998,637 (1999); $8,122,342 (1997)
Gifts Received: $9,210 (2000); $15,746,533 (1999). Note: In 1999, contributions were received from the Estate of Kenneth Gemmill. In 1997, contributions were received from Helen Gemmill.

Typical Recipients

Arts & Humanities: Arts Centers, Historic Preservation, History & Archaeology, Libraries, Museums/Galleries, Music, Opera, Public Broadcasting
Civic & Public Affairs: Botanical Gardens/Parks, Clubs, Professional & Trade Associations, Public Policy, Zoos/Aquariums
Education: Agricultural Education, Arts/Humanities Education, Colleges & Universities, Community & Junior Colleges, Legal Education, Private Education (Precollege), Religious Education, Special Education, Student Aid
Environment: Environment-General, Resource Conservation
Health: Emergency/Ambulance Services, Hospitals
Religion: Churches, Religious Welfare, Seminaries
Science: Science Museums, Scientific Centers & Institutes, Scientific Organizations
Social Services: Camps, Community Service Organizations, People with Disabilities, Shelters/Homelessness, United Funds/United Ways, YMCA/YWCA/YMHA/YWHA, Youth Organizations

Application Procedures

Initial Contact: Send a brief letter of inquiry and a full proposal.
Application Requirements: Include a a description of organization, amount requested, purpose of funds sought, recently audited financial statement, and proof of tax-exempt status.
Deadlines: None.

Restrictions

Grants are not made to individuals.

Foundation Officials

Elizabeth H. Gemmill: trustee B Philadelphia, PA 1945. ED Bryn Mawr College (1967); Boston University (1970). PRIM CORP EMPL vice president, secretary: Tasty Baking Co. CORP AFFIL director: America Water Works Co. Inc.; director: Pennsylvania Facilities Management Corp.
Helen H. Gemmill: trustee

Grants Analysis

Disclosure Period: calendar year ending 2000
Total Grants: $1,127,000*
Number of Grants: 35
Average Grant: $6,676*
Highest Grant: $900,000

Typical Range: $1,000 to $10,000
*Note: Average grant figure excludes highest grant. Giving excludes United Way and scholarship.

Recent Grants

Note: Grants derived from 1999 Form 990.

General

155,000	Heritage Conservancy, Doylestown, PA
60,000	Doylestown Hospital, Doylestown, PA
40,000	Bucks County Historical Society, Doylestown, PA
40,000	Neshaminy Warwick Presbyterian Church, Warminster, PA
40,000	University of Pennsylvania Law School, Philadelphia, PA
26,000	Please Touch Museum, Philadelphia, PA
15,000	Bryn Mawr College, Bryn Mawr, PA -- Helen H. Gemmill Scholarship
15,000	Hamilton College, Clinton, NY -- JK Gemmill Fund
15,000	Princeton Theological Seminary, Princeton, NJ
15,000	Princeton University, Princeton, NJ

WARWICK SAVINGS FOUNDATION

Giving Contact

Timothy A. Dempsey, President
591 RT. 17 M
PO Box 507
Monroe, NY 10950
Phone: (914)782-8605

Description

Founded: 1997
EIN: 061504632
Organization Type: Private Foundation
Grant Types: General Support.

Financial Summary

Total Giving: $148,789 (2001); $112,000 (2000); $150,000 (1999)
Assets: $3,595,494 (2001); $2,244,881 (2000); $1,889,212 (1999)

Typical Recipients

Arts & Humanities: History & Archaeology, Libraries
Civic & Public Affairs: Clubs, Civic & Public Affairs-General, Municipalities/Towns, Safety
Education: Elementary Education (Private), Education-General, Private Education (Precollege)
Health: Clinics/Medical Centers
Religion: Ministries
Social Services: Camps, Day Care, Food/Clothing Distribution, Volunteer Services, YMCA/YWCA/YMHA/YWHA

Foundation Officials

Peter H. Alberghini: director
Arthur W. Budich: vice president, treasurer
Timothy A. Dempsey: president
Ronald J. Gentile: executive vice president
Frances M. Goresh: director
Michael Hoffman: director
Thomas F. Lawrence, Jr.: director
Sister Anne Sakac: director
Robert N. Smith: director
Nancy L. Sobotor-Littell: secretary
Lois E. Ulatowski: assistant secretary

Grants Analysis

Disclosure Period: calendar year ending 2001
Total Grants: $148,789

Number of Grants: 24
Average Grant: $6,200
Highest Grant: $20,000
Lowest Grant: $1,000
Typical Range: $1,000 to $10,000

Recent Grants

Note: Grants derived from 2000 Form 990.

Library-Related

2,500	Albert Wisner Public Library, Warwick, NY
1,000	Friends of the Middletown Thrall Library, Middletown, NY

General

15,000	St. Edward School, Newark, CA
15,000	St. Joseph Parochial School
10,000	Bishop Dunn Memorial School
10,000	Occupations, Inc., Newburgh, NY
10,000	Village of Warwick, Warwick, WI
5,000	Family Health Center of Newburgh, Newburgh, NY
5,000	Food Bank of Hudson Valley
5,000	Kiryas Joel Volunteer EMS, Inc.
5,000	Middletown YMCA, Middletown, NY
5,000	Purple Champions Club

WASHINGTON FORREST FOUNDATION

Giving Contact

Deborah G. Lucckese, Vice President
2300 S. 9th St.
Arlington, VA 22204
Phone: (703)920-2200

Description

Founded: 1968
EIN: 237002944
Organization Type: Private Foundation
Giving Locations: VA: Northern Virginia
Grant Types: Capital, Emergency, General Support, Multiyear/Continuing Support, Operating Expenses, Scholarship, Seed Money.

Donor Information

Founder: the late Benjamin M. Smith

Financial Summary

Total Giving: $614,226 (fiscal year ending June 30, 2002); $510,115 (fiscal 2001); $450,853 (fiscal 2000)
Giving Analysis: Giving for fiscal 2001 includes: foundation grants to United Way ($10,000); fiscal 2000: foundation grants to United Way ($5,000); fiscal 1998: foundation grants to United Way ($5,000);
Assets: $17,630,675 (fiscal 2002); $12,954,863 (fiscal 2001); $12,063,110 (fiscal 2000)
Gifts Received: $457,000 (fiscal 1992). Note: In 1992, contributions were received from the Virginia Smith Charitable Foundation.

Typical Recipients

Arts & Humanities: Arts Associations & Councils, Arts Centers, Arts Outreach, Community Arts, Dance, Ethnic & Folk Arts, Libraries, Music, Opera, Performing Arts, Public Broadcasting, Theater
Civic & Public Affairs: Community Foundations, Economic Development, Civic & Public Affairs-General, Housing, Philanthropic Organizations, Professional & Trade Associations, Public Policy, Urban & Community Affairs, Women's Affairs
Education: Afterschool/Enrichment Programs, Colleges & Universities, Education Funds, Elementary Education (Public), Education-General, Literacy, Medical Education, Minority Education, Private Education (Precollege), Public Education (Precollege),

Religious Education, Secondary Education (Public), Student Aid
Health: AIDS/HIV, Arthritis, Cancer, Children's Health/Hospitals, Clinics/Medical Centers, Emergency/Ambulance Services, Health Organizations, Home-Care Services, Hospices, Mental Health, Research/Studies Institutes, Respiratory
Religion: Churches, Religious Organizations, Religious Welfare
Social Services: Camps, Child Abuse, Child Welfare, Community Service Organizations, Counseling, Delinquency & Criminal Rehabilitation, Domestic Violence, Family Planning, Family Services, Food/Clothing Distribution, Recreation & Athletics, Scouts, Shelters/Homelessness, Substance Abuse, United Funds/United Ways, YMCA/YWCA/YMHA/YWHA, Youth Organizations

Application Procedures

Initial Contact: Request application form.
Deadlines: None.
Review Process: Applications are considered by the foundation board of directors four times annually.

Restrictions

Limited to Northern Virginia.

Additional Information

Publications: Program Policy Statement

Foundation Officials

Leslie S. Ariail: secretary
Allison A. Erdle: trustee
Benjamin C. Gravett: trustee
Deborah G. Lucckese: vice president
David D. Peete, Jr.: trustee
Lindsey D. Peete: executive director
Margaret S. Peete: president
Benjamin M. Smith, Jr.: treasurer

Grants Analysis

Disclosure Period: fiscal year ending June 30, 2002
Total Grants: $614,226
Number of Grants: 112
Average Grant: $5,484
Highest Grant: $25,000
Lowest Grant: $250
Typical Range: $1,000 to $10,000

Recent Grants

Note: Grants derived from fiscal 2000 Form 990.

General

25,000	Arlington Public Schools, Arlington, VA -- first grade at-risk program at Drew School
20,000	Trinity Episcopal Children's Center, Arlington, VA -- support school maintenance
15,000	4-H Character Club of Northern Virginia, Arlington, VA -- after school and summer day camp program
15,000	Alexandria Neighborhood Health Services, Inc, Alexandria, VA -- support the Arlandria Health Center
15,000	Arlington Community Temporary Shelter, Arlington, VA
15,000	Arlington Public Schools, Arlington, VA -- support Wakefield-Kaplan SAT preparatory program
15,000	Arlington United Methodist Church, Arlington, VA -- exterior church painting
15,000	Hospice of Northern Virginia, Falls Church, VA
15,000	Virginia Foundation for Independent Colleges, Richmond, VA
15,000	Virginia United Methodist Homes, Richmond, VA -- support the Samaritan program at he Hermitage in Northern Virginia

DENNIS R. AND PHYLLIS WASHINGTON FOUNDATION

Giving Contact
Russ Ritter, President
PO Box 16630
Missoula, MT 59808-6630
Phone: (406)523-1300
Fax: (406)523-1339
E-mail: lpaulson@washcorp.com
Web: http://www.washcorp.com/Foundation/about.htm

Description
Founded: 1988
EIN: 363606913
Organization Type: Private Foundation
Giving Locations: MT
Grant Types: General Support.

Donor Information
Founder: Montana Rail Link, Montana Resources, Washington Contractors, Envirocon Modern Machinery Co., Western Transport

Financial Summary
Total Giving: $1,328,938 (2000); $1,704,080 (1999); $1,610,382 (1998)
Giving Analysis: Giving for 2000 includes: foundation grants to United Way ($22,000); 1999: foundation grants to United Way ($15,250); foundation scholarships ($39,500) 1998: foundation grants to United Way ($18,500)
Assets: $15,917,240 (2000); $21,942,996 (1999); $15,883,647 (1998)
Gifts Received: $465,999 (2000); $1,490,996 (1999); $1,515,456 (1998). Note: In 2000, contributions were received from Montana Rail Link ($349,999); Dennis & Phyllis Washington ($70,000); Norsk Pacific ($32,700); and various other donors. In 1998, contributions were received from Montana Rail Link ($443,616); Modern Machinery Co. ($22,240); Montana Resources ($16,300); Dennis and Phyllis Washington ($1,000,000); and Envirocon, Inc. ($33,300).

Typical Recipients
Arts & Humanities: Arts Appreciation, Arts & Humanities-General, History & Archaeology, Music, Theater
Civic & Public Affairs: Clubs, Employment/Job Training, Civic & Public Affairs-General, Housing, Women's Affairs, Zoos/Aquariums
Education: Business Education, Colleges & Universities, Engineering/Technological Education, Environmental Education, Private Education (Precollege), Public Education (Precollege), Science/Mathematics Education, Special Education, Student Aid
Health: Cancer, Children's Health/Hospitals, Diabetes, Emergency/Ambulance Services, Health Organizations, Hospitals, Prenatal Health Issues
International: Foreign Arts Organizations
Religion: Bible Study/Translation, Ministries, Religious Welfare
Science: Science Exhibits & Fairs
Social Services: At-Risk Youth, Camps, Child Welfare, Community Centers, Community Service Organizations, Crime Prevention, Delinquency & Criminal Rehabilitation, Food/Clothing Distribution, Homes, People with Disabilities, Recreation & Athletics, Scouts, Sexual Abuse, Shelters/Homelessness, Special Olympics, United Funds/United Ways, YMCA/YWCA/YMHA/YWHA, Youth Organizations

Application Procedures
Initial Contact: Request an application form.
Deadlines: None.
Review Process: Contribution commitee meets quarterly.

Restrictions
Emphasis is on youth and education in areas where the Washington companies operate.

Foundation Officials
William Brodsky: director
Jim Brouelette: secretary
Deborah Brown: treasurer
Frank Gardner: vice president, director
Mike Haight: controller
Helen Miller: director
Dorn Parkinson: director PRIM CORP EMPL chairman: Kasler Holding Co.
Russ Ritter: president
Brian Sheridan: vice president, director
Phyllis Washington: director

Grants Analysis
Disclosure Period: calendar year ending 2000
Total Grants: $1,306,938*
Number of Grants: 95
Average Grant: $13,757
Highest Grant: $75,000
Typical Range: $1,000 to $20,000
*Note: Giving excludes United Way.

Recent Grants
Note: Grants derived from 2000 Form 990.

General
75,000	Shodair Children's Hospital, Helena, MT -- complete outdoor swimming pool
60,000	National Heritage Collector's Society, Westlake Villa, MT -- Young Life Bronzes first payment
56,000	UM Foundation, Missoula, MT -- Dennis and Phyll Washington Presidential Scholarship
50,000	Caring Foundation of Montana, Helena, MT -- mammograms and prostate exams
50,000	Horatio Alger Association, Washington, DC -- scholarship
50,000	Missoula County Stadium Boosters, Missoula, MT -- bleacher/lighting replacement
50,000	Red Cross/Lee Enterprises Fire Fund, Helena, MT -- fire relief for families
50,000	YMCA, Billings, MT -- construction materials
40,000	Jobs for America's Graduates, Helena, MT -- scholarships
33,333	Kidsports, Kalispell, MT -- improvements for the youth complex

WASHINGTON GROUP INTERNATIONAL, INC.

Company Headquarters
720 Park Blvd.
Boise, ID 83712
Web: http://www.wgint.com

Company Description
Founded: 2000
Ticker: WGII
Exchange: NASDAQ
Former Name: Morrison Knudsen (2000);
Acquired: Raytheon (2000).
Operating Revenue: US$3.661 billion (2002)
Profit: US$559.9 million (2002)
Employees: 34000 (2002)
Fortune Rank: 435, per FORTUNE Magazine's list of 500 Largest U.S. Corporations (2002).

Nonmonetary Support
Type: Donated Equipment; In-kind Services; Loaned Employees; Loaned Executives
Contact: Brenda Barnard, Coordinator

Washington Group Foundation, Inc.

Giving Contact
Marlene Puckett, Administrator, Director, Secretary
One Morrison Knudsen Plaza
Boise, ID 83729
Phone: (208)386-5201

Description
EIN: 826005410
Organization Type: Corporate Foundation
Giving Locations: ID: nationally; operating locations.
Grant Types: Employee Matching Gifts.
Note: Employee matching gift ratio: .5 to 1 up to $1,000 annually for educational institutions.

Financial Summary
Total Giving: $346,524 (2001); $372,568 (2000); $419,059 (1998). Note: Contributes through foundation only.
Giving Analysis: Giving for 2000 includes: foundation scholarships ($1,000); foundation ($154,599); foundation gifts to individuals ($216,969); 1998: foundation scholarships ($1,000); foundation grants to United Way ($23,590); foundation ($160,193) foundation gifts to individuals ($234,276)
Assets: $6,250,308 (2001); $6,827,999 (2000); $6,638,628 (1998)
Gifts Received: $84,013 (2001); $2,300 (1998); $150 (1996)

Typical Recipients
Arts & Humanities: Arts Centers, Arts Festivals, Arts Funds, Ballet, Community Arts, Dance, Ethnic & Folk Arts, Arts & Humanities-General, History & Archaeology, Libraries, Museums/Galleries, Music, Opera, Performing Arts, Public Broadcasting, Theater
Civic & Public Affairs: African American Affairs, Business/Free Enterprise, Civil Rights, Community Foundations, Economic Development, Employment/Job Training, Civic & Public Affairs-General, Hispanic Affairs, Housing, Legal Aid, Native American Affairs, Parades/Festivals, Philanthropic Organizations, Professional & Trade Associations, Public Policy, Safety, Urban & Community Affairs, Women's Affairs, Zoos/Aquariums
Education: Arts/Humanities Education, Business Education, Colleges & Universities, Education Associations, Education Funds, Education Reform, Elementary Education (Public), Engineering/Technological Education, Education-General, Minority Education, Private Education (Precollege), Public Education (Precollege), Religious Education, Secondary Education (Private), Student Aid
Environment: Environment-General, Resource Conservation, Wildlife Protection
Health: Alzheimers Disease, Cancer, Children's Health/Hospitals, Clinics/Medical Centers, Diabetes, Emergency/Ambulance Services, Health-General, Health Organizations, Hospices, Hospitals, Long-Term Care, Medical Rehabilitation, Medical Research, Multiple Sclerosis, Public Health, Respiratory, Single-Disease Health Associations
International: Foreign Educational Institutions, International Relations, International Relief Efforts
Religion: Jewish Causes, Religious Organizations, Religious Welfare, Seminaries
Science: Science Museums
Social Services: Animal Protection, At-Risk Youth, Child Welfare, Community Centers, Community Service Organizations, Day Care, Domestic Violence, Family Services, Food/Clothing Distribution, People with Disabilities, Recreation & Athletics, Scouts, Senior Services, Shelters/Homelessness, Social Services-General, United Funds/United Ways, Veterans, YMCA/YWCA/YMHA/YWHA, Youth Organizations

Application Procedures

Initial Contact: Individuals send a written request for a foundation questionnaire. Do not take applications for organizations.

Application Requirements: Completed applications will include activities of the applying organization, specific amount requested, outline of how grant would be used, proof of 501(c)(3) status, and prescribed financial statement and completed questionnaire.

Deadlines: None.

Review Process: Proposals reviewed at regular board meetings.

Evaluative Criteria: Individuals and families requesting aid should reside in the city where the company has a presence, and should be classified as needy. Organizations must have 501(c)(3) status. The importance of the organization to employees, participation of employees in organization, the impact gift will have; and the history of giving to the organization by the foundation and employees, are all taken into consideration.

Restrictions

The foundation is unable to provide grants for business purposes, education such as tuition, legal fees, income taxes, etc.

They are unable to duplicate any services that may be available within the community, and may suggest to applicants other services for which they are qualified.

Additional Information

When approved, limited assistance is distributed as a one-time gift, for which payments are made to service providers or vendors, not given directly to the applicant.

Foundation Officials

Anthony Ferruccio: director
Frank Finlayson: director
Stephen G. Hanks: president, chairman, director, chief executive officer B 1951. ED Brigham Young University BS (1974); University of Utah MBA (1975); University of Idaho JD (1978). PRIM CORP EMPL executive vice president, chief legal officer: Morrison-Knudsen Corp. CORP AFFIL officer: Morrison Knudsen Corp. Delaware Corp.; secretary: Morrison Knudsen Corp. Ohio Corp.; secretary: American Piping Boiler Co.
Betty Hurd: director
James McCallum: director
Mark F. Tavelli: director
Larry R. Thomas: director
Dawn Yantek: director

Grants Analysis

Disclosure Period: calendar year ending 2001
Total Grants: $93,870*
Number of Grants: 311
Average Grant: $300
Highest Grant: $3,622
Lowest Grant: $13
Typical Range: $50 to $1,900
*Note: Giving excludes gifts to individuals.

Recent Grants

Note: Grants derived from 2001 Form 990.

General

15,000	Boise State University Foundation, Boise, ID
5,000	Boys and Girls Club, Davenport, IA
3,622	Women and Children Alliance Crisis Center
3,000	Nampa Shelter Foundation, Nampa, ID
2,500	Hardin Valley Elementary School
2,500	Idaho Fish and Wildlife Foundation, Boise, ID
2,500	Idaho Shakespeare Festival, Inc., Boise, ID
2,500	YMCA, Boise, ID
2,200	University of Wyoming, Laramie, WY
2,000	Boise Public Schools Education Foundation, Boise, ID

WASHINGTON MUTUAL, INC.

Company Headquarters

1201 3rd Avenue, Suite 1500
Seattle, WA 98101
Phone: (206)461-2000
Fax: (206)554-4807
Web: http://www.wamu.com

Company Description

Founded: 1889
Ticker: WM
Exchange: NYSE
Acquired: Bank United Corp. (2001); Dime Savings Bank of New York, FSB (2001).
Assets: US$268.298 billion (2002)
Profit: US$3.896 billion (2002)
Employees: 28798 (2002)
Fortune Rank: 94, per FORTUNE Magazine's list of 500 Largest U.S. Corporations (2002).
SIC(s): 6036 Savings Institutions Except Federal.

Operating Locations

Washington Mutual, Inc. (OR--Medford, Salem; UT--Brigham City, Logan, Ogden, Provo, Roy, St. George, West Jordan; WA--Aberdeen, Seattle)

Nonmonetary Support

Type: Donated Equipment; In-kind Services

Dime Foundation

Giving Contact

Lorraine Whiffen, Assistant Treasurer
Dime Foundation
589 Fifth Avenue
New York, NY 10017
Phone: (516)596-3849

Description

EIN: 112966463
Organization Type: Corporate Foundation
Giving Locations: NJ; NY
Grant Types: General Support, Project.

Financial Summary

Total Giving: $261,500 (2001); $241,500 (2000); $243,500 (1999)
Giving Analysis: Giving for 2001 includes: foundation ($261,500); 2000: foundation ($241,500) 1999: foundation ($243,500)
Assets: $1,007 (2001); $34,640 (2000); $15,763 (1998)
Gifts Received: $245,600 (2001); $261,700 (2000); $205,200 (1999). Note: Contributions were received from Dime Savings Bank of New York FSB.

Typical Recipients

Arts & Humanities: Arts Associations & Councils, Dance, History & Archaeology, Libraries, Music, Theater
Civic & Public Affairs: Asian American Affairs, Community Foundations, Economic Development, Economic Policy, Civic & Public Affairs-General, Hispanic Affairs, Housing, Legal Aid, Urban & Community Affairs
Education: Arts/Humanities Education, Economic Education, Education Reform, Education-General, Literacy
International: International Relief Efforts
Religion: Ministries, Religious Welfare

Social Services: Big Brother/Big Sister, Community Service Organizations, Family Services, Shelters/Homelessness, Social Services-General, Youth Organizations

Application Procedures

Initial Contact: The foundation requests applications be made in writing.
Application Requirements: Include a narrative of the program, list of board members and officers, fiscal information, and proof of tax-exempt status.
Deadlines: April 30 and October 31.

Restrictions

Emphasis is on organizations targeting affordable housing and education programs. Does not support individuals, religious organizations for sectarian purposes, political or lobbying groups, or organizations outside operating areas.

Corporate Officials

Lawrence J. Toal: chairman, chief executive officer PRIM CORP EMPL chairman, chief executive officer: Dime Savings Bank of New York FSB.

Foundation Officials

Richard Dalrymple: president, director
Thomas J. Ducca: treasurer
James Fulton: director
Elizabeth Knoerzer: secretary
Virginia Kopp: director
James M. Lange, Jr.: director
John Morning: director
William Volckhausen: assistant treasurer
Lorraine Whiffen: assistant secretary
Donna Wilson: assistant secretary
Franklin L. Wright, Jr.: assistant treasurer

Grants Analysis

Disclosure Period: calendar year ending 2001
Total Grants: $261,500
Number of Grants: 96
Average Grant: $2,724
Highest Grant: $20,000
Lowest Grant: $1,500
Typical Range: $1,500 to $5,000

Recent Grants

Note: Grants derived from 2001 Form 990.

Library-Related

5,000	Brooklyn Public Library, Brooklyn, NY

General

20,000	Brooklyn Academy of Music, Brooklyn, NY
15,000	Big Brothers and Big Sisters, New York, NY
15,000	Faith Center for Community Development, New York, NY
15,000	Futures in Education Foundation, Douglaston, NY
10,000	Enterprise Foundation, New York, NY
5,000	Boys and Girls Club of America, New York, NY
5,000	Girls Inc., New York, NY
5,000	La Casa de Don Pedro, Newark, NJ
3,500	Louise Wise Services for Children and Families, New York, NY
3,000	Brooklyn Legal Services Corporation, Brooklyn, NY

WASHINGTON MUTUAL, INC.

Company Headquarters

1201 3rd Avenue, Suite 1500
Seattle, WA 98101
Phone: (206)461-2000

Fax: (206)554-4807
Web: http://www.wamu.com

Company Description

Founded: 1889
Ticker: WM
Exchange: NYSE
Acquired: Bank United Corp. (2001); Dime Savings Bank of New York, FSB (2001).
Assets: US$268.298 billion (2002)
Profit: US$3.896 billion (2002)
Employees: 28798 (2002)
Fortune Rank: 94, per FORTUNE Magazine's list of 500 Largest U.S. Corporations (2002).
SIC(s): 6036 Savings Institutions Except Federal.

Operating Locations

Washington Mutual, Inc. (OR--Medford, Salem; UT--Brigham City, Logan, Ogden, Provo, Roy, St. George, West Jordan; WA--Aberdeen, Seattle)

Nonmonetary Support

Value: $2,313,945 (2000 approx)
Type: Donated Equipment; In-kind Services
Volunteer Programs: Employees who work 20 hours or more per week are eligible to receive up to four hours of paid time off each month to do volunteer work through the company's Volunteer Release Time program.
Contact: Lois Harless, Program Manager
Note: Company provides nonmonetary support.

Washington Mutual Foundation

Giving Contact

Washington Mutual Community Relations
999 Third Ave., FIS2913
Seattle, WA 98104
Phone: (206)490-3249
Web: http://wamu.com

Alternate Contact

Phone: 800-258-0543

Description

EIN: 911070920
Organization Type: Corporate Foundation
Former Name: Washington Mutual Bank Foundation.
Giving Locations: AZ; CA; CO; FL; ID; IL; MA; NV; NY; OR; TX; UT; WA: company operating areas.
Grant Types: Capital, Employee Matching Gifts, General Support, Multiyear/Continuing Support, Operating Expenses, Project.
Note: Employee matching gift ratio: 1 to 1, up to $10,000 annually per employee.

Financial Summary

Total Giving: $70,000,000 (2002 approx); $16,712,476 (2001); $41,000,000 (2000 approx). Note: Contributes through corporate direct giving program and foundation.
Giving Analysis: Giving for 2000 includes: foundation matching gifts ($937,277); foundation grants to United Way ($1,332,975); foundation ($9,747,905); corporate direct giving (approx $30,000,000); 1999: foundation matching gifts ($706,443); foundation grants to United Way ($1,328,414); foundation ($6,781,917); 1997: foundation grants to United Way ($415,700); foundation matching gifts ($423,517); foundation ($1,538,222);
Assets: $25,792,633 (2001); $3,369,964 (2000); $3,275,705 (1999)
Gifts Received: $41,255,080 (2001); $12,021,000 (2000); $7,500,000 (1999). Note: Contributions are received from Washington Mutual Bank.

Typical Recipients

Arts & Humanities: Arts Associations & Councils, Arts Centers, Ballet, Community Arts, Ethnic & Folk Arts, Libraries, Museums/Galleries, Music, Performing Arts, Public Broadcasting, Theater
Civic & Public Affairs: Asian American Affairs, Business/Free Enterprise, Community Foundations, Economic Development, Employment/Job Training, Civic & Public Affairs-General, Hispanic Affairs, Housing, Minority Business, Native American Affairs, Public Policy, Urban & Community Affairs, Women's Affairs
Education: Afterschool/Enrichment Programs, Agricultural Education, Arts/Humanities Education, Business Education, Colleges & Universities, Community & Junior Colleges, Economic Education, Education Associations, Education Funds, Education Reform, Education Reform, Elementary Education (Public), Faculty Development, Education-General, Leadership Training, Literacy, Minority Education, Preschool Education, Private Education (Precollege), Public Education (Precollege), Science/Mathematics Education, Special Education
Environment: Environment-General, Resource Conservation
Health: AIDS/HIV, Cancer, Children's Health/Hospitals, Clinics/Medical Centers, Emergency/Ambulance Services, Long-Term Care, Mental Health, Public Health
Religion: Religious Welfare
Science: Scientific Centers & Institutes
Social Services: Camps, Child Welfare, Community Centers, Community Service Organizations, Day Care, Domestic Violence, Family Services, Food/Clothing Distribution, Scouts, Senior Services, United Funds/United Ways, Volunteer Services, YMCA/YWCA/YMHA/YWHA, Youth Organizations

Application Procedures

Initial Contact: Contact the foundation or community relations by letter or phone to request current guidelines and application form.
Application Requirements: Submit a full grant proposal (not to exceed four pages). The proposal should include information about the applicant organization, including organization's name and address; chief executive's name and title; contact person's name, title, phone number, and fax number; counties the organization serves; age, ethnicity, gender, and income demographics of population served by the program, and percentage of people served who are below 80% of median income; names and affiliations of board members; list of Washington Mutual employees who are involved with the organization, and how they support the organization; and proof of tax-exempt status. For school-based programs, include percentage of students eligible for the federal free or reduced lunch program.
A proposal should also include specifics about the funding request, including amount requested; time frame in which funds will be used; the program or project for which you are seeking support and how it relates to your organizational mission; specific program or project goals, objectives, timelines, and anticipated impact; methods for monitoring progress and evaluating success; how the program or project will be funded after the grant period has ended; and letters of agreement or other documentation from any collaborating agencies.
Applicants should include a section on the organization's finances, including total operating budget for the current fiscal year; the organization's sources of revenue for the current and previous fiscal years (with sources and amounts); other sources being solicited for project funding; research; and a detailed budget of the project for which funds are sought, if applicable.
Deadlines: None.
Evaluative Criteria: Preference is given to organizations seeking partial rather than exclusive funding from the foundation. The foundation favors organizations with emphasis on affordable housing, and K-12

public education. A limited number of civic betterment projects are also considered.
Decision Notification: Applicants are generally notified within 60 days.
Notes: Proposals should be sent to the Washington Mutual community relations department serving your area. National grants and those from the states of Washington, Oregon, Idaho, and Illinois should be submitted to the Seattle community relations office listed at the beginning of this entry. Arizona, California, Nevada, Utah, and Colorado requests should be submitted to: Washington Mutual Community Relations, 350 S. Grant Avenue, Los Angeles, CA 90071 (phone 213-217-4088). Florida, Georgia, and South Carolina proposals should be submitted to: Washington Mutual Community Relations, 200 S. Pine Island Road, Suite 206, Plantation, FL 33321 (phone 954-370-0460). New York, New Jersey, Massachusetts, and Pennsylvania proposals should be submitted to: Washington Mutual Community Relations, 589 Fifth Avenue, New York, NY 10017 (phone 212-326-6127). Requests for Texas should be submitted to: Washington Mutual Community Relations, 3200 SW Freeway, Suite 1330, Houston, TX 77027.

Restrictions

Does not support individuals; organizations without tax-exempt status; organizations which discriminate based on race, religion, creed, age, sex, sexual orientation, national origin, or any reason; religious organizations, unless the project to be funded falls within the foundation's guidelines and is for non-religious purposes; or organizations seeking funds for programs or projects outside of Washington Mutual service areas.

Additional Information

Publications: Foundation Annual Report

Corporate Officials

Kerry Kent Killinger: chairman, president, chief executive officer, director B Des Moines, IA 1949. ED University of Iowa BBA (1970); University of Iowa MBA (1971). PRIM CORP EMPL chairman, president, chief executive officer, director: Washington Mutual Inc. CORP AFFIL president: WM Financial Inc.; president, director, chief executive officer, chairman: Washington Mutual Savings Bank; director: Federal Home Loan Bank Seattle. NONPR AFFIL director: Washington Roundtable; director: Washington Savings League; member: Society Financial Analysts; member: Seattle Chamber of Commerce; director: Seattle Repertory Theatre; fellow: Life Management Institute; member: Alliance for Education. CLUB AFFIL Rotary Club.

Foundation Officials

Craig Chapman: board of directors
Daryl David: board of directors
Brad Davis: board of directors
Craig Davis: vice president
Cheryl Di Re: secretary
Bill Ehrlich: board of directors
Robert Flowers: board of directors
Steve Freimuth: board of directors
Kerry Kent Killinger: president (see above)
Marc Kittner: board of directors
Rob Miles: treasurer
Deanna Oppenheimer: vice president
Tim Otani: vice president community relations department
Christine Park: assistant secretary
J. Benson Porter: board of directors

Grants Analysis

Disclosure Period: calendar year ending 2001
Total Grants: $14,839,161*
Number of Grants: 423
Average Grant: $35,081
Highest Grant: $1,139,406
Lowest Grant: $35

Typical Range: $5,000 to $115,000 and $250,000 to $500,000
*Note: Giving excludes scholarship and United Way.

Recent Grants

Note: Grants derived from 2001 Form 990.

Library-Related

250,000	Seattle Public Library Foundation, Seattle, WA

General

588,818	United Way, Seattle, WA
561,118	United Way, Los Angeles, CA
500,000	Los Angeles Annenberg Metropolitan Project, Los Angeles, CA
500,000	Los Angeles Educational Partnership, Los Angeles, CA
500,000	Neighborhood Reinvestment Corporation, Washington, DC
470,000	National Board for Professional Teaching Standards, CA
400,000	Washington State Initiative for National Board Certified Teachers, WA
346,308	United Way, FL
312,500	Urban Economic Empowerment
300,000	Center for the Future of Teaching and Learning, Santa Cruz, CA

WASSERSTEIN PERELLA FOUNDATION

Giving Contact

Edward Golden, Trust Officer
Care of Bankers Trust Co.
PO Box 1297, 7 West
Church Street Station
New York, NY 10008
Phone: (212)454-8602

Alternate Contact

280 Park Ave.
New York, NY 10017

Description

Founded: 1989
EIN: 136916786
Organization Type: Private Foundation
Giving Locations: CA; IL; NY; TX
Grant Types: General Support.

Financial Summary

Total Giving: $777,000 (2001); $698,750 (2000); $657,575 (1999)
Giving Analysis: Giving for 1999 includes: foundation grants to United Way ($2,000)
Assets: $36,037 (2001); $88 (2000); $12,529 (1999)
Gifts Received: $810,000 (2001); $685,060 (2000); $669,000 (1999). Note: In 1999, 2000 and 2001, contributions were received from the Wasserstein Perella Group. In 1995, contributions were received from the Wasserstein Perella Group ($136,000) and Chase NYC ($100,000).

Typical Recipients

Arts & Humanities: Arts Associations & Councils, Arts Festivals, Arts Funds, Ballet, Dance, Film & Video, Libraries, Museums/Galleries, Music, Opera, Performing Arts, Theater
Civic & Public Affairs: African American Affairs, Botanical Gardens/Parks, Civic & Public Affairs-General, Minority Business, Public Policy, Urban & Community Affairs
Education: Business Education, Colleges & Universities, Education-General, Private Education (Precollege)
Environment: Environment-General

Health: Alzheimers Disease, Children's Health/Hospitals, Geriatric Health, Hospitals, Single-Disease Health Associations
International: International Organizations, International Relief Efforts, Trade
Religion: Jewish Causes, Religious Organizations
Social Services: Child Welfare, Recreation & Athletics

Application Procedures

Initial Contact: Send a brief letter of inquiry.
Deadlines: None.

Additional Information

Trust(s): Bankers Trust Co.

Grants Analysis

Disclosure Period: calendar year ending 2001
Total Grants: $777,000
Number of Grants: 79
Average Grant: $8,679*
Highest Grant: $100,000
Lowest Grant: $300
Typical Range: $1,000 to $12,500 and $25,000 to $40,000
*Note: Average grant figure excludes highest grant.

Recent Grants

Note: Grants derived from 2001 Form 990.

Library-Related

100,000	New York Public Library, New York, NY

General

40,000	Ravinia Festival Association, Highland Park, IL
30,000	Kent Waldrep National Paralysis Foundation, Dallas, TX
27,500	Arts Connection, New York, NY
27,500	Arts Connection, New York, NY
25,000	American Council on Germany, New York, NY
25,000	Chicago Urban League, Chicago, IL
25,000	Leo Baeck Institute, New York, NY
25,000	Metropolitan Museum of Art, New York, NY
24,500	Chicago Symphony Orchestra, Chicago, IL
20,000	Michael J Fox Foundation

WATERHOUSE FAMILY FOUNDATION

Giving Contact

128 Todd Lane
Briarcliff Manor, NY 10510-0000

Description

Founded: 1996
EIN: 133914707
Organization Type: Private Foundation

Financial Summary

Assets: $650,434 (1996)

Typical Recipients

Arts & Humanities: Libraries, Museums/Galleries, Theater
Education: Education-General, Preschool Education, Private Education (Precollege), Secondary Education (Private), Student Aid
Health: Cancer, Clinics/Medical Centers, Medical Research
Religion: Churches
Social Services: Recreation & Athletics, Social Services-General, YMCA/YWCA/YMHA/YWHA

Foundation Officials

Christine A. Waterhouse: director
Jennifer A. Waterhouse: director
Kevin C. Waterhouse: director
Lawrence M. Waterhouse, III: director
Lawrence M. Waterhouse, Jr.: president
Patrick R. Waterhouse: director

Recent Grants

Note: Grants derived from 2001 Form 990.

Library-Related

3,000	Bolton Free Library, Bolton Landing, NY

General

450,000	National Theater Workshop of the Handicapped, New York, NY
100,000	Bishop Loughlin High School, New York, NY
100,000	St. Peter's Catholic Church, Chicago, IL
100,000	Villanova College, Villanova, PA
50,000	Morse Foundation
50,000	Westchester Medical Center, Westchester, MA
35,000	Open Door Ossining, Ossining, NY
25,000	Cystic Fibrosis, Cincinnati, OH
10,000	Taft School, Watertown, CT
10,000	Woodlot Christian Preschool

ROBERT S. WATERS CHARITABLE TRUST

Giving Contact

Barbara Robinson, Trust Officer
c/o Mellon Bank NA
PO Box 185
Pittsburgh, PA 15230-9897
Phone: (412)234-5784

Description

Founded: 1952
EIN: 256018986
Organization Type: Private Foundation
Giving Locations: NJ; PA
Grant Types: General Support, Operating Expenses.

Donor Information

Founder: the late Robert S. Waters

Financial Summary

Total Giving: $418,500 (2001); $497,000 (2000); $405,085 (1999)
Giving Analysis: Giving for 2001 includes: foundation grants to United Way ($2,500); 2000: foundation grants to United Way ($2,500); 1999: foundation grants to United Way ($5,000)
Assets: $9,505,527 (2000); $9,936,280 (1999); $9,085,419 (1998)
Gifts Received: $141,865 (2000); $386,865 (1996); $12,808 (1995). Note: In 2000, contributions were received from Nell K. Jones Trust. In 1996, contributions were received from the Robert S. Waters Trust.

Typical Recipients

Arts & Humanities: Arts Associations & Councils, Arts Centers, Arts Institutes, Community Arts, Arts & Humanities-General, Historic Preservation, History & Archaeology, Libraries, Museums/Galleries, Music
Civic & Public Affairs: Community Foundations, Civic & Public Affairs-General
Education: Arts/Humanities Education, Colleges & Universities, Education Funds, Education Reform, Education-General, Literacy, Medical Education, Minority Education, Private Education (Precollege), Special Education
Environment: Air/Water Quality, Environment-General, Resource Conservation, Watershed, Wildlife Protection

Health: Clinics/Medical Centers, Hospitals, Medical Rehabilitation, Public Health
Religion: Religion-General, Ministries, Religious Welfare, Religious Welfare
Science: Scientific Centers & Institutes
Social Services: Community Service Organizations, Family Planning, Family Services, Food/Clothing Distribution, Homes, People with Disabilities, Shelters/Homelessness, United Funds/United Ways

Application Procedures
Initial Contact: Application, deadline, and restriction information provided upon initial contact.

Additional Information
Trust(s): Mellon Bank NA

Foundation Officials
John Davis, Jr. Es: co-trustee

Grants Analysis
Disclosure Period: calendar year ending 2001
Total Grants: $416,000*
Number of Grants: 29
Average Grant: $9,172*
Highest Grant: $150,000
Typical Range: $1,000 to $10,000
*Note: Giving excludes United Way. Average grant excludes highest grant.

Recent Grants
Note: Grants derived from 2001 Form 990.

Library-Related

7,500	Cambria Free Library, Johnstown, PA -- operational

General

150,000	Carnegie Institute, Pittsburgh, PA -- operational
75,000	Historical Society of Western Pennsylvania, Pittsburgh, PA -- operational
20,000	Allegheny Lutheran Home, Holidaysburg, PA -- operational
12,500	Pace School, Pittsburgh, PA -- operational
10,000	Ellis School, Pittsburgh, PA -- operational
10,000	Johnstown Area Heritage Association, Johnstown, PA -- operational
10,000	New Day, Inc., Johnstown, PA -- operational
10,000	Winchester Thurston School, Pittsburgh, PA -- operational
7,500	Christian Home, Johnstown, PA -- operational
7,500	Conamaugh Valley Hospital, Johnstown, PA -- operational

THOMAS J. WATSON FOUNDATION

Giving Contact
Tori Harding-Smith, Executive Director
293 South Main Street
Providence, RI 02903
Phone: (401)274-1952
Fax: (401)274-1954
E-mail: WatsonFoundation@Brown.edu
Web: http://www.WatsonFellowship.org

Description
Founded: 1961
EIN: 136038151
Organization Type: Specialized/Single Purpose Foundation
Giving Locations: nationally.
Grant Types: Fellowship.

Donor Information
Founder: Founded in 1961 by Mrs. Thomas J. Watson, in honor of her husband who died in 1956. In 1914, Mr. Watson became president of a company that manufactured office machines. Ten years later, the company was renamed International Business Machines Corporation (IBM). Thomas Watson served as the company's president for almost forty years and was succeeded by his son, Thomas J. Watson, Jr. No family members are currently associated with IBM. Both Thomas Watson Jr. and his brother, Arthur K. Watson, have donated additional funds to the foundation.

Financial Summary
Total Giving: $2,362,543 (fiscal year ending May 31, 2001); $1,996,692 (fiscal 1998); $1,624,036 (fiscal 1997). Note: 1997 Giving includes fellowships ($945,565); scholarship ($40,711).
Giving Analysis: Giving for fiscal 2001 includes: foundation scholarships ($72,037) foundation fellowships ($1,384,503)
Assets: $72,353,604 (fiscal 2001); $71,086,222 (fiscal 1998); $55,980,961 (fiscal 1997)
Gifts Received: $1,500 (fiscal 1994); $616 (fiscal 1993). Note: Contributions were received from the Arthur K. Watson Trust in New York City.

Typical Recipients
Arts & Humanities: Arts & Humanities-General, History & Archaeology, Libraries, Literary Arts, Museums/Galleries, Music
Civic & Public Affairs: Urban & Community Affairs
Education: Colleges & Universities, Education Associations, Elementary Education (Private), Engineering/Technological Education, Environmental Education, Faculty Development, Education-General, Private Education (Precollege), Public Education (Precollege), Secondary Education (Private), Student Aid
Environment: Air/Water Quality, Environment-General, Resource Conservation, Wildlife Protection
Health: AIDS/HIV, Children's Health/Hospitals
International: Foreign Arts Organizations
Religion: Churches, Religious Welfare
Social Services: Community Service Organizations, YMCA/YWCA/YMHA/YWHA

Application Procedures
Deadlines: Fellowship nominations must be received by the 1st Tuesday in November; nominees' completed applications must arrive by the 1st Tuesday in November.
Review Process: Awards will be announced by 2lMarch 24, 2000.
Notes: Nominations for the Thomas J. Watson Fellowship are open to all graduating seniors of participating colleges and universities. Contact foundation for list of institutions.

Additional Information
Morgan Guaranty Trust Company is listed as corporate trustee of the foundation.
Publications: Fellowship Program Brochure

Foundation Officials
Elizabeth B. Buckner: member advisory board
Walker G. Buckner, Jr.: member advisory board
Frances S. Cox: assistant director
John N. Irwin, III: mem adv board B 1954. ED Princeton University (1976). PRIM CORP EMPL vice president, managing director: Hillside Industries Inc. CORP AFFIL vice president, managing director, director: Hillside Capital Inc. De Corp.
David Ewing McKinney: executive secretary, mem adv board B Harriman, TN 1934. ED Vanderbilt University (1952-1953); University of Tennessee BS (1956). PRIM CORP EMPL president: IBM World Trade America/Far East Corp. CORP AFFIL director: Paxar System Group; director: Paxar Woven Label Group.

Daniel L. Moseley: member executive board
Noreen Tuross: executive director
Thomas John Watson, III: mem adv board B 1944. ED Colby College (1969); Boston University (1972).

Grants Analysis
Disclosure Period: fiscal year ending May 31, 2001
Total Grants: $906,003*
Number of Grants: 91
Average Grant: $9,956
Highest Grant: $43,000
Typical Range: $5,000 to $20,000
*Note: Giving excludes fellowship and scholarships.

Recent Grants
Note: Grants derived from 2000 Form 990.

Library-Related

18,000	New York Society Library, New York, NY -- general operating expenses

General

97,000	Rice University, Houston, TX -- fellowship
88,000	Amherst College, Amherst, MA -- fellowship
66,000	Middlebury College, Middlebury, VT -- for Watson Fellowship Program
44,000	Berea College, Berea, KY -- for Watson Fellowship Program
44,000	Bowdoin College, Brunswick, ME -- fellowship
44,000	California Institute of Technology, Pasadena, CA -- fellowship
44,000	College of Wooster, Wooster, OH -- for Watson Fellowship Program
44,000	Connecticut College, New London, CT -- fellowship
44,000	Earlham College, Richmond, IN -- for Watson Fellowship Program
44,000	Lawrence University, Appleton, WI -- for Watson Fellowship Program

WALTER E. AND CAROLINE H. WATSON FOUNDATION

Giving Contact
Myra Vitto
c/o National City Bank
PO Box 450
Youngstown, OH 44501
Phone: (330)742-4159

Description
Founded: 1964
EIN: 346547726
Organization Type: Private Foundation
Giving Locations: OH
Grant Types: Emergency, General Support, Project.

Donor Information
Founder: Walter E. Watson

Financial Summary
Total Giving: $381,555 (2002); $340,747 (2000); $345,375 (1999)
Giving Analysis: Giving for 2002 includes: foundation grants to United Way ($145,000) 1999: foundation grants to United Way ($66,500)
Assets: $6,711,759 (2002); $8,054,082 (2001); $8,663,243 (2000)

Typical Recipients
Arts & Humanities: Arts Associations & Councils, Arts Centers, Arts Institutes, Community Arts, Arts & Humanities-General, Historic Preservation, History & Archaeology, Libraries, Music, Performing Arts, Public Broadcasting, Theater

Civic & Public Affairs: Botanical Gardens/Parks, Business/Free Enterprise, Chambers of Commerce, Economic Development, Employment/Job Training, Civic & Public Affairs-General, Hispanic Affairs, Public Policy, Urban & Community Affairs

Education: Business Education, Colleges & Universities, Education Funds, Environmental Education, Medical Education, Preschool Education, Private Education (Precollege), Public Education (Precollege), Secondary Education (Public), Special Education, Student Aid

Health: AIDS/HIV, Cancer, Children's Health/Hospitals, Emergency/Ambulance Services, Health Organizations, Heart, Hospices, Hospitals, Long-Term Care, Medical Research, Multiple Sclerosis, Nursing Services, Public Health, Single-Disease Health Associations, Speech & Hearing

International: International Relief Efforts

Religion: Churches, Jewish Causes, Ministries, Religious Welfare

Social Services: Animal Protection, Child Welfare, Community Centers, Community Service Organizations, Day Care, Domestic Violence, Family Planning, Family Services, People with Disabilities, Recreation & Athletics, Scouts, Senior Services, Social Services-General, Substance Abuse, United Funds/United Ways, YMCA/YWCA/YMHA/YWHA, YMCA/YWCA/YMHA/YWHA, Youth Organizations

Application Procedures

Initial Contact: The foundation has no formal grant application procedure or application form.
Deadlines: None.

Restrictions

Grants are limited to public institutions and hospitals in OH.

Additional Information

Trust(s): Natl City Bank

Foundation Officials

Thomas R. Hollern: trustee
Herbert H. Pridham: trustee
Myra Vitto: trustee
John F. Zimmerman, Jr.: trustee

Grants Analysis

Disclosure Period: calendar year ending 2002
Total Grants: $263,055*
Number of Grants: 56
Average Grant: $3,575*
Highest Grant: $62,855
Typical Range: $2,500 to $7,500
*Note: Giving excludes United Way. Average grant excludes highest grant.

Recent Grants

Note: Grants derived from 2001 Form 990.

General

145,500	Youngstown Mahoning Valley United Way, Youngstown, OH
62,855	Forum Health Trumbull Memorial Hospital, Youngstown, OH
13,000	Youngstown State University, Youngstown, PA
12,500	Hospice of the Valley, Youngstown, OH
10,000	PBS 45 and 49, Kent, OH
7,500	Development Potential, Inc., Youngstown, OH
7,500	Monday Musical Club, Youngstown, OH
7,500	YMCA, Youngstown, OH
6,500	Neoucom Foundation, Rootstown, OH
6,000	HELP Hotline Crisis Center, Youngstown, OH

WAUSAU-MOSINEE PAPER CORP.

Company Headquarters

1244 Kronenwetter Dr.
Mosinee, WI 54455
Web: http://www.wausaumosinee.com

Company Description

Founded: 1899
Ticker: WMO
Exchange: NYSE
Former Name: Wausau Paper Mills Co.
Revenue: US$943.8 million (2001)
Employees: 3200 (2001)
SIC(s): 2600 Paper & Allied Products.

Operating Locations

Wausau-Mosinee Paper Corp. (WI--Rhinelander, Wausau)

Wausau Paper Mills Foundation

Giving Contact

Thomas J. Howatt, Foundation Officer
1244 Kronenwetter Drive
Mosinee, WI 54455-9099
Phone: (715)962-2024

Alternate Contact

c/o Mosinee High School Principal
1000 High Street
Mosinee, WI 54455
Phone: (715)693-2550

Description

EIN: 396080502
Organization Type: Corporate Foundation
Former Name: Wausau Paper Mills Foundation, Inc..
Giving Locations: WI
Grant Types: General Support.

Donor Information

Founder: Wausau Paper Mills Co., Rhinelander Paper Mills Co.

Financial Summary

Total Giving: $348,586 (fiscal year ending August 31, 2001); $373,729 (fiscal 2000); $462,115 (fiscal 1999)
Giving Analysis: Giving for fiscal 2000 includes: foundation scholarships ($5,500); foundation matching gifts ($9,635); foundation grants to United Way ($140,650); foundation ($217,944); fiscal 1999: foundation matching gifts ($5,025); foundation scholarships ($5,125); foundation grants to United Way ($193,050); foundation ($258,735); fiscal 1998: foundation matching gifts ($5,130) foundation grants to United Way ($93,625)
Assets: $122,118 (fiscal 2001); $130,345 (fiscal 2000); $470,863 (fiscal 1999)
Gifts Received: $340,000 (fiscal 2001); $480,000 (fiscal 1999); $230,000 (fiscal 1997). Note: In 2001, contributions were received from Wausau-Mosinee Paper Corporation. In fiscal 1996, contributions were received from Wausau Paper Mills Co. ($140,000), Wausau Papers of New Hampshire ($10,000), and Rhinelander Paper Co. ($80,000). In 1997, contributions were received from Wassau Paper Mills Company, Wassau Papers of New Hampshire, and Rhinelander Paper Company.

Typical Recipients

Arts & Humanities: Arts Associations & Councils, Arts Festivals, Community Arts, History & Archaeology, Libraries, Museums/Galleries, Music, Performing Arts, Public Broadcasting, Theater, Visual Arts

Civic & Public Affairs: Botanical Gardens/Parks, Chambers of Commerce, Clubs, Community Foundations, Economic Development, Employment/Job Training, Civic & Public Affairs-General, Housing, Municipalities/Towns, Parades/Festivals, Professional & Trade Associations, Public Policy, Safety, Urban & Community Affairs, Women's Affairs

Education: Arts/Humanities Education, Business Education, Colleges & Universities, Education Funds, Engineering/Technological Education, Education-General, Preschool Education, Public Education (Precollege), Public Education (Precollege), Science/Mathematics Education, Secondary Education (Private), Secondary Education (Public), Special Education, Vocational & Technical Education

Environment: Air/Water Quality, Environment-General, Wildlife Protection

Health: Cancer, Children's Health/Hospitals, Health Organizations, Heart, Hospitals, Public Health, Respiratory

International: International Development, International Relief Efforts

Religion: Religious Organizations, Religious Welfare

Science: Scientific Organizations

Social Services: Community Service Organizations, Emergency Relief, Food/Clothing Distribution, Recreation & Athletics, Scouts, Social Services-General, Special Olympics, United Funds/United Ways, Veterans, YMCA/YWCA/YMHA/YWHA, Youth Organizations

Application Procedures

Initial Contact: Send a brief letter of inquiry.
Application Requirements: Include a description of program, courses completed, rank in class and grade point level.
Deadlines: March 10 for scholarships.
Notes: For scholarships, applications should be addressed to the principal of Mosinee High School, 1000 High St., Mosinee, WI, 54455, (715) 693-2550.

Restrictions

The Norman S. Steve Memorial Scholarship is limited to the field of study of pulp and paper technology or paper science. The Norman S. Steve Memorial Scholarship, the University of Wisconsin- Marathon Center Scholarship and the North Central Technical Institute Scholarship are limited to the graduating students of Mosinee High School only.

Additional Information

Wausau-Mosinee Paper Corp. was formerly Wausau Paper Mills Co.

Corporate Officials

Stuart R. Carlson: executive vice president administration PRIM CORP EMPL executive vice president administration: Wausau-Mosinee Paper Corp.
Scott P. Doescher: senior vice president, secretary, treasurer PRIM CORP EMPL senior vice president, secretary, treasurer: Wausau-Mosinee Paper Corp.
Thomas J. Howatt: president, chief executive officer, director PRIM CORP EMPL president, chief executive officer, director: Wausau-Mosinee Paper Corp.
San Watterson Orr, Jr.: chairman, director B Madison, WI 1941. ED University of Wisconsin BBA (1963); University of Wisconsin JD (1966). PRIM CORP EMPL chairman, director: Wausau-Mosinee Paper Corp. CORP AFFIL president, director: Woodson Fudiciary Corp.; secretary, treasurer, director: Yawkey Lumber Co.; chairman, director: Mosinee Paper Corp.; director: Marshall & Ilsley Corp.; director: MDU Resources Group; director: M & I First America Bank; chairman, director: Marathon Electric Manufacturing Corp.; president, director: Forewood. NONPR

AFFIL director: Leigh Yawkey Woodson Art Museum; vice president, director: YMCA Foundation Wausau; director: WI Taxpayers Alliance; member: WI Bar Association; director: WI Policy Research Institute; director: University Wisconsin Hospital & Clinic; member, board regents: University Wisconsin Systems; director: University Wisconsin Foundation; member: American Law Institute; director: Competitive Wisconsin. CLUB AFFIL Wausau Club.

Richard Louis Radt: vice chairman B Chicago, IL 1932. ED University of Illinois (1956). PRIM CORP EMPL vice chairman: Wausau-Mosinee Paper Corp. NONPR AFFIL director: Leigh Yawkey Woodson Art Museum.

David Byron Smith, Jr.: consultant, director B Chicago, IL 1936. ED Princeton University BSE (1958).

Foundation Officials

San Watterson Orr, Jr.: director (see above)

Grants Analysis

Disclosure Period: fiscal year ending August 31, 2001
Total Grants: $189,381*
Number of Grants: 56
Average Grant: $3,382*
Highest Grant: $40,000
Lowest Grant: $50
Typical Range: $25 to $5,000
***Note:** Giving excludes United Way, scholarships, and matching gifts. Average grant figure excludes highest grant.

Recent Grants

Note: Grants derived from 2001 Form 990.

General

83,650	United Way of Marathon County, Wausau, WI
40,000	Grand Theater Foundation, Inc., Wausau, WI
26,000	Northwoods United Way, Rhinelander, WI
25,000	Wausau Area Community Foundation, Wausau, WI
19,808	American Red Cross, Wausau, WI
16,000	University of Wisconsin Stevens Point Paper Science Foundation, Stevens Point, WI
11,000	Middletown Area United Way, Middletown, OH
11,000	United Way of Mercer County, Inc., Trenton, NJ
10,000	City of Mosinee, Mosinee, WI -- Downtown Redevelopment Project
10,000	Weeks Hospital Association, Lancaster, NH

WAYPOINT FINANCIAL CORP.

Company Headquarters

235 N. 2nd St.
Harrisburg, PA 17101
Web: http://www.waypointbank.com

Company Description

Founded: 2000
Ticker: WYPT
Exchange: NASDAQ
Former Name: York Financial Corp.; Harris Financial.
Assets: US$5.373 billion (2001)
Employees: 890 (2001)
Parent Company: Waypoint Financial Corp., 235 N. 2nd St., Harrisburg, PA, United States

York Federal Savings & Loan Foundation

Giving Contact

Robert W. Pullo, Chairman & Chief Executive Officer
c/o York Federal Savings & Loan Foundation
101 South George Street
York, PA 17401
Phone: (717)815-4501
Fax: (717)846-5590

Description

EIN: 232111139
Organization Type: Corporate Foundation
Giving Locations: PA: York
Grant Types: Employee Matching Gifts, General Support, Scholarship.

Financial Summary

Total Giving: $315,586 (fiscal year ending June 30, 2002); $303,585 (fiscal 2000); $232,633 (fiscal 1999). Note: Contributes through foundation only.
Giving Analysis: Giving for fiscal 2000 includes: foundation grants to United Way ($48,662); foundation ($254,923); fiscal 1999: foundation ($232,633); fiscal 1998: foundation grants to United Way ($68,450); foundation ($213,817);
Assets: $463,303 (fiscal 2002); $157,204 (fiscal 2000); $215,391 (fiscal 1999)
Gifts Received: $328,150 (fiscal 2002); $262,370 (fiscal 2000); $284,650 (fiscal 1998). Note: In fiscal 2002, contributions were received from Waypoint Bank ($294,000), York Container ($5,000), Susquehanna Pfalzgraff ($5,000), Wagaman Construction, Inc. ($5,000), The Wolf Foundation ($10,000), Kinsley Construction ($5,000), and miscellaneous contributions ($4,150). Substantial contributions are received from York Federal Savings & Loan Association.

Typical Recipients

Arts & Humanities: Arts Associations & Councils, Arts Centers, Arts Festivals, Arts Funds, Community Arts, Ethnic & Folk Arts, Arts & Humanities-General, Historic Preservation, History & Archaeology, Libraries, Museums/Galleries, Music, Performing Arts, Theater
Civic & Public Affairs: Business/Free Enterprise, Chambers of Commerce, Clubs, Community Foundations, Employment/Job Training, Civic & Public Affairs-General, Hispanic Affairs, Housing, Minority Business, Municipalities/Towns, Parades/Festivals, Urban & Community Affairs
Education: Business Education, Colleges & Universities, Economic Education, Education Reform, Education-General, Literacy, Preschool Education, Private Education (Precollege), Public Education (Precollege), Student Aid, Vocational & Technical Education
Environment: Environment-General, Resource Conservation
Health: Cancer, Children's Health/Hospitals, Clinics/Medical Centers, Emergency/Ambulance Services, Health-General, Health Organizations, Heart, Hospices, Hospitals, Mental Health, Multiple Sclerosis, Prenatal Health Issues, Public Health, Single-Disease Health Associations
Religion: Churches, Jewish Causes, Religious Welfare, Seminaries
Science: Science Museums
Social Services: Camps, Child Welfare, Community Centers, Community Service Organizations, Counseling, Crime Prevention, Family Services, Food/Clothing Distribution, Homes, People with Disabilities, Recreation & Athletics, Scouts, Sexual Abuse, Social Services-General, Substance Abuse, United Funds/United Ways, YMCA/YWCA/YMHA/YWHA, Youth Organizations

Application Procedures

Initial Contact: Send a written application for funding.
Deadlines: None.

Restrictions

Company does not make grants to religious organizations for sectarian purposes.

Additional Information

Special initiatives are underway to address housing and the needs of low-income communities.

Corporate Officials

Robert W. Pullo: chairman, chief executive officer, director B Cambridge, MA 1939. ED Williams College (1961-1962); Northeastern University (1960-1970). PRIM CORP EMPL chairman, chief executive officer, director: York Federal Savings & Loan Association. CORP AFFIL chairman: Y-F Service Corp.; president, chief executive officer, director: York Financial Corp. NONPR AFFIL director: York County Industrial Development Corp.; director: York Township Water Sewer Authority; member: Pennsylvania Association Savings Institute; director: York Area Enterprise Development Committee; president: Central Pennsylvania Savings Loan League; member: Mayor's Economic Advisory Council.

Foundation Officials

James H. Moss: treasurer B Lancaster, PA 1953. ED Elizabethtown College (1977). PRIM CORP EMPL executive vice president, treasurer: York Federal Savings & Loan Association. CORP AFFIL treasurer: Y-F Service Corp.; vice president: York Financial Corp. NONPR AFFIL member: Financial Executives Institute; member: Financial Managers Society; member: American Institute CPAs.
Robert W. Pullo: president, trustee (see above)

Grants Analysis

Disclosure Period: fiscal year ending June 30, 2002
Total Grants: $266,836*
Number of Grants: 73
Average Grant: $3,655
Highest Grant: $35,000
Lowest Grant: $100
Typical Range: $150 to $10,000
***Note:** Giving excludes United Way.

Recent Grants

Note: Grants derived from fiscal 2002 Form 990.

Library-Related

5,000	Kaltreider Benfer Library, Red Lion, PA
3,333	Hanover Public Library, Hanover, PA
2,556	Martin Library, York, PA -- virtual voyages

General

35,000	Strand Capitol, York, PA
30,000	Penn State York, York, PA
20,000	Sertoma for Hearsay of Central Pennsylvania, PA
17,500	Cultural Alliance of York County, York, PA
16,250	United Way York County, York, PA
16,250	United Way York County, York, PA
16,250	United Way York County, York, PA
15,000	York College of Pennsylvania, York, PA
15,000	York Little Theater, York, PA
10,000	Cultural Alliance of York County, York, PA

RAYMOND JOHN WEAN FOUNDATION

Giving Contact

Raymond J. Wean, Jr., Chairman
PO Box 760
Warren, OH 44482-0760

Phone: (330)394-5600
Fax: (330)394-5601
E-mail: RJWeanFdn@aol.com

Description

Founded: 1949
EIN: 346505038
Organization Type: Family Foundation
Giving Locations: FL: Southeast Florida; OH: Northeast Ohio; PA: Southeast Pennsylvania
Grant Types: Capital, Endowment, General Support, Project, Scholarship.

Donor Information

Founder: Established in 1949 by Raymond J. Wean (1895-1980). Mr. Wean was chairman of Wean United and the Second National Bank of Warren, OH. He also was a trustee of the Community Chest of Palm Beach, American Institute of Economics, Trinity College, and Carnegie-Mellon University.

Financial Summary

Total Giving: $4,437,965 (1999); $3,745,110 (1998); $3,044,710 (1997)
Giving Analysis: Giving for 1998 includes: foundation grants to United Way ($40,000)
Assets: $84,659,513 (1999); $85,998,735 (1998); $76,440,782 (1997)

Typical Recipients

Arts & Humanities: Arts Associations & Councils, Arts Centers, Arts Festivals, Arts Funds, Arts Institutes, Dance, Ethnic & Folk Arts, Arts & Humanities-General, Historic Preservation, History & Archaeology, Libraries, Literary Arts, Museums/Galleries, Music, Opera, Performing Arts, Public Broadcasting, Theater
Civic & Public Affairs: Botanical Gardens/Parks, Clubs, Community Foundations, Economic Development, Employment/Job Training, Civic & Public Affairs-General, Municipalities/Towns, Professional & Trade Associations, Public Policy, Safety, Urban & Community Affairs, Women's Affairs, Zoos/Aquariums
Education: Afterschool/Enrichment Programs, Arts/Humanities Education, Colleges & Universities, Colleges & Universities, Continuing Education, Education Associations, Education Funds, Faculty Development, Education-General, Legal Education, Medical Education, Minority Education, Private Education (Precollege), Public Education (Precollege), Religious Education, Science/Mathematics Education, Student Aid
Environment: Environment-General, Resource Conservation
Health: Cancer, Children's Health/Hospitals, Clinics/Medical Centers, Health Policy/Cost Containment, Health Organizations, Hospices, Hospitals, Long-Term Care, Medical Rehabilitation, Medical Research, Mental Health, Nursing Services, Public Health, Single-Disease Health Associations
International: International Relations
Religion: Churches, Religious Organizations, Religious Welfare, Religious Welfare
Science: Scientific Centers & Institutes, Scientific Research
Social Services: Animal Protection, Child Welfare, Community Service Organizations, Day Care, Family Planning, Family Services, Food/Clothing Distribution, Homes, People with Disabilities, Recreation & Athletics, Scouts, Senior Services, Shelters/Homelessness, Substance Abuse, United Funds/United Ways, YMCA/YWCA/YMHA/YWHA, Youth Organizations

Application Procedures

Initial Contact: Applicants should contact the foundation to request grant application form and procedures.
Application Requirements: Each proposal should include a one to two page cover letter describing the project and the amount of funds being requested. The proposal also should include a copy of the IRS letter confirming Internal Revenue Code 501(c)(3) status; organizational background, including history, mission, etc.; a project description, justification of need, specific goals and objectives, and the project timeline; and a project budget and anticipated expenses, including details about how the funds will be used.
Deadlines: March 1; June 1; September 1.
Review Process: Proposals are considered and reviewed by the board of administrators periodically. Organizations that submit requests for support will receive the board's decision in letter form, within thirty days of grants meeting.

Restrictions

Supports 501(c)(3) organizations only; does not fund individuals. Grants are generally restricted to organizations in Northeast Ohio Southwestern Pennsylvania, and southern Florida.

Additional Information

Publications: Application Form

Foundation Officials

John L. Pogue: member board administrations B 1944. ED DePauw University BA (1966); Indiana University JD (1969). PRIM CORP EMPL attorney: Hoppe, Frey, Hewitt & Milligan. CORP AFFIL director: Therm-O-Link Inc.; secretary: Warren Pump & Supply Co.; director: Second Bancorp Inc.
Gordon B. Wean: mem board admin
Raymond John Wean, III: board administrator B 1948. ED Babson College BA (1973); Babson College BS (1973). CORP AFFIL director: Second Bancorp Inc.
Raymond John Wean, Jr.: chairman board admin B Warren, OH 1921. ED Yale University BA (1943). PRIM CORP EMPL director: Second National Bank Warren OH.

Grants Analysis

Disclosure Period: calendar year ending 2000
Total Grants: $4,430,465*
Number of Grants: 254
Average Grant: $17,443*
Highest Grant: $200,000
Lowest Grant: $150
Typical Range: $1,000 to $5,000 and $5,000 to $50,000
*Note: Giving excludes United Way.

Recent Grants

Note: Grants derived from 2000 Form 990.

Library-Related
50,000	East Cleveland Public Library, Cleveland, OH -- capital expansion

General
200,000	Miss Porter's School, Farmington, CT -- library unrestricted endowment fund
150,000	Pace School, Pittsburgh, PA -- capital campaign
150,000	Shady Side Academy, Pittsburgh, PA -- Five-Year Technology Plan
150,000	University School, Hunting Valley, OH -- construction in arts/technology wing
150,000	Yale University, New Haven, CT -- endowed scholarship fund
125,000	Blair Academy, Blairstown, NJ -- dining hall expansion
125,000	Wooster School, Danbury, CT -- Black Box Theatre
120,000	Deerfield Academy, Deerfield, MA -- financial aid fun
100,000	Middlebury College, Middlebury, VT -- instruction laboratory for Bicentennial Hall
100,000	Palm Beach Day School, Palm Beach, FL -- Food Service Employment Training Program

WEATHERTOP FOUNDATION

Giving Contact

Weathertop Foundation
700 Capital Square
400 Locust Street
Des Moines, IA 50309-2340
Phone: (212)472-1288

Description

Founded: 1996
EIN: 421431036
Organization Type: Private Foundation
Giving Locations: CO: Granby; DC: Washington metro area; HI: Kaoaheo; IA: Des Moines metro area; MA: Boston metro area; Canada
Grant Types: General Support.

Financial Summary

Total Giving: $569,940 (fiscal year ending July 31, 2000)
Giving Analysis: Giving for fiscal 2000 includes: foundation grants to United Way ($10,000)
Assets: $4,768,676 (fiscal 2000); $2,232,642 (fiscal 1996)
Gifts Received: $13,640 (fiscal 2000). Note: In fiscal 2000, contributions were received from Thomas N. Urban, Jr. ($8,992) and Mary B. Urban ($4,648).

Typical Recipients

Arts & Humanities: Arts Centers, Historic Preservation, Libraries, Literary Arts, Public Broadcasting
Civic & Public Affairs: Botanical Gardens/Parks
Education: Colleges & Universities, Science/Mathematics Education
International: International-General
Social Services: Youth Organizations

Foundation Officials

Victoria Urban Broer: director
Cornelia Urban Sawczuk: director
Mary Bright Urban: vice president, secretary
Thomas N. Urban, III: director
Thomas Nelson Urban, Jr.: chairman, president
William G. Urban: treasurer

Grants Analysis

Disclosure Period: fiscal year ending July 31, 2000
Total Grants: $559,940*
Number of Grants: 18
Average Grant: $21,162*
Highest Grant: $200,193
Lowest Grant: $100
Typical Range: $5,000 to $50,000
*Note: Giving excludes United Way. Average grant figure excludes highest grant.

Recent Grants

Note: Grants derived from 2001 Form 990.

Library-Related
5,000	Public Library of Des Moines Foundation, Des Moines, IA

General
354,125	National Tropical Botanical Gardens, Kaoaheo, HI
20,000	Carnegie Institute of Washington, Washington, DC
20,000	Youth Incentives, Inc., Des Moines, IA
10,000	Des Moines National Poetry Festival, Des Moines, IA
10,000	Ridley College, St. Catharines, ON Canada
10,000	United States Central Iowa, Des Moines, IA
5,000	Des Moines Art Center, Des Moines, IA
5,000	Thomas Jefferson Memorial Foundation, Charlottesville, VA

1,000	Drake University, Des Moines, IA
100	Iowa Public Television, Johnston, IA

WEATHERWAX FOUNDATION

Giving Contact

Maria Miceli Dotterweich, Executive Director
c/o Comerica Bank, Trust Dept.
245 W. Michigan Ave., 4th Fl.
Jackson, MI 49204
Phone: (517)787-2117
Web: http://www.lib.msu.edu/harris23/grants/wfbro-chu.htm

Description

Founded: 1981
EIN: 386439807
Organization Type: Private Foundation
Giving Locations: MI: Jackson, Hillsdale, and Lenawee Counties
Grant Types: General Support.

Donor Information

Founder: the K.A. Weatherwax Trust I

Financial Summary

Total Giving: $1,292,667 (fiscal year ending September 30, 2001); $1,219,668 (fiscal 2000); $1,253,778 (fiscal 1999)
Assets: $22,467,745 (fiscal 2001); $25,748,822 (fiscal 2000); $25,167,748 (fiscal 1999)
Gifts Received: $78,296 (fiscal 2000); $4,142,929 (fiscal 1999). Note: In fiscal 1999 and 2000, contributions were received from Estate of Peter Weatherwax. In fiscal 1998, contributions were received from the Estate of Peter Weatherwax. In fiscal 1991, contributions were received from the K. A. Weatherwax Trust I.

Typical Recipients

Arts & Humanities: Arts Festivals, Arts & Humanities-General, Historic Preservation, History & Archaeology, Museums/Galleries, Music, Theater
Civic & Public Affairs: Botanical Gardens/Parks, Clubs, Civic & Public Affairs-General, Housing, Municipalities/Towns, Nonprofit Management, Safety
Education: Arts/Humanities Education, Colleges & Universities, Community & Junior Colleges, Education Associations, Education Funds, Elementary Education (Public), Education-General, International Exchange, Preschool Education, Private Education (Precollege), Public Education (Precollege), Science/Mathematics Education, Secondary Education (Private), Special Education
Environment: Environment-General
Health: Emergency/Ambulance Services, Health Funds, Hospices, Long-Term Care, Mental Health, Public Health, Respiratory, Speech & Hearing
International: Health Care/Hospitals
Religion: Churches, Ministries, Religious Organizations, Religious Welfare
Science: Scientific Centers & Institutes
Social Services: Animal Protection, At-Risk Youth, Child Abuse, Community Centers, Community Service Organizations, Day Care, Family Services, Homes, People with Disabilities, Recreation & Athletics, Scouts, Senior Services, YMCA/YWCA/YMHA/YWHA, Youth Organizations

Application Procedures

Initial Contact: Call or write for application guidelines.
Deadlines: None.

Restrictions

Does not provide grants to individuals or religious organizations for sectarian purposes. Generally does not support the purchase of computers.

Additional Information

Trust(s): Comerica Bank
Publications: Application Guidelines

Foundation Officials

Lawrence Bullen: trust
Nancy Sunday: trust
Peter A. Weatherwax: trustee

Grants Analysis

Disclosure Period: fiscal year ending September 30, 2001
Total Grants: $1,292,667
Number of Grants: 43
Average Grant: $21,650*
Highest Grant: $205,000
Lowest Grant: $1,000
Typical Range: $10,000 to $40,000
*Note: Average grant figure excludes two highest grants ($405,000).

Recent Grants

Note: Grants derived from fiscal 2000 Form 990.

General

270,000	Spring Arbor College, Spring Arbor, MI -- library
125,000	Albion College, Albion, MI -- music facility
100,000	City of Jackson, Jackson, MI -- Nixon Park improvements
70,000	City of Jackson, Jackson, MI -- millennium clock
66,278	Jackson Y Center, Jackson, MI -- customer and data management system
56,050	Starr Commonwealth, Jackson, MI -- street outreach program
52,872	Spring Arbor Township Fire Department, Spring Arbor, MI -- equipment
50,400	Jackson Nonprofit Support Center, Jackson, MI -- operational support
50,000	Boysville of Michigan, Clinton, MI
41,027	Michigan Theater of Jackson, Jackson, MI -- renovations

GIL AND DODY WEAVER FOUNDATION

Giving Contact

Dr. William R. Weaver, Trustee
1845 Woodall Rogers Freeway, Suite 1275
Dallas, TX 75201
Phone: (214)999-9497

Description

Founded: 1980
EIN: 751729449
Organization Type: Private Foundation
Giving Locations: KS; LA; NM; OK; PA; TX; WV
Grant Types: General Support, Multiyear/Continuing Support, Operating Expenses, Project, Research.

Donor Information

Founder: Galbraith Weaver

Financial Summary

Total Giving: $396,100 (fiscal year ending September 30, 2001); $369,700 (fiscal 2000); $292,850 (fiscal 1998)
Assets: $16,088,019 (fiscal 2001); $17,259,801 (fiscal 2000); $10,941,206 (fiscal 1998)
Gifts Received: $2,906,199 (fiscal 2000); $4,825,268 (fiscal 1998); $851,525 (fiscal 1996). Note: In fiscal 1998 and 2000, contributions were received from the estate of G. McF. Weaver. In fiscal 1996, contributions were received from the estate of Eudora J. Weaver.

Typical Recipients

Arts & Humanities: Libraries
Civic & Public Affairs: Economic Development, Civic & Public Affairs-General, Women's Affairs, Zoos/Aquariums
Education: Colleges & Universities, Medical Education, Private Education (Precollege), Special Education, Student Aid
Health: Alzheimers Disease, Cancer, Children's Health/Hospitals, Diabetes, Emergency/Ambulance Services, Health Organizations, Hospitals, Hospitals (University Affiliated), Long-Term Care, Mental Health, Public Health, Research/Studies Institutes, Trauma Treatment
Religion: Churches, Ministries, Missionary Activities (Domestic), Religious Organizations, Religious Welfare, Social/Policy Issues
Science: Science Museums
Social Services: At-Risk Youth, Big Brother/Big Sister, Camps, Child Welfare, Child Welfare, Community Centers, Community Service Organizations, Counseling, Crime Prevention, Family Planning, Family Services, Food/Clothing Distribution, Homes, People with Disabilities, Recreation & Athletics, Scouts, Senior Services, Shelters/Homelessness, Substance Abuse, United Funds/United Ways, YMCA/YWCA/YMHA/YWHA, Youth Organizations

Application Procedures

Initial Contact: The foundation requests applications be made in writing.
Application Requirements: Include a description of organization, amount requested, purpose of funds sought, recently audited financial statement, proof of tax-exempt status, board of directors, and project budget.
Deadlines: July 31.

Restrictions

No grants to individuals or to the arts.

Foundation Officials

John Michener: advisory trustee
Kaethe M. Weaver: advisory trustee
William R. Weaver, MD: trustee

Grants Analysis

Disclosure Period: fiscal year ending September 30, 2001
Total Grants: $396,100
Number of Grants: 30
Average Grant: $8,968*
Highest Grant: $75,000
Lowest Grant: $500
Typical Range: $1,000 to $10,000
*Note: Average grant figures excludes two highest grants ($145,000).

Recent Grants

Note: Grants derived from fiscal 2000 Form 990.

General

50,000	Trinity Christian Academy, Addison, TX -- for capital building fund
33,000	Texas Scottish Rite Hospital, Dallas, TX -- for medical equipment
20,000	Pittsburgh Public Schools, Pittsburgh, PA -- for Galbraith McFadden Weaver scholarship
20,000	Salvation Army, Dallas, TX -- for operating budget
20,000	Tarrant Area Food Bank, Ft. Worth, TX -- for operating funds
19,000	Dallas Theological Seminary, Dallas, TX -- for scholarships
12,500	Southwestern Diabetic Foundation, Gainesville, TX -- for Camp Sweeney
10,000	Cook Children's Medical Center, Ft. Worth, TX -- for uncompensated medical care fund

10,000   MD Anderson Cancer Center, Houston, TX -- for cancer research

10,000   YWCA of Fort Worth and Tarrant County, Ft. Worth, TX -- for child care program for homeless and low income families

WEBBER OIL CO.

Company Headquarters
Bangor, ME
Web: http://www.wenergy.com

Company Description
Revenue: US$30.1 million (2001)
Employees: 200 (2001)
SIC(s): 5100 Wholesale Trade--Nondurable Goods, 5172 Petroleum Products Nec, 5900 Miscellaneous Retail, 5983 Fuel Oil Dealers.

Operating Locations
Webber Oil Co. (ME--Bangor)

Webber Oil Foundation

Giving Contact
Ray Cota
700 Main St.
Bangor, ME 04401
Phone: (207)942-5501
Fax: (207)947-6522

Description
EIN: 237046575
Organization Type: Corporate Foundation
Giving Locations: ME: Bangor
Grant Types: Capital, Scholarship.

Financial Summary
Total Giving: $20,600 (fiscal year ending August 31, 2000); $32,000 (fiscal 1999); $38,600 (fiscal 1998)
Assets: $250,609 (fiscal 2000); $272,438 (fiscal 1999); $234,562 (fiscal 1998)
Gifts Received: $50,000 (fiscal 2000); $25,000 (fiscal 1999); $25,000 (fiscal 1998). Note: In 1999, contributions were received from Sargent, Tyler and West. In fiscal 1997 and 1998, contributions were received from Aroostook Petroleum Products.

Typical Recipients
Arts & Humanities: Dance, Arts & Humanities-General, History & Archaeology, Libraries, Museums/Galleries, Music, Opera, Theater
Civic & Public Affairs: Economic Development, Civic & Public Affairs-General, Municipalities/Towns, Professional & Trade Associations, Urban & Community Affairs
Education: Arts/Humanities Education, Colleges & Universities, Education Funds, Education-General, Private Education (Precollege), Secondary Education (Private), Student Aid, Vocational & Technical Education
Environment: Environment-General
Health: Clinics/Medical Centers, Health-General, Health Organizations, Hospices, Hospitals, Public Health
Religion: Churches
Social Services: Animal Protection, At-Risk Youth, Camps, Child Welfare, Community Service Organizations, Counseling, People with Disabilities, Recreation & Athletics, Scouts, Senior Services, Social Services-General, YMCA/YWCA/YMHA/YWHA, Youth Organizations

Application Procedures
Initial Contact: Request scholarship application information from high school guidance counselor. For non-scholarship grants, send a brief letter of inquiry.

Application Requirements: Include a description of organization, amount requested, and purpose of funds sought.
Deadlines: None.

Restrictions
Recipient must be a student of the high school awarding the scholarship.

Additional Information
Provides scholarships to Bangor, ME, area high school students.

Corporate Officials
Larry K. Mahaney: chairman, president, chief executive officer, director PRIM CORP EMPL chairman, president, chief executive officer, director: Webber Oil Co.
Andy Pease, Jr.: chief financial officer, vice president financial PRIM CORP EMPL chief financial officer, vice president financial: Webber Oil Co.

Foundation Officials
Linda F. Harnum: trustee
Larry K. Mahaney: trustee (see above)
Louise F. Witham: trustee

Grants Analysis
Disclosure Period: fiscal year ending August 31, 2000
Total Grants: $20,600
Number of Grants: 9
Highest Grant: $5,000
Lowest Grant: $500

Recent Grants
Note: Grants derived from 1999 Form 990.

Library-Related

5,000   YMCA Bangor, Camp Jordan Cabin
4,000   Bangor Public Library, Bangor, ME
500   Farmington Public Library, Farmington, ME

General

8,000   Unity College Betterment Fund
3,000   Center for Communications and Learning, Bangor, ME
2,500   Thomas College, Waterville, ME
2,500   YMCA Bar Harbor, Bar Harbor, ME
2,000   Senior Spectrum of Kennebec, Augusta, ME
1,000   Susan Curtis Foundation, Portland, ME
800   Hampden Congregational Church
800   Shaw House, Bangor, ME
700   Abnaki Girl Scout Council, Brewer, ME
700   Boy Scouts of America Katahdin Area Council, Orono, ME

FREDERICK E. WEBER CHARITIES CORP.

Giving Contact
Mary Ann Daily, President
175 Federal Street
Boston, MA 02110
Phone: (617)292-6264

Description
Founded: 1902
EIN: 042133244
Organization Type: Private Foundation
Giving Locations: MA: Boston metropolitan area
Grant Types: Emergency, Endowment, General Support, Scholarship.

Donor Information
Founder: the late Frederick E. Weber

Financial Summary
Total Giving: $381,350 (fiscal year ending March 31, 2002); $420,161 (fiscal 2001); $401,575 (fiscal 2000). Note: Fiscal 1997 Giving includes United Way ($12,500).
Giving Analysis: Giving for fiscal 2002 includes: foundation grants to United Way ($35,000); fiscal 2001: foundation grants to United Way ($30,000) fiscal 1999: foundation grants to United Way ($25,000)
Assets: $8,128,632 (fiscal 2002); $8,364,592 (fiscal 2001); $9,799,701 (fiscal 2000)

Typical Recipients
Arts & Humanities: Libraries, Performing Arts, Public Broadcasting
Civic & Public Affairs: Economic Development, Employment/Job Training, Ethnic Organizations, Civic & Public Affairs-General, Hispanic Affairs, Housing, Law & Justice, Municipalities/Towns, Philanthropic Organizations, Urban & Community Affairs, Women's Affairs
Education: Arts/Humanities Education, Colleges & Universities, Education-General, Minority Education, Private Education (Precollege), Secondary Education (Private), Student Aid, Vocational & Technical Education
Environment: Environment-General
Health: AIDS/HIV, Children's Health/Hospitals, Geriatric Health, Health Organizations, Hospices, Hospitals, Medical Research, Mental Health, Public Health
International: Health Care/Hospitals, International Affairs
Religion: Churches, Religious Organizations, Religious Welfare
Social Services: Camps, Child Welfare, Community Centers, Community Service Organizations, Counseling, Crime Prevention, Domestic Violence, Emergency Relief, Family Planning, Family Services, Food/Clothing Distribution, Homes, People with Disabilities, Recreation & Athletics, Shelters/Homelessness, Social Services-General, Substance Abuse, United Funds/United Ways, YMCA/YWCA/YMHA/YWHA, Youth Organizations

Application Procedures
Initial Contact: Send a brief summarizing letter setting forth the facts and need for funding.
Application Requirements: If a proposal or prospectus is available, it should accompany the letter. Also include a copy of the applicant's balance sheet, proof of tax-exempt status, and a list of board members. All requests should be approved by the president, treasurer, chief executive officer, social services director or other administrative officer of the organization.
Deadlines: None.

Restrictions
Grants are seldom awarded to national organizations or for single-disease projects. Appeals for general support are discouraged.

Additional Information
Publications: Annual Report

Foundation Officials
Lawrence Coolidge: assistant treasurer
Mary Ann Daily: president
Janet W. Eustis: clerk, director
Daniel Anthony Phillips: vice president, treasurer B Boston, MA 1938. ED Harvard University AB (1960); Harvard University MBA (1963). PRIM CORP EMPL president, chief executive officer, director: Fiduciary Trust Co. NONPR AFFIL director: Grimes-King Foundation Elderly; president, member: Harvard University Alumni Association; director: Families International; director: Family Service America; member: Boston

Economic Club; member: Boston Society Security Analysts; president, director: American Memorial Hospital. CLUB AFFIL Commercial Club.
Peter E. Reinhold: director
William C. Swan: director
Daniel P. Wise: director

Grants Analysis

Disclosure Period: fiscal year ending March 31, 2002
Total Grants: $346,350*
Number of Grants: 76
Average Grant: $4,557
Highest Grant: $31,500
Lowest Grant: $100
Typical Range: $1,000 to $10,000
*Note: Giving excludes United Way.

Recent Grants

Note: Grants derived from 2000 Form 990.

General
30,000	Associated Grantmakers of Massachusetts, Boston, MA -- camperships
25,000	United Way of Massachusetts Bay, Boston, MA -- program support
15,000	St. Elizabeth's Hospital, Brighton, MA
10,000	Boston Medical Center, Boston, MA -- revolving fund
10,000	Bridge Over Troubled Waters, Boston, MA -- programs support
10,000	Cambridge College, Cambridge, MA -- program support
10,000	Cambridge Forum, Cambridge, MA -- programs support
10,000	Children's Friend, Worcester, MA
10,000	Children's Hospital, Boston, MA
10,000	Community Care Services, Taunton, MA -- program support

EDWIN S. WEBSTER FOUNDATION

Giving Contact

Michelle Jenney, Foundation Assistant
Grants Management Associates
77 Summer St., Ste. 800
Boston, MA 02110
Phone: (617)426-7172
Fax: (617)426-5441
E-mail: mjenney@grantsmanagement.com
Web: http://www.grantsmanagement.com

Description

Founded: 1948
EIN: 046000647
Organization Type: General Purpose Foundation
Giving Locations: New England.
Grant Types: Capital, Operating Expenses, Project, Research.

Donor Information

Founder: Established in 1948 by the late Edwin S. Webster .

Financial Summary

Total Giving: $2,957,000 (2001); $2,708,000 (2000); $2,242,000 (1998)
Giving Analysis: Giving for 2000 includes: foundation grants to United Way ($100,000); 1998: foundation grants to United Way ($75,000) 1997: foundation grants to United Way ($70,000)
Assets: $38,000,000 (2001); $38,262,511 (2000); $43,269,317 (1998)

Typical Recipients

Arts & Humanities: Arts Centers, Ethnic & Folk Arts, Arts & Humanities-General, Historic Preservation, History & Archaeology, Libraries, Museums/Galleries, Music, Performing Arts, Public Broadcasting, Theater
Civic & Public Affairs: Asian American Affairs, Botanical Gardens/Parks, Clubs, Economic Development, Employment/Job Training, Civic & Public Affairs-General, Housing, Municipalities/Towns, Native American Affairs, Parades/Festivals, Urban & Community Affairs, Women's Affairs, Zoos/Aquariums
Education: Colleges & Universities, Community & Junior Colleges, Education Funds, Education Reform, Engineering/Technological Education, Faculty Development, Leadership Training, Legal Education, Medical Education, Minority Education, Minority Education, Private Education (Precollege), Public Education (Precollege)
Environment: Forestry, Environment-General, Resource Conservation, Wildlife Protection
Health: Cancer, Children's Health/Hospitals, Clinics/Medical Centers, Diabetes, Emergency/Ambulance Services, Eyes/Blindness, Health Organizations, Heart, Hospitals, Hospitals (University Affiliated), Medical Rehabilitation, Medical Research, Mental Health, Public Health, Single-Disease Health Associations, Trauma Treatment
International: Foreign Educational Institutions
Religion: Churches, Jewish Causes, Religious Organizations
Science: Observatories & Planetariums, Science Museums, Scientific Centers & Institutes, Scientific Labs
Social Services: Child Welfare, Emergency Relief, Family Planning, Family Services, Family Services, Food/Clothing Distribution, Homes, People with Disabilities, Recreation & Athletics, Shelters/Homelessness, Substance Abuse, United Funds/United Ways, Youth Organizations

Application Procedures

Initial Contact: Contact foundation in writing or by phone.
Application Requirements: Applicants must provide evidence of their tax-exempt status.
Deadlines: None, but the foundation's preference months are March and September.
Review Process: The trustees meet each year in early June and December to review requests and make distributions. Recipients are notified usually within 15 days of the meeting date.

Restrictions

Grants are not made outside the United States. The foundation does not make grants to individuals, or for loans, seed money, emergency funds, deficit financing, publications, or conferences.

Additional Information

Publications: Application Guidelines

Foundation Officials

Henry Upham Harris, III: trustee CORP AFFIL director: Heritage Bank & Trust.
Henry Upham Harris, Jr.: trustee B New York, NY 1926. ED Stanford University (1951). CORP AFFIL director: Tenneco Inc. NONPR AFFIL chairman emeritus, trustee: Hospital Special Surgery.
Richard Harte, Jr.: trustee PRIM CORP EMPL director: Eaton & Vance Co. PRIM NONPR EMPL chairman, director: Schepens Eye Research Institute. NONPR AFFIL chairman: Schepens Eye Research Institute. CLUB AFFIL president: Hunt Myopia Club.
Edwin W. Hiam: trustee ED California Institute of Technology MA (1948).
Michelle Jenney: foundation assistant

Grants Analysis

Disclosure Period: calendar year ending 2000
Total Grants: $2,608,000*
Number of Grants: 67
Average Grant: $38,925

Highest Grant: $100,000
Lowest Grant: $3,000
Typical Range: $20,000 to $75,000
*Note: Giving excludes United Way.

Recent Grants

Note: Grants derived from 2000 Form 990.

Library-Related
100,000	Boston Athenaeum, Boston, MA
20,000	Bennington Museum, Bennington, VT

General
100,000	Hospital for Special Surgery, New York, NY
100,000	Massachusetts General Hospital, Boston, MA
100,000	Massachusetts Institute of Technology, Cambridge, MA
100,000	Museum of Science, Boston, MA
100,000	New England Aquarium Corporation, Boston, MA
100,000	New York Botanical Garden, Bronx, NY
100,000	United Negro College Fund, Inc., Boston, MA
100,000	United Way of Massachusetts Bay, Boston, MA
100,000	Woods Hole Oceanographic Institution, Woods Hole, MA
80,000	Boys and Girls Clubs of Boston, Inc., Boston, MA

ELEANORE MULLEN WECKBAUGH FOUNDATION

Giving Contact

Therese A. Polakovic, President & Trustee
PO Box 3486
Englewood, CO 80155-3486
Phone: (303)471-1301

Description

Founded: 1975
EIN: 237437761
Organization Type: Private Foundation
Giving Locations: CO
Grant Types: General Support.

Donor Information

Founder: the late Eleanore Mullen Weckbaugh

Financial Summary

Total Giving: $476,966 (fiscal year ending March 31, 2002); $499,235 (fiscal 2001); $436,435 (fiscal 2000)
Assets: $9,974,673 (fiscal 2002); $10,954,787 (fiscal 2001); $11,198,414 (fiscal 2000)

Typical Recipients

Arts & Humanities: Libraries, Music, Opera, Performing Arts, Public Broadcasting
Civic & Public Affairs: Botanical Gardens/Parks, Employment/Job Training, Ethnic Organizations, Civic & Public Affairs-General, Housing, Professional & Trade Associations, Safety, Urban & Community Affairs, Zoos/Aquariums
Education: Afterschool/Enrichment Programs, Arts/Humanities Education, Business Education, Colleges & Universities, Continuing Education, Education Funds, Elementary Education (Public), Private Education (Precollege), Public Education (Precollege), Science/Mathematics Education, Secondary Education (Private), Secondary Education (Public)
Health: Alzheimers Disease, Eyes/Blindness, Heart, Hospitals, Mental Health, Public Health
Religion: Churches, Dioceses, Dioceses, Ministries, Missionary Activities (Domestic), Religious Organizations, Religious Welfare
Science: Science Museums

Social Services: Child Welfare, Community Centers, Community Service Organizations, Counseling, Domestic Violence, Family Planning, Family Services, Food/Clothing Distribution, Homes, People with Disabilities, Scouts, Senior Services, Sexual Abuse, Substance Abuse, Volunteer Services, Youth Organizations

Application Procedures

Initial Contact: Send a brief letter of inquiry.
Application Requirements: purpose of funds sought.
Deadlines: None.

Restrictions

Does not support individuals.

Foundation Officials

Jean Guyton: trustee
Michael Lascor: trustee
Edward J. Limes: treasurer, trustee
Deborah O'Dwyer: trustee
Michael J. Polakovic: vice president, secretary, trustee
Therese A. Polakovic: president, secretary, trustee

Grants Analysis

Disclosure Period: fiscal year ending March 31, 2002
Total Grants: $476,966
Number of Grants: 35
Average Grant: $11,087*
Highest Grant: $100,000
Lowest Grant: $100
Typical Range: $5,000 to $20,000
*Note: Average grant figure excludes highest grant.

Recent Grants

Note: Grants derived from 2000 Form 990.

General

40,000	Mount Saint Vincent Home, Denver, CO -- capital campaign
40,000	St. Mary's Academy, Englewood, CO -- for capital campaign
25,000	Denver Museum of Natural History, Denver, CO
22,000	Sacred Heart House, Denver, CO
20,000	Regis University, Denver, CO
18,860	Archdiocese of Denver, Denver, CO -- for seeds of hope
16,500	Mount Saint Vincent Home, Denver, CO
16,000	Regis High School, Aurora, CO
15,000	St. Joseph Hospital Foundation, Denver, CO
10,500	Archdiocese of Denver, Denver, CO

WEEZIE FOUNDATION

Giving Contact

Shannon Hennessey
JP Morgan Chase Bank
345 Park Ave., 6th Fl.
New York, NY 10154
Phone: (212)464-1936

Description

Founded: 1961
EIN: 136090903
Organization Type: General Purpose Foundation
Giving Locations: Northeastern USA.
Grant Types: General Support.

Donor Information

Founder: Established in 1961 by the late Adelaide T. Corbett .

Financial Summary

Total Giving: $1,371,500 (2001); $1,960,000 (2000); $1,346,000 (1999)
Assets: $27,930,415 (2001); $30,751,342 (2000); $32,660,867 (1999)

Typical Recipients

Arts & Humanities: Libraries, Museums/Galleries, Public Broadcasting
Civic & Public Affairs: Clubs, Community Foundations, Civic & Public Affairs-General, Urban & Community Affairs, Zoos/Aquariums
Education: Agricultural Education, Arts/Humanities Education, Colleges & Universities, Community & Junior Colleges, Education Associations, Education-General, Literacy, Medical Education, Private Education (Precollege), Public Education (Precollege), Religious Education, Science/Mathematics Education, Special Education, Student Aid
Environment: Environment-General
Health: Clinics/Medical Centers, Eyes/Blindness, Hospitals, Hospitals (University Affiliated), Medical Rehabilitation, Mental Health
Religion: Churches, Ministries, Religious Organizations
Science: Scientific Labs
Social Services: Community Service Organizations, Community Service Organizations, Counseling, Family Services, Homes, People with Disabilities, Recreation & Athletics, Substance Abuse, YMCA/YWCA/YMHA/YWHA, Youth Organizations

Application Procedures

Initial Contact: Send a brief letter of inquiry.
Deadlines: None.

Foundation Officials

D. Nelson Adams, Esq.: member advisory committee ED Yale University AB (1932); Harvard University LLB (1935). PRIM CORP EMPL attorney: Davis, Polk & Wardwell. NONPR AFFIL member: New York County Lawyers Association; member: New York State Bar Association; member: New York City Bar Association; member: American Bar Association; member: American Law Institute.
Thomas W. Carroll: advisor
Mrs. George F. Fiske, Jr.: member advisory committee
Mrs. Kirkie T. Hall: member advisory committee
Lucille T. Hays: mem adv comm
Tyler P. Hoffman: member advisory committee
H. S. Graham McBride: adv
William Parsons, Jr.: member advisory committee

Grants Analysis

Disclosure Period: calendar year ending 2001
Total Grants: $1,371,500
Number of Grants: 28
Average Grant: $48,982
Highest Grant: $200,000
Lowest Grant: $2,500
Typical Range: $25,000 to $100,000

Recent Grants

Note: Grants derived from 2001 Form 990.

General

200,000	Massachusetts Horticultural Society, Boston, MA
100,000	Fay School, Southborough, MA
100,000	Nantucket Boys and Girls Club, Nantucket, MA
100,000	Nantucket Cottage Hospital, Nantucket, MA
100,000	Nantucket New School, Nantucket, MA
100,000	Phoenix House Development, New York, NY
81,000	Mission Hill School, Roxbury, MA
75,000	Nantucket Maria Mitchell Association, Nantucket, MA
75,000	Youth Counseling League, New York, NY
50,000	Grymes Memorial School, Orange, VA

WEGE FOUNDATION

Giving Contact

Peter M. Wege, President
PO Box 6388
Grand Rapids, MI 49516
Phone: (616)957-0480

Description

Founded: 1967
EIN: 386124363
Organization Type: Private Foundation
Giving Locations: MI: Greater Kent County, Grand Rapids
Grant Types: General Support.

Donor Information

Founder: Peter M. Wege

Financial Summary

Total Giving: $9,604,259 (2000); $7,032,139 (1999); $4,513,060 (1997)
Giving Analysis: Giving for 2000 includes: foundation grants to United Way ($200,000); 1999: foundation grants to United Way ($100,000) 1997: foundation grants to United Way ($20,000)
Assets: $187,459,935 (2000); $170,090,898 (1999); $8,760,935 (1997)
Gifts Received: $155,000 (1997); $412,000 (1996); $100,000 (1995). Note: In 1996, contributions were received from Peter M. Wege.

Typical Recipients

Arts & Humanities: Arts Associations & Councils, Arts Centers, Community Arts, Libraries, Literary Arts, Museums/Galleries, Music, Public Broadcasting, Theater
Civic & Public Affairs: Botanical Gardens/Parks, Clubs, Economic Development, Employment/Job Training, Civic & Public Affairs-General, Hispanic Affairs, Housing, Municipalities/Towns, Native American Affairs, Philanthropic Organizations, Public Policy, Urban & Community Affairs, Zoos/Aquariums
Education: Arts/Humanities Education, Business Education, Colleges & Universities, Community & Junior Colleges, Education Associations, Education Funds, Environmental Education, Education-General, International Studies, Literacy, Private Education (Precollege), Public Education (Precollege), Secondary Education (Private), Special Education
Environment: Environment-General, Resource Conservation, Wildlife Protection
Health: Cancer, Diabetes, Emergency/Ambulance Services, Health-General, Health Organizations, Hospitals, Medical Rehabilitation, Multiple Sclerosis
International: Foreign Arts Organizations, International Environmental Issues, International Organizations
Religion: Churches, Dioceses, Religious Organizations, Religious Welfare
Social Services: Camps, Child Welfare, Community Service Organizations, Family Planning, Family Services, Homes, Refugee Assistance, Senior Services, Substance Abuse, United Funds/United Ways, Youth Organizations

Application Procedures

Initial Contact: Submit a brief letter of inquiry.
Application Requirements: Include a a description of organization.
Deadlines: September 15 and February 15.

Restrictions

Grants are not made to individuals or political or lobbying groups.

Foundation Officials

Mary Goodwillie Nelson: director
Charles C. Lundstrom: secretary
Ellen Satterlee: treasurer
Diana L. Wege: director
Peter M. Wege, II: vice president PRIM CORP EMPL president: Greylock Inc. CORP AFFIL director: Steelcase Inc.
Peter M. Wege: president B Grand Rapids, MI 1921. ED University of Michigan.

Grants Analysis

Disclosure Period: calendar year ending 2000
Total Grants: $9,404,259*
Number of Grants: 103
Average Grant: $60,540*
Highest Grant: $1,729,670
Typical Range: $30,000 to $100,000
*Note: Giving excludes United Way. Average grant figure excludes two highest grants ($3,289,670).

Recent Grants

Note: Grants derived from 1999 Form 990.

General

1,575,764	Aquinas College, Grand Rapids, MI
615,000	Grand Rapids Art Museum, Grand Rapids, MI
575,000	University of Michigan School of Natural Resources and Environment, Ann Arbor, MI
543,900	St. Stephens Catholic Church, Grand Rapids, MI
450,000	Diocese of Grand Rapids, Grand Rapids, MI
360,000	Land Conservancy of W. Michigan, Grand Rapids, MI
300,000	St. Mary's Health Services, Grand Rapids, MI
284,665	SEED, Grand Rapids, MI
199,500	Frederik Meijer Garden, Grand Rapids, MI
146,000	Grand Rapids Symphony, Grand Rapids, MI

TODD WEHR FOUNDATION

Giving Contact

Ralph G. Schulz, President & Director
111 E. Wisconsin Ave., Suite 2100
Milwaukee, WI 53202
Phone: (414)273-2100

Description

Founded: 1953
EIN: 396043962
Organization Type: Private Foundation
Giving Locations: WI
Grant Types: Project.

Donor Information

Founder: the late C. Frederic Wehr

Financial Summary

Total Giving: $760,000 (2000); $692,825 (1999); $530,000 (1998)
Assets: $15,336,987 (2000); $15,057,697 (1999); $14,688,800 (1998)

Typical Recipients

Arts & Humanities: Museums/Galleries
Civic & Public Affairs: Economic Development, Civic & Public Affairs-General

Education: Colleges & Universities, Engineering/ Technological Education, Environmental Education, Faculty Development, Medical Education, Science/ Mathematics Education, Secondary Education (Public)
Health: Medical Research
Science: Science Museums, Scientific Centers & Institutes
Social Services: Youth Organizations

Application Procedures

Initial Contact: a brief letter of inquiry and full proposal
Deadlines: None.

Restrictions

Does not support individuals.

Foundation Officials

Robert P. Harland: director, vice president
Allan E. Iding: director, treasurer
Ralph G. Schulz: president, director NONPR AFFIL honorary member: Beta Gamma Sigma; member: Masons Shriners; member: American Zoological Society. CLUB AFFIL Milwakee Press Club; Milwaukee Athletic Club.
M. James Termondt: secretary, director

Grants Analysis

Disclosure Period: calendar year ending 2000
Total Grants: $760,000
Number of Grants: 14
Average Grant: $54,286
Highest Grant: $100,000
Typical Range: $20,000 to $100,000

Recent Grants

Note: Grants derived from 1999 Form 990.

General

100,325	Marian College, Fond Du Lac, WI
100,000	Carroll College, Waukesha, WI
100,000	Marquette University, Milwaukee, WI
100,000	Messmer High School, Milwaukee, WI
100,000	Neighborhood Improvement Development Corporation, Milwaukee, WI
50,000	Alverno College, Milwaukee, WI
50,000	Boys and Girls Clubs of Greater Milwaukee, Milwaukee, WI
40,000	Concordia University, Mequon, WI
20,000	Discovery World - The James Lovell Museum of Science, Economics and Technology, Inc., Milwaukee, WI
10,000	Beloit College, Beloit, WI

WEIL, GOTSHAL & MANGES CORP.

Company Headquarters

New York, NY
Web: http://www.weil.com

Company Description

Employees: 1,600
SIC(s): 8111 Legal Services.

Weil, Gotshal & Manges Foundation

Giving Contact

Jesse D. Wolff, Treasurer & Director
Weil, Gotshal & Manges Foundation
767 5th Ave.
New York, NY 10153
Phone: (212)310-8000

Description

Founded: 1983
EIN: 133158325
Organization Type: Corporate Foundation
Giving Locations: NY
Grant Types: General Support.

Donor Information

Founder: Robert Todd Lang, Ira M. Millstein, Harvey R. Miller

Financial Summary

Total Giving: $2,579,705 (2001); $2,427,497 (2000); $1,414,287 (1999). Note: Contributes through foundation only.
Giving Analysis: Giving for 2000 includes: foundation scholarships ($10,000); foundation grants to United Way ($165,000); foundation ($2,252,497); 1999: foundation scholarships ($600); foundation grants to United Way ($167,500); foundation ($1,246,187); 1998: foundation grants to United Way ($160,000); foundation ($1,880,640);
Assets: $2,521,545 (2001); $2,970,795 (2000); $8,344,099 (1997)
Gifts Received: $2,027,834 (2001); $1,500,000 (2000); $1,515,000 (1999). Note: Contributions are received from Weil, Gotshal & Manges LLP.

Typical Recipients

Arts & Humanities: Arts Associations & Councils, Arts Centers, Dance, History & Archaeology, Libraries, Museums/Galleries, Music, Opera, Performing Arts, Public Broadcasting
Civic & Public Affairs: African American Affairs, Botanical Gardens/Parks, Business/Free Enterprise, Chambers of Commerce, Civil Rights, Clubs, Economic Development, Economic Policy, Employment/ Job Training, Ethnic Organizations, Civic & Public Affairs-General, Law & Justice, Legal Aid, Municipalities/Towns, Parades/Festivals, Public Policy, Urban & Community Affairs, Women's Affairs, Zoos/ Aquariums
Education: Arts/Humanities Education, Business Education, Colleges & Universities, Education Associations, Education Reform, Education-General, International Studies, Legal Education, Medical Education, Private Education (Precollege), Secondary Education (Private), Social Sciences Education, Student Aid
Environment: Environment-General
Health: AIDS/HIV, Cancer, Children's Health/Hospitals, Emergency/Ambulance Services, Heart, Medical Research, Prenatal Health Issues, Public Health, Single-Disease Health Associations, Transplant Networks/Donor Banks
International: Foreign Educational Institutions, Human Rights, International Affairs, International Peace & Security Issues, International Relations, Missionary/Religious Activities
Religion: Dioceses, Religion-General, Jewish Causes, Religious Organizations, Religious Welfare
Science: Science Museums, Scientific Centers & Institutes
Social Services: At-Risk Youth, Big Brother/Big Sister, Camps, Child Welfare, Community Service Organizations, Crime Prevention, Emergency Relief, Family Planning, Family Services, Recreation & Athletics, Scouts, Shelters/Homelessness, United Funds/ United Ways, Volunteer Services, YMCA/YWCA/ YMHA/YWHA, Youth Organizations

Application Procedures

Initial Contact: Send a written proposal.
Application Requirements: Include a description of organization; statement of purpose; budget and income; and schedule of activities.
Deadlines: November 1.

Corporate Officials

Ira M. Millstein: partner B New York, NY 1926. ED Columbia University BS (1947); Columbia University LLB (1949). PRIM CORP EMPL partner: Weil, Gotshal & Manges Corp. NONPR AFFIL chairman: New York City Partnership Policy Center; member: New York State Bar Association; member: National Association Corp. Directors; professor, chairman board advisors: Columbia University Center Law Economic Studies; member: Government Cuomo's Task Force on Pension Fund Investment; chairman board trustee: Center Park Conservancy; fellow: American Academy of Arts & Sciences; member: American Bar Association; vice chairman board overseers: Albert Einstein College of Medicine. CLUB AFFIL Metro Club; Quaker Ridge Golf Club.

Foundation Officials

Robert Todd Lang: chairman, director B New York, NY 1924. ED Yale University BA (1945); Yale University LLB (1947). PRIM CORP EMPL senior partner: Weil, Gotshal & Manges Corp. NONPR AFFIL chairman: Task Force Listing Standards Self Regulatory Organizations; member: Task Force Review Federal Securities Law; chairman: Task Force Hedge Funds; member: American Bar Association; member: Committee Federal Regulation Securities.

Harvey R. Miller: chairman, director B Brooklyn, NY 1933. ED Columbia University School of Law (1959). PRIM CORP EMPL partner: Weil, Gotshal & Manges Corp.

Ira M. Millstein: chairman, director (see above)

Grants Analysis

Disclosure Period: calendar year ending 2001
Total Grants: $2,419,705*
Number of Grants: 164
Average Grant: $11,553*
Highest Grant: $300,000
Lowest Grant: $50
Typical Range: $500 to $25,000
*Note: Giving excludes United Way and scholarships. Average grant figure excludes two highest grants ($525,000).

Recent Grants

Note: Grants derived from 2001 Form 990.

General

500,000	United Jewish Appeal - Federation of Jewish Philanthropies of New York, New York, NY
300,000	New York Police and Fire Widows and Children's Benefit, Uniondale, NY
225,000	Twin Tower Fund, New York, NY
155,000	United Way of New York City, New York, NY
150,000	Columbia Law School, New York, NY
100,000	American Red Cross in Greater New York, New York, NY
100,000	Catholic Charities World Trade Center Support Fund, New York, NY
100,000	Citigroup Relief Fund
30,000	Make-A-Wish Foundation of Metro New York, New York, NY
25,000	Health Watch, New York, NY

WEINGART FOUNDATION

Giving Contact

Fred J. Ali, President
1055 West 7th Street, Suite 3050
Los Angeles, CA 90017
Phone: (213)688-7799
Fax: (213)688-1515
E-mail: info@weingartfnd.org
Web: http://www.weingartfnd.org

Alternate Contact

Weingart-Price Fund
San Diego Foundation
1420 Kettner Boulevard, Suite 500
San Diego, CA 92101
Phone: (619)235-2300
Note: For agencies in San Diego and Imperial County.

Description

Founded: 1951
EIN: 956054814
Organization Type: General Purpose Foundation
Giving Locations: CA: seven counties in Southern California
Grant Types: Capital, Employee Matching Gifts, Project, Scholarship, Seed Money.

Donor Information

Founder: Ben Weingart (1888-1980) was a real estate developer in Southern California who helped create a new town, the City of Lakewood, during the 1950s. It was the first planned city in Southern California. Mr. Weingart was born in Atlanta, GA. He attended school through the eighth grade and arrived in Los Angeles when he was 18 years old.

The Weingart Foundation was established in California in 1951 as the B. W. Foundation. The name of the foundation was changed in April 1978. Funds for the foundation's incorporation were donated by the late Ben Weingart and Stella Weingart , who bequeathed their estates to the foundation.

Financial Summary

Total Giving: $36,252,338 (fiscal year ending June 30, 2002); $36,183,031 (fiscal 2001); $38,069,654 (fiscal 2000)
Giving Analysis: Giving for fiscal 1999 includes: foundation matching gifts ($207,387)
Assets: $675,000,000 (fiscal 2002); $779,796,365 (fiscal 2001); $853,000,000 (fiscal 2000 approx)
Gifts Received: $50,000 (fiscal 1992 approx)

Typical Recipients

Arts & Humanities: Arts Centers, Arts Institutes, Arts Outreach, Ballet, Ethnic & Folk Arts, Libraries, Museums/Galleries, Music, Performing Arts, Public Broadcasting, Theater
Civic & Public Affairs: African American Affairs, Clubs, Community Foundations, Civic & Public Affairs-General, Hispanic Affairs, Housing, Law & Justice, Public Policy, Urban & Community Affairs, Zoos/Aquariums
Education: Afterschool/Enrichment Programs, Arts/Humanities Education, Business Education, Colleges & Universities, Community & Junior Colleges, Education Associations, Education Funds, Education Reform, Elementary Education (Private), Engineering/Technological Education, Faculty Development, Education-General, Leadership Training, Legal Education, Literacy, Medical Education, Minority Education, Preschool Education, Private Education (Precollege), Public Education (Precollege), Religious Education, School Volunteerism, Science/Mathematics Education, Secondary Education (Private), Secondary Education (Public), Social Sciences Education, Special Education, Student Aid, Vocational & Technical Education
Environment: Resource Conservation
Health: AIDS/HIV, Cancer, Children's Health/Hospitals, Clinics/Medical Centers, Diabetes, Emergency/Ambulance Services, Eyes/Blindness, Health-General, Health Organizations, Hospices, Hospitals, Long-Term Care, Medical Research, Mental Health, Nursing Services, Outpatient Health Care, Prenatal Health Issues, Prenatal Health Issues, Preventive Medicine/Wellness Organizations, Public Health, Speech & Hearing
International: Foreign Educational Institutions, Missionary/Religious Activities
Religion: Dioceses, Jewish Causes, Religious Welfare, Synagogues/Temples

Science: Science Museums, Scientific Centers & Institutes, Scientific Organizations
Social Services: Animal Protection, At-Risk Youth, Big Brother/Big Sister, Camps, Child Abuse, Child Welfare, Community Centers, Community Service Organizations, Counseling, Crime Prevention, Day Care, Delinquency & Criminal Rehabilitation, Domestic Violence, Emergency Relief, Family Services, Food/Clothing Distribution, Homes, People with Disabilities, Recreation & Athletics, Refugee Assistance, Scouts, Scouts, Senior Services, Shelters/Homelessness, Substance Abuse, Volunteer Services, YMCA/YWCA/YMHA/YWHA, Youth Organizations

Application Procedures

Initial Contact: A qualified organization that believes it meets the foundation's criteria for a grant should first submit a brief, to-the-point "test letter."
Application Requirements: The letter, not to exceed two pages, should contain a concise statement of the need for funds, amount sought, and enough factual information to enable the foundation to determine an initial response. Supporting data may be included. Three copies of the letter and one copy of supporting data are required. If the project meets the foundation's priorities, a formal application will be sent to the organization.
Deadlines: None.
Review Process: Final notification arrives three to four months after receiving the proposal.

Restrictions

The foundation does not make grants for propagandizing, influencing legislation and/or elections, promoting voter registration, for political candidates, political campaigns, or organizations engaged in political activities. The foundation does not make grants to federated appeals or to organizations that collect funds for redistribution to other nonprofit groups. It does not make grants for support of national charities, for operating budgets of agencies served by the United Way or other federated sources (except for approved special projects), for operating expenses of performing arts organizations, or for the benefit of individuals or small groups. The foundation does not consider requests for support of projects that normally would be financed from government funds. It ordinarily does not make grants for endowment funds, contingencies, or deficits. As a general rule, it does not make grants for conferences, seminars, workshops, exhibits, travel, medical research surveys, publishing activities, or films, nor does the foundation encourage applications for funding the projects of environmental, consumer, refugee, or religious programs; international organizations; or governmental or quasi-governmental agencies. The foundation does not approve grants for regular, ongoing, operating support. Applicant organizations must be tax-exempt under section 501(c)(3) of the IRS code.

Additional Information

The foundation expects applicant organizations to show project support from internal sources as well as outside sources. Grants may cover a multiyear period in some cases, but the foundation generally does not make a grant to any organization on an annual basis.
Publications: Annual Report; Guidelines; Application Procedures

Foundation Officials

Fred J. Ali: president, chief administrative officer
Andrew E. Bogen: director
Steven D. Broidy: chairman, chief executive officer, director B 1938. PRIM CORP EMPL vice chairman board, director: City National Bank.
Rosa M. Castillo: program officer
E. Corinne Dela Cruz: assistant treasurer, senior accountant
Murray L. Galinson: director B Minneapolis, MN 1937. ED University of Minnesota (1958); United States International University (1976). PRIM CORP

EMPL chairman, chief executive officer: San Diego National Bank. CORP AFFIL director: Price Enterprises.

John Thomas Gurash: director B Oakland, CA November 25, 1910. ED Loyola University School of Law (1938-1939). CORP AFFIL director: Saint-Gobain Corp. NONPR AFFIL chairman: Horace Mann Educators Corp.; trustee emeritus: Occidental College.

Deborah M. Ives: director finance, controller

Barbara Kaze: program officer

William D. Schulte: director

Steven L. Soboroff: director

Dennis Carothers Stanfill: director B Centerville, TN 1927. ED United States Naval Academy BS (1949); Oxford University MA (1953). PRIM CORP EMPL president: Dennis Stanfill Co. CORP AFFIL director: Dial Corp.; director: Dial Consumer Product Group. NONPR AFFIL trustee: California Institute Technology.

Ann L. Van Dormolen: vice president, treasurer B 1947. ED DePaul University (1968-1973).

Laurence A. Wolfe: vice president admin and real estate, secretary

Jerry C. Yu: program officer

Grants Analysis

Disclosure Period: fiscal year ending June 30, 2002
Total Grants: $36,252,338*
Number of Grants: 356
Average Grant: $101,832
Highest Grant: $3,000,000
Typical Range: $10,000 to $200,000
***Note:** Giving includes matching gifts.

Recent Grants

Note: Grants derived from fiscal 2002 Form 990.

Library-Related
250,000	Library Foundation of Los Angeles, Los Angeles, CA

General
2,250,000	Exposition Park Intergenerational Community Center, Los Angeles, CA
1,000,000	Music Center, Inc., Los Angeles, CA
1,000,000	Occidental College, Los Angeles, CA
1,000,000	St. John's Hospital and Health Center, Los Angeles, CA
1,000,000	USC School of Medicine, Los Angeles, CA
965,000	United Friends of the Children Bridges, Culver City, CA -- for bridges to independence
750,000	Goodwill Industries of Southern California, Los Angeles, CA
600,000	Pediatric and Family Medical Center, Los Angeles, CA
539,000	YMCA Metropolitan Los Angeles, Los Angeles, CA -- for camp fund
500,000	American Red Cross, Los Angeles, CA -- for emergency disaster

J. WEINSTEIN FOUNDATION

Giving Contact

Salvatore Cappuzzo, Secretary & Treasurer
Rockridge Farm, Rte. 52
Carmel, NY 10512
Phone: (914)325-7647

Description

Founded: 1948
EIN: 116003595
Organization Type: Private Foundation
Giving Locations: CT; NY; TN
Grant Types: Endowment, General Support, Multiyear/Continuing Support, Research.

Donor Information

Founder: the late Joe Weinstein, J. W. Mays

Financial Summary

Total Giving: $278,154 (2001); $294,820 (2000); $316,240 (1999)
Assets: $4,964,419 (2001); $4,872,124 (2000); $4,924,802 (1999)
Gifts Received: $50,000 (1993); $50,000 (1992)

Typical Recipients

Arts & Humanities: Libraries, Museums/Galleries
Civic & Public Affairs: Civic & Public Affairs-General, Safety, Urban & Community Affairs, Women's Affairs
Education: Arts/Humanities Education, Colleges & Universities, Education-General, Medical Education, Private Education (Precollege), Secondary Education (Private), Special Education
Health: Cancer, Children's Health/Hospitals, Clinics/Medical Centers, Diabetes, Eyes/Blindness, Geriatric Health, Health Organizations, Hospitals, Hospitals (University Affiliated), Mental Health, Multiple Sclerosis, Research/Studies Institutes, Single-Disease Health Associations
International: Foreign Arts Organizations, Foreign Educational Institutions, International-General, Health Care/Hospitals, International Peace & Security Issues, Missionary/Religious Activities
Religion: Jewish Causes, Religious Organizations
Science: Science Museums, Scientific Centers & Institutes
Social Services: Animal Protection, At-Risk Youth, Camps, Community Service Organizations, Family Planning, People with Disabilities, Recreation & Athletics, Senior Services, Youth Organizations

Application Procedures

Initial Contact: Send a description of organization and the reason for request.
Deadlines: None.

Foundation Officials

Salvatore Cappuzzo: secretary, treasurer

Lloyd J. Shulman: vice president, director PRIM CORP EMPL president, chairman, director: J.W. Mays.

Max L. Shulman: president, director B New York, NY October 18, 1908. ED City University of New York (1924); National University LLB (1930). PRIM CORP EMPL chief executive officer, director: J.W. Mays. CORP AFFIL chairman, president: Weinstein Enterprises. CLUB AFFIL Rotary Club; mem: Harmonie Club.

Sylvia W. Shulman: vice president, director B New York, NY 1918. ED Syracuse University. PRIM CORP EMPL director: J.W. Mays Inc. CORP AFFIL vice president, director: Weinstein Enterprises Inc.

Grants Analysis

Disclosure Period: calendar year ending 2001
Total Grants: $278,154
Number of Grants: 65
Average Grant: $2,356*
Highest Grant: $125,000
Typical Range: $1,000 to $5,000
***Note:** Average grant figure excludes highest grant.

Recent Grants

Note: Grants derived from 2001 Form 990.

General
125,000	New York University Medical Center, New York, NY -- Department of Urology
30,000	New York Methodist Hospital, New York, NY
10,200	American Friends of the Israel Museum, New York, NY
10,000	Breast Cancer Research Foundation, New York, NY
10,000	Ethical Fieldstone Fund, New York, NY
10,000	Memorial Sloan-Kettering Cancer Center, New York, NY
10,000	Temple Beth Shalom, Mahopac, NY
5,500	Brookdale Center on Aging, New York, NY
5,000	American Committee for the Weizmann Institute, New York, NY
5,000	Lighthouse, Inc., New York, NY

CANDACE KING WEIR FOUNDATION

Giving Contact

Candace K. Weir, Trustee
c/o C. L. King & Assocs.
9 Elk St.
Albany, NY 12207
Phone: (518)431-3500

Description

Founded: 1994
EIN: 133797919
Organization Type: Private Foundation
Grant Types: General Support.

Financial Summary

Total Giving: $512,950 (2001); $315,150 (1999); $245,300 (1998)
Assets: $10,720,741 (2001); $9,770,069 (1999); $6,902,085 (1998)
Gifts Received: $999,750 (2001); $1,099,936 (1999); $1,000,000 (1998). Note: In 1998, 1999, and 2001, contributions were received from Candace K. Weir.

Typical Recipients

Arts & Humanities: Arts Institutes, Arts & Humanities-General, Libraries, Literary Arts, Theater
Civic & Public Affairs: Botanical Gardens/Parks, Community Foundations, Economic Development, Civic & Public Affairs-General, Urban & Community Affairs
Education: Colleges & Universities, Medical Education, Private Education (Precollege)
Environment: Environment-General, Resource Conservation
Health: Alzheimers Disease, Hospitals, Medical Research
Religion: Churches, Dioceses, Religious Organizations, Religious Welfare
Social Services: Camps, Community Service Organizations

Application Procedures

Initial Contact: Send letter with supporting attachments to fully disclose charitable purpose of applicant.
Deadlines: None.

Foundation Officials

Meredith Prime: trustee
Amelia F. Weir: trustee
Candace K. Weir: trustee
David A. Weir: trustee

Grants Analysis

Disclosure Period: calendar year ending 2001
Total Grants: $512,950*
Typical Range: $500 to $10,000
***Note:** No grants list available for 2001.

Recent Grants

Note: Grants derived from 2000 Form 990.

Library-Related
3,000	Westport Library, Westport, CT

General

150,000	The Roman Catholic Diocese of Albany, Albany, NY
20,000	The Brown Ledge Foundation, Burlington, VT
10,000	St. Williams Church, Tortola Virgin Islands of the United States
10,000	YADDO, Saratoga Springs, NY
5,000	The Caring Foundation, Derry, NH
5,000	The Committee of 200 Foundation, Chicago, IL
5,000	The Nature Conservancy, Block Island, RI
5,000	WMHT Public Television, Schenectady, NY
4,000	Westport Deport Theatre, Westport, NY
3,000	St. Pius X Building Fund, Loudonville, NY

WILLIAM E. WEISS FOUNDATION

Giving Contact

Tom Miller, President
PO Box 14270
Jackson, WY 83002
Phone: (307)739-8338

Description

Founded: 1955
EIN: 556016633
Organization Type: Private Foundation
Giving Locations: CT; DC: Washington; MT; NY; WV; WY
Grant Types: Capital, General Support, Multiyear/Continuing Support, Project, Scholarship.

Donor Information

Founder: the late William E. Weiss, Jr., the late Helene K Brown

Financial Summary

Total Giving: $512,750 (fiscal year ending March 31, 2002); $536,300 (fiscal 2001); $470,000 (fiscal 2000)
Assets: $10,761,879 (fiscal 2002); $10,562,296 (fiscal 2001); $11,101,844 (fiscal 2000)

Typical Recipients

Arts & Humanities: Arts Associations & Councils, Arts Centers, Dance, Historic Preservation, History & Archaeology, Libraries, Museums/Galleries, Music, Visual Arts
Civic & Public Affairs: Clubs, Civic & Public Affairs-General, Philanthropic Organizations, Safety, Urban & Community Affairs, Women's Affairs, Zoos/Aquariums
Education: Colleges & Universities, Elementary Education (Public), Education-General, Literacy, Minority Education, Preschool Education, Private Education (Precollege), Public Education (Precollege), Science/Mathematics Education, Secondary Education (Private)
Environment: Air/Water Quality, Environment-General, Research, Resource Conservation
Health: Cancer, Emergency/Ambulance Services, Health Organizations, Hospitals, Mental Health
Religion: Churches, Religious Organizations, Religious Welfare
Social Services: Child Welfare, Community Service Organizations, Domestic Violence, Food/Clothing Distribution, Recreation & Athletics, Shelters/Homelessness, Substance Abuse, United Funds/United Ways, Youth Organizations

Application Procedures

Initial Contact: Send a brief letter of inquiry.
Deadlines: in November.

Foundation Officials

Dwyer Brown: secretary
Monte T. Brown: treasurer
Mary Lou Hughes: secretary
Daryl Brown Uber: vice president
William D. Weiss: president
William U. Weiss: treasurer

Grants Analysis

Disclosure Period: fiscal year ending March 31, 2002
Total Grants: $512,750
Number of Grants: 34
Average Grant: $14,023*
Highest Grant: $50,000
Lowest Grant: $750
Typical Range: $5,000 to $25,000
***Note:** Average grant figure excludes highest grant.

Recent Grants

Note: Grants derived from 2000 Form 990.

Library-Related

30,000	Miss Porter's School, Farmington, CT -- library building

General

77,000	Buffalo Bill Historical Center, Cody, WY
50,000	Bethany College, Bethany, WV -- renovation Kirkpatrick Hall of Life Sciences
30,000	Hotchkiss School, Lakeville, CT -- minority student scholarship
30,000	New York Open Center, New York, NY -- minority opportunity programs
28,500	St. John's Episcopal Church -- new organ fund
28,000	Santa Barbara Zoological Gardens, Santa Barbara, CA -- educational outreach zoomobile
25,000	Seattle Art Museum, Seattle, WA -- John Singer Sargent catalogue
20,000	Blues Foundation, The, Memphis, TN -- elementary school education cross-cultural module
20,000	United States Pony Club -- program support academy of excellence
15,000	Asian Art Museum of San Francisco, San Francisco, CA -- new building fund

GEORGE T. WELCH TESTAMENTARY TRUST

Giving Contact

Ted W. Cohan, Trust Officer
c/o Baker Boyer National Bank
PO Box 1796
Walla Walla, WA 99362
Phone: (509)525-2000

Description

Founded: 1938
EIN: 916024318
Organization Type: Private Foundation
Giving Locations: WA: Walla Walla
Grant Types: Project, Scholarship.

Financial Summary

Total Giving: $225,198 (fiscal year ending September 30, 2002); $271,130 (fiscal 2000); $249,965 (fiscal 1999). Note: Fiscal 1997 Giving includes scholarship ($91,832), United Way ($2,000).
Giving Analysis: Giving for fiscal 2002 includes: foundation grants to United Way ($4,000); foundation gifts to individuals ($65,971); foundation scholarships ($75,666); fiscal 2000: foundation gifts to individuals

($71,430); foundation scholarships ($86,300); fiscal 1999: foundation gifts to individuals ($58,208) foundation scholarships ($109,100)
Assets: $3,598,492 (fiscal 2002); $5,683,168 (fiscal 2000); $5,185,240 (fiscal 1999)
Gifts Received: $140 (fiscal 1996); $1,000 (fiscal 1993). Note: In fiscal 1993, contributions were received from Dennis K. L. Kinc.

Typical Recipients

Arts & Humanities: Arts Associations & Councils, Arts Centers, Community Arts, Dance, Arts & Humanities-General, Historic Preservation, Libraries, Museums/Galleries, Music
Civic & Public Affairs: Civic & Public Affairs-General, Housing, Parades/Festivals, Urban & Community Affairs
Education: Afterschool/Enrichment Programs, Arts/Humanities Education, Colleges & Universities, Community & Junior Colleges, Education-General, Gifted & Talented Programs, Literacy, Public Education (Precollege), Student Aid, Vocational & Technical Education
Health: AIDS/HIV, Emergency/Ambulance Services, Hospices, Hospitals, Nursing Services, Prenatal Health Issues
Religion: Religious Welfare
Science: Science Museums
Social Services: Animal Protection, At-Risk Youth, Camps, Camps, Child Abuse, Child Welfare, Community Centers, Community Service Organizations, Day Care, Domestic Violence, Family Planning, Food/Clothing Distribution, Homes, Recreation & Athletics, Senior Services, Shelters/Homelessness, YMCA/YWCA/YMHA/YWHA, Youth Organizations

Application Procedures

Initial Contact: Send an application letter stating academic plans or other need and statement of resources and expenses. Deadlines for medical requests are February 20, May 20, August 20, and November 20; for academic requests, May 1; and for community requests, July 31.

Additional Information

Provides educational grants to students in the Walla Walla, WA, area.
Publications: Application Guidelines
Trust(s): Baker Boyer Natl Bank

Grants Analysis

Disclosure Period: fiscal year ending September 30, 2002
Total Grants: $79,541*
Number of Grants: 29
Average Grant: $2,743
Highest Grant: $10,590
Lowest Grant: $1,000
Typical Range: $1,000 to $5,000
***Note:** Giving excludes scholarships; United Way; gifts to individuals.

Recent Grants

Note: Grants derived from fiscal 2000 Form 990.

General

15,000	Walla Walla Community College, Walla Walla, WA
15,000	YMCA of Walla Walla, Walla Walla, WA
8,500	Blue Mountain Action Council, Walla Walla, WA
7,200	Helpline
7,000	YMCA
3,200	Institute of Forensic Counseling, Walla Walla, WA
3,000	Blue Mountain Arts Reliance
3,000	Carnegie Art Center, Walla Walla, WA
3,000	Center for Sharing, Walla Walla, WA
3,000	Children's Home Society of Washington, Seattle, WA

WELFARE FOUNDATION

Giving Contact

Peter C. Morrow, Executive Secretary
100 W. 10th Street, Suite 1109
Wilmington, DE 19801
Phone: (302)654-2477
Fax: (302)654-2323

Description

Founded: 1930
EIN: 516015916
Organization Type: General Purpose Foundation
Giving Locations: DE: Wilmington including surrounding communities; PA: Southern Chester County
Grant Types: Capital, General Support, Project, Seed Money.

Donor Information

Founder: Established in 1930 by the late Pierre Samuel du Pont (d. 1954) to support initial plans for a public secondary school system. When that project was completed, the foundation turned its support to the community at large.
Du Pont family members are the descendants of Pierre Samuel du Pont de Nemours (1739-1817), a Frenchman who emigrated to America in 1800. His son, Eleuthere Irenee, founded a gunpowder factory in 1801 which was the precursor to E. I. du Pont de Nemours & Company, a manufacturer of chemicals, plastics, fibers, and specialty products. Edward B. du Pont, a treasurer of the foundation, is a director of the company.

Financial Summary

Total Giving: $5,384,250 (2001); $5,229,367 (2000); $5,134,050 (1999)
Giving Analysis: Giving for 2000 includes: foundation grants to United Way ($145,000) 1998: foundation grants to United Way ($115,000)
Assets: $100,158,566 (2001); $117,316,844 (2000); $108,262,039 (1998)

Typical Recipients

Arts & Humanities: Arts Centers, Arts Funds, Arts Institutes, Ballet, Arts & Humanities-General, Historic Preservation, History & Archaeology, Libraries, Museums/Galleries, Music, Opera, Public Broadcasting, Theater, Visual Arts
Civic & Public Affairs: Botanical Gardens/Parks, Community Foundations, Economic Development, Employment/Job Training, Civic & Public Affairs-General, Housing, Law & Justice, Municipalities/Towns, Nonprofit Management, Urban & Community Affairs, Zoos/Aquariums
Education: Arts/Humanities Education, Colleges & Universities, Community & Junior Colleges, Environmental Education, Education-General, Legal Education, Literacy, Medical Education, Minority Education, Private Education (Precollege), Public Education (Precollege), Science/Mathematics Education, Secondary Education (Private), Special Education, Student Aid
Environment: Air/Water Quality, Forestry, Environment-General, Research, Resource Conservation, Watershed, Wildlife Protection
Health: AIDS/HIV, Cancer, Children's Health/Hospitals, Clinics/Medical Centers, Emergency/Ambulance Services, Health Funds, Health Organizations, Hospices, Hospitals, Long-Term Care, Prenatal Health Issues, Preventive Medicine/Wellness Organizations, Public Health, Single-Disease Health Associations
Religion: Churches, Religion-General, Ministries, Religious Organizations, Religious Welfare
Science: Science Museums, Scientific Centers & Institutes, Scientific Research
Social Services: At-Risk Youth, Camps, Child Welfare, Community Centers, Community Service Organizations, Counseling, Day Care, Family Planning, Family Services, Food/Clothing Distribution, Homes,

People with Disabilities, Recreation & Athletics, Scouts, Senior Services, Special Olympics, Substance Abuse, United Funds/United Ways, YMCA/YWCA/YMHA/YWHA, Youth Organizations

Application Procedures

Initial Contact: Applicants should send a request to the foundation.
Application Requirements: Letters should state the reason for the grant request, and include pertinent financial statements, an annual report, and a copy of an IRS tax-exempt status letter.
Deadlines: April 15 and October 15.

Restrictions

The foundation only makes grants to non-profit organizations in Delaware and the greater Wilmington area.

Foundation Officials

Robert H. Bolling, Jr.: president, trustee ED Princeton University (1948). CORP AFFIL director: Wilmington Trust Co.
J. Simpson Dean, Jr.: vice president
Edward Bradford du Pont: treasurer, trustee B Wilmington, DE 1934. ED Yale University ED (1956); Harvard University MBA (1959). PRIM CORP EMPL chairman, director: Atlantic Aviation Corp. CORP AFFIL director: Wilmington Trust Co.; treasurer: Christiana Care Health Services; director: E.I. du Pont de Nemours & Co. NONPR AFFIL president: Eleutherian Mills-Hagley Foundation; treasurer: Wilmington Institute.
Stephen A. Martinenza: assistant treasurer
Peter C. Morrow: executive director PRIM CORP EMPL manager corporate contributions, executive secretary contributions committee: E.I. du Pont de Nemours & Co.
Mrs. W. Laird Stabler, Jr.: secretary, trustee

Grants Analysis

Disclosure Period: calendar year ending 2001
Total Grants: $5,239,250*
Number of Grants: 81
Average Grant: $64,682
Highest Grant: $250,000
Typical Range: $25,000 to $200,000
*Note: Giving excludes United Way.

Recent Grants

Note: Grants derived from 2001 Form 990.

Library-Related
150,000   Friends of the Concord Pike Library, Wilmington, DE -- capital campaign

General
250,000   Boys & Girls Club of Delaware, Wilmington, DE -- capital campaign
200,000   Archmere Academy, Claymont, DE -- science center renovation
200,000   Beebe Medical Foundation, Lewes, DE -- facility expansion/renovation
200,000   Campus Community School, Dover, DE -- land acquisition and renovation
200,000   DE Museum of Natural History, Wilmington, DE -- capital campaign
200,000   Peninsula United Methodist Homes, Hockessin, DE -- capital campaign
200,000   St. Michael's Day Nursery, Wilmington, DE -- acquire/renovate building
200,000   Sanford School, Hockessin, DE -- capital campaign
200,000   Wilmington College, New Castle, DE -- capital campaign
200,000   Wilmington Downtown Business Improvement District, Wilmington, DE -- equipment purchase

WELLMARK BLUE CROSS AND BLUE SHIELD OF IOWA

Company Headquarters

636 Grand Ave.
Des Moines, IA 50309

Company Description

Former Name: Blue Cross & Blue Shield of Iowa.
Employees: 2,000
SIC(s): 6321 Accident & Health Insurance, 6324 Hospital & Medical Service Plans.

Wellmark Foundation

Giving Contact

Dr. Sheila Riggs, Executive Director
Wellmark Foundation
636 Grand Avenue, Station 150
Des Moines, IA 50309-2502
Phone: (515)245-4706
Fax: (515)235-4445
E-mail: wmfoundation@wellmark.com
Web: http://www.wellmark.com/community/wellmark_foundation/wellmark_foundation.htm

Description

Founded: 1991
EIN: 421368650
Organization Type: Corporate Foundation
Giving Locations: IA; SD
Grant Types: General Support, Seed Money.

Donor Information

Founder: Established in 1991 by Blue Cross and Blue Shield of Iowa.

Financial Summary

Total Giving: $1,177,149 (2001); $1,347,225 (2000); $1,660,700 (1999). Note: Contributes through foundation only.
Giving Analysis: Giving for 2001 includes: foundation grants to United Way ($245,113); 2000: foundation grants to United Way ($245,000); foundation ($1,102,225); 1999: foundation grants to United Way ($238,400); foundation ($1,422,300);
Assets: $16,882,705 (2001); $15,935,745 (2000); $16,794,501 (1999)
Gifts Received: $4,336,910 (2001); $4,204,602 (2000); $175,351 (1999). Note: In 1999, 2000, and 2001, contributions were received from Wellmark, Inc. In 1996, contributions were received from Blue Cross and Blue Shield of Iowa.

Typical Recipients

Arts & Humanities: Arts Centers, Libraries, Music, Opera, Theater
Civic & Public Affairs: Clubs, Civic & Public Affairs-General, Public Policy, Rural Affairs, Safety, Women's Affairs, Zoos/Aquariums
Education: Afterschool/Enrichment Programs, Agricultural Education, Business Education, Colleges & Universities, Education-General, Medical Education, Preschool Education, Public Education (Precollege), Student Aid
Environment: Resource Conservation
Health: Alzheimers Disease, Arthritis, Cancer, Children's Health/Hospitals, Clinics/Medical Centers, Emergency/Ambulance Services, Eyes/Blindness, Health-General, Health Organizations, Home-Care Services, Hospices, Hospitals, Hospitals (University Affiliated), Mental Health, Multiple Sclerosis, Nursing Services, Prenatal Health Issues, Preventive Medicine/Wellness Organizations, Public Health, Respiratory
Religion: Religious Organizations, Religious Welfare

Social Services: Child Abuse, Child Welfare, Community Service Organizations, Counseling, Day Care, Domestic Violence, Family Planning, Family Services, Food/Clothing Distribution, People with Disabilities, Recreation & Athletics, Scouts, Senior Services, Social Services-General, Substance Abuse, United Funds/United Ways, YMCA/YWCA/YMHA/YWHA, Youth Organizations

Application Procedures

Initial Contact: See foundation website for detailed application information. Submit a written proposal of ten pages or less. Proposals should be one-sided, 11 point type face or larger, and unbound. The foundation requests one original and 7 copies of the proposal.

Application Requirements: Proposals should include the following information. Cover Page: Agency Information, including primary agency name, address, phone, fax number; contact name, title, and phone number; and other involved entities and contacts. Project Page (1 page): including project name, a project description paragraph (50 words or less), and project abstract (500 words or less). Problem Statement (1-2 pages): statement of need, population served and demographics, and geographic area served. Goals and Measurable Objectives (1-2 pages): including outcome measure, timeline and work plan. Evaluation: include process measures and outcome measures. Budget: include budget narrative and explanation, and sustainability plan for after Wellmark funding ceases.

Proposals must also include two appendices. Appendix 1, 501(c)(3) Organization: must include the organization's IRS letter, recent audited financial statement, and board of directors list. Appendix 2, Grant Appendix must contain letters of support, staff credentials, and any other support documents. Include both appendices in the original proposal only.

Deadlines: First cycle: February 21. Second cycle: June 26. Third cycle: and August 25.

Review Process: Proposals are evaluated by a committee of community health stakeholders and Wellmark staff using a scoring tool. Scoring is divided into sections, with some sections weighted more heavily than others. Description of Need: 20 points maximum. Project Design: 25 points maximum. Feasibility: 20 points maximum. Community Involvement: 10 points maximum. Portability: 5 points maximum. Total possible score is 100.

Evaluative Criteria: Proposals are evaluated based on the following criteria: Need/Relevance, with a demonstration of population's need and prevalence; Project Design, including a scientifically sound proposal, and a program that will generate results that are reproducible, valid, accurate, and can be evaluated; Feasibility, meaning that the project is "do-able," that the activities involved must be detailed in a manner that allows for evaluation, that services must be offered at a reasonable cost, and that patient confidentiality is protected; Portability, so that the program, though aimed at a specific community or population, can be replicated in other areas; Community Involvement, demonstrating broadly-based community involvement, partnerships, coalitions, and collaborations; and Staff Credentials, including education, training, and experience of project manager/coordinators and key personnel.

Decision Notification: Grants approved by the board are disbursed in June 1 for the first cycle, October 1 for the second cycle.

Notes: A postcard is sent to applicant within one week of submission deadline to confirm receipt of proposal.

Additional Information

The foundation hosts grant conferences in both Iowa and South Dakota at least 30 days prior to each submission deadline to review the foundation's guidelines and answer questions relating to the application process. Contact the foundation or visit the foundation's website for additional information.

Publications: Grant Guidelines

Foundation Officials

Janet Griffin: secretary
Mary Elizabeth Kramer: vice president B Burlington, IA 1935. PRIM NONPR EMPL president: Iowa State Senate. NONPR AFFIL member: Rotary International; member: Society Human Resources Management; member: Nexus; member: Greater Des Moines Chamber of Commerce; member: Iowa Management Association.

Grants Analysis

Disclosure Period: calendar year ending 2001
Total Grants: $932,036*
Number of Grants: 38
Average Grant: $23,069*
Highest Grant: $78,500
Lowest Grant: $7,157
Typical Range: $10,000 to $50,000
*Note: Giving excludes United Way. Average grant figure excludes highest grant.

Recent Grants

Note: Grants derived from 2001 Form 990.

General

203,430	United Way of Central Iowa, Des Moines, IA
78,500	Easter Seals of South Dakota, Pierre, SD -- Recycle for Life Project
66,946	Siouxland Human Investment Partnership, Sioux City, IA -- tobacco cessation
51,083	Van Buren County, Keosauqua, IA -- improve health status of men
40,623	Iowa Medical Society Alliance, West Des Moines, IA -- Diabetes
39,360	Iowa Medical Society Alliance, West Des Moines, IA -- Antibiotic Resistance Program
35,793	South Dakota Coalition for Children, Sioux Falls, SD -- youth development
34,390	Healthy Linn Care Network, Cedar Rapids, IA -- asthma incidence, education, awareness and monitoring of treatment compliance
34,158	University of Iowa Foundation, Iowa City, IA -- substance abuse
31,950	Polk County Department of Health, Des Moines, IA -- screen adult population for diabetes

WELLS FARGO BANK NEBRASKA, N.A.

Company Headquarters

1919 Douglas St., Ste. 1
Omaha, NE 68102
Phone: (402)536-2329
Fax: (402)536-2812

Company Description

Employees: 800
SIC(s): 6021 National Commercial Banks.
Parent Company: Wells Fargo & Co., 420 Montgomery Street, San Francisco, CA, United States

Operating Locations

Northwest Bank Nebraska, NA (NE--Omaha)

Nonmonetary Support

Type: Donated Equipment; Donated Products; Loaned Executives; Workplace Solicitation

Giving Contact

Jane Braden, Contributions Administrator
1919 Douglas Street, MAC N8000-020
Omaha, NE 68103
Phone: (402)536-2650
Fax: (402)536-2509

E-mail: Jane.Braden@wellsfargo.com
Web: http://www.wellsfargo.com/about/charitable/index.jhtml

Description

Organization Type: Corporate Giving Program
Giving Locations: operating communities.
Grant Types: Capital, Employee Matching Gifts, General Support, Project, Scholarship.

Financial Summary

Total Giving: $2,000,000 (2002); $650,000 (1998 approx); $600,000 (1996 approx). Note: Contributes through corporate direct giving program only.

Typical Recipients

Arts & Humanities: Arts Associations & Councils, Arts Festivals, Arts Funds, Community Arts, Dance, Libraries, Music, Performing Arts, Theater, Visual Arts
Civic & Public Affairs: Economic Development, Housing, Philanthropic Organizations, Zoos/Aquariums
Education: Agricultural Education, Colleges & Universities, Community & Junior Colleges, Education Funds, Elementary Education (Private), Public Education (Precollege), Religious Education
Health: Health Organizations, Mental Health, Public Health, Single-Disease Health Associations
Religion: Religious Welfare
Social Services: Child Welfare, Community Centers, Counseling, Family Planning, Food/Clothing Distribution, Homes, People with Disabilities, Recreation & Athletics, United Funds/United Ways, Youth Organizations

Application Procedures

Initial Contact: Send a brief letter of inquiry.
Application Requirements: Include a description of organization; proof of tax-exempt status; list of officers and board members; statement outlining the purpose, including timeline and evaluation methods; complete budget for organization or project, including breakdown of programs and administrative expenses; list of contributors and amounts received in current and past year; and a financial statement.
Deadlines: None.
Evaluative Criteria: Organization's responsiveness to community, staff capability, financial management, commitment of board members and volunteers, performance against objectives, internal evaluation process, duplication with existing programs, and stability and range of funding sources.
Decision Notification: Board meets on the last Monday of each month; checks, requests for more information, or letters of refusal are sent within seven to 10 days after proposal is reviewed.

Corporate Officials

Jane Braden: coordinator PRIM CORP EMPL coordinator: Norwest Bank of Nebraska.

WELLS FARGO & CO.

Company Headquarters

420 Montgomery Street
San Francisco, CA 94163
Phone: 800-411-4932
Fax: (415)677-9075
Web: http://www.wellsfargo.com

Company Description

Founded: 1852
Ticker: WFC
Exchange: NYSE
Formed by Merger of: Norwest Corporation (1999);
Acquired: First Security Corp. (2000).
Assets: US$349.259 billion (2002)
Profit: US$5.434 billion (2002)
Employees: 117000 (2002)

Fortune Rank: 46, per FORTUNE Magazine's list of 500 Largest U.S. Corporations (2002).
SIC(s): 6021 National Commercial Banks, 6712 Bank Holding Companies.

Operating Locations
Wells Fargo & Co. (CA; CO--Denver, Englewood; TX--Dallas, San Antonio)

Nonmonetary Support
Type: Donated Equipment; In-kind Services

Wells Fargo Foundation

Giving Contact
Tim Hanlon
550 California St., 7th Floor
San Francisco, CA 94163
Phone: (415)222-5235
Fax: (415)975-6260
Web: http://www.wellsfargo.com/about/charitable.jhtml

Description
EIN: 953288932
Organization Type: Corporate Foundation
Giving Locations: AZ; CA: headquarters and operating communities; CO; ID; NV; NM; OR; TX; UT; WA
Grant Types: Challenge, Employee Matching Gifts, General Support, Project.
Note: Employee matching gift ratio: 1 to 1.

Financial Summary
Total Giving: $12,860 (2001 approx); $21,841,955 (2000); $28,748,106 (1999). Note: Contributes through corporate direct giving program and foundation.
Giving Analysis: Giving for 2000 includes: foundation grants to United Way ($1,901,300) foundation ($19,940,655)
Assets: $15,664 (2001); $6,006 (2000); $21,141,349 (1999).
Gifts Received: $96,659 (2000); $37,126,014 (1999); $1,096,896 (1995). Note: Contributions are received from Wells Fargo & Company. In 1995 contributions were in the form of shares of Intuit, Inc.

Typical Recipients
Arts & Humanities: Arts Centers, Ethnic & Folk Arts, History & Archaeology, Libraries, Museums/Galleries, Music, Opera, Performing Arts, Public Broadcasting, Theater
Civic & Public Affairs: African American Affairs, Chambers of Commerce, Economic Development, Employment/Job Training, Ethnic Organizations, Civic & Public Affairs-General, Hispanic Affairs, Housing, Urban & Community Affairs, Women's Affairs, Zoos/Aquariums
Education: Business Education, Colleges & Universities, Continuing Education, Economic Education, Education Funds, Education Reform, Elementary Education (Private), Engineering/Technological Education, International Studies, Minority Education, Public Education (Precollege), Science/Mathematics Education
Environment: Environment-General
Health: AIDS/HIV, Single-Disease Health Associations
Religion: Jewish Causes
Science: Observatories & Planetariums
Social Services: Child Welfare, Community Centers, Community Service Organizations, Counseling, Family Services, Food/Clothing Distribution, People with Disabilities, Senior Services, United Funds/United Ways, Volunteer Services, YMCA/YWCA/YMHA/YWHA, Youth Organizations

Application Procedures
Initial Contact: Contact information is available from the foundation.
Deadlines: None.
Evaluative Criteria: Nonprofit tax-exempt organizations with 501(c)(3) and 170(b) designations; program capability, sound fiscal policies, responsible financial management, evidence of long-range planning, and effective use of volunteers; benefit to low and moderate income individuals; active board of directors; budget, financial statements, and a plan for funding beyond the period covered by the proposed contributions, particularly in the case of start-up requests; and method of evaluating results of the proposed project.
Decision Notification: Within four to six weeks.
Notes: Incomplete proposals will not be considered and will be returned; binders, videos, and other unrequested materials should not be included and will not be returned if presented.

Restrictions
Applications will not be considered for individuals; including scholarship or fellowship assistance; for-profit entities, including start-up small businesses; endowments; equipment, including computer hardware and software; marketing activities such as sports or athletic groups; hospitals; vehicles; film or video projects, including documentaries; travel expenses, including student trips or tours; or promotional merchandise. The foundation also discourages requests for capital campaigns.

Additional Information
Foundation may require recipient to provide year-end audited financial statements and periodic reports on the project.
United Ways eligible for funding must have at least one full-time Wells Fargo & Company employee in their geographical service territory for funding to occur.
In 1996, Wells Fargo and Company purchased First Interstate Banks of Arizona, California, Oregon, Texas, and Washington.
Publications: Contributions Guidelines

Corporate Officials
Michael J. Gillfillan: vice chairman, chief executive officer B 1948. PRIM CORP EMPL vice chairman: Wells Fargo & Co.
Tim Hanlon: head community development California banks ED University of Detroit. PRIM CORP EMPL head community development California banks: Wells Fargo & Co. NONPR AFFIL member: Barbara Sinatra Childrens Center; member: Yerba Buena Center Arts; member: AIDS Project Los Angeles.
Paul Mandeville Hazen: chairman, chief executive officer, director B Lansing, MI 1941. ED University of Arizona BA (1963); University of California at Berkeley MBA (1964). PRIM CORP EMPL chairman, chief executive officer, director: Wells Fargo & Co. ADD CORP EMPL chairman, chief executive officer: Wells Fargo Bank NA; trustee: Wells Fargo Mortgage & Equity Trust; officer: Wells Fargo Realty Advisors. CORP AFFIL president, chief operating officer, director: Real Estate Industries Group; director: Safeway Inc.; director: Phelps Dodge Corp.; director: AirTouch Communications Inc.; director: Pacific Telesis Group.
Charles M. Johnson: vice chairman B 1942. ED Ohio State University BS (1963); Stanford University MA (1978). PRIM CORP EMPL vice chairman: Wells Fargo & Co.
Richard M. Kovacevich: president, chief executive officer B Tacoma, WA 1943. ED Stanford University BS (1965); Stanford University MBA (1967). PRIM CORP EMPL president, chief executive officer: Wells Fargo Bank NA ADD CORP EMPL president: Anfed Financial Inc. CORP AFFIL director: Northern Studies Power Co.; director: PetSmart Inc.; director: Cargill Inc.; director: Dayton Hudson Corp.

Clyde W. Ostler: vice chairman B 1947. ED University of California, San Diego BA (1968); University of Chicago MBA (1976). PRIM CORP EMPL vice chairman: Wells Fargo & Co.
William F. Zuendt: president, chief executive officer B 1946. ED Rensselaer Polytechnic Institute BA (1968); Stanford University MBA (1973). PRIM CORP EMPL president, chief executive officer: Wells Fargo & Co. CORP AFFIL director: 3Com Corp.; president: Wells Fargo Bank NA.

Foundation Officials
Iris S. Chan: director PRIM CORP EMPL executive vice president: Wells Fargo Bank National Association.
Virginia Arana Greene: director
Tim Hanlon: president (see above)
Patricia Howze: director
Rodney L. Jacobs: chief financial officer B 1940. PRIM CORP EMPL president: Wells Fargo & Co. ADD CORP EMPL vice chairman, chief financial officer: Wells Fargo Bank NA.
Yung Lew: director PRIM CORP EMPL division manager: Wells Fargo Bank NA.
Diane Disney Miller: director B 1933. PRIM CORP EMPL owner, president, director: Retlaw Enterprises ADD CORP EMPL president: Silverado Vineyards.
Karen Wegmann: president, director B 1944. PRIM CORP EMPL executive vice president: Wells Fargo Bank NA.

Grants Analysis
Disclosure Period: calendar year ending 2001
Total Grants: $12,860
Number of Grants: 4
Average Grant: $3,215
Highest Grant: $5,000
Typical Range: $1,000 to $5,000

Recent Grants
Note: Grants derived from 2001 Form 990.

General

5,000	Henry Ohlhoff House, San Francisco, CA -- Women Residential Treatment Program
5,000	Oakland Youth Orchestra, Oakland, CA -- outreach efforts
2,500	Pasadena Junior Chamber of Commerce Foundation, Pasadena, CA -- Operation Santa Claus
360	Hidden Hills Elementary, Phoenix, AZ -- Teacher's Partner Program

FRANKLIN H. AND RUTH L. WELLS FOUNDATION

Giving Contact
Miles J. Gibbons, Jr., Executive Director
4718 Old Gettysburg Rd, Suite 209
Mechanicsburg, PA 17055-8411
Phone: (717)763-1157
Fax: (717)763-1832

Description
Founded: 1983
EIN: 222541749
Organization Type: Private Foundation
Giving Locations: PA: Cumberland County, Dauphin County, Perry County
Grant Types: Emergency, General Support, Project, Seed Money.

Donor Information

Founder: Ruth L. Wells Annuity Trust, Frank Wells Marital Trust

Financial Summary

Total Giving: $238,550 (fiscal year ending May 31, 2002); $210,873 (fiscal 2001); $213,320 (fiscal 2000)
Assets: $5,543,352 (fiscal 2002); $6,272,158 (fiscal 2001); $6,646,926 (fiscal 2000)
Gifts Received: $97,324 (fiscal 1994); $195,898 (fiscal 1992). Note: In fiscal 1994, contributions were received from Ruth L. Wells Charitable Lead Trust.

Typical Recipients

Arts & Humanities: Arts Associations & Councils, Arts Festivals, Community Arts, Arts & Humanities-General, History & Archaeology, Libraries, Museums/Galleries, Music, Opera, Theater
Civic & Public Affairs: Clubs, Community Foundations, Employment/Job Training, Civic & Public Affairs-General, Hispanic Affairs, Housing, Legal Aid, Urban & Community Affairs
Education: Arts/Humanities Education, Business Education, Colleges & Universities, Community & Junior Colleges, Education Funds, Engineering/Technological Education, Environmental Education, Education-General, Leadership Training, Literacy, Medical Education, Minority Education, Private Education (Precollege), Science/Mathematics Education, Special Education
Environment: Resource Conservation, Wildlife Protection
Health: Cancer, Children's Health/Hospitals, Clinics/Medical Centers, Emergency/Ambulance Services, Health Organizations, Hospices, Hospitals, Medical Research, Mental Health, Single-Disease Health Associations
Religion: Ministries, Religious Organizations, Religious Welfare
Science: Science Museums
Social Services: Community Service Organizations, Delinquency & Criminal Rehabilitation, Domestic Violence, Family Planning, Family Services, Food/Clothing Distribution, People with Disabilities, Scouts, Substance Abuse, United Funds/United Ways, Volunteer Services, YMCA/YWCA/YMHA/YWHA, Youth Organizations

Application Procedures

Initial Contact: Submit a brief letter of inquiry stating purpose and goals.
Deadlines: None.

Restrictions

Does not provide support for religious activities, operating expenses, endowments, or debts.

Additional Information

Trust(s): AllFirst Bank

Foundation Officials

Gladys R. Charles: comm mem
William Cramer: comm mem
Miles J. Gibbons, Jr.: executive director B Scranton, PA 1935. ED Dickinson College BA (1957); Georgetown University JD (1964); Harvard University (1966). NONPR AFFIL co-chairman: Foundation Executive Roundtable; member: Rotary Club Harrisburg; director, chairman: Capital Campaign Review Committee.
Julie Thomas: comm mem

Grants Analysis

Disclosure Period: fiscal year ending May 31, 2002
Total Grants: $238,550
Number of Grants: 45
Average Grant: $5,301
Highest Grant: $20,000
Lowest Grant: $250
Typical Range: $1,000 to $10,000

Recent Grants

Note: Grants derived from 2000 Form 990.

General

25,000	River Rescue of Harrisburg, Inc., Harrisburg, PA -- community life team EMS Unification project
25,000	Tri-State University, Angola, IN -- equipment for the physics lab
15,000	Monmouth College, Monmouth, IL -- technology equipment for the new teaching and learning center
12,000	Messiah College, Grantham, PA -- nursing scholarships
11,000	Legal Services, Inc., Carlisle, PA -- child support project
10,000	Susquehanna Housing Initiatives, Harrisburg, PA
5,000	West Perry School District, Elliottsburg, PA
2,000	Harrisburg Area Community College, Harrisburg, PA
2,000	Reading for the Blind and Dyslexic, Princeton, NJ
1,000	Harrisburg Opera Association, Harrisburg, PA

WELSH FAMILY FOUNDATION

Giving Contact

Patrick J. Welsh, Trustee
3 Essex Road
Summit, NJ 07901

Description

Founded: 1996
EIN: 223331136
Organization Type: Private Foundation
Giving Locations: nationally.
Grant Types: General Support.

Donor Information

Founder: Established in 1996 by Patrick J. Welsh.

Financial Summary

Total Giving: $557,000 (2001); $471,000 (2000); $549,500 (1999)
Assets: $7,040,807 (2001); $8,376,962 (2000); $8,437,053 (1999)
Gifts Received: $3,284,299 (1996); $3,371,342 (1994). Note: In 1996, contributions were received from Patrick J. and Carol A. Welsh.

Typical Recipients

Arts & Humanities: Arts Associations & Councils, Libraries, Music
Civic & Public Affairs: Civic & Public Affairs-General, Housing
Education: Colleges & Universities, Education-General, Public Education (Precollege), Secondary Education (Public), Special Education, Student Aid
Environment: Environment-General
Health: Cancer, Children's Health/Hospitals, Heart, Hospitals, Medical Rehabilitation, Single-Disease Health Associations
International: Missionary/Religious Activities
Religion: Religious Welfare
Social Services: Community Service Organizations, Food/Clothing Distribution, United Funds/United Ways, YMCA/YWCA/YMHA/YWHA, Youth Organizations

Application Procedures

Initial Contact: Send a brief letter of inquiry.
Deadlines: None.

Foundation Officials

Carol A. Welsh: trustee
Eric A. Welsh: trustee
Patrick J. Welsh: trustee

Grants Analysis

Disclosure Period: calendar year ending 2001
Total Grants: $557,000
Number of Grants: 18
Average Grant: $18,875*
Highest Grant: $155,000
Lowest Grant: $2,000
Typical Range: $5,000 to $40,000
*Note: Average grant figure excludes two highest grants ($255,000).

Recent Grants

Note: Grants derived from 2000 Form 990.

General

100,000	Overlook Hospital Foundation, Summit, NJ
75,000	PEP Foundation
40,000	Community Food Bank, South Tucson, AZ
40,000	Habitat for Humanity, Wilson, NC
30,000	Memorial Sloan-Kettering Cancer Center, New York, NY
30,000	Valerie Fund
20,000	Salvation Army
15,000	Christopher Reeves Paralysis Foundation, Springfield, NJ
10,000	Anderson School at UCLA, Los Angeles, CA
10,000	Summit Speech School, Summit, NJ

MARGARET L. WENDT FOUNDATION

Giving Contact

Robert J. Kresse, Secretary & Trustee
40 Fountain Plaza, Suite 277
Buffalo, NY 14202-2220
Phone: (716)855-2146
Fax: (716)855-2149

Description

Founded: 1955
EIN: 166030037
Organization Type: General Purpose Foundation
Giving Locations: NY: Western New York state, Buffalo
Grant Types: Capital, Challenge, General Support, Operating Expenses, Project, Research, Seed Money.

Donor Information

Founder: Established in 1955, with funds donated by the late Margaret L. Wendt . The assets of the foundation more than doubled in the period between 1975 and 1980 because of the final distribution of Miss Wendt's bequest.

Financial Summary

Total Giving: $6,680,696 (fiscal year ending January 31, 2001); $3,514,370 (fiscal 1998); $2,589,632 (fiscal 1997)
Giving Analysis: Giving for fiscal 2001 includes: foundation grants to United Way ($163,500) fiscal 1998: foundation grants to United Way ($75,000)
Assets: $118,203,147 (fiscal 2001); $105,765,091 (fiscal 1998); $86,662,480 (fiscal 1997)

Typical Recipients

Arts & Humanities: Arts Associations & Councils, Arts Centers, Arts Institutes, Arts Outreach, Ballet, Dance, Film & Video, Arts & Humanities-General, Historic Preservation, History & Archaeology, Libraries, Literary Arts, Museums/Galleries, Music, Opera, Performing Arts, Public Broadcasting, Theater

Civic & Public Affairs: African American Affairs, Botanical Gardens/Parks, Community Foundations, Economic Development, Employment/Job Training, Civic & Public Affairs-General, Housing, Law & Justice, Legal Aid, Municipalities/Towns, Nonprofit Management, Urban & Community Affairs, Women's Affairs, Zoos/Aquariums

Education: Arts/Humanities Education, Colleges & Universities, Colleges & Universities, Education Funds, Education Reform, Faculty Development, Education-General, Health & Physical Education, Literacy, Medical Education, Preschool Education, Private Education (Precollege), Public Education (Precollege), Science/Mathematics Education, Special Education, Student Aid

Environment: Air/Water Quality, Forestry, Environment-General, Resource Conservation, Wildlife Protection

Health: AIDS/HIV, Alzheimers Disease, Children's Health/Hospitals, Clinics/Medical Centers, Emergency/Ambulance Services, Health Funds, Health Organizations, Heart, Home-Care Services, Hospices, Hospitals, Long-Term Care, Medical Research, Mental Health, Nursing Services, Outpatient Health Care, Research/Studies Institutes, Single-Disease Health Associations, Speech & Hearing

International: Foreign Arts Organizations, Human Rights, International Organizations, Trade

Religion: Churches, Jewish Causes, Ministries, Religious Organizations, Religious Welfare, Seminaries

Science: Science Museums, Scientific Centers & Institutes

Social Services: Animal Protection, Camps, Child Welfare, Community Centers, Community Service Organizations, Counseling, Day Care, Family Planning, Family Services, Food/Clothing Distribution, Homes, People with Disabilities, Recreation & Athletics, Senior Services, Shelters/Homelessness, Social Services-General, Substance Abuse, United Funds/United Ways, United Funds/United Ways, YMCA/YWCA/YMHA/YWHA, Youth Organizations

Application Procedures

Initial Contact: Applicants should send four copies of a letter of request.

Application Requirements: Letters should include a description of the applicant organization, need or problem to be addressed, outline of the proposed project including total budget, specific amount requested, list of the board of directors, audited financial statements for the last three years, and the most recent copy of the organization's IRS determination letter of tax-exempt status.

Deadlines: Submit applications one month prior to the foundation's quarterly meetings.

Restrictions

Grants are not made to individuals.

Foundation Officials

Janet Loew Day: trustee

Robert J. Kresse: secretary, trustee PRIM CORP EMPL partner: Hiscock & Barclay. CORP AFFIL secretary: A. Lunt Design Inc.

Thomas D. Lunt: trustee PRIM CORP EMPL vice president: E. F. Hutton. CORP AFFIL vice president: A. Lunt Design Inc.

Grants Analysis

Disclosure Period: fiscal year ending January 31, 2001

Total Grants: $6,517,196*

Number of Grants: 160

Average Grant: $34,699*

Highest Grant: $1,000,000

Lowest Grant: $500

Typical Range: $3,000 to $35,000

*Note: Giving excludes United Way. Average grant figure excludes highest grant.

Recent Grants

Note: Grants derived from 2001 Form 990.

General

1,000,000	Buffalo and Erie County Historical Society, Buffalo, NY -- to complete the Forest Avenue Resource Center
750,000	Buffalo Seminary, Buffalo, NY -- second half of pledge
750,000	Buffalo Seminary, Buffalo, NY -- for funds to renovate, repair and upgrade the 90-year-old facility
450,000	Western New York Public Broadcasting Association, Buffalo, NY -- to help fund the transition from analog to digital television
450,000	Western New York Public Broadcasting Association, Buffalo, NY -- second half of pledge
250,000	Buffalo and Erie County Historical Society, Buffalo, NY -- to complete the Forest Avenue Resource Center
250,000	D'Youville College, Buffalo, NY -- for "Foundation for the Future" capital campaign for campus expansion
250,000	Niagara Lutheran Home, Buffalo, NY -- capital campaign
250,000	Niagara Lutheran Home, Buffalo, NY -- second half of pledge
190,000	Hilbert College, Hamburg, NY -- renovation of the college's science laboratories

WESSINGER FOUNDATION

Giving Contact

William W. Wessinger, President
121 SW Salmon, Suite 1100
Portland, OR 97204
Phone: (503)274-4051
E-mail: wessinge@gosw.org
Web: http://www.gosw.org/wessinger

Description

Founded: 1979
EIN: 930754224
Organization Type: Private Foundation
Giving Locations: Pacific Northwest, with emphasis on the Tri-County area.
Grant Types: General Support.

Donor Information

Founder: Paul Wessinger Trust

Financial Summary

Total Giving: $525,500 (fiscal year ending September 30, 2001); $590,000 (fiscal 2000); $484,900 (fiscal 1999)

Assets: $7,223,522 (fiscal 2001); $11,004,567 (fiscal 2000); $8,726,592 (fiscal 1999)

Typical Recipients

Arts & Humanities: Arts Associations & Councils, Arts Festivals, Arts Institutes, Ballet, Ethnic & Folk Arts, Historic Preservation, History & Archaeology, Libraries, Literary Arts, Museums/Galleries, Music, Opera, Performing Arts, Public Broadcasting, Theater

Civic & Public Affairs: Botanical Gardens/Parks, Clubs, Community Foundations, Economic Development, Economic Policy, Civic & Public Affairs-General, Housing, Native American Affairs, Zoos/Aquariums

Education: Arts/Humanities Education, Colleges & Universities, Continuing Education, Medical Education, Minority Education, Preschool Education, Private

Education (Precollege), Science/Mathematics Education

Environment: Air/Water Quality, Environment-General, Resource Conservation, Wildlife Protection

Health: AIDS/HIV, Cancer, Children's Health/Hospitals, Clinics/Medical Centers, Emergency/Ambulance Services, Health Funds, Health Organizations, Medical Rehabilitation, Mental Health, Public Health, Speech & Hearing

International: International Environmental Issues

Religion: Ministries, Religious Welfare

Science: Science Museums

Social Services: Animal Protection, At-Risk Youth, Child Welfare, Community Centers, Community Service Organizations, Family Planning, Family Services, Food/Clothing Distribution, People with Disabilities, Scouts, Shelters/Homelessness, Volunteer Services, YMCA/YWCA/YMHA/YWHA, Youth Organizations

Application Procedures

Initial Contact: Send a brief letter of inquiry.
Application Requirements: proof of tax-exempt status and a list of board members.
Deadlines: None.

Restrictions

Preference is given to educational, social welfare, medical, and artistic purposes.

Foundation Officials

Gainor W. Artz: vice president
Anna Boggess: director
Robert D. Geddes: secretary
Thomas B. Stoel: secretary
Julie Vigeland: director
E. Charles Wessinger: director
Henry W. Wessinger: director
Joseph M. Wessinger: director
William W. Wessinger: president
Kathryn W. Withers: director

Grants Analysis

Disclosure Period: fiscal year ending September 30, 2001

Total Grants: $525,500

Number of Grants: 39

Average Grant: $9,068*

Highest Grant: $100,000

Lowest Grant: $1,000

Typical Range: $2,500 to $20,000

*Note: Average grant figure excludes two highest grants ($190,000).

Recent Grants

Note: Grants derived from fiscal 2000 Form 990.

General

165,000	Oregon Community Foundation, Portland, OR -- government for exclusively public purpose
50,000	Friends of the Children's Museum, Portland, OR -- educational
50,000	Portland State University Foundation, Portland, OR -- educational
25,000	National Alliance for the Mentally Ill of Multnomach County, Portland, OR -- medical
25,000	New Avenues for Youth, Portland, OR -- educational
25,000	Pioneer Courthouse Square, Portland, OR -- government for exclusively public purpose
25,000	University of Portland, Portland, OR -- educational
20,000	Audubon Society of Portland, Portland, OR -- scientific
18,000	Providence Child Center Foundation, Portland, OR -- medical
15,000	Hearing and Speech Institute, Portland, OR -- medical

HARRY AND ETHEL WEST FOUNDATION

Giving Contact

Richard G. McBurnie, Manager
PO Box 1825
Bakersfield, CA 93303
Phone: (661)873-0360
Fax: (661)873-0362

Description

Founded: 1972
EIN: 237168492
Organization Type: Private Foundation
Giving Locations: CA: Kern County
Grant Types: Capital, General Support.

Financial Summary

Total Giving: $305,807 (2001); $330,376 (2000); $273,643 (1999)
Giving Analysis: Giving for 1998 includes: foundation grants to United Way ($30) foundation ($336,947)
Assets: $5,304,825 (2001); $5,015,508 (2000); $5,616,468 (1999)

Typical Recipients

Arts & Humanities: Arts Associations & Councils, History & Archaeology, Libraries, Museums/Galleries, Music, Public Broadcasting, Theater
Civic & Public Affairs: Business/Free Enterprise, Clubs, Civic & Public Affairs-General, Hispanic Affairs, Law & Justice, Legal Aid, Native American Affairs, Public Policy, Rural Affairs, Safety, Urban & Community Affairs, Women's Affairs
Education: Colleges & Universities, Education-General, Legal Education, Literacy, Private Education (Precollege), Public Education (Precollege), Secondary Education (Private), Secondary Education (Public), Special Education
Environment: Environment-General, Research, Wildlife Protection
Health: Alzheimers Disease, Arthritis, Cancer, Cancer, Health-General, Health Organizations, Heart, Hospices, Hospitals, Medical Research, Single-Disease Health Associations, Transplant Networks/Donor Banks
Religion: Churches, Religious Welfare
Social Services: Animal Protection, At-Risk Youth, Camps, Child Welfare, Community Service Organizations, Counseling, Crime Prevention, Domestic Violence, Food/Clothing Distribution, Homes, People with Disabilities, Scouts, Senior Services, Shelters/Homelessness, Social Services-General, Substance Abuse, Volunteer Services, YMCA/YWCA/YMHA/YWHA, Youth Organizations

Application Procedures

Initial Contact: Send a brief letter of inquiry.
Deadlines: None.

Restrictions

Generally grants are limited to Kern County, CA.

Foundation Officials

Richard G. McBurnie: president, chief executive officer
Mary C. Means: secretary
Silver D. Sack: treasurer

Grants Analysis

Disclosure Period: calendar year ending 2001
Total Grants: $305,807
Number of Grants: 49
Average Grant: $5,598*
Highest Grant: $31,500
Typical Range: $1,000 to $10,000
*Note: Average grant excludes highest grant.

Recent Grants

Note: Grants derived from 2001 Form 990.

General

31,500	Bakersfield College Foundation, Bakersfield, CA -- capital improvements
27,500	C. S. U. B., Bakersfield, CA -- capital improvements
20,500	Boys & Girls Club, Bakersfield, CA -- capital improvements
20,000	Houchin Blood Bank, Bakersfield, CA -- capital improvements
18,487	Hoffman Hospice, Bakersfield, CA -- capital improvements
17,500	Friends of Mercy Cancer, Bakersfield, CA -- capital improvements
11,700	MARE, Los Angeles, CA -- capital improvements
10,362	Kern High School District Education Foundation, Bakersfield, CA -- capital improvements
9,750	Alliance Against Family Violence, Bakersfield, CA -- capital improvements
8,300	Bright Beginnings Learning Center, Bakersfield, CA -- capital improvements

NEVA AND WESLEY WEST FOUNDATION

Giving Contact

Stuart W. Stedman, Trustee
PO Box 7
Houston, TX 77001-0007
Phone: (713)520-0400
Fax: (713)520-1131

Description

Founded: 1956
EIN: 746039393
Organization Type: Family Foundation
Giving Locations: TX: Houston
Grant Types: Capital, General Support, Operating Expenses, Research.

Donor Information

Founder: Established in 1956 by the late Wesley West and Mrs. Neva Watkins West .

Financial Summary

Total Giving: $1,500,000 (2001); $1,106,000 (2000); $1,238,416 (1998)
Assets: $20,000,000 (2001 approx); $17,324,731 (2000); $20,694,998 (1998)
Gifts Received: $676,438 (1992). Note: In 1992, contributions were received from Neva Watkins West.

Typical Recipients

Arts & Humanities: Ballet, Dance, Arts & Humanities-General, History & Archaeology, Libraries, Museums/Galleries, Music, Opera, Performing Arts, Theater
Civic & Public Affairs: Botanical Gardens/Parks, Clubs, Community Foundations, Civic & Public Affairs-General, Law & Justice, Municipalities/Towns, Public Policy, Zoos/Aquariums
Education: Arts/Humanities Education, Business Education, Colleges & Universities, Community & Junior Colleges, Elementary Education (Private), Engineering/Technological Education, Environmental Education, Education-General, Literacy, Medical Education, Minority Education, Private Education (Precollege), Public Education (Precollege), Religious Education, Science/Mathematics Education, Secondary Education (Private)
Environment: Forestry, Environment-General, Wildlife Protection
Health: Children's Health/Hospitals, Emergency/Ambulance Services, Eyes/Blindness, Health Organizations, Hospitals, Medical Research, Mental Health,

Prenatal Health Issues, Public Health, Speech & Hearing
Religion: Churches, Religious Welfare
Science: Science Museums
Social Services: At-Risk Youth, Camps, Child Welfare, Community Centers, Community Service Organizations, Family Planning, Family Services, Food/Clothing Distribution, Recreation & Athletics, Scouts, Shelters/Homelessness, Youth Organizations

Application Procedures

Initial Contact: Submit a letter or written proposal.
Application Requirements: Include a brief description of the organization's activity, purpose of funds sought, amount requested, and other data considered pertinent to the request.
Deadlines: November 30.

Restrictions

Does not support individuals. Preference is given to Texas charitable organizations.

Additional Information

Publications: Annual Report

Foundation Officials

Randolph L. Pullin: trustee
Betty Ann West Stedman: trustee
Stuart West Stedman: trustee
Neva Watkins West: don, trustee

Grants Analysis

Disclosure Period: calendar year ending 2000
Total Grants: $1,106,000
Number of Grants: 42
Average Grant: $18,813*
Highest Grant: $203,500
Typical Range: $5,000 to $40,000
*Note: Average grant excludes two highest grants ($353,500).

Recent Grants

Note: Grants derived from 2000 Form 990.

Library-Related

25,000	Dimmit County Public Library, Carrizzo Springs, TX -- operating expenses

General

203,500	Texas A & M University, Kingsville, TX -- operating expenses
150,000	St. Luke's United Methodist Church, Houston, TX -- operating expenses
83,500	Houston Grand Opera, Houston, TX -- operating expenses
75,000	St. John School, Houston, TX -- operating expenses
63,000	Museum of Fine Arts - Houston, Houston, TX -- operating expenses
55,000	Texas Children's Hospital Capital Campaign, Houston, TX -- operating expenses
50,000	Baylor College of Medicine Department of Opthalmology, Houston, TX -- research programs in glaucoma
50,000	Houston Music Hall Foundation, Houston, TX -- hobby center construction
50,000	Lady Bird Johnson National Wildflower Center, Austin, TX -- operating expenses
25,000	Fort Worth Zoo, Ft. Worth, TX -- operating expenses

WEST FOUNDATION (TX)

Giving Contact

Reece A. West, President & Treasurer
PO Box 1675
Wichita Falls, TX 76307
Phone: (940)723-2177

Description

Founded: 1973
EIN: 237332105
Organization Type: Private Foundation
Giving Locations: TX: Wichita Falls
Grant Types: Award, General Support, Research, Scholarship.

Donor Information

Founder: the late Gordon T. West, the late Ellen B. West, Gordon T. West, Jr.

Financial Summary

Total Giving: $340,575 (fiscal year ending September 30, 2001); $324,678 (fiscal 2000); $420,000 (fiscal 1998)
Giving Analysis: Giving for fiscal 2001 includes: foundation gifts to individuals ($50,000); foundation scholarships ($75,000); fiscal 2000: foundation gifts to individuals ($50,000); foundation scholarships ($97,714); fiscal 1998: foundation gifts to individuals ($50,000)
Assets: $17,210,238 (fiscal 2001); $8,363,790 (fiscal 2000); $9,002,872 (fiscal 1998)
Gifts Received: $8,101,173 (fiscal 1992). Note: In 1992, contributions were received from Neva Watkins West.

Typical Recipients

Arts & Humanities: Libraries
Civic & Public Affairs: Safety
Education: Business Education, Colleges & Universities, Education Reform, Elementary Education (Private), Elementary Education (Public), Faculty Development, Health & Physical Education, Public Education (Precollege), Science/Mathematics Education, Student Aid, Vocational & Technical Education

Application Procedures

Initial Contact: Submit a brief letter.
Application Requirements: Include name and address of applicant.
Deadlines: None.

Additional Information

Provides awards to public school teachers and teaching institutes and funds for faculty development and research.

Foundation Officials

Joseph Newton Sherrill, Jr.: vice president, trustee B Wichita Falls, TX 1929. ED Massachusetts Institute of Technology (1952); Harvard University (1955). PRIM CORP EMPL president: Sherrill, Crosnoe & Goff. CORP AFFIL general counsel, director: First National Bank Byers; president, director: Wilson Drilling Corp.
Gordon T. West, Jr.: vice president, trustee
Lane T. West: vice president, trustee
Reece A. West: president, trustee

Grants Analysis

Disclosure Period: fiscal year ending September 30, 2001
Total Grants: $215,575*
Number of Grants: 7
Average Grant: $22,263*
Highest Grant: $82,000
Lowest Grant: $6,000
Typical Range: $10,000 to $40,000
*Note: Giving excludes gifts to individuals and scholarships. Average grant figure excludes highest grant.

Recent Grants

Note: Grants derived from fiscal 2000 Form 990.

General

65,217	Midwestern State University, Wichita Falls, TX -- for west foundation elementary coordinator
50,650	Midwestern State University, Wichita Falls, TX -- for scholarships for education students
50,650	Midwestern State University, Wichita Falls, TX -- for faculty development
47,064	Wichita Falls Independent School District, Inc., Wichita Falls, TX -- for faculty scholarship program
34,476	Midwestern State University, Wichita Falls, TX -- for first grade reading cohort program
23,000	Wichita Falls Independent School District, Inc., Wichita Falls, TX -- for early literacy instruction materials
22,200	Wichita Falls Independent School District, Inc., Wichita Falls, TX -- for summer arts festival
10,000	Midwestern State University, Wichita Falls, TX -- for university professors
4,900	Wichita Falls Independent School District, Inc., Wichita Falls, TX -- for conference table and chairs
4,000	Wichita Falls Independent School District, Inc., Wichita Falls, TX -- for MSU/UNT doctoral program

WEST PHARMACEUTICAL SERVICES, INC.

Company Headquarters

101 Gordon Dr.
Lionville, PA 19341-0645
Web: http://www.westpharma.com

Company Description

Founded: 1923
Ticker: WST
Exchange: NYSE
Former Name: West Co. Plastics Group.
Revenue: US$396.9 million (2001)
Employees: 3960 (2001)
SIC(s): 3069 Fabricated Rubber Products Nec, 3089 Plastics Products Nec, 3469 Metal Stampings Nec, 3565 Packaging Machinery.

Operating Locations

West Co. Inc. (FL--Clearwater, St. Petersburg; NE--Kearney; NC--Kinston; PA--Lionville, Lititz, Montgomery, Philadelphia; PR)

Herman O. West Foundation

Giving Contact

Maureen Goebel, Administrator
101 Gordon Drive
Exton, PA 19341
Phone: (610)594-2905
Fax: (610)594-3011
E-mail: maureen.goebel@westpharma.com

Description

EIN: 237173901
Organization Type: Corporate Foundation
Former Name: Herman O. West Foundation (2001).
Giving Locations: FL; NE; NJ; NC; PA: headquarters and operating communities.
Grant Types: Capital, Emergency, General Support, Multiyear/Continuing Support, Scholarship.
Note: Employee matching gift ratio: 1 to 1 up to $750 per employee annually, for secondary and higher education.

Financial Summary

Total Giving: $350,000 (2004 approx); $350,000 (2003 approx); $385,000 (2002). Note: Contributes through foundation only.

Giving Analysis: Giving for 2001 includes: foundation matching gifts ($9,180); foundation scholarships ($60,280); foundation grants to United Way ($110,387); 2000: foundation matching gifts ($15,335); foundation scholarships ($51,507); foundation grants to United Way ($101,125); 1999: foundation matching gifts ($110,139); 1999: foundation scholarships ($58,857); foundation grants to United Way ($95,329); foundation ($153,200);
Assets: $450,000 (2004 approx); $450,000 (2003 approx); $678,000 (2002)
Gifts Received: $648,518 (2001); $4,000 (2000); $381,660 (1999). Note: In 2001, contributions were received from F.H. West and West Pharmaceutical Services.

Typical Recipients

Arts & Humanities: Arts Centers, Community Arts, Arts & Humanities-General, Historic Preservation, History & Archaeology, Libraries, Museums/Galleries, Music, Performing Arts, Theater
Civic & Public Affairs: Business/Free Enterprise, Economic Development, Civic & Public Affairs-General, Public Policy, Safety, Urban & Community Affairs, Zoos/Aquariums
Education: Arts/Humanities Education, Business-School Partnerships, Colleges & Universities, Community & Junior Colleges, Education Associations, Education Funds, Engineering/Technological Education, Faculty Development, Education-General, Literacy, Medical Education, Minority Education, Private Education (Precollege), Public Education (Precollege), Science/Mathematics Education, Secondary Education (Private), Student Aid, Student Aid
Environment: Environment-General
Health: Cancer, Children's Health/Hospitals, Emergency/Ambulance Services, Health Organizations, Hospitals, Medical Rehabilitation, Medical Research, Nursing Services, Prenatal Health Issues, Public Health, Trauma Treatment
International: Health Care/Hospitals, International Organizations
Religion: Religious Welfare
Science: Observatories & Planetariums, Science Museums, Scientific Centers & Institutes, Scientific Organizations
Social Services: Big Brother/Big Sister, Community Centers, Community Service Organizations, Family Planning, People with Disabilities, Recreation & Athletics, Scouts, Senior Services, Social Services-General, Substance Abuse, United Funds/United Ways, YMCA/YWCA/YMHA/YWHA

Application Procedures

Initial Contact: Send a written proposal. For scholarships request an application.
Application Requirements: Include a description of organization, and extent of services provided; recently audited financial statement, indicating sources of funds and how they are disbursed; future needs and services of program; and proof of tax-exempt status.
Deadlines: February 28.

Restrictions

Foundation does not support individuals, political or lobbying groups, or organizations outside operating areas. Scholarship recipients must be dependents of west employees.

Corporate Officials

Steven A. Ellers: executive vice presidento PRIM CORP EMPL chief financial officer: West Co., Inc.
John Robert Gailey, III: vice president, general counsel, secretary B York, PA 1954. ED Haverford College (1976); Temple University (1986). PRIM CORP EMPL vice president, general counsel, secretary: West Co., Inc. CORP AFFIL secretary: Paco Pharmaceutical Services. NONPR AFFIL director: American Society of Corporate Secretaries.

William G. Little: chairman, director B 1942. ED Dunedin Teachers College. PRIM CORP EMPL chairman, president, chief executive officer, director: West Co., Inc.

Donald E. Morel, Jr: president, chief executive officer PRIM CORP EMPL president: West Co., Inc.

Grants Analysis

Disclosure Period: calendar year ending 2002
Total Grants: $384,000
Number of Grants: 55
Average Grant: $4,231 (approx)
Highest Grant: $40,000
Lowest Grant: $500

Recent Grants

Note: Grants derived from 2001 Form 990.

General

36,369	Chester County, Chester, SC
25,000	Delaware County Community College - Downtown, PA
25,000	United Way September 11th Fund
21,148	Pinellas County, FL
18,786	Lenoir County
17,517	Lycoming County, Williamsport, PA
15,000	American Red Cross Disaster Relief Fund, New York, NY
15,000	Franklin Institute of Science Museum, Philadelphia, PA
15,000	Phoenixville YMCA, Phoenixville, PA
10,000	Association of Independent Colleges and Universities, Harrisburg, PA

KATHLEEN PATTON WESTBY FOUNDATION

Giving Contact

John Trygve Westby, Trustee
4815 S. Harvard, Suite 395
Tulsa, OK 74135
Phone: (918)743-8321

Description

Founded: 1991
EIN: 731354412
Organization Type: Private Foundation
Giving Locations: OK: Tulsa
Grant Types: General Support.

Donor Information

Founder: Established in 1991 by Kathleen Patton Westby.

Financial Summary

Total Giving: $122,600 (fiscal year ending June 30, 2002); $36,950 (fiscal 2001); $48,150 (fiscal 2000)
Giving Analysis: Giving for fiscal 2001 includes: foundation grants to United Way ($100); fiscal 2000: foundation grants to United Way ($100) fiscal 1999: foundation grants to United Way ($100)
Assets: $2,005,156 (fiscal 2002); $1,903,762 (fiscal 2001); $1,308,171 (fiscal 2000)
Gifts Received: $518,538 (fiscal 2001); $100,245 (fiscal 1999); $195,088 (fiscal 1997). Note: In fiscal 2001, contributions were received from Kathleen Westby Charitable Lead Trust. In fiscal 1997, contributions were received from Kathleen Patton Westby.

Typical Recipients

Arts & Humanities: Arts Associations & Councils, Arts Centers, Arts Institutes, Ballet, Dance, Historic Preservation, History & Archaeology, Libraries, Museums/Galleries, Music, Opera, Performing Arts
Civic & Public Affairs: Philanthropic Organizations, Public Policy
Education: Colleges & Universities, Education Reform, Student Aid

Environment: Environment-General, Resource Conservation
Religion: Churches
Social Services: Community Service Organizations, Family Planning

Application Procedures

Initial Contact: The foundation has no formal grant application procedure or application form. Send a brief letter of inquiry.
Deadlines: None.

Foundation Officials

Kathleen Patton Westby: trustee
Gerald H. Westby: trustee
John Trygve Westby: trustee

Grants Analysis

Disclosure Period: fiscal year ending June 30, 2002
Total Grants: $122,600*
Number of Grants: 16
Average Grant: $2,507*
Highest Grant: $85,000
Lowest Grant: $100
Typical Range: $1,000 to $5,000
*Note: Average grant figure excludes highest grant.

Recent Grants

Note: Grants derived from fiscal 2000 Form 990.

General

10,000	All Souls Unitarian Church, Tulsa, OK
5,000	Philbrook Museum of Art, Tulsa, OK
5,000	Philbrook Museum of Art, Tulsa, OK
5,000	Tulsa Ballet, Tulsa, OK
5,000	Tulsa Philharmonic, Tulsa, OK
3,000	Tulsa Opera, Inc., Tulsa, OK
2,500	Arts and Humanities Council of Tulsa, Tulsa, OK
2,000	All Souls Unitarian Church, Tulsa, OK
2,000	Light Opera Oklahoma, Tulsa, OK
1,500	Mid-America Art Alliance, Kansas City, MO

WESTERHOFF FAMILY FOUNDATION, INC.

Giving Contact

Garret P. Westerhoff, Trustee
Care of Sax, Macy, Fromm & Co.
855 Valley Road
Clifton, NJ 07013-2441
Phone: (973)472-6250

Description

Founded: 1998
EIN: 223515621
Organization Type: Private Foundation
Grant Types: General Support.

Financial Summary

Total Giving: $57,774 (fiscal year ending April 30, 2001); $43,499 (fiscal 2000); $15,450 (fiscal 1999)
Assets: $206,857 (fiscal 2001); $307,759 (fiscal 2000); $225,818 (fiscal 1999)
Gifts Received: $40,208 (fiscal 2001); $23,151 (fiscal 1999). Note: In fiscal 1999 and 2001, contributions were received from Garrett and Helga Westerhoff.

Typical Recipients

Arts & Humanities: Arts & Humanities-General, Libraries, Music, Public Broadcasting
Civic & Public Affairs: Civic & Public Affairs-General
Education: Arts/Humanities Education, Education-General
Health: Public Health
Religion: Churches

Foundation Officials

Garret P. Westerhoff: trustee
Helga K. Westerhoff: trustee
Katherine Westerhoff: trustee

Grants Analysis

Disclosure Period: fiscal year ending April 30, 2001
Total Grants: $57,774
Number of Grants: 24
Average Grant: $1,323*
Highest Grant: $10,000
Typical Range: $500 to $2,500
*Note: Average grant excludes three highest grants ($30,000).

Recent Grants

Note: Grants derived from fiscal 2001 Form 990.

Library-Related

2,075	Friends of the Kinnelon Library, Kinnelon, NJ
300	Friends of the Kinnelon Library, Kinnelon, NJ

General

10,000	Westerhoff School of Music and Art, Metuchen, NJ
10,000	Westerhoff School of Music and Art, Metuchen, NJ
10,000	Westerhoff School of Music and Art, Metuchen, NJ
5,000	Westerhoff School of Music and Art, Metuchen, NJ
5,000	Westerhoff School of Music and Art, Metuchen, NJ
3,000	Westerhoff School of Music and Art, Metuchen, NJ
2,700	Westerhoff School of Music and Art, Metuchen, NJ
2,500	Rougday Friends of Arts, Phoenix, AZ
1,000	Breckenridge Music Institute, Breckenridge, CO
1,000	KAET - TV, Tempe, AZ

WESTERN NEW YORK FOUNDATION

Giving Contact

Welles V. Moot, Jr., President
237 Main St., Suite 1402
Buffalo, NY 14203
Phone: (716)847-6440
Fax: (716)847-6440

Description

Founded: 1951
EIN: 160845962
Organization Type: Private Foundation
Giving Locations: NY: limited to the 8th Judicial District of NY (Erie, Niagara, Genesee, Wyoming, Allegany, Cattaraugus, and Chautauqua counties)
Grant Types: Capital, Conference/Seminar, Emergency, Endowment, General Support, Loan, Project, Seed Money.

Donor Information

Founder: the late Welles V. Moot

Financial Summary

Total Giving: $596,362 (fiscal year ending July 31, 2002); $650,125 (fiscal 2001); $741,060 (fiscal 2000)
Giving Analysis: Giving for fiscal 2002 includes: foundation grants to United Way ($3,000)
Assets: $10,234,479 (fiscal 2002); $13,348,442 (fiscal 2001); $16,088,247 (fiscal 2000)

Typical Recipients

Arts & Humanities: Arts Associations & Councils, Arts Funds, Arts Institutes, Community Arts, Arts & Humanities-General, Historic Preservation, History & Archaeology, Libraries, Museums/Galleries, Music, Opera, Performing Arts, Public Broadcasting, Theater
Civic & Public Affairs: Botanical Gardens/Parks, Employment/Job Training, Civic & Public Affairs-General, Housing, Legal Aid, Municipalities/Towns, Safety, Urban & Community Affairs, Zoos/Aquariums
Education: Arts/Humanities Education, Business Education, Elementary Education (Private), Preschool Education, Private Education (Precollege), Public Education (Precollege), Science/Mathematics Education, Secondary Education (Public), Student Aid
Environment: Environment-General
Health: Children's Health/Hospitals, Health Organizations, Hospices, Hospitals, Medical Rehabilitation, Mental Health, Public Health, Speech & Hearing
Religion: Religion-General
Science: Science Museums, Scientific Centers & Institutes
Social Services: Child Welfare, Community Centers, Community Service Organizations, Day Care, Family Planning, Family Services, Food/Clothing Distribution, Homes, People with Disabilities, Recreation & Athletics, Scouts, Substance Abuse, United Funds/United Ways, Volunteer Services, YMCA/YWCA/YMHA/YWHA, Youth Organizations

Application Procedures

Initial Contact: Call or write requesting application.
Deadlines: None.

Restrictions

Does not support individuals or organizations for religious purposes.

Additional Information

Publications: Annual Report; Application Form

Foundation Officials

Theodore V. Buerger: assistant treasurer
Anthony S. Johnson: trustee
Cecily M. Johnson: vice president
Jennifer Johnson: trustee
Brenda W. McDuffie: trustee
Trudy A. Mollenberg: trustee
Andrew R. Moot: trustee
John R. Moot: secretary
Richard E. Moot: treasurer
Welles V. Moot, Jr.: president
John N. Walsh, III: trustee

Grants Analysis

Disclosure Period: fiscal year ending July 31, 2002
Total Grants: $593,362*
Number of Grants: 51
Average Grant: $7,944*
Highest Grant: $70,000
Lowest Grant: $500
Typical Range: $1,000 to $10,000
*Note: Giving excludes United Way. Average grant figures excludes four highest grants ($220,000)

Recent Grants

Note: Grants derived from 2000 Form 990.

Library-Related
30,000	Cordelia A. Greene Library, Castile, NY -- for addition to existing building
25,000	Cuba Circulating Library, Cuba, NY -- for construction of addition

General
70,000	United Way of Buffalo and Erie, Buffalo, NY -- for capital renovations
50,000	Greater Niagara Frontier Council, Boy Scouts of America, Buffalo, NY -- for Camp Schoellkopf shower facility
50,000	Irish Classical Theater, Buffalo, NY -- for construction of theater

42,000	Neuroscience Foundation, The, Buffalo, NY -- for Toshiba Stroke Research Center
40,000	Nichols School, Buffalo, NY -- for consolidate campuses
30,000	Hospice Foundation, Buffalo, NY -- for palliative care collaborative
30,000	Success by 6, Buffalo, NY -- to fund program of accreditation for day care centers
30,000	Woman's Christian Association of Fredonia, The, Fredonia, NY -- for expansion project
25,385	Buffalo Museum of Science, Buffalo, NY -- to replace 1984 Chevy dump truck
25,000	Buffalo & Erie County Historical Society, Buffalo, NY -- for patient care

WESTERN & SOUTHERN LIFE INSURANCE CO.

Company Headquarters

400 Broadway St.
Cincinnati, OH 45202
Web: http://www.westernsouthernlife.com

Company Description

Assets: US$32.508 billion (2002)
Employees: 5000 (2002)
SIC(s): 6311 Life Insurance.

Operating Locations

Western & Southern Life Insurance Co. (OH--Cincinnati)

Western-Southern Foundation, Inc.

Giving Contact

Richard K. Taulbee, Assistant Treasurer
Western-Southern Enterprise Fund
400 Broadway
Cincinnati, OH 45202-3341
Phone: (513)629-2121

Description

Founded: 1990
EIN: 311259670
Organization Type: Corporate Foundation
Former Name: Western-Southern Enterprise Fund, Inc..
Giving Locations: OH
Grant Types: General Support, Matching, Scholarship.

Financial Summary

Total Giving: $3,069,459 (2001); $2,855,962 (2000); $2,831,504 (1999). Note: Contributes through foundation only.
Giving Analysis: Giving for 2000 includes: foundation grants to United Way ($173,000); foundation ($2,682,962); 1999: foundation scholarships ($8,000); foundation grants to United Way ($163,000); foundation ($2,660,504); 1997: foundation grants to United Way ($156,240); foundation ($786,760);
Assets: $49,154,305 (2001); $62,345,188 (2000); $56,419,778 (1999)
Gifts Received: $6,985 (2001); $7,900 (2000); $5,355 (1999). Note: Foundation receives contributions from Western-Southern, Columbus Life Charitable Trust, and Continental General.

Typical Recipients

Arts & Humanities: Arts Associations & Councils, Arts Centers, Arts Funds, Arts Institutes, Film & Video, Historic Preservation, Libraries, Museums/Galleries, Music, Performing Arts, Public Broadcasting
Civic & Public Affairs: African American Affairs, Botanical Gardens/Parks, Business/Free Enterprise, Chambers of Commerce, Civil Rights, Clubs, Community Foundations, Economic Development, Economic Policy, Employment/Job Training, Civic & Public Affairs-General, Housing, Municipalities/Towns, Professional & Trade Associations, Public Policy, Urban & Community Affairs, Women's Affairs, Zoos/Aquariums
Education: Business Education, Colleges & Universities, Economic Education, Education Funds, Education-General, Education-General, Minority Education, Private Education (Precollege), Religious Education, Science/Mathematics Education, Secondary Education (Private), Special Education, Student Aid, Vocational & Technical Education
Environment: Environment-General
Health: Cancer, Children's Health/Hospitals, Diabetes, Emergency/Ambulance Services, Health Organizations, Home-Care Services, Hospices, Hospitals, Long-Term Care, Mental Health, Multiple Sclerosis, Prenatal Health Issues, Single-Disease Health Associations
International: International Peace & Security Issues
Religion: Churches, Dioceses, Religious Organizations, Religious Welfare, Seminaries
Social Services: Child Welfare, Community Centers, Community Service Organizations, Crime Prevention, Day Care, Family Services, Homes, People with Disabilities, Recreation & Athletics, Scouts, Senior Services, Shelters/Homelessness, Social Services-General, United Funds/United Ways, YMCA/YWCA/YMHA/YWHA, Youth Organizations

Application Procedures

Initial Contact: Send a brief letter.
Application Requirements: Include a description of organization and project, amount requested, and purpose of funds sought.
Deadlines: None.

Corporate Officials

John F. Barrett: president, chief executive officer, director B 1949. ED University of Cincinnati (1971). PRIM CORP EMPL president, chief executive officer, director: Western & Southern Life Insurance Co. ADD CORP EMPL president: Western Southern Life Assurance Co. CORP AFFIL director: Fifth Third Bank; director: Fifth Third Bancorp; director: Cincinnati Bell Inc.; director: Convergys Corp.; director: Andersons Inc. NONPR AFFIL vice chairmanr: Greater Cincinnati Chamber of Commerce.

Foundation Officials

John F. Barrett: trustee (see above)

Grants Analysis

Disclosure Period: calendar year ending 2002
Total Grants: $680,740*
Number of Grants: 205
Average Grant: $3,321*
Highest Grant: $100,000
Lowest Grant: $25
Typical Range: $50 to $5,000 and $10,000 to $100,000
*Note: Giving excludes United Way. Average grant figure excludes three highest grants totaling $778,237.

Recent Grants

Note: Grants derived from 2001 Form 990.

General
692,010	Xavier University, Cincinnati, OH
337,410	Mount St. Mary's Seminary, Cincinnati, OH

250,000	Cincinnati Development Fund, Cincinnati, OH
190,827	Bayley Place, Cincinnati, OH
105,660	Sisters of Notre Dame De Namur, Cincinnati, OH
103,455	Taft Museum, Cincinnati, OH
100,000	National Underground Railroad Freedom Center, Cincinnati, OH
98,900	United Way, Cincinnati, OH
95,316	United Way, Cincinnati, OH
62,500	Cedar Village, Cincinnati, OH

WESTLB NEW YORK BRANCH

Company Headquarters
New York, NY
Web: http://www.westlb.de

Company Description
SIC(s): 6081 Foreign Banks--Branches & Agencies.
Parent Company: Westdeutsche Landesbank Girozentrale, Herzogstrasse 15, Dusseldorf, Germany

Operating Locations
WestLB Chicago (IL--Chicago); WestLB Los Angeles (CA--Los Angeles); WestLB New York Branch (NY--New York)

Giving Contact
Amy Budd, HR Asst.
1211 Avenue of the Americas, 24th Floor
New York, NY 10036-8701
Phone: (212)852-6000
Fax: (212)921-5494
E-mail: amy_budd@westlb.com

Description
Organization Type: Corporate Giving Program
Giving Locations: NY: New York metropolitan area
Grant Types: General Support.

Typical Recipients
Arts & Humanities: Libraries, Museums/Galleries, Music
Civic & Public Affairs: Professional & Trade Associations
Education: Private Education (Precollege)
Social Services: United Funds/United Ways

Application Procedures
Initial Contact: Send a brief letter of inquiry.
Application Requirements: Include a description of the organization, amount requested, and purpose of funds sought.
Deadlines: November.
Decision Notification: All requests are forwarded to Dusseldorf for approval at the end of the year.

Corporate Officials
John Paul Garber: head US operations PRIM CORP EMPL head US operations: WestLB NY Branch.

WEYERHAEUSER CO.

Company Headquarters
Federal Way, WA
Web: http://www.weyerhaeuser.com

Company Description
Founded: 1900
Ticker: WY
Exchange: NYSE
Acquired: Willamette Industries Inc. (2002).
Revenue: US$18.521 billion (2002)
Profit: US$241 million (2002)

Employees: 56800 (2002)
Fortune Rank: 96, per FORTUNE Magazine's list of 500 Largest U.S. Corporations (2002).
SIC(s): 2411 Logging, 2421 Sawmills & Planing Mills--General, 2431 Millwork, 2435 Hardwood Veneer & Plywood.

Operating Locations
Weyerhaeuser Co. (AL; AR--Hot Springs; CA--Alameda, Altadena, Belmont, City of Commerce, Colton, Emeryville, Los Angeles, Modesto, Oceanside, Pleasanton, Salinas, San Francisco, San Jose, Santa Paula; FL--Miami, Tampa; GA; HI--Honolulu; IL--Belleville, Elgin, Itasca; IA--Waterloo; KY--Franklin; ME--Westbrook; MD--Dorsey, Millersville; MN--Albert Lea, Austin, White Bear Lake; MS--Columbus, Jackson; MO--Clayton, St. Joseph; NJ--Barrington, Marlton, Teaneck; NC--Charlotte, Greensboro, New Bern, Plymouth; OH--Columbus, Mount Vernon; OK--Valliant, Wright City; OR--Beaverton, Eugene, North Bend, Portland, Springfield; PA--Valley Forge; TX--Dallas, Grand Prairie, Houston, McAllen; VA--Richmond; WA--Bellevue, Centralia, Chehalis, Everett, Federal Way, Kent, Longview, Seattle, Tacoma, Union Gap, Vancouver; WI--Rothschild)

Nonmonetary Support
Type: Cause-related Marketing & Promotion; Donated Equipment; Donated Products; Loaned Employees; Loaned Executives; Workplace Solicitation
Contact: Penny Paul, Executive Assistant
Note: Nonmonetary support is contributed directly through the company. Workplace solicitation is for the United Way only.

Weyerhaeuser Co. Foundation

Giving Contact
Elizabeth A. Crossman, Vice President
CH1 L32
PO Box 9777
Federal Way, WA 98063-9777
Phone: (253)924-3159
Fax: (253)924-3658
Web: http://www.weyerhaeuser.com/citizenship/philanthropy/

Description
EIN: 916024225
Organization Type: Corporate Foundation
Giving Locations: AL; AR; MS; NC; OK; OR; WA: nationally, with emphasis on communities, particularly remote communities, in which company has significant numbers of employees.
Grant Types: Award, Capital, Department, Employee Matching Gifts, General Support, Project.
Note: Employee matching gift ratio: 1 to 1 for higher education only.

Financial Summary
Total Giving: $7,364,733 (2001); $6,730,653 (2000); $7,657,506 (1999). Note: Contributes through corporate direct giving program and foundation.
Giving Analysis: Giving for 2000 includes: foundation matching gifts ($202,593); foundation scholarships ($379,285); foundation grants to United Way ($985,330); foundation ($5,163,445); 1999: foundation matching gifts ($198,065); foundation scholarships ($213,157); foundation grants to United Way ($960,625); foundation ($6,285,659); 1997: foundation matching gifts ($134,317); foundation grants to United Way ($1,047,533) foundation ($5,550,506)
Assets: $23,528,514 (2001); $13,931,375 (2000); $5,193,756 (1999)
Gifts Received: $9,668,980 (2001); $7,576,447 (2000); $10,002,888 (1999). Note: Foundation receives contributions from Weyerhaeuser Company.

Typical Recipients
Arts & Humanities: Arts Associations & Councils, Arts Festivals, Arts Funds, Community Arts, Dance, Arts & Humanities-General, Historic Preservation, History & Archaeology, Libraries, Museums/Galleries, Music, Opera, Performing Arts, Public Broadcasting, Theater
Civic & Public Affairs: African American Affairs, Business/Free Enterprise, Chambers of Commerce, Economic Development, Employment/Job Training, Civic & Public Affairs-General, Housing, Legal Aid, Municipalities/Towns, Native American Affairs, Public Policy, Rural Affairs, Safety, Urban & Community Affairs, Zoos/Aquariums
Education: Agricultural Education, Arts/Humanities Education, Business Education, Colleges & Universities, Colleges & Universities, Community & Junior Colleges, Economic Education, Education Associations, Education Funds, Elementary Education (Private), Elementary Education (Public), Engineering/Technological Education, Environmental Education, Education-General, Minority Education, Private Education (Precollege), Public Education (Precollege), Science/Mathematics Education, Social Sciences Education, Student Aid, Vocational & Technical Education
Environment: Forestry, Environment-General, Resource Conservation, Wildlife Protection
Health: Children's Health/Hospitals, Clinics/Medical Centers, Emergency/Ambulance Services, Hospices, Hospitals, Public Health
International: Foreign Educational Institutions, International Affairs, International Development, International Environmental Issues, International Relief Efforts
Religion: Churches
Science: Science Museums, Scientific Centers & Institutes
Social Services: Animal Protection, Child Welfare, Community Centers, Community Service Organizations, Family Services, Food/Clothing Distribution, People with Disabilities, Recreation & Athletics, Scouts, Shelters/Homelessness, Social Services-General, Substance Abuse, United Funds/United Ways, Volunteer Services, YMCA/YWCA/YMHA/YWHA, Youth Organizations

Application Procedures
Initial Contact: Call for application, then send full proposal.
Application Requirements: Completed application includes description of project and sponsoring organization; statement of why project is consistent with foundation guidelines; project cost, sources of funding, and amount requested; evidence of tax-exempt status.
Deadlines: Requests received after September may not be considered until budgets are established for the following year.
Review Process: Appropriate review committee is consulted and request is considered within budget constraints/local priorities.
Evaluative Criteria: Direct relevance to foundation's mission and geographic interests; evidence that project will address important need; innovative and cost-effective approaches; impact consistent with proposed expenditure; evidence that project does not duplicate other efforts; indication that other financial support likely will be available; demonstrated competence of administration and staff.
Decision Notification: Inquiries acknowledged as soon as possible (normally within 30 days); applicants should allow 90 to 120 days for a decision.
Notes: If further consideration is warranted, foundation may ask for additional information or formal proposal; personal meetings or site visits are normally arranged only for projects that have passed initial application.

Restrictions

Does not support religious, sacramental, or theological purposes; political campaigns; to influence legislation; for tickets or tables at fundraising events; individuals; or direct grants to organizations already receiving foundation funds through an umbrella organization.

Discourages applications seeking to cover operating deficits; for services that the public sector should reasonably be expected to provide; to establish endowments or memorials; for research or conferences outside the forest products industry; for hospital building or equipment campaigns that will result in higher costs to healthcare users; for services outside Weyerhaeuser operating area; for general administrative expenses; or for amounts that are clearly unrealistic given the foundation's total annual budget.

The foundation will not consider requests that do not meet its program and geographic criteria. If organizations are unsure about the presence of a Weyerhaeuser facility in their community, write or call the foundation for confirmation before submitting a grant request.

Additional Information

In 1998, the foundation launched a program that supports employee-initiated volunteer projects. Foundation makes cash grants only, with a $1,000 minimum. Normally, support is committed for one year at a time. Grants may be made to umbrella organizations or combined campaigns.

Publications: Biennial Report (includes Current Guidelines); Grant Application; Volunteer Employee Pamphlet

Corporate Officials

William R. Corbin: executive vice president wood products PRIM CORP EMPL executive vice president wood products: Weyerhaeuser Co. ADD CORP EMPL corporate executive: Weyerhaeuser International.

Richard C. Gozon: executive vice president pulp paper & packaging PRIM CORP EMPL executive vice president pulp paper & packaging: Weyerhaeuser Co. CORP AFFIL director: UGI Corp.; director: UGI Utilities Inc.; director: Amerisource Health Corp.

Steven Richard Hill: senior vice president human resources B Oakland, CA 1947. ED University of California at Berkeley BS (1969); University of California, Los Angeles MBA (1971). PRIM CORP EMPL senior vice president human resources: Weyerhaeuser Co. ADD CORP EMPL director: Weyerhaeuser - Canada.

Norman E. Johnson: senior vice president technology B 1933. ED Harvard University Advanced Management Program (1955); Oregon State University MS (1957); University of California at Berkeley PhD (1961). PRIM CORP EMPL senior vice president technology: Weyerhaeuser Co.

Thomas M. Luthy: senior vice president wood products PRIM CORP EMPL senior vice president wood products: Weyerhaeuser Co.

Sandy D. McDade: secretary B Seattle, WA 1952. ED Whitman College (1974); University of Puget Sound (1979). PRIM CORP EMPL senior vice president: Weyerhaeuser Co. NONPR AFFIL member: American Society of Corporate Secretaries.

William Charles Stivers: executive vice president, chief financial officer B Modesto, CA 1938. ED Stanford University BA (1960); University of Southern California MBA (1963); Harvard University Graduate School of Business Administration (1977). PRIM CORP EMPL executive vice president, chief financial officer: Weyerhaeuser Co. CORP AFFIL vice president, director: Weyerhaeuser Real Estate Co.; director: Protection Mutual Insurance Co.; president, director: S&S Land & Cattle Co.; director: First Interstate Bancorp; member national advisory board: Chase Manhattan Corp.; member: Chemical Banking Corp. NONPR AFFIL director: Pacific Rim Finance Center Graduate School Business, University Washington; trustee, chairman: Saint Francis Community

Hospital; trustee: Franciscan Health Systems West; member management & steering committee: American Forest & Paper Association.

George Hunt Weyerhaeuser: director B Seattle, WA 1926. ED Yale University BSIE (1949). CORP AFFIL director: Dietzgen Corp.; director: SAFECO Corp.; director: Boeing Co. NONPR AFFIL member: Business Roundtable; member: Washington State Business Roundtable; member: Business Council.

Foundation Officials

William R. Corbin: trustee (see above)

Elizabeth A. Crossman: president PRIM CORP EMPL director corporate contributions: Weyerhaeuser Co.

Richard C. Gozon: trustee (see above)

Steven Richard Hill: trustee (see above)

Mack L. Hogans: chairman, president, trustee B Abbeville, AL 1949. ED University of Michigan (1971); University of Washington (1976). PRIM CORP EMPL senior vice president corporate affairs: Weyerhaeuser Co.

Norman E. Johnson: trustee (see above)

C. Stephen Lewis: trustee B 1944. PRIM CORP EMPL director: Pacific Northwest Bancorp.

Sandy D. McDade: assistant secretary legal affairs (see above)

Susan M. Mersereau: trustee B Portland, OR 1946. ED Scripps College BA (1968); University of Chicago MA (1971); Antioch College MA (1990). PRIM CORP EMPL vice president: Weyerhaeuser Co. NONPR AFFIL director: King County United Way.

William Charles Stivers: treasurer, trustee (see above)

Linda L. Terrien: assistant treasurer

Karen L. Veitenhans: secretary

George Hunt Weyerhaeuser: trustee (see above)

Robert B. Wilson: trustee

Grants Analysis

Disclosure Period: calendar year ending 2001

Total Grants: $5,927,785*

Number of Grants: 955 (approx)

Average Grant: $6,207

Highest Grant: $200,000

Lowest Grant: $1,000

Typical Range: $1,000 to $10,000

*Note: Giving excludes matching gifts, scholarship, and United Way.

Recent Grants

Note: Grants derived from 2001 Form 990.

General

200,000	International Corrugated Packaging Foundation, Alexandria, VA
187,462	National Merit Scholarship Corporation, Evanston, IL
180,900	United Way of Pierce County, Tacoma, WA
160,000	University of Regina, Newport, RI
154,100	United Way of King County, Seattle, WA
150,000	Boys and Girls Club of Pierce County, Tacoma, WA
117,730	Citizens Scholarship Foundation of America, St. Peter, MN
110,000	Corporate Council for the Arts, Seattle, WA
100,000	Boys and Girls Club of Columbus, Columbus, OH
100,000	Craven County Board of Education, New Bern, NC

CHARLES A. WEYERHAEUSER MEMORIAL FOUNDATION

Giving Contact

Lucy Rosenberry Jones, President & Director
332 Minnesota St., Suite 2100
St. Paul, MN 55101-1308
Phone: (651)228-0935

Description

Founded: 1959

EIN: 416012063

Organization Type: Private Foundation

Giving Locations: MN

Grant Types: General Support, Multiyear/Continuing Support, Project.

Donor Information

Founder: Carl A. Weyerhaeuser Trusts

Financial Summary

Total Giving: $392,525 (fiscal year ending February 28, 2002); $312,900 (fiscal 2001); $71,400 (fiscal 2000)

Giving Analysis: Giving for fiscal 1997 includes: foundation scholarships ($20,000); foundation matching gifts ($60,400) foundation ($78,000).

Assets: $6,482,340 (fiscal 2002); $6,462,579 (fiscal 2001); $6,356,032 (fiscal 2000)

Gifts Received: $77,659 (fiscal 2002); $76,004 (fiscal 2001); $82,161 (fiscal 2000). Note: In fiscal 2002, contributions were received from 1969 IRR Trusts. In fiscal 2000 and 2001, contributions were received from 1969 IRR Trusts and Berkshire Hathaway. In fiscal 1998, contributions were received from Berkshire Hathaway and various others.

Typical Recipients

Arts & Humanities: Arts Centers, Community Arts, History & Archaeology, Libraries, Literary Arts, Museums/Galleries, Music, Opera, Performing Arts, Public Broadcasting

Civic & Public Affairs: Botanical Gardens/Parks, Nonprofit Management, Parades/Festivals, Urban & Community Affairs, Zoos/Aquariums

Education: Colleges & Universities, Elementary Education (Private), Education-General, Religious Education, Social Sciences Education, Student Aid

Environment: Resource Conservation

Health: Mental Health

International: Foreign Educational Institutions

Religion: Churches, Religious Welfare

Science: Science Museums

Social Services: Animal Protection, Community Service Organizations, Family Planning, Family Services, United Funds/United Ways

Application Procedures

Initial Contact: The foundation has no formal grant application procedure or application form.

Deadlines: None.

Decision Notification: Notification of Directors decision is sent as promptly as possible.

Restrictions

Does not support individuals.

Foundation Officials

Elise R. Donohue: director

Gordon E. Hed: assistant secretary, assistant treasurer

Joseph S. Micallef: secretary, treasurer, director B 1933. PRIM CORP EMPL president, chief executive officer, treasurer, director: Fiduciary Counselling Inc. PRIM NONPR EMPL sec-treas: Rock Island Co. CORP AFFIL secretary, treasurer: Rock Island Co.

Charles W. Rosenberry, II: director

Lucy Rosenberry Jones: president, director

Robert J. Sivertsen: vice president, director

Grants Analysis

Disclosure Period: fiscal year ending February 28, 2002

Total Grants: $392,525

Number of Grants: 7

Highest Grant: $300,000

Lowest Grant: $2,000

Typical Range: $6,000 to $20,000

Recent Grants

Note: Grants derived from fiscal 2000 Form 990.

General

35,400	Minnesota Public Radio, St. Paul, MN -- opera underwriting
25,000	Planned Parenthood of Minnesota, St. Paul, MN -- operating support
6,000	Minnesota Historical Society, St. Paul, MN -- operating support
5,000	Morrison County Animal Humane Society, Little Falls, MN -- operating support

WHALLEY CHARITABLE TRUST

Giving Contact

David C. Klementik, Trustee
1210 Graham Ave.
Windber, PA 15963
Phone: (814)467-4000

Description

Founded: 1961
EIN: 237128436
Organization Type: Private Foundation
Giving Locations: IL; PA
Grant Types: General Support.

Donor Information

Founder: John J. Whalley, John Whalley, Jr., Mary Whalley

Financial Summary

Total Giving: $301,064 (2001); $134,632 (2000); $635,012 (1999)
Giving Analysis: Giving for 1998 includes: foundation grants to United Way ($1,000)
Assets: $4,843,837 (2001); $5,553,307 (2000); $6,023,956 (1999)

Typical Recipients

Arts & Humanities: Ethnic & Folk Arts, Arts & Humanities-General, Historic Preservation, History & Archaeology, Libraries, Museums/Galleries, Music, Performing Arts, Visual Arts
Civic & Public Affairs: Botanical Gardens/Parks, Clubs, Civic & Public Affairs-General, Municipalities/Towns, Parades/Festivals, Professional & Trade Associations, Safety, Urban & Community Affairs
Education: Colleges & Universities, Education-General, Private Education (Precollege), Secondary Education (Public), Student Aid
Health: Cancer, Children's Health/Hospitals, Clinics/Medical Centers, Emergency/Ambulance Services, Health-General, Heart, Hospitals, Public Health
Religion: Churches, Jewish Causes, Religious Organizations, Religious Welfare
Social Services: Animal Protection, Child Welfare, Community Service Organizations, Crime Prevention, Homes, People with Disabilities, Recreation & Athletics, Scouts, United Funds/United Ways, Veterans, Volunteer Services, YMCA/YWCA/YMHA/YWHA, Youth Organizations

Application Procedures

Initial Contact: The foundation has no formal grant application procedure or application form.
Deadlines: None.

Foundation Officials

David C. Klementik: trustee
G. Lesko: trustee
John I. Whalley: trustee

Grants Analysis

Disclosure Period: calendar year ending 2001
Total Grants: $301,064
Number of Grants: 59

Average Grant: $3,926*
Highest Grant: $50,000
Typical Range: $1,000 to $5,000
*Note: Average grant figure excludes two highest grants ($95,000).

Recent Grants

Note: Grants derived from 2001 Form 990.

Library-Related

25,000	Windber Public Library, Windber, PA

General

50,000	Windber Medical Center, Windber, PA
45,000	Mount Aloysius College, Cresson, PA
40,000	Penn State University, McKeesport, PA
15,000	Arcadia Performing Arts, Windber, PA
10,000	Windber Volunteer Fire Company 1, Windber, PA
10,000	First Presbyterian Church of Jamestown, Jamestown, NY
10,000	First Presbyterian Church of Jamestown, Jamestown, NY
10,000	St. Francis University, Chicago, IL
10,000	Windber Community, Windber, PA
6,000	Johnstown Symphony Orchestra, Johnstown, PA

WHARTON FOUNDATION

Giving Contact

Jean W. Pettitt, President & Director
1001 Arbolado Road
Santa Barbara, CA 93103
Phone: (805)884-0756
Fax: (805)884-0756
E-mail: jpettitt@homemail.com

Description

Founded: 1954
EIN: 366130748
Organization Type: Private Foundation
Giving Locations: AZ; CA; FL; IL; WA
Grant Types: General Support, Matching, Multiyear/Continuing Support.

Donor Information

Founder: Sara P. Wharton, Joseph B. and Martha W. Wharton

Financial Summary

Total Giving: $134,843 (2001); $160,640 (2000); $162,365 (1998)
Giving Analysis: Giving for 2001 includes: foundation matching gifts ($13,295) 2000: foundation matching gift ($11,100)
Assets: $3,594,914 (2001); $3,817,053 (2000 approx); $3,778,935 (1998)
Gifts Received: $525 (2001); $4,207 (1998); $1,947 (1996). Note: In 1994, contributions were received from Sara P. Wharton ($40,000) and Joseph B. and Martha W. Wharton ($8,500).

Typical Recipients

Arts & Humanities: Arts Funds, Historic Preservation, Libraries, Museums/Galleries, Performing Arts, Public Broadcasting
Civic & Public Affairs: Botanical Gardens/Parks, Community Foundations, Civic & Public Affairs-General, Hispanic Affairs, Housing, Native American Affairs, Parades/Festivals, Zoos/Aquariums
Education: Afterschool/Enrichment Programs, Arts/Humanities Education, Business Education, Colleges & Universities, Elementary Education (Public), Faculty Development, Education-General, Leadership Training, Literacy, Minority Education, Private Education (Precollege), Religious Education, Science/Mathematics Education, Student Aid
Environment: Resource Conservation

Health: Children's Health/Hospitals, Clinics/Medical Centers, Medical Research, Mental Health
Religion: Churches, Ministries, Religious Organizations, Religious Welfare
Science: Science Museums, Scientific Centers & Institutes
Social Services: Animal Protection, Child Welfare, Community Centers, Community Service Organizations, Domestic Violence, Family Services, Recreation & Athletics, Youth Organizations

Application Procedures

Initial Contact: Request application form and guidelines.
Deadlines: May 1 for summer programs and July 1 for all other programs.

Restrictions

Does not support individuals.

Additional Information

Publications: Application Guidelines; Application Form

Foundation Officials

E. W. Barnett: director
M. W. Minnich: vice president, director
C. O'Malley: director
Jean W. Pettitt: president, director
S. D. Pettitt: director
B. Raber: treasurer, director
Kate Schafer: secretary, director
J. G. Wharton: director
Joseph B. Wharton, III: secretary, treasurer
K. B. Wharton: director

Grants Analysis

Disclosure Period: calendar year ending 2001
Total Grants: $121,548*
Number of Grants: 17
Average Grant: $4,597*
Highest Grant: $48,000
Lowest Grant: $500
Typical Range: $1,000 to $10,000
*Note: Giving excludes matching gifts. Average grant figure excludes highest grant.

Recent Grants

Note: Grants derived from 2001 Form 990.

General

48,000	Future Leaders of America, Oxnard, CA -- Latino Youth Leadership Program
20,000	Cleveland Elementary School, Santa Barbara, CA -- support for professional development
10,000	East Bay Conservation Corp, Oakland, CA -- support for EBBC Charter School
10,000	Foundation for Santa Barbara City College, Santa Barbara, CA -- summer program
7,500	Endowment for Youth Committee, Santa Barbara, CA -- support for science, math engineering and technology programs
5,000	Hopi Foundation, Hoteville, AZ -- educational programs
5,000	Santa Barbara Museum of Natural History, Santa Barbara, CA -- Los Marineros
5,000	Santa Maria Valley Discovery Museum, Santa Maria, CA -- Discover After School Success Program
3,800	Future Leaders of America, Oxnard, CA
3,000	Outreach Community Ministries

WHEELER FOUNDATION

Giving Contact
Samuel C. Wheeler, President & Director
1211 SW 5th Ave., Suite 2906
Portland, OR 97204-1911
Phone: (503)228-0261

Description
Founded: 1965
EIN: 930553801
Organization Type: Private Foundation
Giving Locations: NY; OR
Grant Types: General Support, Research, Scholarship.

Donor Information
Founder: the late Coleman H. Wheeler, Cornelia T. Wheeler

Financial Summary
Total Giving: $610,500 (2001); $602,500 (2000); $640,300 (1999)
Giving Analysis: Giving for 2001 includes: foundation scholarships ($10,000); 1998: international subsidiaries ($30,000) foundation ($475,000)
Assets: $15,484,567 (2001); $14,298,606 (2000); $14,596,997 (1999)
Gifts Received: $882,108 (1992). Note: In 1992, contributions were received from Cornelia T. Wheeler ($872,108) and Coleman H. Wheeler ($10,000).

Typical Recipients
Arts & Humanities: Arts Festivals, Historic Preservation, History & Archaeology, Libraries, Museums/Galleries, Music, Opera, Theater
Civic & Public Affairs: Botanical Gardens/Parks, Clubs, Community Foundations, Economic Development, Civic & Public Affairs-General, Municipalities/Towns, Public Policy
Education: Afterschool/Enrichment Programs, Arts/Humanities Education, Colleges & Universities, Continuing Education, Education Funds, Education-General, Health & Physical Education, Minority Education, Private Education (Precollege), Science/Mathematics Education, Secondary Education (Private), Student Aid
Environment: Forestry, Environment-General
Health: Cancer, Children's Health/Hospitals, Clinics/Medical Centers, Emergency/Ambulance Services, Health Funds, Health Organizations, Hospitals, Medical Research, Public Health
International: International Environmental Issues
Religion: Ministries, Religious Organizations, Religious Welfare, Seminaries
Science: Science Museums
Social Services: Child Welfare, Community Service Organizations, Crime Prevention, Day Care, Food/Clothing Distribution, Homes, People with Disabilities, Scouts, Senior Services, Substance Abuse, United Funds/United Ways, YMCA/YWCA/YMHA/YWHA, Youth Organizations

Application Procedures
Initial Contact: Send a brief letter of inquiry.
Application Requirements: Include purpose of funds sought and proof of tax-exempt status.
Deadlines: None.

Restrictions
Grants are not made to individuals.

Foundation Officials
Lil M. Hendrickson: assistant secretary
Charles B. Wheeler: vice president, director
Edward T. Wheeler: secretary, director
John C. Wheeler: vice president, director
Samuel C. Wheeler: president, director
Thomas K. Wheeler: treasurer, director

Grants Analysis
Disclosure Period: calendar year ending 2001
Total Grants: $600,500*
Number of Grants: 54
Average Grant: $9,824*
Highest Grant: $40,000
Typical Range: $1,000 to $10,000
*Note: Giving excludes scholarship. Average grant figure excludes two highest grants ($70,000).

Recent Grants
Note: Grants derived from 2001 Form 990.

General
40,000	World Forestry Center, Portland, OR
30,000	Columbia River Maritime Museum, Astoria, OR
25,000	George Fox University, Newberg, OR
25,000	Providence St. Vincent Medical Foundation, Portland, OR
25,000	YMCA of Columbia-Willamette, Portland, OR
20,000	DePaul Treatment Centers, Portland, OR
20,000	Portland Art Museum, Portland, OR
18,000	Oregon Historical Society, Portland, OR
15,000	Cascade Pacific Council Boy Scouts of America, Portland, OR
15,000	Health Data Research, Inc., Lebanon, OR

JOSEPHINE AND J. A. WHEELER MEMORIAL FOUNDATION

Giving Contact
Gene McLaughlin, Co-Trustee
c/o Security Bank
PO Drawer AA
Ralls, TX 79357-0800
Phone: (806)253-2511

Description
Founded: 1993
EIN: 752485347
Organization Type: Private Foundation
Giving Locations: TX: Ralls
Grant Types: General Support.

Financial Summary
Total Giving: $56,185 (2000); $43,468 (1998); $40,815 (1996)
Assets: $1,047,413 (2000); $1,021,314 (1998); $1,004,194 (1996)

Typical Recipients
Arts & Humanities: History & Archaeology, Libraries, Museums/Galleries
Civic & Public Affairs: Botanical Gardens/Parks, Civic & Public Affairs-General, Municipalities/Towns
Education: Community & Junior Colleges, Education-General, Leadership Training, Public Education (Precollege), Secondary Education (Public)
Health: Emergency/Ambulance Services
Religion: Churches
Social Services: Emergency Relief, Recreation & Athletics, Scouts, Senior Services, Youth Organizations

Application Procedures
Initial Contact: Send a brief letter of inquiry.
Application Requirements: Provide amount requested and purpose of funds sought.
Deadlines: None.

Foundation Officials
Tom J. Brian: co-trustee
Gene McLaughlin: co-trustee
Walker Watkins: co-trustee

Grants Analysis
Disclosure Period: calendar year ending 2000
Total Grants: $56,185
Number of Grants: 7
Average Grant: $4,823*
Highest Grant: $27,250
Lowest Grant: $500
Typical Range: $500 to $3,000
*Note: Average grant figure excludes highest grant.

Recent Grants
Note: Grants derived from 2000 Form 990.

General
27,250	Ralls Ambulance, Ralls, TX
10,145	Ralls VFD, Ralls, TX
6,475	Boy Scouts, Halls, TX
5,000	PMEP, Ralls, TX
4,427	Ralls Independent School District, Ralls, TX
2,388	Ralls High School, Ralls, TX
500	Ralls Historical Museum, Ralls, TX

NATHANIEL WHEELER TRUST

Giving Contact
Stephen Fitch
c/o Fleet National Bank
Fleet Private Clients Group
446 Main Street
Worcester, MA 01608
Phone: (508)793-4205

Description
Founded: 1997
EIN: 046437271
Organization Type: Private Foundation
Giving Locations: MA
Grant Types: General Support.

Financial Summary
Total Giving: $52,170 (2001); $35,966 (2000); $28,283 (1999)
Assets: $1,428,469 (2001); $1,414,039 (2000); $1,295,204 (1999)

Typical Recipients
Arts & Humanities: Libraries
Civic & Public Affairs: Botanical Gardens/Parks, Civic & Public Affairs-General, Urban & Community Affairs
Religion: Churches
Social Services: Senior Services

Application Procedures
Initial Contact: Send a brief letter of inquiry.
Deadlines: None.

Restrictions
Beautification projects in and for the city of Worcester.

Additional Information
Trust(s): Fleet National Bank MA

Grants Analysis
Disclosure Period: calendar year ending 2001
Total Grants: $52,170
Number of Grants: 7
Average Grant: $7,453
Highest Grant: $14,459
Lowest Grant: $1,900

Recent Grants

Note: Grants derived from 2001 Form 990.

Library-Related

11,000	Worcester Public Library, Worcester, MA

General

14,459	Park Spirit of Worcester, Worcester, MA
10,385	Trinity Lutheran Church
6,444	Friends of Worcester Senior Center, Worcester, MA
5,260	Robert H. Goddard Association
2,722	Worcester Common Ground, Worcester, MA
1,900	Tower Hill, Worcester, MA

WHIRLPOOL CORP.

Company Headquarters

Benton Harbor, MI
Web: http://www.whirlpool.com

Company Description

Founded: 1911
Ticker: WHR
Exchange: NYSE
Revenue: US$11.016 billion (2002)
Employees: 68000 (2002)
Fortune Rank: 173, per FORTUNE Magazine's list of 500 Largest U.S. Corporations (2002).
SIC(s): 3582 Commercial Laundry Equipment, 3585 Refrigeration & Heating Equipment, 3631 Household Cooking Equipment, 3633 Household Laundry Equipment.

Operating Locations

Whirlpool Corp. (AR--Fort Smith; IN--Evansville, La Porte; MI--Benton Harbor; OH--Clyde, Findlay, Marion; SC--Columbia; TN--Knoxville, LaVergne)

Whirlpool Foundation

Giving Contact

Barbara Hall, Foundation Contact
Whirlpool Foundation
2000 North M-63
Benton Harbor, MI 49022
Phone: (616)923-5583
Fax: (616)923-3214
Web: http://www.whirlpoolcorp.com/whr/foundation/index.html

Description

EIN: 386077342
Organization Type: Corporate Foundation
Giving Locations: operating locations.
Grant Types: Employee Matching Gifts, Project, Scholarship.
Note: Employee matching gift ratio: 1 to 1. Scholarships are for employees' children only.

Financial Summary

Total Giving: $5,397,553 (fiscal year ending March 31, 2001); $5,630,270 (fiscal 1999); $4,953,489 (fiscal 1997). Note: Contributes through corporate direct giving program and foundation.
Giving Analysis: Giving for fiscal 2001 includes: foundation scholarships ($374,511); foundation matching gifts ($1,086,842); foundation grants to United Way ($1,339,681); foundation ($2,596,519); fiscal 1999: foundation scholarships ($404,200); foundation matching gifts ($689,501); foundation grants to United Way ($1,107,928); foundation ($3,428,641); fiscal 1997: foundation scholarships ($353,000); foundation matching gifts ($779,235); foundation grants to United Way ($939,220) foundation ($2,882,034).
Assets: $14,194,334 (fiscal 2001); $19,261,998 (fiscal 1999); $15,983,268 (fiscal 1997)

Gifts Received: $3,000,000 (fiscal 1999); $2,000,000 (fiscal 1996); $2,000,000 (fiscal 1995).
Note: Foundation receives gifts from Whirlpool Corp.

Typical Recipients

Arts & Humanities: Arts Associations & Councils, Arts Centers, Arts Funds, Arts Institutes, Ballet, Community Arts, Dance, Ethnic & Folk Arts, Arts & Humanities-General, Historic Preservation, History & Archaeology, Libraries, Literary Arts, Museums/Galleries, Music, Opera, Performing Arts, Public Broadcasting, Theater, Visual Arts
Civic & Public Affairs: Botanical Gardens/Parks, Business/Free Enterprise, Civil Rights, Clubs, Community Foundations, Economic Development, Economic Policy, Employment/Job Training, First Amendment Issues, Civic & Public Affairs-General, Hispanic Affairs, Housing, Law & Justice, Municipalities/Towns, Nonprofit Management, Professional & Trade Associations, Public Policy, Safety, Urban & Community Affairs, Women's Affairs
Education: Afterschool/Enrichment Programs, Arts/Humanities Education, Business Education, Colleges & Universities, Community & Junior Colleges, Economic Education, Education Associations, Education Funds, Education Reform, Elementary Education (Private), Elementary Education (Public), Engineering/Technological Education, Education-General, International Studies, Journalism/Media Education, Literacy, Medical Education, Minority Education, Preschool Education, Private Education (Precollege), Public Education (Precollege), Science/Mathematics Education, Secondary Education (Private), Social Sciences Education, Student Aid, Vocational & Technical Education
Environment: Environment-General
Health: Cancer, Clinics/Medical Centers, Emergency/Ambulance Services, Health Organizations, Hospitals, Public Health
International: Foreign Educational Institutions, Health Care/Hospitals, International Development, International Organizations, International Relations
Religion: Religious Welfare
Science: Science Exhibits & Fairs, Scientific Centers & Institutes, Scientific Organizations
Social Services: Animal Protection, Big Brother/Big Sister, Child Welfare, Community Centers, Community Service Organizations, Counseling, Day Care, Delinquency & Criminal Rehabilitation, Domestic Violence, Family Planning, Family Services, Food/Clothing Distribution, Homes, People with Disabilities, Recreation & Athletics, Senior Services, Sexual Abuse, Shelters/Homelessness, Social Services-General, Substance Abuse, United Funds/United Ways, Volunteer Services, YMCA/YWCA/YMHA/YWHA, Youth Organizations

Application Procedures

Initial Contact: Send a brief letter or telephone call for guidelines and application form.
Application Requirements: Submit a letter accompanied by the prescribed application form.
Deadlines: January 1, April 1, July 1, and October 1.

Restrictions

Does not support dinners or special events, fraternal organizations, goodwill advertising, individuals, political or lobbying groups, or religious organizations for sectarian purposes.

Corporate Officials

J. C. Anderson: vice president north americaeo, director PRIM CORP EMPL vice president north america: Whirlpool Corp.
David Ray Whitwam: chairman, president, chief executive officer, director B Madison WI 1942. ED University of Wisconsin BS (1967). PRIM CORP EMPL chairman, president, chief executive officer, director: Whirlpool Corp. CORP AFFIL director: Combustion Engineering Inc.; director: PP&G Industries Inc. NONPR AFFIL member: National Council Housing

Industries; president, director: Soup Kitchen; fellow: Aspen Institute; director: Conference Board. CLUB AFFIL Point O Woods Club.

Foundation Officials

J. C. Anderson: senior vice president (see above)
Nancy T. Snyder: vice president

Grants Analysis

Disclosure Period: fiscal year ending March 31, 2001
Total Grants: $2,596,519*
Number of Grants: 142
Average Grant: $18,285
Highest Grant: $585,841
Typical Range: $1,000 to $50,000
*Note: Giving excludes matching gifts, scholarships, and United Way.

Recent Grants

Note: Grants derived from 2001 Form 990.

General

585,841	Community Economic Development Corp, Benton Harbor, MI
583,134	United Way Southwestern Michigan, MI
500,000	Lake Michigan College Education Fund, Benton Harbor, MI
223,570	University of Notre Dame, South Bend, IN
200,000	Indiana University, Bloomington, IN -- Kelley School of Business
180,815	United Way, Ft. Smith, AR
114,339	United Way Southwestern Indiana, Evansville, IN
107,500	United Way Marion County, Marion, OH
100,000	Lakeland Health Foundation, Benton Harbor, MI
100,000	Montessori House of Children

WHITAKER FOUNDATION

Giving Contact

Peter G. Katona, President
1700 North Moore Street, Suite 2200
Arlington, VA 22209
Phone: (703)528-2430
Fax: (703)528-2431
E-mail: info@whitaker.org
Web: http://www.whitaker.org

Alternate Contact

4718 Old Gettysburg Road, Suite 405
Mechanicsburg, PA 17055-8411
Phone: (717)763-1391
Note: For Harrisburg and Naples regional programs.

Description

Founded: 1975
EIN: 222096948
Organization Type: General Purpose Foundation
Giving Locations: , Harrisburg FL: Naples for regional programs for research, special opportunity, and other grant programs.
Grant Types: Award, Conference/Seminar, Employee Matching Gifts, Fellowship, Research.

Donor Information

Founder: Established as a trust in New York in 1975 by Mr. U. A. Whitaker. Mr. Whitaker founded Aircraft-Marine Products, now known as AMP, Inc., and was the former chairman of both the company and its operating subsidiaries abroad.

Financial Summary

Total Giving: $71,187,397 (2002); $66,489,481 (2001); $47,213,220 (2000)
Giving Analysis: Giving for 2000 includes: foundation fellowships ($5,586,784); 1998: foundation grants

to United Way ($1,200); foundation matching gifts ($136,570) foundation fellowships ($4,570,942)
Assets: $246,225,766 (2002); $370,095,910 (2001); $368,149,320 (2000)

Typical Recipients

Arts & Humanities: Arts Associations & Councils, Arts Centers, Libraries, Museums/Galleries, Music, Opera, Theater

Civic & Public Affairs: Community Foundations, Employment/Job Training, Civic & Public Affairs-General, Housing

Education: Arts/Humanities Education, Business Education, Colleges & Universities, Community & Junior Colleges, Education Associations, Engineering/Technological Education, Education-General, Journalism/Media Education, Legal Education, Medical Education, Private Education (Precollege), Public Education (Precollege), Science/Mathematics Education, Student Aid

Environment: Environment-General

Health: Cancer, Children's Health/Hospitals, Clinics/Medical Centers, Eyes/Blindness, Geriatric Health, Heart, Hospices, Hospitals, Hospitals (University Affiliated), Medical Rehabilitation, Medical Research, Mental Health, Prenatal Health Issues, Preventive Medicine/Wellness Organizations, Public Health, Research/Studies Institutes, Respiratory, Speech & Hearing

International: Foreign Educational Institutions, Health Care/Hospitals, Missionary/Religious Activities

Religion: Churches, Ministries

Science: Science-General, Scientific Centers & Institutes, Scientific Research

Social Services: Community Service Organizations, United Funds/United Ways, YMCA/YWCA/YMHA/YWHA, Youth Organizations

Application Procedures

Initial Contact: Applicants must obtain a copy of the current program guidelines by telephone, email, or letter before submitting an application. Alternatively, program announcements and application forms are available through the Internet.

Deadlines: Varies for each of the program areas. Contact the foundation for specific deadlines.

Review Process: In judging eligibility for research grants, the foundation looks for two factors: the project must significantly involve the use of innovative engineering techniques, and the investigators must be relative beginners in their research careers. Outside the three-county area may apply for outreach or networking grants that would benefit secondary school students residing in the three-county area.

Notes: Most programs at the foundation do not accept new applications. The foundation will close permanently in 2006.

Restrictions

To obtain a biomedical research grant, the principal investigator must be a member of the faculty or research staff of the applicant institution, and have received a doctorate less than eight years prior to submitting a preliminary proposal, or have completed all residencies less than seven years before. Grants generally will not be made to support operating expenses of established programs, nor to finance deficits.

Additional Information

The Whitaker Foundation will spend all of its assets, primarily in support of education and research programs in biomedical engineering, then go out of business at the end of 2006.

Publications: Guidelines; Annual Report; Application Form

Foundation Officials

Dr. William Ralph Brody, PhD: committee member B Stockton, CA 1944. ED Massachusetts Institute of

Technology BSEE (1965); Massachusetts Institute of Technology MSEE (1966); Stanford University MD (1970); Stanford University PhDEE (1972). PRIM NONPR EMPL president: John Hopkins University School of Medicine. CORP AFFIL director: Alza Corp.; directory: Medtronic Inc. NONPR AFFIL member: Institute Sys Science; fellow: NAS; fellow: Institute Medicine and Biomed Engineering; fellow: American Heart Association; fellow: Institute Electrical & Electronic Engineers; fellow: American College Cardiology; fellow: American College Radiology.

G. Burtt Holmes, OD: chairman

Ruth W. Holmes, PhD: committee member

Thomas A. Holmes: committee member

Peter Geza Katona, ScD: president B Budapest, Hungary 1937. ED University of Michigan BS (1960); Massachusetts Institute of Technology SM (1962); Massachusetts Institute of Technology ScD (1965). PRIM NONPR EMPL president, chief executive officer: Whitaker Foundation. NONPR AFFIL senior member: Biomedical Engineering Society; senior member: Institute Electrical & Electronics Engineers; senior member: American Society Engineering Education; fellow: American Institute Medical & Biological Engineering; senior member: American Physiological Society; fellow: American Association Advancement Science.

James E. Kielley, JD: committee member

John H. Linehan, PhD: vice president, vice president biomed engineering

Harold A. McInnes: committee member B Groton, CT 1927. ED Massachusetts Institute of Technology BSME (1949). PRIM CORP EMPL chairman, chief executive officer, director: AMP Inc. CORP AFFIL director: PPG Industries.

Portia W. Shumaker: committee member

Grants Analysis

Disclosure Period: calendar year ending 2002
Total Grants: $71,187,397
Number of Grants: 275 (approx)
Average Grant: $207,954*
Highest Grant: $14,000,000
Lowest Grant: $2,900
Typical Range: $105,000 to $240,000
*Note: Average grant figure excludes highest grant.

Recent Grants

Note: Grants derived from 2001 Form 990.

General

9,038,000	Regents of the University of California, Berkeley, CA -- a leadership program for bioengineering education, research and industrial corporation
4,025,167	Washington University, St. Louis, MO -- Special Grant from Leadership Application
2,708,840	Johns Hopkins University, Baltimore, MD -- Biomedical Engineering Institute at Johns Hopkins
2,390,000	University of Virginia, Charlottesville, VA -- building partnerships between engineering and medicine
2,141,471	Georgia Tech Research Corporation, Atlanta, GA -- An integrated Approach to Biomedical Engineering Education and Research
1,680,932	University of California Davis, Davis, CA -- Sensors Vectors and Systems
1,000,000	Brown University, Providence, RI -- Cellular-and SubCellular-Based Biomedical Engineering at Boston University
1,000,000	University of California Berkeley, Berkeley, CA -- A plan for the Future of Bioengineering
832,500	Greater Harrisburg Foundation, Harrisburg, PA -- March 14, 2001 Awards for 2001 Program

829,545	University of Michigan, Ann Arbor, MI -- reorganization of biomedical engineering

HELEN F. WHITAKER FUND

Giving Contact

Miles J. Gibbons, Jr., Executive Director
4718 Old Gettysburg Road, Suite 209
Mechanicsburg, PA 17055-8411
Phone: (717)763-1600
Fax: (717)763-1832

Description

Founded: 1983
EIN: 222459399
Organization Type: Specialized/Single Purpose Foundation
Giving Locations: FL: Naples; PA: Harrisburg, Philadelphia nationally.
Grant Types: Endowment, Fellowship, General Support, Matching, Multiyear/Continuing Support, Operating Expenses, Project.
Note: Program development support is also offered.

Donor Information

Founder: Established in 1983 by the late Helen F. Whitaker .

Financial Summary

Total Giving: $7,763,808 (fiscal year ending July 31, 2001); $4,458,007 (fiscal 2000); $3,500,000 (fiscal 1999 approx)
Assets: $26,738,852 (fiscal 2001); $33,451,568 (fiscal 2000); $40,000,000 (fiscal 1999 approx)
Gifts Received: $548,044 (fiscal 1993); $34,541 (fiscal 1992)

Typical Recipients

Arts & Humanities: Arts Associations & Councils, Arts Centers, Arts Festivals, Arts Funds, Arts Outreach, Ballet, Arts & Humanities-General, Museums/Galleries, Music, Opera, Performing Arts, Public Broadcasting, Theater

Civic & Public Affairs: Community Foundations

Education: Arts/Humanities Education

International: Foreign Arts Organizations, International Organizations

Application Procedures

Initial Contact: Contact foundation for application guidelines. Preliminary proposals are required.

Application Requirements: Preliminary proposals should include the following: a brief history of the organization; a clear statement of the proposed program's objectives; a brief description of the proposed program; the proposed timetable for the program; a summary budget for each year of the program and the amount of that budget that will be requested from the Whitaker Fund; the identity and affiliation of the contact person for the program; a brief statement of the qualifications of the person who will be responsible for implementing the program; and the criteria for measuring the program's success or failure.

Deadlines: Preliminary proposal deadlines are March 1 for consideration at the June meeting, July 1 for the October meeting, November 1 for the February meeting.

Review Process: Committee meetings are held quarterly, in February, June, and October.

Evaluative Criteria: The Fund considers the following criteria when evaluating proposals: "Quality of the applicant, program participants, and musical content; integrity of program structure; relationship of program to applicant's mission; level of participants (post-conservatory); scope (national in reach, reputation or impact); predominance of American or America-based participants; cost-benefit ratio per direct participant; potential for significant impact." The Fund also examines whether organizations are financially viable, have been in existence for at least five years, employ at least three full-time people, can prove reasonable support from other sources, and primary serve musicians or musical institutions in the United States. "The Helen F. Whitaker Fund: A Summary of Grant Programs"

Restrictions

Grants are made only under announced competitive grant programs that provide support for classical music in the United States. Support is not available for presenting or performing organizations.

Additional Information

The Whitaker Fund plans to spend down all of its assets by the end of 2006. Select organizations are being invited to discuss how The Fund can offer support for programs that would ensure the continued development of Western classical music. The Fund is designing such initiatives to address certain sectors of the classical music scene, rather than aiming them at single organizations. Participation in these initiatives is therefore by invitation only.
Publications: Guidelines

Foundation Officials

Carmelita Biggie: committee member
Miles J. Gibbons, Jr.: executive director, comm mem B Scranton, PA 1935. ED Dickinson College BA (1957); Georgetown University JD (1964); Harvard University (1966). NONPR AFFIL co-chairman: Foundation Executive Roundtable; member: Rotary Club Harrisburg; director, chairman: Capital Campaign Review Committee.
Ruth W. Holmes, PhD: comm mem

Grants Analysis

Disclosure Period: fiscal year ending July 31, 2001
Total Grants: $7,763,808
Number of Grants: 70
Average Grant: $72,497*
Highest Grant: $1,584,000
Lowest Grant: $750
Typical Range: $35,000 to $150,000
*Note: Average grant figure excludes two highest grants ($2,834,000).

Recent Grants

Note: Grants derived from 2001 Form 990.

General

1,584,000	Meet the Composer, New York, NY -- for endowment fund
1,250,000	American Music Center, New York, NY -- for Copying Assistance Program endowment
500,000	Opera America, Washington, DC -- to establish the opera fund
300,000	American Composers Forum, St. Paul, MN -- for Chapter Development Program
250,000	Naples Philharmonic Center for the Arts, Naples, FL -- for endowment for music director chair
225,000	Opera America, Washington, DC -- to establish the opera fund
222,463	Aspen Music Festival and School, Aspen, CO -- for academy of conducting
200,000	American Composers Forum, St. Paul, MN -- for operating expenses
200,000	New World Symphony, Miami Beach, FL -- for Musician Development Program
175,000	American Symphony Orchestra League, Washington, DC -- for orchestra management

W. P. And H. B. White Foundation

Giving Contact

M. Margaret Blanford, Executive Director
540 Frontage Rd., Suite 3240
Northfield, IL 60093
Phone: (847)446-1441

Description

Founded: 1953
EIN: 362601558
Organization Type: Private Foundation
Giving Locations: IL: Chicago metropolitan area
Grant Types: Capital, Emergency, General Support, Multiyear/Continuing Support, Operating Expenses, Professorship, Project, Research, Scholarship.

Donor Information

Founder: the late William P. White, the late Hazel B. White

Financial Summary

Total Giving: $1,732,700 (2002); $2,166,750 (2001); $2,530,295 (2000)
Giving Analysis: Giving for 2002 includes: foundation scholarships ($325,000); 2000: foundation scholarships ($248,750) 1999: foundation scholarships ($225,750)
Assets: $23,134,965 (2002); $33,376,812 (2001); $42,514,312 (2000)

Typical Recipients

Arts & Humanities: Historic Preservation, Libraries, Museums/Galleries, Public Broadcasting, Theater
Civic & Public Affairs: Economic Development, Employment/Job Training, Hispanic Affairs, Housing, Public Policy, Urban & Community Affairs
Education: Afterschool/Enrichment Programs, Arts/Humanities Education, Colleges & Universities, Continuing Education, Education Associations, Education Reform, Education-General, Leadership Training, Literacy, Medical Education, Private Education (Precollege), Public Education (Precollege), Science/Mathematics Education, Secondary Education (Private), Student Aid, Vocational & Technical Education
Health: Cancer, Children's Health/Hospitals, Clinics/Medical Centers, Emergency/Ambulance Services, Heart, Hospitals, Medical Rehabilitation, Medical Research, Mental Health, Prenatal Health Issues, Public Health
Religion: Religious Welfare
Science: Science Museums, Scientific Centers & Institutes
Social Services: At-Risk Youth, Child Abuse, Child Welfare, Community Centers, Community Service Organizations, Emergency Relief, Family Services, Food/Clothing Distribution, People with Disabilities, Scouts, United Funds/United Ways, YMCA/YWCA/YMHA/YWHA, Youth Organizations

Application Procedures

Initial Contact: Send a brief letter of inquiry.
Application Requirements: Include program summary, organization history, and principals involved.
Deadlines: February 1, May 1, August 1, and November 1.

Restrictions

The foundation does not make grants to individuals or for land acquisition, building funds, endowments, publications, conferences, deficit spending, matching gifts, or loans.

Additional Information

Publications: Application Guidelines

Foundation Officials

M. Margaret Blandford: executive director
John H. McCortney: vice president, treasurer
Philip O. White, Jr.: director
Robert P. White: director
Roger B. White: president
Steven R. White: secretary
William P. White, Jr.: director

Grants Analysis

Disclosure Period: calendar year ending 2002
Total Grants: $1,407,700*
Number of Grants: 86
Average Grant: $16,369
Highest Grant: $35,000
Lowest Grant: $5,200
Typical Range: $10,000 to $30,000
*Note: Giving excludes scholarships.

Recent Grants

Note: Grants derived from 2001 Form 990.

General

50,000	Catholic Charities, Chicago, IL
45,000	Ada S. McKinley Community Services, Chicago, IL -- Comprehensive Educational Program
35,000	Golden Apple Foundation, Chicago, IL -- Chicago Golden Apple Scholars
35,000	Holy Trinity High School, Chicago, IL
35,000	Midtown Educational Foundation, Chicago, IL
33,000	Big Shoulders Fund, Chicago, IL -- capital funds
30,000	American Red Cross of Greater Chicago, Chicago, IL
30,000	Cristo Rey Jesuit High School, Chicago, IL
30,000	Cycle, Chicago, IL
25,000	Austin Career Education Center, Chicago, IL

G. R. White Trust

Giving Contact

Don Smith, Trust Officer
c/o Bank One
PO Box 2050
Ft. Worth, TX 76113
Phone: (817)884-4165

Description

EIN: 756094930
Organization Type: Private Foundation
Giving Locations: TX
Grant Types: Capital, General Support, Scholarship.

Donor Information

Founder: G. R. White

Financial Summary

Total Giving: $331,534 (fiscal year ending September 30, 2001); $329,828 (fiscal 2000); $343,360 (fiscal 1999)
Assets: $7,025,838 (fiscal 2001); $6,691,227 (fiscal 2000); $6,769,532 (fiscal 1999)

Typical Recipients

Arts & Humanities: Arts Associations & Councils, History & Archaeology, Libraries, Museums/Galleries
Civic & Public Affairs: Chambers of Commerce, Economic Development, Civic & Public Affairs-General, Municipalities/Towns, Rural Affairs, Safety, Urban & Community Affairs

Education: Agricultural Education, Colleges & Universities, Continuing Education, Engineering/Technological Education, Legal Education, Literacy, Preschool Education, Private Education (Precollege), Religious Education, Science/Mathematics Education, Secondary Education (Private), Special Education, Student Aid

Environment: Resource Conservation, Wildlife Protection

Health: Eyes/Blindness, Hospitals, Medical Rehabilitation, Public Health, Research/Studies Institutes

Religion: Churches, Religious Organizations, Religious Welfare, Seminaries

Social Services: At-Risk Youth, Child Welfare, Community Service Organizations, People with Disabilities, Senior Services, Social Services-General, United Funds/United Ways, YMCA/YWCA/YMHA/YWHA, Youth Organizations

Application Procedures

Initial Contact: Send a brief letter of inquiry.
Application Requirements: Include a description of organization, purpose of funds sought, amount requested, and list of directors.
Deadlines: September 1.

Additional Information

Trust(s): Bank One

Grants Analysis

Disclosure Period: fiscal year ending September 30, 2001
Total Grants: $331,534
Number of Grants: 31
Average Grant: $9,102*
Highest Grant: $58,464
Typical Range: $5,000 to $20,000
*Note: Average grant figure excludes highest grant.

Recent Grants

Note: Grants derived from fiscal 2000 Form 990.

General

58,186	Texas A & M University, College Station, TX -- for student loans
50,000	Texas and Southwestern Cattle Raisers Foundation, Ft. Worth, TX -- for building fund
50,000	University of Texas Law School, Austin, TX -- funding for Fred Wulff Fund
20,000	Casa Care, Inc., Brady, TX -- charitable gift
20,000	Rochelle Volunteer Fire Department, Rochelle, TX -- for purchase of new fire truck
20,000	St. Stephens Episcopal School, Austin, TX -- for science academy
10,000	Baptist General Convention of Texas, Dallas, TX -- for boys and young men camping in Texas
10,000	City of Melvin -- for restoration of Melvin Community Center
10,000	Texas Baptist Missions Foundation, Dallas, TX -- for student center
10,000	VOCA Volunteer Fire Department, Voca, TX -- for fire fighting equipment

WHITECAP FOUNDATION

Giving Contact

800 Wilshire Blvd., Suite 1010
Los Angeles, CA 90017
Phone: (213)624-5401
E-mail: execdirector@Whitecapfdn.org
Web: http://www.whitecapfdn.org

Description

Founded: 1986
EIN: 954111120
Organization Type: Private Foundation

Giving Locations: CA
Grant Types: General Support.

Financial Summary

Total Giving: $1,479,590 (fiscal year ending November 30, 2001); $1,498,171 (fiscal 2000); $1,249,017 (fiscal 1998)
Assets: $9,034,362 (fiscal 2001); $8,674,000 (fiscal 2000); $10,930,131 (fiscal 1998)
Gifts Received: $500,000 (fiscal 2001); $500,000 (fiscal 2000); $200,000 (fiscal 1998). Note: In fiscal 2001, contributions were received from Brack and Elizabeth Duker.

Typical Recipients

Arts & Humanities: Dance, Libraries
Civic & Public Affairs: Asian American Affairs, Civic & Public Affairs-General, Hispanic Affairs, Nonprofit Management, Professional & Trade Associations, Urban & Community Affairs, Women's Affairs
Education: Business Education, Colleges & Universities, Continuing Education, Education Associations, Elementary Education (Public), Education-General, Literacy, Private Education (Precollege), Public Education (Precollege), Religious Education, Special Education
Environment: Environment-General, Resource Conservation, Wildlife Protection
Health: Emergency/Ambulance Services, Mental Health
International: Foreign Educational Institutions, Health Care/Hospitals, International Relief Efforts, Missionary/Religious Activities
Religion: Churches, Religious Organizations, Religious Welfare
Social Services: Child Welfare, Community Centers, Community Centers, Community Service Organizations, Emergency Relief, Family Services, Recreation & Athletics, Scouts, YMCA/YWCA/YMHA/YWHA, Youth Organizations

Application Procedures

Initial Contact: Send a brief letter of inquiry.
Application Requirements: Include a description of organization, a description of the project, and a project budget.
Deadlines: None.

Restrictions

Preference is given to organizations involved with children and families, education, and wildlife conservation.

Foundation Officials

Laura Campobasso: executive director
Brack Duker: chief financial officer, secretary
Elizabeth Duker: president

Grants Analysis

Disclosure Period: fiscal year ending November 30, 2001
Total Grants: $1,479,590
Number of Grants: 56
Average Grant: $19,483*
Highest Grant: $210,692
Lowest Grant: $1,040
Typical Range: $5,000 to $40,000
*Note: Average grant figure excludes four highest grants ($466,456).

Recent Grants

Note: Grants derived from fiscal 2000 Form 990.

Library-Related

25,000	Library Foundation of Los Angeles, Los Angeles, CA

General

136,318	Our Saviour Center/Church of Our Saviour
103,899	Salesian Boys and Girls Club, Los Angeles, CA
100,000	National Aububon Society, CA
76,452	Executive Management Academy
46,800	Mount St. Mary's College, Los Angeles, CA
46,004	P.F. Bresee Foundation, Los Angeles, CA
39,500	Puente Learning Center, Los Angeles, CA
35,000	Valle Lindo School District, CA
30,756	Nature Conservancy, Los Angeles, CA
28,668	Las Familias Del Pueblo, Los Angeles, CA

JOSEPH B. WHITEHEAD FOUNDATION

Giving Contact

Charles H. McTier, President
50 Hurt Plaza, Suite 1200
Atlanta, GA 30303
Phone: (404)522-6755
Fax: (404)522-7026
E-mail: fdns@woodruff.org
Web: http://www.jbwhitehead.org

Description

Founded: 1937
EIN: 586001954
Organization Type: General Purpose Foundation
Giving Locations: GA: Atlanta including metropolitan area
Grant Types: Capital, Challenge, Matching, Multiyear/Continuing Support, Project, Seed Money.
Note: The foundation also provides grants for construction, land acquisition, and equipment.

Donor Information

Founder: Established in 1937 by the will of Joseph B. Whitehead Jr. , in memory of his father, Joseph B. Whitehead, a Tennessee tax lawyer who conceived the idea of bottling Coca-Cola, (then a popular fountain beverage in the South), with friend, Benjamin Thomas, in 1899. The two men were granted an exclusive contract to bottle and sell Coca-Cola in most of the United States, by Asa Candler, president of the Coca-Cola Company. Whitehead moved to Atlanta, with partner John T. Lupton, to establish the Dixie Coca-Cola Bottling Company to serve the southeastern, southwestern and middle western states. The foundation is affiliated with the Lettie Pate Evans Foundation and the Lettie Pate Whitehead Foundation, established by Mr. Whitehead's mother and brother, respectively.

Financial Summary

Total Giving: $16,715,000 (2000); $60,188,725 (1999); $24,923,775 (1998)
Giving Analysis: Giving for 2000 includes: foundation grants to United Way ($6,000,000) 1998: foundation grants to United Way ($400,000)
Assets: $1,076,498,416 (2000); $1,029,531,636 (1999); $1,214,315,536 (1998)

Typical Recipients

Arts & Humanities: Arts Centers, Arts Festivals, Historic Preservation, History & Archaeology, Literary Arts, Performing Arts
Civic & Public Affairs: Botanical Gardens/Parks, Business/Free Enterprise, Community Foundations, Economic Development, Employment/Job Training, Civic & Public Affairs-General, Hispanic Affairs, Housing, Law & Justice, Legal Aid, Nonprofit Management, Philanthropic Organizations, Urban & Community Affairs, Zoos/Aquariums
Education: Afterschool/Enrichment Programs, Colleges & Universities, Economic Education, Education Reform, Elementary Education (Private), Engineering/Technological Education, Environmental Education, Faculty Development, Education-General,

International Studies, Literacy, Preschool Education, Private Education (Precollege), Public Education (Precollege), Public Education (Precollege), School Volunteerism, Science/Mathematics Education, Special Education, Student Aid

Environment: Energy, Environment-General

Health: Alzheimers Disease, Arthritis, Cancer, Children's Health/Hospitals, Clinics/Medical Centers, Health-General, Health Policy/Cost Containment, Health Organizations, Home-Care Services, Hospitals, Kidney, Medical Rehabilitation, Mental Health, Nursing Services, Prenatal Health Issues, Preventive Medicine/Wellness Organizations, Public Health, Respiratory, Single-Disease Health Associations, Trauma Treatment

International: Health Care/Hospitals, International Affairs, International Organizations, International Relief Efforts

Religion: Ministries, Religious Organizations, Religious Welfare, Religious Welfare

Science: Science Museums, Scientific Organizations

Social Services: Animal Protection, At-Risk Youth, Big Brother/Big Sister, Camps, Child Abuse, Child Welfare, Community Centers, Community Service Organizations, Counseling, Delinquency & Criminal Rehabilitation, Domestic Violence, Family Planning, Family Services, Food/Clothing Distribution, Homes, People with Disabilities, Scouts, Senior Services, Shelters/Homelessness, Social Services-General, Substance Abuse, United Funds/United Ways, Volunteer Services, YMCA/YWCA/YMHA/YWHA, Youth Organizations

Application Procedures

Initial Contact: Organizations seeking support should submit a letter of inquiry first. Proposals, when submitted, should be in letter form.

Application Requirements: Description of the organization, its purposes, programs, staffing, and governing board; the organization's latest financial statements, including the most recent audit report; a description of the proposed project and full justification for its funding; an itemized project budget, including other sources of support in hand or anticipated; and evidence from the IRS of the organization's tax-exempt status and that the organization is not a private foundation.

Deadlines: February 1 for the board's April meeting and September 1 for the November meeting.

Review Process: Additional information or a site visit may be requested. Applicants will receive final notification within thirty days of the trustees' meetings, which are held in April and November.

Restrictions

Grants are limited to a selected list of tax-exempt public charities and selected governmental agencies located and operating in metropolitan Atlanta, GA. Preference is given to one-time capital projects; awards for basic operating expenses usually are avoided. No grants to individuals. No loans.

Additional Information

The foundation shares offices and administrative staff with the Robert W. Woodruff Foundation, Lettie Pate Evans Foundation, Lettie Pate Whitehead Foundation, and Ichauway, Inc. Grant inquiries and proposals submitted to the Joseph B. Whitehead Foundation may also be considered by one or more of the associated foundations. It is not necessary to communicate separately with more than one of these foundations in seeking information or requesting grant support.

Publications: Guidelines; Brochure

Foundation Officials

P. Russell Hardin: vice president, secretary PRIM NONPR EMPL vice president-secretary: Ichauway Inc. NONPR AFFIL vice president-secretary: Joseph W Jones Ecological Research Center.

Joseph West Jones: chairman emeritus, trustee B Georgetown, DE 1912. ED Beacom College BA (1932). PRIM CORP EMPL chairman: Ichauway Inc.

Charles Harvey McTier: president B Columbus, GA 1939. ED Emory University BBA (1961). PRIM CORP EMPL president: Ichauway Inc. CORP AFFIL director: SunTrust Bank Georgia Inc.; director: SunTrust Bank Atlanta. NONPR AFFIL trustee: North Georgia United Methodist Foundation; member: President Cir National Academy Sciences Institute Medicine; president: Joseph W Jones Ecological Research Center; member: Management Executives Society; chairman board trustee: Foundation Center; pub member: Joint Commission Accreditation Health Care Organizations; vice chairman, chairman management committee: Council Foundations; member: Association Emory Alumni. CLUB AFFIL Druid Hills Golf Club; Piedmont Driving Club; director: Commerce Club.

James Malcolm Sibley: vice chairman, trustee B Atlanta, GA August 05, 1919. ED Princeton University AB (1941); Woodrow Wilson School of Law (1942); Harvard University Law School (1945-1946). CORP AFFIL director: Summit Industries; director: Rock-Tenn Co.; director: Ichauway Inc. NONPR AFFIL member: Georgia Bar Association; trustee: AG Rhodes Home; member: Atlanta Bar Association; member: American College Probate Counsel; member: American Law Institute; member: American Bar Foundation; member: American Bar Association. CLUB AFFIL Piedmont Driving Club; Commerce Club.

J. Lee Tribble: treasurer PRIM CORP EMPL treasurer: Ichauway Inc. NONPR AFFIL treasurer: Joseph W Jones Ecological Research Center.

James Bryan Williams: trustee B Sewanee, TN 1933. ED Emory University AB (1955). PRIM CORP EMPL chairman, chief executive director, director: SunTrust Banks, Inc. CORP AFFIL director: Sonat Inc.; director: RPC Energy Services Inc.; director: RPC Inc.; director: Georgia-Pacific Corp.; director: Rollins Inc.; director: Coca-Cola Co.; director: Genuine Parts Co.; director: Boral Industries Inc. NONPR AFFIL director: Federal Reserve Bank Atlanta; chairman board trustees: Robert R Woodruff Health Science Center; trustee: Emory University; member: Bankers Roundtable. CLUB AFFIL Piedmont Driving Club; member: Ocean Forest Golf Club; Peachtree Golf Club; Capital City Club; Commerce Club.

Grants Analysis

Disclosure Period: calendar year ending 2000
Total Grants: $10,715,000*
Number of Grants: 20
Average Grant: $535,750
Highest Grant: $1,250,000
Lowest Grant: $15,000
Typical Range: $25,000 to $750,000
*Note: Giving excludes United Way.

Recent Grants

Note: Grants derived from 2000 Form 990.

General

6,000,000	United Way Metropolitan Atlanta, Atlanta, GA -- construction of new child care centers and enhancement of existing programs
2,000,000	YMCA of Metropolitan Atlanta, Inc., Atlanta, GA -- construction of an East Lake Branch of the YMCA
1,750,000	Hillside, Inc. -- acquisition of neighboring property to expand children's home
1,250,000	Georgia Academy for Children and Youth Professionals, Atlanta, GA -- program support
1,000,000	Communities in School of Georgia, Atlanta, GA -- support of Alternative Schools Program
800,000	Atlanta Habitat for Humanity, Atlanta,

	GA -- repair and renovation of headquarters warehouse and establishment of habitat restore
400,000	Link Counseling Center, Atlanta, GA -- campaign for endowment and capital needs
375,000	Sheltering Arms, Atlanta, GA -- acquisition of two child care facilities
350,000	FCS Urban Ministries, Atlanta, GA -- campaign to renovate GlenCastle
350,000	State of Georgia Department of Juvenile Justice, Atlanta, GA -- juvenile detention reform initiative

WHITING FOUNDATION

Giving Contact

Donald E. Johnson, Jr., President & Trustee
Whiting Foundation
901 Citizens Bank Building
Flint, MI 48502
Phone: (810)767-3600

Description

Founded: 1940
EIN: 386056693
Organization Type: Private Foundation
Giving Locations: MI
Grant Types: General Support, Project, Research.

Donor Information

Founder: members of the Johnson family

Financial Summary

Total Giving: $1,136,600 (fiscal year ending June 30, 2001); $1,282,400 (fiscal 2000); $1,126,000 (fiscal 1999)

Giving Analysis: Giving for fiscal 2001 includes: foundation grants to United Way ($17,000) fiscal 1999: foundation grants to United Way ($16,500)

Assets: $22,374,235 (fiscal 2001); $17,617,013 (fiscal 2000); $25,576,584 (fiscal 1999)

Gifts Received: In 1990, contributions were received from the estate of Donald E. Johnson.

Typical Recipients

Arts & Humanities: Arts Associations & Councils, Arts Centers, Arts Institutes, Ballet, Libraries, Museums/Galleries, Music, Theater

Civic & Public Affairs: Community Foundations, Civic & Public Affairs-General, Housing, Parades/Festivals, Safety, Urban & Community Affairs

Education: Arts/Humanities Education, Business Education, Colleges & Universities, Education Funds, Gifted & Talented Programs, Medical Education, Minority Education, Private Education (Precollege), Public Education (Precollege), Religious Education, Secondary Education (Public), Special Education

Environment: Environment-General, Resource Conservation

Health: AIDS/HIV, Cancer, Children's Health/Hospitals, Clinics/Medical Centers, Emergency/Ambulance Services, Eyes/Blindness, Eyes/Blindness, Geriatric Health, Hospitals, Medical Research, Multiple Sclerosis, Public Health, Single-Disease Health Associations, Trauma Treatment

International: Health Care/Hospitals, International Relations

Religion: Churches, Ministries, Religious Welfare

Social Services: Animal Protection, Big Brother/Big Sister, Camps, Child Welfare, Community Service Organizations, Family Planning, Family Services, Food/Clothing Distribution, Homes, People with Disabilities, Recreation & Athletics, Scouts, Senior Services, Shelters/Homelessness, Substance Abuse, United Funds/United Ways, Volunteer Services, YMCA/YWCA/YMHA/YWHA, Youth Organizations

Application Procedures

Initial Contact: Send a brief letter of inquiry.
Application Requirements: Include a description of organization, amount requested, purpose of funds sought, recently audited financial statement, and proof of tax-exempt status.
Deadlines: April 30.

Restrictions

Emphasis is on cancer research, hospital and governmental health programs, public foundations, and educational institutions.

Foundation Officials

Mary Alice J. Heaton: trustee
Donald E. Johnson, Jr.: president, trustee CORP AFFIL president: Advertisers Press.
Marsha A. Kump: executive director
Linda J. LeMieux: trustee
John T. Lindholm: secretary, treasurer, trustee

Grants Analysis

Disclosure Period: fiscal year ending June 30, 2001
Total Grants: $1,119,600*
Number of Grants: 37
Average Grant: $8,878*
Highest Grant: $800,000
Typical Range: $1,000 to $75,000
*Note: Giving excludes United Way. Average grant figure excludes highest grant.

Recent Grants

Note: Grants derived from fiscal 2001 Form 990.

General

800,000	Flint Cultural Center, Flint, MI -- for the Joffrey Ballet
115,000	YWCA of Greater Flint, Flint, MI
25,000	American Red Cross, Flint, MI
25,000	Genesee County Habitat for Humanity, Flint, MI
17,000	United Way of Flint and Lapeer Counties, Flint, MI
10,000	Cancer Research Institute Investigator Program, New York, NY -- investigator program
10,000	Cancer Research Institute Investigator Program, New York, NY
10,000	Humane Society of Genesee County, Burton, MI
10,000	Shelter of Flint, Inc., Flint, MI -- children's program
8,500	Genesee Area Focus Fund, Flint, MI

MACAULEY AND HELEN DOW WHITING FOUNDATION

Giving Contact

Helen Dow Whiting, Treasurer & Trustee
PO Box 1980
Sun Valley, ID 83353
Phone: (208)622-9331

Description

Founded: 1957
EIN: 237418814
Organization Type: Private Foundation
Giving Locations: FL; ID; ME; MA: nationally.
Grant Types: General Support.

Financial Summary

Total Giving: $140,250 (2001); $110,000 (2000); $255,000 (1999)
Assets: $5,064,283 (2001); $5,978,956 (2000); $6,516,092 (1999)

Typical Recipients

Arts & Humanities: Ballet, Dance, Libraries, Music, Public Broadcasting
Civic & Public Affairs: Municipalities/Towns, Zoos/Aquariums
Education: Colleges & Universities, Economic Education, Education Funds, Private Education (Precollege)
Environment: Environment-General, Resource Conservation
Health: Cancer, Clinics/Medical Centers, Hospitals, Hospitals (University Affiliated)
Social Services: Recreation & Athletics

Application Procedures

Initial Contact: Send a brief letter of inquiry describing program or project.
Deadlines: None.

Restrictions

Does not support individuals.

Foundation Officials

Helen Dow Whiting: treasurer, trustee
Macauley Whiting: president, trustee
Mary Macauley Whiting: secretary, trustee
Sara Whiting: trustee

Grants Analysis

Disclosure Period: calendar year ending 2001
Total Grants: $140,250
Number of Grants: 7
Highest Grant: $40,000
Lowest Grant: $5,250

Recent Grants

Note: Grants derived from 2001 Form 990.

General

40,000	Trinity Preparatory School, Winter Park, FL
35,000	H. Lee Moffitt Cancer Center and Research Institute Foundation, Tampa, FL
25,000	Nature Conservancy, Brunswick, MA
15,000	Hotchkiss School, Blue Hill, ME
10,000	Bay School, Blue Hill, ME
10,000	Wood River Land Trust, Ketchum, ID
5,250	Ballet Foundation, Ketchum, ID

CLAUDE R. AND ETHEL B. WHITTENBERGER FOUNDATION

Giving Contact

William J. Rankin, Chairman
PO Box 1073
Caldwell, ID 83605
Phone: (208)459-4649

Description

Founded: 1970
EIN: 237092604
Organization Type: Private Foundation
Giving Locations: ID
Grant Types: General Support, Scholarship.

Donor Information

Founder: the late Ethel B. Whittenberger

Financial Summary

Total Giving: $326,169 (2000); $208,815 (1999); $205,802 (1998)
Giving Analysis: Giving for 2000 includes: foundation scholarships ($69,233) 1999: foundation scholarships ($9,500)
Assets: $6,349,626 (2000); $6,413,814 (1999); $5,957,293 (1998)

Typical Recipients

Arts & Humanities: Arts Associations & Councils, Arts Outreach, Ballet, Community Arts, Dance, Film & Video, Arts & Humanities-General, History & Archaeology, Libraries, Literary Arts, Museums/Galleries, Music, Public Broadcasting
Civic & Public Affairs: Botanical Gardens/Parks, Chambers of Commerce, Community Foundations, Economic Development, Economic Policy, Hispanic Affairs, Housing, Law & Justice, Municipalities/Towns, Nonprofit Management, Zoos/Aquariums
Education: Arts/Humanities Education, Business Education, Colleges & Universities, Economic Education, Education Funds, Education Reform, Elementary Education (Public), Faculty Development, Education-General, Gifted & Talented Programs, Literacy, Minority Education, Public Education (Precollege), Science/Mathematics Education, Secondary Education (Public), Student Aid
Environment: Resource Conservation, Wildlife Protection
Health: Public Health
International: Human Rights
Religion: Churches, Jewish Causes, Religious Welfare
Science: Science Museums, Scientific Centers & Institutes
Social Services: At-Risk Youth, Child Abuse, Child Welfare, Community Service Organizations, Day Care, Family Planning, Family Services, Food/Clothing Distribution, Homes, Recreation & Athletics, Scouts, Social Services-General, Substance Abuse, United Funds/United Ways, Youth Organizations

Application Procedures

Initial Contact: Send outline and budget of project.
Deadlines: None.

Additional Information

Publications: Application Guidelines; Informational Brochure

Foundation Officials

Margaret Gigray: treasurer
D. Whitman Jones: director
Joe Miller: secretary
Donald Price: director
William J. Rankin: chairman

Grants Analysis

Disclosure Period: calendar year ending 2000
Total Grants: $256,936*
Number of Grants: 56
Average Grant: $4,217*
Highest Grant: $25,000
Typical Range: $1,000 to $10,000
*Note: Giving excludes scholarship. Average grant excludes highest grant.

Recent Grants

Note: Grants derived from 1999 Form 990.

Library-Related

3,080	Caldwell Public Library, Caldwell, ID

General

41,763	Albertson College, Caldwell, ID
25,000	St. Dept. of Education, Boise, ID
11,835	Idaho Community Foundation, Boise, ID
8,000	Caldwell Fine Arts, Caldwell, ID
6,000	Planned Parenthood, Boise, ID
5,500	Boise Philharmonic, Boise, ID -- writing project
5,000	Butte View Elementary, Emmett, ID
5,000	Discovery Center, Boise, ID -- museum outreach
5,000	Idaho Suicide Prevention, Boise, ID
5,000	Idaho Zoological Society, Boise, ID

HARVEY RANDALL WICKES FOUNDATION

Giving Contact
James V. Finkbeiner, President
4800 Fashion Square Boulevard
472 Plaza North
Saginaw, MI 48604
Phone: (989)799-1850
Fax: (989)799-3327
E-mail: HRWICKES@concentric.net

Description
Founded: 1945
EIN: 386061470
Organization Type: General Purpose Foundation
Giving Locations: MI: Saginaw County
Grant Types: Capital, Challenge, Scholarship.
Note: The foundation also donates equipment and buildings.

Donor Information
Founder: Established in 1945 in Michigan by the late Harvey Randall Wickes , who was president and later chairman of the Wickes Corporation, which has diversified interests including the merchandising of building supplies.

Financial Summary
Total Giving: $1,849,532 (2001); $1,800,000 (1999 approx); $1,738,667 (1998)
Giving Analysis: Giving for 1998 includes: foundation grants to United Way ($40,000)
Assets: $38,931,839 (2001); $39,721,474 (1998); $36,988,761 (1997)

Typical Recipients
Arts & Humanities: Community Arts, Dance, Arts & Humanities-General, Historic Preservation, History & Archaeology, Libraries, Museums/Galleries, Music, Performing Arts, Theater
Civic & Public Affairs: Botanical Gardens/Parks, Business/Free Enterprise, Chambers of Commerce, Community Foundations, Economic Development, Economic Policy, Employment/Job Training, Civic & Public Affairs-General, Housing, Municipalities/ Towns, Nonprofit Management, Public Policy, Safety, Urban & Community Affairs, Zoos/Aquariums
Education: Business Education, Colleges & Universities, Education Funds, Education-General, Literacy, Minority Education, Public Education (Precollege), Student Aid
Health: Cancer, Clinics/Medical Centers, Emergency/Ambulance Services, Eyes/Blindness, Health Funds, Health Organizations, Hospitals, Medical Rehabilitation, Public Health
Religion: Religion-General, Religious Welfare
Social Services: Big Brother/Big Sister, Camps, Child Abuse, Child Welfare, Community Centers, Community Service Organizations, Crime Prevention, Family Services, Food/Clothing Distribution, Homes, People with Disabilities, Recreation & Athletics, Senior Services, Shelters/Homelessness, Social Services-General, Special Olympics, Substance Abuse, United Funds/United Ways, Volunteer Services, YMCA/YWCA/YMHA/YWHA, Youth Organizations

Application Procedures
Initial Contact: Applications should be in letter form.
Application Requirements: Letters should include specific details as to the proposed use of funds. The foundation will request additional information if necessary.
Deadlines: None.
Review Process: The board of trustees meets in January, April, June, and October.

Restrictions
The foundation does not make grants to individuals, churches, or political organizations. Does not support organizations outside the Saginaw County, Michigan area.

Additional Information
Publications: Guidelines

Foundation Officials
Hugo E. Braun, Jr.: vice president, secretary, trustee B Saginaw, MI 1932. ED Yale University BA (1954); University of Michigan LLB (1957). CORP AFFIL director: Citizens Banking Corp.; director: Wolohan Lumber Co.; director: Citizens Bank Michigan.
Mary Lou Case: trustee PRIM CORP EMPL vice president: W.L. Case & Co.
Kurt Ewend: trustee PRIM CORP EMPL executive vice president, director: Saginaw Bay Underwriters Inc.
James V. Finkbeiner: president, trustee, chairman board B Green Bay, WI 1914. ED University of Michigan BA (1935); University of Michigan JD (1937). PRIM CORP EMPL attorney: Braun Kendrick Finkbeiner Schafer Murphy.
William A. Hendrick: trustee
Richard P. Heuschele, MD: trustee
Craig W. Horn: trustee
Donald E. Juenemann: trustee PRIM CORP EMPL president: Saginaw General Healthcare Corp.
Richard D. Katz: trustee B 1935. PRIM CORP EMPL president, director: Remer Plumbing & Heating Inc.
William F. Nelson, Jr.: trustee PRIM CORP EMPL president: Wm. F. Nelson Electric Inc.
Michele D. Pavlicek: assistant secretary
David F. Wallace: trustee B Brooklyn, NY 1923. ED Michigan State University BSME (1949); Michigan State University MBA (1960). PRIM CORP EMPL chairman board, director: Wolohan Lumber Co.
Lloyd J. Yeo: treasurer, trustee CORP AFFIL director: Great Lakes National Bank.

Grants Analysis
Disclosure Period: calendar year ending 2001
Total Grants: $1,809,532*
Number of Grants: 39
Average Grant: $37,093*
Highest Grant: $400,000
Lowest Grant: $500
Typical Range: $5,000 to $100,000
*Note: Giving excludes United Way. Average grant figure excludes highest grant.

Recent Grants
Note: Grants derived from 2001 Form 990.

General

400,000	Saginaw Valley State University Foundation, University Center, MI
228,334	Saginaw Children's Zoo, Saginaw, MI -- expansion town program
200,000	Council of Foundations -- membership dues
166,666	Saginaw Art Museum, Saginaw, MI -- building program
147,500	Saginaw Valley State University Foundation, University Center, MI
147,500	Saginaw Valley State University Foundation, University Center, MI -- scholarships supporting organization
75,000	Restoration Community Outreach -- renovations and cost overruns for fire stations
60,000	Saginaw Chamber Foundation, Saginaw, MI -- foundation Saginaw County vision 2020
50,000	Child Abuse and Neglect Council -- building expansion
50,000	Pit and Balcony, Inc -- capital improvements

WICKSON-LINK MEMORIAL FOUNDATION

Giving Contact
Lloyd J. Yeo, President & Treasurer
PO Box 3275
3023 Davenport St.
Saginaw, MI 48602
Phone: (517)793-9830
Fax: (517)793-0186

Description
EIN: 386083931
Organization Type: Private Foundation
Giving Locations: MI: Saginaw County
Grant Types: General Support.

Donor Information
Founder: the late James Wickson, the late Meta Wickson

Financial Summary
Total Giving: $288,133 (2001); $315,363 (2000); $329,539 (1999)
Giving Analysis: Giving for 2001 includes: foundation grants to United Way ($6,500); 2000: foundation grants to United Way ($6,000); 1999: foundation grants to United Way ($6,000);
Assets: $5,569,478 (2001); $6,110,376 (2000); $6,180,727 (1999)

Typical Recipients
Arts & Humanities: Arts Associations & Councils, Historic Preservation, History & Archaeology, Libraries, Museums/Galleries, Music, Performing Arts
Civic & Public Affairs: Business/Free Enterprise, Clubs, Community Foundations, Employment/Job Training, Civic & Public Affairs-General, Hispanic Affairs, Housing, Municipalities/Towns, Parades/Festivals, Philanthropic Organizations, Urban & Community Affairs, Zoos/Aquariums
Education: Business Education, Colleges & Universities, Education-General, International Studies, Preschool Education, Private Education (Precollege), Public Education (Precollege), Secondary Education (Private), Secondary Education (Public)
Health: Emergency/Ambulance Services, Geriatric Health, Health Organizations, Hospitals, Nursing Services, Public Health, Single-Disease Health Associations
Religion: Churches, Religion-General, Religious Welfare
Science: Scientific Centers & Institutes
Social Services: At-Risk Youth, Big Brother/Big Sister, Child Abuse, Child Welfare, Community Centers, Community Service Organizations, Domestic Violence, Family Services, Food/Clothing Distribution, People with Disabilities, Recreation & Athletics, Scouts, Shelters/Homelessness, Social Services-General, Special Olympics, United Funds/United Ways, Volunteer Services, YMCA/YWCA/YMHA/YWHA, Youth Organizations

Application Procedures
Initial Contact: Send a brief letter of inquiry describing program or project.
Deadlines: None.

Foundation Officials
Lou Hanisko: director
B. J. Humphreys: vice president, secretary
C. Ward Lauderbach: director
Susan Piesko: director
Lloyd J. Yeo: president, treasurer CORP AFFIL director: Great Lakes National Bank.

Grants Analysis
Disclosure Period: calendar year ending 2001
Total Grants: $281,633*
Number of Grants: 45
Average Grant: $5,003*
Highest Grant: $61,500
Lowest Grant: $500
Typical Range: $1,000 to $10,000
*Note: Giving excludes United Way. Average grant figure excludes highest grant.

Recent Grants
Note: Grants derived from 2000 Form 990.

Library-Related

19,000	Wickson Memorial Library, Frankenmuth, MI

General

29,500	Frankenmuth School District, Frankenmuth, MI
12,600	SVSU Foundation, University Center, MI
10,000	Birch Run Playscape, Birch Run, MI
10,000	Fish Tales, Frankenmuth, MI
10,000	Frankenmuth Rotary Club, Frankenmuth, MI
10,000	Habitat for Humanity, Saginaw, MI
10,000	Saginaw Intermediate School District, Saginaw, MI
10,000	St. Mary's Guardian Angel, Saginaw, MI
9,000	East Side Soup Kitchen, Saginaw, MI
8,750	Saginaw Art Museum, Saginaw, MI

WIDGEON FOUNDATION

Giving Contact
Elizabeth H. Robinson, President
PO Box 1084
Easton, MD 21601
Phone: (610)275-0700

Description
Founded: 1969
EIN: 136113927
Organization Type: Private Foundation
Giving Locations: MD; PA; VA
Grant Types: General Support.

Donor Information
Founder: Elizabeth H. Robinson

Financial Summary
Total Giving: $239,100 (2001); $266,650 (2000); $271,075 (1999)
Assets: $4,876,035 (2001); $5,486,509 (2000); $5,799,517 (1999)

Typical Recipients
Arts & Humanities: Arts Associations & Councils, Arts Centers, Historic Preservation, History & Archaeology, Libraries, Museums/Galleries
Civic & Public Affairs: Botanical Gardens/Parks, Community Foundations, Employment/Job Training, Civic & Public Affairs-General, Public Policy, Safety, Urban & Community Affairs, Zoos/Aquariums
Education: Agricultural Education, Colleges & Universities, Community & Junior Colleges, Education Reform, Engineering/Technological Education, Faculty Development, Education-General, Medical Education, Private Education (Precollege), Public Education (Precollege), Science/Mathematics Education, Secondary Education (Public), Student Aid, Vocational & Technical Education
Environment: Environment-General, Resource Conservation, Wildlife Protection
Health: Alzheimers Disease, Cancer, Children's Health/Hospitals, Diabetes, Emergency/Ambulance Services, Heart, Hospices
International: Foreign Educational Institutions

Religion: Churches, Religious Organizations, Religious Welfare
Social Services: Animal Protection, Community Service Organizations, Homes, People with Disabilities, Recreation & Athletics, Scouts, United Funds/United Ways, YMCA/YWCA/YMHA/YWHA, Youth Organizations

Application Procedures
Initial Contact: Send a brief letter of inquiry.
Application Requirements: Include name, a description of organization, activities, financial statements, and purpose of funds sought.
Deadlines: None.

Restrictions
Emphasis is on medical, religious, environmental, and educational organizations.

Foundation Officials
Jennifer L. Malmberg: treasurer, secretary
Jennifer L. Moyle: secretary/treasurer
Katherine P. Moyle: director
Elizabeth H. Robinson: president, treasurer
Richard M. Robinson: vice president B 1937. ED Harvard University AB (1959). PRIM CORP EMPL chairman, president, chief executive officer, director: Scholastic. CORP AFFIL chairman, president, chief executive officer: SI Holdings.
Susan K. Stoneman: director
George V. Strong, Jr.: secretary

Grants Analysis
Disclosure Period: calendar year ending 2001
Total Grants: $239,100
Number of Grants: 40
Average Grant: $5,978
Highest Grant: $30,000
Lowest Grant: $250
Typical Range: $1,000 to $10,000

Recent Grants
Note: Grants derived from 2001 Form 990.

General

30,000	Community Systems, Bozeman, MT
30,000	Henricus Foundation, Chesterfield, VA
25,000	Lyles Baptist Church, Palmyra, VA
19,000	Salisbury State University, Salisbury, MD
15,000	Cornell Institute for Medical Research, Cherry Hill, NJ
12,500	Naval War College Foundation, Newport, RI
11,000	Dorchester County Historical Society, Cambridge, MD
10,500	Sloan Kettering Cancer Center, New York, NY
10,000	Harvard College, Cambridge, MA
7,500	Campbell University, Buies Creek, NC

E. L. WIEGAND FOUNDATION

Giving Contact
Kristen A. Avansino, President & Executive Director
Wiegand Center
165 West Liberty Street, Suite 200
Reno, NV 89501
Phone: (775)333-0310
Fax: (775)333-0314

Description
Founded: 1982
EIN: 942839372
Organization Type: General Purpose Foundation
Giving Locations: AZ; CA: Northern California; DC: Washington; ID; NV; NY: New York; OR; UT; WA

Grant Types: Project.
Note: Foundation also awards equipment grants.

Donor Information
Founder: Edwin L. Wiegand was born in Dover, OH, in 1891. He experimented with electricity as a boy and concluded that the use of electricity for heating afforded the most important growth potential for the future. In 1915, he obtained his first patent on a metal-sheathed, refractory-insulated electric heating element, and two years later founded the Edwin L. Wiegand Company in Pittsburgh. In a small room with one employee, he manufactured the first successful resistance heating units. Under the trade name "Chromalox," Mr. Wiegand developed and manufactured heating elements for home appliances and industrial uses that are still the heart of many electric appliances today. In 1968, he merged his company with Emerson Electric Company of St. Louis, MO. He moved to Reno, NV, in 1971 and became an active participant in Miami Oil Producers, especially in their development of oil and gas properties. He served on the Miami board until his death at the age of 88.

The foundation was established in 1982 for general charitable purposes. To foster the religious beliefs of E.L. Wiegand, a part of the annual grants are made to Roman Catholic charitable institutions.

Financial Summary
Total Giving: $5,195,200 (fiscal year ending October 31, 2001); $5,100,000 (fiscal 1999 approx); $4,756,301 (fiscal 1998)
Giving Analysis: Giving for fiscal 1998 includes: foundation scholarships ($35,000)
Assets: $116,894,557 (fiscal 2001); $110,000,000 (fiscal 1999 approx); $106,415,022 (fiscal 1998)
Gifts Received: $40,000 (fiscal 1999 approx); $199,657 (fiscal 1998); $24,998 (fiscal 1997 approx)

Typical Recipients
Arts & Humanities: Arts Associations & Councils, Arts Festivals, Ballet, Ethnic & Folk Arts, Film & Video, Arts & Humanities-General, Historic Preservation, History & Archaeology, Libraries, Museums/Galleries, Music, Opera, Performing Arts, Public Broadcasting, Theater
Civic & Public Affairs: Botanical Gardens/Parks, Civil Rights, Economic Policy, Civic & Public Affairs-General, Hispanic Affairs, Law & Justice, Legal Aid, Public Policy, Safety
Education: Agricultural Education, Arts/Humanities Education, Business Education, Colleges & Universities, Education Associations, Elementary Education (Private), Environmental Education, Faculty Development, Education-General, International Exchange, International Studies, Legal Education, Medical Education, Private Education (Precollege), Public Education (Precollege), Religious Education, Science/Mathematics Education, Secondary Education (Private), Secondary Education (Public), Social Sciences Education, Student Aid
Health: Alzheimers Disease, Cancer, Children's Health/Hospitals, Clinics/Medical Centers, Diabetes, Health-General, Health Organizations, Heart, Hospitals, Long-Term Care, Medical Research, Nursing Services, Prenatal Health Issues, Public Health, Respiratory, Single-Disease Health Associations
International: Health Care/Hospitals, Human Rights, International Affairs, Missionary/Religious Activities
Religion: Churches, Dioceses, Religion-General, Religion-General, Religious Organizations, Religious Welfare, Seminaries
Science: Science Museums, Scientific Organizations, Scientific Research
Social Services: Camps, Community Centers, Community Service Organizations, People with Disabilities, Recreation & Athletics, Scouts, Special Olympics, Substance Abuse, YMCA/YWCA/YMHA/YWHA, Youth Organizations

Application Procedures

Initial Contact: Submit a letter of inquiry describing the organization and the proposed request. After a review by foundation staff, a select group is invited to submit a full proposal.

Application Requirements: An original Application for Grant form, a concise description of the project, an itemized budget for the project, project starting date and schedule, qualifications of key personnel, a brief history of the institution, a list of officers and their affiliations, the name of any employee or officer of the foundation who is associated with the applicant, a copy of the IRS tax-exempt determination letter, a copy of current documentary evidence from the organization's state classifying the applicant as tax-exempt, a copy of the most recent 990, current audited financial statements, current interim financial statements, a financial budget for the current year, a statement of the applicant's major sources of support for the last five years, and an indication of how the program will be evaluated upon its completion. All proposals must be in a typewritten format.

Deadlines: Letters of inquiry are accepted throughout the year. Submission deadlines vary depending on the date of the meeting. Upon receiving the Application for Grant Form, applicants are notified of deadlines.

Review Process: Applications are reviewed by the staff and the executive advisory committee before being submitted to the board of trustees. The board meets three times a year, generally in February, June and October. The applicant will be notified if additional information, an interview, or a site inspection is required during the review process.

Restrictions

Grants will not be given for the following purposes: endowments; debt retirement or operating deficits; general, ordinary, and normal operations or their extension, including the repair and maintenance of facilities; emergency funding; general fundraising events, appeals, campaigns, dinners, or mass mailings; loans; distribution of funds to beneficiaries; the influence of legislation or elections; multi-year grants; institutions that use funds to support other institutions; production of documentaries, publications, films, or media presentations; religious institutions for the construction or restoration of buildings; or to institutions that have been in existence for less than five years; federal, state, or local government agencies or institutions; institutions supported by public tax funds; institutions served by the United Way; or individuals.

Additional Information

There are specific geographic restrictions for program areas. Education grants are considered in Nevada, Northern California, Oregon, Idaho, Utah, Washington, and Arizona. Health and medical research grants are considered in Nevada, California, Oregon, Idaho, Utah, and Arizona. Public affairs grants are made in Nevada, California, District of Columbia, and New York City. Civic and community affairs grants are considered in Nevada and California. Arts and cultural affairs grants are also considered in Nevada and California.

A portion of the foundation's fund balance is held as a special fund for the benefit of Roman Catholic charitable organizations.

Publications: Informational Booklet; Application Form; Guidelines

Foundation Officials

Kristen A. Avansino: president, executive director
Raymond C. Avansino, Jr.: chairman, trustee B 1944. PRIM CORP EMPL president, chief operating officer, director: Conrad International Hotels Corp.
James T. Carrico: treasurer
Frank Joseph Fahrenkopf, Jr.: trustee B Brooklyn, NY 1939. ED University of Nevada BA (1962); University of California at Berkeley JD (1965). PRIM CORP EMPL partner, attorney: Hogan & Hartson. NONPR

AFFIL member: Washoe County Bar Association; director: Washoe County Legal Aid Society; director: Babe Ruth Baseball League; member: Northern Nevada Trial Lawyers Association; director: Reno YWCA; director: Nevada Opera Guild; member: Nevada Bar Association; director: Nevada Cancer Society; trustee: National Judicial College Council Future; co-chairman: National Commission Presidential Debates; faculty member: National Judicial College; member: Executives Association Reno; member: National Association Gaming Attorneys; member: Commercial Law League America; member: American Trial Lawyers Association; vice chairman: Center Democracy; president, chief executive officer: American Gaming Association; member: American Judicature Society; member, chairman Coalition for Justice: American Bar Association; member: Alpha Tau Omega. CLUB AFFIL Barristers NV Club.

Harvey C. Fruehauf, Jr.: trustee B Grosse Pointe Park, MI 1929. ED University of Michigan (1952). PRIM CORP EMPL president, director: HCF Enterprises Inc. CORP AFFIL president, treasurer, director: HCF Realty Inc.; chairman, president: Miami Oil Producers Inc.; director: Georgia-Pacific Corp.

Mario Joseph Gabelli: trustee B New York, NY 1942. ED Fordham University BS (1965); Columbia University MBA (1967). PRIM CORP EMPL founder, chairman: Gabelli & Co. CORP AFFIL director: Spinnaker Industries Inc.; director, principal: Lynch Michigan Tele Holding Corp.; chairman: Gamco Investors Inc.; chairman, chief executive officer, director: Lynch Corp.; president: Gabelli Funds Inc.; chairman: Gabelli Securities Inc.; chief investment officer: Gabelli Associates Fund; chairman, president, chief executive officer: Gabelli Equity Trust Inc. NONPR AFFIL director: American Stock Exchange Inc.

Michael J. Melarkey: vice president, secretary
Tina Marie Miller: assistant to president

Grants Analysis

Disclosure Period: fiscal year ending October 31, 2001
Total Grants: $5,192,700*
Number of Grants: 68
Average Grant: $65,498*
Highest Grant: $250,000
Lowest Grant: $1,000
Typical Range: $25,000 to $100,000
***Note:** Giving excludes scholarships. Average grant figure excludes four highest grants ($1,000,800).

Recent Grants

Note: Grants derived from 2001 Form 990.

General

250,800	Bourgarde Catholic High School, Phoenix, AZ -- performing arts complex
250,000	Churchill Arts Council, Fallon, NV -- for theater furnishings
250,000	Nevada Ballet Theatre, Las Vegas, NV -- for Nutcracker production
250,000	Sisters of Our Lady of Mt. Carmel, Reno, NV -- printshop expansion and dormitory extension
227,000	MD Anderson Cancer Center, Houston, TX -- for medical equipment
225,000	Fourth Ward School, Virginia City, NV -- for assembly and performance hall
205,000	DeSales Catholic School, Walla Walla, WA -- science classroom expansion
200,000	Sacred Hearts Academy, Honolulu, HI -- for science lab
200,000	St. Michael's High School, Santa Fe, NM -- for technology network
200,000	University of Nevada Reno Foundation Women's Athletics, Reno, NV -- for facility furnishings and program enhancement

E. F. WILDERMUTH FOUNDATION

Giving Contact

Robert W. Lee, Treasurer
1014 Dublin Rd.
Columbus, OH 43215-1116
Phone: (614)487-0040

Description

Founded: 1962
EIN: 316050202
Organization Type: Private Foundation
Giving Locations: IN; KY; MI; OH; PA; WV
Grant Types: General Support.

Financial Summary

Total Giving: $253,000 (2002); $268,500 (2001); $350,500 (2000)
Assets: $4,808,732 (2002); $6,015,231 (2001); $6,946,812 (2000)
Gifts Received: $50,000 (1997)

Typical Recipients

Arts & Humanities: Ballet, Dance, History & Archaeology, Libraries, Music, Public Broadcasting
Civic & Public Affairs: Civic & Public Affairs-General
Education: Arts/Humanities Education, Business Education, Colleges & Universities, Medical Education, Minority Education, Public Education (Precollege)
Health: Children's Health/Hospitals, Clinics/Medical Centers, Eyes/Blindness, Health-General, Health Organizations, Heart, Hospitals, Mental Health, Single-Disease Health Associations
Religion: Churches, Religion-General, Religious Organizations
Social Services: Animal Protection, Big Brother/Big Sister, Child Welfare, Community Service Organizations, Counseling, People with Disabilities, Youth Organizations

Application Procedures

Initial Contact: The foundation has no formal grant application procedure or application form. Send a brief letter of inquiry.
Application Requirements: Include purpose of funds sought and proof of tax-exempt status.
Deadlines: August 1.

Restrictions

The foundation prefers to fund organizations in Ohio and its contiguous states.

Foundation Officials

Karl Borton: vice president
Thomas Borton: trustee
J. Patrick Campbell: chairman, president
Genevieve Connable: vice president
Bettie A. Kalb: president, secretary
Robert W. Lee: treasurer
David T. Patterson: vice president, legal counsel
Philip N. Phillipson: trustee
Harriet Slaughter: trustee

Grants Analysis

Disclosure Period: calendar year ending 2002
Total Grants: $253,000
Number of Grants: 20
Average Grant: $6,833*
Highest Grant: $75,000
Lowest Grant: $3,000
Typical Range: $5,000 to $30,000
***Note:** Average grant figure excludes two highest grants ($130,000).

Recent Grants

Note: Grants derived from 2002 Form 990.

Library-Related

3,000	Ohioana Library, Columbus, OH

General

75,000	Ballet Metropolitan, Columbus, OH
55,000	Ohio State University Optometry, Columbus, OH
40,000	Wildermuth Community Church, Carroll, OH
30,000	Pennsylvania College of Optometry, Elkins Park, PA
10,000	Buckeye Ranch, Columbus, OH
10,000	Children's Hospital, Boston, MA
10,000	Illinois College of Optometry, Urbana, IL
10,000	Indiana University, Indianapolis, IN
8,000	Kalamazoo College, Kalamazoo, MI
7,500	Community of Holy Rosary St. John, Columbus, OH

JOHN WILEY & SONS, INC.

Company Headquarters

Hoboken, NJ
Web: http://www.wiley.com

Company Description

Ticker: JW
Exchange: OTC
Revenue: US$734.4 million (2002)
Employees: 3100 (2002)
SIC(s): 2721 Periodicals, 2731 Book Publishing.

Operating Locations

John Wiley & Sons (NY--New York)

Nonmonetary Support

Type: Donated Products
Volunteer Programs: Volunteerism is promoted through the Corporate ServiceMatch Program, through which the company provides small grants to organizations where employees volunteer (for 12 to 30 hours in six months, $250; for 30 or more hours, $500). Each employee is limited to two ServiceMatch grants per year.

Giving Contact

Deborah Wiley, Senior Vice President Corp. Comm.
John Wiley & Sons, Inc.
111 River Street
Hoboken, NJ 07030
Phone: (201)748-6000
Fax: (201)748-6940

Description

Organization Type: Corporate Giving Program
Giving Locations: headquarters area only.
Grant Types: Conference/Seminar, Employee Matching Gifts, General Support, Loan, Multiyear/Continuing Support.
Note: The company sponsors a matching gifts program for employee giving.

Financial Summary

Total Giving: $180,230 (fiscal year ending April 30, 2003 approx); $234,300 (fiscal 2002); $185,780 (fiscal 2001). Note: Figures do not include matching gifts or ServiceMatch Program.
Assets: $275,259,000 (fiscal 2002)

Typical Recipients

Arts & Humanities: Ballet, Dance, Libraries, Museums/Galleries, Opera, Performing Arts, Public Broadcasting, Theater
Civic & Public Affairs: Botanical Gardens/Parks, Civil Rights, First Amendment Issues, Professional & Trade Associations, Zoos/Aquariums
Education: Arts/Humanities Education, Business Education, Colleges & Universities, Community & Junior Colleges, Continuing Education, Education Associations, Education Funds, Elementary Education (Private), Elementary Education (Public), Education-General, Legal Education, Literacy, Medical Education, Minority Education, Preschool Education, Private Education (Precollege), Public Education (Precollege), Science/Mathematics Education, Secondary Education (Private), Secondary Education (Public)
Environment: Resource Conservation, Wildlife Protection
Health: AIDS/HIV, Diabetes
Science: Science Museums, Scientific Centers & Institutes, Scientific Organizations
Social Services: Emergency Relief, Shelters/Homelessness

Application Procedures

Initial Contact: Send brief letter of inquiry. For ServiceMatch grants, employees should request application form.
Application Requirements: Include a description of organization, amount requested, purpose of funds sought, and proof of tax-exempt status.
Deadlines: None.

Restrictions

Does not support individuals, film projects, religious organizations for sectarian purposes, or political or lobbying groups. For ServiceMatch grants, support will not be made in lieu of tuition payments; in lieu of payment for tickets, subscription fees, or fundraising events; to provide benefit to the donor or a specified individual of more than a nominal value; to support political, religious, fraternal, social, or athletic organizations; to organizations for which service does not directly and in its entirety benefit the institution (e.g., United Way campaigns or community trusts); in lieu of personal tithes, pledges, or other financial commitments; to separately incorporated fundraising entities such as athletic funds, booster clubs, fraternities and sororities.

Additional Information

Contributions to education are made primarily through matching gift program.
Publications: Contributions Policy Statement

Corporate Officials

William J. Pesce: president, chief executive officer chief financial officer PRIM CORP EMPL president, chief executive officer: John Wiley & Sons.
Robert D. Wilder: executive vice president, chief financial officer PRIM CORP EMPL executive vice president, chief financial officer: John Wiley & Sons.
Bradford Wiley, II: chairman, director B Orange, NJ 1941. ED Columbia University (1965); Johns Hopkins University (1968). PRIM CORP EMPL chairman, director: John Wiley & Sons.
Deborah Wiley: chairman B 1946. ED Pine Manor College AA (1966); Boston University BA (1968); Harvard University (1983). PRIM CORP EMPL chairman: John Wiley & Sons.

Grants Analysis

Disclosure Period: fiscal year ending April 30, 2002
Total Grants: $234,300*
Number of Grants: 51
Average Grant: $4,594
Highest Grant: $20,000
Lowest Grant: $200
Typical Range: $500 to $2,500
*Note: Grants analysis provided by company.

Recent Grants

Note: Grants derived from fiscal 1998 Form 990.

Library-Related

New York Public Library, New York, NY

General

American Institute of Physics, College Park, MD

Association of College and Research Libraries, Newton, MA
Central Park Conservancy, New York, NY
Council for Aid to Education, New York, NY
Juvenile Diabetes Foundation, New York, NY
Library of Congress Center for the Book, Washington, DC
Museum of Modern Art, New York, NY
National Association of Biology Teachers, Reston, VA
Metropolitan Opera, New York, NY

WILKES, ARTIS, HEDRICK & LANE

Company Headquarters

1666 K St. NW, Ste. 1100
Washington, DC 20006

Operating Locations

Wilkes, Artis, Hedrick & Lane (DC--Washington)

Wilkes, Artis, Hedrick & Lane Foundation

Giving Contact

Stanley J. Fineman, President
1150 18th St. NW, Suite 400
Washington, DC 20036
Phone: (202)457-7800
Fax: (202)457-7814

Description

Founded: 1982
EIN: 521272246
Organization Type: Corporate Foundation
Grant Types: General Support.

Donor Information

Founder: Norman M. Glasgow, Sr., Albert L. Ledgard, Jr., Stanley J. Fineman, Whayne S. Quin, Allen Jones, Jr., Robert L. Gorham, Charles A. Camalier III, C. Francis Murphy, Maureen E. Dwyer, Joseph B. Whitebread, Jr.

Financial Summary

Total Giving: $11,450 (fiscal year ending September 30, 2001); $25,880 (fiscal 2000); $72,170 (fiscal 1998)
Assets: $38,479 (fiscal 2001); $48,011 (fiscal 2000); $65,255 (fiscal 1998)
Gifts Received: $51,434 (fiscal 1998); $60,275 (fiscal 1997); $65,364 (fiscal 1996). Note: In 1998, contributions were received from Stanley J. Fineman, Robert L. Gorham, Joseph B. Whitebread, Jr., Christopher H. Collins, Maureen E. Dwyer, Whayne S. Quin, Norman M. Glasglow, Jr., David M. Bond, and John D. Lane. In fiscal 1997, contributions were received from Stanley J. Fineman, Whayne S. Quin, and Robert L. Gorham.

Typical Recipients

Arts & Humanities: Arts Outreach, Historic Preservation, History & Archaeology, Libraries, Museums/Galleries, Opera
Civic & Public Affairs: Business/Free Enterprise, Clubs, Community Foundations, Economic Development, Employment/Job Training, Civic & Public Affairs-General, Housing, Law & Justice, Legal Aid, Parades/Festivals, Professional & Trade Associations, Public Policy, Urban & Community Affairs
Education: Colleges & Universities, International Studies, Legal Education, Secondary Education (Public), Student Aid
Environment: Environment-General

Health: Children's Health/Hospitals, Health-General, Heart, Hospitals, Prenatal Health Issues, Single-Disease Health Associations
Religion: Churches, Jewish Causes, Religious Welfare
Science: Scientific Organizations
Social Services: Community Service Organizations, Family Services, Food/Clothing Distribution, People with Disabilities, Recreation & Athletics, Scouts, Substance Abuse, United Funds/United Ways

Application Procedures

Initial Contact: The foundation has no formal grant application procedure or application form., send a brief letter of inquiry.
Deadlines: None.

Restrictions

Supports only public charities.

Corporate Officials

Stanley J. Fineman: partner PRIM CORP EMPL partner: Wilkes Artis Hedrick & Lane.
Norman M. Glasgow, Jr.: partner PRIM CORP EMPL partner: Wilkes Artis Hedrick & Lane.
Robert L. Gorham: managing partner PRIM CORP EMPL managing partner: Wilkes Artis Hedrick & Lane.
John Salisbury: chief operating officer PRIM CORP EMPL chief operating officer: Wilkes Artis Hedrick & Lane.

Foundation Officials

Charles A. Camalier: vice president, director
Stanley J. Fineman: vice president, director (see above)
Norman M. Glasgow, Jr.: vice president, director (see above)
Robert L. Gorham: president, director (see above)
Eric S. Kassoff: secretary, treasurer, director
Whayne S. Quin: secretary, director
Joseph B. Whitebread, Jr.: treasurer, director

Grants Analysis

Disclosure Period: fiscal year ending September 30, 2001
Total Grants: $11,450
Number of Grants: 12
Average Grant: $586*
Highest Grant: $5,000
Lowest Grant: $100
Typical Range: $200 to $1,000
*Note: Average grant figure excludes highest grant.

Recent Grants

Note: Grants derived from fiscal 2000 Form 990.

General

12,600	DC Bar Public Service Activities Corp, Washington, DC
2,500	Shaw Community Center Food Committee, Washington, DC
1,500	American Heart Association, Washington, DC
1,000	Anti-Defamation League, Washington, DC
1,000	Easter Seal Society, Laytonsville, MD
1,000	H Street Community Development Corporation, Washington, DC
1,000	Jewish Foundation for Group Homes, Rockville, MD
1,000	Rotary Foundation of Washington, DC, Washington, DC
500	Amyotrophic Lateral Sclerosis Association, Washington, DC
500	Baptist Home for Children, Bethesda, MD

EDWARD AND RUTH WILKOF FOUNDATION

Giving Contact

Harry Mestel, President
116 Cleveland Ave. NW, Suite 525
Canton, OH 44702
Phone: (330)452-9788

Description

Founded: 1987
EIN: 341536119
Organization Type: Private Foundation
Giving Locations: FL: Sarasota; OH
Grant Types: General Support.

Donor Information

Founder: Edward and Ruth Wilkof

Financial Summary

Total Giving: $358,450 (fiscal year ending June 30, 2002); $219,684 (fiscal 2001); $232,800 (fiscal 1999)
Giving Analysis: Giving for fiscal 2002 includes: foundation grants to United Way ($10,000); fiscal 2001: foundation grants to United Way ($5,000) fiscal 1999: foundation grants to United Way ($10,000)
Assets: $1,735,368 (fiscal 2002); $1,958,975 (fiscal 2001); $2,095,594 (fiscal 1999)
Gifts Received: $54,750 (fiscal 2002); $28,000 (fiscal 2001); $2,400 (fiscal 1999). Note: In 1999, 2000, and 2002, contributions were received from Edward Wilkof. In fiscal 1990, contributions were received from Edward and Ruth Wilkof.

Typical Recipients

Arts & Humanities: Arts Centers, Arts Funds, Ballet, Libraries, Museums/Galleries, Music, Opera, Performing Arts
Civic & Public Affairs: Clubs, Economic Development, Civic & Public Affairs-General, Philanthropic Organizations, Urban & Community Affairs
Education: Arts/Humanities Education, Colleges & Universities, Education Associations, Education Funds, Private Education (Precollege), Religious Education, Student Aid, Vocational & Technical Education
Environment: Resource Conservation
Health: Clinics/Medical Centers, Emergency/Ambulance Services, Medical Research, Research/Studies Institutes
International: Foreign Educational Institutions, International Peace & Security Issues, Missionary/Religious Activities
Religion: Jewish Causes, Religious Organizations, Religious Welfare, Synagogues/Temples
Social Services: Child Welfare, Community Service Organizations, Day Care, Family Services, Food/Clothing Distribution, United Funds/United Ways, Volunteer Services, Youth Organizations

Application Procedures

Initial Contact: Send a brief letter of inquiry. Send complete information and material relating to request.
Deadlines: None.

Restrictions

Donee must have tax-exempt status by IRS determination.

Foundation Officials

Frank H. Harvey, Jr.: secretary, treasurer
Harry Mestel: president
Michael Sweeney: secretary, treasurer
Richard Wilkof: trustee

Grants Analysis

Disclosure Period: fiscal year ending June 30, 2002
Total Grants: $348,450*
Number of Grants: 44

Average Grant: $5,725*
Highest Grant: $63,000
Lowest Grant: $300
Typical Range: $1,000 to $10,000
*Note: Giving excludes United Way. Average grant figure excludes two highest grants ($108,000).

Recent Grants

Note: Grants derived from fiscal 2000 Form 990.

General

30,000	Sarasota/Manatee Jewish Federation, Sarasota, FL
22,000	Van Wezel Foundation, Sarasota, FL
15,000	Canton Jewish Community Federation, Canton, OH
15,000	Cleveland Orchestra, Cleveland, OH
10,233	Walsh University, Canton, OH
10,000	Florida West Coast Symphony, Sarasota, FL
7,500	Sarasota Memorial Hospital Foundation, Sarasota, FL
5,000	Baylor University Memorial Foundation, Dallas, TX
5,000	Sarasota Child Development Center, Sarasota, FL
5,000	United Way of Central Stark County, Canton, OH

CECILIA YOUNG WILLARD HELPING FUND

Giving Contact

Nancy F. May, Vice President, Trust Officer
c/o Broadway National Bank, Trust Div.
PO Box 17001
San Antonio, TX 78217
Phone: (210)283-6700

Description

Founded: 1987
EIN: 746350893
Organization Type: Private Foundation
Giving Locations: NC
Grant Types: General Support, Operating Expenses, Project.

Donor Information

Founder: Celia Young Willard Trust

Financial Summary

Total Giving: $394,862 (fiscal year ending May 31, 2002); $433,468 (fiscal 2001); $438,414 (fiscal 2000)
Assets: $5,863,804 (fiscal 2002); $6,887,266 (fiscal 2001); $7,564,775 (fiscal 2000)

Typical Recipients

Arts & Humanities: Arts Associations & Councils, Arts Institutes, Community Arts, History & Archaeology, Libraries, Museums/Galleries, Music, Public Broadcasting
Civic & Public Affairs: Community Foundations, Civic & Public Affairs-General, Hispanic Affairs, Housing, Municipalities/Towns, Rural Affairs, Safety
Education: Colleges & Universities, Education-General, Legal Education, Literacy, Medical Education, Private Education (Precollege)
Environment: Environment-General, Resource Conservation, Wildlife Protection
Health: AIDS/HIV, Alzheimers Disease, Cancer, Eyes/Blindness, Health Funds, Heart, Hospices, Hospitals, Long-Term Care, Nursing Services, Prenatal Health Issues
Religion: Churches, Religious Organizations, Religious Welfare
Science: Scientific Centers & Institutes
Social Services: Child Welfare, Community Service Organizations, Family Services, Homes, People with

Disabilities, Senior Services, Volunteer Services, Youth Organizations

Application Procedures

Initial Contact: Send a brief letter of inquiry.
Application Requirements: Include a description of organization, amount requested, purpose of funds sought, proof of tax-exempt status
Deadlines: June 1.

Restrictions

Does not support individuals or political or lobbying groups.

Additional Information

Trust(s): Broadway Natl Bank

Grants Analysis

Disclosure Period: fiscal year ending May 31, 2002
Total Grants: $394,862
Number of Grants: 33
Average Grant: $10,152*
Highest Grant: $70,000
Lowest Grant: $1,000
Typical Range: $5,000 to $20,000
*Note: Average grant figure excludes highest grant.

Recent Grants

Note: Grants derived from 2000 Form 990.

Library-Related

20,000	Comfort Public Library, Inc., Comfort, TX
10,000	Friends of Crockett County Library Inc., Ozona, TX
10,000	New Braunfels Public Library Foundation, New Braunfels, TX

General

60,000	Pickersgill Retirement Community, Towson, MD
50,000	Lenoir-Rhyne College, Hickory, NC
42,292	First Presbyterian Church, Hickory, NC
30,000	Any Baby Can, San Antonio, TX
25,374	Crossnore School, Crossnore, NC
25,374	Grandfather Home for Children, Banner Elk, NC
25,374	Lees-McRae College, Banner Elk, NC
20,000	House of Ruth, Baltimore, MD
15,000	Southwest Texas State University, San Marcos, TX
10,000	Boys Hope Girls Hope, San Antonio, TX

John C. Williams Charitable Trust

Giving Contact

Roberta McCann, Senior Vice President
John C. Williams Charitable Trust
Care of PNC Bank NA
620 Liberty Avenue
Pittsburgh, PA 15222-2705
Phone: (412)762-3779
Fax: (412)762-5439
E-mail: roberta.mccann@pncbank.com

Description

Founded: 1936
EIN: 256024153
Organization Type: Private Foundation
Giving Locations: OH: Steubenville; WV: Weirton
Grant Types: Capital, General Support, Matching, Project, Seed Money.

Donor Information

Founder: the late John C. Williams

Financial Summary

Total Giving: $400,000 (2002 approx); $407,561 (2001); $364,237 (2000). Note: Trust donates 5% of its market value annually.
Assets: $7,405,098 (2001); $8,214,348 (2000); $8,833,121 (1999)

Typical Recipients

Arts & Humanities: Historic Preservation, History & Archaeology, Libraries, Music, Visual Arts
Civic & Public Affairs: Civic & Public Affairs-General, Housing
Education: Colleges & Universities, Community & Junior Colleges, Private Education (Precollege), Science/Mathematics Education
Health: Clinics/Medical Centers, Emergency/Ambulance Services, Health-General, Hospitals, Medical Rehabilitation, Prenatal Health Issues
Religion: Ministries, Religious Welfare
Social Services: Community Centers, Community Service Organizations, Family Planning, Family Services, Homes, People with Disabilities, Recreation & Athletics, Shelters/Homelessness, YMCA/YWCA/YMHA/YWHA, Youth Organizations

Application Procedures

Initial Contact: Send a brief letter of inquiry and a full proposal.
Application Requirements: Include proof of tax-exempt status, latest annual operating budget, recently audited financial statement, amount requested, a description of organization, central planning agency report, history of previous William support and purpose of funds sought.
Deadlines: None.

Restrictions

Grants are not made to individuals, political or lobbying groups, or organizations outside operating areas.

Additional Information

Trust(s): PNC Advisors

Grants Analysis

Disclosure Period: calendar year ending 2001
Total Grants: $407,561
Number of Grants: 8
Average Grant: $43,223*
Highest Grant: $105,000
Lowest Grant: $10,500
Typical Range: $25,000 to $75,000
*Note: Average grant figure excludes highest grant.

Recent Grants

Note: Grants derived from 2000 Form 990.

General

100,000	Brooke Hancock Family Recourse Network, Weirton, WV -- construction of a soccer complex
50,000	All Saints School, Steubenville, OH -- renovation of unused basement room
50,000	Martha Cochrance McConville Home for Aged Women, Steubenville, OH -- restoration and repair of the building
47,900	Weirton Regional Campus, Weirton, WV -- to expand the campus's computer assisted developmental lab facilities
30,000	Northern Panhandle Headstart, Inc., Weirton, WV -- construct a new building to house Head Start children in Weirton Heights
26,000	American Red Cross, Steubenville, OH -- to purchase 2001 passenger van
25,000	AIM Pregnancy Center, Steubenville, OH -- to provide increased safety and comfort for clients

15,337	Catholic Community Center, Steubenville, OH -- to refinish and refurbish gym floor and upgrade public restrooms
10,000	Change, Inc., Weirton, WV -- to renovate a portion of their building to create a second exam room, pharmaceutical room and dental facility
10,000	Women's Health Center of Jefferson County, Steubenville, OH -- to continue to service medically indigent, low income, uninsured/underinsured women and men

Mary Jo Williams Charitable Trust

Giving Contact

Michael E. Collins, Trustee
607 N. 7th
Garden City, KS 67846
Phone: (620)276-3203
Fax: (620)276-3300

Description

Founded: 1988
EIN: 486276428
Organization Type: Private Foundation
Giving Locations: KS: Garden City
Grant Types: Emergency, Endowment, General Support, Scholarship.

Financial Summary

Total Giving: $232,798 (2000); $247,052 (1999); $190,977 (1998)
Giving Analysis: Giving for 1999 includes: foundation grants to United Way ($12,000) 1998: foundation grants to United Way ($12,000)
Assets: $3,723,871 (2000); $3,359,472 (1999); $3,423,394 (1998)

Typical Recipients

Arts & Humanities: Libraries, Music, Public Broadcasting
Civic & Public Affairs: Housing, Professional & Trade Associations, Zoos/Aquariums
Education: Arts/Humanities Education, Community & Junior Colleges, Education Funds, Faculty Development, Education-General, Preschool Education, Public Education (Precollege), Science/Mathematics Education, Student Aid
Environment: Environment-General, Resource Conservation
Health: Emergency/Ambulance Services
Religion: Ministries, Religious Welfare
Social Services: At-Risk Youth, Community Service Organizations, Crime Prevention, Emergency Relief, Food/Clothing Distribution, Senior Services, Shelters/Homelessness, United Funds/United Ways, Veterans, YMCA/YWCA/YMHA/YWHA, Youth Organizations

Application Procedures

Initial Contact: Send a brief letter of inquiry.
Deadlines: None.

Restrictions

Grants are considered for the prevention of cruelty to children and animals. The foundation does not support athletics or athletic competitions.

Foundation Officials

Michael E. Collins: trustee
Leonard Rich: trustee
Jack Williamson: trustee

Grants Analysis

Disclosure Period: calendar year ending 2000
Total Grants: $232,798
Number of Grants: 12

Average Grant: $12,425*
Highest Grant: $59,548
Typical Range: $5,000 to $25,000
*Note: Average grant excludes two highest grants ($108,548).

Recent Grants

Note: Grants derived from 1999 Form 990.

Library-Related

15,000	Finney County Public Library, Garden City, KS -- for education - computer and software for public use

General

75,000	Salvation Army, Garden City, KS -- for aid to the needy
61,000	Nature Conservancy, Topeka, KS
52,500	Mexican American Ministry, Garden City, KS -- for aid to the needy
30,063	Garden City Community College, Garden City, KS -- endowment of reading
25,000	Friends of Lee Richardson Zoo, Garden City, KS -- for education
20,000	Emmaus House, Garden City, KS -- for food and aid to the needy
12,000	Finney County United Way, Garden City, KS -- for various charities
11,610	KANZA Society, Garden City, KS -- for public radio
10,000	Kansas Disaster Services, Newton, KS -- for aid to disaster victims
2,000	Garden City Civic Choral Union, Garden City, KS -- for education

WILLIAMS COMPANIES INC.

Company Headquarters

One Williams Center
Tulsa, OK 74172
Web: http://www.williams.com

Company Description

Ticker: WMB
Exchange: NYSE
Former Name: Transco Energy Co.
Assets: US$34.988 billion (2002)
Employees: 7300 (2002)
Fortune Rank: 196, per FORTUNE Magazine's list of 500 Largest U.S. Corporations (2002).
SIC(s): 1221 Bituminous Coal & Lignite--Surface, 1222 Bituminous Coal--Underground, 1311 Crude Petroleum & Natural Gas, 5172 Petroleum Products Nec.

Operating Locations

Williams (MD; NJ; NY--New York; NC; OH--Lebanon; SC; TX--Houston; VA)

Nonmonetary Support

Type: In-kind Services; Loaned Executives; Workplace Solicitation

The Williams Companies Foundation

Giving Contact

Sylvia Schmidt, Director, Community Relations
One Williams Center
MD 49-3
Tulsa, OK 74172
Phone: (918)573-2106
E-mail: communityrelationstulsa@williams.com
Web: http://www.williams.com/community/

Description

EIN: 237413843
Organization Type: Corporate Foundation
Giving Locations: areas near company headquarters and operating communities.
Grant Types: Capital, Employee Matching Gifts, Endowment, General Support.

Financial Summary

Total Giving: $1,293,942 (2001); $4,806,950 (2000); $6,000,000 (1998 approx). Note: Contributes through corporate direct giving program and foundation.
Giving Analysis: Giving for 2000 includes: foundation scholarships ($200,000); foundation ($4,606,950); 1998: corporate grants to United Way (approx $6,000,000) 1996: corporate direct giving (approx $6,423,000)
Assets: $16,408,829 (2001); $16,068,935 (2000); $20,951,556 (1998)
Gifts Received: $5,000,000 (1995). Note: The foundation receives contributions from The Williams Companies.

Typical Recipients

Arts & Humanities: Arts Associations & Councils, Arts Centers, Arts Institutes, Dance, Historic Preservation, History & Archaeology, Libraries, Museums/Galleries, Music, Opera, Performing Arts, Theater
Civic & Public Affairs: African American Affairs, Botanical Gardens/Parks, Business/Free Enterprise, Clubs, Economic Development, Housing, Law & Justice, Legal Aid, Philanthropic Organizations, Professional & Trade Associations, Public Policy, Rural Affairs, Safety, Urban & Community Affairs, Women's Affairs, Zoos/Aquariums
Education: Afterschool/Enrichment Programs, Agricultural Education, Arts/Humanities Education, Business Education, Colleges & Universities, Community & Junior Colleges, Economic Education, Education Associations, Education Funds, Elementary Education (Private), Education-General, Private Education (Precollege), Public Education (Precollege), Science/Mathematics Education, Secondary Education (Private), Student Aid
Environment: Environment-General, Resource Conservation, Wildlife Protection
Health: AIDS/HIV, Children's Health/Hospitals, Clinics/Medical Centers, Health Funds, Health Organizations, Hospitals, Prenatal Health Issues, Single-Disease Health Associations
International: International Relations
Religion: Social/Policy Issues
Science: Science Exhibits & Fairs, Scientific Organizations
Social Services: At-Risk Youth, Child Welfare, Community Service Organizations, Crime Prevention, Domestic Violence, Emergency Relief, Family Planning, Family Services, Food/Clothing Distribution, Homes, People with Disabilities, Recreation & Athletics, Shelters/Homelessness, Substance Abuse, United Funds/United Ways, YMCA/YWCA/YMHA/YWHA, Youth Organizations

Application Procedures

Initial Contact: Send a brief letter and one copy of a full proposal.
Application Requirements: Include a description of organization, amount requested, purpose of funds sought, recently audited financial statement, and proof of tax-exempt status.
Deadlines: None; board meets in June and December.
Decision Notification: Usually within two weeks of receipt of request.

Restrictions

Does not support fraternal organizations, goodwill advertising, individuals, political or lobbying groups, or religious organizations for sectarian purposes.

Additional Information

Williams Companies acquired Mapco Inc. in 1998/1999.

Grants Analysis

Disclosure Period: calendar year ending 2001
Total Grants: $1,293,942
Number of Grants: 1

Recent Grants

Note: Grants derived from 2001 Form 990.

General

1,293,942	Tulsa Community Foundation, Tulsa, OK

WILLIAMS FAMILY FOUNDATION OF GEORGIA

Giving Contact

Thomas L. Williams, III, President & Director
Williams Family Foundation of Georgia
PO Box 378
Thomasville, GA 31799
Phone: (912)226-8320

Description

Founded: 1980
EIN: 581414850
Organization Type: Private Foundation
Giving Locations: GA: Thomasville
Grant Types: General Support.

Donor Information

Founder: Diane W. Parker, Marguerite N. Williams, Thomas L. Williams III, the late Bennie G. Williams

Financial Summary

Total Giving: $3,279,533 (fiscal year ending November 30, 2000); $577,300 (fiscal 1998); $792,033 (fiscal 1997). Note: 1997 Giving includes United Way ($5,000).
Giving Analysis: Giving for fiscal 2000 includes: foundation grants to United Way ($5,000)
Assets: $71,466,634 (fiscal 2000); $14,755,253 (fiscal 1998); $11,719,234 (fiscal 1997)
Gifts Received: $24,048,556 (fiscal 2000); $311,533 (fiscal 1997); $45,087 (fiscal 1996). Note: In fiscal 2000, contributions were received from Marguerite Williams Estate. In fiscal 1996 and 1997, contributions were received from Bennie G. Williams Charitable Lead Trust.

Typical Recipients

Arts & Humanities: Arts Centers, Community Arts, Historic Preservation, History & Archaeology, Libraries, Museums/Galleries, Music, Public Broadcasting, Theater
Civic & Public Affairs: Botanical Gardens/Parks, Community Foundations, Civic & Public Affairs-General, Housing, Nonprofit Management, Philanthropic Organizations, Women's Affairs
Education: Colleges & Universities, Economic Education, Education-General, Medical Education, Private Education (Precollege), Public Education (Precollege), Science/Mathematics Education
Environment: Forestry, Environment-General, Resource Conservation, Wildlife Protection
Health: Arthritis, Cancer
International: Health Care/Hospitals
Religion: Churches, Religious Welfare
Science: Science Museums, Scientific Research
Social Services: Animal Protection, Camps, Community Centers, Community Service Organizations, Homes, People with Disabilities, Recreation & Athletics, United Funds/United Ways, YMCA/YWCA/YMHA/YWHA, Youth Organizations

Application Procedures

Initial Contact: Send a brief written letter of inquiry.
Application Requirements: Include amount requested, budget, purpose of funds sought, recently audited financial statement, and proof of tax-exempt status.
Deadlines: None.
Review Process: Board meets in May and November to review applications.

Restrictions

Preference given to education and historic preservation primarily in the Thomasville, GA, area.

Foundation Officials

Joseph E. Beverly: director
Frederick Eansor Cooper: director B Thomasville, GA 1942. ED Washington & Lee University BA (1964); University of Georgia JD (1967). PRIM CORP EMPL counsel: Jones, Day, Reavis & Pogue. CORP AFFIL chairman, chief executive officer: Cooper Smith. NONPR AFFIL member: Rotary; member executive committee: University GA Foundation.
Bernard Lanigan, Jr.: treasurer, director
Alston Parker: director
Diane W. Parker: vice president, director
Stephen T. Parker: director
Thomas W. Parker: director
Thomas H. Vann, Jr.: director
Marguerite N. Williams: secretary, director
Thomas L. Williams, III: president, director

Grants Analysis

Disclosure Period: fiscal year ending November 30, 2000
Total Grants: $3,279,533
Number of Grants: 65
Average Grant: $32,094*
Highest Grant: $1,225,500
Typical Range: $10,000 to $50,000
*Note: Average grant excludes highest grant.

Recent Grants

Note: Grants derived from fiscal 1999 Form 990.

Library-Related
5,500	Thomas County Public Library, Thomasville, GA

General
350,000	Boys & Girls Club of Thomas County, Thomasville, GA
111999	Alfred B MacClay State Gardens, Tallahassee, FL
100,000	National Trust for Historic Preservation, Washington, DC
50,000	Project Concern International, San Diego, CA
50,000	Sapelo Island Restoration Foundation, Atlanta, GA
50,000	Thomasville Music and Drama Troupe, Thomasville, GA
47,500	Thomas College, Thomasville, GA
44,000	Vashti Center, The, Thomasville, GA
40,000	Community Foundation of Southwest Georgia, Thomasville, GA
32,000	Thomasville Cultural Center, Thomasville, GA

WILLIS FAMILY FOUNDATION

Giving Contact

Jennie Willis-List, President & Directory
3522 Niblick Court
Denver, NC 28037-8016
Phone: (704)483-1997

Description

Founded: 1997
EIN: 562055841
Organization Type: Private Foundation
Giving Locations: Southeastern United States.
Grant Types: General Support.

Financial Summary

Total Giving: $81,905 (2001); $79,500 (2000); $52,183 (1999)
Assets: $1,194,448 (2001); $1,404,489 (2000); $2,104,233 (1999)
Gifts Received: $994,173 (1997). Note: In 1997, contributions were received from James Richard Willis.

Typical Recipients

Arts & Humanities: Libraries
Civic & Public Affairs: Civic & Public Affairs-General
Education: Public Education (Precollege)
Religion: Ministries
Social Services: Community Service Organizations, YMCA/YWCA/YMHA/YWHA

Application Procedures

Initial Contact: Send in letter form.
Deadlines: None.

Foundation Officials

Michael Willis Good: director
Jeffery Ledward: secretary, director
Jennie List: secretary, director
Evelyn Sayer Willis: vice president, director
James Richard Willis: president, director

Grants Analysis

Disclosure Period: calendar year ending 2001
Total Grants: $81,905
Number of Grants: 7
Average Grant: $2,500*
Highest Grant: $66,905
Lowest Grant: $1,000
Typical Range: $1,000 to $5,000
*Note: Average grant figure excludes highest grant.

Recent Grants

Note: Grants derived from 2001 Form 990.

Library-Related
2,000	East Lincoln Library Fund, Denver, NC

General
66,905	New Direction Ministries, Mars Hill, NC
5,000	Echo, Ft. Myers, FL
3,000	Lee Middle School, Orlando, FL
2,500	Crown Financial Ministries, Gainesville, GA
1,500	Campus Crusade for Christ, Orlando, FL
1,000	YMCA of Greater Charlotte, Charlotte, NC

WILMINGTON TRUST CO.

Company Headquarters

2120 N. Market St.
Wilmington, DE 19802
Web: http://www.wilmingtontrust.com

Company Description

Ticker: WL
Exchange: NYSE
Assets: US$7.518 billion (2001)
SIC(s): 6000 Depository Institutions, 6700 Holding & Other Investment Offices.
Parent Company: Wilmington Trust Corp., Rodney Sq. N, 1100 N. Market Street, Wilmington, DE, United States

Operating Locations

Wilmington Trust Co. (DE--Wilmington)

Wilmington Trust Co. Foundation

Giving Contact

Tim McLaughlin, Corp. Contributions
1100 N. Market St.
Wilmington, DE 19890
Phone: (302)651-1462
Fax: (302)651-8717

Alternate Contact

Tim McCaughlin, Community Relations
Phone: (302)651-8624

Description

EIN: 516021540
Organization Type: Corporate Giving Program
Grant Types: General Support.

Donor Information

Founder: Wilmington Trust Co.

Financial Summary

Total Giving: $57,800 (1998); $87,000 (1992)
Assets: $55,764 (1996); $54,366 (1995); $52,775 (1994)
Gifts Received: $52,497 (1994); $90,392 (1992). Note: In 1992, contributions were received from Wilmington Trust Co.

Typical Recipients

Arts & Humanities: Arts Institutes, Community Arts, Libraries, Museums/Galleries, Music, Opera, Performing Arts, Public Broadcasting, Theater
Civic & Public Affairs: Economic Development, Employment/Job Training, Housing, Municipalities/Towns, Professional & Trade Associations, Public Policy, Zoos/Aquariums
Education: Colleges & Universities
Environment: Environment-General
Health: Clinics/Medical Centers, Health Funds, Health Organizations, Hospitals
Religion: Ministries
Social Services: At-Risk Youth, Community Centers, Community Service Organizations, Day Care, Recreation & Athletics, Senior Services, United Funds/United Ways, Youth Organizations

Application Procedures

Initial Contact: Send a brief letter of inquiry.
Application Requirements: Attach a description of organization including numbers served, purpose of funds sought, recently audited financial statement, operating budget, list of board of directors, funds raised to date and sources, and a list of other corporate support being solicited.
Deadlines: None.

Restrictions

Operating grants are not made to national fund drives, religious organizations for sectarian purposes, educational institutions, or united way agencies. Capital grants are not made to religious organizations for sectarian purposes or private, secondary schools.

Additional Information

Co. no longer gives through the Wilmington Trust Co. Foundation. Its corporate giving program is focused locally.

Corporate Officials

Beryl A. Barmore: vice president, chief operating officer PRIM CORP EMPL vice president: Wilmington Trust Co.

Ted T. Cecala, Jr.: chairman, chief executive officer B Trenton, NJ 1949. ED Florida State University (1971). PRIM CORP EMPL chairman, chief executive officer: Wilmington Trust Co.

David R. Gibson: chief financial officer PRIM CORP EMPL chief financial officer: Wilmington Trust Co.

Robert U. A. Harra, Jr.: president, chief operating officer PRIM CORP EMPL president, chief operating officer: Wilmington Trust Co.

WILSEY FOUNDATION

Giving Contact
Alfred S. Wilsey, Sr., President
Wilsey Foundation
PO Box 3532
San Francisco, CA 94119
Phone: (415)956-2229

Description
EIN: 946098720
Organization Type: Private Foundation
Giving Locations: CA: San Francisco Bay Area
Grant Types: Capital, Endowment, General Support, Scholarship.

Donor Information
Founder: Alfred Wilsey, Jr.

Financial Summary
Total Giving: $561,775 (fiscal year ending March 31, 2001); $335,350 (fiscal 2000); $396,000 (fiscal 1999)
Assets: $4,082,981 (fiscal 2001); $6,047,666 (fiscal 2000); $5,196,956 (fiscal 1999)
Gifts Received: $167,470 (fiscal 1997); $1,076,342 (fiscal 1995); $1,069,376 (fiscal 1994). Note: In fiscal 1997, contributions were received from M. Kathleen Behrens.

Typical Recipients
Arts & Humanities: Arts Centers, Ballet, Arts & Humanities-General, Historic Preservation, Libraries, Museums/Galleries, Music, Opera, Public Broadcasting, Theater
Civic & Public Affairs: Economic Development, Ethnic Organizations, Civic & Public Affairs-General
Education: Colleges & Universities, Continuing Education, Economic Education, Elementary Education (Private), Elementary Education (Public), Education-General, Private Education (Precollege), Religious Education, Secondary Education (Private), Secondary Education (Public)
Health: AIDS/HIV, Clinics/Medical Centers, Emergency/Ambulance Services, Hospitals, Single-Disease Health Associations
International: Missionary/Religious Activities
Religion: Churches, Dioceses, Religion-General, Religious Organizations, Religious Welfare
Social Services: At-Risk Youth, Community Centers, Community Service Organizations, Food/Clothing Distribution, Sexual Abuse, Shelters/Homelessness, Social Services-General, United Funds/United Ways, Volunteer Services, Youth Organizations

Application Procedures
Initial Contact: Apply in writing.
Deadlines: None.

Restrictions
Does not support individuals or political or lobbying groups.

Foundation Officials
Alfred S. Wilsey, Jr.: secretary, treasurer
Diane B. Wilsey: vice president
Michael W. Wilsey: vice president PRIM CORP EMPL chairman, president, director: Wilsey Bennet Co.

Grants Analysis
Disclosure Period: fiscal year ending March 31, 2001
Total Grants: $561,775
Number of Grants: 137
Average Grant: $3,395*
Highest Grant: $100,000
Typical Range: $500 to $5,000
*****Note:** Average grant figure excludes highest grant.

Recent Grants
Note: Grants derived from 2001 Form 990.

General
100,000	Archdiocese of San Francisco, San Francisco, CA
50,000	Archbishop Riordan High School, San Francisco, CA
50,000	University of San Francisco, San Francisco, CA
25,000	ALS Association, San Francisco, CA
25,000	American Center of Wine, Food, and the Arts, Napa, CA
25,000	Fine Arts Museums, San Francisco, CA
12,500	American Irish Fund, San Francisco, CA
10,000	Connecticut College, New London, CT
10,000	Dominican Sisters of Mission San Jose, Oakland, CA
10,000	San Francisco Planning and Urban Research Association (SPUR), San Francisco, CA

ANNE POTTER WILSON FOUNDATION

Giving Contact
Patrick Nelson, Trust Officer
Care of Bank of America
One Bank of America Plaza, M-7
Nashville, TN 37239-1697
Phone: (615)749-3916

Alternate Contact
231 S. LaSalle Street, IL1-231-14-19
Chicago, IL 60697

Description
Founded: 1996
EIN: 626306576
Organization Type: Private Foundation
Giving Locations: DC: Washington; TN: Nashville
Grant Types: General Support.

Donor Information
Founder: Established in 1996 with funds from the Justin and Valere Potter Foundation.

Financial Summary
Total Giving: $1,415,607 (2001); $583,130 (2000); $1,000,000 (1999)
Assets: $26,401,385 (2001); $30,425,343 (2000); $29,774,172 (1999)

Typical Recipients
Arts & Humanities: Historic Preservation, Libraries
Civic & Public Affairs: Botanical Gardens/Parks, Zoos/Aquariums
Education: Colleges & Universities, Secondary Education (Public)
Religion: Religious Welfare
Social Services: Community Service Organizations

Application Procedures
Initial Contact: Submit brief letter with description of organization qualifications, status, and copy of 501(c)(3) determination.
Deadlines: None.

Additional Information
Trust(s): Bank of America

Grants Analysis
Disclosure Period: calendar year ending 2001
Total Grants: $1,415,607
Number of Grants: 8
Average Grant: $59,372*
Highest Grant: $1,000,000
Lowest Grant: $15,000
Typical Range: $25,000 to $100,000
*****Note:** Average grant figure excludes highest grant.

Recent Grants
Note: Grants derived from 2001 Form 990.

Library-Related
50,607	Nashville Public Library, Nashville, TN

General
1,000,000	Vanderbilt University, Nashville, TN
100,000	Nashville Zoo, Nashville, TN
100,000	National Trust for Historic Preservation, Washington, DC
100,000	University School of Nashville, Nashville, TN
25,000	Cheekwood Tennessee Botanical Gardens and Museum of Art, Nashville, TN
25,000	Nashville Rescue Mission, Nashville, TN
15,000	Renewal House, Nashville, TN

H. W. WILSON FOUNDATION

Giving Contact
W. Joyce, III, President, Treasurer
950 University Ave.
Bronx, NY 10452
Phone: (718)588-8400

Description
Founded: 1952
EIN: 237418062
Organization Type: Private Foundation
Giving Locations: CA; DC: Washington; IL; NY; PA nationally.
Grant Types: Research, Scholarship.

Donor Information
Founder: the late H. W. Wilson, the late Mrs. H. W. Wilson, the H. W. Wilson Co.

Financial Summary
Total Giving: $802,600 (fiscal year ending November 30, 2000); $555,900 (fiscal 1999); $576,350 (fiscal 1998)
Giving Analysis: Giving for fiscal 1997 includes: foundation ($588,700)
Assets: $16,703,834 (fiscal 2000); $16,566,705 (fiscal 1999); $15,716,026 (fiscal 1998)

Typical Recipients
Arts & Humanities: Arts Associations & Councils, Dance, Historic Preservation, History & Archaeology, Libraries, Museums/Galleries, Public Broadcasting
Civic & Public Affairs: Botanical Gardens/Parks, Civic & Public Affairs-General, Legal Aid, Nonprofit Management, Public Policy, Urban & Community Affairs, Zoos/Aquariums
Education: Afterschool/Enrichment Programs, Colleges & Universities, Community & Junior Colleges, Literacy, Science/Mathematics Education, Student Aid
Environment: Environment-General, Resource Conservation, Wildlife Protection
Health: Eyes/Blindness, Hospitals
International: Foreign Educational Institutions, Health Care/Hospitals, International Affairs, International Organizations

Religion: Bible Study/Translation, Religious Welfare
Science: Science Museums
Social Services: Child Welfare, Community Centers, Community Service Organizations, Crime Prevention, Delinquency & Criminal Rehabilitation, People with Disabilities, Substance Abuse

Application Procedures

Initial Contact: Send a brief letter of inquiry.
Application Requirements: Including a description of organization and purpose of funds sought.
Deadlines: None.

Restrictions

Focus on is on libraries.

Foundation Officials

James Humphrey, III: president CORP AFFIL director: Wilson (HW) Co.
James F. Phelan: treasurer
Rutherford David Rogers: director B Jesup, IA June 22, 1915. ED University of Northern Iowa BA (1936); Columbia University MA (1937); Columbia University BS (1938); University of Northern Iowa LittD (1977). CORP AFFIL director: Wilson (HW) Co. NONPR AFFIL university lib emeritus: Yale University; board governors: Yale University Press; member: U.S. Advisory Council College Library Resources; member: Sigma Tau Delta; member: Theta Alpha Phi; founder, chairman: Research Libraries Group; chairman program management committee: Intl Federation Library Association; member: Kappa Delta Pi; member: Bibliographical Society America; member: Association College & Reference Library; member: Association Research Libraries; member: American Association University Professors; member: American Librarians Association; fellow: American Academy of Arts & Sciences. CLUB AFFIL Yale Club; New York Lib Club; Grolier Club; Kenwood Country Club; Cosmos Club; Blue Key Club; Columbia University Club.
William Alexander Ziegler: secretary B New York, NY 1924. ED Harvard University AB (1944); Harvard University JD (1949). CORP AFFIL couns: Sullivan & Cromwell; director: HW Wilson Co.; director: Standard Commercial Corp. NONPR AFFIL director: Foreign Policy Association; member: New York City Bar Association; director: Engineering Information. CLUB AFFIL Riverside Country Club; Harvard Fairfield County Club; Harvard New York City Club.

Grants Analysis

Disclosure Period: fiscal year ending November 30, 2000
Total Grants: $802,600
Number of Grants: 4
Highest Grant: $150,000
Lowest Grant: $20,000

Recent Grants

Note: Grants derived from fiscal 1999 Form 990.

Library-Related
25,000	Fund for American Libraries, Chicago, IL
25,000	New Rochelle Public Library, New Rochelle, NY
10,000	Kansas Library Association, KS
10,000	Special Libraries Association, Washington, DC

General
50,000	Iona College, New Rochelle, NY
30,000	Bronx Museum of the Arts, Bronx, NY
30,000	John Henry Newman Foundation, Dallas, TX
30,000	New York Botanical Gardens, New York, NY
25,000	French Institute Alliance Francaise, New York, NY
25,000	New York State Archives Partnership Trust, Albany, NY

25,000	University of Illinois, Chicago, IL
17,500	Rainbow After School Program
15,000	Bronx Council on the Arts, Bronx, NY
15,000	Mount Vernon Ladies Association, Mt. Vernon, VA

HUEY AND ANGELINE WILSON FOUNDATION

Giving Contact

Gregory J. Cotter, Trustee
3636 S. Sherwood Forest Blvd., Suite 650
Baton Rouge, LA 70816-2236
Phone: (225)292-1344
Fax: (225)292-1589

Description

Founded: 1987
EIN: 581714586
Organization Type: Private Foundation
Giving Locations: LA: Baton Rouge metro area
Grant Types: Capital, Emergency, General Support.

Donor Information

Founder: The foundation was established by Huey Wilson and his wife, Angelina Wilson, founders of a catalog showroom business in Baton Rouge, LA. The couple also co-founded an oilfield service business in Houma, LA.

Financial Summary

Total Giving: $228,000 (2001); $226,022 (2000); $155,000 (1999)
Assets: $5,175,532 (2001); $6,328,185 (2000); $4,661,489 (1999)
Gifts Received: $147,785 (2001). Note: In 2001, contributions were received from Huey and Angelina Wilson.

Typical Recipients

Education: Education-General, Public Education (Precollege)
Health: Single-Disease Health Associations
Social Services: Child Welfare, Domestic Violence, Family Services, Food/Clothing Distribution, Volunteer Services, Youth Organizations

Application Procedures

Initial Contact: Submit a written proposal.
Application Requirements: Include a proposal summary, including the following information in the following order: organization name; chief executive officer; brief project summary of 50 words or less; project director; address; phone number; compelling reason for the project expressed in 50 words or less; amount requested; area of interest; mission statement; and service area. Also provide a narrative section including a concise history of the organization and an overview of current programs and activities; description of the challenge to be met by the project; detailed project description, including strategies, measurable objectives, and timetable; plan for continuing the project once foundation support ends; and a methods for evaluating the project. Proposals should be accompanied by the following attachments: copy of the organization's IRS 501(c)(3) determination letter; a statement from the organization's board of directors authorizing the request and agreeing to implement the project if funded; list of board members, including principal occupations and a description of the term of office and rotation schedule for the board; names and qualifications of persons responsible for carrying out the program; detailed project budget and budget narrative, with income sources and expenditures and other sources of potential, pending, and approved funding; financial statements, including the organization's operating budget, balance sheet, and statements of support, revenue and expenses for the last

completed and current fiscal years; and any supporting materials that the applicant wishes to include.
Deadlines: February 23, for notification by May 1; and August 24, for notification by November 1.
Notes: Proposals should be typewritten and stapled, but not bound.

Restrictions

Applicants must be 501(c)(3) tax-exempt organizations. The foundation does not provide seed funding.

Foundation Officials

Gregory J. Cotter: trustee
Angelina M. Wilson: trustee
Huey J. Wilson: trustee

Grants Analysis

Disclosure Period: calendar year ending 2001
Total Grants: $228,000
Number of Grants: 16
Average Grant: $14,250
Highest Grant: $25,000
Lowest Grant: $5,000
Typical Range: $10,000 to $25,000

Recent Grants

Note: Grants derived from 2001 Form 990.

General
41,000	National Hemophilia Foundation - Louisiana Chapter, Baton Rouge, LA
25,000	Family Road of Baton Rouge, Baton Rouge, LA -- program assistant
24,000	Society of St. Vincent de Paul, Baton Rouge, LA -- heart and blood pressure medicine
20,000	Children's Charter School, Baton Rouge, LA -- mobile computer lab
15,000	Volunteers of America Greater Baton Rouge, Inc., Baton Rouge, LA -- funding for community resource coordinator
12,000	Boys & Girls Club, Baton Rouge, LA -- the supreme program
11,000	Baton Rouge Youth, Inc, Baton Rouge, LA -- summer program
10,000	Baton Rouge Alliance for Transitional Living, Baton Rouge, LA -- emergency temporary shelter
10,000	Battered Women's Program, Baton Rouge, LA -- refurbish building
10,000	Cancer Services of Greater Baton Rouge, Baton Rouge, LA -- prescription reimbursement program

MARIE C. AND JOSEPH C. WILSON FOUNDATION

Giving Contact

Ruth H. Fleischmann, Executive Director
Marie C. and Joseph C. Wilson Foundation
160 Allens Creek Road, Suite 206
Rochester, NY 14618
Phone: (716)461-4699
E-mail: mcjcwilsonfdn@juno.com
Web: http://www.mcjcwilsonfoundation.org

Description

Founded: 1963
EIN: 166042022
Organization Type: Private Foundation
Giving Locations: NY: Rochester
Grant Types: Capital, Conference/Seminar, Emergency, Endowment, Fellowship, General Support, Multiyear/Continuing Support, Operating Expenses, Project, Research, Scholarship, Seed Money.

Donor Information

Founder: the late Katherine M. Wilson, the late Joseph C. Wilson

Financial Summary

Total Giving: $815,705 (2001); $630,526 (2000); $816,915 (1999)

Giving Analysis: Giving for 1998 includes: foundation grants to United Way ($2,500)

Assets: $16,915,144 (2001); $17,457,192 (2000); $15,907,486 (1999)

Gifts Received: $15,907,486 (1999); $550 (1998)

Note: In 1998 and 1999, contributions were received from United Way.

Typical Recipients

Arts & Humanities: Arts Associations & Councils, Arts Outreach, Dance, Historic Preservation, History & Archaeology, Museums/Galleries, Performing Arts, Theater

Civic & Public Affairs: African American Affairs, Botanical Gardens/Parks, Community Foundations, Economic Development, Economic Policy, Employment/Job Training, Civic & Public Affairs-General, Housing, Legal Aid, Nonprofit Management, Urban & Community Affairs, Women's Affairs

Education: Afterschool/Enrichment Programs, Arts/Humanities Education, Colleges & Universities, Leadership Training, Literacy, Minority Education, Preschool Education, Private Education (Precollege), Public Education (Precollege), Science/Mathematics Education, Special Education, Student Aid

Environment: Forestry, Environment-General, Environment-General

Health: Adolescent Health Issues, AIDS/HIV, Alzheimers Disease, Children's Health/Hospitals, Clinics/Medical Centers, Diabetes, Eyes/Blindness, Health Organizations, Heart, Hospitals, Long-Term Care, Medical Research, Mental Health, Single-Disease Health Associations

International: International Relations, International Relief Efforts

Religion: Churches, Ministries, Religious Welfare

Social Services: At-Risk Youth, Big Brother/Big Sister, Child Welfare, Community Service Organizations, Domestic Violence, Family Planning, Family Services, Food/Clothing Distribution, People with Disabilities, Recreation & Athletics, Senior Services, Substance Abuse, United Funds/United Ways, Veterans, Volunteer Services, Youth Organizations

Application Procedures

Initial Contact: Send two copies of a succinct, one-page overview of the organization and the program for which funds are being requested.

Deadlines: None.

Notes: For immediate consideration, proposals must be submitted at least four weeks in advance of the board of managers meetings in May and October.

Restrictions

Does not support individuals.

Additional Information

Publications: Annual Report (includes Application Guidelines)

Trust(s): JP Morgan Chase Bank NA

Foundation Officials

R. Thomas Dalbey, Jr.: mgr
Katherine Dalbey Ensign: mgr
Ruth H. Fleischmann: executive director
Deirdre Wilson Garton: mgr
Chris Kling: mgr
Katherine W. Roby: mgr
Mimi D. Tabah: chairperson
Janet C. Wilson: mgr
Joe Wilson: mgr
Joseph R. Wilson: mgr
Scott Wilson: mgr

Grants Analysis

Disclosure Period: calendar year ending 2001
Total Grants: $815,705
Number of Grants: 77
Average Grant: $7,543*
Highest Grant: $150,000
Lowest Grant: $250
Typical Range: $1,000 to $10,000
*Note: Average grant figure excludes two highest grants ($250,000).

Recent Grants

Note: Grants derived from 2000 Form 990.

General

50,000	Smith College, Northampton, MA -- provide financial support to low-income students
48,000	Anthony L. Jordan Health Center, Rochester, NY -- health services for teenagers who have no insurance
20,000	Veteran Outreach Center, Rochester, NY -- salary support
13,000	Alzheimer's Association, Rochester, NY -- establish Marie C. and Joseph C. Wilson Resource Library
11,605	Action for A Better Community, Inc., Rochester, NY -- operating support
10,000	AIDS Rochester, Rochester, NY -- support Daily Bread Program
10,000	Court-Appointed Special Advocates, Rochester, NY -- operating support for program the advocates for children in foster care
10,000	Primary Mental Health Project, Inc., Rochester, NY -- Parent Education and Custody Effectiveness Program
10,000	Rochester Landscape Technicians Program, Inc., Rochester, NY -- operating support
10,000	Southern Partners Fund, Inc., Atlanta, GA -- operating support

MATILDA R. WILSON FUND

Giving Contact

George D. Miller, Jr., President
100 Renaissance Center, 34th Floor
Detroit, MI 48243
Phone: (313)259-7777
Fax: (313)393-7579

Description

Founded: 1954
EIN: 386087665
Organization Type: General Purpose Foundation
Giving Locations: MI: nationally.
Grant Types: Capital, General Support, Multiyear/Continuing Support, Operating Expenses, Project, Seed Money.

Donor Information

Founder: Incorporated in 1944 in Michigan by the late Matilda R. Wilson and Alfred G. Wilson.

Financial Summary

Total Giving: $2,700,000 (2001); $2,759,155 (2000); $2,985,991 (1998)

Giving Analysis: Giving for 2000 includes: foundation grants to United Way ($6,000) 1998: foundation grants to United Way ($8,000)

Assets: $56,000,000 (2001); $56,606,221 (2000); $58,933,168 (1998)

Typical Recipients

Arts & Humanities: Arts Associations & Councils, Arts Centers, Arts Institutes, Ethnic & Folk Arts, Arts & Humanities-General, History & Archaeology, Libraries, Literary Arts, Museums/Galleries, Music, Opera, Performing Arts, Public Broadcasting, Theater

Civic & Public Affairs: Chambers of Commerce, Economic Development, Economic Policy, Civic & Public Affairs-General, Housing, Law & Justice, Legal Aid, Municipalities/Towns, Philanthropic Organizations, Professional & Trade Associations, Public Policy, Urban & Community Affairs, Zoos/Aquariums

Education: Arts/Humanities Education, Colleges & Universities, Education Associations, Elementary Education (Private), Education-General, Leadership Training, Medical Education, Minority Education, Private Education (Precollege), Public Education (Precollege), Science/Mathematics Education, Social Sciences Education

Environment: Environment-General, Resource Conservation

Health: Children's Health/Hospitals, Clinics/Medical Centers, Emergency/Ambulance Services, Eyes/Blindness, Health Organizations, Hospices, Hospitals, Public Health, Research/Studies Institutes

International: Foreign Arts Organizations

Religion: Churches, Religion-General, Religious Organizations, Religious Welfare, Social/Policy Issues

Science: Scientific Centers & Institutes, Scientific Organizations

Social Services: At-Risk Youth, Camps, Child Welfare, Community Service Organizations, Counseling, Delinquency & Criminal Rehabilitation, Family Services, Food/Clothing Distribution, People with Disabilities, Recreation & Athletics, Scouts, Substance Abuse, United Funds/United Ways, Volunteer Services, Youth Organizations

Application Procedures

Initial Contact: Prospective applicants should submit a letter explaining the need and use of requested funds.

Deadlines: None.

Review Process: The board meets quarterly to consider proposals, usually in March, June, September, and December.

Restrictions

The foundation does not make loans or grants to individuals.

Foundation Officials

David M. Hempstead: secretary PRIM CORP EMPL secretary: Detroit Lions Inc. CORP AFFIL secretary: Higbie-Maxon Inc.

George Miller: president B Detroit, MI 1928. ED Amherst College BA (1950); University of Michigan JD (1953). PRIM CORP EMPL partner: Bodman Longley & Dahling. NONPR AFFIL member: Order Coif; member: Phi Beta Kappa; member: Michigan Bar Association; trustee: Henry Ford Health Systems; trustee: Maplegrove Center/Kingswood Hospital; member: American Bar Association; member: Detroit Bar Association. CLUB AFFIL Detroit Athletic Club; Orchard Lake Country Club.

Robert McCellan Surdam: trustee B Albany, NY October 28, 1917. ED Williams College BA (1939). CLUB AFFIL Rolling Rock Club; Yondotega Club; Little Traverse Yacht Club; Jupiter Island Club; Little Harbor Club; Hobe Sound Yacht Club; Jupiter Hills Club; Country Club Detroit; Detroit Club.

Grants Analysis

Disclosure Period: calendar year ending 2000
Total Grants: $2,753,155*
Number of Grants: 43
Average Grant: $50,077*
Highest Grant: $400,000
Typical Range: $10,000 to $50,000 and $100,000 to $200,000

*Note: Giving excludes United Way. Average grant figure excludes two highest grants ($700,000).

Recent Grants

Note: Grants derived from 2000 Form 990.

Library-Related
25,000	Friends of Detroit Public Library, National Automotive History Collection, Detroit, MI -- operating expenses

General
400,000	Michigan State University, East Lansing, MI -- operating expenses
250,000	Detroit Zoological Society, Detroit, MI -- capital
200,000	Michigan State University, East Lansing, MI -- operating expenses
125,000	Detroit Science Center, Detroit, MI -- capital support
100,000	Adrian College, Adrian, MI -- capital
100,000	Center for Creative Studies, Detroit, MI -- operating expenses
100,000	Cranbrook Educational Community, Bloomfield Hills, MI -- capital
100,000	Detroit Symphony Orchestra, Detroit, MI -- operating expenses
100,000	Henry Ford Health System, West Bloomfield, MI -- operating expenses
100,000	Stratford Festival, Toronto, ON Canada -- capital support

THOMAS WILSON SANITARIUM FOR CHILDREN OF BALTIMORE CITY

Giving Contact

Dr. Kenneth S. Schuberth, President
PO Box 2766
250 W. Pratt St., 15th Fl.
Baltimore, MD 21225
Phone: (410)360-9510

Description

Founded: 1879
EIN: 526044885
Organization Type: Private Foundation
Giving Locations: MD: Baltimore
Grant Types: General Support, Research.

Donor Information

Founder: the late Thomas Wilson

Financial Summary

Total Giving: $622,571 (fiscal year ending January 31, 2002); $498,637 (fiscal 2000); $408,763 (fiscal 1999)
Assets: $11,917,749 (fiscal 2002); $12,603,928 (fiscal 2000); $12,673,044 (fiscal 1999)

Typical Recipients

Arts & Humanities: Arts Centers, Museums/Galleries
Civic & Public Affairs: Botanical Gardens/Parks, Zoos/Aquariums
Education: Arts/Humanities Education, Colleges & Universities, Elementary Education (Public), Education-General, Medical Education, Private Education (Precollege), Science/Mathematics Education, Special Education
Health: Adolescent Health Issues, AIDS/HIV, Children's Health/Hospitals, Clinics/Medical Centers, Eyes/Blindness, Hospitals, Medical Rehabilitation, Medical Research, Prenatal Health Issues, Public Health, Respiratory, Single-Disease Health Associations, Speech & Hearing
Science: Science Museums

Social Services: Child Abuse, Child Welfare, Day Care, Family Planning, Family Services, People with Disabilities, Social Services-General, YMCA/YWCA/YMHA/YWHA

Application Procedures

Initial Contact: Send a letter stating the entity to be benefited and services provided.
Deadlines: None.

Restrictions

Limited to grants that benefit the children of Baltimore, MD.

Foundation Officials

Dr. Kenneth S. Schuberth: president
William C. Trimble, Jr.: secretary, treasurer B Buenos Aires, Argentina 1935. ED Princeton University AB (1958); University of Maryland LLB (1964). PRIM CORP EMPL counsel: Semmes Bowen & Semmes. NONPR AFFIL member: Maryland Bar Association; honorary consul: The Netherlands; member: American Bar Association; member: Baltimore Bar Association. CLUB AFFIL Greenspring Valley Hunt Club; Society Cincinnati; Colonial Club.
Kinloch N. Yellott, III: vice president

Grants Analysis

Disclosure Period: fiscal year ending January 31, 2002
Total Grants: $622,571
Number of Grants: 36
Average Grant: $17,294
Highest Grant: $50,000
Lowest Grant: $1,500
Typical Range: $10,000 to $25,000

Recent Grants

Note: Grants derived from 2000 Form 990.

General
29,280	PACT, Baltimore, MD -- purchase of bus
25,000	Kennedy Krieger Research Institute, Baltimore, MD -- methylphenidate treatment in preschool children with ADHD
25,000	National Aquarium in Baltimore, Baltimore, MD -- Baltimore's Youth Program
22,500	Port Discovery, Baltimore, MD
20,000	Johns Hopkins Pediatrics, Baltimore, MD -- intensive diabetes care and education for children with diabetes mellitus
20,000	Living Classrooms Foundation, Baltimore, MD
20,000	Maryland Society for Sight, Baltimore, MD -- pediatric vision screening in Baltimore City
19,980	University of Maryland, Baltimore, MD -- nutrition program
19,302	Johns Hopkins Center for Injury & Research & Policy, Baltimore, MD
15,285	House of Ruth Baltimore, Inc, Baltimore, MD

WINDHAM FOUNDATION

Giving Contact

Arthur Schubert, Vice President
PO Box 70
Grafton, VT 05146
Phone: (802)843-2211
Fax: (802)843-2205
E-mail: winfound@sover.net
Web: http://www.windham-foundation.org
Note: ALT Email:: stephan@sover.net

Description

Founded: 1963
EIN: 136142024
Organization Type: Specialized/Single Purpose Foundation
Giving Locations: VT: emphasis on Windham County
Grant Types: Capital, Challenge, General Support, Matching, Operating Expenses, Project, Scholarship, Seed Money.

Financial Summary

Total Giving: $211,770 (fiscal year ending October 31, 2001); $197,483 (fiscal 1998); $202,688 (fiscal 1997)
Giving Analysis: Giving for fiscal 2001 includes: foundation grants to United Way ($1,000); foundation scholarships ($107,375) fiscal 1998: foundation scholarships ($107,583)
Assets: $53,984,679 (fiscal 2001); $49,132,783 (fiscal 1998); $48,600,694 (fiscal 1997)
Gifts Received: $60,000 (fiscal 2001); $30,000 (fiscal 1997); $30,000 (fiscal 1996). Note: Contributions were received from the Bunbury Co. and the estate of Dean Mathey.

Typical Recipients

Arts & Humanities: Arts Associations & Councils, Arts Festivals, Dance, Ethnic & Folk Arts, Film & Video, Arts & Humanities-General, Historic Preservation, History & Archaeology, Libraries, Museums/Galleries, Music, Public Broadcasting, Theater
Civic & Public Affairs: Clubs, Economic Development, Employment/Job Training, Civic & Public Affairs-General, Housing, Municipalities/Towns, Public Policy, Rural Affairs, Safety, Urban & Community Affairs, Women's Affairs
Education: Afterschool/Enrichment Programs, Arts/Humanities Education, Colleges & Universities, Elementary Education (Public), Environmental Education, Education-General, International Studies, Literacy, Minority Education, Preschool Education, Private Education (Precollege), Public Education (Precollege), Science/Mathematics Education, Secondary Education (Public), Special Education, Student Aid
Environment: Environment-General, Protection, Research, Resource Conservation
Health: Arthritis, Cancer, Diabetes, Emergency/Ambulance Services, Health-General, Health Organizations, Home-Care Services, Hospices, Hospitals, Kidney, Prenatal Health Issues, Public Health, Trauma Treatment
Religion: Churches, Dioceses, Religion-General, Religious Welfare, Seminaries
Science: Observatories & Planetariums
Social Services: Animal Protection, Camps, Community Centers, Community Service Organizations, Day Care, Domestic Violence, Family Planning, Family Services, Food/Clothing Distribution, Recreation & Athletics, Shelters/Homelessness, Social Services-General, United Funds/United Ways, Volunteer Services, Youth Organizations

Application Procedures

Initial Contact: Before submitting a grant request, organizations must first review the foundation's guidelines. Requests for a grant application and guidelines (including an annual report and application cover sheet) can be obtained either by phone or by mail.
Application Requirements: A grant request consists of seven copies of the following: a completed grant application cover sheet; a cover letter, project narrative, and need for assistance, all in five pages or less; and most recent audit, or financial statement if audit is unavailable, and budget for project. Also include one copy of an IRS 501(c)(3) letter of tax free determination. Faxed or e-mailed applications are not accepted.
Deadlines: The grant application deadline changes annually; contact the foundation for further information. Grant applications must arrive at the foundation's

offices before 4:00 pm the day of the designated deadline. Grants received after that time will be included in the following grant cycle.

Review Process: Organizations requesting grants will be notified by mail of the board's decision within eight to ten weeks after the deadline.

Restrictions

As of January 1, 1998, limited its giving to Vermont elementary and secondary education. Grants are not made to individuals.

Foundation Officials

Charles B. Atwater: trustee emeritus
William A. Gilbert: trustee
Samuel Waldron Lambert, III: chairman, trustee B New York, NY 1938. ED Yale University BA (1960); Harvard University LLB (1963). PRIM CORP EMPL partner: Drinker, Biddle & Reath. NONPR AFFIL member: New Jersey Bar Association; member: Princeton Bar Association; member: American Bar Association.
Stephan A. Morse: president, chief executive officer, trustee B 1947. PRIM CORP EMPL president, director: Old Tavern at Grafton Inc. ADD CORP EMPL president, administration, director: Grafton Village Cheese Co. CORP AFFIL director: United Bank; director: Vermont Finance Services.
Robert M. Olmsted: trustee
Arthur Schubert: vice president
Edward Joseph Toohey: treasurer, trustee B Jersey City, NJ 1930. ED Yale University BA (1953). CORP AFFIL vice president: Old Tavern Grafton Inc. NONPR AFFIL director emeritus: New York City Ballet; vice chairman: Peddie School. CLUB AFFIL Yale Club; Sky Club; University Club; Canoe Brook Country Club; Georgetown Club.
Charles C. Townsend, Jr.: trustee PRIM CORP EMPL secretary: The Bunbury Co. CORP AFFIL director: HTI Voice Solutions Inc.; director: Project Orbis International; director: Cary Institutional PRPTS Inc.
Edward R. Zuccaro: vice president, trustee B New York, NY 1943. PRIM CORP EMPL partner: Zuccaro, Willis & Bent. CORP AFFIL clerk, director: Phelps Enterprises; clerk, director: Phelps Real Estate; clerk, director: Music Shop; vice president, secretary, director: Old Tavern Grafton Inc.; treasurer: Grafton Village Cheese Co.; clerk, director: Movie World; clerk, director: Dana Jewelry.

Grants Analysis

Disclosure Period: fiscal year ending October 31, 2001
Total Grants: $104,395*
Number of Grants: 58
Average Grant: $1,568*
Highest Grant: $15,000
Typical Range: $500 to $3,000
***Note:** Giving excludes scholarships and United Way. Average grant figure excludes highest grant.

Recent Grants

Note: Grants derived from 2001 Form 990.

Library-Related

1,000	St. Johnsbury Athenaeum, St. Johnsbury, VT
500	Moore Free Library, Newfane, VT

General

15,000	Vermont Symphony Orchestra, Burlington, VT
10,000	Vermont Diary Farm Sustainable Project, Burlington, VT
5,000	Artemis Wildlife Foundation, Helena, MT
5,000	Brattleboro Arts Initiative, Brattleboro, VT
5,000	Green Mountain Training Center, Brattleboro, VT
5,000	Hilltop Montessori Capital Fund, Brattleboro, VT

5,000	Youth Services, Brattleboro, VT
3,500	Snelling Center for Government, Burlington, VT
3,000	Fairbanks Museum and Planetarium, St. Johnsbury, VT
2,500	Ehtan Allen Homestead Museum, Burlington, VT

WINN-DIXIE STORES INC.

Company Headquarters

Jacksonville, FL
Web: http://www.winn-dixie.com

Company Description

Founded: 1928
Ticker: WIN
Exchange: NYSE
Revenue: US$12.334 billion (2002)
Profit: US$86.9 million (2002)
Employees: 112500 (2002)
Fortune Rank: 149, per FORTUNE Magazine's list of 500 Largest U.S. Corporations (2002).
SIC(s): 5411 Grocery Stores.

Operating Locations

Winn-Dixie Stores Inc. (AL--Montgomery; FL, Jacksonville, Miami, Orlando; GA, Atlanta; KY--Louisville; LA--New Orleans; NC, Charlotte; OH--Cincinnati; SC--Greenville; TX--Fort Worth; VA)

Winn-Dixie Stores Foundation

Giving Contact

August B. Toscano, President & Director, Matching Gifts
Winn-Dixie Stores Foundation
PO Box B
Jacksonville, FL 32203-0297
Phone: (904)783-5000
Fax: (904)783-5235
Web: http://www.winn-dixie.com/company/about_wd/community_commitment.asp

Alternate Contact

5050 Edgewood Court
Jacksonville, FL 32254
Phone: (904)783-5429

Description

EIN: 590995428
Organization Type: Corporate Foundation
Giving Locations: AL; FL; GA; IN; KY; LA; MS; NC; OH; OK; SC; TN; TX; VA: primarily in the company's 14-state trade area; generally within the Southern United States.
Grant Types: Award, Employee Matching Gifts, General Support, Matching, Project, Research, Scholarship.
Note: Employee matching gift ratio: 1 to 1 for educational purposes, art & health facilities, and the United Way.

Financial Summary

Total Giving: $2,000,000 (2002 approx); $1,832,804 (2001); $3,181,436 (2000). Note: Contributes through corporate direct giving program and foundation.
Giving Analysis: Giving for 2002 includes: foundation (approx $2,000,000); 2001: foundation ($1,832,804); 2000: foundation grants to United Way ($25,000); foundation ($1,127,813); foundation matching gifts ($2,028,623);
Assets: $232,494 (2001); $78,837 (2000); $482,576 (1998)
Gifts Received: $2,000,000 (2001); $3,000,000 (2000); $4,000,000 (1998). Note: In 2000 and 1998,

contributions were received from Winn-Dixie Stores, Inc.

Typical Recipients

Arts & Humanities: Arts Associations & Councils, Arts Festivals, History & Archaeology, Libraries, Music, Public Broadcasting
Civic & Public Affairs: African American Affairs, Business/Free Enterprise, Chambers of Commerce, Clubs, Community Foundations, Economic Policy, Civic & Public Affairs-General, Housing, Law & Justice, Legal Aid, Public Policy, Urban & Community Affairs, Women's Affairs, Zoos/Aquariums
Education: Business Education, Colleges & Universities, Education Associations, Education-General, Medical Education, Minority Education, Private Education (Precollege), Science/Mathematics Education, Secondary Education (Public), Student Aid
Health: Alzheimers Disease, Cancer, Children's Health/Hospitals, Clinics/Medical Centers, Clinics/Medical Centers, Diabetes, Emergency/Ambulance Services, Heart, Hospices, Hospitals, Mental Health, Multiple Sclerosis, Prenatal Health Issues, Public Health, Single-Disease Health Associations
Religion: Churches, Religious Organizations, Religious Welfare
Social Services: At-Risk Youth, Big Brother/Big Sister, Child Welfare, Community Service Organizations, Family Services, Food/Clothing Distribution, People with Disabilities, Recreation & Athletics, Scouts, Shelters/Homelessness, Social Services-General, Special Olympics, Substance Abuse, United Funds/United Ways, YMCA/YWCA/YMHA/YWHA, Youth Organizations

Application Procedures

Initial Contact: Submit a letter.
Application Requirements: Provide a description of organization, amount requested, purpose of funds sought, recently audited financial statement, and proof of tax-exempt status.
Deadlines: None. Board meets quarterly.
Notes: Applications should be sent to the nearest division office.

Restrictions

No grants are made to individuals or religious or political organizations. No matching gifts are made to religious, political, fraternal, professional, social, or recreation groups. With the exception of matching gifts, no contributions are made outside the trade territories served by Winn-Dixie.

Additional Information

Publications: Guidelines; Annual Report

Corporate Officials

Andrew Dano Davis: chairman, chief executive officer B Henderson, AR 1945. ED Stetson University. PRIM CORP EMPL chairman: Winn-Dixie Stores Inc.
Frank Lazaran: president, chief executive officer ED California State University, Long Beach BS. PRIM CORP EMPL president, chief executive officer: Winn-Dixie Stores Inc.
Richard P. McCook: senior vice president, chief financial officer B Miami, FL 1953. ED Florida State University BS (1975); Florida State University MS (1976). PRIM CORP EMPL senior vice president, chief financial officer: Winn-Dixie Stores Inc. NONPR AFFIL member: Financial Executives Institute; member: Florida Institute CPAs; member: American Institute CPAs. CLUB AFFIL River Club.

Foundation Officials

Andrew Dano Davis: vice president, director (see above)
Judith Dixon: secretary
Richard P. McCook: vice president (see above)
T. L. Qualls: assistant secretary PRIM CORP EMPL director corporate acctg: Winn-Dixie Stores Inc.
Ellis Zahara: vice president

Grants Analysis

Disclosure Period: calendar year ending 2001
Total Grants: $366,940*
Number of Grants: 100
Average Grant: $2,984*
Highest Grant: $71,500
Lowest Grant: $100
Typical Range: $100 to $5,000
*****Note:** Giving excludes matching gifts and United Way. Average grant figure excludes highest grant.

Recent Grants

Note: Grants derived from 2001 Form 990.

General

71,500	Distributive Education Clubs of America, Reston, VA
40,000	Police Athletic League, Jacksonville, FL
30,000	Ronald McDonald House Charities of Central Florida, Orlando, FL
25,000	National Urban League, New York, NY
25,000	United Way, Montgomery, AL
25,000	Urban League, Jacksonville, FL
20,000	Nassau County Boys and Girls Club, Fernandina Beach, FL
12,500	Community Partnership for the Homeless, Ft. Lauderdale, FL
10,000	American Red Cross, Miami, FL
10,000	JSO Youth Education Program, Jacksonville, FL

WINNEBAGO INDUSTRIES

Company Headquarters

605 W. Crystal Lake Rd.
Forest City, IA 50436
Web: http://www.winnebagoind.com

Company Description

Founded: 1958
Ticker: WGO
Exchange: NYSE
Revenue: US$828.4 million (2002)
Employees: 3685 (2002)
SIC(s): 3355 Aluminum Rolling & Drawing Nec, 3711 Motor Vehicles & Car Bodies, 3792 Travel Trailers & Campers.

Operating Locations

Winnebago Realty Corp. (IA--Forest City)

Winnebago Industries Foundation

Giving Contact

Elsie Felland, Corporate Cashier
PO Box 152
Forest City, IA 50436-0152
Phone: (641)582-3535
Fax: (641)582-6966

Description

EIN: 237174206
Organization Type: Corporate Foundation
Giving Locations: IA
Grant Types: General Support.

Financial Summary

Total Giving: $110,000 (fiscal year ending February 28, 2001); $82,670 (fiscal 2000); $81,620 (fiscal 1999)
Giving Analysis: Giving for fiscal 2000 includes: foundation grants to United Way ($1,000); foundation ($81,670); fiscal 1999: foundation grants to United Way ($1,000) foundation ($80,620)
Assets: $1,565,213 (fiscal 2001); $1,868,580 (fiscal 2000); $1,445,954 (fiscal 1999)
Gifts Received: $250,000 (fiscal 2000)

Typical Recipients

Arts & Humanities: Arts Associations & Councils, Arts Centers, Arts Festivals, Community Arts, History & Archaeology, Libraries, Museums/Galleries, Public Broadcasting
Civic & Public Affairs: Botanical Gardens/Parks, Chambers of Commerce, Clubs, Economic Development, Civic & Public Affairs-General, Housing, Municipalities/Towns, Parades/Festivals, Rural Affairs, Safety, Urban & Community Affairs
Education: Colleges & Universities, Education-General, International Exchange, Private Education (Precollege), Public Education (Precollege), Secondary Education (Public), Student Aid
Environment: Air/Water Quality, Environment-General, Resource Conservation
Health: Cancer, Children's Health/Hospitals, Emergency/Ambulance Services, Eyes/Blindness, Health-General, Health Organizations, Heart, Hospices, Hospitals, Nursing Services
Religion: Jewish Causes, Religious Welfare
Social Services: Animal Protection, Community Centers, Community Service Organizations, Crime Prevention, Day Care, Emergency Relief, Family Planning, Family Services, Food/Clothing Distribution, Recreation & Athletics, Scouts, Special Olympics, Substance Abuse, United Funds/United Ways, YMCA/YWCA/YMHA/YWHA, Youth Organizations

Application Procedures

Initial Contact: Send a full proposal.
Deadlines: None.

Restrictions

Does not support individuals, religious organizations for sectarian purposes, political or lobbying groups, or organizations outside operating areas.

Corporate Officials

Edwin F. Barker: vice president, chief financial officer, chief operating officer B 1947. PRIM CORP EMPL vice president, chief financial officer: Winnebago Industries Inc. ADD CORP EMPL chief financial officer: Winnebago Industries Corp.
Bruce D. Hertzke: president, chief executive officer, chief operating officer PRIM CORP EMPL president, chief executive officer, chief operating officer: Winnebago Industries.

Foundation Officials

Edwin F. Barker: trustee (see above)
Fred G. Dohrmann: manager
Luise V. Hanson: trustee
Bruce D. Hertzke: trustee (see above)

Grants Analysis

Disclosure Period: fiscal year ending February 28, 2001
Total Grants: $110,000
Number of Grants: 144
Average Grant: $764
Highest Grant: $5,000
Typical Range: $250 to $1,500

Recent Grants

Note: Grants derived from fiscal 2001 Form 990.

Library-Related

2,000	Fertile Public Library, Fertile, IA

General

5,000	Hampton Community Christian Daycare, Inc., Hampton, IA
3,000	City of Forest City, Forest City, IA
3,000	Fertile Fire Department, Fertile, IA
3,000	Hancock County Conservation Board, Garner, IA
3,000	Mitchell County Memorial Hospital Fund, Osage, IA
2,500	Hanson Family Life Center, Forest City, IA
2,000	Forest City Ambulance Fund, Forest City, IA
2,000	Habitat for Humanity of North Central Iowa, Mason City, IA
2,000	Iowa Natural Heritage Foundation, Des Moines, IA
2,000	Iowa Natural Heritage Foundation, Des Moines, IA

NORMAN AND ROSITA WINSTON FOUNDATION

Giving Contact

John J. O'Neil, Attorney
1285 Avenue of the Americas
New York, NY 10019-6064
Phone: (212)373-3000
Fax: (212)373-2187

Description

Founded: 1954
EIN: 136161672
Organization Type: General Purpose Foundation
Giving Locations: NY
Grant Types: Fellowship, General Support, Professorship, Project, Research, Scholarship.

Donor Information

Founder: Established in 1954 by the late Norman K. Winston .

Financial Summary

Total Giving: $4,866,000 (2000); $3,600,000 (1997 approx); $3,552,000 (1996)
Giving Analysis: Giving for 2000 includes: foundation scholarships ($340,000)
Assets: $104,446,037 (2000); $75,000,000 (1997 approx); $72,703,380 (1996)

Typical Recipients

Arts & Humanities: Arts Associations & Councils, Arts Centers, Arts Festivals, Arts Outreach, Ballet, Dance, Historic Preservation, Libraries, Museums/Galleries, Music, Opera, Performing Arts, Public Broadcasting, Theater, Visual Arts
Civic & Public Affairs: Botanical Gardens/Parks, Civil Rights, Law & Justice, Public Policy, Urban & Community Affairs
Education: Arts/Humanities Education, Colleges & Universities, Education-General, Education Reform, Leadership Training, Legal Education, Medical Education, Private Education (Precollege), Science/Mathematics Education, Social Sciences Education, Student Aid
Health: Cancer, Geriatric Health, Heart, Hospitals, Long-Term Care, Medical Research, Research/Studies Institutes
International: Foreign Arts Organizations, Foreign Educational Institutions, Human Rights, Missionary/Religious Activities
Religion: Seminaries, Synagogues/Temples
Science: Science-General, Science Museums, Scientific Centers & Institutes
Social Services: Child Welfare, Community Service Organizations, Family Services, Recreation & Athletics, Senior Services, Sexual Abuse, YMCA/YWCA/YMHA/YWHA

Application Procedures

Initial Contact: There is no prescribed form for applications. Proposals should be directed to Julian S. Perlman.
Deadlines: None.

Foundation Officials

Laurie Friedland: director

Grants Analysis

Disclosure Period: calendar year ending 1996
Total Grants: $3,552,000*
Number of Grants: 143
Average Grant: $24,839
Highest Grant: $150,000
Typical Range: $1,000 to $50,000
*Note: Giving excludes scholarships.

Recent Grants

Note: Grants derived from 2000 Form 990.

Library-Related
40,000   New York Public Library, New York, NY

General
250,000   People for the American Way, Washington, DC
240,000   Culture Project, New York, NY -- support director
225,000   Hamilton College, Clinton, NY
150,000   American Friends of Hebrew University, Palm Springs, CA -- Truman Research Institute
150,000   Sloan-Kettering Institute, New York, NY -- for Winston scholarship
150,000   Solomon R. Guggenheim Museum, New York, NY
140,000   Bennington College, Bennington, VT -- renovation
100,000   Brooklyn Academy of Music, Brooklyn, NY -- opera and theater program
100,000   International Rescue Commission, New York, NY
100,000   Lincoln Center for the Performing Arts, New York, NY -- for Great Performances series

WINTER CONSTRUCTION CO.

Company Headquarters

1330 Spring St., NW
Atlanta, GA 30309

Company Description

Employees: 250
SIC(s): 1541 Industrial Buildings & Warehouses, 1542 Nonresidential Construction Nec.

Operating Locations

Winter Construction Co. (GA--Atlanta)

Nonmonetary Support

Type: In-kind Services; Loaned Employees; Loaned Executives

Giving Contact

Leslie Harris, Marketing Vice President
1330 Spring Street, NW, Suite 300
Atlanta, GA 30309-2810
Phone: (404)588-3300
Fax: (404)223-5753
E-mail: lharris@wintercompanies.com
Web: http://www.wintercompanies.com

Description

Organization Type: Corporate Giving Program
Giving Locations: headquarters and operating communities.
Grant Types: Award, General Support.

Financial Summary

Total Giving: $25,000 (1993); $30,000 (1992 approx)

Typical Recipients

Arts & Humanities: Arts Appreciation, Arts Associations & Councils, Arts Centers, Arts Festivals, Arts Funds, Community Arts, Dance, Ethnic & Folk Arts, Historic Preservation, Libraries, Literary Arts, Museums/Galleries, Music, Opera, Performing Arts, Theater, Visual Arts
Civic & Public Affairs: Philanthropic Organizations, Safety, Urban & Community Affairs, Zoos/Aquariums
Education: Arts/Humanities Education, Business Education, Continuing Education
Environment: Environment-General
Social Services: Community Centers, Volunteer Services

Application Procedures

Initial Contact: Send a brief letter of inquiry.
Application Requirements: Include a description of organization, amount requested, and purpose of funds sought.
Deadlines: None.

Restrictions

Does not support individuals.

Corporate Officials

Sean Durkin: chief financial officer, president, chief executive officer PRIM CORP EMPL chief financial officer: Winter Construction Co.
Robert L. Silverman: chairman, president, chief executive officer PRIM CORP EMPL chairman, president, chief executive officer: Winter Construction Co.

Grants Analysis

Typical Range: $1,000 to $2,500

WINTHROP

Giving Contact

Mary D. Damas, President
12625 High Bluff Dr., Suite 215
San Diego, CA 92130
Phone: (858)793-2554

Description

Founded: 1992
EIN: 020453999
Organization Type: Private Foundation
Giving Locations: CA
Grant Types: General Support.

Donor Information

Founder: Established in 1992 by Chatam, Inc.

Financial Summary

Total Giving: $1,189,597 (fiscal year ending May 31, 2002); $1,380,560 (fiscal 2000); $1,195,891 (fiscal 1999)
Giving Analysis: Giving for fiscal 2002 includes: foundation grants to United Way ($37,611); foundation matching gifts ($242,256); fiscal 2000: foundation grants to United Way ($33,500); fiscal 1999: foundation grants to United Way ($30,000)
Assets: $822,588 (fiscal 2002); $2,186,452 (fiscal 2000); $3,399,689 (fiscal 1999)
Gifts Received: $1,400,000 (fiscal 2002); $5,000,000 (fiscal 1992). Note: In 2002, contributions were received from Fisher Scientific Inc.

Typical Recipients

Arts & Humanities: Ethnic & Folk Arts, History & Archaeology, Libraries, Museums/Galleries, Music, Opera, Performing Arts, Public Broadcasting, Theater
Civic & Public Affairs: Botanical Gardens/Parks, Civic & Public Affairs-General, Legal Aid, Philanthropic Organizations, Public Policy, Urban & Community Affairs, Women's Affairs
Education: Business Education, Colleges & Universities, Economic Education, Education Reform, Education-General, Health & Physical Education, Leadership Training, Private Education (Precollege), Public Education (Precollege), Secondary Education (Private), Student Aid
Environment: Resource Conservation
Health: Children's Health/Hospitals, Clinics/Medical Centers, Emergency/Ambulance Services, Eyes/Blindness, Health Funds, Health Organizations, Health Organizations, Heart, Hospitals, Medical Research, Mental Health, Multiple Sclerosis, Public Health, Research/Studies Institutes, Respiratory, Speech & Hearing
International: Foreign Educational Institutions, International Organizations, Missionary/Religious Activities
Religion: Churches, Jewish Causes, Religious Welfare
Science: Science Museums, Scientific Centers & Institutes, Scientific Organizations
Social Services: Big Brother/Big Sister, Child Abuse, Community Service Organizations, Recreation & Athletics, United Funds/United Ways, Volunteer Services, YMCA/YWCA/YMHA/YWHA

Application Procedures

Initial Contact: Send a brief letter of inquiry.
Application Requirements: Include a description of organization, purpose of funds sought, and proof of tax-exempt status.
Deadlines: None.

Foundation Officials

Mary D. Damas: assistant secretary
Paul M. Meister: vice president, treasurer B Kalamazoo, MI 1952. ED University of Michigan BA (1974); Northwestern University MBA (1976). PRIM CORP EMPL chief financial officer, senior vice president finance: Fisher Science International Inc. ADD CORP EMPL managinging director: Latona Associate. CORP AFFIL director: Minerals Technologies Inc.; director: Power Control Technologies; director: MF Worldwide; vice chairman: General Chemical Group Inc.; vice chairman: Gentek Inc.
Paul Michael Montrone: vice president B Scranton, PA 1941. ED University of Scranton BS (1962); Columbia University PhD (1965). PRIM CORP EMPL chief executive officer, chairman: Fisher Science International Inc. ADD CORP EMPL president: Henley Holdings Two Inc. CORP AFFIL advisory board: Zeneca Inc.; advisory board: Sintokagio Ltd.; director: Waste Management Inc.; chairman: Latona Associates; director: Prestolite Wire Corp.; director: Henley Group Inc.; advisory board: ICI Inc.; chairman: Gen Tek Inc.; chairman: General Chemical Group Inc. NONPR AFFIL member dean's advisory council: Columbia University Business School; managing director: Metropolitan Opera Association; member board overseers: Business School Columbia University; member board overseers: Business Roundtable. CLUB AFFIL Lyford Cay Club; University Club; Bald Peak Colony Club; Brook Club.
Allison G. Pellegrino: secretary
Spencer Stokes: president

Grants Analysis

Disclosure Period: fiscal year ending May 31, 2002
Total Grants: $909,730*
Number of Grants: 200
Average Grant: $4,549
Highest Grant: $50,000
Lowest Grant: $90
Typical Range: $1,000 to $10,000
*Note: Giving excludes United Way and metropolitan.

Recent Grants

Note: Grants derived from 2000 Form 990.

General

50,000	Phillips Exeter Academy, Exeter, NH
33,000	Boston Symphony Orchestra, Boston, MA
30,000	Massachusetts General Hospital, Boston, MA
25,000	World War II Memorial Fund, Washington, DC
24,000	Clare Foundation, Inc., Santa Monica, CA
24,000	Fidelity Investments Charitable Gift Fund, Boston, MA
24,000	Michael D. Dingman Foundation, The, Hampton, NH
24,000	Michael D. Dingman Foundation, The, Hampton, NH
24,000	Penates Foundation, Hampton, NH
24,000	Southwestern Oklahoma State University, Weatherford, OK

CLARA B. WINTHROP TRUST

Giving Contact

Richard Olney, III, Trustee
c/o Welch & Forbes
45 School Street
Boston, MA 02108-3204
Phone: (617)523-1635
Fax: (617)742-6243
E-mail: ronly@welchforbes.com

Description

Founded: 1969
EIN: 046039972
Organization Type: Private Foundation
Giving Locations: MA
Grant Types: General Support.

Donor Information

Founder: the late Clara B. Winthrop

Financial Summary

Total Giving: $275,000 (2001); $317,500 (2000); $115,000 (1999)
Assets: $3,855,425 (2001); $4,539,089 (2000); $4,809,844 (1999)

Typical Recipients

Arts & Humanities: Arts Associations & Councils, Community Arts, Historic Preservation, History & Archaeology, Libraries, Museums/Galleries, Music, Public Broadcasting, Theater
Civic & Public Affairs: Civic & Public Affairs-General, Municipalities/Towns, Native American Affairs, Parades/Festivals, Public Policy, Urban & Community Affairs, Zoos/Aquariums
Education: Colleges & Universities, Education Associations, Private Education (Precollege), Secondary Education (Private)
Environment: Environment-General, Resource Conservation
Health: Hospitals, Nursing Services
International: International Organizations
Religion: Churches, Religious Welfare
Science: Science Museums
Social Services: Child Welfare, Community Service Organizations, Family Services, Youth Organizations

Application Procedures

Initial Contact: Applications may be submitted in any form.
Application Requirements: Include purpose of funds sought, the general financial situation of the organization, and proof of tax-exempt status.
Deadlines: None.

Restrictions

Does not support individuals. The Trust makes grants only to charitable organizations within Massachusetts or a state which exempts requests to Massachusetts organizations.

Foundation Officials

F. Murray Forbes, Jr.: trustee
Arthur C. Hodges: trustee
John Lowell: trustee B Westwood, MA September 03, 1919. ED Harvard University (1942). PRIM CORP EMPL partner: Welch & Forbes.
Richard Olney, III: trustee
Oliver A. Spalding: trustee

Grants Analysis

Disclosure Period: calendar year ending 2001
Total Grants: $275,000
Number of Grants: 28
Average Grant: $9,821
Highest Grant: $22,500
Typical Range: $5,000 to $20,000

Recent Grants

Note: Grants derived from 2001 Form 990.

Library-Related

15,000	Manchester by the Sea Conservation Trust, Manchester, MA
10,000	Library of the Boston Athenaeum, Boston, MA
7,500	New England Conservatory of Music, Boston, MA

General

22,500	Peabody Essex Museum, Salem, MA
22,000	New England Aquarium, Boston, MA
15,000	Manchester by the Sea Public Library, Manchester, MA
15,000	Trustees of Reservation, Beverly, MA
15,000	Visiting Nurse Association of the North Shore, Waltham, MA
10,000	Beverly Hospital, Beverly, MA
10,000	Friends of Manchester by the Sea, Manchester, MA
10,000	House of Seven Gables, Salem, MA
10,000	Manchester by the Sea Youth Center, Manchester, MA
10,000	Massachusetts Historical Society, Boston, MA

WIREMOLD CO.

Company Headquarters

West Hartford, CT
Web: http://www.wiremold.com

Company Description

Employees: 681
SIC(s): 3643 Current-Carrying Wiring Devices, 3644 Noncurrent-Carrying Wiring Devices, 3646 Commercial Lighting Fixtures, 3648 Lighting Equipment Nec.

Operating Locations

Wiremold Co. (CT--West Hartford)

Wiremold Foundation

Giving Contact

John D. Murphy, President
60 Woodlawn Street
West Hartford, CT 06110
Phone: (860)233-6251
Fax: (860)523-3699

Description

Founded: 1967
EIN: 066089445
Organization Type: Corporate Foundation
Giving Locations: headquarters area only.
Grant Types: Employee Matching Gifts, General Support.

Donor Information

Founder: The Wiremold Co.

Financial Summary

Total Giving: $289,281 (2001); $261,300 (2000); $223,770 (1999)
Giving Analysis: Giving for 2000 includes: foundation matching gifts ($11,225); foundation grants to United Way ($80,000); foundation ($170,075); 1999: foundation matching gifts ($10,145); foundation ($219,075); 1997: foundation matching gifts ($9,001) foundation ($195,626)
Assets: $434,017 (2001); $439,980 (2000); $418,708 (1999)
Gifts Received: $276,004 (2001); $275,104 (2000); $271,500 (1999)

Typical Recipients

Arts & Humanities: Arts Associations & Councils, Ballet, Arts & Humanities-General, Historic Preservation, History & Archaeology, Libraries, Literary Arts, Museums/Galleries, Music, Performing Arts, Public Broadcasting
Civic & Public Affairs: African American Affairs, Community Foundations, Employment/Job Training, Civic & Public Affairs-General, Housing, Public Policy, Urban & Community Affairs, Women's Affairs
Education: Business Education, Colleges & Universities, Education Funds, Education-General, International Exchange, Literacy, Minority Education, Science/Mathematics Education, Secondary Education (Private), Special Education, Student Aid
Environment: Environment-General, Watershed
Health: AIDS/HIV, Cancer, Children's Health/Hospitals, Clinics/Medical Centers, Emergency/Ambulance Services, Health-General, Health Organizations, Hospitals, Prenatal Health Issues, Public Health
Religion: Churches, Religious Welfare
Science: Science Museums, Scientific Centers & Institutes
Social Services: Camps, Child Welfare, Community Service Organizations, Family Services, Food/Clothing Distribution, Homes, People with Disabilities, Recreation & Athletics, Scouts, Senior Services, Social Services-General, Special Olympics, United Funds/United Ways, YMCA/YWCA/YMHA/YWHA, Youth Organizations

Application Procedures

Initial Contact: Send a letter of inquiry. There is no formal application process.
Application Requirements: Include proof of tax-exempt status.
Deadlines: None.

Restrictions

Preference is given to written requests for capital and/or start-up campaigns over operating funds.

Corporate Officials

Arthur P. Byrne: chairman, president, chief executive officer, director PRIM CORP EMPL chairman, president, chief executive officer, director: Wiremold Co.
Orest J. Fiume: vice president finance, chief financial officer PRIM CORP EMPL vice president finance, chief financial officer: Wiremold Co.

Foundation Officials

Arthur P. Byrne: treasurer (see above)
Jo-Anne Mazzio: secretary
John Davis Murphy: president

Robert H. Murphy: vice president
Michele Sitler: secretary

Grants Analysis

Disclosure Period: calendar year ending 2000
Total Grants: $170,075*
Number of Grants: 62
Average Grant: $2,072*
Highest Grant: $25,750
Lowest Grant: $250
Typical Range: $1,000 to $5,000
***Note:** Giving excludes matching gifts and United Way. Average grant figure excludes two highest grants ($45,750).

Recent Grants

Note: Grants derived from 2001 Form 990.

General

80,000	United Way Combined Health Appeal, Hartford, CT
25,750	Greater Hartford YMCA World Service, Hartford, CT
25,000	Hartford Hospital, Hartford, CT
20,000	Greater Hartford Arts Council, Hartford, CT
10,000	Salvation Army, Hartford, CT
6,000	Doc Hurley Scholarship Foundation, Hartford, CT
5,500	Greater Hartford American Red Cross, Hartford, CT
5,000	Bushnell Memorial, Hartford, CT
5,000	Campaign for St. Francis and Mount Sinai, Glastonbury, CT
5,000	Junior Achievement of Hartford, Hartford, CT

WATSON W. WISE FOUNDATION

Giving Contact

110 N. College, Suite 1002
Tyler, TX 75702
Phone: (903)531-9615

Description

Founded: 1990
EIN: 756064539
Organization Type: Private Foundation
Giving Locations: TX: Tyler
Grant Types: General Support.

Donor Information

Founder: Established in 1990 with funds from the estate of Watson W. Wise.

Financial Summary

Total Giving: $640,000 (2000); $615,000 (1999); $560,000 (1998)
Giving Analysis: Giving for 1998 includes: foundation grants to United Way ($2,000)
Assets: $11,967,186 (2000); $12,278,651 (1999); $11,938,919 (1998)
Gifts Received: $49,160 (1998); $60,932 (1996); $1,199,099 (1994). Note: In 1996 and 1998, contributions were received from the estate of Watson W. Wise.

Typical Recipients

Arts & Humanities: Libraries, Museums/Galleries, Theater
Civic & Public Affairs: Clubs, Community Foundations, Urban & Community Affairs, Women's Affairs
Education: Agricultural Education, Colleges & Universities, Community & Junior Colleges, Engineering/Technological Education, Education-General, Literacy, Minority Education, Private Education (Precollege), Public Education (Precollege), Science/Mathematics Education

Health: Alzheimers Disease, Cancer, Clinics/Medical Centers, Health-General, Health Organizations, Hospices, Hospitals, Hospitals (University Affiliated), Public Health, Respiratory, Transplant Networks/Donor Banks
International: Health Care/Hospitals
Religion: Churches, Dioceses, Religious Welfare
Science: Science Museums, Scientific Centers & Institutes
Social Services: Child Welfare, Community Service Organizations, Day Care, Family Services, Food/Clothing Distribution, People with Disabilities, Scouts, Youth Organizations

Application Procedures

Initial Contact: The foundation has no formal grant application procedure or application form.
Deadlines: None.

Foundation Officials

Calvin N. Clyde, Jr.: vice president
Herman A. Engel: trustee
Will A. Knight: president
Emma F. Wise: trustee

Grants Analysis

Disclosure Period: calendar year ending 2000
Total Grants: $640,000
Number of Grants: 123
Average Grant: $5,204
Highest Grant: $50,000
Typical Range: $1,000 to $10,000

Recent Grants

Note: Grants derived from 1999 Form 990.

General

30,000	Baylor University, Waco, TX -- education
25,000	TISD Foundation, Tyler, TX -- education
20,000	Baylor University, Waco, TX -- education
15,000	Texas Chest Foundation, Tyler, TX -- medical
15,000	Tyler Junior College Foundation, Tyler, TX -- education
15,000	Tyler Junior College Foundation, Tyler, TX -- education
15,000	Tyler Junior College Foundation, Tyler, TX -- education
15,000	Tyler Museum of Art, Tyler, TX
12,400	Stewart Blood Center, Tyler, TX -- medical
10,000	Brookhill School, Bullard, TX -- education

LIN AND ELLA WONG FOUNDATION

Giving Contact

Reuben S. F. Wong, President, Treasurer & Director
220 S. King Street, Suite 2288
Honolulu, HI 96813
Phone: (808)531-3526

Description

Founded: 1991
EIN: 990284508
Organization Type: Private Foundation
Grant Types: General Support.

Financial Summary

Total Giving: $114,050 (2001); $77,450 (2000); $71,150 (1999)
Assets: $1,468,874 (2001); $1,431,552 (2000); $1,564,366 (1999)
Gifts Received: $45,000 (2001); $214,351 (2000); $138,790 (1998). Note: In 2001, contributions were

received from Mr. and Mrs. Henry Chang ($500) and Reuben Wong and Vera Wong ($44,500). In 2000, contributions were received from Mr. and Mrs. Stanley Wong ($144,375), Reuben and Vera Wong ($40,442), Kenneth Huey ($100), Dr. and Mrs. William Wong ($100), and Dr. Alton S. Wong ($29,334). In 1999, contributions were received from Dr. and Mrs. Stanley Wong ($25,000), Reuben and Vera Wong ($86,188), Norwin H.G. Wong ($10,000), and Dr. Alton S. Wong ($28,576). In 1998, contributions were received from Palace Realty, Inc. ($5,500), Mr. and Mrs. Henry Chang ($1,000), Dr. and Mrs. Stanley Wong ($25,000), Dr. Alton S. Wong ($26,032) and Rueben and Vera Wong ($77,638). In 1995, contributions were received from Mr. and Mrs. Henry Chang ($2,000), Dr. and Mrs. Stanley Wong ($37,428), and Reuben and Vera Wong ($101,775).

Typical Recipients

Arts & Humanities: History & Archaeology, Libraries
Civic & Public Affairs: Asian American Affairs, Civic & Public Affairs-General
Education: Colleges & Universities, Education-General, Legal Education, Minority Education, Private Education (Precollege), Secondary Education (Public)
Health: Medical Rehabilitation, Medical Research
Religion: Bible Study/Translation, Churches, Religion-General, Religious Welfare, Synagogues/Temples
Social Services: Scouts, Social Services-General, Special Olympics, YMCA/YWCA/YMHA/YWHA, Youth Organizations

Application Procedures

Initial Contact: Send a brief letter of inquiry.
Application Requirements: a description of organization and purpose of funds sought.
Deadlines: None.

Foundation Officials

Alton S. Wong: director
Reuben S. F. Wong: president, treasurer, director
Stanley S. Wong: director
Vera H. Wong: vice president, secretary, director

Grants Analysis

Disclosure Period: calendar year ending 2001
Total Grants: $114,050
Number of Grants: 30
Average Grant: $2,209*
Highest Grant: $50,000
Lowest Grant: $450
Typical Range: $1,000 to $5,000
***Note:** Average grant figure excludes highest grant.

Recent Grants

Note: Grants derived from 2000 Form 990.

Library-Related

3,000	Friends of Chinatown Library, San Marino, CA -- for library building fund

General

10,000	Commercial Investment Real Estate Foundation, Chicago, IL -- scholarship in real estate education
10,000	Hawaii Rotary Youth Foundation, Honolulu, HI -- for high school students and needy students
10,000	St. Andrew's Cathedral, Honolulu, HI -- for church use
6,000	Chinatown Merchants Association, Honolulu, HI -- scholarship pageant
5,000	Caltech University, Pasadena, CA -- for education program
5,000	Iolani School, Honolulu, HI -- for education fund
5,000	St. Andrew's Priory School for Girls, Honolulu, HI -- for Scholarship Program
2,000	Bible Institute of Hawaii, Honolulu, HI -- for bible training

2,000   Malama Na Keiki Foundation, Honolulu, HI -- for children and families at risk

2,000   Princess Victoria Kaiulana Elementary School, Honolulu, HI -- for educational fund

WOOD FOUNDATION OF CHAMBERSBURG, PA

Giving Contact

Charles O. Wood, III, Trustee
273 Lincoln Way E.
Chambersburg, PA 17201
Phone: (717)267-3174

Description

Founded: 1989
EIN: 251607838
Organization Type: Private Foundation
Giving Locations: CA; DE; MD; MA; PA: Chambersburg County, Franklin County
Grant Types: Capital, Emergency, Endowment, General Support, Multiyear/Continuing Support, Operating Expenses.

Donor Information

Founder: Established in 1989 by Max Zimmer.

Financial Summary

Total Giving: $485,170 (2001); $467,367 (2000); $645,793 (1999)
Giving Analysis: Giving for 2001 includes: foundation grants to United Way ($15,000); 1999: foundation grants to United Way ($15,000); 1998: foundation grants to United Way ($15,000)
Assets: $10,354,620 (2001); $11,931,986 (2000); $12,466,255 (1999)

Typical Recipients

Arts & Humanities: Arts Associations & Councils, Arts Festivals, Arts & Humanities-General, History & Archaeology, Libraries, Literary Arts, Museums/Galleries, Music, Theater
Civic & Public Affairs: Chambers of Commerce, Community Foundations, Economic Development, Employment/Job Training, Civic & Public Affairs-General, Housing, Legal Aid, Municipalities/Towns, Safety, Urban & Community Affairs, Women's Affairs
Education: Colleges & Universities, Continuing Education, Education Funds, Elementary Education (Public), Education-General, Private Education (Precollege), Public Education (Precollege), School Volunteerism, Secondary Education (Public)
Environment: Environment-General
Health: Cancer, Children's Health/Hospitals, Clinics/Medical Centers, Geriatric Health, Heart, Hospices, Hospitals, Long-Term Care, Mental Health, Public Health, Single-Disease Health Associations
Religion: Churches, Religious Welfare
Social Services: Animal Protection, Camps, Community Service Organizations, Counseling, Family Services, Food/Clothing Distribution, Scouts, Senior Services, Shelters/Homelessness, Social Services-General, United Funds/United Ways, YMCA/YWCA/YMHA/YWHA, Youth Organizations

Application Procedures

Initial Contact: Send a brief letter of inquiry and a full proposal.
Deadlines: None.

Restrictions

First consideration will be given to organizations serving the Chambersburg-Franklin Counties, Pennsylvania area.

Foundation Officials

Emilie W. Robinson: trustee
Charles O. Wood, III: trustee
David S. Wood: trustee
Miriam M. Wood: trustee

Grants Analysis

Disclosure Period: calendar year ending 2001
Total Grants: $470,170*
Number of Grants: 68
Average Grant: $6,179*
Highest Grant: $50,000
Typical Range: $1,000 to $10,000
*Note: Giving excludes United Way. Average grant figure excludes highest grant.

Recent Grants

Note: Grants derived from 2001 Form 990.

General

50,000	Boston Celebrity Series, Boston, MA -- annual giving
50,000	Isabella Stewart Gardner Museum, Boston, MA -- pledge
27,201	Financial Counseling Services, Chambersburg, PA -- pledge
25,000	Aurora Theatre Company, Berkeley, CA -- for capital campaign
25,000	Community Foundation of the Eastern Shore, Salisbury, MD -- for Kresge challenge grant
20,000	Community Foundation of the Eastern Shore, Salisbury, MD
18,977	Caledonia Theatre Group, Chambersburg, PA -- pledge
15,000	BOPIC, Chambersburg, PA -- for operations
15,000	Boston Celebrity Series, Boston, MA -- 2001 annual giving
15,000	Chambersburg Area United Way, Chambersburg, PA

WOODCOCK FOUNDATION

Giving Contact

Penny Willgeroot
30 Rockefeller Plz., Rm. 5600
New York, NY 10112
Phone: (212)649-5712

Description

Founded: 1988
EIN: 341606085
Organization Type: Private Foundation
Giving Locations: NY
Grant Types: General Support, Project, Research.

Donor Information

Founder: Polly Guth

Financial Summary

Total Giving: $1,905,508 (fiscal year ending November 30, 2000); $2,795,347 (fiscal 1999); $1,648,846 (fiscal 1998)
Assets: $54,663,727 (fiscal 2000); $51,457,106 (fiscal 1999); $53,148,522 (fiscal 1998)
Gifts Received: $10,907 (fiscal 1995); $155,500 (fiscal 1993). Note: In fiscal 1993, contributions were received from John H. J. Guth ($84,000) and Polly W. Guth ($71,500).

Typical Recipients

Arts & Humanities: Arts Centers, History & Archaeology, Museums/Galleries, Music, Opera, Performing Arts
Civic & Public Affairs: Asian American Affairs, Botanical Gardens/Parks, Economic Development, Ethnic Organizations, Civic & Public Affairs-General, Municipalities/Towns, Philanthropic Organizations,

Public Policy, Urban & Community Affairs, Women's Affairs
Education: Business-School Partnerships, Colleges & Universities, Community & Junior Colleges, Education Funds, Education Reform, Private Education (Precollege), School Volunteerism
Environment: Environment-General, Resource Conservation, Wildlife Protection
Health: Health Organizations
International: International-General, Health Care/Hospitals, International Environmental Issues, International Relations
Social Services: Child Welfare, Community Service Organizations, Day Care, Day Care, Family Planning, Scouts, Youth Organizations

Application Procedures

Initial Contact: Send a brief letter of inquiry.
Deadlines: None.

Foundation Officials

John H. J. Guth: trustee
Polly Guth: trustee
Virginia Montgomery: trustee

Grants Analysis

Disclosure Period: fiscal year ending November 30, 2000
Total Grants: $1,905,508
Number of Grants: 37
Average Grant: $43,672*
Highest Grant: $333,333
Typical Range: $20,000 to $100,000
*Note: Average grant excludes highest grant.

Recent Grants

Note: Grants derived from fiscal 1999 Form 990.

General

334,000	City Year
250,000	Population Council, The, New York, NY
150,000	Ashoka, Arlington, VA
125,000	171 Cedar Arts Center
100,000	Fund for the City of New York, New York, NY
100,000	Glynwood Center, Cold Spring, NY
100,000	Search for Common Ground, Washington, DC
80,000	Corning Community College, Corning, NY
77,000	Glimmerglass Opera, New York, NY
75,000	Calvert Foundation, Katy, TX

ROBERT W. WOODRUFF FOUNDATION

Giving Contact

Charles H. McTier, President
50 Hurt Plz., Suite 1200
Atlanta, GA 30303
Phone: (404)522-6755
Fax: (404)522-7026
E-mail: fdns@woodruff.org
Web: http://www.woodruff.org

Description

Founded: 1937
EIN: 581695425
Organization Type: General Purpose Foundation
Giving Locations: GA: Atlanta some statewide giving
Grant Types: Capital, Challenge, Matching, Multiyear/Continuing Support, Project, Seed Money.
Note: Foundation also gives grants toward land acquisition and equipment costs.

Donor Information

Founder: Established in 1937 by the late Robert W. Woodruff . Mr. Woodruff became president of the Coca-Cola Company in the 1920s and was instrumental in building the soft drink company into an international business. Mr. Woodruff was generally recognized as one of America's leading philanthropists. He was a major benefactor of Emory University in Atlanta. Mr. Woodruff had no children. When he died in 1985, he left almost his entire estate to the foundation.

Financial Summary

Total Giving: $122,831,490 (2002); $113,995,585 (2001); $149,979,270 (2000)

Assets: $2,210,193,890 (2002); $3,139,654,481 (2000); $3,114,438,206 (1999)

Gifts Received: In 1990, the foundation received a gift from the estate of Robert W. Woodruff.

Typical Recipients

Arts & Humanities: Arts Associations & Councils, Arts Centers, Community Arts, Historic Preservation, History & Archaeology, Libraries, Museums/Galleries, Music, Opera, Performing Arts, Public Broadcasting, Theater

Civic & Public Affairs: African American Affairs, Botanical Gardens/Parks, Business/Free Enterprise, Chambers of Commerce, Community Foundations, Economic Development, Civic & Public Affairs-General, Hispanic Affairs, Housing, Law & Justice, Legal Aid, Municipalities/Towns, Nonprofit Management, Public Policy, Safety, Urban & Community Affairs

Education: Agricultural Education, Business Education, Colleges & Universities, Education Associations, Education Funds, Education Reform, Engineering/Technological Education, Education-General, Health & Physical Education, International Studies, Leadership Training, Medical Education, Minority Education, Private Education (Precollege), Science/Mathematics Education, Social Sciences Education, Special Education, Student Aid

Environment: Air/Water Quality, Environment-General, Resource Conservation, Wildlife Protection

Health: Alzheimers Disease, Cancer, Children's Health/Hospitals, Emergency/Ambulance Services, Health-General, Geriatric Health, Health Policy/Cost Containment, Health Organizations, Hospices, Long-Term Care, Medical Rehabilitation, Medical Research, Mental Health, Nursing Services, Public Health, Trauma Treatment

International: Foreign Arts Organizations, Health Care/Hospitals

Religion: Jewish Causes, Religious Welfare

Science: Science Museums, Scientific Centers & Institutes, Scientific Labs, Scientific Research

Social Services: Child Welfare, Community Service Organizations, Counseling, Family Services, Recreation & Athletics, Senior Services, Social Services-General, United Funds/United Ways, YMCA/YWCA/YMHA/YWHA, Youth Organizations

Application Procedures

Initial Contact: Organizations seeking support should submit a letter of inquiry before submitting a proposal.

Application Requirements: Description of the organization, its purposes, staffing, and governing board; the organization's latest financial statements, including the most recent audited report; a description of the proposed project and full justification for its funding; an itemized project budget, including other sources of support in hand or anticipated; and evidence from the IRS of the organization's tax-exempt status and that the organization is not a private foundation.

Deadlines: For consideration at board meetings held in April and November, deadlines are February 1 and September 1, respectively.

Review Process: If the foundation is interested in the program, additional information or a site visit may be requested. Applicants will receive final notification within thirty days of the trustees' meeting.

Restrictions

The foundation does not make grants for general operating expenses or to individuals. The foundation also does not support propaganda or the influencing of legislature. Grants are generally limited to public charities located and operating in Georgia.

Additional Information

The foundation shares a common administrative arrangement with the Lettie Pate Evans Foundation, the Lettie Pate Whitehead Foundation, and the Joseph B. Whitehead Foundation. Applicants do not need to duplicate requests for information or grant funding from these other foundations.

Publications: Guidelines; Brochure; Data Sheet

Foundation Officials

Ivan Allen, Jr.: trustee B Atlanta, GA March 15, 1911. ED Georgia Institute of Technology (1933). PRIM CORP EMPL chairman emeritus: Ivan Allen Co. CORP AFFIL director: Equitable Life Assurance Society. NONPR AFFIL member: National Stationery & Office Equipment Association; member: Sigma Alpha Epsilon; member: Georgia Technology Alumni Association; trustee: Georgia Technology Foundation; member: Atlanta Chamber of Commerce; area president, member national executive board: Boy Scouts America. CLUB AFFIL member: Rotary Club.

Charles H. Ginden: trustee

P. Russell Hardin: vice president, secretary PRIM NONPR EMPL vice president-secretary: Ichauway Inc. NONPR AFFIL vice president-secretary: Joseph W Jones Ecological Research Center.

Joseph W. Jones: chairman emeritus

Wilton D. Looney: trustee B 1919. PRIM CORP EMPL honorary chairman, director: Genuine Parts Co. CORP AFFIL director: RPC Inc.; director: Rollins Inc.; director: Coca-Cola Enterprises Inc.; trustee: Ichauway Inc. NONPR AFFIL trustee: Joseph W Jones Ecological Research Center.

Charles Harvey McTier: president B Columbus, GA 1939. ED Emory University BBA (1961). PRIM CORP EMPL president: Ichauway Inc. CORP AFFIL director: SunTrust Bank Georgia Inc.; director: SunTrust Bank Atlanta. NONPR AFFIL trustee: North Georgia United Methodist Foundation; member: President Cir National Academy Sciences Institute Medicine; president: Joseph W Jones Ecological Research Center; member: Management Executives Society; chairman board trustee: Foundation Center; pub member: Joint Commission Accreditation Health Care Organizations; vice chairman, chairman management committee: Council Foundations; member: Association Emory Alumni. CLUB AFFIL Druid Hills Golf Club; Piedmont Driving Club; director: Commerce Club.

James Malcolm Sibley: vice chairman, trustee B Atlanta, GA August 05, 1919. ED Princeton University AB (1941); Woodrow Wilson School of Law (1942); Harvard University Law School (1945-1946). CORP AFFIL director: Summit Industries; director: Rock-Tenn Co.; director: Ichauway Inc. NONPR AFFIL member: Georgia Bar Association; trustee: AG Rhodes Home; member: Atlanta Bar Association; member: American College Probate Counsel; member: American Law Institute; member: American Bar Foundation; member: American Bar Association. CLUB AFFIL Piedmont Driving Club; Commerce Club.

J. Lee Tribble: treasurer PRIM CORP EMPL treasurer: Ichauway Inc. NONPR AFFIL treasurer: Joseph W Jones Ecological Research Center.

James Bryan Williams: chairman, trustee B Sewanee, TN 1933. ED Emory University AB (1955). PRIM CORP EMPL chairman, chief executive officer, director: SunTrust Banks, Inc. CORP AFFIL director: Sonat Inc.; director: RPC Energy Services Inc.; director: RPC Inc.; director: Georgia-Pacific Corp.; director: Rollins Inc.; director: Coca-Cola Co.; director: Genuine Parts Co.; director: Boral Industries Inc. NONPR AFFIL director: Federal Reserve Bank Atlanta; chairman board trustees: Robert R Woodruff Health Science Center; trustee: Emory University; member: Bankers Roundtable. CLUB AFFIL Piedmont Driving Club; member: Ocean Forest Golf Club; Peachtree Golf Club; Capital City Club; Commerce Club.

Grants Analysis

Disclosure Period: calendar year ending 2002

Total Grants: $122,831,490

Number of Grants: 70

Average Grant: $1,176,253*

Highest Grant: $41,670,000

Lowest Grant: $25,000

Typical Range: $200,000 to $2,000,000

*Note: Average grant figure excludes highest grant.

Recent Grants

Note: Grants derived from 2001 Form 990.

Library-Related

300,000   Council on Library and Information Resources, Atlanta, GA -- for the establishment at Emory University of the Digital Leadership Institute

General

33,778,071 Robert W. Woodruff Health Sciences Center Fund, Atlanta, GA

30,043,080 Robert W. Woodruff Health Sciences Center Fund, Atlanta, GA

25,000,000 Robert W. Woodruff Health Sciences Center Fund, Atlanta, GA

5,500,000 Emory University, Atlanta, GA -- support of the teaching and research mission of the Emory Clinic

5,000,000 Georgia Tech Foundation, Atlanta, GA -- purchase of land

4,000,000 Nature Conservancy, Atlanta, GA -- acquisition of the Chickasawhatchee Swamp

2,500,000 Berry College, Rome, GA -- construction of new science building

2,200,000 Atlanta Neighborhood Development Partnership, Atlanta, GA -- continued support for housing development

2,000,000 Morehouse School of Medicine, Atlanta, GA -- construction of National Center for Primary Care

1,893,750 Ichauway, Inc., Newton, GA -- capital and operating needs

WOODS CHARITABLE FUND

Giving Contact

Pam Baker, Executive Director & Secretary
PO Box 81309
Lincoln, NE 68501
Phone: (402)436-5971
Fax: (402)436-4128
E-mail: pbaker@woodscharitable.org
Web: http://www.woodscharitable.org

Alternate Contact

E-mail: twoods@woodscharitable.org

Description

Founded: 1941
EIN: 476032847
Organization Type: Family Foundation
Giving Locations: NE: Lincoln
Grant Types: Award, General Support, Matching, Multiyear/Continuing Support, Operating Expenses, Project, Seed Money

Donor Information

Founder: Established in 1941 in Nebraska by the late Frank H. Woods , his wife, the late Nelle Cochrane Woods , and their three sons. The fund received substantial support in 1952 from Frank H. Woods before his death later that year. In 1955, the fund received one-third of the net residuary estate of Nelle C. Woods. Over the years, the family-owned Sahara Coal Company has contributed to the fund's assets. Although the five founders are now deceased, other family members continue to serve as officers and trustees of the fund.

At the end of 1993, the fund underwent a major restructuring, resulting in two separate foundations: Woods Charitable Fund, giving in Lincoln, NE, and the Wood's Fund of Chicago.

Financial Summary

Total Giving: $1,600,000 (2001 approx); $1,543,205 (2000); $1,143,900 (1999)
Assets: $37,000,000 (2001 approx); $38,607,912 (2000); $22,383,872 (1999)

Typical Recipients

Arts & Humanities: Arts Associations & Councils, Arts Centers, Arts Outreach, Community Arts, Dance, Arts & Humanities-General, Historic Preservation, Literary Arts, Museums/Galleries, Music, Opera, Performing Arts, Public Broadcasting, Theater, Visual Arts

Civic & Public Affairs: African American Affairs, Asian American Affairs, Civil Rights, Community Foundations, Economic Development, Economic Policy, Employment/Job Training, Ethnic Organizations, Civic & Public Affairs-General, Hispanic Affairs, Housing, Law & Justice, Legal Aid, Municipalities/Towns, Native American Affairs, Nonprofit Management, Public Policy, Rural Affairs, Safety, Urban & Community Affairs, Women's Affairs, Zoos/Aquariums

Education: Arts/Humanities Education, Colleges & Universities, Education Associations, Education Reform, Faculty Development, Education-General, International Studies, Leadership Training, Literacy, Preschool Education, Private Education (Precollege), Public Education (Precollege), Special Education

Health: AIDS/HIV, Alzheimers Disease, Clinics/Medical Centers, Medical Rehabilitation, Mental Health, Public Health, Single-Disease Health Associations

International: International Relief Efforts

Religion: Churches, Religious Welfare, Social/Policy Issues

Science: Science Museums

Social Services: Animal Protection, At-Risk Youth, Big Brother/Big Sister, Child Abuse, Child Welfare, Community Centers, Community Centers, Community Service Organizations, Counseling, Crime Prevention, Day Care, Delinquency & Criminal Rehabilitation, Domestic Violence, Family Planning, Family Services, Food/Clothing Distribution, People with Disabilities, Recreation & Athletics, Scouts, Senior Services, Shelters/Homelessness, Substance Abuse, United Funds/United Ways, Veterans, Volunteer Services, YMCA/YWCA/YMHA/YWHA, Youth Organizations

Application Procedures

Initial Contact: Applicants should contact the fund for a copy of guidelines, procedures, and timetables. Applicants should then send a two-page summary request and budget, or contact the fund by telephone to determine whether the project falls within funding guidelines.

Application Requirements: If the fund requests a full proposal, an organization must provide a completed application form. The fund now accepts the Lincoln/Lancaster County Grantmakers' Association common grant application form. The fund also requires a copy of the IRS determination letter of tax-exempt status; listing of board members, with addresses and phone numbers; audited financial statement for the last fiscal year; income and expense budgets for the current

fiscal year and for the year for which support is sought; organization and project budgets, listing of actual commitments toward projected budget; itemization of other sources of support; and a Form 990 if annual budget exceeds $500,000.

Deadlines: Organizations must submit applications between March 1 and March 15 for the June meeting, between June 1 and June 15 for the September meeting, and between September 1 and September 15 for the December board meeting.

Review Process: Proposals arriving well before a given deadline are given more careful review. An application not clearly within the fund's priorities, but not clearly ineligible, will be reviewed by board members.

Restrictions

The fund supports work in Lincoln, NE, but occasionally reviews proposals from outside of Lincoln, if the proposed activities have statewide impact and can also demonstrate direct impact on Lincoln.

The fund does not make grants for individual needs, endowments, scholarships, fellowships, medical or scientific research, programs for individual schools, residential care and medical clinics, environment programs, recreational programs, fund-raising benefits, program advertising, or religious programs.

Additionally, the Lincoln grant program does not fund capital projects in health-care institutions, or college or university proposals that do not directly involve faculty or students in applied projects that benefit the region.

Buildings and equipment acquisition, expansion, and renovation projects are low priorities for the fund. Applicants should be organizations described in Section 501(c)(3) of the IRS code and have written ruling from the IRS that they also qualify under 509(a)(1), (2), or (3) of the code (publicly supported organizations and their affiliates). The fund occasionally considers proposals from private 501(c)(3) operating foundations; in unusual cases, it may consider fiscal agent and expenditure responsibility grants.

Additional Information

Organizations receiving grants must present written reports informing the board of the use of funds in relation to the original proposal objectives, and the results. Some grantees are asked to participate in a post-grant evaluation to compare program accomplishments with proposed objectives.

The fund offers proposal writing assistance.

Publications: Annual Report; Fund Guidelines; Application Form

Foundation Officials

Pam Baker: executive director, secretary
Joel Gajardo: vice president, director
Marilyn Johnson-Farr: director
Thomas D. Potter: director
Michael John Tavlin: assistant treasurer B Lincoln, NE 1946. ED Oklahoma City University BA (1970); University of Nebraska JD (1973); Washington University LLM (1977). PRIM CORP EMPL treasurer: Aliant Cellular Inc. ADD CORP EMPL treasurer: Aliant Communications Inc.; treasurer: Aliant System Inc.; vice president, section, treasurer: Aliant Midwest Inc.; treasurer: Aliant Network System Inc. CORP AFFIL vice president, secretary, treasurer: Lincoln Tel & Tel Co.; vice president, secretary, treasurer: Prairie Communications Inc.
Avery L. Woods: director
Marjorie Woods: director
Thomas C. Woods, III: president, treasurer B 1945. ED Hiram Scott College (1968). PRIM CORP EMPL chairman: Aliant Communications Inc.

Grants Analysis

Disclosure Period: calendar year ending 2000
Total Grants: $1,543,205
Number of Grants: 83
Average Grant: $18,593
Highest Grant: $100,000

Lowest Grant: $475
Typical Range: $3,000 to $30,000

Recent Grants

Note: Grants derived from 2000 Form 990.

General

100,000	Lincoln Arts Council, Lincoln, NE -- for technology grant
50,000	Child Guidance Center, Bridgeport, CT -- for C.F. STAR - Children and Families Strengthened Through an Array of Resources
50,000	Lincoln Children's Museum, Lincoln, NE -- building acquisition/renovation
50,000	Nebraska Art Association, Lincoln, NE -- for painting acquisition in memory of Thomas C. Woods, III
50,000	People's City Mission, Lincoln, NE -- capital campaign
50,000	People's City Mission, Lincoln, NE -- capital campaign
45,000	Hispanic Community Center, Lincoln, NE -- for changing trends
40,000	Lincoln Community Playhouse, Lincoln, NE -- to establish a Fund Development Office
40,000	Lincoln Medical Education Foundation, Inc., Lincoln, NE -- Center for Family Care Project
40,000	Lincoln Medical Education Foundation, Inc., Lincoln, NE -- Center for Family Care Project

WOODWARD FUND

Giving Contact

Samuel A. Curtis, Jr., Administrator
c/o Fleet National Bank
1 East Ave.
Rochester, NY 14638
Phone: (716)435-7240

Description

Founded: 1965
EIN: 166064221
Organization Type: Private Foundation
Giving Locations: AZ; ME
Grant Types: General Support, Research.

Donor Information

Founder: Florence S. Woodward

Financial Summary

Total Giving: $200,000 (fiscal year ending November 30, 2001); $446,000 (fiscal 2000); $155,000 (fiscal 1998)
Giving Analysis: Giving for fiscal 2000 includes: foundation grants to United Way ($5,000); foundation program-related investments ($241,000); fiscal 1998: foundation grants to United Way ($4,000) foundation ($151,000)
Assets: $3,709,339 (fiscal 2001); $4,224,092 (fiscal 2000); $4,518,055 (fiscal 1998)
Gifts Received: $1,828 (fiscal 1992)

Typical Recipients

Arts & Humanities: Art History, Arts Centers, Arts Funds, History & Archaeology, Libraries, Museums/Galleries, Music, Opera
Civic & Public Affairs: Civic & Public Affairs-General, Housing, Legal Aid, Municipalities/Towns, Nonprofit Management, Urban & Community Affairs, Women's Affairs, Zoos/Aquariums
Education: Colleges & Universities, International Exchange, Minority Education, Preschool Education, Private Education (Precollege), Public Education (Precollege), School Volunteerism, Secondary Education (Public)

Environment: Environment-General, Resource Conservation, Wildlife Protection
Health: Emergency/Ambulance Services, Health Organizations, Hospices, Hospitals, Medical Rehabilitation, Medical Research, Public Health, Single-Disease Health Associations
International: Human Rights, International Development, International Environmental Issues, International Relief Efforts
Religion: Churches, Religious Welfare
Science: Science Museums
Social Services: Animal Protection, At-Risk Youth, Child Welfare, Community Service Organizations, Day Care, Domestic Violence, Family Planning, People with Disabilities, Recreation & Athletics, Shelters/Homelessness, United Funds/United Ways, YMCA/YWCA/YMHA/YWHA, Youth Organizations

Application Procedures

Initial Contact: Foundation does not specify a particular application form.
Deadlines: None.

Restrictions

Does not support individuals.

Additional Information

Trust(s): Fleet Bank NA

Grants Analysis

Disclosure Period: fiscal year ending November 30, 2001
Total Grants: $200,000
Number of Grants: 41
Average Grant: $4,878
Highest Grant: $10,000
Lowest Grant: $1,000
Typical Range: $1,000 to $10,000

Recent Grants

Note: Grants derived from fiscal 2000 Form 990.

General

241,000	Project Mobility, Phoenix, AZ
10,000	College of the Atlantic, Bar Harbor, ME
10,000	Mobius, Boston, MA
10,000	Scottsdale Cultural Council, Scottsdale, AZ
10,000	Scottsdale Cultural Council, Scottsdale, AZ
10,000	United College
8,000	Newton Elementary School
8,000	Newton Elementary School
8,000	Newton Elementary School
8,000	Newton School PTA

WORLD HERITAGE FOUNDATION

Giving Contact

Pat Debone
1 Heritage Pl., Suite 400
Southgate, MI 48195
Phone: (734)246-0015

Description

Founded: 1985
EIN: 382640416
Organization Type: Private Foundation
Giving Locations: MI
Grant Types: General Support.

Donor Information

Founder: Heinz C. Prechter, Heinz Co., Prechter Charitable Lead Trust

Financial Summary

Total Giving: $1,247,600 (2000); $671,622 (1999); $744,833 (1998)
Giving Analysis: Giving for 2000 includes: foundation grants to United Way ($25,000); 1998: foundation grants to United Way ($5,000) 1997: foundation grants to United Way ($5,000)
Assets: $12,976,950 (2000); $13,820,167 (1999); $12,841,861 (1998)
Gifts Received: $26,878 (1995); $75,000 (1994); $100,000 (1993). Note: In fiscal 1995, contributions were received from the Heinz C. Prechter Charitable Lead Trust.

Typical Recipients

Arts & Humanities: Arts Associations & Councils, Arts Institutes, Community Arts, Arts & Humanities-General, History & Archaeology, Libraries, Museums/Galleries, Music, Opera
Civic & Public Affairs: African American Affairs, Clubs, Economic Development, Civic & Public Affairs-General, Parades/Festivals, Public Policy, Urban & Community Affairs, Women's Affairs, Zoos/Aquariums
Education: Arts/Humanities Education, Business Education, Colleges & Universities, Engineering/Technological Education, International Studies, Literacy, Minority Education, Private Education (Precollege), Science/Mathematics Education, Student Aid
Health: AIDS/HIV, Alzheimers Disease, Cancer, Children's Health/Hospitals, Emergency/Ambulance Services, Eyes/Blindness, Health Organizations, Hospitals, Long-Term Care, Public Health, Single-Disease Health Associations
International: International Affairs, International Development, International Relations, International Relief Efforts, Missionary/Religious Activities
Religion: Jewish Causes, Religious Welfare
Science: Scientific Centers & Institutes
Social Services: Child Welfare, Community Service Organizations, Counseling, Food/Clothing Distribution, People with Disabilities, Recreation & Athletics, Scouts, United Funds/United Ways, Volunteer Services, YMCA/YWCA/YMHA/YWHA

Application Procedures

Initial Contact: Send a brief letter of inquiry.
Application Requirements: proof of tax-exempt status.
Deadlines: None.

Foundation Officials

Lori Koenig: treasurer, director
Waltraud Prechter: president, director
David L. Treadwell: secretary, director

Grants Analysis

Disclosure Period: calendar year ending 2000
Total Grants: $1,222,600*
Number of Grants: 153
Average Grant: $5,069*
Highest Grant: $452,183
Lowest Grant: $100
Typical Range: $1,000 to $10,000
***Note:** Giving excludes United Way. Average grant figure excludes highest grant.

Recent Grants

Note: Grants derived from 1999 Form 990.

General

53,753	Center for Public Leadership Studies/TAMU, TX
50,000	Kresge Eye Institute, Detroit, MI
50,000	University of Michigan School of Engineering, Dearborn, MI -- third draw of $500,000 pledge
50,000	University of Michigan School of Engineering, Dearborn, MI -- sixth draw of $500,000 pledge
20,000	Automotive Hall of Fame, Dearborn, MI
20,000	Henry Ford Museum and Greenfield Village, Dearborn, MI -- second draw of $100,000 pledge
18,000	Detroit Renaissance Foundation, Detroit, MI
16,667	Karmanos Cancer Institute, Detroit, MI -- first draw of $50,000 pledge
12,500	Eden Club, Ann Arbor, MI -- second and final draw of $25,000 pledge
11,700	University of Texas M. D. Anderson Cancer Center, Houston, TX

WORNER TRUST

Giving Contact

Jo Ann Harlan
Worner Trust
c/o National City Bank
301 SW Adams
Peoria, IL 61602-1500
Phone: (216)575-2630

Description

Founded: 1996
EIN: 376337761
Organization Type: Private Foundation
Giving Locations: IL
Grant Types: General Support, Project.

Financial Summary

Total Giving: $99,209 (fiscal year ending March 31, 2001)
Assets: $2,405,602 (fiscal 2001); $1,832,834 (fiscal 1996)

Typical Recipients

Civic & Public Affairs: Urban & Community Affairs
Education: Arts/Humanities Education, Colleges & Universities, Elementary Education (Public), Public Education (Precollege), Student Aid
Health: Children's Health/Hospitals
Religion: Churches
Social Services: Child Welfare, Refugee Assistance, Youth Organizations

Application Procedures

Initial Contact: The foundation reports that it has no formal application procedure. Sent a brief letter of inquiry.
Deadlines: None.

Grants Analysis

Disclosure Period: fiscal year ending March 31, 2001
Total Grants: $99,209
Number of Grants: 41
Average Grant: $2,420
Highest Grant: $11,000
Lowest Grant: $250
Typical Range: $400 to $10,000

Recent Grants

Note: Grants derived from 2001 Form 990.

General

11,000	Peoria County Regional Office of Education, Peoria, IL -- for arts in education 2000
10,000	San Jose United Methodist Church, San Jose, IL -- for building addition
8,000	University of Illinois, Peoria, IL -- support for the Peoria Medical Care Craze
7,500	Midwest Central High School, Manito, IL
7,000	WD Boyce Council BSA, Peoria, IL -- for the Peoria Scoutreach Program

5,000	American Near East Refugee Aid, Washington, DC -- support for technology project
5,000	Bradley University, Peoria, IL
5,000	Children's Home Association, Peoria, IL -- for the Totally Integrated Electronic Records Project
5,000	Easter Seals, Peoria, IL -- for Communication Technology Camp
5,000	St. Charles Avenue Presbyterian Church, New Orleans, LA -- for Stair Program

WORONOCO SAVINGS BANK

Company Headquarters

31 Court St.
Westfield, MA 01085-0978
Web: http://www.woronoco.com

Company Description

Founded: 1871
Assets: US$642 billion (2001)
Employees: 142 (2001)
SIC(s): 6036 Savings Institutions Except Federal.
Parent Company: Woronoco Bancorp, Inc., 31 Court St., Westfield, MA, United States

Nonmonetary Support

Volunteer Programs: The company encourages employee volunteerism. Woronoco Savings Bank employees contribute approximately 6,500 volunteer hours annually.

Woronoco Savings Charitable Foundation

Giving Contact

Debra L. Murphy, Senior Vice President & Chief Financial Officer
Woronoco Savings Bank
31 Court Street
Westfield, MA 01086-0978
Phone: (413)564-6241
Web: http://www.woronoco.com/home/sponsors.php
Note: Ms. Murphy is also director and treasurer of the Woronoco Savings Charitable Foundation.

Description

Founded: 2000
EIN: 043458037
Organization Type: Corporate Foundation
Giving Locations: MA: western area
Grant Types: Capital, General Support, Operating Expenses.

Financial Summary

Total Giving: $306,433 (2001); $79,234 (2000)
Giving Analysis: Giving for 2001 includes: foundation matching gifts ($1,320); foundation scholarships ($10,500) foundation ($294,613).
Assets: $7,705,347 (2001); $6,006,034 (2000); $4,315,860 (1999)
Gifts Received: $4,443,600 (1999). Note: In 1999, contributions were received from Woronoco Savings Bank.

Typical Recipients

Arts & Humanities: History & Archaeology, Libraries, Museums/Galleries, Theater
Civic & Public Affairs: Botanical Gardens/Parks, Civic & Public Affairs-General, Housing, Philanthropic Organizations, Safety

Education: Business Education, Colleges & Universities, Secondary Education (Public), Special Education
Health: Hospices, Hospitals
Social Services: Child Welfare, Emergency Relief, Recreation & Athletics, Scouts, Veterans, YMCA/YWCA/YMHA/YWHA, Youth Organizations

Application Procedures

Initial Contact: Contact the company/foundation to request an application form.
Application Requirements: Send written request for application.

Restrictions

Awards are generally limited to western Massachusetts.

Corporate Officials

Cornelius D. Mahoney: chairman, president, chief executive officer
Debra L. Murphy: senior vice president, chief financial officer

Foundation Officials

James A. Adams: director
William G. Aiken: director
Carl J. Antonellis, Jr.: secretary
Barbara Braem: executive director
Agastino J. Calheno: president, director
Neil Mahoney: director
Debra L. Murphy: treasurer, director (see above)
Ann V. Schultz: director
D. Jeffrey Templeton: director

Grants Analysis

Disclosure Period: calendar year ending 2001
Total Grants: $294,613*
Number of Grants: 36
Average Grant: $6,989*
Highest Grant: $50,000
Lowest Grant: $500
Typical Range: $1,000 to $10,000
*Note: Giving excludes matching gifts; scholarships. Average grant figure excludes highest grant.

Recent Grants

Note: Grants derived from 2001 Form 990.

Library-Related
11,000	East Longmeadow Public Library, East Longmeadow, MA -- for renovation and expansion of the current library

General
50,000	Westfield State College, Westfield, MA -- for operating costs
33,333	Boys and Girls Club of Greater Westfield, Westfield, CT -- for operating costs
25,000	Center of Hope, Westfield, MA -- for operating costs
25,000	Center of Hope, Westfield, MA -- for cancer victims
20,000	Noble Hospital, Westfield, MA -- for operating costs
15,000	Discover Westfield Children's Museum, Westfield, MA -- for operating costs
15,000	Westfield High School, Westfield, MA -- to establish a Science Fair Program
10,000	Pioneer Valley Girl Scout Council, Inc., East Longmeadow, MA -- for endowment fund
8,400	Basketball Hall of Fame, Springfield, MA -- for operating costs
6,250	Noble Visiting Nurse and Hospice, Westfield, MA -- for operating costs

WORTHAM FOUNDATION

Giving Contact

Barbara J. Snyder, Grants Administrator
2727 Allen Parkway, Suite 1570
Wortham Tower
Houston, TX 77019
Phone: (713)526-8849
Fax: (713)526-7222

Description

Founded: 1958
EIN: 741334356
Organization Type: General Purpose Foundation
Giving Locations: TX: Houston
Grant Types: Capital, Challenge, Endowment, General Support, Operating Expenses.

Donor Information

Founder: Established in 1958 by Mr. and Mrs. Gus S. Wortham , both deceased. Mr. Wortham was a partner of John L. Wortham & Son, which organized the American General Insurance Company (now American General Corporation). Mr. Wortham was active in civic, educational, and cultural affairs. He was on the board of governors of Rice University and active in fund-raising activities for Rice Stadium, the Houston Symphony Society, Houston Grand Opera, and the Society for the Performing Arts. His wife, Lyndall Finley Wortham , was a member of the board of regents of the University of Houston, and a board member of the Houston Grand Opera Association.

Financial Summary

Total Giving: $12,550,704 (fiscal year ending September 30, 2001); $11,785,651 (fiscal 2000); $11,147,300 (fiscal 1999)
Giving Analysis: Giving for fiscal 1999 includes: foundation grants to United Way ($60,000) fiscal 1998: foundation grants to United Way ($55,000)
Assets: $2,800,000 (fiscal 2001); $247,267,145 (fiscal 2000); $225,388,449 (fiscal 1999)
Gifts Received: $816 (fiscal 1997)

Typical Recipients

Arts & Humanities: Arts Associations & Councils, Arts Outreach, Ballet, Arts & Humanities-General, Historic Preservation, History & Archaeology, Libraries, Literary Arts, Museums/Galleries, Music, Opera, Performing Arts, Public Broadcasting, Theater, Visual Arts
Civic & Public Affairs: Asian American Affairs, Botanical Gardens/Parks, Clubs, Economic Development, Employment/Job Training, Civic & Public Affairs-General, Municipalities/Towns, Parades/Festivals, Urban & Community Affairs, Zoos/Aquariums
Education: Colleges & Universities, Education Reform, Engineering/Technological Education, Education-General, Medical Education, Private Education (Precollege), Science/Mathematics Education
Environment: Environment-General
Health: Cancer, Children's Health/Hospitals, Clinics/Medical Centers, Emergency/Ambulance Services, Hospitals, Public Health
International: Foreign Arts Organizations
Religion: Churches, Religious Welfare
Science: Science-General, Science Museums
Social Services: Animal Protection, Child Welfare, Community Centers, Scouts, Shelters/Homelessness, United Funds/United Ways, YMCA/YWCA/YMHA/YWHA

Application Procedures

Initial Contact: Send one unbound proposal copy. A formal application form can be requested from the foundation.
Application Requirements: The proposal should include purpose of funds sought; project budget;

amount requested and date needed; proof of tax-exempt status; a list of trustees or directors and principal staff; and financial statements for the current fiscal year to date and the last complete fiscal year.
Deadlines: Applications should be received by the first week of January, April, July, or October.
Review Process: Proposals are considered at the foundation's trustee meetings held in February, May, August, and November. The staff will review and respond to requests following scheduled board meetings.

Restrictions

The foundation does not lend or give money to individuals.

Additional Information

Publications: Annual Report Guidelines; Application Form

Foundation Officials

Fred C. Burns: chairman B 1938. ED Rice University (1960). PRIM CORP EMPL managing partner: John L Wortham & Son LLP. CORP AFFIL director: American Indemnity Financial Corp.
Brady F. Carruth: president B 1957. ED University of Texas, Austin BA (1981); University of Texas, Austin MBA (1983). PRIM CORP EMPL vice president, director: Carruth-Doggett Inc. CORP AFFIL president: Gulf Coast Capital Corp.
James A. Elkins, III: trustee B Houston, TX 1952. ED Princeton University BA (1974); University of Texas MBA (1976). PRIM CORP EMPL chairman: Houston Trust Co. CORP AFFIL director: Central Houston Inc. NONPR AFFIL member: Texas Bankers Association; president, trustee: Texas Children's Hospital; member: Robert Morris Associates; vice chairman: Salvation Army; trustee: Menil Foundation; board governors: Rice University; trustee: Houston Zoological Society; trustee: Houston Museum Natural Science; treasurer: Houston Parks Board; member: American Bankers Association; trustee: Childrens Museum. CLUB AFFIL Houston Club; Forum Club.
E. A. Stumpf, III: trustee
R. W. Wortham, III: secretary, treasurer

Grants Analysis

Disclosure Period: fiscal year ending September 30, 2000
Total Grants: $11,716,115*
Number of Grants: 72
Average Grant: $162,724
Highest Grant: $2,000,000
Lowest Grant: $5,000
Typical Range: $10,000 to $25,000 and $100,000 to $300,000
***Note:** Grants analysis provided by foundation. Giving excludes United Way.

Recent Grants

Note: Grants derived from fiscal 2000 Form 990.

General

2,000,000	Houston Music Hall Foundation, Houston, TX
1,060,200	Houston Symphony Society, Houston, TX
1,015,000	Houston Museum of Natural Science, Houston, TX
1,000,000	Museum of Fine Arts - Houston, Houston, TX
750,000	Houston Grand Opera, Houston, TX
500,000	Miller Theater Advisory Council, Houston, TX
500,000	Sam Houston Area Council Boy Scouts, Houston, TX
450,000	Houston Museum of Natural Science, Houston, TX
375,000	Alley Theater, Houston, TX
375,000	Theater Under the Stars, Houston, TX

WORTHINGTON FOODS

Company Headquarters

900 Proprietors Rd.
Worthington, OH 43085
Web: http://www.wfds.com

Company Description

Revenue: US$77 million (2001)
Employees: 350 (2001)
SIC(s): 2000 Food & Kindred Products.

Operating Locations

Worthington Foods (OH--Worthington)

Worthington Foods Foundation

Giving Contact

Allan R. Buller, Chairman
430 E. Dublin-Granville Rd.
Worthington, OH 43085
Phone: (614)885-4426

Alternate Contact

Dale E. Twomley, President, Chief Executive Officer & Director
Note: Contact for direct giving.

Description

EIN: 311286538
Organization Type: Corporate Foundation
Giving Locations: CA; OH: nationally.
Grant Types: Conference/Seminar, Employee Matching Gifts, General Support, Multiyear/Continuing Support, Project, Research, Scholarship.

Financial Summary

Total Giving: $27,500 (fiscal year ending June 30, 2002); $19,000 (fiscal 2001); $39,000 (fiscal 1999 approx)
Giving Analysis: Giving for fiscal 2002 includes: foundation grants to United Way ($5,000)
Assets: $883,524 (fiscal 2002); $849,448 (fiscal 2001); $73,154 (fiscal 1999)
Gifts Received: $65,000 (fiscal 2002); $20,000 (fiscal 2001); $65,000 (fiscal 1997). Note: In fiscal 2002, contributions were received from Allan Buller ($5,000), Dale Twomley ($30,000), and George T. Harding III ($30,000). In fiscal 2000, contributions were received from Allan R. Buller. In fiscal 1994, contributions were received from Worthington Foods.

Typical Recipients

Arts & Humanities: Arts Associations & Councils, History & Archaeology, Libraries
Civic & Public Affairs: Philanthropic Organizations
Education: Colleges & Universities, Education Funds, Faculty Development, Health & Physical Education, International Studies, Medical Education, Minority Education, Private Education (Precollege), Student Aid
Health: Adolescent Health Issues, Alzheimers Disease, Children's Health/Hospitals, Health Organizations, Heart, Nutrition
Religion: Churches, Religious Organizations, Religious Welfare
Social Services: People with Disabilities

Application Procedures

Initial Contact: Send a brief letter of inquiry.
Application Requirements: appropriate support information.
Deadlines: None.

Restrictions

Preference is given to research and education in the fields of health and nutrition.

Corporate Officials

Allan R. Buller: chairman, treasurer, director PRIM CORP EMPL chairman, treasurer, director: Worthington Foods.
William T. Kirkwood: chief financial officer, vice president financial, director PRIM CORP EMPL chief financial officer, vice president financial, director: Worthington Foods.
Dale E. Twomley: president, chief executive officer, director PRIM CORP EMPL president, chief executive officer, director: Worthington Foods.

Foundation Officials

Allan R. Buller: trustee (see above)
George T. Harding, IV: trustee
Dale E. Twomley: trustee (see above)

Grants Analysis

Disclosure Period: fiscal year ending June 30, 2002
Total Grants: $22,500*
Number of Grants: 4
Highest Grant: $10,000
Lowest Grant: $2,500
***Note:** Giving excludes United Way.

Recent Grants

Note: Grants derived from fiscal 2000 Form 990.

General

85,000	Seventh Day Adventist Church, Worthington, OH -- for local church building project
3,000	Loma Linda University, Loma Linda, CA -- for scholarships in field of nutrition
2,000	I Know I Can, Columbus, OH -- for student aid

WPS RESOURCES CORP.

Company Headquarters

700 N. Adams Street
Green Bay, WI 54307-9001
Phone: (920)433-4901
Fax: (920)433-1526
Web: http://www.wpsr.com

Company Description

Founded: 1993
Ticker: WPS
Exchange: NYSE
Assets: US$1.716 billion (2001)
Employees: 2856 (2001)
SIC(s): 4911 Electric Services, 4924 Natural Gas Distribution.

Operating Locations

Wisconsin Public Service Corp. (WI--Green Bay)

Nonmonetary Support

Type: Cause-related Marketing & Promotion; Donated Equipment; Donated Products; Loaned Employees
Volunteer Programs: The company sponsors employee volunteer programs in association with the United Way at Work Committee, Adopt-a-Classroom, and the Lyle Kingston Environmental Group.

WPS Resources Foundation, Inc.

Giving Contact
Larry Weyers, President
Wisconsin Public Service Foundation
PO Box 19001
Green Bay, WI 54307-9001
Phone: (920)433-1103
Fax: (414)433-1693
Web: http://www.wpsr.com/foundat/index.html

Alternate Contact
Wisconsin Public Service Foundation Scholarship Program
College Scholarship Service/Sponsored Scholarship Program
CN 6730
Princeton, NJ 08541
Note: Address for scholarship application form requests.

Description
EIN: 396075016
Organization Type: Corporate Foundation
Former Name: Wisconsin Public Service Foundation, Inc..
Giving Locations: MI: Northern Michigan; WI: Northeast Wisconsin
Grant Types: Capital, Matching, Operating Expenses, Scholarship.
Note: Employee matching gift ratio: 1 to 2.

Financial Summary
Total Giving: $965,599 (2001); $914,437 (2000); $925,000 (1999 approx). Note: Contributes through corporate direct giving program and foundation.
Giving Analysis: Giving for 2000 includes: foundation matching gifts ($29,810); foundation grants to United Way ($127,682); foundation scholarships ($165,350); foundation ($591,595); 1998: foundation matching gifts ($22,461); foundation grants to United Way ($101,610); foundation scholarships ($184,100); 1997: foundation matching gifts ($19,241); foundation grants to United Way ($111,545) foundation scholarships ($176,800)
Assets: $17,718,356 (2001); $18,883,525 (2000); $18,692,832 (1998)
Gifts Received: $50,000 (2001); $230,000 (1998); $95,000 (1997). Note: Contributions are received from Wisconsin Public Service Corp.

Typical Recipients
Arts & Humanities: Arts Festivals, Dance, Arts & Humanities-General, History & Archaeology, Libraries, Museums/Galleries, Music, Opera, Performing Arts, Theater
Civic & Public Affairs: Botanical Gardens/Parks, Business/Free Enterprise, Chambers of Commerce, Clubs, Community Foundations, Economic Development, Civic & Public Affairs-General, Housing, Municipalities/Towns, Philanthropic Organizations, Rural Affairs, Urban & Community Affairs, Women's Affairs, Zoos/Aquariums
Education: Agricultural Education, Business Education, Colleges & Universities, Education Funds, Engineering/Technological Education, Education-General, Medical Education, Minority Education, Public Education (Precollege), Science/Mathematics Education, Science/Mathematics Education, Student Aid
Environment: Environment-General, Wildlife Protection
Health: Children's Health/Hospitals, Clinics/Medical Centers, Emergency/Ambulance Services, Health-General, Health Organizations, Hospitals, Medical Rehabilitation, Mental Health, Prenatal Health Issues, Single-Disease Health Associations
Religion: Religious Welfare
Science: Science Museums

Social Services: Animal Protection, At-Risk Youth, Big Brother/Big Sister, Community Centers, Community Service Organizations, Day Care, Domestic Violence, Family Services, Homes, People with Disabilities, Recreation & Athletics, Scouts, Senior Services, Social Services-General, Special Olympics, Substance Abuse, United Funds/United Ways, Volunteer Services, Volunteer Services, YMCA/YWCA/YMHA/YWHA, Youth Organizations

Application Procedures
Initial Contact: Submit a letter of inquiry.
Application Requirements: Include organization name, a description of organization, amount requested, and reason for request.
Deadlines: None.
Notes: Scholarship applicants should write to request an application form.

Restrictions
Foundation only supports 501(c)(3) organizations.

Corporate Officials
Larry Lee Weyers: chief executive officer, chairman, director services B Tecumseh, NE 1945. ED Doane College BA (1967); Columbia University ME (1971); Harvard University MBA (1975). PRIM CORP EMPL chief executive officer, chairman, director: Wisconsin Public Service Resources Corp. ADD CORP EMPL president, director, chief executive officer, chairman: WPS Resources Corp.; vice president, director: WPS Energy Services Inc.; president, chief executive officer, director: WPS Power Development Inc.
Barth J. Wolf: secretary, manager legal services PRIM CORP EMPL secretary, manager legal services: Wisconsin Public Service Corp.

Foundation Officials
Patrick D. Schrickel: vice president B Green Bay, WI 1944. ED Illinois Institute of Technology (1966); University of Wisconsin (1974). PRIM CORP EMPL executive vice president: Wisconsin Public Service Corp. CORP AFFIL executive vice president: Wisconsin Public Service Resources Corp.
Larry Lee Weyers: president, chief executive officer (see above)
Barth J. Wolf: secretary, assistant treasurer (see above)

Grants Analysis
Disclosure Period: calendar year ending 2001
Total Grants: $625,152*
Number of Grants: 173
Average Grant: $3,614
Highest Grant: $25,000
Lowest Grant: $300
Typical Range: $500 to $20,000
*Note: Giving excludes matching gifts, scholarship, and United Way.

Recent Grants
Note: Grants derived from 2001 Form 990.

General
90,000	United Way Brown County, Green Bay, WI -- operating
60,000	Oshkosh Area United Way, Oshkosh, WI -- operating
37,500	University of Wisconsin-Madison, Madison, WI -- scholarships
25,000	Greater Green Bay Community Foundation, Green Bay, WI -- capital
20,000	Altrusa International Foundation of Green Bay, De Pere, WI -- capital
20,000	Family Services of Northeast Wisconsin Inc., Green Bay, WI -- operating
20,000	National Railroad Museum, Green Bay, WI -- capital
20,000	St. Norbert College, De Pere, WI -- capital
20,000	St. Norbert College, De Pere, WI -- scholarship
20,000	WMC Foundation, Madison, WI -- operating

WRATHER FAMILY FOUNDATION

Giving Contact
Christopher C. Wrather, President & Treasurer
14310 Ventura Blvd, 2nd Fl
Sherman Oaks, CA 91423
Phone: (310)312-8818

Description
EIN: 956100110
Organization Type: Private Foundation
Giving Locations: CA
Grant Types: General Support.

Financial Summary
Total Giving: $315,500 (2000); $164,000 (1999); $272,000 (1997). Note: Fiscal 1996 Giving includes scholarship ($1,000), United Way ($12,500).
Giving Analysis: Giving for 2000 includes: foundation grants to United Way ($10,000) 1997: foundation grants to United Way ($10,000)
Assets: $5,399,884 (2000) $5,193,237 (1999); $4,614,486 (1997)

Typical Recipients
Arts & Humanities: Arts Associations & Councils, Historic Preservation, History & Archaeology, Libraries, Museums/Galleries, Music, Opera, Public Broadcasting, Theater
Civic & Public Affairs: Botanical Gardens/Parks, Civic & Public Affairs-General, Housing, Philanthropic Organizations, Zoos/Aquariums
Education: Business Education, Colleges & Universities, Education Funds, Elementary Education (Public), Education-General, Preschool Education, Private Education (Precollege), Public Education (Precollege), Student Aid
Health: AIDS/HIV, Cancer, Children's Health/Hospitals, Emergency/Ambulance Services, Health Organizations, Hospitals, Long-Term Care, Medical Research, Multiple Sclerosis, Nursing Services, Prenatal Health Issues
International: Health Care/Hospitals, International Relief Efforts
Religion: Churches, Religious Organizations, Religious Welfare
Science: Science Museums
Social Services: At-Risk Youth, Camps, Child Welfare, Community Service Organizations, Day Care, Domestic Violence, Family Services, Food/Clothing Distribution, People with Disabilities, Recreation & Athletics, Scouts, Shelters/Homelessness, Substance Abuse, United Funds/United Ways, Veterans, Youth Organizations

Application Procedures
Initial Contact: The foundation has no formal grant application procedure or application form.
Deadlines: None.

Foundation Officials
Molly W. Dolle: director
Linda W. Finocchiaro: director
Gerald L. Weisberger: secretary
Christopher C. Wrather: president, treasurer

Grants Analysis
Disclosure Period: calendar year ending 2000
Total Grants: $305,500*
Number of Grants: 20
Average Grant: $10,342*
Highest Grant: $109,000
Typical Range: $5,000 to $20,000

*Note: Giving excludes United Way. Average grant figure excludes highest grant.

Recent Grants

Note: Grants derived from 1999 Form 990.

General

50,000	John Wayne Cancer Institute, Santa Monica, CA
25,000	Betty Ford Center at Eisenhower, Rancho Mirage, CA
10,000	Foundation for Santa Barbara City College, Santa Barbara, CA
10,000	Loyola Marymount University, Los Angeles, CA
10,000	Stanford Fund, Stanford, CA
10,000	United Way of Santa Barbara County, Santa Barbara, CA
9,500	Family Service Agency of Santa Barbara, Santa Barbara, CA
7,500	San Gabriel Academy, San Gabriel, CA
5,000	American Red Cross, San Francisco, CA
5,000	Salvation Army, San Francisco, CA

LOLA WRIGHT FOUNDATION

Giving Contact

Patrick H. O'Donnell, Jr., President
404 W. 9th Street
Suite 101-D
Georgetown, TX 78626
Phone: (512)869-2574

Description

Founded: 1954
EIN: 746054717
Organization Type: Private Foundation
Giving Locations: TX
Grant Types: Capital, Endowment, Multiyear/Continuing Support, Project, Research.

Donor Information

Founder: the late Miss Johnie E. Wright

Financial Summary

Total Giving: $741,652 (2002); $666,697 (2000); $461,731 (1999)
Giving Analysis: Giving for 2002 includes: foundation grants to United Way ($17,000); 2000: foundation grants to United Way ($6,000) 1999: foundation grants to United Way ($11,650)
Assets: $13,934,447 (2002); $17,529,676 (2000); $18,358,625 (1999)

Typical Recipients

Arts & Humanities: Ballet, Community Arts, Historic Preservation, History & Archaeology, Libraries, Museums/Galleries, Music, Performing Arts, Theater
Civic & Public Affairs: Botanical Gardens/Parks, Business/Free Enterprise, Community Foundations, Employment/Job Training, Civic & Public Affairs-General, Legal Aid, Nonprofit Management, Urban & Community Affairs, Women's Affairs
Education: Arts/Humanities Education, Colleges & Universities, Continuing Education, Economic Education, Education-General, Literacy, Minority Education, Preschool Education
Environment: Environment-General, Protection
Health: AIDS/HIV, Children's Health/Hospitals, Clinics/Medical Centers, Health-General, Geriatric Health, Heart, Heart, Hospices, Hospitals, Medical Rehabilitation, Mental Health, Research/Studies Institutes, Single-Disease Health Associations
Religion: Religious Welfare
Social Services: At-Risk Youth, Big Brother/Big Sister, Camps, Child Abuse, Child Welfare, Community Centers, Community Service Organizations, Counseling, Domestic Violence, Emergency Relief, Family Planning, Family Services, Food/Clothing Distribution, Homes, People with Disabilities, Recreation & Athletics, Scouts, Senior Services, Sexual Abuse, Shelters/Homelessness, YMCA/YWCA/YMHA/YWHA, Youth Organizations

Application Procedures

Initial Contact: Contact the foundation to request guidelines.
Deadlines: February 28 and August 31.
Review Process: The foundation board typically meets in May and November to consider grant requests.

Restrictions

Does not support individuals. Does not provide grants for operating expenses.

Additional Information

Publications: Application Guidelines; Annual Report
Trust(s): JP Morgan Chase Bank of Texas NA

Foundation Officials

Judge Wilford Flowers: director
Adrian Fowler: director
Raffy Garza-Vizcaino: director
Juan G. Gonzalez: director
Linda H. Guerrero: director
William B. Hilgers: director
Judge James Meyers: director
Patrick H. O'Donnell, Jr.: president
Sandra O'Donnell: president
Ron Oliviera: director
Carole Rylander: director
Vivian E. Todd: director

Grants Analysis

Disclosure Period: calendar year ending 2002
Total Grants: $724,652*
Number of Grants: 61
Average Grant: $11,880
Highest Grant: $30,000
Typical Range: $5,000 to $25,000
*Note: Giving excludes United Way.

Recent Grants

Note: Grants derived from 2002 Form 990.

Library-Related

25,000	Elroy Community Library Association -- portable classroom building

General

30,000	Capital Area Food Bank, Austin, TX -- refrigerated 48 foot trailer
27,795	Hospice Austin, Austin, TX -- beds
25,000	Austin Eastside Story Foundation, Austin, TX -- van
25,000	Capitol Area Homeless Alliance, Austin, TX -- renovation of room and garden terrace
25,000	Hill Country Care
25,000	Seton Fund, Austin, TX -- renovation of patient room
23,625	Greater East Austin Youth Association, Austin, TX -- sports equipment
23,585	Extend-A-Care, Austin, TX -- child care fees
22,618	Austin Groups for the Elderly, Austin, TX -- lighting, plumbing, windows,
22,000	Helping Hand Home for Children, Austin, TX -- van

WURZBURG, INC.

Company Headquarters

710 S. 4th St.
Memphis, TN 38126
Web: http://www.wurzburg.com

Company Description

Employees: 350
SIC(s): 2672 Coated & Laminated Paper Nec, 2761 Manifold Business Forms, 3536 Hoists, Cranes & Monorails, 5112 Stationery & Office Supplies.

Operating Locations

Wurzburg, Inc. (TN--Memphis)

Reginald Wurzburg Foundation

Giving Contact

Minda Wurzburg
Reginald Wurzburg Foundation
710 S. Fourth St.
PO Box 710
Memphis, TN 38101

Description

EIN: 626048546
Organization Type: Corporate Foundation
Giving Locations: TN: Memphis
Grant Types: General Support.

Financial Summary

Total Giving: $145,750 (2000); $224,500 (1999); $84,600 (1998)
Giving Analysis: Giving for 2000 includes: foundation scholarships ($12,000); foundation ($133,750) 1999: foundation ($224,500)
Assets: $2,457,935 (2000); $2,244,939 (1999); $2,581,464 (1998)
Gifts Received: $37,500 (2000); $50,000 (1999); $50,000 (1998). Note: In 1996, 1999 and 2000, contributions were received from Wurzburg Brothers, Inc.

Typical Recipients

Arts & Humanities: Arts Associations & Councils, Ballet, Community Arts, Libraries, Museums/Galleries, Music, Performing Arts, Public Broadcasting, Theater
Civic & Public Affairs: Business/Free Enterprise, Clubs, Civic & Public Affairs-General, Housing, Professional & Trade Associations, Public Policy, Safety, Urban & Community Affairs, Zoos/Aquariums
Education: Business Education, Colleges & Universities, Education-General, Medical Education, Minority Education, Private Education (Precollege), Religious Education
Environment: Wildlife Protection
Health: Alzheimers Disease, Arthritis, Cancer, Children's Health/Hospitals, Clinics/Medical Centers, Diabetes, Emergency/Ambulance Services, Heart, Hospitals, Multiple Sclerosis
International: Missionary/Religious Activities
Religion: Jewish Causes, Religious Organizations, Religious Welfare, Social/Policy Issues, Synagogues/Temples
Social Services: Animal Protection, Big Brother/Big Sister, Community Service Organizations, Crime Prevention, Food/Clothing Distribution, Scouts, Senior Services, Youth Organizations

Application Procedures

Initial Contact: Send a brief letter of inquiry.
Deadlines: None.

Additional Information

Trust(s): National Bank Commerce

Corporate Officials

Bernard Lapides: co-chairman, co-president, director PRIM CORP EMPL co-chairman, co-president, director: Wurzburg Brothers.
Warren Seymour Wurzburg, Sr.: chairman, president, director B Memphis, TN 1926. PRIM CORP EMPL chairman, president, director: Wurzburg.

CORP AFFIL co-chairman, treasurer: Feather Pak Co.; co-chairman, treasurer: Multiform; co-chairman, treasurer: Artcraft Converters; co-chairman, treasurer: Crown Office Furniture.

Grants Analysis
Disclosure Period: calendar year ending 2000
Total Grants: $145,750*
Number of Grants: 53
Average Grant: $2,418*
Highest Grant: $20,000
Typical Range: $1,000 to $5,000
*Note: Average grant excludes highest grant.

Recent Grants
Note: Grants derived from 2000 Form 990.

Library-Related
1,000   Foundation for the Library

General
20,000   Temple Israel
18,000   Memphis Jewish Federation, Memphis, TN
17,000   Houston Jewish Federation, Houston, TX
17,000   Houston Jewish Federation, Houston, TX
15,000   Memphis Jewish Foundation, Memphis, TN
5,000   Memphis Arts Council, Memphis, TN
5,000   University of Memphis, Memphis, TN
4,000   Memphis Jewish Home, Memphis, TN
3,500   Baron Hirsch Congregation
3,000   Christian Brothers University, Memphis, TN

WYMAN-GORDON CO.

Company Headquarters
244 Worcester Street
North Grafton, MA 01536-8001
Web: http://www.wyman-gordon.com

Company Description
Revenue: US$730 million (2001)
Employees: 3400 (2001)
SIC(s): 3462 Iron & Steel Forgings, 3463 Nonferrous Forgings.

Operating Locations
Wyman-Gordon Co. (CA--Mojave, San Leandro; CT--Groton; MA--North Grafton; NV--Carson City; NH--Franklin, Tilton)

Nonmonetary Support
Type: Loaned Executives
Note: Company participates in the United Way Loaned Executive Program.

Wyman-Gordon Foundation

Giving Contact
Warner S. Fletcher, Jr., Director
370 Main Street, Suite 1100
Worcester, MA 01608
Phone: (508)798-8621
Fax: (508)791-6454

Description
EIN: 046142600
Organization Type: Corporate Foundation
Giving Locations: principally near operating locations and to national organizations.
Grant Types: Employee Matching Gifts, Fellowship, General Support, Scholarship, Seed Money.

Financial Summary
Total Giving: $324,725 (2001); $465,836 (2000); $405,097 (1999). Note: Contributes through foundation only.
Giving Analysis: Giving for 2000 includes: foundation matching gifts ($1,936); foundation grants to United Way ($225,000); foundation ($238,900); 1999: foundation matching gifts ($6,170); foundation ($139,680); foundation grants to United Way ($153,000); 1997: foundation grants to United Way ($153,000); foundation ($170,844);
Assets: $7,663,870 (2001); $8,335,268 (2000); $8,984,064 (1999)

Typical Recipients
Arts & Humanities: Arts Appreciation, Ethnic & Folk Arts, Arts & Humanities-General, Historic Preservation, History & Archaeology, Libraries, Museums/Galleries, Music, Public Broadcasting, Theater
Civic & Public Affairs: Business/Free Enterprise, Chambers of Commerce, Clubs, Economic Development, Ethnic Organizations, Civic & Public Affairs-General, Housing, Legal Aid, Parades/Festivals, Professional & Trade Associations, Public Policy, Safety, Urban & Community Affairs
Education: Arts/Humanities Education, Business Education, Business-School Partnerships, Colleges & Universities, Community & Junior Colleges, Economic Education, Education Associations, Education Reform, Engineering/Technological Education, Education-General, Private Education (Precollege), Private Education (Precollege), Science/Mathematics Education, Student Aid, Vocational & Technical Education
Environment: Environment-General
Health: AIDS/HIV, Cancer, Children's Health/Hospitals, Diabetes, Emergency/Ambulance Services, Health-General, Health Organizations, Hospices, Hospitals, Medical Research, Multiple Sclerosis, Nursing Services, Public Health
International: International-General
Religion: Churches, Religious Organizations, Religious Welfare
Science: Science Exhibits & Fairs, Scientific Centers & Institutes, Scientific Research
Social Services: Child Welfare, Community Centers, Community Service Organizations, Family Services, Food/Clothing Distribution, People with Disabilities, Recreation & Athletics, Scouts, Senior Services, Senior Services, Social Services-General, United Funds/United Ways, YMCA/YWCA/YMHA/YWHA, Youth Organizations

Application Procedures
Initial Contact: Submit a formal proposal.
Application Requirements: Include a description of the program and purpose of funds requested.
Deadlines: None.

Restrictions
Does not support individuals, religious organizations for sectarian purposes, or political or lobbying groups.

Foundation Officials
Warner S. Fletcher: director
David P. Gruber: trustee, president B 1941. ED Ohio State University (1965). PRIM CORP EMPL president, chief executive officer, director: Wyman-Gordon Co. CORP AFFIL chief executive officer: Wyman-Gordon Inv Castings; director: State Street Corp.; director: Wyman-Gordon Forgings Inc. NONPR AFFIL trustee: Manufacturer Alliance Productivity & Innovation.

Grants Analysis
Disclosure Period: calendar year ending 2001
Total Grants: $174,350*
Number of Grants: 29
Average Grant: $6,000
Highest Grant: $51,000
Lowest Grant: $350

Typical Range: $1,000 to $15,000
*Note: Giving excludes matching gifts and United Way.

Recent Grants
Note: Grants derived from 2001 Form 990.

General
150,000 United Way Central Massachusetts, Worcester, MA
51,000   Worcester Historic Museum, Worcester, MA
25,000   Age Center of Worcester Area, Worcester, MA
16,000   Worcester Art Museum, Worcester, MA
11,000   Worcester County Food Bank, Worcester, MA
10,000   American Antiquarian Society, Worcester, MA
10,000   Friendly House, Worcester, MA
10,000   Worcester Vocational High School, Worcester, MA
5,000   Barton Center for Diabetes Education, Boylston, MA
5,000   Lutheran Family Services, Portland, OR

WYMAN YOUTH TRUST

Giving Contact
D. E. Wyman, Trustee
Wyman Youth Trust
104 30th Ave. South
Seattle, WA 98144
Phone: (206)682-2256

Description
Founded: 1951
EIN: 916031590
Organization Type: Private Foundation
Giving Locations: NE: Custer County, Lancaster County, York County; WA: King County, Pierce County, Snohomish County
Grant Types: General Support.

Donor Information
Founder: members of the Wyman family

Financial Summary
Total Giving: $651,019 (2000); $405,228 (1998); $372,028 (1997)
Giving Analysis: Giving for 1997 includes: foundation grants to United Way ($40,000)
Assets: $7,028,982 (2000); $8,146,652 (1998); $6,314,795 (1997)

Typical Recipients
Arts & Humanities: Arts Associations & Councils, Arts Centers, Arts Outreach, Ballet, Community Arts, Dance, Ethnic & Folk Arts, Historic Preservation, History & Archaeology, Libraries, Museums/Galleries, Music, Opera, Performing Arts, Theater
Civic & Public Affairs: Business/Free Enterprise, Clubs, Economic Development, Civic & Public Affairs-General, Housing, Parades/Festivals, Urban & Community Affairs, Zoos/Aquariums
Education: Arts/Humanities Education, Business Education, Colleges & Universities, Education Reform, Elementary Education (Private), Education-General, Private Education (Precollege), Public Education (Precollege), Secondary Education (Public), Social Sciences Education, Student Aid
Environment: Protection
Health: AIDS/HIV, Children's Health/Hospitals, Clinics/Medical Centers, Hospitals, Mental Health, Transplant Networks/Donor Banks
International: Foreign Arts Organizations, International Affairs
Religion: Churches, Ministries, Religious Organizations, Religious Welfare
Science: Scientific Centers & Institutes

Social Services: Child Welfare, Community Centers, Community Service Organizations, Counseling, Domestic Violence, Food/Clothing Distribution, Recreation & Athletics, United Funds/United Ways, Volunteer Services, YMCA/YWCA/YMHA/YWHA, Youth Organizations

Application Procedures

Initial Contact: Send a letter of proposal.
Application Requirements: Include a description of organization, a desciption of the proposed project, a statement of financial need, a list of board members, and an annual operating budget.
Deadlines: June 15 for arts and culture grants, September 15 for civic and education, and December 1 for social and health services.

Restrictions

Grants are awarded to support the betterment of all youth and for advancement of civic and cultural development. Grants are not made to individuals.

Additional Information

Publications: Application Guidelines

Foundation Officials

David C. Wyman: trustee
David E. Wyman: trustee
Hal H. Wyman: trustee

Grants Analysis

Disclosure Period: calendar year ending 2000
Total Grants: $651,019
Number of Grants: 161
Average Grant: $3,709*
Highest Grant: $57,500
Typical Range: $1,000 to $5,000
*Note: Average grant figure excludes highest grant.

Recent Grants

Note: Grants derived from 1999 Form 990.

General

50,000	Bush School, Seattle, WA
20,000	YWCA, Birmingham, AL
17,500	PONCHO, Seattle, WA
17,000	Lakeside School, Seattle, WA
16,750	Epiphany School, Seattle, WA
10,400	Pacific Northwest Ballet, Seattle, WA
10,000	Act Theater
10,000	Alliance for Education, Seattle, WA
10,000	Museum of Flight, Seattle, WA
10,000	Seattle Art Museum, Seattle, WA

WYNN FOUNDATION

Giving Contact

Wesley E. Bellwood, President
1280 Bison Ave., Ste. B9-601
Newport Beach, CA 92660
Phone: (949)644-2791

Description

Founded: 1966
EIN: 956136231
Organization Type: Private Foundation
Giving Locations: CA
Grant Types: General Support.

Donor Information

Founder: the late Bee Wynn, the late Carl Wynn

Financial Summary

Total Giving: $1,450,000 (2001); $1,851,000 (2000); $1,348,500 (1999)
Assets: $28,742,040 (2001); $30,331,687 (2000); $21,861,019 (1999)

Gifts Received: $34,414 (1993). Note: In 1993, contributions were received from the estate of Carl E. Wynn.

Typical Recipients

Arts & Humanities: Ballet, History & Archaeology, Libraries, Public Broadcasting
Civic & Public Affairs: Botanical Gardens/Parks, Civic & Public Affairs-General, Hispanic Affairs, Philanthropic Organizations
Education: Business Education, Colleges & Universities, Education Associations, Environmental Education, Education-General, Medical Education, Public Education (Precollege), Science/Mathematics Education, Secondary Education (Public), Special Education
Environment: Research
Health: Alzheimers Disease, Arthritis, Cancer, Children's Health/Hospitals, Clinics/Medical Centers, Health-General, Heart, Hospitals, Hospitals (University Affiliated), Kidney, Medical Research, Mental Health, Prenatal Health Issues, Preventive Medicine/Wellness Organizations, Public Health, Research/Studies Institutes, Single-Disease Health Associations, Trauma Treatment
Religion: Religion-General, Religious Welfare
Science: Science Museums, Scientific Organizations
Social Services: Big Brother/Big Sister, Child Abuse, Child Welfare, Community Service Organizations, Delinquency & Criminal Rehabilitation, Domestic Violence, Family Planning, Family Services, Food/Clothing Distribution, People with Disabilities, Scouts, Shelters/Homelessness, Special Olympics, YMCA/YWCA/YMHA/YWHA, Youth Organizations

Application Procedures

Initial Contact: Application should be submitted in letter form only.
Deadlines: May 15.

Foundation Officials

Wesley E. Bellwood: president B Garfield Township, IA 1923. ED Southwestern University (1948). PRIM CORP EMPL chairman, director: Wynns International.
John D. Borie: secretary
William Christian: assistant treasurer
Billie A. Fischer: vice president
Dorothy L. Frey: treasurer

Grants Analysis

Disclosure Period: calendar year ending 2001
Total Grants: $1,450,000
Number of Grants: 113
Average Grant: $12,832
Highest Grant: $78,000
Typical Range: $5,000 to $30,000

Recent Grants

Note: Grants derived from 2001 Form 990.

General

78,000	Center for Alaskan Coastal Studies, Homer, AK -- Carl E. Wynn Nature Center
68,000	Peppermint Ridge, Corona, CA -- residential program for developmentally disabled
50,000	Citrus Valley Health Foundation, Covina, CA -- hospital programs serving local communities
50,000	City of Hope, Los Angeles, CA -- cancer research
50,000	Foothill Foundation, Glendora, CA -- Hospital Programs
50,000	Loma Linda University Medical Center, Loma Linda, CA -- hospital programs
50,000	Operation Safe House, Grand Terrace, CA -- programs for abused children
40,000	Good Shepherd Shelter, Los Angeles, CA -- serving battered women and their children
40,000	Homer Society of Natural History, Inc., Homer, AK -- Educational Program and Remote Cancer Program
38,000	St. Mary Medical Center, Applevalley, CA -- medical facilities and surgery equipment

WYOMISSING FOUNDATION

Giving Contact

Ned Diefenderfer, Secretary
12 Commerce Drive
Wyomissing, PA 19610
Phone: (610)376-7494
Fax: (610)372-7626

Description

Founded: 1929
EIN: 231980570
Organization Type: General Purpose Foundation
Giving Locations: PA: Berks County and contiguous counties
Grant Types: Capital, Emergency, Multiyear/Continuing Support, Operating Expenses, Seed Money.

Donor Information

Founder: Incorporated in 1929 by the late Ferdinand Thun and members of the Thun family.

Financial Summary

Total Giving: $1,385,676 (2001); $1,146,350 (2000); $2,795,580 (1998)
Giving Analysis: Giving for 2000 includes: foundation grants to United Way ($111,000) 1998: foundation grants to United Way ($103,000)
Assets: $33,641,811 (2001); $37,820,880 (2000); $35,258,419 (1998)

Typical Recipients

Arts & Humanities: Art History, Arts Funds, Arts Institutes, Ballet, Arts & Humanities-General, Historic Preservation, History & Archaeology, Libraries, Museums/Galleries, Music, Performing Arts, Public Broadcasting, Theater
Civic & Public Affairs: Community Foundations, Economic Development, Economic Policy, Civic & Public Affairs-General, Housing, Law & Justice, Legal Aid, Parades/Festivals, Philanthropic Organizations, Public Policy, Urban & Community Affairs, Zoos/Aquariums
Education: Arts/Humanities Education, Business Education, Colleges & Universities, Community & Junior Colleges, Education Funds, Education Reform, Environmental Education, Education-General, Literacy, Minority Education, Special Education
Environment: Air/Water Quality, Environment-General, Resource Conservation, Watershed, Wildlife Protection
Health: AIDS/HIV, Emergency/Ambulance Services, Health Funds, Home-Care Services, Hospitals, Medical Rehabilitation, Nursing Services, Prenatal Health Issues
International: International Affairs, International Relations
Religion: Jewish Causes, Religious Organizations, Religious Welfare
Science: Science Museums, Scientific Centers & Institutes
Social Services: Animal Protection, Community Centers, Community Service Organizations, Counseling, Crime Prevention, Delinquency & Criminal Rehabilitation, Family Planning, Food/Clothing Distribution, Homes, People with Disabilities, Recreation & Athletics, Scouts, Senior Services, Shelters/Homelessness, United Funds/United Ways, YMCA/YWCA/YMHA/YWHA, Youth Organizations

Application Procedures

Initial Contact: The foundation requests applications be made in writing.
Deadlines: None.

Restrictions

The foundation does not make grants to individuals, or for endowments, deficit financing, land acquisition, publications, conferences, scholarships, fellowships, or loans.

Additional Information

Publications: Application Guidelines; Annual Report; Program Policy Statement; Financial Statement

Foundation Officials

Thomas A. Beaver: treasurer PRIM CORP EMPL partner: Reinsel & Co.
Victoria F. Guthrie: trustee
Sidney Delong Kline, Jr.: trustee B West Reading, PA 1932. ED Dickinson College BA (1954); Dickinson School of Law JD (1956). PRIM CORP EMPL chairman, partner: Stevens & Lee PC. CORP AFFIL director: Reading Eagle Co. NONPR AFFIL director: Reading Center City Development Fund; campaign chairman: United Way Berks County; member: Pennsylvania Bar Association; secretary, trustee: Dickinson School Law; fellow: National Society Fund Raising Executives; member: Berks County Bar Association; chairman, trustee: Dickinson College; fellow: American College Trust & Estate Counsel. CLUB AFFIL Pelican Bay Club.
Samuel Alexander McCullough: trustee B Pittsburgh, PA 1938. ED University of Pittsburgh BBA (1960). PRIM CORP EMPL chairman, chief executive officer, president: Meridian Bancorp Inc. CORP AFFIL president: CoreStates Financial Corp.; director: MCGlinn Capital Management. NONPR AFFIL trustee: University Pittsburgh; director: University Pittsburgh Common System Education; chairman: Pennsylvania Chamber Business & Industry; president: Department Community Economic Development; member: International Financial Conference; member: American Bankers Association; member: American Institute Banking; chairman nominating committee: Albright College.
Marlin Miller, Jr.: trustee B 1932. ED Alfred University BS (1954); Harvard University MBA (1956). PRIM CORP EMPL founder, president, chief executive officer, director: Arrow International Inc. ADD CORP EMPL chairman, president, chief executive officer: Arrow Precision Products; president, chief executive officer: Kontron Instruments Inc. CORP AFFIL director: Carpenter Technology Corp.; board member: Connors Investors Services Inc.
Steffen W. Piehn: trustee
Paul Robert Roedel: president B Millville, NJ 1927. ED Rider College BS (1949). CORP AFFIL director: Stainless Steel Industries US; director: GPU Inc.; director: Meridian Bancorp Inc.; director: General Public Utilities Corp.; director: PH Glatfelter Co. NONPR AFFIL member: Financial Executives Institute; trustee: Gettysburg College; chairman: Berks Business Education Coalition.
Hildegarde Ryals: trustee, secretary
Lewis C. Scheffey, Jr.: trustee
Michael J. Thun: trustee

Grants Analysis

Disclosure Period: calendar year ending 2001
Total Grants: $1,254,855*
Number of Grants: 24
Average Grant: $52,286
Highest Grant: $190,000
Lowest Grant: $1,000
Typical Range: $15,000 to $100,000
***Note:** Giving excludes United Way.

Recent Grants

Note: Grants derived from 2001 Form 990.

General

190,000	Berks County Conservancy, Wyomissing, PA -- operating support
176,074	Berks County Community Foundation, Reading, PA -- operating fund
130,821	United Way Berks County, Reading, PA -- annual campaign
125,000	Berkshire Highlands
110,000	Berks County Childcare Initiative, St. Reading, PA -- child care initiative grant
92,781	Hispanic Center of Reading, Reading, PA -- build organizational
85,500	Foundation for the Reading Public Museum and Art Gallery, Reading, PA -- capital campaign
85,500	Hawk Mountain Boy Scouts of America, Reading, PA -- annual campaign
85,000	Performing Arts Center, Reading, PA -- capital campaign
50,000	Police Athletic League, Reading, PA -- capital campaign

WYSS FOUNDATION

Giving Contact

Loren L. Wyss, President & Treasurer
620 SW 5th, Suite 1010
Portland, OR 97204
Phone: (503)294-4485

Description

Founded: 1989
EIN: 931010019
Organization Type: Private Foundation
Giving Locations: OR
Grant Types: Endowment, General Support.

Donor Information

Founder: Established in 1989 by Judith Wyss and Loren L. Wyss.

Financial Summary

Total Giving: $207,200 (fiscal year ending April 30, 2002); $210,150 (fiscal 2001); $222,750 (fiscal 2000)
Assets: $4,095,907 (fiscal 2002); $4,078,681 (fiscal 2001); $4,254,178 (fiscal 2000)

Typical Recipients

Arts & Humanities: Arts Associations & Councils, Arts Outreach, Film & Video, History & Archaeology, Libraries, Literary Arts, Museums/Galleries, Music, Opera, Public Broadcasting, Theater
Civic & Public Affairs: Civic & Public Affairs-General, Hispanic Affairs, Housing, Legal Aid, Women's Affairs
Education: Arts/Humanities Education, Business Education, Colleges & Universities, Literacy, Minority Education, Public Education (Precollege), Science/Mathematics Education, Social Sciences Education
Environment: Environment-General
Health: AIDS/HIV, Clinics/Medical Centers, Health Organizations
International: International Relief Efforts, Missionary/Religious Activities
Religion: Churches, Religion-General, Ministries, Religious Organizations, Religious Welfare, Seminaries
Social Services: Animal Protection, At-Risk Youth, Child Welfare, Community Service Organizations, Counseling, Delinquency & Criminal Rehabilitation, Family Planning, Family Services, Food/Clothing Distribution, Shelters/Homelessness, Youth Organizations

Application Procedures

Initial Contact: Submit a brief letter of inquiry.
Application Requirements: Include a description of organization, amount requested, purpose of funds sought, recently audited financial statement, proof of tax-exempt status, budget, list of board of directors, and organization's history.
Deadlines: None.
Review Process: The board of directors meet in December and April. Preference is given to applicants in the Portland, OR area.

Restrictions

Grants are not made to individuals. No scholarships or medical grants are provided by the foundation.

Foundation Officials

Judith Wyss: secretary, director

Grants Analysis

Disclosure Period: fiscal year ending April 30, 2002
Total Grants: $207,200
Number of Grants: 92
Average Grant: $2,252
Highest Grant: $16,000
Lowest Grant: $350
Typical Range: $1,000 to $4,000

Recent Grants

Note: Grants derived from fiscal 2000 Form 990.

General

30,000	Pacific Northwest College of Art, Portland, OR
30,000	Reed College, Portland, OR
15,950	Dean and Chapter of Ely, Cambs United Kingdom
5,250	Westminster Presbyterian Church, Portland, OR
5,000	Harvard University, Cambridge, MA
5,000	KBPS Public Radio Foundation, Portland, OR
5,000	Multnomah County, Portland, OR
5,000	Portland Opera, Portland, OR
5,000	Self Enhancement, Inc., Portland, OR
4,200	John's Closet Ben Franklin Jr. High School, Daly City, CA

XCEL ENERGY

Company Headquarters

414 Nicollet Mall
Minneapolis, MN 55401-1993
Phone: 800-328-8226
Web: http://www.xcelenergy.com

Company Description

Founded: 2000
Ticker: XEL
Exchange: NYSE
Former Name: Northern States Power (2000);
Acquired: New Century Energy (2000).
Revenue: US$10.341 billion (2002)
Employees: 15812 (2001)
Fortune Rank: 180, per FORTUNE Magazine's list of 500 Largest U.S. Corporations (2002).
SIC(s): 4931 Electric & Other Services Combined, 4932 Gas & Other Services Combined.

Operating Locations

Northern States Power Co. (Minnesota) (DC--Washington; MN--Albany, Brainerd, Excelsior, Farmington, Granite Falls, Mankato, Maple Grove, Minneapolis, Newport, Slayton, St. Cloud, St. Paul, White Bear Lake, Winona, Winthrop; ND--Grand Forks, Mayville, Minot; SD--Sioux Falls; WI--Abbotsford, Eau Claire, Menomonie Falls)

Nonmonetary Support

Type: Donated Equipment; In-kind Services; Loaned Executives

Xcel Energy Foundation

Giving Contact

James D. Rhodes, Contribution Specialist
800 Nicollet Mall Suite 2900
Minneapolis, MN 55402
Phone: (612)330-5500
Fax: (612)330-6947
E-mail: foundation@xcelenergy.com
Web: http://www.xcelenergy.com/XLWEB/CDA/
0,2914,1-1-1_4359_4842-922-0_0_0-0,00.html

Alternate Contact

Phone: (612)330-6933

Description

EIN: 841435965
Organization Type: Corporate Foundation
Giving Locations: near headquarters and service areas only.
Grant Types: Capital, Employee Matching Gifts, General Support, Project.
Note: Employee matching gift ratio: 1 to 1 to education, public broadcasting, and the Minnesota Foodshare Program.

Financial Summary

Total Giving: $7,572,500 (2003 approx); $3,500,000 (2002 approx); $1,771,515 (2000). Note: Contributes through corporate direct giving program only. Giving includes corporate direct giving; domestic subsidiaries; matching gifts.
Giving Analysis: Giving for 2002 includes: foundation matching gifts ($439,892); foundation grants to United Way ($1,545,000); 2000: foundation grants to United Way ($484,833); foundation ($1,286,682); 1998: corporate direct giving ($5,005,208);
Assets: $871,285 (2000)
Gifts Received: $2,000,000 (2000). Note: Contributions were received from Xcel Energy, Inc.

Typical Recipients

Arts & Humanities: Arts Centers, Arts Funds, Arts Institutes, Community Arts, Ethnic & Folk Arts, History & Archaeology, Libraries, Museums/Galleries, Music, Opera, Performing Arts, Public Broadcasting, Theater
Civic & Public Affairs: Botanical Gardens/Parks, Employment/Job Training, Hispanic Affairs, Housing, Legal Aid, Municipalities/Towns, Native American Affairs, Nonprofit Management, Parades/Festivals, Safety, Urban & Community Affairs, Women's Affairs, Zoos/Aquariums
Education: Afterschool/Enrichment Programs, Business Education, Colleges & Universities, Community & Junior Colleges, Education Reform, Elementary Education (Public), Legal Education, Minority Education, Preschool Education, Student Aid
Environment: Environment-General, Wildlife Protection
Health: AIDS/HIV, Cancer, Clinics/Medical Centers, Health Organizations, Hospitals, Mental Health, Nursing Services, Single-Disease Health Associations
Religion: Religious Welfare
Social Services: Child Welfare, Community Centers, Community Service Organizations, Counseling, Day Care, Delinquency & Criminal Rehabilitation, Domestic Violence, Emergency Relief, Family Services, Food/Clothing Distribution, Homes, People with Disabilities, Refugee Assistance, Senior Services, Shelters/Homelessness, Substance Abuse, United Funds/United Ways, Volunteer Services, Youth Organizations

Application Procedures

Initial Contact: Submit the online letter of intent, which is available on the Web site. Company states it wants online applications only.
Deadlines: Each program area has its own deadline for submitting letters of inquiry, and deadlines may vary from year to year. Contact the foundation or check its web site to obtain current deadline information.
Decision Notification: All applicants are notified of the results of its letter of inquiry within three weeks of the submission deadline. For those applicants who are requested to submit a full proposal, the foundation will provide instructions on how to proceed.

Restrictions

Company does not support endowment campaigns; athletic or scholarship competitions; religious, political, veteran or fraternal organizations except for programs these organizations sponsor for direct benefit to the community and not for themselves; benefits or fundraising activities; programs of individual organizations that receive more than 50 percent of their program budget from the United Way or other federated giving drives to which Xcel Energy contributes; disease-specific organizations; sports and athletic programs; or capital projects.

Additional Information

Within one year of receiving grant payment, recipient must submit report detailing the expenditures and results of project.
Addresses and names of the appropriate contact persons are contained in the company's funding guidelines.
First time grants are usually between $1,000 and $5,000.
Publications: Funding Guidelines; Application Form; Corporate Contributions Annual Report

Corporate Officials

Tom Micheletti: vice president public & government affairs PRIM CORP EMPL vice president public & government affairs: Northern States Power Co.

Giving Program Officials

Tom Micheletti: (see above)

Grants Analysis

Disclosure Period: calendar year ending 2002
Total Grants: $3,500,000*
Number of Grants: 600 (approx)
Typical Range: $500 to $1,000 and $10,000 to $20,000
*Note: Giving excludes United Way and matching gifts. Complete grant list not available for 2002.

XEROX CORP.

Company Headquarters

Stamford, CT
Web: http://www.xerox.com

Company Description

Founded: 1906
Ticker: XRX
Exchange: NYSE
Revenue: US$15.849 billion (2002)
Profit: US$91 million (2002)
Employees: 67100 (2002)
Fortune Rank: 116, per FORTUNE Magazine's list of 500 Largest U.S. Corporations (2002).
SIC(s): 3577 Computer Peripheral Equipment Nec, 3578 Calculating & Accounting Equipment, 3579 Office Machines Nec, 5045 Computers, Peripherals & Software.

Operating Locations

Xerox Corp. (CA--Anaheim, El Segundo, Hayward, Los Angeles, Pasadena, Sacramento, San Francisco, Santa Clara; CT--Stamford; DC; GA--Atlanta; IL--Chicago; NY--Rochester, Webster; OK; TX--Dallas; VA--Arlington, Leesburg)

Nonmonetary Support

Value: $1,000,000 (2002 approx)
Type: Donated Equipment; Loaned Employees; Workplace Solicitation
Volunteer Programs: The company encourages employee volunteerism through the Social Service Leave and Community Involvement programs.
Contact: G. L. Watson, Vice President
Note: Nonmonetary support is provided by the company.

Xerox Foundation

Giving Contact

Joseph M. Cahalan, Vice President
The Xerox Foundation
PO Box 1600
800 Long Ridge Road
Stamford, CT 06904
Phone: (203)968-3445
Fax: (203)968-3330

Alternate Contact

800 Long Ridge Road
Stamford, CT 06904

Description

EIN: 060996443
Organization Type: Corporate Foundation
Giving Locations: nationally, with emphasis on operating locations.
Grant Types: Award, Department, Employee Matching Gifts, Fellowship, General Support, Matching, Multiyear/Continuing Support.
Note: Employee matching gift ratio: 1 to 1 for gifts from employees and/or their spouses to institutions of higher learning, up to $1,000 per institution annually.

Financial Summary

Total Giving: $493,383 (2001); $516,000 (2000); $453,440 (1999). Note: Contributes through corporate direct giving program and foundation.
Giving Analysis: Giving for 2000 includes: foundation ($516,000) 1999: foundation ($453,440)
Assets: $765 (2001); $12 (2000); $1,411 (1999)
Gifts Received: $493,000 (2001); $514,830 (2000); $451,388 (1999). Note: Contributions are received from Xerox Corp.

Typical Recipients

Arts & Humanities: Arts Associations & Councils, Arts Centers, Arts Funds, Arts Institutes, Dance, Historic Preservation, Libraries, Museums/Galleries, Music, Opera
Civic & Public Affairs: Civil Rights, Economic Development, Economic Policy, Employment/Job Training, Housing, Professional & Trade Associations, Public Policy, Urban & Community Affairs, Women's Affairs
Education: Business Education, Colleges & Universities, Economic Education, Education Associations, Education Funds, Engineering/Technological Education, Environmental Education, Faculty Development, Literacy, Minority Education, Science/Mathematics Education, Student Aid, Vocational & Technical Education
Environment: Environment-General
Health: Health Policy/Cost Containment
International: Foreign Educational Institutions, International-General, Health Care/Hospitals, International Organizations, International Relations
Science: Scientific Organizations

Social Services: Child Welfare, Community Service Organizations, Domestic Violence, People with Disabilities, Senior Services, Shelters/Homelessness, Substance Abuse, United Funds/United Ways, Youth Organizations

Application Procedures

Initial Contact: Call or see web page for application guidelines. Send a brief letter of inquiry no longer than two or three pages.

Application Requirements: Provide the legal name of organization, official contact person, proof of tax-exempt status, description of activities and programs, purpose of grant, benefits expected, plans for evaluation, projected budget, expected sources, amount of funds needed, and a copy of the latest annual financial statement.

Deadlines: None.

Review Process: The contributions committee reviews submissions collectively on a monthly basis and the board of trustees meets quarterly.

Evaluative Criteria: Application to Xerox focus areas of Employee/Community Affairs, Science/Technology Education, Work Force Preparation, National Affairs, or Culture.

Decision Notification: Within 30 to 60 days of receipt.

Restrictions

Foundation does not support individuals; capital grants; endowments or endowed chairs; political organizations or candidates; religious or sectarian groups; or municipal, county, state, federal, or quasi-governmental agencies.

Additional Information

All requests from organizations that have previously received support will be evaluated based on their accomplishment of the objectives included in the initial request.

Corporate Officials

Allan E. Dugan: senior vice president corporate strategic service B Rochester, NY. ED Pennsylvania State University; University of Toronto. PRIM CORP EMPL senior vice president corporate strategic service: Xerox Corp. CORP AFFIL director: Katun Corp.; director: Rochester Gas & Electric Corp.; director: Greater Rochester Health System Inc. NONPR AFFIL director: National Association Manufacturers; trustee: University Rochester; director: American European Chamber of Commerce.

Anne M. Mulcahy: chairman, chief executive officer B Rockville Centre, NY October 21, 1952. ED Marymount College BA (1974). PRIM CORP EMPL chairman, chief executive officer: Xerox Corp. CORP AFFIL director: Fuji Xerox Co. Ltd.; director: Target Corp.; Fannie Mae; director: Axel Johnson Inc.; director: Catalyst.

Addison Barry Rand: executive vice president operations B Washington, DC 1944. ED American University BS; Stanford University MS. PRIM CORP EMPL executive vice president operations: Xerox Corp. ADD CORP EMPL chairman, chief executive officer: Avis Rent A Car Inc. CORP AFFIL director: Honeywell Inc.; director: Abbott Laboratories; director: Ameritech Corp. NONPR AFFIL member board overseers: Garth Fagan Dance Theatre; member board overseers: Rochester New York Philarmonic Orchestra.

Barry D. Romeril: vice chairman, chief financial officer, director B United Kingdom 1943. ED Oxford University (1966). PRIM CORP EMPL vice chairman, chief financial officer, director: Xerox Corp. ADD CORP EMPL director: Xerox Financial Services Inc.; director: Xerox Credit Corp. CORP AFFIL director: Billiton Plc; director: Fuji Xerox Co. Ltd.

Foundation Officials

Joseph M. Cahalan: vice president
Allan E. Dugan: trustee (see above)
Emerson U. Fullwood: trustee

Anne M. Mulcahy: trustee (see above)
Patricia M. Nazemetz: trustee
Carlos Pascual: trustee
Martin S. Wagner: secretary, general counsel PRIM CORP EMPL assistant secretary: Xerox Corp.

Grants Analysis

Disclosure Period: calendar year ending 2001
Total Grants: $493,383
Number of Grants: 94
Average Grant: $3,477*
Highest Grant: $170,000
Lowest Grant: $1,000
Typical Range: $1,500 to $10,000
*Note: Average grant figure excludes highest grant.

Recent Grants

Note: Grants derived from 2001 Form 990.

General

170,000	European Institute of Business Administration (INSEAD), Fountainbleau France
50,000	Hole in the Wall Gang Camp United Kingdom
35,383	International University of Japan, Niigata Japan
20,000	University of Carlton, Ottawa, ON Canada
20,000	University of Seville, Seville Spain
18,000	McMaster University, Hamilton, ON Canada
15,000	Ecole Polytechnique, Montreal, QC Canada
15,000	University of Toronto, Toronto, ON Canada
15,000	University of York, Toronto, ON Canada
10,000	University of Windsor, Windsor, ON Canada

YAWKEY FOUNDATION Iı

Giving Contact

John L. Harrington, Executive Director & Trustee
990 Washington Street
Dedham, MA 02026
Phone: (781)329-7470
Fax: (781)329-8195
Web: http://www.yawkeyfoundation.org/

Description

Founded: 1983
EIN: 042768239
Organization Type: Private Foundation
Giving Locations: MA, Boston metropolitan area
Grant Types: General Support.

Donor Information

Founder: Established in 1983 by the late Jean R. Yawkey .

Financial Summary

Total Giving: $4,192,734 (fiscal year ending June 30, 2002); $2,073,747 (fiscal 2000); $1,449,673 (fiscal 1998)

Giving Analysis: Giving for fiscal 2000 includes: foundation grants to United Way ($10,000) foundation scholarships ($76,000)

Assets: $367,849,121 (fiscal 2002); $35,925,436 (fiscal 2000); $30,703,066 (fiscal 1998)

Gifts Received: $350,000,000 (fiscal 2002); $517,846 (fiscal 2000); $861,000 (fiscal 1998). Note: In fiscal 2001 and 2002, contributions were received from the Jean R. Yawkey Trust. In fiscal 1998, contributions were received from the estate of Jean R. Yawkey.

Typical Recipients

Arts & Humanities: Arts Centers, Community Arts, Arts & Humanities-General, Libraries, Museums/Galleries, Music, Performing Arts, Public Broadcasting

Civic & Public Affairs: African American Affairs, Business/Free Enterprise, Clubs, Economic Development, Civic & Public Affairs-General, Hispanic Affairs, Housing, Municipalities/Towns, Public Policy, Urban & Community Affairs, Women's Affairs, Zoos/Aquariums

Education: Colleges & Universities, Education Funds, Education-General, International Studies, Literacy, Minority Education, Private Education (Precollege), Public Education (Precollege), Science/Mathematics Education, Secondary Education (Private), Secondary Education (Public), Special Education, Student Aid

Environment: Resource Conservation, Resource Conservation

Health: AIDS/HIV, Alzheimers Disease, Cancer, Children's Health/Hospitals, Clinics/Medical Centers, Emergency/Ambulance Services, Eyes/Blindness, Health Organizations, Hospitals, Medical Research, Single-Disease Health Associations

International: International Affairs

Religion: Religion-General, Jewish Causes, Religious Organizations, Religious Welfare, Seminaries

Social Affairs: At-Risk Youth, Camps, Child Welfare, Community Service Organizations, Family Services, Food/Clothing Distribution, Homes, People with Disabilities, Recreation & Athletics, Scouts, Shelters/Homelessness, Social Services-General, United Funds/United Ways, YMCA/YWCA/YMHA/YWHA, Youth Organizations

Application Procedures

Application Requirements: Foundation is undergoing a significant expansion as a result of the proceeds from the sale of the Yawkey interests in the Boston Red Sox. Foundation is in the process of expanding operations and staff and are also in review of their missions and revisiting guidelines. Accordingly, unsolicited proposals of request are not being accepted at this time.

Foundation Officials

William B. Guttarb: trustee
John Leo Harrington: trustee B Boston, MA 1936. ED Boston College BS (1957); Boston College MBA (1966). PRIM CORP EMPL president: JRY Corp. CORP AFFIL general partner: Boston Red Sox; director: NE Sports Network Inc. NONPR AFFIL member: Massachusetts Society CPA's; director: National Baseball Hall Fame & Museum; trustee: Jimmy Fund; trustee, secretary: Dana Farber Cancer Institute; director: Hospitality Properties Trust; member: American Institute of Certified Public Accountants; member: Beta Gamma Sigma.
Edward F. Kenney: trustee
J. J. McAfferty: trustee

Grants Analysis

Disclosure Period: fiscal year ending June 30, 2002
Total Grants: $3,630,034*
Number of Grants: 120
Average Grant: $17,958*
Highest Grant: $1,005,000
Lowest Grant: $1,000
Typical Range: $5,000 to $30,000
*Note: Giving excludes United Way. Average grant figure excludes two highest grants ($1,511,000).

Recent Grants

Note: Grants derived from fiscal 2001 Form 990.

Library-Related

15,000	Boston Public Library, Boston, MA

General

1,005,000	Massachusetts Hospital School, Boston, MA
562,700	United Way, Boston, MA
505,000	Catholic Charities, Boston, MA
100,000	American Red Cross Massachusetts Bay Chapter, Boston, MA

100,000	Inner City Scholarship Fund, Boston, MA
100,000	National Baseball Hall of Fame, Cooperstown, NY
100,000	National Baseball Hall of Fame, Cooperstown, NY
95,034	Rookie League Baseball, Boston, MA
50,000	Boston College, Chestnut Hill, MA
50,000	Boys and Girls Club of Boston, Boston, MA

LESTER E. YEAGER CHARITABLE TRUST B

Giving Contact
Donald W. Haas, Trustee
PO Box 964
Owensboro, KY 42302-0964
Phone: (270)686-8254

Description
Founded: 1989
EIN: 611159548
Organization Type: Private Foundation
Giving Locations: IN: the Indiana counties bordering Daviess and Henderson Counties, KY; KY: Daviess and Henderson Counties
Grant Types: General Support.

Donor Information
Founder: Established in 1989 with funds from the estate of Lester E. Yeager.

Financial Summary
Total Giving: $186,572 (2000); $191,351 (1999); $215,067 (1998)
Giving Analysis: Giving for 2000 includes: foundation grants to United Way ($1,000); 1999: foundation grants to United Way ($2,000); 1998: foundation grants to United Way ($1,000) foundation ($214,067)
Assets: $5,178,178 (2000); $5,354,226 (1999); $5,318,860 (1998)
Gifts Received: $7,500 (1999); $10,000 (1998). Note: In 1998 contributions were received from the Kellogg Foundation. In 1990, contributions the estate of Lester E. Yeager.

Typical Recipients
Arts & Humanities: Arts Associations & Councils, Arts & Humanities-General, Libraries, Museums/Galleries, Music
Civic & Public Affairs: Botanical Gardens/Parks, Clubs, Civic & Public Affairs-General, Housing, Municipalities/Towns, Urban & Community Affairs, Zoos/Aquariums
Education: Agricultural Education, Arts/Humanities Education, Business Education, Colleges & Universities, Community & Junior Colleges, Education Associations, Education Funds, Elementary Education (Private), Elementary Education (Public), Education-General, Literacy, Private Education (Precollege), Public Education (Precollege), Secondary Education (Public)
Environment: Environment-General
Health: Clinics/Medical Centers, Emergency/Ambulance Services, Health-General, Hospices, Hospitals, Medical Rehabilitation, Single-Disease Health Associations
Religion: Churches, Dioceses, Religious Welfare
Science: Science Museums
Social Services: At-Risk Youth, Child Welfare, Community Centers, Day Care, Family Services, Homes, People with Disabilities, Recreation & Athletics, Senior Services, Shelters/Homelessness, Special Olympics, United Funds/United Ways, Volunteer Services, YMCA/YWCA/YMHA/YWHA, Youth Organizations

Application Procedures
Initial Contact: Send a brief letter of inquiry requesting application form, then send a full proposal.
Application Requirements: Include a description of organization, amount requested, purpose of funds sought, recently audited financial statement, and proof of tax-exempt status.
Deadlines: October 15.

Restrictions
Grants are not made to individuals.

Additional Information
Publications: Application Form; Guidelines

Foundation Officials
Ruth F. Adkins: trustee
Donald W. Haas: trustee
Nancy C. Kennedy: trustee

Grants Analysis
Disclosure Period: calendar year ending 2000
Total Grants: $185,572*
Number of Grants: 44
Average Grant: $3,734*
Highest Grant: $25,000
Typical Range: $1,000 to $10,000
***Note:** Giving excludes United Way. Average grant figure excludes highest grant.

Recent Grants
Note: Grants derived from 2001 Form 990.

General
16,500	Owensboro Board of Education, Owensboro, KY -- school projects
13,000	Owensboro Area Museum of Science and History, Owensboro, KY -- exhibits
10,000	Family YMCA of Henderson County, Henderson, KY -- capital campaign
10,000	Family YMCA of Owensboro/Davies County, Inc., Owensboro, KY -- capital campaign
10,000	Pennyrile Youth Soccer Association, Henderson, KY -- lighting for soccer fields
7,500	St. Anthony's Hospice, Henderson, KY -- computer and program system
6,500	Diocese of Owensboro Educational Institute, Owensboro, KY -- school projects
5,000	Henderson Area Arts Alliance, Henderson, KY -- school programming and sponsorship of arts events
5,000	Kentucky Wesleyan College, Owensboro, KY -- scholarship fund
5,000	Volunteer Center of Owensboro, Owensboro, KY -- Reading Projects

YELLOW CORP.

Company Headquarters
10990 Roe Ave.
Overland Park, KS 66207
Web: http://www.yellowcorp.com

Company Description
Founded: 1924
Ticker: YELL
Exchange: NASDAQ
Revenue: US$3.205 billion (2002)
Employees: 30000 (2001)
Fortune Rank: 474, per FORTUNE Magazine's list of 500 Largest U.S. Corporations (2002).
SIC(s): 4213 Trucking Except Local, 6719 Holding Companies Nec.

Operating Locations
Yellow Corp. (KS)

Nonmonetary Support
Type: In-kind Services; Workplace Solicitation
Note: Nonmonetary Support Range: $35,000 to $40,000. Workplace solicitation is only for the United Way.

Yellow Corp. Foundation

Giving Contact
William Martin, Vice President
10990 Roe Avenue
Overland Park, KS 66211-1213
Phone: (913)696-6123
Fax: (913)696-6116

Description
EIN: 237004674
Organization Type: Corporate Foundation
Giving Locations: MO: Kansas City headquarters and operating communities.
Grant Types: Capital, Employee Matching Gifts, General Support, Multiyear/Continuing Support, Operating Expenses, Project.

Financial Summary
Total Giving: $153,500 (2001); $181,407 (1999); $184,910 (1998). Note: Contributes through corporate direct giving program and foundation. Giving includes foundation.
Giving Analysis: Giving for 2001 includes: foundation ($53,500); foundation grants to United Way ($100,000); 1999: foundation ($81,407) foundation grants to United Way ($100,000)
Assets: $144,854 (2001); $325,424 (1999); $402,433 (1998)
Gifts Received: $125,000 (2001); $60,000 (1999). Note: Contributions were received from Yellow Corporation.

Typical Recipients
Arts & Humanities: Arts Associations & Councils, Arts Centers, Arts Institutes, Ballet, Community Arts, Dance, Arts & Humanities-General, Historic Preservation, History & Archaeology, Libraries, Museums/Galleries, Music, Opera, Performing Arts, Public Broadcasting, Theater, Visual Arts
Civic & Public Affairs: Economic Development, Civic & Public Affairs-General, Urban & Community Affairs, Women's Affairs
Education: Agricultural Education, Arts/Humanities Education, Business Education, Colleges & Universities, Community & Junior Colleges, Economic Education, Environmental Education, Minority Education
Health: Cancer, Children's Health/Hospitals, Health Organizations, Heart, Multiple Sclerosis, Public Health
Religion: Religious Welfare
Social Services: Camps, Child Welfare, Crime Prevention, Domestic Violence, Scouts, Shelters/Homelessness, United Funds/United Ways, Youth Organizations

Application Procedures
Initial Contact: Send a letter.
Application Requirements: Include a description of organization, amount requested, purpose of funds sought, recently audited financial statement, proof of tax-exempt status.
Deadlines: None.
Review Process: Monthly review, follow-up questions, and/or site visits.
Decision Notification: Typically 30 to 60 days from receipt of proposal.

Restrictions

Foundation does not support fraternal organizations, goodwill advertising, individuals, political or lobbying groups, or religious organizations for sectarian purposes.

Additional Information

The foundation reports that they are in the process of reducing their contributions program. In the future, nearly all of the gifts will be issued to the United Way, groups in the Kansas City Area, and organizations that are current recipients of their contributions.

The Yellow Corporate Foundation was formerly known as the Yellow Freight System Foundation.

Foundation Officials

Daniel L. Hornbeck: assistant secretary PRIM CORP EMPL secretary: Yellow Freight System Inc.

Grants Analysis

Disclosure Period: calendar year ending 2001
Total Grants: $53,500*
Number of Grants: 6
Average Grant: $5,700*
Highest Grant: $25,000
Lowest Grant: $1,000
Typical Range: $500 to $20,000
*Note: Giving excludes United Way. Average grant figure excludes highest grant.

Recent Grants

Note: Grants derived from 2001 Form 990.

General
100,000	Heart of America United Way, Kansas City, MO -- community development
25,000	Arizona State University Foundation, Tempe, AZ -- educational
10,000	College Fund/UNCF, St. Louis, MO -- educational
10,000	Scholastic, Inc., New York, NY
5,000	Komen Kansas City Race for the Cure, Kansas City, MO
2,500	Kemper Museum of Contemporary Art, Kansas City, MO
1,000	Kids Walk for Homeless Kids, Inc., Chicago, IL

YIH FAMILY FOUNDATION

Giving Contact

Roy Paxton Yih, President
3000 Danville Blvd., Suite 372
Alamo, CA 94507-1550
Phone: (925)855-4713

Description

Founded: 1997
EIN: 943270705
Organization Type: Private Foundation
Grant Types: General Support.

Financial Summary

Total Giving: $143,498 (fiscal year ending June 30, 2001); $60,800 (fiscal 1999); $56,450 (fiscal 1998)
Assets: $2,380,604 (fiscal 2001); $2,421,021 (fiscal 1999); $1,845,244 (fiscal 1998)

Typical Recipients

Arts & Humanities: Museums/Galleries
Civic & Public Affairs: Civic & Public Affairs-General
Education: Private Education (Precollege), Science/ Mathematics Education
Environment: Wildlife Protection
Health: Cancer
Religion: Churches, Religious Organizations
Social Services: Senior Services

Foundation Officials

Cathy Yih: secretary
Irene C.P. Yih: vice president, treasurer
Roy Paxon Yih: president
Shou-Chen Yih: chairman

Grants Analysis

Disclosure Period: fiscal year ending June 30, 2001
Total Grants: $143,498
Number of Grants: 21
Average Grant: $5,675*
Highest Grant: $30,000
Typical Range: $2,500 to $10,000
*Note: Average grant excludes highest grant.

Recent Grants

Note: Grants derived from fiscal 2001 Form 990.

General
30,000	Seven Hills School, Walnut Creek, CA -- for capital campaign and endowment fund
25,000	Seven Hills School, Walnut Creek, CA -- for capital campaign
10,000	California Alumni Association, Oakland, CA -- for library fund
10,000	Friends of the Sea Otter, Monterey, CA
10,000	Habitot Children's Museum, Berkeley, CA
10,000	Habitot Children's Museum, Berkeley, CA -- for the blast office space exhibit
10,000	St. Anthony's Foundation, San Francisco, CA
10,000	Self Help for the Elderly, San Francisco, CA
7,000	Bayside Community Church, Foster City, CA
5,000	Always Dream Foundation, Oakland, CA -- for breast cancer

J. PAUL YOST TRUST

Giving Contact

Ronald K. Fellheimer, Trustee
c/o Fellheimer Law Firm
210 N. Main Street
Pontiac, IL 61764
Phone: (815)842-3858

Description

Founded: 1991
EIN: 376274704
Organization Type: Private Foundation
Giving Locations: IL: Pontiac
Grant Types: General Support, Scholarship.

Financial Summary

Total Giving: $31,750 (2001); $48,000 (2000); $24,105 (1999)
Giving Analysis: Giving for 2001 includes: foundation grants to United Way ($1,000); foundation scholarships ($6,000); 2000: foundation grants to United Way ($1,000); foundation scholarships ($6,000); 1999: foundation grants to United Way ($1,000); foundation scholarships ($4,105);
Assets: $701,646 (2001); $686,231 (2000); $716,560 (1999)
Gifts Received: $19,563 (1993); $543,323 (1992)

Typical Recipients

Arts & Humanities: History & Archaeology, Libraries, Performing Arts, Theater
Civic & Public Affairs: Civic & Public Affairs-General, Municipalities/Towns, Parades/Festivals
Education: Colleges & Universities, Secondary Education (Public), Student Aid
Health: Clinics/Medical Centers
Religion: Churches

Social Services: Animal Protection, Community Service Organizations, Senior Services, United Funds/ United Ways, Youth Organizations

Application Procedures

Initial Contact: Send a brief letter of inquiry.
Application Requirements: Provide a description of organization, amount requested, and purpose of funds sought.
Deadlines: None.

Restrictions

Grants limited to citizens or organizations in Pontiac, IL.

Foundation Officials

Mary Catherine Dievendorf: trustee
Ronald K. Fellheimer: trustee
Dr. John C. Purnell: trustee
Robert Sear: trustee
Faraday J. Strock: trustee

Grants Analysis

Disclosure Period: calendar year ending 2001
Total Grants: $24,750*
Number of Grants: 7
Average Grant: $3,536
Highest Grant: $6,500
Lowest Grant: $1,000
Typical Range: $1,000 to $5,000
*Note: Giving excludes United Way and scholarships.

Recent Grants

Note: Grants derived from 2000 Form 990.

Library-Related
6,900	Pontiac Public Library, Pontiac, IL

General
9,200	City of Pontiac, Pontiac, IL
6,900	First Presbyterian Church, Pontiac, IL
5,500	Livingston County Historical Society
5,500	Vermillion Players
4,000	Livingston County Humane Society
2,000	Evenglow Lodge Retirement Home
1,000	Proud First Night
1,000	United Way of Pontiac, Pontiac, IL

BILL B. YOUNG FOUNDATION

Giving Contact

Bill B. Young Foundation
c/o Farmers & Drovers Bank
PO Box C
Council Grove, KS 66846-0620
Phone: (316)767-5138

Description

Founded: 1995
EIN: 481161082
Organization Type: Private Foundation
Giving Locations: KS: Council Grove
Grant Types: General Support.

Financial Summary

Total Giving: $15,613 (2001); $44,750 (2000); $39,050 (1999)
Assets: $1,098,262 (2001); $1,080,102 (2000); $910,948 (1999)
Gifts Received: $53,899 (1996); $922,352 (1995).
Note: In 1995, contributions were received from the estate of Bill Young.

Typical Recipients

Civic & Public Affairs: Rural Affairs, Urban & Community Affairs
Health: Hospitals, Public Health

Social Services: Community Centers, Community Service Organizations, Crime Prevention, Recreation & Athletics

Application Procedures

Initial Contact: Request an application form.
Deadlines: None.

Restrictions

Limited to recognized charitable organizations in Council Grove, KS.

Additional Information

Trust(s): Farmers & Drovers Bank

Foundation Officials

Lowell Campbell: trustee
Pat Finney: trustee
Barbara Foster: trustee
Charles Garrett: trustee
Julie Hower: trustee
Henry White, Jr.: trustee
John White: trustee

Grants Analysis

Disclosure Period: calendar year ending 2001
Total Grants: $15,613
Number of Grants: 9
Average Grant: $1,735
Highest Grant: $3,300
Lowest Grant: $225
Typical Range: $500 to $2,500

Recent Grants

Note: Grants derived from 2000 Form 990.

General

20,000	Council Grove Area Foundation, Council Grove, KS -- Wellness Center
4,500	Flint Hills Wind, Council Grove, KS -- youth softball
4,000	Bower Community Center, Council Grove, KS -- community center public rest rooms
3,950	DAR, Council Grove, KS -- repair community statue
3,800	Council Grove Library, Council Grove, KS -- update computers
2,500	Flint Hills Braves, Council Grove, KS -- Baseball Program
2,000	Care and Share, Council Grove, KS -- assist needy
2,000	Crime Stoppers, Council Grove, KS -- youth speakers
2,000	Morris County Fair board, Dwight, KS -- fair building

HUGO H. AND MABEL B. YOUNG FOUNDATION

Giving Contact

Michael C. Bandy
c/o J.P. Morgan Securities Inc.
109 S. Market Street
Loudonville, OH 44842
Phone: (419)994-7015

Description

Founded: 1963
EIN: 346560664
Organization Type: Private Foundation
Giving Locations: OH: Loudonville and Holmes Counties
Grant Types: Capital, Scholarship.

Financial Summary

Total Giving: $348,977 (fiscal year ending April 30, 2001); $403,230 (fiscal 2000); $268,876 (fiscal 1999). Note: Fiscal 1997 Giving includes scholarship ($8,000).
Giving Analysis: Giving for fiscal 2001 includes: foundation grants to United Way ($1,800); foundation scholarships ($13,000) fiscal 2000: foundation scholarships ($8,000)
Assets: $5,957,479 (fiscal 2001); $6,537,981 (fiscal 2000); $6,747,786 (fiscal 1999)

Typical Recipients

Arts & Humanities: Community Arts, Libraries, Music
Civic & Public Affairs: Community Foundations, Economic Development, Municipalities/Towns, Philanthropic Organizations, Professional & Trade Associations, Rural Affairs, Safety, Urban & Community Affairs
Education: Private Education (Precollege), Public Education (Precollege), Student Aid
Health: Cancer, Clinics/Medical Centers, Health Organizations, Hospices, Hospitals
Social Services: Community Service Organizations, People with Disabilities, Recreation & Athletics, Scouts, Senior Services, Youth Organizations

Application Procedures

Initial Contact: Send a brief letter of inquiry. Include a description of organization, amount requested, purpose of funds sought, recently audited financial statement, and proof of tax-exempt status.
Deadlines: None.

Restrictions

Does not support individuals or provide loans.

Foundation Officials

Robert Dubler: trustee
James Dudte: president, trustee
William B. LaPlace: trustee
James S. Lingenfelter: secretary, treasurer
R. D. Mayer: vice president, trustee
Phillip A. Ranney: counsel, trustee CORP AFFIL director: General Housewares Corp.

Grants Analysis

Disclosure Period: fiscal year ending April 30, 2001
Total Grants: $334,177*
Number of Grants: 16
Average Grant: $10,209*
Highest Grant: $109,020
Typical Range: $5,000 to $20,000
*Note: Giving excludes scholarships and United Way. Average grant excludes two highest grants ($191,520).

Recent Grants

Note: Grants derived from fiscal 1999 Form 990.

Library-Related

140,000	Loudonville Public Library, Loudonville, OH

General

85,362	Loudonville Perrysville School, Loudonville, OH -- for scholarship funds
9,500	Village of Perrysville Fire Department, Loudonville, OH
9,000	Ashland Symphony Orchestra Association, Ashland, OH
6,662	Ashland Charities Services, Ashland, OH
6,049	Village of Loudonville - Recreation Department, Loudonville, OH
5,789	Loudonville Police Department, Loudonville, OH
3,500	Loudonville Agricultural Society, Inc., Loudonville, OH
3,000	Mohican Area Community Fund, Loudonville, OH

IRVIN L. YOUNG FOUNDATION

Giving Contact

David S. Fisher, President & Director
15535 St. Therese Blvd.
Brookfield, WI 53005
Phone: (262)495-2485

Description

Founded: 1949
EIN: 396077858
Organization Type: Private Foundation
Giving Locations: CA; WI: nationally.
Grant Types: Capital, General Support, Operating Expenses, Scholarship.

Donor Information

Founder: the late Irvin L. Young

Financial Summary

Total Giving: $205,900 (1999); $620,956 (1996); $613,556 (1995)
Assets: $4,088,665 (1999); $4,142,667 (1996); $4,338,729 (1995)

Typical Recipients

Arts & Humanities: Arts Outreach, Libraries
Civic & Public Affairs: Zoos/Aquariums
Education: Colleges & Universities, Medical Education, Public Education (Precollege), Religious Education, Student Aid
Health: Health Organizations, Hospitals, Nursing Services, Respiratory
International: Health Care/Hospitals, International Development, International Environmental Issues, International Peace & Security Issues, International Relations, International Relief Efforts, Missionary/Religious Activities
Religion: Bible Study/Translation, Churches, Ministries, Missionary Activities (Domestic), Religious Organizations, Religious Welfare, Seminaries
Social Services: Camps, Child Welfare, Community Service Organizations, Food/Clothing Distribution, Scouts, Shelters/Homelessness, Youth Organizations

Application Procedures

Initial Contact: Send a brief letter of inquiry.
Application Requirements: amount requested and purpose of funds sought.
Deadlines: None.

Foundation Officials

Dr. L. Arden Almquist: director
David S. Fisher: president, director
Mary Longbrake: vice president, director
Robert W. Reninger: secretary, director
Mitchell J. Simon: assistant treasurer, director
David A. Voetman: director
Fern D. Young: treasurer, director

Grants Analysis

Disclosure Period: calendar year ending 1996
Total Grants: $620,956
Number of Grants: 16
Average Grant: $8,064*
Highest Grant: $500,000
Typical Range: $500 to $50,000
*Note: Average grant figure excludes highest grant. A more recent grants list was unavailable.

Recent Grants

Note: Grants derived from 1996 Form 990.

General

500,000	Salvation Army, Bakersfield, CA -- for building program

32,000	Berean Mission, St. Louis, MO -- for Vehicle for Katchungu
30,500	Free Methodist Church -- for Kiborgora
23,000	Burundi Scholarships
5,400	McCormick Theological Seminary, Chicago, IL -- for Young Memorial Scholarship
5,000	Evangelical Covenant Church -- for Wasolo Hospital Extension
5,000	Evangelical Covenant Church -- for Wasolo Hospital Solar Panel
5,000	High Adventure Ministries, Simi Valley, CA -- to move Voice of Hope from Lebanon to Israel
5,000	University of Wisconsin, Madison, WI -- for Superior Summer Youth Program
5,000	Zoological Society, Milwaukee, WI

ISAAC HERMAN ZACHARIA FOUNDATION

Giving Contact

Isaac Herman Zacharia, President
1515 Broadway
New York, NY 10036
Phone: (212)869-3333

Description

Founded: 1953
EIN: 510108212
Organization Type: Private Foundation
Giving Locations: NY
Grant Types: General Support.

Donor Information

Founder: Isaac Herman Zacharia

Financial Summary

Total Giving: $145,025 (1996); $147,894 (1995); $27,700 (1994)
Assets: $4,017,405 (1996); $4,105,417 (1995); $3,554,189 (1994)

Typical Recipients

Arts & Humanities: Arts Associations & Councils, Arts Centers, Film & Video, Historic Preservation, Libraries, Literary Arts, Music, Public Broadcasting
Civic & Public Affairs: Clubs, Ethnic Organizations, Civic & Public Affairs-General, Municipalities/Towns, Safety, Urban & Community Affairs
Education: Colleges & Universities, Private Education (Precollege), Religious Education, Secondary Education (Private), Secondary Education (Public)
Health: AIDS/HIV, Clinics/Medical Centers, Emergency/Ambulance Services, Geriatric Health, Health Organizations, Hospices, Hospitals, Long-Term Care, Mental Health, Single-Disease Health Associations
International: Foreign Arts Organizations, International Affairs
Religion: Churches, Jewish Causes, Religious Organizations, Religious Welfare, Synagogues/Temples
Social Services: Community Centers, Community Service Organizations, Crime Prevention, Day Care, Family Services, People with Disabilities, Recreation & Athletics, Senior Services, Veterans, Volunteer Services

Application Procedures

Initial Contact: Send a letter detailing requirements and previous activities.
Deadlines: None.

Foundation Officials

Issac Herman Zacharia: president

Grants Analysis

Disclosure Period: calendar year ending 1996
Total Grants: $145,025
Number of Grants: 24

Average Grant: $1,305*
Highest Grant: $115,000
Typical Range: $100 to $6,000
***Note:** Average grant figure excludes highest grant. A more recent grants list was unavailable.

Recent Grants

Note: Grants derived from 1997 Form 990.

General

130,000	Fidelity Charitable Gift Fund, Portsmouth, OH
85,000	Sephardic Temple
25,000	New York University Medical Center for Urological Research, New York, NY
5,150	Sephardic Old Age Home
5,000	Dr. Henry Janewitz Foundation
3,000	St. Catherine's
2,500	Pro Arte Musical, San Juan, PR
2,000	Columbia Grammar Preparatory, New York, NY
2,000	Jewish Family and Children's Services
1,000	Aventura Turnberry Jewish Center, Miami, FL

H.B. ZACHRY CO.

Company Headquarters

527 Logwood Ave.
San Antonio, TX 78221

Company Description

Employees: 7,000
SIC(s): 1622 Bridge, Tunnel & Elevated Highway.

The Zachry Foundation

Giving Contact

Pamela W. O'Connor, Executive Director
310 South St. Mary's Street, Suite 2500
San Antonio, TX 78205
Phone: (210)554-4663
Fax: (210)554-4605

Description

Founded: 1960
EIN: 741485544
Organization Type: Corporate Foundation
Giving Locations: TX: higher education grants are given throughout the state, San Antonio
Grant Types: Capital, Challenge, Emergency, Multiyear/Continuing Support, Research.

Donor Information

Founder: H. B. Zachry Co. International, H. B. Zachry Co.

Financial Summary

Total Giving: $1,191,500 (2000); $992,801 (1999); $557,225 (1996). Note: Contributes through foundation only.
Giving Analysis: Giving for 2000 includes: foundation ($1,191,500); 1999: foundation grants to United Way ($175,000); foundation ($817,801); 1996: foundation grants to United Way ($100,000) foundation ($457,225)
Assets: $10,494,340 (2000); $10,157,891 (1999); $8,677,759 (1996)
Gifts Received: $1,250,000 (2000); $205,000 (1996); $100,000 (1995). Note: In 2000, contributions were received from Capitol Aggregates ($1,050,000) and the H. B. Zachry Co. ($200,000). In 1995 and 1996, contributions were received from the H. B. Zachry Co.

Typical Recipients

Arts & Humanities: Arts Centers, Arts Outreach, Ethnic & Folk Arts, Arts & Humanities-General, Historic Preservation, Libraries, Museums/Galleries, Music, Performing Arts, Public Broadcasting, Theater
Civic & Public Affairs: Botanical Gardens/Parks, Economic Development, Civic & Public Affairs-General, Housing, Municipalities/Towns, Nonprofit Management, Philanthropic Organizations, Urban & Community Affairs, Zoos/Aquariums
Education: Afterschool/Enrichment Programs, Arts/Humanities Education, Business Education, Business-School Partnerships, Colleges & Universities, Community & Junior Colleges, Continuing Education, Economic Education, Elementary Education (Public), Engineering/Technological Education, Faculty Development, Education-General, Leadership Training, Literacy, Literacy, Medical Education, Private Education (Precollege), Public Education (Precollege), Science/Mathematics Education, Secondary Education (Public), Student Aid, Vocational & Technical Education
Health: Cancer, Children's Health/Hospitals, Clinics/Medical Centers, Diabetes, Emergency/Ambulance Services, Health-General, Health Organizations, Hospices, Hospitals, Hospitals (University Affiliated), Medical Rehabilitation, Medical Research, Public Health, Speech & Hearing
International: Foreign Arts Organizations, International Affairs, Missionary/Religious Activities
Religion: Jewish Causes, Ministries, Religious Organizations, Religious Welfare
Science: Science-General, Observatories & Planetariums, Science Museums, Scientific Centers & Institutes, Scientific Research
Social Services: At-Risk Youth, Big Brother/Big Sister, Camps, Child Welfare, Community Centers, Community Service Organizations, Delinquency & Criminal Rehabilitation, Domestic Violence, Family Services, Homes, People with Disabilities, Recreation & Athletics, Scouts, Senior Services, Social Services-General, Substance Abuse, United Funds/United Ways, YMCA/YWCA/YMHA/YWHA, Youth Organizations

Application Procedures

Initial Contact: a brief letter of inquiry or phone call to request application form, which is required for all proposals
Application Requirements: a description of organization, amount requested, and purpose of funds sought
Deadlines: February 15
Decision Notification: a preliminary review of agency proposals is conducted at the first board meeting held in late spring; organizations denied will be informed at this time and requests receiving interest and meriting further discussion are retained. Respective agencies are considered for funding at the second board meeting in mid-summer; majority of grants are determined and awarded at that time, and all agencies are notified in writing.
Notes: Proposals are accepted only during the first six weeks of the year.

Restrictions

Foundation does not support individuals, endowments, or organizations outside San Antonio for general grants or outside Texas for educational grants.

Corporate Officials

Bruce Benjamin Cloud, Sr.: vice chairman, director vice president B Thomas, OK February 15, 1920. ED Texas A&M University BCE (1940). PRIM CORP EMPL vice chairman, director: H.B. Zachry Co. CORP AFFIL chairman: Bruce Cloud Equipment Co. Inc.; director: Dudley R. Cloud & Son Construction. NONPR AFFIL honorary life board member: Texas State Technology College Foundation; member: Texas Transportation Institute; member: Texas Society Professional Engineers; member: Texas Good Roads-Transportation Association; member: Texas

Hotmix Paving Association; member: Texas Association General Contractors; member: Texas Congress Extension Service; member: San Antonio Chamber of Commerce; member: San Antonio Livestock Association; member: National Asphalt Paving Association; member: Nocturnal Adoration Society; member: Consult Contractors Council America; member: American Institute Management; member: American Management Association; member: Alpha Epsilon Chi; member: American Concrete Paving Association.

Charles E. Ebrom: director, executive vice president B 1931. PRIM CORP EMPL director, executive vice president: H. B. Zachry Co. International.

Peter S. Van Nort: president B 1937. PRIM CORP EMPL president: H.B. Zachry Co.

Henry Bartell Zachry, Jr.: chairman, chief executive officer B Laredo, TX 1933. ED Texas A&M University BScE (1954). PRIM CORP EMPL chairman, chief executive officer: Zachry Inc. CORP AFFIL chairman: H B Zachry Co. NONPR AFFIL director: Southwest Research Institute.

Foundation Officials

Charles E. Ebrom: treasurer, trustee (see above)
Murray Lloyd Johnson, Jr.: secretary, trustee B Lake Charles, LA 1940. ED Austin College (1962); University of Texas (1965). PRIM CORP EMPL vice president, general counsel, director: H.B. Zachry Co. NONPR AFFIL member: American Judicature Society; member: International Association Defense Counsel; member: American Bar Association.
Pamela O'Connor: executive director
Henry Bartell Zachry, Jr.: trustee (see above)
J. P. Zachry: president, trustee B 1937. PRIM CORP EMPL president: Tower Life Insurance Co.
Mollie Steves Zachry: trustee

Grants Analysis

Disclosure Period: calendar year ending 2000
Total Grants: $1,191,500*
Number of Grants: 40
Average Grant: $18,197*
Highest Grant: $250,000
Lowest Grant: $1,500
Typical Range: $2,000 to $25,000
*Note: Giving excludes United Way. Average grant figure excludes two highest grants ($500,000).

Recent Grants

Note: Grants derived from 2000 Form 990.

General

250,000	Cancer Therapy and Research Foundation of South Texas, San Antonio, TX
250,000	Texas A & M Corps Endowment
100,000	Lady Bird Johnson National Wildflower Center, Austin, TX
70,000	St. Mary's University, San Antonio, TX
60,000	San Antonio Symphony, San Antonio, TX
50,000	San Antonio Academy of Texas, San Antonio, TX
50,000	Santa Rosa Children's Hospital Foundation, San Antonio, TX
50,000	Texas A & M Foundation, College Station, TX
25,000	American Red Cross Capital Campaign, Philadelphia, PA
25,000	Boy Scouts of America Alamo Area Council, San Antonio, TX

ANNE AND HENRY ZARROW FOUNDATION

Giving Contact

Judith Z. Kishner, Secretary, Treasurer
401 S. Boston Suite 900
Tulsa, OK 74103
Phone: (918)295-8000

Description

Founded: 1986
EIN: 731286874
Organization Type: Private Foundation
Giving Locations: OK: Tulsa
Grant Types: Emergency, General Support.

Donor Information

Founder: Henry H. Zarrow

Financial Summary

Total Giving: $4,786,395 (2001); $5,778,964 (2000); $3,570,151 (1999)
Giving Analysis: Giving for 2001 includes: foundation grants to United Way ($10,000); 2000: foundation grants to United Way ($13,000); foundation scholarships ($159,067); 1999: foundation grants to United Way ($13,000) foundation scholarships ($98,328)
Assets: $89,709,323 (2001); $93,463,951 (2000); $90,782,321 (1999)
Gifts Received: $1,144,890 (1996); $5,000 (1995); $1,015,825 (1994)

Typical Recipients

Arts & Humanities: Arts Associations & Councils, Arts Funds, Arts Institutes, Ballet, Community Arts, Historic Preservation, History & Archaeology, Libraries, Museums/Galleries, Music, Opera, Theater
Civic & Public Affairs: Community Foundations, Civic & Public Affairs-General, Hispanic Affairs, Housing, Law & Justice, Municipalities/Towns, Native American Affairs, Urban & Community Affairs, Women's Affairs
Education: Colleges & Universities, Education Reform, Education-General, Medical Education, Minority Education, Private Education (Precollege), Public Education (Precollege), Science/Mathematics Education, Secondary Education (Public), Student Aid
Environment: Resource Conservation
Health: Alzheimers Disease, Arthritis, Cancer, Children's Health/Hospitals, Clinics/Medical Centers, Diabetes, Heart, Hospitals, Medical Rehabilitation, Medical Research, Mental Health, Nursing Services, Prenatal Health Issues, Research/Studies Institutes, Respiratory, Single-Disease Health Associations, Speech & Hearing, Transplant Networks/Donor Banks
Religion: Churches, Jewish Causes, Religious Welfare, Synagogues/Temples
Social Services: Child Welfare, Community Service Organizations, Day Care, Domestic Violence, Family Planning, Family Services, Food/Clothing Distribution, People with Disabilities, Recreation & Athletics, Senior Services, Sexual Abuse, Shelters/Homelessness, Substance Abuse, United Funds/United Ways, Volunteer Services, YMCA/YWCA/YMHA/YWHA, Youth Organizations

Application Procedures

Initial Contact: Send a brief letter of inquiry and a full proposal.
Application Requirements: Include a written description of organization amount requested, purpose of funds sought, recently audited financial statement, Form 990 with schedule A and proof of tax-exempt status.
Deadlines: None.

Restrictions

Limited to organizations providing relief to the poor, distressed, or underprivileged in the Tulsa, OK, area.

Additional Information

Provides scholarships for higher education.

Foundation Officials

Steve Cochran: treasurer PRIM CORP EMPL treasurer: Sooner Pipe & Supply Corp.
Julie W. Cohen: director
J. W. Kerby: treasurer PRIM CORP EMPL vice president: Sooner Pipe & Supply Corp.

Judith Z. Kishner: director
Anne S. Zarrow: vice president
Henry H. Zarrow: president B 1929. PRIM CORP EMPL president, chief executive officer: Sooner Pipe & Supply Corp. CORP AFFIL president: A-Z Terminal Corp.; director: Warren Medical Research Institute.
Stuart A. Zarrow: director

Grants Analysis

Disclosure Period: calendar year ending 2001
Total Grants: $4,776,395*
Number of Grants: 148
Average Grant: $22,112*
Highest Grant: $1,548,000
Typical Range: $5,000 to $30,000
*Note: Giving excludes United Way. Average grant figure excludes highest grant.

Recent Grants

Note: Grants derived from 2001 Form 990.

General

1,548,000	Tulsa Community Foundation, Tulsa, OK -- operating
500,000	Mayo Foundation, Scottsdale, AZ -- operating
250,000	Monte Cassino School, Tulsa, OK -- operating
250,000	St. Gregory's University, Shawnee, OK -- operating
205,000	Tulsa Senior Services, Tulsa, OK -- operating
199,474	Tulsa Jewish Retirement and Health Care Center, Tulsa, OK -- operating
100,000	B'nai Emunah Congregation, Tulsa, OK -- operating
100,000	Norman Community Foundation, Norman, OK -- operating
65,500	Tulsa Day Center for the Homeless, Tulsa, OK -- operating
55,000	Community Action Project, Tulsa, OK -- operating

HENRY AND CAROL ZEITER CHARITABLE FOUNDATION

Giving Contact

Henry J. Zeiter, President
255 East Weber Avenue
Stockton, CA 95202
Phone: (209)466-5566

Description

Founded: 1996
EIN: 680369445
Organization Type: Private Foundation
Grant Types: General Support.

Financial Summary

Total Giving: $32,527 (2001); $78,361 (2000); $83,292 (1999)
Giving Analysis: Giving for 2001 includes: foundation scholarships ($10,010); 2000: foundation scholarships ($52,873); 1999: foundation scholarships ($62,280)
Assets: $2,277,789 (2001); $2,802,187 (2000); $2,968,956 (1999)
Gifts Received: $245,575 (2001); $87,883 (2000); $621,479 (1999). Note: In 2001, contributions were received from Henry & Carol Zeiter ($42,400), Joe Zeiter ($40,000), Ed Kahn ($5,000), and John & Lynette ($117,839). In 2000, contributions were received from Henry & Carol Zeiter ($89,250), Joe Zeiter ($15,960), and John & Lynette ($115,917). In 1999, contributions were received from Henry & Carol Zeiter ($379,508), Joe Zeiter ($83,438), and John & Lynette

($158,190). In 1998, contributions were received from Henry and Carol Zeiter ($67,000), Joe Zeiter ($7,500), Anthony Andres ($8,000), John and Lynette Zieter ($115,000), and Buck Lewis Memorial Scholarship ($13,075).

Typical Recipients

Arts & Humanities: Libraries, Music
Civic & Public Affairs: Civic & Public Affairs-General
Education: Education-General, Student Aid
Health: Hospitals
Religion: Religious Organizations, Religious Welfare, Seminaries
Social Services: Shelters/Homelessness

Application Procedures

Initial Contact: Send a written request substantiating need.
Deadlines: None.

Restrictions

Contributions are currently limited to the San Joaquin Valley of CA.

Foundation Officials

Carol Zeiter: secretary
Henry J. Zeiter: president

Grants Analysis

Disclosure Period: calendar year ending 2001
Total Grants: $22,517*
Number of Grants: 22
Average Grant: $796*
Highest Grant: $5,798
Lowest Grant: $95
Typical Range: $200 to $1,000
*Note: Giving excludes scholarships. Average grant figure excludes highest grant.

Recent Grants

Note: Grants derived from 2000 Form 990.

Library-Related

403	St. Anne's School, Stockton, CA -- books for library	
300	St. Anne's School, Stockton, CA	

General

2,500	Stockton Symphony, Stockton, CA
2,000	Stockton Chorale Public Concert, Stockton, CA -- tickets for poor
2,000	Stockton Chorale Public Concert, Stockton, CA -- public concert for shut-ins
1,000	Homeless Shelter
1,000	Salvation Army -- Zeiter Fund for alcoholics
750	Carmel of Thelokos
700	Dameron Hospital Foundation, Stockton, CA -- fund raiser
300	Vincentian Congregation Missions
300	Vincentian Missions and Seminary
295	Homeless Shelter

ZELLERBACH FAMILY FUND

Giving Contact

Linda B. Howe, Program Executive
120 Montgomery Street, Suite 1550
San Francisco, CA 94104
Phone: (415)421-2629
Fax: (415)421-6713

Description

Founded: 1956
EIN: 946069482
Organization Type: Private Foundation
Giving Locations: CA: San Francisco Bay Area
Grant Types: General Support, Project.

Donor Information

Founder: Established in 1956 by the late Jennie B. Zellerbach . The Zellerbach family started a paper business in the latter part of the nineteenth century which, through mergers and acquisitions, became the Crown Zellerbach Corporation.

Financial Summary

Total Giving: $3,923,100 (2001); $3,773,405 (2000); $2,428,074 (1998)
Assets: $94,846,292 (2001); $100,443,383 (2000); $73,893,438 (1998)
Gifts Received: $211,920 (2001); $3,940 (2000); $60,000 (1998). Note: In 2001, contributions were received from Snyder Capital Management ($5,000), Wallace Alexander Gerbode Foundation ($100,000), Levi Strauss Foundation ($5,000), and William and Flora Hewlett Foundation ($100,000).

Typical Recipients

Arts & Humanities: Arts Associations & Councils, Arts Centers, Arts Institutes, Ballet, Community Arts, Dance, Ethnic & Folk Arts, Arts & Humanities-General, History & Archaeology, Literary Arts, Museums/Galleries, Music, Opera, Performing Arts, Theater
Civic & Public Affairs: African American Affairs, Asian American Affairs, Botanical Gardens/Parks, Business/Free Enterprise, Civil Rights, Clubs, Community Foundations, Economic Development, Economic Policy, Employment/Job Training, Civic & Public Affairs-General, Hispanic Affairs, Housing, Law & Justice, Legal Aid, Minority Business, Nonprofit Management, Professional & Trade Associations, Public Policy, Public Policy, Safety, Urban & Community Affairs, Women's Affairs
Education: Afterschool/Enrichment Programs, Arts/Humanities Education, Colleges & Universities, Education-General, Health & Physical Education, Leadership Training, Literacy, Public Education (Precollege), Science/Mathematics Education, Secondary Education (Private), Social Sciences Education, Student Aid
Environment: Environment-General
Health: AIDS/HIV, Cancer, Children's Health/Hospitals, Clinics/Medical Centers, Health Organizations, Mental Health, Prenatal Health Issues, Public Health, Research/Studies Institutes, Trauma Treatment
Religion: Jewish Causes, Religious Welfare, Synagogues/Temples
Social Services: At-Risk Youth, Child Abuse, Child Welfare, Community Centers, Community Service Organizations, Domestic Violence, Emergency Relief, Family Services, Food/Clothing Distribution, Homes, People with Disabilities, Recreation & Athletics, Refugee Assistance, Shelters/Homelessness, Social Services-General, United Funds/United Ways, Volunteer Services, Youth Organizations

Application Procedures

Initial Contact: Initial approach for a grant application may be made by phone or written proposal for community art grants only. All other grants are initiated by the Foundation staff.
Application Requirements: The proposal for an arts project should include a brief summary of the purpose of the program, its goals, number of persons participating, the audience or persons to whom the efforts are directed, and information about the organization's leadership. Press clippings and a few statements from community groups or experts in the field who appreciate the program should also be sent. In addition, requests should include the most recent financial statement, detailed project budget, listing of contributions and grants as well as a list of other groups that have received or will receive a request, and proof of tax-exempt status. have received or will receive a request, and proof of tax-exempt status. have received or will receive a request, and proof of tax-exempt status.
Deadlines: Those seeking art-related grants should call the office to inquire about specific deadlines.
Review Process: Community Arts Distribution Committee meets about every two months. Other board

meetings are held quarterly, in March, June, September, and December.

Restrictions

The fund discourages mail solicitation (except in the San Francisco Bay area community arts projects), and initiates most of its own projects.

Additional Information

The fund is interested in new ideas even though very few new projects can be supported. The fund generally develops its own programs with the guidance of advisory committees.
Publications: Annual Report; Guidelines; Application Form for Community Arts

Foundation Officials

Jeanette Maddux Dunckel: trustee
Philip S. Ehrlich, Jr.: trustee
Sharon Fujii: vice president
Edward A. Nathan: trustee
Cindy Rambo: executive director ED Harvard University MA; Oklahoma State University BA. PRIM NONPR EMPL executive director: Planned Parenthood Alameda-San Francisco.
Louis Saroni, II: vice president, treasurer
Anne Spence: trustee
Mildred Thompson: trustee
Raymond H. Williams: vice president
Charles R. Zellerbach: trustee
John W. Zellerbach: vice president
Thomas H. Zellerbach: trustee
William Joseph Zellerbach: president B San Francisco, CA September 15, 1920. ED University of Pennsylvania Wharton School BS (1942); Harvard University (1958). NONPR AFFIL member: National Paper Trade Association. CLUB AFFIL Villa Taverna Club; Presidio Golf Club; Pacific-Union Club; Peninsula Country Club; Commonwealth Club.
Nancy Zellerbach-Boschwitz: secretary

Grants Analysis

Disclosure Period: calendar year ending 2001
Total Grants: $3,903,100*
Number of Grants: 104
Average Grant: $32,482*
Highest Grant: $557,500
Lowest Grant: $1,000
Typical Range: $10,000 to $50,000
*Note: Giving excludes United Way. Average grant figure excludes highest grant.

Recent Grants

Note: Grants derived from 2001 Form 990.

General

113,000	University of Pennsylvania, Philadelphia, PA
110,000	University of Pennsylvania, Philadelphia, PA
100,000	Regents University of California, Berkeley, CA
95,000	Public Health Institute, Berkeley, CA
89,000	Contra Costa County Integration Program, Martinez, CA
87,000	Art Research and Curriculum, Oakland, CA
80,000	Chinese for Affirmative Action, San Francisco, CA
80,000	Mission Economic Development, San Francisco, CA
80,000	Women's Action to Gain Economic Security, Mountain View, CA
75,000	California Institute of Mental Health, Sacramento, CA

Fran And Irwin Ziegelheim Charitable Foundation

Giving Contact
Frances Ziegelheim, Trustee
19 Woodfield Lane
Saddle River, NJ 07458-3219
Phone: (201)934-6369

Description
Founded: 1989
EIN: 222772946
Organization Type: Private Foundation
Grant Types: General Support, Scholarship.

Financial Summary
Total Giving: $13,123 (2001); $14,430 (2000); $11,678 (1999)
Giving Analysis: Giving for 2001 includes: foundation scholarships ($500) 2000: foundation scholarships ($500)
Assets: $201,768 (2001); $207,921 (2000); $208,752 (1999)

Typical Recipients
Arts & Humanities: Libraries
Civic & Public Affairs: Botanical Gardens/Parks, Clubs, Civic & Public Affairs-General, Public Policy, Safety, Women's Affairs
Education: Education-General, Preschool Education, Private Education (Precollege), Student Aid
Health: Cancer, Diabetes, Emergency/Ambulance Services, Health-General, Hospitals, Long-Term Care, Medical Rehabilitation, Single-Disease Health Associations
Religion: Dioceses, Religion-General, Jewish Causes, Seminaries, Synagogues/Temples
Social Services: Senior Services, Social Services-General, YMCA/YWCA/YMHA/YWHA, Youth Organizations

Application Procedures
Initial Contact: Send a brief letter of inquiry.
Application Requirements: Include a description of organization, amount requested, purpose of funds sought, recently audited financial statement, and proof of tax-exempt status.
Deadlines: None.

Foundation Officials
Joel Bossom: trustee
Frances Ziegelheim: trustee

Grants Analysis
Disclosure Period: calendar year ending 2001
Total Grants: $12,623*
Number of Grants: 20
Average Grant: $631
Highest Grant: $5,005
Lowest Grant: $10
Typical Range: $100 to $1,000
*Note: Giving excludes scholarships.

Recent Grants
Note: Grants derived from 2000 Form 990.

Library-Related
50	Friends of the Fair Lawn Library, Fair Lawn, NJ

General
4,330	Temple Emanuel, Woodcliff Lake, NJ
3,000	J.H.R.C., New Jersey City, NJ
2,650	Arnold B. Gold Foundation, Englewood, NJ
1,275	JCC on the Palisades, Tenafly, NJ
1,000	JCC Association of North America, Tenafly, NJ
500	JCC College Scholarship Fund, Tenafly, NJ
450	Temple Beth Rishon, Wyckoff, NJ
350	Therapeutic Nursery School, Tenafly, NJ
200	Bergen County YWCA, Washington Township, NJ
150	Englewood Hospital and Medical Center, Englewood, NJ

Ziegler Foundation

Giving Contact
Bernard C. Ziegler, President
215 N. Main St.
West Bend, WI 53095
Phone: (262)334-5521

Description
Founded: 1944
EIN: 396044762
Organization Type: Private Foundation
Giving Locations: WI: West Bend and surrounding area
Grant Types: General Support, Scholarship.

Donor Information
Founder: members of the Ziegler family

Financial Summary
Total Giving: $570,190 (2000); $498,630 (1999); $465,700 (1998)
Giving Analysis: Giving for 2000 includes: foundation grants to United Way ($5,775); foundation scholarships ($122,500); 1999: foundation grants to United Way ($5,500); foundation scholarships ($115,460) 1998: foundation grants to United Way ($5,250)
Assets: $11,583,029 (2000); $12,688,733 (1999); $11,286,384 (1998)

Typical Recipients
Arts & Humanities: Arts Funds, Arts Institutes, Arts & Humanities-General, History & Archaeology, Libraries, Literary Arts, Museums/Galleries, Music, Opera, Performing Arts, Public Broadcasting
Civic & Public Affairs: Economic Development, Civic & Public Affairs-General, Hispanic Affairs, Public Policy, Urban & Community Affairs, Zoos/Aquariums
Education: Agricultural Education, Colleges & Universities, Education Funds, Education-General, Health & Physical Education, Literacy, Secondary Education (Public), Student Aid, Vocational & Technical Education
Environment: Environment-General, Resource Conservation
Health: Clinics/Medical Centers, Emergency/Ambulance Services, Eyes/Blindness, Health-General, Hospitals, Medical Research, Public Health, Transplant Networks/Donor Banks
Religion: Churches, Religion-General, Religious Organizations, Religious Welfare
Social Services: Animal Protection, Big Brother/Big Sister, Child Welfare, Community Centers, Community Service Organizations, Family Services, People with Disabilities, Recreation & Athletics, Scouts, Shelters/Homelessness, Substance Abuse, United Funds/United Ways, Volunteer Services, YMCA/YWCA/YMHA/YWHA, Youth Organizations

Application Procedures
Initial Contact: Send written application.
Deadlines: None.

Restrictions
Does not support individuals.

Foundation Officials
Robert J. Bonner: vice president, director
Carolyn Schucht: director
Bernard C. Ziegler, III: assistant secretary, assistant treasurer, director

Bernard C. Ziegler: president, director CORP AFFIL director: Ziegler Co.
Carl H. Ziegler: director
Peter D. Ziegler: assistant secretary, assistant treasurer, director
R. Douglas Ziegler: vice president, secretary, treasurer, director B Milwaukee, WI 1927. ED Northwestern University (1949). CORP AFFIL director: Johnson Controls Inc.; vice president: Ziegler Asset Management Co.

Grants Analysis
Disclosure Period: calendar year ending 2000
Total Grants: $441,915*
Number of Grants: 67
Average Grant: $5,260*
Highest Grant: $50,000
Typical Range: $1,000 to $10,000
*Note: Giving excludes scholarships and United Way. Average grant figure excludes two highest grants ($100,000).

Recent Grants
Note: Grants derived from 1999 Form 990.

General
110,000	West Bend High School, West Bend, WI -- scholarships
60,000	Washington County -- for Fair Park Equestrian Center
30,000	Blood Center of Southeast Wisconsin, Milwaukee, WI -- pledge
25,000	American Red Cross WB Chapter -- pledge for new facility
25,000	Cedar Lakes Conservation Foundation, Milwaukee, WI -- for Everett Smith memorial fund
25,000	Ozaukee Washington Land Trust Inc, Cedarburg, WI -- property purchase
25,000	Ozaukee Washington Land Trust Inc, Cedarburg, WI -- property purchase
25,000	Riveredge Nature Center, Newburg, WI -- pledge
25,000	St. Joseph's Community Hospital, West Bend, WI -- for cancer care center
25,000	WB Athletic Association -- pledge - teamwork 2000 campaign

E. Matilda Ziegler Foundation For The Blind

Giving Contact
William Ziegler, III, President
20 Thorndal Cir.
Darien, CT 06820
Phone: (203)656-8000
Fax: (203)656-8000

Description
Founded: 1928
EIN: 136086195
Organization Type: Private Foundation
Giving Locations: Northeast USA.
Grant Types: General Support, Multiyear/Continuing Support, Research.

Donor Information
Founder: the late Mrs. William Ziegler

Financial Summary
Total Giving: $1,333,300 (2001); $1,006,333 (2000); $1,106,244 (1999)
Giving Analysis: Giving for 2001 includes: foundation scholarships ($350,000)
Assets: $22,802,283 (2001); $25,056,978 (2000); $25,393,541 (1999)
Gifts Received: $2,000 (1997)

Typical Recipients

Arts & Humanities: Arts Outreach, Museums/Galleries, Public Broadcasting, Theater
Civic & Public Affairs: Business/Free Enterprise, Economic Policy
Education: Colleges & Universities, Medical Education, Science/Mathematics Education, Special Education, Vocational & Technical Education
Environment: Environment-General
Health: Eyes/Blindness, Hospitals, Medical Research, Transplant Networks/Donor Banks
International: Health Care/Hospitals, International Relief Efforts
Religion: Religious Organizations
Social Services: Community Centers, People with Disabilities, Recreation & Athletics

Application Procedures

Initial Contact: Send a written proposal.
Application Requirements: Include needs and purpose of funds sought.
Deadlines: June 30.

Restrictions

Limited to programs for the blind.

Foundation Officials

Meredithe L. Applebury: member
Dean Bok: committee member
Cynthia Z. Brighton: director
Charles B. Cook, Jr.: director
Charles C. Cook: director
Johanna Johnson: assistant treasurer
C. Michael Mellor: director
Beatrice H. Page: treasurer, assistant secretary
Dr. Marvin L. Sears: director
Eric M. Steinkraus: director
Helen Ziegler Steinkraus: secretary, vice president CORP AFFIL director: America Fructose Co.
Philip Steinkraus: director
Karl Ziegler: director
William Ziegler, III: president, director B New York, NY 1928. ED Harvard University BA (1950); Columbia University MBA (1962). CORP AFFIL chairman, chairman executive committee: Jon H Swisher & Son; secretary, director: Matilda Ziegler Publishing Co. Blind; chairman, chief executive officer: Lloyd Lumber Division America Maize Products; chairman, chief executive officer, president, chairman executive committee, director: Park Avenue Operating Co.; president, director: GIH Corp.; chairman, chief executive officer: Helme Tobacco Co.; chairman, chief executive officer, chairman executive committee: America Fructose Co.; director: Foresight Industries, Inc. NONPR AFFIL director: Southwest Area Commerce & Industry Association; trustee, director: YMCA Darien Commun; director: Maritime Center Norwalk; director: Project Orbis; member national advisory council: Hampshire College; trustee: Lavelle School Blind. CLUB AFFIL New York Yacht Club; Noroton Yacht Club.

Grants Analysis

Disclosure Period: calendar year ending 2001
Total Grants: $783,300*
Number of Grants: 14
Average Grant: $26,307*
Highest Grant: $415,000
Typical Range: $10,000 to $40,000
*Note: Giving excludes scholarship. Average grant figure excludes highest grant.

Recent Grants

Note: Grants derived from 2001 Form 990.

General

415,000	Matilda Ziegler Publishing Company for the Blind, Inc., Darien, CT -- monthly magazine
250,000	Yale University School of Medicine, New Haven, CT -- basic research
70,000	Cornell University, Ithaca, NY
70,000	Princeton University, Princeton, NJ
70,000	University of Medicine and Dentistry of New Jersey, Newark, NJ
70,000	West Virginia University, Morgantown, WV
70,000	Yale University, New Haven, CT
25,000	Voluntary Services for The Blind of Fairfield County, Stamford, CT -- volunteer services
7,000	Recording for the Blind and Dyslexic, Princeton, NJ -- Library of Recording Textbooks
3,000	Ski for Light, Inc., Minneapolis, MN -- training and volunteer instructor

CHARLOTTE AND ARTHUR ZITRIN FOUNDATION

Giving Contact

Arthur Zitrin, President
56 Ruxton Road
Great Neck, NY 11023

Description

Founded: 1993
EIN: 510337212
Organization Type: Private Foundation
Giving Locations: NY
Grant Types: General Support, Scholarship.

Donor Information

Founder: Established in 1993 by Charlotte and Arthur Zitrin.

Financial Summary

Total Giving: $247,965 (fiscal year ending October 31, 2000); $173,130 (fiscal 1999); $141,775 (fiscal 1998)
Assets: $6,268,895 (fiscal 2000); $5,749,541 (fiscal 1999); $2,266,392 (fiscal 1998)
Gifts Received: $187,584 (fiscal 2000); $428,644 (fiscal 1999); $181,197 (fiscal 1998). Note: Contributions were received from Charlotte and Arthur Zitrin.

Typical Recipients

Arts & Humanities: Arts Outreach, Libraries, Literary Arts, Museums/Galleries, Music, Performing Arts, Public Broadcasting, Visual Arts
Civic & Public Affairs: Botanical Gardens/Parks, Civil Rights, Clubs, Employment/Job Training, Civic & Public Affairs-General, Hispanic Affairs, Legal Aid, Public Policy, Urban & Community Affairs
Education: Colleges & Universities, Education-General, Legal Education, Medical Education, Private Education (Precollege), Public Education (Precollege), School Volunteerism, Student Aid
Environment: Air/Water Quality, Environment-General, Resource Conservation
Health: AIDS/HIV, Cancer, Geriatric Health, Health Organizations, Hospices, Hospitals (University Affiliated), Mental Health, Public Health
International: International Relief Efforts
Religion: Jewish Causes
Science: Scientific Centers & Institutes
Social Services: Child Abuse, Child Welfare, Community Service Organizations, Counseling, Family Services, Food/Clothing Distribution

Application Procedures

Initial Contact: The foundation has no formal grant application procedure or application form. Send a brief letter of inquiry.
Deadlines: None.

Foundation Officials

Arthur Zitrin: president
Charlotte Zitrin: director

Grants Analysis

Disclosure Period: fiscal year ending October 31, 2000
Total Grants: $247,965
Number of Grants: 95
Average Grant: $2,610*
Highest Grant: $25,000
Lowest Grant: $100
Typical Range: $1,000 to $5,000
*Note: Average grant excludes highest grant.

Recent Grants

Note: Grants derived from 2000 Form 990.

General

27,500	University of San Francisco School of Law, San Francisco, CA
25,000	City College 21st Century Foundation, New York, NY
25,000	New York University School of Medicine, New York, NY
12,500	Garden Project, San Francisco, CA
11,000	Bar Association of San Francisco, San Francisco, CA -- Volunteer Legal Services Project
10,000	Bar Association of San Francisco, San Francisco, CA -- scholarship fund
5,000	AAAS, Washington, DC
5,000	Bar Association of San Francisco, San Francisco, CA -- scholarship fund
4,000	Legal Services for Children, San Francisco, CA
4,000	Performing Arts Workshop, San Francisco, CA

ZOLLNER FOUNDATION

Giving Contact

Alice Kopfer, Administrator
c/o Wells Fargo Bank
PO Box 960
Ft. Wayne, IN 46801-6632
Phone: (219)461-6000

Description

Founded: 1983
EIN: 356381471
Organization Type: Private Foundation
Giving Locations: IN: Allen County
Grant Types: General Support.

Donor Information

Founder: the late Fred Zollner

Financial Summary

Total Giving: $557,642 (2000); $498,700 (1999); $407,000 (1998). Note: 1997 Giving includes United Way ($70,000).
Giving Analysis: Giving for 2000 includes: foundation grants to United Way ($70,000); 1999: foundation grants to United Way ($70,000) 1998: foundation grants to United Way ($70,000)
Assets: $12,444,053 (2000); $12,693,944 (1999); $11,598,571 (1998)
Gifts Received: $1,777 (1997); $300,500 (1995). Note: In 1995 and 1997, contributions were received from the Fred Zollner Irrevocable Trust.

Typical Recipients

Arts & Humanities: Libraries, Museums/Galleries, Public Broadcasting
Civic & Public Affairs: Botanical Gardens/Parks, Clubs, Community Foundations, Economic Development, Civic & Public Affairs-General, Philanthropic

Organizations, Professional & Trade Associations, Urban & Community Affairs, Zoos/Aquariums
Education: Business Education, Colleges & Universities, Engineering/Technological Education, Education-General, Science/Mathematics Education, Secondary Education (Private), Vocational & Technical Education
Health: Health Organizations, Hospitals, Public Health
Science: Scientific Centers & Institutes
Social Services: Food/Clothing Distribution, Scouts, Shelters/Homelessness, United Funds/United Ways, YMCA/YWCA/YMHA/YWHA, Youth Organizations

Application Procedures
Initial Contact: brief letter of inquiry
Deadlines: None.

Restrictions
Contributions are not made to organizations for retarded people; liberal arts colleges; philharmonic or other similar organizations; fine arts organizations or fine arts departments or classes at any educational organization; for the renovation of old buildings which have suffered deterioration of more than ten percent of the structure; for the renovation, reconstruction, or replacement of historic buildings, sites, or landmarks; any churches, except those having a hospital division; any minority group that directly or indirectly receives any subsidy from the U.S., state, county, or municipal government; organizations that limit their benefits to the members of particular ethnic groups; and any school that does not follow an open admissions policy.

Additional Information
Trust(s): Wells Fargo Bank

Grants Analysis
Disclosure Period: calendar year ending 2000
Total Grants: $487,642*
Number of Grants: 21
Average Grant: $15,091*
Highest Grant: $80,000
Typical Range: $5,000 to $30,000
*Note: Giving excludes United Way. Average grant figure exludes three highest grants ($216,000).

Recent Grants
Note: Grants derived from 2001 Form 990.

General

72,700	United Way of Allen County, Ft. Wayne, IN

70,000	Junior Achievement, Ft. Wayne, IN
55,000	Indiana Institute of Technology, Ft. Wayne, IN
50,000	University of Saint Francis, Ft. Wayne, IN
45,000	Anthony Wayne Area Council Boy Scouts of America, Ft. Wayne, IN
41,000	IPFW, Ft. Wayne, IN
30,000	Indiana Vocational Technical College, Ft. Wayne, IN
30,000	Tri State University, Angola, IN
25,000	Northeast Indiana Innovation Center, Ft. Wayne, IN
25,000	YMCA, Ft. Wayne, IN

HERBERT G. AND DOROTHY ZULLIG FOUNDATION

Giving Contact
Robert W. Koester, President
Herbert G. and Dorothy Zullig Foundation
PO Box 603
Sheridan, WY 82801
Phone: (307)672-6494

Description
Founded: 1987
EIN: 830282365
Organization Type: Private Foundation
Giving Locations: WY: Sheridan County
Grant Types: General Support, Scholarship.

Financial Summary
Total Giving: $40,000 (2001); $54,500 (2000)
Giving Analysis: Giving for 2001 includes: foundation scholarships ($4,000)
Assets: $737,175 (2001); $1,041,531 (2000)

Typical Recipients
Arts & Humanities: Libraries
Education: Colleges & Universities
Health: Hospitals, Mental Health, Preventive Medicine/Wellness Organizations
Religion: Religious Welfare
Social Services: Child Abuse, Child Welfare, Community Centers, Community Service Organizations, Social Services-General, YMCA/YWCA/YMHA/YWHA, Youth Organizations

Application Procedures
Initial Contact: Submit a letter of request.
Application Requirements: Include purpose of funds sought and financial statements.
Deadlines: None.

Foundation Officials
Robert W. Koester: president
Richard Kraft: vice president
John Pradere: secretary, treasurer

Grants Analysis
Disclosure Period: calendar year ending 2001
Total Grants: $36,000*
Number of Grants: 8
Highest Grant: $10,000
Lowest Grant: $1,000
Typical Range: $2,000 to $10,000
*Note: Giving excludes scholarship.

Recent Grants
Note: Grants derived from 2000 Form 990.

Library-Related

5,000	Sheridan County Library Foundation, Sheridan, WY -- purchase books and subscriptions

General

15,000	Genesis Foundation, Inc., Sheridan, WY -- salvation army
15,000	Memorial Hospital Foundation, Sheridan, WY -- new hospital construction
5,000	Sheridan College Foundation, Sheridan, WY -- Zullig scholarship
5,000	Sheridan County YMCA, Sheridan, WY -- partnership with youth program operating
4,000	Wellness Council, Sheridan, WY -- operating community health education and safe community program
2,500	Life Link of Sheridan County, Sheridan, WY -- operating
2,000	Advocacy and Resource Center, Sheridan, WY -- building fund, general operating
1,000	Sheridan County CASA, Sheridan, WY -- operating abused and neglected children

Arranges funders by the state in which their main office is located. Within each state, foundation names are listed in alphabetical order. Defunct or inactive organizations are not included in this list.

Alabama

Alabama Power Co.
Bedsole Foundation (J. L.)
Bennett Family Foundation (Claude)
Blount Educational and Charitable Foundation (Mildred Weedon)
Bruno Charitable Foundation (Joseph S.)
Comer Foundation (AL)
Crampton Trust
Daniel Foundation of Alabama
Ebsco Industries, Inc.
Energen Corp.
Figtree Foundation
Hill Crest Foundation
Johnson Charitable Trust (Terry Wayne and Sheron B.)
Kaul Foundation Trust (Hugh)
McGregor Foundation (Thomas and Frances)
McWane Corp.
Meyer Foundation (Robert R.)
Robert Charitable Trust 2 (John A. and Delia T.)
Shook Foundation (Barbara Ingalls)
Smith, Jr. Foundation (M. W.)
Tennessee Valley Printing Co.
Tractor & Equipment Co.
Vulcan Materials Co.

Alaska

Nolan Charitable Trust (James and Elise)
Usibelli Coal Mine, Inc.

Arizona

Fear Not Foundation
Kieckhefer Foundation (J. W.)
Long Foundation (John F.)
Marshall Foundation
McDonald Foundation (Armstrong)
Morris Foundation (Margaret T.)
Mulcahy Foundation
Phelps Dodge Corp.
Research Corp.
Spalding Foundation (Eliot)
Stardust Foundation

Arkansas

Altheimer Charitable Foundation (Ben J.)
Cabe Foundation (C. Louis and Mary C.)
De Queen Regional Medical Center
Frueauff Foundation (Charles A.)

Jones Foundation (Harvey and Bernice)
McKinney Charitable Trust (Carl and Alleen)
Murphy Foundation
Ottenheimer Brothers Foundation
Sturgis Charitable and Educational Trust (AR) (Roy and Christine)

California

Adobe Systems
Ahmanson Foundation
Amado Foundation (Maurice)
American Honda Motor Company, Inc.
Appelbaum-Kahn Foundation
Arata Brothers Trust
Argyros Foundation
Arkelian Foundation (Ben H. and Gladys)
Arrillaga Foundation (John)
AT&T National Pro-Am Youth Fund
Atkinson Foundation
Autry Foundation
Baker Foundation (R. C.)
Baker Street Foundation
Bandai America, Inc.
Bay View Bank
Bechtel Group, Inc.
Beckman Foundation (Arnold and Mabel)
Benbough Foundation (Legler)
Berger Foundation (H. N. and Frances C.)
Bettingen Corp. (Burton G.)
Beynon Foundation (Kathryne)
Borchard Foundation (Albert and Elaine)
The Bothin Foundation
Bourns, Inc.
Bradford Foundation (George and Ruth)
Bright Family Foundation
Broderbund LLC
Buck Foundation (Frank H. and Eva B.)
Buckley & Sperling, Inc.
Burnand Medical and Educational Foundation (Alphonse A.)
California Bank & Trust
Campini Foundation (Frank A.)
Charles Schwab Corp.
Chartwell Foundation
ChevronTexaco Corp.
Cisco Systems, Inc.
Clorox Co.
Colburn Fund
Columbia Foundation
Connell Foundation (Michael J.)
Copley Press, Inc.
Cowell Foundation (S. H.)
Crail-Johnson Foundation

Crocker Trust (Mary A.)
Crummer Foundation (Roy E.)
Darling Foundation (Hugh and Hazel)
Day Foundation (Willametta K.)
Dr. Seuss Foundation
Doheny Foundation Trust (Carrie Estelle)
Drown Foundation (Joseph)
Ducommun, Inc.
Duffield Family Foundation
Durfee Foundation
Edison International
Ellis Foundation
Essick Foundation
Exchange Bank
Feintech Family Foundation
Fireman's Fund Insurance Co.
Fleishhacker Foundation
Fluor Corp.
Friedhofer Charitable Trust (Virginia)
Friedman Family Foundation
Fujitsu America
Fuller Foundation (DE)
Furthur Foundation
Gaia Fund
Gallo Foundation (Ernest)
Gamble Foundation
Gap, Inc.
Gellert Family Foundation (Fred)
Gellert Foundation (Carl Gellert and Celia Berta)
Geschke Foundation (Charles M. and Nancy A.)
Getty Trust (J. Paul)
Ghidotti Foundation
Gilmore Foundation (William G.)
Goel Foundation
Gold Foundation (David B.)
Goldman Fund (Richard and Rhoda)
Green Foundation (Robert and Susan)
Greenville Foundation
Griswold Foundation (Lillian Sherwood)
Gumbiner Foundation (Josephine)
Haas Fund (Miriam and Peter)
Haas Fund (Walter and Elise)
Haas, Jr. Fund (Evelyn and Walter)
Hafif Family Foundation
Haigh-Scatena Foundation
Hale Foundation (Crescent Porter)
Hammer Foundation (Armand)
Han Charitable Foundation (Edna and Yu-Shan)
Hanover Foundation
Harden Foundation

Haynes Foundation (John Randolph and Dora)
Hedco Foundation
Heller Charitable Foundation (Clarence E.)
Hewlett Foundation (William and Flora)
Hoag Family Foundation (George)
Hodges Foundation (Bess J.)
Hoffman & Elaine S. Hoffman Foundation (H. Leslie)
Howe and Mitchell B. Howe Foundation (Lucille Horton)
Hume Foundation (Jaquelin)
Irvine Foundation (The James)
Irwin Charity Foundation (William G.)
Ishiyama Foundation
Jackson Family Foundation (Ann)
Jameson Foundation (J. W. and Ida M.)
Jewett Foundation (George Frederick)
Johnson Charitable Educational Trust (James Hervey)
Johnson Foundation (Charles and Ann)
Jones Foundation (Fletcher)
Kajima Engineering and Construction, Inc.
Katz Family Foundation
Keck Foundation (W. M.)
Keck, Jr. Foundation (William M.)
Kelly Foundation
Knapp Foundation (CA)
Koret Foundation
Lane Family Charitable Trust
Langendorf Foundation (Stanley S.)
Lantz Foundation (Walter)
Latkin Charitable Foundation (Herbert and Gertrude)
Lavine Family Foundation (Richard and Ruth)
Leavey Foundation (Thomas and Dorothy)
LEF Foundation
Lesher Foundation (Dean and Margaret)
Lin Foundation (T. Y.)
Long Foundation (J. M.)
Ludwick Family Foundation
Lurie Foundation (Louis R.)
Lux Foundation (Miranda)
Lytel Foundation (Bertha Russ)
Management Compensation Group/Dulworth, Inc.
Mattel Inc.
McAlister Charitable Foundation (Harold)
McBean Charitable Trust (Alletta Morris)
McBean Family Foundation
McClatchy Co.

McConnell Foundation
McMahan Foundation (Catherine L. and Robert O.)
Mead Foundation (Giles W. and Elise G.)
Miller Foundation (Earl B. and Loraine H.)
Mitsubishi Motor Sales of America, Inc.
Moldaw Family Foundation
Mosbacher, Jr. Foundation (Emil)
Mosher Foundation (Samuel B.)
Murphey Foundation (Lluella Morey)
Nakamichi Foundation (E.)
Newhall Foundation (Henry Mayo)
Norris Foundation (Kenneth T. and Eileen L.)
Norton Family Foundation (Peter)
Oak Tree Charitable Foundation
Odell Fund (Robert Stewart and Helen Pfeiffer)
Osher Foundation (Bernard)
Pacific Life Insurance Co.
Packard Foundation (David and Lucile)
Parsons Foundation (Ralph M.)
Parvin Foundation (Albert)
Patron Saints Foundation
Pell Family Foundation
Peppers Foundation (Ann)
Peters Foundation (Leon S.)
Pickford Foundation (Mary)
Ralph's Grocery Co.
Rosenberg Foundation
Rosenberg, Jr. Family Foundation (Louise and Claude)
Ryan Foundation (David Claude)
Sandy Foundation (George H.)
Schermer Charitable Trust (Frances)
Schwab-Rosenhouse Memorial Foundation
Scott Foundation (Virginia Steele)
Sempra Energy
Setzer Foundation
Seven Springs Foundation
S.G. Foundation
Sierra Health Foundation
Sierra Pacific Industries
Silver Lining Foundation
Skaggs Foundation (L. J. Skaggs and Mary C.)
Smith Trust (May and Stanley)
Stamps Foundation (James L.)
Stans Foundation
Stauffer Charitable Trust (John)

Steele Foundation (Harry and Grace)
Stillwell Charitable Trust (Glen and Dorothy)
Strauss Foundation (Leon)
Stulsaft Foundation (Morris)
Swig Foundation (The)
Taube Family Foundation
Teichert & Sons (A.)
Thornton Foundation
Thornton Foundation (Flora L.)
Trust Funds
Ueberroth Family Foundation
United Paramount Network
Universal Studios
Unocal Corp.
Valley Foundation
Valley Foundation (Wayne and Gladys)
Walt Disney Co.
Weingart Foundation
Wells Fargo & Co.
West Foundation (Harry and Ethel)
Wharton Foundation
Whitecap Foundation
Wilsey Foundation
Winthrop
Wrather Family Foundation
Wynn Foundation
Yih Family Foundation
Zeiter Charitable Foundation (Henry and Carol)
Zellerbach Family Fund

Colorado

Anschutz Family Foundation
Bacon Foundation (E. L. and Oma)
Boettcher Foundation
Bonfils-Stanton Foundation
Buell Foundation (Temple Hoyne)
Castle Rock Foundation
Clark Fund (Lynn and Helen)
Coors Foundation (Adolph)
Copic Medical Foundation
Crowell Trust (Henry P. and Susan C.)
Dominic Foundation
Duncan Trust (John G.)
El Pomar Foundation
Fairchild-Meeker Charitable Trust (Freeman E.)
Fishback Foundation Trust (Harmes C.)
Forest Oil Corp.
Gates Family Foundation
Great-West Life and Annuity Insurance Co.
Hewit Family Foundation
JJJ Foundation
Johns Manville
Johnson Foundation (Helen K. and Arthur E.)
Joslin-Needham Family Foundation
King Foundation (Kenneth Kendal)
Kitzmiller/Bales Trust
Krieble Foundation (Vernon K.)
McDonald Foundation (J. M.)
McKee Charitable Trust (Thomas M.)
Monfort Family Foundation
Morrison Charitable Trust (Pauline A. and George R.)
Muchnic Foundation

Mullen Foundation (J. K.)
Norgren Foundation (Carl A.)
Petteys Memorial Foundation (Jack)
Pittsburg & Midway Coal Mining Co.
Schooler Family Foundation (Ohio)
Security Life of Denver Insurance Co.
Stone Trust (H. Chase)
Storage Technology Corp.
Weckbaugh Foundation (Eleanore Mullen)

Connecticut

AmBase Corp.
American Optical Corp.
Barden Precision Bearings
Barnes Foundation
Barnes Group, Inc.
Brace Foundation (Donald C.)
Braitmayer Foundation
Collis Foundation
Contempo Communications
Crane Co.
Crompton Corp.
Culpeper Memorial Foundation (Daphne Seybolt)
Dibner Fund
Dime Bank of Norwich Connecticut
Eastern Savings and Loan Foundation
Educational Foundation of America
Ensign-Bickford Industries
Fischbach Foundation
Fisher Foundation
GE Capital Corp.
General Electric Co.
Goodnow Fund
Griffis Foundation
Harcourt Foundation (Ellen Knowles)
Hartford Courant Foundation
Hartford Financial Services Group, Inc.
Hexcel Corp.
Hoffman Foundation (Maximilian E. and Marion O.)
Huisking Foundation
International Paper Co.
Jones and Bessie D. Phelps Foundation (Cyrus W. and Amy F.)
Kohn-Joseloff Foundation
Koopman Fund
Kreitler Foundation
Larsen Fund
Lingnan Foundation
Lydall, Inc.
Masterpool Foundation
Matthies Foundation (Katharine)
Mazer Foundation (Jacob and Ruth)
Meadwestvaco Corp.
Moore Charitable Foundation (Marjorie)
Muhlethaler Foundation, Inc. (Jane T.)
NEBCO Evans
New Haven Savings Bank
Newman's Own, Inc.
NewMil Bancorp
Noble Foundation, Inc. (Edward John)
Olin Corp.
Palmer Fund (Frank Loomis)

Phoenix Home Life Mutual Insurance Co.
Price Foundation (Lucien B. and Katherine E.)
Rich Foundation Inc.
Rogow Birken Foundation
Saunders Charitable Foundation Trust (Helen M.)
Smart Family Foundation
Stanley Works
Stone Foundation
Sun Hill Foundation
Tauck Foundation (Arthur C. and Lee Anne)
Tetley U.S.A., Inc.
Valentine Foundation (Lawson)
Vance Charitable Foundation (Robert C.)
Vanderbilt Trust (R. T.)
Wiremold Co.
Xerox Corp.
Ziegler Foundation for the Blind (E. Matilda)

Delaware

Arguild Foundation
Barra Foundation
Borkee-Hagley Foundation
Crestlea Foundation
Crystal Trust
CTW Foundation, Inc.
Dell Foundation (Hazel)
duPont Foundation (Chichester)
E.I. du Pont de Nemours & Co.
Fair Play Foundation
Glencoe Foundation
Good Samaritan
Kent-Lucas Foundation
Kutz Foundation (Milton and Hattie)
Laffey-McHugh Foundation
Longwood Foundation
Marmot Foundation
MBNA Corp.
Raskob Foundation for Catholic Activities, Inc.
Vale Foundation (Ruby R.)
Welfare Foundation
Wilmington Trust Co.

District of Columbia

Arca Foundation
Arcana Foundation
Bender Foundation
Benton Foundation
Bloedorn Foundation (Walter A.)
Cafritz Foundation (Morris and Gwendolyn)
Cohen Foundation (Naomi and Nehemiah)
Davis Foundation (Evelyn Y.)
Fannie Mae
Fowler Memorial Foundation (John Edward)
Freed Foundation
Graham Fund (Philip L.)
Higginson Trust (Corina)
Himmelfarb Foundation (Paul and Annetta)
Kennedy, Jr. Foundation (Joseph P.)
Kiplinger Foundation
Kiplinger Washington Editors, Inc.
Lea Foundation (Helen Sperry)

Loughran Foundation (Mary and Daniel)
Marpat Foundation
McGowan Charitable Fund (William G.)
M.E. Foundation
Mead Family Foundation (Gilbert and Jaylee)
Meyer Foundation (Eugene and Agnes E.)
Moriah Fund, Inc.
Pepco Holdings, Inc.
Public Welfare Foundation
Strong Foundation (Hattie M.)
Wilkes, Artis, Hedrick & Lane

Florida

Appleby Trust (Scott B. and Annie P.)
BankAtlantic Bancorp
BCR Foundation
Beattie Foundation (Cordelia Lee)
Beveridge Foundation, Inc. (Frank Stanley)
Bush Charitable Foundation, Inc. (Edyth)
Carnival Corp.
Chatlos Foundation
Cheatham Foundation (Owen)
Cobb Family Foundation
Davis Foundations (Arthur Vining)
Dettman Foundation (Leroy E.)
Doyle Foundation
Dunspaugh-Dalton Foundation
duPont Foundation (Alfred I.)
Florida Rock Industries, Inc.
Florida Rock & Tank Lines
Gulf Power Co.
Houck Foundation (May Kay)
Kennedy Family Foundation (Ethel and W. George)
Kennedy Foundation (Ethel)
Knight Foundation (John S. and James L.)
Koch Foundation, Inc.
Landegger Charitable Foundation
Lattner Foundation (Forrest C.)
Lowe Foundation (Joe and Emily)
Magruder Foundation (Chesley G.)
Martin Foundation
Mendel Foundation
Metal Industries, Inc.
Morgan Foundation (Louie R. and Gertrude)
Peterson Charitable Foundation (Folke H.)
Publix Supermarkets
Rayonier, Inc.
Royal Foundation (May Mitchell)
Selby and Marie Selby Foundation (William G.)
Simon Foundation (Sidney, Milton, and Leoma)
Speer Foundation (Roy M.)
SunTrust Banks of Florida
Swisher Foundation (Carl S.)
United States Sugar Corp.
Wahlert Foundation
Winn-Dixie Stores Inc.

Georgia

Arnold Fund
BellSouth Corp.
Bowman Foundation (Wayne and Ida)
Callaway Foundation, Inc.
Campbell Foundation (J. Bulow)
Citizens Union Bank
Clary Foundation, Inc. (Eugene M.)
Coca-Cola Co.
Community Enterprises
Cox Enterprises, Inc.
Equifax, Inc.
Evans Foundation, Inc. (Lettie Pate)
Georgia-Pacific Corp.
Georgia Power Co.
Haley Foundation (W. B.)
Harland Charitable Foundation (John H. and Wilhelmina D.)
ING North America Insurance Corp.
Martin Charitable Trust (Margaret Lee)
McCarty Foundation (John and Margaret)
Morris Communications Corp.
National Service Industries, Inc.
Porter Testamentary Trust (James Hyde)
Rich Foundation
Smith Foundation (William R. and Sara Babb)
SunTrust Bank Atlanta
SunTrust Banks, Inc.
Trippe Trust (William D.)
Whitehead Foundation (Joseph B.)
Williams Family Foundation of Georgia
Winter Construction Co.
Woodruff Foundation (Robert W.)

Hawaii

Atherton Family Foundation
Atherton Foundation (Leburta)
Baldwin Memorial Foundation (Fred)
Castle Foundation (Harold K. L.)
Castle Foundation (Samuel N. and Mary)
Cooke Foundation
First Hawaiian, Inc.
Frear Eleemosynary Trust (Mary D. and Walter F.)
McInerny Foundation
Resco, Inc.
Wong Foundation (Lin and Ella)

Idaho

Albertson's Inc.
Boise Cascade Corp.
CHC Foundation
Cimino Foundation (James and Barbara)
Engl Family Foundation (Michael S.)
Intermountain Gas Co.
Morrison Foundation (Harry W.)
Ore-Ida Foods

Washington Group International, Inc.
Whiting Foundation (Macauley and Helen Dow)
Whittenberger Foundation (Claude R. and Ethel B.)

Illinois
Abbott Laboratories
Akzo Nobel Chemicals
AMCORE Financial, Inc.
Aon Corp.
Archer-Daniels-Midland Co.
Bank One Corp.
Bere Foundation
Blowitz-Ridgeway Foundation
Blum Foundation (Harry and Maribel G.)
Blum-Kovler Foundation
Boothroyd Foundation (Charles H. and Bertha L.)
BP Amoco Corp.
Brach Foundation (Helen)
Brunswick Corp.
Burnett Co. (Leo)
Butz Foundation
Caestecker Foundation (Charles and Marie)
Camp and Bennet Humiston Trust (Apollos)
Caterpillar Inc.
Cheney Foundation (Elizabeth F.)
Chicago Board of Trade
Chicago Rawhide Co.
Chicago Title Corp.
Chicago Tribune Direct Marketing
Citizens First National Bank
CLARCOR, Inc.
Claypool Foundation (Silas and Ruth)
CNA Financial Corp.
Coleman Foundation (IL)
Commonwealth Edison Co.
Cox Charitable Trust (A. G.)
Crown Memorial (Arie and Ida)
Cudahy Fund (Patrick and Anna M.)
Cuneo Foundation
Deere & Co.
Demos Foundation (N.)
Dillon Foundation
Duchossois Family Foundation
Exelon
Field Foundation of Illinois
Fischer Foundation (Sonja and F. Conrad)
Florsheim Group Co.
Fortune Brands, Inc.
Fry Foundation (Lloyd A.)
Galvin Foundation (Robert)
GATX Corp.
Geifman Family Foundation
Genius Charitable Trust (Elizabeth Morse)
Graham Foundation for Advanced Studies in the Fine Arts
Haffner Foundation
Hartmarx Corp.
Heath Foundation (Mary)
Hegeler II Foundation (Julius W.)
Hermann Foundation (Grover)
Ideal Industries, Inc.
Illinois Tool Works, Inc.

Integra Bank
Johnson Foundation (A.D.)
Kemper National Insurance Companies
Kern Foundation Trust
Korte Construction Co.
Lederer Foundation (Francis L.)
Lehmann Foundation (Otto W.)
MacArthur Foundation (John D. and Catherine T.)
McCormick Foundation (Chauncey and Marion Deering)
McCormick Tribune Foundation (Robert R.)
Mellinger Educational Foundation (Edward Arthur)
Meyer Family Foundation
Meyers Charitable Family Fund
Moore and Arletta E. Moore Foundation (Kenneth S.)
Morrill Charitable Foundation
Motorola, Inc.
Myers Charitable Trust
National Manufacturing Co.
Norris Foundation (Dellora A. and Lester J.)
Northern Trust Corp.
Norton Memorial Corp. (Geraldi)
Nuveen Co. (The John)
Offield Family Foundation (The)
Ohio National Life Insurance Co.
Ondeo Nalco Co.
Payne Foundation (Frank E. and Seba B.)
Peoples Energy Corp.
Pick, Jr. Fund (Albert)
Polk Brothers Foundation, Inc.
Prentice Foundation (Abra)
Quincy Newspapers
Regenstein Foundation
Retirement Research Foundation
Rice Foundation
R.R. Donnelley & Sons Co.
Russell Charitable Foundation (Tom)
Saemann Foundation (Franklin I.)
Sang Foundation (Elsie O. and Philip D.)
Sara Lee Corp.
Scherer Foundation (Karla)
Scholl Foundation (Dr.)
Seabury Foundation
Southwest News Herald
Square D Co.
State Farm Mutual Automobile Insurance Co.
Stuart Foundation (Elbridge and Evelyn)
Swift Print Communications Tribune Co.
Tyndale House Foundation
UAL Corp.
USG Corp.
Vermilion Healthcare Foundation
White Foundation (W. P. and H. B.)
Worner Trust
Yost Trust (J. Paul)

Indiana
1st Source Corp.
American General Finance
American United Life Insurance Co.
Anderson Foundation (John W.)
Anthem Inc.
Auburn Foundry
Ayres Foundation
Ball Brothers Foundation
Ball Foundation (George and Frances)
Bowsher-Booher Foundation
Central Soya Co.
Clowes Fund
Cole Foundation (Olive B.)
Conseco, Inc.
Cummins, Inc.
Decio Foundation (Arthur J.)
Eli Lilly & Co.
Foellinger Foundation
Ford Meter Box Co.
Glick Foundation (Eugene and Marilyn)
Griffith Foundation (W. C.)
Indianapolis Newspapers, Inc.
Journal-Gazette Co.
Kuhne Foundation Trust (Charles W.)
Lilly Endowment
McFarland Charitable Trust (H. Richard)
McMillen Foundation
National City Bank of Indiana
Noyes, Jr. Memorial Foundation (Nicholas H.)
Oliver Memorial Trust Foundation
Ontario Corp.
Pulliam Charitable Trust (Nina Mason)
Raker Foundation (M. E.)
Rieke Corp.
Schneider Foundation (Dr. Louis A. and Anne B.)
Simon Charitable Foundation Number One (Melvin and Bren)
South Bend Tribune Corp.
TCB Bank
Tobias Foundation (Randall L.)
Vann Family Foundation
Zollner Foundation

Iowa
Ahrens Foundation (Claude W. and Dolly)
Amerus Group Co.
Audubon State Bank
Bechtel Charitable Remainder Uni-Trust (Marie H.)
Carver Charitable Trust (Roy J.)
Employers Mutual Casualty Co.
Fiserve
Forster Charitable Trust (James W. and Ella B.)
Gazette Co.
Grinnell Mutual Reinsurance Co.
Guaranty Bank & Trust Co.
Hall-Perrine Foundation
Harper Brush Works
HON Industries, Inc.
Iowa Savings Bank
Kinney-Lindstrom Foundation

Kuyper Foundation (Peter H. and E. Lucille Gaass)
Lee Endowment Foundation
Lee Enterprises, Inc.
Lisle Corp.
Maytag Family Foundation (Fred)
McDonald Manufacturing Co. (A.Y.)
McElroy Trust (R. J.)
Mid-Iowa Health Foundation
Owen Industries
Pella Corp.
Principal Financial Group
Sheaffer Pen Corp.
Stebens Charitable Foundation (Bertha)
Van Buren Foundation
Weathertop Foundation
Wellmark Blue Cross and Blue Shield of Iowa
Winnebago Industries

Kansas
Baehr Foundation (Louis W. and Dolpha)
Baughman Foundation
Bryden Foundation (Blanche)
Central National Bank
Cessna Aircraft Co.
Cray Residuary Charitable Trust (Evah C.)
Davis Foundation (James A. and Juliet L.)
DeVore Foundation
Excel Corp.
Gault-Hussey Charitable Trust
Hansen Foundation (Dane G.)
Hauptli Charitable Foundation (A. John and Barbara A.)
Kansas Health Foundation
Koch Industries, Inc.
Mingenback Foundation (Julia J.)
Powell Family Foundation
Ross Foundation
Schowalter Foundation
Security Benefit Life Insurance Co.
Smoot Charitable Foundation
Sunderland Foundation
Williams Charitable Trust (Mary Jo)
Yellow Corp.
Young Foundation (Bill B.)

Kentucky
Abercrombie Foundation
Blood-Horse Charitable Foundation
Brown Foundation, Inc. (James Graham)
Brown Foundation (W. L. Lyons)
Brown & Williamson Tobacco Corp.
C. E. and S. Foundation
Community Trust Bancorp, Inc.
Cooke Foundation Corp. (V. V.)
Cralle Foundation
Duncan Trust (Louise Head)
Gheens Foundation
Houchens Foundation (Ervin G.)
Humana, Inc.
LG&E Energy Corp.

Masland Trust No. 2 (Maurice H.)
Norton Foundation
Thomas Foundation (Joan and Lee)
Thomas Industries
Vogt Machine Co. (Henry)
Yeager Charitable Trust B (Lester E.)

Louisiana
Freeport-McMoRan Copper & Gold, Inc.
German Protestant Orphan Asylum Association Foundation
Keller Family Foundation
Powers Foundation
RosaMary Foundation
Saia Foundation (Louis P.)
Schlieder Educational Foundation (Edward G.)
Southwestern Electric Power Co.
Wilson Foundation (Huey and Angeline)

Maine
Brook Family Foundation
Burnham Charitable Trust (Margaret E.)
Central Maine Power Co.
Davenport Trust Fund
Davies Benevolent Fund (Edward H.)
Gardiner Savings Institution
Hannaford Brothers Co.
Key Bank of Maine
Mulford Trust (Clarence E.)
Oak Grove School
Orchard Foundation
Webber Oil Co.

Maryland
Abell Foundation
Alexander Edwards Trust (Margaret)
Baker, Jr. Memorial Fund (William G.)
Baker Trust (Clayton)
Baltimore Equity Society
Broomfield Charitable Foundation
Campbell Foundation (MD)
Casey Foundation (Eugene B.)
Chase Charitable Foundation (Richard Allen)
COMSAT International
Constellation Energy Group, Inc.
Darby Foundation
Denit Trust for Charitable and Educational Purposes (Helen Pumphrey)
Fairchild Foundation, Inc. (Sherman)
Giant Food, Inc.
Goldseker Foundation of Maryland (Morris)
Gordon Charitable Trust (Peggy and Yale)
Gudelsky Family Foundation (Homer and Martha)
Hecht-Levi Foundation
Henson Foundation (Richard A.)
Hughes Medical Institute (Howard)
Kerr Fund (Grayce B.)
Knapp Foundation, Inc. (MD)

Knott Foundation (Marion I. and Henry J.)
Leidy Foundation (John J.)
Lockhart Vaughan Foundation
McCormick & Company, Inc.
Mechanic Foundation (Morris A.)
Middendorf Foundation
Morgan and Samuel Tate Morgan, Jr. Foundation (Marietta McNeill)
Perdue Farms
Price Associates (T. Rowe)
Procter & Gamble Company, Cosmetics Division
Rollins-Luetkemeyer Foundation
Rouse Co.
Sinnisen Foundation (Albert E. and Naomi B.)
Smith Foundation (Gordon V. and Helen C.)
Unger Foundation (Aber D.)
Wallis Trust (Dorothy Wagner)
Warfield Memorial Fund (Anna Emory)
Widgeon Foundation
Wilson Sanitarium for Children of Baltimore City (Thomas)

Massachusetts

Acushnet Foundation
Alden Trust (George I.)
Alden Trust (John W.)
Allmerica Financial Corp.
Ansin Foundation (Ronald M.)
Arakelian Foundation (Mary Alice)
Ash Charitable Corp.
Azadoutioun Foundation
Babson Foundation (Paul and Edith)
Balfour Foundation (L. G.)
Barrington Foundation
Bay State Bancorp, Inc.
Beaucourt Foundation
Bendit Charitable Foundation (Leo H.)
Boston Globe (The)
Bright Charitable Trust (Alexander H.)
Building 19 Foundation
Cabot Corp.
Cabot Family Charitable Trust
Cambridge Mustard Seed Foundation
Campbell and Adah E. Hall Charity Fund (Bushrod H.)
Chase Trust (Alice P.)
Childs Charitable Foundation (Roberta M.)
Country Curtains, Inc.
Cove Charitable Trust
Cox Charitable Trust (Jessie B.)
Daniels Foundation (Fred Harris)
Davis Foundation (Irene E. and George A.)
Demoulas Supermarkets, Inc.
Dunkin' Donuts, Inc.
East Cambridge Savings Bank
Eastern Bank

Ellsworth Foundation (Ruth H. and Warren A.)
Erving Industries
Fidelity Investments
FleetBoston Financial Corp.
Fletcher Foundation
Friendship Fund
Fuller Foundation (George F. and Sybil H.)
Gillette Co.
Goldberg Family Foundation
Grimshaw-Gudewicz Charitable Foundation
Hamilton Charitable Corp.
Harrington Foundation (Francis A. and Jacquelyn H.)
Henderson Foundation
Henderson Foundation (George B.)
Hershey Family Foundation
Higgins Foundation (John W. and Clara C.)
Hoche-Scofield Foundation
Home for Aged Men in the City of Brockton
Hopedale Foundation
Hornblower Fund (Henry)
Hyde Manufacturing Co.
Island Foundation (MA)
Jaffe Foundation
John Hancock Financial Services
Johnson Fund (Edward C.)
Keel Foundation
Kelley and Elza Kelley Foundation (Edward Bangs)
Kendall Foundation (Henry P.)
Killam Trust (Constance)
Kilmartin Industries
Ladd Charitable Corp. (Helen and George)
Levy Foundation (June Rockwell)
M/A-COM, Inc.
Massachusetts Mutual Life Insurance Co.
McCarthy Memorial Trust Fund (Catherine)
McEvoy Foundation (Mildred H.)
Memorial Foundation for the Blind
Merck Family Fund
Mifflin Memorial Fund (George H. and Jane A.)
Millipore Corp.
New England Business Service
Norcross Wildlife Foundation
NSTAR
Pappas Charitable Foundation (Thomas Anthony)
Parametric Technology Corp.
Pardoe Foundation (Samuel P.)
Peabody Charitable Fund (Amelia)
Peabody Foundation (Amelia)
Phillips Foundation (Ellis L.)
Pierce Charitable Trust (Harold Whitworth)
Poitras Charitable Trust (Dorothy W.)
Polaroid Corp.
Poorvu Foundation (William J. and Lia G.)
Proctor Foundation (Mattina R.)
Prouty Foundation (Olive Higgins)

Provident Community Foundation
Rabb Charitable Foundation (Sidney and Esther)
Rabb Charitable Trust (Sidney R.)
Ratshesky Foundation (A. C.)
Riley Foundation (Mabel Louise)
Roddy Foundation (Fred M.)
Rogers Family Foundation
Rubin Family Fund (Cele H. and William B.)
Russell Trust (Josephine G.)
Saltonstall Charitable Foundation (Richard)
Sawyer Charitable Foundation
Shatz, Schwartz & Fentin PC
Shaw's Supermarkets, Inc.
Sherman Trust (Margaret E.)
Small Business Service Bureau
Smith Family Foundation (Richard and Susan)
State Street Corp.
Stearns Trust (Artemas W.)
Steiger Memorial Fund (Albert)
Stevens Foundation (Abbot and Dorothy H.)
Stevens Foundation (Nathaniel and Elizabeth P.)
Stoddard Charitable Trust
Thompson Trust (Thomas)
TJX Companies, Inc.
Tupancy-Harris Foundation of 1986
Van Buren Foundation (Elsie Procter)
Wallace Foundation (George R.)
Walsh Charity Trust (Blanche)
Weber Charities Corp. (Frederick E.)
Webster Foundation (Edwin S.)
Wheeler Trust (Nathaniel)
Winthrop Trust (Clara B.)
Woronoco Savings Bank
Wyman-Gordon Co.
Yawkey Foundation II

Michigan

Abrams Foundation (Talbert and Leota)
Ash Foundation (Stanley P. and Blanche E.)
Barstow Foundation
Batts Foundation
Bauervic Foundation (Charles M.)
Bauervic-Paisley Foundation
Besser Foundation
Bishop Charitable Trust (A. G.)
Boutell Memorial Fund
Carls Foundation
Chamberlain Foundation
Comerica Inc.
Consumers Energy Co.
Delano Foundation (Mignon Sherwood)
DeRoy Testamentary Foundation
DeVos Foundation (Richard and Helen)
Dow Corning Corp.
Dow Foundation (Herbert H. and Grace A.)

DTE Energy Co.
Dura Automotive Systems Inc.
Earhart Foundation
Eddy Family Memorial Fund (C. K.)
Ewald Foundation (H. T.)
Farmer Jack Supermarkets
Farwell Foundation (Drusilla)
Ford Fund (Walter and Josephine)
Ford Fund (William and Martha)
Ford II Fund (Edsel B.)
Ford II Fund (Henry)
Ford Motor Co.
Fruehauf Foundation
General Motors Corp.
Gerber Products Co.
Gerstacker Foundation (Rollin M.)
Gilmore Foundation (Irving S.)
Herrick Foundation
Holnam, Inc.
Hudson-Webber Foundation
Hurst Foundation
Interkal, Inc.
JSJ Corp.
Kantzler Foundation
Kaufman Endowment Fund (Louis G.)
Kaufman Foundation
Keeler Foundation
Keller Foundation
Kresge Foundation
La-Z-Boy, Inc.
Lee Scholarship Fund Trust (Whilma B.)
Loutit Foundation
Magna International of America, Inc.
McGregor Fund
Merkley Charitable Trust
Miller Foundation
Mills Fund (Frances Goll)
Morley Foundation
Mott Foundation (Charles Stewart)
National Standard Co.
Newman Family Foundation
Oleson Foundation
Plym Foundation
R&B Machine Tool Co.
Ratner Foundation (Milton M.)
Sage Foundation
Scottsman Industries
Sebastian Foundation
Skillman Foundation
Spartan Stores, Inc.
Steelcase Inc.
Strosacker Foundation (Charles J.)
Taubman Foundation (A. Alfred)
Thoman Foundation (W. B. and Candace)
Tiscornia Foundation
Todd Co. (A.M.)
Towsley Foundation (Harry A. and Margaret D.)
Upjohn Foundation (Harold and Grace)
Upton Foundation (Frederick S.)
Van Andel Foundation (Jay and Betty)
Vicksburg Foundation
Vollbrecht Foundation (Frederick A.)
Weatherwax Foundation

Wege Foundation
Whirlpool Corp.
Whiting Foundation
Wickes Foundation (Harvey Randall)
Wickson-Link Memorial Foundation
Wilson Fund (Matilda R.)
World Heritage Foundation

Minnesota

ADC Telecommunications
Allianz Life Insurance Company of North America
Andersen Corp.
Andersen Foundation
Andersen Foundation (Hugh J.)
Bell Foundation (James Ford)
Bemis Company, Inc.
Bigelow Foundation (F. R.)
Blandin Foundation
Bremer Foundation (Otto)
Bush Foundation
Butler Family Foundation (Patrick and Aimee)
Cargill, Inc.
Carlson Companies, Inc.
Carolyn Foundation
Davis Foundation (Edwin W. and Catherine M.)
Donaldson Company, Inc.
Driscoll Foundation
Ecolab, Inc.
Federated Mutual Insurance Co.
Fuller Co. (H.B.)
General Mills, Inc.
Griggs and Mary Griggs Burke Foundation (Mary Livingston)
Grotto Foundation
Hallett Charitable Trust (E. W.)
Heilmaier Charitable Foundation (Anna M.)
Hickory Tech Corp.
Homecrest Industries, Inc.
HRK Foundation
Hubbard Broadcasting, Inc.
International Multifoods Corp.
Jostens, Inc.
Land O'Lakes, Inc.
Lilly Foundation (Richard Coyle)
Marbrook Foundation
Mardag Foundation
McNeely Foundation
Medtronic, Inc.
Metris Companies, Inc.
Midcontinent Media, Inc.
Minnesota Mining & Manufacturing Co.
Minnesota Mutual Life Insurance Co.
Neilson Foundation (George W.)
O'Shaughnessy Foundation (I. A.)
Phillips Family Foundation (The Jay and Rose)
Rahr Malting Co.
Red Wing Shoe Company, Inc.
Regis Corp.
Saint Croix Foundation
St. Paul Companies, Inc.
Schmoker Family Foundation
Southways Foundation
Specialty Manufacturing Co.

Stearns Foundation
Target Corp.
TCF National Bank Minnesota
Tozer Foundation
U.S. Bancorp Piper Jaffray
Weyerhaeuser Memorial Foundation (Charles A.)
Xcel Energy

Mississippi

Bryan Foods
Hardin Foundation (Phil)
Sullivan Foundation (Algernon Sydney)
Walker Foundation

Missouri

ACF Industries
Ameren Corp.
Andrews McMeel Universal
Anheuser-Busch Companies, Inc.
Bakewell Corp.
Barrows Foundation (Geraldine and R. A.)
Bartlett & Co.
Bromley Residuary Trust (Guy I.)
Burns & McDonnell
Commerce Bancshares, Inc.
Cowden Foundation (Louetta M.)
Dula Educational and Charitable Foundation (Caleb C. and Julia W.)
Francis Families Foundation
Garvey Memorial Foundation (Edward Chase)
GenAmerica Financial Corp.
Green Foundation (Allen P. and Josephine B.)
Hall Family Foundation (The)
H&R Block, Inc.
Jordan and Ettie A. Jordan Charitable Foundation (Mary Ranken)
Kansas City Southern Railway
Kauffman Foundation (Ewing Marion)
Kemper Foundation (William T.)
Loose Trust (Harry Wilson)
Lowe Family Foundation
Maritz, Inc.
McGee Foundation (MO)
Messing Family Charitable Foundation
Miller-Mellor Association
Monsanto Co.
Morgan Charitable Residual Trust (W. and E.)
Moss Charitable Trust (Finis M.)
Nestle Purina PetCare Co.
Olin Foundation (Spencer T. and Ann W.)
Oppenstein Brothers Foundation
Pott Foundation (Herman T. and Phenie R.)
Pulitzer, Inc.
Reliable Life Insurance Co.
Schutte Foundation (Victor E. and Caroline E.)
Shaw Foundation (Arch W.)
Shelter Mutual Insurance Co.
Slusher Charitable Foundation (Roy W.)
Smith Foundation (Ralph L.)

Speas Foundation (Victor E.)
Speas Memorial Trust (John W. and Effie E.)
Steadley Memorial Trust (Kent D. and Mary L.)
Stupp Foundation (Norman J.)
Sunnen Foundation
Turner Charitable Trust (Courtney S.)
Van Evera Foundation (Dewitt)

Montana

Allen Foundation (Nibs and Edna)
Anderson Foundation (L. P. and Teresa)
Bair Family Trust (Charles M.)
Boe Brothers Foundation
Washington Foundation (Dennis R. and Phyllis)

Nebraska

Ameritas Life Insurance Corp.
Baright Foundation (Hollis and Helen)
Cooper Foundation
Farr Trust (Frank M. and Alice M.)
Giger Foundation (Paul and Oscar)
Heuermann Foundation (Bernard K. and Norma F.)
Hitchcock Foundation (Gilbert M. and Martha H.)
Kawasaki Motors Manufacturing Corporation U.S.A.
Kiewit Foundation (Peter)
Livingston Foundation (Milton S. and Corinne N.)
Pamida, Inc.
Peter Kiewit Sons' Inc.
Physicians Mutual Insurance Co.
Quivey-Bay State Foundation
Reynolds Foundation (Edgar & Francis)
Scoular Co.
Union Pacific Corp.
Valmont Industries, Inc.
Wells Fargo Bank Nebraska, N.A.
Woods Charitable Fund

Nevada

Bretzlaff Foundation
Buck Foundation (Carol Franc)
Cord Foundation (E. L.)
Harris Foundation (William H. and Mattie Wattis)
Hawkins Foundation (Robert Z.)
Lied Foundation Trust
Pennington Foundation (William N. and Myriam)
Ray Foundation
Redfield Foundation (Nell J.)
Reynolds Foundation (Donald W.)
Sierra Pacific Resources
Stout Foundation (Charles H.)
Wiegand Foundation (E. L.)

New Hampshire

Barker Foundation Inc.

Bean Foundation (Norwin S. and Elizabeth N.)
Benz Trust (Doris L.)
Byrne Foundation
Cogswell Benevolent Trust
Dingman Foundation (Michael D.)
Foundation for Seacoast Health
Fuller Foundation (MA)
Henney Trust (Keith)
Hunt Foundation (Samuel P.)
Jameson Trust (Oleonda)
Kingsbury Corp.
Mascoma Savings Bank
Monadnock Paper Mills, Inc.
National Grange Mutual Insurance Co.
Putnam Foundation
Smyth Trust (Marion C.)
Unitrode Corp.

New Jersey

American Standard Inc.
Ballet Makers
Brady Foundation
Brundage Charitable, Scientific, and Wildlife Conservation Foundation (Charles E. and Edna T.)
Bunbury Co., Inc.
Campbell Soup Co.
Cape Branch Foundation
Carillon Importers, Ltd.
Caspersen Foundation for Aid to Health and Education (O. W.)
Church & Dwight Company, Inc.
CIT Group, Inc.
Clover Foundation
Colt Foundation (James J.)
Conway Scholarship Foundation (Carle C.)
Cowles Charitable Trust
Crames Family Foundation (Arthur)
D&B
DBH Foundation for Law, Land, and the Felicitous Environment
Dodge Foundation (Geraldine R.)
Edison Fund (Charles)
Formosa Plastics Corporation, USA
Fund for New Jersey
Hoffmann-La Roche, Inc.
Holzer Memorial Foundation (Richard H.)
Huber Foundation
Hyde and Watson Foundation
Jaqua Foundation
Jaydor Corp.
Jockey Hollow Foundation
Johnson & Johnson
Kajima International, Inc.
Kalkus Foundation
Kaplen Foundation
Kirby Foundation (F. M.)
Klipstein Foundation (Ernest Christian)
Lazarus Charitable Trust
Lipton Co.
Maneely Fund
Martini Foundation (Nicholas)
New Jersey Natural Gas Co.
Newcombe Foundation (Charlotte W.)
Oki America, Inc.

Pond Foundation (C. Northrop Pond and Alethea Marder)
Prudential Insurance Co. of America
Public Service Electric & Gas Co.
Read Foundation (Charles L.)
Red Devil
Sandy Hill Foundation
Schenck Charitable Foundation (L. P.)
Schering-Plough Corp.
Schumann Fund for New Jersey
Schwartz Foundation (Arnold A.)
Simon Foundation (William E.)
Snyder Foundation (Harold B. and Dorothy A.)
Subaru of America, Inc.
Terumo Medical Corp.
Tsumura International, Inc.
Turrell Fund
Upton Charitable Foundation (Lucy and Eleanor S.)
Van Houten Memorial Fund (Edward W. and Stella C.)
Victoria Foundation
Welsh Family Foundation
Westerhoff Family Foundation, Inc.
Wiley & Sons, Inc. (John)
Ziegelheim Charitable Foundation (Fran and Irwin)

New Mexico

Chamiza Foundation
Daniels Foundation (Edgar Foster)
Fab Steel Products Co.
Holt Foundation (William Knox)
Hubbard Foundation (R. D. and Joan Dale)
Maddox Foundation (J. F.)
McCune Charitable Foundation (Marshall L. and Perrine D.)
PNM Resources, Inc.
Seidman Family Foundation
Stockman Family Foundation Trust

New York

ABC, Inc.
Achelis Foundation
Air France
AKC Fund
Alavi Foundation
Alexander Foundation (Joseph)
Allen Brothers Foundation
Allyn Foundation
Altman Foundation
Ambrose Monell Foundation (The)
Anderson Foundation (NY)
AOL Time Warner
Archbold Charitable Trust (Adrian and Jessie)
Arkell Hall Foundation
AT&T Corp.
Atran Foundation, Inc.
August Family Foundation (Charles J. and Burton S.)

Avery Arts Foundation (Milton and Sally)
Avon Products, Inc.
Backus Foundation (Beatrice and Roy)
Badgeley Residuary Charitable Trust (Rose M.)
Bailey Family Foundation (William O. and Carole P.)
Baird Foundation
Baker Trust (George F.)
The Bank of Greene County
Bank of New York Company, Inc.
Barker Foundation (J.M.R.)
Barker Welfare Foundation
Barth Foundation, Inc. (The Theodore H.)
Bat Hanadiv Foundation No. 3
Bauer Family Foundation
Bausch & Lomb, Inc.
Bay Foundation
Becher Foundation (Hildegarde D.)
Benenson Foundation (Frances and Benjamin)
Benetton U.S.A. Corp.
Bernhard Foundation (Arnold)
Bingham Second Betterment Fund (William)
Birds Eye Foods, Inc.
Bismarck Charitable Trust (Mona)
Bodman Foundation
Boehm Foundation
Booth Ferris Foundation
Bowne Foundation (Robert)
Bristol-Myers Squibb Co.
Brookdale Foundation
Brooks Foundation (Gladys)
Burchfield Foundation (Charles E.)
Bydale Foundation
Calder Foundation (Louis)
Candlesticks, Inc.
Canon U.S.A., Inc.
Carnahan-Jackson Foundation
Carnegie Corp. of New York
Carvel Foundation (Thomas and Agnes)
Cary Charitable Trust (Mary Flagler)
CBS Corp.
Central Hudson Gas & Electric Corp.
Chadwick Fund (Dorothy Jordan)
Chapman Charitable Corp. (Howard and Bess)
Charitable Venture Foundation
Chazen Foundation
Cheek Family Foundation (Trust for the)
Cheever Porter Foundation (Mrs.)
Children's Foundation of Erie County
Chisholm Foundation (M. A.)
Christian Dior Perfumes, Inc.
CIBC World Markets
Citigroup Inc.
City National Bank & Trust Co.
Claiborne and Art Ortenberg Foundation (Liz)
Clark Foundation (NY)

Coleman Foundation (George E.)
Commonwealth Fund (The)
ContiGroup Companies, Inc.
Cook Foundation (Louella)
Cornell Trust (Peter C.)
Corning Inc.
Crary Foundation (Bruce L.)
Credit Suisse First Boston Corp.
Crosswicks Foundation
Cummings Foundation (James H.)
Cummings Memorial Fund (The Frances L. and Edwin L.)
Daily News, L.P.
Dana Charitable Trust (Eleanor Naylor)
Dana Foundation (Charles A.)
Davenport-Hatch Foundation
de Coizart Perpetual Charitable Trust (Sarah K.)
DeCamp Foundation (Ira W.)
Decker Foundation (Dr. G. Clifford and Florence B.)
Dedalus Foundation
Delmas Foundation (Gladys Krieble)
Dewar Foundation
Dickenson Foundation (Harriet Ford)
Dickler Family Foundation
Dodge Foundation (Cleveland H.)
Doherty Charitable Foundation (Henry L. and Grace)
Donaldson Charitable Trust (Oliver S. and Jennie R.)
Dorot Foundation
Dow Jones & Company, Inc.
Dreyfus Corp.
Dreyfus Foundation, Inc. (Max and Victoria)
Dreyfus Foundation (Jean and Louis)
Ducommun and Gross Foundation
Duke Foundation (Doris)
Dyson Foundation
Eastman Kodak Co.
Eckman Charitable Foundation (Samuel and Rae)
Edmonds Foundation (Dean S.)
Emerson Foundation, Inc. (Fred L.)
Erpf Fund (Armand G.)
Everett Charitable Trust
Farash Charitable Foundation (Max and Marian)
Faulkner Trust (Marianne G.)
Ferkauf Foundation (Eugene and Estelle)
Ferriday Fund Charitable Trust
Fink Foundation (NY)
Ford Foundation
Fortis, Inc.
Foundation for Child Development
Frankel Foundation (Evan)
Freeman Charitable Trust (Samuel)
French Foundation (D.E.)
Frese Foundation (Arnold D.)
Fribourg Foundation
Fromkes Foundation (Saul)
Garfinkle-Minard Foundation, Inc.
Gebbie Foundation

Gifford Charitable Corp. (Rosamond)
Gilman Foundation (Howard)
Gleason Foundation
Goldman Foundation (Herman)
Golub Corp.
Goodman Family Foundation
Gould Foundation (The Florence)
Grant Foundation (Charles M. and Mary D.)
Greentree Foundation
Greenwall Foundation
Guardian Life Insurance Company of America
Guggenheim Foundation (Harry Frank)
Gund Foundation (Geoffrey)
Guttman Foundation (Stella and Charles)
Hagedorn Fund
Handy & Harman
Harkness Foundation for Dance
HarperCollins Publishers, Inc.
Harriman Foundation (Gladys and Roland)
Harriman Foundation (Mary W.)
Hartford Foundation, Inc. (The John A.)
Hatch Charitable Trust (Margaret Milliken)
Hayden Foundation (Charles)
Hazen Foundation (Edward W.)
Hearst Foundation, Inc. (The)
Hearst Foundation (William Randolph)
Hebrew Technical Institute
Heckscher Foundation for Children
Heinz Trust (Drue)
Heyward Memorial Fund (DuBose and Dorothy)
Hill Foundation (Sandy)
Hilliard Corp.
Hino Diesel Trucks (U.S.A.)
Holmberg Foundation
Holtzmann Foundation (Jacob L. and Lillian)
Homeland Foundation (NY)
Hopkins Foundation (Josephine Lawrence)
Howard and Bush Foundation
Hudson River Bancorp, Inc.
Hughes Foundation (Geoffrey C.)
Hugoton Foundation
Hulbert Foundation (Nila B.)
Hultquist Foundation
Icahn Foundation (Carl C.)
International Business Machines
Iscol Family Foundation
Ittleson Foundation
Jenjo Foundation
JM Foundation
Johnson Charitable Trust (Keith Wold)
Johnson Endeavor Foundation (Christian A.)
Johnson Foundation (Howard)
Johnson Foundation (Willard T. C.)
Johnson Memorial Trust (John Alfred and Oscar)
Jones Foundation (Daisy Marquis)

Joukowsky Family Foundation
Joy Family Foundation
J.P. Morgan Chase & Co.
Jurzykowski Foundation (Alfred)
Kahn, Lucas-Lancaster, Inc. Children's Wear
Kaplan Fund (J. M.)
Kaplun Foundation (Morris J. and Betty)
Katzenberger Foundation
Kaufmann Foundation (Henry)
KeySpan Corp.
King Family Foundation (Charles and Lucille)
Kinney Memorial Foundation
Klee Foundation (Conrad and Virginia)
Klingenstein Fund, Inc. (Esther A. and Joseph)
Klingestein Fund
Klock and Lucia Klock Kingston Foundation (Jay E.)
Klosk Fund (Rose and Louis)
Knox Foundation (Seymour H.)
Kornfeld Foundation (Emily Davie and Joseph S.)
Kovarik Foundation for Poetry (Henry P.)
Kranes Charitable Trust (Sidney and Judith)
Kress Foundation (Samuel H.)
Kurz Family Foundation
L and L Foundation
Lake Placid Education Foundation
Lang Foundation (Eugene M.)
Lasdon Foundation (William and Mildred)
Lauder Foundation
Lemberg Foundation
Lenna Foundation (Reginald A. and Elizabeth S.)
Liberman Foundation (Bertha and Isaac)
Link, Jr. Foundation (George)
List Foundation (Albert A.)
Littauer Foundation (Lucius N.)
Liz Claiborne, Inc.
Loews Corp.
Loewy Family Foundation
Long Island Lighting Co.
Lowenstein Foundation (Leon)
LSR Fund
Luce Foundation (Henry)
Lurcy Charitable and Educational Trust (Georges)
Macy, Jr. Foundation (Josiah)
Macy's East, Inc.
Mailman Family Foundation (A. L.)
Mandeville Foundation
Markle Foundation (John and Mary R.)
Marx Foundation (Virginia and Leonard)
Mather Fund (Richard)
Mathers Charitable Foundation (G. Harold and Leila Y.)
Mathis-Pfohl Foundation
MBIA, Inc.
McCann Foundation
McCarthy Charities

McGonagle Foundation (Dextra Baldwin)
McGraw-Hill Companies, Inc.
Meier Foundation (Richard)
Mellon Foundation (Andrew W.)
Memton Fund
Mercury Aircraft, Inc.
Merrill Lynch & Company, Inc.
Metropolitan Life Insurance Co.
Mex-Am Cultural Foundation
Millbrook Tribute Garden
MONY Group, Inc.
Morris Family Foundation
Morris Foundation (Norman M.)
Morris Foundation (William T.)
Moses Fund, Inc. (Henry and Lucy)
Neuberger Foundation (Roy R. and Marie S.)
New-Land Foundation
New York Foundation
New York Life Insurance Co.
New York Mercantile Exchange
New York State Electric & Gas Corp.
New York Stock Exchange, Inc.
New York Times Co.
New Yorker Magazine (The)
Newman Assistance Fund (Jerome A. and Estelle R.)
Niagara Mohawk Holdings, Inc.
NLI International, Inc.
Norman Foundation
Normandie Foundation
O'Connor Foundation (A. Lindsay and Olive B.)
Oestreicher Foundation (Sylvan and Ann)
Oishei Foundation (The John R.)
Olin Foundation (John M.)
Oneida Savings Bank
L'Oreal U.S.A.
Osborn Charitable Trust (Edward B.)
Paley Foundation, Inc. (William S.)
Palisades Educational Foundation
Park Foundation
Parshelsky Foundation (Moses L.)
Paul and C. Michael Paul Foundation (Josephine Bay)
PepsiCo Inc.
Pfizer Inc.
Pforzheimer Foundation, Inc. (The Carl and Lily)
Piankova Foundation (Tatiana)
Pinkerton Foundation
Price Foundation (Louis and Harold)
Prospect Hill Foundation
Prudential Securities, Inc.
Raymond Corp.
Reader's Digest Association, Inc.
Reed Foundation (NY)
Reuss Memorial Trust (Allene)

Revson Foundation (Charles H.)
Reynolds Foundation (Christopher)
Rheinstrom Hill Community Foundation
Rich Products Corp.
Richardson Fund (Ann S.)
Riedman Foundation
Robinson-Broadhurst Foundation
Robinson Fund (Maurice R.)
Rockefeller Brothers Fund, Inc.
Rockefeller Fund (David)
Rohatyn Foundation (Felix and Elizabeth)
Rose Foundation (Billy)
Rosenthal Foundation (Ida and William)
Rossi Foundation (William and Alice)
Rothschild Foundation (Judith)
Rubin Foundation (Samuel)
Rubinstein Foundation (Helena)
Rudin Foundation
Rudin Foundation (Samuel and May)
Russer Foods
St. Giles Foundation
Salomon Smith Barney Holdings, Inc.
Samuels Foundation (Fan Fox and Leslie R.)
Sasco Foundation
Scherman Foundation
Scheuer Family Foundation Inc. (S. H. and Helen R.)
Schieffelin Residuary Trust (Sarah I.)
Schiff Foundation (Dorothy)
Schlumberger Ltd.
Schmitt Foundation (Kilian J. and Caroline F.)
Schwartz Fund for Education and Health Research (Arnold and Marie)
Seherr-Thoss Foundation
Seneca Foods Corp.
Sharp Foundation (Evelyn)
Sheldon Foundation Inc. (Ralph C.)
Shubert Foundation
Slater Trust (Lillian M.)
Snow Foundation (John Ben)
Snow Memorial Trust (John Ben)
Snyder Charitable Trust (Harrison C. and Margaret A.)
Solow Foundation
Sound Shore Foundation
Sperandio Family Foundation
Spewack Article 5th Trust (Bella)
Sprague Educational and Charitable Foundation (Seth)
Starr Foundation
Statler Foundation
Steele-Reese Foundation
Sulzberger Foundation
Summerfield Foundation, Inc. (Solon E.)
Taconic Foundation
Teagle Foundation
Thanksgiving Foundation
Thompson Co. (J. Walter)
Tinker Foundation
Trust for Mutual Understanding

Tuch Foundation (Michael)
UBS PaineWebber, Inc.
Unilever United States, Inc.
United Armenian Charities
United States-Japan Foundation
United States Trust Co. of New York
Utica National Insurance Group
Verizon Communications Inc.
Vernon Foundation (Miles Hodsdon)
Vetlesen Foundation (G. Unger)
Viyu Foundation
Vogler Foundation (Laura B.)
Wallace-Reader's Digest Fund (DeWitt)
Wallace-Reader's Digest Fund (Lila)
Warhol Foundation for the Visual Arts (The Andy)
Warner Fund (Albert and Bessie)
Warren and Beatrice W. Blanding Foundation (Riley J. and Lillian N.)
Warwick Savings Foundation
Wasserstein Perella Foundation
Waterhouse Family Foundation
Weezie Foundation
Weil, Gotshal & Manges Corp.
Weinstein Foundation (J.)
Weir Foundation (Candace King)
Wendt Foundation (Margaret L.)
Western New York Foundation
WestLB New York Branch
Wilson Foundation (H. W.)
Wilson Foundation (Marie C. and Joseph C.)
Winston Foundation (Norman and Rosita)
Woodcock Foundation
Woodward Fund
Zacharia Foundation (Isaac Herman)
Zitrin Foundation (Charlotte and Arthur)

North Carolina

Acme-McCrary Corp./Sapona Manufacturing Co.
Babcock Foundation (Mary Reynolds)
Bank of America Corp.
Belk Stores Services, Inc.
Bergen Foundation (Frank and Lydia)
Biddle Foundation (Mary Duke)
Blue Bell, Inc.
Blumenthal Foundation
Broyhill Family Foundation
Burlington Industries, Inc.
Cannon Foundation, Inc. (The)
CCB Financial Corp.
Cemala Foundation
Dalton Foundation (Harry L.)
Dover Foundation
Duke Endowment
Duke Energy Corp.
Finch Foundation (Doak)

Finch Foundation (Thomas Austin)
Franklin Foundation Inc. (John and Mary)
Freas Foundation
Fredrickson Foundation (Ambrose and Ida)
Goodrich Corp.
Hanes Foundation (John Wesley and Anna Hodgin)
Harvey Foundation (C. Felix)
Hillsdale Fund
Interstate/Johnson Lane
Janirve Foundation
Lowe's Companies
Miller Brewing Co. (Eden, NC)
Mitsubishi Semiconductor America
Moore & Sons (B.C.)
Ohl, Jr. Trust (George A.)
Progress Energy Inc.
RBC Centura
Reichhold Chemicals, Inc.
Rexam, Inc.
R.J. Reynolds Tobacco
Royal & SunAlliance USA, Inc.
Smith Horticultural Trust (Stanley)
SPX Corp.
Stonecutter Mills Corp.
Tanner Companies (Rutherfordton, NC)
Thomasville Furniture Industries, Inc.
Tri-County Telephone Foundation
Wachovia Bank of North Carolina NA
Willis Family Foundation

North Dakota

MDU Resources Group, Inc.

Ohio

AK Steel Holding Corp.
Alms Trust (Eleanora)
Amcast Industrial Corp.
Andersons, Inc.
Andrews Foundation
Ashtabula Foundation
Baird Brothers Co. Foundation
Bardes Corp.
Beasley Charitable Trust (Lucy and Emily)
Beecher Foundation (Florence Simon)
Berkman Foundation (Louis and Sandra)
Berry Foundation (Loren M.)
Bicknell Fund
Bingham Foundation (William)
Borden, Inc.
Britton Fund
Bruening Foundation (Eva L. and Joseph M.)
Brush Foundation
Calhoun Charitable Trust (Kenneth L.)
Cayuga Foundation
Cinergy Corp.
Cleveland-Cliffs, Inc.
Codrington Charitable Foundation (George W.)
Columbus Dispatch Printing Co.

Commercial Intertech Foundation
Cooper Tire & Rubber Co.
Corbett Foundation
Crandall Memorial Foundation (J. Ford)
Dater Foundation (Charles H.)
Dayton Power and Light Co.
Deuble Foundation (George H.)
Eaton Corp.
Eaton Foundation (Cyrus)
Emery Memorial (Thomas J.)
Evans Foundation (Thomas J.)
Farmer Family Foundation
Fifth Third Bancorp
Figgie Educational Foundation
Firestone, Jr. Foundation (Harvey)
Firman Fund
Flowers Charitable Trust (Albert W. and Edith V.)
Forest City Enterprises, Inc.
Fox Charitable Trust (Emma R.)
French Oil Mill Machinery Co.
Frohring Foundation (Paul and Maxine)
GAR Foundation
Grimes Foundation
Griswold Foundation (John C.)
Gund Foundation (George)
H. C. S. Foundation
Haman Family Foundation
Haskell Fund
Hershey Foundation
Honda of America Manufacturing, Inc.
Hoover Foundation (The)
Hoover Foundation (Herbert W.)
Hoover Trust Fund (W. Henry)
Humphrey Fund (George M. and Pamela S.)
Huntington Bancshares, Inc.
Ingalls Foundation (Louise H. and David S.)
Jarson Kaplan Foundation
Jennings Foundation (Martha Holden)
Kenridge Fund
Ketrow Foundation
Kettering Fund
Key Bank NA
KeyCorp
Kilcawley Fund (William H.)
Kilworth Charitable Trust (Florence B.)
Kroger Co.
Mandel Foundation (Jack N. and Lilyan)
Markey Charitable Fund (John C.)
Massie Trust (David Meade)
Mather Charitable Trust (S. Livingston)
Mather and William Gwinn Mather Fund (Elizabeth Ring)
Mayerson Foundation (Manuel D. and Rhoda)
McFawn-The Sisler McFawn Foundation (L. Sisler)
McMaster Foundation (Harold and Helen)
Minster Machine Co.

Morgan Foundation (Burton D.)
Musson Charitable Foundation (R. C. and Katharine M.)
National City Corp.
National Machinery Co.
Nord Family Foundation
Nordson Corp.
O'Bleness Foundation (Charles)
Peterloon Foundation
Pollock Co. Foundation (William B.)
Reeves Foundation (OH)
Reinberger Foundation
Ritter Charitable Trust (George and Mary)
Rosenberry Tuscarawas County Foundation (Harold C. and Marjorie Q.)
Rosenthal Foundation (Lois and Richard)
Ross Products Division, Abbott Laboratories
Rupp Foundation (Fran and Warren)
Russell Charitable Trust (Josephine S.)
Schlink Foundation (Albert G. and Olive H.)
Schmidlapp Trust No. 1 (Jacob G.)
Schmidlapp Trust No. 2 (Jacob G.)
Scott Fetzer Co.
Scripps Co. (E.W.)
Second Foundation
Semple Foundation (Louise Taft)
Sherwin-Williams Co.
Slemp Foundation
Smith Foundation (Kelvin and Eleanor)
South Waite Foundation
Spahr Family Foundation
Stocker Foundation
Stone Foundation (France)
Straker Charitable Foundation (J. William and Mary Helen)
Stranahan Foundation
Timken Foundation of Canton
Toledo Blade Co.
Trumbull County Scholarship Foundation
Van Wert County Foundation
Watson Foundation (Walter E. and Caroline H.)
Wean Foundation (Raymond John)
Western & Southern Life Insurance Co.
Wildermuth Foundation (E. F.)
Wilkof Foundation (Edward and Ruth)
Worthington Foods
Young Foundation (Hugo H. and Mabel B.)

Oklahoma

Aldridge Charitable and Educational Trust (Tom S. and Marye Kate)
American Fidelity Assurance Co.
Beatty Trust (Cordelia Lunceford)

Bernsen Foundation (Grace and Franklin)
Bovaird Foundation (Mervin)
Broadhurst Foundation
Chapman Charitable Trust (H. A. and Mary K.)
Collins Foundation (George and Jennie)
Collins, Jr. Foundation (George Fulton)
Goddard Foundation (Charles B.)
Harmon Foundation (Pearl M. and Julia J.)
Helmerich Foundation
Inasmuch Foundation
Kerr Foundation, Inc.
Kirkpatrick Foundation, Inc.
Lyon Foundation
Mabee Foundation, Inc. (J. E. and L. E.)
McCasland Foundation
McMahon Foundation
Meinders Foundation
Merrick Foundation
Noble Foundation (Samuel Roberts)
OG&E Electric Services
Puterbaugh Foundation
Sarkeys Foundation
Share Trust (Charles Morton)
Titus Foundation (C. W.)
Westby Foundation (Kathleen Patton)
Williams Companies Inc.
Zarrow Foundation (Anne and Henry)

Oregon

Ackerman Trust (Anna Keesling)
Adler Trust (Leo)
Bloch Foundation (Rene)
Braemar Charitable Trust
Carpenter Foundation
Chiles Foundation
Collins Foundation
Collins Medical Trust
Faith Foundation
Ford Family Foundation
Frank Family Foundation (A. J.)
Hunt Charitable Trust (C. Giles)
Jackson Foundation (OR)
Jeld-Wen, Inc.
Johnson Foundation (Samuel S.)
Lamb Foundation
Louisiana-Pacific Corp.
McKay Family Foundation
Meyer Memorial Trust
Mitsubishi Silicon America
Northwest Natural Gas Co.
PacifiCorp
Pioneer Trust Bank, NA
Templeton Foundation (Herbert A.)
Tucker Charitable Trust (Rose E.)
W. A. Woodard Foundation
Wessinger Foundation
Wheeler Foundation
Wyss Foundation

Pennsylvania

Air Products and Chemicals, Inc.
Alcoa Inc.
Alexander Stewart MD Foundation Trust

Allegheny Foundation
AMETEK, Inc.
AMP, Inc.
Annenberg Foundation
Arcadia Foundation
Arronson Foundation
Asplundh Foundation
Baird Trust (Gladys)
Baker Foundation (Dexter F. and Dorothy H.)
Bard Foundation (Robert)
Beneficia Foundation
Berwind Group
Betts Industries
Binney & Smith, Inc.
Binswanger Companies
Bishop Foundation (Vernon and Doris)
Bowman Proper Charitable Trust (J.)
Brossman Charitable Foundation (William and Jemima)
Bryn Mawr Bank Corp.
Buhl Foundation (PA)
Carpenter Foundation (E. Rhodes and Leona B.)
Cassett Foundation (Louis N.)
CertainTeed Corp.
Charity Randall Foundation
CIGNA Corp.
Claneil Foundation
Clapp Charitable and Educational Trust (George H. and Anne L.)
Clemens Markets
Coen Family Foundation (Charles S. and Mary)
Colonial Oaks Foundation
Connelly Foundation
Connemara Fund
Crawford Estate Trust Fund A (E. R.)
Dendroica Foundation
Dentsply International, Inc.
Dietrich Foundation (William B.)
Douty Foundation (Alfred and Mary)
Dynamet, Inc.
Eberly Foundation
Eccles Foundation (Ralph M. and Ella M.)
Eden Hall Foundation
Elf Atochem North America, Inc.
Ellis Grant and Scholarship Fund (Charles E.)
Fair Oaks Foundation
Falk Medical Fund (Maurice)
Fels Fund (Samuel S.)
FMC Corp.
Foster Charitable Trust
Foster Co. (L.B.)
Freeport Brick Co.
G/S/M Industrial, Inc.
Garver Charity Fund (David B.)
Giant Eagle, Inc.
Giant Food Stores
Grable Foundation
Graham Engineering Corp.
Greenfield Foundation (Albert M.)
Grundy Foundation
Hamer Foundation
Harsco Corp.
Heinz Endowment (Howard)
Heinz Endowment (Vira I.)
Heinz Family Foundation
Henkel Corp.

Hershey Foods Corp.
High Foundation
Hillman Foundation
H.J. Heinz Co.
Hoch Foundation (Charles H.)
Holt Family Foundation
Hopwood Charitable Trust (John M.)
Hulme Charitable Foundation (Milton G.)
Hunt Corp.
Hunt Foundation (Roy A.)
Huston Charitable Trust (Stewart)
Huston Foundation
Independence Foundation
Jacobs Charitable Trust (Margaret G.)
J&L Specialty Steel, Inc.
Jennings Foundation (Mary Hillman)
Jewish Healthcare Foundation
Johnson Foundation (Thomas Phillips and Jane Moore)
Justus Trust (Edith C.)
Kardon Foundation (Samuel and Rebecca)
Kavanagh Foundation (T. James)
Kline Foundation (Charles and Figa)
Kline Foundation (Josiah W. and Bessie H.)
Knudsen Charitable Foundation (Earl)
Kunkel Foundation (John Crain)
Lamco Communications
Laurel Foundation
Lebanon Mutual Insurance Co.
Lebovitz Fund
Lefton Co. (Al Paul)
Lehigh Cement Co.
Levitt Foundation (NY)
Love Foundation (George H. and Margaret McClintic)
Ludwick Foundation (Christopher)
Massey Charitable Trust
McCausland Foundation
McCormick Charitable Trust (Margaret Ogilvie)
McCormick Trust (Anne)
McCune Charitable Trust (John R.)
McCune Foundation
McFeely-Rogers Foundation
McKenna Foundation (Katherine Mabis)
McKenna Foundation (Philip M.)
McLean Contributionship
McShain Charities (John)
Mellon Family Foundation (R. K.)
Mellon Foundation (Richard King)
Mengle Foundation (Glenn and Ruth)
Miller Charitable Foundation (Howard E. and Nell E.)
Mine Safety Appliances Co.
Morris Charitable Trust (Charles M.)
Murphy Co. Foundation (G.C.)
Oxford Foundation

Patterson Charitable Fund (W. I.)
Penn Foundation (William)
Peters Charitable Trust (Edward V. and Jessie L.)
Peters Foundation (Charles F.)
Pew Charitable Trusts
Phillips Charitable Trust (Dr. and Mrs. Arthur William)
Pine Tree Foundation
Pitt-Des Moines, Inc.
Pittsburgh Child Guidance Foundation
Plankenhorn Foundation (Harry)
PNC Financial Services Group, Inc.
PPG Industries, Inc.
Quaker Chemical Corp.
Reidler Foundation
Rider-Pool Foundation
Robertshaw Charitable Foundation
Robinson Family Foundation (Donald and Sylvia)
S&T Bancorp, Inc.
Scaife Family Foundation
Schoonmaker J-Sewkly Valley Hospital Trust
Seton Co.
Seybert Institution for Poor Boys and Girls (Adam and Maria Sarah)
Sharon Steel Corp.
Sheary Trust for Charity (Edna M.)
Shore Fund
Smith Charitable Foundation (Arlene H.)
Smith Memorial Fund (Ethel Sergeant Clark)
Snayberger Memorial Foundation (Harry E. and Florence W.)
Snee-Reinhardt Charitable Foundation
Snyder Foundation (William I. and Patricia S.)
Sordoni Foundation
Sovereign Bank
Spang & Co.
Speyer Foundation (Alexander C. and Tillie S.)
Stabler Foundation (Donald B. and Dorothy L.)
Stackpole-Hall Foundation
Standard Steel
Standard Steel Speciality Co.
Staunton Farm Foundation
Steinman Foundation (James Hale)
Steinman Foundation (John Frederick)
Stott Foundation (Louis L.)
Strauss Foundation
Strawbridge Foundation of Pennsylvania II (Margaret Dorrance)
Stuart Charitable Foundation (G. B.)
Susquehanna-Pfaltzgraff Co.
Teleflex, Inc.
TMC Investment Co.
Trees Charitable Trust (Edith L.)
Trexler Trust (Harry C.)
U.S. Steel Corp.
Vanguard Group
Vesuvius Foundation
Warwick Foundation

Waters Charitable Trust (Robert S.)
Waypoint Financial Corp.
Wells Foundation (Franklin H. and Ruth L.)
West Pharmaceutical Services, Inc.
Whalley Charitable Trust
Whitaker Fund (Helen F.)
Williams Charitable Trust (John C.)
Wood Foundation of Chambersburg, PA
Wyomissing Foundation

Rhode Island

Adams Trust (Charles E. and Caroline J.)
Adelson Trust (Diana S.)
Champlin Foundation
Chase Charity Foundation (Alfred E.)
Citizens Financial Group, Inc.
Clarke Trust (John)
Cranston Print Works Co.
Dexter Charitable Trust (Henrietta)
Dimeo Construction Co.
Feinstein Foundation
Hasbro, Inc.
Hathaway Memorial Charitable Trust
Heydt Fund (Nan and Matilda)
Kimball Foundation (Horace A. Kimball and S. Ella)
Littlefield Memorial Trust (Ida Ballou)
Long Foundation (George A. and Grace)
North Family Trust
Providence Gas Co.
Providence Journal-Bulletin Co.
Rice Charitable Foundation (Albert W.)
Textron, Inc.
Trimix Foundation
Watson Foundation (Thomas J.)

South Carolina

Bell Foundation (S. Lewis and Lucia B.)
Bowater, Inc.
Chapin Foundation of Myrtle Beach, South Carolina
Colonial Life & Accident Insurance Co.
Evening Post Publishing Co.
Fullerton Foundation
Gregg-Graniteville Foundation
Jacobs Family Foundation
Liberty Corp.
Self Family Foundation
Sonoco Products Co.
Spring/Close Foundation
Springs Foundation, Inc.
Symmes Foundation (F. W.)

South Dakota

IBP
Vucurevich Foundation (John T.)

Tennessee

Ansley Foundation (Dantzler Bond)
Benwood Foundation

Bridgestone Americas Holding, Inc.
Christy-Houston Foundation
Davis Foundation (Joe C.)
First Tennessee National Corp.
Frist Foundation
Joyce Family Foundation
Lyndhurst Foundation
North American Royalties
Pattee Foundation
Plough Foundation
Sedgwick, Inc.
Thompson Charitable Foundation
Toms Foundation (The)
Tonya Memorial Foundation
Tucker Foundation
Wilson Foundation (Anne Potter)
Wurzburg, Inc.

Texas

Abell-Hanger Foundation
Alcon Laboratories, Inc.
Alexander Foundation (Robert D. and Catherine R.)
Amgen, Inc.
AMR Corp.
Anderson Foundation (M. D.)
Apteckar Foundation (Marian Meaker)
Argyle Foundation
Beal Foundation
Belo Corp.
Bertha Foundation
Brackenridge Foundation (George W.)
Bragg Charitable Trust (R. B. O.)
Brown Foundation
Brown Foundation (M. K.)
Burlington Northern Santa Fe Corp.
Burlington Resources Inc.
Burnett Foundation (The)
Cain Foundation (Effie and Wofford)
Cain Foundation (Gordon and Mary)
Carter Foundation (Amon G.)
Cauthorn Charitable Trust (John and Mildred)
CenterPoint Energy, Inc.
CH Foundation
Clayton Fund
Clements Foundation
Cockrell Foundation
Contran Corp.
Cook, Sr. Charitable Foundation (Kelly Gene)
Cooper Industries Ltd.
Coy Foundation (Dave)
Cullen Foundation (The)
Decherd Foundation
Dibrell Charitable Trust (Volney E.)
Dishman Charitable Foundation Trust (H. E. and Kate)
Doak Charitable Trust (Clifton C. and Henryetta C.)
Dodge Jones Foundation and Subsidiary
Doss Foundation, Inc. (M. S.)
Dougherty, Jr. Foundation (James R.)
Dunagan Foundation
Duncan Foundation (L. H. and C. W.)
Early Foundation

ECG Foundation
El Paso Corp.
Elkins, Jr. Foundation (Margaret and James A.)
ExxonMobile Corp.
Farish Fund (William Stamps)
Fasken Foundation
Fikes Foundation (Leland)
Fish Foundation (Ray C.)
Fleming Foundation
Fondren Foundation
Frost National Bank
Gage Foundation (Alfred S.)
Garvey Texas Foundation
George Foundation
Griffin Foundation (Rosa May)
Gulf Coast Medical Foundation
Halff Foundation (G. A. C.)
Hallberg Foundation (E. L. and R. F.)
Halliburton Co.
Halsell Foundation (Ewing)
Hamman Foundation (George and Mary Josephine)
Hawn Foundation
Heath Foundation (Ed and Mary)
Herd Foundation (Bob L.)
Herzstein Charitable Foundation (Albert and Ethel)
Hillcrest Foundation
Hobby Family Foundation
Hoblitzelle Foundation
Hoglund Foundation
Houston Endowment
Huthsteiner Fine Arts Trust
Jamail Foundation (Lee and Joseph D.)
Johnson Foundation (Burdine)
Johnson Foundation (M. G. and Lillie A.)
Jones Foundation (Helen)
Kayser Foundation
Kempner Fund (Harris and Eliza)
Kilroy Foundation (William S. and Lora Jean)
Kimberly-Clark Corp.
Kinder Morgan
King Foundation (Carl B. and Florence E.)
Kleberg Foundation (Robert J. Kleberg, Jr. and Helen C.)
Knox, Sr., and Pearl Wallis Knox Charitable Foundation (Robert W.)
Koehler Foundation (Marcia and Otto)
Lard Trust (Mary Potishman)
Lennox Foundation (Martha, David and Bagby)
Luse Foundation (W. P. and Bulah)
Masters Family Foundation
Mayer Foundation (James and Eva)
Mayor Foundation (Oliver Dewey)
Mays Foundation
McDermott Foundation (The Eugene)
McGovern Foundation (John P.)
McGovern Fund
McKee Foundation (Robert E. and Evelyn)

McMillan, Jr. Foundation (Bruce)
McNutt Charitable Trust (Amy Shelton)
McQueen Foundation (Adeline and George)
Meadows Foundation (The)
Meyer Family Foundation (Paul J.)
Meyer Foundation (Alice Kleberg Reynolds)
Moody Foundation
Munson Foundation Trust (W. B.)
Norman Foundation (Summers A.)
O'Connor Foundation (Kathryn)
O'Donnell Foundation
O'Quinn Foundation (John M.)
Overlake Foundation
Owsley Foundation (Alvin and Lucy)
Pelz Trust (H.E. and Ruby)
Peterson Foundation (Hal and Charlie)
Pineywoods Foundation
Piper Foundation (Minnie Stevens)
Potts and Sibley Foundation
Powell Foundation
The Prairie Foundation
Priddy Foundation
Quanex Corp.
Rachal Foundation (Ed)
RGK Foundation
Richardson Foundation (Sid W.)
Roberts Foundation (Dora)
Rockwell Fund, Inc.
Rogers Fund for the Arts (Russell Hill)
Sams Foundation (Earl C.)
SBC Communications Inc.
Scott Foundation (William E.)
Scurlock Foundation
Semmes Foundation
Shell Oil Co.
Smith and W. Aubrey Smith Charitable Foundation (Clara Blackford)
South Plains Foundation
Stark Foundation (Nelda C. and H. J. Lutcher)
Steinhagen Benevolent Trust (B. A. and Elinor W.)
Stemmons Foundation
Sterling-Turner Foundation
Strake Foundation
Sturgis Charitable and Educational Trust (TX) (Roy and Christine)
Summerlee Foundation
Swalm Foundation
Temple Foundation (T. L. L.)
Temple-Inland, Inc.
Texas Instruments Inc.
Thornton Charitable Trust (Anna W. Thornton and Alexander P.)
Trull Foundation (The)
Vale-Asche Foundation
Vaughan Foundation (Rachael and Ben)
Vaughn Foundation (Jim M.)
Vaughn, Jr. Foundation Fund (James M.)
Waggoner Charitable Trust (Crystelle)
Walsh Foundation

Ward Heritage Foundation (Mamie McFaddin)
Weaver Foundation (Gil and Dody)
West Foundation (Neva and Wesley)
West Foundation (TX)
Wheeler Memorial Foundation (Josephine and J. A.)
White Trust (G. R.)
Willard Helping Fund (Cecilia Young)
Wise Foundation (Watson W.)
Wortham Foundation
Wright Foundation (Lola)
Zachry Co. (H.B.)

Utah

Bamberger Memorial Foundation (John Ernest Bamberger and Ruth Eleanor)
Burton Private Foundation (Robert Harold)
Daugherty Foundation
Dee Foundation (Lawrence T. and Janet T.)
Dumke Foundation (Ezekiel R. and Edna Wattis)
Eccles Charitable Foundation (Willard L.)
Eccles Foundation (George S. and Dolores Dore)
Eccles Foundation (Marriner S.)
Michael Foundation (Herbert I. and Elsa B.)
Novell
Stewart Educational Foundation (Donnell B. and Elizabeth Dee Shaw)
Swanson Family Foundation, Inc. (Dr. W. C.)

Vermont

Ben & Jerry's Homemade, Inc.
Carris Reels
Central Vermont Public Service Corp.
Cone-Blanchard Corp.
Fleming and Jane Howe Patrick Foundation (Robert)
Proctor Trust (Mortimer R.)
Windham Foundation

Virginia

Beazley Foundation
Bryant Foundation (The)
Cabell III and Maude Morgan Cabell Foundation (Robert G.)
Camp Younts Foundation
Campbell Foundation (Ruth and Henry)
Carter Foundation (Beirne)
Chesapeake Corp.
Cole Trust (Quincy)
Dominion
Easley Trust (Andrew H. and Anne O.)
Ethyl Corp.
Evans Foundation (Edward P.)
Gray Foundation (Garland and Agnes Taylor)
Joco Foundation
Landmark Communications, Inc.
Lane Foundation (Minnie and Bernard)

McDougall Charitable Trust (Ruth Camp)
Norfolk Shipbuilding & Drydock Corp.
North Shore Foundation
Old Dominion Box Co.
Olmsted Foundation (George and Carol)
Olsson Memorial Foundation (Elis)
Perry Foundation
Phipps Foundation (Columbus)
Portsmouth General Hospital Foundation
Reynolds Foundation (Richard S.)
Richardson Benevolent Foundation (C. E.)
Scott Foundation (William H., John G., and Emma)
Seay Memorial Trust (George and Effie)
Shenandoah Life Insurance Co.
Shenandoah Telecommunications Co.
Treakle Foundation (J. Edwin)
Vaughan Furniture Co.
Virginia Environmental Endowment
Washington Forrest Foundation
Whitaker Foundation

Washington

Archibald Charitable Foundation (Norman)
Avista Corp.
Bishop Foundation (E. K. and Lillian F.)
Cheney Foundation (Ben B.)
Dimmer Family Foundation
Fehsenfeld Charitable Foundation (Frank B. and Virginia V.)
Forest Foundation
Foster Foundation
Fuchs Foundation (Gottfried and Mary)
Gates Foundation (Bill and Melinda)
Glaser Foundation
Howarth Trust Fund
Johnston-Hanson Foundation
Kawabe Memorial Fund
Kongsgaard-Goldman Foundation
Medina Foundation
Microsoft Corp.
Murdock Charitable Trust (M. J.)
Nesholm Family Foundation
Norcliffe Foundation
Petrie Trust (Lorene M.)
SAFECO Corp.
Shepherd Foundation (Harold and Helen)
Simpson Investment Co.
Snyder Foundation (Frost and Margaret)
Stewardship Foundation
Stubblefield (Estate of Joseph L.)
US Bank
Washington Mutual, Inc.
Welch Testamentary Trust (George T.)
Weyerhaeuser Co.
Wyman Youth Trust

West Virginia

Bowen Foundation (Ethel N.)
Carter Family Foundation
Clay Foundation
Daywood Foundation
Fenton Foundation
Hunnicutt Foundation (H. P. and Anne S.)
Huntington Foundation
Jacobson Foundation (Bernard H. and Blanche E.)
McDonough Foundation (Bernard)
One Valley Bank NA
Shott, Jr. Foundation (Hugh I.)
Smoot Charitable Trust (Frank Litz)
Teubert Charitable Trust (James H. and Alice)

Wisconsin

Alexander Foundation (Walter)
Alliant Energy Corp.
Andres Charitable Trust (Frank G.)
Appleton Papers, Inc.
Aylward Family Foundation
Badger Meter, Inc.
Banta Corp.
Bemis Manufacturing Co.
Bradley Foundation (Lynde and Harry)
Brillion Iron Works
Brodbeck Enterprises
Bucyrus International, Inc.
Carter Trust (Evelyn C.)
Christensen Charitable and Religious Foundation (L. C.)
Cleary Foundation
Cremer Foundation
CUNA Mutual Group
DEC International, Inc. SMS/Nelles Cheese Equipment
First Financial Bank
Firstar Bank Milwaukee NA
Fortis Health
Giddings & Lewis
Grede Foundries
Harley-Davidson Co.
Helfaer Foundation (Evan and Marion)
Johnson Controls Inc.
Johnson Foundation
Johnson & Son (S.C.)
Joy Global, Inc.
Kikkoman Foods
Kohler Foundation
Lunda Charitable Trust
Marcus Corp.
Marshall & Ilsley Corp.
McBeath Foundation (Faye)
MGE Energy, Inc.
Miller Foundation (Steve J.)
Mosinee Paper Corp.
Oshkosh B'Gosh, Inc.
Park Bank
Peters Foundation (R. D. and Linda)
Peterson Charitable Foundation (Ellsworth and Carla)
Phillips Family Foundation (L. E.)
Rockwell Automation Inc.
Ross Memorial Foundation (Will)
Saint Francis Bank
Schoenleber Foundation

Schroeder Foundation
    (Walter)
Sentry Insurance, A Mutual
    Co.
Smith Corp. (A.O.)
Stackner Family Foundation
Steigleder Charitable Trust
    (Bert L. and Patricia S.)

Stora Enso
United Wisconsin Services
Vogel Foundation
VPI Foundation Inc.
Wausau-Mosinee Paper
    Corp.
Wehr Foundation (Todd)
WPS Resources Corp.

Young Foundation (Irvin L.)
Ziegler Foundation

Wyoming

Goodstein Foundation
Patterson Memorial Trust
    (Hazel)

Sargent Foundation (Newell
    B.)
Surrena Memorial Fund
    (Harry and Thelma)
Weiss Foundation (William
    E.)
Zullig Foundation (Herbert G.
    and Dorothy)

FUNDERS BY OPERATING LOCATIONS

Arranges corporations by the states of their major operating locations. Within each state, company names are listed in alphabetical order.

Alabama

Air Products and Chemicals, Inc.
Akzo Nobel Chemicals
Alabama Power Co.
Alcoa Inc.
Amcast Industrial Corp.
American Honda Motor Company, Inc.
Belk Stores Services, Inc.
Blue Bell, Inc.
Boise Cascade Corp.
Bowater, Inc.
Caterpillar Inc.
CLARCOR, Inc.
Clorox Co.
Crompton Corp.
Cummins, Inc.
Eastman Kodak Co.
Eaton Corp.
Ecolab, Inc.
E.I. du Pont de Nemours & Co.
Elf Atochem North America, Inc.
Eli Lilly & Co.
Employers Mutual Casualty Co.
Equifax, Inc.
Fannie Mae
FMC Corp.
Forest City Enterprises, Inc.
Fortune Brands, Inc.
General Motors Corp.
Georgia Power Co.
Gerber Products Co.
Halliburton Co.
Harsco Corp.
Hartmarx Corp.
Humana, Inc.
Hunt Corp.
Johnson Controls Inc.
Kimberly-Clark Corp.
Lehigh Cement Co.
Liberty Corp.
Louisiana-Pacific Corp.
Meadwestvaco Corp.
Minnesota Mining & Manufacturing Co.
New York Times Co.
Olin Corp.
Pittsburg & Midway Coal Mining Co.
Sara Lee Corp.
Scripps Co. (E.W.)
Square D Co.
State Farm Mutual Automobile Insurance Co.
Steelcase Inc.
Texas Instruments Inc.
Unocal Corp.
USG Corp.
Vulcan Materials Co.
Weyerhaeuser Co.
Winn-Dixie Stores Inc.

Alaska

AT&T Corp.
Carnival Corp.
ChevronTexaco Corp.
Eastman Kodak Co.

Fluor Corp.
FMC Corp.
General Mills, Inc.
Minnesota Mining & Manufacturing Co.
Ondeo Nalco Co.
PacifiCorp
Unocal Corp.
Usibelli Coal Mine, Inc.

Arizona

Abbott Laboratories
Air Products and Chemicals, Inc.
Albertson's Inc.
American General Finance
AT&T Corp.
Badger Meter, Inc.
Ben & Jerry's Homemade, Inc.
Boise Cascade Corp.
Caterpillar Inc.
Cox Enterprises, Inc.
Crane Co.
Dow Jones & Company, Inc.
Eastman Kodak Co.
Edison International
Eli Lilly & Co.
Equifax, Inc.
Evening Post Publishing Co.
Fannie Mae
Federated Mutual Insurance Co.
Fifth Third Bancorp
Firstar Bank Milwaukee NA
FMC Corp.
Fortis, Inc.
Fujitsu America
Gerber Products Co.
Henkel Corp.
Hexcel Corp.
H.J. Heinz Co.
Humana, Inc.
Johns Manville
J.P. Morgan Chase & Co.
Kimberly-Clark Corp.
Kroger Co.
Lee Enterprises, Inc.
McClatchy Co.
McCormick & Company, Inc.
Meadwestvaco Corp.
Minnesota Mining & Manufacturing Co.
Northern Trust Corp.
Olin Corp.
Phelps Dodge Corp.
Prudential Insurance Co. of America
Pulitzer, Inc.
Sara Lee Corp.
Scoular Co.
Scripps Co. (E.W.)
Stanley Works
State Farm Mutual Automobile Insurance Co.
Texas Instruments Inc.
Thompson Co. (J. Walter)
U.S. Bancorp Piper Jaffray

Arkansas

Air Products and Chemicals, Inc.

Albertson's Inc.
Alcoa Inc.
Amcast Industrial Corp.
Anheuser-Busch Companies, Inc.
Belk Stores Services, Inc.
Bridgestone Americas Holding, Inc.
CenterPoint Energy, Inc.
Dow Jones & Company, Inc.
Eastman Kodak Co.
E.I. du Pont de Nemours & Co.
Equifax, Inc.
Gerber Products Co.
Hartmarx Corp.
Holnam, Inc.
Illinois Tool Works, Inc.
Johnson Controls Inc.
Johnson & Son (S.C.)
Kimberly-Clark Corp.
La-Z-Boy, Inc.
Liberty Corp.
Magna International of America, Inc.
Meadwestvaco Corp.
Phelps Dodge Corp.
PPG Industries, Inc.
Prudential Insurance Co. of America
Quanex Corp.
Reliable Life Insurance Co.
Rouse Co.
R.R. Donnelley & Sons Co.
Sara Lee Corp.
Schering-Plough Corp.
Smith Corp. (A.O.)
Southwestern Electric Power Co.
Union Pacific Corp.
Weyerhaeuser Co.
Whirlpool Corp.

California

Abbott Laboratories
ABC, Inc.
Air France
Air Products and Chemicals, Inc.
Akzo Nobel Chemicals
Albertson's Inc.
Alcoa Inc.
Allianz Life Insurance Company of North America
American General Finance
American Honda Motor Company, Inc.
American United Life Insurance Co.
AMETEK, Inc.
Amgen, Inc.
AMP, Inc.
Anheuser-Busch Companies, Inc.
AT&T Corp.
Avon Products, Inc.
Banta Corp.
Barnes Group, Inc.
Bausch & Lomb, Inc.
Bay View Bank
Bechtel Group, Inc.
Belo Corp.

Ben & Jerry's Homemade, Inc.
Boise Cascade Corp.
Bourns, Inc.
BP Amoco Corp.
Bridgestone Americas Holding, Inc.
Brunswick Corp.
Bucyrus International, Inc.
Burlington Industries, Inc.
Burnett Co. (Leo)
California Bank & Trust
Campbell Soup Co.
Canon U.S.A., Inc.
Cargill, Inc.
CertainTeed Corp.
ChevronTexaco Corp.
Church & Dwight Company, Inc.
CIBC World Markets
CIT Group, Inc.
Citizens Financial Group, Inc.
CLARCOR, Inc.
Clorox Co.
Comerica Inc.
Copley Press, Inc.
Cox Enterprises, Inc.
Crane Co.
Crompton Corp.
CUNA Mutual Group
Daily News, L.P.
D&B
Donaldson Company, Inc.
Dow Corning Corp.
Dow Jones & Company, Inc.
Ducommun, Inc.
Dunkin' Donuts, Inc.
Eastman Kodak Co.
Eaton Corp.
Ecolab, Inc.
Edison International
E.I. du Pont de Nemours & Co.
Elf Atochem North America, Inc.
Eli Lilly & Co.
Equifax, Inc.
Exchange Bank
Fannie Mae
FleetBoston Financial Corp.
Fluor Corp.
FMC Corp.
Forest City Enterprises, Inc.
Fortis, Inc.
Fujitsu America
Fuller Co. (H.B.)
Gap, Inc.
GATX Corp.
GE Capital Corp.
General Mills, Inc.
General Motors Corp.
Gerber Products Co.
Giant Food, Inc.
Gillette Co.
Halliburton Co.
HarperCollins Publishers, Inc.
Harsco Corp.
Hasbro, Inc.
Henkel Corp.
Hershey Foods Corp.
Hexcel Corp.
H.J. Heinz Co.

Hoffmann-La Roche, Inc.
HON Industries, Inc.
Hubbard Broadcasting, Inc.
Hunt Corp.
Illinois Tool Works, Inc.
International Multifoods Corp.
Johns Manville
Johnson Controls Inc.
Johnson & Johnson
Johnson & Son (S.C.)
Jostens, Inc.
J.P. Morgan Chase & Co.
Kajima International, Inc.
Kawasaki Motors Manufacturing Corporation U.S.A.
Kemper National Insurance Companies
Kimberly-Clark Corp.
La-Z-Boy, Inc.
Land O'Lakes, Inc.
Lee Enterprises, Inc.
Lehigh Cement Co.
Lipton Co.
Liz Claiborne, Inc.
Louisiana-Pacific Corp.
M/A-COM, Inc.
Macy's East, Inc.
Mattel Inc.
McCormick & Company, Inc.
Meadwestvaco Corp.
Metropolitan Life Insurance Co.
Microsoft Corp.
Minnesota Mining & Manufacturing Co.
Mitsubishi Motor Sales of America, Inc.
Mitsubishi Silicon America
Nestle Purina PetCare Co.
New York Times Co.
NLI International, Inc.
Nordson Corp.
Northern Trust Corp.
Oki America, Inc.
Olin Corp.
Ondeo Nalco Co.
Oshkosh B'Gosh, Inc.
Pacific Life Insurance Co.
PepsiCo Inc.
Pfizer Inc.
Phelps Dodge Corp.
Pitt-Des Moines, Inc.
Polaroid Corp.
Prudential Insurance Co. of America
Quaker Chemical Corp.
Ralph's Grocery Co.
Reichhold Chemicals, Inc.
Rich Products Corp.
R.J. Reynolds Tobacco
Rockwell Automation Inc.
Rouse Co.
R.R. Donnelley & Sons Co.
SAFECO Corp.
Salomon Smith Barney Holdings, Inc.
Sara Lee Corp.
Schering-Plough Corp.
Schlumberger Ltd.
Scoular Co.
Scripps Co. (E.W.)

Security Life of Denver Insurance Co.
Sempra Energy
Shell Oil Co.
Sherwin-Williams Co.
Smith Corp. (A.O.)
Square D Co.
Stanley Works
State Farm Mutual Automobile Insurance Co.
Steelcase Inc.
Subaru of America, Inc.
Teichert & Sons (A.)
Teleflex, Inc.
Texas Instruments Inc.
Thompson Co. (J. Walter)
Union Pacific Corp.
U.S. Bancorp Piper Jaffray
United States Trust Co. of New York
Unitrode Corp.
Universal Studios
Unocal Corp.
USG Corp.
Walt Disney Co.
Wells Fargo & Co.
WestLB New York Branch
Weyerhaeuser Co.
Wyman-Gordon Co.
Xerox Corp.

Colorado

ABC, Inc.
Air Products and Chemicals, Inc.
Akzo Nobel Chemicals
Albertson's Inc.
Alcoa Inc.
American United Life Insurance Co.
AMETEK, Inc.
Amgen, Inc.
Anheuser-Busch Companies, Inc.
AT&T Corp.
Bemis Company, Inc.
Ben & Jerry's Homemade, Inc.
Boise Cascade Corp.
Caterpillar Inc.
ChevronTexaco Corp.
Church & Dwight Company, Inc.
D&B
Dow Jones & Company, Inc.
Eastman Kodak Co.
Ecolab, Inc.
E.I. du Pont de Nemours & Co.
Eli Lilly & Co.
Evening Post Publishing Co.
Fluor Corp.
FMC Corp.
Forest Oil Corp.
Fortis, Inc.
Fujitsu America
General Mills, Inc.
Gerber Products Co.
Great-West Life and Annuity Insurance Co.
Hoffmann-La Roche, Inc.
Holnam, Inc.
Illinois Tool Works, Inc.
International Multifoods Corp.
Kemper National Insurance Companies
Kimberly-Clark Corp.
Kinder Morgan
Kroger Co.
Louisiana-Pacific Corp.
Meadwestvaco Corp.

Microsoft Corp.
Minnesota Mining & Manufacturing Co.
Nestle Purina PetCare Co.
Pfizer Inc.
Rockwell Automation Inc.
Rouse Co.
R.R. Donnelley & Sons Co.
SAFECO Corp.
St. Paul Companies, Inc.
Scoular Co.
Scripps Co. (E.W.)
Security Life of Denver Insurance Co.
State Farm Mutual Automobile Insurance Co.
Storage Technology Corp.
Subaru of America, Inc.
Texas Instruments Inc.
Union Pacific Corp.
U.S. Bancorp Piper Jaffray
Valmont Industries, Inc.
Wells Fargo & Co.

Connecticut

ABC, Inc.
Air Products and Chemicals, Inc.
AMETEK, Inc.
Barden Precision Bearings
Barnes Group, Inc.
Bausch & Lomb, Inc.
Ben & Jerry's Homemade, Inc.
Campbell Soup Co.
CIGNA Corp.
Citizens Financial Group, Inc.
Country Curtains, Inc.
Cox Enterprises, Inc.
Crompton Corp.
Eaton Corp.
Ecolab, Inc.
E.I. du Pont de Nemours & Co.
Eli Lilly & Co.
Fannie Mae
FleetBoston Financial Corp.
Fujitsu America
General Motors Corp.
Handy & Harman
Harsco Corp.
Hershey Foods Corp.
Hunt Corp.
Illinois Tool Works, Inc.
International Multifoods Corp.
Johnson & Johnson
Marcus Corp.
Massachusetts Mutual Life Insurance Co.
McClatchy Co.
McCormick & Company, Inc.
Metropolitan Life Insurance Co.
Microsoft Corp.
Minnesota Mining & Manufacturing Co.
Mitsubishi Silicon America
Nestle Purina PetCare Co.
New York Life Insurance Co.
New York Times Co.
Olin Corp.
Pacific Life Insurance Co.
Pfizer Inc.
Phoenix Home Life Mutual Insurance Co.
Rayonier, Inc.
Reader's Digest Association, Inc.
R.R. Donnelley & Sons Co.
St. Paul Companies, Inc.

Salomon Smith Barney Holdings, Inc.
Sara Lee Corp.
Schlumberger Ltd.
Shaw's Supermarkets, Inc.
Shell Oil Co.
Stanley Works
Teleflex, Inc.
Tetley U.S.A., Inc.
Wiremold Co.
Wyman-Gordon Co.
Xerox Corp.

Delaware

Akzo Nobel Chemicals
AMETEK, Inc.
Avon Products, Inc.
CertainTeed Corp.
CIBC World Markets
Country Curtains, Inc.
Dentsply International, Inc.
Duke Energy Corp.
E.I. du Pont de Nemours & Co.
Equifax, Inc.
GE Capital Corp.
General Motors Corp.
Johnson Controls Inc.
J.P. Morgan Chase & Co.
Kimberly-Clark Corp.
New York Life Insurance Co.
St. Paul Companies, Inc.
Sara Lee Corp.
Schering-Plough Corp.
Sovereign Bank
Wilmington Trust Co.

District of Columbia

Air Products and Chemicals, Inc.
American Honda Motor Company, Inc.
Amgen, Inc.
Bechtel Group, Inc.
Ben & Jerry's Homemade, Inc.
BP Amoco Corp.
Burlington Industries, Inc.
Caterpillar Inc.
COMSAT International
Dow Corning Corp.
Dow Jones & Company, Inc.
Eastman Kodak Co.
Ecolab, Inc.
Ethyl Corp.
Fluor Corp.
FMC Corp.
GE Capital Corp.
General Mills, Inc.
Gerber Products Co.
Giant Food, Inc.
Halliburton Co.
Humana, Inc.
Kimberly-Clark Corp.
Kiplinger Washington Editors, Inc.
Meadwestvaco Corp.
Microsoft Corp.
Minnesota Mining & Manufacturing Co.
Niagara Mohawk Holdings, Inc.
Pepco Holdings, Inc.
Pfizer Inc.
Progress Energy Inc.
Prudential Insurance Co. of America
Rouse Co.
Scripps Co. (E.W.)
Shell Oil Co.

Thompson Co. (J. Walter)
TJX Companies, Inc.
Wilkes, Artis, Hedrick & Lane
Xcel Energy
Xerox Corp.

Florida

Air France
Air Products and Chemicals, Inc.
Alcoa Inc.
American United Life Insurance Co.
AMETEK, Inc.
Anheuser-Busch Companies, Inc.
AT&T Corp.
Bausch & Lomb, Inc.
Belk Stores Services, Inc.
Bemis Company, Inc.
Ben & Jerry's Homemade, Inc.
Blue Bell, Inc.
Bridgestone Americas Holding, Inc.
Burnett Co. (Leo)
Canon U.S.A., Inc.
Cargill, Inc.
Carnival Corp.
Caterpillar Inc.
CertainTeed Corp.
ChevronTexaco Corp.
Chicago Tribune Direct Marketing
Church & Dwight Company, Inc.
CNA Financial Corp.
Coca-Cola Co.
Comerica Inc.
Constellation Energy Group, Inc.
Cox Enterprises, Inc.
Crane Co.
D&B
Donaldson Company, Inc.
Dow Jones & Company, Inc.
Eastman Kodak Co.
Eaton Corp.
Ecolab, Inc.
E.I. du Pont de Nemours & Co.
Eli Lilly & Co.
Equifax, Inc.
Fannie Mae
Fifth Third Bancorp
Firstar Bank Milwaukee NA
Florida Rock Industries, Inc.
Florida Rock & Tank Lines
FMC Corp.
Forest City Enterprises, Inc.
Fortis, Inc.
Fuller Co. (H.B.)
GATX Corp.
GE Capital Corp.
General Mills, Inc.
General Motors Corp.
Gerber Products Co.
Halliburton Co.
Harsco Corp.
H.J. Heinz Co.
Hubbard Broadcasting, Inc.
Humana, Inc.
Huntington Bancshares, Inc.
International Multifoods Corp.
Johnson Controls Inc.
Johnson & Johnson
J.P. Morgan Chase & Co.
Kimberly-Clark Corp.
Land O'Lakes, Inc.
Lipton Co.
Louisiana-Pacific Corp.

Macy's East, Inc.
Marcus Corp.
McCormick & Company, Inc.
Meadwestvaco Corp.
Metropolitan Life Insurance Co.
Microsoft Corp.
Minnesota Mining & Manufacturing Co.
Mitsubishi Motor Sales of America, Inc.
Morris Communications Corp.
New York Times Co.
Northern Trust Corp.
Olin Corp.
Ondeo Nalco Co.
L'Oreal U.S.A.
Pacific Life Insurance Co.
Phelps Dodge Corp.
Prudential Insurance Co. of America
Publix Supermarkets
Rockwell Automation Inc.
Rouse Co.
R.R. Donnelley & Sons Co.
St. Paul Companies, Inc.
Sara Lee Corp.
Schering-Plough Corp.
Scoular Co.
Scripps Co. (E.W.)
Security Life of Denver Insurance Co.
Shell Oil Co.
Sherwin-Williams Co.
Smith Corp. (A.O.)
Square D Co.
Stanley Works
Storage Technology Corp.
Subaru of America, Inc.
SunTrust Banks of Florida
Teleflex, Inc.
Terumo Medical Corp.
Tetley U.S.A., Inc.
Texas Instruments Inc.
Thompson Co. (J. Walter)
TJX Companies, Inc.
United States Sugar Corp.
United States Trust Co. of New York
Universal Studios
USG Corp.
Walt Disney Co.
West Pharmaceutical Services, Inc.
Weyerhaeuser Co.
Winn-Dixie Stores Inc.

Georgia

Air Products and Chemicals, Inc.
Akzo Nobel Chemicals
Alcoa Inc.
American Honda Motor Company, Inc.
American United Life Insurance Co.
Anheuser-Busch Companies, Inc.
Appleton Papers, Inc.
Barnes Group, Inc.
Bausch & Lomb, Inc.
Belk Stores Services, Inc.
Birds Eye Foods, Inc.
Bridgestone Americas Holding, Inc.
Brunswick Corp.
Burlington Industries, Inc.
California Bank & Trust
Campbell Soup Co.
Caterpillar Inc.

Central Soya Co.
CertainTeed Corp.
ChevronTexaco Corp.
Chicago Tribune Direct Marketing
Church & Dwight Company, Inc.
CIBC World Markets
CIT Group, Inc.
Citizens Financial Group, Inc.
CLARCOR, Inc.
Clorox Co.
Cox Enterprises, Inc.
CUNA Mutual Group
Deere & Co.
Dow Corning Corp.
Dow Jones & Company, Inc.
Eastman Kodak Co.
Ecolab, Inc.
E.I. du Pont de Nemours & Co.
Elf Atochem North America, Inc.
Eli Lilly & Co.
Equifax, Inc.
Fannie Mae
Federated Mutual Insurance Co.
FMC Corp.
Fortis, Inc.
Fuller Co. (H.B.)
GE Capital Corp.
GenAmerica Financial Corp.
General Motors Corp.
Georgia Power Co.
Gerber Products Co.
Gillette Co.
Harsco Corp.
Hartmarx Corp.
Henkel Corp.
H.J. Heinz Co.
HON Industries, Inc.
ING North America Insurance Corp.
International Multifoods Corp.
Interstate/Johnson Lane
Johnson Controls Inc.
Johnson & Johnson
Johnson & Son (S.C.)
Kajima International, Inc.
Kawasaki Motors Manufacturing Corporation U.S.A.
Kimberly-Clark Corp.
Kroger Co.
Liz Claiborne, Inc.
Louisiana-Pacific Corp.
Macy's East, Inc.
Magna International of America, Inc.
Meadwestvaco Corp.
Minnesota Mining & Manufacturing Co.
National Service Industries, Inc.
New York Life Insurance Co.
Nordson Corp.
Oki America, Inc.
Olin Corp.
Ondeo Nalco Co.
Pfizer Inc.
Phelps Dodge Corp.
Polaroid Corp.
Prudential Insurance Co. of America
Quaker Chemical Corp.
Reader's Digest Association, Inc.
Rexam, Inc.
Rich Products Corp.
Rockwell Automation Inc.
Rouse Co.
R.R. Donnelley & Sons Co.

SAFECO Corp.
Salomon Smith Barney Holdings, Inc.
Sara Lee Corp.
Schering-Plough Corp.
Schlumberger Ltd.
Scottsman Industries
Scripps Co. (E.W.)
Security Life of Denver Insurance Co.
Shell Oil Co.
Sherwin-Williams Co.
Sonoco Products Co.
SPX Corp.
Square D Co.
Stanley Works
State Farm Mutual Automobile Insurance Co.
Subaru of America, Inc.
Tetley U.S.A., Inc.
Texas Instruments Inc.
Thompson Co. (J. Walter)
TJX Companies, Inc.
USG Corp.
Vulcan Materials Co.
Weyerhaeuser Co.
Winn-Dixie Stores Inc.
Winter Construction Co.
Xerox Corp.

Hawaii

ChevronTexaco Corp.
Eastman Kodak Co.
Ecolab, Inc.
First Hawaiian, Inc.
General Mills, Inc.
Gerber Products Co.
Kimberly-Clark Corp.
Lee Enterprises, Inc.
Meadwestvaco Corp.
Metropolitan Life Insurance Co.
Minnesota Mining & Manufacturing Co.
Ondeo Nalco Co.
Shell Oil Co.
Subaru of America, Inc.
Unocal Corp.
Weyerhaeuser Co.

Idaho

Albertson's Inc.
American Honda Motor Company, Inc.
Anheuser-Busch Companies, Inc.
Avista Corp.
Boise Cascade Corp.
Cargill, Inc.
Eastman Kodak Co.
Equifax, Inc.
Evening Post Publishing Co.
FMC Corp.
General Mills, Inc.
Gerber Products Co.
H.J. Heinz Co.
Intermountain Gas Co.
Kimberly-Clark Corp.
Land O'Lakes, Inc.
Louisiana-Pacific Corp.
Meadwestvaco Corp.
St. Paul Companies, Inc.
Union Pacific Corp.
U.S. Bancorp Piper Jaffray

Illinois

Abbott Laboratories
ABC, Inc.
Air Products and Chemicals, Inc.
Akzo Nobel Chemicals

Albertson's Inc.
Alcoa Inc.
American Standard Inc.
American United Life Insurance Co.
AMETEK, Inc.
AMP, Inc.
Anheuser-Busch Companies, Inc.
Archer-Daniels-Midland Co.
Avon Products, Inc.
Bank of New York Company, Inc.
Barnes Group, Inc.
Bausch & Lomb, Inc.
Bemis Company, Inc.
Ben & Jerry's Homemade, Inc.
Birds Eye Foods, Inc.
Borden, Inc.
Bowater, Inc.
BP Amoco Corp.
Bridgestone Americas Holding, Inc.
Brunswick Corp.
Burlington Industries, Inc.
California Bank & Trust
Campbell Soup Co.
Canon U.S.A., Inc.
Cargill, Inc.
Caterpillar Inc.
Chicago Rawhide Co.
Chicago Tribune Direct Marketing
CIBC World Markets
CIT Group, Inc.
CLARCOR, Inc.
Clorox Co.
Coca-Cola Co.
Comerica Inc.
Commonwealth Edison Co.
Copley Press, Inc.
Cox Enterprises, Inc.
Crane Co.
Crompton Corp.
D&B
Donaldson Company, Inc.
Dow Jones & Company, Inc.
Eastman Kodak Co.
Eaton Corp.
Ebsco Industries, Inc.
Ecolab, Inc.
E.I. du Pont de Nemours & Co.
Employers Mutual Casualty Co.
Equifax, Inc.
Fannie Mae
Firstar Bank Milwaukee NA
Florsheim Group Co.
Fluor Corp.
FMC Corp.
Fortis, Inc.
Fortune Brands, Inc.
Fuller Co. (H.B.)
GATX Corp.
GE Capital Corp.
General Mills, Inc.
General Motors Corp.
Gerber Products Co.
Gillette Co.
HarperCollins Publishers, Inc.
Harsco Corp.
Hartmarx Corp.
Henkel Corp.
H.J. Heinz Co.
Ideal Industries, Inc.
Illinois Tool Works, Inc.
International Multifoods Corp.
J&L Specialty Steel, Inc.
Johns Manville
Johnson Controls Inc.

Johnson & Johnson
Johnson & Son (S.C.)
Jostens, Inc.
J.P. Morgan Chase & Co.
Kajima International, Inc.
Kemper National Insurance Companies
Kimberly-Clark Corp.
Korte Construction Co.
Lee Enterprises, Inc.
Louisiana-Pacific Corp.
Magna International of America, Inc.
Marcus Corp.
Maritz, Inc.
Mattel Inc.
McCormick & Company, Inc.
McWane Corp.
Meadwestvaco Corp.
Metropolitan Life Insurance Co.
Microsoft Corp.
Minnesota Mining & Manufacturing Co.
Mitsubishi Motor Sales of America, Inc.
Mitsubishi Silicon America
New York Times Co.
NLI International, Inc.
Northern Trust Corp.
Olin Corp.
Ondeo Nalco Co.
Pamida, Inc.
Peoples Energy Corp.
Pfizer Inc.
Polaroid Corp.
Prudential Insurance Co. of America
Prudential Securities, Inc.
Quanex Corp.
Quincy Newspapers
Reichhold Chemicals, Inc.
Rexam, Inc.
Rockwell Automation Inc.
R.R. Donnelley & Sons Co.
SAFECO Corp.
St. Paul Companies, Inc.
Sara Lee Corp.
Schering-Plough Corp.
Scottsman Industries
Scoular Co.
Shell Oil Co.
Sherwin-Williams Co.
Smith Corp. (A.O.)
Southwest News Herald
SPX Corp.
Square D Co.
State Farm Mutual Automobile Insurance Co.
Stora Enso
Storage Technology Corp.
Subaru of America, Inc.
Swift Print Communications
Texas Instruments Inc.
Thompson Co. (J. Walter)
Universal Studios
USG Corp.
Valmont Industries, Inc.
Vulcan Materials Co.
WestLB New York Branch
Weyerhaeuser Co.
Xerox Corp.

Indiana

1st Source Corp.
Air Products and Chemicals, Inc.
Alcoa Inc.
Amcast Industrial Corp.
American Honda Motor Company, Inc.

American United Life Insurance Co.
AMP, Inc.
Andersons, Inc.
Archer-Daniels-Midland Co.
Auburn Foundry
Ben & Jerry's Homemade, Inc.
Bridgestone Americas Holding, Inc.
Campbell Soup Co.
Caterpillar Inc.
Central Soya Co.
ChevronTexaco Corp.
Chicago Rawhide Co.
CLARCOR, Inc.
Conseco, Inc.
Crompton Corp.
Cummins, Inc.
Donaldson Company, Inc.
Dow Jones & Company, Inc.
Eaton Corp.
Ecolab, Inc.
E.I. du Pont de Nemours & Co.
Eli Lilly & Co.
Fifth Third Bancorp
Ford Meter Box Co.
Fuller Co. (H.B.)
GATX Corp.
General Motors Corp.
Gerber Products Co.
Harsco Corp.
Hartmarx Corp.
Huntington Bancshares, Inc.
Indianapolis Newspapers, Inc.
International Multifoods Corp.
Johnson Controls Inc.
Kroger Co.
Lehigh Cement Co.
Liberty Corp.
Marcus Corp.
McCormick & Company, Inc.
Meadwestvaco Corp.
Microsoft Corp.
Minnesota Mining & Manufacturing Co.
Ondeo Nalco Co.
L'Oreal U.S.A.
Pfizer Inc.
Phelps Dodge Corp.
Pulitzer, Inc.
Rexam, Inc.
R.R. Donnelley & Sons Co.
St. Paul Companies, Inc.
Sara Lee Corp.
Schering-Plough Corp.
Scripps Co. (E.W.)
Shell Oil Co.
Sherwin-Williams Co.
South Bend Tribune Corp.
SPX Corp.
Square D Co.
Stanley Works
State Farm Mutual Automobile Insurance Co.
Subaru of America, Inc.
Texas Instruments Inc.
USG Corp.
Valmont Industries, Inc.
Vulcan Materials Co.
Whirlpool Corp.

Iowa

Air Products and Chemicals, Inc.
Alcoa Inc.
American Honda Motor Company, Inc.
Appleton Papers, Inc.

Archer-Daniels-Midland Co.
Birds Eye Foods, Inc.
Bridgestone Americas Holding, Inc.
CertainTeed Corp.
Chesapeake Corp.
Citizens First National Bank
Cox Enterprises, Inc.
Crompton Corp.
Cummins, Inc.
CUNA Mutual Group
Deere & Co.
Donaldson Company, Inc.
Dow Corning Corp.
Dow Jones & Company, Inc.
Eaton Corp.
Ecolab, Inc.
E.I. du Pont de Nemours & Co.
Elf Atochem North America, Inc.
Eli Lilly & Co.
Employers Mutual Casualty Co.
Fannie Mae
Firstar Bank Milwaukee NA
FMC Corp.
Fortune Brands, Inc.
Gazette Co.
General Mills, Inc.
General Motors Corp.
Harsco Corp.
Hickory Tech Corp.
H.J. Heinz Co.
Holnam, Inc.
HON Industries, Inc.
Iowa Savings Bank
Land O'Lakes, Inc.
Lee Enterprises, Inc.
Lipton Co.
Lisle Corp.
Magna International of America, Inc.
Marcus Corp.
McWane Corp.
Minnesota Mining & Manufacturing Co.
Ondeo Nalco Co.
Owen Industries
Pamida, Inc.
Pella Corp.
Pitt-Des Moines, Inc.
Principal Financial Group
Quanex Corp.
Rockwell Automation Inc.
Rouse Co.
Sara Lee Corp.
Sheaffer Pen Corp.
Square D Co.
U.S. Bancorp Piper Jaffray
USG Corp.
Vulcan Materials Co.
Weyerhaeuser Co.
Winnebago Industries

Kansas

Abbott Laboratories
Air Products and Chemicals, Inc.
American United Life Insurance Co.
Appleton Papers, Inc.
Archer-Daniels-Midland Co.
Bemis Company, Inc.
Blue Bell, Inc.
BP Amoco Corp.
Burlington Industries, Inc.
CertainTeed Corp.
Chicago Rawhide Co.
Crompton Corp.
Deere & Co.

Donaldson Company, Inc.
Eastman Kodak Co.
Eaton Corp.
Ecolab, Inc.
E.I. du Pont de Nemours & Co.
Equifax, Inc.
Excel Corp.
FMC Corp.
Fortis, Inc.
General Mills, Inc.
General Motors Corp.
Humana, Inc.
International Multifoods Corp.
Johns Manville
Johnson Controls Inc.
Jostens, Inc.
Koch Industries, Inc.
Macy's East, Inc.
Maritz, Inc.
McCormick & Company, Inc.
Metropolitan Life Insurance Co.
Morris Communications Corp.
Ondeo Nalco Co.
Pamida, Inc.
PepsiCo Inc.
PPG Industries, Inc.
Royal & SunAlliance USA, Inc.
St. Paul Companies, Inc.
Sara Lee Corp.
Scoular Co.
Security Benefit Life Insurance Co.
Security Life of Denver Insurance Co.
Sherwin-Williams Co.
Smith Corp. (A.O.)
Stanley Works
Texas Instruments Inc.
Union Pacific Corp.
U.S. Bancorp Piper Jaffray
Yellow Corp.

Kentucky

Air Products and Chemicals, Inc.
Akzo Nobel Chemicals
Alcoa Inc.
American General Finance
American Standard Inc.
American United Life Insurance Co.
Amgen, Inc.
Appleton Papers, Inc.
Ben & Jerry's Homemade, Inc.
Berwind Group
Borden, Inc.
BP Amoco Corp.
Chesapeake Corp.
CLARCOR, Inc.
Community Trust Bancorp, Inc.
Dow Corning Corp.
Eastman Kodak Co.
E.I. du Pont de Nemours & Co.
Elf Atochem North America, Inc.
Eli Lilly & Co.
Fidelity Investments
Fifth Third Bancorp
Fluor Corp.
Fortune Brands, Inc.
Fuller Co. (H.B.)
General Motors Corp.
Harsco Corp.
Hartmarx Corp.

Hershey Foods Corp.
HON Industries, Inc.
Humana, Inc.
Hunt Corp.
Huntington Bancshares, Inc.
International Multifoods Corp.
Johnson Controls Inc.
LG&E Energy Corp.
Liberty Corp.
Marcus Corp.
Meadwestvaco Corp.
Minnesota Mining & Manufacturing Co.
Mosinee Paper Corp.
National City Corp.
Nestle Purina PetCare Co.
New York Times Co.
Oshkosh B'Gosh, Inc.
PepsiCo Inc.
Phelps Dodge Corp.
Pulitzer, Inc.
Rockwell Automation Inc.
Rouse Co.
R.R. Donnelley & Sons Co.
Sara Lee Corp.
Shell Oil Co.
Smith Corp. (A.O.)
Square D Co.
Texas Instruments Inc.
Thomas Industries
Vogt Machine Co. (Henry)
Vulcan Materials Co.
Weyerhaeuser Co.
Winn-Dixie Stores Inc.

Louisiana

Air Products and Chemicals, Inc.
Alcoa Inc.
Anheuser-Busch Companies, Inc.
Belo Corp.
Blue Bell, Inc.
Boise Cascade Corp.
Borden, Inc.
CertainTeed Corp.
ChevronTexaco Corp.
Cox Enterprises, Inc.
Cranston Print Works Co.
Crompton Corp.
D&B
Donaldson Company, Inc.
Eastman Kodak Co.
Ecolab, Inc.
E.I. du Pont de Nemours & Co.
Eli Lilly & Co.
FMC Corp.
Freeport-McMoRan Copper & Gold, Inc.
GATX Corp.
General Motors Corp.
Harsco Corp.
Holnam, Inc.
Johnson Controls Inc.
Kansas City Southern Railway
Louisiana-Pacific Corp.
New York Times Co.
Olin Corp.
Ondeo Nalco Co.
Phelps Dodge Corp.
PPG Industries, Inc.
Prudential Insurance Co. of America
Rockwell Automation Inc.
Rouse Co.
Schering-Plough Corp.
Shell Oil Co.
Southwestern Electric Power Co.

State Farm Mutual Automobile Insurance Co.
Union Pacific Corp.
Unocal Corp.
USG Corp.
Vulcan Materials Co.
Winn-Dixie Stores Inc.

Maine

Bausch & Lomb, Inc.
Bowater, Inc.
Central Maine Power Co.
Corning Inc.
Ecolab, Inc.
Hannaford Brothers Co.
Johns Manville
Kimberly-Clark Corp.
Louisiana-Pacific Corp.
New York Times Co.
Ondeo Nalco Co.
Rexam, Inc.
Royal & SunAlliance USA, Inc.
R.R. Donnelley & Sons Co.
Shaw's Supermarkets, Inc.
U.S. Bancorp Piper Jaffray
Webber Oil Co.
Weyerhaeuser Co.

Maryland

Air Products and Chemicals, Inc.
Alcon Laboratories, Inc.
American United Life Insurance Co.
Aon Corp.
Belk Stores Services, Inc.
Borden, Inc.
BP Amoco Corp.
Chesapeake Corp.
ChevronTexaco Corp.
Clorox Co.
COMSAT International
Constellation Energy Group, Inc.
Country Curtains, Inc.
D&B
Dow Jones & Company, Inc.
Eastman Kodak Co.
Eaton Corp.
Ebsco Industries, Inc.
Ecolab, Inc.
Eli Lilly & Co.
Equifax, Inc.
FMC Corp.
Fortis, Inc.
Fuller Co. (H.B.)
General Motors Corp.
Gerber Products Co.
Giant Food, Inc.
Giant Food Stores
Halliburton Co.
Harsco Corp.
Johnson Controls Inc.
Johnson & Son (S.C.)
J.P. Morgan Chase & Co.
Kimberly-Clark Corp.
Kiplinger Washington Editors, Inc.
M/A-COM, Inc.
McCormick & Company, Inc.
Minnesota Mining & Manufacturing Co.
Pepco Holdings, Inc.
Perdue Farms
Peter Kiewit Sons' Inc.
Price Associates (T. Rowe)
Procter & Gamble Company, Cosmetics Division
Rexam, Inc.
Rouse Co.

Royal & SunAlliance USA, Inc.
Scripps Co. (E.W.)
Shell Oil Co.
Sherwin-Williams Co.
Smith Corp. (A.O.)
Subaru of America, Inc.
Terumo Medical Corp.
Texas Instruments Inc.
USG Corp.
Weyerhaeuser Co.
Williams Companies Inc.

Massachusetts

Abbott Laboratories
ABC, Inc.
Air Products and Chemicals, Inc.
Allmerica Financial Corp.
American Honda Motor Company, Inc.
American Optical Corp.
AMP, Inc.
Anheuser-Busch Companies, Inc.
Bausch & Lomb, Inc.
Ben & Jerry's Homemade, Inc.
Berwind Group
Boston Globe (The)
Bridgestone Americas Holding, Inc.
Cabot Corp.
Cargill, Inc.
CertainTeed Corp.
Church & Dwight Company, Inc.
Citizens Financial Group, Inc.
Corning Inc.
Country Curtains, Inc.
Cox Enterprises, Inc.
Cranston Print Works Co.
Demoulas Supermarkets, Inc.
Dow Jones & Company, Inc.
Dunkin' Donuts, Inc.
Eastern Bank
Eastman Kodak Co.
Eaton Corp.
Ecolab, Inc.
E.I. du Pont de Nemours & Co.
Elf Atochem North America, Inc.
Eli Lilly & Co.
Equifax, Inc.
Erving Industries
Fannie Mae
Fidelity Investments
FleetBoston Financial Corp.
Fortis, Inc.
Fortune Brands, Inc.
Fuller Co. (H.B.)
General Mills, Inc.
General Motors Corp.
Gerber Products Co.
Giant Food Stores
Gillette Co.
Golub Corp.
HarperCollins Publishers, Inc.
H.J. Heinz Co.
Hyde Manufacturing Co.
Illinois Tool Works, Inc.
International Multifoods Corp.
John Hancock Financial Services
Johnson Controls Inc.
Johnson & Johnson
Kimberly-Clark Corp.
M/A-COM, Inc.
Marcus Corp.
Meadwestvaco Corp.

Microsoft Corp.
Millipore Corp.
Minnesota Mining & Manufacturing Co.
New York Times Co.
NLI International, Inc.
NSTAR
Ondeo Nalco Co.
Pacific Life Insurance Co.
Pfizer Inc.
Phoenix Home Life Mutual Insurance Co.
Polaroid Corp.
Providence Gas Co.
Providence Journal-Bulletin Co.
Prudential Insurance Co. of America
Prudential Securities, Inc.
Rayonier, Inc.
Rexam, Inc.
Rockwell Automation Inc.
Rouse Co.
Royal & SunAlliance USA, Inc.
R.R. Donnelley & Sons Co.
St. Paul Companies, Inc.
Salomon Smith Barney Holdings, Inc.
Security Life of Denver Insurance Co.
Shaw's Supermarkets, Inc.
Shell Oil Co.
Square D Co.
Stanley Works
Subaru of America, Inc.
Texas Instruments Inc.
TJX Companies, Inc.
United States Trust Co. of New York
USG Corp.
Wyman-Gordon Co.

Michigan

Abbott Laboratories
ABC, Inc.
Air Products and Chemicals, Inc.
Akzo Nobel Chemicals
Alcoa Inc.
Amcast Industrial Corp.
American Honda Motor Company, Inc.
American United Life Insurance Co.
AMETEK, Inc.
AMP, Inc.
Andersons, Inc.
Archer-Daniels-Midland Co.
Barnes Group, Inc.
Bausch & Lomb, Inc.
Bemis Company, Inc.
Berwind Group
Birds Eye Foods, Inc.
BP Amoco Corp.
Bridgestone Americas Holding, Inc.
Campbell Soup Co.
Carris Reels
CertainTeed Corp.
Cleveland-Cliffs, Inc.
Comerica Inc.
Cox Enterprises, Inc.
Crompton Corp.
CUNA Mutual Group
Donaldson Company, Inc.
Dow Corning Corp.
Dow Jones & Company, Inc.
Eastman Kodak Co.
Eaton Corp.
Ecolab, Inc.

E.I. du Pont de Nemours & Co.
Elf Atochem North America, Inc.
Equifax, Inc.
Ethyl Corp.
Fannie Mae
Farmer Jack Supermarkets
FMC Corp.
Fortis, Inc.
Fuller Co. (H.B.)
General Motors Corp.
Gerber Products Co.
Handy & Harman
HarperCollins Publishers, Inc.
Hexcel Corp.
H.J. Heinz Co.
Holnam, Inc.
Huntington Bancshares, Inc.
Illinois Tool Works, Inc.
Interkal, Inc.
International Multifoods Corp.
Johnson Controls Inc.
JSJ Corp.
Kawasaki Motors Manufacturing Corporation U.S.A.
Kimberly-Clark Corp.
Kroger Co.
La-Z-Boy, Inc.
Louisiana-Pacific Corp.
Magna International of America, Inc.
Marcus Corp.
Maritz, Inc.
McCormick & Company, Inc.
Meadwestvaco Corp.
Metropolitan Life Insurance Co.
Minnesota Mining & Manufacturing Co.
Mitsubishi Motor Sales of America, Inc.
Ondeo Nalco Co.
Pamida, Inc.
Pfizer Inc.
Prudential Insurance Co. of America
Quaker Chemical Corp.
Quanex Corp.
R&B Machine Tool Co.
Reichhold Chemicals, Inc.
Rockwell Automation Inc.
Rouse Co.
Sara Lee Corp.
Schlumberger Ltd.
Scottsman Industries
Scripps Co. (E.W.)
Shell Oil Co.
Sherwin-Williams Co.
Simpson Investment Co.
Smith Corp. (A.O.)
SPX Corp.
Stanley Works
State Farm Mutual Automobile Insurance Co.
Steelcase Inc.
Teleflex Inc.
Texas Instruments Inc.
Thompson Co. (J. Walter)
Todd Co. (A.M.)
Universal Studios
Vulcan Materials Co.
Whirlpool Corp.

Minnesota

ABC, Inc.
ADC Telecommunications
American United Life Insurance Co.
Anheuser-Busch Companies, Inc.

Archer-Daniels-Midland Co.
Banta Corp.
Bausch & Lomb, Inc.
Boise Cascade Corp.
Bridgestone Americas Holding, Inc.
Cargill, Inc.
CenterPoint Energy, Inc.
CertainTeed Corp.
Church & Dwight Company, Inc.
Clorox Co.
Cummins, Inc.
Deere & Co.
Eastman Kodak Co.
Ebsco Industries, Inc.
Ecolab, Inc.
Elf Atochem North America, Inc.
Eli Lilly & Co.
Equifax, Inc.
Excel Corp.
Fannie Mae
Federated Mutual Insurance Co.
Firstar Bank Milwaukee NA
FMC Corp.
Forest City Enterprises, Inc.
Fortis, Inc.
Fuller Co. (H.B.)
General Mills, Inc.
Gerber Products Co.
Gillette Co.
Harsco Corp.
Hickory Tech Corp.
Homecrest Industries, Inc.
Hubbard Broadcasting, Inc.
International Multifoods Corp.
Jostens, Inc.
Land O'Lakes, Inc.
Lee Enterprises, Inc.
Lehigh Cement Co.
Marcus Corp.
McClatchy Co.
Meadwestvaco Corp.
Microsoft Corp.
Minnesota Mining & Manufacturing Co.
Morris Communications Corp.
Nestle Purina PetCare Co.
Ondeo Nalco Co.
L'Oreal U.S.A.
Pfizer Inc.
Rahr Malting Co.
Regis Corp.
Rexam, Inc.
Rouse Co.
R.R. Donnelley & Sons Co.
St. Paul Companies, Inc.
Sara Lee Corp.
Scoular Co.
Seneca Foods Corp.
Shell Oil Co.
Stanley Works
State Farm Mutual Automobile Insurance Co.
TCF National Bank Minnesota
Texas Instruments Inc.
U.S. Bancorp Piper Jaffray
USG Corp.
Weyerhaeuser Co.
Xcel Energy

Mississippi

Air Products and Chemicals, Inc.
Akzo Nobel Chemicals
Alcoa Inc.
Barnes Group, Inc.

Belk Stores Services, Inc.
Blue Bell, Inc.
Borden, Inc.
Caterpillar Inc.
ChevronTexaco Corp.
Clorox Co.
Crompton Corp.
D&B
Eastman Kodak Co.
E.I. du Pont de Nemours & Co.
Eli Lilly & Co.
Fannie Mae
FMC Corp.
General Motors Corp.
Holnam, Inc.
Kansas City Southern Railway
Kimberly-Clark Corp.
La-Z-Boy, Inc.
Louisiana-Pacific Corp.
Magna International of America, Inc.
Mosinee Paper Corp.
New York Times Co.
Ondeo Nalco Co.
Prudential Insurance Co. of America
Quanex Corp.
R.R. Donnelley & Sons Co.
Sara Lee Corp.
Shell Oil Co.
SPX Corp.
Stanley Works
Thomasville Furniture Industries, Inc.
USG Corp.
Weyerhaeuser Co.

Missouri

ABC, Inc.
Air Products and Chemicals, Inc.
Alcoa Inc.
Ameren Corp.
American United Life Insurance Co.
Anheuser-Busch Companies, Inc.
Bakewell Corp.
Bank of New York Company, Inc.
Banta Corp.
Bausch & Lomb, Inc.
Chicago Rawhide Co.
Church & Dwight Company, Inc.
Clorox Co.
Commerce Bancshares, Inc.
Cox Enterprises, Inc.
Crane Co.
Deere & Co.
Donaldson Company, Inc.
Dow Jones & Company, Inc.
Eastman Kodak Co.
Eaton Corp.
Ecolab, Inc.
Elf Atochem North America, Inc.
Eli Lilly & Co.
Fannie Mae
Fluor Corp.
Fortis, Inc.
GenAmerica Financial Corp.
General Mills, Inc.
General Motors Corp.
Hartmarx Corp.
Humana, Inc.
International Multifoods Corp.
Johnson Controls Inc.

Kansas City Southern Railway
Kimberly-Clark Corp.
Korte Construction Co.
Magna International of America, Inc.
Marcus Corp.
Maritz, Inc.
McCormick & Company, Inc.
Meadwestvaco Corp.
Microsoft Corp.
Minnesota Mining & Manufacturing Co.
Morris Communications Corp.
Nestle Purina PetCare Co.
New England Business Service
Olin Corp.
Ondeo Nalco Co.
Pamida, Inc.
Prudential Insurance Co. of America
Pulitzer, Inc.
Rexam, Inc.
Rockwell Automation Inc.
Rouse Co.
SAFECO Corp.
Sara Lee Corp.
Schering-Plough Corp.
Scoular Co.
Scripps Co. (E.W.)
Shell Oil Co.
Shelter Mutual Insurance Co.
Square D Co.
Stanley Works
State Farm Mutual Automobile Insurance Co.
Swift Print Communications
Tetley U.S.A., Inc.
Texas Instruments Inc.
Thompson Co. (J. Walter)
Union Pacific Corp.
U.S. Bancorp Piper Jaffray
USG Corp.
Weyerhaeuser Co.

Montana

American General Finance
Boise Cascade Corp.
Evening Post Publishing Co.
General Mills, Inc.
Land O'Lakes, Inc.
Lee Enterprises, Inc.
Louisiana-Pacific Corp.
PacifiCorp
Pamida, Inc.
St. Paul Companies, Inc.
U.S. Bancorp Piper Jaffray

Nebraska

Air Products and Chemicals, Inc.
Archer-Daniels-Midland Co.
Bausch & Lomb, Inc.
Bemis Company, Inc.
Campbell Soup Co.
CLARCOR, Inc.
Commerce Bancshares, Inc.
Cox Enterprises, Inc.
Crompton Corp.
Eaton Corp.
Ecolab, Inc.
Eli Lilly & Co.
Fannie Mae
FMC Corp.
Hershey Foods Corp.
IBP
Kinder Morgan
Land O'Lakes, Inc.
Lee Enterprises, Inc.

Magna International of America, Inc.
Marcus Corp.
Minnesota Mining & Manufacturing Co.
Pamida, Inc.
Pfizer Inc.
Physicians Mutual Insurance Co.
Principal Financial Group
Prudential Insurance Co. of America
Pulitzer, Inc.
Rockwell Automation Inc.
Schering-Plough Corp.
Scoular Co.
Square D Co.
State Farm Mutual Automobile Insurance Co.
Union Pacific Corp.
U.S. Bancorp Piper Jaffray
Valmont Industries, Inc.
Wells Fargo Bank Nebraska, N.A.
West Pharmaceutical Services, Inc.

Nevada

American Standard Inc.
Bechtel Group, Inc.
Crompton Corp.
Eastman Kodak Co.
Ecolab, Inc.
FMC Corp.
General Mills, Inc.
Landmark Communications, Inc.
Louisiana-Pacific Corp.
Meadwestvaco Corp.
R.R. Donnelley & Sons Co.
Sara Lee Corp.
Shell Oil Co.
Sherwin-Williams Co.
Sierra Pacific Resources
USG Corp.
Wyman-Gordon Co.

New Hampshire

Anheuser-Busch Companies, Inc.
Bausch & Lomb, Inc.
Clorox Co.
Demoulas Supermarkets, Inc.
Ecolab, Inc.
Forest City Enterprises, Inc.
General Motors Corp.
J&L Specialty Steel, Inc.
Johnson Controls Inc.
Kingsbury Corp.
Lydall, Inc.
Millipore Corp.
New England Business Service
Royal & SunAlliance USA, Inc.
Shaw's Supermarkets, Inc.
Stanley Works
Teleflex, Inc.
Unitrode Corp.
Wyman-Gordon Co.

New Jersey

Abbott Laboratories
Air Products and Chemicals, Inc.
Akzo Nobel Chemicals
American General Finance
American Standard Inc.
American United Life Insurance Co.

Anheuser-Busch Companies, Inc.
Aon Corp.
AT&T Corp.
Ballet Makers
Barnes Group, Inc.
Bausch & Lomb, Inc.
Bechtel Group, Inc.
Bemis Company, Inc.
Berwind Group
Birds Eye Foods, Inc.
Borden, Inc.
BP Amoco Corp.
Canon U.S.A., Inc.
Chesapeake Corp.
CIT Group, Inc.
Country Curtains, Inc.
Crompton Corp.
D&B
Dow Corning Corp.
Dow Jones & Company, Inc.
Dreyfus Corp.
Eastman Kodak Co.
Ebsco Industries, Inc.
E.I. du Pont de Nemours & Co.
Eli Lilly & Co.
Equifax, Inc.
Exelon
FleetBoston Financial Corp.
Fluor Corp.
FMC Corp.
Fortis, Inc.
Fujitsu America
General Motors Corp.
Gerber Products Co.
Handy & Harman
Harsco Corp.
Hasbro, Inc.
H.J. Heinz Co.
Hoffmann-La Roche, Inc.
Illinois Tool Works, Inc.
International Multifoods Corp.
J&L Specialty Steel, Inc.
Jaydor Corp.
Johns Manville
Johnson Controls Inc.
Johnson & Johnson
Johnson & Son (S.C.)
Kajima International, Inc.
Kimberly-Clark Corp.
Lipton Co.
Liz Claiborne, Inc.
Macy's East, Inc.
McCormick & Company, Inc.
Metropolitan Life Insurance Co.
Minnesota Mining & Manufacturing Co.
Mitsubishi Motor Sales of America, Inc.
MONY Group, Inc.
New York Life Insurance Co.
New York Times Co.
Oki America, Inc.
Olin Corp.
Ondeo Nalco Co.
Phelps Dodge Corp.
Polaroid Corp.
Prudential Insurance Co. of America
Prudential Securities, Inc.
Public Service Electric & Gas Co.
Rayonier, Inc.
Reichhold Chemicals, Inc.
Rexam, Inc.
Rich Products Corp.
R.J. Reynolds Tobacco
Rockwell Automation Inc.
Rouse Co.

Royal & SunAlliance USA, Inc.
St. Paul Companies, Inc.
Sara Lee Corp.
Schering-Plough Corp.
Shaw's Supermarkets, Inc.
Shell Oil Co.
Sherwin-Williams Co.
Sovereign Bank
Square D Co.
Subaru of America, Inc.
Terumo Medical Corp.
Thompson Co. (J. Walter)
U.S. Bancorp Piper Jaffray
Universal Studios
USG Corp.
Walt Disney Co.
Weyerhaeuser Co.
Williams Companies Inc.

New Mexico

Air Products and Chemicals, Inc.
Borden, Inc.
ChevronTexaco Corp.
Ecolab, Inc.
E.I. du Pont de Nemours & Co.
Equifax, Inc.
FMC Corp.
Hershey Foods Corp.
Hubbard Broadcasting, Inc.
International Multifoods Corp.
Lee Enterprises, Inc.
Marcus Corp.
Phelps Dodge Corp.
Pittsburg & Midway Coal Mining Co.
PNM Resources, Inc.
Pulitzer, Inc.
Sara Lee Corp.
Scripps Co. (E.W.)
Unocal Corp.

New York

Abbott Laboratories
ABC, Inc.
Air Products and Chemicals, Inc.
Akzo Nobel Chemicals
Alcoa Inc.
American Standard Inc.
AMETEK, Inc.
Anheuser-Busch Companies, Inc.
Appleton Papers, Inc.
AT&T Corp.
Avon Products, Inc.
Bank of New York Company, Inc.
Barnes Group, Inc.
Bausch & Lomb, Inc.
Bemis Company, Inc.
Ben & Jerry's Homemade, Inc.
Berwind Group
Birds Eye Foods, Inc.
BP Amoco Corp.
Bridgestone Americas Holding, Inc.
Burlington Industries, Inc.
Burnett Co. (Leo)
California Bank & Trust
Campbell Soup Co.
Canon U.S.A., Inc.
CertainTeed Corp.
Chesapeake Corp.
Chicago Tribune Direct Marketing
Christian Dior Perfumes, Inc.
CIBC World Markets

CIT Group, Inc.
Citizens Financial Group, Inc.
ContiGroup Companies, Inc.
Corning Inc.
Country Curtains, Inc.
Cox Enterprises, Inc.
Crane Co.
Cranston Print Works Co.
Credit Suisse First Boston Corp.
Crompton Corp.
Cummins, Inc.
CUNA Mutual Group
D&B
Deere & Co.
Donaldson Company, Inc.
Dow Jones & Company, Inc.
Eastman Kodak Co.
Eaton Corp.
Ecolab, Inc.
E.I. du Pont de Nemours & Co.
Elf Atochem North America, Inc.
Eli Lilly & Co.
Equifax, Inc.
Ethyl Corp.
Evening Post Publishing Co.
Fannie Mae
FleetBoston Financial Corp.
FMC Corp.
Forest City Enterprises, Inc.
Fortis, Inc.
Fortune Brands, Inc.
Fujitsu America
Fuller Co. (H.B.)
GATX Corp.
GE Capital Corp.
General Motors Corp.
Gerber Products Co.
Giant Food Stores
Golub Corp.
Handy & Harman
HarperCollins Publishers, Inc.
Harsco Corp.
Hartmarx Corp.
Hasbro, Inc.
Hilliard Corp.
Hino Diesel Trucks (U.S.A.)
HON Industries, Inc.
Illinois Tool Works, Inc.
International Multifoods Corp.
J&L Specialty Steel, Inc.
Johnson & Johnson
Jostens, Inc.
J.P. Morgan Chase & Co.
Kahn, Lucas-Lancaster, Inc. Children's Wear
Kajima International, Inc.
Kawasaki Motors Manufacturing Corporation U.S.A.
Kimberly-Clark Corp.
Long Island Lighting Co.
Lydall, Inc.
Macy's East, Inc.
Maritz, Inc.
Mattel Inc.
Metropolitan Life Insurance Co.
Microsoft Corp.
Minnesota Mining & Manufacturing Co.
Mitsubishi Motor Sales of America, Inc.
Mitsubishi Silicon America
MONY Group, Inc.
Nestle Purina PetCare Co.
Niagara Mohawk Holdings, Inc.
NLI International, Inc.
Oki America, Inc.
Olin Corp.

Ondeo Nalco Co.
L'Oreal U.S.A.
Oshkosh B'Gosh, Inc.
PepsiCo Inc.
Pfizer Inc.
Phelps Dodge Corp.
Phoenix Home Life Mutual Insurance Co.
Prudential Insurance Co. of America
Prudential Securities, Inc.
Raymond Corp.
Reader's Digest Association, Inc.
Reichhold Chemicals, Inc.
R.J. Reynolds Tobacco
Rouse Co.
Royal & SunAlliance USA, Inc.
Russer Foods
St. Paul Companies, Inc.
Sara Lee Corp.
Schlumberger Ltd.
Scoular Co.
Seneca Foods Corp.
Sheaffer Pen Corp.
Shell Oil Co.
State Farm Mutual Automobile Insurance Co.
Stora Enso
Subaru of America, Inc.
Sumitomo Mitsui Banking Corp.
Tetley U.S.A., Inc.
Texas Instruments Inc.
Thompson Co. (J. Walter)
TJX Companies, Inc.
United States Trust Co. of New York
Universal Studios
USG Corp.
Utica National Insurance Group
Walt Disney Co.
WestLB New York Branch
Wiley & Sons, Inc. (John)
Williams Companies Inc.
Xerox Corp.

North Carolina

Abbott Laboratories
ABC, Inc.
Air Products and Chemicals, Inc.
Akzo Nobel Chemicals
American Honda Motor Company, Inc.
American Standard Inc.
American United Life Insurance Co.
AMP, Inc.
Archer-Daniels-Midland Co.
Bausch & Lomb, Inc.
Bechtel Group, Inc.
Belk Stores Services, Inc.
Benetton U.S.A. Corp.
Bridgestone Americas Holding, Inc.
Brown & Williamson Tobacco Corp.
Burlington Industries, Inc.
Campbell Soup Co.
Carris Reels
Caterpillar Inc.
Chesapeake Corp.
Cox Enterprises, Inc.
Crane Co.
Cranston Print Works Co.
Cummins, Inc.
D&B
Donaldson Company, Inc.

Dow Corning Corp.
Dow Jones & Company, Inc.
Duke Energy Corp.
Eastman Kodak Co.
Eaton Corp.
Ecolab, Inc.
E.I. du Pont de Nemours & Co.
Eli Lilly & Co.
Equifax, Inc.
Fannie Mae
FMC Corp.
Fortis, Inc.
Fortune Brands, Inc.
Fujitsu America
Fuller Co. (H.B.)
General Motors Corp.
Gerber Products Co.
Hannaford Brothers Co.
Harsco Corp.
Henkel Corp.
Hoffmann-La Roche, Inc.
HON Industries, Inc.
International Multifoods Corp.
Johns Manville
Kimberly-Clark Corp.
La-Z-Boy, Inc.
Landmark Communications, Inc.
Louisiana-Pacific Corp.
Lowe's Companies
Lydall, Inc.
Marcus Corp.
Meadwestvaco Corp.
Microsoft Corp.
Minnesota Mining & Manufacturing Co.
National Service Industries, Inc.
New York Times Co.
Pacific Life Insurance Co.
Phelps Dodge Corp.
Prudential Insurance Co. of America
Pulitzer, Inc.
Reichhold Chemicals, Inc.
Rexam, Inc.
R.J. Reynolds Tobacco
Rockwell Automation Inc.
Royal & SunAlliance USA, Inc.
R.R. Donnelley & Sons Co.
Sara Lee Corp.
Scottsman Industries
Smith Corp. (A.O.)
Sonoco Products Co.
Square D Co.
Stanley Works
Steelcase Inc.
Stonecutter Mills Corp.
Tanner Companies (Rutherfordton, NC)
Texas Instruments Inc.
Thomasville Furniture Industries, Inc.
Unitrode Corp.
Vulcan Materials Co.
Wachovia Bank of North Carolina NA
West Pharmaceutical Services, Inc.
Weyerhaeuser Co.
Williams Companies Inc.
Winn-Dixie Stores Inc.

North Dakota

Bucyrus International, Inc.
Employers Mutual Casualty Co.
Lee Enterprises, Inc.
Pamida, Inc.

St. Paul Companies, Inc.
U.S. Bancorp Piper Jaffray
Xcel Energy

Ohio

Abbott Laboratories
ABC, Inc.
Air Products and Chemicals, Inc.
Akzo Nobel Chemicals
Alcoa Inc.
Amcast Industrial Corp.
American Honda Motor Company, Inc.
American Standard Inc.
American United Life Insurance Co.
AMETEK, Inc.
Andersons, Inc.
Anheuser-Busch Companies, Inc.
Appleton Papers, Inc.
Avon Products, Inc.
Banta Corp.
Barnes Group, Inc.
Bemis Company, Inc.
Birds Eye Foods, Inc.
Borden, Inc.
BP Amoco Corp.
Bridgestone Americas Holding, Inc.
Broderbund LLC
Campbell Soup Co.
CertainTeed Corp.
Cessna Aircraft Co.
Chesapeake Corp.
Church & Dwight Company, Inc.
CLARCOR, Inc.
Clorox Co.
Coca-Cola Co.
Columbus Dispatch Printing Co.
Comerica Inc.
Cox Enterprises, Inc.
Crane Co.
Crompton Corp.
Cummins, Inc.
Dentsply International, Inc.
Donaldson Company, Inc.
Dow Jones & Company, Inc.
Eastman Kodak Co.
Eaton Corp.
Ecolab, Inc.
E.I. du Pont de Nemours & Co.
Elf Atochem North America, Inc.
Eli Lilly & Co.
Fannie Mae
Fidelity Investments
Fifth Third Bancorp
Fluor Corp.
Forest City Enterprises, Inc.
Fortis, Inc.
Fortune Brands, Inc.
French Oil Mill Machinery Co.
Fuller Co. (H.B.)
GATX Corp.
General Mills, Inc.
General Motors Corp.
Gerber Products Co.
Giant Food Stores
Gillette Co.
Handy & Harman
Harsco Corp.
Henkel Corp.
Hexcel Corp.
H.J. Heinz Co.

Honda of America Manufacturing, Inc.
Humana, Inc.
Illinois Tool Works, Inc.
International Multifoods Corp.
Johns Manville
Johnson Controls Inc.
Johnson & Johnson
Johnson & Son (S.C.)
Kemper National Insurance Companies
Key Bank NA
Kimberly-Clark Corp.
Kroger Co.
Liberty Corp.
Louisiana-Pacific Corp.
Macy's East, Inc.
Marcus Corp.
McWane Corp.
Meadwestvaco Corp.
Microsoft Corp.
Minnesota Mining & Manufacturing Co.
Mosinee Paper Corp.
National City Corp.
Nestle Purina PetCare Co.
Nordson Corp.
Ondeo Nalco Co.
Pacific Life Insurance Co.
Phelps Dodge Corp.
PPG Industries, Inc.
Prudential Insurance Co. of America
Reichhold Chemicals, Inc.
Rich Products Corp.
Rockwell Automation Inc.
Rouse Co.
R.R. Donnelley & Sons Co.
SAFECO Corp.
St. Paul Companies, Inc.
Sara Lee Corp.
Scott Fetzer Co.
Scoular Co.
Scripps Co. (E.W.)
Shell Oil Co.
Sherwin-Williams Co.
Smith Corp. (A.O.)
Spartan Stores, Inc.
SPX Corp.
Square D Co.
Stanley Works
State Farm Mutual Automobile Insurance Co.
Teleflex, Inc.
Texas Instruments Inc.
Thompson Co. (J. Walter)
Unocal Corp.
USG Corp.
Western & Southern Life Insurance Co.
Weyerhaeuser Co.
Whirlpool Corp.
Williams Companies Inc.
Winn-Dixie Stores Inc.
Worthington Foods

Oklahoma

Air Products and Chemicals, Inc.
Akzo Nobel Chemicals
Albertson's Inc.
Anheuser-Busch Companies, Inc.
Badger Meter, Inc.
Belo Corp.
Blue Bell, Inc.
Bridgestone Americas Holding, Inc.
Chicago Rawhide Co.
Cox Enterprises, Inc.
Crompton Corp.

Donaldson Company, Inc.
Dow Jones & Company, Inc.
Eaton Corp.
Ecolab, Inc.
E.I. du Pont de Nemours & Co.
Elf Atochem North America, Inc.
Equifax, Inc.
Fluor Corp.
FMC Corp.
Fuller Co. (H.B.)
General Motors Corp.
Halliburton Co.
Handy & Harman
Harsco Corp.
Johnson Controls Inc.
Kimberly-Clark Corp.
Meadwestvaco Corp.
Metropolitan Life Insurance Co.
Minnesota Mining & Manufacturing Co.
Ondeo Nalco Co.
Prudential Insurance Co. of America
Quaker Chemical Corp.
Rockwell Automation Inc.
Scripps Co. (E.W.)
State Farm Mutual Automobile Insurance Co.
Union Pacific Corp.
USG Corp.
Valmont Industries, Inc.
Weyerhaeuser Co.
Xerox Corp.

Oregon

ABC, Inc.
Air Products and Chemicals, Inc.
Albertson's Inc.
American Honda Motor Company, Inc.
AMP, Inc.
Appleton Papers, Inc.
Avista Corp.
Berwind Group
Boise Cascade Corp.
Borden, Inc.
ChevronTexaco Corp.
Crompton Corp.
D&B
Deere & Co.
Eastman Kodak Co.
Equifax, Inc.
Fannie Mae
FleetBoston Financial Corp.
Forest City Enterprises, Inc.
Fortis, Inc.
Fujitsu America
Fuller Co. (H.B.)
GATX Corp.
General Mills, Inc.
H.J. Heinz Co.
Johnson Controls Inc.
Land O'Lakes, Inc.
Lee Enterprises, Inc.
Louisiana-Pacific Corp.
Metropolitan Life Insurance Co.
Minnesota Mining & Manufacturing Co.
Mitsubishi Silicon America
Northwest Natural Gas Co.
Oki America, Inc.
Ore-Ida Foods
Pacific Life Insurance Co.
PacifiCorp
Pioneer Trust Bank, NA
Rexam, Inc.

R.R. Donnelley & Sons Co.
St. Paul Companies, Inc.
Schlumberger Ltd.
Scottsman Industries
Simpson Investment Co.
Stanley Works
State Farm Mutual Automobile Insurance Co.
Subaru of America, Inc.
Union Pacific Corp.
U.S. Bancorp Piper Jaffray
Unocal Corp.
Washington Mutual, Inc.
Weyerhaeuser Co.

Pennsylvania

ABC, Inc.
Air Products and Chemicals, Inc.
Albertson's Inc.
Alcoa Inc.
Alcon Laboratories, Inc.
Amcast Industrial Corp.
American General Finance
American United Life Insurance Co.
AMETEK, Inc.
AMP, Inc.
Anheuser-Busch Companies, Inc.
Appleton Papers, Inc.
AT&T Corp.
Barnes Group, Inc.
Bausch & Lomb, Inc.
Bechtel Group, Inc.
Bemis Company, Inc.
Berwind Group
Birds Eye Foods, Inc.
Borden, Inc.
Brunswick Corp.
Bryn Mawr Bank Corp.
Campbell Soup Co.
Caterpillar Inc.
CertainTeed Corp.
ChevronTexaco Corp.
CNA Financial Corp.
Coca-Cola Co.
Constellation Energy Group, Inc.
Cox Enterprises, Inc.
Crane Co.
Crompton Corp.
CUNA Mutual Group
D&B
Donaldson Company, Inc.
Dow Jones & Company, Inc.
Dynamet, Inc.
Eastman Kodak Co.
Eaton Corp.
Ebsco Industries, Inc.
Ecolab, Inc.
E.I. du Pont de Nemours & Co.
Elf Atochem North America, Inc.
Eli Lilly & Co.
Equifax, Inc.
Exelon
Fannie Mae
FleetBoston Financial Corp.
FMC Corp.
Forest City Enterprises, Inc.
Forest Oil Corp.
Fortis, Inc.
Foster Co. (L.B.)
Freeport Brick Co.
GATX Corp.
General Motors Corp.
Giant Eagle, Inc.
Giant Food Stores
Golub Corp.

Guardian Life Insurance Company of America
Halliburton Co.
Harley-Davidson Co.
Harsco Corp.
Hartmarx Corp.
Henkel Corp.
Hershey Foods Corp.
Hexcel Corp.
H.J. Heinz Co.
HON Industries, Inc.
Hunt Corp.
Illinois Tool Works, Inc.
Integra Bank
J&L Specialty Steel, Inc.
Johnson Controls Inc.
Johnson & Johnson
Jostens, Inc.
Kahn, Lucas-Lancaster, Inc. Children's Wear
Kimberly-Clark Corp.
Lamco Communications
Lebanon Mutual Insurance Co.
Lehigh Cement Co.
Lipton Co.
Louisiana-Pacific Corp.
McClatchy Co.
McCormick & Company, Inc.
Meadwestvaco Corp.
Metropolitan Life Insurance Co.
Millipore Corp.
Minnesota Mining & Manufacturing Co.
New York Times Co.
Ondeo Nalco Co.
Pepco Holdings, Inc.
Pfizer Inc.
Pitt-Des Moines, Inc.
PPG Industries, Inc.
Prudential Insurance Co. of America
Quaker Chemical Corp.
Rockwell Automation Inc.
Rouse Co.
Royal & SunAlliance USA, Inc.
R.R. Donnelley & Sons Co.
S&T Bancorp, Inc.
Sara Lee Corp.
Schlumberger Ltd.
Sharon Steel Corp.
Shell Oil Co.
Sherwin-Williams Co.
Sovereign Bank
Spang & Co.
SPX Corp.
Square D Co.
Standard Steel
Standard Steel Speciality Co.
Stanley Works
Susquehanna-Pfaltzgraff Co.
Teleflex, Inc.
Tetley U.S.A., Inc.
Union Pacific Corp.
Universal Studios
Vanguard Group
West Pharmaceutical Services, Inc.
Weyerhaeuser Co.

Puerto Rico

Amgen, Inc.
Credit Suisse First Boston Corp.
Ecolab, Inc.
Gerber Products Co.
Johnson & Johnson
Millipore Corp.
Polaroid Corp.

R.J. Reynolds Tobacco
Schering-Plough Corp.
Sherwin-Williams Co.
Sonoco Products Co.
Storage Technology Corp.
West Pharmaceutical Services, Inc.

Rhode Island

ABC, Inc.
Ben & Jerry's Homemade, Inc.
Borden, Inc.
Citizens Financial Group, Inc.
Country Curtains, Inc.
Cox Enterprises, Inc.
Cranston Print Works Co.
Dow Jones & Company, Inc.
FleetBoston Financial Corp.
Louisiana-Pacific Corp.
McCormick & Company, Inc.
Mine Safety Appliances Co.
New York Times Co.
Providence Gas Co.
Providence Journal-Bulletin Co.
Sheaffer Pen Corp.
Stanley Works

South Carolina

Air Products and Chemicals, Inc.
Alcoa Inc.
Bausch & Lomb, Inc.
Bechtel Group, Inc.
Belk Stores Services, Inc.
Bowater, Inc.
Burlington Industries, Inc.
CCB Financial Corp.
CertainTeed Corp.
Church & Dwight Company, Inc.
Cox Enterprises, Inc.
Cummins, Inc.
Deere & Co.
Dow Corning Corp.
Duke Energy Corp.
Eastman Kodak Co.
Eaton Corp.
Ecolab, Inc.
E.I. du Pont de Nemours & Co.
Elf Atochem North America, Inc.
Equifax, Inc.
Evening Post Publishing Co.
FleetBoston Financial Corp.
Fluor Corp.
FMC Corp.
Giant Food Stores
Hasbro, Inc.
Johnson Controls Inc.
Jostens, Inc.
Kimberly-Clark Corp.
La-Z-Boy, Inc.
Liberty Corp.
Louisiana-Pacific Corp.
Marcus Corp.
Meadwestvaco Corp.
Minnesota Mining & Manufacturing Co.
New York Times Co.
Ondeo Nalco Co.
Progress Energy Inc.
Pulitzer, Inc.
Rexam, Inc.
Rockwell Automation Inc.
R.R. Donnelley & Sons Co.
Sara Lee Corp.
Scoular Co.
Scripps Co. (E.W.)

Shell Oil Co.
Smith Corp. (A.O.)
Sonoco Products Co.
Square D Co.
Vulcan Materials Co.
Whirlpool Corp.
Williams Companies Inc.
Winn-Dixie Stores Inc.

South Dakota

American United Life Insurance Co.
Chicago Rawhide Co.
FMC Corp.
Land O'Lakes, Inc.
Midcontinent Media, Inc.
Minnesota Mining & Manufacturing Co.
Morris Communications Corp.
Ondeo Nalco Co.
Royal & SunAlliance USA, Inc.
U.S. Bancorp Piper Jaffray
Xcel Energy

Tennessee

Air Products and Chemicals, Inc.
Akzo Nobel Chemicals
Albertson's Inc.
Alcoa Inc.
American General Finance
Anheuser-Busch Companies, Inc.
Aon Corp.
Archer-Daniels-Midland Co.
Banta Corp.
Barnes Group, Inc.
Bechtel Group, Inc.
Berwind Group
Bowater, Inc.
Bridgestone Americas Holding, Inc.
Burlington Industries, Inc.
Cargill, Inc.
CLARCOR, Inc.
CNA Financial Corp.
Crompton Corp.
Cummins, Inc.
D&B
Eastman Kodak Co.
Eaton Corp.
Ecolab, Inc.
E.I. du Pont de Nemours & Co.
Eli Lilly & Co.
First Tennessee National Corp.
Fluor Corp.
Fuller Co. (H.B.)
General Mills, Inc.
General Motors Corp.
Gerber Products Co.
Harsco Corp.
Illinois Tool Works, Inc.
Johns Manville
Johnson Controls Inc.
Jostens, Inc.
Kimberly-Clark Corp.
Kroger Co.
La-Z-Boy, Inc.
Magna International of America, Inc.
Marcus Corp.
Meadwestvaco Corp.
Minnesota Mining & Manufacturing Co.
Nestle Purina PetCare Co.
New York Times Co.
Olin Corp.

Ondeo Nalco Co.
L'Oreal U.S.A.
Oshkosh B'Gosh, Inc.
Pacific Life Insurance Co.
Progress Energy Inc.
Prudential Insurance Co. of America
Rich Products Corp.
Rockwell Automation Inc.
R.R. Donnelley & Sons Co.
SAFECO Corp.
Sara Lee Corp.
Schering-Plough Corp.
Scripps Co. (E.W.)
Sedgwick, Inc.
Shell Oil Co.
Smith Corp. (A.O.)
Square D Co.
Stanley Works
State Farm Mutual Automobile Insurance Co.
Texas Instruments Inc.
Thomasville Furniture Industries, Inc.
Vulcan Materials Co.
Whirlpool Corp.
Wurzburg, Inc.

Texas

Abbott Laboratories
ABC, Inc.
Air France
Air Products and Chemicals, Inc.
Akzo Nobel Chemicals
Albertson's Inc.
Alcoa Inc.
Alcon Laboratories, Inc.
Allianz Life Insurance Company of North America
American Standard Inc.
American United Life Insurance Co.
AMP, Inc.
AMR Corp.
Anheuser-Busch Companies, Inc.
Aon Corp.
Bank of New York Company, Inc.
Barnes Group, Inc.
Bausch & Lomb, Inc.
Belk Stores Services, Inc.
Belo Corp.
Bemis Company, Inc.
Birds Eye Foods, Inc.
Blue Bell, Inc.
Borden, Inc.
BP Amoco Corp.
Bridgestone Americas Holding, Inc.
Broderbund LLC
California Bank & Trust
Campbell Soup Co.
Caterpillar Inc.
CenterPoint Energy, Inc.
CertainTeed Corp.
ChevronTexaco Corp.
Chicago Tribune Direct Marketing
Church & Dwight Company, Inc.
CIBC World Markets
CIT Group, Inc.
CLARCOR, Inc.
Cleveland-Cliffs, Inc.
Clorox Co.
Comerica Inc.
COMSAT International
Constellation Energy Group, Inc.

Cox Enterprises, Inc.
Crompton Corp.
Cummins, Inc.
CUNA Mutual Group
Deere & Co.
Donaldson Company, Inc.
Dow Jones & Company, Inc.
Eastman Kodak Co.
Eaton Corp.
Ebsco Industries, Inc.
Ecolab, Inc.
E.I. du Pont de Nemours & Co.
El Paso Corp.
Elf Atochem North America, Inc.
Eli Lilly & Co.
Equifax, Inc.
Ethyl Corp.
Fannie Mae
Fidelity Investments
Fluor Corp.
FMC Corp.
Fortis, Inc.
Fortune Brands, Inc.
Frost National Bank
Fujitsu America
Fuller Co. (H.B.)
GATX Corp.
GE Capital Corp.
General Mills, Inc.
General Motors Corp.
Gerber Products Co.
Harsco Corp.
Hasbro, Inc.
Hexcel Corp.
H.J. Heinz Co.
Holnam, Inc.
HON Industries, Inc.
Humana, Inc.
Hunt Corp.
Illinois Tool Works, Inc.
International Multifoods Corp.
Johns Manville
Johnson Controls Inc.
Johnson & Johnson
Johnson & Son (S.C.)
Jostens, Inc.
J.P. Morgan Chase & Co.
Kajima International, Inc.
Kimberly-Clark Corp.
Kroger Co.
Liz Claiborne, Inc.
Louisiana-Pacific Corp.
Magna International of America, Inc.
Management Compensation Group/Dulworth, Inc.
Marcus Corp.
Maritz, Inc.
Mattel Inc.
McCormick & Company, Inc.
Metropolitan Life Insurance Co.
Microsoft Corp.
Minnesota Mining & Manufacturing Co.
Mitsubishi Motor Sales of America, Inc.
Mitsubishi Silicon America
New York Life Insurance Co.
Northern Trust Corp.
Ondeo Nalco Co.
L'Oreal U.S.A.
Oshkosh B'Gosh, Inc.
Pacific Life Insurance Co.
Pepco Holdings, Inc.
PepsiCo Inc.
Phelps Dodge Corp.
Prudential Insurance Co. of America
Quaker Chemical Corp.

Quanex Corp.
Reichhold Chemicals, Inc.
Reliable Life Insurance Co.
Rockwell Automation Inc.
Rouse Co.
Royal & SunAlliance USA, Inc.
R.R. Donnelley & Sons Co.
SAFECO Corp.
St. Paul Companies, Inc.
Salomon Smith Barney Holdings, Inc.
Sara Lee Corp.
Schering-Plough Corp.
Schlumberger Ltd.
Scottsman Industries
Scripps Co. (E.W.)
Security Life of Denver Insurance Co.
Shell Oil Co.
Sherwin-Williams Co.
Smith Corp. (A.O.)
Southwestern Electric Power Co.
Square D Co.
Stanley Works
State Farm Mutual Automobile Insurance Co.
Storage Technology Corp.
Subaru of America, Inc.
Teleflex, Inc.
Texas Instruments Inc.
Thompson Co. (J. Walter)
Union Pacific Corp.
Unocal Corp.
USG Corp.
Valmont Industries, Inc.
Vulcan Materials Co.
Wells Fargo & Co.
Weyerhaeuser Co.
Williams Companies Inc.
Winn-Dixie Stores Inc.
Xerox Corp.

Utah

Abbott Laboratories
Air Products and Chemicals, Inc.
Albertson's Inc.
AT&T Corp.
Banta Corp.
Barnes Group, Inc.
Boise Cascade Corp.
ChevronTexaco Corp.
D&B
Dow Jones & Company, Inc.
Ecolab, Inc.
GATX Corp.
Kimberly-Clark Corp.
La-Z-Boy, Inc.
Land O'Lakes, Inc.
Meadwestvaco Corp.
Minnesota Mining & Manufacturing Co.
Novell
Ondeo Nalco Co.
Pacific Life Insurance Co.
Quanex Corp.
Royal & SunAlliance USA, Inc.
Thompson Co. (J. Walter)
U.S. Bancorp Piper Jaffray
USG Corp.
Valmont Industries, Inc.
Washington Mutual, Inc.

Vermont

Ben & Jerry's Homemade, Inc.
Carris Reels
Central Vermont Public Service Corp.
General Motors Corp.
Golub Corp.
Johnson Controls Inc.
McCormick & Company, Inc.
Stanley Works

Virgin Islands

Raymond Corp.

Virginia

Abbott Laboratories
Air Products and Chemicals, Inc.
Alcoa Inc.
American Honda Motor Company, Inc.
American Standard Inc.
American United Life Insurance Co.
AMP, Inc.
Anheuser-Busch Companies, Inc.
AT&T Corp.
Banta Corp.
Bausch & Lomb, Inc.
Belk Stores Services, Inc.
Belo Corp.
Ben & Jerry's Homemade, Inc.
Burlington Industries, Inc.
Chesapeake Corp.
COMSAT International
Country Curtains, Inc.
Cox Enterprises, Inc.
D&B
Dow Jones & Company, Inc.
Eastman Kodak Co.
Ecolab, Inc.
E.I. du Pont de Nemours & Co.
Equifax, Inc.
Fluor Corp.
FMC Corp.
Fortune Brands, Inc.
General Motors Corp.
Giant Food, Inc.
Giant Food Stores
Hershey Foods Corp.
HON Industries, Inc.
Illinois Tool Works, Inc.
Johns Manville
Kroger Co.
Landmark Communications, Inc.
Lehigh Cement Co.
Lipton Co.
Lydall, Inc.
McCormick & Company, Inc.
Meadwestvaco Corp.
Old Dominion Box Co.
Ondeo Nalco Co.
Prudential Insurance Co. of America
Rockwell Automation Inc.
Royal & SunAlliance USA, Inc.
R.R. Donnelley & Sons Co.
SAFECO Corp.
Sara Lee Corp.
Scripps Co. (E.W.)
Shell Oil Co.
Shenandoah Life Insurance Co.
Stanley Works

State Farm Mutual Automobile Insurance Co.
Texas Instruments Inc.
Thomasville Furniture Industries, Inc.
USG Corp.
Vaughan Furniture Co.
Vulcan Materials Co.
Weyerhaeuser Co.
Williams Companies Inc.
Winn-Dixie Stores Inc.
Xerox Corp.

Washington

ABC, Inc.
Adobe Systems
Air Products and Chemicals, Inc.
Albertson's Inc.
Alcoa Inc.
American United Life Insurance Co.
AMETEK, Inc.
AT&T Corp.
Avista Corp.
Banta Corp.
Barnes Group, Inc.
Belo Corp.
Birds Eye Foods, Inc.
Boise Cascade Corp.
Borden, Inc.
Burlington Industries, Inc.
California Bank & Trust
Carnival Corp.
Caterpillar Inc.
CertainTeed Corp.
ChevronTexaco Corp.
Church & Dwight Company, Inc.
Cox Enterprises, Inc.
CUNA Mutual Group
Donaldson Company, Inc.
Dow Corning Corp.
Dow Jones & Company, Inc.
Eastman Kodak Co.
Eaton Corp.
Ecolab, Inc.
Elf Atochem North America, Inc.
Eli Lilly & Co.
Equifax, Inc.
Fannie Mae
FMC Corp.
Fortune Brands, Inc.
Fuller Co. (H.B.)
GATX Corp.
GE Capital Corp.
Guardian Life Insurance Company of America
HON Industries, Inc.
Hubbard Broadcasting, Inc.
International Multifoods Corp.
Johnson Controls Inc.
Johnson & Son (S.C.)
Kimberly-Clark Corp.
Land O'Lakes, Inc.
Louisiana-Pacific Corp.
Macy's East, Inc.
McCormick & Company, Inc.
Meadwestvaco Corp.
Microsoft Corp.
Minnesota Mining & Manufacturing Co.
Oki America, Inc.
Olin Corp.
Ondeo Nalco Co.
Pacific Life Insurance Co.
PacifiCorp
Prudential Insurance Co. of America

Rayonier, Inc.
Rockwell Automation Inc.
Rouse Co.
R.R. Donnelley & Sons Co.
St. Paul Companies, Inc.
Sara Lee Corp.
Simpson Investment Co.
Smith Corp. (A.O.)
Square D Co.
Texas Instruments Inc.
Union Pacific Corp.
U.S. Bancorp Piper Jaffray
Unocal Corp.
US Bank
USG Corp.
Washington Mutual, Inc.
Weyerhaeuser Co.

West Virginia

Air Products and Chemicals, Inc.
Belk Stores Services, Inc.
Berwind Group
E.I. du Pont de Nemours & Co.
Eli Lilly & Co.
FMC Corp.
General Motors Corp.
Giant Food Stores
Harsco Corp.
Johns Manville
Lee Enterprises, Inc.
Metropolitan Life Insurance Co.
Minnesota Mining & Manufacturing Co.
Olin Corp.
Ondeo Nalco Co.
PacifiCorp
Phelps Dodge Corp.
PPG Industries, Inc.
Scripps Co. (E.W.)

Wisconsin

Air Products and Chemicals, Inc.
Akzo Nobel Chemicals
Alliant Energy Corp.
Amcast Industrial Corp.
American Standard Inc.
American United Life Insurance Co.
Andersen Corp.
Anheuser-Busch Companies, Inc.
Appleton Papers, Inc.
Bank of New York Company, Inc.
Banta Corp.
Barnes Group, Inc.
Bemis Company, Inc.
Bucyrus International, Inc.
Campbell Soup Co.
Cargill, Inc.
Caterpillar Inc.
Chesapeake Corp.
Cox Enterprises, Inc.
Crompton Corp.
DEC International, Inc. SMS/Nelles Cheese Equipment
Donaldson Company, Inc.
Dow Jones & Company, Inc.
Eastman Kodak Co.
Eaton Corp.
Ecolab, Inc.
Elf Atochem North America, Inc.

Equifax, Inc.
First Financial Bank
Firstar Bank Milwaukee NA
Fluor Corp.
FMC Corp.
Fortis, Inc.
Fortune Brands, Inc.
General Motors Corp.
Gerber Products Co.
Giddings & Lewis
Guardian Life Insurance Company of America
Handy & Harman
Henkel Corp.
Hunt Corp.
Johnson Controls Inc.
Joy Global, Inc.
JSJ Corp.
Kemper National Insurance Companies
Kimberly-Clark Corp.
Land O'Lakes, Inc.
Lee Enterprises, Inc.
Louisiana-Pacific Corp.
Marcus Corp.
Marshall & Ilsley Corp.
Meadwestvaco Corp.
Midcontinent Media, Inc.
Minnesota Mining & Manufacturing Co.
Mosinee Paper Corp.
Nordson Corp.
Olin Corp.
Ondeo Nalco Co.
Ore-Ida Foods
Pamida, Inc.
Pitt-Des Moines, Inc.
PPG Industries, Inc.
Quanex Corp.
Rexam, Inc.
R.J. Reynolds Tobacco
Rockwell Automation Inc.
Rouse Co.
Saint Francis Bank
St. Paul Companies, Inc.
Sara Lee Corp.
Sentry Insurance, A Mutual Co.
Smith Corp. (A.O.)
Square D Co.
Stora Enso
Texas Instruments Inc.
U.S. Bancorp Piper Jaffray
Unocal Corp.
USG Corp.
Vulcan Materials Co.
Wausau-Mosinee Paper Corp.
Weyerhaeuser Co.
WPS Resources Corp.
Xcel Energy

Wyoming

American General Finance
ChevronTexaco Corp.
FMC Corp.
Kinder Morgan
Land O'Lakes, Inc.
Ondeo Nalco Co.
Pamida, Inc.
Pittsburg & Midway Coal Mining Co.
U.S. Bancorp Piper Jaffray
Unocal Corp.

The following index lists alphabetically grants given to libraries and other library-related projects by the state in which the library and/or project is located. Within each state, grants are listed in alphabetical order. When several grants have been given to the same organization, such as the New York Public Library, individual grants are listed in descending order by the grant amount.

Alabama

B.B. Comer Memorial School -- library operations and expansion of facility (180,000) see Comer Foundation (AL)

Birmingham Public Library (25,000) see Hugh Kaul Foundation Trust

Birmingham Public Library (5,000) see John A. and Delia T. Robert Charitable Trust 2

Emmet O'Neal Library (50,000) see McWane Corp.

Emmet O'Neal Library -- education (10,000) see Joseph S. Bruno Charitable Foundation

Grove Hill Public Library (10,000) see J. L. Bedsole Foundation

Mobile County Public Library (100,000) see J. L. Bedsole Foundation

Mobile County Public Library (10,000) see J. L. Bedsole Foundation

Mobile Public Library -- new equipment (100,000) see Crampton Trust

Mountain Brook Library Foundation -- expansion of facility (50,000) see Comer Foundation (AL)

Mountain Brook Library Foundation (5,000) see Barbara Ingalls Shook Foundation

Mountain Brook Library Foundation (5,000) see Tractor & Equipment Co.

Wheeler Basin Regional Library (2,635) see Tennessee Valley Printing Co.

Alaska

Friends of the Library -- for landscaping and exterior modifications (22,264) see James and Elise Nolan Charitable Trust

Irene Ingle Public Library -- for computer purchases (5,600) see James and Elise Nolan Charitable Trust

Newton County Library (3,600) see Mays Foundation

Searcy County Library (3,600) see Mays Foundation

Arizona

Desert Foothills Library (25,000) see Sarah K. de

Coizart Perpetual Charitable Trust

Friends of the Library (160) see Research Corp.

Friends of the Library (120) see Research Corp.

Libraries LTD (3,000) see Eliot Spalding Foundation

Prescott Public Library (5,000) see V. V. Cooke Foundation Corp.

Sedona Public Library (50,000) see The Offield Family Foundation

Town of Jerome Library (18,000) see Phelps Dodge Corp.

Tucson-Pima Public Library, Inc. -- create four teen centers (126,600) see DeWitt Wallace-Reader's Digest Fund

Arkansas

Barton Library (17,400) see Murphy Foundation

Booneville Library (2,500) see Spang & Co.

Central Arkansas Library (31,250) see Ottenheimer Brothers Foundation

California

Academy Foundation (30,000) see Mary Pickford Foundation

Alameda County Library Foundation -- for the Reading for Life Program (211,000) see Richard and Rhoda Goldman Fund

Bancroft Library (10,000) see T. Y. Lin Foundation

Berkeley Public Library (100,000) see Bernard Osher Foundation

Berkeley Public Library Foundation (100,000) see Koret Foundation

Braille Institute of Orange County -- support of orange county library services (10,000) see Glen and Dorothy Stillwell Charitable Trust

California State Library Foundation (25,000) see Kikkoman Foods

California State Library Foundation -- for school Library Enrichment Program (10,000) see Ralph's Grocery Co.

Carmel Public Library (15,000) see Harold McAlister Charitable Foundation

Community Health Library of Los Gatos -- for operating support (55,000) see Valley Foundation

David Hale Library (2,500) see Ducommun and Gross Foundation

David Hale Library (2,500) see Ducommun, Inc.

Ferndale Library (12,786) see Bertha Russ Lytel Foundation

Fresno County Library -- funds for operation and administration (2,000) see Leon S. Peters Foundation

Friends and Foundation of San Francisco Public Library (1,000) see Robert and Susan Green Foundation

Friends of Chinatown Library -- for library building fund (3,000) see Lin and Ella Wong Foundation

Friends of the Bancroft Library (225,000) see William Randolph Hearst Foundation

Friends of the Esparto Regional Library (10,000) see A. Teichert & Sons

Friends of the Guadalupe Public Library -- library expansion (16,000) see S.G. Foundation

Friends of the Guadalupe Public Library -- to assist the following the Guadalupe Public Library (8,654) see Herbert and Gertrude Latkin Charitable Foundation

Henry E. Huntington Library and Art Gallery -- book acquisitions (500,000) see Ahmanson Foundation

Henry E. Huntington Library and Art Gallery (25,000) see J. W. and Ida M. Jameson Foundation

Henry E. Huntington Library and Art Gallery -- purchase of stereo microscopes (19,200) see Stanley Smith Horticultural Trust

Henry E. Huntington Library and Art Gallery -- design exhibition for the field lab station (10,000) see George Hoag Family Foundation

Huntington Library (3,500,000) see Virginia Steele Scott Foundation

Huntington Library (210,000) see Virginia Steele Scott Foundation

Huntington Library (97,300) see Essick Foundation

Huntington Library (53,333) see Walter Lantz Foundation

Huntington Library -- William Morris Collection (50,000) see Fletcher Jones Foundation

Huntington Library (40,500) see Virginia Steele Scott Foundation

Huntington Library -- for history fellowships (22,000) see John Randolph and Dora Haynes Foundation

Huntington Library -- to cataloging the papers of Edmund D Edelman papers (10,000) see John Randolph and Dora Haynes Foundation

Huntington Library (10,000) see L. J. Skaggs and Mary C. Skaggs Foundation

Huntington Library (5,000) see H. Leslie Hoffman & Elaine S. Hoffman Foundation

Huntington Library -- school tours (5,000) see Ann Peppers Foundation

Jewish Community Library of Los Angeles (15,000) see Maurice Amado Foundation

Library Foundation (25,000) see Walter Lantz Foundation

Library Foundation (10,000) see McGraw-Hill Companies, Inc.

Library Foundation (3,000) see Rene Bloch Foundation

Library Foundation of Los Angeles (344,800) see Tribune Co.

Library Foundation of Los Angeles (250,000) see Weingart Foundation

Library Foundation of Los Angeles -- reading enrichment programs (200,000) see Ahmanson Foundation

Library Foundation of Los Angeles (25,000) see Michael J. Connell Foundation

Library Foundation of Los Angeles -- Grandparents and Books reading enrichment program for children (25,000) see

George Hoag Family Foundation

Library Foundation of Los Angeles (25,000) see Whitecap Foundation

Library Foundation of Los Angeles -- electronic neighborhood (16,712) see John Randolph and Dora Haynes Foundation

Library Foundation of Los Angeles (1,500) see Albert Parvin Foundation

Long Beach Public Library Foundation -- family learning center (50,000) see Earl B. and Loraine H. Miller Foundation

Long Beach Public Library Foundation (25,000) see Leburta Atherton Foundation

Long Beach Public Library Foundation (25,000) see BP Amoco Corp.

Long Beach Public Library Foundation (11,700) see Josephine Gumbiner Foundation

Long Beach Public Library Foundation (5,000) see Bess J. Hodges Foundation

Los Angeles County Public Library Foundation -- Homework Help Center (50,000) see American Honda Motor Company, Inc.

Mendocino County Library Foundation -- education (5,000) see George and Ruth Bradford Foundation

Oakland Public Library Foundation -- PASS Program (10,000) see Clorox Co.

Otis Library -- financial assistance for microfilming archived local newspaper (2,800) see Dime Bank of Norwich Connecticut

Performing Arts Center of Los Angeles -- to fund construction of the Children's Amphitheater at the new Disney Concert Hall (954,391) see W. M. Keck Foundation

Performing Arts Center of Los Angeles County -- construction of the Walt Disney Concert Hall (1,000,000) see SBC Communications Inc.

Project Read (5,000) see Rich Foundation

Rancho Mirage Public Library (2,000,000) see Annenberg Foundation

Richard Nixon Library (5,000) see Stans Foundation

Richard Nixon Library and Birthplace Foundation (59,200) see Argyros Foundation

Rohnert Park/Cotati Library Committee -- support construction costs for new library (5,000) see Exchange Bank

Sacramento Public Library Foundation -- to update computers in branches (5,000) see Kelly Foundation

Sacto Public Library Foundation -- for Scholarship Resource Center (12,500) see Schwab-Rosenhouse Memorial Foundation

San Diego County Library -- charitable (5,000) see Alphonse A. Burnand Medical and Educational Foundation

San Diego Public Library (10,000) see Ellis Foundation

San Francisco Library Foundation (200,000) see Baker Street Foundation

San Francisco Public Library (25,000) see Bernard Osher Foundation

San Francisco Public Library (25,000) see Bernard Osher Foundation

San Francisco Public Library -- Wallace Stegner Environmental Center (15,000) see Mary A. Crocker Trust

School of the Sacred Heart (10,000) see Moldaw Family Foundation

Sherman Library and Gardens -- capital campaign (15,000) see Pacific Life Insurance Co.

Siskiyou County Public Library -- expansion and remodeling (41,617) see McConnell Foundation

South San Francisco Public Library -- for Homework Assistance Program (10,000) see Atkinson Foundation

St. Anne's School -- books for library (403) see Henry and Carol Zeiter Charitable Foundation

St. Anne's School (300) see Henry and Carol Zeiter Charitable Foundation

St. Barnabas School Library (5,000) see Bess J. Hodges Foundation

Take Home Library (200,000) see Silver Lining Foundation

Take Home Library (100,000) see Silver Lining Foundation

U.M.C.A. Library (5,000) see John F. Long Foundation

United Friends of Children (5,000) see Kathryne Beynon Foundation

Woodbury University (10,000) see Carle C.

Conway Scholarship Foundation

Zen Library Project (25,000) see Katz Family Foundation

Colorado

Auraria Library -- for purchasing additional equipment for the computer commons area (20,000) see Kenneth Kendal King Foundation

Denver Public Library (5,000) see Hewit Family Foundation

Denver Public Library see Security Life of Denver Insurance Co.

East Morgan County Library (43,800) see Joslin-Needham Family Foundation

Grover Regional Library Association (10,000) see Monfort Family Foundation

Hotchkiss Public Library (90,000) see Gates Family Foundation

Lake County Public Library -- support remodel and reroofing of the library (10,000) see Anschutz Family Foundation

Mesa County Public Library -- lift for van (1,565) see E. L. and Oma Bacon Foundation

Mesa County Public Library Foundation -- capital campaign (25,000) see Cox Enterprises, Inc.

Pikes Peak Library (20,000) see H. Chase Stone Trust

Pikes Peak Library District -- Carnegie Library restoration (265,000) see El Pomar Foundation

Pikes Peak Library District (100,000) see Gates Family Foundation

Pikes Peak Library District -- to provide funds for restoration of 1095 Carnegie Library Building (5,000) see Inasmuch Foundation

Connecticut

Berlin-Peck Memorial Library -- support salary for library science staff (27,500) see Marjorie Moore Charitable Foundation

Cornwall Public Library (33,750) see Harriet Ford Dickenson Foundation

Darien Library (10,000) see Joe and Emily Lowe Foundation

East Greenwich Free Library (500) see Trimix Foundation

Ferguson Library Foundation (1,000) see Rich Foundation Inc.

Friends of Darien Library (20,000) see Goodnow Fund

Greenwich Library (130,000) see Leon Lowenstein Foundation

Greenwich Library -- for Peterson Business Award Dinner (10,000) see Crane Co.

Greenwich Library (1,000) see William S. Paley Foundation, Inc.

Greenwich Library (500) see Figgie Educational Foundation

Greenwich Library Development Foundation (50,000) see Norman M. Morris Foundation

Greenwich Library, The (10,000) see Harvey Firestone, Jr. Foundation

Greenwich Library, The (1,000) see AmBase Corp.

Gunn Memorial Library (2,500) see Rene Bloch Foundation

Miss Porter's School -- library building (30,000) see William E. Weiss Foundation

New Milford Public Library -- for dedication room for USA veteran (4,000) see Ellen Knowles Harcourt Foundation

Norfolk Library (5,000) see AKC Fund

Oliver Walcott Library (5,715) see Seherr-Thoss Foundation

Peck Memorial Library of Berlin -- purchase large print books and audio taped books (1,500) see Robert C. Vance Charitable Foundation

Southern Connecticut Library Council (2,500) see New Haven Savings Bank

Stonington Free Library -- contribution to support organization (1,000) see Blood-Horse Charitable Foundation

Voluntown Public Library -- expand and re-do youth biography section of library (1,000) see Eastern Savings and Loan Foundation

Wadsworth Athenaeum (88,000) see Hartford Financial Services Group, Inc.

Wadsworth Athenaeum -- Michael Sweerts exhibition (30,000) see Helen M. Saunders Charitable Foundation Trust

Wadsworth Athenaeum -- Sol LeWitt Cube Show (20,000) see Helen M. Saunders Charitable Foundation Trust

Wadsworth Athenaeum -- Gauguin exhibit (15,000) see Helen M. Saunders Charitable Foundation Trust

Wadsworth Athenaeum (11,000) see Kohn-Joseloff Foundation

Wadsworth Athenaeum -- for Docent Program (10,000) see Maximilian E. and Marion O. Hoffman Foundation

Wadsworth Athenaeum -- annual fund (10,000) see Larsen Fund

Wadsworth Athenaeum (6,000) see William O. and Carole P. Bailey Family Foundation

Western Connecticut Library Council (25,000) see Reader's Digest Association, Inc.

Westport Library (5,000) see Arthur C. and Lee Anne Tauck Foundation

Westport Library (3,000) see Candace King Weir Foundation

Westport Public Library (100,000) see Arnold Bernhard Foundation

Wilton Public Library (2,000) see Dibner Fund

Windsor Library Association (1,000) see Cone-Blanchard Corp.

Yale University -- support for the revision of Redesigning the American Lawn (36,500) see Mary Flagler Cary Charitable Trust

Delaware

Friends of the Concord Pike Library -- capital campaign (200,000) see Crystal Trust

Friends of the Concord Pike Library -- capital campaign (150,000) see Welfare Foundation

Friends of the Concord Pike Library (15,000) see Marmot Foundation

Hagley Museum and Library -- operating support (5,000) see Crestlea Foundation

Intercollegiate Studies Institute (105,000) see Jaquelin Hume Foundation

Intercollegiate Studies Institute, Inc. -- community service (500) see Dentsply International, Inc.

St. Andrew's School (10,000) see Pattee Foundation

Wilmington Library -- restoration and hanging of North Carolina Wyeth paintings (25,000) see Fair Play Foundation

District of Columbia

Columbia Public Library (200) see Kahn, Lucas-Lancaster, Inc. Children's Wear

Council on Library and Information Resources -- distance learning initiative (220,000) see Henry Luce Foundation

Folger Shakespeare Library -- for renovation

(100,000) see Arcana Foundation

Folger Shakespeare Library (25,000) see Georges Lurcy Charitable and Educational Trust

Folger Shakespeare Library (20,000) see Marpat Foundation

Folger Shakespeare Library -- operating support (15,000) see Memton Fund

Folger Shakespeare Library -- operating support (15,000) see Memton Fund

Library of Congress (525,000) see Naomi and Nehemiah Cohen Foundation

Library of Congress (227,000) see Liz Claiborne and Art Ortenberg Foundation

Library of Congress -- support acquisition and fellowship (185,000) see Henry Luce Foundation

Library of Congress -- for Library's Fall 2001 Exhibition of Japanese Art and Literature (142,500) see United States-Japan Foundation

Library of Congress -- education and training (141,000) see J. Paul Getty Trust

Library of Congress (100,000) see Shell Oil Co.

Library of Congress -- special event fund (50,000) see Fortis Health

Library of Congress -- Kissinger chair (33,333) see Freeport-McMoRan Copper & Gold, Inc.

Library of Congress (25,000) see AOL Time Warner

Library of Congress (20,000) see ContiGroup Companies, Inc.

Library of Congress (10,000) see Reed Foundation (NY)

Richard Nixon Library and Birthplace Foundation (50,000) see Sylvan and Ann Oestreicher Foundation

Special Libraries Association (10,000) see H. W. Wilson Foundation

Florida

Broward Public Library Foundation (25,000) see Rogow Birken Foundation

Broward Public Library Foundation (19,350) see Leroy E. Dettman Foundation

Broward Public Library Foundation (19,200) see Leroy E. Dettman Foundation

Broward Public Library Foundation (13,000) see Folke H. Peterson Charitable Foundation

Dade Public Education Fund -- Citibank Family Tech Program (150,000) see Citigroup Inc.

Delray Beach Library (29,000) see Forrest C. Lattner Foundation

Fau Foundation (22,039) see Leroy E. Dettman Foundation

Fau Foundation (15,789) see Leroy E. Dettman Foundation

Florida College -- west wing of the William F. Chatlos Library (50,000) see Chatlos Foundation

Friends of the Crestview Library (1,000) see Gulf Power Co.

Friends of the Library -- for program services (5,000) see May Kay Houck Foundation

Friends of the Palm Beach Count Public Library, Inc. (1,000) see United States Sugar Corp.

Friends of the Pensacola Library (4,000) see BCR Foundation

Friends of the Winter Haven Public Library -- for library support (4,500) see Dorothy W. Poitras Charitable Trust

Germany Public Library -- for program services (15,000) see May Kay Houck Foundation

Greater Clearwater Public Library Foundation (10,000) see Doyle Foundation

Jacksonville Library (5,000) see Carl S. Swisher Foundation

Navarre Public Library (10,000) see Tom S. and Marye Kate Aldridge Charitable and Educational Trust

South Florida Center for Theological Studies -- for library expansion (100,000) see Hugoton Foundation

Washington County Public Library -- capital funds (5,000) see Gulf Power Co.

Georgia

Atlanta Fulton Public Library (3,000) see Whilma B. Lee Scholarship Fund Trust

Council on Library and Information Resources -- for the establishment at Emory University of the Digital Leadership Institute (300,000) see Robert W. Woodruff Foundation

Greene County Library (250) see Citizens Union Bank

Liberty County Public Library -- operating support (20,714) see Margaret Lee Martin Charitable Trust

Nancy Quinn Memorial Library (3,000) see Scottsman Industries

Newton County Library (64,379) see James Hyde Porter Testamentary Trust

Thomas County Public Library (5,500) see Williams Family Foundation of Georgia

Troup Harris Coweta Regional Library -- integrated library computer system (93,176) see Callaway Foundation, Inc.

Idaho

Caldwell Public Library (3,080) see Claude R. and Ethel B. Whittenberger Foundation

Community Library Association (5,000) see James and Barbara Cimino Foundation

Eastern Idaho Library Network Consortium (28,000) see Steele-Reese Foundation

Illinois

American Library Association (257,000) see Verizon Communications Inc.

American Library Association (250,000) see Verizon Communications Inc.

American Library Association (250,000) see Verizon Communications Inc.

American Library Association (200,000) see Verizon Communications Inc.

American Library Association -- to develop and support a national network to build capacity and sustain public libraries (200,000) see Lila Wallace-Reader's Digest Fund

American Library Association -- Young Adult Reading Project (12,000) see Margaret Alexander Edwards Trust

American Library Association -- Young Adult Reading Project (10,000) see Margaret Alexander Edwards Trust

American Library Association (10,000) see Scott Fetzer Co.

American Library Association -- Young Adult Reading Project (7,625) see Margaret Alexander Edwards Trust

Chicago Public Library (75,000) see Elizabeth Morse Genius Charitable Trust

Chicago Public Library Foundation -- Tyrannosaurus Reads (100,000) see Albert Pick, Jr. Fund

Chicago Public Library Foundation -- for the Family Computer Center

(50,000) see Barker Welfare Foundation

Chicago Public Library Foundation -- for Teacher in the Library (10,000) see Field Foundation of Illinois

Chicago Public Library Foundation (5,000) see Southwest News Herald

Coffeen Community Library -- purchase of books (2,000) see Mary Heath Foundation

Decatur Public Library (60,000) see Archer-Daniels-Midland Co.

Forrest Library (2,500) see Quanex Corp.

Fund for American Libraries (25,000) see H. W. Wilson Foundation

Geneseo Public Library District -- for equipment (20,655) see Myers Charitable Trust

Loyola Academy (5,000) see Cele H. and William B. Rubin Family Fund

Newberry Library -- fund current operating expenses (100,000) see Smart Family Foundation

Newberry Library (50,000) see Illinois Tool Works, Inc.

Newberry Library -- funding for endowment (50,000) see Dr. Scholl Foundation

Newberry Library (30,000) see Haffner Foundation

Newberry Library -- capital support (25,000) see Northern Trust Corp.

Newberry Library (20,000) see Chauncey and Marion Deering McCormick Foundation

Newberry Library (15,000) see FMC Corp.

Newberry Library (10,000) see Abra Prentice Foundation

Newberry Library (5,000) see Ondeo Nalco Co.

Newberry Library (2,500) see Charles H. and Bertha L. Boothroyd Foundation

Newberry Library (2,000) see Regenstein Foundation

North Suburban Library Foundation -- operating support (7,500) see Chicago Tribune Direct Marketing

Northwestern University -- funding for heart research (93,513) see Dr. Scholl Foundation

Palestine Public Library District -- library lighting (400) see Mary Heath Foundation

Pontiac Public Library (6,900) see J. Paul Yost Trust

Rantoul Public Library (100,000) see Jeld-Wen, Inc.

Rockford Public Library (3,000) see AMCORE Financial, Inc.

Sterling Public Library (11,500) see Dillon Foundation

Sterling Rock Falls Day Care Agency, Inc. (429,250) see Dillon Foundation

Urban Libraries Council -- provide technical assistance and coordination for public libraries (270,100) see DeWitt Wallace-Reader's Digest Fund

Westville Public Library (25,000) see Julius W. Hegeler II Foundation

Indiana

Allen County Public Library (1,000) see Vann Family Foundation

Allen County Public Library Foundation (6,000) see Journal-Gazette Co.

Eckhart Public Library (7,000) see Rieke Corp.

Eckhart Public Library -- young adult program (2,500) see Olive B. Cole Foundation

Friends of the Library (125) see Dr. Louis A. and Anne B. Schneider Foundation

Indiana University Foundation (250,000) see Randall L. Tobias Foundation

Indiana University Foundation (150,000) see Randall L. Tobias Foundation

Indianapolis Marion County Public Library Foundation -- for support toward creating the Indianapolis Special Collections Room (750,000) see Nina Mason Pulliam Charitable Trust

Indianapolis-Marion County Public Library Foundation (2,500) see KeyCorp

Junior Achievement of Central Indiana -- for operations (3,000) see George and Frances Ball Foundation

Kentucky Mountain Bible College -- construction funds to complete town house apartment complex (50,000) see Chatlos Foundation

Muncie Public Library -- capital campaign (100,000) see George and Frances Ball Foundation

Muncie Public Library (50,000) see Ball Brothers Foundation

Muncie Public Library (5,000) see Ontario Corp.

Notre Dame Library Architecture Endowment -- college library (25,000) see Plym Foundation

Red Trail Conservancy, Inc. -- for operations (15,000) see George and Frances Ball Foundation

West Jay Community Center, Inc. (5,000) see Andersons, Inc.

West Jay Community Center, Inc. -- capital campaign (5,000) see George and Frances Ball Foundation

Iowa

Allison Public Library -- new library and community room (25,000) see R. J. McElroy Trust

Anamosa Public Library -- Anamosa Library and Learning Center (15,000) see R. J. McElroy Trust

Audubon Public Library (1,375) see Audubon State Bank

Belmond Public Library (25,000) see Eaton Corp.

Bettendorf Public Library (55,000) see Roy J. Carver Charitable Trust

Birmingham Public Library -- Ralph Shott Memorial (595) see Van Buren Foundation

Carver Youth Recreation Program (50,000) see Roy J. Carver Charitable Trust

Carver Youth Recreation Program (50,000) see Roy J. Carver Charitable Trust

Clear Lake Public Library (50,000) see Lee Endowment Foundation

Fertile Public Library (2,000) see Winnebago Industries

Friends of Sioux City Public Library -- purchase bilingual children's books (1,000) see IBP

Glidden Public Library (1,500) see Iowa Savings Bank

Greater Cedar Rapids Foundation -- for Skate, Inc., campaign (40,000) see Alliant Energy Corp.

Greater Cedar Rapids Foundation -- for Skate, Inc., campaign (10,000) see Alliant Energy Corp.

Keosauqua Public Library -- computerize circulation system (4,125) see Van Buren Foundation

Marion Public Library -- construction of new facility (8,000) see Alliant Energy Corp.

Public Library of Des Moines Foundation (5,000) see Weathertop Foundation

Public Library of Des Moines Foundation (1,500) see Amerus Group Co.

Rock Rapids Public Library -- establish "The Serendipity Club" (6,000) see James W. and Ella B. Forster Charitable Trust

Southeastern Library Services -- software upgrade for county libraries (1,689) see Van Buren Foundation

Stewart Library -- automation of library equipment (25,000) see Claude W.

and Dolly Ahrens Foundation

Stewart Library (1,000) see Grinnell Mutual Reinsurance Co.

Waverly Public Library (5,000) see CUNA Mutual Group

Kansas

Atchison County Library -- audio books (3,500) see W. and E. Morgan Charitable Residual Trust

Atchison Library (8,000) see Muchnic Foundation

Dodge City Public Library -- Literacy Training Program (11,505) see Baughman Foundation

Finney County Public Library -- for education - computer and software for public use (15,000) see Mary Jo Williams Charitable Trust

Hays Public Library Trust (5,000) see Ross Foundation

Kansas Library Association (10,000) see H. W. Wilson Foundation

Liberal Memorial Library -- internet access equipment and augment book budget (17,320) see Baughman Foundation

Library Foundation (10,000) see Security Benefit Life Insurance Co.

Pittsburgh State University (10,000) see Louis W. and Dolpha Baehr Foundation

Topeka and Shawnee County Public Library (500) see Blanche Bryden Foundation

Kentucky

Library Foundation (1,000) see PPG Industries, Inc.

Louisville Free Public Library (15,000) see LG&E Energy Corp.

Louisville Free Public Library Foundation -- for Youth Summer Reading Program (15,000) see Humana, Inc.

Louisiana

Ascension Parish Library Board (20,000) see Vulcan Materials Co.

Maine

Auburn Public Library (50,000) see Gladys and Roland Harriman Foundation

Auburn Public Library (5,000) see Hannaford Brothers Co.

Bangor Public Library (4,000) see Webber Oil Co.

Blue Hill Library -- pledge payment for capital campaign (25,000) see Britton Fund

Brown Memorial Library (25,000) see William Bingham Second Betterment Fund

Brown Memorial Library (5,000) see Margaret E. Burnham Charitable Trust

Falmouth Memorial Library (5,000) see Margaret E. Burnham Charitable Trust

Farmington Public Library (500) see Webber Oil Co.

Gardiner Library (1,000) see Gardiner Savings Institution

Library Club of Lovell -- for public library purposes (3,300) see Clarence E. Mulford Trust

Ludden Memorial Library (105,000) see Meadwestvaco Corp.

Ludden Memorial Library (25,000) see William Bingham Second Betterment Fund

Maine Community Foundation (50,000) see William Bingham Second Betterment Fund

Maine Community Foundation (25,000) see William Bingham Second Betterment Fund

Northeast Harbor Library -- operating support (5,000) see Crestlea Foundation

Norway Medical Library (25,000) see William Bingham Second Betterment Fund

Norway Memorial Library (25,000) see William Bingham Second Betterment Fund

Oakland Public Library -- expand and strengthen an educational enrichment program (141,900) see DeWitt Wallace-Reader's Digest Fund

Oakland Public Library -- educational (30,000) see Brook Family Foundation

Maryland

Baltimore County Public Library -- capital campaign (5,000) see Campbell Foundation (MD)

Boonsboro Ambulance and Rescue Service, Inc. -- for external defibrilation (9,700) see Albert E. and Naomi B. Sinnisen Foundation

Enoch Pratt Free Library -- provide opportunities for low income youth (130,900) see DeWitt Wallace-Reader's Digest Fund

Enoch Pratt Free Library (43,000) see Marion I. and Henry J. Knott Foundation

Enoch Pratt Free Library (25,000) see William G. Baker, Jr. Memorial Fund

Enoch Pratt Free Library (25,000) see John J. Leidy Foundation

Enoch Pratt Free Library -- for youth development, After-School Program at Roland Park Public School (20,000) see Clayton Baker Trust

Enoch Pratt Free Library (20,000) see T. Rowe Price Associates

Enoch Pratt Free Library -- family place program (10,000) see Baltimore Equity Society

Enoch Pratt Free Library (5,000) see Hecht-Levi Foundation

Frederick County Public Libraries -- construction (15,000) see John Ben Snow Memorial Trust

Kennedy Krieger Institute -- capital campaign (20,000) see Constellation Energy Group, Inc.

Kennedy Krieger Institute (1,666) see Giant Food, Inc.

National First Ladies Library (15,000) see Forest City Enterprises, Inc.

Reach, Inc -- for office equipment (2,354) see Albert E. and Naomi B. Sinnisen Foundation

Roland Park Library Initiative, Inc. -- for community development (40,000) see Lockhart Vaughan Foundation

St. James School Library Fund (8,000) see Lucien B. and Katherine E. Price Foundation

University of Maryland Foundation (350,000) see Foundation for Child Development

Village Learning Place, Inc (25,000) see William G. Baker, Jr. Memorial Fund

Village Learning Place, Inc. -- for community development and capital campaign (50,000) see Clayton Baker Trust

Washington County Free Library -- construction funding (5,000) see Albert E. and Naomi B. Sinnisen Foundation

Massachusetts

American Antiquarian Society -- research library (9,000) see Margaret E. Sherman Trust

Bancroft Memorial Library -- for historic renovations (13,000) see Hopedale Foundation

Beaman Memorial Public Library (3,000) see Margaret E. Sherman Trust

Boston Athenaeum (100,000) see Edwin S. Webster Foundation

Boston Athenaeum (10,000) see Constance Killam Trust

Boston Public Library -- for education (75,000) see Richard and Susan Smith Family Foundation

Boston Public Library (15,000) see Yawkey Foundation II

Boston Public Library Foundation (300,000) see Fidelity Investments

Boston Public Library Foundation (165,000) see Mabel Louise Riley Foundation

Boston Public Library Foundation (17,000) see Sidney R. Rabb Charitable Trust

Boston Public Library Foundation (8,000) see Sidney and Esther Rabb Charitable Foundation

Boston Public Library Foundation (5,000) see William J. and Lia G. Poorvu Foundation

Boston Public Library Foundation (2,000) see Sawyer Charitable Foundation

Brookline Public Library (12,500) see Sulzberger Foundation

Brookline Public Library (1,000) see Hamilton Charitable Corp.

Brookline Public Library (1,000) see Hamilton Charitable Corp.

Brooks School (7,550) see Catherine McCarthy Memorial Trust Fund

Cambridge Public library -- for 2000 Summer Reading Program (5,000) see East Cambridge Savings Bank

Chicopee Public Library (10,000) see Dow Jones & Company, Inc.

East Longmeadow Public Library -- for expansion and renovation of the East Longmeadow Public Library (250,000) see Irene E. and George A. Davis Foundation

East Longmeadow Public Library -- for renovation and expansion of the current library (11,000) see Woronoco Savings Bank

French Library and Cultural Center (85,000) see Beaucourt Foundation

French Library and Cultural Center (70,000) see Beaucourt Foundation

French Library and Cultural Center -- operating support (1,000) see Chiles Foundation

Friends of Newburyport Library (25,000) see Eastern Bank

Friends of Newburyport Library (20,000) see Mary Alice Arakelian Foundation

Friends of the Hopedale Library (2,000) see Hopedale Foundation

Friends of the Milton Public Library (100,000) see Longwood Foundation

Friends of the Worcester Public Library -- towards renovation to Worcester Public Library (250,000) see Stoddard Charitable Trust

Friends of the Worcester Public Library -- capital project for the expansion and renovation of Salem Square (30,000) see Ruth H. and Warren A. Ellsworth Foundation

Friends of the Worcester Public Library -- expansion and renovation of library (20,000) see Francis A. and Jacquelyn H. Harrington Foundation

Hingham Public Library (10,000) see Orchard Foundation

Hingham Public Library (1,000) see Building 19 Foundation

John F. Kennedy Library (200,000) see Joseph P. Kennedy, Jr. Foundation

John F. Kennedy Library (200,000) see Joseph P. Kennedy, Jr. Foundation

Lenox Library Association (5,000) see Country Curtains, Inc.

Library of the Boston Athenaeum (50,000) see Cabot Family Charitable Trust

Library of the Boston Athenaeum (10,000) see Clara B. Winthrop Trust

Manchester by the Sea Conservation Trust (15,000) see Clara B. Winthrop Trust

Morse Institute Library (10,000) see TJX Companies, Inc.

Nantucket Athenaeum (150,000) see Tupancy-Harris Foundation of 1986

Nantucket Athenaeum (25,000) see Allegheny Foundation

Nantucket Athenaeum (500) see McCausland Foundation

New England Conservatory of Music (7,500) see Clara B. Winthrop Trust

Northboro Public Library (3,000) see Margaret E. Sherman Trust

Plymouth Public Library (5,000) see Henry Hornblower Fund

Proprietors of the Boston Athenaeum (25,000) see Sun Hill Foundation

Randall Library (12,500) see Joe and Emily Lowe Foundation

Somerset Public Library (1,800) see Hathaway Memorial Charitable Trust

South Dennis Library Fund (4,000) see C. Northrop

Pond and Alethea Marder
Pond Foundation

Springfield Libraries and Museums (4,000) see Albert
Steiger Memorial Fund

Springfield Library & Museums (15,000) see Textron, Inc.

Springfield Library and Museums Association -- support for public libraries
and museums (2,050)
see Shatz, Schwartz &
Fentin PC

Talking Book Library (6,600)
see Memorial Foundation
for the Blind

Thomas Crane Public Library -- for April 2001
grants (10,000) see Oliver S. and Jennie R. Donaldson Charitable Trust

Wellesley Free Library
(1,000) see Cele H. and
William B. Rubin Family
Fund

Worcester Public Library
(250,000) see George I.
Alden Trust

Worcester Public Library
(150,000) see George F.
and Sybil H. Fuller Foundation

Worcester Public Library
(30,000) see Hoche-Scofield Foundation

Worcester Public Library
(11,000) see Nathaniel
Wheeler Trust

Michigan

Brother Rice High School
(5,000) see Drusilla Farwell Foundation

Crooked Tree District Library
(250) see Chamberlain
Foundation

Detroit Public Library -- for
operating support
(2,500,000) see Skillman
Foundation

Fremont Area District Library
(50,000) see Gerber Products Co.

Friends of Detroit Public Library, National Automotive History Collection --
operating expenses
(25,000) see Matilda R.
Wilson Fund

Grand Rapids Public Library
(12,500) see Keller Family Foundation

Hespena Library -- heritage
giving (75,000) see
Gerber Products Co.

Library of Michigan Foundation (195,000) see Talbert and Leota Abrams
Foundation

Peter White Library (5,000)
see Cleveland-Cliffs, Inc.

Ryerson Library Foundation
(84,186) see Keeler Foundation

Ryerson Library Foundation -- support annual
fund (25,000) see Sebastian Foundation

Ryerson Library Foundation -- annual support

(2,000) see Frank B. and
Virginia V. Fehsenfeld
Charitable Foundation

Saline Public Library (5,000)
see R&B Machine Tool
Co.

Sanilac District Library -- for
building expansion and
renovation project
(75,000) see Herrick
Foundation

Vicksburg District Library --
equipment (4,207) see
Vicksburg Foundation

Warner Baird District Library -- capital campaign
(25,000) see JSJ Corp.

Wickson Memorial Library
(19,000) see Wickson-
Link Memorial Foundation

Minnesota

Friends of Pelican Rapid Library -- capital construction (5,000) see MDU Resources Group, Inc.

Friends of the Minneapolis
Public Library (2,500) see
Metris Companies, Inc.

Friends of the St. Paul Public
Library (52,000) see Hubbard Broadcasting, Inc.

Friends of the St. Paul Public
Library -- system renewal
(30,000) see Mary Livingston Griggs and Mary
Griggs Burke Foundation

Friends of the St. Paul Public
Library (10,000) see
Anna M. Heilmaier Charitable Foundation

Friends of the St. Paul Public
Library (10,000) see U.S.
Bancorp Piper Jaffray

Friends of the St. Paul Public
Library -- for the Saint
Paul Public Library's Summer Reading Program
(7,500) see H.B. Fuller
Co.

Friends of the St. Paul Public
Library -- renewal capital
campaign (5,000) see
Land O'Lakes, Inc.

Hennepin County Library
Foundation (5,000) see
Jostens, Inc.

James J. Hill Reference Library -- operating support
(5,000) see Driscoll Foundation

Library Foundation of Hennepin County (2,500) see
Schmoker Family Foundation

Owatonna Public Library
(4,500) see Federated
Mutual Insurance Co.

The Friends of the St. Paul
Public Library -- support
for the renewal campaign
(75,000) see Patrick and
Aimee Butler Family
Foundation

West Tisbury Library (500)
see Louis L. Stott Foundation

Mississippi

Yazoo Library Association --
restoration of the B.S.
Ricks Memorial Library
(40,000) see Charles M.
and Mary D. Grant Foundation

Missouri

Daniel Boone Regional Library Foundation (2,000)
see Shelter Mutual Insurance Co.

Forsyth Library Friends
(3,500) see Roy W.
Slusher Charitable Foundation

Friends of the Saint Louis
Public Library -- operating funds (1,000) see
Bakewell Corp.

Harry S. Truman Library Institute (5,000) see Andrews
McMeel Universal

Harry S. Truman Library Institute for National and International Affairs (62,500)
see William T. Kemper
Foundation

Kirkwood Public Library Foundation (8,500) see Edward Chase Garvey Memorial Foundation

Law Library Association of
St. Louis (12,000) see Edward Chase Garvey Memorial Foundation

Lebanon Public Library -- library project (10,000)
see Lowe Family Foundation

Linda Hall Library (10,000)
see Bartlett & Co.

Maryville Public Library
(5,000) see Kawasaki Motors Manufacturing Corporation U.S.A.

Missouri Botanical Gardens -- toward costs of a
program of ecological research and training
(900,000) see Andrew W.
Mellon Foundation

Missouri Development Finance Board -- for Adult
Rehabilitation Center
(1,800,000) see The Hall
Family Foundation

Missouri Development Finance Board -- classroom for democracy campaign support (20,000)
see Courtney S. Turner
Charitable Trust

St. Louis Mercantile Library
Association (80,000) see
Herman T. and Phenie R.
Pott Foundation

Truman Library Institute
(125,000) see Francis
Families Foundation

Truman Library Institute
(120) see Small Business
Service Bureau

Webb City Library -- for children's library (80,000)
see C. W. Titus Foundation

Montana

Miles City Public Library
Foundation (3,000) see
L. P. and Teresa Anderson Foundation

Nebraska

Bloomfield Library Foundation (103,000) see Peter
Kiewit Sons' Inc.

City of Ralston (100,000) see
Peter Kiewit Sons' Inc.

Friends of Libraries (1,500)
see NEBCO Evans

Fullerton Public Library
(3,000) see John C. Markey Charitable Fund

Lincoln Public Schools Library (6,220) see Liz
Claiborne and Art Ortenberg Foundation

Omaha Public Library (5,000)
see Paul and Oscar
Giger Foundation

Omaha Public Library Foundation (1,000) see Valmont Industries, Inc.

Osmond Public Library -- for
book shelves, computers
and furniture for library
(75,000) see Lied Foundation Trust

Ralston Public Library Foundation (103,350) see Hollis and Helen Baright
Foundation

Tilden Library Foundation --
furnishings and equipment for auditorium in
new library (36,000) see
Lied Foundation Trust

Nevada

Museum Library & Arts Foundation -- purchase of collections (10,000) see
Charles H. Stout Foundation

Washoe County Library System -- develop teen action teams (106,700) see
DeWitt Wallace-Reader's
Digest Fund

Washoe Library Foundation -- to construct Verdi
Nature Center (50,000)
see E. L. Cord Foundation

New Hampshire

Concord Public Library Foundation -- for children's
room renovation (25,000)
see Samuel P. Hunt
Foundation

Concord Public Library Foundation -- children's Room
Project (20,000) see
Oleonda Jameson Trust

Cook Memorial Library
(10,000) see Doris L.
Benz Trust

Elm Research Institute
(10,000) see Elsie Procter Van Buren Foundation

Gilmanton Year Round Library (25,000) see Doris
L. Benz Trust

Stephenson Memorial Library
(5,000) see Monadnock
Paper Mills, Inc.

Stephenson Memorial Library
(5,000) see Morrill Charitable Foundation

Stephenson Memorial Library
(5,000) see Morrill Charitable Foundation

Tuck Library (25,000) see
George R. Wallace Foundation

University of New Hampshire
at Manchester -- for new
library (100,000) see
Samuel P. Hunt Foundation

New Jersey

Arnold Schwartz Memorial Library (20,000) see Arnold
A. Schwartz Foundation

Bernardsville Public Library --
for books (52,000) see
Jockey Hollow Foundation

Fort Lee Public Library see
Oki America, Inc.

Friends of the Fair Lawn Library (50) see Fran and
Irwin Ziegelheim Charitable Foundation

Friends of the Kinnelon Library (2,075) see Westerhoff Family Foundation,
Inc.

Friends of the Kinnelon Library (300) see Westerhoff Family Foundation,
Inc.

New Jersey Historical Society -- toward construction
of a new library (50,000)
see Prospect Hill Foundation

Newark Public Library
(10,000) see Lucy and Eleanor S. Upton Charitable Foundation

North Plain Field Library
(10,000) see Saul
Fromkes Foundation

Princeton Public Library
(10,000) see Dow
Jones & Company, Inc.

South Brunswick Public Library Foundation
(10,000) see Dow
Jones & Company, Inc.

New York

Albany Public Library -- support library campaign
(2,000) see Hudson River
Bancorp, Inc.

Albany Public Library -- library donation (2,000)
see Hudson River Bancorp, Inc.

Albany Public Library see Microsoft Corp.

Albert Wisner Public Library
(2,500) see Warwick Savings Foundation

American Foundation for
Blind -- educational material for special library services (10,000) see Knapp
Foundation, Inc. (MD)

American Friends of the Medem Library, Inc. -- archives project (10,000) see Lucius N. Littauer Foundation

American Trust for the British Library (15,000) see Reed Foundation (NY)

Aurora Free Library Association (6,000) see Cayuga Foundation

Bolton Free Library (3,000) see Waterhouse Family Foundation

Brooklyn Public Library -- toward construction of the Technology Loft in their new youth wind. (150,000) see Charles Hayden Foundation

Brooklyn Public Library (150,000) see J. M. Kaplan Fund

Brooklyn Public Library -- provide low-income teenagers after-school educational enrichment, job readiness, career planning and leadership development (105,600) see De-Witt Wallace-Reader's Digest Fund

Brooklyn Public Library -- for an initiative aimed at promoting reading readiness and making life longer readers for children (50,000) see Louis Calder Foundation

Brooklyn Public Library (15,000) see Greentree Foundation

Brooklyn Public Library (15,000) see Henry and Lucy Moses Fund, Inc.

Brooklyn Public Library (12,500) see KeySpan Corp.

Brooklyn Public Library (10,000) see Daily News, L.P.

Brooklyn Public Library (6,000) see Michael Tuch Foundation

Brooklyn Public Library (5,000) see Washington Mutual, Inc.

Brooklyn Public Library -- for the Ready to Read Educational Program for children (2,500) see Moses L. Parshelsky Foundation

Broome Library Foundation (100,000) see A. Lindsay and Olive B. O'Connor Foundation

Buffalo 7 Erie County Public Library (1,000) see Viyu Foundation

Canajoharie Library and Art Gallery -- conservation of works in the art collection of the gallery (12,000) see Stockman Family Foundation Trust

Canajoharie Library and Art Gallery -- operating support (10,000) see Arkell Hall Foundation

Castleton Public Library -- library donation (1,000)

see Hudson River Bancorp, Inc.

Catskill Mountain Crafts Collective -- color and crafts festival (20,000) see A. Lindsay and Olive B. O'Connor Foundation

Chautauqua Catteraugus Library System -- new bookmobile (70,000) see Ralph C. Sheldon Foundation Inc.

Chautauqua-Cattaraugus Library System -- Gates Foundation partnership (184,047) see Gebbie Foundation

Chautauqua-Cattaraugus Library System (70,000) see Hultquist Foundation

Chautauqua-Cattaraugus Library System -- book plan and subscriptions (27,763) see Gebbie Foundation

Chautauqua-Cattaraugus Library System -- Alexander Finley Library (15,000) see Gebbie Foundation

Columbia University Rare Book and Manuscript Library (2,000) see Bella Spewack Article 5th Trust

Cordelia A. Greene Library -- for addition to existing building (30,000) see Western New York Foundation

Cuba Circulating Library -- for construction of addition (25,000) see Western New York Foundation

Cuba Circulating Library (5,000) see Carnahan-Jackson Foundation

East Greenbush Community Library -- library donation (1,000) see Hudson River Bancorp, Inc.

Field Library (8,449) see Reader's Digest Association, Inc.

Fort Plain Free Library -- program support (1,500) see Arkell Hall Foundation

Foundation Center (2,000) see Ittleson Foundation

Foundation Center -- for the Philanthropic Center (1,000) see Virginia Environmental Endowment

Foundation Center, The (1,500) see Phil Hardin Foundation

Frick Collection -- historic archives (40,000) see Gladys Krieble Delmas Foundation

Frick Collection (10,000) see Edward B. Osborn Charitable Trust

Frick Collection -- charitable and educational purposes (10,000) see Sage Foundation

Friends of the Library (135,700) see Ishiyama Foundation

Friends of the Library (15,000) see Ghidotti Foundation

Friends of the Middletown Thrall Library (1,000) see Warwick Savings Foundation

Friends of the Shelter Island Public Library Society (10,000) see Gladys Brooks Foundation

Galway Public Library (2,500) see Arthur Crames Family Foundation

Genesis Foundation -- library (50,000) see Bender Foundation

Geneva Free Library -- for community preservation (7,500) see John Ben Snow Foundation

George Bush Presidential Library Foundation (600,000) see MBNA Corp.

Hamilton Public Library (12,000) see Howard and Bess Chapman Charitable Corp.

Hamilton Public Library -- building fund (10,000) see Oneida Savings Bank

Hammondsport Public Library (5,000) see Mercury Aircraft, Inc.

Hillsdale Public Library (2,500) see Rheinstrom Hill Community Foundation

Hudson Area Association Library -- children's room improvement project (5,000) see Hudson River Bancorp, Inc.

Hudson Area Association Library -- library donation (2,000) see Hudson River Bancorp, Inc.

Hudson Day Care Center -- insulation of infant room (2,500) see Hudson River Bancorp, Inc.

James Prendergast Free Library -- purchase of books (30,000) see Gebbie Foundation

James Prendergast Library (100,000) see Carnahan-Jackson Foundation

James Prendergast Library -- for computer resources and senior services (14,500) see John Alfred and Oscar Johnson Memorial Trust

James Prendergast Library -- educational (7,000) see Holmberg Foundation

Jewish Braille Institute -- for library (2,000) see Jerome A. and Estelle R. Newman Assistance Fund

Katonah Village Library (2,500) see William S. Paley Foundation, Inc.

Katonah Village Library (2,500) see William S. Paley Foundation, Inc.

Kingston Area Library (8,000) see Jay E. Klock and Lucia Klock Kingston Foundation

Lake Placid Public Library -- building fund (40,000)

see Loewy Family Foundation

Lake Placid Public Library -- debt servicing (25,500) see Lake Placid Education Foundation

Larchmont Public Library -- operating needs (20,000) see Huisking Foundation

Libraries for the Future (150,000) see Metropolitan Life Insurance Co.

Libraries for the Future -- for Bay Area Education ACCESS (75,000) see Walter and Elise Haas Fund

Library Foundation of Buffalo and Erie County -- support the Western New York rare book consortium (200,000) see The John R. Oishei Foundation

Library Foundation of Buffalo and Erie County -- support rare book expansion project (200,000) see The John R. Oishei Foundation

Long Lake Library -- education (7,410) see Lake Placid Education Foundation

Longwood Public Library (3,950) see Henry P. Kovarik Foundation for Poetry

Louise Adelia Read Memorial Library (10,000) see Charles L. Read Foundation

Manhattan College -- for library and endowment (500,000) see Starr Foundation

Metropolitan Museum of Art -- Thomas J. Watson, Jr. Memorial Library (100,000) see Achelis Foundation

Miles City Public Library (10,000) see Nibs and Edna Allen Foundation

Millbrook Free Library (120,000) see Millbrook Tribute Garden

Millbrook Free Library (8,000) see Adrian and Jessie Archbold Charitable Trust

Millbrook Library (50,000) see McCann Foundation

Mind-Builders Creative Arts Co., Inc. -- toward renovation of basement and courtyard space at their Bronx facility (75,000) see Charles Hayden Foundation

Morgan Library -- for digitalize collection of medieval and renaissance illuminated manuscripts (400,000) see Homeland Foundation (NY)

Morgan Library (100,000) see Burlington Resources Inc.

Morgan Library (25,000) see M. A. Chisholm Foundation

Morgan Library (10,000) see M. A. Chisholm Foundation

Morgan Library (10,000) see James J. Colt Foundation

Morgan Library (5,000) see Crane Co.

Museum of Modern Art -- for a capital project (4,000,000) see Evelyn and Walter Haas, Jr. Fund

Museum of Modern Art (20,000) see Sarah K. de Coizart Perpetual Charitable Trust

Museum of Modern Art (15,000) see Adrian and Jessie Archbold Charitable Trust

Museum of Modern Art (2,500) see Kajima Engineering and Construction, Inc.

Museum of Modern Art (2,500) see Richard Meier Foundation

Nassau Free Library -- library donation (1,000) see Hudson River Bancorp, Inc.

New Rochelle Public Library (25,000) see H. W. Wilson Foundation

New York Botanical Gardens (20,000) see Samuel Freeman Charitable Trust

New York Botanical Gardens (5,000) see Dendroica Foundation

New York Library Association -- library purposes and fellowships (20,000) see Lake Placid Education Foundation

New York Public Library (1,088,361) see The Carl and Lily Pforzheimer Foundation, Inc.

New York Public Library (800,000) see Dorot Foundation

New York Public Library (500,000) see Esther A. and Joseph Klingenstein Fund, Inc.

New York Public Library -- for South Court Programs (500,000) see Starr Foundation

New York Public Library (500,000) see UBS Paine-Webber, Inc.

New York Public Library (325,000) see Scherman Foundation

New York Public Library (200,000) see The Florence Gould Foundation

New York Public Library (200,000) see Helena Rubinstein Foundation

New York Public Library (100,000) see The Ambrose Monell Foundation

New York Public Library (100,000) see Felix and Elizabeth Rohatyn Foundation

New York Public Library (100,000) see Wasserstein Perella Foundation

New York Public Library (90,000) see Allene Reuss Memorial Trust

New York Public Library (75,000) see Felix and Elizabeth Rohatyn Foundation

New York Public Library -- for program support (50,000) see Corning Inc.

New York Public Library (50,000) see Gladys and Roland Harriman Foundation

New York Public Library (50,000) see Hebrew Technical Institute

New York Public Library (49,585) see Frances and Benjamin Benenson Foundation

New York Public Library (40,000) see Norman and Rosita Winston Foundation

New York Public Library (25,000) see The Theodore H. Barth Foundation, Inc.

New York Public Library (25,000) see CBS Corp.

New York Public Library -- for research (25,000) see Hagedorn Fund

New York Public Library (25,000) see McGraw-Hill Companies, Inc.

New York Public Library -- toward the conservation treatment laboratory (25,000) see Prospect Hill Foundation

New York Public Library (25,000) see Rudin Foundation

New York Public Library (25,000) see Sarah I. Schieffelin Residuary Trust

New York Public Library (25,000) see Dorothy Schiff Foundation

New York Public Library (21,210) see Country Curtains, Inc.

New York Public Library -- for Page Program (20,000) see Barker Welfare Foundation

New York Public Library -- for specific programs (15,000) see Mary Livingston Griggs and Mary Griggs Burke Foundation

New York Public Library -- support of the research libraries (15,000) see Alfred Jurzykowski Foundation

New York Public Library (15,000) see New York Life Insurance Co.

New York Public Library (15,000) see New York Stock Exchange, Inc.

New York Public Library (15,000) see Prudential Securities, Inc.

New York Public Library (12,500) see Hebrew Technical Institute

New York Public Library (10,000) see Cowles Charitable Trust

New York Public Library (10,000) see Dow Jones & Company, Inc.

New York Public Library (10,000) see Armand G. Erpf Fund

New York Public Library (10,000) see Mary W. Harriman Foundation

New York Public Library -- for business research libraries (10,000) see Hugoton Foundation

New York Public Library (10,000) see Millipore Corp.

New York Public Library (10,000) see United States Trust Co. of New York

New York Public Library (5,300) see Sylvan and Ann Oestreicher Foundation

New York Public Library (5,000) see Atran Foundation, Inc.

New York Public Library (5,000) see Harriet Ford Dickenson Foundation

New York Public Library -- support of public libraries in Greenwich Village area (5,000) see Sidney and Judith Kranes Charitable Trust

New York Public Library (5,000) see Eugene M. Lang Foundation

New York Public Library (5,000) see William and Mildred Lasdon Foundation

New York Public Library (5,000) see Bertha and Isaac Liberman Foundation

New York Public Library -- to support the Jewish Division of the library (4,000) see Moses L. Parshelsky Foundation

New York Public Library (2,000) see Crane Co.

New York Public Library (1,250) see Garfinkle-Minard Foundation, Inc.

New York Public Library (1,000) see Ballet Makers

New York Public Library (1,000) see Bella Spewack Article 5th Trust

New York Public Library -- for Employee Matching Gift Program (200) see Daily News, L.P.

New York Public Library see Dreyfus Corp.

New York Public Library see John Wiley & Sons, Inc.

New York Public Library Astor Lenox and Tilden Foundation (100,000) see Anheuser-Busch Companies, Inc.

New York Society Library -- general operating expenses (18,000) see

Thomas J. Watson Foundation

New York University -- Grey Art Gallery (35,000) see The Andy Warhol Foundation for the Visual Arts

North Greenbush Public Library -- library donation (1,000) see Hudson River Bancorp, Inc.

Olive Free Library -- permanent endowment (200,000) see A. Lindsay and Olive B. O'Connor Foundation

Ossining Public Library (10,500) see Reader's Digest Association, Inc.

Patrons Program -- Library Connections Program (100,000) see Louis Calder Foundation

Patterson Library (25,000) see Carnahan-Jackson Foundation

Pencil, Inc. (500) see Richard Meier Foundation

Pierpont Morgan Library -- for endowment (250,000) see Rockefeller Brothers Fund, Inc.

Pierpont Morgan Library (100,000) see The Ambrose Monell Foundation

Pierpont Morgan Library -- towards the building fund (100,000) see Margaret T. Morris Foundation

Pierpont Morgan Library -- for challenge grant (71,000) see Arcana Foundation

Pierpont Morgan Library (20,000) see Drue Heinz Trust

Pierpont Morgan Library (5,000) see Harriet Ford Dickenson Foundation

Pius XII Foundation -- to support the reconfiguration of the library (50,000) see Ira W. DeCamp Foundation

Queens Borough Public Library (10,000) see Billy Rose Foundation

Queens Library Foundation (110,000) see J. M. Kaplan Fund

Queens Library Foundation -- toward renovation of the second floor children's area of the Steinway Branch (75,000) see Charles Hayden Foundation

Queens Library Foundation (40,000) see J. M. Kaplan Fund

Rensselaer Public Library -- library donation (1,000) see Hudson River Bancorp, Inc.

Replications -- toward replication of KIPP Academy in IS 148 in Community Schools District Nine (90,000) see Charles Hayden Foundation

Replications, Inc. -- for capacity building (75,000) see

Ira W. DeCamp Foundation

Ripley Free Library -- educational (7,000) see Holmberg Foundation

River Street Park -- preservation in the Village of Valatie (2,000) see Hudson River Bancorp, Inc.

Rogers Memorial Library (3,000) see Tatiana Piankova Foundation

Rogers Memorial Library (1,000) see Albert and Bessie Warner Fund

Roman Athenaeum Foundation (158,471) see Clover Foundation

Rundel Library Foundation (25,000) see Riedman Foundation

Rundel Library Foundation -- computer upgrade, program and restoration of Rundel building (25,000) see Kilian J. and Caroline F. Schmitt Foundation

Rye Free Reading Room (15,000) see Henry L. and Grace Doherty Charitable Foundation

Rye Free Reading Room (5,000) see Scott B. and Annie P. Appleby Trust

Rye Free Reading Room (2,000) see Sound Shore Foundation

Seymour Library -- new books and periodical fund (10,000) see D.E. French Foundation

Sinclairville Free Library (57,500) see Ralph C. Sheldon Foundation Inc.

Sinclairville Free Library (25,000) see Carnahan-Jackson Foundation

Skaneateles Library Association -- for operating support (28,500) see Allyn Foundation

South Salem Library Association (75,000) see Dextra Baldwin McGonagle Foundation

Standing Tall, Inc. (5,000) see Eugene and Estelle Ferkauf Foundation

Steele Memorial Library -- A. Marshall Lowman and Charles A. Winding Material Fund (20,000) see Anderson Foundation (NY)

Syracuse Children's Chorus, Inc. (2,000) see Richard Mather Fund

The New York Public Library (223,000) see New York Life Insurance Co.

Tompkins County Public Library (15,000) see J. M. McDonald Foundation

Town of Clinton Library (1,000) see McCann Foundation

Troy Public Library -- library donation (2,000) see Hudson River Bancorp, Inc.

Troy Public Library Foundation (25,000) see McCarthy Charities

Ulysses Philmathic Library (25,000) see J. M. McDonald Foundation

White Plains Public Library Foundation (10,500) see Reader's Digest Association, Inc.

White Plains Public Library Foundation (10,000) see Virginia and Leonard Marx Foundation

North Carolina

Alamance County Public Library (7,500) see AMETEK, Inc.

Alamance Public Library (15,000) see AMETEK, Inc.

Belhaven Public Library (5,000) see Tri-County Telephone Foundation

Cleveland County Library System (10,000) see Dover Foundation

Conservation Trust for North Carolina -- for operations (25,000) see Cemala Foundation

Currituck County Library -- for computer equipment (6,000) see Knapp Foundation, Inc. (MD)

East Lincoln Library Fund (2,000) see Willis Family Foundation

Echo Foundation (20,000) see Goodrich Corp.

Forsyth County Public Library -- establish bilingual mini-libraries (5,000) see R.J. Reynolds Tobacco

Friends of Boonville Library -- construction of Boonville library (10,000) see John Wesley and Anna Hodgin Hanes Foundation

Friends of Madison County Library (450,000) see Janirve Foundation

Friends of Madison County Library -- construction of a new library (25,000) see The Cannon Foundation, Inc.

Gibsonville Public Library (15,000) see AMETEK, Inc.

Jesse Helms Center Foundation (10,000) see Broyhill Family Foundation

North Carolina School of Arts Foundation (2,000) see Edgar Foster Daniels Foundation

Public Library of Charlotte and Mecklenburg (3,000) see Harry L. Dalton Foundation

Public Library of Charlotte and Mecklenburg County -- create Teens Succeed (157,000) see DeWitt Wallace-Reader's Digest Fund

UNC - Chapel Hill Friends of the Library (2,500) see Tanner Companies (Rutherfordton, NC)

Ohio

Bainbridge Public Library (5,000) see Paul and Maxine Frohring Foundation

Case Western Reserve University Library (1,740,000) see Second Foundation

Cleveland Public Library (15,000) see Cyrus Eaton Foundation

Coonskin Library Association (9,000) see Charles O'Bleness Foundation

Dover Public Library -- building addition (2,500) see Haman Family Foundation

East Cleveland Public Library -- to renovate and expand the main library (150,000) see Eva L. and Joseph M. Bruening Foundation

East Cleveland Public Library -- capital campaign (50,000) see Key Bank NA

East Cleveland Public Library -- capital expansion (50,000) see Raymond John Wean Foundation

Foundation Center Library (3,000) see Second Foundation

Foundation Center, The -- library services expenses (1,000) see Burton D. Morgan Foundation

Friends of Cleveland Public Library (1,000) see Second Foundation

Library Legacy Foundation (200,000) see Harold and Helen McMaster Foundation

Library Legacy Foundation (25,000) see France Stone Foundation

Loudonville Public Library (140,000) see Hugo H. and Mabel B. Young Foundation

Loudonville Public Library -- capital campaign (25,000) see Fran and Warren Rupp Foundation

Main Street Mansfield -- Richland County Rail-Trail Commission (35,000) see Fran and Warren Rupp Foundation

Mechanicsburg Public Library -- Support for general programming (2,000) see Honda of America Manufacturing, Inc.

Mercantile Library (15,000) see Lois and Richard Rosenthal Foundation

Minerva Public Library (25,000) see Herbert W. Hoover Foundation

National First Ladies Library (215,000) see The Hoover Foundation

National First Ladies Library (75,000) see Herbert W. Hoover Foundation

National First Ladies Library (50,000) see George H. Deuble Foundation

National First Ladies Library (1,000) see Jack N. and Lilyan Mandel Foundation

Newcomerstown Public Library -- elevator for new public library (35,000) see Harold C. and Marjorie Q. Rosenberry Tuscarawas County Foundation

North Canton Library Association (575,000) see The Hoover Foundation

Norwalk Public Library (24,510) see Albert G. and Olive H. Schlink Foundation

Oberlin Public Library (33,750) see Nord Family Foundation

Oberlin Public Library (15,000) see Nordson Corp.

Ohioana Library (3,000) see E. F. Wildermuth Foundation

Old Trail School -- construct a new admissions building (100,000) see Burton D. Morgan Foundation

Public Library of Cincinnati and Hamilton County -- for Westwood Branch expansion (90,000) see Charles H. Dater Foundation

Public Library of Cincinnati and Hamilton County -- for expansion of the Westwood branch (30,000) see Charles H. Dater Foundation

Richmond Academy of the Arts -- capital campaign (50,000) see Fran and Warren Rupp Foundation

Ritter Library (52,073) see George and Mary Ritter Charitable Trust

St. Paris Public Library (5,000) see Dayton Power and Light Co.

Tiffin-Seneca Public Library (8,655) see National Machinery Co.

Toledo Lucas County Public Library -- community service (20,000) see Toledo Blade Co.

Way Public Library Foundation -- operating (37,000) see Stranahan Foundation

Western Reserve Academy (20,125) see Goodrich Corp.

Oklahoma

Blackwell High School -- computerized library book (9,220) see Cordelia Lunceford Beatty Trust

Blackwell Public Library -- children's books (1,000) see Cordelia Lunceford Beatty Trust

Cartwright Memorial Library -- for the construction of a new facility

(50,000) see Sarkeys Foundation

Nowata City County Library -- contribution (13,743) see Pearl M. and Julia J. Harmon Foundation

Nowata City County Library -- contribution (2,000) see Pearl M. and Julia J. Harmon Foundation

Nowata City County Library -- contribution (1,500) see Pearl M. and Julia J. Harmon Foundation

Nowata City-County Library -- maintain grounds, Nowata library (19,380) see Pearl M. and Julia J. Harmon Foundation

Tulsa City County Library -- contribution Hardesty Library (5,000) see Pearl M. and Julia J. Harmon Foundation

Tulsa City County Library -- contribution Hardesty Library (5,000) see Pearl M. and Julia J. Harmon Foundation

Oregon

Coos County Library Service District -- Coos Connections (140,000) see Ford Family Foundation

Coos County Library Service District -- upgrade the computer network serving all Coos County libraries (43,000) see Ben B. Cheney Foundation

Douglas County Library Foundation -- national board certified teachers (65,100) see Ford Family Foundation

Eugene Public Library Foundation -- construction of new library (100,000) see Collins Foundation

Friends of The Coos Bay Public Library -- education (8,000) see Braemar Charitable Trust

Glendale Library Branch of the Douglas County (6,425) see C. Giles Hunt Charitable Trust

Jackson County Library Foundation -- site acquisition (125,000) see Ford Family Foundation

Jackson County Library Foundation (25,000) see Carpenter Foundation

Jackson Education Service District -- Southern Oregon Online School (79,242) see Ford Family Foundation

Junior Achievement of Western Oregon -- program expansion (42,000) see Ford Family Foundation

Lewis and Clark College -- to expand and modernize the Northwestern School

of Law Library (750,000) see Meyer Memorial Trust

Reedsport Branch Library (6,000) see C. Giles Hunt Charitable Trust

Salem Public Library Foundation (1,150) see Pioneer Trust Bank, NA

Southern Oregon Library Information System -- for a shared automated catalog system (300,000) see Meyer Memorial Trust

Winston Branch Library (6,800) see C. Giles Hunt Charitable Trust

Pennsylvania

Abington Township Public Library -- library renovation and automation project (10,000) see McLean Contributionship

Adams Memorial Library (59,200) see McFeely-Rogers Foundation

Agnes Irwin School (500) see Subaru of America, Inc.

Allegheny County Library -- for eiNetwork (200,000) see Grable Foundation

Allentown Public Library -- debt reduction (206,000) see Harry C. Trexler Trust

Allentown Public Library (4,000) see Dexter F. and Dorothy H. Baker Foundation

Altoona Area Public Library (5,000) see Harrison C. and Margaret A. Snyder Charitable Trust

American Philosophical Society -- to increase number of and extend the trial period for fellowships for faculty members (1,475,000) see Andrew W. Mellon Foundation

Annville Free Library (500) see Lebanon Mutual Insurance Co.

Athenaeum of Philadelphia -- toward the Philadelphia architects and buildings project (329,950) see William Penn Foundation

Athenaeum of Philadelphia -- conference seating (50,000) see Barra Foundation

Athenaeum of Philadelphia -- for book fund (10,000) see Albert M. Greenfield Foundation

Athenaeum of Philadelphia -- conference seating (7,500) see Barra Foundation

Bala Cynwyd Library (9,000) see Maurice Amado Foundation

Bethlehem Area Public Library (92,000) see Frank E. and Seba B. Payne Foundation

Bethlehem Area Public Library -- reference and audio visual renovation

(59,500) see Reidler Foundation

Bosler Free Library (15,000) see G. B. Stuart Charitable Foundation

Braddock's Field Historical Society -- capital (125,000) see U.S. Steel Corp.

Braddock's Field Historical Society -- Braddock Carnegie Library restoration (40,000) see Allegheny Foundation

Butler Public Library (5,000) see Spang & Co.

Cambria Free Library -- operational (7,500) see Robert S. Waters Charitable Trust

Cameron County Public Library (500) see AK Steel Holding Corp.

Carnegie Free Library of McKeesport (30,000) see E. R. Crawford Estate Trust Fund A

Carnegie Free Library of McKeesport (5,000) see Charles F. Peters Foundation

Carnegie Institute (20,000) see Cleveland H. Dodge Foundation

Carnegie Institute -- Scientific research (10,000) see Dynamet, Inc.

Carnegie Institute -- Powdermill Natural Program (1,000) see Dynamet, Inc.

Carnegie Institute -- for museum of art (1,000) see William I. and Patricia S. Snyder Foundation

Carnegie Library -- to improve building systems in the Homewood Branch (250,000) see McCune Foundation

Carnegie Library for the Blind and Physically Handicapped (10,000) see Milton G. Hulme Charitable Foundation

Carnegie Library of Pittsburgh -- for expansion of the eNetwork (1,000,000) see Vira I. Heinz Endowment

Carnegie Library of Pittsburgh -- for support of customer research component of "Agenda for Change: Planning for the Future" (250,000) see Buhl Foundation (PA)

Carnegie Library of Pittsburgh -- for public library system (51,935) see W. I. Patterson Charitable Fund

Carnegie Second Century Fund (12,000) see Milton G. Hulme Charitable Foundation

Citizens Library (3,000) see Charles S. and Mary Coen Family Foundation

Clarion Free Library -- purchase new copier (7,870) see Dr. and Mrs. Arthur

William Phillips Charitable Trust

Corry Public Library (2,350) see Arlene H. Smith Charitable Foundation

Cranberry Public Library -- for education purposes (5,000) see Charity Randall Foundation

Dauphin County Library System -- support construction (50,000) see Josiah W. and Bessie H. Kline Foundation

Easttown Library Foundation (50,000) see Arronson Foundation

Eccles Lesher Memorial Library (117,778) see Ralph M. and Ella M. Eccles Foundation

Ephrata Public Library (505) see G/S/M Industrial, Inc.

Franklin County Library System (10,000) see Alexander Stewart MD Foundation Trust

Franklin Library Association (3,000) see Edward V. and Jessie L. Peters Charitable Trust

Frederickson Library (10,000) see Donald B. and Dorothy L. Stabler Foundation

Fredrickson Public Library -- for building fund (50,000) see John Crain Kunkel Foundation

Free Library (5,000) see Vanguard Group

Free Library of Philadelphia -- collaborate with key community partnership to develop young library leaders (124,400) see DeWitt Wallace-Reader's Digest Fund

Free Library of Philadelphia (50,000) see AMETEK, Inc.

Free Library of Philadelphia (50,000) see Pine Tree Foundation

Free Library of Philadelphia (10,000) see AMETEK, Inc.

Free Library of Philadelphia -- Summer Reading Program (5,000) see AMETEK, Inc.

Free Library of Philadelphia -- for cultural and educational programming (5,000) see Alfred and Mary Douty Foundation

Friends of Southhampton Free Library (25,000) see Grundy Foundation

Greensburg Hempfield Area Library -- toward library technology upgrades (5,000) see Robertshaw Charitable Foundation

Hanover Public Library (6,000) see Susquehanna-Pfaltzgraff Co.

Hanover Public Library (3,333) see Waypoint Financial Corp.

Hellertown Area Library (5,000) see Frank E. and

Seba B. Payne Foundation

Hollidaysburg Free Public Library (4,639) see Harrison C. and Margaret A. Snyder Charitable Trust

Hollidaysburg Free Public Library (2,139) see Harrison C. and Margaret A. Snyder Charitable Trust

James Prendergast Library Association -- air conditioner system (100,000) see Ralph C. Sheldon Foundation Inc.

James Prendergast Library Association -- books and tapes (65,000) see Ralph C. Sheldon Foundation Inc.

James V. Brown Library -- for bookmobile and operations (20,000) see Harry Plankenhorn Foundation

James V. Brown Library -- for large print books (5,000) see Harry Plankenhorn Foundation

James V. Brown Library (2,000) see Lamco Communications

Jersey Shore Public Library (500) see Susquehanna-Pfaltzgraff Co.

Kaltreider Benfer Library (10,000) see Susquehanna-Pfaltzgraff Co.

Kaltreider Benfer Library (5,000) see Waypoint Financial Corp.

Kaltreider Benfer Library -- capital campaign (2,000) see Graham Engineering Corp.

La Roche College -- for support of integrated online library system for the college library (131,050) see Buhl Foundation (PA)

Lancaster County Library (500) see G/S/M Industrial, Inc.

Lauri Ann West Memorial Library (12,000) see Milton G. Hulme Charitable Foundation

Lebanon Community Library (3,000) see Vernon and Doris Bishop Foundation

Lebanon Valley College -- finish and equip classroom (50,000) see Josiah W. and Bessie H. Kline Foundation

Library Company -- operating support (5,000) see Crestlea Foundation

Library Company (1,500) see Quaker Chemical Corp.

Library Company of Philadelphia -- International Fellow Program (500,000) see Barra Foundation

Library Company of Philadelphia -- towards the creation of a Conservation Endowment Fund (150,000) see McLean Contributionship

Library Company of Philadelphia -- retrospective conversion (50,000) see Barra Foundation

Library Company of Philadelphia -- dissertation fellowship (50,000) see Gladys Krieble Delmas Foundation

Ligonier Valley Library (25,000) see Katherine Mabis McKenna Foundation

Lower Merion Library Foundation -- collection development project (57,900) see McLean Contributionship

Martin Library (5,000) see Freas Foundation

Martin Library -- virtual voyages (2,556) see Waypoint Financial Corp.

Mary S. Biesecker Library (5,000) see Dominic Foundation

Marysville - Rye Library Association -- painting improvements to main floor (2,000) see Josiah W. and Bessie H. Kline Foundation

Mengle Memorial Library (35,000) see Glenn and Ruth Mengle Foundation

Mifflin County Library (5,000) see Standard Steel

Mifflin County Library (1,000) see Standard Steel

Newtown Public Library (5,000) see T. James Kavanagh Foundation

Oil City Library (20,000) see Edith C. Justus Trust

Pittsburgh Technology Institute (1,000) see Trumbull County Scholarship Foundation

Point Park College -- towards project: teach designed to train K-12 teachers to meet anticipated teacher shortage (100,000) see Hillman Foundation

Rebecca M. Arthurs Memorial Library (1,200) see S&T Bancorp, Inc.

Rosenbach Museum and Library -- restoration of two historic buildings that house the museum on Delancey Place (150,000) see Connelly Foundation

Rosenbach Museum and Library (1,000) see Binswanger Companies

Sewickley Academy (41,100) see William I. and Patricia S. Snyder Foundation

Sewickley Public Library -- community (40,000) see Mary Hillman Jennings Foundation

Sleighton School -- refurbishing library and purchase appliances (25,000) see Ethel Sergeant Clark Smith Memorial Fund

Southern Lehigh Public Library (50,000) see Frank

E. and Seba B. Payne Foundation

Southern York County Library (15,000) see Susquehanna-Pfaltzgraff Co.

Warren Library Association (14,586) see Gladys Baird Trust

William Jeanes Memorial Library (2,500) see Margaret G. Jacobs Charitable Trust

William Jeanes Memorial Library (2,000) see Quaker Chemical Corp.

Windber Public Library (25,000) see Whalley Charitable Trust

Rhode Island

Company of the Redwood Library and Athenaeum -- implementation consultant and sponsor exhibits (35,000) see Frank Stanley Beveridge Foundation, Inc.

Harmony Library (500) see Kilmartin Industries

John Carter Brown Library (250,000) see CTW Foundation, Inc.

John Carter Brown Library (40,000) see Reed Foundation (NY)

John Carter Brown Library (16,100) see George E. Coleman Foundation

John Carter Brown Library -- addition to endowment (10,000) see Lucius N. Littauer Foundation

Memorial and Library Association Westerly (2,000) see Morris Family Foundation

Newport Public Library -- renovation and construction project (200,000) see Alletta Morris McBean Charitable Trust

Providence Athenaeum -- architects' fees (10,000) see June Rockwell Levy Foundation

Providence Athenaeum (6,667) see Providence Journal-Bulletin Co.

Providence Public Library (15,400) see Textron, Inc.

Providence Public Library -- program for young readers (10,000) see Collis Foundation

Providence Public Library -- support for a new program called Teen Power (10,000) see June Rockwell Levy Foundation

Providence Public Library (5,000) see John Clarke Trust

Redwood Library Athenaeum -- restoration and renovation of the library (400,000) see Alletta Morris McBean Charitable Trust

Redwood Library and Athenaeum (5,000) see Oliver

S. and Jennie R. Donaldson Charitable Trust

Ruth Woolf Adelson Medical Library Fund (1,500) see Diana S. Adelson Trust

South Carolina

Chapin Memorial Library (135,600) see Chapin Foundation of Myrtle Beach, South Carolina

St. Andrews School Library (6,000) see Chapin Foundation of Myrtle Beach, South Carolina

Tennessee

Chattanooga-Hamilton County Bicentennial Library (100,000) see Benwood Foundation

City of Lavergne -- for the Promise Project (124,000) see Blandin Foundation

Cleveland Public Library (150,000) see Tucker Foundation

Foundation for The Memphis/ Shelby County Public Library -- building (325,000) see Plough Foundation

Foundation for The Memphis/ Shelby County Public Library -- building (150,000) see Plough Foundation

Foundation for the Blount County Public Library (11,250) see First Tennessee National Corp.

Foundation for the Memphis-Shelby County Public Library -- for building and renovation (385,000) see Plough Foundation

Foundation for the Memphis-Shelby County Public Library (20,000) see First Tennessee National Corp.

Linebaugh Public Library -- equipment for expansion of genealogy section (56,000) see Christy-Houston Foundation

Metropolitan Nashville Library (50,000) see Joyce Family Foundation

Nashville Public Library (50,607) see Anne Potter Wilson Foundation

Nashville Public Library Foundation -- capital campaign (525,000) see Joe C. Davis Foundation

Nashville Public Library Foundation (250,000) see Bridgestone Americas Holding, Inc.

Tennessee Voices for Children -- program support (1,000) see Thompson Charitable Foundation

Texas

Austin Public Library (5,000) see ECG Foundation

Bryan City Library -- for educational purposes

(12,500) see Clifton C. and Henryetta C. Doak Charitable Trust

Canyon Library (3,333) see Mays Foundation

Civil War Preservation Trust -- support for the Land and Water Conservation Fund (15,000) see Martha, David and Bagby Lennox Foundation

Cold Spring Area Public Library -- for operations (5,000) see Pineywoods Foundation

Comfort Public Library, Inc. (20,000) see Cecilia Young Willard Helping Fund

Dallas Education Center -- equip and furnish virtual library (100,000) see Hillcrest Foundation

Dimmit County Public Library -- contribution toward new library and museum construction (60,000) see Ewing Halsell Foundation

Dimmit County Public Library -- operating expenses (25,000) see Neva and Wesley West Foundation

East Dallas Community School -- toward campus development (300,000) see Hoblitzelle Foundation

East Dallas Community School -- facility restoration (50,000) see Hoblitzelle Foundation

El Paso Public Library (7,767) see Marian Meaker Apteckar Foundation

El Progreso Memorial Library -- for capital campaign (5,000) see Frost National Bank

Fairfield Library Association -- for charitable purposes (5,889) see R. B. O. Bragg Charitable Trust

Floyd Co. Library Friends -- build public library in Floydada (30,000) see Paul J. Meyer Family Foundation

Fort Bend County Libraries -- provide high quality after-school educational enrichment and career development programs for low income youth (123,500) see DeWitt Wallace-Reader's Digest Fund

Fort Worth Public Library Foundation -- Provide office space for Library Foundation in new facility (175,000) see Sid W. Richardson Foundation

Fort Worth Public Library Foundation (25,000) see Burlington Northern Santa Fe Corp.

Fort Worth Public Library Foundation (20,000) see AMR Corp.

Fort Worth Public Library Foundation (5,000) see Anna W. Thornton and Alexander P. Thornton Charitable Trust

Friends of Crockett County Library Inc. (10,000) see Cecilia Young Willard Helping Fund

Friends of Public Library of Buda, Texas -- operating funds (2,500) see Burdine Johnson Foundation

Friends of the Dallas Public Library -- renovation of The J Erik Jonsson Library (400,000) see The Eugene McDermott Foundation

Friends of the Dallas Public Library -- renovate the J. Erik Jonsson Central Library's Genealogy Reference Collections (100,000) see Hillcrest Foundation

Friends of the Dallas Public Library -- for eighth floor renovation (50,000) see Leland Fikes Foundation

Friends of the Dallas Public Library (1,000) see Decherd Foundation

Friends of the Katy Trail, Inc. -- support building of the Katy Trail (100,000) see Hillcrest Foundation

Friends of the Texas Medical Center Library (30,000) see John P. McGovern Foundation

George Bush Presidential Library (30,000) see John P. McGovern Foundation

George Bush Presidential Library Foundation (1,000,000) see Annenberg Foundation

George Bush Presidential Library Foundation -- for endowment or program support (500,000) see Starr Foundation

Goliad County Library -- capital campaign for building renovation (25,000) see Rockwell Fund, Inc.

Harris County Public Library (10,000) see Powell Foundation

Houston Public Library (5,000) see Scurlock Foundation

J.R. Huffman Public Library -- for furnishings (55,467) see T. L. L. Temple Foundation

Jacksonville College -- library (170,000) see Summers A. Norman Foundation

Junior Achievement of South Texas (500) see Argyle Foundation

Kaufman County Library (40,000) see Edna M. Sheary Trust for Charity

Kaufman County Library (2,795) see Clements Foundation

Kountze Library (10,000) see Gilbert M. and Martha H. Hitchcock Foundation

Kurth Memorial Library -- construct new library facility (464,460) see T. L. L. Temple Foundation

Kurth Memorial Library -- for operations (6,825) see Pineywoods Foundation

Library of Congress (20,000) see Margaret and James A. Elkins, Jr. Foundation

Lone Oak Area Public Library (10,000) see Tom S. and Marye Kate Aldridge Charitable and Educational Trust

Marshall Public Library -- operations (500) see H.E. and Ruby Pelz Trust

Medina Community Library -- to assist with renovations of building for new library (45,000) see Hal and Charlie Peterson Foundation

New Braunfels Public Library Foundation (10,000) see Cecilia Young Willard Helping Fund

Palacios Library -- for new roof (15,000) see Gulf Coast Medical Foundation

Recording Library for the Blind (6,000) see Potts and Sibley Foundation

Rice University Friends of Fondren Library (5,000) see Lee and Joseph D. Jamail Foundation

Rosenberg Library (3,450) see Moody Foundation

Rube Sessions Memorial Library -- for operations (5,025) see Pineywoods Foundation

Rusk County Library System -- literary endowment program (32,000) see Bruce McMillan, Jr. Foundation

San Antonio Library Foundation -- purchase of books (50,000) see Ewing Halsell Foundation

San Antonio Public Library -- toward an innovative three-year pilot program to reduce the rate of illiteracy in the San Antonio community (400,000) see Houston Endowment

San Antonio Public Library (10,000) see G. A. C. Halff Foundation

San Antonio Public Library Foundation -- endowment for visual impairment (350,000) see Semmes Foundation

San Antonio Public Library Foundation -- Latino Leadership for the Library (250,000) see Brown Foundation

San Antonio Public Library Foundation -- Latino Leadership for the Library Initiative (250,000) see James Graham Brown Foundation, Inc.

San Antonio Public Library Foundation -- promotion

of the arts (170,000) see Russell Hill Rogers Fund for the Arts

San Antonio Public Library Foundation (5,000) see Minnie Stevens Piper Foundation

Stella Link Redevelopment Association -- contribution for campus park (1,600,000) see McGovern Fund

T.L.L. Temple Memorial Library (40,975) see Temple-Inland, Inc.

Temple Memorial Library and Archives -- for archives budget (154,261) see T. L. L. Temple Foundation

Temple Memorial Library and Archives -- for budget deficit (117,520) see T. L. L. Temple Foundation

Texas College -- choral scholarship fund (28,000) see Effie and Wofford Cain Foundation

Texas Tech Museum -- for Southwest Collection Library (31,500) see CH Foundation

Texas Tech University -- for library (45,000) see CH Foundation

Tyler County Public Library -- expansion project (25,000) see T. L. L. Temple Foundation

Utah

Provo City Library (200,000) see Willard L. Eccles Charitable Foundation

Vermont

Bennington Museum (20,000) see Edwin S. Webster Foundation

Brooks Memorial Library -- for Collection Improvement Program (14,200) see Thomas Thompson Trust

Brown Public Library (2,500) see Robert Fleming and Jane Howe Patrick Foundation

Fairlee Public Library -- for renovations (2,300) see Mascoma Savings Bank

Green Mountain College -- fund to establish a chaplaincy program (25,000) see Lillian M. Slater Trust

Kellogg-Hubbard Library -- construction and renovations of the children's library (50,000) see Turrell Fund

Kellogg-Hubbard Library (2,000) see Seidman Family Foundation

Moore Free Library (500) see Windham Foundation

Norman Williams Public Library (75,000) see LSR Fund

St. Johnsbury Athenaeum (1,000) see Windham Foundation

Virginia

Alexandria Library (5,000) see The Bryant Foundation

Alexandria Library (1,000) see Koopman Fund

Braille Circulating Library -- headquarter renovations (15,000) see William H., John G., and Emma Scott Foundation

Charles P. Jones Memorial Library -- expansion and renovation of the library (10,000) see Beirne Carter Foundation

Elis Olsson Memorial Library Fund (1,000) see Chesapeake Corp.

Fort Valley Community Library (500) see Shenandoah Telecommunications Co.

Friends of the Mathews Memorial Library -- renovation and expansion (50,000) see Robert G. Cabell III and Maude Morgan Cabell Foundation

Friends of the Waverly Public Library (75,000) see Garland and Agnes Taylor Gray Foundation

Gloucester Library Endowment Foundation (18,000) see J. Edwin Treakle Foundation

Haysi Public Library (2,600) see Columbus Phipps Foundation

Jonnie B. Deel Memorial Library (3,000) see Columbus Phipps Foundation

Library Gallery -- education art workshops (1,000) see Slemp Foundation

Library Gallery (1,000) see Slemp Foundation

Library of Virginia Foundation (20,000) see SunTrust Banks, Inc.

Lonesome Pine Regional Library -- addition to library (100,000) see Slemp Foundation

Mathews Memorial Library, Friends of (18,000) see J. Edwin Treakle Foundation

Mount Jackson Community Library (500) see Shenandoah Telecommunications Co.

National Sporting Library (125,000) see Edward P. Evans Foundation

National Sporting Library -- acquisition fund endowment (10,000) see McBean Family Foundation

New Market Area Library (500) see Shenandoah Telecommunications Co.

Randolph-Macon College -- audio-visual classroom (50,000) see Richard S. Reynolds Foundation

Ruth Camp Campbell Memorial Library (12,000) see

Ruth Camp McDougall Charitable Trust

Shenandoah County Central Library (40,000) see Shenandoah Telecommunications Co.

Steward School -- grant for construction of a new library (25,000) see Quincy Cole Trust

Strasburg Community Library (500) see Shenandoah Telecommunications Co.

Tazewell County Public Library -- technical expense (25,000) see Thompson Charitable Foundation

Thomas Jefferson Memorial Foundation -- Jefferson Research Library (500,000) see Robert G. Cabell III and Maude Morgan Cabell Foundation

Thomas Jefferson Memorial Foundation (5,000) see Trust for the Cheek Family Foundation

Thomas Jefferson Memorial Foundation Inc -- construction of Jefferson Research Library (75,000) see Marietta McNeill Morgan and Samuel Tate Morgan, Jr. Foundation

Washington

Ezra Meeker Historical Society Foundation Center -- install a new heating system (38,000) see Ben B. Cheney Foundation

Garfield County -- memorial library and fairgrounds (20,000) see Harold and

Helen Shepherd Foundation

King County Library System -- provide educational and employment opportunities for low-income teenagers (182,200) see DeWitt Wallace-Reader's Digest Fund

Pierce County Library Foundation -- purchase and equip a kids bookmobile (50,000) see Ben B. Cheney Foundation

Seattle Public Library -- for program fund (10,000) see Kawabe Memorial Fund

Seattle Public Library Foundation (500,000) see Foster Foundation

Seattle Public Library Foundation (335,179) see Norcliffe Foundation

Seattle Public Library Foundation (250,000) see Washington Mutual, Inc.

Seattle Public Library Foundation (50,000) see E. K. and Lillian F. Bishop Foundation

Seattle Public Library Foundation (12,500) see Foster Foundation

Tacoma Public Library -- programs (10,000) see Howarth Trust Fund

West Virginia

Bridgeport Public Library (18,199) see Evelyn C. Carter Trust

Craft Memorial Library (50,000) see Hugh I. Shott, Jr. Foundation

Greenbrier County Library -- for program support (10,000) see Daywood Foundation

Kanawha County Library Foundation (2,500) see One Valley Bank NA

Kanawha County Schools -- library automation (7,620) see Clay Foundation

Library Foundation of Kanawha County -- library automation (80,000) see Clay Foundation

Library Foundation of Kanawha County (15,000) see Bernard H. and Blanche E. Jacobson Foundation

Pleasants County Public Library (5,000) see Charles S. and Mary Coen Family Foundation

Wisconsin

Abbotsford Library -- for 10 books on CD format and encyclopedias (5,000) see L. C. Christensen Charitable and Religious Foundation

Brillion Public Library (5,000) see R. D. and Linda Peters Foundation

Caestecker Public Library Foundation (25,000) see Charles and Marie Caestecker Foundation

City of Wisconsin Rapids McMallan Memorial Library (100,000) see Stora Enso

Cudahy Public Library Expansion Committee (200,000) see Patrick and Anna M. Cudahy Fund

Friends of the Bruce Public Library (50,000) see Jeld-Wen, Inc.

Friends of the Butler Library, Inc. (5,000) see Park Bank

General Library System, UW-Madison (15,000) see Schoenleber Foundation

La Crosse Public Library -- public library association (1,000) see Cleary Foundation

MSOE/Walter Schroeder Library Endowment Fund (19,680) see Walter Schroeder Foundation

Manitowoc Public Library (4,000) see VPI Foundation Inc.

Merrill Area Public Library (30,000) see Metal Industries, Inc.

Milwaukee Public Library (5,000) see Baird Brothers Co. Foundation

Milwaukee Public Library see Microsoft Corp.

Milwaukee Public Library Foundation (100,000) see Schoenleber Foundation

Milwaukee Public Library Foundation -- technical assistance grant McBeath Community Partners (25,000) see Faye McBeath Foundation

Milwaukee Public Library Foundation (10,000) see Joy Global, Inc.

Milwaukee Public Library Foundation -- program support (5,600) see Marcus Corp.

Milwaukee Public Library Foundation (5,000) see Fortis Health

Milwaukee Public Library Foundation (5,000) see Grede Foundries

Monona Library -- building fund (10,000) see MGE Energy, Inc.

Neenah Public Library (25,000) see Aylward Family Foundation

Riverfront, Inc. -- capital campaign (3,000) see JSJ Corp.

Riverfront, Inc. -- employment for developmentally handicapped (1,000) see Cleary Foundation

St. Francis Public Library Foundation (26,000) see Saint Francis Bank

Tomah Public Library -- air conditioning for computer room (3,660) see Frank G. Andres Charitable Trust

Wisconsin Library Association Foundation, Inc. (2,500) see Banta Corp.

Wyoming

Sheridan County Library Foundation -- purchase books and subscriptions (5,000) see Herbert G. and Dorothy Zullig Foundation

Story Library (5,000) see Harry and Thelma Surrena Memorial Fund

Washakie County Library (2,500) see Newell B. Sargent Foundation

OFFICERS AND DIRECTORS BY NAME

Arranges officers, trustees, directors, managers, and staff in alphabetical order by last name, along with the name of the funder.

A

Abbott, David T.: executive director, Gund Foundation (George)

Abbott, Kyle C.: director, Abrams Foundation (Talbert and Leota)

Abbs, Jan P.: secretary, Ontario Corp. Foundation

Abel, Alice: director, Abel Foundation

Abel, James P.: president, Abel Foundation; president, director, NEBCO Evans

Abel, John C.: director, Abel Foundation

Abeles, Charles Calvert: trustee, Higginson Trust (Corina)

Abell, William Shepherdson, Jr.: trustee, Abell Foundation

Abendshein, Nancy I.: trustee, Brown Foundation

Abercrombie, George: trustee, Hoffmann-La Roche Foundation

Abercrombie, Josephine E.: donor, president, trustee, Abercrombie Foundation

Abney, Cary M.: secretary, Pelz Trust (H.E. and Ruby)

Abney, Ruben K.: co-trustee, Pelz Trust (H.E. and Ruby)

Abney, William A.: co-trustee, Pelz Trust (H.E. and Ruby)

Abplanalp, Robert H.: director, Carvel Foundation (Thomas and Agnes)

Abrams, Spence, Sr.: director, Stebens Charitable Foundation (Bertha)

Aceves, Ann N.: vice president, Neuberger Foundation (Roy R. and Marie S.)

Acker, Janet: secretary, Giger Foundation (Paul and Oscar)

Ackerman, Asche: vice president, Vale-Asche Foundation

Ackerman, F. Duane: chief executive officer, BellSouth Corp.

Ackerman, Lisa Marilyn: vice president, Kress Foundation (Samuel H.)

Acklin, Robert G.: secretary, treasurer, Bicknell Fund

Acosta, Thomas I.: vice chairman, New York Foundation

Acton, Elizabeth S.: vice president, treasurer, Ford Motor Co.

Acton, Evelyn Meadows: director emeritus, Meadows Foundation (The)

Acuff, A. Marshall, Jr.: trustee, Mott Foundation (Charles Stewart)

Adam, J. Marc: president, director, 3M Foundation; vice president marketing, Minnesota Mining & Manufacturing Co.

Adam, Milton F.: secretary, CHC Foundation

Adams, Alicia: secretary, BellSouth Foundation

Adams, Carolyn T.: director, Penn Foundation (William)

Adams, Caryl W.: secretary, French Foundation (D.E.)

Adams, D. Nelson, Esq.: member advisory committee, Weezie Foundation

Adams, James A.: director, Woronoco Savings Charitable Foundation

Adams, John: director, Honda of America Foundation

Adams, Lloyd: secretary, treasurer, Tractor & Equipment Co. Foundation

Adams, Louise B.: trustee, Barnes Foundation

Adams, Melissa J.: corporate donations officer, Frost National Bank

Adams, Michael T.: secretary, AK Steel Foundation

Adams, Peter Webster: trustee, Humphrey Fund (George M. and Pamela S.)

Adams, R. E.: vice president, Conway Scholarship Foundation (Carle C.)

Adams, Robert Merrihew: trustee, Newcombe Foundation (Charlotte W.)

Adams, Thomas B.: mem, Henderson Foundation (George B.)

Adamson, Roland: executive director, George Foundation

Addison, Brian M.: trustee, Dentsply International Foundation

Adelman, Linda M.: director, Eastern Savings and Loan Foundation

Adger, Joyce T.: manager, Hanes Foundation (John Wesley and Anna Hodgin)

Adisek, Valerie: admin secretary, Johnson Controls Foundation

Adkins, Albert G.: assistant comptroller, U.S. Steel Foundation

Adkins, Ruth F.: trustee, Yeager Charitable Trust B (Lester E.)

Adler, Arlene: board chair, Hazen Foundation (Edward W.)

Adler, Herbert S.: director, Research Corp.

Adriance, Bryan: member, Cranston Foundation; vice president, finance & administration, Cranston Print Works Co.

Agger, David: director, Osher Foundation (Bernard)

Agnew, Dan F.: president, director, Grinnell Mutual Group Foundation; president, chief executive officer, Grinnell Mutual Reinsurance Co.

Agnich, Richard John: director, Texas Instruments Foundation; senior vice president, secretary, general counsel, Texas Instruments Inc.

Agon, Jean-Paul: president, chief executive officer, director, L'Oreal U.S.A.

Ahlers, Linda L.: president, Target Corp.

Ahlstrom, R. W.: trustee, Andres Charitable Trust (Frank G.)

Ahmadi, Hoshang: director, Alavi Foundation

Ahmanson, Howard Fieldstead, Jr.: chairman, Ahmanson Foundation

Ahmanson, Robert H.: president, trustee, Ahmanson Foundation

Ahmanson, William H.: vice president, trustee, Ahmanson Foundation

Ahnert, Edward F.: president, Exxon Mobil Foundation; corporate contribution manager, ExxonMobile Corp.

Ahrens, Chad: trustee, Ahrens Foundation (Claude W. and Dolly)

Ahrens, Claude W.: trustee, Ahrens Foundation (Claude W. and Dolly)

Ahrens, John: trustee, Ahrens Foundation (Claude W. and Dolly)

Ahrens, Richard: trustee, Ahrens Foundation (Claude W. and Dolly)

Aiken, J. Kirby: auxiliary director, Russell Charitable Foundation (Tom)

Aiken, William G.: director, Woronoco Savings Charitable Foundation

Ainsworth, Laine: director, Hedco Foundation

Akel, Ferris G.: chairman, Decker Foundation (Dr. G. Clifford and Florence B.)

Akeroyd, Richard: executive director, libraries & public access to information, Gates Foundation (Bill and Melinda)

Akers, Carolyn Bailey: secretary, second vice president, Bailey Family Foundation (William O. and Carole P.)

Akers, John Fellows: member, director, New York Times Co.

Akin, Judy S.: assistant secretary, Holt Foundation (William Knox)

Akre, Charles Thomas: vice president, director, Marpat Foundation

Alberghini, Peter H.: director, Warwick Savings Foundation

Albers, C. Hugh: chairman, Coleman Foundation (IL)

Albert, Daniel: director, AT&T National Pro-Am Youth Fund

Alberts, Bruce Michael, PhD: trustee, Carnegie Corp. of New York

Albertson, Don, MD: trustee, Foundation for Seacoast Health

Albrecht, Kenneth: trustee emeritus, Blandin Foundation

Albrecht, Leslie: grants assistant, Cowell Foundation (S. H.)

Albrecht, Randal A.: secretary, DEC International-Albrecht Foundation

Alcock, Gudrun: vice president, Boothroyd Foundation (Charles H. and Bertha L.)

Alcott, Kent: chief financial officer, Chicago Rawhide Co.

Alda, Alan: trustee, Jenjo Foundation

Alda, Arlene: trustee, Jenjo Foundation

Alda, Beatrice: trustee, Jenjo Foundation

Alda, Elizabeth: trustee, Jenjo Foundation

Aldax, Gary: director, Sierra Pacific Resources Charitable Foundation

Alden, Alison: senior vice president sales, service, human resources, NSTAR; trustee, NSTAR Foundation

Aldridge, Elizabeth A.: secretary, Noble Foundation (Samuel Roberts)

Aldridge, Karen B.: program officer, Mott Foundation (Charles Stewart)

Aldridge, Kimberly F.: director, Aldridge Charitable and Educational Trust (Tom S. and Marye Kate)

Aldridge, Laverne R.: director, Aldridge Charitable and Educational Trust (Tom S. and Marye Kate)

Aldridge, M. L.: director, Aldridge Charitable and Educational Trust (Tom S. and Marye Kate)

Aldridge, Robert S.: director, Aldridge Charitable and Educational Trust (Tom S. and Marye Kate)

Aldridge, Tom S.: director, Aldridge Charitable and Educational Trust (Tom S. and Marye Kate)

Alewine, Betty L.: president, chief executive officer, COMSAT International

Alexander, Catherine R.: trustee, Alexander Foundation (Robert D. and Catherine R.)

Alexander, Cleopatra B.: executive director, Pick, Jr. Fund (Albert)

Alexander, Helen C.: vice president, director, Kleberg Foundation (Robert J. Kleberg, Jr. and Helen C.)

Alexander, Jack H.: secretary, Peppers Foundation (Ann)

Alexander, James: co-trustee, Genius Charitable Trust (Elizabeth Morse)

Alexander, John D., Jr.: secretary, vice president, Kleberg Foundation (Robert J. Kleberg, Jr. and Helen C.)

Alexander, John R.: secretary, trustee, Hilliard Foundation

Alexander, R. Denny: investment counsel, trustee, Alexander Foundation (Robert D. and Catherine R.)

Alexander, Rex: director, Hammer Foundation (Armand)

Alexander, Richard G.: trustee, Douty Foundation (Alfred and Mary)

Alexander, Stephen: chief executive, Dunkin' Donuts, Inc.

Alexander, Susan H.: director, Cabot Corp. Foundation

Alfert, Arthur S.: vice president, director, Alexander Foundation (Joseph)

Alford, L. E.: president, Hale Foundation (Crescent Porter)

Alhart, Donald E.: treasurer, Johnson Fund (Edward C.)

Ali, Fred J.: president, chief administrative officer, Weingart Foundation

Alkire, Durwood: adv, Archibald Charitable Foundation (Norman)

Allaire, Paul A.: director, Sara Lee Corp.

Allaire, Paul Arthur: trustee, Ford Foundation

Allan, Karen C.: secretary, trustee, Carpenter Foundation

Allardyce, Fred A.: director, American Standard Foundation; senior vice president chairman, chief financial officer, American Standard Inc.

Allday, Doris Fondren: board of directors, Fondren Foundation

Allday, R. Edwin: board of directors, Fondren Foundation

Allen, Alvena: director, Kennedy Family Foundation (Ethel and W. George)

Allen, Barbara Powell: secretary, Powell Family Foundation

Allen, Corinne A.: executive director, Benwood Foundation

Allen, Edna R.: president, Allen Foundation (Nibs and Edna)

Allen, Ivan, Jr.: trustee, Woodruff Foundation (Robert W.)

Allen, Leigh B., III: secretary, Walker Foundation

Allen, Leon: chairman, Tetley U.S.A., Inc.

Allen, Lew, Jr.: director, member directors grant program committee, Keck Foundation (W. M.)

Allen, Richard: director, Sordoni Foundation

Allen, Samuel R.: director, Deere Foundation (John)

Allen, Shirley: vice president, Berger Foundation (H. N. and Frances C.)

Allen, Thomas F.: secretary, Bingham Foundation (William); treasurer, assistant secretary, Spahr Family Foundation

Allen, Thomas R.: vice president, chief financial officer, Dodge Jones Foundation and Subsidiary

Allen, Wells, Jr.: director, Klee Foundation (Conrad and Virginia)

Allin, William B.: treasurer, Self Family Foundation

Allison, Diane M.: executive director, Educational Foundation of America

Allison, Donn: secretary, De Queen Regional Medical Center

Allison, Ethelyn: trustee, Snyder Foundation (Harold B. and Dorothy A.)

Allison, Walter W.: vice president, assistant treasurer, Lyon Foundation

Allman, Edward Lee: trustee, Edison Fund (Charles)

Allman, George P.: senior vice president, New England Business Service

Allocco, Nancy A.: grant administrator, assistant secretary, Hyde and Watson Foundation

Allsbrook, Bethany: program officer, Hall-Perrine Foundation

Allton, John D.: treasurer, Schlink Foundation (Albert G. and Olive H.)

Allyn, Amy: director, Allyn Foundation

Allyn, David: director, Allyn Foundation

Allyn, Dawn N.: secretary, Allyn Foundation

Allyn, Eric R.: director, Allyn Foundation

Allyn, Janet J.: director, Allyn Foundation

Allyn, Laura Austin: director, Allyn Foundation

Allyn, Lew F.: president, Allyn Foundation

Allyn, Scott: director, Allyn Foundation

Allyn, William Finch: treasurer, Allyn Foundation; director, Emerson Foundation, Inc. (Fred L.)

Allyn, William G.: hon officer, Allyn Foundation

Allyn, William Scott: director, Allyn Foundation

Alm, John Richard: director, Coca-Cola Foundation

Alm, Robert: president, First Hawaiian Foundation

Alman, Larry: board of directors, Ottenheimer Brothers Foundation

Almeida, Richard: chairman, chief executive officer, GE Capital Corp.

Almquist, L. Arden: director, Young Foundation (Irvin L.)

Alphin, J. S. (Steele): trustee, Bank of America Foundation

Alsdorf, Marilynn Bruder: director, Rice Foundation

Alsip, John F., III: president, chief executive officer, director, Rahr Malting Co.

Altamore, Ellen: adv, Delano Foundation (Mignon Sherwood)

Altermatt, Paul B.: president, director, Harcourt Foundation (Ellen Knowles)

Altheide, Paul D.: secretary, treasurer, Rachal Foundation (Ed)

Althof, Timothy D.: vice president investor relations, New England Business Service

Altman, Lawrence Kimball, MD: director, Macy, Jr. Foundation (Josiah)

Alton, Robert D., Jr.: trustee, Hickory Tech Corp. Foundation

Altschuler, Alan: trustee, New York Foundation

Altshuler, Sharman B.: secretary, trustee, Merck Family Fund

Alvarez, Cesar: trustee, Knight Foundation (John S. and James L.)

Alves, Wendi: director, Lesher Foundation (Dean and Margaret)

Amado, Bernice: vice president, secretary, director, Amado Foundation (Maurice)

Amado, Ralph A.: director, Amado Foundation (Maurice)

Amado, Ralph D.: director, Amado Foundation (Maurice)

Ambach, Gordon M.: director, Wallace-Reader's Digest Fund (DeWitt)

Ambach, Lucy E.: trustee, Sasco Foundation

Amboian, John P.: executive vice president, chief financial officer, Nuveen Co. (The John)

Ambrozy, Sandra McAlister: senior program officer, Kresge Foundation

Ambuel, Helen B.: director, Mead Witter Foundation, Inc.

Amemiya, Koichi: president, chief executive officer, director, American Honda Motor Company, Inc.

Amemiya, Minoru: chairman, chief executive officer, Interkal, Inc.

Ames, Aubin Z.: trustee, Schumann Fund for New Jersey

Ames, Edward A.: trustee, Cary Charitable Trust (Mary Flagler)

Ames, Kathleen L.F.: vice president, Harriman Foundation (Mary W.)

Ames, Morgan P.: treasurer, Price Foundation (Lucien B. and Katherine E.)

Amoroso, Joseph A., Jr.: director, East Cambridge Savings Charitable Foundation

Amsterdam, Gustave G.: trustee, Greenfield Foundation (Albert M.)

Amundson, Joyce: president, chief executive officer Ross Products Division, Ross Products Division, Abbott Laboratories

Andersen, Christine E.: vice president, Andersen Foundation (Hugh J.)

Andersen, Kathy: administrator, AMR/American Airlines Foundation

Andersen, Sarah J.: president, Andersen Foundation (Hugh J.)

Anderson, Alice Childs: vice president, AKC Fund

Anderson, Andrew E.: secretary, treasurer, trustee, Stone Foundation (France)

Anderson, Anne Heller: secretary, trustee, Heller Charitable Foundation (Clarence E.)

Anderson, Carl T.: secretary, Markey Charitable Fund (John C.)

Anderson, Carmen: trustee, Pittsburgh Child Guidance Foundation

Anderson, Charles D.: trustee, Anderson Foundation

Anderson, D. Kent: chairman, director, Houston Endowment

Anderson, David: trustee, CLARCOR Foundation

Anderson, Deb: manager, St. Paul Companies, Inc.

Anderson, Esperanza Guerro: director, Bush Foundation

Anderson, Eugene Karl: vice president, Contran Corp.; treasurer, Simmons Foundation, Inc. (Harold)

Anderson, Fred C.: director, Norcross Wildlife Foundation

Anderson, Gary E.: chairman, president, chief executive officer, Dow Corning Corp.

Anderson, J. C.: vice president north america, Whirlpool Corp.; senior vice president, Whirlpool Foundation

Anderson, James D.: director, Vermilion Healthcare Foundation

Anderson, Jeffrey W.: trustee, Anderson Foundation

Anderson, John: chairman, Florida Rock & Tank Lines

Anderson, John Firth: chairman, Pineywoods Foundation

Anderson, Judy M.: senior vice president charitable giving, Georgia Power Co.; executive director, secretary, assistant treasurer, Georgia Power Foundation

Anderson, Kenneth G.: president, trustee, Swisher Foundation (Carl S.)

Anderson, Kevin: trustee, Anderson Foundation

Anderson, Kristin: secretary, contact, Burnett Co. Charitable Foundation

(Leo); vice president, director community affairs, Burnett Co. (Leo)

Anderson, Lisa: trustee, Norcliffe Foundation

Anderson, Mary: trustee, Anderson Foundation

Anderson, Mary A.: vice president, Stearns Foundation

Anderson, Michael Scott: director, Overlake Foundation

Anderson, Peter A.: treasurer, Trust Foundation

Anderson, Richard: treasurer, Fribourg Foundation

Anderson, Robert P., PhD: secretary, treasurer, South Plains Foundation

Anderson, Roger E.: vice chairman, Fry Foundation (Lloyd A.)

Anderson, Sandra K.: president, Anderson Foundation (L. P. and Teresa)

Anderson, Stefan Stolen: director, Ball Foundation (George and Frances)

Anderson, Steven Craig: director, Overlake Foundation

Anderson, Steven L.: president, Reynolds Foundation (Donald W.)

Anderson, Thomas Harold: chairman, trustee, Anderson Foundation; chairman, director, Andersons, Inc.

Anderson, Wilbur L.: trustee, Ashtabula Foundation

Anderson, William J.: treasurer, Kuyper Foundation (Peter H. and E. Lucille Gaass)

Andreas, G. Allen: chairman, chief executive officer, Archer-Daniels-Midland Co.

Andrew, Phoebe Haffner: director, Haffner Foundation

Andrews, Christie F.: vice president, director, Hewit Family Foundation

Andrews, David R.: president, PepsiCo Foundation, Inc.; senior vice president and general counsel, PepsiCo Inc.

Andrews, Edward C., Jr.: honorary director, Dana Foundation (Charles A.)

Andrews, Harry C.: executive vice president, Minnesota Mining & Manufacturing Co.

Andrews, Hugh T.: director, Andrews McMeel Universal Foundation

Andrews, James C.: director, Andrews McMeel Universal Foundation

Andrews, Kathleen W.: vice president, secretary, Andrews McMeel Universal Foundation

Andrews, Paul R. P.: adjunct director, Educational Foundation of America

Andrews, Richard J.: director, Hewit Family Foundation

Andriessen, Frans H.J.J.: director, Sara Lee Corp.

Andrus, John E., III: trustee, Marbrook Foundation

Angelastro, Linda W.: executive director, Ensign-Bickford Foundation; director corporate communications, Ensign-Bickford Industries

Angelica, Robert: treasurer, AT&T Foundation

Angell, Christopher C.: president, director, Kornfeld Foundation (Emily Davie and Joseph S.)

Anglin, Richard: chief financial officer, Florsheim Group Co.

Angood, Arthur W.: president, chief executive officer, trustee, Miller Foundation

Angus, Jeffrey W.: senior vice president information system, New England Business Service

Anlyan, William George: trustee, Duke Endowment

Anneberg, A. Lee, MD: director, Copic Medical Foundation

Annenberg, Leonore A.: president, director, Annenberg Foundation

Annenberg, Wallis: vice president, Annenberg Foundation

Annette, Kathleen: vice chairman, trustee, Blandin Foundation

Anschutz, Elizabeth S.: trustee, Anschutz Family Foundation

Anschutz-Rodgers, Sue: donor, president, executive director, trustee, Anschutz Family Foundation

Ansin, Ronald M.: trustee, Ansin Foundation (Ronald M.)

Anthony, Barbara Cox: chairman, Cox Foundation (James M.)

Anthony, Frederick W.: secretary, Palisades Educational Foundation

Anthony, Nancy: advisor, Kirkpatrick Foundation, Inc.

Anthony, Ralph F.: president, director, Palisades Educational Foundation

Anti, Janet McCune Edwards: member dispensing committee, McCune Charitable Trust (John R.)

Antonelli, Edward A.: president, chief executive officer, director, Morris Foundation (William T.)

Antonellis, Carl J., Jr.: secretary, Woronoco Savings Charitable Foundation

Antrim, Joseph L., III: director, Cabell III and Maude Morgan Cabell Foundation (Robert G.)

Apolinsky, Harold I.: trustee, Bennett Family Foundation (Claude)

Appel, Gloria W.: president, trustee, Price Foundation (Louis and Harold)

Appel, John: trustee, Forster Charitable Trust (James W. and Ella B.)

Appel, Robert J.: treasurer, Levitt Foundation (NY)

Appell, Lloyd: director, Vicksburg Foundation

Appell, Louis J., Jr.: president, Susquehanna-Pfaltzgraff Co.

Applebury, Meredithe L.: member, Ziegler Foundation for the Blind (E. Matilda)

Appleton, James: director, Hedco Foundation

Apraxine, Pierre: director, Gilman Foundation (Howard)

Apregan, Craig: director, Peters Foundation (Leon S.)

April, Anne M.: trustee, Barker Foundation Inc.

Arant, R.: vice president, trustee, Johns Manville Fund

Arbor, Patrick H.: chairman, Chicago Board of Trade

Arbury, Julie Carol: trustee, donor great granddaughter, Dow Foundation (Herbert H. and Grace A.)

Archbold, Armar A.: trustee, McNeely Foundation

Archer, W. C., III: senior vice president external affairs, Georgia Power Co.

Arensberg, Frank L., II: trustee, Vesuvius Foundation

Argyros, George L.: secretary, trustee, Argyros Foundation; chairman, director, Beckman Foundation (Arnold and Mabel)

Argyros, Julie A.: president, trustee, Argyros Foundation

Ariail, Leslie S.: secretary, Washington Forrest Foundation

Ariail, Lester: manager, Porter Testamentary Trust (James Hyde)

Arias, Ron R.: trustee, Miller Foundation (Earl B. and Loraine H.)

Arison, M. Micky: trustee, Arison Foundation; chairman, chief executive officer, director, Carnival Corp.

Arison, Madeleine: trustee, Arison Foundation

Arison, Marilyn: trustee, Arison Foundation

Arison, Shari: president, Arison Foundation; director, Carnival Corp.

Arkwright, Richard T.: president, St. Giles Foundation

Armacost, Samuel Henry: director, Irvine Foundation (The James)

Armbruster, John D.: treasurer, Metris Companies Foundation

Armbruster, Timothy D.: governor, Baker, Jr. Memorial Fund (William G.); president, Goldseker Foundation of Maryland (Morris)

Armour, Laurance H., III: director, Gulf Coast Medical Foundation

Armour, Laurance Hearne, Jr.: director, Gulf Coast Medical Foundation

Armstrong, Bill: director, South Plains Foundation

Armstrong, C. Michael: chairman, chief executive officer, director, AT&T Corp.

Armstrong, Robert E.: director, new programs and major grants member, Luce Foundation (Henry)

Armstrong, T. G.: president, chief executive officer, director, Standard Steel Speciality Co.

Arnn, Nancy Miller: trustee, Edison Fund (Charles)

Arnold, David J.: trustee, Strosacker Foundation (Charles J.)

Arnold, Fred E.: chairman advisory committee, Jordan and Ettie A. Jordan Charitable Foundation (Mary Ranken)

Arnold, Isaac, Jr.: vice president, trustee, Cullen Foundation (The)

Arnold, James C.: vice president, Jones Foundation (Helen)

Arnold, Louise Willson: president, executive secretary, director, Jones Foundation (Helen)

Arnold, Martha G.: president, trustee, Strosacker Foundation (Charles J.)

Arnold, Peter: director, Roddy Foundation (Fred M.)

Arnold, Phyllis H.: mem, trustee, One Valley Bank Foundation; president, chief executive officer, director, One Valley Bank NA

Arnold, Robert Neff: vice president, secretary, director, Jones Foundation (Helen)

Arnold, Roland R.: trustee, Halff Foundation (G. A. C.)

Arone, Vincent J.: treasurer, director, Hopedale Foundation

Aronson, Edgar D.: director, Pforzheimer Foundation, Inc. (The Carl and Lily)

Aronson, Nancy P.: vice president, director, Pforzheimer Foundation, Inc. (The Carl and Lily)

Arpey, Gerard J.: president, chief executive officer, AMR Corp.

Arrillaga, Frances C.: vice president, director, Arrillaga Foundation (John)

Arrillaga, John: president, secretary, director, Arrillaga Foundation (John)

Arrillaga, John, Jr.: treasurer, director, Arrillaga Foundation (John)

Arrillaga, Laura: secretary, director, Arrillaga Foundation (John)

Arrington, David J.: trustee, Niagara Mohawk Foundation

Arsenian, Deana: senior program officer international peace, Carnegie Corp. of New York

Arthur, Michael: secretary, trustee, Chiles Foundation

Artz, Gainor W.: vice president, Wessinger Foundation

Arundel, Edward M.: off, Neilson Foundation (George W.)

Asch, George: trustee, Price Foundation (Louis and Harold)

Asche Russell, Vale: president, Vale-Asche Foundation

Ash, Blanche E.: vice president, Ash Foundation (Stanley P. and Blanche E.)

Ash, Jennifer K.: director, Ash Foundation (Stanley P. and Blanche E.)

Ash, Stanley P.: president, Ash Foundation (Stanley P. and Blanche E.)

Ashe, Carol: secretary, general counsel, Global Community Partnerships

Ashen, Nancy: fiscal officer, New York Foundation

Asher, James M.: section, Hearst Foundation (William Randolph)

Asher, Thomas J.: vice president, secretary, Rich Foundation

Ashkettle, Phillip D.: president, chief executive officer, director, Reichhold Chemicals, Inc.

Ashley, Duane T.: trustee, Pittsburgh Child Guidance Foundation

Ashley, W. Seaborn, Jr.: director, Citizens Union Bank Foundation

Ashmun, Candace McKee: vice president, trustee, Fund for New Jersey

Ashmus, Kenneth Allen: secretary supervisory

board, Codrington Charitable Foundation (George W.)

Ashton, Clifford L.: mem, Bamberger Memorial Foundation (John Ernest Bamberger and Ruth Eleanor)

Ashton, Dore: director, Dedalus Foundation

Ashton, Robert W.: secretary, Bay Foundation

Askey, William Hartman: treasurer, secretary, Clayton Fund

Askow, Irwin J.: vice president, trustee, Graham Foundation for Advanced Studies in the Fine Arts

Asplundh, Barr E.: vice president, director, Asplundh Foundation

Asplundh, Brent D.: director, Asplundh Foundation

Asplundh, Carl H. J., Jr.: director, Asplundh Foundation

Asplundh, Christopher B.: president, director, Asplundh Foundation

Asplundh, E. Boyd: secretary, treasurer, director, Asplundh Foundation

Asplundh, Edward K.: president, Asplundh Foundation

Asplundh, Gregg G.: director, Asplundh Foundation

Asplundh, Ian L.: director, Asplundh Foundation

Asplundh, Paul S.: director, Asplundh Foundation

Asplundh, Robert H.: director, Asplundh Foundation

Asplundh, Scott M.: director, Asplundh Foundation

Asplundh, Steven G.: director, Asplundh Foundation

Asplundh, Stewart L.: director, Asplundh Foundation

Atcheson, Elizabeth: trustee, Crocker Trust (Mary A.)

Atherton, Frank C.: vice president, treasurer, director, Atherton Family Foundation; director, Atherton Foundation (Leburta)

Atherton, Geary: director, Holt Foundation (William Knox)

Atherton, Holt: director, Holt Foundation (William Knox)

Atherton, Leburta G.: president, director, Atherton Foundation (Leburta)

Atkins, Frederick J.: director, French Foundation (D.E.)

Atkins, John B.: treasurer, director, Heuermann Foundation (Bernard K. and Norma F.)

Atkinson, Duane E.: president, director, Atkinson Foundation

Atkinson, Gail: program manager, Braemar Charitable Trust

Atkinson, Harold S., Jr.: trustee, Camp Younts Foundation

Atkinson, Ray N.: vice president, director, Atkinson Foundation

Attaway, John: secretary, Publix Supermarkets Charities

Attfield, Gillian: advisory committee member, Dickenson Foundation (Harriet Ford)

Atwater, Charles B.: director, Bunbury Co., Inc.; trustee emeritus, Windham Foundation

Atwater, Edward C.: secretary, treasurer, Gleason Foundation

Atwater, William E.: secretary, director, First Hawaiian Foundation

Atwood, Marjorie: trustee, Donaldson Charitable Trust (Oliver S. and Jennie R.)

Au, Tung: trustee, Lingnan Foundation

Auchincloss, Lou Stanton: honorary director, Macy, Jr. Foundation (Josiah)

Auen, Joan C.: secretary-treasurer, director, Berger Foundation (H. N. and Frances C.)

Auen, Ronald M.: president, director, Berger Foundation (H. N. and Frances C.)

Auer, Albert J.: director, Hoag Family Foundation (George)

Aufieror, Charles: director, East Cambridge Savings Charitable Foundation

August, Andrew: trustee, August Family Foundation (Charles J. and Burton S.)

August, Bruce A.: secretary, director, Morris Foundation (William T.)

August, Burton S., Sr.: trustee, August Family Foundation (Charles J. and Burton S.)

August, Charles J.: trustee, August Family Foundation (Charles J. and Burton S.)

August, Jan Lise: trustee, August Family Foundation (Charles J. and Burton S.)

August, Jean B.: trustee, August Family Foundation (Charles J. and Burton S.)

August, John W.: trustee, August Family Foundation (Charles J. and Burton S.)

August, Robert W.: trustee, August Family Foundation (Charles J. and Burton S.)

Auguste, MacDonald: treasurer, Rayonier Foundation

Augustine, Avery: director, Noyes, Jr. Memorial Foundation (Nicholas H.)

Aull, William C.: director, Castle Foundation (Harold K. L.)

Aupperle, Tammy B.: program director, Heinz Co. Foundation (H.J.)

Austen, W. Gerald, MD: chairman, trustee, Knight Foundation (John S. and James L.)

Austermiller, Judy: trustee, Boehm Foundation

Austin, Ann W.: member, Staunton Farm Foundation

Austin, Carlos: secretary, director, Tribune New York Foundation

Austin, Edward H., Jr.: trustee, Halsell Foundation (Ewing)

Austin, Gary: director, Brillion Foundation

Austin, H. Brent: executive vice president, chief financial officer, director, El Paso Corp.

Austin, Leroy: corporator, Oak Grove School

Austin, Sabrina: executive director, Duke Energy Foundation

Autry, Jacqueline: vice president, director, Autry Foundation

Autry, Rebecca: secretary, Bardes Fund

Auw, Pierre E.: trustee, Hodges Foundation (Bess J.)

Avampato, Charles M.: president, Clay Foundation

Avansino, Kristen A.: president, executive director, Wiegand Foundation (E. L.)

Avansino, Raymond C., Jr.: chairman, trustee, Wiegand Foundation (E. L.)

Avedisian, James R.: director, Atkinson Foundation

Avery, Caroline: president, Durfee Foundation

Avery, Halina: trustee, director, Durfee Foundation

Avery, William Joseph: trustee, Connelly Foundation

Axelrod, Margaret G.: treasurer, director, mem, Katzenberger Foundation

Axtell, Clayton M., III: director, Klee Foundation (Conrad and Virginia)

Axtell, Clayton M., Jr.: president, Klee Foundation (Conrad and Virginia)

Axworthy, Lloyd: director, MacArthur Foundation (John D. and Catherine T.)

Ayaub, John J.: vice president, secretary, trustee, Sage Foundation

Ayer, Everett L.: mem, Gardiner Savings Institution Charitable Foundation

Ayer, Ramani: chairman, president, chief executive officer, Hartford Financial Services Group, Inc.

Ayers, Jule: director, Sordoni Foundation

Aylesworth, William Andrew: treasurer, Texas Instruments Foundation; chief financial officer, treasurer, senior vice president, Texas Instruments Inc.

Aylmer, John F.: director, Kelley and Elza Kelley Foundation (Edward Bangs)

Aylward, A. A.: vice president, Aylward Family Foundation

Aylward, E. W.: president, Aylward Family Foundation

Aylward, R.J.: director, Aylward Family Foundation

Ayres, Nancy: president, director, Noyes, Jr. Memorial Foundation (Nicholas H.)

Azoulay, Bernard: trustee, Atofina Chemicals Foundation; president, chief executive officer, Elf Atochem North America, Inc.

B

Baack, Margaret: vice president, Ideal Industries Foundation

Babbio, Lawrence T., Jr.: vice chairman, president, Verizon Communications Inc.

Babcock, Bruce M.: director, Babcock Foundation (Mary Reynolds)

Babicka, Jerry: director, Educational Foundation of America

Babicka, Laren: adjunct director, Educational Foundation of America

Babicka, Shelley E.: adjunct director, Educational Foundation of America

Babington, Catherine V.: president, director, Abbott Laboratories Fund

Babs, Douglas: director, Burlington Northern Santa Fe Foundation

Babson, Donald Paul: trustee, Babson Foundation (Paul and Edith)

Babson, James A.: trustee, Babson Foundation (Paul and Edith)

Babson, Katherine L.: trustee, Babson Foundation (Paul and Edith)

Bacal, Michael: treasurer, Hexcel Foundation

Bach, Neil C.: chairman, trustee, Camp and Bennet Humiston Trust (Apollos)

Bachman, C. William: director, Utica National Foundation

Bachman, Dale: trustee, Cooke Foundation

Bachman, Mark: director, National Service Foundation

Bachmann, Bruce R.: director, Polk Brothers Foundation, Inc.

Bachmann, Tom: director, Grinnell Mutual Group Foundation

Bacigalupi, Jean: president, Haigh-Scatena Foundation

Backus, Candace Carlucci: secretary, trustee, program officer, Kerr Fund (Grayce B.)

Bacon, Carolyn R.: chief executive director, O'Donnell Foundation

Bacon, Herbert L.: president, Bacon Foundation (E. L. and Oma)

Bacon, Kenneth J.: senior vice president, Fannie Mae; director, Fannie Mae Foundation

Bacon, Laura May: treasurer, Bacon Foundation (E. L. and Oma)

Bacot, John Carter: director, Macy, Jr. Foundation (Josiah)

Badman, Benjamin, Jr.: assistant secretary, assistant treasurer, Sordoni Foundation

Baer, Timothy: vice president, Target Corp.; secretary, Target Foundation

Bagley, Nancy R.: vice president, Arca Foundation

Bagley, Nicole: director, Arca Foundation

Bagley, Smith: president, Arca Foundation

Bahrt, Fred R.: president, director, Gellert Foundation (Carl Gellert and Celia Berta)

Bailey, Andrew C., Esq.: trustee, Riley Foundation (Mabel Louise)

Bailey, Anita Lamb: director, Lamb Foundation

Bailey, Barbara Sue: trustee, Claypool Foundation (Silas and Ruth)

Bailey, Ben: director, Lamb Foundation

Bailey, D. P.: trustee, Exxon Mobil Foundation

Bailey, Dan: president, Selby and Marie Selby Foundation (William G.)

Bailey, George P.: secretary, second vice president, Bailey Family Foundation (William O. and Carole P.)

Bailey, Hoyt Q.: president, Dover Foundation

Bailey, James D.: director, Cudahy Fund (Patrick and Anna M.)

Bailey, Joanne: assistant secretary, Claneil Foundation

Bailey, Toff: director, Lamb Foundation

Bailey, William O.: president, Bailey Family Foundation (William O. and Carole P.)

Baillon, Austin J.: director, Grotto Foundation

Baillon, Peter M.: director, Grotto Foundation

Bains, Harrison MacKellar, Jr.: vice president, treasurer, Bristol-Myers Squibb Co.; treasurer, Bristol-Myers Squibb Foundation Inc.

Baird, Dugald Euan: chairman, president, chief executive officer, Schlumberger Ltd.

Baird, Joni E.: vice president, fund administrator, Johns Manville Fund

Baird, Nolan H., Jr.: trustee, Steele Foundation (Harry and Grace)

Baird, Philip F., Jr.: trustee, McKay Family Foundation

Baird, Richard A.: president, Giant Food, Inc.

Baird, Zoe: president, Markle Foundation (John and Mary R.)

Bakalis, Desi: director, Demos Foundation (N.)

Baker, Ann Cassidy: chairman, Broadhurst Foundation

Baker, Anne: manager corporate contributions

Baker, Anthony K.: trustee, Baker Trust (George F.)

Baker, Benjamin M., III: director, Lockhart Vaughan Foundation

Baker, C. Allen: trustee, Alcon Foundation; executive vice president, Alcon Laboratories, Inc.

Baker, David S.: trustee, Rich Foundation

Baker, Dennis J.: vice president, director, CertainTeed Corp.; director, Saint-Gobain Corporation Foundation

Baker, Dexter Farrington: trustee, Baker Foundation (Dexter F. and Dorothy H.)

Baker, Dorothy H.: trustee, Baker Foundation (Dexter F. and Dorothy H.)

Baker, Douglas J.: president, chief operating officer, Ecolab, Inc.

Baker, Edward L.: president, Florida Rock Industries Foundation; chairman, director, Florida Rock Industries, Inc.; president, Florida Rock & Tank Lines Foundation

Baker, George F., III: trustee, Baker Trust (George F.)

Baker, James Addison, III: trustee, Hughes Medical Institute (Howard)

Baker, Joeseph, Jr.: committee member, Smith, Jr. Foundation (M. W.)

Baker, Julia Clayton: trustee, Baker Trust (Clayton)

Baker, Kane K.: trustee, Baker Trust (George F.)

Baker, Larry: vice president employee relations, National Machinery Co.; secretary, treasurer, trustee, National Machinery Foundation, Inc.

Baker, Leslie Mayo, Jr.: chairman, Wachovia Bank of North Carolina NA

Baker, Norman D., Jr.: secretary, treasurer, trustee, Kimball Foundation (Horace A. Kimball and S. Ella)

Baker, Pam: executive director, secretary, Woods Charitable Fund

Baker, Paula W.: vice president, IBM International Foundation; director corporate support plans & programs, International Business Machines

Baker, Richard W.: trustee, Speer Foundation (Roy M.)

Baker, Robert W.: senior vice president, deputy general counsel, El Paso Corporate Foundation

Baker, Thomas E.: executive director, secretary, Oishei Foundation (The John R.)

Baker, Tracy A.: trustee, Gerber Foundation

Baker, William C.: trustee, Baker Trust (Clayton)

Baker, William O.: chairman emeritus, Mellon Foundation (Andrew W.)

Baker, William Oliver: trustee, Fund for New Jersey; director, Guggenheim Foundation (Harry Frank)

Bakewell, Edward L., III: chairman, chief executive officer, Bakewell Corp.; president, director, Bakewell, Jr. Family Foundation (Edward L.)

Bakken, Douglas Adair: executive director, Ball Brothers Foundation

Bakkensen, Ralph V. G.: secretary, M/A-COM Foundation

Balaban, Donald: director, Kirkpatrick Foundation, Inc.

Balderston, Frederick Emery: director, Osher Foundation (Bernard)

Baldree, Edwin M.: president, Tri-County Telephone Foundation

Baldwin, Bennet M.: assistant treasurer, trustee, Baldwin Memorial Foundation (Fred)

Baldwin, John C.: secretary, trustee, Baldwin Memorial Foundation (Fred); secretary, director, Castle Foundation (Harold K.

L.); president, Castle Foundation (Samuel N. and Mary)

Baldwin, Robert Hayes Burns: chairman, director, Dodge Foundation (Geraldine R.)

Bales, Dane G.: president, trustee, Hansen Foundation (Dane G.)

Balgooyen, Warren: director, Norcross Wildlife Foundation

Ball, Anne F.: trustee, Firestone, Jr. Foundation (Harvey)

Ball, Frank E.: vice president, director, Ball Brothers Foundation

Ballard, A. L.: secretary, treasurer, Hale Foundation (Crescent Porter)

Ballentine, George W., Jr.: trustee, Self Family Foundation

Ballmer, Steven Anthony: president, chief executive officer, director, Microsoft Corp.

Balloun, James S.: chairman, chief executive officer, president, National Service Industries, Inc.

Balsama, Maybelle L.: trustee, Bean Foundation (Norwin S. and Elizabeth N.)

Baltz, Ellen L.: director, trustee, Baker Foundation (Dexter F. and Dorothy H.)

Bamberger, Clarence, Jr.: mem, Bamberger Memorial Foundation (John Ernest Bamberger and Ruth Eleanor)

Banach, Joan: secretary, Dedalus Foundation

Banbury, Hunter: president, chief executive officer, treasurer, Cone-Blanchard Corp.

Banfield, Dick: president, Magna International of America, Inc.

Banis, Richard P.: treasurer, Pennington Foundation (William N. and Myriam)

Bankowski, Elizabeth: secretary, Ben & Jerry's Foundation

Banner, Matthew R., III: director, King Foundation (Kenneth Kendal)

Bannister, Thomas J., Jr.: president, Bakewell Corp.

Banno, Tetsuji: president, Oki America, Inc.

Bannon, Mel B.: trustee, Beynon Foundation (Kathryne)

Bannon, Robert D.: trustee, Beynon Foundation (Kathryne)

Barbato, Randall: treasurer, Nord Family Foundation

Barbera, Rosalie N.: vice president, director, Banta Corp. Foundation

Barbutes, Tracy: executive director, Katz Family Foundation

Bard, D. L., Jr.: trustee, Exxon Mobil Foundation

Bardes, Judith L.: executive director, trustee, Douty Foundation (Alfred and Mary); mgr, Seybert Institution for Poor Boys and Girls (Adam and Maria Sarah)

Bardes, Merrilyn B.: president, Bardes Corp.

Bardige, Betty S.: chairman, director, Mailman Family Foundation (A. L.)

Bardin, Mary Beth: executive vice president public affairs & communications, Verizon Communications Inc.

Bardoff, Ralph: vice president, director, Ishiyama Foundation

Bardusch, William E., Jr.: president, trustee, Sullivan Foundation (Algernon Sydney)

Bardwell, Stanley, M.D.: treasurer, Hudson River Bancorp Inc. Foundation

Bare, John: director evaluation, Knight Foundation (John S. and James L.)

Barhoum, Ann F.: director, executive committee, Francis Families Foundation

Bark, Dennis L.: chairman, trustee, Earhart Foundation

Barkeley, Norman A.: chairman emeritus, Ducommun, Inc.

Barker, Allan M.: treasurer, trustee, Barker Foundation Inc.

Barker, Ann S.: director, mem, Barker Foundation (J.M.R.)

Barker, Dorothy A.: trustee, Barker Foundation Inc.

Barker, Douglas M.: secretary, Barker Foundation Inc.

Barker, Edwin F.: vice president, chief financial officer, Winnebago Industries; trustee, Winnebago Industries Foundation

Barker, Elizabeth S.: vice president, director, mem, Barker Foundation (J.M.R.)

Barker, James R.: mem, Barker Foundation (J.M.R.)

Barker, Judith: president, Avon Products Foundation, Inc.

Barker, Mary L.: trustee, Stewart Educational Foundation (Donnell B. and Elizabeth Dee Shaw)

Barker, Norman, Jr.: director, member audit committee, member grant committee, Keck Foundation (W. M.)

Barker, Peter Keefe: treasurer, director, member executive committee, member grant, Keck Foundation (W. M.)

Barker, Robert R.: president, director, mem, Barker Foundation (J.M.R.)

Barker, Stella: trustee, Surrena Memorial Fund (Harry and Thelma)

Barker, William Benjamin: director, mem, Barker Foundation (J.M.R.)

Barker, William P.: trustee, McFeely-Rogers Foundation

Barletta, Robert: treasurer, Prospect Hill Foundation

Barlow, Gregory P.: executive director, Medina Foundation

Barmore, Beryl A.: vice president, Wilmington Trust Co.

Barnes, Carlyle Fuller: president, Barnes Foundation

Barnes, Corbin: treasurer, Cook, Sr. Charitable Foundation (Kelly Gene)

Barnes, Judith A.: director, Howard and Bush Foundation

Barnes, Thomas O.: secretary, Barnes Group Foundation Inc.; board chairman, Barnes Group, Inc.

Barnes, W. Michael: senior vice president finance & planning, chief financial officer, Rockwell Automation Inc.; member trust committee, Rockwell International Corp. Trust

Barnes, Wallace W.: director, Barnes Group Foundation Inc.

Barnett, Carol: chairman, chief executive officer, Publix Supermarkets Charities

Barnett, E. W.: director, Wharton Foundation

Barney, Marlene S.: director, Exchange Bank Foundation

Barnhart, Lorraine: director, Freed Foundation; vice president, trustee, Huber Foundation

Baron, Blue: secretary, Mechanic Foundation (Morris A.)

Baron, Jules M.: director, Goldman Foundation (Herman)

Baron, Richard K.: executive director, Goldman Foundation (Herman)

Baron, Thomas H.: trustee, Niagara Mohawk Foundation

Baronner, Robert Francis: director, One Valley Bank Foundation

Barr, John H.: vice president, Oak Tree Charitable Foundation

Barrett, Allen M., Jr.: vice president corporate communications, McCormick & Company, Inc.

Barrett, John F.: treasurer, Emery Memorial (Thomas J.); trustee,

Western-Southern Foundation, Inc.; president, chief executive officer, director, Western & Southern Life Insurance Co.

Barron, John H. C.: secretary, Cafritz Foundation (Morris and Gwendolyn)

Barron, M. P.: director, Audubon State Bank Charitable Foundation

Barroso, Carmen: director population, new partnerships, MacArthur Foundation (John D. and Catherine T.)

Barrow, Steve: program officer, Sierra Health Foundation

Barrows, J. Craig: assistant secretary, trustee, M/A-COM Foundation; general counsel, secretary, New England Business Service

Barry, Elizabeth T.: director, Gazette Foundation

Barry, Tina S.: vice president corporate communications, Kimberly-Clark Corp.; president, director, Kimberly-Clark Foundation

Barsky, Barbara: vice president, PNM Foundation

Barsness, W. E. Bye: vice chairman, trustee, McNeely Foundation

Barstow, David O.: trustee, Barstow Foundation

Barstow, Frederick E.: president, Barstow Foundation

Barstow, John C.: trustee, Barstow Foundation

Barstow, Richard G.: trustee, Barstow Foundation

Barstow, Robert G.: trustee, Barstow Foundation

Barstow, Robert O.: trustee, Barstow Foundation

Bartelt, Sarah Caswell: director, Beveridge Foundation, Inc. (Frank Stanley)

Barth, John: member advisory board, Johnson Controls Foundation; president, chief executive officer, Johnson Controls Inc.

Bartha, Louis A.: secretary, director, The Prairie Foundation

Bartl, James F.: secretary, director, Phillips Family Foundation (L. E.)

Bartlett, Paul Dana, Jr.: chairman, director, Bartlett & Co.; trustee, Bartlett & Co. Grain Charitable Foundation

Bartlett, Thomas Alva: chairman, United States-Japan Foundation

Bartley, Charles R., Sr.: vchairman, Exchange Bank Foundation

Barton, Glen A.: chairman, chief executive officer, Caterpillar Foundation

Barton, Shannon: program officer, Davis Foundation (Joe C.)

Barton, Willis H., Jr.: vice president, director, New Milford Savings Bank Foundation

Bartos, John: trustee, Strosacker Foundation (Charles J.)

Bartwink, Theodore S.: treasurer, secretary, Harkness Foundation for Dance

Barwick, Kent L.: director, Clark Foundation (NY)

Basner, Ruth H.: mem, Hoover Foundation (Herbert W.)

Bass, Edward Perry: vice president, director, Richardson Foundation (Sid W.)

Bass, F. W.: trustee, Exxon Mobil Foundation

Bass, John T.: vice chairman, treasurer, Crowell Trust (Henry P. and Susan C.)

Bass, Lee M.: vice president, director, Richardson Foundation (Sid W.)

Bass, Nancy Lee: vice president, director, Richardson Foundation (Sid W.)

Bass, Perry Richardson: president, director, Richardson Foundation (Sid W.)

Bass, Sid Richardson: vice president, director, Richardson Foundation (Sid W.)

Bastian, Frank W.: secretary, director, Schoenleber Foundation

Batchelor, Karen: director, Comerica Charitable Foundation

Bateman, Janey: secretary, director, Hawn Foundation

Bateman, Mary Michael: vice chairman, Vermilion Healthcare Foundation

Bates, Arthur: trustee, Charitable Venture Foundation

Bates, James C.: vice president, chief financial officer, ACF Industries

Bates, Jeanne M.: vice president, program officer, Hall Family Foundation (The)

Bates, R. K.: director, Hegeler II Foundation (Julius W.)

Bates, Ronnie L.: sen vice president external affairs, Georgia Power Co.; director, Georgia Power Foundation

Batkin, Jonathan: director, Chamiza Foundation

Batte, G. A., Jr.: director, member, Cannon Foundation, Inc. (The)

Batten, Frank, Jr.: executive vice president, Landmark Communications, Inc.

Batten, Frank, Sr.: chairman, director, Landmark

Communications Foundation; chairman, Landmark Communications, Inc.

Battinelli, Salvatore: finance manager, Kendall Foundation (Henry P.)

Batts, James L.: director, Batts Foundation

Batts, John H.: president, director, Batts Foundation

Batts, John T.: director, Batts Foundation

Batts, Julie: secretary, Gilmore Foundation (Irving S.)

Batts, Michael A.: director, Batts Foundation

Batts, Robert H.: director, Batts Foundation

Battye, Kenneth: trustee, Gordon Charitable Trust (Peggy and Yale)

Bauder, Lillian: chairman, trustee, Skillman Foundation

Bauer, David P.: trustee, Bauer Family Foundation

Bauer, Douglas F.: secretary, treasurer, trustee, Bowne Foundation (Robert)

Bauer, Lisa M.: trustee, Bauer Family Foundation

Bauer, Mary Grace: trustee, Bauer Family Foundation

Bauer, Paul D.: trustee, Bauer Family Foundation

Bauervic-Wright, Rose: vice president, Bauervic Foundation (Charles M.)

Baukol, Ronald Oliver: director, executive vice president, Minnesota Mining & Manufacturing Co.

Baum, Alexio R.: trustee, Gerstacker Foundation (Rollin M.)

Baum, Steven: secretary, treasurer, Dorot Foundation

Bauman, Steve: secretary, Ottenheimer Brothers Foundation

Baumann, Lawra: vice president, Fifth Third Foundation; foundation officer, Schmidlapp Trust No. 1 (Jacob G.)

Baumblatt, Stanley: assistant secretary, Merrill Lynch & Co. Foundation Inc.

Baumgardner, Anita A.: secretary, trustee, Copley Foundation (James S.)

Baumgartner, Howard E.: trustee, Schowalter Foundation

Bausch, Elizabeth: trustee, Nord Family Foundation

Bawek, Rick: chief executive officer, Red Wing Shoe Co. Foundation

Baxter, Barbara J.: vice president, trustee, Andrews Foundation

Baxter, Joe E.: secretary, treasurer, director, Meyer Family Foundation (Paul J.)

Bay, Frederick: chairman, Bay Foundation

Bay, Mogens C.: trustee, Kiewit Foundation (Peter); chairman, chief executive officer, Valmont Industries, Inc.

Bayless, Mary C.: director, Connell Foundation (Michael J.)

Bayliss, Harry G.: treasurer, trustee, Alden Trust (George I.)

Bayne, J. E.: treasurer, Exxon Mobil Foundation

Beach, Clarence E.: director, Broyhill Family Foundation

Beach, E. D.: secretary, treasurer, director, Broyhill Family Foundation

Beach, Ross: trustee, Hansen Foundation (Dane G.)

Beal, Barry A.: trustee, Beal Foundation

Beal, Carlton E., Jr.: trustee, Beal Foundation

Beal, Keleen H.: chairman, Beal Foundation

Beal, Kelly S.: trustee, Beal Foundation

Beal, Richard M.: treasurer, Gallo Foundation (Ernest)

Beal, Spencer E.: trustee, Beal Foundation

Beale, Susan M.: vice president, secretary, DTE Energy Co.; member, DTE Energy Foundation

Beall, Carolyn C.: assistant treasurer, Campbell Foundation (MD)

Beall, Donald Ray: director, executive committee, Rockwell Automation Inc.

Beall, Kenneth S., Esq.: secretary, Fuller Foundation (DE)

Bean, Roy H.: trustee, Ashtabula Foundation

Bear, Stephen E.: director, Bristol-Myers Squibb Foundation Inc.

Beard, Anson McCook, Jr.: trustee, Hartford Foundation, Inc. (The John A.)

Beard, Ellanor Allday: board of directors, Fondren Foundation

Beard, Peter: vice president national philanthropy, Fannie Mae Foundation

Beardsley, George B.: trustee, Gates Family Foundation

Beardsley, Pamela: trustee, Boettcher Foundation

Bearn, Alexander Gordon, MD: trustee, Hughes Medical Institute (Howard); director honorary, Macy, Jr. Foundation (Josiah)

Bearse, Stacy V.: treasurer, Blood-Horse Charitable Foundation

Beason, Jeffrey I.: senior vice president, controller, El Paso Corporate Foundation

Beattie, Art P.: vice president, secretary, treasurer, Alabama Power Co.; treasurer, director, Alabama Power Foundation

Beattie, Catherine Hamrick: director, Fullerton Foundation

Beaulieu, Rita H.: treasurer, director, Vance Charitable Foundation (Robert C.)

Beauvais, Pamela McCarthy: president, McCarthy Charities

Beaver, Thomas A.: treasurer, Wyomissing Foundation

Beaz, Marianne: vice president client service & pension investments, Pacific Life Insurance Co.

Bechdel, Donna: executive director, Decker Foundation (Dr. G. Clifford and Florence B.)

Becht, Loretta J.: assistant secretary, Hyde and Watson Foundation

Bechtel, Robert W.: co-trustee, mgr, director, Potts and Sibley Foundation

Beck, Audrey Jones: director, Houston Endowment

Beck, Barbara: vice president, director, Cisco Systems Foundation

Beck, Joyce M.: administrative assistant, Ball Foundation (George and Frances)

Beck, Nancy: trustee, The MBNA Foundation

Beck, Phyllis Whitman: chairman, Independence Foundation

Beck, Susan K.: member distribution committee, trustee, Kettering Fund

Becker, Allen: trustee, Schowalter Foundation

Becker, Gerald R.: vice president, treasurer, Lytel Foundation (Bertha Russ)

Becker, Harold M.: chairman, chief executive officer, Guaranty Bank & Trust Co.; director, Guaranty Bank and Trust Co. Charitable Trust

Becker, Howard C.: trustee, Ohio National Foundation; vice president, Ohio National Life Insurance Co.

Becker, John A.: director, Firstar Bank Milwaukee NA

Becker, Katrina H.: vice president, secretary, director, Barker Welfare Foundation

Becker, Richard K.A.: assistant secretary, Loughran Foundation (Mary and Daniel)

Becker, Robert A.: president, Provident Community Foundation

Becker, Robert D.: director, Guaranty Bank and Trust Co. Charitable Trust

Becker, Steve: chief executive officer, chief financial officer, Kawasaki Motors Manufacturing Corporation U.S.A.

Becket, MacDonald G.: trustee, Unocal Foundation

Beckett, Steven J.: trustee, American Optical Foundation

Beckman, Arnold W.: director, Beckman Foundation (Arnold and Mabel)

Beckman, G. Patricia: director, Beckman Foundation (Arnold and Mabel)

Beckner, Lou: assistant secretary, Houchens Foundation (Ervin G.)

Beckworth, Laura H.: vice president, Hobby Family Foundation

Bediones, Delores: trustee, Locations Foundation

Bedsole, M. Palmer: member distribution committee, Bedsole Foundation (J. L.)

Bedsole, T. Massey: chairman distribution committee, trustee, Bedsole Foundation (J. L.)

Bedsole, Travis M., Jr.: member distribution committee, Bedsole Foundation (J. L.)

Beebe, Lydia I.: corporate secretary, ChevronTexaco Corp.

Beeby, Thomas H.: trustee, Graham Foundation for Advanced Studies in the Fine Arts

Beech, Thomas Foster: executive vice president, Burnett Foundation (The)

Beer, Robert A.: trustee, Brace Foundation (Donald C.)

Beers, Julius H.: treasurer, Oleson Foundation

Beeston, John J., MD: board mem, Brush Foundation

Beetle, Vivian: admin director, Hoffmann-La Roche Foundation; director community affairs, Hoffmann-La Roche, Inc.

Behrend, Catherine H.: director, Hebrew Technical Institute

Behrenhausen, Richard A.: president, chief executive officer, McCormick Tribune Foundation (Robert R.)

Behrens, Roger: vice president, HON Industries Charitable Foundation

Beinecke, Elizabeth G.: vice president, director, Prospect Hill Foundation

Beinecke, Frederick William: trustee, Kress Foundation (Samuel H.); vice president, director, Prospect Hill Foundation

Beinecke, John B.: vice president, director, Prospect Hill Foundation

Beinecke, William Sperry: president, director, Prospect Hill Foundation

Beisler, Ralph: secretary, trustee, Robinson-Broadhurst Foundation

Beistline, Earl Hoover: director, Usibelli Foundation

Beland, Elizabeth A.: administrator, Stevens Foundation (Abbot and Dorothy H.)

Belcher, Dennis Irl: treasurer, trustee, Olsson Memorial Foundation (Elis)

Belcher, Donald David: chairman, president, chief executive officer, director, Banta Corp.; vice president, director, Banta Corp. Foundation

Belda, Alain J. P.: chairman, chief executive officer, director, Alcoa Inc.; trustee, Ford Foundation

Belda, Ricardo E.: director, Alcoa Foundation

Beldecos, J. Nicholas: trustee, Scaife Family Foundation

Belden, Frederick H., Jr.: mem, trustee, One Valley Bank Foundation; executive vice president, One Valley Bank NA

Belin, Daniel N.: trustee, Ahmanson Foundation; vice chairman, trustee, Kress Foundation (Samuel H.)

Belin, Oscar F.: president, trustee, Bryden Foundation (Blanche); trustee, Hansen Foundation (Dane G.)

Beling, Betty: assoc director, Borchard Foundation (Albert and Elaine)

Beling, Willard A.: chairman, director, Borchard Foundation (Albert and Elaine)

Belinkie, Julie Bender: president, Bender Foundation

Belk, John Montgomery: member board advisors, Belk Foundation; chairman, chief executive officer, Belk Stores Services, Inc.

Bell, David L.: trustee, Self Family Foundation

Bell, Diane Fisher: vice president, Fisher Foundation

Bell, Ford W.: trustee, Bell Foundation (James Ford)

Bell, Judy: trustee, El Pomar Foundation

Bell, Larry: trustee, Beal Foundation

Bell, Lawrence T.: vice president law, general counsel, Ecolab, Inc.

Bell, R. Terry: president, trustee, Rockwell Fund, Inc.

Bell, Richard A.: trustee, vice president, Sarkeys Foundation

Bell, Robert Morrall: president, director, Gregg-Graniteville Foundation

Bell, Samuel H., Jr.: trustee, Bell Foundation (James Ford)

Bell, Samuel P.: vice president, trustee, Jones Foundation (Fletcher)

Bell, Susan M.: senior supervisor-corporate communications, Ameren Corp.

Bellairs, Robert J.: co-trustee, Bishop Charitable Trust (A. G.)

Bellamy, George E.: director, Morgan Foundation (Louie R. and Gertrude)

Belles, Lawrence L.: president, director, Cheney Foundation (Elizabeth F.)

Bellinger, Susan: trustee, New York Foundation

Belloff, Frederick: director, Bush Charitable Foundation, Inc. (Edyth)

Belloff, Mary Gretchen: vice chairman, director, Bush Charitable Foundation, Inc. (Edyth)

Bellor, Mary: president, secretary, Graham Fund (Philip L.)

Bellwood, Wesley E.: president, Wynn Foundation

Belt, John L.: director, Kirkpatrick Foundation, Inc.

Belton, Sharon Sayles: director, Bush Foundation

Beltz, Susan W.: director, Pine Tree Foundation

BeMiller, Linda P.: program officer, Forest Foundation

Bemis, Richard A.: president, Bemis Family Foundation (F.K.); president, chief executive officer, director, Bemis Manufacturing Co.

Benard, Michael P.: vice president, director communications & public affairs, Eastman Kodak Co.

Benbough, Legler: president, Benbough Foundation (Legler)

Benckenstein, Eunice R.: vice chairman, trustee, Stark Foundation (Nelda C. and H. J. Lutcher)

Bender, Christine: secretary, treasurer, director, Cimino Foundation (James and Barbara)

Bender, David S.: vice president, Bender Foundation

Bender, Howard Marvin: executive vice president, Bender Foundation

Bender, Sondra D.: chairwoman, Bender Foundation

Bender, Stanley Seymour: secretary, Bender Foundation

Bender-Laskow, Barbara: vice president, Bender Foundation

Bendheim, John M.: vice president, director, Lowenstein Foundation (Leon)

Bendheim, John M., Jr.: director, Lowenstein Foundation (Leon)

Bendheim, Robert Austin: president, director, Lowenstein Foundation (Leon)

Bendheim-Thoman, Lynn: director, Lowenstein Foundation (Leon)

Benedict, Kennette: director peace & international cooperation, MacArthur Foundation (John D. and Catherine T.)

Benenson, Charles B.: president, Benenson Foundation (Frances and Benjamin)

Benenson, Lawrence A.: director, Hebrew Technical Institute

Benetton, Luciano: chairman, president, chief executive officer, director, Benetton U.S.A. Corp.

Benjamin, Adelaide Wisdom: trustee, RosaMary Foundation

Benjamin, Andrew: trustee, RosaMary Foundation

Bennack, Frank Anthony, Jr.: director, board chairman, Hearst Foundation, Inc. (The); vice president, director, Hearst Foundation (William Randolph)

Bennett, Charles: director, German Protestant Orphan Asylum Association Foundation

Bennett, Clark: trustee, Bennett Family Foundation (Claude)

Bennett, Franklin: trustee, Pollock Co. Foundation (William B.)

Bennett, Joann: treasurer, Argyle Foundation

Bennett, John J., Jr.: secretary, St. Giles Foundation

Bennett, Nancy: trustee, Bennett Family Foundation (Claude)

Bennett, Robert B.: trustee, Statler Foundation

Bennett O'Leary, Katherine: trustee, Bennett Family Foundation (Claude)

Bennington, Ronald Kent: trustee, Hoover Foundation (The)

Bensen, M. James: trustee, Blandin Foundation

Benson, Bill R.: executive vice president, chief financial officer, Physicians Mutual Insurance Co.; vice president, director, Physicians Mutual Insurance Co. Foundation

Benson, Donald: trustee, Share Trust (Charles Morton)

Benson, Gregory L.: director, treasurer, Andersen Foundation

Benson, James M.: president, Metropolitan Life Insurance Co.

Benson, John W.: executive vice president health care, Minnesota Mining & Manufacturing Co.

Benson, Keith W., III: president, chief executive officer, National Manufacturing Co.

Benson, Keith W., Jr.: chairman, director, National Manufacturing Co.

Benson, Lee-Hoon: program officer, Bush Foundation

Benson, Martha L.: vice president, treasurer, chief financial officer, Meadows Foundation (The)

Benson, Peter M.: director, NMC Foundation

Benson, Steve R.: director administration, El Pomar Foundation

Benten, R. Anthony: assistant treasurer, New York Times Co. Foundation

Bentley, Greg: director, Trust Foundation

Bentley, Maria C.: treasurer, director, Gellert Foundation (Carl Gellert and Celia Berta)

Benton, Charles: chairman, Benton Foundation

Benton, Craig: director, Benton Foundation

Benton, Marjorie Craig: trustee, Benton Foundation

Bentson, Nathan L.: chairman, president, Midcontinent Media Foundation; chairman, chief executive officer, director, Midcontinent Media, Inc.

Bentzen, Michael P.: secretary, trustee, Fowler Memorial Foundation (John Edward)

Bere, Barbara Van Dellen: president, director, Bere Foundation

Bere, David L.: secretary, treasurer, Bere Foundation

Bere, James Frederick, Jr.: vice president, director, Bere Foundation

Bere, Robert P.: vice president, director, Bere Foundation

Berelson, Ellen S.: vice president, director, Barth Foundation, Inc. (The Theodore H.)

Berelson, Thelma D.: secretary, director, Barth Foundation, Inc. (The Theodore H.)

Berenato, Joseph C.: president, chief executive officer, Ducommun, Inc.

Berey, Mark H.: senior vice president, chief financial officer, treasurer, Giant Food, Inc.

Berg, Alan: vice president, Becher Foundation (Hildegarde D.)

Berg, Anne P.: grant consultant, Rich Foundation

Berg, Lois: secretary, Johnson Foundation

Berg, Sue M.: secretary, CLARCOR Foundation

Bergenfield, Burt: trustee, Simon Foundation (Sidney, Milton, and Leoma)

Bergent, Nancy W.: trustee, Kunkel Foundation (John Crain)

Berger, Claudia: secretary, Lin Foundation (T. Y.)

Berger, Gretchen: director, Patron Saints Foundation

Berger, John N.: vice president, director, Berger Foundation (H. N. and Frances C.)

Berger, Miles Lee: director, Graham Foundation for Advanced Studies in the Fine Arts

Bergeron, Peter L.: trustee, Foundation for Seacoast Health

Bergethon, K. Roald: trustee, Newcombe Foundation (Charlotte W.)

Bergquist, Renee: director investor relations, Albertson's Inc.

Bergreen, Bernard D.: president, Gilman Foundation (Howard)

Bergsteinsson, Paul: vice president, CIGNA Foundation

Bergtold, Susanna: director, Scherman Foundation

Berilgen, Bulent A.: vice president, chief operating officer, director, Forest Oil Corp.

Berk, Sam: secretary, trustee, Nord Family Foundation

Berk, Tony B.: trustee, Parshelsky Foundation (Moses L.)

Berkenstadt, James A.: admin, Cremer Foundation

Berkman, Andrew: director, Hebrew Technical Institute

Berkman, Louis: president, trustee, Berkman Foundation (Louis and Sandra); chairman, trustee, Fair Oaks Foundation

Berkopec, Robert N.: treasurer, assistant secretary, Bradley Foundation (Lynde and Harry)

Berkowitz, Martin A.: comptroller, Prudential Foundation

Berlamino, Betty Ellen: president, director, Tribune New York Foundation

Berlanti, Merryl A.: vice president, Dominic Foundation

Berlanti, Richard A.: president, Dominic Foundation

Berlanti, Todd A.: secretary, treasurer, Dominic Foundation

Berliant, Jennie D.: trustee, Rosenthal Foundation (Lois and Richard)

Berliantt, Mark H.: trustee, Rosenthal Foundation (Lois and Richard)

Berlin, Charles, PhD: director, Littauer Foundation (Lucius N.)

Bermas, Stephen: president, Conway Scholarship Foundation (Carle C.)

Bernadotte, Christian C.: vice president, Nordson Corp.

Bernard, Carolyn K.: trustee, Hawkins Foundation (Robert Z.)

Bernard, Leslie M.: program officer, Kresge Foundation

Bernard, Lewis W.: trustee, Getty Trust (J. Paul); chairman, Markle Foundation (John and Mary R.); trustee, Mellon Foundation (Andrew W.)

Bernard, Robert: member grantmaking committee, Claiborne Foundation (Liz); senior vice president international sales, Liz Claiborne, Inc.

Berndt, Richard O.: director, Baltimore Equitable Insurance Foundation

Bernhardson, Ivy S.: treasurer, Bush Foundation

Bernhardt, Stephen J.: president, treasurer, Baltimore Equitable Insurance Foundation; chairman, president, chief executive officer, chief financial officer, Baltimore Equity Society

Bernstein, Alan S.: trustee, Lurcy Charitable and Educational Trust (Georges)

Bernstein, Alison: vice president, education, media, arts, & culture, Ford Foundation

Bernstein, Alison R.: vice president, knowledge, creativity and freedom, Ford Foundation

Bernstein, Daniel Lewis: trustee, Lurcy Charitable and Educational Trust (Georges)

Bernstein, Erik P.: trustee, Phillips Family Foundation (The Jay and Rose)

Bernstein, George Lurcy: trustee, Lurcy Charitable and Educational Trust (Georges)

Bernstein, Henry B.: director finance, Pew Charitable Trusts

Bernstein, Jay S.: trustee, Lawrence Foundation

Bernstein, Lawrence: trustee, Lawrence Foundation

Bernstein, Leonard S.: chairman, president, chief executive officer, Candlesticks, Inc.; trustee, Lawrence Foundation

Bernstein, Loraine: trustee, assistant director, concert coordinator, Gordon Charitable Trust (Peggy and Yale)

Bernstein, Morton J.: director, Samuels Foundation (Fan Fox and Leslie R.)

Bernstein, Paula P.: trustee, Phillips Family Foundation (The Jay and Rose)

Bernstein, R. L.: vice president, Dr. Seuss Foundation

Bernstein, William E.: trustee, Phillips Family Foundation (The Jay and Rose)

Berresford, Susan Vail: president, Ford Foundation

Berrier, Ronald G.: vice president, treasurer, assistant secretary, Thomasville Furniture Industries, Inc.

Berry, Archie: corporator, Oak Grove School

Berry, Charles D.: trustee, Berry Foundation (Loren M.)

Berry, David L.: trustee, Berry Foundation (Loren M.)

Berry, Donald C., Jr.: treasurer, trustee, McDonald Foundation (J. M.)

Berry, George W.: trustee, Berry Foundation (Loren M.)

Berry, John William, Jr.: president, trustee, Berry Foundation (Loren M.)

Berry, Karen R.: secretary, Kornfeld Foundation (Emily Davie and Joseph S.)

Berry, Sharon: director, M.E. Foundation

Berry, Thomas Eugene: assistant secretary, trustee, Sterling-Turner Foundation

Berry, Thomas W.: director, treasurer, Hyde and Watson Foundation

Berry, William S.: director, Rayonier Foundation; executive vice president forest resources & wood products, Rayonier, Inc.

Berryhill, John: co-trustee, Latkin Charitable Foundation (Herbert and Gertrude)

Bersoff, Edward H., PhD: vice chair, Meyer Foundation (Eugene and Agnes E.)

Berthold, James K.: director, Sunnen Foundation

Bertran, David R.: senior vice president manufacturing & logistics, Ondeo Nalco Co.; director, ONDEO Nalco Foundation

Bertrand, Frederic Howard: chairman, Central Vermont Public Service Corp.

Berwald, John: director, Crail-Johnson Foundation

Berylson, Amy S.: trustee, Smith Family Foundation (Richard and Susan)

Berylson, John G.: trustee, Smith Family Foundation (Richard and Susan)

Bescherer, Edwin A., Jr.: trustee, Dun & Bradstreet Corp. Foundation, Inc.

Beschloss, Afsaneh M.: trustee, Ford Foundation

Bessant, Catherine P.: trustee, Bank of America Foundation

Bessemer, Mary T.: director emeritus, Holmberg Foundation

Besser, John Edward: director, Barnes Group Foundation Inc.; senior vice president finance & law, Barnes Group, Inc.

Bessette, Andy: director, vice chairman, St. Paul Companies Inc. Foundation

Best, Barbara D.: director, Dana Foundation (Charles A.)

Betten, Michael G.: director, Dime Savings Bank of Norwich Foundation

Bettis, Bernice A.: secretary, director, King Foundation (Kenneth Kendal)

Betts, C. R.: trustee, Betts Foundation

Betts, I. R.: trustee, Betts Foundation

Betts, R. E.: trustee, Betts Foundation

Betts, Richard T.: trustee, Betts Foundation; chairman, president, director, Betts Industries

Betz, Bill B.: director, Jameson Foundation (J. W. and Ida M.)

Beukema, Henry S.: executive director, McCune Foundation

Beverly, Joseph E.: director, Williams Family Foundation of Georgia

Bevona, Devra A.: assistant secretary, treasurer, Seneca Foods Foundation

Bewley, Peter D.: senior vice president, general counsel, secretary, Clorox Co.; vice president, secretary, Clorox Co. Foundation

Beyer, Joanne B.: president, Allegheny Foundation; vice president, secretary, treasurer, Scaife Family Foundation

Bezik, Cynthia B.: senior vice president finance, Cleveland-Cliffs, Inc.

Bianchini, Thomas J.: secretary, treasurer, Kirby Foundation (F. M.)

Bianco, Richard A.: president, chief executive officer, director, AmBase Corp.

Bibb, Thomas F.: vice president, treasurer, trustee, Halff Foundation (G. A. C.)

Biber, David D.: secretary, treasurer, Lilly Endowment

Bickel, Bruce: senior vice president, manager, Hopwood Charitable Trust (John M.)

Bicknell, Warren, III: vice president, trustee, Bicknell Fund

Bicknell, Wendy H.: trustee, Bicknell Fund

Biemer, Linda: director, Klee Foundation (Conrad and Virginia)

Bienz, Walt: trustee, Auburn Foundry Foundation

Bifulco, Frank P., Jr.: director, Coca-Cola Foundation

Bigelow, T. William: trustee, Smyth Trust (Marion C.)

Biggers, Covella H.: treasurer, Houchens Foundation (Ervin G.)

Biggers, Erin: director, Houchens Foundation (Ervin G.)

Biggers, Gil E.: director, Houchens Foundation (Ervin G.)

Biggers, Gil M.: president, Houchens Foundation (Ervin G.)

Biggie, Carmelita: committee member, Whitaker Fund (Helen F.)

Biggs, John Herron: trustee, Getty Trust (J. Paul)

Biggs, Victor: assistant vice president, Brookdale Foundation

Bigham, James John: executive vice president, chief financial officer, director, ContiGroup Companies, Inc.

Bihary, Kristen: vice president, Eaton Corp.

Bilezikian, Doreen: director, Kelley and Elza Kelley Foundation (Edward Bangs)

Billegsly, James R.: director, Doherty Charitable Foundation (Henry L. and Grace)

Billings, Peter, Jr.: trustee, Michael Foundation (Herbert I. and Elsa B.)

Billingsley, Helen Lee: director, Doherty Charitable Foundation (Henry L. and Grace)

Billingsley, James Ray: vice president, treasurer, Doherty Charitable Foundation (Henry L. and Grace)

Bilski, Berthold: director, Littauer Foundation (Lucius N.)

Bilton, Stuart Douglas: president, chief executive officer, Chicago Title Corp.; trustee, Chicago Title and Trust Co. Foundation

Bing, Dave: trustee, McGregor Fund

Binswanger, David R.: president, chief executive officer, Binswanger Companies; treasurer, Binswanger Foundation

Binswanger, Frank G., III: secretary, Binswanger Foundation

Binswanger, Frank G., Jr.: co-chairman, director, Binswanger Companies

Binswanger, John K.: co-chairman, director, Binswanger Companies; chairman, Binswanger Foundation

Binswanger, Robert B.: vice chairman, Binswanger Foundation

Birch, Edward: trustee, Mosher Foundation (Samuel B.)

Birchenough, David: vice president, Klee Foundation (Conrad and Virginia)

Birckhead, Toni: trustee, Rosenthal Foundation (Lois and Richard)

Bircumshaw, Colin: vice president, Price Foundation (Lucien B. and Katherine E.)

Bircumshow, Colin: director, Price Foundation (Lucien B. and Katherine E.)

Bird, Hobart M.: trustee, Braemar Charitable Trust

Bird, Marian A.: trustee, Braemar Charitable Trust

Bird, Peter F., Jr.: executive director, chief executive officer, Frist Foundation

Bischoff, Manfred: aerospace and industrial businesses, DaimlerChrysler AG

Bisesi, James T.: director, Glick Foundation (Eugene and Marilyn)

Bisgrove, Debra: director, Stardust Foundation

Bisgrove, Gerald: president, Stardust Foundation

Bishop, Donald F., II: president, executive director, O'Connor Foundation (A. Lindsay and Olive B.)

Bishop, John L.: auxiliary director, Russell Charitable Foundation (Tom)

Bishop, Kim: director, Simpson Fund

Bishop, Leslie R.: assistant secretary/treasurer, director, Russell Charitable Foundation (Tom)

Bishop, Margaret: gov, Munson Foundation Trust (W. B.)

Bishop, Robert L., II: chairman, member advisory committee, O'Connor Foundation (A. Lindsay and Olive B.)

Bishop, Timothy R.: treasurer, Collins Foundation

Bishop, Vernon: trustee, Bishop Foundation (Vernon and Doris)

Bittner, R. Richard: trustee, director, Bechtel Charitable Remainder Uni-Trust (Marie H.)

Bittorf, Joseph L.: chairperson, NMC Foundation

Bjornson, Donald R., MD: director, CHC Foundation

Bjornson, Edith Cameron: vice president, senior program officer, Markle Foundation (John and Mary R.)

Black, Creed Carter: trustee, Knight Foundation (John S. and James L.)

Black, Gary, Jr.: chairman, trustee, Abell Foundation

Black, Gary E.: president, director, Fireman's Fund Foundation; president claims division, director, Fireman's Fund Insurance Co.

Black, Isabelle E.: vice president, Miller Foundation (Steve J.)

Black, Lennox K.: president, Teleflex Foundation; chairman, director, Teleflex, Inc.

Black, Natalie A.: vice president, director, Kohler Foundation

Black, Thomas F., III: president, trustee, Kimball Foundation (Horace A. Kimball and S. Ella)

Blackburn, Richard W.: trustee, Duke Energy Foundation

Blackburn, Sharon L.: member advisory committee, Meyer Foundation (Robert R.)

Blackford, Robert N.: trustee, Magruder Foundation (Chesley G.)

Blackwell, Anna Derby: trustee, Cooke Foundation

Blackwell, Jean: vice president, human resources, Cummins, Inc.

Blaine, Anne B.: member distribution committee, Bruening Foundation (Eva L. and Joseph M.)

Blair, Gary J.: treasurer, trustee, Blade Foundation

Blair, Ian D.: trustee, Todd Co. Foundation (A.M.)

Blair, Pat: pub trustee, Carpenter Foundation

Blake, Benjamin L.: director, The Prairie Foundation

Blake, Jonathan D.: director, Daniels Foundation (Fred Harris)

Blake, Lucy: trustee, Crocker Trust (Mary A.)

Blamey, Richard L.: secretary, treasurer, director, VPI Foundation Inc.

Blanchard, Larry: assistant secretary, treasurer, CUNA Mutual Group Foundation, Inc.

Blandford, M. Margaret: executive director, White Foundation (W. P. and H. B.)

Blanding, Stephen P.: secretary, treasurer, Lesher Foundation (Dean and Margaret)

Blaney, Carolyn E.: director, Eberly Foundation

Blanke, Gail Ann: vice president, Avon Products Foundation, Inc.

Blanton, Eddy S.: vice president, director, Scurlock Foundation

Blanton, Jack S., Jr.: vice president, director, Scurlock Foundation

Blanton, Jack Sawtelle: chairman, director, Houston Endowment

Blanton, Laura L.: president, director, Scurlock Foundation

Blasdale, William: trustee, Acushnet Foundation

Blass, Gus, III: board of directors, Ottenheimer Brothers Foundation

Blass, Noland, Jr.: board director, Ottenheimer Brothers Foundation

Blaxter, H. Vaughan, III: director, secretary, Hillman Foundation

Blaylock, Marcia: trustee, CLARCOR Foundation

Blazedale, Bill: trustee, Acushnet Foundation

Blazek, Frank A.: president, secretary, Giger Foundation (Paul and Oscar)

Bleck, Eugene Edmund, MD: director, Hale Foundation (Crescent Porter)

Bletzner, John: vice president, treasurer, Dingman Foundation (Michael D.)

Bleustein, Jeffrey L.: chief executive officer, chairman, Harley-Davidson Co.

Blevins, Kerrie: program officer, Butler Family Foundation (Patrick and Aimee)

Bliss, Paul: adv comm mem, Moore and Arletta E. Moore Foundation (Kenneth S.)

Bliumis, Sarah W.: trustee, Bydale Foundation

Bloch, Donald B.: trustee, Bendit Charitable Foundation (Leo H.)

Bloch, Kenneth D.: trustee, Bendit Charitable Foundation (Leo H.)

Bloch, Kurt Julius: trustee, Bendit Charitable Foundation (Leo H.)

Bloch, Mary: member disbursement committee, Oppenstein Brothers Foundation

Bloch, Robert L.: secretary, program officer, H&R Block Foundation

Block, Allan James: vice president, trustee, Blade Foundation; director, Toledo Blade Co.

Block, John Robinson: vice president, trustee, Blade Foundation; co-publisher, editor-in-chief, european corresp, Toledo Blade Co.

Block, Leonard Nathan: vice president, director,

Kaufmann Foundation (Henry)

Block, William: vice president, trustee, Blade Foundation; chairman, director, Toledo Blade Co.

Block, William, Jr.: president, trustee, Blade Foundation; president, director, Toledo Blade Co.

Bloedorn, John H., Jr.: trustee, Bloedorn Foundation (Walter A.)

Blohm, Donald E.: administrator, La-Z-Boy Foundation

Blood, Francis J.: director, Provident Community Foundation

Bloodworth, Carolyn A.: secretary-trs, Consumers Energy Co.; secretary-treasurer, Consumers Energy Foundation

Bloom, Larry L.: chief financial officer, Lee Enterprises, Inc.

Bloomquist, Keith: controller, Sheaffer Pen Corp.

Blossom, C. Bingham: trustee, president, chairman investment committee, Bingham Foundation (William)

Blossom, C. Perry: trustee, treasurer, Bingham Foundation (William)

Blossom, Laurel: trustee, chairman grant eval committee, Bingham Foundation (William)

Blossom, Robin Dunn: trustee, chairman education committee, Bingham Foundation (William)

Blount, William Houston: trustee, Kaul Foundation Trust (Hugh)

Blow, Timothy: chief financial officer, Hudson River Bancorp, Inc.

Bluemle, Lewis William, Jr.: senior vice president, trustee, Connelly Foundation

Blum, Frank: admin comm mem, Bowman Proper Charitable Trust (J.)

Blum, Paul: admin comm mem, Bowman Proper Charitable Trust (J.)

Blumenthal, Alan: trustee, Blumenthal Foundation

Blumenthal, Anita: trustee, Blumenthal Foundation

Blumenthal, Philip: trustee, Blumenthal Foundation

Blumenthal, Samuel, PhD: trustee, Blumenthal Foundation

Blumenthal, Yvonne: vice president & manager, community investment, US Bank

Blummer, William E.: secretary, treasurer, Vale-Asche Foundation

Blystone, John B.: chairman, president, chief executive officer, director, SPX Corp.

Blyth, Jon R.: program director, Mott Foundation (Charles Stewart)

Boatman, Dennis: director, Hall-Perrine Foundation

Bobins, Norman: trustee, Chicago Title and Trust Co. Foundation

Bocko, Mindy: trustee, Fuller Foundation (MA)

Bocko, Miranda Fuller: trustee, Fuller Foundation (MA)

Bockway, Jerome: trustee, Ashtabula Foundation

Boddie, J. Herbert: trustee emeritus, Blount Educational and Charitable Foundation (Mildred Weedon)

Bodine, Jean: trustee, McLean Contributionship

Boeckman, Duncan Eugene: director, O'Donnell Foundation

Boeckmann, Alan L.: chairman, chief executive officer, Fluor Corp.; trustee, Fluor Foundation

Boedeker, Lucy: office manager, Bechtel Charitable Remainder Uni-Trust (Marie H.)

Boehl, Kenneth F.: treasurer, trustee, The MBNA Foundation

Boehm, Diane: trustee, Boehm Foundation

Boehm, Frances: trustee, Boehm Foundation

Boehm, Robert L.: trustee, Boehm Foundation

Boer, William: vice president, assistant secretary, DeVos Foundation (Richard and Helen)

Boesel, Charles: contributions committee, CNA Foundation

Boesel, Stephen W.: vice president, secretary, treasurer, trustee, Price Associates Foundation (T. Rowe)

Boesen, James M.: treasurer, director, Dillon Foundation

Boettiger, John R.: director, Reynolds Foundation (Christopher)

Bogen, Andrew E.: director, Weingart Foundation

Bogert, Jeremiah Milbank: member, JM Foundation

Bogert, Margaret Milbank: vice president, JM Foundation

Boggess, Anna: director, Wessinger Foundation

Bogle, John C.: senior chairman, Vanguard Group; chairman, Vanguard Group Foundation

Bohart, Barbara: director, Educational Foundation of America

Bohart, James, Jr.: adjunct director, Educational Foundation of America

Bohlin, Daniel J.: director, Olmsted Foundation (George and Carol)

Bohling, John A.: senior vice president, PacifiCorp; board member, PacifiCorp Foundation

Bohne, Phillip W.: director, German Protestant Orphan Asylum Association Foundation

Boisi, Geoffrey T.: trustee, Carnegie Corp. of New York

Boitano, Caroline O.: executive director, Bank of America Foundation

Boivin, David: director, vice president, Saint-Gobain Corporation Foundation

Bok, Dean: committee member, Ziegler Foundation for the Blind (E. Matilda)

Boklund, Thomas B.: trustee, Gilmore Foundation (William G.)

Bokor, Peter: director, Kornfeld Foundation (Emily Davie and Joseph S.)

Bolesky, Edward M.: senior vice president, New England Business Service

Bolliger, Ralph: vice president, trustee, Collins Foundation

Bollinder, Lee C.: trustee, Kresge Foundation

Bolling, Carol: 2nd vice president, community relations, John Hancock Financial Services

Bolling, Robert H., Jr.: president, trustee, Welfare Foundation

Bolt, John F.: secretary, Landegger Charitable Foundation

Bolton, Archer L., Jr.: trustee, Russell Trust (Josephine G.)

Boman, Keith G.: trustee, Reynolds Foundation (Donald W.)

Bomberger, Carolyn L.: president, Koch Foundation, Inc.

Bomberger, Dorothy C.: assistant treasurer, director, Koch Foundation, Inc.

Bomberger, Matthew A.: director, Koch Foundation, Inc.

Bomberger, Michelle H.: director, Koch Foundation, Inc.

Bomberger, Rachel A.: secretary, board member, Koch Foundation, Inc.

Bomberger, William A.: assistant secretary, board member, Koch Foundation, Inc.

Bon, Lauren: trustee, Annenberg Foundation

Bonachi, Edward J.: senior vice president, treasurer, chief financial officer, Allianz Life Insurance Company of North America

Bonansinga, Joseph: director, Oakley-Lindsay Foundation of Quincy Newspapers and Its Subsidiaries

Bond, Arthur D., III: president, director, Green

Foundation (Allen P. and Josephine B.)

Bond, Christopher Samuel: director, Green Foundation (Allen P. and Josephine B.)

Bond, Ina B. Hamilton: president, trustee, Brown Foundation (W. L. Lyons)

Boney, Sion A.: trustee, Hillsdale Fund

Boney, Sion A., III: trustee, Hillsdale Fund

Bonner, Betty: secretary, Smith Foundation (William R. and Sara Babb)

Bonner, Henry M.: director, Lake Placid Education Foundation

Bonner, Marsha: trustee, Hazen Foundation (Edward W.)

Bonner, Robert J.: vice president, director, Ziegler Foundation

Bonner, Sarah H.: vice president, trustee, Dunspaugh-Dalton Foundation

Bonno, Anthony J.: senior vice president human resources, Pacific Life Insurance Co.

Bonvino, Frank W.: vice president, secretary, general counsel, International Multifoods Corp.

Bonzani, A.: secretary, IBM International Foundation

Booker, W. Wayne: vice chairman, Ford Motor Co.

Booker, William W.: secretary, treasurer, Daywood Foundation

Boone, D. William: trustee, Seabury Foundation

Boone, Rick: trustee, Priddy Foundation

Boone, Robert S.: trustee, Seabury Foundation

Boorstin, Daniel Joseph: director, Cafritz Foundation (Morris and Gwendolyn)

Booth, Margaret Ann: trustee, New York Foundation

Borchers, Judith: executive director, Cudahy Fund (Patrick and Anna M.)

Borden, Noel M.: vice chairman, director, Shenandoah Telecommunications Co.; secretary, ShenTel Foundation

Borek, JoAnne: executive director, trustee, Peabody Charitable Fund (Amelia)

Borer, Jeffrey: director, Gilman Foundation (Howard)

Borgelt, Burton C.: trustee, Dentsply International Foundation

Borie, John D.: secretary, Wynn Foundation

Borman, Paul: president, director, Borman's Inc. Fund; chief executive officer, Farmer Jack Supermarkets

Borton, Karl: vice president, Wildermuth Foundation (E. F.)

Borton, Thomas: trustee, Wildermuth Foundation (E. F.)

Bosacker, Lyle T.: director, Hickory Tech Corp.; trustee, Hickory Tech Corp. Foundation

Boskin, Michael J.: director, Koret Foundation

Boss, W. Andrew: president, director, Boss Foundation

Bossom, Joel: trustee, Ziegelheim Charitable Foundation (Fran and Irwin)

Boswell, Robert S.: president, chief executive officer, director, Forest Oil Corp.

Bosworth, Arthur H., II: trustee, Buell Foundation (Temple Hoyne)

Botania, Celeste: trustee, Mosher Foundation (Samuel B.)

Botham, Lydia: vice chairman, secretary, Land O'Lakes Foundation; director test kitchens, Land O'Lakes, Inc.

Bothwell, Henry J.: fund comm mem, Kaufman Endowment Fund (Louis G.)

Bott, Thomas: chairman, Vermilion Healthcare Foundation

Bottemiller, Donald L.: trustee, Homecrest Foundation; president, Homecrest Industries, Inc.

Bottemiller, Mark: secretary, treasurer, Homecrest Foundation

Bottemiller, Nancy: trustee, Homecrest Foundation

Bottomley, George T.: honorary trustee, Fuller Foundation (MA)

Bottomley, John T.: executive director, trustee, Fuller Foundation (MA)

Bottomley, Lydia Fuller: trustee, Fuller Foundation (MA)

Bottomley, Stephen D.: treasurer, Fuller Foundation (MA)

Bottorff, Mary Kay: president, Brunswick Foundation

Bouchard, Mike: secretary, treasurer, McDonald Foundation (Armstrong)

Bouchard, Ryan: vice president, McDonald Foundation (Armstrong)

Boudjakdji, Millicent Hearst: director, Hearst Foundation, Inc. (The); president, director, Hearst Foundation (William Randolph)

Boudouris, William: chief financial officer, Korte Construction Co.

Boudreau, Donald L.: executive vice president, J.P. Morgan Chase & Co.; vice president, trustee, J.P. Morgan Chase Foundation

Bouldin, Granville S. R.: director, Christy-Houston Foundation

Bouligny, James A.: trustee, Johnson Foundation (M. G. and Lillie A.)

Boulware, C. Diane: director, Sunnen Foundation

Bouma, Mary: trustee, Ghidotti Foundation

Bouque, Roy L.: director, Stulsaft Foundation (Morris)

Bourchard, Laurie: vice president, McDonald Foundation (Armstrong)

Bourdeau, Paul: secretary, Rogow Birken Foundation

Bourns, Gordon L.: president, trustee, Bourns Foundation; chairman, Bourns, Inc.

Bouscaren, Helen Hunt: trustee, Hunt Foundation (Roy A.)

Boutault, Delores J.: manager, Stamps Foundation (James L.)

Boutault, E. C.: president, trustee, Stamps Foundation (James L.)

Boven, Thomas: vice president, Loutit Foundation

Bovender, Jack Oliver, Jr.: president, chief executive officer, Frist Foundation

Bowden, Travis J.: chairman, president, chief executive officer, director, Gulf Power Co.

Bowen, Arthur H., Jr.: trustee, Cowden Foundation (Louetta M.)

Bowen, Henry: director, Bowen Foundation (Ethel N.)

Bowen, Otis R., MD: director, Lilly Endowment

Bowen, William G.: president, trustee, Mellon Foundation (Andrew W.)

Bowen, William H.: vice president, assistant secretary, Altheimer Charitable Foundation (Ben J.)

Bowes, Donald C.: director, Howard and Bush Foundation

Bowles, Beatrice: secretary, treasurer, Lux Foundation (Miranda)

Bowles, Crandall C.: director, Springs Foundation, Inc.

Bowles, Erskine B.: trustee, Duke Endowment

Bowles, Margaret C.: secretary, Clowes Fund

Bowlin, Michael Ray: chairman, director, ARCO Foundation; chairman, chief executive officer, director, BP Amoco Corp.

Bowman, Bob: secretary, Pineywoods Foundation

Bowman, David S.: director, Bowman Foundation (Wayne and Ida)

Bowman, Dick D.: treasurer, ShenTel Foundation

Bowman, Donald W.: president, director, Bowman Foundation (Wayne and Ida)

Bowman, George A., Jr.: vice president community affairs, State Street Corp.; foundation manager, vice president, State Street Foundation

Bowman, Jocelyn: director, Kelley and Elza Kelley Foundation (Edward Bangs)

Bowman, Mayne J.: vice president, Bowman Foundation (Wayne and Ida)

Bowman, Roberta B.: vice president, Duke Energy Foundation

Bowman, Susan D.: secretary, treasurer, director, Ralph and Donna Korte Family Charitable Foundation

Bowman, William H.: secretary, director, Bowman Foundation (Wayne and Ida)

Boxx, Linda McKenna: director, McKenna Foundation (Katherine Mabis)

Boxx, T. William: chairman, McKenna Foundation (Katherine Mabis); secretary, treasurer, officer, McKenna Foundation (Philip M.)

Boyce, Ann Allston: vice president, trustee, Price Associates Foundation (T. Rowe)

Boyce, Doreen Elizabeth: president, Buhl Foundation (PA)

Boyce, Phillip R.: chairman, Valley Foundation

Boyd, David E.: member, Campbell Foundation (J. Bulow)

Boyd, F. J.: president, director, Audubon State Bank Charitable Foundation

Boyd, Hallam, Jr.: trustee, Plough Foundation

Boyd, Morton: trustee, Gheens Foundation

Boyd, Willard Lee: trustee, Carver Charitable Trust (Roy J.)

Boyette, John G.: treasurer, Cox Foundation (James M.)

Boylan, Elizabeth J.: vice president, Maneely Fund

Boyle, Beverly: executive director, Fisher Foundation

Boyle, Dennis: director, Vicksburg Foundation

Boyle, Douglas J.: vice president, Edmonds Foundation (Dean S.)

Boyle, Judy: secretary, AUL Foundation Inc.

Boyle, Richard James: trustee, J.P. Morgan Chase Foundation

Bozman, William H.: vice president, director, Marpat Foundation

Brace, Robert P.: trustee, Duke Energy Foundation

Bracht, Chuck: president, Management Compensation Group/Dulworth, Inc.

Bracken, Frank A.: president, director, Ball Foundation (George and Frances)

Bracken, William M.: director, Ball Brothers Foundation

Brackett, Norman E.: trustee, National Grange Mutual Charitable Trust

Bradburn, Thomas J.: chief executive officer, president, Norfolk Shipbuilding & Drydock Corp.

Brademas, John: trustee, United States-Japan Foundation

Braden, Jane: coordinator, Wells Fargo Bank Nebraska, N.A.

Braden, Katherine F.: vice president, treasurer, Castle Foundation (Harold K. L.)

Bradford, Hilary P.: trustee, Children's Foundation of Erie County

Bradford, Pamela: executive director, PacifiCorp Foundation

Bradford, Robert: director, Bradford Foundation (George and Ruth)

Bradlee, Dudley H., II: director, Hornblower Fund (Henry)

Bradley, Darby: trustee, Friendship Fund

Bradley, James: director, Spring/Close Foundation

Bradley, Jane C.: trustee, Cabot Family Charitable Trust

Bradley, John F.: trustee, Stillwell Charitable Trust (Glen and Dorothy)

Bradley, Joseph S.: trustee, Cord Foundation (E. L.)

Bradley, Thomas: director, treasurer, St. Paul Companies Inc. Foundation

Bradley, William O.: trustee, Cord Foundation (E. L.)

Bradshaw, Wilson: director, Bush Foundation

Brady, Heather: administrative assistant, Kerr Fund (Grayce B.)

Brady, James C., Jr.: president, treasurer, trustee, Brady Foundation

Brady, Katherine D.: trustee, Darby Foundation

Brady, Nicholas Frederick: trustee, Brady Foundation

Braem, Barbara: executive director, Woronoco Savings Charitable Foundation

Bragg, C. Bartley: adjunct director, Educational Foundation of America

Bragg, Carole P.: adjunct director, Educational Foundation of America

Braitmayer, Eric A.: trustee, Braitmayer Foundation

Braitmayer, John W.: trustee, Braitmayer Foundation

Braitmayer, Karen L.: trustee, Braitmayer Foundation

Brake, Joni C.: board, McKinney Charitable Trust (Carl and Alleen)

Braly, Hugh C.: secretary, trustee, Anschutz Family Foundation

Bramble, Forrest F., Jr.: vice president, trustee, Middendorf Foundation

Branch, J. Read: president, treasurer, Cabell III and Maude Morgan Cabell Foundation (Robert G.)

Branch, J. Read, Jr.: director, Cabell III and Maude Morgan Cabell Foundation (Robert G.)

Branch, Patteson, Jr.: director, Cabell III and Maude Morgan Cabell Foundation (Robert G.)

Brand, Elizabeth D.: secretary, vice president, Dalton Foundation (Harry L.)

Brand, Michael M.: trustee, Morley Foundation

Brand, R. Alfred, III: vice president, director, Dalton Foundation (Harry L.)

Brandenburg, R. N.: president, Glaser Foundation

Brandman, Etta: vice president, assistant treasurer, secretary, Harkness Foundation for Dance

Brandt, E. N.: vice president, assistant secretary, trustee, Gerstacker Foundation (Rollin M.)

Branly, Maura J.: director, Koch Foundation, Inc.

Brant, Theresa: assistant executive secretary, Raymond Foundation

Brantley, Rena: secretary, director, Hedco Foundation

Branum, Frances Daniel: director, Daniel Foundation of Alabama

Brasel, Susan S.: director, Sunnen Foundation

Brashear, Albert R.: director public affairs, Motorola Foundation; senior vice president, director corporate communications, Motorola, Inc.

Bratton, Dennis: vice president finance, treasurer, French Oil Mill Machinery Co.

Brauer, Rhonda L.: secretary, New York Times Co. Foundation

Braught, Barbara: executive director, McCasland Foundation

Braun, Hugo E., Jr.: vice president, secretary, trustee, Wickes Foundation (Harvey Randall)

Braun, Jan: program manager, Reader's Digest Foundation

Braun, Mary Connolly: president, Arguild Foundation

Brauner, David A.: vice president, director, Goldman Foundation (Herman)

Brawer, Catherine Coleman: president, director, Rosenthal Foundation (Ida and William)

Brawer, Robert A.: vice president, director, Rosenthal Foundation (Ida and William)

Bray, Thomas Joseph: trustee, Earhart Foundation

Brecher, Howard A.: vice president, director, Bernhard Foundation (Arnold)

Breckenridge, Charles: vice president, director, Murphy Co. Foundation (G.C.)

Breckenridge, Isabella: director, Marpat Foundation

Breen, Marion I.: vice president, director, Starr Foundation

Breene, William E.: trustee, Phillips Charitable Trust (Dr. and Mrs. Arthur William)

Bregar, H. H.: secretary, director, Blum Foundation (Harry and Maribel G.); secretary, Blum-Kovler Foundation

Breitmeyer, Julie F.: trustee, Keller Family Foundation

Bremekamp, Theodore H., III: trustee, Raskob Foundation for Catholic Activities, Inc.

Brennan, Anthony L.: director, Baltimore Equitable Insurance Foundation

Brennan, David P.: chairman, Chicago Board of Trade Foundation

Brennan, John Joseph: director, president, Vanguard Group; president, Vanguard Group Foundation

Brennan, Leo Joseph, Jr.: vice president, executive director, Ford Motor Co. Fund

Brennan, Michael J.: chief financial officer, executive vice president, Binswanger Companies

Brennan, Virginia S.: trustee, chairman, Self Family Foundation

Brenner, Charles S.: director, Guttman Foundation (Stella and Charles)

Brenner, Edgar H.: president, Guttman Foundation (Stella and Charles)

Brenner, Paul R.: trustee, Calder Foundation (Louis)

Breon, Willard S.: vice president, Schooler Family Foundation (Ohio)

Bresko, Andrew G.: trustee, Crandall Memorial Foundation (J. Ford)

Brest, Paul: president, Hewlett Foundation (William and Flora)

Brett, Thomas R.: trustee, Mabee Foundation, Inc. (J. E. and L. E.)

Brevig, Yasue: mem allocations comm, Kawabe Memorial Fund

Brewer, Herman: director Chicago working group, MacArthur Foundation (John D. and Catherine T.)

Brewer, Sebert, Jr.: secretary-treasurer, Benwood Foundation

Brian, Tom J.: co-trustee, Wheeler Memorial Foundation (Josephine and J. A.)

Bricker, Phyllis F.: secretary, Portsmouth General Hospital Foundation

Bridgeland, James Ralph, Jr.: secretary, trustee, Semple Foundation (Louise Taft)

Bridgeman, Gary: director, American Optical Foundation

Bridgeman, Jeannette C.: treasurer, assistant secretary, Beazley Foundation

Bridges, Kenneth: trustee, McMahon Foundation

Briggs, Eleanor: director, Griggs and Mary Griggs Burke Foundation (Mary Livingston)

Briggs, Robert: trustee, Knight Foundation (John S. and James L.)

Briggs, Robert W.: co-trustee, executive director, GAR Foundation

Bright, Calvin E.: president, Bright Family Foundation

Bright, James R.: assistant secretary, Ingalls Foundation (Louise H. and David S.)

Bright, Lyn: secretary, treasurer, Bright Family Foundation

Bright, Marjorie: vice president, Bright Family Foundation

Brighton, Cynthia Z.: director, Ziegler Foundation for the Blind (E. Matilda)

Briloff, Abraham Jacob: assistant secretary, assistant treasurer, Eckman Charitable Foundation (Samuel and Rae)

Brimner, David: chairman, Shaw's Supermarkets, Inc.

Brind, Ira: trustee, Connelly Foundation

Brinkman, Robert J.: director, Davenport-Hatch Foundation

Brinn, Mildred Cunningham: president, treasurer, director, L and L Foundation

Brinzo, John S.: trustee, Cleveland-Cliffs Foundation (The); president,

chief executive officer, Cleveland-Cliffs, Inc.

Brisbane, Paul: trustee, Fairchild-Meeker Charitable Trust (Freeman E.)

Briselli, Iso: board member, Fels Fund (Samuel S.)

Bristol, Barbara F.: vice president, Fruehauf Foundation

Bristow, Elliott B.: treasurer, Barnes Foundation

Brittenham, Raymond L.: secretary, Tinker Foundation

Britton, John E., Esq.: director, Smith Charitable Foundation (Arlene H.)

Britton, Lynda R.: president, trustee, Britton Fund

Britton, Terence B.: vice president, trustee, Britton Fund

Britton, Timothy C.: vice president, trustee, Britton Fund

Broader, Shelley: director, Hannaford Charitable Foundation

Broadfoot, John W., Jr.: director, Meadows Foundation (The)

Brock, M. H.: president, trustee, Johnson Foundation (M. G. and Lillie A.)

Brock, Marissa J.: trustee, Johnson Foundation (Howard)

Brock, Rodney G.: trustee, Foundation for Seacoast Health

Brockert, C.: trustee, Snyder Foundation (Frost and Margaret)

Brockington, Randolph W.: trustee, Pittsburgh Child Guidance Foundation

Brockmeyer, Alison: director, Stuart Charitable Foundation (G. B.)

Brockway, Eleanor: director, Memorial Foundation for the Blind

Brodbeck, Barry J.: vice president, treasurer, Brodbeck Foundation

Brodbeck, Helen S.: director, Brodbeck Foundation

Brodbeck, Robert J.: president, chief executive officer, director, Brodbeck Enterprises; secretary, Brodbeck Foundation

Broder, Hans: president, Smith Foundation (William R. and Sara Babb)

Broderick, Catharine O.: trustee, Rockefeller Brothers Fund, Inc.

Brodhead, William McNulty: trustee, Skillman Foundation

Brodsky, William: director, Washington Foundation (Dennis R. and Phyllis)

Brody, William Ralph, PhD: committee member, Whitaker Foundation

Broer, Victoria Urban: director, Weathertop Foundation

Broidy, Steven D.: chairman, chief executive officer, director, Weingart Foundation

Brom, Joseph P.: vice president, trustee, Ohio National Foundation

Broman, Susan: executive director, Steelcase Foundation

Bronson, Edgerton: treasurer, Saint Croix Foundation

Bronson, Eleanor D.: director, Daniels Foundation (Fred Harris)

Bronstein, Lenore: trustee, Ferkauf Foundation (Eugene and Estelle)

Bronstein, Robert: trustee, Ferkauf Foundation (Eugene and Estelle)

Brook, Jacqueline C.: director, Brook Family Foundation

Brook, Paul F.: secretary, treasurer, Brook Family Foundation

Brook, Robert L.: director, Brook Family Foundation

Brook, Shirley W.: director, Brook Family Foundation

Brooking, Garland M.: founder, Trull Foundation (The)

Brooking, Gladys Trull: founder, Trull Foundation (The)

Brooks, Balbi A.: treasurer, director, Atherton Foundation (Leburta)

Brooks, Bruce M.: director community affairs, Microsoft Corp.

Brooks, Conley, Jr.: trustee, Marbrook Foundation

Brooks, Conley, Sr.: trustee, Marbrook Foundation

Brooks, E. R.: chairman, Southwestern Electric Power Co.

Brooks, Frank J.: trustee, Kavanagh Foundation (T. James)

Brooks, John G., Esq.: trustee, Mifflin Memorial Fund (George H. and Jane A.)

Brooks, Julie B. A.: grants coordinator, Sara Lee Foundation

Brooks, Lynn A.: president, chief executive officer, Rieke Corp.

Brooks, Markell: trustee, Marbrook Foundation

Brooks, Roger Kay: chairman, Amerus Group Co.

Brooks, William C.: trustee, Hudson-Webber Foundation

Broomfield, Jane: vice president, secretary, treasurer, Broomfield Charitable Foundation

Broomfield, William S.: president, Broomfield Charitable Foundation

Broomfield Aiken, Nancy: director, Broomfield Charitable Foundation

Broomfield Shaffer, Barbara: director, Broomfield Charitable Foundation

Brostowitz, James M.: treasurer, Harley-Davidson Foundation

Brouelette, Jim: secretary, Washington Foundation (Dennis R. and Phyllis)

Brovitz, Cortland L.: trustee, August Family Foundation (Charles J. and Burton S.)

Brower, Sam R.: secretary, treasurer, Owen Foundation

Browman, Brett: assistant vice president, American Fidelity Assurance Co.; member, American Fidelity Corp. Founders Fund

Brown, Ann Noble: trustee, Noble Foundation (Samuel Roberts)

Brown, Barbara: president, Ingalls Foundation (Louise H. and David S.)

Brown, Barbara J.: president, director, Abrams Foundation (Talbert and Leota)

Brown, Bertram S., MD: trustee, Falk Medical Fund (Maurice)

Brown, Bruce E.: vice president, Boothroyd Foundation (Charles H. and Bertha L.)

Brown, Carol R.: director, Heinz Endowment (Howard)

Brown, Catherine: director communities programs, McCormick Tribune Foundation (Robert R.)

Brown, Charles Foster, III: trustee, Meyer Family Foundation

Brown, Clarence J., Jr.: trustee, Grimes Foundation

Brown, Craig C.: treasurer, director, Abrams Foundation (Talbert and Leota)

Brown, David Lloyd: director, Phillips Foundation (Ellis L.)

Brown, David R., MD: trustee, Noble Foundation (Samuel Roberts)

Brown, Deborah: treasurer, Washington Foundation (Dennis R. and Phyllis)

Brown, Diane Solomon: vice president, Cohen Foundation (Naomi and Nehemiah)

Brown, Dwyer: secretary, Weiss Foundation (William E.)

Brown, Forrest C., MD: trustee, Lattner Foundation (Forrest C.)

Brown, Frances Carroll: vice president, treasurer, director, M.E. Foundation

Brown, Frank C.: president, Rexam Foundation

Brown, Fred E.: director, Lake Placid Education Foundation

Brown, Gifford E.: global vice president, chief financial officer, Dow Corning Corp.

Brown, Gloria Primm: senior program officer international development, Carnegie Corp. of New York

Brown, Harold: president, treasurer, director, Hamilton Charitable Corp.

Brown, Harold, PhD: chairman, Mattel Foundation

Brown, Hillary: director, Scherman Foundation

Brown, James Knight: secretary, Clay Foundation

Brown, Jeanette Grasselli: trustee, Jennings Foundation (Martha Holden)

Brown, John Carter: director, Cafritz Foundation (Morris and Gwendolyn)

Brown, John Seely: director, MacArthur Foundation (John D. and Catherine T.)

Brown, Joseph Warner, Jr.: chairman, chief executive officer, MBIA, Inc.

Brown, Keith A.: trustee, Morgan Foundation (Burton D.)

Brown, Kiyoko O.: director, Doherty Charitable Foundation (Henry L. and Grace)

Brown, Margarite: secretary, treasurer, trustee, Crummer Foundation (Roy E.)

Brown, Martin S.: trustee, Brown Foundation (W. L. Lyons)

Brown, Mickey A.: senior vice president distribution, Georgia Power Co.; director, Georgia Power Foundation

Brown, Monte T.: treasurer, Weiss Foundation (William E.)

Brown, Nancy Juckett: trustee, Hill Foundation (Sandy)

Brown, Neil A.: secretary, Firman Fund

Brown, Owsley, II: treasurer, trustee, Brown Foundation (W. L. Lyons)

Brown, Patricia: assistant secretary, McDermott Foundation (The Eugene)

Brown, Patricia A.: secretary, treasurer, executive director, director, Bettingen Corp. (Burton G.)

Brown, Philip: co-trustee, Jacobs Charitable Trust (Margaret G.)

Brown, Prudence: trustee, Levitt Foundation (NY)

Brown, Robert C.: director, Valley Foundation (Wayne and Gladys)

Brown, Robert S.: director, Hewit Family Foundation

Brown, Robert William, MD: vice president, director, Carter Foundation (Amon G.)

Brown, Samuel H.: trustee, Medina Foundation

Brown, Tammy: secretary, Progress Energy Foundation; manager community relations, Progress Energy Inc.

Brown, Theodore Lawrence: secretary, director, Beckman Foundation (Arnold and Mabel)

Brown, Timothy Charles: president, Thomas Foundation; chairman, president, chief executive officer, director, Thomas Industries

Brown, W. L. Lyons: secretary, trustee, Brown Foundation (W. L. Lyons)

Brown, Walter R.: president, Doherty Charitable Foundation (Henry L. and Grace)

Brown, Wanda W.: secretary, Bovaird Foundation (Mervin)

Brown, William Hill, III: director, Scott Foundation (William H., John G., and Emma)

Brown, William J.: trustee, Mex-Am Cultural Foundation

Brown, William Lee Lyons, Jr.: trustee, Brown Foundation (W. L. Lyons)

Browne, Rodney M.: mgr, Porter Testamentary Trust (James Hyde)

Brownell, John R.: secretary, Reynolds Foundation (Edgar & Francis)

Brownfield, Roberta F.: trustee, Perry Foundation

Browning, Kent C.: trustee, Miller Foundation (Earl B. and Loraine H.)

Browning, Peter C.: chief executive officer, president, director, Sonoco Products Co.

Brownlee, Susan: executive director, Grable Foundation

Brownlie, Edward Carter: assistant secretary, assistant treasurer, duPont Foundation (Alfred I.)

Broyhill, Faye A.: director, Broyhill Family Foundation

Broyhill, M. Hunt: president, director, Broyhill Family Foundation

Broyhill, Paul Hunt: chairman, director, Broyhill Family Foundation

Brozyna, Jeffry H.: vice president, general counsel, Lehigh Cement Co.

Bruce, Carole W.: director, Cemala Foundation

Bruce, Donald: director, Gilman Foundation (Howard)

Brucia, Charles J.: vice president, treasurer, director, King Family Foundation (Charles and Lucille)

Bruehler, Carol: secretary, McNutt Charitable Trust (Amy Shelton)

Bruen, William D., Jr.: trustee, Sullivan Foundation (Algernon Sydney)

Brumback, Charles T.: director, McCormick Tribune Foundation (Robert R.)

Brumback, D. L., Jr.: trustee, Van Wert County Foundation

Brumberg, Pamela Ween: program officer, Littauer Foundation (Lucius N.)

Brumm, Paul Michael: executive vice president, chief financial officer, Fifth Third Bancorp

Brusati, Peter J.: executive director, secretary, Gellert Foundation (Carl Gellert and Celia Berta)

Brush Wright, Barbara: president, Brush Foundation

Brusseau, Carolyn J.: trustee, Bigelow Foundation (F. R.)

Bryan, James L.: president, CUNA Mutual Group Foundation, Inc.

Bryan, John, III: chairman, president, chief executive officer, Bryan Foods

Bryant, Arthur Herbert, II: president, treasurer, Bryant Foundation (The)

Bryant, Douglas E.: secretary, treasurer, Cockrell Foundation

Bryson, James E.: trustee, member, Templeton Foundation (Herbert A.)

Bryson, Jane T.: vice president, trusteem member, Templeton Foundation (Herbert A.)

Bryson, John D., Jr.: president, Ross Memorial Foundation (Will)

Bryson, John E.: chairman, chief executive officer, Edison International; director, member executive committee, member grant committee, Keck Foundation (W. M.); member, Templeton Foundation (Herbert A.)

Bryson, Louise Henry: trustee, Getty Trust (J. Paul)

Buchanan, Carol P.: trustee, Phipps Foundation (Columbus)

Buchanan, Valda M.: secretary, Merrick Foundation

Buchholz, William E.: senior vice president, chief financial officer, Ondeo Nalco Co.

Buck, Carol: president, Buck Foundation (Frank H. and Eva B.)

Buck, Carol F.: trustee, Buck Foundation (Carol Franc)

Buck, James E.: secretary, New York Stock Exchange Foundation, Inc.;

senior vice president, secretary, New York Stock Exchange, Inc.

Buck, Paul: director, Buck Foundation (Frank H. and Eva B.)

Buck, Walter: secretary, Buck Foundation (Frank H. and Eva B.)

Buck, Winthrop Lawrence: trustee, Children's Foundation of Erie County

Buckler, Robert J.: chief executive officer, president, DTE Energy Co.; director, DTE Energy Foundation

Buckless, Shawn P.: clerk, Roddy Foundation (Fred M.)

Buckley, Francis J., Jr.: director, Dime Savings Bank of Norwich Foundation

Buckley, Jerome M., MD: director, chairman, Copic Medical Foundation

Buckley, Jerry S.: senior vice president public affairs, Campbell Soup Co.; trustee, Campbell Soup Foundation

Buckman, Ed: mem, Teubert Charitable Trust (James H. and Alice)

Buckmaster, Raleigh D.: trustee, McElroy Trust (R. J.)

Bucknam, Elizabeth M.: president, trustee, Barker Foundation Inc.

Buckner, Bill: president, chief executive officer, Excel Corp.

Buckner, Elizabeth B.: member advisory board, Watson Foundation (Thomas J.)

Buckner, Linda: secretary, treasurer, Dodge Jones Foundation and Subsidiary

Buckner, Walker G., Jr.: member advisory board, Watson Foundation (Thomas J.)

Budd, MacDonald: secretary, director, Cheatham Foundation (Owen)

Budd, Wayne A.: executive vice president, general counsel, John Hancock Financial Services

Budich, Arthur W.: vice president, treasurer, Warwick Savings Foundation

Budig, Gene Arthur: board member, Kauffman Foundation (Ewing Marion)

Budney, Albert J., Jr.: trustee, Niagara Mohawk Foundation; president, director, Niagara Mohawk Holdings, Inc.

Buechel, Kathleen W.: president, treasurer, Alcoa Foundation

Buechner, Thomas S.: trustee, Corning Inc. Foundation

Buerger, Theodore V.: assistant treasurer, Western New York Foundation

Buford, Georgia L.: secretary, Copic Medical Foundation

Bugg, Wendell: director, Honda of America Foundation

Bugliarello, George, MD: director, Teagle Foundation

Buhler, Amy: secretary, treasurer, Old Dominion Box Co. Foundation

Buhler, Frank H.: chairman, Old Dominion Box Co.; president, Old Dominion Box Co. Foundation

Buhler, Michael O.: president, director, Old Dominion Box Co.; vice president, Old Dominion Box Co. Foundation

Buhlman, Karla: vice president music and film, Autry Foundation

Buhrmaster, Robert C.: president, chief executive officer, chairman, Jostens, Inc.

Buhsmer, John Henry: trustee emeritus, McLean Contributionship

Buice, William T., III: cotrustee, Steele-Reese Foundation

Bukowski, Gerard T., Jr.: secretary, Burns & McDonnell Foundation

Bukstein, Roy: cfo, director, Baker Street Foundation

Buldak, Gerald E.: vice president, Bank One Foundation

Bulkley, Maureen: foundation administrator, Kinder Morgan Foundation

Bullard, Robert L.: chairman, trustee, Bigelow Foundation (F. R.)

Bullen, Lawrence: trust, Weatherwax Foundation

Buller, Allan R.: chairman, treasurer, director, Worthington Foods; trustee, Worthington Foods Foundation

Bullion, J. W.: trustee, director, Meadows Foundation (The)

Bullis, Eugene: chief financial officer, Parametric Technology Corp.

Bullitt, William C.: president, trustee, Seybert Institution for Poor Boys and Girls (Adam and Maria Sarah)

Bullock, Ellis F.: secretary, executive director, director, Grotto Foundation

Bullock, Herbert E.: director, New Milford Savings Bank Foundation

Bullock, Maurice Randolph: co-trustee, director, Potts and Sibley Foundation

Bultena, John: secretary, treasurer, O'Shaughnessy Foundation (I. A.)

Bumsted, William J.: director, Lake Placid Education Foundation

Bunch, Charles E.: director, PPG Industries Foundation

Bundschuh, George August William: trustee, New York Life Foundation

Bundy, Charles Alan: director, consult, Spring/Close Foundation; director, Springs Foundation, Inc.

Bunnen, Melissa: director, treasurer, Norman Foundation

Bunnen, Robert L., Jr.: director, Norman Foundation

Bunting, George L.: director, Baltimore Equitable Insurance Foundation

Bunting, George Lloyd, Jr.: trustee, Abell Foundation

Bunting, Josiah, III: director, Guggenheim Foundation (Harry Frank)

Bunting, Susan R., EdD: president, Foundation for Seacoast Health

Bunton, Mary Anne: vice president, Liberty Corp.

Burch, Ken L.: director, ShenTel Foundation

Burchfield, Albert H., III: member, Staunton Farm Foundation

Burchfield, C. Arthur: president, director, Burchfield Foundation (Charles E.)

Burchfield, Violet P.: director, Burchfield Foundation (Charles E.)

Burd, Loretta M.: chairman, CUNA Mutual Group; vice president, CUNA Mutual Group Foundation, Inc.

Burdge, Jeffrey John: director, Kline Foundation (Josiah W. and Bessie H.)

Burenga, Kenneth L.: president, chief operating officer, chief executive officer, Dow Jones & Company, Inc.

Buresh, Ernest J.: director, Hall-Perrine Foundation

Burger, Edward A.: secretary, treasurer, director, Hubbard Foundation (R. D. and Joan Dale)

Burger, Gary: co-director community partners program, Knight Foundation (John S. and James L.)

Burger, Jane C.: trustee, Pittsburgh Child Guidance Foundation

Burgess, Christopher R.: assistant vice president, Chesapeake Corp.

Burgher, Bedford L.: treasurer, Garvey Texas Foundation

Burke, Charles R.: chairman, director, Grable Foundation

Burke, Charles R., Jr.: associate director, board director, Grable Foundation

Burke, Daniel W.: board member, Fels Fund (Samuel S.)

Burke, F. William: director, secretary, Loughran Foundation (Mary and Daniel)

Burke, James M.: trustee, Altman Foundation

Burke, Judith A.: trustee, Gordon Charitable Trust (Peggy and Yale)

Burke, Kathleen J.: trustee, Bank of America Foundation

Burke, Mary Griggs: president, director, Griggs and Mary Griggs Burke Foundation (Mary Livingston)

Burke, Patricia G.: director, Grable Foundation

Burke, Steven E.: director, treasurer, Grable Foundation

Burke, Thomas C.: trustee emeritus, Altman Foundation

Burke, Thomas R.: secretary, Hitchcock Foundation (Gilbert M. and Martha H.)

Burke, Walter: treasurer, director, Fairchild Foundation, Inc. (Sherman)

Burke, Walter F., III: director, chairman, Fairchild Foundation, Inc. (Sherman)

Burke, Ward R.: trustee, Temple Foundation (T. L. L.)

Burke, William L.: trustee, Merrill Lynch & Co. Foundation Inc.

Burkett, Radford: adv board comm mem, Heath Foundation (Mary)

Burkett, Robert L.: director, Gilman Foundation (Howard)

Burkey, Kathy: pub trustee, Carpenter Foundation

Burkholder, Robert E.: secretary, treasurer, Gooding Group Foundation

Burkle, Ron: chairman, Ralph's-Food 4 Less Foundation

Burks, Lawrence E.: treasurer, trustee, Strosacker Foundation (Charles J.)

Burleigh, William Robert: chairman, Scripps Co. (E.W.); member, Scripps Howard Foundation

Burlingame, Harold W.: executive vice president wireless group, AT&T Corp.; trustee, AT&T Foundation

Burlinson, R. F.: treasurer, trust, Handy & Harman Foundation

Burnand, Alphonse A., III: president, Burnand Medical and Educational Foundation (Alphonse A.); vice president, treasurer, Steele Foundation (Harry and Grace)

Burnand, Audrey Steele: treasurer, Burnand Medical and Educational Foundation (Alphonse A.); president, Steele Foundation (Harry and Grace)

Burner, David L.: chairman, Goodrich Corp.

Burnes, Kennett F.: chairman, chief executive officer, president, Cabot Corp.

Burnett, James F.: vice president, trustee, Fair Play Foundation

Burnett, Nancy Ann Packard: trustee, vice chairman, Packard Foundation (David and Lucile)

Burnett, Rebecca: adv, Delano Foundation (Mignon Sherwood)

Burnett, Stephanie S.: treasurer, Memorial Foundation for the Blind

Burnham, Alice B.: trustee, Humphrey Fund (George M. and Pamela S.)

Burnham, Duane L.: director, Sara Lee Corp.

Burnham, Patricia R.: trustee, Plough Foundation

Burns, Ann B.: officer, Neilson Foundation (George W.)

Burns, Edward W.: assistant treasurer, Morris Foundation (William T.)

Burns, Fred C.: chairman, Wortham Foundation

Burns, John: trustee, AT&T National Pro-Am Youth Fund

Burns, Rex: vice chairman, Mid-Iowa Health Foundation

Burns, Ruth Ann: director, Foundation for Child Development

Burns, Ruthelen Griffith: adv, Griffith Foundation (W. C.)

Burns, Sara J.: president, director, Central Maine Power Co.

Burns, Valerie: secretary board designators, Henderson Foundation (George B.)

Burr, Robert B., Jr.: trustee, Mellon Family Foundation (R. K.); treasurer, trustee, Mellon Foundation (Richard King)

Burrage, Darrell: vice president, Berger Foundation (H. N. and Frances C.)

Burrell, Jack: co-trustee, Luse Foundation (W. P. and Bulah)

Burrell, Jack L., Jr.: co-trustee, Luse Foundation (W. P. and Bulah)

Burrill, W. Gregory: secretary, director, Hopedale Foundation

Burris, Berlean M.: director, Field Foundation of Illinois

Burroughs, Hugh: director philanthropy program,

Packard Foundation (David and Lucile)

Burrows, Robert Lee, Jr.: vice president, Harvey Foundation (C. Felix)

Burrows, Sunny Harvey: secretary, treasurer, Harvey Foundation (C. Felix)

Burson, Glenda: vice president, treasurer, McWane Corp.

Burt, Barbara: president, treasurer, Foellinger Foundation

Burton, Edson: trustee, Chicago Title and Trust Co. Foundation

Burton, Richard R.: chairman, Burton Private Foundation (Robert Harold)

Burton, Sally F.: vice president, director, Brush Foundation

Bury, Anita: assistant secretary, Regenstein Foundation

Buscarino, Carolyn M.: director, New York Life Foundation

Busch, August Adolphus, III: chairman, Anheuser-Busch Companies, Inc.

Busch, Lawrence S.: assistant treasurer, Mellon Family Foundation (R. K.); trustee, assistant treasurer, Mellon Foundation (Richard King)

Busch, Paul: trustee, Dibner Fund

Bush, Antoinette Cook: partner, CNA Financial Corp.

Bush, Bonnie: assistant trustee, BellSouth Foundation

Bush, Michael J.: vice president real estate, Giant Food, Inc.

Bushyeager, Peter J.: president, director, New York Life Foundation

Butcher, Gary: president, chief executive officer, Chicago Rawhide Co.

Buthman, Mark A.: senior vice president, chief financial officer, Kimberly-Clark Corp.

Butler, Brigid M.: trustee, Butler Family Foundation (Patrick and Aimee)

Butler, Carol H.: president, trustee, Humphrey Fund (George M. and Pamela S.)

Butler, Catherine: trustee, Butler Family Foundation (Patrick and Aimee)

Butler, Cecelia M.: trustee, Butler Family Foundation (Patrick and Aimee)

Butler, Dixon M.: president, director, Virginia Environmental Endowment

Butler, Eugene W.: treasurer, Norris Foundation (Dellora A. and Lester J.)

Butler, Henry King: director, Christy-Houston Foundation

Butler, Herbert Johnston: director, Johnston-Hanson Foundation

Butler, John D.: executive vice president, chief human resources officer, Textron, Inc.

Butler, John K.: treasurer, trustee, Butler Family Foundation (Patrick and Aimee)

Butler, John R.: chairman, JJJ Foundation

Butler, Katharine: trustee, Brace Foundation (Donald C.)

Butler, Patricia M.: trustee, Butler Family Foundation (Patrick and Aimee)

Butler, Patrick: vice president, trustee, Butler Family Foundation (Patrick and Aimee)

Butler, Paul S.: trustee, Butler Family Foundation (Patrick and Aimee)

Butler, Peter M.: president, trustee, Butler Family Foundation (Patrick and Aimee)

Butler, Sandra K.: trustee, Butler Family Foundation (Patrick and Aimee)

Buttner, Jean Bernhard: president, director, Bernhard Foundation (Arnold)

Butz, Barbara T.: director, Butz Foundation

Butz, Elvira M.: vice president, Butz Foundation

Butz, Theodore H.: president, Butz Foundation

Butz, Thompson H.: treasurer, Butz Foundation

Butzer, Bart: executive president, Target Stores, Target Corp.

Buzzard, James A.: president, Meadwestvaco Corp.

Byers, Fritz: assistant secretary, Blade Foundation

Byers, Karen D.: chief financial officer, Markle Foundation (John and Mary R.)

Byers, R. A.: vice president finance, treasurer, Pitt-Des Moines, Inc.; trustee, Pitt-Des Moines Inc. Charitable Trust

Byom, John: chief financial officer, International Multifoods Corp.

Byrd, Benjamin F., Jr.: director, Joyce Family Foundation

Byrd, D. Harold, Jr.: trustee, Hillcrest Foundation

Byrd, Edward R.: chief financial officer, Pacific Life Foundation

Byrne, Arthur P.: chairman, president, chief executive officer, director, Wiremold Co.; treasurer, Wiremold Foundation

Byrne, Brendan T.: director, Carvel Foundation (Thomas and Agnes)

Byrne, Dorothy M.: president, Byrne Foundation

Byrne, John J., III: director, Byrne Foundation

Byrne, Mark J.: director, Byrne Foundation

Byrne, Patricia: vice president, Citigroup Foundation

Byrne, Patrick M.: director, Byrne Foundation

Byrne, Stephen J.: director, Haley Foundation (W. B.)

Byrnes, Maureen K.: director health human services program, Pew Charitable Trusts

Byrns, Priscilla U.: trustee, Upton Foundation (Frederick S.)

Bzdak, Michael J.: director corporate contributions, Johnson & Johnson Family of Companies Contribution Fund

C

Caamano, Rafael F.: trustee, Homeland Foundation (NY)

Cabe, Anita B.: secretary, treasurer, director, Cabe Foundation (C. Louis and Mary C.)

Cabe, Charles L., Jr.: president, director, Cabe Foundation (C. Louis and Mary C.)

Cabe, Mary C.: vice president, director, Cabe Foundation (C. Louis and Mary C.)

Cabe Long, Marianne: vice president, director, Cabe Foundation (C. Louis and Mary C.)

Cabell, Charles L.: secretary, Cabell III and Maude Morgan Cabell Foundation (Robert G.)

Cabell, John Branch: director, Cabell III and Maude Morgan Cabell Foundation (Robert G.)

Cabell, Royal E., Jr.: vice president, secretary, Cabell III and Maude Morgan Cabell Foundation (Robert G.); president, Scott Foundation (William H., John G., and Emma)

Cabell, Susan M.: trustee, Perry Foundation

Cable, Howard: adv, Beasley Charitable Trust (Lucy and Emily)

Cabot, John Godfrey Lowell: trustee, Cabot Family Charitable Trust

Cabot, Louis Wellington: trustee, Cabot Family Charitable Trust

Caestecker, Thomas E.: trustee, Caestecker Foundation (Charles and Marie)

Caffrey, Thomas F., Esq.: co-trustee, McCarthy Memorial Trust Fund (Catherine)

Cafritz, Calvin: chairman, president, chief executive officer, Cafritz Foundation (Morris and Gwendolyn)

Caggiano, Ida: clerk, Home for Aged Men in the City of Brockton

Cagle, Ronald E., MD: trustee, McMahon Foundation

Cahalan, Joseph M.: vice president, Xerox Foundation

Cahill, George Francis, Jr.: director, Greenwall Foundation

Cahill, Robert V.: vice president, Chartwell Foundation

Cahners, Nancy L.: trustee, Rabb Charitable Trust (Sidney R.)

Cahners-Kaplan, Helene R.: trustee, Rabb Charitable Foundation (Sidney and Esther)

Cahouet, Frank Vondell: director, Heinz Endowment (Howard)

Caimi, Gina: secretary, Erpf Fund (Armand G.)

Cain, Effie Marie: honorary president, director, Cain Foundation (Effie and Wofford)

Cain, James B.: vice president, director, Cain Foundation (Effie and Wofford)

Cain, John C.: director, vice president, Cain Foundation (Effie and Wofford)

Cain, Mary H.: vice president, Cain Foundation (Gordon and Mary)

Calabresi, Anne T.: trustee, Carolyn Foundation

Calabresi, Guido: trustee emeritus, Carolyn Foundation

Calder, Frederick C.: vice president, Lake Placid Education Foundation

Calder, Peter D.: trustee, Calder Foundation (Louis)

Calderon, Stanley J.: vice president, Bank One Foundation

Caldwell, Barry: trustee, Alcon Foundation

Caldwell, Blake W.: assistant secretary, trustee, Sterling-Turner Foundation

Caldwell, Royce S.: director, SBC Foundation

Caldwell-Johnson, Terry: director, Mid-Iowa Health Foundation

Calgaro, Annette: assistant vice president, Clapp Charitable and Educational Trust (George H. and Anne L.)

Calheno, Agastino J.: president, director, Woronoco Savings Charitable Foundation

Calhoun, Essie L.: vice president, Eastman Kodak Charitable Trust

Calhoun, Lawrence E.: secretary, treasurer, Homecrest Foundation; secretary, treasurer, vice president finance, Homecrest Industries, Inc.

Caligiuri, Mark: trustee, Jenjo Foundation

Calil, Cassio A.: treasurer, IBM International Foundation

Calise, William Joseph, Junior: senior vice president, secretary, general counsel, Rockwell Automation Inc.

Call, Curtis: treasurer, Central Maine Power Co.

Call, Robert V., Jr.: chairman, trustee, Agrilink Foods/Pro-Fac Foundation

Callahan, Daniel J., III: director vice chairman treasurer, Cafritz Foundation (Morris and Gwendolyn)

Callahan, Eugene J., Esq.: trustee, Plough Foundation

Callard, David Jacobus: trustee, Rockefeller Brothers Fund, Inc.

Callaway, Mark Clayton: trustee, Callaway Foundation, Inc.

Calligaris, Alfred E.: director, Utica National Foundation

Callum, Brian: director, Building 19 Foundation

Calvert, Lloyd P.: mem, trustee, One Valley Bank Foundation

Camalier, Charles A.: vice president, director, Wilkes, Artis, Hedrick & Lane Foundation

Cambell, Colin G.: director, Rockefeller Fund (David)

Cambrom, Joe Carroll: member, American Fidelity Corp. Founders Fund

Cambrom, Laura: member, American Fidelity Corp. Founders Fund

Cambrom, William M.: chairman, American Fidelity Corp. Founders Fund

Cameron, John J.: director, Provident Community Foundation

Cameron, Paul E.: assistant secretary, assistant treasurer, Gamble Foundation

Cammarata, Bernard: chairman, TJX Companies, Inc.

Camp, John M., Jr.: director, trustee, Camp Younts Foundation; director, Campbell Foundation (Ruth and Henry)

Camp, Paul D., III: director, Campbell Foundation (Ruth and Henry)

Campanaro, Leonard A.: treasurer, Harsco Corp. Fund

Campbell, Benjamin K.: vice president, treasurer, Knox Foundation (Seymour H.)

Campbell, Bert Louis: trustee, Cullen Foundation (The)

Campbell, Beth: director, Gumbiner Foundation (Josephine)

Campbell, Beth Newlands: director, Hannaford Charitable Foundation

Campbell, Bruce S., III: treasurer, Campbell Foundation (MD)

Campbell, C. David: president, assistant secretary, McGregor Fund

Campbell, Carol: director, Argyros Foundation

Campbell, Charles J.: chairman, president, chief executive officer, Florsheim Group Co.

Campbell, Cole C.: director, Pulitzer Foundation; editor, Pulitzer, Inc.

Campbell, Donald G.: executive vice president, chief financial officer, TJX Companies, Inc.; treasurer, director, TJX Foundation, Inc.

Campbell, Douglas: vice president, Erpf Fund (Armand G.)

Campbell, Elizabeth: secretary, trustee, Howarth Trust Fund

Campbell, George: director, Gebbie Foundation

Campbell, Hazard K.: chairman, treasurer, Knox Foundation (Seymour H.)

Campbell, J. Patrick: chairman, president, Wildermuth Foundation (E. F.)

Campbell, J. Tyler: director, Campbell Foundation (MD)

Campbell, Jack D.: trustee, Cooper Foundation

Campbell, John L.: trustee, Peterloon Foundation

Campbell, Keith M.: vice president, director, Minnesota Mutual Foundation

Campbell, King: chairman, Smith and W. Aubrey Smith Charitable Foundation (Clara Blackford)

Campbell, Kleber A., III: director, Memorial Foundation for the Blind

Campbell, Lowell: trustee, Young Foundation (Bill B.)

Campbell, Lynette E.: trustee, Douty Foundation (Alfred and Mary)

Campbell, Martha S.: director of evaluation, program director, Irvine Foundation (The James)

Campbell, Mary: director program development and eval, Irvine Foundation (The James)

Campbell, Mary Jo: assistant treasurer, Campbell Foundation (MD)

Campbell, Nelson D.: trustee, Lyndhurst Foundation

Campbell, Robert Henderson: director, Pew Charitable Trusts

Campbell, Sallie G.: associate director, Newcombe Foundation (Charlotte W.)

Campbell, Sarah P.: director, Plym Foundation

Campbell, True Miller: director, Meadows Foundation (The)

Campbell, William B.: president, Campbell Foundation (MD)

Campion, Ashley: trustee, Johnson Foundation (Helen K. and Arthur E.)

Campion, Berit: trustee, Johnson Foundation (Helen K. and Arthur E.)

Campion, Lynn H.: vice president, treasurer, trustee, Johnson Foundation (Helen K. and Arthur E.)

Campion, Thomas B., Jr.: trustee, Johnson Foundation (Helen K. and Arthur E.)

Campobasso, Laura: executive director, Whitecap Foundation

Canales, James E.: president, chief executive officer, Irvine Foundation (The James)

Candler, Peter M.: member, Campbell Foundation (J. Bulow)

Canfield, Charles F.: director, ONDEO Nalco Foundation

Cann, Samuel A.: trustee, Huston Charitable Trust (Stewart)

Canning, John Beckman: secretary, Rayonier Foundation

Cannon, Charles G.: trustee, Gates Family Foundation

Cannon, Ted: secretary, treasurer, Quivey-Bay State Foundation

Cannon, W. C., Jr.: director, member, Cannon Foundation, Inc. (The)

Canoles, Leroy T., Jr.: trustee, Beazley Foundation

Canon, Joseph E.: executive vice president, executive director, Dodge Jones Foundation and Subsidiary

Canter, Lisa: board member, Roberts Foundation (Dora)

Canter, Roger: board member, Roberts Foundation (Dora)

Canzonetta, Margaret M.: administration director, GAR Foundation

Capehart, Thomas R.: vice president, Oak Tree Charitable Foundation

Capo, Thomas Patrick: director, DaimlerChrysler AG

Cappelloni, Robert: trustee, Lux Foundation (Miranda)

Cappuzzo, Salvatore: secretary, treasurer, Weinstein Foundation (J.)

Capranica, Ruth M.: vice president, Knapp Foundation, Inc. (MD)

Capranica, Steven F.: treasurer, Knapp Foundation, Inc. (MD)

Capron, Jeffery P.: treasurer, trustee, Fowler Memorial Foundation (John Edward)

Carano, Donald L.: trustee, Pennington Foundation (William N. and Myriam)

Caraway, R. B., MD: director, Gulf Coast Medical Foundation

Cardinale, Ruth A.: secretary, Sunnen Foundation

Cardinali, Albert J.: trustee, Heyward Memorial Fund (DuBose and Dorothy)

Cardman, Thomas: executive director, Gebbie Foundation

Carey, C. M.: director, Frank Family Foundation (A. J.)

Carey, Claire Z., PhD: trustee, The MBNA Foundation

Carey, Kathryn Ann: foundation manager, American Honda Foundation

Carlberg, Scott C.: assistant vice president, Duke Energy Foundation

Carlin, E. Taylor: director, AMCORE Foundation

Carlisle, Ann C.: secretary, treasurer, manager, Stemmons Foundation

Carlson, Arleen M.: emeritus director, Carlson Family Foundation (Curtis L.)

Carlson, Cheryl C.: secretary, director, Vance Charitable Foundation (Robert C.)

Carlson, Herbert E., Jr.: chairman, president, director, Vance Charitable Foundation (Robert C.)

Carlson, Herbert E., Sr.: treasurer, trustee, Vance Charitable Foundation (Robert C.)

Carlson, Joseph, II: director, New Milford Savings Bank Foundation

Carlson, Marjorie: trustee, Gund Foundation (George)

Carlson, Stuart R.: executive vice president administration, Mosinee Paper Corp.

Carlston, Douglas G.: chairman, Broderbund LLC; president, director, Carlston Family Foundation

Carlston, Erin G.: director, Carlston Family Foundation

Carlstrom, R. William: secretary, Glaser Foundation

Carlton, Jerry W.: president, trustee, Day Foundation (Willametta K.)

Carmichael, Barbara S.: trustee, Dow Corning Foundation

Carmichael, Daniel P.: director, Lilly Endowment

Carmichael, David R.: senior vice president, general counsel, director, Pacific Life Insurance Co.

Carney, Victoria Butler: director, Johnston-Hanson Foundation

Carothers, Andre: director, Furthur Foundation

Carothers, Suzanne: trustee, Bowne Foundation (Robert)

Carp, Daniel A.: chairman, chief executive officer, Eastman Kodak Co.

Carpenter, Carroll M.: vice president, Good Samaritan

Carpenter, David: secretary, Figgie Educational Foundation

Carpenter, Dunbar: treasurer, trustee, Carpenter Foundation

Carpenter, Edmund Mogford: president, chief executive officer, Barnes Group, Inc.

Carpenter, Edmund Nelson, II: secretary, treasurer, Good Samaritan

Carpenter, Edward: trustee, Claypool Foundation (Silas and Ruth)

Carpenter, G. Paul: president, Howarth Trust Fund

Carpenter, Jane H.: president, trustee, Carpenter Foundation

Carpin, John: director, Illinois Tool Works Foundation

Carr, Cassandra Colvin: director, SBC Foundation

Carr, Diane E.: grant administrator, MacArthur Foundation (John D. and Catherine T.)

Carr, F. William, Jr.: trustee, Dougherty, Jr. Foundation (James R.)

Carr, James H.: senior vice president, Fannie Mae Foundation

Carr, Rachael: trustee, Dougherty, Jr. Foundation (James R.)

Carr, Robert, MD: president, Global Community Partnerships

Carr, Robert F., III: director, Prentice Foundation (Abra)

Carr, Robert O.: director, Capezio/Ballet Makers Dance Foundation

Carrico, James T.: treasurer, Wiegand Foundation (E. L.)

Carriere, Margaret E.: vice president, secretary, trustee, Halliburton Foundation, Inc.

Carrigg, James A.: trustee, Decker Foundation (Dr. G. Clifford and Florence B.)

Carrington, Lisa: director, Noyes, Jr. Memorial Foundation (Nicholas H.)

Carrion, Gladys: trustee, New York Foundation

Carris, Barbara T.: vice president, Carris Corp. Foundation

Carris, William H.: president, Carris Corp. Foundation; chairman, president, chief executive officer, Carris Reels

Carroll, Cindie: board mem, Brush Foundation

Carroll, Daniel B.: trustee, Massey Charitable Trust

Carroll, Dennis P.: assistant treasurer, Bank One Foundation

Carroll, Francis R.: president, director, Small Business Service Bureau; trustee, Small Business Service Bureau Charitable Foundation

Carroll, Mary M.: trustee, Small Business Service Bureau Charitable Foundation

Carroll, Milton: director, Houston Endowment

Carroll, R. J.: controller, IBM International Foundation

Carroll, Thomas W.: advisor, Weezie Foundation

Carroll, Walter J.: executive director, trustee, Massey Charitable Trust

Carruth, Brady F.: president, Wortham Foundation

Carsky, Katherine: vice president, Robinson Fund (Maurice R.)

Carswell, Robert: secretary, Greentree Foundation

Carter, Hodding, III: president, chief executive officer, trustee, Knight Foundation (John S. and James L.)

Carter, James J., Jr.: director, Trippe Trust (William D.)

Carter, John Boyd, Jr.: director, Kleberg Foundation (Robert J. Kleberg, Jr. and Helen C.)

Carter, Larry R.: trustee, Cisco Systems Foundation

Carter, Lee A.: president, trustee, Emery Memorial (Thomas J.)

Carter, M. A.: director, Bayport Foundation

Carter, Michael C.: board mem, Brush Foundation

Carter, Richard J., Jr.: trustee, Ferriday Fund Charitable Trust

Carter, Ruth Ann: director, Eberly Foundation

Carter, Susan M.: director, secretary, assistant treasurer, Georgia Power Foundation

Carter, Virginia P.: board mem, Brush Foundation

Cartmill, Molly: director corporate contributions, Sempra Energy

Carttar, Paul: chief operating officer, Kauffman Foundation (Ewing Marion)

Cartwright, Cheri D.: executive director, assistant secretary-treasurer, Sarkeys Foundation

Cartwright, Herbert L., III: comptroller, Abell-Hanger Foundation

Caruso, Anthony: director, Bay State Federal Savings Charitable Foundation

Carver, Lucille Avis: secretary, trustee, Carver Charitable Trust (Roy J.)

Carver, Roy James, Jr.: vice chairman, trustee, Carver Charitable Trust (Roy J.)

Casady, Simon: director, Mid-Iowa Health Foundation

Case, Mary Lou: trustee, Wickes Foundation (Harvey Randall)

Case, Richard G.: assistant secretary, Gifford Charitable Corp. (Rosamond)

Case, Stephen M.: chairman, AOL Time Warner

Case, Weldon Wood: trustee, Morgan Foundation (Burton D.)

Casey, A. Michael: vice president, treasurer, The Bothin Foundation

Casey, Betty Brown: chairman, president, treasurer, trustee, Casey Foundation (Eugene B.)

Casey, Coleman H.: trustee, Saunders Charitable Foundation Trust (Helen M.)

Casey, Douglas R.: trustee, Casey Foundation (Eugene B.)

Casey, John P.: treasurer, Altman Foundation

Casey, Lyman H.: executive director, The Bothin Foundation

Casey, William L.: assistant secretary, Johnson Foundation (Thomas Phillips and Jane Moore)

Cashman, Elizabeth E.: trustee, Goddard Foundation (Charles B.)

Casper, Bonnie B.: director, Staunton Farm Foundation

Caspersen, Barbara M.: vice president, treasurer, Caspersen Foundation for Aid to Health and Education (O. W.)

Caspersen, Erik Michael Westby: vice president, director, Caspersen Foundation for Aid to Health and Education (O. W.)

Caspersen, Finn M. W., Jr.: vice president, director, Caspersen Foundation for Aid to Health and Education (O. W.)

Clement, Ronald W.: executive director, Haigh-Scatena Foundation

Clemente, C. Lou: chairman, Pfizer Foundation; executive vice president corporate affairs, secretary, corporate counsel, Pfizer Inc.

Clements, B. Gill: vice president, Clements Foundation

Clements, Keith R.: president, director, Andersen Foundation

Clements, Rita C.: vice president, O'Donnell Foundation

Clements, William P., Jr.: president, Clements Foundation

Cleveland, Cotton Mather: trustee, National Grange Mutual Charitable Trust

Clevenger, Raymond C., III: director, Markle Foundation (John and Mary R.)

Cliff, Ursula: director, Hughes Foundation (Geoffrey C.)

Cliff, Walter Conway: assistant treasurer, secretary, director, Gould Foundation (The Florence)

Clifford, Charles H.: treasurer, Langendorf Foundation (Stanley S.)

Clifford, Charles H., Jr.: director, Langendorf Foundation (Stanley S.)

Clifford, Cliff: manager, IBM International Foundation

Clifford, Ed: trustee, McKinney Charitable Trust (Carl and Alleen)

Clifford, Patrick A.: program assistant, Portsmouth General Hospital Foundation

Clive, Winifred J.: trustee, Johnson Foundation (Thomas Phillips and Jane Moore)

Cloherty, Patricia M.: director, Kauffman Foundation (Ewing Marion)

Cloniger, Kermit: mem, Finch Foundation (Thomas Austin)

Cloonan, Brian: assistant comptroller, Prudential Foundation

Close, Anne Springs: chairman, director, Spring/Close Foundation; donor, chairwoman, director, Springs Foundation, Inc.

Close, Derick Springsteen: director, Spring/Close Foundation

Close, Elliott Springs: director, Spring/Close Foundation

Close, Frances A.: director, Spring/Close Foundation

Close, Hugh William, Jr.: director, Spring/Close Foundation; president, director, Springs Foundation, Inc.

Close, Katherine Anne, MD: director, Spring/Close Foundation

Close, Leroy Springs: director, Spring/Close Foundation

Close, Pat: director, Springs Foundation, Inc.

Close, Patricia: director, Spring/Close Foundation

Cloud, Bruce Benjamin, Sr.: vice chairman, director, Zachry Co. (H.B.)

Clough, William P., III: trustee, Bingham Second Betterment Fund (William)

Clougherty, Coleman F.: vice president, director, Link, Jr. Foundation (George)

Clowes, Alexander W.: president, Clowes Fund

Clowes, Jonathan J.: director, Clowes Fund

Clowes, Margaret J.: vice president, Clowes Fund

Clowes, Thomas J.: director, Clowes Fund

Clutterbuck, Robert T.: vice president, KeyCorp

Clyde, Calvin N., Jr.: vice president, Wise Foundation (Watson W.)

Cobb, Charles E., Jr.: president, Cobb Family Foundation

Cobb, Christian M.: vice president, Cobb Family Foundation

Cobb, K. W.: chief tax officer, General Motors Foundation

Cobb, Sara B.: vice president education, Lilly Endowment

Cobb, Sue M.: vice president, Cobb Family Foundation

Cobb, Tobin T.: vice president, Cobb Family Foundation

Coblentz, William Kraemer: director, Koret Foundation

Coburn, Jean Crummer: president, trustee, Crummer Foundation (Roy E.)

Coburn, Milton: vice president, trustee, Crummer Foundation (Roy E.)

Cochran, John R., III: president & chief operating officer MBNA America Bank, MBNA Corp.; trustee, The MBNA Foundation

Cochran, Peyton S., Jr.: director, Guggenheim Foundation (Harry Frank)

Cochran, Steve: treasurer, Zarrow Foundation (Anne and Henry)

Cochrane, Eugene W., Jr.: vice president and director health care division, Duke Endowment

Cocke, Dudley: director, Bush Foundation

Cockerham, Haven E.: senior vice president human resources, R.R. Donnelley & Sons Co.

Cockrell, Ernest Harris: president, director, Cockrell Foundation

Cockrell, Janet S.: director, Cockrell Foundation

Coe, Charles R., Jr.: trustee, Merrick Foundation

Coe, Elizabeth Merrick: president, trustee, Merrick Foundation

Coe, Ross M.: trustee, Merrick Foundation

Coe, Walter S.: trustee, Gheens Foundation

Coe, Ward I.: trustee, Merrick Foundation

Coen, Charles R.: trustee, Coen Family Foundation (Charles S. and Mary)

Coen, Kent: trustee, Reynolds Foundation (Edgar & Francis)

Coffey, Deeda: secretary, director, Dalton Foundation (Harry L.)

Coffey, Eve Alda: trustee, Jenjo Foundation

Coffey, James: trustee, Jenjo Foundation

Coffey, John: vice president programs, State Farm Companies Foundation; senior vice president, State Farm Mutual Automobile Insurance Co.

Coffey, Robert L.: treasurer, O'Connor Foundation (Kathryn)

Coffin, Dwight C.: vice president, secretary, director, ContiGroup Companies Foundation; vice president human resources, ContiGroup Companies, Inc.; secretary, Fribourg Foundation

Cogan, James Richard: treasurer, director, Bunbury Co., Inc.

Cohen, Bluma D.: vice president, executive director, foundation manager, trustee, Jurzykowski Foundation (Alfred)

Cohen, Charlotte McKee: vice president, trustee, McKee Foundation (Robert E. and Evelyn)

Cohen, Eileen Phillips: director, Phillips Family Foundation (L. E.)

Cohen, Julie W.: director, Zarrow Foundation (Anne and Henry)

Cohen, Ken P.: chairman, trustee, Exxon Mobil Foundation

Cohen, Kenneth P.: director, Teagle Foundation

Cohen, Martin: trustee, treasurer, Graham Fund (Philip L.)

Cohen, Maryjo Rose: vice president, treasurer, director, Phillips Family Foundation (L. E.)

Cohen, Melvin Samuel: president, director, Phillips Family Foundation (L. E.)

Cohen, Michael I.: director, Foundation for Child Development

Cohen, Sandra: secretary, Bank of America Foundation

Cohen, Sharon: chief communications officer, Kauffman Foundation (Ewing Marion)

Cohen, Stephen M.: vice president, chief financial officer, Hughes Medical Institute (Howard)

Cohen-Solomon, Lillian: president, Cohen Foundation (Naomi and Nehemiah)

Cohl, Claudia: vice president, Robinson Fund (Maurice R.)

Cohn, Richard: director, Bruno Charitable Foundation (Joseph S.)

Coit, Barbara E.: committee member, Eccles Charitable Foundation (Willard L.)

Coit, Benton C.: director, Drown Foundation (Joseph)

Coit, Susan E.: committee member, Eccles Charitable Foundation (Willard L.)

Coit, William E.: committee member, Eccles Charitable Foundation (Willard L.)

Coker, Charles W.: director, Sara Lee Corp.

Coker, Charles Westfield: trustee, Sonoco Foundation; vice president, Sonoco Products Co.

Colage, Vera L.: vice president, director, Hopkins Foundation (Josephine Lawrence)

Colburn, Frances Haffner: director, Haffner Foundation

Colburn, Richard Dunton: director, Colburn Fund

Colby, Benjamin N.: trustee, Appleby Trust (Scott B. and Annie P.)

Colby, F. Jordan: trustee, Appleby Trust (Scott B. and Annie P.)

Colby, Jonathan E.: trustee, Lingnan Foundation

Colby Pierce, Sarah Rob: trustee, Appleby Trust (Scott B. and Annie P.)

Cole, Elizabeth: corporator, Oak Grove School

Cole, Franklin Alan: chairman, director, Aon Foundation

Cole, Kathleen: president, chief executive officer, Parametric Technology Corp.

Cole, Margaret Ann: trustee, Seidman Family Foundation

Cole, Ralph A.: vice president, trustee, Strosacker Foundation (Charles J.)

Colello, Joan: secretary, executive director, trustee, Pinkerton Foundation

Coleman, Burlin: chairman, president, chief executive officer, Community Trust Bancorp, Inc.

Coleman, J. Reed: trustee, Kemper Foundation (James S.)

Coleman, John A.: assistant secretary, Rockwell International Corp. Trust

Coleman, Leonard S., Jr.: director, Clark Foundation (NY); trustee, Schumann Fund for New Jersey

Coleman, Reed: director, Bradley Foundation (Lynde and Harry)

Coletti, Brynne F.: president, treasurer, trustee, Farmer Family Foundation

Coletti, Robert E.: trustee, Farmer Family Foundation

Colgan, Celeste: vice president, secretary, Halliburton Foundation, Inc.

Collesano, Marguerite: trustee, Statler Foundation

Collette, Claire M.: assistant secretary, assistant treasurer, Hume Foundation (Jaquelin)

Collette, Gay: secretary, McGovern Foundation (John P.)

Collier, Carol R.: director, Penn Foundation (William)

Collier, Jean: comptroller, Arison Foundation

Collins, Anne Childs: director, AKC Fund

Collins, Arthur D., Jr.: chairman, chief executive officer, Medtronic, Inc.

Collins, Dennis Arthur: president, director, chief executive officer, Irvine Foundation (The James)

Collins, Donald A.: trustee, Scaife Family Foundation

Collins, Frances R.: trustee, Collins Foundation (George and Jennie)

Collins, Fulton: trustee, Collins Foundation (George and Jennie); chairman, Collins, Jr. Foundation (George Fulton)

Collins, James: executive director, member advisory committee, Pott Foundation (Herman T. and Phenie R.)

Collins, James H.: president, Deere Foundation (John)

Collins, James W.: director, Oakley-Lindsay Foundation of Quincy Newspapers and Its Subsidiaries

Collins, John P., Jr.: trustee, Smith Horticultural Trust (Stanley)

Collins, Lawrence A., Jr.: trustee, Miller Foundation (Earl B. and Loraine H.)

Collins, Leland: manager, Porter Testamentary Trust (James Hyde)

Collins, Maribeth Wilson: president, trustee, Collins Foundation; trustee, Collins Medical Trust

Collins, Maureen A.: director, Unilever United States Foundation

Collins, Michael E.: trustee, Williams Charitable Trust (Mary Jo)

Collins, Paul John: vice chairman, director, Citigroup Inc.

Collins, R. M.: trustee, Smith Horticultural Trust (Stanley)

Collins, Robert R.: director, Green Foundation (Allen P. and Josephine B.)

Collins, Roger B.: chairman, Collins Foundation (George and Jennie); treasurer, Collins, Jr. Foundation (George Fulton)

Collins, Suzanne M.: secretary, Collins, Jr. Foundation (George Fulton)

Collins, Truman W., Jr.: vice president, trustee, Collins Foundation; trustee, Collins Medical Trust

Collins, William R., Jr.: trustee, Snyder Charitable Trust (Harrison C. and Margaret A.)

Collis, Charles A.: director, Collis Foundation

Collis, Elfried A.: director, Collis Foundation

Collision, Arthur R: trustee, Blowitz-Ridgeway Foundation

Collister, Richard A.: president, Comerica Charitable Foundation

Collyer, Michael, Esq.: director, King Family Foundation (Charles and Lucille)

Colodny, Edwin I.: chairman, COMSAT International

Colson, Charles Wendell: acting president, M.E. Foundation

Colten, M.: vice president, secretary, treasurer, Conway Scholarship Foundation (Carle C.)

Colton, S. David: vice president, general counsel, Phelps Dodge Corp.

Colvard, Karen: program officer, Guggenheim Foundation (Harry Frank)

Comai, Barbara L.: trustee, Miller Foundation

Comay, Estelle: secretary, treasurer, Falk Medical Fund (Maurice)

Combs, W. G.: vice president, trustee, Long Foundation (J. M.)

Comer, Richard J., Jr.: chairman, Comer Foundation (AL)

Comfort, William: trustee, Hartford Foundation, Inc. (The John A.)

Commes, Thomas Allen: president, chief operating officer, director, Sherwin-Williams Co.

Compton, Bruce C.: grants information manager, Pew Charitable Trusts

Compton, Gary: board, McKinney Charitable Trust (Carl and Alleen)

Compton, Kelly Hoglund: secretary, treasurer, Hoglund Foundation

Compton, Michael S.: president, Pioneer Trust Bank, NA

Compton, Robert: trustee, Plough Foundation

Compton, Robert A.: board member, Kauffman Foundation (Ewing Marion)

Comstock, Henry W., Jr.: clerk, director, Beaucourt Foundation

Conant, Colleen Christner: branch manager, Scripps Co. (E.W.)

Conant, Douglas R.: president, chief executive officer, director, Campbell Soup Co.

Conant, John A.: secretary, Harland Charitable Foundation (John H. and Wilhelmina D.)

Conant, Miriam Harland: president, Harland Charitable Foundation (John H. and Wilhelmina D.)

Conaty, William J.: director, Arison Foundation; chairperson, director, GE Foundation

Concino, Frank, Jr.: president, chief executive officer, Lamco Communications

Condos, Barbara S.: mng trustee, Rogers Fund for the Arts (Russell Hill)

Condron, Christopher M.: president, chief executive officer, Dreyfus Corp.

Cone, Ashley E.: secretary, Cemala Foundation

Cone, Ceasar, III: president, director, Cemala Foundation

Cone, Janet G.: director, Cemala Foundation

Cone, Walter C.: director, Cemala Foundation

Coniglio, Peter J.: trustee, AT&T National Pro-Am Youth Fund

Conkling, Phillip W.: trustee, The MBNA Foundation

Conley, R. E.: chief financial officer, secretary, treasurer, director, Standard Steel Speciality Co.; director, Standard Steel Specialty Co. Foundation

Conn, James P.: trustee, Odell Fund (Robert Stewart and Helen Pfeiffer)

Conn, Michael K.: vice president, secretary, National Standard Foundation

Connable, Genevieve: vice president, Wildermuth Foundation (E. F.)

Connell, Michael J.: president, director, Connell Foundation (Michael J.)

Connell, Richard: vice president, treasurer, chief information officer, Skillman Foundation

Connelly, Christine C.: trustee, Connelly Foundation

Connelly, Daniele: trustee, Connelly Foundation

Connelly, Martha L.: chairman, trustee, Lattner Foundation (Forrest C.)

Connelly, Thomas M.: senior vice president, chief science & technology officer, E.I. du Pont de Nemours & Co.

Connelly, Thomas S.: trustee, donor son, Connelly Foundation

Conner, Claudia: grant associate, Foundation for Child Development

Conner, Robert P.: treasurer, director, Barker Foundation (J.M.R.)

Connery, Cristin H.: director, Harriman Foundation (Gladys and Roland)

Connick, Frances S.: trustee, Lingnan Foundation

Connolly, Arthur G., Jr. Es: secretary, Arguild Foundation

Connolly, Arthur Gould, Jr.: president, Laffey-McHugh Foundation

Connolly, Arthur Guild, Sr.: president, Arguild Foundation; vice president, Laffey-McHugh Foundation

Connolly, Francis H.: secretary, treasurer, Perdue Foundation (Arthur W.)

Connolly, John J.: director corporate relations, NSTAR; director, NSTAR Foundation

Connolly, Robert M.: trustee, Massey Charitable Trust

Connolly, Sherry S.: secretary, treasurer, director, Vann Family Foundation

Connolly, Thomas A., Esq.: treasurer, Arguild Foundation

Connor, James W.: president, Lyon Foundation

Connor, Richard L.: president, publisher, ABC, Inc.

Connor, Walter Robert: president, chief executive officer, Teagle Foundation

Connors, John: senior vice president finance & administration, chief financial officer, Microsoft Corp.

Conomikes, John G.: director, Hearst Foundation, Inc. (The); vice president, director, Hearst Foundation (William Randolph)

Conover, Charles W.: trustee, Anderson Foundation (John W.)

Conover, Joseph I.: director, Oakley-Lindsay Foundation of Quincy Newspapers and Its Subsidiaries

Conover, Robert V.: director, Kikkoman Foundation

Conrad, William C.: executive secretary, Stackpole-Hall Foundation

Conroy, Patrick F.: vice president, New York Mercantile Exchange

Considine, Terry: director, Bradley Foundation (Lynde and Harry)

Contino, Francis A.: executive vice president, chief financial officer, McCormick & Company, Inc.

Conway, Jill Kathryn Ker: vice chairman, trustee, Knight Foundation (John S. and James L.); chairwoman, Kresge Foundation

Conway, John H., Jr.: vice chairman, Mabee Foundation, Inc. (J. E. and L. E.)

Conway, John K.: secretary, Kemper Foundation (James S.)

Conway, John Paul: vice president, secretary, director, Dillon Foundation

Conway, Maribeth: vice president, trustee, Nolan Charitable Trust (James and Elise)

Conway, William G.: director, Noble Foundation, Inc. (Edward John)

Cook, Charlene: admin assistant, Davis Foundations (Arthur Vining)

Cook, Charles B., Jr.: director, Ziegler Foundation for the Blind (E. Matilda)

Cook, Charles C.: director, Ziegler Foundation for the Blind (E. Matilda)

Cook, Charles W.: treasurer, assistant secretary, trustee, Sullivan Foundation (Algernon Sydney)

Cook, Floyd P., Jr.: chief financial officer, Hanover Foundation

Cook, John W.: president, Luce Foundation (Henry)

Cook, Kim: trustee, Fairchild-Meeker Charitable Trust (Freeman E.)

Cook, Mary Lola: vice president, Finch Foundation (Doak)

Cook, Mary McDermott: president, McDermott Foundation (The Eugene)

Cook, Melvin: trustee, Snyder Foundation (Harold B. and Dorothy A.)

Cook, Mildred: chief financial officer, treasurer, secretary, Freeport Brick Co.

Cook, Phyllis: director, Osher Foundation (Bernard)

Cook, Wallace Lawrence: director, Dana Foundation (Charles A.)

Cooke, John F.: executive vice president external affairs, trustee, Getty Trust (J. Paul)

Cooke, John Warren: president, mgr, Treakle Foundation (J. Edwin)

Cooke, Richard A., Jr.: trustee, Cooke Foundation

Cooke, Samuel A.: president, trustee, Cooke Foundation

Cooke, Tracy A.: director, Cooke Foundation Corp. (V. V.)

Cooke, V. V., Jr.: president, Cooke Foundation Corp. (V. V.)

Coolidge, Lawrence: trustee, Mifflin Memorial Fund (George H. and Jane A.); assistant treasurer, Weber Charities Corp. (Frederick E.)

Coombs, Frederick A.: trustee, Fredrickson Foundation (Ambrose and Ida)

Coombs, John Wendell: trustee, Davenport Trust Fund

Coon, Jerome J.: treasurer, Physicians Mutual Insurance Co. Foundation

Coon, Marcia M.: trustee, Mercury Aircraft Foundation

Cooney, Daniel P.: assistant secretary, Bank One Foundation

Cooper, Aldrage B.: vice president community relations, Johnson & Johnson; member corporate contributions committee, Johnson & Johnson Family of Companies Contribution Fund

Cooper, Barry: trustee, Klosk Fund (Rose and Louis)

Cooper, Deborah: administrator assistant, Scripps Howard Foundation

Cooper, Douglas C.: chairman, Gardiner Savings Institution; mem, Gardiner Savings Institution Charitable Foundation

Cooper, Frank G., Esq.: secretary, assistant treasurer, Dietrich Foundation (William B.)

Cooper, Frederick Eansor: director, Williams Family Foundation of Georgia

Cooper, Marsh Alexander: vice president, director, member grant program committee, Keck Foundation (W. M.)

Cooper, Nathan: trustee, Klosk Fund (Rose and Louis)

Cooper, Richard Casey: president, trustee, Bovaird Foundation (Mervin)

Cooper, Ronald F.: assistant secretary, assistant treasurer, Tri-County Telephone Foundation

Cooper, William Allen: chairman, director, TCF National Bank Minnesota

Coors, Holland H.: ambassador, Castle Rock Foundation; trustee, Coors Foundation (Adolph)

Coors, Jeffrey H.: treasurer, Castle Rock Foundation; treasurer, trustee, Coors Foundation (Adolph)

Coors, William K.: trustee, Castle Rock Foundation; president, Coors Foundation (Adolph)

Cope, Andrew G.: trustee, Tucker Foundation

Copeland, Gerret van Sweringen: trustee, Longwood Foundation

Copeland, Margot: non-voting trustee, McDonald Investments Foundation

Copley, David C.: president, trustee, Copley Foundation (James S.); president, chief executive officer, director, senior management board, Copley Press, Inc.

Copley, Edward Alvin: director, Hawn Foundation

Copley, Helen K.: chairman, Copley Foundation (James S.)

Copp, Eugenie T.: trustee, Carolyn Foundation

Coppock, P. C.: trustee, Harsco Corp. Fund

Coppola, Joseph R.: chairman, president, chief executive officer, director, Giddings & Lewis

Corbally, Richard V.: secretary, director, McCann Foundation

Corbett, Cornelia Gerry: trustee, Farish Fund (William Stamps)

Corbett, Patricia A.: chairman, president, Corbett Foundation

Corbett, Thomas R.: trustee, Corbett Foundation

Corbin, Hunter W.: director, president, principal officer, Hyde and Watson Foundation

Corbin, Lee Harrison: assistant secretary, assistant treasurer, director, Hopkins Foundation (Josephine Lawrence)

Corbin, William R.: executive vice president wood products, Weyerhaeuser Co.; trustee, Weyerhaeuser Co. Foundation

Corcoran, John J.: assistant secretary, CIGNA Foundation

Corcoran, Martha: trustee, Anderson Foundation

Corcoran, William W., Esq.: co-trustee, Clarke Trust (John)

Cordaro, Nancy Anne: director, Alexander Foundation (Walter)

Corey, William G., MD: medical advisor, trustee, Norris Foundation (Kenneth T. and Eileen L.)

Corken, Wilton C., Jr.: trustee, Higginson Trust (Corina)

Corkery, Nancy W.: trustee, Braitmayer Foundation

Corley, A. Wayne: executive director, Temple Foundation (T. L. L.)

Corley, Mary Jo Ratner: president, trustee, Ratner Foundation (Milton M.)

Cormier, Robert: ex-officio member, Henderson Foundation (George B.)

Cornell, Jennifer: giving contact, Charitable Venture Foundation

Cornwall, John W.: trustee, Fund for New Jersey

Cornwall, Joseph C.: chairman emeritus, treasurer, Fund for New Jersey

Cornwall, Mary: secretary, treasurer, Ray Foundation

Cornwell, Diane: administrative director, Haynes Foundation (John Randolph and Dora)

Cornwell, W. Don: director, Wallace-Reader's Digest Fund (DeWitt)

Corpus, Janet: trustee, Azadoutioun Foundation

Corrigan, Ann G.: trustee, Goddard Foundation (Charles B.)

Cortese, Arline Snyder: trustee, Snyder Foundation (Harold B. and Dorothy A.)

Cortines, Ramon C.: trustee, Getty Trust (J. Paul)

Cortner, Nancy: trustee, Sullivan Foundation (Algernon Sydney)

Corvin, Adele: president, Stulsaft Foundation (Morris)

Corvin, Dana: director, Stulsaft Foundation (Morris)

Corvin, Dorothy S.: director, Stulsaft Foundation (Morris)

Corwin, Laura J.: secretary, New York Times Co. Foundation

Cory, William F.: trustee, Carver Charitable Trust (Roy J.)

Cosgriff, Robert H.: vice president, Allen Brothers Foundation

Cosgrove, Michael J.: treasurer, Arison Foundation

Cosper, Judith McBean: vice president, director, McBean Family Foundation; director, Newhall Foundation (Henry Mayo)

Costa, Paulo F.: member corporate contributions committee, Johnson & Johnson Family of Companies Contribution Fund

Costas, Elizabeth: administration director, Cummings Memorial Fund (The Frances L. and Edwin L.)

Costello, James P.: director, French Foundation (D.E.)

Costello, John T.: vice president corporate relations, Commonwealth Edison Co.

Costello, Michael J.: director, Patron Saints Foundation

Costley, Gary E.: chairman, president, chief executive officer, director, International Multifoods Corp.

Costley, Gary Edward: trustee, Miller Foundation

Costley, Lew: trustee, Swanson Family Foundation, Inc. (Dr. W. C.)

Coti, Ralph: secretary, director, Clover Foundation

Cotsen, Lloyd Edward: trustee, Ahmanson Foundation

Cotter, Gregory J.: trustee, Wilson Foundation (Huey and Angeline)

Cotter, Jeffrey L.: secretary, treasurer, S.G. Foundation

Cotter, Patrick William: secretary, director, Stackner Family Foundation

Cottingham, Patty: executive director, secretary, Scripps Howard Foundation

Cottle, John I., III: secretary, Blount Educational and Charitable Foundation (Mildred Weedon)

Coughenour, Katherine N.: trustee, Quaker Chemical Foundation

Coughlan, Gary Patrick: chief financial officer, senior vice president finance, Abbott Laboratories; director, Abbott Laboratories Fund

Coughlin, Barring: assistant secretary, trustee, Eaton Foundation (Cyrus)

Coughlin, Brian T.: executive director, assistant secretary, AK Steel Foundation

Coulter, George S.: trustee, Swisher Foundation (Carl S.)

Coulthard, Diana S.: trustee, Smoot Charitable Trust (Frank Litz)

Courts, R. W., II: chairman, Campbell Foundation (J. Bulow)

Courts, Richard Winn, II: trustee, Franklin Foundation Inc. (John and Mary)

Coury, Maxime: director, Grand Marnier Foundation

Couzens, Melinda A. Rodgers: trustee, Anschutz Family Foundation

Covington, Joe S., MD: director, Hardin Foundation (Phil)

Covitt, Regina: assistant treasurer, Bettingen Corp. (Burton G.)

Cowan, James R.: vice president, director, Stonecutter Foundation; chairman, president, chief executive officer, director, Stonecutter Mills Corp.

Cowan, Keith O.: vice president corporate development, BellSouth Corp.

Cowan, Kim: program officer, Bruening Foundation (Eva L. and Joseph M.)

Cowan, William Maxwell, MD,PhD: vice president, chief scientific officer, Hughes Medical Institute (Howard)

Coward, Ira E.: director, board member, Gregg-Graniteville Foundation

Cowden, W. H., Jr.: vice president, Peterson Foundation (Hal and Charlie)

Cowen, Robert J.: trustee, Beal Foundation

Cowgill, Bruce H.: president, CertainTeed Corp.

Cowin, Peter G.: trustee, Hill Crest Foundation

Cowles, Charles: trustee, Cowles Charitable Trust

Cowles, Gardner, III: president, trustee, Cowles Charitable Trust

Cowles, Jan S.: trustee, Cowles Charitable Trust

Cox, C. Richard: vice president programs, Penn Foundation (William)

Cox, Clint V.: trustee, Broadhurst Foundation

Cox, Daniel T.: chairman, Aon Corp.

Cox, Frances S.: assistant director, Watson Foundation (Thomas J.)

Cox, Kenneth: trustee, McGowan Charitable Fund (William G.)

Cox, Martha B.: trustee, Braemar Charitable Trust

Cox, Morgan: board, McKinney Charitable Trust (Carl and Alleen)

Cox, Phillip R.: director, Cinergy Foundation

Cox, Robert T.: director, Shelter Insurance Foundation

Cox, William Coburn, Jr.: trustee, Cox Charitable Trust (Jessie B.)

Coy, Oona: trustee, Merck Family Fund

Coyne, Ava: secretary, Hanover Foundation

Coyte, Julia D.: director, Hubbard Foundation

Cradick, Susan J.: secretary, treasurer, HON Industries Charitable Foundation

Craig, Albert, III: director, Staunton Farm Foundation

Craig, Debbie F.: trustee, Meyer Memorial Trust

Craig, Gregory L.: member, Staunton Farm Foundation

Craig, H. Curtis: trustee, Brown Foundation, Inc. (James Graham)

Craig, James P.: trustee, Bonfils-Stanton Foundation

Craig, Jane Alice: trustee, Callaway Foundation, Inc.

Craig, John Edwin, Jr.: executive vice president, treasurer, Commonwealth Fund (The); director, Greenwall Foundation

Craig, Lee C.: director, East Cambridge Savings Charitable Foundation

Crain, James T., Jr.: executive director, Cralle Foundation

Crain, John W.: program director, vice president, Summerlee Foundation

Cram, Katharine Neilson: off, Neilson Foundation (George W.)

Cramb, Charles W.: senior vice president finance, chief financial officer, Gillette Co.

Cramer, Theiline: trustee, Norcliffe Foundation

Cramer, William: comm mem, Wells Foundation (Franklin H. and Ruth L.)

Crames, Arthur: director, Crames Family Foundation (Arthur)

Crames, Dale: director, Crames Family Foundation (Arthur)

Crampton, Stuart Jessup Bigelow: director, Research Corp.

Crane, Charles M.: trustee, Friendship Fund

Crane, Diane: trustee, Friendship Fund

Crane, Jonathan: trustee, McDonald Investments Foundation

Crane, Marjorie Knight: trustee, Knight Foundation (John S. and James L.)

Crane, Sylvia E.: trustee, Friendship Fund

Crane, Thomas: treasurer, Friendship Fund

Craner, Ernest C.: director, CHC Foundation

Crank, Celia Whitfield: board of directors, Fondren Foundation

Cranston, H. Stephen: secretary, Knapp Foundation (CA)

Craven, David Leigh: trustee, Longwood Foundation

Crawford, Alan, Jr.: mgr, Ludwick Foundation (Christopher)

Crawford, Donald D., Jr.: treasurer, director, Skaggs Foundation (L. J. Skaggs and Mary C.)

Crawford, Helen: director, Huisking Foundation

Crawford, James C., Jr.: chairman, president, chief executive officer, director, Moore & Sons (B.C.)

Crawford, John: vice president, director, VPI Foundation Inc.

Crawford, Kirk: chief financial officer, Moore & Sons (B.C.)

Crawford, Lucy: executive director, Norton Foundation

Crawford, Patricia Bates: trustee, Johnson Foundation (Howard)

Cray, Cloud: co-trustee, Cray Residuary Charitable Trust (Evah C.)

Crays, Thomas: director, Vermilion Healthcare Foundation

Crean, Eilean: assistant secretary, Dorot Foundation

Creason, Karen K.: director, Johnson Foundation (Samuel S.)

Creason, Kennard: trustee, Loutit Foundation

Creedon, John F.: president, Home for Aged Men in the City of Brockton

Creek, Wallace W.: chief financial funds officer, trustee, General Motors Foundation

Cremer, Frances H.: president, Cremer Foundation

Cremer, Holly L.: treasurer, Cremer Foundation

Cresci, Andrew A.: director, Gellert Foundation (Carl Gellert and Celia Berta)

Crew, Donald W.: treasurer, director, Greenville Foundation

Crew, Herb: director, chairman, Greenville Foundation

Crew, John: director, treasurer, Greenville Foundation

Crew, Richard A.: chairman, director, Greenville Foundation

Crim, Alonzo A.: trustee, Mott Foundation (Charles Stewart)

Criscuoli, Phyllis M.: administration director, treasurer, Dodge Foundation (Cleveland H.)

Crisp, Peter O.: director, Teagle Foundation

Critchlow, Paul W.: president, trustee, Merrill Lynch & Co. Foundation Inc.; senior vice president

marketing & communications, Merrill Lynch & Company, Inc.

Croce, Robert W.: group chairman, Johnson & Johnson

Crockard, Francis H.: trustee, Comer Foundation (AL)

Crocker, Charles: trustee, Crocker Trust (Mary A.)

Croft, Mary: secretary, treasurer, Cowles Charitable Trust

Cromwell, Carol: program manager, International Business Machines

Cromwell, M. Jenkins, Jr.: director, Baltimore Equitable Insurance Foundation

Cronin, George T.: trustee, Irwin Charity Foundation (William G.)

Cronin, James P.: director, Dime Savings Bank of Norwich Foundation

Cronson, Mary: president, trustee, Sharp Foundation (Evelyn)

Cronson, Paul: secretary, trustee, Sharp Foundation (Evelyn)

Crooke, Edward A.: director, Baltimore Equitable Insurance Foundation

Crooks, David W.: assistant secretary, Scotsman Industries Foundation

Crooks, Richard M.: director, Allen Brothers Foundation

Cropper, Steve: director, Gilman Foundation (Howard)

Crory, Elizabeth L.: trustee, Mascoma Savings Bank Foundation

Crosbie, Stewart: secretary, Physicians Mutual Insurance Co. Foundation

Crosby, Edwin L.: chairman, trustee, Carolyn Foundation

Crosby, Ella P.: trustee emeritus, Southways Foundation

Crosby, Franklin M., III: trustee, Carolyn Foundation

Crosby, G. Christian: trustee, Carolyn Foundation

Crosby, Harriett: trustee, Carolyn Foundation

Crosby, Robert C.: board member, Frist Foundation

Crosby, Sumner McKnight, Jr.: vice chairman, trustee, Carolyn Foundation

Crosby, Thomas Manville, Jr.: trustee, Carolyn Foundation

Cross, Jane C.: vice president, trustee, Cooke Foundation Corp. (V. V.)

Cross, Joe D., Jr.: director, Cooke Foundation Corp. (V. V.)

Cross, Michael R.: vice president finance, treasurer,

Bush Charitable Foundation, Inc. (Edyth)

Cross, Michael T.: director, Van Wert County Foundation

Cross, Travis: trustee emeritus, Meyer Memorial Trust

Crossman, Elizabeth A.: president, Weyerhaeuser Co. Foundation

Crouch, Robert F.: vice president, trustee, Copley Foundation (James S.)

Crouter, Henry E.: mgr, Ludwick Foundation (Christopher)

Crow, Jon K.: vice president, treasurer, Southways Foundation

Crow-Johnson, Shelli: secretary, treasurer, Bryden Foundation (Blanche)

Crowe, Timothy J.: vice president, chief financial officer, Knight Foundation (John S. and James L.)

Crowley, Caroline M.: trustee, Connelly Foundation

Crowley, Samantha K.: trustee, Bicknell Fund

Crown, Arie Steven: vice president, director, Crown Memorial (Arie and Ida)

Crown, James S.: director, Sara Lee Corp.

Crown, James Schine: vice president, director, Crown Memorial (Arie and Ida)

Crown, Lester: treasurer, director, Crown Memorial (Arie and Ida)

Crown, Rebecca: vice president, director, Crown Memorial (Arie and Ida)

Crown, Susan: president, director, Crown Memorial (Arie and Ida)

Crown, William: director, vice president, Crown Memorial (Arie and Ida)

Crown Star, Sara: director, vice president, Crown Memorial (Arie and Ida)

Crowther, A. B.: co-trustee, Coy Foundation (Dave)

Croxton, William M.: vice president, Jameson Foundation (J. W. and Ida M.)

Crozier, Daniel G., Jr.: trustee, McFeely-Rogers Foundation

Crozier, James Brooks: trustee, McFeely-Rogers Foundation

Crozier, Nancy R.: vice president, trustee, McFeely-Rogers Foundation

Cruikshank, Robert J.: vice president, assistant secretary, trustee, Fish Foundation (Ray C.)

Crump, Suzanne B.: director, Scott Foundation (William H., John G., and Emma)

Cruz, Frank H.: director, Irvine Foundation (The James)

Cryer, Arthur W.: trustee, Baird Foundation

Csaszar, Bernice: administrator, Bridgestone/Firestone Trust Fund (The)

Cudahy, Janet S., MD: president, director, donor daughter-in-law, Cudahy Fund (Patrick and Anna M.)

Cudahy, Richard D.: chairman, director, donor son, Cudahy Fund (Patrick and Anna M.)

Cudahy, Richard D., Jr.: director, donor grandson, Cudahy Fund (Patrick and Anna M.)

Cudlip, Brittain B.: chairman, Bardes Corp.

Culbertson, Judy B.: director, trustee, Meadows Foundation (The)

Cullen, James D., Esq.: secretary, director, Smith Charitable Foundation (Arlene H.)

Cullen, Roy Henry: president, trustee, Cullen Foundation (The)

Cullum, Charles: vice president, trustee, McDermott Foundation (The Eugene)

Cullum, William Bennett: secretary, treasurer, Decherd Foundation

Culpepper, Jerry: advisor, director, Smith and W. Aubrey Smith Charitable Foundation (Clara Blackford)

Culver, Ellsworth: vice president, Arca Foundation

Culver, Margaret S.: secretary, treasurer, Vogt Foundation (Henry)

Culver, Robert L.: director, Cabot Corp. Foundation

Cummings, Douglas R.: honorary director, Kirkpatrick Foundation, Inc.

Cummings, Helen K.: board member, Frist Foundation

Cummings, Patricia A.: executive director, Phillips Family Foundation (The Jay and Rose)

Cummings, Robert: trustee, North Family Trust

Cummings, Susan Hurd: trustee, Payne Foundation (Frank E. and Seba B.)

Cundiff, Richard M.: treasurer, Ford Fund (Walter and Josephine); treasurer,, Ford II Fund (Henry)

Cuneo, Herta: director, Cuneo Foundation

Cuneo, John F., Jr.: president, director, Cuneo Foundation

Cunin, Marilyn: chairman distribution committee, Bruening Foundation (Eva L. and Joseph M.)

Cunningham, Betty: adv board comm mem, Heath Foundation (Mary)

Cunningham, Helen: executive director, Fels Fund (Samuel S.)

Cunningham, John W.: vice president, board member, director, Gregg-Graniteville Foundation

Cunningham, M.: trustee, Snyder Foundation (Frost and Margaret)

Cunningham, Michael W.: chief financial officer, ING North America Insurance Corp.

Cunningham, Richard: vice president, director, Fleming and Jane Howe Patrick Foundation (Robert)

Cunningham, Thomas P.: director, Chicago Board of Trade Foundation

Cunningham, William J., Jr.: trustee, Statler Foundation

Cunnisse, Maurice: chairman, president, American Optical Corp.

Cuny, Lynn: director, Summerlee Foundation

Cuomo, Ralph: treasurer, Hearst Foundation, Inc. (The)

Curi, John L.: director, Hoag Family Foundation (George)

Curl, Paul T.: director, Piper Foundation (Minnie Stevens)

Curler, Jeffrey H.: president, chief executive officer, Bemis Company, Inc.

Curley, Charles: trustee, Strauss Foundation (Leon)

Curley, Walter Joseph Patrick, Jr.: trustee, Achelis Foundation

Curley, Walter W.: president, Lake Placid Education Foundation

Curnes, Thomas J.: treasurer, trustee, Buell Foundation (Temple Hoyne)

Curran, Carol Cockrell: director, Cockrell Foundation

Curran, Charles: director, Francis Families Foundation

Curran, Charles E.: director, H&R Block Foundation

Curran, Richard B.: director, Cockrell Foundation

Currie, John Thornton "Jack": vice chairman, trustee, Kempner Fund (Harris and Eliza)

Curry, Anna A.: trustee, Alexander Edwards Trust (Margaret)

Curry, Elizabeth R.: director, Hyde and Watson Foundation

Curry, Jennifer: trustee, Huber Foundation

Curry, Monty M.: gov, Mayor Foundation (Oliver Dewey)

Curry, Nancy E.: trustee, Pittsburgh Child Guidance Foundation

Curry, Natalie H.: trustee, Hulme Charitable Foundation (Milton G.)

Curry, R. Boykin, Jr.: trustee emeritus, Self Family Foundation

Curtis, Barron W.: assistant treasurer, Deere Foundation (John)

Curtis, Carlton L.: director, Coca-Cola Foundation

Curtis, Diane: director, Barker Welfare Foundation

Curtis, Elizabeth H.: director, admin, Atkinson Foundation

Curtis, Gerald L.: trustee, United States-Japan Foundation

Curvin, Robert, PhD: trustee, Victoria Foundation

Cushman, John C.: secretary, Howe and Mitchell B. Howe Foundation (Lucille Horton)

Cuthrie, Sarah Walker: trustee, Metal Industries Foundation

Cutino, Peter: director, AT&T National Pro-Am Youth Fund

Cutlip, Randall Brower: trustee, McNutt Charitable Trust (Amy Shelton)

Cutter, Nancy L.: admin assistant, Foundation for Seacoast Health

Cuzzort, Pamela K.: treasurer, Tucker Foundation

Cyphers, Judith B.: secretary, director grants, office, Strong Foundation (Hattie M.)

D

D'Agnes, Glenn: chief financial officer, HarperCollins Publishers, Inc.

D'Alessandro, David F.: president, chief operating officer, John Hancock Financial Services

D'Amato, Domenico Donald: president, director, Vogler Foundation (Laura B.)

D'Amato, Lawrence L.: treasurer, director, Vogler Foundation (Laura B.)

D'Andrade, Hugh Alfred: trustee, member, Schering-Plough Foundation

D'Arata, Joy E.: vice president, trustee, Chatlos Foundation

D'Elia, Lorraine: director, Gellert Foundation (Carl Gellert and Celia Berta)

d'Harnoncourt, Anne: director, administration committee, Luce Foundation (Henry)

D'Mara, John M.: trustee, Heckscher Foundation for Children

D'Olier, Henry Mitchell: president, director, Castle Foundation (Harold K. L.)

D'Unger, Claude: vice president, Rachal Foundation (Ed)

Daberko, David A.: officer, National City Corp. Charitable Foundation II

Dadourian, Alexander: vice president, United Armenian Charities

Dadourian, Haig: president, United Armenian Charities

Dadourian, Peter: treasurer, United Armenian Charities

Daft, Douglas N.: chairman, chief executive officer, Coca-Cola Co.

Daggett, Christopher J.: chairman, Schumann Fund for New Jersey

Dahan, Rene: senior vice president, ExxonMobile Corp.

Dahlstrom, Donald F.: communications officer, Mott Foundation (Charles Stewart)

Daie, Jaleh: director science program, Packard Foundation (David and Lucile)

Daily, Mary Ann: president, Weber Charities Corp. (Frederick E.)

Dajao, R. Faith, MD: director, Portsmouth General Hospital Foundation

Dalbey, R. Thomas, Jr.: mgr, Wilson Foundation (Marie C. and Joseph C.)

Dale, Kenneth: trustee, Baker Foundation (R. C.)

Daley, Pamela: director, Arison Foundation

Dalhouse, Warner Norris: director, Shenandoah Life Insurance Co.

Dalneoff, Stanley: treasurer, Fink Foundation (NY)

Dalrymple, Elizabeth T.: trust, Anderson Foundation (NY)

Dalrymple, Richard: president, director, Dime Foundation

Dalton, Mary K.: president, treasurer, director, Dalton Foundation (Harry L.)

Daly, Denis G.: secretary, Amcast Industrial Corp.

Daly, James J.: member board governors, Brooks Foundation (Gladys)

Daly, Robert P.: director, Huisking Foundation

Damas, Mary D.: assistant secretary, Winthrop

Dame, W. Page, Jr.: trustee, Warfield Memorial Fund (Anna Emory)

Dammerman, Dennis Dean: vice chairman, director, General Electric Co.

Dampeer, John Lyell: chairman, treasurer, trustee, Smith Foundation (Kelvin and Eleanor)

Dana, Alden P.: trustee, Cone Automatic Machine Co. Charitable Foundation

Danenhauer, Edwin H.: assistant secretary, Dingman Foundation (Michael D.)

Danforth, Richard M.: mem, Gardiner Savings Institution Charitable Foundation

Daniel, Barbara Fish: president, trustee, Fish Foundation (Ray C.)

Daniel, Charles W.: president, Daniel Foundation of Alabama

Daniel, Christopher J.: vice president, treasurer, trustee, Fish Foundation (Ray C.)

Daniel, David Ronald: director, Markle Foundation (John and Mary R.)

Daniel, Frank, MD: director, De Queen Regional Medical Center

Daniel, James L., Jr.: vice president, trustee, Fish Foundation (Ray C.)

Daniel, M. C.: chairman, Daniel Foundation of Alabama

Daniel, Robert A.: assistant treasurer, Kemper Foundation (James S.)

Daniels, Bill: trustee, Priddy Foundation

Daniels, Bruce G.: president, Daniels Foundation (Fred Harris)

Daniels, Edgar F.: president, director, Daniels Foundation (Edgar Foster)

Daniels, Fred H., II: director, Daniels Foundation (Fred Harris)

Daniels, Janet B.: director, Daniels Foundation (Fred Harris)

Daniels, Lillian I.: secretary, treasurer, Memton Fund

Daniels, Mitchell E., Jr.: senior vice president, Eli Lilly & Co.; chairman, treasurer, Lilly Foundation (Eli)

Daniels, Ron: trustee, Boehm Foundation

Daniels, Thomas E.: trustee, George Foundation

Danielson, John G.: vice president, treasurer, Albertson's Inc.

Danis, Ross: program officer, Dodge Foundation (Geraldine R.)

Dann, Jesse: trustee, Viyu Foundation

Dann, Marion: trustee, Viyu Foundation

Dann, William: trustee, Viyu Foundation

Dann, William R., Jr.: trustee, Viyu Foundation

Danner, Douglas: trustee, Riley Foundation (Mabel Louise)

Danser, Gordon O.: trustee, Cape Branch Foundation

Dantzscher, Adam B.: executive director, Fleming and Jane Howe Patrick Foundation (Robert)

Darden, Constance S. duPont: director, North Shore Foundation

Darden, Joshua P., Jr.: president, director, North Shore Foundation

Dargene, Carl J.: director, AMCORE Foundation

Darland, Tye: secretary, Koch Foundation, Inc. (Fred C. and Mary R.)

Darling, Robert Edward, Jr.: chairman, Ensign-Bickford Foundation

Darnieder, Gregory M.: secretary, Pick, Jr. Fund (Albert)

Darrell, John S.: director, Ray Foundation

Darrow, Jill C.: executive director, Fry Foundation (Lloyd A.)

Dascoli, D. Paul: chief financial officer, vice president, Thomasville Furniture Industries, Inc.

Dass, Ram: director, Furthur Foundation

Dattilo, Thomas A.: chairman, president, chief executive officer, Cooper Tire & Rubber Co.

Daughdrill, James M., III: president, Walker Foundation

Daugherty, David M.: treasurer, Kiplinger Foundation

Daugherty, Robert B.: director, Valmont Industries, Inc.

Dauphin, Richard B.: assistant secretary, Reliant Resources Foundation

Davenport, Judith M.: trustee, Pittsburgh Child Guidance Foundation

Davenport, Margaret: trustee, Golub Foundation

Davenport, Palmer: director, Kelley and Elza Kelley Foundation (Edward Bangs)

David, Daryl: board of directors, Washington Mutual Foundation

Davidson, Brad: trustee, Kaplan Fund (J. M.)

Davidson, Denise S.: secretary, Jamail Foundation (Lee and Joseph D.)

Davidson, Elizabeth: trustee, Kaplan Fund (J. M.)

Davidson, Endicott P.: trustee, Ingalls Foundation (Louise H. and David S.)

Davidson, James E.: director, Mardag Foundation

Davidson, John: member admin committee, Selby and Marie Selby Foundation (William G.)

Davidson, John Matthew: trustee, Kaplan Fund (J. M.)

Davidson, Peter W.: chairman, Kaplan Fund (J. M.)

Davidson, Phyllis: mem, Phipps Foundation (Columbus)

Davidson, William M., IV: treasurer, mgr, Ludwick Foundation (Christopher)

Davies, Robert N.: director, Goldman Foundation (Herman)

Davies, Trevor C.: chief financial officer treasurer, assistant secretary, Coleman Foundation (IL)

Davis, Andrew: assistant vice president, Fredrickson Foundation (Ambrose and Ida)

Davis, Andrew Dano: vice president, director, Winn-Dixie Stores Foundation; chairman, Winn-Dixie Stores Inc.

Davis, Brad: board of directors, Washington Mutual Foundation

Davis, Brigit Ann: program manager, Johnson Foundation (Helen K. and Arthur E.)

Davis, Charles, Jr.: treasurer, Gulf Coast Medical Foundation

Davis, Craig: vice president, Washington Mutual Foundation

Davis, Donald H., Jr.: president, chief executive officer, chairman, Rockwell Automation Inc.; chairman trust committee, Rockwell International Corp. Trust

Davis, Eddie L.: trustee, Hartford Courant Foundation

Davis, Edward: secretary, director, mem, Katzenberger Foundation

Davis, Edwin W.: secretary, administrator, director, Murphy Co. Foundation (G.C.)

Davis, Eleanor L.: trustee, Connelly Foundation

Davis, Elizabeth K.: trustee, Kunkel Foundation (John Crain)

Davis, Erroll Brown, Jr.: chairman, president, chief executive officer, Alliant Energy Corp.

Davis, Evelyn Y.: trustee, Davis Foundation (Evelyn Y.)

Davis, F. A.: president, director, Starr Foundation

Davis, F. Elwood: trustee, Bloedorn Foundation (Walter A.)

Davis, Frederick W., II: secretary, director, Davis Foundation (Edwin W. and Catherine M.)

Davis, G. Gordon, Esq.: secretary, gov, trustee, Crary Foundation (Bruce L.)

Davis, Gale Lansing: director, Griggs and Mary Griggs Burke Foundation (Mary Livingston)

Davis, Gilbert S.: director, Memorial Foundation for the Blind

Davis, Holbrook R.: trustee, Davis Foundations (Arthur Vining)

Davis, J. H. Dow: chairman, Davis Foundations (Arthur Vining)

Davis, James N.: executive director, Gheens Foundation

Davis, Jane C.: vice president, director, Skaggs Foundation (L. J. Skaggs and Mary C.)

Davis, Joel P.: trustee, Davis Foundations (Arthur Vining)

Davis, John, Jr. Es: co-trustee, Waters Charitable Trust (Robert S.)

Davis, John B., MD: director, Physicians Mutual Insurance Co. Foundation

Davis, John H.: trustee, Davis Foundation (Irene E. and George A.)

Davis, Karen: director, Hasbro Charitable Trust Inc.

Davis, Karen Padgett: president, director, Commonwealth Fund (The)

Davis, Karyll A.: trustee, Heinz Co. Foundation (H.J.)

Davis, Laurianne T.: president, Tiscornia Foundation

Davis, Margaret C. W.: treasurer, Campbell Foundation (MD)

Davis, Mary E.: vice president, director, Davis Foundation (Edwin W. and Catherine M.); trustee, Davis Foundation (Irene E. and George A.)

Davis, Michael M.: trustee, Kendall Foundation (Henry P.)

Davis, Milton Austin: director, Field Foundation of Illinois

Davis, Robert Edwin: trust, Bloedorn Foundation (Walter A.)

Davis, Robert M.: trustee, Barden Foundation, Inc.

Davis, Robert S.: president, director, Saint Croix Foundation; president, chairman, Tozer Foundation

Davis, Sam H.: director, Kohler Foundation

Davis, Stephen A.: trustee, Davis Foundation (Irene E. and George A.)

Davis, Ted C.: trustee, Gerber Foundation

Davis, Ulla Z.: executive director, Hale Foundation (Crescent Porter)

Davis, Virginia: director, Snee-Reinhardt Charitable Foundation

Davis, William E.: trustee, Niagara Mohawk Foundation; chairman, chief executive officer, Niagara Mohawk Holdings, Inc.

Davis, William L.: chairman, president, chief executive officer, R.R. Donnelley & Sons Co.

Davis, Willie D.: director, Sara Lee Corp.

Davis, Winifred S.: trustee, Harland Charitable Foundation (John H. and Wilhelmina D.)

Davison, Daniel Pomeroy: vice president, treasurer, ast secretary, director, Gould Foundation (The Florence)

Dawley, Gary: trustee, Besser Foundation

Dawson, Brennan: vice president external affairs, Brown & Williamson Tobacco Corp.

Dawson, Judith: vice president, secretary, director, Atherton Family Foundation

Day, Ann B.: president, director, Carpenter Foundation (E. Rhodes and Leona B.)

Day, Antonia Scott: vice president, director, secretary, Powell Foundation

Day, Betty T.: assistant secretary, assistant treasurer, Cemala Foundation

Day, Dorothy W.: trustee, Day Foundation (Willametta K.)

Day, Fred N., IV: vice president, director, Progress Energy Foundation

Day, H. Corbin: director, Hyde and Watson Foundation

Day, Howard M.: vice president, trustee, Day Foundation (Willametta K.); vice president, director, member director grant program committee, Keck Foundation (W. M.)

Day, Janet Loew: trustee, Wendt Foundation (Margaret L.)

Day, Matthew, Jr.: member, Carnegie Corp. of New York

Day, Paul B., Jr.: vice president, secretary, treasurer, Carpenter Foundation (E. Rhodes and Leona B.)

Day, Robert A., Jr.: chairman, trustee, Day Foundation (Willametta K.); chairman, president, chief executive officer, Keck Foundation (W. M.)

Day, Susan C., MD: vice president, trustee, Seybert Institution for Poor Boys and Girls (Adam and Maria Sarah)

Day, Tammis M.: vice president, trustee, Day Foundation (Willametta K.); director, Keck Foundation (W. M.)

Day, Theodore J.: vice president, trustee, Day Foundation (Willametta K.); director, member audit committee, Keck Foundation (W. M.)

Days, Drew Saunders, III: director, MacArthur Foundation (John D. and Catherine T.)

De Bakcsy, Alex: vice president, trustee, Copley Foundation (James S.)

De Boer, Richard G.: treasurer, Scotsman Industries Foundation

De Gaetano, Peter F.: secretary, director, Piankova Foundation (Tatiana)

de Garne, Lilo Navales: foundation officer, State Street Foundation

de Lone, Madeline: trustee, Hazen Foundation (Edward W.)

De Raismes, Ann D.: member, Hartford Financial Services Group, Inc.

de Rham, Casimir, Jr.: trustee, Campbell and Adah E. Hall Charity Fund (Bushrod H.)

De Witt, William: trustee, Semple Foundation (Louise Taft)

Deacy, Jean: trustee, Halsell Foundation (Ewing)

Deal, Janet J.: trustee, Upjohn Foundation (Harold and Grace)

Dean, Anthony M.: treasurer, trustee, Blowitz-Ridgeway Foundation

Dean, Anthony Taylor: president, chief operating officer, Nuveen Co. (The John)

Dean, J. Simpson, Jr.: vice president, Welfare Foundation

Dean, Roger W.: controller, chief administrative officer, Fifth Third Bancorp

Dean, Sarah M.: executive director, McBeath Foundation (Faye)

Dearstyne, William D., Jr.: group chairman, Johnson & Johnson; member corporate contributions committee, Johnson & Johnson Family of Companies Contribution Fund

Deatherage, Marie: special programs officer, Meyer Memorial Trust

DeBacker, Lois R.: program officer, Mott Foundation (Charles Stewart)

Debevoise, Dickinson Richards: trustee, Fund for New Jersey

Debs, Barbara Knowles: trustee, Dodge Foundation (Geraldine R.)

Decherd, Maureen H.: president, Decherd Foundation

Decherd, Robert William: chairman, president, chief executive officer, director, Belo Corp.; trustee, Belo Foundation; chairman, Decherd Foundation

Decio, Arthur J.: trustee, Decio Foundation (Arthur J.)

Decio, Patricia C.: trustee, Decio Foundation (Arthur J.)

Decio, Terrence M.: trustee, Decio Foundation (Arthur J.)

Decker, A. Dean: adv comm mem, trustee, Moore and Arletta E. Moore Foundation (Kenneth S.)

Decker, C. Arnold: chairman emeritus, Decker Foundation (Dr. G. Clifford and Florence B.)

Decker, Janet: gov, Crary Foundation (Bruce L.)

Decker, Mary L.: vice president, Bank One Foundation

Decker, Robert W.: president, treasurer, director, Scott Foundation (William E.)

DeCotis, Deborah: director, Rubinstein Foundation (Helena)

DeCrona, Bruce: chief financial officer, controller, vice president finance, Exchange Bank

Dee, David L.: vice chairman, Dee Foundation (Lawrence T. and Janet T.)

Dee, Shelly Louise Hoglund: trustee, Hoglund Foundation

Dee, Thomas D., II: chairman, Dee Foundation (Lawrence T. and Janet T.)

Dee, Thomas D., III: vchairman, Dee Foundation (Lawrence T. and Janet T.)

Deegan-Day, Joseph: trustee, Day Foundation (Willametta K.)

Deems, Richard Emmet: director, Hearst Foundation, Inc. (The); vice president, director, Hearst Foundation (William Randolph)

Deen, R. B., Jr.: secretary, director, Hardin Foundation (Phil)

Deering, Anthony W.: chairman, chief executive officer, Rouse Co.; chairman, president, trustee, Rouse Co. Foundation

DeGaetano, Peter F.: secretary, director, L and L Foundation

DeGive, Josephine: trustee, Friendship Fund

DeGraan, Edward F.: president, chief operating officer, director, Gillette Co.

Degrange, Vivianne V.: secretary, clerk, Kilmartin Industries Charitable Foundation

DeGroot, Dana Riley: director, Engl Family Foundation (Michael S.)

Deitrick, Scott R.: vice president, Hammer Foundation (Armand)

DeKruif, Robert M.: trustee, Ahmanson Foundation

del Sol, Carlos: vice president, trustee, Campbell Soup Foundation

Dela Cruz, E. Corinne: assistant treasurer, senior accountant, Weingart Foundation

Delahaye, Michael T.: director, New York Life Foundation

Deland, Emme Levin: director, Kornfeld Foundation (Emily Davie and Joseph S.)

Delaney, Wayne E.: director, advisor, Smith and W. Aubrey Smith Charitable Foundation (Clara Blackford)

Delattre, Edwin J.: trustee, Quaker Chemical Foundation

DeLauder, William B.: trustee, The MBNA Foundation

DeLauro, Debra: secretary, Greenfield Foundation (Albert M.)

Delbridge, Ed: director, Christy-Houston Foundation

Delgado, Gloria: president, SBC Foundation

Delgado, Jane L.: trustee, Kresge Foundation

DeLissio, Janet: treasurer, Ensign-Bickford Foundation

Delli Carpini, Michael X.: director public policy program, Pew Charitable Trusts

DeLoach, Harris E., Junior: president, chief executive officer, Sonoco Products Co.

DeLoache, Bond D.: co-trustee, Davis Foundation (Joe C.)

DeLoache, William R.: co-trustee, Davis Foundation (Joe C.)

DeLoache, William R., Jr.: co-trustee, Davis Foundation (Joe C.)

DeLordo, Ellen B.: president, ONDEO Nalco Foundation

Delori, Rosamond P.: trustee, secretary, Putnam Foundation

Delouvrier, Philippe: trustee, Connelly Foundation

DeMaio, Susan M.: assistant secretary, Barker Welfare Foundation

DeMajistre, Robert: trustee, Seton Co. Foundation

Demarest, Daniel Anthony: treasurer, Bay Foundation; secretary, treasurer, Paul and C. Michael Paul Foundation (Josephine Bay)

Demer, Elmer G.: trustee, Second Foundation

Demeritt, Stephen R.: vice chairman, General Mills, Inc.

Deming, Winifred: vice president, Benbough Foundation (Legler)

Demorest, Byron, MD: director, Sierra Health Foundation

DeMott, Alfred E.: director, Hoch Foundation (Charles H.)

Dempsey, James Howard, Jr.: secretary, trustee, Andrews Foundation

Dempsey, Timothy A.: president, Warwick Savings Foundation

Denham, Robert E.: director, MacArthur Foundation (John D. and Catherine T.)

Denison, Harriet S.: mgr, Smith Foundation (Ralph L.)

Denison, Martha: director, Smith Foundation (Ralph L.)

Denius, F. Wofford: vice president, director, Cain Foundation (Effie and Wofford)

Denius, Frank W.: executive vice president, director, Cain Foundation (Effie and Wofford)

Denk, Fred: secretary, PPG Industries Foundation

Denkers, Julie: committee member, Eccles Charitable Foundation (Willard L.)

Denkers, Stephen G.: committee member, Eccles Charitable Foundation (Willard L.)

Denkers, Susan E.: committee member, Eccles Charitable Foundation (Willard L.)

Denman, Gilbert M., Jr.: trustee, Brackenridge Foundation (George W.); trustee, chairman, Halsell Foundation (Ewing)

Denman, Leroy G., Jr.: trustee, Brackenridge Foundation (George W.)

Denman, Mary Ellen: vice president, Howarth Trust Fund

Dennis, Andre L., Esq.: director, Independence Foundation

Denworth, Joanne R.: director, Penn Foundation (William)

Denworth, Raymond K., Jr.: vice president, director, Fels Fund (Samuel S.)

DePopolo, Margaret: mem, Henderson Foundation (George B.)

Derisley, Arthur: president, treasurer, trustee, Carls Foundation

Derrer, Suzanne: director, Reynolds Foundation (Christopher)

Derrickson, Lloyd J.: secretary, director, Freed Foundation

Derry, R. Michael: vice president, HON Industries Charitable Foundation

Derry, William S.: trustee, Van Wert County Foundation

DeSalva, AnnaMaria: director, Bristol-Myers Squibb Foundation Inc.

Deschamps, Bruno: president, chief operating officer, Ecolab, Inc.

Deschenes, Joseph E.: treasurer, Provident Community Foundation

Deschepper, James L.: director, Oakley-Lindsay Foundation of Quincy Newspapers and Its Subsidiaries

Deshotel, Adrian B.: secretary, treasurer, American Standard Foundation; vice president human resources, American Standard Inc.

Desoer, Barbara J.: trustee, Bank of America Foundation

DeSoto, Pete: chairman, president, chief executive officer, Metal Industries, Inc.

Dessingue, William: executive director, Charitable Venture Foundation

Destruel, Jean E.: director, Exchange Bank Foundation

Detlefs, Suzanne H.: trustee, vice president, BellSouth Foundation

Dettman, Douglas R.: president, director, Dettman Foundation (Leroy E.)

Dettman, Gregory L.: secretary, director, Dettman Foundation (Leroy E.)

Deubel, George: director, Sierra Health Foundation

Deuble, Andrew H.: secretary, trustee, Deuble Foundation (George H.)

Deuble, Steven G.: president, trustee, Deuble Foundation (George H.)

Deuble, Walter C.: trustee, Deuble Foundation (George H.)

Deuble, Walter J.: trustee, Deuble Foundation (George H.)

Devaney, Phyllis: director, Building 19 Foundation

Devine, John M.: vice chairman, chief financial officer, General Motors Corp.

Devine, Nancy: director communities programs, Wallace-Reader's Digest Fund (Lila)

DeVita, M. Christine: president, director, Wallace-Reader's Digest Fund (DeWitt); president, secretary, director, Wallace-Reader's Digest Fund (Lila)

DeVitt Jones, Helen: hon chairman, trustee, CH Foundation

DeVore, Richard A.: president, secretary, DeVore Foundation

DeVore, Ronald: chairman, president, chief executive officer, Terumo Medical Corp.

DeVore, William O.: vice president, treasurer, DeVore Foundation

DeVos, Helen June (Van Wesep): president, DeVos Foundation (Richard and Helen)

Dewar, Robert: director, Claiborne and Art Ortenberg Foundation (Liz)

Dewey, Francis H., III: chairman, trustee, Alden Trust (George I.)

Dewey, Henry Bowen, Esq.: co-trustee, Hoche-Scofield Foundation

Dewey, Robert F.: president, trustee, Gifford Charitable Corp. (Rosamond)

Dewing, Merlin E.: director, Bush Foundation

DeWoody, Beth Rudin: president, director, Rudin Foundation

Dexel, Albert: assistant secretary, assistant treasurer, Tiscornia Foundation

Deyo, R.: president, trustee, Johnson & Johnson Family of Companies Contribution Fund

Di Re, Cheryl: secretary, Washington Mutual Foundation

di San Faustino, Genevieve Bothin Lyman: president, director, donor granddaughter, The Bothin Foundation

Diamond, Lorraine: secretary, Vogler Foundation (Laura B.)

Diaz, Angela: trustee, New York Foundation

Dibner, Brent: trustee, Dibner Fund

Dibner, David: president, treasurer, trustee, Dibner Fund

Dibner, Frances K.: vice president, treasurer, trustee, Dibner Fund

Dick, Rollin M.: executive vice president, chief financial officer, Conseco, Inc.

Dicke, Richard M., Esq.: trustee, Ferkauf Foundation (Eugene and Estelle)

Dickenson, Gwen: administrative assistant, Self Family Foundation

Dickes, Don D.: secretary, treasurer, trustee, Timken Foundation of Canton

Dickey, E. D.: secretary, CTW Foundation, Inc.

Dickler, Ruth: president, Dickler Family Foundation

Dickler, Susan: executive vice president, Dickler Family Foundation

Dickman, J. Jerry: trustee, Chapman Charitable Trust (H. A. and Mary K.)

Dickman, Norbert J.: vice president, director, The Prairie Foundation

Dickoff, Gil A.: treasurer, Crane Co.

Dickson, Margaret C.: vice president, treasurer, Harland Charitable Foundation (John H. and Wilhelmina D.)

Dickson, Michael M.: trustee, Harland Charitable Foundation (John H. and Wilhelmina D.)

Dickson, Robert T.: president, director, The Prairie Foundation

Dickson, Stanley: trustee, Brown Foundation, Inc. (James Graham)

Didden, George A., III: director, Arcana Foundation

Diehl, Betty: director, Lytel Foundation (Bertha Russ)

Diehl, John E.: director, Grotto Foundation

Dienst, Edward J.: trustee, Niagara Mohawk Foundation

Dietl, Wally: secretary, Holzer Memorial Foundation (Richard H.)

Dietler, Cortland S.: trustee, El Pomar Foundation

Dietrich, G. Phillip: adv, Delano Foundation (Mignon Sherwood)

Dietrich, William B.: president, treasurer, Dietrich Foundation (William B.)

Dietz, Carolyn Emmerson: chairman, president, Sierra Pacific Foundation

Dievendorf, Mary Catherine: trustee, Yost Trust (J. Paul)

Diez-Morales, Luis: trustee, Hartford Courant Foundation

Diggs, James C.: vice president, PPG Industries Foundation

Dikeou, George D., Esq.: director, Copic Medical Foundation

DiLeo, Victor: trustee, Schwartz Foundation (Arnold A.)

Dill, Agnes M.: director, Chamiza Foundation

Diller, Whitney Clay: treasurer, Clay Foundation

Dillon, Ann: trustee, Bonfils-Stanton Foundation

Dillon, David Brian: chief executive officer, Kroger Co.

Dillon, Francis B.: trustee, Arata Brothers Trust

Dillon, John T.: chairman, chief executive officer, director, International Paper Co.

Dillon, Margo: assistant secretary, director, Dillon Foundation

Dillon, Peter W.: president, director, Dillon Foundation

Dillon, Ray E., III: trustee, Davis Foundation (James A. and Juliet L.)

Dillon, Tanya: director, Allyn Foundation

Dills, Joan Nelson: administrator, Stulsaft Foundation (Morris)

Dills, Max J.: director, Shelter Mutual Insurance Co.

DiMaggio, Jacqueline: treasurer, Niagara Mohawk Foundation

DiMarco, James F.: senior vice president, Johnson & Son (S.C.)

Dimeo, Bradford S.: vice president, Dimeo Construction Co.

Dimeo, Thomas P.: chairman, president, chief executive officer, director, Dimeo Construction Co.

Dimmer, Carolyn J.: vice president, Dimmer Family Foundation

Dimmer, Diane C.: secretary, Dimmer Family Foundation

Dimmer, John B.: treasurer, Dimmer Family Foundation

Dimmer, John C.: president, Dimmer Family Foundation

Dimmer, Marilyn J.: vice president, Dimmer Family Foundation

DiNardo, Joseph: trustee, Statler Foundation

Dinerstein, Martha L.: managing director, head marketing & corporate communications, United States Trust Co. of New York

Dingell, Deborah I.: president, trustee, General Motors Foundation

Dingle, Doris B.: board member, Brush Foundation

Dingman, Elizabeth T.: vice president, Dingman Foundation (Michael D.)

Dingman, Michael David: president, Dingman Foundation (Michael D.)

Dingus, Mary Anne Duncan: director, Duncan Foundation (L. H. and C. W.)

Dinner, Joan Withers: director, Hale Foundation (Crescent Porter)

Dinner, Richard S.: trustee, Swig Foundation (The)

DiNome, Anthony J.: secretary, treasurer, Benenson Foundation (Frances and Benjamin)

Dinse, Ann G.: trustee, Turrell Fund

DiPilla, Betty: secretary, Maneely Fund

Disney, Anthea: president, chief executive officer, HarperCollins Publishers, Inc.

Disney, Roy Edward: trustee, vice president, Disney Co. Foundation (Walt); vice chairman, director, Walt Disney Co.

Divers-White, Beverly: trustee, Hazen Foundation (Edward W.)

Dix, Lawrence: treasurer, Becher Foundation (Hildegarde D.)

Dix, Ronald H.: director, Badger Meter Foundation; vice president administration & human resources, Badger Meter, Inc.

Dixon, Ashley M.: director, Fear Not Foundation

Dixon, Judith: secretary, Winn-Dixie Stores Foundation

Dixon, Marcus K.: trustee, Dentsply International Foundation

Dixon, Paul Edward: secretary, trustee, Handy & Harman Foundation

Dixon, Ruth B.: chairman, Barstow Foundation

Dixon, Thomas F.: vice president, director, Harriman Foundation (Gladys and Roland)

Dixon, Thomas H.: director, Oneida Savings Bank Charitable Foundation

Dixon, William R.: trustee, Barstow Foundation

Dmitrieff, Alexander: director, Griffis Foundation

Doan, Herbert Dow: chairman, Dow Foundation (Herbert H. and Grace A.)

Doane, Ken: program officer education, Cowell Foundation (S. H.)

Dobbins, Allen L., EdD: director, Hedco Foundation

Dobbs, David L.: trustee, Nolan Charitable Trust (James and Elise)

Dobbs, W. L.: mgr, Porter Testamentary Trust (James Hyde)

Doberstein, Stephen C.: director, Crystal Trust

Dobkin, Kendal Kennedy: director, Kennedy Family Foundation (Ethel and W. George)

Dobras, Mary Ann: trustee, Stocker Foundation

Dobras, Wendy: trustee, Stocker Foundation

Dobrof, Rose: secretary, New York Foundation

Dobron, Eugenia: proposal coord, Pew Charitable Trusts

Dobson, Charles C.: trustee, Carolyn Foundation

Dobson, Douglas R.: trustee, vice chairman, Stackpole-Hall Foundation

Dockson, Robert Ray: 1st vice president, trustee, Haynes Foundation (John Randolph and Dora)

Dodd, Ruth E.: secretary, Connell Foundation (Michael J.)

Dodge, Cleveland Earl, Jr.: president, chairman executive committee, member

finance committee, Dodge Foundation (Cleveland H.)

Dodge, David S.: mem executive comm, director, Dodge Foundation (Cleveland H.)

Dodge, James H.: chairman, chief executive officer, president, director, Providence Gas Co.

Dodson, Betty Jo: mem, Phipps Foundation (Columbus)

Doefler, Ronald J.: assistant treasurer, Hearst Foundation (William Randolph)

Doerr, Henry: off, Neilson Foundation (George W.)

Doescher, Scott P.: senior vice president, secretary, treasurer, Mosinee Paper Corp.

Doherty, Janice L.: secretary, Smoot Charitable Foundation

Dohrmann, Fred G.: manager, Winnebago Industries Foundation

Doiron, Mark: director, Hannaford Charitable Foundation

Dolan, James F.: trustee, Heinz Trust (Drue)

Dolan, Joseph S.: executive director, secretary, Achelis Foundation

Dolan, Peter R.: chairman, chief executive officer, Bristol-Myers Squibb Co.

Dolan, Regina A.: trustee, Paine Webber Foundation; chief financial officer, vice president, UBS PaineWebber, Inc.

Dolan, Ronald J.: trustee, Ohio National Foundation; senior vice president, chief financial officer, director, Ohio National Life Insurance Co.

Dolden, Roger: chief financial officer, L'Oreal U.S.A.

Doll, A. Robert: president, C. E. and S. Foundation

Doll, Thomas J.: trustee, Subaru of America Foundation; vice president, chief financial officer, Subaru of America, Inc.

Dolle, Guy: chairman, J&L Specialty Steel, Inc.

Dolle, Molly W.: director, Wrather Family Foundation

Dolvin, Neal: director, Citizens Union Bank Foundation

Domke, Doreta: director, McConnell Foundation

Donahue, Frank R., Jr.: secretary, director, Barra Foundation

Donahue, Jeffrey H.: senior vice president, chief financial officer, Rouse Co.

Donahue, Josephine C.: director administration, Dana Foundation (Charles A.)

Donaldson, Don: vice president, assistant secretary, Lyon Foundation

Donaldson, Richard Miesse: treasurer, Brush Foundation

Donaly, Joyce: treasurer, CNA Foundation

Donati, John: director, S.G. Foundation

Donelson, Harold L.: assistant secretary, assistant treasurer, McMillen Foundation

Donley, Edward J.: trustee, Rider-Pool Foundation

Donnelley, James R.: vice president, treasurer, Griswold Foundation (John C.); director, R.R. Donnelley & Sons Co.

Donnelly, John L.: treasurer, director, Gazette Foundation

Donofrio, Nicholas M.: senior vice president technology manufacturing, International Business Machines

Donoghue, Norman E., II: trustee, Bard Foundation (Robert)

Donohoe, John C.: trustee, Walsh Charity Trust (Blanche)

Donohue, Elise R.: director, Weyerhaeuser Memorial Foundation (Charles A.)

Donough, Robert J.: member, Oishei Foundation (The John R.)

Donovan, Anne Fuller: trustee, Fuller Foundation (MA)

Donovan, David E.: director, vice president, Bank One Foundation

Donovan, James E.: treasurer, Bank One Foundation

Donovan, Thomas F.: trustee, Connelly Foundation

Donovan, Thomas J.: trustee, Bean Foundation (Norwin S. and Elizabeth N.)

Donovan, Thomas Roy: president, chief executive officer, Chicago Board of Trade

Dooley, Eugene: director, Kovarik Foundation for Poetry (Henry P.)

Dooner, Marie E.: secretary, Maneely Fund

Doordan, Helen R.: first vice president, Raskob Foundation for Catholic Activities, Inc.

Dopson, Arnold B.: chairman, Blount Educational and Charitable Foundation (Mildred Weedon)

Dor, Barbara: trustee, Ferkauf Foundation (Eugene and Estelle)

Dor, Benny: trustee, Ferkauf Foundation (Eugene and Estelle)

Dorman, David W.: president, director, AT&T Corp.

Dorn, David F.: trustee, Glendorn Foundation

Dorn, Frederick M.: trustee, Glendorn Foundation

Dorn, Gail J.: vice president communications, Target Corp.; trustee, Target Foundation

Dorn, John C.: trustee, Glendorn Foundation

Dorn, William L.: chairman, chief executive officer, director, Forest Oil Corp.

Dornsife, David H.: vice president, director, Hedco Foundation

Dornsife, Ester M.: president, director, Hedco Foundation

Dornsife, Harold W.: cfo, director, Hedco Foundation

Dorsey, Bob Rawls: director emeritus, Keck Foundation (W. M.)

Dorskind, Albert A.: vice president, chief financial officer, director, Parsons Foundation (Ralph M.)

Dossman, Curley M., Junior: president, Georgia-Pacific Foundation

Double, William F.: director, St. Francis Bank Foundation

Dougherty, Kevin: trustee, Dougherty, Jr. Foundation (James R.)

Dougherty, Mary Patricia: secretary, treasurer, trustee, Dougherty, Jr. Foundation (James R.)

Douglas, Laurinda L.: trustee, Hillsdale Fund

Douglas, Walter E.: trustee, Skillman Foundation

Douglass, Robert Royal: trustee, J.P. Morgan Chase Foundation

Douglass, William Birch, III: secretary, Gray Foundation (Garland and Agnes Taylor)

Douthat, Anne S.: mgr, Smith Foundation (Ralph L.)

Douthat, E. M., III: director, Smith Foundation (Ralph L.)

Douthat, Neil T.: trustee, Smith Foundation (Ralph L.)

Douthat, Paul N.: director, Smith Foundation (Ralph L.)

Douthitt, Jane: secretary, treasurer, director, Daniels Foundation (Edgar Foster)

Dover, Vera M.: secretary, Butz Foundation

Dow, Michael Lloyd: treasurer, Dow Foundation (Herbert H. and Grace A.)

Dow, Peggy Anne: secretary, chief financial officer, director, Silver Lining Foundation

Dowd, Hector G.: secretary, Frese Foundation (Arnold D.)

Dowdle, James C.: director, McCormick Tribune Foundation (Robert R.)

Dowling, Edward C.: senior vice president, operations, Cleveland-Cliffs, Inc.

Dowling, Thomas: secretary, Carris Corp. Foundation

Downer, Edwin E.: director, Hardin Foundation (Phil)

Downes, Laurence M.: president, chief executive officer, director, chairman, New Jersey Natural Gas Co.; trustee, New Jersey Natural Gas Foundation

Downey, Thelma L.: assistant secretary, assistant treasurer, Olsson Memorial Foundation (Elis)

Downing, Danna: director, Vicksburg Foundation

Downing, Kathryn M.: vice chairman, Times Mirror Foundation; executive vice president, Tribune Co.

Downs, John H., Jr.: director, Coca-Cola Foundation

Doyle, Allen: trustee, Valentine Foundation (Lawson)

Doyle, Daniel M.: president, director, Doyle Foundation

Doyle, Daniel M., Jr.: director, Doyle Foundation

Doyle, Donald W.: vice president, trustee, Gheens Foundation

Doyle, Janice C.: assistant secretary, CUNA Mutual Group Foundation, Inc.

Doyle, L. F. Boker: trustee, Taconic Foundation

Doyle, Michael P., PhD: vice president, secretary, Research Corp.

Doyle, Robert A.: director, AMCORE Foundation

Doyle, Rosaleen J.: vice president, director, Doyle Foundation

Doyle, Terence N.: secretary, Butler Family Foundation (Patrick and Aimee); co-trustee, Heilmaier Charitable Foundation (Anna M.)

Doyle, Valentine: trustee, Valentine Foundation (Lawson)

Doyle Carter, Margaret: director, Doyle Foundation

Dragon, Robert E., MD: director, Vance Charitable Foundation (Robert C.)

Drain, Randall G.: director, Joukowsky Family Foundation

Dramis, Fran: trustee, Bell-South Foundation

Drasner, Fred: co-founder, president, chief executive officer, co-publisher, director, Daily News, L.P.

Dray, James R.: director, Schmitt Foundation (Kilian J. and Caroline F.)

Drebin, Allan I.: treasurer, director, Cheney Foundation (Elizabeth F.)

Drees, Charles F.: director, Gulf Coast Medical Foundation

Dresser, Joyce G.: trustee, Arkell Hall Foundation

Drew, Francis J.: vice president, Amcast Industrial Foundation

Drew, Helen Hall: trustee, Stackpole-Hall Foundation

Drexel, Noreen: president, trustee, McBean Charitable Trust (Alletta Morris)

Drexler, Millard S.: trustee, Gap Foundation; president, chief executive officer, director, Gap, Inc.

Drinkwater, Clover M.: assistant secretary, Anderson Foundation (NY)

Driscoll, Elizabeth S.: director, Driscoll Foundation

Driscoll, Rudolph Weyerhaeuser: vice president, director, Driscoll Foundation

Driscoll, Walter John: president, director, Driscoll Foundation

Driscoll, William P., Junior: vice president, officer, General Electric Co.

Droege, Mark E.: trustee, BellSouth Foundation

Drossman, Mitchell A.: assistant secretary, Kaufmann Foundation (Henry)

Drost, Carolyn Jill: director, Eberly Foundation

Drowota, Frank F., III: trustee, Ansley Foundation (Dantzler Bond); board member, Frist Foundation

Druckenmiller, Bruce: trustee, Plankenhorn Foundation (Harry)

Druliner, Kathryn: trustee, Cooper Foundation

Drumwright, Elenita M.: president, Memton Fund

Drumwright, Elizabeth: director, Memton Fund

Drury, Lynn E.: president, Bank of America Foundation

Drushel, William H., Jr.: trustee, Cullen Foundation (The)

Dryfoos, Jacqueline H.: chairman, director, New York Times Co. Foundation

Drymalski, Raymond Hibner: assistant treasurer, assistant secretary, Offield Family Foundation (The)

du Pont, Christopher T.: vice president, trustee, duPont Foundation (Chichester)

du Pont, Edward Bradford: vice president, trustee, Longwood Foundation;

treasurer, trustee, Welfare Foundation

du Pont, Irenee, Jr.: trustee, Crystal Trust

du Pont, Lammot Joseph: trustee, Marmot Foundation

du Pont, Miren de Amezola: trustee, Marmot Foundation

du Pont, Pete, IV: director, Bradley Foundation (Lynde and Harry)

du Pont, Willis Harrington: president, trustee, Marmot Foundation

Dubiel, Robert S.: trustee, Acushnet Foundation

Dubin, Seth Harris: director, Hebrew Technical Institute

Dubler, Robert: trustee, Young Foundation (Hugo H. and Mabel B.)

DuBose, Suzanne A.: president, Verizon Foundation

DuBose, Vivian Noble: trustee, Noble Foundation (Samuel Roberts)

Ducca, Thomas J.: treasurer, Dime Foundation

Duchossois, Craig J.: chief executive officer,

Duchossois, Dayle Paige: director, Duchossois Family Foundation

Duchossois, Kimberly: president, Duchossois Family Foundation

Duchossois, Richard Louis: chairman, chief executive officer, director; secretary, Duchossois Family Foundation

Ducommun, Robert E.: president, Ducommun and Gross Foundation

Ducommun Depeyster, Electra: vice president, treasurer, Ducommun and Gross Foundation

Dudgeon, Clair: trustee, Van Wert County Foundation

Dudley, Joan R.: assistant treasurer, Brown Foundation, Inc. (James Graham)

Dudnick, Andrew: secretary, director, Baker Street Foundation

Dudte, James: president, trustee, Young Foundation (Hugo H. and Mabel B.)

Duello, J. Donald: president, treasurer, director, Shelter Insurance Foundation

Duff, Charles F.: vice president, trustee, Gray Foundation (Garland and Agnes Taylor)

Duffell, Carol: secretary, treasurer, Semmes Foundation

Duffield, Cheryl D.: director, Duffield Family Foundation

Duffield, David A.: director, Duffield Family Foundation

Duffield, Laurie E.: director, Duffield Family Foundation

Duffield, Michael D.: director, Duffield Family Foundation

Duffy, Bernard J., Jr.: mem, McGee Foundation (MO)

Duffy, Edward W.: director, Utica National Foundation

Duffy, Michael G.: trustee at large, Raskob Foundation for Catholic Activities, Inc.

Duffy, Vivien Stiles: executive director, Rohatyn Foundation (Felix and Elizabeth)

Dugan, Allan E.: senior vice president corporate strategic service, Xerox Corp.; trustee, Xerox Foundation

Duggan, Robert D.: chairman, S&T Bancorp Charitable Foundation; chairman, chief executive officer, S&T Bancorp, Inc.

Dugger, Albia: director, Norcross Wildlife Foundation

Duhaime, William E.: pub trustee, Carpenter Foundation

Duke, Anthony Drexel, Sr.: trustee, Achelis Foundation

Duke, Robin Chandler Tippett: trustee, Packard Foundation (David and Lucile)

Duker, Brack: chief financial officer, secretary, Whitecap Foundation

Duker, Elizabeth: president, Whitecap Foundation

Dukess, A. Carleton: chair, New York Foundation

Dulaney, Jane Norton: president, Norton Foundation

Dulaney, Robert W.: vice president, Norton Foundation

Dulle, Mary: chairman, Alcon Foundation

Dullea, Charles, SJ: director, Hale Foundation (Crescent Porter)

Duman, Louis J., MD: trustee, Bonfils-Stanton Foundation

Dumas, Kevin L.: director, New Milford Savings Bank Foundation

Dumke, Edmund E.: treasurer, director, invest adv, Dumke Foundation (Ezekiel R. and Edna Wattis)

Dumke, Ezekiel R., Jr.: president, director, Dumke Foundation (Ezekiel R. and Edna Wattis)

Dumke, Valerie: assistant secretary, director, Dumke Foundation (Ezekiel R. and Edna Wattis)

Dunagan, John C.: vice president, Dunagan Foundation

Dunagan, Kathleen: secretary, Dunagan Foundation

Dunagan, Kathlyn C.: president, Dunagan Foundation

Dunbar, C. Wendell: treasurer, trustee, Towsley Foundation (Harry A. and Margaret D.)

Duncan, Anne S.: director, Duncan Foundation (L. H. and C. W.)

Duncan, Brenda: director, Duncan Foundation (L. H. and C. W.)

Duncan, C. W., III: director, Duncan Foundation (L. H. and C. W.)

Duncan, Charles William, Jr.: chairman, director, Duncan Foundation (L. H. and C. W.)

Duncan, George T.: trustee, Franklin Foundation Inc. (John and Mary)

Duncan, John D., Esq.: trustee, Davies Benevolent Fund (Edward H.)

Duncan, John H., Jr.: director, Duncan Foundation (L. H. and C. W.)

Duncan, John H., Sr.: president, director, Duncan Foundation (L. H. and C. W.)

Duncan, Sam: president, Ralph's-Food 4 Less Foundation; president, chief executive officer, Ralph's Grocery Co.

Duncan, William G., Jr.: trustee, Gheens Foundation

Dunckel, Jeanette Maddux: director, Haigh-Scatena Foundation; trustee, Zellerbach Family Fund

Dunford, Betty P.: vice president, trustee, Cooke Foundation

Dunlap, Richard Lowell: senior program officer, Kresge Foundation

Dunlop, Joy S.: president, director, Dell Foundation (Hazel)

Dunmire, Cyril C., Jr.: director, Stabler Foundation (Donald B. and Dorothy L.)

Dunn, Edward K., Jr.: director, Baltimore Equitable Insurance Foundation; treasurer, trustee, Warfield Memorial Fund (Anna Emory)

Dunn, Harry E.: vice president, Treakle Foundation (J. Edwin)

Dunn, Norma F.: president, El Paso Corporate Foundation; vice president investor & public relations, El Paso Corp.

Dunn, Peter M., Esq.: secretary, general counsel, Chapman Charitable Corp. (Howard and Bess)

Dunnington, Patricia: trustee, Sprague Educational and Charitable Foundation (Seth)

Dunnington, Walter Grey, Jr.: trustee, Sullivan Foundation (Algernon Sydney)

Dunstan, Christopher T.: member, director, Oishei Foundation (The John R.)

Dunton, Gary C.: president, chief operating officer, MBIA, Inc.

Dunworth, Gerald J.: treasurer, director, Palisades Educational Foundation

Duplessie, David: corporator, Oak Grove School

DuPont, Augustus I.: vice president, general counsel, secretary, Crane Co.; vice president, secretary, director, Crane Foundation

DuPont, Elizabeth Lee: vice president, Good Samaritan

DuPont, Lea C.: vice president, Good Samaritan

Duquette, Ernest A.: trustee, American Optical Foundation

Durand, H. Whitney: treasurer, trustee, Tonya Memorial Foundation

Durbin, Vaughn: secretary, Colt Foundation (James J.)

Durden, J. C.: vice president, director, Tractor & Equipment Co. Foundation

Durein, Nancy: trustee, AT&T National Pro-Am Youth Fund

Durham, Earl: vice chair, trustee, Hazen Foundation (Edward W.)

Durham, Shirley: contributions manager, Ford Motor Co. Fund

Durkin, Sean: chief financial officer, Winter Construction Co.

Duronio, Carolyn D.: secretary, Pittsburgh Child Guidance Foundation

Durrett, Joseph P.: chief executive officer, Broderbund LLC

Durrett, William E.: senior chairman, American Fidelity Assurance Co.; president, American Fidelity Corp. Founders Fund

Dury, Joseph D., Jr.: director, Staunton Farm Foundation

Dutcher, Judi: president Minnesota community, Bigelow Foundation (F. R.)

Dutton, J. C.: board of directors, Meadwestvaco Corp. Foundation

Dutton, Uriel E.: trustee, Anderson Foundation (M. D.)

Duvick, Dave: secretary, Ecolab Foundation

Evans, Nancy H.: director, Guaranty Bank and Trust Co. Charitable Trust

Evans, Richard G.: secretary, Metris Companies Foundation

Evans, Richard W., Jr.: chairman, chief executive officer, Frost National Bank

Evans, Robert E.: director, McDonough Foundation (Bernard)

Evans, Robert Sheldon: chairman, Crane Co.; chairman, director, Crane Foundation

Evans, Thomas H.: trustee, Henson Foundation (Richard A.)

Evarts, William Maxwell, Jr.: director, Clark Foundation (NY)

Everbach, O. George: director, Kimberly-Clark Foundation

Everett, C. Taylor: trustee, Gray Foundation (Garland and Agnes Taylor)

Everett, Wendy: director, Sierra Health Foundation

Ewald, Carolyn T.: vice president, Ewald Foundation (H. T.)

Ewald, Holly: vice president, Ewald Foundation (H. T.)

Ewald, John Clifford: vice president, Ewald Foundation (H. T.)

Ewald, Kristi: vice president, Ewald Foundation (H. T.)

Ewend, Kurt: trustee, Wickes Foundation (Harvey Randall)

Ewing, George H.: director, Chamiza Foundation

Ewing, Stephen E.: trustee, Skillman Foundation

Eychaner, Barbara: director, WPWR-TV Channel 50 Foundation

Eychaner, Fred: president, WPWR-TV Channel 50 Foundation

F

Fabens, Andrew Lawrie, III: assistant secretary, Smith Foundation (Kelvin and Eleanor)

Facini, Deborah L.: trustee, Kunkel Foundation (John Crain)

Fad, Otto C.: vice president, Crestlea Foundation

Fadim, Melissa Sage Booth: chairwoman, president, treasurer, trustee, Sage Foundation

Faechner, Allen D.: trustee, Boe Brothers Foundation

Fahey, Christine: assistant secretary, Schering-Plough Foundation

Fahrenkopf, Frank Joseph, Jr.: trustee, Wiegand Foundation (E. L.)

Fair, F. Doyle: trustee, Hansen Foundation (Dane G.)

Fair, Jewell L.: secretary, Landegger Charitable Foundation

Fair, Russell B.: vice president pharmacy operations, Giant Food, Inc.

Fairbanks, J. Nelson: president, chief executive officer, director, United States Sugar Corp.

Fairbanks, John: senior vice president, New England Business Service

Faircloth, Karen E.: secretary, treasurer, Stuart Charitable Foundation (G. B.)

Faith, Marshall E.: chairman, director, Scoular Co.; trustee, Scoular Foundation

Faith, Richard G.: president, director, Faith Foundation

Falahee, William: controller, Kaplan Fund (J. M.)

Falberg, Kathryn E.: senior vice president finance, chief financial officer, Amgen, Inc.

Falcone, Tasha A.: director, Allyn Foundation

Falconer, Barbara E.: president, Stuart Charitable Foundation (G. B.)

Falconer, Keith D.: director, Stuart Charitable Foundation (G. B.)

Falencki, Karin: trustee, Jurzykowski Foundation (Alfred)

Fales, Nancy C.: trustee, Laurel Foundation

Falk, Harvey L.: member grantmaking committee, Claiborne Foundation (Liz); president, vice chairman, Liz Claiborne, Inc.

Falk, Sigo: chairman, Falk Medical Fund (Maurice)

Falk, Thomas J.: chairman, president, chief executive officer, Kimberly-Clark Corp.

Fallon, Elena: director, Andrews McMeel Universal Foundation

Fallon, Gail A.: secretary, director, Dell Foundation (Hazel)

Fallon, James P.: vice president, trustee, Frueauff Foundation (Charles A.)

Falsgraf, William Wendell: secretary, trustee, Frohring Foundation (Paul and Maxine)

Fanning, Karl P.: trustee, Frueauff Foundation (Charles A.)

Fanning, Katherine Woodruff: trustee, Mott Foundation (Charles Stewart)

Fanton, Jonathan Foster: president, chief executive officer, MacArthur Foundation (John D. and Catherine T.); trustee, Rockefeller Brothers Fund, Inc.

Farabee, Mary Margaret: director, ECG Foundation

Faraci, John V.: director, International Paper Co. Foundation

Farash, Marian M.: trustee, Farash Charitable Foundation (Max and Marian)

Farash, Max M.: trustee, Farash Charitable Foundation (Max and Marian)

Farkouh, Fred C.: treasurer, Dickler Family Foundation

Farley, James Duncan: chairman, trustee, Hartford Foundation, Inc. (The John A.)

Farley, Terrence Michael: director, Harriman Foundation (Gladys and Roland)

Farmer, Charles Albert: trustee, National Grange Mutual Charitable Trust

Farrar, Elizabeth S.: director, Memton Fund

Farrar, Marjorie M.: vice president, Memton Fund

Farrar-Wellman, Olivia: director, Memton Fund

Farrell, Bruce C.: off, Seherr-Thoss Foundation

Farrell, W. James: chairman, chief executive officer, Illinois Tool Works, Inc.

Farrington, Hugh G.: president, chief executive officer, director, Hannaford Brothers Co.

Farrington, Jerry S.: director, Hoblitzelle Foundation

Farrow, William M.: vice president, Bank One Foundation

Farver, Charles: vice president, Kuyper Foundation (Peter H. and E. Lucille Gaass); chairman, Pella Corp.; treasurer, director, Pella Rolscreen Foundation

Farver, Joan Kuyper: president, director, Kuyper Foundation (Peter H. and E. Lucille Gaass); chairman emeritus, director, Pella Corp.; director, Pella Rolscreen Foundation

Fasenmyer, Janet: controller, Metal Industries, Inc.

Fasken, F. Andrew: vice president, Fasken Foundation

Fasken, Steven P.: trustee, Fasken Foundation

Fast, Eric C.: president, chief executive officer, Crane Co.; director, Crane Foundation

Fatone, Joseph A.: director, Eastern Savings and Loan Foundation

Fatzinger, Walter Robert, Jr.: director, Loughran Foundation (Mary and Daniel)

Faude, Janet Bailey: assistant treasurer, second vice president, Bailey Family Foundation (William O. and Carole P.)

Faust, Drew G.: trustee, Mellon Foundation (Andrew W.)

Faust, Mary Lou: trustee, Decker Foundation (Dr. G. Clifford and Florence B.)

Faust, Michael L.: administrator, Kiewit Companies Foundation

Faust, Robert J.: secretary, treasurer, director, Duncan Foundation (L. H. and C. W.)

Favret, John A.: member distribution committee, Bruening Foundation (Eva L. and Joseph M.)

Fawcett, Daniel W.: trustee, Thompson Trust (Thomas)

Fawley, Dan: assistant treasurer, Reynolds Tobacco Company Foundation (R. J.)

Fay, Lawrence: director, Carvel Foundation (Thomas and Agnes)

Fay, Patricia R.: director, Lurie Foundation (Louis R.)

Fay, Paul B., Jr.: trustee, Odell Fund (Robert Stewart and Helen Pfeiffer)

Fay, Ray M.: trustee, Alexander Edwards Trust (Margaret)

Fayard, Gary P.: treasurer, director, Coca-Cola Foundation

Fazendeiro, Anne: trustee, Grimshaw-Gudewicz Charitable Foundation

Fazzolari, Salvatore D.: treasurer, secretary, trustee, Harsco Corp. Fund

Fearn, Jeff: section, treasurer, Koret Foundation

Fearon, Janet A.: executive director, trustee, Newcombe Foundation (Charlotte W.)

Fearon, Robert H., Jr.: vice president, Chapman Charitable Corp. (Howard and Bess)

Feather-Francis, Carol: vice president, trustee, Baughman Foundation

Featherman, Sandra, PhD: vice president, director, Fels Fund (Samuel S.)

Federal, Joseph L.: director, Price Foundation (Lucien B. and Katherine E.)

Fee, Allen K.: trustee, Davis Foundation (James A. and Juliet L.)

Feeney, Christine: grantmaking associate, Rice Charitable Foundation (Albert W.)

Feeney, Thomas J., Esq.: trustee, Sandy Foundation (George H.)

Feese Guyette, Phillis: trustee, Plankenhorn Foundation (Harry)

Fegan, Ann B.: president, Reidler Foundation

Fegan, Howard D.: trustee, Reidler Foundation

Fegan, John H.: trustee, Reidler Foundation

Fehsenfeld, Frank B.: vice president, treasurer, Fehsenfeld Charitable Foundation (Frank B. and Virginia V.)

Fehsenfeld, John A.: trustee, Fehsenfeld Charitable Foundation (Frank B. and Virginia V.)

Fehsenfeld, Thomas V.: trustee, Fehsenfeld Charitable Foundation (Frank B. and Virginia V.)

Fehsenfeld, Virginia V.: president, secretary, Fehsenfeld Charitable Foundation (Frank B. and Virginia V.)

Fehsenfeld, William S.: trustee, Fehsenfeld Charitable Foundation (Frank B. and Virginia V.)

Fehsenfeld Smith, Nancy: trustee, Fehsenfeld Charitable Foundation (Frank B. and Virginia V.)

Feidner, Robert J.: fin officer, Jewish Healthcare Foundation

Feinblatt, Eugene M.: president, treasurer, Unger Foundation (Aber D.)

Feinblatt, John: director, Unger Foundation (Aber D.)

Feinblatt, Marjorie W.: director, Unger Foundation (Aber D.)

Feinerman, James V.: trustee, Lingnan Foundation

Feinstein, Alan Shawn: president, director, Feinstein Foundation

Feinstein, Karen Wolk, PhD: president, Jewish Healthcare Foundation

Feintech, Evelyn M.: director, Feintech Family Foundation

Feintech, Irving: vice president, Feintech Family Foundation

Feintech, Norman: president, Feintech Family Foundation

Feith, Susan: vice president, executive director, Mead Witter Foundation, Inc.

Fejes, Frank S.: director, Hugoton Foundation

Felderstein, Sandra: distribution trustee, Schwab-Rosenhouse Memorial Foundation

Feldman, Roberta: trustee, Graham Foundation for Advanced Studies in the Fine Arts

Fella, Leon: director, Schmitt Foundation (Kilian J. and Caroline F.)

Fella, Robert H.: president, Schmitt Foundation (Kilian J. and Caroline F.)

Feller, James R.: secretary, director, Hoch Foundation (Charles H.)

Feller, Nancy P.: assistant secretary Assoc Gen Counc, Ford Foundation

Feller, Robert J.: vice president, Shelter Mutual Insurance Co.

Fellheimer, Ronald K.: trustee, Yost Trust (J. Paul)

Felsinger, Donald E.: president, chief executive officer, Sempra Energy

Fenlon, Thomas B., Esq.: trustee, Schieffelin Residuary Trust (Sarah I.)

Fennessy, Jacquie: executive director, Patron Saints Foundation

Fentin, Gary S.: trustee, Shatz, Schwartz & Fentin Charitable Foundation; senior partner, Shatz, Schwartz & Fentin PC

Fenton, Elinor P.: secretary, director, Fenton Foundation

Fenton, Frank M.: treasurer, director, Fenton Foundation

Fenton, Thomas K.: vice president, director, Fenton Foundation

Fenton, Wilmer C.: president, director, Fenton Foundation

Fergerson, Anne: contact, Davis Foundation (Joe C.)

Ferguson, James M., III: trustee, Trees Charitable Trust (Edith L.)

Ferguson, Parris R.: director, Aldridge Charitable and Educational Trust (Tom S. and Marye Kate)

Ferguson, Sanford Barnett: president, trustee, Scaife Family Foundation

Ferkauf, Estelle: trustee, Ferkauf Foundation (Eugene and Estelle)

Ferkauf, Eugene: trustee, Ferkauf Foundation (Eugene and Estelle)

Ferland, E. James: chairman, president, chief executive officer, Public Service Electric & Gas Co.

Fernandes, Alvin C., Jr.: secretary, director, Ayres Foundation

Fernandez, Michael: president, CIGNA Foundation

Fernandez-Palmer, Lydia: director, Patron Saints Foundation

Ferranti, Anthony L.: comptroller, Pforzheimer Foundation, Inc. (The Carl and Lily)

Ferraro, Jim: chief financial officer, Giant Food Stores

Ferrasci, Frank E.: treasurer, Harden Foundation

Ferruccio, Anthony: director, Washington Group Foundation, Inc.

Fetters, David: vice president, director, Midcontinent Media Foundation

Fetzer, Carol J.: fdn admin, secretary, trustee, Carolyn Foundation; assistant secretary, Southways Foundation

Feurt, Suzanne L.: program officer, Mott Foundation (Charles Stewart)

Fey, Eugene E.: treasurer, trustee, Pinkerton Foundation

Fick, Jeffrey D.: vice president, HON Industries Charitable Foundation

Fidel, Arthur: dist committee member, Morris Charitable Trust (Charles M.)

Fiedl, Arthur: dist committee member, Morris Charitable Trust (Charles M.)

Field, Arthur Norman: director, Brookdale Foundation

Field, Benjamin R., III: senior vice president, chief financial officer, treasurer, Bemis Company, Inc.

Field, Marshall, IV: director, Field Foundation of Illinois

Fields, Candice: Distribution trustee, Schwab-Rosenhouse Memorial Foundation

Fields, Curtland E.: trustee, Turrell Fund

Fields, Gregory F.: secretary, duPont Foundation (Chichester)

Fields, Laura Kemper: mem disbursement comm, Oppenstein Brothers Foundation

Fields, Randolph: treasurer, Farwell Foundation (Drusilla)

Fierce, Hughlyn F.: trustee, J.P. Morgan Chase Foundation

Fiery, Michael A.: mem, Teubert Charitable Trust (James H. and Alice)

Fies, Larry R.: chief financial officer, treasurer, Irvine Foundation (The James)

Fiez, Terri: manager community relations, CUNA Mutual Group; executive director, CUNA Mutual Group Foundation, Inc.

Fife, Francis: vice president, trustee, Perry Foundation

Fife, Jesse, Junior: trustee, Pittsburgh Child Guidance Foundation

Fifield, Helen D.: director, Memorial Foundation for the Blind

Figgie, Harry E., Jr.: president, trustee, Figgie Educational Foundation

Figgie, Nancy F.: assistant secretary, trustee, Figgie Educational Foundation

Fikes, Amy L.: vice president, trustee, Fikes Foundation (Leland)

Fikes, Lee: president, treasurer, trustee, chairman, Fikes Foundation (Leland)

Fillius, Milton Franklin, Jr.: chairman, director, Drown Foundation (Joseph)

Fillo, Stephen W.: director, Markle Foundation (John and Mary R.)

Finch, Edward Ridley, Jr.: general counsel, trustee, St. Giles Foundation

Finch, Thomas Austin, Jr.: manager, Finch Foundation (Thomas Austin)

Findlay, Marjorie M.: director, Claneil Foundation

Findlay, Robert W.: trustee, Morrison Charitable Trust (Pauline A. and George R.)

Findley, Barry B.: trustee, Sturgis Charitable and Educational Trust (AR) (Roy and Christine)

Fine, Roger Seth: vice president, general counsel, Johnson & Johnson; president, Johnson & Johnson Family of Companies Contribution Fund

Fineman, Stanley J.: partner, Wilkes, Artis, Hedrick & Lane; vice president, director, Wilkes, Artis, Hedrick & Lane Foundation

Fink, David: president, Auburn Foundry

Fink, Harold: secretary, Fink Foundation (NY)

Fink, Richard H.: director, Koch Foundation, Inc. (Fred C. and Mary R.)

Fink, William E.: chairman, Auburn Foundry; trustee, Auburn Foundry Foundation

Finkbeiner, James V.: president, trustee, chairman board, Wickes Foundation (Harvey Randall)

Finkelstein, Bernard: trustee, Altman Foundation

Finkelstein, Michael: assistant treasurer, Fisher Foundation

Finkle, H. Michael: director, Vermilion Healthcare Foundation

Finkle, Leon: trustee, City National Bank Foundation

Finlayson, Frank: director, Washington Group Foundation, Inc.

Finlayson, John L.: vice president finance & administration, Susquehanna-Pfaltzgraff Co.

Finley, Louis M., Jr.: comm mem, Smith, Jr. Foundation (M. W.)

Finley, Warren: trustee, Argyros Foundation

Finneran, Laurey: trustee, LEF Foundation

Finney, Graham Stanley: trustee, Seybert Institution for Poor Boys and Girls (Adam and Maria Sarah)

Finney, Jon: vice chairmanr, Van Buren Foundation

Finney, Pat: trustee, Young Foundation (Bill B.)

Finocchiaro, Linda W.: director, Wrather Family Foundation

Fiola, Janet S.: senior vice president human resources, Medtronic, Inc.

Fiorani, R. P.: vice president, director, Square D Foundation

Fiorella, Peter J., Jr.: trustee, Statler Foundation

Firestine, Larry: adv, Ritter Charitable Trust (George and Mary)

Firman, Pamela H.: president, Firman Fund

Firman, Royal: trustee, Firman Fund

Firman, Stephanie: trustee, Firman Fund

First, Carole P. Bailey: vice president, treasurer, Bailey Family Foundation (William O. and Carole P.)

Firth, Edmee de Montmollin: executive director, Dreyfus Foundation (Jean and Louis)

Firth, Katherine V.: vice president, Dreyfus Foundation (Jean and Louis)

Firth, Nicholas L. D.: president, Dreyfus Foundation (Jean and Louis)

Fischbach, Beatrice: secretary, Fischbach Foundation

Fischer, Billie A.: vice president, Wynn Foundation

Fischer, Diane: corporate secretary, Atran Foundation, Inc.

Fischer, Duane A.: president, chief executive officer, director, Scoular Co.; trustee, Scoular Foundation

Fischer, F. Conrad: trustee, Fischer Foundation (Sonja and F. Conrad)

Fischer, Richard Lawrence: director, Alcoa Foundation; executive vice president, chairman counsel, Alcoa Inc.

Fischer, Sonja: trustee, Fischer Foundation (Sonja and F. Conrad)

Fish, Brian: director, Greenville Foundation

Fish, Eugene C., Esq.: vice president, Independence Foundation; trustee, Reidler Foundation

Fish, John: trustee, Stauffer Communications Foundation

Fish, Lawrence K.: trustee, Citizens Charitable Foundation; chairman, chief executive officer, president, Citizens Financial Group, Inc.

Fish-Sadin, Susanne: director, secretary, Greenville Foundation

Fishbein, Donna Jaffe: trustee, Jaffe Foundation

Fisher, David I.: trustee, Getty Trust (J. Paul)

Fisher, David J.: director, Chicago Board of Trade Foundation

Fisher, David S.: president, director, Young Foundation (Irvin L.)

Fisher, Donald George: director, Gap Foundation; founder, chairman, director, Gap, Inc.

Fisher, Doris F.: director, Gap Foundation

Fisher, Francis M., Jr.: trustee, Gulf Power Foundation

Fisher, Frederick E.: secretary, director, Doyle Foundation

Fisher, Grace Pond: trustee, Pond Foundation (C. Northrop Pond and Alethea Marder)

Fisher, Hinda N.: president, treasurer, Fisher Foundation

Fisher, John Wesley: president, director, Ball Brothers Foundation

Fisher, Kenneth: secretary, treasurer, director, Scurlock Foundation

Fisher, Robert J.: vice president, Gap Foundation

Fisher, W. S.: vice president, director, member, Cannon Foundation, Inc. (The)

Fishman, Janet: contact, Beneficia Foundation

Fishman, Jay: director, chairman, St. Paul Companies Inc. Foundation

Fishman, Joseph L.: vice president, director, treasurer, secretary, Moses Fund, Inc. (Henry and Lucy)

Fishman, Steven S.: chairman, president, chief executive officer, Pamida, Inc.

Fisk, Robert D.: trustee, Seabury Foundation

Fiske, George F., Jr.: member advisory committee, Weezie Foundation

Fitz-Gerald, David: treasurer, Carris Corp. Foundation; chief financial officer, Carris Reels

Fitzgerald, Dennis M.: vice president, secretary, director, Vernon Foundation (Miles Hodsdon)

Fitzgerald, J. T.: vice president, Price Foundation (Lucien B. and Katherine E.)

FitzGerald, John R.: director, Eastern Savings and Loan Foundation

Fitzgerald, Margaret Boles: director, new programs and major grants committee, Luce Foundation (Henry)

Fitzgerald, Michael C.: director, Vernon Foundation (Miles Hodsdon)

FitzGibbon, David J.: president, chief executive officer, Bardes Corp.

Fitzpatrick, Fenton J.: trustee, McShain Charities (John)

Fitzpatrick, Jack: director, Gellert Foundation (Carl Gellert and Celia Berta)

Fitzpatrick, Jane P.: chairman, chief executive officer, treasurer, Country Curtains, Inc.; chairman, High Meadow Foundation

Fitzpatrick, John H.: president, High Meadow Foundation

Fitzsimmons, Hugh A., Jr.: trustee, Halsell Foundation (Ewing)

Fitzsimmons, Mark D.: associate director fellows program, MacArthur Foundation (John D. and Catherine T.)

Fitzsimonds, Roger Leon: chairman emeritus, Firstar Foundation, Inc.

FitzSimons, Dennis J.: director, McCormick Tribune Foundation (Robert R.)

FitzSimons, John S.: secretary, Dyson Foundation

Fiume, Orest J.: vice president finance, chief financial officer, Wiremold Co.

Fix, Duard: trustee, Kitzmiller/Bales Trust

Fizdale, Richard B.: chairman, chief executive officer, director, Burnett Co. (Leo)

Fizer, Don: secretary, director, Mathers Charitable Foundation (G. Harold and Leila Y.)

Flad, Eleanor Beecher: chairman, Beecher Foundation (Florence Simon)

Flad, Erle L.: director, Beecher Foundation (Florence Simon)

Flad, Ward Beecher: director, Beecher Foundation (Florence Simon)

Flaherty, William: president, Polaroid Foundation

Flake, Floyd Harold: director, Fannie Mae Foundation

Flam, Jack: director, Dedalus Foundation

Flanagan, Edward P.: secretary, Price Foundation (Lucien B. and Katherine E.)

Flanagan, Sheila: treasurer, Price Foundation (Lucien B. and Katherine E.)

Flanagin, Neil: director, Scholl Foundation (Dr.)

Flanders, Grame L.: trustee, Acushnet Foundation

Flanigan, Peter Magnus: trustee, Olin Foundation (John M.)

Flaville, Victoria K.: vice president, secretary, Connelly Foundation

Flaws, James B.: executive vice president, chief financial officer, director, Corning Inc.

Fleischer, Henry: trustee, Carls Foundation

Fleischmann, Ruth H.: executive director, Wilson Foundation (Marie C. and Joseph C.)

Fleishhacker, David: president, Fleishhacker Foundation

Fleishhacker, Edie: director, Fleishhacker Foundation

Fleishhacker, Mortimer, III: treasurer, Fleishhacker Foundation

Fleishhacker, William: director, Fleishhacker Foundation

Fleishman, Ernest B.: first vice president, Robinson Fund (Maurice R.)

Fleishman, Joel Lawrence: director, Markle Foundation (John and Mary R.)

Fleming, Barbara Jane: vice president, director, Dettman Foundation (Leroy E.)

Fleming, David, MD: director global health strategies program, Gates Foundation (Bill and Melinda)

Fleming, David D.: president, Mellinger Educational Foundation (Edward Arthur)

Fleming, Richard Harrison: executive vice president, chief financial officer, USG Corp.

Fleming, Samuel C.: director, Commonwealth Fund (The)

Fleming-McGrath, Lucy: trustee, Homeland Foundation (NY)

Fletcher, Allen W.: chairman, trustee, Fletcher Foundation; trustee, Stoddard Charitable Trust

Fletcher, Earnest P., Jr.: treasurer, trustee, Robinson-Broadhurst Foundation

Fletcher, Mary F.: trustee, Fletcher Foundation

Fletcher, Maureen T.: assistant secretary, Hayden Foundation (Charles)

Fletcher, Nina M.: trustee, Fletcher Foundation

Fletcher, Patricia A.: trustee, Fletcher Foundation

Fletcher, Warner S.: secretary, trustee, Alden Trust (George I.); secretary, treasurer, trustee, Fletcher Foundation; chairman, trustee, Stoddard Charitable Trust; director, Wyman-Gordon Foundation

Flippin, Doreen A.: grants administrator, Davis Foundations (Arthur Vining)

Flood, Al: chairman, chief executive officer, CIBC World Markets

Floren, Kari: foundation administrator, DeCamp Foundation (Ira W.)

Flores-New, Fernando: trustee, Gerber Foundation

Florie, Walter M., Jr.: president, Miller Foundation (Earl B. and Loraine H.)

Florino, Joanne V.: executive director, Park Foundation

Florio, Carl A.: president, chief executive officer, Hudson River Bancorp, Inc.; director, Hudson River Bancorp Inc. Foundation

Florio, Thomas: chairman, president, chief executive officer, director, New Yorker Magazine (The)

Flournoy, Houston I.: vice president, Jones Foundation (Fletcher)

Flower, Allen E.: chief financial officer, vice president, COMSAT International

Flower, Walter C., III: secretary, German Protestant Orphan Asylum Association Foundation

Flowers, Robert: board of directors, Washington Mutual Foundation

Flowers, Thomas J.: president, Hultquist Foundation

Flowers, Wilford: director, Wright Foundation (Lola)

Floyd, James M., Sr.: trustee, Martin Charitable Trust (Margaret Lee)

Floyd, Joseph H.: vice president, director, Midcontinent Media Foundation; president, director, Midcontinent Media, Inc.

Fluor, John Robert, II: vice president corporate & public affairs, Fluor Corp.; president, trustee, Fluor Foundation

Flynn, Edward M.: trustee, Statler Foundation

Flynn, James T.: executive vice president, chief operating officer, Long Island Lighting Co.

Flynn, Joan B.: secretary, Barnes Foundation

Focht, Jack: mem, Kansas Health Foundation

Foege, William H., MD: director, MacArthur Foundation (John D. and Catherine T.)

Foerster, Barbara: director, Aldridge Charitable and Educational Trust (Tom S. and Marye Kate)

Foerstner, George C.: director, Hall-Perrine Foundation

Foley, Eileen D.: trustee, Foundation for Seacoast Health

Foley, Janet B.: director, Memorial Foundation for the Blind

Foley, Karen: president, director, CNA Foundation

Foley, William: vice chairman, Chicago Title and Trust Co. Foundation

Folger, Peter: director, McBean Family Foundation

Fondren, Bentley B.: board of directors, Fondren Foundation

Fondren, Leland T.: chairman, Fondren Foundation

Fondren, Robert E.: board of directors, Fondren Foundation

Fondren, Walter W., III: board of directors, Fondren Foundation

Fondren, Walter W., IV: board of directors, Fondren Foundation

Fonseca, Caio: trustee, Kaplan Fund (J. M.)

Fonseca, Elizabeth K.: trustee, Kaplan Fund (J. M.)

Fonseca, Isabel: trustee, Kaplan Fund (J. M.)

Fonseca, Quina: trustee, Kaplan Fund (J. M.)

Fonstad, Eric: assistant secretary, Harnischfeger Industries Foundation

Fontaine, George R.: trustee, Lyndhurst Foundation

Fontaine, John C.: chairman, trustee, Kress Foundation (Samuel H.)

Fonteyne, Herman J.: president, chief executive officer, director, Ensign-Bickford Industries

Fooks, Thomas H., V: trustee, Fair Play Foundation

Foord, Deborah C.: officer, Seherr-Thoss Foundation

Forbes, Dorothy L.: executive director, Cabot Corp. Foundation

Forbes, F. Murray, Jr.: trustee, Winthrop Trust (Clara B.)

Forbes, Orcilia Zuniga: trustee, Meyer Memorial Trust

Ford, Alfred B.: trustee, Ford Motor Co. Fund

Ford, Cynthia N.: trustee, McGregor Fund

Ford, Daniel: vice chairman, Ford Meter Box Foundation

Ford, Edsel B., II: president, director, member, Ford II Fund (Edsel B.); president, trustee, mem, Ford II Fund (Henry); trustee, Skillman Foundation

Ford, Frank I., Jr.: cfo, secretary, treasurer, director, Arkelian Foundation (Ben H. and Gladys)

Ford, Joanne C.: president, director, ONDEO Nalco Foundation

Ford, Josephine Clay: president, trustee, mem, Ford Fund (Walter and Josephine)

Ford, Martha F.: trustee, Firestone, Jr. Foundation (Harvey); trustee, mem, Ford Fund (William and Martha)

Ford, Michael C.: trustee, The MBNA Foundation

Ford, Richard: secretary, Oleson Foundation

Ford, Richard Edmond: vice president, Daywood Foundation

Ford, Susan B.: trustee, Spahr Family Foundation

Ford, Thomas A.: trustee, Spahr Family Foundation

Ford, Virginia: trustee, Agrilink Foods/Pro-Fac Foundation

Ford, William Clay, Jr.: chairman, chief executive officer, Ford Motor Co.

Ford, William Clay, Sr.: president, trustee, mem, Ford Fund (William and Martha)

Fordyce, Michael J.: director, Grinnell Mutual Group Foundation; chairman, director, Grinnell Mutual Reinsurance Co.

Foreman, Robert B.: vice president, trustee, SPX Foundation

Forer, Lois G.: vice president, trustee, Seybert Institution for Poor Boys and Girls (Adam and Maria Sarah)

Forkner, Joanne S.: vice president, Jockey Hollow Foundation

Forlini, Rina: secretary, Macy, Jr. Foundation (Josiah)

Formica, Mark J.: trustee, Citizens Charitable Foundation; vice president, director, Citizens Financial Group, Inc.

Formisano, Roger: vice president, United Wisconsin Services Foundation

Forrester, Margaretta: co-trustee, Van Evera Foundation (Dewitt)

Fors, Richard D.: director, Oishei Foundation (The John R.)

Forsyte, Carol: assistant secretary, Motorola Foundation

Forsyth, Stephen C.: senior vice president finance & administration, chief financial officer, Hexcel Corp.

Forsythe, Carl S., III: trustee, de Coizart Perpetual Charitable Trust (Sarah K.)

Forsythe, John G.: vice president tax and public affairs, Ecolab, Inc.

Fort, John F., III: secretary, trustee, Brown Foundation

Forte, D. A.: vice president, Johns Manville Fund

Forte, Linda: director, Comerica Charitable Foundation

Fortier, Albert M.: trustee, Thompson Trust (Thomas)

Fortson, Benjamin J.: trustee, Burnett Foundation (The)

Foshee, D. L.: trustee, Halliburton Foundation, Inc.

Foshee, Douglas L.: president, chief executive officer, El Paso Corp.

Foskett, Nettie: admin, Prospect Hill Foundation

Fosmark, Mike: member administrative committee, Swanson Family Foundation, Inc. (Dr. W. C.)

Foster, Barbara: trustee, Young Foundation (Bill B.)

Foster, Charles E.: director, SBC Foundation

Foster, D. S.: secretary, Eden Hall Foundation

Foster, David G.: vice president, corporate controller, New England Business Service

Foster, Diana: trustee, Stranahan Foundation

Foster, Evelyn W.: trustee, Foster Foundation

Foster, F. Jay: acct, Hegeler II Foundation (Julius W.)

Foster, Howard K., MD: member, Staunton Farm Foundation

Foster, J. R.: trustee, Foster Charitable Trust

Foster, Jay L.: trustee, Foster Charitable Trust

Foster, Joe C., Jr.: secretary, director, Abrams Foundation (Talbert and Leota)

Foster, Karen C.: secretary, treasurer, Sierra Pacific Resources Charitable Foundation

Foster, Lee B.: trustee, Foster Charitable Trust; membership, Foster Co. Charitable Trust (L.B.); president, chief executive officer, director, Foster Co. (L.B.)

Foster, Louise M.: chief financial officer, Penn Foundation (William)

Foster, Michael G., Jr.: director, Foster Foundation

Foster, Michael G., Sr.: trustee, Foster Foundation

Foster, Richard N.: director, Keck Foundation (W. M.)

Foster, Tyler H.: director, East Cambridge Savings Charitable Foundation

Foti, Samuel J.: president, chief executive officer, MONY Foundation; president, chief operating officer, director, MONY Group, Inc.

Foulkrod, Fred A.: vice president, treasurer, Plankenhorn Foundation (Harry)

Fountain, W. Frank, Jr.: vice president government affairs, DaimlerChrysler AG; president, DaimlerChrysler Corp. Fund

Fournier, Lucinda: trustee, Day Foundation (Willametta K.); director, Keck Foundation (W. M.)

Fowler, Adrian: director, Wright Foundation (Lola)

Fowler, Elizabeth P.: treasurer, Park Foundation

Fowler, Fred J.: group president, Energy Transmission, Duke Energy Corp.

Fowler, Robert F., III: trustee, Arnold Fund

Fox, Bernard Michael: trustee, Hartford Courant Foundation

Fox, Daryl K.: admin, J&L Specialty Steel Charitable Foundation

Fox, Eric R.: trustee, Farash Charitable Foundation (Max and Marian)

Fox, Jerry D.: secretary, treasurer, director, Journal-Gazette Foundation, Inc.

Fox, Joseph Carter: chairman, president, chief executive officer, Chesapeake Corp.

Fox, Lewis M.: director, Piper Foundation (Minnie Stevens)

Foy, Douglas J.: treasurer, assistant secretary, director, Ball Brothers Foundation; treasurer, assistant secretary, Ball Foundation (George and Frances)

Fraedrich, David S.: director, Baird Brothers Co. Foundation

Fraenkel, Fabian I.: director, Kline Foundation (Charles and Figa)

Fraenkel, George Kessler: treasurer, Atran Foundation, Inc.

Fraher, Paula J.: corporate initiatives executive, Bank of America Foundation

Fraim, Martha B.: trustee, Berry Foundation (Loren M.)

Fraim, William L.: trustee, Berry Foundation (Loren M.)

France, Donald R.: trustee, Lee Scholarship Fund Trust (Whilma B.)

Franceschelli, Anthony D.: vice president, Emerson Foundation, Inc. (Fred L.)

Francis, Cheryl A.: executive vice president, chief financial officer, R.R. Donnelley & Sons Co.

Francis, David V.: director, executive committee, Francis Families Foundation

Francis, Frank: trustee, Ghidotti Foundation

Francis, J. Scott: director, executive committee,

Francis Families Foundation

Francis, John B.: director, honorary chairman, Francis Families Foundation

Francis, Mary Harris: director, honorary vice chairman, Francis Families Foundation

Francis, R. Lewis: vice president, chief financial officer; secretary, treasurer, Old Dominion Box Co. Foundation

Franco, Francisco Gomez: president, director, Clover Foundation

Frank, Dennis D.: director, Frank Family Foundation (A. J.)

Frank, J. T.: director, Frank Family Foundation (A. J.)

Frank, John V.: president, trustee, Morgan Foundation (Burton D.)

Frank, Michael J.: committee partner, vice president, City National Bank & Trust Co.

Frank, Paul C.: vice president, director, Chamiza Foundation

Frank, Seth E.: trustee, Lurcy Charitable and Educational Trust (Georges)

Frank, Stanley J., Jr.: vice president, trustee, Dater Foundation (Charles H.)

Frank, Stephen E.: president, chief operating officer, director, Edison International

Frankel, Ernest: president, director, Frankel Foundation (Evan)

Frankel, Joan Murtagh: assistant secretary, assistant treasurer, Hughes Foundation (Geoffrey C.)

Franklin, Alice: director, vice president, Norman Foundation

Franklin, Andrew D.: director, Norman Foundation

Franklin, Audrey Fishman: member, Norman Foundation

Franklin, Bion: treasurer, Crosswicks Foundation

Franklin, Carl M.: chairman, Stauffer Charitable Trust (John)

Franklin, H. Allen: president, chief executive officer, Georgia Power Co.

Franklin, John Hope: trustee, Duke Endowment

Franklin, Laurie: secretary, Crosswicks Foundation

Franklin, Marc Scott: senior vice president strategic planning, Pacific Life Insurance Co.

Franklin, William P.: trustee, Fasken Foundation

Frantz, Susan C.: program officer, Sarkeys Foundation

Fraser, Robert W.: director, Provident Community Foundation

Fraser, Russell: director, S.G. Foundation

Frazier, J. Phillip: trustee, Niagara Mohawk Foundation

Freas, Arthur K.: mgr, Freas Foundation

Freas, Margery H.: mgr, Freas Foundation

Frederick, Catherine H.: trustee, Harmon Foundation (Pearl M. and Julia J.)

Frederick, David C.: member, Staunton Farm Foundation

Frederick, Richard, III: member, Staunton Farm Foundation

Fredericksen, Jay A.: vice president, director, Rayonier Foundation

Fredrickson, Robert R.: secretary, treasurer, trustee, Mosher Foundation (Samuel B.)

Freed, Elizabeth Ann: president, director, Freed Foundation

Freeman, Annette Stoddard: director, Cudahy Fund (Patrick and Anna M.)

Freeman, David Forgan: special advisor, Scherman Foundation

Freeman, Houghton: director, Starr Foundation

Freeman, James D.: vp, Schurz Communications Foundation

Freeman, Jim: vice president, chairman corporate contributions committee, American United Life Insurance Co.

Freeman, Nancy S.: secretary, Fisher Foundation

Freeman, Richard W., Jr.: chairman, trustee, Rosa-Mary Foundation

Freeman, Robert: director, Virginia Environmental Endowment

Freeman, Tina: trustee, RosaMary Foundation

Frehse, Robert M., Jr.: executive director, Hearst Foundation, Inc. (The); vice president, executive director, Hearst Foundation (William Randolph)

Freimuth, Steve: board of directors, Washington Mutual Foundation

Frelinghuysen, George L. K.: assistant treasurer, director, Pforzheimer Foundation, Inc. (The Carl and Lily)

Frelinghuysen, Peter: vice president, trustee, Achelis Foundation

French, Christopher E.: president, director, Shenandoah Telecommunications Co.; president, ShenTel Foundation

French, Daniel P.: chairman, president, chief executive officer, director, French Oil Mill Machinery Co.

French, Fuller: treasurer, Fuller Foundation (DE)

French, Jerry: director, Shelter Insurance Foundation

French, Linda Jean: secretary, treasurer, Francis Families Foundation

French, Warren B., Jr.: chairman, director, Shenandoah Telecommunications Co.; director, ShenTel Foundation

Frenchman, Gerald: vice president, ContiGroup Companies Foundation

Frenzel, William: trustee, United States-Japan Foundation

Frerichs, Ernest S.: executive director, Dorot Foundation

Frese, Ines: chairman, Frese Foundation (Arnold D.)

Freund, Frederick W.: executive director, trustee, Gilmore Foundation (Irving S.)

Frey, Dorothy L.: treasurer, Wynn Foundation

Frey, Eugene U.: trustee, Bigelow Foundation (F. R.)

Fribourg, Charles: director, Fribourg Foundation

Fribourg, Mary Ann: mem, director, Fribourg Foundation

Fribourg, Paul J.: chairman, president, chief executive officer, ContiGroup Companies, Inc.; vice president, Fribourg Foundation

Frick, David R.: chairman, Anthem Foundation, Inc.

Fricke, Howard R.: chairman, Security Benefit Life Insurance Co.; trustee, Security Benefit Life Insurance Co. Charitable Trust

Fricks, William Peavy: chairman, chief executive officer, Norfolk Shipbuilding & Drydock Corp.

Friedberg, Bruce: board member, Fireman's Fund Foundation

Friede, Barbara: director, Fireman's Fund Foundation

Friedlaender, Helmut N.: director, AMETEK Foundation

Friedland, Laurie: director, Winston Foundation (Norman and Rosita)

Friedlander, W. John: director, Lake Placid Education Foundation

Friedman, Alan D.: co-trustee, Lard Trust (Mary Potishman)

Friedman, Bayard H.: co-trustee, Lard Trust (Mary Potishman)

Friedman, David A.: secretary, Friedman Family Foundation

Friedman, David G.: assistant secretary, Fribourg Foundation

Friedman, Eleanor: vice president, Friedman Family Foundation

Friedman, Harold Edward: secretary, Fox Charitable Trust (Emma R.)

Friedman, Marjorie N.: director, Harriman Foundation (Mary W.)

Friedman, Nancy: trustee, Fox Charitable Trust (Emma R.)

Friedman, Phyllis C.: trustee, Gordon Charitable Trust (Peggy and Yale)

Friedman, Phyllis K.: president, Friedman Family Foundation

Friedman, Robert E.: treasurer, Friedman Family Foundation

Friedman, Robert F.: director, Rosenberg Foundation

Friedman, Robert S.: secretary, treasurer, Rubinstein Foundation (Helena)

Friedman, Saul: co-trustee, Schermer Charitable Trust (Frances)

Friedman, Sidney O.: trustee, Lurcy Charitable and Educational Trust (Georges)

Friedman, Walker C.: co-trustee, Lard Trust (Mary Potishman)

Friedrich, Richard A., Sr.: vice president, Eastern Savings and Loan Foundation

Friend, Eugene L.: vice chairman, director, Koret Foundation

Friend, Robert: director, Osher Foundation (Bernard)

Frisch, Maureen: president, director, Simpson Fund; vice president public affairs, Simpson Investment Co.

Frist, Thomas Fearn, Jr.: chairman, chief executive officer,

Frist, Thomas Fearn, Sr.: trustee, Ansley Foundation (Dantzler Bond)

Fritch, Sandra: adv, Cayuga Foundation

Fritsche, E. Alan: executive director, Hamman Foundation (George and Mary Josephine)

Fritze, Steven L.: vice president, controller, Ecolab, Inc.

Fritzson, Paul A.: executive vice president , chief executive officer, Hannaford Brothers Co.; president, director, Hannaford Charitable Foundation

Frizen, Edwin L., Jr.: chairman, trustee, Crowell

Trust (Henry P. and Susan C.); president, Tyndale House Foundation

Froelich, Georgia A.: treasurer, Hershey Foundation

Frohring, Paul Robert: president, trustee, Frohring Foundation (Paul and Maxine)

Fromkes, Otto: director, Fromkes Foundation (Saul)

Fronterhouse, Gerald W.: chairman, director, Hoblitzelle Foundation

Frost, Herbert G., Jr.: director, Jones Foundation (Harvey and Bernice)

Frost, Robert D.: director, Littauer Foundation (Lucius N.)

Frost, William Lee: president, treasurer, director, Littauer Foundation (Lucius N.)

Frueauff, David: president, Frueauff Foundation (Charles A.)

Frueauff, Sue M.: program officer, trustee, Frueauff Foundation (Charles A.)

Frueauff-Grace, Anna Kay: trustee, Frueauff Foundation (Charles A.)

Fruehauf, Harvey C., Jr.: president, Fruehauf Foundation; trustee, Wiegand Foundation (E. L.)

Fry, Lloyd A., III: vice president, Fry Foundation (Lloyd A.)

Frye, Clayton Wesley, Jr.: trustee, LSR Fund

Fryling, Victor J.: director, Consumers Energy Foundation

Frymoyer, John W., MD: director, Macy, Jr. Foundation (Josiah)

Fuemmeler, Carl D.: vice president, director, Green Foundation (Allen P. and Josephine B.)

Fuhrman, Susan C.: trustee, Fund for New Jersey

Fujii, Sharon: vice president, Zellerbach Family Fund

Fujiki, Yasuo: trustee, Subaru of America Foundation; chairman, chief executive officer, director, Subaru of America, Inc.

Fukukawa, Shinji: trustee, United States-Japan Foundation

Fukunaga, Mark H.: alternate mem distribution comm, McInerny Foundation

Fuller, Carl W.: trustee, Blount Educational and Charitable Foundation (Mildred Weedon)

Fuller, Charles A., Jr.: fdn mgr, Slusher Charitable Foundation (Roy W.)

Fuller, Cynthia Q.: trustee, Fund for New Jersey

Fuller, Geraldine: president, Fuller Foundation (DE)

Fuller, Gillian: vice president, Fuller Foundation (DE)

Fuller, Jack W.: director, McCormick Tribune Foundation (Robert R.)

Fuller, Joyce I.: assistant treasurer, trustee, Fuller Foundation (George F. and Sybil H.)

Fuller, Kathryn Scott: trustee, Ford Foundation

Fuller, Lincoln E.: trustee, Fuller Foundation (George F. and Sybil H.)

Fuller, Mark W.: vice chairman, trustee, Fuller Foundation (George F. and Sybil H.)

Fuller, Peter, Jr.: president, Fuller Foundation (MA)

Fuller, Peter D., Sr.: trustee, Fuller Foundation (MA)

Fuller, Russell E.: chairman, treasurer, trustee, Fuller Foundation (George F. and Sybil H.)

Fullinwider, Jerome M.: trustee, Abell-Hanger Foundation

Fullwood, Emerson U.: trustee, Xerox Foundation

Fulstone, Georgia: vice president, director, Skaggs Foundation (L. J. Skaggs and Mary C.)

Fulton, James: director, Dime Foundation

Fulton, Richard: chief financial officer, Iowa Savings Bank

Fulton, V. Neil: assistant secretary, Gilmore Foundation (William G.)

Funaro, Patricia P.: program manager, U.S. Steel Foundation

Funderburk, Charles B.: trustee, Blount Educational and Charitable Foundation (Mildred Weedon)

Funnell, James D., Jr.: secretary, Muhlethaler Foundation, Inc. (Jane T.)

Fuqua, Doylene: board, McKinney Charitable Trust (Carl and Alleen)

Furichi, Takeshi: president, chief executive officer, NLI International, Inc.

Furlaud, Richard Mortimer: trustee, Olin Foundation (John M.)

Furlong, R. Michael: director, Coleman Foundation (IL)

Furman, Jeffrey: treasurer, trustee, Ben & Jerry's Foundation

Furmansky, Stewart: director, Kline Foundation (Charles and Figa)

Furness, Adrianne: secretary, Benton Foundation

Furtado, Eydie A.: adv, Hathaway Memorial Charitable Trust

Furth, John L.: director, treasurer, chairman fin committee, mbr executive

committee, Foundation for Child Development

Fusscas, Amanda: director, Krieble Foundation (Vernon K.)

Fusscas, Christopher: director, Krieble Foundation (Vernon K.)

Fusscas, Frederick: director, Krieble Foundation (Vernon K.)

Fusscas, Helen K.: president, Krieble Foundation (Vernon K.)

Futamura, Hiroshi: director, Kikkoman Foundation

Futo, Kyle Monfort: vice president, Monfort Family Foundation

Futter, Ellen Victoria: director, Noble Foundation, Inc. (Edward John)

Futterknecht, James O., Jr.: chairman, president, chief executive officer, chief operating officer, director, Dura Automotive Systems Inc.; president, Dura Automotive Systems Inc. Charitable Foundation

Fynboe, Carl T.: board member, Stewardship Foundation

G

Gabelli, Mario Joseph: trustee, Wiegand Foundation (E. L.)

Gaberman, Barry D.: senior vice president, Ford Foundation

Gabier, Russell L.: secretary, trustee, Gilmore Foundation (Irving S.)

Gable, Robert L.: director, NEBS Foundation; chairman, director, Unitrode Corp.

Gabriel, Nicholas M.: treasurer, director financial services, Ford Foundation

Gackle, George D.: treasurer, director, Rahr Foundation

Gadosik, Barbara: director corporate contributions, Sherwin-Williams Foundation

Gaffney, Joseph M.: director, Nesholm Family Foundation

Gage, Barbara C: director, Carlson Companies, Inc.; president, Carlson Family Foundation (Curtis L.)

Gage, Jack D.: director, Rahr Foundation

Gagnier, Charles E.: chairman, AMCORE Financial, Inc.; president, director, AMCORE Foundation

Gagnon, Pierre: chief operating officer, president, Mitsubishi Motor Sales of America, Inc.

Gahagan, Alexis duPont: trustee, duPont Foundation (Chichester)

Gahagan, Katharine G.: president, duPont Foundation (Chichester)

Gailey, John Robert, III: vice president, general counsel, secretary, West Pharmaceutical Services, Inc.

Gaines, Sharon: trust, Morgan Charitable Residual Trust (W. and E.)

Gaines, Thomas W., Jr.: adv comm, Duncan Trust (Louise Head)

Gaines, Tyler B.: trustee, Hitchcock Foundation (Gilbert M. and Martha H.)

Gainey, W. W., Jr.: treasurer, Dover Foundation

Gaither, James C.: director, Hewlett Foundation (William and Flora)

Gajardo, Joel: vice president, director, Woods Charitable Fund

Galbraith, James: director, Scott Foundation (Virginia Steele)

Galik, Jeffrey: assistant treasurer, Bristol-Myers Squibb Foundation Inc.

Galinson, Murray L.: director, Weingart Foundation

Gallagher, Daniel J.: treasurer, Knott Foundation (Marion I. and Henry J.)

Gallagher, Donald J.: vice president, sales, Cleveland-Cliffs, Inc.

Gallagher, Edward: director, Norcross Wildlife Foundation

Gallagher, J. Peter: trustee, Hillsdale Fund

Gallagher, James J.: director, Haigh-Scatena Foundation

Gallagher, Lindsay R.: trustee, Knott Foundation (Marion I. and Henry J.)

Gallagher, Margaret W.: trustee, Hillsdale Fund

Gallagher, Michael L.: trustee, Kiewit Foundation (Peter)

Gallagher, Terence Joseph: secretary, director, Pfizer Foundation

Galler, Ida E.: secretary, Starr Foundation

Gallo, Ernest: president, Gallo Foundation (Ernest)

Gallo, Joseph E.: vice president, Gallo Foundation (Ernest)

Gallo, Mary I.: vice president, Gallo Foundation (Ernest)

Gallwas, Gerald E.: director, Beckman Foundation (Arnold and Mabel)

Galvin, Christopher B.: director, Motorola Foundation; president, chief executive officer, director, Motorola, Inc.

Galvin, Mary G.: secretary, treasurer, Galvin Foundation (Robert)

Galvin, Robert William: president, Galvin Foundation (Robert)

Gambet, Daniel George: trustee, Trexler Trust (Harry C.)

Gambill, Malcolm W.: president, trustee, Harsco Corp. Fund

Gamble, George F.: vice president, Gamble Foundation

Gamble, Launce E.: president, Gamble Foundation

Gamble, Mark D.: vice president, treasurer, Gamble Foundation

Gamble, Mary S.: vice president, Gamble Foundation

Gamble, Robert: executive director, Goldman Fund (Richard and Rhoda)

Gamble Price, Aimee: vice president, secretary, Gamble Foundation

Gambrel, Amy H.: trustee, Crandall Memorial Foundation (J. Ford)

Gamerman, Carolyn: administrator, Arca Foundation

Games, Robert W.: executive secretary, Van Wert County Foundation

Gamper, Albert R., Jr.: president, chief executive officer, director, CIT Group Foundation; president, chief executive officer, chairman, CIT Group, Inc.

Gamron, W. Anthony: treasurer, director, Kimberly-Clark Foundation

Gancer, Donald Charles: president, Boothroyd Foundation (Charles H. and Bertha L.)

Ganci, Paul J.: president, chief operating officer, Central Hudson Gas & Electric Corp.

Gannett, William B.: president, director, Hopedale Foundation

Ganzi, Victor F.: director, Hearst Foundation, Inc. (The); vice president, secretary, Hearst Foundation (William Randolph)

Garber, John Paul: head US operations, WestLB New York Branch

Garber, Karlene Beal: trustee, Beal Foundation

Garcia, Jaime: director, pac northwest giving, Gates Foundation (Bill and Melinda)

Garcia, Pedro: trustee, Chiles Foundation

Gardener, Robert: trust, Smith Foundation (William R. and Sara Babb)

Gardner, D. L.: vice president, assistant treasurer, Cleveland-Cliffs Foundation (The)

Gardner, David Pierpont: chairman, director, Eccles Foundation (George S. and Dolores Dore); vice chairman, trustee, Getty Trust (J. Paul)

Gardner, Dorsey: trustee, Evans Foundation (Edward P.)

Gardner, Emerson N.: director, Olmsted Foundation (George and Carol)

Gardner, Frank: vice president, director, Washington Foundation (Dennis R. and Phyllis)

Gardner, James L.: trustee, Fluor Foundation

Gardner, James Richard: vice president, Pfizer Foundation

Gardner, Joan L.: trustee, Bigelow Foundation (F. R.)

Gardner, Patricia: trustee, Besser Foundation

Gardner, Roger L.: president, trustee, Jones Foundation (Daisy Marquis)

Gardner, William: vice president, Rossi Foundation (William and Alice)

Gareau, Joseph A.: executive vice president, chief investment officer, Hartford Financial Services Group, Inc.

Garey, Gerard S.: president, ex-officio trustee, Raskob Foundation for Catholic Activities, Inc.

Garfinkel, Steven R.: secretary, treasurer, trustee, Seybert Institution for Poor Boys and Girls (Adam and Maria Sarah)

Garfinkle, Gillian: director, Garfinkle-Minard Foundation, Inc.

Garfinkle, Nicholas: director, Garfinkle-Minard Foundation, Inc.

Garfinkle, Norton: director, Garfinkle-Minard Foundation, Inc.

Garfinkle, Sally Minard: director, Garfinkle-Minard Foundation, Inc.

Garrett, Charles: trustee, Young Foundation (Bill B.)

Garrett, Joseph H., Junior: vice president government & international operations, Rockwell Automation Inc.

Garrett, Judith M.: president, executive director, Belo Foundation

Garrett, Michael D.: director, Alabama Power Foundation

Garrett, Robert: trustee, Abell Foundation

Garrett, Wendy: trustee, Owsley Foundation (Alvin and Lucy)

Garrison, Lisa: program officer, Dodge Foundation (Geraldine R.)

Garrison, Milton: director, Lebanon Mutual Foundation

Garron, Dynell: director, Gap, Inc.

Garside, Elizabeth Ransome: director, AKC Fund

Garst, Mary: director, Audubon State Bank Charitable Foundation

Garst, Stephen: director, Audubon State Bank Charitable Foundation

Gartland, John J., Jr.: president, director, McCann Foundation

Gartland, Michael G.: assistant secretary, director, McCann Foundation

Gartner, Peggy: admin, Blumenthal Foundation

Garton, Deirdre Wilson: mgr, Wilson Foundation (Marie C. and Joseph C.)

Garvey, James Sutherland: vice president, Garvey Texas Foundation

Garvey, Richard F.: trustee, Garvey Texas Foundation

Garvey, Shirley F.: president, Garvey Texas Foundation

Garwood, William L., Jr.: vice president, Clayton Fund; vice president, secretary, director, ECG Foundation

Garza-Vizcaino, Raffy: director, Wright Foundation (Lola)

Gasparinetti, Luigi: director, Gilman Foundation (Howard)

Gassaway, James M.: trustee, Grundy Foundation

Gassman, Robert S.: treasurer, director, Guttman Foundation (Stella and Charles)

Gast, Aaron E.: trustee, Newcombe Foundation (Charlotte W.)

Gaston, Karen H.: chief executive officer, Equifax, Inc.

Gates, Carol W.: vice president, treasurer, Oxford Foundation

Gates, Charles Cassius, Jr.: trustee, Gates Family Foundation

Gates, Melinda French: co-founder, Gates Foundation (Bill and Melinda)

Gates, Valerie: vice president, Gates Family Foundation

Gates, William H., Sr.: co-chair, chief executive officer, Gates Foundation (Bill and Melinda)

Gates, William Henry, III: co-founder, Gates Foundation (Bill and Melinda); co-founder, chairman, chief software architect, Microsoft Corp.

Gaudiani, Claire L.: director, Luce Foundation (Henry)

Gault, Stanley Carleton: trustee, Morgan Foundation (Burton D.)

Gaus, William Thomas: treasurer, Miller Foundation (Steve J.); vice president, director, Schroeder Foundation (Walter)

Gavin, Robert Michael, Jr.: director, Research Corp.

Gay, Frank William: trustee, Hughes Medical Institute (Howard)

Gayle, Gibson, Jr.: president, trustee, Anderson Foundation (M. D.)

Gayle, Helene, MPH: director HIV, TB and reprod health program, Gates Foundation (Bill and Melinda)

Gayle, Karla: vice president, trust officer, Kaul Foundation Trust (Hugh)

Gaynor, George N.: vice president, Norris Foundation (Dellora A. and Lester J.)

Gebert, J. J.: vice president, treasurer, trustee, Johns Manville Fund

Gebhard, Elizabeth R.: director, Demos Foundation (N.)

Geddes, Robert D.: secretary, Wessinger Foundation

Gehrke, Patrice: trustee, Gilmore Foundation (William G.)

Geier, Vickie: secretary, Midcontinent Media Foundation

Geifman, Geraldine: secretary, director, Geifman Family Foundation

Geifman, Stephen L.: president, Geifman Family Foundation

Geifman, Terri: assistant treasurer, director, Geifman Family Foundation

Geiger, Linda: assistant secretary, Reliant Resources Foundation

Geillser, Thomas: board member, Fireman's Fund Foundation

Geisel, Audrey S.: president, assistant secretary, Dr. Seuss Foundation

Geisel, Jean F.: secretary, Bausch & Lomb Foundation, Inc.

Geissinger, Frederick Wallace: president, vice chairman, chief executive officer, American General Finance; president, American General Finance Foundation

Geist, Carol Berg: trustee, Bingham Second Betterment Fund (William)

Gelbman, Ronald G.: chairman diagnostics group, Johnson & Johnson; member corporate contributions committee, Johnson & Johnson Family of Companies Contribution Fund

Gell, Carl L.: director, Loughran Foundation (Mary and Daniel)

Gellert, Annette: director, Gellert Family Foundation (Fred)

Gellert, Fred, Jr.: chairman, Gellert Family Foundation (Fred)

Gellert, Michael E.: director, Humana Foundation

Gelman, Michael C.: director, Goldman Fund (Richard and Rhoda)

Gelman, Susan R.: director, member executive committee, Goldman Fund (Richard and Rhoda)

Gemmill, Elizabeth H.: trustee, Warwick Foundation

Gemmill, Helen H.: trustee, Warwick Foundation

Genega, Stanley G.: director, Olmsted Foundation (George and Carol)

Gentile, Ronald J.: executive vice president, Warwick Savings Foundation

Gentle, William J.: trustee, treasurer, Retirement Research Foundation

Gentry, Nolden: director, Mid-Iowa Health Foundation

Geogheghan, Jack: secretary, Becher Foundation (Hildegarde D.)

George, A. Fred: trustee, Campbell Soup Foundation

George, Donald A.: clerk, trustee, Ash Charitable Corp.

George, Helen A.: secretary, Cremer Foundation

George, Henrietta A.: director, Kleberg Foundation (Robert J. Kleberg, Jr. and Helen C.)

George, Margaret E.: director, Eberly Foundation

George, Pamela L.: secretary, Hobby Family Foundation

Georgiadis, Patricia: director, Bristol-Myers Squibb Foundation Inc.

Gerace, Frank: trustee, Gerstacker Foundation (Rollin M.)

Geramian, Mohammad: president, Alavi Foundation

Gerard, Jamie K.: attorney, Newman's Own Foundation

Gerard, Karen N.: vice chairman, director, vice chairman executive committee, mbr fin committee, Foundation for Child Development

Gerber, Harry: director, First Source Foundation

Gerber, Margaret L.: trustee, Lyndhurst Foundation

Gerber, Mary E.: secretary, AMCORE Foundation

Gerken, Walter Bland: vice president, director, chairman audit comm, Keck Foundation (W. M.)

Gerry, Elbridge Thomas: president, Harriman Foundation (Gladys and Roland); director, Harriman Foundation (Mary W.)

Gerry, Elbridge Thomas, Jr.: president, director, Harriman Foundation (Gladys and Roland)

Gerry, Martha Farish: president, trustee, Farish Fund (William Stamps)

Gershowitz, Diane M.: director, Marcus Corp. Foundation

Gerst, Christopher: assistant corporate secretary, St. Paul Companies Inc. Foundation

Gerstacker, Esther S.: vice president, trustee, Gerstacker Foundation (Rollin M.)

Gerstacker, Lisa J.: vice president, secretary, assistant treasurer, trustee, Gerstacker Foundation (Rollin M.)

Gerstein, David: trustee, Price Foundation (Louis and Harold)

Gerstle, Mark R.: director, Cummins Foundation; vice president, cummins business services, Cummins, Inc.

Gerstley-Hofheimer, Carol: trustee, Cassett Foundation (Louis N.)

Gerstung, Sandra L.: president, director, Hecht-Levi Foundation

Gerth, Robert L.: adv, Archibald Charitable Foundation (Norman)

Geschke, Charles Matthew: co-chairman, Adobe Systems; president, Geschke Foundation (Charles M. and Nancy A.)

Geschke, Kathleen A.: director, Geschke Foundation (Charles M. and Nancy A.)

Geschke, Nancy A.: secretary, treasurer, Geschke Foundation (Charles M. and Nancy A.)

Getman, Frank W., Esq.: president, director, Dewar Foundation

Getman, Michael F.: treasurer, director, Dewar Foundation

Getz, Barbara: executive director, Gerber Foundation

Getz, Dennis A.: secretary, Steinman Foundation (James Hale)

Gherty, John E.: president, chief executive officer, Land O'Lakes, Inc.

Ghisalbert, Adele F.: director, Harcourt Foundation (Ellen Knowles)

Giacoio, Anthony: chief executive officer, director, Ballet Makers; secretary, Capezio/Ballet Makers Dance Foundation

Gianas, Peter T.: secretary, director, trustee, Spalding Foundation (Eliot)

Giannini, Vincent: treasurer, assistant secretary, director, Tribune New York Foundation

Gibbons, Boyd M., III: president, Johnson Foundation

Gibbons, John Joseph: trustee, Fund for New Jersey

Gibbons, Miles J., Jr.: executive director, Wells Foundation (Franklin H. and Ruth L.); executive director, comm mem, Whitaker Fund (Helen F.)

Gibbs, George: director, Doheny Foundation Trust (Carrie Estelle)

Gibbs, James Ronald: trustee, Smith Horticultural Trust (Stanley)

Gibbs, Joseph E.: trustee, Shook Foundation (Barbara Ingalls)

Gibbs, Larry: trustee, Rosenberry Tuscarawas County Foundation (Harold C. and Marjorie Q.)

Giberson, Robert C.: trustee, Johnson Foundation (Burdine)

Gibson, Darryl R.: adv comm mem, Moore and Arletta E. Moore Foundation (Kenneth S.)

Gibson, David R.: chief financial officer, Wilmington Trust Co.

Gibson, Edgar A.: adv, Ritter Charitable Trust (George and Mary)

Gibson, Kay: trustee, Morgan Charitable Residual Trust (W. and E.)

Gibson, Rose: assistant secretary, Heinz Family Foundation

Gibson, Roxanne: director, Lesher Foundation (Dean and Margaret)

Gicking, Robert K.: vice president, Reidler Foundation

Giddens, Paul J.: vice president human resources, Quanex Corp.; director, president, Quanex Foundation

Giefer, Michael J.: treasurer, Driscoll Foundation

Giffin, John H., Jr.: trustee, Smyth Trust (Marion C.)

Gigray, Margaret: treasurer, Whittenberger Foundation (Claude R. and Ethel B.)

Gilbert, Jeffrey R.: executive director, PPG Industries Foundation

Gilbert, Lee: co-trustee, Moss Charitable Trust (Finis M.)

Gilbert, Richard: vice president, Bretzlaff Foundation

Gilbert, S. Parker: advisory director, Macy, Jr. Foundation (Josiah)

Gilbert, Terry: secretary, Copley Foundation (James S.)

Gilbert, William A.: trustee, Windham Foundation

Gilbertson, Laura H.: director, Bingham Foundation (William)

Gildred, Lynn R.: secretary, S.G. Foundation

Gildred, Stuart C.: president, director, S.G. Foundation

Giles, Clark P.: committee member, Eccles Charitable Foundation (Willard L.)

Gilford, Steve, Esq.: admin comm mem, Bowman Proper Charitable Trust (J.)

Gill, Barbara E.: vice president public affairs, Dana Foundation (Charles A.)

Gill, Deborah R.: director, Meadows Foundation (The)

Gill, Elisabeth Childs: president, AKC Fund

Gill, Lawrence: vice president, Dodge Jones Foundation and Subsidiary

Gill, Sherry B.: trustee, Gordon Charitable Trust (Peggy and Yale)

Gill, Thomas I.: assistant secretary, Andrews McMeel Universal Foundation

Gillem, Christopher: program director, Murdock Charitable Trust (M. J.)

Gilles, Michael O.: senior vice president, treasurer, Bay State Federal Savings Charitable Foundation

Gillespie, George Joseph, III: president, treasurer, Olin Foundation (John M.); director, Paley Foundation, Inc. (William S.); president, trustee, Pinkerton Foundation

Gillespie, Tyrone W.: grant comm, Royal Foundation (May Mitchell)

Gillette, Marilyn: director information technology services, Getty Trust (J. Paul)

Gillfillan, Michael J.: vice chairman, Wells Fargo & Co.

Gillheeney, Gary S.: chief financial officer, Providence Gas Co.

Gilliam, James Howard, Jr.: trustee, Hughes Medical Institute (Howard)

Gillies, Archibald L.: president, director, Warhol Foundation for the Visual Arts (The Andy)

Gillstrom, Mary: assistant secretary, Andersen Foundation

Gillum, R. D.: chairperson, General Motors Foundation

Gilman, E. Atwill: trustee, Boettcher Foundation

Gilman, Richard H.: director, Boston Globe Foundation

Gilmour, Allan Dana: vice chairman, chief financial officer, Ford Motor Co.

Gilpin, Larry V.: trustee, Target Foundation

Gilreath, Deborah Vann: director, Vann Family Foundation

Gimon, Eleanor H.: director, Hewlett Foundation (William and Flora)

Gimon, Eleanor Hewlett: director, Hewlett Foundation (William and Flora)

Gin McGowan, Sue: president, McGowan Charitable Fund (William G.)

Ginden, Charles H.: trustee, Woodruff Foundation (Robert W.)

Gioia, Lucy: office administrator, Dreyfus Foundation, Inc. (Max and Victoria)

Giordano, Alexandra: director, Memton Fund

Gipson, Fred: trustee, Sarkeys Foundation

Girard, Linda M.: trustee, member, Templeton Foundation (Herbert A.)

Gische, Samuel R.: fin director, controller, Hartford Foundation, Inc. (The John A.)

Gisel, William George: president, director, Cummings Foundation (James H.)

Gitlin, Paul, Esq.: trustee, Brace Foundation (Donald C.)

Given, Davis: trustee, Davis Foundations (Arthur Vining)

Given, Tasha: hon director, Allyn Foundation

Gladden, Gordon D.: trustee, Henson Foundation (Richard A.)

Glade, Fred M., Jr.: trustee, Reynolds Foundation (Edgar & Francis)

Gladstone, Henry A.: trustee, Strauss Foundation

Glancy, Alfred Robinson, III: trustee, treasurer, Hudson-Webber Foundation

Glancy, Ruth R.: trustee, McGregor Fund

Glaser, Robert Joy, MD: honorary emeritus trustee, Packard Foundation (David and Lucile)

Glasgow, Norman M., Jr.: partner, Wilkes, Artis, Hedrick & Lane; vice president, director, Wilkes, Artis, Hedrick & Lane Foundation

Glasscock, Larry G.: director, Anthem Foundation, Inc.; chairman, chief executive officer, Anthem Inc.

Glassmoyer, Thomas P.: trustee, Newcombe Foundation (Charlotte W.)

Glaubig, J. C.: trustee, Exxon Mobil Foundation

Glaudel, Robert H.: senior vice president human resources, New England Business Service

Glaze, Nancy: director arts program, Packard Foundation (David and Lucile)

Gleason, Edward M.: secretary-treasurer, Alliant Energy Foundation, Inc.

Gleason, James S.: director, chairman, Gleason Foundation

Gleason, Janis F.: director, Gleason Foundation

Gleason, Tracy R.: president, director, Gleason Foundation

Glebocki, Geoffrey: senior program officer, Gund Foundation (George)

Glenn, James K., Jr.: member board advisors, Belk Foundation

Glenn, M. Virginia: director, Fab Steel Products Foundation

Glenn, Stanley: president, chief executive officer, Fab Steel Products Co.

Glick, Darwin: director, Lebanon Mutual Foundation

Glick, Eugene B.: president, trustee, Glick Foundation (Eugene and Marilyn)

Glick, Madeline Einhorn: treasurer, New York Foundation

Glick, Marilyn K.: trustee, secretary, treasurer, Glick Foundation (Eugene and Marilyn)

Gloyd, Lawrence Eugene: trustee, CLARCOR Foundation

Glynn, Gary Allen: president, U.S. Steel Corp.; vice president, investment, U.S. Steel Foundation

Glynn, William C.: president, chief executive officer, director, Intermountain Gas Co.; director, Intermountain Gas Industries Foundation

Goble, Gary F.: assistant treasurer, Fleming Foundation

Goddard, Samuel P., Jr.: vice president, director, trustee, Spalding Foundation (Eliot)

Goddard, William R., Jr.: trustee, Goddard Foundation (Charles B.)

Godfrey, Crawford: trustee, Norman Foundation (Summers A.)

Godfrey, Dudley J., Jr.: director, Cudahy Fund (Patrick and Anna M.)

Godfrey, Marian A.: director culture program, Pew Charitable Trusts

Godfrey, Thomas: director, Kikkoman Foundation

Godlasky, Tom: executive vice president, chief investment officer, Amerus Group Co.

Goel, Poonam: president, Goel Foundation

Goel, Prabhu: secretary, Goel Foundation

Goertz, Ruth: committee member, Haman Family Foundation

Goettler, Ralph H.: trustee, Allegheny Foundation

Goings, Lanetta: vice president, trustee, Blade Foundation

Gold, Elaine: secretary, treasurer, director, Gold Foundation (David B.)

Gold, Emily: director, Gold Foundation (David B.)

Gold, Steven A.: director, Gold Foundation (David B.)

Gold-Bubier, Diane: director, Gold Foundation (David B.)

Gold-Lurie, Barbara: president, Gold Foundation (David B.)

Goldberg, Amy: vice president, Arronson Foundation

Goldberg, Avram J.: trustee, Rabb Charitable Foundation (Sidney and Esther)

Goldberg, Avram Jacob: trustee, Goldberg Family Foundation

Goldberg, Carol Rabb: trustee, Goldberg Family Foundation

Goldberg, Deborah B.: trustee, Rabb Charitable Foundation (Sidney and Esther)

Goldberg, Deborah Beth: trustee, Goldberg Family Foundation

Goldberg, Edward Jay: vice president, Macy's East, Inc.

Goldberg, Joel: president, Rich Foundation

Goldberg, Joshua R.: trustee, Rabb Charitable Foundation (Sidney and Esther)

Goldberg, Joshua Rabb: trustee, Goldberg Family Foundation

Golden, Charles E.: executive vice president, chief financial officer, Eli Lilly & Co.

Golden, Gail: secretary, assistant treasurer, ACF Foundation; vice president, Icahn Foundation (Carl C.)

Golden, Michael: senior vice president, director, New York Times Co. Foundation

Golden, Rebecca: director, Ben & Jerry's Foundation

Golden, Robert C.: trustee, Prudential Foundation

Golden, Terence C.: director, Cafritz Foundation (Morris and Gwendolyn)

Golden, William T.: treasurer, director, Kaufmann Foundation (Henry)

Goldman, David: director, Feinstein Foundation

Goldman, Douglas E.: director, member executive committee, Goldman Fund (Richard and Rhoda); trustee, Haas Fund (Walter and Elise)

Goldman, John D.: trustee, member executive committee, Goldman Fund (Richard and Rhoda); trustee, Haas Fund (Walter and Elise)

Goldman, Lisa: trustee, Goldman Fund (Richard and Rhoda)

Goldman, Marcia L.: trustee, Goldman Fund (Richard and Rhoda)

Goldman, Neal: secretary-treasurer, Polaroid Foundation

Goldman, Peter: president, Kongsgaard-Goldman Foundation

Goldman, Richard Nathaniel: president, director, member executive committee, Goldman Fund (Richard and Rhoda)

Goldschmid, Harvey J.: director, Greenwall Foundation

Goldseker, Sheldon: chairman, trustee, member, Goldseker Foundation of Maryland (Morris)

Goldseker, Simon: vice chairman, trustee, member, Goldseker Foundation of Maryland (Morris)

Goldsmith, Stephen: director, Fannie Mae Foundation

Goldstein, Bruce D.: secretary, Haigh-Scatena Foundation

Goldstein, Diane R.: trustee, Plough Foundation

Goldstein, Joseph L., MD: trustee, Hughes Medical Institute (Howard)

Goldstein, Michael L.: director, Goldman Foundation (Herman)

Goldstein, Robert H.: president, trustee, Ash Charitable Corp.

Goldstein, Steven: chief financial officer, RBC Centura

Golieb, Abner J.: president, director, mem, Katzenberger Foundation

Gollihue, Alan E.: executive director, Portsmouth General Hospital Foundation

Golston, Allan C., CPA: chief financial officer, chief administrative officer, Gates Foundation (Bill and Melinda)

Golub, Lewis: chairman, chief executive officer, director, Golub Corp.

Golub, Mona: trustee, Golub Foundation

Gomer, Adelaide P.: second vice president, secretary, Park Foundation

Gomer, Alicia P.: jr. advisory, Park Foundation

Gomez, Begona Laresgoitide: vice president, director, Clover Foundation

Gomez, Ernesto: tax officer, Burlington Resources Foundation

Gomez, Oscar C.: director, Verizon Foundation

Gonthier, Laurie G.: director, New Milford Savings Bank Foundation

Gonthier, Robert A., Jr.: director, Provident Community Foundation

Gonzales, David L.: vice president community affairs, PepsiCo Inc.

Gonzalez, Bethaida C.: trustee, Gifford Charitable Corp. (Rosamond)

Gonzalez, Jose: program director health, Bush Foundation

Gonzalez, Juan G.: director, Wright Foundation (Lola)

Gonzelez, Rosa: trustee, Children's Foundation of Erie County

Good, Michael Willis: director, Willis Family Foundation

Good, Robert Alan, MD: trustee, Dana Charitable Trust (Eleanor Naylor)

Goodale, Irene E.: trustee, Peterloon Foundation

Goodban, Nicholas: senior vice president philanthropy, McCormick Tribune Foundation (Robert R.)

Gooding, John S.: chairman, director, G/S/M Industrial, Inc.; president, Gooding Group Foundation

Goodman, Barbara F.: trustee, Goodman Family Foundation

Goodman, Carroll R.: assistant secretary, trustee, Sterling-Turner Foundation

Goodman, Charles: vice president, director, Crown Memorial (Arie and Ida)

Goodman, Harold S.: trustee, Messing Family Charitable Foundation

Goodman, Helen G.: senior vice president, Hartford Financial Services Group, Inc.

Goodman, Roy Matz: trustee, Goodman Family Foundation

Goodmanson, Richard: executive vice president, chief operating officer, E.I. du Pont de Nemours & Co.

Goodnight, Cecil L.: vice president, director, Progress Energy Foundation

Goodnow, Edward B.: trustee, Goodnow Fund

Goodrich, Gillian C.: trustee, Comer Foundation (AL)

Goodsell, Jill: admin, trustee, Foster Foundation

Goodspeed, Lisa: trustee, Huber Foundation

Goodstein, Les: president, Daily News, L.P.

Goodstein, Lucy M.: vice president, Goodstein Foundation

Goodwillie Nelson, Mary: director, Wege Foundation

Goodwin, Catherine R.: trustee, Foundation for Seacoast Health

Goodwin, David P.: trustee, Cogswell Benevolent Trust

Goodwin, Neva R.: vice chairman, trustee, Rockefeller Brothers Fund, Inc.

Goodwin, Richard L.: mem, Gardiner Savings Institution Charitable Foundation

Goodwin, William Maxwell: vice president commun devel, Lilly Endowment

Goodyear, William M.: trustee, Bank of America Foundation

Goolsby, John L.: trustee, Reynolds Foundation (Donald W.)

Gordon, Bruce S.: executive director, Verizon Foundation

Gordon, C. Leonard: director, Frankel Foundation (Evan)

Gordon, Ellen Rubin: president, director, Rubin Family Fund (Cele H. and William B.)

Gordon, Hunter R.: advisory trustee, McLean Contributionship

Gordon, Jonathan R.: director, Mailman Family Foundation (A. L.)

Gordon, Joseph K.: trustee, McLean Contributionship

Gordon, Lois: director, Fleishhacker Foundation

Gordon, Melvin Jay: vice president, director, Rubin Family Fund (Cele H. and William B.)

Gordon, Raymond J.: trustee, real estate mgr, Gordon Charitable Trust (Peggy and Yale)

Gordon, Susan: assistant treasurer, Icahn Foundation (Carl C.)

Gordon, Thomas Christian, Jr.: assistant secretary, trustee, Gray Foundation (Garland and Agnes Taylor)

Gore, Ruth T.: director, Chapin Foundation of Myrtle Beach, South Carolina

Gorelick, Jamie Shona: vice chair, Fannie Mae; director, MacArthur Foundation (John D. and Catherine T.)

Goresh, Frances M.: director, Warwick Savings Foundation

Gorham, John: chairman distribution comm, mem investigating comm, Champlin Foundation

Gorham, Robert L.: managing partner, Wilkes, Artis, Hedrick & Lane; president, director, Wilkes, Artis, Hedrick & Lane Foundation

Goriup, Mary A.: mgr, Hedco Foundation

Gorman, Mary V.: chief financial officer, Newhall Foundation (Henry Mayo)

Gorman, Michael R.: executive director, Irwin Charity Foundation (William G.)

Gormisky, Paul J.: director, Cabot Corp. Foundation

Gormley, Patrick A.: vice president, Bacon Foundation (E. L. and Oma)

Gorsuch, Joan: secretary, Regenstein Foundation

Gosney, Timothy J.: trustee, Stillwell Charitable Trust (Glen and Dorothy)

Gottlieb, Art: secretary, Gumbiner Foundation (Josephine)

Gottwald, Thomas E.: president, chief executive officer, Ethyl Corp.

Gougeon, Meade A.: trustee, Kantzler Foundation

Gould, Brian: controller, treasurer, Interkal, Inc.

Gould, Jay E.: director, Provident Community Foundation

Gould, Paul A.: vice president, director, Allen Brothers Foundation

Gould, Russell S.: senior vice president finance investments, Getty Trust (J. Paul)

Gow, Ian F.: director, trustee, Crummer Foundation (Roy E.)

Gozon, Richard C.: executive vice president pulp paper & packaging, Weyerhaeuser Co.; trustee, Weyerhaeuser Co. Foundation

Gozonsky, Edwin S.: trustee, Adelson Trust (Diana S.)

Graber, Samuel W.: gov, Mayor Foundation (Oliver Dewey)

Graber, Thomas H., II: trustee, Ketrow Foundation

Grabois, Neil R.: vice president/director for strategic planning, Carnegie Corp. of New York

Grado, John, Jr.: trustee, Wallace Foundation (George R.)

Grady, Stafford Robert: vchairman, Mead Foundation (Giles W. and Elise G.)

Grady, Thomas M.: member, director, Cannon Foundation, Inc. (The)

Graf, Don: president, trustee, CH Foundation

Grafe, Tim: trustee, Donaldson Foundation

Grafer, W. D.: vice president finance, National Standard Co.; treasurer, National Standard Foundation

Graff, David: chief financial officer, controller, Quincy Newspapers

Graham, Barbara L.: assistant secretary, Burns & McDonnell Foundation

Graham, Colleen: secretary, Rich Foundation Inc.

Graham, Donald Edward: trustee, Graham Fund (Philip L.)

Graham, George E., Jr.: director, Asplundh Foundation

Graham, James E.: director, Asplundh Foundation

Graham, Mary: director, MacArthur Foundation (John D. and Catherine T.)

Graham, Patricia Albjerg, PhD: vice president, Johnson Foundation

Graham, Robert M.: treasurer, Eccles Foundation (George S. and Dolores Dore)

Graham, Stanley E.: trustee, Hill Crest Foundation

Grainger, Joseph C.: executive director, Harden Foundation

Gralnek, Ann D.: senior advisor, Jewett Foundation (George Frederick)

Granadillo, Pedro P.: director, Lilly Foundation (Eli)

Grandon, Carleen M.: director, Hall-Perrine Foundation

Grange, David L.: executive vice president, chief operating officer, McCormick Tribune Foundation (Robert R.)

Granger, John C.: trustee, Blount Educational and Charitable Foundation (Mildred Weedon)

Grano, Joseph J., Jr.: chairman, chief executive officer, UBS PaineWebber, Inc.

Granoff, Mark Howard: vice president, United Wisconsin Services Foundation

Grant, David: executive director, Dodge Foundation (Geraldine R.)

Grant, Hugh: president, chief executive officer, Monsanto Co.

Grant, Maria O.: director, Scott Foundation (Virginia Steele)

Grant, R. Gene: director, Cheney Foundation (Ben B.)

Grant, Richard A.: vice president, director, Connell Foundation (Michael J.)

Grant, William West, III: trustee, Gates Family Foundation

Granucci-Tufo, Judy: charitable contributions analyst, Bank of America Foundation

Grasley, Michael Howard: senior vice president, Shell Oil Co.

Grasmere, Robert H.: trustee, Turrell Fund

Grassilli, Robert J.: treasurer, director, Gellert Foundation (Carl Gellert and Celia Berta)

Grasso, Richard A.: chairman, chief executive officer, New York Stock Exchange, Inc.

Graunke, James W.: secretary, director, Patron Saints Foundation

Gravelle, Peter W.: president, chief operating officer, Scotsman Industries Foundation; president, chief operating officer, director, Scottsman Industries

Graven, Dennis L.: chief financial officer, vice president finance, Brillion Iron Works

Graves, Ann P.: assistant treasurer, Burlington Resources Foundation

Graves, Herbert C.: chairman, Standard Steel

Graves, Howard: director, Guggenheim Foundation (Harry Frank)

Graves, Milton T.: vice president, director, Cockrell Foundation

Gravett, Benjamin C.: trustee, Washington Forrest Foundation

Gray, Becki: executive director, Usibelli Foundation

Gray, Bruce B.: assistant treasurer, trustee, Gray Foundation (Garland and Agnes Taylor)

Gray, Catherine: member investment committee, Goldseker Foundation of Maryland (Morris)

Gray, Charles M.: president, Demos Foundation (N.)

Gray, Constance F.: trustee, Duke Endowment

Gray, D. L.: assistant secretary, treasurer, director, member, Cannon Foundation, Inc. (The)

Gray, Elizabeth B.: trustee, Berry Foundation (Loren M.)

Gray, Elmon T.: president, treasurer, trustee, Gray Foundation (Garland and Agnes Taylor)

Gray, Garland, II: assistant secretary, trustee, Gray Foundation (Garland and Agnes Taylor)

Gray, Hanna Holborn, PhD: chairman, Hughes Medical Institute (Howard); chairman, trustee, Mellon Foundation (Andrew W.)

Gray, Harry Barkus: director, Beckman Foundation (Arnold and Mabel)

Gray, James E.: president, chief operating officer, Macy's East, Inc.

Gray, Janet: member, Northern Trust Co. Charitable Trust

Gray, Lloyd H., Jr.: director, Trippe Trust (William D.)

Graybill, Charles S., MD: chairman, trustee, McMahon Foundation

Grealis, William J.: vice president, Cinergy Corp.; director, Cinergy Foundation

Grebe, Michael W.: president, Bradley Foundation (Lynde and Harry)

Green, Bennie: treasurer, trustee, Rockwell Fund, Inc.

Green, Bill: trustee, Taconic Foundation

Green, Don C.: secretary, treasurer, Mid-Iowa Health Foundation

Green, Edward S.: assistant treasurer, Gifford Charitable Corp. (Rosamond)

Green, Ernestine R.: chairwoman, trustee, Statler Foundation

Green, Lois B.: co-trustee, Hoche-Scofield Foundation

Green, Margaret H: trustee, chairman, BellSouth Foundation

Green, Michael: vice president, director, Loewy Family Foundation

Green, Richard C.: director, Hall Family Foundation (The)

Green, Robert L.: president, Green Foundation (Robert and Susan)

Greenawalt, W. Eileen: secretary, trustee, Bonfils-Stanton Foundation

Greenbaum, Maurice Coleman: secretary, director, Mandeville Foundation

Greenberg, Eileen Bender: vice president, Bender Foundation

Greenberg, Gary: vice president, Rogow Birken Foundation

Greenberg, Maurice Raymond: chairman board, director, Starr Foundation

Greenberg, Michael: treasurer, director, Newman Assistance Fund (Jerome A. and Estelle R.)

Greenberg, Sidney: president, Rogow Birken Foundation

Greene, John K.: trustee, Kaul Foundation Trust (Hugh)

Greene, Marion E.: president, LEF Foundation

Greene, Paul F.: trustee, Levy Foundation (June Rockwell)

Greene, Richard L.: director, Koret Foundation

Greene, Roger W.: director, Memorial Foundation for the Blind

Greene, Virginia Arana: director, Wells Fargo Foundation

Greener, Chuck: director, Fannie Mae Foundation

Greenewalt, David: adv trustee, Crystal Trust

Greenfield, Albert M., III: trustee, Greenfield Foundation (Albert M.)

Greenfield, Bruce Harold: trustee, Greenfield Foundation (Albert M.)

Greenfield, Jerry: cofounder, vice chairman, Ben & Jerry's Homemade, Inc.

Greenfield, Stewart: trustee, Dibner Fund

Greenlaw, Patricia A.: trustee, Small Business Service Bureau Charitable Foundation

Greenleaf, Arline Ripley: trustee, Sprague Educational and Charitable Foundation (Seth)

Greenlee, Paul, Jr.: trustee, Anderson Foundation (NY)

Greenstein, Andrew M.: trustee, August Family Foundation (Charles J. and Burton S.)

Greenwall, Francis M.: director, Greenwall Foundation

Greenway, Lumina V.: trustee, Verney Foundation (Gilbert)

Greer, David S.: trustee, Jaffe Foundation

Greer, George C.: chairman, Eden Hall Foundation

Greer, Margaret Weyerhaeuser Jewett: trustee, Jewett Foundation (George Frederick)

Greer, William Hershey, Jr.: trustee, Jewett Foundation (George Frederick)

Greevy, Charles F., III: president, Plankenhorn Foundation (Harry)

Grefenstette, Carl G.: director, vice president, Hillman Foundation

Gregorian, Vartan: president, Carnegie Corp. of New York

Gregory, Theophilus: director outreach programs, El Pomar Foundation

Greiner, Amelia: trustee, Gifford Charitable Corp. (Rosamond)

Greisman, Stuart L., D.O.: director, Copic Medical Foundation

Gremer, David C.: assistant treasurer, U.S. Steel Foundation

Grenz, M. Kay: director, 3M Foundation; vice president human resources, Minnesota Mining & Manufacturing Co.

Gresham, James Thomas: president, general manager, Callaway Foundation, Inc.

Gresham, Mary: secretary, director, Rahr Foundation

Gretta, John W.: assistant treasurer, Scott & Fetzer Foundation

Greve, John H.: trustee, Kinney-Lindstrom Foundation

Grey, John: director, Rice Foundation

Grieder, Jerome B.: trustee, Lingnan Foundation

Grier-Miller, Brenda: trustee, Nord Family Foundation

Griffin, Diane P.: trustee, Beazley Foundation

Griffin, Donald Redfield: director, Guggenheim Foundation (Harry Frank)

Griffin, Janet: secretary, Wellmark Foundation

Griffin, Leslie: director, Boston Globe Foundation

Griffin, Sandra L.: admin, Bernsen Foundation (Grace and Franklin)

Griffin, Sandy: scholarship administration, Moody Foundation

Griffin, Stuart L.: assistant secretary, Alabama Power Foundation

Griffin, William E.: president, director, Carvel Foundation (Thomas and Agnes)

Griffis, Hughes: president, director, Griffis Foundation

Griffith, Alan Richard: vice chairman, Bank of New York Company, Inc.

Griffith, Charles P., Jr.: adv, Griffith Foundation (W. C.)

Griffith, Chip: vice president, Kuyper Foundation (Peter H. and E. Lucille Gaass)

Griffith, J. Larry: trustee, Carver Charitable Trust (Roy J.)

Griffith, Mary: vice president, Kuyper Foundation (Peter H. and E. Lucille Gaass)

Griffith, Walter S.: adv, Griffith Foundation (W. C.)

Griffith, William C., III: adv, Griffith Foundation (W. C.)

Griffiths, Andrea Q.: vice president, Staunton Farm Foundation

Griffiths, Clark A.: chairman, Mascoma Savings Bank

Griffiths, Mary Elizabeth: member, Staunton Farm Foundation

Griggs, Alfred L.: director, Beveridge Foundation, Inc. (Frank Stanley)

Griggs, C. E. Bayliss: vice president, director, Griggs and Mary Griggs

Burke Foundation (Mary Livingston)

Grijalva, Norbert R.: tax officer, El Paso Corporate Foundation

Grimes, Anne Windfohr: trustee, Burnett Foundation (The)

Grimes, L. E.: treasurer, trustee, Fair Play Foundation

Grimes, Perley H., Jr.: officer, Seherr-Thoss Foundation

Grimes, Steve: chief financial officer, Bandai America, Inc.

Grimm, Janet L.: trustee, Toms Foundation (The)

Grimm, R. Brett: trustee, Toms Foundation (The)

Grimm, Ronald L.: chairman, Toms Foundation (The)

Grisanti, Eugene P.: director, Ambrose Monell Foundation (The)

Grisham, Don: fund committee member, Kaufman Endowment Fund (Louis G.)

Griswold, D. Ross, Jr.: vice president, Griswold Foundation (John C.)

Griswold, David E.: off, Griswold Foundation (Lillian Sherwood)

Grogan, Paul: trustee, Knight Foundation (John S. and James L.)

Groom, Bruce M.: secretary, trustee, Barstow Foundation

Gross, Bert M.: senior vice president, general council, secretary, Regis Foundation

Gross, Charles: assistant secretary, WPWR-TV Channel 50 Foundation

Gross, Cornelia B.: secretary, treasurer, McCausland Foundation

Gross, Courtlandt D.: adv director, Ducommun and Gross Foundation

Grosser, Steven E.: executive director, treasurer, Midcontinent Media Foundation

Grossman, Roberta: vice president, Badgeley Residuary Charitable Trust (Rose M.)

Grotjohn, Mo: executive director, treasurer, Meinders Foundation

Grousbeck, H. Irving: director, Hewlett Foundation (William and Flora)

Grove, William: trustee, McDonald Investments Foundation

Grover, Carol: president, director, VPI Foundation Inc.

Grover, R. Bruce: vice president, director, VPI Foundation Inc.

Grover Scott, Karen: director, VPI Foundation Inc.

Grubb, Dale B.: trustee, Glendorn Foundation

Gruber, David P.: trustee, president, Wyman-Gordon Foundation

Gruenberg, Jennifer: director, Marx Foundation (Virginia and Leonard)

Gruetner, Donald W.: secretary, treasurer, South Waite Foundation

Grumman, Cornelia: director, Phillips Foundation (Ellis L.)

Grumman, David L.: director, mem, Phillips Foundation (Ellis L.)

Grundfest, Judy: board director, Ottenheimer Brothers Foundation

Grundfest, Julianne D.: board of directors, Ottenheimer Brothers Foundation

Grune, George Vincent: chairman, director, Wallace-Reader's Digest Fund (DeWitt)

Gubert, Walter: vice chairman, J.P. Morgan Chase & Co.

Gudelsky, John: secretary, director, Gudelsky Family Foundation (Homer and Martha)

Gudelsky, Martha: president, director, Gudelsky Family Foundation (Homer and Martha)

Gudelsky, Medda: secretary, director, Gudelsky Family Foundation (Homer and Martha)

Guenther, Jack Egon: trustee, McNutt Charitable Trust (Amy Shelton)

Guenther, Paul Bernard: trustee, Cary Charitable Trust (Mary Flagler)

Guerrero, Anthony R., Jr.: executive vice president, First Hawaiian Foundation

Guerrero, Linda H.: director, Wright Foundation (Lola)

Guerrero, Reynaldo R.: trustee, Boehm Foundation

Guggenhime, Richard Johnson: president, trustee, Langendorf Foundation (Stanley S.)

Guidi, Marcello: director, Gilman Foundation (Howard)

Guidone, Rosemary: executive vice president, trustee, Price Foundation (Louis and Harold)

Guild, Henry Rice, Jr.: trustee, Henderson Foundation (George B.)

Guin, James M.: vice president human resources & public relations, Burlington Industries, Inc.

Guiterrez, Sigfredo: secretary, manager, trustee, Bucyrus-Erie Foundation

Gula, Richard: president, director, Boston Globe Foundation

Gulick, Alice J.: trustee, Eaton Foundation (Cyrus)

Gulick, Henry W.: president, trustee, Eaton Foundation (Cyrus)

Gully, Philip G.: member, Staunton Farm Foundation

Gumbiner, Alis: cfo, vp, Gumbiner Foundation (Josephine)

Gumbiner, Burke F.: chief financial officer, Gumbiner Foundation (Josephine)

Gumbiner, Lee: vice president, Gumbiner Foundation (Josephine)

Gumprecht, Pamela (Howard): trustee, Scripps Howard Foundation

Guna, Edward F.: vice president, treasurer, U.S. Steel Foundation

Gund, Agnes: trustee, Getty Trust (J. Paul)

Gund, Ann Landreth: secretary, trustee, Gund Foundation (George)

Gund, Catherine: trustee, Gund Foundation (George)

Gund, Geoffrey de Conde: trustee, Gund Foundation (Geoffrey); president, treasurer, trustee, Gund Foundation (George)

Gund, George, III: trustee, Gund Foundation (George)

Gund, Llura A.: vice president, trustee, Gund Foundation (George)

Gunderson, Harold: president, Howarth Trust Fund

Gunn, Barbara: director, Glick Foundation (Eugene and Marilyn)

Gunn, Colin: director, Palisades Educational Foundation

Gunn, Mary: director Pueblo, CO program, Packard Foundation (David and Lucile)

Gunter, Margaret C.: trustee, Dula Educational and Charitable Foundation (Caleb C. and Julia W.)

Gunther, Donald J.: director, Bechtel Group, Inc.

Gupta, Geeta Rao: director, Moriah Fund, Inc.

Gurash, John Thomas: director, Weingart Foundation

Guren, Debra S.: president, Hershey Foundation

Gurieva, Diana M.: executive vice president, Dyson Foundation

Gussin, Robert Zalmon, PhD: vice president science & technology, Johnson & Johnson; member corporate contributions committee, Johnson & Johnson Family of Companies Contribution Fund

Gust, Anne: executive vice president human resources, legal, administration, Gap, Inc.

Gust, Anne B.: executive vice president, chief administrative officer, Gap, Inc.

Gustafson, James E.: president, chief operating officer, St. Paul Companies, Inc.

Gustafson, Karl W.: treasurer, Stockman Family Foundation Trust

Guster, Timothy S.: vice president, secretary, Scott & Fetzer Foundation

Guth, Bernard M.: trustee, Greenfield Foundation (Albert M.)

Guth, Janet: trustee, Greenfield Foundation (Albert M.)

Guth, John E., Jr.: chairman, director, National Standard Co.

Guth, John H. J.: trustee, Woodcock Foundation

Guth, Polly: trustee, Woodcock Foundation

Guthman, Sandra P.: president, chief executive officer, Polk Brothers Foundation, Inc.

Guthridge, Charles M.: trustee, Scott Foundation (William H., John G., and Emma)

Guthrie, Victoria F.: trustee, Wyomissing Foundation

Gutierrez, Ernest B.: sr program officer, Kresge Foundation

Gutman, Roberta W.: program administrator, Motorola Foundation

Guttarb, William B.: trustee, Yawkey Foundation II

Guttmacher, Richard: vice president, Oak Grove School

Guttowsky, Lois K.: secretary, Morley Foundation

Guyton, Jean: trustee, Weckbaugh Foundation (Eleanore Mullen)

Gvozdjak, John M.: secretary, treasurer, NMC Foundation

Gwyn, John E.: director, Klee Foundation (Conrad and Virginia)

H

Haar, Charles M.: director, DBH Foundation for Law, Land, and the Felicitous Environment

Haar, Susan E.: director, DBH Foundation for Law, Land, and the Felicitous Environment

Haas, David W.: vice chairman, secretary, Penn Foundation (William)

Haas, Donald W.: trustee, Yeager Charitable Trust B (Lester E.)

Haas, Duncan: director, Penn Foundation (William)

Haas, Evelyn Danzig: don, co-chairman, trustee, Haas, Jr. Fund (Evelyn and Walter)

Haas, Frederick R.: director, Penn Foundation (William)

Haas, Janet F.: president, director, Penn Foundation (William)

Haas, John O.: director, Penn Foundation (William)

Haas, Leonard C.: director, Penn Foundation (William)

Haas, Miriam Lurie: don, president, trustee, Haas Fund (Miriam and Peter)

Haas, Nancy B.: director, Penn Foundation (William)

Haas, Peter Edgar, Jr.: president, Haas Fund (Walter and Elise)

Haas, Peter Edgar, Sr.: honorary president, Haas Fund (Walter and Elise)

Haas, Robert Douglas: trustee, Haas, Jr. Fund (Evelyn and Walter)

Haas, Thomas W.: director, Penn Foundation (William)

Haas, William D.: director, Penn Foundation (William)

Haase, Herman A.: admin, Peters Foundation (Charles F.)

Haasen, Adolf: director, Backus Foundation (Beatrice and Roy)

Habegger, Gary L.: vice president human resources, Goodrich Corp.; president, Goodrich Foundation, Inc. (B.F.)

Habermeier, Juergen: vice chairman, Hexcel Corp.

Habermeyer, H. William, Jr.: vice president, director, Progress Energy Foundation

Hackett, James P.: trustee, Steelcase Foundation; president, chief executive officer, Steelcase Inc.

Haefner, Lloyd: director, Bradford Foundation (George and Ruth)

Haensel, Peter C.: president, director, Schoenleber Foundation

Hafer, Anne M.: director, Bair Family Trust (Charles M.)

Haffenreffer, T. C., Jr.: vice chairman, director, Rahr Malting Co.

Haffner, Charles Christian, III: president, treasurer, director, Haffner Foundation

Hafif, Herbert: director, Hafif Family Foundation

Hagan, David I.: trustee, Seybert Institution for Poor Boys and Girls (Adam and Maria Sarah)

Hansen, Maxine: director, Autry Foundation

Hansen, Nancy Huston: vice president evangelical relations, Huston Foundation

Hansen, Robert: director, Petteys Memorial Foundation (Jack)

Hansen, Robert U.: trustee, Kitzmiller/Bales Trust

Hansen, Robert V.: director, Joslin-Needham Family Foundation

Hanshaw, Frank E., Jr.: vice president, Huntington Foundation

Hansler, John F.: secretary, director, Cheney Foundation (Ben B.)

Hanson, Elizabeth J.: chp, secretary, treasurer, Johnston-Hanson Foundation

Hanson, Eric: director, Johnston-Hanson Foundation

Hanson, Erik A.: vice president, director, Loewy Family Foundation

Hanson, Fred L.: vice president, Johnston-Hanson Foundation

Hanson, John Nils: president, Harnischfeger Industries Foundation; chairman, president, chief executive officer, Joy Global, Inc.

Hanson, Jon F.: trustee, Prudential Foundation

Hanson, Luise V.: trustee, Winnebago Industries Foundation

Hanson, P. A.: controller, Exxon Mobil Foundation

Hanson, Richard E.: vice president, director, 3M Foundation

Hanson, Stan: vice president, Kawasaki Motors Manufacturing Corporation U.S.A.

Hanson, Terry: secretary, treasurer, Madison Gas & Electric Foundation; chief financial officer, MGE Energy, Inc.

Hanson, Virginia Wilson: trustee, director, Meadows Foundation (The)

Hanssen, Marty Voelkel: trustee, secretary, Knott Foundation (Marion I. and Henry J.)

Hanway, H. Edward: chairman, chief executive officer, CIGNA Corp.

Hapgood, Elaine P.: president, Educational Foundation of America

Haqq, Constance T.: executive director, Nordson Corp. Foundation

Harckham, Peter B.: secretary, trustee, Heller Charitable Foundation (Clarence E.)

Harden, Glen: treasurer, Progress Energy Foundation; executive vice president, chief financial officer, Progress Energy Inc.

Harden, O. C., Jr.: trustee, Blount Educational and Charitable Foundation (Mildred Weedon)

Harden, Oleta J.: secretary, New Jersey Natural Gas Foundation

Hardenbergh, Gabrielle: secretary, Saint Croix Foundation

Harder, Henry U.: trustee emeritus, Dodge Foundation (Geraldine R.)

Harder, Willis: president, Schowalter Foundation

Hardin, Jacob C., Jr.: director, Doherty Charitable Foundation (Henry L. and Grace)

Hardin, P. Russell: vice president, secretary, Evans Foundation, Inc. (Lettie Pate)

Hardin, Vaughn C.: trustee, The MBNA Foundation

Harding, David R.: trustee, Camp and Bennet Humiston Trust (Apollos)

Harding, George T., IV: trustee, Worthington Foods Foundation

Harding, Leslie: director, Portsmouth General Hospital Foundation

Harding, Louis: vice president, Schwartz Foundation (Arnold A.)

Hardwick, Charles: executive director foundation, Pfizer Foundation

Hardy, Gene M.: director, La-Z-Boy Foundation

Hardy, Joan J.: trustee, McBeath Foundation (Faye)

Hardy, Richard B.: trustee, Hyde Charitable Foundation; chairman, chief executive officer, director, Hyde Manufacturing Co.

Hardy, Thomas B.: trustee, Hyde Charitable Foundation

Hargrave, Karen: trustee, Houck Foundation (May Kay)

Hargrave, Louis W.: vice president, trustee, Warfield Memorial Fund (Anna Emory)

Hargrow, Ralph: senior vice president Human Resources, International Multifoods Corp.

Harkins, James F., Jr.: treasurer, Saint-Gobain Corporation Foundation

Harl, Sidney W.: director, Paley Foundation, Inc. (William S.)

Harland, Robert P.: director, vice president, Wehr Foundation (Todd)

Harlem, Robert A.: trustee, Warren and Beatrice W. Blanding Foundation (Riley J. and Lillian N.)

Harless, Katherine J.: director, Verizon Foundation

Harleston, Bernard Warren, PhD: director, senior associates,, Macy, Jr. Foundation (Josiah)

Harley, Patricia R.: secretary, Johnson Fund (Edward C.)

Harmon, Brenda S.: treasurer, AK Steel Foundation

Harmon, John J.: chairperson, Raskob Foundation for Catholic Activities, Inc.

Harmony, Jane E.: director, Baird Brothers Co. Foundation

Harms, Richard: secretary, treasurer, director, Audubon State Bank Charitable Foundation

Harngan, Karen: contributions committee, CNA Foundation

Harnum, Linda F.: trustee, Webber Oil Foundation

Harper, Barry: president, chief executive officer, Harper Brush Works

Harper, Bill: trustee, Gifford Charitable Corp. (Rosamond)

Harper, Ralph E.: secretary, treasurer, director, Gleason Foundation

Harper, Valerie: admin, Dana Charitable Trust (Eleanor Naylor)

Harra, Robert U. A., Jr.: president, chief operating officer, Wilmington Trust Co.

Harrell, Dorothy: executive director, Bonfils-Stanton Foundation

Harrell, Pauline Chase: mem, Henderson Foundation (George B.)

Harrer, Donald G.: president, Lee Endowment Foundation

Harrington, Charles M.: trustee, Mascoma Savings Bank Foundation

Harrington, Deborah Weil: director, Norman Foundation

Harrington, Earl W., Jr.: mem distribution comm, Champlin Foundation

Harrington, Francis A., Jr.: trustee, Harrington Foundation (Francis A. and Jacquelyn H.)

Harrington, George S.: trustee, Marmot Foundation

Harrington, James H.: trustee, Harrington Foundation (Francis A. and Jacquelyn H.)

Harrington, John Leo: trustee, Yawkey Foundation II

Harrington, Kathleen B.: assistant treasurer, Earhart Foundation

Harrington, Phyllis: trustee, Harrington Foundation (Francis A. and Jacquelyn H.)

Harrington, Samuel P.: member, Norman Foundation

Harris, Ellen H.: trustee, Callaway Foundation, Inc.

Harris, Elmer Beseler: chairman, Alabama Power Foundation; member advisory committee, Meyer Foundation (Robert R.)

Harris, George: assistant secretary, assistant treasurer, director, Littauer Foundation (Lucius N.)

Harris, George R.: trustee, Schumann Fund for New Jersey

Harris, Henry Upham, III: trustee, Webster Foundation (Edwin S.)

Harris, Henry Upham, Jr.: trustee, Webster Foundation (Edwin S.)

Harris, J. Ira: vice president, Polk Brothers Foundation, Inc.

Harris, Kelly L.: trustee, Knott Foundation (Marion I. and Henry J.)

Harris, Lindsay: trustee, Knott Foundation (Marion I. and Henry J.)

Harris, Lisa: administrator, Sierra Pacific Resources Charitable Foundation

Harris, Marilyn A.: trustee, U.S. Steel Foundation

Harris, Martin R.: treasurer, Piper Foundation (Minnie Stevens)

Harris, O. Ben: director, assistant secretary, Georgia Power Foundation

Harris, Paul W.: executive vice president, Hoblitzelle Foundation

Harris, Richard M.: trustee, Lattner Foundation (Forrest C.)

Harris, Robert C.: president, Gilmore Foundation (William G.)

Harris, Roland J.: director, Dime Savings Bank of Norwich Foundation

Harris, Suzanne C.: assistant treasurer, Clemens Foundation

Harris, T. Britton, IV: chief information officer, Verizon Foundation

Harris, T. G.: trustee, Chesapeake Corp. Foundation

Harris, Thomas K.: trustee, Knott Foundation (Marion I. and Henry J.)

Harris, Thomas L.: chief administrative officer, director finance, Irvine Foundation (The James)

Harris, W. Patrick: executive vice president investments, Carter Foundation (Amon G.)

Harris, William C.: trustee, Camp and Bennet Humiston Trust (Apollos)

Harrison, Carl: vice president finance, chief financial officer, Owen Industries

Harrison, Lois Cowles: trustee, Cowles Charitable Trust

Harrison, Lois Eleanor: trustee, Cowles Charitable Trust

Harrison, Marian P.: director, assistant treasurer, Powell Foundation

Harrison, Ronald E.: senior vice president global diversity, community affairs, PepsiCo Inc.

Harrison, William B., Jr.: director, New York Stock Exchange Foundation, Inc.

Hart, Barbara: director, Publix Supermarkets Charities

Hart, Dehler: director, Springs Foundation, Inc.

Hart, George G.: secretary, Lake Placid Education Foundation

Hart, Joseph T. C.: treasurer, Ambrose Monell Foundation (The); secretary, Vetlesen Foundation (G. Unger)

Hart, William D., Jr.: secretary, general counsel, trustee, Heckscher Foundation for Children

Harte, Richard, Jr.: trustee, Webster Foundation (Edwin S.)

Hartley, Barbara: chairperson, Johnson Foundation (Helen K. and Arthur E.)

Hartley, Richard O.: chairman grant comm, Royal Foundation (May Mitchell)

Hartley, Susan J.: grant committee, Royal Foundation (May Mitchell)

Hartman, Betty Regenstein: vice president, director, Regenstein Foundation

Hartman, Jerry J.: director, Utica National Foundation

Hartmann, David B.: trustee, Pittsburgh Child Guidance Foundation

Hartshorne, Harold, Jr.: director, Chapin Foundation of Myrtle Beach, South Carolina

Hartung, Suzanne R.: vice president, Rupp Foundation (Fran and Warren)

Hartwell, David B.: trustee, Bell Foundation (James Ford)

Harvey, A. Mosby, Jr.: secretary, HON Industries Charitable Foundation; vice president, secretary, general counsel, HON Industries, Inc.

Harvey, Ann: director, Harvey Foundation (C. Felix)

Harvey, C. Felix: vice president, Harvey Foundation (C. Felix)

Harvey, Charlene: director, vice chair, Rosenberg Foundation

Harvey, Constance: program director, Shubert Foundation

Harvey, Frank H., Jr.: secretary, treasurer, Wilkof Foundation (Edward and Ruth)

Harvey, James D.: adv, Ritter Charitable Trust (George and Mary)

Harvey, Joan: director, New-Land Foundation

Harvey, Joseph: director, New-Land Foundation

Harvey, Margaret B.: president, Harvey Foundation (C. Felix)

Harvey, Robert W.: vice chairman, CenterPoint Energy, Inc.

Harvey, Thomas B., Esq.: trustee, Douty Foundation (Alfred and Mary)

Harvey, Thomas Hal: president, New-Land Foundation

Harvey, Tom: assistant treasurer, BellSouth Foundation

Harwich, A. Peter: secretary, Unilever United States Foundation

Hasbargen, Vernae: trustee emeritus, Blandin Foundation

Hashim, Carlisle V.: trustee, Knott Foundation (Marion I. and Henry J.)

Haskell, Antoinette M.: treasurer, Public Welfare Foundation

Haskell, Coburn: president, trustee, Haskell Fund

Haskell, Eric T.: trustee, Haskell Fund

Haskell, John G.: president, Chapman Charitable Corp. (Howard and Bess)

Haskell, Mark: trustee, Haskell Fund

Haskell, Mary E.: trustee, Haskell Fund

Haskell, Melville H., Jr.: trustee, Haskell Fund

Haskell, Robert G.: president, director, Pacific Life Foundation; senior vice president public affairs, Pacific Life Insurance Co.

Haskell, Robert H.: vice chairman, director, Public Welfare Foundation

Haskell, Schuyler A.: vice president, trustee, Haskell Fund

Haskell-Green, Sarah: trustee, Haskell Fund

Haslam, Anne S.: secretary, Teichert Foundation

Hassan, Fred: chairman, chief executive officer, Schering-Plough Corp.

Hasten, Andrea: director, Cuneo Foundation

Hasting, Carl D.: vice president, secretary, treasurer, director, Keck, Jr. Foundation (William M.)

Hastings, Alfred B., Jr.: trustee, Murphey Foundation (Lluella Morey)

Hastings, David R., II: trustee, Mulford Trust (Clarence E.)

Hastings, Peter G.: trustee, Mulford Trust (Clarence E.)

Hatayama, Kuniki: chief financial officer, Kikkoman Foods; director, Kikkoman Foundation

Hatch, Francis W., III: president, trustee, Merck Family Fund

Hatch, Rakia I.: trustee, Hatch Charitable Trust (Margaret Milliken)

Hatch, Richard L.: trustee, Hatch Charitable Trust (Margaret Milliken)

Hatcher, Dottie: senior director, Gap Foundation

Hathaway, D. C.: trustee, Harsco Corp. Fund

Hathaway, Derek C.: director, Kline Foundation (Josiah W. and Bessie H.)

Hathaway, E. Phillips: president, trustee, Middendorf Foundation

Hathaway, Richard E.: trustee, City National Bank Foundation

Hattler, Robert L.: treasurer, German Protestant Orphan Asylum Association Foundation

Hattox, Brock Alan: director, National Service Foundation; executive vice president, chief financial officer, National Service Industries, Inc.

Haubein, Robert H., Jr.: director, Georgia Power Foundation

Hauben, David: vice president, treasurer, Lowe Foundation (Joe and Emily)

Hauptfuhrer, Robert Paul: director, Barra Foundation

Hauptli, Barbara A.: trust, Hauptli Charitable Foundation (A. John and Barbara A.)

Hausmann, Carl L.: chairman, president, chief executive officer, Central Soya Co.

Hauswirth, Lisa G.: director, Langendorf Foundation (Stanley S.)

Haviland, David Sands: director, Howard and Bush Foundation

Hawk, Daniel D.: vice president, treasurer, Burlington Resources Foundation

Hawk, Dennis Dale: member, Norman Foundation

Hawkins, Chaille W.: assistant secretary, trustee, Sterling-Turner Foundation

Hawkins, Prince A.: trustee, Hawkins Foundation (Robert Z.)

Hawkins, William: general tax council, Coca-Cola Foundation

Hawkinson, John: trustee, Blandin Foundation

Hawley, Philip Metschan: trustee, Haynes Foundation (John Randolph and Dora)

Hawley, Wendell C.: director, Tyndale House Foundation

Hawn, Bruce Sams: president, chief executive officer, director, Sams Foundation (Earl C.)

Hawn, Gates Helms: director, Clark Foundation (NY)

Hawn, J. Verne: director, Hawn Foundation

Hawn, Jim J.: director, Hawn Foundation

Hawn, Joe Verne, Jr.: director, Hawn Foundation

Hawn, Nancy: director, Sams Foundation (Earl C.)

Hawn, W. A., Jr.: president, Hawn Foundation

Hawn, William Russell, Jr.: director, Hawn Foundation

Haxo, John V., MD: director, New Milford Savings Bank Foundation

Hay, Susan: manager, National Grange Mutual Charitable Trust

Hayakawa, Y.: chairman, president, chief executive officer, Hino Diesel Trucks (U.S.A.)

Hayama, John: vice president, Locations Foundation

Hayashi, Kazuya: director, Kikkoman Foundation

Hayes, Arthur H., Jr.: director, Macy, Jr. Foundation (Josiah)

Hayes, Carol: general counsel, Coca-Cola Foundation

Hayes, John: director, secretary, Hermann Foundation (Grover)

Hayes, Mariam C.: president, director, member, Cannon Foundation, Inc. (The)

Hayes, Patricia Ann: trustee, RGK Foundation

Hayes, R. C.: director, member, Cannon Foundation, Inc. (The)

Hayes, Rob: director, Mid-Iowa Health Foundation

Hayes, Synnova Bay: president, Bay Foundation

Haygood, Paul: trustee, German Protestant Orphan Asylum Association Foundation

Hayne, Roxana Catto: vice president, secretary, Gage Foundation (Alfred S.)

Hayner, Herman Henry: trustee, Shepherd Foundation (Harold and Helen)

Hayner, James K.: trustee, Stubblefield (Estate of Joseph L.)

Haynes, Larry N.: director, Christy-Houston Foundation

Haynes, Noris R., Jr.: executive director, trustee, Plough Foundation

Hays, Frances McKee: senior vice president, McKee Foundation (Robert E. and Evelyn)

Hays, Lucille T.: mem adv comm, Weezie Foundation

Hays, Thomas Chandler: chairman, chief executive officer, director, Fortune Brands, Inc.

Haywood, T. C.: director, Cannon Foundation, Inc. (The)

Hazard, Eileen: program officer, Verizon Foundation

Hazard, Susan J.: trustee, Lantz Foundation (Walter)

Hazel, John T., Jr.: director, Loughran Foundation (Mary and Daniel)

Hazel, Lewis F.: treasurer, Children's Foundation of Erie County

Hazelett, Susie: executive director, Tobias Foundation (Randall L.)

Hazelrigg, Charles R.: trustee, Johnson Foundation (Helen K. and Arthur E.)

Hazelton, Robert L.: senior vice president, McKee Foundation (Robert E. and Evelyn)

Hazen, Kathy: executive director, Buck Foundation (Frank H. and Eva B.)

Hazen, Paul Mandeville: chairman, chief executive officer, director, Wells Fargo & Co.

Head, Beverly P., III: trustee, Kaul Foundation Trust (Hugh)

Head, Deidra: director, McBean Family Foundation

Head, Sheila McBean: director, McBean Family Foundation

Heafey, Edwin Austin, Jr.: director, Valley Foundation (Wayne and Gladys)

Healey, Louis: chief financial officer, Jaydor Corp.

Healy, James T.: president, Trust Funds

Healy, Jo Ann: administrator, Alliant Energy Foundation, Inc.

Heard, Drew R.: chairman, McMillan, Jr. Foundation (Bruce)

Heard, Jane: director, Colt Foundation (James J.)

Heard, Karen: director, Colt Foundation (James J.)

Heard, Thomas H.: vice president, director, Colt Foundation (James J.)

Hearn, Thomas A.: vice president, treasurer, director, Russell Charitable Foundation (Tom)

Hearst, George Randolph, Jr.: president, director, Hearst Foundation, Inc. (The); vice president, director, Hearst Foundation (William Randolph)

Hearst, John Randolph, Jr.: director, Hearst Foundation, Inc. (The); vice president, director, Hearst Foundation (William Randolph)

Hearst, William R., III: president, director, Hearst Foundation, Inc. (The); vice president, director, Hearst Foundation (William Randolph)

Heasley, Karen L.: director, Snee-Reinhardt Charitable Foundation

Heasley, Paul A.: off, Snee-Reinhardt Charitable Foundation

Heasley, Timothy: director, Snee-Reinhardt Charitable Foundation

Heath, Ruth: assistant secretary, Harvey Foundation (C. Felix)

Heaton, Mary Alice J.: trustee, Whiting Foundation

Hebenstreit, James B.: president, Bartlett & Co.; trustee, Bartlett & Co. Grain Charitable Foundation

Hecht, John: chief financial officer, AMCORE Financial, Inc.

Heckel, Ben: co-trustee, Swift Co. Inc. Charitable Trust (John S.)

Hed, Gordon E.: assistant secretary, assistant treasurer, Weyerhaeuser Memorial Foundation (Charles A.)

Hedberg, Douglas A.: trustee, Ashtabula Foundation

Hedberg, S. Anders, Ph.D.: director, Bristol-Myers Squibb Foundation Inc.

Heddens, B. Spencer: director, Francis Families Foundation

Hedemark, N. Charles: executive vice president, chief operating officer, director, Intermountain Gas Co.; director, Intermountain Gas Industries Foundation

Hedges, James R., III: vice president, trustee, Tonya Memorial Foundation

Hedges, M. D.: trustee, Betts Foundation

Heeg, Peggy A.: executive vice president, general counsel, director, El Paso Corporate Foundation

Heegaard, Peter A.: chairman, member executive committee, Blandin Foundation

Heemstra, Linda R.: trustee, Kantzler Foundation

Heenan, Earl I., Jr.: vchairman, trustee, Earhart Foundation

Heeter, Chris R.: secretary, Stardust Foundation

Hefferan, Pat: vice president, Mitsubishi Semiconductor America, Inc. Funds

Hefferline, Arline: secretary, Norcliffe Foundation

Heffern, Gordon Emory: trustee, Knight Foundation (John S. and James L.)

Heffernan, E. Mary: treasurer, Noble Foundation, Inc. (Edward John)

Heffernan, Elizabeth Blossom: vice president, trustee, chairman public information committee, Bingham Foundation (William)

Heffner, Jane E.: vice president, Salomon Smith Barney Holdings, Inc.

Hefty, Noel M.: trustee, Messing Family Charitable Foundation

Hefty, Terrance: trustee, Messing Family Charitable Foundation

Hefty, Thomas R.: chairman, president, chief executive officer, United Wisconsin Services

Hegarty, Neal R.: program officer, Mott Foundation (Charles Stewart)

Hegeler, Alix S.: director, Hegeler II Foundation (Julius W.)

Hegeler, Julius W., II: director, Hegeler II Foundation (Julius W.)

Hegeler, Madelle G.: mgr, Hegeler II Foundation (Julius W.)

Hehl, David K.: director, La-Z-Boy, Inc.

Heidt, Jill: director, Lesher Foundation (Dean and Margaret)

Heidt, Julia Scripps: trustee, Scripps Howard Foundation

Heil, Mark: committee member, Haman Family Foundation

Heilala, John A.: trustee, Vulcan Materials Co. Foundation

Heill, Mark: committee member, Haman Family Foundation

Heilman, Susan B.: executive assistant, Huston Foundation

Heim, Ed: secretary advisory committee, Blue Bell Foundation

Heimbold, Charles Andreas, Jr.: president, chief executive officer, Bristol-Myers Squibb Co.

Heimerman, Quentin O.: vice president, Saint Croix Foundation

Heinecke, James O.: director, Associated Banc-Corp Foundation

Heineman, Benjamin W., Jr.: director, Arison Foundation

Heineman, Benjamin Walter, Jr.: director, GE Foundation

Heinemen, Melvin L.: secretary, treasurer, director, Rohatyn Foundation (Felix and Elizabeth)

Heinen, Stacy: director, Grinnell Mutual Group Foundation

Heintz, Stephen B.: president, Rockefeller Brothers Fund, Inc.

Heinz, Andre: director, Heinz Family Foundation

Heinz, Andre T.: director, Heinz Endowment (Vira I.)

Heinz, Drue: director emeritus, Heinz Endowment (Howard); trustee, Heinz Trust (Drue)

Heinz, H. John, IV: director, Heinz Endowment (Howard)

Heinz, Teresa: trustee, Carnegie Corp. of New York; chairwoman, Heinz Endowment (Howard); director, Heinz Endowment (Vira I.); chairperson, chief executive officer, Heinz Family Foundation

Heisen, JoAnn Heffernan: vice president, chief information officer, Johnson & Johnson; treasurer, Johnson & Johnson Family of Companies Contribution Fund

Heiser, James S.: chief financial officer, Ducommun, Inc.

Heiskell, Marian Sulzberger: president, director, Sulzberger Foundation

Heller, Alfred E.: president, trustee, Heller Charitable Foundation (Clarence E.)

Heller, Helen H.: secretary, treasurer, director, Davenport-Hatch Foundation

Heller, Katherine: secretary, trustee, Heller Charitable Foundation (Clarence E.)

Heller, Miranda: vice president, trustee, Heller Charitable Foundation (Clarence E.)

Hellie, Thomas L.: executive director, Kemper Foundation (James S.)

Helm, George T.: trustee, Levy Foundation (June Rockwell)

Helm, John: director, Johnson Foundation (Samuel S.)

Helmerich, Walter Hugo, III: trustee, Helmerich Foundation

Helmick, Walter E.: vice president, Stans Foundation

Helmig, Albert: director, New York Mercantile Exchange Charitable Foundation

Helmke, Walter Paul: vice president, secretary, Foellinger Foundation

Helms, Ann Marie: program associate, assistant secretary, Mellon Family Foundation (R. K.); assistant secretary, Mellon Foundation (Richard King)

Helsby, Keith R.: treasurer, New York Stock Exchange Foundation, Inc.

Helseth, Nancy L.: admin, Collins Medical Trust

Helzner, Judith F.: director population & reprod health, MacArthur Foundation (John D. and Catherine T.)

Hemme, Dennis: vice president, CNA Foundation

Hemphill, Caroline M.: director special programs, assistant secretary-treasurer, Olin Foundation (John M.)

Hemphill, William L.: director, Cemala Foundation

Hempstead, David M.: secretary, trustee, Ford Fund (Walter and Josephine); secretary, trustee, member, Ford Fund (William and Martha); secretary, Ford II Fund (Edsel B.); secretary, trustee, Ford II Fund (Henry); secretary, Wilson Fund (Matilda R.)

Henderson, Barclay G. S.: trustee, Henderson Foundation

Henderson, Darryl K.: trustee, Lowe's Charitable and Educational Foundation

Henderson, Delores: director, Mardag Foundation

Henderson, Ernest, III: trustee, Henderson Foundation

Henderson, George: treasurer, Pineywoods Foundation

Henderson, George W., III: director, Burlington Industries Foundation; chief executive officer, chairman, Burlington Industries, Inc.

Henderson, Gerald C.: trustee, Henderson Foundation (George B.)

Henderson, James D.: trustee, Fuller Foundation (MA)

Henderson, Rhoe B., III: director, Gebbie Foundation

Henderson, Robert P.: director, Fairchild Foundation, Inc. (Sherman)

Henderson, Thomas J.: vice president, director, Atkinson Foundation

Henderson, William M.: trustee, Edison Fund (Charles)

Hendrick, William A.: trustee, Wickes Foundation (Harvey Randall)

Hendricks, Ben F.: mgr, Porter Testamentary Trust (James Hyde)

Hendrickson, Lil M.: assistant secretary, Wheeler Foundation

Hendrix, C. E., Jr.: president, De Queen Regional Medical Center

Heningburg, Gustav: trustee, Fund for New Jersey

Henkels, Alexander Ardley, Jr.: president, Staunton Farm Foundation

Henley, Arlene S.: co-trustee, Robert Charitable Trust 2 (John A. and Delia T.)

Henneman, Larry R.: officer, Neilson Foundation (George W.)

Hennessey, Frank Martin: trustee, Hudson-Webber Foundation

Hennessy, Marilyn: president, Retirement Research Foundation

Hennessy, Michael W.: president, chief executive officer, director, Coleman Foundation (IL)

Henney, Jane E., MD: member, Kansas Health Foundation

Henning, Leo T.: director, Oakley-Lindsay Foundation of Quincy Newspapers and Its Subsidiaries

Henrich, William J., Jr.: secretary, general counsel, Annenberg Foundation

Henrickson, C. Robert: director, MetLife Foundation

Henrickson, Patricia K.R.: vice president, Atherton Family Foundation

Henry, Brent: director, Public Welfare Foundation

Henry, C. L.: chairman, president, chief executive officer, Johns Manville

Henry, Carl F.H.: director, M.E. Foundation

Henry, Dorothy J.: trustee, Johnson Foundation (Howard)

Henry, Douglas: director, Joyce Family Foundation

Henry, Leland W.: trustee, Berry Foundation (Loren M.)

Henry, Patricia: plant manager, Miller Brewing Co. (Eden, NC)

Henry, Patricia M.: trustee, Medina Foundation

Henry, Robert A., MD: director, AMCORE Foundation

Henry, Shauna I.: director, Rosenberg Foundation

Henry Wood, Margaret: chairperson, Joyce Family Foundation

Henry-Williams, Dee: grants program assistant, Target Foundation

Henseler, Gerald A.: executive vice president, chief financial officer, director, Banta Corp.; president, Banta Corp. Foundation

Henson, Jackson W.: director, secretary, Reynolds Tobacco Company Foundation (R. J.)

Henson, Richard A.: chairman, trustee, Henson Foundation (Richard A.)

Henson, William C.: treasurer, trustee, Foundation for Seacoast Health

Herald, James E.: vice president finance, Mine Safety Appliances Co.; secretary, Mine Safety Appliances Co. Charitable Foundation

Herbert, Gavin Shearer, Jr.: director, Beckman Foundation (Arnold and Mabel)

Herbert, John K., III: trustee, Henderson Foundation (George B.)

Herbert, Peter A.: vice president, director, Guttman Foundation (Stella and Charles)

Herbold, Robert J.: executive vice president, Microsoft Corp.

Herbst, Linda Vitti: trustee, Price Foundation (Louis and Harold)

Herd, Bob L.: president, Herd Foundation (Bob L.)

Herd, Patsy L.: vice president, Herd Foundation (Bob L.)

Herd, Tevis: trustee, Abell-Hanger Foundation

Herder, Charles: trustee, George Foundation

Hereford, J.: vice president, Conway Scholarship Foundation (Carle C.)

Hergenhan, Joyce: director, Arison Foundation; director, president, GE Foundation

Herlich, Harold N., Jr.: secretary, Kaufman Endowment Fund (Louis G.)

Herlin, Cara: advisory trustee, Trull Foundation (The)

Herlin, Jean Trull: founder, trustee emeritus, Trull Foundation (The)

Herman, Bruce: treasurer, Hexcel Foundation

Herman, Iving, Ph.D.: Distribution trustee, Schwab-Rosenhouse Memorial Foundation

Herman, Ronald D.: treasurer, Employers Mutual Charitable Foundation

Herman, Tom: director, Hedco Foundation

Herman, William A., III: secretary, treasurer, director, Morris Communications Corp.

Hermance, Frank S.: president, director, AMETEK Foundation; chairman, chief executive officer, director, AMETEK, Inc.

Hermanson, Everett J.: trustee, Kinney-Lindstrom Foundation

Hernandez, Colleen: director, Fannie Mae Foundation

Hernandez, Robert M.: vice chairman, chief financial

officer, director, U.S. Steel Corp.; chief financial officer, U.S. Steel Foundation

Herndon, Herschel: director, Global Communication, Stanley Works

Herr, Earl Binkley, Jr.: director, Lilly Endowment

Herrell, John E.: treasurer, assistant secretary, Atkinson Foundation

Herrera, Julia: director, Chamiza Foundation

Herrera, Sharon Hays: vice president, trustee, McKee Foundation (Robert E. and Evelyn)

Herrigel, Fred, III: president, Read Foundation (Charles L.)

Herrigel, Rodger K.: secretary, Read Foundation (Charles L.)

Herriman, M. Davis, Junior: vice president, grocery operations, Giant Food, Inc.

Herring, Leonard Gray: vice president, Lowe's Charitable and Educational Foundation

Herrington, Ed: vice president, Rheinstrom Hill Community Foundation

Herrington, Marilyn A.: president, Hudson River Bancorp Inc. Foundation

Hershberger, Howard: trustee, Schowalter Foundation

Hershey, Barry J.: trustee, Hershey Family Foundation

Hershey, Connie: trustee, Hershey Family Foundation

Hershey, Loren W.: chairman, Hershey Foundation

Herterich, Karen Kennedy: director, Kennedy Family Foundation (Ethel and W. George)

Hertzke, Bruce D.: president, chief executive officer, chief operating officer, Winnebago Industries; trustee, Winnebago Industries Foundation

Herweg, Darlynn: director, Union Pacific Corp.; assistant secretary, Union Pacific Foundation

Herzstein, Stanley: director, Koret Foundation

Hesdorffer, Lisa S.: vice president, director, Schmoker Family Foundation

Heselton, George W.: mem, Gardiner Savings Institution Charitable Foundation

Hess, Bev: secretary, treasurer, Mingenback Foundation (Julia J.)

Hess, Donald E.: secretary-treasurer, Figtree Foundation

Hess, Donald Marc: secretary, treasurer, Figtree Foundation

Hess, George B., Jr.: director, Baltimore Equitable Insurance Foundation

Hess, William C.: vice president, director, Audubon State Bank Charitable Foundation; chief executive officer, Iowa Savings Bank; secretary, treasurer, director, Iowa Savings Bank Charitable Foundation

Hessinger, Carl John William: trustee, Trexler Trust (Harry C.)

Hessler, Deborah: secretary, Bush Charitable Foundation, Inc. (Edyth)

Hesson, Jeffrey L.: director, Ray Foundation

Hester, James McNaughton: president, director, Guggenheim Foundation (Harry Frank)

Heston, W. Craig: president, director, Utica National Foundation; chairman, chief executive officer, director, Utica National Insurance Group

Hetherington, Eileen Mavis: director, Foundation for Child Development

Heuer, Laura Baxter: assistant secretary, treasurer, trustee, Andrews Foundation

Heuermann, Bernard K.: president, director, Heuermann Foundation (Bernard K. and Norma F.)

Heuermann, Norma F.: vice president, director, Heuermann Foundation (Bernard K. and Norma F.)

Heuschele, Richard P., MD: trustee, Wickes Foundation (Harvey Randall)

Heuser, Henry V.: chairman, director, Vogt Machine Co. (Henry)

Heuser, Henry V., Jr.: president, director, Vogt Foundation (Henry)

Hewey, Kristina B.: trustee, Braitmayer Foundation

Hewit, Betty Ruth: vice president, director, Hewit Family Foundation

Hewit, William D.: president, treasurer, director, Hewit Family Foundation

Hewitt, Steven J.: senior vice president, chief financial officer

Hewlett, Walter B.: chairman, Hewlett Foundation (William and Flora)

Heyler, David B., Jr.: trustee, McAlister Charitable Foundation (Harold)

Heyman, Joseph S.: president, trustee, Stone Foundation (France)

Hiam, Edwin W.: trustee, Webster Foundation (Edwin S.)

Hibben, Seabury J.: trustee, Seabury Foundation

Hibberd, William F.: secretary, Harriman Foundation (Gladys and Roland)

Hickey, James H.: trustee, Baker Foundation (R. C.)

Hickox, Charles C.: director, Barker Welfare Foundation

Hickox, John B.: director, Barker Welfare Foundation

Hickox, Linda J.: director, Barker Welfare Foundation

Hicks, Kenneth W.: member, Kansas Health Foundation

Hiddeman, J.: trustee, Alcon Foundation

Hieber, Carl O.: trustee, Plankenhorn Foundation (Harry)

Higgins, Barbara: director, Memorial Foundation for the Blind

Higgins, Eunice O.: secretary, trustee, Olin Foundation (Spencer T. and Ann W.)

Higgins, Michael R.: treasurer, Amcast Industrial Foundation

Higgins, Paul M.: director, Dime Savings Bank of Norwich Foundation

Higgins, Ralph P.: treasurer, trustee, Eaton Foundation (Cyrus)

Higgins, Richard: trustee, Higgins Foundation (John W. and Clara C.)

Higgins, Walter M.: chairman, president, chief executive officer, Sierra Pacific Resources

High, Calvin G.: trustee, High Foundation

High, Gregory A.: trustee, High Foundation

High, Janet C.: trustee, High Foundation

High, Richard L.: trustee, High Foundation

High, S. Dale: trustee, High Foundation

High, Sadie H.: trustee, High Foundation

High, Steven D.: trustee, High Foundation

High, Suzanne M.: trustee, High Foundation

Hightower, George H., Jr.: vice president, trustee, Community Enterprises

Hightower, Neil Hamilton: secretary, treasurer, trustee, Community Enterprises

Hightower, William H., Jr.: president, trustee, Community Enterprises

Higie, William F.: secretary, mgr, Glendorn Foundation

Higley, Robert A.: secretary, treasurer, O'Quinn Foundation (John M.)

Hilbert, Robert: secretary, treasurer, vice president admin, trustee, El Pomar Foundation

Hilbert, Stephen C.: founder, chairman, president, chief executive officer, Conseco, Inc.

Hilbrich, Gerald F.: director, Bush Charitable Foundation, Inc. (Edyth)

Hildebrandt, A. Thomas: director, Davenport-Hatch Foundation

Hildebrandt, Austin E.: president, director, Davenport-Hatch Foundation

Hildebrandt, Mary: director, Davenport-Hatch Foundation

Hilgers, William B.: director, Wright Foundation (Lola)

Hilinski, Chester C.: trustee emeritus, Connelly Foundation

Hill, Allen M.: president, chief executive officer, Dayton Power and Light Co.

Hill, Bill J.: secretary, treasurer, Beal Foundation

Hill, Bonnie Guiton: president, chief executive officer, Times Mirror Foundation; vice president, Tribune Co.

Hill, C. Dennis: director, Fleming and Jane Howe Patrick Foundation (Robert)

Hill, Charlotte Bishop: vchairwoman, mem adv comm, O'Connor Foundation (A. Lindsay and Olive B.)

Hill, David N.: president, Newhall Foundation (Henry Mayo)

Hill, Gisele N.: secretary, Arison Foundation

Hill, James: senior vice president corporate affairs, GlaxoSmithKline Plc

Hill, John P., Jr.: administrator, Dominic Foundation

Hill, Karra Mays: director, Mays Foundation

Hill, Kent: president, Gulf Coast Medical Foundation

Hill, Linda Bourns: vice president, trustee, Bourns Foundation

Hill, Louis Fors: vice president, Grotto Foundation

Hill, Louis Shea: director, Grotto Foundation

Hill, Marion: vice president, Newhall Foundation (Henry Mayo)

Hill, Pamela: executive secretary, O'Connor Foundation (A. Lindsay and Olive B.)

Hill, Sally R.: vice president, director, Burchfield Foundation (Charles E.)

Hill, Steven Richard: senior vice president human resources, Weyerhaeuser Co.; trustee, Weyerhaeuser Co. Foundation

Hill, Thomas: treasurer, Ecolab Foundation

Hill Johnson, Elizabeth: president, director, Johnson Foundation (Samuel S.)

Hillenbrand, John A., II: chairman, president, Cinergy Foundation

Hiller, William: executive director, Jennings Foundation (Martha Holden)

Hilliard, Frank P.: director, Cooke Foundation Corp. (V. V.)

Hilliard, Robert Glenn: chairman, ING North America Insurance Corp.

Hilliker, Don: secretary, WPWR-TV Channel 50 Foundation

Hillman, Elsie Hilliard: director, Hillman Foundation

Hillman, Henry Lea, Jr.: chairman, Hillman Foundation

Hillmer, Patricia: trustee, National Machinery Foundation, Inc.

Hillson, David R.: executive director, secretary, Robinson-Broadhurst Foundation

Hillyard, Gerald R., Jr.: trustee, Johnson Foundation (Helen K. and Arthur E.)

Hiltz, Francie S.: trustee, H. C. S. Foundation

Hiltz, L. Thomas: trustee, H. C. S. Foundation

Hilyard, James E.: vice president, director, Saint-Gobain Corporation Foundation

Himle, Karen: vice president corporate committee, St. Paul Companies, Inc.

Himmelfarb, Paul: secretary, director, Himmelfarb Foundation (Paul and Annetta)

Himmelman, Bonnie: president, director, Fairchild Foundation, Inc. (Sherman)

Hindley, George: mgr, Lytel Foundation (Bertha Russ)

Hines, Rodney: program manager, Microsoft Corp.

Hines, Tony: director, Honda of America Foundation

Hing, Bill Ong: chair, Rosenberg Foundation

Hinrichs, Horst: vice chairman, director, American Standard Inc.

Hintz, Gregory J.: mgr, Mercury Aircraft Foundation; treasurer, Mercury Aircraft, Inc.

Hipp, William Hayne: president, chief executive officer, director, Liberty Corp.; chairman, president, director, Liberty Corp. Foundation

Hiraki, Phyllis: trustee, Priddy Foundation

Hirano, Irene Y.: trustee, Kresge Foundation

Hirsch, Bruce A.: executive director, Heller Charitable Foundation (Clarence E.)

(Edward V. and Jessie L.)

Hughes, Timothy W.: senior vice president, Cox Enterprises, Inc.; vice president, trustee, Cox Foundation (James M.)

Hughey, Richard M., Jr.: program officer, Gilmore Foundation (Irving S.)

Hughey, Richard M., Sr.: program officer, Gilmore Foundation (Irving S.)

Hugo, Richard: assistant secretary, assistant treasurer, Peters Foundation (R. D. and Linda)

Huhn, Les M.: president, Jameson Foundation (J. W. and Ida M.)

Huisking, Frank R.: treasurer, director, Huisking Foundation

Huisking, Richard V., Jr.: secretary, director, Huisking Foundation

Huisking, Richard V., Sr.: director, Huisking Foundation

Huisking, William W., Jr.: vice president, director, Huisking Foundation

Huitt, J. Fred: vice chairman board trustees, member investment committee, Trull Foundation (The)

Huizenga, Raymond: trustee, National Grange Mutual Charitable Trust

Hulbert, Henry L.: trustee, Hulbert Foundation (Nila B.); mng trustee, Warren and Beatrice W. Blanding Foundation (Riley J. and Lillian N.)

Hulbert, J. Burton: trustee, Hulbert Foundation (Nila B.)

Hulbert, Maureen: trustee, Warren and Beatrice W. Blanding Foundation (Riley J. and Lillian N.)

Hulbert, William H.: trustee, Hulbert Foundation (Nila B.)

Hull, John: vice president finance, Mellon Foundation (Andrew W.)

Hullet, Diane D.: trustee, Dow Foundation (Herbert H. and Grace A.)

Hulme, Aura P.: trustee, Hulme Charitable Foundation (Milton G.)

Hulme, Helen C.: trustee, Hulme Charitable Foundation (Milton G.)

Hultgren, Dennis N.: director, Appleton Papers, Inc.

Hume, Caroline H.: president, trustee, Hume Foundation (Jaquelin)

Hume, George H.: first vice president, secretary, trustee, Hume Foundation (Jaquelin)

Hume, William J.: second vice president, treasurer, trustee, Hume Foundation (Jaquelin)

Humleker, Margaret Banta: vice president, director, Banta Corp. Foundation

Hummel, Richard J.: president, treasurer, Hoch Foundation (Charles H.)

Hummer, Philip Wayne: director, Field Foundation of Illinois

Humphrey, Deborah L.: director, Bowater, Inc.

Humphrey, G. Watts, Jr.: president, Blood-Horse Charitable Foundation

Humphrey, James, III: president, Wilson Foundation (H. W.)

Humphrey, William R., Jr.: trustee, Marbrook Foundation

Humphreys, B. J.: vice president, secretary, Wickson-Link Memorial Foundation

Hund, Thomas N.: executive vice president, chief financial officer, Burlington Northern Santa Fe Corp.

Hundrup, Rick: vice president finance, chief financial officer, Usibelli Coal Mine, Inc.

Hunia, Edward Mark: sr vice president, treasurer, secretary, Kresge Foundation

Hunkin, John: president, CIBC World Markets

Hunnewell, Catherine S.: vice president, director, assistant secretary, Schmoker Family Foundation

Hunt, Andrew McQ.: trustee, Hunt Foundation (Roy A.)

Hunt, Cathryn J.: trustee, Hunt Foundation (Roy A.)

Hunt, Christopher M., MD: trustee, Hunt Foundation (Roy A.)

Hunt, Daniel K.: trustee, Hunt Foundation (Roy A.)

Hunt, Gary H.: director, Beckman Foundation (Arnold and Mabel)

Hunt, James B.: trustee, Carnegie Corp. of New York

Hunt, James L.: secretary, Lurie Foundation (Louis R.)

Hunt, John Bankson: trustee, Hunt Foundation (Roy A.)

Hunt, Linda: board member, Smith and W. Aubrey Smith Charitable Foundation (Clara Blackford)

Hunt, Natasha: director, McBean Family Foundation

Hunt, Penny: executive director staff, Medtronic Foundation

Hunt, Richard M.: trustee, donor son, Hunt Foundation (Roy A.)

Hunt, Roy A., III: trustee, Hunt Foundation (Roy A.)

Hunt, Sarah Anschutz: trustee, Anschutz Family Foundation

Hunt, Torrence M.: trustee, donor son, Hunt Foundation (Roy A.)

Hunt, Torrence M., Jr.: president, trustee, Hunt Foundation (Roy A.)

Hunt, William Edwards: trustee, Hunt Foundation (Roy A.)

Hunt Badiner, Marion: trustee, Hunt Foundation (Roy A.)

Hunter, Hugh V.: director, Howe and Mitchell B. Howe Foundation (Lucille Horton)

Hunter, J. Philip: secretary, Anderson Foundation (NY)

Hunter, Robert D.: trustee, J.P. Morgan Chase Foundation

Hunter, Timothy M.: treasurer, Smith Charitable Foundation (Arlene H.)

Hunter, William O.: trustee, Crawford Estate Trust Fund A (E. R.)

Hunting, David Dyer, Jr.: trustee, Steelcase Foundation; director, Steelcase Inc.

Huntington, Lawrence Smith: chairman finance committee, director, Commonwealth Fund (The); chairman emeritus, Macy, Jr. Foundation (Josiah)

Hupfer, Charles J.: trustee, Sonoco Foundation

Huplits, W. N.: assistant controller, Exxon Mobil Foundation

Hurd, Betty: director, Washington Group Foundation, Inc.

Hurd, Terri: administrator, Kettering Fund

Hurlbutt, Jacqueline A.: vice president, Bank One Foundation

Hurley, Joseph G.: president, director, Parsons Foundation (Ralph M.)

Hurley, Webster H.: trustee, Retirement Research Foundation

Hurley, Willard L.: trustee, Hill Crest Foundation

Hurley, William P.: vice president, secretary, assistant treasurer, director, Hopkins Foundation (Josephine Lawrence)

Hurst, Anthony P.: president, Hurst Foundation

Hurst, Dean W.: off, Stewart Educational Foundation (Donnell B. and Elizabeth Dee Shaw)

Hurst, Ronald F.: vice president, Hurst Foundation

Hurston, Patricia: vice president, Bank One Foundation

Hurwitz, Charles Edwin: trustee, RGK Foundation

Hurwitz, Roger T.: mem disbursement comm, Oppenstein Brothers Foundation

Hurwitz, Samuel: assistant secretary, Iscol Family Foundation

Husarik, Ernest Alfred: member advisory & distribution committee, Jennings Foundation (Martha Holden)

Husbands, Thomas F.: assistant treasurer, Borkee-Hagley Foundation

Hussein, Claudia L.: trustee, Pittsburgh Child Guidance Foundation

Hussing, Howard: president, chief executive officer, director, Olmsted Foundation (George and Carol)

Hustad, Paul A.: director, Burns & McDonnell Foundation

Huston, Charles L., IV: treasurer, Huston Foundation

Huston, Charles Lukens, III: trustee, Huston Charitable Trust (Stewart); director operations, vice president community relations, Huston Foundation

Huston, Rebecca L.: secretary, Huston Foundation

Huston, Scott G.: executive director, Huston Charitable Trust (Stewart)

Hutcheson, Mary Ross Carter: president, Carter Foundation (Beirne)

Hutcheson, Suzanne Lilly: director, Lilly Foundation (Richard Coyle)

Hutchings, Peter Lounsbery: executive vice president, chief financial officer, Guardian Life Insurance Company of America

Hutchings, Richard S.: trustee, Johnson Fund (S.C.)

Hutchins, William Bruce, III: president, director, Alabama Power Foundation

Hutchinson, Frederick E., PhD: trustee, The MBNA Foundation

Hutchinson, Herman R.: vice president, director, Barra Foundation

Hutchison, S. L.: chief financial officer, director, Crail-Johnson Foundation

Hutta, Jane: secretary, SMBC Global Foundation, Inc.; general counsel, assistant treasurer, staff attorney, Sumitomo Mitsui Banking Corp.

Hutterly, Jane M.: executive vice president, Johnson Fund (S.C.)

Hyatt, Linda S.: vice president, executive director, Landmark Communications Foundation

Hyatt, Richard: trustee, National Grange Mutual Charitable Trust

Hybl, William J.: chairman, chief executive officer, trustee, El Pomar Foundation

Hyde, Douglas W.: chairman, president, chief executive officer, Oshkosh B'Gosh, Inc.

Hyde, Henry B.: director, Erpf Fund (Armand G.)

I

I'Anson, Lawrence W., Jr.: president, executive director, Beazley Foundation

Iakovos, Metropolitan: director, Demos Foundation (N.)

Iakvos, Bishop: director, Demos Foundation (N.)

Ibbotson, Robert D.: trustee, Morrison Charitable Trust (Pauline A. and George R.)

Icahn, Carl Celian: president, treasurer, ACF Foundation; owner, chairman, director, ACF Industries; president, director, Icahn Foundation (Carl C.)

Icahn, Liba: treasurer, director, Icahn Foundation (Carl C.)

Ice, Carl R.: executive vice president, chief operating officer, Burlington Northern Santa Fe Corp.

Iding, Allan E.: director, treasurer, Wehr Foundation (Todd)

Ifezue, Ta'Lisa J.: trust associate, Van Houten Memorial Fund (Edward W. and Stella C.)

Iger, Robert A.: trustee, Disney Co. Foundation (Walt)

Ignat, Joseph N.: president, trustee, Nord Family Foundation

Ignat, Pam: trustee, Nord Family Foundation

Iijima, Hirao: chairman, Mitsubishi Motor Sales of America, Inc.

Imboden, Connie: governor, Baker, Jr. Memorial Fund (William G.)

Imeson, Tom: chairman, director, PacifiCorp Foundation

Immelt, Jeffrey R.: chairman, chief executive officer, General Electric Co.

Ince, Max L.: president, director, South Plains Foundation

Infanger, Marie W.: hon officer, Allyn Foundation

Ingalls, Louise H.: trustee, Ingalls Foundation (Louise H. and David S.)

Ingalls, Rebekah: secretary, trustee, Ingalls Foundation (Louise H. and David S.)

Ingalls, Walter H.: director, Bank of Greene County Charitable Foundation

Inglee, Gale: assistant treasurer, director, Dillon Foundation

Inglis, Timothy M.: treasurer, Laurel Foundation

Ingram, Beverly: vice president, Giger Foundation (Paul and Oscar)

Ingwersen, James C.: secretary, assistant treasurer, director, Atkinson Foundation

Inouye, Minoru: vchairman, trustee, United States-Japan Foundation

Inskeep, Harriet J.: director, Journal-Gazette Foundation, Inc.

Inskeep, Richard G.: owner, president, public, Journal-Gazette Co.; president, director, Journal-Gazette Foundation, Inc.

Inskip, Gregory A.: director, Glencoe Foundation

Ireland, Cornelia W.: trustee, Mather and William Gwinn Mather Fund (Elizabeth Ring)

Ireland, George R.: treasurer, Mather and William Gwinn Mather Fund (Elizabeth Ring)

Ireland, Gregg A.: trustee, Stauffer Communications Foundation

Ireland, James D., III: president, Mather and William Gwinn Mather Fund (Elizabeth Ring)

Irish, Ann K.: trustee, Earhart Foundation

Irvin, Nathaniel, II: director, Babcock Foundation (Mary Reynolds)

Irvin, Patricia L.: vice president, operations and planning, Mellon Foundation (Andrew W.)

Irwin, Jane G.: director, chairman compensation committee, Luce Foundation (Henry)

Irwin, John N., III: chairman, chief executive officer, treasurer, trustee, Achelis Foundation; mem adv board, Watson Foundation (Thomas J.)

Irwin, Robert James Armstrong: trustee, Baird Foundation; treasurer, director, Cummings Foundation (James H.)

Irwin, William Baird: trustee, Baird Foundation

Isakower, Glorie: vice president, Kaplun Foundation (Morris J. and Betty)

Iscol, Jill: president, treasurer, director, Iscol Family Foundation

Iscol, Kenneth H.: vice president, secretary, director, Iscol Family Foundation

Isdaner, Scott Rosen: trustee, Strauss Foundation

Iselin, John Jay, PhD: director, Macy, Jr. Foundation (Josiah)

Ishiyama, George I.: president, director, Ishiyama Foundation

Ishiyama, Jean: assistant secretary, Ishiyama Foundation

Ishiyama, Setsuko: secretary, treasurer, director, Ishiyama Foundation

Isom, Ralph: director, CHC Foundation

Isonaga, Robert: treasurer, Locations Foundation

Ittleson, Henry Anthony: chairman, president, director, Ittleson Foundation

Ittleson, Marianne S.: director, Ittleson Foundation

Ivens, Barbara J.: president, trustee, Gerber Foundation

Iversen, Robert C.: chief operating officer, Air France

Iverson, Kenneth A.: vice president, corporate secretary, Ecolab, Inc.

Ives, Deborah M.: director finance, controller, Weingart Foundation

Ivey, Harriet M.: president, chief executive officer, Pulliam Charitable Trust (Nina Mason)

Ivey, M. K.: assistant secretary, Exxon Mobil Foundation

Ivey, Susan: president, chief executive officer, Brown & Williamson Tobacco Corp.

Iwanicki, John: member, Northern Trust Co. Charitable Trust

Iwata, Ruth S.: mem allocations comm, Kawabe Memorial Fund

Izzo, Scott D.: program associate, secretary, Mellon Foundation (Richard King)

J

Jaber, Paul N.: director, New Milford Savings Bank Foundation

Jackman, J. Warren: trustee, Bernsen Foundation (Grace and Franklin)

Jackson, Basil L.: vice president, Bowen Foundation (Ethel N.)

Jackson, Blaine: trustee, McKinney Charitable Trust (Carl and Alleen)

Jackson, Charles: president, Marshall Foundation

Jackson, David D.: president, Summerlee Foundation

Jackson, Edgar R.: vice president, director, Parsons Foundation (Ralph M.)

Jackson, Herrick: trustee, Connemara Fund

Jackson, Jack: vice chairman, secretary, treasurer, Heath Foundation (Ed and Mary)

Jackson, James W.: secretary, trustee, Blowitz-Ridgeway Foundation

Jackson, John E.: trustee, Nordson Corp. Foundation

Jackson, Kenneth T.: director, Luce Foundation (Henry)

Jackson, Maria: trustee, Connemara Fund

Jackson, Palmer G.: cfo, director, Jackson Family Foundation (Ann)

Jackson, Peggy E.: trustee, Lantz Foundation (Walter)

Jackson, Peter: vice president, director, Jackson Family Foundation (Ann)

Jackson, Polly B.: trustee, Connemara Fund

Jackson, Richard E.: trustee, Davenport Trust Fund

Jackson, William R.: trustee, Pitt-Des Moines Inc. Charitable Trust

Jacobs, Brett S.: secretary, trustee, Jacobs Family Foundation

Jacobs, Bruce E.: vice president, director, Grede Foundation; president, chief executive officer, Grede Foundries

Jacobs, Clay S.: treasurer, trustee, Jacobs Family Foundation

Jacobs, Debra M.: administration agent, Beattie Foundation (Cordelia Lee); president, member administration committee, Selby and Marie Selby Foundation (William G.)

Jacobs, Frank D.: assistant secretary, McMaster Foundation (Harold and Helen)

Jacobs, Henry D., Jr.: chairman, trustee, Jacobs Family Foundation

Jacobs, Linda E.: vice president, Rockefeller Brothers Fund, Inc.

Jacobs, Rodney L.: chief financial officer, Wells Fargo Foundation

Jacobs, Susan C.: trustee, Jacobs Family Foundation

Jacobs, Terry S.: trustee, National Grange Mutual Charitable Trust

Jacobson, Lyle Gordon: treasurer, Hickory Tech Corp. Foundation

Jacobson, Malcolm B.: trustee, Cassett Foundation (Louis N.)

Jacobson, Richard J.: vice president, treasurer, Cox Enterprises, Inc.

Jacobson, Sibyl C.: president, chief executive officer, director, MetLife Foundation

Jacoby, Jennifer: associate director, Crown Memorial (Arie and Ida)

Jaffe, Edwin A.: chairman, Jaffe Foundation

Jaffe, Ira J.: trustee, McGregor Fund

Jaffe, Lola: vchairman, Jaffe Foundation

Jaffe, Mary Hewlett: director, Hewlett Foundation (William and Flora)

Jaffe, Robert: trustee, Jaffe Foundation

Jaffe, Ruth M.: trustee, Kantzler Foundation

Jaffe, Suzanne Denbo: treasurer, Research Corp.

Jaffrey, Jonathan D.: vice president, secretary, Day Foundation (Willametta K.); vice president, chief admin officer, Keck Foundation (W. M.)

Jagow, Elmer: trustee, Frohring Foundation (Paul and Maxine)

Jalkut, Thomas P.: trustee, Killam Trust (Constance)

Jamail, Joseph D., III: vice president, Jamail Foundation (Lee and Joseph D.)

Jamail, Lee H.: president, Jamail Foundation (Lee and Joseph D.)

Jamail, Randall Hage: vice president, Jamail Foundation (Lee and Joseph D.)

Jamail, Robert Lee: secretary, treasurer, Jamail Foundation (Lee and Joseph D.)

James, Diana L.: secretary, treasurer, Reidler Foundation

James, Donald M.: chairman, Vulcan Materials Co. Foundation

James, Jean Butz: director, Butz Foundation

James, John J., Esq.: trustee, Gerber Foundation

James, Lynda: secretary, The Prairie Foundation

James, Ronald E.: director, Butz Foundation

James, Wilmot G.: trustee, Ford Foundation

James-Brown, Christine: board member, Fels Fund (Samuel S.)

Jameson, Kelly J.: assistant secretary, El Paso Corporate Foundation

Jammal, Eleanor A.: president, trustee, Ashtabula Foundation

Jander, Steve M.: trustee, Campbell Soup Foundation

Janik, Mary C.: mgr, Scotsman Industries Foundation

Janke, Lucinda P.: trustee, Kiplinger Foundation

Janney, Mary D.: director, Strong Foundation (Hattie M.)

Jansen, Larry: director, Grinnell Mutual Group Foundation

Jansing, Caroline C.: trustee, Cook Foundation (Louella)

Jansing, Christopher C.: trustee, Cook Foundation (Louella)

Jansing, John Cook: trustee, Cook Foundation (Louella)

Jantz, Sue Ann: trustee, Schowalter Foundation

Jaquay, Robert: associate director, Gund Foundation (George)

Jarcho, Fredrica: program officer, Greenwall Foundation

Jarrells, Judy: director, Joco Foundation

Jaskol, Leonard R.: chairman, president, chief executive officer, director, Lydall, Inc.

Jastrow, Kenneth M., II: chairman, chief executive officer, Temple-Inland Foundation

Javitch, Jonathan: director, Lebovitz Fund

Jean, Raymond A.: chairman, president, chief executive officer, director, Quanex Corp.

Jeannero, Jane M.: secretary, trustee, Gerber Foundation

Jeffrey, Katharine M.: member, Mather Charitable Trust (S. Livingston)

Jelinek, Don: trustee, Reynolds Foundation (Edgar & Francis)

Jelley, Philip M.: secretary, director, Skaggs Foundation (L. J. Skaggs and Mary C.)

Jellison, William R.: trustee, Dentsply International Foundation

Jenkins, David H., DVM: director, Bank of Greene County Charitable Foundation

Jenkins, Deborah: director, CHC Foundation

Jenkins, Douglas A.: director, Bair Family Trust (Charles M.)

Jenkins, Greg G.: director, El Paso Corporate Foundation

Jenkins, James R.: director, Deere Foundation (John)

Jenkins, John E., Jr.: director, Huntington Foundation

Jenkins, John S.: director, Walker Foundation

Jenks, John R.: treasurer, chief information officer, Irvine Foundation (The James)

Jenks, Rodney P.: secretary, Hexcel Foundation

Jenney, Michelle: foundation assistant, Webster Foundation (Edwin S.)

Jennings, Christina W.: director, Jennings Foundation (Mary Hillman)

Jennings, Cynthia: director, Jennings Foundation (Mary Hillman)

Jennings, Elizabeth Cabell: director, Cabell III and

Johnston, Chapman: president, chief executive officer, Tanner Companies (Rutherfordton, NC); vice president, Tanner Foundation

Johnston, Charles H.: director, Peterson Foundation (Hal and Charlie)

Johnston, Gerald E.: president, chief executive officer, Clorox Co.; trustee, Clorox Co. Foundation

Johnston, James W.: director, La-Z-Boy, Inc.

Johnston, Lawrence R.: chairman, chief executive officer, director, Albertson's Inc.

Johnston, S. K., Jr.: trustee, Tucker Foundation

Johnston, William R.: director, New York Stock Exchange Foundation, Inc.

Jokiel, Peter E.: senior vice president, chief financial officer, CNA Financial Corp.

Jones, B. L.: executive director, Fasken Foundation

Jones, Bernice: director, Jones Foundation (Harvey and Bernice)

Jones, Boisfeuillet, Jr.: director, Meyer Foundation (Eugene and Agnes E.)

Jones, Charles N., MD: vice president, De Queen Regional Medical Center

Jones, Christopher: senior program officer, Microsoft Corp.; chief executive officer, Thompson Co. (J. Walter)

Jones, D. Whitman: director, Whittenberger Foundation (Claude R. and Ethel B.)

Jones, David A., Jr.: director, Humana Foundation

Jones, David Allen: chairman, chief executive officer, director, Humana Foundation; co-founder, chairman, director, Humana, Inc.

Jones, Edward A.: director, Crosswicks Foundation

Jones, Emily J.: assistant vice president, corporate secretary, Meadows Foundation (The)

Jones, Ernest E.: director, Penn Foundation (William)

Jones, Farrell: president, Levitt Foundation (NY)

Jones, Helen DeVitt: director, Jones Foundation (Helen)

Jones, Helen Jeane: director, Redfield Foundation (Nell J.)

Jones, Howard D., III: secretary, Baltimore Equitable Insurance Foundation

Jones, Ingrid Saunders: chairman, director, Coca-Cola Foundation

Jones, James H.: section, assistant treasurer,, Coleman Foundation (IL)

Jones, James W.: board chair, Meyer Foundation (Eugene and Agnes E.)

Jones, Jill: assistant secretary, State Farm Companies Foundation

Jones, JoAnn: trustee, Cauthorn Charitable Trust (John and Mildred)

Jones, John M.: adv, O'Bleness Foundation (Charles)

Jones, John P., III: chairman, president, chief executive officer, Air Products and Chemicals, Inc.; trustee, Rider-Pool Foundation

Jones, Johnny C.: trustee, Share Trust (Charles Morton)

Jones, Joseph W.: chairman emeritus, Woodruff Foundation (Robert W.)

Jones, Joseph West: secretary, director, Coca-Cola Foundation; chairman emeritus, Evans Foundation, Inc. (Lettie Pate); chairman emeritus, trustee, Whitehead Foundation (Joseph B.)

Jones, Josephine: vice president, Crosswicks Foundation

Jones, Kathy: president, Honda of America Foundation

Jones, Kenneth W.: controller, Liberty Corp.; controller, treasurer, Liberty Corp. Foundation

Jones, Leslie A.: chairman, Dentsply International, Inc.

Jones, M. Steve: gov, Mayor Foundation (Oliver Dewey)

Jones, Mary Duke Trent: second vchairman, assistant secretary, assistant treasurer, trustee, Biddle Foundation (Mary Duke); trustee, Duke Endowment

Jones, Melissa A.: director, Houston Endowment

Jones, Nathan J.: director, Deere Foundation (John)

Jones, O. D.: trustee, Long Foundation (J. M.)

Jones, Owen: chief executive officer, chief operating officer, director, Sheaffer Pen Corp.

Jones, Patrick: chief financial officer, Noble Foundation (Samuel Roberts)

Jones, Raymond E.: secretary, director, Shelter Insurance Foundation; executive vice president, secretary, Shelter Mutual Insurance Co.

Jones, Robert G.: trustee, McDonald Investments Foundation

Jones, Robert T.: vice president, trustee, Anderson Foundation (NY)

Jones, Samuel L., III: director, Exchange Bank Foundation

Jones, Scott D.A.: grants administration assistant, Knight Foundation (John S. and James L.)

Jones, Stephen N.: vice president, secretary, trustee, Casey Foundation (Eugene B.)

Jones, Steve: gov, Munson Foundation Trust (W. B.)

Jones, Sumner: executive vice president, Eastern Bank

Jones, Tony: chairman, Hudson River Bancorp, Inc.

Jones, William H.: vice president, Hudson River Bancorp Inc. Foundation

Jones Joyce, Alexis: director, Joyce Family Foundation

Jonklaas, Anthony: trustee, Kenridge Fund

Jonklaas, Clair Hanna B.: president, trustee, Kenridge Fund

Jonsen, Albert R.: director, Sierra Health Foundation

Joos, David W.: president, chief executive officer electric, executive vice president, Consumers Energy Co.

Joralemon, Jane G.: president, trustee, Anderson Foundation (NY)

Jordan, Ann K.: fund comm mem, Kaufman Endowment Fund (Louis G.)

Jordan, Barbara M.: director, Claneil Foundation

Jordan, Grady: director, Hawn Foundation

Jordan, Henry A.: secretary, director, Claneil Foundation

Jordan, Marie I.: secretary, Bank One Foundation

Jordan, Vernon E., Jr.: director, Sara Lee Corp.

Jose, Kathanni P.: trustee, Southways Foundation

Joseph, Amy: vice president, secretary, trustee, Farmer Family Foundation

Joseph, Robert L.: comptroller, Scotsman Industries Foundation

Joslin, David C.: trustee, Gerber Foundation

Joslin, Roger Scott: treasurer, State Farm Companies Foundation

Joslyn, Robert B.: trustee, Fruehauf Foundation

Joukowsky, Artemis A. W.: director, Joukowsky Family Foundation

Joukowsky, Martha Content: director, Joukowsky Family Foundation

Joy, Joan H.: trustee, Joy Family Foundation

Joy, Paul W.: don, trustee, Joy Family Foundation

Joy, Stephen T.: trustee, Joy Family Foundation

Joy Reinhold, Paula: trustee, Joy Family Foundation

Joy Sullivan, Marsha: trustee, Joy Family Foundation

Joyce, Bernard F.: vice president, secretary, director, Link, Jr. Foundation (George)

Joyce, Michael Stewart: trustee, Pinkerton Foundation

Juarez, Steve: director financial management, Getty Trust (J. Paul)

Jubb, Marilyn Sue: vice president, Anderson Foundation (L. P. and Teresa)

Juday, David W.: president, Ideal Industries Foundation; chairman, director, Ideal Industries, Inc.

Judge, James J.: senior vice president corporate service business unit, treasurer, NSTAR; trustee, NSTAR Foundation

Juenemann, Donald E.: trustee, Wickes Foundation (Harvey Randall)

Juett, Katherine L.: trustee, Lyndhurst Foundation

Juhl, Randy: trustee, Ahrens Foundation (Claude W. and Dolly)

Juilfs, George C.: president, chief executive officer, director, Cinergy Foundation

Jukosky, James A.: vice president, trustee, Brundage Charitable, Scientific, and Wildlife Conservation Foundation (Charles E. and Edna T.)

Jukosky, Susan: trustee, Brundage Charitable, Scientific, and Wildlife Conservation Foundation (Charles E. and Edna T.)

Junck, Mary E.: trustee, Hartford Courant Foundation

Jung, Andrea: president, chief executive officer, Avon Products, Inc.

Junius, Daniel M.: senior vice president, chief financial officer, treasurer, New England Business Service

Jurzykowski, M. Christine: secretary, treasurer, trustee, Jurzykowski Foundation (Alfred)

Jurzykowski, Yolande L.: executive vice president, trustee, Jurzykowski Foundation (Alfred)

Justice, Larry: mgr, Porter Testamentary Trust (James Hyde)

Justice, Melody: director, Coca-Cola Foundation

Justice, Rita F.: mem, Phipps Foundation (Columbus)

K

Kaden, Ellen O.: senior vice president, Campbell Soup Foundation

Kaemmer, Arthur W., MD: chairman, treasurer, HRK Foundation

Kaemmer, Martha H.: vice president, HRK Foundation

Kaesemeyer, Tom: executive director, secretary, Gates Family Foundation

Kahler, Judy: director, Land O'Lakes Foundation

Kahler, Michael E.: director, chairman, ONDEO Nalco Foundation

Kahn, Andrew: director, Kahn Foundation; chief executive officer, Kahn, Lucas-Lancaster, Inc. Children's Wear

Kahn, Michael: president, director, Reynolds Foundation (Christopher)

Kahn, Peggy Anne: director, Kahn Foundation

Kahn, Richard D.: assistant secretary, director, Barker Foundation (J.M.R.)

Kailbourne, Erland E.: director,

Kain, Herbert, MD: trustee, Valley Foundation

Kaiser, Ferdinand C.: vice president, secretary, trustee, Arkell Hall Foundation

Kakabadse, Yolanda: trustee, Ford Foundation

Kakita, Edward Y.: director, Nakamichi Foundation (E.)

Kalaher, Richard A.: president, American Standard Foundation; vice president, secretary, general counsel, American Standard Inc.

Kalainov, Sam Charles: chairman, president, chief executive officer, Amerus Group Co.

Kalb, Bettie A.: president, secretary, Wildermuth Foundation (E. F.)

Kalis, David B.: senior vice president communications, International Business Machines

Kalish, Daniel M.: executive director, Jennings Foundation (Martha Holden)

Kalish, Katherine M.: mgr, Porter Testamentary Trust (James Hyde)

Kalisman, Gayle T.: president, Taubman Foundation (A. Alfred)

Kalkus, June: vice president, Kalkus Foundation

Kalkus, Mark: secretary, Kalkus Foundation

Kalkus, Peter: president, Kalkus Foundation

Kallaus, Kurt J.: director, Sunnen Foundation

Kallet, Michael R.: president, Oneida Savings

Bank Charitable Foundation

Kaltenbacher, Philip David: chairman, president, chief executive officer, director, Seton Co.; trustee, Seton Co. Foundation

Kamen, Harry Paul: chairman, president, chief executive officer, Metropolitan Life Insurance Co.

Kamphuis, Robert D.: president, Giddings & Lewis Foundation

Kamprath, Stan: president, executive director, Johnson Foundation (Helen K. and Arthur E.)

Kamras, Marvin: distribution trustee, Schwab-Rosenhouse Memorial Foundation

Kane, Charles J.: board member, Frist Foundation

Kane, Douglas C.: vice president, director, MDU Resources Foundation; executive vice president, chief operating officer, director, MDU Resources Group, Inc.

Kane, John F.: treasurer, Lyon Foundation

Kaneshiro, Steven: grant administrator, Atherton Family Foundation

Kangisser, Dianne: vice president, executive director, trustee, Bowne Foundation (Robert)

Kann, Peter Robert: chairman, chief executive officer, director, Dow Jones & Company, Inc.; member advisory committee, Dow Jones Foundation

Kanner, Abraham Pascal: vice president, Rosenthal Foundation (Ida and William)

Kantor, Gregg: vice president, Northwest Natural Gas Co.

Kaplan, Berton B.: vice president, Pick, Jr. Fund (Albert)

Kaplan, Helene L.: chairman, trustee, Carnegie Corp. of New York; director, vice chairman, Commonwealth Fund (The); vice chairman, trustee, Getty Trust (J. Paul)

Kaplan, Mary E.: trustee, Kaplan Fund (J. M.)

Kaplan, Myran J.: trustee, Jarson Kaplan Foundation

Kaplan, Renee T.: director, Amado Foundation (Maurice)

Kaplan, Richard D.: trustee, Kaplan Fund (J. M.)

Kaplan, Richard J.: director grants mgmt, res and info, MacArthur Foundation (John D. and Catherine T.)

Kaplan, Stanley Meisel, MD: trustee, Jarson Kaplan Foundation

Kaplen, Alexander: trustee, Kaplen Foundation

Kaplen, Lawrence: trustee, Kaplen Foundation

Kaplen, Margaret: fdn mgr, trustee, Kaplen Foundation

Kaplen, Wilson R.: trustee, Kaplen Foundation

Karaba, Frank Andrew: trustee, Caestecker Foundation (Charles and Marie)

Karatsu, Jeanne: trustee, Miller Foundation (Earl B. and Loraine H.)

Karbowiak, Christine: chairman, Bridgestone/Firestone Trust Fund (The)

Kardon, Emanuel S.: president, trustee, Kardon Foundation (Samuel and Rebecca)

Karl, Rosemary M.: trustee, Fredrickson Foundation (Ambrose and Ida)

Karlstrom, Paul Johnson: director, Scott Foundation (Virginia Steele)

Karmel, Roberta S.: trustee, Kemper Foundation (James S.)

Karr, Kathie L.: director, Bristol-Myers Squibb Foundation Inc.

Karvellas, Steven: director, New York Mercantile Exchange Charitable Foundation

Kassel, Sylvia: director, Schwartz Fund for Education and Health Research (Arnold and Marie)

Kassoff, Eric S.: secretary, treasurer, director, Wilkes, Artis, Hedrick & Lane Foundation

Kassouf, Susan: special projects director, Johnson Endeavor Foundation (Christian A.)

Katayama, Ayao: president, trustee, Kajima Foundation

Katch, Kim: secretary, Trust Foundation

Katchadourian, Herant, MD: director, Hewlett Foundation (William and Flora)

Katigan, Carrie McCune: member dispensing committee, McCune Charitable Trust (John R.)

Katona, Peter Geza, ScD: president, Whitaker Foundation

Katz, Bruce: trustee, Katz Family Foundation

Katz, Richard D.: trustee, Wickes Foundation (Harvey Randall)

Katz, Roger: trustee, Katz Family Foundation

Katz, Saul: trustee, Katz Family Foundation

Katzowitz, Lauren: secretary, Dickler Family Foundation

Kaufman, Clementine: officer, Hecht-Levi Foundation

Kaufman, Iva: program director, Sun Hill Foundation

Kaufman, James: secretary, Neuberger Foundation (Roy R. and Marie S.)

Kaufman, Marvin A.: chairman, director, Samuels Foundation (Fan Fox and Leslie R.)

Kaufman, Michael: fund committee member, Kaufman Endowment Fund (Louis G.)

Kaufman, Peter: chairman, fund comm mem, Kaufman Endowment Fund (Louis G.)

Kaufman, Richard F.: trustee, Kaufman Foundation

Kaufman, Ron: director, Osher Foundation (Bernard)

Kaufman, Sylvia C.: trustee, Kaufman Foundation

Kaufmann, Barbara W.: director, Minnesota Mining & Manufacturing Co.

Kaufmann, Thomas C.: vice president, Boothroyd Foundation (Charles H. and Bertha L.)

Kavanagh, Thomas E.: trustee, Kavanagh Foundation (T. James)

Kavanaugh, Edward: vice president, treasurer, secretary, Dingman Foundation (Michael D.)

Kay, David R.: treasurer, director, Goldman Foundation (Herman)

Kay, Herma Hill: director, Rosenberg Foundation

Kayajan, John M.: director, Kelley and Elza Kelley Foundation (Edward Bangs)

Kayden, Jerold: director, DBH Foundation for Law, Land, and the Felicitous Environment

Kaye, Brian T.: secretary, St. Francis Bank Foundation

Kaylor, Howard S.: trustee, Sinnisen Foundation (Albert E. and Naomi B.)

Kaylor, Omer T.: contact person, Sinnisen Foundation (Albert E. and Naomi B.)

Kayne, Barry: director, Kutz Foundation (Milton and Hattie)

Kayser, Kraig H.: president, chief executive officer, director, Seneca Foods Corp.

Kaze, Barbara: program officer, Weingart Foundation

Kazlauskas, Deborah: secretary, Trimix Foundation

Keane, Thomas M.: vice chairman, trustee, Foundation for Seacoast Health

Kear, Joseph G.: trustee, Massie Trust (David Meade)

Kearney, Christopher J.: trustee, SPX Foundation

Kearney, Lynn: director, Dedalus Foundation

Kearney, R. Wynn, Jr.: director, Hickory Tech Corp.; trustee, Hickory Tech Corp. Foundation

Kearns, David Todd: trustee, Ford Foundation

Kearns, Fred M., Jr.: president, Acme-McCrary and Sapona Foundation

Keating, Kevin: treasurer, Pfizer Foundation

Keating, Phillip: chairman, Rieke Corp.

Keator, William C.: program director, Davis Foundations (Arthur Vining)

Keck, Erin A.: director, member directors grant program committee, Keck Foundation (W. M.)

Keck, Howard B., Jr.: vice president, director, member audit & executive committees, Keck Foundation (W. M.)

Keck, Katherine Cone: director, Mead Foundation (Giles W. and Elise G.)

Keck, William M., II: vice president, director, membership audit & executive committee, Keck Foundation (W. M.); president, director, Keck, Jr. Foundation (William M.)

Keck, William M., III: director, Keck Foundation (W. M.)

Keckher, Kelly J.: trustee, Pittsburgh Child Guidance Foundation

Kedash, David B.: chief financial officer, The MBNA Foundation

Keefe, Catherine G.: assistant secretary, treasurer, McFeely-Rogers Foundation

Keefe, Pamela B.: trustee, Humphrey Fund (George M. and Pamela S.)

Keegan, John Phillip: president, treasurer, Edison Fund (Charles)

Keegan, Peter: senior vice president, Loews Foundation

Keeler, Issac S.: trustee, Keeler Foundation

Keeler, John: advisory committee member, Dickenson Foundation (Harriet Ford)

Keeler, Mary Ann: trustee, Keeler Foundation

Keeler, Miner S., II: trustee, Keeler Foundation

Keeler, Shirley: advisory committee member, Dickenson Foundation (Harriet Ford)

Keeley, Warner: trustee, AT&T National Pro-Am Youth Fund

Keeling, Rudolph W.: vice president, LG&E Energy Foundation

Keen, Gordon L., Jr.: director, McCausland Foundation

Keenan, Frances Murray: vice president finance, Abell Foundation

Keenan, James F.: secretary, Plym Foundation

Keene, Starling Anderson: secretary, AKC Fund

Keesee, Christian Kirkpatrick: vice president, director, Kirkpatrick Foundation, Inc.

Kefauver, Horace D.: trustee, Sinnisen Foundation (Albert E. and Naomi B.)

Keibaum, Jack: general manager, Cone-Blanchard Corp.

Keir, Gerald J.: director, First Hawaiian Foundation

Keiser, Ann T.: mgr fin admin, Davis Foundation (Irene E. and George A.)

Keith, Garnett L.: trustee, Hughes Medical Institute (Howard)

Keith, M. Langhorne: assistant secretary, Loughran Foundation (Mary and Daniel)

Kelleher, D. William: director, Eastern Savings and Loan Foundation

Kelleher, Joan N.: vice president, treasurer, Gage Foundation (Alfred S.)

Keller, Bernedine J.: vice president, Keller Foundation

Keller, Betsy: trustee, Lux Foundation (Miranda)

Keller, Fred M.: president, Keller Foundation

Keller, Frederick P.: treasurer, Keller Foundation

Keller, Linn Maxwell: director, Keller Foundation

Keller, Lorissa K.: director, Keller Foundation

Keller, Rayford L.: president, assistant treasurer, Overlake Foundation

Keller, Susan: director, Keller Foundation

Keller, Suzanne: chairman, DBH Foundation for Law, Land, and the Felicitous Environment

Keller, Thomas L.: vice president, treasurer, assistant secretary, Overlake Foundation

Keller, William B.: director, Alabama Power Foundation

Kelley, Barbara M.: vice president, Bausch & Lomb Foundation, Inc.

Kelley, Bruce Gunn: vice president, director, Employers Mutual Charitable Foundation

Kelley, Donald E.: trustee, Rieke Corp. Foundation

Kelley, Natalie R.: director, Robertshaw Charitable Foundation

Kelley, Ruth B.: hon director, Kelley and Elza Kelley Foundation (Edward Bangs)

Kelley, Thomas J.: director, Trust Funds

Kelling, Robert S., Jr.: director, Hale Foundation (Crescent Porter)

Kelly, A. William: director, Sordoni Foundation

Kelly, Anastasia: secretary, director, Fannie Mae Foundation

Kelly, D. C.: treasurer, trustee, Handy & Harman Foundation

Kelly, Daniel J.: vice president, Smith and W. Aubrey Smith Charitable Foundation (Clara Blackford)

Kelly, Ernest M.: trustee, Magruder Foundation (Chesley G.)

Kelly, Flaminia Odescalchi: trustee, Bonfils-Stanton Foundation

Kelly, Hugh Rice: secretary, Reliant Resources Foundation

Kelly, Jon S.: chief executive officer, director, Kelly Foundation

Kelly, Joseph: director, King Foundation (Kenneth Kendal)

Kelly, Lorraine A.: vice president, director, Park Bank Foundation

Kelly, Michael J.: vice president, director, Park Bank Foundation

Kelly, Raymond B., III: vice president, secretary, director, Scott Foundation (William E.)

Kelly, Robert E.: director, Kelly Foundation

Kelly, Thomas E.: trustee, Fasken Foundation

Kelly, William J.: vice president, treasurer, Holmberg Foundation

Kelly, William M.: trustee, New York Foundation

Kelman, Deborah Sloss: director, Fleishhacker Foundation

Kelson, Richard B.: director, Alcoa Foundation

Kemper, David Woods: chairman, president, chief executive officer, director, Commerce Bancshares, Inc.

Kemper, Jonathan McBride: director, Commerce Bancshares Foundation; vice chairman, Commerce Bancshares, Inc.; co-trustee, contributions committee, Kemper Foundation (William T.)

Kemper, Talfourd H.: secretary, treasurer, Carter Foundation (Beirne)

Kempner, Carl L.: treasurer, Erpf Fund (Armand G.)

Kempner, Hetta Ellen Towler: trustee, Kempner Fund (Harris and Eliza)

Kempner, Isaac Herbert, III: trustee, Kempner Fund (Harris and Eliza)

Kempton, George Roger: chief executive officer, Scotsman Industries Foundation; chairman, chief executive officer, director, Scottsman Industries

Kemsey, Esther J.: trustee, Chatlos Foundation

Kenan, James G., III: trustee, Hartford Foundation, Inc. (The John A.)

Kenan, Thomas Stephen, III: secretary, treasurer, trustee, secretary investments committee, Biddle Foundation (Mary Duke); trustee, Duke Endowment

Kendall, Donald M.: co-founder, PepsiCo Inc.

Kendall, Henry Way: trustee, Kendall Foundation (Henry P.)

Kendall, Janet: associate vice president, SBC Communications Inc.; chairman, SBC Foundation

Kendall, John P.: trustee, Kendall Foundation (Henry P.)

Kendall, Rebecca O.: director, Lilly Foundation (Eli)

Keniry, Joseph P.: vice president, Rexam Foundation

Kennan, Christopher J.: director, Rockefeller Fund (David)

Kennan, Joan Elisabeth: executive director, Arcana Foundation

Kennedy, Bruce C.: trustee, Van Wert County Foundation

Kennedy, David Boyd: president, Earhart Foundation

Kennedy, Derek: chief financial officer, Excel Corp.

Kennedy, Edward Moore: president, trustee, Kennedy, Jr. Foundation (Joseph P.)

Kennedy, Holly: secretary, Arcana Foundation

Kennedy, Jack E.: director, Hewit Family Foundation

Kennedy, James Cox: chairman, chief executive officer, director, Cox Enterprises, Inc.

Kennedy, Janice: program director, Murdock Charitable Trust (M. J.)

Kennedy, Kenneth: director, Cheatham Foundation (Owen)

Kennedy, Kimberly: director, Kennedy Family Foundation (Ethel and W. George)

Kennedy, Nancy C.: trustee, Yeager Charitable Trust B (Lester E.)

Kennedy, Thomas J.: vice president, Smoot Charitable Foundation

Kennedy, Wayne G.: president, director, Kennedy Family Foundation (Ethel and W. George)

Kennedy, William: director, Kennedy Family Foundation (Ethel and W. George)

Kennedy Olsen, Kathleen P.: director, Kennedy Family Foundation (Ethel and W. George)

Kennel, Russel R.: secretary, director, Lee Foundation

Kennerly, Michael: grant committee, Royal Foundation (May Mitchell)

Kenney, Edward F.: trustee, Yawkey Foundation II

Kenny, John J.: treasurer, Loews Corp.; secretary, treasurer, trustee, Loews Foundation

Kent, Katherine G.: trustee, Bryden Foundation (Blanche)

Kentz, Frederick C., III: trustee, Hoffmann-La Roche Foundation; vice president, secretary, general counsel, Hoffmann-La Roche, Inc.

Kenyon, Robert W.: mem distribution comm, Champlin Foundation

Kerby, J. W.: treasurer, Zarrow Foundation (Anne and Henry)

Kerlin, Gilbert: secretary, mem executive & fin comms, director, Dodge Foundation (Cleveland H.)

Kerlin, William H., Jr.: chairman, Graham Engineering Corp.; trustee, Graham Foundation

Kerly, Diane M.: trustee, Hamer Foundation

Kern, John C.: trustee, Kern Foundation Trust

Kerr, Breene M.: chairman, treasurer, life trustee, Kerr Fund (Grayce B.)

Kerr, Cody T.: trustee, Kerr Foundation, Inc.

Kerr, Daniel L.: secretary, treasurer, Faith Foundation

Kerr, Darlene D.: trustee, Niagara Mohawk Foundation

Kerr, Lou C.: vice president, secretary, Kerr Foundation, Inc.

Kerr, Marcy S.: adv trustee, Kerr Fund (Grayce B.)

Kerr, Robert Samuel, Jr.: president, Kerr Foundation, Inc.

Kerr, Sharon: trustee, Kerr Foundation, Inc.

Kerr, Sheryl V.: president, life trustee, Kerr Fund (Grayce B.)

Kerr, Steven: vice president corporate leadership development, General Electric Co.; assistant treasurer, trustee, Kerr Foundation, Inc.

Kerstein, Ruth: secretary, director, Schwartz Fund for Education and Health Research (Arnold and Marie)

Kersten, Katherine: director, vice president, Cargill Foundation

Kesler, Robert: secretary, treasurer, Vermilion Healthcare Foundation

Kessler, Emily R.: executive director, Joukowsky Family Foundation

Kessler, James Lee: trustee, Kempner Fund (Harris and Eliza)

Ketcham, Geoff C.: executive vice president, treasurer, chief financial officer, Energen Corp.

Ketcherside, James Lee: director, Mingenback Foundation (Julia J.)

Ketelsen, James L.: director, Sara Lee Corp.

Kettering, Virginia W.: trustee, Kettering Fund

Keune, Donald J.: adv, Cayuga Foundation

Keuthen, Catherine J.: legal adv, NSTAR Foundation

Key, Amy Bronson: director, Daniels Foundation (Fred Harris)

Key, Martha: co-trustee, Pelz Trust (H.E. and Ruby)

Keydel, Frederick R.: trustee, Fruehauf Foundation

Keyes, James Henry: advisor, Johnson Controls Foundation

Keyser, Alan J.: trustee, Quaker Chemical Foundation

Keyser, F. Ray, Jr.: chairman, director, Central Vermont Public Service Corp.

Keyte, David H.: vice president, chief financial officer, Forest Oil Corp.

Khoury, Eileen M.: trustee, Russell Trust (Josephine G.)

Khoury, Kenneth F.: vice president, Georgia-Pacific Foundation

Kibbe, Barbara: director organizational effectiveness program, Packard Foundation (David and Lucile)

Kibbe, Sharon: director, Glick Foundation (Eugene and Marilyn)

Kick, Frank J.: treasurer, Bydale Foundation

Kidder, C. Robert: chairman, president, chief executive officer, director, Borden, Inc.

Kidder, Rushworth Moulton: trustee, Mott Foundation (Charles Stewart)

Kieckhefer, John I.: trustee, Kieckhefer Foundation (J. W.)

Kieckhefer, Robert H.: trustee, Kieckhefer Foundation (J. W.)

Kieding, Richard: president, S.G. Foundation

Kielley, James E., JD: committee member, Whitaker Foundation

Kienker, James W.: senior vice president, chief financial officer, Maritz, Inc.

Kiernan, Donald E., Sr.: senior vice president, chief financial officer, treasurer, SBC Communications Inc.; director, SBC Foundation

Kiernat, Elizabeth M.: trustee, Bigelow Foundation (F. R.)

Kiewit, Eve: trustee, Kiewit Foundation (Peter)

Kiewit, Peter, Jr.: chairman, trustee, Kiewit Foundation (Peter)

Kiker, John D.: vice president corporate communications, UAL Corp.

Kilbride, Marc: treasurer, Reliant Resources Foundation

Kilen, C. Bruce: trustee, McKay Family Foundation

Kilgus, Amy C.: trustee, Saemann Foundation (Franklin I.)

Kilgus, Joann A.: trustee, Saemann Foundation (Franklin I.)

Killinger, Kerry Kent: president, Washington Mutual Foundation; chairman, president, chief executive officer, director, Washington Mutual, Inc.

Killinger, William: director, Joco Foundation

Kilmartin, David F.: chairman, president, chief executive officer, director, Kilmartin Industries; president, director, Kilmartin Industries Charitable Foundation

Kilroy, Lora Jean: trustee, Kilroy Foundation (William S. and Lora Jean)

Kilroy, Mari Angela: trustee, Kilroy Foundation (William S. and Lora Jean)

Kilroy, William S.: trustee, Kilroy Foundation (William S. and Lora Jean)

Kilts, James M.: chairman, chief executive officer, director, Gillette Co.

Kimball, Ray: director, De Queen Regional Medical Center

Kimball, Richard W.: director, Teagle Foundation

Kime, Jack E.: chief financial officer, Heinz Endowment (Vira I.)

Kimelman, Donald: director venture fund, Pew Charitable Trusts

Kimmet, Gary J.: director, Gleason Foundation

Kin, Donna J.: executive secretary, National Machinery Foundation, Inc.

Kindler, Jeffrey B.: senior vice president, general counsel, Pfizer Inc.

Kindred, John J., III: trustee, Hagedorn Fund

King, Betty S.: secretary, Richardson Benevolent Foundation (C. E.)

King, David A.: executive director, mem distribution & investigating comm, Champlin Foundation

King, Diana: president, director, King Family Foundation (Charles and Lucille)

King, Jodie W.: secretary, Hearst Foundation, Inc. (The); assistant secretary, Hearst Foundation (William Randolph)

King, Judith S.: trustee, treasurer, Stoddard Charitable Trust

King, Lee E.: director, Portsmouth General Hospital Foundation

King, Mary E.: secretary, Arca Foundation

King, Maxwell: executive director, Heinz Endowment (Vira I.)

King, May Dougherty: chairman, trustee, Dougherty, Jr. Foundation (James R.)

King, Michael J.: director, Gellert Foundation (Carl Gellert and Celia Berta)

King, Pam: director Pueblo, CO program, Packard Foundation (David and Lucile)

King, Randall C.: treasurer, PNC Financial Services Group, Inc.

King, Richard S.: assistant treasurer, Alabama Power Foundation

King, Sharon B.: trustee, assistant secretary, Altman Foundation

King, Susan Robinson: vice president public affairs, Carnegie Corp. of New York

King, Thomas A.: president, Lilly Foundation (Eli)

King, Wendall: director, Harper Brush Works Foundation

King, William Joseph: vice president, treasurer, director, Kline Foundation (Josiah W. and Bessie H.); chairman, Stabler Foundation (Donald B. and Dorothy L.)

Kinghorn, John: assistant treasurer, Prudential Foundation

Kingsland, Richard M.: chief financial officer, secretary, Valley Foundation (Wayne and Gladys)

Kingsley, Alfred D.: vice president, assistant secretary, ACF Foundation

Kingsley, Mitchell: trustee, Schowalter Foundation

Kinnamon, David Lucas: secretary, director, Ross Memorial Foundation (Will)

Kinney, George R.: trustee, Kinney Memorial Foundation

Kinney, Josephine J.: trustee, Kinney Memorial Foundation

Kinney, Richard J.: president, Schering-Plough Foundation

Kintzel, Lee: co-trustee, Roddy Foundation (Fred M.)

Kiplinger, Austin Huntington: president, trustee, Kiplinger Foundation; chairman, director, Kiplinger Washington Editors, Inc.

Kiplinger, Knight Austin: trustee, Kiplinger Foundation; president, publisher, director, Kiplinger Washington Editors, Inc.

Kiplinger, Todd Lawrence: trustee, Kiplinger Foundation; vice chairman, director, Kiplinger Washington Editors, Inc.

Kipp, Robert Almy: director, Hall Family Foundation (The)

Kirby, Fred M., III: director, Kirby Foundation (F. M.)

Kirby, Fred Morgan: president, director, Kirby Foundation (F. M.)

Kirby, Jefferson Walker: director, Kirby Foundation (F. M.)

Kirby, John L.: chief administrative officer, executive vice president, United States Trust Co. of New York

Kirby, Nancy J.: trustee, Douty Foundation (Alfred and Mary)

Kirby, S. Dillard: vice president, director, Kirby Foundation (F. M.)

Kirby, Walker D.: vice president, director, Kirby Foundation (F. M.)

Kirchner, Audrey: secretary, Bemis Co. Foundation

Kirk, Ann: director, Portsmouth General Hospital Foundation

Kirker, James M.: director, Dime Savings Bank of Norwich Foundation

Kirkham, Kate B.: president, trustee, Bicknell Fund

Kirklin, Starr J.: director, Hickory Tech Corp.; trustee, Hickory Tech Corp. Foundation

Kirkman, Harry: secretary, director, Benton Foundation

Kirkpatrick, Joan E.: chairman, Kirkpatrick Foundation, Inc.

Kirkpatrick, John Elson: honorary chairman, director, Kirkpatrick Foundation, Inc.

Kirkpatrick, Ken: president, US Bank

Kirkwood, Gloria: secretary, Britton Fund

Kirkwood, William T.: chief financial officer, vice president financial, director, Worthington Foods

Kiser, Gerald L.: president, chief executive officer, director, La-Z-Boy, Inc.

Kishner, Judith Z.: director, Zarrow Foundation (Anne and Henry)

Kissinger, Thomas F.: secretary, director, Marcus Corp. Foundation

Kissling, Walter: chief financial officer, Fuller Co. (H.B.)

Kissner, Naida: program assistant, Fuller Co. Foundation (H.B.)

Kita, John J.: vice president, treasurer, controller, Smith Corp. (A.O.); treasurer, Smith Foundation, Inc. (A.O.)

Kitabjian, Mary: assistant secretary, Pforzheimer Foundation, Inc. (The Carl and Lily)

Kitajima, Terry (Terunori): vice president, Kawasaki Good Times Foundation

Kitchen, Michael B.: president, chief executive officer, director, CUNA Mutual Group; secretary, treasurer, executive officer, CUNA Mutual Group Foundation, Inc.

Kitko, Paulette F.: secretary, treasurer, Haskell Fund

Kittner, David: president, trustee, Kardon Foundation (Samuel and Rebecca)

Kittner, Marc: board of directors, Washington Mutual Foundation

Kiuchi, Michio: director, Kikkoman Foundation

Kizer, John Oscar: secretary, treasurer, Daywood Foundation

Klatman, Michael: president, StorageTek Foundation

Klausner, Richard D., MD: executive director, global health, Gates Foundation (Bill and Melinda)

Klebba, Kenneth J.: president, treasurer, Vollbrecht Foundation (Frederick A.)

Kleeman, R. Henry: assistant secretary, Sara Lee Foundation

Kleh, Jack: trustee, Bloedorn Foundation (Walter A.)

Klein, Bruce A.: trustee, CLARCOR Foundation; chief financial officer, vice president, CLARCOR, Inc.

Klein, Charles T.: vice president, trustee, Frueauff Foundation (Charles A.)

Klein, David M.: vice president, Hartford Financial Services Group, Inc.

Klein, Donald: vice president, Liberman Foundation (Bertha and Isaac)

Klein, Edith Miller: director, Morrison Foundation (Harry W.)

Klein, Jeffrey: president, Liberman Foundation (Bertha and Isaac)

Klein, Raphael: director, Bank of Greene County Charitable Foundation

Klein, Ray: trustee, Kerr Foundation, Inc.

Kleiner, Charlene: secretary, McBean Family Foundation

Klementik, David C.: trustee, Whalley Charitable Trust

Kleven, Cynthia F.: secretary, director, 3M Foundation; director community affairs, Minnesota Mining & Manufacturing Co.

Kline, Daniel L.: vice president, trustee, Blowitz-Ridgeway Foundation

Kline, Darrell: trustee, Share Trust (Charles Morton)

Kline, Gary H.: secretary, Field Foundation of Illinois

Kline, Lowell L.: executive director, president, Crowell Trust (Henry P. and Susan C.)

Kline, Sidney Delong, Jr.: trustee, Wyomissing Foundation

Kline, Thomas J., Jr.: trustee, New York Foundation

Kling, Chris: mgr, Wilson Foundation (Marie C. and Joseph C.)

Kling, Donalyn G.: off, Griswold Foundation (Lillian Sherwood)

Klingenstein, Frederick A.: first vice president, secretary, director, Klingenstein Fund, Inc. (Esther A. and Joseph)

Klingenstein, John: president, treasurer, director, Klingenstein Fund, Inc. (Esther A. and Joseph)

Klinger, Andrew M.: trustee, Mex-Am Cultural Foundation

Klinger, Linda L.: executive director, McElroy Trust (R. J.)

Klingstein, Alan L.: treasurer, Klingestein Fund

Klingestein, Lee P.: president, Klingestein Fund

Klingestein, Paul H.: vice president, Klingestein Fund

Klingner, Linda: secretary, treasurer, Morrison Foundation (Harry W.)

Klipstein, David C.: vice president, Klipstein Foundation (Ernest Christian)

Klipstein, David H.: president, Klipstein Foundation (Ernest Christian)

Klipstein, Pamela: treasurer, Klipstein Foundation (Ernest Christian)

Kloenhammer, Janet S.: director, Fireman's Fund Foundation

Kloska, Ronald Frank: trustee, Decio Foundation (Arthur J.)

Kluge, John Werner: director, Shubert Foundation

Kluge, Patricia: vice president, director, Virginia Environmental Endowment

Klugman, Craig: editor, Journal-Gazette Co.

Knapp, Anthony: vice president, Motorola Foundation

Knapp, Cleon Talboys: president, Knapp Foundation (CA)

Knapp, Elizabeth W.: vice president, Knapp Foundation (CA)

Knapp, William A.: vice president, McDonald Manufacturing Co. Charitable Foundation (A.Y.)

Knell, Theresa N.: secretary, trustee, Middendorf Foundation

Kneppler, Robert B., Jr.: director, Cook, Sr. Charitable Foundation (Kelly Gene)

Knese, William F.: chairman, trustee, CLARCOR Foundation; vice president, treasurer, CLARCOR, Inc.

Knez, Brian J.: trustee, Smith Family Foundation (Richard and Susan)

Knez, Debra S.: trustee, Smith Family Foundation (Richard and Susan)

Knight, Charles Field: trustee, Olin Foundation (John M.)

Knight, Dale: director, McDonough Foundation (Bernard)

Knight, Kathleen C.: member, Staunton Farm Foundation

Knight, Will A.: president, Wise Foundation (Watson W.)

Knighton, Elizabeth: director, Tyndale House Foundation

Knoble, Lindsey: director, Davenport-Hatch Foundation

Knoell, John: trustee, Grundy Foundation

Knoerzer, Elizabeth: secretary, Dime Foundation

Knorr, Eric T.: director, Kansas Health Foundation

Knott, David L.: trustee, Knott Foundation (Marion I. and Henry J.)

Knott, Henry Joseph, Jr: president, chairman, director, Knott Foundation (Marion I. and Henry J.)

Knott, Marion I.: chairman, Knott Foundation (Marion I. and Henry J.)

Knott, Martin G.: trustee, Knott Foundation (Marion I. and Henry J.)

Knott, Patty L.: trustee, Knott Foundation (Marion I. and Henry J.)

Knott, Teresa A.: trustee, Knott Foundation (Marion I. and Henry J.)

Knowles, Jeremy R., PhD: trustee, Hughes Medical Institute (Howard)

Knowles, Marie L.: executive vice president, chief financial officer, BP Amoco Corp.

Knowles, Rachel Hunt: trustee, Hunt Foundation (Roy A.)

Knox, Northrup Rand, Jr.: president, Knox Foundation (Seymour H.)

Knox, Seymour Horace, IV: vice president, secretary, Knox Foundation (Seymour H.)

Knox, Wendell J.: trustee, Eastern Bank Charitable Foundation

Knudson, John E., Jr.: vice president, chief financial officer, Henkel Corp.

Kobusch, Margaret M.: trustee, Dula Educational and Charitable Foundation (Caleb C. and Julia W.)

Koch, Charles de Ganahl: chairman, chief executive officer, director, Koch Industries, Inc.

Koch, Curtis J.: vice president, Schlink Foundation (Albert G. and Olive H.)

Koch, David Hamilton: trustee, Koch Foundation, Inc. (Fred C. and Mary R.)

Koch, Elizabeth B.: president, director, Koch Foundation, Inc. (Fred C. and Mary R.)

Koch, Justine: accountant, Altman Foundation

Koch, Kenneth: trustee, Van Wert County Foundation

Kochheiser, George W.: vice president, Employers Mutual Charitable Foundation

Kodama, Ryuzo: director, SMBC Global Foundation, Inc.; director, head Americas Division, Sumitomo Mitsui Banking Corp.

Koehn, Elwood: trustee, Schowalter Foundation

Koelbel, Gene N.: vice president, trustee, Norgren Foundation (Carl A.)

Koenemann, Carl F.: chief financial officer, executive vice president, Motorola, Inc.

Koenig, Lori: treasurer, director, World Heritage Foundation

Koenigsberger, Joseph A.: treasurer, Guggenheim Foundation (Harry Frank)

Koepke, James E.: trustee, Farr Trust (Frank M. and Alice M.)

Koeppe, Alfred C.: senior vice president corporate services & external affairs, Public Service Electric & Gas Foundation

Koerner, Philip D.: trustee, National Grange Mutual Charitable Trust; chairman, president, chief executive officer, National Grange Mutual Insurance Co.

Koester, Robert W.: president, Zullig Foundation (Herbert G. and Dorothy)

Kohler, Ruth DeYoung, II: president, chief operating officer, director, Kohler Foundation

Kohn, Bernhard L., Jr.: vice president, Kohn-Joseloff Foundation

Kohn, Bernhard L., Sr.: president, Kohn-Joseloff Foundation

Kohn, Edith: vice president, secretary, Arronson Foundation

Kohn, Ellen: vice president, Arronson Foundation

Kohn, Joan J.: secretary, treasurer, Kohn-Joseloff Foundation

Kohn, Joseph C.: vice president, Arronson Foundation

Kohnen, Theodore J.: treasurer, New York Life Foundation

Kohnstamm, Abby V.: vice chairman, director, IBM International Foundation

Koike, Wayne: treasurer, Haigh-Scatena Foundation

Kojima, K.: chairman, chief executive officer, Fujitsu America

Kokjer, Ralph L., Jr.: president, director, Harden Foundation

Kokot, Eugene V.: secretary, director, King Family Foundation (Charles and Lucille)

Kolb, John E.: director, mem executive committee, chairman legal committee, Keck Foundation (W. M.)

Komansky, David H.: trustee, vice president, Merrill Lynch & Co. Foundation Inc.; chairman, chief executive officer, Merrill Lynch & Company, Inc.

Konek, Jana L.: grants manager, Kansas Health Foundation

Kongsgaard, Martha: vice president, Kongsgaard-Goldman Foundation

Kononowitz, Thomas J.: vice president, New Jersey Natural Gas Foundation

Koontz, Richard Harvey: trustee, Bowne Foundation (Robert)

Koop, Dick W.: trustee, Johnson Foundation (M. G. and Lillie A.)

Koopman, Beatrice F.: trustee, Koopman Fund

Koopman, Dorothy B.: trustee, Koopman Fund

Koopman, Georgette A.: president, trustee, Koopman Fund

Koopman, Rena B.: secretary, trustee, Koopman Fund

Koopman, Richard, Jr.: trustee, Koopman Fund

Kopczick, Elise M.: vice president human resources, Crane Co.; vice president, Crane Foundation

Kopp, Bonnie: secretary, treasurer, Loutit Foundation

Kopp, Virginia: director, Dime Foundation

Koprulu, Nina Joukowsky: director, Joukowsky Family Foundation

Koren, John: secretary, trustee, Berkman Foundation (Louis and Sandra)

Koren, Tony: director programs, El Pomar Foundation

Koret, Susan: chairman, director, Koret Foundation

Korgenski, Marcy: member administration committee, Swanson Family Foundation, Inc. (Dr. W. C.)

Kornegay, S. Dock: director, secretary, Duke Energy Foundation

Korniczky, Anna T.: treasurer, Harriman Foundation (Gladys and Roland)

Kornmeier, Richard K.: trustee, Peterson Charitable Foundation (Folke H.)

Korstange, Jason: president, TCF Foundation

Kortbein, Donald: trustee, Andres Charitable Trust (Frank G.)

Korte, Greg O.: director, Ralph and Donna Korte Family Charitable Foundation

Korte, Ralph F.: chairman, Korte Construction Co.; president, director, Ralph and Donna Korte Family Charitable Foundation

Korte, Todd J.: vice president, director, Ralph and Donna Korte Family Charitable Foundation

Korte Solheim, Vicki: director, Ralph and Donna Korte Family Charitable Foundation

Kortendick, Russel L., Sr.: vice president, Christensen Charitable and Religious Foundation (L. C.)

Kortepeter, Wendy Griffith: adv, Griffith Foundation (W. C.)

Kosai, Aizo: mem allocations comm, Kawabe Memorial Fund

Kosak, Stephen P.: consultant, Bowman Proper Charitable Trust (J.)

Kosche, Peter C.: senior vice president corporate affairs, Olin Corp.; trustee, Olin Corp. Charitable Trust

Koskey, Richard P.: secretary, Rheinstrom Hill Community Foundation

Koskinas, Helen: director, Memorial Foundation for the Blind

Koskinen, Jean A.: director, Alexander Foundation (Walter)

Koskinen, Walter: vice president, director, Alexander Foundation (Walter)

Kosminsky, Jay P.: president, Pfizer Foundation

Kostishack, John: executive director, Bremer Foundation (Otto)

Kountze, Charles Denman: trustee, Hitchcock Foundation (Gilbert M. and Martha H.)

Kountze, Denman: president, trustee, Hitchcock Foundation (Gilbert M. and Martha H.)

Kountze, Edward H.: trustee, Hitchcock Foundation (Gilbert M. and Martha H.)

Kountze, Mary: trustee, Hitchcock Foundation (Gilbert M. and Martha H.)

Kountze, Neely: trustee, Hitchcock Foundation (Gilbert M. and Martha H.)

Koupal, Raymond: vice president, chief financial officer,

Koutsky, Lori J.: foundation manager, Minnesota Mutual Foundation

Kovacevich, Richard M.: president, chief executive officer, Wells Fargo & Co.

Koven, Joan Follin Hughes: secretary, treasurer, director, Marpat Foundation

Kovler, Everett: president, Blum Foundation (Harry and Maribel G.)

Kovler, H. Jonathan: vice president, treasurer, Blum Foundation (Harry and Maribel G.)

Kovler, Peter: assistant secretary, Blum Foundation (Harry and Maribel G.); treasurer, assistant secretary, Blum-Kovler Foundation

Kowalke, Stephen C.: treasurer, Target Foundation

Kowert, Marie F.: assistant secretary, Steele Foundation (Harry and Grace)

Koziar, Stephen F., Jr.: president, trustee, Dayton Power and Light Co. Foundation

Kozmetsky, Cynthia: trustee, treasurer, vice president, secretary, RGK Foundation

Kozmetsky, Gregory Allen: president, chairman, trustee, RGK Foundation

Kozmetsky, Ronya: don, trustee, RGK Foundation

Kozusko, Donald: trustee, Gund Foundation (Geoffrey)

Kraen, Donald P.: trustee, Patterson Memorial Trust (Hazel)

Kraft, Richard: vice president, Zullig Foundation (Herbert G. and Dorothy)

Krakora, Joseph: vice president, director, Marpat Foundation

Krakower, Victor: mgr, McGregor Foundation (Thomas and Frances)

Kramarsky, Sara Ann: secretary, Schiff Foundation (Dorothy)

Kramer, Irwin H.: vice president, Allen Brothers Foundation

Kramer, Katie S.: vice president grants/scholarships, Boettcher Foundation

Kramer, Lawrence I., Jr.: executive director, Lux Foundation (Miranda)

Kramer, Mary Elizabeth: vice president, Wellmark Foundation

Krantez, Leo: president, chief executive officer, Integra Bank

Kraus, John P.: trustee, Anderson Foundation

Kraus, Rick: administrator, Federated Mutual Insurance Foundation

Krause, Charles A.: vice chairman, trustee, McBeath Foundation (Faye)

Krause, Jim L.: director grants administration, assistant treasurer, Mott Foundation (Charles Stewart)

Krause, Sandra S.: trustee, Strauss Foundation

Krause, Steve: member, Northern Trust Co. Charitable Trust

Krauter, Donald W.: trustee, Slater Trust (Lillian M.)

Krave, Helmuth: secretary, Farwell Foundation (Drusilla)

Krave, Hugo: president, Farwell Foundation (Drusilla)

Kreamer, Janice C.: trustee, Johnson Foundation

Kredel, Richard S.: secretary, treasurer, trustee, Stamps Foundation (James L.)

Kreiner, Charles F., Jr.: director, Cummings Foundation (James H.)

Kreitler, Hobart C.: president, Kreitler Foundation

Kreitler, James S.: director, Kreitler Foundation

Kreitler, John M.: director, Kreitler Foundation

Kreitler, Karen R.: director, Kreitler Foundation

Kreitler, Sally S.: secretary, Kreitler Foundation

Kreitler, Thomas S.: vice president, Kreitler Foundation

Kreps, Juanita Morris: trustee, Duke Endowment

Kresa, Kent: trustee, Haynes Foundation (John Randolph and Dora); director, member executive committee, member grant committee, Keck Foundation (W. M.)

Kresge, Bruce Anderson, MD: vice president, trustee, Kresge Foundation

Kresse, Robert J.: secretary, trustee, Wendt Foundation (Margaret L.)

Kressley, Larry: executive director, Public Welfare Foundation

Krieble, Collette C.: vice president, Krieble Foundation (Vernon K.)

Krieble, Frederick B.: director, Krieble Foundation (Vernon K.)

Krieble, Frederick K.: vice president, Krieble Foundation (Vernon K.)

Krieble, Helen E.: president, Krieble Foundation (Vernon K.)

Krieble, Nancy B.: secretary, Krieble Foundation (Vernon K.)

Krieger, Theresa: trustee, Carls Foundation

Krinsky, Josephine B.: trustee, Parshelsky Foundation (Moses L.)

Krinsky, Robert Daniel: trustee, Parshelsky Foundation (Moses L.)

Krone, Bruce A.: secretary, trustee, Dater Foundation (Charles H.)

Krone, Dorothy G.: vice president, trustee, Dater Foundation (Charles H.)

Kroner, Herbert: president, Becher Foundation (Hildegarde D.)

Kronstadt, Annette: director, Himmelfarb Foundation (Paul and Annetta)

Kronstadt, Lillian: executive director, Himmelfarb Foundation (Paul and Annetta)

Kropf, Susan J.: director, Wallace-Reader's Digest Fund (DeWitt)

Krukowski, Francis V.: president, Price Foundation (Lucien B. and Katherine E.)

Krulak, Allan C.: vice president, Forest City Enterprises Charitable Foundation, Inc.; vice president corporate & public affairs, director, Forest City Enterprises, Inc.

Kubasak, Thomas F.: chief financial officer, Trust Funds

Kuechle, Scott E.: vice president treasurer, Goodrich Corp.; treasurer, Goodrich Foundation, Inc. (B.F.)

Kuehn, Henry: trustee, Graham Foundation for Advanced Studies in the Fine Arts

Kuehn, Ronald L., Jr.: chairman, chief executive officer, El Paso Corp.

Kuester, Dennis J.: president, director, Marshall & Ilsley Corp.; vice president, director, Marshall & Ilsley Foundation, Inc.

Kugler, Marianne: program officer, Mott Foundation (Charles Stewart)

Kuljian, Christa: program officer, Mott Foundation (Charles Stewart)

Kully, Robert I.: president, trust, Livingston Foundation (Milton S. and Corinne N.)

Kulp, Jill Clemens: trustee, Clemens Foundation

Kulynych, Petro: chairman, treasurer, Lowe's Charitable and Educational Foundation

Kumm, L. Hope: director, Cleary Foundation

Kummer, Robert W., Jr.: vice president, trustee, Jones Foundation (Fletcher)

Kump, Marsha A.: executive director, Whiting Foundation

Kunce, Marquita L.: assistant treasurer, Olin Foundation (Spencer T. and Ann W.)

Kunin, Constance: trustee, Bigelow Foundation (F. R.)

Kunin, Myron: chairman, director, Regis Corp.; president, Regis Foundation

Kunkel, John C., II: trustee, Kunkel Foundation (John Crain)

Kunkel, Paul A.: trustee, Kunkel Foundation (John Crain)

Kunkel, W. Minster, MD: trustee, Kunkel Foundation (John Crain)

Kunkle, Gary: president, chief operating officer, Dentsply International, Inc.

Kuntz, Jean M.: trustee, Harmon Foundation (Pearl M. and Julia J.)

Kunzman, Edward D.: president, Schwartz Foundation (Arnold A.)

Kunzman, Steven: secretary, treasurer, Schwartz Foundation (Arnold A.)

Kupferberg, Max: trustee, Vogler Foundation (Laura B.)

Kuprenski, Shelagh: secretary, Ewald Foundation (H. T.)

Kurczewski, Walter W.: vice president, secretary, general counsel, Square D Co.; president, director, Square D Foundation

Kurth, Jeri: co-trustee, Cray Residuary Charitable Trust (Evah C.)

Kurtz, Samuel B.: director, Lebanon Mutual Foundation

Kurtz, Samuel G.: chairman, director, Lebanon Mutual Insurance Co.

Kury, Mark C.: executive vice president, director, McDonough Foundation (Bernard)

Kurz, Ellen: director, Kurz Family Foundation

Kurz, Herbert: president, Kurz Family Foundation

Kurz, Leonard: director, Kurz Family Foundation

Kurzman, H. Michael: vice president, director, Lurie Foundation (Louis R.)

Kushlan, James: director, Frohring Foundation (Paul and Maxine)

Kushlan, Paula Frohring: trustee, Frohring Foundation (Paul and Maxine)

Kustosz, Susan N.: director, Harcourt Foundation (Ellen Knowles)

Kutella, Ronald J.: president, Sedgwick, Inc.

Kuth, Byron: vice president, LEF Foundation

Kuth, Lyda Ebert: cfo, secretary, LEF Foundation

Kwoh, Stewart: director, Fannie Mae Foundation

Kwong, Peter: trustee, New York Foundation

L

L'Engle Franklin, Madeleine: president, Crosswicks Foundation

La Boon, Robert Bruce: vice president, Kayser Foundation

La Force, James Clayburn: director, Bradley Foundation (Lynde and Harry)

La Valley, Frederick J. M.: trustee, Grundy Foundation

LaBahn, Mary Ann: vice president, treasurer, Ross Memorial Foundation (Will)

LaBahn, Mary Ann W.: director, Bucyrus-Erie Foundation

Labalme, Patricia Hochschild: trustee, Delmas Foundation (Gladys Krieble)

LaBelle, Jenijoy: secretary, Essick Foundation

Labik, Nancy: foundation coord, Chicago Title and Trust Co. Foundation

Laboutin Bannon, Alexandra: trustee, Beynon Foundation (Kathryne)

Labrato, Ronnie R.: secretary, Gulf Power Foundation

Labrecque, Thomas Goulet: president, chief operating officer, director, J.P. Morgan Chase & Co.; president, J.P. Morgan Chase Foundation

Labutka, Carolyn E.: vice president, executive director, Aon Foundation

Lachman, Marguerite Leanne: trustee, Chicago Title and Trust Co. Foundation

Lackey, S. Allen: director, Shell Oil Co. Foundation

Lackland, David: trustee, Schwartz Foundation (Arnold A.)

LaCounte, Maage E.: director, Johnston-Hanson Foundation

Lacourse, Julien: executive vice president, Demoulas Supermarkets, Inc.

Lacy, Benjamin H.: treasurer, clerk, director, NEBS Foundation

Lacy, Jill: corporate secretary, Bay State Federal Savings Charitable Foundation

Ladd, Edward: trustee, Forster Charitable Trust (James W. and Ella B.)

Ladd, George E., III: director, Ladd Charitable Corp. (Helen and George)

Ladd, Lincoln F.: director, Ladd Charitable Corp. (Helen and George)

Ladd, Robert M.: director, Ladd Charitable Corp. (Helen and George)

Ladds, Herbert P., Jr.: director, Utica National Foundation

Lady, David C.: administration, Kauffman Foundation (Ewing Marion)

Lafferty, Bernard: president, director, Duke Foundation (Doris)

Lafleur, Richard B.: treasurer, Roddy Foundation (Fred M.)

Lafond, Colette: advisory board, Van Evera Foundation (Dewitt)

LaFond, Laura J. Van Evera: co-trustee, Van Evera Foundation (Dewitt)

Lafond, Susan G.: trustee, Bean Foundation (Norwin S. and Elizabeth N.)

LaFreniere, Norma B.: member distribution comm, Champlin Foundation

Lagasse, Raymond A.: chairman, Mascoma Savings Bank Foundation

Lagemann, Ellen Condliffe: director, Markle Foundation (John and Mary R.)

Lagerlof, Stanley C.: trustee, Stillwell Charitable Trust (Glen and Dorothy)

Lagomasino, Maria Elena: trustee, J.P. Morgan Chase Foundation

Laird, Walter Jones, Jr.: director, Glencoe Foundation

Laitman, Nanette L.: trustee, Lasdon Foundation (William and Mildred)

Lakin, Charles: director, Lytel Foundation (Bertha Russ)

Lally, Joachim: trustee, Russell Trust (Josephine G.)

Lamade, Howard: adv comm, Lamco Foundation

Lamade, J. Robert: adv comm, Lamco Foundation

Lamade, James S.: adv comm, Lamco Foundation

LaMarche, Gerald: director, ONDEO Nalco Foundation

Lamb, Barbara: director, Lamb Foundation

Lamb, Carl: director, Lamb Foundation

Lamb, Dana: gov, Mayor Foundation (Oliver Dewey)

Lamb, Dorothy: director, Lamb Foundation

Lamb, Frank: chairman, Lamb Foundation

Lamb, Greg: director, Lamb Foundation

Lamb, Helen: director, Lamb Foundation

Lamb, Isabelle Smith: director, Bishop Foundation (E. K. and Lillian F.)

Lamb, Maryann: treasurer, Lamb Foundation

Lamb, Paula L.: vchairman, Lamb Foundation

Lamb, Peter: director, Lamb Foundation

Lambe, James F.: senior vice president human resources, Ondeo Nalco Co.; director, ONDEO Nalco Foundation

Lambert, Greg: director, Sierra Pacific Resources Charitable Foundation

Lambert, Joseph: treasurer, S.G. Foundation

Lambert, Linda P.: director, Kirkpatrick Foundation, Inc.; trustee, Reynolds Foundation (Donald W.)

Lambert, Samuel Waldron, III: president, trustee, Bunbury Co., Inc.; chairman, trustee, Windham Foundation

Lampros, Jack D.: off, Stewart Educational Foundation (Donnell B. and Elizabeth Dee Shaw)

Lanahan, W. Wallace, Jr.: member investment committee, Goldseker Foundation of Maryland (Morris)

Lancaster, Rose C.: trustee, member contributions committee, Trull Foundation (The)

Lancaster, Sally Rhodus, PhD: director emeritus, Meadows Foundation (The)

Land, Lillie S.: secretary, director, duPont Foundation (Alfred I.)

Landegger, Carl Clement: treasurer, director, Landegger Charitable Foundation

Landegger, George Francis: president, director, Landegger Charitable Foundation

Landman, Carole: trustee, Heckscher Foundation for Children

Landry, Edward A.: assistant secretary, assistant treasurer, Hume Foundation (Jaquelin); trustee, Lantz Foundation (Walter)

Landry, Margaret: adv, Patron Saints Foundation

Landvater, Carrie: secretary, treasurer, Ray Foundation

Lane, Bernard Bell: director, Lane Foundation (Minnie and Bernard)

Lane, Eileen: secretary, Jewish Healthcare Foundation

Lane, Joan: trustee, Lane Family Charitable Trust

Lane, Joan Fletcher: director, Irvine Foundation (The James)

Lane, Lynn L.: director, treasurer, Reynolds Tobacco Company Foundation (R. J.)

Lane, Minnie B.: director, Lane Foundation (Minnie and Bernard)

Lane, Nancy Wolfe: vice president, Wolfe Associates, Inc.

Lane, Ralph: trustee, Lane Family Charitable Trust

Lane, Robert: president, Ideal Industries, Inc.

Lane, Robert W.: vice president, director, Deere Foundation (John)

Lane, Thomas H.: trustee, Dow Corning Foundation

Lane, William A., Jr.: president, trustee, Dunspaugh-Dalton Foundation

Laney, James Thomas: director, chairman nominations committee, Luce Foundation (Henry)

Laney, John: vice president, program officer, Hall Family Foundation (The)

Lang, David: trustee, Lang Foundation (Eugene M.)

Lang, Eugene Michael: donor, trustee, Lang Foundation (Eugene M.)

Lang, Jane: trustee, Lang Foundation (Eugene M.)

Lang, Keith H.: member dist committee, member investigating committee, Champlin Foundation

Lang, Robert Todd: chairman, director, Weil, Gotshal & Manges Foundation

Lang, Sherry: vice president & director investor relations, TJX Companies, Inc.; director, TJX Foundation, Inc.

Lang, Stephen: trustee, Lang Foundation (Eugene M.)

Lang, Theresa: trustee, Lang Foundation (Eugene M.)

Langdon, George Dorland, Jr.: trustee, Kresge Foundation

Lange, Beverly J.: secretary, Anderson Foundation

Lange, James M., Jr.: director, Dime Foundation

Lange, Terry L.: treasurer, Thomas Foundation

Langemann, Ellen Condliffe, PhD: director, Greenwall Foundation

Langfitt, Thomas W., MD: director, Pew Charitable Trusts

Langford, J. Beverly: treasurer, trustee, Ratner Foundation (Milton M.)

Langford, Thomas A.: trustee, Duke Endowment

Langland, Marc: director, Usibelli Foundation

Langner, Jay B.: director, Mailman Family Foundation (A. L.)

Langstaff, Carol: director, Guggenheim Foundation (Harry Frank)

Lanier, John E.: trustee, Peterloon Foundation

Lanier, Linda L.: director, Atkinson Foundation

Lanier, Melissa Emery: vice president, trustee, Peterloon Foundation

Lanier, Richard S.: director, Trust for Mutual Understanding

Lanigan, Bernard, Jr.: treasurer, director, Williams Family Foundation of Georgia

Lankenship, Robert: director, McConnell Foundation

Lanning, Donald R.: vice president grocery operations, Campbell Soup Co.

Lanphear, Gail E.: president, trustee, Gerstacker Foundation (Rollin M.)

Lansaw, Judy W.: secretary, trustee, Dayton Power and Light Co. Foundation

Lansing, John S.: executive director, Lake Placid Education Foundation

Lant, Steven V.: chief financial officer, Central Hudson Gas & Electric Corp.

Lanterman, A. Kirk: director, Usibelli Foundation

Lantz, Joanne Baldwin: director, Foellinger Foundation

Lapeyre, Pierre S.: executive consult, assistant secretary, Schlieder Educational Foundation (Edward G.)

Lapham, Lewis: director, Guggenheim Foundation (Harry Frank)

Lapides, Bernard: co-chairman, co-president, director, Wurzburg, Inc.

LaPierre, Susan: vice president community relations, East Cambridge Savings Charitable Foundation

LaPlace, William B.: vice president, trustee, Second Foundation; trustee, Young Foundation (Hugo H. and Mabel E.)

LaRich, Jeffrey: trustee, Frohring Foundation (Paul and Maxine)

Lark, Carolyn: vice president, Donaldson Charitable Trust (Oliver S. and Jennie R.)

Lark, J. Andrew: co-trustee, Cummings Memorial Fund (The Frances L. and Edwin L.)

Larkin, Al: president, Boston Globe Foundation

Larkin, Frank Y.: vice chairman, director, Noble Foundation, Inc. (Edward John)

Larkin, June Noble: chairwoman, director, Noble Foundation, Inc. (Edward John)

Larkins, Michealle: program officer, Ratshesky Foundation (A. C.)

Larouche, Carol A.: assistant secretary, Barker Foundation Inc.

Larsen, Brent: director, Grinnell Mutual Group Foundation

Larsen, Christopher: second vice president, Larsen Fund

Larsen, John O.: director, Alliant Energy Foundation, Inc.

Larsen, Jonathan Zerbe: secretary, Larsen Fund

Larsen, Marshall O.: president, chief executive officer, director, Goodrich Corp.

Larsen, Nancy D.: secretary, treasurer, Allen Foundation (Nibs and Edna)

Larsen, Robert R.: president, Larsen Fund

Larson, Carol S.: vice president, director programs, Packard Foundation (David and Lucile)

Larson, Marie: secretary, Offield Family Foundation (The)

Larson, Peter N.: chairman, chief executive officer, director, Brunswick Corp.

Larson, Richard: director, Brillion Foundation

Larson, Robert C.: trustee, Kresge Foundation

LaRussa, Anne: director, Bruno Charitable Foundation (Joseph S.)

LaRussa, Benny M., Jr.: vice president, treasurer, Bruno Charitable Foundation (Joseph S.)

Lascor, Michael: trustee, Weckbaugh Foundation (Eleanore Mullen)

Lasdon, Mildred D.: trustee, Lasdon Foundation (William and Mildred)

Lashley, Elinor Huston: vice president ed and cultural rels, Huston Foundation

Laske, Arthur Charles, Jr.: treasurer, director, Morris Foundation (William T.)

Lasley, Robert: co-trustee, Moss Charitable Trust (Finis M.)

Lasota, Kathleen: secretary, Quaker Chemical Foundation

Lassalle, Honor: president, Norman Foundation

Lassalle, Nancy Norman: member, Norman Foundation; vice president, secretary, Normandie Foundation

Lassalle, Philip E.: director, Norman Foundation

Lasser, Miles L.: executive director, Sheldon Foundation Inc. (Ralph C.)

Lassiter, Reynolds: director, Babcock Foundation (Mary Reynolds)

Lasurdo, I. Jerry: director, Vogler Foundation (Laura B.)

Latham, David: admin assistant, Reed Foundation (NY)

Latham, John Brace: trustee, Brace Foundation (Donald C.)

Latham, Robert C.: second vice chairman, director, Grinnell Mutual Reinsurance Co.

Lathan, Roger D.: director, Schmitt Foundation (Kilian J. and Caroline F.)

Lathem, Edward: director, Dr. Seuss Foundation

Latta, Courtney E.: senior program officer, Reynolds Foundation (Donald W.)

Laub, Russell K.: first vice president, Hoch Foundation (Charles H.)

Laube, F. H., III: chairman, chief executive officer, president, Freeport Brick Co.; secretary, Freeport Brick Co. Charitable Trust

Laube, Harry R.: assistant secretary, assistant treasurer, Freeport Brick Co. Charitable Trust

Lauchert, F. H.: trustee, Atofina Chemicals Foundation

Lauck, Joseph: director, Lebanon Mutual Foundation

Lauder, Estee: president, Lauder Foundation

Lauder, Leonard Alan: secretary-treasurer, Lauder Foundation

Lauder, Norma J.: vice president, Bank One Foundation

Lauder, Ronald Stephen: vice president, Lauder Foundation

Lauderbach, C. Ward: director, Wickson-Link Memorial Foundation

Laughon, Kenneth C.: director, Carter Foundation (Beirne)

Launius, Leigh Ann (Korns): assistant secretary, Cox Foundation (James M.)

Lauren, Charles B.: trustee, Hagedorn Fund

Lautz, Terrill E.: trustee, Lingnan Foundation; vice president, secretary,, Luce Foundation (Henry)

LaVeque, Edgar G., MD: trustee, Valley Foundation

Lavezzo, Janette: trustee, Arata Brothers Trust

LaVigne, Gregory P.: trustee, Reliable Life Insurance Co. Foundation

Lavine, Gary J.: trustee, Niagara Mohawk Foundation

Lavine, Ruth J.: president, director, Lavine Family Foundation (Richard and Ruth)

Lavis, Stella Amado: director, Amado Foundation (Maurice)

Law, D. Brian: trustee, Kantzler Foundation

Lawford, Patricia Kennedy: trustee, Kennedy, Jr. Foundation (Joseph P.)

Lawin, Bruce A.: president, chief executive officer, Specialty Manufacturing Co.

Lawler, John J.: director, Cabot Corp. Foundation

Lawless, Robert J.: chairman, president, chief executive officer, chief operating officer, director, McCormick & Company, Inc.

Lawliss, Donald E.: director, Provident Community Foundation

Lawrence, Anne I.: vice president, Ingalls Foundation (Louise H. and David S.)

Lawrence, Anne T.: trustee, Semple Foundation (Louise Taft)

Lawrence, Barbara Childs: president, AKC Fund

Lawrence, Belinda Turner: director administration, Knight Foundation (John S. and James L.)

Lawrence, Carol: assistant secretary, Daniels Foundation (Fred Harris)

Lawrence, Charles M.: president, Lytel Foundation (Bertha Russ)

Lawrence, Elizabeth Atwood: trustee, Donaldson Charitable Trust (Oliver S. and Jennie R.)

Lawrence, J. Vinton: vice president, AKC Fund

Lawrence, James A.: chief financial officer, executive vice president, General Mills, Inc.

Lawrence, John T., Jr.: vice president, trustee, Emery Memorial (Thomas J.); treasurer, Ingalls Foundation (Louise H. and David S.); treasurer, trustee, Semple Foundation (Louise Taft)

Lawrence, Keith: secretary, Pickford Foundation (Mary)

Lawrence, Ralph: president, chief operating officer, Hyde Manufacturing Co.

Lawrence, Richard Wesley, Jr.: president, gov, trustee, Crary Foundation (Bruce L.)

Lawrence, Robert Ashton: trustee, Saltonstall Charitable Foundation (Richard)

Lawrence, Sull: secretary, Pickford Foundation (Mary)

Lawrence, Thomas F., Jr.: director, Warwick Savings Foundation

Lawrence, Warren: director, Vicksburg Foundation

Lawrenz, Ruthmarie M.: director, Schroeder Foundation (Walter)

Laws, Donald P.: member advisory committee, Blue Bell Foundation

Lawson, A. E.: executive director, Exxon Mobil Foundation

Lawson, A. Peter: vice president, Motorola Foundation

Lawson, Floyd: director, Klee Foundation (Conrad and Virginia)

Lawson, John K.: senior vice president, Deere & Co.; director, Deere Foundation (John)

Lawson-Johnston, Peter Orman: chairman, director, Guggenheim Foundation (Harry Frank)

Laybourne, Everett Broadstone: vice president, director, Parsons Foundation (Ralph M.)

Layden, Mark: director, Vermilion Healthcare Foundation

Layman, Sandy: secretary, trustee, Blandin Foundation

Lazaran, Frank: president, chief executive officer, Winn-Dixie Stores Inc.

Lazarus, Charles P.: trustee, Lazarus Charitable Trust

Lazarus, Leonard: secretary, Solow Foundation

Le Grand, Clay: trustee, Carver Charitable Trust (Roy J.)

Lea, Anna L.: vice president, treasurer, director, Lea Foundation (Helen Sperry)

Lea, Helena A.: vice president, director, Lea Foundation (Helen Sperry)

Lea, R. Brooke, II: vice president, director, Lea Foundation (Helen Sperry)

Lea, Sperry: president, director, Lea Foundation (Helen Sperry)

Leach, Willis R.: trustee, Stamps Foundation (James L.)

Leaders, Rance: secretary, treasurer, trustee, Miller Foundation

Leahey, William E., Jr.: director, Alcoa Foundation

Leahy, Charles F.: trustee, Jameson Trust (Oleonda)

Leahy, Edwin D., OSB: trustee, The MBNA Foundation

Leahy, Eileen: manager corporate contributions, Public Service Electric & Gas Foundation

Leahy, Richard: trustee, Peabody Charitable Fund (Amelia)

Leape, Jim: director, conservation and science program, Packard Foundation (David and Lucile)

Leary, Hugh K.: executive director, treasurer, Scott Foundation (William H., John G., and Emma)

Leath, Berneice R.: secretary, treasurer, Priddy Foundation

Leavey, Joseph James: trustee, Leavey Foundation (Thomas and Dorothy)

Lebedoff, Randy Miller: vice president, general counsel, McClatchy Co.; secretary, Star Tribune Foundation

Lebedun, Barbara: president, H&R Block Foundation

Lebens, Jeffrey Kent: senior vice president financial & administration, treasurer, Intermountain Gas Co.; director, Intermountain Gas Industries Foundation

LeBlanc, Robert: president, chief operating officer, Handy & Harman

LeBoeuf, Raymond W.: director, PPG Industries Foundation; director, chairman, chief executive officer, PPG Industries, Inc.

Lebovitz, Herbert C.: president, treasurer, Lebovitz Fund

Lebovitz, James: director, Lebovitz Fund

Lebow, Jane: vice president, Dickler Family Foundation

LeBreton, Pierre R., PhD: trustee, Blowitz-Ridgeway Foundation

LeBuhn, Robert: president, trustee, Dodge Foundation (Geraldine R.)

Lechleiter, John C.: director, Lilly Foundation (Eli)

LeClerc, Paul: trustee, Mellon Foundation (Andrew W.)

Leder, Philip: director, chairman, Revson Foundation (Charles H.)

Lederer, Adrienne: president, director, Lederer Foundation (Francis L.)

Ledes, John G.: assistant treasurer, assistant secretary, director, Hopkins Foundation (Josephine Lawrence)

Ledgett, Ronald A.: senior vice president, NSTAR; trustee, NSTAR Foundation

Ledward, Jeffery: secretary, director, Willis Family Foundation

Lee, C. T.: president, Formosa Plastics Corporation, USA

Lee, Donna: trustee, BellSouth Foundation

Lee, Dwight E.: vice president, director, Barker Foundation (J.M.R.)

Lee, George Ludlow, Jr.: trustee, Red Devil Foundation

Lee, H. Clifford: chairman, director, Bush Charitable Foundation, Inc. (Edyth)

Lee, Hali Hae Kyung: trustee, Bowne Foundation (Robert)

Lee, James R.: director, Patron Saints Foundation

Lee, Jane T.: chairman, director, Red Devil; trustee, Red Devil Foundation

Lee, John J.: chairman, president, chief executive officer, director, Hexcel Corp.; trustee, Hexcel Foundation

Lee, Madeline: executive director, New York Foundation

Lee, Mary: trustee, Red Devil Foundation

Lee, Richard H.: president, trustee, Fowler Memorial Foundation (John Edward)

Lee, Robert W.: treasurer, Wildermuth Foundation (E. F.)

Leemputte, Peter: trustee, Chicago Title and Trust Co. Foundation

Leeson, Cathy: treasurer, Hobby Family Foundation

LeFeber, Marilyn Stein: vice president communications, Mott Foundation (Charles Stewart)

Lefevour, Suzanne A.: trustee, Butler Family Foundation (Patrick and Aimee)

Leffall, LaSalle D., Jr.: director, Dana Foundation (Charles A.)

Lefton, Al Paul, Jr.: president, chief executive officer, director, Lefton Co. (Al Paul); trustee, Lefton Co. Foundation (Al Paul)

Legare, Richard J.: director, Dime Savings Bank of Norwich Foundation

Legg, Louis E.: vice president, Thoman Foundation (W. B. and Candace)

Leggat, John E., Esq.: trustee, Walsh Charity Trust (Blanche)

Legner, Theresa M.: assistant secretary, Mosinee Paper Corp. Foundation

Lehner, Carl P.: president, chief executive officer; trustee, Orchard Foundation

Lehner, Philip: chairman,

Lehr, Gustav J.: vice president, director, Shelter Insurance Foundation; chairman, director, Shelter Mutual Insurance Co.

Lehr, Ronald L.: trustee, Johnson Foundation (Helen K. and Arthur E.)

Leiberman, Patricia S.: vice chair, Mailman Family Foundation (A. L.)

Leibowitz, Martin L.: vice chairman, Carnegie Corp. of New York

Leibrock, Robert C.: president, Abell-Hanger Foundation

Lemaster, James: president, Anthem Foundation, Inc.

LeMieux, Linda J.: trustee, Whiting Foundation

Lemke, Carl R.: secretary, Mead Witter Foundation, Inc.

Lemle, Stuart: director, JJJ Foundation

Lemole, Emily Jane: secretary, treasurer, Asplundh Foundation

Lemons, Wishard: trustee, Broadhurst Foundation

Lenahan, Joan O.: secretary, Humana Foundation

Lenhard, John E.: secretary, associate general counsel, Cleveland-Cliffs, Inc.

Lenhart, Carole S.: treasurer, Beveridge Foundation, Inc. (Frank Stanley)

Lenihan, F. Thomas, Esq.: trustee, Kimball Foundation (Horace A. Kimball and S. Ella)

Lenkowsky, Leslie, PhD: trustee, Achelis Foundation

Lenna, Elizabeth S.: director, Lenna Foundation (Reginald A. and Elizabeth S.)

Lenna, Reginald A.: director, Lenna Foundation (Reginald A. and Elizabeth S.)

Lennartz, Ann: vice president, Kuyper Foundation (Peter H. and E. Lucille Gaass)

Lenny, Richard H.: president, chief executive officer, Hershey Foods Corp.

Lenox, John W.: director, Shelter Insurance Foundation

Lents, Max R.: director, chairman medical research committee, Keck Foundation (W. M.)

Leonard, Anna B.: 2nd vice president, Vale-Asche Foundation

Leonard, Joan S., Esq.: vice president, general counsel, Hughes Medical Institute (Howard)

Leonard, Kathryn: treasurer, Bauervic Foundation (Charles M.)

Leonard, Patricia A.: president, secretary, Bauervic Foundation (Charles M.)

Leonard, Theodore J.: director, Bauervic Foundation (Charles M.)

Leonard, Timothy J.: director, Bauervic Foundation (Charles M.)

Leone, Daniel A.: director, East Cambridge Savings Charitable Foundation

Lepak, Robert R.: trustee, Davis Foundation (Irene E. and George A.)

Lerman, Philip: director, Cudahy Fund (Patrick and Anna M.)

Lerner, Ralph E.: secretary, trustee, Lingnan Foundation

Lerner, Randolph D., Esq.: chairman, director, MBNA Corp.

Leroux, Robert J.: vice president, controller, Cleveland-Cliffs, Inc.

Lesar, David J.: chairman, president, chief executive officer, Halliburton Co.; trustee, Halliburton Foundation, Inc.

Lesher, Cynthia: director, Lesher Foundation (Dean and Margaret)

Lesher, Margaret L.: president, director, Lesher Foundation (Dean and Margaret)

Lesher, Melinda: director, Lesher Foundation (Dean and Margaret)

Lesher, Stephen: vice president, Lesher Foundation (Dean and Margaret)

Lesko, G.: trustee, Whalley Charitable Trust

Leslie, Gaylord E.: trustee, Van Wert County Foundation

Lesser, Richard G.: executive vice president, chief operating officer, director, TJX Companies, Inc.; chief operating officer, director, TJX Foundation, Inc.

Lessersohn, James C.: vice president, treasurer, New York Times Co. Foundation

Letbetter, R. Steve: chairman, president, chief executive officer, CenterPoint Energy, Inc.

Letcher, Edith Gilmore: trustee, Phillips Charitable Trust (Dr. and Mrs. Arthur William)

Letrillart, Thierry: president, chief executive officer, Christian Dior Perfumes, Inc.

Leung, Sandra: secretary, Bristol-Myers Squibb Foundation Inc.

Levan, Alan: chairman, president, chief executive officer, BankAtlantic Bancorp; president, trustee, BankAtlantic Foundation

Levan, B. W.: vice president, director, Shell Oil Co. Foundation

Levan, Shelley: treasurer, trustee, BankAtlantic Foundation

Levavy, Zvi: president, Kaplun Foundation (Morris J. and Betty)

Leveille, Raymond G., Jr.: trustee, Levy Foundation (June Rockwell)

Levenson, Beatrice: secretary, Fischbach Foundation

Leverenz, Robert H.: director, VPI Foundation Inc.

Leverett, Allen L.: executive vice president, chief financial officer, Georgia Power Co.; director, Georgia Power Foundation

Levett, Edith: secretary emeritus, Greenwall Foundation

Levi, Alexander H.: vice president, director, Hecht-Levi Foundation

Levi, Richard H.: vice president, treasurer, director, Hecht-Levi Foundation

Levi, Ryda H.: vice president, director, Hecht-Levi Foundation

Levin, Gail C.: executive director, Annenberg Foundation

Levin, Jack I.: trustee, Phillips Family Foundation (The Jay and Rose)

Levin, John P.: trustee, Phillips Family Foundation (The Jay and Rose)

Levin, John P., Jr.: director, Rosenberg, Jr. Family Foundation (Louise and Claude)

Levin, Richard C.: director, Hewlett Foundation (William and Flora)

Levin, Robert J.: director, Fannie Mae Foundation

Levin, Suzan: trustee, Phillips Family Foundation (The Jay and Rose)

Levine, Arnold J.: director, Kaufmann Foundation (Henry)

Levine, Kenneth M.: director, MONY Foundation; executive vice president, chief investment officer, director, MONY Group, Inc.

Levine, Richard E.: secretary, Rollins-Luetkemeyer Foundation

Levine, Sidney: director, Dewar Foundation

Levine, Victoria M.: director, Barra Foundation

Levitan, David Maurice: vice president, Fink Foundation (NY)

Levitt, Alvin T., Esq.: secretary, treasurer, Seven Springs Foundation

Levy, Andrew H.: director, Newman Assistance Fund (Jerome A. and Estelle R.)

Levy, David: trustee, National Service Foundation

Levy, David B.: treasurer, director, Rudin Foundation

Levy, H. George: director, La-Z-Boy, Inc.

Levy, Richard: chief financial officer, Community Trust Bancorp, Inc.

Levy, Roberta Morse: secretary, Ratshesky Foundation (A. C.)

Levy, Susan M.: director community relations, R.R. Donnelley & Sons Co.

Levy, William R.: co-trustee, Jacobs Charitable Trust (Margaret G.)

Lew, Yung: director, Wells Fargo Foundation

Lewin, John: vice president, director, Rudin Foundation

Lewis, C. Stephen: trustee, Weyerhaeuser Co. Foundation

Lewis, Craig: treasurer, trustee, Middendorf Foundation

Lewis, Diana D.: vice president human resources, Ecolab, Inc.

Lewis, Emily S.: trustee, Saltonstall Charitable Foundation (Richard)

Lewis, George Ralph: trustee, Kemper Foundation (James S.)

Lewis, Hunter: trustee, Rockefeller Brothers Fund, Inc.

Lewis, Jeffrey R.: executive director, chief operating officer, Heinz Family Foundation

Lewis, Joanna M.: director, Barra Foundation

Lewis, John: Distribution trustee, Schwab-Rosenhouse Memorial Foundation

Lewis, John D.: vice chairman, Comerica Inc.

Lewis, Kenneth D.: chairman, president, chief executive officer, Bank of America Corp.

Lewis, Laurie M.: member dispensing committee, McCune Charitable Trust (John R.)

Lewis, Marilyn Ware: vice president, secretary, Oxford Foundation

Lewis, Merwin: vice president, Oestreicher Foundation (Sylvan and Ann)

Lewis, Priscilla: director communications, special assistant to the president, Rockefeller Brothers Fund, Inc.

Lewis, Russell T.: president, chief executive officer, New York Times Co.

Lewis, Sharon: trustee, Harris Foundation (William H. and Mattie Wattis)

Lewis, W. Ashton: secretary, trustee, Beazley Foundation

Lewis, Warren: director, Lebanon Mutual Foundation

Lewy, Ralph I.: treasurer, Pick, Jr. Fund (Albert)

Ley, Watson: trustee, Van Wert County Foundation

Leydorf, Frederick Leroy: director, Jameson Foundation (J. W. and Ida M.)

Libin, Jerome B.: director, Park Foundation

Lichtman, Judith: 1st vice president, treasurer, Moriah Fund, Inc.

Liddy, Richard A.: chairman, president, chief executive officer, GenAmerica Financial Corp.

Lidvall, John Gabrielson: treasurer, director, Hall-Perrine Foundation

Lieberman, Leonard: chairman, trustee, Fund for New Jersey

Liebich, Donald H.: trustee, Charitable Venture Foundation

Liebich, Herbert K.: trustee, Charitable Venture Foundation

Liebich, Kurt: trustee, Charitable Venture Foundation

Liebich, Richard C.: trustee, Charitable Venture Foundation

Liebler, Arthur C.: vice president communications, DaimlerChrysler AG; trustee, DaimlerChrysler Corp. Fund

Liebman, Kate: program officer, Altman Foundation

Liebman, Seymour: executive vice president finance, chief financial officer, Canon U.S.A., Inc.

Lien, Tracy K.: assistant secretary, CUNA Mutual Group Foundation, Inc.

Lieser, W. E.: secretary, treasurer, trustee, Reeves Foundation (OH)

Lifton, Robert: director, chairman, Pick, Jr. Fund (Albert)

Light, Christopher Upjohn: vice president, Upjohn Foundation (Harold and Grace)

Lightfoot, Sara Lawrence: chairman, MacArthur Foundation (John D. and Catherine T.)

Ligon, Bill A., Jr.: trustee, Hawkins Foundation (Robert Z.)

Lilley, Jack: director, Smith and W. Aubrey Smith Charitable Foundation (Clara Blackford)

Lillios, Paul C.: director, Demos Foundation (N.)

Lilly, Bruce A.: director, Lilly Foundation (Richard Coyle)

Lilly, David M.: president, Lilly Foundation (Richard Coyle)

Lilly, David M., Jr.: president, Lilly Foundation (Richard Coyle)

Lilly, Eli, II: director, Lilly Endowment

Lilly, Elizabeth M.: vice president, Lilly Foundation (Richard Coyle)

Lilly, Katherine V.: vice president, director, Mardag Foundation

Liman, Ellen: president, Lowe Foundation (Joe and Emily)

Limbert, G. Christian, Jr.: chief financial officer, treasurer, Clemens Markets

Limes, Edward J.: treasurer, trustee, Weckbaugh Foundation (Eleanore Mullen)

Lincoln, William T.: treasurer, trustee, Berry Foundation (Loren M.)

Lindberg, Jerome L.: vice president, trustee, Buell Foundation (Temple Hoyne)

Lindberg, Mark: senior program officer, Bremer Foundation (Otto)

Linde, Robert R.: mng trustee, Rogers Fund for the Arts (Russell Hill)

Lindenauer, Arthur: executive vice president, chief financial officer, Schlumberger Ltd.

Lindheim, Elaine L.: president, Amado Foundation (Maurice)

Lindholm, John T.: secretary, treasurer, trustee, Whiting Foundation

Lindley, F. Haynes, Jr.: president emeritus, trustee, Haynes Foundation (John Randolph and Dora)

Lindquist, David S.: auxiliary director, Russell Charitable Foundation (Tom)

Lindquist, John N., MD: president, director, Russell Charitable Foundation (Tom)

Lindsay, David J.: trustee, CLARCOR Foundation; vice president, CLARCOR, Inc.

Lindsay, F. M., Jr.: director, Oakley-Lindsay Foundation of Quincy Newspapers and Its Subsidiaries

Lindsay, Gary J.: secretary, treasurer, Schmitt Foundation (Kilian J. and Caroline F.)

Lindsay, Nancy D.: trustee, Dodge Foundation (Geraldine R.)

Lindsey, Handy L., Jr.: president, Field Foundation of Illinois

Lindsey, John: trustee, Swisher Foundation (Carl S.)

Lindsey, Paul F.: vice president, trust officer, Myers Charitable Trust

Lindt, Gillian: director, Guggenheim Foundation (Harry Frank)

Lindwall, Ronald L.: treasurer, Hubbard Foundation

Linebarger, Thomas: vice president, chief financial officer, Cummins, Inc.

Linehan, John H., PhD: vice president, vice president biomed engineering, Whitaker Foundation

Lingenfelter, James S.: secretary, treasurer, Young Foundation (Hugo H. and Mabel B.)

Lingenfelter, Paul Eugene: vice president human and community dev, MacArthur Foundation (John D. and Catherine T.)

Link, Eleanor Irene Higgins: chairman, director, Link, Jr. Foundation (George)

Link, Robert Emmett: vchairman, director, Link, Jr. Foundation (George)

Linke, Curtis G.: chairman, director, Deere Foundation (John)

Linnell, John W.: mem distribution comm, Champlin Foundation

Linnell, Norman C.: vice president, general counsel, Donaldson Company, Inc.; president, trustee, Donaldson Foundation

Linnen, Mary Lou: director, Barker Welfare Foundation

Linowes, R. Robert: director, Loughran Foundation (Mary and Daniel)

Linz, Andrew: president, director, Loewy Family Foundation

Lione, Gail A.: secretary, Harley-Davidson Foundation

Lipetz, Marcia: executive director, WPWR-TV Channel 50 Foundation

Lipkowitz, Irving: director, Hebrew Technical Institute

Lipschultz, William H.: trustee, Bremer Foundation (Otto)

Lipsitz, Michael: assistant secretary, Bank One Foundation

Lipton, Harvey L.: director, Hearst Foundation, Inc. (The); vice president, director, Hearst Foundation (William Randolph)

Lisher, Mary K.: director, Lilly Endowment

Lishman, Ruth C.: grant comm, Royal Foundation (May Mitchell)

Liska, Paul J.: executive vice president, chief financial officer, St. Paul Companies, Inc.

Lisle, Edwin: chairman, Lisle Corp.; trustee, Lisle Foundation

Lisle, John C.: president, chief executive officer, Lisle Corp.; trustee, Lisle Foundation

Lisle, Larry D.: trustee, Markey Charitable Fund (John C.)

Lisle, Lorance W.: trustee, Markey Charitable Fund (John C.)

List, Jennie: secretary, director, Willis Family Foundation

List, Jo: treasurer, List Foundation (Albert A.)

List, Thomas E.: trustee, Saemann Foundation (Franklin I.)

List, Viki: president, List Foundation (Albert A.)

Lister, William H.: trustee, Robinson-Broadhurst Foundation

Litow, Stanley S.: president, IBM International Foundation

Littejohn, Myrl: advisory board, committee member, Heath Foundation (Mary)

Littenberg, Celia: director, Feintech Family Foundation

Little, Dan: trustee, Sarkeys Foundation

Little, H. Timothy: director, Portsmouth General Hospital Foundation

Little, James S.: director, Hedco Foundation

Little, Lew: treasurer, director, ECG Foundation

Little, William A.: trustee, George Foundation

Little, William G.: chairman, director, West Pharmaceutical Services, Inc.

Littlejohn, Carl W., Jr.: director, board mem, Gregg-Graniteville Foundation

Littrell, Harold U.: co-trustee, Ackerman Trust (Anna Keesling)

Litvack, Sanford M.: member, director, Walt Disney Co.

Litwin, Gordon: director, Scherman Foundation

Litzenberg, Jack A.: program officer, Mott Foundation (Charles Stewart)

Livingston, John H.: vice president, St. Giles Foundation

Livingston, Johnston R.: vice president, trustee, Bonfils-Stanton Foundation

Llosa, Patricia: director, Kornfeld Foundation (Emily Davie and Joseph S.)

Lloyd, Susan L.: president, secretary, trustee, Lattner Foundation (Forrest C.)

Lo, Karl: trustee, Lingnan Foundation

Lobbia, John E.: trustee, Hudson-Webber Foundation

Locher, John J.: treasurer, Barnes Group Foundation Inc.; vice president, treasurer, Barnes Group, Inc.

Locke, Elizabeth Hughes: president and director education division, Duke Endowment

Lockwood, Glenn C.: senior vice president, chief financial officer, New Jersey Natural Gas Co.; treasurer, New Jersey Natural Gas Foundation

Lockwood, Theodore Davidge: director, Guggenheim Foundation (Harry Frank)

Loeb, Charles W.: trustee, Jacobson Foundation (Bernard H. and Blanche E.)

Loehr, Sarita: vice president, PNM Foundation

Loers, Lloyd: vice president, Lee Endowment Foundation

Loewenstern, Richard: director, Herzstein Charitable Foundation (Albert and Ethel)

Loflin, Clyatt E., Jr.: trustee officer, Wachovia Bank of North Carolina NA

Loflin, Ed: assistant treasurer, Wachovia Bank of North Carolina NA

Lofrese, Anke: assistant secretary, Hyde and Watson Foundation

Lofton, Thomas M.: chairman, Lilly Endowment

Logan, Wendy B.: member corporate contributions committee, Johnson & Johnson Family of Companies Contribution Fund

Lohse, Ashby I.: secretary, Mulcahy Foundation

Lohse, Florence: vice president, Mulcahy Foundation

Lohse, Kathy: treasurer, Mulcahy Foundation

Lohse, Linda: secretary, treasurer, Mulcahy Foundation

Lohse, Robert D.: president, Mulcahy Foundation

Lomb, Chris: director, Ideal Industries Foundation

Lombard, Jane K.: mem distribution comm, trustee, Kettering Fund

Lombardi, Thomas J.: treasurer, Merrill Lynch & Co. Foundation Inc.

Loncto, Denis: trustee, Coleman Foundation (George E.)

Long, Jacob F.: trustee, Long Foundation (John F.)

Long, John F.: director, Long Foundation (John F.)

Long, Mary P.: director, Long Foundation (John F.)

Long, Michael Thomas: director, Ensign-Bickford Foundation

Long, Milton: trustee, Long Foundation (J. M.)

Long, Robert A.: mem, McGee Foundation (MO)

Long, Robert Merrill: president, trustee, Long Foundation (J. M.)

Long, Robert R.: trustee, Camp Younts Foundation; chairman, SunTrust Bank Atlanta

Longacre, Joseph M.: trustee, Mascoma Savings Bank Foundation

Longbrake, Mary: vice president, director, Young Foundation (Irvin L.)

Longenecker, Kent: trustee, Davis Foundation (James A. and Juliet L.)

Longley, Elizabeth A.: vice president corporate affairs, Prudential Securities Foundation; 1st vice president, Prudential Securities, Inc.

Longwell, Harry J.: senior vice president, Exxon-Mobile Corp.

Looker, Charles: director, Kaufmann Foundation (Henry)

Loomis, Lois C.: contact, McInerny Foundation

Loomis, Worth: president, trustee,

Looney, Wilton D.: trustee, Evans Foundation, Inc. (Lettie Pate)

Loos, Henry J.: trustee, Steigleder Charitable Trust (Bert L. and Patricia S.)

Lopdrup, Kim: board member, Dunkin' Donuts, Inc.

Loper, Graham B.: vice president, trustee, Brown Foundation, Inc. (James Graham)

Loper, Ray: trustee, Brown Foundation, Inc. (James Graham)

Lopez, A. M.: trustee, Exxon Mobil Foundation

Lopez, Owen: executive director, McCune Charitable Foundation (Marshall L. and Perrine D.)

Lord, John S.: director, Bush Charitable Foundation, Inc. (Edyth)

Loren, Allan Z.: chairman, chief executive officer, director, D&B

Loring, Jonathan B.: president, trustee, Levy Foundation (June Rockwell)

Loring, Karl H., CPA: chief financial officer, Knapp Foundation (CA)

Loring, Peter B.: trustee, Mifflin Memorial Fund (George H. and Jane A.)

Loring, Valerie S.: trustee, Stoddard Charitable Trust

Losinger, Sarah McCune: chairman, McCune Charitable Foundation (Marshall L. and Perrine D.); member dispensing committee, McCune Charitable Trust (John R.)

Louden, G. Malcolm: treasurer, secretary, general manager, Fleming Foundation

Loufek, Joseph R.: director, Hall-Perrine Foundation

Loughlin, Caroline: trustee, RosaMary Foundation

Loughlin, Caroline K.: treasurer, trustee, Keller Family Foundation

Loughlin, Elizabeth M.: director, Keller Family Foundation

Loughman, Thomas F.: secretary, treasurer, trustee, Barden Foundation, Inc.

Loughrey, F. Joseph: director, Cummins Foundation; group president worldwide operations & technology, vice president, Cummins, Inc.

Louis, Kenneth C.: president, chief operating officer, director, Ameritas Life Insurance Corp.

Louise, Stella: trustee, Retirement Research Foundation

Love, Howard McClintic: director, Heinz Endowment (Howard)

Love, Jeff: vice president, Kayser Foundation

Love, Sherwood L.: assistant treasurer, Duke Energy Foundation

Lovejoy, Joseph Ensign: chairman, director, Ensign-Bickford Industries

Lovelace, John G.: trustee, Pittsburgh Child Guidance Foundation

Lovett, D. M.: president, director, Spalding Foundation (Eliot)

Lovett, Tiffany W.: trustee, Mott Foundation (Charles Stewart)

Lowe, Albert: director, Patron Saints Foundation

Lowe, Derrick C.: vice president, Lowe Family Foundation

Lowe, Elizabeth H.: director, Parsons Foundation (Ralph M.)

Lowe, Kenneth W.: president, chief executive officer, director, Scripps Co. (E.W.)

Lowe, Walter M.: director, French Foundation (D.E.)

Lowell, John: trustee, Winthrop Trust (Clara B.)

Lowell, William A.: trustee, Peabody Charitable Fund (Amelia)

Lower, James Paul: director, mem legal comm, Keck Foundation (W. M.)

Lower, Judith A.: secretary, Keck Foundation (W. M.)

Lowet, Henry A.: vice president, secretary, director, Littauer Foundation (Lucius N.)

Lowry, David B.: vice president, Freeport-McMoRan Foundation

Lowry, Robert L.: chief financial officer, Pulliam Charitable Trust (Nina Mason)

Loyd, Kurt: trustee, McKinney Charitable Trust (Carl and Alleen)

Loyd, Mary Jo: corp secretary, trustee, Rockwell Fund, Inc.

Lubar, Sheldon B.: director, Firstar Foundation, Inc.

Lubchenco, Jane: trustee, Packard Foundation (David and Lucile)

Lubin, Arline J.: trustee, Morris Foundation (Norman M.)

Lubin, Emanuel: vice president, Benenson Foundation (Frances and Benjamin)

Lubin, Kenneth A.: trustee, Morris Foundation (Norman M.)

Lubin, Marvin: vice president, Morris Foundation (Norman M.)

Lubow, Mary Ellen: trustee, Beynon Foundation (Kathryne)

Lucas, Colin: trustee, Mellon Foundation (Andrew W.)

Lucas, Herbert L., Jr.: trustee, Getty Trust (J. Paul)

Lucas, Robert C.: vice president, Allen Foundation (Nibs and Edna)

Lucckese, Deborah G.: vice president, Washington Forrest Foundation

Luce, H. Christopher: director, finance, new programs and grants committee, Luce Foundation (Henry)

Luce, Henry, III: chairman, chief executive officer, Luce Foundation (Henry)

Luce, Priscilla: chairperson, Greenfield Foundation (Albert M.)

Ludington, Cassandra V. A.: trustee, Kent-Lucas Foundation

Ludington, John Samuel: assistant treasurer, trustee, Strosacker Foundation (Charles J.)

Ludington, Thomas L.: trustee, Gerstacker Foundation (Rollin M.)

Ludwick, Arthur J.: cfo, director, Ludwick Family Foundation

Ludwick, Erik Arthur: director, Ludwick Family Foundation

Ludwick, Heidi Ann: director, Ludwick Family Foundation

Ludwick, Sarah Lynne: president, director, Ludwick Family Foundation

Ludwick Warner, Sharon Lynne: secretary, director, Ludwick Family Foundation

Luers, William Henry: advisory trustee, Rockefeller Brothers Fund, Inc.

Luetkemeyer, Anne A.: secretary, director, Rollins-Luetkemeyer Foundation

Luetkemeyer, John A., Jr.: president, Rollins-Luetkemeyer Foundation

Luff, Paula: senior program officer, Pfizer Foundation

Luftglass, Rick: associate director corporate philanthropy, Pfizer Foundation

Lugo, Luis E.: director religion program, Pew Charitable Trusts

Lukas, John: director, Gilman Foundation (Howard)

Lukaszewicz, Peter: treasurer, Bemis Family Foundation (F.K.); treasurer, director, Bemis Manufacturing Co.

Luke, David Lincoln, III: retired chairman board,, Macy, Jr. Foundation (Josiah)

Luke, John A., Jr.: treasurer, Tinker Foundation

Luke, Kathleen Allen: vice president, PepsiCo Foundation, Inc.

Luke, Monica: manager, Thompson Charitable Foundation

Lukins, Scott: assistant treasurer, assistant secretary, Johnston-Hanson Foundation

Lukowski, Stanley J.: chairman, chief executive officer, Eastern Bank

Luljak, Tom: executive director, United Wisconsin Services Foundation

Lummis, Isabel S.: trustee, Brown Foundation

Lummis, William R., Esq.: trustee, Hughes Medical Institute (Howard)

Lund, Margaret McKee: senior vice president, McKee Foundation (Robert E. and Evelyn)

Lunda, Larry: trustee, Lunda Charitable Trust

Lunda, Lydia: trustee, Lunda Charitable Trust

Lunda, Milton: trustee, Lunda Charitable Trust

Lundback, Lee C.: director, Staunton Farm Foundation

Lundberg, Minnie P.: treasurer, director, King Foundation (Kenneth Kendal)

Lundgren, H. David: director, Fireman's Fund Foundation

Lundgren, Kenneth: trustee, director, Blandin Foundation

Lundstrom, Charles C.: secretary, Wege Foundation

Lundy, Marjorie W.: secretary contributions committee, Northern Trust Co. Charitable Trust

Lunger, Francis: chief financial officer, corporate vice president, Millipore Corp.

Lunsford, David H.: mem, Teubert Charitable Trust (James H. and Alice)

Lunt, Thomas D.: trustee, Wendt Foundation (Margaret L.)

Lupton, T. Cartter, II: trustee, Lyndhurst Foundation

Lurcott, Robert: president, chief executive officer, Henkel Corp.

Lurie, Robert Alfred: president, donor, director, Lurie Foundation (Louis R.)

Lustberg, Lawrence S.: trustee, Fund for New Jersey

Luthy, Thomas M.: senior vice president wood products, Weyerhaeuser Co.

Luttgens, Leslie L.: director, Rosenberg Foundation

Lutz, Theodore M.: trustee, Graham Fund (Philip L.)

Lyall, Katharine Culbert: trustee, Kemper Foundation (James S.)

Lyddon, Grant: vice president, Seven Springs Foundation

Lyddon, John Knight: trustee, Seven Springs Foundation

Lyddon, Martha D.: president, Seven Springs Foundation

Lyle, Paul: trustee, Mayer Foundation (James and Eva)

Lyman, Carol: director, O'Shaughnessy Foundation (I. A.)

Lynch, Harry H.: director, Maddox Foundation (J. F.)

Lynch, Luba H.: executive director, secretary, Mailman Family Foundation (A. L.)

Lynch, Michael: director, Illinois Tool Works Foundation

Lynch, Nancy Ann: secretary, director, Dewar Foundation

Lynch, Peter L.: president, chief operating officer, Albertson's Inc.

Lynch, Robert L. K.: chairman, Kempner Fund (Harris and Eliza)

Lynch, Thomas C.: trustee, J.P. Morgan Chase Foundation

Lynch, Thomas P.: chairman, trustee, Stamps Foundation (James L.)

Lynham, John Marmaduke, Jr.: director, Strong Foundation (Hattie M.)

Lynn, June: co-trustee, Cray Residuary Charitable Trust (Evah C.)

Lyon, Kathryn F.: secretary, Raskob Foundation for Catholic Activities, Inc.

Lyon, Marina: director public affairs, U.S. Bancorp Piper Jaffray

Lyons, Bernard E.: director, Colburn Fund

Lyons, Kristina E.: trustee, Baldwin Memorial Foundation (Fred)

Lyons, Louis: trustee, Camp and Bennet Humiston Trust (Apollos)

Lyons, Melanie: director, member grant committee, Claiborne Foundation (Liz)

Lyons, Michael H., II: president, trustee, Baldwin Memorial Foundation (Fred)

Lyons, Shaun L.: vice president, assistant secretary, trustee, Baldwin Memorial Foundation (Fred)

Lyons, Tony J.: gov, Mayor Foundation (Oliver Dewey)

M

Maas, Suzanne W.: executive director, Boston Globe Foundation

Mabbett, John R., III: president, chief executive officer, Florida Rock & Tank Lines

Mabee, Joe: vice chairman, trustee, Mabee Foundation, Inc. (J. E. and L. E.)

Mabee, Joseph Guy, Jr.: trustee, Mabee Foundation, Inc. (J. E. and L. E.)

Mabry, Rhett N.: director child care division, Duke Endowment

Mac Kimm, Margaret (Pontius) "Mardie": trustee, Chicago Title and Trust Co. Foundation

MacAffer, Kenneth S., Jr.: director, Kelley and Elza Kelley Foundation (Edward Bangs)

MacAlister, Patricia A.: trustee, Blowitz-Ridgeway Foundation

MacAllaster, Archie F.: director, Clark Foundation (NY)

MacAllaster, David S.: assistant secretary, Morris Foundation (William T.)

Macauley, Victoria J.: vice president, Stuart Charitable Foundation (G. B.)

MacBeth, Anita L.: trustee, Bourns Foundation

MacCaul, Cathleen: communications manager, Microsoft Corp.

MacColl, John: director, St. Paul Companies Inc. Foundation

MacColl, Stephanie: director, The Bothin Foundation

MacConnell, Diane: director, Memorial Foundation for the Blind

MacConnell, Gary: director, Memorial Foundation for the Blind

MacConnell, Jocelyn H.: trustee, Hulme Charitable Foundation (Milton G.)

MacDonald, Harold C.: comptroller, Moody Foundation

MacDonald, John A.: vice president, treasurer, Hall Family Foundation (The)

MacDonald, Susanne Fuller: trustee, Fuller Foundation (MA)

MacElree, Jane Cox: trustee, Cox Charitable Trust (Jessie B.)

Macfie, Valerie A.: board member, Snow Foundation (John Ben)

MacGregor, David Lee: treasurer, director, Stackner Family Foundation

Machado, Edward J.: senior vice president, chief financial officer, Shenandoah Life Insurance Co.

MacInnes, Gordon A.: trustee, Fund for New Jersey

Mack, John E., III: chairman, chief executive officer, Central Hudson Gas & Electric Corp.

Mack, John J.: chief executive officer, Credit Suisse First Boston Corp.

Mack, Olga List: secretary, List Foundation (Albert A.)

Mackay, Clader M.: secretary, treasurer, Mead Foundation (Giles W. and Elise G.)

Mackay, Richard N.: vice president, Mead Foundation (Giles W. and Elise G.)

Mackay, Robert Battin: trustee, St. Giles Foundation

Mackell, John: trustee, Pennington Foundation (William N. and Myriam)

MacKenzie, Tod J.: senior vice president, corporate communications, PepsiCo Inc.

Mackenzie, Wendy Jacobus: secretary, Heinz Family Foundation

Mackey, Mary Ann: foundation accountant, PPG Industries Foundation

Mackey, William R.: trustee, Gilmore Foundation (William G.)

Mackler, Harvey A.: director, Alexander Foundation (Joseph)

Mackler, Helen: secretary, director, Alexander Foundation (Joseph)

Macklin, B. G.: trustee, Exxon Mobil Foundation

MacLeod, Gary: trustee, Medina Foundation

MacNeary, John D.: trustee, Heckscher Foundation for Children

MacPhee, Chester R., Jr.: trustee, Sandy Foundation (George H.)

MacPherson, D. R.: president, chief executive officer, director, Red Devil

Madding, Claudia: president, Archer-Daniels-Midland Foundation

Maddox, Don: president, Maddox Foundation (J. F.)

Maddox, James M.: vice president, Maddox Foundation (J. F.)

Maddox, Thomas M.: director, Maddox Foundation (J. F.)

Maddux, Thomas H.: trustee, Warfield Memorial Fund (Anna Emory)

Madhavpeddi, Kalidas: vice president, Phelps Dodge Foundation

Madiera, Anthony G.: treasurer, Eastern Savings and Loan Foundation

Madigan, John W.: chairman, director, McCormick Tribune Foundation (Robert R.)

Madison, Michael H.: president, chief executive officer, chief financial officer, Southwestern Electric Power Co.

Maerki, Max H.: senior vice president, PNM Resources, Inc.

Maffucci, David G.: executive vice president, chief financial officer, Bowater, Inc.

Mafreci, August: trustee, August Family Foundation (Charles J. and Burton S.)

Magaram, Philip S.: secretary, treasurer, director, Drown Foundation (Joseph)

Magary, Susan B., Esq.: officer, Seherr-Thoss Foundation

Magee, Wayne E.: grants analyst, Moody Foundation

Maggi, Darius: gov, Mayor Foundation (Oliver Dewey)

Magpantay, Glenn: trustee, Boehm Foundation

Magruder, G. Brock: trustee, Magruder Foundation (Chesley G.)

Mahaney, Larry K.: chairman, president, chief executive officer, director, Webber Oil Co.; trustee, Webber Oil Foundation

Maher, Francesca M.: senior vice president, general counsel, secretary, UAL Corp.

Mahon, Arthur Joseph: trustee, Archbold Charitable Trust (Adrian and Jessie)

Mahon, Myra: director, Archbold Charitable Trust (Adrian and Jessie); trustee, New York Foundation

Mahone, Andrea Torres: member, Staunton Farm Foundation

Mahoney, Cornelius D.: chairman, president, chief executive officer, Woronoco Savings Bank

Mahoney, Elaine: director, Drown Foundation (Joseph)

Mahoney, Joseph A.: director, New York Stock Exchange Foundation, Inc.

Mahoney, Neil: director, Woronoco Savings Charitable Foundation

Mahoney, P. Michael: chairman, president, chief executive officer, director, Park Bank; president, director, Park Bank Foundation

Mahoney, Richard: director, Benton Foundation

Mahoney, Stephen J.: president, director, Smith Charitable Foundation (Arlene H.)

Maidenberg, Michael: trustee, Knight Foundation (John S. and James L.)

Maider, Robert L.: trustee, City National Bank Foundation

Maine, Jerry I.: trustee, Morrison Charitable Trust (Pauline A. and George R.)

Maisano, Lise Einfeld: senior program officer, Cowell Foundation (S. H.)

Maitland, Peter K.: president, director, USG Foundation

Makowski, Bob: chief financial officer, Park Bank

Makupson, Amyre: trustee, Skillman Foundation

Malaquias, Stephen W., MD: director, Kelley and Elza Kelley Foundation (Edward Bangs)

Malcolm, Allen R.: president, Snow Foundation (John Ben); trustee, Snow Memorial Trust (John Ben)

Malcolm, Bruce L.: board member, Snow Foundation (John Ben)

Malcom, Shirley M.: director, Heinz Endowment (Howard)

Mali, Adair Price: director, AKC Fund

Mallahan, Mary Ann: secretary, Illinois Tool Works Foundation

Mallick, Craig D.: general manager, U.S. Steel Foundation

Malloy, Mary T.: secretary, Sara Lee Foundation

Malloy, Susan R.: president, Sun Hill Foundation

Malloy, Timon J.: secretary, Sun Hill Foundation

Malloy Combs, Jennifer: treasurer, Sun Hill Foundation

Malmberg, Jennifer L.: treasurer, secretary, Widgeon Foundation

Malmloff, Cheryl: community relations administrator, R.R. Donnelley & Sons Co.

Malo, J. Kenneth, Jr.: director, Mullen Foundation (J. K.)

Malo, John F.: president, director, Mullen Foundation (J. K.)

Malo, Kathleen: director, Mullen Foundation (J. K.)

Malone, Donna: assistant trustee, BellSouth Foundation

Malone, Frank M., Jr.: trustee, Franklin Foundation Inc. (John and Mary)

Maloni, William R.: senior vice president policy & public affairs, Fannie Mae; director, Fannie Mae Foundation

Malouf, Donald J.: vice president, secretary, Overlake Foundation

Malquist, Malyn K.: senior vice president, chief financial officer, Avista Corp.

Malti, George M.: director, Holt Foundation (William Knox)

Malvaso, James J.: president, chief executive officer, director, Raymond Corp.

Manapat, Christine: assistant secretary, treasurer, United States-Japan Foundation

Mancasola, John A.: executive vice president, secretary, treasurer, McConnell Foundation

Mandel, Deborah: assistant treasurer, MetLife Foundation

Mandel, Jack N.: trustee, Mandel Foundation (Jack N. and Lilyan)

Mandel, Ruth: director, Revson Foundation (Charles H.)

Mandell, Elizabeth H.: president, trustee, Heller Charitable Foundation (Clarence E.)

Mandell, Sarah Coade: secretary, trustee, Heller Charitable Foundation (Clarence E.)

Mandelstam, Charles L.: secretary, Rubin Foundation (Samuel)

Mandeville, Hubert T.: president, treasurer, director, Mandeville Foundation

Mandeville, Josephine C.: chairman, chief executive officer, president, trustee, donor daughter, Connelly Foundation

Mandeville, Matthew T.: director, Mandeville Foundation

Mandeville, P. Kempton: vice president, director, Mandeville Foundation

Mandeville, Peter O.: trustee, Connelly Foundation

Mangan, Lawrence T.: vice president, treasurer, Connelly Foundation

Mangino, Terri C.: executive director, assistant secretary, Rose Foundation (Billy)

Manigault, Peter: chairman, Evening Post Publishing Co.; president, Post and Courier Foundation

Manilow, Barbara Goodman: vice president, director, Crown Memorial (Arie and Ida)

Mankiller, Wilma Pearl: trustee, Ford Foundation

Manley, Joan D.: director, Sara Lee Corp.

Manley, Terrell S.: assistant treasurer, Stans Foundation

Manley, William: vice president, Stans Foundation

Mann, Robert M.: vice president, secretary, CNA Foundation

Manne, Larry R.: director, Oakley-Lindsay Foundation of Quincy Newspapers and Its Subsidiaries

Mannion, Geraldine P.: program chair U.S. democracy, Carnegie Corp. of New York

Mannion, Patrick A.: vice president, trustee, Gifford Charitable Corp. (Rosamond)

Manns, Andrew: vice president financial, treasurer, Monadnock Paper Mills, Inc.

Manny, Carter Hugh, Jr.: director emeritus, Graham Foundation for Advanced Studies in the Fine Arts

Mansell, Edmona Lyman: vice president, director, The Bothin Foundation

Manske, Susan E.: vice president, chief investment officer, MacArthur Foundation (John D. and Catherine T.)

Mantell, Lester J.: vice president, treasurer, contr, director, AmBase Foundation

Manton, Edwin Alfred Grenville: director, Starr Foundation

Manuel, Mary: director, Grotto Foundation

Maples, Roger C.: director, Christy-Houston Foundation

Marangi, Leonard M.: trustee, Murphey Foundation (Lluella Morey)

Marbut, Margo: trustee, Argyle Foundation

Marbut, Mike: director, Argyle Foundation

Marbut, Robert: trustee, Argyle Foundation

Marcantonio, Richard L.: vice president, chairman, Ecolab, Inc.

Marcela, Paul A.: secretary, Dow Corning Foundation

Marcotte, Erin: trustee, Dougherty, Jr. Foundation (James R.)

Marcus, Lorraine: secretary, Boothroyd Foundation (Charles H. and Bertha L.)

Marcus, Stephen Howard: chairman, chief executive officer, Marcus Corp.; president, director, Marcus Corp. Foundation

Marcuse, Edgar K., MD: director, Nesholm Family Foundation

Margenthaler, Donald R.: president, director, Deere & Co.; executive officer, director, Deere Foundation (John)

Margotta, Gisela L.: treasurer, East Cambridge Savings Charitable Foundation

Marin, Lawrence: vice president, Kaplun Foundation (Morris J. and Betty)

Marion, Anne W.: president, trustee, Burnett Foundation (The)

Marion, John Louis: trustee, Burnett Foundation (The)

Maritz, W. Stephen: president, chief executive officer, Maritz, Inc.

Mark, Sarah E.: trustee, Greenfield Foundation (Albert M.)

Markel, Charles A., III: vice president finance, treasurer, LG&E Energy Corp.; vice president, treasurer, LG&E Energy Foundation

Markel, Larry G., MD: assistant secretary, Lyon Foundation

Markela, June: trustee, Boehm Foundation

Markey, John Clifton, II: trustee, Markey Charitable Fund (John C.)

Markey, John R.: president, treasurer, Markey Charitable Fund (John C.)

Markham, Marianna: director, Jones Foundation (Helen)

Markham, Sharon F.: vice president, Retirement Research Foundation

Markman, Joanne W.: director, Pine Tree Foundation

Markos, Arthur C.: president, chief executive officer, Gardiner Savings Institution; president, director, Gardiner Savings Institution Charitable Foundation

Marks, Dennis A.: vice president, Boothroyd Foundation (Charles H. and Bertha L.)

Marks, Nancy: trustee, Priddy Foundation

Marks, Paul C.: director, trustee, Camp Younts Foundation

Marks, Paul Camp: director, Campbell Foundation (Ruth and Henry)

Marks, Randolph A.: director, Knox Foundation (Seymour H.)

Marks, Raymond: secretary, treasurer, Stulsaft Foundation (Morris)

Marlar, Donald F.: trustee, Bernsen Foundation (Grace and Franklin)

Marley, James Earl: director, Kline Foundation (Josiah W. and Bessie H.)

Marmer, Lynn: president, The Kroger Co. Foundation

Marmion, William H.: trustee, Miller Foundation (Earl B. and Loraine H.)

Maroney, Eleanor Silliman: secretary, Borkee-Hagley Foundation; trustee, advisory, Crystal Trust

Marosek, Edwin P.: trustee, Anderson Foundation (NY)

Marquardt, Robert: mem admin comm, Swanson Family Foundation, Inc. (Dr. W. C.)

Marram, Ellen R.: director, New York Times Co. Foundation

Marran, Elizabeth: vice president, Kennedy Foundation (Ethel)

Marran, Ethel K.: president, treasurer, Kennedy Foundation (Ethel)

Marran, Laura: secretary, Kennedy Foundation (Ethel)

Marron, Donald Baird: director, Dana Foundation (Charles A.)

Marrone, Lynda: grants mgr, Bremer Foundation (Otto)

Marrow, Deborah: director Getty Grant Program, Getty Trust (J. Paul)

Mars, Bernard S.: trustee, Foster Charitable Trust

Mars, Peter F.: trustee, Foster Charitable Trust

Marsh, Edward W.: secretary, treasurer, Murphy Foundation

Marsh, Harold N., III: treasurer, Fireman's Fund Foundation

Marsh, Helsel R., Jr.: member, Staunton Farm Foundation

Marsh, Jeaneane Duncan: vice president, director, Duncan Foundation (L. H. and C. W.)

Marsh, Larry R.: director, Olmsted Foundation (George and Carol)

Marsh, R. Bruce: general tax counsel, ChevronTexaco Corp.

Marsh, Richard S. T.: director, Strong Foundation (Hattie M.)

Marshall, Collin S., Esq.: trustee, Van Buren Foundation (Elsie Procter)

Marshall, David B.: president, director, Contempo Communications Foundation for the Arts, Inc.

Marshall, David L.: secretary, treasurer, director, Contempo Communications Foundation for the Arts, Inc.

Marshall, Jim: manager, Porter Testamentary Trust (James Hyde)

Marshall, Joan F.: president, Contempo Communications; vice president, director, Contempo Communications Foundation for the Arts, Inc.

Marshall, John Elbert, III: president, chief executive officer, trustee, Kresge Foundation

Marshall, Rose M.: co-trustee, Arakelian Foundation (Mary Alice)

Marshall, Siri M.: trustee, General Mills Foundation; senior vice president, general counsel, General Mills, Inc.

Marshall, Stephanie Pace, PhD: vice president, Fry Foundation (Lloyd A.)

Marshall, Thomas C.: vice president, director, Drown Foundation (Joseph)

Marshall, William H.: treasurer, Clowes Fund

Marshall, William M.: trustee, Crandall Memorial Foundation (J. Ford)

Marsico, Louis J., Jr.: vice president finance and administration, McCormick Tribune Foundation (Robert R.)

Martin, C. Alan: director, Alabama Power Foundation

Martin, C. Cecil: director, Houchens Foundation (Ervin G.)

Martin, Carmel C., Jr.: secretary, treasurer, AT&T National Pro-Am Youth Fund

Martin, Casper: treasurer, secretary, director, Martin Foundation

Martin, Dan M.: director world resources & population programs, MacArthur Foundation (John D. and Catherine T.)

Martin, Don: manager, Porter Testamentary Trust (James Hyde)

Martin, Elizabeth: co-president, Martin Foundation

Martin, George: treasurer, Anthem Foundation, Inc.

Martin, Geraldine F.: chairman, Martin Foundation

Martin, Glenn R.: vice president, director, Reynolds Foundation (Richard S.)

Martin, J. Landis: trustee, Bonfils-Stanton Foundation

Martin, JoAnn M.: controller, Ameritas Charitable Foundation; senior vice president, partner, chief financial officer, Ameritas Life Insurance Corp.

Martin, John: comm mem, Smith, Jr. Foundation (M. W.)

Martin, John W.: chief financial officer, Ontario Corp.; treasurer, Ontario Corp. Foundation

Martin, Joseph W., Jr.: treasurer, director, Skaggs Foundation (L. J. Skaggs and Mary C.)

Martin, Karen C.: program officer, Corning Inc. Foundation

Martin, Lauralee: chief financial officer, GE Capital Corp.

Martin, Lee: director, Martin Foundation

Martin, Lois Lynne: secretary, Houchens Foundation (Ervin G.)

Martin, Mary Ann: trustee, New Jersey Natural Gas Foundation

Martin, Maurice H.: president, trustee, Tonya Memorial Foundation

Martin, N. E.: trustee, National Machinery Foundation, Inc.

Martin, Rex: director, Martin Foundation

Martin, Richard J.: executive vice president public relations employee communications, AT&T Corp.; chairman, trustee, AT&T Foundation

Martin, Robert E., Jr.: treasurer, Ashtabula Foundation

Martin, Susan Fasken: trustee, Fasken Foundation

Martin, Vincent L.: director, Bucyrus-Erie Foundation

Martin, Webb Franklin: trustee, Mott Foundation (Charles Stewart)

Martin-Brown, Jennifer: co-president, Martin Foundation

Martinenza, Stephen A.: treasurer, Crestlea Foundation; assistant secretary, assistant treasurer, Longwood Foundation; assistant treasurer, Welfare Foundation

Martinez, Jorge: director information, Knight Foundation (John S. and James L.)

Martini, Gloria: vice president, Martini Foundation (Nicholas)

Martini, William J.: trustee, Martini Foundation (Nicholas)

Martiny, Mary Anne: assistant secretary, Harley-Davidson Foundation

Marty, Mary: assistant treasurer, Boston Globe Foundation

Marx, Leonard: vice president, Marx Foundation (Virginia and Leonard)

Marx, Leonard, Jr.: treasurer, Marx Foundation (Virginia and Leonard)

Marx, Robert: director, vice president, Samuels Foundation (Fan Fox and Leslie R.)

Marx, Virginia: president, Marx Foundation (Virginia and Leonard)

Mary, Pauline: president, McShain Charities (John)

Marzio, Peter C.: director, Wallace-Reader's Digest Fund (DeWitt)

Masaoka, Jan: treasurer, Haigh-Scatena Foundation

Mascotte, John P.: director, Hall Family Foundation (The)

Masi, Wendy S.: vice president, Mailman Family Foundation (A. L.)

Masin, Michael Terry: director, chairman legal committee, member executive committee, Keck Foundation (W. M.); vice chairman, president, Verizon Communications Inc.; director, secretary, treasurer, Verizon Foundation

Masket, Steven N.: assistant secretary, Rosenthal Foundation (Ida and William)

Mason, Cheryl White: director, Irvine Foundation (The James)

Mason, Emma Newby: trustee, Nord Family Foundation

Mason, Frederick T.: assistant secretary, assistant treasurer, Sulzberger Foundation

Mason, Jack Arliss: 2nd vice president, Tri-County Telephone Foundation

Mason, James C.: director, Bishop Foundation (E. K. and Lillian F.)

Mason, James L.: vice president, director public affairs, Eaton Charitable Fund

Massar, Mike: director, Heath Foundation (Ed and Mary)

Massey, Joe B.: trustee, Massey Charitable Trust

Massey, Morris: secretary, Goodstein Foundation

Massey, Walter Eugene: director, Commonwealth Fund (The); trustee, Mellon Foundation (Andrew W.)

Masters, James L., IV: president, Masters Family Foundation

Masters, Jane J.: assistant secretary, assistant treasurer, Mather and William Gwinn Mather Fund (Elizabeth Ring)

Masters, Mickey Jo: chairman, Masters Family Foundation

Masuda, Shigeru: chairman, director, Mitsubishi Silicon America

Masumoto, Davis Mas: director, Irvine Foundation (The James)

Matheny, N. D.: trustee, Smith Horticultural Trust (Stanley)

Mather, Karen W.: grants manager, program officer, Gates Family Foundation

Matherne, Louis K.: treasurer, Chesapeake Corp.

Mathes, Stephen Jon, Esq.: secretary, Levitt Foundation (NY)

Matheson, Alline: director, Barker Welfare Foundation

Matheson, Bonnie B.: trustee, Dow Foundation (Herbert H. and Grace A.)

Mathews, Odonna: vice president consumer affairs, Giant Food, Inc.

Mathews, Paul: vice president, Tyndale House Foundation

Mathews, Sharron: director operations, Chiles Foundation

Mathews, Sylvia M.: chief operating officer, executive director, libraries, pac northwest, Gates Foundation (Bill and Melinda)

Mathias, Charles McCurdy, Jr.: director, Tinker Foundation

Mathiasen, Karl: secretary, Moriah Fund, Inc.

Mathis, David B.: chief executive officer, chairman, Kemper Foundation (James S.)

Mathis, William Nelson: trustee, Brown Foundation

Mathisen, Mark E.: director, vice president, Saint-Gobain Corporation Foundation

Mathison, William A.: member corporate contributions committee, Ecolab, Inc.

Mathruni, Arjun K.: executive vice president, chief financial officer, J.P. Morgan Chase & Co.; trustee, J.P. Morgan Chase Foundation

Matosziuk, Edward J.: trustee, Hamer Foundation

Matsui, Takashi: mem allocations comm, Kawabe Memorial Fund

Matsuzaki, Motoyasu: executive vice president, chief financial officer, Fujitsu America

Matte, Christopher: adv, Hathaway Memorial Charitable Trust

Matteson, William B.: trustee, Hartford Foundation, Inc. (The John A.)

Matthews, Allan: program officer, Moody Foundation

Matthews, David: adv comm mem, Moore and Arletta E. Moore Foundation (Kenneth S.)

Matthews, E. E.: director, Starr Foundation

Matthews, Janice C.: treasurer, CHC Foundation

Matthews, Joseph B.: director, Dodge Jones Foundation and Subsidiary

Matthews, Julia Jones: president, director, Dodge Jones Foundation and Subsidiary

Matthews, Kade L.: director, Dodge Jones Foundation and Subsidiary

Matthews, Robert: member advisory committee, Blue Bell Foundation

Matthews, Westina Lomax: secretary, trustee, Merrill Lynch & Co. Foundation Inc.; senior director, first vice president corporate respons, Merrill Lynch & Company, Inc.

Matthews, William: director, Oneida Savings Bank Charitable Foundation

Mattocks, David M., PhD: program officer general grants, Ford Family Foundation

Mattox, Martha L.: trustee, Johnson Foundation (Burdine)

Mattson, Bradford C.: executive vice president exterior building products, CertainTeed Corp.

Mattson, David C.: director, Shelter Mutual Insurance Co.

Mattson, Ellwood: fund comm mem, Kaufman Endowment Fund (Louis G.)

Matz, Dorothy A.: director, Kleberg Foundation (Robert J. Kleberg, Jr. and Helen C.)

Maughan, Deryck C.: vice chairman, Citigroup Inc.; director, New York Stock Exchange Foundation, Inc.

Maurer, Eleanor Johnson: treasurer, director, Kirkpatrick Foundation, Inc.

Maurer, Gilbert Charles: director, Hearst Foundation, Inc. (The); vice president, director, Hearst Foundation (William Randolph)

Maurer, Jeffrey Stuart: president, chief operating officer, director, United States Trust Co. of New York

Maurin, Christian: chairman, chief executive officer, Ondeo Nalco Co.

Mauro, Margaret: executive director, secretary, trustee, Rouse Co. Foundation

Mavec, Ellen S.: vchpn, trustee, Smith Foundation (Kelvin and Eleanor)

May, Carolyn A.: director, Niagara Mohawk Foundation

May, Cordelia Scaife: chairman, trustee, donor, Laurel Foundation

May, Irenee du Pont, Jr.: secretary, trustee, Longwood Foundation

Maybee, Terri R.: assistant treasurer, Hall Family Foundation (The)

Mayer, Charles B.: vice president, German Protestant Orphan Asylum Association Foundation

Mayer, George J.: director, German Protestant Orphan Asylum Association Foundation

Mayer, John A. "Tony", Jr.: board member, Kauffman Foundation (Ewing Marion)

Mayer, R. D.: vice president, trustee, Young Foundation (Hugo H. and Mabel B.)

Mayer, Robert L.: trustee, Vesuvius Foundation

Mayerson, Arlene B.: vice president, Mayerson Foundation (Manuel D. and Rhoda)

Mayerson, Donna: secretary, Mayerson Foundation (Manuel D. and Rhoda)

Mayerson, Fred: trust, Mayerson Foundation (Manuel D. and Rhoda)

Mayerson, Manuel D.: trustee, Mayerson Foundation (Manuel D. and Rhoda)

Mayerson, Neal H.: president, treasurer, Mayerson Foundation (Manuel D. and Rhoda)

Mayerson, Rhoda: trustee, Mayerson Foundation (Manuel D. and Rhoda)

Mayfield, Nelda: trustee, Cauthorn Charitable Trust (John and Mildred)

Mayhew, Eva: assistant trustee, BellSouth Foundation

Maynard, Olivia P.: trustee, Mott Foundation (Charles Stewart)

Mayo, Andy: director, Hannaford Charitable Foundation

Mayo, James Otis: vice chairman, secretary, director, Kiplinger Washington Editors, Inc.

Mayo, Joanna M.: director, Peters Foundation (Charles F.)

Mayr, Gerhard: director, Lilly Foundation (Eli)

Mays, Alfred T.: member corporate contributions committee, Johnson & Johnson Family of Companies Contribution Fund

Mays, Armon: director, Mays Foundation

Mays, Robert: vice president, Camp Younts Foundation

Mays, Troy M.: director, Mays Foundation

Maytag, Frederick L., III: trustee, Maytag Family Foundation (Fred)

Maytag, Kenneth P.: trustee, Maytag Family Foundation (Fred)

Maza, Bruce A.: executive director, C. E. and S. Foundation

Mazer, David: vice president, treasurer, Mazer Foundation (Jacob and Ruth)

Mazer, Richard: vice president, secretary, Mazer Foundation (Jacob and Ruth)

Mazmanian, Daniel A.: trustee, Haynes Foundation (John Randolph and Dora)

Mazur, John: treasurer, Eden Hall Foundation

Mazzilli, Philip J.: trustee, Equifax Foundation

Mazzio, Jo-Anne: secretary, Wiremold Foundation

McAfee, Emily Jean H.: director, Haley Foundation (W. B.)

McAfferty, J. J.: trustee, Yawkey Foundation II

McAlister, Consuela Cuneo: director, Cuneo Foundation

McAlister, Fern Smith: vice president, trustee, McAlister Charitable Foundation (Harold)

McAlister, James P.: president, McAlister Charitable Foundation (Harold)

McAlister, Tim: director, Cuneo Foundation

McAllister, Leo: secretary, director, Sierra Health Foundation

McArthur, Daniel E.: assistant treasurer, Mead Foundation (Giles W. and Elise G.)

McAuliffe, Stephanie: director organizational effectiveness, Packard Foundation (David and Lucile)

McBean, Nancy H.: director, McBean Family Foundation

McBratney, R. Bruce: trustee, Sullivan Foundation (Algernon Sydney)

McBride, H. S. Graham: adv, Weezie Foundation

McBryde, Nowlin: director, Peterson Foundation (Hal and Charlie)

McBurnie, Richard G.: president, director, Arkelian Foundation (Ben H. and Gladys); president, chief executive officer, West Foundation (Harry and Ethel)

McCabe, Barry E.: executive vice president, chief operating officer, Mascoma Savings Bank Foundation

McCall, Dorothy R.: vice president, Doherty Charitable Foundation (Henry L. and Grace)

McCall, John: vice president, LG&E Energy Foundation

McCallie, Allen L.: secretary, Lyndhurst Foundation

McCallister, Beth: secretary, Badger Meter Foundation

McCallum, James: director, Washington Group Foundation, Inc.

McCallum, William T.: president, chief executive officer, Great-West Life and Annuity Insurance Co.

McCalmont, Susan: executive director, Kirkpatrick Foundation, Inc.

McCalpin, William F.: trustee, Lingnan Foundation; executive vice president, chief operating officer, Rockefeller Brothers Fund, Inc.

McCandless, June: director, Hughes Foundation (Geoffrey C.)

McCandless, O. Carlysle: executive vice president, assistant secretary, treasurer, director, Hughes Foundation (Geoffrey C.)

McCandliss, Len: president, director, Sierra Health Foundation

McCann, James: trustee, Mosher Foundation (Samuel B.)

McCann, Linda: assistant trustee, BellSouth Foundation

McCart, Thomas R.: chairman, president, chief executive officer, director, TCB Bank; president, TCB Bank Foundation

McCarthy, Charles: president, chief executive officer, Tetley U.S.A., Inc.

McCarthy, Denis: vice president, McCarthy Charities

McCarthy, Gerald Patrick: executive director, secretary, Virginia Environmental Endowment

McCarthy, John Peters: trustee, Olin Foundation (Spencer T. and Ann W.)

McCarthy, Kathleen Leavey: acting chairman, Leavey Foundation (Thomas and Dorothy)

McCarthy, Peter John: trustee, Atofina Chemicals Foundation; vice president public affairs, Elf Atochem North America, Inc.

McCarthy, Robert J.: director, New Milford Savings Bank Foundation

McCarthy, Robert P.: treasurer, McCarthy Charities

McCarthy, Thomas F.: chairman, trustee, Henson Foundation (Richard A.)

McCartor, Alice: program officer, Meyer Memorial Trust

McCarty, Marilu H.: executive secretary, Franklin Foundation Inc. (John and Mary)

McCasland, Thomas H., Jr.: trustee, McCasland Foundation

McCauley, Joan D.: director, Heinz Family Foundation

McCausland, Bonnie: president, McCausland Foundation

McCausland, Peter: vice president, McCausland Foundation

McClain, David H.: assistant secretary, PPG Industries Foundation

McClain, John David: president, Brillion Foundation; president, chief executive officer, Brillion Iron Works

McClain, Terry James: director, Valmont Foundation; senior vice president, chief financial officer, Valmont Industries, Inc.

McClanahan, David M.: director, Reliant Resources Foundation

McClay, Paul F.: mem, Gardiner Savings Institution Charitable Foundation

McCleery, Tania L-J.: trustee, Guggenheim Foundation (Harry Frank)

McClenahan, Carol T.: member, Staunton Farm Foundation

McClimon, Timothy J.: executive director, AT&T Foundation

McClintock, John R. D.: trustee, Childs Charitable Foundation (Roberta M.)

McCloskey, Geoffrey: assistant treasurer, CUNA Mutual Group Foundation, Inc.

McCluskey, Lynn A.: assistant secretary, assistant treasurer, Dyson Foundation

McCluski, Stephen C.: president, director, Bausch & Lomb Foundation, Inc.

McConn, Christiana R.: secretary, trustee, Sterling-Turner Foundation

McConnell, Doug C.: president, Tyndale House Foundation

McCook, Richard P.: vice president, Winn-Dixie Stores Foundation; senior vice president, chief financial officer, Winn-Dixie Stores Inc.

McCord, Kathy: secretary, Kirkpatrick Foundation, Inc.

McCormack, Elizabeth J.: trustee, Trust for Mutual Understanding

McCormack, Kristen J.: vice president, trustee, Hayden Foundation (Charles)

McCormick, Brooks: chairman, director, McCormick Foundation (Chauncey and Marion Deering)

McCormick, Charlotte Deering: vice president, McCormick Foundation (Chauncey and Marion Deering)

McCormick, Thomas P.: treasurer, Barker Welfare Foundation

McCormick, William Thomas, Jr.: chairman, chief executive officer, director, Consumers Energy Co.; chairman, Consumers Energy Foundation

McCortney, John H.: vice president, treasurer, White Foundation (W. P. and H. B.)

McCown, J. Ross: vice president, secretary, Abel Foundation

McCoy, Alan: trustee, AK Steel Foundation

McCoy, Dena Woodard: director, W. A. Woodard Foundation

McCoy, Joseph P.: vice president, controller, Burlington Resources Foundation

McCoy, Louise Boney: trustee, Hillsdale Fund

McCracken, Paul Winston: trustee, Earhart Foundation

McCrary, C.W., III: director, Acme-McCrary and Sapona Foundation

McCrary, Charles D.: director, Alabama Power Foundation

McCrary, Charles W., Jr.: chairman, chief executive officer, director, Acme-McCrary Corp./Sapona Manufacturing Co.; vice president, Acme-McCrary and Sapona Foundation

McCraven, Paul: vice president, secretary, trustee, New Haven Savings Bank Foundation, Inc.

McCray, Ron: secretary, Kimberly-Clark Foundation

McCrodden, Bruce: senior vice president, corp. public affairs, National City Corp.

McCue, Howard McDowell, III: secretary, director, Cheney Foundation (Elizabeth F.); vice president, secretary, director, chairman, Fry Foundation (Lloyd A.)

McCullar, J. Bryan: manager grants administrator, Knight Foundation (John S. and James L.)

McCullough, F. E.: mem distribution comm, Flowers Charitable Trust (Albert W. and Edith V.)

McCullough, Hubert: director, Christy-Houston Foundation

McCullough, P. Michael: director, trustee, Meadows Foundation (The)

McCullough, Samuel Alexander: trustee, Wyomissing Foundation

McCullough, W. R.: trustee, Cone Automatic Machine Co. Charitable Foundation

McCully, A. C.: trustee, Frueauff Foundation (Charles A.)

McCully, George E.: director, Phillips Foundation (Ellis L.)

McCune, John R., VI: member, McCune Charitable Foundation (Marshall L. and Perrine D.); member dispensing committee, McCune Charitable Trust (John R.); member distribution committee, McCune Foundation

McCusker, Francis C.: director, McDonough Foundation (Bernard)

McDade, Sandy D.: secretary, Weyerhaeuser Co.; assistant secretary legal affairs, Weyerhaeuser Co. Foundation

McDaniel, Glen P.: trustee, Thornton Foundation (Flora L.)

McDermott, Margaret M.: trustee, McDermott Foundation (The Eugene)

McDonagh, William M.: president, chief operating officer, Broderbund LLC; director, Carlston Family Foundation

McDonald, Anne E.: trustee, Stout Foundation (Charles H.)

McDonald, Charles R.: vice president, secretary, trustee, Ratner Foundation (Milton M.)

McDonald, Charline: program officer, Meyer Memorial Trust

McDonald, Douglas B.: vice president, treasurer, Stout Foundation (Charles H.)

McDonald, Ellice, Jr.: president, director, Glencoe Foundation

McDonald, Frank J.: vice president, quality, Cummins, Inc.

McDonald, James, IV: vice president, McDonald Foundation (Armstrong)

McDonald, James M., III: president, McDonald Foundation (Armstrong)

McDonald, John E.: director, Exchange Bank Foundation

McDonald, John M., III: chairman, president, director, McDonald Manufacturing Co. (A.Y.); vice president, McDonald Manufacturing Co. Charitable Foundation (A.Y.)

McDonald, Katherine: secretary, treasurer, McDonald Foundation (Armstrong)

McDonald, M. B.: secretary, McDonald Manufacturing Co. Charitable Foundation (A.Y.)

McDonald, Malcolm S.: trustee, Ford Motor Co. Fund

McDonald, Malcolm W.: treasurer, Grotto Foundation; secretary, treasurer, trustee, McNeely Foundation

McDonald, Mike: chief financial officer, McDonald Manufacturing Co. (A.Y.)

McDonald, Nellie Jane: director, Schwartz Fund for Education and Health Research (Arnold and Marie)

McDonald, Peter M.: president, Davis Foundation (James A. and Juliet L.)

McDonald, Robert Delos: chairman, chief executive officer, McDonald Manufacturing Co. (A.Y.); president, McDonald Manufacturing Co. Charitable Foundation (A.Y.)

McDonald, Rosa H.: vice president, director, Glencoe Foundation

McDonald, Thomas: trustee, McDonald Investments Foundation

McDonald, William E.: mem supervisory board, Codrington Charitable Foundation (George W.)

McDonnell, Archie R., Sr.: treasurer, director, Hardin Foundation (Phil)

McDonough, Gerald C.: trustee, Commercial Intertech Foundation

McDonough, Otto C.: director, mgr, Stebens Charitable Foundation (Bertha)

McDonough, William: trustee, Carnegie Corp. of New York

McDowell, Deborah E.: trustee, Kresge Foundation

McDowell, J. Walter: president, chief executive officer, director, Wachovia Bank of North Carolina NA; director, Wachovia Foundation, Inc. (The)

McDuffie, Brenda W.: trustee, Western New York Foundation

McElhinny, C.A.: vice president, director, Murphy Co. Foundation (G.C.)

McElroy, Dee: executive vice president, foundation manager, Gulf Coast Medical Foundation

McEvoy, George H.: trustee, McEvoy Foundation (Mildred H.)

McEvoy, Rosemary: director, Cuneo Foundation

McFadden, Harry W., Jr. MD: assistant treasurer, director, Physicians Mutual Insurance Co. Foundation

McFadden, Maureen: director, CHC Foundation

McFadden, R. Bruce: trustee, Mosher Foundation (Samuel B.)

McFaddin, Eugene H. B.: trustee, Ward Heritage Foundation (Mamie McFaddin)

McFaddin, James L. C., Jr.: trustee, Ward Heritage Foundation (Mamie McFaddin)

McFadyen, Barbara N.: director, Grable Foundation

McFall, William R.: trustee, Phipps Foundation (Columbus)

McFarland, Catherine M.: executive off, secretary, Victoria Foundation

McFarland, H. Richard: trustee, McFarland Charitable Trust (H. Richard)

McFarland, Sarah F.: trustee, McFarland Charitable Trust (H. Richard)

McFarland, William J.: executive director, secretary, Cummings Foundation (James H.)

McFate, William J.: trustee, Phillips Charitable Trust (Dr. and Mrs. Arthur William)

McFillin, Patricia J.: trustee, McShain Charities (John)

McGann, John P.: clerk, Cabot Corp. Foundation

McGavick, Michael: director, CNA Foundation

McGee, Gary C.: secretary, trustee, Perry Foundation

McGee, Joseph John, Jr.: president, chairman, mem, director, McGee Foundation (MO)

McGee, Thomas F., Sr.: vchairman, mem, director, McGee Foundation (MO)

McGee, Thomas R.: treasurer, mem, director, McGee Foundation (MO)

McGee, Thomas R., Jr.: mem, McGee Foundation (MO)

McGehee, Robert B.: trustee, Progress Energy Foundation; executive vice president, general counsel, Progress Energy Inc.

McGill, Charmaine D.: director, vice president, Cain

Foundation (Effie and Wofford)

McGill, Joe K.: president, chairman, trustee, Doss Foundation, Inc. (M. S.)

McGilvreay, William F.: president, director, East Cambridge Savings Charitable Foundation

McGinnis, Kermit E.: secretary, treasurer, Huntington Foundation

McGinnis, W. Patrick: chief executive officer, Nestle Purina PetCare Co.

McGlinn, Barbara T.: assistant secretary, Colonial Oaks Foundation

McGlinn, John F., II: assistant treasurer, Colonial Oaks Foundation

McGlinn, Terrence J.: president, Colonial Oaks Foundation

McGlinn, Terrence J., Jr.: director, Colonial Oaks Foundation

McGlinn Auman, Christine R.: executive director, secretary, Colonial Oaks Foundation

McGoldrick, John: director, Bristol-Myers Squibb Foundation Inc.

McGough, W. Thomas, Jr.: secretary, Pittsburgh Child Guidance Foundation

McGovern, John Phillip, MD: president, McGovern Fund

McGovern, Kathrine G.: vice president, treasurer, McGovern Foundation (John P.)

McGrath, Barry G.: chairman, president, Pittsburg & Midway Coal Mining Co.

McGrath, Joan S.: contributions administrator, Fortune Brands, Inc.

McGraw, Dave: trustee, Fairchild-Meeker Charitable Trust (Freeman E.)

McGraw, Michael J.: senior vice president law & human resources, Brown & Williamson Tobacco Corp.

McGregor, Douglas A.: trustee, Rouse Co. Foundation

McGregor, Mark: vice president, treasurer, Storage Technology Corp.

McGrew, Margery: director, Meyers Charitable Family Fund

McGuigan, William: assistant treasurer, Bunbury Co., Inc.

McGuire, Allen G.: director, co-trustee, Potts and Sibley Foundation

McGuire, Christopher M.: vice president, assistant secretary, director, Berger Foundation (H. N. and Frances C.)

McGuire, Grant: chairman, Teubert Charitable Trust (James H. and Alice)

McGuire, Patricia A.: director, Meyer Foundation (Eugene and Agnes E.)

McHenry, James F.: director, Green Foundation (Allen P. and Josephine B.)

McHugh, Ann: vice president, treasurer, director, Carvel Foundation (Thomas and Agnes)

McHugh, Katherine S.: director, Cox Charitable Trust (Jessie B.)

McHugh, Marie L.: vice president, director, Laffey-McHugh Foundation

McIninch, Douglas A.: co-trustee, Hunt Foundation (Samuel P.)

McInnes, Harold A.: committee member, Whitaker Foundation

McIntosh, DeCourcy Eyre: mem, Central Charities Foundation

McIntosh, James C.: director, Castle Foundation (Harold K. L.); trustee, Castle Foundation (Samuel N. and Mary)

McIntosh, Robert E.: assistant secretary, assistant treasurer, director, Green Foundation (Allen P. and Josephine B.)

McIntyre, Brett J.: vice president, treasurer, Humana Foundation

McIntyre, David I.: clerk, Roddy Foundation (Fred M.)

McIntyre, John W., Esq.: co-trustee, Roddy Foundation (Fred M.)

McIntyre, Mark: member, Norman Foundation

McIntyre, Susan: assistant secretary, Fribourg Foundation

McJunkin, Donald R.: president, trustee, McDonald Foundation (J. M.)

McJunkin, Eleanor F.: vice president, trustee, McDonald Foundation (J. M.)

McJunkin, Reed L.: secretary, trustee, McDonald Foundation (J. M.)

McKay, Shawn: director, Grinnell Mutual Group Foundation

McKean, John R.: chairman, director, Bay View Bank

McKee, C. Steven: trustee, McKee Foundation (Robert E. and Evelyn)

McKee, David C.: secretary, assistant treasurer, trustee, McKee Foundation (Robert E. and Evelyn)

McKee, E. Marie: senior vice president, Corning Inc.; chairman, trustee, Corning Inc. Foundation

McKee, John S.: senior vice president, McKee Foundation (Robert E. and Evelyn)

McKee, Louis B.: president-treasurer, trustee, McKee Foundation (Robert E. and Evelyn)

McKee, Michael: director, Jones Foundation (Fletcher)

McKee, Nelson D.: vice president, trustee, McKee Foundation (Robert E. and Evelyn)

McKee, Philip Russell: vice president, trustee, McKee Foundation (Robert E. and Evelyn)

McKee, R. Brian: trustee, McKee Foundation (Robert E. and Evelyn)

McKee, Raymond M.: trustee, Bank of America Foundation

McKee, Robert E., III: trustee, treasurer, McKee Foundation (Robert E. and Evelyn)

McKee, Susan J.: vice president, trustee, McKee Foundation (Robert E. and Evelyn)

McKee, Timothy E.: director, Kansas Health Foundation

McKee, W. W.: president, chief executive officer, director, Pitt-Des Moines, Inc.

McKelvey, Patricia E.: secretary, Strosacker Foundation (Charles J.)

McKenna, Andrew James: director, Aon Foundation; trustee, Decio Foundation (Arthur J.)

McKenna, Matthew M.: secretary, PepsiCo Foundation, Inc.; senior vice president of finance, PepsiCo Inc.

McKenna, Thomas M.: director, Penn Foundation (William)

McKenna, William P.: vice president finance, chief financial officer, treasurer, Bourns, Inc.

McKenna, Wilma F.: vchairman, director, McKenna Foundation (Katherine Mabis)

McKenzie, Charles: trustee, Robinson-Broadhurst Foundation

McKenzie, D. Ray, Jr.: vice president, Callaway Foundation, Inc.

McKenzie, Dorma J.: trustee, Brown Foundation, Inc. (James Graham)

McKenzie, Floretta Dukes: trustee, Higginson Trust (Corina)

McKenzie, Wendy Jacobus: director, Heinz Endowment (Vira I.)

McKeown, Dan: treasurer, Boss Foundation

McKeown, Heidi: vice president, secretary, director, Boss Foundation

McKim, Karen P.: secretary, executive director, Corbett Foundation

McKinnell, Henry A., PhD: chairman, chief executive officer, director, Pfizer Inc.

McKinney, David B.: vice president, treasurer, trustee, Bovaird Foundation (Mervin)

McKinney, David Ewing: executive secretary, mem adv board, Watson Foundation (Thomas J.)

McKinnon, John Q.: vice president, Bank One Foundation

McKinzie, Philip S. L.: gov, Mayor Foundation (Oliver Dewey)

McKnight-Crosby, Sumner, III: trustee, Carolyn Foundation

McKonly, Donald E.: director, Kahn Foundation; chief financial officer, Kahn, Lucas-Lancaster, Inc. Children's Wear

McKown, C. H.: director, Huntington Foundation

McLain, Sandy: 2nd vice president, Van Buren Foundation

McLane, Derek: adjunct director, Educational Foundation of America

McLane, John P.: director, French Foundation (D.E.)

McLane, Malcolm: trustee, Jameson Trust (Oleonda)

McLane-Bradley, Elizabeth: trustee, Friendship Fund

McLaren, Ross: chief executive officer, Shaw's Supermarkets, Inc.

McLaughlin, Ann: director, Dana Foundation (Charles A.)

McLaughlin, Ann D.: director, Fannie Mae Foundation

McLaughlin, Gene: co-trustee, Wheeler Memorial Foundation (Josephine and J. A.)

McLaughlin, Loretta: director, Boston Globe Foundation

Mclaughlin, Marcie: trustee, Blandin Foundation

McLaughlin, Michael John: secretary, New York Life Foundation; senior vice president, deputy general counsel, New York Life Insurance Co.

McLaughlin, Michael T.: general counsel, Pacific Life Foundation

McLaughlin, Wendy A., MD: trustee, Foundation for Seacoast Health

McLean, Don: treasurer, Toms Foundation (The)

McLean, Sandra L.: executive drc, advisory trustee, McLean Contributionship

McLean, William L., III: chairman, trustee, McLean Contributionship

McLean, William L., IV: vice chairman, trustee, McLean Contributionship

McLeod, E. Douglas: director/development, Moody Foundation

McMahan, Michael L.: chief financial officer, McMahan Foundation (Catherine L. and Robert O.)

McMahan, Neal W.: executive director, McMahan Foundation (Catherine L. and Robert O.)

McMahan, Nicki Wilson: director, McMahan Foundation (Catherine L. and Robert O.)

McMahon, Ian: treasurer, New Milford Savings Bank Foundation; chief financial officer, treasurer, NewMil Bancorp

McMahon, John J., Jr.: chairman, president, chief executive officer, treasurer, McWane Corp.; trustee, McWane Foundation

McMahon, Kevin: trustee, CH Foundation

McManus, Joseph, Esq.: secretary, treasurer, Olmsted Foundation (George and Carol)

McManus, Patrick J.: treasurer, Raymond Foundation

McMaster, Harold A.: president, treasurer, McMaster Foundation (Harold and Helen)

McMaster, Helen E.: vice president, secretary, McMaster Foundation (Harold and Helen)

McMaster, Ronald A.: trustee, McMaster Foundation (Harold and Helen)

McMeel, Bridget J.: director, Andrews McMeel Universal Foundation

McMeel, John Paul: president, treasurer, Andrews McMeel Universal Foundation

McMeel, Susan S.: director, Andrews McMeel Universal Foundation

McMeel, Suzanne E.: director, Andrews McMeel Universal Foundation

McMeel Jackoboice, Maureen: director, Andrews McMeel Universal Foundation

McMenamin, Joan B. S.: director, Clark Foundation (NY)

McMenamin, Louise A.: secretary, treasurer, director, Cudahy Fund (Patrick and Anna M.)

McMillan, C. Steven: president, chief executive officer, Sara Lee Corp.; director, Sara Lee Foundation

McMillan, Cary D.: executive vice president, chief financial officer, chief administrative officer, Sara Lee Corp.

McMillan, Elizabeth H., M.D.: member, Mather Charitable Trust (S. Livingston)

McMillan, Elizabeth Mather: member, Mather Charitable Trust (S. Livingston)

McMillan, S. Sterling, III: member, Mather Charitable Trust (S. Livingston)

McMillan, S. Sterling, PhD: member, Mather Charitable Trust (S. Livingston); trustee, Mather Fund (Richard)

McMillen, Dale W., III: director, McMillen Foundation

McMillen, John F.: president, director, McMillen Foundation

McMillion, R.D.: vice president, secretary, National Standard Foundation

McMinn, Robert J.: grants administrator, Greenwall Foundation

McMinn, William A.: vice president, Cain Foundation (Gordon and Mary)

McMullen, Melinda: president, Bank One Foundation

McMurray, Sharon: director, Comerica Charitable Foundation

McNamara, James D.: treasurer, ARCO Foundation

McNamara, Julia: vice chairman, trustee, New Haven Savings Bank Foundation, Inc.

McNamara, Michael William: chairman, president, chief executive officer, director, Key Bank of Maine

McNamee, George C.: chairman, director, New York Stock Exchange Foundation, Inc.

McNeely, Gregory: trustee, McNeely Foundation

McNeely, Harry G., III: trustee, McNeely Foundation

McNeely, Harry G., Jr.: chairman, trustee, McNeely Foundation

McNeer, Charles Selden: treasurer, Johnson Foundation

McNeil, Collin F.: director, Barra Foundation

McNeil, Lois F.: president, director, Claneil Foundation

McNeil, Robert D.: director, Claneil Foundation

McNeil, Robert L., III: director, Barra Foundation

McNeil, Robert L., Jr.: president, treasurer, director, Barra Foundation

McNeill, Corbin Asahel, Jr.: president, chief executive officer, director, chairman, Exelon

McNerney, W. James, Jr.: chairman, chief executive officer, director, Minnesota Mining & Manufacturing Co.

McParland, Nathaniel P., MD: trustee, Retirement Research Foundation

McPhail, Gary: president emeritus, Amerus Group Co.

McPhee, Penelope: vice president, chief program officer, Knight Foundation (John S. and James L.)

McPherson, Mary Patterson, PhD: director, Macy, Jr. Foundation (Josiah); vice president, Mellon Foundation (Andrew W.)

McQuiston, W. James: chairman, trustee, Miller Foundation

McTier, Charles Harvey: president, Evans Foundation, Inc. (Lettie Pate)

McWilliams, D. Bradley: vice president, Cooper Industries Foundation; chief financial officer, senior vice president finance, Cooper Industries Ltd.

Meachum, Bruce: director, Vermilion Healthcare Foundation

Meachum, Clyde: director, Vermilion Healthcare Foundation

Mead, Elizabeth: president, treasurer, director, Mead Family Foundation (Gilbert and Jaylee)

Mead, George Wilson, II: president, director, Mead Witter Foundation, Inc.; chairman, director, Stora Enso

Mead, Gilbert Dunbar: chairman, director, Mead Family Foundation (Gilbert and Jaylee)

Mead, Giles W., Jr.: president, Mead Foundation (Giles W. and Elise G.)

Mead, Jane W.: director, Mead Foundation (Giles W. and Elise G.)

Mead, Jaylee M.: vice president, director, Mead Family Foundation (Gilbert and Jaylee)

Mead, Marilyn K.: director, Mead Family Foundation (Gilbert and Jaylee)

Mead, Parry W.: vice president, Mead Foundation (Giles W. and Elise G.)

Mead, Walter Russell: director, Arca Foundation

Mead-Siohan, Diana: secretary, director, Mead Family Foundation (Gilbert and Jaylee)

Meade, Joseph F., III: trustee, Mercury Aircraft Foundation; president, Mercury Aircraft, Inc.

Meade, Joseph F., Jr.: trustee, Mercury Aircraft

Foundation; chairman, director, Mercury Aircraft, Inc.

Meader, Mary U.: trustee, Upjohn Foundation (Harold and Grace)

Meador, David E.: senior vice president, chief financial officer, DTE Energy Co.

Meadowcroft, William Howarth: trustee, Howarth Trust Fund

Meadows, Curtis W., Jr.: director emeritus, Meadows Foundation (The)

Meadows, Eric R.: director, Meadows Foundation (The)

Meadows, John M.: trustee, director, Meadows Foundation (The)

Meadows, Mark L.: trustee, director, Meadows Foundation (The)

Meadows, Robert A.: chairman, trustee, vice president, director, Meadows Foundation (The)

Means, Hugh: director, Jones Foundation (Harvey and Bernice)

Means, Mary C.: vice president, assistant secretary, director, Arkelian Foundation (Ben H. and Gladys); secretary, West Foundation (Harry and Ethel)

Mebane, David Cummins: chairman, president, Madison Gas & Electric Foundation; chairman, president, chief executive officer, director, MGE Energy, Inc.

Mebane, John G., Jr.: trustee, mem investments comm, Biddle Foundation (Mary Duke)

Mecca, Robert A.: vice president, director, treasurer, Regenstein Foundation

Mechanic, Clarisse B.: president, Mechanic Foundation (Morris A.)

Medley, Carl F., Jr.: director, Portsmouth General Hospital Foundation

Medlin, John Grimes, Jr.: trustee, Duke Endowment

Medovitch, J. Terry: treasurer, Freeport Brick Co. Charitable Trust

Medvin, Harvey Norman: executive vice president, treasurer, chief financial officer, Aon Corp.; treasurer, Aon Foundation

Meehan, Dorothy A.: vice president, Sierra Health Foundation

Meehan, William P.: trustee, Hexcel Foundation

Meenan, Julie: executive director, Gumbiner Foundation (Josephine)

Meeusen, Richard A.: vice president, chief financial officer, treasurer, Badger Meter, Inc.

Meggers, Steph: manager, Grinnell Mutual Group Foundation

Meier, Richard: trustee, Meier Foundation (Richard)

Meier, Richard W.: director, secretary, Bakewell, Jr. Family Foundation (Edward L.)

Meier, Stephen Charles: vice chairman, Tribune Co.

Meilahn, J. E.: secretary, treasurer, Federated Mutual Insurance Foundation

Meinders, Herman: president, trustee, Meinders Foundation

Meinders, LaDonna: vice president, trustee, Meinders Foundation

Meinders, Robert: secretary, trustee, Meinders Foundation

Meine, D. L.: assistant secretary, Meadwestvaco Corp. Foundation

Meister, Paul M.: vice president, treasurer, Winthrop

Melarkey, Michael J.: treasurer, Bretzlaff Foundation; vice president, secretary, Wiegand Foundation (E. L.)

Melican, James Patrick, Jr.: executive vice president, International Paper Co.

Melley, Maura L.: trustee, Hartford Courant Foundation

Mellon, Richard Prosser: chairman, trustee, Mellon Foundation (Richard King)

Mellon, Seward Prosser: don, director, trustee, Mellon Family Foundation (R. K.); president, chairman executive comm, trustee, Mellon Foundation (Richard King)

Mellon, Thomas J., Jr.: vice president, Hale Foundation (Crescent Porter)

Mellon, Timothy: trustee, Mellon Foundation (Andrew W.)

Mellor, C. Michael: director, Ziegler Foundation for the Blind (E. Matilda)

Melnicoff, David C.: board member, Fels Fund (Samuel S.)

Melton, Rollan D.: vice president, Snow Foundation (John Ben); trustee, Snow Memorial Trust (John Ben)

Melton-Williams, Emelie: assistant secretary, Snow Foundation (John Ben)

Meltzer, Jay J.: director, Hebrew Technical Institute

Menagvale, Sandy Nalbone: trustee, Snyder Foundation (Harold B. and Dorothy A.)

Menapace, John J.: director, Sordoni Foundation

Menard, Raymond N.: trustee, Levy Foundation (June Rockwell)

Mendel, Audre D.: vice president, Mendel Foundation

Mendel, Herbert D.: president, Mendel Foundation

Mendel, Jon B.: director, Metris Companies Foundation

Mendel, Julie: director, Mendel Foundation

Mendelovitz, Mark C.: secretary, trustee, Swalm Foundation

Mengebier, David G.: president, Consumers Energy Foundation

Mengel, Andre, PhD: director, Independence Foundation

Menges, Carl Braun: director, Greenwall Foundation

Menke, John R.: director, Hebrew Technical Institute

Menton, Deborah A.: executive director, secretary, Noble Foundation, Inc. (Edward John)

Mentzer, Edward W.: director, St. Francis Bank Foundation

Menzies, John: member, Cranston Foundation

Menzies, Julia Baker: director, Lockhart Vaughan Foundation

Merced, Victor: program officer, Meyer Memorial Trust

Mercer, Henry D., Jr.: trustee, Frese Foundation (Arnold D.)

Merck, Adele Shook: trustee, Shook Foundation (Barbara Ingalls)

Merck, Antony M.: treasurer, trustee, Merck Family Fund

Merck, Josephine A.: vice president, trustee, Merck Family Fund

Merck, Wilhelm M.: trustee, Merck Family Fund

Merdek, Andrew Austin: vice president legal affairs, secretary, Cox Enterprises, Inc.; secretary, Cox Foundation (James M.)

Merin, Kenneth D.: president, chief executive officer, trustee, Hayden Foundation (Charles)

Merkle, K. A.: secretary, General Motors Foundation

Merlotti, Frank Henry: trustee, Steelcase Foundation; director, Steelcase Inc.

Merrick, Frank W.: trustee, Merrick Foundation

Merrick, Robert B.: trustee, Merrick Foundation

Merrick, Ward S., Jr.: trustee, Merrick Foundation

Merrill, Thomas M.: vice president, director, Harden Foundation

Merritt, Pamela M.: secretary, McMillan, Jr. Foundation (Bruce)

Mersereau, Susan M.: trustee, Weyerhaeuser Co. Foundation

Merthan, Claudia Boettcher: chairman, trustee, Boettcher Foundation

Meserow, J. Tod: secretary, director, Russell Charitable Foundation (Tom)

Mesher, John R.: assistant secretary, Saint-Gobain Corporation Foundation

Messier, Andre J., Jr.: director, Eastern Savings and Loan Foundation

Messing, Roswell, III: trustee, Messing Family Charitable Foundation

Messing, Wilma E.: trustee, Messing Family Charitable Foundation

Messman, Jack L.: president, chief executive officer, Novell

Messner, Robert T.: vice president, director, Murphy Co. Foundation (G.C.)

Mestel, Harry: president, Wilkof Foundation (Edward and Ruth)

Metts, Harold: director, Houston Endowment

Metz, Mary Seawell: president, director, Cowell Foundation (S. H.)

Metzger, Michael D.: vice president, chief financial officer, JSJ Corp.

Meuleman, Robert Joseph: director, AMCORE Foundation

Meyer, Alex Alfred: director, Hall-Perrine Foundation

Meyer, Alice Jane: vice president, director, Meyer Family Foundation (Paul J.)

Meyer, Alice K.: president, treasurer, Meyer Foundation (Alice Kleberg Reynolds)

Meyer, Henry L., III: trustee, Bicknell Fund

Meyer, L. D.: assistant treasurer, Exxon Mobil Foundation

Meyer, Lawrence H. (Bud): commun director, Knight Foundation (John S. and James L.)

Meyer, Patricia: secretary, Argyle Foundation

Meyer, Paul J., Sr.: president, director, Meyer Family Foundation (Paul J.)

Meyer, Roger F.: president, Laurel Foundation

Meyer, Ronald: president, chief executive officer, Universal Studios

Meyer, Sarah: senior program officer, Microsoft Corp.

Meyer, Vaughan B.: vice president, secretary, Meyer Foundation (Alice Kleberg Reynolds)

Meyer, William A.: vice president, director, Meyer Family Foundation (Paul J.)

Meyers, David R.: president, director, Meyers Charitable Family Fund

Meyers, Evan A.: vice president, chief financial officer, Kansas Health Foundation

Meyers, Frederick C.: secretary, treasurer, Meyers Charitable Family Fund

Meyers, Gail: trustee, Heckscher Foundation for Children

Meyers, James: director, Wright Foundation (Lola)

Meyerson, Marvin: trustee, Retirement Research Foundation

Meysman, Frank L.: director, Sara Lee Corp.

Micallef, Joseph S.: assistant secretary, director, Davis Foundation (Edwin W. and Catherine M.); secretary, Driscoll Foundation; secretary, treasurer, director, Weyerhaeuser Memorial Foundation (Charles A.)

Michaelis, Mary F.: trustee, McCasland Foundation

Michaels, Jack D.: secretary, HON Industries Charitable Foundation; chairman, chief executive officer, director, HON Industries, Inc.

Michalis, Clarence F.: chairman, Macy, Jr. Foundation (Josiah)

Michel, Betsy S.: trustee, Dodge Foundation (Geraldine R.); president, Jockey Hollow Foundation

Michel, Clifford Lloyd: treasurer, Jockey Hollow Foundation

Michel, Sally J.: trustee, Abell Foundation

Micheletti, Tom: vice president public & government affairs, Xcel Energy

Michelson, Gertrude Geraldine: director, Markle Foundation (John and Mary R.); chairman, Rubinstein Foundation (Helena)

Michener, John: advisory trustee, Weaver Foundation (Gil and Dody)

Michler, John F.: treasurer, director, Alexander Foundation (Walter)

Mickelson, P. Gregory: director, VPI Foundation Inc.

Mida, Richard E.: vice president, secretary, Vollbrecht Foundation (Frederick A.)

Middeleer, William P.: vice president, Muhlethaler

Foundation, Inc. (Jane T.)

Middleton, Reginald: vice president, Strauss Foundation

Midkiff, Robert Richards: president, director, Atherton Family Foundation

Mifflan, Robert B.: executive director, Christy-Houston Foundation

Mihori, James S.: trustee, Grimes Foundation

Mikell, Ray S.: vice president, Cook, Sr. Charitable Foundation (Kelly Gene)

Mikush, Sandra H.: assistant director, Babcock Foundation (Mary Reynolds)

Milband, David L.: director, Memton Fund

Milbank, Jeremiah, III: director, Guggenheim Foundation (Harry Frank); mem, JM Foundation

Milbank, Jeremiah, Jr.: president, JM Foundation

Milbank, Michelle: director, Memton Fund

Milbank, Samuel L.: director, Memton Fund

Milbank, Thomas L.: director, Memton Fund

Milberger, Edith: assistant treasurer, Foundation for Child Development

Milby, Charles D., Jr.: treasurer, Hamman Foundation (George and Mary Josephine)

Miles, Diane Day: secretary, Demos Foundation (N.)

Miles, John: trustee, Homecrest Foundation

Miles, John C., II: trustee, Dentsply International Foundation; president, chief executive officer, director, Dentsply International, Inc.

Miles, Nancy: trustee, Homecrest Foundation

Miles, Pat: secretary, director, Greenville Foundation

Miles, Rob: treasurer, Washington Mutual Foundation

Miles, William: director, Greenville Foundation

Milfs, Audrey L.: secretary, Pacific Life Foundation; vice president, corporate secretary, director, Pacific Life Insurance Co.

Millan, Jacqueline R.: vice president, manager corporate contributions, PepsiCo Foundation, Inc.; director, PepsiCo Inc.

Millender, Edith Morse: assistant secretary, Ratshesky Foundation (A. C.)

Miller, Allen L.: trustee, Miller Foundation

Miller, Carl: director, Brillion Foundation

Miller, Diana: trustee, Valentine Foundation (Lawson)

Miller, Diane Disney: director, Wells Fargo Foundation

Miller, Dolores E.: secretary, Markle Foundation (John and Mary R.)

Miller, Donn Biddle: vice chairman, director, Irvine Foundation (The James); president, trustee, Pacific Life Foundation

Miller, Edmund J.: program officer, Mott Foundation (Charles Stewart)

Miller, Edward A.: director, Stulsaft Foundation (Morris)

Miller, Eugene A.: chairman, trustee, McGregor Fund

Miller, George: president, Wilson Fund (Matilda R.)

Miller, Gerald W.: trustee, Stranahan Foundation

Miller, Gordon E.: director, The Bothin Foundation

Miller, Harlan: treasurer, trustee, Miller Foundation (Earl B. and Loraine H.)

Miller, Harvey R.: chairman, director, Weil, Gotshal & Manges Foundation

Miller, Harvey S. Shipley: treasurer, Arcadia Foundation

Miller, Harvey Shipley: officer, Avery Arts Foundation (Milton and Sally)

Miller, Helen: director, Washington Foundation (Dennis R. and Phyllis)

Miller, I. Clinton: director, ShenTel Foundation

Miller, James C.: president, S&T Bancorp Charitable Foundation; president, director, S&T Bancorp, Inc.

Miller, James D.: trustee, Richardson Benevolent Foundation (C. E.)

Miller, James H., III: senior vice president, Alabama Power Co.; director, Alabama Power Foundation

Miller, James Ludlow: secretary, treasurer, Miller-Mellor Association

Miller, Jeffrey W.: trustee, Glendorn Foundation

Miller, JoZach, IV: vice president, Miller-Mellor Association

Miller, Joe: secretary, Whittenberger Foundation (Claude R. and Ethel B.)

Miller, John C.: trustee, City National Bank Foundation

Miller, Joyce G.: executive director, Amado Foundation (Maurice)

Miller, Loren: member, Northern Trust Co. Charitable Trust

Miller, Lucy: trustee, Valentine Foundation (Lawson)

Miller, Mark F.: director, Hearst Foundation, Inc. (The); vice president, director, Hearst Foundation (William Randolph)

Miller, Marlin, Jr.: trustee, Wyomissing Foundation

Miller, Mary Frances: trustee, Mellinger Educational Foundation (Edward Arthur)

Miller, Mary J.: vice president, trustee, Price Associates Foundation (T. Rowe)

Miller, Nancy A.: director, Harcourt Foundation (Ellen Knowles)

Miller, Norman C.: president, Miller Foundation (Steve J.)

Miller, Patricia Hillman: director, Eberly Foundation

Miller, Robert Branson, Jr.: trustee, Miller Foundation

Miller, Robert Branson, Sr.: trustee emeritus, Miller Foundation

Miller, Sally C.: director emeritus, Meadows Foundation (The)

Miller, Theodore W.: trustee, Miller Foundation (Steve J.)

Miller, Tina Marie: assistant to president, Wiegand Foundation (E. L.)

Miller, Wilford: committee member, Haman Family Foundation

Miller, William: director, South Plains Foundation

Miller, William Irwin: director, Cummins Foundation

Millhouse, Barbara B.: vice president, director, Babcock Foundation (Mary Reynolds)

Millican, S. A.: assistant secretary, Exxon Mobil Foundation

Milligan, Donald: assistant treasurer, Sun Hill Foundation

Milliken, W. Dickerson: secretary, director, Hoag Family Foundation (George)

Millman, Paul: director, Mattel Foundation

Mills, Carlotta R.: program officer, Kresge Foundation

Mills, John T.: trustee, U.S. Steel Foundation

Mills, Kelly L.: assistant secretary, Noyes, Jr. Memorial Foundation (Nicholas H.)

Mills, Linda S.: director, SBC Foundation

Mills, Phyllis J.: trustee, Cary Charitable Trust (Mary Flagler)

Mills, Rick J.: president, fleetguard, Cummins, Inc.

Millspaugh, Gordon A., Jr.: assistant treasurer, trustee, Victoria Foundation

Millstein, Ira M.: partner, Weil, Gotshal & Manges Corp.; chairman, director, Weil, Gotshal & Manges Foundation

Milne, Garth Leroy: senior vice president, treasurer, Motorola, Inc.

Milner, John C.: secretary, treasurer, Glencoe Foundation

Milski, Mark: director, Littauer Foundation (Lucius N.)

Milstein, Richard Sherman: clerk, Steiger Memorial Fund (Albert)

Miltenberger, Arthur D.: vice president, Mellon Foundation (Richard King)

Minard, Sally: president, director, Garfinkle-Minard Foundation, Inc.

Miner, Joshua L., IV: trustee, Stevens Foundation (Nathaniel and Elizabeth P.)

Miner, Justine: director, Baker Street Foundation

Miner, Mary: president, director, Baker Street Foundation

Miner, Nicola: director, Baker Street Foundation

Miner, Phoebe S.: trustee, Stevens Foundation (Abbot and Dorothy H.)

Minnema, John: vice president, Jaqua Foundation

Minnich, M. W.: vice president, director, Wharton Foundation

Minnis, Ann: grants administrator, director, Texas Instruments Foundation

Minow, Martha Louise: director, Revson Foundation (Charles H.)

Minter-Dowd, Christine: vice president, Marpat Foundation

Minton, Dwight Church: chairman, director, Church & Dwight Company, Inc.

Miori, Sylvan: director, Gulf Coast Medical Foundation

Miracle, Robert Warren: president, Goodstein Foundation

Mirakhor, Abbas: treasurer, Alavi Foundation

Mirikitani, Cora: senior program director, Irvine Foundation (The James)

Miro, Jeffrey H.: secretary, Taubman Foundation (A. Alfred)

Mirsky, Burton M.: vice president finance, Dana Foundation (Charles A.)

Mister, Melvin: trustee, Taconic Foundation

Mitchell, Betsy: trustee, Children's Foundation of Erie County

Mitchell, Braxton D.: vice president, trustee, Warfield Memorial Fund (Anna Emory)

Mitchell, Charlotte: assistant trustee, BellSouth Foundation

Mitchell, David: trustee, August Family Foundation (Charles J. and Burton S.)

Mitchell, Donald D.: co-trustee, Arakelian Foundation (Mary Alice)

Mitchell, James: director, Texas Instruments Foundation; vice president for human resources, Texas Instruments Inc.

Mitchell, Janet A.: trustee, Smoot Charitable Trust (Frank Litz)

Mitchell, John A.: trustee, Cornell Trust (Peter C.)

Mitchell, John Daniel: director, Beneficia Foundation

Mitchell, John Francis: vice chairman, director, Motorola, Inc.

Mitchell, Joseph C.: trustee, Delmas Foundation (Gladys Krieble); president, director, Samuels Foundation (Fan Fox and Leslie R.)

Mitchell, Judith M.: trustee, Peterloon Foundation

Mitchell, Kim S.: assistant secretary, Van Andel Foundation (Jay and Betty)

Mitchell, Lucy C.: trustee, Carolyn Foundation; assistant treasurer, trustee, Southways Foundation

Mitchell, M.: vice president, trustee, Johns Manville Fund

Mitchell, Miriam Pitcairn: vice president, director, Beneficia Foundation

Mitchell, Robert J.: treasurer, ACF Industries

Mitchnick, Les: vice president, secretary, executive director, Nakamichi Foundation (E.)

Mixer, David P.: treasurer, Trimix Foundation

Mixer, Gail S.: president, Trimix Foundation

Mixon, Bobby C.: president, Morgan Foundation (Louie R. and Gertrude)

Miyakoshi, Takeshi: president, director, Kawasaki Good Times Foundation

Mize, Ann: director, Muchnic Foundation

Mize, David C.: secretary, Muchnic Foundation

Mobley, E. B.: president, Griffin Foundation (Rosa May)

Mobley, Ebb: vice president, Griffin Foundation (Rosa May)

Mobley, Ernestine L.: manager, Finch Foundation (Thomas Austin)

Mobley, M. D.: treasurer, General Motors Foundation

Mobley, Stacey J.: senior vice president, chief administrative officer, general counsel, E.I. du Pont de Nemours & Co.

Mochon, Margaret: director, Howard and Bush Foundation

Moe, Henrik: president, DEC International, Inc. SMS/

Nelles Cheese Equipment

Moe, James D.: corporate vice president, general counsel, secretary, Cargill, Inc.

Moe, Richard: trustee, Ford Foundation

Moeller, Joseph W.: president, chief operating officer, Koch Industries, Inc.

Moeller, Lisa Robertshaw: director, Robertshaw Charitable Foundation

Moen, Stephanie S.: director, Vann Family Foundation

Moen, Timothy P.: vice president, Bank One Foundation

Moffat, William R.: trustee, Carpenter Foundation

Moffett, F. Wesley, Jr.: trustee, Houck Foundation (May Kay)

Moffitt, James F.: trustee, Kerr Fund (Grayce B.)

Mogi, Yozaburo: chairman, president, chief executive officer, Kikkoman Foods; director, Kikkoman Foundation

Mogilnik, Nina B.: senior program officer, Altman Foundation

Mohn, Richard E.: chairman, director, Sovereign Bank; director, Sovereign Bank Foundation

Mohraz, Judy J.: director, Baltimore Equitable Insurance Foundation

Moldaw, Carol A.: director, Moldaw Family Foundation

Moldaw, Phyllis: vice president, treasurer, Moldaw Family Foundation

Moldaw, Stuart G.: president, Moldaw Family Foundation

Moldaw, Susan J.: director, Moldaw Family Foundation

Molella, Salvador: vice president, treasurer, Carvel Foundation (Thomas and Agnes)

Molina, Mario J.: director, MacArthur Foundation (John D. and Catherine T.)

Moline, Carmen: treasurer, Mulcahy Foundation

Moline, Kenneth A.: president, Taube Family Foundation

Moll, Curtis E.: member supervisory board, Codrington Charitable Foundation (George W.)

Mollenberg, Trudy A.: trustee, Western New York Foundation

Moltz, James E.: trustee, Rockefeller Brothers Fund, Inc.

Molyneux, Richard A.: chairman, director, Key Bank of Maine

Monahan, Michael J.: vice president external affairs, Ecolab, Inc.

Monastiere, Dominic: president, Kantzler Foundation

Moncla, Jean: vice president, trust officer, Ward Heritage Foundation (Mamie McFaddin)

Monell, Ambrose K.: director, Ambrose Monell Foundation (The)

Monello, Joseph D.: vice president finance, Kansas City Southern Railway

Monfort, Myra: secretary, Monfort Family Foundation

Monsied, Charles, III: trustee, German Protestant Orphan Asylum Association Foundation

Montalvo, Elba: trustee, New York Foundation

Monte, Jeffery P.: secretary, Burlington Resources Foundation

Monteith, Edgar W.: secretary, trustee, Brown Foundation

Montera, Kaye C. Monfort: president, Monfort Family Foundation

Montgomery, J. R.: secretary, director, Bertha Foundation

Montgomery, Mary Louise: clerk, director, Kelley and Elza Kelley Foundation (Edward Bangs)

Montgomery, Philip O'Bryan, Jr.: director, O'Donnell Foundation

Montgomery, Virginia: trustee, Woodcock Foundation

Montoya, Maria: director, Avon Products Foundation, Inc.

Montoya, Robert: treasurer, Chamiza Foundation

Montrone, Paul Michael: vice president, Winthrop

Moody, Frances A.: executive director, Moody Foundation

Moody, Natalie: director, Gilman Foundation (Howard)

Moody, Ross R.: trustee, Moody Foundation

Mooney, Brian P.: trustee, New York Foundation

Moore, Albert W.: director, Gleason Foundation

Moore, Bob: board mem, Roberts Foundation (Dora)

Moore, Charles R., Jr.: trustee, Long Foundation (George A. and Grace)

Moore, E. Kevin: treasurer, Schering-Plough Foundation

Moore, Gregory: trustee, Grimes Foundation

Moore, Hannah T. C.: treasurer, Island Foundation (MA)

Moore, Hardy: president, Lennox Foundation (Martha, David and Bagby)

Moore, Harvin, IV: director, Powell Foundation

Moore, Irving, Jr.: secretary, Gulf Coast Medical Foundation

Moore, Jack: vice president, Gulf Coast Medical Foundation

Moore, Jacqueline G.: president, Griswold Foundation (John C.)

Moore, Jim S., PhD: director, South Plains Foundation

Moore, John E.: executive vice president human resources, Cessna Aircraft Co.; vice president, Cessna Foundation, Inc.

Moore, John H.: trustee, Brackenridge Foundation (George W.)

Moore, Kevin S.: treasurer, director, Clark Foundation (NY)

Moore, L. W.: adv, Beasley Charitable Trust (Lucy and Emily)

Moore, Lewis B.: trustee, Grimes Foundation

Moore, Linda J.: membership, Foster Co. Charitable Trust (L.B.)

Moore, Margaret D.: senior vice president, human resources, PepsiCo Inc.

Moore, Martin L., Jr.: trustee, Patterson Charitable Fund (W. I.)

Moore, Mary: vice president & manager, community relations, US Bank

Moore, Michael J.: director, Island Foundation (MA)

Moore, Nancy Powell: foundation manager, director, president, treasurer, Powell Foundation

Moore, Peter M.: grants director, Moody Foundation

Moore, Randolph G.: director, Castle Foundation (Harold K. L.)

Moore, Robert: trustee, Gulf Power Foundation; chairman, Standard Steel Speciality Co.

Moore, Robert P.: trustee, Barden Foundation, Inc.

Moore, Stephen O.: director, vice president, Hardin Foundation (Phil)

Moore, Steven: president, Oklahoma Gas & Electric Co. Foundation

Moore, T. Justin, Jr.: vice president, Scott Foundation (William H., John G., and Emma)

Moore, Thomas R.: secretary, counsel, PNC Foundation

Moorman, Bette D.: president, director, Davis Foundation (Edwin W. and Catherine M.)

Moot, Andrew R.: trustee, Western New York Foundation

Moot, John R.: secretary, Western New York Foundation

Moot, Richard E.: treasurer, Western New York Foundation

Moot, Welles V., Jr.: president, Western New York Foundation

Mora, Susan: assistant administration, Stulsaft Foundation (Morris)

Moran, Cynthia S.: trustee, Spahr Family Foundation

Moran, Edward P., Jr.: trustee, Barker Foundation Inc.

Moran, Elizabeth A.: trustee, The MBNA Foundation

Moran, Harry J.: executive vice president, Sonoco Products Co.

Moran, Susan B.: vice president, trustee, Barker Foundation Inc.

Moran, Tina: secretary, Niagara Mohawk Foundation

Moravitz, Edward: trustee, Giant Eagle Foundation

Morby, Carolyn R.: trustee, Gerber Foundation

Morel, Donald E., Jr: president, chief executive officer, West Pharmaceutical Services, Inc.

Moreland, Jeffrey: director, Burlington Northern Santa Fe Foundation

Moreno, Albert F.: director, Rosenberg Foundation

Moreton, Fred A., Jr.: member, Burton Private Foundation (Robert Harold)

Morf, Darrel Arle: vice president, attorney, director, Hall-Perrine Foundation

Morgan, Alethia, M.D.: director, Copic Medical Foundation

Morgan, Anne Hodges: board member, Kauffman Foundation (Ewing Marion); vice president, director, Kirkpatrick Foundation, Inc.

Morgan, Carol: chairperson, National Service Foundation

Morgan, Charles O., Jr.: trustee, Chatlos Foundation

Morgan, Davis: mgr, Porter Testamentary Trust (James Hyde)

Morgan, Edward L.: group senior vice president, Hartford Financial Services Group, Inc.

Morgan, Gayle: program director music, Cary Charitable Trust (Mary Flagler)

Morgan, George A.: trustee, City National Bank Foundation; executive vice president, City National Bank & Trust Co.

Morgan, Glenn R.: executive vice president, chief financial officer, treasurer, member, Hartmarx Corp.

Morgan, James F., Jr.: vice president, director, Atherton Family Foundation

Morgan, James H.: chairman, president, chief executive officer, director, Interstate/Johnson Lane

Morgan, John A.: chairman disbursement comm, Oppenstein Brothers Foundation

Morgan, Michael: director, Koch Foundation, Inc. (Fred C. and Mary R.)

Morgan, Michael C.: director, Kinder Morgan Foundation

Morgan, Paul F.: vice president, director, Atherton Family Foundation

Morgan, Paul S.: co-trustee, Hoche-Scofield Foundation

Morgan, R. Scott: director, Portsmouth General Hospital Foundation

Morgan, Roy E.: director, Sordoni Foundation

Morgridge, John P.: trustee, Cisco Systems Foundation

Morian, Wilhelmina Cullen Robertson: secretary-treasurer, trustee, Cullen Foundation (The)

Moriarty, Brunilda: assistant secretary, Hyde and Watson Foundation

Morley, Burrows, Jr.: trustee, Morley Foundation

Morley, Christopher: trustee, Morley Foundation

Morley, David H.: trustee, Morley Foundation

Morley, Edward B., Jr.: past president, trustee, Morley Foundation

Morley, George B., Jr.: trustee, Morley Foundation

Morley, Katharyn M.: trustee, Morley Foundation

Morley, Mark B.: treasurer, Morley Foundation

Morley, Peter B., Jr.: trustee, Morley Foundation

Morley, Robert S.: president, Morley Foundation

Morley Beck, Carol: trustee, Morley Foundation

Morning, John: director, Dime Foundation; trustee, Mott Foundation (Charles Stewart)

Morns, Katherine B.: member board advisors, Belk Foundation

Moroney, James McQueen, Jr.: trustee, Belo Foundation

Morrell, Michael W.: vice president, Verizon Foundation

Morrill, Amy B.: trustee, Morrill Charitable Foundation

Morrill, Richard L.: director, Teagle Foundation

Mulcahy, Betty Jane: trustee, H. C. S. Foundation

Mulcahy, Michael J.: director, Vermilion Healthcare Foundation

Mulderrig, Steve: director, Tribune New York Foundation

Mulhern, Mark: assistant treasurer, Progress Energy Foundation

Mulhern, Timothy P.: trustee, Shatz, Schwartz & Fentin Charitable Foundation; partner, Shatz, Schwartz & Fentin PC

Mulkey, Kim: director, Technology program, Bell-South Foundation

Mullen, Dennis M.: president, chief executive officer, director, Birds Eye Foods, Inc.

Mullendore, Stuart L.: trustee, Sinnisen Foundation (Albert E. and Naomi B.)

Muller, George T.: president, trustee, Subaru of America Foundation; president, chief operating officer, director, Subaru of America, Inc.

Mullin, Jack Shan: adv, Archibald Charitable Foundation (Norman)

Mullins, Charles H.: trustee, McKinney Charitable Trust (Carl and Alleen)

Mullins, Terrell: trustee, Johnson Foundation (M. G. and Lillie A.)

Mulroney, John P.: director, Penn Foundation (William)

Mulroy, Thomas M., Esq.: trustee, Miller Charitable Foundation (Howard E. and Nell E.)

Mulvahill, Karen: director, Comerica Charitable Foundation

Mulzer, Kenneth: secretary, treasurer, TCB Bank Foundation

Munder, Barbara A.: senior vice president new initiatives, McGraw-Hill Companies, Inc.

Mundy, George E.: director, Trippe Trust (William D.)

Mundy, Rodney O.: director, Alabama Power Foundation

Munger, Molly: director, Irvine Foundation (The James)

Munitz, Barry: president, chief executive officer, Getty Trust (J. Paul)

Munson, Ben, IV: gov, Munson Foundation Trust (W. B.)

Munson, David, Jr.: gov, Munson Foundation Trust (W. B.)

Munson, David M., Sr.: gov, Munson Foundation Trust (W. B.)

Munson, Edwin Palmer: assistant secretary, Scott Foundation (William H., John G., and Emma)

Munson, John K.: gov, Munson Foundation Trust (W. B.)

Munson, Peter: gov, Munson Foundation Trust (W. B.)

Munyon, Wendy Nelson: secretary, Grinnell Mutual Group Foundation

Murase, Haruo: chairman, president, chief executive officer, Canon U.S.A., Inc.

Murchison, George M.: trustee, Hodges Foundation (Bess J.)

Murfree, Matt B., III: director, Christy-Houston Foundation

Murguia, Ramon: director, Francis Families Foundation

Murphy, Arthur: director, Eckman Charitable Foundation (Samuel and Rae)

Murphy, Bart: trustee, Retirement Research Foundation

Murphy, Charles H., Jr.: director, Murphy Foundation

Murphy, Christopher J., III: president, chief executive officer, director, 1st Source Corp.; director, First Source Foundation

Murphy, D. P., Jr.: president trustee, Handy & Harman Foundation

Murphy, Debra L.: senior vice president, chief financial officer, Woronoco Savings Bank; treasurer, director, Woronoco Savings Charitable Foundation

Murphy, Diana E.: director, Bush Foundation

Murphy, Frank H.: trustee, The MBNA Foundation

Murphy, Gerald B.: chairman, Bair Family Trust (Charles M.)

Murphy, Henry L., Jr.: vice president, admin mgr, director, Kelley and Elza Kelley Foundation (Edward Bangs)

Murphy, John: trustee, Self Family Foundation

Murphy, John Davis: president, Wiremold Foundation

Murphy, John E.: chairman, president, chief executive officer, Bay State Federal Savings Charitable Foundation

Murphy, Johnie W.: president, director, Murphy Foundation

Murphy, Mark M.: secretary, executive director, Fund for New Jersey

Murphy, Patsy: secretary, director, Carlston Family Foundation

Murphy, R. Madison: president, director, Murphy Foundation

Murphy, Robert F., Jr.: trustee, Walsh Charity Trust (Blanche)

Murphy, Robert H.: vice president, Wiremold Foundation

Murphy, Tern C.: trustee, The MBNA Foundation

Murphy, Terry M.: vice president finance, chief financial officer, Quanex Corp.; vice president, director, Quanex Foundation

Murphy, William J.: director, mem adv comm, O'Connor Foundation (A. Lindsay and Olive B.)

Murrah, Jack: president, trustee, Lyndhurst Foundation

Murray, Archibald R.: director, Scherman Foundation

Murray, Arthur W.: trustee, Mellinger Educational Foundation (Edward Arthur)

Murray, Catherine Fondren Underwood: secretary, treasurer, Fondren Foundation

Murray, Daniel T.: secretary, Gallo Foundation (Ernest)

Murray, Diana T.: director, Markle Foundation (John and Mary R.)

Murray, Douglas P.: president, trustee, Lingnan Foundation

Murray, J. Terrance: treasurer, Demos Foundation (N.)

Murray, James E.: chief operating officer, Humana Foundation

Murray, Linda T.: assistant secretary, director, Vernon Foundation (Miles Hodsdon)

Murray, Robert E.: vice president, Edison Fund (Charles)

Murray, Robert J.: chairman, president, chief executive officer, New England Business Service

Murray, William E.: trustee, Donaldson Charitable Trust (Oliver S. and Jennie R.)

Murrin, Evelyn L.: trustee, Pittsburgh Child Guidance Foundation

Murtagh, Robert J.: co-trustee, Booth Ferris Foundation

Murtaugh, James: program director, Claiborne and Art Ortenberg Foundation (Liz)

Musarra, Arthur F.: trustee, Statler Foundation

Muse, Martha Twitchell: chairman, Tinker Foundation

Musgrave, Colleen: administrator, Simpson Fund

Musgrave, David L.: trustee, Claypool Foundation (Silas and Ruth)

Musgrave, Todd: adv board committee member, Heath Foundation (Mary)

Musser, William L.: director, Barker Foundation (J.M.R.)

Musson, Irvin J., III: trustee, Musson Charitable Foundation (R. C. and Katharine M.)

Musson, Irvin J., Jr.: trustee, Musson Charitable Foundation (R. C. and Katharine M.)

Mustain, Phyllis S.: director, Burchfield Foundation (Charles E.)

Mustain, Robert D.: secretary, director, Burchfield Foundation (Charles E.)

Myer, David: trustee, Andres Charitable Trust (Frank G.)

Myers, Gertrude: trustee, Share Trust (Charles Morton)

Myers, Jo Ann Morrison: president, Figtree Foundation

Myers, Lynn Howe: chairman, vice president, Howe and Mitchell B. Howe Foundation (Lucille Horton)

Myers, Marilyn B.: adv, Kirkpatrick Foundation, Inc.

Myers, Michele Tolela: director, Fairchild Foundation, Inc. (Sherman)

Myers, Mitchell C.: director, Howe and Mitchell B. Howe Foundation (Lucille Horton)

Myers, Stanley Thomas: president, chief executive officer, director, Mitsubishi Silicon America

Myers, Toni: admin, Rosa-Mary Foundation

Myszka, Michele: vice president, director, Pacific Life Foundation; community relations director, public affairs, Pacific Life Insurance Co.

N

Nabers, Hugh C., Jr.: trustee, Comer Foundation (AL)

Nadel, Susan Bryson: mem, Templeton Foundation (Herbert A.)

Nadler, Charles, Ph.D.: Distribution trustee, Schwab-Rosenhouse Memorial Foundation

Naeve, Stephen W.: vice chairman, executive vice president, chief financial officer, CenterPoint Energy, Inc.

Nagel, Robert D.: director investments, Wallace-Reader's Digest Fund

(DeWitt); director investments, treasurer, Wallace-Reader's Digest Fund (Lila)

Nagle, James: trustee, Graham Foundation for Advanced Studies in the Fine Arts

Nagy, Julia Ann: treasurer, Huber Foundation

Naiman, Norma Lee: director, Himmelfarb Foundation (Paul and Annetta)

Najarian, Richard: trustee, Raymond Foundation

Nakano, Tsuyoshi: mem allocations comm, Kawabe Memorial Fund

Nalbach, Kay C.: president, Hartmarx Charitable Foundation

Nalbone, Ray: trustee, Snyder Foundation (Harold B. and Dorothy A.)

Nally, Joseph: director, Doheny Foundation Trust (Carrie Estelle)

Nalty, Donald J.: chairman, director, Schlieder Educational Foundation (Edward G.)

Nalty, Elizabeth S.: president, director, Schlieder Educational Foundation (Edward G.)

Nalty, Jill: treasurer, director, Schlieder Educational Foundation (Edward G.)

Nanon, Patricia: vice president, director, Newman Assistance Fund (Jerome A. and Estelle R.)

Naples, Ronald James: president, chief executive officer, director, Quaker Chemical Corp.

Napp, Laurie: director, Provident Community Foundation

Nardi, Nicholas J.: secretary, treasurer, Culpeper Memorial Foundation (Daphne Seybolt)

Narten, Janet E.: executive director, Bruening Foundation (Eva L. and Joseph M.)

Narvarte, Julia: assistant treasurer, trustee, Doss Foundation, Inc. (M. S.)

Naschke, Arlene M.: trustee, Messing Family Charitable Foundation

Nash, Lucia S.: corp chairman, trustee, Smith Foundation (Kelvin and Eleanor)

Nash, Martin: director, Kennedy Family Foundation (Ethel and W. George)

Nash, Regina F.: administrative assistant, Frist Foundation

Nash, Robert: director, Klee Foundation (Conrad and Virginia)

Nathan, David, MD: director, Dyson Foundation

Nathan, Edward A.: trustee, Zellerbach Family Fund

Nation, Robert F.: president, director, Kline Foundation

(Josiah W. and Bessie H.)

Naughton, John Patrick, MD: director, Cummings Foundation (James H.)

Naus, Laura: secretary, Ambrose Monell Foundation (The)

Navick, Jerald I.: director, Eastern Savings and Loan Foundation

Naylor, Robert E.: director, Penn Foundation (William)

Nazemetz, Patricia M.: trustee, Xerox Foundation

Neal, Diane: president, Mervyns, Target Corp.

Neal, Monica: contact,

Nebeker, Carolyn: mem admin comm, Swanson Family Foundation, Inc. (Dr. W. C.)

Nedley, Robert E.: president, duPont Foundation (Alfred I.)

Neeleman, Stanley Duane: trustee, Johnson Foundation (Helen K. and Arthur E.)

Neff, Wheeler K.: assistant secretary, director, CTW Foundation, Inc.

Neff, Zane: director, ShenTel Foundation

Negley, Leslie N.: trustee, Brown Foundation

Negley, Nancy B.: vice president, trustee, Brown Foundation

Negley, W. Walter: trustee, Brown Foundation

Neiger, John: vice president financial, Auburn Foundry

Neill, Rolfe: trustee, Knight Foundation (John S. and James L.)

Neimann, Diane B.: executive director, Bell Foundation (James Ford)

Neish, Francis E., Jr.: trustee, Crawford Estate Trust Fund A (E. R.)

Nejes, Roger: senior vice president financial & administration, chief financial officer, Foster Co. (L.B.)

Nelson, Anne: secretary, treasurer, Marshall Foundation

Nelson, Betsy: director, Baltimore Equitable Insurance Foundation

Nelson, Charles E.: chairman, director, Kirkpatrick Foundation, Inc.

Nelson, Clark: treasurer, McBean Family Foundation

Nelson, David: president, director, Honda of America Foundation

Nelson, David L.: vice president, grant director, Houston Endowment

Nelson, Donald: director, Allyn Foundation

Nelson, Elizabeth: co-trustee, Stuart Foundation (Elbridge and Evelyn)

Nelson, Fredric C.: secretary, director, Cowell Foundation (S. H.)

Nelson, H. Joe, III: president, director, Houston Endowment

Nelson, John M.: co-trustee, Hoche-Scofield Foundation

Nelson, Kirk N.: vice president, Federated Mutual Insurance Foundation

Nelson, Leonard B.: director, McConnell Foundation

Nelson, Marilyn Carlson: chairman, chief executive officer, Carlson Companies, Inc.

Nelson, Virginia: corporate communications manager, TJX Companies, Inc.

Nelson, Wilbur, Jr.: co-trustee, Clarke Trust (John)

Nelson, William E.: director, Kikkoman Foundation

Nelson, William F., Jr.: trustee, Wickes Foundation (Harvey Randall)

Nelson, William O.: director, AMCORE Foundation

Nemirow, Arnold M.: chairman, president, chief executive officer, Bowater, Inc.

Neppl, Walter J.: trustee emeritus, Dodge Foundation (Geraldine R.)

Nero, Vivian: secretary, AT&T Foundation

Nesbeda, Peter J.: corporator, Island Foundation (MA)

Nesbitt, Robert: director, Patron Saints Foundation

Nesbitt, William A.: trustee, director, Meadows Foundation (The)

Neshek, Milton E.: director, Kikkoman Foundation

Nesholm, John F.: director, Nesholm Family Foundation

Nesholm, Laurel: executive director, Nesholm Family Foundation

Nestor, Alexander R.: vice president, trustee, Jones and Bessie D. Phelps Foundation (Cyrus W. and Amy F.)

Netzer, Leon: chairman, Jewish Healthcare Foundation

Neuberger, James A.: vice president, Neuberger Foundation (Roy R. and Marie S.)

Neuberger, Marie S.: vice president, Neuberger Foundation (Roy R. and Marie S.)

Neuberger, Roy R.: president, treasurer, director, Neuberger Foundation (Roy R. and Marie S.)

Neuberger, Roy S.: vice president, Neuberger Foundation (Roy R. and Marie S.)

Neuenfeldt, Bonnie: executive director, Land O'Lakes Foundation

Neustadt, Richard M.: director, Benton Foundation

Nevers, Tom: grant mgr, Bishop Foundation (E. K. and Lillian F.)

Neves, Susan: director, executive committee, Francis Families Foundation

Nevins, Jane: vice president, Dana Press editor, Dana Foundation (Charles A.)

Newberry, Edith McBean: president, director, McBean Family Foundation

Newburger, May W.: trustee, Levitt Foundation (NY)

Newcom, Jennings Jay: assistant secretary, director, Hubbard Foundation (R. D. and Joan Dale)

Newcombe, Margaret P.: trustee, Knapp Foundation, Inc. (MD)

Newell, Marjory A.: vice president, director, Atherton Foundation (Leburta)

Newell, Wanda Y.: director education programs, McCormick Tribune Foundation (Robert R.)

Newhall, Anthony: secretary, Newhall Foundation (Henry Mayo)

Newhall, David S.: president, Newhall Foundation (Henry Mayo)

Newhall, George A.: director, Newhall Foundation (Henry Mayo)

Newhall, Henry K.: director, McBean Family Foundation

Newhall, Jane: director, Newhall Foundation (Henry Mayo)

Newhall, John Breed: trustee, Killam Trust (Constance)

Newhall, Jon: director, Newhall Foundation (Henry Mayo)

Newhall, Roger: director, Newhall Foundation (Henry Mayo)

Newhall Woods, Edwin: director, Newhall Foundation (Henry Mayo)

Newkirk, Diana: trustee, Durfee Foundation

Newkirk, Jonathan: secretary, Durfee Foundation

Newkirk, Judith A.: chairman, Durfee Foundation

Newkirk, Michael A.: vice president, treasurer, Durfee Foundation

Newman, David: trustee, Arnold Fund

Newman, Donald L.: vice president, Newman Family Foundation

Newman, Frances Moody: chairman, trustee, Moody Foundation

Newman, Howard A.: chairman, director, Newman Assistance Fund (Jerome A. and Estelle R.)

Newman, K. Sidney: secretary, Snyder Foundation (William I. and Patricia S.)

Newman, Martha: executive director, Fisher Foundation

Newman, Max K.: president, Newman Family Foundation

Newman, Michael: vice president, St. Paul Companies Inc. Foundation

Newman, Murray H.: vice president, trust, Livingston Foundation (Milton S. and Corinne N.)

Newman, Patricia: trustee, Livingston Foundation (Milton S. and Corinne N.)

Newman, Paul L.: president, Newman's Own Foundation

Newman, Steven E.: secretary, Newman Family Foundation

Newman, William C.: president, director, Newman Assistance Fund (Jerome A. and Estelle R.)

Newnham, Dennis: president, chief executive officer, Tsumura International, Inc.

Newsted, Richard E.: executive vice president, AK Steel Holding Corp.

Newton, J. Michael: director, ONDEO Nalco Foundation

Newton, Jane Norton: vice president, Norton Foundation

Ney, Lillian V.: president, director, Gebbie Foundation

Neys, Alan: director, Campini Foundation (Frank A.)

Neys, Hendrika C.: director, Campini Foundation (Frank A.)

Neys, Patricia: secretary, treasurer, Campini Foundation (Frank A.)

Ng, Ho Yan J.: supervisor administration and budget, Sara Lee Foundation

Niblack, John F., PhD: vice chairman, president global research & development, director, Pfizer Inc.

Niblock, W. Robert: president, director, Porter Paint Foundation, Inc.

Nichols, Barrett: trustee, Brown Foundation, Inc. (James Graham)

Nichols, James R.: trustee, Babson Foundation (Paul and Edith)

Nichols, Kate Cowles: trustee, Cowles Charitable Trust

Nichols, Scott G.: secretary, treasurer, Kelly Foundation

Nichols, William Ford, Jr.: treasurer, Hewlett Foundation (William and Flora)

Nicholson, David A.: director, Daniels Foundation (Fred Harris)

Nicholson, Jan: president, Grable Foundation

Nicholson, Mamie W.: program officer, Self Family Foundation

Nicholson, Marion G.: director, Grable Foundation

Nicholson, William B.: director, Grable Foundation

Nicholson, William S.: director, Daniels Foundation (Fred Harris)

Nickenson, Betty: secretary, trustee, BCR Foundation

Nickerson, E. Carlton: hon director, Kelley and Elza Kelley Foundation (Edward Bangs)

Nickerson, Frank L.: hon director, Kelley and Elza Kelley Foundation (Edward Bangs)

Nickerson, Joshua A., Jr.: director, Kelley and Elza Kelley Foundation (Edward Bangs)

Nides, Tom: treasurer, director, Fannie Mae Foundation

Niekamp, Cynthia A.: senior vice president, chief financial officer, Meadwestvaco Corp.

Nielsen, Jeffrey M.: secretary, treasurer, Good Samaritan

Nielsen, Willard D.: vice president public affairs, Johnson & Johnson; member corporate contributions committee, Johnson & Johnson Family of Companies Contribution Fund

Niemeyer, Ken: trustee, Bedsole Foundation (J. L.)

Niffenegger, Joyce U.: trustee, Hoover Foundation (The)

Niles, Clayton E.: treasurer, director, Spalding Foundation (Eliot)

Niles, Clayton N.: president, Spalding Foundation (Eliot)

Nimick, Francis B., Jr.: chairman board directors, Buhl Foundation (PA)

Nishizawa, Tetsuro: trustee, Subaru of America Foundation

Nisita, Maurizio: senior vice president global operations, Ecolab, Inc.

Nisselson, Allan: director, Goldman Foundation (Herman)

Noble, C.: director, ARCO Foundation

Noble, Edward E.: trustee, Noble Foundation (Samuel Roberts)

Noble, Maria: trustee, Noble Foundation (Samuel Roberts)

Noble, Mary Jane: trustee, Noble Foundation (Samuel Roberts)

Noble, Ted: director, Tyndale House Foundation

Nobles, G. Edmund: director, Haley Foundation (W. B.)

Noda, Hiroshi: director, Kawasaki Good Times Foundation

Noel, Brenda: director, Kurz Family Foundation

Nogales, Luis Guerrero: trustee, Ford Foundation

Nogueira, Gilda M.: clerk, East Cambridge Savings Charitable Foundation

Noha, Edward J.: chairman, CNA Foundation

Nojima, Paul: chairman, president; chief executive officer, Bandai America, Inc.

Nolan, Arthur A., Jr.: chairman, director, Rice Foundation

Nolan, Daniel P.: trustee, Charitable Venture Foundation

Nolan, James: director, Cuneo Foundation

Nolan, Patricia: vice president, treasurer, director, Rice Foundation

Nolan, Peter G.: president, director, secretary, Rice Foundation

Noland, Mariam C.: trustee, Knight Foundation (John S. and James L.)

Noon, Prudence J.: president, Newhall Foundation (Henry Mayo)

Noonan, James W.: secretary, trustee, Levy Foundation (June Rockwell)

Noonan, John: trustee, Schumann Fund for New Jersey

Noonan, T. M.: vice president taxes, Crane Co.; vice president, Crane Foundation

Nooyi, Indra K.: president, chief financial officer, director, PepsiCo Inc.

Norcross, Arthur D., Jr.: director, Norcross Wildlife Foundation

Norcross, Elizabeth: trustee, Baldwin Memorial Foundation (Fred)

Nord, Cynthia W.: vice president, trustee, Nord Family Foundation

Nord, Eric Thomas: trustee, Nord Family Foundation

Nord, Richard: trustee, Nord Family Foundation

Nord, Shannon: trustee, Nord Family Foundation

Norden, William Benjamin, Esq.: secretary, treasurer, director, Eckman

Charitable Foundation (Samuel and Rae)

Nordhoff, Carroll D.: executive vice president, McCormick & Company, Inc.

Nored, Anita: secretary, treasurer, Gardiner Savings Institution Charitable Foundation

Norfleet, Robert Fillmore, Jr.: trustee, Scott Foundation (William H., John G., and Emma)

Norgren, Donald K.: trustee, Norgren Foundation (Carl A.)

Norgren, Leigh H.: president, treasurer, trustee, Norgren Foundation (Carl A.)

Norman, Abigail: director, Norman Foundation

Norman, Andrew E.: member, Norman Foundation; president, treasurer, Normandie Foundation

Norman, Margaret: director, secretary, Norman Foundation

Norman, Rebecca: director, Norman Foundation

Norman, Sarah E.: director, Norman Foundation

Norquist, Helena Miller: president, Miller-Mellor Association

Norris, Bradley K.: trustee, Norris Foundation (Kenneth T. and Eileen L.)

Norris, Harlyne J.: medical advisory, trustee, Norris Foundation (Kenneth T. and Eileen L.)

Norris, John D.: director, Norris Foundation (Dellora A. and Lester J.)

Norris, P. C.: secretary, Meadwestvaco Corp. Foundation

Norris, Robert C.: chairman, Norris Foundation (Dellora A. and Lester J.)

Norris-Szanto, Gillian: program officer, Annenberg Foundation

Northcutt, G.R.: president, National Standard Foundation

Northridge, Mark: trustee, Cogswell Benevolent Trust

Northrup, Sharon: trustee, Gifford Charitable Corp. (Rosamond)

Northrup, Wilhem E.: director, Harriman Foundation (Gladys and Roland)

Norton, Benjamin P.: trustee, Stocker Foundation

Norton, Eileen: vice president, Norton Family Foundation (Peter)

Norton, Patrick H.: chairman, director, La-Z-Boy, Inc.

Norton, Peter: president, Norton Family Foundation (Peter)

Norton, Sara Jane: executive director, Stocker Foundation

Norwood, Ralph M.: president, treasurer, Polaroid Foundation

Nosbush, Mark: chief financial officer, Specialty Manufacturing Co.

Noski, Charles H.: vice chairman, chief financial officer, director, AT&T Corp.

Noss, Stanley: trustee, Barden Foundation, Inc.

Noumair, George: trustee, Heckscher Foundation for Children

Novak, Richard F.: vice president human resources, Cleveland-Cliffs, Inc.

Nowak, Carole M.: treasurer, Firman Fund

Nowell, Lionel L., III: treasurer, PepsiCo Foundation, Inc.

Nowicki, Douglas R.: trustee, McFeely-Rogers Foundation

Nowicki, Sandra G.: president, director, Bettingen Corp. (Burton G.)

Nowland, Frankie: president, director social responsibilities, Borden Foundation, Inc.

Noyes, Elizabeth H.: director, Noyes, Jr. Memorial Foundation (Nicholas H.)

Noyes, Evan L., Jr.: director, Noyes, Jr. Memorial Foundation (Nicholas H.)

Noyes, Henry S.: director, Noyes, Jr. Memorial Foundation (Nicholas H.)

Noyes, Nicholas S.: director, Noyes, Jr. Memorial Foundation (Nicholas H.)

Nozari, Mohamed S.: executive vice president, Minnesota Mining & Manufacturing Co.

Nozzolillo, Anthony: senior vice president financial, chief financial officer, Long Island Lighting Co.

Nuce, Michael: member, Teubert Charitable Trust (James H. and Alice)

Nuernberger, W. W.: trustee, Cooper Foundation

Nunan, Caroline S.: chairman, Steinman Foundation (James Hale)

Nunn, Sam: trustee, Carnegie Corp. of New York

Nunn, Warne Harry: trustee, Meyer Memorial Trust

Nussbaum, Samuel R., MD: executive vice president, chief medical officer, Anthem Inc.

Nutter, Wallace L.: director, Rayonier Foundation; president, chief executive officer, director, Rayonier, Inc.

Nye, Elizabeth: vice president, director, Griffis Foundation

Nyheim, John: director, Penn Foundation (William)

Nylander, Jane C.: ex-officio mem, Henderson Foundation (George B.)

Nystrom, William B.: board chairman, McConnell Foundation

O

O'Brien, Donal Clare, Jr.: trustee, LSR Fund

O'Brien, Francis X.: secretary, trustee, Brundage Charitable, Scientific, and Wildlife Conservation Foundation (Charles E. and Edna T.); trustee, Upton Charitable Foundation (Lucy and Eleanor S.)

O'Brien, John Francis, Jr.: president, chief executive officer, Allmerica Financial Corp.

O'Brien, John M.: senior vice president, New York Times Co. Foundation

O'Brien, Julia P.: trustee, Lockhart Vaughan Foundation

O'Brien, Lallie L.: trustee, Seybert Institution for Poor Boys and Girls (Adam and Maria Sarah)

O'Brien, Michael A.: chairman, McInerny Foundation

O'Brien, Richard T.: executive vice president, chief operating officer, PacifiCorp; member, PacifiCorp Foundation

O'Brien, Robert S.: mem, Hoover Foundation (Herbert W.)

O'Brien, William J., III: trustee, DaimlerChrysler Corp. Fund

O'Connell, Brian: director, Kauffman Foundation (Ewing Marion)

O'Connell, Jane B.: president, trustee, Altman Foundation

O'Connell, Margaret Mary: executive director, Allyn Foundation

O'Connor, Brennan J.: treasurer, Portsmouth General Hospital Foundation

O'Connor, Dennis: president, director, O'Connor Foundation (Kathryn)

O'Connor, Edward J.: secretary, director, Smith Foundation, Inc. (A.O.)

O'Connor, George R.: trustee, Brown Foundation

O'Connor, James John: vice president, director, Brach Foundation (Helen)

O'Connor, Kristen K.: treasurer, Ahmanson Foundation

O'Connor, Maconda Brown: president,

trustee, Brown Foundation

O'Connor, Pamela: executive director, Zachry Foundation (The)

O'Connor, Roxana: trustee, secretary, Andres Charitable Trust (Frank G.)

O'Connor, Sally A.: vice president, executive director, Barnes Foundation

O'Connor, Sarane R.: director, Barker Welfare Foundation

O'Connor, Thomas, Jr.: vice president, O'Connor Foundation (Kathryn)

O'Connor, Timothy M.: secretary, director, Mullen Foundation (J. K.)

O'Dell, Lisa: mem, Teubert Charitable Trust (James H. and Alice)

O'Donnell, Doris: trustee, Allegheny Foundation

O'Donnell, Edith Jones: secretary, treasurer, O'Donnell Foundation

O'Donnell, Francis X.: director, Chicago Board of Trade Foundation

O'Donnell, James E.: president, treasurer, Maneely Fund

O'Donnell, Kerry J.: president, Falk Medical Fund (Maurice)

O'Donnell, Patrick H., Jr.: president, Wright Foundation (Lola)

O'Donnell, Paul J.: trustee, Dodge Foundation (Geraldine R.)

O'Donnell, Peter, Jr.: president, O'Donnell Foundation

O'Donnell, Sandra: president, Wright Foundation (Lola)

O'Dwyer, Deborah: trustee, Weckbaugh Foundation (Eleanore Mullen)

O'Flynn, Thomas M.: executive vice president, chief financial officer, Public Service Electric & Gas Co.

O'Grady, Dennis R.: director, Bank of Greene County Charitable Foundation

O'Hanlon, Helen J.: trustee, Buck Foundation (Carol Franc)

O'Hara, Bonnie: admin, Long Foundation (John F.)

O'Hara, James: trustee, Gund Foundation (Geoffrey)

O'Hara, Margaret E.: vice president, Bank One Foundation

O'Healy, Quill: chairman, chief executive officer, director, Sedgwick, Inc.

O'Keefe, Ann: senior program officer, Davis Foundations (Arthur Vining)

O'Leary, Patrick J.: vice president finance, treasurer, chief financial officer, SPX Corp.; secretary, treasurer, SPX Foundation

O'Maley, David B.: president, trustee, Ohio National Foundation; chairman, president, chief executive officer, director, Ohio National Life Insurance Co.

O'Malley, C.: director, Wharton Foundation

O'Neal, Thelma K.: secretary, Warfield Memorial Fund (Anna Emory)

O'Neil, James E.: vice president technology, Kingsbury Corp.; executive trustee, Kingsbury Fund

O'Neil, John J., Esq.: director, Scherman Foundation

O'Neil, Robert Marchant: director, Commonwealth Fund (The)

O'Neil, Thomas J.: trustee, Cleveland-Cliffs Foundation (The); president, chief operating officer, Cleveland-Cliffs, Inc.

O'Neill, Abby Milton Rockefeller: advisory trustee, Rockefeller Brothers Fund, Inc.

O'Quinn, John M.: president, O'Quinn Foundation (John M.)

O'Reilly, David J.: chairman, chief executive officer, director, ChevronTexaco Corp.

O'Reilly, William M.: secretary, Sentry Insurance Foundation Inc.

O'Rourke, Eileen: treasurer, Abell Foundation

O'Rourke, Joan C.: director, Trust Funds

O'Shanna, Dick: treasurer, vice president, director, Square D Foundation

O'Shaughnessy, Barbara: director, O'Shaughnessy Foundation (I. A.)

O'Shaughnessy, Daniel J.: director, O'Shaughnessy Foundation (I. A.)

O'Shaughnessy, Eileen: director, O'Shaughnessy Foundation (I. A.)

O'Shaughnessy, J. Michael: director, O'Shaughnessy Foundation (I. A.)

O'Shaughnessy, John F., Jr.: director, O'Shaughnessy Foundation (I. A.)

O'Shaughnessy, Lawrence M.: president, director, O'Shaughnessy Foundation (I. A.)

O'Shaughnessy, Mary Kay: director, O'Shaughnessy Foundation (I. A.)

O'Sullivan, Benjamin C., Esq.: trustee, Holtzmann Foundation (Jacob L. and Lillian)

O'Toole, Robert Joseph: chairman, president, chief executive officer, director, Smith Corp. (A.O.); director, Smith Foundation, Inc. (A.O.)

Oakley, Allen M.: director, Oakley-Lindsay Foundation of Quincy Newspapers and Its Subsidiaries

Oakley, David R.: director, Oakley-Lindsay Foundation of Quincy Newspapers and Its Subsidiaries

Oakley, Donald M.: director, Oakley-Lindsay Foundation of Quincy Newspapers and Its Subsidiaries

Oakley, Jimmy: trustee, Priddy Foundation

Oakley, Peter Anthony: secretary, Oakley-Lindsay Foundation of Quincy Newspapers and Its Subsidiaries

Oakley, Ralph M.: director, Oakley-Lindsay Foundation of Quincy Newspapers and Its Subsidiaries

Oakley, Thomas A.: president, treasurer, Oakley-Lindsay Foundation of Quincy Newspapers and Its Subsidiaries; president, chief executive officer, publisher, editor, Quincy Newspapers

Ober, Gayle M.: president, Mardag Foundation

Ober, Richard B.: director, Mardag Foundation

Ober, Timothy M.: treasurer, director, Mardag Foundation

Oberbeck, Christian L.: trustee, Sharon Steel Foundation

Obolensky, Ivan: president, treasurer, director, Hopkins Foundation (Josephine Lawrence)

Obrow, Norman C.: president, director, Drown Foundation (Joseph)

Obser, Fred: trustee, Heckscher Foundation for Children

Ochiltree, Ned A., Jr.: trustee, Meyer Family Foundation

Ochsner, Ronald C., M.D.: director, Copic Medical Foundation

Odahowski, David A.: president, director, Bush Charitable Foundation, Inc. (Edyth)

Oddo, Nancy E.: vice president, director, Dreyfus Foundation, Inc. (Max and Victoria)

Odlozil, Becky W.: executive director, Belo Foundation

Oechsle, Vernon E.: chairman, director, Quanex Corp.; vice president, director, Quanex Foundation

Oehmig, Margaret W.: vice president, Cain Foundation (Gordon and Mary)

Oehmig, William C.: secretary, treasurer, Cain Foundation (Gordon and Mary)

Oelman, Robert S.: trustee, Grimes Foundation

Oestreicher, Ann: president, Oestreicher Foundation (Sylvan and Ann)

Oetzel, Anita: adv comm mem, Moore and Arletta E. Moore Foundation (Kenneth S.)

Offield, Edna Jean: chairman, director, Offield Family Foundation (The)

Offield, James S.: vice president, treasurer, director, Offield Family Foundation (The)

Offield, Paxson H.: president, director, Offield Family Foundation (The)

Offutt, James A.: director, Shelter Insurance Foundation

Offutt, Thomas W., III: secretary, Mather Charitable Trust (S. Livingston)

Ogilvie, Donna Brace: trustee, Brace Foundation (Donald C.)

Ogle, Laura Kerr: trustee, Kerr Foundation, Inc.

Ogletree, Sandy: vice president, director, South Plains Foundation

Ohm, Paul: trustee, Miller Foundation

Ohnmacht, Susan: secretary, Sams Foundation (Earl C.)

Ohnstad, Samuel J.: secretary, treasurer, Anderson Foundation (L. P. and Teresa)

Okada, Natsuo: president, director, SMBC Global Foundation, Inc.; president, Sumitomo Mitsui Banking Corp.

Oken, Loretta M.: program director, Heinz Co. Foundation (H.J.)

Okonak, James R.: executive director, secretary, trustee, McFeely-Rogers Foundation

Olander, Chris K.: executive director, assistant treasurer, JM Foundation

Olberding, David L.: vice president, trustee, Dater Foundation (Charles H.)

Olds, William Lee, III: trustee, Irwin Charity Foundation (William G.)

Olds, William Lee, Jr.: president, trustee, Irwin Charity Foundation (William G.)

Oleson, Donald W.: vice president, Oleson Foundation

Oleson, Gerald W.: president, Oleson Foundation

Olfers, Sarah: advisory trustee, Trull Foundation (The)

Olin, Kent Oliver: trustee, El Pomar Foundation

Oliver, Charles R.: trustee, Fluor Foundation

Oliver, Daniel: trustee, Coleman Foundation (George E.)

Oliver, Louise: trustee, Coleman Foundation (George E.)

Oliver, Melvin: vice president, asset building & community development, Ford Foundation

Olivett, John M.: treasurer, Bank of Greene County Charitable Foundation

Oliviera, Ron: director, Wright Foundation (Lola)

Olmstead, Tommy: manager, Porter Testamentary Trust (James Hyde)

Olmsted, Robert M.: director, Bunbury Co., Inc.; trustee, Windham Foundation

Olney, Richard, III: trustee, Winthrop Trust (Clara B.)

Olofson, Elizabeth: executive director, Guttman Foundation (Stella and Charles)

Olrogg, Elgin E.: vice president, director, Cheney Foundation (Ben B.)

Olsen, Kenneth Harry: trustee, Keel Foundation

Olsen, Thomas S.: treasurer, director, Kelley and Elza Kelley Foundation (Edward Bangs)

Olson, Beverly Knight: trustee, Knight Foundation (John S. and James L.)

Olson, C. T.: vice president, Exxon Mobil Foundation

Olson, Jim: chief financial officer, controller, vice president financial, Rahr Malting Co.

Olson, Neil D.: vice president, treasurer, Verizon Foundation

Olson, Paul M.: president, Blandin Foundation

Olson, R. Thomas: mem, Glaser Foundation

Olsson, John E.: trustee, Cooper Foundation

Olsson, Shirley: vice president, trustee, Olsson Memorial Foundation (Elis)

Olsson, Sture Gordon: president, trustee, Olsson Memorial Foundation (Elis)

Olvany, Karen L.: contact, Guardian Life Insurance Company of America

Olwell, Margaret D.: chairperson, Bamberger Memorial Foundation (John Ernest Bamberger and Ruth Eleanor)

Olwell, William H.: secretary, treasurer, Bamberger Memorial Foundation (John Ernest Bamberger and Ruth Eleanor)

Omachinski, David L.: chief financial officer, treasurer, vice president, Oshkosh B'Gosh, Inc.

Oman, Richard Heer: trustee, Reinberger Foundation

Omohundro, William D.: trustee, Patterson Memorial Trust (Hazel)

Oneglia, Roderic M.: officer, Seherr-Thoss Foundation

Ong, John Doyle: trustee, Knight Foundation (John S. and James L.)

Ono, Masatoshi: chairman, chief executive officer, Bridgestone Americas Holding, Inc.

Opie, John D.: vice chairman, executive officer, director, General Electric Co.

Oppenheim, David Jerome: chairman, director, Dreyfus Foundation, Inc. (Max and Victoria)

Oppenheimer, Deanna: vice president, Washington Mutual Foundation

Oppenheimer, James Richard: director, Tozer Foundation

Oppenheimer, Jesse Halff: assistant secretary, Meyer Foundation (Alice Kleberg Reynolds)

Oran, Stuart I.: president, chief executive officer, United Airlines Foundation

Orders, William H.: trustee, Symmes Foundation (F. W.)

Oreffice, Paul Fausto: trustee, Gerstacker Foundation (Rollin M.)

Oresman, Donald: treasurer, Colt Foundation (James J.)

Orlando, Philip A.: assistant vice president taxation, M/A-COM Foundation

Orlikoff, Richard: secretary, Herald Newspapers Foundation, Inc.; vice president, Southwest News Herald

Ormsby, David G.: president, director, AmBase Foundation

Ormseth, Milo E.: co-trustee, Jackson Foundation (OR); trustee, Tucker Charitable Trust (Rose E.)

Orosz, Florence U.: president, Upjohn Foundation (Harold and Grace)

Orr, Franklin M., Jr.: trustee, Packard Foundation (David and Lucile)

Orr, Michael P.: director, Deere Foundation (John)

Orr, San Watterson, Jr.: chairman, director, Mosinee Paper Corp.; vice president, director, Mosinee Paper Corp. Foundation; chairman, director, Wausau-Mosinee Paper Corp.; director, Wausau Paper Mills Foundation

Orr, Susan Packard: chairman, trustee, Packard

Foundation (David and Lucile)

Orser, William Stanley: executive vice president energy supply, Progress Energy Inc.

Ortenberg, Arthur: don, trustee, director, Claiborne and Art Ortenberg Foundation (Liz)

Ortenberg, Elisabeth Claiborne: donor, director, trustee, Claiborne and Art Ortenberg Foundation (Liz)

Ortiz, Pat: senior vice president, general counsel, secretary, PNM Foundation

Ortwein, Linda G.: trustee, Ratshesky Foundation (A. C.)

Osborn, June Elaine, MD: president, Macy, Jr. Foundation (Josiah)

Osborne, Burl: president publishing division, director, Belo Corp.; chairman, trustee, Belo Foundation

Osborne, Katherine: director, Powell Foundation

Osborne, Richard J.: trustee, Duke Energy Foundation

Osborne, Robert T.: chief operating officer, Icahn Foundation (Carl C.)

Osgood, Edward H.: trustee, Levy Foundation (June Rockwell)

Osher, Barbro: president, Osher Foundation (Bernard)

Osher, Bernard A.: treasurer, Osher Foundation (Bernard)

Ostergard, Paul Michael: president, Citigroup Foundation; vice president, director corporate contributions, Citigroup Inc.

Ostler, Clyde W.: vice chairman, Wells Fargo & Co.

Ostrov, Gerlad M.: member corporate contributions committee, Johnson & Johnson Family of Companies Contribution Fund

Oswald, Ellen: director, member, Smart Family Foundation

Oswalt, William: president, Vicksburg Foundation

Otani, Tim: vice president community relations department, Washington Mutual Foundation

Otero, Carlos: executive director, assistant secretary-treasurer, Piper Foundation (Minnie Stevens)

Ott, Alan Wayne: treasurer, trustee, Gerstacker Foundation (Rollin M.)

Ottaway, James Haller, Jr.: senior vice president, director, Dow Jones & Company, Inc.; member advisory committee, Dow Jones Foundation

Otteman, Merlin G., M.D.: director, Copic Medical Foundation

Otunnu, Olara A.: trustee, Carnegie Corp. of New York

Ouichi, Sadamori: mem allocations comm, Kawabe Memorial Fund

Outlaw, Karen: director, Norcross Wildlife Foundation

Overholt, J. C.: vchairman, Freeport Brick Co. Charitable Trust

Ovrom, Arthur P.: chairman, Van Buren Foundation

Owen, Dolores C.: trustee, Owen Foundation

Owen, Gene V.: trustee, Mayer Foundation (James and Eva)

Owen, Mary Jane: trust, Smith Foundation (William R. and Sara Babb)

Owen, Richard F.: vice president, trustee, Owen Foundation

Owen, Robert E.: president, trustee, Owen Foundation; chairman, president, chief executive officer, Owen Industries

Owen, Rosalyn: secretary, Medina Foundation

Owen-Jones, Lindsay: chairman, director, L'Oreal U.S.A.

Owens, Charlotte Kay: trustee, officer mgr, Harmon Foundation (Pearl M. and Julia J.)

Owens, Samuel H.: treasurer, St. Giles Foundation

Owens, William A.: trustee, Carnegie Corp. of New York

Owings, John R.: vice president, chief financial officer, Air Products and Chemicals, Inc.

Owsley, Alvin Mansfield, Jr.: trustee, Owsley Foundation (Alvin and Lucy)

Owsley, David Thomas: trustee, Owsley Foundation (Alvin and Lucy)

Oxnam, Robert B.: director, Erpf Fund (Armand G.); trustee, Rockefeller Brothers Fund, Inc.

Ozark, Edward L.: vice president administration, assistant secretary, JSJ Corp.

P

Pace, Joann N.: president, Norris Foundation (Dellora A. and Lester J.)

Pacheco, Albert M.: director, East Cambridge Savings Charitable Foundation

Pachon, Harry P.: trustee, Haynes Foundation (John Randolph and Dora)

Packard, Charles E.: trustee, Argyros Foundation

Packard, George R.: trustee, United States-Japan Foundation

Packard, Julie Elizabeth: vice chairman, trustee, Packard Foundation (David and Lucile)

Packard, Ralph K.: director, chief financial officer, Vanguard Group; treasurer, Vanguard Group Foundation

Pacocha, Betty F.: secretary, New Milford Savings Bank Foundation

Padewer, Harvey J.: group president, Energy Services, Duke Energy Corp.

Padgett, Melissa A. Rodgers: trustee, Anschutz Family Foundation

Padilla, Eddie: senior vice president, treasurer, PNM Foundation

Paganucci, Paul Donnelly: director, Fairchild Foundation, Inc. (Sherman)

Page, Arthur B.: trustee, Campbell and Adah E. Hall Charity Fund (Bushrod H.)

Page, Beatrice H.: treasurer, assistant secretary, Ziegler Foundation for the Blind (E. Matilda)

Page, David Keith: trustee, Kresge Foundation

Paine, Walter C.: director, Phillips Foundation (Ellis L.)

Paisley, Beverly: president, director, Bauervic-Paisley Foundation

Paisley, Bonnie: director, Bauervic-Paisley Foundation

Paisley, Charles: director, Bauervic-Paisley Foundation

Paisley, Martha: vice president, director, Bauervic-Paisley Foundation

Paisley, Peter, Jr.: director, Bauervic-Paisley Foundation

Paisley, Peter W.: director, Bauervic-Paisley Foundation

Palantoni, Frank: chief executive officer, Gerber Products Co.

Palenchar, David J.: vice president programs, trustee, El Pomar Foundation

Paley, William Cushing: director, Paley Foundation, Inc. (William S.)

Pallotti, Marianne Marguerite: vice president, corp secretary, Hewlett Foundation (William and Flora)

Palmer, Denise: vice president, strategy & finance, Chicago Tribune Direct Marketing

Palmer, George C., II: president, trustee, Perry Foundation

Palmer, Ian Campbell: director, Beveridge Foundation, Inc. (Frank Stanley)

Palmer, Joseph Beveridge: director, Beveridge Foundation, Inc. (Frank Stanley)

Palmer, L. Guy, II: director, Dana Foundation (Charles A.)

Palmer, Patricia S.: grants admin, Larsen Fund

Palmer, Ralph W.: co-trustee, Baright Foundation (Hollis and Helen)

Palmisano, Samuel J.: president, chief operating officer, director, International Business Machines

Palmore, Roderick A.: vice president, secretary, Sara Lee Foundation

Palumbo, Lillian, PhD: trustee, Snyder Foundation (Harold B. and Dorothy A.)

Pampusch, Anita Marie, PhD: president, Bush Foundation

Panagulias, Robert G.: assistant treasurer, Charity Randall Foundation

Panaritis, Andrea: executive director, secretary, Reynolds Foundation (Christopher)

Panazzi, Donna M.: vice president, secretary, Laurel Foundation

Pancoast, Terrence Russell: secretary, treasurer, trustee, member, Templeton Foundation (Herbert A.)

Pang, Gerald M.: executive vice president, First Hawaiian Foundation

Pansini, F. David: director, Doheny Foundation Trust (Carrie Estelle)

Papasan, Larry: trustee, Plough Foundation

Pappas, Helen K.: director, Pappas Charitable Foundation (Thomas Anthony)

Pappas, John C.: director, Pappas Charitable Foundation (Thomas Anthony)

Pappas, Sophia H.: director, Pappas Charitable Foundation (Thomas Anthony)

Pappert, E. Thomas: trustee, DaimlerChrysler Corp. Fund

Paquet, Joseph F., MD: trustee, Collins Medical Trust

Paras, Philip G.: treasurer, assistant secretary, Seneca Foods Foundation

Pardoe, Charles E.: treasurer, Pardoe Foundation (Samuel P.)

Pardoe, Charles H., II: president, Pardoe Foundation (Samuel P.)

Pardoe, Prescott Bruce: vice president, Pardoe Foundation (Samuel P.)

Pardoe Ballou, E. Spencer: secretary, Pardoe Foundation (Samuel P.)

Pardoe Gray, Elizabeth E.: assistant treasurer,

Pardoe Foundation (Samuel P.)

Parenti, Marlies H.: senior program officer, Kresge Foundation

Parenti, Renato R.: trustee, Arata Brothers Trust

Parisi, Franklin Joseph: chairman, Star Tribune Foundation

Park, Bernard G.: director, Eastern Savings and Loan Foundation

Park, Christine: director, Target Foundation; assistant secretary, Washington Mutual Foundation

Park, Dorothy D.: president, Park Foundation

Park, James Charles: trustee, Besser Foundation

Park, Roy H., III: jr. advisory, Park Foundation

Park, Roy H., Jr.: first vice president, Park Foundation

Parke, Jennifer H.: trustee, Hudson-Webber Foundation

Parker, Alston: director, Williams Family Foundation of Georgia

Parker, Arthur: trustee, Grimshaw-Gudewicz Charitable Foundation

Parker, Bertram B.: director, Gebbie Foundation

Parker, Carol Himmelfarb: director, Himmelfarb Foundation (Paul and Annetta)

Parker, Diane W.: vice president, director, Williams Family Foundation of Georgia

Parker, Franklin E., IV: trustee, Victoria Foundation

Parker, Geraldine M.: secretary, director, Gebbie Foundation

Parker, John: trustee, Victoria Foundation

Parker, Maclyn T., Esq.: president, director, Cole Foundation (Olive B.)

Parker, Margaret H.: vice president, trustee, Victoria Foundation

Parker, Michael D.: trustee, Dow Foundation (Herbert H. and Grace A.)

Parker, Renee: advisory board, Vucurevich Foundation (John T.)

Parker, Scott: president, Peterson Foundation (Hal and Charlie)

Parker, Stephen T.: director, Williams Family Foundation of Georgia

Parker, Tara Biggers: director, Houchens Foundation (Ervin G.)

Parker, Thomas W.: director, Williams Family Foundation of Georgia

Parkinson, Dorn: director, Washington Foundation (Dennis R. and Phyllis)

Parks, Carol S.: mgr, trustee, Sawyer Charitable Foundation

Parks, Floyd L.: vice president, treasurer, trustee, Gilmore Foundation (Irving S.)

Parks, Martin A.: trustee, Robinson-Broadhurst Foundation

Parmelee, David W.: trustee, Howard and Bush Foundation

Parrott, John C., Jr.: director, Audubon State Bank Charitable Foundation

Parrs, Marianne: director, International Paper Co. Foundation

Parrs, Marianne M.: executive vice president, International Paper Co.

Parry, Frances: trustee, Stranahan Foundation

Parry, Gwyn: director, Hoag Family Foundation (George)

Parry, William E.: vice president, general counsel, Ondeo Nalco Co.

Parsley, Georganna S.: vice president, secretary, Strake Foundation

Parsons, Donald: director, Kutz Foundation (Milton and Hattie)

Parsons, Donald, Esq.: director, Kaufman Endowment Fund (Louis G.)

Parsons, Richard D.: advisory trustee, Rockefeller Brothers Fund, Inc.

Parsons, Robert W., Jr.: director, vice chairman, assistant treasurer, section, Hyde and Watson Foundation

Parsons, Roger B.: director, assistant treasurer, Hyde and Watson Foundation

Parsons, William, Jr.: member advisory committee, Weezie Foundation

Partee, Sue Garrett: board mem, Roberts Foundation (Dora)

Partridge, George, Jr.: director, McDonough Foundation (Bernard)

Parvin, Phyllis: president, Parvin Foundation (Albert)

Parvin, Stanley: director, Parvin Foundation (Albert)

Pascoe, William T., III: vice president, treasurer, Oak Tree Charitable Foundation

Pascual, Carlos: trustee, Xerox Foundation

Pasqual, Leandro: director, Harcourt Foundation (Ellen Knowles)

Pastin, Max: president, trustee, Blowitz-Ridgeway Foundation

Pastrana, Glenn M.: research assistant, matching gifts coordinator, ARCO Foundation

Pate, Galen T.: trustee, Bigelow Foundation (F. R.)

Pate, William C.: chairman, BellSouth Foundation

Patel, Homi Burjor: president, chief operating officer, director, Hartmarx Corp.

Paterson, Allan G., Jr.: mng trustee, Rogers Fund for the Arts (Russell Hill)

Patino, Douglas Xavier: trustee, Mott Foundation (Charles Stewart)

Paton, Leland B.: president capital marketings, director, member executive committee, Prudential Securities, Inc.

Patram, Bruce T.: chief financial officer, Acme-McCrary Corp./Sapona Manufacturing Co.; secretary, treasurer, Acme-McCrary and Sapona Foundation

Patrick, Charles F.: treasurer, trustee, Copley Foundation (James S.); executive vice president, chief operating officer, senior management board, Copley Press, Inc.

Patrick, Deval Laurdine: trustee, Ford Foundation

Patrick, Harriet S.: president, director, Fleming and Jane Howe Patrick Foundation (Robert)

Patrick, Michael: director, Norcross Wildlife Foundation

Patrick, Michael E.: vice president, chief investment officer, Meadows Foundation (The)

Patrone, Mary Jane: director, clerk, Boston Globe Foundation

Pattee, Anne L.: secretary, director, Pattee Foundation

Pattee, Dorothy E.: director, Pattee Foundation

Pattee, Gordon B.: president, director, Pattee Foundation

Patten, George: director, Harper Brush Works Foundation

Patterson, Dana L.: chief financial officer, Standard Steel

Patterson, David K.: secretary, Klee Foundation (Conrad and Virginia)

Patterson, David T.: vice president, legal counsel, Wildermuth Foundation (E. F.)

Patterson, James Randolph: trustee, Collins Medical Trust

Patterson, Jennifer: office administrator, Charitable Venture Foundation

Patterson, Marvin Breckinridge: president, director, Marpat Foundation

Patterson, Michael E.: vice chairman, J.P. Morgan Chase & Co.

Patterson, Richard L.: president, Interkal, Inc.

Pattillo, Frank: vice chairman, RBC Centura

Patton, Henry: mgr, Porter Testamentary Trust (James Hyde)

Patton, Thomas V.: trustee, Reeves Foundation (OH)

Patton Westby, Kathleen: trustee, Westby Foundation (Kathleen Patton)

Patzer, Shane A.: director, Abrams Foundation (Talbert and Leota)

Patzer, Tiffany L.: director, Abrams Foundation (Talbert and Leota)

Patzner, Faye A.: assistant secretary, CUNA Mutual Group Foundation, Inc.

Paukstis, John J.: vice president, New England Business Service

Paul, Robert Arthur: vice president, assistant secretary, assistant treasurer, trustee, Berkman Foundation (Louis and Sandra); president, trustee, Fair Oaks Foundation; treasurer, Jewish Healthcare Foundation

Paulaula, Michelle: vice president, trustee, Mosher Foundation (Samuel B.)

Paulick, Raymond S.: secretary, Blood-Horse Charitable Foundation

Paulis, Raymond: trustee, Andres Charitable Trust (Frank G.)

Pauly, Robert L.: chairman, Gellert Foundation (Carl Gellert and Celia Berta)

Pavlicek, Michele D.: assistant secretary, Wickes Foundation (Harvey Randall)

Paxton, Lawrence: vice president financial, Shenandoah Telecommunications Co.; vice president fin, ShenTel Foundation

Payne, James O.: trustee, Berry Foundation (Loren M.)

Payne, John F.: adv comm, Duncan Trust (Louise Head)

Payne, John L. D.: mem, trustee, One Valley Bank Foundation

Payne, Tommy J.: director, vice president, Reynolds Tobacco Company Foundation (R. J.)

Payson, Mary Stone: trustee, Stone Foundation

Payton, Sylvia: program officer, Boston Globe Foundation

Pazol, James L.: co-trustee, Schermer Charitable Trust (Frances)

Peace, N. Brian: secretary, Lowe's Charitable and Educational Foundation

Peacock, John E. D.: president, director, Ayres Foundation

Peacock, John E. D., Jr.: vice president, treasurer, director, Ayres Foundation

Pear, Henry E.: treasurer, Leidy Foundation (John J.)

Pear, Ruth C.: vice president, Leidy Foundation (John J.)

Pearce, Harry J.: vice chairman, General Motors Corp.

Pearce, Jim: treasurer, De Queen Regional Medical Center

Pearce, Thomas: adv board comm mem, Heath Foundation (Mary)

Pearl, Mary Corliss: director, Claiborne and Art Ortenberg Foundation (Liz)

Pearlstine, Jules: assistant secretary, Clemens Foundation

Pearson, Maida S.: chairman, Smith, Jr. Foundation (M. W.)

Pease, Andy, Jr.: chief financial officer, vice president financial, Webber Oil Co.

Peck, Judd: director, Vermilion Healthcare Foundation

Peck, Marni: director, Wahlert Foundation

Peck, Sidney: trustee, Azadoutioun Foundation

Peckham, Eugene E.: secretary, Decker Foundation (Dr. G. Clifford and Florence B.); director, mem adv comm, O'Connor Foundation (A. Lindsay and Olive B.)

Peconi, Maurice V.: vice president, PPG Industries Foundation

Pederson, O. N.: trustee, Griffin Foundation (Rosa May)

Pederson, Sally: director, Mid-Iowa Health Foundation

Pedley, J. Douglas: president, director, French Foundation (D.E.)

Peeke, Richard L.: director, Provident Community Foundation

Peel, Michael A.: trustee, General Mills Foundation; senior vice president human resources, General Mills, Inc.

Peelor, Pamela K., Esq.: co-trustee, Knudsen Charitable Foundation (Earl)

Peeps, Claire: executive director, Durfee Foundation

Peery, Richard Taylor: director, Arrillaga Foundation (John)

Peete, David D., Jr.: trustee, Washington Forrest Foundation

Peete, Lindsey D.: executive director, Washington Forrest Foundation

Peete, Margaret S.: president, Washington Forrest Foundation

Pegues, Elizabeth: director, Grotto Foundation

Pegues-Smart, Elizabeth: 1st vice president, director, Grotto Foundation

Pell, Christopher T.H.: trustee, Hartford Foundation, Inc. (The John A.)

Pell, Eda: president, Pell Family Foundation

Pell, Joseph: chief executive officer, Pell Family Foundation

Pellegrini, Maria: director science engineering and lib arts programs, Keck Foundation (W. M.)

Pellegrino, Allison G.: secretary, Winthrop

Pellegrom, Daniel Earl: board mem, Brush Foundation

Pelphrey, Stephen: trustee, McKinney Charitable Trust (Carl and Alleen)

Pemberton, Gayle: board member, Greenwall Foundation

Pence, Margaret H.: director, Hall Family Foundation (The)

Pendergast, Edward G.: trustee, Bigelow Foundation (F. R.); director, Mardag Foundation

Pendergraft, Neal R.: trustee, Reynolds Foundation (Donald W.)

Penick, Edward M.: board director, Ottenheimer Brothers Foundation

Penn, Milton L.: president, director, Kelley and Elza Kelley Foundation (Edward Bangs)

Pennington, Malcolm: director, Kikkoman Foundation

Pennington, Myriam: trustee, Pennington Foundation (William N. and Myriam)

Pennington, William N.: chairman, Pennington Foundation (William N. and Myriam)

Pennink, Eshowe P.: director, Beneficia Foundation

Pennink, Mark J.: treasurer, director, Beneficia Foundation

Pennoyer, Russell Parsons: president, trustee, Achelis Foundation

Penny, Sylvia V.: trustee, Knapp Foundation, Inc. (MD)

Penrose, S. B.L.: treasurer, Exxon Mobil Foundation

Penta, Phyllis: director, Bay State Federal Savings Charitable Foundation

Peppel, Alan S.: trustee, Hyde Charitable Foundation

Perabo, Fred H.: secretary board control, Ralston Purina Trust Fund

Perachio, Elaine: executive director, Kempner Fund (Harris and Eliza)

Perdue, Franklin P.: president, Perdue Foundation (Arthur W.)

Perdue, James Arthur: chairman, chief executive officer, Perdue Farms; vice president, Perdue Foundation (Arthur W.)

Pereira, Jeanette: secretary, treasurer, Brookdale Foundation

Perella, Frederick J., Jr.: executive vice president, ex-officio trustee, Raskob Foundation for Catholic Activities, Inc.

Perenchio, Andrew Jerrold: president, Chartwell Foundation

Perenchio, John: vice president, Chartwell Foundation

Peretz, Anne Labouisse: director, Clark Foundation (NY)

Perez, Arnaldo: assistant vice president, secretary, Arison Foundation; vice president, general counsel, secretary, Carnival Corp.

Perez, Elsa Vega: program officer, Bremer Foundation (Otto)

Perez, William D.: vice chairman, trustee, Johnson Fund (S.C.); president, chief executive officer, director, Johnson & Son (S.C.)

Perfetto, Carlo M.: trustee, Statler Foundation

Perille, Toni: associate director, Brach Foundation (Helen)

Perkin, Gordon W., MD: senior fellow, global health program, Gates Foundation (Bill and Melinda)

Perkins, Arnold X. C.: director, Haigh-Scatena Foundation

Perkins, Mary T. Bryan: vice president, Carter Foundation (Beirne)

Perkins, Richard C.: director, Holt Foundation (William Knox)

Perkins, Robert E.: admin agent, Beattie Foundation (Cordelia Lee)

Perkins, Roswell Burchard: honorary director, Commonwealth Fund (The)

Perkins, Shirley L.: secretary, Red Wing Shoe Co. Foundation

Perkins Moffett, Jane: board mem, Brush Foundation

Perlmuth, William Alan: president, Harkness Foundation for Dance

Perlow, Charles: dist committee member, Morris Charitable Trust (Charles M.)

Permaul, Jane S.: trustee, Lingnan Foundation

Pero, Perry R.: senior executive vice president, chief financial officer, Northern Trust Corp.

Perpich, Joseph George, MD, JD: director, Greenwall Foundation; vice president grants & special programs, Hughes Medical Institute (Howard)

Perrella, Frank E.: trustee, City National Bank Foundation

Perrin, Joe: controller, Tennessee Valley Printing Co.

Perry, Carrolle F.: trustee, Douty Foundation (Alfred and Mary)

Perry, Marilyn: president, trustee, Kress Foundation (Samuel H.)

Perry, Martha J.: mng director, McCune Foundation

Perry, Mary Mayne: trustee, Toms Foundation (The)

Perry, Robert: program officer, Dodge Foundation (Geraldine R.)

Pershan, Richard, Esq.: trustee, Reuss Memorial Trust (Allene)

Person, Conrad: manager international programs & product giving, Johnson & Johnson Family of Companies Contribution Fund

Pertschuk, Michael: director, Benton Foundation

Pertzik, Marvin J.: secretary, treasurer, director, Griggs and Mary Griggs Burke Foundation (Mary Livingston)

Peru, Ramiro G.: senior vice president, chief financial officer, Phelps Dodge Corp.

Peruski, Charles A.: assistant treasurer, Bank One Foundation

Perz, Thomas R.: president, chief executive officer, Saint Francis Bank; vice president, director, St. Francis Bank Foundation

Pesce, William J.: president, chief executive officer, Wiley & Sons, Inc. (John)

Petas, John: vice president, director, American Honda Foundation

Peters, Alice A.: president, chief financial officer, Peters Foundation (Leon S.)

Peters, Alton Emil: director, Cheever Porter Foundation (Mrs.)

Peters, Darrell: director, Peters Foundation (Leon S.)

Peters, Kenneth: director, Peters Foundation (Leon S.)

Peters, Peter P.: vice president, secretary, Peters Foundation (Leon S.)

Peters, Phillip: vice president administration, secretary-treasurer, Mott Foundation (Charles Stewart)

Peters, Ronald: director, Peters Foundation (Leon S.)

Peters, Ronald Edward: trustee, Pittsburgh Child Guidance Foundation

Petersen, Raymond Joseph: director, Hearst Foundation, Inc. (The); vice president, director, Hearst Foundation (William Randolph)

Petersen, Robert E.: director, Sierra Health Foundation

Peterson, C. D.: director, Peterson Foundation (Hal and Charlie)

Peterson, Carla J.: trustee, Peterson Charitable Foundation (Ellsworth and Carla)

Peterson, David W.: trustee, Lehmann Foundation (Otto W.)

Peterson, Edward M.: Corporate responsibility manager, Commonwealth Edison Co.

Peterson, Ellsworth Lorin: trustee, Peterson Charitable Foundation (Ellsworth and Carla)

Peterson, Jeffrey T.: secretary, treasurer, Lilly Foundation (Richard Coyle); secretary, director, Saint Croix Foundation

Peterson, John S.: secretary, director, Crail-Johnson Foundation

Peterson, Jude M.: trustee, Butler Family Foundation (Patrick and Aimee)

Peterson, Kate B.: trustee, Butler Family Foundation (Patrick and Aimee)

Peterson, Lucille S.: trustee, Lehmann Foundation (Otto W.)

Peterson, Mary E.: officer, Lehmann Foundation (Otto W.)

Peterson, Pam L.: secretary, Swig Foundation (The)

Peterson, Richard J.: trustee, Lehmann Foundation (Otto W.)

Peterson, Robert L.: chairman, chief executive officer, director, IBP

Peterson, Samuel R.: controller, PNC Foundation

Peterson, Wendy Rice: trustee, Baldwin Memorial Foundation (Fred)

Peterson, William E.: general counsel, Sierra Pacific Resources

Peterson, William L.: secretary, director, Ball Brothers Foundation

Petracca, Kim: trustee, Foster Charitable Trust

Petrie, Elizabeth M.: trustee, Greenfield Foundation (Albert M.)

Petrites, Mary E.: grant administrator, MacArthur Foundation (John D. and Catherine T.)

Petrizzo, John: vice president, chief financial officer, Tetley U.S.A., Inc.

Petrone, Joseph Carlton, Jr.: trustee, Henderson Foundation

Petrone, Victor: director, Patron Saints Foundation

Petteys, Robert: director, Joslin-Needham Family Foundation

Petteys, Robert A.: director, Petteys Memorial Foundation (Jack)

Pettinato, Fred: trustee, Alcon Foundation

Pettit, William O., Jr.: treasurer, director, Daniels Foundation (Fred Harris)

Pettitt, Jean W.: president, director, Wharton Foundation

Pettitt, S. D.: director, Wharton Foundation

Pettker, Jack: member, Scott Foundation (Virginia Steele)

Petty, Marty: trustee, Hartford Courant Foundation

Pew, Arthur E., III: director, Pew Charitable Trusts

Pew, J. Howard, II: director, Pew Charitable Trusts

Pew, J. N., III: director, Pew Charitable Trusts

Pew, Joseph N., IV, MD: director, Pew Charitable Trusts

Pew, Mary Catharine, MD: director, Pew Charitable Trusts

Pew, Robert Anderson: director, Pew Charitable Trusts

Pew, Robert C.: trustee, Steelcase Foundation

Pew, Robert Cunningham, II: trustee, Steelcase Foundation

Pew, Sandy: director, Pew Charitable Trusts

Pfaff, Christian J.: president, chief executive officer, Thomasville Furniture Industries, Inc.

Pfaltz, Hugo M.: trustee, Fredrickson Foundation (Ambrose and Ida)

Pfeifer, Shirley E.: vice president, Ewald Foundation (H. T.)

Pfenning, Wayne E.: trustee, Cone Automatic Machine Co. Charitable Foundation

Pfenninger, Elizabeth M.: adv, Cayuga Foundation

Pfohl, James M.: president, Mathis-Pfohl Foundation

Pforzheimer, Carl A.: director, Pforzheimer Foundation, Inc. (The Carl and Lily)

Pforzheimer, Carl Howard, III: president, treasurer, director, Pforzheimer Foundation, Inc. (The Carl and Lily)

Pforzheimer, Carol K.: director, Pforzheimer Foundation, Inc. (The Carl and Lily)

Pforzheimer, Elizabeth S.: director, Pforzheimer Foundation, Inc. (The Carl and Lily)

Pfotenhauer, James: treasurer, Ideal Industries Foundation; chief financial officer, Ideal Industries, Inc.

Phelan, James F.: treasurer, Wilson Foundation (H. W.)

Phelizon, Jean-Francois: chairman, chief executive officer, director, CertainTeed Corp.; president, director, Saint-Gobain Corporation Foundation

Phelps, Don C.: mng trustee, Puterbaugh Foundation

Phelps, Mary E.: secretary, Buckley & Sperling Law Firm Foundation

Phelps, W. H.: trustee, McCasland Foundation

Phibbs, Joan F.: director, member board, Gregg-Graniteville Foundation

Phillippe, Gilbert: adv board comm mem, Heath Foundation (Mary)

Phillips, Blaine T.: president, trustee, Fair Play Foundation

Phillips, Charles R.: vice president finance, National Manufacturing Co.

Phillips, Dan: secretary, treasurer, Griffin Foundation (Rosa May)

Phillips, Daniel Anthony: vice president, treasurer, Weber Charities Corp. (Frederick E.)

Phillips, Edith: vice president, director, Phillips Family Foundation (L. E.)

Phillips, Edward Jay: trustee, Phillips Family Foundation (The Jay and Rose)

Phillips, Ellis Laurimore, III: president, director, mem, Phillips Foundation (Ellis L.)

Phillips, Ellis Laurimore, Jr.: vice president, director, mem, Phillips Foundation (Ellis L.)

Phillips, Gifford: president, director, Chamiza Foundation

Phillips, James: chief executive officer, Management Compensation Group/Dulworth, Inc.

Phillips, James L.: director, Chamiza Foundation

Phillips, Jeanne: trustee, Phillips Family Foundation (The Jay and Rose)

Phillips, Joann K.: secretary, assistant treasurer, director, Chamiza Foundation

Phillips, Morton B.: trustee, Phillips Family Foundation (The Jay and Rose)

Phillips, Pauline: trustee emeritus, Phillips Family

Foundation (The Jay and Rose)

Phillips, Robert G.: director, El Paso Corporate Foundation

Phillips, Rose: trustee, Phillips Family Foundation (The Jay and Rose)

Phillips, Russell Alexander, Jr.: trustee, Lingnan Foundation

Phillips, T. Ward: director, Mid-Iowa Health Foundation

Phillipson, Philip N.: trustee, Wildermuth Foundation (E. F.)

Phipps, Howard, Jr.: director, Noble Foundation, Inc. (Edward John)

Phipps, Mary Stone: vice president, trustee, Achelis Foundation

Piacentini, Carmella V.: administrator, Olin Corp. Charitable Trust

Piano, Evelyn: president, vice president community affairs, Star Tribune Foundation

Picard, William: director, Hedco Foundation

Pichler, Joseph A.: chairman, Kroger Co.

Pichon, Emily E.: secretary, Cole Foundation (Olive B.)

Pichon, John N.: director, Raker Foundation (M. E.)

Pichon, John N., Jr.: chairman, Cole Foundation (Olive B.)

Pick, Albert, III: vice president, director, Pick, Jr. Fund (Albert)

Pickard, Mary: vice president committee affairs, St. Paul Companies, Inc.

Pickering, Thomas R.: trustee, Carnegie Corp. of New York

Pidherny, Dennis N.: assistant treasurer, Dun & Bradstreet Corp. Foundation, Inc.

Piedrahita, Jorge: assistant treasurer, Ford Motor Co. Fund

Piehn, Steffen W.: trustee, Wyomissing Foundation

Piepel, J. D.: director, Bayport Foundation

Pierce, A. Kenneth, Jr.: vice president, chief financial officer, director, Columbus Dispatch Printing Co.; vice president, secretary, treasurer, Wolfe Associates, Inc.

Pierce, C. Fenning: secretary, Schooler Family Foundation (Ohio)

Pierce, John: trustee, Fuller Foundation (MA)

Pierce, Larry S.: director, Kinder Morgan Foundation

Pierce, Thomas M.: trustee, Burnham Charitable Trust (Margaret E.)

Piereson, James, PhD: section, trustee, Olin Foundation (John M.); director, Simon Foundation (William E.)

Piersall, Rick: sr vice president, Roberts Foundation (Dora)

Pierskalla, William Peter: director, Bush Foundation

Piersol, Catherine V.: director, Bush Foundation

Pierson, Joseph A.: trustee, Rockefeller Brothers Fund, Inc.

Pierson, Robert L.: secretary, Leidy Foundation (John J.)

Pierson, W. Michel: president, Leidy Foundation (John J.)

Pierson, Wayne George: treasurer, Meyer Memorial Trust

Pierz, Ann K.: director, Oneida Savings Bank Charitable Foundation

Piesko, Susan: director, Wickson-Link Memorial Foundation

Pifer, Alan Jay Parrish: director, Guggenheim Foundation (Harry Frank)

Piggott, J. Miller: trustee, Bennett Family Foundation (Claude)

Pigott, Dana: trustee, Norcliffe Foundation

Pigott, James C.: trustee, Norcliffe Foundation

Pigott, Mary P.: trust, Norcliffe Foundation

Pildner, Henry, Jr.: trustee, Steinman Foundation (John Frederick)

Pillsbury, George Sturgis, Jr.: trustee, Southways Foundation

Pillsbury, John S., III: president, trustee, Southways Foundation

Pillsbury, John S., Jr.: trustee emeritus, Southways Foundation

Pillsbury, Marnie S.: executive director, Rockefeller Fund (David)

Pinckney, C. Cotesworth: secretary, Scott Foundation (William H., John G., and Emma)

Pincus, Lionel Irwin: director, Ittleson Foundation

Pindroh, Corene L.: trustee, Murphey Foundation (Lluella Morey)

Pineda, Patricia S.: director, Irvine Foundation (The James)

Pinover, Bruce M.: trustee, Chesapeake Corp. Foundation

Piper, William H.: vice chairman, trustee, Mott Foundation (Charles Stewart)

Pirayandeh, Mohammad: director, Alavi Foundation

Pirkle, Linda: assistant secretary, Berkman Foundation (Louis and Sandra)

Pisano, Jane G.: chairman comm res & grants,

trustee, Haynes Foundation (John Randolph and Dora)

Pisarczyk, R. V.: trustee, Exxon Mobil Foundation

Pissocra, Ronald L.: trustee, Reeves Foundation (OH)

Piszel, Anthony: comptroller, Prudential Foundation

Pitcairn, Feodor Urban: executive secretary, director, Beneficia Foundation

Pitcairn, Kirstin Odhner: director, Beneficia Foundation

Pitcairn, Laren: president, director, Beneficia Foundation

Pitcairn, Mary Eleanor: director, Beneficia Foundation

Piteleski, Dan N.: executive vice president, chief information officer, Metris Companies, Inc.

Pitluk, Marvin J., PhD: trustee, Blowitz-Ridgeway Foundation

Pitman, Donne W.: trustee, Chapman Charitable Trust (H. A. and Mary K.)

Pittman, Nancy: executive director, Brown Foundation

Pittman, W. Dayton: director, Hammer Foundation (Armand)

Pitts, C. L.: secretary, Callaway Foundation, Inc.

Pivnick, Isadore: vice president, director, Stulsaft Foundation (Morris)

Pizzey, G. John: director, Alcoa Foundation

Plaeger, Frederick J., II: senior vice president, assistant secretary, general counsel, Burlington Resources Foundation

Planitzer, Russell E.: chairman, Parametric Technology Corp.

Platt, Lewis Emmett: trustee, Packard Foundation (David and Lucile)

Platts, Robin: executive director, Knott Foundation (Marion I. and Henry J.)

Player, Willa B.: trustee emeritus, Mott Foundation (Charles Stewart)

Pledger, Pauline: secretary, Trippe Trust (William D.)

Plimpton, Anne W.: trustee, Kendall Foundation (Henry P.)

Plummer, Michelle M.: chief financial officer, Bank of Greene County Charitable Foundation

Plummer, Roberta S.: director, Holt Foundation (William Knox)

Plym, Andrew J.: director, Plym Foundation

Plym, J. Eric: president, Plym Foundation

Poff, W. Herbert, III: secretary, Plankenhorn Foundation (Harry)

Pogue, John L.: member board administrations,

Wean Foundation (Raymond John)

Pohl, Rachel L.: program officer, Cox Charitable Trust (Jessie B.)

Pohl, Susan Wyckoff: trustee, Norcliffe Foundation

Poindexter, Christian Herndon: chairman, president

Poissant, Gerald R.: assistant treasurer, Taubman Foundation (A. Alfred)

Poitras, Edward: trustee, Poitras Charitable Trust (Dorothy W.)

Poitras, James: trustee, Poitras Charitable Trust (Dorothy W.)

Poitras, Kay: trustee, Poitras Charitable Trust (Dorothy W.)

Poitras, Patricia: trustee, Poitras Charitable Trust (Dorothy W.)

Pokorny, Gene: director, Benton Foundation

Polakovic, Michael J.: vice president, secretary, trustee, Weckbaugh Foundation (Eleanore Mullen)

Polakovic, Therese A.: president, secretary, trustee, Weckbaugh Foundation (Eleanore Mullen)

Polisi, Joseph W.: director, Noble Foundation, Inc. (Edward John)

Politeo, Janet L.: vice president, Glaser Foundation

Polk, Cheryl: executive director, Haas Fund (Miriam and Peter)

Polk, Eugene P.: admin off, trustee, Kieckhefer Foundation (J. W.); trustee, Morris Foundation (Margaret T.)

Polk, Howard: director, Polk Brothers Foundation, Inc.

Pollano, John T., Esq.: treasurer, trustee, Ash Charitable Corp.

Pollard, David R.: director, Fireman's Fund Foundation; officer, Fireman's Fund Insurance Co.

Pollay, Richard L.: vice chairman emeritus, director, Chicago Title Corp.; trustee, Chicago Title and Trust Co. Foundation

Pollock, Davis E.: president, Van Buren Foundation

Pollock, John Phleger: president, Jones Foundation (Fletcher)

Pollock, Robert B.: trustee, Fortis Foundation

Pollock, Samuel: trustee, Jaqua Foundation

Pomeroy, Ellen R.C.: trustee, LSR Fund

Pomeroy, Gay M.: trustee, Mather Fund (Richard)

Pond, Alethea Marder: trustee, Pond Foundation (C. Northrop Pond and Alethea Marder)

Pond, Byron O., Jr.: president, Amcast Industrial Foundation

Pond, Charles N., Jr.: trustee, Pond Foundation (C. Northrop Pond and Alethea Marder)

Pond, Dale C.: trustee, Lowe's Charitable and Educational Foundation

Pontarelli, Tom: director, CNA Foundation

Pool, Peggy Cook: president, Cook, Sr. Charitable Foundation (Kelly Gene)

Poole, Steven W.: trustee, Gerber Foundation

Poorvu, Lia G.: trustee, Poorvu Foundation (William J. and Lia G.)

Poorvu, William J.: trustee, Poorvu Foundation (William J. and Lia G.)

Pope, John Rogers: vice chairman, McMillan, Jr. Foundation (Bruce)

Popoff, Jean U.: trustee, Gerstacker Foundation (Rollin M.)

Popott, Frank: trustee, Dow Foundation (Herbert H. and Grace A.)

Popovich, J. Kristoffer: trustee, Hoffman & Elaine S. Hoffman Foundation (H. Leslie)

Popovich, Jane H.: trustee, Hoffman & Elaine S. Hoffman Foundation (H. Leslie)

Poppleton, Jay K.: trustee, Metal Industries Foundation

Portenoy, Norman S.: vice president, director, Dreyfus Foundation, Inc. (Max and Victoria)

Portenoy, Winifred Riggs: president, director, Dreyfus Foundation, Inc. (Max and Victoria)

Porter, Donald E.: director, Bucyrus-Erie Foundation

Porter, J. Benson: board of directors, Washington Mutual Foundation

Porter, Joann O.: trustee, Knott Foundation (Marion I. and Henry J.)

Porter, John W.: trustee, Mott Foundation (Charles Stewart)

Porter, Martin S.: trustee, Knott Foundation (Marion I. and Henry J.)

Porter, Russell M.: trustee, Bismarck Charitable Trust (Mona)

Portlock, Carver A.: trustee, Seybert Institution for Poor Boys and Girls (Adam and Maria Sarah)

Posley, Steven: trustee, Grimes Foundation

Post, David A.: vice president, Equifax Foundation; corporate vice president, chief financial officer, Equifax, Inc.

Post, Jeffery H.: executive vice president, chief financial officer, chief actuary, Fireman's Fund Insurance Co.

Poston, Met R.: chairman adv comm, Janirve Foundation

Poteat-Flores, Jennifer: trustee, Towsley Foundation (Harry A. and Margaret D.)

Potter, Thomas D.: director, Woods Charitable Fund

Pottruck, David Steven: president, co-chief executive officer, director, Charles Schwab Corp.

Pouliot, Raymond E.: director, Provident Community Foundation

Powell, Ben H., V: director, vice president, Powell Foundation

Powell, Brentnall M.: trustee, Lockhart Vaughan Foundation

Powell, E. Bryson: trustee, Scott Foundation (William H., John G., and Emma)

Powell, John B., Jr.: trustee, Baker Trust (Clayton)

Powell, John Brentnall, Jr.: director, Lockhart Vaughan Foundation

Powell, Joseph B., Jr.: director, Haley Foundation (W. B.)

Powell, Kitty King: director, Powell Foundation

Powell, Myrtis H.: director, Public Welfare Foundation

Powell, Nancy: administrative assistant, Treakle Foundation (J. Edwin)

Powell, Nicholas K.: vice president, Powell Family Foundation

Powell, Paul: director, Intermountain Gas Industries Foundation

Powell, Susan Baker: director, Lockhart Vaughan Foundation

Powers, Edward: foundation managing, trustee, Acushnet Foundation

Powers, John P.: senior director, Educational Foundation of America

Powers, Suzanne L.: director, New Milford Savings Bank Foundation

Pradere, John: secretary, treasurer, Zullig Foundation (Herbert G. and Dorothy)

Prager, William W., Jr.: vice president, Summerfield Foundation, Inc. (Solon E.)

Pramberg, John H., Jr.: co-trustee, Arakelian Foundation (Mary Alice)

Pratt, Abby: vice president, Dickler Family Foundation

Pratt, G. Gerald: trustee, Meyer Memorial Trust

Pratt, Harold I.: trustee, Pierce Charitable Trust (Harold Whitworth)

Pratt, Mitchell C.: treasurer, program officer, Scherman Foundation

Pray, Donald E.: trustee, Bernsen Foundation (Grace and Franklin)

Prechter, Waltraud: president, director, World Heritage Foundation

Prendergast, G. Joseph: chairman, Wachovia Bank of North Carolina NA; director, Wachovia Foundation, Inc. (The)

Prendergast, S. Larry: trustee, chairman, Turrell Fund

Prescott, Ann: treasurer, Brown Foundation

Prescott, Claudia: chief financial officer, Dr. Seuss Foundation

Pressler, Paul S.: trustee, Disney Co. Foundation (Walt)

Preston, Carole: director, Himmelfarb Foundation (Paul and Annetta)

Preston, Jenny Childs: secretary, AKC Fund

Preston, Seymour S., III: director, Barra Foundation

Prestrud, Stuart H.: adv, Archibald Charitable Foundation (Norman)

Price, Allen R.: trustee, Claypool Foundation (Silas and Ruth)

Price, Ann Sage: trustee, Sage Foundation

Price, Carry: director public relations, Liberty Corp.

Price, Charles H.: vice president, Hultquist Foundation

Price, Clement A.: president, trustee, Fund for New Jersey

Price, David B., Jr.: vice president, Goodrich Foundation, Inc. (B.F.)

Price, Donald: director, Whittenberger Foundation (Claude R. and Ethel B.)

Price, Harold: chairman, treasurer, trustee, Price Foundation (Louis and Harold)

Price, Helen Smith: executive director, officer, Coca-Cola Foundation

Price, Morton L.: secretary, Crosswicks Foundation

Price, Pauline: vice president, secretary, trustee, Price Foundation (Louis and Harold)

Price, Samuel P.: director, Lenna Foundation (Reginald A. and Elizabeth S.)

Price, Steven F.: assistant treasurer, Alliant Energy Foundation, Inc.

Price, William James, IV: trustee, Casey Foundation (Eugene B.)

Price, William W.: trustee, Slater Trust (Lillian M.)

Prickett, Caroline J. du Pont: trustee, duPont Foundation (Chichester)

Priddy, Betsy: adv director, Priddy Foundation

Priddy, Randy: adv director, Priddy Foundation

Priddy, Robert T.: trustee emeritus, Priddy Foundation

Priddy, Ruby N.: advisory trustee, Priddy Foundation

Pridham, Herbert H.: trustee, Watson Foundation (Walter E. and Caroline H.)

Priest Rose, Sandra: director, Hebrew Technical Institute

Prime, Meredith: gov, Crary Foundation (Bruce L.); director, Lake Placid Education Foundation; trustee, Weir Foundation (Candace King)

Primus, Melvin R., Jr.: trustee, Fund for New Jersey

Prince, Larry L.: trustee, Campbell Foundation (J. Bulow)

Prince, Robert: treasurer, Home for Aged Men in the City of Brockton

Principi, Amy: director, Wahlert Foundation

Printz, Albert: mem distribution comm, Flowers Charitable Trust (Albert W. and Edith V.)

Priory, Richard B.: chairman, president, chief executive officer, Duke Energy Corp.

Pritchard, Lee E.: assistant secretary, assistant treasurer, Broyhill Family Foundation

Pritchard, Marc S.: president, Procter & Gamble Cosmetics Foundation

Pritzlaff, John C., Jr.: board member, trustee, Olin Foundation (Spencer T. and Ann W.)

Privette, Ray: treasurer, director, Nakamichi Foundation (E.)

Proctor, Mattina R.: trustee, Proctor Foundation (Mattina R.)

Proctor, Venable B.: secretary, O'Connor Foundation (Kathryn)

Proczko, Taras R.: secretary, director, Hartmarx Charitable Foundation

Prohofsky, Dennis E.: secretary, Minnesota Mutual Foundation; senior vice president, general counsel, secretary, Minnesota Mutual Life Insurance Co.

Prosser, Cynthia Phillips: secretary, director, Phillips Foundation (Ellis L.)

Prothro, Caren H.: treasurer, director, Hoblitzelle Foundation

Prothro, Vincent: secretary, treasurer, McDermott Foundation (The Eugene)

Protsch, Eliot G.: director, Alliant Energy Foundation, Inc.

Prout, Curtis, MD: trustee, Campbell and Adah E.

Hall Charity Fund (Bushrod H.)

Prouty, Hillary: trustee, Prouty Foundation (Olive Higgins)

Prouty, Lewis I.: president, Prouty Foundation (Olive Higgins)

Prouty, Richard: trustee, Prouty Foundation (Olive Higgins)

Pruis, John J.: director, Ball Brothers Foundation; executive vice president, director, Ball Foundation (George and Frances)

Pruitt, Gary B.: director, Irvine Foundation (The James)

Prussian, Gordon S.: secretary, Polk Brothers Foundation, Inc.

Pruzansky, Joshua Murdock: secretary, director, Frankel Foundation (Evan)

Pryor, Jeff W.: assistant executive director, Anschutz Family Foundation

Pryor, Millard H., Jr.: managing director,

Puerto, Mariella: project director, Boston Globe Foundation

Puff, Randy A.: vice president, trustee, Gerber Foundation

Pugnetti, Wendy: assistant secretary, Rayonier Foundation

Pulatie, David L.: senior vice president human resources, Phelps Dodge Corp.

Pullen, Dave E.: president, Johns Manville Fund

Pulles, Gregory J.: vice chairman, TCF Financial Corp., TCF National Bank Minnesota

Pulley, Cassandra M.: director, Sara Lee Foundation

Pulliam, Eugene S.: senior vice president, publisher, Indianapolis Newspapers, Inc.

Pulliam, Larry: executive vice president, Noble Foundation (Samuel Roberts)

Pullin, Randolph L.: trustee, West Foundation (Neva and Wesley)

Pulling, Thomas Leffingwell: director, finance, nominations committee member, Luce Foundation (Henry)

Pullo, Robert W.: chairman, chief executive officer, director, Waypoint Financial Corp.; president, trustee, York Federal Savings & Loan Foundation

Purcell, Cindy: member admin committee, executive director operations, Swanson Family Foundation, Inc. (Dr. W. C.)

Purcell, Nancy L.: secretary, Anthem Foundation, Inc.

Purchase, Lara: vice president, Kalkus Foundation

Purkey, Sheila L.: secretary, treasurer, Goldseker Foundation of Maryland (Morris)

Purmort, Francis W., III: director, Van Wert County Foundation

Purmort, Paul W., Jr.: trustee, Van Wert County Foundation

Purnell, John C.: trustee, Yost Trust (J. Paul)

Puryear, Mary: program officer culture & arts, Prudential Foundation

Putman, Gerald: executive director, Decker Foundation (Dr. G. Clifford and Florence B.)

Putnam, David F.: trustee, Putnam Foundation

Putnam, James A.: trustee, Putnam Foundation

Putnam, Rosamond: trustee, Putnam Foundation

Putnam, Theodore I., MD: director, Cummings Foundation (James H.)

Pyle, Edwin T.: director, Mingenback Foundation (Julia J.)

Pyle, Ida M.: trustee, Ward Heritage Foundation (Mamie McFaddin)

Pyne, Eben Wright: director, AmBase Foundation

Pytte, Agnar: director, Fairchild Foundation, Inc. (Sherman)

Q

Quackenbush, Karen: director, Memton Fund

Qualls, T. L.: assistant secretary, Winn-Dixie Stores Foundation

Quammen, David: director, Claiborne and Art Ortenberg Foundation (Liz)

Queenan, Charles J., Jr.: trustee, Evans Foundation (Edward P.)

Queller, Robert L.: trustee, Earhart Foundation

Quick, Elizabeth L.: director, member, Cannon Foundation, Inc. (The)

Quick, Yvonne: secretary, Campbell Foundation (J. Bulow)

Quin, Whayne S.: secretary, director, Wilkes, Artis, Hedrick & Lane Foundation

Quinn, James W.: assistant secretary, Allen Brothers Foundation

Quinn, Jane Bryant: program director, Wallace-Reader's Digest Fund (DeWitt)

Quinn, John: treasurer, Robinson Fund (Maurice R.)

Quinn, Mary: program officer, Avon Products Foundation, Inc.

Quinn, Mary S.: mgr, Sawyer Charitable Foundation

Quintal, Janet: assistant treasurer, Reynolds Tobacco Company Foundation (R. J.)

Quisenberry, Cynthia: trustee, Castle Foundation (Samuel N. and Mary)

R

Rabbino, Robert A., Jr.: director, SMBC Global Foundation, Inc.; joint general manager, Sumitomo Mitsui Banking Corp.

Raber, B.: treasurer, director, Wharton Foundation

Raber, Chester A.: trustee, High Foundation

Rabinovich, Regina, MPH: director, infectious disease program, Gates Foundation (Bill and Melinda)

Radcliffe, R. Stephen: executive vice president, American United Life Insurance Co.

Radcliffe, Sandra: trustee, Providence Journal Charitable Foundation

Rader, I. Andrew: director, Bradley Foundation (Lynde and Harry)

Radosevich, Carol: president, director, PNM Foundation

Radt, Richard Louis: vice chairman, Mosinee Paper Corp.; treasurer, director, Mosinee Paper Corp. Foundation; vice chairman, Wausau-Mosinee Paper Corp.

Raffin, Margaret: director, Ishiyama Foundation

Ragan, Michael: contributions committee, CNA Foundation

Ragone, David Vincent: director, Luce Foundation (Henry)

Rahjes, Doyle Dean: trustee, Hansen Foundation (Dane G.)

Rahr, Frederick W.: president, director, Rahr Foundation

Rahr, Guido R., Jr.: vice president, director, Rahr Foundation; chairman, director, Rahr Malting Co.

Rainbolt, Harold E.: vice president, secretary, SBC Foundation

Raines, Franklin Delano: chairman, chief executive officer, Fannie Mae; chairman, Fannie Mae Foundation

Rainey, Esther: treasurer, Callaway Foundation, Inc.

Rainey, Martha R.: assistant treasurer, Liberty Corp. Foundation

Rainwater, Betty Gregg: president, treasurer, trustee, BCR Foundation

Raisler, Herbert A.: director, Hebrew Technical Institute

Raithel, M. L.: vice president, director, Crane Foundation

Raley, J. Gary: trustee, Johnson Fund (S.C.)

Rambo, Cindy: executive director, Zellerbach Family Fund

Ramo, Simon: director, member executive committee, member grant committee, Keck Foundation (W. M.)

Ramsay, Scott W.: trustee, Shaw's Supermarkets Charitable Foundation; executive vice president administration, treasurer, director, Shaw's Supermarkets, Inc.

Ramsey, David: secretary, director, Trust Funds

Ramsey, Diane H.: vice president, Alliant Energy Foundation, Inc.

Ramsey, Flora J.: president, director, Jackson Family Foundation (Ann)

Ramsey, JoElla: secretary, American Fidelity Corp. Founders Fund

Ramsey, Sam: manager, Porter Testamentary Trust (James Hyde)

Ramsey, Thomas R.: secretary, Toms Foundation (The)

Ramseyer, Roger: vice president, Koch Foundation, Inc. (Fred C. and Mary R.); director community relations, Koch Industries, Inc.

Ramsland, Jane B.: trustee, Beal Foundation

Ranck, Richard G.: trustee, Fredrickson Foundation (Ambrose and Ida)

Rand, Addison Barry: executive vice president operations, Xerox Corp.

Randall, Brett R.: treasurer, Charity Randall Foundation

Randall, James A.: director, board mem, Gregg-Graniteville Foundation

Randall, Rita M.: secretary, Charity Randall Foundation

Randall, Robert P.: treasurer, Charity Randall Foundation

Randall, Robin S.: secretary, Charity Randall Foundation

Randall, Sandra Fleishhacker: director, Fleishhacker Foundation

Randall, William B.: president, Grotto Foundation

Randall, William Lovis: chairman, trustee, McBeath Foundation (Faye)

Randall-Dana, Nancy: director, Grotto Foundation

Randle, Kathryn A.: chairman, trustee, Chatlos Foundation

Randolph, Susan R.: vice president, Benwood Foundation

Randt, Virginia H.: director, Hearst Foundation, Inc. (The); vice president, director, Hearst Foundation (William Randolph)

Rankin, Alex: trustee, Brown Foundation, Inc. (James Graham)

Rankin, William J.: chairman, Whittenberger Foundation (Claude R. and Ethel B.)

Ranney, George A., Jr.: director, Field Foundation of Illinois

Ranney, Phillip A.: secretary, treasurer, director, Second Foundation; counsel, trustee, Young Foundation (Hugo H. and Mabel B.)

Rapaport, Bernard R.: secretary, treasurer, Lowenstein Foundation (Leon)

Rapoport, Leonard: director, Kline Foundation (Charles and Figa)

Rappaport, Daniel: chairman, director, New York Mercantile Exchange; president, director, New York Mercantile Exchange Charitable Foundation

Rappleye, Richard Kent: vice president field services, Mott Foundation (Charles Stewart)

Rappleyea, Holly: secretary, treasurer, Hudson River Bancorp Inc. Foundation

Rapport, Carmi: vice president, Rheinstrom Hill Community Foundation

Rarig, Cynthia K.: trustee, Patterson Charitable Fund (W. I.)

Rarogiewicz, Rick L.: vice president, Eastern Savings and Loan Foundation

Raskob, Anthony W., Jr.: trustee, Raskob Foundation for Catholic Activities, Inc.

Raskob, B. Russell: treasurer, Raskob Foundation for Catholic Activities, Inc.

Raskob, Jakob T.: trustee, Raskob Foundation for Catholic Activities, Inc.

Raspberry, William J.: trustee, Johnson Foundation

Raspe, Phillip A., Jr.: assistant treasurer, Paley Foundation, Inc. (William S.)

Rassas, George: director, Cuneo Foundation

Rassi, Alan J.: vice president, Caterpillar Foundation

Rast, L. Edmund: trustee, member executive committee, chairman, Franklin Foundation Inc. (John and Mary)

Ratchford, Daniel J.: trustee, Snyder Charitable Trust (Harrison C. and Margaret A.)

Ratcliffe, David M.: chief financial officer, treasurer, director, Georgia Power Co.

Rath, Frank E., Jr.: chairman, president, chief executive officer, director, Spang & Co.; trustee, Spang & Co. Charitable Trust

Ratliff, Eugene F.: director, Lilly Endowment

Rau, John E.: trustee, Chicago Title and Trust Co. Foundation

Raub, Philip J.: director, Baltimore Equitable Insurance Foundation

Rawlins, Charles O.: treasurer, assistant secretary, Georgia Power Foundation

Rawls, John P.: trustee, Hyde Charitable Foundation

Ray, Gilbert T.: trustee, Haynes Foundation (John Randolph and Dora)

Ray, James C.: president, Ray Foundation

Ray, John L.: trustee, Jacobson Foundation (Bernard H. and Blanche E.)

Ray, June M.: director, Ray Foundation

Ray, Smith K.: trustee, Beal Foundation

Raymond, Carolyn M.: trustee, McLean Contributionship

Raymond, Charles V.: president, chief executive officer, Citigroup Foundation

Raymond, George G., III: executive secretary, Raymond Foundation

Raymond, Larry: vice president, Memorial Foundation for the Blind

Raymond, Lee R.: chairman, president, chief executive officer, ExxonMobile Corp.

Raymond, Louise: director corporate contributions, McGraw-Hill Companies, Inc.

Rayport, Jeffrey F.: director, Andrews McMeel Universal Foundation

Rea, Paul: trustee, Beal Foundation

Rea, William H.: vchairman, Buhl Foundation (PA); director, Heinz Endowment (Howard)

Reagan, Richard: president, treasurer, director, Norcross Wildlife Foundation

Reak, David R.: director, Metris Companies Foundation

Reali, Joseph A.: secretary, counsel, MetLife Foundation

Reardon, Daniel C.: trustee, Bremer Foundation (Otto)

Reardon, Edward J.: secretary, mem, director, McGee Foundation (MO)

Reardon, Edward J., II: director, Commerce Bancshares Foundation

Reavis, Lincoln: trustee, Smith Foundation (Kelvin and Eleanor)

Reber, Brett: director, Mingenback Foundation (Julia J.)

Rebl, Joseph W.: senior vice president finance, Bryn Mawr Bank Corp.

Reckling, Isla C.: treasurer, trustee, Sterling-Turner Foundation

Reckling, James S.: assistant secretary, trustee, Sterling-Turner Foundation

Reckling, John P.: assistant secretary, trustee, Sterling-Turner Foundation

Reckling, Stephen M.: assistant secretary, trustee, Sterling-Turner Foundation

Reckling, T. R., III: president, trustee, Sterling-Turner Foundation

Reckling, Thomas R., IV: assistant secretary, trustee, Sterling-Turner Foundation

Records, George Jeffrey: director, Kirkpatrick Foundation, Inc.

ReDavid, Suzanne: administration, Publix Supermarkets Charities

Redden, Virgil F.: trustee, Blount Educational and Charitable Foundation (Mildred Weedon)

Redding, S. Steele: vice president, Acme-McCrary and Sapona Foundation

Redding, William H., Jr.: president, director, Acme-McCrary Corp./Sapona Manufacturing Co.; vice president, Acme-McCrary and Sapona Foundation

Reddy, Lata N.: vice president, Prudential Foundation

Redgrave, Martyn R.: executive vice president, chief financial officer, Carlson Companies, Inc.

Redies, Dennis M.: president, Redies Foundation (Edward F.)

Redman, Manville: vchairman, McMahon Foundation

Redpath, Frederick L.: vice president, trustee, Sullivan Foundation (Algernon Sydney)

Reece Tacha, Deanell: director, Kansas Health Foundation

Reed, Barbara, M.D.: director, Copic Medical Foundation

Reed, Charles E., Esq.: consultant, Hathaway Memorial Charitable Trust

Reed, Cynthia: assistant secretary, Hasbro Charitable Trust Inc.; senior vice president, general counsel, Hasbro, Inc.

Reed, George W.: secretary, treasurer, director, Duke Foundation (Doris)

Reed, Hariett: trustee, McBean Charitable Trust (Alletta Morris)

Reed, Marsha L.: secretary, Disney Co. Foundation (Walt)

Reed, Richard W., Jr.: director, Staunton Farm Foundation

Reed, Robert A.: president, chief executive officer, Physicians Mutual Insurance Co.; president, director, Physicians Mutual Insurance Co. Foundation

Reed, Samuel L.: director, Ball Foundation (George and Frances)

Reed, Vincent Emory: trustee, Graham Fund (Philip L.); director emeritus, Strong Foundation (Hattie M.)

Reed, William Garrard, Jr.: director, Simpson Fund

Reeder, Robert M.: trustee, Plankenhorn Foundation (Harry)

Reekie, Robert: director, Tyndale House Foundation

Rees, Samuel: secretary, Amcast Industrial Foundation

Reese, J. Gilbert: chairman, chief executive officer, Evans Foundation (Thomas J.)

Reese, Louella H.: vice president, treasurer, Evans Foundation (Thomas J.)

Reese, Lowell O.: vice president, director, Brillion Foundation; director, Peters Foundation (R. D. and Linda)

Reeves, Charles B., Jr.: president, trustee, Warfield Memorial Fund (Anna Emory)

Reeves, J. Paul: vice president, board mem, director, Gregg-Graniteville Foundation

Reeves, Ken: vice president, administrator, director, International Paper Co. Foundation

Reeves, Margaret H.: president, trustee, Reeves Foundation (OH)

Regan, Lois M.: admin, program officer urban environment, Cary Charitable Trust (Mary Flagler)

Regan, Timothy J.: chief financial officer, Scoular

Co.; trustee, Scoular Foundation

Regenstein, Joseph, Jr.: president, director, Regenstein Foundation

Regino, Rita: vice president, director, Gudelsky Family Foundation (Homer and Martha)

Reich, Charles: executive vice president, Minnesota Mining & Manufacturing Co.

Reich, Laurence: assistant secretary, Brundage Charitable, Scientific, and Wildlife Conservation Foundation (Charles E. and Edna T.)

Reichert, Joshua S.: director environment program, Pew Charitable Trusts

Reichl, Alexander: president, director, Alexander Foundation (Walter)

Reid, J. Marshall: governor, chair, Baker, Jr. Memorial Fund (William G.)

Reid, John A.: trustee, Slemp Foundation

Reid, Robert J.: executive director, secretary, Maddox Foundation (J. F.)

Reidler, Carl J.: trustee, Reidler Foundation

Reidler, Paul G.: president emeritus, Reidler Foundation

Reidy, Janet: director, Memorial Foundation for the Blind

Reidy, Joseph: director, Memorial Foundation for the Blind

Reigle, Thomas J.: vice president, executive director, secretary, Johnson Fund (S.C.)

Reilly, Edward Arthur: vice president, treasurer, Cheatham Foundation (Owen)

Reilly, Marilyn L.: secretary, mgr, Miller Foundation (Earl B. and Loraine H.)

Reilly, William Kane: trustee, Packard Foundation (David and Lucile)

Rein, Catherine Amelia: director, MetLife Foundation; vice president, Metropolitan Life Insurance Co.

Reinberg, Jeffrey D.: senior vice president, Maritz, Inc.

Reinberger, Robert N.: co-director, trustee, Reinberger Foundation

Reinberger, William C.: co-director, trustee, Reinberger Foundation

Reinemund, Steve S.: chairman, chief executive officer, director, PepsiCo Inc.

Reiner, John P.: secretary, treasurer, director, Loewy Family Foundation

Reinhart, M. H.: director, Carpenter Foundation (E. Rhodes and Leona B.)

Reinhold, Peter E.: director, Weber Charities Corp. (Frederick E.)

Reinhold, Roger C.: president, Portsmouth General Hospital Foundation

Reinking, C. William: president, chief executive officer, director, Exchange Bank; director, Exchange Bank Foundation

Reis, Jean S.: vice president, treasurer, trustee, Corbett Foundation

Reischmann, Janis A.: giving contact, Baldwin Memorial Foundation (Fred)

Reising, Richard P.: senior vice president, general counsel, secretary, Archer-Daniels-Midland Co.; vice president, Archer-Daniels-Midland Foundation

Reiss, Vicki: executive director, Shubert Foundation

Reister, Raymond A.: director, Saint Croix Foundation

Reiten, Richard G.: president, chief executive officer, chairman, Northwest Natural Gas Co.

Reitz, Carl F.: secretary, Besser Foundation

Renaghan, Denise M.: executive vice president, director, Bay State Federal Savings Charitable Foundation

Renchof, Sharon A.: assistant treasurer, Bank One Foundation

Reneker, Emily: director, Harper Brush Works Foundation

Reninger, Robert W.: secretary, director, Young Foundation (Irvin L.)

Renken, Susan: trustee, Cooper Foundation

Renner, Tom: director, Lytel Foundation (Bertha Russ)

Renner, Trevor: adjunct director, Educational Foundation of America

Rennie, Renate: president, Tinker Foundation

Rennolds, Edmund A., Jr.: director, Cabell III and Maude Morgan Cabell Foundation (Robert G.)

Reno, Robert H.: trustee, Jameson Trust (Oleonda)

Renyi, Thomas A.: chairman, chief executive officer, director, Bank of New York Company, Inc.

Renzi, Elaine: secretary, Hornblower Fund (Henry)

Repine, John E., MD: trustee, Bonfils-Stanton Foundation

Resnick, Alan H.: treasurer, Bausch & Lomb Foundation, Inc.; vice president, treasurer, Bausch & Lomb, Inc.

Resnick, Sydney: treasurer, Valley Foundation

Resor, James P.: trustee, Southways Foundation

Respess, Gary: director, Tri-County Telephone Foundation

Reuben, Don Harold: secretary, Prentice Foundation (Abra)

Reusch, Belinda Bunnen: director, Norman Foundation

Reusch, Kendrick: member, Norman Foundation

Reusche, Robert F.: chairman, Demos Foundation (N.)

Reusing, Vincent P.: director, MetLife Foundation

Reuter, Carol Joan: chief executive officer, director, New York Life Foundation; vice president, New York Life Insurance Co.

Reutter, James L.: treasurer, Thoman Foundation (W. B. and Candace)

Reveley, Walter Taylor, III: trustee, Mellon Foundation (Andrew W.)

Revere, Elspeth: director general program, MacArthur Foundation (John D. and Catherine T.)

Revson, Charles H., Jr.: secretary, treasurer, Revson Foundation (Charles H.)

Rex, John: president, American Fidelity Assurance Co.; treasurer, American Fidelity Corp. Founders Fund

Reyna, Diane: director, Chamiza Foundation

Reynolds, David Parham: president, director, Reynolds Foundation (Richard S.)

Reynolds, Harold: chairman, chief executive officer, Citizens Union Bank

Reynolds, Heather C.: director, Beneficia Foundation

Reynolds, Jim: board, McKinney Charitable Trust (Carl and Alleen)

Reynolds, Joyce: assistant secretary, Cain Foundation (Effie and Wofford)

Reynolds, Karen M.: manager, McNeely Foundation

Reynolds, Richard Samuel, III: secretary, director, Reynolds Foundation (Richard S.)

Reynolds, Robert Hugh: vice president, secretary, Noyes, Jr. Memorial Foundation (Nicholas H.)

Reynolds, Sigrid S.: director, Strong Foundation (Hattie M.)

Reynolds, Thomas A., Jr.: trustee, Hartford Foundation, Inc. (The John A.)

Reynolds, Timothy T.: trustee, Titus Foundation (C. W.)

Reynolds, William Gray, Jr.: treasurer, director, Reynolds Foundation (Richard S.)

Reznick, Marilyn: vice president education program, AT&T Foundation

Rhees, Carol A.: secretary, Lea Foundation (Helen Sperry)

Rheinstrom, Carrol: president, Rheinstrom Hill Community Foundation

Rheinstrom, Majorie: vice president, Rheinstrom Hill Community Foundation

Rhinehart, M. K.: treasurer, Johns Manville Fund

Rhoads, Edward: trustee, Lingnan Foundation

Rhoads, Katheryn V.: executive director, Hermann Foundation (Grover)

Rhoads, Paul Kelly: president, director, Hermann Foundation (Grover)

Rhoads, R. Carl: trustee, Clemens Foundation

Rhoads, Richard H.: director, NEBS Foundation

Rhodes, Lanier: director, Citizens Union Bank Foundation

Rhodes, Skip: manager corporate contributions, ChevronTexaco Corp.

Rhodes, Thomas L.: director, vice chairman, Bradley Foundation (Lynde and Harry)

Rhodes, William Reginald: vice chairman, Citigroup Inc.

Rhodus, G. Tom: director, trustee, Meadows Foundation (The)

Ribeiro, Carl: trustee, Acushnet Foundation

Ribikawskis, Mary: assistant vice president, assistant secretary, CNA Foundation

Riccobene, Mary: vice president, director, McDonough Foundation (Bernard)

Rice, Charles M.: vice president, CHC Foundation

Rice, Elisabeth: executive director, Fletcher Foundation

Rice, Henry F.: treasurer, trustee, Baldwin Memorial Foundation (Fred)

Rice, J. Elisabeth: trustee, Peabody Charitable Fund (Amelia)

Rice, John W.: director, Unilever United States Foundation

Rice, Liston Michael, Jr.: president, director public affairs, Texas Instruments Foundation

Rice, Lois Dickson: director, Guggenheim Foundation (Harry Frank)

Rice, Mary H.: vice president, HRK Foundation

Rice, Patricia E.: trustee, Peabody Charitable Fund (Amelia)

Rice, Robert V.: director, St. Francis Bank Foundation

Rice, Sheila K.: program mgr, Kemper Foundation

(William T.); program officer, Oppenstein Brothers Foundation

Rich, Frank D., Jr.: president, Rich Foundation Inc.

Rich, Leonard: trustee, Williams Charitable Trust (Mary Jo)

Rich, Marsha E.: trustee, Russell Trust (Josephine G.)

Rich, Robert E., Jr.: secretary, Rich Family Foundation; president, director, Rich Products Corp.

Rich, Robert N.: vice president, Rich Foundation Inc.

Rich, Robert S., Esq.: trustee, Anschutz Family Foundation

Rich, Thomas L.: vice president, Rich Foundation Inc.

Rich, Zan McKenna: director, McKenna Foundation (Katherine Mabis)

Richards, Bruce C., M.D.: director, Copic Medical Foundation

Richards, J. Stephen: grant department administrator, MacArthur Foundation (John D. and Catherine T.)

Richards, Joel, III: vice president, director, El Paso Corporate Foundation

Richards, Thomas W.: vice president, Marpat Foundation

Richards, Yale: asst secy, Livingston Foundation (Milton S. and Corinne N.)

Richardson, Alan: executive director, PacifiCorp Foundation

Richardson, Beatrix W.: trustee, Hillsdale Fund

Richardson, Eudora L.: trustee, Hillsdale Fund

Richardson, Gale: trustee, Priddy Foundation

Richardson, George E., Jr.: chairman contributions, Northwest Natural Gas Co.

Richardson, Joan: director, Bradford Foundation (George and Ruth)

Richardson, Lunsford, Jr.: president, trustee, Hillsdale Fund

Richardson, Robert: president, chief executive officer, director, Unitrode Corp.

Richardson, Sarah Beinecke: director, Prospect Hill Foundation

Richardson, Susan H.: trustee, Holtzmann Foundation (Jacob L. and Lillian)

Richenthal, Arthur: director, Fromkes Foundation (Saul)

Richie, Beth: trustee, Boehm Foundation

Richman, John M.: trustee, Johnson Foundation

Richman, Martin Franklin: secretary, Pforzheimer Foundation, Inc. (The Carl and Lily)

Richmond, Frederick Alexander: secretary, Ducommun and Gross Foundation

Richmond, Charles P.: co-trustee, Arakelian Foundation (Mary Alice)

Richmond, Henry R.: assistant scr, trustee, member, Templeton Foundation (Herbert A.)

Richmond, John: treasurer, Cemala Foundation

Richmond, Julius Benjamin: director, Foundation for Child Development

Richmond, Katherine K.: director, Cemala Foundation

Richmond, Matthew D.: director, Cemala Foundation

Richmond, Merritt: treasurer, Cemala Foundation

Richmond, Ruth B.: president, trustee, member, Templeton Foundation (Herbert A.)

Richwine, Marilyn: secretary, treasurer, Cessna Foundation, Inc.

Rickert, Elizabeth S.: trustee, Sperandio Family Foundation

Rickman, Ronald L.: vice president, director, Lee Foundation

Riddell, Janice B.: program officer, Olin Foundation (John M.)

Ridder, Bernard J.: vice president, Oak Tree Charitable Foundation

Ridgway, Ronald H.: secretary, treasurer, director, Pulitzer Foundation; senior vice president, Pulitzer, Inc.

Ridgway, Rozanne L.: director, Sara Lee Corp.

Ridings, Dorothy Sattes: director, Benton Foundation

Ridler, Gregory L.: director, Beecher Foundation (Florence Simon)

Riecker, John E.: secretary, Towsley Foundation (Harry A. and Margaret D.)

Riecker, Margaret Ann: president, donor granddaughter, Dow Foundation (Herbert H. and Grace A.); president, trustee, Towsley Foundation (Harry A. and Margaret D.)

Riecker, Steven: trustee, Towsley Foundation (Harry A. and Margaret D.)

Riedel, Walter G., III: secretary, treasurer, Stark

Foundation (Nelda C. and H. J. Lutcher)

Rieder, Corrine H., EdD: executive director, treasurer, Hartford Foundation, Inc. (The John A.)

Riedman, John R.: manager, Riedman Foundation

Rieger, Kathryn K.: vice president, Kohn-Joseloff Foundation

Riehl, Margaret K.: trustee, Knott Foundation (Marion I. and Henry J.)

Rieke, Blaine: member advisory board, Johnson Controls Foundation

Rieke, Glenn T.: trustee, Rieke Corp. Foundation

Rieke, Mahlon E.: trustee, Rieke Corp. Foundation

Rieke, William Oliver, MD: executive director, Cheney Foundation (Ben B.)

Riepe, James S.: director, Baltimore Equitable Insurance Foundation

Rifkind, Robert Singer: chairman, Revson Foundation (Charles H.)

Riggs, Judson T.: director, Teichert Foundation

Riggs, Louis V.: chairman, president, chief executive officer, Teichert & Sons (A.)

Riggs, William R.: director, AUL Foundation Inc.

Riker, Bernard: adv, Delano Foundation (Mignon Sherwood)

Riley, Emily C.: executive vice president, trustee, Connelly Foundation

Riley, H. John, Jr.: chairman, president, chief executive officer, Cooper Industries Foundation; chairman, president, chief executive officer, director, Cooper Industries Ltd.

Riley, John: trustee, Raymond Foundation

Riley, Kathleen K.: assistant secretary, assistant treasurer, Mather and William Gwinn Mather Fund (Elizabeth Ring)

Riley, Richard T.: senior vice president, New England Business Service

Riley-Chen, Dottye: secretary, Cummings Memorial Fund (The Frances L. and Edwin L.)

Rimel, Rebecca Webster: president, chief executive officer, director, Pew Charitable Trusts

Rimer, Edward S.: treasurer, Muhlethaler Foundation, Inc. (Jane T.)

Ring, Lucy A.: director, Murphy Foundation

Rintamaki, John M.: group vice president, chief of staff, Ford Motor Co.; secretary, Ford Motor Co. Fund

Rios, Sara: trustee, Boehm Foundation

Rios, F. A.: trustee, Exxon Mobil Foundation

Riser, Mary M.: secretary, Smith, Jr. Foundation (M. W.)

Risner, Ollie J.: vice president, trustee, Stone Foundation (France)

Rissinger, Rollin: president, director, Lebanon Mutual Insurance Co.

Rissinger, Rollin, Jr.: director, Lebanon Mutual Foundation

Ristine, Kenneth I.: program officer, Cheney Foundation (Ben B.)

Ritchey, S(amuel) Donley, Jr.: director, Rosenberg Foundation

Ritchie, Daniel Lee: president, trustee, Buell Foundation (Temple Hoyne)

Ritchie, Kathryn A.: assistant secretary, Greentree Foundation

Ritchin, Hyman B.: director, Hebrew Technical Institute

Ritter, Russ: president, Washington Foundation (Dennis R. and Phyllis)

Ritzen, Evy Kay: director, Meadows Foundation (The)

Rives, S. Bradford: vice president, treasurer, director, LG&E Energy Foundation

Rizley, Robert S.: trustee, Sarkeys Foundation

Rizner, Dean B.: secretary, treasurer, Citizens Union Bank Foundation

Rizzi, Gary: secretary, director, New York Mercantile Exchange Charitable Foundation

Rizzo, Anthony M.: director, New Milford Savings Bank Foundation

Rizzo, Frank M.: trustee, Fox Charitable Trust (Emma R.)

Rizzo, Guy: director, Kennedy Family Foundation (Ethel and W. George)

Rizzo, Robert J.: senior coordinator, Sara Lee Foundation

Roach, Michele C.: assistant secretary, assistant treasurer, trustee, Chatlos Foundation

Roark, Margaret E.: assistant secretary, El Paso Corporate Foundation

Roath, S. D.: trustee, Long Foundation (J. M.)

Robb, Richard G.: director, Park Foundation

Robbins, Barry: trustee, Grimshaw-Gudewicz Charitable Foundation

Robbins, Cathy O.: advisory committee member, Inasmuch Foundation

Robbins, Dianne: secretary, trustee, Fuller Foundation (George F. and Sybil H.)

Robbins, Gerald: corporator, Oak Grove School

Robbins, Jack K.: vice president, secretary, Oak Tree Charitable Foundation

Robbins, N. Clay: president, director, Lilly Endowment

Robers, Ignatius H.: director, Associated Banc-Corp Foundation

Roberson, Dennis: vice president, director, Motorola Foundation

Roberts, Bernadette: program associate, Arca Foundation

Roberts, C. Reid: director, Memorial Foundation for the Blind

Roberts, Dolores A.: director, Hegeler II Foundation (Julius W.)

Roberts, Eugene Leslie, Jr.: director, Andrews McMeel Universal Foundation

Roberts, Frank H.: honorary emeritus trustee, Packard Foundation (David and Lucile)

Roberts, John Joseph: director, Starr Foundation

Roberts, Judith V.: vice president, Morrison Foundation (Harry W.)

Roberts, Kenneth Lewis: president, board member, Frist Foundation

Roberts, Morris S.: treasurer, director, Kornfeld Foundation (Emily Davie and Joseph S.)

Roberts-Lambert, Melanie: program director, secretary, Summerlee Foundation

Robertshaw, Anne B.: director, Robertshaw Charitable Foundation

Robertshaw, John A., III: director, Robertshaw Charitable Foundation

Robertshaw, John A., Jr.: chairman, Robertshaw Charitable Foundation

Robertshaw, Karen: trustee, Locations Foundation

Robertshaw, Marc B.: director, Robertshaw Charitable Foundation

Robertson, Ann: assistant secretary, Francis Families Foundation

Robertson, E. Lorrie: member distribution committee, Bruening Foundation (Eva L. and Joseph M.)

Robertson, Gloria J.: trustee, Miller Foundation

Robertson, Stuart: treasurer, trustee, Doss Foundation, Inc. (M. S.)

Robinett, P. Ward, Jr.: trustee, Beazley Foundation

Robinson, Barbara: treasurer, Staunton Farm Foundation

Robinson, Barbara K.: director, Heinz Endowment (Howard)

Robinson, Barbara Paul: chairman, chairman executive committee, member audit committee, Foundation for Child Development

Robinson, Brent: member, trustee, One Valley Bank Foundation

Robinson, Carol: trustee, Robinson Family Foundation (Donald and Sylvia)

Robinson, Charles N.: director, Kelley and Elza Kelley Foundation (Edward Bangs)

Robinson, Danita M.H.: secretary, Hall Family Foundation (The)

Robinson, Donald: trustee, Robinson Family Foundation (Donald and Sylvia)

Robinson, Elizabeth H.: president, treasurer, Widgeon Foundation

Robinson, Emilie W.: trustee, Wood Foundation of Chambersburg, PA

Robinson, J. Douglas: president, director, Utica National Foundation

Robinson, Jean A.: vice chairman, Buhl Foundation (PA)

Robinson, John F.: trustee, Crowell Trust (Henry P. and Susan C.)

Robinson, John H.: executive vice president, Carter Foundation (Amon G.)

Robinson, Joseph A.: chief financial officer, secretary, treasurer, director, Dura Automotive Systems Inc.; secretary, Dura Automotive Systems Inc. Charitable Foundation

Robinson, Kristy Kay Hoglund: trustee, Hoglund Foundation

Robinson, Leroy: member board advisors, Belk Foundation

Robinson, Lori E.: director, Emerson Foundation, Inc. (Fred L.)

Robinson, Michael J.: treasurer, Illinois Tool Works Foundation

Robinson, Peter A.: trustee at large, Raskob Foundation for Catholic Activities, Inc.

Robinson, Ralph C.: trustee, Surrena Memorial Fund (Harry and Thelma)

Robinson, Richard M.: vice president, Widgeon Foundation

Robinson, Russell M., II: trustee, Duke Endowment

Robinson, Stephen: trustee, Robinson Family Foundation (Donald and Sylvia)

Robinson, Sylvia: trustee, Robinson Family Foundation (Donald and Sylvia)

Robinson, Walter G.: hon director, Kelley and Elza Kelley Foundation (Edward Bangs)

Robinson, Warren L.: secretary, treasurer, director, MDU Resources Foundation; exe vice president, treasurer, chief financial officer, MDU Resources Group, Inc.

Robinson, Winnie M.: president, trustee, Robinson-Broadhurst Foundation

Robison, B. J.: vice president, Pfizer Foundation

Robison, David: trustee, Houck Foundation (May Kay)

Robison, Earl F.: trustee, Houck Foundation (May Kay)

Roby, Katherine W.: mgr, Wilson Foundation (Marie C. and Joseph C.)

Rocco, Anthony: director, Vermilion Healthcare Foundation

Roche, Blanche: trust officer, Hecht-Levi Foundation

Rochelle, Deborah: secretary, Cook, Sr. Charitable Foundation (Kelly Gene)

Rockefeller, David, Jr.: trustee, Rockefeller Brothers Fund, Inc.

Rockefeller, David, Sr.: advisory trustee, Rockefeller Brothers Fund, Inc.

Rockefeller, Laurance Spelman: trustee, LSR Fund; advisory trustee, Rockefeller Brothers Fund, Inc.

Rockefeller, Richard Gilder: trustee, Rockefeller Brothers Fund, Inc.

Rockefeller, Steven Clark: chairman, trustee, Rockefeller Brothers Fund, Inc.

Rockey, Travis O.: vice president, director, Evening Post Publishing Co.

Rockway, Dennis: director, Gumbiner Foundation (Josephine)

Rodecker, Arthur: president, trustee, DeRoy Testamentary Foundation

Rodes, Joe M.: president, trustee, Brown Foundation, Inc. (James Graham)

Rodgers, James R.: trustee, Beatty Trust (Cordelia Lunceford)

Rodgers, William W.: trustee, Beatty Trust (Cordelia Lunceford)

Rodgers Drumm, Susan E.: program ofr, trustee, Anschutz Family Foundation

Rodriguez, Janet: program officer, Dodge Foundation (Geraldine R.)

Rodriguez, Javier G.: cfo, treasurer, Day Foundation (Willametta K.)

Rodriguez, Jay: president, Hafif Family Foundation

Rodriguez, Ramon L.: associate director grantmaking, BellSouth Foundation

Rodriguez, Soraya: director foundation operations & national programs, Verizon Foundation

Roe, Larry C.: director, Oakley-Lindsay Foundation of Quincy Newspapers and Its Subsidiaries

Roedel, Paul Robert: president, Wyomissing Foundation

Roeder, R. Kent: director, Oakley-Lindsay Foundation of Quincy Newspapers and Its Subsidiaries

Roff, John Hugh, Jr.: trustee, Inasmuch Foundation

Rogers, Charles B.: treasurer, Pickford Foundation (Mary)

Rogers, Christopher W.: trustee, Stevens Foundation (Abbot and Dorothy H.)

Rogers, Desiree Glapion: senior vice president, Peoples Energy Corp.

Rogers, Fred McFeely: president, trustee, McFeely-Rogers Foundation

Rogers, Irving E., III: trustee, Rogers Family Foundation

Rogers, Irving E., Jr.: trustee, Rogers Family Foundation

Rogers, Jacqueline H.: trustee, Rogers Family Foundation

Rogers, James B.: trustee, McFeely-Rogers Foundation

Rogers, James E., Jr.: vice chairman, president, chief executive officer, director, Cinergy Corp.; chairman, director, Cinergy Foundation

Rogers, Jeffrey B.: chief financial officer, Indianapolis Newspapers, Inc.

Rogers, Jesse: trustee, Priddy Foundation

Rogers, John F.: trustee, McFeely-Rogers Foundation

Rogers, John W., Jr.: trustee, Knight Foundation (John S. and James L.)

Rogers, Nancy: member grantmaking committee, Claiborne Foundation (Liz)

Rogers, Rutherford David: director, Wilson Foundation (H. W.)

Rogers, Samuel S.: mng trustee, Stevens Foundation (Abbot and Dorothy H.); trustee, Stevens Foundation (Nathaniel and Elizabeth P.)

Rogers, Stephen Hitchcock: trustee, Rogers Family Foundation

Rogers, William R.: director, Cemala Foundation

Rogers-Rice, Gail: gov, Crary Foundation (Bruce L.)

Rogow, Bruce: executive vice president, Rogow Birken Foundation

Rogow, Helen: vice president, Rogow Birken Foundation

Rohatyn, Elizabeth: vice president, director, Rohatyn Foundation (Felix and Elizabeth)

Rohatyn, Felix George: president, director, Rohatyn Foundation (Felix and Elizabeth)

Rohatyn, Nicholas: secretary, treasurer, director, Rohatyn Foundation (Felix and Elizabeth)

Rohlfing, Joan H.: vice president, director, Atherton Family Foundation

Rohm, Robert F., Jr.: secretary, treasurer, Hultquist Foundation

Rohr, James Edward: chairman, chief executive officer, president, director, PNC Financial Services Group, Inc.

Rohrbach, Matthew A.: mem, Teubert Charitable Trust (James H. and Alice)

Rohrback, William: trustee, Harris Foundation (William H. and Mattie Wattis)

Roland, Peter F.: director, Lake Placid Education Foundation

Rolfe, Lee W.: trustee, Norcliffe Foundation

Rolfs, Edward C.: mem, Central Charities Foundation; chairman, president, chief executive officer, director, Central National Bank

Rolfs, Edward J.: mem, Central Charities Foundation

Rolfsen, Carl D.: chairman board, Foellinger Foundation

Romano, Linda E.: director, Utica National Foundation

Romeril, Barry D.: vice chairman, chief financial officer, director, Xerox Corp.

Roof, Donald C.: executive vice president, chief financial officer, treasurer, Joy Global, Inc.

Rooks, Charles S.: executive director, Meyer Memorial Trust

Rooney, Maria R.: vice president, Crosswicks Foundation

Rooney, Patrick T.: advisory committee member, Inasmuch Foundation

Root, Kimberly Lowe: secretary, Lowe Family Foundation

Rooze, M. Ellen: assistant secretary, Anthem Foundation, Inc.

Roper, John L., IV: executive vice president, chief operating officer, secretary, director, Norfolk Shipbuilding & Drydock Corp.

Roper, John Lonsdale, III: president, chief executive officer, director, Norfolk Shipbuilding & Drydock Corp.

Roper, Wayne J.: secretary, director, Bradley Foundation (Lynde and Harry)

Roque, Marcia: member, Staunton Farm Foundation

Rosa, Karen L.: vice president, executive director, Altman Foundation

Rosacker, Jo Helen: secretary, associate director, Richardson Foundation (Sid W.)

Rosand, David: director, Dedalus Foundation

Rosario, Donna: assistant treasurer, Barker Foundation (J.M.R.)

Roscitt, Richard R.: chairman, chief executive officer, ADC Telecommunications

Rose, Deborah H.: trustee, City National Bank Foundation

Rose, Evans, Jr.: trustee, Vesuvius Foundation

Rose, Frances: trustee, Figgie Educational Foundation

Rose, Frederick Phineas: director, Kaufmann Foundation (Henry)

Rose, Karen M.: group vice president, chief financial officer, Clorox Co.

Rose, Matthew K.: president, chief executive officer, director, Burlington Northern Santa Fe Corp.

Rose, Thomas F.: vice president, chief financial officer, Todd Co. (A.M.)

Rosebrock, Charles A.: director, Ladd Charitable Corp. (Helen and George)

Roselle, David P., PhD: trustee, The MBNA Foundation

Rosen, Bruce T.: trustee, Peters Charitable Trust (Edward V. and Jessie L.)

Rosen, Louis: board director, Ottenheimer Brothers Foundation

Rosenbaum, Howard: assistant treasurer, trustee, Heckscher Foundation for Children

Rosenberg, Claude Newman, Jr.: secretary, Rosenberg, Jr. Family Foundation (Louise and Claude)

Rosenberg, Louise J.: president, Rosenberg, Jr. Family Foundation (Louise and Claude)

Rosenberg, Sonia: director, Guttman Foundation (Stella and Charles)

Rosenberger, A. R.: board of directors, Meadwestvaco Corp. Foundation

Rosenberry, Charles W., II: director, Weyerhaeuser Memorial Foundation (Charles A.)

Rosenberry Jones, Lucy: president, director, Weyerhaeuser Memorial Foundation (Charles A.)

Rosenblatt, Roger: director, Greenwall Foundation

Rosenblatt, Toby: director, Irvine Foundation (The James)

Rosenburg, Norman: director, Moriah Fund, Inc.

Rosenfield, Allan, MD: trustee, Packard Foundation (David and Lucile)

Rosenfield, Patricia L.: chair Carnegie Scholars program, Carnegie Corp. of New York

Rosenthal, Alan: trustee, Schumann Fund for New Jersey

Rosenthal, David S.: trustee, Rosenthal Foundation (Lois and Richard)

Rosenthal, Lois R.: trustee, Rosenthal Foundation (Lois and Richard)

Rosenthal, Richard H.: trustee, Rosenthal Foundation (Lois and Richard)

Rosenthal, Robert, Esq.: director, Hebrew Technical Institute

Rosenzweig, Elias: director, Goldman Foundation (Herman)

Rosin, Axel G.: director, chairman emeritus, Scherman Foundation

Rosin, Katharine S.: secretary, director, Scherman Foundation

Rosloniec, James J.: treasurer, trustee, Van Andel Foundation (Jay and Betty)

Ross, Alexander B.: director, Barker Welfare Foundation

Ross, D. P., Jr.: trustee, Fair Play Foundation

Ross, David P.: bank rep, contact, Speas Foundation (Victor E.); trust officer, Turner Charitable Trust (Courtney S.)

Ross, Dickinson C.: vice president, trustee, Jones Foundation (Fletcher)

Ross, Eleanor: assistant secretary, assistant treasurer, Oxford Foundation

Ross, Hal: vice president, Ross Foundation

Ross, John: director, Davenport-Hatch Foundation

Ross, Katherine: executive director, Scherer Foundation (Karla)

Ross, Ralph: vchairman, Valley Foundation

Ross, Robert D.: vice president, Lee Endowment Foundation

Ross, Robert J.: advisory committee member, Inasmuch Foundation

Ross, Samuel D., Jr.: trustee, Kline Foundation (Josiah W. and Bessie H.)

Ross, Sarane H.: president, Barker Welfare Foundation

Ross, Sharryn: trustee, Azadoutioun Foundation

Ross, Tom: secretary, treasurer, American Honda Foundation

Ross, William Jarboe: trustee, Inasmuch Foundation

Rossellini, Isabella: director, Gilman Foundation (Howard)

Rossi, Alice: vice president, secretary, Rossi Foundation (William and Alice)

Rossi, William: president, treasurer, Rossi Foundation (William and Alice)

Rossi-Landi, Beatrice: trustee, Dougherty, Jr. Foundation (James R.)

Rossin, Alan: materials director, Dynamet, Inc.

Rossley, Paul Robert: trustee, McEvoy Foundation (Mildred H.)

Rossway, Melvin: fund comm mem, Kaufman Endowment Fund (Louis G.)

Rosta, Fannie: trustee, Martini Foundation (Nicholas)

Rostad, Lee B.: vchairman, Bair Family Trust (Charles M.)

Rostow, Sheilah B.: vice president, Palmer Fund (Frank Loomis)

Rotan, Caroline P.: secretary, Farish Fund (William Stamps)

Roth, Janet E.: program assoc, Trexler Trust (Harry C.)

Roth, Michael I.: director, MONY Foundation; chairman, chief executive officer, director, MONY Group, Inc.

Rothenberg, Laraine S.: director, Wallace-Reader's Digest Fund (DeWitt)

Rothhammer, Amilu S., M.D.: director, Copic Medical Foundation

Rotholz, Max: director, Gulf Coast Medical Foundation

Rothschild, Walter N., Jr.: hon director, Macy, Jr. Foundation (Josiah)

Rounsavall, Robert, III: trustee, Brown Foundation, Inc. (James Graham)

Rountree, Stephen D.: trustee, Ahmanson Foundation; executive vice president, chief operating officer, Getty Trust (J. Paul)

Rourke, Floyd H.: trustee, Hill Foundation (Sandy)

Rouse, Eloise Meadows: director emeritus, Meadows Foundation (The)

Rout, Robert E.: senior vice president, chief financial officer, S&T Bancorp, Inc.

Routt, J. Robert: vice president, controller, Scripps Co. (E.W.); trustee, Scripps Howard Foundation

Roux, Michel: president, chief executive officer, director, Carillon Importers, Ltd.; president, director, Grand Marnier Foundation

Rover, Edward F.: president, Dana Foundation (Charles A.)

Rovira, Luis Dario: trustee, sociology, Buell Foundation (Temple Hoyne)

Rowe, George, Jr.: president, Ambrose Monell Foundation (The); president, treasurer, director, Vetlesen Foundation (G. Unger)

Rowe, John W.: chairman, chief executive officer, president, director, Commonwealth Edison Co.

Rowland, Jennifer: vice president, Faith Foundation

Rowland, Landon Hill: president, chief executive officer, director, Kansas City Southern Railway

Roy, Madeleine J.: treasurer, Crosswicks Foundation

Royalty, David L.: treasurer, director, Scholl Foundation (Dr.)

Royer, David L.: vice president, treasurer, chief financial officer, director, National Grange Mutual Insurance Co.

Royer, Robert Lewis: trustee, Brown Foundation, Inc. (James Graham)

Rozett, Martha: vice president, Tuch Foundation (Michael)

Rubacka, Kristen E.: director, Emerson Foundation, Inc. (Fred L.)

Rubenstein, Ernest: secretary, director, Guttman Foundation (Stella and Charles)

Rubenstein, Michael: trustee, Valley Foundation

Rubenstein, William H.: secretary, treasurer, Andersen Foundation (Hugh J.)

Rubin, Carolyn D.: treasurer, director, Dettman Foundation (Leroy E.)

Rubin, Donald S.: senior vice president investor relations, McGraw-Hill Companies, Inc.

Rubin, Jane Lockhart Gregory: treasurer, Reed Foundation (NY)

Rubin, Lara R.: director, Reed Foundation (NY)

Rubin, Maia A.: treasurer, Reed Foundation (NY)

Rubin, Pearl W.: trustee, Jones Foundation (Daisy Marquis)

Rubin, Peter L.: director, Reed Foundation (NY)

Rubin, Reed: president, Reed Foundation (NY)

Rubin, Richard: president, Dedalus Foundation

Rubin, Steve: treasurer, Copic Medical Foundation

Rubin, Steven M.: member, trustee, One Valley Bank Foundation

Rubin, Wendy H.: vice chairman, trustee, Bigelow Foundation (F. R.)

Ruby, Paul J.: director, Campini Foundation (Frank A.)

Rude, N. Jean: co-trustee, Hallett Charitable Trust (E. W.)

Rudin, Eric C.: secretary, treasurer, director, Rudin Foundation (Samuel and May)

Rudin, Jack: chairman, director, Rudin Foundation

Rudin, Jeffrey: vice president, general counsel, Millipore Corp.; trustee, Millipore Foundation (The)

Rudin, Katherine L.: vice president, director, Rudin Foundation (Samuel and May)

Rudin, Lewis: vchairman, director, Rudin Foundation; vice president, director, Rudin Foundation (Samuel and May)

Rudin, Mary C.: director, Parvin Foundation (Albert)

Rudin, William: vice president, director, Rudin Foundation (Samuel and May)

Ruding, Herman Onno: vice chairman, Citigroup Inc.

Rudner, Jocelyn P.: trustee, Plough Foundation

Rudy, Dale: corporate trustee rep, Kern Foundation Trust

Ruebhausen, Oscar Melick: chairman emeritus, Greenwall Foundation

Rueckert, William Dodge: chairman fin comm, mem executive comm, director, Dodge Foundation (Cleveland H.)

Ruelle, Mark A.: senior vice president, chief financial officer, treasurer, Sierra Pacific Resources

Ruemenapp, Harold A.: trustee, Besser Foundation

Ruf, Dave G., Jr.: chairman, president, chief executive officer, director, Burns &

McDonnell; chairman, president, director, Burns & McDonnell Foundation

Ruff, Edward C.: executive vice president, chief operating officer, Interstate/Johnson Lane

Ruff, Scott T.: director, Oakley-Lindsay Foundation of Quincy Newspapers and Its Subsidiaries

Ruge, Lois Fisher: vice president, Fisher Foundation

Ruggiero, Anthony W.: executive vice president, chief financial officer, Olin Corp.

Ruh, Ronald R.: trustee, Hitchcock Foundation (Gilbert M. and Martha H.)

Rummel, Mason: executive director, secretary, Brown Foundation, Inc. (James Graham)

Runnells, Clive: director, Gulf Coast Medical Foundation

Runnells, Clive, III: director, Gulf Coast Medical Foundation

Runser, C. Allan: trustee, Van Wert County Foundation

Rupp, Sheron Adeline: vice president, Rupp Foundation (Fran and Warren)

Ruppert, Barbara L.: assistant secretary, Bunbury Co., Inc.

Rupple, Brenton H.: director, Bucyrus-Erie Foundation

Ruslander, Julian, Esq.: trustee, Falk Medical Fund (Maurice)

Russ, Jack: director, Lytel Foundation (Bertha Russ)

Russ, Susan: trustee, Children's Foundation of Erie County

Russack, Richard A.: president, Burlington Northern Santa Fe Foundation

Russell, C. Edward, Jr.: secretary, Portsmouth General Hospital Foundation

Russell, Charles P.: vice president, board of director, Columbia Foundation

Russell, Christine Haas: secretary, program consult, donor, Columbia Foundation; chief executive officer, director, Gaia Fund

Russell, Donald B.: co-trustee, Moss Charitable Trust (Finis M.)

Russell, Frank Eli: trustee, Pulliam Charitable Trust (Nina Mason)

Russell, Fred McFerrin: trustee, Ansley Foundation (Dantzler Bond)

Russell, G. Richard: chairman, trustee, Kiewit Foundation (Peter)

Russell, Jenny D.: executive director, Merck Family Fund

Russell, John A.: director, Kline Foundation (Josiah W. and Bessie H.)

Russell, John G.: director, Consumers Energy Foundation

Russell, Madeleine Haas: president, donor, Columbia Foundation

Russell, Nancy M.: trustee, Pulliam Charitable Trust (Nina Mason)

Russell, Rush L.: vice president programs, Penn Foundation (William)

Russell, Timothy M.: manager community initiatives program, Sara Lee Foundation

Russell-Shapiro, Alice: treasurer, board directors, Columbia Foundation

Russo, Steven: director, Fear Not Foundation

Russom, Mary S.: secretary, treasurer, Vulcan Materials Co.

Rust, Edward Barry, Jr.: chairman, president, director, State Farm Companies Foundation; chairman, president, chief executive officer, director, State Farm Mutual Automobile Insurance Co.

Rust, Judge Lloyd: trustee, Johnson Foundation (M. G. and Lillie A.)

Ruszin, Thomas E., Jr.: treasurer

Rutherfurd, Guy G.: honorary chairman, assistant treasurer, trustee, Achelis Foundation

Rutledge, Jessica L.: administrative assistant, Brooks Foundation (Gladys)

Rutstein, David W.: secretary, Giant Food Foundation; senior vice president, general counsel, chief administrative officer, Giant Food, Inc.

Ryals, Hildegarde: trustee, secretary, Wyomissing Foundation

Ryan, Arthur Frederick: trustee, J.P. Morgan Chase Foundation; chairman, chief executive officer, Prudential Insurance Co. of America

Ryan, Bob: board chairman, Medtronic Foundation

Ryan, Gladys B.: vice president, secretary, treasurer, Ryan Foundation (David Claude)

Ryan, James M.: director, Exchange Bank Foundation

Ryan, Jerome D.: president, Ryan Foundation (David Claude)

Ryan, John Thomas, III: chairman, chief executive officer, Mine Safety Appliances Co.

Ryan, Mark: trustee, Providence Journal Charitable Foundation

Ryan, Patrick G.: chairman, president, chief executive officer, Aon Corp.; president, director, Aon Foundation

Ryan, Stephen J.: director, member executive committee, member grant committee, Keck Foundation (W. M.)

Ryan, Stephen M.: vice president, secretary, treasurer, Ryan Foundation (David Claude)

Ryan Simmonds, Patricia: director, Lesher Foundation (Dean and Margaret)

Ryberg, Claire Dumke: vice president, director, Dumke Foundation (Ezekiel R. and Edna Wattis)

Rylander, Carole: director, Wright Foundation (Lola)

Ryskamp, Charles Andrew: trustee, Mellon Foundation (Andrew W.)

S

Saal, William Dunne: trustee, H. C. S. Foundation

Sabia, Arthur V.: trustee, Statler Foundation

Sabin, Andrew E.: treasurer, director, Frankel Foundation (Evan)

Sachs, Carolyn: director, Benton Foundation

Sack, Kelly: community affairs officer, TCF National Bank Minnesota

Sack, Silver D.: treasurer, West Foundation (Harry and Ethel)

Sackett, John I.: director, CHC Foundation

Sadler, Gale: secretary, treasurer, McMahon Foundation

Sadusky, Gaylord: trust, Citizens First National Bank Foundation

Saeki, Takehiko: director, Kawasaki Good Times Foundation; president, Kawasaki Motors Manufacturing Corporation U.S.A.

Saffold, Gordon E., Jr.: past president, Portsmouth General Hospital Foundation

Safire, William L.: chairman, Dana Foundation (Charles A.)

Sagan, Bruce: president, Herald Newspapers Foundation, Inc.

Saia, Ann M., Jr.: trustee, Saia Foundation (Louis P.)

Saia, Louis P., Jr.: trustee, Saia Foundation (Louis P.)

Saia, Lyndon, Jr.: trustee, Saia Foundation (Louis P.)

Saint-Amand, Cynthia C.: trustee, Chisholm Foundation (M. A.)

Sais, Pat: assistant secretary, Harden Foundation

Sakac, Anne: director, Warwick Savings Foundation

Sakaguchi, Russell G.: president, ARCO Foundation

Sakahara, Toru: mem allocations comm, Kawabe Memorial Fund

Sakrison, James: director, Spalding Foundation (Eliot)

Salanitri, Marie: trustee, Martini Foundation (Nicholas)

Salisbury, John: chief operating officer, Wilkes, Artis, Hedrick & Lane

Salisbury, Lois: director children & families program, Packard Foundation (David and Lucile)

Salizzoni, Frank L.: vice chairman, director, H&R Block Foundation; chairman, director, H&R Block, Inc.

Salomon, Richard E.: secretary, treasurer, director, Rockefeller Fund (David)

Salstrom, Heidi: program manager, Microsoft Corp.

Salter, Lee W.: president, chief executive officer, McConnell Foundation

Salvadore, Eugene Anthony: chairman, administrator, J&L Specialty Steel Charitable Foundation; president, chief executive officer, J&L Specialty Steel, Inc.

Salyer, Richard: vice president, Stamps Foundation (James L.)

Salzer, Richard L., Jr, MD: director, Greenwall Foundation

Sama, Doriann: administrative assistant, Altman Foundation

Samelson, Judy Y.: vice president communications, Mott Foundation (Charles Stewart)

Sampson, Glenda: adv comm mem, Moore and Arletta E. Moore Foundation (Kenneth S.)

Samson, D. H.: assistant treasurer, Exxon Mobil Foundation

Samuels, Victoria Woolner: director, Newman Assistance Fund (Jerome A. and Estelle R.)

Sanborn, J. Gregg: trustee, Foundation for Seacoast Health

Sanborn, Lorraine: director, Provident Community Foundation

Sandalls, William Thomas, Jr.: senior vice president, chief financial officer, Dreyfus Corp.

Sandbach, George A.: director, Borkee-Hagley Foundation

Sandberg, Nancy B.: chairman, director, Boss Foundation

Sandberg, Paul W.: treasurer, director, Gebbie Foundation

Sanders, Charles Addison: chairman board directors, Commonwealth Fund (The)

Sanders, D. Faye: senior vice president, Citizens Charitable Foundation

Sanders, John W.: trustee, Cleveland-Cliffs Foundation (The); senior vice president, international development, Cleveland-Cliffs, Inc.

Sanders, Wayne R.: chairman, Kimberly-Clark Corp.

Sandler, David P.: secretary, Arcadia Foundation

Sandler, Malvin Gustav: trustee, Sharon Steel Foundation

Sandman, Dan D.: senior vice president human resources, secretary, general counsel, U.S. Steel Corp.; trustee, U.S. Steel Foundation

Sandman, John B.: executive vice president, chief operating officer, Teichert & Sons (A.)

Sando, Joe: director, Chamiza Foundation

Sanford, Claire C.: trustee, Baldwin Memorial Foundation (Fred)

Sanford, Kay: trustee, CH Foundation

Sanford, Laura: president, SBC Foundation

Sanford, Mary Cameron: trustee, Baldwin Memorial Foundation (Fred)

Sang, Bernard: secretary, Sang Foundation (Elsie O. and Philip D.)

Sang, Donald: assistant secretary, Sang Foundation (Elsie O. and Philip D.)

Sang, Elsie O.: president, Sang Foundation (Elsie O. and Philip D.)

Sanger, Michael: member, JM Foundation

Sanger, Stephen W.: chairman, chief executive officer, General Mills Foundation; chairman, chief executive officer, director, General Mills, Inc.

Sanobe, Takashi: senior chief executive officer, chairman, Mitsubishi Motor Sales of America, Inc.

Santangelo, Joseph A.: vice president, treasurer, Arkell Hall Foundation

Santos, John F., PhD: trustee, Retirement Research Foundation

Sapp, Charles: vice president, Kayser Foundation

Saraya, Yusuke: trustee, board secretary, United States-Japan Foundation

Sargent, Allison: grant program manager, Calder Foundation (Louis)

Sargent, Hugh A. A., Esq.: president, mgr, Ludwick Foundation (Christopher)

Sargent, John A.: trustee, Bloedorn Foundation (Walter A.)

Sargent, Joseph Dudley: president, chief executive officer, director, Guardian Life Insurance Company of America

Sargent, Kevin J.: director, Oakley-Lindsay Foundation of Quincy Newspapers and Its Subsidiaries

Sargent, Newell B.: trustee, Sargent Foundation (Newell B.)

Sarofim, Christopher B.: trustee, Brown Foundation

Sarofim, Louisa Stude: vice president, trustee, Brown Foundation

Saroni, Louis, II: vice president, treasurer, Zellerbach Family Fund

Sarrow, Robert D.: secretary, Kantzler Foundation

Sartwelle, James D., Sr.: chairman, George Foundation

Sarver, James H.: vice president, Hunnicutt Foundation (H. P. and Anne S.)

Sarver, James H., II: treasurer, Hunnicutt Foundation (H. P. and Anne S.)

Sasakawa, Yohei: trustee, United States-Japan Foundation

Sasiela, Joseph: vice president, Kantzler Foundation

Sasser, Barbara Weston: secretary, Kempner Fund (Harris and Eliza)

Sasso, John: director, Fannie Mae Foundation

Sato, Suzanne M.: vice president arts & culture program, AT&T Foundation

Satterfield, Byron K.: treasurer, Bowen Foundation (Ethel N.)

Satterlee, Ellen: treasurer, Wege Foundation

Sauer, William: vice president, S.G. Foundation

Saul, Bernard Francis, II: mem, Olmsted Foundation (George and Carol)

Saunders, Sarah W.: clerk, Cabot Corp. Foundation

Saunders, Theresa J.: treasurer, Portsmouth General Hospital Foundation

Sauvayre, Sara Chubb: trustee, Victoria Foundation

Savage, Arthur V., Esq.: treasurer, gov, trustee, Crary Foundation (Bruce L.)

Savage, Horace S., Jr.: director, Portsmouth General Hospital Foundation

Savage, Toy D., Jr.: secretary, treasurer, director, North Shore Foundation

Savageau, Judy: director, Memorial Foundation for the Blind

Schornack, John James: trustee, Graham Foundation for Advanced Studies in the Fine Arts

Schorrak, Walter: director, Schoenleber Foundation

Schott, Milton B., Jr.: trustee, H. C. S. Foundation

Schram, Earl: director, Hudson River Bancorp Inc. Foundation

Schram, Earl, Jr.: director, Hudson River Bancorp Inc. Foundation

Schramm, Carl J.: president, chief executive officer, director, Kauffman Foundation (Ewing Marion)

Schrempp, Jurgen E.: chairman, DaimlerChrysler AG

Schrickel, Patrick D.: vice president, WPS Resources Foundation, Inc.

Schroeder, Charles Edgar: president, director, McCormick Foundation (Chauncey and Marion Deering)

Schroeder, Diane: director, Dell Foundation (Hazel)

Schroeder, W. Craig: executive director, trustee, The MBNA Foundation

Schroth, Virginia Cowles: trustee, Cowles Charitable Trust

Schubert, Arthur: vice president, Windham Foundation

Schubert, James, MD: director, Sierra Health Foundation

Schuberth, Kenneth S.: president, Wilson Sanitarium for Children of Baltimore City (Thomas)

Schucht, Carolyn: director, Ziegler Foundation

Schueler, John R.: publisher, president, McClatchy Co.

Schuette, William D.: vice president, trustee, Gerstacker Foundation (Rollin M.)

Schuh, Dale R.: president, chief executive officer, chairman, Sentry Insurance, A Mutual Co.

Schullinger, John N., MD: trustee, Edison Fund (Charles)

Schulte, Anthony M.: director, Scherman Foundation

Schulte, Stephanie J.: secretary, trustee, Spahr Family Foundation

Schulte, William D.: director, Weingart Foundation

Schulten, Warren R.: vice president, Miller Foundation (Earl B. and Loraine H.)

Schultz, Ann V.: director, Woronoco Savings Charitable Foundation

Schultz, Larry G.: vice president, comptroller, U.S. Steel Foundation

Schultz, Randy: director, Intermountain Gas Industries Foundation

Schultz, Rhoda: director, The Bothin Foundation

Schulz, Ralph G.: president, director, Wehr Foundation (Todd)

Schumacher, J. Donald: trustee, Cornell Trust (Peter C.)

Schumacher, Katharina E.: secretary, treasurer, Buhl Foundation (PA)

Schumacher, Robert: trustee, Smoot Charitable Trust (Frank Litz)

Schuman, Allan L.: chairman, chief executive officer, director, Ecolab, Inc.

Schundler, Eloise: assistant secretary, director, Vernon Foundation (Miles Hodsdon)

Schurz, James Montgomery: president, Schurz Communications Foundation

Schurz, Todd F.: vice president, Schurz Communications Foundation; president, publisher, editor, director, South Bend Tribune Corp.

Schwab, Charles R.: chairman, co-chief executive officer, director, Charles Schwab Corp.; chairman, Schwab Corp. Foundation (Charles)

Schwab, Cindy A.: vice president, Abbott Laboratories Fund

Schwab, Roger: director, Hedco Foundation

Schwabacher, Christopher C.: director, Goldman Foundation (Herman)

Schwander, Stephen S.: director, Vogler Foundation (Laura B.)

Schwanfelder, Nancy Healy: secretary, director, Dumke Foundation (Ezekiel R. and Edna Wattis)

Schwanke, Jodie: vice president, Faith Foundation

Schwanke, Lawrence E.: trustee, Bemis Co. Foundation

Schwartz, Arthur L.: vice president, Landegger Charitable Foundation

Schwartz, Carol Levitt: director, Strong Foundation (Hattie M.)

Schwartz, Carol List: director, List Foundation (Albert A.)

Schwartz, Marie D.: president, Schwartz Fund for Education and Health Research (Arnold and Marie)

Schwartz, Milton: trustee, Mex-Am Cultural Foundation

Schwartz, Renee Gerstler: secretary-treasurer, director, New-Land Foundation

Schwartz, Stephen L.: president, Brookdale Foundation

Schwartz, Steven J.: trustee, Shatz, Schwartz & Fentin Charitable Foundation; senior partner, Shatz, Schwartz & Fentin PC

Schwarz, H. Marshall: chairman, chief executive officer, United States Trust Co. of New York

Schwarzkopf, Kurt: corporate secretary, St. Paul Companies Inc. Foundation

Schweid, Edward: chairman, Fox Charitable Trust (Emma R.)

Schweitzer, Catherine F.: foundation manager, Baird Foundation

Schweitzer, Peter A.: president, Thompson Co. (J. Walter)

Schweizer, Paul A.: trustee, Hilliard Foundation

Schwendener, Benjamin O., Jr.: president, secretary, Thoman Foundation (W. B. and Candace)

Schwertfeger, Timothy R.: chairman, chief executive officer, Nuveen Co. (The John)

Scicutella, John Vincent: trustee, J.P. Morgan Chase Foundation

Scirica, Anthony J.: director, Penn Foundation (William)

Scott, Bruce K.: director, Olmsted Foundation (George and Carol)

Scott, Cornell: chairman, trustee, New Haven Savings Bank Foundation, Inc.

Scott, D. Dwight: executive vice president, El Paso Corporate Foundation; executive vice president, chief financial officer, El Paso Corp.

Scott, Edgar, Jr.: director, Cheever Porter Foundation (Mrs.)

Scott, Eileen: treasurer, assistant secretary, Mellon Foundation (Andrew W.)

Scott, Frank L.: chairman board trustees, Baker Foundation (R. C.)

Scott, George A.: president,

Scott, Mark J.: director, vice president, Saint-Gobain Corporation Foundation

Scott, Nadya Ann Kozmetsky: vice president, trustee, RGK Foundation

Scott, Peter M., III: treasurer, director, Progress Energy Foundation

Scott, Sally: program director, Goldseker Foundation of Maryland (Morris)

Scott, Tom: director, Potts and Sibley Foundation

Scott, Walter, Jr.: chairman emeritus, Kiewit Companies Foundation

Scott, Wesley L.: director, Cudahy Fund (Patrick and Anna M.)

Scott, William C.: director, Newman Assistance Fund (Jerome A. and Estelle R.)

Scoville, Thomas W.: director, Public Welfare Foundation

Scribner, Beth: program officer, Educational Foundation of America

Scribner, Charles, III: vice president, trustee, Homeland Foundation (NY)

Scripps, Charles Edward: chairman executive committee, director, Scripps Co. (E.W.); member, Scripps Howard Foundation

Scripps, Edward Wyllis, II: member, Scripps Howard Foundation

Scripps, Maggie: trustee, Scripps Howard Foundation

Scripps, Paul K.: vice president, director, Scripps Co. (E.W.); trustee, Scripps Howard Foundation

Scsaurszki, Tamas A.: program officer, Mott Foundation (Charles Stewart)

Seabury, Charlene Brown: executive secretary, trustee, Seabury Foundation

Seabury, David D.: trustee, Seabury Foundation

Seale, Pete: trust, Elkins, Jr. Foundation (Margaret and James A.)

Seaman, Elizabeth D.: consult, Morgan and Samuel Tate Morgan, Jr. Foundation (Marietta McNeill)

Seaman, Irving, Jr.: director, Demos Foundation (N.)

Sear, Robert: trustee, Yost Trust (J. Paul)

Sear, Timothy R. G.: trustee, Alcon Foundation; president, chief executive officer, Alcon Laboratories, Inc.

Sears, Marvin L.: director, Ziegler Foundation for the Blind (E. Matilda)

Seay, Nancy Clements: vice president, Clements Foundation

Sebastian, Audrey M.: trustee, Sebastian Foundation

Sebastian, David S.: trustee, Sebastian Foundation

Sebastian, John O.: trustee, Sebastian Foundation

Sebastiano, Patrick A.: director, Beecher Foundation (Florence Simon)

Sebesta, Carol A.: treasurer, Abbott Laboratories Fund

Sebree, Michael M.K.: assistant secretary, director, Skaggs Foundation (L. J. Skaggs and Mary C.)

Sedgwick, Jeanne: director conservation program, Packard Foundation (David and Lucile)

Sedwick, Helen: secretary, director, Baker Street Foundation

Seelbach, William Robert: mem supervisory board, Codrington Charitable Foundation (George W.)

Seely, Christopher W.: trustee, Huber Foundation

Segal, Beth Ann: vice president, secretary, Lebovitz Fund

Segal, Marilyn Mailman: chairman emeritus, Mailman Family Foundation (A. L.)

Segal, Richard D.: president, director, Mailman Family Foundation (A. L.)

Segal, Susan L.: director, Tinker Foundation

Segel, Kenneth T.: senior program officer, Jewish Healthcare Foundation; director, Staunton Farm Foundation

Segers, Ben: trustee, Musson Charitable Foundation (R. C. and Katharine M.)

Segers, Robert S.: trustee, Musson Charitable Foundation (R. C. and Katharine M.)

Seherr-Thoss, Henry W.: officer, Seherr-Thoss Foundation

Seherr-Thoss, Sonia P.: officer, Seherr-Thoss Foundation

Seidel, Arnold: trustee, Friedhofer Charitable Trust (Virginia)

Seidenberg, Ivan G.: president, chief executive officer, director, Verizon Communications Inc.

Seidler, James F.: trustee, Reliable Life Insurance Co. Foundation

Seidler, Lee J.: treasurer, director, Shubert Foundation

Seidler, Terry: director, Doheny Foundation Trust (Carrie Estelle)

Seidman, B. Thomas: trustee, Seidman Family Foundation

Seidman, Jane R.: trustee, Seidman Family Foundation

Seidman, Lewis William: trustee, Seidman Family Foundation

Seidman, Nancy Caroline: trustee, Seidman Family Foundation

Seidman, Sarah B.: trustee, Seidman Family Foundation

Seidman, Sarah L.: trustee, Seidman Family Foundation

Seidman, Tracy H.: trustee, Seidman Family Foundation

Sherbrooke, Ross E.: trustee, Fidelity Foundation

Sheridan, Brian: vice president, director, Washington Foundation (Dennis R. and Phyllis)

Sheridan, John J.: secretary, treasurer, director, Brach Foundation (Helen)

Sherin, Keith S.: director, Arison Foundation; senior vice president finance, chief financial officer, General Electric Co.

Sherman, Alison A.: director, Pforzheimer Foundation, Inc. (The Carl and Lily)

Sherman, Bruce: co-trustee, Schermer Charitable Trust (Frances)

Sherman, Bruce R.: treasurer, St. Francis Bank Foundation

Sherman, LeRoy J.: president, chief operating officer, McDonald Manufacturing Co. (A.Y.); vice president, McDonald Manufacturing Co. Charitable Foundation (A.Y.)

Sherman, Susan Elizabeth: president, chief executive officer, Independence Foundation

Sherr, Sidney S.: trustee, Gordon Charitable Trust (Peggy and Yale)

Sherrets, Amelia: trustee, Children's Foundation of Erie County

Sherrill, Edmund K., II: director, Good Samaritan

Sherrill, H. Sinclair: director, Good Samaritan

Sherrill, Henry W.: president, Good Samaritan

Sherrill, Hugh Virgil: director, Kleberg Foundation (Robert J. Kleberg, Jr. and Helen C.)

Sherrill, Joseph Newton, Jr.: vice president, trustee, West Foundation (TX)

Sherry, Judith K.: director, Staunton Farm Foundation

Sherry, Peter J., Jr.: secretary, Ford Motor Co. Fund

Sherwell, Jon: trustee, Henson Foundation (Richard A.)

Sherwin, Brian: president, South Waite Foundation

Sherwin, Dennis: mem, South Waite Foundation

Sherwin, Douglas F.: vice president, Lee Endowment Foundation

Sherwin, Margaret H.: vice president, South Waite Foundation

Sherwin, Peter: mem, South Waite Foundation

Sherwood, Lynne: corporate secretary, JSJ Corp.; secretary, treasurer, trustee, JSJ Foundation

Shields, Margaret M.: treasurer, Colonial Oaks Foundation

Shields, Shirley M.: secretary, Commercial Intertech Foundation

Shifler, E. H.: director, Eden Hall Foundation

Shiflett, B. B.: founder, Trull Foundation (The)

Shiflett, Laura Trull: founder, Trull Foundation (The)

Shine, Warren: trustee, Dibner Fund

Shineman, Edward W., Jr.: president, trustee, Arkell Hall Foundation

Shinners, William L.: vice president, McShain Charities (John)

Shinoda, Shunji: director, Nakamichi Foundation (E.)

Shipley, Larry: chief financial officer, IBP

Shipley, Walter Vincent: mem, director, Wallace-Reader's Digest Fund (DeWitt)

Shipley Miller, Harvey S.: trustee, Rothschild Foundation (Judith)

Shippee, Patricia Morel: director, Griffis Foundation

Shirk, Susan: trustee, United States-Japan Foundation

Shirley, Betsy B.: vice president, Jockey Hollow Foundation

Shirley, Paul V., Jr.: trustee, Hitchcock Foundation (Gilbert M. and Martha H.)

Shoaff, Thomas Mitchell: director, McMillen Foundation

Shoffner, Gary E.: director, Pickford Foundation (Mary)

Shojai, Tracie M.: trustee, McKay Family Foundation

Shook, Barbara Ingalls: chairman, treasurer, Shook Foundation (Barbara Ingalls)

Shook, Elesabeth Ridgely: trustee, Shook Foundation (Barbara Ingalls)

Shook, Robert P.: president, secretary, Shook Foundation (Barbara Ingalls)

Shore, Alastair: president, board member, Fireman's Fund Foundation

Short, Harry: director, Portsmouth General Hospital Foundation

Short, Randall K.: assistant treasurer, Boston Globe Foundation

Shott, Scott: vice president, Shott, Jr. Foundation (Hugh I.)

Shoup, Helen H.: trustee, Hulme Charitable Foundation (Milton G.)

Shriver, Eunice Kennedy: executive vice president, trustee, Kennedy, Jr. Foundation (Joseph P.)

Shriver, Sargent: officer, Kennedy, Jr. Foundation (Joseph P.)

Shuey, John Henry: chairman, president, chief executive officer, director, Amcast Industrial Corp.; president, Amcast Industrial Foundation

Shuford, Harry A.: trustee, Hillcrest Foundation

Shulman, Lloyd J.: vice president, director, Weinstein Foundation (J.)

Shulman, Max L.: president, director, Weinstein Foundation (J.)

Shulman, Sylvia W.: vice president, director, Weinstein Foundation (J.)

Shumaker, Portia W.: committee member, Whitaker Foundation

Shuman, D. Ellen: vice president, chief investment officer, Carnegie Corp. of New York

Shuman, Stanley S.: director, Allen Brothers Foundation

Shumway, Forrest Nelson: director, Irvine Foundation (The James)

Shust, Robert B.: trustee, Patterson Charitable Fund (W. I.)

Shuster, George Whitcomb: trustee, Cranston Foundation; president, chief executive officer, director, Cranston Print Works Co.

Shute, Benjamin R., Jr.: secretary, Rockefeller Brothers Fund, Inc.

Shutis, Larry: trustee, Fairchild-Meeker Charitable Trust (Freeman E.)

Shyer, Marlene: trustee, Heckscher Foundation for Children

Sibera, Helen Mary: director, Sordoni Foundation

Sibert, Leslie R.: vice president transmission, Georgia Power Co.

Sibley, D. J.: director, Potts and Sibley Foundation

Sibley, Hiram: chairman, Potts and Sibley Foundation

Sibley, James Malcolm: trustee, Evans Foundation, Inc. (Lettie Pate); vice chairman, trustee, Whitehead Foundation (Joseph B.)

Sibol, Mike: director, Susquehanna-Pfaltzgraff Co.

Sichler, Edward H., III: treasurer, Earhart Foundation

Siddall, David L.: vice president, associate general counsel, El Paso Corporate Foundation

Sidford, Holly: program director, Wallace-Reader's Digest Fund (Lila)

Sidhu, Jay S.: president, chief executive officer, chairman, Sovereign Bank; director, Sovereign Bank Foundation

Siebert, Sara: trustee, Alexander Edwards Trust (Margaret)

Siegel, Bernard L.: president, Kutz Foundation (Milton and Hattie)

Siegel, Herbert: chairman, Statler Foundation

Siegel, Herbert Jay: director, Dana Foundation (Charles A.)

Sieve, Richard, MD: secretary, Valley Foundation

Siewert, Penny: vice president regional services, United Wisconsin Services; vice president, secretary, treasurer, United Wisconsin Services Foundation

Sigfusson, Becky B.: vice president, director, Bere Foundation

Sigman, Stan: director, SBC Foundation

Signorile, A. J.: treasurer, trustee, Dana Charitable Trust (Eleanor Naylor)

Sikkema, Karen Ann: president, trustee, Unocal Foundation

Silas, Cecil Jesse: director, Wallace-Reader's Digest Fund (DeWitt)

Silberman, Sidney J., Esq.: treasurer, Scheuer Family Foundation Inc. (S. H. and Helen R.)

Silberman, Walter, MD: trustee, Valley Foundation

Silbert, Bernard: director, Parvin Foundation (Albert)

Silbert, Steven: director, Parvin Foundation (Albert)

Silk, Dorothy: trustee, Thoman Foundation (W. B. and Candace)

Silliman, Henry Harper, Jr.: president, Borkee-Hagley Foundation; treasurer, trustee, Longwood Foundation

Silliman, John E.: vice president, Borkee-Hagley Foundation

Silliman, Perry: secretary-treasurer, Murphy Foundation

Silliman, Robert M.: vice president, treasurer, Borkee-Hagley Foundation

Sills, John Leland: director, Rudin Foundation

Silvati, John Donald: vice president, trustee, Dater Foundation (Charles H.)

Silver, Stanley: president, Kahn, Lucas-Lancaster, Inc. Children's Wear

Silver-Parker, Esther: president, trustee, AT&T Foundation

Silverman, Barry S.: chairman, director, Jaydor Corp.; trustee, Jaydor Foundation

Silverman, Jeffrey: trustee, Jaydor Foundation

Silverman, Lawrence D.: treasurer, director, Lederer Foundation (Francis L.)

Silverman, Michael David: president, chief executive officer, director, Jaydor Corp.; trustee, Jaydor Foundation

Silverman, Robert L.: chairman, president, chief executive officer, Winter Construction Co.

Silverman, Sandra: president, executive director, assistant secretary, Scherman Foundation

Silverstein, Duane: executive director, Goldman Fund (Richard and Rhoda)

Simi, Jean: executive assistant, corporate assistant secretary, Mott Foundation (Charles Stewart)

Simmons, Glenn Reuben: vice chairman, Contran Corp.

Simmons, Hardwick: chairman, chief executive officer, Prudential Securities, Inc.

Simmons, Harold Clark: chairman, director, Simmons Foundation, Inc. (Harold)

Simmons, Hildy J.: managing director, Morgan Charitable Trust (J.P.)

Simmons, L. E.: director, Houston Endowment

Simmons, Roy William: mem, Bamberger Memorial Foundation (John Ernest Bamberger and Ruth Eleanor)

Simmons, Ruth J.: trustee, Carnegie Corp. of New York

Simmons, Tom: assistant secretary, director, Midcontinent Media Foundation

Simock, Debbie: manager community relations, Avista Corp.

Simon, Allison S.: president, Stemmons Foundation

Simon, Eleanor A.: secretary, Mendel Foundation

Simon, Heinz K.: vice president, Stemmons Foundation

Simon, J. Peter: vice president, treasurer, director, Simon Foundation (William E.)

Simon, John: director, Allen Brothers Foundation

Simon, John Gerald: trustee, Taconic Foundation

Simon, Kenneth: secretary, treasurer, Kayser Foundation

Simon, Mitchell J.: assistant treasurer, director, Young Foundation (Irvin L.)

Simon, Paul: trustee, Strauss Foundation (Leon)

Simon, R. Matthew: director, Brach Foundation (Helen)

Simon, Ralph: trustee, Strauss Foundation (Leon)

Simon, Raymond F.: president, executive director, Brach Foundation (Helen); vice president, Polk Brothers Foundation, Inc.

Simon, William: trustee, Strauss Foundation (Leon)

Simon, William Edward, Jr.: president, director, Simon Foundation (William E.)

Simon-Morris, Johanna K.: director, Simon Foundation (William E.)

Simonet, John Thomas: vice president, Tozer Foundation

Simons, Anne M.: trustee, Medina Foundation

Simons, Bren: trustee, Simon Charitable Foundation Number One (Melvin and Bren)

Simons, John Farr: director, Marpat Foundation

Simons, Melvin J.: trustee, Simon Charitable Foundation Number One (Melvin and Bren)

Simonson, Anne Larsen: first vice president, Larsen Fund

Simpkins, Jacqueline De-Neuflize: trustee, Sprague Educational and Charitable Foundation (Seth)

Simpson, Betty: clerk, Memorial Foundation for the Blind

Simpson, Phyllis T.: secretary, Duke Energy Corp.; assistant secretary, Duke Energy Foundation

Simpson, William H.: president, chief executive officer, Susquehanna-Pfaltzgraff Co.; secretary, Susquehanna-Pfaltzgraff Foundation

Sims, Don: director, Sierra Pacific Resources Charitable Foundation

Sims, Frank: director, vice president, Cargill Foundation

Sims, Robert L.: trustee, Cord Foundation (E. L.)

Sims, Sally: director, Patron Saints Foundation

Sinclair, John P., Esq.: director, Glencoe Foundation

Sinclair, K. Richard C.: mem, trustee, One Valley Bank Foundation

Singer, Suzanne: secretary, trust, Livingston Foundation (Milton S. and Corinne N.)

Singleton, Matt: vice president, chief executive officer, director, CIBC World Markets

Singley Koontz, Frederick: trustee, Wallis Trust (Dorothy Wagner)

Sinisi, Andrea: executive director, contributions committee, CNA Foundation

Sinnett, Clifford H.: trustee, Burnham Charitable Trust (Margaret E.)

Sinon, Frank A., Esq.: secretary, Stabler Foundation (Donald B. and Dorothy L.)

Sircy, Melissa Smith: trustee, Slemp Foundation

Sirek, John: director citizenship programs, McCormick Tribune Foundation (Robert R.)

Sirota, Wilbert H., Esq.: secretary, director, Hecht-Levi Foundation

Sisco, Jean Head: trustee, Higginson Trust (Corina)

Sisk, John F.: trustee, Donaldson Charitable Trust (Oliver S. and Jennie R.)

Siska, Nancy P.: member contributions committee, Cargill, Inc.

Sitler, Michele: secretary, Wiremold Foundation

Sitnick, Irving: president, director, Moses Fund, Inc. (Henry and Lucy)

Sittenfeld, Paul George: secretary, trustee, Peterloon Foundation

Sittinger, Tammy: coord, Square D Foundation

Sivertsen, Robert J.: vice president, director, Weyerhaeuser Memorial Foundation (Charles A.)

Six, Julie G.: treasurer, Greenfield Foundation (Albert M.)

Skadon, Janet T.: director, Bishop Foundation (E. K. and Lillian F.)

Skaggs, Mary C.: president, director, Skaggs Foundation (L. J. Skaggs and Mary C.)

Skarbek, Cynthia: director, Smith Foundation (Gordon V. and Helen C.)

Skelton, Anne: trustee, Reliable Life Insurance Co. Foundation

Skidmore, Brenda L.: trustee, Chesapeake Corp. Foundation; president, Crestar Foundation

Skiles, Win: vice president, Texas Instruments Foundation; senior vice president, Texas Instruments Inc.

Skilling, Raymond Inwood: executive vice president, chief counsel, director, Aon Corp.; director, Aon Foundation

Skinner, Frank: director, vice president, Reynolds

Tobacco Company Foundation (R. J.)

Skinner, William L.: director, Ball Brothers Foundation

Sklar, Eric: treasurer, Arca Foundation

Skott, Allen: director, American Optical Foundation

Skule, John L., III: senior vice president public affairs, Bristol-Myers Squibb Co.; director, Bristol-Myers Squibb Foundation Inc.

Skulsky, Craig S.: treasurer, Newman Family Foundation

Slade, Jodie H.: director, Tri-County Telephone Foundation

Slamar, Charles, Jr.: trustee, Mellinger Educational Foundation (Edward Arthur)

Slaughter, Harriet: trustee, Wildermuth Foundation (E. F.)

Slaughter, Ken: chief financial officer, Gazette Co.; vice president, director, Gazette Foundation

Slaughter, Michie P.: director, Kauffman Foundation (Ewing Marion)

Slavin, Morton A.: clerk, director, Housen Foundation

Slavitt, Lesley D.: vice president, Bank One Foundation

Slaymaker, Eugene W.: president, trustee, Baughman Foundation

Slesh, Cristin: program officer, Bruening Foundation (Eva L. and Joseph M.)

Slesin, Louis E.: director, Rubinstein Foundation (Helena)

Slesin, Suzanne: director, Rubinstein Foundation (Helena)

Slifka, Marlee: trustee, Lunda Charitable Trust

Sligar, James S.: trustee, LSR Fund

Slizewski, Beatrice B.: vice president corporate communications, Birds Eye Foods, Inc.

Sloan, Sue: senior program officer, PPG Industries Foundation

Sloane, Ann Brownell: assistant treasurer, Rosenthal Foundation (Ida and William)

Sloane, Howard Grant: chairman, Heckscher Foundation for Children

Sloane, Virginia: president, trustee, Heckscher Foundation for Children

Slosburg, Stanley J.: trust, Livingston Foundation (Milton S. and Corinne N.)

Sloss, Hillary: director, Fleishhacker Foundation

Sloss, Laura: director, Fleishhacker Foundation

Slutzky, Paul: director, Bank of Greene County Charitable Foundation

Sly, Helen S.: president, director, fdr daughter, Sunnen Foundation

Smadbeck, Arthur J.: trustee, Heckscher Foundation for Children

Smadbeck, Louis, Jr.: trustee, Heckscher Foundation for Children

Smadbeck, Mina: trustee, Heckscher Foundation for Children

Smadbeck, Paul: trustee, Heckscher Foundation for Children

Smaldone, Laurie: director, Bristol-Myers Squibb Foundation Inc.

Small, Malinda B.: director national-state affairs & corporate contributions, Constellation Energy Group, Inc.

Smallwood, Thomas L.: secretary, director, Bradley Foundation (Lynde and Harry); co-trustee, admin, Helfaer Foundation (Evan and Marion)

Smart, George M.: trustee, Commercial Intertech Foundation

Smart, Mary: secretary, Smart Family Foundation

Smith, Alexander Wyly, Jr.: trustee, member executive committee, Franklin Foundation Inc. (John and Mary)

Smith, Alice: chairman, trustee, Lyndhurst Foundation

Smith, Alice T.: vchairman, Brown Foundation (M. K.)

Smith, Allen C.: trustee, Hilliard Foundation

Smith, Alson H., Jr.: sr vice president, director, Virginia Environmental Endowment

Smith, Arthur K.: trustee, Michael Foundation (Herbert I. and Elsa B.)

Smith, Arthur O.: president, Smith Foundation, Inc. (A.O.)

Smith, Benjamin M., Jr.: treasurer, Washington Forrest Foundation

Smith, Bill: chief executive officer, City National Bank & Trust Co.

Smith, Bob: director, Bradley Foundation (Lynde and Harry)

Smith, Bradford K.: vice president, peace & social justice, Ford Foundation; director, Noble Foundation, Inc. (Edward John)

Smith, Brenda J.: trustee, El Pomar Foundation

Smith, Brian J.: secretary, Abbott Laboratories Fund

Smith, Bruce G.: director, Smith Foundation (Gordon V. and Helen C.)

Smith, Cecil O.: director, Tri-County Telephone Foundation

Smith, Charles W.: trustee, Sargent Foundation (Newell B.)

Smith, Cherida C.: vice president, trustee, Collins Foundation

Smith, D. Scarborough, III: director, SMBC Global Foundation, Inc.; joint general manager, Sumitomo Mitsui Banking Corp.

Smith, David A.: director, Kline Foundation (Josiah W. and Bessie H.)

Smith, David Byron, Jr.: consultant, director, Wausau-Mosinee Paper Corp.

Smith, David L.: executive director, trustee, Abell-Hanger Foundation

Smith, David S., Jr.: director, Noble Foundation, Inc. (Edward John)

Smith, David Shiverick: chairman, director, Olmsted Foundation (George and Carol)

Smith, Diane M.: president, director, Bank One Foundation

Smith, Donald E.: president, Rupp Foundation (Fran and Warren)

Smith, Douglas I.: director, Smith Foundation (Gordon V. and Helen C.)

Smith, E. Berry: secretary, treasurer, Schurz Communications Foundation

Smith, E. Sue: assistant secretary, Amcast Industrial Foundation

Smith, E.J. Noble: president, director, Noble Foundation, Inc. (Edward John)

Smith, Eaton: director, King Foundation (Kenneth Kendal)

Smith, Ervie L.: executive director, Valley Foundation

Smith, Francis Street: secretary, treasurer, North American Royalties Foundation

Smith, Frank K.: vice president, director, Smith Charitable Foundation (Arlene H.)

Smith, Fred W.: chairman, Reynolds Foundation (Donald W.)

Smith, Gavin H.: president, director, Burlington Resources Foundation

Smith, Geoffrey: treasurer, Brunswick Foundation

Smith, Gerald C.: manager, director, Redfield Foundation (Nell J.)

Smith, Gerald J.: program officer, Moody Foundation

Smith, Gordon H.: director, Demos Foundation (N.)

Smith, Gordon L., Jr.: trustee, North American Royalties Foundation

Smith, Gordon Victor: president, Smith Foundation (Gordon V. and Helen C.)

Smith, Gregory M.: investment analyst, Kresge Foundation

Smith, H. I.: treasurer, director, Bush Foundation

Smith, H. Warren: vice president, Fehsenfeld Charitable Foundation (Frank B. and Virginia V.)

Smith, Harold Byron, Jr.: president, Illinois Tool Works Foundation

Smith, Harold W.: vice president, trustee, Swisher Foundation (Carl S.)

Smith, Helen C.: vice president, Smith Foundation (Gordon V. and Helen C.)

Smith, Howard W., Jr.: secretary, Bryant Foundation (The)

Smith, J. Burleson: director, Piper Foundation (Minnie Stevens)

Smith, J. Kay: vice president, Corp. Communications/Public Policy, Ameren Corp.

Smith, Jack: director, Lytel Foundation (Bertha Russ)

Smith, Jack A.: senior vice president, Reader's Digest Association, Inc.

Smith, James: trustee, Slemp Foundation

Smith, James C.: director, Slemp Foundation

Smith, James S.: president, treasurer, Frese Foundation (Arnold D.)

Smith, Jean Kennedy: trustee, Kennedy, Jr. Foundation (Joseph P.)

Smith, Jeanne H.: adv comm mem, Inasmuch Foundation

Smith, Jeremy T.: director, Noble Foundation, Inc. (Edward John)

Smith, John Francis, Jr.: chairman, General Motors Corp.

Smith, Jon D., Jr.: assistant treasurer, Hearst Foundation (William Randolph)

Smith, Jonathan, OD: trustee, Reynolds Foundation (Donald W.)

Smith, Joseph A.: manager, executive director, Employers Mutual Charitable Foundation

Smith, Kathleen D.: trustee, Raskob Foundation for Catholic Activities, Inc.

Smith, Kenneth M.: director, Phipps Foundation (Columbus)

Smith, L. Edwin: treasurer, director, Jones Foundation (Helen)

Smith, Langhorne B.: treasurer, director, Claneil Foundation

Smith, Laura: trustee, Frese Foundation (Arnold D.)

Smith, Lewis W.: director, Morgan Foundation (Louie R. and Gertrude)

Smith, Lunsford Richardson: trustee, Hillsdale Fund

Smith, M. Munson: trustee, secretary, Johnson Foundation (M. G. and Lillie A.)

Smith, Margaret: director, Heath Foundation (Ed and Mary)

Smith, Mark C.: president, Ontario Corp. Foundation

Smith, Martin C.: director, Bank of Greene County Charitable Foundation

Smith, Mary Mills Abel: trustee, duPont Foundation (Chichester)

Smith, Mary Welles Mooers: vice president, trustee, Hilliard Foundation

Smith, May: trustee, Smith Horticultural Trust (Stanley)

Smith, Melinda Hoag: president, director, Hoag Family Foundation (George)

Smith, Michael J.: assistant vice president investments, Mott Foundation (Charles Stewart)

Smith, Michael L.: director, Anthem Foundation, Inc.; executive vice president, chief financial officer, Anthem Inc.

Smith, Michael S.: vice president, Metris Companies Foundation

Smith, Molly R.: trustee, Hillsdale Fund

Smith, Nancey E.: trustee, Slemp Foundation

Smith, Nancy: vice president, Smith Foundation (William R. and Sara Babb)

Smith, Nancy DuVergne: treasurer, trustee, Levy Foundation (June Rockwell)

Smith, Nancy Z.: treasurer, SMBC Global Foundation, Inc.; vice president, Sumitomo Mitsui Banking Corp.

Smith, Neil T.: trustee, Smith Foundation (Ralph L.)

Smith, Nickie Beth: director, Aldridge Charitable and Educational Trust (Tom S. and Marye Kate)

Smith, Norman J.: president, Ford Family Foundation

Smith, Olcott D.: hon trustee, Hartford Courant Foundation

Smith, Orville D.: trustee, McMahon Foundation

Smith, Pamela Klipstein: vice president, Klipstein Foundation (Ernest Christian)

Smith, Philip J.: director, Shubert Foundation

Smith, Phyllis W.: trustee, Masland Trust No. 2 (Maurice H.)

Smith, Ralph L., Jr.: mgr, Smith Foundation (Ralph L.)

Smith, Raymond W.: trustee, Carnegie Corp. of New York

Smith, Richard G., III: trustee, Hillsdale Fund

Smith, Richard M.: trustee, Pinkerton Foundation

Smith, Robert A.: trustee, Smith Family Foundation (Richard and Susan)

Smith, Robert A., III: director, Doheny Foundation Trust (Carrie Estelle)

Smith, Robert N.: director, Warwick Savings Foundation

Smith, S. Garry: secretary, treasurer, foundation manager, executive director, Daniel Foundation of Alabama

Smith, Sara Babb: vice chairman, Smith Foundation (William R. and Sara Babb)

Smith, Stephen Byron: director, Illinois Tool Works Foundation

Smith, Stephen J.: secretary, Christensen Charitable and Religious Foundation (L. C.)

Smith, Steve C.: trustee, McBeath Foundation (Faye)

Smith, Susan F.: trustee, Smith Family Foundation (Richard and Susan)

Smith, Thelma G.: president, director, Second Foundation

Smith, Theodore M.: executive director, Kendall Foundation (Henry P.)

Smith, Timothy S.: secretary, treasurer, Rupp Foundation (Fran and Warren)

Smith, Tracy D.: trustee, Michael Foundation (Herbert I. and Elsa B.)

Smith, Van P.: chairman, Ontario Corp.

Smith, W. Keith: chairman, Dreyfus Corp.

Smith, W. R.: director, Heath Foundation (Ed and Mary)

Smith, Walt: treasurer, Glaser Foundation

Smith, Wes: trustee, Reynolds Foundation (Donald W.)

Smith, William C.: trustee, Cooper Foundation

Smith, William D.: chief executive officer, Kemper Foundation (James S.)

Smith, William F.: assistant treasurer, Alabama Power Foundation

Smith, William Mason, III: treasurer, Prouty Foundation (Olive Higgins)

Smith, William N.: president, trustee, City National Bank Foundation; president, chief executive officer, director, City National Bank & Trust Co.

Smith, William R.: chairman, Smith Foundation (William R. and Sara Babb)

Smith, Win C.: director, Vermilion Healthcare Foundation

Smith, Zachary Taylor, II: director, secretary, Babcock Foundation (Mary Reynolds)

Smith Campbell, Barbara: trustee, Reynolds Foundation (Donald W.)

Smith Magness, Debby: trustee, Reynolds Foundation (Donald W.)

Smitson, Robert M.: director, Ball Foundation (George and Frances)

Smoley, Sandra R., RN: director, Sierra Health Foundation

Smoot, J. Thomas, Jr.: trustee, Edison Fund (Charles)

Smyth, Geralynn D.: trustee, Knott Foundation (Marion I. and Henry J.)

Smyth, John C.: vice president, director, Knott Foundation (Marion I. and Henry J.)

Smyth, Maureen H.: vice president programs, Mott Foundation (Charles Stewart)

Smyth, Patricia K.: trustee, Knott Foundation (Marion I. and Henry J.)

Smythe, John W.: executive director, treasurer, Jones Foundation (Fletcher)

Sneag, Lawrence O.: treasurer, Ittleson Foundation

Snider, Richard C.: secretary, director, Rudin Foundation

Snider, Timothy R.: senior vice president, Phelps Dodge Corp.

Snow, David H.: vice president, treasurer, Snow Foundation (John Ben)

Snow, Jonathan L.: secretary, Snow Foundation (John Ben); trustee, Snow Memorial Trust (John Ben)

Snow, Ronald: trustee, Jameson Trust (Oleonda)

Snowball, Julie: president, Swanson Family Foundation, Inc. (Dr. W. C.)

Snyder, Abram M.: vice president, Plankenhorn Foundation (Harry)

Snyder, Audrey: executive director, trustee, Snyder Foundation (Harold B. and Dorothy A.)

Snyder, Carroll E.: director, Vermilion Healthcare Foundation

Snyder, Leonard N.: trustee, Grundy Foundation

Snyder, Molly Sue: trustee, Braemar Charitable Trust

Snyder, Nancy T.: vice president, Whirlpool Foundation

Snyder, Patricia: admin, Graham Foundation for Advanced Studies in the Fine Arts

Snyder, Patricia S.: vice president, Snyder Foundation (William I. and Patricia S.)

Snyder, Phyllis Johnson: trustee, Snyder Foundation (Harold B. and Dorothy A.)

Snyder, Robert E.: vice president, secretary, treasurer, Byrne Foundation

Snyder, William I.: president, Snyder Foundation (William I. and Patricia S.)

Sobol, Thomas: director, Pforzheimer Foundation, Inc. (The Carl and Lily)

Soboroff, Steven L.: director, Weingart Foundation

Sobotor-Littell, Nancy L.: secretary, Warwick Savings Foundation

Socolow, Daniel J.: director fellows program, MacArthur Foundation (John D. and Catherine T.)

Soderberg, Elsa A.: vice president, Allyn Foundation

Soderberg, Jon: director, Allyn Foundation

Soderberg, Libby: director, Allyn Foundation

Soderberg, Peer: director, Allyn Foundation

Soderberg, Peter: director, Allyn Foundation

Soderberg, Robert C.: director, Allyn Foundation

Soiefer, Ronald M.: director, Unilever United States Foundation

Solana, Nancy: vice president, secretary, Fikes Foundation (Leland)

Solano, Patrick: director, Sordoni Foundation

Sollins, Karen R.: chairman, director, Scherman Foundation

Solnit, Albert Jay: director, New-Land Foundation

Solomon, Daniel: secretary, Cohen Foundation (Naomi and Nehemiah)

Solomon, David: treasurer, Cohen Foundation (Naomi and Nehemiah)

Solomon, Larry R.: secretary, Florsheim Shoe Foundation

Solomon, Milton D.: vice president, secretary, trustee, Bydale Foundation

Solomon, Peter J.: director, Littauer Foundation (Lucius N.)

Solomon, Richard: director, Graham Foundation for Advanced Studies in the Fine Arts

Stapleton, Katharine H.: trustee, Fishback Foundation Trust (Harmes C.)

Stark, Jay W.: trustee, Kunkel Foundation (John Crain)

Stark, John K.: trustee, Kunkel Foundation (John Crain)

Stark, K. R.: trustee, Kunkel Foundation (John Crain)

Stark, Nathan Julius: trustee, Allegheny Foundation

Stark, Nelda Childers: chairman, Stark Foundation (Nelda C. and H. J. Lutcher)

Starkey, Cathy A.: administration assistant, Bruening Foundation (Eva L. and Joseph M.)

Starkins, Clifford E.: director, Cheever Porter Foundation (Mrs.)

Starr, Arthur F.: trustee, Bean Foundation (Norwin S. and Elizabeth N.)

Starr, Karen: senior program officer, Bremer Foundation (Otto)

Starr, Lori: director communications, Getty Trust (J. Paul)

Starr, Sally: clerk, Hamilton Charitable Corp.

Staszak, Thomas A.: contr, assistant treasurer, Regenstein Foundation

Staton, Jimmy: trustee, Norman Foundation (Summers A.)

Stauffer, John H.: trustee, Stauffer Communications Foundation

Stauffer Lyddon, Dorothy: chairman, Seven Springs Foundation

Stavro, William: vice president, Mattel Foundation

Stavropoulos, William S.: trustee, Gerstacker Foundation (Rollin M.)

Stawarz, Raymond R.: chief financial officer, Federated Mutual Insurance Co.; treasurer, Federated Mutual Insurance Foundation

Steadman, Michael W.: assistant vice president, Kilworth Charitable Trust (Florence B.)

Stearns, Nancy: trustee, Plankenhorn Foundation (Harry)

Stearns, Robert H.: president, Stearns Foundation

Stearns, Roger R.: secretary, Stearns Foundation

Stebbins, Richard A.: director, Beveridge Foundation, Inc. (Frank Stanley)

Stecher, Patsy Palmer: director, Beveridge Foundation, Inc. (Frank Stanley)

Stedman, Betty Ann West: trustee, West Foundation (Neva and Wesley)

Stedman, Stuart West: trustee, West Foundation (Neva and Wesley)

Steeger, Dean H.: secretary, trustee, Hayden Foundation (Charles)

Steel, Corrine: director, Bay Foundation

Steel, John: trustee, Warner Fund (Albert and Bessie)

Steel, Kitty: trustee, Warner Fund (Albert and Bessie)

Steel, Lewis M.: trustee, Warner Fund (Albert and Bessie)

Steel, Ruth M.: trustee, Warner Fund (Albert and Bessie)

Steele, Elizabeth R.: member advisory committee, Dow Jones Foundation; secretary, Steele Foundation (Harry and Grace)

Steele, Finley M.: trustee, Hilliard Foundation

Steele, George: vice president, Marshall Foundation

Steele, James M.: committee member, Eccles Foundation (Marriner S.)

Steele, Lela Emery: president, treasurer, trustee, Peterloon Foundation

Steele, Susan J.: acting executive director, Buell Foundation (Temple Hoyne)

Steele, William G., Jr.: chairman, Bean Foundation (Norwin S. and Elizabeth N.)

Steele Hoyt, Elizabeth: trustee, Peterloon Foundation

Steever, Jerry: vice president, director, Midcontinent Media Foundation

Steffen, Phyllis: director, Grinnell Mutual Group Foundation

Steffens, John Laundon: executive vice president, Merrill Lynch & Company, Inc.

Steffens, Marian I.: secretary, Robinson Fund (Maurice R.)

Steffens, Roger S.: treasurer, Georgia Power Foundation

Steffes, Don C.: president, Mingenback Foundation (Julia J.)

Stehling, James: director, Peterson Foundation (Hal and Charlie)

Steiger, Albert E., III: director, Steiger Memorial Fund (Albert)

Steiger, Albert E., Jr.: president, Steiger Memorial Fund (Albert)

Steiger, Allen: treasurer, Steiger Memorial Fund (Albert)

Steiger, Philip C., Jr.: director, Steiger Memorial Fund (Albert)

Steiger, Ralph A., II: vice president, director, Steiger Memorial Fund (Albert)

Stein, Christine D.: program director, Price Associates Foundation (T. Rowe)

Stein, Mary Ann Efroymson: president, Moriah Fund, Inc.

Steinberg, Robert A.: trustee, Gordon Charitable Trust (Peggy and Yale)

Steinbright, Marilyn L.: president, Arcadia Foundation

Steinhafel, Gregg: president, Target Stores, Target Corp.

Steinhauer, Bruce W., MD: trustee, vice chairman, McGregor Fund

Steinhause, Mitchell: vice president, director, New York Mercantile Exchange Charitable Foundation

Steinkraus, Eric M.: director, Ziegler Foundation for the Blind (E. Matilda)

Steinkraus, Helen Ziegler: secretary, vice president, Ziegler Foundation for the Blind (E. Matilda)

Steinkraus, Philip: director, Ziegler Foundation for the Blind (E. Matilda)

Steinman, Beverly R.: vchairman, Steinman Foundation (James Hale)

Steinman, Jeffrey: executive vice president, director, Rudin Foundation

Steinschneider, Jean M.: director, Huisking Foundation

Steinweg, Bernard: mem, director, Fribourg Foundation

Stemberg, Sy: chairman, director, New York Life Foundation

Stemmons, Jean H.: vice president, Stemmons Foundation

Stemmons, John M., Sr.: vice president, Stemmons Foundation

Stemmons, Ruth T.: vice president, Stemmons Foundation

Stemple, Ernest Edward: director, Starr Foundation

Stender, Bruce W.: chairman, member executive committee, Blandin Foundation

Stepanian, Tania W.: chairperson, Crocker Trust (Mary A.)

Stephanoff, Kathryn A.: chairwoman, Trexler Trust (Harry C.)

Stephans, William W. T.: chief financial officer, Scott Fetzer Co.; vice president, treasurer, Scott & Fetzer Foundation

Stephens, Alice: trustee, McKinney Charitable Trust (Carl and Alleen)

Stephens, Christopher H.: vice president, director, Backus Foundation (Beatrice and Roy)

Stephens, Elton Bryson: founder, chairman, Ebsco Industries, Inc.

Stephens, Gene: member, Bridgestone/Firestone Trust Fund (The)

Stephens, Inge T.: treasurer, director, Backus Foundation (Beatrice and Roy)

Stephens, James T.: president, director, Ebsco Industries, Inc.

Stephens, Louis Cornelius, Jr.: vchairman, trustee, Duke Endowment

Stephens, Robert: trustee, Packard Foundation (David and Lucile)

Stephens, Thomas J.: president, director, Backus Foundation (Beatrice and Roy)

Stephenson, John W.: executive director, Campbell Foundation (J. Bulow)

Sterba, Jeffry: chairman, president, chief executive officer, PNM Resources, Inc.

Sterling, Helen N.: trustee emerita, Rockwell Fund, Inc.

Sterling, Sonja J.: secretary, Deere Foundation (John)

Stern, Henry: vice president, secretary, Lowe Foundation (Joe and Emily)

Stern, John N.: chairman, Altheimer Charitable Foundation (Ben J.)

Stern, William: vice president, director, Atran Foundation, Inc.

Sternheim, Marci B.: executive director, Dibner Fund

Stettinius, Wallace: vice president, trustee, Gray Foundation (Garland and Agnes Taylor)

Steuart, Guy T., II: director, Cafritz Foundation (Morris and Gwendolyn)

Steuert, D. Michael: senior vice president, chief financial officer, Fluor Corp.

Stevens, E. W. Dann: trustee, Viyu Foundation

Stevens, Gregory W.: vice president, treasurer, Phelps Dodge Corp.

Stevens, James P.: trustee, Swisher Foundation (Carl S.)

Stevens, James W.: trustee, Dodge Foundation (Geraldine R.)

Stevens, Lorne G.: director, La-Z-Boy, Inc.

Stevens, Melissa Jones: director, Houston Endowment

Stevens, Robert L.: chairman, president, chief executive officer, Bryn Mawr Bank Corp.

Stevens, Rowland: trustee, Chapman Charitable Corp. (Howard and Bess)

Stevens, Tamara: administrator, High Meadow Foundation

Stevenson, Ruth Carter: president, director, donor daughter, Carter Foundation (Amon G.)

Stewart, Alan M.: executive director, Cullen Foundation (The)

Stewart, Cynthia: secretary, Texas Instruments Foundation

Stewart, Donald M.: director, New York Times Co. Foundation

Stewart, Donnell B.: off, Stewart Educational Foundation (Donnell B. and Elizabeth Dee Shaw)

Stewart, Elizabeth D.: off, Stewart Educational Foundation (Donnell B. and Elizabeth Dee Shaw)

Stewart, Jerry L.: director, Alabama Power Foundation

Stewart, John T., III: chairman, Kansas Health Foundation

Stewart, Marise M.M.: trustee, Mott Foundation (Charles Stewart)

Stewart, Stacey Davis: president, chief executive officer, director, Fannie Mae Foundation

Steyer, Hume R.: trustee, Sharon Steel Foundation

Stickels, Eric E.: treasurer, secretary, Oneida Savings Bank Charitable Foundation

Stieg, Elizabeth A.: assistant secretary, trustee, Carls Foundation

Stieg, Harold E.: vice president, secretary, trustee, Carls Foundation

Stiles, Robert: director, Bausch & Lomb Foundation, Inc.

Stimson, Bruce: chief financial officer, Teichert Foundation

Stine, Lynn B.: vice president, director, Bere Foundation

Stine, Thomas Henry: trustee, Thanksgiving Foundation

Stinnett, J. Daniel: director, Commerce Bancshares Foundation

Stinson, Kenneth E.: member contributions committee, Kiewit Companies Foundation; chairman, chief executive officer, director, Peter Kiewit Sons' Inc.

Stirn, Cara S.: vice president, trustee, Smith Foundation (Kelvin and Eleanor)

Stivers, William Charles: executive vice president, chief financial officer, Weyerhaeuser Co.; treasurer, trustee, Weyerhaeuser Co. Foundation

Stock, John P.: director, Valley Foundation (Wayne and Gladys)

Stocker, Beth K.: president, Stocker Foundation

Stockly, Doris Silliman: director, Borkee-Hagley Foundation

Stockman, Hervey S.: president, Stockman Family Foundation Trust

Stockman, Hervey S., Jr.: vice president, Stockman Family Foundation Trust

Stockman, Sarah A.: chairman, secretary, Stockman Family Foundation Trust

Stockwell, Lance: trustee, Bovaird Foundation (Mervin)

Stoddard, James A.: executive director, Hubbard Foundation (R. D. and Joan Dale)

Stoel, Thomas B.: trustee, Tucker Charitable Trust (Rose E.); secretary, Wessinger Foundation

Stokes, Jerome W. D.: director, Public Welfare Foundation

Stokes, Patrick T.: president, chief executive officer, Anheuser-Busch Companies, Inc.

Stokes, Samuel N.: vice president, Marpat Foundation

Stokes, Spencer: president, Winthrop

Stokes, Thomas C.: trustee, treasurer, Gates Family Foundation

Stokesbary, Terry: program director, Murdock Charitable Trust (M. J.)

Stone, Anne L.: vice president, Rollins-Luetkemeyer Foundation

Stone, Charles Lynn, Jr.: president, trustee, Stone Foundation

Stone, Edward Carroll, Jr.: director, chairman science engineering liberal arts committee, Keck Foundation (W. M.)

Stone, Edward Eldredge: vice president, trustee, Stone Foundation

Stone, Holly: vice president, director, Gudelsky Family Foundation (Homer and Martha)

Stone, J. Jacques: secretary, treasurer, Tuch Foundation (Michael)

Stone, James D.: director, Rollins-Luetkemeyer Foundation

Stone, Larry D.: chairman, Lowe's Charitable and Educational Foundation

Stone, Robert A.: admin, Peters Foundation (Charles F.)

Stone, Robert G.: director, Exchange Bank Foundation

Stone, Roger David: director, Erpf Fund (Armand G.)

Stone, Sara S.: trustee, Stone Foundation

Stoneman, Susan K.: director, Widgeon Foundation

Stonesifer, Patty: co-chair, president, Gates Foundation (Bill and Melinda)

Stookey, John Hoyt: director, Clark Foundation (NY)

Stookey, Katherine Emory: trustee, Sasco Foundation

Stopher, Joseph E.: president, trustee, Gheens Foundation

Storch, Gerald L.: senior vice president strategic business, Target Corp.

Storey, Charles Porter: trustee, Hillcrest Foundation

Storey, Robert Davis: trustee, Gund Foundation (George)

Stotsenberg, Edward: president, chief financial officer, Pickford Foundation (Mary)

Stotsenberg, Henry: president, Pickford Foundation (Mary)

Stott, Benjamin W.: trustee, Stott Foundation (Louis L.)

Stott, Edward B.: trustee, Stott Foundation (Louis L.)

Stott, Francis: director, Educational Foundation of America

Stott, Kristine: trustee, Stott Foundation (Louis L.)

Stottlemyer, Charles E.: chairman, mem admin comm, Selby and Marie Selby Foundation (William G.)

Stout, Elizabeth West: president, trustee, Stout Foundation (Charles H.)

Stout, Jean C.: treasurer, director, Hugoton Foundation

Stout, Joan K.: president, managing director, Hugoton Foundation

Stout, Joan M.: secretary, director, Hugoton Foundation

Stout, John K.: director, Hugoton Foundation

Stout, Ray E., III: vice president, director, Hugoton Foundation

Stout, Richard M.: treasurer, trustee, Stout Foundation (Charles H.)

Stout, William J.: assistant secretary, treasurer, Ayres Foundation

Stout Gilweit, Martha: trustee, secretary, Stout Foundation (Charles H.)

Stovall, David: director, Gulf Coast Medical Foundation

Stovall, Guy F., III: director, Gulf Coast Medical Foundation

Stracener, J. O.: director, Tractor & Equipment Co. Foundation

Strachan, Camilee: trustee, German Protestant Orphan Asylum Association Foundation

Strait, Agnes: director national programs, Verizon Foundation

Strait, Rex: vice president, Van Buren Foundation

Straitor, George A.: assistant treasurer, Ford Fund (Walter and Josephine)

Strake, George W., Jr.: director, Herzstein Charitable Foundation (Albert and Ethel); president, treasurer, Strake Foundation

Straker, John W., Jr.: secretary, Straker Charitable Foundation (J. William and Mary Helen)

Straker Henderson, Susan: president, treasurer, Straker Charitable Foundation (J. William and Mary Helen)

Stranahan, Duane, Jr.: trustee, Stranahan Foundation

Stranahan, Julie: trustee, Fruehauf Foundation

Stranahan, Mark: trustee, Stranahan Foundation

Stranahan, Stephen: trustee, Stranahan Foundation

Strand, Allan E.: trustee, Sullivan Foundation (Algernon Sydney)

Strassler, David H.: president, Barrington Foundation

Strassler, Robert B.: secretary, treasurer, Barrington Foundation

Straton, Suzanne J.: trustee, Perry Foundation

Stratton, Robert A.: director, Olmsted Foundation (George and Carol)

Strausburg, Virginia M.: executive director, Dayton Power and Light Co. Foundation

Strauss, Benjamin: trustee, Strauss Foundation

Strauss, Robert Perry: trustee, Strauss Foundation

Strauss, Sam B., Jr.: board director, Ottenheimer Brothers Foundation

Strausse, Donald: trustee, Wahlert Foundation

Strecker, A. M.: executive vice president, chief operating officer, Oklahoma Gas & Electric Co. Foundation

Streep, Mary B. Simon: director, Simon Foundation (William E.)

Street, Alice Ann: president, director, Bertha Foundation

Street, E. Bruce: director, Bertha Foundation

Street, Gordon P., Jr.: chairman, president, chief executive officer, director,

North American Royalties; trustee, North American Royalties Foundation

Street, J. O.: trustee, Halff Foundation (G. A. C.)

Street, James E.: director, Kinder Morgan Foundation

Street, M. Boyd: director, Bertha Foundation

Street, M. Boyd, Jr.: director, Bertha Foundation

Street, Ruth L.: vice president, North American Royalties Foundation

Street, S. H.: trustee, Halff Foundation (G. A. C.)

Streeter, Margaret B.: trust, Anderson Foundation (NY)

Streng, William Paul: secretary, treasurer, Lennox Foundation (Martha, David and Bagby)

Stresser, Chris: director, Norcross Wildlife Foundation

Stribling, Jera G.: executive director, Bruno Charitable Foundation (Joseph S.)

Strickland, Carol A.: chairman corporate contributions committee, U.S. Trust Corp. Foundation

Strickland, David J.: assistant secretary, Unilever United States Foundation

Strickland, Frances: director, Citizens Union Bank Foundation

Strickland, Robert Louis: vice president, Lowe's Charitable and Educational Foundation

Stringfellow, Ladson: trustee, Bell Foundation (S. Lewis and Lucia B.)

Strobel, Pamela B.: chief executive officer, Commonwealth Edison Co.

Strock, Faraday J.: trustee, Yost Trust (J. Paul)

Strom, Lee D.: director, Crummer Foundation (Roy E.)

Stromberg, Burle U.: director, Portsmouth General Hospital Foundation

Stromberg, C. W.: off, Stewart Educational Foundation (Donnell B. and Elizabeth Dee Shaw)

Stromberg, Jean G.: director, Hewlett Foundation (William and Flora)

Strong, Bente: director, Strong Foundation (Hattie M.)

Strong, George V., Jr.: secretary, Widgeon Foundation

Strong, Gregory S.: treasurer, Minnesota Mutual Foundation; vice president actuary, Minnesota Mutual Life Insurance Co.

Strong, Henry: chairman, president, officer, Strong Foundation (Hattie M.)

Strong, Henry L.: vice president, officer, Strong Foundation (Hattie M.)

Strong, John D., Jr.: trustee, Bernsen Foundation (Grace and Franklin)

Strother, Jack W., Jr.: co-trustee, Commercial Bank Foundation

Strother, Jack W., Sr.: co-trustee, Commercial Bank Foundation

Stroud, Douglas A.: vice president, director, Bertha Foundation

Stroud, Robert R.: vice president, Cremer Foundation

Strovers, Clifford L.: vice president, director, Grinnell Mutual Group Foundation; director, Grinnell Mutual Reinsurance Co.

Strudwick, Barry: trustee, Warfield Memorial Fund (Anna Emory)

Strudwick, Lewis C.: trustee, Warfield Memorial Fund (Anna Emory)

Strumpf, Linda B.: vice president, chief investment officer, Ford Foundation

Stryker, Jon L.: trust, Upjohn Foundation (Harold and Grace)

Stuart, Susan W.: director, Seneca Foods Foundation

Stubblefield, Joel R.: trustee, Reynolds Foundation (Donald W.)

Stubblefield, Nelson: trustee, Cauthorn Charitable Trust (John and Mildred)

Stubing, William C.: president, director, Greenwall Foundation

Stuckeman, Herman Campbell: trustee, Vesuvius Foundation

Stude, Elisa J.: trustee, Brown Foundation

Stude, Herman L.: assistant secretary, Brown Foundation

Stude, Mike S.: chairman, trustee, Brown Foundation

Stuecker, Phillip James: vice president, chief financial officer, secretary, Thomas Foundation

Stuker, Robert: trustee, Chicago Title and Trust Co. Foundation

Stumler, David J.: assistant secretary, Thomas Foundation

Stumpf, E. A., III: trustee, Wortham Foundation

Sturgeon, Barry M.: trustee, Davenport Trust Fund

Sturges, Caren: trustee, Ingalls Foundation (Louise H. and David S.)

Sturges, Carrie Trammell: board of directors, Fondren Foundation

Sturges, Robert: vice president, Arison Foundation

Sturgis, Christine: program officer, Mott Foundation (Charles Stewart)

Suarez, Rocio: executive director, Baker Trust (George F.)

Subik, Clark D.: trustee, City National Bank Foundation

Subourne, Mary Lee: trustee, Red Devil Foundation

Sudderth, Robert J., Jr.: president, Benwood Foundation

Sudhoff, Robert J.: vice president financial, chief financial officer, Minster Machine Co.; vice president, secretary, Minster Machine Co. Foundation

Sugasawa, Kiyoshi: chief financial officer, Kajima International, Inc.

Sugges, Elizabeth: student board mem, Marshall Foundation

Sullivan, Antony T.: secretary, program officer, Earhart Foundation

Sullivan, Austin Padraic, Junior: trustee, General Mills Foundation; senior vice president corporate relations, General Mills, Inc.

Sullivan, Barbara D., Esq: president, Robinson Fund (Maurice R.)

Sullivan, Bradley J.: assistant treasurer, Dime Savings Bank of Norwich Foundation

Sullivan, Dennis: assistant comptroller, Prudential Foundation

Sullivan, Elizabeth C.: vice president program, Kresge Foundation

Sullivan, Frank P.: vice president sales & marketing, Square D Co.; vice president, director, Square D Foundation

Sullivan, G. Craig: chairman, Clorox Co.

Sullivan, John: group vice president, CNA Foundation

Sullivan, John M.: assistant secretary, treasurer, Cain Foundation (Gordon and Mary)

Sullivan, Kerry H.: trustee officer, director grant making, Balfour Foundation (L. G.); director grant making, Chase Charity Foundation (Alfred E.)

Sullivan, Kevin F.: vice president, PPG Industries Foundation

Sullivan, Kevin I.: trustee, Children's Foundation of Erie County

Sullivan, Laura P.: vice president, secretary, director, State Farm Companies Foundation; vice president, secretary, counsel, State Farm Mutual Automobile Insurance Co.

Sullivan, Peter B.: treasurer, assistant secretary, Sheldon Foundation Inc. (Ralph C.)

Sullivan, Richard J.: trustee, Fund for New Jersey

Sullivan, Roger L.: secretary, Bair Family Trust (Charles M.)

Sullivan, Susan: program officer, Verizon Foundation

Sullivan, T. Dennis: vice president fin, Mellon Foundation (Andrew W.)

Sullivan, Timothy B.: vice chairperson, NMC Foundation

Sullivan, Walter H., Jr.: trustee, Hume Foundation (Jaquelin)

Sullivan, William J.: treasurer, director, Dell Foundation (Hazel)

Sullivan, Wilma J.: secretary, Dime Savings Bank of Norwich Foundation

Sulzberger, Arthur Ochs, Junior: director, chairman, publisher, New York Times Co.

Sulzberger, Arthur Ochs, Sr.: vice president, secretary, Sulzberger Foundation

Sulzberger, Judith P., MD: vice president, director, Sulzberger Foundation

Sulzer, Joseph P.: trustee, Massie Trust (David Meade)

Sumida, Sheila M.: director, First Hawaiian Foundation

Summerall, Robert, Jr.: director, Morgan Foundation (Louie R. and Gertrude)

Summerfield, Esthel: secretary, Abell Foundation

Summers, Mark: trustee, McDonald Investments Foundation

Summers, Stuart G.: senior vice president, general counsel, Ohio National Foundation

Summers, William B., Jr.: chairman, chief executive officer, president, KeyCorp; trustee, McDonald Investments Foundation

Summerville, Frances M.: trustee, Slater Trust (Lillian M.)

Sumter, John: trustee, Bloedorn Foundation (Walter A.)

Sunada, Chris: grant manager, Atherton Family Foundation

Sunday, Nancy: trust, Weatherwax Foundation

Sunderland, Charles T.: vice president, Sunderland Foundation

Sunderland, James P.: director, Francis Families Foundation; chairman, president, Sunderland Foundation

Sunderland, Kenton W.: vice president, secretary, Sunderland Foundation

Sunderland, Robert: vice president, treasurer, director, Sunderland Foundation

Sung, Patsy: co-trustee, Han Charitable Foundation (Edna and Yu-Shan)

Sung, Robert: co-trustee, Han Charitable Foundation (Edna and Yu-Shan)

Suomi, Marvin J.: secretary, Kajima Foundation

Surdam, Robert McCellan: trustee, Wilson Fund (Matilda R.)

Surrey, Mary P.: secretary, treasurer, director, Dreyfus Foundation, Inc. (Max and Victoria)

Suttles, William Maurrelle: trustee, Franklin Foundation Inc. (John and Mary)

Sutton, Donald C.: trustee, Van Wert County Foundation

Sutton, Howard: president, chief executive officer, Providence Journal Charitable Foundation; trustee, Steelcase Foundation

Sutton, Thomas C.: chairman, director, Pacific Life Foundation; chairman, chief executive officer, director, Pacific Life Insurance Co.

Suwyn, Mark A.: chairman, president, Louisiana-Pacific Foundation

Suzaki, Takeshi: secretary, treasurer, Kawasaki Good Times Foundation

Suzuki, Kari: program associate, Bremer Foundation (Otto)

Swain, Kristin A.: president, Corning Inc. Foundation

Swalm, David C.: vice president, trustee, Swalm Foundation

Swalm, Jo Beth Camp: president, trustee, Swalm Foundation

Swan, Barbara J.: director, Alliant Energy Foundation, Inc.

Swan, Philip V.: vice president, treasurer, Peppers Foundation (Ann)

Swan, Robert W.: trustee, Hilliard Foundation

Swan, Robert C.: vice president, secretary, Phelps Dodge Corp.; president, Phelps Dodge Foundation

Swan, William C.: director, Weber Charities Corp. (Frederick E.)

Swander, Dan: president, chief operating officer, International Multifoods Corp.

Swaney, Robert E., Jr.: vice president, chief investment officer, Mott Foundation (Charles Stewart)

Swann, Roy W.: trustee, Smith Foundation (William R. and Sara Babb)

Swanson, E. William: director, Hale Foundation (Crescent Porter)

Swanson, Earl: director, member, Katzenberger Foundation

Swanson, Linda: director, Gebbie Foundation

Swanson, Lynwood W.: trustee, Murdock Charitable Trust (M. J.)

Swanson, W. Charles: chairman, Swanson Family Foundation, Inc. (Dr. W. C.)

Swasey, Frederick W.: honorary trustee, Fuller Foundation (MA)

Swasey, Hope Halsey: trustee, Fuller Foundation (MA)

Sweasy, William J.: president, Red Wing Shoe Co. Foundation

Sweat, Carol G.: trustee, Garvey Texas Foundation

Sweeney, Michael: secretary, treasurer, Wilkof Foundation (Edward and Ruth)

Sweeney, Robert: president, director, King Foundation (Kenneth Kendal)

Sweeney, Thomas Joseph, Jr.: vice president, treasurer, Dreyfus Foundation (Jean and Louis); co-trustee, Kranes Charitable Trust (Sidney and Judith); trustee, Pinkerton Foundation

Sweet, Adele Hall: president, Schiff Foundation (Dorothy)

Swenson, Hal: trustee, Michael Foundation (Herbert I. and Elsa B.)

Swift, Bryan: president, Swift Print Communications

Swift, E. Clinton: director, Phillips Foundation (Ellis L.)

Swift, Hampden M.: co-trustee, Swift Co. Inc. Charitable Trust (John S.)

Swig, Kent: trustee, Swig Foundation (The)

Swig, Richard L.: trustee, Swig Foundation (The)

Swig, Robert: trustee, Swig Foundation (The)

Swig, Steven L.: trustee, Swig Foundation (The)

Swindoll, B. Carver: director, Mingenback Foundation (Julia J.)

Swinney, Caroline T.: assistant secretary, Motorola Foundation

Switz, Robert E.: senior vice president, chief financial officer, ADC Telecommunications

Swygert, H. Patrick: director, Fannie Mae Foundation

Sykes, James T.: president, Cremer Foundation

Syrmis, Pamela L.: vice president, director, Ittleson Foundation

Syrmis, Victor P., MD: director, Ittleson Foundation

Szabad, George Michael: secretary, treasurer, trustee, Dibner Fund

Szabo, Raymond: secretary, trustee, Eaton Foundation (Cyrus)

Szutu, Gene: hon trustee, Lingnan Foundation

T

Tabah, Mimi D.: chairperson, Wilson Foundation (Marie C. and Joseph C.)

Tabankin, Margery: director, Arca Foundation

Taff, Reuvin: distribution trustee, Schwab-Rosenhouse Memorial Foundation

Tafoya, Linda S.: secretary, Castle Rock Foundation; executive director, secretary, Coors Foundation (Adolph)

Taft, Dudley S.: chairman, trustee, Semple Foundation (Louise Taft)

Taft, Robert A., II: trustee, Semple Foundation (Louise Taft)

Taggart, Richard: vice president financial, chief financial officer, Brodbeck Enterprises

Tail, Norbert: secretary, director, McKenna Foundation (Philip M.)

Takahara, Sumiko: trustee, United States-Japan Foundation

Takamatsu, Hiroshi: director, Kikkoman Foundation

Takanishi, Ruby: president, member executive committee, director, Foundation for Child Development

Takehara, Masataka: chairman, president, chief executive officer, Mitsubishi Semiconductor America; president, director, Mitsubishi Semiconductor America, Inc. Funds

Takeuchi, Seiichi: secretary, treasurer, Bandai Foundation

Talbot, Deborah L.: trustee, J.P. Morgan Chase Foundation

Talbrook, Philip Mark: board member, Jacobs Family Foundation

Taleff, Lynne: director, Hardin Foundation (Phil)

Talen, Polly M.: senior program officer, social action, Target Corp.

Tallent, Charles J.: trustee, Arkell Hall Foundation

Talley, Rebecca: trustee, McDonald Investments Foundation

Tallon, James J., Jr.: director, Commonwealth Fund (The)

Tanaka, Ted: director, Nakamichi Foundation (E.)

Tanner, Harold: president, Revson Foundation (Charles H.)

Tanner, Henry J.: director, Scott Foundation (Virginia Steele)

Tanner, James T.: chairman, Tanner Companies (Rutherfordton, NC); president, Tanner Foundation

Tanner, L. Gene: treasurer, Noyes, Jr. Memorial Foundation (Nicholas H.)

Tanner, Michael S.: secretary, Tanner Foundation

Tanner, Pell: director, Tanner Foundation

Tanner, Robin C.: treasurer, director loans, office, Strong Foundation (Hattie M.)

Tapp, Frances Carr: trustee, Dougherty, Jr. Foundation (James R.)

Taradash, Bernard A. G.: trustee, Grimshaw-Gudewicz Charitable Foundation

Tarica, Regina Amado: vice president, cfo, director, Amado Foundation (Maurice)

Tarica, Samuel R.: vice president, director, Amado Foundation (Maurice)

Tarnok, Robert C.: controller, MetLife Foundation

Tata, Ratan Naval: trustee, Ford Foundation

Tate, Linda Crowe: vice president, director, McMillen Foundation

Tate, Warren E.: section, treasurer, Gulf Power Foundation

Tatlock, Anne M.: trustee, Hughes Medical Institute (Howard); director, Teagle Foundation

Tatro, Wayne S.: director, Provident Community Foundation

Tatum, Jacquelyn: assistant trustee, BellSouth Foundation

Tatum, Linda: secretary, treasurer, Lesher Foundation (Dean and Margaret)

Taube, Thaddeus N.: president, director, Koret Foundation; chairman, Taube Family Foundation

Taubman, A. Alfred: chairman, treasurer, trustee, Taubman Foundation (A. Alfred)

Taubman, Judith M.: trustee, Taubman Foundation (A. Alfred)

Taubman, Nancy: president, Fischbach Foundation

Taubman, Robert S.: trustee, Skillman Foundation

Taubman, Selwyn: treasurer, Fischbach Foundation

Taubman, William S.: trustee, Taubman Foundation (A. Alfred)

Tauck, Arthur C.: trustee, Tauck Foundation (Arthur C. and Lee Anne)

Tauke, Thomas J.: executive vice president, Verizon Foundation

Taurel, Sidney: chairman, president, chief executive officer, Eli Lilly & Co.

Tavelli, Mark F.: director, Washington Group Foundation, Inc.

Taveras, Barbara: president, Hazen Foundation (Edward W.)

Tavlin, Michael John: assistant treasurer, Woods Charitable Fund

Taylor, Alexander S., II: trustee, Bicknell Fund

Taylor, Alfred Hendricks, Jr.: trustee, Kresge Foundation

Taylor, Alice: director, Memorial Foundation for the Blind

Taylor, Allen M.: chairman, director, Bradley Foundation (Lynde and Harry)

Taylor, Barbara Olin: board member, trustee, Olin Foundation (Spencer T. and Ann W.)

Taylor, Benjamin B.: director, Boston Globe Foundation

Taylor, Brett M., Junior: director, Hickory Tech Corp.; president, Hickory Tech Corp. Foundation

Taylor, David H.: vice president, director, Davenport-Hatch Foundation

Taylor, Douglas F.: director, Davenport-Hatch Foundation

Taylor, F. Morgan, Jr.: board member, trustee, Olin Foundation (Spencer T. and Ann W.)

Taylor, Frederick B.: vice chairman, chief investment officer, United States Trust Co. of New York

Taylor, Irby N.: director, Hawn Foundation

Taylor, J. P.: board mem, Roberts Foundation (Dora)

Taylor, Jean: assistant secretary, Cisco Systems Foundation

Taylor, John R.: investment officer, Heinz Family Foundation

Taylor, Kenneth Nathaniel: director, Tyndale House Foundation

Taylor, Margaret L.: treasurer, chief financial officer, Duffield Family Foundation

Taylor, Margaret W.: secretary, treasurer, Tyndale House Foundation

Taylor, Mark: vice president, Burns & McDonnell

Taylor, Mark Douglas: assistant secretary, Tyndale House Foundation

Taylor, Mary E.: vice president, trustee, Merrill Lynch & Co. Foundation Inc.

Taylor, Nick R.: co-trustee, Baright Foundation (Hollis and Helen)

Taylor, Penelope J.: trustee, The MBNA Foundation

Taylor, Peter J.: director, Irvine Foundation (The James)

Taylor, Peter W.: director, Tyndale House Foundation

Taylor, Philip E.: president, chief executive officer, JSJ Corp.

Taylor, Priscilla P.: executive director, Cemala Foundation

Taylor, R. E. (Gene): trustee, Bank of America Foundation

Taylor, S. Martin: senior vice president human resources & corporate affairs, DTE Energy Co.; president, director, DTE Energy Foundation

Taylor, Steven W.: trustee, Puterbaugh Foundation

Taylor, Teddy O.: trustee, Blount Educational and Charitable Foundation (Mildred Weedon)

Taylor, Terrence J.: treasurer, ONDEO Nalco Foundation

Taylor, William G.: director, Springs Foundation, Inc.

Taylor Hansen, Susan: director, Portsmouth General Hospital Foundation

Tchen, Tina: director, Field Foundation of Illinois

Teaff, Bob: trustee, Cauthorn Charitable Trust (John and Mildred)

Teagle, Walter C., III: director, Teagle Foundation

Teague, Barry L.: member, Campbell Foundation (J. Bulow)

Teague, Lawrence Barry: trustee, Campbell Foundation (J. Bulow)

Teague, William J.: trustee, Mabee Foundation, Inc. (J. E. and L. E.)

Tedesco, Ralph: member, NYSEG Foundation, Inc.

Teichert, Frederick A.: executive director, Teichert Foundation

Teichert, Melita M.: director, Teichert Foundation

Teitz, Jeffrey J.: trustee, Adelson Trust (Diana S.)

Tellalian, Aram H., Jr.: president, trustee, Jones and Bessie D. Phelps Foundation (Cyrus W. and Amy F.)

Tellalian, Robert S.: secretary, trustee, Jones and Bessie D. Phelps Foundation (Cyrus W. and Amy F.)

Tellez, Cora M.: vice president, director, Cowell Foundation (S. H.)

Tellez, Luis E.: treasurer, director, Clover Foundation

Tempas, Jeffrey J.: director, Ray Foundation

Temple, Arthur, III: trustee, Temple Foundation (T. L. L.); chairman, chief executive officer, Temple-Inland Foundation

Temple, Arthur, Jr.: chairman, trustee, Temple Foundation (T. L. L.)

Templeton, D. Jeffrey: director, Woronoco Savings Charitable Foundation

Templeton, Edward O.: director, St. Francis Bank Foundation

Templeton, Robert: mem, Templeton Foundation (Herbert A.)

Templin, Gary A.: director, Haigh-Scatena Foundation

Ten Pas, Paul H.: secretary, director, Kohler Foundation

Tengi, Frank R.: treasurer, Starr Foundation

Tenney, Daniel Gleason, Jr.: secretary, JM Foundation

Tennison, Raymond P.: director, Simpson Fund

Tenny, Barron M.: executive vice president, secretary, general counsel, Ford Foundation

Tepner, Ronald: member, Bridgestone/Firestone Trust Fund (The)

Terlizzi, Donald: director, Capezio/Ballet Makers Dance Foundation

Terlizzi, Nick, Jr.: chairman, director, Ballet Makers; vice president, Capezio/Ballet Makers Dance Foundation

Termondt, M. James: president, treasurer, Fry Foundation (Lloyd A.); secretary, director, Wehr Foundation (Todd)

Terpenning, Linda M.: membership, Foster Co. Charitable Trust (L.B.)

Terrien, Linda L.: assistant treasurer, Weyerhaeuser Co. Foundation

Terry, Charles R., Sr.: chairman, Hill Crest Foundation

Terry, Mary: assistant secretary, Reader's Digest Foundation

Terry, Thomas T.: trustee, Mascoma Savings Bank Foundation

Tessler, C.: secretary, Long Foundation (J. M.)

Testa, Linda: program manager, Microsoft Corp.

Testa, Richard J.: president, treasurer, director, Beaucourt Foundation; trustee, Keel Foundation

TeStrake, Harvey D.: mgr, secretary, Miller Foundation (Steve J.)

Tetterton, Clarence E.: secretary, treasurer, Tri-County Telephone Foundation

Thacher, Michael: general manager public relations & communications, Unocal Corp.

Thacker, Frank: chairman, AT&T National Pro-Am Youth Fund

Thakkar, Kelly L.: trustee, McKay Family Foundation

Thatcher, Gerald D.: trustee, Van Wert County Foundation

Thaxter, Sidney F.: clerk, Barker Foundation Inc.

Thayer, Tyrone K.: corp. vice president, Cargill, Inc.

Theisen, Herbert J.: assistant secretary, general counsel, Johnson Foundation (A.D.)

Thelander, B. L.: director, ARCO Foundation

Thelen, Cynthia A.: coordinator, General Mills Foundation

Theobald, Jon A.: trustee, Bigelow Foundation (F. R.); vice president, Tozer Foundation

Theobald, Thomas Charles: director, MacArthur Foundation (John D. and Catherine T.)

Thieman, Frederick W.: director, Heinz Endowment (Howard)

Thier, Samuel O., MD: director, Commonwealth Fund (The)

Thies, Richard Henry: assistant treasurer, Madison Gas & Electric Foundation

Thomas, David A.: director, member legal committee, Keck Foundation (W. M.)

Thomas, Dennis: director, International Paper Co. Foundation

Thomas, Gladys R.: vice president, Starr Foundation

Thomas, Glenn E.: director, Thomas Foundation (Joan and Lee)

Thomas, J. G.: trustee, Fortis Foundation

Thomas, James A.: director, Parsons Foundation (Ralph M.)

Thomas, Jane R.: trustee, Skillman Foundation

Thomas, Joan E.: director, Thomas Foundation (Joan and Lee)

Thomas, Julie: comm mem, Wells Foundation (Franklin H. and Ruth L.)

Thomas, L. Newton, Jr.: president, Daywood Foundation; trustee, Jacobson Foundation (Bernard H. and Blanche E.)

Thomas, Larry R.: director, Washington Group Foundation, Inc.

Thomas, Lee B.: director, Thomas Foundation (Joan and Lee)

Thomas, Lowell S., Jr.: director, Barra Foundation

Thomas, Lyda Ann Quinn: trustee, Kempner Fund (Harris and Eliza)

Thomas, Margaret Jean: executive director, secretary, Grotto Foundation

Thomas, Michael E.: director, Morrison Foundation (Harry W.)

Thomas, Richard L.: director, Sara Lee Corp.

Thompson, Billie: secretary, trustee, Doss Foundation, Inc. (M. S.)

Thompson, Christine: secretary, Marshall Foundation

Thompson, Donald L.: chairman, chief executive officer, Hunt Corp.

Thompson, E. Arthur: president, Cooper Foundation

Thompson, E. N.: chairman, Cooper Foundation

Thompson, Frederic: trustee, Davies Benevolent Fund (Edward H.)

Thompson, Gene: director, Jones Foundation (Harvey and Bernice)

Thompson, George: trustee, Blandin Foundation

Thompson, Harry A.: trustee, Vesuvius Foundation

Thompson, J. K.: director, ARCO Foundation

Thompson, Jack Edward: trustee, Cooper Foundation

Thompson, Jane A.: trustee, Vesuvius Foundation

Thompson, Janice: secretary, treasurer, Herd Foundation (Bob L.)

Thompson, Jesse J.: director, Thompson Charitable Foundation

Thompson, Jim: president, chief executive officer, ING North America Insurance Corp.

Thompson, Kirby A.: trustee, Equifax Foundation

Thompson, Leonora Kempner: chairman emeritus, Kempner Fund (Harris and Eliza)

Thompson, Marcia T.: director, Scherman Foundation

Thompson, Margaret E.: trustee, Dow Foundation (Herbert H. and Grace A.)

Thompson, Margaret E., MD: trustee, Towsley Foundation (Harry A. and Margaret D.)

Thompson, Melinda: treasurer, director, Patron Saints Foundation

Thompson, Mildred: trustee, Zellerbach Family Fund

Thompson, Mona: trustee, Coen Family Foundation (Charles S. and Mary)

Thompson, Nelda: secretary, trustee, CH Foundation

Thompson, Peter K., MD: treasurer, Kempner Fund (Harris and Eliza)

Thompson, Ralph LaSalle: treasurer, Grinnell Mutual Group Foundation

Thompson, Richard L.: director, Bristol-Myers Squibb Foundation Inc.

Thompson, Roger K.: trustee, Van Wert County Foundation

Thompson, Sylvia M.: director, Thompson Charitable Foundation

Thomsen, C. J.: trustee, McDermott Foundation (The Eugene)

Thomson, Lucy M.: vice president, trustee, Morley Foundation

Thomson, R. Patrick: president, director, New York Mercantile Exchange

Thomson, Richard B., Jr.: trustee, Morley Foundation

Thomson, Robert C., Jr.: president, treasurer, director, Vernon Foundation (Miles Hodsdon)

Thoreen, John F.: director, Tozer Foundation

Thorn, Therese M.: trustee, Ratner Foundation (Milton M.)

Thornburgh, Richard E.: chief financial officer, member, Credit Suisse First Boston Foundation Trust

Thorne, Daniel Kempner: trustee, Kempner Fund (Harris and Eliza)

Thorne, Felicitas Selter: vice president, Millbrook Tribute Garden

Thorne, Jane W.: trustee emeritus, Fund for New Jersey

Thorne, Oakleigh: trustee, Millbrook Tribute Garden

Thorne, Oakleigh Blakeman: president, trustee, Millbrook Tribute Garden

Thornton, B. H.: trustee, Share Trust (Charles Morton)

Thornton, Charles B., Jr.: president, Thornton Foundation

Thornton, Flora L.: trustee, Thornton Foundation (Flora L.)

Thornton, Thomas N.: director, Andrews McMeel Universal Foundation

Thornton, William Laney: vice president, Thornton Foundation; trustee, Thornton Foundation (Flora L.)

Thorpe, Brendan: secretary, Keck Foundation (W. M.)

Thorpe, Neal O.: executive director, trustee, Murdock Charitable Trust (M. J.)

Thorson, Steven J., M.D.: director, Copic Medical Foundation

Thorstenson, T.: vice president, Caterpillar Foundation

Thrall, Gordon: trustee, Norman Foundation (Summers A.)

Thralls, Sharon: director, Patron Saints Foundation

Throop, William M., Jr.: trustee, Bingham Second Betterment Fund (William)

Thrower, Larry W.: vice president, director, Copic Medical Foundation

Thrune, Charles J.: assistant vice president, trustee, Strosacker Foundation (Charles J.)

Thun, Michael J.: trustee, Wyomissing Foundation

Thurber, Peter Palms: trustee, McGregor Fund

Thurston, Samuel E.: senior vice president distribution, Giant Food, Inc.

Thye, Pamela M.: chairman, Steinman Foundation (John Frederick)

Tibitts, Daniel: director, AT&T National Pro-Am Youth Fund

Tice, Mark Randolph: director, Lebanon Mutual Foundation

Ticknor, David: adv, Delano Foundation (Mignon Sherwood)

Tieken, Theodore D.: director, Demos Foundation (N.)

Tienda, Marta, PhD: trustee, Carnegie Corp. of New York

Tifft, Kenneth A.: assistant secretary, trustee, Anderson Foundation (NY)

Tiger, Edith: trustee, Boehm Foundation

Tilleman, Paul J.: treasurer, director, Stackner Family Foundation

Tillman, Robert L.: chairman, president, chief executive officer, Lowe's Companies

Tilton, Glenn F.: vice chairman, director, ChevronTexaco Corp.

Tilton, Sumner B., Jr.: trustee, Ellsworth Foundation (Ruth H. and Warren A.)

Timken, William Robert, Jr.: vice president, trustee, Timken Foundation of Canton

Timmerman, Robert P.: board mem, director, Gregg-Graniteville Foundation

Tippett, Henry H.: secretary, treasurer, Tiscornia Foundation

Tippins, Carolyn H.: trustee, Tippins Foundation

Tippins, George W.: trustee, Tippins Foundation

Tippitt, Anna: vice president, Vale-Asche Foundation

Tipton, Gwendlyn I.: scholarship admin, director, Cole Foundation (Olive B.)

Tipton, Ronald D.: director, MDU Resources Foundation

Tisch, Andrew H.: trustee, Loews Foundation

Tisch, James S.: president, chief executive officer, director, Loews Corp.

Tisch, Laurence Alan: senior vice president, director, CNA Foundation; co-chairman, director, Loews Corp.; trustee, Loews Foundation

Tisch, Preston Robert: co-chairman, co-chief executive officer, director, CBS Corp.; president, donor, director, CNA Foundation; co-chairman, director, Loews Corp.; trustee, Loews Foundation

Tiscornia, Bernice: first vice president, Tiscornia Foundation

Tiscornia, James: second vice president, Tiscornia Foundation

Tiscornia, Lester C.: president, trustee, Tiscornia Foundation

Toal, Lawrence J.: chairman, chief executive officer, Washington Mutual, Inc.

Tobias, Barry: treasurer, trustee, Sharp Foundation (Evelyn)

Tobias, Randall L.: president, treasurer, Tobias Foundation (Randall L.)

Tobias, Todd C.: vice president, Tobias Foundation (Randall L.)

Tobias-Button, Paige N.: vice president, secretary, Tobias Foundation (Randall L.)

Tobin, Gerald C.: assistant treasurer, assistant secretary, director, Hopkins Foundation (Josephine Lawrence)

Tobisman, Stuart Paul: vice president, director, counsel, Bettingen Corp. (Burton G.)

Todd, A. J., III: chairman, president, chief executive officer, Todd Co. (A.M.); trustee, Todd Co. Foundation (A.M.)

Todd, Sandra: trustee, Patterson Memorial Trust (Hazel)

Todd, Vivian E.: director, Wright Foundation (Lola)

Toft, Richard Paul: chairman, Chicago Title Corp.; trustee, Chicago Title and Trust Co. Foundation

Toledano, John O. H.: vice chairman, secretary, director, Acme-McCrary

Corp./Sapona Manufacturing Co.; vice president, Acme-McCrary and Sapona Foundation

Toledano, John O.H., Jr.: director, Acme-McCrary and Sapona Foundation

Tomas, Kay: secretary, Gilmore Foundation (Irving S.)

Tomer, Richard S.: president, trustee, Andrews Foundation; treasurer, Figgie Educational Foundation

Tomisek, John: secretary, treasurer, director, Cuneo Foundation

Tompkins, Mary K.: secretary-treasurer, McShain Charities (John)

Toms, William: trustee, Ghidotti Foundation

Toohey, Edward Joseph: president, director, Bunbury Co., Inc.; treasurer, trustee, Windham Foundation

Tookmanian, Donna: treasurer, Mailman Family Foundation (A. L.)

Topek, Nathan: director, Herzstein Charitable Foundation (Albert and Ethel)

Toppeta, William J.: director, MetLife Foundation

Torcivia, Carolyn: secretary, Park Bank Foundation

Torgerson, William T.: vice president, cfo, Pepco Holdings, Inc.

Torkildsen, John: assistant controller, IBM International Foundation

Toronto, Shannon K.: executive director, Eccles Foundation (Marriner S.)

Torrance, Susan: assistant secretary, Greenfield Foundation (Albert M.)

Torray, Robert E.: director, Kirkpatrick Foundation, Inc.

Torregrossa, Bernice C.: grants analyst, Moody Foundation

Tosh, Dennis A.: assistant treasurer, Ford Motor Co. Fund

Totten, H. W., Jr.: director, Smith and W. Aubrey Smith Charitable Foundation (Clara Blackford)

Touchton, J. Thomas: director, Beveridge Foundation, Inc. (Frank Stanley)

Toussaint, Carol: Interim executive director, Alliant Energy Foundation, Inc.

Tower, Caroline: director, Haigh-Scatena Foundation

Towers, James K., III: vice president, Gooding Group Foundation

Townsend, Charles C., Jr.: secretary, director, Bunbury Co., Inc.; trustee, Windham Foundation

Townsend, John W., IV: vice president, trustee, Altman Foundation

Townsend, Katie A.: treasurer, ONDEO Nalco Foundation

Townsend, Wilbur L.: director, Allyn Foundation

Trachtenberg, Bruce: director commun, Wallace-Reader's Digest Fund (DeWitt)

Tracy, Charles S.: director, Allyn Foundation

Tracy-Nagle, Patricia: senior vice president, Osher Foundation (Bernard)

Traeger, Michelle O'Shaughnessy: director, O'Shaughnessy Foundation (I. A.)

Train, Russell E.: advisory trustee, Rockefeller Brothers Fund, Inc.

Tran, Khanh T.: executive vice president, chief financial officer, director, Pacific Life Insurance Co.

Trapani, Cosmo S.: executive vice president, chief financial officer, Unitrode Corp.

Trapp, George J.: secretary, director, New York Life Foundation

Trask, Frederick K., III: vice president, assistant secretary, Boettcher Foundation

Trask, Robert B.: president, chief operating officer, director, Country Curtains, Inc.; clerk, trustee, High Meadow Foundation

Traylor, Fasaha M.: senior program officer, Foundation for Child Development

Treadway, Lyman H., III: trustee, Bicknell Fund

Treadwell, David L.: secretary, director, World Heritage Foundation

Treat, Charles O.: vice president, Dime Savings Bank of Norwich Foundation

Treckelo, Richard M.: trustee, Decio Foundation (Arthur J.)

Treeger, Clarence R.: president, trustee, Summerfield Foundation, Inc. (Solon E.)

Treeger, Thomas C.: treasurer, secretary, Summerfield Foundation, Inc. (Solon E.)

Treiber, John A.: vice president, director, Stackner Family Foundation

Treiber, Patricia S.: president, director, Stackner Family Foundation

Tremblay, Wade: trustee, Perry Foundation

Trencher, Lewis J.: chairman, director, Thompson Co. Fund (J. Walter); chief operating officer, director, Thompson Co. (J. Walter)

Trethewey, James A.: senior vice president, operations services, Cleveland-Cliffs, Inc.

Tribble, J. Lee: treasurer, Evans Foundation, Inc. (Lettie Pate)

Trice, Thomas L., IV: treasurer, trustee, Henson Foundation (Richard A.)

Trimble, William C., Jr.: secretary, treasurer, Wilson Sanitarium for Children of Baltimore City (Thomas)

Tripp, Sharon: director, Griffis Foundation

Trobster, Glenn: trustee, Fairchild-Meeker Charitable Trust (Freeman E.)

Trone, George A.: program officer, Mott Foundation (Charles Stewart)

Trosino, Vincent Joseph: assistant secretary, State Farm Companies Foundation; executive vice president, vice chairman, chief operating officer, director, State Farm Mutual Automobile Insurance Co.

Trost, Carlisle Albert H.: director, Olmsted Foundation (George and Carol)

Trost, Cathy: director, member nonmonetary committee, Foundation for Child Development

Trotter, Ann: secretary-treasurer, Anderson Foundation (M. D.)

Trotter, Jack T.: vice president, trustee, Anderson Foundation (M. D.)

Trotter, Lloyd G.: director, Arison Foundation

Trout, David M., Jr.: mgr, Freas Foundation

Trout, Rebecca F.: mgr, Freas Foundation

Trower, Thomas H.: trustee, Bovaird Foundation (Mervin)

True, Lawrence Y.: trustee, Johnson Charitable Educational Trust (James Hervey)

Trull, R. Scott: trustee, Trull Foundation (The)

Trull, Robert B.: founder, trustee emeritus, Trull Foundation (The)

Trussell, Philip A.: director, East Cambridge Savings Charitable Foundation

Tryloff, Robin: executive director community relations, Sara Lee Corp.; president, executive director, director, Sara Lee Foundation

Tse, E. S.: director, Starr Foundation

Tsui, John K.: vice president, director, First Hawaiian Foundation

Tsuji, Masaaki: chairman, president, Bandai Foundation

Tsumura, Monty: chairman, Tsumura International, Inc.

Tubergen, Jerry L.: vice president, secretary, chief operating officer, DeVos Foundation (Richard and Helen)

Tuchler, John E.: president, Marx Foundation (Virginia and Leonard)

Tuck, Daniel H.: director, Tuch Foundation (Michael)

Tuck, Eugene, Esq.: president, Tuch Foundation (Michael)

Tuck, Jonathan S.: director, Tuch Foundation (Michael)

Tucker, Elmer D.: comm mem, Eccles Foundation (Marriner S.)

Tucker, Robert A.: president, director, CTW Foundation, Inc.

Tugwell, Franklin: executive director, Heinz Endowment (Vira I.)

Tullidge, Thomas H.: vice president, trustee, Gray Foundation (Garland and Agnes Taylor)

Tullius, Raymond L., Jr.: trustee, Mabee Foundation, Inc. (J. E. and L. E.)

Tully, Ellen D. B. F.: president, Friendship Fund

Tunheim, Kathryn H.: director, Bush Foundation

Tunioli, Carlo: vice president, general manager, Benetton U.S.A. Corp.

Tunney, Debra L.: program associate, Reynolds Foundation (Donald W.)

Tunney, James J.: vice president, Florsheim Shoe Foundation

Tupper, Christopher N.: corporator, Island Foundation (MA)

Turcik, John J.: controller, Mellon Family Foundation (R. K.)

Turissini, Christina H.: comptroller, Gates Family Foundation

Turk, James C.: trustee, Richardson Benevolent Foundation (C. E.)

Turletes, Vincent N.: trustee, Millbrook Tribute Garden

Turley, Bob: president, chief operating officer, director, Perdue Farms

Turnbull, Kenneth W.: trustee, Schwartz Foundation (Arnold A.)

Turnbull, William: trustee, Victoria Foundation

Turner, Diana Lassalle: director, Norman Foundation

Turner, Frank B.: trustee, Arnold Fund

Turner, Laura Jennings: director, Cockrell Foundation

Turner, Richard: manager corporate contributions, Peoples Energy Corp.

Turner, Roger: member, Norman Foundation

Turner, Ronald G.: vice chairman board trustees, Baker Foundation (R. C.)

Turner, Vivian L.: president, Reynolds Tobacco Company Foundation (R. J.)

Tuross, Noreen: executive director, Watson Foundation (Thomas J.)

Turtell, Dan: chief financial officer, Harper Brush Works

Tusch, Carol: treasurer, International Paper Co. Foundation

Tuthill, Howard S., III: secretary, Norris Foundation (Dellora A. and Lester J.)

Tutt, Russell Thayer, Jr.: president, trustee, El Pomar Foundation

Tuttle, Thomas N., Jr.: treasurer, secretary, Miller Foundation (Steve J.)

Twigg-Smith, Thurston: alternate member, McInerny Foundation

Twomley, Dale E.: president, chief executive officer, director, Worthington Foods; trustee, Worthington Foods Foundation

Tyburski, Charles: member distribution committee, Flowers Charitable Trust (Albert W. and Edith V.)

Tyler, Kenneth: trustee, Leavey Foundation (Thomas and Dorothy)

Tyler, Ronnie Curtis: director, Summerlee Foundation

Tyler, William B.: trustee, Alden Trust (John W.)

Tynan, Ronald B.: chairman, Flowers Charitable Trust (Albert W. and Edith V.)

Tynan-Chapman, Patricia: secretary, director, Harden Foundation

Tyrie, James C.: co-trustee, Hunt Foundation (Samuel P.)

Tyson, Janice C.: secretary, Clemens Foundation

Tysse, John W.: trustee, Strosacker Foundation (Charles J.)

Tytus, John: trustee, Semple Foundation (Louise Taft)

U

Uber, Daryl Brown: vice president, Weiss Foundation (William E.)

Uchida, Hisashi: senior executive vice president administration, Mitsubishi Silicon America

Ueberroth, Joseph: treas, Ueberroth Family Foundation

Ueberroth, Peter Victor: vice president, Ueberroth Family Foundation

Ueberroth, Virginia: president, Ueberroth Family Foundation

Ueberroth Booth, Vicki: secretary, Ueberroth Family Foundation

Ughetta, William C.: trustee, Corning Inc. Foundation

Uihlein, David V., Jr.: director, Bradley Foundation (Lynde and Harry)

Ukropina, James R.: director, member legal committee, Keck Foundation (W. M.)

Ulatowski, Lois E.: assistant secretary, Warwick Savings Foundation

Ulf, Franklin E.: director, Parsons Foundation (Ralph M.)

Ulrich, Don A.: executive director, Reeves Foundation (OH)

Ulrich, Robert J.: chairman, chief executive officer, director, Target Corp.; chairman, trustee, Target Foundation

Ulsh, Sandy: vice president, executive director, Ford Motor Co.

Ummer, James Walter, Esq.: director, Snee-Reinhardt Charitable Foundation

Underhill, Evelyn: trustee, Norman Foundation (Summers A.)

Underwood, Cecil H.: president, Huntington Foundation

Underwood, David M.: board of directors, Fondren Foundation

Underwood, David M., Jr: board of directors, Fondren Foundation

Underwood, Frank D.: executive director, member, Forest Foundation

Underwood, Lynda Knapp: board of directors, Fondren Foundation

Unger, James J.: vice chairman, chief executive officer, ACF Industries

Unger, Leonard: secretary, treasurer, director, Lavine Family Foundation (Richard and Ruth)

Unger, Ruth Halls: trustee, Ghidotti Foundation

Ungerland, Thomas J.: trustee, Edison Fund (Charles)

Ungerleider, Jeane: president, Dorot Foundation

Ungerleider, Steven: vice president, Dorot Foundation

Unkrur, Theresa: contributions committee, CNA Foundation

Unruh, Eugene: trustee, Schowalter Foundation

Upton, David F.: trustee, Upton Foundation (Frederick S.)

Upton, Stephen E., LHD: chairman board trustees, Upton Foundation (Frederick S.)

Urahn, Susan: director education, Pew Charitable Trusts

Urban, Henry Zellar: director, Knox Foundation (Seymour H.)

Urban, Mary Bright: vice president, secretary, Weathertop Foundation

Urban, Thomas N., III: director, Weathertop Foundation

Urban, Thomas Nelson, Jr.: chairman, president, Weathertop Foundation

Urban, William G.: treasurer, Weathertop Foundation

Urda, Linda V., PhD: assoc director, GAR Foundation

Uribe de Mena, Joanna: vice president, Haigh-Scatena Foundation

Urkowitz, Michael: senior vice president, J.P. Morgan Chase & Co.; trustee, J.P. Morgan Chase Foundation

Ursu, John Joseph: director, 3M Foundation; general counsel, senior vice president legal affairs, Minnesota Mining & Manufacturing Co.

Ury, Robert I.: vice president, secretary, director, Lederer Foundation (Francis L.)

Usdan, Adam: vice president, Lemberg Foundation

Usdan, John: treasurer, Lemberg Foundation

Usdan, Suzanne: president, Lemberg Foundation

Usher, Thomas J.: chairman, chief executive officer, U.S. Steel Corp.; chairman board trustees, U.S. Steel Foundation

Ushio, Jiro: vchairman board trustee, United States-Japan Foundation

Usibelli, Joseph E., Jr.: president, chief executive officer, director, Usibelli Coal Mine, Inc.; director, Usibelli Foundation

Usibelli, Joseph E., Sr.: chairman, Usibelli Coal Mine, Inc.; director, Usibelli Foundation

Utley, L.: president, General Motors Foundation

Utterback, Ann M.: director, Maddox Foundation (J. F.)

V

Vagelos, Pindaros Roy: trustee, Prudential Insurance Co. of America

Vahlberg, Vivian: director journalism program, McCormick Tribune Foundation (Robert R.)

Vaimberg, Mitzi: vice president civic community services, AT&T Foundation

Valade, Gary C.: executive vice president, chief financial officer, DaimlerChrysler AG; trustee, DaimlerChrysler Corp. Fund

Vale, Beverly: director, Feinstein Foundation

Vale, Richard T.: director, Snee-Reinhardt Charitable Foundation

Valentine, E. Massey: trustee, Chesapeake Corp. Foundation

Valentine, J. E.: chief financial officer, Bardes Corp.

Valentine, Joan Selverstone: director, Research Corp.

Valentine, Joseph: director, Stulsaft Foundation (Morris)

Valentine, Katrina: secretary, McDonough Foundation (Bernard)

Valentine, Volina Cline: secretary, director, Fullerton Foundation

Valentino, Nick: treasurer, Britton Fund

Valla, Eugene L.: cfo, director, Lurie Foundation (Louis R.)

Vallene, Joseph A., III: trustee, Snyder Foundation (Harold B. and Dorothy A.)

Valley, Tamara A.: chairman, Valley Foundation (Wayne and Gladys)

Valliant, John R.: trustee, Kerr Fund (Grayce B.)

Vallier, Marjorie A.: secretary, director, Schroeder Foundation (Walter)

Van Alen, Elizabeth K.: president, treasurer, trustee, Kent-Lucas Foundation

Van Alen, James L., II: trustee, Kent-Lucas Foundation

Van Alen, William L.: vice president, trustee, Kent-Lucas Foundation

Van Allen, Hazel C. (Bretzlaff): president, Bretzlaff Foundation

Van Allen, William G.: secretary, Bretzlaff Foundation

Van Andel, David: vice president, trustee, Van Andel Foundation (Jay and Betty)

Van Andel, Jay: president, trustee, Van Andel Foundation (Jay and Betty)

Van Atten, Carol: assistant secretary, Hayden Foundation (Charles)

Van Benschoten, David: vice president, treasurer, General Mills Foundation

Van Berkel, Thomas M.: trustee, National Grange Mutual Charitable Trust

van Beuren, John A.: trustee, McBean Charitable Trust (Alletta Morris)

Van Bronkhorst, Edwin E.: honorary emeritus trustee, Packard Foundation (David and Lucile)

Van Buren, Elsie Proctor: trustee, Van Buren Foundation (Elsie Procter)

Van Clief, Mary Ann: vice president, director, Brookdale Foundation

Van de Bovenkamp, Sue Erpf: president, director, Erpf Fund (Armand G.)

Van De Maele, Joan G.: director, Guggenheim Foundation (Harry Frank)

Van den Berg, Margaret: administration assistant, Kerr Fund (Grayce B.)

van den Blink, Jan: trustee, Hilliard Foundation

van den Blink, Nelson Mooers: chairman, chief executive officer, treasurer, director, Hilliard Corp.; president, trustee, Hilliard Foundation

Van Doren, James E.: trustee, Sage Foundation

Van Dormolen, Ann L.: vice president, treasurer, Weingart Foundation

Van Dusen, Albert Clarence: vchairman, Buhl Foundation (PA)

Van Dyk, Alison Jackson: trustee, Connemara Fund

Van Dyke, Clifford D.: vice president, Kantzler Foundation

Van Dyke, John W.: senior vice president, chief financial officer, director, American Optical Corp.

Van Dyke, William Grant: chairman, president, chief executive officer, director, Donaldson Company, Inc.

Van Ee, Henry: admin, Seidman Family Foundation

Van Evera, William P.: co-trustee, Van Evera Foundation (Dewitt)

Van Gorden, Mary: trustee, Lunda Charitable Trust

Van Gorder, John Frederic: executive director, Lowenstein Foundation (Leon)

Van Liemt, Hans B.: director, Sara Lee Corp.

Van Loan, Katherine R.: trustee at large, Raskob Foundation for Catholic Activities, Inc.

Van Ness, Stanley C.: trustee, Prudential Foundation

Van Nort, Peter S.: president, Zachry Co. (H.B.)

Van Pelt, Lester, Jr.: secretary-treasurer, trustee, Abell-Hanger Foundation

Van Rees, Linda: financial trustee, Schwab-Rosenhouse Memorial Foundation

Van Riper, Jeffrey L.: secretary, Seneca Foods Foundation

Van Sant, Nadine: president, Pick, Jr. Fund (Albert)

Van Soelen, Ted: president, director, Fab Steel Products Foundation

Van Vliet, Emily: trustee, Peterson Charitable Foundation (Folke H.)

Van Vliet, Frank: trustee, Peterson Charitable Foundation (Folke H.)

Van Zante, Mary: secretary, Pella Rolscreen Foundation

Van Zyl, Gyte: vice president, director, Bettingen Corp. (Burton G.)

Van Zyl, Jane: director, Bettingen Corp. (Burton G.)

Van Zytveld, John: senior program director, Murdock Charitable Trust (M. J.)

Vance, Douglass: vice president, director, Berger Foundation (H. N. and Frances C.)

Vandagriff, Judy A.: senior vice president, El Paso Corporate Foundation

vanden Henvel, Melinda F.: trustee, Fuller Foundation (MA)

Vander Ark, Tom: executive director education, Gates Foundation (Bill and Melinda)

Vanderbilt, Hugh Bedford, Jr.: trustee, Vanderbilt Trust (R. T.)

Vanderbilt, Hugh Bedford, Sr.: chairman, trustee, Vanderbilt Trust (R. T.)

Vanderbilt, P.: trustee, Vanderbilt Trust (R. T.)

Vanderbilt, Robert T., Jr.: trustee, Vanderbilt Trust (R. T.)

VanderRoest, Stan M.: treasurer, trustee, Gerber Foundation

Vandiver, Susan T.: vice president grant programs, Cowell Foundation (S. H.)

Vangelis, Damon A.: program associate, Olin Foundation (John M.)

Vanison, Richard C.: assistant treasurer, Clark Foundation (NY)

Vann, James M.: chairman, director, Vann Family Foundation

Vann, James M., III: director, Vann Family Foundation

Vann, Marjorie Lee: president, director, Vann Family Foundation

Vann, Thomas H., Jr.: director, Williams Family Foundation of Georgia

Vanosdol, Thomas: chairman, Ford Meter Box Foundation

Vanz, Robert: trustee, Acushnet Foundation

Vargas, Arturo: trustee, Hazen Foundation (Edward W.)

Varner, Durward B.: trustee, Cooper Foundation

Vasquez, Anthony A.: computer specialist, Bremer Foundation (Otto)

Vaughan, Anne V.: assistant secretary, Burlington Resources Foundation

Vaughan, Ben F., III: trustee, Dougherty, Jr. Foundation (James R.); president, trustee, Vaughan Foundation (Rachael and Ben)

Vaughan, Ben F., IV: vice president, trustee, Vaughan Foundation (Rachael and Ben)

Vaughan, Daphne duPont: secretary, treasurer, trustee, Vaughan Foundation (Rachael and Ben)

Vaughan, Genevieve: trustee, Dougherty, Jr. Foundation (James R.); vice president, trustee, Vaughan Foundation (Rachael and Ben)

Vaughan, John B.: president, director, Vaughan Foundation; chairman, chief executive officer, Vaughan Furniture Co.

Vaughan, William B.: president, Vaughan Furniture Co.

Vaughn, James M.: director, Vaughn Foundation (Jim M.)

Vaughn, James M., Jr.: director, Vaughn Foundation (Jim M.); president, Vaughn, Jr. Foundation Fund (James M.)

Vaughn, Sally: vice president, Vaughn, Jr. Foundation Fund (James M.)

Vaun, William S., MD: vice president, director, Greenwall Foundation

Vawter, Paul E.: trustee, Valentine Foundation (Lawson)

Veitenhans, Karen L.: secretary, Weyerhaeuser Co. Foundation

Venteicher, Louis: chairman, president, chief executive officer, Audubon State Bank

Vera, George: director finance and administration, Packard Foundation (David and Lucile)

Verenes, George: treasurer, director, Harcourt Foundation (Ellen Knowles)

Vergas, Sophia: secretary, administrator, Liberty Corp. Foundation

Vergin, Brian: trustee, Blandin Foundation

Verity, C. William, Jr.: director emeritus, Keck Foundation (W. M.)

Verney, E. Geoffrey: trustee, Verney Foundation (Gilbert)

Verney, Richard Greville: chairman, chief executive officer, director, Monadnock Paper Mills, Inc.; president, Verney Foundation (Gilbert)

Vernon, Russell O.: director, Hebrew Technical Institute

Verrecchia, Alfred J.: treasurer, trustee, Hasbro Charitable Trust Inc.; executive, director, Hasbro, Inc.

Verret, Paul A.: secretary, treasurer, Bigelow Foundation (F. R.); secretary, Mardag Foundation

Verville, Norbert J.: treasurer, Bucyrus-Erie Foundation; vice president, chief financial officer, treasurer, director, Bucyrus International, Inc.

Vetrovec, Pauline: secretary, director, Jameson Foundation (J. W. and Ida M.)

Vett, Thomas W.: secretary, treasurer, King Foundation (Carl B. and Florence E.)

Viall, William A.: trustee, Littlefield Memorial Trust (Ida Ballou)

Viault, Raymond: vice chairman, director, General Mills, Inc.

Vierk, Richard: trustee, Cooper Foundation

Vigeland, Julie: co-trustee, Jackson Foundation (OR); director, Wessinger Foundation

Vilcot, Gerard: treasurer, IBM International Foundation

Villani, Edmond D.: trustee, Rockefeller Brothers Fund, Inc.

Vincent, Kirk F.: executive vice president, J&L Specialty Steel, Inc.

Vincent, Luci Daley: director, Hamilton Charitable Corp.

Vinney, Les C.: senior vice president, chief financial officer, Goodrich Corp.

Vinolus, Peter: vice chairman, trustee, Statler Foundation

Vinovich, William N.: vice chairman, trustee, Anderson Foundation (John W.)

Viola, Vincent: chairman, director, New York Mercantile Exchange Charitable Foundation

Virch, Claus: trustee, Sharp Foundation (Evelyn)

Visbal, J. Malcolm: director, Gellert Foundation (Carl Gellert and Celia Berta)

Vitarelli, Robert: program officer, Reynolds Foundation (Christopher)

Vitto, Myra: trustee, Watson Foundation (Walter E. and Caroline H.)

Vliet, Marni: president, chief executive officer, Kansas Health Foundation

Voegeli, William: program officer, Olin Foundation (John M.)

Voelkel, Alice K.: trustee, Knott Foundation (Marion I. and Henry J.)

Voelte, D. R.: director, ARCO Foundation

Voetman, David A.: director, Young Foundation (Irvin L.)

Vogel, Daniel C.: vice president, Vogel Foundation

Vogel, David L.: president, Vogel Foundation

Vogel, Judith: director, Mid-Iowa Health Foundation

Vogel, Peter C.: secretary, Vogel Foundation

Vogt, David: adv, O'Bleness Foundation (Charles)

Vogt, Martha: senior program officer, Rockwell Fund, Inc.

Vogt, Theodore: adv, O'Bleness Foundation (Charles)

Voilleque, Anne S.: director, CHC Foundation

Vojvoda, Antoinette P.: president, Knapp Foundation, Inc. (MD)

Volanakis, Peter F.: president Corning technologies, Corning Inc.

Volckhausen, William: assistant treasurer, Dime Foundation

Volden, Mary Ellen: director global philanthropy, Binney & Smith, Inc.

Volk, Norman Hans: president, trustee, Hartford Foundation, Inc. (The John A.)

Volk, Stephen R.: chairman, Credit Suisse First Boston Corp.

Volland, Patricia J.: trustee, Altman Foundation

Von Boecklin, August: trustee, Snyder Foundation (Frost and Margaret)

von Habsburg-Lothringen, Inmaculada: trustee, Kress Foundation (Samuel H.)

von Hoffmann, Beatrix: vice president, Arcana Foundation

von Hoffmann, Ladislaus: president, treasurer, Arcana Foundation

von Kalinowski, Julian Onesime: director, member legal committee, Keck Foundation (W. M.)

von Ziegesar, Franz: vice president, trustee, Bowne Foundation (Robert)

Vora, Sonia: assistant secretary, Bristol-Myers Squibb Foundation Inc.

Vorchheimer, Neal P.: director, Unilever United States Foundation

Vorhees, Charles A.: director, Brach Foundation (Helen)

Vorhees, Charles M.: chairman, director, Brach Foundation (Helen)

Vorous, Steve: chief financial officer, Sierra Health Foundation

Vossler, Robert P.: trustee, Strauss Foundation (Leon)

Vout, Murray C.: trustee, AT&T National Pro-Am Youth Fund

Voyles, Bobby: president, Citizens Union Bank; chairman, Citizens Union Bank Foundation

Vraney, Inge: vice president, board member, Koch Foundation, Inc.

Vraney, Lawrence: treasurer, Koch Foundation, Inc.

Vucurevich, Alex: adv board, Vucurevich Foundation (John T.)

Vucurevich, Connie L.: adv board, Vucurevich Foundation (John T.)

Vucurevich, Thomas: adv board, Vucurevich Foundation (John T.)

Vujovich, Christina M.: director, Cummins Foundation; vice president environmental policy, Cummins, Inc.

W

Wabich, James A.: assistant secretary, Sara Lee Foundation

Wacaster, C. Thompson: vice president, Hardin Foundation (Phil)

Wachenfeld, Howard: trustee, Hayden Foundation (Charles)

Wachenfeld, William: director, Simon Foundation (William E.)

Wachtel, Michael D.: president, Oshkosh B'Gosh Foundation Inc.; chief operating officer, Oshkosh B'Gosh, Inc.

Wackerman, Dorothy C.: director, vice president, secretary, Saint-Gobain Corporation Foundation

Wade, Charles N.: treasurer, Dunagan Foundation

Wade, William: manager, Porter Testamentary Trust (James Hyde)

Wade, Wyatt R.: president, Memorial Foundation for the Blind

Wadleigh, Theodore: trustee, Cogswell Benevolent Trust

Wagabaza, Helen M.: assistant secretary, CUNA Mutual Group Foundation, Inc.

Wagele, James: senior vice president, Bank of America Foundation

Waggoner, Robert E.: director, Bush Charitable Foundation, Inc. (Edyth)

Wagner, Ann: secretary, trustee, Langendorf Foundation (Stanley S.)

Wagner, Jeffrey T.: trustee, Reeves Foundation (OH)

Wagner, Lawrence M.: treasurer, director, Hillman Foundation

Wagner, Lucinda A.: trustee, Plankenhorn Foundation (Harry)

Wagner, Martin S.: secretary, general counsel, Xerox Foundation

Wagner, Sally E.: director, Emerson Foundation, Inc. (Fred L.)

Wagoner, G. Richard, Jr.: president, chief executive officer, director, General Motors Corp.

Wahlert, Alan: director, Wahlert Foundation

Wahlert, Celeste: trustee, Wahlert Foundation

Wahlert, David: trustee, Wahlert Foundation

Wahlert, Donna: trustee, Wahlert Foundation

Wahlert, James: trustee, Wahlert Foundation

Wahlert, Mark: director, Wahlert Foundation

Wahlert, Nancy: director, Wahlert Foundation

Wahlert, R. C., II: trustee, Wahlert Foundation

Wahlert, Robert H.: president, treasurer, Wahlert Foundation

Wahlert, Susan: director, Wahlert Foundation

Wahlig, George C.: treasurer, director, Lee Foundation

Wahlig, Michael J.: assistant secretary, Target Foundation

Wainscott, James L.: treasurer, AK Steel Foundation

Wainwright, Carroll Livingston, Jr.: director, Noble Foundation, Inc. (Edward John)

Wainwright, Stuyvesant, III: treasurer, trustee, Lingnan Foundation

Waitzman, James W., Jr.: chairman, president, chief executive officer, Tractor & Equipment Co.; president, director, Tractor & Equipment Co. Foundation

Wakefield, Thomas: secretary, treasurer, trustee, Dunspaugh-Dalton Foundation

Wakley, James T.: president, director, McDonough Foundation (Bernard)

Walacky, Mary E.: executive director, Davis Foundation (Irene E. and George A.)

Walch, W. Stanley: mem adv comm, Jordan and Ettie A. Jordan Charitable Foundation (Mary Ranken)

Walcott, Eustis: vice president, MassMutual Foundation for Hartford, Inc. (The)

Walcott, Leonard E., Jr.: vice president, managing director, Ahmanson Foundation

Walda, Julie Inskeep: director, Journal-Gazette Foundation, Inc.

Waldbauer, Robert T.: director, Vogler Foundation (Laura B.)

Waldrop, Keith: adv board committee member, Heath Foundation (Mary)

Walenczyk, Elizabeth: assistant secretary, International Paper Co. Foundation

Wales, Alice: vchairman, Decker Foundation (Dr. G. Clifford and Florence B.)

Walker, Claire: executive director, Pittsburgh Child Guidance Foundation

Walker, Courtney Johnson: trustee, McNutt Charitable Trust (Amy Shelton)

Walker, Donna Lee: vice president, PPG Industries Foundation

Walker, Gary: director, Penn Foundation (William)

Walker, Harry W., III: director, Campbell Foundation (Ruth and Henry)

Walker, Harry Webster, II: director, trustee, Camp Younts Foundation; director, McDougall Charitable Trust (Ruth Camp)

Walker, Harvey L.: executive director, secretary, treasurer, Cain Foundation (Effie and Wofford)

Walker, James T.: trustee, Metal Industries Foundation

Walker, Kenneth G.: director, Redfield Foundation (Nell J.)

Walker, Mallory: director, Heinz Endowment (Howard)

Walker, Mary H.: trustee, Haskell Fund

Walker, Michael Charles, Sr: vice president, Schmitt Foundation (Kilian J. and Caroline F.)

Walker, Nancy: trustee, Corbett Foundation

Walker, Robert L.: vice president, Rachal Foundation (Ed)

Walker, W. E., III: trustee, Walker Foundation

Walker, William: director, Jones Foundation (Harvey and Bernice)

Wall, Irving M.: director, Shubert Foundation

Wall, Jenai Sullivan: alternate member, McInerny Foundation

Wall, John C.: vice president, chief technical office, Cummins, Inc.

Wall, John W.: trustee, Providence Journal Charitable Foundation

Wallace, Ann Fowler: program office, Cox Charitable Trust (Jessie B.)

Wallace, Charlie F.: 1st vice president, Tri-County Telephone Foundation

Wallace, David F.: trustee, Wickes Foundation (Harvey Randall)

Wallace, Dennis: general manager, Tri-County Telephone Foundation

Wallace, George R., III: trustee, Wallace Foundation (George R.)

Wallace, Sarah R.: president, secretary, Evans Foundation (Thomas J.)

Wallace, William H.: chairman, Hawkins Foundation (Robert Z.)

Wallach, Diane Gates: vice president, Gates Family Foundation

Waller, Jeffrey M.: treasurer, trustee, Johnson Fund (S.C.)

Waller, June: trustee, Saemann Foundation (Franklin I.)

Waller, Katherine A.: trustee, Saemann Foundation (Franklin I.)

Waller, Michael E.: trustee, Hartford Courant Foundation

Waller, Pete: trustee, Fairchild-Meeker Charitable Trust (Freeman E.)

Waller, William S.: assistant treasurer, Reliant Resources Foundation

Wallman, Joel: program officer, Guggenheim Foundation (Harry Frank)

Wallman, Susan A.: manager corporate contributions, McGraw-Hill Companies, Inc.

Walmsley, Cheryl M.: grant administrator, Hunt Corp.

Walsh, Edward F., Jr.: secretary, trustee, Children's Foundation of Erie County

Walsh, Edward J., Jr.: secretary, Rose Foundation (Billy)

Walsh, F. Howard, Jr.: trustee, Fleming Foundation; assistant secretary, assistant treasurer, Walsh Foundation

Walsh, Frank E., III: vice president, Sandy Hill Foundation

Walsh, Frank E., Jr.: chairman, Sandy Hill Foundation

Walsh, Gary W.: tax counsel, U.S. Steel Foundation

Walsh, Jeffrey R.: secretary, treasurer, Sandy Hill Foundation

Walsh, John: vice president and director, J Paul Getty Museum, Getty Trust (J. Paul)

Walsh, John N., III: trustee, Western New York Foundation

Walsh, John N., Jr.: vice president, Cummings Foundation (James H.)

Walsh, Joseph: president, Sandy Hill Foundation

Walsh, Karen R.: vice president, Sandy Hill Foundation

Walsh, Mary D.: vice president, Sandy Hill Foundation

Walsh, Mary D. Fleming: president, trustee, Fleming Foundation; vice president, Walsh Foundation

Walsh, Mason, Jr.: vice chairman, trustee, Mellon Family Foundation (R. K.)

Walsh, Michael J.: vice president, CertainTeed Corp.

Walsh, Sandy: director, Sierra Pacific Resources Charitable Foundation

Walsh, Semmes Guest: governor, Baker, Jr. Memorial Fund (William G.); member investment committee, Goldseker Foundation of Maryland (Morris)

Walsh, William J.: director corporate responsibility, Public Service Electric & Gas Co.; president, Public Service Electric & Gas Foundation

Walter, Donald F.: vice president, treasurer, Plym Foundation

Walter, Mary K.: assistant secretary, Bank One Foundation

Walter, William G.: chairman, chief executive officer, director, FMC Corp.

Walters, Carole H.: vice president, Hershey Foundation

Walters, Clarence: trustee, Reynolds Foundation (Edgar & Francis)

Walters, Geoffrey King: director, Research Corp.

Walters, John Alexander: trustee, Alcon Foundation

Walters, Sumner J.: trustee, Van Wert County Foundation

Walther, Larry: chairman, SBC Foundation

Walton, Edward: director, Feinstein Foundation

Walton, James Mellon: chairman, Heinz Endowment (Vira I.); trustee, Scaife Family Foundation

Walton, Joseph Carroll: trustee, Scaife Family Foundation

Walton, O. B., III: assistant secretary, Walker Foundation

Waltrip, William H.: chairman, director, Bausch & Lomb, Inc.

Wamhoff, Richard M.: president, chief executive officer, director, Ore-Ida Foods

Wang, Susan: executive, president, Formosa Plastics Corporation, USA

Wang, Yung-ching: chairman, Formosa Plastics Corporation, USA

Warburg, James P., Jr.: trustee, Bydale Foundation

Warburg, Jennifer J.: trustee, Bydale Foundation

Warburg, Joan M.: president, trustee, Bydale Foundation

Warburg, Philip N.: trustee, Bydale Foundation

Ward, Anthony C.: adv director, Ducommun and Gross Foundation

Ward, John M.: director, secretary, Schlieder Educational Foundation (Edward G.)

Ward, Lane: trustee, George Foundation

Ward, Laysha L.: director, Target Foundation

Ward, Mabel B.: executive director, Bedsole Foundation (J. L.); member, Crampton Trust

Ward, Ralph, Jr.: president, treasurer, McMillan, Jr. Foundation (Bruce)

Ward, Robert F.: president, director, Hardin Foundation (Phil)

Ward, T. Bestor, III: mem distribution comm, Bedsole Foundation (J. L.)

Ward, Terry W.: vice president, treasurer, Farish Fund (William Stamps)

Ward, William R.: trustee, El Pomar Foundation

Ward, William R., Jr.: assistant secretary, treasurer, Vaughan Foundation (Rachael and Ben)

Warden, William C., Jr.: secretary, Lowe's Charitable and Educational Foundation

Wardley, George P.: secretary, Utica National Foundation

Wardley, George P., III: secretary, Utica National Foundation

Wardrop, Richard M., Jr.: chairman, chief executive officer, director, AK Steel Holding Corp.

Ware, John H., IV: vice president, Oxford Foundation

Ware, Marian S.: chairman, president, Oxford Foundation

Ware, Paul W.: vice president, Oxford Foundation

Ware, Richard Anderson: president emeritus, trustee, Earhart Foundation

Wareing, Elizabeth B.: president, Scurlock Foundation

Warfield, Guy: trustee, Warfield Memorial Fund (Anna Emory)

Wargo, Bruce W.: secretary, treasurer, Anderson Foundation (John W.)

Warhola, John: vice president, director, Warhol Foundation for the Visual Arts (The Andy)

Waring, Bayard D.: co-managing trustee, Peabody Foundation (Amelia)

Waring, Philip B.: vice president grant making, Peabody Foundation (Amelia)

Wark, Robert Rodgers: president, Scott Foundation (Virginia Steele)

Warman, Michele S.: secretary, general counsel, Mellon Foundation (Andrew W.)

Warner, Glen W.: treasurer, trust, Ashtabula Foundation

Warner, Joseph C.: trustee, Simon Foundation (Sidney, Milton, and Leoma)

Warner, Marianne R.: president, Rachal Foundation (Ed)

Warner, Meryll: trustee, Simon Foundation (Sidney, Milton, and Leoma)

Warner, Norton: trustee, Cooper Foundation

Warner, Theodore Kugler, Jr.: secretary, treasurer, Independence Foundation

Warnock, John E.: co-chairman, chief technology officer, Adobe Systems

Warren, Ingrid R.: mem executive comm, director, Dodge Foundation (Cleveland H.)

Warren, Robert D.: senior vice president business management development, New England Business Service

Warren, Shirley: director, Davenport-Hatch Foundation

Warren, Wilbert W., Jr.: director, Baird Brothers Co. Foundation

Warren, William Michael, Jr.: chairman, president, chief executive officer, chief operating officer, director, Energen Corp.

Warsaw, James: president, chief executive officer, director, AMCORE Financial, Inc.

Warwin, Jason: trustee, New York Foundation

Wascoe, Thomas M.: director, Abbott Laboratories Fund

Washington, Nancy D.: president, Pittsburgh Child Guidance Foundation

Washington, Phyllis: director, Washington Foundation (Dennis R. and Phyllis)

Watanabe, August M.: director, Lilly Foundation (Eli)

Waterbury, James B.: trustee, chairman, McElroy Trust (R. J.)

Waterhouse, Christine A.: director, Waterhouse Family Foundation

Waterhouse, Jennifer A.: director, Waterhouse Family Foundation

Waterhouse, Kevin C.: director, Waterhouse Family Foundation

Waterhouse, Lawrence M., III: director, Waterhouse Family Foundation

Waterhouse, Lawrence M., Jr.: president, Waterhouse Family Foundation

Waterhouse, Patrick R.: director, Waterhouse Family Foundation

Waters, Bill W.: chairman, Brown Foundation (M. K.)

Waters, Frank: director, Tri-County Telephone Foundation

Waters, James R.: member, Central Charities Foundation

Waters, John: chief financial officer, Guaranty Bank & Trust Co.

Watkins, Gregory W.: vice president, El Paso Corporate Foundation

Watkins, Ruth Ann: secretary, trustee, Retirement Research Foundation

Watkins, Walker: co-trustee, Wheeler Memorial Foundation (Josephine and J. A.)

Watrous, Helen C.: director, Petteys Memorial Foundation (Jack)

Watson, Alonzo Wallace, Jr.: secretary, director, Eccles Foundation (George S. and Dolores Dore); committee member, Eccles Foundation (Marriner S.)

Watson, Daniel E.: director, Kinder Morgan Foundation

Watson, Jane W.: assistant secretary, assistant treasurer, Ingalls Foundation (Louise H. and David S.)

Watson, Jerome P.: director, Oakley-Lindsay Foundation of Quincy Newspapers and Its Subsidiaries

Watson, JoAnn: corporator, Island Foundation (MA)

Watson, Michael B.: vice president, director, Mellon Family Foundation (R. K.); vice president, trustee, Mellon Foundation (Richard King)

Watson, Raymond L.: vice chairman, Pacific Life Insurance Co.

Watson, Solomon Brown, IV: senior vice president, general counsel, New York Times Co. Foundation

Watson, Steven L.: president, director, Contran Corp.; vice president, secretary, director, Simmons Foundation, Inc. (Harold)

Watson, Stuart G.: secretary, Haley Foundation (W. B.)

Werbel, Robert H.: secretary, director, Allen Brothers Foundation

Werderman, Del V.: treasurer, Hoag Family Foundation (George)

Werner, Jan: secretary, treasurer, Vaughn, Jr. Foundation Fund (James M.)

Werner, John B.: executive director, Cabell III and Maude Morgan Cabell Foundation (Robert G.)

Werner, Vanda N.: secretary, trustee, Norgren Foundation (Carl A.)

Wertenberger, Maurice R.: vice president, Batts Foundation

Wertich, Richard: secretary, Morgan Foundation (Louie R. and Gertrude)

Wertz, Ronald W.: president, Hillman Foundation

Wesby, Meridith D.: director, Daniels Foundation (Fred Harris)

Wescombe, Gary: treasurer, Beckman Foundation (Arnold and Mabel)

Wesley, Norman H.: president, chief operating officer, Fortune Brands, Inc.

Wesselink, David D.: president, director, Metris Companies Foundation; chairman, chief executive officer, Metris Companies, Inc.

Wessely, Boris: treasurer, Rockefeller Brothers Fund, Inc.

Wessinger, E. Charles: director, Wessinger Foundation

Wessinger, Henry W.: director, Wessinger Foundation

Wessinger, Joseph M.: director, Wessinger Foundation

Wessinger, William W.: president, Wessinger Foundation

West, A. Stanley: trustee, Cleveland-Cliffs Foundation (The); senior vice president, sales & commercial planning, Cleveland-Cliffs, Inc.

West, David M., M.D.: director, Copic Medical Foundation

West, Gordon T., Jr.: vice president, trustee, West Foundation (TX)

West, Lane T.: vice president, trustee, West Foundation (TX)

West, Neva Watkins: don, trustee, West Foundation (Neva and Wesley)

West, Reece A.: president, trustee, West Foundation (TX)

West, Ronald D.: executive director, secretary, Emerson Foundation, Inc. (Fred L.); director, French Foundation (D.E.)

West, Terry W.: trustee, Sarkeys Foundation

West, Thomas H., Jr.: director, Hopedale Foundation

West, W. Richard, Jr.: secretary, Bush Foundation; trustee, Ford Foundation

Westby, Gerald H.: trustee, Westby Foundation (Kathleen Patton)

Westby, John Trygve: trustee, Westby Foundation (Kathleen Patton)

Westerhoff, Garret P.: trustee, Westerhoff Family Foundation, Inc.

Westerhoff, Helga K.: trustee, Westerhoff Family Foundation, Inc.

Westerhoff, Katherine: trustee, Westerhoff Family Foundation, Inc.

Western, David: director, Claiborne and Art Ortenberg Foundation (Liz)

Westfeldt, Thomas J.: director, vice president, Schlieder Educational Foundation (Edward G.)

Westmoreland, William C.: director, Guggenheim Foundation (Harry Frank)

Wetter, Larry V.: trustee, Jeld-wen Foundation; vice chairman, director, Jeld-Wen, Inc.

Wettingfeld, Robert F., MD: president, Holmberg Foundation

Wetz, P. A.: trustee, Exxon Mobil Foundation

Wetzel, Joy: trustee, Ellsworth Foundation (Ruth H. and Warren A.)

Wetzel, Mark R.: trustee, Ellsworth Foundation (Ruth H. and Warren A.)

Wetzel, Todd H.: trustee, Ellsworth Foundation (Ruth H. and Warren A.)

Weyerhaeuser, Annette Thayer Black: vice president, director, member, Forest Foundation; board member, Stewardship Foundation

Weyerhaeuser, Gail T.: president, treasurer, director, Forest Foundation

Weyerhaeuser, George Hunt: director, Weyerhaeuser Co.; trustee, Weyerhaeuser Co. Foundation

Weyerhaeuser, William Toycen: director, member, Forest Foundation; chairman, Stewardship Foundation

Weyers, Larry Lee: chief executive officer, chairman, director, WPS Resources Corp.; president, chief executive officer, WPS Resources Foundation, Inc.

Weyland, Wendell P.: trustee, Benz Trust (Doris L.)

Weymouth, George A.: trustee, Allegheny Foundation

Whalen, George T., Jr.: trustee, Millbrook Tribute Garden

Whalen, Gertrude: director, Vernon Foundation (Miles Hodsdon)

Whalen, Michael S.: co-trustee, Stauffer Charitable Trust (John)

Whalen, Robert W.: trustee, Millbrook Tribute Garden

Whalen, Timothy P.: director Conservation Institute, Getty Trust (J. Paul)

Whalley, John I.: trustee, Whalley Charitable Trust

Wharton, J. G.: director, Wharton Foundation

Wharton, Joseph B., III: secretary, treasurer, Wharton Foundation

Wharton, K. B.: director, Wharton Foundation

Wheatley, Bruce C.: vice president, Commercial Intertech Foundation

Wheeler, Arnold: chief financial officer, Bartlett & Co.

Wheeler, Charles B.: vice president, director, Wheeler Foundation

Wheeler, Edward T.: secretary, director, Wheeler Foundation

Wheeler, John C.: vice president, director, Wheeler Foundation

Wheeler, Kathryn Lillard: honorary director, Irvine Foundation (The James)

Wheeler, Margaret S.: senior program officer, Bruening Foundation (Eva L. and Joseph M.)

Wheeler, Ruth B.: trustee, Dow Foundation (Herbert H. and Grace A.)

Wheeler, Samuel C.: president, director, Wheeler Foundation

Wheeler, Thomas K.: treasurer, director, Wheeler Foundation

Wheeler, Wilmot Fitch, Jr.: vice president, director, Morris Foundation (William T.)

Wheelock, Ann Marie: president, chief executive officer, Fannie Mae Foundation

Whelan, Tim: trustee, Morgan Charitable Residual Trust (W. and E.)

Whetzel, William: director, Staunton Farm Foundation

Whiffen, Lorraine: assistant secretary, Dime Foundation

Whipple, William Perry: board chairman, director, Hall-Perrine Foundation

Whisler, J. Steven: chairman, president, chief executive officer, Phelps Dodge Corp.

Whitacre, Edward E., Jr.: chairman, director, chief executive officer, SBC Communications Inc.

Whitaker, Shannon McNeely: trustee, McNeely Foundation

White, A. Dennis: vice president, MetLife Foundation

White, C. Cody, Jr.: president, treasurer, Powers Foundation

White, Charles H., Jr.: director, Heath Foundation (Ed and Mary)

White, Claire Mott: trustee, Mott Foundation (Charles Stewart)

White, Clare W.: trustee, McKee Charitable Trust (Thomas M.)

White, Clayton A.: trustee, Homecrest Foundation

White, Edward D., III: trustee, Boettcher Foundation

White, Henry, Jr.: trustee, Young Foundation (Bill B.)

White, J. Randall: director, Sara Lee Foundation

White, James M., Jr.: trustee, Levy Foundation (June Rockwell)

White, James R.: secretary, director, Square D Foundation

White, James S.: director, Penn Foundation (William)

White, John: director, Rachal Foundation (Ed); trustee, Young Foundation (Bill B.)

White, John P.: chairman, director, Kornfeld Foundation (Emily Davie and Joseph S.)

White, Karen: secretary, treasurer, McDonald Investments Foundation

White, Lynn T.: vice president, trustee, Towsley Foundation (Harry A. and Margaret D.)

White, Margaret R.: trustee, Hillsdale Fund

White, Marion C.: secretary, Klipstein Foundation (Ernest Christian)

White, Miles D.: chairman, chief executive officer, Abbott Laboratories

White, Nancy G.: director, Green Foundation (Allen P. and Josephine B.)

White, Pamela: director, Memton Fund

White, Philip O., Jr.: director, White Foundation (W. P. and H. B.)

White, Richard K.: trustee, Trexler Trust (Harry C.)

White, Robert B.: secretary, treasurer, Cemala Foundation

White, Robert P.: director, White Foundation (W. P. and H. B.)

White, Roger B.: president, White Foundation (W. P. and H. B.)

White, Ronald M.: program officer, Mott Foundation (Charles Stewart)

White, Sara Margaret: vice president, secretary, Powers Foundation

White, Stephen C.: vice president, Powers Foundation

White, Steven R.: secretary, White Foundation (W. P. and H. B.)

White, William Bew, Jr.: trustee, Shook Foundation (Barbara Ingalls)

White, William P., Jr.: director, White Foundation (W. P. and H. B.)

White, William Samuel: chairman, president, chief executive officer, trustee, chairman several com, Mott Foundation (Charles Stewart)

Whitebread, Joseph B., Jr.: treasurer, director, Wilkes, Artis, Hedrick & Lane Foundation

Whitehead, Dane E.: vice president, Burlington Resources Foundation

Whitehead, John C.: chairman emeritus, Mellon Foundation (Andrew W.)

Whitelaw, Essie M.: president, chief operating officer, United Wisconsin Services; vice president, United Wisconsin Services Foundation

Whitestone, Barbara: secretary, Furthur Foundation

Whitfield, Sue Trammell: board of directors, Fondren Foundation

Whitfield, Susan T.: board of directors, Fondren Foundation

Whitfield, W. Trammell: board of directors, Fondren Foundation

Whitfield, William F., Jr.: board of directors, Fondren Foundation

Whitfield, William F., Sr.: board of directors, Fondren Foundation

Whitford, Thomas K.: executive director, PNC Foundation

Whiting, Eleanor W.: assistant treasurer, Plankenhorn Foundation (Harry)

Whiting, Helen Dow: treasurer, trustee, Whiting Foundation (Macauley and Helen Dow)

Whiting, Macauley: secretary, Dow Foundation (Herbert H. and Grace A.); president, trustee, Whiting Foundation (Macauley and Helen Dow)

Whiting, Mary Macauley: secretary, trustee, Whiting Foundation (Macauley and Helen Dow)

Whiting, Sara: trustee, Whiting Foundation (Macauley and Helen Dow)

Whitlow, Sally: trustee, Spahr Family Foundation

Whitney, Charles L.: atty, secretary, director, Heuermann Foundation (Bernard K. and Norma F.)

Whitney, Donald W.: chairman, Jones Foundation (Daisy Marquis)

Whitney, Kate R.: president, Greentree Foundation

Whitridge, Fredrick W.: trustee, Crocker Trust (Mary A.)

Whitridge, Serena H.: trustee, Merck Family Fund

Whittaker, E. William: treasurer, trustee, Anderson Foundation (NY)

Whittaker, Ethel A.: vice president, trustee, Anderson Foundation (NY)

Whittaker, J. Bruce: president, Bank of Greene County Charitable Foundation

Whittelsey, Lucia: clerk, Oak Grove School

Whittemore, Clark M., Jr.: secretary, treasurer, director, Dana Foundation (Charles A.)

Whittenburg, James V.: trustee, Snyder Foundation (Harold B. and Dorothy A.)

Whittman, Iris: chief financial officer, TCB Bank

Whitton, Roger: contr, Thomas Foundation

Whitwam, David Ray: chairman, president, chief executive officer, director, Whirlpool Corp.

Whyel, George S.: trustee emeritus, Mott Foundation (Charles Stewart)

Whyel, Rosalie A.: director, Usibelli Foundation

Whyte, Joseph L.: director, Loughran Foundation (Mary and Daniel)

Wiatr, Francis J.: director, New Milford Savings Bank Foundation; president, chief executive officer, director, NewMil Bancorp

Wice, David Herschel: board member, Fels Fund (Samuel S.)

Wickham, Woodward A., Jr.: vice president general program, MacArthur Foundation (John D. and Catherine T.)

Wideman, Frank J., III: president, Self Family Foundation

Widener, Mary Lee: director, Cowell Foundation (S. H.)

Wiedemann, Dorothy E.: trustee, Schlink Foundation (Albert G. and Olive H.)

Wiedemann, Robert A.: president, secretary, Schlink Foundation (Albert G. and Olive H.)

Wiegley, Allan R.: treasurer, director, Oishei Foundation (The John R.)

Wiens, Harold J.: executive vice president, Minnesota Mining & Manufacturing Co.

Wierichs, James R.: secretary, trustee, Morgan Foundation (Louie R. and Gertrude)

Wiertelak, James B.: senior vice president, chief financial officer, director, Sedgwick, Inc.

Wierzba, Thomas M.: trustee, Johnson Fund (S.C.)

Wiese, Barbara P.: trustee, Ashtabula Foundation

Wigdale, James B.: chairman, director, Marshall & Ilsley Corp.; president, director, Marshall & Ilsley Foundation, Inc.

Wightman, Orrin S., III: trustee, Dula Educational and Charitable Foundation (Caleb C. and Julia W.)

Wilbanks, Daniel P.: vchairman, Blount Educational and Charitable Foundation (Mildred Weedon)

Wilboith, Bert M.: director, Ayres Foundation

Wilbur, Colburn S.: trustee, Packard Foundation (David and Lucile)

Wilcock, James William: chairman, director, Foster Co. (L.B.)

Wilcox, Diane E. H., Esq.: director, Joco Foundation

Wilde, Alexander: vice president communications, Ford Foundation

Wildenstein, Daniel Leopold: vice president, director, Gould Foundation (The Florence)

Wilder, Daren R.: assistant secretary, assistant treasurer, Dougherty, Jr. Foundation (James R.)

Wilder, David: trustee, Mayer Foundation (James and Eva)

Wilder, Robert D.: executive vice president, chief financial officer, Wiley & Sons, Inc. (John)

Wilderson, Frank B., Jr.: first vice chair, Bush Foundation

Wilding White, Mary Louise: trustee, Higgins Foundation (John W. and Clara C.)

Wilding White, Philip Q.: trustee, Higgins Foundation (John W. and Clara C.)

Wile, Sarah W.: director, Hardin Foundation (Phil)

Wiley, Bradford, II: chairman, director, Wiley & Sons, Inc. (John)

Wiley, Deborah: chairman, Wiley & Sons, Inc. (John)

Wiley, Donna J.: director, Clowes Fund

Wiley, S. Donald: director, H.J. Heinz Co.

Wilford, Sara R.: vice president, treasurer, Greentree Foundation

Wilkening, Laurel Lynn: director, Research Corp.

Wilkerson, Thomas D.: mem, trustee, One Valley Bank Foundation

Wilkes, Andrea: secretary, trustee, Kiplinger Foundation

Wilkes, Corbin M.: vice president finance, Kiplinger Washington Editors, Inc.

Wilkes, Susan Cornell: trustee, Cornell Trust (Peter C.)

Wilkie, Valleau, Jr.: executive vice president, executive director, Wallace-Reader's Digest Fund (DeWitt)

Wilkin, Abra Prentice: president, Prentice Foundation (Abra)

Wilkin, George: co-trustee, Luse Foundation (W. P. and Bulah)

Wilkins, Wilfred G.: chairman, trustee, Anderson Foundation (John W.)

Wilkinson, Darla J.: secretary, assistant treasurer, trustee, Sullivan Foundation (Algernon Sydney)

Wilkinson, F. McKinnon: trustee, Symmes Foundation (F. W.)

Wilkinson, Frank W.: secretary, Bowen Foundation (Ethel N.)

Wilkinson, Richard W.: president, Bowen Foundation (Ethel N.)

Wilkof, Richard: trustee, Wilkof Foundation (Edward and Ruth)

Wille, Robert H.: vice president, trustee, Arkell Hall Foundation

Willes, Mark Hinckley: chairman, Times Mirror Foundation

Willet, Daniel J.: treasurer, ContiGroup Companies Foundation

Willhardt, Gary, PhD: trustee, Mellinger Educational Foundation (Edward Arthur)

Williams, A. Morris, Jr.: president, director, Pine Tree Foundation

Williams, Allison F.: trustee, Harland Charitable Foundation (John H. and Wilhelmina D.)

Williams, Dale: trustee, McKay Family Foundation

Williams, David: chief financial officer, North American Royalties

Williams, David R.: trustee, Heinz Co. Foundation (H.J.); executive vice president, director, H.J. Heinz Co.

Williams, E. Belvin: executive director, trustee, Turrell Fund

Williams, E. Grainger: board director, Ottenheimer Brothers Foundation

Williams, Elizabeth A. W.: director administration, Pew Charitable Trusts

Williams, Elynor Alberta: director, Sara Lee Foundation

Williams, Eugene Flewellyn, Jr.: chairman, trustee, Olin Foundation (John M.)

Williams, Gary S.: treasurer, Bank of America Foundation

Williams, Gayle: executive director, Babcock Foundation (Mary Reynolds)

Williams, Gray, Jr.: trustee, Sullivan Foundation (Algernon Sydney)

Williams, James Bryan: trustee, Evans Foundation, Inc. (Lettie Pate); chairman, trustee, Woodruff Foundation (Robert W.)

Williams, Jane: trustee, Quaker Chemical Foundation

Williams, John: member, trustee, One Valley Bank Foundation

Williams, John O.: assistant secretary, treasurer, Caspersen Foundation for Aid to Health and Education (O. W.); director, CTW Foundation, Inc.

Williams, Karen Hastie: director, Fannie Mae Foundation

Williams, M. Nancy: executive vice president, Cockrell Foundation

Williams, Marguerite N.: secretary, director, Williams Family Foundation of Georgia

Williams, Martha G.: director, Liberty Corp. Foundation

Williams, Marty: chief financial officer, Lisle Corp.

Williams, Mary C.: vice president, director, New Milford Savings Bank Foundation

Williams, Nathaniel: program officer, New York Foundation

Williams, Neil: trustee, Duke Endowment

Williams, Raymond H.: vice president, Zellerbach Family Fund

Williams, Robert: member distribution committee, Bedsole Foundation (J. L.)

Williams, Robert G.: director, Pew Charitable Trusts

Williams, Robert M.: assistant secretary, Progress Energy Foundation

Williams, Ruth W.: secretary, treasurer, director, Pine Tree Foundation

Williams, Samuel C., Jr.: trustee, Upton Charitable Foundation (Lucy and Eleanor S.)

Williams, Sarah: assistant director, Pfizer Inc.

Williams, Sarah P.: trustee, Appleby Trust (Scott B. and Annie P.)

Williams, Stella R.: assistant secretary, Kent-Lucas Foundation

Williams, Stephen J.: director, Raker Foundation (M. E.)

Williams, Thomas L., III: president, director, Williams Family Foundation of Georgia

Williamson, Anne: executive director, Keller Foundation

Williamson, Beverly: trustee, Priddy Foundation

Williamson, Charles R.: chief executive officer, chairman, director, Unocal Corp.

Williamson, Harold: director, Copic Medical Foundation

Williamson, Jack: trustee, Williams Charitable Trust (Mary Jo)

Williamson, Richard: trustee, Chicago Title and Trust Co. Foundation

Williamson, Susan K.: mem distribution comm, trustee, Kettering Fund

Williamson, W. Bland: secretary, trustee, Bernsen Foundation (Grace and Franklin)

Willis, Dudley H.: trustee, Saltonstall Charitable Foundation (Richard)

Willis, Evelyn Sayer: vice president, director, Willis Family Foundation

Willis, James Richard: president, director, Willis Family Foundation

Willis, Jo Ellyn: vice president, director, Square D Foundation

Willis, Mark A.: president, J.P. Morgan Chase Foundation

Willis, Sally S.: trustee, Saltonstall Charitable Foundation (Richard)

Willis, Steve: director, Trust Foundation

Willner, Robin: member, International Business Machines

Willock, Ashley M.: director, Fear Not Foundation

Willock, Katheryne: director, Fear Not Foundation

Willock, Norman A.: director, Fear Not Foundation

Willock, Scott: director, Fear Not Foundation

Willoughby, Donald E.: executive director, IBP Foundation

Wills, Rosemary C.: assistant secretary, assistant treasurer, duPont Foundation (Alfred I.)

Willson, George C., III: president, director, Green

Foundation (Allen P. and Josephine B.)

Willson, Harry: director, Haley Foundation (W. B.)

Willumstad, Robert B.: president, director, Citigroup Inc.

Wilmot, Carol B.: secretary, Champlin Foundation

Wilsey, Alfred S., Jr.: secretary, treasurer, Wilsey Foundation

Wilsey, Diane B.: vice president, Wilsey Foundation

Wilsey, Michael W.: vice president, Wilsey Foundation

Wilson, Angelina M.: trustee, Wilson Foundation (Huey and Angeline)

Wilson, Blenda Jacqueline: trustee, Getty Trust (J. Paul)

Wilson, Donna: assistant secretary, Dime Foundation

Wilson, Dorothy B.: vice chairman, Toms Foundation (The)

Wilson, Dorothy Cheney: director emeritus, Meadows Foundation (The)

Wilson, Eugene R.: senior vice president development, Kauffman Foundation (Ewing Marion)

Wilson, Faye C.: secretary, Gilmore Foundation (William G.)

Wilson, Gayle: director, Parsons Foundation (Ralph M.)

Wilson, George E.: director, East Cambridge Savings Charitable Foundation

Wilson, Howard O.: treasurer, Peppers Foundation (Ann)

Wilson, Huey J.: trustee, Wilson Foundation (Huey and Angeline)

Wilson, Isabel Brown: first vice president, trustee, Brown Foundation

Wilson, J. Richard: president, Besser Foundation

Wilson, Janet C.: mgr, Wilson Foundation (Marie C. and Joseph C.)

Wilson, Joe: mgr, Wilson Foundation (Marie C. and Joseph C.)

Wilson, John H., II: president, Piper Foundation (Minnie Stevens)

Wilson, Joseph R.: mgr, Wilson Foundation (Marie C. and Joseph C.)

Wilson, Kevin: director, Portsmouth General Hospital Foundation

Wilson, Kirke P.: president, secretary, Rosenberg Foundation

Wilson, Larry: president, director, CUNA Mutual Group Foundation, Inc.

Wilson, Lee Anne: trustee, Sarkeys Foundation

Wilson, Mary Jane: secretary, ONDEO Nalco Foundation

Wilson, Peter: director, CNA Foundation

Wilson, Peter A.: trustee, Keel Foundation

Wilson, Richard A.: treasurer, director, Connell Foundation (Michael J.)

Wilson, Robert B.: trustee, Weyerhaeuser Co. Foundation

Wilson, Robert F.: treasurer, Rollins-Luetkemeyer Foundation

Wilson, Rosine M.: trustee, Ward Heritage Foundation (Mamie McFaddin)

Wilson, Sandra C.: vice president administration, director, International Paper Co. Foundation

Wilson, Scott: mgr, Wilson Foundation (Marie C. and Joseph C.)

Wilson, T. J.: director, McDonough Foundation (Bernard)

Wilson, Ted: director, Norcross Wildlife Foundation

Wilson Arnold, Louise: treasurer, trustee, CH Foundation

Winawer, Gail T.: director, Crames Family Foundation (Arthur)

Winch, David C.: treasurer, Minster Machine Co. Foundation

Winch, Harold S.: president, Minster Machine Co. Foundation

Winch, Heather E.: secretary, Minster Machine Co. Foundation

Winch, John: president, chief operating officer, director, Minster Machine Co.; vice president, Minster Machine Co. Foundation

Winch, Nancy E.: president, Minster Machine Co. Foundation

Winchell, Jean Rogers: mng trustee, Rogers Fund for the Arts (Russell Hill)

Winchester, David P.: director, Rice Foundation

Windsor, Robert G.: trustee, Castle Rock Foundation

Winford, Benny F.: secretary, treasurer, director, Tractor & Equipment Co. Foundation

Winkel, John: director, Bloedorn Foundation (Walter A.)

Winkelman, Edie C.: chairman, Trust Foundation

Winkhaus, Hans Dietrich: chairman, director, Henkel Corp.

Winkler, Charles E.: director, Kansas Health Foundation

Winkler, Virginia: co-trustee, Hallberg Foundation (E. L. and R. F.)

Winkley, V. Carol: assistant secretary, assistant treasurer, Davis Foundation (James A. and Juliet L.)

Winmill, Mark C.: trustee, Thanksgiving Foundation

Winship, William B.: trustee, Bingham Second Betterment Fund (William)

Winsor, Frank: director, Morrison Foundation (Harry W.)

Winston, Bert F., Jr.: vice president, trustee, Sterling-Turner Foundation

Winston, Eleanor C.: secretary, trustee, Southways Foundation

Winston, Harold R., Sr.: director, Stebens Charitable Foundation (Bertha)

Winston, L. David: assistant secretary, trustee, Sterling-Turner Foundation

Winston, Melinda: hon director, Patron Saints Foundation

Winston, Samuel G.: trustee, Blowitz-Ridgeway Foundation

Winter, Alison: treasurer, Demos Foundation (N.)

Winter, William Bergford: chairman, president, director, Bucyrus-Erie Foundation; president, Bucyrus International, Inc.

Winton, Nanette B.: secretary, treasurer, director, Fab Steel Products Foundation

Wisdom, Betty: trustee, RosaMary Foundation

Wisdom, Scott: member, Grotto Foundation

Wise, Bradford A.: director, Hannaford Charitable Foundation

Wise, Daniel P.: director, Weber Charities Corp. (Frederick E.)

Wise, Emma F.: trustee, Wise Foundation (Watson W.)

Wise, Kathryn E.: secretary, Norton Memorial Corp. (Geraldi)

Wise, Leslie: treasurer, Farwell Foundation (Drusilla)

Wise, Robert Edward, MD: trustee, Dana Charitable Trust (Eleanor Naylor)

Wiseman, Ronald D.: assistant secretary, Thomas Foundation

Wishnia, Steven: trustee, Plough Foundation

Wishnick, Lisa: director, Wishnick Foundation (Robert I.)

Wishnick, William: president, director, Wishnick Foundation (Robert I.)

Wiskowski, Carol A.: secretary, Madison Gas & Electric Foundation; assistant vice president administration, MGE Energy, Inc.

Wislow, Robert A.: trustee, Graham Foundation for Advanced Studies in the Fine Arts

Wisner, Frank: trustee, Rockefeller Brothers Fund, Inc.

Wisnom, David, Jr.: president, Lux Foundation (Miranda)

Wisnosky, Karen: secretary, Brady Foundation

Wister, Diana S.: president, Strawbridge Foundation of Pennsylvania II (Margaret Dorrance)

Wit, Harold Maurice: director, Allen Brothers Foundation

Witham, John A.: executive vice president, chief financial officer, Metris Companies, Inc.

Witham, Louise F.: trustee, Webber Oil Foundation

Withers, Kathryn W.: director, Wessinger Foundation

Witherspoon, Douglas C.: director, Scholl Foundation (Dr.)

Withington, Nathan N.: president, Hornblower Fund (Henry)

Withum, Lawrence A., Jr.: trustee, Coen Family Foundation (Charles S. and Mary)

Wittmann, Lin: director, Brillion Foundation

Wlahofsky, Jeffrey A.: trustee, Pittsburgh Child Guidance Foundation

Wobst, Frank: chairman, director, Huntington Bancshares, Inc.

Wohlert, Roger W.: vice president, treasurer, SBC Foundation

Wohlstetter, John: vice president, director, Rose Foundation (Billy)

Wojchik, Larry: chairman, Land O'Lakes Foundation

Wolcott, Arthur S.: chairman, director, Seneca Foods Corp.

Wolf, Barth J.: secretary, manager legal services, WPS Resources Corp.; secretary, assistant treasurer, WPS Resources Foundation, Inc.

Wolf, Don: director, Foellinger Foundation

Wolf, Harold: director, Peters Foundation (R. D. and Linda)

Wolf, Harold J.: secretary, treasurer, director, Brillion Foundation

Wolf, John M., Sr.: director, Kaufmann Foundation (Henry)

Wolf, Robert B.: trustee, Patterson Charitable Fund (W. I.)

Wolfe, Kenneth L.: chairman, director, Hershey Foods Corp.

Wolfe, Laurence A.: vice president admin and real estate, secretary, Weingart Foundation

Wolfe, Merle D.: president, director, Thompson Charitable Foundation

Wolfe, William C., Jr.: vice president, Wolfe Associates, Inc.

Wolfert, Rick: president, chief operating officer, GE Capital Corp.

Wolff, Paula: trustee, Johnson Foundation

Wolff, Rosalie S.: vice president, Solow Foundation

Wolfrom, Howard E., Jr.: treasurer, assistant secretary, Burns & McDonnell Foundation

Wollen, Carolyn S.: trustee, Bingham Second Betterment Fund (William)

Woller, Basil R.: senior vice president, El Paso Corporate Foundation

Wollseiffen, Shelley: member, Cranston Foundation

Wolman, J. Martin: vice president, treasurer, Lee Endowment Foundation

Wolman, Paul C., III: director, Unger Foundation (Aber D.)

Woloshyn, Sonyia: treasurer, Turrell Fund

Wolter, Gary J.: vice president, Madison Gas & Electric Foundation; senior vice president administration, MGE Energy, Inc.

Wolters, Kate Pew: trustee, Steelcase Foundation

Wolverton, David: president, Priddy Foundation

Womack, Chris: senior vice president, Georgia Power Co.; director, Georgia Power Foundation

Womble, Astrid C.: executive director, president, director, Collis Foundation

Womble, Ralph H.: trustee, Hanes Foundation (John Wesley and Anna Hodgin)

Wondergem, Casey: contact, Van Andel Foundation (Jay and Betty)

Woner, Bruce J.: member, Central Charities Foundation

Wong, Alton S.: director, Wong Foundation (Lin and Ella)

Wong, Reuben S. F.: president, treasurer, director, Wong Foundation (Lin and Ella)

Wong, Stanley S.: director, Wong Foundation (Lin and Ella)

Wong, Vera H.: vice president, secretary, director, Wong Foundation (Lin and Ella)

Wood, Anthony C.: executive director, secretary, Ittleson Foundation

Wood, Barbara M. J.: director, Rice Foundation

Wood, Charles O., III: trustee, Wood Foundation of Chambersburg, PA

Wood, David S.: trustee, Wood Foundation of Chambersburg, PA

Wood, James F.: director, McMahon Foundation

Wood, Kate B.: director, Hyde and Watson Foundation

Wood, Miriam M.: trustee, Wood Foundation of Chambersburg, PA

Wood, Paul W.: president, director, Unilever United States Foundation

Wood, Robert A.: director, Green Foundation (Allen P. and Josephine B.)

Wood, Stephen R.: president, LG&E Energy Corp.

Wood, Susannah C. L.: director, AKC Fund

Wood, Sylvia Upton: secretary, trustee, Upton Foundation (Frederick S.)

Wood, Willis B., Jr.: trustee, Haynes Foundation (John Randolph and Dora)

Wood Knight, Elizabeth: director, Green Foundation (Allen P. and Josephine B.)

Woodard, Andrew: director, W. A. Woodard Foundation

Woodard, Carlton: president, W. A. Woodard Foundation

Woodard, Joy: director, W. A. Woodard Foundation

Woodard, Kim C.: director, W. A. Woodard Foundation

Woodard, Kristen A.: director, W. A. Woodard Foundation

Woodard, Tod Casey: vice president, W. A. Woodard Foundation

Woodbury, John D., MD: director, Physicians Mutual Insurance Co. Foundation

Woodbury, Susan B.: trustee, Alden Trust (George I.)

Wooden, Douglas: senior vice president, chief financial officer, Great-West Life and Annuity Insurance Co.

Woodling, Ann: trustee, Stocker Foundation

Woodling, Nancy Elizabeth: trustee, Stocker Foundation

Woodruff, Fred M., Jr.: trustee, Miller Foundation

Woodruff, Judy: trustee, Carnegie Corp. of New York

Woods, Avery L.: director, Woods Charitable Fund

Woods, David F.: clerk, director, Beveridge Foundation, Inc. (Frank Stanley)

Woods, Dick H.: co-trustee, Schutte Foundation (Victor E. and Caroline E.)

Woods, Gloria: contributions committee, CNA Foundation

Woods, H.A. (Al): trustee, McKee Foundation (Robert E. and Evelyn)

Woods, Jerry Dean: treasurer, Grinnell Mutual Group Foundation; vice president financial, Grinnell Mutual Reinsurance Co.

Woods, Marjorie: director, Woods Charitable Fund

Woods, Robert F.: director, IBM International Foundation

Woods, Thomas C., III: president, treasurer, Woods Charitable Fund

Woodside, Blair C., Jr.: member, Hoover Foundation (Herbert W.)

Woodson, C. E., MD: director, Gulf Coast Medical Foundation

Woodson, Robert Ray: trustee, Campbell Foundation (J. Bulow)

Woodward, Joanne Gignilliat: director, Newman's Own Foundation

Woodward, Sharon V.: president, treasurer, Baltimore Equitable Insurance Foundation

Woollcott, James: mem adv comm, Janirve Foundation

Word, Joanne Whittaker: trustee, Anderson Foundation (NY)

Worfel, C. Christopher: secretary, treasurer, Loutit Foundation

Wortham, R. W., III: secretary, treasurer, Wortham Foundation

Worthington, Dave: chief financial officer, Rieke Corp.

Wortman, Judy B.: executive secretary, Kutz Foundation (Milton and Hattie)

Wraase, Dennis: president, chief executive officer, Pepco Holdings, Inc.

Wrather, Christopher C.: president, treasurer, Wrather Family Foundation

Wren, Nancy G.: vice chairman, Portsmouth General Hospital Foundation

Wright, Alan M.: director, Consumers Energy Foundation

Wright, Arnold W., Jr.: vice president, executive director, CIGNA Foundation

Wright, Barbara: secretary, Packard Foundation (David and Lucile)

Wright, Charles E.: trustee, Arkell Hall Foundation

Wright, Donald Franklin: director, Times Mirror Foundation

Wright, Franklin L., Jr.: assistant treasurer, Dime Foundation

Wright, Gay: trust officer, trustee, Cray Residuary Charitable Trust (Evah C.)

Wright, Glen A.: director, Fleming and Jane Howe Patrick Foundation (Robert)

Wright, Hasbrouck S.: executive trustee, Kunkel Foundation (John Crain)

Wright, James: director, Fairchild Foundation, Inc. (Sherman)

Wright, James O.: president, director, Badger Meter Foundation; chairman, director, Badger Meter, Inc.

Wright, James W.: treasurer, director, Park Bank Foundation

Wright, Lawrence A.: director, Atkinson Foundation

Wright, Martha C.: vice president, director, Cemala Foundation

Wright, Norma G.: member, Teubert Charitable Trust (James H. and Alice)

Wright, Randell: director, De Queen Regional Medical Center

Wright, Randy L.: treasurer, Jones Foundation (Helen)

Wright, Rick: trustee, Fund for New Jersey

Wright, Thomas G.: executive editor, Tennessee Valley Printing Co.

Wright, Vernon H.C.: executive vice chairman, chief financial officer, MBNA Corp.

Wright, William Bigelow: director, Bunbury Co., Inc.

Wright, William L.: vice president, Hultquist Foundation

Wright, William R.: trustee, Davis Foundations (Arthur Vining)

Wright, William T., II: trustee, Kunkel Foundation (John Crain)

Wriston, Kathryn Dineen: secretary, trustee, Hartford Foundation, Inc. (The John A.)

Wulf, Clark J.: assistant treasurer, Bank One Foundation

Wulf, Gene C.: vice president, controller, Bemis Co. Foundation

Wulf, Jerold W.: director, Andersen Foundation

Wurtele, C. Angus: director, Bush Foundation

Wurzburg, Warren Seymour, Sr.: chairman, president, director, Wurzburg, Inc.

Wyatt, Jane C.: director, Trippe Trust (William D.)

Wyatt, Judy: secretary, trustee, Dayton Power and Light Co. Foundation

Wyckoff, Ann Pigott: president, Norcliffe Foundation

Wyckoff, Ed Lisk, Jr.: president, treasurer, trustee, Homeland Foundation (NY)

Wyeth, Phyllis Mills: trustee, duPont Foundation (Chichester)

Wylie, D. C., Jr.: trustee, Bell Foundation (S. Lewis and Lucia B.)

Wylie, Jean: regional grants director, Moody Foundation

Wyman, David C.: trustee, Wyman Youth Trust

Wyman, David E.: trustee, Wyman Youth Trust

Wyman, Hal H.: trustee, Wyman Youth Trust

Wynia, Ann: chair, Bush Foundation

Wynkoop, Roger D.: president, ACF Industries

Wynne, Richard B.: mem adv comm, Janirve Foundation

Wyron, Dorothy F.: vice president, Portsmouth General Hospital Foundation

Wysong, Kathryn: director, O'Shaughnessy Foundation (I. A.)

Wyss, Judith: secretary, director, Wyss Foundation

Wyss, Loren L.: trustee, Templeton Foundation (Herbert A.)

Wyszomierski, Jack L.: executive vice president, chief financial officer, Schering-Plough Corp.; trustee, member, Schering-Plough Foundation

Y

Yalich, Barbara L.: advisory committee member, Inasmuch Foundation

Yamada, Albert M.: director, First Hawaiian Foundation

Yamada, Tadataka, MD: trustee, Rockefeller Brothers Fund, Inc.

Yamasaki, Ken: director, Nakamichi Foundation (E.)

Yamasaki, Koichi: director, Nakamichi Foundation (E.)

Yamazaki, Yashiro: president, director, Nakamichi Foundation (E.)

Yamba, A. Zachary: trustee, Victoria Foundation

Yancey, Helen Lund: vice president, trustee, McKee Foundation (Robert E. and Evelyn)

Yanchura, Marc P.: treasurer, MacArthur Foundation (John D. and Catherine T.)

Yancy, Howard: president, director, ECG Foundation

Yancy, Mary Garwood: president, director, ECG Foundation

Yang, Y. C.: chairman, Lin Foundation (T. Y.)

Yantek, Dawn: director, Washington Group Foundation, Inc.

Yantz, Jerome: treasurer, Kantzler Foundation

Yao, Lily K.: president, director, First Hawaiian Foundation; director, First Hawaiian, Inc.

Yarnevich, George W.: vice president, Smoot Charitable Foundation

Yastine, Barbara: chief financial officer, Credit Suisse First Boston Corp.

Yasui, Lise: director, Penn Foundation (William)

Yasutake, Chiyoko: member allocations committee, Kawabe Memorial Fund

Yasutake, Webster T.: member allocations committee, Kawabe Memorial Fund

Yates, Edward D.: trustee, Dentsply International Foundation; senior vice president, chief financial officer, Dentsply International, Inc.

Yates, H. Roy: vice president, Howarth Trust Fund

Yates, Mary-Alice: secretary, Guggenheim Foundation (Harry Frank)

Yeager, Charles G.: trustee, Stranahan Foundation

Yeager, Jane Meseck: program manager, Microsoft Corp.

Yeatman, C. Perry: director, Unilever United States Foundation

Yeckel, Carl: president, director, King Foundation (Carl B. and Florence E.)

Yedlin, Joseph: treasurer, director, Gudelsky Family Foundation (Homer and Martha)

Yee, Robert B.: treasurer, Lin Foundation (T. Y.)

Yehle, Eugene C.: chairman, trustee, Strosacker Foundation (Charles J.)

Yehling, Mary Kleine: executive director, Tyndale House Foundation

Yellin, Ira E.: trustee, Getty Trust (J. Paul)

Yellott, Kinloch N., III: vice president, Wilson Sanitarium for Children of Baltimore City (Thomas)

Yeo, Lloyd J.: treasurer, trustee, Wickes Foundation (Harvey Randall); president, treasurer, Wickson-Link Memorial Foundation

Yeomans, Janet L.: treasurer, director, 3M Foundation; vice president, treasurer, Minnesota Mining & Manufacturing Co.

Yhouse, Paul A.: president, chief executive officer, director, Holnam, Inc.

Yih, Cathy: secretary, Yih Family Foundation

Yih, Irene C.P.: vice president, treasurer, Yih Family Foundation

Yih, Roy Paxon: president, Yih Family Foundation

Yih, Shou-Chen: chairman, Yih Family Foundation

Yingling, John Edward, Jr.: chief administrative and financial officer, Dodge Foundation (Geraldine R.)

Yocum, Robert G.: secretary, Harsco Corp. Fund

Yoder, Diane: trustee, Schowalter Foundation

Yoder, Elvin D.: trustee, Schowalter Foundation

Yonkman, Mark: director, Comerica Charitable Foundation

Yontz, Merle R.: vice president, trustee, Mellinger Educational Foundation (Edward Arthur)

York, Glen T.: president, Trippe Trust (William D.)

York, Michael H., Sr.: director, Trippe Trust (William D.)

Yost, Karen M.: director, Vogler Foundation (Laura B.)

Young, Chad: director, Masters Family Foundation

Young, Donald J.: director, Pappas Charitable Foundation (Thomas Anthony)

Young, Emily B.: trustee, Baldwin Memorial Foundation (Fred)

Young, Fern D.: treasurer, director, Young Foundation (Irvin L.)

Young, Francis B.: adv, Beasley Charitable Trust (Lucy and Emily)

Young, Frank: director, Vermilion Healthcare Foundation

Young, George F., Jr.: trustee, Crawford Estate Trust Fund A (E. R.)

Young, Gerald T.: secretary, treasurer, trustee, Bourns Foundation

Young, John R.: president, Gould Foundation (The Florence); president, director, Hughes Foundation (Geoffrey C.); director, Mathers Charitable Foundation (G. Harold and Leila Y.)

Young, Leslie D.: trustee, Glendorn Foundation

Young, Lindsay: director, Thompson Charitable Foundation

Young, Mary K.: director, Hughes Foundation (Geoffrey C.)

Young, Merrilynn: comptroller, Grable Foundation

Young, Richard B.: trustee, Acushnet Foundation

Young, Richard C.: trustee, McElroy Trust (R. J.)

Young, Robert C.: trustee, Van Wert County Foundation

Young, Robert Harris: president, chief executive officer, Central Vermont Public Service Corp.

Young, Toni P.: director, Kutz Foundation (Milton and Hattie)

Young, William: trustee, Acushnet Foundation

Youngberg, Francey Lim: director, Meyer Foundation (Eugene and Agnes E.)

Younger, Charles M., MD: trustee, Abell-Hanger Foundation

Younglove, Eileen M.: contributions manager, UAL Corp.; secretary, United Airlines Foundation

Yoxall, James R.: secretary, treasurer, trustee, Baughman Foundation

Yu, Jerry C.: program officer, Weingart Foundation

Yuen, Cheryl L.: consultant - cultural program, Sara Lee Foundation

Yuras, Susan Hawn: chairman, vice president, director, Sams Foundation (Earl C.)

Z

Zabel, William D.: trustee, Valentine Foundation (Lawson)

Zabotin, Mischa A.: secretary, director, Loewy Family Foundation

Zaccaria, Adrian: vice chairman, president, director, Bechtel Group, Inc.

Zacharia, Issac Herman: president, Zacharia Foundation (Isaac Herman)

Zachry, Henry Bartell, Jr.: chairman, chief executive officer, Zachry Co. (H.B.); trustee, Zachry Foundation (The)

Zachry, J. P.: president, trustee, Zachry Foundation (The)

Zachry, Mollie Steves: trustee, Zachry Foundation (The)

Zahara, Ellis: vice president, Winn-Dixie Stores Foundation

Zahr, Andrew A.: treasurer, Hartmarx Charitable Foundation

Zales, William E., Jr.: secretary, Alabama Power Foundation

Zamora-Cope, Rosie: director, Houston Endowment

Zandueta, Lilibeth D.: director, Bristol-Myers Squibb Foundation Inc.

Zanino, Walter J.: controller, trustee, Norris Foundation (Kenneth T. and Eileen L.)

Zante, Mary Van: secretary, treasurer, Kuyper Foundation (Peter H. and E. Lucille Gaass)

Zanze, Anthony Olds: trustee, Irwin Charity Foundation (William G.)

Zanze, J.: trustee, Irwin Charity Foundation (William G.)

Zapanta, Edward, MD: director, Irvine Foundation (The James)

Zapisek, John R.: treasurer, Utica National Foundation; senior vice president financial, chief financial officer, treasurer, director, Utica National Insurance Group

Zarrow, Anne S.: vice president, Zarrow Foundation (Anne and Henry)

Zarrow, Henry H.: president, Zarrow Foundation (Anne and Henry)

Zarrow, Stuart A.: director, Zarrow Foundation (Anne and Henry)

Zeagler, M. F.: assistant executive director, Temple Foundation (T. L. L.)

Zech, Ronald H.: chairman, president, chief executive officer, chief operating officer, GATX Corp.

Zedaker, Michael R.: trustee, Van Wert County Foundation

Zeftel, Leo: director, Kutz Foundation (Milton and Hattie)

Zeglis, John D.: chairman and chief executive officer wireless group, AT&T Corp.; director, Sara Lee Corp.

Zeidman, Elizabeth G.: trustee, Greenfield Foundation (Albert M.)

Zeifang, Amy D.: secretary, Duffield Family Foundation

Zeigler, Kenneth B.: director, Brunswick Foundation

Zeigon, James W.: executive vice president, J.P. Morgan Chase & Co.; trustee, J.P. Morgan Chase Foundation

Zeiter, Carol: secretary, Zeiter Charitable Foundation (Henry and Carol)

Zeiter, Henry J.: president, Zeiter Charitable Foundation (Henry and Carol)

Zellerbach, Charles R.: trustee, Zellerbach Family Fund

Zellerbach, John W.: vice president, Zellerbach Family Fund

Zellerbach, Thomas H.: trustee, Zellerbach Family Fund

Zellerbach, William Joseph: president, Zellerbach Family Fund

Zellerbach-Boschwitz, Nancy: secretary, Zellerbach Family Fund

Zelus, Marsha: director, McMahan Foundation (Catherine L. and Robert O.)

Zemelman, David: trustee, CBS Foundation

Zemsky, Howard: president, Russer Foods; trustee, Russer Foods/Zemsky Family Trust

Zemsky, Sam: chairman, director, Russer Foods; trustee, Russer Foods/Zemsky Family Trust

Zemsky, Shirley: trustee, Russer Foods/Zemsky Family Trust

Zenner, Patrick J.: trustee, Hoffmann-La Roche Foundation; president, chief executive officer, director, Hoffmann-La Roche, Inc.

Zerhusen, David E.: senior vice president, El Paso Corporate Foundation

Zerkel, James E., II: director, ShenTel Foundation

Zervigon, Carlos: trustee, RosaMary Foundation

Zervigon, Luis C.: secretary, director, Keller Family Foundation

Zervigon, Mary K.: secretary, trustee, Keller Family Foundation; trustee, RosaMary Foundation

Zeugner, Mary Z. (Rennolds): director, Cabell III and Maude Morgan Cabell Foundation (Robert G.)

Zezima, Stephen P.: vice president taxation, M/A-COM Foundation

Ziegelheim, Frances: trustee, Ziegelheim Charitable Foundation (Fran and Irwin)

Ziegenbein, Lyn Wallin: executive director, secretary, Kiewit Foundation (Peter)

Ziegler, Arthur P., Jr.: trustee, Allegheny Foundation

Ziegler, Bernard C.: president, director, Ziegler Foundation

Ziegler, Bernard C., III: assistant secretary, assistant treasurer, director, Ziegler Foundation

Ziegler, Carl H.: director, Ziegler Foundation

Ziegler, Karl: director, Ziegler Foundation for the Blind (E. Matilda)

Ziegler, Peter D.: assistant secretary, assistant treasurer, director, Ziegler Foundation

Ziegler, R. Douglas: advisor, Johnson Controls Foundation; vice president, secretary, treasurer, director, Ziegler Foundation

Ziegler, William, III: president, director, Ziegler Foundation for the Blind (E. Matilda)

Ziegler, William Alexander: secretary, Wilson Foundation (H. W.)

Ziemer, James L.: president, Harley-Davidson Foundation

Ziesing, Joanne K.: secretary, Klingestein Fund

Zigas, Barry: senior vice president, Fannie Mae; director, Fannie Mae Foundation

Zimbalist, Efram, III: trustee, Hartford Courant Foundation

Zimmerman, Joel: distribution trustee, Schwab-Rosenhouse Memorial Foundation

Zimmerman, John F., Jr.: trustee, Watson Foundation (Walter E. and Caroline H.)

Zimmerman, L. Wilbur: office, vice president, mgr, Ludwick Foundation (Christopher)

Zimmerman, Martin B.: trustee, Ford Motor Co. Fund

Zimmerman, Michael David: trustee, Michael Foundation (Herbert I. and Elsa B.)

Zimmerman, Richard Anson: director, Stabler Foundation (Donald B. and Dorothy L.)

Zimmerman, S. LaNette: senior vice president human resources, Chicago Title Corp.; trustee, Chicago Title and Trust Co. Foundation

Zimmerman, W. E.: executive vice president, trustee, Reeves Foundation (OH)

Zimmermann, K. Noel P.: secretary, director, Phillips Foundation (Ellis L.)

Zinn, Douglas C.: executive director, Biddle Foundation (Mary Duke)

Zionts, Nancy: sr program officer, Jewish Healthcare Foundation

Zippert, Carol Prejean: director, Babcock Foundation (Mary Reynolds)

Zippiroli, Lorraine: director children families communities program, Packard Foundation (David and Lucile)

Zises, Seymour: director, Fink Foundation (NY)

Zitrin, Arthur: president, Zitrin Foundation (Charlotte and Arthur)

Zitrin, Charlotte: director, Zitrin Foundation (Charlotte and Arthur)

ZoBell, Karl: vice president, trustee, Copley Foundation (James S.); secretary, Dr. Seuss Foundation

Zuber, Harold L., Jr.: vice president, chief financial officer, Teleflex, Inc.

Zuccaro, Edward R.: director, Bunbury Co., Inc.; vice president, trustee, Windham Foundation

Zuccaro, Richard W.: vice president, New York Life Foundation

Zuckerberg, Roy J.: director, Brookdale Foundation

Zuckerman, Harriet: senior vice president, Mellon Foundation (Andrew W.)

Zuendt, William F.: president, chief executive officer, Wells Fargo & Co.

Zutz, Denise M.: member advisory board, Johnson Controls Foundation; vice president corporate communications, Johnson Controls Inc.

Zweibel, Nancy, PhD: program officer, Retirement Research Foundation

Zwetsch, Gil A.: director, Johnston-Hanson Foundation

MASTER INDEX

Arranges in alphabetical order the foundations profiled in this directory and includes the page number on which the profile appears. Also listed are former names of funders. These citations also include the page number of the profile in which this information is located.

D

G

Master Index